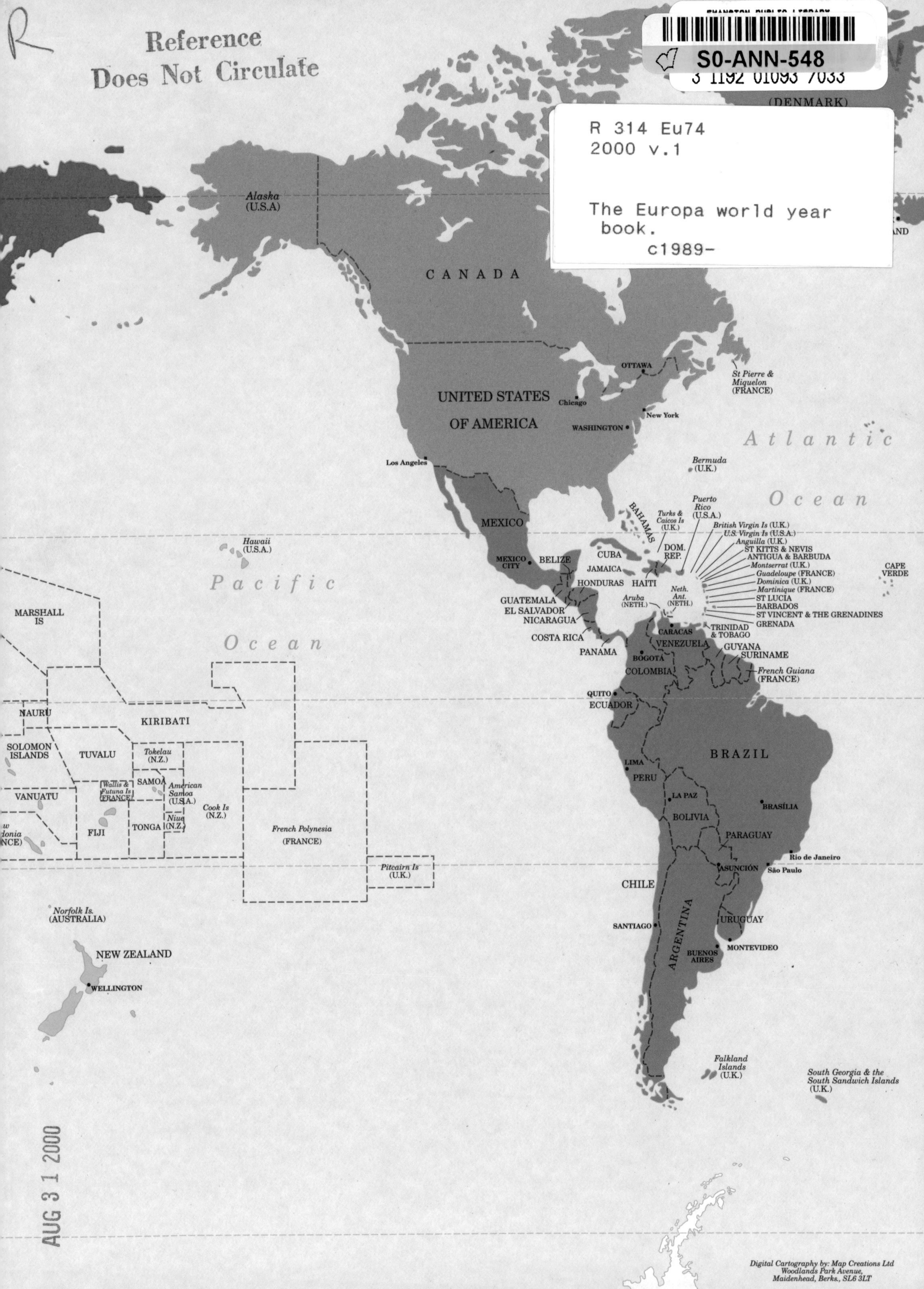
(DENMARK)
Alaska
(U.S.A)
CANADA
OTTAWA
St Pierre &
Miquelon
(FRANCE)
UNITED STATES
OF AMERICA
Chicago
New York
WASHINGTON
Atlantic
Ocean
Los Angeles
Bermuda
(U.K.)
Puerto
Rico
(U.S.A.)
Turks &
Caicos Is
(U.K.)
BAHAMAS
British Virgin Is (U.K.)
U.S. Virgin Is (U.S.A.)
Anguilla (U.K.)
ST KITTS & NEVIS
ANTIGUA & BARBUDA
Montserrat (U.K.)
Guadeloupe (FRANCE)
Dominica (U.K.)
Martinique (FRANCE)
ST LUCIA
BARBADOS
ST VINCENT & THE GRENADINES
GRENADA
CAPE
VERDE
MEXICO
Hawaii
(U.S.A.)
MEXICO
CITY
BELIZE
CUBA
DOM.
REP.
JAMAICA
HAITI
HONDURAS
Pacific
Ocean
GUATEMALA
EL SALVADOR
NICARAGUA
COSTA RICA
PANAMA
Aruba
(NETH.)
Neth.
Ant.
(NETH.)
TRINIDAD
& TOBAGO
CARACAS
VENEZUELA
GUYANA
SURINAME
French Guiana
(FRANCE)
BOGOTA
COLOMBIA
QUITO
ECUADOR
MARSHALL
IS
NAURU
KIRIBATI
SOLOMON
ISLANDS
TUVALU
Tokelau
(N.Z.)
SAMOA
Wallis &
Futuna Is
(FRANCE)
American
Samoa
(U.S.A.)
VANUATU
FIJI
TONGA
Niue
(N.Z.)
Cook Is
(N.Z.)
French Polynesia
(FRANCE)
Pitcairn Is
(U.K.)
BRAZIL
LIMA
PERU
LA PAZ
BOLIVIA
BRASÍLIA
PARAGUAY
Rio de Janeiro
São Paulo
ASUNCIÓN
CHILE
Norfolk Is.
(AUSTRALIA)
SANTIAGO
ARGENTINA
URUGUAY
MONTEVIDEO
BUENOS
AIRES
NEW ZEALAND
WELLINGTON
Falkland
Islands
(U.K.)
South Georgia & the
South Sandwich Islands
(U.K.)
Digital Cartography by: Map Creations Ltd
Woodlands Park Avenue,
Maidenhead, Berks., SL6 3LT

# THE EUROPA WORLD YEAR BOOK 2000

# THE EUROPA WORLD YEAR BOOK 2000

VOLUME I

PART ONE: INTERNATIONAL ORGANIZATIONS
PART TWO: AFGHANISTAN–JORDAN

**First published 1926**


11 New Fetter Lane, London, EC4P 4EE, England
(A member of the Taylor & Francis Group)



ISBN 1-85743-075-1 (The Set)
1-85743-076-X (Vol. I)
ISSN 0956-2273
Library of Congress Catalog Card Number 59-2942

Typeset by UBL International and printed by Unwin Brothers Limited
The Gresham Press
Old Woking, Surrey

# FOREWORD

THE EUROPA WORLD YEAR BOOK (formerly THE EUROPA YEAR BOOK: A WORLD SURVEY) was first published in 1926. Since 1960 it has appeared in annual two-volume editions, and has become established as an authoritative reference work, providing a wealth of detailed information on the political, economic and commercial institutions of the world.

Volume I contains a comprehensive listing of more than 1,650 international organizations and the first part of the alphabetical survey of countries of the world, from Afghanistan to Jordan. Following the re-establishment of sovereignty over Macau by the People's Republic of China on 19 December 1999, Macau appears as a Special Administrative Region of China, for the first time, in this edition. There is also a new chapter on the UN-administered territory of East Timor. Volume II contains countries from Kazakhstan to Zimbabwe.

The International Organizations section gives extensive coverage to the United Nations and its related agencies and bodies. There are also detailed articles concerning some 60 other major international and regional organizations (including the World Trade Organization, the European Union and the North Atlantic Treaty Organization—NATO); entries for many affiliated organizations appear within these articles. In addition, briefer details of more than 1,000 other international organizations appear in a separate section which starts on page 279. A comprehensive Index of International Organizations can be found at the end of Volume I.

Each country is covered by an individual chapter, containing: an introductory survey including recent history, economic affairs, government, defence, social welfare, education, and public holidays; an economic and demographic survey using the latest available statistics on area and population, agriculture, forestry, fishing, industry, finance, trade, transport, tourism, the media, and education; and a directory section containing names, addresses and other useful facts about government, political parties, diplomatic representation, judiciary, religious groups, the media, telecommunications, banks, insurance, trade and industry, development organizations, chambers of commerce, industrial and trade associations, utilities, trade unions, transport and tourism.

Any important government changes (e.g. ministerial reorganizations and election results) that occur during the final stages of the production of the book and cannot, therefore, be incorporated in the appropriate chapters, may be found in Late Information, see p. xv–xvi.

Readers are referred to our eight regional surveys, AFRICA SOUTH OF THE SAHARA, CENTRAL AND SOUTH-EASTERN EUROPE, EASTERN EUROPE, RUSSIA AND CENTRAL ASIA, THE FAR EAST AND AUSTRALASIA, THE MIDDLE EAST AND NORTH AFRICA, SOUTH AMERICA, CENTRAL AMERICA AND THE CARIBBEAN, THE USA AND CANADA and WESTERN EUROPE, for additional information on the geography, history and economy of these areas. More detailed coverage of international organizations may be found in THE EUROPA DIRECTORY OF INTERNATIONAL ORGANIZATIONS.

The information is extensively revised and updated annually by a variety of methods, including direct mailing to all the institutions listed. Many other sources are used, such as national statistical offices, government departments and diplomatic missions. The editors thank the innumerable individuals and organizations throughout the world whose generous co-operation in providing current information for this edition is invaluable in presenting the most accurate and up-to-date material available.

March 2000.

# ACKNOWLEDGEMENTS

The editors gratefully acknowledge particular indebtedness for permission to reproduce material from the following publications: the United Nations' *Demographic Yearbook*, *Statistical Yearbook* and *Industrial Commodity Statistics Yearbook*; the United Nations Educational, Scientific and Cultural Organization's *Statistical Yearbook*; the Food and Agriculture Organization of the United Nations' *Production Yearbook*, *Yearbook of Fishery Statistics* and *Yearbook of Forest Products*; the International Labour Office's *Yearbook of Labour Statistics*; the World Bank's *World Bank Atlas*, *Global Development Finance*, *World Development Report* and *World Development Indicators*; the International Monetary Fund's *International Financial Statistics* and *Government Finance Statistics Yearbook*; the World Tourism Organization's *Yearbook of Tourism Statistics*; and *The Military Balance 1999–2000*, a publication of the International Institute for Strategic Studies, 23 Tavistock Street, London, WC2E 7NQ.

# CONTENTS



* A complete Index of International Organizations is to be found on p. 2071.

## PART TWO
## Afghanistan–Jordan



An Index of Territories is to be found at the end of Volume II.

# ABBREVIATIONS

AB Aktiebolag (Joint-Stock Company); Alberta
Abog. Abogado (Lawyer)
Acad. Academician; Academy
ACP African, Caribbean and Pacific (countries)
ACT Australian Capital Territory
AD anno Domini
ADB African Development Bank; Asian Development Bank
ADC aide-de-camp
Adm. Admiral
admin. administration
AfDB African Development Bank
AG Aktiengesellschaft (Joint-Stock Company)
AH anno Hegirae
a.i. ad interim
AID (US) Agency for International Development
AIDS Acquired Immunodeficiency Syndrome
AK Alaska
Al. Aleja (Alley, Avenue)
AL Alabama
ALADI Asociación Latinoamericana de Integración
Alt. Alternate
AM Amplitude Modulation
a.m. ante meridiem (before noon)
amalg. amalgamated
Apdo Apartado (Post Box)
APEC Asia-Pacific Economic Co-operation
approx. approximately
Apt Apartment
AR Arkansas
AŞ Anonim Şirketi (Joint-Stock Company)
A/S Aktieselskab (Joint-Stock Company)
ASEAN Association of South East Asian Nations
asscn association
assoc. associate
ASSR Autonomous Soviet Socialist Republic
asst assistant
Aug. August
auth. authorized
Ave Avenue
Avda Avenida (Avenue)
Avv. Avvocato (Lawyer)
AZ Arizona

BC British Columbia
BC before Christ
Bd Board
Bd, Bld, Blv., Blvd Boulevard
b/d barrels per day
BFPO British Forces' Post Office
Bhd Berhad (Public Limited Company)
Bldg Building
Blvr Bulevar
BP Boîte postale (Post Box)
br.(s) branch(es)
Brig. Brigadier
BSE Bovine spongiform encephalopathy
BSEC (Organization of) Black Sea Economic Co-operation
bte boîte (box)
BTN Brussels Tariff Nomenclature
bul. bulvar (boulevard)

C Centigrade
c. circa; cuadra(s) (block(s) )

CA California
CACM Central American Common Market
Cad. Caddesi (Street)
CAP Common Agricultural Policy
cap. capital
Capt. Captain
CARICOM Caribbean Community and Common Market
CBSS Council of Baltic Sea States
CCL Caribbean Congress of Labour
Cdre Commodore
CEMAC Communauté économique et monétaire de l'Afrique centrale
Cen. Central
CEO Chief Executive Officer
CFA Communauté Financière Africaine; Co-opération Financière en Afrique centrale
CFP Common Fisheries Policy; Communauté française du Pacifique; Comptoirs français du Pacifique
Chair. Chairman/person/woman
Chih. Chihuahua
CI Channel Islands
Cia Companhia
Cía Compañía
CICP Centre for International Crime Prevention
Cie Compagnie
c.i.f. cost, insurance and freight
C-in-C Commander-in-Chief
circ. circulation
CIS Commonwealth of Independent States
CJD Creutzfeldt-Jakob disease
cm centimetre(s)
cnr corner
CO Colorado
Co Company; County
c/o care of
Coah. Coahuila
Col Colonel
Col. Colima; Colonia
COMESA Common Market for Eastern and Southern Africa
Comm. Commission; Commendatore
Commdr Commander
Commdt Commandant
Commr Commissioner
Cond. Condiminio
Confed. Confederation
Cont. Contador (Accountant)
Corp. Corporate
Corpn Corporation
CP Case Postale; Caixa Postal; Casella Postale (Post Box); Communist Party
CPSU Communist Party of the Soviet Union
Cres. Crescent
CSCE Conference on Security and Co-operation in Europe
CSTAL Confederación Sindical de los Trabajadores de América Latina
CT Connecticut
CTCA Confederación de Trabajadores Centro-americanos
Cttee Committee
cu cubic
cwt hundredweight

DC District of Columbia; Distrito Capital; Distrito Central
DE Departamento Estatal; Delaware

Dec. December
Del. Delegación
Dem. Democratic; Democrat
Dep. Deputy
dep. deposits
Dept Department
devt development
DF Distrito Federal
Dgo Durango
Diag. Diagonal
Dir Director
Div. Division(al)
DM Deutsche Mark
DMZ demilitarized zone
DN Distrito Nacional
Doc. Docent
Dott. Dottore
Dr Doctor
Dr. Drive
Dra Doctora
Dr Hab. Doktor Habilitowany (Assistant Professor)
dr.(e) drachma(e)
Drs Doctorandus
dwt dead weight tons

E East; Eastern
EBRD European Bank for Reconstruction and Development
EC European Community
ECA (United Nations) Economic Commission for Africa
ECE (United Nations) Economic Commission for Europe
ECLAC (United Nations) Economic Commission for Latin America and the Caribbean
ECO Economic Co-operation Organization
Econ. Economist; Economics
ECOSOC (United Nations) Economic and Social Council
ECOWAS Economic Community of West African States
ECU European Currency Unit
Edif. Edificio (Building)
edn edition
EEA European Economic Area
EFTA European Free Trade Association
e.g. exempli gratia (for example)
EIB European Investment Bank
eKv electron kilovolt
EMS European Monetary System
EMU economic and monetary union
eMv electron megavolt
Eng. Engineer; Engineering
ERM exchange rate mechanism
ESACA Emisora de Capital Abierto Sociedad Anónima
Esc. Escuela; Escudos; Escritorio
ESCAP (United Nations) Economic and Social Commission for Asia and the Pacific
ESCWA (United Nations) Economic and Social Commission for Western Asia
esq. esquina (corner)
est. established; estimate; estimated
etc. et cetera
EU European Union
eV eingetragener Verein
excl. excluding
exec. executive
Ext. Extension

F Fahrenheit
f. founded
FAO Food and Agriculture Organization
f.a.s. free alongside ship
Feb. February
Fed. Federation; Federal
FL Florida
FM frequency modulation
fmr(ly) former(ly)
f.o.b. free on board
Fr Father
Fr. Franc
Fri. Friday
FRY Federal Republic of Yugoslavia
ft foot (feet)
FYRM former Yugoslav republic of Macedonia

g gram(s)
GA Georgia
GATT General Agreement on Tariffs and Trade
GCC Gulf Co-operation Council
Gdns Gardens
GDP gross domestic product
Gen. General
GeV giga electron volts
GmbH Gesellschaft mit beschränkter Haftung (Limited Liability Company)
GMT Greenwich Mean Time
GNP gross national product
Gov. Governor
Govt Government
Gro Guerrero
grt gross registered tons
Gto Guanajuato
GWh gigawatt hours

ha hectares
HE His/Her Eminence; His/Her Excellency
hf hlutafelag (Limited Company)
HI Hawaii
HIV human immunodeficiency virus
hl hectolitre(s)
HM His/Her Majesty
Hon. Honorary, Honourable
hp horsepower
HQ Headquarters
HRH His/Her Royal Highness

IA Iowa
IBRD International Bank for Reconstruction and Development (World Bank)
ICC International Chamber of Commerce
ICFTU International Confederation of Free Trade Unions
ICRC International Committee of the Red Cross
ID Idaho
IDA International Development Association
IDB Inter-American Development Bank
i.e. id est (that is to say)
IFC International Finance Corporation
IL Illinois
ILO International Labour Organization/Office
IMF International Monetary Fund
in (ins) inch (inches)
IN Indiana
Inc, Incorp. Incd Incorporated
incl. including
Ind. Independent
INF Intermediate-Range Nuclear Forces
Ing. Engineer
Insp. Inspector
Int. International
Inzå. Engineer
IPU Inter-Parliamentary Union
Ir Engineer
IRF International Road Federation
irreg. irregular
Is Islands
ISIC International Standard Industrial Classification
ITU International Telecommunication Union
Iur. Lawyer

Jal. Jalisco
Jan. January
Jnr Junior
Jr Jonkheer (Netherlands); Junior
Jt Joint

kg kilogram(s)
KG Kommandit Gesellschaft (Limited Partnership)
kHz kilohertz
KK Kaien Kaisha (Limited Company)
km kilometre(s)
Kom. Komnata (Room)
kor. korpus (block)
KS Kansas
kv. kvartal (apartment block); kvartira (apartment)
kW kilowatt(s)
kWh kilowatt hours
KY Kentucky

LA Louisiana
lauk laukums (square)
lb pound(s)
Lic. Licenciado
Licda Licenciada
LNG liquefied natural gas
LPG liquefied petroleum gas
Lt, Lieut Lieutenant
Ltd Limited

m metre(s)
m. million
MA Massachusetts
Maj. Major
Man. Manager; managing
MB Manitoba
mbH mit beschränkter Haftung (with limited liability)
Mc/s megacycles per second
MD Maryland
ME Maine
Me Maître
mem.(s) member(s)
MEP Member of the European Parliament
Mercosul Mercado Comum do Sul (Southern Common Market)
Mercosur Mercado Común del Sur (Southern Common Market)
MEV, MeV mega electron volts
Méx. México
MFN most favoured nation
mfrs manufacturers
Mgr Monseigneur; Monsignor
MHz megahertz
MI Michigan
MIA missing in action
Mich. Michoacán
MIGA Multilateral Investment Guarantee Agency
Mil. Military
Mlle Mademoiselle
mm millimetre(s)
Mme Madame
MN Minnesota
MO Missouri
Mon. Monday
Mor. Morelos
MP Member of Parliament
MS Mississippi
MSS Manuscripts
MT Montana
MW megawatt(s); medium wave
MWh megawatt hour(s)

N North; Northern
n.a. not available
nab. naberezhnaya (embankment, quai)
NAFTA North American Free Trade Agreement
nám. náměstí (square)
Nat. National
NATO North Atlantic Treaty Organization
Nay. Nayarit
NB New Brunswick
NC North Carolina
NCO non-commissioned officer
ND North Dakota
NE Nebraska; North-East
NF Newfoundland
NGO non-governmental organization
NH New Hampshire
NJ New Jersey
NL Nuevo León
NM New Mexico
NMP net material product
no numéro, número (number)
no. number
Nov. November
nr near
nrt net registered tons
NS Nova Scotia
NSW New South Wales
NV Naamloze Vennootschap (Limited Company); Nevada
NW North-West
NY New York
NZ New Zealand

OAPEC Organization of Arab Petroleum Exporting Countries
OAS Organization of American States
OAU Organization of African Unity
Oax. Oaxaca
Oct. October
OECD Organisation for Economic Co-operation and Development
OECS Organisation of Eastern Caribbean States
Of. Oficina (Office)
OH Ohio
OHCR Office of the United Nations High Commissioner of Human Rights
OIC Organization of the Islamic Conference
OK Oklahoma
ON Ontario
OPEC Organization of the Petroleum Exporting Countries
opp. opposite
OR Oregon
Org. Organization
ORIT Organización Regional Interamericana de Trabajadores
OSCE Organization for Security and Co-operation in Europe

p. page
p.a. per annum
PA Pennsylvania
Parl. Parliament(ary)
pas. passazh (passage)
per. pereulok (lane, alley)
PE Prince Edward Island
Perm. Rep. Permanent Representative

PF Postfach (Post Box)
PK Post Box (Turkish)
Pl. Plac (square)
pl. platz; place; ploshchad (square)
PLC Public Limited Company
PLO Palestine Liberation Organization
p.m. post meridiem (after noon)
PMB Private Mail Bag
PNA Palestinian National Authority
POB Post Office Box
pp. pages
PQ Québec
PR Puerto Rico
pr. prospekt (avenue)
Pres. President
Prin. Principal
Prof. Professor
Propr Proprietor
Prov. Province; Provincial; Provinciale (Dutch)
prov. provulok (lane)
PT Perseroan Terbatas (Limited Company)
Pte Private; Puente (Bridge)
Pty Proprietary
p.u. paid up
publ. publication; published
Publr Publisher
Pue. Puebla
Pvt. Private

Qld Queensland
Qro Querétaro
Q. Roo Quintana Roo
q.v. quod vide (to which refer)

Rag. Ragioniere (Accountant)
Rd Road
R(s) rand; rupee(s)
reg., regd register; registered
reorg. reorganized
Rep. Republic; Republican; Representative
Repub. Republic
res reserve(s)
retd retired
Rev. Reverend
RI Rhode Island
RJ Rio de Janeiro
Rm Room
RN Royal Navy
ro-ro roll-on roll-off
RP Recette principale
Rp.(s) rupiah(s)
RSFSR Russian Soviet Federative Socialist Republic
Rt Right

S South; Southern; San
SA Société Anonyme, Sociedad Anónima (Limited Company); South Australia
SAARC South Asian Association for Regional Co-operation
SAECA Sociedad Anónima Emisora de Capital Abierto
SADC Southern African Development Community
SAR Special Administrative Region
SARL Sociedade Anônima de Responsabilidade Limitada (Joint-Stock Company of Limited Liability)
Sat. Saturday
SC South Carolina
SD South Dakota
Sdn Bhd Sendirian Berhad (Private Limited Company)
SDR(s) Special Drawing Right(s)
SE South-East
Sec. Secretary
Secr. Secretariat
Sen. Senior; Senator
Sept. September
SER Sua Eccellenza Reverendissima (His Eminence)
SFRY Socialist Federal Republic of Yugoslavia
Sin. Sinaloa
SITC Standard International Trade Classification
SJ Society of Jesus
SK Saskatchewan
SLP San Luis Potosí
SMEs small and medium-sized enterprises
s/n sin número (without number)
Soc. Society
Sok. Sokak (Street)
Son. Sonora
Şos. Şosea (Road)
SP São Paulo
SpA Società per Azioni (Joint-Stock Company)
Sq. Square
sq square (in measurements)
Sr Senior; Señor
Sra Señora
Srl Società a Responsabilità Limitata (Limited Company)
SSR Soviet Socialist Republic
St Saint, Sint; Street
Sta Santa
Ste Sainte
str. strada, stradă (street)
str-la stradelă (street)
subs. subscriptions; subscribed
Sun. Sunday
Supt Superintendent
sv. Saint
SW South-West

Tab. Tabasco
Tamps Tamaulipas
TAŞ Turkiye Anonim Şirketi (Turkish Joint-Stock Company)
Tas Tasmania
TD Teachta Dàla (Member of Parliament)
tech., techn. technical
tel. telephone
TEU 20-ft equivalent unit
Thur. Thursday
TN Tennessee
Treas. Treasurer
Tue. Tuesday
TV television
TX Texas

u. utca (street)
u/a unit of account
UAE United Arab Emirates
UEE Unidade Económica Estatal
UEMOA Union économique et monetaire ouest-africaine
UK United Kingdom
ul. ulica, ulitsa (street)
UM ouguiya
UN United Nations
UNCTAD United Nations Conference on Trade and Development
UNDCP United Nations International Drug Control Programme
UNDP United Nations Development Programme
UNEP United Nations Environment Programme
UNESCO United Nations Educational, Scientific and Cultural Organization
UNHCR United Nations High Commissioner for Refugees
UNICEF United Nations Children's Fund
Univ. University
UNRWA United Nations Relief and Works Agency for Palestine Refugees in the Near East
USA United States of America
USAID United States Agency for International Development
USSR Union of Soviet Socialist Republics
UT Utah

VA Virginia
VAT Value-added Tax
VEB Volkseigener Betrieb (Public Company)
Ven. Venerable
Ver. Veracruz
VHF Very High Frequency
VI (US) Virgin Islands
Vic Victoria
viz. videlicet (namely)
Vn Veien (Street)
vol.(s) volume(s)
VT Vermont
vul. vulitsa (street)

W West; Western
WA Western Australia; Washington (State)
WCL World Confederation of Labour
Wed. Wednesday
WEU Western European Union
WFP World Food Programme
WFTU World Federation of Trade Unions
WHO World Health Organization
WI Wisconsin
WTO World Trade Organization
WV West Virginia
WY Wyoming

yr year
YT Yukon Territory
Yuc. Yucatán

# INTERNATIONAL TELEPHONE CODES

To make international calls to telephone and fax numbers listed in *The Europa World Year Book*, dial the international code of the country from which you are calling, followed by the appropriate country code for the organization you wish to call (listed below), followed by the area code (if applicable) and telephone or fax number listed in the entry.

| | Country code | + or – GMT* |
|---|---|---|
| Afghanistan | 93 | +4½ |
| Albania | 355 | +1 |
| Algeria | 213 | +1 |
| Andorra | 376 | +1 |
| Angola | 244 | +1 |
| Antigua and Barbuda | 1 268 | –4 |
| Argentina | 54 | –3 |
| Armenia | 374 | +4 |
| Australia | 61 | +7 to +10 |
| Australian External Territories: | | |
| Australian Antarctic Territory | 672 | +3 to +10 |
| Christmas Island | 61 | +10 |
| Cocos (Keeling) Islands | 61 | +10 |
| Norfolk Island | 672 | +11½ |
| Austria | 43 | +1 |
| Azerbaijan | 994 | +5 |
| The Bahamas | 1 242 | –5 |
| Bahrain | 973 | +3 |
| Bangladesh | 880 | +6 |
| Barbados | 1 246 | –4 |
| Belarus | 375 | +2 |
| Belgium | 32 | +1 |
| Belize | 501 | –6 |
| Benin | 229 | +1 |
| Bhutan | 975 | +6 |
| Bolivia | 591 | –4 |
| Bosnia and Herzegovina | 387 | +1 |
| Botswana | 267 | +2 |
| Brazil | 55 | –3 to –4 |
| Brunei | 673 | +8 |
| Bulgaria | 359 | +2 |
| Burkina Faso | 226 | 0 |
| Burundi | 257 | +2 |
| Cambodia | 855 | +7 |
| Cameroon | 237 | +1 |
| Canada | 1 | –3 to –8 |
| Cape Verde | 238 | –1 |
| The Central African Republic | 236 | +1 |
| Chad | 235 | +1 |
| Chile | 56 | –4 |
| China, People's Republic | 86 | +8 |
| Special Administrative Regions: | | |
| Hong Kong | 852 | +8 |
| Macau | 853 | +8 |
| China (Taiwan) | 886 | +8 |
| Colombia | 57 | –5 |
| The Comoros | 269 | +3 |
| Congo, Democratic Republic | 243 | +1 |
| Congo, Republic | 242 | +1 |
| Costa Rica | 506 | –6 |
| Côte d'Ivoire | 225 | 0 |
| Croatia | 385 | +1 |
| Cuba | 53 | –5 |
| Cyprus | 357 | +2 |
| 'Turkish Republic of Northern Cyprus' | 90 392 | +2 |
| Czech Republic | 420 | +1 |
| Denmark | 45 | +1 |
| Danish External Territories: | | |
| Faroe Islands | 298 | 0 |
| Greenland | 299 | –1 to –4 |
| Djibouti | 253 | +3 |

| | Country code | + or – GMT* |
|---|---|---|
| Dominica | 1 767 | –4 |
| The Dominican Republic | 1 809 | –4 |
| East Timor | 670 | +8 |
| Ecuador | 593 | –5 |
| Egypt | 20 | +2 |
| El Salvador | 503 | –6 |
| Equatorial Guinea | 240 | +1 |
| Eritrea | 291 | +3 |
| Estonia | 372 | +2 |
| Ethiopia | 251 | +3 |
| Fiji | 679 | +12 |
| Finland | 358 | +2 |
| Finnish External Territory: | | |
| Åland Islands | 358 | +2 |
| France | 33 | +1 |
| French Overseas Departments: | | |
| French Guiana. | 594 | –3 |
| Guadeloupe | 590 | –4 |
| Martinique | 596 | –4 |
| Réunion | 262 | +4 |
| French Overseas Collectivités Territoriales: | | |
| Mayotte | 269 | +3 |
| Saint Pierre and Miquelon | 508 | –3 |
| French Overseas Territories: | | |
| French Polynesia | 689 | –10 |
| New Caledonia | 687 | +11 |
| Wallis and Futuna Islands | 681 | +12 |
| Gabon | 241 | +1 |
| The Gambia | 220 | 0 |
| Georgia | 995 | +4 |
| Germany | 49 | +1 |
| Ghana | 233 | 0 |
| Greece | 30 | +2 |
| Grenada | 1 473 | –4 |
| Guatemala | 502 | –6 |
| Guinea | 224 | 0 |
| Guinea-Bissau | 245 | 0 |
| Guyana | 592 | –4 |
| Haiti | 509 | –5 |
| Honduras | 504 | –6 |
| Hungary | 36 | +1 |
| Iceland | 354 | 0 |
| India | 91 | +5½ |
| Indonesia | 62 | +7 to +8 |
| Iran | 98 | +3½ |
| Iraq | 964 | +3 |
| Ireland | 353 | 0 |
| Israel | 972 | +2 |
| Italy | 39 | +1 |
| Jamaica | 1 876 | –5 |
| Japan | 81 | +9 |
| Jordan | 962 | +2 |
| Kazakhstan | 7 | +6 |
| Kenya | 254 | +3 |
| Kiribati | 686 | +12 |
| Korea, Democratic People's Republic (North Korea) | 850 | +9 |
| Korea, Republic (South Korea) | 82 | +9 |
| Kuwait | 965 | +3 |
| Kyrgyzstan | 996 | +5 |

| | Country code | + or – GMT* |
|---|---|---|
| Laos | 856 | +7 |
| Latvia | 371 | +2 |
| Lebanon | 961 | +2 |
| Lesotho | 266 | +2 |
| Liberia | 231 | 0 |
| Libya | 218 | +1 |
| Liechtenstein | 423 | +1 |
| Lithuania | 370 | +2 |
| Luxembourg | 352 | +1 |
| Macedonia, former Yugoslav republic | 389 | +1 |
| Madagascar | 261 | +3 |
| Malawi | 265 | +2 |
| Malaysia | 60 | +8 |
| Maldives | 960 | +5 |
| Mali | 223 | 0 |
| Malta | 356 | +1 |
| The Marshall Islands | 692 | +12 |
| Mauritania | 222 | 0 |
| Mauritius | 230 | +4 |
| Mexico | 52 | –6 to –7 |
| Micronesia, Federated States | 691 | +10 to +11 |
| Moldova | 373 | +2 |
| Monaco | 377 | +1 |
| Mongolia | 976 | +8 |
| Morocco | 212 | 0 |
| Mozambique | 258 | +2 |
| Myanmar | 95 | +6½ |
| Namibia | 264 | +2 |
| Nauru | 674 | +12 |
| Nepal | 977 | +5¾ |
| The Netherlands | 31 | +1 |
| Netherlands Dependencies: | | |
| Aruba | 297 | –4 |
| Netherlands Antilles | 599 | –4 |
| New Zealand | 64 | +12 |
| New Zealand's Dependent and Associated Territories: | | |
| Cook Islands | 682 | –10½ |
| Niue | 683 | –11 |
| Nicaragua | 505 | –6 |
| Niger | 227 | +1 |
| Nigeria | 234 | +1 |
| Norway | 47 | +1 |
| Norwegian External Territory: | | |
| Svalbard | 47 | +1 |
| Oman | 968 | +4 |
| Pakistan | 92 | +5 |
| Palau | 680 | +9 |
| Panama | 507 | –5 |
| Papua New Guinea | 675 | +10 |
| Paraguay | 595 | –4 |
| Peru | 51 | –5 |
| The Philippines | 63 | +8 |
| Poland | 48 | +1 |
| Portugal | 351 | 0 |
| Qatar | 974 | +3 |
| Romania | 40 | +2 |
| The Russian Federation | 7 | +2 to +12 |
| Rwanda | 250 | +2 |
| Saint Christopher and Nevis | 1 869 | –4 |
| Saint Lucia | 1 758 | –4 |
| Saint Vincent and the Grenadines | 1 784 | –4 |
| Samoa | 685 | –11 |
| San Marino | 378 | +1 |
| São Tomé and Príncipe | 239 | 0 |
| Saudi Arabia | 966 | +3 |
| Senegal | 221 | 0 |

| | Country code | + or – GMT* |
|---|---|---|
| Seychelles | 248 | +4 |
| Sierra Leone | 232 | 0 |
| Singapore | 65 | +8 |
| Slovakia | 421 | +1 |
| Slovenia | 386 | +1 |
| Solomon Islands | 677 | +11 |
| Somalia | 252 | +3 |
| South Africa | 27 | +2 |
| Spain | 34 | +1 |
| Sri Lanka | 94 | +5½ |
| Sudan | 249 | +2 |
| Suriname | 597 | –3 |
| Swaziland | 268 | +2 |
| Sweden | 46 | +1 |
| Switzerland | 41 | +1 |
| Syria | 963 | +2 |
| Tajikistan | 7 | +5 |
| Tanzania | 255 | +3 |
| Thailand | 66 | +7 |
| Togo | 228 | 0 |
| Tonga | 676 | +13 |
| Trinidad and Tobago | 1 868 | –4 |
| Tunisia | 216 | +1 |
| Turkey | 90 | +2 |
| Turkmenistan | 993 | +5 |
| Tuvalu | 688 | +12 |
| Uganda | 256 | +3 |
| Ukraine | 380 | +2 |
| United Arab Emirates | 971 | +4 |
| United Kingdom | 44 | 0 |
| United Kingdom Crown Dependencies | 44 | 0 |
| United Kingdom Overseas Territories: | | |
| Anguilla | 1 264 | –4 |
| Ascension Island | 247 | 0 |
| Bermuda | 1 441 | –4 |
| British Virgin Islands | 1 284 | –4 |
| Cayman Islands | 1 345 | –5 |
| Diego Garcia (British Indian Ocean Territory) | 246 | +5 |
| Falkland Islands | 500 | –4 |
| Gibraltar | 350 | +1 |
| Montserrat | 1 664 | –4 |
| Saint Helena | 290 | 0 |
| Tristan da Cunha | 2 897 | 0 |
| Turks and Caicos Islands | 1 649 | –5 |
| United States of America | 1 | –5 to –10 |
| United States Commonwealth Territories: | | |
| Northern Mariana Islands | 1 670 | +10 |
| Puerto Rico | 1 787 | –4 |
| United States External Territories: | | |
| American Samoa | 684 | –11 |
| Guam | 1 671 | +10 |
| United States Virgin Islands | 1 340 | –4 |
| Uruguay | 598 | –3 |
| Uzbekistan | 998 | +5 |
| Vanuatu | 678 | +11 |
| Vatican City | 39 | +1 |
| Venezuela | 58 | –4 |
| Viet Nam | 84 | +7 |
| Yemen | 967 | +3 |
| Yugoslavia | 381 | +1 |
| Zambia | 260 | +2 |
| Zimbabwe | 263 | +2 |

* Time difference in hours + or – Greenwich Mean Time (GMT). The times listed compare the standard (winter) times. Some countries adopt Summer (Daylight Saving) Time — i.e. + 1 hour — for part of the year.

# LATE INFORMATION

**AFGHANISTAN** (p.363)

**Taliban Government Changes**
(March 2000)

**Minister of Education:** MOLA AMIR KHAN MOTAQI.

**Minister of Finance:** MOLA ABDOL WASAY AGHAJAN MOTASEM.

**Minister of Haj and Endowment Affairs:** Alhaj SAYD GHAYSODDIN AGHA.

**ALBANIA** (p.380)

**Government Changes**
(January 2000)

**Minister of the Public Economy and Privatization:** MUSTAFA MUCI.

**Minister of State in the Office of the President:** ILIR ZELA.

**ANTIGUA AND BARBUDA** (p. 438)

**Government Change**
(February 2000)

In mid-February 2000 the Minister of Labour, Home Affairs and Co-operatives, STEADROY BENJAMIN, assumed the Social Improvement portfolio from the Minister of Health, BERNARD PERCIVAL.

**ARGENTINA** (p. 456)

**Cámara de Diputados**
(Chamber of Deputies)
(December 1999)

**President:** RAFAEL MANUEL PASCUAL.

**Senado**
(Senate)
(December 1999)

**President:** CARLOS 'CHACHO' ALVAREZ.

**ARMENIA** (p.479)

**Government Changes**
(February 2000)

**Minister of Finance and the Economy:** LEVON BARKHOUDRIAN.

**Minister for Territorial Administration and Urban Development:** LEONID AKOPIAN.

**Minister of Health and Social Security:** ARARAT MKRTCHIAN.

**Minister of Agriculture and Ecology:** ZAVEN GEVORKIAN.

**Minister of Transport and Communications:** ROBERT NAZARIAN.

**Minister of State Property:** DAVID VARDANIAN.

**Chief of Staff of the Government and Senior Adviser to the Prime Minister:** SHAGEN KARAMANOUKIAN.

**BELARUS** (p.616)

On 14 March 2000 ULADZIMIR YERMOSHIN was confirmed as Chairman of the Cabinet of Ministers by 95 votes to one in the House of Representatives.

**Government Changes**
(March 2000)

**First Deputy Chairman:** ANDREY KABYAKOW.

**Chairman of the State Control Committee:** (vacant).

**BOLIVIA** (p. 694)

**Government Change**
(March 2000)

The Minister without Portfolio, responsible for Government Information, JOSÉ LANDÍVAR ROCA, presented his resignation.

**BOSNIA AND HERZEGOVINA** (p.716)

**Serb Republic Government Changes**
(February 2000)

**Deputy Prime Minister and Minister for War Veterans and Casualties, and Labour Affairs:** NENAD SUZIĆ.

**CANADA** (p. 871)

**Provincial Legislatures**
(February 2000)

**British Columbia**

**Premier:** UJJAL DOSANJH.

**CHILE** (p. 938)

**HEAD OF STATE**

**President:** RICARDO LAGOS ESCOBAR (officially inaugurated 10 March 2000).

**NEW CABINET**
(March 2000)

A coalition of parties represented in the Concertación de los Partidos de la Democracia (CPD), including the Partido Demócrata Cristiano (PDC), the Partido Socialista de Chile (PS), the Partido por la Democracia (PPD) and the Partido Radical Socialdemócrata (PRSD).

**Minister of Agriculture:** JAIME CAMPOS QUIROGA (PRSD).

**Minister of the Economy, Mining and Energy:** JOSÉ DE GREGORIO REVECO (PDC).

**Minister of Finance:** NICOLÁS EYZAGUIRRE GUZMÁN (PPD).

**Minister of Foreign Affairs:** SOLEDAD ALVEAR VALENZUELA (PDC).

**Minister of Housing and National Properties:** CLAUDIO ORREGO LARRAÍN (PDC).

**Minister of the Interior:** JOSÉ MIGUEL INSULZA SALINAS (PS).

**Minister of Justice:** JOSÉ ANTONIO GÓMEZ URRUTIA (PRSD).

**Minister of Labour and Social Security:** RICARDO SOLARI SAAVEDRA (PS).

**Minister of National Defence:** MARIO FERNÁNDEZ BAEZA (PDC).

**Minister of the National Women's Service (Senam):** ADRIANA DELPIANO PUELMA (PS).

**Minister of Planning and Co-operation (MIDEPLAN):** ALEJANDRA KRAUSS VALLE (PDC).

**Minister of Public Education:** MARIANA AYLWIN OYARZUN (PDC).

**Minister of Public Health:** MICHELLE BACHELET JERIA (PS).

**Minister of Public Works, Transport and Telecommunications:** CARLOS CRUZ LORENZEN (PPD).

**Minister, Secretary-General of Government:** CLAUDIO HUEPE GARCÍA (PDC).

**Minister, Secretary-General of the Presidency:** ALVARO GARCÍA HURTADO (PPD).

**CHINA (TAIWAN)** (p. 1035)

**President**

**Election, 18 March 2000***

| Candidate | Votes | % of Votes |
|---|---|---|
| CHEN SHUI-BIAN (Democratic Progressive Party—DPP) | 4,977,737 | 39.3 |
| JAMES SOONG (Independent) | 4,664,922 | 36.8 |
| LIEN CHAN (Kuomintang—KMT) | 2,925,513 | 23.1 |
| HSU HSIN-LIANG (Independent) | 79,429 | 0.6 |
| LI AO (Independent) | 16,782 | 0.1 |

* Results are provisional.

**THE DEMOCRATIC REPUBLIC OF THE CONGO** (p.1091)

**New Provincial Governor**
(December 1999)

**Equateur:** CHRISTIAN ELOKO BOTOLO.

**CÔTE D'IVOIRE** (p. 1135)

**Government Change**
(March 2000)

**Minister of Foreign Affairs:** CHARLES PROVIDENCE GOMIS.

## EL SALVADOR (p. 1345)

### Asamblea Nacional
(National Assembly)

**General Election, 12 March 2000**

| Party | Seats |
|---|---|
| Frente Farabundo Martí para la Liberación Nacional (FMLN) | 31 |
| Alianza Republicana Nacionalista (ARENA) | 29 |
| Partido de Conciliación Nacional (PCN) | 13 |
| Partido Demócrata Cristiano (PDC) | 6 |
| Centro Democrático Unido (CDU)* | 3 |
| Partido Acción Nacional (PAN) | 2 |
| **Total** | 84 |

* Electoral alliance comprising the Convergencia Democrática (CD) and the Partido Social Demócrata (PSD).

## THE GAMBIA (p.1552)

### Government Change
(March 2000)

**Secretary of State for Justice, Attorney-General:** PAP CHEYASSIN SECKA.

# PART ONE
# International Organizations

# THE UNITED NATIONS

**Address:** United Nations Plaza, New York, NY 10017, USA.

**Telephone:** (212) 963-1234; **fax:** (212) 963-4879; **internet:** www.un.org.

The United Nations was founded in 1945 to maintain international peace and security and to develop international co-operation in economic, social, cultural and humanitarian problems.

The United Nations was a name devised by President Franklin D. Roosevelt of the USA. It was first used in the Declaration by United Nations of 1 January 1942, when representatives of 26 nations pledged their governments to continue fighting together against the Axis powers.

The United Nations Charter (see p. 17) was drawn up by the representatives of 50 countries at the United Nations Conference on International Organization, which met at San Francisco from 25 April to 26 June 1945. The representatives deliberated on the basis of proposals put forward by representatives of China, the USSR, the United Kingdom and the USA at Dumbarton Oaks in August–October 1944. The Charter was signed on 26 June 1945. Poland, not represented at the Conference, signed it later but nevertheless became one of the original 51 members.

The United Nations officially came into existence on 24 October 1945, when the Charter had been ratified by China, France, the USSR, the United Kingdom and the USA, and by a majority of other signatories. United Nations Day is now celebrated annually on 24 October.

The UN's chief administrative officer is the Secretary-General, elected for a five-year term by the General Assembly on the recommendation of the Security Council. He acts in that capacity at all meetings of the General Assembly, the Security Council, the Economic and Social Council, and the Trusteeship Council, and performs such other functions as are entrusted to him by those organs. He is required to submit an annual report to the General Assembly and may bring to the attention of the Security Council any matter which, in his opinion, may threaten international peace.

**Secretary-General** (1997–2001): KOFI ANNAN (Ghana).

## Membership

### MEMBERS OF THE UNITED NATIONS

(with assessments for percentage contributions to the UN budget for 1998, and year of admission)

| Member | Assessment | Year |
|---|---|---|
| Afghanistan | 0.004 | 1946 |
| Albania | 0.003 | 1955 |
| Algeria | 0.116 | 1962 |
| Andorra | 0.004 | 1993 |
| Angola | 0.010 | 1976 |
| Antigua and Barbuda | 0.002 | 1981 |
| Argentina | 0.768 | 1945 |
| Armenia | 0.027 | 1992 |
| Australia | 1.471 | 1945 |
| Austria | 0.935 | 1955 |
| Azerbaijan | 0.060 | 1992 |
| Bahamas | 0.015 | 1973 |
| Bahrain | 0.018 | 1971 |
| Bangladesh | 0.010 | 1974 |
| Barbados | 0.008 | 1966 |
| Belarus[1] | 0.164 | 1945 |
| Belgium | 1.096 | 1945 |
| Belize | 0.001 | 1981 |
| Benin | 0.002 | 1960 |
| Bhutan | 0.001 | 1971 |
| Bolivia | 0.008 | 1945 |
| Bosnia and Herzegovina[2] | 0.005 | 1992 |
| Botswana | 0.010 | 1966 |
| Brazil | 1.514 | 1945 |
| Brunei | 0.020 | 1984 |
| Bulgaria | 0.045 | 1955 |
| Burkina Faso | 0.002 | 1960 |
| Burundi | 0.001 | 1962 |
| Cambodia | 0.001 | 1955 |
| Cameroon | 0.014 | 1960 |
| Canada | 2.825 | 1945 |
| Cape Verde | 0.001 | 1975 |
| Central African Republic | 0.002 | 1960 |
| Chad | 0.001 | 1960 |
| Chile | 0.113 | 1945 |
| China, People's Republic[3] | 0.901 | 1945 |
| Colombia | 0.108 | 1945 |
| Comoros | 0.001 | 1975 |
| Congo, Democratic Republic (formerly Zaire) | 0.008 | 1960 |
| Congo, Republic | 0.003 | 1960 |
| Costa Rica | 0.017 | 1945 |
| Côte d'Ivoire | 0.012 | 1960 |
| Croatia[2] | 0.056 | 1992 |
| Cuba | 0.039 | 1945 |
| Cyprus | 0.034 | 1960 |
| Czech Republic[4] | 0.169 | 1993 |
| Denmark | 0.687 | 1945 |
| Djibouti | 0.001 | 1977 |
| Dominica | 0.001 | 1978 |
| Dominican Republic | 0.016 | 1945 |
| Ecuador | 0.022 | 1945 |
| Egypt | 0.069 | 1945 |
| El Salvador | 0.012 | 1945 |
| Equatorial Guinea | 0.001 | 1968 |
| Eritrea | 0.001 | 1993 |
| Estonia | 0.023 | 1991 |
| Ethiopia | 0.007 | 1945 |
| Fiji | 0.004 | 1970 |
| Finland | 0.538 | 1955 |
| France | 6.494 | 1945 |
| Gabon | 0.018 | 1960 |
| The Gambia | 0.001 | 1965 |
| Georgia | 0.058 | 1992 |
| Germany | 9.630 | 1973 |
| Ghana | 0.007 | 1957 |
| Greece | 0.368 | 1945 |
| Grenada | 0.001 | 1974 |
| Guatemala | 0.019 | 1945 |
| Guinea | 0.003 | 1958 |
| Guinea-Bissau | 0.001 | 1974 |
| Guyana | 0.001 | 1966 |
| Haiti | 0.002 | 1945 |
| Honduras | 0.004 | 1945 |
| Hungary | 0.119 | 1955 |
| Iceland | 0.032 | 1946 |
| India | 0.305 | 1945 |
| Indonesia | 0.173 | 1950 |
| Iran | 0.303 | 1945 |
| Iraq | 0.087 | 1945 |
| Ireland | 0.223 | 1955 |
| Israel | 0.329 | 1949 |
| Italy | 5.394 | 1955 |
| Jamaica | 0.006 | 1962 |
| Japan | 17.981 | 1956 |
| Jordan | 0.008 | 1955 |
| Kazakhstan | 0.124 | 1992 |
| Kenya | 0.007 | 1963 |
| Kiribati | n.a. | 1999 |
| Korea, Democratic People's Republic | 0.031 | 1991 |
| Korea, Republic | 0.955 | 1991 |
| Kuwait | 0.154 | 1963 |
| Kyrgyzstan | 0.015 | 1992 |
| Laos | 0.001 | 1955 |
| Latvia | 0.046 | 1991 |
| Lebanon | 0.016 | 1945 |
| Lesotho | 0.002 | 1966 |
| Liberia | 0.002 | 1945 |
| Libya | 0.160 | 1955 |
| Liechtenstein | 0.005 | 1990 |
| Lithuania | 0.045 | 1991 |
| Luxembourg | 0.066 | 1945 |
| Macedonia, former Yugoslav republic[2] | 0.005 | 1993 |
| Madagascar | 0.003 | 1960 |
| Malawi | 0.002 | 1964 |
| Malaysia | 0.168 | 1957 |
| Maldives | 0.001 | 1965 |
| Mali | 0.003 | 1960 |
| Malta | 0.014 | 1964 |
| Marshall Islands | 0.001 | 1991 |
| Mauritania | 0.001 | 1961 |
| Mauritius | 0.009 | 1968 |
| Mexico | 0.941 | 1945 |
| Micronesia, Federated States | 0.001 | 1991 |
| Moldova | 0.043 | 1992 |
| Monaco | 0.003 | 1993 |
| Mongolia | 0.002 | 1961 |

| | | |
|---|---|---|
| Morocco | 0.041 | 1956 |
| Mozambique | 0.002 | 1975 |
| Myanmar | 0.009 | 1948 |
| Namibia | 0.007 | 1990 |
| Nauru | n.a. | 1999 |
| Nepal | 0.004 | 1955 |
| Netherlands | 1.619 | 1945 |
| New Zealand | 0.221 | 1945 |
| Nicaragua | 0.002 | 1945 |
| Niger | 0.002 | 1960 |
| Nigeria | 0.070 | 1960 |
| Norway | 0.605 | 1945 |
| Oman | 0.050 | 1971 |
| Pakistan | 0.060 | 1947 |
| Palau | 0.001 | 1994 |
| Panama | 0.016 | 1945 |
| Papua New Guinea | 0.007 | 1975 |
| Paraguay | 0.014 | 1945 |
| Peru | 0.085 | 1945 |
| Philippines | 0.077 | 1945 |
| Poland | 0.251 | 1945 |
| Portugal | 0.368 | 1955 |
| Qatar | 0.033 | 1971 |
| Romania | 0.102 | 1955 |
| Russia[5] | 2.873 | 1945 |
| Rwanda | 0.002 | 1962 |
| Saint Christopher and Nevis | 0.001 | 1983 |
| Saint Lucia | 0.001 | 1979 |
| Saint Vincent and the Grenadines | 0.001 | 1980 |
| Samoa (formerly Western Samoa) | 0.001 | 1976 |
| San Marino | 0.002 | 1992 |
| São Tomé and Príncipe | 0.001 | 1975 |
| Saudi Arabia | 0.594 | 1945 |
| Senegal | 0.006 | 1960 |
| Seychelles | 0.002 | 1976 |
| Sierra Leone | 0.001 | 1961 |
| Singapore | 0.167 | 1965 |
| Slovakia[4] | 0.053 | 1993 |
| Slovenia[2] | 0.060 | 1992 |
| Solomon Islands | 0.001 | 1978 |
| Somalia | 0.001 | 1960 |
| South Africa | 0.365 | 1945 |
| Spain | 2.571 | 1955 |
| Sri Lanka | 0.013 | 1955 |
| Sudan | 0.009 | 1956 |
| Suriname | 0.004 | 1975 |
| Swaziland | 0.002 | 1968 |
| Sweden | 1.099 | 1946 |
| Syria | 0.062 | 1945 |
| Tajikistan | 0.008 | 1992 |
| Tanzania[6] | 0.004 | 1961 |
| Thailand | 0.158 | 1946 |
| Togo | 0.002 | 1960 |
| Tonga | n.a. | 1999 |
| Trinidad and Tobago | 0.018 | 1962 |
| Tunisia | 0.028 | 1956 |
| Turkey | 0.440 | 1945 |
| Turkmenistan | 0.015 | 1992 |
| Uganda | 0.004 | 1962 |
| Ukraine[1] | 0.678 | 1945 |
| United Arab Emirates | 0.177 | 1971 |
| United Kingdom | 5.076 | 1945 |
| USA | 25.000 | 1945 |
| Uruguay | 0.049 | 1945 |
| Uzbekistan | 0.077 | 1992 |
| Vanuatu | 0.001 | 1981 |
| Venezuela | 0.235 | 1945 |
| Viet Nam | 0.010 | 1977 |
| Yemen[7] | 0.010 | 1947/67 |
| Yugoslavia[2] | 0.060 | 1945 |
| Zambia | 0.003 | 1964 |
| Zimbabwe | 0.009 | 1980 |

**Total Membership:** 188 (17 February 2000)

[1] Until December 1991 both Belarus and Ukraine were integral parts of the USSR and not independent countries, but had separate UN membership.

[2] Bosnia and Herzegovina, Croatia and Slovenia, previously republics within the Socialist Federal Republic of Yugoslavia, were each granted full UN membership in May 1992. Yugoslavia continued to exist (changing its official title to the Federal Republic of Yugoslavia in April 1992) but comprised only the two republics of Serbia and Montenegro. The remaining republic, Macedonia, declared itself a sovereign state in November 1991, and was admitted to the UN in April 1993 under the name of the former Yugoslav republic of Macedonia. In September 1992 the UN General Assembly voted to suspend Yugoslavia from participation in its proceedings until the new Yugoslav state had applied and been accepted to fill the seat in the UN occupied by the former Yugoslavia. Yugoslavia was still permitted, however, to participate in the work of UN organs other than Assembly bodies.

[3] From 1945 until 1971 the Chinese seat was occupied by the Republic of China (confined to Taiwan since 1949).

[4] Czechoslovakia, which had been a member of the UN since 1945, ceased to exist as a single state on 31 December 1992. In January 1993, as Czechoslovakia's legal successors, the Czech Republic and Slovakia were granted UN membership, and seats on subsidiary bodies that had previously been held by Czechoslovakia were divided between the two successor states.

[5] Russia assumed the USSR's seat in the General Assembly and its permanent seat on the Security Council (see p. 00) in December 1991, following the USSR's dissolution.

[6] Tanganyika was a member of the United Nations from December 1961 and Zanzibar was a member from December 1963. From April 1964 the United Republic of Tanganyika and Zanzibar continued as a single member, changing its name to United Republic of Tanzania in November 1964.

[7] The Yemen Arab Republic (admitted to the UN as Yemen in 1947) and the People's Democratic Republic of Yemen (admitted as Southern Yemen in 1967) merged to form the Republic of Yemen in May 1990.

### SOVEREIGN COUNTRIES NOT IN THE UNITED NATIONS

(17 February 2000)

China (Taiwan)
Switzerland
Tuvalu
Vatican City (Holy See)

Note: On 17 February 2000 the Security Council approved the admission to the UN of Tuvalu; the decision required official endorsement by the General Assembly.

# Diplomatic Representation

### MEMBER STATES' PERMANENT MISSIONS TO THE UNITED NATIONS

(with Permanent Representatives—December 1999)

**Afghanistan:** 360 Lexington Ave, 11th Floor, New York, NY 10017; tel. (212) 972-1212; fax (212) 972-1216; e-mail afgwatan@aol.com; Dr Ravan A. G. Farhâdi.

**Albania:** 320 East 79th St, New York, NY 10021; tel. (212) 249-2059; fax (212) 535-2917; e-mail albun@undp.org; Agim Nesho.

**Algeria:** 326 East 48th St, New York, NY 10017; tel. (212) 750-1960; fax (212) 759-9538; e-mail dzaun@undp.org; Abdallah Baali.

**Andorra:** 2 United Nations Plaza, 25th Floor, New York, NY 10017; tel. (212) 750-8064; fax (212) 750-6630; e-mail andorra@un.int; Juli Minoves Triquell.

**Angola:** 125 East 73rd St, New York, NY 10021; tel. (212) 861-5656; fax (212) 861-9295; Afonso van-Dúnem 'Mbinda'.

**Antigua and Barbuda:** 610 Fifth Ave, Suite 311, New York, NY 10020; tel. (212) 541-4117; fax (212) 757-1607; e-mail atgun@undp.org; Dr Patrick Albert Lewis.

**Argentina:** 1 United Nations Plaza, 25th Floor, New York, NY 10017; tel. (212) 688-6300; fax (212) 980-8395; e-mail argentina@un.int; Fernando Enrique Petrella.

**Armenia:** 119 East 36th St, New York, NY 10016; tel. (212) 686-9079; fax (212) 686-3934; e-mail armun@undp.org; Dr Movses Abelian.

**Australia:** 150 42nd St, 33rd Floor, New York, NY 10017; tel. (212) 351-6600; fax (212) 351-6610; e-mail australia@un.org; Penelope Anne Wensley.

**Austria:** 823 United Nations Plaza, 8th Floor, New York, NY 10017; tel. (212) 949-1840; fax (212) 953-1302; e-mail autun@undp.org; Dr Ernst Sucharipa.

**Azerbaijan:** 866 United Nations Plaza, Suite 560, New York, NY 10017; tel. (212) 371-2672; fax (212) 371-2784; e-mail azerbaijan@un.int; Eldar G. Kouliev.

**Bahamas:** 231 East 46th St, New York, NY 10017; tel. (212) 421-6925; fax (212) 759-2135; e-mail bsun@undp.org; Maurice Moore.

**Bahrain:** 2 United Nations Plaza, 25th Floor, New York, NY 10017; tel. (212) 223-6300; fax (212) 319-0687; e-mail bhrun@undp.org; Jassim Mohammed Buallay.

**Bangladesh:** 821 United Nations Plaza, 8th Floor, New York, NY 10017; tel. (212) 867-3434; fax (212) 972-4038; e-mail bangladesh@un.int; internet www.un.int/bangladesh; Anwarul Karim Chowdhury.

**Barbados:** 800 Second Ave, 2nd Floor, New York, NY 10017; tel. (212) 867-8431; fax (212) 986-1030; e-mail brbun@undp.org; June Yvonne Clarke.

**Belarus:** 136 East 67th St, New York, NY 10021; tel. (212) 535-3420; fax (212) 734-4810; e-mail blrun@undp.org; Alyaksandr N. Sychov.

**Belgium:** 823 United Nations Plaza, 4th Floor, New York, NY 10017; tel. (212) 378-6300; fax (212) 681-7618; e-mail belgium@un.int; internet www.un.int/belgium; ANDRÉ ADAM.

**Belize:** 800 Second Ave, Suite 400G, New York, NY 10017; tel. (212) 593-0999; fax (212) 593-0932; e-mail blzun@un.int; MICHAEL ANTHONY ASHCROFT.

**Benin:** 4 East 73rd St, New York, NY 10021; tel. (212) 249-6014; fax (212) 734-4735; e-mail benun@undp.org; JOËL WASSI ADECHI.

**Bhutan:** 2 United Nations Plaza, 27th Floor, New York, NY 10017; tel. (212) 826-1919; fax (212) 826-2998; e-mail pmbnewyork@aol.com; Lyonpo OM PRADHAN.

**Bolivia:** 211 East 43rd St, 8th Floor (Room 802), New York, NY 10017; tel. (212) 682-8132; fax (212) 682-8133; e-mail bolnu@aol.com; Dr ROBERTO JORDÁN-PANDO.

**Bosnia and Herzegovina:** 866 United Nations Plaza, Suite 580, New York, NY 10017; tel. (212) 751-9015; fax (212) 751-9019; e-mail bihnyun@aol.com; MUHAMED SACIRBEY.

**Botswana:** 103 East 37th St, New York, NY 10016; tel. (212) 889-2277; fax (212) 725-5061; e-mail bwaun@nywork2.undp.org; LEGWAILA JOSEPH LEGWAILA.

**Brazil:** 747 Third Ave, 9th Floor, New York, NY 10017; tel. (212) 372-2600; fax (212) 371-5716; e-mail braun@undp.org; GELSON FONSECA, Jr.

**Brunei:** 866 United Nations Plaza, Room 248, New York, NY 10017; tel. (212) 838-1600; fax (212) 980-6478; e-mail brun@undp.org; JEMAT Haji AMPAL.

**Bulgaria:** 11 East 84th St, New York, NY 10028; tel. (212) 737-4790; fax (212) 472-9865; e-mail bgrun@undp.org; Chargé d'affaires a.i. Dr VLADIMIR C. SOTIROV.

**Burkina Faso:** 115 East 73rd St, New York, NY 10021; tel. (212) 288-7515; fax (212) 772-3562; e-mail bfoun@undp.org; MICHEL KAFANDO.

**Burundi:** 336 East 45th St, 12th Floor, New York, NY 10017; tel. (212) 499-0001; fax (212) 499-0006; e-mail bdiun@undp.org; MARC NTETURUYE.

**Cambodia:** 866 United Nations Plaza, Suite 420, New York, NY 10017; tel. (212) 223-0676; fax (212) 223-0425; e-mail cambodia@un.int; BORITH OUCH.

**Cameroon:** 22 East 73rd St, New York, NY 10021; tel. (212) 794-2295; fax (212) 249-0533; MARTIN BELINGA EBOUTOU.

**Canada:** 1 Dag Hammarskjöld Plaza, 885 Second Ave, 14th Floor, New York, NY 10017; tel. (212) 848-1100; fax (212) 848-1195; e-mail canada@un.int; internet www.un.int/canada; ROBERT R. FOWLER.

**Cape Verde:** 27 East 69th St, New York, NY 10021; tel. (212) 472-0333; fax (212) 794-1398; e-mail cpvun@undp.org; JOSÉ LUIS BARBOSA LEÃO MONTEIRO.

**Central African Republic:** 386 Park Ave South, Suite 1114, New York, NY 10016; tel. (212) 679-8089; fax (212) 545-8326; ANTONIO DEINDE FERNANDEZ.

**Chad:** 211 East 43rd St, Suite 1703, New York, NY 10017; tel. (212) 986-0980; fax (212) 986-0152; e-mail tcdun@undp.org; AHMAT A. HAGGAR.

**Chile:** 3 Dag Hammarskjöld Plaza, 305 East 47th St, 10th/11th Floor, New York, NY 10017; tel. (212) 832-3323; fax (212) 832-8714; e-mail chile@un.int; JUAN LARRAÍN.

**China, People's Republic:** 350 East 35th St, New York, NY 10016; tel. (212) 655-6100; fax (212) 634-7626; e-mail chnun@undp.org; internet www.un.int/china; QIN HUASAN.

**Colombia:** 140 East 57th St, 5th Floor, New York, NY 10022; tel. (212) 355-7776; fax (212) 371-2813; e-mail colun@undp.org; ALFONSO VALDIVIESO.

**Comoros:** 420 East 50th St, New York, NY 10022; tel. (212) 972-8010; fax (212) 983-4712; e-mail comun@undp.org; Chargé d'affaires a.i. MAHMOUD MOHAMED ABOUD.

**Congo, Democratic Republic:** 866 United Nations Plaza, Suite 511, New York, NY 10017; tel. (212) 319-8061; fax (212) 319-8232; e-mail drcun@undp.org; ANDRÉ MWAMBA KAPANGA.

**Congo, Republic:** 14 East 65th St, New York, NY 10021; tel. (212) 744-7840; fax (212) 744-7975; BASILE IKOUEBE.

**Costa Rica:** 211 East 43rd St, Room 903, New York, NY 10017; tel. (212) 986-6373; fax (212) 986-6842; e-mail missioncr@aol.com; BERND NIEHAUS.

**Côte d'Ivoire:** 46 East 74th St, New York, NY 10021; tel. (212) 717-5555; fax (212) 717-4492; e-mail civun@undp.org; CLAUDE STANISLAS BOUAH-KAMON.

**Croatia:** 820 Second Ave, 19th Floor, New York, NY 10017; tel. (212) 986-1585; fax (212) 986-2011; Dr IVAN ŠIMONOVIĆ.

**Cuba:** 315 Lexington Ave and 38th St, New York, NY 10016; tel. (212) 689-7215; fax (212) 779-1697; e-mail cuba@un.int; BRUNO RODRÍGUEZ PARRILLA.

**Cyprus:** 13 East 40th St, New York, NY 10016; tel. (212) 481-6023; fax (212) 685-7316; e-mail cyprus@un.int; SOTIRIOS ZACKHEOS.

**Czech Republic:** 1109–1111 Madison Ave, New York, NY 10028; tel. (212) 535-8814; fax (212) 772-0586; e-mail czeun@undp.org; VLADIMÍR GALUŠKA.

**Denmark:** 1 Dag Hammarskjöld Plaza, 885 Second Ave, 18th Floor, New York, NY 10017; tel. (212) 308-7009; fax (212) 308-3384; e-mail denmark@un.int; JØRGEN BØJER.

**Djibouti:** 866 United Nations Plaza, Suite 4011, New York, NY 10017; tel. (212) 753-3163; fax (212) 223-1276; e-mail djiboutiun@aol.com; ROBLE OLHAYE.

**Dominica:** 800 Second Ave, Suite 400H, New York, NY 10017; tel. (212) 949-0853; fax (212) 808-4975; e-mail dmaun@undp.org; SIMON PAUL RICHARDS.

**Dominican Republic:** 144 East 44th St, 4th Floor, New York, NY 10017; tel. (212) 867-0833; fax (212) 986-4694; e-mail undomrep@aol.com; CRISTINA AGUIAR.

**Ecuador:** 866 United Nations Plaza, Room 516, New York, NY 10017; tel. (212) 935-1680; fax (212) 935-1835; e-mail ecuador@un.int; MARIO ALEMÁN.

**Egypt:** 304 East 44th St, New York, NY 10017; tel. (212) 503-0300; fax (212) 949-5999; e-mail egypt@un.int; AHMED ABOUL GHEIT.

**El Salvador:** 46 Park Ave, New York, NY 10016; tel. (212) 679-1616; fax (212) 725-7831; e-mail gbeneke@missions.un.org; Dr RICARDO G. CASTAÑEDA-CORNEJO.

**Equatorial Guinea:** 57 Magnolia Ave, Mount Vernon, NY 10553; tel. (914) 664-1882; fax (914) 667-6838; e-mail gnqun@undp.org; Pastor MICHA ONDO BILE.

**Eritrea:** 800 Second Ave, 18th Floor, New York, NY 10017; tel. (212) 687-3390; fax (212) 687-3138; e-mail eriun@undp.org; HAILE MENKERIOS.

**Estonia:** 600 Third Ave, 26th Floor, New York, NY 10016; tel. (212) 883-0640; fax (212) 883-0648; e-mail estun@undp.org; SVEN JÜRGENSON.

**Ethiopia:** 866 Second Ave, 3rd Floor, New York, NY 10017; tel. (212) 421-1830; fax (212) 754-0360; Dr DURI MOHAMMED.

**Fiji:** 630 Third Ave, 7th Floor, New York, NY 10017; tel. (212) 687-4130; fax (212) 687-3963; e-mail fiji@un.int; AMRAIYA NAIDU.

**Finland:** 866 United Nations Plaza, Suite 222, New York, NY 10017; tel. (212) 355-2100; fax (212) 759-6156; MARJATTA RASI.

**France:** 1 Dag Hammarskjöld Plaza, 245 East 47th St, 44th Floor, New York, NY 10017; tel. (212) 308-5700; fax (212) 421-6889; e-mail france@un.int; ALAIN DEJAMMET.

**Gabon:** 18 East 41st St, 9th Floor, New York, NY 10017; tel. (212) 686-9720; fax (212) 689-5769; DENIS DANGUE RÉWAKA.

**The Gambia:** 800 Second Ave, Suite 400F, New York, NY 10017; tel. (212) 949-6640; fax (212) 856-9820; e-mail gambia@un.int; BABOUCARR-BLAISE ISMAILA JAGNE.

**Georgia:** 1 United Nations Plaza, 26th Floor, New York, NY 10021; tel. (212) 759-1949; fax (212) 759-1832; e-mail geoun@undp.org; Dr PETER P. CHKHEIDZE.

**Germany:** 871 United Nations Plaza, New York, NY 10017; tel. (212) 940-0400; fax (212) 940-0402; e-mail germany@un.int; Prof. Dr DIETER KASTRUP.

**Ghana:** 19 East 47th St, New York, NY 10017; tel. (212) 832-1300; fax (212) 751-6743; e-mail ghana@un.int; Chargé d'affaires a.i. KOBINA SEKYI.

**Greece:** 866 Second Ave, New York, NY 10017; tel. (212) 888-6900; fax (212) 888-4440; e-mail greece@un.int; ELIAS GOUNARIS.

**Grenada:** 800 Second Ave, Suite 400K, New York, NY 10017; tel. (212) 599-0301; fax (212) 599-1540; e-mail grdun@undp.org; Dr LAMUEL A. STANISLAUS.

**Guatemala:** 57 Park Ave, New York, NY 10016; tel. (212) 679-4760; fax (212) 685-8741; e-mail guatemala@un.int; GERT ROSENTHAL.

**Guinea:** 140 East 39th St, New York, NY 10016; tel. (212) 687-8115; fax (212) 687-8248; MAHAWA BANGOURA CAMARA.

**Guinea-Bissau:** 211 East 43rd St, Room 604, New York, NY 10017; tel. (212) 338-9394; fax (212) 573-6094; e-mail gnbun@undp.org; Chargé d'affaires a.i. JOÃO SOARES.

**Guyana:** 866 United Nations Plaza, Suite 555, New York, NY 10017; tel. (212) 527-3232; fax (212) 935-7548; e-mail guyun@undp.org; SAMUEL R. INSANALLY.

**Haiti:** 801 Second Ave, Room 600, New York, NY 10017; tel. (212) 370-4840; fax (212) 661-8698; e-mail haiti@un.int; PIERRE LELONG.

**Honduras:** 866 United Nations Plaza, Suite 417, New York, NY 10017; tel. (212) 752-3370; fax (212) 223-0498; ANGEL EDMUNDO ORELLANA MERCADO.

**Hungary:** 227 East 52nd St, New York, NY 10022; tel. (212) 752-0209; fax (212) 755-5395; e-mail hungary@un.int; ANDRÉ ERDŐS.

**Iceland:** 800 Third Ave, 36th Floor, New York, NY 10017; tel. (212) 593-2700; fax (212) 593-6269; THORSTEINN INGÓLFSSON.

**India:** 235 East 43rd St, New York, NY 10017; tel. (212) 490-9660; fax (212) 490-9656; e-mail indiaun@mcimail.com; KAMALESH SHARMA.

**Indonesia:** 325 East 38th St, New York, NY 10016; tel. (212) 972-8333; fax (212) 972-9780; e-mail idnun@undp.org; MAKARIM WIBISONO.

**Iran:** 622 Third Ave, 34th Floor, New York, NY 10017; tel. (212) 687-2020; fax (212) 867-7086; e-mail iran@un.int; internet www.un.int; SEYED MOHAMMAD HADI NEJAD-HOSSEINIAN.

**Iraq:** 14 East 79th St, New York, NY 10021; tel. (212) 737-4433; fax (212) 772-1794; e-mail irqun@undp.org; Dr SAEED HASAN.

**Ireland:** 1 Dag Hammarskjöld Plaza, 885 Second Ave, 19th Floor, New York, NY 10017; tel. (212) 421-6934; fax (212) 752-4726; e-mail irlun@undp.org; RICHARD RYAN.

**Israel:** 800 Second Ave, New York, NY 10017; tel. (212) 499-5510; fax (212) 499-5515; e-mail isrun@undp.org; DORE GOLD.

**Italy:** 2 United Nations Plaza, 24th Floor, New York, NY 10017; tel. (212) 486-9191; fax (212) 486-1036; e-mail itaun@undp.org; FRANCESCO PAOLO FULCI.

**Jamaica:** 767 Third Ave, 9th Floor, New York, NY 10017; tel. (212) 935-7509; fax (212) 935-7607; e-mail jamun@undp.org; internet www.undp.org/missions/jamaica; PATRICIA DURRANT.

**Japan:** 866 United Nations Plaza, 2nd Floor, New York, NY 10017; tel. (212) 223-4300; fax (212) 751-1966; e-mail jpnun@undp.org; YUKIO SATO.

**Jordan:** 866 United Nations Plaza, 4th Floor, New York, NY 10017; tel. (212) 832-9553; fax (212) 832-5346; HASAN ABU-NIMAH.

**Kazakhstan:** 866 United Nations Plaza, Suite 586, New York, NY 10017; tel. (212) 230-1900; fax (212) 230-1172; e-mail kazun@nygate.undp.org; Chargé d'affaires a.i. YERZHAN KH. KAZYKHANOV.

**Kenya:** 866 United Nations Plaza, Room 486, New York, NY 10017; tel. (212) 421-4740; fax (212) 486-1985; e-mail kenun@undp.org; NJUGUNA M. MAHUGU.

**Korea, Democratic People's Republic:** 335 East 45th St, New York, NY 10017; tel. (212) 972-3105; fax (212) 972-3154; LI HYONG-CHOL.

**Korea, Republic:** 866 United Nations Plaza, Suite 300, New York, NY 10017; tel. (212) 371-1280; fax (212) 371-8873; e-mail korun@undp.org; LEE SEE-YOUNG.

**Kuwait:** 321 East 44th St, New York, NY 10017; tel. (212) 973-4300; fax (212) 370-1733; e-mail kwtun@undp.org; internet www.undp.org/missions/kuwait; MOHAMMAD A. ABULHASAN.

**Kyrgyzstan:** 866 United Nations Plaza, Suite 477, New York, NY 10017; tel. (212) 486-4214; fax (212) 486-5259; e-mail kyrgyzstan@un.int; ELMIRA IBRAIMOVA.

**Laos:** 317 East 51st St, New York, NY 10022; tel. (212) 832-2734; fax (212) 750-0039; e-mail laoun@undp.org; ALOUNKÈO KITTIKHOUN.

**Latvia:** 333 East 50h St, New York, NY 10022; tel. (212) 838-8877; fax (212) 838-8920; e-mail latun@undp.org; Dr JANIS PRIEDKALNS.

**Lebanon:** 866 United Nations Plaza, Room 531–533, New York, NY 10017; tel. (212) 355-5460; fax (212) 838-2819; e-mail lbnun@undp.org; Chargé d'affaires a.i. Dr HIGHAM HAMDAN.

**Lesotho:** 204 East 39th St, New York, NY 10016; tel. (212) 661-1690; fax (212) 682-4388; e-mail les@missions.un.org; PERCY METSING MANGOAELA.

**Liberia:** 820 Second Ave, 13th Floor, New York, NY 10017; tel. (212) 687-1033; fax (212) 687-1035; NEH DUKULY-TOLBERT.

**Libya:** 309-315 East 48th St, New York, NY 10017; tel. (212) 752-5775; fax (212) 593-4787; ABUZED O. DORDA.

**Liechtenstein:** 633 Third Avenue, 27th Floor, New York, NY 10017; tel. (212) 599-0220; fax (212) 599-0064; e-mail liechtenstein@un.int; CLAUDIA FRITSCHE.

**Lithuania:** 420 Fifth Ave, 3rd Floor, New York, NY 10018; tel. (212) 354-7820; fax (212) 354-7833; e-mail lithuania@un.int; Dr OSKARAS JUSYS.

**Luxembourg:** 17 Beekman Pl., New York, NY 10022; tel. (212) 935-3589; fax (212) 935-5896; e-mail luxembourg@un.int; HUBERT WURTH.

**Macedonia, former Yugoslav republic:** 866 United Nations Plaza, Suite 517, New York, NY 10017; tel. (212) 308-8504; fax (212) 308-8724; e-mail mkdun@undp.org; NASTE CALOVSKI.

**Madagascar:** 820 Second Ave, Suite 800, New York, NY 10017; tel. (212) 986-9491; fax (212) 986-6271; e-mail mdgun@undp.org; JEAN DELACROIX BAKONIARIVO.

**Malawi:** 600 Third Ave, 30th Floor, New York, NY 10016; tel. (212) 949-0180; fax (212) 599-5021; e-mail mwiun@undp.org; Prof. DAVID RUBADIRI.

**Malaysia:** 313 East 43rd St, New York, NY 10017; tel. (212) 986-6310; fax (212) 490-8576; e-mail mysun@undp.org; AGAM HASMY.

**Maldives:** 800 Second Ave, Suite 400E, New York, NY 10017; tel. (212) 599-6195; fax (212) 661-6405; e-mail mdvun@undp.org; HUSSAIN SHIHAB.

**Mali:** 111 East 69th St, New York, NY 10021; tel. (212) 737-4150; fax (212) 472-3778; MOCTAR OUANE.

**Malta:** 249 East 35th St, New York, NY 10016; tel. (212) 725-2345; fax (212) 779-7097; e-mail mltun@undp.org; WALTER BALZAN.

**Marshall Islands:** 800 Second Ave, 18th Floor, New York, NY 10017; tel. (212) 983-3040; fax (212) 983-3202; e-mail mhlun@undp.org; Chargé d'affaires a.i. JAKEO A. RELANG.

**Mauritania:** 211 East 43rd St, Suite 2000, New York, NY 10017; tel. (212) 986-7963; fax (212) 986-8419; e-mail mauritania@un.int; MAHFOUDH OULD DEDDACH.

**Mauritius:** 211 East 43rd St, 15th Floor, New York, NY 10017; tel. (212) 949-0190; fax (212) 697-3829; e-mail twwan@undp.org; ANUND PRIYAY NEEWOOR.

**Mexico:** 2 United Nations Plaza, 28th Floor, New York, NY 10017; tel. (212) 752-0220; fax (212) 688-8862; e-mail mexicoun@aol.com; MANUEL TELLO.

**Micronesia, Federated States:** 820 Second Ave, Suite 17A, New York, NY 10017; tel. (212) 697-8370; fax (212) 697-8295; e-mail fsmun@fsmgov.org; MASAO NAKAYAMA.

**Moldova:** 573-577 Third Ave, New York, NY 10016; tel. (212) 682-3523; fax (212) 682-6274; e-mail unmoldova@aol.com; Dr ION BOTNARU.

**Monaco:** 866 United Nations Plaza, Suite 520, New York, NY 10017; tel. (212) 832-0721; fax (212) 832-5358; e-mail mcoun@undp.org; JACQUES LOUIS BOISSON.

**Mongolia:** 6 East 77th St, New York, NY 10021; tel. (212) 861-9460; fax (212) 861-9464; e-mail mngun@nywork2.undp.org; JARGALSAIKHANY ENKHSAIKHAN.

**Morocco:** 866 Second Ave, 6th and 7th Floors, New York, NY 10017; tel. (212) 421-1580; fax (212) 980-1512; e-mail marun@undp.org; AHMED SNOUSSI.

**Mozambique:** 420 East 50th St, New York, NY 10022; tel. (212) 644-5965; fax (212) 644-5972; e-mail mozun@undp.org; CARLOS DOS SANTOS.

**Myanmar:** 10 East 77th St, New York, NY 10021; tel. (212) 535-1310; fax (212) 737-2421; e-mail mmrun@undp.org; WIN MRA.

**Namibia:** 135 East 36th St, New York, NY 10016; tel. (212) 685-2003; fax (212) 685-1561; e-mail namibia@un.int; MARTIN ANDJABA.

**Nepal:** 820 Second Ave, Suite 17B, New York, NY 10017; tel. (212) 370-3988; fax (212) 953-2038; e-mail nepal@un.int; NARENDRA BIKRAM SHAH.

**Netherlands:** 235 East 45th St, 16th Floor, New York, NY 10017; tel. (212) 697-5547; fax (212) 370-1954; e-mail nldun@undp.org; PETER VAN WALSUM.

**New Zealand:** 1 United Nations Plaza, 25th Floor, New York, NY 10017; tel. (212) 826-1960; fax (212) 758-0827; e-mail nz@un.int; internet www.missions.un.int/newzealand; MICHAEL JOHN POWLES.

**Nicaragua:** 820 Second Ave, 8th Floor, New York, NY 10017; tel. (212) 490-7997; fax (212) 286-0815; e-mail nicaragua@un.int; ALFONSO ORTEGA URBINA.

**Niger:** 417 East 50th St, New York, NY 10022; tel. (212) 421-3260; fax (212) 753-6931; OUSMANE MOUTARI.

**Nigeria:** 828 Second Ave, New York, NY 10017; tel. (212) 953-9130; fax (212) 697-1970; e-mail ngaun@undp.org; ARTHUR C. I. MBANEFO.

**Norway:** 825 Third Ave, 39th Floor, New York, NY 10022; tel. (212) 421-0280; fax (212) 688-0554; e-mail norun@undp.org; OLE PETER KOLBY.

**Oman:** 866 United Nations Plaza, Suite 540, New York, NY 10017; tel. (212) 355-3505; fax (212) 644-0070; e-mail omnun@undp.org; FUAD MUBARAK AL-HINAI.

**Pakistan:** 8 East 65th St, New York, NY 10021; tel. (212) 879-8600; fax (212) 744-7348; e-mail pakistan@undp.org; INAMUL HAQUE.

**Palau:** New York; e-mail plwun@undp.org.

**Panama:** 866 United Nations Plaza, Suite 4030, New York, NY 10017; tel. (212) 421-5420; fax (212) 421-2694; e-mail pan@missions.un.org; RAMÓN A. MORALES.

**Papua New Guinea:** 201 East 42nd St, Suite 405, New York, NY 10017; tel. (212) 832-0043; fax (212) 832-0918; e-mail png@un.int; PETER DICKSON DONIGI.

**Paraguay:** 211 East 43rd St, Suite 400, New York, NY 10017; tel. (212) 687-3490; fax (212) 818-1282; e-mail paraguay@un.int; Chargé d'affaires a.i. GENARO PAPPALARDO.

**Peru:** 820 Second Ave, Suite 1600, New York, NY 10017; tel. (212) 687-3336; fax (212) 972-6975; e-mail onuper@aol.com; FRANCISCO A. TUDELA.

**Philippines:** 556 Fifth Ave, 5th Floor, New York, NY 10036; tel. (212) 764-1300; fax (212) 840-8602; e-mail misunphi@idt.net; (vacant).

**Poland:** 9 East 66th St, New York, NY 10021; tel. (212) 744-2506; fax (212) 517-6771; e-mail polun@undp.org; EUGENIUSZ WYZNER.

**Portugal:** 866 Second Ave, 9th Floor, New York, NY 10017; tel. (212) 759-9444; fax (212) 355-1124; e-mail prtun@undp.org; internet www.undp.org/missions/portugal; ANTÓNIO MONTEIRO.

**Qatar:** 747 Third Ave, 22nd Floor, New York, NY 10017; tel. (212) 486-9335; fax (212) 758-4952; e-mail qatun@undp.org; Chargé d'affaires a.i. JAMAL NASSIR SULTAN AL-BADER.

**Romania:** 573–577 Third Ave, New York, NY 10016; tel. (212) 682-3273; fax (212) 682-9746; e-mail romun@undp.org; ION GORITA.

**Russia:** 136 East 67th St, New York, NY 10021; tel. (212) 861-4900; fax (212) 628-0252; e-mail rusun@undp.org; SERGEI V. LAVROV.

**Rwanda:** 124 East 39th St, New York, NY 10016; tel. (212) 679-9010; fax (212) 679-9133; e-mail rwaun@undp.org; JOSEPH W. MUTABOBA.

**Saint Christopher and Nevis:** 414 East 75th St, 5th Floor, New York, NY 10021; tel. (212) 535-1234; fax (212) 535-6854; e-mail sknmission@aol.com; Sir LEE MOORE.

**Saint Lucia:** 800 Second Ave, 9th Floor, New York, NY 10017; tel. (212) 697-9360; fax (212) 697-4993; e-mail slumission@aol.com; JULIAN ROBERT HUNTE.

**Saint Vincent and the Grenadines:** 801 Second Ave, 21st Floor, New York, NY 10017; tel. (212) 687-4490; fax (212) 949-5946; e-mail vctun@undp.org; DENNIE M. J. WILSON.

**Samoa:** 800 Second Ave, Suite 400D, New York, NY 10017; tel. (212) 599-6196; fax (212) 599-0797; e-mail samoa@un.int; TUILOMA NERONI SLADE.

**San Marino:** 327 East 50th St, New York, NY 10022; tel. (212) 751-1234; fax (212) 751-1436; e-mail smrun@undp.org; GIAN NICOLA FILIPPI BALESTRA.

**São Tomé and Príncipe:** 400 Park Ave, 7th Floor, New York, NY 10022; tel. (212) 317-0533; fax (212) 317-0580; e-mail stpun@undp.org; Chargé d'affaires a.i. DOMINGOS AUGUSTO FERREIRA.

**Saudi Arabia:** 405 Lexington Ave, 56th Floor, New York, NY 10017; tel. (212) 697-4830; fax (212) 983-4895; e-mail saudiarabia@un.int; FAWZI BIN ABDUL MAJEED SHOBOKSHI.

**Senegal:** 238 East 68th St, New York, NY 10021; tel. (212) 517-9030; fax (212) 517-3032; IBRA DEGUÈNE KA.

**Seychelles:** 800 Second Ave, Room 400C, New York, NY 10017; tel. (212) 972-1785; fax (212) 972-1786; CLAUDE MOREL.

**Sierra Leone:** 245 East 49th St, New York, NY 10017; tel. (212) 688-1656; fax (212) 688-4924; e-mail sierraleone@un.int; IBRAHIM M'BABA KAMARA.

**Singapore:** 231 East 51st St, New York, NY 10022; tel. (212) 826-0840; fax (212) 826-2964; e-mail sgpun@undp.org; KISHORE MAHBUBANI.

**Slovakia:** 866 United Nations Plaza, Suite 494, New York, NY 10017; tel. (212) 980-1558; fax (212) 980-3295; e-mail svkun@undp.org; PETER TOMKA.

**Slovenia:** 600 Third Ave, 24th Floor, New York, NY 10016; tel. (212) 370-3007; fax (212) 370-1824; e-mail slovenia@un.int; (vacant).

**Solomon Islands:** 800 Second Ave, Suite 400L, New York, NY 10017; tel. (212) 599-6193; fax (212) 661-8925; e-mail simny@solomons.com; REX STEPHEN HOROI.

**Somalia:** 425 East 61st St, Suite 702, New York, NY 10021; tel. (212) 688-9410; fax (212) 759-0651; e-mail somun@undp.org; Chargé d'affaires a.i. FATUN MUHAMMAD HASSAN.

**South Africa:** 333 East 38th St, 9th Floor, New York, NY 10016; tel. (212) 213-5583; fax (212) 692-2498; e-mail soafun@undp.org; DUMISANA SHADRACK KUMALO.

**Spain:** 823 United Nations Plaza, 9th Floor, New York, NY 10017; tel. (212) 661-1050; fax (212) 949-7247; e-mail spain@un.int; internet www.spainun.org; INOCENCIO F. ARIAS.

**Sri Lanka:** 630 Third Ave, 20th Floor, New York, NY 10017; tel. (212) 986-7040; fax (212) 986-1838; e-mail srilanka@un.int; JOHN DE SARAM.

**Sudan:** 655 Third Ave, Suite 500-510, New York, NY 10017; tel. (212) 573-6033; fax (212) 573-6160; e-mail sdnun@undp.org; ELFATIH MOHAMED AHMED ERWA.

**Suriname:** 866 United Nations Plaza, Suite 320, New York, NY 10017; tel. (212) 826-0660; fax (212) 980-7029; e-mail surun@undp.org; SUBHAS CHANDRA MUNGRA.

**Swaziland:** 408 East 50th St, New York, NY 10022; tel. (212) 371-8910; fax (212) 754-2755; e-mail swzun@undp.org; MOSES MATHENDELE DLAMINI.

**Sweden:** 1 Dag Hammarskjöld Plaza, 885 Second Ave, 46th Floor, New York, NY 10017; tel. (212) 583-2500; fax (212) 832-0389; e-mail sweun@undp.org; internet www.undp.org/missions/sweden; HANS DAHLGREN.

**Syria:** 820 Second Ave, 15th Floor, New York, NY 10017; tel. (212) 661-1313; fax (212) 983-4439; e-mail syrun@undp.org; Dr MIKHAIL WEHBE.

**Tajikistan:** 136 East 67th St, New York, NY 10021; tel. (212) 744-2196; fax (212) 472-7645; e-mail tjkun@undp.org; RASHID ALIMOV.

**Tanzania:** 205 East 42nd St, 13th Floor, New York, NY 10017; tel. (212) 972-9160; fax (212) 682-5232; e-mail tzrepny@aol.com; DAUDI NGELAUTWA MWAKAWAGO.

**Thailand:** 351 East 52nd St, New York, NY 10022; tel. (212) 754-2230; fax (212) 754-2535; e-mail thaun@undp.org; ASDA JAYANAMA.

**Togo:** 112 East 40th St, New York, NY 10016; tel. (212) 490-3455; fax (212) 983-6684; e-mail togoun@undp.org; ROLAND YAO KPOTSRA.

**Trinidad and Tobago:** 820 Second Ave, 5th Floor, New York, NY 10017; tel. (212) 697-7620; fax (212) 682-3580; e-mail ttoun@undp.org; GEORGE W. MCKENZIE.

**Tunisia:** 31 Beekman Pl., New York, NY 10022; tel. (212) 751-7503; fax (212) 751-0569; e-mail tunun@undp.org; ALI HACHANI.

**Turkey:** 821 United Nations Plaza, 11th Floor, New York, NY 10017; tel. (212) 949-0150; fax (212) 949-0086; e-mail turkun@aol.com; VOLKAN VURAL.

**Turkmenistan:** 866 United Nations Plaza, Suite 424, New York, NY 10021; tel. (212) 486-8908; fax (212) 486-2521; AKSOLTAN T. ATAEVA.

**Uganda:** 336 East 45th St, New York, NY 10017; tel. (212) 949-0110; fax (212) 687-4517; e-mail ugaun@undp.org; Prof. MATIA MULAMBA SEMAKULA KIWANUKA.

**Ukraine:** 220 East 51st St, New York, NY 10022; tel. (212) 759-7003; fax (212) 355-9455; e-mail ukrun@undp.org; VOLODYMYR YELCHENKO.

**United Arab Emirates:** 747 Third Ave, 36th Floor, New York, NY 10017; tel. (212) 371-0480; fax (212) 371-4923; MOHAMMAD JASIM SAMHAN.

**United Kingdom:** 1 Dag Hammarskjöld Plaza, 885 2nd Ave, New York, NY 10017; tel. (212) 745-9200; fax (212) 745-9316; e-mail uk@un.int; Sir JEREMY GREENSTOCK.

**USA:** 799 United Nations Plaza, New York, NY 10017; tel. (212) 415-4000; fax (212) 415-4443; e-mail usaun@undp.org; RICHARD C. HOLBROOKE.

**Uruguay:** 747 Third Ave, 21st Floor, New York, NY 10017; tel. (212) 752-8240; fax (212) 593-0935; e-mail uruguay@un.int; JORGE PÉREZ-OTERMIN.

**Uzbekistan:** 866 United Nations Plaza, Suite 326, New York, NY 10017; tel. (212) 486-4242; fax (212) 486-7998; e-mail uzbun@undp.org; ALISHER VOHIDOV.

**Vanuatu:** 866 United Nations Plaza, 3rd Floor, New York, NY 10017; tel. (212) 593-0144; fax (212) 593-0219; e-mail vutun@undp.org; Chargé d'affaires a.i. SELWYN ARUTANGAI.

**Venezuela:** 335 East 46th St, New York, NY 10017; tel. (212) 557-2055; fax (212) 557-3528; e-mail venun@undp.org; IGNACIO ARCAYA.

**Viet Nam:** 866 United Nations Plaza, Suite 435, New York, NY 10017; tel. (212) 644-0594; fax (212) 644-5732; e-mail vietnamun@aol.com; NGO QUANG XUAN.

**Yemen:** 413 East 51st St, New York, NY 10022; tel. (212) 355-1730; fax (212) 750-9613; e-mail yemun@undp.org; ABDALLA SALEH AL-ASHTAL.

**Yugoslavia:** 854 Fifth Ave, New York, NY 10021; tel. (212) 879-8700; fax (212) 879-8705; e-mail yugun@undp.org; Chargé d'affaires a.i. VLADISLAV JOVANOVIĆ.

**Zambia:** 800 Second Ave, 9th Floor, New York, NY 10017; tel. (212) 972-7200; fax (212) 972-7360; e-mail zmbun@undp.org; PETER LESA KASANDA.

**Zimbabwe:** 128 East 56th St, New York, NY 10022; tel. (212) 980-9511; fax (212) 308-6705; T. J. B. JOKONYA.

## OBSERVERS

Non-member states, inter-governmental organizations, etc., which have received an invitation to participate in the sessions and the work of the General Assembly as Observers, maintaining permanent offices at the UN.

### Non-member states

**Holy See:** 25 East 39th St, New York, NY 10016; tel. (212) 370-7885; fax (212) 370-9622; e-mail hsmission@holyseemission.org; Most Rev. RENATO RAFFAELE MARTINO, Titular Archbishop of Segermes.

**Switzerland:** 633 Third Ave, 29th Floor, New York, NY 10017; tel. (212) 286-1540; fax (212) 286-1555; e-mail vertretung-un@nyc.rep.admin.ch.

### Inter-governmental organizations*

**Asian-African Legal Consultative Committee:** 404 East 66th St, Apt 12c, New York, NY 10021; tel. (212) 734-7608; e-mail 102077.27512@compuserve.com; K. Bhagwat-Singh.

**Caribbean Community:** 97-40 62nd Drive, 15K, Rego Park, NY 11374–1336; tel. and fax (718) 896-1179; Hamid Mohammed.

**Commonwealth Secretariat:** 800 Second Ave, 4th Floor, New York, NY 10017; tel. (212) 599-6190; fax (212) 972-3970; e-mail chogrm@aol.com.

**European Union:** Delegation of the European Commission, 3 Dag Hammarskjöld Plaza, 12th Floor, 305 East 47th St, New York, NY 10017; tel. (212) 371-3804; fax (212) 758-2718; e-mail bneven@usany.eudel.com; Liaison Office of the General Secretariat of the Council of Ministers of the European Union, 345 East 46th St, 6th Floor, New York, NY 10017; tel. (212) 292-8600; fax (212) 681-6266; the Observer is the Permanent Representative to the UN of the country currently exercising the Presidency of the Council of Ministers of the European Union.

**La Francophonie:** 801 Second Ave, Suite 605, New York, NY 10017; tel. (212) 867-6771; fax (212) 867-3840; e-mail ny-acct@iamdigex.net; Ridha Bouabid.

**International Organization for Migration:** 122 East 42nd St, Suite 1610, New York, NY 10168; tel. (212) 681-7000; fax (212) 867-5887; e-mail unobserver@iom.int; Robert G. Paiva.

**International Seabed Authority:** 1 United Nations Plaza, Room 1140, New York, NY 10017; tel. (212) 963-6470; fax (212) 963-0908.

**International Tribunal for the Law of the Sea:** 1 United Nations Plaza, Room 1140, New York, NY 10017, tel. (212) 963-6480; fax (212) 963-0908.

**Latin American Economic System:** 820 Second Ave, Suite 1601, New York, NY 10017; tel. (212) 972-1096; fax (212) 922-1683; Allan Wagner.

**League of Arab States:** 747 Third Ave, 35th Floor, New York, NY 10017; tel. (212) 838-8700; fax (212) 355-3909; Dr Hussein A. Hassouna.

**Organization of African Unity:** 346 East 50th St, New York, NY 10022; tel. (212) 319-5490; fax (212) 319-7135; Amadou Kébé.

**Organization of the Islamic Conference:** 130 East 40th St, 5th Floor, New York, NY 10016; tel. (212) 883-0140; fax (212) 883-0143; e-mail oicun@undp.org; Mokhtar Lamani.

* The following inter-governmental organizations have a standing invitation to participate as Observers, but do not maintain permanent offices at the United Nations:

African, Caribbean and Pacific Group of States
African Development Bank
Agency for the Prohibition of Nuclear Weapons in Latin America and the Caribbean
Andean Community
Association of Caribbean States
Central American Integration System
Commonwealth of Independent States
Council of Europe
Economic Co-operation Organization
International Criminal Police Organization (Interpol)
Latin American Economic System
Latin American Parliament
Organisation for Economic Co-operation and Development
Organization for Security and Co-operation in Europe
Organization of American States
Permanent Court of Arbitration
South Pacific Forum

### Other observers

**International Committee of the Red Cross:** 801 Second Ave, 18th Floor, New York, NY 10017; tel. (212) 599-6021; fax (212) 599-6009; e-mail mail@icrc.delnyc.org; Sylvie Junod.

**International Federation of Red Cross and Red Crescent Societies:** 630 Third Ave, Suite 2104, New York, NY 10017; tel. (212) 338-0161; fax (212) 338-9832; e-mail ifrcny@nygate.undp.org; Entcho Gospodinov.

**Palestine:** 115 East 65th St, New York, NY 10021; tel. (212) 288-8500; fax (212) 517-2377; e-mail mission@palestine-un.org; Dr Nasser al-Kidwa.

**Sovereign Military Order of Malta:** 416 East 47th St, 8th Floor, New York, NY 10017; tel. (212) 355-6213; fax (212) 355-4014; e-mail smom@tiac.com; José Antonio Linati-Bosch.

# United Nations Information Centres/Services

**Afghanistan:** (temporarily inactive).

**Algeria:** 9a rue Emile Payen, Hydra, Algiers; tel. (2) 744902; fax (2) 748505.

**Argentina:** Junín 1940, 1°, 1113 Buenos Aires; tel. (1) 803-7671; fax (1) 804-7545; e-mail buenosaires@ccmail.unicc.org (also covers Uruguay).

**Australia:** POB 4045, 46-48 York St, 5th Floor, Sydney, NSW 2001; tel. (2) 9262-5111; fax (2) 9262-5886; e-mail unsyd@ozemail.com.au (also covers Fiji, Kiribati, Nauru, New Zealand, Samoa, Tonga, Tuvalu and Vanuatu).

**Austria:** POB 500, Vienna International Centre, 1400 Vienna; tel. (1) 26060-4266; fax (1) 26060-5899; e-mail unis@unov.un.or.at (also covers Hungary, Slovakia and Slovenia).

**Bahrain:** POB 26004, Villa 131, Rd 2803, Segaya, Manama (also covers Qatar and the United Arab Emirates).

**Bangladesh:** POB 3658, House 60, Rd 11A, Dhanmondi, Dhaka 1209; tel. (2) 818600; fax (2) 812343.

**Belgium:** 40 ave de Broqueville, 1200 Brussels; tel. (2) 289-28-90; e-mail unicbel@mbox.unicc.org (also covers Luxembourg and the Netherlands).

**Bolivia:** Apdo 9072, Avda Mariscal, Santa Cruz No. 1350, La Paz; tel. (2) 358590; fax (2) 391368; e-mail unicbol@cos.pnud.bo.

**Brazil:** Palacio Itamaraty, Avda Marechal Floriano 196, 20080-002 Rio de Janeiro; tel. (21) 253-2211; fax (21) 233-5753; e-mail nacoes.unidas@openlink.com.br.

**Burkina Faso:** PB 135, ave Georges Konseiga, Secteur no 4, Ouagadougou; tel. (3) 306076; fax (3) 311322 (also covers Chad, Mali and Niger).

**Burundi:** PB 2160, ave de la Révolution 117, Bujumbura; tel. (2) 25018; fax (2) 25850.

**Cameroon:** PB 836, Immeuble Kamdem, rue Joseph Clère, Yaoundé; tel. 22-50-43; fax 23-51-73 (also covers the Central African Republic and Gabon).

**Chile:** Edif. Naciones Unidas, Avda Dag Hammarskjöld, Casilla 179-D, Santiago; tel. (2) 210-2000; fax (2) 208-1946; e-mail dpisantiago@eclac.cl.

**Colombia:** Apdo Aéreo 058964; Calle 100, No. 8a–55, Of. 815, Santafé de Bogotá 2; tel. (1) 257-6044; fax (1) 257-6244; e-mail santafe@ccmail.unicc.org (also covers Ecuador and Venezuela).

**Congo, Democratic Republic:** PB 7248, Batîment Deuxième République, blvd du 30 juin, Kinshasa; tel. (12) 33431; fax (871) 150-3261.

**Congo, Republic:** POB 13210, ave Foch, Case ORTF 15, Brazzaville; tel. 835090; fax 836140.

**Czech Republic:** Panská 5, 110 00 Prague 1; e-mail unicprg@terminal.cz; internet www.unicprague.cz.

**Denmark:** Midtermolen 3, 2100 Copenhagen Ø; tel. 35-46-73-00; fax 35-46-73-01; e-mail unic@un.dk; internet www.un.dk (also covers Finland, Iceland, Norway and Sweden).

**Egypt:** POB 982, World Trade Centre, 1191 Corniche El Nil, Boulak, Cairo; tel. (2) 769595; fax (2) 769393 (also covers Saudi Arabia).

**El Salvador:** (temporarily inactive).

**Ethiopia:** POB 3001, Africa Hall, Addis Ababa; tel. (1) 510172; fax (1) 516027.

**France:** 1 rue Miollis, 75732 Paris Cédex 15; tel. 1-45-68-10-00; fax 1-43-06-46-78.

**Germany:** 53175 Bonn, Haus Cartanjen, Martin-Luther-King-Str. 8; 53153 Bonn; tel. (228) 815-2770; fax (228) 815-2777; e-mail unic@uno.de; internet www.uno.de.

**Ghana:** POB 2339, Gamel Abdul Nassar/Liberia Roads, Accra; tel. (21) 666851; fax (21) 665578 (also covers Sierra Leone).

**Greece:** 36 Amalia Ave, 105 58; Athens; tel. (1) 5230640; fax (1) 5233639; e-mail athens@ccmail.unicc.org (also covers Cyprus and Israel).

**India:** 55 Lodi Estate, New Delhi 110 003; tel. (11) 462-3439; fax (11) 462-0293 (also covers Bhutan).

**Indonesia:** Gedung Dewan Pers, 5th Floor, 32–34 Jalan Kebon Sirih, Jakarta; tel. (21) 3800292; fax (21) 3800274.

**Iran:** POB 15875-4557; 185 Ghaem Magham Farahani Ave, Teheran 15868; tel. (21) 873-1534; fax (21) 204-4523.

**Italy:** Palazzetto Venezia, Piazza San Marco 50, 00186 Rome; tel. (06) 6785907; fax (06) 6789907; fax (06) 6997337; e-mail dpi-roma-cc@un.org (also covers the Holy See, Malta and San Marino).

**Japan:** UNU Bldg, 8th Floor, 53-70 Jingumae S-chome, Shibuya-ku, Tokyo 150 0001; tel. (3) 5467-4451; fax (3) 5467-4455; e-mail unictok@orange.ifnet.or.jp (also covers Palau).

**Kenya:** POB 30552, United Nations Office, Gigiri, Nairobi; tel. (2) 623292; fax (2) 624349 (also covers Seychelles and Uganda).

**Lebanon:** Riad es-Solh Sq., POB 4656, Chouran, Beirut; tel. (1) 981301; fax (1) 740230 (also covers Jordan, Kuwait and Syria).

**Lesotho:** POB 301; Letsie Rd, Food Aid Compound, behind Hotel Victoria, Maseru 100; tel. 312496; fax 310042.

**Libya:** POB 286, Shara Muzzafar al-Aftas, Hay al-Andalous, Tripoli; tel. (21) 4777885; fax (21) 4777343 .

**Madagascar:** PB 1348, 22 rue Rainitovo, Antasahavola, Antananarivo; tel. (2) 24115; fax (2) 33315.

**Mexico:** Presidente Masaryk 29, 6°, México 11 570, DF; tel. (5) 250-1364; fax (5) 203-8638; e-mail dpi-mexico@un.org (also covers Cuba and the Dominican Republic).

**Morocco:** PB 601, zankat Tarik Ibnou Zind (Angle rue Roudana) 6, Rabat; tel. (77) 686-33; fax (77) 683-77; e-mail unicmor@mbox .unicc.org.

**Myanmar:** POB 230, 6 Natmauk Rd, Yangon; tel. (1) 292619; fax (1) 292911.

**Namibia:** Private Bag 13351, Paratus Bldg, 372 Independence Ave, Windhoek; tel. (61) 233034; fax (61) 233036; e-mail unic@un.na.

**Nepal:** POB 107, UN House, Kathmandu; tel. (1) 524366; fax (1) 523991.

**Nicaragua:** Apdo 3260, Palacio de la Cultura, Managua; tel. (2) 664253; fax (2) 222362.

**Nigeria:** POB 1068, 17 Kingsway Rd, Ikoyi, Lagos; tel. 269-4886; fax (1) 269-934; e-mail uniclag@unic.org.ng.

**Pakistan:** POB 1107, House No. 26, 88th St, G-6/3, Islamabad; tel. (51) 270610; fax (51) 271856.

**Panama:** POB 6-9083, El Dorado; Banco Central Hispano Edif., Calle Gerardo Ortega y Av. Samuel Lewis, Panama City; tel. (7) 233-0557; fax (7) 223-2198; e-mail cinup@sinfo.net.

**Paraguay:** Casilla de Correo 1107, Edif. City, 3°, Asunción; tel. (21) 493025; fax (21) 449611; e-mail unic@undp.org.py.

**Peru:** POB 14-0199, Lord Cochrane 130, San Isidro, Lima 27; tel. (1) 441-8745; fax (1) 441-8735; e-mail lima@ccmail.unicc.org.

**Philippines:** NEDA Bldg, Ground Floor, 106 Amorsolo St, Legaspi Village, Makati City, Manila; tel. (2) 8920611; fax (2) 8163011 (also covers Papua New Guinea and Solomon Islands).

**Poland:** 00-608 Warsaw, Al. Niepodległości 186; 02-514 Warsaw, POB 1; tel. (22) 8259245; fax (22) 8255785; e-mail registry.pl@ undp.org.

**Portugal:** Rua Latino Coelho No. 1, Edif. Aviz, Bloco A1, 10°, 1000 Lisbon; tel. (1) 319-0790; fax (1) 352-0559; e-mail lisbon@ccmail.unicc .org.

**Romania:** POB 1-701, 16 Aurel Vlaic St, Bucharest; tel. (1) 2113242; fax (1) 2113506; e-mail fo.rom@undp.org.

**Russia:** 4/16 Glazovsky Per., Moscow; tel. (095) 241-2894; fax (095) 230-2138; e-mail dpi-moscow@un.org.

**Senegal:** PB 154, Immeuble UNESCO, 12 ave Roume, Dakar; tel. 823-30-70; fax 822-26-79 (also covers Cape Verde, Côte d'Ivoire, The Gambia, Guinea, Guinea-Bissau and Mauritania).

**South Africa:** Metro Park Bldg, 351 Schoeman St, POB 12677, Pretoria 0126; tel. (12) 320-1110; fax (12) 320-1122.

**Spain:** Avda General Perón 32-1°, 28020 Madrid; tel. (91) 5558087; fax (91) 5971231; e-mail madrid@ccmail.unicc.org.

**Sri Lanka:** POB 1505, 202–204 Bauddhaloka Mawatha, Colombo 7; tel. (1) 580691; fax (1) 581116.

**Sudan:** POB 913, UN Compound, Gamma'a Ave, Khartoum; tel. (11) 777816; fax (871) 1516741 (also covers Somalia).

**Switzerland:** Palais des Nations, 1211 Geneva 10; tel. (22) 917-2300, fax (22) 917-0030; e-mail dpi_geneva@unog.ch; internet www.unog.ch.

**Tanzania:** POB 9224, Old Boma Bldg, Morogoro Rd/Sokoine Drive, Dar es Salaam; tel. (51) 119510; fax (51) 112923; e-mail unic.urt@ raha.com.

**Thailand:** ESCAP, United Nations Bldg, Rajdamnern Ave, Bangkok 10200; tel. (2) 288-1866; fax (2) 288-1052 (also covers Cambodia, Hong Kong, Laos, Malaysia, Singapore and Viet Nam).

**Togo:** PB 911, 107 blvd du 13 janvier, Lomé; tel. and fax 212306 (also covers Benin).

**Trinidad and Tobago:** POB 130, Bretton Hall, 16 Victoria Ave, Port of Spain; tel. 623-4813; fax 623-4332; e-mail dpi-porspa@un.org (also covers Antigua and Barbuda, the Bahamas, Barbados, Belize, Dominica, Grenada, Guyana, Jamaica, the Netherlands Antilles, Saint Christopher and Nevis, Saint Lucia, Saint Vincent and the Grenadines and Suriname).

**Tunisia:** PB 863, 61 blvd Bab-Benat, Tunis; tel. (1) 560-203; fax (1) 568-811.

**Turkey:** PK 407, 197 Atatürk Bulvarı, Ankara; tel. (312) 4268113; fax (312) 4689719; e-mail unic@un.org.tr.

**United Kingdom:** Millbank Tower, 21st Floor, 21-24 Millbank, London, SW1P 4QH; tel. (2) 7630-1981; fax (2) 7976-6478; e-mail info@uniclondon.org (also covers Ireland).

**USA:** 1775 K St, NW, Washington, DC 20006; tel. (202) 331-8670; fax (202) 331-9191; e-mail dpi-washington@un.org.

**Yemen:** POB 237, Handhal St, 4 Al-Boniya Arca, San'a; tel. (1) 274000; fax (1) 274043; e-mail unicyem@ynet.ye.

**Zambia:** POB 32905, Lusaka 10101; tel. (1) 228487; fax (1) 222958 (also covers Botswana, Malawi and Swaziland).

**Zimbabwe:** POB 4408, Sanders House, 2nd Floor, First St/Jason Moyo Ave, Harare; tel. (4) 777060; fax (4) 750476.

### OTHER UNITED NATIONS OFFICES

**Armenia:** 375001 Yerevan, 14 Karl Libknekht St, 1st Floor; tel. and fax (2) 15-16-47.

**Azerbaijan:** Baku, 3 Isteglialiyat St; tel. and fax (12) 98-32-35.

**Belarus:** 220050 Minsk, 17 Kirov St, 6th Floor; tel. 2278149; fax 22260340; e-mail un_undp@un.minsk.by.

**Eritrea:** POB 5366, Andinet St, Zone 4 Admin. 07, Airport Rd, Asmara; tel. (1) 182166; fax (1) 182573.

**Georgia:** 380079 Tbilisi, Eristavi St 9; tel. (32) 998558; fax (32) 250271; e-mail registry.ge@undp.org.ge; internet www.undp.org.ge.

**Kazakhstan:** 480100 Almaty, c/o KIMEP, 4 Abai Ave; tel. (3272) 64-26-18; fax (3272) 64-26-08; e-mail vp@un.almaty.kz.

**Ukraine:** 252020 Kiev, 6 Klovsky Uzviz, 1; tel. (44) 293-34-12; fax (44) 293-26-07; e-mail fo.ukr@undp.org.

**Uzbekistan:** 700029 Tashkent, 4 Taras Shevchenko St; tel. (371) 139-48-35; fax (371) 120-62-91; e-mail fouzb@fouzb.undp.org; internet www.undp.uz.

## Finance

The majority of the UN's peace-keeping operations (q.v.) are financed separately from the UN's regular budget by assessed contributions from member states.

In recent years the UN has suffered financial difficulties, owing to an expansion of the UN's political and humanitarian activities and delay on the part of member states in paying their contributions. In 1993 the UN Secretary-General formulated a series of economy measures to be applied throughout the organization, in order to avert a financial crisis. However, the fragility of the organization's financial situation persisted, partly owing to delays in the process between approval of a peace-keeping operation and receipt of contributions for that budget. In 1997 a US business executive announced a donation of US $1,000m., to be paid in regular instalments over a 10-year period, to finance humanitarian and environmental programmes. A UN International Partnership Trust Fund was established to administer the donation. At 30 September 1999 members owed the UN some $2,510m., of which $644m. was for the regular budget, $1,831m. for peace-keeping operations and $35m. for international tribunals. Almost two-thirds of the unpaid contributions was owed by the USA.

In 1997 the UN Secretary-General pledged to implement administrative reforms of the UN and to reduce the organization's budget. The budget for the two-year period 1998–99 amounted to US $2,532m., compared with the 1996–97 total of $2,712m. (later revised to $2,542m.). The Secretary-General's reform programme included a proposal to establish a Development Account, through which administrative savings could be used to finance development projects. The Account was established by the General Assembly in December.

**TWO-YEAR BUDGET OF THE UNITED NATIONS (US $'000)**

| | 1998-99* |
|---|---|
| Overall policy-making, direction and co-ordination | 478,283.7 |
| Political affairs | 206,100.1 |
| International justice and law | 53,514.7 |
| International co-operation for development | 272,593.9 |
| Regional co-operation for development | 370,368.9 |
| Human rights and humanitarian affairs | 127,362.9 |
| Public information | 138,040.4 |
| Common support services | 446,190.7 |
| Internal oversight | 18,359.6 |
| Jointly-financed activities and special expenses | 58,464.4 |
| Capital expenditures | 34,550.3 |
| Staff assessment | 315,436.7 |
| Development Account | 13,065.0 |
| **Total** | 2,532,331.2 |

* Revised figures.

## United Nations Publications

*Africa Recovery* (quarterly).

*Annual Report of the Secretary-General on the Work of the Organization.*

*Basic Facts About the United Nations.*

*Demographic Yearbook.*

*Development Update* (2 a month).

*Energy Statistics Yearbook.*

*Index to Proceedings* (of the General Assembly; the Security Council; the Economic and Social Council; the Trusteeship Council).

*Monthly Bulletin of Statistics.*

*Population and Vital Statistics Report* (quarterly).

*Statistical Yearbook.*

*The UN Chronicle* (quarterly).

*United Nations Disarmament Yearbook.*

*United Nations Juridical Yearbook.*

*World Economic and Social Survey.*

*Yearbook of the International Law Commission.*

*Yearbook of the United Nations.*

Other UN publications are listed in the chapters dealing with the agencies concerned.

# Secretariat

According to the UN Charter the Secretary-General is the chief administrative officer of the organization, and he may appoint further Secretariat staff as required. The principal departments and officers of the Secretariat are listed below. The chief administrative staff of the UN Regional Commissions and of all the subsidiary organs of the UN are also members of the Secretariat staff and are listed in the appropriate chapters. The Secretariat staff also includes a number of special missions and special appointments, including some of senior rank.

In June 1998 the total number of staff of the Secretariat holding appointments continuing for a year or more was approximately 13,543, including those serving away from the headquarters, but excluding staff working for the UN specialized agencies and subsidiary organs.

In July 1997 the Secretary-General initiated a comprehensive reform of the administration of the UN and abolished some 1,000 Secretariat posts. A Senior Management Group was established as part of a new Secretariat leadership and management structure, to enhance day-to-day efficiency and accountability. The reforms aimed to restructure the Secretariat's substantive work programme around the UN's five core missions, i.e. peace and security, economic and social affairs, development co-operation, humanitarian affairs and human rights. During 1997 the Centre for Human Rights and the Office of the High Commissioner for Human Rights were consolidated into a single office under the reform process, while a new Office for Drug Control and Crime Prevention was established, within the framework of the UN Office in Vienna, to integrate efforts to combat crime, drug abuse and terrorism. A new Office of the Iraq Programme was established in October to undertake and co-ordinate activities relating to the oil-for-food programme (see Security Council, p. 13). In December the General Assembly endorsed a recommendation of the Secretary-General to create the position of Deputy Secretary-General, who was to assist in the management of Secretariat operations, in particular the ongoing reform process, and represent the Secretary-General as required.

### SECRETARY-GENERAL

Kofi Annan (Ghana).

### DEPUTY SECRETARY-GENERAL

Louise Fréchette (Canada).

### EXECUTIVE OFFICE OF THE SECRETARY-GENERAL

**Under-Secretary-General, Chief of Staff:** S. Iqbal Riza (Pakistan).

**Assistant Secretary-General, Special Adviser:** John G. Ruggie.

**Assistant Secretary-General, External Relations:** Gillian Sorensen (USA).

### DEPARTMENT FOR DISARMAMENT AFFAIRS

**Under-Secretary-General:** Jayantha Dhanapala (Sri Lanka).

### DEPARTMENT OF ECONOMIC AND SOCIAL AFFAIRS

**Under-Secretary-General:** Nitin Desai (India).

**Assistant Secretary-General, Special Adviser on Gender Issues and the Advancement of Women:** Angela King (Jamaica).

**Assistant Secretary-General, Policy Co-ordination:** Patrizio Civili (Italy).

### DEPARTMENT OF GENERAL ASSEMBLY AFFAIRS AND CONFERENCE SERVICES

**Under-Secretary-General:** Jin Yongjian (China).

**Assistant Secretary-General:** Federico Riesco (Chile).

### DEPARTMENT OF MANAGEMENT

**Under-Secretary-General:** Joseph E. Connor (USA).

**Assistant Secretary-General, Controller:** Jean-Pierre Halbwachs (Mauritius).

**Assistant Secretary-General, Human Resources:** Rafiah Salim (Malaysia).

**Assistant Secretary-General, Central Support:** Toshiyuki Niwa (Japan).

### DEPARTMENT OF PEACE-KEEPING OPERATIONS

**Under-Secretary-General:** Bernard Miyet (France).

**Assistant Secretary-General:** Hédi Annabi (Tunisia).

**Assistant Secretary-General:** Young-jin Choi (Republic of Korea).

### DEPARTMENT OF POLITICAL AFFAIRS

**Under-Secretary-General:** Sir Kieran Prendergast (United Kingdom).

**Assistant Secretary-General:** Danilo Türk (Slovenia).

**Assistant Secretary-General:** Ibrahima Fall (Senegal).

### DEPARTMENT OF PUBLIC INFORMATION

**Under-Secretary-General:** Kensaku Hogen (Japan).

### OFFICE FOR THE CO-ORDINATION OF HUMANITARIAN AFFAIRS

**Under-Secretary-General for Humanitarian Affairs and Emergency Relief Co-ordinator:** Sérgio Vieira de Mello (Brazil).

**Officer-in-Charge:** Ross Mountain.

### OFFICE FOR DRUG CONTROL AND CRIME PREVENTION

**Under-Secretary-General:** PINO ARLACCHI (Italy).

### OFFICE OF INTERNAL OVERSIGHT SERVICES

**Under-Secretary-General:** DILEEP NAIR (Singapore).

### OFFICE OF THE IRAQ PROGRAMME

**Assistant Secretary-General:** BENON V. SEVAN (Cyprus).

### OFFICE OF LEGAL AFFAIRS

**Under-Secretary-General, The Legal Counsel:** HANS CORELL (Sweden).

### OFFICE OF SECURITY CO-ORDINATION

**Assistant Secretary-General:** BENON V. SEVAN (Cyprus).

### OFFICE OF THE UNITED NATIONS HIGH COMMISSIONER FOR HUMAN RIGHTS

**Address:** Palais des Nations, 1211 Geneva 10, Switzerland.

**Telephone:** (22) 9173134; **fax:** (22) 9170245; **internet:** www.unhchr.ch.

**High Commissioner:** MARY ROBINSON (Ireland).

### GENEVA OFFICE

**Address:** Palais des Nations, 1211 Geneva 10, Switzerland.

**Telephone:** (22) 9171234; 412962; **fax:** (22) 9170123; **internet:** www.unog.ch.

**Director-General:** VLADIMIR PETROVSKY (Russia).

### NAIROBI OFFICE

**Address:** POB 30552, Nairobi, Kenya.

**Telephone:** (2) 623292; **fax:** (2) 624349.

**Director-General:** KLAUS TÖPFER (Germany).

### VIENNA OFFICE

**Address:** Vienna International Centre, POB 500, 1400 Vienna, Austria.

**Telephone:** (1) 26060-4266; **fax:** (1) 26060-5866; **internet:** www.un.or.at.

**Director-General:** PINO ARLACCHI (Italy).

# General Assembly

The General Assembly was established as a principal organ of the United Nations under the UN Charter (see p. 18). It first met on 10 January 1946. It is the main deliberative organ of the United Nations, and the only one composed of representatives of all the UN member states. Each delegation consists of not more than five representatives and five alternates, with as many advisers as may be required. The Assembly meets regularly for three months each year, and special sessions may also be held. It has specific responsibility for electing the Secretary-General and members of other UN councils and organs, and for approving the UN budget and the assessments for financial contributions by member states. It is also empowered to make recommendations (but not binding decisions) on questions of international security and co-operation.

After the election of its President and other officers, the Assembly opens its general debate, a three-week period during which the head of each delegation makes a formal statement of his or her government's views on major world issues. The Assembly then begins examination of the principal items on its agenda: it acts directly on a few agenda items, but most business is handled by the six Main Committees (listed below), which study and debate each item and present draft resolutions to the Assembly. After a review of the report of each Main Committee, the Assembly formally approves or rejects the Committee's recommendations. On designated 'important questions', such as recommendations on international peace and security, the admission of new members to the United Nations, or budgetary questions, a two-thirds majority is needed for adoption of a resolution. Other questions may be decided by a simple majority. In the Assembly, each member has one vote. Voting in the Assembly is sometimes replaced by an effort to find consensus among member states, in order to strengthen support for the Assembly's decisions: the President consults delegations in private to find out whether they are willing to agree to adoption of a resolution without a vote; if they are, the President can declare that a resolution has been so adopted. A list of major decisions of the Assembly, according to which an international agreement, convention or declaration was adopted, is given below.

Special sessions of the Assembly may be held to discuss issues which require particular attention (e.g. illicit drugs) and 'emergency special sessions' may also be convened to discuss situations on which the UN Security Council has been unable to reach a decision (for example, Israel's construction of new settlements in east Jerusalem in 1997). In June 1997 a special session was held to review the state of the environment and to renew commitment to the objectives of the UN Conference on Environment and Development, held five years previously in Rio de Janeiro, Brazil. In June 1998 a special session was convened to consider strategies to counter the world drug problem.

In September 1992 the Federal Republic of Yugoslavia (which in April had formally replaced the Socialist Federal Republic of Yugoslavia, although comprising only two of the six former Yugoslav republics) was suspended from the proceedings of the General Assembly. The Assembly required the new Yugoslav state to apply to occupy the former Yugoslavia's seat in the UN. Following the successful conclusion of democratic elections, South Africa was readmitted to the General Assembly in June 1994.

**President of 54th Session** (from September 1999): THEO-BEN GURIRAB (Namibia).

### MAIN COMMITTEES

There are six Main Committees, on which all members have a right to be represented. Each Committee includes an elected Chairperson and two Vice-Chairs.

**First Committee:** Disarmament and International Security.

**Second Committee:** Economic and Financial.

**Third Committee:** Social, Humanitarian and Cultural.

**Fourth Committee:** Special Political and Decolonization.

**Fifth Committee:** Administrative and Budgetary.

**Sixth Committee:** Legal.

### OTHER SESSIONAL COMMITTEES

**General Committee:** f. 1946; composed of 28 members, including the Assembly President, the 21 Vice-Presidents of the Assembly and the Chairs of the six Main Committees.

**Credentials Committee:** f. 1946; composed of nine members elected at each Assembly session.

### POLITICAL AND SECURITY MATTERS

**Special Committee on Peace-keeping Operations:** f. 1965; 34 appointed members.

**Disarmament Commission:** f. 1978 (replacing body f. 1952); 61 members.

**UN Scientific Committee on the Effects of Atomic Radiation:** f. 1955; 21 members.

**Committee on the Peaceful Uses of Outer Space:** f. 1959; 61 members; has a Legal Sub-Committee and a Scientific and Technical Sub-Committee.

**Ad Hoc Committee on the Indian Ocean:** f. 1972; 44 members.

**Committee on the Exercise of the Inalienable Rights of the Palestinian People:** f. 1975; 23 members.

**Special Committee on the Implementation of the Declaration on Decolonization:** f. 1961; 23 members.

### DEVELOPMENT

**Commission on Science and Technology for Development:** f. 1992; 53 members.

**Committee on New and Renewable Sources of Energy and on Energy for Development:** f. 1992; 24 members.

**United Nations Environment Programme (UNEP) Governing Council:** f. 1972; 58 members (see p. 47).

### LEGAL QUESTIONS

**International Law Commission:** f. 1947; 34 members elected for a five-year term; originally established in 1946 as the Committee on the Progressive Development of International Law and its Codification.

**Advisory Committee on the UN Programme of Assistance in Teaching, Study, Dissemination and Wider Appreciation of International Law:** f. 1965; 25 members.

**UN Commission on International Trade Law:** f. 1966; 36 members.

**Special Committee on the Charter of the United Nations and on the Strengthening of the Role of the Organization:** f. 1975; composed of all UN members.

There is also a UN Administrative Tribunal and a Committee on Applications for Review of Administrative Tribunal Judgments.

### ADMINISTRATIVE AND FINANCIAL QUESTIONS

**Advisory Committee on Administrative and Budgetary Questions:** f. 1946; 16 members appointed for three-year terms.

**Committee on Contributions:** f. 1946; 18 members appointed for three-year terms.

**International Civil Service Commission:** f. 1972; 15 members appointed for four-year terms.

**Committee on Information:** f. 1978, formerly the Committee to review UN Policies and Activities; 89 members.

There is also a Board of Auditors, Investments Committee, UN Joint Staff Pension Board, Joint Inspection Unit, UN Staff Pension Committee, Committee on Conferences, and Committee for Programme and Co-ordination.

# Security Council

The Security Council was established as a principal organ under the United Nations Charter (see p. 19); its first meeting was held on 17 January 1946. Its task is to promote international peace and security in all parts of the world. Significant resolutions adopted by the Council are documented below.

### MEMBERS

Permanent members:

People's Republic of China, France, Russia, United Kingdom, USA.

The remaining 10 members are normally elected (five each year) by the General Assembly for two-year periods (five countries from Africa and Asia, two from Latin America, one from eastern Europe, and two from western Europe and others).

Non-permanent members as at 1 January 2000:

Argentina, Canada, Malaysia, Namibia, the Netherlands (term expires 31 December 2000);
Bangladesh, Jamaica, Mali, Tunisia, Ukraine (term expires 31 December 2001).

### ORGANIZATION

The Security Council has the right to investigate any dispute or situation which might lead to friction between two or more countries, and such disputes or situations may be brought to the Council's attention either by one of its members, by any member state, by the General Assembly, by the Secretary-General or even, under certain conditions, by a state which is not a member of the United Nations.

The Council has the right to recommend ways and means of peaceful settlement and, in certain circumstances, the actual terms of settlement. In the event of a threat to or breach of international peace or an act of aggression, the Council has powers to take 'enforcement' measures in order to restore international peace and security. These include severance of communications and of economic and diplomatic relations and, if required, action by air, land and sea forces.

All members of the United Nations are pledged by the Charter to make available to the Security Council, on its call and in accordance with special agreements, the armed forces, assistance and facilities necessary to maintain international peace and security. These agreements, however, have not yet been concluded.

The Council is organized to be able to function continuously. The Presidency of the Council is held monthly in turn by the member states in English alphabetical order. Each member of the Council has one vote. On procedural matters decisions are made by the affirmative vote of any nine members. For decisions on other matters the required nine affirmative votes must include the votes of the five permanent members. This is the rule of 'great power unanimity' popularly known as the 'veto' privilege. In practice, an abstention by one of the permanent members is not regarded as a veto. Any member, whether permanent or non-permanent, must abstain from voting in any decision concerning the pacific settlement of a dispute to which it is a party. Any member of the UN that is party to a dispute under consideration by the Council may participate in the Council's discussions without a vote.

### ACTIVITIES

In January 1992 the first ever summit meeting of the Security Council was convened, and was attended by the heads of state or government of 13 of its 15 members, and by the ministers of foreign affairs of the remaining two. The subject of the summit meeting, which was presented in a report drafted by the Secretary-General (entitled 'An Agenda for Peace') was the UN's role in preventive diplomacy, peace-keeping and peace-making.

Consideration of reform of the Security Council commenced in 1993 at the 48th Session of the General Assembly, which established a Working Group to assess the issue. In October 1994 a general debate of the General Assembly revealed widespread support for expanding the Security Council to 20 seats and awarding permanent membership to Japan and Germany. The issue continued to be under consideration by an open-ended working group of the General Assembly in 1997. In March the President of the General Assembly formally introduced a proposal for reform, which envisaged a Council consisting of 24 members, including five new permanent members and four new non-permanent members. In September 1998 the General Assembly agreed to continue discussions on reform of the Council during its 53rd session; it subsequently remained an issue of ongoing debate.

During 1999 the Security Council continued to monitor closely all existing peace-keeping missions and the situations in countries where missions were being undertaken, and to authorize extensions of their mandates accordingly. In February the mandate of the UN Preventive Deployment Force (UNPREDEP), along the borders of the former Yugoslav republic of Macedonia, and of the UN Observer Mission in Angola (MONUA) were terminated. In June the Council authorized the establishment of a UN Interim Administration in Kosovo (UNMIK) and a UN Mission in East Timor (UNAMET) (see below). In October the functions of UNAMET were subsumed into a new UN Transitional Administration in East Timor (UNTAET). In the same month the Council approved the establishment of the UN Mission in Sierra Leone (UNAMSIL) to succeed the previous observer mission in that country. (For details of UN observer missions and peace-keeping operations, see pp. 57–63.) During 1999 the Council also continued to monitor and support efforts to secure peace in Afghanistan, Cyprus, Georgia, Central Africa, the Middle East, Somalia, Tajikistan and Western Sahara.

In July 1998 a new series of sanctions, which had been authorized by the Council in June, entered into effect against the UNITA authorities in Angola, owing to their failure to implement earlier Council resolutions demanding compliance with the obligations of the peace process in that country. Accordingly, states were required to freeze all UNITA funds held within their territory, to prevent any official contacts with UNITA leaders, and to prohibit the receipt or sale of diamonds from areas not under government control. In subsequent resolutions the Council continued to blame UNITA for the impasse in the peace process in Angola. In mid-1999 the Council established two expert panels to consider UNITA's banking arrangements and sources of funding, and to investigate its supplies of armaments and use of foreign mercenaries. In September 1998 a special meeting of the Council adopted a resolution to strengthen the effectiveness of arms embargoes imposed against countries in Africa, which at that time were in force against Libya, Liberia, UNITA in Angola, Somalia, former combatants in Rwanda, and former members of the military regime in Sierra Leone. In March the Council voted to impose an arms embargo against the Federal Republic of Yugoslavia, in order to accelerate a dialogue between the Serbian authorities and separatist forces in the province of Kosovo and Metohija, with regard to its political status. In September, following an escalation of hostilities in Kosovo, the Council reiterated previous demands for an immediate cease-fire, and called for the withdrawal of Serbian forces, provision for the safe return of civilians who had been displaced by the recent fighting, and the initiation of negotiations on self-rule for the ethnic Albanians in

Kosovo. The Council also determined to consider further action if its demands were ignored, but omitted any explicit authorization for military intervention in that region. In March the Security Council held an open meeting to discuss the sanctions imposed against Libya following that country's refusal to extradite for trial two people suspected of bombing a US passenger airline over the United Kingdom in 1988. In August 1998 the Council endorsed a proposal to convene a trial under Scottish jurisdiction at a court in the Netherlands, and resolved to suspend all punitive measures against Libya once the authorities in that country had surrendered the suspects. In April 1999, following a period of intensive negotiations, facilitated by the South African President, Nelson Mandela, and representatives of the Saudi Arabian Government, Libya released the two suspects, who were escorted to the Netherlands by the UN's Legal Counsel. On their arrival, and transfer to Scottish custody, the suspension of sanctions against Libya came into effect. In February the Council urged countries to impose a voluntary embargo on the sale or supply of armaments to Eritrea or Ethiopia, owing to an escalation in the conflict between those countries.

In late March 1999 an emergency meeting of the Council was convened following the initiation of an aerial offensive by NATO against the Federal Republic of Yugoslavia, which aimed to accelerate a peace settlement on the political future of Kosovo. A draft resolution, presented by Russia, condemning the action and demanding an immediate end to the bombing was rejected by a majority of Council members. In May the Council expressed regret at the bombing of the embassy of the People's Republic of China in Belgrade, the Federal Republic of Yugoslavia, by NATO military aircraft, and urged NATO to conduct a full investigation. In June the Council approved Resolution 1244, which served as the legal basis of an international agreement to end the conflict in Kosovo. The resolution provided for the withdrawal of Yugoslav forces from the province under the supervision of a new international security presence, which was to co-ordinate the demilitarization of Kosovo and establish a safe environment for the returning population. It also provided for the establishment of a civilian operation to co-ordinate humanitarian assistance and economic rehabilitation, maintain law and order, and supervise the establishment of new democratic institutions. Also in June the Council urged all parties in the conflict in the Democratic Republic of the Congo (DRC) to maintain a cease-fire and participate in a new round of negotiations for a peaceful settlement, and called for a cease-fire in the conflict between Eritrea and Ethiopia following a warning of impending drought in the region. In July the Council declared its support for peace agreements signed between conflicting parties in the DRC and in Sierra Leone. In the following month the Council authorized the deployment of up to 90 military personnel to assist parties to implement the cease-fire accord in the DRC and authorized the provisional expansion of the existing UN mission in Sierra Leone. Also in August the Council adopted its first resolution concerned exclusively with the welfare of children in armed conflict, and in September adopted a resolution on the protection of civilians in armed conflict. In mid-June the Council formally established a UN mission to organize and supervise a popular consultation on the political future of East Timor, which was initially scheduled to be held on 8 August. At the end of June the Council endorsed a decision of the UN Secretary-General to postpone the vote owing to the unstable security situation in the territory. In early September the Council met in emergency session in response to the escalation of violence that had followed the referendum, held on 30 August. The Council demanded that Indonesian forces restore order in the territory, and resolved to send a high-level delegation to discuss the peaceful implementation of the outcome of the referendum with the Indonesian authorities. In mid-September, following the Indonesian Government's agreement to allow foreign troops into East Timor, the Council authorized the establishment of a multinational force to restore peace and security in the territory, to protect and support UN personnel, and to facilitate humanitarian assistance operations. In October the Council established the UN Transitional Administration in East Timor (UNTAET) as the sole legitimate authority in the territory with responsibility to supervise the period of transition to independence. The existing UN mission was incorporated into UNTAET, while it was anticipated that the international force would be replaced by a military component of UNTAET within a period of a few months. In October the Council also authorized a new UN Mission in Sierra Leone (UNAMSIL) to replace the observer mission in that country, and approved the establishment of a UN Office in Angola to assist capacity-building, to promote human rights, and to liaise with the political, military and civilian authorities. In mid-October the Council issued a resolution in which it condemned the suspected illegal training and other terrorist-related activities undertaken in Taliban-controlled areas of Afghanistan, and, in particular, the shielding of those suspected of organizing the bomb attacks against the US embassies in Kenya and Tanzania in August 1998. The Council demanded that the main suspects be extradited for trial and resolved to impose punitive measures against the Taliban authorities if these conditions were not met within one month. Consequently, an embargo on all Taliban-controlled overseas funds and international flights of the national airline entered into effect on 14 November 1999.

In December 1996 the Council approved the implementation of Resolution 986, which was adopted in April 1995, to provide for the limited sale of Iraqi petroleum to enable the purchase of humanitarian supplies and the provision of contributions to the UN Compensation Committee (which had been established to settle claims against Iraq resulting from the Gulf War). Exports of petroleum up to a value of US $1,000m. every 90 days were to be permitted under the agreement; the Council was responsible for renewing the mandate of the agreement and for approving contracts for the sale of petroleum and the purchase of food and medical goods. The Council monitored the situation in Iraq throughout 1997 and received regular reports from the UN Special Commission (UNSCOM), which had been established in 1991 to monitor the disposal of weapons. In mid-1997 the Council criticized Iraqi interference and non-compliance with UNSCOM activities. In October UNSCOM proposed that further punitive measures be imposed on Iraq to force the Government to disclose its weapons programme. The Council adopted a resolution to threaten the imposition of new sanctions; however, the People's Republic of China, France and Russia abstained from the vote. A few days later Iraq announced that all US members of UNSCOM were obliged to leave the country, and rejected the use of US surveillance aircraft in the inspection programme. The Council issued a condemnation of the expulsion order, but was divided on the means of retaliation. In mid-November the Council voted unanimously to impose a travel ban on all Iraqi officials deemed to be responsible for disrupting UNSCOM's operations. Iraq responded by implementing the expulsion of the US element of UNSCOM (having postponed the order pending negotiations), prompting the UN to withdraw almost all of the 97-member inspection team from the country in protest. UNSCOM resumed its activities in late November, following intensive diplomatic efforts. However, by early 1998 the contentious issues regarding the composition of UNSCOM, and Iraq's refusal to grant unrestricted access to a substantial number of sensitive sites throughout the country, remained unresolved. In late January the Iraqi Government requested a suspension of UNSCOM activities, pending a technical evaluation of Iraq's weaponry by a multinational team of experts. The US and United Kingdom Governments attempted to generate support among Security Council members and other Governments in the Gulf region for the use of force, in the event of Iraq's continued refusal to co-operate with the inspection process, in order to destroy any Iraqi facilities for the manufacture of chemical, biological and nuclear weapons. In mid-February the Security Council authorized the UN Secretary-General to visit Iraq, in an attempt to resolve the escalating diplomatic crisis without resort to military confrontation. The Secretary-General concluded a Memorandum of Understanding (MoU) with the Iraqi authorities allowing UNSCOM inspectors unrestricted access to the disputed sites within Iraq. The Security Council endorsed the agreement in early March, but threatened the 'severest measures' if Iraq failed to comply with the MoU. In February the Council approved a resolution expanding the so-called oil-for-food programme to allow for sales of petroleum up to a value of $5,256m. every 180 days (superseding a resolution to extend the programme at its existing level, which was authorized in December 1997). The new agreement entered into force on 1 June 1998, following the Secretary-General's approval of a new distribution plan. At the end of June the Council adopted a resolution permitting states to authorize the limited export of essential equipment to enable Iraq to increase its petroleum production. In August the Council criticized Iraq's decision to suspend co-operation with UN weapons inspectors, owing to renewed concern on the part of the Iraqi Government that UNSCOM was obstructing the removal of UN sanctions. UNSCOM resolved to continue to monitor sites already inspected, but suspended all new inspection activities. At the end of October a diplomatic crisis again arose following an announcement by the Iraq authorities that they would end all co-operation with UNSCOM until the Security Council had reviewed the sanctions measures in force against Iraq and removed the current UNSCOM Chairman, as part of a complete restructuring of that body. The Council condemned Iraq's action as a violation of earlier resolutions, and of the MoU concluded in February, but reiterated its willingness to conduct a comprehensive review of sanctions, as proposed by the UN Secretary-General, if Iraq resumed co-operation. With no agreement having been reached, all UN personnel were withdrawn from Iraq in mid-November. The anticipated military strikes against Iraq, however, were averted at the last minute following Iraq's decision to allow UNSCOM to resume normal tasks. At the end of November there were reports that Iraq was continuing to withhold requested documents and to restrict access to certain military sites. In mid-December UNSCOM's chairman, Richard Butler, reported to the Security Council of Iraq's continued failure to co-operate with UN inspectors and ordered the withdrawal of all UNSCOM personnel from Iraq. The US and United Kingdom Governments responded to Butler's report by conducting extensive airstrikes against Iraqi military targets; however, their action was condemned by some governments for having been undertaken without explicit Security Council authorization. In early 1999 US and British military aircraft continued to patrol no-fly zones in northern and southern Iraq and conducted several airstrikes against military sites. The future of UNSCOM remained uncertain, amidst allegations that it was used illegally to provide intelligence information to the US Government. In January the Security Council decided to establish three panels to review the disarmament process in Iraq, to assess the impact of UN sanctions on the Iraqi people and to investigate Kuwaiti civilians still unaccounted for having been taken hostage in 1990. In October 1999 the Council agreed to permit Iraq to generate a further $3,040m. in the next 180-day period of the oil-for-food agreement, accounting for the shortfall of authorized revenue that had not yet been generated. In November Iraq temporarily suspended its exports of petroleum under the oil-for-food agreement, in protest at the short-term extensions of the programme granted by the Security Council. In mid-December the Council approved a six-month extension of the programme. A few days later it adopted a resolution establishing a new policy towards Iraq. The resolution provided for an unlimited ceiling on petroleum exports under the agreed humanitarian programme, and for a suspension of sanctions pending Iraq's co-operation with a new arms inspection body, the UN Monitoring, Verification and Inspection Commission, which was to replace UNSCOM.

## COMMITTEES

In early 1999 there were two **Standing Committees**, each composed of representatives of all Council member states:

Committee of Experts on Rules of Procedure (studies and advises on rule of procedure and other technical matters);

Committee on the Admission of New Members;

***Ad hoc* Committees**, which are established as needed, comprise all Council members and meet in closed session:

Security Committee on Council Meetings away from Headquarters.

Security Council Committee established pursuant to Resolution 1267 (1999) concerning Afghanistan;

Security Council Committee established pursuant to Resolution 1160 (1998) concerning Kosovo;

Security Council Committee established pursuant to Resolution 1132 (1997) concerning Sierra Leone;

Security Council Committee established pursuant to Resolution 985 (1995) concerning Liberia;

Security Council Committee established pursuant to Resolution 918 (1994) concerning Rwanda;

Security Council Committee established pursuant to Resolution 864 (1993) concerning Angola;

Security Council Committee established pursuant to Resolution 751 (1992) concerning Somalia;

Security Council Committee established pursuant to Resolution 748 (1992) concerning Libya;

Governing Council of the UN Compensation Commission established by Security Council Resolution 692 (1991);

Security Council Committee established pursuant to Resolution 661 (1990) concerning the situation between Iraq and Kuwait.

## INTERNATIONAL TRIBUNALS

In May 1993 the Security Council, acting under Article VII of the UN Charter, adopted Resolution 827, which established an *ad hoc* 'war crimes' tribunal. The so-called International Tribunal for the Prosecution of Persons Responsible for Serious Violations of International Humanitarian Law Committed in the Territory of the Former Yugoslavia (also referred to as the International Criminal Tribunal for the former Yugoslavia—ICTY) was inaugurated in The Hague, Netherlands, in November, comprising a prosecutor and 11 judges sitting in two trial chambers and one appeals chamber. In May 1998 the Security Council authorized the establishment of a third trial chamber, and the election of three new judges, in order to expand the capacity of the Tribunal. Public hearings were initiated in November 1994. The first trial proceedings commenced in May 1996, and the first sentence was imposed by the Tribunal in November. In July and November 1995 the Tribunal formally charged the Bosnian Serb political and military leaders Radovan Karadžić and Gen. Ratko Mladić, on two separate indictments, with genocide and crimes against humanity, and in July 1996 issued international warrants for their arrest. The enforcement of arrests has become one of the principal difficulties confronting the ICTY. By August 1998 28 people were being held in custody, of whom 13 had surrendered voluntarily, seven had been arrested and eight had been detained by multinational forces in the former Yugoslavia; at that time a further 60 people had been indicted by the Tribunal. In mid-1998 the ICTY began investigating reported acts of violence against civilians committed by both sides in the conflict in the southern Serbian province of Kosovo and Metohija. In early 1999 there were reports of large-scale, organized killings, rape and expulsion of the local Albanian population by Serbian forces. In April ICTY personnel visited refugee camps in neighbouring countries in order to compile evidence of the atrocities, and obtained intelligence information from NATO members regarding those responsible for the incidents. In May the President of the Federal Republic of Yugoslavia, Slobodan Milošević was indicted, along with three senior government ministers and the chief-of-staff of the army, charged with crimes against humanity and violations of the customs of war committed in Kosovo since 1 January 1999. In June, following the establishment of an international force to secure peace in Kosovo, the ICTY established teams of experts to investigate alleged atrocities at 529 identified grave sites. By late October 91 individuals had been publicly indicted by the Tribunal (including 18 whose charges were subsequently removed), of whom 34 were in custody. Five trials had been completed at that time.

**President of the ICTY:** CLAUDE JORDA (France).

**Address:** Public Information Unit, POB 13888, 2501 The Hague, Netherlands.

**Telephone:** (70) 416-5233; **fax:** (70) 416-5355; **internet:** www.un.org/icty.

In November 1994 the Security Council adopted Resolution 955, establishing an International Criminal Tribunal for Rwanda (ICTR) to prosecute persons responsible for genocide and other serious violations of humanitarian law that had been committed in Rwanda and by Rwandans in neighbouring states. The Tribunal was to consist of two three-member trial chambers and one appeals chamber with five additional judges, and was to be served by the same Prosecutor as that of the ICTY. Its temporal jurisdiction was limited to the period 1 January to 31 December 1994. In April 1998 the Security Council authorized the establishment of a third three-member trial chamber. The first plenary session of the Tribunal was held in The Hague in June 1995; formal proceedings at its permanent headquarters in Arusha, Tanzania, were initiated in November. The first trial of persons charged by the Tribunal commenced in January 1997, and sentences were imposed in July. During the year the proceedings of the ICTR were undermined by reports of mismanagement and the need for administrative reforms. In September 1998 the former Rwandan Prime Minister, Jean Kambanda, and a former mayor of Taba, Jean-Paul Akayesu, both Hutu extremists, were found guilty of genocide and crimes against humanity; Kambanda subsequently became the first person ever to be sentenced under the 1948 Convention on the Prevention and Punishment of the Crime of Genocide. By October 1999 48 people had been indicted by the Tribunal, of whom 38 were being detained in custody. In November the Rwandan Government temporarily suspended co-operation with the Tribunal in protest at a decision of the appeals chamber to release an indicted former government official owing to procedural delays.

**President of the ICTR:** NAVANETHEM PILLAY (South Africa).

**Address:** Arusha International Conference Centre, POB 6016, Arusha, Tanzania.

**Telephone:** (57) 4207; **fax:** (57) 4000; **e-mail:** public@un.org; **internet:** www.un.org/ictr.

Both Tribunals are supported by teams of investigators and human rights experts working in the field to collect forensic and other evidence in order to uphold indictments. Evidence of mass graves resulting from large-scale unlawful killings has been uncovered in both regions.

**Chief Prosecutor:** CARLA DEL PONTE (Switzerland).

# Trusteeship Council

The Trusteeship Council (comprising the People's Republic of China—a non-active member until May 1989—France, Russia, the United Kingdom and the USA) has supervised United Nations Trust Territories through the administering authorities to promote the political, economic, social and educational advancement of the inhabitants towards self-government or independence (see Charter, p. 23). On 1 October 1994 the last territory remaining under UN trusteeship, the Republic of Palau (part of the archipelago of the Caroline Islands), declared its independence under a compact of free association with the USA, its administering authority. The Security Council terminated the Trusteeship Agreement on 10 November, having determined that the objectives of the agreement had been fully attained. On 1 November the Trusteeship Council formally suspended its operations; in the future it was to be convened on an extraordinary basis as required.

# Economic and Social Council—ECOSOC

ECOSOC promotes world co-operation on economic, social, cultural and humanitarian problems. (See Charter, p. 21.)

### MEMBERS

Fifty-four members are elected by the General Assembly for three-year terms: 18 are elected each year. Membership is allotted by regions as follows: Africa 14 members, western Europe and others 13, Asia 11, Latin America 10, eastern Europe 6.

**President:** MAKARIM WIBISONO (Indonesia).

### ORGANIZATION

The Council, which meets annually for four to five weeks between May and July, alternately in New York and Geneva, is mainly a central policy-making and co-ordinating organ. It has a co-ordinating function between the UN and the specialized agencies, and also makes consultative arrangements with approved voluntary or non-governmental organizations which work within the sphere of its activities. The Council has functional and regional commissions to carry out much of its detailed work.

In November 1997 the General Assembly endorsed a series of recommendations of the Secretary-General to reform the management of the UN, which included plans to consolidate and strengthen the work of ECOSOC. Under the reforms, the Committees on New and Renewable Sources of Energy and Energy for Development and on Natural Resources were to be consolidated into the Commission on Sustainable Development, while the Commissions on Crime Prevention and Criminal Justice and on Narcotic Drugs were to be combined, and the Committee on Economic, Social and Cultural Rights was to report to the Council through the Commission on Human Rights.

During 1999 ECOSOC pursued discussions with the IMF and World Bank regarding the socio-economic aspects of globalization and increased co-operation for development.

### SESSIONAL COMMITTEES

Each sessional committee comprises the 54 members of the Council: there is a First (Economic) Committee, a Second (Social) Committee and a Third (Programme and Co-ordination) Committee.

### FUNCTIONAL COMMISSIONS

**Commission on Crime Prevention and Criminal Justice:** f. 1992; aims to formulate an international convention on crime prevention and criminal justice; 40 members.

**Commission on Human Rights:** f. 1946; seeks greater respect for the basic rights of man, the prevention of discrimination and the protection of minorities; reviews specific instances of human rights violation and dispatches rapporteurs to investigate allegations of abuses in particular countries; provides policy guidance; works on declarations, conventions and other instruments of international law; meets annually for six weeks; 53 members. There is a Sub-Commission on Prevention of Discrimination and Protection of Minorities, comprising working groups on issues such as slavery, indigenous populations, detention and communications.

**Commission on Narcotic Drugs:** f. 1946; mainly concerned in combating illicit traffic; 53 members. There is a Sub-Commission on Illicit Drug Traffic and Related Matters in the Near and Middle East.

**Commission on Population and Development:** f. 1946; advises the Council on population matters and their relation to socio-economic conditions; 47 members.

**Commission on Science and Technology for Development:** f. 1992; works on the restructuring of the UN in the economic, social and related fields; 53 members.

**Commission for Social Development:** f. 1946 as the Social Commission; advises ECOSOC on issues of social and community development; 46 members.

**Commission on the Status of Women:** f. 1946; aims at equality of political, economic and social rights for women, and supports the right of women to live free of violence; 45 members.

**Commission on Sustainable Development:** f. 1993 to oversee integration into the UN's work of the objectives set out in 'Agenda 21', the programme of action agreed by the UN Conference on Environment and Development in June 1992; 53 members.

**Statistical Commission:** Standardizes terminology and procedure in statistics and promotes the development of national statistics; 24 members.

### COMMITTEES AND SUBSIDIARY BODIES

**Commission on Human Settlements:** f. 1977.

**Committee for Development Planning:** f. 1965.

**Committee on Economic, Social and Cultural Rights:** f. 1976.

**Committee of Experts on the Transport of Dangerous Goods:** f. 1953.

**Committee on Natural Resources:** f. 1992.

**Committee on Negotiations with Intergovernmental Agencies:** f. 1946.

**Committee on New and Renewable Sources of Energy and Energy for Development:** f. 1992.

**Committee on Non-Governmental Organizations:** f. 1946.

**Committee for Programme and Co-ordination:** f. 1962.

### REGIONAL COMMISSIONS

(see pp. 26–35)

**Economic Commission for Africa—ECA.**

**Economic Commission for Europe—ECE.**

**Economic Commission for Latin America and the Caribbean—ECLAC.**

**Economic and Social Commission for Asia and the Pacific—ESCAP.**

**Economic and Social Commission for Western Asia—ESCWA.**

### RELATED BODIES

**Board of Trustees of the International Research and Training Institute for Women (INSTRAW):** 11 members (see p. 67).

**International Narcotics Control Board:** f. 1964; 13 members.

**UNDP/UNFPA Executive Board:** 36 members, elected by ECOSOC (see p. 44).

**UNHCR Executive Committee:** 53 members, elected by ECOSOC (see p. 50).

**UNICEF Executive Board:** 36 members, elected by ECOSOC (see p. 40).

**WFP Executive Board:** one-half of the 36 members are elected by ECOSOC, one-half by the FAO; governing body of the World Food Programme (see p. 68).

# International Court of Justice

**Address:** Peace Palace, Carnegieplein 2, 2517 KJ The Hague, Netherlands.

**Telephone:** (70) 302-23-23; **fax:** (70) 364-99-28; **e-mail:** mail@icj-cij.org; **internet:** www.icj–cij.org.

Established in 1945, the Court is the principal judicial organ of the UN. All members of the UN, and also Switzerland, are parties to the Statute of the Court. (See Charter, p. 23.)

## THE JUDGES

(February 2000; in order of precedence)

| | Term Ends* |
|---|---|
| **President:** GILBERT GUILLAUME (France) | 2009 |
| **Vice-President:** SHI JIUYONG (People's Republic of China) | 2003 |
| **Judges:** | |
| SHIGERU ODA (Japan) | 2003 |
| MOHAMMED BEDJAOUI (Algeria) | 2006 |
| RAYMOND RANJEVA (Madagascar) | 2009 |
| GÉZA HERCZEGH (Hungary) | 2003 |
| CARL-AUGUST FLEISCHHAUER (Germany) | 2003 |
| ABDUL G. KOROMA (Sierra Leone) | 2003 |
| VLADLEN S. VERESHCHETIN (Russia) | 2006 |
| ROSALYN HIGGINS (United Kingdom) | 2009 |
| GONZALO PARRA-ARANGUREN (Venezuela) | 2009 |
| PIETER H. KOOIJMANS (Netherlands) | 2006 |
| JOSÉ FRANCISCO REZEK (Brazil) | 2006 |
| AWN SHAWKAT AL-KHASAWNEH (Jordan) | 2009 |
| (vacant) | |

**Registrar:** PHILIPPE COUVREUR (Belgium)

* Each term ends on 5 February of the year indicated.

The Court is composed of 15 judges, each of a different nationality, elected with an absolute majority by both the General Assembly and the Security Council. Representation of the main forms of civilization and the different legal systems of the world are borne in mind in their election. Candidates are nominated by national panels of jurists.

The judges are elected for nine years and may be re-elected; elections for five seats are held every three years. The Court elects its President and Vice-President for each three-year period. Members may not have any political, administrative, or other professional occupation, and may not sit in any case with which they have been otherwise connected than as a judge of the Court. For the purposes of a case, each side—consisting of one or more States—may, unless the Bench already includes a judge with a corresponding nationality, choose a person from outside the Court to sit as a judge on terms of equality with the Members. Judicial decisions are taken by a majority of the judges present, subject to a quorum of nine Members. The President has a casting vote.

## FUNCTIONS

The International Court of Justice operates in accordance with a Statute which is an integral part of the UN Charter. Only States may be parties in cases before the Court; those not parties to the Statute may have access in certain circumstances and under conditions laid down by the Security Council.

The Jurisdiction of the Court comprises:

1. All cases which the parties refer to it jointly by special agreement (indicated in the list below by a stroke between the names of the parties).

2. All matters concerning which a treaty or convention in force provides for reference to the Court. About 700 bilateral or multilateral agreements make such provision. Among the more noteworthy: Treaty of Peace with Japan (1951), European Convention for Peaceful Settlement of Disputes (1957), Single Convention on Narcotic Drugs (1961), Protocol relating to the Status of Refugees (1967), Hague Convention on the Suppression of the Unlawful Seizure of Aircraft (1970).

3. Legal disputes between States which have recognized the jurisdiction of the Court as compulsory for specified classes of dispute. Declarations by the following 62 States accepting the compulsory jurisdiction of the Court are in force: Australia, Austria, Barbados, Belgium, Botswana, Bulgaria, Cambodia (Kampuchea), Cameroon, Canada, Colombia, the Democratic Republic of the Congo, Costa Rica, Cyprus, Denmark, the Dominican Republic, Egypt, Estonia, Finland, The Gambia, Georgia, Greece, Guinea, Guinea-Bissau, Haiti, Honduras, Hungary, India, Japan, Kenya, Liberia, Liechtenstein, Luxembourg, Madagascar, Malawi, Malta, Mauritius, Mexico, Nauru, the Netherlands, New Zealand, Nicaragua, Nigeria, Norway, Pakistan, Panama, Paraguay, the Philippines, Poland, Portugal, Senegal, Somalia, Spain, Sudan, Suriname, Swaziland, Sweden, Switzerland, Togo, Uganda, the United Kingdom, Uruguay, and the Federal Republic of Yugoslavia.

Disputes as to whether the Court has jurisdiction are settled by the Court.

Judgments are without appeal, but are binding only for the particular case and between the parties. States appearing before the Court undertake to comply with its Judgment. If a party to a case fails to do so, the other party may apply to the Security Council, which may make recommendations or decide upon measures to give effect to the Judgment.

Advisory opinions on legal questions may be requested by the General Assembly, the Security Council or, if so authorized by the Assembly, other United Nations organs or specialized agencies.

Rules of Court governing procedure are made by the Court under a power conferred by the Statute.

In July 1993 the Court established a seven-member Chamber for Environmental Matters, in view of the world-wide expansion of environmental law and protection.

## CONSIDERED CASES

### Judgments

Since 1946 more than 80 cases have been referred to the Court by States. Some were removed from the list as a result of settlement or discontinuance, or on the grounds of a lack of basis for jurisdiction. Cases which have been the subject of a Judgment by the Court include: Monetary Gold Removed from Rome in 1943 (Italy *v.* France, United Kingdom and USA); Sovereignty over Certain Frontier Land (Belgium/Netherlands); Arbitral Award made by the King of Spain on 23 December 1906 (Honduras *v.* Nicaragua); Temple of Preah Vihear (Cambodia *v.* Thailand); South West Africa (Ethiopia and Liberia *v.* South Africa); Northern Cameroons (Cameroon *v.* United Kingdom); North Sea Continental Shelf (Federal Republic of Germany/Denmark and Netherlands); Appeal relating to the Jurisdiction of the ICAO Council (India *v.* Pakistan); Fisheries Jurisdiction (United Kingdom *v.* Iceland; Federal Republic of Germany *v.* Iceland); Nuclear Tests (Australia *v.* France; New Zealand *v.* France); Aegean Sea Continental Shelf (Greece *v.* Turkey); United States of America Diplomatic and Consular Staff in Teheran (USA *v.* Iran); Continental Shelf (Tunisia/Libya); Delimitation of the Maritime Boundary in the Gulf of Maine Area (Canada/USA); Continental Shelf (Libya/Malta); Application for revision and interpretation of the Judgment of 24 February 1982 in the case concerning the Continental Shelf (Tunisia *v.* Libya); Military and Paramilitary Activities in and against Nicaragua (Nicaragua *v.* USA); Frontier Dispute (Burkina Faso/Mali); Delimitation of Maritime Boundary (Denmark *v.* Norway); Maritime Boundaries (Guinea-Bissau *v.* Senegal); Elettronica Sicula SpA (USA *v.* Italy); Land, Island and Maritime Frontier Dispute (El Salvador/Honduras) (in one aspect of which Nicaragua was permitted to intervene); Delimitation of Maritime Boundary in the area between Greenland and Jan Mayen island (Denmark *v.* Norway); Maritime Delimitation and Territorial Questions between Qatar and Bahrain (Qatar *v.* Bahrain), aspects of which were still under consideration in 1999; Territorial Dispute (Libya/Chad); East Timor (Portugal *v.* Australia); the Gabčíkovo-Nagymaros Hydroelectric Project (Hungary *v.* Slovakia), aspects of which were still under consideration in 1999; and Fisheries Jurisdiction (Spain *v.* Canada).

Other cases remaining under consideration, or pending before the Court, at the end of 1999 were: cases brought by Libya against the United Kingdom and the USA concerning questions of interpretation and application of the 1971 Montreal Convention arising from the aerial incident at Lockerbie, United Kingdom, in 1988; a case brought by Iran against the USA concerning the destruction of oil platforms; cases brought by Bosnia and Herzegovina and Croatia against the Federal Republic of Yugoslavia concerning the application of the Convention on the Prevention and Punishment of the Crime of Genocide; a case brought by Cameroon against Nigeria concerning the land and maritime boundary between those two states, as well as a case concerning the interpretation of the Judgment of the Court on its jurisdiction in that case; a case concerning the boundary around Kasikili/Sedudu Island brought by Botswana and Namibia; a case concerning sovereignty over Pulau Ligatan and Pulau Sipadan brought by Indonesia and Malaysia; a case brought by Guinea against the Democratic Republic of the Congo concerning the treatment of a Guinean business executive, Ahmadou Sadio Diallo; a case brought by Germany against the USA concerning alleged violations of the 1963 Vienna Convention on Consular Relations with respect to the treatment of two German nationals; cases concerning the legality of the use of force brought by the Federal Republic of Yugoslavia against Belgium, Canada, France, Germany, Italy, the Netherlands, Portugal and the United Kingdom; cases brought by the Democratic Republic of the Congo (DRC) against Burundi, Rwanda, and Uganda, regarding armed activities on the territory of the DRC; a case brought by Pakistan against India concerning an aerial incident in August 1999; and a dispute between Nicaragua and Honduras concerning maritime delimitation in the Caribbean Sea.

**Advisory Opinions**

Matters on which the Court has delivered an Advisory Opinion at the request of the United Nations General Assembly, or an organ thereof, include the following: Condition of Admission of a State to Membership in the United Nations; Competence of the General Assembly for the Admission of a State to the United Nations; Interpretation of the Peace Treaties with Bulgaria, Hungary and Romania; International Status of South West Africa; Reservations to the Convention on the Prevention and Punishment of the Crime of Genocide; Effect of Awards of Compensation Made by the United Nations Administrative Tribunal (UNAT); Western Sahara; Application for Review of UNAT Judgment No. 333; Applicability of the Obligation to Arbitrate under Section 21 of the United Nations Headquarters Agreement of 26 June 1947 (relating to the closure of the Observer Mission to the United Nations maintained by the Palestine Liberation Organization).

An Advisory Opinion has been given at the request of the Security Council: Legal Consequences for States of the continued presence of South Africa in Namibia (South West Africa) notwithstanding Security Council resolution 276 (1970). In 1989 (at the request of the UN Economic and Social Council—ECOSOC) the Court gave an Advisory Opinion on the Applicability of Article 6, Section 22, of the Convention on the Privileges and Immunities of the United Nations. The Court has also, at the request of UNESCO, given an Advisory Opinion on Judgments of the Administrative Tribunal of the ILO upon Complaints made against UNESCO, and on the Constitution of the Maritime Safety Committee of the Inter-Governmental Maritime Consultative Organization, at the request of IMCO. In July 1996 the Court delivered Advisory Opinions on the Legality of the Use by a State of Nuclear Weapons in Armed Conflict, requested by WHO, and on the Legality of the Use or Threat of Nuclear Weapons, requested by the UN General Assembly. In August 1998 ECOSOC requested an Advisory Opinion on the Difference Relating to Immunity from Legal Prosecution of a Special Rapporteur of the Commission on Human Rights.

## Finance

The annual budget for the Court amounts to approximately US $11m. financed entirely by the United Nations.

## Publications

*Acts and Documents, No. 5* (contains Statute and Rules of the Court, the Resolution concerning its internal judicial practice and other documents).

*Bibliography* (annually).

*Pleadings* (Written Pleadings and Statements, Oral Proceedings, Correspondence): series.

*Reports* (Judgments, Opinions and Orders): series.

*Yearbook*.

# Charter of the United Nations

(Signed 26 June 1945)

We the peoples of the United Nations determined

to save succeeding generations from the scourge of war, which twice in our lifetime has brought untold sorrow to mankind, and

to reaffirm faith in fundamental human rights, in the dignity and worth of the human person, in the equal rights of men and women and of nations large and small, and

to establish conditions under which justice and respect for the obligations arising from treaties and other sources of international law can be maintained, and

to promote social progress and better standards of life in larger freedom,

And for these ends

to practise tolerance and live together in peace with one another as good neighbours, and

to unite our strength to maintain international peace and security, and

to ensure, by the acceptance of principles and the institution of methods, that armed force shall not be used, save in the common interest, and

to employ international machinery for the promotion of the economic and social advancement of all peoples,

Have resolved to combine our efforts to accomplish these aims.

Accordingly, our respective Governments, through representatives assembled in the city of San Francisco, who have exhibited their full powers found to be in good and due form, have agreed to the present Charter of the United Nations and do hereby establish an international organization to be known as the United Nations.

### I. PURPOSES AND PRINCIPLES

*Article 1*

The Purposes of the United Nations are:

1. To maintain international peace and security, and to that end: to take effective collective measures for the prevention and removal of threats to the peace, and for the suppression of acts of aggression or other breaches of the peace, and to bring about by peaceful means, and in conformity with the principles of justice and international law, adjustment or settlement of international disputes or situations which might lead to a breach of the peace:

2. To develop friendly relations among nations based on respect for the principle of equal rights and self-determination of peoples, and to take other appropriate measures to strengthen universal peace;

3. To achieve international co-operation in solving international problems of an economic, social, cultural, or humanitarian character, and in promoting and encouraging respect for human rights and for fundamental freedoms for all without distinction as to race, sex, language, or religion; and

4. To be a centre for harmonizing the accusations of nations in the attainment of these common ends.

*Article 2*

The Organization and its Members, in pursuit of the Purposes stated in Article 1, shall act in accordance with the following Principles.

1. The Organization is based on the principle of the sovereign equality of all its Members.

2. All Members, in order to ensure to all of them the rights and benefits resulting from membership, shall fulfil in good faith the obligations assumed by them in accordance with the present Charter.

3. All Members shall settle their international disputes by peaceful means in such a manner that international peace and security, and justice, are not endangered.

4. All Members shall refrain in their international relations from the threat or use of force against the territorial integrity or political independence of any state, or in any manner inconsistent with the Purposes of the United Nations.

5. All Members shall give the United Nations every assistance in any action it takes in accordance with the present Charter, and shall refrain from giving assistance to any state against which the United Nations is taking preventive or enforcement action.

6. The Organization shall ensure that states which are not Members of the United Nations act in accordance with these Principles so far

as may be necessary for the maintenance of international peace and security.

7. Nothing contained in the present Charter shall authorize the United Nations to intervene in matters which are essentially within the domestic jurisdiction of any state or shall require the Members to submit such matters to settlement under the present Charter; but this principle shall not prejudice the application of enforcement measures under Chapter VII.

## II. MEMBERSHIP

*Article 3*

The original Members of the United Nations shall be the states which, having participated in the United Nations Conference on International Organization at San Francisco, or having previously signed the Declaration by United Nations of January 1, 1942, sign the present Charter and ratify it in accordance with Article 110.

*Article 4*

1. Membership in the United Nations is open to all other peace-loving states which accept the obligations contained in the present Charter and, in the judgement of the Organization, are able and willing to carry out these obligations.

2. The admission of any such state to membership in the United Nations will be effected by a decision of the General Assembly upon the recommendation of the Security Council.

*Article 5*

A member of the United Nations against which preventive or enforcement action has been taken by the Security Council may be suspended from the exercise of the rights and privileges of membership by the General Assembly upon the recommendation of the Security Council. The exercise of these rights and privileges may be restored by the Security Council.

*Article 6*

A Member of the United Nations which has persistently violated the Principles contained in the present Charter may be expelled from the Organization by the General Assembly upon the recommendation of the Security Council.

## III. ORGANS

*Article 7*

1. There are established as the principal organs of the United Nations: a General Assembly, a Security Council, an Economic and Social Council, a Trusteeship Council, an International Court of Justice, and a Secretariat.

2. Such subsidiary organs as may be found necessary may be established in accordance with the present Charter.

*Article 8*

The United Nations shall place no restrictions on the eligibility of men and women to participate in any capacity and under conditions of equality in its principal and subsidiary organs.

## IV. THE GENERAL ASSEMBLY

### Composition

*Article 9*

1. The General Assembly shall consist of all the Members of the United Nations.

2. Each Member shall have not more than five representatives in the General Assembly.

### Functions and Powers

*Article 10*

The General Assembly may discuss any questions or any matters within the scope of the present Charter or relating to the powers and functions of any organs provided for in the present Charter, and, except as provided in Article 12, may make recommendations to the Members of the United Nations or to the Security Council or to both on any such questions or matters.

*Article 11*

1. The General Assembly may consider the general principles of co-operation in the maintenance of international peace and security, including the principles governing disarmament and the regulation of armaments, and may make recommendations with regard to such principles to the Members or to the Security Council or to both.

2. The General Assembly may discuss any questions relating to the maintenance of international peace and security brought before it by any Member of the United Nations, or by the Security Council, or by a state which is not a Member of the United Nations in accordance with Article 35, paragraph 2, and, except as provided in Article 12, may make recommendations with regard to any such question to the state or states concerned or to the Security Council or both. Any such question on which action is necessary shall be referred to the Security Council by the General Assembly either before or after discussion.

3. The General Assembly may call the attention of the Security Council to situations which are likely to endanger international peace and security.

4. The powers of the General Assembly set forth in this Article shall not limit the general scope of Article 10.

*Article 12*

1. While the Security Council is exercising in respect of any dispute or situation the functions assigned to it in the present Charter, the General Assembly shall not make any recommendations with regard to that dispute or situation unless the Security Council so requests.

2. The Secretary-General, with the consent of the Security Council, shall notify the General Assembly at each session of any matters relative to the maintenance of international peace and security which are being dealt with by the Security Council and shall similarly notify the General Assembly, or the Members of the United Nations if the General Assembly is not in session, immediately the Security Council ceases to deal with such matters.

*Article 13*

1. The General Assembly shall initiate studies and make recommendations for the purpose of:

(a) promoting international co-operation in the political field and encouraging the progressive development of international law and its codification;

(b) promoting international co-operation in the economic, social, cultural, educational, and health fields, and assisting in the realization of human rights and fundamental freedoms for all without distinction as to race, sex, language, or religion.

2. The further responsibilities, functions and powers of the General Assembly with respect to matters mentioned in paragraph 1(b) above are set forth in Chapters IX and X.

*Article 14*

Subject to the provision of Article 12, the General Assembly may recommend measures for the peaceful adjustment of any situation, regardless of origin, which it deems likely to impair the general welfare or friendly relations among nations, including situations resulting from a violation of the provisions of the present Charter setting forth the Purposes and Principles of the United Nations.

*Article 15*

1. The General Assembly shall receive and consider annual and special reports from the Security Council; these reports shall include an account of the measures that the Security Council has decided upon or taken to maintain international peace and security.

2. The General Assembly shall receive and consider reports from the other organs of the United Nations.

*Article 16*

The General Assembly shall perform such functions with respect to the international trusteeship system as are assigned to it under Chapters XII and XIII, including the approval of the trusteeship agreements for areas not designated as strategic.

*Article 17*

1. The General Assembly shall consider and approve the budget of the Organization.

2. The expenses of the Organization shall be borne by the Members as apportioned by the General Assembly.

3. The General Assembly shall consider and approve any financial and budgetary arrangements with specialized agencies referred to in Article 57 and shall examine the administrative budgets of such specialized agencies with a view to making recommendations to the agencies concerned.

### Voting

*Article 18*

1. Each Member of the General Assembly shall have one vote.

2. Decisions of the General Assembly on important questions shall be made by a two-thirds majority of the members present and voting. These questions shall include: recommendations with respect to the maintenance of international peace and security, the election of the non-permanent Members of the Security Council, the election of the Members of the Economic and Social Council, the election of Members of the Trusteeship Council in accordance with paragraph 1(c) of Article 86, the admission of new Members to the United Nations, the suspension of the rights and privileges of membership, the expulsion of Members, questions relating to the operation of the trusteeship system, and budgetary questions.

3. Decisions on other questions, including the determination of additional categories of questions to be decided by a two-thirds majority, shall be made by a majority of the members present and voting.

*Article 19*

A Member of the United Nations which is in arrears in the payment of its financial contributions to the Organization shall have no vote in the General Assembly if the amount of its arrears equals or exceeds the amount of the contributions due from it for the preceding two full years. The General Assembly may, nevertheless, permit such a Member to vote if it is satisfied that the failure to pay is due to conditions beyond the control of the Member.

**Procedure**

*Article 20*

The General Assembly shall meet in regular annual sessions and in such special sessions as occasion may require. Special sessions shall be convoked by the Secretary-General at the request of the Security Council or of a majority of the members of the United Nations.

*Article 21*

The General Assembly shall adopt its own rules of procedure. It shall elect its President for each session.

*Article 22*

The General Assembly may establish such subsidiary organs as it deems necessary for the performance of its functions.

## V. THE SECURITY COUNCIL

**Composition**

*Article 23*

1. The Security Council shall consist of 11 Members of the United Nations. The Republic of China*, France, the Union of Soviet Socialist Republics†, the United Kingdom of Great Britain and Northern Ireland, and the United States of America shall be permanent members of the Security Council. The General Assembly shall elect six other Members of the United Nations to be non-permanent members of the Security Council, due regard being specially paid, in the first instance to the contribution of Members of the United Nations to the maintenance of international peace and security and to the other purposes of the Organization, and also to equitable geographical distribution.

2. The non-permanent members of the Security Council shall be elected for a term of two years. In the first election of the non-permanent members, however, three shall be chosen for a term of one year. A retiring member shall not be eligible for immediate re-election.

3. Each member of the Security Council shall have one representative.

* From 1971 the Chinese seat in the UN General Assembly and its permanent seat in the Security Council were occupied by the People's Republic of China.

† In December 1991 Russia assumed the former USSR's seat in the UN General Assembly and its permanent seat in the Security Council.

**Functions and Powers**

*Article 24*

1. In order to ensure prompt and effective action by the United Nations, its Members confer on the Security Council primary responsibility for the maintenance of international peace and security, and agree that in carrying out its duties under this responsibility the Security Council acts on their behalf.

2. In discharging these duties the Security Council shall act in accordance with the Purposes and Principles of the United Nations. The specific powers granted to the Security Council for the discharge of these duties are laid down in Chapters VI, VII, VIII and XII.

3. The Security Council shall submit annual and, when necessary, special reports to the General Assembly for its consideration.

*Article 25*

The Members of the United Nations agree to accept and carry out the decisions of the Security Council in accordance with the present Charter.

*Article 26*

In order to promote the establishment and maintenance of international peace and security with the least diversion for armaments of the world's human and economic resources, the Security Council shall be responsible for formulating, with the assistance of the Military Staff Committee referred to in Article 47, plans to be submitted to the Members of the United Nations for the establishment of a system for the regulation of armaments.

**Voting**

*Article 27*

1. Each member of the Security Council shall have one vote.

2. Decisions of the Security Council on procedural matters shall be made by an affirmative vote of seven members.

3. Decisions of the Security Council on all other matters shall be made by an affirmative vote of seven members including the concurring votes of the permanent members; provided that, in decisions under Chapter VI, and under paragraph 3 of Article 52, a party to a dispute shall abstain from voting.

**Procedure**

*Article 28*

1. The Security Council shall be so organized as to be able to function continuously. Each member of the Security Council shall for this purpose be represented at all times at the seat of the Organization.

2. The Security Council shall hold periodic meetings at which each of its members may, if it so desires, be represented by a member of the government or by some other specially designated representative.

3. The Security Council may hold meetings at such places other than the seat of the Organization as in its judgment will best facilitate its work.

*Article 29*

The Security Council may establish such subsidiary organs as it deems necessary for the performance of its functions.

*Article 30*

The Security Council shall adopt its own rules of procedure, including the method of selecting its President.

*Article 31*

Any Member of the United Nations which is not a member of the Security Council may participate, without vote, in the discussion of any question brought before the Security Council whenever the latter considers that the interests of that Member are specially affected.

*Article 32*

Any Member of the United Nations which is not a member of the Security Council or any state which is not a Member of the United Nations, if it is a party to a dispute under consideration by the Security Council, shall be invited to participate, without vote, in the discussion relating to the dispute. The Security Council shall lay down such conditions as it deems just for the participation of a state which is not a Member of the United Nations.

## VI. PACIFIC SETTLEMENT OF DISPUTES

*Article 33*

1. The parties to any dispute, the continuance of which is likely to endanger the maintenance of international peace and security, shall, first of all, seek a solution by negotiation, enquiry, mediation, conciliation, arbitration, judicial settlement, resort to regional agencies or arrangements, or other peaceful means of their own choice.

2. The Security Council shall, when it deems necessary, call upon the parties to settle their disputes by such means.

*Article 34*

The Security Council may investigate any dispute, or any situation which might lead to international friction or give rise to a dispute, in order to determine whether the continuance of the dispute or situation is likely to endanger the maintenance of international peace and security.

*Article 35*

1. Any Member of the United Nations may bring any dispute, or any situation of the nature referred to in Article 34, to the attention of the Security Council or of the General Assembly.

2. A state which is not a Member of the United Nations may bring to the attention of the Security Council or of the General Assembly any dispute to which it is a party if it accepts in advance, for the purposes of the dispute, the obligations of pacific settlement provided in the present Charter.

3. The proceedings of the General Assembly in respect of matters brought to its attention under this Article will be subject to the provisions of Articles 11 and 12.

*Article 36*

1. The Security Council may, at any stage of a dispute of the nature referred to in Article 33 or of a situation of like nature, recommend appropriate procedures or methods of adjustment.

2. The Security Council should take into consideration any procedures for the settlement of the dispute which have already been adopted by the parties.

3. In making recommendations under this Article the Security Council should also take into consideration that legal disputes should as a general rule be referred by the parties to the International Court of Justice in accordance with the provisions of the statute of the Court.

*Article 37*

1. Should the parties to a dispute of the nature referred to in Article 33, fail to settle it by the means indicated in that Article, they shall refer it to the Security Council.

2. If the Security Council deems that the continuance of the dispute is in fact likely to endanger the maintenance of international peace and security, it shall decide whether to take action under Article 36 or to recommend such terms of settlement as it may consider appropriate.

*Article 38*

Without prejudice to the provisions of Articles 33 to 37, the Security Council may, if all the parties to any dispute so request, make recommendations to the parties with a view to a pacific settlement of the dispute.

## VII. ACTION WITH RESPECT TO THREATS TO THE PEACE, BREACHES OF THE PEACE, AND ACTS OF AGGRESSION

*Article 39*

The Security Council shall determine the existence of any threat to the peace, breach of the peace, or act of aggression and shall make recommendations, or decide what measures shall be taken in accordance with Articles 41 and 42, to maintain or restore international peace and security.

*Article 40*

In order to prevent an aggravation of the situation, the Security Council may, before making the recommendations or deciding upon the measures provided for in Article 39, call upon the parties concerned to comply with such provisional measures as it deems necessary or desirable. Such provisional measures shall be without prejudice to the rights, claims, or position of the parties concerned. The Security Council shall duly take account of failure to comply with such provisional measures.

*Article 41*

The Security Council may decide what measures not involving the use of armed force are to be employed to give effect to its decisions, and it may call upon the Members of the United Nations to apply such measures. These may include complete or partial interruption of economic relations and of rail, sea, air, postal, telegraphic, radio, and other means of communication, and the severance of diplomatic relations.

*Article 42*

Should the Security Council consider that measures provided for in Article 41 would be inadequate or have proved to be inadequate, it may take such action by air, sea, or land forces as may be necessary to maintain or restore international peace and security. Such action may include demonstrations, blockade, and other operations by air, sea, or land forces of Members of the United Nations.

*Article 43*

1. All Members of the United Nations, in order to contribute to the maintenance of international peace and security, undertake to make available to the Security Council, on its call and in accordance with a special agreement or agreements, armed forces, assistance, and facilities, including rights of passage, necessary for the purpose of maintaining international peace and security.

2. Such agreement or agreements shall govern the numbers and types of forces, their degree of readiness and general location, and the nature of the facilities and assistance to be provided.

3. The agreement or agreements shall be negotiated as soon as possible on the initiative of the Security Council. They shall be concluded between the Security Council and Members or between the Security Council and groups of Members and shall be subject to ratification by the signatory states in accordance with their respective constitutional processes.

*Article 44*

When the Security Council has decided to use force it shall, before calling upon a Member not represented on it to provide armed forces in fulfilment of the obligations assumed under Article 43, invite that Member, if the Member so desires, to participate in the decisions of the Security Council concerning the employment of contingents of that Member's armed forces.

*Article 45*

In order to enable the United Nations to take urgent military measures, Members shall hold immediately available national air-force contingents for combined international enforcement action. The strength and degree of readiness of these contingents and plans for their combined action shall be determined, within the limits laid down in the special agreement and agreements referred to in Article 43, by the Security Council with the assistance of the Military Staff Committee.

*Article 46*

Plans for the application of armed force shall be made by the Security Council with the assistance of the Military Staff Committee.

*Article 47*

1. There shall be established a Military Staff Committee to advise and assist the Security Council on all questions relating to the Security Council's military requirements for the maintenance of international peace and security, the employment and command of forces placed at its disposal, the regulation of armaments, and possible disarmament.

2. The Military Staff Committee shall consist of the Chiefs of Staff of the permanent members of the Security Council or their representatives. Any Member of the United Nations not permanently represented on the Committee shall be invited by the Committee to be associated with it when the efficient discharge of the Committee's responsibilities requires the participation of that Member in its work.

3. The Military Staff Committee shall be responsible under the Security Council for the strategic direction of any armed forces placed at the disposal of the Security Council. Questions relating to the command of such forces shall be worked out subsequently.

4. The Military Staff Committee, with the authorization of the Security Council and after consultation with appropriate regional agencies, may establish regional sub-committees.

*Article 48*

1. The action required to carry out the decisions of the Security Council for the maintenance of international peace and security shall be taken by all the Members of the United Nations or by some of them, as the Security Council may determine.

2. Such decisions shall be carried out by the Members of the United Nations directly and through their action in the appropriate international agencies of which they are members.

*Article 49*

The Members of the United Nations shall join in affording mutual assistance in carrying out the measures decided upon by the Security Council.

*Article 50*

If preventive or enforcement measures against any state are taken by the Security Council, any other state, whether a Member of the United Nations or not, which finds itself confronted with special economic problems arising from the carrying out of those measures shall have the right to consult the Security Council with regard to a solution of those problems.

*Article 51*

Nothing in the present Charter shall impair the inherent right of individual or collective self-defence if an armed attack occurs against a Member of the United Nations, until the Security Council has taken measures necessary to maintain international peace and security. Measures taken by Members in the exercise of this right of self-defence shall be immediately reported to the Security Council and shall not in any way affect the authority and responsibility of the Security Council under the present Charter to take at any time such action as it deems necessary in order to maintain or restore international peace and security.

## VIII. REGIONAL ARRANGEMENTS

*Article 52*

1. Nothing in the present Charter precludes the existence of regional arrangements or agencies for dealing with such matters relating to the maintenance of international peace and security as are appropriate for regional action, provided that such arrangements or agencies and their activities are consistent with the Purposes and Principles of the United Nations.

2. The Members of the United Nations entering into such arrangements or constituting such agencies shall make every effort to achieve pacific settlement of local disputes through such regional agencies before referring them to the Security Council.

3. The Security Council shall encourage the development of pacific settlement of local disputes through such regional arrangements or by such regional agencies either on the initiative of the states concerned or by reference from the Security Council.

4. This Article in no way impairs the application of Articles 34 and 35.

*Article 53*

1. The Security Council shall, where appropriate, utilize such regional arrangements or agencies for enforcement action under its authority. But no enforcement action shall be taken under regional arrangements or by regional agencies without the authorization of the Security Council, with the exception of measures against any enemy state, as defined in paragraph 2 of this Article, provided for pursuant to Article 107 or in regional arrangements directed against renewal of aggressive policy on the part of any such state, until such time as the Organization may, on request of the Governments concerned, be charged with the responsibility for preventing further aggression by such a state.

2. The term enemy state as used in paragraph 1 of this Article applies to any state which during the Second World War has been an enemy of any signatory of the present Charter.

*Article 54*

The Security Council shall at all times be kept fully informed of activities undertaken or in contemplation under regional arrangements or by regional agencies for the maintenance of international peace and security.

## IX. INTERNATIONAL ECONOMIC AND SOCIAL CO-OPERATION

*Article 55*

With a view to the creation of conditions of stability and well-being which are necessary for peaceful and friendly relations among nations based on respect for the principle of equal rights and self-determination of peoples, the United Nations shall promote:

(a) higher standards of living, full employment, and conditions of economic and social progress and development;

(b) solutions of international economic, social, health, and related problems; and international cultural and educational co-operation; and

(c) universal respect for, and observance of, human rights and fundamental freedoms for all without distinction as to race, sex, language, or religion.

*Article 56*

All Members pledge themselves to take joint and separate action in co-operation with the Organization for the achievement of the purposes set forth in Article 55.

*Article 57*

1. The various specialized agencies, established by intergovernmental agreement and having wide international responsibilities, as defined in their basic instruments, in economic, social, cultural, educational, health, and related fields, shall be brought into relationship with the United Nations in accordance with the provisions of Article 63.

2. Such agencies thus brought into relationship with the United Nations are hereinafter referred to as specialized agencies.

*Article 58*

The Organization shall make recommendations for the co-ordination of the policies and activities of the specialized agencies.

*Article 59*

The Organization shall, where appropriate, initiate negotiations among the states concerned for the creation of any new specialized agencies required for the accomplishment of the purposes set forth in Article 55.

*Article 60*

Responsibility for the discharge of the functions of the Organization set forth in this Chapter shall be vested in the General Assembly and, under the authority of the General Assembly, in the Economic and Social Council, which shall have for this purpose the powers set forth in Chapter X.

## X. THE ECONOMIC AND SOCIAL COUNCIL

### Composition

*Article 61*

1. The Economic and Social Council shall consist of 18 Members of the United Nations elected by the General Assembly.

2. Subject to the provisions of paragraph 3, six members of the Economic and Social Council shall be elected each year for a term of three years. A retiring member shall be eligible for immediate re-election.

3. At the first election, 18 members of the Economic and Social Council shall be chosen. The term of office of six members so chosen shall expire at the end of one year, and of six other members at the end of two years, in accordance with arrangements made by the General Assembly.

4. Each member of the Economic and Social Council shall have one representative.

### Functions and Powers

*Article 62*

1. The Economic and Social Council may make or initiate studies and reports with respect to international economic, social, cultural, educational, health, and related matters and may make recommendations with respect to any such matters to the General Assembly, to the Members of the United Nations, and to the specialized agencies concerned.

2. It may make recommendations for the purpose of promoting respect for, and observance of, human rights and fundamental freedoms for all.

3. It may prepare draft conventions for submission to the General Assembly, with respect to matters falling within its competence.

4. It may call, in accordance with the rules prescribed by the United Nations, international conferences on matters falling within its competence.

*Article 63*

1. The Economic and Social Council may enter into agreements with any of the agencies referred to in Article 57, defining the terms on which the agency concerned shall be brought into relationship with the United Nations. Such agreements shall be subject to approval by the General Assembly.

2. It may co-ordinate the activities of the specialized agencies through consultation with and recommendations to such agencies and through recommendations to the General Assembly and to the Members of the United Nations.

*Article 64*

1. The Economic and Social Council may take appropriate steps to obtain regular reports from the specialized agencies. It may make arrangements with the Members of the United Nations and with specialized agencies to obtain reports on the steps taken to give effect to its own recommendations and to recommendations on matters falling within its competence made by the General Assembly.

2. It may communicate its observations on these reports to the General Assembly.

*Article 65*

The Economic and Social Council may furnish information to the Security Council and shall assist the Security Council upon its request.

*Article 66*

1. The Economic and Social Council shall perform such functions as fall within its competence in connection with the carrying out of the recommendations of the General Assembly.

2. It may, with the approval of the General Assembly, perform services at the request of Members of the United Nations and at the request of specialized agencies.

3. It shall perform such other functions as are specified elsewhere in the present Charter or as may be assigned to it by the General Assembly.

### Voting

*Article 67*

1. Each member of the Economic and Social Council shall have one vote.

2. Decisions of the Economic and Social Council shall be made by a majority of the members present and voting.

### Procedure

*Article 68*

The Economic and Social Council shall set up commissions in economic and social fields and for the promotion of human rights, and such other commissions as may be required for the performance of its functions.

*Article 69*

The Economic and Social Council shall invite any Member of the United Nations to participate, without vote, in its deliberations on any matter of particular concern to that Member.

*Article 70*

The Economic and Social Council may make arrangements for representatives of the specialized agencies to participate, without vote, in its deliberations and in those of the commissions established by it, and for its representatives to participate in the deliberations of the specialized agencies.

*Article 71*

The Economic and Social Council may make suitable arrangements for consultation with non-governmental organizations which are concerned with matters within its competence. Such arrangements may be made with international organizations and, where appropriate, with national organizations after consultation with the Member of the United Nations concerned.

*Article 72*

1. The Economic and Social Council shall adopt its own rules of procedure, including the method of selecting its President.

2. The Economic and Social Council shall meet as required in accordance with its rules, which shall include provision for the convening of meetings on the request of a majority of its members.

## XI. NON-SELF-GOVERNING TERRITORIES

*Article 73*

Members of the United Nations which have or assume responsibilities for the administration of territories whose peoples have not yet attained a full measure of self-government recognize the principle that the interests of the inhabitants of these territories are paramount, and accept as a sacred trust the obligation to promote to the utmost, within the system of international peace and security established by the present Charter, the well-being of the inhabitants of these territories, and, to this end:

(a) to ensure, with due respect for the culture of the peoples concerned, their political, economic, social, and educational advancement, their just treatment, and their protection against abuses;

(b) to develop self-government, to take due account of the political aspirations of the peoples, and to assist them in the progressive development of their free political institutions, according to the particular circumstances of each territory and its peoples and their varying stages of advancement;

(c) to further international peace and security;

(d) to promote constructive measures of development, to encourage research, and to co-operate with one another and, when and where appropriate, with specialized international bodies with a view to the practical achievement of the social, economic, and scientific purposes set forth in this Article; and

(e) to transmit regularly to the Secretary-General for information purposes, subject to such limitations as security and constitutional considerations may require, statistical and other information, of a technical nature relating to economic, social, and educational conditions in the territories for which they are respectively responsible other than those territories to which Chapters XII and XIII apply.

*Article 74*

Members of the United Nations also agree that their policy in respect of the territories to which this Chapter applies, no less than in respect of their metropolitan areas, must be based on the general principles of good-neighbourliness, due account being taken of the interests and well-being of the rest of the world, in social, economic, and commercial matters.

## XII. INTERNATIONAL TRUSTEESHIP SYSTEM

*Article 75*

The United Nations shall establish under its authority an international trusteeship system for the administration and supervision of such territories as may be placed thereunder by subsequent individual agreements. These territories are hereinafter referred to as trust territories.

*Article 76*

The basic objectives of the trusteeship system, in accordance with the Purposes of the United Nations laid down in Article 1 of the present Charter, shall be:

(a) to further international peace and security;

(b) to promote the political, economic, social, and educational advancement of the inhabitants of the trust territories, and their progressive development towards self-government or independence as may be appropriate to the particular circumstances of each territory and its peoples and the freely expressed wishes of the peoples concerned, and as may be provided by the terms of each trusteeship agreement;

(c) to encourage respect for human rights and for fundamental freedoms for all without distinction as to race, sex, language, or religion, and to encourage recognition of the interdependence of the peoples of the world; and

(d) to ensure equal treatment in social, economic, and commercial matters for all Members of the United Nations and their nationals, and also equal treatment for the latter in the administration of justice, without prejudice to the attainment of the foregoing objectives and subject to the provisions of Article 80.

*Article 77*

1. The trusteeship system shall apply to such territories in the following categories as may be placed thereunder by means of trusteeship agreements.

(a) territories now held under mandate;

(b) territories which may be detached from enemy states as a result of the Second World War; and

(c) territories voluntarily placed under the system by states responsible for their administration.

2. It will be a matter for subsequent agreement as to which territories in the foregoing categories will be brought under the trusteeship system and upon what terms.

*Article 78*

The trusteeship system shall not apply to territories which have become Members of the United Nations, relationship among which shall be based on respect for the principle of sovereign equality.

*Article 79*

The terms of trusteeship for each territory to be placed under the trusteeship system, including any alteration or amendment, shall be agreed upon by the states directly concerned, including the mandatory power in the case of territories held under mandate by a Member of the United Nations, and shall be approved as provided for in Articles 83 and 85.

*Article 80*

1. Except as may be agreed upon in individual trusteeship agreements, made under Articles 77, 79, and 81, placing each territory under the trusteeship system, and until such agreements have been concluded, nothing in this Chapter shall be construed in or of itself to alter in any manner the rights whatsoever of any states or any peoples or the terms of existing international instruments to which Members of the United Nations may respectively be parties.

2. Paragraph 1 of this Article shall not be interpreted as giving grounds for delay or postponement of the negotiation and conclusion of agreements for placing mandated and other territories under the trusteeship system as provided for in Article 77.

*Article 81*

The trusteeship agreement shall in each case include the terms under which the trust territory will be administered and designate the authority which will exercise the administration of the trust territory. Such authority, hereinafter called the administering authority, may be one or more states or the Organization itself.

*Article 82*

There may be designated, in any trusteeship agreement, a strategic area or areas which may include part or all of the trust territory to which the agreement applies, without prejudice to any special agreement or agreements made under Article 43.

*Article 83*

1. All functions of the United Nations relating to strategic areas, including the approval of the terms of the trusteeship agreements and of their alteration or amendment, shall be exercised by the Security Council.

2. The basic objectives set forth in Article 76 shall be applicable to the people of each strategic area.

3. The Security Council shall, subject to the provisions of the trusteeship agreements and without prejudice to security considerations, avail itself of the assistance of the Trusteeship Council to perform those functions of the United Nations under the trusteeship system relating to political, economic, social, and educational matters in the strategic areas.

*Article 84*

It shall be the duty of the administering authority to ensure that the trust territory shall play its part in the maintenance of international peace and security. To this end the administering authority may make use of volunteer forces, facilities, and assistance from the trust territory in carrying out the obligations towards the Security Council undertaken in this regard by the administering authority, as well as for local defence and the maintenance of law and order within the trust territory.

*Article 85*

1. The functions of the United Nations with regard to trusteeship agreements for all areas not designated as strategic, including the approval of the terms of the trusteeship agreements and of their alteration or amendment, shall be exercised by the General Assembly.

2. The Trusteeship Council, operating under the authority of the General Assembly, shall assist the General Assembly in carrying out these functions.

## XIII. THE TRUSTEESHIP COUNCIL*

### Composition

*Article 86*

1. The Trusteeship Council shall consist of the following Members of the United Nations:

(a) those Members administering trust territories:

(b) such of those Members mentioned by name in Article 23 as are not administering trust territories; and

(c) as many other Members elected for three-year terms by the General Assembly as may be necessary to ensure that the total number of members of the Trusteeship Council is equally divided between those Members of the United Nations which administer trust territories and those which do not.

2. Each member of the Trusteeship Council shall designate one specially qualified person to represent it therein.

### Functions and Powers

*Article 87*

The General Assembly and, under its authority, the Trusteeship Council, in carrying out their functions, may:

(a) consider reports submitted by the administering authority;

(b) accept petitions and examine them in consultation with the administering authority;

(c) provide for periodic visits to the respective trust territories at times agreed upon with the administering authority; and

(d) take these and other actions in conformity with the terms of the trusteeship agreements.

*Article 88*

The Trusteeship Council shall formulate a questionnaire on the political, economic, social, and educational advancement of the inhabitants of each trust territory, and the administering authority for each trust territory within the competence of the General Assembly shall make an annual report to the General Assembly upon the basis of such questionnaire.

### Voting

*Article 89*

1. Each member of the Trusteeship Council shall have one vote.

2. Decisions of the Trusteeship Council shall be made by a majority of the members present and voting.

### Procedure

*Article 90*

1. The Trusteeship Council shall adopt its own rules of procedure, including the method of selecting its President.

2. The Trusteeship Council shall meet as required in accordance with its rules, which shall include provision for the convening of meetings on the request of a majority of its members.

*Article 91*

The Trusteeship Council shall, when appropriate, avail itself of the assistance of the Economic and Social Council and of the specialized agencies in regard to matters with which they are respectively concerned.

* On 1 October 1994 the Republic of Palau, the last remaining territory under UN trusteeship, became independent. The Trusteeship Council formally suspended operations on 1 November; subsequently it was to be convened, as required, on an extraordinary basis.

## XIV. THE INTERNATIONAL COURT OF JUSTICE

*Article 92*

The International Court of Justice shall be the principal judicial organ of the United Nations. It shall function in accordance with the annexed Statute, which is based upon the Statute of the Permanent Court of International Justice and forms an integral part of the present Charter.

*Article 93*

1. All Members of the United Nations are *ipso facto* parties to the Statute of the International Court of Justice.

2. A state which is not a Member of the United Nations may become a party to the Statute of the International Court of Justice on condition to be determined in each case by the General Assembly upon the recommendation of the Security Council.

*Article 94*

1. Each Member of the United Nations undertakes to comply with the decision of the International Court of Justice in any case to which it is a party.

2. If any party to a case fails to perform the obligations incumbent upon it under a judgment rendered by the Court, the other party may have recourse to the Security Council, which may, if it deems necessary, make recommendations or decide upon measures to be taken to give effect to the judgment.

*Article 95*

Nothing in the present Charter shall prevent Members of the United Nations from entrusting the solution of their differences to other tribunals by virtue of agreements already in existence or which may be concluded in the future.

*Article 96*

1. The General Assembly or the Security Council may request the International Court of Justice to give an advisory opinion on any legal question.

2. Other organs of the United Nations and specialized agencies, which may at any time be so authorized by the General Assembly, may also request advisory opinions of the Court on legal questions arising within the scope of their activities.

## XV. THE SECRETARIAT

*Article 97*

The Secretariat shall comprise a Secretary-General and such staff as the Organization may require. The Secretary-General shall be appointed by the General Assembly upon the recommendation of the Security Council. He shall be the chief administrative officer of the Organization.

*Article 98*

The Secretary-General shall act in that capacity in all meetings of the General Assembly, of the Security Council, of the Economic and Social Council, and of the Trusteeship Council, and shall perform such other functions as are entrusted to him by these organs. The Secretary-General shall make an annual report to the General Assembly on the work of the Organization.

*Article 99*

The Secretary-General may bring to the attention of the Security Council any matter which in his opinion may threaten the maintenance of international peace and security.

*Article 100*

1. In the performance of their duties the Secretary-General and the staff shall not seek or receive instructions from any government or from any other authority external to the Organization. They shall refrain from any action which might reflect on their position as international officials responsible only to the Organization.

2. Each Member of the United Nations undertakes to respect the exclusively international character of the responsibilities of the Secretary-General and the staff and not to seek to influence them in the discharge of their responsibilities.

*Article 101*

1. The staff shall be appointed by the Secretary-General under regulations established by the General Assembly.

2. Appropriate staffs shall be permanently assigned to the Economic and Social Council, the Trusteeship Council, and, as required, to other organs of the United Nations. These staffs shall form a part of the Secretariat.

3. The paramount consideration in the employment of the staff and in the determination of the conditions of service shall be the necessity of securing the highest standards of efficiency, competence, and

integrity. Due regard shall be paid to the importance of recruiting the staff on as wide a geographical basis as possible.

### XVI. MISCELLANEOUS PROVISIONS

*Article 102*

1. Every treaty and every international agreement entered into by any Member of the United Nations after the present Charter comes into force shall as soon as possible be registered with the Secretariat and published by it.

2. No party to any such treaty or international agreement which has not been registered in accordance with the provisions of paragraph 1 of this Article may invoke that treaty or agreement before any organ of the United Nations.

*Article 103*

In the event of a conflict between the obligations of the Members of the United Nations under the present Charter and their obligations under any other international agreement, their obligations under the present Charter shall prevail.

*Article 104*

The Organization shall enjoy in the territory of each of its Members such legal capacity as may be necessary for the exercise of its functions and the fulfilment of its purposes.

*Article 105*

1. The Organization shall enjoy in the territory of each of its Members such privileges and immunities as are necessary for the fulfilment of its purposes.

2. Representatives of the Members of the United Nations and officials of the Organization shall similarly enjoy such privileges and immunities as are necessary for the independent exercise of their functions in connection with the Organization.

3. The General Assembly may make recommendations with a view to determining the details of the application of paragraphs 1 and 2 of this Article or may propose conventions to the Members of the United Nations for this purpose.

### XVII. TRANSITIONAL SECURITY ARRANGEMENTS

*Article 106*

Pending the coming into force of such special agreements referred to in Article 43 as in the opinion of the Security Council enable it to begin the exercise of its responsibilities under Article 42, the parties to the Four-Nation Declaration signed at Moscow, October 30, 1943, and France, shall, in accordance with the provisions of paragraph 5 of that Declaration, consult with one another and as occasion requires with other Members of the United Nations with a view to such joint action on behalf of the Organization as may be necessary for the purpose of maintaining international peace and security.

*Article 107*

Nothing in the present Charter shall invalidate or preclude action, in relation to any state which during the Second World War has been an enemy of any signatory to the present Charter, taken or authorized as a result of that war by the Governments having responsibility for such action.

### XVIII. AMENDMENTS

*Article 108*

Amendments to the present Charter shall come into force for all Members of the United Nations when they have been adopted by a vote of two-thirds of the members of the General Assembly and ratified in accordance with their respective constitutional processes by two-thirds of the Members of the United Nations, including all the permanent members of the Security Council.

*Article 109*

1. A General Conference of the Members of the United Nations for the purpose of reviewing the present Charter may be held at a date and place to be fixed by a two-thirds vote of the members of the General Assembly and by a vote of any seven members of the Security Council. Each Member of the United Nations shall have one vote in the conference.

2. Any alteration of the present Charter recommended by a two-thirds vote of the conference shall take effect when ratified in accordance with their respective constitutional processes by two-thirds of the Members of the United Nations including all the permanent members of the Security Council.

3. If such a conference has not been held before the tenth annual session of the General Assembly following the coming into force of the present Charter, the proposal to call such a conference shall be placed on the agenda of that session of the General Assembly, and the conference shall be held if so decided by a majority vote of the members of the General Assembly and by a vote of any seven members of the Security Council.

### XIX. RATIFICATION AND SIGNATURE

*Article 110*

1. The present Charter shall be ratified by the signatory states in accordance with their respective constitutional processes.

2. The ratifications shall be deposited with the Government of the United States of America, which shall notify all the signatory states of each deposit as well as the Secretary-General of the Organization when he has been appointed.

3. The present Charter shall come into force upon the deposit of ratifications by the Republic of China, France, the Union of Soviet Socialist Republics, the United Kingdom of Great Britain and Northern Ireland, and the United States of America, and by a majority of the other signatory states. A protocol of the ratifications deposited shall thereupon be drawn up by the Government of the United States of America which shall communicate copies thereof to all the signatory states.

4. The states signatory to the present Charter which ratify it after it has come into force will become original Members of the United Nations on the date of the deposit of their respective ratifications.

*Article 111*

The present Charter, of which the Chinese, French, Russian, English, and Spanish texts are equally authentic, shall remain deposited in the archives of the Government of the United States of America. Duly certified copies thereof shall be transmitted by that Government to the Governments of the other signatory states.

In Faith Whereof the representatives of the Governments of the United Nations have signed the present Charter.

Done at the city of San Francisco the twenty-sixth day of June, one thousand nine hundred and forty-five.

## Amendments

The following amendments to Articles 23 and 27 of the Charter came into force in August 1965.

*Article 23*

1. The Security Council shall consist of 15 Members of the United Nations. The Republic of China, France, the Union of Soviet Socialist Republics, the United Kingdom of Great Britain and Northern Ireland, and the United States of America shall be permanent members of the Security Council. The General Assembly shall elect 10 other Members of the United Nations to be non-permanent members of the Security Council, due regard being specially paid, in the first instance to the contribution of Members of the United Nations to the maintenance of international peace and security and to the other purposes of the Organization, and also to equitable geographical distribution.

2. The non-permanent members of the Security Council shall be elected for a term of two years. In the first election of the non-permanent members after the increase of the membership of the Security Council from 11 to 15, two of the four additional members shall be chosen for a term of one year. A retiring member shall not be eligible for immediate re-election.

3. Each member of the Security Council shall have one representative.

*Article 27*

1. Each member of the Security Council shall have one vote.

2. Decisions of the Security Council on procedural matters shall be made by an affirmative vote of nine members.

3. Decisions of the Security Council on all other matters shall be made by an affirmative vote of nine members including the concurring votes of the permanent members; provided that, in decisions under Chapter VI and under paragraph 3 of Article 52, a party to a dispute shall abstain from voting.

The following amendments to Article 61 of the Charter came into force in September 1973.

*Article 61*

1. The Economic and Social Council shall consist of 54 Members of the United Nations elected by the General Assembly.

2. Subject to the provisions of paragraph 3, 18 members of the Economic and Social Council shall be elected each year for a term of three years. A retiring member shall be eligible for immediate re-election.

3. At the first election after the increase in the membership of the Economic and Social Council from 27 to 54 members, in addition to

the members elected in place of the nine members whose term of office expires at the end of that year, 27 additional members shall be elected. Of these 27 additional members, the term of office of nine members so elected shall expire at the end of one year, and of nine other members at the end of two years, in accordance with arrangements made by the General Assembly.

4. Each member of the Economic and Social Council shall have one representative.

The following amendment to Paragraph 1 of Article 109 of the Charter came into force in June 1968.

*Article 109*

1. A General Conference of the Members of the United Nations for the purpose of reviewing the present Charter may be held at a date and place to be fixed by a two-thirds vote of the members of the General Assembly and by a vote of any nine members of the Security Council. Each Member of the United Nations shall have one vote in the conference.

# UNITED NATIONS REGIONAL COMMISSIONS

## Economic Commission for Europe—ECE

**Address:** Palais des Nations, 1211 Geneva 10, Switzerland.

**Telephone:** (22) 9174444; **fax:** (22) 9170505; **e-mail:** info.ece@unece.org; **internet:** www.unece.org.

The UN Economic Commission for Europe was established in 1947. Representatives of all European countries, the USA, Canada, Israel and central Asian republics study the economic, environmental and technological problems of the region and recommend courses of action. ECE is also active in the formulation of international legal instruments and the setting of international standards.

### MEMBERS

| | |
|---|---|
| Albania | Liechtenstein |
| Andorra | Lithuania |
| Armenia | Luxembourg |
| Austria | Macedonia, former Yugoslav republic |
| Azerbaijan | Malta |
| Belarus | Moldova |
| Belgium | Monaco |
| Bosnia and Herzegovina | Netherlands |
| Bulgaria | Norway |
| Canada | Poland |
| Croatia | Portugal |
| Cyprus | Romania |
| Czech Republic | Russia |
| Denmark | San Marino |
| Estonia | Slovakia |
| Finland | Slovenia |
| France | Spain |
| Georgia | Sweden |
| Germany | Switzerland |
| Greece | Tajikistan |
| Hungary | Turkey |
| Iceland | Turkmenistan |
| Ireland | Ukraine |
| Israel | United Kingdom |
| Italy | USA |
| Kazakhstan | Uzbekistan |
| Kyrgyzstan | Yugoslavia |
| Latvia | |

## Organization

(December 1999)

### COMMISSION

ECE, with ECAFE (now ESCAP), was the earliest of the five regional economic commissions set up by the UN Economic and Social Council. The Commission holds an annual plenary session and several informal sessions, and meetings of subsidiary bodies are convened throughout the year.

**President:** MIROSLAV SOMOL (Czech Republic).

### SECRETARIAT

The secretariat services the meetings of the Commission and its subsidiary bodies and publishes periodic surveys and reviews, including a number of specialized statistical bulletins on timber, steel, chemicals, housing, building, and transport (see list of publications below). It maintains close and regular liaison with the United Nations Secretariat in New York, with the secretariats of the other UN regional commissions and of other UN organizations, including the UN Specialized Agencies, and with other intergovernmental organizations. The Executive Secretary also carries out secretarial functions for the executive body of the 1979 Convention on Long-range Transboundary Air Pollution and its protocols. The ECE and UN Secretariats also service the ECOSOC Committee of Experts on the Transport of Dangerous Goods.

**Executive Secretary:** YVES BERTHELOT (France).

## Activities

The guiding principle of ECE activities is the promotion of sustainable development. Within this framework, ECE's main objectives are to provide assistance to countries of central and eastern Europe in their transition from centrally-planned to market economies and to achieve the integration of all members into the European and global economies. Environmental protection, transport, statistics, trade facilitation and economic analysis are all principal topics in the ECE work programme, which also includes activities in the fields of timber, energy, trade, industry, and human settlements.

The 50th annual session of the ECE, held in April 1997, introduced a programme of reform, reducing the number of principal subsidiary bodies from 14 to seven, in order to concentrate resources on the core areas of work listed below, assisted by sub-committees and groups of experts. The Commission also determined to strengthen economic co-operation within Europe and to enhance co-operation and dialogue with other sub-regional organizations. In April 1998 the Commission decided to establish an *ad hoc* working group to consider and develop practices for relations with the business community.

**Committee on Environmental Policy:** Provides policy direction for the ECE region and promotes co-operation among member governments in developing and implementing policies for environmental protection, rational use of natural resources, and sustainable development; supports the integration of environmental policy into sectoral policies; seeks solutions to environmental problems, particularly those of a transboundary nature; assists in strengthening environmental management capabilities, particularly in countries in transition; prepares ministerial conferences (normally held every four years—1998: Århus, Denmark); develops and promotes the implementation of international agreements on the environment; and assesses national policies and legislation.

**Committee on Human Settlements:** Reviews trends and policies in the field of human settlements; undertakes studies and organizes seminars; promotes international co-operation in the field of housing and urban and regional research; assists the countries of central and eastern Europe, which are currently in the process of economic transition, in reformulating their policies relating to housing, land management, sustainable human settlements, and planning and development.

**Committee on Sustainable Energy:** Exchanges information on general energy problems; work programme comprises activities including labelling classification systems and related legal and policy frameworks; liberalization of energy markets, pricing policies and supply security; development of regional sustainable energy strategies for the 21st century; rational use of energy, efficiency and conservation; energy infrastructure including interconnection of electric power and gas networks; coal and thermal power generation in the context of sustainable energy development; Energy Efficiency 2000 project; promotion and development of a market-based Gas Industry in Economics in Transition—Gas Centre project; and technical assistance and operational activities in energy for the benefit of countries with economies in transition.

**Committee for Trade, Industry and Enterprise Development:** A forum for studying means of expanding and diversifying trade among European countries, as well as with countries in other regions, and for drawing up recommendations on how to achieve these ends. Analyses trends, problems and prospects in intra-European trade; explores means of encouraging the flow of international direct investment, including joint ventures, into the newly opening economies of central and eastern Europe; promotes new or improved methods of trading by means of marketing, industrial co-operation, contractual guides, and the facilitation of international trade procedures (notably by developing and diffusing electronic data interchange standards and messages for administration, commerce and transport—UNEDIFACT). In March 1997 ECE's Working Party on the Facilitation of International Trade Procedures was transformed into the Centre for the Facilitation of Procedures and Practices for Administration, Commerce and Trade, which was intended to develop harmonized procedures for international transactions and to promote private sector activities.

**Conference of European Statisticians:** Promotes improvement of national statistics and their international comparability in economic, social, demographic and environmental fields; promotes co-ordination of statistical activities of European international organizations; and responds to the increasing need for international statistical co-operation both within the ECE region and between the region and other regions. Works very closely with the OECD and the EU.

**Inland Transport Committee:** Promotes a coherent, efficient, safe and sustainable transport system through the development of international agreements, conventions and other instruments covering a wide range of questions relating to road, rail, inland water and combined transport, including infrastructure, border-crossing facilitation, road traffic safety, requirements for the construction of road vehicles and other transport regulations, particularly in the fields of transport of dangerous goods and perishable foodstuffs. Also considers transport trends and economics and compiles transport statistics. Assists central and eastern European countries in developing their transport systems and infrastructures.

**Timber Committee:** Regularly reviews markets for forest products; analyses long-term trends and prospects for forestry and timber; keeps under review developments in the forest industries, including environmental and energy-related aspects. Subsidiary bodies run jointly with the FAO deal with forest technology, management and training and with forest economics and statistics.

### SUB-REGIONAL PROGRAMMES

**Southeast European Co-operation Initiative—SECI:** initiated in December 1996, in order to encourage co-operation among countries of the sub-region and to facilitate their access to the process of European integration. Nine *ad hoc* Project Groups have been established to undertake preparations for the following selected projects: trade facilitation; transport infrastructure, in particular road and rail networks; financial policies to promote small and medium-sized enterprises; co-operation to combat crime and corruption; energy efficiency demonstration zone networks; interconnection of natural gas networks; co-operation among securities markets; and the Danube recovery programme, incorporating the Danube River Basin and other international waterways and lakes. Activities are overseen by a SECI Agenda Committee and a SECI Business Advisory Council. Participating countries: Albania, Bosnia and Herzegovina, Bulgaria, Croatia, Greece, Hungary, the former Yugoslav republic of Macedonia, Moldova, Romania, Slovenia and Turkey.

**Special Programme for the Economies of Central Asia—SPECA:** initiated in March 1998 as a joint programme of the ECE and ESCAP. Aims to strengthen sub-regional co-operation, in particular in the following areas: the development of transport infrastructure and facilitation of cross-border activities; the rational use of energy and water; regional development and attraction of foreign investment; and development of multiple routes for pipeline transportation of hydrocarbons to global markets. Participating countries: Kazakhstan, Kyrgyzstan, Tajikistan, Turkmenistan and Uzbekistan.

## Finance

ECE's budget for the two years 1998-99 was US $44m.

## Publications

*ECE Annual Report.*

*Annual Bulletin of Housing and Building Statistics for Europe.*

*Annual Bulletin of Steel Statistics for Europe.*

*Annual Bulletin of Transport Statistics for Europe.*

*The Chemical Industry.*

*Directory of Chemical Producers and Products.*

*Economic Survey of Europe* (3 a year).

*Statistics of Road Traffic Accidents in Europe.*

*Statistics of World Trade in Steel.*

*The Steel Market.*

*Timber Bulletin for Europe.*

*Transport Information.*

*Trends in Europe and North America: Statistical Yearbook of the ECE.*

*UN Manual of Tests and Criteria of Dangerous Goods.*

*UN Recommendations on the Transport of Dangerous Goods.*

Series of studies on air pollution, the environment, forestry and timber, water, trade facilitation, industrial co-operation, energy, joint ventures, and economic reforms in eastern Europe.

Reports, proceedings of meetings, technical documents, codes of conduct, codes of practice, guide-lines to governments, etc.

# Economic and Social Commission for Asia and the Pacific—ESCAP

**Address:** United Nations Bldg, Rajdamnern Ave, Bangkok 10200, Thailand.

**Telephone:** (2) 288-1866; **fax:** (2) 288-1052; **e-mail:** unisbkk.unescap@un.org; **internet:** www.unescap.org.

The Commission was founded in 1947 to encourage the economic and social development of Asia and the Far East; it was originally known as the Economic Commission for Asia and the Far East (ECAFE). The title ESCAP, which replaced ECAFE, was adopted after a reorganization in 1974.

### MEMBERS

Afghanistan
Armenia
Australia
Azerbaijan
Bangladesh
Bhutan
Brunei
Cambodia
China, People's Republic
Fiji
France
India
Indonesia
Iran
Japan
Kazakhstan
Kiribati
Korea, Democratic People's Republic
Korea, Republic
Kyrgyzstan
Laos
Malaysia
Maldives
Marshall Islands
Micronesia, Federated States
Mongolia
Myanmar
Nauru
Nepal
Netherlands
New Zealand
Pakistan
Palau
Papua New Guinea
Philippines
Russia
Samoa
Singapore
Solomon Islands
Sri Lanka
Tajikistan
Thailand
Tonga
Turkey
Turkmenistan
Tuvalu
United Kingdom
USA
Uzbekistan
Vanuatu
Viet Nam

### ASSOCIATE MEMBERS

American Samoa
Cook Islands
French Polynesia
Guam
Hong Kong
Macau
New Caledonia
Niue
Northern Mariana Islands

## Organization

(December 1999)

### COMMISSION

The Commission meets annually at ministerial level to examine the region's problems, to review progress, to establish priorities and to decide upon the recommendations of the Executive Secretary or the subsidiary bodies of the Commission.

Ministerial and intergovernmental conferences on specific issues may be held on an *ad hoc* basis with the approval of the Commission, although, from 1998, no more than one ministerial conference and five intergovernmental conferences may be held during one year.

### COMMITTEES AND SPECIAL BODIES

The following advise the Commission and help to oversee the work of the Secretariat:

**Committee on the Environment and Natural Resources Development:** meets annually.

**Committee on Regional Economic-Co-operation:** meets every two years, with a high-level Steering Group, which meets annually to discuss and develop policy options.

**Committee on Socio-economic Measures to Alleviate Poverty in Rural and Urban Areas:** meets annually.

**Committee on Statistics:** meets every two years.

**Committee on Transport, Communications, Tourism and Infrastructure Development:** meets annually.

**Special Body on Least-Developed and Land-locked Developing Countries:** meets every two years.

**Special Body on Pacific Island Developing Countries:** meets every two years.

In addition, an Advisory Committee of permanent representatives and other representatives designated by members of the Commission functions as an advisory body.

### SECRETARIAT

The Secretariat operates under the guidance of the Commission and its subsidiary bodies. It consists of two servicing divisions, covering administration and programme management, in addition to the following substantive divisions: International trade and economic co-operation (scheduled to merge with the industry and technology division, with effect from 1 January 2000, in order to form a single trade and industry division); Industry and technology; Environment and natural resources management; Social development; Population and rural and urban development; Transport, communications, tourism and infrastructure development; Statistics; and Development research and policy analysis.

The Secretariat also includes the ESCAP/UNCTAD Joint Unit on Transnational Corporations and the UN information services.

**Executive Secretary:** Dr ADRIANUS MOOY (Indonesia).

### SUB-REGIONAL OFFICE

**ESCAP Pacific Operations Centre (ESCAP/POC):** Port Vila, Vanuatu; tel. 23458; fax 23921; e-mail escap@vanuatu.com.vu; f. 1984, to provide effective advisory and technical assistance at a sub-regional level and to identify the needs of island countries. Dir SAVENACA SIWATIBAU.

## Activities

ESCAP acts as a UN regional centre, providing the only intergovernmental forum for the whole of Asia and the Pacific, and executing a wide range of development programmes through technical assistance, advisory services to governments, research, training and information.

In 1992 ESCAP began to reorganize its programme activities and conference structures in order to reflect and serve the region's evolving development needs. The approach that was adopted focused on regional economic co-operation, poverty alleviation through economic growth and social development, and environmental and sustainable development.

**Regional Economic Co-operation: Trade and investment.** Provides technical assistance and advisory services, and aims to promote the exchange of experience and specialist knowledge in the trade and investment sector. ESCAP continues to assess issues arising from the implementation of World Trade Organization commitments and to assist least developed countries to undertake trade liberalization measures in accordance with national priorities. ESCAP promotes regional co-operation for enhancing trade efficiency, including electronic commerce, and increasing the exports of developing countries, in particular in the areas of commodities, textiles and products of small and medium-sized enterprises. Special emphasis is given to the needs of least developed, land-locked and island developing countries, and to economies in transition (such as those of the former USSR) in furthering their integration into the region's economy. In addition, the sub-programme aims to enhance institutional capacity-building, to promote private capital flows for trade-related investment, and to strengthen information services in the region relating to trade and investment.

**Regional Economic Co-operation: Research and policy analysis.** Aims to increase the understanding of the economic and social development situation in the region, with particular attention given to sustainable economic growth, poverty alleviation, the integration of environmental concerns into macroeconomic decisions and policy-making processes, and enhancing the position of the region's disadvantaged economies. The sub-programme is responsible for the provision of technical assistance, and the production of relevant documents and publications.

**Regional Economic Co-operation: Industry and technology.** Aims to assist countries (and, in particular, least developed, land-locked and island developing countries) to formulate policies for accelerated industrial and technological development and to promote the use and development of environmentally-sound technologies in industry. Concerned with strengthening national capabilities in areas such as capital flows, the involvement of women in manufacturing, strengthening industrial and technological infrastructure, and access to new and emerging technologies, and with strengthening institutional capacities to identify, adapt and transfer appropriate technologies. ESCAP aims to enhance the participation of the private sector in the development of human resources in this area.

**Environment and natural resources development.** Concerned with strengthening national capabilities to achieve environmentally-sound and sustainable development by integrating economic concerns, such as the sustainable management of natural resources, into economic planning and policies. The sub-programme was responsible for implementation of the Regional Action Programme for Environmentally Sound and Sustainable Development for the period 1996–2000, adopted in November 1995. Other activities included the promotion of integrated water resources development and management, including water quality and a reduction in water-related natural disasters; strengthening the formulation of policies in the sustainable development of land and mineral resources; the consideration of energy resource options, such as rural energy supply, energy conservation and the planning of power networks; and promotion of the use of space technology applications for environmental management, natural disaster monitoring and sustainable development.

**Social development.** The main objective of the sub-programme was to assess and respond to regional trends and challenges in social policy and human resources development, with particular attention to the planning and delivery of social services and training programmes for disadvantaged groups, including the poor, youths, women, the disabled, and the elderly. Implements global and regional mandates, such as the Programme of Action of the World Summit for Social Development and the Jakarta Plan of Action on Human Resources Development and Action for the Asian and Pacific Decade of Disabled Persons 1993–2002. In addition, the sub-programme aims to strengthen the capacity of public and non-government institutions to address the problems of marginalized social groups and to foster partnerships between governments, the private sector, community organizations and all other involved bodies.

**Population and rural and urban development.** Aims to assess and strengthen the capabilities of local institutions in rural and urban development, as well as increasing the capacity of governmental and non-government organizations to develop new approaches to poverty alleviation and to support food security for rural households. Promotes the correct use of agro-chemicals in order to increase food supply and to achieve sustainable agricultural development and administers the Fertilizer Advisory Development and Information Network for Asia and the Pacific (FADINAP). Rural employment opportunities and the access of the poor to land, credit and other productive assets are also considered by the subprogramme. Undertakes technical co-operation and research in the areas of ageing, female economic migration and reproductive health, and prepares specific publications relating to population. Implements global and regional mandates, such as the Programme of Action of the International Conference on Population and Development. The Secretariat co-ordinates the Asia-Pacific Population Information Network (POPIN).

**Transport, communications, tourism and infrastructure development.** Aims to develop inter- and intra-regional transport links to enhance trade and tourism, mainly through implementation of an Asian Land Transport Infrastructure Development project. Other activities are aimed at improving the planning process in developing infrastructure facilities and services, in accordance with the regional action programme of the New Delhi Action Plan on Infrastructure Development in Asia and the Pacific, which was adopted at a ministerial conference held in October 1996, and at enhancing private sector involvement in national infrastructure development through financing, management, operations and risk-sharing. Aims to reduce the adverse environmental impact of the provision of infrastructure facilites and to promote more equitable and easier access to social amenities. Tourism concerns include the development of human resources, improved policy planning for tourism development, greater investment in the industry, and minimizing the environmental impact of tourism.

**Statistics.** Provides training and advice in priority areas, including national accounts statistics, gender statistics, population censuses and surveys, and the management of statistical systems. Supports co-ordination throughout the region of the development, implementation and revision of selected international statistical standards. Disseminates comparable socio-economic statistics, with increased use of the electronic media, promotes the use of modern information technology in the public sector and trains senior-level officials in the effective management of information technology.

Throughout all the sub-programmes, ESCAP aimed to focus particular attention on the needs and concerns of least developed, land-locked and island developing nations in the region.

### CO-OPERATION WITH THE ASIAN DEVELOPMENT BANK

In July 1993 a memorandum of understanding was signed by ESCAP and the Asian Development Bank (ADB—q.v.), outlining priority areas of co-operation between the two organizations. These were: regional and sub-regional co-operation; issues concerning the least-developed, land-locked and island developing member countries; poverty alleviation; women in development; population; human resource development; the environment and natural resource management; statistics and data bases; economic analysis; transport and communications; and industrial restructuring and privatization. The two organizations were to co-operate in organizing workshops, seminars and conferences, in implementing joint projects, and in exchanging information and data on a regular basis.

### ASSOCIATED BODIES

**Asian and Pacific Centre for Transfer of Technology:** Off New Mehrauli Rd, POB 4575, New Delhi 110 016, India; tel. (11) 6856276; fax (11) 6856274; e-mail postmaster@apctt.org; internet www.apctt.org; f. 1977 to assist countries of the ESCAP region by strengthening their capacity to develop, transfer and adopt technologies relevant to the region, and to identify and to promote regional technology development and transfer. Dir Dr JÜRGEN H. BISCHOFF. Publs *Asia Pacific Tech Monitor, VATIS Updates on Biotechnology, Food Processing, Ozone Layer Protection, Non-Conventional Energy,* and *Waste Technology* (each every 2 months), *International Technology and Business Opportunities Update* (quarterly).

**ESCAP/WMO Typhoon Committee:** c/o UNDP, POB 7285, ADC, Pasay City, Metro Manila, Philippines; tel. (2) 9228055; fax (2) 9228413; e-mail tcs@cyber.cyb-live.com; f. 1968; an intergovernmental body sponsored by ESCAP and WMO for mitigation of typhoon damage. It aims at establishing efficient typhoon and flood warning systems through improved meteorological and telecommunication facilities. Other activities include promotion of disaster preparedness, training of personnel and co-ordination of research. The committee's programme is supported from national resources and also by UNDP and other international and bilateral assistance. Mems: Cambodia, People's Republic of China, Hong Kong, Japan, Democratic People's Republic of Korea, Republic of Korea, Laos, Macau, Malaysia, Philippines, Thailand, Viet Nam. Co-ordinator of Secretariat: Dr ROMAN L. KINTANAR.

**Regional Co-ordination Centre for Research and Development of Coarse Grains, Pulses, Roots and Tuber Crops in the Tropics of Asia and the Pacific (CGPRT Centre):** Jalan Merdeka 145, Bogor 16111, Indonesia; tel. (251) 343277; fax (251) 336290; e-mail cgprt@server.indo.net.id; internet www.cgprt.org.sg; f. 1981; initiates and promotes research, training and publications on the production, marketing and use of these crops. Dir HARUO INAGAKI. Publs *Palawija News* (quarterly), working paper series and monograph series.

**Statistical Institute for Asia and the Pacific:** Akasaka POB 13, Tokyo 107–8691, Japan; tel. (3) 3357-8351; fax (3) 3356-8305; e-mail unsiap@ma.kcom.ne.jp; internet www1.kcom.ne.jp/~unsiap; f. 1970; trains government statisticians; prepares teaching materials, provides facilities for special studies and research of a statistical nature, assists in the development of statistical education and training at all levels in national and sub-regional centres. Dir LAU KAK EN.

**WMO/ESCAP Panel on Tropical Cyclones:** Technical Support Unit, Abhawa Bhaban, Agargon, Dhaka 1207, Bangladesh; f. 1973 to mitigate damage caused by tropical cyclones in the Bay of Bengal and the Arabian Sea; mems: Bangladesh, India, Maldives, Myanmar, Pakistan, Sri Lanka, Thailand.

## Finance

For the two-year period 1996–97 ESCAP's regular budget, an appropriation from the UN budget, was US $67.5m. The regular budget is supplemented annually by funds from various sources for technical assistance.

## Publications

*Annual Report.*
*Agro-chemicals News in Brief* (quarterly).
*Asia-Pacific Development Journal* (2 a year).
*Asia-Pacific in Figures* (annually).
*Asia-Pacific Population Journal* (quarterly).
*Asia-Pacific Remote Sensing and GIS Journal* (2 a year).
*Atlas of Mineral Resources of the ESCAP Region.*
*Confluence* (water resources newsletter, 2 a year).
*Economic and Social Survey of Asia and the Pacific* (annually).
*Environmental News Briefing* (every 2 months).
*ESCAP Energy News* (2 a year).
*ESCAP Human Resources Development Newsletter* (2 a year).
*ESCAP Population Data Sheet* (annually).
*ESCAP Tourism Newsletter* (2 a year).
*Fertilizer Trade Information Monthly Bulletin.*
*Foreign Trade Statistics of Asia and the Pacific* (annually).
*Government Computerization Newsletter* (irregular).
*Industry and Technology Development News for Asia and the Pacific* (annually).
*Poverty Alleviation Initiatives* (quarterly).
*Regional Network for Agricultural Machinery Newsletter* (3 a year).
*Small Industry Bulletin for Asia and the Pacific* (annually).
*Social Development Newsletter* (2 a year).
*Space Technology Applications Newsletter* (quarterly).
*Statistical Indicators for Asia and the Pacific* (quarterly).
*Statistical Newsletter* (quarterly).
*Statistical Yearbook for Asia and the Pacific.*
*Trade and Investment Information Bulletin* (monthly).
*Transport and Communications Bulletin for Asia and the Pacific* (annually).
*Water Resources Journal* (quarterly).
Bibliographies; country and trade profiles; commodity prices; statistics.

# Economic Commission for Latin America and the Caribbean—ECLAC

**Address:** Edif. Naciones Unidas, Avda Dag Hammarskjöld, Casilla 179D, Santiago, Chile.

**Telephone:** (2) 2102000; **fax:** (2) 2080252; **e-mail:** webmaster@eclac.cl; **internet:** www.eclac.org.

The UN Economic Commission for Latin America was founded in 1948 to co-ordinate policies for the promotion of economic development in the Latin American region. The current name of the Commission was adopted in 1984.

### MEMBERS

Antigua and Barbuda
Argentina
Bahamas
Barbados
Belize
Bolivia
Brazil
Canada
Chile
Colombia
Costa Rica
Cuba
Dominica
Dominican Republic
Ecuador
El Salvador
France
Grenada
Guatemala
Guyana
Haiti
Honduras
Italy
Jamaica
Mexico
Netherlands
Nicaragua
Panama
Paraguay
Peru
Portugal
Saint Christopher and Nevis
Saint Lucia
Saint Vincent and the Grenadines
Spain
Suriname
Trinidad and Tobago
United Kingdom
USA
Uruguay
Venezuela

### ASSOCIATE MEMBERS

Anguilla
Aruba
British Virgin Islands
Montserrat
Netherlands Antilles
Puerto Rico
United States Virgin Islands

## Organization

(December 1999)

### COMMISSION

The Commission normally meets every two years in one of the Latin American capitals. The 27th session of the Commission was held in Oranjestad, Aruba in May 1998. The Commission has established the following permanent bodies:

**Caribbean Development and Co-operation Committee.**

**Central American Development and Co-operation Committee.**

**Committee of High-Level Government Experts.**

**Committee of the Whole.**

**Regional Conference on the Integration of Women into the Economic and Social Development of Latin America and the Caribbean.**

**Regional Council for Planning.**

### SECRETARIAT

The Secretariat employs more than 500 staff and comprises the Office of the Executive Secretary; the Programme Planning and Operations Division; and the Office of the Secretary of the Commission. ECLAC's work programme is carried out by the following divisions: Economic Development; Social Development; International Commerce, Finance and Transportation; Productive and Entrepreneurial Development; Statistics and Economic Projections; Environment and Development; and Population. There is also a Woman and Development Unit, support divisions of documents and publications, and of administration, and an Economic and Social Documentation Centre (CLADES).

ECLAC has two sub-regional headquarters: one in Mexico, covering Central America and the Spanish-speaking Caribbean; and the other in Port of Spain, Trinidad and Tobago, covering the remainder of the Caribbean. There are also five national offices: in Santafé de Bogotá, Brasília, Buenos Aires, Montevideo and Washington.

**Executive Secretary:** José Antonio Ocampo (Colombia).

**Secretary of the Commission:** Ernesto Ottone.

## Activities

ECLAC collaborates with regional governments in the investigation and analysis of regional and national economic problems, and provides guidance in the formulation of development plans. Its activities include research; analysis; publication of information; provision of technical assistance; participation in seminars and conferences; training courses; and co-operation with national, regional and international organizations.

The 26th session of the Commission, which was held in San José, Costa Rica, in April 1996, considered means of strengthening the economic and social development of the region, within the framework of a document prepared by ECLAC's Secretariat, and adopted a resolution which defined ECLAC as a centre of excellence, charged with undertaking an analysis of specific aspects of the development process, in collaboration with member governments. The meeting also reviewed the impact on ECLAC of the ongoing process of reform throughout the UN system. The Commission agreed to establish an *ad hoc* working group to recommend a strategic framework for the Commission, to define priorities for a future work programme and to improve working relations between the Commission and member states. In May 1998 the 27th Commission, held in Oranjestad, Aruba, approved the ongoing reform programme, and in particular efforts to enhance the effectiveness and transparency of ECLAC's activities. The main topics of debate at the meeting were public finances, fiscal management and social and economic development. The Commission adopted a Fiscal Covenant, incorporating measures to consolidate fiscal adjustment and to strengthen public management, democracy and social equity, which was to be implemented throughout the region and provide the framework for further debate at national and regional level.

ECLAC works closely with other agencies within the UN system and with other regional and multinational organizations. ECLAC is co-operating with the OAS and the Inter-American Development Bank in the servicing of intergovernmental groups undertaking preparatory work for the establishment of a Free Trade Area of the Americas.

**Latin American and Caribbean Institute for Economic and Social Planning—ILPES:** Edif. Naciones Unidas, Avda Dag Hammarskjöld, Casilla 1567, Santiago, Chile; tel. (2) 2102506; fax (2) 2066104; e-mail pdekock@eclac.cl; f. 1962; supports regional governments through the provision of training, advisory services and research in the field of public planning policy and co-ordination. Dir José Antonio Ocampo.

**Latin American Demographic Centre—CELADE:** Edif. Naciones Unidas, Avda Dag Hammarskjöld, Casilla 179-D, Santiago, Chile; tel. (2) 2102002; fax (2) 2080252; e-mail dblanchard@eclac.cl; f. 1957, became an integral part of ECLAC in 1975; provides technical assistance to governments, universities and research centres in demographic analysis, population policies, integration of population factors in development planning, and data processing; conducts three-month courses on demographic analysis for development and various national and regional seminars; provides demographic estimates and projections, documentation, data processing, computer packages and training. Dir Daniel S. Blanchard.

## Finance

ECLAC receives an appropriation from the regular budget of the UN, as well as extrabudgetary contributions from governments, other organizations and UN agencies, including UNDP, UNFPA and UNICEF. For the two-year period 1998–99 ECLAC's regular budget amounted to US $93.3m., while voluntary donations and contributions totalled $15.9m.

## Publications

*Boletín del Banco de Datos del CELADE* (annually).

*Boletín demográfico* (2 a year).

*Boletín de Facilitación del Comercio y el Transporte* (every 2 months).

*CEPAL Review* (Spanish and English, 3 a year).

*CEPALINDEX* (annually).

*Co-operation and Development* (Spanish and English, quarterly).

*DOCPAL Resúmenes* (population studies, 2 a year).

*ECLAC Notes / Notas de la CEPAL* (every 2 months).

*Economic Panorama of Latin America* (annually).

*Economic Survey of Latin America and the Caribbean* (Spanish and English, annually).

*Foreign Investment in Latin America and the Caribbean.*

*Notas de Población* (2 a year).

*PLANINDEX* (2 a year).

*Preliminary Overview of the Economy of Latin America and the Caribbean* (annually).

*Social Panorama of Latin America* (annually).

*Statistical Yearbook for Latin America and the Caribbean* (Spanish and English).

Studies, reports, bibliographical bulletins.

# Economic Commission for Africa—ECA

**Address:** Africa Hall, POB 3001, Addis Ababa, Ethiopia.

**Telephone:** (1) 515826; **fax:** (1) 512233; **e-mail:** ecainfo@un.org; **internet:** www.un.org/depts/eca.

The UN Economic Commission for Africa was founded in 1958 by a resolution of ECOSOC to initiate and take part in measures for facilitating Africa's economic development.

### MEMBERS

| | | |
|---|---|---|
| Algeria | Eritrea | Niger |
| Angola | Ethiopia | Nigeria |
| Benin | Gabon | Rwanda |
| Botswana | The Gambia | São Tomé and Príncipe |
| Burkina Faso | Ghana | Senegal |
| Burundi | Guinea | Seychelles |
| Cameroon | Guinea-Bissau | Sierra Leone |
| Cape Verde | Kenya | Somalia |
| Central African Republic | Lesotho | South Africa |
| Chad | Liberia | Sudan |
| Comoros | Libya | Swaziland |
| Congo, Democratic Republic | Madagascar | Tanzania |
| Congo, Republic | Malawi | Togo |
| Côte d'Ivoire | Mali | Tunisia |
| Djibouti | Mauritania | Uganda |
| Egypt | Mauritius | Zambia |
| Equatorial Guinea | Morocco | Zimbabwe |
| | Mozambique | |
| | Namibia | |

## Organization

(December 1999)

### COMMISSION

The Commission may only act with the agreement of the government of the country concerned. It is also empowered to make recommendations on any matter within its competence directly to the government of the member or associate member concerned, to governments admitted in a consultative capacity, and to the UN Specialized Agencies. The Commission is required to submit for prior consideration by ECOSOC any of its proposals for actions that would be likely to have important effects on the international economy.

### CONFERENCE OF MINISTERS

The Conference, which meets every two years, is attended by ministers responsible for economic or financial affairs, planning and development of governments of member states, and is the main deliberative body of the Commission.

The Commission's responsibility to promote concerted action for the economic and social development of Africa is vested primarily in the Conference, which considers matters of general policy and the priorities to be assigned to the Commission's programmes, considers inter-African and international economic policy, and makes recommendations to member states in connection with such matters.

### OTHER POLICY-MAKING BODIES

A Conference of Ministers of Finance and a Conference of Ministers responsible for economic and social development and planning meet in alternate years to formulate policy recommendations. Each is served by a committee of experts. Five intergovernmental committees of experts attached to the Sub-regional Development Centres (see below) meet annually and report to the Commission through a Technical Preparatory Committee of the Whole, which was established in 1979 to deal with matters submitted for the consideration of the Conference.

Seven other committees meet regularly to consider issues relating to the following policy areas: women and development; development information; sustainable development; human development and civil society; industry and private sector development; natural resources and science and technology; and regional co-operation and integration.

### SECRETARIAT

The Secretariat provides the services necessary for the meeting of the Conference of Ministers and the meetings of the Commission's subsidiary bodies, carries out the resolutions and implements the programmes adopted there. It comprises an Office of the Executive Secretary, the African Centre for Women and the following eight divisions: Food Security and Sustainable Development; Development Management; Development Information Services; Regional Co-operation and Integration; Programme Planning, Finance and Evaluation; Economic and Social Policy; Human Resources and System Management; Conference and General Services.

**Executive Secretary:** KINGSLEY Y. AMOAKO (Ghana).

### SUB-REGIONAL DEVELOPMENT CENTRES

Multinational Programming and Operational Centres (MULPOCs) were established, in 1977, to implement regional development programmes. In May 1997 the Commission decided to transform the MULPOCs into Sub-regional Development Centres (SRDCs) in order to enable member states to play a more effective role in the process of African integration and to facilitate the integration efforts of the other UN agencies active in the sub-regions. In addition, the SRDCs were to act as the operational arms of ECA at national and sub-regional levels: to ensure harmony between the objectives of sub-regional and regional programmes and those defined by the Commission; to provide advisory services; to facilitate sub-regional economic co-operation, integration and development; to collect and disseminate information; to stimulate policy dialogue; and to promote gender issues. In July 1997 it was reported that ECA intended to deploy 25% of its professional personnel in the SRDCs (up from 9%) and to allocate approximately 40% of its budget to the Centres.

**Central Africa:** POB 836, Yaoundé, Cameroon; tel. 23-14-61; fax 23-31-85; e-mail casrdc@camnet.cm; Dir ABDOULAYE NIANG.

**Eastern Africa:** c/o UNDP, ave de l'Armée 12, BP 445, Kigali, Rwanda; tel. 77822; fax 76263; Dir HALIDOU OUÉDRAOGO.

**North Africa:** POB 316, Tangier, Morocco; tel. (9) 322346; fax (9) 340357; e-mail srdc@cybermania.net.ma; Dir S. JUGESSUR.

**Southern Africa:** POB 30647, Lusaka, Zambia; tel. (1) 228503; fax (1) 236949; e-mail uneca@zamnet.zm; Dir Dr ROBERT M. OKELLO.

**West Africa:** POB 744, Niamey, Niger; tel. 72-29-61; fax 72-28-94; Dir HENRI SOUMAH.

## Activities

The Commission's activities are designed to encourage sustainable socio-economic development in Africa and to increase economic co-operation among African countries and between Africa and other parts of the world. The Secretariat is guided in its efforts by major regional strategies including the Abuja Treaty establishing the African Economic Community signed under the aegis of the Organization of African Unity and the UN New Agenda for the Development of Africa covering the period 1991–2000. ECA's main programme areas for the period 1996–2001 were based on an Agenda for Action, which was announced by the OAU Council of Ministers in March 1995 and adopted by African heads of state in June, with the stated aim of 'relaunching Africa's economic and social development'. The five overall objectives were to facilitate economic and social policy analysis and implementation; to ensure food security and sustainable development; to strengthen development management; to harness information for development; and to promote regional co-operation and integration. In all its activities ECA aimed to promote the themes of capacity-building and of fostering leadership and the empowerment of women in Africa. In May 1998 ECA's African Centre for Women inaugurated a new Fund for African Women's Development to support capacity-building activities.

### DEVELOPMENT INFORMATION SYSTEMS

The Pan-African Documentation and Information Service (PADIS) was established in 1980. The main objectives of PADIS are: to provide access to numerical and other information on African social, economic, scientific and technological development issues; to assist African countries in their efforts to develop national information handling capabilities through advisory services and training; to establish a data communication network to facilitate the timely use of information on development; and to design sound technical specifications, norms and standards to minimize technical barriers in the exchange of information. ECA is promoting the use of electronic systems to disseminate information throughout the region, under its commitment for the period 1996–2001 to harness information for development purposes. ECA aims to co-ordinate the implementation of the African Information Society Initiative (AISI), a framework for creating an information and communications infrastructure. In addition, ECA encourages member governments to liberalize the telecommunications sector and stimulate imports of computers in order to enable the expansion of information technology throughout Africa.

ECA also promotes the development and co-ordination of national statistical services in the region and undertakes the collection, evaluation and dissemination of statistical information. ECA's work in the field of statistics has been concentrated in five main areas: the African Household Survey Capability Programme, which aims to assist in the collection and analysis of demographic, social and economic data on households; the Statistical Training Programme for Africa, which aims to make the region self-sufficient in statistical personnel at all levels; the Technical Support Services, which provide technical advisory services for population censuses, demographic surveys and civil registration; the National Accounts Capability Programme, which aims at improving economic statistics generally by building up a capability in each country for the collection, processing and analysis of economic data; and the ECA-Regional Statistical Data Base, part of PADIS, which provides on-line statistical information to users. In 1997 ECA planned to upgrade its statistical database in order to provide a data services centre for the region.

ECA assists its member states in (i) population data collection and data processing; (ii) analysis of demographic data obtained from censuses or surveys; (iii) training demographers at the Regional Institute for Population Studies (RIPS) in Accra, Ghana, and at the Institut de formation et de recherche démographiques (IFORD) in Yaoundé, Cameroon; (iv) formulation of population policies and integrating population variables in development planning, through advisory missions and through the organization of national seminars on population and development; and (v) dissemination of information through its *Newsletter, Demographic Handbook for Africa,* the *African Population Studies* series and other publications. The strengthening of national population policies was an important element of ECA's objective of ensuring food security in African countries. The Ninth Joint Conference of African Planners, Statisticians and Demographers was held in March 1996, in Addis Ababa, Ethiopia.

## DEVELOPMENT MANAGEMENT

ECA aims to assist governments, public corporations, universities and the private sector in improving their financial management; strengthening policy-making and analytical capacities; adopting measures to redress skill shortages; enhancing human resources development and utilization; and promoting social development through programmes focusing on youth, people with disabilities and the elderly. The Secretariat organizes training workshops, seminars and conferences at national, subregional and regional levels for ministers, public administrators and senior policy-makers, as well as for private and non-governmental organizations. ECA aims to increase the participation of women in economic development and incorporates this objective into its administrative activities and work programmes.

Following the failure to implement many of the proposals under the UN Industrial Development Decade for Africa (IDDA, 1980–90) and the UN Programme of Action for African Economic Recovery and Development (1986–90), a second IDDA was adopted by the Conference of African Ministers of Industry in July 1991. The main objectives of the second IDDA include the consolidation and rehabilitation of existing industries, the expansion of new investments, and the promotion of small-scale industries and technological capabilities. In June 1996 a conference, organized by ECA, was held in Accra, Ghana, with the aim of reviving private investment in Africa in order to stimulate the private sector and promote future economic development. In October 1999 the first African Development Forum (ADF) was held in Addis Ababa, Ethiopia. The ADF process was initiated by ECA to formulate an agenda for effective, sustainable development in African countries through dialogue and partnership between governments, academics, the private sector, donor agencies etc. It was intended that the process would focus towards an annual meeting concerned with a specific development issue. The first Forum was convened on the theme 'The Challenge to Africa of Globalization and the Information Age'. It reviewed the AISI (see above) and formulated country action plans and work programmes for 2000. The four issues addressed were: strengthening Africa's information infrastructure; Africa and the information economy; information and communication technologies for improved governance; and democratizing access to the information society.

In 1997 ECA hosted the first of a series of meetings on good governance, in the context of the UN system-wide Special Initiative on Africa. The second African Governance Forum (AGF II) was held in Accra, Ghana, in June 1998. The Forum focused on accountability and transparency, which participants agreed were essential elements in promoting development in Africa and should involve commitment from both governments and civil organizations. A third AGF was to be held in Mali, in 1999, to consider issues relating to conflict prevention, management and governance.

## ECONOMIC AND SOCIAL POLICY

The Economic and Social Policy division concentrates on the following areas: economic policy analysis, social policy and poverty analysis, and the co-ordination and monitoring of special issues and programmes. Monitoring economic and social trends in the African region and studying the development problems concerning it are among the fundamental tasks of the Commission, while the special issues programme updates legislative bodies regarding the progress made in the implementation of initiatives affecting the continent. Every year the Commission publishes the *Survey of Economic and Social Conditions in Africa* and the *Economic Report on Africa*.

The Commission gives assistance to governments in general economic analysis, fiscal, financial and monetary management, trade liberalization, regional integration and planning. The ECA's work on economic planning has been broadened in recent years, in order to give more emphasis to macro-economic management in a mixed economy approach: a project is being undertaken to develop short-term forecasting and policy models to support economic management. The Commission has also undertaken a major study of the informal sector in African countries. Special assistance is given to least-developed, land-locked and island countries which have a much lower income level than other countries and which are faced with heavier constraints. Studies are also undertaken to assist longer-term planning.

In May 1994 ECA ministers of economic and social development and of planning, meeting in Addis Ababa, adopted a *Framework Agenda for Building and Utilizing Critical Capacities in Africa*. The agenda aimed to identify new priority areas to stimulate development by, for example, strengthening management structures, a more efficient use of a country's physical infrastructure and by expanding processing or manufacturing facilities.

ECA aims to strengthen African participation in international negotiations. To this end, assistance has been provided to member states in the ongoing multilateral trade negotiations under the World Trade Organization; in the annual conferences of the IMF and the World Bank; in negotiations with the EU; and in meetings related to economic co-operation among developing countries. Studies have been prepared on problems and prospects likely to arise for the African region from the implementation of the Common Fund for Commodities and the Generalized System of Trade Preferences (both supervised by UNCTAD); the impacts of exchange-rate fluctuations on the economies of African countries; and on the long-term implications of different debt arrangements for African economies. ECA assists individual member states by undertaking studies on domestic trade, expansion of inter-African trade, transnational corporations, integration of women in trade and development, and strengthening the capacities of state-trading organizations. ECA encourages the diversification of production, the liberalization of cross-border trade and the expansion of domestic trade structures, within regional economic groupings, in order to promote intra-African trade. ECA also helps to organize regional and 'All-Africa' trade fairs.

In March/April 1997 the Conference of African Ministers of Finance, meeting in Addis Ababa, reviewed a new initiative of the World Bank and IMF to assist the world's 41 most heavily indebted poor countries, of which 33 were identified as being in sub-Saharan Africa. While the Conference recognized the importance of the involvement of multilateral institutions in assisting African economies to achieve a sustainable level of development, it criticized aspects of the structural adjustment programmes imposed by the institutions and advocated more flexible criteria to determine eligibility for the new initiative.

In 1997, with regard to social policy, ECA focused upon improving the socio-economic prospects of women through the promotion of social and legal equality, increasing opportunities for entering higher education and monitoring the prevalence of poverty.

## FOOD SECURITY AND SUSTAINABLE DEVELOPMENT

In the early 1990s reports were compiled on the development, implementation and sound management of environmental programmes at national, sub-regional and regional levels. ECA members adopted a common African position for the UN Conference on Environment and Development, held in June 1992. In 1995 ECA published its first comprehensive report and statistical survey of human development issues in African countries. The *Human Development in Africa Report*, which was to be published every two years, aimed to demonstrate levels of development attained, particularly in the education and child health sectors, to identify areas of concern and to encourage further action by policy-makers and development experts. In 1997 ECA was actively involved in the promotion of food security in African countries and the study of the relationship between population, food security, the environment and sustainable development.

### PROGRAMME PLANNING, FINANCE AND EVALUATION

ECA provides guidance in the formulation of policies towards the achievement of Africa's development objectives to the policy-making organs of the UN and OAU. It contributes to the work of the General Assembly and other specialized agencies by providing an African perspective in the preparation of development strategies. In March 1996 the UN announced a system-wide Special Initiative on Africa to mobilize resources and to implement a series of political and economic development objectives over a 10-year period. ECA's Executive Secretary is the Co-Chair, with the Administrator of the UNDP, of the Steering Committee for the Initiative.

### REGIONAL CO-OPERATION AND INTEGRATION

The Regional Co-operation and Integration Division administers the transport and communications and mineral and energy sectors, in addition to its activities concerning the Sub-regional Development Centres (SRDCs—see above), the integrated development of transboundary water resources, and facilitating and enhancing the process of regional economic integration.

ECA was appointed lead agency for the second United Nations Transport and Communications Decade in Africa (UNTACDA II), covering the period 1991–2000. The principal aim of UNTACDA II is the establishment of an efficient, integrated transport and communications system in Africa. The specific objectives of the programme include: (i) the removal of physical and non-physical barriers to intra-African trade and travel, and improvement in the road transport sector; (ii) improvement in the efficiency and financial viability of railways; (iii) development of Africa's shipping capacity and improvement in the performance of Africa's ports; (iv) development of integrated transport systems for each lake and river basin; (v) improvement of integration of all modes of transport in order to carry cargo in one chain of transport smoothly; (vi) integration of African airlines, and restructuring of civil aviation and airport management authorities; (vii) improvement in the quality and availability of transport in urban areas; (viii) development of integrated regional telecommunications networks; (ix) development of broadcasting services, with the aim of supporting socio-economic development; and (x) expansion of Africa's postal network. ECA is the co-ordinator, with the World Bank, of a regional Road Maintenance Initiative, which was launched in 1988. By early 1996 13 African countries were receiving assistance under the initiative, which sought to encourage a partnership between the public and private sectors to manage and maintain road infrastructure more efficiently and thus to improve country-wide communications and transportation activities. The third African road safety congress was held in April 1997, in Pretoria, South Africa. The congress, which was jointly organized by ECA and the OECD, aimed to increase awareness of the need to adopt an integrated approach to road safety problems. During 1998/99 transport activities included consideration of a new African air transport policy, workshops on port restructuring, and regional and country analyses of transport trends and reforms.

The Fourth Regional Conference on the Development and Utilization of Mineral Resources in Africa, held in March 1991, adopted an action plan that included the formulation of national mineral exploitation policies; and the promotion of the gemstone industry, small-scale mining and the iron and steel industry. ECA supports the Southern African Mineral Resources Development Centre in Dar-es-Salaam, Tanzania, and the Central African Mineral Development Centre in Brazzaville, Republic of the Congo, which provide advisory and laboratory services to their respective member states.

ECA's Energy Programme provides assistance to member states in the development of indigenous energy resources and the formulation of energy policies to extricate member states from continued energy crises. In 1997 ECA strengthened co-operation with the World Energy Council and agreed to help implement the Council's African Energy Programme.

ECA assists member states in the assessment and use of water resources and the development of river and lake basins common to more than one country. ECA encourages co-operation between countries with regard to water issues and collaborates with other UN agencies and regional organizations to promote technical and economic co-operation in this area. A meeting of chief executives of river and lake basin organizations in Africa was scheduled to be held, under ECA auspices, in July 1999. ECA has been particularly active in efforts to promote the integrated development of the water resources of the Zambezi river basin and of Lake Victoria.

In all of its activities ECA aims to strengthen institutional capacities in order to support the process of regional integration, and aims to assist countries to implement existing co-operative agreements, for example by promoting the harmonization of macroeconomic and taxation policies and the removal of non-tariff barriers to trade.

## Finance

For the two-year period 1998–99 ECA's regular budget, an appropriation from the UN budget, was an estimated US $89.6m.

## Publications

*Annual Report of the ECA.*
*Africa Index* (2 a year).
*African Population Newsletter* (2 a year).
*African Population Studies* series (irregular).
*African Socio-Economic Indicators* (annually).
*African Statistical Yearbook.*
*African Trade Bulletin* (2 a year).
*African Women Report* (annually).
*Compendium of Intra-African and Related Foreign Trade Statistics.*
*Demographic Handbook for Africa* (irregular).
*Devindex Africa* (quarterly).
*Directory of African Statisticians* (every 2 years).
*ECA Development Policy Review.*
*ECA Environment Newsletter* (3 a year).
*Flash on Trade Opportunities* (quarterly).
*Focus on African Industry* (2 a year).
*Human Development in Africa Report* (every 2 years).
*PADIS Newsletter* (quarterly).
*People First* (2 a year).
*Report of the Executive Secretary* (every 2 years).
*Rural Progress* (2 a year).
*Statistical Newsletter* (2 a year).
*Survey of Economic and Social Conditions in Africa* (annually).

# Economic and Social Commission for Western Asia—ESCWA

**Address:** Riad es-Solh Sq., POB 11-8575, Beirut, Lebanon.
**Telephone:** (1) 981301; **fax:** (1) 981510; **internet:** www.escwa.org.lb.

The UN Economic Commission for Western Asia was established in 1974 by a resolution of the UN Economic and Social Council (ECOSOC), to provide facilities of a wider scope for those countries previously served by the UN Economic and Social Office in Beirut (UNESOB). The name 'Economic and Social Commission for Western Asia' (ESCWA) was adopted in 1985.

### MEMBERS

| | |
|---|---|
| Bahrain | Palestine |
| Egypt | Qatar |
| Iraq | Saudi Arabia |
| Jordan | Syria |
| Kuwait | United Arab Emirates |
| Lebanon | Yemen |
| Oman | |

## Organization

(December 1999)

### COMMISSION

The sessions of the Commission (held every two years) are attended by delegates from member states. Representatives of UN bodies and specialized agencies, regional organizations, other UN member states, and non-governmental organizations having consultative status with ECOSOC may attend as observers.

### PREPARATORY COMMITTEE

The Committee, formerly the Technical Committee, has the task of reviewing programming issues and presenting recommendations in that regard to the sessions of the Commission. It is the principal subsidiary body of the Commission and functions as its policy-making structure. Six specialized inter-governmental committees have been established to consider specific areas of activity, to report on these to the Preparatory Committee and to assist the Committee in formulating ESCWA's medium-term work programmes.

**Statistical Committee:** first session convened in 1995; meets every two years.

**Committee on Social Development:** established in 1994; meets every two years.

**Committee on Energy:** established in 1995; meets every two years.

**Committee on Water Resources:** established in 1995; meets annually.

**Committee on Transport:** established in 1997; meets every two years.

**Committee on Liberalization of Foreign Trade and Economic Globalization:** established in 1997; meets annually.

### SECRETARIAT

The Secretariat comprises an Executive Secretary, a Deputy Executive Secretary, a Senior Advisor and Secretary of the Commission, an Information Services Unit and a Programme Planning and Co-ordination Unit. ESCWA's technical and substantive activities are undertaken by the following divisions: energy, natural resources and environment; social development issues and policies; economic development issues and policies; sectoral issues and policies; statistics; and technical co-operation.

**Executive Secretary:** Dr HAZEM ABD EL-AZIZ EL-BEBLAWI (Egypt).

## Activities

ESCWA is responsible for proposing policies and actions to support development and to further economic co-operation and integration in western Asia. ESCWA undertakes or sponsors studies of economic social and development issues of the region, collects and disseminates information, and provides advisory services to member states in various fields of economic and social development. It also organizes conferences and intergovernmental and export group meetings and sponsors training workshops and seminars.

Much of ESCWA's work is carried out in co-operation with other UN bodies, as well as with other international and regional organizations, for example the League of Arab States (q.v.) the Co-operation Council for the Arab States of the Gulf (q.v.) and the Organization of the Islamic Conference (OIC, q.v.).

ESCWA works within the framework of medium-term plans, which are divided into two-year programmes of action and priorities. The biennium 1994–95 was considered to be a transitional period during which the Commission restructured its work programme. This restructuring focused ESCWA activities from 15 to five sub-programmes. A further reorganization of the sub-programmes was implemented in 1997 to provide the framework for activities in the medium-term period 1998–2001.

### MANAGEMENT OF NATURAL RESOURCES AND ENVIRONMENT

The main objective of the sub-programme was to promote regional co-ordination and co-operation in the management of natural resources, in particular water resources and energy, and the protection of the environment. The sub-programme aimed to counter the problem of an increasing shortage of freshwater resources and deterioration in water quality resulting from population growth, agricultural land-use and socio-economic development, by supporting measures for more rational use and conservation of water resources, and by promoting public awareness and community participation in water and environmental protection projects. In addition, ESCWA aimed to assist governments in the formulation and implementation of capacity-building programmes and the development of surface and groundwater resources.

ESCWA supports co-operation in the establishment of electricity distribution and supply networks throughout the region and promotes the use of alternative sources of energy and the development of new and renewable energy technologies. Similarly, ESCWA promotes the application of environmentally sound technologies in order to achieve sustainable development, as well as measures to recycle resources, minimize waste and reduce the environmental impact of transport operations and energy use. Under the sub-programme ESCWA was to collaborate with national, regional and international organizations in monitoring and reporting on emerging environmental issues and to pursue implementation of Agenda 21, which was adopted at the June 1992 UN conference on Environment and Development, with particular regard to land and water resource management and conservation.

### IMPROVEMENT OF THE QUALITY OF LIFE

ESCWA's key areas of activity in this sub-programme were population, human development, the advancement of women and human settlements, and, in particular, to pursue the implementation of recommendations relevant to the region of the four UN world conferences held on these themes during the mid-1990s.

ESCWA's objectives with regard to population were to increase awareness and understanding of links between population factors and poverty, human rights and the environment, and to strengthen the capacities of member states to analyse and assess demographic trends and migration. The main aim in the area of human development was to further the alleviation of poverty and to generate a sustainable approach to development through, for example, greater involvement of community groups in decision-making and projects to strengthen production and income-generating capabilities. The sub-programme incorporated activities to ensure all gender-related recommendations of the four world conferences could be pursued in the region, including support for the role of the family and assistance to organizations for monitoring and promoting the advancement of women. With regard to human settlements, the objectives of the sub-programme were to monitor and identify problems resulting from rapid urbanization and social change, to promote understanding and awareness of the problems and needs of human settlements, and to strengthen the capacity of governments in the region in formulating appropriate policies and strategies for sustainable human settlement development.

### ECONOMIC DEVELOPMENT AND GLOBAL CHANGES

During the period 1998–2001 ESCWA aimed to support member states in their understanding of the process of globalization of the world economy and their participation in international trading negotiations and arrangements. ESCWA also aimed to strengthen the capacity of members in implementing economic reform policies, financial management and other structural adjustment measures, and to facilitate intra-regional trade, investment and capital movements.

### CO-ORDINATION OF POLICIES AND HARMONIZATION OF NORMS AND REGULATIONS FOR SECTORAL DEVELOPMENT

This sub-programme was concerned with the harmonization of standards throughout the region in the areas of transport, industry, agriculture and technology. ESCWA aimed to promote co-operation among member states in transport and infrastructure policies and greater uniformity of safety and legal standards, the latter with a view to facilitating border crossings between countries in the region. ESCWA, similarly, aimed to assist local industries to meet regional and international standards and regulations, as well as to improve the competitiveness of industries through the development of skills and policies and greater co-operation with other national and regional support institutions. ESCWA strategies to develop the agricultural potential of member states included resource conservation activities, agricultural management, institution-building and harmonization of regulations and norms. In the field of technology the sub-programme was designed to strengthen the capabilities of member states, to promote the transfer of technologies, research and development activities, and to enhance collaboration in the production sector.

### DEVELOPMENT, CO-ORDINATION AND HARMONIZATION OF STATISTICS AND INFORMATION

In the medium-term ESCWA aimed to develop the statistical systems of member states in order to improve the relevance and accuracy of economic and social data, and to implement measures to make the information more accessible to planners and researchers. ESCWA also intended to promote the comparability of statistics, through implementation of various standard international systems and programmes, particularly focusing on a series of national population and housing censuses scheduled to be conducted in the region in 2000.

## Finance

ESCWA's share of the UN budget for the two years 1998–99 was US $49.5m., compared with $33.2m. for the previous biennium.

## Publications

All publications are annual, unless otherwise indicated.

*Agriculture and Development in Western Asia.*

*External Trade Bulletin of the ESCWA Region.*

*National Accounts Studies of the ESCWA Region.*

*Population Bulletin of the ESCWA Region.*

*Prices and Financial Statistics in the ESCWA Region.*

*Socio-economic Data Sheet* (every 2 years).

*Statistical Abstract of the ESCWA Region.*

*Survey of Economic and Social Developments in the ESCWA Region.*

*Transport Bulletin.*

# OTHER UNITED NATIONS BODIES

## Office for the Co-ordination of Humanitarian Affairs—OCHA

**Address:** United Nations Plaza, New York, NY 10017, USA.

**Telephone:** (212) 963-1234; **fax:** (212) 963-1312; **e-mail:** ochany@un.org; **internet:** www.reliefweb.int.

OCHA was established in January 1998 as part of the UN Secretariat, with a mandate to co-ordinate international humanitarian assistance and to provide policy and other advice on humanitarian issues. It replaced the Department of Humanitarian Affairs, established in 1992.

### Organization

(December 1999)

OCHA has headquarters in New York, and in Geneva, Switzerland, and it maintains a field presence in 22 locations. In 1999 there were 137 staff at the headquarters (of whom 50 were regular staff and 87 were extrabudgetary) and 57 field staff.

**Under Secretary-General for Humanitarian Affairs and Emergency Relief Co-ordinator:** SÉRGIO VIEIRA DE MELLO (Brazil).

### Activities

OCHA's mandate is to work with UN agencies, governments, intergovernmental humanitarian organizations and non-governmental organizations to ensure that a co-ordinated and effective response to emergency situations is provided. OCHA reaches agreement with other UN bodies regarding the division of responsibilities, which may include field missions to assess requirements, organizing Consolidated Inter-agency Appeals for financial assistance, and mobilizing other resources. The Emergency Relief Co-ordinator is the principal adviser to the UN Secretary-General on humanitarian issues. He chairs an Inter-Agency Standing Committee (IASC), which co-ordinates and administers the international response to humanitarian disasters and to the development of relevant policies. The Co-ordinator also acts as Convener of the Executive Committee for Humanitarian Affairs, which provides a forum for humanitarian agencies, as well as the political and peace-keeping departments of the UN Secretariat, to exchange information on emergency situations and humanitarian issues.

OCHA monitors developments throughout the world and undertakes contingency planning to enable it to respond immediately to emergency situations. A Humanitarian Early Warning System (HEWS) has been established to assess indicators in order to identify the likelihood of a humanitarian crisis occurring in a certain area. An Integrated Regional Information Network (IRIN) was created in 1995 in Nairobi, Kenya, to disseminate information on the humanitarian situation in central and east Africa. Additional IRINs have since been established in Abidjan, Côte d'Ivoire, and Johannesburg, South Africa, in order to provide accurate information concerning developments in western and southern Africa. An IRIN for central Asia and central and eastern Europe, which had been scheduled to open in Ankara, Turkey, in mid-1998, was postponed, owing to a lack of funding. A complementary service, ReliefWeb, which was launched in 1996, monitors crises and publishes the information obtained on the internet. IRIN and ReliefWeb together form part of OCHA's Policy, Analysis and Information Division, based in New York. In addition, OCHA holds a number of conferences and workshops.

OCHA administers a Disaster Response System, which monitors field situations, liaises with UN Resident Co-ordinators worldwide and undertakes disaster-preparedness activities. UN Disaster Assessment and Co-ordination (UNDAC) teams, established by OCHA with the aid of donor governments, are available for immediate deployment to help to determine requirements and to co-ordinate assistance in those countries affected by disasters, for example by establishing reliable telecommunications and securing other logistical support. OCHA maintains a Central Register of Disaster Management Capacities, which may be available for international assistance. In addition, emergency equipment and supplies are held in a warehouse in Pisa, Italy, ready for emergency dispatch. OCHA also issues Situation Reports to inform the international community of any emergency situation, the type and level of assistance required and action being undertaken.

In 1998 OCHA appealed for some US $2,160m. of assistance to support 12.8m. people in need of emergency relief. By the end of that year the international community had provided some $1,061m. in aid (including bilateral aid), of which $33m. was for OCHA's co-ordination activities in the field. The Consolidated Inter-agency Appeal Process (CAP) was established to organize a co-ordinated response to resource mobilization following humanitarian crises. Between 1992 and mid-1999 108 CAP appeals were launched, generating some US $13,300m. A Central Emergency Revolving Fund (CERF), under the authority of the Emergency Relief Co-ordinator, enables humanitarian agencies to provide an immediate response to emergencies, before donor contributions become available. Agencies borrowing from the fund are required to reimburse the amount loaned within a certain period of time, which is not to exceed one year. Between 1992 and mid-1999 the CERF was used 61 times, making disbursements totalling $135.7m.

### Finance

OCHA's budgetary requirements for 1999–2000 were an estimated US $42.4m., of which about $18.4m. was to be provided from the regular budget of the UN.

### Publication

*OCHANews* (weekly).

## Office for Drug Control and Crime Prevention—ODCCP

**Address:** Vienna International Centre, POB 500, 1400 Vienna, Austria.

**Telephone:** (1) 26060-4266; **fax:** (1) 26060-5866; **internet:** www.odccp.org.

The Office was established in November 1997 to strengthen the UN's integrated approach to issues relating to drug control, crime prevention and international terrorism. It comprises two principal components: the United Nations International Drug Control Programme and the Centre for International Crime Prevention, both headed by the ODCCP Executive Director.

A new UN Global Programme against Money Laundering was established within the framework of the ODCCP to provide technical and legal assistance to Governments in monitoring financial transactions and establishing appropriate frameworks to counter the problem. The Programme, in collaboration with other governmental organizations, law enforcement agencies and academic institutions, aimed to establish a comprehensive database on money-laundering legislation throughout the world, and constituted a key element in ODCCP activities in support of the elaboration of an International Convention against Transnational Organized Crime. In March 1999 the Programme inaugurated an Offshore Initiative with a proposed set of guide-lines for the acceptable operation of offshore centres.

**Executive Director:** PINO ARLACCHI (Italy).

## UNITED NATIONS INTERNATIONAL DRUG CONTROL PROGRAMME—UNDCP

UNDCP was established in 1991 to co-ordinate the activities of all UN specialized agencies and programmes in matters of international drug control. The structures of the former Division of Narcotic Drugs, the UN Fund for Drug Abuse Control and the secretariat of the International Narcotics Control Board (see below) were integrated into the new body. Accordingly, UNDCP became the focal point for promoting the UN Decade Against Drug Abuse (1991–2000) and for assisting member states to implement the Global Programme of Action that was adopted by the General Assembly in 1990 with the objective of achieving an international society free of illicit drugs and drug abuse. At a special summit meeting of the UN General Assembly, held in June 1998, heads of state and representatives of some 150 countries adopted a global strategy, formulated on the basis of UNDCP proposals, to reduce significantly the production of illicit substances, by 2008, and to strengthen drug prevention, treatment and rehabilitation programmes, by 2003.

UNDCP serves as an international centre of expertise and information on drug abuse control, with the capacity to provide legal and technical assistance in relevant concerns. The Programme supports governments in efforts to strengthen their institutional capacities for drug control (for example, drug identification and drug law enforcement training) and to prepare and implement national drug control 'master plans'. Efforts to enhance regional co-operation in the control of narcotics are also supported. Through these national and regional strategies. UNDCP aims to reduce the demand for illicit drugs, to suppress trafficking in these substances and to reduce the production of drugs, for example by creating alternative sources of income for farmers economically dependent on the production of illicit narcotic crops. This latter approach has been successfully applied in Laos, reducing the levels of opium cultivation, and in the coca-growing regions of Peru, Bolivia and Colombia.

UNDCP sponsors activities to generate public awareness of the harmful effects of drug abuse, as part of its efforts to reduce the demand for illicit drugs. Preventive education programmes, reaching some 650,000 schoolchildren, have been undertaken in 13 Latin American and Caribbean countries and territories. UNDCP also works with governments, as well as non-governmental and private organizations, in the treatment, rehabilitation and social reintegration of drug addicts. UNDCP undertakes research to monitor the drugs problem: for example, assessing the characteristics of drug-users and the substances being used, to help identify people at risk of becoming drug users and to enhance the effectiveness of national programmes to address the issue. More recent specific concerns of UNDCP include the damaging environmental effects of the illicit cultivation of drugs, in particular in the Andean region of Latin America and in South and East Asia, and the abuse of drugs in sport. In February 1995 a memorandum of understanding was signed by the Programme and the International Olympic Committee, initiating a joint campaign entitled 'Sport against drugs'.

UNDCP promotes implementation of the following major treaties which govern the international drug control system: the Single Convention on Narcotic Drugs (1961) and a Protocol amending the Convention (1972); the Convention on Psychotropic Substances (1971); and the UN Convention against Illicit Traffic in Narcotic Drugs and Psychotropic Substances (1988). Among other important provisions, these treaties aim to restrict severely the production of narcotic drugs, while ensuring an adequate supply for medical and scientific purposes, to prevent profits obtained from the illegal sale of drugs being diverted into legal usage and to secure the extradition of drug-traffickers and the transfer of proceedings for criminal prosecution. UNDCP assists countries to adapt their national legislation and drug policies to facilitate their compliance with these conventions and to enhance co-ordinated efforts with other governments to control the movement of drugs. UNDCP services meetings of the International Narcotics Control Board, an independent body responsible for promoting and monitoring government compliance with the provisions of the drug control treaties, and of the Commission on Narcotic Drugs, which, as a functional committee of ECOSOC (q.v.), is the main policy-making organ within the UN system on issues relating to international drug abuse control.

In April 1999 UNDCP became the seventh co-sponsor of the Joint UN Programme on HIV and AIDS (UNAIDS), which was established on 1 January 1996 by UNICEF, UNDP, UNFPA, UNESCO, WHO and the World Bank. UNDCP's participation was in recognition of the importance of international drug control efforts in preventing the spread of HIV/AIDS.

### Finance

The UNDCP Fund receives an allocation from the regular budget of the UN, although voluntary contributions from member states and private organizations represent the majority of its resources. The regular budget for the two year period 1998–99 amounted to US $16.3m., while the proposed voluntary funded budget totalled $148.6m.

### Publications

*Bulletin on Narcotics* (quarterly).

*Global Illicit Drug Trends.*

*ODCCP Update* (quarterly).

*Technical Series.*

## CENTRE FOR INTERNATIONAL CRIME PREVENTION—CICP

The CICP is the UN body responsible for crime prevention, criminal justice and criminal law reform. It assists members in the use and application of international standards and norms relating to these areas, for example the Minimum Rules for the Treatment of Prisoners, Conventions against Torture, and Other Cruel, Inhuman or Degrading Treatment or Punishment, and Safeguards Guaranteeing the Protection of the Rights of Those Facing the Death Penalty. The Centre is also responsible for technical co-operation activities and aims to strengthen national capacities to reform and establish appropriate legal and criminal justice systems. In 1999 the CICP was designated to conduct technical studies in support of a new Global Programme against Corruption, a three-year Global Programme against Trafficking in Human Beings, and Global Studies on Organized Crime, which aimed to analyse emerging transnational criminal organizations and assist countries to formulate strategies to combat the problem. During 1999 the CICP continued to undertake preparations for the 10th UN Congress on the Prevention of Crime and Treatment of Offenders, which was to be convened in April 2000 specifically to consider the challenges of the 21st century.

The CICP promotes research and undertakes studies of new forms of crime prevention, in collaboration with the UN Interregional Crime and Justice Research Institute (UNICRI, q.v.). It also maintains a UN Crime and Justice Information Network database (UNCJIN), which provides information on national crime statistics, publications and links to other relevant intergovernmental agencies and research and academic institutes.

### Finance

The Centre has an annual administrative budget of US $2.5m.

# Office of the United Nations High Commissioner for Human Rights—OHCHR

**Address:** Palais des Nations, 1211 Geneva 10, Switzerland.

**Telephone:** (22) 9177900; **fax:** (22) 9179012; **e-mail:** scrt.hchr@unog.ch; **internet:** www.unhchr.ch.

The Office is a body of the UN Secretariat and is the focal point for UN human rights activities. Since September 1997 it has incorporated the Centre for Human Rights.

## Organization

(December 1999)

### HIGH COMMISSIONER

In December 1993 the UN General Assembly decided to establish the position of a United Nations High Commissioner for Human Rights (UNHCHR) following a recommendation of the World Conference on Human Rights, held in Vienna, Austria, in June of that year. The High Commissioner, who is the UN official with principal responsibility for UN human rights activities, is appointed by the UN Secretary-General, with the approval of the General Assembly, for a four-year term in office, renewable for one term.

**High Commissioner:** MARY ROBINSON (Ireland).

**Deputy to the High Commissioner:** BERTRAND GANGAPERSAND RAMCHARAN (Guyana).

### ADMINISTRATION

The work of the Office is conducted by the following branches: Research and Right to Development, responsible for human rights policy development, undertaking research and providing information to the High Commissioner and other human rights experts, working groups, etc.; Support Services, which provides administrative support to UN human rights mechanisms, including the Commission on Human Rights and its working groups, and the Subcommission on the Prevention of Discrimination and Protection of Minorities and its working groups; and Activities and Programmes, which conducts field operations, provides advice and technical assistance to governments, and implements special procedures relating to human rights concerns. The Office also comprises a Staff Office, an Administrative Section and a branch office in New York, USA.

### FIELD PRESENCES

As the Office's involvement in field work has expanded, a substantial structure of field presences has developed to strengthen this aspect of the Office's work. In 1999 there were 22 field presences, covering the following areas: Abkhazia (Georgia), Angola, Burundi, Central African Republic, Colombia, the Democratic Republic of the Congo, El Salvador, Gaza (Emerging Palestinian Autonomous Areas), Guatemala, Liberia, Malawi, Mongolia, Rwanda, Sierra Leone, South Africa, Southern Africa, Togo and the former Yugoslavia.

## Activities

The mandate of the OHCHR incorporates the following functions and responsibilities: the promotion and protection of human rights throughout the world; the reinforcement of international co-operation in the field of human rights; the promotion of universal ratification and implementation of international standards; the establishment of a dialogue with governments to ensure respect for human rights; and co-ordination of efforts by other UN programmes and organs to promote respect for human rights. The Office may study and react to cases of serious violations of human rights, and may undertake diplomatic efforts to prevent violations. It also produces educational and other information material to enhance understanding of human rights. The Office is the lead agency in undertaking preparations for the World Conference against Racism, Racial Discrimination, Xenophobia and Related Intolerance, scheduled to be convened in South Africa in July 2001.

OHCHR field offices and operations ('field presences'—see above) undertake a variety of activities, such as training and other technical assistance, support for Special Rapporteurs (usually appointed by the Commission on Human Rights), monitoring and fact-finding, and are increasingly a regular component of the Office's activities. In response to this development, the OHCHR has initiated a process of reviewing its activities in the field and of integrating them more effectively into the Office's overall structure and objectives.

During 1999 the High Commissioner investigated reports of gross violations of human rights in Kosovo and Metohija (the Federal Republic of Yugoslavia), Sierra Leone and East Timor, and issued reports to the Commission on Human Rights. In September the High Commissioner recommended the establishment of an international commission of inquiry to pursue consideration of the alleged abuses of human rights committed by the Indonesian authorities in East Timor during 1999. Within the framework of the interim administration in Kosovo, OHCHR was responsible for chairing a Joint Commission on Prisoners and Detainees, which met for the first time in September.

### TECHNICAL CO-OPERATION PROGRAMME

The UN Technical Co-operation Programme in the Field of Human Rights has been operational since 1955 to assist states, at their request, to strengthen their capacities in the observance of democracy, human rights, and the rule of law. The Programme has expanded significantly in recent years and is one of the key components of OHCHR's activities. Examples of work undertaken within the framework of the programme include training courses and workshops on good governance and the observance of human rights, expert advisory services on the incorporation of international human rights standards into national legislation and policies and on the formulation of national plans of action for the promotion and protection of human rights, fellowships, the provision of information and documentation, and consideration of promoting a human rights culture.

## Finance

The Office is financed from the regular budget of the UN.

## Publications

*Fact sheet series.*

*Human Rights Quarterly.*

*Human rights study series.*

*Professional training series.*

Other reference material, reports, proceedings of conferences, workshops, etc.

# United Nations Centre for Human Settlements—UNCHS (Habitat)

**Address:** POB 30030, Nairobi, Kenya.

**Telephone:** (2) 621234; **fax:** (2) 624266; **e-mail:** habitat@unchs.org; **internet:** www.unchs.org.

UNCHS (Habitat) was established in October 1978 to service the intergovernmental Commission on Human Settlements, and to serve as a focus for human settlements activities in the UN system.

## Organization

(December 1999)

### UN COMMISSION ON HUMAN SETTLEMENTS

The Commission (see ECOSOC, p. 15) is the governing body of UNCHS (Habitat). It meets every two years and has 58 members, serving for four years. Sixteen members are from Africa, 13 from Asia, six from eastern European countries, 10 from Latin America and 13 from western Europe and other countries.

### CENTRE FOR HUMAN SETTLEMENTS

The Centre services the Commission on Human Settlements, implements its resolutions and ensures the integration and co-ordination of technical co-operation, research and policy advice. Its Work Programme incorporates the following priority areas, as defined by the Commission: Shelter and social services; Urban management; Environment and infrastructure; and Assessment, information and monitoring.

In 1992 the UN General Assembly designated UNCHS (Habitat) as the *ad hoc* secretariat for the Second UN Conference on Human Settlements, Habitat II, which was held in Istanbul, Turkey, in June 1996. As a result, most of the Centre's activities in recent years have been concerned with servicing and stimulating participation in the preparatory process for the Conference at global, regional, national and local levels.

**Executive Director:** Dr KLAUS TÖPFER (Germany) (acting).

## Activities

UNCHS (Habitat) supports and conducts capacity-building and operational research, provides technical co-operation and policy advice, and disseminates information with the aim of strengthening the development and management of human settlements.

In June 1996 representatives of 171 national governments and of more than 500 municipal authorities attending Habitat II adopted a Global Plan of Action (the 'Habitat Agenda'), which incorporated detailed programmes of action to realize economic and social development and environmental sustainability, and endorsed the conference's objectives of ensuring 'adequate shelter for all' and 'sustainable human settlements development in an urbanizing world'. UNCHS (Habitat) was expected to provide the leadership and serve as a focal point for the implementation of the Agenda. It has consequently undertaken a process of restructuring its working methods and organization, which was still ongoing in 1998. In 1999 UNCHS (Habitat) approved a set of 23 resolutions to reduce poverty, improve shelter and environmental conditions, promote good governance, and improve the status of women. A special session of the UN General Assembly was to be held in 2001 to report on the implementation of the recommendations of the Habitat II conference.

Following the June 1996 conference, UNCHS (Habitat) established a Global Urban Observatory to monitor implementation of the Habitat Agenda and to report on local and national plans of action, international and regional support programmes and ongoing research and development. The Observatory, which incorporates the Best Practices and Local Leadership Programme and the Urban Indicators Programme, operates through an international network of regional and national institutions, all of which provide local training in appropriate data collection methods and in the development, adoption and maintenance of reliable information systems.

UNCHS (Habitat) is the co-ordinating agency for the implementation of the Global Strategy for Shelter to the Year 2000 (GSS), adopted by the General Assembly in 1988. The GSS aims to facilitate the construction and improvement of housing for all, in particular by and for the poorest in society, and promotes the use of legal and other incentives to encourage non-governmental parties to become engaged in housing and urban development.

Through its Women in Human Settlements Development Programme, which was established in 1990, UNCHS (Habitat) ensured that the issue of human settlements was included in the agenda of the UN Fourth World Conference on Women, which was held in Beijing, People's Republic of China, in September 1995, and successfully incorporated the right of women to ownership of land and property into the Global Platform for Action which resulted from the conference. An advisory board, the Huairou Commission, comprising women from 'grass-roots' groups, non-governmental organizations (NGOs), the UN and research and political institutions, has since been established to ensure a link between the Beijing and Habitat Agendas and the inclusion of gender issues in the follow-up to Habitat II.

The Centre participates in implementing the human settlements component of Agenda 21, which was adopted at the UN Conference on Environment and Development in June 1992, and is also responsible for the chapter of Agenda 21 that refers to solid waste management and sewage-related issues. UNCHS (Habitat) implements a programme entitled 'Localizing Agenda 21', to assist local authorities in developing countries to address local environmental and infrastructure-related problems. It also collaborates with national governments, private-sector and non-governmental institutions and UN bodies to achieve the objectives of Agenda 21. The Settlement Infrastructure and Environment Programme was initiated in 1992 to support developing countries in improving the environment of human settlements through policy advice and planning, infrastructure management and enhancing awareness of environmental and health concerns in areas such as water, sanitation, waste management and transport. An Urban Management Programme aims to strengthen the contribution of cities and towns in developing countries towards human development, including economic growth, social advancements, the reduction of poverty and the improvement of the environment. The Programme is an international technical co-operation project, of which UNCHS (Habitat) is the executing agency, the World Bank is an associated agency, while UNDP provides core funding and monitoring. The Programme is operated through regional offices, in collaboration with bilateral and multilateral support agencies, and brings together national and local authorities, community leaders and representatives of the private sector to consider specific issues and solutions to urban problems. A Sustainable Cities Programme, operated jointly with UNEP, is concerned with incorporating environmental issues into urban planning and management, in order to ensure sustainable and equitable development. The Programme is active in some 20 cities worldwide, although a prepared series of policy guide-lines is used in many others. Some 95% of the Programme's resources are spent at city level to strengthen the capacities of municipal authorities and their public-, private- and community-sector partners in the field of environmental planning and management, with the objective that the concepts and approaches of the Programme are replicated throughout the region. UNCHS (Habitat) provides the secretariat of the Urban Environment Forum, which has been developed as a global network of city authorities, international agencies and other bodies concerned with exchanging information and policies in order to improve the urban environment. In addition, UNCHS (Habitat) supports training and other activities designed to strengthen management development (in particular in the provision and maintenance of services and facilities) at local and community level.

Increasingly UNCHS (Habitat) is being called upon to contribute to the relief, rehabilitation and development activities undertaken by the UN in areas affected by regional and civil conflict. UNCHS (Habitat) has been actively involved in the reconstruction of human settlements and other development activities in Afghanistan, and in 1997/98 was also contributing to reconstruction programmes in Angola, Iraq, Rwanda and Somalia. In November 1999 it was announced that UNCHS (Habitat) was to administer a new Housing and Property Directorate in post-conflict Kosovo and Metohija, within the framework of the UN's interim administration in the province.

## Finance

The Centre's work programme is financed from the UN regular budget, the Habitat and Human Settlements Foundation and from extra-budgetary resources. The approved budget for the two-year period 2000–01 amounted to US $23m.

## Publications

*Global Report on Human Settlements.*

*Habitat Debate* (quarterly).

Technical reports and studies, occasional papers, bibliographies, directories.

# United Nations Children's Fund—UNICEF

**Address:** 3 United Nations Plaza, New York, NY 10017, USA.

**Telephone:** (212) 326-7000; **fax:** (212) 888-7465; **e-mail:** netmaster@unicef.org; **internet:** www.unicef.org.

UNICEF was established in 1946 by the UN General Assembly as the UN International Children's Emergency Fund, to meet the emergency needs of children in post-war Europe and China. In 1950 its mandate was changed to respond to the needs of children in developing countries. In 1953 the General Assembly decided that UNICEF should continue its work, as a permanent arm of the UN system, with an emphasis on programmes giving long-term benefits to children everywhere, particularly those in developing countries. In 1965 UNICEF was awarded the Nobel Peace Prize.

## Organization

(December 1999)

### EXECUTIVE BOARD

The Executive Board, as the governing body of UNICEF, establishes policy, reviews programmes and approves expenditure. Membership comprises 36 governments from all regions, elected in rotation for a three-year term by ECOSOC.

### SECRETARIAT

The Executive Director of UNICEF is appointed by the UN Secretary-General in consultation with the Executive Board. The administration of UNICEF and the appointment and direction of staff are the responsibility of the Executive Director, under policy directives laid down by the Executive Board, and under a broad authority delegated to the Executive Director by the Secretary-General. At October 1999 there were some 5,600 UNICEF staff positions, of whom more than 86% were in the field.

**Executive Director:** CAROL BELLAMY (USA).

### UNICEF REGIONAL OFFICES

UNICEF has a network of eight regional and 125 field offices serving more than 160 countries and territories. Its offices in Tokyo, Japan and Brussels, Belgium support fund-raising activities; UNICEF's supply division is administered from the office in Copenhagen, Demark. A research centre concerned with child development is based in Florence, Italy.

**The Americas and the Caribbean:** Apdo 89829, Santafé de Bogotá, Colombia; tel. (1) 6357255; fax (1) 6357337; e-mail tacro@unicef.org.

**Central and Eastern Europe, Commonwealth of Independent States and Baltic States:** Palais des Nations, 1211 Geneva, Switzerland; tel. (22) 9095605; fax (22) 9095909; e-mail ceecisro@unicef.ch.

**East Asia and the Pacific:** POB 2-154, Bangkok 10200, Thailand; tel. (2) 2805931; fax (2) 2803563; e-mail eapro@unicef.org.

**Eastern and Southern Africa:** POB 44145, Nairobi, Kenya; tel. (2) 621234; fax (2) 622678; e-mail nairobiro@unicef.org.

**Europe:** Palais des Nations, 1211 Geneva 10, Switzerland; tel. (22) 9095111; fax (22) 9095900.

**Middle East and North Africa:** POB 840028, 11181 Amman, Jordan; tel. (6) 4629571; fax (6) 4640049; e-mail menaro@unicef.org.jo.

**South Asia:** POB 5815, Leknath Marg, Kathmandu, Nepal; tel. 1417082; fax 1419479; e-mail rosa@unicef.org.

**West and Central Africa:** BP 443, Abidjan 04, Côte d'Ivoire; tel. 213131; fax 227607; e-mail wcaro@unicef.org.

### OTHER UNICEF OFFICES

**International Child Development Centre:** Piazza SS. Annunziata 12, 50122 Florence, Italy; tel. (055) 2345258; fax (055) 244817; e-mail florence@unicef-icdc.it.

**Belgium:** POB 104, 1000 Brussels; tel. (2) 5132251; fax (2) 5132290.

**Denmark:** UNICEF Plads, Freeport 2100, Copenhagen; tel. (45) 35273527; fax (45) 35269421; e-mail supply@unicef.dk.

**Japan:** UN Bldg, 8th Floor, 53-70, Jingumae 5-chome, Shibuya-ku, Tokyo 150, Japan; tel. (3) 5467-4431; fax (3) 5467-4437; e-mail unicef@sh0.po.iijnet.or.jp.

### NATIONAL COMMITTEES

UNICEF is supported by 37 National Committees, mostly in industrialized countries, whose volunteer members, numbering more than 100,000, raise money through various activities, including the sale of greetings cards. The Committees also undertake advocacy and awareness campaigns on a number of issues and provide an important link with the general public.

## Activities

UNICEF is dedicated to the well-being of children and women and works for the realization and protection of their rights within the frameworks of the Convention on the Rights of the Child, which was adopted by the UN General Assembly in 1989 and by 1998 was almost universally ratified, and of the Convention on the Elimination of All Forms of Discrimination Against Women, adopted by the UN General Assembly in 1979. UNICEF promotes the full implementation of the Conventions. It also continues to provide relief and rehabilitation assistance in emergencies. Through its extensive field network in some 161 developing countries, areas and territories, UNICEF undertakes, in co-ordination with governments, local communities and other aid organizations, programmes in health, nutrition, education, water and sanitation, the environment, women in development, and other fields of importance to children. Emphasis is placed on low-cost, community-based programmes. UNICEF programmes are increasingly focused on supporting children and women during critical periods of their life, when intervention was determined to make a lasting difference i.e. early childhood, the primary school years, adolescence and the reproductive years.

UNICEF was instrumental in organizing the World Summit for Children, held in September 1990 and attended by representatives from more than 150 countries, including 71 heads of state or government. The Summit produced a Plan of Action which recognized the rights of the young to 'first call' on their countries' resources and formulated objectives for the year 2000, including: (i) a reduction of the 1990 mortality rates for infants and children under five years by one-third, or to 50–70 per 1,000 live births, whichever is lower; (ii) a reduction of the 1990 maternal mortality rate by one-half; (iii) a reduction by one-half of the 1990 rate for severe malnutrition among children under the age of five; (iv) universal access to safe drinking water and to sanitary means of excreta disposal; and (v) universal access to basic education and completion of primary education by at least 80% of children. UNICEF supports the efforts of governments to achieve these objectives. In 2000 UNICEF planned to launch a new global initiative to promote a comprehensive approach to children's well-being which included survival, growth and development in early childhood, quality basic education for all, and adolescent health, development and participation.

UNICEF co-sponsored (with UNESCO, UNDP and the World Bank) the World Conference on Education for All, which was held in Thailand in March 1990, and has made efforts to achieve the objectives formulated by the conference, which include the elimination of disparities in education between boys and girls. Since the Conference an estimated 50m. more children had enrolled in primary schools in developing countries by 1999, however there was still concern at the lack of access to basic education and the drop-out rate. UNICEF, in co-operation with the World Bank and UNDP, promotes quality education for all and aims to achieve universal access to basic education and completion of primary school education by at least 80% of children by the end of 2000. UNICEF supports education projects in sub-Saharan Africa, South Asia and countries in the Middle East and North Africa. UNICEF implements a Girls' Education Programme in more than 50 developing countries, which aimed to increase the enrolment of girls in primary schools. In 1998 the African Girls' Education Initiative supported 4,200 schools and literacy centres in West and Central Africa.

Through UNICEF's efforts the needs and interests of children were incorporated into Agenda 21, which was adopted as a plan of action for sustainable development at the UN Conference on Environment and Development, held in June 1992. In mid-1997, at the UN General Assembly's Special Session on Sustainable Development, UNICEF highlighted the need to improve safe water supply, sanitation and hygiene as fundamental to fulfilment of child rights. In 1999 UNICEF continued to work with the World Bank to bring the benefits of safe water, sanitation and hygiene education to more than 250m. people in Africa. UNICEF also works with UNEP to promote environment issues of common concern and with the World Wide Fund for Nature to support the conservation of local ecosystems.

UNICEF aims to increase the level of development aid to developing countries, to ensure access to basic social services, and to help poor countries to obtain debt relief. UNICEF is the leading agency in promoting the 20/20 initiative, which was endorsed at the World Summit for Social Development, which took place in Copenhagen,

Denmark, in March 1995. It aimed to encourage the governments of developing and donor countries to allocate at least 20% of their domestic budgets and official development aid respectively, to health care, primary education and low-cost safe water and sanitation. In October 1998 the progress of the initiative was discussed at a meeting held in Hanoi, Viet Nam. Representatives of UNICEF, other UN and international agencies and of governments attending the meeting also considered measures to improve the quality and impact of these basic social services and of using resources more efficiently and equitably.

UNICEF supports special projects to provide education, counselling and care for the estimated 250m. children between the ages of five and 14 years working in developing countries, many of whom were thought to be engaged in hazardous or exploitative labour. UNICEF played a major role at the World Congress against Commercial Sexual Exploitation of Children, held in Stockholm, Sweden, in 1996, which adopted a Declaration and Agenda for Action to end the sexual exploitation of children. UNICEF also actively participated in the International Conference on Child Labour held in Oslo, Norway, in November 1997. The Conference adopted an Agenda for Action to eliminate the worst forms of child labour, including slavery-like practices, forced labour, commercial sexual exploitation and the use of children in drugs-trafficking and other hazardous forms of work. UNICEF supports the 1999 ILO Worst Forms of Child Labour Convention, which aims at the prohibition and immediate elimination of the worst forms of child labour. In 1999 UNICEF launched a global initiative, Education as a Preventive Strategy Against Child Labour, with the aim of providing schooling to millions of children forced to work full time.

Child health is UNICEF's largest programme sector, accounting for some 32% of programme expenditure in 1998. An estimated 11m. children under five years of age in developing countries die each year from largely preventable causes. UNICEF has worked with WHO and other partners to increase global immunization coverage against the following six diseases: measles, poliomyelitis, tuberculosis, diphtheria, whooping cough and tetanus. By 1999 more than 120 countries had achieved the objective of immunizing 80% of children against these diseases before their first birthday (compared with less than 5% in 1980), preventing more than 3m. child deaths each year. UNICEF and WHO also work in conjunction on the Integrated Management of Childhood Illness programme to control diarrhoeal dehydration, one of the largest causes of death among children under five years of age in the developing world. UNICEF-assisted programmes for the control of diarrhoeal diseases promote the low-cost manufacture and distribution of pre-packaged salts or home-made solutions. The use of 'oral rehydration therapy' rose from 17% in 1985 to nearly 70% in 1998, and is believed to prevent approximately 1.5m. child deaths each year. To control acute respiratory infections, which kill more than 1.9m. children under five years old each year, UNICEF works with WHO in training health workers to diagnose and treat the associated diseases in many developing countries. As a result, child deaths from pneumonia and other respiratory infections have been reduced by one-half since 1990. In October 1998 UNICEF, together with WHO, UNDP and the World Bank, inaugurated a new global campaign, Roll Back Malaria, to fight the disease which kills more than 1m. people each year. By 1999 there were control programmes in more than 30 countries.

According to UNICEF estimates, almost one-third of children under five years of age, or some 166m., are underweight, while each year malnutrition contributes to the deaths of almost 6m. children in that age group and leaves millions of others with physical and mental disabilities. UNICEF supports national efforts to reduce malnutrition, for example, fortifying staple foods with micronutrients, widening women's access to education, improving household food security and basic health services, and promoting sound child-care and feeding practices. By 1999 almost 15,000 hospitals in 132 countries had implemented the recommendations of UNICEF and WHO, entitled '10 steps to successful breast-feeding', to become 'baby-friendly'. In 1996 UNICEF expressed its concern at the impact of international economic embargoes on child health, citing as an example the extensive levels of child malnutrition recorded in Iraq. In early 1998 UNICEF remained actively concerned at the levels of child malnutrition and accompanying diseases in Iraq and in the Democratic People's Republic of Korea, which had suffered severe food shortages. During that year UNICEF worked to strengthen child-care facilities in those countries and operated nutritional rehabilitation centres. In October UNICEF published a report which highlighted the increasing incidence of poverty and child malnutrition throughout South and South-East Asia. In April UNICEF published a report entitled Generation in Jeopardy, concerned with the suffering of children as a result of war, poverty, disease and other social blights, particulary in areas of Africa and Eastern Europe.

UNICEF estimates that almost 600,000 women die every year during pregnancy or child birth, largely because of inadequate maternal health care, while some 300m. women live with permanent injuries or chronic disabilities resulting from complications during pregnancy or childbirth. With its partners in the Safe Motherhood Initiative—UNFPA, WHO, the World Bank, the International Planned Parenthood Federation, the Population Council, and Family Care International—UNICEF promotes measures to reduce maternal mortality and morbidity, including improving access to quality reproductive health services, educating communities about safe motherhood and the rights of women, training midwives, and expanding access to family planning services.

During 1998 an estimated 2.5m. young people, aged 15 to 24 years, were infected with the human immunodeficiency virus (HIV), while some 1,300 children under 15 died as a result of AIDS every day. UNICEF attempts to reduce the risk of transmission during pregnancy and childbirth, and promotes HIV/AIDS education and prevention programmes, particularly among young people. It also supports programmes to assist the estimated 11m. children who have lost one or both parents to AIDS since the epidemic began. UNICEF works closely in this field with governments and co-operates with other UN agencies in the Joint UN Programme on HIV/AIDS (UNAIDS), which became operational on 1 January 1996.

UNICEF provides assistance to countries affected by violence and social disintegration, in particular to assist the estimated 1m. children orphaned or separated from their parents and the 15m. children made homeless as a result of armed conflict in the past decade. In 1998 UNICEF extended emergency humanitarian assistance, including food, safe water, medicine and shelter to 26 countries affected by armed conflict. UNICEF also aims to assist ongoing development by supporting activities such as immunization and education (through 'Edukits') in refugee camps and the reconstruction of school buildings. Special programmes assist traumatized children and help unaccompanied children to be reunited with parents or extended families. In 1999 UNICEF mobilized humanitarian response teams to assist the thousands of ethnic Albanians fleeing the conflict in Kosovo and Metohija, southern Serbia. By mid-April UNICEF had delivered medicines, clothing and other essential items, valued at US $1.7m. The Fund pledged to support the enrolment of all refugee children into makeshift schools, and at the end of April initiated an immunization programme for all children under five years of age in camps in the former Yugoslav republic of Macedonia. UNICEF has subsequently worked to support the returning populations through mine-awareness campaigns, the provision of services to local hospitals for women and babies, and the distribution of school materials and other supplies. UNICEF-supported programmes help to rehabilitate former child soldiers in several countries, including Sierra Leone and Afghanistan, through counselling, education and job training. UNICEF continues to campaign to increase the minimum legal age for combatants from 15 to 18 years. UNICEF was an active participant in the so-called 'Ottawa' process (supported by the Canadian Government) to negotiate an international ban on anti-personnel land-mines which, it was estimated, kill and maim between 8,000 and 10,000 childen every year. The so-called Convention on the Prohibition of the Use, Stockpiling, Production and Transfer of Anti-Personnel Mines and on their Destruction, was signed by 123 countries in December 1997, and entered into force in March 1999. By October the Convention had been ratified by 89 countries. UNICEF was committed to campaigning for its universal ratification and implementation.

## Finance

UNICEF is funded by voluntary contributions from governments and non-governmental and private-sector sources. Total income in 1998 amounted to US $966m., of which 62% was from governments. Total expenditure in 1998 amounted to $882m.

UNICEF's income is divided between contributions for general resources, for supplementary funds and for emergencies. General resources are the funds available to fulfil commitments for co-operation in country programmes approved by the Executive Board, and to meet administrative and programme support expenditures. These funds amounted to US $571m. in 1998. Contributions for supplementary funds are those sought by UNICEF from governments and intergovernmental organizations to support projects for which general resources are insufficient, or for relief and rehabilitation programmes in emergency situations. Supplementary funding in 1998 amounted to $279m. Funding for emergencies in 1998 amounted to $116m.

## Publications

*Facts and Figures* (annually, in English, French and Spanish).

*The Progress of Nations* (annually, in Arabic, English, French, Russian, Spanish and more than 20 other national languages).

*The State of the World's Children* (annually, in Arabic, English, French, Russian and Spanish and about 30 other national languages).

*UNICEF Annual Report* (in English, French and Spanish).

*UNICEF at a Glance* (annually, in English, French and Spanish).

# United Nations Conference on Trade and Development—UNCTAD

**Address:** Palais des Nations, 1211 Geneva 10, Switzerland.

**Telephone:** (22) 9071234; **fax:** (22) 9070057; **e-mail:** ers@unctad.org; **internet:** www.unctad.org.

UNCTAD was established in December 1964. It is the principal instrument of the UN General Assembly concerned with trade and development, and is the focal point within the UN system for integrated activities relating to trade, finance, technology, investment and sustainable development. It aims to maximize the trade and development opportunities of developing countries, in particular least-developed countries, and to assist them to adapt to the increasing globalization and liberalization of the world economy.

## Organization

(December 1999)

### CONFERENCE

The Conference is the organization's highest policy-making body and normally meets every four years at ministerial level in order to formulate major policy guide-lines and to decide on UNCTAD's forthcoming programme of work. Ninth session: Midrand, South Africa, April/May 1996; 10th session: Bangkok, Thailand, February 2000. UNCTAD has 188 members, including all the UN member states, and many intergovernmental and non-governmental organizations participate in its work as observers.

### SECRETARIAT

The secretariat comprises the following Divisions: Globalization and Development Strategies; International Trade in Goods and Services and Commodities; Investment, Technology and Enterprise Development; Services Infrastructure for Development and Trade Efficiency. It also incorporates the Office of the Special Co-ordinator for Least Developed, Land-locked, and Small Island Developing States.

As well as servicing the Conference, the UNCTAD secretariat undertakes policy analysis; monitoring, implementation and follow-up of decisions of intergovernmental bodies; technical co-operation in support of UNCTAD's policy objectives; and information exchanges and consultations of various types. In October 1998 some 390 staff were employed at the secretariat.

**Secretary-General:** RUBENS RICÚPERO (Brazil).

### TRADE AND DEVELOPMENT BOARD

The Trade and Development Board is the executive body of UNCTAD. It comprises elected representatives from 144 UNCTAD member states and is responsible for ensuring the overall consistency of UNCTAD's activities, as well as those of its subsidiary bodies. The Board meets for a regular annual session lasting about 10 days, at which it examines global economic issues. It also reviews the implementation of the Programme of Action for the Least-Developed Countries and the UN New Agenda for the Development of Africa in the 1990s, with particular attention given to lessons that may be drawn from successful development experiences. The Board may also meet a further three times a year in order to address management or institutional matters.

### COMMISSIONS

The 1996 Conference approved the establishment of three Commissions to replace existing committees and working groups: the Commission on Trade in Goods and Services and Commodities; the Commission on Investment, Technology and Related Financial Issues; and the Commission on Enterprise, Business Facilitation and Development. UNCTAD also services the ECOSOC Commission on Science and Technology for Development (see below).

## Activities

During the 1980s one of UNCTAD's major roles was providing a forum for the negotiation of international agreements on commodities. These agreements were designed to ensure the stabilization of conditions in the trade of the commodities concerned. Agreements were negotiated on tin (1981), jute (1982), cocoa (1986), olive oil (1986) and rubber (1987). The establishment of the Common Fund for Commodities was agreed by UNCTAD in 1980, and the Fund came into operation in September 1989 (see p. 287). In 1994 the members of the International Tropical Timber Organization (see p. 288), meeting under UNCTAD auspices, decided to replace the International Tropical Timber Agreement of 1983 with ITTA 1994. The new agreement entered into force in January 1997.

By the early 1990s most of the commodity agreements had lapsed and the conclusion of the GATT Uruguay Round of trade talks in December 1993 and the changes in international trading structures that had already taken place were deemed to necessitate a substantial reorientation of UNCTAD's role. Following restructuring agreed at the eighth session of the Conference in Cartagena, Colombia, in February 1992, further changes to UNCTAD's focus and organization were approved at the ninth Conference that was held in Midrand, South Africa, in April/May 1996. In particular, UNCTAD was to give special attention to assisting developing countries in taking advantage of the increased liberalization of world trade under the GATT and World Trade Organization agreements (see p. 274). Concern was expressed that the world's poorest countries would be even further marginalized if they were not given additional support to enable them to begin to compete with more successful economies. During 1996 a Trust Fund for the Least Developed Countries was established, with an initial target figure of US $5m., with the aim of assisting those countries to become integrated into the world economy. UNCTAD has been mandated as the organ within the UN system responsible for negotiating a multilateral framework governing direct foreign investment that would protect the interests of the poorest countries, taking account of the work already undertaken by OECD in this area. In UNCTAD's revised approach, encouragement of foreign direct investment and of domestic private enterprise in developing countries and countries in transition have become central to the agency's work. UNCTAD is increasingly seeking the input and participation of non-governmental groups, such as academics, non-governmental organizations (NGOs) and business representatives, in its intergovernmental machinery, where appropriate. In November 1998 UNCTAD organized a Partners for Development summit meeting, with the aim of identifying development projects of interest to the private sector and facilitating co-operation between private companies, banks and development bodies. Some 2,700 representatives of the private sector, NGOs, academic institutions and governments from 172 countries attended the conference, which was held in Lyon, France. During the meeting the UNCTAD secretariat concluded 18 partnership agreements with private and public organizations, covering the following areas of activity: international transport; investment promotion; electronic commerce; the promotion of small and medium-sized enterprises and of entrepreneurship; conservation of biodiversity and sustainable development; and agricultural commodities.

The Commission on Trade in Goods and Services and Commodities examines ways of maximizing the positive impact of globalization and liberalization on sustainable development by assisting in the effective integration of developing countries into the international trading system. In the field of services, where developing countries suffer from deficiencies in the customs, financial and communications sectors, the Commission recommends ways for countries to overcome problems in these areas. In the field of commodities, the Commission promotes diversification, to reduce dependence on single commodities, transparency in commodity markets and the sustainable management of commodity resources. During the 1990s UNCTAD undertook research into the design and implementation of a multilateral system to trade emissions of so-called greenhouse gases. In June 1997, in co-operation with the Earth Council, UNCTAD established a Greenhouse Gas Emissions Trading Policy Forum. In October 1998 UNCTAD and the Earth Council sponsored the establishment of an International Emissions Trade Association (IETA), which was envisaged as a successor to the Forum, comprising multinational companies, international organizations and non-government organizations, government agencies, and industry associations. The IETA was to serve as a forum for the exchange of information and ideas relating to international emissions trading and as a means of developing the market in emission permit trading, which was scheduled to be launched in 2008.

The Commission on Investment, Technology and Related Financial Issues provides a forum to help general understanding of trends in the flow of foreign direct investment, which is considered one of the principal instruments for the integration of developing economies into the global system, and assists developing countries in improving their overall investment climate. The Commission examines issues related to competition law and assists developing countries in formulating competition policies. The Commission also undertakes the functions of the former ECOSOC Commission on International Investment and Transnational Corporations, which aimed to provide an understanding of the nature of foreign direct investment and transnational corporations, to secure effective international agreements and to strengthen the capacity of developing countries in their dealings with transnational corporations through an integrated approach, including research, information and technical assistance. A subsidiary body—the Intergovernmental Group of Experts on International Standards of Accounting and Reporting—aimed to improve the availability of information disclosed by transnational corporations. In November 1997 the UN General Assembly endorsed a proposal of the UN Secretary-General that the Group report directly through the UNCTAD Commission on Investment, Technology and Related Financial Issues.

The Commission on Enterprise, Business Facilitation and Development advises countries on policy-related issues and training activities concerning the development of entrepreneurship. It facilitates the exchange of experiences on the formulation and implementation of enterprise development strategies, including privatization, public-sector co-operation and the special problems relating to enterprise development in countries in economic transition.

UNCTAD is responsible for the Generalized System of Preferences (GSP), initiated in 1971, whereby a proportion of both agricultural and manufactured goods that are exported by developing countries receive preferential tariff treatment by certain developed countries, Russia and several central European countries. UNCTAD monitors changes in and amendments to national GSP schemes and reviews the use of these schemes by beneficiary developing countries. In addition, the Commission on Trade in Goods and Services and Commodities (see above) is responsible for providing a forum to examine the operation of schemes, the benefits they offer and the future role of the GSP. At November 1998 15 national GSP schemes were in operation, offered by 29 countries (including the 15 member countries of the European Union). Following the signing of the GATT Uruguay Round trade agreement in April 1994, UNCTAD estimated that the value of trade preferences for developing countries would be reduced, owing to a general reduction of tariffs. It advocated maintaining preferential margins for developing countries and extending GSP benefits to agricultural products and textiles from those countries after import quotas were eliminated, in accordance with the trade agreement.

Trade efficiency was discussed for the first time at the 1992 Conference, with computer-based technologies capable of substantially reducing the cost of transactions providing the focus. In 1994 a Global Trade Point Network (GTPNet), comprising an electronic network of trade-related information, was launched. The scheme, in which 120 countries were participating at November 1998, is monitored by the Commission on Enterprise, Business Facilitation and Development.

UNCTAD's work in the field of shipping and maritime activity resulted in the adoption of the UN Convention on a Code of Conduct for Liner Conferences (effective from 1983), which provides for the national shipping lines of developing countries to participate on an equal basis with the shipping lines of developed countries. Other UNCTAD initiatives have resulted in the adoption of the UN Convention on the Carriage of Goods by Sea (Hamburg Rules—1978), the UN Convention on International Multimodal Transport (1980), the UN Convention on Conditions for Registration of Ships (1986), and the International Convention on Maritime Liens and Mortgages. This last Convention was adopted in May 1993 in Geneva by a UN International Maritime Organization Conference of Plenipotentiaries, and its objectives were to encourage international uniformity in the field of maritime liens and mortgages and to improve conditions for ship financing. Technical co-operation and training projects, financed by UNDP and additional funds from bilateral donors, constitute an important component of UNCTAD's work in the fields of ports and multimodal transport and have resulted in the development of specialized courses. A software package Advance Cargo Information System (ACIS), enables shipping lines and railway companies to track the movement of cargo. Through the use of ACIS and the Automated System for Customs Data (ASYCUDA), operational in more than 75 countries, UNCTAD aims to enhance the effective exchange of information in order to counter customs fraud.

UNCTAD aims to give particular attention to the needs of the world's 48 least developed countries (LDCs—as defined by the UN). The eighth session of the Conference requested that detailed analyses of the socio-economic situations and domestic policies of the LDCs, their resource needs, and external factors affecting their economies be undertaken as part of UNCTAD's work programme. The ninth session determined that particular attention be given to the problems of the LDCs in all areas of UNCTAD's work.

UNCTAD provides assistance to developing countries in the area of debt-management, and in seeking debt relief from their creditors. UNCTAD and the World Bank have begun a joint programme to extend technical co-operation to developing countries in the field of debt management, where UNCTAD is responsible for the software component of the project. The assistance is based on the development and distribution of software (the Debt Management and Financial Analysis System—DMFAS) designed to enable debtor countries to analyse data, make projections, and to plan strategies for debt repayment and reorganization. UNCTAD provides training for operators in the use of the software, and for senior officials, to increase their awareness of institutional reforms which might be necessary for effective debt management.

The Secretariat provided technical assistance to developing countries in connection with the Uruguay Round of multilateral trade negotiations (see WTO). The International Trade Centre in Geneva is operated jointly by WTO and UNCTAD.

Since May 1993 UNCTAD has serviced the ECOSOC Commission on Science and Technology for Development, which provides a forum for discussion of the following issues relating to science and technology for development: technology for small-scale economic activities to address the basic needs of low-income countries; gender implications of science and technology for developing countries; science and technology and the environment; the contribution of technologies to industrialization in developing countries; and the role of information technologies, in particular in relation to developing countries. The Commission meets every two years.

# Finance

The operational expenses of UNCTAD are borne by the regular budget of the UN, and amount to approximately US $55m. annually. Technical co-operation activities, financed from extra-budgetary resources, amount to some $22m. annually.

# Publications

*Advanced Technology Assessment System Bulletin* (occasional).

*Guide to UNCTAD Publications* (annually).

*Handbook of International Trade and Development Statistics* (annually).

*The Least Developed Countries Report* (annually).

*Monthly Commodity Price Bulletin.*

*Review of Maritime Transport* (annually).

*Trade and Development Report* (annually).

*Transnational Corporations* (3 a year).

*UNCTAD Commodity Yearbook.*

*UNCTAD News* (6 a year).

*World Investment Report* (annually).

# United Nations Development Programme—UNDP

**Address:** One United Nations Plaza, New York, NY 10017, USA.

**Telephone:** (212) 906-5315; **fax:** (212) 906-5364; **e-mail:** hq@undp.org; **internet:** www.undp.org.

The Programme was established in 1965 by the UN General Assembly. Its central mission is to help countries to eradicate poverty and achieve a sustainable level of human development.

## Organization

(December 1999)

UNDP is responsible to the UN General Assembly, to which it reports through ECOSOC.

### EXECUTIVE BOARD

The Executive Board is responsible for providing intergovernmental support to, and supervision of, the activities of UNDP and the UN Population Fund (UNFPA). It comprises 36 members: eight from Africa, seven from Asia, four from eastern Europe, five from Latin America and the Caribbean and 12 from western Europe and other countries.

### SECRETARIAT

Offices and divisions at the Secretariat include: Planning and Resource Management; Development Policy Resources and External Affairs; Evaluation, Audit and Performance Review; and the Office of the Human Development Report. Five regional bureaux, all headed by an assistant administrator, cover: Africa; Asia and the Pacific; the Arab states; Latin America and the Caribbean; and Europe and the Commonwealth of Independent States.

**Administrator:** MARK MALLOCH BROWN (United Kingdom).

**Associate Administrator:** DR ZÉPHIRIN DIABRÉ (Burkina Faso).

### COUNTRY OFFICES

In almost every country receiving UNDP assistance there is an office, headed by the UNDP Resident Representative, who co-ordinates all UN technical assistance, advises the Government on formulating the country programme, ensures that field activities are undertaken, and acts as the leader of the UN team of experts working in the country. Resident Representatives are normally designated as co-ordinators for all UN operational development activities; the offices function as the primary presence of the UN in most developing countries.

## Activities

As the world's largest source of grant technical assistance in developing countries, UNDP works with more than 150 governments and 40 international agencies in efforts to achieve faster economic growth and better standards of living throughout the developing world. Most of the work is undertaken in the field by the various United Nations agencies, or by the government of the country concerned. UNDP is committed to allocating some 87% of its core resources to low-income countries with an annual income per caput of less than US $750. Assistance is mostly non-monetary, comprising the provision of experts' services, consultancies, equipment and fellowships for advanced study abroad. In 1996 35% of spending on projects was for the services of personnel, 25% for subcontracts, 18% for equipment and 16% for training; the remainder was for other costs, such as maintenance of equipment. Most UNDP projects incorporate training for local workers. Developing countries themselves provide 50% or more of the total project costs in terms of personnel, facilities, equipment and supplies. At December 1996 there were 3,240 UN volunteer specialists and field workers, as well as 4,501 international experts and 5,703 national experts serving under UNDP. In that year UNDP awarded 13,393 fellowships for nationals of developing countries to study abroad.

In 1993 UNDP began to examine its role and effectiveness in promoting sustainable human development, an approach to economic growth that encompasses individual well-being and choice, equitable distribution of the benefits of development and conservation of the environment. In June 1994 the Executive Board endorsed a proposal of the UNDP Administrator to make sustainable human development the guiding principle of the organization. Within this framework there were to be the following priority objectives: poverty elimination; sustainable livelihoods; good governance; environmental protection and regeneration; and the advancement and empowerment of women. The allocation of programming resources has subsequently reflected UNDP's new agenda, with 26% of resources directed towards poverty eradication and livelihoods for the poor, 25% to capacity-building and governance, 24% to projects concerned with environmental resources and food security, and 23% to public resources management for sustainable human development (with 2% to other activities).

In 1994 the Executive Board also determined that UNDP should assume a more active and integrative role within the UN development system. This approach has been implemented by UNDP Resident Representatives, who aim to co-ordinate UN policies to achieve sustainable human development, in consultation with other agencies, in particular UNEP, FAO and UNHCR. UNDP has subsequently allocated more resources to training and skill-sharing programmes in order to promote this co-ordinating role. In late 1997 the UNDP Administrator was appointed to chair a UN Development Group, which was established as part of a series of structural reform measures initiated by the UN Secretary-General and which aimed to strengthen collaboration between some 20 UN funds, programmes and other development bodies. UNDP's leading role within the process of UN reform was also to be reflected in its own internal reform process, 'UNDP 2001', which was scheduled to be completed in early 2000.

UNDP aims to help governments to reassess their development priorities and to design initiatives for sustainable development. UNDP country officers support the formulation of national human development reports (NHDRs), which aim to facilitate activities such as policy-making, the allocation of resources and monitoring progress towards poverty eradiction and sustainable development. In addition, the preparation of Advisory Notes and Country Co-operation Frameworks by UNDP officials help to highlight country-specific aspects of poverty eradiction and national strategic priorities. In January 1998 the Executive Board adopted eight guiding principles relating to sustainable human development that were to be implemented by all country offices, in order to ensure a focus to UNDP activities. A network of Sub-regional Resource Facilities (SURFs) has been established to strengthen and co-ordinate UNDP's technical assistance services.

UNDP's activities to facilitate poverty eradication include support for capacity-building programmes and initiatives to generate sustainable livelihoods, for example by improving access to credit, land and technologies. In March 1996 UNDP launched the Poverty Strategies Initiative (PSI) to strengthen national capacities to assess and monitor the extent of poverty and to combat the problem. By May 1997 80 projects had been approved for funding under the PSI. All PSI projects were intended to involve representatives of governments, the private sector, social organizations and research institutions in policy debate and formulation. In early 1997 a UNDP scheme to support private-sector and community-based initiatives to generate employment opportunities, MicroStart, became operational with some US $41m. in initial funds. UNDP supports the Caribbean Project Development Facility and the Africa Project Development Facility, which are administered by the International Finance Corporation (q.v.) and which aim to develop the private sector in these regions in order to generate jobs and sustainable livelihoods.

Approximately one-quarter of all UNDP programme resources support national efforts to ensure efficient governance and to build effective relations between the state, the private sector and civil society, which are essential to achieving sustainable development. UNDP undertakes assessment missions to help ensure free and fair elections and works to promote human rights, an accountable and competent public sector, a competent judicial system and decentralized government and decision-making. Within the context of the UN Special Initiative on Africa, UNDP supports the Africa Governance Forum which convenes annually to consider aspects of governance and development. In July 1997 UNDP organized an International Conference on Governance for Sustainable Growth and Equity, which was held in New York, USA, and attended by more than 1,000 representatives of national and local authorities and the business and non-governmental sectors. At the Conference UNDP initiated a four-year programme to promote activities and to encourage new approaches in support of good governance. In May/June 1999 a World Conference on Governance was held in Manila, the Philippines, attended by some 1,000 government officials and representatives of the private sector and non-governmental organizations. UNDP sponsored a series of meetings held on the subject of Building Capacities for Governance. In April UNDP and the Office of the High Commissioner for Human Rights launched a joint programme to strengthen capacity-building in order to promote the integration of human rights issues into activities concerned with sustainable human development.

Within UNDP's framework of urban development activities the Local Initiative Facility for Urban Environment (LIFE) undertakes small-scale environmental projects in low-income communities, in collaboration with local authorities and community-based groups. Recent initiatives include canal and river improvement projects in Thailand, improvement of the urban environment in a suburb of Cairo, Egypt, and public-health improvements and the environmental rehabilitation of precipitous housing areas in Brazil. Other initiatives include the Urban Management Programme and the Public-Private Partnerships Programme for the Urban Environment which aimed to generate funds, promote research and support new technologies to enhance sustainable environments in urban areas. In November 1996 UNDP initiated a process of collaboration between city authorities world-wide to promote implementation of the commitments made at the 1995 Copenhagen summit for social development (see below) and to help to combat aspects of poverty and other urban problems, such as poor housing, transport, the management of waste disposal, water supply and sanitation. The first Forum of the so-called World Alliance of Cities Against Poverty was convened in October 1998, in Lyon, France. UNDP supports the development of national programmes that emphasize the sustainable management of natural resources, for example through its Sustainable Energy Initiative, which promotes more efficient use of energy resources and the introduction of renewable alternatives to conventional fuels. UNDP is also concerned with forest management, the aquatic environment and sustainable agriculture and food security.

In the mid-1990s UNDP expanded its role in countries in crisis and with special circumstances, working in collaboration with other UN agencies to promote relief and development efforts. In particular, UNDP was concerned to achieve reconciliation, reintegration and reconstruction in affected countries, as well as to support emergency interventions and management and delivery of programme aid. In 1995 the Executive Board decided that 5% of total UNDP core resources be allocated to countries in 'special development situations'. During 1996–97 special development initiatives to promote peace and national recovery were undertaken in more than 32 countries. Activities included strengthening democratic institutions in Guatemala, the clearance of anti-personnel land-mines in Cambodia and Laos, socio-economic rehabilitation in Lebanon and the rehabilitation of communities for returning populations in some 20 countries. UNDP has established a mine action unit within its Emergency Response Division, in order to strengthen national demining capabilities. In December 1996 UNDP launched the Civilian Reconstruction Teams programme, creating some 5,000 jobs for former combatants in Liberia to work on the rehabilitation of the country's infrastructure. UNDP has extended its Disaster Management Training Programme, in order, partly, to help countries to attain the objectives of the International Decade for Natural Disaster Reduction (announced in 1990).

UNDP is a co-sponsor, jointly with WHO, the World Bank, UNICEF, UNESCO, UNDCP and UNFPA, of a Joint UN Programme on HIV and AIDS, which became operational on 1 January 1996. UNAIDS co-ordinates UNDP's HIV and Development Programme. Within the UN system UNDP also has responsibility for co-ordinating activities following global UN conferences. In March 1995 government representatives attending the World Summit for Social Development, which was held in Copenhagen, Denmark, adopted the Copenhagen Declaration and a Programme of Action, which included initiatives to promote the eradication of poverty, to increase and reallocate official development assistance to basic social programmes and to promote equal access to education. With particular reference to UNDP, the Programme of Action advocated that UNDP support the implementation of social development programmes, co-ordinate these efforts through its field offices and organize efforts on the part of the UN system to stimulate capacity-building at local, national and regional levels. A review conference to consider implementation of the Summit's objectives was scheduled to be convened in 2000. Following the UN Fourth World Conference on Women, held in Beijing, People's Republic of China, in September 1995, UNDP led inter-agency efforts to ensure the full participation of women in all economic, political and professional activities, and assisted with further situation analysis and training activities. (UNDP also created a Gender in Development Office to ensure that women participate more fully in UNDP-sponsored activities.) UNDP played an important role, at both national and international levels, in preparing for the second UN Conference on Human Settlements (Habitat II), which was held in Istanbul, Turkey, in June 1996 (see the UN Centre for Human Settlements, p. 38). At the conference UNDP announced the establishment of a new facility, which was designed to promote private-sector investment in urban infrastructure. The facility was to be allocated initial resources of US $10m., with the aim of generating a total of $1,000m. from private sources for this sector.

Since 1990 UNDP has published an annual *Human Development Report*, incorporating a Human Development Index, which ranks countries in terms of human development, using three key indicators: life expectancy, adult literacy and basic income required for a decent standard of living. In 1997 a Human Poverty Index and a Gender-related Development Index, which assesses gender equality on the basis of life expectancy, education and income, were introduced into the Report for the first time. In 1996 UNDP implemented its first corporate communications and advocacy strategy, which aimed to generate public awareness of the activities of the UN system, to promote debate on development issues and to mobilize resources by increasing public and donor appreciation of UNDP. A series of national and regional workshops was held, while media activities focused on the publication of the annual *Human Development Report* and the International Day for the Eradication of Poverty, held on 17 October. UNDP aims to use the developments in information technology to advance its communications strategy and to disseminate guide-lines and technical support throughout its country office network.

In October 1999 UNDP, in collaboration with an international communications company, Cisco Systems, organized NetAid, a series of international concerts held to improve awareness of Third World poverty, and broadcast live on the internet. Proceeds and donations generated by the initiative were to assist Kosovo refugees and the poorest African nations.

## Finance

UNDP is financed by the voluntary contributions of members of the United Nations and the Programme's participating agencies. Contributions from recipient governments, or third-party sources, to share the cost of projects constitute an increasingly significant portion of UNDP's total income. In 1996 total voluntary contributions amounted to US $2,186m., compared with some $1,842m. in 1995. Contributions to UNDP's core resources amounted to $844m. in 1996, compared with $927m. in 1995, while contributions to non-core funds, including cost-sharing arrangements, amounted to $1,342m. In 1996 estimated field programme expenditure under UNDP's core programme totalled $1,211m., of which $544m. was from general resources and $667m. cost-sharing contributions.

**UNDP FIELD PROGRAMME EXPENDITURE BY REGION**
(1996, UNDP core programme, US $ million)

| | |
|---|---|
| Africa | 248 |
| Asia and the Pacific | 196 |
| Latin America and the Caribbean | 613 |
| Arab states | 61 |
| Europe and the CIS | 43 |
| Global and interregional | 50 |
| **Total** | 1,211* |

* Including government cash counterpart contributions.

## Publications

*Annual Report.*

*Choices* (quarterly).

*Co-operation South* (2 a year).

*Human Development Report* (annually).

## Associated Funds and Programmes

UNDP is the central funding, planning and co-ordinating body for technical co-operation within the UN system. A number of associated funds and programmes, financed separately by means of voluntary contributions, provide specific services through the UNDP network. In April 1996 the UNDP Administrator signed an agreement on the establishment of a new trust fund to promote economic and technical co-operation among developing countries.

Total expenditure of funds and programmes administered by UNDP amounted to an estimated US $263.3m. in 1996. The principal funds and programmes are listed below.

### CAPACITY 21

UNDP initiated Capacity 21 at the UN Conference on Environment and Development, which was held in June 1992, to support developing countries in preparing and implementing policies for sustainable development. Capacity 21 promotes new approaches to development, through national development strategies, community-based management and training programmes. During 1998 programmes funded by Capacity 21 were under way in 52 countries.

### GLOBAL ENVIRONMENT FACILITY—GEF

The GEF, which is managed jointly by UNDP, the World Bank and UNEP, began operations in 1991, with funding of US $1,500m. over a three-year period. Its aim is to support projects for the prevention of climate change, conserving biological diversity, protecting international waters, and reducing the depletion of the ozone layer in the atmosphere. UNDP is responsible for capacity-building, targeted research, pre-investment activities and technical assistance. UNDP also administers the Small Grants Programme of the GEF, which supports community-based activities by local non-governmental organizations. During the pilot phase of the GEF, in the period 1991–94, $242.5m. in funding was approved for 55 UNDP projects. In March 1994 representatives of 87 countries agreed to provide $2,000m. to replenish GEF funds for a further three-year period from July of that year. At 30 June 1997 the GEF portfolio comprised 69 projects, with financing of almost $675m. In November 33 donor countries committed themselves to a target figure of $2,750m. for the next replenishment of GEF funds.

## MONTREAL PROTOCOL

UNDP assists countries to eliminate the use of ozone-depleting substances (ODS), in accordance with the Montreal Protocol to the Vienna Convention for the Protection of the Ozone Layer (see p. 48), through the design, monitoring and evaluation of ODS phase-out projects and programmes. In particular, UNDP provides technical assistance and training, national capacity-building and demonstration projects and technology transfer investment projects. The latter accounted for more than 75% of UNDP's activities in this area in 1994. In 1996, through the Executive Committee of the Montreal Protocol, UNDP provided US $27.0m. to assist 28 countries in eliminating ozone-depleting substances.

## OFFICE TO COMBAT DESERTIFICATION AND DROUGHT—UNSO

The Office was established following the conclusion, in October 1994, of the UN Convention to Combat Desertification in Those Countries Experiencing Serious Drought and/or Desertification, Particularly in Africa. It replaced the former UN Sudano-Sahelian Office (UNSO), while retaining the same acronym. UNSO is responsible for UNDP's role in desertification control and dryland management. Special emphasis is given to strengthening the environmental planning and management capacities of national institutions. During 1998 UNSO, in collaboration with other international partners, supported the implementation of the UN Convention in 55 designated countries.

**Director:** PHILIP DOBIE.

## PROGRAMME OF ASSISTANCE TO THE PALESTINIAN PEOPLE—PAPP

PAPP is committed to strengthening newly-created institutions in the Israeli-occupied Territories and emerging Palestinian autonomous areas, to creating employment opportunities and to stimulating private and public investment in the area to enhance trade and export potential. Examples of PAPP activities include the following: construction of sewage collection networks and systems in the northern Gaza Strip; provision of water to 500,000 people in rural and urban areas of the West Bank and Gaza; construction of schools, youth and health centres; support to vegetable and fish traders through the construction of cold storage and packing facilities; and provision of loans to strengthen industry and commerce. Field programme expenditure in 1996 totalled US $47.1m.

## UNITED NATIONS CAPITAL DEVELOPMENT FUND—UNCDF

The Fund was established in 1966 and became fully operational in 1974. It invests in poor communities in least-developed countries by providing economic and social infrastructure, credit for both agricultural and small-scale entrepreneurial activities, and local development funds which encourage people's participation as well as that of local governments in the planning and implementation of projects. UNCDF aims to promote the interests of women in community projects and to enhance their earning capacities. A Special Unit for Microfinance was established in 1997 as a joint UNDP/UNCDF operation, to facilitate co-ordination between microcredit initiatives of the UN, and to support UNDP's MicroStart initiative. In May 1996 stable funding for the Fund was pledged by eight donors for a three-year period. UNCDF's annual programming budget amounts to some US $40m.

**Internet:** www.undp.org/uncdf.

**Executive Secretary:** POUL GROSEN.

## UNITED NATIONS DEVELOPMENT FUND FOR WOMEN—UNIFEM

UNIFEM is the UN's lead agency in addressing the issues relating to women in development and promoting the rights of women worldwide. The Fund provides direct financial and technical support to enable low-income women in developing countries to increase earnings, gain access to labour-saving technologies and otherwise improve the quality of their lives. It also funds activities that include women in decision-making related to mainstream development projects. UNIFEM has supported the preparation of national reports in 30 countries and used the priorities identified in these reports and in other regional initiatives to formulate a Women's Development Agenda for the 21st century. Through these efforts, UNIFEM played an active role in the preparation for the UN Fourth World Conference on Women, which was held in Beijing, People's Republic of China, in September 1995. Programme expenditure in 1997 totalled US $13.8m.

**Headquarters:** 304 East 45th St, New York, NY 10017, USA; tel. (212) 906-6400; fax (212) 906-6705; internet www.unifem.undp.org.

**Director:** NOELEEN HEYZER (Singapore).

## UNITED NATIONS REVOLVING FUND FOR NATURAL RESOURCES EXPLORATION—UNRFNRE

The UNRFNRE was established in 1974 to provide risk capital to finance exploration for natural resources (particularly minerals) in developing countries and, when discoveries are made, to help to attract investment. The revolving character of the Fund lies in the undertaking of contributing governments to make replenishment contributions to the Fund when the projects it finances lead to commercial production. UNRFNRE publishes *Environmental Guidelines for the Mineral Sector* to encourage the sustainable development of resources. In 1996 voluntary contributions to the Fund amounted to US $1.3m.

**Director:** SHIGEAKI TOMITA (Japan).

## UNITED NATIONS VOLUNTEERS—UNV

The United Nations Volunteers is an important source of middle-level skills for the UN development system supplied at modest cost, particularly in the least-developed countries. Volunteers expand the scope of UNDP project activities by supplementing the work of international and host-country experts and by extending the influence of projects to local community levels. UNV also supports technical co-operation within and among the developing countries by encouraging volunteers from the countries themselves and by forming regional exchange teams comprising such volunteers. UNV is involved in areas such as peace-building, elections, human rights, humanitarian relief and community-based environmental programmes, in addition to development activities.

The UN International Short-term Advisory Programme, which is the private-sector development arm of UNV, has increasingly focused its attention on countries in the process of economic transition. Since 1994 UNV has administered UNDP's Transfer of Knowledge Through Expatriate Nationals (TOKTEN) programme, which was initiated in 1977 to enable specialists and professionals from developing countries to contribute to development efforts in their countries of origin through short-term technical assignments.

At 31 October 1998 2,262 UNVs were serving in 129 countries, while the total number of people who had served under the initiative amounted to 17,740.

**Headquarters:** POB 260111, 53153 Bonn, Germany; tel. (228) 8152000; fax (228) 8152001; e-mail hq@unv.org; internet www.unv.org.

**Executive Co-ordinator:** SHARON CAPELING-ALAKIJA.

# United Nations Environment Programme—UNEP

**Address:** POB 30552, Nairobi, Kenya.

**Telephone:** (2) 621234; **fax:** (2) 226890; **e-mail:** painfo@unep.org; **internet:** www.unep.org.

The United Nations Environment Programme was established in 1972 by the UN General Assembly, following recommendations of the 1972 UN Conference on the Human Environment, in Stockholm, Sweden, to encourage international co-operation in matters relating to the human environment.

## Organization

(January 2000)

### GOVERNING COUNCIL

The main functions of the Governing Council, which meets every two years, are to promote international co-operation in the field of the environment and to provide general policy guidance for the direction and co-ordination of environmental programmes within the UN system. It comprises representatives of 58 states, elected by the UN General Assembly, for four-year terms, on a regional basis. The Council is assisted in its work by a Committee of Permanent Representatives.

### HIGH-LEVEL COMMITTEE OF MINISTERS AND OFFICIALS IN CHARGE OF THE ENVIRONMENT

The Committee was established by the Governing Council in April 1997, with a mandate to consider the international environmental agenda and to make recommendations to the Council on reform and policy issues. In addition, the Committee, comprising 36 elected members, was to provide guidance and advice to the Executive Director, to enhance UNEP's collaboration and co-operation with other multilateral bodies and to help to mobilize financial resources for UNEP.

### SECRETARIAT

The Secretariat serves as a focal point for environmental action within the UN system. At October 1999 UNEP had 618 members of staff, of whom 284 were based at the organization's headquarters and 334 at regional and other offices.

**Executive Director:** Dr KLAUS TÖPFER (Germany).

### REGIONAL OFFICES

**Africa:** POB 30552, Nairobi, Kenya; tel. (2) 624283; fax (2) 623928.

**Asia and the Pacific:** UN Bldg, 10th Floor, Rajdamnern Ave, Bangkok 10200, Thailand; tel. (2) 288-1870; fax (2) 280-3829.

**Europe:** CP 356, 15 chemin des Anémones, 1219 Châtelaine, Geneva, Switzerland; tel. (22) 9799111; fax (22) 7973420.

**Latin America and the Caribbean:** Blvd de los Virreyes 155, Lomas Virreyes, 11000 México, DF, Mexico; tel. (5) 2024841; fax (5) 2020950.

**North America:** DC-2 Bldg, Room 0803, 2 United Nations Plaza, New York, NY 10017, USA; tel. (212) 963-8210; fax (212) 963-7341; e-mail uneprona@un.org; internet www.rona.unep.org.

**West Asia:** Sheikh Rashid Bldg, 1st Floor, 244 Road No 2904, Area 329, Manama, Bahrain; tel. 276072; fax 276075; e-mail uneprowa@batelco.com.bh.

### OTHER OFFICES

**Convention on International Trade in Endangered Species of Wild Fauna and Flora (CITES):** 15 chemin des Anémones, 1219 Châtelaine, Geneva, Switzerland; tel. (22) 9178139; fax (22) 7973417; e-mail cites@unep.ch; internet www.cites.org; Sec.-Gen. WILLEM WOUTER WIJNSTEKERS (Netherlands).

**Global Programme of Action for the Protection of the Marine Environment from Land-based Activities:** POB 16227, 2500 The Hague, The Netherlands; tel. (70) 4114460; fax (70) 3456648; e-mail gpa@unep.nl; Co-ordinator VEERLE VANDEWEERD.

**Regional Co-ordinating Unit for East Asian Seas:** UN Bldg, 10th Floor, Rajdamnern Ave, Bangkok 10200, Thailand; tel. (2) 288-1860; fax (2) 281-2428; e-mail kirkman.unescap@un.org; Co-ordinator HUGH KIRKMAN.

**Regional Co-ordinating Unit for the Caribbean Environment Programme:** 14-20 Port Royal St, Kingston, Jamaica; tel. 9229267; fax 9229292; internet www.cep.unep.org; Co-ordinator NELSON ANDRADE.

**Secretariat of the Basel Convention:** CP 356, 15 chemin des Anémones, 1219 Châtelaine, Geneva, Switzerland; tel. (22) 9178218; fax (22) 7973454; e-mail sbc@unep.ch; internet www.unep.ch/basel; Officer-in-Charge PER BAKKEN.

**Secretariat of the Convention on Biological Diversity:** World Trade Centre, 393 St Jacques St West, Suite 300, Montréal, Québec, Canada H2Y 1N9; tel. (514) 288-2220; fax (514) 288-6588; e-mail secretariat@biodiv.org; internet www.biodiv.org; Exec. Sec. HAMDALLAH ZEDAN (acting).

**Secretariat of the Multilateral Fund for the Implementation of the Montreal Protocol:** 1800 McGill College Ave, 27th Floor, Montréal, Québec, Canada H3A 3J6; tel. (514) 282-1122; fax (514) 282-0068; e-mail secretariat@unmfs.org; Chief OMAR EL-ARINI.

**UNEP Arab League Liaison Office:** 24 Iraq St, Mohandessin, Cairo, Egypt; tel. (2) 3361349; fax (2) 3370658.

**UNEP/CMS** (Convention on the Conservation of Migratory Species of Wild Animals) **Secretariat:** Martin-Luther-King-Str. 8, 53175 Bonn, Germany; tel. (228) 8152401; fax (228) 8152449; e-mail cms@unep.de; internet www.wcmc.org.uk/cms; Exec. Sec. ARNULF MÜLLER-HELMBRECHT.

**UNEP Chemicals:** CP 356, 11–13 chemin des Anémones, 1219 Châtelaine, Geneva, Switzerland; tel. (22) 9178111; fax (22) 7943460; e-mail jwillis@unep.ch; internet www.chem.unep.ch/irptc/; Dir JAMES B. WILLIS.

**UNEP Co-ordinating Unit for the Mediterranean Action Plan (MEDU):** Leoforos Vassileos Konstantinou 48, POB 18019, 11610 Athens, Greece; tel. (1) 7273100; fax (1) 7253196; e-mail unepmedu@unepmap.gr; internet www.unepmap.org; Co-ordinator LUCIEN CHABASON.

**UNEP Division of Technology, Industry and Economics:** Tour Mirabeau, 39–43, Quai André Citroën, 75739 Paris Cédex 15, France; tel. 1-44-37-14-50; fax 1-44-37-14-74; e-mail unepie@unep.fr; internet www.unepie.org/; Dir JACQUELINE ALOISI DE LARDEREL.

**UNEP International Environmental Technology Centre:** 2-110 Ryokuchi koen, Tsurumi-ku, Osaka 538-0036, Japan; tel. (6) 6915-4581; fax (6) 6915-0304; e-mail ietc@unep.or.jp; Officer-in-Charge LILIA G. C. CASANOVA.

**UNEP Ozone Secretariat:** POB 30552, Nairobi, Kenya; tel. (2) 623885; fax (2) 623913; e-mail ozoneinfo@unep.org; internet www.unep.ch/ozone/; Exec. Sec. K. MADHAVA SARMA.

**UNEP Secretariat for the UN Scientific Committee on the Effects of Atomic Radiation:** Vienna International Centre, Wagramerstrasse 5, POB 500, 1400 Vienna, Austria; tel. (1) 26060-4330; fax (1) 26060-5902; e-mail burton.bennett@unvienna.un.or.at; Sec. BURTON G. BENNETT.

## Activities

UNEP aims to maintain a constant watch on the changing state of the environment; to analyse the trends; to assess the problems using a wide range of data and techniques; and to promote projects leading to environmentally sound development. It plays a catalytic and co-ordinating role within and beyond the UN system. Many UNEP projects are implemented in co-operation with other UN agencies, particularly UNDP, the World Bank group, FAO, UNESCO and WHO. About 45 intergovernmental organizations outside the UN system and 60 international non-governmental organizations have official observer status on UNEP's Governing Council, and, through the Environment Liaison Centre in Nairobi, UNEP is linked to more than 6,000 non-governmental bodies concerned with the environment. UNEP also sponsors international conferences, programmes, plans and agreements regarding all aspects of the environment.

In February 1997 the Governing Council, at its 19th session, adopted a ministerial declaration (the Nairobi Declaration) on UNEP's future role and mandate, which recognized the organization as the principal UN body working in the field of the environment and as the leading global environmental authority, setting and overseeing the international environmental agenda. In June a Special Session of the UN General Assembly, referred to as the 'Earth Summit + 5', was convened to review the state of the environment and progress achieved in implementing the objectives of the UN Conference on Environment and Development (UNCED) in Rio de Janeiro, Brazil, in June 1992. The meeting adopted a Programme for Further Implementation of Agenda 21 (a programme of activities to promote sustainable development, adopted by UNCED) in order to intensify efforts in areas such as energy, freshwater resources and technology transfer. The meeting confirmed UNEP's essential role in advancing the Programme and as a global authority promoting a coherent legal and political approach to the environmental challenges of sustainable development. An extensive process of restructuring and realignment of functions was subsequently initiated by UNEP, and a new organizational structure reflecting the decisions of the Nairobi Declaration was implemented during 1999.

## ENVIRONMENTAL ASSESSMENT AND EARLY WARNING

The Nairobi Declaration resolved that the strengthening of UNEP's information, monitoring and assessment capabilities was a crucial element of the organization's restructuring, in order to help establish priorities for international, national and regional action, and to ensure the efficient and accurate dissemination of emerging environmental trends and emergencies.

UNEP has developed an extensive network of collaborating centres to assist in its analysis of the state of the global environment. The outcome of its work, the first Global Environment Outlook (GEO-I), was published in January 1997. A second process of global assessment resulted in the publication of GEO-II in September 1999. UNEP has initiated a major Global International Waters Assessment to consider all aspects of the world's water-related issues, in particular problems of shared transboundary waters, and of future sustainable management of water resources. UNEP is also a sponsoring agency of the Joint Group of Experts on the Scientific Aspects of Marine Environmental Pollution and contributes to the preparation of reports on the state of the marine environment and on the impact of land-based activities on that environment. In November 1995 UNEP published a Global Biodiversity Assessment, which was the first comprehensive study of biological resources throughout the world.

UNEP's environmental information network includes the Global Resource Information Database (GRID), which converts collected data into information usable by decision-makers. The INFOTERRA programme facilitates the exchange of environmental information through an extensive network of national 'focal points'. By the end of 1998 178 countries were participating in the network. UNEP promotes public access to environmental information, as well as participation in environmental concerns, through the INFOTERRA initiative. UNEP aims to establish in every developing region an Environment and Natural Resource Information Network (ENRIN) in order to make available technical advice and manage environmental information and data for improved decision-making and action-planning in countries most in need of assistance. UNEP aims to integrate all its information resources in order to improve access to information and to promote the international exchange of information. This was to be achieved through the design and implementation of UNEPNET, which was to operate throughout the UN system and be fully accessible through the world-wide information networks. In addition, by late 1998, 15 so-called Mercure satellite systems were operational world-wide, linking UNEP offices and partner agencies.

UNEP's information, monitoring and assessment structures also serve to enhance early-warning capabilities and to provide accurate information during an environmental emergency. In 1997 and 1998 UNEP organized a series of meetings to assess the environmental damage resulting from forest fires in Indonesia and to consider measures to respond effectively to further incidents. In April 1998 an international meeting, convened under UNEP auspices in Geneva, Switzerland, approved US $10m. to finance an immediate package of measures aimed at extinguishing the most dangerous fires, preventing others from spreading and improving Indonesia's fire-fighting capabilities. UNEP was also concerned with other 'man-made' fires, in particular in Brazil where an extensive conflagration was threatening an indigenous reserve and a number of endangered species.

## POLICY DEVELOPMENT AND LAW

UNEP aims to promote the development of policy tools and guidelines in order to achieve the sustainable management of the world environment. At a national level it assists governments to develop and implement appropriate environmental instruments and aims to co-ordinate policy initiatives. Training workshops in various aspects of environmental law and its applications are conducted. UNEP supports the development of new legal, economic and other policy instruments to improve the effectiveness of existing environmental agreements.

UNEP was instrumental in the drafting of a Convention on Biological Diversity (CBD) to preserve the immense variety of plant and animal species, in particular those threatened with extinction. The Convention entered into force at the end of 1993; by mid-1998 174 countries were parties to the CBD. UNEP supports co-operation for biodiversity assessment and management in selected developing regions and for the development of strategies for the conservation and sustainable exploitation of individual threatened species (e.g. the Global Tiger Action Plan). UNEP also provides assistance for the preparation of individual country studies and strategies to strengthen national biodiversity management and research. In 1996 an *ad hoc* working group on biosafety was established to negotiate the conclusion of a protocol to the CBD to regulate international trade in living modified organisms (including genetically modified—GM—seeds and crops and pharmaceutical derivatives), in order to reduce any potential adverse effects on biodiversity and human health. An extraordinary session of the conference of parties to the CBD was convened in Cartagena, Colombia, in February 1999, to consider the provisional text formulated by the group and, if approved, to adopt its legally-binding provisions. The meeting, however, was suspended, owing to outstanding differences between the main producer countries and developing nations regarding the implications of the protocol on principles of free trade. An agreement on the so-called Cartagena Protocol was finally concluded at a meeting of parties to the CBD, held in Montreal, Canada, in January 2000. The Protocol permitted countries to ban imports of GM products if there were outstanding safety concerns, and provided for greater transparency in the description of products containing GM organisms, through a limited labelling system.

In October 1994 87 countries, meeting under UN auspices, signed a Convention to Combat Desertification (see UNSO, p. 46), which aimed to provide a legal framework to counter the degradation of drylands. An estimated 75% of all drylands have suffered some land degradation, affecting approximately 1,000m. people in 110 countries. A second conference of the parties to the Convention was held in Dakar, Senegal, in December 1998. UNEP continues to support the implementation of the Convention, as part of its efforts to protect land resources. UNEP also aims to improve the assessment of dryland degradation and desertification in co-operation with governments and other international bodies, as well as identifying the causes of degradation and measures to overcome these.

UNEP estimates that one-third of the world's population will suffer chronic water shortages by 2025, owing to rising demand for drinking water as a result of growing populations, decreasing quality of water because of pollution, and increasing requirements of industries and agriculture. UNEP provides scientific, technical and administrative support to facilitate the implementation and co-ordination of regional seas conventions and plans of action. UNEP promotes international co-operation in the management of river basins and coastal areas and for the development of tools and guidelines to achieve the sustainable management of freshwater and coastal resources. In particular, UNEP aims to control land-based activities, principally pollution, which affect freshwater resources, marine biodiversity and the coastal ecosystems of small-island developing states. In November 1995 110 governments adopted a Global Programme of Action for the Protection of the Marine Environment from Land-based Activities. UNEP aims to develop a similar global instrument to ensure the integrated management of freshwater resources, in order to address current and future needs.

In 1996 UNEP, in collaboration with FAO, began to work towards promoting and formulating a legally-binding international convention on prior informed consent (PIC) for hazardous chemicals and pesticides in international trade, extending a voluntary PIC procedure of information exchange undertaken by more than 100 governments since 1991. The Convention was adopted at a conference held in Rotterdam, Netherlands, in September 1998, and was to enter into force on being ratified by 50 signatory states. It aimed to reduce risks to human health and the environment by restricting the production, export and use of hazardous substances and enhancing information exchange procedures.

In conjunction with UNCHS (Habitat), UNDP, the World Bank and other regional organizations and institutions, UNEP promotes environmental concerns in urban planning and management through the Sustainable Cities Programme, as well as regional workshops concerned with urban pollution and the impact of transportation systems. In January 1994 UNEP inaugurated an International Environmental Technology Centre (IETC), with offices in Osaka and Shiga, Japan, in order to strengthen the capabilities of developing countries and countries with economies in transition to promote environmentally-sound management of cities and freshwater reservoirs through technology co-operation and partnerships.

UNEP has played a key role in global efforts to combat risks to the ozone layer, resultant climatic changes and atmospheric pollution. UNEP worked in collaboration with the World Meteorological Organization to formulate a Framework Convention on Climate Change, with the aim of reducing the emission of gases that have a warming effect on the atmosphere, and has remained an active participant in the ongoing process to review and enforce its implementation (see WMO, p. 112, for further details). UNEP was the lead agency in formulating the 1987 Montreal Protocol to the Vienna Convention for the Protection of the Ozone Layer (1985), which provided for a 50% reduction in the production of chlorofluorocarbons (CFCs) by 2000. An amendment to the Protocol was adopted in 1990, which required complete cessation of the production of CFCs by 2000 in industrialized countries and by 2010 in developing countries; these deadlines were advanced to 1996 and 2006, respectively, in November 1992. In 1997 the ninth Conference of the Parties to the Vienna Convention adopted a further amendment which aimed to introduce a licensing system for all controlled substances.

A Multilateral Fund for the Implementation of the Montreal Protocol was established in June 1990 to promote the use of suitable technologies and the transfer of technologies to developing countries. UNEP, UNDP, the World Bank and UNIDO are the sponsors of the Fund, which by early 1997 had financed 1,800 projects in 106 developing countries at a cost of US $565m. In November 1996 the Fund was replenished, with commitments totalling $540m. for the three-year period 1997–99.

### POLICY IMPLEMENTATION

UNEP's Division of Environmental Policy Implementation incorporates two main functions: technical co-operation and response to environmental emergencies.

With the UN Office for the Co-ordination of Humanitarian Assistance, UNEP has established an Environmental Emergencies Unit to mobilize and co-ordinate international assistance and expertise to countries facing disasters. It undertakes initial assessments of the situation, as well as post-conflict analysis, as required. During 1998 the Unit provided assistance to Armenia and Georgia, following extensive flooding, to Chile, to combat acute river pollution, to Madagascar, following a serious chemical fire, to Moldova, threatened with underground water pollution, and to Somalia, to investigate an alleged dumping of hazardous substances. Other major environmental emergencies occurred during that year as a result of the floods and heavy rain in Bangladesh, the People's Republic of China, Mexico and parts of East Africa, and as the result of drought caused by the El Niño weather phenomenon in Brazil, Cuba and Indonesia. In mid-1999 UNEP established a Balkan Task Force to assess the environmental impact of NATO's aerial offensive against the Federal Republic of Yugoslavia.

UNEP, together with UNDP and the World Bank, is an implementing agency of the Global Environment Facility (GEF, see p. 45), which was established in 1991 as a mechanism for international co-operation in projects concerned with biological diversity, climate change, international waters and depletion of the ozone layer. UNEP services the Scientific and Technical Advisory Panel, which was established to provide expert advice on GEF programmes and operational strategies.

### TECHNOLOGY, INDUSTRY AND ECONOMICS

The use of inappropriate industrial technologies and the widespread adoption of unsustainable production and consumption patterns have been identified as being inefficient in the use of renewable resources and wasteful, in particular in the use of energy and water. UNEP aims to encourage governments and the private sector to develop and adopt policies and practices that are cleaner and safer, make efficient use of natural resources, incorporate environmental costs, ensure the environmentally sound management of chemicals, and reduce pollution and risks to human health and the environment. In collaboration with other organizations and agencies UNEP works to define and formulate international guide-lines and agreements to address these issues. UNEP also promotes the transfer of appropriate technologies and organizes conferences and training workshops to provide sustainable production practices. Relevant information is disseminated through the International Cleaner Production Information Clearing House. UNEP, together with UNIDO, has established eight National Cleaner Production Centres to promote a preventive approach to industrial pollution control. In May 1999 representatives of some 33 countries signed an International Declaration on Cleaner Production, launched by UNEP in 1998, with a commitment to implement cleaner and more sustainable production methods and to monitor results.

UNEP provides institutional servicing to the Basel Convention on the Control of Transboundary Movements of Hazardous Wastes and their Disposal, which was adopted in 1989 with the aim of preventing the disposal of wastes from industrialized countries in countries that have no processing facilities. In March 1994 the second meeting of parties to the Convention agreed to ban exportation of hazardous wastes between OECD and non-OECD countries by the end of 1997. The amendment of the Convention required ratification by three-quarters of signatory states before it could enter into effect, and was not achieved by December 1997. The fourth full meeting of parties to the Convention, held in February 1998, attempted to clarify the classification and listing of hazardous wastes, which was expected to stimulate further ratifications. In December 1999 132 states adopted a Protocol to the Convention to address issues relating to liability and compensation for damages from waste exports. The governments also agreed to establish a multilateral fund to finance immediate clean-up operations following any environmental accident.

The UNEP Chemicals office was established to promote the sound management of hazardous substances, central to which was the International Register of Potentially Toxic Chemicals (IRPTC). UNEP aims to facilitate access to data on chemicals and hazardous wastes, in order to assess and control health and environmental risks, by using the IRPTC as a clearing house facility of relevant information and by publishing information and technical reports on the impact of the use of chemicals.

UNEP's OzonAction Programme works to promote information exchange, training and technological awareness. Its objective is to strengthen the capacity of governments and industry in developing countries to undertake measures towards the cost-effective phasing-out of ozone-depleting substances. UNEP also encourages the development of alternative and renewable sources of energy. To achieve this, UNEP is supporting the establishment of a network of centres to research and exchange information of environmentally-sound energy technology resources.

### REGIONAL CO-OPERATION AND REPRESENTATION

UNEP maintains six regional offices. These work to initiate and promote UNEP objectives and to ensure that all programme formulation and delivery meets the specific needs of countries and regions. They also provide a focal point for building national, sub-regional and regional partnership and enhancing local participation in UNEP initiatives. Following UNEP's reorganization a co-ordination office was established at headquarters to promote regional policy integration, to co-ordinate programme planning, and to provide necessary services to the regional offices.

UNEP provides administrative support to several regional conventions, for example the Lusaka Agreement on Co-operative Enforcement Operations Directed at Illegal Trade in Wild Flora and Fauna, which entered into force in December 1996 having been concluded under UNEP auspices in order to strengthen the implementation of the Convention on Biological Diversity and the Convention on International Trade in Endangered Species (CITES) in Eastern and Central Africa. UNEP also organizes conferences, workshops and seminars at national and regional levels, and may extend advisory services or technical assistance to individual governments.

### CONVENTIONS

UNEP aims to develop and promote international environmental legislation in order to pursue an integrated response to global environmental issues, to enhance collaboration among existing convention secetariats, and to co-ordinate support to implement the work programmes of international instruments.

UNEP has been an active participant in the formulation of several major conventions (see above). The Division of Environmental Conventions is mandated to assist the Division of Policy Development and Law in the formulation of new agreements or protocols to existing conventions. Following the successful adoption of the Rotterdam Convention in September 1998, UNEP is working to formulate a multilateral agreement to reduce and ultimately eliminate the manufacture and use of Persistent Organic Pollutants (POPs), which are considered to be a major global environmental hazard. UNEP sponsored the first meeting of an Intergovernmental Negotiating Committee on POPs, which was held in Montreal, Canada, in June 1998. An agreement on POPs was expected to be ready for signature in 2000.

UNEP has been designated to provide secretariat functions to a number of global and regional environmental conventions (see above for list of offices).

### COMMUNICATION AND PUBLIC INFORMATION

UNEP's public education campaigns and outreach programmes promote community involvement in environmental issues. Further communication of environmental concerns is undertaken through the media, an information centre service and special promotional events, including World Environment Day, photograph competitions and the awarding of the Sasakawa Prize to recognize distinguished service to the environment by individuals and groups. In 1996 UNEP initiated a Global Environment Citizenship Programme to promote acknowledgment of the environmental responsibilities of all sectors of society.

## Finance

UNEP derives its finances from the regular budget of the United Nations and from voluntary contributions to the Environment Fund. In February 1999 the Governing Council authorized a budget of US $120m. for the two-year period 2000–01, of which $100m. was for programme activities (see below), $14.4m. for management and administration, and $5m. for fund programme reserves.

**APPROVED BUDGET FOR FUND PROGRAMME ACTIVITIES, 2000–01**

| | (US $'000) |
|---|---|
| Environmental Assessment and Early Warning | 24,000 |
| Policy Development and Law | 13,000 |
| Policy Implementation | 7,000 |
| Technology, Industry and Economics | 23,000 |
| Regional Co-operation and Representation | 20,500 |
| Environment Conventions | 6,775 |
| Communications and Public Information | 5,725 |
| **Total** | 100,000 |

## Publications

*Annual Report.*
*APELL Newsletter* (2 a year).
*Cleaner Production Newsletter* (2 a year).
*Climate Change Bulletin* (quarterly).
*Connect* (UNESCO-UNEP newsletter on environmental degradation, quarterly).
*Desertification Control Bulletin* (2 a year).
*EarthViews* (quarterly).
*Environment Forum* (quarterly).
*Environmental Law Bulletin* (2 a year).
*Financial Services Initiative* (2 a year).
*GEF News* (quarterly).
*GPA Newsletter.*
*IETC Insight* (3 a year).
*Industry and Environment Review* (quarterly).
*Leave it to Us* (children's magazine, 2 a year).
*Managing Hazardous Waste* (2 a year).
*Our Planet* (quarterly).
*OzonAction Newsletter* (quarterly).
*Tierramerica* (4–6 a year).
*Tourism Focus* (2 a year).
*UNEP Chemicals Newsletter* (2 a year).
*UNEP Update* (monthly).
*World Atlas of Desertification.*
Studies, reports, legal texts, technical guide-lines, etc.

# United Nations High Commissioner for Refugees—UNHCR

**Address:** CP 2500, 1211 Geneva 2 dépôt, Switzerland.
**Telephone:** (22) 7398502; **fax:** (22) 7397312; **e-mail:** hqpi00@unhcr.ch; **internet:** www.unhcr.ch.

The Office of the High Commissioner was established in 1951 to provide international protection for refugees and to seek durable solutions to their problems.

## Organization

(December 1999)

### HIGH COMMISSIONER

The High Commissioner is elected by the United Nations General Assembly on the nomination of the Secretary-General, and is responsible to the General Assembly and to the UN Economic and Social Council (ECOSOC).

**High Commissioner:** SADAKO OGATA (Japan).
**Deputy High Commissioner:** FREDERICK BARTON (USA).

### EXECUTIVE COMMITTEE

The Executive Committee of the High Commissioner's Programme, established by ECOSOC, gives the High Commissioner policy directives in respect of material assistance programmes and advice in the field of international protection. In addition, it oversees UNHCR's general policies and use of funds. The Committee, which comprises representatives of 53 states, both members and non-members of the UN, meets once a year.

### ADMINISTRATION

Headquarters includes the Executive Office, comprising the offices of the High Commissioner, the Deputy High Commissioner and the Assistant High Commissioner. There are separate offices for the Inspector General, the Special Envoy in the former Yugoslavia, and the Director of the UNHCR liaison office in New York. The other principal administrative units are the Division of Communication and Information, the Department of International Protection, the Division of Resource Management, and the Department of Operations, which is responsible for the five regional bureaux covering Africa; Asia and the Pacific; Europe; the Americas and the Caribbean; and Central Asia, South-West Asia, North Africa and the Middle East. At July 1999 there were 274 UNHCR field offices in 120 countries. At that time UNHCR employed 5,155 people, including short-term staff, of whom 4,265 (or 83%) were working in the field.

## Activities

The competence of the High Commissioner extends to any person who, owing to well-founded fear of being persecuted for reasons of race, religion, nationality or political opinion, is outside the country of his or her nationality and is unable or, owing to such fear or for reasons other than personal convenience, remains unwilling to accept the protection of that country; or who, not having a nationality and being outside the country of his or her former habitual residence, is unable or, owing to such fear or for reasons other than personal convenience, is unwilling to return to it. Refugees who are assisted by other United Nations agencies, or who have the same rights or obligations as nationals of their country of residence, are outside the mandate of UNHCR.

In recent years there has been a significant shift in UNHCR's focus of activities. Increasingly UNHCR is called upon to support people who have been displaced within their own country (i.e. with similar needs to those of refugees but who have not crossed an international border) or those threatened with displacement as a result of armed conflict. In addition, it is providing greater support to refugees who have returned to their country of origin, to assist their reintegration, and is working to enable the local community to support the returnees. At December 1998 the refugee population world-wide totalled 11.5m. and UNHCR was concerned with a further 1.3m. asylum-seekers, 1.9m. recently returned refugees and 6.7m. others (of whom an estimated 4.9m. were internally displaced persons—IDPs).

### INTERNATIONAL PROTECTION

As laid down in the Statute of the Office, one of the two primary functions of UNHCR is to extend international protection to refugees. In the exercise of this function, UNHCR seeks to ensure that refugees and asylum-seekers are protected against *refoulement* (forcible return), that they receive asylum, and that they are treated according to internationally recognized standards. UNHCR pursues these objectives by a variety of means which include promoting the conclusion and ratification by states of international conventions for the protection of refugees. UNHCR promotes the adoption of liberal practices of asylum by states, so that refugees and asylum-seekers are granted admission, at least on a temporary basis.

The most comprehensive instrument concerning refugees that has been elaborated at the international level is the 1951 United Nations Convention relating to the Status of Refugees. This Convention, the scope of which was extended by a Protocol adopted in 1967, defines the rights and duties of refugees and contains provisions dealing with a variety of matters which affect the day-to-day lives of refugees (see below). The application of the Convention and its Protocol is supervised by UNHCR. Important provisions for the treatment of refugees are also contained in a number of instruments adopted at the regional level. These include the OAU Convention of 1969 Governing the Specific Aspects of Refugee Problems, the European Agreement on the Abolition of Visas for Refugees, and the 1969 American Convention on Human Rights.

UNHCR has actively encouraged states to accede to the 1951 United Nations Refugee Convention and the 1967 Protocol: 137 states had acceded to either or both of these basic refugee instruments by 31 July 1999. An increasing number of states have also adopted domestic legislation and/or administrative measures to implement the international instruments, particularly in the field of procedures for the determination of refugee status. Such measures provide an important guarantee that refugees will be accorded the standards of treatment which have been internationally established for their benefit. In recent years UNHCR has formulated a strategy designed to address the fundamental causes of refugee flows.

UNHCR has attempted to deal with the problem of military attacks on refugee camps, by formulating and encouraging the acceptance of a set of principles to ensure the safety of refugees. It also seeks to address the specific needs of refugee women and children.

## ASSISTANCE ACTIVITIES

UNHCR assistance activities are divided into General Programmes (which include a Programme Reserve, a General Allocation for Voluntary Repatriation and an Emergency Fund) and Special Programmes. The latter are undertaken at the request of the UN General Assembly, the Secretary-General of the UN or member states, in response to a particular crisis.

The first phase of an assistance operation uses UNHCR's capacity of emergency preparedness and response. This enables UNHCR to address the immediate needs of refugees at short notice, for example, by employing specially-trained emergency teams and maintaining stockpiles of basic equipment, medical aid and materials. A significant proportion of UNHCR expenditure is allocated to the next phase of an operation, providing 'care and maintenance' in stable refugee circumstances. This assistance can take various forms, including the provision of food, shelter, medical care and essential supplies. Also covered in many instances are basic services, including education and counselling.

**POPULATIONS OF CONCERN TO UNHCR BY REGION*** ('000 persons, at 31 December 1998)

| | Refugees | Asylum-seekers | Returned refugees† | Others of concern‡ | Total |
|---|---|---|---|---|---|
| Africa | 3,271 | 63 | 1,297 | 1,654 | 6,285 |
| Asia | 4,745 | 28 | 317 | 2,385 | 7,475 |
| Europe | 2,668 | 577 | 286 | 2,682 | 6,213 |
| Latin America | 74 | 0 | 8 | 20 | 102 |
| North America | 660 | 646 | — | — | 1,305 |
| Oceania | 74 | 5 | — | — | 80 |
| **Total** | 11,492 | 1,319 | 1,907 | 6,742 | 21,460 |

* In accordance with the regional classification of the UN's Department for Economic and Social Affairs, under which Africa includes countries of North Africa, and Asia incorporates Cyprus and Turkey and all countries of the Middle East not located on the African continent; Latin America covers Central and South America and the Caribbean.

† Refugees who have returned to their place of origin and remain of concern to UNHCR for a maximum period of two years.

‡ Mainly internally displaced persons (IDPs) and IDPs of concern to UNHCR who have returned to their place of origin and who remain of concern to UNHCR for a maximum of two years; also includes people who have received temporary protection and assistance outside their country, but who have not been formally recognized as refugees, as well as certain groups of war-affected populations and of countries of the former USSR who have not been granted a new nationality.

**POPULATIONS OF CONCERN TO UNHCR BY COUNTRY*** ('000 persons, at 31 December 1998)

| | Refugees | Asylum-seekers | Returned refugees† | Others of concern† |
|---|---|---|---|---|
| **Africa** | | | | |
| Algeria | 165.2 | 0.1 | — | 0.1 |
| Burundi | 25.1 | 0.3 | 114.6 | 110.6 |
| Congo, Democratic Republic | 240.3 | 0.1 | 111.3 | — |
| Côte d'Ivoire | 119.9 | 0.5 | — | — |
| Ethiopia | 262.0 | 0.1 | 22.8 | — |
| Guinea | 413.7 | — | — | — |
| Guinea-Bissau | 6.6 | — | — | 195.6 |
| Kenya | 238.2 | 6.4 | 0.0 | — |
| Liberia | 103.1 | 0.0 | 251.4 | |
| Rwanda | 33.4 | 0.8 | 231.8 | 626.1 |
| Sierra Leone | 9.9 | — | 198.4 | 670.0 |
| Somalia | 0.3 | — | 103.3 | 51.6 |
| Sudan | 391.5 | 0.1 | 63.4 | — |
| Tanzania | 543.9 | 14.1 | — | — |
| Uganda | 204.5 | 0.1 | 2.3 | — |
| Zambia | 168.6 | 1.2 | — | — |
| **Asia** | | | | |
| Afghanistan | — | — | 193.7 | 343.7 |
| Armenia | 310.0 | — | 0.0 | — |
| Azerbaijan | 221.6 | 0.3 | — | 576.3 |
| China, People's Republic‡ | 292.3 | — | — | — |
| Cyprus | 0.1 | 0.1 | — | 265.0 |
| Georgia | 0.0 | — | — | 277.0 |
| India | 185.5 | 0.0 | — | — |
| Iran | 1,931.3 | — | — | — |
| Iraq | 104.1 | 1.6 | 22.5 | — |
| Kuwait | 4.2 | 0.2 | — | 138.0 |
| Nepal | 126.1 | 0.1 | — | — |
| Pakistan | 1,202.5 | 0.2 | — | — |
| Sri Lanka | 0.0 | 0.0 | 0.1 | 717.6 |
| Thailand | 138.3 | 0.8 | — | 1.2 |
| **Europe** | | | | |
| Belarus | 0.1 | 16.4 | — | 160.0 |
| Bosnia and Herzegovina | 40.0 | — | 242.4 | 924.3 |
| Croatia | 29.0 | — | 41.1 | 114.7 |
| France | 140.2 | — | — | — |
| Germany | 949.2 | 370.0 | — | — |
| Netherlands | 131.8§ | — | — | — |
| Russia | 128.6 | 11.3 | 0.1 | 1,025.2 |
| Sweden | 178.8§ | — | — | — |
| Switzerland | 81.9 | 44.7 | — | — |
| Ukraine | 6.1 | 0.2 | — | 105.7 |
| United Kingdom | 116.1§ | 81.0§ | — | — |
| Yugoslavia | 502.0 | 6.0 | 1.9 | 335.0 |
| **North America** | | | | |
| Canada | 135.7§ | 23.3§ | — | — |
| USA | 524.1§ | 622.3§ | — | — |

* The list includes only those countries having 100,000 or more persons of concern to UNHCR.

† See table above for definitions.

‡ Excluding Hong Kong Special Administrative Region.

§ Figure estimated by UNHCR.

As far as possible, assistance is geared towards the identification and implementation of durable solutions to refugee problems—this being the second statutory responsibility of UNHCR. Such solutions generally take one of three forms: voluntary repatriation, local integration or resettlement in another country. Voluntary repatriation is increasingly the preferred solution, given the easing of political tension in many regions from which refugees have fled. Where voluntary repatriation is feasible, the Office assists refugees to overcome obstacles preventing their return to their country of origin. This may be done through negotiations with governments involved, or by providing funds either for the physical movement of refugees or for the rehabilitation of returnees once back in their own country.

**ORIGIN OF MAJOR REFUGEE POPULATIONS AND PERSONS IN REFUGEE-LIKE SITUATIONS*** ('000 persons, estimated at 31 December 1998)

| Origin | Refugees |
|---|---|
| Afghanistan | 2,633.9 |
| Iraq | 590.8 |
| Burundi | 500.0 |
| Somalia | 480.8 |
| Bosnia and Herzegovina | 471.6 |
| Sierra Leone | 411.0 |
| Sudan | 374.2 |
| Eritrea | 345.4 |
| Croatia | 334.6 |
| Azerbaijan | 328.5 |

* Information on the origin of refugees is not available for a number of, mainly industrialized, countries. Data exclude some 3.2m. Palestinian refugees who come under the mandate of UNRWA (q.v.). Palestinians who are outside the UNRWA area of operation, for example those in Iraq and Libya, are considered to be of concern to UNHCR.

When voluntary repatriation is not an option, efforts are made to assist refugees to integrate locally and to become self-supporting in their countries of asylum. This may be done either by granting loans to refugees, or by assisting them, through vocational training or in other ways, to learn a skill and to establish themselves in gainful occupations. One major form of assistance to help refugees re-establish themselves outside camps is the provision of housing. In cases where resettlement through emigration is the only viable solution to a refugee problem, UNHCR negotiates with governments in an endeavour to obtain suitable resettlement opportunities, to encourage liberalization of admission criteria and to draw up special immigration schemes. During 1997 25,179 refugees were resettled under UNHCR auspices.

In the early 1990s UNHCR aimed to consolidate efforts to integrate certain priorities into its programme planning and implementation, as a standard discipline in all phases of assistance. The considerations include awareness of specific problems confronting refugee women, the needs of refugee children, the environmental impact of refugee programmes and long-term development objectives. In an effort to improve the effectiveness of its programmes, UNHCR has initiated a process of delegating authority, as well as responsibility for operational budgets, to its regional and field representatives, increasing flexibility and accountability.

### ASIA AND THE PACIFIC

In June 1989 an international conference was convened by UNHCR in Geneva to discuss the ongoing problem of refugees and displaced persons in and from the Indo-Chinese peninsula. The participants adopted the Comprehensive Plan of Action (CPA) for Indo-Chinese Refugees, which provided for the 'screening' of all Vietnamese arrivals in the region to determine their refugee status, the resettlement of 'genuine' refugees and the repatriation (described as voluntary 'in the first instance') of those deemed to be economic migrants. A steering committee of the international conference, representing 15 nations, met regularly to supervise the plan. In March 1996 UNHCR confirmed that it was to terminate funding for the refugee camps (except those in Hong Kong) on 30 June to coincide with the formal conclusion of the CPA; however, it pledged to support transitional arrangements regarding the completion of the repatriation process and maintenance of the remaining Vietnamese 'non-refugees' during the post-CPA phase-out period, as well as to continue its support for the reintegration and monitoring of returning nationals in Viet Nam and Laos. The prospect of forcible repatriation provoked rioting and violent protests in many camps throughout the region. By early July 16,800 Vietnamese remained in camps in Hong Kong, 4,000 in Indonesia, 3,700 in Thailand and 1,900 in the Philippines, with Malaysia and Singapore having completed the repatriation process. (At that time more than 88,000 Vietnamese and 22,000 Laotians had returned to their countries of origin under the framework of the CPA.) In late July the Philippines Government agreed to permit the remaining camp residents to settle permanently in that country. In September the remaining Vietnamese refugees detained on the island of Galang, in Indonesia, were repatriated, and in February 1997 the last camp for Vietnamese refugees in Thailand was formally closed. In mid-June of that year the main Vietnamese detention camp in Hong Kong was closed. However, the scheduled repatriation of all remaining Vietnamese (estimated at some 1,600 people qualifying as refugees and 700 non-refugees) before the transfer of sovereignty of the territory to the People's Republic of China on 30 June failed to be achieved. In early 1998 the Hong Kong authorities formally terminated the policy of granting a port of first asylum to Vietnamese 'boat people'. At the end of that year some 1,000 refugees and 20 asylum-seekers remained in Hong Kong. UNHCR proposed the integration of the remaining Vietnamese as a final durable solution to the situation. At 31 December 1998 UNHCR was providing assistance to a further 292,300 Vietnamese refugees in mainland People's Republic of China. In 1995, in accordance with an agreement concluded with the Chinese Government, UNHCR initiated a programme to redirect its local assistance to promote long-term self-sufficiency in the poorest settlements, including support for revolving-fund rural credit schemes.

The conclusion of a political settlement of the conflict in Cambodia in October 1991 made possible the eventual repatriation of some 370,000 Cambodian refugees and displaced persons. A land-mine survey was undertaken in order to identify the risk to returnees posed by unexploded mines (mine clearance was subsequently undertaken under UN auspices). The actual repatriation operation began in March 1992 and was completed in April 1993. At the same time, however, thousands of ethnic Vietnamese (of whom there were estimated to be 200,000 in Cambodia) were fleeing to Viet Nam, as a result of violence perpetrated against them by Cambodian armed groups. In March 1994 25,000 supporters of the Khmers Rouges in Cambodia fled across the border into Thailand, following advances by government forces. The refugees were immediately repatriated by the Thai armed forces into Khmer Rouge territory, which was inaccessible to aid agencies. In July 1997 armed conflict between opposing political forces in northern Cambodia resulted in large-scale population movements. A voluntary repatriation programme was initiated in October to assist any refugee wishing to return. By 30 June 1998 some 5,595 Cambodians had been repatriated with UNHCR support, while a substantial number of others had returned in a spontaneous movement following a lull in the fighting in some border areas. In late March 1999 UNHCR announced that the last Cambodian refugees had left camps in Thailand, the majority having been repatriated to north-western Cambodia. A new UNHCR programme was initiated to monitor the welfare of returnees and assist in their reintegration.

A temporary cessation of hostilities between the Sri Lankan Government and Tamil separatists in early 1995 greatly facilitated UNHCR's ongoing efforts to repatriate Sri Lankan Tamils who had fled to India. However, later in that year an offensive by Sri Lankan government troops in the northern Jaffna peninsula caused a massive displacement of the local Tamil population and effectively ended the repatriation process. In India UNHCR had been concerned with verifying the voluntary nature of the repatriations, while in Sri Lanka itself UNHCR operated two 'Open Relief Centres' (established in 1990) to provide food, water and medical assistance and secure shelter for people unable to return to their home area. By 31 December 1998 there were more than 600,000 Sri Lankan IDPs of concern to UNHCR, as well as 114,600 IDPs who had recently returned to their home areas, and an estimated 70,300 Sri Lankan refugees remaining in India owing to the country's persisting political instability. India's total refugee population, of some 185,000 at December 1998, also included 98,000 refugees from the People's Republic of China (mainly Tibetans), and 16,100 Afghans.

In 1991–92 thousands of people of Nepalese ethnic origin living in Bhutan sought refuge from alleged persecution by fleeing to Nepal. By the end of 1998 their number totalled 105,700, of whom 95,700 were receiving UNHCR assistance in the form of food, shelter, medical care, water and camp assistance. UNHCR has agreed to maintain its funding of the refugee camps, provided that negotiations between the two Governments, under the auspices of a high-level joint committee (established in 1993), continue. UNHCR has also made known its willingness to provide technical support for the verification of citizenship of the refugees, which was the principal issue precluding a resolution of the situation. In September 1999 negotiations on the repatriation of refugees, which resumed at the start of that year, again stalled owing to disagreements regarding a verification mechanism. At 31 December 1998 Nepal was also hosting some 20,400 refugees from Tibet.

From April 1991 increasing numbers of Rohingya Muslims in Myanmar fled into Bangladesh to escape the brutality and killings perpetrated by the Myanma armed forces. UNHCR launched an international appeal for financial aid for the refugees, at the request of Bangladesh, and collaborated with other UN agencies in providing humanitarian assistance. In May 1993 UNHCR and Bangladesh signed a memorandum of understanding, whereby UNHCR would be able to monitor the repatriation process of the estimated 270,000 Myanmar refugees and ensure that people were returning of their own free will. In November a memorandum of understanding, signed with the Myanma Government, secured UNHCR access to the returnees. The first refugees returned to Myanmar with UNHCR assistance at the end of April 1994. They were provided with a small amount of cash, housing grants and two months' food rations, and were supported by several small-scale reintegration projects. Despite disruption to the repatriation process owing to cyclone damage to repatriation facilities and attempts to prevent the spread of disease, by the end of December 1996 the Myanma refugee population in Bangladesh had declined to 30,578. UNHCR continued to monitor the estimated 219,282 returnees in Myanmar and to support their reintegration, for example through community-based agricultural activities and literacy and other education programmes. In January 1997 the Bangladesh and Myanma Governments agreed to conclude the mass repatriation programme by 31 March, later extended to August. In July, in advance of the revised deadline, Rohingya activists initiated a hunger-strike in protest at alleged efforts by the Bangladesh authorities to repatriate forcibly the remaining refugees. In early 1998 UNHCR attempted to resume the repatriation process and to find a local solution for those unwilling to return to Myanmar. At the end of that year there were some 22,200 refugees remaining in camps in Bangladesh.

In the early 1990s members of ethnic minorities in Myanmar attempted to flee attacks by government troops into Thailand; however, the Thai Government refused to recognize them as refugees or to offer them humanitarian assistance. Throughout 1997 the border camps were vulnerable to attacks by rival Karen (Kayin) factions and by Myanma Government forces. In December Thailand and Myanmar agreed to commence 'screening' the refugees to determine those who had fled persecution and those who were economic migrants. By the end of 1998 there were 101,700 people in camps along the Myanma–Thai border, the majority of whom were Karen refugees.

In April 1999, following the announcement by the Indonesian Government, in January, that it would consider a form of autonomy or independence for East Timor, some 26,000 Indonesian settlers left their homes as a result of clashes between opposing groups and uncertainty regarding the future of the territory. The popular referendum on the issue, conducted in late August, and the resulting victory for the independence movement, provoked a violent reaction by pro-integration militia. UNHCR staff, along with other international personnel, were forced to evacuate the territory in early September. At that time there were reports of forced mass deportations of Timorese to West Timor, while a large number of others fled their homes into remote mountainous areas of East Timor. In mid-September UNHCR staff visited West Timor to review the state of refugee camps, allegedly under the control of militia, and to persuade the authorities to permit access for humanitarian personnel. At the end of September there were 230,000 East Timorese registered in 28 camps in West Timor. At that time there were also an estimated 190,000–300,000 people displaced within East Timor, although the International Committee of the Red Cross estimated that a total of 800,000 people, or some 94% of the population, had been displaced, or deported, during the crisis. The arrival of multinational troops, from 20 September, helped to stabilize the region and enable the safe receipt and distribution of food supplies, prompting several thousands to return from hiding. Most homes, however, along with almost all other buildings in the capital, Dili, had been destroyed. At the end of September UNHCR was leading inter-agency humanitarian operations in the territory; it planned to open seven offices throughout East Timor and to register all returning refugees and displaced persons in order to determine the precise figures of those missing or deported. In October UNHCR, together with the International Organization for Migration, initiated a repatriation programme for the refugees in West Timor. By the end of November an estimated 103,000 East Timorese had returned to the territory.

In early 1999 fighting between Muslim separatists and government forces in the autonomous Mindanao region of southern Philippines resulted in an estimated displaced population of 41,000.

## CENTRAL ASIA, SOUTH-WEST ASIA, NORTH AFRICA AND THE MIDDLE EAST

From 1979, as a result of civil strife in Afghanistan, there was a massive movement of refugees from that country into Pakistan and Iran, creating the world's largest refugee population, which reached a peak of almost 6.3m. people in 1992. In 1988 UNHCR agreed to provide assistance for the voluntary repatriation of refugees, both in ensuring the rights of the returning population and in providing material assistance such as transport, immunization, and supplies of food and other essentials. In April 1992, following the establishment of a new Government in Afghanistan, refugees began to return in substantial numbers (hitherto only a small number had returned), although large numbers of people continued to flee into Pakistan as a result of the fighting that persisted. UNHCR efforts to facilitate the process of voluntary repatriation and to provide emergency assistance to camps within Afghanistan were disrupted in early 1994 by a renewal of serious hostilities, which also resulted in a further 76,000 Afghans fleeing to Pakistan during that year. However, repatriation of refugees to areas unaffected by the conflict continued. From October 1996 renewed hostilities in northern and western regions of Afghanistan resulted in further massive population displacement and in November UNHCR suspended its relief activities in the Afghan capital, Kabul, owing to mounting security concerns. Relief operations continued in other parts of the country. In Afghanistan UNHCR, with other UN agencies, has attempted to meet the immediate needs of IDPs and recent returnees (totalling 193,700 returned refugees, 27,900 returned IDPs and 315,800 IDPs as at 31 December 1998), for example, by increasing rural water supply, initiating income-generation projects and providing food and tools. In Iran UNHCR has worked to ensure the voluntary nature of repatriation, while in Pakistan it has focused activities on strengthening refugees' capacity for self-sufficiency. During 1997 UNHCR operated a pilot scheme to organize group repatriations to specific areas in Afghanistan, under the protection of international observers, and in early 1998 UNHCR initiated a new monitoring system to evaluate the situation of returnees in Afghanistan. By 30 June 59,070 refugees had returned, with UNHCR assistance, from Pakistan and 753 from Iran since the start of the year, bringing the total number of returnees to more than 4m. since 1988 (2.7m. from Pakistan and 1.3m. from Iran). However, the ongoing civil conflict and new population displacement precluded a settlement of the Afghan refugee situation and continued to cause immense difficulties in undertaking a comprehensive humanitarian operation in that country. At the end of 1998 a total of 1.4m. Afghan refugees remained in Iran, 1.2m. in Pakistan, 16,100 in India and 11,700 in countries of the former USSR.

In late 1992 people began to flee civil conflict in Tajikistan and to seek refuge in Afghanistan. In 1993 an emergency UNHCR operation established a reception camp to provide the 60,000 Tajik refugees with basic assistance, and began to move them away from the border area to safety. In December a tripartite agreement was signed by UNHCR and the Tajik and Afghan Governments regarding the safety of refugees returning to Tajikistan. UNHCR monitored the repatriation process and provided materials for the construction of almost 20,000 homes. The repatriation process was concluded by the end of 1997. At the end of 1998, however, there were still more than 40,000 Tajik refugees remaining in other countries of the former USSR.

In March–May 1991, following the war against Iraq by a multinational force, and the subsequent Iraqi suppression of resistance in Kurdish areas in the north of the country, there was a massive movement of some 1.5m., mainly Kurdish, refugees, into Iran and Turkey. UNHCR was designated the principal UN agency to seek to alleviate the crisis. In May the refugees began to return to Iraq in huge numbers, and UNHCR assisted in their repatriation, establishing relief stations along their routes from Iran and Turkey. By the end of the year, however, negotiations between the Kurds and the Iraqi Government had broken down and refugees were once again entering Iran in large numbers, following the resumption of the violent suppression of Kurdish activists. In April 1994 UNHCR initiated a programme to provide food and relief assistance to Turkish Kurds who had fled into northern Iraq. In September 1996 fighting escalated among the Kurdish factions in northern Iraq. By the time a cease-fire agreement was concluded in November some 65,000 Iraqi Kurds had fled across the border into Iran. UNHCR, together with the Iranian Government, provided these new refugees with basic humanitarian supplies. By the end of the year, however, the majority of refugees had returned to Iraq, owing to poor conditions in the temporary settlements, security concerns at being located in the border region and pressure from the Iranian authorities. UNHCR announced its intention to withdraw from the Atroush camp, which housed an estimated 15,000 Turkish Kurds, following several breaches of security in the camp, and expressed its concern at the political vacuum in the region resulting from the factional conflict. UNHCR proceeded to transfer 4,000 people to other local settlements and to provide humanitarian assistance to those refugees who had settled closer to Iraqi-controlled territory but who had been refused asylum. At 31 December 1998 the refugee population in Iraq totalled 104,100, of whom 62,600 were Palestinians, 29,100 Iranians and 11,300 were from Turkey. In addition, there were 22,500 recently returned refugees in Iraq of concern to UNHCR. At that time there was still a substantial Iraqi refugee population in the region, totalling an estimated 590,800 of whom 530,600 were in Iran. At the end of 1998 Iran remained the principal country of asylum in the world, hosting some 1,931,300 refugees, mainly from Afghanistan and Iraq.

UNHCR co-ordinates humanitarian assistance for the estimated 165,000 Sahrawis registered as refugees in the Tindouf area of Algeria. Approximately 80,000 most vulnerable members of the Sahrawi refugee population receive direct assistance from UNHCR. In September 1997 an agreement was reached on implementing the 1991 Settlement Plan for the Western Sahara. Accordingly, UNHCR was to help organize the registration and safe return of up to 135,000 Sahrawi refugees who had been identified as eligible to vote in the referendum on the future of the territory, scheduled to be conducted in early December 1998 (subsequently postponed). In addition, UNHCR was to facilitate the reintegration of the returnees and monitor their rehabilitation.

In June 1992 people fleeing the civil war and famine in Somalia began arriving in Yemen in large numbers. UNHCR set up camps to accommodate some 50,000 refugees, providing them with shelter, food, water and sanitation. As a result of civil conflict in Yemen in mid-1994 a large camp in the south of the country was demolished and other refugees had to be relocated, while the Yemeni authorities initiated a campaign of forcible repatriation. During early 1998 the refugee population in Yemen expanded owing to the influx of Somalis fleeing the ongoing civil conflict and the effects of heavy flooding which had devastated areas in the south of that country. At the end of 1998 Yemen was hosting 61,400 refugees, of whom 57,400 were from Somalia, and a further 28,500 people in a refugee-like situation of concern to UNHCR.

## AFRICA

During the 1990s UNHCR provided assistance to refugee populations in many parts of the continent where civil conflict, drought, extreme poverty, violations of human rights or environmental degradation had forced people to flee their countries. The majority of African refugees and returnees are located in countries that are themselves suffering major economic problems and are thus unable to provide the basic requirements of the uprooted people. Furthermore, UNHCR has often failed to receive adequate international financial support to implement effective relief programmes.

### East Africa

The Horn of Africa, afflicted in the late 1980s and early 1990s by famine, separatist violence and ethnic conflict, experienced large-scale population movements. In 1992 UNHCR initiated a repatriation programme for the massive Somali and Ethiopian refugee populations in Kenya, which included assistance with reconstruction projects and the provision of food to returnees and displaced persons. The implementation by UNHCR of community-based projects, for example seed distribution, the establishment of a women's bakery co-operative and support for a brick production initiative, served as important instruments of assistance and of bringing stability to areas of returnee settlements. However, the continuing instability in north-western Somalia prevented a completion of the repatriation process, and resulted in further population displacement. From October 1997 severe flooding in southern areas of Somalia further hindered the repatriation of refugees. None the less, UNHCR and the authorities in north-western Somalia agreed to proceed with the repatriation process, with the aim of facilitating the speedy return of 100,000 Somalis, and to initiate projects to aid their reintegration. During 1998 an estimated 48,100 Somali refugees were repatriated from Ethiopia under UNHCR auspices. Some spontaneous repatriation also took place, leaving a total Somali refugee population of 480,800, of whom 249,200 were in Ethiopia and 174,000 were in Kenya. At the end of 1998 Ethiopia was still hosting a total of 262,000 refugees, while Kenya was hosting 238,200.

During the 1980s more than 900,000 Ethiopians fled to neighbouring countries. By November 1997 UNHCR estimated that some 600,000 Ethiopians had repatriated, either by spontaneous or organized movements. The voluntary repatriation operation of the estimated 50,000 Ethiopians remaining in Sudan was concluded in mid-1998. In September 1999 UNHCR announced that the automatic refugee status of Ethiopians who left their country before 1991 was to be withdrawn with effect from 1 March 2000. UNHCR was to provide transportation and rehabilitation assistance until that date.

From 1992 some 500,000 Eritreans took refuge in Sudan as a result of separatist conflicts; however, by 1995 an estimated 125,000 had returned spontaneously, in particular following Eritrea's accession to independence in May 1993. A UNHCR repatriation programme to assist the remaining refugees, which had been delayed for various political, security and funding considerations, was initiated in November 1994. However, its implementation was hindered by a shortfall in donor funding and by disputes between the Eritrean and Sudanese Governments. At the end of 1998 Sudan still hosted a total of 391,500 refugees including 342,300 from Eritrea and 35,600 from Ethiopia. Renewed conflict between Ethiopia and Eritrea, which commenced in 1998, had, by mid-1999, resulted in the displacement of some 350,000 Eritreans and 300,000 Ethiopians. Meanwhile, UNHCR continued to negotiate with the Eritrean Government to permit an organized, voluntary repatriation of refugees from Sudan. At 31 December 1998 some 374,000 Sudanese remained as refugees, mainly in the Central African Republic, the Democratic Republic of the Congo, Ethiopia, Kenya and Uganda, owing to continuing civil unrest. The Ugandan Government, hosting an estimated 189,800 of these refugees, has provided new resettlement sites and has supported refugee efforts to construct homes and cultivate crops in order to achieve some degree of self-sufficiency.

### West Africa

In West Africa the refugee population increased by one-third during 1992 and the first half of 1993, with the addition of new refugees fleeing Togo, Liberia and Senegal. In accordance with a peace agreement, signed in July 1993, UNHCR was responsible for the repatriation of Liberian refugees who had fled to Guinea, Côte d'Ivoire and Sierra Leone during the civil conflict. The voluntary repatriation programme was to include substantial assistance to rebuild Liberia's infrastructure; UNHCR also began to provide emergency relief to displaced persons within the country. Persisting political insecurity prevented large-scale repatriation of Liberian refugees, and in mid-1996 UNHCR suspended its preparatory activities for a repatriation and reintegration operation, owing to an escalation in hostilities. At February 1997 the Liberian refugee population in West Africa totalled 758,000; however, the prospect of a peaceful settlement in Liberia, with preparations under way for a general election to be conducted in July, prompted a movement of refugees returning home, and in April UNHCR initiated an organized repatriation of Liberian refugees from Ghana. Improved security conditions in the country, following the establishment of a democratically-elected government and the consolidation of the peace settlement, were expected to accelerate the return of refugees and other displaced persons during 1998. In the event the process was hindered slightly by logistical difficulties and the persisting volatility of some border regions. In April UNHCR operations in northern Liberia were temporarily suspended as a result of attacks by anti-government militia and clashes between rebel and government forces which prompted 6,000 Liberians to flee to Guinea. During the year UNHCR assisted a total of 75,700 Liberian refugees to return home and organized quick impact projects to facilitate their reintegration. A further 160,000 Liberians were estimated to have returned without assistance. At the end of 1998 there were still some 258,700 Liberian refugees, of whom 117,700 were in Côte d'Ivoire and 114,300 in Guinea. At that time there were also some 251,400 recently returned Liberian refugees of concern to UNHCR.

Further large-scale population displacement in West Africa followed an escalation of violence in Sierra Leone in early 1995. By December 1996 there were 120,000 Sierra Leonean refugees in Liberia and 248,827 in Guinea, while a further 654,600 internally displaced Sierra Leoneans were of concern to UNHCR. The repatriation of Sierra Leonean refugees from Liberia was initiated in February 1997; however, the programme was suspended in May, owing to renewed political violence, which forced UNHCR staff to evacuate the country, and the seizure of power by military forces. Thousands of people fled to other parts of the country, as well as to Guinea and Liberia, to escape the hostilities. Following the intervention of the ECOMOG multinational force (see ECOWAS p. 165) and the conclusion of a peace agreement in October, residents of the Sierra Leone capital, Freetown, who had been displaced by the conflict, began to return. In February 1998 ECOMOG troops took control of Freetown from the rebel military forces, and in the following month the elected President, Ahmed Tejan Kabbah, was reinstated as Head of State. None the less, large numbers of Sierra Leoneans continued to cross the border into neighbouring countries, owing to ongoing violence in the northern and eastern regions of the country and severe food shortages. At 31 December 1998 there were some 297,200 Sierra Leonean refugees in Guinea and 103,000 in Liberia. There were also 198,400 recently returned refugees in Sierra Leone of concern to UNHCR and an estimated displaced population of 670,000. In early 1999 anti-government forces again advanced on Freetown, prompting heavy fighting with ECOMOG troops and the displacement of thousands more civilians. In February a reported 200,000 people fled the town of Kenema in south-eastern Sierra Leone following attacks by rebel militia. In May a cease-fire agreement was concluded between the Government and opposition forces, and a formal peace accord was signed in early July. By November, however, UNHCR noted that few Sierra Leonean refugees had repatriated, owing to persisting security concerns.

In June 1998 UNHCR expressed concern at the outbreak of fighting in Guinea-Bissau, which had prompted the majority of the capital's population of some 300,000 to flee into the surrounding countryside and generated concern for the safety of the estimated 15,000 Senegalese refugees who had been based in camps in Guinea-Bissau since 1992. UNHCR staff attempted to monitor the movements of the population, and, despite the border between Guinea and Guinea-Bissau officially being declared closed, estimated that some 12,000 people crossed into the neighbouring country during June 1998. A cease-fire was agreed between the conflicting forces in August; however there was renewed conflict in October prompting further population displacement. UNHCR staff attempted to distribute mosquito nets and other non-food supplies to the displaced population, but, along with other humanitarian personnel, they were repeatedly obliged to evacuate the country owing to the ongoing violence. A peace accord was concluded in November. In early 1999 UNHCR began preparations to implement a repatriation programme and continued to provide assistance to some 150,000 IDPs. In early 1994 some 40,000 Tuareg nomads, who had fled from northern Mali into Burkina Faso, received protection and material assistance from two newly-established UNHCR field offices. During 1995 large numbers of the Malian refugee population (totalling some 175,000) returned spontaneously from camps in Mauritania, Burkina Faso and Algeria, owing to political developments in Mali. An organized repatriation of the remaining refugees was initiated in 1996. In November UNHCR signed an agreement with the Malian and Nigerien Governments establishing the conditions of repatriation of 25,000 Tuareg refugees living in Niger. By 31 December 1998 almost all Malian refugees in the region had repatriated, and there were 61,400 recently returned refugees of concern to UNHCR.

### Central Africa

Since 1993 the Great Lakes region of Central Africa has experienced massive population displacement, causing immense operational challenges and demands on the resources of international humanitarian and relief agencies. In October of that year a military coup in Burundi prompted some 580,000 people to flee into Rwanda and Tanzania, although many had returned by early 1994. By May, however, an estimated 860,000 people from Burundi and Rwanda had fled to neighbouring states (following a resurgence of ethnic violence in both countries), including 250,000 mainly Rwandan Tutsi refugees who entered Tanzania over a 24-hour period in late April. In May UNHCR began an immediate operation to airlift emergency supplies to the refugees. Despite overcrowding in camps and a high incidence of cholera and dysentery (particularly in camps in eastern Zaire, where many thousands of Rwandan Hutus had sought refuge following the establishment of a new Rwandan Government in July) large numbers of refugees refused to accept UNHCR-assisted repatriation, owing to fears of reprisal ethnic killings. In September reports of mass ethnic violence, which were disputed by some UN agencies, continued to disrupt UNHCR's policy of repatriation and to prompt returnees to cross the border back into Zaire. Security in the refugee camps, which was undermined by the presence of military and political elements of the former Rwandan Government, remained an outstanding concern of UNHCR. A resurgence of violence in Burundi, in February 1995, provoked further mass population movements. However, in March the Tanzanian authorities, reportedly frustrated at the lack of international assistance for the refugees and the environmental degradation resulting from the camps, closed Tanzania's border with Burundi, thus preventing the admission into the country of some 100,000 Rwandan Hutu refugees who were fleeing camps in Burundi. While persisting disturbances in Rwanda disrupted UNHCR's repatriation programme, in April Rwandan government troops employed intimidation tactics to force some 90,000 internally displaced Hutus to leave a heavily-populated camp in the south-west of the country; other small camps were closed. In August the Zairean Government initiated a programme of forcible repatriation of the estimated 1m. Rwandan and 70,000 Burundian Hutu refugees remaining in the country, which prompted as many as 100,000 refugees to flee the camps into the surrounding countryside. Following widespread international condemnation of the forcible repatriation and expressions of concern for the welfare of the remaining refugees, the Zairean Government suspended the programme, having first received an assurance that UNHCR would assume responsibility for the repatriation of all the refugees by the end of 1995 (although in December the Government accepted that its deadline could not be achieved). In September Rwanda agreed to strengthen its reception facilities and to provide greater security and protection for returnees, in collaboration with UNHCR, in order to prepare for any large-scale repatriation. UNHCR, meanwhile, expanded its information campaign, to promote the return of refugees, and enhanced its facilities at official border entry points. In December UNHCR negotiated an agreement between the Rwandan and Tanzanian authorities concerning the repatriation of the estimated 500,000 Rwandans remaining in camps in Tanzania. UNHCR agreed to establish a separate camp in north-west Tanzania in order to accommodate elements of the refugee population that might disrupt the repatriation programme. The repatriation of Rwandan refugees from all host countries was affected by reports of reprisals against Hutu returnees by the Tutsi-dominated Government in Rwanda. In February 1996 the Zairean Government renewed its efforts to accelerate the repatriation process, owing to concerns that the camps were becoming permanent settlements and that they were being used to train and rearm a Hutu militia. In July the Burundian Government forcibly repatriated 15,000 Rwandan refugees, having announced the closure of all remaining refugee camps. The repatriation programme, which was condemned by UNHCR, was suspended by the country's new military authorities, but only after many more thousands of refugees had been obliged to return to Rwanda and up to 30,000 had fled to Tanzania.

In October 1996 an escalation of hostilities between Zairean government forces, accused by Rwanda of arming the Hutu *Interahamwe* militia, and Zairean (Banyamulenge) Tutsis, who had been the focus of increasingly violent assaults, resulted in an extreme humanitarian crisis. Some 250,000 refugees fled 12 camps in the east of the country, including 90,000 Burundians who returned home. An estimated 500,000 refugees regrouped in Muganga camp, west of Goma, although with insufficient relief assistance, following the temporary evacuation of international aid workers. UNHCR appealed to all Rwandan Hutu refugees to return home, and issued assurances of the presence of human rights observers in Rwanda to enhance their security. In mid-November, with the apparent withdrawal of *Interahamwe* forces, and the advance of the Tutsi-dominated Alliance des forces démocratiques pour la libération du Congo–Zaïre (AFDL), more than 600,000 refugees unexpectedly returned to Rwanda; however, concern remained on the part of the international community for the substantial number of Rwandan Hutu refugees at large in eastern Zaire. Further mass movement of Ruwandan refugee populations occurred in December, owing to the threat of forcible repatriation by the Tanzanian Government, which had announced its intention of closing all camps by the end of the year. UNHCR initiated a repatriation programme; however, 200,000 refugees, unwilling to return to Rwanda, fled their camps. The majority of the refugees were later identified by the Tanzanian national army and escorted to the Rwandan border. By the end of December some 483,000 refugees had returned to Rwanda from Tanzania.

In February 1997 violence in Zaire escalated, prompting some 56,000 Zaireans to flee into Tanzania and disrupting the distribution of essential humanitarian supplies to refugees remaining in Zaire. An estimated 170,000 refugees abandoned their temporary encampment at Tingi-Tingi, fearing attacks by the advancing AFDL forces. About 75,000 reassembled at Ubundu, south of Kisangani, while the fate of the other refugees remained uncertain. In March and April reports of attacks on refugee camps, by AFDL forces and local Zaireans, resulted in large numbers of people fleeing into the surrounding countryside, with the consequent deaths of many of the most vulnerable members of the refugee population from disease and starvation. At the end of April the leader of the AFDL, Laurent-Désiré Kabila, ordered the repatriation of all Rwandan Hutu refugees by the UN within 60 days. Emergency air and land operations to evacuate some 185,000 refugees who had regrouped into temporary settlements were initiated a few days later. The repatriation process, however, was hindered by administrative and logistical difficulties and lack of co-operation on the part of the AFDL forces. By June an estimated 215,000 Rwandans were still missing or dispersed throughout the former Zaire (renamed the Democratic Republic of the Congo—DRC—by the AFDL in May). In the following months relations between the Kabila Government and UNHCR deteriorated as a result of several incidences of forcible repatriations of refugees to Rwanda and reports that the authorities were hindering a UN investigation into alleged abuses of the human rights of Rwandan Hutu refugees by AFDL forces. In August an agreement was concluded to provide for the voluntary repatriation of some 75,000 Congolese refugees remaining in Tanzania, under UNHCR supervision, and in December a tripartite agreement was signed to provide for the organized repatriation of the remaining Congolese refugees in Rwanda, with both Governments agreeing to observe strict conditions of security for the refugees on both sides of the border. Meanwhile, an estimated 40,000 refugees from the Republic of the Congo fled to the DRC in mid-1997, following the outbreak of civil conflict. In December a memorandum of understanding was signed by representatives of the two Governments and of UNHCR, providing for their immediate repatriation. UNHCR's concerns in the Great Lakes region in 1998 were to ensure the security of the returning refugee populations and to assist their reintegration and national reconciliation. UNHCR also resolved to work, in co-operation with UNDP and WFP, to rehabilitate areas previously inhabited by refugees in countries of asylum and undertook to repair roads, bridges and other essential transport infrastructure, improve water and sanitation facilities, and strengthen the education sector. However, the political stability of the region remained uncertain. In August fighting between rebel and government forces again broke out in the DRC, which forced UNHCR temporarily to evacuate, and prompted substantial numbers of people to flee to neighbouring countries. At 31 December the major populations of concern to UNHCR in the Great Lakes region were as follows: 231,800 returned refugees, and a further 625,000 IDPs, in Rwanda; 240,300 refugees, and some 111,300 recently returned refugees, in the DRC; 100,000 IDPs in Burundi, as well as 114,600 returned refugees; and a refugee population of 543,900 remaining in Tanzania.

From late 1998 intense fighting in the Republic of the Congo disrupted UNHCR humanitarian efforts in that country and left some 200,000 people displaced south-west of the capital, Brazzaville. A further 27,500 people fled across the border to the DRC, while there were up to 100,000 people displaced within the country. Fighting continued during 1999, and in July an estimated 25,000 Congolese refugees fled to Gabon. In the same month some 14,000 refugees from the DRC crossed into the Central African Republic, bringing the total number of refugees since the resumption of conflict in August 1998 to some 100,000 (the majority of whom were in Tanzania), while a further 100,000 people were thought to have been displaced. In August 1999 the security situation in Burundi deteriorated, and there were reports of a steady flow of Burundians fleeing to camps in Tanzania. In October UNHCR, along with other agencies, suspended its non-essential operations in Burundi as a result of the deaths of two UN personnel.

### Southern Africa

In 1994 continuing civil conflict in Angola caused some 370,000 people to leave their home areas. Prior to the signing of a peace settlement in November, UNHCR provided assistance to 112,000 IDPs and returnees, although military activities, which hindered accessibility, undermined the effectiveness of the assistance programme. In mid-1995, following a consolidation of the peace process in Angola, UNHCR appealed for US $44m. to support the voluntary repatriation of Angolan refugees over a two-and-a-half-year operation. Implementation of the repatriation programme was delayed, however, reportedly owing to poor accommodation and other facilities for returnees, limited progress in confining and disarming opposition troops and the continued hazard of land-mines throughout the country. During 1997 an estimated 53,000 Angolans voluntarily returned from the DRC and Zambia, bringing the total returnees since mid-1995 to some 130,000. In November 1997 UNHCR resolved to implement an operation to provide for the repatriation and reintegration of the remaining 240,000 Angolan refugees by June 1999, of whom 160,000 were to return during 1998 and 80,000 in 1999. UNHCR allocated $15.7m. to support the repatriation process and other activities in Angola, including strengthening the country's road infrastructure, monitoring areas of return, reintegration projects and promoting links with other development programmes. In May 1998, however, the security situation in Angola deteriorated, and at the end of June UNHCR declared a temporary suspension of the repatriation operation. The renewed violence also resulted in further population displacement: by December at least 90,000 people had been displaced within Angola and 40,000 had fled to the DRC. At that time the total Angolan refugee population amounted to some 315,900, while there were 75,800 recently returned Angolan refugees of concern to UNHCR. Heavy fighting in central Angola in early 1999 resulted in massive population displacement in and around the city of Huambo, and, by April, a further 21,500 refugees had arrived in the DRC.

### THE AMERICAS AND THE CARIBBEAN

The International Conference on Central American Refugees (CIREFCA), held in Guatemala in May 1989, adopted a plan of action for the voluntary repatriation of refugees in the region, and established national co-ordinating committees to assist in this process. At that time there were some 150,000 refugees receiving UNHCR assistance, and a further estimated 1.8m. other refugees and displaced persons. The repatriation process initiated by CIREFCA was formally concluded in June 1994. UNHCR's efforts in the region have subsequently emphasized legal issues and refugee protection, while assisting governments to formulate national legislation on asylum and refugees. At the end of 1998 the outstanding populations of concern to UNHCR in Central America were the 28,300 mainly Guatemalan refugees remaining in Mexico and some 7,500 recently returned Guatemalan refugees. At that time Costa Rica was hosting a refugee population of some 23,000, the majority of whom were from Nicaragua.

In early 1997 UNHCR was monitoring the situation in Colombia, where ongoing internal conflict and alleged human rights abuses, committed by armed groups, had resulted in massive population displacement. UNHCR was also providing basic legal and medical assistance to some 200 refugees in Colombia, although the actual refugee population in that country was estimated to be more than 5,000. By late 1998 there were reports of 500,000 Colombians living in the border regions of Venezuela and a further 30,000 in Ecuador. During that year UNHCR undertook fact-finding missions and, in particular, implemented a pilot documentation project for 1,000 Colombian refugees and conducted training programmes for Ecuadorean police working in the border areas.

Canada and the USA are major countries of resettlement for refugees. UNHCR provides counselling and legal services for asylum-seekers in these countries. At 31 December 1998 the estimated refugee populations totalled 135,700 in Canada and 524,100 in the USA, while asylum-seekers numbered 23,300 and 622,300 respectively.

### EUROPE

The political changes in eastern and central Europe during the early 1990s resulted in a dramatic increase in the number of asylum-seekers and displaced people in the region. UNHCR was the agency designated by the UN Secretary-General to lead the UN relief operation to assist those affected by the conflict in the former Yugoslavia. It was responsible for the supply of food and other humanitarian aid to the besieged capital of Bosnia and Herzegovina, Sarajevo, and to Muslim and Croatian enclaves in the country, under the armed escort of the UN Protection Force. Assistance was provided not only to Bosnian refugees in Croatia and displaced people within Bosnia and Herzegovina's borders, but also, in order to forestall further movements of people, to civilians whose survival was threatened. The operation was often seriously hampered by armed attacks (resulting, in some cases, in fatalities), distribution difficulties and underfunding from international donors. The Dayton peace agreement, which was signed in December 1995 bringing an end to the conflict, secured the right for all refugees and displaced persons freely to choose their place of residence within the new territorial arrangements of Bosnia and Herzegovina. Thus, the immediate effect of the peace accord was further population displacement, including a mass exodus of almost the entire Serb population of Sarajevo. Under the peace accord, UNHCR was responsible for planning and implementing the repatriation of all Bosnian refugees and displaced persons, estimated at 2m.; however, there were still immense obstacles to freedom of movement, in particular for minorities wishing to return to an area dominated by a different politico-ethnic faction. By the end of 1998 there was still a Bosnian refugee population of some 597,000, the majority of whom were in Germany, Austria and the Federal Republic of Yugoslavia (FRY). In addition, there were 242,400 recently returned refugees and 87,900 returned IDPs of concern to UNHCR in Bosnia and Herzegovina and 836,400 IDPs who had yet to return home. Plans to accelerate reconstruction and rehabilitation efforts during 1999 were disrupted by events in the FRY (see below).

From March 1998 attacks by Serbian forces against members of a separatist movement in the southern Serbian province of Kosovo and Metohija resulted in large-scale population displacement. Of particular concern were some 50,000 people who had fled to the surrounding mountains, close to the Albanian border, without shelter or adequate provisions. In October the withdrawal of Serbian troops and the involvement of the international community in the provision of aid and monitoring of the situation in Kosovo was thought to have prompted substantial numbers to have returned home. However, in December there were reports of renewed attacks by Serbian forces on the local Albanian population, which persisted into 1999. The failure of peace negotiations prompted further displacement, and in late March an estimated 95,000 people fled their homes following the withdrawal of international observers of the OSCE and the commencement of a NATO operation, which aimed to halt the Serbian attacks and compel the FRY to agree to a peace settlement. By mid-April UNHCR estimated that up to 1.3m. Kosovar Albanians had been displaced since the fighting began in 1998, with reports that thousands had been forcibly expelled by Serbian troops in recent weeks. UNHCR attempted to provide emergency relief to the thousands of refugees who fled to neighbouring countries, and expressed concern for those remaining in the province, of whom up to 400,000 were thought to be living without shelter. In early April UNHCR condemned the decision of the authorities in the former Yugoslav republic of Macedonia (FYRM) forcibly to evacuate some 30,000 refugees from camps in Blace, near the FRY border, and subsequently to close the border to further refugees. At that time UNHCR helped to co-ordinate an international effort to evacuate substantial numbers of the refugees to third countries, and issued essential identity and travel documents. In Albania UNHCR funded transport to relocate an estimated 250,000 people from the border town of Kukës, where resources and the local infrastructure were strained by the massive population influx, to other sites throughout the country. At the start of June the Kosovar refugee population totalled some 443,300 people in Albania, 247,800 in the FYRM, 69,300 in Montenegro, and 21,700 in Bosnia and Herzegovina, while at least 40,000 had been temporarily resettled in more than 20 other countries. In mid-June, following a cease-fire accord and an agreement by the FRY to withdraw all forces and paramilitary units, UNHCR initiated a large-scale registration operation of Kosovar refugees and began to deliver emergency provisions to assist the displaced population within Kosovo. Despite warnings of anti-personnel devices and lack of shelter, UNHCR estimated that some 477,000 refugees had returned in a spontaneous repatriation movement by the end of June. Meanwhile, local Serbs began to move out of the province; by August an estimated 137,000 Serbs had left Kosovo, fearing reprisal attacks by returning ethnic Albanians. In September UNHCR estimated that one-third of all homes in Kosovo had been destroyed or seriously damaged during the conflict, prompting concerns regarding the welfare of returning refugees and IDPs in the coming winter months. UNHCR began to distribute 'shelter kits' to assist the process of reconstruction of homes, and proceeded to accelerate the distribution of blankets and winter clothing, as well as of fuel and other essential supplies, throughout Serbia and Montenegro.

In December 1992 UNHCR dispatched teams to establish offices in both Armenia and Azerbaijan to assist people displaced as a result of the war between the two countries and to provide immediate relief. A cease-fire was signed between the two sides in May 1994, although violations of the accord were subsequently reported and relations between the two countries remained tense. At the end of 1998 the region was still supporting a massive displaced population: including 310,000 Azerbaijani refugees in Armenia and 188,400 Armenians in Azerbaijan (of whom 150,000 and 8,500, respectively, were receiving UNHCR assistance) and 576,300 IDPs of concern to UNHCR in Azerbaijan. UNHCR's humanitarian activities have focused on improving shelter, in particular for the most vulnerable among the refugee population, and promoting economic self-sufficiency and stability. In Georgia, where almost 300,000 people have left their homes as a result of civil conflict since 1991, UNHCR has attempted to encourage income-generating activities among the displaced population, to increase the Georgian Government's capacity to support those people and to assist the rehabilitation of people returning to their areas of origin. During 1995 UNHCR pursued a process, initiated in the previous year, to establish a comprehensive approach to the problems of refugees, returnees, IDPs and migrants in the Commonwealth of Independent States. A regional conference convened in Geneva, Switzerland, in May 1996, endorsed a framework of activities aimed at managing migratory flows and at developing institutional capacities to prevent mass population displacements. At that time it was estimated that more than 9m. former citizens of the USSR had relocated since its disintegration as a result of conflict, economic pressures and ecological disasters.

In March 1995 UNHCR initiated an assistance programme for people displaced as a result of conflict in the separatist republic of Chechnya (Russian Federation), as part of a UN inter-agency relief effort, in collaboration with the International Committee of the Red Cross (ICRC, q.v.). UNHCR continued its activities in 1996, at the request of the Russian Government, at which time the displaced population within Chechnya and in the surrounding republics totalled 490,000. During 1997 UNHCR provided reintegration assistance to 25,000 people who returned to Chechnya, despite reports of sporadic violence. The security situation in the region deteriorated sharply in mid-1999, following a series of border clashes and incursions by Chechen separatist forces into the neighbouring republic of Dagestan. In September Russian military aircraft began an aerial offensive against suspected rebel targets in Chechnya, and at the end of the month ground troops moved into the republic. By November an estimated 225,000 Chechens had fled to neighbouring Ingushetia. UNHCR dispatched food supplies to assist the refugees, but was awaiting security guarantees before deploying emergency teams to the region.

### CO-OPERATION WITH OTHER ORGANIZATIONS

UNHCR works closely with other UN agencies, intergovernmental organizations and non-governmental organizations (NGOs) to increase the scope and effectiveness of its emergency operations. Within the UN system UNHCR co-operates, principally, with the World Food Programme in the distribution of food aid, UNICEF and the World Health Organization in the provision of family welfare and child immunization programmes, and UNDP in development-related activities and the preparation of guide-lines for the continuum of emergency assistance to development programmes. UNHCR also has close working relationships with the International Committee of the Red Cross and the International Organization for Migration. In 1999 UNHCR worked with 513 NGOs as 'implementing partners', enabling UNHCR to broaden the use of its resources while maintaining a co-ordinating role in the provision of assistance.

### TRAINING

UNHCR organizes training programmes and workshops to enhance the capabilities of field workers and non-UNHCR staff, in the following areas: the identification and registration of refugees; people-orientated planning; resettlement procedures and policies; emergency response and management; security awareness; stress management; and the dissemination of information through the electronic media.

## Finance

UNHCR's administrative expenditure is mostly financed as part of the United Nations' regular budget. General Programmes of material assistance are financed from voluntary contributions made by governments and also from non-governmental sources. In addition, UNHCR undertakes a number of Special Programmes, as requested by the UN General Assembly, the Secretary-General of the UN or a member state, to assist returnees and, in some cases, displaced persons. The 1999 budget amounted to US $914.8m., including $413m. allocated to finance General Programmes, $482m. for Special Programmes, and $19.8m. for the administrative budget. The total budget for 1999 was subsequently revised to $1,700m. as a result of the conflict in Kosovo.

## Publications

*Refugees* (quarterly, in English, French, German, Italian, Japanese and Spanish).

*Refugee Survey Quarterly.*

*The State of the World's Refugees* (every 2 years).

*UNHCR Handbook for Emergencies.*

Press releases, reports.

# United Nations Peace-keeping Operations

**Address:** Department of Peace-keeping Operations, Room S-3727-B, United Nations, New York, NY 10017, USA.

**Telephone:** (212) 963-8079; **fax:** (212) 963-9222; **internet:** www.un.org/Depts/dpko/.

United Nations peace-keeping operations have been conceived as instruments of conflict control. The UN has used these operations in various conflicts, with the consent of the parties involved, to maintain international peace and security, without prejudice to the positions or claims of parties, in order to facilitate the search for political settlements through peaceful means such as mediation and the good offices of the Secretary-General. Each operation is established with a specific mandate, which requires periodic review by the Security Council. United Nations peace-keeping operations fall into two categories: peace-keeping forces and observer missions.

Peace-keeping forces are composed of contingents of military and civilian personnel, made available by member states. These forces assist in preventing the recurrence of fighting, restoring and maintaining peace, and promoting a return to normal conditions. To this end, peace-keeping forces are authorized as necessary to undertake negotiations, persuasion, observation and fact-finding. They conduct patrols and interpose physically between the opposing parties. Peace-keeping forces are permitted to use their weapons only in self-defence.

Military observer missions are composed of officers (usually unarmed), who are made available, on the Secretary-General's request, by member states. A mission's function is to observe and report to the Secretary-General (who, in turn, informs the UN Security Council) on the maintenance of a cease-fire, to investigate violations and to do what it can to improve the situation.

Peace-keeping forces and observer missions must at all times maintain complete impartiality and avoid any action that might affect the claims or positions of the parties. In January 1995 the UN Secretary-General presented a report to the Security Council, reassessing the UN's role in peace-keeping. The document stipulated that UN forces in conflict areas should not be responsible for peace-enforcement duties, and included a proposal for the establishment of a 'rapid reaction' force which would be ready for deployment within a month of being authorized by the Security Council. In September 1997 the UN Secretary-General established a staff to plan and organize the establishment of the so-called UN Stand-by Forces High Readiness Brigade. At that time, however, only seven countries—Austria, Canada, Denmark, the Netherlands, Norway, Poland and Sweden—had formally committed troops to the force, which was expected to be fully operational in 1999. A Stand-by Arrangements System has been operational since 1994, to which some 80 countries had identified 104,300 troops as available for peace-keeping duties, as well as other services and equipment, by April 1999.

The UN's peace-keeping operations are financed by assessed contributions from member states (with the exception of two operations that are ongoing and financed through the regular budget of the UN). A significant expansion in the UN's peace-keeping activities during the early 1990s was accompanied by a perpetual financial crisis within the organization, as a result of the increased financial burden and the failure of member states to pay outstanding contributions. By mid-September 1999 unpaid contributions to the peace-keeping accounts amounted to US $1,830m.

By October 1999 the UN had undertaken a total of 53 peace-keeping operations, of which 13 were authorized in the period 1948–88 and 40 since 1988, reaching a peak in 1993 with a total deployment of more than 80,000 troops from 77 countries.

## UNITED NATIONS CIVILIAN POLICE MISSION IN HAITI—MIPONUH

**Headquarters:** Port-au-Prince, Haiti.

**Special Representative of the UN Secretary-General and Head of Mission:** ALFREDO LOPES CABRAL (Guinea-Bissau).

**Police Commissioner:** Col GEORGES GABBARDO (France).

MIPONUH was established by the Security Council in late November 1997, as a successor mission to the four-month UN Transition Mission in Haiti (UNTMIH), and marked the end of UN military involvement, which had commenced in September 1993 with the deployment of the original UN Mission in Haiti. MIPONUH, with a mandate for a period of one year, was to support the process of national reconciliation and complete UNTMIH's mandate of undertaking training activities and providing other law enforcement expertise in order to strengthen Haiti's national police force. MIPONUH was also to work closely with the joint civilian mission of the UN and Organization of American States (MICIVIH). In November 1998 the Security Council extended MIPONUH's mandate for a further year, to 30 November 1999. In November 1999 the Council resolved to maintain MIPONUH until 15 March 2000, when it was to be succeeded by an International Civilian Support Mission in Haiti (MICAH).

At 30 September 1999 MIPONUH comprised 286 civilian police officers, assisted by additional international and local support staff. The General Assembly appropriation for the mission for the 12-month period July 1999–June 2000 was US $18.6m.

## UNITED NATIONS DISENGAGEMENT OBSERVER FORCE—UNDOF

**Headquarters:** Damascus, Syria.

**Commander:** Maj.-Gen. CAMERON ROSS (Canada).

UNDOF was established for an initial period of six months by a UN Security Council resolution in May 1974, following the signature in Geneva of a disengagement agreement between Syrian and Israeli forces. The mandate has since been extended by successive resolutions. The initial task of the Force was to take over territory evacuated in stages by the Israeli troops, in accordance with the disengagement agreement, to hand over territory to Syrian troops, and to establish an area of separation on the Golan Heights.

UNDOF continues to monitor the area of separation; it carries out inspections of the areas of limited armaments and forces; uses its best efforts to maintain the cease-fire; and undertakes activities of a humanitarian nature, such as arranging the transfer of prisoners and war-dead between Syria and Israel. The Force operates exclusively on Syrian territory.

At 30 September 1999 the Force comprised 1,035 troops; it is assisted by approximately 80 military observers of UNTSO's Observer Group Golan. Further UNTSO military observers help UNDOF in the performance of its tasks, as required. The General Assembly appropriated US $35.4m. to cover the cost of the operation for the period 1 July 1999–30 June 2000.

## UNITED NATIONS INTERIM ADMINISTRATION MISSION IN KOSOVO—UNMIK

**Headquarters:** Priština, Kosovo, Yugoslavia.

**Special Representative of the UN Secretary-General and Head of Mission:** Dr BERNARD KOUCHNER (France).

**Principal Deputy Special Representative of the UN Secretary-General:** JAMES P. COVEY (USA).

In June 1999 NATO suspended a 10-week aerial offensive against the Federal Republic of Yugoslavia, following an agreement by the Serbian authorities to withdraw all security and paramilitary forces from the southern province of Kosovo and Metohija, where Serbian repression of a separatist movement had prompted a humanitarian crisis and co-ordinated international action to resolve the conflict. On 10 June the UN Security Council adopted Resolution 1244, which outlined the terms of a political settlement for Kosovo and provided for the deployment of international civilian and security personnel. The security presence, termed the Kosovo Peace Implementation Force (KFOR), was to be led by NATO, while the UN was to oversee all civilian operations. UNMIK was established under the terms of Resolution 1244 as the supreme legal and executive authority in Kosovo, with responsibility for all civil administration and for facilitating the reconstruction and rehabilitation of the province as an autonomous region. For the first time in a UN operation other organizations were mandated to co-ordinate aspects of the mission in Kosovo, under the UN's overall jurisdiction. The four key elements of UNMIK were the interim civil administration; humanitarian affairs (led by UNHCR); democratization and institution-building (OSCE); and economic reconstruction (EU). An advance team, under a temporary interim administrator, accompanied the first deployment of KFOR troops, and civilian police officers began arriving in the province at the end of June. UNMIK and KFOR immediately established a Joint Implementation Commission to co-ordinate and supervise the demilitarization of the Kosovo Liberation Army. UNMIK initiated a mass information campaign (and later administered new radio stations in Kosovo) to urge co-operation with the international personnel in the province and tolerance for all ethnic communities. A Mine Co-ordinating Centre supervised efforts to deactivate anti-personnel devices and to ensure the safety of the returning ethnic Albanian population. In mid-July the UN Secretary-General's permanent Special Representative took office, and chaired the first meeting of the Kosovo Transitional Council (KTC), which had been established by the UN as a multi-ethnic consultative organ, the highest political body under UNMIK, to help to restore law and order in the province and to reintegrate the local administrative infrastructure. In August a Joint Advisory Council on Legislative Matters was constituted, with representatives of UNMIK and the local judiciary, in order to consider measures to eliminate discrimination from the province's legal framework. At the end of July UNMIK personnel began to supervise customs controls at Kosovo's international borders. Other developments in the first few months of UNMIK's deployment included the establishment of joint commissions on energy and public utilities, education, and health, a Technical Advisory Commission on establishing a judiciary and prosecution service, and, in October, the establishment of a Fuel Supervisory Board to administer the import, sale and distribution of petroleum. Central financial institutions for the province were inaugurated in November. In the same month UNMIK established a Housing and Property Directorate and Claims Commission in order to resolve residential property disputes. In September the KTC agreed to establish a Joint Security Committee, in response to concerns at the escalation of violence in the province, in particular attacks on remaining Serbian civilians. In mid-October a UN worker was murdered, reportedly by ethnic Albanians who had identified him as a local Serb. In November the Special Representative appealed for additional funds and police officers to counter further ethnic violence. In mid-December the leaders of the three main political groupings in Kosovo agreed on a provisional power-sharing arrangement with UNMIK for the administration of Kosovo until the holding of elections, scheduled for 2000. The agreement on the so-called Kosovo-UNMIK Joint Interim Administrative Structure established an eight-member executive Interim Administrative Council and a framework of administrative departments. The KTC was to maintain its consultative role.

At 30 September 1999 UNMIK comprised 1,552 civilian police officers, 34 military personnel and an additional 436 international civilian personnel. At that time a formal budget for the mission had yet to be approved. However, the General Assembly had apportioned US $125m. among member states as a special assessment.

## UNITED NATIONS INTERIM FORCE IN LEBANON—UNIFIL

**Headquarters:** Naqoura, Lebanon.

**Commander:** Maj.-Gen. SETH KEFI OBENG (Ghana).

UNIFIL was established by a UN Security Council resolution in March 1978, following an invasion of Lebanon by Israeli forces. The mandate of the force is to confirm the withdrawal of Israeli forces, to restore international peace and security, and to assist the Government of Lebanon in ensuring the return of its effective authority in southern Lebanon. UNIFIL has also extended humanitarian assistance to the population of the area, particularly since the second Israeli invasion of Lebanon in 1982. By 1999 Security Council Resolution 425, requiring the unconditional withdrawal of Israeli troops from southern Lebanon, had yet to be implemented. In April 1992, however, in accordance with its mandate, UNIFIL completed the transfer of part of its zone of operations to the control of the Lebanese army. UNIFIL's monitoring activities are confined to the staffing of checkpoints and observation posts, which are designed to deter hostilities. UNIFIL provides civilians with food, water, medical supplies, fuel and escorts to farmers. UNIFIL medical centres and mobile teams provide care to an average 3,000 civilian patients each month, and a field dental programme has been established.

In April 1996 Israel initiated a large-scale offensive against suspected targets pertaining to the Hezbollah militia in southern Lebanon. During the offensive Israeli artillery shells struck a UNIFIL base at Qana, which was temporarily being used to shelter civilians displaced by the hostilities, resulting in the deaths of some 100 people. The UN Security Council condemned the attack and demanded the respect by all sides for UNIFIL's mandate and for the safety and freedom of movement of its troops. In May a UN inquiry concluded that the UN site had been deliberately targeted during the offensive, owing to the presence of Hezbollah activists in the camp. In June 1997 the UN General Assembly resolved that Israel should contribute US $1.8m. towards UNIFIL's operational costs, as compensation for the Qana incident.

At 30 September 1999 the Force comprised 4,459 troops, assisted by some 60 military observers of UNTSO's Observer Group Lebanon, and other international and local civilian staff. The General Assembly appropriation for the operation for the period July 1999–June 2000 amounted to US $148.9m.

## UNITED NATIONS IRAQ-KUWAIT OBSERVATION MISSION—UNIKOM

**Headquarters:** Umm Qasr, Kuwait.

**Commander:** Maj.-Gen. JOHN VISE (Ireland).

UNIKOM was established by a UN Security Council resolution (initially for a six-month period) in April 1991, to monitor a 200-km demilitarized zone along the border between Iraq and Kuwait. The task of the mission was to deter violations of the border, to monitor the Khawr 'Abd Allah waterway between Iraq and Kuwait, and to prevent military activity within the zone. In February 1993 the Security Council adopted a resolution to strengthen UNIKOM, following incursions into Kuwaiti territory by Iraqi personnel. The resolution also expanded the mission's mandate to include the capacity to take physical action to prevent violations of the demilitarized zone and of the newly-defined boundary between Iraq and Kuwait. UNIKOM provides technical support to other UN operations in the area, particularly the Iraq–Kuwait Boundary Demarcation

Commission, and has assisted with the relocation of Iraqi citizens from Kuwait, which was completed in February 1994.

At 31 May 1999 UNIKOM comprised 908 troops and 194 military observers, assisted by some 200 international and local civilian support staff. In June 1999 the UN General Assembly appropriated US $54.0m. for the maintenance of the mission for a period of one year; two-thirds of UNIKOM's total costs are funded by voluntary contributions from Kuwait.

## UNITED NATIONS MILITARY OBSERVER GROUP IN INDIA AND PAKISTAN—UNMOGIP

**Headquarters:** Rawalpindi, Pakistan (November–April), Srinagar, India (May–October).

**Chief Military Observer:** Maj.-Gen. JOZSEF BALI (Hungary).

The Group was established in 1948 by UN Security Council resolutions aiming to restore peace in the region of Jammu and Kashmir, the status of which had become a matter of dispute between the Governments of India and Pakistan. Following a cease-fire which came into effect in January 1949, the military observers of UNMOGIP were deployed to assist in its observance. There is no periodic review of UNMOGIP's mandate. In 1971, following the signature of a new cease-fire agreement, India claimed that UNMOGIP's mandate had lapsed, since it was originally intended to monitor the agreement reached in 1949. Pakistan, however, regarded UNMOGIP's mission as unchanged, and the Group's activities have continued, although they have been somewhat restricted on the Indian side of the 'line of control', which was agreed by India and Pakistan in 1972.

At 31 October 1999 there were 45 military observers deployed on both sides of the 'line of control'. The cost of the operation in 1999 was estimated to amount to US $7.3m., which was to be covered by the regular budget of the UN.

## UNITED NATIONS MISSION FOR THE REFERENDUM IN WESTERN SAHARA—MINURSO

**Headquarters:** el-Aaiún, Western Sahara.

**Special Representative of the UN Secretary-General:** WILLIAM EAGLETON (USA).

**Personal Envoy of the UN Secretary-General:** JAMES A. BAKER, III (USA).

**Chairman of the Identification Commission:** EDUARDO VETERE (Italy).

**Chief Military Observer:** Brig.-Gen. BERND LUBENIK (Austria).

In April 1991 the UN Security Council endorsed the establishment of MINURSO to verify a cease-fire in the disputed territory of Western Sahara (claimed by Morocco), which came into effect in September 1991, to implement a programme of repatriation of Western Saharan refugees (in co-ordination with UNHCR), to secure the release of all Sahrawi political prisoners, and to organize a referendum on the future of the territory. The referendum, originally envisaged for January 1992, was, however, postponed indefinitely. In 1992 and 1993 the Secretary-General's Special Representative organized negotiations between the Frente Popular para la Liberación de Saguia el Hamra y Río de Oro (Frente Polisario) and the Moroccan Government, who were in serious disagreement regarding criteria for eligibility to vote in the referendum (in particular, the Moroccan Government insisted that more than 100,000 members of ethnic groups who had been forced to leave the territory under Spanish rule prior to the last official census in 1974, the results of which were to be used as a basis for voter registration, should be allowed to participate in a referendum). Nevertheless, in March 1993 the Security Council advocated that further efforts should be made to compile a satisfactory electoral list and to resolve the outstanding differences on procedural issues. An Identification Commission was consequently established to begin the process of voter registration, although this was obstructed by the failure of the Moroccan Government and the Frente Polisario to pursue political dialogue. The identification and registration operation was formally initiated in August 1994; however, the process was complicated by the dispersed nature of the Western Saharan population. In December the Secretary-General expressed his intention to commence the transitional period of the settlement plan, during which time MINURSO was to oversee a reduction of Moroccan government troops in the region, a confinement of Frente Polisario troops, the release of political prisoners and the exchange of other prisoners and refugees, with effect from 1 June 1995. While this date was later reviewed, in June 1995 a Security Council mission visited the region to assess the referendum process. The mission recognized legitimate difficulties in conducting the identification process; however, it urged all parties to co-operate with MINURSO and suggested that the operation's future would be reconsidered in the event of further delays. In December the UN Secretary-General reported that the identification of voters had stalled, owing to persistent obstruction of the process on the part of the Moroccan and Frente Polisario authorities. By May 1996 all efforts to resume the identification process had failed, as a result of the ongoing dispute regarding the number of potentially eligible voters, as well as the Frente Polisario's insistence on reviewing those already identified (a demand rejected by Morocco). Three registration offices in Western Sahara and one in Mauritania were closed. At the end of May the Security Council endorsed a recommendation of the Secretary-General to suspend the identification process until all sides demonstrate their willingness to co-operate with the mission. The Security Council decided that MINURSO's operational capacity should be reduced by 20%, with sufficient troops retained to monitor and verify the cease-fire. The Secretary-General's acting Special Representative pursued efforts to maintain political dialogue in the region; however, no significant progress was achieved in furthering the identification process.

In early 1997 the new Secretary-General of the UN, Kofi Annan, attempted to revive the possibility of an imminent resolution of the dispute, amid increasing concerns that the opposing authorities were preparing for a resumption of hostilities in the event of a collapse of the existing cease-fire, and appointed James Baker, a former US Secretary of State, as his Personal Envoy to the region. In June Baker obtained the support of Morocco and the Frente Polisario, as well as Algeria and Mauritania (which border the disputed territory), to conduct further negotiations in order to advance the referendum process. Direct talks between senior representatives of the Moroccan Government and the Frente Polisario authorities were initiated later in that month, in Lisbon, Portugal, under the auspices of the UN, and attended by Algeria and Mauritania in an observer capacity. In September the two sides concluded an agreement which aimed to resolve the outstanding issues of contention and enable the referendum to be conducted in late 1998. The agreement included a commitment by both parties to identify eligible Sahrawi voters on an individual basis, in accordance with the results of the 1974 census, and a code of conduct to ensure the impartiality of the poll. In October 1997 the Security Council extended MINURSO's mandate to 20 April 1998 and endorsed a recommendation of the Secretary-General to increase the strength of the mission to supervise nine identification centres. The process of voter identification resumed in December 1997. The timetable for the settlement plan envisaged the identification process as being completed by 31 May 1998, a final list of voters to be published, after a process of appeal, in late July, followed by a transitional period, under UN authority, during which all Sahrawi refugees were to be repatriated. The referendum was scheduled to be conducted on 7 December, and MINURSO was expected to withdraw from the region in January 1999. In January 1998 the Security Council approved the deployment of an engineering unit to support MINURSO in its demining activities. In April the Council extended MINURSO's mandate for a three-month period. At that time there were already significant delays apparent in the identification process, owing to ongoing disputes regarding the eligibility of members of three Saharan tribal groups. In July the Security Council extended MINURSO's mandate until 21 September, but warned that it would be terminated if either side significantly obstructed implementation of the settlement plan.

By early September 1998 the initial identification process had been completed, with a total of 147,350 voters identified, including 87,238 since December 1997. However, the issue of the eligibility of 65,000 members of the three disputed tribal groups remained unresolved. Later in September the UN Security Council extended MINURSO's mandate by 30 days, to enable the Personal Envoy of the Secretary-General to attempt to negotiate a solution to the problem. At the end of October the Council, extending MINURSO's mandate until 17 December, endorsed a series of measures proposed by the Secretary-General to advance the referendum process and urged both sides to agree to the plans by mid-November. The measures provided for a strengthened Identification Commission to consider requests from any applicant from the disputed tribal groups on an individual basis, with effect from 1 December. On that date a provisional list of voters was to be published and the appeals process initiated. The proposals also incorporated the need for an agreement by both sides with UNHCR with regard to arrangements for the repatriation of refugees. In early November the Secretary-General visited the region to promote his proposals for a peaceful settlement. At that time it was anticipated that the new timetable could allow for the identification process to be completed by mid-April 1999, a transitional period to commence in June or July, with the referendum to be conducted in December. By early December the Frente Polisario, Algeria and Mauritania were reported to have accepted the proposals, while the position of the Moroccan

Government remained uncertain, placing the future of MINURSO in doubt. Negotiations ensued between representatives of the UN and the Moroccan Government, and in late January 1999 an agreement was reached on the proposals, which included the establishment of a new UNHCR office in Western Sahara. In mid-March Morocco signed an agreement with the UN to secure the legal basis of the MINURSO operation, which was subsequently extended by the Security Council. In May the Council extended the mandate until mid-September in order to resume the identification process and implement the settlement plan. At the same time the Moroccan Government and the Frente Polisario agreed in principle to a draft plan of action for cross-border confidence measures. A new timetable envisaged the referendum being held on 31 July 2000. In July 1999 the UN published a provisional list of 85,000 qualified voters. In September the Mission's mandate was extended until mid-December. In late November almost 200 Moroccan prisoners of war were released by the Frente Polisario authorities, following a series of negotiations led by the Special Representative of the UN Secretary-General. In December the UN Security Council extended MINURSO's mandate until 29 February 2000. However, the Council acknowledged that the ongoing difficulties regarding voter admissibility precluded any possibility of conducting the referendum before 2002.

The mission has headquarters in the north and south of the disputed territory, and there is a liaison office in Tindouf, Algeria, which was established in order to maintain contact with the Frente Polisario (which is based in Algeria) and the Algerian Government.

At 30 September 1999 MINURSO comprised 231 military personnel and 80 civilian police officers. The General Assembly appropriation to cover the cost of the mission for the period 1 July 1999–30 June 2000 amounted to US $52.1m.

## UNITED NATIONS MISSION IN BOSNIA AND HERZEGOVINA—UNMIBH

**Headquarters:** Sarajevo, Bosnia and Herzegovina.

**Special Representative of the Secretary-General and Co-ordinator of UN Operations in Bosnia and Herzegovina:** JACQUES PAUL KLEIN (USA).

**Commissioner of the UN International Police Task Force:** Col. DETLEF BUWITT (Germany).

In February 1992 the UN established a Protection Force (UNPROFOR), in response to the escalating conflict in the former Yugoslavia, which became one of the largest operations ever mounted by the UN. UNPROFOR assumed responsibility for monitoring the withdrawal of anti-aircraft and heavy weapons by both Bosnian Muslims and Serbs to agreed locations within Bosnia and Herzegovina, the delivery of humanitarian assistance and monitoring compliance with the prohibition on military flights in Bosnian airspace. In December 1995 leaders of the warring parties in the former Yugoslavia signed a peace accord, which had been concluded in the previous month in Dayton, USA. UNPROFOR's mandate was terminated a few days later, when a new multinational force under NATO command (the Implementation Force—IFOR) assumed authority for implementation of the peace accord, for a 12-month period, on 20 December.

On 21 December 1995 the Security Council agreed on the establishment of the UN International Police Task Force (IPTF) and a UN civilian office, in accordance with the Dayton peace agreement. The operation subsequently became known as the UN Mission in Bosnia and Herzegovina (UNMIBH). The IPTF's tasks included: monitoring, observing and inspecting law enforcement activities in Bosnia and Herzegovina; the training of police officers and personnel; assessing threats to public order and advising on the capability of law enforcement agencies to deal with such threats; and accompanying the Bosnian police forces in the execution of their duties. The UN Co-ordinator was to exercise authority over the IPTF Commissioner and to co-ordinate other UN activities in Bosnia and Herzegovina relating to humanitarian relief and refugees, de-mining, elections and economic reconstruction. UNMIBH was to co-operate closely with IFOR and, later, with its successor operation, the Stabilization Force (SFOR), which became operational in December 1996. In early 1996 the UN was criticized for slow deployment of the IPTF: at the start of February fewer than 300 out of a total authorized strength of 1,721 police officers had arrived in the country. The Force was charged with maintaining an observer presence in Serb-dominated suburbs of Sarajevo that were due to come under the administration of the Bosnian Federation in March, a presence that was intended to provide encouragement to Serbs to stay in these areas. However, the vast majority of the Serbs took flight into the Republika Srpska prior to the transition of authority. In March the Security Council authorized the deployment of five military liaison officers, in order to strengthen liaison arrangements with IFOR. In August the mission reported failure on the part of Bosnian Federation police to protect political opponents of the Muslim nationalist Party of Democratic Action (PDA) from attacks by PDA loyalists in advance of the forthcoming all-Bosnia legislative elections. Prior to and during the elections, which were held on 14 September, the IPTF assisted IFOR in providing protection to refugees and displaced people returning to vote in their towns of origin. At the international conference to review implementation of the Dayton agreement, which was held in mid-November, it was agreed that the IPTF's mandate was to be strengthened, granting it enhanced powers to investigate the Bosnian police in both sectors of the country. In mid-December the Security Council extended UNMIBH's mandate until 21 December 1997. In February 1997 the IPTF criticized police officers for using excessive force against civilians during recent unrest between the Muslim and Croat populations in Mostar. In the following month the Security Council demanded that the Mostar authorities suspend and prosecute those officers responsible for the attacks. Also in March the Council authorized the strengthening of the IPTF by an additional 186 police officers and 11 civilian monitors in order to monitor, restructure and train the local police force in the contested north-eastern city of Brčko, which was temporarily under international supervision. In August UNMIBH criticized the forcible evacuation of some 500 Bosniaks from the Muslim Croat Federation and initiated an investigation into the role of the local police in the incident. In Brčko, in August, 58 IPTF monitors had to be evacuated by SFOR troops after coming under attack by Bosnian Serbs demanding control of the local police station. In September UNMIBH co-operated with SFOR and an election monitoring group to assist safe and democratic voting in municipal elections in the Bosnian Federation, and monitored the movement of voters within the region and across boundary lines. UNMIBH's mandate, and that of the IPTF, was extended in December until 21 June 1998, and subsequently for a further 12-month period. In May the Security Council authorized the deployment of an additional 30 IPTF monitors to conduct a series of intensive training programmes for the local police in Bosnia and Herzegovina. In July the Security Council endorsed the establishment of a new programme, within UNMIBH's mandate, to assess and monitor the judicial system in Bosnia and Herzegovina and to promote the rule of law. The Council authorized the deployment of 26 legal experts to undertake the programme. In June 1999 the Council extended UNMIBH's mandate, including that of the IPTF, until 21 June 2000.

At 30 September 1999 UNMIBH comprised 1,700 civilian police officers. The General Assembly appropriation for the period 1 July 1999 to 30 June 2000, which included the budgets of the UN Mission of Observers in Prevlaka and of UN liaison offices in Belgrade and Zagreb, amounted to US $178.2m.

## UNITED NATIONS MISSION IN SIERRA LEONE—UNAMSIL

**Headquarters:** Freetown, Sierra Leone.

**Special Representative of the Secretary-General and Chief of Mission:** OLUYEMI ADENIJI (Nigeria).

**Commander:** Maj.-Gen. VIJAY KUMAR JETLEY (India).

In July 1998 the Security Council established a UN observer mission in Sierra Leone (UNOMSIL) to monitor the military and security situation in that country following the restoration of a democratically-elected government. UNOMSIL was authorized to oversee the disarmament and demobilization of former combatants, as well as the voluntary disarmament of members of the civilian defence force, and to assist in monitoring respect for international humanitarian law. The Special Representative, with the civilian component of the mission, was authorized to advise the Sierra Leonean authorities on police practice, training and reform, and to help to address the country's human rights needs. UNOMSIL was to work closely with forces of the Economic Community for West African States (ECOWAS) in promoting peace and national reconciliation. In January 1999, following a sudden escalation of hostilities, the UN Security Council extended the mandate of UNOMSIL for a further two months, although acknowledged that several UNOMSIL military observers, together with civilian support staff, would withdraw to Conakry, Guinea, until the security situation improved. In March the Security Council condemned the ongoing violation of human rights in Sierra Leone and urged all neighbouring countries to prevent the cross-border supply of armaments to anti-government forces. None the less, the Council extended the mission's mandate until mid-June and, subsequently, until mid-December. In August the Security Council authorized a provisional expansion of UNOMSIL of up to 210 military observers, in order to support the implementation of a peace agreement which had been signed in July, in Lomé, Togo. In October the Council authorized the establishment of the UN Mission in Sierra Leone (UNAMSIL), comprising up to 6,000 military personnel, to help to consolidate peace in that country. UNAMSIL was mandated to co-operate with the Sierra Leonean Government and all other parties to enforce the cease-fire accord and Lomé peace agreement, to implement a plan for the disarmament and demobilization of all former combatants, and to facilitate the delivery of humanitarian assistance. The Mission was to assume responsibility for all civilian, political and military components of UNOMSIL, the mandate of which was to terminate with immediate effect. In February 2000 the Council approved an expanded mandate for the Mission, and enlarged its authorized strength from 6,000 to 11,100 military personnel.

At 5 January 2000 UNAMSIL comprised 4,288 troops and 220 military observers. The proposed budget for the Mission, which remained under consideration by the UN General Assembly in December 1999, amounted to US $208.5m. for the period until 30 June 2000.

## UNITED NATIONS MISSION IN THE CENTRAL AFRICAN REPUBLIC—MINURCA

**Headquarters:** Bangui, Central African Republic.

**Commander:** Brig.-Gen. BARTHÉLÉMY RATANGA (Gabon).

In August 1997 the UN Security Council authorized the activities of the Inter-African Mission to Monitor the Bangui Accords (MISAB), to which responsibility for peace-keeping activities in the Central African Republic (CAR) had been transferred from the Elements français d'assistance opérationelle (EFAO) in February, by overseeing an agreement signed by the conflicting parties in January and undertaking efforts to disarm rebel soldiers and other combatants. MISAB comprised some 800 troops from Burkina Faso, Chad, Gabon and Mali (and later from Senegal and Togo), with logistical support from a small contingent of French troops. In November the Security Council requested the UN Secretary-General to report on the efforts to restore stability in the country and to make recommendations on further measures to support the process after the expiry of the MISAB mandate in February 1998 (although this was subsequently extended until mid-April). In March the Security Council authorized the establishment of the UN Mission in the Central African Republic (MINURCA), which assumed responsibility from MISAB on 15 April, with an initial three month mandate. MINURCA's mandate was to maintain and enhance stability and security in the country, help to restore law and order and freedom of movement in the capital, Bangui, supervise the disarmament process, assist in the training of the national police force, and provide technical support in preparations for new legislative elections, scheduled to be conducted in August and September 1998. A national electoral commission was formally established in May; however, it remained ineffective owing to disagreements between the political parties regarding its composition. A compromise agreement was finally concluded, following negotiations held under the auspices of the UN Special Representative. In July the UN Security Council agreed to extend MINURCA's mandate to late October. Also in July the Government announced a new electoral timetable, providing for polls to take place in September and October. However, this was suspended in August owing to delays in electoral preparations, in particular with logistical difficulties in registering voters. A UN radio station was established in July, broadcasting on issues relating to MINURCA's mandate and informing voters on the electoral process. MINURCA also established a joint committee, with the CAR Government, to address the issue of restructuring the country's armed forces. In October the Security Council endorsed the decision to conduct legislative elections on 22 November and 13 December, and agreed to expand MINURCA's mandate to cover support for the conduct of elections, including the supervision of security of international observers and of electoral equipment. The Council also extended the mission's mandate to 28 February 1999, when it was to be terminated. In February, however, the Council determined to extend MINURCA's mandate to enable it to supervise the conduct of presidential elections and to continue to assist with the implementation of political and social reforms. The mission was to be withdrawn no later than 15 November. Presidential elections were successfully conducted in September. In October the Security Council agreed to extend MINURCA's mandate for a final three-month period, in order to ensure a smooth transition to a new post-conflict UN presence in the country. Accordingly, the Mission was concluded on 15 February 2000; it was to be superseded by the UN Peace-building Support Office in the CAR (BONUCA).

At 30 September 1999 MINURCA comprised 1,349 military personnel and 24 civilian police officers. The General Assembly appropriation for the mission for the period 1 July 1999–30 June 2000 amounted to US $33.3m.

## UNITED NATIONS MISSION IN THE DEMOCRATIC REPUBLIC OF THE CONGO—MONUC

**Headquarters:** Kinshasa, Democratic Republic of the Congo.

**Special Envoy of the UN Secretary-General:** KAMEL MORJANE (Tunisia).

**Commander:** JAMES BAXTER (United Kingdom).

In August 1999 the UN Security Council authorized the deployment of up to 90 military liaison personnel to support implementation of a cease-fire agreement for the Democratic Republic of the Congo (DRC) which had been signed in Lusaka, Zambia, in July. Technical officers were also to be dispatched to Namibia, Rwanda, Uganda and Zimbabwe, all signatories of the Lusaka accord, to assess the security of any future UN presence in the sub-region. The Security Council approved the establishment of MONUC in late November. With an initial mandate until 1 March 2000, the mission was to continue to establish contacts with all signatories to the cease-fire agreement and to liaise with the newly-established Joint Military Commission in the DRC in order to uphold implementation of the agreement. MONUC was also mandated to plan for the observation of the cease-fire and disengagement of forces, to facilitate the delivery of humanitarian assistance, and to report on local security conditions. MONUC was to comprise liaison and technical assessment officers, as well as other multidisciplinary personnel, previously authorized by the Council; however, the Council requested that up to 500 military observers be equipped ready for deployment pending further recommendations on the security situation in the DRC by the UN Secretary-General.

## UNITED NATIONS MISSION OF OBSERVERS IN PREVLAKA—UNMOP

**Headquarters:** Cavtat, Croatia.

**Chief Military Observer:** Col GRAEME ROGER WILLIAMS (New Zealand).

UNMOP was authorized by the Security Council in January 1996, following the termination of the mandate of the UN Confidence Restoration Operation, to assume responsibility for monitoring the demilitarization of the Prevlaka peninsula in Croatia, which had been occupied by the Serbian-dominated Yugoslav People's Army. UNMOP became operational on 1 February. While political tensions persisted throughout 1996, the UN Secretary-General reported that UNMOP's presence in the region had facilitated the process of bilateral negotiations between Croatia and the Federal Republic of Yugoslavia. In authorizing extensions of UNMOP's mandate in January and April 1997, the Security Council urged both parties to refrain from provocative actions in Prevlaka, to cease any violations of the demilitarized zone and to co-operate fully with UNMOP. The Council also reiterated the urgency of removing anti-personnel landmines from areas patrolled by UNMOP in order to improve the safety and security of the region and ensure freedom of movement to enable UNMOP to implement its mandate. By December it was reported that the demining process had been completed in the entire UN-controlled territory. UNMOP's mandate has subsequently been extended for six-month periods, most recently, despite concerns at the lack of substantive progress towards a settlement of the Prevlaka issue, until mid-July 2000.

At 30 September 1999 UNMOP comprised 28 military observers. The annual cost of UNMOP is included in the budget of the UN Mission in Bosnia and Herzegovina (see above).

## UNITED NATIONS MISSION OF OBSERVERS IN TAJIKISTAN—UNMOT

**Headquarters:** Dushanbe, Tajikistan.

**Special Representative of the UN Secretary-General and Head of Mission:** IVO PETROV (Bulgaria).

**Chief Military Observer:** Brig.-Gen. JOHN HVIDEGAARD (Denmark).

In December 1994 the UN Security Council authorized the establishment of UNMOT to monitor a cease-fire that had been agreed by the Tajik Government and opposition forces in September. The mission had an initial mandate of six months, which was conditional on an extension of the cease-fire agreement beyond February 1995. UNMOT's mandate was to assist a Tajik Joint Commission to monitor the cease-fire; to investigate and report on violations of the cease-fire; to provide good offices, as stipulated in the cease-fire agreement; to maintain close contact with the parties to the conflict, as well as close liaison with the mission of the OSCE and with the peace-keeping forces of the Commonwealth of Independent States; to provide political liaisons and co-ordination to facilitate humanitarian assistance by the international community; and to support the offices of the UN Secretary-General. In April 1995 there was an escalation of military activities on the Tajik-Afghan border, which threatened the conditions necessary for the continued deployment of the UN observers. In June the mission's mandate was extended for a further six months. However, the Security Council demanded that substantive progress be made by all sides on institutional and political issues and that they demonstrate commitment to the promotion of democracy and national reconciliation. In November 1996 UNMOT expressed concern at the outbreak of renewed hostilities in central Tajikistan and urged both sides to observe the agreed cease-fire. In early December UNHCR and UNMOT protested to the leadership of the Tajik opposition in exile over the alleged brutal treatment of Tajik refugees in northern Afghanistan. In mid-December a new cease-fire agreement was concluded by the Government and the opposition (which was violated almost immediately), and later in the month two new peace accords were signed in the presence of the UN Special Representative. Inter-Tajik peace talks continued in early 1997 in Teheran, Iran, with the Special Representative's participation. However, in February the UN Secretary-General authorized the suspension of all UN activities in the country, with the exception of a small UNMOT team to be retained in Dushanbe, as a result of a deterioration in the security situation and, in particular, following an incident in which five UNMOT observers were taken hostage, along with seven other international personnel, by Tajik rebel Islamic forces. In March the two sides concluded an agreement on the integration of the country's armed forces and other confidence-building measures. In mid-March the Security Council authorized a six-month extension of UNMOT's mandate. In May the Tajik Government and opposition forces signed a protocol ending hostilities and guaranteeing implementation of the December 1996 peace accord. At the end of June 1997 the leaders of the two sides signed a Peace and National Reconciliation Accord formally ending the country's civil war. UNMOT's mandate was extended in June and again in September. It was to encourage co-operation within the country in implementing the peace accords and to supervise the return of Tajik refugees from Afghanistan and the reintegration of rebel soldiers. In November the Security Council agreed to strengthen the operation by 45 observers to monitor the implementation of the military aspects of the June accord, including the demobilization of opposition troops, and to investigate any reported violations of the cease-fire agreement. UNMOT was to continue to provide good offices and expert advice and to co-operate with the Commissions on National Reconciliation and on Elections and Holding of a Referendum. In early 1998 the peace process was disrupted by clashes between the conflicting factions, and in May the UN Secretary-General reported that conditions suitable for the holding of elections were unlikely to be achieved in 1998. None the less, the Council extended UNMOT's mandate. During 1999 a series of political and constitutional reforms was implemented, which helped to consolidate the peace process and further democratization measures. UNMOT's mandate was extended for six-month periods in May and again in November.

At 30 September 1999 UNMOT comprised 33 military observers and two civilian police officers. The General Assembly budget appropriation for the period 1 July 1999–30 June 2000 amounted to US $18.7m.

## UNITED NATIONS OBSERVER MISSION IN GEORGIA—UNOMIG

**Headquarters:** Sukhumi, Georgia.

**Special Representative of the UN Secretary-General and Head of Mission:** LIVIU BOTA (Romania).

**Chief Military Observer:** Maj.-Gen. TARIQ WASEEM GHAZI (Pakistan).

UNOMIG was established in August 1993 to verify compliance with a cease-fire agreement, signed in July between the Government of Georgia and Abkhazian forces. The mission was the UN's first undertaking in the former USSR. In October the UN Secretary-General stated that a breakdown in the cease-fire agreement had invalidated UNOMIG's mandate. He proposed, however, to maintain, for information purposes, the eight-strong UNOMIG team in the city of Sukhumi, which had been seized by Abkhazian separatist forces in late September. In late December the Security Council authorized the deployment of additional military observers in response to the signing of a memorandum of understanding by the conflicting parties earlier that month. Further peace negotiations, which were conducted in January–March 1994 under the authority of the UN Secretary-General's Special Envoy, achieved no political consensus. While the Security Council approved new resolutions to prolong the existence of UNOMIG, the full deployment of a peace-keeping force remained dependent on progress in the peace process. In July the Security Council endorsed the establishment of a peace-keeping force, consisting of 3,000 troops from the Commonwealth of Independent States (CIS, q.v.), to verify a cease-fire agreement that had been signed in May. At the same time the Security Council increased the authorized strength of the mission from 88 to 136 military observers and expanded UNOMIG's mandate to incorporate the following tasks: to monitor and verify the implementation of the agreement and to investigate reported violations; to observe the CIS forces; to verify that troops and heavy military equipment remain outside the security zone and the restricted weapons zone; to monitor the storage of the military equipment withdrawn from the restricted zones; to monitor the withdrawal of Georgian troops from the Kodori Gorge region to locations beyond the Abkhazian frontiers; and to patrol regularly the Kodori Gorge. Peace negotiations were pursued in 1995, despite periodic outbreaks of violence in Abkhazia. In July 1996 the Security Council, extending UNOMIG's mandate, expressed its concern at the lack of progress being made towards a comprehensive political settlement in the region. The Council also urged the Abkhazian side to accelerate significantly the process of voluntary return of Georgian refugees and displaced persons to Abkhazia. In October the Council decided to establish a human rights office as part of UNOMIG. In May 1997 the Security Council issued a Presidential Statement urging greater efforts towards achieving a peaceful solution to the dispute. The Statement endorsed a proposal of the UN Secretary-General to strengthen the political element of UNOMIG to enable the mission to assume a more active role in furthering a negotiated settlement. In July direct discussions between representatives of the Georgian and Abkhazian authorities, the first in more than two years, were held under UN auspices. In early 1998 the security situation in Abkhazia deteriorated. Following an outbreak of violence in May the conflicting parties signed a cease-fire accord, which incorporated an agreement that UNOMIG and CIS forces would continue to work to create a secure environment to allow for the return of displaced persons to the Gali region of Abkhazia. In addition, the UN Security Council urged both parties to establish a protection unit to ensure the safety of UN military observers. In October 1999 seven UN personnel were held hostage for a short period in the Kodor Gorge area of Abkhazia. UNOMIG's mandate has been granted successive six-monthly extensions, the most recent of which was until 31 July 2000.

At 30 September 1999 UNOMIG comprised 96 military observers. The General Assembly budget appropriation for the mission for the period 1 July 1999–30 June 2000 amounted to US $31.0m.

## UNITED NATIONS PEACE-KEEPING FORCE IN CYPRUS—UNFICYP

**Headquarters:** Nicosia, Cyprus.

**Special Adviser to the Secretary-General:** ALVARO DE SOTO (Peru).

**Acting Special Representative of the UN Secretary-General and Chief of Mission:** JAMES HOLGER (Chile).
land).

**Commander:** Maj.-Gen. EVERGISTO ARTURO DE VERGARA (Argentina).

UNFICYP was established in March 1964 by a UN Security Council resolution (for a three-month period, subsequently extended) to prevent a recurrence of fighting between the Greek and Turkish Cypriot communities, and to contribute to the maintenance of law and order and a return to normal conditions. The Force controls a 180-km buffer zone, established (following the Turkish intervention in 1974) between the cease-fire lines of the Turkish forces and the Cyprus National Guard. The Force also performs humanitarian functions, such as facilitating the supply of electricity and water across the cease-fire lines, and offering emergency medical services. In August 1996 serious hostilities between elements of the two communities in the UN-controlled buffer zone resulted in the deaths of two people and injuries to many others, including 12 UN personnel. Following further intercommunal violence, UNFICYP advocated the prohibition of all weapons and military posts along the length of the buffer zone. The Force also proposed additional humanitarian measures to improve the conditions of minority groups living in the two parts of the island. A new series of direct negotiations between the leaders of the two communities was initiated, under the auspices of the Secretary-General's Special Adviser, in July 1997; however, the talks were suspended at the end of that year. In November 1999 the leaders of the two communities agreed to resume proximity negotiations, the first round of which took place in New York, in December.

At 30 September 1999 UNFICYP had an operational strength of 1,228 military personnel and 35 civilian police officers, supported by international and local civilian staff. The 1999 budget appropriation for the force amounted to US $45.6m., of which some $24.5m. was to be met by assessed contributions from UN member states, with voluntary contributions from the Governments of Cyprus and of Greece to amount to $14.6m. and $6.5m. respectively.

## UNITED NATIONS TRANSITIONAL ADMINISTRATION IN EAST TIMOR—UNTAET

**Headquarters:** Dili, East Timor.

**Special Representative of the UN Secretary-General and Chief of Mission:** SÉRGIO VIEIRA DE MELLO (Brazil).

**Commander:** Gen. JAIME DE LOS SANTOS (Philippines).

**Chief Military Observer:** Brig.-Gen. REZAQUL HAIDER (Bangladesh).

In May 1999 Indonesia and Portugal signed an accord, under UN auspices, providing for a 'popular consultation' to determine the future status of East Timor, a former Portuguese colony which had been governed by Indonesia since 1976. The poll was to be organized by the UN, offering eligible voters a form of political autonomy or full independence from Indonesia, the outcome of which would then be endorsed by the Indonesian Government and implemented by a UN transitional authority. Under the agreement, Indonesia was to be responsible for maintaining peace and security in the territory and to ensure that voting was conducted without intimidation or violence, while the UN was to provide additional unarmed civilian and police personnel. In June the Security Council formally authorized the establishment of a UN Mission in East Timor (UNAMET), which was to comprise up to 280 police advisers and 50 military liaison officers, with an initial mandate until 31 August (later extended). The poll, which had been scheduled to be held on 8 August, was twice postponed, owing to security concerns; however, registration of voters commenced in mid-July. In late August the UN Security Council condemned the violent attacks and intimidatory tactics of militia groups favouring support for Indonesia, and acknowledged reports that Indonesian officers had failed to prevent the decline in law and order, but determined that the vote should proceed. The Council also resolved to expand UNAMET's presence in September to 460 police officers and 300 military liaison officers. The popular poll was conducted on 30 August. International and local UN staff supervised some 800 polling stations, established by UNAMET in 200 locations throughout the territory, and estimated that votes were cast by 98.6% of the 451,792 East Timorese who had been registered. The security situation in the territory declined dramatically following the popular consultation, and on 1 September the Security Council convened an emergency meeting to condemn, and demand the arrest of, those responsible for violent attacks on UN staff, pro-independence supporters and foreign journalists. The civil unrest and indiscriminate killings escalated after the announcement of the results of the poll, which identified some 78.5% of Timorese voters in favour of independence, and resulted in mass population displacement. A further meeting of Security Council members, held on 5 September, resolved to send a five-member mission to discuss the situation with the Indonesian Government. The failure of a curfew, imposed by the Indonesian authorities a few days later, to restore security prompted the UN to evacuate almost all its remaining staff. In mid-September, following international condemnation of the situation and intense diplomatic pressure, the Indonesian Government reversed its earlier opposition to a proposal by the Australian Government and agreed to permit foreign troops to help restore order in East Timor. The Security Council subsequently authorized the establishment of a multinational force, under unified command, with a mandate to restore peace and security in the territory, until replaced by a UN peace-keeping operation. The so-called International Force for East Timor (Interfet) was also mandated to protect and support UNAMET and to facilitate humanitarian operations; it was expected to total 7,500 from some 20 countries. The first multinational troops, from Australia, New Zealand and the United Kingdom, arrived on 20 September. A week later Interfet assumed formal control of the territory, while UNAMET re-established its headquarters in Dili. In late October, following ratification of the results of the popular poll by the Indonesian People's Consultative Assembly, the Security Council voted to establish a UN Transitional Administration in East Timor (UNTAET) to oversee the transition to independence and govern the territory on an interim basis. UNTAET, with an initial mandate until 31 January 2001, was to exercise all judicial and executive authority in East Timor. Its mandate authorized UNTAET to provide security and maintain law and order in the territory; to assume responsibility for the co-ordination and provision of humanitarian assistance; to establish an effective administration; to assist in the development of civil and social services and to promote capacity-building for self-government; and to assist in the creation of conditions for sustainable development. The responsibilities and personnel of UNAMET were incorporated into UNTAET. Interfet's mandate was to continue until the military component of UNTAET had been established.

UNTAET had an authorized strength of 8,950 troops, 200 military observers, and 1,640 civilian police officers. It was to be funded mainly from assessed contributions, although a Trust Fund was established to channel voluntary contributions for specific purposes.

## UNITED NATIONS TRUCE SUPERVISION ORGANIZATION—UNTSO

**Headquarters:** Government House, Jerusalem.

**Chief-of-Staff:** Maj.-Gen. TIMOTHY R. FORD (Australia).

UNTSO was established initially to supervise the truce called by the UN Security Council in Palestine in May 1948 and has assisted in the application of the 1949 Armistice Agreements. Its activities have evolved over the years, in response to developments in the Middle East and in accordance with the relevant resolutions of the Security Council. There is no periodic renewal procedure for UNTSO's mandate.

UNTSO observers assist the UN peace-keeping forces in the Middle East (see above), UNIFIL and UNDOF. In addition, UNTSO operates six outposts in the Sinai region of Egypt to maintain a UN presence there, and one at Ismailia, Egypt, in the area of the Suez canal. There is also a small detachment of observers in Beirut, Lebanon and liaison offices in Amman, Jordan, and Gaza. UNTSO observers have been available at short notice to form the nucleus of other peace-keeping operations.

The operational strength of UNTSO at 30 September 1999 was 141 military observers, supported by international and local civilian staff. UNTSO expenditures are covered by the regular budget of the United Nations. The cost of the operation in 1999 was estimated to be US $23.7m.

# United Nations Population Fund—UNFPA

**Address:** 220 East 42nd St, New York, NY 10017, USA.

**Telephone:** (212) 297-5020; **fax:** (212) 557-6416; **internet:** www.unfpa.org.

Created in 1967 as the Trust Fund for Population Activities, the UN Fund for Population Activities (UNFPA) was established as a Fund of the UN General Assembly in 1972 and was made a subsidiary organ of the UN General Assembly in 1979, with the UNDP Governing Council (now the Executive Board) designated as its governing body. In 1987 UNFPA's name was changed to the United Nations Population Fund (retaining the same acronym).

## Organization

(December 1999)

### EXECUTIVE DIRECTOR

The Executive Director, who has the rank of Under-Secretary-General of the UN, is responsible for the overall direction of the Fund, working closely with governments, other United Nations bodies and agencies, and non-governmental and international organizations to ensure the most effective programming and use of resources in population activities.

**Executive Director:** Dr NAFIS SADIK (Pakistan).

### EXECUTING AGENCIES

UNFPA provides financial and technical assistance to developing countries at their request. In many projects assistance is extended through member organizations of the UN system (in particular, FAO, ILO, UNESCO, WHO), although projects are executed increasingly by national governments themselves. The Fund may also call on the services of international, regional and national non-governmental and training organizations, as well as research institutions. In addition, eight UNFPA regional technical support teams, composed of experts from the UN, its specialized agencies and non-governmental organizations, assist countries at all stages of project/programme development and implementation.

### FIELD ORGANIZATION

UNFPA operates field offices, each headed by an UNFPA Representative, in 66 countries. In other countries UNFPA uses UNDP's field structure of Resident Representatives as the main mechanism for performing its work. The field offices assist governments in formulating requests for aid and co-ordinate the work of the executing agencies in any given country or area. UNFPA has eight regional technical support teams (see above). At 1 January 1997 there were 677 UNFPA staff members in the field, of a world-wide total of 919.

## Activities

The major functions of UNFPA, according to its mandate, are: to build up the capacity to respond to needs in population and family planning; to promote awareness of population problems in developed and developing countries and possible strategies to deal with them; to assist countries, at their request, in dealing with their population problems, in the forms and means best suited to the individual countries' needs; and to play a leading role in the UN system in promoting population programmes, and to co-ordinate projects supported by the Fund.

In co-operation with the UN Population Division, UNFPA played an important role in preparing for and conducting the International Conference on Population and Development (ICPD), held in Cairo, Egypt, in September 1994. UNFPA's Executive Director, Dr Nafis Sadik, acted as Secretary-General of the Conference, which was attended by representatives of 182 countries. The ICPD adopted a Programme of Action, establishing the objectives to be pursued for the next 20 years (despite reservations recorded by the representatives of some predominantly Roman Catholic and Islamic countries, concerning sections which they regarded as endorsing abortion and sexual promiscuity). The Programme's objectives envisaged universal access to reproductive health and family planning services, a reduction in infant, child and maternal mortality, a life expectancy at birth of 75 years or more, and universal access to primary education for all children by 2015. The Programme emphasized the necessity of empowering and educating women, in order to achieve successful sustainable human development. Annual expenditure required for the implementation of the objectives was estimated to amount to US $17,000m. in 2000, increasing to $21,700m. in 2015: of these amounts, the international community or donor countries would need to contribute about one-third. During 1995 UNFPA undertook to redefine its programme directions, resource allocations and policy guide-lines in order to implement effectively the recommendations of the Cairo Conference Programme of Action. The Executive Board subsequently endorsed the following as core programme areas: Reproductive Health, including Family Planning and Sexual Health; Population and Development Strategies; and Advocacy (for example, human rights, education, basic health services and the empowerment of women). A special session of the UN General Assembly was held in June/July 1999 to assess progress in achieving the objectives of the ICPD and to identify priorities for future action. In February UNFPA organized a forum, held in The Hague, Netherlands, and attended by delegates from 177 countries, to review implementation of the ICPD Programme of Action in preparation for the special session. The forum's recommendations included greater funding for UNFPA activities, in particular for the prevention of HIV and AIDS, from governments as well as the private sector and non-governmental organizations, the incorporation of gender issues into social and development policies, greater involvement of women in decision-making processes, and strengthened political commitment to the reproductive health of adolescents.

UNFPA recognizes that improving reproductive health is an essential requirement for improving the general welfare of the population and the basis for empowering women and achieving sustainable social and economic development. The ICPD succeeded in raising the political prominence of reproductive health issues and stimulating consideration by governments of measures to strengthen and restructure their health services and policies. UNFPA encourages the integration of family planning into all maternal, child and other reproductive health care. Its efforts to improve the quality of these services include support for the training of health-care personnel and promoting greater accessibility. Many reproductive health projects focus on the reduction of maternal mortality, which was included as a central objective of the ICPD Programme and recognized as a legitimate element of international human rights instruments concerning the right to life/survival. The ICPD reported that the leading cause of maternal deaths (i.e. those related to pregnancy, which amount to some 585,000 each year) was unsafe abortions, and urged governments to confront the issue as a major public health concern. UNFPA is also concerned with reducing the use of abortion (i.e. its use as a means of family planning), and with preventing infertility, reproductive tract infections and sexually-transmitted diseases, including HIV and AIDS. Special attention is given to the specific needs of adolescents, for example through education and counselling initiatives, and to women in emergency situations. UNFPA also supports research into contraceptives and training in contraceptive technology. During the early 1990s UNFPA's Global Initiative on Contraceptive Requirements and Logisitics Management Needs in Developing Countries organized in-depth studies on contraceptive requirements in certain developing countries (including Brazil, Bangladesh and Egypt). In April 1998 UNFPA formally inaugurated a new pilot rural population control programme in the People's Republic of China, with a redefined emphasis on education and other methods to promote voluntary contraceptive use and reduce birth rates.

UNFPA helps countries to formulate and implement comprehensive population policies as a central part of any strategies to achieve sustainable development. The Fund aims to ensure that the needs and concerns of women are incorporated into development and population policies. Under this programme area UNFPA provides assistance and training for national statistical offices in undertaking basic data collection, for example censuses and demographic surveys. UNFPA also provides assistance for analysis of demographic and socio-economic data, for research on population trends and for the formulation of government policies. It supports a programme of fellowships in demographic analysis, data processing and cartography.

UNFPA's advocacy role is incorporated into all its programming activities in support of the objectives of the ICPD. Consequently, the Fund aims to encourage the participation of women at all levels of decision- and policy-making and supports programmes that improve the access of all girls and women to education and grant women equal access to land, credit and employment opportunities. UNFPA's 1997 *State of World Population Report* defined the improved welfare of women as an issue of basic human rights, which included the eradication of all forms of gender discrimination, reproductive choice and the protection of women from sexual and domestic violence. UNFPA helps to promote awareness of these objectives and to incorporate them into national programmes. In 1997 UNFPA appointed a special ambassador to generate international awareness of the dangers of female genital mutilation. UNFPA also has special programmes on youth, on ageing, and on AIDS, and is currently increasing educational and research activities in the area of population and the environment. UNFPA attempts to increase awareness of the issue of population through regional and national seminars, publications (see below) and audio-visual aids, participation in conferences, and through a pro-active relationship with the mass media. In 1999 UNFPA promoted observance of 12 October as the symbolic day on which the world's population was estimated to reach 6,000m.

In 1995 UNFPA actively participated in the World Summit for Social Development, an international conference held in Copenhagen, Denmark, in March, and the UN Fourth World Conference on Women, held in Beijing, People's Republic of China, in September, at which the key concepts of the ICPD Programme were emphasized and reinforced. In 1996 UNFPA contributed to the second UN Conference on Human Settlements (Habitat II), which was held in Istanbul, Turkey, in June, by reporting on current trends in urbanization and population distribution and their link to human settlements. UNFPA is participating in the Special Initiative on Africa that was initiated by the UN Secretary-General in March 1996. UNFPA's principal involvement is to assist countries to implement efforts for reproductive health and to promote the integration of population considerations into development planning. UNFPA's Executive Director chairs the inter-agency Task Force on Basic Social Services for All, which was initially established to strengthen collaboration on implementing the ICPD Programme of Action through the UN Resident Co-ordinator System. In 1996 the Task Force assumed its current name with an expanded mandate to co-ordinate the follow-up to other global conferences. UNFPA also collaborates with other UN agencies and international experts to develop a reliable, multidisciplinary set of indicators to measure progress towards achieving the objectives of different conferences and to help formulate reproductive health programmes and monitor their success.

## Finance

UNFPA is supported entirely by voluntary contributions from donor countries. In 1997 UNFPA's provisional income totalled US $319.9m. of which $290.1m. was for regular resources and $29.8m. for multi- and bilateral co-financing activities. Provisional project expenditure in 1997 totalled $214m., compared with $216.5m. in 1996. The income for 1998 was expected to total $290m.

## Publications

*Annual Report.*

*AIDS Update* (annually).

*Dispatches* (10 a year, in English, French and Spanish).

*Inventory of Population Projects in Developing Countries around the World* (annually in English and French).

*Populi* (quarterly, in English, French and Spanish).

*State of World Population Report* (annually).

Reports and reference works; videotapes and radio programmes.

# United Nations Relief and Works Agency for Palestine Refugees in the Near East—UNRWA

**Addresses:** Gamal Abd an-Nasser St, Gaza City; Bayader Wadi Seer, POB 140157, Amman 11814, Jordan.

**Telephone** (Gaza City): (7) 6777333; **fax:** (7) 6777555.

**Telephone** (Amman): (6) 5826171; **fax:** (6) 5826177.

**E-mail:** unrwapio@unrwa.org; **internet:** www.unrwa.org.

UNRWA was established by the UN General Assembly to provide relief, health, education and welfare services for Palestine refugees in the Near East, initially on a short-term basis. UNRWA began operations in May 1950 and, in the absence of a solution to the refugee problem, its mandate has subsequently been extended by the General Assembly, most recently until 30 June 2002.

## Organization

(December 1999)

UNRWA employs an international staff of about 130 and more than 21,000 local staff, mainly Palestine refugees. In mid-1996 the agency's headquarters were relocated, from Vienna, Austria, to Gaza and Jordan. The Commissioner-General is the head of all UNRWA operations and reports directly to the UN General Assembly. UNRWA has no governing body, but its activities are reviewed annually by a 10-member Advisory Commission comprising representatives of the governments of:

| | | |
|---|---|---|
| Belgium | Jordan | Turkey |
| Egypt | Lebanon | United Kingdom |
| France | Syria | USA |
| Japan | | |

**Commissioner-General:** PETER HANSEN (Denmark).

### FIELD OFFICES

Each field office is headed by a director and has departments responsible for education, health and relief and social services programmes, finance, administration, supply and transport, legal affairs and public information.

**Gaza:** POB 61; Al Azhar Rd, Rimal Quarter, Gaza City; tel. (7) 2824508; fax (7) 6777444.

**Jordan:** POB 484; Al Zubeidi Bldg, Mustafa Bin Abdullah St, Tla'a Al-Ali, Amman; tel. (6) 5607194; fax (6) 5685476.

**Lebanon:** POB 947; Bir Hassan, Ghobeiri, Beirut; tel. (1) 603437; fax (1) 603443.

**Syria:** POB 4313; UN Compound, Mezzah Highway/Beirut Rd, Damascus; tel. (11) 6133035; fax (11) 6133047.

**West Bank:** POB 19149; Sheik Jarrah Qtr, Jerusalem; tel. (2) 5890400; fax (2) 5322714.

### LIAISON OFFICES

**Egypt:** 2 Dar-el-Shifa St, Garden City, POB 227, Cairo; tel. (2) 354-8502; fax (2) 354-8504.

**USA:** 2 United Nations Plaza, Room DC 2-1755, New York, NY 10017; tel. (212) 963-2255; fax (212) 935-7899.

## Activities

### ASSISTANCE ACTIVITIES

Since 1950 UNRWA has been the main provider of relief, health, education and social services for Palestine refugees in Lebanon, Syria, Jordan, the West Bank and the Gaza Strip. For UNRWA's purposes, a Palestine refugee is one whose normal residence was in Palestine for a minimum of two years before the 1948 conflict and who, as a result of the Arab–Israeli hostilities, lost his or her home and means of livelihood. To be eligible for assistance, a refugee must reside in one of the five areas in which UNRWA operates and be in need. A refugee's descendants who fulfil certain criteria are also eligible for UNRWA assistance. At 31 December 1998 UNRWA was providing essential services to 3,573,382 registered refugees (see table). Of these, an estimated 1,159,669 (33%) were living in 59 camps serviced by the Agency, while the remaining refugees had settled in the towns and villages already existing.

UNRWA's three principal areas of activity are education; health services; and relief and social services. Some 77% of the Agency's 1999 regular budget was devoted to these three operational programmes.

Education accounted for 47% of UNRWA's 1999 budget. In the 1998/99 school year there were 458,716 pupils enrolled in 650 UNRWA schools, and 13,915 educational staff. UNRWA also operated eight vocational and teacher-training centres, which provided a total of 4,632 training places. UNRWA awarded 891 scholarships for study at Arab universities in 1998/99. Technical co-operation for the Agency's education programme is provided by UNESCO.

Health services accounted for 18% of UNRWA's 1999 general fund budget. At the end of 1998 there were 122 primary health care units providing outpatient medical care, disease prevention and control, maternal and child health care and family planning services, of which 82 also offered dental care. At that time annual patient visits to UNRWA medical units numbered 7.0m., while the number of health staff totalled 3,484. UNRWA also operates a small hospital in the West Bank and offers assistance towards emergency and other secondary treatment, mainly through contractual agreements with non-governmental and private hospitals Technical assistance for the health programme is provided by WHO.

Relief and social services accounted for 12% of UNRWA's general fund budget for 1999. These services comprise the distribution of food rations, the provision of emergency shelter and the organization of welfare programmes for the poorest refugees (at 31 December 1998 195,359 refugees, or 5.5% of the total registered refugee population, were eligible to receive special hardship assistance). In 1998 UNRWA provided technical and financial support to 70 women's programmes, 26 youth activity centres and 32 community-based rehabilitation centres.

In order to encourage Palestinian self-reliance the Agency issues grants to ailing businesses and loans to families who qualify as special hardship cases. Between 1983 and early 1993 608 such grants and loans were made. In 1991 UNRWA launched an income generation programme, which provides capital loans to small businesses and micro-enterprises with the objective of creating sustainable employment and eliminating poverty, particularly in the Occupied Territories. By 31 December 1998 18,053 loans, with a total estimated value of US $30.1m., had been issued to new and existing Palestinian-owned enterprises.

Following the signing of the Declaration of Principles by the Palestine Liberation Organization and the Israeli Government in September 1993, UNRWA initiated a Peace Implementation Programme (PIP) to improve services and infrastructure for Palestinian refugees. In September 1994 the first phase of the programme (PIP I) was concluded after the receipt of US $93.2m. in pledged donations. PIP I projects included the construction of 33 schools and 24 classrooms and specialized education rooms, the rehabilitation of 4,700 shelters, the upgrading of solid waste disposal facilities throughout the Gaza Strip and feasibility studies for two sewerage systems. It was estimated that these projects created more than 5,500 jobs in the Gaza Strip for an average period of four months each. By mid-1998 the total number of PIP projects, including those under the second phase of the programme (PIP II), amounted to 369, while funds received or pledged to the Programme totalled $221.7m.

Since 1993 UNRWA has been engaged in the construction, equipping and commissioning of a 232-bed hospital in Gaza, with funds from the European Union and its member states. Construction was finished in 1996. The hospital and an affiliated nursing college were to be integrated into the health care system of the Palestinian National Authority, once the process of commissioning had been completed.

### AID TO DISPLACED PERSONS

After the renewal of Arab–Israeli hostilities in the Middle East in June 1967, hundreds of thousands of people fled from the fighting and from Israeli-occupied areas to east Jordan, Syria and Egypt. UNRWA provided emergency relief for displaced refugees and was additionally empowered by a UN General Assembly resolution to provide 'humanitarian assistance, as far as practicable, on an emergency basis and as a temporary measure' for those persons other than Palestine refugees who were newly displaced and in urgent need. In practice, UNRWA lacked the funds to aid the other displaced persons and the main burden of supporting them devolved on the Arab governments concerned. The Agency, as requested by the Government of Jordan in 1967 and on that Government's behalf, distributes rations to displaced persons in Jordan who are not registered refugees of 1948.

**RECENT EMERGENCIES**

Since 1982 UNRWA has managed a specially-funded operation in Lebanon, aimed at assisting refugees displaced by the continued civil conflict. In late 1986 and early 1987 fighting caused much destruction to Palestinian housing and UNRWA facilities in Lebanon, and an emergency relief operation was undertaken. In April 1996 UNRWA dispatched emergency supplies to assist some of the estimated 500,000 people displaced by renewed military activities in southern Lebanon.

In January 1991 (following the outbreak of war between Iraq and a multinational force whose aim was to enforce the withdrawal of Iraqi forces from Kuwait) the Israeli authorities imposed a curfew on Palestinians in the Israeli-occupied territories, and in February UNRWA began an emergency programme of food distribution to Palestinians who had thereby been prevented from earning a living. Following the conflict, Jordan absorbed more than 300,000 people fleeing Kuwait and other Gulf countries. Many of these people are eligible for UNRWA services.

In September 1992 an UNRWA mission was sent to Kuwait, following allegations of abuses of human rights perpetrated by the Kuwaiti authorities against Palestinian refugees living there. The mission was, however, limited to assessing the number of Palestinians from the Gaza Strip in Kuwait, who had been unable to obtain asylum in Jordan, since Jordan did not recognize Gazan identity documents.

**STATISTICS**

**Refugees Registered with UNRWA** (31 December 1998)

| Country | Number | % of total |
|---|---|---|
| Jordan | 1,487,449 | 41.6 |
| Gaza Strip | 785,551 | 22.0 |
| West Bank | 562,737 | 15.7 |
| Syria | 370,035 | 10.4 |
| Lebanon | 367,610 | 10.3 |
| **Total** | 3,573,382 | 100.0 |

## Finance

UNRWA is financed almost entirely by voluntary contributions from governments and the European Union, the remainder being provided by UN bodies, non-governmental organizations, business corporations and private sources, which also contribute to extra-budgetary activities. UNRWA's general fund budget for 1999 amounted to US $352.8m.

## Publication

*Annual Report of the Commissioner-General of UNRWA.*

# United Nations Training and Research Institutes

## UNITED NATIONS INSTITUTE FOR DISARMAMENT RESEARCH—UNIDIR

**Address:** Palais des Nations, 1211 Geneva 10, Switzerland.

**Telephone:** (22) 9173186; **fax:** (22) 9170176; **e-mail:** plewis@unog.ch; **internet:** www.unog.ch/unidir.

UNIDIR is an autonomous institution within the United Nations. It was established by the General Assembly in 1980 for the purpose of undertaking independent research on disarmament and related problems, particularly international security issues. UNIDIR's statute became effective on 1 January 1985.

The work of the Institute is based on the following objectives: to provide the international community with more diversified and complete data on problems relating to international security, the armaments race and disarmament in all fields, so as to facilitate progress towards greater global security and towards economic and social development for all peoples; to promote informed participation by all states in disarmament efforts; to assist ongoing negotiations on disarmament, and continuing efforts to ensure greater international security at a progressively lower level of armaments, in particular nuclear weapons, by means of objective studies and analyses; and to conduct long-term research on disarmament in order to provide a general insight into the problems involved and to stimulate new initiatives for negotiations.

The work programme of UNIDIR is reviewed annually and is subject to approval by its Board of Trustees. In 1999 UNIDIR conducted research and organized workshops or conferences on a range of issues, including: South Asian nuclear testing; trust and confidence-building measures in South Asia; the development of information and telecommunications in the context of international security; biological warfare and disarmament; the use of commercial satellite technology in the Middle East; and peace-keeping in Africa. Research projects are conducted within the Institute, or commissioned to individual experts or research organizations. For some major studies, multinational groups of experts are established. The Institute offers internships, in connection with its research programme.

The Institute's budget for 1997 amounted to US $900,000. It is financed mainly by voluntary contributions from governments and public or private organizations. A contribution to the costs of the Director and staff may be provided from the UN regular budget.

The Director of UNIDIR reports annually to the General Assembly on the activities of the Institute. The UN Secretary-General's Advisory Board on Disarmament Studies functions as UNIDIR's Board of Trustees.

**Director:** Patricia Lewis (United Kingdom).

**Publications:** *Disarmament Forum* (quarterly), *UNIDIR Newsletter* (quarterly); research reports (6 a year); research papers (irregular).

## UNITED NATIONS INSTITUTE FOR TRAINING AND RESEARCH—UNITAR

**Address:** Palais des Nations, 1211 Geneva 10, Switzerland.

**Telephone:** (22) 9171234; **fax:** (22) 9178047; **e-mail:** info@unitar.org; **internet:** www.unitar.org.

UNITAR was established in 1963, as an autonomous body within the United Nations, in order to enhance the effectiveness of the latter body in achieving its major objectives. In recent years the main focus of the Institute has shifted to training, with basic research being conducted only if extra-budgetary funds are made available. Training is provided at various levels for personnel on assignments under the United Nations and its specialized agencies or under organizations operating in related fields. Training programmes comprise courses on multilateral diplomacy and the management of international affairs. Other training and capacity-building programmes, which are funded by special-purpose grants, are offered in issues relating to economic and social development, such as the application of environmental law, the legal aspects of debt, economic and financial management and public administration, chemicals and waste management, and disaster control. Most training programmes are designed and conducted in Geneva.

UNITAR offers a fellowship programme in peace-making and preventive diplomacy to provide advanced training for international and national civil servants in conflict analysis and mediation. It also organizes, jointly with the UN Office for Legal Affairs, an annual fellowship programme in international law.

By the end of September 1995 more than 24,000 participants from 180 countries had attended courses, seminars or workshops organized by UNITAR. Each year approximately 3,000 people participate in UNITAR training programmes.

UNITAR is financed by voluntary contributions from UN member states, by donations from foundations and other non-governmental sources, and by income generated by its Reserve Fund.

**Executive Director:** Marcel A. Boisard (Switzerland).

## UNITED NATIONS INTERNATIONAL RESEARCH AND TRAINING INSTITUTE FOR THE ADVANCEMENT OF WOMEN—INSTRAW

**Address:** Calle César Nicolás Pensón 102-A, POB 21747, Santo Domingo, Dominican Republic.

**Telephone:** (809) 685-2111; **fax:** (809) 685-2117; **e-mail:** instraw.hq.sd@codetel.net.do; **internet:** www.un.org/instraw.

The Institute was established by ECOSOC, and endorsed by the General Assembly, in 1976, following a recommendation of the World Conference on the International Women's Year (1975). INSTRAW provides training, conducts research and collects and disseminates relevant information in order to stimulate and to assist the advancement of women and their integration in the development process, both as participants and beneficiaries. During the two year period 1998–99 INSTRAW's research programme was to focus on the following issues: engendering the political agenda; the temporary labour migration of women; development of a database on water-resources management; and development and implementation of a database on gender-related training materials. INSTRAW's training programme for the same period incorporated activities in statistics and indicators on gender issues; women, environmental management and sustainable development; and a workshop on human rights and trafficking in women.

INSTRAW is an autonomous body of the UN, funded by voluntary contributions from UN member states, inter- and non-governmental organizations, foundations and other private sources. An 11-member Board of Trustees meets annually to formulate the principles and guide-lines for the activities of INSTRAW and to consider the current work progamme and budget proposals, and reports to ECOSOC. INSTRAW maintains a liaison office at the UN Secretariat in New York.

**Director:** YAKIN ERTÜRK.

**Publications:** *INSTRAW News* (2 a year); training materials, research studies.

## UNITED NATIONS INTERREGIONAL CRIME AND JUSTICE RESEARCH INSTITUTE—UNICRI

**Address:** Via Giulia 52, 00186 Rome, Italy.

**Telephone:** (06) 6877437; **fax:** (06) 6892638; **e-mail:** unicri@unicri.it; **internet:** www.unicri.it.

The Institute was established in 1968 as the United Nations Social Defence Research Institute. Its present name was adopted by a resolution of ECOSOC in 1989. The Institute undertakes research, training and information activities in the fields of crime prevention and criminal justice, at international, regional and national levels.

In collaboration with national governments, UNICRI aims to establish a reliable base of knowledge and information on organized crime; to identify strategies for the prevention and control of crime, within the framework of contributing to socio-economic development and protecting human rights; and to design systems to support policy formulation, implementation and evaluation. UNICRI organizes workshops and conferences, and promotes the exchange of information through its international documentation centre on criminology.

UNICRI is funded by the United Nations Crime Prevention and Criminal Justice Fund, which is financed by voluntary contributions from UN member states, non-governmental organizations, academic institutions and other concerned bodies.

**Officer-in-Charge:** ALBERTO BRADANINI (Italy).

## UNITED NATIONS RESEARCH INSTITUTE FOR SOCIAL DEVELOPMENT—UNRISD

**Address:** Palais des Nations, 1211 Geneva 10, Switzerland.

**Telephone:** (22) 7988400; **fax:** (22) 7400791; **e-mail:** info@unrisd.org; **internet:** www.unrisd.org.

UNRISD was established in 1963 as an autonomous body within the United Nations, to conduct multi-disciplinary research into the social dimensions of contemporary problems affecting development.

The Institute aims to provide governments, development agencies, grass-roots organizations and scholars with a better understanding of how development policies and processes of economic, social and environmental change affect different social groups.

UNRISD research is undertaken in collaboration with a network of national research teams drawn from local universities and research institutions. UNRISD aims to promote and strengthen research capacities in developing countries. In late 1998 its research programme included the following projects: Business responsibility for sustainable development; community perspectives on urban governance—volunteer action and local democracy: a partnership for a better urban future; emerging mass tourism in the South; gender, poverty and well-being; technical co-operation and women's lives: integrating gender into development policy; globalization and citizenship; grassroots initiatives and knowledge networks for land reform in developing countries; information technologies and social development; public sector reform and crisis-ridden states; research, exchange and action on social development in sub-Saharan Africa; and war-torn societies.

The Institute is supported by voluntary grants from governments, and also receives financing from other UN organizations, and from various other national and international agencies.

**Director:** THANDIKA MKANDAWIRE (Sweden).

**Publications:** *UNRISD Social Development News* (quarterly), discussion papers and monographs.

## UNITED NATIONS UNIVERSITY—UNU

**Address:** 53–70, Jingumae 5-chome, Shibuya-ku, Tokyo 150-8925, Japan.

**Telephone:** (3) 3499-2811; **fax:** (3) 3499-2828; **e-mail:** mbox@hq.unu.edu; **internet:** www.unu.edu.

The University is sponsored jointly by the United Nations and UNESCO. It is an autonomous institution within the United Nations, guaranteed academic freedom by a charter approved by the General Assembly in 1973. It is governed by a 28-member University Council of scholars and scientists, of whom 24 are appointed by the Secretary-General of the UN and the Director-General of UNESCO (who, together with the Executive Director of UNITAR, are ex-officio members of the Council; the Rector is also on the Council). The University is not traditional in the sense of having students or awarding degrees, but works through networks of collaborating institutions and individuals. These include Associated Institutions (universities and research institutes linked with the UNU under general agreements of co-operation). The UNU undertakes multi-disciplinary research on problems of human survival, development and welfare that are the concern of the United Nations and its agencies, and works to strengthen research and training capabilities in developing countries. It provides post-graduate fellowships for scientists and scholars from developing countries, and conducts various training activities in association with its programme.

The UNU's research and training centres and programmes include the World Institute of Development Economics Research (UNU/WIDER) in Helsinki, Finland, the Institute for New Technologies (UNU/INTECH) in Maastricht, the Netherlands, the International Institute for Software Technology (UNU/IIST) in Macau, the UNU Institute for Natural Resources in Africa in Accra, Ghana (UNU/INRA—with a mineral resources unit in Lusaka, Zambia), the UNU Programme for Biotechnology in Latin America and the Caribbean (UNU/BIOLAC), based in Caracas, Venezuela, the UNU International Leadership Academy (UNU/ILA) in Amman, Jordan, the Institute of Advanced Studies (UNU/IAS), based in Tokyo, Japan, and the UNU International Network on Water, Environment and Health (UNU/INWEH) in Ontario, Canada.

The UNU is financed by voluntary contributions from UN member states. By May 1999 US $350m. had been pledged.

**Rector:** Prof. HANS J. A. VAN GINKEL (Netherlands).

**Publication:** *UNU Nexions* (regular newsletter).

## UNIVERSITY FOR PEACE

**Address:** POB 138, Ciudad Colón, Costa Rica.

**Telephone:** 249-1072; **fax:** 249-1929.

The University for Peace was established by the United Nations in 1980 to conduct research on, *inter alia*, disarmament, mediation, the resolution of conflicts, the preservation of the environment, international relations, peace education and human rights. In 1999 the Council of the University met for the first time since 1994.

**Rector:** MAURICE STRONG (Canada).

**Publications:** *Dialogue*, *Infopaz*.

# World Food Programme—WFP

**Address:** Via Cesare Giulio Viola 68, Parco dei Medici, 00148 Rome, Italy.

**Telephone:** (06) 6513-1; **fax:** (06) 6590-632; **e-mail:** wfpinfo@wfp.org; **internet:** www.wfp.org.

WFP, the food aid organization of the United Nations, became operational in 1963. It provides relief assistance to victims of natural and man-made disasters, and supplies food aid to people in developing countries with the aim of stimulating self-reliant communities.

## Organization

(December 1999)

### EXECUTIVE BOARD

At the end of 1995 the governing body of WFP, the 42-member Committee on Food Aid Policies and Programmes (CFA), was transformed into the WFP Executive Board, in accordance with a resolution of the UN General Assembly. The Board, comprising 36 members, held its first session in January 1996. It was to meet in three regular sessions each year.

### SECRETARIAT

WFP's Executive Director is appointed jointly by the UN Secretary-General and the Director-General of FAO and is responsible for the management and administration of the Programme. In 1998 there were 5,021 WFP staff members, of whom some 81% were working in the field. WFP administers nine regional offices to provide operational, financial and management support at a more local level.

**Executive Director:** CATHERINE A. BERTINI (USA).

## Activities

WFP is the only multilateral organization with a mandate to use food aid as a resource. It is the second largest source of assistance in the UN, after the World Bank group, in terms of actual transfers of resources, and the largest source of grant aid in the UN system. WFP handles more than one-third of the world's food aid. WFP is also the largest contributor to South–South trade within the UN system, through the purchase of food and services from developing countries. WFP's mission is to provide food aid to save lives in refugee and other emergency situations, to improve the nutrition and quality of life of vulnerable groups and to help to develop assets and promote the self-reliance of poor families and communities. WFP aims to focus its efforts on the world's poorest countries and to provide at least 90% of its total assistance to those designated as 'low-income food-deficit'. It also endeavours to address the specific nutritional needs of women and to increase their access to food and development resources. At the World Food Summit, held in November 1996, WFP endorsed the commitment to reduce by 50% the number of undernourished people, no later than 2015. In 1998 WFP delivered some 2.8m. metric tons of food assistance, reaching an estimated 74.8m. people in 80 countries.

In the early 1990s there was a substantial shift in the balance between emergency relief and development assistance provided by WFP, owing to the growing needs of victims of drought and other natural disasters, refugees and displaced persons. By 1994 two-thirds of all food aid was for relief assistance and one-third for development, representing a direct reversal of the allocations five years previously. In addition, there was a noticeable increase in aid given to those in need as a result of civil war, compared with commitments for victims of natural disasters. WFP has undertaken efforts to be prepared for emergency situations and to improve its capacity for responding effectively to situations as they arise. Through its Vulnerability Analysis and Mapping (VAM) project, WFP aims to identify potentially vulnerable groups by providing information on food security and the capacity of different groups for coping with shortages, and to enhance emergency contingency-planning and long-term assistance objectives. By 1999 VAM field units were operational in Angola, Bangladesh, Burkina Faso, Cambodia, the People's Republic of China, Ecuador, Ethiopia, India, Indonesia, Mozambique, Nicaragua, Pakistan, Sudan and Uganda. The key elements of WFP's emergency response capacity are its strategic stores of food and logistics equipment (maintained in Nairobi, Kenya, and Pisa, Italy), stand-by arrangements to enable the rapid deployment of personnel, communications and other essential equipment, and the Augmented Logistics Intervention Team for Emergencies (ALITE), which undertakes capacity assessments and contingency-planning. A Crisis Support Facility was established at WFP Headquarters in 1996 in order to process information and assist co-ordination between WFP and other UN agencies working in Liberia. The Facility was reactivated in November to ensure an effective response to the humanitarian crisis in the former Zaire.

In 1998 some 56.4m. people received WFP humanitarian relief, of whom 16.3m. were refugees and internally displaced persons, and 40.1m. were victims of earthquakes, drought, floods and other natural disasters. In that year sub-Saharan Africa accounted for the largest share, some 59%, of total relief operational expenditure. The main populations of concern were in Angola, the Great Lakes region, Liberia and Sierra Leone, which were affected by civil conflict, and in east Africa, where the people were affected by extreme climatic conditions and renewed conflict. In July WFP established a special task force to co-ordinate a massive delivery of food aid by air, which aimed to reach 1.8m. people in southern Sudan, affected by famine resulting from poor harvests, fighting and floods. The cost of WFP relief operations in Sudan totalled US $160m. In September WFP initiated its largest ever emergency operations to assist more than 19m. victims of flooding in Bangladesh. In the same month WFP approved its first emergency relief operation for the People's Republic of China, following severe flooding in that country. The operation assisted some 5.8m. people, at a cost of $87m., through the construction of temporary shelters, the provision of drinking water and rehabilitation of roads. In November, following the devastation caused by 'Hurricane Mitch', WFP undertook an immediate emergency distribution of food, using existing local reserves, reaching some 600,000 people in El Salvador, Guatemala, Honduras and Nicaragua. WFP subsequently approved a six-month operation, totalling $62.7m., to provide food to 1.1m. people who had been displaced from their homes and land as a result of the hurricane. During 1998 WFP remained actively concerned with the food situation in the Democratic People's Republic of Korea (DPRK), which had required substantial levels of emergency food supplies in recent years, owing to natural disasters and consistently poor harvests. In 1998 WFP provided food for an estimated 5m. people in that country at a cost of $126m. In September/October WFP, together with UNICEF and the EU, conducted the first random nation-wide nutritional survey in the DPRK, which identified some 16% of young children as suffering acute malnutrition and 60% suffering long-term malnutrition. By mid-1999 an estimated 1.5m.–3.5m. people had died of starvation in the DPRK since 1995. At that time WFP appealed for $260m. to provide assistance to some 8m. people in that country for a further 12-month period.

In accordance with a Security Council resolution providing for the limited sale of petroleum by the Iraqi Government in exchange for the purchase of essential humanitarian supplies, which came into effect in December 1996, WFP was mandated to establish an observation system to ensure the fair and efficient distribution of food throughout the country. WFP was also required to transport and distribute the food supplies to local populations in the north of Iraq. In October 1997 a joint FAO/WFP mission to Iraq reported extensive levels of malnutrition. In March 1998 WFP conducted a nutritional survey of children and women in Iraq, in an operation organized with the Iraqi Government and UNICEF. During 1998 WFP supervised the distribution of 4.8m. metric tons of food under the special operation in Iraq, at a cost of US $13.3m.

Through its development activities, WFP aims to alleviate poverty in developing countries by promoting self-reliant families and communities. Food is supplied, for example, as an incentive in development self-help schemes and as part-wages in labour-intensive projects of many kinds. In all its projects WFP aims to assist the most vulnerable groups and to ensure that beneficiaries have an adequate and balanced diet. Activities supported by the Programme include the settlement and resettlement of groups and communities; land reclamation and improvement; irrigation; forestry; dairy development; road construction; training of hospital staff; community development; and human resources development such as feeding expectant or nursing mothers and schoolchildren, and support for education, training and health programmes. At the end of 1998 WFP was supporting 125 development projects, which benefited some 18.4m. people during that year. Projects included income diversification training in Egypt, school feeding programmes in Morocco, the provision of essential items to support girls in Bhutan living away from home in order to pursue full-time education, a project to increase self-reliance among women in the poorest communities in Bangladesh, and food production assistance in Tajikistan and Bosnia and Herzegovina.

Following a comprehensive evaluation of its activities, WFP is increasingly focused on linking its relief and development activities to provide a continuum between short-term relief and longer-term rehabilitation and development. In order to achieve this objective, WFP aims to integrate elements that strengthen disaster mitigation into development projects, including soil conservation, reafforestation, irrigation infrastructure and transport construction and rehabilitation and to promote capacity-building elements within relief operations, e.g. training, income-generating activities and environmental protection measures. In 1998 WFP approved 12 new 'protracted refugee and displaced persons operations', where the emphasis is on fostering stability, rehabilitation and long-term development after an emergency. In all these operations, which are undertaken in collaboration with UNHCR and other international agencies, WFP is responsible for mobilizing basic food commoditities and for related transport, handling and storage costs.

**OPERATIONAL EXPENDITURE IN 1998, BY REGION AND TYPE*** (US $ '000, provisional figures)

| Region | Development | Relief | Special operations | Total (incl. others†) |
|---|---|---|---|---|
| Sub-Saharan Africa | 81,035 | 538,551 | 19,100 | 646,925 |
| Asia | 102,006 | 294,244 | 1,063 | 400,976 |
| Latin America and the Caribbean | 49,259 | 11,323 | – | 63,853 |
| North Africa and the Middle East | 22,012 | 15,282 | 13,305 | 58,949 |
| Europe and the CIS | – | 56,099 | 640 | 57,139 |
| **Total** | 254,315 | 915,504 | 34,111 | 1,237,549‡ |

* Excludes programme support and administrative costs.
† Trust fund expenditures.
‡ Includes operational expenditures that cannot be apportioned by project operation.

## Finance

The Programme is funded by voluntary contributions from donor countries and intergovernmental bodies such as the European Union. Contributions are made in the form of commodities, finance and services (particularly shipping). Commitments to the International Emergency Food Reserve (IEFR), from which WFP provides the majority of its food supplies, and to the Immediate Response Account of the IEFR (IRA) are also made on a voluntary basis by donors. WFP's total expenditure in 1998 (including non-operational costs) amounted to some US $1,348m.

## Publications

*Annual Report.*
*WFP in Action.*

# SPECIALIZED AGENCIES WITHIN THE UN SYSTEM

## Food and Agriculture Organization of the United Nations—FAO

**Address:** Viale delle Terme di Caracalla, 00100 Rome, Italy.

**Telephone:** (06) 57051; **fax:** (06) 5705-3152; **e-mail:** telex-room@fao.org; **internet:** www.fao.org.

FAO, the first specialized agency of the UN to be founded after the Second World War, was established in Québec, Canada, in October 1945. The Organization aims to alleviate malnutrition and hunger, and serves as a co-ordinating agency for development programmes in the whole range of food and agriculture, including forestry and fisheries. It helps developing countries to promote educational and training facilities and the creation of appropriate institutions.

#### MEMBERS

181 members (including the European Union as a member organization): see Table on pp. 114–116.

### Organization

(December 1999)

#### CONFERENCE

The governing body is the FAO Conference of member nations. It meets every two years, formulates policy, determines the Organization's programme and budget on a biennial basis, and elects new members. It also elects the Director-General of the Secretariat and the Independent Chairman of the Council. Every other year, FAO also holds conferences in each of its five regions (see below).

#### COUNCIL

The FAO Council is composed of representatives of 49 member nations, elected by the Conference for staggered three-year terms. It is the interim governing body of FAO between sessions of the Conference. The most important standing Committees of the Council are: the Finance and Programme Committees, the Committee on Commodity Problems, the Committee on Fisheries, the Committee on Agriculture and the Committee on Forestry.

#### SECRETARIAT

The total number of staff at FAO headquarters in September 1999 was 2,278, of whom 67 were associate experts, while staff in field, regional and country offices numbered 1,865, including 132 associate experts. Work is supervised by the following Departments: Administration and Finance; General Affairs and Information; Economic and Social Policy; Agriculture; Forestry; Fisheries; Sustainable Development; and Technical Co-operation.

**Director-General:** JACQUES DIOUF (Senegal).

#### REGIONAL OFFICES

**Africa:** UN Agency Bldg, North Maxwell Rd, POB 1628, Accra, Ghana; tel. (21) 666851; fax (21) 668427; e-mail fao-raf@fao.org; Regional Rep. B. F. DADA.

**Asia and the Pacific:** Maliwan Mansion, Phra Atit Rd, Bangkok 10200, Thailand; tel. (2) 281-7844; fax (2) 280-0445; e-mail fao-rap@fao.org; Regional Rep. PREM NATH.

**Europe:** Viale delle Terme di Caracalla, Room A-304, 00100 Rome, Italy; tel. (06) 570-54241; fax (06) 570-55634; Regional Rep. M. LINDAU.

**Latin America and the Caribbean:** Avda Dag Hammarskjöld 3241, Casilla 10095, Vitacura, Santiago, Chile; tel. (2) 337-2100; fax (2) 337-2101; e-mail fao-rlc-registry@field.fao.org; internet www.rlc.fao.org; Regional Rep. GUSTAVO GORDILLO.

**Near East:** 11 El-Eslah el-Zerai St, Dokki, POB 2223, Cairo, Egypt; tel. (2) 3372229; fax (2) 3495981; e-mail fao-rne@field.fao.org; Regional Rep. ATIF YEHEYA BUKHARI.

In addition, the following Sub-regional Offices are operational: in Harare, Zimbabwe (for Southern and Eastern Africa); in Bridgetown, Barbados (for the Caribbean); in Tunis, Tunisia (for North Africa); in Budapest, Hungary (for Central and Eastern Europe); and in Apia, Samoa (for the Pacific Islands).

#### JOINT DIVISIONS AND LIAISON OFFICES

**Joint ECA/FAO Agriculture Division:** Africa Hall, POB 3001, Addis Ababa, Ethiopia; tel. (1) 510406; fax (1) 514416.

**Joint ECE/FAO Timber Section:** Palais des Nations, 1211 Geneva 10, Switzerland; tel. (22) 917-2874; fax (22) 917-0041.

**Joint ESCWA/FAO Agriculture Division:** POB 927115, Amman, Jordan; tel. (6) 606847; fax (6) 674261.

**Joint IAEA/FAO Division of Nuclear Techniques in Food and Agriculture:** Wagramerstrasse 5, 1400 Vienna, Austria; tel. (1) 2060-21610; fax (1) 2060-29946.

**European Union:** 21 ave du Boulevard, 1210 Brussels, Belgium; tel. (2) 203-8852; e-mail fao-lobr@field.fao.org; Dir M. R. DE MONTALEMBERT.

**Japan:** 6F Yokohama International Organizations Centre, Pacifico-Yokohama, 1-1-1, Minato Mirai, Nishi-ku, Yokohama 220-0012; tel. (45) 222-1101; fax (45) 222-1103.

**North America:** Suite 300, 2175 K St, NW, Washington, DC 20437, USA; tel. (202) 653-2400; fax (202) 653-5760; e-mail fao-lowa@fao.org; Dir C. H. RIEMENSCHNEIDER.

**United Nations:** Suite DC1-1125, 1 United Nations Plaza, New York, NY 10017, USA; tel. (212) 963-6036; fax (212) 888-6188; Dir B. TOURÉ.

### Activities

FAO aims to raise levels of nutrition and standards of living, by improving the production and distribution of food and other commodities derived from farms, fisheries and forests. FAO provides technical information, advice and assistance by disseminating information; acting as a neutral forum for discussion of food and agricultural issues; advising governments on policy and planning; and developing capacity directly in the field.

In November 1999 the FAO Conference identified the following areas of activity as FAO priorities for 2000–01: the Special Programme for Food Security; transboundary animal and plant pests and diseases; forest conservation; promotion of the Codex Alimentarius code on food standards; strengthening the technical co-operation programme (which funds 12% of FAO's field programme expenditure); and the implementation of a Programme Against African Trypanosomiasis. In October 1997 FAO organized its first televised fund-raising event 'TeleFood', broadcast to an estimated 500m. viewers in some 70 countries. This has subsequently been organized on an annual basis in order to raise public awareness of the problems of hunger and malnutrition. In December 1999 a TeleFood concert was held in Jamaica, which was broadcast around the world and on the internet. Since 1997 public donations to TeleFood have totalled more than US $4m., financing some 476 'grass-roots' projects in nearly 100 countries. The projects provided tools, seeds and other essential supplies directly to small-scale farmers, and were especially aimed at helping women.

In November 1996 FAO hosted the World Food Summit, which was held in Rome and was attended by heads of state and senior government representatives of 186 countries. Participants approved the Rome Declaration on World Food Security and the World Food Summit Plan of Action, with the aim of halving the number of people afflicted by undernutrition, at that time estimated to total 828m. world-wide, no later than 2015.

FAO's total field programme expenditure for 1998 was US $278m., compared with $260m. in 1997. An estimated 33% of field projects were in Africa, 22% in Asia and the Pacific, 12% in the Near East, 10% in Latin America and the Caribbean, 4% in Europe, and 19% were inter-regional or global.

#### AGRICULTURE

FAO's most important area of activity is crop production which annually accounts for about 24% of FAO's Field Programme expenditure. FAO assists developing countries in increasing agricultural production, by means of a number of methods, including improved seeds and fertilizer use, soil conservation and reforestation, better water resource management techniques, upgrading storage facilities, and improvements in processing and marketing. FAO places special emphasis on the cultivation of under-exploited traditional food crops, such as cassava, sweet potato and plantains.

In 1985 the FAO Conference approved an International Code of Conduct on the Distribution and Use of Pesticides, and in 1989 the

Conference adopted an additional clause concerning 'Prior Informed Consent' (PIC), whereby international shipments of newly banned or restricted pesticides should not proceed without the agreement of importing countries. Under the clause, FAO aims to inform governments about the hazards of toxic chemicals and to urge them to take proper measures to curb trade in highly toxic agrochemicals while keeping the pesticides industry informed of control actions. In mid-1996 FAO, in collaboration with UNEP, publicized a new initiative which aimed to increase awareness of, and to promote international action on, obsolete and hazardous stocks of pesticides remaining throughout the world. In September 1998 a new legally-binding treaty on trade in hazardous chemicals and pesticides was adopted at an international conference held in Rotterdam, the Netherlands. The so-called Rotterdam Convention required that hazardous chemicals and pesticides banned or severely restricted in at least two countries should not be exported unless explicitly agreed by the importing country. It also identified certain pesticide formulations as too dangerous to be used by farmers in developing countries, and incorporated an obligation that countries halt national production of those hazardous compounds. The treaty was to enter into force on being ratified by 50 signatory states. FAO was co-operating with UNEP to provide an interim secretariat for the Convention. In July 1999 a conference on the Rotterdam Convention, held in Rome, established an Interim Chemical Review Committee with responsibility for recommending the inclusion of chemicals or pesticide formulations in the PIC procedure. By September the treaty had been signed by 60 states. As part of its continued efforts to reduce the environmental risks posed by over-reliance on pesticides, FAO has extended to other regions its Integrated Pest Management (IPM) programme in Asia and the Pacific on the adoption of safer and more effective methods of pest control, such as biological control methods and natural predators, such as spiders and wasps, to avert pests.

FAO's Joint Division with the International Atomic Energy Agency (IAEA) tests controlled-release formulas of pesticides and herbicides that gradually free their substances and can limit the amount of agrochemicals needed to protect crops. The Joint FAO-IAEA Division is engaged in exploring biotechnologies and in developing non-toxic fertilizers (especially those that are locally available) and improved strains of food crops (especially from indigenous varieties). In the area of animal production and health, the Joint Division has developed progesterone-measuring and disease diagnostic kits, of which thousands have been delivered to developing countries. FAO's plant nutrition activities aim to promote nutrient management, such as the Integrated Plant Nutritions Systems (IPNS), which are based on the recycling of nutrients through crop production and the efficient use of mineral fertilizers.

The conservation and sustainable use of plant and animal genetic resources are promoted by FAO's Global System for Plant Genetic Resources, which includes five databases, and the Global Programme for Animal Genetic Resources. An FAO programme supports the establishment of gene banks, designed to maintain the world's biological diversity by preserving animal and plant species threatened with extinction. FAO, jointly with UNEP, has published a document listing the current state of global livestock genetic diversity. In June 1996 representatives of more than 150 governments convened in Leipzig, Germany, at a meeting organized by FAO (and hosted by the German Government) to consider the use and conservation of plant genetic resources as an essential means of enhancing food security. The meeting adopted a Global Plan of Action, which included measures to strengthen the development of plant varieties and to promote the use and availability of local varieties and locally-adapted crops to farmers, in particular following a natural disaster, war or civil conflict.

An Emergency Prevention System for Transboundary Animal and Plant Pests and Diseases (EMPRES) was established in 1994 to strengthen FAO's activities in the prevention, control and, where possible, eradication of highly contagious diseases and pests. EMPRES's initial priorities were locusts and rinderpest. During 1994 EMPRES published guide-lines on all aspects of desert locust monitoring, commissioned an evaluation of recent control efforts and prepared a concept paper on desert locust management. FAO has assumed responsibility for technical leadership and co-ordination of the Global Rinderpest Eradication Campaign, which has the objective of eliminating the disease by 2010. In 1996/97 EMPRES helped to combat rinderpest outbreaks in five countries and desert locust outbreaks in North Africa, the Sahel and Red Sea basin. In November 1997 FAO initiated a Programme Against African Trypanosomiasis, which aimed to counter the disease affecting cattle in almost one-third of Africa.

## ENVIRONMENT

At the UN Conference on Environment and Development (UNCED), held in Rio de Janeiro, Brazil, in June 1992, FAO participated in several working parties and supported the adoption of Agenda 21, a programme of activities to promote sustainable development. FAO is responsible for the chapters of Agenda 21 concerning water resources, forests, fragile mountain ecosystems and sustainable agriculture and rural development.

## FISHERIES

FAO's Fisheries Department consists of a multi-disciplinary body of experts who are involved in every aspect of fisheries development from coastal surveys, improvement of production, processing and storage, to the compilation of statistics, development of computer databases, improvement of fishing gear, institution-building and training. In November 1993 the FAO Conference adopted an agreement to improve the monitoring and control of fishing vessels operating on the high seas that are registered under 'flags of convenience'. These ships, amounting to an estimated 20% of all fishing vessels, are often able to avoid compliance with internationally accepted marine conservation and management measures. In March 1995 a ministerial meeting of fisheries adopted a Rome Consensus on World Fisheries, which identified a need for immediate action to eliminate overfishing and to rebuild and enhance depleting fish stocks. In November the FAO Conference adopted a Code of Conduct for Responsible Fishing, which incorporated many global fisheries and aquaculture issues (including fisheries resource conservation and development, fish catches, seafood and fish processing, commercialization, trade and research) to promote the sustainable development of the sector. In February 1999 the FAO Committee on Fisheries adopted new international measures, within the framework of the Code of Conduct, in order to reduce over-exploitation of the world's fish resources, as well as plans of action for the conservation and management of sharks and the reduction in the incidental catch of seabirds in longline fisheries. The voluntary measures were endorsed at a ministerial meeting, held in March and attended by representatives of some 126 countries, which issued a declaration to promote the implementation of the Code of Conduct and to achieve sustainable management of fisheries and aquaculture. In October a new Sustainable Fisheries Livelihoods Programme was initiated to assist 24 African countries to implement the Code of Conduct and to promote small-scale artisanal fishing projects. FAO promotes aquaculture as a valuable source of animal protein, and as an income-generating activity for rural communities. A new Programme of Fisheries Assistance for Small Island Developing States, which had been formulated by FAO in consultation with South Pacific member states and with the Alliance of Small Island States, was approved at a session of the Committee on Fisheries in March 1997. In 1996/97 FAO took part in 21 technical consultations on the management of marine resources. In addition, work on aquatic genetic resources was strengthened and studies were undertaken to monitor the impact of 'El Niño', a periodic warming of the tropical Pacific Ocean, on aquaculture in Latin America and Africa. In 1999 FAO collaborated with the Network of Aquaculture Centres in Asia and the Pacific (NACA) in preparations for a Conference on Aquaculture in the Third Millennium, which was scheduled to be held in Bangkok, Thailand, in February 2000. The Conference was to consider global trends in aquaculture and future policy measures to ensure the sustainable development of the sector.

## FORESTRY

FAO focuses on the contribution of forestry to food security, on effective and responsible forest management and on maintaining a balance between the economic, ecological and social benefits of forest resources. The Organization has helped to develop national forestry programmes and to promote the sustainable development of all types of forest. FAO's Forests, Trees and People Programme promotes the sustainable management of tree and forest resources, based on local knowledge and management practices, in order to improve the livelihoods of rural people in developing countries. A draft strategic plan for the sustainable management of trees and forests was formulated in 1997, the main objectives of which were to maintain the environmental diversity of forests, to realise the economic potential of forests and trees within a sustainable framework, and to establish broad social networks of interested parties to manage and develop forest environments. A series of meetings of the regional forestry commissions was held during 1998 to consider the plan.

## NUTRITION

The International Conference on Nutrition, sponsored by FAO and WHO, took place in Rome in December 1992. It approved a World Declaration on Nutrition and a Plan of Action, aimed at promoting efforts to combat malnutrition as a development priority. Since the conference, more than 100 countries have formulated national plans of action for nutrition, many of which were based on existing development plans such as comprehensive food security initiatives, national poverty alleviation programmes and action plans to attain the targets set by the World Summit for Children in September 1990. In October 1996 FAO jointly organized the first World Congress on Calcium and Vitamin D in Human Life, held in Rome. The Congress discussed methods to increase the intake of calcium and vitamin D by all members of the population in order to promote growth during childhood and adolescence and to reduce the prevalence of diseases such as osteoporosis, cancer and hypertension.

### PROCESSING AND MARKETING

An estimated 20% of all food harvested is lost before it can be consumed, and in some developing countries the proportion is much higher. FAO helps reduce immediate post-harvest losses, with the introduction of improved processing methods and storage systems. It also advises on the distribution and marketing of agricultural produce and on the selection and preparation of foods for optimum nutrition. Many of these activities form part of wider rural development projects. Many developing countries rely on agricultural products as their main source of foreign earnings, but the terms under which they are traded are usually more favourable to the industrialized countries. FAO continues to favour the elimination of export subsidies and related discriminatory practices, such as protectionist measures that hamper international trade in agricultural commodities. By late 1997 FAO had organized 18 regional workshops and 44 national projects in order to help member states to implement World Trade Organization regulations, in particular with regard to agricultural policy, intellectual property rights, sanitary and phytosanitary measures, technical barriers to trade and the international standards of the Codex Alimentarius, and to consider the impact on member states of the ministerial decision concerning the possible negative effects of the reform programme on least-developed and net-food importing developing countries. FAO evaluates new market trends and helps to develop improved plant and animal quarantine procedures. In November 1997 the FAO Conference adopted new guide-lines on surveillance and on export certification systems in order to harmonize plant quarantine standards. In August 1999 FAO announced the establishment of a new forum, PhAction, to promote post-harvest research and the development of effective post-harvest services and infrastructure.

### FOOD SECURITY

FAO's policy on food security aims to encourage the production of adequate food supplies, to maximize stability in the flow of supplies, and to ensure access on the part of those who need them. In 1994 FAO initiated a Special Programme for Food Security, which was designed to assist low-income countries with a food deficit to increase food production and productivity as rapidly as possible, primarily through the widespread adoption by farmers of improved production technologies, with emphasis on areas of high potential. At December 1999 83 countries were categorized as 'low-income food-deficit', of which 42 were in Africa, while the Special Programme was engaged in projects in 54 countries. A budget of US $10m. was allocated to the Programme for the two-year period 1998–99. In 1996 FAO was actively involved in the formulation of a Plan of Action on food security, adopted at the World Food Summit in November, and was to be responsible for monitoring and promoting its implementation. In March 1999, FAO signed agreements with the International Fund for Agricultural Development (IFAD) and WFP which aimed to increase co-operation within the framework of the Special Programme for Food Security. The Programme promotes South-South co-operation to improve food security and the exchange of knowledge and experience. By mid-1999 10 bilateral co-operation agreements were in force, for example, between Viet Nam and Senegal, and India and Eritrea.

FAO's Global Information and Early Warning System (GIEWS), which become operational in 1975, monitors the crop and food outlook at global and national levels in order to detect emerging food supply difficulties and disasters and to ensure rapid intervention in countries experiencing food supply shortages. It publishes regular reports on the weather conditions and crop prospects in sub-Saharan Africa and in the Sahel region and issues special alerts which describe the situation in countries or sub-regions experiencing food difficulties and recommends an appropriate international response. In October 1999 FAO published the first *State of Food Insecurity in the World*, based on data compiled by a new Food Insecurity and Vulnerability Information and Mapping Systems programme.

### FAO INVESTMENT CENTRE

The Investment Centre was established in 1964 to help countries to prepare viable investment projects that will attract external financing. The Centre focuses its evaluation of projects on two fundamental concerns: the promotion of sustainable activities for land management, forestry development and environmental protection, and the alleviation of rural poverty. In 1998 44 projects were approved, representing a total investment of some US $3,000m.

### EMERGENCY RELIEF

FAO works to rehabilitate agricultural production following natural and man-made disasters by providing emergency seed, tools, and technical and other assistance. Jointly with the United Nations, FAO is responsible for the World Food Programme (q.v.), which provides emergency food supplies and food aid in support of development projects. In 1997 more than 60 countries suffered the effects of heavy flooding or severe drought (occasionally, as in the case of Indonesia, followed by extensive forest fires), caused wholly or partially by the El Niño weather phenomenon. FAO attempted to help assess the damage to agricultural systems, to provide rehabilitation assistance and to initiate efforts to strengthen the resistance of agricultural sectors against future weather anomalies. In 1998 FAO was concerned at the possible effects of a converse climatic occurence, 'La Niña', caused by upswelling of cold water in areas of the Pacific Ocean. By 30 November FAO's Special Relief Operations Service had undertaken 96 new projects in 45 countries during that year, at a cost of US $93.3m. (53% in Africa, 23% in Asia and the Pacific, 10% in the Near East, 7% in Europe, and 7% in Latin America and the Caribbean).

### INFORMATION

FAO functions as an information centre, collecting, analysing, interpreting and disseminating information through various media, including an extensive internet site. It issues regular statistical reports, commodity studies, and technical manuals in local languages (see list of publications below). Other materials produced by the FAO include information booklets, reference papers, reports of meetings, training manuals and audiovisuals.

FAO compiles and co-ordinates an extensive range of international databases on agriculture, fisheries, forestry, food and statistics, the most important of these being AGRIS (the International Information System for the Agricultural Sciences and Technology) and CARIS (the Current Agricultural Research Information System). Statistical databases include the GLOBEFISH databank and electronic library, FISHDAB (the Fisheries Statistical Database), FORIS (Forest Resources Information System), and GIS (the Geographic Information System). In addition, AGROSTAT PC has been designed to provide access to updated figures in six agriculture-related topics via personal computer. In 1996 FAO established a World Agricultural Information Centre (WAICENT), which offers wide access to agricultural data through the electronic media.

## FAO Councils and Commissions

(Based at the Rome headquarters unless otherwise indicated.)

**African Commission on Agricultural Statistics:** c/o FAO Regional Office for Africa, POB 1628, Accra, Ghana: f. 1961 to advise member countries on the development and standardization of food and agricultural statistics; 37 member states.

**African Forestry and Wildlife Commission:** f. 1959 to advise on the formulation of forest policy and to review and co-ordinate its implementation on a regional level; to exchange information and advise on technical problems; 42 member states.

**Asia and Pacific Commission on Agricultural Statistics:** c/o FAO Regional Office, Maliwan Mansion, Phra Atit Rd, Bangkok 10200, Thailand; f. 1962 to review the state of food and agricultural statistics in the region and to advise member countries on the development and standardization of agricultural statistics; 25 member states.

**Asia and Pacific Plant Protection Commission:** c/o FAO Regional Office, Maliwan Mansion, Phra Atit Rd, Bangkok 10200, Thailand; f. 1956 (new title 1983) to strengthen international co-operation in plant protection to prevent the introduction and spread of destructive plant diseases and pests; 25 member states.

**Asia-Pacific Fishery Commission:** c/o FAO Regional Office, Maliwan Mansion, Phra Atit Rd, Bangkok 10200, Thailand; f. 1948 to develop fisheries, encourage and co-ordinate research, disseminate information, recommend projects to governments, propose standards in technique and management measures; 20 member states.

**Asia-Pacific Forestry Commission:** f. 1949 to advise on the formulation of forest policy, and review and co-ordinate its implementation throughout the region; to exchange information and advise on technical problems; 29 member states.

**Caribbean Plant Protection Commission:** f. 1967 to preserve the existing plant resources of the area.

**Commission on African Animal Trypanosomiasis:** f. 1979 to develop and implement programmes to combat this disease; 39 member states.

**Commission for Controlling the Desert Locust in the Eastern Region of its Distribution Area in South West Asia:** f. 1964 to carry out all possible measures to control plagues of the desert locust in Afghanistan, India, Iran and Pakistan.

**Commission for Controlling the Desert Locust in the Near East:** c/o FAO Regional Office for the Near East, POB 2223, Cairo, Egypt; f. 1967 to promote national and international research and action with respect to the control of the desert locust in the Near East.

**Commission for Controlling the Desert Locust in North-West Africa:** f. 1971 to promote research on control of the desert locust in NW Africa.

**Commission on Fertilizers:** f. 1973 to provide guidance on the effective distribution and use of fertilizers.

**Commission for Inland Fisheries of Latin America:** f. 1976 to promote, co-ordinate and assist national and regional fishery and limnological surveys and programmes of research and development leading to the rational utilization of inland fishery resources.

**Commission on Plant Genetic Resources:** f. 1983 to provide advice on programmes dealing with crop improvement through plant genetic resources.

**European Commission on Agriculture:** f. 1949 to encourage and facilitate action and co-operation in technological agricultural problems among member states and between international organizations concerned with agricultural technology in Europe.

**European Commission for the Control of Foot-and-Mouth Disease:** f. 1953 to promote national and international action for the control of the disease in Europe and its final eradication.

**European Forestry Commission:** f. 1947 to advise on the formulation of forest policy and to review and co-ordinate its implementation on a regional level; to exchange information and to make recommendations; 27 member states.

**European Inland Fisheries Advisory Commission:** f. 1957 to promote improvements in inland fisheries and to advise member governments and FAO on inland fishery matters.

**FAO Regional Commission on Farm Management for Asia and the Far East:** c/o FAO Regional Office, Maliwan Mansion, Phra Atit Rd, Bangkok 10200, Thailand; f. 1959 to stimulate and co-ordinate farm management research and extension activities and to serve as a clearing-house for the exchange of information and experience among the member countries in the region.

**FAO/WHO Codex Alimentarius Commission:** f. 1962 to make proposals for the co-ordination of all international food standards work and to publish a code of international food standards; 158 member states.

**General Fisheries Council for the Mediterranean—GFCM:** f. 1952 to develop aquatic resources, to encourage and co-ordinate research in the fishing and allied industries, to assemble and publish information, and to recommend the standardization of equipment, techniques and nomenclature.

**Indian Ocean Fishery Commission:** f. 1967 to promote national programmes, research and development activities, and to examine management problems; 41 member states.

**International Poplar Commission:** f. 1947 to study scientific, technical, social and economic aspects of poplar and willow cultivation; to promote the exchange of ideas and material between research workers, producers and users; to arrange joint research programmes, congresses, study tours; to make recommendations to the FAO Conference and to National Poplar Commissions.

**International Rice Commission:** f. 1948 to promote national and international action on production, conservation, distribution and consumption of rice, except matters relating to international trade; 61 member states.

**Joint FAO/WHO/OAU Regional Food and Nutrition Commission for Africa:** c/o FAO Regional Office for Africa, POB 1628, Accra, Ghana; f. 1962 to provide liaison in matters concerning food and nutrition, and to review food and nutritional problems in Africa; 43 member states.

**Latin American and Caribbean Forestry Commission:** f. 1948 to advise on formulation of forest policy and review and co-ordinate its implementation throughout the region; to exchange information and advise on technical problems; 31 member states.

**Near East Forestry Commission:** f. 1953 to advise on formulation of forest policy and review and co-ordinate its implementation throughout the region; to exchange information and advise on technical problems; 20 member states.

**Near East Regional Commission on Agriculture:** c/o FAO Regional Office, POB 2223, Cairo, Egypt; f. 1983 to conduct periodic reviews of agricultural problems in the region; to promote the formulation and implementation of regional and national policies and programmes for improving production of crops and livestock; to strengthen the management of crops, livestock and supporting services and research; to promote the transfer of technology and regional technical co-operation; and to provide guidance on training and human resources development.

**North American Forestry Commission:** f. 1959 to advise on the formulation and co-ordination of national forest policies in Canada, Mexico and the USA; to exchange information and to advise on technical problems; three member states.

**Regional Animal Production and Health Commission for Asia and the Pacific:** c/o FAO Regional Office, Maliwan Mansion, Phra Atit Rd, Bangkok 10200, Thailand; f. 1973 to promote livestock development in general, and national and international research and action with respect to animal health and husbandry problems in the region; 14 member states.

**Regional Commission on Land and Water Use in the Near East:** f. 1967 to review the current situation with regard to land and water use in the region; to identify the main problems concerning the development of land and water resources which require research and study and to consider other related matters.

**Regional Fisheries Advisory Commission for the Southwest Atlantic:** f. 1961 to advise FAO on fisheries in the South-west Atlantic area, to advise member countries (Argentina, Brazil and Uruguay) on the administration and rational exploitation of marine and inland resources; to assist in the collection and dissemination of data, in training, and to promote liaison and co-operation.

**Western Central Atlantic Fishery Commission:** f. 1973 to assist international co-operation for the conservation, development and utilization of the living resources, especially shrimps, of the Western Central Atlantic.

## Finance

FAO's Regular Programme, which is financed by contributions from member governments, covers the cost of the FAO's Secretariat, its Technical Co-operation Programme (TCP) and part of the cost of several special action programmes. The budget for the two years 2000–2001 was maintained at US $650m., the same amount as was approved for the previous biennium. Much of FAO's technical assistance programme is funded from extra-budgetary sources. The single largest contributor is the United Nations Development Programme (UNDP), which in 1998 accounted for $33m., or 12% of field project expenditures. More important are the trust funds that come mainly from donor countries and international financing institutions. They totalled $208m., or 75% of field project expenditures in 1998. FAO's contribution under the TCP (FAO's regular budgetary funds for the Field Programme) was $34m., or 12% of field project expenditures, while the Organization's contribution under the Special Programme for Food Security was $3m., or some 1% of the total $278m.

## Publications

*Animal Health Yearbook.*
*Commodity Review and Outlook* (annually).
*Environment and Energy Bulletin.*
*Fertilizer Yearbook.*
*Food Crops and Shortages* (6 a year).
*Food Outlook* (5 a year).
*Plant Protection Bulletin* (quarterly).
*Production Yearbook.*
*Quarterly Bulletin of Statistics.*
*The State of Food and Agriculture* (annually).
*The State of World Fisheries and Aquaculture* (annually).
*The State of the World's Forests* (every 2 years).
*Trade Yearbook.*
*Unasylva* (quarterly).
*Yearbook of Fishery Statistics.*
*Yearbook of Forest Products.*
*World Animal Review* (quarterly).
*World Watch List for Domestic Animal Diversity.*
Commodity reviews; studies; manuals.

# International Atomic Energy Agency—IAEA

**Address:** POB 100, Wagramerstrasse 5, 1400 Vienna, Austria.
**Telephone:** (1) 26000; **fax:** (1) 26007; **e-mail:** official.mail@iaea.org; **internet:** www.iaea.or.at.

The International Atomic Energy Agency (IAEA) is an intergovernmental organization, established in 1957 in accordance with a decision of the General Assembly of the United Nations. Although it is autonomous, the IAEA is administratively a member of the United Nations, and reports on its activities once a year to the UN General Assembly. Its main objectives are to enlarge the contribution of atomic energy to peace, health and prosperity throughout the world and to ensure, so far as it is able, that assistance provided by it or at its request or under its supervision or control is not used in such a way as to further any military purpose.

### MEMBERS

131 members: see Table on pp. 114–116.

## Organization

(December 1999)

### GENERAL CONFERENCE

The Conference, comprising representatives of all member states, convenes each year for general debate on the Agency's policy, budget and programme. It elects members to the Board of Governors, and approves the appointment of the Director-General; it admits new member states.

### BOARD OF GOVERNORS

The Board of Governors consists of 35 member states: 22 elected by the General Conference for two-year periods and 13 designated by the Board from among member states which are advanced in nuclear technology. It is the principal policy-making body of the Agency and is responsible to the General Conference. Under its own authority, the Board approves all safeguards agreements, important projects and safety standards. In 1999 the General Conference adopted a resolution on expanding the Board's membership to 43, to include 18 states designated as the most advanced in nuclear technology. The resolution required ratification by two-thirds of member states to come into effect.

### SECRETARIAT

The Secretariat, comprising about 2,100 staff, is headed by the Director-General, who is assisted by six Deputy Directors-General. The Secretariat is divided into six departments: Technical Co-operation; Nuclear Energy; Nuclear Safety; Nuclear Sciences and Applications; Safeguards; Administration. A Standing Advisory Group on Safeguards Implementation advises the Director-General on technical aspects of safeguards.

**Director-General:** Dr MOHAMMAD EL-BARADEI (Egypt).

## Activities

The IAEA's functions can be divided into two main categories: technical co-operation (assisting research on and practical application of atomic energy for peaceful uses); and safeguards (ensuring that special fissionable and other materials, services, equipment and information made available by the Agency or at its request or under its supervision are not used for any military purpose).

### TECHNICAL CO-OPERATION AND TRAINING

The IAEA provides assistance in the form of experts, training and equipment to technical co-operation projects and applications worldwide, with an emphasis on radiation protection and safety-related activities. Training is provided to scientists, and experts and lecturers are assigned to provide specialized help on specific nuclear applications.

### FOOD AND AGRICULTURE

In co-operation with FAO (q.v.), the Agency conducts programmes of applied research on the use of radiation and isotopes in fields including: efficiency in the use of water and fertilizers; improvement of food crops by induced mutations; eradication or control of destructive insects by the introduction of sterilized insects (radiation-based Sterile Insect Technique); improvement of livestock nutrition and health; studies on improving efficacy and reducing residues of pesticides, and increasing utilization of agricultural wastes; and food preservation by irradiation. The programmes are implemented by the Joint FAO/IAEA Division of Nuclear Techniques in Food and Agriculture and by the FAO/IAEA Agriculture Biotechnology Laboratory, based at Seibersdorf, Austria. A new laboratory at Seibersdorf, which was to serve as a Training and Reference Centre for food and pesticide-control activities, opened in mid-1999. The Centre was to support the implementation of national legislation and trade agreements ensuring the quality and safety of food products in international trade.

### LIFE SCIENCES

In co-operation with the World Health Organization (WHO, q.v.), IAEA promotes the use of nuclear techniques in medicine, biology and health-related environmental research, provides training, and conducts research on techniques for improving the accuracy of radiation dosimetry.

In 1999 IAEA/WHO Network of Secondary Standard Dosimetry Laboratories (SSDLs) comprised 87 laboratories in 58 member states. The Agency's Dosimetry Laboratory performs dose intercomparisons for both SSDLs and radiotherapy centres. The IAEA undertakes maintenance plans for nuclear laboratories; national programmes of quality control for nuclear medicine instruments; quality control of radioimmunoassay techniques; radiation sterilization of medical supplies; and improvement of cancer therapy.

### PHYSICAL SCIENCES AND LABORATORIES

The Agency's programme in physical sciences includes industrial applications of isotopes and radiation technology; application of nuclear techniques to mineral exploration and exploitation; radiopharmaceuticals; and hydrology, involving the use of isotope techniques for assessment of water resources. Nuclear data services are provided, and training is given for nuclear scientists from developing countries. The IAEA Laboratory at Seibersdorf, Austria, supports the Agency's research, radio-isotope and agriculture programmes, while the Safeguards Analytical Laboratory analyses nuclear fuel-cycle samples collected by IAEA safeguards inspectors. The IAEA Marine Environment Laboratory, in Monaco, studies radionuclides and other ocean pollutants. In July 1992 the EC, Japan, Russia and the USA signed an agreement to co-operate in the engineering design of an International Thermonuclear Experimental Reactor (ITER). The project aimed to demonstrate the scientific and technological feasibility of fusion energy, with the aim of providing a source of clean, abundant energy in the 21st century. An Extension Agreement, signed in 1998, provided for the continuation of the project.

### NUCLEAR POWER

At the end of 1998 there were 434 nuclear power plants in operation in 32 countries throughout the world, with a total generating capacity of 348,864 MW, providing about 17% of total electrical energy generated during the year. There were also 36 reactors under construction, in 14 countries. The Agency helps developing member states to introduce nuclear-powered electricity-generating plants through assistance with planning, feasibility studies, surveys of manpower and infrastructure, and safety measures. It publishes books on numerous aspects of nuclear power, and provides training courses on safety in nuclear power plants and other topics. An energy data bank collects and disseminates information on nuclear technology, and a power-reactor information system monitors the technical performance of nuclear power plants. There is increasing interest in the use of nuclear reactors for seawater desalination and radiation hydrology techniques to provide potable water.

### RADIOACTIVE WASTE MANAGEMENT

The Agency provides practical help to member states in the management of radioactive waste. The Waste Management Advisory Programme (WAMAP) was established in 1987, and undertakes advisory missions in member states. A code of practice to prevent the illegal dumping of radioactive waste was drafted in 1989, and another on the international trans-boundary movement of waste was drafted in 1990. A ban on the dumping of radioactive waste at sea came into effect in February 1994, under the Convention on the Prevention of Marine Pollution by Dumping of Wastes and Other Matters (see IMO, p. 90). The IAEA was to determine radioactive levels, for purposes of the Convention, and provide assistance to countries for the safe disposal of radioactive wastes.

In September 1997 a Joint Convention on the Safety of Spent Fuel Management and on the Safety of Radioactive Waste Management was opened for signature. The first internationally-binding legal device to address such issues, the Convention was to ensure the safe storage and disposal of nuclear and radioactive waste, during both the construction and operation of a nuclear power plant, as well as following its closure. The Convention was to come into force 90 days after being ratified by 25 member states, 15 of which were to be in possession of an operational nuclear reactor. By November 1999 40 states had signed the Convention, of which 13 had become parties to it.

## NUCLEAR SAFETY

The IAEA's nuclear safety programme encourages international co-operation in the exchange of information, promoting implementation of its safety standards and providing advisory safety services. It includes the IAEA International Nuclear Event Scale; the Incident Reporting System; an emergency preparedness programme; operational safety review teams; the 15-member International Nuclear Safety Advisory Group (INSAG); the Radiation Protection Advisory Team; and a safety research co-ordination programme. The safety review teams provide member states with advice on achieving and maintaining a high level of safety in the operation of nuclear power plants, while research programmes establish risk criteria for the nuclear fuel cycle and identify cost-effective means to reduce risks in energy systems. By the end of 1998 the review teams had conducted studies of operational safety at 100 plants. At that time 53 member states had agreed to report all nuclear events, incidents and accidents according to the International Nuclear Event Scale. In May the Director-General initiated a review of the Agency's nuclear strategy, proposing the development of national safety profiles, more active promotion of safety services and improved co-operation at governmental and non-governmental levels.

The revised edition of the Basic Safety Standards for Radiation Protection (IAEA Safety Series No. 9) was approved in 1994. The Nuclear Safety Standards programme, initiated in 1974 with five codes of practice and more than 60 safety guides, was revised in 1987 and again in 1995.

During 1998 there were some 250 technical co-operation projects under way in the field of nuclear safety and radiation protection. Missions visited about 50 countries to assist with radiation protection.

Following a serious accident at the Chornobyl (Chernobyl) nuclear power plant in Ukraine (then part of the USSR) in April 1986, two conventions were formulated by the IAEA and entered into force in October. The first, the Convention on Early Notification of a Nuclear Accident, commits parties to provide information about nuclear accidents with possible trans-boundary effects at the earliest opportunity (it had 84 parties by November 1999); and the second commits parties to endeavour to provide assistance in the event of a nuclear accident or radiological emergency (it had 79 parties by November 1999). During 1990 the IAEA organized an assessment of the consequences of the Chernobyl accident, undertaken by an international team of experts, who reported to an international conference on the effects of the accident, convened at the IAEA headquarters in Vienna in May 1991. In February 1993 INSAG published an updated report on the Chernobyl incident, which emphasized the role of design factors in the accident, and the need to implement safety measures in the RBMK-type reactor. In March 1994 an IAEA expert mission visited Chernobyl and reported continuing serious deficiencies in safety at the defunct reactor and the units remaining in operation. An international conference reviewing the radiological consequences of the accident, 10 years after the event, was held in April 1996, co-sponsored by the IAEA, WHO and the European Commission. Concerns over the reactor's safety persisted in 1998.

At the end of September 1999 the IAEA activated an Emergency Response Centre, following a serious incident at a fuel conversion facility in Tokaimura, Japan. The Centre was used to process information from the Japanese authorities and to ensure accurate reporting of the event. In mid-October a three-member IAEA team of experts visited the site to undertake a preliminary investigation into the causes and consequences of the accident.

An International Convention on Nuclear Safety was adopted at an IAEA conference in June 1994. The Convention applies to land-based civil nuclear power plants: adherents commit themselves to fundamental principles of safety, and maintain legislative frameworks governing nuclear safety. The Convention entered into force in October 1996, after having been signed by 65 states and ratified or otherwise approved by 26 states. The first Review Meeting of Contracting Parties to the Convention was held in mid-April 1999. By November 52 states had ratified the Convention.

In September 1997 more than 80 member states adopted a protocol to revise the 1963 Vienna Convention on Civil Liability for Nuclear Damage, fixing the minimum limit of liability for the operator of a nuclear reactor at 300m. Special Drawing Rights (SDRs, the accounting units of the IMF) in the event of an accident. The amended protocol also extended the length of time during which claims may be brought for loss of life or injury. The amended protocol had been signed by 14 countries and ratified by two by November 1999. A Convention on Supplementary Funding established a further compensatory fund to provide for the payment of damages following an accident; contributions to the Fund were to be calculated on the basis of the nuclear capacity of each member state. The Convention had 13 signatories and two contracting states by November 1999.

In July 1996 the IAEA co-ordinated a study on the radiological situation at the Mururoa and Fangatauta atolls, following the French nuclear test programmes in the South Pacific. Results published in May 1998 concluded there was no radiological health risk and that neither remedial action nor continued environmental monitoring was necessary.

## DISSEMINATION OF INFORMATION

The International Nuclear Information System (INIS), which was established in 1970, provides a computerized indexing and abstracting service. Information on the peaceful uses of atomic energy is collected by member states and international organizations and sent to the IAEA for processing and dissemination (see list of publications below). The IAEA also co-operates with the FAO in an information system for agriculture (AGRIS) and with the World Federation of Nuclear Medicine and Biology, and the non-profit Cochrane Collaboration, in maintaining an electronic database of best practice in nuclear medicine. The IAEA Nuclear Data Section provides cost-free data centre services and co-operates with other national and regional nuclear and atomic data centres in the systematic world-wide collection, compilation, dissemination and exchange of nuclear reaction data, nuclear structure and decay data, and atomic and molecular data for fusion.

## SAFEGUARDS

The Treaty on the Non-Proliferation of Nuclear Weapons (known also as the Non-Proliferation Treaty or NPT), which entered into force in 1970, requires each non-nuclear-weapon state (one which had not manufactured and exploded a nuclear weapon or other nuclear explosive device prior to 1 January 1967) which is a party to the Treaty to conclude a safeguards agreement with the IAEA. Under such an agreement, the state undertakes to accept IAEA safeguards on all nuclear material in all its peaceful nuclear activities for the purpose of verifying that such material is not diverted to nuclear weapons or other nuclear explosive devices. In May 1995 the Review and Extension Conference of parties to the NPT agreed to extend the NPT indefinitely, and reaffirmed support for the IAEA's role in verification and the transfer of peaceful nuclear technologies. By June 1998 181 non-nuclear-weapon states and the five nuclear-weapon states had ratified and acceded to the Treaty, but a number of non-nuclear-weapon states had not complied, within the prescribed time-limit, with their obligations under the Treaty regarding the conclusion of the relevant safeguards agreement with the Agency.

Five nuclear-weapon states, the People's Republic of China, France, Russia, the United Kingdom and the USA, have concluded safeguards agreements with the Agency that permit the application of IAEA safeguards to all their nuclear activities, excluding those with 'direct national significance'. A Comprehensive Nuclear Test Ban Treaty (CTBT) was opened for signature in September 1996, having been adopted by the UN General Assembly. The Treaty was to enter into international law upon ratification by all 44 nations with known nuclear capabilities. A separate verification organization was to be established, based in Vienna. A Preparatory Commission for the treaty organization became operational in 1997. By June 1999 152 countries had signed the CTBT and 37 had ratified it, including 18 of the 44 states with nuclear capabilities. However, in October 1999 the US Senate rejected ratification of the CTBT.

The IAEA administers full applications of safeguards in relation to the Treaty for the prohibition of Nuclear Weapons in Latin America (Tlatelolco Treaty). By late 1998 31 of the 32 states party to the Tlatelolco Treaty had concluded safeguards agreements with the IAEA, as had all 11 signatories of the South Pacific Nuclear-Free Zone Treaty (Rarotonga Treaty). NPT safeguards agreements were in force with seven of the nine States party to the Treaty in the South-East Asia Nuclear-Weapon Free Zone (Treaty of Bangkok). In April 1996 an African Nuclear-Weapon Free Zone Treaty (the Pelindaba Treaty) was signed by 43 states at a ceremony in Cairo, Egypt. The IAEA provided technical and legal advice during the negotiations on the Treaty, which committed countries to renouncing the development, acquisition, testing or stationing of nuclear arms on their territories and prohibited all dumping of imported radioactive waste. The Treaty, as with the NPT and the other regional treaties, required and relied upon the IAEA safeguards systems. At the end of 1998 safeguards agreements were in force with 138 states. Of these, 69 states had declared nuclear activities and were under inspection.

In April 1992 the Democratic People's Republic of Korea (DPRK) ratified a safeguards agreement with the IAEA. In late 1992 and early 1993, however, the IAEA unsuccessfully requested access to two non-declared sites in the DPRK, where it was suspected that material capable of being used for the manufacture of nuclear weapons was stored. In March 1993 the DPRK announced its intention of withdrawing from the NPT: it suspended its withdrawal in June, but continued to refuse full access to its nuclear facilities for IAEA inspectors. In May 1994 the DPRK began to refuel an experimental nuclear power reactor at Yongbyon, but refused to allow the IAEA to analyse the spent fuel rods in order to ascertain whether plutonium had been obtained from the reactor for possible military use. In June the IAEA Board of Governors halted IAEA technical assistance to the DPRK (except medical assistance) because of continuous violation of the NPT safeguards agreements. In the same month the DPRK withdrew from the IAEA (though not from the NPT): however, it allowed IAEA inspectors to remain at the Yongbyon site to conduct safeguards activites. In October the Governments of the DPRK and the USA concluded an agreement whereby the former agreed to halt construction of two new nuclear reactors, on condition that it received international aid for the construction of two 'light water' reactors (which could not produce materials for the manufacture of nuclear weapons). The DPRK also agreed to allow IAEA inspections of all its nuclear sites, but only after the installation of one of the 'light water' reactors had been completed, a time lapse of at least five years. In November IAEA inspectors visited the DPRK to initiate verification of the suspension of the country's nuclear programme, in accordance with the agreement concluded in the previous month. Since 1995 the IAEA has pursued technical discussions with the DPRK authorities as part of the Agency's efforts to achieve the full compliance of the DPRK with the IAEA safeguards agreement. By the end of 1999 the canning of spent fuel rods from the Yongbyon nuclear power reactor was completed. However, little overall progress had been achieved, owing to the obstruction of inspectors by the authorities in that country, including their refusal to provide samples for analysis. The IAEA was unable to verify the suspension of the nuclear programme and declared that the DPRK continued to be in non-compliance with its NPT safeguards agreement. In March 1999 the USA concluded an accord with the DPRK to provide for inspection of a suspected nuclear facility near Yongbyon. Further negotiations were to be pursued to restrict the country's missile production programme.

In April 1991 the UN Security Council requested the IAEA to conduct investigations into Iraq's capacity to produce nuclear weapons, following the end of the war between Iraq and the UN-authorized, US-led multinational force. The IAEA was to work closely with a UN Special Commission of experts (UNSCOM, q.v.), established by the Security Council, whose task was to inspect and dismantle Iraq's weapons of mass destruction (including chemical and biological weapons). In July the IAEA declared that Iraq had violated its safeguards agreement with the IAEA by not submitting nuclear material and relevant facilities in its uranium-enrichment programme to the Agency's inspection. This was the first time that a state party to the NPT had been condemned for concealing a programme of this nature. In October the sixth inspection team, composed of UNSCOM and representatives of the IAEA, was reported to have obtained conclusive documentary evidence that Iraq had a programme for developing nuclear weapons. By February 1994 all declared stocks of nuclear-weapons-grade material had been removed from Iraq. Subsequently, the IAEA pursued a programme of long-term surveillance of nuclear activity in Iraq, under a mandate issued by the UN Security Council. In September 1996 Iraq submitted to the IAEA a 'full, final and complete' declaration of its nuclear activities. However, in September–October 1997 the IAEA recommended that Iraq disclose further equipment, materials and information relating to its nuclear programme. In April 1998 IAEA technical experts were part of a special group that entered eight presidential sites in Iraq to collect baseline data, in accordance with a Memorandum of Understanding concluded between the UN Secretary-General and the Iraqi authorities in February. The accord aimed to ensure full Iraqi co-operation with UNSCOM and IAEA personnel. In August, however, Iraq suspended co-operation with UN inspectors, which prevented IAEA from implementing its programme of ongoing monitoring and verification (OMV) activities. Iraq's action was condemned by the IAEA General Conference in September. In October IAEA reported that while there was no evidence of Iraq having produced nuclear weapons or having retained or obtained a capability for the production of nuclear weapons, the Agency was unable to guarantee that all items had been found. All IAEA inspectors were temporarily relocated from Iraq to Bahrain in November, in accordance with a decision to withdraw UNSCOM personnel owing to Iraq's failure to agree to resume co-operation.

In late 1997 the IAEA began inspections in the USA to verify the conversion for peaceful uses of nuclear material released from the military sector. In 1998 the United Kingdom announced that substantial quantities of nuclear material previously in its military programme would become available for verification under its voluntary offer safeguards agreement.

At the end of 1998 there were 1,085 nuclear facilities and locations containing nuclear material subject to IAEA safeguards. Of these, 636 were inspected in 1998, in a total of 2,507 inspections. Expenditure on the Safeguards Regular Budget for that year was US $98.5m., including extrabudgetary funds of $18.2m.

In June 1995 the Board of Governors approved measures to strengthen the safeguards system, including allowing inspection teams greater access to suspected nuclear sites and to information on nuclear activities in member states, reducing the notice time for inspections by removing visa requirements for inspectors and using environmental monitoring (i.e. soil, water and air samples) to test for signs of radioactivity. In April 1996 the IAEA initiated a programme to prevent and combat illicit trafficking of nuclear weapons, and in May 1998 the IAEA and the World Customs Organization (q.v.) signed a Memorandum of Understanding to enhance co-operation in the prevention of illicit nuclear trafficking. In May 1997 the Board of Governors adopted a protocol approving measures to strengthen safeguards further, in order to ensure the compliance of non-nuclear-weapon states with IAEA commitments. The new protocol compelled member states to provide inspection teams with improved access to information concerning existing and planned nuclear activities, and to allow access to locations other than known nuclear sites within that country's territory. The protocol was opened for signature in September 1997 and had 35 signatories by mid-January 1999.

### NUCLEAR FUEL CYCLE

The Agency promotes the exchange of information between member states on technical, safety, environmental, and economic aspects of nuclear fuel cycle technology, including uranium prospecting and the treatment and disposal of radioactive waste; it provides assistance to member states in the planning, implementation and operation of nuclear fuel cycle facilities and assists in the development of advanced nuclear fuel cycle technology. Every two years, in collaboration with the OECD, the Agency prepares estimates of world uranium resources, demand and production.

## Finance

The Agency is financed by regular and voluntary contributions from member states. Expenditure approved under the regular budget for 2000 amounted to some US $221.7m., and the target for voluntary contributions to finance the IAEA technical assistance and co-operation programme in 2000 was $73m.

## Publications

*Annual Report.*
*IAEA Bulletin* (quarterly).
*IAEA Newsbriefs* (every 2 months).
*IAEA Yearbook.*
*INIS Atomindex* (bibliography, 2 a month).
*INIS Reference Series.*
*INSAG Series.*
*Legal Series.*
*Meetings on Atomic Energy* (quarterly).
*The Nuclear Fuel Cycle Information System: A Directory of Nuclear Fuel Cycle Facilities.*
*Nuclear Fusion* (monthly).
*Nuclear Safety Review* (annually).
*Panel Proceedings Series.*
*Publications Catalogue* (annually).
*Safety Series.*
*Technical Directories.*
*Technical Reports Series.*

# International Bank for Reconstruction and Development—IBRD (World Bank)

**Address:** 1818 H St, NW, Washington, DC 20433, USA.

**Telephone:** (202) 477-1234; **fax:** (202) 477-6391; **e-mail:** pic@worldbank.org; **internet:** www.worldbank.org.

The IBRD was established in December 1945. Initially it was concerned with post-war reconstruction in Europe; since then its aim has been to assist the economic development of member nations by making loans where private capital is not available on reasonable terms to finance productive investments. Loans are made either direct to governments, or to private enterprises with the guarantee of their governments. The World Bank, as it is commonly known, comprises the IBRD and the International Development Association (IDA, q.v.). The affiliated group of institutions, comprising the IBRD, the IDA, the International Finance Corporation (IFC, q.v.), the Multilateral Investment Guarantee Agency (MIGA, q.v.) and the International Centre for Settlement of Investment Disputes (ICSID, see below), is now referred to as the World Bank Group.

### MEMBERS

There are 181 members: see Table on pp. 114–116. Only members of the International Monetary Fund (IMF, q.v.) may be considered for membership in the World Bank. Subscriptions to the capital stock of the Bank are based on each member's quota in the IMF, which is designed to reflect the country's relative economic strength. Voting rights are related to shareholdings.

## Organization

(December 1999)

Officers and staff of the IBRD serve concurrently as officers and staff in the IDA. The World Bank has offices in Brussels, New York, Paris, London and Tokyo; regional missions in Nairobi (for eastern Africa) and Abidjan (for western Africa); and resident missions in more than 70 countries.

### BOARD OF GOVERNORS

The Board of Governors consists of one Governor appointed by each member nation. Typically, a Governor is the country's finance minister, central bank governor, or a minister or an official of comparable rank. The Board normally meets once a year.

### EXECUTIVE DIRECTORS

With the exception of certain powers specifically reserved to them by the Articles of Agreement, the Governors of the Bank have delegated their powers for the conduct of the general operations of the World Bank to a Board of Executive Directors which performs its duties on a full-time basis at the Bank's headquarters. There are 24 Executive Directors (see table below); each Director selects an Alternate. Five Directors are appointed by the five members having the largest number of shares of capital stock, and the rest are elected by the Governors representing the other members. The President of the Bank is Chairman of the Board.

The Executive Directors fulfil dual responsibilities. First, they represent the interests of their country or groups of countries. Second, they exercise their authority as delegated by the Governors in overseeing the policies of the Bank and evaluating completed projects. Since the Bank operates on the basis of consensus (formal votes are rare), this dual role involves frequent communication and consultations with governments so as to reflect accurately their views in Board discussions.

The Directors consider and decide on Bank policy and on all loan and credit proposals. They are also responsible for presentation to the Board of Governors at its Annual Meetings of an audit of accounts, an administrative budget, the *Annual Report* on the operations and policies of the World Bank, and any other matter that, in their judgement, requires submission to the Board of Governors. Matters may be submitted to the Governors at the Annual Meetings or at any time between Annual Meetings.

### OFFICE OF THE PRESIDENT

**President and Chairman of Executive Directors:** JAMES D. WOLFENSOHN (USA).

**Managing Directors:** SVEN SANDSTRÖM (Sweden), SHENGMAN ZHANG (People's Republic of China), PETER L. WOICKE (Germany), JEFFREY GOLDSTEIN (USA), Dr MAMPHELA RAMPHELE (South Africa) (designate).

**Corporate Secretary:** CHEIKH IBRAHIMA FALL (Senegal).

### OFFICES

**New York Office and World Bank Mission to the United Nations:** 809 United Nations Plaza, Suite 900, New York, NY 10017, USA; Special Rep. to UN CARLSTON B. BOUCHER.

**European Office:** 66 ave d'Iéna, 75116 Paris, France.

**Brussels Office:** 10 rue Montoyer, bte 16, 1000 Brussels, Belgium.

**London Office:** New Zealand House, 15th Floor, Haymarket, London, SW1Y 4TE, United Kingdom; Special Rep. to the UK, Ireland and OECD ANDREW ROGERSON.

**Regional Mission in Eastern Africa:** POB 30577, Nairobi; Hill Park Bldg, Upper Hill, Nairobi, Kenya; Chief HAROLD E. WACKMAN.

**Regional Mission in Western Africa:** angle rues Booker Washington/Jacques Aka, Cocody, BP 1850, Abidjan 01, Côte d'Ivoire; Chief SHIGEO KATSU.

**Tokyo Office:** Fukoku Seimei Bldg, 10th Floor, 2-2-2 Uchisaiwaicho, Chiyoda-ku, Tokyo 100-0011, Japan; Dir SHUZO NAKAMURA.

## Activities

### FINANCIAL OPERATIONS

IBRD capital is derived from members' subscriptions to capital shares, the calculation of which is based on their quotas in the International Monetary Fund (q.v.). At 30 June 1999 the total subscribed capital of the IBRD was US $188,220m., of which the paid-in portion was $11,395m. (6.1%); the remainder is subject to call if required. Most of the IBRD's lendable funds come from its borrowing, on commercial terms, in world capital markets, and also from its retained earnings and the flow of repayments on its loans. IBRD loans carry a variable interest rate, rather than a rate fixed at the time of borrowing.

IBRD loans usually have a 'grace period' of five years and are repayable over 15 years or fewer. Loans are made to governments, or must be guaranteed by the government concerned, and are normally made for projects likely to offer a commercially viable rate of return. In 1980 the World Bank introduced structural adjustment lending, which (instead of financing specific projects) supports programmes and changes necessary to modify the structure of an economy so that it can restore or maintain its growth and viability in its balance of payments over the medium term.

The IBRD and IDA together made 276 new lending and investment commitments totalling US $28,994.1m. during the year ending 30 June 1999, compared with 286 (amounting to $28,593.9m.) in the previous year. During 1998/99 the IBRD alone approved commitments totalling $22,182.3m. (compared with $21,086.2m. in the previous year), of which $8,754.8m. was allocated to East Asia and the Pacific and $7,133.3m. to Latin America and the Caribbean (see table). The largest borrower of IBRD funds in 1998/99 was Argentina ($3,226m. for eight projects), followed by Indonesia ($2,605m. for 10 projects) and the Republic of Korea ($2,048m. for two projects). Disbursements by the IBRD in the year ending 30 June 1999 amounted to $18,205m., compared with $19,232m. in the previous year. (For details of IDA operations, see separate chapter on IDA.)

IBRD operations are supported by medium- and long-term borrowings in international capital markets. During the year ending 30 June 1999 the IBRD's net income amounted to US $1,518m.

The World Bank's primary objectives are the achievement of sustainable economic growth and the reduction of poverty in developing countries. In the context of stimulating economic growth the Bank promotes both private-sector development and human resource development and has attempted to respond to the growing demands by developing countries for assistance in these areas. The Bank's efforts to reduce poverty comprise two main elements: the compiling of country-specific assessments and the formulation of country assistance strategies (CASs) to review and guide the Bank's country programmes. Since August 1998 the Bank has published CASs, with the approval of the government concerned. In 1996/97 the Bank established a Poverty Sector Board, within the Poverty Reduction and Economic Management Network (see below), to direct the implementation of its poverty reduction efforts. A Committee on Development Effectiveness addresses issues relating to the relevance and effectiveness of operations and monitors implementation of decisions taken by the Board of Governors on these matters.

In March 1997 the Board of Executive Directors endorsed a 'Strategic Compact', providing for a programme of reforms, to be implemented over a period of 30 months, to increase the effectiveness of the Bank in achieving its central objective of poverty reduction.

**EXECUTIVE DIRECTORS AND THEIR VOTING POWER** (30 June 1999)

| Executive Director | Casting Votes of | IBRD Total votes | IBRD % of total | IDA Total votes | IDA % of total |
|---|---|---|---|---|---|
| **Appointed:** | | | | | |
| JAN PIERCY | USA | 265,219 | 16.53 | 1,745,962 | 14.99 |
| SATORU MIYAMURA | Japan | 127,250 | 7.93 | 1,252,764 | 10.75 |
| HELMUT SCHAFFER | Germany | 72,649 | 4.53 | 820,259 | 7.04 |
| JEAN-CLAUDE MILLERON | France | 69,647 | 4.34 | 497,297 | 4.27 |
| STEPHEN PICKFORD | United Kingdom | 69,647 | 4.34 | 582,514 | 5.00 |
| **Elected:** | | | | | |
| RUTH BACHMAYER (Austria) | Austria, Belarus*, Belgium, Czech Republic, Hungary, Kazakhstan, Luxembourg, Slovakia, Slovenia, Turkey | 76,720 | 4.78 | 498,386 | 4.28 |
| PIETER STEK (Netherlands) | Armenia, Bosnia and Herzegovina, Bulgaria*, Croatia, Cyprus, Georgia, Israel, the former Yugoslav republic of Macedonia, Moldova, Netherlands, Romania*, Ukraine* | 72,208 | 4.50 | 420,880 | 3.61 |
| FEDERICO FERRER (Spain) | Costa Rica, El Salvador, Guatemala, Honduras, Mexico, Nicaragua, Panama, Spain, Venezuela* | 68,475 | 4.27 | 244,522 | 2.10 |
| TERRIE O'LEARY (Canada) | Antigua and Barbuda*, The Bahamas*, Barbados*, Belize, Canada, Dominica, Grenada, Guyana, Ireland, Jamaica*, Saint Christopher and Nevis, Saint Lucia, Saint Vincent and the Grenadines | 62,217 | 3.88 | 478,284 | 4.11 |
| MURILO PORTUGAL (Brazil) | Brazil, Colombia, Dominican Republic, Ecuador, Haiti, Philippines, Suriname*, Trinidad and Tobago | 58,124 | 3.62 | 330,694 | 2.84 |
| NEIL HYDEN (Australia)† | Australia, Cambodia, Kiribati, Republic of Korea, Marshall Islands, Federated States of Micronesia, Mongolia, New Zealand, Papua New Guinea, Samoa, Solomon Islands, Vanuatu | 55,800 | 3.48 | 342,480 | 2.94 |
| GODFREY GAOSEB (Namibia) | Angola, Botswana, Burundi, Eritrea, Ethiopia, The Gambia, Kenya, Lesotho, Liberia, Malawi, Mozambique, Namibia*, Nigeria, Seychelles*, Sierra Leone, South Africa, Sudan, Swaziland, Tanzania, Uganda, Zambia, Zimbabwe | 55,190 | 3.44 | 465,400 | 4.00 |
| FRANCO PASSACANTANDO (Italy) | Albania, Greece, Italy, Malta*, Portugal | 55,093 | 3.43 | 458,030 | 3.93 |
| B. P. SINGH (India)† | Bangladesh, Bhutan, India, Sri Lanka | 54,945 | 3.43 | 496,937 | 4.27 |
| INAAMUL HAQUE (Pakistan) | Algeria, Ghana, Iran, Iraq, Morocco, Pakistan, Tunisia | 54,052 | 3.37 | 237,322 | 2.04 |
| ILKKA NIEMI (Finland) | Denmark, Estonia*, Finland, Iceland, Latvia, Lithuania*, Norway, Sweden | 50,839 | 3.17 | 565,573 | 4.86 |
| MATTHIAS MEYER (Switzerland) | Azerbaijan, Kyrgyzstan, Poland, Switzerland, Tajikistan, Turkmenistan*, Uzbekistan | 46,096 | 2.87 | 404,736 | 3.47 |
| ZHU XIAN | People's Republic of China | 45,049 | 2.81 | 219,696 | 1.89 |
| KHALID H. ALYAHYA | Saudi Arabia | 45,045 | 2.81 | 412,982 | 3.55 |
| ANDREI BUGROV | Russia | 45,045 | 2.81 | 31,593 | 0.27 |
| KHALID AL-SAAD (Kuwait) | Bahrain*, Egypt, Jordan, Kuwait, Lebanon, Libya, Maldives, Oman, Qatar*, Syria, United Arab Emirates, Yemen | 43,984 | 2.74 | 262,432 | 2.25 |
| JANNES HUTAGALUNG (Indonesia) | Brunei*, Fiji, Indonesia, Laos, Malaysia, Myanmar, Nepal, Singapore*, Thailand, Tonga, Viet Nam | 41,096 | 2.56 | 311,463 | 2.67 |
| VALERIANO F. GARCÍA (Argentina) | Argentina, Bolivia, Chile, Paraguay, Peru, Uruguay* | 37,499 | 2.34 | 220,223 | 1.89 |
| BASSARY TOURÉ (Mali) | Benin, Burkina Faso, Cameroon, Cape Verde, Central African Republic, Chad, Comoros, Democratic Republic of the Congo, Republic of the Congo, Côte d'Ivoire, Djibouti, Equatorial Guinea, Gabon, Guinea, Guinea-Bissau, Madagascar, Mali, Mauritania, Mauritius, Niger, Rwanda, São Tomé and Príncipe, Senegal, Togo | 32,252 | 2.01 | 348,156 | 2.99 |

Note: Afghanistan (550 votes in IBRD and 13,557 in IDA) and Somalia (802 votes in IBRD and 10,506 in IDA) did not participate in the 1998 regular election of Executive Directors; Palau (266 votes in IBRD and 504 in IDA) became a member after that election.
* Member of IBRD only (not IDA).
† Took office 1 August 1999.

The reforms, which aimed to increase the proportion of projects rated as satisfactory in development terms from 66% to 75% included greater decentralization of decision-making, and investment in front-line operations, enhancing the administration of loans, and improving access to information and co-ordination of Bank activities through a knowledge management system comprising four thematic networks: the Human Development Network; the Environmentally and Socially Sustainable Development Network; the Finance, Private Sector and Infrastructure Development Network; and the Poverty Reduction and Economic Management Network. In July the World Bank initiated a review to assess the economic and social impact of its work in developing countries. During 1997/98 the extreme financial difficulties confronting several Asian economies tested the Bank's capactity to respond effectively to major financial challenges and accelerated its process of internal reform. A Special Financial Operations Unit was established to help to alleviate the consequences of the crisis in all affected countries, while collaboration with external partners was enhanced. In 1998/99 the Bank's Executive Directors endorsed a Comprehensive Development Framework (CDF) to effect a new approach to development assistance based on partnerships and country responsibility, with an emphasis on the interdependence of the social, structural, human, governmental, economic and environmental elements of development. The Framework, which aimed to enhance the overall effectiveness of development assistance, was formulated after a series of consultative meetings, organized by the Bank and attended by representatives of governments, donor agencies, financial institutions, non-governmental organizations, the private sector and academics. By June 1999 12 countries were implementing pilot projects based on the CDF concept.

In June 1995 the World Bank joined other international donors (including regional development banks, other UN bodies, Canada, France, the Netherlands and the USA) in establishing a Consultative Group to Assist the Poorest (CGAP), which was to channel funds to the most needy through grass-roots agencies. An initial credit of approximately US $200m. was committed by the donors. The Bank manages the CGAP Secretariat, which is responsible for the administration of external funding and for the evaluation and approval of project financing. In addition, the CGAP was to provide training and information services on microfinance for policy-makers and practitioners.

In September 1996 the World Bank/IMF Development Committee endorsed a joint initiative to assist heavily indebted poor countries (HIPCs) to reduce their debt burden to a sustainable level, in order to make more resources available for poverty reduction and economic growth. A new Trust Fund was established by the World Bank in

November to finance the initiative. The Fund, consisting of an initial allocation of US $500m. from the IBRD surplus and other contributions from multilateral creditors, was to be administered by IDA. Of the 41 HIPCs identified by the Bank, 33 were in sub-Saharan Africa. In the majority of cases a sustainable level of debt was targeted at 200%–250% of the net present value (NPV) of the debt in relation to total annual exports. Other countries with a lower debt-to-export ratio were to be eligible for assistance under the initiative, providing that their export earnings were more than 40% of GDP and government revenue at least 20% of GDP. In April 1997 the World Bank and the IMF announced that Uganda was to be the first beneficiary of the initiative, enabling the Ugandan Government to reduce its external debt by some 20%, or an estimated $338m. The Bank's approved loan of $160m. was to be disbursed in April 1998, conditional on the contribution by other official creditors and multinational institutions of their share of the debt relief and on Uganda's pursuing its programme of economic and social development reforms. A grant of $75m. was to be made available to the Ugandan authorities in the interim year. In September 1997 assistance valued at $448m. in NPV terms (as at the 'completion point' of the process to ensure eligibility to receive debt relief) was approved for Bolivia, of which the Bank's share totalled $54m. In the same month assistance amounting to $115m., with $44m. to be provided by the Bank, was approved for Burkina Faso. A package of assistance totalling $256m. was approved for Guyana in December. In March 1998 Côte d'Ivoire qualified for assistance to reduce its external debt by $345m., of which the Bank was to contribute $91m., and in April an agreement was approved for Mozambique totalling $1,442m. in assistance (increased to $1,716m., with $381m. from the Bank, when Mozambique reached completion point in June 1999). In September 1998 assistance totalling $128m. was approved for Mali. At 30 June 1999 a total of $3,355m. of debt relief in NPV terms had been agreed under the initiative, of which the Bank's share was $801m. At that time, two countries, Benin and Senegal, had been assessed as having a sustainable level of external debt and, therefore, not eligible for assistance. Ethiopia, Guinea-Bissau and Mauritania were under consideration as the next beneficiaries of debt relief (although the approval of assistance for Ethiopia and Guinea-Bissau was later postponed, owing to the outbreak of armed conflict in those countries). In early 1999 the World Bank and IMF initiated a comprehensive review of the HIPC initiative. By April meetings of the Group of Seven industrialized nations (G-7) and of the governing bodies of the Bank and IMF indicated a consensus that the scheme needed to be amended and strengthened, in order to allow more countries to benefit from the initiative, to accelerate the process by which a country may qualify for assistance, and to enhance the effectiveness of debt relief. In June the G-7 and Russia, meeting in Cologne, Germany, agreed to increase contributions to the HIPC Trust Fund and to cancel substantial amounts of outstanding debt, and proposed more flexible terms for eligibility. In September the Bank and IMF reached an agreement on an enhanced HIPC scheme, with further revenue to be generated through the revaluation of a percentage of IMF gold reserves.

## TECHNICAL ASSISTANCE

The provision of technical assistance to member countries has become a major component of World Bank activities. The economic sector and project analysis undertaken by the Bank in the normal course of its operations is the vehicle for considerable technical assistance. In addition, project loans and credits may include funds earmarked specifically for feasibility studies, resource surveys, management or planning advice, and training.

The Bank serves as an executing agency for projects financed by the UN Development Programme. It also administers projects financed by various trust funds.

Technical assistance (usually reimbursable) is also extended to countries that do not need Bank financial support, e.g. for training and transfer of technology. The Bank encourages the use of local consultants to assist with projects and stimulate institutional capability.

The Project Preparation Facility (PPF) was established in 1975 to provide cash advances to prepare projects that may be financed by the Bank. In December 1994 the PPF's commitment authority was increased from US $220m. to $250m. In 1992 the Bank established an Institutional Development Fund (IDF), which became operational on 1 July; the purpose of the Fund was to provide rapid, small-scale financial assistance, to a maximum value of $500,000, for capacity-building proposals.

In 1993 a task force was established to consider measures to reduce poverty in sub-Saharan Africa, in consultation with local and national experts, non-governmental organizations and government officials. The task force published its assessment of the situation in December 1996 and recommended that the Bank revise its lending strategy to emphasize poverty-reduction objectives and strengthen systematic monitoring of the poverty situation in all sub-Saharan African countries receiving World Bank assistance.

In March 1996 a new programme to co-ordinate development efforts in Africa was announced by the UN Secretary-General. The World Bank was to facilitate the mobilization of the estimated US $25,000m. required to achieve the objectives of the Special Initiative over a 10-year period. In addition, the Bank was to provide technical assistance to enable countries to devise economic plans (in particular following a period of civil conflict), agricultural development programmes and a common strategy for African countries to strengthen the management capacities of the public sector.

In April 1999 the World Bank and the IMF convened an international meeting of governments and agencies to review the immediate response of the international community to meet the humanitarian, economic and financial needs of the six Balkan countries most affected by the conflict in Kosovo and Metohija, a southern province of Serbia (Federal Republic of Yugoslavia). The meeting also aimed to consider areas for future co-operation and measures to promote economic recovery and growth in those countries.

## ECONOMIC RESEARCH AND STUDIES

In the 1990s the World Bank's research, conducted by its own research staff, was increasingly concerned with providing information to reinforce the Bank's expanding advisory role to developing countries and to improve policy in the Bank's borrowing countries. The principal areas of current research focus on issues such as maintaining sustainable growth while protecting the environment and the poorest sectors of society, encouraging the development of the private sector, and reducing and decentralizing government activities.

**Consultative Group on International Agricultural Research—CGIAR:** founded in 1971 under the sponsorship of the World Bank, FAO and UNDP. The Bank is chairman of the Group (which includes governments, private foundations and multilateral development agencies) and provides its secretariat. In February 1995 UNEP was invited to become the fourth sponsoring member. The Group was formed to raise financial support for international agricultural research work for improving crops and animal production in the developing countries; it supports 16 research centres. Donations to the group's core research agenda totalled US $340m. in 1998. Exec. Sec. ALEXANDER VON DER OSTEN.

## CO-OPERATION WITH OTHER ORGANIZATIONS

The World Bank co-operates closely with other UN bodies, at the project level, particularly in the design of social funds and social action programmes. It collaborates with the IMF in implementing economic adjustment programmes in developing countries. The Bank holds regular consultations with the European Union and OECD on development issues, and the Bank-NGO Committee provides an annual forum for discussion with non-governmental organizations (NGOs). In September 1995 the Bank initiated the Information for Development Programme (InfoDev) with the aim of fostering partnerships between governments, multilateral institutions and private-sector experts in order to promote reform and investment in developing countries through improved access to information technology. In 1997 a Partnerships Group was established to strengthen the Bank's work with development institutions, representatives of civil society and the private sector. The Group established a new Development Grant Facility, which became operational in October, to support partnership initiatives and to co-ordinate all of the Bank's grant-making activities. Also in 1997 the Bank, in partnership with the IMF, UNCTAD, UNDP, the World Trade Organization (WTO) and International Trade Commission, established an Integrated Framework for Trade-related Assistance to Least Developed Countries, at the request of the WTO, to assist those countries to integrate into the global trading system and improve basic trading capabilities.

Strengthening co-operation with external partners was a fundamental element of the Comprehensive Development Framework, which was adopted in 1998/99 (see above). During that year the Bank consolidated new partnerships in order to extend an effective international response to the financial crises which had affected several Asian countries from mid-1997. The Bank administered a US $40m. Trust Fund, established by the Asia-Europe Meeting (ASEM, see p. 130) and collaborated closely with the Japanese Government in its provision of assistance under the so-called Miyazawa initiative. In July 1999 the World Bank and European Commission organized an international conference to mobilize funds for post-conflict rehabilitation in Kosovo.

The Bank conducts co-financing and aid co-ordination projects with official aid agencies, export credit institutions, and commercial banks. During the year ending 30 June 1999 a total of 103 IBRD and IDA projects involved co-financers' contributions amounting to US $11,350m.

**Global Environment Facility—GEF:** founded in 1990 by the World Bank, UNDP and the UN Environment Programme, as a three-year pilot programme designed to provide grants for investment projects and technical assistance. The aim of the GEF is to assist developing countries in implementing projects that benefit the global (not just the local) environment. At the UN Conference on Environment and Development in June 1992, the GEF was recognized, in Agenda 21, as a source of funds to assist with activities benefiting the global environment, and was designated as the operator of the financial mechanism serving the conventions on climate change and biological diversity. In March 1994 87 industrialized and developing countries agreed to restructure and replenish the GEF for a further three-year period from July of that year. Funds amounting to US $2,000m. were to be made available by 26 donor countries. In November 1997 33 donor countries committed themselves to a target figure of $2,750m. for the next replenishment of GEF funds. The replenishment was approved by the Bank's Executive Board in July 1998. CEO and Chair. MOHAMMED EL-ASHRY.

### EVALUATION

The World Bank's Operations Evaluation Department studies and publishes the results of projects after a loan has been fully disbursed, so as to identify problems and possible improvements in future activities. A Quality Assurance Group monitors the effectiveness of the Bank's operations and performance.

In September 1993 the Bank's Board of Executive Directors agreed to establish an independent Inspection Panel, consistent with the Bank's objective of improving project implementation and accountability. The panel, which became operational in September 1994, was to conduct independent investigations and report on complaints concerning the design, appraisal and implementation of development projects supported by the Bank. By the end of 1999 the panel had received 14 formal requests for inspection. The three projects reviewed in 1999 concerned land reforms in Brazil, diamond mining in Lesotho and a poverty reduction scheme in the People's Republic of China.

### IBRD INSTITUTIONS

**World Bank Institute—WBI:** founded in March 1999 by merger of the Bank's Learning and Leadership Centre, previously responsible for internal staff training, and the Economic Development Institute (EDI), which had been established in 1955 to train government officials concerned with development programmes and policies. The new Institute aimed to emphasize the Bank's priority areas through the provision of training courses and seminars relating to poverty, crisis response, good governance and anti-corruption strategies. The Institute was also to take the lead in co-ordinating a process of consultation and dialogue with researchers and other representatives of civil society to examine poverty for a forthcoming *World Development Report*. Activities of the Institute in 1998/99 included a Clean Air Initiative for Latin American Cities, a new training programme for public officials responsible for financial sector supervision, and the establishment of a World Bank Learning Network. Under the EDI a World Links for Development programme was initiated to connect schools in developing countries with partner establishments in industrialized nations via the internet. Dir VINOD THOMAS (India).

**International Centre for Settlement of Investment Disputes—ICSID:** founded in 1966 under the Convention of the Settlement of Investment Disputes between States and Nationals of Other States. The Convention was designed to encourage the growth of private foreign investment for economic development, by creating the possibility, always subject to the consent of both parties, for a Contracting State and a foreign investor who is a national of another Contracting State to settle any legal dispute that might arise out of such an investment by conciliation and/or arbitration before an impartial, international forum. The governing body of the Centre is its Administrative Council, composed of one representative of each Contracting State, all of whom have equal voting power. The President of the World Bank is (*ex officio*) the non-voting Chairman of the Administrative Council.

At mid-1999 131 countries had signed and ratified the Convention to become ICSID Contracting States. During 1998/99 11 new cases were registered, bringing the total number of cases registered to 65. Sec.-Gen. IBRAHIM F. I. SHIHATA.

## Publications

*Abstracts of Current Studies: The World Bank Research Program* (annually).
*Annual Report on Operations Evaluation.*
*Annual Report on Portfolio Performance.*
*Annual Review of Development Effectiveness.*
*EDI Annual Report.*
*Global Commodity Markets* (quarterly).
*Global Development Finance* (annually, also on CD-Rom).
*Global Economic Prospects and Developing Countries* (annually).
*ICSID Annual Report.*
*ICSID Review—Foreign Investment Law Journal* (2 a year).
*Joint BIS-IMF-OECD-World Bank Statistics on External Debt* (quarterly, also available on the internet at www.worldbank.org/data/jointdebt.html).
*New Products and Outreach* (EDI, annually).
*News from ICSID* (2 a year).
*Research News* (quarterly).
*South Asia Rural Development Series.*
*Staff Working Papers.*
*Transition* (every 2 months).
*World Bank Annual Report.*
*World Bank Atlas* (annually).
*World Bank Catalog of Publications.*
*World Bank Economic Review* (3 a year).
*The World Bank and the Environment* (annually).
*World Bank Research Observer.*
*World Development Indicators* (annually, also on CD-Rom).
*World Development Report* (annually, also on CD-Rom).

# World Bank Statistics

**LENDING OPERATIONS, BY PURPOSE**
(projects approved, year ending 30 June 1999; US $ million)

| | IBRD | IDA | Total |
|---|---|---|---|
| Agriculture | 1,787.7 | 1,020.1 | 2,807.8 |
| Education | 804.4 | 539.8 | 1,344.3 |
| Electric power and other energy | 340.0 | 100.0 | 440.0 |
| Environment | 311.0 | 228.3 | 539.3 |
| Finance | 2,574.9 | 301.5 | 2,876.4 |
| Health, nutrition and population | 514.2 | 592.5 | 1,106.7 |
| Industry | 590.0 | 87.0 | 677.0 |
| Mining and other extractive activities | 300.0 | 15.0 | 315.0 |
| Petroleum and gas | — | 17.5 | 17.5 |
| Public-sector management | 1,042.1 | 387.8 | 1,430.0 |
| Social sector | 2,235.9 | 442.7 | 2,678.6 |
| Telecommunications | — | 10.8 | 10.8 |
| Transportation | 2,040.5 | 981.3 | 3,021.8 |
| Urban development | 319.9 | 386.6 | 706.5 |
| Water supply and sanitation | 509.8 | 242.9 | 752.7 |
| Multisector | 8,811.7 | 1,457.9 | 10,269.6 |
| **Total** | 22,182.3 | 6,811.8 | 28,994.1 |

**IBRD INCOME AND EXPENDITURE**
(US $ million, year ending 30 June)

| Revenue | 1998 | 1999 |
|---|---|---|
| Income from loans: | | |
| Interest | 6,775 | 7,535 |
| Commitment charges | 106 | 114 |
| Income from investments and securities | 1,622 | 1,975 |
| Other income | 10 | 18 |
| **Total income** | 8,513 | 9,642 |

| Expenditure | 1998 | 1999 |
|---|---|---|
| Interest on borrowings | 6,000 | 6,703 |
| Amortization of issuance and prepayment costs | 144 | 143 |
| Interest on securities sold under repurchase agreements and payable-for-cash collateral received | 100 | 36 |
| Administrative expenses | 813 | 859 |
| Provision for loan losses | 251 | 246 |
| Other financial expenses | 10 | 8 |
| **Total** | 7,318 | 7,995 |
| **Operating income** | 1,195 | 1,647 |
| Effects of accounting change | 160 | — |
| *less* Contributions to special programmes | 112 | 129 |
| **Net income** | 1,243 | 1,518 |

**IBRD LOANS AND IDA CREDITS APPROVED, BY SECTOR AND REGION** (1 July 1998–30 June 1999; US $million)

| Sector | Africa | East Asia and Pacific | South Asia | Europe and Central Asia | Latin America and the Caribbean | Middle East and North Africa | Total |
|---|---|---|---|---|---|---|---|
| Agriculture | 188.1 | 1,011.8 | 390.6 | 242.9 | 520.4 | 454.0 | 2,807.8 |
| Education | 194.1 | 557.2 | 98.2 | 41.1 | 398.6 | 55.0 | 1,344.3 |
| Electric power and other energy | — | 100.0 | 210.0 | 46.0 | 30.0 | 54.0 | 440.0 |
| Environment | 15.0 | 304.0 | 138.6 | 27.4 | 54.3 | — | 539.3 |
| Finance | 79.9 | 826.0 | 119.0 | 362.0 | 1,330.5 | 159.0 | 2,876.4 |
| Health, nutrition and population | 172.1 | 104.7 | 32.0 | 94.5 | 309.4 | 101.0 | 1,106.7 |
| Industry | — | 100.0 | 325.0 | 470.0 | 40.0 | 35.0 | 677.0 |
| Mining and other extractive activities | 15.0 | — | — | 300.0 | — | — | 315.0 |
| Petroleum and gas | 17.5 | — | — | — | — | — | 17.5 |
| Public-sector management | 108.8 | 203.5 | — | 616.9 | 97.2 | 403.5 | 1,430.0 |
| Social sector | 129.6 | 990.0 | — | 229.1 | 1,279.9 | 50.0 | 2,678.6 |
| Telecommunications | 10.8 | — | — | — | — | — | 10.8 |
| Transportation | 236.6 | 1,041.5 | 561.3 | 638.0 | 544.5 | — | 3,021.8 |
| Urban development | 110.9 | 264.7 | 105.0 | 59.1 | 102.8 | 64.0 | 706.5 |
| Water supply and sanitation | 75.0 | 149.8 | 32.4 | 385.5 | 30.0 | 80.0 | 752.7 |
| Multisector | 715.1 | 4,112.0 | 550.0 | 1,773.5 | 2,999.0 | 120.0 | 10,269.6 |
| **Total** | 2,068.5 | 9,765.2 | 2,562.0 | 5,286.0 | 7,736.8 | 1,575.5 | 28,994.1 |
| of which: IBRD | 5.0 | 8,754.8 | 750.0 | 4,350.3 | 7,133.3 | 1,189.0 | 22,182.3 |
| IDA | 2,063.5 | 1,010.4 | 1,812.0 | 935.7 | 603.6 | 386.5 | 6,811.8 |
| Number of operations | 56 | 55 | 18 | 74 | 51 | 22 | 276 |

**IBRD OPERATIONS AND RESOURCES, 1995–99** (US $ million, years ending 30 June)

| | 1994/95 | 1995/96 | 1996/97 | 1997/98 | 1998/99 |
|---|---|---|---|---|---|
| Loans approved | 16,853 | 14,656* | 14,525 | 21,086 | 22,182 |
| Gross disbursements | 12,672 | 13,372* | 13,998 | 19,232 | 18,205 |
| Net disbursements† | 897 | 1,213 | 2,094 | n.a. | n.a. |
| New medium- to long-term borrowings | 9,026 | 10,883 | 15,139 | n.a. | n.a. |
| Net income | 1,354 | 1,187 | 1,285 | 1,243 | 1,518 |
| Subscribed capital | 176,438 | 180,630 | 182,426 | 186,436 | 188,220 |
| Statutory lending limit | 195,248 | 197,785 | 198,705 | 202,209 | 205,292 |
| Loans and callable guarantees outstanding | 123,676 | 110,369 | 105,954 | 106,947 | 117,694 |

* Including refinanced/rescheduled overdue charges of US $167.8m. for Bosnia and Herzegovina.

† Including disbursements, repayments and prepayments to/from all members, including third-party repayments.

Source: *World Bank Annual Report 1999*.

# International Development Association—IDA

**Address:** 1818 H Street, NW, Washington, DC 20433, USA.

**Telephone:** (202) 477-1234; **fax:** (202) 477-6391; **internet:** www.worldbank.org/ida.

The International Development Association began operations in November 1960. Affiliated to the IBRD (see above), IDA advances capital to the poorer developing member countries on more flexible terms than those offered by the IBRD.

### MEMBERS

160 members: see Table on pp. 114–116.

## Organization

(December 1999)

Officers and staff of the IBRD serve concurrently as officers and staff of IDA.

**President and Chairman of Executive Directors:** JAMES D. WOLFENSOHN (*ex officio*).

## Activities

IDA assistance is aimed at the poorer developing countries, (i.e. those with an annual GNP per head of less than US $925 in 1997 dollars in 1998/99). Under IDA lending conditions, credits can be extended to countries whose balance of payments could not sustain the burden of repayment required for IBRD loans. Terms are more favourable than those provided by the IBRD; credits are for a period of 35 or 40 years, with a 'grace period' of 10 years, and carry no interest charges. At 30 June 1999 81 countries were eligible for IDA assistance, including several small-island economies with a GNP per head greater than $925, but which would otherwise have little or no access to Bank funds.

IDA's total development resources, consisting of members' subscriptions and supplementary resources (additional subscriptions and contributions), are replenished periodically by contributions from the more affluent member countries. In November 1998 representatives of 39 donor countries agreed to provide $11,600m. for the 12th replenishment of IDA funds, enabling total lending to amount to an estimated $20,500m. in the period July 1999–June 2002. The new IDA-12 resources were to be directed towards the following objectives: investing in people; promoting good governance; promoting broad-based growth; and protecting the environment.

During the year ending 30 June 1999 IDA credits totalling US $6,811.8m. (excluding a development grant of $150m.) were approved. Of total IDA assistance during that year, $2,063.5m. (30.3%) was for Africa, and $1,812.0m. (26.6%) for South Asia (see table on p. 81). The largest borrowers of IDA credits were Bangladesh ($1,020.7m. for six projects) and India ($654.8m. for four projects). IDA administers a Trust Fund, which was established in November 1996 as part of a World Bank/IMF initiative to assist heavily indebted poor countries (HIPCs, see IBRD). During 1998/99 an IDA development grant of $150m. was extended to Mozambique under the HIPC initiative in support of an economic management project.

## Publication

*Annual Report.*

**IDA OPERATIONS AND RESOURCES, 1994–99** (US $ million, years ending 30 June)

| | 1993/94 | 1994/95 | 1995/96 | 1996/97 | 1997/98 | 1998/99 |
|---|---|---|---|---|---|---|
| Commitments | 6,592 | 5,669 | 6,861 | 4,622 | 7,508* | 6,812* |
| Disbursements | 5,532 | 5,703 | 5,884 | 5,979 | 5,630 | 6,023 |

* Excluding HIPC development grants.

Source: *World Bank Annual Report 1999.*

# International Finance Corporation—IFC

**Address:** 2121 Pennsylvania Ave, NW, Washington, DC 20433, USA.

**Telephone:** (202) 477-1234; **fax:** (202) 974-4384; **e-mail:** information@ifc.org; **internet:** www.ifc.org.

IFC was founded in 1956 as a member of the World Bank Group to stimulate economic growth in developing countries by financing private-sector investments, mobilizing capital in international financial markets, and providing technical assistance and advice to governments and businesses.

### MEMBERS

174 members: see Table on pp. 114–116.

## Organization

(December 1999)

IFC is a separate legal entity in the World Bank Group. Executive Directors of the World Bank also serve as Directors of IFC. The President of the World Bank is *ex officio* Chairman of the IFC Board of Directors, which has appointed him President of IFC. Subject to his overall supervision, the day-to-day operations of IFC are conducted by its staff under the direction of the Executive Vice-President.

### PRINCIPAL OFFICERS

**President:** JAMES D. WOLFENSOHN (USA).

**Executive Vice-President:** PETER L. WOICKE (Germany).

### REGIONAL AND INDUSTRY DEPARTMENTS

Seven Regional Departments cover: East Asia and the Pacific; South and Southeast Asia; Central Asia, the Middle East and North Africa; Central and Southern Europe; Europe; Latin America and the Caribbean; and sub-Saharan Africa. These aim to develop strategies for member countries, promote businesses, and strengthen relations with governments and the private sector. Industry Departments cover agribusiness; financial markets; chemicals, petrochemicals and fertilizers; corporate finance services; petroleum, gas and mining; power; and telecommunications, transportation and utilities.

### REGIONAL AND RESIDENT MISSIONS

There are Regional and Resident Missions in Argentina, Australia, Brazil (for Latin America and the Caribbean), Cameroon (for Central Africa), People's Republic of China, Côte d'Ivoire (for West Africa), Egypt (for the Middle East), Ghana, Guatemala, India (for South and Southeast Asia), Kenya (for East Africa), Republic of Korea, Mexico, Morocco (for North Africa), Nigeria, Pakistan, the Philippines, Russia (for Europe), South Africa (for Southern Africa), Thailand, Turkey, Viet Nam and Zimbabwe. There are also Special Representatives in France, Germany, Japan and the United Kingdom, and other programme co-ordinators, managers and investment officers in more than 30 additional countries.

## Activities

IFC provides financial support and advice for private-sector ventures and projects, and assists governments in creating conditions that stimulate the flow of domestic and foreign private savings and investment. Increasingly, IFC has worked to mobilize additional capital from other financial institutions. In all its activities IFC is guided by three major principles:

(i) The catalytic principle. IFC should seek above all to be a catalyst in helping private investors and markets to make good investments.

(ii) The business principle. IFC should function like a business in partnership with the private sector and take the same commercial risks, so that its funds, although backed by public sources, are transferred under market disciplines.

(iii) The principle of the special contribution. IFC should participate in an investment only when it makes a special contribution that supplements or complements the role of market operators.

IFC's authorized capital is US $2,450m. At 30 June 1999 paid-in capital was $2,349.8m. The World Bank was originally the principal source of borrowed funds, but IFC also borrows from private capital markets. IFC's net income amounted to $249.3m. in 1998/99, compared with $245.8m. in the previous year.

To be eligible for financing, projects must be profitable for investors, must benefit the economy of the country concerned, and must comply with IFC's environmental guide-lines. IFC may provide finance for a project that is partly state-owned, provided that there is participation by the private sector and that the project is operated on a commercial basis.

In the year ending 30 June 1999 project financing approved by IFC amounted to US $5,280m. for 255 projects (compared with $5,905m. for 304 projects in the previous year). Of the total approved, $3,505m. was for IFC's own account, while $1,775m. was in the form of loan syndications and underwriting of securities issues and investment funds by more than 100 participant banks and institutional investors. Generally, the IFC limits its financing to 5%–15% of the total cost of a project, but may take up to a 35% stake in a venture (although never as a majority shareholder). Disbursements for IFC's account amounted to $2,102m. (compared with $2,054m. in the previous year).

Projects approved during 1998/99 were located in 77 countries and regions. During that year IFC approved its largest ever project allocation, totalling some US $250m., in support of the establishment of a $750m. Asia Opportunity Fund, which aimed to assist corporate restructuring in Asian companies affected by financial instability. IFC also approved an investment for the first time in Saint Christopher and Nevis. The largest proportion of total financing by IFC was allocated to Latin America and the Caribbean (46%); Asia and the Pacific received 20%, Europe 17%, Central Asia, the Middle East and North Africa 9% and sub-Saharan Africa 7%. The Corporation invests in a wide variety of business and financial institutions in a broad range of sectors. In 1998/99 more than one-third of total financing approved (37%) was for financial services. Other financing was for infrastructure (15%), petroleum, gas and mining (15%), chemicals and petrochemicals (7%), cement and construction materials (6%), food and agribusiness (5%), manufacturing (4%) and others (11%).

During 1996/97 IFC inaugurated a three year pilot programme, 'Extending IFC's Reach', which aimed to encourage private investment in 16 countries and regions (expanded to 20 in 1998/99) where adverse political conditions had previously limited IFC intervention. IFC has expanded its field-based activities in those countries in order to enhance local knowledge, strengthen relationships with government authorities and local businesses and improve access to IFC products and services. By 30 June 1999 IFC had approved 160 projects in 'Outreach' countries amounting to some US $1,000m., of which 67 investments, totalling $68.3m., were through a Small Enterprise Fund (SEF).

IFC offers risk-management services, assisting institutions in avoiding financial risks that arise from changes in interest rates, in exchange rates or in commodity prices. In 1998/99 IFC approved eight risk-management projects for companies and banks, bringing the total number of projects approved since the introduction of the service in 1990 to 83 in 35 countries.

IFC provides advisory services, particularly in connection with privatization and corporate restructuring, private infrastructure, and the development of capital markets. Under the Technical Assistance Trust Funds Program (TATF), established in 1988, IFC manages resources contributed by various governments and agencies to provide finance for feasibility studies, project identification studies and other types of technical assistance relating to project preparation. By 30 June 1999 the TATF had mobilized US $87m. through 26 trust funds, financing more than 700 technical assistance projects. The Foreign Investment Advisory Service (FIAS), established in 1986, is operated jointly by IFC and the IBRD: it provides advice on promoting foreign investment and strengthening the country's investment framework at the request of governments. During 1998/99 FIAS undertook projects and assignments in 33 countries.

IFC has helped to establish several regional facilities which aim to assist small-scale entrepreneurs to develop business proposals and generate funding for their projects. For each of the facilities listed below IFC is the executing agency. The Africa Project Development Facility (APDF) was established in 1986 by IFC, UNDP and the African Development Bank, and maintains offices in Cameroon, Côte d'Ivoire, Ghana, Kenya, South Africa and Zimbabwe. The South Pacific Project Facility, based in Sydney, Australia, was established in 1991. A separate office in Port Moresby, Papua New Guinea, was opened in 1997. The Facility is complemented by a Pacific Island Investment Fund, which was established by IFC in 1995. A Mekong Project Development Facility was inaugurated in 1995, specifically to support the development of small and medium-sized enterprises in Cambodia, Laos and Viet Nam. IFC also administers the Business Advisory Service for the Caribbean and Central America (BAS). In 1992 two locally-owned affiliates of the BAS were established—the Asesoría Empresarial Centroamericana in Costa Rica, to serve Central America, and Enterprise Development Ltd in Trinidad and Tobago, to serve the southern Caribbean and Guyana.

In 1989 IFC (with UNDP, the African Development Bank and other agencies and governments) began operating a new facility, the African Management Services Company (AMSCO), which helps to find qualified senior executives from around the world to work with African companies, assist in the training of local managers, and provide supporting services. By 31 December 1996 AMSCO had signed management contracts with companies in 19 countries. IFC's Africa Enterprise Fund (AEF) provides financial assistance to small and medium-sized enterprises. In 1995 a new facility, Enterprise Support Services for Africa (ESSA), was established, to provide technical and production assistance to businesses after they have secured financing. ESSA commenced operations in February 1996 for an initial three-year period. In 1998/99 ESSA was expanded to be available throughout sub-Saharan Africa as part of APDF.

The dissolution of the USSR in 1991, and the transition to market economies there and in other central and eastern European countries, led to an increase in IFC activities in the region during the 1990s. In order to facilitate the privatization process in that region, the IFC has conducted several single-enterprise advisory assignments and has undertaken work to formulate models that can be easily replicated, notably for small-scale privatization and the privatization of agricultural land in Russia, Ukraine and Belarus.

## Publications

*Annual Report.*

*Emerging Stock Markets Factbook* (annually).

*Global Agribusiness* (series of industry reports).

*Impact* (quarterly).

*Lessons of Experience* (series).

*Results on the Ground* (series).

Discussion papers and technical documents.

**IFC OPERATIONS AND RESOURCES, 1990–99** (fiscal years ending 30 June)

| | 1990 | 1991 | 1992 | 1993 | 1994 | 1995 | 1996 | 1997 | 1998 | 1999 |
|---|---|---|---|---|---|---|---|---|---|---|
| **Approved investments** | | | | | | | | | | |
| Number of new projects | 122 | 152 | 167 | 185 | 231 | 213 | 264 | 276 | 304 | 255 |
| Total financing (US $ million) | 2,201 | 2,846 | 3,226 | 3,936 | 4,287 | 5,467 | 8,118 | 6,722 | 2,905 | 5,280 |
| Total project costs* (US $ million) | 9,490 | 10,683 | 12,000 | 17,422 | 15,839 | 19,352 | 19,633 | 17,945 | 15,726 | 15,578 |
| **Disbursements** (IFC's own account, US $ million) | 1,001 | 1,249 | 1,114 | 1,106 | 1,537 | 1,808 | 2,053 | 2,003 | 2,054 | 2,102 |
| **Resources and income** (US $ million) | | | | | | | | | | |
| Borrowings | 3,580 | 4,130 | 5,114 | 5,565 | 6,531 | 7,993 | 8,956 | 10,123 | 11,162 | 12,429 |
| Paid-in capital | 1,072 | 1,145 | 1,251 | 1,423 | 1,658 | 1,875 | 2,076 | 2,229 | 2,337 | 2,350 |
| Retained earnings | 792 | 957 | 1,138 | 1,280 | 1,538 | 1,726 | 2,071 | 2,503 | 2,749 | 2,998 |
| Net income | 157.0 | 165.9 | 180.2 | 141.7 | 258.2 | 188.0 | 345.8 | 431.9 | 245.8 | 249.3 |

* Including investment mobilized from other sources.

Source: *IFC Annual Report 1999*.

# Multilateral Investment Guarantee Agency—MIGA

**Address:** 1818 H Street, NW, Washington, DC 20433, USA.

**Telephone:** (202) 473-6163; **fax:** (202) 522-2630; **internet:** www.miga.org.

MIGA was founded in 1988 as an affiliate of the World Bank. Its mandate is to encourage the flow of foreign direct investment to, and among, developing member countries, through the provision of political risk insurance and investment marketing services to foreign investors and host governments, respectively.

### MEMBERS

At December 1999 MIGA had 151 member countries. Membership is open to all countries that are members of the World Bank.

## Organization

(December 1999)

MIGA is legally and financially separate from the World Bank. It is supervised by a Council of Governors (comprising one Governor and one Alternate of each member country) and an elected Board of Directors (of no less than 12 members).

**President:** JAMES D. WOLFENSOHN (USA).

**Executive Vice-President:** MOTOMICHI IKAWA (Japan).

## Activities

The convention establishing MIGA took effect in April 1988. Authorized capital was US $1,082m. In April 1998 the Board of Directors approved an increase in MIGA's capital base. A grant of $150m. was transferred from the IBRD as part of the package, while the capital increase (totalling $700m. callable capital and $150m. paid-in capital) was approved by MIGA's Council of Governors in April 1999.

MIGA's purpose is to guarantee eligible investments against losses resulting from non-commercial risks, under four main categories:

(i) transfer risk resulting from host government restrictions on currency conversion and transfer;

(ii) risk of loss resulting from legislative or administrative actions of the host government;

(iii) repudiation by the host government of contracts with investors in cases in which the investor has no access to a competent forum;

(iv) the risk of armed conflict and civil unrest.

Before guaranteeing any investment, MIGA must ensure that it is commercially viable, contributes to the development process and is not harmful to the environment. During the fiscal year 1998/99 MIGA and IFC appointed the first Compliance Advisor and Ombudsman to consider the concerns of local communities directly affected by MIGA or IFC sponsored projects. In February 1999 the Board of Directors approved an increase in the amount of political risk insurance available for each project, from US $75m. to $200m., and increased the amount available to each host government from $350m. to $620m.

During the year ending 30 June 1999 MIGA issued 72 investment insurance contracts in 29 countries with a value of US $1,310m., compared with 55 contracts valued at $831m. in 1997/98. The amount of direct investment associated with the contracts totalled approximately $5,200m. (compared with $6,100m. in the previous year).

MIGA also provides policy and advisory services to promote foreign investment in developing countries and in transitional economies, and to disseminate information on investment opportunities. In October 1995 MIGA established a new network on investment opportunities, which connected investment promotion agencies (IPAs) throughout the world on an electronic information network. The so-called IPA*net* aimed to encourage further investments among developing countries, to provide access to comprehensive information on investment laws and conditions and to strengthen links between governmental, business and financial associations and investors. A new version of IPA*net* was launched in 1997 (and it can be accessed at www.ipanet.net). In June 1998 MIGA initiated a new internet-based facility, 'PrivatizationLink', to provide information on investment opportunities resulting from the privatization of industries in emerging economies.

## Publications

*Annual Report.*

*MIGA News* (quarterly).

# International Civil Aviation Organization—ICAO

**Address:** 999 University St, Montreal, PQ H3C 5H7, Canada.
**Telephone:** (514) 954-8219; **fax:** (514) 954-6077; **e-mail:** icaohq@icao.int; **internet:** www.icao.int.

The Convention on International Civil Aviation was signed in Chicago in 1944. As a result, ICAO was founded in 1947 to develop the techniques of international air navigation and to help in the planning and improvement of international air transport.

### MEMBERS

185 members: see Table on pp. 114–116.

## Organization

(December 1999)

### ASSEMBLY

Composed of representatives of all member states, the Assembly is the organization's legislative body and meets at least once every three years. It reviews the work of the organization, sets out the work programme for the next three years, approves the budget and determines members' contributions.

### COUNCIL

Composed of representatives of 33 member states, elected by the Assembly. It is the executive body, and establishes and supervises subsidiary technical committees and makes recommendations to member governments; meets in virtually continuous session; elects the President, appoints the Secretary-General, and administers the finances of the organization. The Council is assisted by the Air Navigation Commission (on technical matters), the Air Transport Committee (on economic matters), the Committee on Joint Support of Air Navigation Services and the Finance Committee. The functions of the Council are:

(i) to adopt international standards and recommended practices and incorporate them as annexes to the Convention on International Civil Aviation;

(ii) to arbitrate between member states on matters concerning aviation and implementation of the Convention;

(iii) to investigate any situation which presents avoidable obstacles to development of international air navigation;

(iv) to take whatever steps are necessary to maintain safety and regularity of operation of international air transport;

(v) to provide technical assistance to the developing countries under the UN Development Programme and other assistance programmes.

**President of the Council:** Dr Assad Kotaite (Lebanon).

### SECRETARIAT

The Secretariat, headed by a Secretary-General, is divided into five main divisions: the Air Navigation Bureau, the Air Transport Bureau, The Technical Co-operation Bureau, the Legal Bureau, and the Bureau of Administration and Services.

**Secretary-General:** Renato Claudio Costa Pereira (Brazil).

### REGIONAL OFFICES

**Asia and Pacific:** POB 11, 252/1 Vipavadee Rangsit Rd, Ladyao, Chatuchak, Bangkok 10900, Thailand.

**Eastern and Southern Africa:** POB 46294, Nairobi, Kenya.

**Europe:** 3 bis, Villa Emile-Bergerat, 92522 Neuilly-sur-Seine Cédex, France.

**Middle East:** Egyptian Civil Aviation Complex, Cairo Airport Rd, Cairo, Egypt.

**North America, Central America and the Caribbean:** Apdo Postal 5-377, CP 11590, México 5, DF, Mexico.

**South America:** Apdo 4127, Lima 100, Peru.

**Western and Central Africa:** BP 2356, Dakar, Senegal.

## Activities

ICAO aims to ensure the safe and orderly growth of civil aviation; to encourage skills in aircraft design and operation; to improve airways, airports and air navigation; to prevent the waste of resources in unreasonable competition; to safeguard the rights of each contracting party to operate international air transport; and to prevent discriminatory practices. ICAO collects and publishes statistics relating to civil aviation. In the late 1990s ICAO implemented a Year 2000 Programme in order to address potential malfunctions, resulting from the date change at the start of the new century, of systems affecting the safety, regularity and efficiency of international civil aviation operations. All states were to publish information on the compliance of their aeronautical, air navigation and aerodrome services by 1 July 1999, and the situation was to be regularly assessed by the ICAO Secretariat.

### SAFETY AND SECURITY

ICAO aims to enhance all aspects of air safety and security. In 1998 a Global Aviation Safety Plan was initiated to promote new safety measures, and a Programme for the Prevention of Controlled Flights into Terrain continued to be implemented. ICAO assists member countries to develop appropriate educational and training activities. It also supports programmes to assist the victims of aircraft accidents. The 32nd Assembly, held in September/October 1998, endorsed the establishment of a Safety Oversight Programme, to provide for mandatory, systematic and harmonized safety audits regularly to be undertaken in member states. The Programme became operational on 1 January 1999 with the aim of auditing all member states over an initial three-year period. On 1 October 1998 a protocol to the Convention, prohibiting the use of weapons against civil aircraft in flight, entered into effect, having been adopted in 1984 following an attack on a Korean Airlines passenger flight.

### NAVIGATION

ICAO projects relating to navigation have included automated data interchange systems, all-weather navigation, obstacle clearances and the use of space technology in air navigation. In May 1998 an international conference was held in Rio de Janeiro, Brazil, to consider implementation of the Communications, Navigation, Surveillance, and Air Traffic Management (CNS/ATM) systems. The conference urged greater financing and co-operation between states to ensure that the CNS/ATM becomes the basis of a global ATM system. An Air Traffic Management Operational Concept Panel, which was to develop standards and recomended procedures for the development of an integrated ATM system, was convened for the first time in March/April 1999. In October 1998 the Assembly adopted a Charter on the Rights and Obligations of States relating to Global Navigation Satellite Systems (GNSS) to serve as an interim framework on the GNSS. A long-term legal framework on principles governing the GNSS, including a new international convention, remained under consideration.

### ENVIRONMENT

International standards and guide-lines for noise certification of aircraft and international provisions for the regulation of aircraft engine emissions have been adopted and published in Annex 16 to the Chicago Convention. However, these remained under consideration in the late 1990s. ICAO was recognized in the Kyoto Protocol to the Framework Convention on Climate Change as the global body through which industrialized nations were to pursue the limitation or reduction of so-called greenhouse gas emissions. In 1998 ICAO's Committee on Aviation Environmental Protection recommended a reduction of 16% in the permissible levels of nitrogen oxides emitted by aircraft engines. The new limits, to be applicable to new engine designs from 2003, were adopted by the ICAO Council in early 1999.

### ICAO SPECIFICATIONS

These are contained in annexes to the Chicago Convention, and in three sets of Procedures for Air Navigation Services (PANS Documents). The specifications are periodically revised in keeping with developments in technology and changing requirements. The 18 annexes to the Convention include personnel licensing, rules relating to the conduct of flights, meteorological services, aeronautical charts, air–ground communications, safety specifications, identification, air-traffic control, rescue services, environmental protection, security and the transporting of dangerous goods. Technical Manuals and Circulars are issued to facilitate implementation.

### ICAO REGIONAL PLANS

These set out the technical requirements for air navigation facilities in the nine ICAO regions; Regional Offices offer assistance (see addresses above). Because of growth in air traffic and changes in the pattern of air routes, the Plans are periodically amended. ICAO maintains a structure of Planning and Implementation Regional Groups.

**TECHNICAL CO-OPERATION**

ICAO's Technical Co-operation Bureau promotes the implementation of ICAO Standards and Recommended Practices, including the CNS/ATM and Safety Oversight Programmes, and assists developing countries in the execution of various projects, financed by UNDP and other sources.

ICAO works in close co-operation with other UN bodies, such as the World Meteorological Organization, the International Telecommunication Union, the Universal Postal Union, the World Health Organization and the International Maritime Organization. Non-governmental organizations which also participate in ICAO's work include the International Air Transport Association (q.v.), the Airports Council International (q.v.), the International Federation of Air Line Pilots' Associations (q.v.), and the International Council of Aircraft Owner and Pilot Associations.

## Finance

ICAO is financed mainly by contributions from member states; the 32nd Session of the Assembly, held in September/October 1998, approved budgets of US $52.7m. for 1999, $53.8m. for 2000, and $55.4m. for 2001.

## Publications

*Aircraft Accident Digest.*

*Annual Civil Aviation Report.*
*Civil Aviation Statistics of the World* (annually).

*ICAO Journal* (10 a year, in English, French and Spanish; quarterly digest in Russian).

Lexicon of Terms.

Regional Air Navigation Plans.

Transition (CNS/ATM newsletter, quarterly).
Conventions, agreements, rules of procedures, regulations, technical publications and manuals.

# International Fund for Agricultural Development—IFAD

**Address:** Via del Serafico 107, 00142 Rome, Italy.
**Telephone:** (06) 54591; **fax:** (06) 5043463; **e-mail:** ifad@ifad.org; **internet:** www.ifad.org.

IFAD was established in 1977, following a decision by the 1974 UN World Food Conference, with a mandate to combat hunger and eradicate poverty on a sustainable basis in the low-income, food-deficit regions of the world. Funding operations began in January 1978.

**MEMBERS**

161 members: see Table on pp. 114–116.

## Organization

(December 1999)

**GOVERNING COUNCIL**

Each member state is represented in the Governing Council (the Fund's highest authority) by a Governor and an Alternate. Sessions are held annually with special sessions as required. The Governing Council elects the President of the Fund (who also chairs the Executive Board) by a two-thirds majority for a four-year term. The President is eligible for re-election.

**EXECUTIVE BOARD**

Consists of 18 members and 18 alternates, elected by the Governing Council, who serve for three years. The Executive Board is responsible for the conduct and general operation of IFAD and approves loans and grants for projects; it holds three regular sessions each year.

Following agreement on the fourth replenishment of the Fund's resources in February 1997, the governance structure of the Fund was amended. Former Category I countries (i.e. industrialized donor countries) were reclassified as List A countries and were awarded a greater share of the 1,800 votes in the Governing Council and Executive Board, in order to reflect their financial contributions to the Fund. Former Category II countries (petroleum-exporting developing donor countries) were reclassified as List B countries, while recipient developing countries, formally Category III countries, were termed as List C countries, and divided into three regional Sub-Lists. Where previously each category was ensured equal representation on the Executive Board, the new allocation of seats was as follows: eight List A countries, four List B, and two of each Sub-List C group of countries.

**President and Chairman of Executive Board:** FAWZI HAMAD AL-SULTAN (Kuwait).

**Vice-President:** JOHN WESTLEY (USA).

**DEPARTMENTS**

IFAD has three main administrative departments: the Economic Policy and Resource Strategy Department, the Programme Management Department (with five regional Divisions and a Technical Advisory Division); and the Management and Personnel Services Department (including Office of the Secretary, Management Information Systems, Personnel Division, and Administrative Services). At 1 December 1998 IFAD had 276 regular staff.

## Activities

The Fund's objective is to mobilize additional resources to be made available on concessionary terms for agricultural development in developing member states. IFAD provides financing primarily for projects designed to improve food production systems and to strengthen related policies, services and institutions. In allocating resources IFAD is guided by: the need to increase food production in the poorest food-deficit countries; the potential for increasing food production in other developing countries; and the importance of improving the nutrition, health and education of the poorest people in developing countries, i.e. small-scale farmers, artisanal fishermen, nomadic pastoralists, indigenous populations, rural women, and the rural landless. All projects emphasize the participation of beneficiaries in development initiatives, both at the local and national level. IFAD is a leading repository in the world of knowledge, resources and expertise in the field of rural hunger and poverty alleviation. Through its technical assistance grants, IFAD aims to promote research and capacity-building in the agricultural sector, as well as the development of technologies to increase production and alleviate rural poverty. In the late 1990s IFAD was increasingly involved in promoting the use of communication technology to facilitate the exchange of information and experience among rural communities, specialized institutions and organizations and IFAD-sponsored projects.

IFAD is empowered to make both grants and loans. Grants are limited to 7.5% of the resources committed in any one financial year. Loans are available on highly concessionary, intermediate and ordinary terms. Highly concessionary loans carry no interest but have an annual service charge of 0.75% and a repayment period of 40 years. Intermediate term loans are subject to a variable interest charge, equivalent to 50% of the interest rate charged on World Bank loans, and are repaid over 20 years. Ordinary loans carry a variable interest charge equal to that charged by the World Bank, and are repaid over 15–18 years. Highly concessionary loans form about two-thirds of the total lent annually by IFAD. To avoid duplication of work, the administration of loans, for the purposes of disbursements and supervision of project implementation, is entrusted to competent international financial institutions, with the Fund retaining an active interest. In order to increase the impact of its lending resources on food production, the Fund seeks as much as possible to attract other external donors and beneficiary governments as co-financiers of its projects.

At the end of 1998 total IFAD loans approved since 1978 amounted to US $6,056.5m. for 518 projects. During the same period the Fund approved 1,209 research and technical assistance grants, at a cost of $319.1m. In 1998 IFAD approved $413.2m. for 30 projects, as follows: $143.9m. for 12 projects in sub-Saharan Africa, (or 34.8% of the total committed in that year), $104.6m. for seven operations in Asia and the Pacific (25.3%), $74.0m. for five projects in Latin America and the Caribbean (17.9%) and $90.7m. for six projects in the Near East and North Africa (22.0%). Technical assistance grants amounting to $30.2m. (for research, training and project preparation and development), were awarded, bringing the total financial assistance approved in 1998 to $443.4m., compared with $429.9m. in 1997.

IFAD's development projects usually include a number of components, such as infrastructure (e.g. improvement of water supplies, small-scale irrigation and road construction); input supply (e.g. improved seeds, fertilizers and pesticides); institutional support (e.g. research, training and extension services); and producer incentives (e.g. pricing and marketing improvements). IFAD also attempts to enable the landless to acquire income-generating assets: by increasing the provision of credit for the rural poor, it seeks to free them from dependence on the capital market and to generate productive activities.

The Fund supports projects that are concerned with environmental conservation, in an effort to alleviate poverty that results from the deterioration of natural resources. In addition, it extends environmental assessment grants to review the environmental consequences of projects under preparation.

In addition to its regular efforts to identify projects and programmes, IFAD organizes special programming missions to certain selected countries to undertake a comprehensive review of the constraints affecting the rural poor, and to help countries to design strategies for the removal of these constraints. In general, projects based on the recommendations of these missions tend to focus on institutional improvements at the national and local level to direct inputs and services to small farmers and the landless rural poor. Monitoring and evaluation missions are also sent to check the progress of projects.

In November 1995 IFAD organized a Conference on Hunger and Poverty, which was held in Brussels, Belgium, together with the World Bank, the European Commission, FAO, WFP and several European governments. The conference was attended by representatives from some 300 non-governmental organizations, and approved a programme of action to combat hunger and poverty.

In October 1997 IFAD was appointed to administer the Global Mechanism of the Convention to Combat Desertification in those Countries Experiencing Drought and Desertification, particularly in Africa, which entered into force in December 1996. The Mechanism was envisaged as a means of mobilizing and channelling resources for implementation of the Convention. A series of collaborative institutional arrangements were to be concluded between IFAD, UNDP and the World Bank in order to facilitate the effective functioning of the Mechanism.

In February 1998 IFAD inaugurated a new Trust Fund to complement the multilateral debt initiative for Heavily Indebted Poor Countries (HIPCs—see World Bank p. 78). The Fund was intended to assist IFAD's poorest members deemed to be eligible under the initiative to channel resources from debt repayments to communities in need. Also in 1998 the Executive Board endorsed a policy framework for the Fund's provision of assistance in post-conflict situations, with the aim of achieving a continuum from emergency relief to a secure basis from which to pursue sustainable development. At that time IFAD was involved in projects to combat problems resulting from civil conflict in Angola, El Salvador, Rwanda, and the West Bank and Gaza Strip, and in a project to rehabilitate crops and livestock after severe flooding in the Democratic People's Republic of Korea.

## Finance

In accordance with the Articles of Agreement establishing IFAD, the Governing Council periodically undertakes a review of the adequacy of resources available to the Fund and may request members to make additional contributions. In 1997 the fourth replenishment of the Fund's resources, amounting to US $460m. over a three-year period, was successfully concluded. The administrative budget approved for 1998 amounted to $51.1m. The provisional budget for 1999 amounted to $55.0m.

## Publications

*Annual Report.*
*IFAD Update* (2 a year).
*Staff Working Papers* (series).
*The State of World Rural Poverty.*

# International Labour Organization—ILO

**Address:** 4 route des Morillons, 1211 Geneva 22, Switzerland.

**Telephone:** (22) 7996111; **fax:** (22) 7988685; **internet:** www.ilo.org.

ILO was founded in 1919 to work for social justice as a basis for lasting peace. It carries out this mandate by promoting decent living standards, satisfactory conditions of work and pay and adequate employment opportunities. Methods of action include the creation of international labour standards; the provision of technical co-operation services; and research and publications on social and labour matters. In 1946 ILO became a specialized agency associated with the UN. It was awarded the Nobel Peace Prize in 1969.

### MEMBERS

174 members: see Table on pp. 114–116.

## Organization

(December 1999)

### INTERNATIONAL LABOUR CONFERENCE

The supreme deliberative body of ILO, the Conference meets annually in Geneva, with a session devoted to maritime questions when necessary; it is attended by about 2,000 delegates, advisers and observers. National delegations are composed of two government delegates, one employers' delegate and one workers' delegate. Non-governmental delegates can speak and vote independently of the views of their national government. The conference elects the Governing Body and adopts International Labour Conventions and Recommendations. Every two years the Conference adopts the ILO Budget.

The President and Vice-Presidents hold office for the term of the Conference only.

### GOVERNING BODY

ILO's executive council meets three times a year in Geneva to decide policy and programmes. It is composed of 28 government members, 14 employers' members and 14 workers' members. Ten seats are reserved for 'states of chief industrial importance': Brazil, the People's Republic of China, France, Germany, India, Italy, Japan, Russia, the United Kingdom and the USA. The remaining 18 are elected from other countries every three years. Employers' and workers' members are elected as individuals, not as national candidates.

Among the Committees formed by the Governing Body are: the Committee on Freedom of Association; the Programme, Financial and Administrative Committee; the Building Sub-Committee; the Committee on Legal Issues and International Labour Standards; the Sub-Committee on Multinational Enterprises; the Working Party on Policy regarding the Revision of Standards; the Committee on Employment and Social Policy; the Committee on Sectoral and Technical Meetings and Related Issues; the Committee on Technical Co-operation; and the Working Party on the Social Dimensions of the Liberalization of International Trade.

**Chairman** (1999–2000): JACQUES ELMIGER (Switzerland).

**Employers' Vice-Chairman:** ROLF THÜSING (Germany).

**Workers' Vice-Chairman:** WILLIAM BRETT (United Kingdom).

### INTERNATIONAL LABOUR OFFICE

The International Labour Office is ILO's secretariat, operational headquarters and publishing house. It is staffed in Geneva and in the field by about 1,700 people of some 115 nationalities. Operations are decentralized to regional, area and branch offices in nearly 40 countries.

**Director-General:** JUAN O. SOMAVÍA (Chile).

### REGIONAL OFFICES

**Regional Office for Africa:** 01 BP 3960, Abidjan 01, Côte d'Ivoire.

**Regional Office for the Americas:** Apdo Postal 3638, Lima 1, Peru.

**Regional Office for Arab States:** POB 11-4088, Beirut, Lebanon.

**Regional Office for Asia and the Pacific:** POB 2-349, Bangkok 10200, Thailand.

## Activities

In 1999 ILO identified the following four principal themes as strategic objectives for its 2000–01 work programme: to promote and realize fundamental principles and rights at work; to create greater opportunities for women and men to secure decent employment and income; to enhance the coverage and effectiveness of social protection for all; and to strengthen tripartism and social dialogue.

### FUNDAMENTAL PRINCIPLES AND RIGHTS AT WORK

One of ILO's primary functions is the adoption by the International Labour Conference of conventions and recommendations setting minimum labour standards. Through ratification by member states, conventions create binding obligations to put their provisions into effect. Recommendations provide guidance as to policy and practice. At June 1999 a total of 182 conventions and 190 recommendations had been adopted, ranging over a wide field of social and labour matters, including basic human rights such as freedom of association, abolition of forced labour, elimination of discrimination in employment promotion, training and the protection of workers. Together they form the International Labour Code. By 1999 more than 6,600 ratifications of the conventions had been registered by member states. The Committee of Experts on the Application of Conventions and Recommendations and the Conference Committee on the Application of Standards monitor the adoption of international labour standards. In June 1998 a Declaration establishing seven fundamental labour standards was adopted by the Conference. All member states were obliged to observe the four principles upon which these standards were based (see above), whether or not they had ratified the corresponding international conventions.

From 1996 ILO resolved to strengthen its efforts, working closely with UNICEF, to encourage member states to ratify and to implement relevant international standards on child labour. By late 1999 some 90 countries were taking part in ILO's International Programme for the Elimination of Child Labour (IPEC, established in 1992), with emphasis placed on the elimination of the most severe forms of labour such as hazardous working conditions and occupations, child prostitution and trafficking of children. In addition, IPEC gives special attention to children who are particularly vulnerable, for example those under 12 years of age.

### DECENT EMPLOYMENT AND INCOME

ILO aims to monitor, examine and report on the situation and trends in employment throughout the world, and considers the effects on employment and social justice of economic trade, investment and related phenomena. In 1998 ILO estimated that some 1,000m. workers, or one-third of the world's labour force, were unemployed or underemployed. It was particularly concerned with the impact on employment and related social issues of the financial crisis that had affected several Asian economies from mid-1997.

ILO's Employment and Training Department analyses and develops policies to promote the following objectives: full, productive and freely-chosen employment; a labour market that combines flexibility in the use of labour with employment security; enhanced employment opportunities for workers by adapting and improving their skills and competence through training; and the protection and access to employment of specific groups, such as women, youths, migrant workers and disabled persons; and the rehabilitation of workers exposed to drug and alcohol abuse.

ILO maintains technical relations with the IMF, the World Bank, OECD, the WTO and other international organizations on global economic issues, international and national strategies for employment, structural adjustment, and labour market and training policies. A number of employment policy reviews have been carried out by the ILO within the framework of the UN Administrative Committee on Co-ordination Task Force on Full Employment and Sustainable Livelihoods.

### SOCIAL PROTECTION FOR ALL

Access to an adequate level of social protection is recognized in ILO's 1944 Declaration of Philadelphia, as well as in a number of international labour standards, as a basic right of all individuals. ILO aims to enable countries to extend social protection to all groups in society and to improve working conditions and safety at work. The fundamental premise of ILO's new programme sector on economic and social security was that adequate security was essential for productive work and human dignity in the future global economy. It was to address the following concerns: why certain individuals and groups lack decent social security; how new schemes may be initiated in member countries to complement or replace existing social security systems; means of improving the governance and coverage of social protection programmes; identifying the constitutive elements of social security; and creating a balance between the flexible needs of the labour market with adequate social protection.

ILO extends direct technical assistance to member states in order to improve occupational safety and health, for example, through the development of management tools, monitoring and information services designed to prevent occupational accidents and diseases, and measures to protect the health and welfare of workers and the environment. ILO has also established a series of alliances and partnerships with governments, non-governmental organizations, social groups and human rights organizations to reinforce health and safety advocacy campaigns.

### TRIPARTISM AND SOCIAL DIALOGUE

This area was identified as one of the four strategic objectives in order to concentrate and reinforce ILO's support for strengthening the process of tripartism, the role and activities of its tripartite constituents (i.e. governments, employers and workers' organizations), and, in particular, their capacity to engage in and to promote the use of social dialogue. ILO recognizes that the enactment of labour laws, and ensuring their effective enforcement, collective bargaining and other forms of co-operation are important means of promoting social justice. It aims to assist governments and employers' and workers' organizations to establish sound labour relations, to adapt labour laws to meet changing economic and social needs, and to improve labour administration.

### INTERNATIONAL LABOUR CONFERENCE

86th Session: June 1998. Adopted the Declaration of Fundamental Principles and Rights at Work, committing members to respect and promote seven core labour standards, based on the principles of: freedom of association and the effective right to collective bargaining; the abolition of forced or compulsory labour; the abolition of child labour; and the elimination of discrimination in employment. Adopted a resolution on the development of employment opportunities and employment protection for young people. Adopted a recommendation on the general conditions necessary for the stimulation of employment in small and medium-sized enterprises. Referred a proposed international convention on contract labour to the Governing Body for further consideration. Held a first discussion on the abolition of severe forms of child labour; a proposed convention and recommendations on the issue were to be discussed in the following session.

87th Session: June 1999. Adopted the Worst Forms of Child Labour Convention, requiring signatory states to secure the prohibition and elimination of the most severe or hazardous forms of child labour. Also adopted a Recommendation urging any ratifying state to declare those activities to be criminal offences and to impose penal sanctions against the perpetrators. Adopted a Resolution condemning Myanmar for consistent violations of the Forced Labour Convention, which prevented that country from attending meetings or receiving technical assistance. Agreed that a revision of the Maternity Protection Convention (No 103) was appropriate, but referred the issue for further discussion in the 88th session. The situation of migrant workers remained under consideration.

### MEETINGS

Among meetings held during 1999, in addition to the regular International Labour Conference and the Governing Body sessions, were the Meeting of Experts on Ambient Factors at the Workplace; the Tripartite Meeting on Voluntary Initiatives Affecting Training and Education on Safety; Health and Environment in the Chemical Industries; the Tripartite Meeting on Managing the Privatization and Restructuring of Public Utilities; the International Symposium on the Future of Employers' Organizations; the Tripartite Meeting on Social and Labour Issues in Small-scale Mines; the Meeting of Experts on Labour Inspection and Child Labour; the Tripartite Meeting on the Human Resource Implications of Globalization and Restructuring in Commerce; and the Tripartite Meeting on Safety and Health in the Fishing Industry.

### INTERNATIONAL INSTITUTE FOR LABOUR STUDIES

Established in 1960 and based at ILO's Geneva headquarters, the Institute promotes the study and discussion of policy issues of concern to ILO and its constituents, i.e. government, employers and workers. The core theme of the Institute's activities is the interaction between labour institutions, development and civil society in a global economy. It identifies emerging social and labour issues by developing new areas for research and action, and encourages dialogue on social policy between the tripartite constituency of the ILO and the international academic community and other experts. The Institute maintains research networks, conducts courses, seminars and social policy forums, and supports internships and visiting scholar and internship programmes.

### INTERNATIONAL TRAINING CENTRE OF ILO

**Address:** Corso Unità d'Italia 125, 10127 Turin, Italy.

The Centre became operational in 1965. The ILO Director-General is Chairman of the Board of the Centre. It provides programmes for directors in charge of technical and vocational institutions, training officers, senior and middle-level managers in private and public enterprises, trade union leaders, and technicians, primarily from the developing regions of the world. Since 1991 the Centre has been increasingly used by UN agencies to provide training for improving the management of development and for building national capacities to sustain development programmes. In January 1996 a UN Staff College was established to improve staff training and to enhance collaboration among the various agencies and programmes of the UN.

## Finance

The regular budget for the two years 2000–01 was US $467.5m.

## Publications

(in English, French and Spanish unless otherwise indicated)

*Bulletin of Labour Statistics* (quarterly).

*International Labour Review* (quarterly).

*International studies, surveys, works of practical guidance or reference* on questions of social policy, manpower, industrial relations, working conditions, social security, training, management development, etc.

*Key Indicators of the Labour Market.*

*Labour Law Documents* (selected labour and social security laws and regulations; 3 a year).

*Official Bulletin* (3 a year).

*Reports* for the annual sessions of the International Labour Conference, etc. (also in Arabic, Chinese and Russian).

*World Employment Report* (every 2 years).

*World Labour Report* (every 2 years).

*World of Work* (magazine issued in several languages; 5 a year).

*Yearbook of Labour Statistics.*

Also maintains a database on international labour standards, ILOLEX, and a database on national labour law, NATLEX, in electronic form.

# International Maritime Organization—IMO

**Address:** 4 Albert Embankment, London, SE1 7SR, United Kingdom.

**Telephone:** (20) 7735-7611; **fax:** (20) 7587-3210; **e-mail:** info@imo.org; **internet:** www.imo.org.

The Inter-Governmental Maritime Consultative Organization (IMCO) began operations in 1959, as a specialized agency of the UN to facilitate co-operation among governments on technical matters affecting international shipping. Its main functions are the achievement of safe and efficient navigation, and the control of pollution caused by ships and craft operating in the marine environment. IMCO became IMO in 1982.

### MEMBERS

157 members and two associate members: see Table on pp. 114–116.

## Organization

(December 1999)

### ASSEMBLY

The Assembly consists of delegates from all member countries, who each have one vote. Associate members and observers from other governments and the international agencies are also present. Regular sessions are held every two years. The Assembly is responsible for the election of members to the Council and approves the appointment of the Secretary-General of the Secretariat. It considers reports from all subsidiary bodies and decides the action to be taken on them; it votes the agency's budget and determines the work programme and financial policy. The 21st regular session of the Assembly was held in London in November 1999.

The Assembly also recommends to members measures to promote maritime safety and to prevent and control maritime pollution from ships.

### COUNCIL

The Council is the governing body of the Organization between the biennial sessions of the Assembly. Its members, representatives of 32 states, are elected by the Assembly for a term of two years. The Council appoints the Secretary-General; transmits reports by the subsidiary bodies, including the Maritime Safety Committee, to the Assembly, and reports on the work of the Organization generally; submits budget estimates and financial statements with comments and recommendations to the Assembly. The Council normally meets twice a year.

**Facilitation Committee:** Constituted by the Council in May 1972 as a subsidiary body, this Committee deals with measures to facilitate maritime travel and transport and matters arising from the 1965 Facilitation Convention. Membership open to all IMO member states.

### MARITIME SAFETY COMMITTEE

The Maritime Safety Committee is open to all IMO members. The Committee meets at least once a year and submits proposals to the Assembly on technical matters affecting shipping, including prevention of marine pollution.

**Sub-Committees:**

Bulk Liquids and Gases*.
Carriage of Dangerous Goods, Solid Cargoes and Containers.
Fire Protection.
Flag State Implementation*.
Radiocommunications and Search and Rescue.
Safety of Navigation.
Ship Design and Equipment.
Stability and Load Lines and Fishing Vessel Safety.
Standards of Training and Watchkeeping.

* Also sub-committees of the Marine Environment Protection Committee.

### LEGAL COMMITTEE

Established by the Council in June 1967 to deal initially with problems connected with the loss of the tanker *Torrey Canyon*, and subsequently with any legal problems laid before IMO. Membership open to all IMO member states.

### MARINE ENVIRONMENT PROTECTION COMMITTEE

Established by the eighth Assembly (1973) to co-ordinate IMO's work on the prevention and control of marine pollution from ships, and to assist IMO in its consultations with other UN bodies, and with international organizations and expert bodies in the field of marine pollution. Membership is open to all IMO members.

### TECHNICAL CO-OPERATION COMMITTEE

Constituted by the Council in May 1972, this Committee evaluates the implementation of UN Development Programme projects for which IMO is the executing agency, and generally reviews IMO's technical assistance programmes. Its membership is open to all IMO member states.

### SECRETARIAT

The Secretariat consists of the Secretary-General and a staff appointed by the Secretary-General and recruited on as wide a geographical basis as possible.

**Secretary-General:** WILLIAM A. O'NEIL (Canada).

**Divisions of the Secretariat:**

Administrative
Conference
Legal Affairs and External Relations
Marine Environment
Maritime Safety
Technical Co-operation

## Activities

In addition to the work of its committees and sub-committees, the organization works in connection with the following Conventions, of which it is the depository:

International Convention for the Prevention of Pollution of the Sea by Oil, 1954. IMO took over administration from the United Kingdom in 1959.

Convention on Facilitation of International Maritime Traffic, 1965. Came into force in March 1967.

International Convention on Load Lines, 1966. Came into force in July 1968.

International Convention on Tonnage Measurement of Ships, 1969. Convention embodies a universal system for measuring ships' tonnage. Came into force in 1982.

International Convention relating to Intervention on the High Seas in Cases of Oil Pollution Casualties, 1969. Came into force in May 1975. A Protocol adopted in 1973 came into force in 1983.

International Convention on Civil Liability for Oil Pollution Damage, 1969. Came into force in June 1975.

Intenational Convention on the Establishment of an International Fund for Compensation for Oil Pollution Damage, 1971. Came into force in October 1978.

Convention relating to Civil Liability in the Field of Maritime Carriage of Nuclear Material, 1971. Came into force in 1975.

Special Trade Passenger Ships Agreement, 1971. Came into force in 1974.

Convention on the International Regulations for Preventing Collisions at Sea, 1972. Came into force in July 1977.

Convention on the Prevention of Marine Pollution by Dumping of Wastes and Other Matter, 1972. Came into force in August 1975. Extended to include a ban on low-level nuclear waste in November 1993; came into force in February 1994.

International Convention for Safe Containers, 1972. Came into force in September 1977.

International Convention for the Prevention of Pollution from Ships, 1973 (as modified by the Protocol of 1978). Came into force in October 1983. Extended to include a ban on air pollution in September 1997; amendments will come into force 12 months after 15 countries whose combined fishing fleets constitute 50% of the world's merchant fleet have become parties thereto.

International Convention on Safety of Life at Sea, 1974. Came into force in May 1980. A Protocol drawn up in 1978 came into force in May 1981. Extended to include an International Safety Management (ISM) Code in October 1997.

Athens Convention relating to the Carriage of Passengers and their Luggage by Sea, 1974. Came into force in April 1987.

Convention on the International Maritime Satellite Organization, 1976. Came into force in July 1979.

Convention on Limitation of Liability for Maritime Claims, 1976. Came into force in December 1986.

International Convention for the Safety of Fishing Vessels, Torremolinos, 1977. Will come into force 12 months after 15 countries whose combined fishing fleets constitute 50% of world fishing fleets of 24 metres in length and over have become parties thereto.

International Convention on Standards of Training, Certification and Watchkeeping for Seafarers, 1978. Came into force in April 1984; restructured in February 1997.

International Convention on Maritime Search and Rescue, 1979. Came into force in June 1985.

Paris Memorandum of Understanding on Port State Control, 1982.

International Convention for the Suppression of Unlawful Acts against the Safety of International Shipping, 1988. Came into force in March 1992.

Protocol for the Suppression of Unlawful Acts against the Safety of Fixed Platform located on the Continental Shelf, 1988. Came into force in March 1992.

International Convention on Salvage, 1989. Came into force in July 1996.

International Convention on Oil Pollution, Preparedness, Response and Co-operation, 1990. Came into force on 13 May 1995.

International Convention on Liability and Compensation for Damage in Connection with the Carriage of Hazardous and Noxious Substances by Sea, 1996.

### ASSOCIATED INSTITUTES

**IMO Maritime Law Institute—IMLI:** POB 31, Msida, MSD 01, Malta; tel. 319343; fax 343092; e-mail imli@maltanet.net; provides training for maritime lawyers. Dir Prof. DAVID ATTARD.

**Regional Marine Pollution Emergency Response Centre for the Mediterranean Sea—REMPEC:** Manoel Island, GZR 03, Malta; tel. 337296; fax 339951; e-mail rempecdirector@waldonet.mt; f. 1976 as the Regional Oil Comnbating Centre for the Mediterranean Sea. Administered by IMO in conjunction with the Regional Seas Programme of the UN Environment Programme. Aims to develop measures to combat pollution in the Mediterranean. Dir ROBERTO PATRUNO.

**World Maritime University—WMU:** POB 500, Citadellsvägen 29, 201 24 Malmö, Sweden; tel. (40) 356300; fax (40) 128442; e-mail info@wmu.se; internet www.wmu.se; f. by IMO in 1983. It offers postgraduate courses in various maritime disciplines, mainly for students from developing countries. Rector K. LAUBSTEIN. Publs *WMU Newsletter*, *WMU Handbook*.

## Finance

Contributions are received from the member states. The budget appropriation for the two years 2000–01 amounted to £36.61m.

## Publications

*IMO News* (quarterly).

Numerous specialized publications, including international conventions of which IMO is depositary.

# International Monetary Fund—IMF

**Address:** 700 19th St, NW, Washington, DC 20431, USA.

**Telephone:** (202) 623-7300; **fax:** (202) 623-6220; **internet:** www.imf.org.

The IMF was established at the same time as the World Bank in December 1945, to promote international monetary co-operation, to facilitate the expansion and balanced growth of international trade and to promote stability in foreign exchange.

### MEMBERS

182 members: see Table on pp. 114–116.

## Organization

(December 1999)

**Managing Director:** MICHEL CAMDESSUS (France) (until Feb. 2000).

**First Deputy Managing Director:** STANLEY FISCHER (USA).

**Deputy Managing Directors:** SHIGEMITSU SUGISAKI (Japan); EDUARDO ANINAT (Chile).

### BOARD OF GOVERNORS

The highest authority of the Fund is exercised by the Board of Governors, on which each member country is represented by a Governor and an Alternate Governor. The Board of Governors meets once a year, but the Governors may take votes by mail or other means between annual meetings. The Board of Governors has delegated many of its powers to the Executive Directors. However, the conditions governing the admission of new members, adjustment of quotas and the election of Executive Directors, as well as certain other important powers, remain the sole responsibility of the Board of Governors. The voting power of each member on the Board of Governors is related to its quota in the Fund (see p. 94).

The Interim Committee of the Board of Governors, established in 1974, usually meets twice a year. It comprises 24 members, representing the same countries or groups of countries as those on the Board of Executive Directors (see below). It reviews the international monetary system and advises the Board of Governors, but has no decision-making authority. In September 1999 the Board of Governors adopted a resolution to transform the Committee into the International Monetary and Financial Committee of the Board of Governors.

The Development Committee (the Joint Ministerial Committee of the Boards of Governors of the World Bank and the IMF on the Transfer of Real Resources to Developing Countries) was also created in 1974, with a structure similar to that of the Interim Committee, to review development policy issues and financing requirements.

### BOARD OF EXECUTIVE DIRECTORS

The 24-member Board of Executive Directors, responsible for the day-to-day operations of the Fund, is in continuous session in Washington, under the chairmanship of the Fund's Managing Director or Deputy Managing Directors. The USA, the United

Kingdom, Germany, France and Japan each appoint one Executive Director, while the other 19 Executive Directors are elected by groups of the remaining countries. As in the Board of Governors, the voting power of each member is related to its quota in the Fund, but in practice the Executive Directors normally operate by consensus.

The Managing Director of the Fund serves as head of its staff, which is organized into departments by function and area. At 31 December 1998 the Fund staff employed 2,196 staff members (with a further 428 additional authorized staff positions) from 123 countries. In mid-1994 two new positions of Deputy Managing Director were created, bringing the total to three. This major structural development was approved by the Executive Board and reflected the increase in reponsibilities of that position, owing to the IMF's greatly enlarged membership.

## Activities

The purposes of the IMF, as defined in the Articles of Agreement, are:

(i) To promote international monetary co-operation through a permanent institution which provides the machinery for consultation and collaboration on monetary problems.

(ii) To facilitate the expansion and balanced growth of international trade, and to contribute thereby to the promotion and maintenance of high levels of employment and real income and to the development of members' productive resources.

(iii) To promote exchange stability, to maintain orderly exchange arrangements among members, and to avoid competitive exchange depreciation.

(iv) To assist in the establishment of a multilateral system of payments in respect of current transactions between members and in the elimination of foreign exchange restrictions which hamper the growth of trade.

(v) To give confidence to members by making the general resources of the Fund temporarily available to them, under adequate safeguards, thus providing them with the opportunity to correct maladjustments in their balance of payments, without resorting to measures destructive of national or international prosperity.

(vi) In accordance with the above, to shorten the duration of and lessen the degree of disequilibrium in the international balances of payments of members.

In joining the Fund, each country agrees to co-operate with the above objectives. In accordance with its objective of facilitating the expansion of international trade, the IMF encourages its members to accept the obligations of Article VIII, Sections two, three and four, of the Articles of Agreement. Members that accept Article VIII undertake to refrain from imposing restrictions on the making of payments and transfers for current international transactions and from engaging in discriminatory currency arrangements or multiple currency practices without IMF approval. By December 1999 147 members had accepted Article VIII status.

In October 1995 the Interim Committee of the Board of Governors endorsed recent decisions of the Executive Board to strengthen IMF financial support to members requiring exceptional assistance. An Emergency Financing Mechanism was established to enable the IMF to respond to potential or actual financial crises, while additional funds were made available for short-term currency stabilization. (The Mechanism was activated for the first time in July 1997, in response to a request by the Philippines Government to reinforce the country's international reserves, and was subsequently used during that year to assist Thailand, Indonesia and the Republic of Korea, and, in July 1998, Russia.) Emergency assistance was also to be available to countries in a post-conflict situation, in addition to existing arrangements for countries having been affected by natural disasters, to facilitate the rehabilitation of their economies and to improve their eligibility for further IMF concessionary arrangements. During 1998/99 the IMF extended emergency assistance totalling SDR 221m. to seven countries. Following the earthquake that took place in Turkey in August 1999, the IMF extended its largest ever emergency loan, amounting to SDR 362m.

In December 1996 the IMF and the World Trade Organization (q.v.) signed a co-operation agreement which provided for increased consultation and exchanges of information and data between the two organizations, and granted each organization observer status at certain of the other's decision-making bodies. In April 1997 the Interim Committee of the Board of Governors endorsed proposals to amend the Articles of Agreement to include the promotion of capital-account liberalization as a specific objective of the IMF and to extend the Fund's mandate to cover capital movements. The proposed amendment remained under consideration in 1999.

In mid-1997 the devaluation of the Thai baht, following intense speculation of the currency and market losses, initiated a period of severe financial and economic turmoil in several Asian countries. The widespread effect of the crisis dominated the work of the IMF in 1997/98 and placed a substantial strain on its financial resources: by August 1998 the Fund had disbursed approximately US $26,000m. to assist the countries most affected by the Asian crisis, i.e. Indonesia, the Republic of Korea and Thailand. The IMF led efforts to mobilize additional funding from international sources, and aimed to help restore confidence in those economies, to support structural reforms, including the reform of financial systems, and to address governance issues, such as links between commerce and government and the question of economic transparency. In April 1998 the Executive Board attempted to focus on discussions concerning the strengthening of the international monetary system by identifying the following fundamental approaches: reinforcing international and domestic financial systems; strengthening IMF surveillance; promoting greater availability and transparency of information regarding member countries' economic data and policies; emphasizing the central role of the IMF in crisis management; and establishing effective procedures to involve the private sector in forestalling or resolving financial crises. The Fund pursued its review and reform of the international financial architecture during 1998/99. Demands on IMF resources, however, remained heavy owing to the ongoing effects of the Asian financial crisis and economic upheavals in Russia, in mid-1998, and in Brazil, at the end of that year.

### SURVEILLANCE

Under its Articles of Agreement, the Fund is mandated to oversee the effective functioning of the international monetary system. Accordingly, the Fund aims to exercise firm surveillance over the exchange rate policies of member states and to assess whether a country's economic situation and policies are consistent with the objectives of sustainable development and domestic and external stability. The Fund's main tools of surveillance are regular, bilateral consultations with member countries conducted in accordance with Article IV of the Articles of Agreement, which cover fiscal and monetary policies, balance of payments and external debt developments, as well as policies that affect the economic performance of a country, such as the labour market, social and environmental issues and good governance, and aspects of the country's capital accounts, and finance and banking sectors. In addition, World Economic Outlook discussions are held, normally twice a year, by the Executive Board to assess policy implications from a multilateral perspective and to monitor global developments. The rapid decline in the value of the Mexican peso in late 1994 and the financial crisis in Asia, which became apparent in mid-1997, focused attention on the importance of IMF surveillance of the economies and financial policies of member states and prompted the Fund to enhance the effectiveness of its surveillance and to encourage the full and timely provision of data by member countries in order to maintain fiscal transparency. In April 1996 the IMF established the Special Data Dissemination Standard, which was intended to improve access to reliable economic statistical information for member countries that have, or are seeking, access to international capital markets. In March 1999 the IMF undertook to strengthen the Standard by the introduction of a new reserves data template. By September 47 countries had subscribed to the Standard. In December 1997 the Executive Board approved a new General Data Dissemination System (GDDS), to encourage all member countries to improve the production and dissemination of core economic data. The operational phase of the GDDS was scheduled to commence in early 2000. In April 1997, in an effort to improve the value of surveillance by means of increased transparency, the Executive Board agreed to the voluntary issue of Press Information Notices (PINs) (on the internet and in *IMF Economic Reviews*), following each member's Article IV consultation with the Board, to those member countries wishing to make public the Fund's views. Other background papers providing information on and analysis of economic developments in individual countries continued to be made available. In April 1998 the Interim Committee adopted a voluntary Code of Good Practices on Fiscal Transparency: Declaration of Principles, which aimed to increase the quality and promptness of official reports on economic indicators, and in September 1999 adopted a Code of Good Practices on Transparency in Monetary and Financial Policies: Declaration of Principles.

### SPECIAL DRAWING RIGHTS

The special drawing right (SDR) was introduced in 1970 as a substitute for gold in international payments. It was intended eventually to become the principal reserve asset in the international monetary system, although by 1999 this appeared unlikely to happen. SDRs are allocated to members in proportion to their quotas. The IMF has allocated a total of SDR 21,433m. since the SDR was created in 1970. In October 1996 the Executive Board agreed to a new allocation of SDRs in order to achieve their equitable distribution among member states (i.e. all members would have an equal number of SDRs relative to the size of their quotas). In particular, this was deemed necessary since 38 countries that had

**BOARD OF EXECUTIVE DIRECTORS** (September 1999)

| Director | Casting Votes of | Total Votes | % |
|---|---|---|---|
| **Appointed:** | | | |
| KARIN LISSAKERS | USA | 371,743 | 17.35 |
| YUKIO YOSHIMURA | Japan | 133,378 | 6.23 |
| BERND ESDAR | Germany | 130,332 | 6.08 |
| JEAN-CLAUDE MILLERON | France | 107,635 | 5.02 |
| STEPHEN PICKFORD | United Kingdom | 107,635 | 5.02 |
| **Elected:** | | | |
| WILLY KIEKENS (Belgium) | Austria, Belarus, Belgium, Czech Republic, Hungary, Kazakhstan, Luxembourg, Slovakia, Slovenia, Turkey | 111,696 | 5.21 |
| J. DE BEAUFORT WIJNHOLDS (Netherlands) | Armenia, Bosnia and Herzegovina, Bulgaria, Croatia, Cyprus, Georgia, Israel, the former Yugoslav republic of Macedonia, Moldova, Netherlands, Romania, Ukraine | 105,412 | 4.92 |
| AGUSTÍN CARSTENS (Mexico) | Costa Rica, El Salvador, Guatemala, Honduras, Mexico, Nicaragua, Spain, Venezuela | 92,425 | 4.32 |
| RICCARDO FAINI (Italy) | Albania, Greece, Italy, Malta, Portugal, San Marino | 90,636 | 4.23 |
| THOMAS A. BERNES (Canada) | Antigua and Barbuda, Bahamas, Barbados, Belize, Canada, Dominica, Grenada, Ireland, Jamaica, Saint Christopher and Nevis, Saint Lucia, Saint Vincent and the Grenadines | 80,205 | 3.74 |
| KAI AAEN HANSEN (Denmark) | Denmark, Estonia, Finland, Iceland, Latvia, Lithuania, Norway, Sweden | 76,276 | 3.56 |
| GREGORY F. TAYLOR (Australia) | Australia, Kiribati, Republic of Korea, Marshall Islands, Federated States of Micronesia, Mongolia, New Zealand, Palau, Papua New Guinea, Philippines, Samoa, Seychelles, Solomon Islands, Vanuatu | 72,397 | 3.38 |
| ABDULRAHMAN A. AL-TUWAIJRI | Saudi Arabia | 70,105 | 3.27 |
| KLEO-THONG HETRAKUL (Thailand) | Brunei, Cambodia, Fiji, Indonesia, Laos, Malaysia, Myanmar, Nepal, Singapore, Thailand, Tonga, Viet Nam | 68,229 | 3.19 |
| JOSÉ PEDRO DE MORAIS, Jnr (Angola) | Angola, Botswana, Burundi, Eritrea, Ethiopia, The Gambia, Kenya, Lesotho, Liberia, Malawi, Mozambique, Namibia, Nigeria, Sierra Leone, South Africa, Swaziland, Tanzania, Uganda, Zambia, Zimbabwe | 68,021 | 3.18 |
| A. SHAKOUR SHAALAN (Egypt) | Bahrain, Egypt, Iraq, Jordan, Kuwait, Lebanon, Libya, Maldives, Oman, Qatar, Syria, United Arab Emirates, Yemen | 61,242 | 2.87 |
| ALEKSEI V. MOZHIN | Russia | 59,704 | 2.79 |
| ROBERTO F. CIPPA (Switzerland) | Azerbaijan, Kyrgyzstan, Poland, Switzerland, Tajikistan, Turkmenistan, Uzbekistan | 56,628 | 2.64 |
| MURILO PORTUGAL (Brazil) | Brazil, Colombia, Dominican Republic, Ecuador, Guyana, Haiti, Panama, Suriname, Trinidad and Tobago | 53,422 | 2.49 |
| VIJAY L. KELKAR (India) | Bangladesh, Bhutan, India, Sri Lanka | 52,112 | 2.43 |
| ABBAS MIRAKHOR (Iran) | Algeria, Ghana, Iran, Morocco, Pakistan, Tunisia | 51,793 | 2.42 |
| WEI BENHUA | People's Republic of China | 47,122 | 2.20 |
| NICOLÁS EYZAGUIRRE (Chile) | Argentina, Bolivia, Chile, Paraguay, Peru, Uruguay | 43,395 | 2.03 |
| ALEXANDRE BARRO CHAMBRIER (Gabon) | Benin, Burkina Faso, Cameroon, Cape Verde, Central African Republic, Chad, Comoros, Republic of the Congo, Côte d'Ivoire, Djibouti, Equatorial Guinea, Gabon, Guinea, Guinea-Bissau, Madagascar, Mali, Mauritania, Mauritius, Niger, Rwanda, São Tomé and Príncipe, Senegal, Togo | 25,169 | 1.17 |

Note: At 1 September 1999 member countries' votes totalled 2,148,188, while votes in the Board of Executive Directors totalled 2,140,042. The latter total does not include the votes of Afghanistan and Somalia, which did not participate in the 1998 election of Executive Directors; it also excludes the votes of the Democratic Republic of the Congo and Sudan, whose voting rights were suspended with effect from 2 June 1994 and 9 August 1993 respectively.

joined the Fund since the last allocation of SDRs in 1981 had not yet received any of the units of account. In September 1997 at the annual meeting of the Executive Board, a resolution approving a special allocation of SDR 21,400m. was passed, in order to ensure an SDR to quota ratio of 29.32%, for all member countries. The resolution was to come into effect following its acceptance by 60% of member countries, having 85% of the total voting power. At the end of 1999 50 members (30.6% of the voting power) had ratified the amendment.

From 1974 to 1980 the SDR was valued on the basis of the market exchange rate for a basket of 16 currencies, belonging to the members with the largest exports of goods and services; since 1981 it has been based on the currencies of the five largest exporters (France, Germany, Japan, the United Kingdom and the USA), although the list of currencies and the weight of each in the SDR valuation basket is revised every five years. In January 1999 the IMF incorporated the new currency of the European Economic and Monetary Union, the euro, into the valuation basket; it replaced the French and German currencies, on the basis of their conversion rates with the euro as agreed by the EU. The value of the SDR averaged US $1.3565 during 1998, and at 30 November 1999 stood at $1.3696.

The Second Amendment to the Articles of Agreement (1978) altered and expanded the possible uses of the SDR in transactions with other participants. These 'prescribed holders' of the SDRs have the same degree of freedom as Fund members to buy and sell SDRs and to receive or use them in loans, pledges, swaps, donations or settlement of financial obligations. In 1998/99 there were 15 'prescribed holders': the African Development Bank and the African Development Fund, the Arab Monetary Fund, the Asian Development Bank, the Bank of Central African States, the Bank for International Settlements, the Central Bank of West African States, the East African Development Bank, the Eastern Caribbean Central Bank, the International Bank for Reconstruction and Development and the International Development Association, the International Fund for Agricultural Development, the Islamic Development Bank, the Latin American Reserve Fund and the Nordic Investment Bank.

## QUOTAS

Each member is assigned a quota related to its national income, monetary reserves, trade balance and other economic indicators. A member's subscription is equal to its quota and is payable partly in SDRs and partly in its own currency. The quota determines a member's voting power, which is based on one vote for each

SDR 100,000 of its quota *plus* the 250 votes to which each member is entitled. A member's quota also determines its access to the financial resources of the IMF, and its allocation of SDRs.

Quotas are reviewed at intervals of not more than five years, to take into account the state of the world economy and members' different rates of development. General increases were made in 1959, 1966, 1970, 1978, 1980 and 1984, while special increases were made for the People's Republic of China in April 1980, for a group of 11 members in December 1980, and for Saudi Arabia in April 1981. In June 1990 the Board of Governors authorized proposals for a Ninth General Review of quotas. Total quotas were to be increased by roughly 50% (depending on various factors). At the same time the Board of Governors stipulated that the quota increase could occur only after the Third Amendment of the IMF's Articles of Agreement had come into effect. The amendment provides for the suspension of voting and other related rights of members that do not fulfil their obligations under the Articles. By September 1992 the necessary proportion of IMF members had accepted the amendment, and it entered into force in November. The Tenth General Review of quotas was concluded in December 1994, with the Board recommending no further increase in quotas. However, the Board resolved to monitor closely the Fund's liquidity. In October 1996 the Fund's Managing Director advocated an increase in quotas under the latest review of at least two-thirds in the light of the IMF's reduced liquidity position. (The IMF had extended unprecedentedly large amounts in stand-by arrangements during the period 1995–96, notably to Mexico and Russia.) In January 1998 the Board of Governors adopted a resolution in support of an increase in quotas of 45%, subject to approval by member states constituting 85% of total quotas (as at December 1997). Sufficient consent had been granted by January 1999 to enable the Eleventh General Review of Quotas to enter into effect. At 2 December 1999 total quotas in the Fund amounted to SDR 210,245.9m.

## RESOURCES

Members' subscriptions form the basic resource of the IMF. They are supplemented by borrowing. Under the General Arrangements to Borrow (GAB), established in 1962, the 'Group of Ten' industrialized nations (G-10—Belgium, Canada, France, Germany, Italy, Japan, the Netherlands, Sweden, the United Kingdom and the USA) and Switzerland (which became a member of the IMF in May 1992 but which had been a full participant in the GAB from April 1984) undertake to lend the Fund as much as SDR 17,000m. in their own currencies, to assist in fulfilling the balance-of-payments requirements of any member of the group, or in response to requests to the Fund from countries with balance-of-payments problems that could threaten the stability of the international monetary system. In 1983 the Fund entered into an agreement with Saudi Arabia, in association with the GAB, making available SDR 1,500m., and other borrowing arrangements were completed in 1984 with the Bank for International Settlements, the Saudi Arabian Monetary Agency, Belgium and Japan, making available a further SDR 6,000m. In 1986 another borrowing arrangement with Japan made available SDR 3,000m. In May 1996 GAB participants concluded an agreement in principle to expand the resources available for borrowing to SDR 34,000m., by securing the support of 25 countries with the financial capacity to support the international monetary system. The so-called New Arrangements to Borrow (NAB) was approved by the Executive Board in January 1997. It was to enter into force, for an initial five-year period, as soon as the five largest potential creditors participating in NAB had approved the initiative and the total credit arrangement of participants endorsing the scheme had reached at least SDR 28,900m. While the GAB credit arrangement was to remain in effect, the NAB was expected to be the first facility to be activated in the event of the Fund's requiring supplementary resources. In July 1998 the GAB was activated for the first time in more than 20 years in order to provide funds totalling US $6,300m. in support of an IMF emergency assistance package for Russia (the first time the GAB had been used for a non-participant). The NAB became effective in November, and was used for the first time as part of an extensive programme of support for Brazil, which was adopted by the IMF in early December.

## DRAWING ARRANGEMENTS

Exchange transactions within the Fund take the form of members' purchases (i.e. drawings) from the Fund of the currencies of other members for the equivalent amounts of their own currencies. Fund resources are available to eligible members on an essentially short-term and revolving basis to provide members with temporary assistance to contribute to the solution of their payments problems. Before making a purchase, a member must show that its balance of payments or reserve position makes the purchase necessary. Apart from this requirement, reserve tranche purchases (i.e. purchases that do not bring the Fund's holdings of the member's currency to a level above its quota) are permitted unconditionally.

With further purchases, however, the Fund's policy of 'conditionality' means that a member requesting assistance must agree to adjust its economic policies, as stipulated by the IMF. All requests other than for use of the reserve tranche are examined by the Executive Board to determine whether the proposed use would be consistent with the Fund's policies, and a member must discuss its proposed adjustment programme (including fiscal, monetary, exchange and trade policies) with IMF staff. Purchases outside the reserve tranche are made in four credit tranches, each equivalent to 25% of the member's quota; a member must reverse the transaction by repurchasing its own currency (with SDRs or currencies specified by the Fund) within a specified time. A credit tranche purchase is usually made under a 'Stand-by Arrangement' with the Fund, or under the Extended Fund Facility. A Stand-by Arrangement is normally of one or two years' duration, and the amount is made available in instalments, subject to the member's observance of 'performance criteria'; repurchases must be made within three-and-a-quarter to five years. An Extended Arrangement is normally of three years' duration, and the member must submit detailed economic programmes and progress reports for each year; repurchases must be made within four-and-a-half to 10 years. A member whose payments imbalance is large in relation to its quota may make use of temporary facilities established by the Fund using borrowed resources, namely the 'enlarged access policy' established in 1981, which helps to finance Stand-by and Extended Arrangements for such a member, up to a limit of between 90% and 110% of the member's quota annually. Repurchases are made within three-and-a-half to seven years. In October 1994 the Executive Board approved a temporary increase in members' access to IMF resources, on the basis of a recommendation by the Interim Committee. The annual access limit under IMF regular tranche drawings, Stand-by Arrangements and Extended Fund Facility credits was increased from 68% to 100% of a member's quota, with the cumulative access limit remaining at 300% of quota. The arrangements were extended, on a temporary basis, in November 1997.

In addition, there are special-purpose arrangements, all of which are subject to the member's co-operation with the Fund to find an appropriate solution to its difficulties. The Buffer Stock Financing Facility (BSFF) was established in 1969 in order to enable members to pay their contributions to the buffer stocks which were intended to stabilize markets for primary commodities. The BSFF has not been used since 1984. In 1988 the Fund established the Compensatory and Contingency Financing Facility (CCFF), which replaced and expanded a previous facility. The CCFF provides compensation to members whose export earnings are reduced as a result of circumstances beyond their control, or which are affected by excess costs of cereal imports. Contingency financing is provided to help members to maintain their efforts at economic adjustment even when affected by a sharp increase in interest rates or other externally-derived difficulties. Repurchases are made within three-and-a-quarter to five years. No members used the CCFF in 1997/98. In July 1998, however, the IMF approved US $2,157m. under the CCFF as part of a programme of assistance for Russia, in particular to compensate for reduced export earnings relating to a decline in petroleum prices. A further SDR 443m. was drawn under the CCFF during 1998/99 by Azerbaijan, Jordan and Pakistan. In December 1997 the Executive Board established a new Supplemental Reserve Facility (SRF) to provide short-term assistance to members experiencing exceptional balance-of-payments difficulties resulting from a sudden loss of market confidence. Repayments were to be made within one to one-and-a-half years of the purchase, unless otherwise extended by the Board. The SRF was activated immediately to provide SDR 9,950m. to the Republic of Korea, as part of Stand-by Arrangement amounting to SDR 15,550m., the largest amount ever committed by the Fund. (With additional financing from governments and international institutions, the total assistance 'package' for the Republic of Korea reached an estimated $57,000m.) In July 1998 SDR 4,000m. was made available to Russia under the SRF and, in December, some SDR 9,100m. was extended to Brazil under the SRF as part of a new Stand-by Arrangement. In April 1999 an additional facility was established, for a two-year period, to provide short-term financing on similar terms to the SRF in order to prevent more stable economies being affected by adverse international financial developments and to maintain investor confidence. Under the Contingent Credit Lines (CCL) member countries were to have access to up to 500% of their quota, subject to meeting various economic criteria stipulated by the Fund.

In April 1993 the Fund established the systemic transformation facility (STF) to assist countries of the former USSR and other economies in transition. The STF was intended to be a temporary facility to enable member countries to draw on financial assistance for balance-of-payments difficulties resulting from severe disruption of their normal trade and payments arrangements. Access to the facility was limited to not more than 50% of a member's quota, and repayment terms were equal to those for the extended Fund facility. The expiry date for access to resources under this facility was extended by one year from 31 December 1994, to the end of 1995. During the STF's period of operations purchases amounting to SDR 3,984m. were made by 20 countries.

In 1986 the Fund established a Structural Adjustment Facility (SAF) to provide balance-of-payments assistance on concessionary terms to low-income developing countries. In November 1993 the Executive Board agreed that no new commitments would be made under the SAF. In 1987 the Fund established an Enhanced Structural Adjustment Facility (ESAF), which was to provide new resources of SDR 6,000m. (in addition to any amounts remaining undisbursed under the SAF), to assist the adjustment efforts of, in particular, heavily indebted countries. Eligible members must develop a three-year adjustment programme (with assistance given jointly by staff of the Fund and of the World Bank) to strengthen the balance-of-payments situation and foster sustainable economic growth. Maximum access is set at 190% (255% in exceptional circumstances) of the member's quota. ESAF loans carry an interest rate of 0.5% per year and are repayable within 10 years, including a five-and-a-half-year grace period. In February 1994 a new period of operations of the ESAF became effective, following an agreement to enlarge the ESAF Trust (the funding source for ESAF arrangements) by transferring the bulk of resources from the Special Disbursement Account (SDA) of the SAF. The enlarged ESAF came into effect on 23 February 1994, when the Executive Board accepted that sufficient contributions had been committed to the Loan and Subsidy Accounts of the ESAF Trust. The terms and conditions of the new Trust facility remained the same as those under the original ESAF, although the list of countries eligible for assistance was enlarged by six to 78 (subsequently extended to 80). The commitment period for lending from the ESAF Trust expired on 31 December 1996, with disbursements to be made through to the end of 1999. In September 1996 the Interim Committee of the Board of Governors endorsed measures to finance the ESAF for a further five-year (2000–2004) period, after which the facility was to become self-sustaining. The interim period of the ESAF was to be funded mainly from bilateral contributions, but drawing on the Fund's additional resources as necessary. In September 1999 it was announced that the successor facility to the ESAF was to be a Poverty Reduction and Growth Facility, with greater emphasis on poverty reduction as a key element of growth-orientated economic strategies.

The ESAF was to support, through long-maturity loans and grants, IMF participation in a joint initiative, with the World Bank, to provide exceptional assistance to heavily indebted poor countries (HIPCs), in order to help them to achieve a sustainable level of debt management. The initiative was formally approved at the September 1996 meeting of the Interim Committee, having received the support of the 'Paris Club' of official creditors, which agreed to increase the relief on official debt from 67% to 80%. In February 1997 the Executive Board established an ESAF-HIPC Trust, through which the IMF was to channel resources for the HIPC initiative and interim ESAF operations. In all, 41 HIPCs were identified, 33 of which were in sub-Saharan Africa. In April 1997 Uganda was approved as the first beneficiary of the initiative (see World Bank, p. 79). The Fund was to provide assistance worth US $70m. in April 1998, on the condition that other official creditors contributed their agreed proportion of debt relief and that Uganda pursued a programme of economic and social policy reform. In September 1997 assistance was approved for Bolivia and Burkina Faso under the HIPC initiative. Assistance was approved for Guyana in December 1997, and for Côte d'Ivoire, Mozambique and Mali in March, April and September 1998 respectively. At September 1999 IMF assistance under the scheme in net present value terms amounted to $305m. of a total of $3,355m. of assistance committed, which had a nominal debt relief value of $6,770m. In early 1999 the IMF and World Bank initiated a comprehensive review of the HIPC scheme, in order to consider modifications of the initiative and to strengthen the link between debt relief and poverty reduction. A consensus emerged among the financial institutions and leading industralized nations to enhance the scheme, in order to make it available to more countries, and to accelerate the process of providing debt relief. In September the IMF Board of Governors expressed its commitment to undertaking an off-market transaction of a percentage of the Fund's gold reserves (i.e. a sale, at market prices, to central banks of member countries with repayment obligations to the Fund, which were then to be made in gold), as part of the funding arrangements of the enhanced HIPC scheme.

During 1998/99 the IMF approved funding commitments amounting to SDR 29,413m. in new arrangements. Of the total amount, SDR 14,325m. was committed under seven Stand-by Arrangements (including SDR 13,025m. for Brazil), SDR 14,090m. under five Extended Arrangements, and SDR 998m. under 10 new and six augmented ESAF arrangements. During 1998/99 members' purchases from the general resources account amounted to SDR 21,414m., compared with SDR 18,951m. in 1997/98, with the main users of IMF resources being Brazil, Indonesia and Russia. Outstanding IMF credit at 30 April 1999 totalled SDR 67,175m., compared with SDR 56,026m. as at the previous year.

### TECHNICAL ASSISTANCE

This is provided by special missions or resident representatives who advise members on every aspect of economic management. Specialized technical assistance is provided by the IMF's various departments, and accounted for some 15% of the administrative budget in 1998/99. The IMF Institute, founded in 1964, trains officials from member countries in financial analysis and policy, balance-of-payments methodology and public finance: it also gives assistance to national and regional training centres. The IMF is co-sponsor of the Joint Vienna Institute, which was opened in the Austrian capital in October 1992 and which trains officials from former centrally-planned economies in various aspects of economic management and public administration. In May 1998 an IMF–Singapore Regional Training Institute was inaugurated, in collaboration with the Singaporean Government, in order to provide training for officials from the Asia-Pacific region. In January 1999 the IMF, in co-operation with the African Development Bank and the World Bank, announced the establishment of a Joint Africa Institute, in Abidjan, Côte d'Ivoire, which was to offer training to officials from African countries from the second half of the year. The IMF Institute also co-operates with other established regional training centres and institutes in order to refine its delivery of technical assistance and training services.

## Publications

*Annual Report.*

*Balance of Payments Statistics Yearbook.*

*Direction of Trade Statistics* (quarterly and annually).

*Finance and Development* (quarterly, published jointly with the World Bank).

*Government Finance Statistics Yearbook.*

*IMF Economic Reviews* (3 a year).

*IMF Survey* (2 a month).

*International Capital Markets: Developments, Prospects and Key Policy Issues.*

*International Financial Statistics* (monthly and annually, also on CD-ROM).

*Joint BIS-IMF-OECD-World Bank Statistics on External Debt* (quarterly).

*Staff Papers* (quarterly).

*World Economic Outlook* (2 a year).

Occasional papers, economic and financial surveys, pamphlets, booklets.

## Statistics

**QUOTAS** (SDR million)

| | 1 December 1999 |
|---|---|
| Afghanistan* | (161.9) 120.4 |
| Albania | 48.7 |
| Algeria | 1,254.7 |
| Angola | 286.3 |
| Antigua and Barbuda | 13.5 |
| Argentina | 2,117.1 |
| Armenia | 92.0 |
| Australia | 3,236.4 |
| Austria | 1,872.3 |
| Azerbaijan | 160.9 |
| Bahamas | 130.3 |
| Bahrain | 135.0 |
| Bangladesh | 533.3 |
| Barbados | 67.5 |
| Belarus | 386.4 |
| Belgium | 4,605.2 |
| Belize | 18.8 |
| Benin | 61.9 |
| Bhutan | 6.3 |
| Bolivia | 171.5 |
| Bosnia and Herzegovina | 169.1 |
| Botswana | 63.0 |
| Brazil | 3,036.1 |
| Brunei† | (215.2) 150.0 |
| Bulgaria | 640.2 |
| Burkina Faso | 60.2 |
| Burundi | 77.0 |
| Cambodia | 87.5 |
| Cameroon | 185.7 |
| Canada | 6,369.2 |
| Cape Verde | 9.6 |

| *— continued* | 1 December 1999 |
|---|---|
| Central African Republic | 55.7 |
| Chad | 56.0 |
| Chile | 856.1 |
| China, People's Republic | 4,687.2 |
| Colombia | 774.0 |
| Comoros | 8.9 |
| Congo, Democratic Republic* | (533.0) 291.0 |
| Congo, Republic | 84.6 |
| Costa Rica | 164.1 |
| Côte d'Ivoire | 325.2 |
| Croatia | 365.1 |
| Cyprus | 139.6 |
| Czech Republic | 819.3 |
| Denmark | 1,642.8 |
| Djibouti | 15.9 |
| Dominica | 8.2 |
| Dominican Republic | 218.9 |
| Ecuador | 302.3 |
| Egypt | 943.7 |
| El Salvador | 171.3 |
| Equatorial Guinea | 32.6 |
| Eritrea | 15.9 |
| Estonia | 65.2 |
| Ethiopia | 133.7 |
| Fiji | 70.3 |
| Finland | 1,263.8 |
| France | 10,738.5 |
| Gabon | 154.3 |
| The Gambia | 31.1 |
| Georgia | 150.3 |
| Germany | 13,008.2 |
| Ghana | 369.0 |
| Greece | 823.0 |
| Grenada | 11.7 |
| Guatemala | 210.2 |
| Guinea | 107.1 |
| Guinea-Bissau | 14.2 |
| Guyana | 90.9 |
| Haiti† | (81.9) 60.7 |
| Honduras | 129.5 |
| Hungary | 1,038.4 |
| Iceland | 117.6 |
| India | 4,158.2 |
| Indonesia | 2,079.3 |
| Iran | 1,497.2 |
| Iraq* | (1,188.4) 504.0 |
| Ireland | 838.4 |
| Israel | 928.2 |
| Italy | 7,055.5 |
| Jamaica | 273.5 |
| Japan | 13,312.8 |
| Jordan | 170.5 |
| Kazakhstan | 365.7 |
| Kenya | 271.4 |
| Kiribati | 5.6 |
| Korea, Republic | 1,633.6 |
| Kuwait | 1,381.1 |
| Kyrgyzstan | 88.8 |
| Laos† | (52.9) 39.1 |
| Latvia | 126.8 |
| Lebanon | 203.0 |
| Lesotho | 34.9 |
| Liberia* | (129.2) 73.3 |
| Libya | 1,123.7 |
| Lithuania | 144.2 |
| Luxembourg | 279.1 |
| Macedonia, former Yugoslav republic | 68.9 |
| Madagascar | 122.2 |
| Malawi | 69.4 |
| Malaysia | 1,486.6 |
| Maldives | 8.2 |
| Mali | 93.3 |
| Malta | 102.0 |
| Marshall Islands† | (3.5) 2.5 |
| Mauritania | 64.4 |
| Mauritius | 101.6 |
| Mexico | 2,585.8 |
| Micronesia, Federated States | 5.1 |
| Moldova | 123.2 |
| Mongolia | 51.1 |
| Morocco | 588.2 |

| *— continued* | 1 December 1999 |
|---|---|
| Mozambique | 113.6 |
| Myanmar | 258.4 |
| Namibia | 136.5 |
| Nepal | 71.3 |
| Netherlands | 5,162.4 |
| New Zealand | 894.6 |
| Nicaragua | 130.0 |
| Niger | 65.8 |
| Nigeria | 1,753.2 |
| Norway | 1,671.7 |
| Oman | 194.0 |
| Pakistan | 1,033.7 |
| Palau | 3.1 |
| Panama | 206.6 |
| Papua New Guinea | 131.6 |
| Paraguay | 99.9 |
| Peru | 638.4 |
| Philippines | 879.9 |
| Poland | 1,369.0 |
| Portugal | 867.4 |
| Qatar | 263.8 |
| Romania | 1,030.2 |
| Russia | 5,945.4 |
| Rwanda | 80.1 |
| Saint Christopher and Nevis | 8.9 |
| Saint Lucia | 15.3 |
| Saint Vincent and the Grenadines† | (8.3) 6.0 |
| Samoa | 11.6 |
| San Marino | 17.0 |
| São Tomé and Príncipe | 7.4 |
| Saudi Arabia | 6,985.5 |
| Senegal | 161.8 |
| Seychelles | 8.8 |
| Sierra Leone | 103.7 |
| Singapore | 862.5 |
| Slovakia | 357.5 |
| Slovenia | 231.0 |
| Solomon Islands | 10.4 |
| Somalia* | (81.7) 44.2 |
| South Africa | 1,868.5 |
| Spain | 3,048.9 |
| Sri Lanka | 413.4 |
| Sudan* | (315.1) 169.7 |
| Suriname | 92.1 |
| Swaziland | 50.7 |
| Sweden | 2,395.5 |
| Switzerland | 3,458.5 |
| Syria | 293.6 |
| Tajikistan | 87.0 |
| Tanzania | 198.9 |
| Thailand | 1,081.9 |
| Togo | 73.4 |
| Tonga | 6.9 |
| Trinidad and Tobago | 335.6 |
| Tunisia | 286.5 |
| Turkey | 964.0 |
| Turkmenistan | 75.2 |
| Uganda | 180.5 |
| Ukraine | 1,372.0 |
| United Arab Emirates | 611.7 |
| United Kingdom | 10,738.5 |
| USA | 37,149.3 |
| Uruguay | 306.5 |
| Uzbekistan | 275.6 |
| Vanuatu | 17.0 |
| Venezuela | 2,659.1 |
| Viet Nam | 329.1 |
| Yemen | 243.5 |
| Zambia | 489.1 |
| Zimbabwe | 353.4 |

* At 1 December 1999 these members had overdue obligations and were therefore ineligible to consent to the increase in quotas under the Eleventh General Review (which came into effect in January). The figures listed are those determined under previous reviews, while the figures in parentheses are the proposed Eleventh General Review quotas.

† At 1 December 1999 these members had not yet consented to their increased quotas under the Eleventh General Review. The proposed quotas are those in parentheses.

**FINANCIAL ACTIVITIES** (SDR million, year ending 30 April)

| Type of Transaction | 1994 | 1995 | 1996 | 1997 | 1998 | 1999 |
|---|---|---|---|---|---|---|
| Total disbursements | 5,903 | 11,178 | 12,303 | 5,644 | 19,924 | 22,240 |
| Purchases by facility (General Resources Account)* | 5,241 | 10,592 | 10,826 | 4,939 | 18,951 | 21,414 |
| Stand-by and first credit tranche | 1,052 | 7,587 | 9,127 | 1,836 | 16,127 | 12,868 |
| Compensatory and Contingency Financing Facility | 718 | 287 | 9 | 282 | — | 2,600 |
| Extended Fund Facility | 746 | 1,595 | 1,554 | 2,820 | 2,824 | 5,947 |
| Systemic Transformation Facility | 2,725 | 1,123 | 136 | — | — | — |
| Loans under SAF/ESAF arrangements | 662 | 587 | 1,477 | 705 | 973 | 826 |
| Special Disbursement Account resources | 68 | 19 | 185 | — | — | — |
| ESAF Trust resources | 594 | 568 | 1,292 | 705 | 973 | 826 |
| By region: | | | | | | |
| Africa | 1,185 | 1,022 | 2,304 | 992 | 876 | 542 |
| Asia | 690 | 383 | 367 | 181 | 16,446 | 8,918 |
| Europe | 3,258 | 2,896 | 5,156 | 3,381 | 2,170 | 5,169 |
| Middle East | 11 | 76 | 129 | 153 | 148 | 157 |
| Western Hemisphere | 758 | 6,801 | 4,427 | 937 | 283 | 7,454 |
| Repurchases and repayments | 4,509 | 4,231 | 7,100 | 7,196 | 4,385 | 11,091 |
| Repurchases | 4,343 | 3,984 | 6,698 | 6,668 | 3,789 | 10,465 |
| Trust Fund and SAF/ESAF loan repayments | 166 | 247 | 402 | 528 | 596 | 626 |
| Total outstanding credit provided by Fund (end of year) | 29,889 | 36,837 | 42,040 | 40,488 | 56,026 | 67,175 |
| *Of which:* | | | | | | |
| General Resources Account | 25,533 | 32,140 | 36,268 | 34,539 | 49,701 | 60,651 |
| Special Disbursement Account | 1,835 | 1,651 | 1,545 | 1,220 | 922 | 677 |
| Administered Accounts | | | | | | |
| Trust Fund | 105 | 102 | 95 | 90 | 90 | 89 |
| ESAF Trust† | 2,416 | 2,944 | 4,132 | 4,639 | 5,314 | 5,758 |

* Excluding reserve tranche purchases.
† Including Saudi Fund for Development associated loans.
Source: *International Monetary Fund Annual Report 1999.*

# International Telecommunication Union—ITU

**Address:** Place des Nations, 1211 Geneva 20, Switzerland.
**Telephone:** (22) 7305111; **fax:** (22) 7337256; **e-mail:** itumail@itu.int; **internet:** www.itu.int.

Founded in 1865, ITU became a specialized agency of the UN in 1947. It acts to encourage world co-operation in the use of telecommunication, to promote technical development and to harmonize national policies in the field.

### MEMBERS

189 member states: see Table on pp. 114–116. A further 363 scientific and technical companies, public and private operators, broadcasters and other organizations are also ITU members.

## Organization

(December 1999)

### PLENIPOTENTIARY CONFERENCE

The supreme organ of ITU; normally meets every four years. The main tasks of the Conference are to elect ITU's leadership, establish policies, revise the Convention (see below) and approve limits on budgetary spending.

### WORLD CONFERENCES ON INTERNATIONAL TELECOMMUNICATIONS

The World Conferences on International Telecommunications are held at the request of members and after approval by the Plenipotentiary Conference. The World Conferences are authorized to review and revise the regulations applying to the provision and operation of international telecommunications services. As part of the 1993 restructuring of ITU, separate Conferences were to be held by three sectors (see below): Radiocommunication Conferences (to be held every two years); Telecommunication Standardization Conferences (to be held every four years or at the request of one-quarter of ITU members); and Telecommunication Development Conferences (to be held every four years).

### ITU COUNCIL

The Council meets annually in Geneva and is composed of 46 members elected by the Plenipotentiary Conference.

The Council ensures the efficient co-ordination and implementation of the work of the Union in all matters of policy, administration and finance, in the interval between Plenipotentiary Conferences, and approves the annual budget. It also co-ordinates the efforts of ITU to assist developing countries in the improvement of telecommunications equipment and networks.

### GENERAL SECRETARIAT

The Secretary-General is elected by the Plenipotentiary Conference, and is responsible to it for the General Secretariat's work, and for the Union's administrative and financial services. The General Secretariat's staff totals about 712, representing 74 nationalities; the working languages are Arabic, Chinese, English, French, Russian and Spanish.

**Secretary-General:** Yoshio Utsumi (Japan).

**Deputy Secretary-General:** Roberto Blois (Brazil).

## Convention

The International Telecommunication Convention is the definitive convention of the Union, member countries being those that signed it in 1932 or acceded to it later. Since 1932 it has been superseded by new versions adopted at successive Plenipotentiary Conferences. At the Additional Plenipotentiary Conference held in December 1992, in Geneva, Switzerland, a new constitution and convention were signed. They entered into force on 1 July 1994, but the provisions relating to the new structure and functioning of ITU became effective on 1 March 1993. The Constitution contains the fundamental provisions of ITU, whereas the Convention contains other provisions which complement those of the Constitution and which, by their nature, require periodic revision.

The Constitution and Convention establish the purposes and structure of the Union, contain the general provisions relating to telecommunications and special provisions for radio, and deal with relations with the UN and other organizations. Both instruments are further complemented by the administrative regulations listed below.

### INTERNATIONAL TELECOMMUNICATIONS REGULATIONS

The International Telecommunications Regulations were adopted in 1988 and entered into force in 1990. They establish the general principles relating to the provision and operation of international telecommunication services offered to the public. They also establish rules applicable to administrations and recognized private operating agencies. Their provisions are applied to both wire and wireless telegraph and telephone communications in so far as the Radio Regulations do not provide otherwise.

### RADIO REGULATIONS

The Radio Regulations, which first appeared in 1906, include general rules for the assignment and use of frequencies and the associated orbital positions for space stations. They include a Table of Frequency Allocations (governing the use of radio frequency bands between 9 kHz and 400 GHz) for the various radio services (*inter alia* radio broadcasting, television, radio astronomy, navigation aids, point-to-point service, maritime mobile, amateur).

The 1979 World Administrative Radio Conference undertook a complete revision of the radio spectrum allocation. Partial revisions were also made by subsequent world and regional administrative radio conferences, particularly with reference to space radiocommunications, using satellites.

## Activities

In December 1992 an Additional Plenipotentiary Conference was held in Geneva, Switzerland, which agreed on reforms to the structure and functioning of ITU. As a result, ITU comprised three sectors corresponding to its main functions: standardization; radiocommunication; and development. In October 1994 the ordinary Plenipotentiary Conference, held in Kyoto, Japan, adopted ITU's first strategic plan. A second strategic plan, for the period 1999–2003, was adopted by the conference, convened in Minneapolis, USA, in October/November 1998. The plan recognized new trends and developments in the world telecommunication environment, such as globalization, liberalization, and greater competition, assessed their implications for ITU, and proposed new strategies and priorities to enable ITU to function effectively. The conference approved the active involvement of ITU in governance issues relating to the internet, and recommended that a World Summit on the Information Society be convened, given the rapid developments in that field. During 1999 an ITU Year 2000 Task Force pursued efforts to ensure that communications companies complied with measures to prevent any potential difficulties resulting from the millennium date change.

### RADIOCOMMUNICATION SECTOR

The role of the sector is to ensure an equitable and efficient use of the radio-frequency spectrum by all radiocommunication services. The Radio Regulations are reviewed and revised by the sector's conferences. The technical work on issues to be considered by conferences is conducted by Radiocommunication Assemblies, on the basis of recommendations made by Study Groups. These groups of experts study technical questions relating to radiocommunications, according to a study programme formulated by the Assemblies. The Assemblies may approve, modify or reject any recommendations of the Study Groups, and are authorized to establish new groups and to abolish others. The Sector administers ITU's 'International Mobile Telecommunication-2000' initiative, which aimed to provide wireless access to the global telecommunication infrastructure through satellite and terrestrial systems. The 1998 Plenipotentiary Conference resolved to establish a working group open to members of the Sector to prepare recommendations concerning the submission and processing of charges of satellite networking filings. A World Radiocommunication Conference was scheduled to be held in İstanbul, Turkey, in May/June 2000.

The procedural rules used in the application of the Radio Regulations were to be considered by a nine-member Radio Regulations Board, which may also perform duties relating to the allocation and use of frequencies and consider cases of interference.

The administrative work of the sector is the responsibility of the Radiocommunication Bureau, which is headed by an elected Director. The Bureau co-ordinates the work of Study Groups, provides administrative support for the Radio Regulations Board, and works alongside the General Secretariat to prepare conferences and to provide relevant assistance to developing countries. The Director is assisted by an Advisory Group.

**Director:** ROBERT W. JONES (Canada).

### TELECOMMUNICATION STANDARDIZATION SECTOR

The sector was established to study technical, operational and tariff issues in order to standardize telecommunications throughout the world. The sector's conferences consider draft standards, referred to as Recommendations, which, if approved, establish ITU guidelines to guarantee the effective provision of telecommunication services. According to the priority given to different issues concerning draft standards, the conferences may maintain, establish or abolish Study Groups. Recommendations may be approved outside of the four-year interval between conferences if a Study Group concludes such action to be urgent. According to the 1999–2003 strategic plan, one of the priorities for the sector was to be the formulation of recommendations relating to Internet Protocol-based networks, as well as more general recommendations to keep pace with the rapid technological developments and expansion of market demand. A World Telecommunication Standardization Assembly was scheduled to be held in Montréal, Canada, in 2000, to consider settlement rates for international connections. In June 1999 an ITU Study Group recommended implementing a scaled system of accounting rates based on telephone densities.

Preparations for conferences and other meetings of the sector are made by the Telecommunication Standardization Bureau (ITU-T). It administers the application of conference decisions, as well as relevant provisions of the International Telecommunications Regulations. The ITU-T is headed by an elected Director, who is assisted by an Advisory Group. The Director reports to conferences and to the ITU Council on the activities of the sector.

**Director:** HOULIN ZHAO (People's Republic of China).

### TELECOMMUNICATION DEVELOPMENT SECTOR

The sector's objectives are to promote the development of telecommunication networks and services in developing countries, to facilitate the transfer of appropriate technologies and the use of resources by preferential credit arrangements, and to provide advice on issues specific to telecommunications. The sector operates as an executing agency for projects under the UN development system or other funding arrangements. In 1995 the ITU supported the establishment of an independent company, *World Tel*, which aimed to provide funding, technology and management assistance to telecommunications projects in low-income countries. The company's first large-scale project, finalized in 1997, aimed to provide local telephone services in Mexico.

The sector holds conferences regularly to encourage international co-operation in the development of telecommunications, and to determine strategies for development. Conferences consider the result of work undertaken by Study Groups on issues of benefit to developing countries, including development policy, finance, network planning and operation of services. The sector aims to hold one world conference and one regional conference each in Africa, Asia and the Pacific, the Americas, Europe, and the Arab States every four years. The first World Telecommunications Development Conference was held in Buenos Aires, Argentina, in 1994; the second was convened in Valletta, Malta, in March 1998. The 1999–2003 strategic plan emphasized the need for the sector to enhance collaboration with the private sector and relevant organizations, especially at regional and sub-regional levels, and to promote new and more effective partnership arrangements in and between the public and private sectors.

The administrative work of the sector is conducted by the Telecommunication Development Bureau, which may also study specific problems presented by a member state. The Director of the Bureau reports to conferences and the ITU Council, and is assisted by an Advisory Board.

**Director:** HAMEDOU I. TOURÉ (Mali).

### INFORMATION

ITU issues numerous technical and statistical publications (see below) and maintains a library and archives. It also offers the use of an on-line computer-based Telecom information exchange service (TIES), which provides access to ITU databases, document exchange, and other telecommunication information.

## Finance

The 1998 Plenipotentiary Conference approved a maximum budget of 333.2m. Swiss francs for the two-year period 2000–01.

## Publications

*List of Publications* (2 a year).

*Telecommunication Journal* (monthly in English, French and Spanish).

*World Telecommunication Development Report*.

Conventions, statistics, regulations, technical documents and manuals, conference documents.

# United Nations Educational, Scientific and Cultural Organization—UNESCO

**Address:** 7 place de Fontenoy, 75352 Paris 07 SP, France.

**Telephone:** 1-45-68-10-00; **fax:** 1-45-67-16-90; **internet:** www.unesco.org.

UNESCO was established in 1946 'for the purpose of advancing, through the educational, scientific and cultural relations of the peoples of the world, the objectives of international peace and the common welfare of mankind'.

### MEMBERS

188 members, and four associate members: see Table on pp. 114–116.

## Organization

(December 1999)

### GENERAL CONFERENCE

The supreme governing body of the Organization, the Conference meets in ordinary session once in two years and is composed of representatives of the member states.

### EXECUTIVE BOARD

The Board, comprising 58 members, prepares the programme to be submitted to the Conference and supervises its execution; it meets twice or sometimes three times a year.

### SECRETARIAT

**Director-General:** Koichiro Matsuura (Japan).

**Director of the Executive Office:** Georges Malempré (Belgium).

### CO-OPERATING BODIES

In accordance with UNESCO's constitution, national Commissions have been set up in most member states. These help to integrate work within the member states and the work of UNESCO.

### PRINCIPAL REGIONAL OFFICES

#### Africa

**Regional Office for Education in Africa:** 12 ave Roume, BP 3311, Dakar, Senegal; tel. 823-50-82; fax 823-83-93; e-mail uhdak@unesco.org; Dir P. Obanya.

**Regional Office for Science and Technology for Africa:** POB 30592, Nairobi, Kenya; tel. (2) 621234; fax (2) 215991; e-mail nairobi@unesco.org; internet www.unesco-nairobi.unon.org; f. 1965 to execute UNESCO's regional science programme, and to assist in the planning and execution of national programmes. Dir P. B. Vitta.

#### Arab States

**Regional Office for Education in the Arab States:** POB 5244, ave Cité Sportive, Beirut, Lebanon; tel. (1) 850075; fax (1) 824854; e-mail uhbei@unesco.org; internet www.unesco.org.lb; Dir V. Billeh.

**Regional Office for Science and Technology in the Arab States:** 8 Abdel Rahman Fahmy St, Garden City, Cairo 11511, Egypt; tel. (2) 3543036; fax (2) 3545296; e-mail uhcai@unesco.org; Dir Dr Mohamed el-Deek (acting).

#### Asia and the Pacific

**Principal Regional Office for Asia and the Pacific:** 920 Sukhumvit Rd, POB 967, Bangkok 10110, Thailand; tel. (2) 391-0789; fax (2) 391-0866; e-mail uhbgk@unesco.org; Dir Víctor Ordóñez.

**Regional Office for Book Development in Asia and the Pacific:** POB 2034, Islamabad 44000, Pakistan; tel. (51) 813308; fax (51) 825341; Dir M. M. Kaseju.

**Regional Office for Science and Technology for South-East Asia:** UN Building (2nd Floor), Jalan M. H. Thamrin 14, Tromol Pos 1273/JKT, Jakarta 10002, Indonesia; tel. (21) 3141308; fax (21) 3150382; e-mail uhjak@unesco.org; Dir Prof. Stephen Hill.

#### Europe and North America

**European Centre for Higher Education (CEPES):** Palatul Kretulescu, Stirbei Voda 39, 70732 Bucharest, Romania; tel. (1) 3159956; fax (1) 3123567; e-mail cepes@cepes.ro; internet www.cepes.ro; Dir Jan Sadlak.

**Regional Office for Science and Technology for Europe:** Palazzo Loredan degli Ambasciatori, 1262/A Dorsoduro, 30123 Venice, Italy; tel. (041) 522-5535; fax (041) 528-9995; e-mail roste@unesco.org; Dir Prof. Pierre Lasserre.

#### Latin America and the Caribbean

**Caribbean Network of Educational Innovation for Development:** POB 423, Bridgetown, St Michael, Barbados; tel. 4274771; fax 4360094; e-mail uhbri@unesco.org; Head of Office R. Colleen Winter-Braithwaite.

**Regional Centre for Higher Education in Latin America and the Caribbean (CRESALC):** Ave Los Chorros, c/c Calle Aceuducto, Edif. Asovincar, Altos de Sebucan, Apdo 68394, Caracas 1062 A, Venezuela; tel. (2) 286-0721; fax (2) 286-2039; e-mail uhcar@unesco.org; Dir L. Yarzabal.

**Regional Office for Culture in Latin America and the Caribbean:** Apdo 4158, Havana 4, Cuba; tel. (7) 32-7741; fax (7) 33-3144; e-mail uhldo@unesco.org; Dir Gloria López Morales.

**Regional Office for Education in Latin America and the Caribbean:** Calle Enrique Delpiano 2058, Plaza Pedro de Valdivia, Casilla 3187, Santiago, Chile; tel. (2) 2049032; fax (2) 2091875; e-mail uhstg@unesco.org; Dir A. Machado Pinheiro.

**Regional Office for Science and Technology for Latin America and the Caribbean:** Avda Brasil 2697 P. 4, Casilla 859, 11300 Montevideo, Uruguay; tel. (2) 7072023; fax (2) 7072140; e-mail orcyt@unesco.org.uy; internet www.unesco.org.uy; Dir Francisco José Lecayo.

## Activities

UNESCO's overall work programme for 1998–99 comprised the following four major programmes: Education for All Throughout Life; the Sciences in the Service of Development; Cultural Development: Heritage and Creativity; and Communication, Information and Informatics. It also incorporated two transdisciplinary projects—Education for a Sustainable Future and Towards a Culture of Peace—which encompassed UNESCO's fundamental objectives of promoting peace, international understanding, respect for human rights, and sustainable development, through education, training and awareness-generating activities. In implementing the work programme UNESCO was to target four priority groups, identified as being women, young people, African member states and least-developed countries. UNESCO is responsible for co-ordinating activities relating to the International Year for the Culture of Peace, designated by the UN General Assembly to be observed in 2000. A core element of the programme of activities was to be the signing by individuals of a Manifesto 2000 for a Culture of Peace and Non-violence, which was inaugurated in December 1998 at a celebration of the 50th anniversary of the Universal Declaration of Human Rights. In November 1999 the UNESCO General Conference confirmed that Education for All Throughout Life was to be UNESCO's main priority in its work programme for 2000–01. The other major programme areas of the previous biennium were also to be pursued.

### EDUCATION

Since its establishment UNESCO has devoted itself to promoting education in accordance with principles based on democracy and respect for human rights.

In March 1990 UNESCO, with other UN agencies, sponsored the World Conference on Education for All. 'Education for All' was subsequently adopted as a guiding principle of UNESCO's contribution to development. The promotion of access to learning opportunities throughout an individual's life is a priority for UNESCO's 1996–2001 programme of activities: Education for All Throughout Life was a key element of the 1998–99 work programme and was allocated a budget of US $104.6m. UNESCO aims, initially, to foster basic education for all. The second part of its strategy is to renew and diversify education systems, including updating curricular programmes in secondary education, strengthening science and technology activities and ensuring equal access to education for girls and women. In December 1993 the heads of government of nine highly-populated developing countries (Bangladesh, Brazil, the People's Republic of China, Egypt, India, Indonesia, Mexico, Nigeria and Pakistan), meeting in Delhi, India, agreed to co-operate with the objective of achieving comprehensive primary education for all children and of expanding further learning opportunities for children and adults. By September 1999 all nine countries had officially signed the so-called Delhi Declaration. In November the General Conference urged for further support for new basic education projects targeting marginalized groups, including orphans, indigenous populations, refugees and the disabled. In endorsing the education programme for 2000–01 the Conference also emphasized the importance of information technologies, and the need to train teachers in the use of these, with the objective of providing educational opportunities to all.

Within the UN system, UNESCO is responsible for providing technical assistance and educational services within the context of emergency situations. This includes providing education to refugees and displaced persons, as well as assistance for the rehabilitation of national education systems. In Palestine, UNESCO collaborates with UNRWA (q.v.) to assist with the training of teachers, educational planning and rehabilitation of schools.

UNESCO is concerned with improving the quality, relevance and efficiency of higher education. It assists member states in reforming their national systems, organizes high-level conferences for Ministers of Education and other decision-makers, and disseminates research papers. A World Conference on Higher Education was convened in October 1998 in Paris, France. The Conference adopted a World Declaration on Higher Education for the 21st Century, incorporating proposals to reform higher education, with emphasis on access to education, and educating for individual development and active participation in society. The Conference also approved a framework for Priority Action for Change and Development of Higher Education, which comprised guide-lines for governments and institutions to meet the objectives of greater accessibility, as well as improved standards and relevancy of higher education.

The International Institute for Educational Planning and the International Bureau of Education (see below) undertake training, research and the exchange of information on aspects of education. A UNESCO Institute for Education, based in Hamburg, Germany, researches literacy activities and the evolution of adult learning systems.

## SCIENCE AND SOCIAL SCIENCES

In November 1999 the General Conference identified the following as priority areas of UNESCO science initiatives in 2000–01: combating poverty; science education; support for the integration of women in all fields of science and technology; the need for a future generations approach; environment and sustainable development; promotion of cultural diversity; the elaboration of an ethical framework for the application of scientific results; and access to scientific information. UNESCO was to continue to implement projects under the programme of the Sciences in the Service of Development, which was initiated in the previous biennium in order to foster the advancement, transfer and exchange of knowledge in the physical, natural, social and human sciences and to promote their application with the objective of improving the social and natural environment. The Conference also endorsed a Declaration on Science and the Use of Scientific Knowledge and an agenda for action, which had been adopted at the World Conference on Science, held in June/July, in Budapest, Hungary.

UNESCO aims to improve the level of university teaching of the basic sciences through training courses, establishing national and regional networks and centres of excellence, and fostering co-operative research. In carrying out its mission, UNESCO relies on partnerships with non-governmental organizations and the world scientific communities. With the International Council of Scientific Unions and the Third World Academy of Sciences, UNESCO operates a short-term fellowship programme in the basic sciences and an exchange programme of visiting lecturers. In September 1996 UNESCO initiated a 10-year World Solar Programme, which aimed to promote the application of solar energy and to increase research, development and public awareness of all forms of ecologically-sustainable energy use.

In May 1997 the International Bioethics Committee, a group of 36 specialists who meet under UNESCO auspices, approved a draft version of a Universal Declaration on the Human Genome and Human Rights, in an attempt to provide ethical guide-lines for developments in human genetics. The Declaration, which identified some 100,000 hereditary genes as 'common heritage', was adopted by the UNESCO General Conference in November and committed states to promoting the dissemination of relevant scientific knowledge and co-operating in genome research. The November Conference also resolved to establish an 18-member World Commission on the Ethics of Scientific Knowledge and Technology to serve as a forum for the exchange of information and ideas and to promote dialogue between scientific communities, decision-makers and the public.

UNESCO has over the years established various forms of intergovernmental co-operation concerned with the environmental sciences and research on natural resources, in order to support the recommendations of the June 1992 UN Conference on Environment and Development and, in particular, the implementation of 'Agenda 21' to promote sustainable development. The International Geological Correlation Programme, undertaken jointly with the International Union of Geological Sciences, aims to improve and facilitate global research of geological processes. In the context of the International Decade for Natural Disaster Reduction (declared in 1990), UNESCO has conducted scientific studies of natural hazards and means of mitigating their effects and has organized several disaster-related workshops. The International Hydrological Programme considers scientific aspects of water resources assessment and management; and the Intergovernmental Oceanographic Commission (IOC, q.v.) focuses on issues relating to oceans, shorelines and marine resources, in particular the role of the ocean in climate and global systems. The IOC has been actively involved in the establishment of a Global Coral Reef Monitoring Network. An initiative on Environment and Development in Coastal Regions and in Small Islands is concerned with ensuring environmentally-sound and sustainable development by strengthening management of the following key areas: freshwater resources; the mitigation of coastline instability; biological diversity; and coastal ecosystem productivity.

UNESCO's Man and the Biosphere Programme supports a world-wide network of biosphere reserves (comprising 356 sites in 90 countries in 1998), which aim to promote environmental conservation and research, education and training in biodiversity and problems of land use (including the fertility of tropical soils and the cultivation of sacred sites). Following the signing of the Convention to Combat Desertification in October 1994, UNESCO initiated an International Programme for Arid Land Crops, based on a network of existing institutions, to assist implementation of the Convention.

In 1994 UNESCO initiated an international social science research programme, the Management of Social Transformations (MOST), to promote capacity-building in social planning at all levels of decision-making. UNESCO sponsors several research fellowships in the social sciences. In other activities UNESCO promotes the rehabilitation of underprivileged urban areas, the research of socio-cultural factors affecting demographic change, and the study of family issues.

UNESCO aims to assist the building and consolidation of peaceful and democratic societies. An international network of institutions and centres involved in research on conflict resolution is being established to support the promotion of peace. Other training, workshop and research activities have been undertaken in countries that have suffered conflict. The Associated Schools Project (comprising more than 5,200 institutions in 158 countries at December 1998) has, for more than 40 years, promoted the principles of peace, human rights, democracy and international co-operation through education. An International Youth Clearing House and Information Service (INFOYOUTH) aims to increase and consolidate the information available on the situation of young people in society, and to heighten awareness of their needs, aspirations and potential among public and private decision-makers. UNESCO's programme also focuses on the educational and cultural dimensions of physical education and sport and their capacity to preserve and improve health.

Fundamental to UNESCO's mission is the rejection of all forms of discrimination. It disseminates scientific information aimed at combating racial prejudice, works to improve the status of women and their access to education, and promotes equality between men and women.

**Abdus Salam International Centre for Theoretical Physics:** based in Trieste, Italy, the Centre brings together scientists from the developed and developing countries. With support from the Italian Government, the Centre has been operated jointly by the IAEA and UNESCO since 1970. At the end of 1995 administrative responsibility for the Centre was transferred to UNESCO, although IAEA remained a partner in the operations of the Centre. Each year it offers seminars followed by a research workshop, as well as short topical seminars, training courses, symposia and panels. Independent research is also carried out. The programme concentrates on solid-state physics, high-energy and elementary particle physics, physics of nuclear structure and reactions, applicable mathematics and, to a lesser extent, on physics of the earth and the environment, physics of energy, biophysics, microprocessors and physics of technology; Dir Prof. MIGUEL A. VIRASORO (Argentina).

## CULTURE

In undertaking efforts to preserve the world's cultural and natural heritage UNESCO has attempted to emphasize the link between culture and development. The 2000–01 programme Cultural Development: Heritage and Creativity was to pursue UNESCO's objectives relating to the preservation and enhancement of cultural and natural heritage and promoting living cultures, in particular through the formulation of new national and international legislation (including an instrument on underwater cultural heritage), efforts to counter the illicit trafficking of cultural property, and the promotion of all forms of creativity.

UNESCO's World Heritage Programme, inaugurated in 1978, aims to protect historic sites and natural landmarks of outstanding universal significance, in accordance with the 1972 UNESCO Convention Concerning the Protection of the World Cultural and Natural Heritage, by providing financial aid for restoration, technical assistance, training and management planning. By December 1999 the 'World Heritage List' comprised 630 sites in 118 countries: for example, the Great Barrier Reef in Australia, the Galapagos Islands (Ecuador), Chartres Cathedral (France), the Taj Mahal at Agra (India), Auschwitz concentration camp (Poland), the historic sanctuary of Machu Picchu (Peru), Robben Island (South Africa), and the Serengeti National Park (Tanzania). UNESCO also maintains a 'List of World Heritage in Danger', comprising 27 sites at November 1999, in order to attract international attention to sites particularly at risk from the environment or human activities. In 1992 a World Heritage Centre was established to enable rapid mobilization of international technical assistance for the preservation of cultural sites. In addition, UNESCO supports efforts for the collection and safeguarding of humanity's non-material heritage, including oral traditions, music, dance and medicine. In co-operation with the International Council for Philosophy and Humanistic Studies, UNESCO is compiling a directory of endangered languages.

UNESCO encourages the translation and publication of literary works, publishes albums of art, and produces records, audiovisual programmes and travelling art exhibitions. It supports the development of book publishing and distribution, including the free flow of books and educational material across borders, and the training of editors and managers in publishing. UNESCO is active in preparing and encouraging the enforcement of international legislation on copyright.

In December 1992 UNESCO established the World Commission on Culture and Development, to strengthen links between culture and development and to prepare a report on the issue. Within the context of the UN's World Decade for Cultural Development (1988–97) UNESCO launched the Silk Roads Project, as a multidisciplinary study of the interactions among cultures and civilizations along the routes linking Asia and Europe, and established an International Fund for the Promotion of Culture, awarding two annual prizes for music and the promotion of arts. In April 1999 UNESCO celebrated the completion of a major international project, the *General History of Africa*.

### COMMUNICATION, INFORMATION AND INFORMATICS

UNESCO's communications programme comprises three interrelated components concerned with the flow of information: a commitment to ensuring the wide dissemination of information, through the development of communications infrastructures and without impediments to freedom of expression or of the press; promotion of greater access to knowledge through international co-operation in the areas of information, libraries and archives; and efforts to harness informatics for development purposes and strengthen member states' capacities in this field. Within this framework, activities include assistance towards the development of legislation, training programmes and infrastructures for the media in countries where independent and pluralistic media are in the process of emerging; assistance, through professional organizations, in the monitoring of media independence, pluralism and diversity; promotion of exchange programmes and study tours, especially for young communications professionals from the least developed countries and central and eastern Europe; and improving access and opportunities for women in the media. UNESCO's fourth major work programme for 2000–01 was entitled Towards a Communication and Information Society for All.

In regions affected by conflict UNESCO supports efforts to establish and maintain an independent media service. This strategy is largely implemented through an International Programme for the Development of Communication (IPDC—see below). In Cambodia, Haiti and Mozambique UNESCO participated in the restructuring of the media in the context of national reconciliation and in Bosnia and Herzegovina assisted in the development of independent media. In December 1998 the Israeli–Palestinian Media Forum was established, to foster professional co-operation between Israeli and Palestinian journalists. IPDC provides support to communication and media development projects in the developing world, including the establishment of news agencies and newspapers and training editorial and technical staff. Since its establishment in 1982 IPDC has provided more than US $75m. to finance some 600 projects.

The General Information Programme (PGI), which was established in 1976, provides a focus for UNESCO's activities in the fields of specialized information systems, documentation, libraries and archives. Under PGI, UNESCO aims to facilitate the elaboration of information policies and plans to modernize libraries and archives services; to encourage standardization; to train information specialists; and to establish specialized information networks. The objectives of the programme are accomplished by improving access to scientific literature; the holding of national seminars on information policies; the furthering of pilot projects, and preservation and conservation efforts under the Records and Archives Management Programme (RAMP); and the training of users of library and information services. UNESCO is participating in the reconstruction of the National and University Library in Bosnia and Herzegovina and in several national and regional projects to safeguard documentary heritage. PGI's mandate extends to trends and societal impacts of information technologies. In March 1997 the first International Congress on Ethical, Legal and Societal Aspects of Digital Information ('InfoEthics') was held in Monte Carlo, Monaco. At the second 'InfoEthics' Congress, held in October 1998, experts discussed issues concerning privacy, confidentiality and security in the electronic transfer of information. A World Commission on the Ethics of Scientific Knowledge and Technology, which had been approved by the 1997 General Conference, met for the first time in April 1999, in Oslo, Norway.

UNESCO supports the development of computer networking and the training of informatics specialists, in particular through its Intergovernmental Informatics Programme. The Programme's priorities include training in informatics, software development and research, the modernization of public administration and informatics policies, and the development of regional computer networks.

## Finance

UNESCO's activities are funded through a regular budget provided by contributions from member states and extrabudgetary funds from other sources, particularly UNDP, the World Bank, regional banks and other bilateral Funds-in-Trust arrangements. UNESCO co-operates with many other UN agencies and international non-governmental organizations.

UNESCO's Regular Programme budget for the two years 2000–01 was US $544.4m., the same as for the previous biennium.

## Publications

(mostly in English, French and Spanish editions; Arabic, Chinese and Russian versions are also available in many cases)

*Copyright Bulletin* (quarterly).

*International Review of Education* (quarterly).

*International Social Science Journal* (quarterly).

*Museum International* (quarterly).

*Nature and Resources* (quarterly).

*Prospects* (quarterly review on education).

*UNESCO Courier* (monthly, in 27 languages).

*UNESCO Sources* (monthly).

*UNESCO Statistical Yearbook*.

*World Communication Report*.

*World Educational Report* (every 2 years).

*World Heritage Review* (quarterly).

*World Information Report*.

*World Science Report* (every 2 years).

Books, databases, video and radio documentaries, statistics, scientific maps and atlases.

## INTERGOVERNMENTAL COMMITTEE FOR PHYSICAL EDUCATION AND SPORT

**Address:** 7 place de Fontenoy, 75352 Paris, France.

Established by UNESCO in 1978 to serve as a permanent intergovernmental body in the field of physical education and sport.

The Committee is composed of 30 representatives of member states of UNESCO, elected by the General Conference.

Among its many activities aimed at further development of physical education and sport throughout the world, the Committee is responsible for supervising the planning and implementation of UNESCO's programme of activities in physical education and sport, promoting international co-operation in this area and facilitating the adoption and implementation of an International Charter of physical education and sport.

## INTERNATIONAL BUREAU OF EDUCATION—IBE

**Address:** POB 199, 1211 Geneva 20, Switzerland.

**Telephone:** (22) 9177800; **fax:** (22) 9177801; **e-mail:** doc.centre@ibe.unesco.org; **internet:** www.ibe.unesco.org.

Founded in 1925, the IBE became an intergovernmental organization in 1929 and was incorporated into UNESCO in 1969. The Bureau's fundamental mission is to deal with matters concerning educational content, methods, and teaching/learning strategies. In addition, the IBE, as an observatory of educational trands and innovations, has assumed responsibilities in the field of educational information. It publishes a quarterly review of education and newsletter, in addition to various monographs and reference works. The Council of the IBE is composed of representatives of 28 member states of UNESCO, designated by the General Conference. The International Conference on Education is held periodically.

**Director:** JACQUES HALLAK (acting).

## INTERNATIONAL INSTITUTE FOR EDUCATIONAL PLANNING—IIEP

**Address:** 7–9 rue Eugène Delacroix, 75116 Paris, France.

**Telephone:** 1-45-03-77-00; **fax:** 1-40-72-83-66; **e-mail:** information@iiep.unesco.org; **internet:** www.unesco.org/iiep.

The Institute was established by UNESCO in 1963 to serve as a world centre for advanced training and research in educational planning. Its purpose is to help all member states of UNESCO in their social and economic development efforts, by enlarging the fund of knowledge about educational planning and the supply of competent experts in this field.

Legally and administratively a part of UNESCO, the Institute is autonomous, and its policies and programme are controlled by its own Governing Board, under special statutes voted by the General Conference of UNESCO.

A satellite office of the IIEP was opened in Buenos Aires, Argentina, in June 1998.

**Director:** GUDMUND HERNES.

# United Nations Industrial Development Organization—UNIDO

**Address:** Vienna International Centre, POB 300, 1400 Vienna, Austria.

**Telephone:** (1) 260260; **fax:** (1) 2692669; **e-mail:** unido-pinfo@unido.org; **internet:** www.unido.org.

UNIDO began operations in 1967, as an autonomous organization within the UN Secretariat, and became a specialized agency of the UN on 1 January 1986. Its objective is to promote and accelerate sustainable industrial development in developing countries. UNIDO aims to contribute to the stability of the global socio-economic system and promote equitable and sustainable industrialization.

### MEMBERS

168 members: see Table on pp. 114–116.

## Organization

(December 1999)

### GENERAL CONFERENCE

The General Conference, which consists of representatives of all member states, meets once every two years. It is the chief policy-making body of the Organization, and reviews UNIDO's policy concepts, strategies on industrial development and budget. The eighth General Conference was held in Vienna, Austria, in November/December 1999.

### INDUSTRIAL DEVELOPMENT BOARD

The Board consists of 53 members elected by the General Conference for a three-year period. It reviews the implementation of the approved work programme, the regular and operational budgets and other General Conference decisions.

### PROGRAMME AND BUDGET COMMITTEE

The Committee, consisting of 27 members elected by the General Conference for a two-year term, assists the Industrial Development Board in preparing work programmes and budgets.

### SECRETARIAT

The Secretariat comprises the office of the Director-General and three divisions, each headed by a Managing Director: Investment Promotion and Institutional Capacity Building; Sectoral Support and Environmental Sustainability; and Field Operations and Administration. At December 1999 the Secretariat comprised 603 staff members.

**Director-General:** CARLOS ALFREDO MAGARIÑOS (Argentina).

### FIELD REPRESENTATION

UNIDO field officers work in developing countries, at the level of Country Director, National Director, National Programme Officer and Junior Programme Officer. At the end of 1999 there were 29 field offices. The Business Plan that was adopted in December 1997 (see below) envisaged greater decentralization of activities and a strengthened field representation.

## Activities

In its efforts to promote the advancement and integration of industry, UNIDO provides a global forum for addressing common obstacles to sustainable industrialization, for developing and assessing conventions, codes, norms and regulations, for disseminating new advances, policies and experiences in sustainable industrialization, for establishing international partnerships and networks and for developing comparable statistics and measures to provide criteria for industrial performance. In addition, UNIDO provides a range of services to governments, institutes and enterprises to enhance their capabilities to achieve UNIDO's overall aim of environmentally sustainable and equitable industrial development. The following three core competencies form the basis of UNIDO's services to promote sustainable industrialization, undertaken at policy, institutional and enterpreneural level: the encouragement of competitive economies; the development of a sound environment; and the promotion of productive employment. Client countries may select relevant aspects from these core elements to design an integrated and specific approach to a problem.

Between 1993 and 1998 UNIDO implemented a major restructuring programme in order to respond to changes in the global economy and industrial development. In December 1995 the General Conference, meeting in Vienna, Austria, approved the following set of development priorities, which formed the basis of a new conceptual and substantive framework for UNIDO activities:

(i) Promotion of economic co-operation between both developing and industrialized countries;
(ii) Dissemination of environmentally sustainable and energy-efficient industrial growth;
(iii) Development of small and medium-sized enterprises (SMEs);
(iv) Growth of global industrial competitiveness;
(v) Dissemination of new technologies;
(vi) Industrial development in rural areas;
(vii) Promotion of agro-industry in least-developed countries.

The seventh General Conference, held in December 1997, endorsed a Business Plan on the Future Role and Functions of UNIDO, which further defined the organization's functions and future priorities. The Plan regrouped UNIDO's activities into two main areas—Strengthening of industrial capacities and Cleaner and sustainable industrial development—which, together with an administrative component, was reflected in a revision of the organizational structure (see above). According to the Plan, activities were to be concentrated in support of the development and mainstreaming of SMEs (identified as the principal means for achieving equitable and sustainable industrial development) in support of agro-based industries and their integration into national industrial structures, and in least-developed countries, in particular in Africa, with emphasis on service provision at regional and sub-regional level. In December 1999 the General Conference approved a new approach of developing integrated industrial service packages designed specifically for individual countries.

In 1996 UNIDO implemented a number of normative activities that aimed to assist the industrial sector in developing countries and in countries with economies in transition to compete for international business. Some of the activities undertaken were: co-operation with the International Organization for Standardization to establish internationally-recognized accreditation bodies in developing countries; the construction of a UNIDO Industrial Development Index to measure industrial development on the basis of various indicators; the preparation of UNIDO guide-lines for the classification and certification of industrial science and technology parks; and the assessment of industrial performance through the use of existing technological, environmental and social parameters.

Since 1993 much of UNIDO's assistance to governments, agencies and private industrial institutions has aimed at developing a strong private sector. The percentage of UNIDO's private-sector counterparts doubled between 1993 and 1996 to reach some 50%, while technical co-operation projects involving the private sector accounted for some 80% of all projects undertaken in 1996. UNIDO also works with the private sector in an advisory and co-operative function. In 1996 UNIDO launched the International Business Advisory Council (IBAC), composed of international industrialists whose role it is to advise UNIDO on means of approaching industrialization and promoting awareness of the Organization's work. In the same year UNIDO undertook an initiative to establish National Industrial Business Councils in 12 developing countries. The Councils aim to assist UNIDO in developing and funding joint programmes with the private sector and in recognizing industrial business achievements through the use of international standards and conventions. In the period 1996–98 UNIDO trained 7,505 people, assisted 38,477 small and medium-sized enterprises, and generated US $506m. in industrial investments, through some 634 projects. The first UNIDO Forum on Sustainable Industrial Development was held in December 1999.

UNIDO provides advice to governmental agencies and industrial institutions to improve the management of human resources. The Organization also undertakes training projects to develop human resources in specific industries, and aims to encourage the full participation of women in economic progress through gender awareness programmes and practical training to improve women's access to employment and business opportunities.

The 1995 Conference resolved that special attention was to be given to the industrialization of developing countries in Africa, and in October 1996 UNIDO formally inaugurated the Alliance for Africa's Industrialization, which constituted the industrial sector element of the UN system-wide special initiative on Africa. The programme was to promote development of the continent's natural resources, strengthen labour resources and build government capacities in order to exploit new global markets, in particular in the agro-industrial sector. During 1997 UNIDO helped to organize a number of conferences and forums to promote industrialization in developing countries. UNIDO supported the 13th Conference of African Ministers of Industry (Cami-13), held in Accra, Ghana, in May, which discussed methods to increase Africa's industrial development in the 21st century and to encourage greater participation by the private sector. UNIDO also sponsored an investment forum held in Yaoundé, Cameroon, in June, and a further UNIDO-sponsored forum was held in Abidjan, Côte d'Ivoire, in November, which concentrated on the potential impact of the Asian economic crisis on African economies.

UNIDO is increasingly involved in general environmental projects. As one of the four implementing agencies of the Multilateral Fund for the Implementation of the Montreal Protocal, UNIDO assists developing countries in efforts gradually to reduce the use of ozone-depleting substances. It is also involved in implementing the Kyoto Protocol of the Framework Convention on Climate Change (relating to greenhouse gas emissions) in old factories world-wide. In 1997 UNIDO established a Cleaner Production Centre in Budapest, Hungary, to encourage increased industrial efficiency and to reduce health risks and environmental pollution from production methods in that country.

UNIDO also supports collaborative efforts between countries with complementary experience or resources in specific sectors. A network of Investment and Technology Promotion Offices in 12 countries publicize investment opportunities, provide information to investors and promote business contacts between industrialized and developing countries and economies in transition. UNIDO also maintains a Centre for International Industrial Co-operation in Russia. UNIDO is increasingly working to achieve investment promotion and transfer of technology and knowledge among developing countries.

UNIDO supports regional networks and centres of excellence, including the International Centre for Genetic Engineering and Biotechnology, based in Trieste (Italy) and New Delhi (India), the International Centre for Sciences and High Technology, in Trieste, and the Centre for the Application of Solar Energy, in Perth, Australia.

## Finance

The regular budget for the two years 1998–99 amounted to approximately US $129.5m. There was an operational budget of some $11.4m. for the same period. The approved regular budget for 2000–01 amounted to $132.9m. In 1998 UNIDO's technical co-operation expenditure amounted to $81m. Allocations were received from UNDP, the Multilateral Fund for the Implementation of the Montreal Protocol on Substances that Deplete the Ozone Layer, and the Common Fund for Commodities. In addition, voluntary contributions from 31 member states amounted to $34m. The Industrial Development Fund is used by UNIDO to finance development projects which fall outside the usual systems of multilateral funding. In 1998 a total of $15.1m. was approved by the Fund.

## Publications

*Annual Report.*

*Environmental Technology Monitor* (quarterly).

*Industrial Africa* (every 2 months).

*Industrial Development Global Report* (annually).

*International Yearbook of Industrial Statistics* (annually).

*The Globalization of Industry: Implications for Developing Countries Beyond 2000.*

*UNIDOScope* (monthly).

*World Information Directory of Industrial Technology and Investment Support Services.*

Several other publications and databases; numerous working papers and reports (listed in *UNIDO Links* as they appear).

# Universal Postal Union—UPU

**Address:** Case postale, 3000 Berne 15, Switzerland.

**Telephone:** (31) 3503111; **fax:** (31) 3503110; **e-mail:** info@upu.int; **internet:** www.upu.int.

The General Postal Union was founded by the Treaty of Berne (1874), beginning operations in July 1875. Three years later its name was changed to the Universal Postal Union. In 1948 the UPU became a specialized agency of the UN.

### MEMBERS

189 members: see Table on pp. 114–116.

## Organization

(December 1999)

### CONGRESS

The supreme body of the Union is Congress, which meets, in principle, every five years. It focuses on general principles and broad policy issues. It is responsible for the Constitution and its General Regulations, changes in the provision of the Universal Postal Convention and Agreements, approval of the strategic plan and budget parameters, formulation of overall policy on technical co-operation and for elections and appointments. The 22nd Congress was held in Beijing, the People's Republic of China, in August/September 1999; the 23rd Congress was to be held in Côte d'Ivoire in 2004.

### COUNCIL OF ADMINISTRATION

The Council, created by the Seoul Congress, 1994, to replace the existing Executive Council, meets annually at Berne. It is composed of a Chairman and representatives of 40 member countries of the Union elected by Congress on the basis of an equitable geographical distribution. It is responsible for supervising the affairs of the Union between Congresses, including the approval of proposals to modify provisions in the Universal Postal Convention and Special Agreements. The Council also considers policies that may affect other sectors, such as standardization and quality of service, provides a forum for considering the implications of governmental policies with respect to competition, deregulation, and trade-in-service issues for international postal services, and considers intergovernmental aspects of technical co-operation. The Council approves the Union's budget, supervises the activities of the International Bureau and takes decisions regarding UPU contacts with other international agencies and bodies. It is also responsible for promoting and co-ordinating all aspects of technical assistance among member countries.

### POSTAL OPERATIONS COUNCIL (POC)

As the technical organ of the UPU, the Council, comprising 40 elected member countries, is responsible for the operational, economic and commercial aspects of international postal services. It promotes the studies undertaken by some postal services and the introduction of new postal products. It also prepares and issues recommendations for member countries concerning uniform standards of practice for technological, operational or other processes within its competence. The POC aims to assist national postal services to modernize postal products, including letter and parcel post, financial services and expedited mail services.

### INTERNATIONAL BUREAU

The day-to-day administrative work of UPU is executed through the International Bureau, which provides secretariat and support facilities for the UPU's bodies. It serves as an instrument of liaison, information and consultation for the postal administration of the member countries and promotes technical co-operation among Union members. It also acts as a clearing house for the settlement of accounts between postal administrations for inter-administration charges related to the exchange of postal items and international reply coupons. The Bureau supports the technical assistance programmes of the UPU and serves as an intermediary between the UPU, the UN, its agencies and other international organizations, customer organizations and private delivery services. Increasingly the Bureau has assumed a greater role in certain areas of postal administration, for example, the application of Electronic Data Interchange (EDI) technology and the monitoring of quality of postal services world-wide.

**Director-General of the International Bureau:** THOMAS E. LEAVEY (USA).

## Activities

The essential principles of the Union are the following:

(i) to develop social, cultural and commercial communication between people through the efficient operation of the postal services;

(ii) to guarantee freedom of transit and free circulation of postal items;

(iii) to ensure the organization, development and modernization of the postal services;

(iv) to promote and participate in postal technical assistance between member countries;

(v) to ensure the interoperability of postal networks by implementing a suitable policy of standardization;

(vi) to meet the changing needs of customers; and

(vii) to improve the quality of service.

The common rules applicable to the international postal service and to the letter-post provisions are contained in the Universal Postal Convention and its Detailed Regulations. Owing to their importance in the postal field and their historical value, these two Acts, together with the Constitution and the General Regulations, constitute the compulsory Acts of the Union. It is therefore not possible to be a member country of the Union without being a party to these Acts and applying their provisions.

The activities of the international postal service, other than letter mail, are governed by Special Agreements. These are binding only for the countries that have acceded to them. There are four such Agreements:

1. Agreement concerning Postal Parcels.
2. Agreement concerning Postal Money Orders.
3. Agreement concerning Giro Transfers.
4. Agreement concerning Cash on Delivery Items.

## Finance

The 1999 approved budget amounted to 35.7m. Swiss francs. The Council agreed to maintain the regular budget at 35.7m. Swiss francs for 2000. All of the UPU's regular budget expenses are financed by member countries, based on a contribution class system. Members are listed in 11 classes, establishing the proportion that they should pay.

## Publications

*Postal Statistics.*

*Union Postale* (quarterly, in French, German, English, Arabic, Chinese, Spanish and Russian).

Other UPU publications are listed in *Liste des publications du Bureau international*; all are in French and English, some also in Arabic and Spanish.

# World Health Organization—WHO

**Address:** Ave Appia, 1211 Geneva 27, Switzerland.

**Telephone:** (22) 7912111; **fax:** (22) 7910746; **e-mail:** inf@who.ch; **internet:** www.who.int.

WHO, established in 1948, is the lead agency within the UN system concerned with the protection and improvement of public health.

### MEMBERS

191 members and two associate members: see Table on pp. 114–116.

## Organization

(January 2000)

### WORLD HEALTH ASSEMBLY

The Assembly meets in Geneva, once a year; it is responsible for policy making and the biennial programme and budget; appoints the Director-General, admits new members and reviews budget contributions.

### EXECUTIVE BOARD

The Board is composed of 32 health experts designated by, but not representing, their governments; they serve for three years, and the World Health Assembly elects 10–12 member states each year to the Board. It meets at least twice a year to review the Director-General's programme, which it forwards to the Assembly with any recommendations that seem necessary. It advises on questions referred to it by the Assembly and is responsible for putting into effect the decisions and policies of the Assembly. It is also empowered to take emergency measures in case of epidemics or disasters.

**Chairman:** A. J. M. SULAIMAN (Oman).

### SECRETARIAT

**Director-General:** Dr GRO HARLEM BRUNDTLAND (Norway).

**Executive Directors:** Dr JIE CHEN (People's Republic of China), Dr JULIO J. FRENK (Mexico), Dr DAVID L. HEYMANN (USA), ANN KERN (Australia), Dr POONAM KHETRAPAL SINGH (India), Dr SOUAD LYAGOUBI-OUAHCHI (Tunisia), Dr MICHAEL SCHOLTZ (Germany), Dr OLIVE SHISANA (South Africa), Dr YASUHIRO SUZUKI (Japan).

### REGIONAL OFFICES

Each of WHO's six geographical regions has its own organization consisting of a regional committee representing the member states and associate members in the region concerned, and a regional office staffed by experts in various fields of health.

**Africa:** (temporary office) Parirenyatwa Hospital, Mazoe St, POB BE 773, Belvedere, Harare, Zimbabwe; tel. (4) 4707494; fax (4) 4728998; e-mail regafro@whoafr.org; internet www.whoafr.org; Dir Dr EBRAHIM MALICK SAMBA (The Gambia).

**Americas:** Pan-American Sanitary Bureau, 525 23rd St, NW, Washington, DC 20037, USA; tel. (202) 861-3200; fax (202) 974-3663; e-mail postmaster@paho.org; internet www.paho.org; Dir Sir GEORGE ALLEYNE (Barbados).

**Eastern Mediterranean:** POB 1517, Alexandria 21563, Egypt; tel. (3) 4820223; fax (3) 4838916; e-mail emro@who.sci.eg; internet www.who.sci.eg; Dir Dr HUSSEIN ABDUL-RAZZAQ GEZAIRY.

**Europe:** 8 Scherfigsvej, 2100 Copenhagen Ø, Denmark; tel. (1) 39-17-17-17; fax (1) 39-17-18-18; e-mail postmaster@who.dk; internet www.who.dk; Dir Dr MARC DANZON (France).

**South-East Asia:** World Health House, Indraprastha Estate, Mahatma Gandhi Rd, New Delhi 110 002, India; tel. (11) 3317804; fax (11) 3318607; e-mail postmaster@who.ernet.in; internet www.who.ernet.in; Dir Dr UTON MUCHTAR RAFEI (Indonesia).

**Western Pacific:** POB 2932, Manila 1000, Philippines; tel. (2) 5288001; fax (2) 5211036; e-mail postmaster@who.org.ph; internet www.who.org.ph; Dir Dr SHIGERU OMI (Japan).

## Activities

WHO's objective is stated in the constitution as 'the attainment by all peoples of the highest possible level of health'. 'Health' is defined as 'a state of complete physical, mental and social well-being and not merely the absence of disease and infirmity'.

It acts as the central authority directing international health work, and establishes relations with professional groups and government health authorities on that basis.

It supports, on request from member states, programmes to promote health, prevent and control health problems, control or eradicate disease, train health workers best suited to local needs and strengthen national health systems. Aid is provided in emergencies and natural disasters.

A global programme of collaborative research and exchange of scientific information is carried out in co-operation with about 1,000 national institutions. Particular stress is laid on the widespread communicable diseases of the tropics, and the countries directly concerned are assisted in developing their research capabilities.

It keeps communicable and non-communicable diseases and other health problems under constant surveillance, promotes the exchange of prompt and accurate information and of notification of outbreaks of diseases, and administers the International Health Regulations. It sets standards for the quality control of drugs, vaccines and other substances affecting health.

It collects and disseminates health data and carries out statistical analyses and comparative studies in such diseases as cancer, heart disease and mental illness.

It receives reports on drugs observed to have shown adverse reactions in any country, and transmits the information to other member states.

It promotes improved environmental conditions, including housing, sanitation and working conditions. All available information on effects on human health of the pollutants in the environment is critically reviewed and published.

Co-operation among scientists and professional groups is encouraged, and the organization may propose international conventions and agreements. It assists in developing an informed public opinion on matters of health.

## HEALTH FOR ALL

In May 1981 the 34th World Health Assembly adopted a Global Strategy in support of 'Health for all by the year 2000'. Through a broad consultation process involving all its partners, WHO reviews the attainment by all citizens of the world of a level of health that will permit them to lead a socially and economically productive life. Primary health care is seen as the key to 'Health for all', with the following as minimum requirements:

- Safe water in the home or within 15 minutes' walking distance, and adequate sanitary facilities in the home or immediate vicinity;
- Immunization against diphtheria, pertussis (whooping cough), tetanus, poliomyelitis, measles and tuberculosis;
- Local health care, including availability of at least 20 essential drugs, within one hour's travel;
- Trained personnel to attend childbirth, and to care for pregnant mothers and children up to at least one year old.

The Ninth General Programme of Work, for the period 1996–2000, defined a policy framework for world action on health and the management and programme development of WHO itself. In May 1998 the World Health Assembly agreed that a new global strategy should be effected, through regional and national health policies. The so-called 'Health for all in the 21st century' initiative was to build on the primary health care approach of the 'Health for all' strategy, but was to strengthen the emphasis on quality of life, equity in health and access to health services.

In July 1998 Dr Gro Harlem Brundtland officially took office as the new Director-General of WHO. She immediately announced an extensive reform of the organization, including restructuring the WHO technical programmes into nine groups, or 'clusters', each headed by an Executive Director (see above). The groups were established within the framework of the following four main areas of activity: Combating ill health, incorporating Communicable Diseases and Non-communicable Diseases; Building healthy populations and communities, comprising the groups Health Systems and Community Health, Sustainable Development and Healthy Environments and Social Change and Mental Health; Sustained health, including the groups Health Technology and Pharmaceuticals and Evidence and Information for Policy; and Internal support—reaching out, comprising External affairs and Governing Bodies, and General Management.

## COMMUNICABLE DISEASES

The Communicable Diseases group works to reduce the impact of infectious diseases world-wide through surveillance and response; prevention and control; eradication and elimination; and research and development. The group seeks to strengthen global monitoring of important communicable disease problems and to increase the organization's capacity to provide an effective response to those problems. WHO also aims to reduce the impact of other communicable diseases through intensive, routine, prevention and control and, where possible, through the elimination or eradication of specific infections. The group advocates a functional approach to disease control collaborating with other groups at all stages to provide an integrated response.

One of WHO's major achievements was the eradication of smallpox. Following a massive international campaign of vaccination and surveillance (begun in 1958 and intensified in 1967), the last case was detected in 1977 and the eradication of the disease was declared in 1980. In May 1996 the World Health Assembly resolved that, pending a final endorsement, all remaining stocks of the smallpox virus were to be destroyed on 30 June 1999, although 500,000 doses of smallpox vaccine were to remain, along with a supply of the smallpox vaccine seed virus, in order to ensure that a further supply of the vaccine could be made available if required. In May 1999, however, the Assembly authorized a temporary retention of stocks of the virus until 2002. In 1988 the World Health Assembly declared its commitment to the similar eradication of poliomyelitis by the end of 2000 and launched the Global Polio Eradication Initiative. In August 1996 WHO, UNICEF and Rotary International, together with other national and international partners, initiated a campaign to 'Kick Polio out of Africa', with the aim of immunizing more than 100m. children in 46 countries against the disease over a three-year period. By 1998 the number of cases of polio had been reduced from 35,000, in 1988, to just over 5,000. At the end of 1998 50 countries were still known or suspected of being polio endemic. During 1999 and 2000 efforts to achieve the target date for eradication were intensified, in particular through the organization of large-scale national immunization days.

The objective of providing immunization for all children by 1990 was adopted by the World Health Assembly in 1977. Six diseases (measles, whooping cough, tetanus, poliomyelitis, tuberculosis and diphtheria) became the target of the Expanded Programme on Immunization (EPI), in which WHO, UNICEF and many other organizations collaborated. As a result of massive international and national efforts, the global immunization coverage increased from 20% in the early 1980s to the targeted rate of 80% by the end of 1990. This coverage signified that more than 100m. children in the developing world under the age of one had been successfully vaccinated against the targeted diseases, the lives of about 3m. children had been saved every year, and 500,000 annual cases of paralysis as a result of polio had been prevented. In 1992 the Assembly resolved to reach a new target of 90% immunization coverage with the six EPI vaccines; to introduce hepatitis B as a seventh vaccine (with the aim of an 80% reduction in the incidence of the disease in children by 2001); and to introduce the yellow fever vaccine in areas where it occurs endemically.

In 1995 WHO established the Division of Emerging, Viral and Bacterial ('other communicable') Diseases Surveillance and Control to promote the development of national and international infrastructure and resources to recognize, monitor, prevent and control communicable diseases and emerging and re-emerging health problems, including anti-microbial resistance. WHO also aimed to promote applied research on the diagnosis, epidemiology, prevention and control of communicable diseases and emerging health problems. In July 1996 WHO launched an interagency initiative to control an outbreak of cerebrospinal meningitis in Africa, which caused some 15,000 deaths in the first half of that year. In January 1997 an International Co-ordinating Group (ICG) was established to ensure the optimum use and rapid provision of the 14m. doses of vaccine available for epidemic control in 1997, following the enormous demand of the previous year.

As a result of the reforms of the organization implemented from mid-1998, the Division of Control of Tropical Diseases was integrated into the Communicable Diseases cluster, providing active support for planning and implementing control programmes (based on global strategies for integrated tropical disease control) at regional, sub-regional and national levels. It assists with the mobilization of resources for disease control and the co-ordination of national and international participation. The group also promotes research and training that are directly relevant to control needs, and promotes the monitoring and evaluation of control measures.

A Special Programme for Research and Training in Tropical Diseases, sponsored jointly by WHO, UNDP and the World Bank, as well as by contributions from donor countries, was established in 1975, and involves a world-wide network of some 5,000 scientists working on the development and application of vaccines, new drugs, diagnostic kits and preventive measures, and an applied field research on practical community issues affecting the target diseases.

The Onchocerciasis Control Programme in West Africa (OCP) was initiated in 1974 to eliminate onchocerciasis, which can cause blindness, as a major public health problem and an impediment to socio-economic development in 11 countries of the region. In January 1996 a new initiative, the African Programme for Onchocerciasis Control (APOC), covering 19 countries outside West Africa, became operational, with funding co-ordinated by the World Bank and with WHO as the executing agency. In December 1994 WHO announced that the OCP was to be terminated by the end of 2002, by which time it was estimated that 40m. people would have been protected from the disease and 600,000 people prevented from blindness. In May 1999 WHO reported that the OCP, based in Ouagadougou, Burkina Faso, was to be transformed into a Multi-disease Surveillance Centre. The Onchocerciasis Elimination Programme in the Americas (OEPA), launched in 1992, co-ordinates work to control the disease in six endemic countries of Latin America. In January 1998 a new 20-year programme to eliminate lymphatic filariasis was initiated, with substantial funding and support from two major pharmaceutical companies, and in collaboration with the World Bank, the Arab Fund for Economic and Social Development and the governments of Japan, the United Kingdom and the USA. In early 1997 WHO determined that South American trypanosomiasis ('Chagas disease'), which causes the deaths of some 45,000 people each year and infects a further 16m.–18m., could be eliminated from the Southern Cone region of Latin America by 2000, owing to the enhanced political commitment of the governments of those countries concerned and improved control measures. The countries of the Andean region of Latin America initiated a plan for the elimination of transmission of Chagas disease in February 1997; a similar plan was launched by Central American governments in October.

A Ministerial Conference on Malaria, organized by WHO, was held in October 1992, attended by representatives from 102 member countries. The Conference adopted a plan of action for the 1990s for the control of the disease, which kills an estimated 1m. people every year and affects a further 300m.–500m. Some 90% of all cases are in sub-Saharan Africa. WHO assists countries where malaria is endemic to prepare national plans of action for malaria control in accordance with WHO's Global Malaria Control Strategy, which emphasized strengthening local capabilities, for example through training, for effective health control. In July 1998 WHO declared the control of malaria a priority concern, and in October formally launched the 'Roll Back Malaria' programme, in conjunction with UNICEF, the World Bank and UNDP. Emphasis was to be placed on strengthening local health systems and on the promotion of inexpensive preventative measures, including the use of bednets treated with insecticides. WHO also supported the development of more effective anti-malaria drugs and vaccines through the 'New Medicines for Malaria' venture. A new African Initiative for Malaria Control in the 21st Century aimed to reduce the prevalence of malaria in 42 African countries by as much as 50% by 2010.

In July 1994 WHO, together with the Sasakawa Memorial Health Foundation, organized an international conference on the elimination of leprosy. The conference adopted a declaration on their commitment to the elimination of leprosy (the reduction of the prevalence of leprosy to less than one case per 10,000 population) by 2000 and WHO established a Special Programme devoted to this objective. In September 1998 WHO announced that the use of a combination of three drugs (known as multi-drug therapy—MDT) had resulted in a reduction in the number of leprosy cases worldwide from 10m.–12m. in 1988, to 1.15m. in 1997. Moreover, in April 1999 WHO announced that the number of countries having more than one case of leprosy per 10,000 had declined from 122 in 1985 to 28. However, concern was expressed at the feasibility of the elimination target, in particular, given the large numbers of undetected cases of the disease. WHO reported that the continued use of MDT treatment over a period of five–10 years would result in an end to all transmission of the disease, except in India, which had more than one-half of the global total of active leprosy cases. In November 1999 WHO launched a new initiative, in collaboration with several governments and a major pharmaceutical company, to eradicate leprosy by the end of 2005. In July 1998 the Director-General of WHO and representatives of more than 20 countries, meeting in Yamoussoukro, Côte d'Ivoire, signed a declaration on the control of another emerging mycobacterial disease, Buruli ulcer.

According to WHO estimates, one-third of the world's population is infected with TB, and 2m.–3m. people die from the disease each year, prompting WHO, in 1993, to declare TB a global emergency. In 1995 WHO established a Global Tuberculosis Programme to address the challenges of the TB epidemic. WHO provides technical support to all member countries, with special attention given to those with high TB prevalence, to establish effective national tuberculosis control programmes. WHO's strategy for TB control includes the use of DOTS (direct observation treatment, short-course), standardized treatment guide-lines, and result accountability through routine evaluation of treatment outcomes. Simultaneously, WHO is encouraging research with the aim of further disseminating DOTS, adapting DOTS for wider use, developing new tools for prevention, diagnosis and treatment, and containing new threats such as the HIV/TB co-epidemic. In March 1997 WHO reported that even limited use of DOTS was resulting in the stabilization of the TB epidemic. However, inadequate control of DOTS in some areas was resulting in the development of drug-resistant and, often, incurable strains of the disease. By late 1998 WHO estimated that 8m. new cases of TB were occurring world-wide each year, of which more than one-half were in Asia. In March 1999 WHO announced the launch of a new initiative, 'Stop TB', in co-operation with the World Bank, the US Government and a coalition of non-governmental organizations, which aimed to promote DOTS to ensure its use in 85% of cases by 2005, compared with some 16% in the late 1990s.

## NON-COMMUNICABLE DISEASES

The Non-communicable Diseases group comprises three departments responsible for the surveillance, prevention and management of uninfectious diseases (such as those arising from an unhealthy diet).

'Inter-Health', an integrated programme to combat non-communicable diseases, was initiated in 1990, with the particular aim of preventing an increase in the incidence of such diseases in developing countries.

WHO's programmes for diabetes mellitus, chronic rheumatic diseases and asthma assist with the development of national initiatives, based upon goals and targets for the improvement of early detection, care and reduction of long-term complications. They also monitor the global epidemiological situation and co-ordinate multinational research activities concerned with the prevention and care of non-communicable diseases. In mid-1998 WHO adopted a resolution on measures to be taken to combat these diseases, the prevalence of which was anticipated to increase, particularly in developing countries, owing to rising life expectancy and changes in lifestyles. For example, between 1995 and 2025 the number of adults affected by diabetes was projected to increase from 135m. to 300m. In February 1999 WHO initated a new programme, 'Vision 2020: the Right to Sight', which aimed to eliminate avoidable blindness (estimated to be as much as 80% of all cases) by 2020. Blindness was otherwise predicted to increase by as much as twofold, owing to the increased longevity of the global population.

WHO's Cardiovascular Diseases Programme aims to prevent and control the major cardiovascular diseases, which are responsible for more than 14m. deaths each year. It is estimated that one-third of these deaths could have been prevented with existing scientific knowledge.

The Global Cancer Control Programme is concerned with the prevention of cancer, improving its detection and cure and ensuring care of all cancer patients in need. In 1998 a five-year programme to improve cancer care in developing countries was established, sponsored by private enterprises.

The WHO Human Genetics Programme manages genetic approaches for the prevention and control of common hereditary diseases and of those with a genetic predisposition representing a major health importance. The Programme also concentrates on the further development of genetic approaches suitable for incorporation into health care systems, as well as developing a network of international collaborating programmes.

## HEALTH SYSTEMS AND COMMUNITY HEALTH

During 1998 WHO integrated its programmes relating to the health and development of children and adolescents, reproductive health and research (including HIV/AIDS and sexually transmitted diseases), women's health, and health systems within the Health Systems and Community Health group. The group's aim is to improve access to sustainable health care for all by strengthening health systems and fostering individual, family and community development. Activities include newborn care; child health, including promoting and protecting the health and development of the child through such approaches as promotion of breast-feeding and use of the mother-baby package, as well as care of the sick child, including diarrhoeal and acute respiratory disease control and support to women and children in difficult circumstances; the promotion of safe motherhood and maternal health; adolescent health, including the promotion and development of young people and the prevention of specific health problems; women, health and development, including addressing issues of gender, sexual violence, and harmful traditional practices; and human reproduction, including research related to contraceptive technologies and effective methods. In addition, WHO aims to provide technical leadership and co-ordination on reproductive health and to support countries in their efforts to ensure that people: experience healthy sexual development and maturation; have the capacity for healthy, equitable and responsible relationships; can achieve their reproductive intentions safely and healthily; avoid illnesses, diseases and injury related to sexuality and reproduction; and receive appropriate counselling, care and rehabilitation for diseases and conditions related to sexuality and reproduction.

In September 1997 WHO, in collaboration with UNICEF, formally launched a programme advocating the Integrated Management of Childhood Illness (IMCI), following successful regional trials in more than 20 developing countries during 1996–97. IMCI recognizes that pneumonia, diarrhoea, measles, malaria and malnutrition cause some 70% of the 11m. childhood deaths each year, and recommends screening sick children for all five conditions, to obtain a more accurate diagnosis than may be achieved from the results of a single assessment. WHO's Division of Diarrhoeal and Acute Respiratory Disease Control encourages national programmes aimed at reducing childhood deaths as a result of diarrhoea, particularly through the use of oral rehydration therapy and preventive measures. The Division is also seeking to reduce deaths from pneumonia in infants through the use of a simple case-management strategy involving the recognition of danger signs and treatment with an appropriate antibiotic.

In December 1995 WHO's Global Programme on AIDS (Acquired Immunodeficiency Syndrome), which began in 1987, was concluded. A Joint UN Programme on the human immunodeficiency virus (HIV) and AIDS—UNAIDS—became operational on 1 January 1996, sponsored jointly by WHO, the World Bank, UNICEF, UNDP, UNESCO and UNFPA. (The UN International Drug Control Programme became the seventh sponsoring agency of UNAIDS in 1999.) WHO established an Office of HIV/AIDS and Sexually Transmitted Diseases in order to ensure the continuity of its global response to the problem, which included support for national control and education plans, improving the safety of blood supplies and improving the care and support of AIDS patients. In addition, the Office was to liaise with UNAIDS, which has its secretariat at WHO headquarters, and to make available WHO's research and technical expertise. At December 1999 an estimated 50m. adults and children world-wide had contracted HIV/AIDS (including some 16m. who had since died), of whom 5.6m. were newly infected during that year.

By the late 1990s many countries had failed significantly to reduce inequalities in healthcare, to improve the health of poor and disadvantaged people or to improve the sustainability of health systems, owing to weak national health systems and the insufficient use of evidence-based, cost-effective treatment methods. In addition, there was a lack of systems to monitor improvements in health services and to determine overall changes in health. The Health Systems and Community Health group, therefore, aims to address these problems and works to ensure that treatment concerning children, adolescents and women, and reproductive health, HIV/AIDS and other sexually transmitted infections, is effectively provided. WHO assists countries to expand and improve the functioning of their health infrastructure in order to ensure wider access to care, hospital services and health education. It works with countries to ensure continuity and quality of care at all levels, by well-trained health personnel.

In March 1996 WHO's Centre for Health Development opened at Kobe, Japan. The Centre was to research health developments and other determinants to strengthen policy decision-making within the health sector.

### SUSTAINABLE DEVELOPMENT AND HEALTHY ENVIRONMENTS

The Sustainable Development and Healthy Environment group comprises four departments that concentrate on: health in sustainable development; nutrition for health and development; protection of the human environment; and emergency and humanitarian action.

The group seeks to monitor the advantages and disadvantages for health, nutrition, environment and development arising from the process of globalization; to integrate the issue of health into poverty reduction programmes; and to promote human rights and equality. Adequate and safe food and nutrition is a priority programme area. WHO collaborates with FAO, the World Food Programme, UNICEF and other UN agencies in pursuing its objectives relating to nutrition and food safety. An estimated 780m. world-wide cannot meet basic needs for energy and protein, more than 2,000m. people lack essential vitamins and minerals, and 170m. children are estimated to be malnourished. In December 1992 WHO and FAO hosted an international conference on nutrition, at which a World Declaration and Plan of Action on Nutrition was adopted to make the fight against malnutrition a development priority. Following the conference, WHO promoted the elaboration and implementation of national plans of action on nutrition. WHO aims to support the enhancement of member states' capabilities in dealing with their nutrition situations, and addressing scientific issues related to preventing, managing and monitoring protein-energy malnutrition; micronutrient malnutrition, including iodine deficiency disorders, vitamin A deficiency, and nutritional anaemia; and diet-related non-communicable diseases such as cancer and heart disease. In 1990 the World Health Assembly resolved to eliminate iodine deficiency (causing mental handicap) by 2000. In collaboration with other international agencies, WHO is implementing a comprehensive strategy for promoting appropriate infant, young child and maternal nutrition, and for dealing effectively with nutritional emergencies in large populations. Areas of emphasis include promoting health-care practices that enhance successful breast-feeding; appropriate complementary feeding; refining the use and interpretation of body measurements for assessing nutritional status; relevant information, education and training; and action to give effect to the International Code of Marketing of Breast-milk Substitutes. WHO's food safety programme aims to protect human health against risks associated with biological and chemical contaminants and additives in food. With FAO, WHO establishes food standards (through the work of the Codex Alimentarius Commission and its subsidiary committees) and evaluates food additives, pesticide residues and other contaminants and their implications for health. The programme provides expert advice on such issues as food-borne pathogens (e.g. listeria), production methods (e.g. aquaculture) and food biotechnology (e.g. genetic modification).

WHO's Programme for the Promotion of Environmental Health undertakes a wide range of initiatives to tackle the increasing threats to health and well-being from a changing environment, especially in relation to air pollution, water quality, sanitation, protection against radiation, management of hazardous waste, chemical safety and housing hygiene. Some 1,200m. people world-wide have no access to clean drinking water, while a further 2,900m. people are denied suitable sanitation systems. WHO helped launch the Water Supply and Sanitation Council in 1990 and regularly updates its *Guidelines for Drinking Water Quality*. In rural areas, the emphasis continues to be on the provision and maintenance of safe and sufficient water supplies and adequate sanitation, the health aspects of rural housing, vector control in water resource management, and the safe use of agrochemicals. In urban areas, assistance is provided to identify local environmental health priorities and to improve municipal governments' ability to deal with environmental conditions and health problems in an integrated manner; promotion of the 'Healthy City' approach is a major component of the Programme. Other Programme activities include environmental health information development and management, human resources development, environmental health planning methods, research and work on problems relating to global environment change, such as UV-radiation. A report considering the implications of climate change on human health, prepared jointly by WHO, WMO and UNEP, was published in July 1996. The WHO Global Strategy for Health and Environment, developed in response to the WHO Commission on Health and Environment which reported to the UN Conference on Environment and Development in June 1992, provides the framework for Programme activities.

WHO's work in the promotion of chemical safety is undertaken in collaboration with ILO and UNEP through the International Programme on Chemical Safety (IPCS), the Central Unit for which is located in WHO. The Programme provides internationally-evaluated scientific information on chemicals, promotes the use of such information in national programmes, assists member states in establishment of their own chemical safety measures and programmes, and helps them strengthen their capabilities in chemical emergency preparedness and response and in chemical risk reduction. In 1995 an Inter-organization Programme for the Social Management of Chemicals was established by UNEP, ILO, FAO, WHO, UNIDO and OECD, in order to strengthen international co-operation in the field of chemical safety. In 1998 WHO led an international assessment of the health risk from bendocine disruptors (chemicals which disrupt hormonal activities).

Within the UN system, WHO's Division of Emergency and Humanitarian Action co-ordinates the international response to emergencies and natural disasters in the health field, in close co-operation with other agencies and within the framework set out by the UN's Office for the Co-ordination of Humanitarian Affairs. In this context, WHO provides expert advice on epidemiological surveillance, control of communicable diseases, public health information and health emergency training. Its emergency preparedness activities include co-ordination, policy-making and planning, awareness-building, technical advice, training, publication of standards and guide-lines, and research. Its emergency relief activities include organizational support, the provision of emergency drugs and supplies and conducting technical emergency assessment missions. The Division's objective is to strengthen the national capacity of member states to reduce the adverse health consequences of disasters. In responding to emergency situations, WHO always tries to develop projects and activities that will assist the national authorities concerned in rebuilding or strengthening their own capacity to handle the impact of such situations. In late 1998 WHO was a major participant in international relief efforts to assist countries in Central America affected by a severe hurricane. A supply management (SUMA) system was used by WHO for the first time to co-ordinate the management and distribution of relief items and supplies. During 1999 emergency and humanitarian activities included the provision of emergency medical supplies to refugees fleeing the conflict in Kosovo and Metohija (Federal Republic of Yugoslavia) and support for the health authorities in neighbouring host countries; post-conflict surveillance of the public health situation in Kosovo, together with the co-ordination of agencies providing health care and preparation of a plan of action for the rehabilitation and improvement of health services in the region; emergency aid and an assessment of health priorities following a major earthquake in Turkey; and technical support to restore health facilities and establish an effective communicable diseases surveillance system in East Timor.

### SOCIAL CHANGE AND MENTAL HEALTH

The Social Change and Mental Health group comprises four departments: Health Promotion; Disability, Injury Prevention and Rehabilitation; Mental Health; and Substance Abuse. The group works to assess the impact of injuries, violence and sensory impairments on health, and formulates guide-lines and protocols for the prevention and management of mental problems. The Health Promotion department promotes decentralized and community-based health programmes and is concerned with developing new approaches to population ageing and encouraging healthy life-styles and self-care. It also seeks to relieve the negative impact of social changes such as urbanization, migration and changes in family structure upon health. Several health promotion projects have been undertaken, in collaboration between WHO regional and country offices and other relevant organizations, including: the Global School Health Initiative, to bridge the sectors of health and education and to promote the health of school-age children; the Global Strategy for Occupational Health, to promote the health of the working population and the control of occupational health risks; Community-based Rehabilitation, which aimed to provide a more enabling environment for people with disabilities; and a communication strategy to provide training and support for health communications personnel and initiatives.

In July 1997 the fourth International Conference on Health Promotion (ICHP) was held in Jakarta, Indonesia, where a declaration on 'Health Promotion into the 21st Century' was agreed. The fifth ICHP was scheduled to be convened in June 2000, in Mexico City, Mexico.

Mental health problems, which include unipolar and bipolar affective disorders, psychosis, epilepsy, dementia, Parkinson's disease, multiple sclerosis, drug and alcohol dependency, and neuropsychiatric disorders such as post-traumatic stress disorder, obsessive compulsive disorder and panic disorder, have been identified by WHO as significant global health problems. Although, overall, physical health has improved, mental, behavioural and social health problems are increasing, owing to extended life expectancy and improved child mortality rates, and factors such as war and poverty. WHO aims to address mental problems by increasing awareness of mental health issues and promoting improved mental health services and primary care.

The Substance Abuse department is concerned with problems of alcohol, drugs and other substance abuse. Within its Programme on Substance Abuse (PSA), which was established in 1990 in response to the global increase in substance abuse, WHO provides technical support to assist countries in formulating policies with regard to the prevention and reduction of the health and social effects of psychoactive substance abuse. PSA's sphere of activity includes epidemiological surveillance and risk assessment, advocacy and the dissemination of information, strengthening national and regional prevention and health promotion techniques and strategies, the development of cost-effective treatment and rehabilitation approaches, and also encompasses regulatory activities as required under the international drugs-control treaties in force.

The Tobacco or Health Programme, which was incorporated into the PSA in May 1994, aims to reduce the use of tobacco, by educating tobacco-users and preventing young people from adopting the habit. In 1996 WHO published its first report on the tobacco situation world-wide. According to WHO, about one-third of the world's population aged over 15 years smoke tobacco, which causes approximately 3.5m. deaths each year (through lung cancer, heart disease, chronic bronchitis and other effects). In 1998 the 'Tobacco Free Initiative', a major global anti-smoking campaign, was established. In May 1999 the World Health Assembly endorsed the formulation of a Framework Convention on Tobacco Control (FCTC) to help to combat the increase in tobacco use (although a number of tobacco growers expressed concerns about the effect of the convention on their livelihoods). The greatest increase in tobacco use was forecast to occur in developing countries.

### HEALTH TECHNOLOGY AND PHARMACEUTICALS

WHO's Health Technology and Pharmaceuticals group is made up of three departments: Essential Drugs and Other Medicines; Vaccines and Other Biologicals; and Blood Safety and Clinical Technology. It promotes the development of drugs and vaccines, the self-sufficiency of immunization programmes and world-wide co-operation on blood safety.

The Department of Essential Drugs and Other Medicines promotes public health through the development of national drugs policies and global guide-lines and through collaboration with member countries to promote access to essential drugs, the rational use of medicines and compliance with international drug-control requirements. The department comprises four teams: Policy Access and Rational Use; the Drug Action Programme; Quality, Safety and the Regulation of Medicines; and Traditional Medicine.

The Policy Access and Rational Use team and the Drug Action Programme assist in the development and implementation by member states of pharmaceutical policies, in ensuring a supply of essential drugs of good quality at low cost, and in the rational use of drugs. Other activities include global and national operational research in the pharmaceutical sector, and the development of technical tools for problem solving, management and evaluation. The Policy Access and Rational Use team also has a strong advocacy and information role, promulgated through a periodical, the *Essential Drugs Monitor*, an extensive range of technical publications, and an information dissemination programme targeting developing countries.

The Quality, Safety and Regulation of Medicines team supports national drug-regulatory authorities and drug-procurement agencies and facilitates international pharmaceutical trade through the exchange of technical information and the harmonization of internationally respected norms and standards. In particular, it publishes the *International Pharmacopoeia*, the *Consultative List of International Nonproprietary Names for Pharmaceutical Substances*, and annual and biennial reports of Expert Committees responsible for determining relevant international standards for the manufacture and specification of pharmaceutical and biological products in international commerce. It provides information on the safety and efficacy of drugs, with particular regard to counterfeit and substandard projects, to health agencies and providers of health care, and it maintains the pharmaceuticals section of the UN *Consolidated List of Products whose Consumption and/or Sale have been Banned, Withdrawn, Severely Restricted or Not Approved by Governments*. The *WHO Model List of Essential Drugs* is updated every two years and is complemented by corresponding model prescribing information; the 10th *Model List* was published in 1998 and identified 306 essential drugs.

The Traditional Medicine team encourages and supports member states in the integration of traditional medicine into national health-care systems and in the appropriate use of traditional medicine, in particular through the provision of technical guide-lines, standards and methodologies.

In January 1999 the Executive Board adopted a resolution on WHO's Revised Drug Strategy which placed emphasis on the inequalities of access to pharmaceuticals, and also covered specific aspects of drugs policy, quality assurance, drug promotion, drug donation, independent drug information and rational drug use. Plans of action involving co-operation with member states and other international organizations were to be developed to monitor and analyse the pharmaceutical and public health implications of international agreements, including trade agreements.

In September 1991 the Children's Vaccine Initiative (CVI) was launched, jointly sponsored by the Rockefeller Foundation, UNDP, UNICEF, the World Bank and WHO, to facilitate the development and provision of children's vaccines. The CVI has as its ultimate goal the development of a single oral immunization shortly after birth that will protect against all major childhood diseases. In 1998 the CVI reported that 4m. children die each year of diseases for which there were existing common vaccines. An International Vaccine Institute was established in Seoul, Republic of Korea, as part of the CVI, to provide scientific and technical services for the production of vaccines for developing countries. In September 1996 WHO, jointly with UNICEF, published a comprehensive survey, entitled *State of the World's Vaccines and Immunization*.

### HEALTH DAYS

World Health Day is observed on 7 April every year, and is used to promote awareness of a particular health topic ('Active Ageing makes the Difference', in 1999). World TB Day is held every year on 24 March, World No Tobacco Day on 31 May, World Diabetes Day, in association with the International Diabetes Federation, on 14 November, World AIDS Day on 1 December, and World Asthma Day on 11 December.

### ASSOCIATED AGENCY

**International Agency for Research on Cancer:** 150 Cours Albert Thomas, 69372 Lyon Cédex 08, France; tel. 4-72-73-85-67; fax 4-72-73-85-75; e-mail gaudin@iarc.fr. Established in 1965 as a self-governing body within the framework of WHO, the Agency organizes international research on cancer. It has its own laboratories and runs a programme of research on the environmental factors causing cancer. Members: Australia, Belgium, Canada, Denmark, Finland, France, Germany, Italy, Japan, Netherlands, Norway, Russia, Sweden, Switzerland, United Kingdom, USA. Dir Dr Paul Kleihues (Germany).

## Finance

WHO's regular budget is provided by assessment of member states and associate members. An additional fund for specific projects is provided by voluntary contributions from members and other sources, including UNDP and UNFPA.

A regular budget of US $842.7m. was approved for the two years 1998–99. In May 1999 the Assembly approved a regular budget of

$842.64m. for the 2000–01 biennium, with a further $15m. to be available to fund priority programmes.

**WHO budget appropriations by region, 1998–99**

| Region | Amount (US dollars) | % of total budget |
|---|---|---|
| Africa | 157,413,000 | 18.68 |
| Americas | 82,686,000 | 9.81 |
| South-East Asia | 99,251,000 | 11.78 |
| Europe | 49,823,000 | 5.91 |
| Eastern Mediterranean | 90,249,000 | 10.71 |
| Western Pacific | 80,279,000 | 9.53 |
| Global and inter-regional | 282,953,000 | 33.58 |
| **Total** | 842,654,000 | 100.00 |

## Publications

*Bulletin of WHO* (monthly).

*Environmental Health Criteria.*

*International Digest of Health Legislation* (quarterly).

*International Statistical Classification of Diseases and Related Health Problems,* Tenth Revision, 1992–1994 (versions in 37 languages).

*Weekly Epidemiological Record.*

*WHO Drug Information* (quarterly).

*World Health Statistics Annual.*

Technical report series; catalogues of specific scientific, technical and medical fields available.

# World Intellectual Property Organization—WIPO

**Address:** 34 chemin des Colombettes, 1211 Geneva 20, Switzerland.
**Telephone:** (22) 3389111; **fax:** (22) 7335428; **e-mail:** wipo.mail@wipo.int; **internet:** www.wipo.int.

WIPO was established by a Convention signed in Stockholm in 1967, which came into force in 1970. It became a specialized agency of the UN in December 1974.

### MEMBERS

171 members: see Table on pp. 114–116.

## Organization

(December 1999)

### GENERAL ASSEMBLY

The General Assembly is one of the three WIPO governing bodies, and is composed of all states that are party to the WIPO Convention and that are also members of any of the WIPO-administered Unions (see below). In October 1999 the Assembly comprised 158 members. The Assembly meets in ordinary session once every two years to agree on programmes and budgets. It elects the Director-General, who is the executive head of WIPO.

### CONFERENCE

All member states are represented in the Conference, which meets in ordinary session once every two years to adopt budgets and programmes.

### CO-ORDINATION COMMITTEE

Countries belonging to the Committee are elected from among the member states of WIPO, the Paris and Berne Unions, and, *ex officio*, Switzerland. At October 1999 there were 72 members of the Committee. It meets in ordinary session once a year.

### INTERNATIONAL BUREAU

The International Bureau, as WIPO's secretariat, prepares the meetings of the various bodies of WIPO and the Unions, mainly through the provision of reports and working documents. It organizes the meetings, and sees that the decisions are communicated to all concerned, and, as far as possible, that they are carried out.

The International Bureau implements projects and initiates new ones to promote international co-operation in the field of intellectual property. It acts as an information service and publishes reviews. It is also the depositary of most of the treaties administered by WIPO.

**Director-General:** Dr Kamil Idris (Sudan).

## Activities

WIPO is responsible for promoting the protection of intellectual property throughout the world. Intellectual property comprises two principal branches: industrial property (patents and other rights in technological inventions, rights in trademarks, industrial designs, appellations of origin, etc.) and copyright and neighbouring rights (in literary, musical, artistic, photographic and audiovisual works).

WIPO administers international treaties relating to intellectual property, of which the most important are the Paris Convention for the Protection of Industrial Property (1883) and the Berne Convention for the Protection of Literary and Artistic Works (1886). WIPO's main areas of activity are progressive development of international intellectual property law, global protection systems and services, and co-operation for development.

### CO-OPERATION FOR DEVELOPMENT

WIPO carries out a substantial programme of development co-operation for the benefit of developing countries. The programme is directed towards: human resources, in particular the training of officials, lawyers, researchers and the private sector; the formulation or improvement of new national laws and regulations, regional treaties and different types of regional co-operation structures encouraging local inventive and artistic-creative activity; the teaching of intellectual property; the creation of measures to establish or expand the profession of intellectual property specialists; promoting exchange of experience and information among legislators and members of the judicial branch; giving advice on how to acquire access and disseminate information in patent documents; and promoting awareness of the importance of obtaining protection for inventions, trademarks, industrial designs and literary and artistic works.

In the field of copyright, WIPO aims to encourage and increase the creation of literary and artistic works by nationals in developing countries, and thereby to maintain their national culture in their own languages and/or corresponding to their own ethnic and social traditions and aspirations; and to improve the conditions of acquisition of the right to use or enjoy the literary and artistic works in which copyright is owned by foreigners.

In both industrial property and copyright, WIPO's development co-operation consists mainly of advice, training and the furnishing of documents and equipment. The advice is given by the staff of WIPO, experts chosen by WIPO or international meetings called by WIPO. The training is individual (on-the-job) or collective (courses, seminars and workshops). In 1998 a WIPO Worldwide Academy was established to strengthen human resource development programmes in intellectual property systems at national and regional levels. It maintains a Distance Learning Centre using the electronic media.

WIPO advises countries on obligations under the World Trade Organization's agreement on Trade-Related Aspects of Intellectual Property Rights (TRIPS). The two organizations have agreed on a joint technical co-operation initiative to assist developing countries to harmonize their national legislative and administrative structures in compliance with the TRIPS accord, by 1 January 2000.

In 1998, in response to the growth of electronic commerce, WIPO established a new administrative section to co-ordinate programmes and activities relating to the intellectual property aspects of electronic commerce. In September 1999 WIPO organized the first International Conference on Electronic Commerce and Intellectual Property.

### LEGAL AND TECHNICAL

WIPO prepares new treaties concerning the protection of intellectual property and undertakes the revision of existing treaties administered by the Organization. WIPO also carries out studies on issues in the field of intellectual property that could be the subject of model laws or guide-lines for implementation at the national or international levels.

WIPO administers international classifications established by treaties and relating to inventions, marks and industrial designs.

Those classifications are subject to periodical revisions to ensure their improvement in terms of coverage and precision.

**WIPO Permanent Committee on Industrial Property Information:** composed of representatives of 118 states and five intergovernmental organizations (July 1997); encourages co-operation between national and regional industrial property offices; and monitors all matters concerning patent, trademark, documentation and information on industrial property.

### GLOBAL PROTECTION SYSTEMS AND SERVICES

WIPO maintains international registration services, which facilitate obtaining protection of intellectual property in the various countries of the world which participate in the international system for the administration of those services.

**International registration of trademarks:** operating since 1893; during 1998 there were 20,020 registrations and renewals of trademarks; publ. *WIPO Gazette of International Marks* (monthly).

**International deposit of industrial designs:** operating since 1928; during 1998 6,464 deposits, renewals and prolongations of industrial designs were made; publ. *International Designs Bulletin* (monthly).

**International registration of appellations of origin:** operating since 1966; by 30 September 1997 740 appellations had been registered; publ. *Les appellations d'origine* (irreg.).

**International applications for patents:** operating since 1978; during 1998 67,007 record copies of international applications for patents under the Patent Co-operation Treaty (PCT) were received.

WIPO also maintains the WIPO Arbitration and Mediation Centre, which became operational on 1 October 1994, to facilitate the settlement of intellectual property disputes between private parties. The Centre also organizes arbitrator and mediator workshops and assists in the development of WIPO model contract clauses and industry-specific resolution schemes. In 1999 the Centre established an internet-based resolution facility to accelerate and enhance its dispute resolution capabilities, and to consider internet-related disputes.

### PARIS AND BERNE CONVENTIONS

**International Union for the Protection of Industrial Property (Paris Convention):** the treaty was signed in Paris in 1883, and last revised in 1967; there were 153 members of the Union's Assembly at December 1999. Member states must accord to nationals and residents of other member states the same advantages under their laws relating to the protection of inventions, trademarks and other subjects of industrial property as they accord to their own nationals.

**International Union for the Protection of Literary and Artistic Works (Berne Union):** the treaty was signed in Berne in 1886 and last revised in 1971; there were 137 member states at December 1999. Members of the Union's Assembly must accord the same protection to the copyright of nationals of other member states as to their own. The treaty also prescribes minimum standards of protection, for example, that copyright protection generally continues throughout the author's life and for 50 years after. It includes special provision for the developing countries.

### OTHER AGREEMENTS

(Status as on 19 October 1999, unless otherwise indicated)

**International Protection of Industrial Property:**

Madrid Agreement of 14 April 1891, for the Repression of False or Deceptive Indications of Source on Goods; 31 states party to the Agreement.

Madrid Agreement of 14 April 1891, Concerning the International Registration of Marks; 62 states party to the Agreement.

The Hague Agreement of 6 November 1925, Concerning the International Deposit of Industrial Designs; 29 states party to the Agreement.

Nice Agreement of 15 June 1957, Concerning the International Classification of Goods and Services for the Purposes of the Registration of Marks; 60 states party to the Agreement.

Lisbon Agreement of 31 October 1958, for the Protection of Appellations of Origin and their International Registration; 19 states party to the Agreement.

Locarno Agreement of 8 October 1968, Establishing an International Classification for Industrial Designs; 37 states party to the Agreement.

Patent Co-operation Treaty of 19 June 1970 (PCT); 104 states party to the Treaty.

Strasbourg Agreement of 24 March 1971, Concerning the International Patent Classification (IPC); 44 states party to the Agreement.

Vienna Agreement of 12 June 1973, Establishing an International Classification of the Figurative Elements of Marks; 15 states party to the Agreement.

Budapest Treaty of 28 April 1977, on the International Recognition of the Deposit of Micro-organisms for the Purposes of Patent Procedure; 47 states party to the Treaty.

Nairobi Treaty of 26 September 1981, on the Protection of the Olympic Symbol; 39 states party to the Treaty.

Trademark Law Treaty of 27 October 1994; 25 states party to the Treaty.

Protocol Relating to the Madrid Agreement Concerning the International Registration of Marks, signed on 28 June 1989; 37 contracting states.

Treaty on Intellectual Property in Respect of Integrated Circuits, 1989; not yet entered into force.

Copyright Treaty, 1996; not yet entered into force.

**Special International Protection of the Rights of Performers, Producers of Phonograms and Broadcasting Organizations ('Neighbouring Rights'):**

Rome Convention, 26 October 1961, for the Protection of Performers, Producers of Phonograms and Broadcasting Organizations; 63 states party to the Convention.

Geneva Convention, 29 October 1971, for the Protection of Producers of Phonograms against Unauthorized Duplication of their Phonograms; 59 states party to the Convention.

Brussels Convention, 21 May 1974, Relating to the Distribution of Programme-carrying Signals Transmitted by Satellite; 24 states party to the Convention.

Performancs and Phonograms Treaty, 1996; not yet entered into force.

## Finance

The budget for the two years 2000–2001 amounted to 409.7m. Swiss francs, compared with 383m. Swiss francs in 1998–99.

## Publications

*Annual Report.*

*Les appellations d'origine* (irregular, in French).

*Industrial Property and Copyright* (monthly in English and French; bimonthly in Spanish).

*Intellectual Property in Asia and the Pacific* (quarterly in English).

*International Designs Bulletin* (monthly in English and French, also on CD-Rom).

*Newsletter* (irregular in Arabic, English, French, Portuguese, Russian and Spanish).

*PCT Gazette* (weekly in English and French).

*PCT Newsletter* (monthly in English).

*WIPO Gazette of International Marks* (monthly, in English and French, also on CD-Rom).

A collection of industrial property and copyright laws and treaties; a selection of publications related to intellectual property.

# World Meteorological Organization—WMO

**Address:** 7 bis, ave de la Paix, CP 2300, 1211 Geneva 2, Switzerland.
**Telephone:** (22) 7308111; **fax:** (22) 7308181; **e-mail:** ipa@gateway.wmo.ch; **internet:** www.wmo.ch.

The WMO started activities and was recognized as a Specialized Agency of the UN in 1951, operating in the fields of meteorology, climatology, operational hydrology and related fields, as well as their applications.

### MEMBERS

185 members: see Table on pp. 114–116.

## Organization

(December 1999)

### WORLD METEOROLOGICAL CONGRESS

The supreme body of the Organization, the Congress, is convened every four years and represents all members; it adopts regulations, and determines policy, programme and budget. Thirteenth Congress: May 1999.

### EXECUTIVE COUNCIL

The Council has 36 members and meets at least yearly to prepare studies and recommendations for the Congress; it supervises the implementation of Congress resolutions and regulations, informs members on technical matters and offers advice.

### SECRETARIAT

The secretariat acts as an administrative, documentary and information centre; undertakes special technical studies; produces publications; organizes meetings of WMO constituent bodies; acts as a link between the meteorological and hydrometeorological services of the world, and provides information for the general public.

**Secretary-General:** Prof. G. O. P. Obasi (Nigeria).

### REGIONAL ASSOCIATIONS

Members are grouped in six Regional Associations (Africa, Asia, Europe, North and Central America, South America and South-West Pacific), whose task is to co-ordinate meteorological activity within their regions and to examine questions referred to them by the Executive Council. Sessions are held at least once every four years.

### TECHNICAL COMMISSIONS

The Technical Commissions are composed of experts nominated by the members of the Organization. Sessions are held at least once every four years. The Commissions cover the following areas: Basic Systems; Climatology; Instruments and Methods of Observation; Atmospheric Sciences; Aeronautical Meteorology; Agricultural Meteorology; Hydrology; Marine Meteorology.

## Activities

### WORLD WEATHER WATCH PROGRAMME

Combining facilities and services provided by the members, the Programme's primary purpose is to make available meteorological and related geophysical and environmental information enabling them to maintain efficient meteorological services. Facilities in regions outside any national territory (outer space, ocean areas and Antarctica) are maintained by members on a voluntary basis.

**Antarctic Activities:** co-ordinate WMO activities related to the Antarctic, in particular the surface and upper-air observing programme, plan the regular exchange of observational data and products needed for operational and research purposes, study problems related to instruments and methods of observation peculiar to the Antarctic, and develop appropriate regional coding practices. Contacts are maintained with scientific bodies dealing with Antarctic research and with other international organizations on aspects of Antarctic meteorology.

**Data Management:** This aspect of the Programme monitors the integration of the different components of the World Weather Watch (WWW) Programme, with the intention of increasing the efficiency of, in particular, the Global Observing System, the Global Data Processing System and the Global Telecommunication System. The Data Management component of the WWW Programme develops data handling procedures and standards for enhanced forms of data representation, in order to aid member countries in processing large volumes of meteorological data. It also supports the co-ordinated transfer of expertise and technology to developing countries.

**Emergency Response Activities:** assist national meteorological services to respond effectively to man-made environmental emergencies, particularly nuclear accidents, through the development, co-ordination and implementation of WMO/IAEA established procedures and response mechanisms for the provision and exchange of observational data and specialized transport model products.

**Global Data Processing System:** consists of World Meteorological Centres (WMCs) at Melbourne (Australia), Moscow (Russia) and Washington, DC (USA), 35 Regional/Specialized Meteorological Centres (RSMCs) and 183 National Meteorological Centres. The WMCs and RSMCs provide analyses, forecasts and warnings for exchange on the Global Telecommunications System. Some centres concentrate on the monitoring and forecasting of environmental quality and special weather phenomena, such as tropical cyclones, monsoons, droughts, etc., which have a major impact on human safety and national economies. These analyses and forecasts are designed to assist the members in making local and specialized forecasts.

**Global Observing System:** Simultaneous observations are made at more than 10,000 land stations. Meteorological information is also received from 3,000 aircraft, 7,000 ships, 300 fixed and drifting buoys and 10 polar orbiting and geostationary meteorological satellites. About 160 members operate some 1,100 ground stations equipped to receive picture transmissions from geostationary and polar-orbiting satellites.

**Global Telecommunication System:** provides telecommunication services for the rapid collection and exchange of meteorological information and related data; consists of (a) the Main Telecommunication Network (MTN), (b) six Regional Meteorological Telecommunication networks, and (c) the national telecommunication networks. The system operates through 174 National Meteorological Centres, 15 Regional Telecommunications Hubs and the three WMCs.

**Instruments and Methods of Observation Programme:** promotes the world-wide standardization of meteorological and geophysical instruments and methods of observation and measurement to meet agreed accuracy requirements. It provides related guidance material and training assistance in the use and maintenance of the instruments.

**System Support Activity:** provides guidance and support to members in the planning, establishment and operation of the WWW. It includes training, technical co-operation support, system and methodology support, operational WWW evaluations, advanced technology support, an operations information service, and the WWW referral catalogue.

**Tropical Cyclone Programme:** established in response to UN General Assembly Resolution 2733 (XXV), aims at the development of national and regionally co-ordinated systems to ensure that the loss of life and damage caused by tropical cyclones and associated floods, landslides and storm surges are reduced to a minimum. The programme supports the transfer of technology, and includes five regional tropical cyclone bodies covering more than 60 countries, to improve warning systems and for collaboration with other international organizations in activities related to disaster mitigation.

### WORLD CLIMATE PROGRAMME

Adopted by the Eighth World Meteorological Congress (1979), the World Climate Programme (WCP) comprises the following components: World Climate Data and Monitoring Programme (WCDMP), World Climate Applications and Services Programme (WCASP), World Climate Impact Assessment and Response Strategies Programme (WCIRP), World Climate Research Programme (WCRP). The WCP is supported by the Global Climate Observing System (GCOS), which provides comprehensive observation of the global climate system, involving a multi-disciplinary range of atmospheric, oceanic, hydrologic, cyrospheric and biotic properties and processes. In 1997/98 the GCOS was particularly active in monitoring the impact of the El Niño weather phenomenon on the climate system. The objectives of the WCP are: to use existing climate information to improve economic and social planning; to improve the understanding of climate processes through research, so as to determine the predictability of climate and the extent of man's influence on it; and to detect and warn governments of impending climate variations or changes, either natural or man-made, which may significantly affect critical human activities.

Co-ordination of the overall Programme is the responsibility of the WMO, along with direct management of the WCDMP and WCASP. The UN Environment Programme (UNEP, q.v.) has accepted responsibility for the WCIRP, while the WCRP is jointly administered by WMO, the International Council of Scientific

Unions (ICSU, q.v.) and UNESCO's Intergovernmental Oceanographic Commission. Other organizations involved in the Programme include FAO, WHO, and the Consultative Group on International Agricultural Research (CGIAR). The WCP Co-ordinating Committee co-ordinates the activities of the four components of the Programme and liaises with other international bodies concerned with climate. In addition, the WCP supports the WMO/UNEP Intergovernmental Panel on Climate Change and the implementation of international agreements, such as the UN Framework Convention on Climate Change (see below).

**World Climate Applications and Services Programme (WCASP):** promotes applications of climate knowledge in the areas of food production, water, energy (especially solar and wind energy), urban planning and building, human health, transport, tourism and recreation.

**World Climate Data and Monitoring Programme (WCDMP):** aims to make available reliable climate data for detecting and monitoring climate change for both practical applications and research purposes. The major projects are: the Climate Change Detection Project (CCDP); development of climate data bases; computer systems for climate data management (CLICOM); the World Data and Information Referral Service (INFOCLIMA); the Climate Monitoring System; and the Data Rescue (DARE) project.

**World Climate Impact Assessment and Response Strategies Programme (WCIRP):** aims to make reliable estimates of the socio-economic impact of climate changes, and to assist in forming national policies accordingly. It concentrates on: study of the impact of climate variations on national food systems; assessment of the impact of man's activities on the climate, especially through increasing the amount of carbon dioxide and other radiatively active gases in the atmosphere; and developing the methodology of climate impact assessments.

**World Climate Research Programme (WCRP):** organized jointly with the Intergovernmental Oceanographic Commission of UNESCO and the ICSU, to determine to what extent climate can be predicted, and the extent of man's influence on climate. Its three specific objectives are: establishing the physical basis for weather predictions over time ranges of one to two months; understanding and predicting the variability of the global climate over periods of several years; and studying the long-term variations and the response of climate to natural or man-made influence over periods of several decades. Studies include: changes in the atmosphere caused by emissions of carbon dioxide, aerosols and other gases; the effect of cloudiness on the radiation balance; the effect of ground water storage and vegetation on evaporation; the Arctic and Antarctic climate process; and the effects of oceanic circulation changes on the global atmosphere. The 10-year Tropical Ocean and Global Atmosphere Project, which ended in 1994, developed forecasting techniques used to monitor the climate phenomenon, El Niño, in 1997–98.

## ATMOSPHERIC RESEARCH AND ENVIRONMENT PROGRAMME

This major programme aims to help members to implement research projects; to disseminate relevant scientific information; to draw the attention of members to outstanding research problems of major importance, such as atmospheric composition and environment changes; and to encourage and help members to incorporate the results of research into operational forecasting or other appropriate techniques, particularly when such changes of procedure require international co-ordination and agreement.

**Global Atmosphere Watch (GAW):** This is a world-wide system that integrates most monitoring and research activities involving the measurement of atmospheric composition, and is intended to serve as an early warning system to detect further changes in atmospheric concentrations of 'greenhouse' gases, changes in the ozone layer and in long-range transport of pollutants, including acidity and toxicity of rain, as well as the atmospheric burden of aerosols. The instruments of these globally standardized observations and related research are a set of 20 global stations in remote areas and, in order to address regional effects, some 200 regional stations measuring specific atmospheric chemistry parameters, such as ozone and acid deposition. GAW is the main contributor of data on chemical composition and physical characteristics of the atmosphere to the GCOS. Through GAW, WMO has collaborated with the UN Economic Commission for Europe (ECE) and has been responsible for the meteorological part of the Monitoring and Evaluation of the Long-range Transmission of Air Pollutants in Europe. In this respect, WMO has arranged for the establishment of two Meteorological Synthesizing Centres (Oslo, Norway, and Moscow, Russia) which provide daily analysis of the transport of pollution over Europe. The GAW also gives attention to atmospheric chemistry studies, prepares scientific assessments and encourages integrated environmental monitoring. Quality Assurance Science Activities Centres have been established to ensure an overall level of quality in GAW.

**Physics and Chemistry of Clouds and Weather Modification Research Programme:** encourages scientific research on cloud physics and chemistry, with special emphasis on interaction between clouds and atmospheric chemistry, as well as weather modification such as precipitation enhancement ('rain-making') and hail suppression. It provides information on world-wide weather modification projects, and guidance in the design and evaluation of experiments. It also studies the chemistry of clouds and their role in the transport, transformation and dispersion of pollution.

**Tropical Meteorology Research Programme:** aims at the promotion and co-ordination of members' research efforts into such important problems as monsoons, tropical cyclones, meteorological aspects of droughts in the arid zones of the tropics, rain-producing tropical weather systems, and the interaction between tropical and mid-latitude weather systems. This should lead to a better understanding of tropical systems and forecasting, and thus be of economic benefit to tropical countries.

**Weather Prediction Research Programmes:** The programmes assist members in exchanging the results of research on weather prediction and long-range forecasting by means of international conferences and technical reports and progress reports on numerical weather prediction, in order to improve members' weather services. The Programme on Very Short- and Short-range Weather Prediction Research is designed to promote and co-ordinate research activities by members, with a view to improving forecast accuracy over a period extending to three or four days. The Programme on Medium- and Long-range Weather Prediction Research is aimed at the improvement and better co-ordination of members' research activities in weather prediction beyond day four, including monthly and seasonal forecasting.

## APPLICATIONS OF METEOROLOGY PROGRAMME

**Agricultural Meteorology Programme:** the study of weather and climate as they affect agriculture and forestry, the selection of crops and their protection from disease and deterioration in storage, soil conservation, phenology and physiology of crops and productivity and health of farm animals; the Commission for Agricultural Meteorology supervises the applications projects and also advises the Secretary-General in his efforts to co-ordinate activities in support of food production. There are also special activities in agrometeorology to monitor and combat drought and desertification, to apply climate and real-time weather information in agricultural planning and operations, and to help improve the efficiency of the use of human labour, land, water and energy in agriculture; close co-operation is maintained with FAO, centres of CGIAR and UNEP.

**Aeronautical Meteorology Programme:** to provide operational meteorological information required for safe, regular and efficient air navigation, as well as meteorological assistance to non-real-time activities of the aviation industry. The programme is implemented at global, regional and national levels by the Commission for Aeronautical Meteorology (CAeM) playing a major role, taking into account relevant meteorological developments in science and technology, studying aeronautical requirements for meteorological services, promoting international standardization of methods, procedures and techniques, and considering requirements for basic and climatological data as well as aeronautical requirements for meteorological observations and specialized instruments. Activities under this programme are carried out, where relevant, with the International Civil Aviation Organization (ICAO, q.v.) and in collaboration with users of services provided to aviation.

**Marine Meteorology and Related Oceanographic Activities Programme:** operational monitoring of the oceans and the maritime atmosphere; collection, exchange, archival recording and management of marine data; processing of marine data, and the provision of marine meteorological and oceanographic services in support of the safety of life and property at sea and of the efficient and economic operation of all sea-based activities. The Commission for Marine Meteorology (CMM) has broad responsibilities in the overall management of the programme. Certain programme elements are undertaken, jointly with the Intergovernmental Oceanographic Commission, within the context of the Integrated Global Ocean Services System (IGOSS), the Global Ocean Observing System (GOOS) and the work of the Data Buoy Co-operation Panel (DBCP). Close co-operation also occurs with the International Maritime Organization (IMO, q.v.), as well as with other bodies both within and outside the UN system.

**Public Weather Services Programme:** assists members in providing reliable and effective weather and related services for the benefit of the public. The main objectives of the programme are: to strengthen members' capabilities to meet the needs of the community through the provision of comprehensive weather and related services, with particular emphasis on public safety and welfare; and to foster a better understanding by the public of the capabilities of national meteorological services and how best to use their services.

### HYDROLOGY AND WATER RESOURCES PROGRAMME

The overall objective of this major programme is to apply hydrology to meet the needs of sustainable development and use of water and related resources, for the mitigation of water-related disasters and for effective environment management at national and international levels. The Programme promotes the standardization of hydrological observations and the efficient transfer of techniques and methods. It consists of three mutually supporting component programmes:

**Operational Hydrology Programme (OHP)—Basic Systems:** Deals with rational development and operation of hydrological services of members; water resources assessment; technology in operational hydrology; and capacity building in hydrology and water resources.

**Operational Hydrology Programme (OHP)—Applications and Environment:** Concentrates on water-related aspects of disaster mitigation through forecasting and hazard assessment; studies of the impact of climate change on water resources; effective use of operational hydrology in support of sustainable development, including the protection of the aquatic environment.

The above are both planned and executed under the auspices of the Commission for Hydrology (CHy), which brings together representatives of the world's hydrological and hydrometeorological services.

**Programme on Water-Related Issues:** ensures co-operation between WMO and other international organizations that have water-related programmes, including work related to water resources assessment and natural disaster reduction. It maintains particularly close links with UNESCO.

Specific suppport for the transfer of operational technology is provided through the Hydrological Operational Multipurpose System (HOMS).

Other WMO programmes contain hydrological elements, which are closely co-ordinated with the Hydrology and Water Resources Programme. These include the Tropical Cyclone Programme, the World Climate Programme, and the Global Energy and Water Budget Experiment of the World Climate Research Programme.

### EDUCATION AND TRAINING PROGRAMME

The overall objective of this programme is to assist members in developing adequately trained staff to meet their responsibilities for providing meteorological and hydrological information services.

Activities include surveys of the training requirements of member states, the development of appropriate training programmes, the monitoring and improvement of the network of WMO Regional Meteorological Training Centres, the organization of training courses, seminars and conferences and the preparation of training materials. The Programme also arranges individual training programmes and the provision of fellowships. There are about 500 trainees in any one year. About 300 fellowships are awarded annually. Advice is given on training materials, resources and expertise between members. A Panel of Experts on Education and Training was set up by the Executive Council to serve as an advisory body on all aspects of technical and scientific education and of training in meteorology and operational hydrology.

### TECHNICAL CO-OPERATION PROGRAMME

The objective of the WMO Technical Co-operation Programme is to assist developing countries in improving their meteorological and hydrological services so that they can serve the needs of their people more effectively. This is through improving, *inter alia*, their early warning systems for severe weather; their agricultural-meteorological services, to assist in more reliable and fruitful food production; and the assessment of climatological factors for economic planning. At a regional level the Programme concentrates on disaster prevention and mitigation. In 1995 the cost of the assistance to developing countries, administered or arranged by the Technical Co-operation Programme, was US $15.7m.

**United Nations Development Programme (UNDP):** WMO provides assistance in the development of national meteorological and hydrological services, in the application of meteorological and hydrological data to national economic development, and in the training of personnel. Assistance in the form of expert missions, fellowships and equipment was provided to 70 countries in 1995 at a cost of US $1.6m., financed by UNDP.

**Voluntary Co-operation Programme (VCP):** WMO assists members in implementing the World Weather Watch Programme to develop an integrated observing and forecasting system. Member governments contribute equipment, services and fellowships for training, in addition to cash donations. In 1995 79 projects for equipment and 100 projects for fellowships were approved under this programme. The total cost of all VCP projects in 1995 was US $6.0m.

WMO also carries out assistance projects under Trust Fund arrangements, financed by national authorities, either for activities in their own country or in a beneficiary country and managed by UNDP, the World Bank and UNEP. Such arrangements provided almost one-half of total Programme funds in 1996.

Financial support from WMO's regular budget for fellowships, group training, technical conferences and study tours amounted to US $1.3m. in 1995.

### CO-OPERATION WITH OTHER BODIES

As a Specialized Agency of the UN, WMO is actively involved in the activities of the UN system. In addition, WMO has concluded a number of formal agreements and working arrangements with international organizations both within and outside the UN system, at the intergovernmental and non-governmental level. As a result, WMO participates in major international conferences convened under the auspices of the UN or other organizations.

**Intergovernmental Panel on Climate Change (IPCC):** established in 1988 by UNEP and WMO; comprises some 2,500 scientists who meet regularly to assess scientific information on changes in climate. The IPCC aims to formulate a realistic response to climate change, based on a global scientific consensus, in order to influence governmental action. In December 1995 the IPCC presented evidence to 120 governments, demonstrating 'a discernible human influence on global climate'. The IPCC supports the adoption of legally-binding commitments to reduce the emission of so-called 'greenhouse' gases and works closely with a subsidiary body of the Conference of the Parties to the UN Framework Convention on Climate Change (UNFCCC) to provide information on the state of the world's climate and on assessing the infrastructure required to monitor the climate system.

**Secretariat of the UN Framework Convention on Climate Change:** Haus Carstanjen, Martin-Luther-King-Strasse 8, 53175 Bonn, Germany; tel. (228) 815-1000; fax (228) 815-1999; e-mail secretariat@unfccc.de; internet www.unfccc.de. WMO and UNEP worked together to formulate the Convention, in response to the first report of the IPCC, issued in August 1990, which predicted an increase in the concentration of 'greenhouse' gases (i.e. carbon dioxide and other gases that have a warming effect on the atmosphere) owing to human activity. The UNFCCC was signed in May 1992 and formally adopted at the UN Conference on Environment and Development, held in June. It entered into force in March 1994. It commits countries to submitting reports on measures being taken to reduce the emission of greenhouse gases and recommends stabilizing these emissions at 1990 levels by 2000; however, this was not legally-binding. In July 1996, at the second session of the Conference of the Parties (COP) of the Convention, representatives of developed countries declared their willingness to commit to legally-binding objectives for emission limitations in a specified timetable. Multilateral negotiations ensued to formulate a mandatory treaty on greenhouse gas emissions. At the third COP, held in Kyoto, Japan, in December 1997, 38 industrial nations endorsed mandatory reductions of emissions of the six most harmful gases by an average of 5.2% from 1990 levels, between 2008 and 2012. The agreement was to enter into force on being ratified by countries representing 55% of the world's carbon dioxide emissions in 1990. The fourth COP, convened in Buenos Aires, Argentina, in November 1998, adopted a plan of action to promote implementation of the Kyoto Protocol, through further detailed consideration of measures designed to reduce gas emissions. These included the Clean Development Mechanism, by which industrialized countries may obtain credits towards achieving their reduction targets by assisting developing countries to implement emission-reducing measures, and a system of trading emission quotas. The meeting also agreed on the need to formulate an effective compliance mechanism; however, discussion on the voluntary participation by developing countries in the Kyoto Protocol was postponed. The fifth COP to pursue negotiations on implementation of the Kyoto Protocol was held in Bonn, Germany, in November 1999.

### INTERNATIONAL DAY

World Meteorological Day is observed every year on 23 March. The theme in 1999 was 'Weather, Climate and Health'.

## Finance

WMO is financed by contributions from members on a proportional scale of assessment. The assessed regular budget for the four years 2000–03 was 248.8m. Swiss francs; additional expenditure of 3.5m. Swiss francs was also authorized to be used for high priority activities. Outside this budget, WMO implements a number of projects as executing agency for the UNDP or else under trust-fund arrangements.

## Publications

*Annual Report.*

*Statements on the Status of the Global Climate.*

*WMO Bulletin* (quarterly in English, French, Russian and Spanish).

Reports, technical regulations, manuals and notes and training publications.

# Membership of the United Nations and its Specialized Agencies

(at December 1999, unless otherwise indicated)

| | UN | IAEA | IBRD | IDA | IFC | IMF | FAO[1] | IFAD[2] | IMO[3] | ICAO[4] | ILO | ITU[5] | UNESCO[6] | UNIDO | UPU[7] | WHO[8] | WMO[9] | WIPO[10] |
|---|---|---|---|---|---|---|---|---|---|---|---|---|---|---|---|---|---|---|
| Afghanistan | x | x | x | x | x | x | x | x | | x | x | x | x | x | x | x | x | |
| Albania | x | x | x | x | x | x | x | x | x | x | x | x | x | x | x | x | x | |
| Algeria | x | x | x | x | x | x | x | x | x | x | x | x | x | x | x | x | x | x |
| Andorra | x | | | | | | | | | | | x | x | | | x | | x |
| Angola | x | x | x | x | x | x | x | x | x | x | x | x | x | x | x | x | x | x |
| Antigua and Barbuda | x | | x | | x | x | x | x | x | x | x | x | x | | x | x | x | |
| Argentina | x | x | x | x | x | x | x | x | x | x | x | x | x | x | x | x | x | x |
| Armenia | x | x | x | x | x | x | x | x | | x | x | x | x | x | x | x | x | x |
| Australia | x | x | x | x | x | x | x | x | x | x | x | x | x | | x | x | x | x |
| Austria | x | x | x | x | x | x | x | x | x | x | x | x | x | x | x | x | x | x |
| Azerbaijan | x | | x | x | x | x | x | x | x | x | x | x | x | x | x | x | x | x |
| Bahamas | x | | x | | x | x | x | | x | x | x | x | x | x | x | x | x | x |
| Bahrain | x | | x | | x | x | x | | x | x | x | x | x | x | x | x | x | x |
| Bangladesh | x | x | x | x | x | x | x | x | x | x | x | x | x | x | x | x | x | x |
| Barbados | x | | x | | x | x | x | x | x | x | x | x | x | x | x | x | x | x |
| Belarus | x | x | x | | x | x | | | | x | x | x | x | x | x | x | x | x |
| Belgium | x | x | x | x | x | x | x | x | x | x | x | x | x | x | x | x | x | x |
| Belize | x | | x | x | x | x | x | x | x | x | x | x | x | x | x | x | x | |
| Benin | x | x | x | x | x | x | x | x | x | x | x | x | x | x | x | x | x | x |
| Bhutan | x | | x | x | | x | x | x | | x | | x | x | x | x | x | | x |
| Bolivia | x | x | x | x | x | x | x | x | x | x | x | x | x | x | x | x | x | x |
| Bosnia and Herzegovina | x | x | x | x | x | x | x | x | x | x | x | x | x | x | x | x | x | x |
| Botswana | x | | x | x | x | x | x | x | | x | x | x | x | x | x | x | x | x |
| Brazil | x | x | x | x | x | x | x | x | x | x | x | x | x | x | x | x | x | x |
| Brunei | x | | x | | | x | | | x | x | | x | | | x | x | x | x |
| Bulgaria | x | x | x | | x | x | x | | x | x | x | x | x | x | x | x | x | x |
| Burkina Faso | x | x | x | x | x | x | x | x | | x | x | x | x | x | x | x | x | x |
| Burundi | x | | x | x | x | x | x | x | | x | x | x | x | x | x | x | x | x |
| Cambodia | x | x | x | x | x | x | x | x | x | x | x | x | x | x | x | x | x | x |
| Cameroon | x | x | x | x | x | x | x | x | x | x | x | x | x | x | x | x | x | x |
| Canada | x | x | x | x | x | x | x | x | x | x | x | x | x | | x | x | x | x |
| Cape Verde | x | | x | x | x | x | x | x | x | x | x | x | x | x | x | x | x | x |
| Central African Republic | x | | x | x | x | x | x | x | | x | x | x | x | x | x | x | x | x |
| Chad | x | | x | x | x | x | x | x | | x | x | x | x | x | x | x | x | x |
| Chile | x | x | x | x | x | x | x | x | x | x | x | x | x | x | x | x | x | x |
| China, People's Republic | x | x | x | x | x | x | x | x | x | x | x | x | x | x | x | x | x | x |
| Colombia | x | x | x | x | x | x | x | x | x | x | x | x | x | x | x | x | x | x |
| Comoros | x | | x | x | x | x | x | x | | x | x | x | x | x | x | x | x | |
| Congo, Democratic Republic | x | x | x | x | x | x | x | x | x | x | x | x | x | x | x | x | x | x |
| Congo, Republic | x | | x | x | x | x | x | x | x | x | x | x | x | x | x | x | x | x |
| Costa Rica | x | x | x | x | x | x | x | x | x | x | x | x | x | x | x | x | x | x |
| Côte d'Ivoire | x | x | x | x | x | x | x | x | x | x | x | x | x | x | x | x | x | x |
| Croatia | x | x | x | x | x | x | x | x | x | x | x | x | x | x | x | x | x | x |
| Cuba | x | x | | | | | x | x | x | x | x | x | x | x | x | x | x | x |
| Cyprus | x | x | x | x | x | x | x | x | x | x | x | x | x | x | x | x | x | x |
| Czech Republic | x | x | x | x | x | x | x | | x | x | x | x | x | x | x | x | x | x |
| Denmark | x | x | x | x | x | x | x | x | x | x | x | x | x | x | x | x | x | x |
| Djibouti | x | | x | x | x | x | x | x | x | x | x | x | x | x | x | x | x | |
| Dominica | x | | x | x | x | x | x | x | x | | x | x | x | x | x | x | x | x |
| Dominican Republic | x | x | x | x | x | x | x | x | x | x | x | x | x | x | x | x | x | |
| Ecuador | x | x | x | x | x | x | x | x | x | x | x | x | x | x | x | x | x | x |
| Egypt | x | x | x | x | x | x | x | x | x | x | x | x | x | x | x | x | x | x |
| El Salvador | x | x | x | x | x | x | x | x | x | x | x | x | x | x | x | x | x | x |
| Equatorial Guinea | x | | x | x | x | x | x | x | x | x | x | x | x | x | x | x | | x |
| Eritrea | x | | x | x | x | x | x | x | x | x | x | x | x | x | x | x | x | x |
| Estonia | x | x | x | | x | x | x | | x | x | x | x | x | | x | x | x | x |
| Ethiopia | x | x | x | x | x | x | x | x | x | x | x | x | x | x | x | x | x | x |
| Fiji | x | | x | x | x | x | x | x | x | x | x | x | x | x | x | x | x | x |
| Finland | x | x | x | x | x | x | x | x | x | x | x | x | x | x | x | x | x | x |
| France | x | x | x | x | x | x | x | x | x | x | x | x | x | x | x | x | x | x |
| Gabon | x | x | x | x | x | x | x | x | x | x | x | x | x | x | x | x | x | x |
| The Gambia | x | | x | x | x | x | x | x | x | x | x | x | x | x | x | x | x | x |
| Georgia | x | x | x | x | x | x | x | x | x | x | x | x | x | x | x | x | x | x |
| Germany | x | x | x | x | x | x | x | x | x | x | x | x | x | x | x | x | x | x |
| Ghana | x | x | x | x | x | x | x | x | x | x | x | x | x | x | x | x | x | x |
| Greece | x | x | x | x | x | x | x | x | x | x | x | x | x | x | x | x | x | x |
| Grenada | x | | x | x | x | x | x | x | x | x | x | x | x | x | x | x | | x |
| Guatemala | x | x | x | x | x | x | x | x | x | x | x | x | x | x | x | x | x | x |

*continued*

| | UN | IAEA | IBRD | IDA | IFC | IMF | FAO[1] | IFAD[2] | IMO[3] | ICAO[4] | ILO | ITU[5] | UNESCO[6] | UNIDO | UPU[7] | WHO[8] | WMO[9] | WIPO[10] |
|---|---|---|---|---|---|---|---|---|---|---|---|---|---|---|---|---|---|---|
| Guinea | x | | x | x | x | x | x | x | x | x | x | x | x | x | x | x | x | x |
| Guinea-Bissau | x | | x | x | x | x | x | x | x | x | x | x | x | x | x | x | x | x |
| Guyana | x | | x | x | x | x | x | x | x | x | x | x | x | x | x | x | x | x |
| Haiti | x | x | x | x | x | x | x | x | x | x | x | x | x | x | x | x | x | x |
| Honduras | x | x | x | x | x | x | x | x | x | x | x | x | x | x | x | x | x | x |
| Hungary | x | x | x | x | x | x | x | | x | x | x | x | x | x | x | x | x | x |
| Iceland | x | x | x | x | x | x | x | | x | x | x | x | x | | x | x | x | x |
| India | x | x | x | x | x | x | x | x | x | x | x | x | x | x | x | x | x | x |
| Indonesia | x | x | x | x | x | x | x | x | x | x | x | x | x | x | x | x | x | x |
| Iran | x | x | x | x | x | x | x | x | x | x | x | x | x | x | x | x | x | |
| Iraq | x | x | x | x | x | x | x | x | x | x | x | x | x | x | x | x | x | x |
| Ireland | x | x | x | x | x | x | x | x | x | x | x | x | x | x | x | x | x | x |
| Israel | x | x | x | x | x | x | x | x | x | x | x | x | x | x | x | x | x | x |
| Italy | x | x | x | x | x | x | x | x | x | x | x | x | x | x | x | x | x | x |
| Jamaica | x | x | x | | x | x | x | x | x | x | x | x | x | x | x | x | x | x |
| Japan | x | x | x | x | x | x | x | x | x | x | x | x | x | x | x | x | x | x |
| Jordan | x | x | x | x | x | x | x | x | x | x | x | x | x | x | x | x | x | x |
| Kazakhstan | x | x | x | x | x | x | x | x | x | x | x | x | x | x | x | x | x | x |
| Kenya | x | x | x | x | x | x | x | x | x | x | x | x | x | x | x | x | x | x |
| Kiribati | x | | x | x | x | x | x | | | x | | x | x | | x | x | | |
| Korea, Democratic People's Republic | x | | | | | | x | x | x | x | | x | x | x | x | x | x | x |
| Korea, Republic | x | x | x | x | x | x | x | x | x | x | x | x | x | x | x | x | x | x |
| Kuwait | x | x | x | x | x | x | x | x | x | x | x | x | x | x | x | x | x | x |
| Kyrgyzstan | x | | x | x | x | x | x | x | | x | x | x | x | x | x | x | x | x |
| Laos | x | | x | x | x | x | x | x | | x | x | x | x | x | x | x | x | x |
| Latvia | x | x | x | x | x | x | x | | x | x | x | x | x | | x | x | x | x |
| Lebanon | x | x | x | x | x | x | x | x | x | x | x | x | x | x | x | x | x | x |
| Lesotho | x | | x | x | x | x | x | x | | x | x | x | x | x | x | x | x | x |
| Liberia | x | x | x | x | x | x | x | x | x | x | x | x | x | x | x | x | x | x |
| Libya | x | x | x | x | x | x | x | x | x | x | x | x | x | x | x | x | x | x |
| Liechtenstein | x | x | | | | | | | | | | x | | | x | x | | x |
| Lithuania | x | x | x | | x | x | x | | x | x | x | x | x | x | x | x | x | x |
| Luxembourg | x | x | x | x | x | x | x | x | x | x | x | x | x | x | x | x | x | x |
| Macedonia, former Yugoslav republic | x | | x | x | x | x | x | x | x | x | x | x | x | x | x | x | x | x |
| Madagascar | x | x | x | x | x | x | x | x | x | x | x | x | x | x | x | x | x | x |
| Malawi | x | | x | x | x | x | x | x | x | x | x | x | x | x | x | x | x | x |
| Malaysia | x | x | x | x | x | x | x | x | x | x | x | x | x | x | x | x | x | x |
| Maldives | x | | x | x | x | x | x | x | x | x | | x | x | x | x | x | x | |
| Mali | x | x | x | x | x | x | x | x | | x | x | x | x | x | x | x | x | x |
| Malta | x | x | x | | | x | x | x | x | x | x | x | x | x | x | x | x | x |
| Marshall Islands | x | x | x | x | x | x | x | | x | x | | x | x | | | x | | |
| Mauritania | x | | x | x | x | x | x | x | x | x | x | x | x | x | x | x | x | x |
| Mauritius | x | x | x | x | x | x | x | x | x | x | x | x | x | x | x | x | x | x |
| Mexico | x | x | x | x | x | x | x | x | x | x | x | x | x | x | x | x | x | x |
| Micronesia, Federated States of | x | | x | x | x | x | | | | x | | x | x | | | x | x | |
| Moldova | x | x | x | x | x | x | x | x | | x | x | x | x | x | x | x | x | x |
| Monaco | x | x | | | | | | | x | x | | x | x | | x | x | x | x |
| Mongolia | x | x | x | x | x | x | x | x | x | x | x | x | x | x | x | x | x | x |
| Morocco | x | x | x | x | x | x | x | x | x | x | x | x | x | x | x | x | x | x |
| Mozambique | x | | x | x | x | x | x | x | x | x | x | x | x | x | x | x | x | x |
| Myanmar | x | x | x | x | x | x | x | x | x | x | x | x | x | x | x | x | x | |
| Namibia | x | | x | | x | x | x | x | x | x | x | x | x | x | x | x | x | x |
| Nauru | x | | | | | | | | | x | | x | x | | x | x | | |
| Nepal | x | | x | x | x | x | x | x | x | x | x | x | x | x | x | x | x | x |
| Netherlands | x | x | x | x | x | x | x | x | x | x | x | x | x | x | x | x | x | x |
| New Zealand | x | x | x | x | x | x | x | x | x | x | x | x | x | x | x | x | x | x |
| Nicaragua | x | x | x | x | x | x | x | x | x | x | x | x | x | x | x | x | x | x |
| Niger | x | x | x | x | x | x | x | x | | x | x | x | x | x | x | x | x | x |
| Nigeria | x | x | x | x | x | x | x | x | x | x | x | x | x | x | x | x | x | x |
| Norway | x | x | x | x | x | x | x | x | x | x | x | x | x | x | x | x | x | x |
| Oman | x | | x | x | x | x | x | x | x | x | x | x | x | x | x | x | x | x |
| Pakistan | x | x | x | x | x | x | x | x | x | x | x | x | x | x | x | x | x | x |
| Palau | x | | x | x | x | x | x | | x | x | | | x | | | x | | |
| Panama | x | x | x | x | x | x | x | x | x | x | x | x | x | x | x | x | x | x |
| Papua New Guinea | x | | x | x | x | x | x | x | x | x | x | x | x | x | x | x | x | x |
| Paraguay | x | x | x | x | x | x | x | x | x | x | x | x | x | x | x | x | x | x |
| Peru | x | x | x | x | x | x | x | x | x | x | x | x | x | x | x | x | x | x |
| Philippines | x | x | x | x | x | x | x | x | x | x | x | x | x | x | x | x | x | x |
| Poland | x | x | x | x | x | x | x | | x | x | x | x | x | x | x | x | x | x |
| Portugal | x | x | x | x | x | x | x | x | x | x | x | x | x | x | x | x | x | x |
| Qatar | x | x | x | | | x | x | x | x | x | x | x | x | x | x | x | x | x |
| Romania | x | x | x | | x | x | x | x | x | x | x | x | x | x | x | x | x | x |
| Russia | x | x | x | x | x | x | | | x | x | x | x | x | x | x | x | x | x |
| Rwanda | x | | x | x | x | x | x | x | | x | x | x | x | x | x | x | x | x |
| Saint Christopher and Nevis | x | | x | x | x | x | x | x | | | x | | x | x | x | x | | x |

*continued*

| | UN | IAEA | IBRD | IDA | IFC | IMF | FAO[1] | IFAD[2] | IMO[3] | ICAO[4] | ILO | ITU[5] | UNESCO[6] | UNIDO | UPU[7] | WHO[8] | WMO[9] | WIPO[10] |
|---|---|---|---|---|---|---|---|---|---|---|---|---|---|---|---|---|---|---|
| Saint Lucia | x | | x | x | x | x | x | x | x | x | x | x | x | x | x | x | x | x |
| Saint Vincent and the Grenadines | x | | x | x | | x | x | x | x | x | x | x | x | x | x | x | | x |
| Samoa | x | | x | x | x | x | x | x | x | x | | x | x | | x | x | | x |
| San Marino | x | | | | | x | x | | | x | x | x | x | | x | x | x | x |
| São Tomé and Príncipe | x | | x | x | | x | x | x | x | x | x | x | x | x | x | x | x | x |
| Saudi Arabia | x | x | x | x | x | x | x | x | x | x | x | x | x | x | x | x | x | x |
| Senegal | x | x | x | x | x | x | x | x | x | x | x | x | x | x | x | x | x | x |
| Seychelles | x | | x | | x | x | x | x | | x | x | x | x | x | x | x | x | |
| Sierra Leone | x | x | x | x | x | x | x | x | x | x | x | x | x | x | x | x | x | x |
| Singapore | x | x | x | | x | x | | | x | x | x | x | | | x | x | x | x |
| Slovakia | x | x | x | x | x | x | x | | x | x | x | x | x | x | x | x | x | x |
| Slovenia | x | x | x | x | x | x | x | | x | x | x | x | x | x | x | x | x | x |
| Solomon Islands | x | | x | x | x | x | x | x | x | x | x | x | x | | x | x | x | |
| Somalia | x | | x | x | x | x | x | x | x | x | x | x | x | x | x | x | x | x |
| South Africa | x | x | x | x | x | x | x | x | x | x | x | x | x | | x | x | x | x |
| Spain | x | x | x | x | x | x | x | x | x | x | x | x | x | x | x | x | x | x |
| Sri Lanka | x | x | x | x | x | x | x | x | x | x | x | x | x | x | x | x | x | x |
| Sudan | x | x | x | x | x | x | x | x | x | x | x | x | x | x | x | x | x | x |
| Suriname | x | | x | | | x | x | x | x | x | x | x | x | x | x | x | x | x |
| Swaziland | x | | x | x | x | x | x | x | | x | x | x | x | x | x | x | x | x |
| Sweden | x | x | x | x | x | x | x | x | x | x | x | x | x | x | x | x | x | x |
| Switzerland | | x | x | x | x | x | x | x | x | x | x | x | x | x | x | x | x | x |
| Syria | x | x | x | x | x | x | x | x | x | x | x | x | x | x | x | x | x | |
| Tajikistan | x | | x | x | x | x | x | x | | x | x | x | x | x | x | x | x | x |
| Tanzania | x | x | x | x | x | x | x | x | x | x | x | x | x | x | x | x | x | x |
| Thailand | x | x | x | x | x | x | x | x | x | x | x | x | x | x | x | x | x | x |
| Togo | x | | x | x | x | x | x | x | x | x | x | x | x | x | x | x | x | x |
| Tonga | x | | x | x | x | x | x | x | | x | | x | x | x | x | x | x | |
| Trinidad and Tobago | x | | x | x | x | x | x | x | x | x | x | x | x | x | x | x | x | x |
| Tunisia | x | x | x | x | x | x | x | x | x | x | x | x | x | x | x | x | x | x |
| Turkey | x | x | x | x | x | x | x | x | x | x | x | x | x | x | x | x | x | x |
| Turkmenistan | x | | x | | x | x | x | | x | x | x | x | x | x | x | x | x | x |
| Tuvalu | | | | | | | | | | | | x | x | | x | x | | |
| Uganda | x | x | x | x | x | x | x | x | | x | x | x | x | x | x | x | x | x |
| Ukraine | x | x | x | | x | x | | | x | x | x | x | x | x | x | x | x | x |
| United Arab Emirates | x | x | x | x | x | x | x | x | x | x | x | x | x | x | x | x | x | x |
| United Kingdom | x | x | x | x | x | x | x | x | x | x | x | x | x | x | x | x | x | x |
| USA | x | x | x | x | x | x | x | x | x | x | x | x | | | x | x | x | x |
| Uruguay | x | x | x | | x | x | x | x | x | x | x | x | x | x | x | x | x | x |
| Uzbekistan | x | x | x | x | x | x | | | | x | x | x | x | x | x | x | x | x |
| Vanuatu | x | | x | x | x | x | x | | x | x | | x | x | x | x | x | x | |
| Vatican City | | x | | | | | | | | | | x | | | x | | | x |
| Venezuela | x | x | x | | x | x | x | x | x | x | x | x | x | x | x | x | x | x |
| Viet Nam | x | x | x | x | x | x | x | x | x | x | x | x | x | x | x | x | x | x |
| Yemen | x | x | x | x | x | x | x | x | x | x | x | x | x | x | x | x | x | x |
| Yugoslavia[11] | x | x | | | | | x | x | x | x | x | x | x | x | x | x | x | x |
| Zambia | x | x | x | x | x | x | x | x | | x | x | x | x | x | x | x | x | x |
| Zimbabwe | x | x | x | x | x | x | x | x | x | x | x | x | x | x | x | x | x | x |

[1] The Cook Islands, Niue and the European Union are members of FAO.

[2] The Cook Islands is a member of IFAD.

[3] Hong Kong and Macau are associate members of IMO.

[4] The Cook Islands is a member of ICAO.

[5] Members also include British Overseas Territories, French Overseas Territories and United States Territories.

[6] The Cook Islands and Niue are members of UNESCO; Aruba, the British Virgin Islands, Macau and the Netherlands Antilles are associate members.

[7] Members also include British Overseas Territories and the Netherlands Antilles and Aruba.

[8] The Cook Islands and Niue are members of WHO; Puerto Rico and Tokelau are associate members.

[9] Members also include British Caribbean Territories, the Cook Islands, French Polynesia, Hong Kong, Macau, the Netherlands Antilles and Aruba, New Caledonia and Niue.

[10] Membership as at October 1999.

[11] See p. 4 for details on Yugoslavia's status in the UN.

# AFRICAN DEVELOPMENT BANK—ADB

**Address:** rue Joseph Anoma, 01 BP 1387, Abidjan 01, Côte d'Ivoire.
**Telephone:** 20-44-44; **fax:** 20-40-06; **e-mail:** afdb@afdb.org; **internet:** www.afdb.org.

Established in 1964, the Bank began operations in July 1966, with the aim of financing economic and social development in African countries.

### AFRICAN MEMBERS

| | | |
|---|---|---|
| Algeria | Equatorial Guinea | Namibia |
| Angola | Eritrea | Niger |
| Benin | Ethiopia | Nigeria |
| Botswana | Gabon | Rwanda |
| Burkina Faso | The Gambia | São Tomé and Príncipe |
| Burundi | Ghana | Senegal |
| Cameroon | Guinea | Seychelles |
| Cape Verde | Guinea-Bissau | Sierra Leone |
| Central African Republic | Kenya | Somalia |
| Chad | Lesotho | South Africa |
| Comoros | Liberia | Sudan |
| Congo, Democratic Republic | Libya | Swaziland |
| Congo, Republic | Madagascar | Tanzania |
| Côte d'Ivoire | Malawi | Togo |
| Djibouti | Mali | Tunisia |
| Egypt | Mauritania | Uganda |
| | Mauritius | Zambia |
| | Morocco | Zimbabwe |
| | Mozambique | |

There are also 24 non-African members.

## Organization

(January 2000)

### BOARD OF GOVERNORS

The highest policy-making body of the Bank. Each member country nominates one Governor, usually its Minister of Finance and Economic Affairs, and an alternate Governor or the Governor of its Central Bank. The Board meets once a year. It elects the Board of Directors and the President.

### BOARD OF DIRECTORS

The Board consists of 18 members (of whom six are non-African), elected by the Board of Governors for a term of three years, renewable once; it is responsible for the general operations of the Bank. The Board meets on a weekly basis.

### OFFICERS

The President is responsible for the organization and the day-to-day operations of the Bank under guidance of the Board of Directors. The President is elected for a five-year term and serves as the Chairman of the Board of Directors. Three Vice-Presidents are responsible for Operations, Finance and Planning, and Corporate Management.

The Bank's operational activities are divided into five regional departments (for northern, southern, eastern, western and central Africa), departments for central operations and for the private sector, and units for co-operation and for environment and sustainable development.

**Executive President and Chairman of Board of Directors:** OMAR KABBAJ (Morocco).

**Vice-President** (Finance and Planning): AHMED M. F. BAHGAT (Egypt).

**Vice-President** (Administration and Corporate Management): CHANEL BOUCHER (Canada).

**Vice-President** (Operations): CYRIL ENWEZE (Nigeria).

**Secretary-General:** PHILIBERT AFRIKA (Rwanda).

### FINANCIAL STRUCTURE

The ADB Group of development financing institutions comprises the African Development Fund (ADF) and the Nigeria Trust Fund (NTF), which provide concessionary loans, and the African Development Bank itself. The group uses a unit of account (UA), which, at 1 February 1999, was valued at US $1.38977.

The capital stock of the Bank was at first exclusively open for subscription by African countries, with each member's subscription consisting of an equal number of paid-up and callable shares. In 1978, however, the Governors agreed to open the capital stock of the Bank to subscription by non-regional states on the basis of nine principles aimed at maintaining the African character of the institution. The decision was finally ratified in May 1982, and the participation of non-regional countries became effective on 30 December. It was agreed that African members should still hold two-thirds of the share capital, that all loan operations should be restricted to African members, and that the Bank's President should always be an African national. In 1997 the ADB's authorized capital was US $21,858m. At the end of 1997 subscribed capital was $21,529m. (of which the paid-up portion was $2,644m.). In May 1998 the Board of Governors approved an increase in capital of 35%, and resolved that the non-African members' share of the capital be increased from 33.3% to 40%.

## Activities

At the end of 1997 total loan and grant approvals by the ADB Group since the beginning of its operations amounted to US $32,525m. Of that amount agriculture received the largest proportion of assistance (23.5%), while public utilities received 20.7%, transport 16.8%, industry 16.4%, multi-sector activities 12.8%, and social projects 9.7%. In 1997 the group approved 105 loans and grants amounting to $1,777m., compared with 31 loans and grants valued at $803m. in 1996.

A new credit policy, adopted in May 1995, effectively disqualified 39 low-income regional members, deemed to be non-creditworthy, from receiving non-concessional ADB financing, in an attempt to reduce the accumulation of arrears. The ADB Group estimated that its capital requirements for the period 1997–2001 would amount to US $46,500m. to allow for greater flexibility in its lending. During 1996 the Bank supported international efforts to address the problem of heavily indebted poor countries (HIPCs), and agreed to participate in a six-year initiative which aimed to encourage economic prospects in those countries while reducing outstanding debt and preventing its recurrence (see World Bank, p. 78). The ADB's initial contribution to the HIPC initiative, approved in April 1997, was an amount up to UA 230m., to be generated over the period 1997–2003. In September 1997 the Bank approved an initial UA 133m. to establish a Supplementary Financing Mechanism, which aimed to assist countries eligible for ADF funds to meet interest payments on outstanding Bank debt.

The ADB contributed funds for the establishment in 1986 of the Africa Project Development Facility, which assists the private sector in Africa by providing advisory services and finance for entrepreneurs: it is managed by the International Finance Corporation (IFC—see p. 83). In 1989 the ADB, in co-ordination with IFC and UNDP, created the African Management Services Company (AMSCo) which provides management support and training to private companies in Africa.

The Bank also provides technical assistance to regional member countries in the form of experts' services, pre-investment feasibility studies, and staff training; much of this assistance is financed through bilateral aid funds contributed by non-African member states. The Bank's African Development Institute provides training for officials of regional member countries in order to enhance the management of Bank-financed projects and, more broadly, to strengthen national capacities for promoting sustainable development. In 1990 the ADB established the African Business Round Table (ABR), which is composed of the chief executives of Africa's leading corporations. The ABR aims to strengthen Africa's private sector, promote intra-African trade and investment, and attract foreign investment to Africa. The ABR is chaired by the ADB's Executive President. At its fourth annual meeting, held in Arusha, Tanzania, in March 1994, the ABR resolved to establish an African Investment Bank, in co-operation with the ADB, which was to provide financial services to African companies. In November 1999 a Joint Africa Institute, which had been established by the Bank, the World Bank and the IMF, was formally inaugurated in Abidjan, Côte d'Ivoire. The Institute aimed to enhance training opportunities in economic policy and management and to strengthen capacity-building in the region.

In 1990 a Memorandum of Understanding for the Reinforcement of Co-operation between the Organization of African Unity (OAU—q.v.), the UN's Economic Commission for Africa (q.v.) and the ADB was signed by the three organizations. A joint secretariat supports co-operation activities between the organizations.

### AFRICAN DEVELOPMENT BANK (ADB)

The Bank makes loans at a variable rate of interest, which is adjusted twice a year (the rate was 7.39% per year at December 1997), plus a commitment fee of 1% (to be reduced to 0.75% following a decision by the Board of Governors in May 1998). Loan approvals

**Group Loan and Grant Approvals by Country**
(millions of UA)

| Country | 1996 | 1997 | Cumulative total* |
|---|---|---|---|
| Algeria | 250.00 | — | 1,336.50 |
| Angola | | | 294.14 |
| Benin | 18.00 | 19.33 | 265.26 |
| Botswana | — | — | 324.93 |
| Burkina Faso | — | 32.76 | 278.52 |
| Burundi | — | — | 267.37 |
| Cameroon | — | 29.40 | 533.94 |
| Cape Verde | — | 8.47 | 145.09 |
| Central African Republic | — | — | 139.39 |
| Chad | — | 37.22 | 260.13 |
| Comoros | — | — | 64.74 |
| Congo, Democratic Republic | — | — | 936.20 |
| Congo, Republic | — | — | 277.83 |
| Côte d'Ivoire | 29.00 | 6.07 | 917.79 |
| Djibouti | — | — | 83.90 |
| Egypt | — | 44.47 | 1,399.25 |
| Equatorial Guinea | — | — | 64.99 |
| Eritrea | 14.03 | 22.49 | 36.52 |
| Ethiopia | 19.50 | 28.00 | 925.61 |
| Gabon | — | 19.81 | 579.71 |
| Gambia | 4.00 | 11.03 | 168.98 |
| Ghana | 7.53 | 58.00 | 555.01 |
| Guinea | — | 29.94 | 456.33 |
| Guinea Bissau | — | 18.50 | 157.26 |
| Kenya | 15.94 | 1.10 | 485.10 |
| Lesotho | — | 0.80 | 246.50 |
| Liberia | — | — | 153.25 |
| Madagascar | — | 34.61 | 348.80 |
| Malawi | 5.00 | 39.08 | 439.44 |
| Mali | — | 61.13 | 388.07 |
| Mauritania | 16.70 | 4.02 | 238.06 |
| Mauritius | — | 9.30 | 151.95 |
| Morocco | 60.41 | 151.48 | 2,463.28 |
| Mozambique | 24.36 | 76.00 | 568.86 |
| Namibia | — | — | 26.92 |
| Niger | — | 0.70 | 164.42 |
| Nigeria | 2.09 | — | 1,902.87 |
| Rwanda | — | 1.50 | 231.77 |
| São Tomé and Príncipe | 2.60 | 1.88 | 89.58 |
| Senegal | 12.00 | 20.00 | 398.05 |
| Seychelles | — | 8.36 | 82.40 |
| Sierra Leone | — | 12.15 | 158.75 |
| Somalia | — | — | 150.40 |
| South Africa | — | 114.20 | 114.20 |
| Sudan | — | — | 349.80 |
| Swaziland | — | — | 188.93 |
| Tanzania | — | 108.16 | 587.63 |
| Togo | — | 12.20 | 157.30 |
| Tunisia | 27.35 | 168.46 | 2,051.91 |
| Uganda | 22.03 | 27.77 | 506.87 |
| Zambia | 15.00 | 17.78 | 536.91 |
| Zimbabwe | 13.00 | 80.57 | 607.92 |
| Total | 558.54 | 1,316.74 | 24,259.34 |

* Since the initial operation of the three institutions (1967 for ADB, 1974 for ADF and 1976 for NTF).

amounted to US $771.1m. for 17 loans in 1997. Since October 1997 new fixed and floating rate loans have also been made available.

## AFRICAN DEVELOPMENT FUND (ADF)

The Fund commenced operations in 1974. It grants interest-free loans to low-income African countries for projects with repayment over 50 years (including a 10-year grace period) and with a service charge of 0.75% per annum. Grants for project feasibility studies are made to the poorest countries.

In 1987 donor countries agreed on a fifth replenishment of the Fund's resources, amounting to US $2,800m. for 1988–90. In future 85% of available resources was to be reserved for the poorest countries (those with annual GDP per caput of less than $510, at 1985 prices). In 1991 a sixth replenishment of the Fund's resources amounting to $3,340m. was approved for 1991–93. Negotiations for the seventh replenishment of the Fund's resources commenced in May 1993. However, in May 1994, donor countries withheld any new funds owing to dissatisfaction with the Bank's governance. In May 1996, following the implementation of various institutional reforms to strengthen the Bank's financial management and decision-making capabilities and to reduce its administrative costs, an agreement was concluded on the seventh replenishment of the ADF. Donor countries pledged some $2,690m. for the period 1996–98. An additional allocation of $420m. was endorsed at a special donors' meeting held in Osaka, Japan, in June. The ADF aimed to offer concessional assistance to 42 African countries over the period 1996–98. In January 1999 negotiations on the eighth replenishment of the Fund were concluded with an agreement to provide additional resources amounting to $3,437m. The replenishment was approved by the Board of Governors in May.

In 1997 88 ADF loans and grants were approved amounting to US $1,006m., compared with 19 operations for $286m. approved in 1996.

**Summary of Bank Group Activities** (US $ million)

| | 1996 | 1997 | Cumulative total* |
|---|---|---|---|
| ADB loans | | | |
| Number | 11 | 17 | 742 |
| Amount approved | 508.18 | 771.12 | 20,712.51 |
| Disbursements | 1,007.94 | 925.74 | 14,234.26 |
| ADF loans and grants | | | |
| Number | 19 | 88 | 1,271 |
| Amount approved | 286.36 | 1,005.47 | 11,492.69 |
| Disbursements | 626.45 | 646.08 | 7,601.65 |
| NTF loans | | | |
| Number | 1 | — | 58 |
| Amount approved | 8.63 | — | 320.27 |
| Disbursements | 7.18 | 4.85 | 210.50 |
| Group total | | | |
| Number | 31 | 105 | 2,071 |
| Amount approved | 803.16 | 1,776.59 | 32,525.47 |
| Disbursements | 1,641.57 | 1,576.67 | 22,046.41 |

* Since the initial operations of the three institutions (1967 for ADB, 1974 for ADF and 1976 for NTF).

Source: *Annual Report 1997*.

**Group Loan and Grant Approvals by Sector, 1996–97**
(millions of UA)

| Sector | 1996 | % | 1997 | % |
|---|---|---|---|---|
| Agriculture | 72.45 | 13.0 | 165.11 | 12.5 |
| Transport | 110.34 | 19.8 | 181.12 | 13.8 |
| Public utilities | 75.60 | 13.5 | 133.62 | 10.1 |
| Industry | 117.16 | 21.0 | 229.18 | 17.4 |
| Social | 23.80 | 4.3 | 178.38 | 13.5 |
| Multisector | 159.19 | 28.5 | 429.30 | 32.6 |
| Total | 558.54 | 100.0 | 1,316.74 | 100.0 |

## NIGERIA TRUST FUND (NTF)

The Agreement establishing the Nigeria Trust Fund was signed in February 1976 by the Bank and the Government of Nigeria. The Fund is administered by the Bank and its loans are granted for up to 25 years, including grace periods of up to five years, and carry 0.75% commitment charges and 4% interest charges. The loans are intended to provide financing for projects in co-operation with other lending institutions. The Fund also aims to promote the private sector and trade between African countries by providing information on African and international financial institutions able to finance African trade.

In 1996 the fund approved one loan amounting to US $8.63m., bringing the total amount committed since operations began to $320.27m. for 58 loans. There were no NTF loan approvals in 1997.

## ASSOCIATED INSTITUTIONS

The ADB actively participated in the establishment of five associated institutions:

**Africa Reinsurance Corporation–Africa-Re:** Reinsurance House, 46 Marina, PMB 12765, Lagos, Nigeria; tel. (1) 2663323; fax (1) 2668802; e-mail africare@hyperia.com; f. 1977; started operations in 1978; its purpose is to foster the development of the insurance and reinsurance industry in Africa and to promote the growth of national and regional underwriting capacities; auth. cap. US $50m., of which the ADB holds 10%. There are 12 directors, one appointed by the Bank. Mems: 41 countries, the ADB, and some 90 insurance and reinsurance cos. Man. Dir BAKARY KAMARA.

**African Export-Import Bank–Afreximbank:** POB 404 Gezira, Cairo 11568; World Trade Centre Bldg, 1191 Corniche el-Nil, Cairo 11221, Egypt; tel. (2) 5780282; fax (2) 5780277; e-mail mail@afreximbank.com; internet www.afreximbank.com; f. 1993; aims to increase the volume of African exports and to expand intra-African trade by financing exporters and importers directly and indirectly through trade finance institutions, such as commercial banks; auth.

cap. US $750m.; paid-up cap. $145.4m. (Dec. 1998). Pres. CHRISTOPHER C. EDORDU; Exec. Vice-Pres. JEAN-LOUIS EKRA. Publ. *Annual Report*.

**Association of African Development Finance Institutions–AADFI:** c/o ADB, 01 BP 1387, Abidjan 01, Côte d'Ivoire; tel. 20-40-90; fax 22-73-44; e-mail adfi@africaonline.co.ci; f. 1975; aims to promote co-operation among financial institutions in the region in matters relating to economic and social development, research, project design, financing and the exchange of information. Mems: 92 in 43 African and non-African countries. Pres. GERSHOM MUMBA; Sec.-Gen. Dr MAGATTE WADE.

**Shelter-Afrique** (Société pour l'habitat et le logement territorial en Afrique): Longonot Rd, POB 41479, Nairobi, Kenya; tel. (2) 722305; fax (2) 722024; e-mail info@shelter.co.ke; f. 1982 to finance housing in ADB mem. countries. Share cap. is US $300m., held by 39 African countries, the ADB, Africa-Re and the Commonwealth Development Corpn; Chair. P. M. N'KOUE N'KONGO; Man. Dir P. M'BAYE.

**Société Internationale Financière pour les Investissements et le Développement en Afrique–SIFIDA:** 22 rue François-Perréard, BP 310, 1225 Chêne-Bourg/Geneva, Switzerland; tel. (22) 8692000; fax (22) 8692001; e-mail sifida@cortex.ch; internet www.sifida.com; f. 1970 by 120 financial and industrial institutions, including the ADB and the IFC. Following a restructuring at the end of 1995, the main shareholders are the Banque Nationale de Paris (BNP), SFOM (itself owned by BNP and Dresdner Bank) and the six banking affiliates of BNP/SFOM in West and Central Africa. SIFIDA is active in the fields of project and trade finance in Africa and also provides financial advisory services, notably in the context of privatizations and debt conversion; auth. cap. US $75m., subscribed cap. $12.5m. Chair. VIVIEN LÉVY-GARBOUA; Man. Dir PHILIPPE SÉCHAUD. Publ. *African Banking Directory* (annually).

## Publications

*Annual Report.*

*ADB Today* (every 2 months).

*African Development Report* (annually).

*African Development Review.*

*Basic Information* (annually).

*Economic Research Papers.*

*Quarterly Operational Summary.*

*Statistical Handbook* (annually).

Summaries of operations in each member country and various background documents.

# ANDEAN COMMUNITY OF NATIONS

## (COMUNIDAD ANDINA DE NACIONES—CAN)

**Address:** Avda Paseo de la República 3895, San Isidro, Lima 27; Casilla 18-1177, Lima 18, Peru.

**Telephone:** (1) 4111400; **fax:** (1) 2213329; **e-mail:** contacto@comunidadandina.org; **internet:** www.comunidadandina.org.

The organization, officially known as the Acuerdo de Cartagena (the Cartagena Agreement) and also known as the Grupo Andino (Andean Group) or the Pacto Andino (Andean Pact), was established in 1969. In March 1996 member countries signed a Reform Protocol of the Cartagena Agreement, according to which the Group was to be superseded by the Andean Community of Nations (CAN, generally referred to as the Andean Community), in order to promote greater economic, commercial and political integration, under a new Andean Integration System (Sistema Andino de Integración). The group covers an area of 4,710,000 sq km, with some 105m. inhabitants (in 1998).

### MEMBERS

| Bolivia | Colombia | Ecuador | Peru | Venezuela |
|---|---|---|---|---|

Note: Chile withdrew from the Group in 1976. Panama has observer status with the Community.

## Organization

(January 2000)

### ANDEAN PRESIDENTIAL COUNCIL

The presidential summits, which had been held annually since 1989, were formalized under the 1996 Reform Protocol of the Cartagena Agreement as the Andean Presidential Council. The Council provides the political leadership of the Community.

### COMMISSION

The Commission consists of a plenipotentiary representative from each member country, with each country holding the presidency in turn. The Commission is the main policy-making organ of the Andean Community, and is responsible for co-ordinating Andean trade policy.

### COUNCIL OF FOREIGN MINISTERS

The Council of Foreign Ministers meets annually or whenever it is considered necessary, to formulate common external policy and to co-ordinate the process of integration.

### GENERAL SECRETARIAT

The General Secretariat (formerly the Junta) is the body charged with implementation of all guide-lines and decisions issued by the bodies listed above. It submits proposals to the Commission for facilitating the fulfilment of the Community's objectives. Members are appointed for a three-year term. They supervise technical officials assigned to the following Departments: External Relations, Agricultural Development, Press Office, Economic Policy, Physical Integration, Programme of Assistance to Bolivia, Industrial Development, Programme Planning, Legal Affairs, Technology. Under the reforms agreed in March 1996 the Secretary-General is elected by the Council of Foreign Ministers and has enhanced powers to adjudicate in disputes arising between member states.

**Secretary-General:** SEBASTIÁN ALEGRETT (Venezuela).

### PARLIAMENT

**Parlamento Andino:** Carrera 7ª, No. 13–58, Oficina 401, Santafé de Bogotá, Colombia; tel. (1) 284-4191; fax (1) 284-3270; e-mail correo@parlamentoandino.org; internet www.parlamentoandino.org; f. 1979; comprises five members from each country, and meets in each capital city in turn; makes recommendations on regional policy. In April 1997 a new protocol was adopted which provided for the election of members by direct and universal voting. Sec.-Gen. Dr RUBÉN VÉLEZ NÚÑEZ.

### COURT OF JUSTICE

**Tribunal de Justicia de la Comunidad Andina:** Calle Roca 450 y 6 de deciembre, Quito, Ecuador; tel. (2) 529990; fax (2) 509404; e-mail tjca@impsat.net.ec; internet www.altesa.net/tribunal; f. 1979, began operating in 1984; a protocol approved in May 1996 modified the Court's functions; its main responsibilities are to resolve disputes among member countries and interpret community legislation. It comprises five judges, one from each member country, appointed for a renewable period of six years. The Presidency is assumed annually by each judge in turn, by alphabetical order of country. Pres. RUBÉN HERDOIZA MERA (Ecuador)

## Activities

In May 1979, at Cartagena, Colombia, the Presidents of the five member countries signed the 'Mandate of Cartagena', which envisaged greater economic and political co-operation, including the establishment of more sub-regional development programmes (especially in industry). In May 1989 the Group undertook to revitalize the process of Andean integration, by withdrawing measures that obstructed the programme of trade liberalization, and by complying with tariff reductions that had already been agreed upon. In May 1991, in Caracas, Venezuela, a summit meeting of the Andean Group agreed the framework for the establishment of a free-trade area on 1 January 1992 and for an Andean common market by 1995 (see below, under Trade).

In March 1996 heads of state, meeting in Trujillo, Peru, affirmed member countries' commitment to combating drugs-trafficking and indirectly condemned the decision of the USA to 'decertify' the

Colombian anti-narcotics campaign (and thus to suspend financial assistance to that country). At the same meeting, member countries agreed to a substantial restructuring of the Andean Group. The heads of state signed the Reform Protocol of the Cartagena Agreement, establishing the Andean Community of Nations, which was to have more ambitious economic and political objectives than the previous Group. A new General Secretariat was to replace the existing Junta as the body responsible for implementing the Community's decision and was to be headed by a Secretary-General with greater executive and decision-making powers than at present. The initiation of these reforms was also designed to accelerate harmonization in economic matters, particularly the achievement of a common external tariff. However, the commitment of member countries to the Community was brought into question later in 1996: in June the Bolivian President attended the summit meeting of the Mercado Común del Sur (Mercosur—see p. 267) and agreed the framework of a free-trade agreement with Mercosur on a unilateral basis (thus becoming an associate member of that grouping). Nevertheless in September the five countries agreed to negotiate with Mercosur as a bloc. In April 1997 the Peruvian Government announced its intention to withdraw from the Cartagena Agreement, owing to the group's failure to agree on the terms of Peru's full integration into the Community's trading system. Later in that month the heads of state of the four other Community members attended a summit meeting, in Sucre, Bolivia, and reiterated their commitment to strengthening regional integration. A high-level group of representatives was established to pursue negotiations with Peru regarding its future relationship with the Community (agreement was reached in June—see below).

The 10th presidential summit, held in Guayaquil, Ecuador, in April 1998, reiterated the objective of creating a common market by 2005 and defined specific measures to achieve this, including efforts to promote the Community, to strengthen joint institutions and physical infrastructure, and to formulate a common foreign policy.

## TRADE

Trade within the group increased by about 37% annually between 1978 and 1980. A council for customs affairs met for the first time in January 1982, aiming to harmonize national legislation within the group. In December 1984 the member states launched a new common currency, the Andean peso, aiming to reduce dependence on the US dollar and to increase regional trade. The new currency was to be backed by special contributions to the Fondo Andino de Reservas (now the Fondo Latinoamericano de Reservas) amounting to US $80m., and was to be 'pegged' to the US dollar, taking the form of financial drafts rather than notes and coins. In May 1986 a new formula for trade among member countries was agreed, in order to restrict the number of products exempted from trade liberalization measures to 40 'sensitive' products.

The 'Caracas Declaration' of May 1991 established an Andean free-trade zone, which was to commence on 1 January 1992. Ecuador, with its highly protectionist system, was given a special dispensation whereby it was to abolish 50% of its tariffs by January 1992, with the remainder being removed by June of the same year. Heads of state also agreed in May 1991 to create a common external tariff (CET), to standardize member countries' trade barriers in their dealings with the rest of the world. In December heads of state defined four main levels of external tariffs (between 5% and 20%), with the intention that these would enter into effect in January 1992, but the conclusion of negotiations was delayed by Ecuador's request for numerous exceptions. Following the Peruvian Government's suspension of the Peruvian Constitution in April 1992, Venezuela suspended its diplomatic relations with Peru, and negotiations on the CET were halted. In August a request by Peru for a suspension of its rights and obligations under the Pact was approved. The other members then ratified the four-level CET (although Bolivia was to retain a two-level system).

In May 1994 an agreement was reached to introduce a four-tier structure of external tariffs from 1 January 1995; however, differences within the group remained. In November 1994 ministers of trade and integration, meeting in Quito, Ecuador, concluded a final agreement on the CET. The agreement, which came into effect in February 1995, covered 90% of the region's imports (the remainder to be incorporated by 1999 later extended to June 2000), which were to be subject to the following tariff bands: 5% for raw materials; 10%–15% for semi-manufactured goods; and 20% for finished products. In order to reach an agreement, special treatment and exemptions were granted, while Peru, initially, was to remain a 'non-active' member of the accord: Bolivia was to maintain external tariffs of 5% and 10%, Ecuador was permitted to apply the lowest rate of 5% to an initial 800 industrial items, and Colombia and Venezuela were granted 230 items to be subject to special treatment for four years. In June 1997 an agreement was concluded to ensure Peru's continued membership of the Community, which provided for that country's integration into the group's free-trade zone. The Peruvian Government agreed to eliminate customs duties on some 2,500 products with immediate effect, and it was agreed that the process be completed by 2005. However, negotiations were to continue with regard to the replacement of Peru's single tariff on products from outside the region with the Community's scale of external duties.

## EXTERNAL RELATIONS

In September 1995 heads of state of member countries identified the formulation of common positions on foreign relations as an important part of the process of relaunching the integration initiative. A Protocol Amending the Cartagena Agreement was signed in June 1997 to confirm the formulation of a common foreign policy. During 1998 the General Secretariat held consultations with government experts, academics, representatives of the private sector and other interested parties to help formulate a document on guidelines for a common foreign policy. The guide-lines, establishing the principles, objectives and mechanisms of a common foreign policy, were approved by the Council of Foreign Ministers in 1999. A Council on Trade and Industry between the Andean Community and the USA has been established to strengthen the trading relations between the two sides. A co-operation agreement between the European Union and Andean Group was signed in April 1993. A Euro-Andean Forum is held periodically to promote co-operation, trade and investment between the two communities. In February 1998 the Community signed a co-operation and technical assistance agreement with the EU in order to combat drugs-trafficking.

In April 1998, at the 10th Andean presidential summit, an agreement was signed with Panama establishing a framework for negotiations providing for the conclusion of a free-trade accord by the end of 1998 and Panama's eventual associate membership of the Community. Also in April 1998 the Community signed a framework agreement with Mercosur on the establishment of a free-trade accord. The process of extending trade preferences was to commence in October 1998, and the agreement was to become fully effective on 1 January 2000. Negotiations between the two sides, however, were delayed during 1998, owing to differences regarding tariff reductions and the items to be covered by the accord. Bilateral agreements between the countries of the two groupings were extended. In January 1999 representatives of the Community and Mercosur pledged to work towards completing the first stage of negotiations of the free-trade agreement by 31 March; however, this failed to be achieved. It was agreed, in March, that bilateral trade arrangements would be extended and that the Community would initiate negotiations to conclude a free-trade area with Brazil. A preferential tariff agreement was concluded between Brazil and the Community in July; the accord entered into effect, for a period of two years, in mid-August.

In March 1998 ministers of trade from 34 countries, meeting in San José, Costa Rica, concluded an agreement on the structure of negotiations for the establishment of a Free Trade Area of the Americas (FTAA). The process was formally initiated by heads of state, meeting in Santiago, Chile, in the following month. The Community negotiated as a bloc to obtain chairmanship of three of the nine negotiating groups: on market access (Colombia), on competition policy (Peru), and on intellectual property (Venezuela). The Community insisted that the final declaration issued by the meeting include recognition that the varying levels of development of the participating countries had to be taken into consideration throughout the negotiating process.

In August 1999 the Secretary-General of the Community visited Guyana in order to promote bilateral trading opportunities and to strengthen relations with the Caribbean Community.

## INDUSTRY

Negotiations began in 1970 for the formulation of joint industrial programmes, particularly in the petrochemicals, metal-working and motor vehicle industries, but disagreements over the allocation of different plants, and the choice of foreign manufacturers for co-operation, prevented progress and by 1984 the more ambitious schemes had been abandoned. Instead, emphasis was to be placed on assisting small and medium-sized industries, particularly in the agro-industrial and electronics sectors, in co-operation with national industrial organizations.

An Andean Agricultural Development Programme was formulated in 1976 within which 22 resolutions aimed at integrating the Andean agricultural sector were approved. In 1984 the Andean Food Security System was created to develop the agrarian sector, replace imports progressively with local produce, and improve rural living conditions. In April 1998 the Presidential Council instructed the Commission, together with ministers of agriculture, to formulate an Andean Common Agricultural Policy, including measures to harmonize trade policy instruments and legislation on animal and plant health. The policy, and a plan of action for its implementation, were scheduled to be concluded in 2000.

In May 1987 member countries signed the Quito Protocol, modifying the Cartagena Agreement, to amend the strict rules that had formerly been imposed on foreign investors in the region. The Protocol entered into force in May 1988. Accordingly, each government was to decide which sectors were to be closed to foreign participation, and the period within which foreign investors must transfer a majority shareholding to local investors was extended to 30 years (37 years in Bolivia and Ecuador). In March 1991 the provisions of the Protocol (Decision 220) was replaced by Decision 291, with the aim of further liberalizing foreign investment and stimulating an inflow of foreign capital and technology. External and regional investors were to be permitted to repatriate their profits (in accordance with the laws of the country concerned) and there was no stipulation that a majority share-holding must eventually be transferred to local investors. A further directive, adopted in March, covered the formation of 'Empresas Multinacionales Andinas' (multinational enterprises) in order to ensure that at least two member countries have a shareholding of 15% or more of the capital, including the country where the enterprise was to be based. These enterprises were entitled to participate in sectors otherwise reserved for national enterprises, subject to the same conditions as national enterprises in terms of taxation and export regulations, and to gain access to the markets of all member countries.

In November 1988 member states established a bank, the Banco Intermunicipal Andino, which was to finance public works.

In May 1995 the Group initiated a programme to promote the use of cheap and efficient energy sources and greater co-operation in the energy sector. The programme planned to develop a regional electricity grid.

## TRANSPORT AND COMMUNICATIONS

In 1983 the Commission formulated a plan to assist Bolivia by giving attention to its problems as a land-locked country, particularly through improving roads connecting it with the rest of the region and with the Pacific. The Community has pursued efforts to improve infrastructure throughout the region. An 'open skies' agreement, giving airlines of member states equal rights to airspace and airport facilities within the grouping, was signed in May 1991. In June 1998 the Commission approved the establishment of an Andean Commission of Land Transportation Authorities, which was to oversee the operation and development of land transportation services. Similarly, an Andean Committee of Water Transportation Authorities has been established to ensure compliance with Community regulations regarding ocean transportation activities. The Community aims to facilitate the movement of goods throughout the region by the use of different modes of transport ('multimodal transport') and to guarantee operational standards. It also intends to harmonize Community transport regulations and standards with those of Mercosur countries.

In August 1996 the Community approved a regulatory framework for the development of a commercial Andean satellite system. In December 1997 the General Secretariat approved regulations for granting authorization for the use of the system; the Commission subsequently granted the first Community authorization to an Andean multinational enterprise, comprising 44 companies from all five member states. The system was expected to be fully operational in 2002. Since 1994 the Community has undertaken efforts to establish a digital technology infrastructure throughout the Community. By the end of 1998 a series of cross-border interconnections between the countries had been established and the process had been almost completed. In May 1999 the Andean Committee of Telecommunications Authorities agreed to remove all restrictions to free trade in telecommunications services (excluding sound broadcasting and television) by 1 January 2002. The Committee also determined to formulate provisions on interconnection and the safeguarding of free competition and principles of transparency within the sector.

**Asociación de Empresas de Telecomunicaciones de la Comunidad Andina—ASETA:** Calle La Pradera 510 y San Salvador, Casilla 10-1106042, Quito, Ecuador; tel. (2) 563-812; fax (2) 562-499; internet www.aseta.org.ec; recommends to its members measures to improve telecommunications services, in order to contribute to the further integration of the countries of the Andean Group. Sec.-Gen. MARCELO LÓPEZ ARJONA.

## SOCIAL INTEGRATION

Several formal agreements and institutions have been established within the framework of the grouping to enhance social development and welfare (see below). The Community aimed to incorporate these bodies into the process of enhanced integration and to promote greater involvement of representatives of the civil society.

## INSTITUTIONS

**Consejo Consultivo Empresarial Andino** (Andean Business Advisory Council): Edif. Cámara de Comercio de Guayaquil, Av. Olmeda 414 y Boyacá, Guayaquil, Ecuador; tel. (4) 323130; fax (4) 323478; e-mail presid@gye.satnet.net; first meeting held in November 1998; a consultative institution within the framework of the Sistema Andino de Integración; comprises elected representatives of business organizations; advises Community ministers and officials on integration activities affecting the business sector.

**Consejo Consultivo Laboral Andino** (Andean Labour Advisory Council): Calle 39, No 26-23, Santafé de Bogotá, Colombia; tel. (1) 2697119; fax (1) 2688576; a consultative institution within the framework of the Sistema Andino de Integración; comprises elected representatives of labour organizations; advises Community ministers and officers on related labour issues.

**Convenio Andrés Bello** (Andrés Bello Agreement): Paralela Autopista Norte, Avda 13 85–60, Santafé de Bogotá, Colombia; tel. (1) 6181701; fax (1) 6100139; e-mail ecobello@coll.telecom.com.co; internet www.cab.int.co; f. 1970, modified in 1990; aims to promote integration in the educational, technical and cultural sectors. Mems: Bolivia, Chile, Colombia, Ecuador, Panama, Peru, Spain, Venezuela.

**Convenio Hipólito Unanue** (Hipólito Unanue Agreement): Edif. Cartagena, Paseo de la República 3832, 3°, Lima, Peru; tel. (1) 2210074; fax (1) 4409285; e-mail postmaster@conhu.org.pe; internet www.conhu.org.pe; f. 1971 on the occasion of the first meeting of Andean ministers of health; aims to enhance the development of health services, and to promote regional co-ordination in areas such as environmental health, disaster preparedness and the prevention and control of drug abuse.

**Convenio Simón Rodríguez** (Simón Rodríguez Agreement): Luis Felipe Borja s/n, Edif. Géminis, 9°, Quito, Ecuador; tel. (2) 5453774; organization to promote a convergence of social and labour conditions throughout the Community, for example, working hours and conditions, employment and social security policies, and to promote the participation of workers and employers in the subregional integration process.

**Corporación Andina de Fomento—CAF** (Andean Development Corporation): Torre CAF, Avda Luis Roche, Altamira, Apdo 5086, Caracas, Venezuela; tel. (2) 209-2111; fax (2) 209-2394; e-mail sede@caf.com; internet www.caf.com; f. 1968, began operations in 1970; aims to encourage the integration of the Andean countries by specialization and an equitable distribution of investments. It conducts research to identify investment opportunities, and prepares the resulting investment projects; gives technical and financial assistance; and attracts internal and external credit. Auth. cap. US $3,000m., subscribed or underwritten by the governments of member countries, or by public-, semi-public and private-sector institutions authorized by those governments. The Board of Directors comprises representatives of each country at ministerial level. Mems: the Andean Community, Brazil, Chile, Jamaica, Mexico, Panama, Paraguay, Trinidad and Tobago, and 22 private banks in the Andean region. Exec. Pres. ENRIQUE GARCÍA RODRÍGUEZ (Bolivia).

**Fondo Latinoamericano de Reservas—FLAR** (Latin American Reserve Fund): Edif. Banco de Occidente, Carrera 13, No. 27–47, 10°, Santafé de Bogotá, Colombia; tel. (1) 2858511; fax (1) 2881117; e-mail agamarra@bloomberg.net; f. 1978 as the Fondo Andino de Reservas to support the balance of payments of member countries, provide credit, guarantee loans, and contribute to the harmonization of monetary and financial policies; adopted present name in 1991, in order to allow the admission of other Latin American countries. In 1992 the Fund began extending credit lines to commercial for export financing. It is administered by an Assembly of the ministers of finance and economy of the member countries, and a Board of Directors comprising the Presidents of the central banks of the member states. In October 1995 it was agreed to expand the Fund's capital from US $800m. to $1,000m.; the increase became effective on 30 June 1997. Exec. Pres. MIGUEL VELASCO BOSSHARD (Peru); Sec.-Gen. MANUEL MARTÍNEZ (Colombia).

**Universidad Andina Simón Bolívar** (Simón Bolívar Andean University): Calle Real Audiencia 73, POB 608-33, Sucre, Bolivia; tel. (64) 60265; fax (64) 60833; e-mail uasb@uasb.edu.bo; internet www.uasb.edu.bo; f. 1985; institution for post-graduate study and research; promotes co-operation between other universities in the Andean region.

# ASIA-PACIFIC ECONOMIC CO-OPERATION—APEC

**Address:** 438 Alexandra Rd, 19th Floor, Alexandra Point, Singapore 119958.

**Telephone:** 2761880; **fax:** 2761775; **e-mail:** info@mail.apecsec.org.sg; **internet:** www.apecsec.org.sg.

Asia-Pacific Economic Co-operation (APEC) was initiated in November 1989, in Canberra, Australia, as an informal consultative forum. Its aim is to promote multilateral economic co-operation on issues of trade and investment.

### MEMBERS

| | | |
|---|---|---|
| Australia | Japan | Philippines |
| Brunei | Korea, Republic | Russia |
| Canada | Malaysia | Singapore |
| Chile | Mexico | Taiwan* |
| China, People's Republic | New Zealand | Thailand |
| Hong Kong | Papua New Guinea | USA |
| Indonesia | Peru | Viet Nam |

* Admitted as Chinese Taipei.

## Organization

(January 2000)

### ECONOMIC LEADERS' MEETINGS

The first meeting of APEC heads of government was convened in November 1993, in Seattle, USA. Subsequently, each annual meeting of APEC ministers of foreign affairs and of economic affairs has been followed by an informal gathering of the leaders of the APEC economies, at which the policy objectives of the grouping are discussed and defined. The 1999 meeting was held in Auckland, New Zealand, in September, and the 2000 meeting was scheduled to be held in Brunei, in November.

### MINISTERIAL MEETINGS

APEC ministers of foreign affairs and ministers of economic affairs meet annually. These meetings are hosted by the APEC Chair, which rotates each year, although it was agreed, in 1989, that alternate Ministerial Meetings were to be convened in an ASEAN member country. Senior officials meet regularly between Ministerial Meetings to co-ordinate and to administer the budgets and work programmes of APEC's committees and working groups. Other meetings of ministers are also held on a regular basis to enhance co-operation in specific areas.

### SECRETARIAT

In 1992 the Ministerial Meeting, held in Bangkok, Thailand, agreed to establish a permanent secretariat to support APEC activities, and approved an annual budget of US $2m. The Secretariat became operational in February 1993. The Executive Director is appointed from the member economy chairing the group and serves a one-year term. A Deputy Executive Director is appointed by the member economy designated to chair APEC in the following year.

**Executive Director:** SERBINI ALI (Brunei).

**Deputy Executive Director:** ZHANG YAN (People's Republic of China).

### COMMITTEES AND GROUPS

**Agricultural Technical Co-operation Experts' Group (ATC):** f. 1995, recognized as a formal APEC grouping in October 1996; aims to promote co-operation in the following areas: conservation and utilization of plant and animal genetic resources; research, development and extension of agricultural biotechnology; marketing, processing and distribution of agricultural products; plant and animal quarantine and pest management; development of an agricultural finance system; sustainable agriculture; and agricultural technology transfer and training.

**Budget and Administrative Committee (BAC):** f. 1993 to advise APEC senior officials on budgetary, administrative and managerial issues. The Committee reviews the operational budgets of APEC committees and groups, evaluates their effectiveness and conducts assessments of group projects.

**Committee on Trade and Investment (CTI):** f. 1993 on the basis of a Declaration signed by ministers meeting in Seattle, USA, in order to facilitate the expansion of trade and the development of a liberalized environment for investment among member countries. The CTI undertakes initiatives to improve the flow of goods, services and technology in the region. In May 1997 an APEC Tariff Database was inaugurated, with sponsorship from the private sector. A new Market Access Group was established in 1998 to administer CTI activities concerned with non-tariff measures.

**Economic Committee:** f. 1994 following an agreement, in November, to transform the existing *ad hoc* group on economic trends and issues into a formal committee. The Committee aims to enhance APEC's capacity to analyse economic trends and to research and report on issues affecting economic and technical co-operation in the region. In addition, the Committee is considering the environmental and development implications of expanding population and economic growth.

**Ad Hoc Policy Level Group on Small and Medium Enterprises (PLG-SME):** f. 1995 to oversee all APEC activities relating to SMEs; supported the establishment of an APEC Centre for Technical Exchange and Training for Small and Medium Enterprises, which was inaugurated at Los Baños, near Manila, the Philippines, in September 1996.

In addition, the following Working Groups promote and co-ordinate practical co-operation between member countries in different activities: Trade and investment data review; Trade promotion; Industrial science and technology; Human resources development; Energy; Marine resource conservation; Telecommunications; Transport; Tourism; and Fisheries. (See below for more detailed information.)

### ADVISORY COUNCIL

**APEC Business Advisory Council (ABAC):** Manila, Philippines; tel. (2) 8436001; fax (2) 8454832; e-mail abacsec@equitable.equicom.com; an agreement to establish ABAC, comprising up to three representatives of the private sector from each APEC member economy, was concluded at the Ministerial Meeting held in November 1995. The first meeting of ABAC was convened in June 1996 in Manila, the Philippines. At the meeting, ABAC resolved to accelerate the liberalization of regional trade and agreed to focus its activities on infrastructure, SMEs and human resource development, regional communications and finance and cross-border investment. In 1998 ABAC focused on measures to alleviate the effects of the financial crisis in Asia, in particular by enhancing confidence in the private sector, as well as other efforts to support SMEs, to develop electronic commerce in the region and to advise on APEC plans of action. In 1999 ABAC was to continue to promote capital flows into Asia, to restructure unpaid corporate debts, to recapitalize banks and to develop an Asian debt or bond market. Other priorities were to include the development of policies to revive private investment in economies affected by recession, proposals for a food system for member countries, and methods to strengthen the capacity of economies to benefit from trade liberalization. Chair. PHILIP BURDON (New Zealand).

## Activities

APEC was initiated in 1989 as a forum for informal discussion between the six ASEAN members and their six dialogue partners in the Pacific, and, in particular, to promote trade liberalization in the Uruguay Round of negotiations, which were being conducted under the General Agreement on Tariffs and Trade (GATT). The Seoul Declaration, adopted by ministers meeting in the Republic of Korea in November 1991, defined the objectives of APEC.

ASEAN countries were initially reluctant to support any more formal structure of the forum, or to admit new members, owing to concerns that it would undermine ASEAN's standing as a regional grouping and be dominated by powerful non-ASEAN economies. In August 1991 it was agreed to extend membership to the People's Republic of China, Hong Kong and Taiwan (subject to conditions imposed by the People's Republic of China, including that a Taiwanese official of no higher than vice-ministerial level should attend the annual meeting of ministers of foreign affairs). Mexico and Papua New Guinea acceded to the organization in November 1993, and Chile joined in November 1994. The summit meeting held in November 1997 agreed that Peru, Russia and Viet Nam should be admitted to APEC at the 1998 meeting, but imposed a 10-year moratorium on further expansion of the grouping.

In September 1992 APEC ministers agreed to establish a permanent secretariat. In addition, the meeting created an 11-member non-governmental Eminent Persons Group (EPG), which was to assess trade patterns within the region and propose measures to promote co-operation. At the Ministerial Meeting in Seattle, USA, in November 1993, members agreed on a framework for expanding trade and investment among member countries, and to establish a permanent committee (the CTI, see above) to pursue these objectives.

In August 1994 the EPG proposed the following timetable for the liberalization of all trade across the Asia-Pacific region: negotiations for the elimination of trade barriers were to commence in 2000 and be completed within 10 years in developed countries, 15 years in newly-industrialized economies and by 2020 in developing countries. Trade concessions could then be extended on a reciprocal basis to non-members in order to encourage world-wide trade liberalization rather than isolate APEC as a unique trading bloc. In November 1994 the meeting of APEC heads of government adopted the Bogor Declaration of Common Resolve, which endorsed the EPG's timetable for free and open trade and investment in the region by the year 2020. Malaysia expressed its dissension, however, by proposing that the timetable for the elimination of trade barriers be non-binding. Other issues incorporated into the Declaration included the implementation of GATT commitments in full and strengthening the multilateral trading system through the forthcoming establishment of the World Trade Organization (WTO), intensifying development co-operation in the Asia-Pacific region and expanding and accelerating trade and investment programmes.

During 1995 meetings of APEC officials and other efforts to substantiate the trade liberalization agreement revealed certain differences among members regarding the timetable and means of implementing the measures, which were to be agreed upon at the 1995 Economic Leaders' Meeting. The principal concern, expressed notably by the USA, focused on whether tariff reductions were to be achieved by individual trade liberalization plans or based on some reciprocal or common approach. In August the EPG issued a report, to be considered at the November Leaders' Meeting, which advocated acceleration of tariff reductions and other trade liberalization measures agreed under GATT, the establishment of a dispute mediation service to reduce and settle regional trade conflicts and a review of new trade groupings within the APEC region. Further proposals for the implementation of the Bogor Declaration objectives were presented, in September, by the Pacific Business Forum, comprising APEC business representatives. The recommendations included harmonization of product quality, the establishment of one-stop investment agencies in each APEC country, training and technology transfers and the implementation of visa-free business travel by 1999. In November 1995 the Ministerial Meeting decided to dismantle the EPG, and to establish an APEC Business Advisory Council consisting of private-sector representatives.

In November 1995 APEC heads of government, meeting in Osaka, Japan, adopted an Action Agenda as a framework to achieve the commitments of the Bogor Declaration. Part One of the Agenda identified action areas for the liberalization of trade and investment and the facilitation of business, for example customs procedures, rules of origin and non-tariff barriers. It incorporated agreements that the process was to be comprehensive, consistent with WTO commitments, comparable among all APEC economies and non-discriminatory. Each member economy was to ensure the transparency of its laws, regulations and procedures that affect the flow of goods, services and capital among APEC economies and to refrain from implementing any trade protection measures. A second part of the Agenda was to provide a framework for further economic and technical co-operation between APEC members in areas such as energy, transport, infrastructure, SMEs and agricultural technology. In order to resolve a disagreement concerning the inclusion of agricultural products in the trade liberalization process, a provision for flexibility was incorporated into the Agenda, taking into account diverse circumstances and different levels of development in APEC member economies. Liberalization measures were to be implemented from January 1997 (i.e. three years earlier than previously agreed) and were to be subject to annual reviews. A Trade and Investment Liberalization and Facilitation Special Account was established to finance projects in support of the implementation of the Osaka Action Agenda. In May 1996 APEC senior officials met in Cebu, the Philippines, to consider the medium-term Individual Action Plans (IAPs) of tariff reductions, which had been submitted by all members, and to achieve some coherent approach to tariff liberalization prior to the Leaders' Meeting in November.

In November 1996 the Economic Leaders' Meeting, held in Subic Bay, the Philippines, approved the Manila Action Plan for APEC (MAPA), which had been formulated at the preceding Ministerial Meeting, held in Manila. MAPA incorporated the IAPs and other collective measures aimed at achieving the trade liberalization and co-operation objectives of the Bogor Declaration (see above), as well as the joint activities specified in the second part of the Osaka Agenda. Heads of government also endorsed a US proposal to eliminate tariffs and other barriers to trade in information technology products by 2000 and determined to support efforts to conclude an agreement to this effect at the forthcoming WTO conference; however, they insisted on the provision of an element of flexibility in achieving trade liberalization in this sector.

The 1997 Economic Leaders' Meeting, held in Vancouver, Canada, in November, was dominated by concern at the financial instability that had affected several Asian economies during 1997. The final declaration of the summit meeting endorsed a framework of measures which had been agreed by APEC deputy ministers of finance and central bank governors at an emergency meeting convened in the previous week in Manila, the Philippines (the so-called Manila Framework for Enhanced Asian Regional Co-operation to Promote Financial Stability). The meeting, attended by representatives of the IMF, the World Bank and the Asian Development Bank, committed all member economies receiving IMF assistance to undertake specified economic and financial reforms, and supported the establishment of a separate Asian funding facility to supplement international financial assistance (although this was later rejected by the IMF). The meeting urged APEC ministers of finance and governors of central banks to accelerate efforts for the development of the region's financial and capital markets and to liberalize capital flows in the region. Measures were to include strengthening financial market supervision and clearing and settlement infrastructure, the reform of pension systems, and promoting co-operation among export credit agencies and financing institutions. The principal item on the Vancouver summit agenda was an initiative to enhance trade liberalization, which, the grouping insisted, should not be undermined by the financial instability in Asia. At the earlier Ministerial Meeting the following nine economic sectors had been identified for 'early voluntary sectoral liberalization' ('EVSL'): environmental goods and services; fish and fish products; forest products; medical equipment and instruments; toys; energy; chemicals; gems and jewellery; and telecommunications. The heads of government subsequently requested the authorities in each member state to formulate details of tariff reductions in these sectors by mid-1998, with a view to implementing the measures in 1999. (In June 1998, however, ministers of trade, meeting in Malaysia, failed to conclude an agreement on early tariff reductions, in part owing to Japan's reluctance to liberalize trade in fish and forest products.) In Vancouver APEC Economic Leaders declared their support for an agreement to liberalize financial services (which was successfully negotiated under the auspices of the WTO in December 1997) and for the objective of reducing the emission of 'greenhouse gases', which was under consideration at a global conference, held in Kyoto, Japan, in December.

In May 1998 APEC finance ministers met in Canada to consider the ongoing financial and economic crisis in Asia and to review progress in implementing efforts to alleviate the difficulties experienced by several member economies. The ministers agreed to pursue activities in the following three priority areas: capital market development, capital account liberalization and strengthening financial systems (including corporate governance). The region's economic difficulties remained the principal topic of discussion at the Economic Leaders' Meeting, which was held in Kuala Lumpur, Malaysia, in November. A final declaration reiterated their commitment to co-operation in pursuit of sustainable economic recovery and growth, in particular through the restructuring of financial and corporate sectors, promoting and facilitating private-sector capital flows, and efforts to strengthen the global financial system. The meeting endorsed a proposal of ABAC to establish a partnership for equitable growth, which aimed to enhance business involvement in APEC's programme of economic and technical co-operation. Other initiatives approved included an Agenda of APEC Science and Technology Industry Co-operation into the 21st Century (for which the People's Republic of China announced it was to establish a special fund), an Action Programme on Skills and Development in APEC, and a public awareness campaign on the envisaged technological problems associated with the date change to 2000. Japan's persisting opposition to a reduction of tariffs in the fish and forestry sectors prevented final approval of the EVSL scheme, and it was agreed to refer the proposals to the WTO for consideration. Substantive progress at the meeting was further hindered by political differences within the grouping regarding human rights, and in particular, the treatment by the Malaysian authorities of the imprisoned former Deputy Prime Minister, Anwar Ibrahim. A declaration of support for the democratic reform movement in Malaysia by the US representative, Vice-President Gore, dominated discussions at the start of the summit meeting and provoked a formal complaint from the Malaysian Government.

In September 1999 political dialogue regarding the civil conflict in East Timor dominated the start of the annual meetings of the grouping, held in Auckland, New Zealand, although the issue remained separate from the official agenda. Ministers of foreign affairs, convened in emergency session, declared their support for the establishment of a multinational force, under UN auspices, to restore peace in the territory and determined to provide humanitarian and technical assistance to facilitate the process of reconstruction and rehabilitation. The Leaders' Meeting considered measures to sustain the economic recovery in Asia and endorsed the APEC Principles to Enhance Competition and Regulatory Reform (for example, transparency, accountability, non-discrimination) as a framework to strengthen APEC markets and to enable further integration and implementation of the IAPs. Also under discussion was the forthcoming round of multilateral trade negotiations, scheduled to be initiated by the WTO in Seattle, USA, in November. The heads of government proposed the objective of completing a single package of trade agreements within three years and endorsed the abolition of export subsidies for agricultural products. The meeting determined to support the efforts of the People's Republic of China, Russia, Taiwan and Viet Nam to accede to WTO membership.

## WORKING GROUPS

APEC's structure of working groups aims to promote practical and technical co-operation in specific areas, and to help to implement individual and collective action plans in response to the directives of the Economic Leaders. APEC recognizes sustainable development as a key issue cross-cutting all forum activities. In 1997 APEC leaders declared their commitment to the integration of women into the mainstream of APEC activities.

**Energy:** Responsible for the development of the energy component of the 1995 Action Agenda. APEC ministers responsible for energy convened for the first time in 1996 to discuss major energy challenges confronting the region and to provide guidance for the working group. Accordingly, the group's main objectives were determined as being to enhance regional energy security and to improve the fuel supply market for the power sector; to develop and implement programmes of work for promoting the adoption of environmentally-sound energy technologies and promoting private sector investment in regional power infrastructure; to develop energy efficiency guide-lines; and to standardize testing facilities and results. In March 1999 the group resolved to establish a business network to improve relations and communications with the private sector. The first meeting of the network took place in April. In October 1998 energy ministers, meeting in Okinawa, Japan, emphasized the role of the sector in stimulating economic activity and the need to develop infrastructure, to improve energy efficiency and to accelerate the development of natural gas reserves.

**Fisheries:** Aims to maximize the economic benefits and sustainability of fisheries resources for all APEC members. In 1996 the group initiated a four-year study on trade and investment liberalization in the sector, in the areas of tariffs, non-tariff barriers and investment measures and subsidies. In 1997 the group organized two technical workshops on seafood inspection systems, and conducted a workshop addressing destructive fishing techniques, in particular cyanide fishing, in an effort to conserve natural resources and to protect the marine environment. The first APEC Aquaculture Forum, which considered the sustainable development of aquaculture in the region and the development of new markets for APEC fish products, was held in Taipei, Taiwan, in June 1998. In May 1999 new guide-lines were adopted to encourage the participation of the private sector in the activities of the working group.

**Human Resources Development:** Comprises five networks which promote co-operation in different areas of human resources, training and education: the Business Management Network, with a focus on executive education and development; the Human Resources in Industrial Technology Network, concerned with technical and professional standards and identification of skill shortages; the Network for Economic Development Management; the Education Forum, concerned with the performance of education systems in preparing people for the changing labour market; and a Labour Market Information Group. The working group undertakes activities through these networks to implement ministerial and leaders' directives and the 'Medium Term Strategic Priorities', which were formulated in January 1997. A voluntary network of APEC Study Centers links higher education and research institutions throughout member economies concerned with the APEC process. In January 1998 the working group established a Task Force on the Human Resource and Social Impacts of the Financial Crisis. Other projects in 1998 were concerned with recognition and development of vocational standards and qualifications, labour market information and analysis, and the establishment of a network of APEC senior executives responsible for human resources management.

**Industrial Science and Technology:** Aims to contribute to sustainable development in the region, improve the availability of information, enhance human resources development in the sector, improve the business climate, promote policy dialogue and review and facilitate networks and partnerships. Accordingly, the group has helped to establish an APEC Virtual Centre for Environmental Technology Exchange in Japan, a Science and Technology Industry Parks Network, an International Molecular Biology Network for the APEC Region, and an APEC Centre for Technology Foresight, based in Thailand.

**Marine Resource Conservation:** Promotes initiatives within APEC to protect the marine environment and its resources. In 1996 a five-year project was initiated for the management of red tide and harmful algal blooms in the APEC region. An APEC Action Plan for Sustainability of the Marine Environment was adopted by ministers responsible for the environment, meeting in June 1997. The Plan aimed to promote regional co-operation and an integrated approach to coastal management, the prevention, reduction and control of marine pollution, and sustainable development. The group promotes these objectives through research, training, information exchange and the promotion of partnerships with the private sector. It also supports efforts to establish an Ocean Research Network of centres of excellence in the Pacific. In December 1997 the group organized a workshop, in Hong Kong, on the impact of destructive fishing practices on the marine environment. In April 1998 a workshop was held in Australia on preventing maritime accidents and pollution in the Pacific region. In April 1999 the group organized a training course, held in Hong Kong, on the satellite remote sensing of algal blooms.

**Telecommunications:** Incorporates four steering groups concerned with different aspects of the development and liberalization of the sector—Liberalization; Business facilitation; Development co-operation; and Human resource development. Activities guided by directives of ministers responsible for telecommunications, who first met in 1995, in the Republic of Korea, and adopted a Seoul Declaration on Asia Pacific Infrastructure Information (APII). The second ministerial meeting, held in Gold Coast, Australia, in September 1996, adopted more detailed proposals for liberalization of the sector in member economies. In June 1998 ministers, meeting in Singapore, agreed to remove technical barriers to trade in telecommunications equipment (although Chile and New Zealand declined to sign up to the arrangement). In March 1999 the working group concluded an APEC Framework for Telecommunications Interconnection.

**Tourism:** Aims to achieve long-term sustainability of the tourism industry, in environmental and social terms, through human resources development, greater involvement of the private sector in policy formation, liberalizing trade in services associated with tourism to facilitate investment and movement within the region, and using tourism to achieve sustainable economic development. In 1998 the group initiated a project to assess the impact of the Asian financial crisis on regional tourism and to identify strategies to counter any negative effects. The first meeting of APEC ministers of tourism was scheduled to be held in the Republic of Korea, in July 2000.

**Trade and Investment Data Review:** Mainly concerned with improving the comparability of data in trade products, services and international investment among member economies, and with the development of an APEC database to store and process this information.

**Trade Promotion:** Aims to promote trade, as a key aspect of regional economic co-operation, through activities to enhance trade financing, skills and training, information and networking (for example, through the establishment of APEC Net, providing information to the business community via the internet, accessible at www.apecnet.org.sg), and co-operation with the private sector and public agencies, including trade promotion organizations. Organizes an APEC International Trade Fair, the third of which was held in Kuala Lumpur, Malaysia, in November 1998. The fourth Trade Fair was scheduled to be held in Jakarta, Indonesia, in October 2000.

**Transportation:** Undertakes initiatives to enhance the efficiency and safety of the regional transportation system, in order to facilitate the development of trade. A Road Transportation Harmonization Project aims to provide the basis for common standards in the automotive industry in the Asia-Pacific region. In 1998 the group focused on three main areas: improving the competitiveness of the transportation industry; safe and environmentally-sound transportation systems; and human resources development, including training, research and education. The group has published surveys, directories and manuals on all types of transportation systems, and has compiled an inventory on regional co-operation on oil spills preparedness and response arrangements.

# Publications

*APEC Business Travel Handbook.*

*APEC Economic Outlook* (annually).

*APEC Energy Statistics* (annually).

*Foreign Direct Investment and APEC Economic Integration* (irregular).

*Guide to the Investment Regimes of the APEC Member Economies.*

*Selected APEC Documents* (annually).

*The State of Economic and Technical Co-operation in APEC.*

*Who is Who in Fish Inspection of APEC Economies* (irregular).

Working group reports, regional directories, other irregular surveys.

# ASIAN DEVELOPMENT BANK—ADB

**Address:** 6 ADB Ave, Mandaluyong City 0401, Metro Manila, Philippines; POB 789, 0980 Manila, Philippines.

**Telephone:** (2) 6324444; **fax:** (2) 6362444; **e-mail:** information@mail.asiandevbank.org; **internet:** www.adb.org.

The Bank commenced operations in December 1966. The Bank's principal functions are to provide loans and equity investments for the economic and social advancement of its developing member countries, to give technical assistance for the preparation and implementation of development projects and programmes and advisory services, to promote investment of public and private capital for development purposes, and to respond to requests from developing member countries for assistance in the co-ordination of their development policies and plans.

### MEMBERS

There are 41 member countries and territories within the ESCAP region and 16 others (see list of subscriptions below).

## Organization

(January 2000)

### BOARD OF GOVERNORS

All powers of the Bank are vested in the Board, which may delegate its powers to the Board of Directors except in such matters as admission of new members, changes in the Bank's authorized capital stock, election of Directors and President, and amendment of the Charter. One Governor and one Alternate Governor are appointed by each member country. The Board meets at least once a year.

### BOARD OF DIRECTORS

The Board of Directors is responsible for general direction of operations and exercises all powers delegated by the Board of Governors, which elects it. Of the 12 Directors, eight represent constituency groups of member countries within the ESCAP region (with about 65% of the voting power) and four represent the rest of the member countries. Each Director serves for two years and may be re-elected.

Three specialized committees (the Audit Committee, the Budget Review Committee and the Inspection Committee), each comprising six members, assist the Board of Directors to exercise its authority with regard to supervising the Bank's financial statements, approving the administrative budget, and reviewing and approving policy documents and assistance operations.

The President of the Bank, though not a Director, is Chairman of the Board.

**Chairman of Board of Directors and President:** TADAO CHINO (Japan).

**Vice-President** (Region East): PETER H. SULLIVAN (USA).

**Vice-President** (Finance and Administration): JOHN LINTJER (Netherlands).

**Vice-President** (Region West): MYOUNG-HO SHIN (Republic of Korea).

### ADMINISTRATION

The Bank had 1,966 staff at the end of 1998.

A major reorganization of the Bank's administrative and operational structure came into effect on 1 January 1995, in order to strengthen the Bank's regional and country focus. The offices of the General Auditor, Operations Evaluation, Strategy and Policy, and Environment and Social Development report directly to the President of the Bank. The three Vice-Presidents are responsible for the following departments and divisions: Programmes (West), Agriculture and Social Sectors, Infrastructure, Energy and Financial Sectors, the Private Sector Group, the Economics and Development Resource Centre; Programmes (East), Agriculture and Social Sectors, Infrastructure, Energy and Financial Sectors, the Office of Co-financing Operations, the Office of Pacific Operations, Central Operations Services; and, the Office of the Secretary, the Office of the General Counsel, Budget, Personnel and Management Systems, Office of Administrative Services, Controller's Department, Treasurer's Department, the Office of External Relations, the Office of Information Systems and Technology, and the North American, European and Japanese Representative Offices.

There are Resident Missions in Bangladesh, Cambodia, India, Indonesia, Kazakhstan, Nepal, Pakistan, Sri Lanka, Uzbekistan and Viet Nam. In addition, there is a Bank Regional Mission in Vanuatu (for the South Pacific) and Representative Offices in Tokyo, Japan, Frankfurt am Main, Germany (for Europe), and Washington, DC, USA (for North America). Resident Missions in Laos and Kyrgyzstan were scheduled to be opened in early 2000.

**Secretary:** R. SWAMINATHAN.

**General Counsel:** BARRY METZGER (USA).

### INSTITUTE

**ADB Institute—ADBI:** Kasumigaseki Bldg, 8th Floor, 2–5 Kasumigaseki 3-Chome, Chiyoda-ku, Tokyo 100, Japan; tel. (3) 3593-5500; fax (3) 3593-5571; e-mail webmaster@adbi.org; internet www.adbi.org; f. 1997 as a subsidiary body of the ADB to research and analyse long-term development issues and to disseminate development practices through training and other capacity-building activities. Dean MASARU YOSHITOMI.

### FINANCIAL STRUCTURE

The Bank's ordinary capital resources (which are used for loans to the more advanced developing member countries) are held and used entirely separately from its Special Funds resources (see below). A fourth General Capital Increase (GCI IV), amounting to US $26,318m. (or some 100%), was authorized in May 1994. At the final deadline for subscription to GCI IV, on 30 September 1996, 55 member countries had subscribed shares amounting to $24,675.4m.

At 31 December 1998 the position of subscriptions to the capital stock was as follows: authorized US $49,154m.; subscribed $48,456m.

The Bank also borrows funds from the world capital markets. Total borrowings during 1998 amounted to US $9,617m. (compared with $5,588m. in 1997).

In July 1986 the Bank abolished the system of fixed lending rates, under which ordinary operations loans had carried interest rates fixed at the time of loan commitment for the entire life of the loan. Under the new system the lending rate is adjusted every six months, to take into account changing conditions in international financial markets.

### SPECIAL FUNDS

The Asian Development Fund (ADF) was established in 1974 in order to provide a systematic mechanism for mobilizing and administering resources for the Bank to lend on concessionary terms to the least-developed member countries. In 1998 the Bank revised the terms of ADF. With effect from 1 January 1999 all new project loans were to be repayable within 32 years, including an eight-year grace period, while quick-disbursing programme loans had a 24-year maturity, including an eight-year grace period. The previous annual service charge was redesignated as an interest charge, including a portion to cover administrative expenses. The new interest charges on all loans were 1%–1.5% per annum. At 31 December 1998 cumulative disbursements from ADF resources totalled US $13,135.5m.

Successive replenishments of the Fund's resources amounted to US $809m. for the period 1976–78, $2,150m. for 1979–82, $3,214m. for 1983–86, and $3,600m. for 1987–90. A further replenishment (ADF VI) was approved in December 1991, providing $4,200m. for the four years 1992–95. In January 1997 donor countries concluded an agreement for a seventh replenishment of the Fund's resources, which incorporated an agreed figure of $6,300m. for ADF operations during the period 1997–2000 and recommendations that new donor contributions initially amount to $2,610m. and that the commitment authority from non-donor resources total $3,300m., almost double the level set in the previous replenishment.

The Bank provides technical assistance grants from its Technical Assistance Special Fund (TASF). By the end of 1998, the Fund's total resources amounted to US $734.0m., of which $624.5m. had been utilized or committed. The Japan Special Fund (JSF) was established in 1988 to provide finance for technical assistance by means of grants, in both the public and private sectors. The JSF aims to help developing member countries restructure their economies, enhance the opportunities for attracting new investment, and recycle funds. The Japanese Government had committed a total of 80,700m. yen (equivalent to $696.4m.) to the JSF by the end of 1998 (of which $537.7m. had been utilized). In March 1997 the Japanese Government made the first contribution to the ADB Institute Special Fund, which had been established to finance the initial operations of the new Institute (see above). By 31 December 1998 cumulative commitments to the Special Fund amounted to 3,500m. yen (or $28.1m.).

## Activities

Loans by the Bank are usually aimed at specific projects. In responding to requests from member governments for loans, the

Bank's staff assesses the financial and economic viability of projects and the way in which they fit into the economic framework and priorities of development of the country concerned. In 1987 the Bank adopted a policy of lending in support of programmes of sectoral adjustment, not limited to specific projects; such lending was not to exceed 15% of total Bank lending. In 1985 the Bank decided to expand its assistance to the private sector, hitherto comprising loans to development finance institutions, under government guarantee, for lending to small and medium-sized enterprises; a programme was formulated for direct financial assistance, in the form of equity and loans without government guarantee, to private enterprises. In addition, the Bank was to increase its support for financial institutions and capital markets and, where appropriate, give assistance for the privatization of public sector enterprises. In 1992 a Social Dimensions Unit was established as part of the central administrative structure of the Bank, which contributed to the Bank's increasing awareness of the importance of social aspects of development as essential components of sustainable economic growth. During the early 1990s the Bank also aimed to expand its role as project financier by providing assistance for policy formulation and review and promoting regional co-operation, while placing greater emphasis on individual country requirements.

Under the Bank's Medium-Term Strategic Framework for the period 1995–98 the following concerns were identified as strategic development objectives: promoting economic growth; reducing poverty; supporting human development (including population planning); improving the status of women; and protecting the environment. Accordingly, the Bank resolved to promote sound development management, by integrating into its operations and projects the promotion of governance issues, such as capacity-building, legal frameworks and openness of information. During 1995 the Bank introduced other specific policy initiatives including a new co-financing and guarantee policy to extend the use of guarantees and to provide greater assistance to co-financiers in order to mobilize more effectively private resources for development projects; a commitment to assess development projects for their impact on the local population and to avoid all involuntary resettlement where possible; the establishment of a formal procedure for grievances, under which the Board may authorize an inspection of a project, by an independent panel of experts, at the request of the affected community or group; and a policy to place greater emphasis on the development of the private sector, through the Bank's lending commitments and technical assistance activities. During 1997 the Bank attempted to refine its policy on good governance by emphasizing the following two objectives: assisting the governments of developing countries to create conditions conducive to private-sector investment, for example through public-sector management reforms; and assisting those governments to identify and secure large-scale and long-term funding, for example through the establishment of joint public-private ventures and the formulation of legal frameworks.

The currency instability and ensuing financial crises affecting many Asian economies in the second half of 1997 and in 1998 prompted the Bank to reflect on its role in the region. The Bank resolved to strengthen its activities as a broad-based development institution, rather than solely as a project financier, through lending policies, dialogue, co-financing and technical assistance. A Task Force on Financial Sector Reform was established to review the causes and effects of the regional financial crisis. The Task Force identified the Bank's initial priorities as being to accelerate banking and capital market reforms in member countries, to promote market efficiency in the financial, trade and industrial sectors, to promote good governance and sound corporate management, and to alleviate the social impact of structural adjustments. In mid-1999 the Bank approved a technical assistance grant to establish an internet-based Asian Recovery Information Centre, which aimed to facilitate access to information regarding the economic and social impact of the Asian financial crisis, analyses of economic needs of countries, reform programmes and monitoring of the economic recovery process. In November the Board of Directors approved a new overall strategy objective of poverty reduction, which was to be the principal consideration for all future Bank lending, project financing and technical assistance.

In 1998 the Bank approved 66 loans in 57 projects amounting to US $5,982.5m. (compared with $9,414.0m. for 91 loans in 75 projects in 1997). Loans from ordinary capital resources totalled $4,995.4m., while loans from the ADF amounted to $987.1m. in 1998. Private-sector operations approved amounted to $198.5m., which included direct loans without government guarantee of $136.1.m. and equity investments of $62.4m. The financial sector continued to account for the largest proportion of assistance, following the financial crisis in Asia, although this declined from 49.5% in 1997 to 28.0% in 1998. The Bank's primary objective in 1998 was to support economic growth in the region. Some 25% of lending was allocated to transport and communications infrastructure. Disbursements of loans during 1998 amounted to $6,766.3m., bringing cumulative disbursements to a total of $49,451.4m.

**SUBSCRIPTIONS AND VOTING POWER**
(31 December 1998)

| Country | Subscribed capital (% of total) | Voting power (% of total) |
|---|---|---|
| **Regional:** | | |
| Afghanistan | 0.035 | 0.379 |
| Australia | 5.949 | 5.110 |
| Bangladesh | 1.050 | 1.191 |
| Bhutan | 0.006 | 0.356 |
| Cambodia | 0.051 | 0.392 |
| China, People's Republic | 6.625 | 5.651 |
| Cook Islands | 0.003 | 0.353 |
| Fiji | 0.070 | 0.407 |
| Hong Kong | 0.560 | 0.799 |
| India | 6.509 | 5.558 |
| Indonesia | 5.599 | 4.830 |
| Japan | 16.046 | 13.188 |
| Kazakhstan | 0.829 | 1.014 |
| Kiribati | 0.004 | 0.354 |
| Korea, Republic | 5.179 | 4.494 |
| Kyrgyzstan | 0.307 | 0.597 |
| Laos | 0.014 | 0.362 |
| Malaysia | 2.800 | 2.591 |
| Maldives | 0.004 | 0.354 |
| Marshall Islands | 0.003 | 0.353 |
| Micronesia, Federated States | 0.004 | 0.354 |
| Mongolia | 0.015 | 0.363 |
| Myanmar | 0.560 | 0.799 |
| Nauru | 0.004 | 0.354 |
| Nepal | 0.151 | 0.472 |
| New Zealand | 1.579 | 1.614 |
| Pakistan | 2.240 | 2.143 |
| Papua New Guinea | 0.096 | 0.428 |
| Philippines | 2.434 | 2.298 |
| Samoa | 0.003 | 0.354 |
| Singapore | 0.350 | 0.631 |
| Solomon Islands | 0.007 | 0.356 |
| Sri Lanka | 0.596 | 0.828 |
| Taiwan | 1.120 | 1.247 |
| Tajikistan | 0.294 | 0.586 |
| Thailand | 1.400 | 1.471 |
| Tonga | 0.004 | 0.354 |
| Tuvalu | 0.001 | 0.352 |
| Uzbekistan | 0.693 | 0.905 |
| Vanuatu | 0.007 | 0.356 |
| Viet Nam | 0.351 | 0.632 |
| **Sub-total** | 63.555 | 65.230 |
| **Non-regional:** | | |
| Austria | 0.350 | 0.631 |
| Belgium | 0.350 | 0.631 |
| Canada | 5.378 | 4.653 |
| Denmark | 0.350 | 0.631 |
| Finland | 0.350 | 0.631 |
| France | 2.393 | 2.265 |
| Germany | 4.448 | 3.909 |
| Italy | 1.627 | 1.652 |
| Netherlands | 1.055 | 1.195 |
| Norway | 0.350 | 0.631 |
| Spain | 0.350 | 0.631 |
| Sweden | 0.350 | 0.631 |
| Switzerland | 0.600 | 0.831 |
| Turkey | 0.350 | 0.631 |
| United Kingdom | 2.100 | 2.031 |
| USA | 16.046 | 13.188 |
| **Sub-total** | 36.445 | 34.770 |
| **Total** | 100.000 | 100.000 |

In 1998 grants approved for technical assistance (e.g. project preparation, consultant services and training) amounted to US $163.2m. for 248 projects, with $54.7m. deriving from the Bank's ordinary resources and the TASF, $89.2m. from the JSF and $19.3m. from bilateral and multilateral sources. The Bank's Operations Evaluation Office prepares reports on completed projects, in order to assess achievements and problems. In 1997 the Bank adopted several new initiatives to evaluate and classify project performance and to assess the impact on development of individual projects.

The Bank co-operates with other international organizations active in the region, particularly the World Bank group, the IMF, UNDP and APEC, and participates in meetings of aid donors for developing member countries. In 1996 the Bank signed a memorandum of understanding with the UN Industrial Development

Organization (UNIDO), in order to strengthen co-operation between the two organizations. A new policy concerning co-operation with non-governmental organizations was approved by the Bank in 1998.

## Finance

Internal administrative expenses amounted to US $193.8m. in 1998, and were projected to total $207.0m. in 1999.

## Publications

*ADB Business Opportunities* (monthly).

*ADB Research Bulletin* (2 a year).

*ADB Review* (6 a year).

*Annual Report.*

*Asian Development Outlook* (annually).

*Asian Development Review* (2 a year).

*The Bank's Medium-Term Strategic Framework.*

*Key Indicators of Developing Asian and Pacific Countries* (annually).

*Law and Development Bulletin* (2 a year).

*Loan, Technical Assistance and Private Sector Operations Approvals* (monthly).

*Loan and Technical Assistance Statistics Yearbook.*

*Project Profiles for Commercial Co-financing* (quarterly).

Studies and reports, guide-lines, sample bidding documents, staff papers.

## Statistics

**BANK ACTIVITIES BY SECTOR**

| | Loan Approvals (US $ million) | | |
|---|---|---|---|
| | 1998 | | 1968–98 |
| Sector | Amount | % | % |
| Agriculture and natural resources | 420.86 | 7.04 | 19.40 |
| Energy | 440.00 | 7.35 | 21.91 |
| Finance | 1,675.50 | 28.01 | 16.42 |
| Industry and non-fuel minerals | 4.42 | 0.07 | 3.09 |
| Social infrastructure | 705.04 | 11.78 | 15.48 |
| Transport and communications | 1,496.70 | 25.02 | 19.45 |
| Multi-sector and others | 1,240.00 | 20.73 | 4.24 |
| **Total** | 5,982.52 | 100.00 | 100.00 |

**LENDING ACTIVITIES BY COUNTRY** (US $ million)

| | Loans approved in 1998 | | |
|---|---|---|---|
| Country | Ordinary Capital | ADF | Total |
| Bangladesh | 16.70 | 183.60 | 200.30 |
| Bhutan | — | 5.70 | 5.70 |
| China, People's Republic | 1,202.00 | — | 1,202.00 |
| India | 250.00 | — | 250.00 |
| Indonesia | 1,836.00 | — | 1,836.00 |
| Kiribati | — | 10.24 | 10.24 |
| Kyrgyzstan | — | 65.00 | 65.00 |
| Laos | — | 20.00 | 20.00 |
| Maldives | — | 6.30 | 6.30 |
| Nauru | 5.00 | — | 5.00 |
| Nepal | — | 105.00 | 105.00 |
| Papua New Guinea | 14.10 | — | 14.10 |
| Philippines | 846.58 | 8.80 | 855.38 |
| Samoa | — | 7.50 | 7.50 |
| Solomon Islands | — | 26.00 | 26.00 |
| Sri Lanka | 5.00 | 185.00 | 190.00 |
| Tajikistan | — | 20.00 | 20.00 |
| Thailand | 630.00 | — | 630.00 |
| Uzbekistan | 120.00 | — | 120.00 |
| Vanuatu | — | 20.00 | 20.00 |
| Viet Nam | — | 184.00 | 184.00 |
| Regional | 70.00 | 140.00 | 210.00 |
| **Total** | 4,995.38 | 987.14 | 5,982.52 |

**LENDING ACTIVITIES** (in %)

| | 1993–97 | | 1998 | |
|---|---|---|---|---|
| Country | Ordinary Capital | ADF | Ordinary Capital | ADF |
| Bangladesh | 0.2 | 21.0 | 0.3 | 18.6 |
| Bhutan | — | 0.3 | — | 0.6 |
| Cambodia | — | 2.5 | — | 4.1 |
| China, People's Republic | 23.3 | — | 24.1 | — |
| Cook Islands | — | 0.2 | — | — |
| Fiji | 0.2 | — | — | — |
| India | 13.2 | — | 5.0 | — |
| Indonesia | 22.2 | 3.6 | 36.8 | — |
| Kazakhstan | 1.6 | 0.8 | — | — |
| Kiribati | — | — | — | 1.0 |
| Korea, Republic | 18.3 | — | — | — |
| Kyrgyzstan | — | 3.4 | — | 6.6 |
| Laos | — | 5.8 | — | 2.0 |
| Malaysia | 0.9 | — | — | — |
| Maldives | — | 0.2 | — | 0.7 |
| Marshall Islands | — | 0.5 | — | — |
| Micronesia, Federated States | — | 0.5 | — | — |
| Mongolia | — | 4.8 | — | — |
| Nauru | — | — | 0.1 | — |
| Nepal | 0.2 | 5.1 | — | 10.6 |
| Pakistan | 4.1 | 21.2 | — | — |
| Papua New Guinea | 0.2 | 0.6 | 0.3 | — |
| Philippines | 6.7 | 3.0 | 16.9 | 0.9 |
| Samoa | — | 0.0 | — | 0.8 |
| Solomon Islands | — | 0.0 | — | 2.6 |
| Sri Lanka | 0.0 | 7.8 | 0.1 | 18.7 |
| Tajikistan | — | — | — | 2.0 |
| Thailand | 8.5 | — | 12.6 | — |
| Tonga | — | 0.3 | — | — |
| Uzbekistan | 0.3 | 0.3 | 2.4 | — |
| Vanuatu | — | 0.1 | — | 2.0 |
| Viet Nam | 0.1 | 18.0 | — | 28.8 |
| Regional | — | — | 1.4 | — |
| **Total** | 100.0 | 100.0 | 100.0 | 100.0 |
| **Value** (US $ million) | 21,903.8 | 7,214.4 | 4,995.4 | 987.1 |

Source: *ADB Annual Report 1998*.

# ASSOCIATION OF SOUTH EAST ASIAN NATIONS—ASEAN

**Address:** 70A Jalan Sisingamangaraja, POB 2072, Jakarta 12110, Indonesia.

**Telephone:** (21) 7262991; **fax:** (21) 7398234; **e-mail:** public@asean.or.id; **internet:** www.aseansec.org.

ASEAN was established in August 1967 at Bangkok, Thailand, to accelerate economic progress and to increase the stability of the South-East Asian region.

### MEMBERS

| | | |
|---|---|---|
| Brunei | Malaysia | Thailand |
| Cambodia | Myanmar | Viet Nam |
| Indonesia | Philippines | |
| Laos | Singapore | |

## Organization

(January 2000)

### SUMMIT MEETING

The highest authority of ASEAN, bringing together the heads of government of member countries. The first meeting was held in Bali, Indonesia, in February 1976. In 1992 it was agreed that summit meetings were to be held every three years, with an interim informal gathering of heads of government convened at least once. The 30th anniversary of the founding of ASEAN was commemorated at an informal summit meeting held in Kuala Lumpur, Malaysia, in December 1997. The sixth summit meeting was convened in Hanoi, Viet Nam, in December 1998 and the seventh meeting was scheduled to be held in Brunei, in 2001. An informal summit was convened in Manila, Philippines, in November 1999.

### MINISTERIAL MEETINGS

The ASEAN Ministerial Meeting (AMM), comprising ministers of foreign affairs of member states, meets annually, in each member country in turn, to formulate policy guidelines and to co-ordinate ASEAN activities. These meetings are followed by 'post-ministerial conferences' (PMCs), where ASEAN ministers of foreign affairs meet with their counterparts from countries that are 'dialogue partners' (see below) as well as from other countries. Ministers of economic affairs also meet once a year, to direct ASEAN economic co-operation. Joint Ministerial Meetings, consisting of ministers of foreign affairs and of economic affairs are convened prior to a summit meeting, and may be held at the request of either group of ministers. Other ministers meet regularly to promote co-operation in different sectors. Ministerial meetings are serviced by the committees described below.

### STANDING COMMITTEE

The Standing Committee normally meets every two months. It consists of the minister of foreign affairs of the host country and ambassadors of the other members accredited to the host country.

### SECRETARIATS

A permanent secretariat was established in Jakarta, Indonesia, in 1976 to form a central co-ordinating body. The Secretariat comprises the following four bureaux: economic co-operation; functional co-operation; ASEAN co-operation and dialogue relations; and AFTA. The Secretary-General holds office for a five-year term, and is assisted by two Deputy Secretaries-General. In each member country day-to-day work is co-ordinated by an ASEAN National Secretariat.

**Secretary-General:** RODOLFO SEVERINO (Philippines).

**Deputy Secretary-General:** SUTHAD SETBOONSARNG.

### COMMITTEES AND SENIOR OFFICIALS' MEETINGS

Relevant ministerial meetings are serviced by the following three Committees: Culture and Information; Science and Technology; and Social Development. ASEAN political co-operation is directed by a Senior Officials' Meeting. Economic co-operation activities are administered by a Senior Economic Officials' Meeting. Other groups of senior officials meet to direct ASEAN activities concerned with drug issues and the environment. Matters relating to the civil service are considered by an ASEAN Conference (held every two years). ASEAN's various work programmes and activities are also supported by a network of subsidiary technical bodies comprising sub-committees, expert groups, *ad hoc* working groups and working parties.

To support the conduct of relations with other countries and international organizations, ASEAN committees (composed of heads of diplomatic missions) have been established in 15 foreign capitals: those of Australia, Belgium, Canada, the People's Republic of China, France, Germany, India, Japan, the Republic of Korea, New Zealand, Pakistan, Russia, Switzerland, the United Kingdom and the USA.

## Activities

ASEAN was established in 1967 with the signing of the ASEAN Declaration, otherwise known as the Bangkok Declaration, by the ministers of foreign affairs of Indonesia, Malaysia, the Philippines, Singapore and Thailand. Brunei joined the organization in January 1984, shortly after attaining independence. Viet Nam was admitted as the seventh member of ASEAN in July 1995. Laos and Myanmar joined in July 1997 and Cambodia was formally admitted in April 1999, fulfilling the organization's ambition to incorporate all 10 countries in the sub-region.

### TRADE

A Basic Agreement on the Establishment of ASEAN Preferential Trade Arrangements was concluded in 1977, but by mid-1987 the system covered only about 5% of trade between member states, since individual countries were permitted to exclude any 'sensitive' products from preferential import tariffs. In December 1987 the meeting of ASEAN heads of government resolved to reduce such exclusions to a maximum of 10% of the number of items traded and to a maximum of 50% of the value of trade, over the next five years (seven years for Indonesia and the Philippines).

In January 1992 heads of government, meeting in Singapore, signed an agreement to create an 'ASEAN Free Trade Area' (AFTA), by 2008. In accordance with the agreement, a common effective preferential tariff (CEPT) scheme came into effect in January 1993. The CEPT covered all manufactured products, including capital goods, and processed agricultural products (which together accounted for two-thirds of intra-ASEAN trade), but was to exclude unprocessed agricultural products. Tariffs were to be reduced to a maximum of 20% within a period of five to eight years and to 0%–5% during the subsequent seven to 10 years. Fifteen categories were designated for accelerated tariff reduction, including vegetable oils, rubber products, textiles, cement and pharmaceuticals. Member states were, however, still to be permitted exclusion for certain 'sensitive' products. In October 1993 ASEAN trade ministers agreed to modify the CEPT, with only Malaysia and Singapore having adhered to the original tariff reduction schedule. The new AFTA programme, under which all member countries except Brunei were scheduled to begin tariff reductions from 1 January 1994, substantially enlarged the number of products to be included in the tariff-reduction process and reduced the list of products eligible for protection. In September 1994 ASEAN ministers of economic affairs agreed to accelerate the implementation of AFTA: tariffs were to be reduced to 0%–5% within seven to 10 years, or within five to eight years for products designated for accelerated tariff cuts. In July 1995 Viet Nam was admitted as a member of ASEAN and was granted until 2006 to implement the AFTA trade agreements. In September 1995 ASEAN economy ministers, meeting in Brunei, advocated a further acceleration of the tariff reduction deadline, to 2000. The ministers emphasized the importance of maintaining momentum in trade liberalization, in order to ensure ASEAN's continued relevance in relation to other regional groupings. In December 1995 heads of government, convened in Bangkok, agreed to maintain the objective of achieving AFTA by 2003, while pursuing efforts to eliminate or reduce tariffs to less than 5% on the majority of products by 2000. Liberalization was to be extended to certain service industries, including banking, telecommunications and tourism. In July 1997 Laos and Myanmar became members of ASEAN and were granted a 10-year period, from 1 January 1998, to comply with the AFTA schedule. In December 1997 ASEAN heads of government again agreed to accelerate the implementation of AFTA, but without specifying any new target date. In October 1998 ASEAN ministers of economic affairs, reiterating their commitment to reducing restrictions to intra-ASEAN trade, estimated that by 2000 some 85.2% of all products would be subject to tariffs of 0%–5%. In December 1998 heads of state, meeting in Hanoi, Viet Nam, approved a Statement on Bold Measures, detailing ASEAN's strategies to deal with the economic crisis in the region. These included incentives to attract investors, for example a three-year exemption on corporate taxation, accelerated implementation of the ASEAN Investment Area (see below), and advancing the AFTA deadline, for the original six members, to 2002, with some 90% of products to be covered by the arrangements by 2000. The Hanoi Plan of Action, which was also adopted at the meeting as a framework for the development of the organization over the period 1999–2004, incorporated a series of measures aimed at strengthening macroeconomic and financial co-operation and enhancing greater economic integration. In April 1999 Cambodia, on being admitted as a full member of ASEAN, signed an agreement to implement the tariff reduction programme over a 10-year period, commencing 1 January 2000. Cambodia also signed a declaration endorsing the commitments of the 1998 Statement on Bold Measures.

In June 1996 ASEAN's Working Group on Customs Procedures completed a draft legal framework for regional co-operation in order to simplify and to harmonize customs procedures, legislation and product classification. The customs agreement was to complement AFTA in facilitating intra-ASEAN trade. It was signed in March 1997 at the inaugural meeting of ASEAN finance ministers.

During 1991 ASEAN ministers discussed a proposal made by the Malaysian Government for the formation of an economic grouping, to be composed of ASEAN members, the People's Republic of China, Hong Kong, Japan, the Republic of Korea and Taiwan. In July 1993 ASEAN ministers of foreign affairs agreed a compromise, whereby the grouping was to be a caucus within APEC, although it was to be co-ordinated by ASEAN's meeting of economy ministers. In July 1994 ministers of foreign affairs of nine prospective members of the group held their first informal collective meeting; however, no progress was made towards forming the so-called East Asia Economic Caucus (EAEC). Japan's position on joining the EAEC remained to be established, owing to Japan's unwillingness to offend the USA, whose Government had expressed concerns that the grouping might undermine APEC by dividing the Asia-Pacific region. There was renewed speculation on the formation of an East Asian grouping following the informal meeting of heads of state of ASEAN countries, China, Japan and the Republic of Korea, held in November 1999 at which all parties agreed to strengthen regional unity and discussed the long-term possibility of establishing an East Asian common market and currency.

## SECURITY

In 1971 ASEAN members endorsed a declaration envisaging the establishment of a Zone of Peace, Freedom and Neutrality (ZOPFAN) in the South-East Asian region. This objective was incorporated in the Declaration of ASEAN Concord, which was adopted at the first summit meeting of the organization, held in Bali, Indonesia, in February 1976. (The Declaration also issued guidelines for co-operation in economic development and the promotion of social justice and welfare.) Also in February 1976 a Treaty of Amity and Co-operation was signed by heads of state, establishing principles of mutual respect for the independence and sovereignty of all nations, non-interference in the internal affairs of one another and settlement of disputes by peaceful means. The Treaty was amended in December 1987 by a protocol providing for the accession of Papua New Guinea and other non-member countries in the region; it was reinforced by a second protocol, signed in July 1998.

In January 1992 ASEAN leaders agreed that there should be greater co-operation on security matters within the grouping, and that ASEAN's post-ministerial conferences (PMCs) should be used as a forum for discussion of questions relating to security with its dialogue partners and other countries. In July 1992 the ASEAN Ministerial Meeting issued a statement calling for a peaceful resolution of the dispute concerning the Spratly Islands in the South China Sea, which are claimed, wholly or partly, by the People's Republic of China, Viet Nam, Taiwan, Brunei, Malaysia and the Philippines. (In February China had introduced legislation that defined the Spratly Islands as belonging to its territorial waters.) The ministers proposed a code of international conduct for the South China Sea, to be based on the principles contained in ASEAN's Treaty of Amity and Co-operation. At the ensuing PMC ASEAN requested the USA to maintain a military presence in the region, to compensate for the departure of its forces from the Philippines. The USA affirmed its commitment to maintaining the balance of security in South-East Asia. However, the issue of sovereignty of the Spratly Islands remained unresolved, and tensions in the region heightened in early 1995 owing to Chinese occupation of part of the disputed territory. Viet Nam's accession to ASEAN in July 1995, bringing all the Spratly Islands claimants except China and Taiwan into the grouping, was expected to strengthen ASEAN's position of negotiating a multilateral settlement on the Islands. In mid-1999 ASEAN established a special committee to formulate a code of conduct to be observed by all claimants to the Spratly Islands. Proposals under consideration were a ban on the building of all new structures, which had been the cause of escalating tensions in 1998, and a declaration rejecting the use of force to resolve disputes. A draft code of conduct was reported to have been formulated and approved by senior officials meeting in November 1999. China, however, refused to endorse the document, although it agreed to pursue discussions on the future of the islands on the basis of the proposed code and resolved not to attempt to strengthen its presence on the islands.

In December 1995 ASEAN heads of government, meeting in Bangkok, signed a treaty establishing a South-East Asia Nuclear-Weapon Free Zone (SEANWFZ). The treaty was also signed by Cambodia, Myanmar and Laos. It was extended to cover the offshore economic exclusion zones of each country. On ratification by all parties, the Treaty was to prohibit the manufacture or storage of nuclear weapons within the region. Individual signatories were to decide whether to allow port visits or transportation of nuclear weapons by foreign powers through territorial waters. The Treaty entered into force on 27 March 1997. ASEAN senior officials were mandated to oversee implementation of the Treaty pending the establishment of a permanent monitoring committee. In July 1999 the People's Republic of China and India agreed to observe the terms of the SEANWFZ.

In July 1997 ASEAN ministers of foreign affairs reiterated their commitment to the principle of non-interference in the internal affairs of other countries. However, the group's efforts in Cambodia (see below) marked a significant shift in diplomatic policy towards one of 'constructive intervention', which had been proposed by Malaysia's Deputy Prime Minister in recognition of the increasing interdependence of the region. At the Ministerial Meeting, held in July 1998, Thailand's Minister of Foreign Affairs, supported by his Philippine counterpart, proposed that the grouping formally adopt a policy of 'flexible engagement'. The proposal, based partly on concerns that the continued restrictions imposed by the Myanma authorities on dissident political activists was damaging ASEAN relations with its dialogue partners, was to provide for the discussion of the affairs of other member states when they have an impact on neighbouring countries. While rejecting the proposal, other ASEAN ministers agreed to pursue a more limited version, referred to as 'enhanced interaction', and to maintain open dialogue within the grouping. In September 1999 the violence surrounding a popular referendum in East Timor and the resulting humanitarian crisis highlighted the unwillingness of some ASEAN countries to intervene in member countries and undermined the political unity of the grouping. A compromise agreement, whereby countries acted on an individual basis rather than as representatives of ASEAN, was formulated prior to an emergency meeting of ministers of foreign affairs, held during the APEC meetings in Auckland, New Zealand. Malaysia, the Philippines, Singapore and Thailand declared their support for the establishment of a multinational force to restore peace in East Timor and committed troops to participate in the Australian-led operation. Myanmar and Viet Nam, however, remained opposed to any intervention in the territory.

**ASEAN Regional Forum (ARF):** In July 1993 the meeting of ASEAN ministers of foreign affairs sanctioned the establishment of a forum that was to discuss and co-operate on security issues within the region, and in particular was to ensure the involvement of the People's Republic of China in regional dialogue. The ARF was informally initiated during that year's PMC, comprising the ASEAN countries, its dialogue partners (at that time—Australia, Canada, the EC, Japan, the Republic of Korea, New Zealand and the USA), as well as the People's Republic of China, Laos, Papua New Guinea, Russia and Viet Nam. The first formal meeting of the ARF was conducted in July 1994, following the Ministerial Meeting held in Bangkok, Thailand, and it was agreed that the ARF be convened on an annual basis. The 1995 meeting, held in Brunei, in August, attempted to define a framework for the future of the ARF. It was perceived as evolving in three stages: the promotion of confidence-building (including disaster relief and peace-keeping activities); the development of preventive diplomacy; and the elaboration of approaches to conflict. The 19 ministers of foreign affairs attending the meeting (Cambodia participated for the first time) recognized that the ARF was still in the initial stage of implementing confidence-building measures. The ministers, having conceded to a request by China not to discuss explicitly the Spratly Islands, expressed concern at overlapping sovereignty claims in the region. In a further statement, the ministers urged an 'immediate end' to the testing of nuclear weapons, then being undertaken by the French Government in the South Pacific region. The third ARF, convened in July 1996, which was attended for the first time by India and Myanmar, agreed a set of criteria and guiding principles for the future expansion of the grouping. In particular, it was decided that the ARF would only admit as participants countries that have a direct influence on the peace and security of the East Asia and Pacific region. The meeting supported the efforts of all claimants to territories in the South China Sea to resolve any disputes in accordance with international law, and recognized the importance of ending all testing of nuclear weapons in the region. The ARF that was held in July 1997 reviewed progress being made in developing the first two 'tracks' of the ARF process, through the structure of inter-sessional working groups and meetings. The Forum's consideration of security issues in the region was dominated by concern at the political situation in Cambodia; support was expressed for ASEAN mediation to restore stability within that country. Myanmar and Laos attended the ARF for the first time. Mongolia was admitted into the ARF at its meeting in July 1998. The meeting condemned the recent testing of nuclear weapons in the region, but declined to criticize specifically India and Pakistan as the two countries involved. In July 1999 the ARF warned the Democratic People's Republic of Korea not to conduct any further testing of missiles over the Pacific.

## EXTERNAL RELATIONS

**European Union:** In March 1980 a co-operation agreement was signed between ASEAN and the European Community (EC, as the EU was known prior to its restructuring on 1 November 1993), which provided for the strengthening of existing trade links and increased co-operation in the scientific and agricultural spheres. A Joint Co-operation Committee met in November (and annually thereafter); it drew up a programme of scientific and technological co-operation, approved measures to promote contacts between industrialists from the two regions, and agreed on EC financing of ASEAN regional projects. An ASEAN-EC Business Council was launched in December 1983 to provide a forum for business representatives from the two regions and to identify joint projects. Three European Business Information Councils have since been established, in Malaysia, the Philippines and Thailand, in order to promote private sector co-operation. The first meeting of ministers of economic affairs from ASEAN and EC member countries took place in October 1985. In 1986 a joint group of experts on trade was set up, to examine problems of access to ASEAN markets and similar matters, and in 1987 joint investment committees were established in all the ASEAN capital cities. In December 1990 the Community adopted new guidelines on development co-operation, with an increase in assistance to Asia, and a change in the type of aid given to ASEAN members, emphasizing training, science and technology and venture capital, rather than assistance for rural development. In October 1992 the EC and ASEAN agreed to promote further trade between the regions, as well as bilateral investment, and made a joint declaration in support of human rights. The agreement was reached in spite of Portugal's threat to veto it in protest at the killing of demonstrators in East Timor by Indonesian security forces in November 1991. In May 1995 ASEAN and EU senior officials endorsed an initiative to convene an Asia-Europe Meeting (ASEM) in order to strengthen links between the two economic regions. A second ASEM was convened in April 1998 (see EU, p. 194). In October 1995 an ASEAN-EU Eminent Persons Group was established to consider the future direction of ASEAN-EU relations. In November 1996 an EU-ASEAN Junior Managers Exchange Programme was initiated, as part of efforts to promote co-operation and understanding between the industrial and business sectors in both regions. In February 1997 a Ministerial Meeting was held in Singapore. Despite ongoing differences regarding human rights, in particular ASEAN's granting of full membership status to Myanmar and the situation in East Timor (which precluded the conclusion of a new co-operation agreement), the meeting issued a final joint declaration, committing both sides to strengthening co-operation and dialogue on economic, international and bilateral trade, security and social issues. A protocol to the 1980 co-operation agreement was signed, enabling the participation of Viet Nam in the dialogue process. In November 1997 a meeting of the Joint Co-operation Committee was postponed and later cancelled, owing to a dispute concerning the participation of Myanmar in the meeting as an observer. A compromise agreement allowing Myanma officials to attend meetings in an observer capacity, was concluded in November 1998. However, the first meeting of the Joint Co-operation Committee, scheduled to take place in Bangkok, Thailand, in January 1999, was again cancelled, owing to controversy over perceived discrimination by the EU against Myanmar's status. The meeting was finally convened in late May.

**People's Republic of China:** Efforts to develop consultative relations between ASEAN and China were initiated in 1993. Joint Committees on economic and trade co-operation and on scientific and technological co-operation were subsequently established. The first formal consultations between senior officials of the two sides were held in April 1995. ASEAN representatives expressed serious concern at China's recent aggressive action in the Spratly Islands, in particular permitting illegal fishing activities and constructing a semi-permanent naval installation on one of the disputed reefs. In July China assured ASEAN ministers of foreign affairs that it would seek a peaceful resolution to the sovereignty dispute over the Islands, in accordance with international law. At the same time China reasserted its own territorial claims to the Islands. Despite ASEAN's continued concern at China's claims in the South China Sea, efforts have been pursued to strengthen relations between the two sides, and in July 1996 China was admitted to the PMC as a full dialogue partner. In February 1997 a Joint Co-operation Committee was established to co-ordinate the China-ASEAN dialogue and all aspects of relations between the two sides. In April, at a meeting of ASEAN-Chinese senior officials, for the first time China agreed to discuss issues relating to the South China Sea at a multilateral forum, rather than limiting discussions to a bilateral basis. Relations between the two sides were further strengthened by China's expression of support for the expansion of the ASEAN grouping, by granting membership to Cambodia, Laos and Myanmar, and the decision to establish a joint business council to promote bilateral trade and investment. China participated in the informal summit meeting that was held in December, at the end of which both sides issued a joint statement affirming their commitment to resolving regional disputes through peaceful means. A second meeting of the Joint Co-operation Committee was held in March 1999.

**Japan:** The ASEAN-Japan Forum was established in 1977 to discuss matters of mutual concern in trade, investment, technology transfer and development assistance. The first ever meeting between ASEAN economic ministers and the Japanese Minister of International Trade and Industry was held in October 1992. At this meeting, and subsequently, ASEAN requested Japan to increase its investment in member countries and to make Japanese markets more accessible to ASEAN products in order to reduce the trade deficit with Japan. Japan agreed to extend ASEAN's privileges under its generalized system of tariffs until 2001. Since 1993 ASEAN-Japanese development and cultural co-operation has expanded under schemes including the Inter-ASEAN Technical Exchange Programme, the Japan-ASEAN Co-operation Promotion Programme and the ASEAN-Japan Friendship Programme. In December 1997 Japan, attending the informal summit meeting in Malaysia, agreed to improve market access for ASEAN products and to provide training opportunities for more than 20,000 young people in order to help develop local economies. A joint statement, issued after the meeting, committed both sides to greater co-operation and to the promotion of regional peace and stability. In December 1998 ASEAN heads of government welcomed a Japanese initiative, announced in October, to allocate US $30,000m. to promote economic recovery in the region. At the same time the Japanese Prime Minister announced a further package of $5,000m. to be available as concessionary loans for infrastructure projects. In November 1999 Japan, along with the People's Republic of China and the Republic of Korea, attending an informal summit meeting of ASEAN, agreed to strengthen economic and political co-operation with the ASEAN countries, to enhance political and security dialogue, and to implement joint infrastructure and social projects.

**Other countries:** Under the ASEAN-Australia Economic Co-operation Programme, Australia gives financial support for ASEAN activities, and a joint Business Council was set up in 1980. A third phase of the Programme was initiated in mid-1994, with assistance amounting to $A32m. for the period to June 1998, which was to concentrate on projects in the environmental management, telecommunications, transport and agro-industrial sectors. Co-operation relations with New Zealand are based on the Inter-Institutional Linkages Programme and the Trade and Investment Promotion Programme, which mainly provide assistance in forestry development, dairy technology, veterinary management and legal aid training. An ASEAN-New Zealand Joint Management Committee was initiated in November 1993, in order to oversee the implementation of co-operation projects. The USA gives assistance for the development of small- and medium-sized businesses and other projects, and supports a Center for Technology Exchange. In 1990 ASEAN and the USA established an ASEAN-US Joint Working Group, whose purpose is to review ASEAN's economic relations with the USA and to identify measures by which economic links could be strengthened. ASEAN-Canadian co-operation projects include fisheries technology, the telecommunications industry, use of solar energy, and a forest seed centre. A Joint Planning and Monitoring Committee was established in 1994 (and met for the first time in October 1995) to oversee projects at the planning and implementation levels. In July 1991 the Republic of Korea was accepted as a 'dialogue partner', and in December a joint ASEAN-Korea Chamber of Commerce was established. During 1995 co-operation projects concerned with human resources development, science and technology, agricultural development and trade and investment policies were implemented. The Republic of Korea participated in ASEAN's informal summit meetings in December 1997 and November 1999 (see above).

In July 1993 both India and Pakistan were accepted as sectoral partners: sectoral partners can participate in ASEAN meetings on certain sectors such as trade, transport and communications and tourism. An ASEAN-India Business Council was established, and met for the first time, in New Delhi, in February 1995. In December 1995 the ASEAN summit meeting agreed to enhance India's status to that of a full dialogue partner; India was formally admitted to the PMC in July 1996. In July 1998 India rejected a proposal that Pakistan attend that month's ARF to discuss issues relating to both countries' testing of nuclear weapons.

**Indo-China:** In 1981 ASEAN sponsored a UN conference on Kampuchea, and gave assurances that it would not, as a group, supply arms to any faction. In 1988–89 'informal' meetings were held by representatives of Viet Nam, Laos, ASEAN and the Kampuchean factions to discuss a possible political settlement in Kampuchea. ASEAN participated in the international conference on Cambodia (as it was now known) which was held in Paris, France, in July/August 1989, and in further negotiations held in Jakarta, Indonesia in February 1990, neither of which achieved a political settlement. In July ASEAN ministers urged the formation of a Supreme National Council (SNC), on which the Vietnamese-supported Government of Cambodia and the three opposition groups would be represented. A UN proposal for the formation of an SNC and the holding of elections, under UN supervision, was accepted by all the Cambodian factions in September. Following the mass return of Cambodian refugees and displaced people in 1992–93, ASEAN and Japan provided technical experts to assist in the resettlement of the returnees. In July 1994 ASEAN ministers of foreign affairs and their dialogue partner counterparts agreed to provide military training in order to assist the Cambodian Government to consolidate its position. In July 1995 Cambodia was accorded observer status. Co-operation between the two sides subsequently focused on issues relating to Cambodia's future admission to the grouping as a full member. In May 1997 ASEAN ministers of foreign affairs confirmed that Cambodia, together with Laos and Myanmar, was to be admitted to the grouping in July of that year. In mid-July, however, Cambodia's membership was postponed owing to the deposition of Prince Ranariddh, and the resulting civil unrest. Later in that month Cambodia's *de facto* leader, Second Prime Minister Hun Sen, agreed to ASEAN's pursuit of a mediation role in restoring stability in the country and in preparing for democratic elections. In early August the ministers of foreign affairs of Indonesia, the Philippines and Thailand, representing ASEAN, met Hun Sen to confirm these objectives. In January 1998 Hun Sen refused to meet with ASEAN's three-member delegation. However, a team of observers from the grouping joined an international monitoring mission to supervise the election held in Cambodia in July. International approval of the conduct of the election, and consequently of Hun Sen's victory, prompted ASEAN to agree to reconsider Cambodia's admission into the Association. In December, following the establishment of a coalition administration in Cambodia, the country was welcomed, by the Vietnamese Government, as the 10th member of ASEAN, despite an earlier meeting of ministers of foreign affairs which failed to reach a consensus decision. Its formal admission took place on 30 April 1999.

In July 1992 Viet Nam and Laos signed ASEAN's Treaty on Amity and Co-operation: subsequently, the two countries participated in ASEAN meetings and committees as observers. Viet Nam was admitted as a full member of ASEAN in July 1995. In July 1994 an official delegation from Myanmar attended the annual Ministerial Meeting, having been invited by the host Thai Government on the basis of ASEAN's policy of pursuing limited 'constructive engagement' with Myanmar in order to encourage democracy in that country. In July 1995 Myanmar signed ASEAN's Treaty on Amity and Co-operation. In July 1996 ASEAN granted Myanmar observer status and admitted it to the ARF, despite the expression of strong reservations by (among others) the Governments of Australia, Canada and the USA, owing to the human rights situation in Myanmar. In November ASEAN heads of government, attending an informal summit meeting in Jakarta, Indonesia, agreed to admit Myanmar as a full member of the grouping at the same time as Cambodia and Laos. While Cambodia's membership was postponed, Laos and Myanmar were admitted to ASEAN in July 1997.

In June 1996 ministers of ASEAN countries, and of the People's Republic of China, Cambodia, Laos and Myanmar adopted a framework for ASEAN-Mekong Basin Development Co-operation. The initiative aimed to strengthen the region's cohesiveness, with greater co-operation on issues such as drugs-trafficking, labour migration and terrorism, and to facilitate the process of future expansion of ASEAN. Groups of experts and senior officials were to be convened to consider funding issues and proposals to link the two regions, including a gas pipeline network, rail links and the establishment of a common time zone. In December 1996 the working group on rail links appointed a team of consultants to conduct a feasibility study of the proposals.

## INDUSTRY

The ASEAN Industrial Complementation programme, initiated in 1981, encourages member countries to produce complementary products in specific industrial sectors for preferential exchange among themselves, for example components to be used in the automobile industry (under the Brand-to-Brand Complementation scheme—BBC—established in 1988). The ASEAN-Chambers of Commerce and Industry (CCI) aims to enhance ASEAN economic and industrial co-operation, and the participation in these activities of the private sector. In 1994/95 it was agreed to establish a permanent ASEAN-CCI secretariat at the ASEAN Secretariat. An ASEAN industrial joint venture (AIJV), established in 1983, sets up projects with at least 40% participation by private sector companies from two or more ASEAN member states, to receive preferential trade treatment (in the form of tariff reductions of up to 90%) within the region. In September 1994 changes to the AIJV scheme were formulated by ASEAN economic officials to bring it into line with tariff reductions anticipated under the CEPT arrangement and to maintain its margin of preference. In April 1995 a meeting of ASEAN economic ministers resolved to phase out the AIJV and the BBC. The ASEAN Consultative Committee on Standards and Quality (ACCSQ) aims to promote the understanding and implementation of quality concepts, which are considered to be important in strengthening the economic development of a member state and in helping to eliminate trade barriers. ACCSQ comprises three working groups: standards and information, conformance and assessment, and testing and calibration. In September 1994 the ACCSQ was recognized by the International Organization for Standardization as the standards organization for South-East Asia. In 1995 ACCSQ began to consider the elimination of technical barriers to trade, in order to facilitate the implementation of AFTA. In September 1994 an *ad hoc* Working Group on Intellectual Property Co-operation was established, with a mandate to formulate a framework agreement on intellectual property co-operation and to strengthen ASEAN activities towards intellectual property protection in the region. ASEAN aimed to establish, by 2004, a regional electronic database to strengthen the administration of intellectual property.

In 1988 the ASEAN Fund was established, with capital of US $150m. (of which $15m. was contributed by the Asian Development Bank), to provide finance for portfolio investments in ASEAN countries, in particular for small and medium-sized enterprises (SMEs). The Hanoi Plan of Action, which was adopted by ASEAN heads of state in December 1998, incorporated a series of initiatives to enhance the development of SMEs, including training and technical assistance, co-operation activities and greater access to information.

## FINANCE, BANKING AND INVESTMENT

In 1987 heads of government agreed to accelerate regional co-operation in this field, in order to support intra-ASEAN trade and investment; they adopted measures to increase the role of ASEAN currencies in regional trade, to assist negotiations on the avoidance of double taxation, and to improve the efficiency of tax and customs administrators. An ASEAN Reinsurance Corporation was established in 1988, with initial authorized capital of US $10m. In December 1995 the summit meeting proposed the establishment of an ASEAN Investment Area (AIA). Other measures to attract greater financial resource flows in the region, including an ASEAN Plan of Action for the Promotion of Foreign Direct Investment and Intra-ASEAN Investment, were implemented during 1996. In February 1997 ASEAN central bank governors agreed to strengthen efforts to combat currency speculation through the established network of foreign-exchange repurchase agreements. However, from mid-1997 several Asian currencies were undermined by speculative activities. Subsequent unsuccessful attempts to support the foreign-exchange rates contributed to a collapse in the value of financial markets in some countries and to a reversal of the region's economic growth, at least in the short term, while governments undertook macro-economic structural reforms. In early December ASEAN ministers of finance, meeting in Malaysia, agreed to liberalize markets for financial services and to strengthen surveillance of member country economies in order to help prevent further deterioration of the regional economy. The ministers also endorsed a proposal for the establishment of an Asian funding facility to provide emergency assistance in support of international credit and structural reform programmes. At the informal summit meeting held later in December ASEAN leaders issued a joint statement in which they expressed the need for mutual support to counter the region's financial crisis and urged greater international assistance to help overcome the situation and address the underlying problems. The heads of government also resolved to accelerate the implementation of the AIA in order to promote intra-ASEAN trade and to attract foreign direct investment. In July 1998 the ASEAN Ministerial Meeting endorsed the decisions of finance ministers, taken in February, to promote greater use of regional currencies for trade payments and to establish an economic surveillance mechanism. In October ministers of economic affairs, meeting in Manila, the Philippines, signed a framework agreement on the AIA, which was expected to provide for equal treatment of domestic and other ASEAN direct investment proposals within the grouping by 2010, and of all foreign investors by 2020. The meeting also confirmed that the proposed surveillance system to monitor the economic stability and financial systems of member states would be implemented with immediate effect, and would require the voluntary submission of economic information by all members to a monitoring committee, to be based in Jakarta, Indonesia. The ASEAN surveillance process and the framework agreement on the AIA were incorporated into the Hanoi Plan of Action, adopted by heads of state in December 1998. The AIA was to be implemented by means of individual and collective action plans according to the following schedules: Co-operation and facilitation; Promotion and awareness;

and Liberalization. The summit meeting also resolved to accelerate reforms, particularly in the banking and financial sectors, in order to strengthen the region's economies, and to promote the liberalization of the financial services sector. In March 1999 ASEAN ministers of trade and industry, meeting in Phuket, Thailand, as the AIA Council, agreed to open their manufacturing, agriculture, fisheries, forestry and mining industries to foreign investment. Investment restrictions affecting those industries were to be eliminated by 2003 in most cases, although Laos and Viet Nam were granted until 2010 to eliminate restrictions. In addition, ministers adopted a number of measures to encourage investment in the region, including access to three-year corporate income-tax exemptions, and tax allowances of 30% for investors. The AIA agreement formally entered into force in June 1999, having been ratified by all member countries.

## AGRICULTURE AND FORESTRY

In October 1983 a ministerial agreement on fisheries co-operation was concluded, providing for the joint management of fish resources, the sharing of technology, and co-operation in marketing. In July 1994 a Conference on Fisheries Management and Development Strategies in the ASEAN region, held in Bangkok, Thailand, resolved to enhance fish production through the introduction of new technologies, aquaculture development, improvements of product quality and greater involvement by the private sector.

Co-operation in forestry is focused on joint projects, funded by ASEAN's dialogue partners, which include a Forest Tree Seed Centre, an Institute of Forest Management and the ASEAN Timber Technology Centre. In April 1995 representatives of the ASEAN Secretariat and private-sector groups met to co-ordinate the implementation of a scheme to promote the export of ASEAN agricultural and forestry products.

ASEAN holds an emergency rice reserve, amounting to 53,000 metric tons, as part of its efforts to ensure food security in the region. There is an established ASEAN programme of training and study exchanges for farm workers, agricultural experts and members of agricultural co-operatives. During 1998 ASEAN was particularly concerned with the impact of the region's economic crisis on the agricultural sector, and of the possible effects of climatic change. In September ministers of agriculture and forestry, meeting in Hanoi, Viet Nam, endorsed a Strategic Plan of Action on ASEAN Co-operation in Food, Agriculture and Forestry for the period 1999–2004. The Plan focused on programmes and activities aimed at enhancing food security, and the international competitiveness of ASEAN food, agriculture and forestry products, promoting the sustainable use and conservation of natural resources, encouraging greater involvement by the private sector in the food and agricultural industry, and strengthening joint approaches on international and regional issues. An ASEAN Task Force has been established to harmonize regulations on agricultural products derived from biotechnology by 2000. In December 1998 heads of state resolved further to improve food security in the region by establishing an ASEAN Food Security Information Service to enhance the capacity of member states to forecast and manage food supplies and the use of basic commodities.

## MINERALS AND ENERGY

In April 1994, a meeting of the ASEAN economic ministers on energy co-operation recognized the significance of energy and power development in sustaining the overall growth of the region's economies. A medium-term programme of action on energy co-operation, for the period 1995–99, included measures to promote energy efficiency, the diversification of energy sources, training and research activities, and the exchange of information on energy policies among ASEAN members. In 1990 efforts to establish an ASEAN electricity grid were initiated. In July 1996 ASEAN ministers of energy, meeting in Kuala Lumpur, Malaysia, discussed the construction of a gas pipeline network linking all member countries. The ASEAN-EC Energy Management, Training and Research Centre (AEEMTRC), a co-operation project implemented with funding from the EU, based in Jakarta, Indonesia, conducts research, information, management and training activities in all aspects of energy, and publishes reference materials for the exchange of energy information. An ASEAN energy business forum is held annually and attended by representatives of the energy industry in the private and public sectors.

A Framework of Co-operation in Minerals was adopted by an ASEAN working group of experts in August 1993. The group has also developed a programme of action for ASEAN co-operation in the development and utilization of industrial minerals to promote the exploration and development of mineral resources in ASEAN member countries, the transfer of mining technology and expertise, the participation of the private sector in industrial mineral production. The programme of action is implemented by an ASEAN Regional Development Centre for Mineral Resources, which also conducts workshops and training programmes relating to the sector.

## TRANSPORT AND COMMUNICATIONS

ASEAN aims to promote greater co-operation in the transport and communications sector, and in particular to develop multi-modal transport; achieve interoperability and interconnectivity in telecommunications; harmonize road transport laws and regulations; improve air space management; develop ASEAN legislation for the carriage of dangerous goods and waste by land and sea; and human resources development. The summit meeting, held in December 1998, agreed to develop a trans-ASEAN transportation network by 2000, comprising principal routes for the movement of goods and people. In September 1999 ASEAN ministers of transport and communications resolved to establish working groups to strengthen co-operation within the sector and adopted a programme of action for further development of the sector in the period 1999–2004.

## SCIENCE AND TECHNOLOGY

In February 1994 ASEAN ministers of science and technology adopted a Plan of Action which was to be a framework for ASEAN co-operation in this sector for the period 1994–98. The Plan aimed to achieve a high-level of intra-ASEAN co-operation, with the involvement of the private sector; to establish a network of science and technology centres, infrastructure and programmes for human resources; to promote technology transfer; to enhance public awareness of the importance of science and technology for economic development; and to increase the level of co-operation in science and technology with the international community. ASEAN supports co-operation in food science and technology, meteorology and geophysics, microelectronics and information technology, biotechnology, non-conventional energy research, materials science and technology and marine science. There is an ASEAN Science Fund, used to finance policy studies in science and technology and to support information exchange and dissemination.

## ENVIRONMENT

A ministerial meeting on the environment, held in April 1994, approved an ASEAN Strategic Plan of Action on the Environment for the period 1994–98, which established long-term objectives on environmental quality and standards for the ASEAN region and aimed to enhance joint action to address environmental concerns. At the same time the ministers adopted standards for air quality and river water which were to be achieved by all ASEAN member countries by 2010. In June 1995 ministers agreed to co-operate in order to counter the problems of transboundary pollution. During 1997 efforts continued to establish an ASEAN Regional Centre for Biodiversity Conservation, which was to be based in the Philippines. In December ASEAN heads of state endorsed a Regional Haze Action Plan to address the environmental problems resulting from forest fires, which had afflicted several countries in the region throughout that year. A Haze Technical Task Force undertook to implement the plan in 1998, with assistance from the UN Environment Programme, and was to assist members to formulate national haze action plans. In March ministers of the environment requested international financial assistance to help to mitigate the dangers of forest fires in Indonesia, which had suffered an estimated US $1,000m. in damages in 1997 as a result of the fires (of an estimated total of $1,300m. suffered by the region as a whole, mainly resulting from health problems and the effects on tourism). Sub-regional fire-fighting arrangement working groups for Sumatra and Borneo were established in April 1998, and in May the Task Force organized a regional workshop to strengthen ASEAN capacity to prevent and alleviate the haze caused by the extensive fires. A pilot project of aerial surveillance of the areas in the region most at risk of forest fires was initiated in July. In December heads of government resolved to establish an ASEAN Regional Research and Training Centre for Land and Forest Fire Management by 2004. Other environmental objectives approved at the meeting included: implementation of a water conservation programme by 2001; greater co-operation in the integrated protection and management of coastal zones; establishment of a regional centre or network for the promotion of environmentally-sound technologies by 2004; and formation and adoption of an ASEAN protocol on access to genetic resources by 2003.

## SOCIAL DEVELOPMENT

ASEAN concerns in social development include youth development, the role of women, health and nutrition, education, labour affairs and disaster management. In December 1993 ASEAN ministers responsible for social affairs adopted a Plan of Action for Children, which provided a framework for regional co-operation for the survival, protection and development of children in member countries. An ASEAN task force on AIDS has been created, and its first meeting was held in Jakarta in March 1993.

ASEAN supports efforts to combat drug abuse and illegal drugs-trafficking. It aims to promote education and drug-awareness campaigns throughout the region, and administers a project to strengthen the training of personnel involved in combating drug concerns. In October 1994 a meeting of ASEAN Senior Officials on Drug Matters approved a three-year plan of action on drug abuse, which provided a framework for co-operation in four priority areas: preventive drug education; treatment and rehabilitation; law enforcement; and research. In July 1998 ASEAN ministers of foreign affairs signed a Joint Declaration for a Drug-Free ASEAN, which envisaged greater co-operation among member states, in particular in information exchange, educational resources and legal procedures, in order to eliminate the illicit production, processing and trafficking of narcotic substances by 2020.

In December 1998 ASEAN leaders approved a series of measures aimed at mitigating the social impact of the financial and economic crises which had affected many countries in the region. Plans of Action were to be implemented on ASEAN Rural Development and Poverty Eradication, and Social Safety Nets, which aimed to protect the most vulnerable members of society. The summit meeting also emphasized the need to promote job generation as a key element of strategies for economic recovery and growth.

### TOURISM

National Tourist Organizations from ASEAN countries meet regularly to assist in co-ordinating the region's tourist industry. In January 1995 the Organizations agreed to participate in a new tourism body, which was to include ASEAN private-sector organizations involved in the industry. A Tourism Forum is held annually to promote ASEAN's tourist industry. The first formal meeting of ASEAN ministers of tourism was held in January 1998, in Cebu, the Philippines. The meeting adopted a Plan of Action on ASEAN Co-operation in Tourism, which aimed to promote intra-ASEAN travel, greater investment in the sector, joint marketing of the region as a tourist destination and environmentally sustainable tourism. The second meeting of ASEAN ministers of tourism was held in Singapore in January 1999. Ministers agreed to appoint country co-ordinators to implement various initiatives, including the designation of 2002 as 'Visit ASEAN Millennium Year'; research to promote the region as a tourist destination in the 21st century, and to develop a cruise-ship industry; and the establishment of a network of ASEAN Tourism Training Centres to develop new skills and technologies in the tourism industry by 2001.

### CULTURE AND INFORMATION

Regular workshops and festivals are held in visual and performing arts, youth music, radio, television and films, and print and interpersonal media. In addition, ASEAN administers a News Exchange and provides support for the training of editors, journalists and information officers. In July 1997 ASEAN ministers of foreign affairs endorsed the establishment of an ASEAN Foundation to promote awareness of the organization and greater participation in its activities.

## Publications

*Annual Report of the ASEAN Standing Committee.*

*ASEAN Insurance Journal.*

*ASEAN Journal on Science and Technology for Development* (2 a year).

*ASEAN Update* (every 2 months).

*Information Series* and *Documents Series.*

# BANK FOR INTERNATIONAL SETTLEMENTS—BIS

**Address:** Centralbahnplatz 2, 4002 Basel, Switzerland.

**Telephone:** (61) 2808080; **fax:** (61) 2809100; **e-mail:** emailmaster@bis.org; **internet:** www.bis.org.

The Bank for International Settlements was founded pursuant to the Hague Agreements of 1930 to promote co-operation among national central banks and to provide additional facilities for international financial operations.

## Organization

(January 2000)

### GENERAL MEETING

The General Meeting is held annually in June and is attended by representatives of the central banks of countries in which shares have been subscribed. At 31 March 1999 the central banks of the following authorities were entitled to attend and vote at General Meetings of the BIS: Australia, Austria, Belgium, Brazil, Bulgaria, Canada, the People's Republic of China, the Czech Republic, Denmark, Estonia, Finland, France, Germany, Greece, Hong Kong, Hungary, Iceland, India, Ireland, Italy, Japan, the Republic of Korea, Latvia, Lithuania, Mexico, the Netherlands, Norway, Poland, Portugal, Romania, Russia, Saudi Arabia, Singapore, Slovakia, South Africa, Spain, Sweden, Switzerland, Turkey, the United Kingdom and the USA. The legal status of the Yugoslav issue of the Bank's capital remains in suspense. However, new shares have been issued, on an interim basis, to the central banks of four of the successor states of the former Yugoslavia, i.e. Bosnia and Herzegovina, Croatia, the former Yugoslav republic of Macedonia and Slovenia, pending a comprehensive settlement of all outstanding issues.

### BOARD OF DIRECTORS

The Board of Directors is responsible for the conduct of the Bank's operations at the highest level, and comprises the Governors in office of the central banks of Belgium, France, Germany, Italy, the United Kingdom and the USA, each of whom appoints another member of the same nationality. The statutes also provide for the election to the Board of not more than nine Governors of other member central banks: those of Canada, Japan, the Netherlands, Sweden and Switzerland are also members of the Board.

**Chairman of the Board and President of the Bank:** URBAN BÄCKSTRÖM (Sweden).

### MANAGEMENT

**General Manager:** ANDREW CROCKETT (United Kingdom).

The Bank has a staff of about 485 employees, from 32 countries. In July 1998 the BIS inaugurated its first overseas administrative unit, the Representative Office for Asia and the Pacific, which was based in Hong Kong.

## Activities

The BIS is an international financial institution whose special role is to promote the co-operation of central banks, and to fulfil the function of a 'central banks' bank'. Although it has the legal form of a company limited by shares, it is an international organization governed by international law, and enjoys special privileges and immunities in keeping with its role (a Headquarters Agreement was concluded with Switzerland in 1987). The participating central banks were originally given the option of subscribing the shares themselves or arranging for their subscription in their own countries: thus the BIS also has some private shareholders, but they have no right of participation in the General Meeting. Some 86% of the total share capital is in the hands of central banks and 14% is held by private shareholders.

### FINANCE

The authorized capital of the Bank is 1,500m. gold francs, divided into 600,000 shares of 2,500 gold francs each.

**Statement of Account***
(In gold francs; units of 0.29032258 . . . gram of fine gold—Art. 4 of the Statutes; 31 March 1999)

| Assets | | % |
|---|---|---|
| Gold (bars) | 2,801,471,476 | 4.23 |
| Cash on hand and on sight a/c with banks | 8,289,300 | 0.01 |
| Treasury bills | 7,314,049,359 | 11.04 |
| Time deposits and advances | 33,500,158,974 | 50.58 |
| Securities at term | 22,443,860,437 | 33.88 |
| Miscellaneous | 169,247,504 | 0.26 |
| **Total** | 66,237,077,050 | 100.00 |

| Liabilities | | % |
|---|---|---|
| Authorized cap.: 1,500,000,000 | | |
| Issued cap.: 1,292,912,500 | | |
| viz. 517,165 shares of which | | |
| 25% paid up . . . . . | 323,228,125 | 0.49 |
| Reserves. . . . . . | 2,605,641,703 | 3.93 |
| Deposits (gold) . . . . . | 3,192,576,626 | 4.82 |
| Deposits (currencies). . . . | 57,827,234,298 | 87.30 |
| Miscellaneous . . . . . | 2,231,030,139 | 3.37 |
| Dividend payable on 1 July . . | 57,366,159 | 0.09 |
| **Total** . . . . . . . | 66,237,077,050 | 100.0 |

* Assets and liabilities in US dollars are converted at US $208 per fine ounce of gold (equivalent to 1 gold franc = $1.94149 . . .) and all other items in currencies on the basis of market rates against the US dollar.

## BANKING OPERATIONS

The BIS assists central banks in managing and investing their monetary reserves: in 1999 some 120 international financial institutions and central banks from all over the world had deposits with the BIS, which managed around 7% of world foreign exchange reserves.

The BIS uses the funds deposited with it partly for lending to central banks. Its credit transactions may take the form of swaps against gold; covered credits secured by means of a pledge of gold or marketable short-term securities; credits against gold or currency deposits of the same amount and for the same duration held with the BIS; unsecured credits in the form of advances or deposits; or standby credits, which in individual instances are backed by guarantees given by member central banks. In addition, the Bank undertakes operations in foreign exchange and in gold, both with central banks and with the markets.

In 1982, faced with the increasingly critical debt situation of some Latin American countries and the resultant threat to the viability of the international financial system, the BIS granted comparatively large-scale loans to central banks that did not number among its shareholders: the central banks of Argentina, Brazil and Mexico were granted bridging loans pending the disbursement of balance-of-payments credits extended by the IMF. These facilities amounted to almost US $3,000m., all of which had been repaid by the end of 1983. The Bank subsequently made similar loans, but with decreasing frequency. Since 1990 the BIS has contributed funds to bridging facilities arranged for the central banks of Venezuela, Guyana, Hungary, Romania, the former Yugoslav republic of Macedonia, Mexico (in 1995) and Thailand (in August 1997). Within the framework of an international financial programme, approved in support of the Brazilian economy in late 1998, the Bank was to co-ordinate a credit facility of up to $13,280m. in favour of the Banco Central do Brasil. Funds were provided with the backing or guarantee of 19 central banks.

The BIS also engages in traditional types of investment: funds not required for lending to central banks are placed in the market as deposits with commercial banks and purchases of short-term negotiable paper, including Treasury bills. Such operations constitute a major part of the Bank's business.

Because the central banks' monetary reserves must be available at short notice, they can only be placed with the BIS at short term, for fixed periods and with clearly defined repayment terms. The BIS has to match its assets to the maturity structure and nature of its commitments, and must therefore conduct its business with special regard to maintaining a high degree of liquidity.

The Bank's operations must be in conformity with the monetary policy of the central banks of the countries concerned. It is not permitted to make advances to governments or to open current accounts in their name. Real estate transactions are also excluded.

## INTERNATIONAL MONETARY CO-OPERATION

Governors of central banks meet for regular discussions at the BIS to co-ordinate international monetary policy and ensure orderly conditions on the international financial markets. There is close co-operation with the IMF and the World Bank. The BIS participates in meetings of the so-called Group of 10 (G-10) industrialized nations (see IMF p. 93), which has been a major forum for discussion of international monetary issues since its establishment in 1962. Governors of central banks of the G-10 countries convene for regular Basle Monthly Meetings. In 1971 a Standing Committee of the G-10 central banks was established at the BIS to consider aspects of the development of Euro-currency markets. In February 1999 the G-10 renamed the body as the Committee on the Global Financial System, and approved a revised mandate to undertake systematic short-term monitoring of global financial system conditions; longer-term analysis of the functioning of financial markets; and the articulation of policy recommendations aimed at improving market functioning and promoting stability. The Committee was to meet four times a year.

In 1974 the Governors of central banks of the G-10 set up the Basle Committee on Banking Supervision (whose secretariat is provided by the BIS) to co-ordinate banking supervision at the international level. The Committee pools information on banking supervisory regulations and surveillance systems, including the supervision of banks' foreign currency business, identifies possible danger areas and proposes measures to safeguard the banks' solvency and liquidity. An International Conference of Banking Supervisors is held every two years. In 1997 the Committee published new guide-lines, entitled Core Principles for Effective Banking Supervision, that were intended to provide a comprehensive set of standards to ensure sound banking. In 1998 the Committee was concerned with the development and implementation of the Core Principles, particularly given the ongoing financial and economic crisis affecting several Asian countries and instability of other major economies. A Financial Stability Institute was established in 1998, jointly by the BIS and Basle Committee, to enhance the capacity of central banks and supervisory bodies to implement aspects of the Core Principles, through the provision of training programmes and other policy workshops. In 1999 the Committee was to undertake a key role in a Joint Year 2000 Council, which aimed to ensure an effective response to the technological difficulties resulting from the millennium date change and to supervise banks' compliance with adopted strategies.

In February 1999 ministers of finance and governors of the central banks of the Group of Seven (G-7) industrialized nations approved the establishment of a Financial Stability Forum to strengthen co-operation among the world's largest economies and economic bodies, to improve the monitoring of international finance and to prevent a recurrence of the economic crises of 1997 and 1998. The General Manager of the BIS was appointed to chair the Forum for an initial three-year term. The first meeting of the Forum, comprising representatives of G-7 ministries of finance and central banks, and of international financial institutions and regulatory bodies, took place at the headquarters of the IMF in Washington, DC, USA, in April 1999. Three working groups were established to study aspects of highly leveraged, or unregulated, institutions, offshore financial centres, and short-term capital flows. In November the Forum constituted additional groups to review deposit insurance schemes and to consider measures to promote implementation of international standards.

The Bank organizes and provides the secretariat for periodic meetings of experts, such as the Group of Computer Experts, the Group of Experts on Payment Systems, the Group of Experts on Monetary and Economic Data Bank Questions, which aims to develop a data bank service for the G-10 central banks and the BIS, and the Committee of Experts on Gold and Foreign Exchange, which monitors financial market developments.

Since January 1998 the BIS has hosted the secretariat of the International Association of Insurance Supervisors, established in 1994. The Association aims to promote co-operation within the insurance industry with regard to effective supervision and the development of domestic insurance markets.

## RESEARCH

The Bank's Monetary and Economic Department conducts research, particularly into monetary and financial questions; collects and publishes data on securities markets and international banking developments; and organizes a data bank for central banks. The BIS Annual Report provides an independent analysis of monetary and economic developments. Statistics on international banking and on external indebtedness are also published regularly.

## AGENCY AND TRUSTEE FUNCTIONS

Throughout its history the BIS has undertaken various duties as Trustee Fiscal Agent or Depository with regard to international loan agreements. From October 1986 the BIS performed the functions of Agent for the private European Currency Unit (ECU) clearing and settlement system, in accordance with the provisions of successive agreements concluded between the then ECU Banking Association (now Euro Banking Association—EBA), based in Paris, and the BIS. This arrangement was terminated following the introduction of the euro on 1 January 1999, when the ECU clearing system was replaced by a new euro clearing system of the EBA. At that time 62 banks had been granted the status of clearing bank by the EBA.

In April 1994 the BIS assumed new functions in connection with the rescheduling of Brazil's external debt, which had been agreed by the Brazilian Government in November 1993. In accordance with two collateral pledge agreements, the BIS acts in the capacity of Collateral Agent to hold and invest collateral for the benefit of the holders of certain US dollar-denominated bonds, maturing in 15 or 30 years, which have been issued by Brazil under the rescheduling arrangements. The Bank acts in a similar capacity for Peru, in accordance with external debt agreements concluded in November 1996 and a collateral agreement signed with the BIS in March 1997, and for Côte d'Ivoire, under a restructuring agreement signed in May 1997 and collateral agreement signed in March 1998.

## Publications

*Annual Report* (in English, French, German and Italian).

*Quarterly Review: International Banking and Financial Market Developments* (English, French, German and Italian).

*The BIS Consolidated International Banking Statistics* (every 6 months).

*Joint BIS-IMF-OECD-World Bank Statistics on External Debt* (quarterly).

*Regular OTC Derivatives Market Statistics* (every 6 months).

*Central Bank Survey of Foreign Exchange and Derivatives Market Activity* (3 a year).

# BLACK SEA ECONOMIC CO-OPERATION—BSEC

**Address:** İstinye Cad. Müşir Fuad Paşa Yalısı, Eski Tersane 80860 İstinye-İstanbul, Turkey.

**Telephone:** (212) 229-63-30; **fax:** (212) 229-63-36; **e-mail:** bsec@turk.net; **internet:** www.bsec.gov.tr.

The Black Sea Economic Co-operation (BSEC) was established in 1992 to strengthen regional co-operation, particularly in the field of economic development. In June 1998, at a summit meeting held in Yalta, Ukraine, participating countries signed the BSEC Charter, thereby officially elevating the BSEC to regional organization status. The Charter entered into force on 1 May 1999, at which time the BSEC formally became the Organization of the Black Sea Economic Co-operation, retaining the same acronym.

### MEMBERS

| | | |
|---|---|---|
| Albania | Georgia | Russia |
| Armenia | Greece | Turkey |
| Azerbaijan | Moldova | Ukraine |
| Bulgaria | Romania | |

Note: Observer status has been granted to Austria, Egypt, France, Germany, Israel, Italy, Poland, Slovakia and Tunisia. The BSEC Business Council, International Black Sea Club, and the Energy Charter Conference also have observer status.

## Organization

(January 2000)

### PRESIDENTIAL SUMMIT

The presidential summit, comprising the heads of state and of government of member states, represents the highest authority of the body.

### COUNCIL

The council of ministers of foreign affairs is BSEC's principal decision-making organ. Ministers meet at least once a year to review progress and to define new objectives.

### PARLIAMENTARY ASSEMBLY

The parliamentary assembly, consisting of the representatives of the national parliaments of member states, was created in February 1993 to provide a legal basis for the implementation of decisions within the BSEC framework. It comprises three committees concerning economic, commercial, technological and environmental affairs; legal and political affairs; and cultural, educational and social affairs.

### SECRETARIAT

The Secretariat commenced operations in March 1994. Its tasks are, primarily, of an administrative and technical nature, and include the maintenance of archives, and the preparation and distribution of documentation.

**Secretary-General:** VASSIL BAYTCHEV.

## Activities

In June 1992, at a summit meeting held in İstanbul, heads of state and of government signed the summit declaration on BSEC, which established a regional structure for economic co-operation. The organization's main areas of co-operation include transport and communications; information technology; the standardization and certification of products; energy; the mining and processing of raw materials; tourism; agriculture and agro-industry; health care and pharmaceuticals; sustainable development; environmental protection; and science and technology. In order to promote regional co-operation, the organization also aims to strengthen the business environment by providing support for small and medium-sized enterprises; facilitating closer contacts between businesses in member countries; progressively eliminating obstacles to the expansion of trade; creating appropriate conditions for investment and industrial co-operation, in particular through the avoidance of double taxation and the promotion and protection of investments; encouraging the dissemination of information concerning international tenders organized by member states; and promoting economic co-operation in free-trade zones.

A BSEC Business Council was established in İstanbul in December 1992 by the business communities of member states. It has observer status at the BSEC, and aims to identify private and public investment projects, maintain business contacts and develop programmes in various sectors. A Black Sea Trade and Development Bank was inaugurated in early 1998, in Thessaloniki, Greece, as the organization's main funding institution, to finance and implement joint regional projects. It began operations on 1 July 1999. The European Bank for Reconstruction and Development (EBRD, see p. 168) was entrusted as the depository for all capital payments made prior to its establishment. A BSEC Co-ordination Centre, located in Ankara, Turkey, aims to promote the exchange of statistical and economic information. In September 1998 a Black Sea International Studies Centre was inaugurated in Athens, Greece, in order to undertake research concerning the BSEC, in the fields of economics, industry and technology.

A Strategic Action Plan to reduce pollution in the Black Sea was signed by Bulgaria, Georgia, Romania, Russia, Turkey and Ukraine in November 1996. The Black Sea Environment Programme, implementation of which was to amount to some US $750m., was to be reviewed in 2001. The Programme was expected to be funded by international agencies such as the World Bank.

# CARIBBEAN COMMUNITY AND COMMON MARKET—CARICOM

**Address:** Bank of Guyana Building, POB 10827, Georgetown, Guyana.

**Telephone:** (2) 69281; **fax:** (2) 67816; **e-mail:** carisec3@caricom.org; **internet:** www.caricom.org.

CARICOM was formed in 1973 by the Treaty of Chaguaramas, signed in Trinidad, as a movement towards unity in the Caribbean; it replaced the Caribbean Free Trade Association (CARIFTA), founded in 1965. A revision of the Treaty of Chaguaramas (by means of nine separate Protocols) was undertaken in the 1990s, to institute greater regional integration and to establish a single Caribbean market and economy.

### MEMBERS

| | |
|---|---|
| Anguilla* | Jamaica |
| Antigua and Barbuda | Montserrat |
| Bahamas† | Saint Christopher and Nevis |
| Barbados | Saint Lucia |
| Belize | Saint Vincent and the Grenadines |
| British Virgin Islands* | Suriname |
| Dominica | Trinidad and Tobago |
| Grenada | Turks and Caicos Islands* |
| Guyana | |

* The British Virgin Islands and the Turks and Caicos Islands were granted associate membership in 1991; Anguilla's application for associate membership was approved in July 1998 and formally implemented in July 1999.

† The Bahamas is a member of the Community but not the Common Market.

Note: Haiti was accepted as a full member of the Community in July 1997, although the final terms and conditions of its accession had yet to be concluded; it was invited to participate in the deliberations of all the organs and bodies of the Community in the interim. The terms for Haiti's accession were agreed in July 1999. Aruba, Bermuda, the Cayman Islands, Colombia, the Dominican Republic, Mexico, the Netherlands Antilles, Puerto Rico and Venezuela have observer status with the Community.

## Organization

(January 2000)

### HEADS OF GOVERNMENT CONFERENCE AND BUREAU

The Conference is the final authority of the Community and determines policy. It is responsible for the conclusion of treaties on behalf of the Community and for entering into relationships between the Community and international organizations and states. Decisions of the Conference are generally taken unanimously. Heads of government meet annually.

At a special meeting of the Conference, held in Trinidad and Tobago in October 1992, participants decided to establish a Heads of Government Bureau, with the capacity to initiate proposals, to update consensus and to secure the implementation of CARICOM decisions. The Bureau became operational in December, comprising the Chairman of the Conference, as Chairman, as well as the incoming and outgoing Chairmen of the Conference, and the Secretary-General of the Conference, in the capacity of Chief Executive Officer.

### COMMUNITY COUNCIL OF MINISTERS

In October 1992 CARICOM heads of government agreed that a Caribbean Community Council of Ministers should be established to replace the existing Common Market Council of Ministers as the second highest organ of the Community. Protocol I amending the Treaty of Chaguaramas, to restructure the organs and institutions of the Community, was formally adopted at a meeting of CARICOM heads of government in February 1997 and was signed by all member states in July. The inaugural meeting of the Community Council of Ministers was held in Nassau, the Bahamas, in February 1998. The Council consists of ministers responsible for community affairs, as well as other government ministers designated by member states, and is responsible for the development of the Community's strategic planning and co-ordination in the areas of economic integration, functional co-operation and external relations.

### MINISTERIAL COUNCILS

The principal organs of the Community are assisted in their functions by the following bodies, established under Protocol I amending the Treaty of Chaguaramas: the Council for Trade and Economic Development (COTED); the Council for Foreign and Community Relations (COFCOR); the Council for Human and Social Development (COHSOD); and the Council for Finance and Planning (COFAP). The Councils are responsible for formulating policies, promoting their implementation and supervising co-operation in the relevant areas.

### SECRETARIAT

The Secretariat is the main administrative body of the Caribbean Community. The functions of the Secretariat are: to service meetings of the Community and of its Committees; to take appropriate follow-up action on decisions made at such meetings; to carry out studies on questions of economic and functional co-operation relating to the region as a whole; to provide services to member states at their request in respect of matters relating to the achievement of the objectives of the Community.

**Secretary-General:** Edwin W. Carrington (Trinidad and Tobago).

**Deputy Secretary-General:** Dr Carla Barnett (Belize).

## Activities

### REGIONAL INTEGRATION

In 1989 CARICOM heads of government established the 15-member West Indian Commission to study regional political and economic integration. The Commission's final report, submitted in July 1992, recommended that CARICOM should remain a community of sovereign states (rather than a federation), but should strengthen the integration process and expand to include the wider Caribbean region. It recommended the formation of an Association of Caribbean States (ACS), to include all the countries within and surrounding the Caribbean Basin (see p. 290). The Heads of Government Conference that was held in October 1992 established an Inter-Governmental Task Force, which was to undertake preparations for a reorientation of CARICOM. In February 1993 it presented a draft Charter of Civil Society for the Community, which set out principles in the areas of democracy, government, parliament, freedom of the press and human rights. The Charter was signed by Community heads of government in February 1997. Suriname was admitted to the organization in July 1995. In July 1997 the Heads of Government Conference agreed to admit Haiti as a member, although the terms and conditions of its accession to the organization had yet to be negotiated. In November the Secretaries-General of CARICOM and the ACS signed a Co-operation Agreement to formalize the reciprocal procedures through which the organizations work to enhance and facilitate regional integration.

In August 1998 CARICOM signed a free-trade accord with the Dominican Republic. The agreement, covering trade in goods and services, technical barriers to trade, government procurement, and sanitary and phytosanitary measures and standards, was to enter into effect on 1 January 1999. In November 1998, however, formal negotiations on the implementation of the agreement were suspended, and the date of the entry into force postponed, owing to differences regarding items to be excluded from the provisions of the accord.

In July 1999 CARICOM heads of government endorsed proposals to establish a Caribbean Court of Justice, which, it was provisionally agreed, would be located in Port of Spain, Trinidad and Tobago. The Court was intended to replace the Judicial Committee of the Privy Council as the Court of Final Appeal for those countries recognizing its jurisdiction, and was also to adjudicate on trade disputes and on the interpretation of the CARICOM Treaty.

### CO-ORDINATION OF FOREIGN POLICY

The co-ordination of foreign policies of member states is listed as one of the main objectives of the Community in its founding treaty. Activities include: strengthening of member states' position in international organizations; joint diplomatic action on issues of particular interest to the Caribbean; joint co-operation arrangements with third countries and organizations; and the negotiation of free-trade agreements with third countries and other regional groupings. This last area of activity has assumed increasing importance since the agreement in 1994 by almost all the governments of countries in the Americas to establish a 'Free Trade Area of the Americas' (FTAA) by 2005. In April 1997 CARICOM inaugurated a Regional Negotiating Machinery body to co-ordinate the region's external negotiations. The main focus of activities was to be the establishment of the FTAA, as well as other aspects of the forthcoming second summit meeting of the Americas (held in April 1998), ACP relations with the EU after the expiry of the Lomé IV Convention in 2000, and multilateral trade negotiations under the WTO.

In 1990 a working group was established with Brazil, Colombia and Venezuela to consider ways of developing regional economic co-operation, including greater self-sufficiency in food, joint exploration for mineral resources, joint trading policies, and co-operation in communications and transport systems. In July 1991 Venezuela applied for membership of CARICOM, and offered a non-reciprocal free-trade agreement for CARICOM exports to Venezuela, over an initial five-year period. In October 1993 the newly-established Group of Three (Colombia, Mexico and Venezuela) signed joint agreements with CARICOM and Suriname on combating drugs-trafficking and environmental protection. In June 1994 CARICOM and Colombia concluded an agreement on trade, economic and technical co-operation, which, *inter alia* gives special treatment to the least-developed CARICOM countries. CARICOM has observer status in the Latin American Rio Group (see p. 302).

In 1992 Cuba applied for observer status within CARICOM, and in July 1993 a joint commission was inaugurated to establish closer ties between CARICOM and Cuba. In July 1997 the heads of government agreed to pursue consideration of a free-trade accord between the Community and Cuba. In February 1992 ministers of foreign affairs from CARICOM and Central American states met to discuss future co-operation, in view of the imminent conclusion of the North American Free Trade Agreement (NAFTA, see p. 224) between the USA, Canada and Mexico. It was agreed that a consultative forum would be established to discuss the possible formation of a Caribbean and Central American free-trade zone. In October 1993 CARICOM declared its support for NAFTA, but requested a 'grace period', during which the region's exports would have parity with Mexican products, and in March 1994 requested that it should be considered for early entry into NAFTA. In July 1996 the heads of government expressed strong concern over the complaint lodged with the World Trade Organization (WTO) by the USA, Ecuador, Guatemala and Honduras regarding the European Union's import regime on bananas, which gives preferential access to bananas from the ACP countries (see the EU, p. 197). CARICOM requested the US Government to withdraw its complaint and to negotiate a settlement. Nevertheless, WTO panel hearings on the complaint were initiated in September. Banana producers from the ACP countries were granted third-party status, at the insistence of the Eastern Caribbean ambassador to the EU, Edwin Laurent. In December a special meeting of the Heads of Government Conference was convened, in Barbados, in order to formulate a common position on relations with the USA, in particular with respect to measures to combat illegal drugs-trafficking, following reports that the US Government was planning to impose punitive measures against certain regional authorities, owing to their perceived failure to implement effective controls on illicit drugs. The Conference confirmed the need for comprehensive co-operation and technical assistance to combat the problem, but warned that any adverse measures implemented by the USA would undermine CARICOM–US relations. The Conference decided to establish a Caribbean Security Task Force to help formulate a single regional agreement on maritime interdiction, incorporating agreements already concluded by individual members.

In May 1997 CARICOM heads of government met the US President, Bill Clinton, to discuss issues of mutual concern. A partnership for prosperity and security was established at the meeting, and arrangements were instituted for annual consultations between the ministers of foreign affairs of CARICOM countries and the US Secretary of State. However, the Community failed to secure a commitment by the USA to grant the region's exports 'NAFTA-parity' status, or to guarantee concessions to the region's banana industry, following a temporary ruling of the WTO, issued in March, upholding the US trade complaint. The WTO ruling was confirmed in May and endorsed by the WTO dispute settlement body in September. The USA's opposition to a new EU banana policy (which was to terminate the import licensing system, extending import quotas to 'dollar' producers, while maintaining a limited duty-free quota for Caribbean producers) was strongly criticized by CARICOM leaders, meeting in July 1998. In March 1999 the 10th Inter-Sessional meeting of the Conference of Heads of Government, held in Paramaribo, Suriname, issued a statement condemning the imposition by the USA of sanctions against a number of EU imports, in protest at the revised EU banana regime, and the consequences of this action on Caribbean economies, and agreed to review its co-operation with the USA under the partnership for prosperity and security.

In July 1998 heads of government expressed concern at the hostility between the Government and opposition groupings in Guyana. The two sides signed an agreement, under CARICOM auspices, and in September a CARICOM mediation mission visited Guyana to promote further dialogue. Also in 1998 CARICOM was particularly concerned by the movement within Nevis to secede from its federation with Saint Christopher. In July heads of government agreed to dispatch a mediation team to the country (postponed until September). The Heads of Government Conference held in March 1999 welcomed the establishment of a Constitutional Task Force by the local authorities to prepare a draft constitution, on the basis of recommendations of a previous constitutional commission and the outcome of a series of public meetings.

## ECONOMIC CO-OPERATION

The Caribbean Community's main field of activity is economic integration, by means of a Caribbean Common Market which replaced the former Caribbean Free Trade Association. The Secretariat and the Caribbean Development Bank carry out research on the best means of facing economic difficulties, and meetings of the Chief Executives of commercial banks and of central bank officials are also held with the aim of strengthening regional co-operation. In October 1998 the CARICOM Bureau requested an urgent assessment of the impact on the region of the financial and economic instability apparent in several major economies.

During the 1980s the economic difficulties of member states hindered the development of intra-regional trade. At the annual Conference held in June/July 1987, the heads of government agreed to dismantle all obstacles to trade within CARICOM by October 1988. This was implemented as planned, but a three-year period was permitted during which 17 products from the member countries of the Organisation of Eastern Caribbean States (OECS, see p. 292) would be allowed protection.

In July 1984 heads of government agreed to establish a common external tariff (CET) on certain products, in order to protect domestic industries, although implementation of the CET was considerably delayed (see below). They also urged the necessity of structural adjustment in the economies of the region, including measures to expand production and reduce imports. In 1989 the Conference of Heads of Government agreed to implement, by July 1993, a series of measures to encourage the creation of a single Caribbean market. These included the establishment of a CARICOM Industrial Programming Scheme; the bringing into operation of the CARICOM Enterprise Regime; abolition of passport requirements for CARICOM nationals travelling within the region; full implementation of the rules of origin and the revised scheme for the harmonization of fiscal incentives; free movement of skilled workers; removal of all remaining regional barriers to trade; establishment of a regional system of air and sea transport; and the introduction of a scheme for regional capital movement. In November 1989 a CARICOM Export Development Council was established, and undertook a three-year export development project to stimulate trade within CARICOM and to promote exports outside the region.

In August 1990 CARICOM heads of government mandated the governors of CARICOM members' central banks to begin a study of the means to achieve a monetary union within CARICOM; they also institutionalized meetings of CARICOM ministers of finance and senior finance officials, to take place twice a year.

The deadline of 1 January 1991 for the establishment of a CET was not achieved, and in July a new deadline of 1 October was set for those members which had not complied—Antigua and Barbuda, Belize, Montserrat, Saint Christopher and Nevis and Saint Lucia, whose governments feared that the tariff would cause an increase in the rate of inflation and damage domestic industries. This deadline was later (again unsuccessfully) extended to February 1992. The tariff, which imposed a maximum level of duty of 45% on imports (compared with a maximum rate of 20% imposed by members of the Andean Group and the Central American Common Market), was also criticized by the World Bank, the IMF and the US Government as being likely to reduce the region's competitiveness. At a special meeting, held in October 1992, CARICOM heads of government agreed to reduce the maximum level of tariffs to between 30% and 35%, to be in effect by 30 June 1993 (the level was to be further lowered, to 25%–30% by 1995). The Bahamas, however, was not party to these trading arrangements (since it is a member of the Community but not of the Common Market), and Belize was granted an extension for the implementation of the new tariff levels. At the Heads of Government Conference, held in July 1995 in Guyana, Suriname was admitted as a full member of CARICOM and acceded to the treaty establishing the common market. It was granted until 1 January 1996 for implementation of the tariff reductions.

The 1995 Heads of Government Conference approved additional measures to promote the single market. The free movement of skilled workers (mainly graduates from recognized regional institutions) was to be permitted from 1 January 1996. At the same time an agreement on the mutual protection and provision of social security benefits was to enter into force. The meeting also agreed to implement the 'open-sky' agreement enabling all CARICOM-owned and -controlled airlines to operate freely within the region.

In July 1996 the heads of government decided that CARICOM ministers of finance, central bank governors and planning agencies should meet more frequently to address single market issues and agreed to extend the provisions of free movement to sports people, musicians and others working in the arts and media. In July 1997 the heads of government, meeting in Montego Bay, Jamaica, agreed to accelerate economic integration, with the aim of completing a single market by 1999. It was noted that, as of 1 July 1997, all member states except Antigua and Barbuda had implemented the second phase of the CET, while four countries had implemented phase three, comprising a tariff of 0%–25%. At the meeting 11 member states signed Protocol II amending the Treaty of Chaguaramas, which constituted a central element of a CARICOM single market and economy, providing for the right to establish enterprises, the provision of services and the free movement of capital and labour throughout participating countries. By September 1999 13 member states had signed and provisionally applied Protocol II.

In July 1998, at the meeting of heads of government, held in St Lucia, an agreement was signed with the Insurance Company of the West Indies to accelerate the establishment of a Caribbean Investment Fund, which was to mobilize foreign currency from extra-regional capital markets for investment in new or existing enterprises in the region. Some 60% of all funds generated were to be used by CARICOM countries and the remainder by non-CARICOM members of the ACS. By July 1999 US $40m. had been mobilized for the fund, which was expected to become operational, with funds of $150m., by early 2000.

## INDUSTRY AND ENERGY

CARICOM aims to promote the development of joint ventures in exporting industries (particularly the woodwork, furniture, ceramics and foundry industries) through an agreement (reached in 1989) on an industrial programming scheme. Work on an investors' guide for each member state was completed in 1984. CARICOM's Export Development Council gives training and consultancy services to regional manufacturers. Regional manufacturers' exhibitions (CARIMEX) are held every three years. The Caribbean Trade Information System (CARTIS) comprises computer databases covering country and product profiles, trade statistics, trade opportunities, institutions and bibliographical information; it links the national trade centres of CARICOM members. A protocol relating to the CARICOM Industrial Programming Scheme (CIPS), approved in 1988, is the Community's instrument for promoting the co-operative development of industry in the region. Protocol III amending the Treaty of Chaguaramas, with respect to industrial policy, was opened for signature in July 1998. By September 1999 it had been signed by 11 member states.

The Secretariat has established a national standards bureau in each member country to harmonize technical standards, and supervises the metrication of weights and measures. In 1999 CARICOM members agreed to establish a new Regional Organization of Standards and Quality to develop common regional standards and resolve disputes.

The CARICOM Alternative Energy Systems Project provides training, assesses energy needs and conducts energy audits. Efforts in regional energy development are directed at the collection and analysis of data for national energy policy documents. A project document for the development of geothermal energy in the region was completed in 1990, and a reconnaissance study was started in the same year.

## TRANSPORT, COMMUNICATIONS AND TOURISM

A Caribbean Confederation of Shippers' Councils represents the interests of regional exporters and importers. In July 1990 the Caribbean Telecommunications Union was established to oversee developments in regional telecommunications.

In 1988 a Consultative Committee on Caribbean Regional Information Systems (CCCRIS) was established to evaluate and monitor the functioning of existing information systems and to seek to co-ordinate and advise on the establishment of new systems.

A Summit of Heads of Government on Tourism, Trade and Transportation was held in Trinidad and Tobago, in August 1995, to which all members of the ACS and regional tourism organizations were invited. In 1997 CARICOM heads of government considered a number of proposals relating to air transportation, tourism, human resource development and capital investment, which had been identified by Community ministers of tourism as critical issues in the sustainable development of the tourist industry. The heads of government requested ministers to meet regularly to develop tourism policies, and in particular to undertake an in-depth study of human resource development issues in early 1998. A new fund to help train young people from the region in aspects of the tourist industry was inaugurated in July 1997, in memory of the former Prime Minister of Jamaica, Michael Manley. In July 1999 heads of government signed Protocol VI amending the Treaty of Chaguaramas providing for a common transportation policy.

## AGRICULTURE

In 1985 the New Marketing Arrangements for Primary Agricultural Products and Livestock were instituted, with the aim of increasing the flow of agricultural commodities within the region. A computer-based Caribbean Agricultural Marketing Information System was initiated in 1987.

At the CARICOM summit meeting in July 1996 it was agreed to undertake wide-ranging measures in order to modernize the agricultural sector and to increase the international competitiveness of Caribbean agricultural produce. The CARICOM Secretariat was to support national programmes with assistance in policy formulation, human resource development and the promotion of research and technology development in the areas of productivity, marketing, agri-business and water resources management. During 1997 CARICOM Governments continued to lobby against a complaint lodged at the WTO with regard to the EU's banana import regime (offering favourable conditions to ACP producers—see above) and to generate awareness of the economic and social importance of the banana industry to the region. Protocol V amending the Treaty of Chaguaramas, which was concerned with agricultural policy, was opened for signature by heads of government in July 1998. By September 1999 it had been signed and provisionally applied by 11 member states.

## HEALTH AND EDUCATION

In 1986 CARICOM and the Pan-American Health Organization launched 'Caribbean Co-operation in Health' with projects to be undertaken in six main areas: environmental protection, including the control of disease-bearing pests; development of human resources; chronic non-communicable diseases and accidents; strengthening health systems; food and nutrition; maternal and child health care; and population activities. In early 1996 the Japanese Government approved a loan of US $0.5m. to assist CARICOM in the implementation of a health care programme aimed at children. A Caribbean Environmental Health Institute (see below) aims to promote collaboration among member states in all areas of environmental management and human health.

CARICOM educational programmes have included the improvement of reading in schools through assistance for teacher-training; and ensuring the availability of low-cost educational material throughout the region. A strategy for developing and improving technical and vocational education and training within each member state and throughout the region was completed and published in 1990. In July 1997 CARICOM heads of government adopted the recommendations of a ministerial committee, which identified priority measures for implementation in the education sector. These included the objective of achieving universal, quality secondary education and the enrolment of 15% of post-secondary students in tertiary education by 2005, as well as improved training in foreign languages and science and technology.

## EMERGENCY ASSISTANCE

A Caribbean Disaster Emergency Response Agency (CDERA) was established in 1991 to co-ordinate immediate disaster relief, primarily in the event of hurricanes (see Institutions below). During 1997 CARICOM Governments remained actively concerned with the situation in Montserrat, which had suffered a series of massive volcanic eruptions. At the Heads of Government Conference in July, the Community pledged humanitarian, economic and technical assistance and resolved to help mobilize external assistance from regional and international donor countries and institutions. In March 1998 CARICOM heads of government agreed to establish a team, comprising representatives of the CARICOM secretariat, CDERA and the Caribbean Development Bank, to assist the Montserrat Government in formulating programmes to provide a secure future for the island. In November the Community determined to support the countries of Central America in their reconstruction and rehabilitation efforts following the devastation caused by 'Hurricane Mitch', and to co-ordinate the provision of immediate humanitarian assistance by CARICOM member countries.

## INSTITUTIONS

The following are among the institutions formally established within the framework of CARICOM.

**Assembly of Caribbean Community Parliamentarians:** c/o CARICOM Secretariat; an intergovernmental agreement on the establishment of a regional parliament entered into force in August 1994; inaugural meeting held in Barbados, in May 1996. Comprises up to four representatives of the parliaments of each member country, and up to two of each associate member. It aims to provide a forum for wider community involvement in the process of integration and for enhanced deliberation on CARICOM affairs; authorized to issue recommendations for the Conference of Heads of Government and to adopt resolutions on any matter arising under the Treaty of Chaguaramas.

**Caribbean Agricultural Research and Development Institute—CARDI:** UWI Campus, St Augustine, Trinidad and Tobago; tel. 645-1205; fax 645-1208; e-mail infocentre@cardi.org; internet www.cardi.org; f. 1975; aims to support the development of profitable and sustainable business systems and enterprises through its scientific, technological and information activities; provides training, a Caribbean agricultural information service, and technology and business advisory services. Exec. Dir HAYDEN BLADES. Publs *CARDI Update, Procicaribe News, CARDI Annual Report*, technical bulletin series.

**Caribbean Centre for Development Administration—CARICAD:** ICB Bldg, Roebuck St, St Michael, Barbados; tel. 4278535; fax 4361709; e-mail caricad@caribsurf.com; f. 1980; aims to assist governments in the reform of the public sector and to strengthen their managerial capacities for public administration; promotes the involvement of the private sector, non-governmental organizations and other bodies in all decision-making processes. Exec. Dir Dr I. GOMES.

**Caribbean Disaster Emergency Response Agency—CDERA:** The Garrison, St Michael, Barbados; tel. 436-9651; fax 437-7649; e-mail cdera@caribsurf.com; internet www.cdera.org. For activities, see Emergency Assistance above. Regional Co-ordinator JEREMY COLLYMORE.

**Caribbean Environmental Health Institute—CEHI:** POB 1111, The Morne, Castries, St Lucia; tel. 4522501; fax 4532721; e-mail cehi@candw.lc; internet www.cehi.org.lc; f. 1980 (began operations in 1982); provides technical and advisory services to member states in formulating environmental health policy legislation and in all areas of environmental management (for example, solid waste management, water supplies, beach and air pollution, and pesticides control); promotes, collates and disseminates relevant research; conducts courses, seminars and workshops throughout the region. Exec. Dir VINCENT SWEENEY.

**Caribbean Food and Nutrition Institute:** UWI Campus, St Augustine, Trinidad and Tobago; tel. 662-7025; fax 662-5511; f. 1967 to serve the governments and people of the region and to act as a catalyst among persons and organizations concerned with food and nutrition through research and field investigations, training in nutrition, dissemination of information, advisory services and production of educational material. Mems: all English-speaking Caribbean territories, including the mainland countries of Belize and Guyana. Dir Dr FITZROY HENRY. Publs *Cajanus* (quarterly), *Nyam News* (monthly), *Nutrient-Cost Tables* (quarterly), educational material.

**Caribbean Food Corporation—CFC:** 30 Queen's Park West, Post Office Bag 264B, Port of Spain, Trinidad and Tobago; tel. 622-5827; fax 622-4430; e-mail cfc@trinidad-net; f. 1976 (began operations in 1979); implements joint-venture projects with investors from the private and public sectors to enhance regional food self-sufficiency and reduce the need for food imports. Man. Dir E. C. CLYDE PARRIS.

**Caribbean Meteorological Organization:** POB 461, Port of Spain, Trinidad and Tobago; tel. 624-4481; fax 623-3634; e-mail cebcmo@carib-link.net; f. 1951 to co-ordinate regional activities in meteorology, operational hydrology and allied sciences; became an associate institution of CARICOM in 1983. Comprises a headquarters unit, a Council of Government Ministers, the Caribbean Meteorological Foundation and the Caribbean Institute of Meteorology and Hydrology, located in Barbados. Mems: govts of 16 countries and territories represented by the National Meteorological and Hydrometeorological Services. Co-ordinating Dir T. W. SUTHERLAND.

### ASSOCIATE INSTITUTIONS

**Caribbean Development Bank:** POB 408, Wildey, St Michael, Barbados; tel. 431-1600; fax 426-7269; e-mail info@caribank.org; internet www.caribank.org; f. 1969 to stimulate regional economic growth through support for agriculture, industry, transport and other infrastructure, tourism, housing and education; subscribed cap. US $566.7m. (1998). In 1998 net approvals totalled $121.8m.; at the end of 1998 grant and loan disbursements totalled $1,162.3m. The Special Development Fund was replenished in 1996. Mems: CARICOM states, and Anguilla, Canada, Cayman Islands, the People's Republic of China, Colombia, France, Germany, Italy, Mexico, United Kingdom, Venezuela. Pres. Sir NEVILLE NICHOLLS.

**Caribbean Law Institute:** University of the West Indies, Cave Hill Campus, POB 64, Bridgetown, Barbados; tel. 417-4560; fax 417-4138.

Other Associate Institutions of CARICOM, in accordance with its constitution, are the University of Guyana and the University of the West Indies.

## Publication

*Annual Report.*

# CENTRAL AMERICAN INTEGRATION SYSTEM

## (SISTEMA DE LA INTEGRACIÓN CENTROAMERICANA—SICA)

**Address:** blvd de la Orden de Malta 470, Santa Elena, Antiguo Cuscatlán, San Salvador, El Salvador.

**Telephone:** 289-6131; **fax:** 289-6124; **e-mail:** sgsica@sicanet.org.sv; **internet:** www.sicanet.org.sv.

Founded in December 1991, when the heads of state of six Central American countries signed the Protocol of Tegucigalpa to the agreement establishing the Organization of Central American States (f. 1951), creating a new framework for regional integration. A General Secretariat of the Sistema de la Integración Centroamericana (SICA) was inaugurated in February 1993 to co-ordinate the process of political, economic, social cultural and environmental integration and to promote democracy and respect for human rights throughout the region.

### MEMBERS

| | | |
|---|---|---|
| Costa Rica | Guatemala | Nicaragua |
| El Salvador | Honduras | Panama |

### OBSERVERS

| | |
|---|---|
| Belize | Dominican Republic |

## Organization

(January 2000)

### SUMMIT MEETINGS

The meetings of heads of state of member countries serve as the supreme decision-making organ of SICA.

### COUNCIL OF MINISTERS

Ministers of Foreign Affairs of member states meet regularly to provide policy direction for the process of integration.

### CONSULTATIVE COMMITTEE

The Committee comprises representatives of business organizations, trade unions, academic instituions and other federations concerned with the process of integration in the region. It is an integral element of the integration system and assits the Secretary-General in determining the policies of the organization.

### GENERAL SECRETARIAT

The General Secretariat of SICA was established in February 1993 to co-ordinate the process of enhanced regional integration. It comprises the following divisions: inter-institutional relations; research and co-operation; legal and political affairs; economic affairs; and communications and information.

In September 1997 CACM heads of state, meeting in the Nicaraguan capital, signed the Managua Declaration in support of further regional integration and the establishment of a political union. A commission was to be established to consider all aspects of the policy and to formulate a timetable for the integration process. In February 1998 SICA heads of state resolved to establish a Unified General Secretariat to integrate the institutional aspects of SICA (see below) in a single office, to be located in San Salvador. The process was ongoing in 1999.

**Secretary-General:** ERNESTO LEAL SÁNCHEZ (Nicaragua).

### SPECIALIZED TECHNICAL SECRETARIATS

**Secretaría Ejecutiva de la Comisión Centroamericana de Ambiente y Desarrollo:** blvd de la Orden de Malta 470, Santa

Elena, Antiguo Cuscatlán, San Salvador, El Salvador; tel. 289-6131; fax 289-6124; internet www.ccad.org.gt; f. 1989 to enhance collaboration in the promotion of sustainable development and environmental protection. Exec. Sec. MAURICIO CASTRO.

**Secretaría General de la Coordinación Educativa y Cultural Centroamericana:** 175m. norte de la esquina oeste del ICE, Sabana Norte, San José, Costa Rica; tel. 232-3783; fax 231-2366; f. 1982; promotes development of regional programmes in the fields of education and culture. Sec.-Gen. MERVIN HERRERA ARAYA.

**Secretaría Permanente del Tratado General de Integración Económica Centroamericana—SIECA:** 4a Avda 10–25, Zona 14, Apdo Postal 1237, 01901 Guatemala City, Guatemala; tel. (2) 3682151; fax (2) 3681071; e-mail sieca@pronet.net.gt; internet www.sieca.org; f. 1960 to assist the process of economic integration and the establishment of a Central American Common Market (see below). Sec.-Gen. HAROLDO RODAS MELGAR.

**Secretaría Técnica del Consejo de Integración Social—SISCA:** blvd de la Orden de Malta 470, Santa Elena, Antiguo Cuscatlán, San Salvador, El Salvador; tel. 289-6131; fax 289-6124; Dir-Gen. Dr HUGO MORGADO.

## OTHER SPECIALIZED SECRETARIATS

**Dirección General de Turismo de la Secretaria General del SICA:** blvd de la Orden de Malta 470, Santa Elena, Antiguo Cuscatlán, San Salvador, El Salvador; tel. 289-6131; fax 289-6124; e-mail econtreras@sicanet.org.sv; Sec.-Gen. EDGARDO CONTRERAS SCHNEIDER.

**Secretaría del Consejo Agropecuario Centroamericano:** Apdo Postal 55-2200 Coronado, Costa Rica; tel. 216-0303; fax 216-0285; e-mail rguillen@iica.ac.cr; f. 1991 to determine and co-ordinate regional policies and programmes relating to agriculture and agro-industry. Sec-Gen. ROGER GUILLEN BUSTOS.

**Secretaría Ejecutiva del Consejo Monetario Centroamericano—CMCA** (Central American Monetary Council): Apdo 5438-, 1000 San José, Costa Rica; tel. 233-6044; fax 221-5643; e-mail secma@sol.racsa.co.cr; internet www.cmca.or.ca; f. 1964 by the presidents of Central American central banks, to co-ordinate monetary policies. Exec. Sec. MANUEL FONTECHA FERRARI. Publs *Boletín Estadístico* (annually), *Informe Económico* (annually).

**Secretaría Ejecutiva de la Comisión Centroamericana de Transporte Marítimo—COCATRAM:** Cine Cabrera 2c. arriba y 2½ al sur, Apdo 2423, Managua, Nicaragua; tel. (2) 222754; fax (2) 222759; e-mail cocatram@ibw.com.ni; f. 1981; Exec. Sec. LIANA ZÚÑIGA DE CÁCERES.

## PARLIAMENT

**Address:** 12a Avda 33-04, Zona 5, Guatemala City, Guatemala.

**Telephone:** (2) 339-0466; **fax:** (2) 334-6670; **e-mail:** cdpar@parlacen.org.gt; **internet:** www.parlacen.org.gt.

Founded 1989 within the framework of the Central American Common Market. Comprises representatives of El Salvador, Guatemala, Honduras, Nicaragua and Panama. In February 1998 heads of state of member countries resolved to limit the number of deputies to 10–15 from each country.

**President:** JOSÉ ERNESTO SOMARRIBA SOSA (Nicaragua).

## COURT OF JUSTICE

**Address:** Kilómetro 17½ carretera norte, contiguo a la TANIC, Managua, Nicaragua.

**Telephone:** 233-2128; **fax:** 233-2135; **e-mail:** cortecen@tmx.com.ni; **internet:** www.ccj.org.ni.

Tribunal authorized to consider disputes relating to treaties agreed within the regional integration system. In February 1998 Central American heads of state agreed to limit the number of magistrates in the Court to one per country.

## *AD HOC* INTERGOVERNMENTAL SECRETARIATS

**Comisión para el Desarrollo Científico y Tecnológico de Centroamérica y Panamá** (Comission for the Scientific and Technological Development of Central America and Panama): Apdo Postal 4458, Col Palmira, Avda República de Brasil 2231, Tegucigalpa, Honduras; tel. and fax 232-5669; f. 1976; Pres. GERARDO ZEPEDA.

**Consejo Centroamericano de Instituciones de Seguridad Social—COCISS:** Apdo Postal 1649, Frente al Catastro, Managua, tel. 249-6663; fax 249-0418; f. 1992; Pres. Dr MARIANELA MORALES.

**Consejo del Istmo Centroamericano de Deportes y Recreación:** 5009-1000 San José, Costa Rica; tel. 257-8770; fax 227-5003; f. 1992; Pres. HILDA GONZÁLEZ.

**Secretaría Ejecutiva del Consejo Centroamericana de Vivienda y Asentamientos Humanos** (Central American Council on Housing and Human Settlements): Avda la Paz 244, Tegucigalpa, Honduras; tel. 236-5804; fax 236-6560; f. 1992; Dir CONCEPCIÓN RAMOS.

**Secretaría Ejecutiva del Consejo de Electrificación de América Central:** Apdo Postal 10032, San José, Costa Rica; tel. 220-7562; fax 220-8232; e-mail ceac@ns.ice.go.cr; f. 1985; Dir LUIS BUJÁN.

## OTHER REGIONAL INSTITUTIONS

### Finance

**Banco Centroamericano de Integración Económica—BCIE** (Central American Bank for Economic Integration): Apdo Postal 772, Tegucigalpa, Honduras; tel. 228-2243; fax 228-2185; f. 1961 to promote the economic integration and balanced economic development of member countries; finances public and private development projects, particularly those related to industrialization and infrastructure. By June 1993 cumulative lending amounted to US $3,217m., mainly for roads, hydroelectricity projects, housing and telecommunications. Auth. cap. $2,000m. Pres. JOSÉ MANUEL PACAS. Publs *Annual Report, Revista de la Integración y el Desarrollo de Centroamérica*.

### Public Administration

**Centro de Coordinación para la Prevención de Desastres Naturales en América Central:** Apdo Postal 6-3232, Calle Arzobispo Makarios III, La Alameda, Edif. SEVENM 2, El Dorado, Panama; tel. 2361680; fax 2361393; e-mail cepreden@sinfo.net; Dir LUIS ROLANDO DURÁN VARGAS.

**Comisión Centroamericana Permanente para la Erradicación de la Producción, Tráfico, Consumo y Uso Ilícitos de Estupefacientes y Sustancias Psicotrópicas—CCP:** Edif. de Comisiones, 1°, Tegucigalpa, Honduras; tel. and fax 238-3960. Pres. Dr CARLOS SOSA COELLO.

**Instituto Centroamericano de Administración Pública—ICAP** (Central American Institute of Public Administration): POB 10025-1000, De la Heladería Pops en Curridabat 100 mts sur y 50 oeste, San José, Costa Rica; tel. 234-1011; fax 225-2049; e-mail icapcr@sol.racsa.co.cr; internet www.icap.ac.cr; f. 1954 by the five Central American Republics and the United Nations, with later participation by Panama. The Institute aims to train the region's public servants, provide technical assistance and carry out research leading to reforms in public administration. Dir Dr HUGO ZELAYA CÁLIX.

**Secretaría Ejecutiva de la Comisión Regional de Recursons Hidráulicos:** Apdo Postal 21-2300, Curridabat, San José, Costa Rica; tel. 231-5791; fax 296-0047; e-mail crrher@sol.racas.co.cr; f. 1962; Exec. Dir ELADIO ZÁRATE.

### Education and Health

**Comité Coordinador Regional de Instituciones de Agua Potable y Saneamiento de Centro América, Panamá y República Dominicana—CAPRE:** Avda Central, Calles 3 y 5, Edif. la Llancuna 15°, Apdo Postal 5120-1000, San José, Costa Rica; tel. 257-6054; fax 222-3941; e-mail capregtz@sol.racsa.co.cr; Dir ILIANA ARCE UMAÑA.

**Confederación Universitaria Centroamericana** (Central American University Confederation): Apdo 37, Ciudad Universitaria Rodrigo Facio, 2060 San José, Costa Rica; tel. 225-2744; fax 234-0071; e-mail secretaria@sp.csuca.ac.cr; internet www.csuca.ac.cr; f. 1948 to guarantee academic, administrative and economic autonomy for universities and to encourage regional integration of higher education; maintains libraries and documentation centres; Council of 32 mems. Mems: 16 universities, in Belize, Costa Rica (four), El Salvador, Guatemala, Honduras (two), Nicaragua (four) and Panama (three). Sec.-Gen. Dr RICARDO SOL ARRIAZA (El Salvador). Publs *Estudios Sociales Centroamericanas* (quarterly), *Cuadernos de Investigación* (monthly), *Carta Informativa de la Secretaría General* (monthly).

**Instituto de Nutrición de Centroamérica y Panamá—INCAP** (Institute of Nutrition of Central America and Panama): Apdo 1188, Carretera Roosevelt, Zona 11, 01901 Guatemala City, Guatemala; tel. (2) 4723762; fax (2) 4736529; e-mail hdelgado@incap.org.gt; f. 1949 to promote the development of nutritional sciences and their application and to strengthen the technical capacity of member countries to reach food and nutrition security; provides training and technical assistance for nutrition education and planning; conducts applied research; disseminates information. Maintains library (including about 600 periodicals). Administered by the Pan American Health Organization (PAHO) and the World Health Organization. Mems: CACM mems and Belize and Panama. Dir Dr HERNÁN L. DELGADO. Publ. Annual Report.

**Organismo Internacional Regional de Sanidad Agropecuaria—OIRSA** (International Regional Organization of Plant Protection and Animal Health): Calle Ramón Belloso, Final Pasaje Isolde, Col Escalón, Apdo Postal 61, San Salvador, El Salvador; tel. 263-

1123; fax 263-1128; e-mail oirsa@ns1.oirsa.org.sv; internet www.ns1.oirsa.org.sv; f. 1953 for the prevention of the introduction of animal and plant pests and diseases unknown in the region; research, control and eradication programmes of the principal pests present in agriculture; technical assistance and advice to the ministries of agriculture and livestock of member countries; education and qualification of personnel. Mems: Belize, Costa Rica, Dominican Republic, El Salvador, Guatemala, Honduras, Mexico, Nicaragua, Panama. Exec. Dir Dr CELIO HUMBERTO BARRETO.

### Transport and Communications

**Comisión Centroamericana de Ferrocarriles—COCAFER** (Central American Railways Commission): c/o SIECA, 4A Avda 10–25, Zona 14, Apdo Postal 1237, 01901 Guatemala City, Guatemala; tel. (2) 368-2151; fax (2) 368-1071.

**Comisión Técnica de las Telecomunicaciones de Centroamérica—COMTELCA** (Technical Commission for Telecommunications in Central America): Apdo 1793, Tegucigalpa, Honduras; tel. 220-6666; fax 220-1197; e-mail dgeneral@comtelca.hn; internet www.comtelca.hn; f. 1966 to co-ordinate and improve the regional telecommunications network. Dir-Gen. HÉCTOR L. RODRÍGUEZ MILLA.

**Corporación Centroamericana de Servicios de Navegación Aérea—COCESNA** (Central American Air Navigation Service Corporation): Apdo 660, Aeropuerto de Toncontín, Tegucigalpa, Honduras; tel. 233-1143; fax 233-1219; e-mail gergral@cocesna.hn; f. 1960; offers radar air traffic control services, aeronautical telecommunications services, flight inspections and radio assistance services for air navigation; administers the Central American Aeronautical School. Gen. Man. EDUARDO MARÍN J.

# Central American Common Market—CACM (Mercado Común Centroamericano)

CACM was established by the Organization of Central American States under the General Treaty of Central American Economic Integration (Tratado General de Integración Económica Centroamericana) signed in Managua on 13 December 1960. It was ratified by all countries by September 1963. It now forms a subsystem of the Sistema de la Integración Centroamericana (SICA, see above).

### MEMBERS

| | | |
|---|---|---|
| Costa Rica | El Salvador | Nicaragua |
| Guatemala | Honduras | |

## Organization

(January 2000)

### MINISTERIAL MEETINGS

The organization's policy is formulated by regular meetings of the Council of Ministers for Economic Integration (COMIECO), meetings of other ministers, and of presidents of central banks, also play an important part.

### PERMANENT SECRETARIAT

**Secretaría Permanente del Tratado General de Integración Económica Centroamericana—SIECA:** provides institutional support for the Common Market, supervises the correct implementation of the legal instruments of economic integration, carries out relevant studies at the request of the Common Market authorities, and arranges meetings. There are departments covering the working of the Common Market; negotiations and external trade policy; external co-operation; systems and statistics; finance and administration. There is also a unit for co-operation with the private sector and finance institutions and a legal consultative committee.

## Activities

The General Treaty envisaged the eventual liberalization of intra-regional trade and the establishment of a free-trade area and a customs union. Economic integration in the region, however, has been hampered by ideological differences between governments, difficulties in internal supply, protectionist measures by overseas markets, external and intra-regional debts, adverse rates of exchange and high interest rates. Regular meetings of senior customs officials aim to increase co-operation, to develop a uniform terminology, and to recommend revisions of customs legislation. CACM member-countries also aim to pursue a common policy in respect of international trade agreements on commodities, raw materials and staples.

Under the Convention for Fiscal Incentives for Industrial Development, which came into operation in 1969, a wide range of tax benefits are applied to various categories of industries in the region, to encourage productivity. SIECA carries out studies on the industrial sector, compiles statistics, and provides information to member governments. It also analyses energy consumption in the region and assists governments in drawing up energy plans, aiming to reduce dependence on imported petroleum.

A co-ordinating commission supervises the marketing of four basic crops (maize, rice, beans and sorghum), recording and forecasting production figures and recommending minimum guarantee prices. Information on other crops is also compiled. A permanent commission for agricultural research and extension services monitors and co-ordinates regional projects in this field.

An agreement to establish a Central American Monetary Union was signed in 1964, with the eventual aim of establishing a common currency and aligning foreign exchange and monetary policies. The Central American Monetary Council, comprising the presidents of the member states' central banks, meets regularly to consider monetary policy and financial affairs. A Fund for Monetary Stabilization provides short-term financial assistance to members facing temporary balance-of-payments difficulties.

Trade within the region increased in value from US $33m. in 1960 to $1,129m. in 1980, but subsequently diminished every year until 1986, when it amounted to $406m. The decline was due to a number of factors: low prices for the region's main export commodities, and heavy external debts, both resulting in a severe shortage of foreign exchange, and intra-regional trade 'freezes' provoked by debts amounting to $700m. at mid-1986 (Guatemala and Costa Rica being the chief creditors, and Nicaragua and El Salvador the main debtors). In January 1986 a new CACM tariff and customs agreement came into effect, imposing standard import duties for the whole region (aimed at discouraging the import of non-essential goods from outside the region), and a uniform tariff nomenclature. Honduras, however, continued to insist on bilateral tariff agreements with other member countries. Honduras subsequently signed a temporary free-trade agreement with all the other member states. From 1987 intra-regional trade increased steadily and reached an estimated $1,840m. in 1997.

In June 1990 the presidents of the five CACM countries signed a declaration welcoming peace initiatives in El Salvador, Guatemala and Nicaragua, and appealing for a revitalization of CACM, as a means of promoting lasting peace in the region. In December the presidents committed themselves to the creation of an effective common market, proposing the opening of negotiations on a comprehensive regional customs and tariffs policy by March 1991, and the introduction of a regional 'anti-dumping' code by December 1991. They requested the support of multilateral lending institutions through investment in regional development, and the cancellation or rescheduling of member countries' debts.

In February 1993 the European Community (EC) signed a new framework co-operation agreement with the CACM member states extending the programme of economic assistance and political dialogue initiated in 1984; a further co-operation agreement with the European Union (as the EC had become) was signed in early 1996.

In October 1993 the presidents of the CACM countries and Panama signed a protocol to the 1960 General Treaty, committing themselves to full economic integration in the region (with a common external tariff of 20% for finished products and 5% for raw materials and capital goods) and creating conditions for increased free trade. The countries agreed to accelerate the removal of internal non-tariff barriers, but no deadline was set. Full implementation of the protocol was to be 'voluntary and gradual', owing to objections on the part of Costa Rica and Panama. In May 1994, however, Costa Rica committed itself to full participation in the protocol. In March 1995 a meeting of the Central American Monetary Council discussed and endorsed a reduction in the tariff levels from 20% to 15% and from 5% to 1%. However, efforts to adopt this as a common policy were hindered by the implementation of these tariff levels by El Salvador on a unilateral basis, from 1 April, and the subsequent modifications by Guatemala and Costa Rica of their external tariffs.

In May 1997 the heads of state of CACM member countries, together with the Prime Minister of Belize, conferred with the US President, Bill Clinton, in San José, Costa Rica. The leaders resolved to establish a Trade and Investment Council to promote trade relations; however, Clinton failed to endorse a request from CACM members that their products receive preferential access to US markets, on similar terms to those from Mexico agreed under the NAFTA accord. During the year the Central American Governments pursued negotiations to conclude free-trade agreements with Mexico, Panama and the members of the Caribbean Community and Common Market (CARICOM). Nicaragua signed a bilateral accord with Mexico in December (Costa Rica already having done so in 1994). In November 1997, at a special summit meeting of CACM heads of state, an agreement was reached with the President of the Dominican Republic to initiate a gradual process of incorporating that country into the process of Central American integration, with the aim of promoting sustainable development throughout the region. The first sectors for increased co-operation between the two sides were to be tourism, health, investment promotion and air transport. A free-trade accord with the Dominican Republic was concluded in April 1998, and formally signed in November.

In November 1998 Central American heads of state held an emergency summit meeting to consider the devastation in the region caused by 'Hurricane Mitch'. The Presidents urged international creditors to write off the region's estimated debts of US $16,000m. to assist in the economic recovery of the countries worst-affected. They also reiterated requests for preferential treatment for the region's exports within the NAFTA framework. In October 1999 heads of state adopted a strategic framework to strengthen the capacity for the physical, social, economic and environmental infrastructure of Central American countries to withstand the impact of natural disasters. In particular, programmes for the integrated management and conservation of water resources, and for the prevention of forest fires were to be implemented.

## Publications

*Anuario Estadístico Centroamericano de Comercio Exterior.*

*Carta Informativa* (monthly).

*Cuadernos de la SIECA* (2 a year).

*Estadísticas Macroeconómicas de Centroamérica* (annually).

*Series Estadísticas Seleccionadas de Centroamérica* (annually).

# COMMON MARKET FOR EASTERN AND SOUTHERN AFRICA—COMESA

**Address:** COMESA Centre, Ben Bella Rd, POB 30051, 10101 Lusaka, Zambia.

**Telephone:** (1) 229726; **fax:** (1) 225107; **e-mail:** comesa@comesa.zm; **internet:** www.comesa.int.

COMESA was formally inaugurated in 1994 as a successor to the Preferential Trade Area for Eastern and Southern Africa (PTA), which was established in 1981.

### MEMBERS

| | |
|---|---|
| Angola | Mauritius |
| Burundi | Namibia |
| Comoros | Rwanda |
| Congo, Democratic Republic | Seychelles |
| Djibouti | Sudan |
| Egypt | Swaziland |
| Eritrea | Tanzania* |
| Ethiopia | Uganda |
| Kenya | Zambia |
| Madagascar | Zimbabwe |
| Malawi | |

* In July 1999 announced intention to withdraw membership.

## Organization

(January 2000)

### AUTHORITY

The Authority of the Common Market is the supreme policy organ of COMESA, comprising heads of state or of government of member countries. The inaugural meeting of the Authority took place in Lilongwe, Malawi, in December 1994. The second summit meeting was held in Lusaka, Zambia, in April 1997, the third in Kinshasa, Democratic Republic of the Congo, in June 1998, and the fourth was held in Nairobi, Kenya, in May 1999.

### COUNCIL OF MINISTERS

Each member government appoints a minister to participate in the Council. The Council monitors COMESA activities, including supervision of the Secretariat, recommends policy direction and development, and reports to the Authority.

A Committee of Governors of Central Banks advises the Authority and the Council of Ministers on monetary and financial matters.

### COURT OF JUSTICE

The COMESA treaty envisaged the establishment of a sub-regional Court of Justice, to replace the former PTA Tribunal, with authority to settle disputes between member states and to adjudicate on matters concerning the interpretation of the treaty. In June 1998 COMESA heads of state announced the appointment of seven judges to serve in the Court.

**President:** JOSEPHAT KANYWANYI (Tanzania).

### SECRETARIAT

In 1998 the administrative structure of COMESA was undergoing a process of restructuring, according to which the existing 12 divisional areas were to be consolidated into the following four divisions: Trade, customs and monetary affairs; Investment promotion and private sector development; Infrastructure development; and Information.

**Secretary-General:** J. E. O. MWENCHA (Kenya).

## Activities

The COMESA treaty was signed by member states of the PTA in November 1993 and was scheduled to come into effect on being ratified by 10 countries. COMESA formally succeeded the PTA in December 1994 (by which time it had received 12 ratifications), with the aim of strengthening the process of regional economic integration that had been initiated under the PTA, in order to help member states achieve sustainable economic growth.

COMESA aims to establish a free-trade area by 31 October 2000, requiring full liberalization of trading practices, including the elimination of non-tariff barriers, to ensure the free movement of goods, services and capital within the Common Market. In April 1997 COMESA heads of state agreed that a common external tariff would be implemented by 2004, to strengthen the establishment of a regional customs union, with a zero tariff on products originating from within the Common Market. COMESA aimed to formulate a common investment procedure to promote domestic, cross-border and direct foreign investment by ensuring the free movement of capital, services and labour. In April 1999 12 countries were reported to have reduced tariff rates on goods originating within the Common Market by 60%–90%. In May heads of state agreed to establish a Free Trade Area Committee, comprising representatives of the Democratic Republic of the Congo, Egypt, Kenya, Malawi, Mauritius, Uganda, Zambia and Zimbabwe, to facilitate and co-ordinate preparations for the establishment of the free-trade zone.

The PTA aimed to facilitate intra-regional trade by establishing a clearing house to deal with credit arrangements and balance of payments issues. The clearing house became operational in February 1984 using the unit of account of the PTA (UAPTA) as its currency. (The UAPTA was valued at the rate of the IMF special drawing rights.) The clearing house, based in Harare, Zimbabwe, remained an integral part of the COMESA infrastructure, although its role was diminished by the liberalisation of foreign exchange markets in the majority of member countries. In April 1997 the Authority endorsed a proposal to replace UAPTA with a COMESA dollar (CMD), to be equivalent to the value of the US currency. An Automated System of Customs Data (ASYCUDA) has been established to facilitate customs administration in all COMESA member states. Through support for capacity-building activities and the establishment of other specialized institutions (see below) COMESA aims to reinforce its objectives of regional integration. Preparations for the establishment of a COMESA Telecommunications Company were underway in 1999.

Co-operation programmes have been implemented by COMESA in the industrial, agricultural, energy and transport and communications sectors. A regional food security programme aimed to ensure adequate food supplies at all times. In 1997 COMESA Heads of State advocated that the food sector be supported by the immediate implementation of an irrigation action plan for the region. The organization also supports the establishment of common agricultural standards and phytosanitary regulations throughout the region in order to stimulate trade in food crops. Other initiatives include a road customs declaration document, a regional customs bond guarantee scheme, third party motor vehicle insurance scheme and travellers cheques in the UAPTA unit of currency. A Trade Information Network, established under the PTA to disseminate information on the production and marketing of goods manufactured and traded in the region, was scheduled to be transformed into the COMESA Information Network (COMNET). The first meeting of representatives of business communities in COMESA countries was held in November 1997, and the first COMESA trade fair was held in Nairobi, Kenya, in May 1999.

Since its establishment there have been concerns on the part of member states, as well as other regional non-member countries, in particular South Africa, of adverse rivalry between COMESA and the Southern African Development Community (SADC, q.v.) and of a duplication of roles. In December 1996 and January 1997 respectively, Lesotho and Mozambique suspended their membership of COMESA and announced their intention to withdraw from the organization owing to concerns that their continued participation in COMESA was incompatible with their SADC membership. Lesotho subsequently terminated its membership. In July 1999 Tanzania declared its intention to withdraw from COMESA, reportedly in opposition to further proposed tariff reductions.

### COMESA INSTITUTIONS

**COMESA Association of Commercial Banks:** 101 Union Ave, POB 2940, Harare, Zimbabwe; tel. (4) 793911; fax (4) 730819; aims to strengthen co-operation between banks in the region; organizes training activities; conducts studies to harmonize banking laws and operations. Mems: commercial banking orgs in Burundi, Kenya, Malawi, Sudan, Tanzania, Uganda.

**COMESA Leather and Leather Products Institute—LLPI:** POB 5538, Addis Ababa, Ethiopia; tel (1) 510361; fax (1) 615755; e-mail comesa.llpi@telecom.net.et; internet www.leathernet.com/comesa/llpi; f. 1990 as the PTA Leather Institute. Mems: Govts of 17 COMESA mem. states; Dir Dr Robert Arunga.

**COMESA Metallurgical Technology Centre:** c/o 101 Union Ave, Harare, Zimbabwe; tel. (1) 793911; fax (1) 730819; conducts research, testing and evaluation of raw materials, training and the exchange of appropriate technologies in order to promote the local mineral resources sectors.

**Compagnie de réassurance de la Zone d'échanges préférentiels—Zep-re** (PTA Reinsurance Co): Anniversary Towers, University Way, POB 42769, Nairobi, Kenya; tel. (2) 212792; fax (2) 224102; e-mail zep-re@africaonline.co.ke; f. 1992 (began operations on 1 January 1993); provides local reinsurance services and training to personnel in the insurance industry; auth. cap. CMD 27.3m.; Man. Dir S. M. Lubasi.

**Eastern and Southern African Trade and Development Bank:** NSSF Bldg, 23rd Floor, Bishop's Rd, POB 48596, Nairobi, Kenya; tel. (2) 712260; fax (2) 711510; e-mail infoserv@ptabank.co.ke; internet www.ptabank.co.ke; f. 1983 as PTA Development Bank; aims to mobilize resources and finance COMESA activities to foster regional integration; promotes investment and co-financing within the region; shareholders 16 COMESA mem. states and the African Development Bank; cap. p.u. SDR 63.7m. (Dec. 1998); Pres. Dr Michael Gondwe (acting).

**Federation of National Associations of Women in Business—FEMCOM:** c/o COMESA Secretariat; f. 1993 to provide links between female business executives throughout the region and to promote greater awareness of relevant issues at policy level. FEMCOM was to be supported by a Revolving Fund for Women in Business.

## Finance

COMESA is financed by member states. Its administrative budget for 1996 amounted to US $4m. In April 1997 COMESA heads of state concluded that the organization's activities were being undermined by lack of resources, and determined to expel countries which fail to pay membership dues over a five-year period.

## Publications

*Annual Report of the Council of Ministers.*
*Asycuda Newsletter.*
*COMESA Journal.*
*COMESA Trade Directory* (annually).
*COMESA Trade Information Newsletter* (monthly).
Demand/supply surveys, catalogues and reports.

# THE COMMONWEALTH

**Address:** Commonwealth Secretariat, Marlborough House, Pall Mall, London, SW1Y 5HX, United Kingdom.

**Telephone:** (20) 7839-3411; **fax:** (20) 7930-0827; **e-mail:** info@commonwealth.int; **internet:** www.thecommonwealth.org.

The Commonwealth is a voluntary association of 54 independent states, comprising about one-quarter of the world's population. It includes the United Kingdom and most of its former dependencies, and former dependencies of Australia and New Zealand (themselves Commonwealth countries).

The evolution of the Commonwealth began with the introduction of self-government in Canada in the 1840s; Australia, New Zealand and South Africa became independent before the First World War. At the Imperial Conference of 1926 the United Kingdom and the Dominions, as they were then called, were described as 'autonomous communities within the British Empire, equal in status', and this change was enacted into law by the Statute of Westminster, in 1931.

The modern Commonwealth began with the entry of India and Pakistan in 1947, and of Sri Lanka (then Ceylon) in 1948. In 1949, when India decided to become a republic, the Commonwealth Heads of Government agreed to replace allegiance to the British Crown with recognition of the British monarch as Head of the Commonwealth, as a condition of membership. This was a precedent for a number of other members (see Heads of State and Heads of Government, below).

### MEMBERS*

Antigua and Barbuda
Australia
Bahamas
Bangladesh
Barbados
Belize
Botswana
Brunei
Cameroon
Canada
Cyprus
Dominica
Fiji
The Gambia
Ghana
Grenada
Guyana
India
Jamaica
Kenya
Kiribati
Lesotho
Malawi
Malaysia
Maldives
Malta
Mauritius
Mozambique
Namibia
Nauru
New Zealand
Nigeria
Pakistan
Papua New Guinea
Saint Christopher and Nevis
Saint Lucia
Saint Vincent and the Grenadines
Samoa
Seychelles
Sierra Leone
Singapore
Solomon Islands
South Africa
Sri Lanka
Swaziland
Tanzania
Tonga
Trinidad and Tobago
Tuvalu†
Uganda
United Kingdom
Vanuatu
Zambia
Zimbabwe

* Ireland, South Africa and Pakistan withdrew from the Commonwealth in 1949, 1961 and 1972 respectively. In October 1987 Fiji's membership was declared to have lapsed (following the proclamation of a republic there); it was readmitted on 1 October 1997. Pakistan rejoined the Commonwealth in October 1989; however, it was suspended from participation in meetings of the Commonwealth in October 1999. South Africa rejoined in June 1994. Nigeria's membership was suspended in November 1995; it formally resumed membership on 29 May 1999, when a new civilian government was inaugurated.

† Tuvalu is a special member of the Commonwealth; it has the right to participate in all activities except full Meetings of Heads of Government.

#### Dependencies and Associated States

Australia:
- Ashmore and Cartier Islands
- Australian Antarctic Territory
- Christmas Island
- Cocos (Keeling) Islands
- Coral Sea Islands Territory
- Heard Island and the McDonald Islands
- Norfolk Island

New Zealand:
- Cook Islands
- Niue
- Ross Dependency
- Tokelau

United Kingdom:
- Anguilla
- Bermuda
- British Antarctic Territory
- British Indian Ocean Territory
- British Virgin Islands
- Cayman Islands
- Channel Islands
- Falkland Islands
- Gibraltar
- Isle of Man
- Montserrat
- Pitcairn Islands
- St Helena
  - Ascension
  - Tristan da Cunha
- South Georgia and the South Sandwich Islands
- Turks and Caicos Islands

### HEADS OF STATE AND HEADS OF GOVERNMENT

At January 2000 21 member countries were monarchies and 33 were republics. All Commonwealth countries accept Queen Elizabeth II as the symbol of the free association of the independent member nations and as such the Head of the Commonwealth. Of the 33 republics, the offices of Head of State and Head of Government were combined in 22: Botswana, Cameroon, Cyprus, The Gambia, Ghana, Guyana, Kenya, Kiribati, Malawi, Maldives, Mozambique, Namibia, Nauru, Nigeria, Seychelles, Sierra Leone, South Africa, Sri Lanka, Tanzania, Uganda, Zambia and Zimbabwe. The two offices were separated in the remaining 11: Bangladesh, Dominica, Fiji, India, Malta, Mauritius, Pakistan, Samoa, Singapore, Trinidad and Tobago and Vanuatu.

Of the monarchies, the Queen is Head of State of the United Kingdom and of 15 others, in each of which she is represented by a Governor-General: Antigua and Barbuda, Australia, the Bahamas, Barbados, Belize, Canada, Grenada, Jamaica, New Zealand, Papua New Guinea, Saint Christopher and Nevis, Saint Lucia, Saint Vincent and the Grenadines, Solomon Islands and Tuvalu. Brunei, Lesotho, Malaysia, Swaziland and Tonga are also monarchies, where the traditional monarch is Head of State.

The Governors-General are appointed by the Queen on the advice of the Prime Ministers of the country concerned. They are wholly independent of the Government of the United Kingdom.

### HIGH COMMISSIONERS

Governments of member countries are represented in other Commonwealth countries by High Commissioners, who have a status equivalent to that of Ambassadors.

## Organization

(January 2000)

The Commonwealth is not a federation: there is no central government nor are there any rigid contractual obligations such as bind members of the United Nations.

The Commonwealth has no written constitution but its members subscribe to the ideals of the Declaration of Commonwealth Principles unanimously approved by a meeting of heads of government in Singapore in 1971. Members also approved the 1977 statement on apartheid in sport (the Gleneagles Agreement); the 1979 Lusaka Declaration on Racism and Racial Prejudice; the 1981 Melbourne Declaration on relations between developed and developing countries; the 1983 New Delhi Statement on Economic Action; the 1983 Goa Declaration on International Security; the 1985 Nassau Declaration on World Order; the Commonwealth Accord on Southern Africa (1985); the 1987 Vancouver Declaration on World Trade; the Okanagan Statement and Programme of Action on Southern Africa (1987); the Langkawi Declaration on the Environment (1989); the Kuala Lumpur Statement on Southern Africa (1989); the Harare Commonwealth Declaration (1991); the Ottawa Declaration on Women and Structural Adjustment (1991); the Limassol Statement on the Uruguay Round of multilateral trade negotiations (1993); the Millbrook Commonwealth Action Programme on the Harare Declaration (1995); the Edinburgh Commonwealth Economic Declaration (1997); and the Fancourt Commonwealth Declaration on Globalization and People-centred Development.

### MEETINGS OF HEADS OF GOVERNMENT

Meetings are private and informal and operate not by voting but by consensus. The emphasis is on consultation and exchange of views for co-operation. A communiqué is issued at the end of every meeting. Meetings are held every two years in different capitals in the Commonwealth. The 1999 meeting was held in Durban, South Africa, in November, and the 2001 meeting was to be held in Australia.

### OTHER CONSULTATIONS

Meetings at ministerial and official level are also held regularly. Since 1959 finance ministers have met in a Commonwealth country in the week prior to the annual meetings of the IMF and the World Bank. Meetings on education, legal, women's and youth affairs are held at ministerial level every three years. Ministers of health hold annual meetings, with major meetings every three years, and ministers of agriculture meet every two years. Ministers of trade, labour and employment, industry, science and the environment also hold periodic meetings.

Senior officials—cabinet secretaries, permanent secretaries to heads of government and others—meet regularly in the year between meetings of heads of government to provide continuity and to exchange views on various developments.

### COMMONWEALTH SECRETARIAT

The Secretariat, established by Commonwealth heads of government in 1965, operates as an international organization at the service of all Commonwealth countries. It organizes consultations between governments and runs programmes of co-operation. Meetings of heads of government, ministers and senior officials decide these programmes and provide overall direction.

The Secretariat is headed by a secretary-general (elected by heads of government), assisted by three deputy secretaries-general. One deputy is responsible for political affairs, one for economic and social affairs, and one for development co-operation (including the Commonwealth Fund for Technical Co-operation—see below). The Secretariat comprises 12 Divisions in the fields of political affairs; legal and constitutional affairs; information and public affairs; administration; economic affairs; human resource development; gender and youth affairs; science and technology; economic and legal advisory services; export and industrial development; management and training services; and general technical assistance services. It also includes a non-governmental organizations desk and a unit for strategic planning and evaluation.

**Secretary-General:** Chief E. CHUKWUEMEKA (EMEKA) ANYAOKU (Nigeria); (from April 2000) DONALD MCKINNON (New Zealand).

**Deputy Secretary-General (Political):** KRISHNAN SRINIVASAN (India).

**Deputy Secretary-General (Economic and Social):** Dame VERONICA SUTHERLAND (United Kingdom).

**Deputy Secretary-General (Development Co-operation):** (vacant).

## Activities

### INTERNATIONAL AFFAIRS

In October 1991 heads of government, meeting in Harare, Zimbabwe, issued the Harare Commonwealth Declaration, in which they reaffirmed their commitment to the Commonwealth Principles declared in 1971, and stressed the need to promote sustainable development and the alleviation of poverty. The Declaration placed emphasis on the promotion of democracy and respect for human rights and resolved to strengthen the Commonwealth's capacity to assist countries in entrenching democratic practices. The meeting also welcomed the political reforms introduced by the South African Government to end the system of apartheid and urged all South African political parties to commence negotiations on a new constitution as soon as possible. The meeting endorsed measures on the phased removal of punitive measures against South Africa. 'People-to-people' sanctions (including consular and visa restrictions, cultural and scientific boycotts and restrictions on tourism promotion) were removed immediately, with economic sanctions to remain in place until a constitution for a new democratic, non-racial state had been agreed. A sports boycott, first imposed in 1977, would continue to be repealed on a sport-by-sport basis, as each sport in South Africa became integrated and non-racial. The embargo on the supply of armaments would remain in place until a post-apartheid, democratic regime had been firmly established in South Africa. In December a group of six eminent Commonwealth citizens was dispatched to observe multi-party negotiations on the future of South Africa and to assist the process where possible. In October 1992, in a fresh attempt to assist the South African peace process, a Commonwealth team of 18 observers was sent to monitor political violence in the country. A second phase of the Commonwealth Mission to South Africa (COMSA) began in February 1993, comprising 10 observers with backgrounds in policing, the law, politics and public life. COMSA issued a report in May in which it urged a concerted effort to build a culture of political tolerance in South Africa. In a report on its third phase, issued in December, COMSA appealed strongly to all political parties to participate in the transitional arrangements leading to democratic elections. In October the Commonwealth heads of government, meeting in Limassol, Cyprus, agreed that a democratic and non-racial South Africa would be invited to join the organization. They endorsed the removal of all economic sanctions against South Africa, but agreed to retain the arms embargo until a post-apartheid, democratic government had been established.

In November 1995 Commonwealth heads of government, convened in New Zealand, formulated and adopted the Millbrook Commonwealth Action Programme on the Harare Declaration, to promote adherence by member countries to the fundamental principles of democracy and human rights (as proclaimed in the 1991 Declaration). The Programme incorporated a framework of measures to be pursued in support of democratic processes and institutions, and actions to be taken in response to violations of the Harare Declaration principles, in particular the unlawful removal of a democratically-elected government. A Commonwealth Ministerial Action Group on the Harare Declaration (CMAG) was to be established to implement this process and to assist the member country involved to comply with the Harare principles. On the basis of this Programme, the leaders suspended Nigeria from the Commonwealth with immediate effect, following the execution by that country's military Government of nine environmental and human rights protesters and a series of other violations of human rights. The meeting determined to expel Nigeria from the Commonwealth if no 'demonstrable progress' had been made towards the establishment of a democratic authority by the time of the next summit meeting. In addition, the Programme formulated measures to promote sustainable development in member countries, which was considered to be an important element in sustaining democracy, and to facilitate consensus-building within the international community. Earlier in the meeting a statement was issued declaring the 'overwhelming majority' of Commonwealth governments to be opposed to nuclear-testing programmes being undertaken in the South Pacific region. However, in view of events in Nigeria, the issue of nuclear testing and disagreement among member countries did not assume the significance anticipated.

In December 1995 CMAG convened for its inaugural meeting in London. The Group, comprising the ministers of foreign affairs of Canada, Ghana, Jamaica, Malaysia, New Zealand, South Africa, the United Kingdom and Zimbabwe, commenced by considering efforts to restore democratic government in the three Commonwealth countries under military regimes, i.e. The Gambia, Nigeria and Sierra Leone. At the second meeting of the Group, in April 1996, ministers commended the conduct of presidential and parliamentary elections in Sierra Leone and the announcement by The Gambia's military leaders to proceed with a transition to civilian rule. In June a three-member CMAG delegation visited The Gambia to reaffirm Commonwealth support of the transition process in that country and to identify possible areas of further Commonwealth assistance. In August the Gambian authorities issued a decree removing the ban on political activities and parties, although shortly afterwards prohibited certain parties and candidates involved in political life prior to the military take-over from contesting the elections. CMAG recommended that in such circumstances there should be no Commonwealth observers sent to either the presidential or parliamentary elections, which were held in September 1996 and January 1997 respectively. Following the restoration of a civilian Government in early 1997, CMAG requested the Commonwealth Secretary-General to extend technical assistance to The Gambia in order to consolidate the democratic transition process. In April 1996 it was noted that the human rights situation in Nigeria had continued to deteriorate. CMAG, having pursued unsuccessful efforts to initiate dialogue with the Nigerian authorities, outlined a series of punitive and restrictive measures (including visa restrictions on members of the administration, a cessation of sporting contacts and an embargo on the export of armaments) that it would recommend for collective Commonwealth action in order to exert further pressure for reform in Nigeria. Following a meeting of a high-level delegation of the Nigerian Government and CMAG in June, the Group agreed to postpone the implementation of the sanctions, pending progress on the dialogue. (Canada, however, determined, unilaterally, to impose the measures with immediate effect; the United Kingdom did so in accordance with a decision of the European Union to implement limited sanctions against Nigeria.) A proposed CMAG mission to Nigeria was postponed in August, owing to restrictions imposed by the military authorities on access to political detainees and other civilian activists in that country. In September the Group agreed to proceed with the visit and to delay further a decision on the implementation of sanction measures. CMAG, without the participation of the representative of the Canadian Government, undertook its ministerial mission in November. In July 1997 the Group reiterated the Commonwealth Secretary-General's condemnation of a military coup in Sierra Leone in May, and decided to suspend that country's participation in meetings of the Commonwealth pending the restoration of a democratic government.

In October 1997 Commonwealth heads of government, meeting in Edinburgh, the United Kingdom, endorsed CMAG's recommendation that the imposition of sanctions against Nigeria be held in abeyance pending the scheduled completion of a transition programme towards democracy by October 1998. It was also agreed that CMAG be formally constituted as a permanent organ to investigate abuses of human rights throughout the Commonwealth. Jamaica and South Africa were to be replaced as members of CMAG by Barbados and Botswana, respectively.

In March 1998 CMAG, at its ninth meeting, commended the efforts of the Economic Community of West African States in restoring the democratically-elected Government of President Ahmed Tejan Kabbah in Sierra Leone, and agreed to remove all restrictions on

Sierra Leone's participation in Commonwealth activities. Later in that month, a representative mission of CMAG visited Sierra Leone to express its support for Kabbah's administration and to consider the country's needs in its process of reconstruction. At the CMAG meeting held in October members agreed that Sierra Leone should no longer be considered under the Group's mandate; however, they urged the Secretary-General to continue to assist that country in the process of national reconciliation and to facilitate negotiations with opposition forces to ensure a lasting cease-fire.

In April 1998 the Nigerian military leader, Gen. Sani Abacha, confirmed his intention to conduct a presidential election in August, but indicated that, following an agreement with other political organizations, he was to be the sole candidate. In June, however, Abacha died suddenly. His successor, Gen. Abdulsalam Abubakar, immediately released several prominent political prisoners, and in early July agreed to meet with the Secretaries-General of the UN and the Commonwealth to discuss the release of the imprisoned opposition leader, Chief Moshood Abiola. Abubakar also confirmed his intention to abide by the programme for transition to civilian rule by October. Shortly before his intended release, in mid-July, Abiola died of heart failure. The Commonwealth Secretary-General subsequently endorsed a new transition programme, which provided for the election of a civilian leader in May 1999. In October 1998 CMAG, convened for its 10th formal meeting, acknowledged Abubakar's efforts towards restoring a democratic government and recommended that member states begin to remove sanctions against Nigeria and that it resume participation in certain Commonwealth activities. The Commonwealth Secretary-General subsequently announced a programme of technical assistance to support Nigeria in the planning and conduct of democratic elections. Staff teams from the Commonwealth Secretariat observed local government, and state and governorship elections, held in December and in January 1999, respectively. A 23-member Commonwealth Observer Group was also dispatched to Nigeria to participate in international and local efforts to monitor the preparations and conduct of legislative and presidential elections, held in late February. While the Group reported several deficiencies and irregularities in the conduct of the polling, it confirmed that, in general, the conditions had existed for free and fair elections and that the elections were a legitimate basis for the transition of power to a democratic, civilian government. In April CMAG voted to readmit Nigeria to full membership on 29 May, upon the installation of the new civilian administration.

In 1999 the Commonwealth Secretary-General appointed a Special Envoy to broker an agreement in order to end a civil dispute in Honiara, the Solomon Islands. An accord was signed in late June, and it was envisaged that the Commonwealth would monitor its implementation. Also in June an agreement was concluded between opposing political groups in Zanzibar, having been facilitated by the good offices of the Secretary-General.

In mid-October 1999 a special meeting of CMAG was convened to consider the overthrow of the democratically-elected Government in Pakistan by the military. The meeting condemned the action as a violation of Commonwealth principles and urged the new authorities to declare a timetable for the return to democratic rule. CMAG also resolved to send a four-member delegation, comprising the ministers of foreign affairs of Barbados, Canada, Ghana and Malaysia, to discuss this future course of action with the military regime. Pakistan was suspended from participation in meetings of the Commonwealth with immediate effect. The suspension, pending the restoration of a democratic government, was endorsed by heads of government, meeting in November, who requested that CMAG keep the situation in Pakistan under review. At the meeting, held in Durban, South Africa, CMAG was reconstituted to comprise the ministers of foreign affairs of Australia, Bangladesh, Barbados, Botswana, Canada, Malaysia, Nigeria and the United Kingdom. It was agreed that no country would serve for more than two consecutive two-year terms. CMAG was requested to remain actively involved in the post-conflict development and rehabilitation of Sierra Leone and the process of consolidating peace. It was also urged to monitor persistent violations of the Harare Declaration principles in all countries. Its future mandate was to be considered by a Commonwealth High Level Group, which was established by heads of government to review the role and activities of the Commonwealth.

**Political Affairs Division:** assists consultation among member governments on international and Commonwealth matters of common interest. In association with host governments, it organizes the meetings of heads of government and senior officials. The Division services committees and special groups set up by heads of government dealing with political matters. The Secretariat has observer status at the United Nations, and the Division manages a joint office in New York to enable small states, which would otherwise be unable to afford facilities there, to maintain a presence at the United Nations. The Division monitors political developments in the Commonwealth and international progress in such matters as disarmament, the concerns of small states, dismantling of apartheid and the Law of the Sea. It also undertakes research on matters of common interest to member governments, and reports back to them. The Division is involved in diplomatic training and consular co-operation.

In 1990 Commonwealth heads of government mandated the Division to support the promotion of democracy by monitoring the preparations for and conduct of parliamentary, presidential or other elections in member countries at the request of national governments. In March 1998 the Commonwealth undertook its first joint mission with La Francophonie, to observe elections in Seychelles. In the same month representatives of the Commonwealth Secretary-General were present at elections held in Vanuatu. In May an observer mission was dispatched to monitor the electoral process in Lesotho. Further observer missions were undertaken in Nigeria, in February 1999, in Antigua and Barbuda, in March, and in Malawi and South Africa, in June.

A new expert group on good governance and the elimination of corruption in economic management convened for its first meeting in May 1998. In November 1999 Commonwealth heads of government endorsed a Framework for Principles for Promoting Good Governance and Combating Corruption, which had been drafted by the group.

## LAW

**Legal and Constitutional Affairs Division:** promotes and facilitates co-operation and the exchange of information among member governments on legal matters. It administers, jointly with the Commonwealth of Learning, a distance training programme for legislative draftsmen and assists governments to reform national laws to meet the obligations of international conventions. The Division organizes the triennial meeting of ministers, Attorneys General and senior ministry officials concerned with the legal systems in Commonwealth countries. It has also initiated four Commonwealth schemes for co-operation on extradition, the protection of material cultural heritage, mutual assistance in criminal matters and the transfer of convicted offenders within the Commonwealth. It liaises with the Commonwealth Magistrates' and Judges' Association, the Commonwealth Legal Education Association, the Commonwealth Lawyers' Association (with which it helps to prepare the triennial Commonwealth Law Conference for the practising profession), the Commonwealth Association of Legislative Counsel, and with other international non-governmental organizations. The Division provides in-house legal advice for the Secretariat. The quarterly *Commonwealth Law Bulletin* reports on legal developments in and beyond the Commonwealth.

The Division's Commercial Crime Unit assists member countries to combat financial and organized crime, in particular transborder criminal activities, and promotes the exchange of information regarding national and international efforts to combat serious commercial crime through a quarterly publication, *Commonwealth Legal Assistance News,* and the *Crimewatch* bulletin. A Human Rights Unit aims to assist governments to strengthen national institutions and other mechanisms for the protection for human rights. It also organizes training workshops and promotes the exchange of relevant information among member countries.

## ECONOMIC CO-OPERATION

In October 1997 Commonwealth heads of government, meeting in Edinburgh, the United Kingdom, signed an Economic Declaration that focused on issues relating to global trade, investment and development and committed all member countries to free-market economic principles. The Declaration also incorporated a provision for the establishment of a Trade and Investment Access Facility within the Secretariat in order to assist developing member states in the process of international trade liberalization and promote intra-Commonwealth trade.

In May 1998 the Commonwealth Secretary-General appealed to the Group of Eight industrialized nations to accelerate and expand the initiative to ease the debt burden of the most heavily indebted poor countries (HIPCs) (see World Bank and IMF). However, the Group failed to endorse the so-called 'Mauritius Mandate', adopted by Commonwealth finance ministers, meeting in Mauritius, in September 1997, which stipulated that by 2000 all eligible HIPCs should have in progress measures to reduce their external debt. In October 1998 Commonwealth finance ministers, convened in Ottawa, Canada, reiterated their appeal to international financial institutions to accelerate the HIPC initiative. The meeting also issued a Commonwealth Statement on the global economic crisis and endorsed several proposals to help to counter the difficulties experienced by several countries. These measures included a mechanism to enable countries to suspend payments on all short-term financial obligations at a time of emergency without defaulting, assistance to governments to attract private capital and to manage capital market volatility, and the development of international codes of conduct regarding financial and monetary policies and corporate governance. In March 1999 the Commonwealth Secretariat hosted a joint IMF-World Bank conference to review the HIPC scheme and initiate a process of reform. In November 1999 Commonwealth heads of government, meeting in South Africa, declared their support for measures undertaken by the World Bank and IMF to enhance the HIPC initiative. At the end of an informal retreat the leaders adopted the Fancourt Commonwealth Declaration on Globalization and People-Centred Development, which emphasized the need for a more equitable spread of wealth generated by the process of globalization, and expressed a renewed commitment to the elimination of all forms of discrimination, the promotion of people-centred development and capacity-building, and efforts to ensure developing countries benefit from future multilateral trade liberalization measures.

In October 1998 ministers of finance agreed to establish a Commonwealth Y2K (Year 2000) Preparedness facility to help countries to deal with the technical difficulties resulting from the millennium date change.

**Economic Affairs Division:** organizes and services the annual meetings of Commonwealth ministers of finance and the ministerial group on small states and assists in servicing the biennial meetings of heads of government and periodic meetings of environment ministers. It engages in research and analysis on economic issues of interest to member governments and organizes seminars and conferences of government officials and experts. The Division undertook a major programme of technical assistance to enable developing Commonwealth countries to participate in the Uruguay Round of multilateral trade negotiations and has assisted the African, Caribbean and Pacific (ACP) group of countries in their trade negotiations with the European Union. It continues to help developing countries to strengthen their links with international capital markets and foreign investors. The Division also services groups of experts on economic affairs that have been commissioned by governments to report on, among other things, protectionism; obstacles to the North-South negotiating process; reform of the international financial and trading system; the debt crisis; management of technological change; the special needs of small states; the impact of change on the development process; environmental issues; women and structural adjustment; and youth unemployment. The Division co-ordinates the Secretariat's environmental work and manages the Iwokrama International Rainforest Programme.

The Division played a catalytic role in the establishment of a Commonwealth Equity Fund, initiated in September 1990, to allow developing member countries to improve their access to private institutional investment, and promoted a Caribbean Investment Fund. The Division supported the establishment of a Commonwealth Private Investment Initiative (CPII) to mobilize capital, on a regional basis, for investment in newly-privatized companies and in small and medium-sized businesses in the private sector. The first regional fund under the CPII was launched in July 1996. The Commonwealth Africa Investment Fund (Comafin), was to be managed by the United Kingdom's official development institution, the Commonwealth Development Corporation, to assist businesses in 19 countries in sub-Saharan Africa, with initial resources of US $63.5m. In August 1997 a fund for the Pacific Islands was launched, with an initial capital of $15.0m. A $200m. South Asia Regional Fund was established at the Heads of Government Meeting in October. In October 1998 a fund for the Caribbean states was inaugurated, at a meeting of Commonwealth finance ministers.

## HUMAN RESOURCES

**Human Resource Development Division:** consists of two departments concerned with education and health. The Division co-operates with member countries in devising strategies for human resource development.

The **Education Department** arranges specialist seminars, workshops and co-operative projects and commissions studies in areas identified by ministers of education, whose three-yearly meetings it also services. Its present areas of emphasis include improving the quality of and access to basic education; strengthening the culture of science, technology and mathematics education in formal and non-formal areas of education; improving the quality of management in institutions of higher learning and basic education; improving the performance of teachers; strengthening examination assessment systems; and promoting the movement of students between Commonwealth countries. The Department also promotes multi-sectoral strategies to be incorporated in the development of human resources. Emphasis is placed on ensuring a gender balance, the appropriate use of technology, promoting good governance, addressing the problems of scale particular to smaller member countries, and encouraging collaboration between governments, the private sector and other non-governmental organizations.

The **Health Department** organizes ministerial, technical and expert group meetings and workshops, to promote co-operation on health matters, and the exchange of health information and expertise. The Department commissions relevant studies and provides professional and technical advice to member countries and to the Secretariat. It also supports the work of regional health organizations and promotes health for all people in Commonwealth countries.

**Gender and Youth Affairs Division:** consists of the Gender Affairs Department and the Commonwealth Youth Affairs Department.

The **Gender Affairs Department** is responsible for the implementation of the 1995 Commonwealth Plan of Action on Gender and Development, which was endorsed by the Heads of Government in order to achieve gender equality in the Commonwealth. The main objective of the Plan is to ensure that gender is incorporated into all policies, programmes, structures and procedures of member states and of the Commonwealth Secretariat. The Department is also addressing specific concerns such as the integration of gender issues into national budgetary processes, increasing the participation of women in politics and conflict prevention and resolution, and the promotion of human rights, including the elimination of violence against women and girls.

The **Youth Affairs Department** administers the Commonwealth Youth Programme (CYP), funded through separate voluntary contributions from governments, which seeks to promote the involvement of young people in the economic and social development of their countries. The CYP was awarded a budget of £2.1m. for 1998/99. It provides policy advice for governments and operates regional training programmes for youth workers and policy-makers through its centres in Africa, Asia, the Caribbean and the Pacific. It conducts a Youth Study Fellowship scheme, a Youth Project Fund, a Youth Exchange Programme (in the Caribbean), and a Youth Service Awards Scheme, holds conferences and seminars, carries out research and disseminates information. In May 1995 a Commonwealth Youth Credit Initiative was launched, in order to provide funds, training and advice to young entrepreneurs. In May 1998 a Commonwealth ministerial meeting, held in Kuala Lumpur, Malaysia, approved a new Plan of Action on Youth Empowerment to the Year 2005, which was to be presented to the 1999 meeting of heads of government.

## SCIENCE

**Science and Technology Division:** is partially funded and governed by the Commonwealth Science Council, consisting of 35 member governments, which aims to enhance the scientific and technological capabilities of member countries, through co-operative research, training and the exchange of information. Current priority areas of work are concerned with the promotion of sustainable development and cover biological diversity and genetic resources, water resources, and renewable energy.

## TECHNICAL CO-OPERATION

**Commonwealth Fund for Technical Co-operation (CFTC):** f. 1971 to facilitate the exchange of skills between member countries and to promote economic and social development. It is administered by the Commonwealth Secretariat and financed by voluntary subscriptions from member governments. The CFTC responds to requests from member governments for technical assistance, such as the provision of experts for short or medium-term projects, advice on economic or legal matters, in particular in the areas of natural resources management and public-sector reform, and training programmes. The CFTC also administers the Langkawi awards for the study of environmental issues, which is funded by the Canadian Government. The CFTC budget for 1998/99 amounted to £20.5m. During 1995–97 more than 9,000 nationals from 49 Commonwealth developing countries trained under CFTC programmes, while more than 700 experts and consultants were assigned to projects in 45 countries. During that time CFTC also assisted six countries to define their maritime boundaries, 17 countries to develop their mineral and petroleum resources and undertook 84 export-promotion programmes.

CFTC activities are implemented by the following divisions:

**Economic and Legal Advisory Services Division:** serves as an in-house consultancy, offering advice to governments on macroeconomic and financial management, capital market and private-sector development, debt management, the development of natural resources, and the negotiation of maritime boundaries and fisheries access agreements;

**Export and Industrial Development Division:** advises on all aspects of export marketing and the development of tourism, industry, small businesses and enterprises. Includes an Agricultural Development Unit, which provides technical assistance in agriculture and renewable resources;

**General Technical Assistance Services Division:** provides short- and long-term experts in all fields of development;

**Management and Training Services Division:** provides integrated packages of consultancy and training to enhance skills in areas such as public sector reform and the restructuring of enterprises, and arranges specific country and overseas training programmes.

The Secretariat also includes an Administration Division, a Strategic Planning and Evaluation Unit, and an Information and Public Affairs Division, which produces information publications, and radio and television programmes, about Commonwealth co-operation and consultation activities.

## Finance

The Secretariat's budget for 1998/99 was £10.5m. Member governments meet the cost of the Secretariat through subscriptions on a scale related to income and population.

## Publications

*Commonwealth Currents* (quarterly).
*Commonwealth Declarations 1971–91*.
*Commonwealth Organisations* (directory).
*The Commonwealth Today*.
*In Common* (quarterly newsletter of the Youth Programme).
*International Development Policies* (quarterly).
*Link In to Gender and Development* (2 a year)
*Notes on the Commonwealth* (series of reference leaflets).
*Report of the Commonwealth Secretary-General* (every 2 years).
*The Commonwealth Yearbook*.
Numerous reports, studies and papers (catalogue available).

# Commonwealth Organizations

(In the United Kingdom, unless otherwise stated.)

### AGRICULTURE AND FORESTRY

**Commonwealth Forestry Association:** c/o Oxford Forestry Institute, South Parks Rd, Oxford, OX1 3RB; tel. (1865) 271037; fax (1865) 275074; e-mail cfa@plants.ox.ac.uk; f. 1921; produces, collects and circulates information relating to world forestry and promotes good management, use and conservation of forests and forest lands throughout the world. Mems: 900. Chair. Dr J. S. Maini. Publs *International Forestry Review* (quarterly), *Commonwealth Forestry News* (quarterly), *Commonwealth Forestry Handbook* (irregular).

**Standing Committee on Commonwealth Forestry:** Forestry Commission, 231 Corstorphine Rd, Edinburgh, EH12 7AT; tel. (131) 314-6137; fax (131) 334-0442; e-mail libby.jones@forestry.gov.uk; f. 1923 to provide continuity between Confs, and to provide a forum for discussion on any forestry matters of common interest to mem. govts which may be brought to the Cttee's notice by any member country or organization; 54 mems. 1997 Conference: Victoria Falls, Zimbabwe; 2001 Conference: Perth, Australia. Sec. Libby Jones. Publ. *Newsletter* (quarterly).

### COMMONWEALTH STUDIES

**Institute of Commonwealth Studies:** 28 Russell Sq., London, WC1B 5DS; tel. (20) 7862-8844; fax (20) 7862-8820; e-mail ics@sas.ac.uk; internet www.sas.ac.uk/commonwealthstudies/; f. 1949 to promote advanced study of the Commonwealth; provides a library and meeting place for postgraduate students and academic staff engaged in research in this field; offers postgraduate teaching. Dir Prof. Pat Caplan. Publs *Annual Report, Collected Seminar Papers, Newsletter, Theses in Progress in Commonwealth Studies*.

### COMMUNICATIONS

**Commonwealth Telecommunications Organisation:** Clareville House, 26–27 Oxendon St, London, SW1Y 4EL; tel. (20) 7930-5516; fax (20) 7930-4248; e-mail info@cto.int; f. 1967; aims to enhance the development of telecommunications in Commonwealth countries and contribute to the communications infrastructure required for economic and social devt, through a devt and training programme. Exec. Dir Dr David Souter. Publ. *CTO Briefing* (3 a year).

### EDUCATION AND CULTURE

**Association of Commonwealth Universities (ACU):** John Foster House, 36 Gordon Sq., London, WC1H 0PF; tel. (20) 7387-8572; fax (20) 7387-2655; e-mail info@acu.ac.uk; internet www.acu.ac.uk; f. 1913; organizes major meetings of Commonwealth universities and their representatives; publishes factual information about Commonwealth universities and access to them; acts as a liaison office and general information centre and provides a recruitment advertising and publicity service; hosts a management consultancy service; supplies secretariats for the Commonwealth Scholarship Comm., the Marshall Aid Commemoration Comm. and the Commonwealth Universities Study Abroad Consortium; administers various other fellowship and scholarship programmes. Mems: 486 universities in 36 Commonwealth countries or regions. Sec.-Gen. Prof. Michael Gibbons. Publs include: *Commonwealth Universities Yearbook, ACU Bulletin of Current Documentation* (5 a year), *ACU: Aims and Functions* (annually), *Report of the Council of the ACU* (annually), *Awards for University Teachers and Research Workers, Awards for Postgraduate Study at Commonwealth Universities, Awards for First Degree Study at Commonwealth Universities, Awards for University Administrators and Librarians, Who's Who of Executive Heads: Vice-Chancellors, Presidents, Principals and Rectors,* Student Information Papers (study abroad series).

**Commonwealth Association for Education in Journalism and Communication—CAEJAC:** c/o Faculty of Law, University of Western Ontario, London, ON N6A 3K7, Canada; tel. (519) 6613348; fax (519) 6613790; e-mail caejc@julian.uwo.ca; f. 1985; aims to foster high standards of journalism and communication education and research in Commonwealth countries and to promote co-operation among institutions and professions. c. 700 mems in 32 Commonwealth countries. Pres. Prof. Syed Arabi Idid (Malaysia); Sec. Prof. Robert Martin. Publ. *CAEJAC Journal* (annually).

**Commonwealth Association of Science, Technology and Mathematics Educators—CASTME:** c/o Education Dept, Human Resource Development Division, Commonwealth Secretariat, Marlborough House, Pall Mall, London, SW1Y 5HX; tel. (20) 7747-6282; fax (20) 7747-6287; f. 1974; special emphasis is given to the social significance of education in these subjects. Organizes an Awards Scheme to promote effective teaching and learning in these subjects, and biennial regional seminars. Pres. Sir Hermann Bondi; Hon. Sec. Dr Ved Goel. Publ. *CASTME Journal* (quarterly).

**Commonwealth Council for Educational Administration and Management:** c/o International Educational Leadership Centre, School of Management, Lincoln University Campus, Brayford Pool, Lincoln, LN6 7TS; tel. (1522) 886071; fax (1522) 886023; e-mail athody@lincoln.ac.uk; f. 1970; aims to foster quality in professional development and links among educational administrators; holds nat. and regional confs, as well as visits and seminars. Mems: 24 affiliated groups representing 3,000 persons. Pres. Prof. Angela Thody; Sec. Geraldine Bristow. Publs *Managing Education Matters* (2 a year), *International Studies in Educational Administration* (2 a year).

**Commonwealth Institute:** Kensington High St, London, W8 6NQ; tel. (20) 7603-4535; fax (20) 7602-7374; e-mail info@commonwealth.org.uk; internet www.commonwealth.org.uk; f. 1893 as the Imperial Institute; the Inst. houses a Commonwealth Resource and Literature Library and a Conference and Events Centre; organizes visual arts exhibitions and supplies educational resource materials and training; a new five-year strategic plan, entitled 'Commonwealth 21', was inaugurated in 1998. Chair. David A. Thompson; Dir-Gen. David French. Publ. *Annual Review*.

**The Commonwealth of Learning:** 1285 West Broadway, Suite 600, Vancouver, British Columbia V6H 3X8, Canada; tel. (604) 775-8200; fax (604) 775-8210; e-mail info@col.org; internet www.col.org; f. 1987 by Commonwealth Heads of Government to promote and develop distance education and open learning. Pres. Dato' Prof. Gajaraj Dhanarajan.

**League for the Exchange of Commonwealth Teachers:** 7 Lion Yard, Tremadoc Rd, London, SW4 7NQ; tel. (20) 7498-1101; fax (20) 7720-5403; e-mail 100745.1501@compuserve.com; internet ourworld.compuserve.com/homepages/lectcom_exchange; f. 1901; promotes educational exchanges for a period of one year between teachers in Australia, the Bahamas, Barbados, Bermuda, Canada, Guyana, India, Jamaica, Kenya, Malawi, New Zealand, Pakistan, South Africa and Trinidad and Tobago. Dir Patricia Swain. Publs *Annual Report, Exchange Teacher* (annually), *Commonwealth Times* (2 a year).

### HEALTH

**Commonwealth Medical Association:** BMA House, Tavistock Sq., London, WC1H 9JP; tel. (20) 7383-6095; fax (20) 7383-6195; e-mail com_med_assn@compuserve.com; internet www.coma.co.za; f. 1962 for the exchange of information; provision of tech. co-operation and advice; formulation and maintenance of a code of ethics; provision of continuing medical education; devt and promotion of health education programmes; and liaison with WHO and the UN on health issues; meetings of its Council are held every three years. Mems: medical asscns in Commonwealth countries. Dir Marianne Haslegrave; Sec. Dr J. D. J. Havard. Publ. *CommonHealth* (quarterly).

**Commonwealth Pharmaceutical Association:** 1 Lambeth High St, London, SE1 7JN; tel. (20) 7820-3399 ext. 303; fax (20) 7582-3401; e-mail eharden@rpsgb.org.uk; f. 1970 to promote the interests of pharmaceutical sciences and the profession of pharmacy in the

Commonwealth; to maintain high professional standards, encourage links between members and the creation of nat. asscns; and to facilitate the dissemination of information. Holds confs (every four years) and regional meetings. Mems: 39 pharmaceutical asscns. Sec. PHILIP E. GREEN. Publ. *Quarterly Newsletter*.

**Commonwealth Society for the Deaf:** 34 Buckingham Palace Rd, London, SW1W 0RE; tel. (20) 7233-5700; fax (20) 7233-5800; e-mail sound.seekers@btinternet.com; promotes the health, education and general welfare of the deaf in developing Commonwealth countries; encourages and assists the development of educational facilities, the training of teachers of the deaf, and the provision of support for parents of deaf children; organizes visits by volunteer specialists to developing countries; provides audiological equipment and organises the training of audiological maintenance technicians; conducts research into the causes and prevention of deafness. CEO Brig. J. A. DAVIS. Publ. *Annual Report*.

**Sight Savers International (Royal Commonwealth Society for the Blind):** Grosvenor Hall, Bolnore Rd, Haywards Heath, West Sussex, RH16 4BX; tel. (1444) 446600; fax (1444) 446688; e-mail information@sightsaversint.org.uk; internet www.sightsavers .org.uk; f. 1950 to prevent blindness and restore sight in developing countries, and to provide education and community-based training for incurably blind people; operates in collaboration with local partners, with high priority given to training local staff; Chair. DAVID THOMPSON; Dir RICHARD PORTER. Publ. *Horizons* (newsletter, 3 a year).

## INFORMATION AND THE MEDIA

**Commonwealth Broadcasting Association:** 17 Fleet St, London, EC4Y 1AA; tel. (20) 7583-5550; fax (20) 7583-5549; e-mail cba@cba.org.uk; internet www.oneworld.org/cba; f. 1945; gen. confs are held every two years. Mems: 100 in 57 countries. Sec.-Gen. ELIZABETH SMITH. Publs *Commonwealth Broadcaster* (quarterly), *Commonwealth Broadcaster Directory* (annually).

**Commonwealth Institute:** see under Education.

**Commonwealth Journalists Association:** 17 Nottingham St, London, W1M 3RD; tel. (20) 7486-3844; fax (20) 7486-3822; f. 1978 to promote co-operation between journalists in Commonwealth countries, organize training facilities and confs, and foster understanding among Commonwealth peoples. Pres. MURRAY BURT; Exec. Dir LAWRIE BREEN.

**Commonwealth Press Union** (Asscn of Commonwealth Newspapers, News Agencies and Periodicals): 17 Fleet St, London, EC4Y 1AA; tel. (20) 7583-7733; fax (20) 7583-6868; e-mail 106156.3331@compuserve.com; f. 1950; promotes the welfare of the Commonwealth press; provides training for journalists and organizes biennial confs. Mems: c. 1,000 newspapers, news agencies, periodicals in 42 Commonwealth countries. Dir ROBIN MACKICHAN. Publs *CPU News, Annual Report*.

## LAW

**Commonwealth Lawyers' Association:** c/o The Law Society, 114 Chancery Lane, London, WC2A 1PL; tel. (20) 7320-5772; fax (20) 7831-0057; e-mail cla@lawsociety.org.uk; internet www .commonwealthlawyers.com; f. 1983 (fmrly the Commonwealth Legal Bureau); seeks to maintain and promote the rule of law throughout the Commonwealth, by ensuring that the people of the Commonwealth are served by an independent and efficient legal profession; upholds professional standards and promotes the availability of legal services; assists in organizing the triennial Commonwealth law confs. Pres. (1999–2001) CYRUS DAS; Exec. Sec. HELEN POTTS. Publs *The Commonwealth Lawyer, Clarion*.

**Commonwealth Legal Advisory Service:** c/o British Institute of International and Comparative Law, Charles Clore House, 17 Russell Sq., London, WC1B 5DR; tel. (20) 7636-5802; fax (20) 7323-2016; e-mail biicl@dial.pipex.com; financed by the British Institute and by contributions from Commonwealth govts; provides research facilities for Commonwealth govts and law reform commissions. Sec. MICHAEL MAUNSELL.

**Commonwealth Legal Education Association:** c/o Legal and Constitutional Affairs Division, Commonwealth Secretariat, Marlborough House, Pall Mall, London, SW1Y 5HX; tel. (20) 7747-6415; fax (20) 7747-6406; e-mail clea@commonwealth.int; internet www.clea.com.uk; f. 1971 to promote contacts and exchanges and to provide information regarding legal education. Gen. Sec. JOHN HATCHARD. Publs *Commonwealth Legal Education Association Newsletter* (3 a year), *Directory of Commonwealth Law Schools* (every 2 years).

**Commonwealth Magistrates' and Judges' Association:** Uganda House, 58/59 Trafalgar Sq., London, WC2N 5DX; tel. (20) 7976-1007; fax (20) 7976-2395; e-mail cmja@btinternet.com; f. 1970 to advance the administration of the law by promoting the independence of the judiciary, to further education in law and crime prevention and to disseminate information; confs and study tours; corporate membership for asscns of the judiciary or courts of limited jurisdiction; assoc. membership for individuals. Pres. DAVID ARMATI; Sec.-Gen. Dr KAREN BREWER. Publ. *Commonwealth Judicial Journal* (2 a year).

## PARLIAMENTARY AFFAIRS

**Commonwealth Parliamentary Association:** Westminster House, Suite 700, 7 Millbank, London, SW1P 3JA; tel. (20) 7799-1460; fax (20) 7222-6073; e-mail hq.sec@comparlhq.org.uk; internet www.comparlhq.org.uk; f. 1911 to promote understanding and co-operation between Commonwealth parliamentarians; organization: Exec. Cttee of 32 MPs responsible to annual Gen. Assembly; 147 brs throughout the Commonwealth; holds annual Commonwealth Parliamentary Confs and seminars; also regional confs and seminars; Sec.-Gen. ARTHUR DONAHOE. Publ. *The Parliamentarian* (quarterly).

## PROFESSIONAL AND INDUSTRIAL RELATIONS

**Commonwealth Association of Architects:** 66 Portland Pl., London, W1N 4AD; tel. (20) 7490-3024; fax (20) 7253-2592; e-mail caa@gharchitects.demon.co.uk; f. 1964; an asscn of 38 socs of architects in various Commonwealth countries. Objects: to facilitate the reciprocal recognition of professional qualifications; to provide a clearing house for information on architectural practice, and to encourage collaboration. Plenary confs every three years; regional confs are also held. Exec. Dir TONY GODWIN. Publs *Handbook, Objectives and Procedures: CAA Schools Visiting Boards, Architectural Education in the Commonwealth* (annotated bibliography of research), *CAA Newsnet* (2 a year), a survey and list of schools of architecture.

**Commonwealth Association for Public Administration and Management—CAPAM:** 1075 Bay St, Suite 402, Toronto, ON M5S 2B1, Canada; tel. (416) 920-3337; fax (416) 920-6574; e-mail capam@compuserve.com; internet www.comnet.mt/capam/; f. 1994; aims to promote sound management of the public sector in Commonwealth countries and to assist those countries undergoing political or financial reforms. An international awards programme to reward innovation within the public sector was introduced in 1997, and was to be awarded every 2 years. Pres. Dr ZOLA SKWEYIYA (South Africa); Exec. Dir ART STEVENSON (Canada).

**Commonwealth Foundation:** Marlborough House, Pall Mall, London, SW1Y 5HY; tel. (20) 7930-3783; fax (20) 7839-8157; e-mail geninfo@commonwealth.int; internet www.commonwealth foundation.com; f. 1966; promotes people-to-people interaction, and collaboration within the non-governmental sector of the Commonwealth; supports non-governmental organizations, professional associations and Commonwealth arts and culture. Awards an annual Commonwealth Writers' Prize. Funds are provided by Commonwealth govts. Chair. DONALD O. MILLS (Jamaica); Dir Dr HUMAYUN KHAN (Pakistan).

**Commonwealth Trade Union Council:** Congress House, 23–28 Great Russell St, London, WC1B 3LS; tel. (20) 7631-0728; fax (20) 7436-0301; e-mail info@commonwealthtuc.org; internet www .commonwealthtuc.org; f. 1979; links trade union national centres (representing more than 30m. trade union mems) throughout the Commonwealth; promotes the application of democratic principles and core labour standards, works closely with other international trade union orgs. Dir ANNIE WATSON. Publ. *Annual Report*.

## SCIENCE AND TECHNOLOGY

**Commonwealth Engineers' Council:** c/o Institution of Civil Engineers, One Great George St, London, SW1P 3AA; tel. (20) 7222-7722; fax (20) 7222-7500; e-mail international@ice.org.uk; f. 1946; the Council meets every two years to provide an opportunity for engineering institutions of Commonwealth countries to exchange views on collaboration; there is a standing cttee on engineering education and training; organizes seminars on related topics. Sec. J. A. WHITWELL.

**Commonwealth Geological Surveys Consultative Group:** c/o Commonwealth Science Council, CSC Earth Sciences Programme, Marlborough House, Pall Mall, London, SW1Y 5HX; tel. (20) 7839-3411; fax (20) 7839-6174; e-mail comsci@gn.apc.org; f. 1948 to promote collaboration in geological, geochemical, geophysical and remote sensing techniques and the exchange of information. Geological Programme Officer Dr SIYAN MALOMO; Publ. *Earth Sciences Newsletter*.

## SPORT

**Commonwealth Games Federation:** Walkden House, 3–10 Melton St, London, NW1 2EB; tel. (20) 7383-5596; fax (20) 7383-5506; e-mail commonwealthgamesfederation@btinternet.com; internet www.commonwealthgames-fed.org; the Games were first held in 1930 and are now held every four years; participation is limited to competitors representing the mem. countries of the Commonwealth; to be held in Manchester, United Kingdom, in 2002.

Mems: 72 affiliated bodies. Pres. HRH The Earl of WESSEX; Chair. MICHAEL FENNELL.

### YOUTH

**Commonwealth Youth Exchange Council:** 7 Lion Yard, Tremadoc Rd, London, SW4 7NQ; tel. (20) 7498-6151; fax (20) 7720-5403; e-mail mail@cyec.demon.co.uk; f. 1970; promotes contact between groups of young people of the United Kingdom and other Commonwealth countries by means of educational exchange visits, provides information for organizers and allocates grants; 224 mem. orgs. Dir V. S. G. CRAGGS. Publs *Contact* (handbook), *Exchange* (newsletter), *Safety and Welfare* (guide-lines for Commonwealth Youth Exchange groups).

**Duke of Edinburgh's Award International Association:** Award House, 7-11 St Matthew St, London, SW1P 2JT; tel. (20) 7222-4242; fax (20) 7222-4141; e-mail sect@intaward.org; internet www.theaward.org; f. 1956; offers a programme of leisure activities for young people, comprising Service, Expeditions, Physical Recreation, and Skills; operates in more than 90 countries (not confined to the Commonwealth). International Sec.-Gen. PAUL ARENGO-JONES; Dir Vice-Adm. MICHAEL GRETTON. Publs *Award World* (2 a year), *Annual Report*, handbooks and guides.

### MISCELLANEOUS

**British Commonwealth Ex-Services League:** 48 Pall Mall, London, SW1Y 5JG; tel. (20) 7973-7200; fax (20) 7973-7308; links the ex-service orgs in the Commonwealth, assists ex-servicemen of the Crown and their dependants who are resident abroad; holds triennial confs. Grand Pres. HRH The Duke of EDINBURGH; Sec.-Gen. Lt-Col S. POPE. Publ. *Annual Report.*

**Commonwealth Countries League:** 14 Thistleworth Close, Isleworth, Middlesex, TW7 4QQ; tel. (20) 8737-3572; fax (20) 8568-2495; f. 1925 to secure equal opportunities and status between men and women in the Commonwealth, to act as a link between Commonwealth women's orgs, and to promote and finance secondary education of disadvantaged girls of high ability in their own countries, through the CCL Educational Fund; holds meetings with speakers and an annual Conf., organizes the annual Commonwealth Fair for fund-raising; individual mems and affiliated socs in the Commonwealth. Sec.-Gen. SHEILA O'REILLY. Publ. *CCL Newsletter* (3 a year).

**Commonwealth War Graves Commission:** 2 Marlow Rd, Maidenhead, Berks, SL6 7DX; tel. (1628) 634221; fax (1628) 771208; e-mail general.enq@cwgc.org; internet www.cwgc.org; f. 1917 (as Imperial War Graves Commission); responsible for the commemoration in perpetuity of the 1.7m. members of the Commonwealth Forces who died during the wars of 1914–18 and 1939–45; provides for the marking and maintenance of war graves and memorials at some 23,000 locations in 150 countries. Mems: Australia, Canada, India, New Zealand, South Africa, United Kingdom. Pres. HRH The Duke of KENT; Dir-Gen. D. KENNEDY.

**Joint Commonwealth Societies' Council:** c/o Royal Commonwealth Society, 18 Northumberland Ave, London, WC2N 5BJ; tel. (20) 7930-6733; fax (20) 7930-9705; e-mail jcsc@rcsint.org; internet www.rcsint.org; f. 1947; provides a forum for the exchange of information regarding activities of mem. orgs which promote understanding among countries of the Commonwealth; co-ordinates the distribution of the Commonwealth Day message by Queen Elizabeth and organizes the observance of the Commonwealth Day and produces educational materials relating to the occasion; mems: 16 unofficial Commonwealth orgs and four official bodies. Chair. Sir PETER MARSHALL; Sec. EMMA ARMSTRONG.

**Royal Commonwealth Society:** 18 Northumberland Ave, London, WC2N 5BJ; tel. (20) 7930-6733; fax (20) 7930-9705; e-mail info@rcsint.org; internet www.rcsint.org; f. 1868; to promote international understanding of the Commonwealth and its people; organizes meetings and seminars on topical issues, and cultural and social events; library housed by Cambridge University Library. Chair. Sir MICHAEL MCWILLIAM; Dir PETER LUFF. Publs *Annual Report, Newsletter* (3 a year), conference reports.

**Royal Over-Seas League:** Over-Seas House, Park Place, St James's St, London, SW1A 1LR; tel. (20) 7408-0214; fax (20) 7499-6738; f. 1910 to promote friendship and understanding in the Commonwealth; club houses in London and Edinburgh; membership is open to all British subjects and Commonwealth citizens. Chair. Sir GEOFFREY ELLERTON; Dir-Gen. ROBERT F. NEWELL. Publ. *Overseas* (quarterly).

**The Victoria League for Commonwealth Friendship:** 55 Leinster Sq., London, W2 4PW; tel. (20) 7243-2633; fax (20) 7229-2994; f. 1901; aims to further personal friendship among Commonwealth peoples and to provide hospitality for visitors; maintains Student House, providing accommodation for students from Commonwealth countries; has brs elsewhere in the UK and abroad. Pres. HRH Princess MARGARET, Countess of SNOWDON; Chair. COLIN WEBBER; Gen. Sec. JOHN ALLAN. Publ. *Annual Report.*

# THE COMMONWEALTH OF INDEPENDENT STATES—CIS

**Address:** 220000 Minsk, Kirava 17, Belarus.
**Telephone:** (172) 22-35-17; **fax:** (172) 27-23-39; **e-mail:** postmaster@www.cis.minsk.by; **internet:** www.cis.minsk.by.

The Commonwealth of Independent States is a voluntary association of 12 (originally 11) states, established at the time of the collapse of the USSR in December 1991.

### MEMBERS

| | |
|---|---|
| Armenia | Moldova |
| Azerbaijan | Russia |
| Belarus | Tajikistan |
| Georgia | Turkmenistan |
| Kazakhstan | Ukraine |
| Kyrgyzstan | Uzbekistan |

Note: Azerbaijan signed the Alma-Ata Declaration (see below), but in October 1992 the Azerbaijan legislature voted against ratification of the foundation documents (see below) by which the Commonwealth of Independent States had been founded in December 1991. Azerbaijan, however, formally became a member of the CIS in September 1993, after the legislature voted in favour of membership. Georgia was admitted to the CIS in December 1993.

## Organization

(January 2000)

### COUNCIL OF HEADS OF STATE

This is the supreme body of the CIS, on which all the member states of the Commonwealth are represented at the level of head of state, for discussion of issues relating to the co-ordination of Commonwealth activities and the development of the Minsk Agreement. Decisions of the Council are taken by common consent, with each state having equal voting rights. The Council meets no less than twice a year, although an extraordinary meeting may be convened on the initiative of the majority of Commonwealth heads of state.

### COUNCIL OF HEADS OF GOVERNMENT

This Council convenes for meetings no less than once every three months; an extraordinary sitting may be convened on the initiative of a majority of Commonwealth heads of government. The two Councils may discuss and take necessary decisions on important domestic and external issues and may hold joint sittings.

Working and auxiliary bodies, composed of authorized representatives of the participating states, may be set up on a permanent or interim basis on the decision of the Council of Heads of State and the Council of Heads of Government.

### CIS EXECUTIVE COMMITTEE

The Committee was established by the Council of Heads of State in April 1999 to supersede the existing Secretariat, the Inter-state Economic Committee and other working bodies and committees, in order to improve the efficient functioning of the organization.

**Executive Secretary and Chairman of the Executive Committee:** YURII YAROV.

## Activities

On 8 December 1991 the heads of state of Belarus, Russia and Ukraine signed the Minsk Agreement, providing for the establishment of a Commonwealth of Independent States. Formal recognition of the dissolution of the USSR was incorporated in a second treaty, signed by 11 heads of state in the Kazakh capital, Alma-Ata (Almaty), later in that month.

In March 1992 a meeting of the CIS Council of Heads of Government decided to establish a commission to examine the resolution that 'all CIS member states are the legal successors of the rights and obligations of the former Soviet Union'. Documents relating to the legal succession of the Soviet Union were signed at a meeting of Heads of State in July. In April an agreement establishing an Inter-parliamentary Assembly (IPA), signed by Armenia, Belarus, Kazakhstan, Kyrgyzstan, Russia, Tajikistan and Uzbekistan, was published. The first Assembly was held in Bishkek, Kyrgyzstan, in September, attended by delegates from all these countries, with the exception of Uzbekistan.

A CIS Charter was formulated at the meeting of the heads of state in Minsk, Belarus, in January 1993. The Charter, providing for a defence alliance, an inter-state court and an economic co-ordination committee, was to serve as a framework for closer co-operation and was signed by all of the members except Moldova, Turkmenistan and Ukraine.

In November 1995, at the Council of Heads of Government meeting, Russia expressed concern at the level of non-payment of debts by CIS members (amounting to an estimated US $5,800m.), which, it said, was hindering further integration. At the meeting of the Council in April 1996 a long-term plan for the integrated development of the CIS, incorporating measures for further socio-economic, military and political co-operation was approved.

In March 1997 the Russian President, Boris Yeltsin, admitted that the CIS institutional structure had failed to ameliorate the severe economic situation of certain member states. Nevertheless, support for the CIS as an institution was reaffirmed by the participants during the meeting. At the heads of state meeting held in Chişinău, Moldova, in October, Russia was reportedly criticized by the other country delegations for failing to implement CIS agreements, for hindering development of the organization and for failing to resolve regional conflicts. Russia, for its part, urged all member states to participate more actively in defining, adopting and implementing CIS policies. In 1998 the issue of reform of the CIS was seriously addressed. The necessity of improving the activities of the CIS and of reforming its bureaucratic structure was emphasized at the meeting of heads of state in April. However, little in the way of reform was achieved at the meeting and it was decided not to adopt any declaration relating to the discussions. Reform of the CIS was also the main item on the agenda of the eleventh IPA, held in June. It was agreed that an essentially new institution needed to be created, taking into account the relations between the states in a new way. The IPA approved a decision to sign the European Social Charter; a declaration of co-operation between the Assembly and the OSCE Parliamentary Assembly (q.v.) was also signed. In the same month the first plenary meeting of a special forum, convened to address issues of restructuring the CIS, was held. Working groups were to be established to co-ordinate proposals and draft documents. However, in October reform proposals drawn up by 'experienced specialists' and presented by the Executive Secretary were unanimously rejected as inadequate by the 12 member states. In March 1999 Boris Yeltsin, acting as Chairman of the Council of Heads of State, dismissed the Executive Secretary, Boris Berezovskii, owing to alleged misconduct and neglect of duties. The decision was endorsed by the Council of Heads of State meeting in early April. The Council also adopted guide-lines for restructuring the CIS and for the future development of the organization. Economic co-operation was to be a priority area of activity, and in particular, the establishment of a free-trade zone.

Alliances of various kinds have been formed by CIS member states among themselves, which, some observers considered as having undermined the Commonwealth and rendered it redundant. In March 1996 Belarus, Kazakhstan, Kyrgyzstan and the Russian Federation signed the Quadripartite Treaty for greater integration. This envisaged the establishment of a 'New Union', based, initially on a common market and customs union and was to be open to all CIS members and the Baltic states. In April 1996 Belarus and Russia signed the Treaty on the Formation of a Community of Sovereign Republics (CSR), which provided for extensive economic, political and military co-operation. In April 1997 the two countries signed a further Treaty of Union and, in addition, initialled the Charter of the Union, which detailed the procedures and institutions designed to develop a common infrastructure, a single currency and a joint defence policy within the CSR, with the eventual aim of 'voluntary unification of the member states'. The Charter was signed in May and ratified by the respective legislatures the following month. The Union's Parliamentary Assembly, comprising 36 members from the legislature of each country, convened in official session for the first time shortly afterwards.

## ECONOMIC AFFAIRS

At a meeting of the Council of Heads of Government in March 1992 agreement was reached on repayment of the foreign debt of the former USSR. Agreements were also signed on pensions, joint tax policy and the servicing of internal debt. In May an agreement on repayment of inter-state debt and the issue of balance-of-payments statements was signed by the heads of government, meeting in Tashkent, Uzbekistan. In July it was decided to establish an economic court in Minsk.

The CIS Charter, formulated in January 1993 and signed by seven of the 10 member countries, provided for the establishment of an economic co-ordination committee. In February, at a meeting of the heads of foreign economic departments, a Foreign Economic Council was formed. All states, with the exception of Turkmenistan, signed a declaration of support for increased economic union at a meeting of the heads of state in May. At a further meeting, held in September, agreement on a framework for economic union, including the gradual removal of tariffs and creation of a currency union was reached, although Ukraine and Turkmenistan did not sign the accord. Turkmenistan was subsequently admitted as a full member of the economic union in December 1993 and Ukraine as an associate member in April 1994.

At the Council of Heads of Government meeting in September 1994 all member states, except Turkmenistan, agreed to establish an Inter-state Economic Committee to implement economic treaties adopted within the context of an economic union. The establishment of a payments union to improve the settlement of accounts was also agreed. Heads of state, meeting in the following month, resolved that the Inter-state Economic Committee would be located in Moscow, with Russia contributing the majority of administrative costs in exchange for 50% of the voting rights. The first session of the Committee was held in November. In April 1998 CIS heads of state resolved to incorporate the functions of the Committee, along with those of other working bodies and sectional committees, into a new CIS Executive Committee.

In October 1997 seven heads of government signed a document on implementing the 'concept for the integrated economic development of the CIS' which had been approved in March. The development of economic co-operation between the member states was a priority task of the special forum on reform held in June 1998. In the same month an economic forum, held in St Petersburg, Russia, acknowledged the severe economic conditions prevailing in certain CIS states.

## BANKING AND FINANCIAL AFFAIRS

In February 1992 CIS heads of state agreed to retain the rouble as the common currency for trade between the republics. However, in July 1993, in an attempt to control inflation, notes printed before 1993 were withdrawn from circulation and no new ones were issued until January 1994. Despite various agreements to recreate the 'rouble zone', including a protocol agreement signed in September 1993 by six states, it effectively remained confined to Tajikistan, which joined in January 1994, and Belarus, which joined in April. Both those countries proceeded to introduce national currencies in May 1995. In January 1993, at the signing of the CIS Charter, all 10 member countries endorsed the establishment of an inter-state bank to facilitate payments between the republics and to co-ordinate monetary-credit policy. Russia was to hold 50% of shares in the bank, but decisions were to be made only with a two-thirds majority approval.

## TRADE

Agreement was reached on the free movement of goods between republics at a meeting of the Council of Heads of State in February 1992, and in April 1994 an agreement on the creation of a free-trade zone within the CIS was signed. In July a council of the heads of customs committees, meeting in Moscow, approved a draft framework for customs legislation in CIS countries, to facilitate the establishment of a free-trade zone. The framework was approved by all the participants, with the exception of Turkmenistan. In April 1999 CIS heads of state signed a protocol to the 1994 free-trade area accord, which aimed to accelerate economic co-operation.

At the first session of the Inter-state Economic Committee in November 1994 draft legislation regarding a customs union was approved. In March 1998 Russia, Belarus, Kazakhstan and Kyrgyzstan signed an agreement establishing a customs union, which was to be implemented in two stages: firstly, the removal of trade restrictions and the unification of trade and customs regulations; followed by the integration of economic, monetary and trade policies (see above). The establishment of a customs union and the doubling of intra-CIS trade by 2000 were objectives endorsed by all participants, with the exception of Georgia, at the Council of Heads of Government meeting held in March 1997. In February 1999 Tajikistan signed the 1996 agreement to become the fifth member of the customs union. In October 1999 the heads of state of the five member states reiterated their political determination to implement the customs union and approved a programme to harmonize national legislation to create a single economic space.

## DEFENCE

An Agreement on Armed Forces and Border Troops was concluded on 30 December 1991, at the same time as the Agreement on Strategic Forces. This confirmed the right of member states to set up their own armed forces and appointed Commanders-in-Chief of the Armed Forces and of the Border Troops, who were to elaborate joint security procedures. In February 1992 an agreement was signed stipulating that the commander of the strategic forces was subordinate to the Council of Heads of States. Eight states agreed on a unified command for general-purpose (i.e. non-strategic) armed forces for a transitional period of two years. Azerbaijan, Moldova and Ukraine resolved to establish independent armed forces.

In January 1992 Commissions on the Black Sea Fleet (control of which was disputed by Russia and Ukraine) and the Caspian Flotilla (the former Soviet naval forces on the Caspian Sea) were established. The defence and stability of CIS external borders and the status of strategic and nuclear forces were among topics discussed at the meeting of heads of state and of government, in Bishkek, in October. The formation of a defence alliance was provided for in the CIS Charter formulated in January 1993 and signed by seven of the 10 member countries; a proposal by Russia to assume control of all nuclear weapons in the former USSR was rejected at the same time.

In June 1993 CIS defence ministers agreed to abolish CIS joint military command and to abandon efforts to maintain a unified defence structure. The existing CIS command was to be replaced, on a provisional basis, by a 'joint staff for co-ordinating military co-operation between the states of the Commonwealth'. It was widely reported that Russia had encouraged the decision to abolish the joint command, owing to concerns at the projected cost of a CIS joint military structure and support within Russia's military leadership of bilateral military agreements with the country's neighbours. In December the Council of Defence Ministers agreed to establish a secretariat to co-ordinate military co-operation as a replacement to the joint military command. In November 1995 the Council of Defence Ministers authorized the establishment of a Joint Air Defence System, to be co-ordinated largely by Russia. By early 1998 all member states, except Azerbaijan and Moldova, were participating in the system (Armenia, Georgia, Kyrgyzstan and Uzbekistan joined in January). Air defence forces were to be set up in Tajikistan in 1998 and a CIS combat duty system was to be created in 1999–2005. A meeting of the Council of Defence Ministers in Moscow, in December 1998, approved a plan for further development of the system. Russia and Belarus were also in the process of establishing a joint air-defence unit in the context of the CSR (see above).

In August 1996 the Council of Defence Ministers condemned what it described as the political, economic and military threat implied in any expansion of NATO (q.v.). The statement was not signed by Ukraine. The eigthth plenary session of the IPA, held in November, urged NATO countries to abandon plans for the organization's expansion. In September the first meeting of the inter-state commission for military economic co-operation was held; a draft agreement on the export of military projects and services to third countries was approved.

The basic principles of a programme for greater military and technical co-operation were approved by the Council of Defence Ministers in March 1997. In April 1998 the Council proposed drawing up a draft programme for military and technical co-operation between member countries and also discussed procedures advising on the use and maintenance of armaments and military hardware. Draft proposals relating to information security for the military were approved by the Council in December. It was remarked that the inadequate funding of the Council was a matter for concern and that the CIS states had failed to fulfil their military co-operation plan for 1998.

## REGIONAL SECURITY

At a meeting of heads of government in March 1992 agreements on settling inter-state conflicts were signed by all participating states (except Turkmenistan). At the same meeting an agreement on the status of border troops was signed by five states. In May a five-year Collective Security Agreement was signed. In July further documents were signed on collective security and it was agreed to establish joint peacemaking forces to intervene in CIS disputes. In April 1999 Armenia, Belarus, Kazakhstan, Kyrgyzstan, Russia and Tajikistan signed a protocol to extend the Collective Security Agreement for a further five-year period.

In September 1993 the Council of Heads of State agreed to establish a Bureau of Organized Crime, to be based in Moscow. A meeting of the Council of Border Troop Commanders in January 1994 prepared a report on the issue of illegal migration and drug trade across the extenal borders of the CIS; Moldova, Georgia and Tajikistan did not attend. A programme to combat organized crime within the CIS was approved by heads of government, meeting in Moscow, in April 1996.

In February 1995 a non-binding memorandum on maintaining peace and stability was adopted by heads of state, meeting in Almaty. Signatories were to refrain from applying military, political, economic or other pressure on another member country, to seek the peaceful resolution of border or territorial disputes and not to support or assist separatist movements active in other member countries. In April 1998 the Council of Defence Ministers approved a draft document proposing that coalition forces be provided with technical equipment to enhance collective security.

In June 1998, at a session of the Council of Border Troop Commanders, some 33 documents were signed relating to border co-operation. A framework protocol on the formation and expedient use of a border troops reserve in critical situations was discussed and signed by several participants. A register of work in scientific and engineering research carried out in CIS countries in the interests of border troops was also adopted.

The fourth plenary session of the IPA in March 1994 established a commission for the resolution of the conflicts in the secessionist regions of Nagornyi Karabakh (Azerbaijan) and Abkhazia (Georgia) and endorsed the use of CIS peace-keeping forces. In the following month Russia agreed to send peace-keeping forces to Georgia, and the dispatch of peace-keeping forces was approved by the Council of Defence Ministers in October. The subsequent session of the IPA in October adopted a resolution to send groups of military observers to Abkhazia and to Moldova. The inter-parliamentary commission on the conflict between Abkhazia and Georgia proposed initiating direct negotiations with the two sides in order to reach a peaceful settlement.

In December 1994 the Council of Defence Ministers enlarged the mandate of the commander of the CIS collective peace-keeping forces in Tajikistan: when necessary CIS military contingents were permitted to engage in combat operations without the prior consent of individual governments. At the Heads of State meeting in Moscow in January 1996 Georgia's proposal to impose sanctions against Abkhazia was approved, in an attempt to achieve a resolution of the conflict. Provisions on arrangements relating to collective peace-keeping operations were approved at the meeting; the training of military and civilian personnel for these operations was to commence in October. In March 1997 the Council of Defence Ministers agreed to extend the peace-keeping mandates for CIS forces in Tajiskistan and Abkhazia (following much disagreement, the peace-keepers' mandate in Abkhazia was renewed once more in October). At a meeting of the Council in January 1998 a request from Georgia that the CIS carry out its decisions to settle the conflict with Abkhazia was added to the agenda. The Council discussed the promotion of military co-operation and the improvement of peace-making activities, and declared that there was progress in the formation of the collective security system, although the situation in the North Caucasus remained tense. In April President Yeltsin requested that the Armenian and Azerbaijani presidents sign a document to end the conflict in Nagornyi Karabakh; the two subsequently issued a statement expressing their support for a political settlement of the conflict. A document proposing a settlement of the conflict in Abkhazia was also drawn up, but the resolutions adopted were not accepted by Abkhazia. Against the wishes of the Abkhazian authorities, the mandate for the CIS troops in the region was extended to cover the whole of the Gali district. The mandate expired in July 1998, but the forces remained in the region while its renewal was debated. In April 1999 the Council of Heads of State agreed to extend the operation's mandate by six months.

An emergency meeting of heads of state in October 1996 discussed the renewed fighting in Afghanistan and the threat to regional security. The participants requested the UN Security Council to adopt measures to resolve the conflict. The eighth plenary session of the IPA in November reiterated the call for a cessation of hostilities in the country. In June 1998 the IPA approved the Kyrgyzstan parliament's appeal for a peace settlement in Afghanistan.

A meeting of the Council of Ministers of Internal Affairs was held in Tashkent, Uzbekistan, in June 1998; President Leonid Kuchma of Ukraine signed a decree approving his country's membership of the Council. A number of co-operation agreements were signed, including a framework for the exchange of information between CIS law-enforcement agencies. The Council also decided to maintain its contact with Interpol.

## LEGISLATIVE CO-OPERATION

An agreement on legislative co-operation was signed at an Inter-Parliamentary Conference in January 1992; joint commissions were established to co-ordinate action on economy, law, pensions, housing, energy and ecology. The CIS Charter, formulated in January 1993, provided for the establishment of an inter-state court. In October 1994 a Convention on the rights of minorities was adopted at the meeting of the Heads of State. In May 1995, at the sixth plenary session of the IPA, several acts to improve co-ordination of legislation were approved, relating to migration of labour, consumer rights, and the rights of prisoners of war.

The creation of a Council of Ministers of Internal Affairs was approved at the Heads of State meeting in January 1996; the Council was to promote co-operation between the law-enforcement bodies of member states. At the 10th plenary session of the IPA in December 1997 14 laws, relating to banking and financial services, education, ecology and charity were adopted. At the IPA session held in June

1998 10 model laws relating to social issues were approved, including a law on obligatory social insurance against production accidents and occupational diseases, and on the general principles of regulating refugee problems.

### OTHER ACTIVITIES

The CIS has held a number of discussions relating to the environment. In July 1992 agreements were concluded to establish an Inter-state Ecological Council. The 10th plenary session of the IPA in December 1997 appealed to international organizations, parliaments and governments to participate in defeating an international convention on ecological safety.

In July 1992 it was agreed to establish an Inter-state Television and Radio Company (ITRC). In February 1995 the IPA established a Council of Heads of News Agencies, in order to promote the concept of a single information area. In December 1997 the IPA expressed concern about the dissemination of misleading or inaccurate information, particularly via the internet.

A Petroleum and Gas Council was created at a Heads of Government meeting in March 1993, to guarantee energy supplies and to invest in the Siberian petroleum industry. The Council was to have a secretariat based in Tyumen, Siberia. In the field of civil aviation, the inter-state economic committee agreed in February 1997 to establish an Aviation Alliance to promote co-operation between the countries' civil aviation industries.

# CO-OPERATION COUNCIL FOR THE ARAB STATES OF THE GULF

**Address:** POB 7153, Riyadh 11462, Saudi Arabia.

**Telephone:** (1) 482-7777; **fax:** (1) 482-9089; **internet:** www.gcc-sg.org.

More generally known as the Gulf Co-operation Council (GCC), the organization was established on 25 May 1981 by six Arab states.

### MEMBERS

| | | |
|---|---|---|
| Bahrain | Oman | Saudi Arabia |
| Kuwait | Qatar | United Arab Emirates |

## Organization

(January 2000)

### SUPREME COUNCIL

The Supreme Council is the highest authority of the GCC, comprises the heads of member states and meets annually in ordinary session, and in emergency session if demanded by two or more members. The Presidency of the Council is undertaken by each state in turn, in alphabetical order. The Supreme Council draws up the overall policy of the organization; it discusses recommendations and laws presented to it by the Ministerial Council and the Secretariat General in preparation for endorsement. The GCC's charter provides for the creation of a commission for the settlement of disputes between member states, to be attached to and appointed by the Supreme Council. In December 1997 the Supreme Council authorized the establishment of a 30-member Consultative Council, appointed by member states, to act as an advisory body.

### MINISTERIAL COUNCIL

The Ministerial Council consists of the foreign ministers of member states, meeting every three months, and in emergency session if demanded by two or more members. It prepares for the meetings of the Supreme Council, and draws up policies, recommendations, studies and projects aimed at developing co-operation and co-ordination among member states in various spheres.

### SECRETARIAT GENERAL

The Secretariat assists member states in implementing recommendations by the Supreme and Ministerial Councils, and prepares reports and studies, budgets and accounts. The Secretary-General is appointed by the Supreme Council for a renewable three-year term. In March 1996 the Ministerial Council approved a proposal that, in future, the position of Secretary-General be rotated among member states, in order to ensure equal representation. Assistant Secretary-Generals are appointed by the Ministerial Council upon the recommendation of the Secretary General. All member states contribute in equal proportions towards the budget of the Secretariat.

**Secretary-General:** Sheikh JAMIL IBRAHIM ALHEJAILAN (Saudi Arabia).

**Assistant Secretary-General for Political Affairs:** Dr HAMAD ALI AS-SULAYTI (Bahrain).

**Assistant Secretary-General for Economic Affairs:** AJLAN ALI AL-KUWARI (Qatar).

**Assistant Secretary-General for Military Affairs:** Maj.-Gen. FALEH ABDULLAH ASH-SHATTI (Kuwait).

## Activities

The GCC was set up following a series of meetings of foreign ministers of the states concerned, culminating in an agreement on the basic details of its charter on 10 March 1981. The Charter was signed by the six heads of state on 25 May. It describes the organization as providing 'the means for realizing co-ordination, integration and co-operation' in all economic, social and cultural affairs.

### ECONOMIC CO-OPERATION

In November 1982 GCC ministers drew up a 'unified economic agreement' covering freedom of movement of people and capital, the abolition of customs duties, technical co-operation, harmonization of banking regulations and financial and monetary co-ordination. At the same time GCC heads of state approved the formation of a Gulf Investment Corporation, to be based in Kuwait (see below). Customs duties on domestic products of the Gulf states were abolished in March 1983, and new regulations allowing free movement of workers and vehicles between member states were also introduced. A common minimum customs levy (of between 4% and 20%) on foreign imports was imposed in 1986. In May 1992 GCC trade ministers announced the objective of establishing a GCC common market by 2000. In September 1992 GCC ministers reached agreement on the application of a unified system of tariffs by March 1993. A meeting of the Supreme Council, held in December 1992, however, decided to mandate GCC officials to formulate a plan for the introduction of common external tariffs, to be presented to the Council in December 1993. Only the tax on tobacco products was to be standardized from March 1993, at a rate of 50% (later increased to 70%). In April 1994 ministers of finance agreed to pursue a gradual approach to unifying tariffs, which was to be achieved according to a schedule over two to three years. A technical committee, which had been constituted to consider aspects of establishing a customs union, met for the first time in June 1998. In December the Supreme Council requested that ministers of finance conclude an agreement on a unified customs tariff before the end of 1999, and resolved that a customs union become effective in March 2001. In November 1999 the Supreme Council concluded an agreement to establish a customs union by 1 March 2005. The arrangement required all member states to amend their tariff levels to 5.5% on basic commodities and 7.5% on other commodities. The Council also requested that members implement a unified legal system for customs by the end of 2000.

In February 1987 the governors of the member states' central banks agreed in principle to co-ordinate their rates of exchange, and this was approved by the Supreme Council in November. It was subsequently agreed to link the Gulf currencies to a 'basket' of other currencies. In April 1993 GCC central bank governors agreed to establish a joint banking supervisory committee, in order to devise rules for GCC banks to operate in other member states. They also decided to allow Kuwait's currency to become part of the GCC monetary system that was established following Iraq's invasion of Kuwait in order to defend the Gulf currencies. In December 1997 GCC heads of state authorized the guide-lines that had been formulated to enable national banks to establish operations in other GCC states. These were to apply only to banks established at least 10 years previously with a share capital of more than US $100m.

### TRADE AND INDUSTRY

In 1982 a ministerial committee was formed to co-ordinate trade policies and development in the region. Technical subcommittees were established to oversee a strategic food reserve for the member states, and joint trade exhibitions (which were generally held every year until responsibility was transferred to the private sector in 1996). In November 1986 the Supreme Council approved a measure whereby citizens of GCC member states were enabled to undertake certain retail trade activities in any other member state, with effect from 1 March 1987. The ministerial committee in charge of trade also forms the board of directors of the GCC Authority for Standards and Metrology, which approves minimum standards for goods produced in or imported to the region.

In 1985 the Supreme Council endorsed a common industrial strategy for the GCC states. It approved regulations stipulating that priority should be given to imports of GCC industrial products, and permitting GCC investors to obtain loans from GCC industrial development banks. In November 1986 resolutions were adopted on the protection of industrial products, and on the co-ordination of industrial projects, in order to avoid duplication. In March 1989 the Ministerial Council approved the Unified GCC Foreign Capital Investment Regulations, which aimed to attract foreign investment and to co-ordinate investments amongst GCC countries. Further guide-lines to promote foreign investment in the region were formulated during 1997. In December 1999 the Supreme Council amended the conditions determining rules of origin on industrial products in order to promote direct investment and intra-Community trade. In December 1992 the Supreme Council endorsed Patent Regulations for GCC member states to facilitate regional scientific and technological research. A GCC Patent Office for the protection of intellectual property in the region, was established in 1998.

In December 1998 the Supreme Council discussed the effect on members' economies of the decline in petroleum prices. The Council urged members to comply with the petroleum production cuts pledged earlier in the year (see OPEC, p. 252) and agreed to extend the reductions until June 1999 in an attempt to promote market stability. Other petroleum producing countries were requested to make similar production commitments.

## AGRICULTURE

A unified agricultural policy for GCC countries was endorsed by the Supreme Council in November 1985. Between 1983 and 1990 ministers also approved proposals for harmonizing legislation relating to water conservation, veterinary vaccines, insecticides, fertilizers, fisheries and seeds. A permanent committee on fisheries aims to co-ordinate national fisheries policies, to establish designated fishing periods and to undertake surveys of the fishing potential in the Arabian (Persian) Gulf. Co-operation in the agricultural sector also extends to consideration of the water resources in the region.

## TRANSPORT, COMMUNICATIONS AND INFORMATION

During 1985 feasibility studies were undertaken on new rail and road links between member states, and on the establishment of a joint coastal transport company. A scheme to build a 1,700-km railway to link all the member states and Iraq (and thereby the European railway network) was postponed, owing to its high cost (estimated at US $4,000m.). In November 1993 ministers agreed to request assistance from the International Telecommunication Union on the establishment of a joint telecommunications network, which had been approved by ministers in 1986. The region's telecommunications systems were to be integrated through underwater fibre-optic cables and a satellite-based mobile telephone network. In the mid-1990s GCC ministers of information began convening on a regular basis with a view to formulating a joint external information policy. In November 1997 GCC interior ministers approved a simplified passport system to facilitate travel between member countries.

## ENERGY

In 1982 a ministerial committee was established to co-ordinate hydrocarbons policies and prices. Ministers adopted a petroleum security plan to safeguard individual members against a halt in their production, to form a stockpile of petroleum products, and to organize a boycott of any non-member country when appropriate. In December 1987 the Supreme Council adopted a plan whereby a member state whose petroleum production was disrupted could 'borrow' petroleum from other members, in order to fulfil its export obligations.

During the early 1990s proposals were formulated to integrate the electricity networks of the six member countries. In the first stage of the plan the networks of Saudi Arabia, Bahrain, Kuwait and Qatar would be integrated; those of the United Arab Emirates (UAE) and Oman would be interconnected and finally linked to the others in the second stage, to be completed by 2003. In December 1997 GCC heads of state declared that work should commence on the first stage of the plan, under the management of an independent authority. The estimated cost of the project was more than US $6,000m. However, it was agreed not to invite private developers to participate in construction of the grid, but that the first phase of the project be financed by member states (to contribute 35% of the estimated $2,000m. required), and by loans from commercial banking and international monetary institutions. The so-called Gulf Council Interconnection Authority was established in mid-1999, with its headquarters in Dammam, Saudi Arabia.

## REGIONAL SECURITY

Although no mention of defence or security was made in the original charter, the summit meeting which ratified the charter also issued a statement rejecting any foreign military presence in the region. The Supreme Council meeting in November 1981 agreed to include defence co-operation in the activities of the organization: as a result, defence ministers met in January 1982 to discuss a common security policy, including a joint air defence system and standardization of weapons. In November 1984 member states agreed to form the Peninsula Shield Force for rapid deployment against external aggression, comprising units from the armed forces of each country under a central command to be based in Saudi Arabia.

In October 1987 (following an Iranian missile attack on Kuwait, which supported Iraq in its war against Iran) GCC ministers of foreign affairs issued a statement declaring that aggression against one member state was regarded as aggression against them all. In December the Supreme Council approved a joint pact on regional co-operation in matters of security. In August 1990 the Ministerial Council condemned Iraq's invasion of Kuwait as a violation of sovereignty, and demanded the withdrawal of all Iraqi troops from Kuwait. During the crisis and the ensuing war between Iraq and a multinational force which took place in January and February 1991, the GCC developed closer links with Egypt and Syria, which, together with Saudi Arabia, played the most active role among the Arab countries in the anti-Iraqi alliance. In March the six GCC nations, Egypt and Syria formulated the 'Declaration of Damascus', which announced plans to establish a regional peace-keeping force. The Declaration also urged the abolition of all weapons of mass destruction in the area, and recommended the resolution of the Palestinian question by an international conference. In June Egypt and Syria, whose troops were to have formed the largest proportion of the peace-keeping force, announced their withdrawal from the project, reportedly as a result of disagreements with the GCC concerning the composition of the proposed force and the remuneration involved. A meeting of ministers of foreign affairs of the eight countries took place in July, but agreed only to provide mutual military assistance when necessary. In September 1992 the signatories of the Damascus Declaration adopted a joint statement on regional questions, including the Middle East peace process and the dispute between the UAE and Iran (see below), but rejected an Egyptian proposal to establish a series of rapid deployment forces which could be called upon to defend the interests of any of the eight countries. A meeting of GCC ministers of defence in November agreed to maintain the Peninsula Shield Force. In November 1993 GCC ministers of defence approved a proposal to expand the force from 8,000 to 17,000 troops and incorporate air and naval units. Ministers also agreed to strengthen the defence of the region by developing joint surveillance and early warning systems. A GCC military committee was established, and convened for the first time in April 1994, to discuss the implementation of the proposals. Joint military training exercises were conducted by forces of five GCC states (excluding Qatar) in northern Kuwait in March 1996. In December 1997 the Supreme Council approved plans that had been authorized by defence ministers in November for linking the region's military telecommunications networks and establishing a common early warning system.

In 1992 Iran extended its authority over the island of Abu Musa, which it had administered under a joint arrangement with the UAE since 1971. In September 1992 the GCC Ministerial Council condemned Iran's continued occupation of the island and efforts to consolidate its presence, and reiterated support of UAE sovereignty over Abu Musa, as well as the largely uninhabited Greater and Lesser Tunb islands (also claimed by Iran). In December 1994 the GCC supported the UAE's request that the dispute be referred to the International Court of Justice.

In late September 1992 a rift within the GCC was caused by an incident on the disputed border between Saudi Arabia and Qatar. Qatar's threat to boycott a meeting of the Supreme Council in December was allayed at the last minute as a result of mediation efforts by the Egyptian President. At the meeting, which was held in UAE, Qatar and Saudi Arabia agreed to establish a joint commission to demarcate the disputed border. The resolution of border disputes was the principal concern of GCC heads of state when they convened for their annual meeting in December 1994, in Bahrain. The Kuwaiti leader proposed the establishment of a GCC framework for resolving border disputes, consisting of bilateral negotiations between the concerned parties, mediated by a third GCC state.

In November 1994 a security agreement, to counter regional crime and terrorism, was concluded by GCC states. The pact, however, was not signed by Kuwait, which claimed that a clause concerning the extradition of offenders was in contravention of its constitution;

Qatar did not attend the meeting, held in Riyadh, owing to its ongoing dispute with Saudi Arabia (see above). At the summit meeting in December GCC heads of state expressed concern at the increasing incidence of Islamic extremist violence throughout the region. In April 1995 GCC interior ministers convened to discuss ongoing civil unrest in Bahrain; the ministers collectively supported measures adopted by the Bahraini Government to secure political and civil stability. The continuing unrest in Bahrain and the involvement of the Iranian Government in Bahraini domestic affairs remained issues of concern for the GCC throughout 1995 and 1996.

During 1995 the deterioration of relations between Qatar and other GCC states threatened to undermine the Council's solidarity. In December Qatar publicly displayed its dissatisfaction at the appointment, without a consensus agreement, of Saudi Arabia's nominee as the new Secretary-General by failing to attend the final session of the Supreme Council, held in Muscat, Oman. However, at a meeting of ministers of foreign affairs in March 1996, Qatar endorsed the new Secretary-General, following an agreement on future appointment procedures, and reasserted its commitment to the organization. In June Saudi Arabia and Qatar agreed to reactivate a joint technical committee in order to finalize the demarcation of their mutual border. In December Qatar hosted the annual GCC summit meeting; however, Bahrain refused to attend, owing to Qatar's 'unfriendly attitude' and the long-standing territorial dispute over the Hawar islands. The issue dominated the meeting, which agreed to establish a four-member committee to resolve the conflicting sovereignty claims. In January 1997 the ministers of foreign affairs of Kuwait, Oman, Saudi Arabia and the UAE, meeting in Riyadh, formulated a seven-point memorandum of understanding to ease tensions between Bahrain and Qatar. The two countries refused to sign the agreement; however, in March both sides announced their intention to establish diplomatic relations at ambassadorial level.

In May 1997 the Ministerial Council, meeting in Riyadh, expressed concern at Turkey's cross-border military operation in northern Iraq and urged a withdrawal of Turkish troops from Iraqi territory. In December the Supreme Council reaffirmed the need to ensure the sovereignty and territorial integrity of Iraq. At the same time, however, the Council expressed concern at the escalation of tensions in the region, owing to Iraq's failure to co-operate with the UN Special Commission (UNSCOM). The Council also noted the opportunity to strengthen relations with Iran, in view of political developments in that country. In mid-February 1998 the US Defense Secretary visited each of the GCC countries in order to generate regional support for any punitive military action against Iraq, given that country's obstruction of UN weapons inspectors. Kuwait was the only country to declare its support for the use of force (and to permit the use of its bases in military operations against Iraq), while other member states urged a diplomatic solution to the crisis. Qatar pursued a diplomatic initiative to negotiate directly with the Iraqi authorities, and in mid-February the Qatari Minister of Foreign Affairs became the most senior GCC government official to visit Iraq since 1990. The GCC supported an agreement concluded between the UN Secretary-General and the Iraqi authorities at the end of February 1998, and urged Iraq to co-operate with UNSCOM in order to secure an end to the problem and a removal of the international embargo against the country. This position was reiterated at meetings of the Ministerial Council in March, and of the Supreme Council in December. In March 1999 the Ministerial Council expressed concern at Iraq's persistent refusal to co-operate with the UN. Other outstanding issues of concern in 1998 and 1999 continued to be the progress of the Middle East peace process and Iran's ongoing claim to sovereignty over Abu Musa and the Greater and Lesser Tunb islands. In March 1999 ministers condemned the military exercises being conducted by Iran in the waters around the islands as a threat to regional security and a violation of the UAE's sovereignty. Nevertheless, member countries continued to pursue efforts to strengthen relations with Iran, and in May President Khatami undertook a state visit to Qatar, Saudi Arabia and Syria, prompting concern on the part of the UAE that its support within the GCC and the solidarity of the grouping were being undermined. In June a meeting of GCC ministers of foreign affairs was adjourned, owing to reported disagreements between Saudi Arabia and the UAE. Diplomatic efforts secured commitments, issued by both countries later in that month, to co-operate fully within the GCC. In early July the Ministerial Council reasserted GCC support of the UAE's sovereignty claim over the disputed islands and determined to establish a committee, comprising the ministers of foreign affairs of Oman, Qatar and Saudi Arabia and the GCC Secretary-General, to resolve the dispute. In December the Supreme Council extended the mandate of the committee to establish a mechanism for direct negotiations between UAE and Iran.

## EXTERNAL RELATIONS

In June 1988 an agreement was signed by GCC and European Community (EC) ministers on economic co-operation (with effect from January 1990): the EC agreed to assist the GCC states in developing their agriculture and industry. In March 1990, at the first annual meeting of a Joint Co-operation Council, established under the accord, GCC and EC ministers of foreign affairs undertook to hold negotiations on a free-trade agreement. Discussions began in October, although any final accord would require the GCC to adopt a unified structure of customs duties. In early 1992 the agreement was jeopardized by the GCC's opposition to the EC's proposed tax on fossil fuels (in order to reduce pollution), which would have raised the price of a barrel of petroleum by an estimated US $10 by 2000. With the new US administration proposing a similar energy tax, in March 1993 GCC oil ministers threatened to restrict the supply of petroleum (the GCC countries control some 45% of the world's petroleum reserves) in retaliation. In October 1995 a conference was held in Muscat, Oman, which aimed to strengthen economic co-operation between European Union (EU, as the restructured EC was now known) and GCC member states, and to promote investment in both regions. In April 1996 the Joint Council advocated the conclusion of free-trade negotiations by 1998. In December 1997 GCC heads of state condemned statements issued by the European Parliament, as well as by other organizations, regarding human rights issues in member states and insisted they amounted to interference in GCC judicial systems. In October 1998 the Joint Council again resolved to accelerate discussions on the conclusion of a free-trade agreement, although no new deadline was set. It was agreed that the most contentious issue at that time, concerning the EU's imposition of duties on aluminium exports by Gulf states, was to be determined during the negotiations, in order to prevent further delays.

In December 1991 GCC ministers of finance and of foreign affairs approved the establishment of an Arab Development Fund, which aimed to create greater political and economic stability in the region, and in particular was intended to assist Egypt and Syria, as a reward for their active military part in the Gulf War and their major role in the security force envisaged by the Declaration of Damascus. A starting capital of US $10,000m. was originally envisaged for the Fund, although by mid-1992 only $6,500m. had been pledged, with reports that the project had been scaled down. In May 1993 ministers of finance from the GCC states, Egypt and Syria, meeting in Qatar, failed to agree on the level of contributions to the Fund.

In September 1994 GCC ministers of foreign affairs decided to end the secondary and tertiary embargo on trade with Israel. In February 1995 a ministerial meeting of signatories of the Damascus Declaration adopted a common stand, criticizing Israel for its refusal to renew the nuclear non-proliferation treaty. In December 1996 the foreign ministers of the Damascus Declaration states, convened in Cairo, requested the USA to exert financial pressure on Israel to halt the construction of settlements on occupied Arab territory.

In late June 1997 ministers of foreign affairs of the Damascus Declaration states agreed to pursue efforts to establish a free-trade zone throughout the region, which was to form the basis of a future Arab common market.

## INVESTMENT CORPORATION

**Gulf Investment Corporation (GIC):** Joint Banking Center, Kuwait Real Estate Bldg, POB 3402, Safat 13035, Kuwait; tel. 2431911; fax 2448894; e-mail gic@gic.com.kw; internet www.gic.com.kw; f. 1983 by the six member states of the GCC, each contributing US $350m. of the total capital of $2,100m.; total assets $10,245m., dep. $8,135m. (1995); investment chiefly in the Gulf region, financing industrial projects (including pharmaceuticals, chemicals, steel wire, aircraft engineering, aluminium, dairy produce and chicken-breeding). GIC provides merchant banking and financial advisory services, and in 1992 was appointed to advise the Kuwaiti Government on a programme of privatization. Chair. AHMAD BIN HUMAID AT-TAYER; Gen. Man. HISHAM A. RAZZUQI. Publ. *The GIC Gazetteer* (annually).

**Gulf International Bank:** POB 1017, Al-Dowali Bldg, 3 Palace Ave, Manama 317, Bahrain; tel. 534000; fax 522633; internet www.gibonline.com; f. 1976 by the six GCC states and Iraq; became a wholly-owned subsidiary of the GIC (without Iraqi shareholdings) in 1991; in April 1999 a merger with Saudi Investment Bank was concluded; cap. US $450m., dep. $8,491m., total assets $10,209m. (Dec. 1998). Chair. IBRAHIM ABD AL-KARIM; Gen. Man. ABDULLAH AL-KUWAIZ.

# Publications

*GCC News* (monthly).

*At-Ta'awun* (periodical).

# COUNCIL OF ARAB ECONOMIC UNITY

**Address:** 1191 Corniche en-Nil, 12th Floor, POB 1, Mohammed Fareed, Cairo, Egypt.

**Telephone:** (2) 5755321; **fax:** (2) 5754090.

Established in 1957 by the Economic Council of the Arab League. The first meeting of the Council was held in 1964.

### MEMBERS

| | |
|---|---|
| Egypt | Palestine |
| Iraq | Somalia |
| Jordan | Sudan |
| Kuwait | Syria |
| Libya | United Arab Emirates |
| Mauritania | Yemen |

## Organization

(January 2000)

### COUNCIL

The Council consists of representatives of member states, usually ministers of economy, finance and trade. It meets twice a year; meetings are chaired by the representative of each country for one year.

### GENERAL SECRETARIAT

Entrusted with the implementation of the Council's decisions and with proposing work plans, including efforts to encourage participation by member states in the Arab Economic Unity Agreement. The Secretariat also compiles statistics, conducts research and publishes studies on Arab economic problems and on the effects of major world economic trends.

**General Secretary:** HASSAN IBRAHIM.

### COMMITTEES

There are seven standing committees: preparatory, follow-up and Arab Common Market development; Permanent Delegates; budget; economic planning; fiscal and monetary matters; customs and trade planning and co-ordination; statistics. There are also seven *ad hoc* committees, including meetings of experts on tariffs, trade promotion and trade legislation.

## Activities

The Council undertakes to co-ordinate measures leading to a customs union subject to a unified administration; conduct market and commodity studies; assist with the unification of statistical terminology and methods of data collection; conduct studies for the formation of new joint Arab companies and federations; and to formulate specific programmes for agricultural and industrial co-ordination and for improving road and railway networks.

### ARAB COMMON MARKET

**Members:** Egypt, Iraq, Jordan, Libya, Mauritania, Syria and Yemen.

Based on a resolution passed by the Council in August 1964; its implementation is supervised by the Council and does not constitute a separate organization. Customs duties and other taxes on trade between the member countries were eliminated in annual stages, the process being completed in 1971. The second stage was to be the adoption of a full customs union, and ultimately all restrictions on trade between the member countries, including quotas, and restrictions on residence, employment and transport, were to be abolished. In practice, however, the trading of national products has not been freed from all monetary, quantitative and administrative restrictions.

Between 1978 and 1989, the following measures were undertaken by the Council for the development of the Arab Common Market: introduction of flexible membership conditions for the least developed Arab states (Mauritania, Somalia, Sudan and Yemen); approval in principle of a fund to compensate the least developed countries for financial losses incurred as a result of joining the Arab Common Market; approval of legal, technical and administrative preparations for unification of tariffs levied on products imported from non-member countries; formation of a committee of ministerial deputies to deal with problems in the application of market rulings and to promote the organization's activities and adoption of unified customs legislation and of an integrated programme aimed at enhancing trade between member states and expanding members' productive capacity.

### MULTILATERAL AGREEMENTS

The Council has initiated the following multilateral agreements aimed at achieving economic unity:

Agreement on Basic Levels of Social Insurance.

Agreement on Reciprocity in Social Insurance Systems.

Agreement on Labour Mobility.

Agreement on Organization of Transit Trade.

Agreement on Avoidance of Double Taxation and Elimination of Tax Evasion.

Agreement on Co-operation in Collection of Taxes.

Agreement on Capital Investment and Mobility.

Agreement on Settlement of Investment Disputes between Host Arab Countries and Citizens of Other Countries.

### JOINT VENTURES

A number of multilateral organizations in industry and agriculture have been formed on the principle that faster development and economies of scale may be achieved by combining the efforts of member states. In industries that are new to the member countries, Arab Joint Companies are formed, while existing industries are co-ordinated by the setting up of Arab Specialized Unions. The unions are for closer co-operation on problems of production and marketing, and to help companies deal as a group in international markets. The companies are intended to be self-supporting on a purely commercial basis; they may issue shares to citizens of the participating countries. The joint ventures are:

**Arab Joint Companies** (cap. = capital; figures in Kuwaiti dinars unless otherwise stated):

Arab Company for Drug Industries and Medical Appliances: POB 925161, Amman, Jordan; tel. (6) 5821618; fax (6) 5821649; e-mail acdima@go.com.jo; internet www.arabla.com.com/Acdima; f. 1976; cap. 60m.

Arab Company for Industrial Investment: POB 3385, Alwiyah, Baghdad, Iraq; tel. 718-9215; fax 718-0710; auth. cap. 150m.

Arab Company for Livestock Development: POB 5305, Damascus, Syria; tel. 666037; cap. 60m.

Arab Mining Company: POB 20198, Amman, Jordan; tel. (6) 663148; fax (6) 684114; cap. 120m.

**Specialized Arab Unions and Federations:**

Arab Co-operative Federation: POB 57640, Baghdad, Iraq; tel. (1) 888-8121.

Arab Federation for Paper, Printing and Packaging Industries: POB 5456, Baghdad, Iraq; tel. (1) 887-2384; fax (1) 886-9639; f. 1977; 250 mems.

Arab Federation of Chemical Fertilizers Producers: POB 23696, Kuwait.

Arab Federation of Engineering Industries: POB 509, Baghdad, Iraq; tel. (1) 776-1101.

Arab Federation of Shipping: POB 1161, Baghdad, Iraq; tel. (1) 717-4540; fax (1) 717-7243; f. 1979; 22 mems.

Arab Federation of Leather Industries: POB 2188, Damascus, Syria.

Arab Federation of Textile Industries: POB 620, Damascus, Syria.

Arab Federation of Travel Agents: POB 7090, Amman, Jordan.

Arab Seaports Federation: Basrah, Iraq; tel. (1) 413211.

Arab Sugar Federation: POB 195, Khartoum, Sudan.

Arab Union for Cement and Building Materials: POB 9015, Damascus, Syria; tel. (11) 6665070; fax (11) 6621525; e-mail aucbm@go .com.jo; f. 1977; 18 mems.

Arab Union of Fish Producers: POB 15064, Baghdad, Iraq; tel. (1) 551-1261.

Arab Union of Food Industries: POB 13025, Baghdad, Iraq.

Arab Union of Land Transport: POB 926324, Amman 11110, Jordan; tel. (6) 5663153; fax (6) 5664232.

Arab Union of the Manufacturers of Pharmaceuticals and Medical Appliances: POB 81150, Amman 11181, Jordan; tel. (6) 4654306; fax (6) 4648141; f. 1986.

Arab Union of Railways: POB 6599, Aleppo, Syria; tel. (21) 220302.

General Arab Insurance Federation: POB 611, 11511 Cairo, Egypt; tel. (2) 5743177; fax (2) 5762310; f. 1964.

## Publications

*Annual Bulletin for Arab Countries' Foreign Trade Statistics.*
*Annual Bulletin for Official Exchange Rates of Arab Currencies.*
*Arab Economic Unity Bulletin* (2 a year).
*Demographic Yearbook for Arab Countries.*
*Economic Report of the General Secretary* (2 a year).
*Guide to Studies prepared by Secretariat.*
*Progress Report* (2 a year).
*Statistical Yearbook for Arab Countries.*
*Yearbook for Intra-Arab Trade Statistics.*
*Yearbook of National Accounts for Arab Countries.*

# COUNCIL OF BALTIC SEA STATES—CBSS

**Address:** Strömsberg, POB 2010, 103 11 Stockhölm, Sweden.

**Telephone:** (8) 440-19-20; **fax:** (8) 440-19-44; **e-mail:** cbss@baltinfo.org; **internet:** www.baltinfo.org/CBSS.htm.

The Council of Baltic Sea States (CBSS) was established in 1992 to intensify co-operation between member states.

### MEMBERS

| | | |
|---|---|---|
| Denmark | Iceland | Poland |
| Estonia | Latvia | Russia |
| Finland | Lithuania | Sweden |
| Germany | Norway | |

The European Commission also has full membership status.

## Organization

(January 2000)

### PRESIDENCY

The presidency is occupied by heads of government for one year, on a rotating basis. Informal summit meetings of heads of government take place on an irregular basis, according to requirements.

### COUNCIL

The Council comprises the ministers of foreign affairs of each member state and a representative of the European Commission. The Council meets annually and aims to serve as a forum for guidance and overall co-ordination among participating states. The minister of foreign affairs of the presiding country is responsible for co-ordinating the Council's activities between ministerial sessions.

### COMMITTEE OF SENIOR OFFICIALS—CSO

The Committee consists of senior officials of the ministries of foreign affairs of the member states and of the European Commission. It serves as a discussion forum for matters relating to the work of the Council and undertakes inter-sessional activities. The Chairman of the Committee, from the same country serving as President of the CBSS, meets regularly with the previous and future Chairmen. The so-called Troika aims to maintain information co-operation, promote better exchange of information, and ensure more effective decision-making.

### SECRETARIAT

In June 1998 the presidency agreed to establish a permanent secretariat in Stockholm. The tasks of the secretariat include the preparation of summit meetings, annual sessions of ministers of foreign affairs, and other meetings of high-level officials and experts, the provision of technical support to the presidency regarding the implementation of plans, maintaining contacts with other sub-regional organizations, and strengthening awareness of the Council and its activities.

**Secretary-General:** JACEK STAROSCIAK (Poland).

### COMMISSIONER

**Address:** Amagertorv 14², POB 1165, 1010 Copenhagen K, Denmark.

**Telephone:** 33-91-22-88; **fax:** 33-91-22-96; **e-mail:** mail@cbss-commissioner.org; **internet:** www.cbss-commissioner.org.

The ministerial session held in May 1994 agreed to appoint an independent Commissioner on democratic institutions and human rights to serve a three-year term of office, from October of that year. In July 1997, at the sixth ministerial session held in Riga, the Commissioner's term of office was extended by a further three years. The Commissioner is based in Copenhagen, Denmark.

**Commissioner:** Dr OLE ESPERSEN (Denmark).

## Activities

The CBSS was established in March 1992 as a forum to enhance and strengthen co-operation between countries in the Baltic Sea region. At a meeting of the Council in Kalmar, Sweden, in July 1996, ministers adopted an Action Programme as a guide-line for CBSS activities. The main programme areas covered stable and participatory political development; economic integration and prosperity; and protection of the environment.

At the summit meeting held in Visby, Sweden, in May 1996, heads of government agreed to establish a Task Force on organized crime to counter drugs-trafficking, strengthen judicial co-operation, increase the dissemination of information, impose regional crime-prevention measures, improve border controls and provide training. In January 1998 the second Baltic Sea States Summit, convened in Riga, Latvia, agreed to extend the mandate of the Task Force until the end of 2000 and to enhance co-operation in the areas of civic security and border control.

The Council has founded a number of working groups, comprising experts in specific fields, which aim to report on and recommend action on issues of concern to the Council. In 1999 there were three groups working under the auspices of the CSO: the working group on assistance to democratic institutions, based in Riga, Latvia; the working group on economic co-operation, based in Bonn, Germany; and the working group on nuclear and radiation safety, based in Helsinki, Finland. The Swedish Special Group originated as a working group with a mandate to support the elimination of the sexual exploitation of children for commercial purposes in the Baltic Sea region. The Group helped to organize a conference on the subject held in Tallinn, Estonia, in September 1998.

In July 1998 ministers of trade of member states met in Vilnius, Lithuania, to discuss the development of small and medium-sized enterprises. Ministers agreed to strengthen links between member states, to implement measures to increase access to information in the region and to improve procedures for commercial border crossings by 2000.

## Finance

The Council is financed by contributions of the governments of its 11 member states.

## Publication

*Newsletter* (monthly).

# THE COUNCIL OF EUROPE

**Address:** 67075 Strasbourg Cédex, France.

**Telephone:** 3-88-41-20-00; **fax:** 3-88-41-27-81; **e-mail:** point_i@coe.int; **internet:** www.coe.int.

The Council was founded in May 1949 to achieve a greater unity between its members, to facilitate their social progress and to uphold the principles of parliamentary democracy, respect for human rights and the rule of law. Membership has risen from the original 10 to 41.

### MEMBERS*

| | |
|---|---|
| Albania | Lithuania |
| Andorra | Luxembourg |
| Austria | Macedonia, former Yugoslav republic |
| Belgium | Malta |
| Bulgaria | Moldova |
| Croatia | Netherlands |
| Cyprus | Norway |
| Czech Republic | Poland |
| Denmark | Portugal |
| Estonia | Romania |
| Finland | Russia |
| France | San Marino |
| Georgia | Slovakia |
| Germany | Slovenia |
| Greece | Spain |
| Hungary | Sweden |
| Iceland | Switzerland |
| Ireland | Turkey |
| Italy | Ukraine |
| Latvia | United Kingdom |
| Liechtenstein | |

* Armenia, Azerbaijan, Bosnia and Herzegovina and Monaco have applied for full membership. In addition, Belarus and the Federal Republic of Yugoslavia have applied for membership; however, at January 2000, their applications were not under consideration owing to the political situation in those countries. The Holy See, Canada, Japan, Mexico and the USA have observer status with the organization.

## Organization

(January 2000)

### COMMITTEE OF MINISTERS

The Committee consists of the ministers of foreign affairs of all member states (or their deputies); it decides with binding effect all matters of internal organization, makes recommendations to governments and draws up conventions and agreements; it also discusses matters of political concern, such as European co-operation, compliance with member states' commitments, in particular concerning the protection of human rights, and considers possible co-ordination with other institutions, such as the European Union (EU) and the Organization for Security and Co-operation in Europe (OSCE). The Committee usually meets in May and November each year.

### CONFERENCES OF SPECIALIZED MINISTERS

There are 19 Conferences of specialized ministers, meeting regularly for intergovernmental co-operation in various fields.

### PARLIAMENTARY ASSEMBLY

**President:** Lord Russell-Johnston (United Kingdom).

**Chairman of the Socialist Group:** Peter Schieder (Austria).

**Chairman of the Group of the European People's Party:** René van der Linden (Netherlands).

**Chairman of the European Democratic (Conservative) Group:** David Atkinson (United Kingdom).

**Chairman of the Liberal Democratic and Reformers' Group:** Kriistina Ojuland (Estonia).

**Chairman of the Unified European Left Group:** Jaakko Laakso (Finland).

Members are elected or appointed by their national parliaments from among the members thereof; political parties in each delegation follow the proportion of their strength in the national parliament. Members do not represent their governments; they speak on their own behalf. At January 2000 the Assembly had 291 members (and 291 substitutes): 18 each for France, Germany, Italy, Russia and the United Kingdom; 12 each for Poland, Spain, Turkey and Ukraine; 10 for Romania; seven each for Belgium, the Czech Republic, Greece, Hungary, the Netherlands and Portugal; six each for Austria, Bulgaria, Sweden and Switzerland; five each for Croatia, Denmark, Finland, Georgia, Moldova, Norway and Slovakia; four each for Albania, Ireland and Lithuania; three each for Cyprus, Estonia, Iceland, Latvia, Luxembourg, the former Yugoslav republic of Macedonia, Malta and Slovenia; and two each for Andorra, Liechtenstein and San Marino. Israel, Canada and Mexico have permanent observer status, while Armenia, Azerbaijan, Belarus and Bosnia and Herzegovina have been granted special 'guest status'. (Belarus's special status was suspended in January 1997.)

The Assembly meets in ordinary session once a year. The session is divided into four parts, held in the last full week of January, April, June and September. The Assembly submits Recommendations to the Committee of Ministers, passes Resolutions, and discusses reports on any matters of common European interest. It is also a consultative body to the Committee of Ministers, and elects the Secretary-General, the Deputy Secretary-General, the Clerk of the Assembly, the Council's Commissioner for Human Rights, and the members of the European Court of Human Rights.

**Standing Committee:** Represents the Assembly when it is not in session, and may adopt Recommendations to the Committee of Ministers and Resolutions on behalf of the Assembly. Consists of the President, Vice-Presidents, Chairmen of the Political Groups, Chairmen of the Ordinary Committees and Chairmen of national delegations. Meets usually three times a year.

**Ordinary Committees:** political; economic and development; social, health and family affairs; legal and human rights; culture and education; science and technology; environment, regional planning and local authorities; migration, refugees and demography; rules of procedure and immunities; agriculture; parliamentary and public relations; budget; monitoring; equal opportunities.

### CONGRESS OF LOCAL AND REGIONAL AUTHORITIES OF EUROPE—CLRAE

The Congress was established in 1994, incorporating the former Standing Conference of Local and Regional Authorities, in order to protect and promote the political, administrative and financial autonomy of local and regional European authorities by encouraging central governments to develop effective local democracy. The Congress comprises two chambers—a Chamber of Local Authorities and a Chamber of Regions—with a total membership of 291 elected representatives. Annual sessions are mainly concerned with local government matters, regional planning, protection of the environment, town and country planning, and social and cultural affairs. A Standing Committee, drawn from all national delegations, meets between plenary sessions of the Congress; other working groups, appointed by the Chambers, meet regularly to consider specific issues: for example, inner city problems, education, rural development, and unemployment. *Ad hoc* conferences and steering committees are also held.

The Congress advises the Council's Committee of Ministers and the Parliamentary Assembly on all aspects of local and regional policy and co-operates with other national and international organizations representing local government. The Congress monitors implementation of the European Charter of Local Self-Government, which was opened for signature in 1985 and provides common standards for effective local democracy. Other legislative guide-lines for the activities of local authorities and the promotion of democracy at local level include the 1980 European Outline Convention on Transfrontier Co-operation, and its Additional Protocol which was opened for signature in 1995, a Convention on the Participation of Foreigners in Public Life at Local Level (1992), and the European Charter for Regional or Minority Languages (1992). In addition, the European Urban Charter defines citizens' rights in European towns and cities, for example in the areas of transport, urban architecture, pollution and security.

**President:** Alain Chenard (France).

### SECRETARIAT

**Secretary-General:** Dr Walter Schwimmer (Austria).

**Deputy Secretary-General:** Hans Christian Krüger (Germany).

**Clerk of the Parliamentary Assembly:** Bruno Haller (France).

## Activities

In an effort to harmonize national laws, to put the citizens of member countries on an equal footing and to pool certain resources and facilities, the Council has concluded a number of conventions and agreements covering particular aspects of European co-operation. Since 1989 the Council has undertaken to increase co-operation with all countries of the former Eastern bloc and to facilitate their accession to the organization. In October 1997 heads of state or government of member countries convened for only the second time (the first meeting took place in Vienna, in October 1993—see below) with the aim of formulating a new social model to consolidate democracy throughout Europe. The meeting endorsed a Final Declaration and an Action Plan, which established priority areas for future Council activities, including fostering social cohesion; protecting civilian security; promoting human rights; enhancing joint measures to counter cross-border illegal trafficking; and strengthening democracy through education and other cultural activities. In addition, the meeting generated renewed political commitment to the Programme of Action against Corruption, which has become a key element of Council activities.

## HUMAN RIGHTS

The promotion and development of human rights is one of the major tasks of the Council of Europe. The European Convention for the Protection of Human Rights and Fundamental Freedoms was opened for signature in 1950. The Steering Committee for Human Rights is responsible for inter-governmental co-operation in human rights and fundamental freedoms; it works to strengthen the effectiveness of systems for protecting human rights, to identify potential threats and challenges to human rights, and to encourage education and provide information on the subject. It was responsible for the preparation of the European Ministerial Conference on Human Rights (1985), and an informal European Ministerial Conference on Human Rights (1990) and the elaboration of the European Convention for the Prevention of Torture (1987), which entered into force in February 1989. At the Council's first meeting of heads of state and of government, held in Vienna, Austria, in October 1993, members agreed to draw up a new Protocol to the European Convention on Human Rights to establish cultural rights of minorities and to draw up a new Framework Convention for the protection of national minorities. (Work on the Additional Protocol, however, was suspended in 1996.) The Framework Convention was adopted by the Council's Committee of Ministers in November 1994 and opened for signature on 1 February 1995. It entered into force on 1 February 1998 as the first ever legally-binding instrument devoted to the general protection of national minorities. In addition, the Convention obliged all parties to implement domestic legislation and programmes to fulfil the objectives of the instrument and to submit regular reports, to an 18-member Advisory Committee, on their implementation of the Convention.

The 1993 Vienna summit meeting also agreed to restructure the control mechanism for the protection of human rights, mainly the procedure for the consideration of cases, in order to reduce the length of time before a case is concluded. As a result, a new Protocol (No. 11) to the European Convention on Human Rights was opened for signature by member states in May 1994. The existing institutions (i.e. the European Commission of Human Rights and the European Court of Human Rights) were to be replaced by a single Court, working on a full-time basis. This was formally established on 1 November 1998, when Protocol 11 entered into force. The Commission was to continue to deal with applications declared admissible before 1 November, for a 12-month period.

In January 1999 the Parliamentary Assembly endorsed the appointment of a Council of Europe Commissioner for Human Rights to help prevent human rights abuses.

### European Court of Human Rights

The Court has compulsory jurisdiction and is competent to consider complaints lodged by states party to the European Convention and by individuals, groups of individuals or non-governmental organizations claiming to be victims of breaches of the Convention's guarantees. The Court comprises one judge for each contracting state (i.e. 41 in 1999). The Court sits in three-member Committees, empowered to declare applications inadmissible in the event of unanimity and where no further examination is necessary, seven-member Chambers, and a 17-member Grand Chamber. Chamber judgments become final three months after delivery, during which period parties may request a rehearing before the Grand Chamber, subject to acceptance by a panel of five judges. Grand Chamber judgments are final. Contracting parties are bound by the Court's final judgments; responsibility for supervising their execution is vested in the Council's Committee of Ministers. At the end of 1999 12,635 applications were pending before the Court.

**President:** LUZIUS WILDHABER (Switzerland).

**Registrar:** MICHELE DE SALVIA (Italy).

### European Committee for the Prevention of Torture and Inhuman or Degrading Treatment or Punishment—CPT

The Committee was established under the 1987 Convention for the Prevention of Torture as an integral part of the Council of Europe's system for the protection of human rights. The Committee, comprising independent experts, aims to examine the treatment of persons deprived of their liberty with a view to strengthening, if necessary, the protection of such persons from torture and from inhuman or degrading treatment or punishment. It conducts periodic visits to prisons, detention centres, and all other sites where persons are deprived of their liberty by a public authority, in all states parties to the Convention, and may also undertake *ad hoc* visits when the Committee considers them necessary. By January 2000 the Committee had undertaken 67 periodic visits and 29 *ad hoc* visits. After each visit the Committee drafts a report of its findings and any further advice or recommendations, based on dialogue and co-operation.

**President:** IVAN ZAKINE (France).

### European Social Charter

The European Social Charter, in force since 1965, is the counterpart of the European Convention on Human Rights, in the field of protection of economic and social rights. A revised Charter, which amended existing guarantees and incorporated new rights, was opened for signature in May 1996, and entered into force on 1 July 1999. At December 1999 the Charters were applied in 26 member states guaranteeing fundamental rights in all aspects of national social policies. These relate to conditions of employment (such as the prohibition on the employment of children, non-discrimination in employment, the right to decent working conditions and a fair remuneration and trade union rights), and of social cohesion (such as the right to social security and assistance, and the rights of families, migrants and elderly persons to legal, social and economic protection). A supervisory procedure provides for the examination of each contracting party's practical application of the rights guaranteed. A European Committee of Social Rights, composed of independent experts undertakes a legal assessment of national legislation, regulations and practices within the content of the Charter. The Committee of Ministers may then, if it considers it to be appropriate given economic and social factors, address a recommendation to the state concerned, asking it to comply with the Charter. Decisions are prepared by a Governmental Committee, composed of representatives of each Contracting Party. An Additional Protocol (1995), providing for a system of collective complaints, entered into force on 1 July 1998 and aimed to reinforce the Charter's control mechanism.

**President of the Committee of Independent Experts:** MATTI MIKKOLA (Finland).

**President of the Governmental Committee:** WILLEM VAN DE REE (Netherlands).

## RACISM AND INTOLERANCE

In October 1993 heads of state and of government, meeting in Vienna, resolved to reinforce a policy to combat all forms of intolerance, in response to the increasing incidence of racial hostility and intolerance towards minorities in European societies. A European Commission against Racism and Intolerance (ECRI) was established by the summit meeting to analyse and assess the effectiveness of legal, policy and other measures taken by member states to combat these problems. It became operational in March 1996. Members of ECRI are designated by governments on the basis of their recognized expertise in the field, although participate in the Commission in an independent capacity. ECRI undertakes activities in three programme areas: country-by-country approach; work on general themes; and ECRI and civil society. In the first area of activity, ECRI analyses the situation regarding racism and intolerance in each of the member states, in order to advise governments on measures to combat these problems. In December 1998 ECRI completed a first round of reports for all Council members. A follow-up series of reports were to be prepared during the four-year period 1999–2002. ECRI's work on general themes includes the preparation of policy recommendations and guide-lines on issues of importance to combating racism and intolerance. ECRI also collects and disseminates examples of good practices relating to these issues. Under the third programme area ECRI aims to disseminate information and raise awareness of the problems of racism and intolerance among the general public.

A Committee on the Rehabilitation and Integration of People with Disabilities supports co-operation between member states in this field and undertakes studies in order to promote legislative and administrative action.

## MEDIA AND COMMUNICATIONS

Article 10 of the European Convention on Human Rights (freedom of expression and information) forms the basis for the Council of Europe's mass media activities. Implementation of the Council of Europe's work programme concerning the media is undertaken by the Steering Committee on the Mass Media (CDMM), which comprises senior government officials and representatives of professional organizations, meeting in plenary session twice a year. The CDMM is mandated to devise concerted European policy measures and appropriate legal instruments. Its underlying aims are to further freedom of expression and information in a pluralistic democracy, and to promote the free flow of information and ideas. The CDMM is assisted by various specialist groups and committees. Policy and legal instruments have been developed on subjects including: exclusivity rights; media concentrations and transparency of media ownership; protection of journalists in situations of conflict and tension; independence of public-service broadcasting, protection of rights holders; legal protection of encrypted television services; and media and elections. These policy and legal instruments (mainly in the form on non-binding recommendations addressed to member governments) are complemented by the publication of studies, analyses and seminar proceedings on topics of media law and policy. The CDMM has also prepared a number of international binding legal instruments, including the European Convention on Transfrontier Television (adopted in 1989 and ratified by 21 countries by December 1999) and the European Convention relating to questions on copyright law and other rights in the context of transfrontier broadcasting by satellite (ratified by two countries and signed by seven other member states and the European Community by December 1999). CDMM areas of activity in 1999 included: new communications technologies and their impact on human rights and democratic values; the protection of journalists' sources; media reporting on legal proceedings; the independence and functions of regulatory authorities for the broadcasting sector; and the legal protection of conditional access services.

## SOCIAL COHESION

In June 1998, the Committee of Ministers established the European Committee for Social Cohesion (CDCS). The CDCS has the following responsibilities: to prepare proposals for a strategy for social cohesion, to co-ordinate, guide and stimulate co-operation between member States with a view to promoting social cohesion in Europe (by, for example, the regular exchange of views, information and good practice) and to promoting the social standards embodied in the European Social Charter and other Council of European instruments, including the European Code of Social Security. The CDCS is also responsible for executing the terms of reference of the European Code of Social Security, the European Convention on Social Security and the European Agreement on 'au pair' Placement. The CDCS initiated a series of activities in 1999, in particular to promote social standards, and to facilitate access to social rights (such as rights to employment, housing, social protection) and a Programme for Children.

The European Code of Social Security and its Protocol entered into force in 1968; by 1999 the Code and Protocol had been ratified by Belgium, Germany, Luxembourg, the Netherlands, Norway, Portugal and Sweden, while the Code alone had been ratified by Cyprus, Denmark, France, Greece, Ireland, Italy, Spain, Switzerland, Turkey and the United Kingdom. These instruments set minimum standards for medical care and the following benefits: sickness, old-age, unemployment, employment injury, family, maternity, invalidity and survivor's benefit. A revision of these instruments, aiming to provide higher standards and greater flexibility, was completed for signature in 1990 and had been signed by 14 states by 1999.

The European Convention on Social Security, in force since 1977, now applies in Austria, Belgium, Italy, Luxembourg, the Netherlands, Portugal, Spain and Turkey; most of the provisions apply automatically, while others are subject to the conclusion of additional multilateral or bilateral agreements. The Convention is concerned with establishing the following four fundamental principles of international law on social security: equality of treatment, unity of applicable legislation, conservation of rights accrued or in course of acquisition, and payment of benefits abroad. In 1994 a Protocol to the Convention, providing for the enlargement of the personal scope of the Convention, was opened for signature. By the end of 1998 it had been signed by Austria, Greece and Luxembourg.

## HEALTH

Through a series of expert committees, the Council aims to ensure constant co-operation in Europe in a variety of health-related fields, with particular emphasis on patients' rights, for example: equity in access to health care, quality assurance, health services for institutionalized populations (prisoners, elderly in homes), discrimination resulting from health status and education for health. These efforts are supplemented by the training of health personnel.

Improvement of blood transfusion safety and availability of blood and blood derivatives has been ensured through European Agreements and guide-lines. Advances in this field and in organ transplantation are continuously assessed by expert committees.

Eighteen states co-operate in a Partial Agreement to protect the consumer from potential health risks connected with commonplace or domestic activities. The committees of experts of the Public Health Committee provide the scientific base for national and international regulations regarding products which have a direct or indirect impact on the human food chain, pesticides, pharmaceuticals and cosmetics.

In the co-operation group to combat drug abuse and illicit drugs trafficking (Pompidou Group), 31 states work together, through meetings of ministers, officials and experts, to counteract drug abuse. The Group follows a multidisciplinary approach embracing in particular legislation, law enforcement, prevention, treatment, rehabilitation and data collection.

The Convention on the Elaboration of a European Pharmacopoeia (establishing legally binding standards for medicinal substances, auxiliary substances, pharmaceutical preparations and other articles) entered into force in eight signatory states in May 1974: in 1999 27 states and the European Union were parties to the Convention. WHO and 16 European and non-European states participate as observers in the sessions of the European Pharmacopoeia Commission. A network of official control laboratories for human and veterinary medicines was established in 1995, open to all signatory countries to the Convention and observers at the Pharmacopoeia Commission. The third edition of the European Pharmacopoeia includes some 1,550 harmonized European standards, or 'monographs', 250 general methods of analysis and 1,000 reagents.

In April 1997 the first international convention on biomedicine was opened for signature at a meeting of health ministers of member states, in Oviedo, Spain. The so-called Convention for the Protection of Human Rights and the Dignity of Human Beings with Respect to the Applications of Biology and Medicine incorporated provisions on scientific research, the principle of informed patient consent, organ and tissue transplants and the prohibition of financial gain and disposal of a part of the human body. It entered into force on 1 November 1999. An Additional Protocol to the Convention, with regard to the prohibition of medical cloning of human beings, was approved by Council heads of state and government in October 1997 and was opened for signature in January 1998. In early 2000 work was ongoing to draft protocols relating to the transplantation of human organs and tissue, medical research, protection of the human embryo and foetus and genetics.

## POPULATION AND MIGRATION

The European Convention on the Legal Status of Migrant Workers, in force since 1983, was applicable by 1995 to France, Italy, the Netherlands, Norway, Portugal, Spain, Sweden and Turkey. The Convention is based on the principle of equality of treatment for migrant workers and the nationals of the host country as to housing, working conditions, and social security. The Convention also upholds the principle of the right to family reunion. An international consultative committee, representing the parties to the Convention, monitors the application of the Convention.

In 1996 the European Committee on Migration concluded work on a project entitled 'The Integration of Immigrants: Towards Equal Opportunities' was concluded and the results were presented at the sixth conference of European ministers responsible for migration affairs, held in Warsaw, Poland. At the conference a new project, entitled 'Tensions and Tolerance: Building better integrated communities across Europe' was initiated; it was concluded in 1999. The Committee was responsible for activities concerning Roma/ Gypsies in Europe, in co-ordination with other relevant Council of Europe bodies. The Committee is also jointly responsible, with the *ad hoc* Committee of Experts on the legal aspects of territorial asylum, refugees and stateless persons, for the examination of migration issues arising at the pan-European level.

The European Population Committee, an intergovernmental committee of scientists and government officials responsible for population matters, monitors and analyses population trends throughout Europe and informs governments, research centres and the public of demographic developments and their impact on policy decisions. It compiles an annual statistical review of demographic developments (covering 46 European states) and publishes the results of studies on population issues, such as the demographic characteristics of national minorities in certain European states (Vol. I—1998), internal migration and regional population dynamics (1999), fertility and new types of households and family formation in Europe, and demographic trends and the labour market (both to be published in 2000). Future publications were to include studies on trends in mortality and differential mortality in Europe, the demographic characteristics of immigrant populations, the demographic consequences of economic transition in the countries of central and eastern Europe, and the demographic implications of social exclusion.

## COUNCIL OF EUROPE DEVELOPMENT BANK

A Council of Europe Social Development Fund was created in 1956 (as the Resettlement Fund). Its primary aim was to finance projects to benefit refugees, migrants and displaced persons, and victims of natural or ecological disasters. As a secondary objective, it also funds social projects involving job creation, vocational training, social housing, education, health, the protection of the environment, and the protection and rehabilitation of the historic heritage. In November 1999 the Fund was renamed the Council of Europe Development Bank. At September subscribed capital amounted to €1,401m., while total loans granted since the Fund's inception amounted to €12,210m.

## EQUALITY BETWEEN WOMEN AND MEN

The Steering Committee for Equality between Women and Men (CDEG—an intergovernmental committee of experts) is responsible for encouraging action at both national and Council of Europe level to promote equality of rights and opportunities between the two sexes. Assisted by various specialist groups and committees, the CDEG is mandated to establish analyses, studies and evaluations, to examine national policies and experiences, to work out concerted policy strategies and measures for implementing equality and, as necessary, to prepare appropriate legal and other instruments. It is also responsible for preparing the European Ministerial Conferences on Equality between Women and Men. The main areas of CDEG activities are the comprehensive inclusion of the rights of women (for example, violence against women, forced prostitution, reproductive rights) within the context of human rights; the issue of equality and democracy, including the promotion of the participation of women in political and public life; projects aimed at studying the specific equality problems related to cultural diversity, migration and minorities; positive action in the field of equality between men and women and the mainstreaming of equality into all policies and programmes at all levels of society. In October 1998 the Committee of Ministers adopted a recommendation to member states on gender mainstreaming.

## LEGAL MATTERS

The European Committee on Legal Co-operation develops co-operation between member states in the field of law, with the objective of harmonizing and modernizing public and private law, including administrative law and the law relating to the judiciary. The Committee is responsible for expert groups which consider issues relating to administrative law, efficiency of justice, family law, nationality, information technology and data protection. Numerous conventions and Recommendations have been adopted, and followed up by appropriate committees or groups of experts, on matters which include: information on foreign law; children born out of wedlock; adoption; nationality; animal protection; administrative law; custody of children; data protection; legal aid; and the legal status of non-governmental organizations.

An *ad hoc* Committee of Legal Advisors on Public and International Law (CAHDI), comprising the legal advisors of ministers of foreign affairs of member states and of several observer states, is authorized to examine questions of public international law, and to exchange and, if appropriate, to co-ordinate the views of member states. Recent activities of the CAHDI include the preparation of a Recommendation on reaction to inadmissible reservations to international treaties, and publication of a report on a pilot project relating to state practice with regard to state succession and recognition in the period 1989–1994. An *ad hoc* Committee of Experts on the Legal Aspects of Territorial Asylum, Refugees and Stateless Persons (CAHAR) proposes solutions to practical and legal problems relating to its area of expertise, formulates appropriate legal instruments, reviews relevant national and international developments and adopts Recommendations. The CAHAR has adopted a series of opinions for the Committee of Ministers on the situation of refugees and displaced persons in the CIS, on access to asylum by EU citizens, and on the human rights of refugees and asylum-seekers in Europe. It works closely with other international bodies, in particular UNHCR and the Council's Parliamentary Assembly.

With regard to crime, the European Committee on Crime Problems has prepared conventions on such matters as extradition, mutual assistance, recognition and enforcement of foreign judgments, the transfer of proceedings, the suppression of terrorism, the transfer of prisoners, the compensation to be paid to victims of violent crime, and search, seizure and confiscation of the proceeds from crime. A new Criminal Convention on Corruption was opened for signature in January 1999, while a Civil Law Convention against Corruption was opened for signature in November. In May a new monitoring organ, the Group of States against Corruption (GRECO), became operational.

A Criminological Scientific Council, composed of specialists in law, psychology, sociology and related sciences, advises the Committee and organizes criminological research conferences and colloquia. A Council for Penological Co-operation organizes regular high-level conferences of directors of prison administration and is responsible for collating statistical information on detention and community sanctions in Europe. The Council prepared new European Prison Rules in 1987 and European Rules on Community Sanctions (alternatives to imprisonment) in 1992.

In May 1990 the Committee of Ministers adopted a Partial Agreement to establish the European Commission for Democracy through Law, to be based in Venice, Italy. The Commission is composed of legal and political experts and is concerned with the guarantees offered by law in the service of democracy. In particular, it may supply opinions upon request, made through the Committee of Ministers, by the Parliamentary Assembly, the Secretary-General or any member states of the Council of Europe. Other states and international organizations may request opinions with the consent of the Committee of Ministers. The Commission may also conduct research on its own initiative. In 1999 the Commission was working on the following issues: constitutional justice; constitutional reforms; electoral law and national minorities; self-determination and secession in constitutional law; federated and regional entities and international treaties; and the prohibition of political parties. The Commission has pursued its activities through the UniDem (University for Democracy) programme of seminars and maintains its own website (at venice.coe.int/).

The promotion of local and regional democracy and of decentralized transfrontier co-operation constitutes a major aim of the Council's intergovernmental programme of activities. The Steering Committee on Local and Regional Democracy (CDLR) serves as a forum for representatives of member states to exchange information and pursue co-operation in order to promote the decentralization of powers, in accordance with the European Charter on Local Self-Government. The CDLR aims to improve the legal, institutional and financial framework of local democracy and to encourage citizen participation in local and regional communities. It prepares comparative studies and national reports, and issues guide-lines to promote the implementation of the principles of subsidiarity and solidarity, and is responsible for formulating or finalizing drafts of legal texts in the field of local and regional democracy. The work of the CDLR constitutes a basis for the provision of aid to central and eastern European countries under the ADACS-Local Government Programme. The policy of the Council of Europe on transfrontier co-operation between territorial communities or authorities is implemented through two committees. A Select Committee of Experts on Transfrontier Co-operation (LR-R-CT), composed of national experts, aims to monitor the implementation of the European Outline Convention on Transfrontier Co-operation between Territorial Communities or Authorities; to make proposals for the elimination of obstacles, in particular of a legal nature, to transfrontier and interterritorial co-operation; and to compile 'best practice' examples of transfrontier co-operation in various fields of activity. A Committee of Advisers for the development of transfrontier co-operation in central and eastern Europe is composed of three members representing, respectively, the Secretary General, the Committee of Ministers and the Congress of Local and Regional Authorities of Europe. Its task is to guide the promotion of transfrontier co-operation in central and eastern European countries, with a view to fostering good neighbourly relations between the frontier populations, especially in particularly sensitive regions. Its programme comprises: conferences and colloquies designed to raise awareness on the Outline Convention; meetings in border regions between representatives of local communities with a view to strengthening mutual trust; and restricted meetings with national and local representatives responsible for preparing the legal texts for ratification and/or implementation of the Outline Convention.

## EDUCATION, CULTURE AND HERITAGE

The European Cultural Convention covers education, culture, heritage, sport and youth. Programmes on education, higher education, culture and cultural heritage are managed by the Council for Cultural Co-operation, assisted by four specialized committees.

The education programme consists of projects on 'Education for democratic citizenship', 'Learning and teaching about the history of Europe in the 20th century', 'Language policies for a multilingual and multicultural Europe', and 'Education strategies for social cohesion and democratic security'. Other activities include: the annual European Schools Day Competition, organized in co-operation with the EU; the In-service Educational Staff Training Programme; the Network for School Links and Exchanges; and the European Secondary School Students Exchange Programme. The Council's main contribution in the field of higher education is its activity on the recognition of qualifications and mobility of students and staff. The Council of Europe/UNESCO Convention on the Recognition of Qualifications Concerning Higher Education in the European Region was adopted in 1997 and entered into force on 1 February 1999. Practical recognition work is conducted within the framework of a European Network of National Information Centres (ENIC) network on academic recognition and mobility. Other activities include a legislative reform programme; lifelong learning for equity and social cohesion; universities as sites of citizenship and civic responsibility; and techical co-operation and assistance to South-East Europe, in particular Bosnia and Herzegovina and Kosovo and Metohija.

In the field of cultural policy, a series of surveys of national policies are conducted (for example, on Croatia and Portugal in 1998 and Romania in 1999). Since 1998 this series has been complemented by 'transversal' policy reviews, for example on national cultural institutions and on cultural policy and cultural diversity. A Research and Development Unit for cultural policies became operational in 1997 with responsibility for the improvement, accuracy and circulation of information concerning European cultural policies. During 1999 reviews of national book policies were undertaken in Albania, Estonia and Lithuania. Guide-lines have been formulated on library legislation and policy in Europe, and in early 2000 work was ongoing on the preparation of guide-lines on book development and electronic publishing, and on a European policy on access to archives. Two main archive projects were being undertaken at early 2000—the computerization of the Komintern Archives in Moscow, Russia, and the reconstitution of archival sources relating to Polish history. In 1998 the Council initiated a new four-year assistance programme to support cultural development in South-East Europe (the MOSAIC project). A similar plan, the STAGE project, for countries of the Caucasus was scheduled to become operational in 2000.

The European Convention on Cinematographic Co-production was opened for signature in October 1992. The Eurimages support fund helps to finance co-production of films. Conventions for the Protection of the Architectural Heritage and the Protection of the Archaeological Heritage provide a legal framework for European co-operation in these areas. The Cultural Heritage Committee promotes discussion on measures relating to heritage and consolidating democracy in Europe, the formulation of strategies for sustainable development, and on national experience and policies concerning conservation and enhancement of the European cultural heritage. In September 1999 a new campaign was inaugurated to promote co-operation and to generate awareness of the common heritage of Europe. In 1996 the European Conference of Ministers responsible for cultural heritage resolved to establish a network for the dissemination of information, using the electronic media, on heritage policies in states party to the European Cultural Convention. The network was initiated as a pilot scheme, covering six countries, in 1999. It was being developed by the European Foundation for Heritage Skills, which aimed to develop practical co-operation among professionals of all European countries.

### YOUTH

In 1972 the Council of Europe established the European Youth Centre (EYC) in Strasbourg. A second residential centre was created in Budapest in 1995. The centres, run with and by international non-governmental youth organizations representing a wide range of interests, provide about 50 residential courses a year (study sessions, training courses, symposia) and a programme of 10 language courses. A notable feature of the EYC is its decision-making structure, by which decisions on its programme and general policy matters are taken by a Programming Committee composed of an equal number of youth organizations and government representatives.

The European Youth Foundation (EYF) aims to provide financial assistance to European activities of non-governmental youth organizations and began operations in 1973. Since that time more than 350 organizations have received financial aid for carrying out international activities, while more than 210,000 young people have participated in meetings supported by the Foundation. The European Steering Committee for Intergovernmental Co-operation in the Youth Field conducts research in youth-related matters and prepares for ministerial conferences.

### SPORT

The Committee for the Development of Sport, founded in November 1977, administers the Sports Fund. Its activities concentrate on the implementation of the European Sports Charter; the role of sport in society (e.g. medical, political, ethical and educational aspects); the provision of assistance in sports reform to new member states in central and eastern Europe; the practice of sport (activities, special projects, etc.); the diffusion of sports information; and co-ordination of sports research. The Committee is also responsible for preparing the conference of European ministers responsible for sport. In 1985 the Committee of Ministers adopted the European Convention on Spectator Violence and Misbehaviour at Sports Events. A Charter on Sport for Disabled Persons was adopted in 1986, an Anti-Doping Convention in 1989, and a Code of Sports Ethics in 1992. In 1996 the Committee for the Development of Sport adopted an Action Plan for Bosnia and Herzegovina, entitled 'Rehabilitation through Sport'.

### ENVIRONMENT AND SUSTAINABLE DEVELOPMENT

In 1995 a pan-European biological and landscape diversity strategy, formulated by the Committee of Ministers, was endorsed at a ministerial conference of the UN Economic Commission for Europe, which was held in Sofia, Bulgaria. The strategy was to be implemented jointly by the Council of Europe and UNEP, in close co-operation with the European Community. In particular, it provided for implementation of the Convention on Biological Diversity.

At January 2000 40 states and the European Community had ratified a Convention on the Conservation of European Wildlife and Natural Habitats, which entered into force in June 1982 and gives total protection to 693 species of plants, 89 mammals, 294 birds, 43 reptiles, 21 amphibians, 115 freshwater fishes, 111 invertebrates and their habitats. The Convention established a network of protected areas known as the 'Emerald Network'. The Council's NATUROPA Centre provides information and documentation on the environment, through periodicals and campaigns such as the Europe Nature Conservation Year (1995). The Council awards the European Diploma for protection of areas of European significance, supervises a network of biogenetic reserves, and maintains 'red lists' of threatened animals and plants.

Regional disparities constitute a major obstacle to the process of European integration. Conferences of ministers of regional planning are held to discuss these issues. In 1997 they adopted a set of principles concerning the outlook for sustainable development and its implication for Europe beyond the year 2000.

### EXTERNAL RELATIONS

Agreements providing for co-operation and exchange of documents and observers have been concluded with the United Nations and its agencies, and with most of the European inter-governmental organizations and the Organization of American States. Particularly close relations exist with the EU, OECD, and the OSCE. Relations with non-member states, other organizations and non-governmental organizations are co-ordinated by the Directorate General of Political Affairs.

Israel, Canada and Mexico are represented in the Parliamentary Assembly by observer delegations, and certain European and other non-member countries participate in or send observers to certain meetings of technical committees and specialized conferences at intergovernmental level. Full observer status with the Council was granted to the USA in 1995, to Canada and Japan in 1996 and to Mexico in 1999. The Holy See has had a similar status since 1970.

The European Centre for Global Interdependence and Solidarity (the 'North–South Centre') was established in Lisbon, Portugal, in 1990, in order to provide a framework for European co-operation in this area and to promote pluralist democracy and respect for human rights. The Centre is co-managed by parliamentarians, governments, non-governmental organizations and local and regional authorities. Its activities are divided into three programmes: public information and media relations; education and training for global interdependence; and dialogue for global partnership. The Centre organizes workshops, seminars and training courses on global interdependence and convenes international colloquies on human rights.

During the early 1990s the Council of Europe established a structure of programmes to assist the process of democratic reform in central and eastern European countries that had formerly been under communist rule. In October 1997 the meeting of heads of state or of government of Council members agreed to extend the programmes as the means by which all states are assisted to meet their undertakings as members of the Council. In 1998 the co-operation programmes were renamed the 'activities for developing and consolidating democratic stability' (ADACS), which were mainly concerned with the development of the rule of law; the protection and promotion of human rights; and strengthening local democracy. In 1999 bilateral joint programmes, established with the support of the European Commission, within the framework of ADACS, covered Albania, Armenia, Azerbaijan, Georgia, Moldova, Russia and Ukraine. Multilateral joint programmes have been implemented in the fields of protection of national minorities, the fight against organized crime (the OCTOPUS programme), and bio-ethics (DEBRA). A scheme of Democratic Leadership Programmes has also been established for the training of political leaders. Within the framework of the co-operation programme 19 information and documentation centres have been established in 14 countries of Central and Eastern Europe. Council offices in Sarajevo and Tirana support the implementation of the ADACS programmes in Bosnia and Herzegovina and Albania, respectively. A secretariat representation to co-ordinate the Council's contribution to the UN operation in Kosovo was established in the capital of Kosovo and Metohija, Priština, in mid-1999.

## Finance

The budget is financed by contributions from members on a proportional scale of assessment (using population and gross domestic product as common indicators). The 1999 budget totalled £159.5m.

## Publications

*Activities and achievements* (in 17 languages).

*Activities Report* (in French and English).

*Annual Report of the Council for Cultural Co-operation.*

*Catalogue of Publications* (annually).
*Congress of Local and Regional Authorities of Europe Newsletter* (6 a year).
*Europa40plus* (electronic newsletter, monthly, in English and French).
*European Cultural Diary* (annually).
*European Heritage* (2 a year, in English, French and German).
*The Europeans* (electronic bulletin of the Parliamentary Assembly).
*Naturopa* (3 a year, in 4 languages).
*Official Gazette of the Council of Europe* (monthly, in English and French).
*Sports Information Bulletin* (quarterly).
*Strategy Bulletin* (6 a year, in 5 languages).

# ECONOMIC COMMUNITY OF WEST AFRICAN STATES—ECOWAS

**Address:** ECOWAS Secretariat and Conference Centre, 60 Yakubu Gowon Crescent, Asokoro, Abuja, Nigeria.

**Telephone and fax:** (9) 2347648; **e-mail:** info@ecowas.net; **internet:** www.ecowas.net.

The Treaty of Lagos, establishing ECOWAS, was signed in May 1975 by 15 states, with the object of promoting trade, co-operation and self-reliance in West Africa. Outstanding protocols bringing certain key features of the Treaty into effect were ratified in November 1976. Cape Verde joined in 1977. A revised ECOWAS treaty, designed to accelerate economic integration and to increase political co-operation, was signed in July 1993.

### MEMBERS

| | | |
|---|---|---|
| Benin | Guinea | Niger |
| Burkina Faso | Guinea-Bissau | Nigeria |
| Cape Verde | Liberia | Senegal |
| Côte d'Ivoire | Mali | Sierra Leone |
| The Gambia | Mauritania | Togo |
| Ghana | | |

## Organization

(January 2000)

### AUTHORITY OF HEADS OF STATE AND GOVERNMENT

The Authority is the supreme decision-making organ of the Community, with responsibility for its general development and realization of its objectives.The Chairman is drawn from the member states in turn. In August 1997 ECOWAS heads of state decided that the Authority should be convened twice each year (previously on an annual basis) to enhance monitoring and co-ordination of the Community's activities.

### COUNCIL OF MINISTERS

The Council consists of two representatives from each country; a chairman is drawn from each country in turn. It meets twice a year, and is responsible for the running of the Community.

### EXECUTIVE SECRETARIAT

The Executive Secretary is elected for a four-year term, which may be renewed once only.

**Executive Secretary:** Lansana Kouyaté (Guinea).

### SPECIALIZED TECHNICAL COMMISSIONS

There are eight commissions, comprising representatives of each member state, which prepare Community projects and programmes in the following areas:

(i) Food and Agriculture;
(ii) Industry, Science and Technology, and Energy;
(iii) Environment and Natural Resources;
(iv) Transport, Communications, and Tourism;
(v) Trade, Customs, Taxation, Statistics, and Money and Payments;
(vi) Political, Judicial and Legal Affairs, Regional Security, and Integration;
(vii) Human Resources, Information, and Social and Cultural Affairs; and
(viii) Administration and Finance.

### ECOWAS FUND FOR CO-OPERATION, COMPENSATION AND DEVELOPMENT

**Address:** BP 2704, blvd du 13 Janvier, Lomé, Togo.

**Telephone and fax:** 216864.

The Fund is administered by a Board of Directors. The chief executive of the Fund is the Managing Director, who holds office for a renewable term of four years. There is a staff of 100. The authorized cap. of the Fund is US $500m.; paid-up cap. totalled $66.5m. (at Dec. 1997). In 1988 agreements were reached with the African Development Bank and the Islamic Development Bank on the co-financing of projects and joint training of staff. Efforts are currently being undertaken to enhance the Fund's financial resources, by opening its capital to non-regional participants.

**Managing Director:** Drabo D. Barthelamy (acting).

## Activities

ECOWAS aims to promote co-operation and development in economic, social and cultural activity, particularly in the fields for which specialized technical commissions (see above) are appointed, to raise the standard of living of the people of the member countries, increase and maintain economic stability, improve relations among member countries and contribute to the progress and development of Africa.

The treaty provides for compensation for states whose import duties are reduced through trade liberalization and contains a clause permitting safeguard measures in favour of any country affected by economic disturbances through the application of the treaty.

The treaty also contains a commitment to abolish all obstacles to the free movement of people, services and capital, and to promote: harmonization of agricultural policies; common projects in marketing, research and the agriculturally based industries; joint development of economic and industrial policies and elimination of disparities in levels of development; and common monetary policies.

Lack of success in many of ECOWAS' aims has been attributed to the existence of numerous other intergovernmental organizations in the region (in particular the francophone Communauté économique de l'Afrique de l'ouest, replaced by the Union économique et monétaire ouest-africaine in 1994, q.v.) and to member governments' lack of commitment, shown by their reluctance to implement policies at the national level, their failure to provide the agreed financial resources, and the absence of national links with the Secretariat. During the 1990s ECOWAS activities were increasingly dominated by its efforts to secure peace in Liberia, and later in Sierra Leone (see below).

A revised treaty for the Community was drawn up by an ECOWAS Committee of Eminent Persons in 1991–92, and was signed at the ECOWAS summit conference that took place in Cotonou, Benin, in July 1993. The treaty, which was to extend economic and political co-operation among member states, designates the achievement of a common market and a single currency as economic objectives, while in the political sphere it envisages the establishment of a West African Parliament, an economic and social council and an ECOWAS Court of Justice to replace the existing Tribunal and enforce Community decisions. The treaty also formally assigned the Community with the responsibility of preventing and settling regional conflicts. At the summit meeting, held in Abuja, Nigeria, in August 1994, ECOWAS heads of state and government signed a protocol agreement for the establishment of a regional parliament; however, no timetable was specified for this to be achieved. The meeting also adopted a Convention on Extradition of non-political offenders. At the end of July 1995 the new ECOWAS treaty was reported to have entered into effect, having received the required number of ratifications.

## TRADE AND MONETARY UNION

Elimination of tariffs and other obstructions to trade among member states, and the establishment of a common external tariff, were planned over a transitional period of 15 years. At the 1978 Conference of Heads of State and Government it was decided that from May 1979 no member state might increase its customs tariff on goods from another member. This was regarded as the first step towards the abolition of customs duties within the Community. During the first two years import duties on intra-community trade were to be maintained, and then eliminated in phases over the next eight years. Quotas and other restrictions of equivalent effect were to be abolished in the first 10 years. In the remaining five years all differences between external customs tariffs were to be abolished.

The 1980 meeting of heads of state and government decided to establish a free-trade area for unprocessed agricultural products and handicrafts from May 1981. Tariffs on industrial products made by specified community enterprises were also to be abolished from that date, but implementation was delayed by difficulties in defining the enterprises. From 1 January 1990 tariffs were eliminated on 25 listed items manufactured in ECOWAS member states. Over the ensuing decade, tariffs on other industrial products were to be eliminated as follows: the 'most-developed' countries of ECOWAS (Côte d'Ivoire, Ghana, Nigeria and Senegal) were to abolish tariffs on 'priority' products within four years and on 'non-priority' products within six years; the second group (Benin, Guinea, Liberia, Sierra Leone and Togo) were to abolish tariffs on 'priority' products within six years, and on 'non-priority' products within eight years; and the 'least-developed' members (Burkina Faso, Cape Verde, The Gambia, Guinea-Bissau, Mali, Mauritania and Niger) were to abolish tariffs on 'priority' products within eight years and on 'non-priority' products within 10 years. By 1997 an estimated 400 industrial goods had been approved under the trade liberalization scheme.

In 1990 ECOWAS heads of state and government agreed to adopt measures that would create a single monetary zone and remove barriers to trade in goods that originated in the Community. ECOWAS regards monetary union as necessary to encourage investment in the region, since it would greatly facilitate capital transactions with foreign countries. In September 1992 it was announced that, as part of efforts to enhance monetary co-operation and financial harmonization in the region, the West African Clearing House was to be restructured as the West African Monetary Agency (WAMA, see p. 295). As a specialized agency of ECOWAS, WAMA was to be responsible for administering an ECOWAS exchange rate system (EERS) and for establishing the single monetary zone. A credit guarantee scheme and travellers' cheque system were to be established in association with the EERS. The agreement establishing WAMA was signed by the Governors of the central banks of ECOWAS member states, meeting in Banjul, The Gambia, in March 1996. In July the Authority agreed to impose a common value-added tax (VAT) on consumer goods, in order to rationalize indirect taxation and to stimulate greater intra-Community trade. In August 1997 ECOWAS heads of state and government appointed an *ad hoc* monitoring committee to promote and oversee the implementation of trade liberalization measures and the establishment of a single monetary zone by 2000. The meeting also authorized the introduction of the regional travellers' cheque scheme. In March 1998 senior customs officials of ECOWAS countries agreed to harmonize customs policies and administrations, in order to facilitate intra-Community trade, and to pursue the objective of establishing a common external tariff by 2000. In October 1998 the travellers' cheque scheme was formally inaugurated at a meeting of ECOWAS heads of state. The cheques were to be issued by WAMA in denominations of a West African Unit of Account and convertible into each local currency at the rate of one Special Drawing Right (SDR—see IMF p. 91). The cheques entered into circulation on 1 July 1999.

In December 1992 ECOWAS ministers agreed on the institutionalization of an ECOWAS trade fair, in order to promote trade liberalization and intra-Community trade. The first trade fair, which was held in Dakar, Senegal in May/June 1995, was attended by some 400 private businesses from the 16 member states. A second trade fair was scheduled to be held in Accra, Ghana, in 1999.

## TRAVEL, TRANSPORT AND COMMUNICATIONS

In 1979 ECOWAS heads of state signed a Protocol relating to free circulation of the region's citizens and to rights of residence and establishment of commercial enterprises. The first provision (the right of entry without a visa) came into force in 1980. The second provision, allowing unlimited rights of residence, was signed in 1986 (although Nigeria indicated that unskilled workers and certain categories of professionals would not be allowed to stay for an indefinite period) and came into force in 1989. The third provision, concerning the right to establish a commercial enterprise in another member state was signed in 1990. In July 1992 the ECOWAS Authority formulated a Minimum Agenda for Action for the implementation of Community agreements regarding the free movement of goods and people, for example the removal of non-tariff barriers, the simplification of customs and transit procedures and a reduction in the number of control posts on international roads. By mid-1996 the ECOWAS summit meeting observed that few measures had been adopted by member states to implement the Minimum Agenda, and emphasized that it remained a central element of the Community's integration process. In April 1997 the Gambian and Senegalese finance and trade officials concluded an agreement on measures to facilitate the export of goods via Senegal to neighbouring countries, in accordance with ECOWAS protocols relating to inter-state road transit arrangements. A Brown Card scheme, providing a recognized third-party liability insurance throughout the region, was operational in 1998.

In August 1996 the initial phase of a programme to improve regional telecommunications was reported to have been completed. Some US $35m. had been granted for project financing in eight ECOWAS countries. A second phase of the programme (INTELCOM II), which aimed to modernize and expand the region's telecommunications services, was initiated by ECOWAS heads of state in August 1997.

A programme for the development of an integrated regional road network was adopted in 1980. Under the programme, two major trans-regional roads were to be completed: the Trans-Coastal Highway, linking Lagos, Nigeria, with Nouackchott, Mauritania (4,767 km); and the Trans-Sahelian Highway, linking Dakar, Senegal, with N'Djamena, Chad (4,633 km). By mid-1998 about 83% of the trans-coastal route was complete, and about 87% of the trans-Sahelian route.

## ECONOMIC AND INDUSTRIAL DEVELOPMENT

In November 1984 ECOWAS heads of state and government approved the establishment of a private regional investment bank, to be known as Ecobank Transnational Inc. The bank, which was based in Lomé, Togo, opened in March 1988. ECOWAS has a 10% share in the bank. By mid-1999 Ecobank affiliates were operating in Benin, Burkina Faso, Côte d'Ivoire, Ghana, Mali, Nigeria and Togo. At that time plans were underway to commence operations in Guinea, Liberia, Niger and Senegal.

The West African Industrial Forum, sponsored by ECOWAS, is held every two years to promote regional industrial investment. The Secretariat is formulating a West African Industrial Master Plan. The first phase involved the compilation of an inventory of industrial enterprises, while the second phase was to comprise study of important industrial sub-sectors, prior to the drawing up of the Master Plan.

In September 1995 Nigeria, Ghana, Togo and Benin resolved to develop a gas pipeline to connect Nigerian gas supplies to the other countries. In August 1999 the participating countries, together with two petroleum companies operating in Nigeria, signed an agreement on the financing and construction of the pipeline, which was expected to become operational in 2002. During 1997 a Community initiative to connect the electricity supply networks throughout the region was under consideration.

In August 1997 the Authority of Heads of State and Government urged all member states to co-ordinate their long-term development programmes in order to formulate common objectives and to encourage greater economic growth in the region as a whole.

## REGIONAL SECURITY

In 1990 a Standing Mediation Committee was formed to mediate in disputes between member states. Member states reaffirmed their commitment to refrain from aggression against one another at a summit conference in 1991. The revised ECOWAS treaty, signed in July 1993, incorporates a separate provision for regional security, requiring member states to work towards the maintenance of peace, stability and security.

In December 1997 an extraordinary meeting of ECOWAS heads of state and government was convened in Lomé, Togo, to consider the future stability and security of the region. It was agreed that a permanent mechanism be established for conflict prevention and the maintenance of peace. ECOWAS leaders also reaffirmed their commitment to pursuing dialogue to prevent conflicts, co-operating in the early deployment of peace-keeping forces and implementing measures to counter trans-border crime and the illegal trafficking of armaments and drugs. At the meeting ECOWAS leaders acknowledged ECOMOG's role in restoring constitutional order in Liberia and expressed their appreciation of the force's current efforts in Sierra Leone. In March 1998 ECOWAS ministers of foreign affairs, meeting in Yamoussoukro, Côte d'Ivoire, resolved that ECOMOG should become the region's permanent peace-keeping force, and upheld the decision of heads of state regarding the establishment of a new body, which should be used to observe, analyse and monitor the security situation in the West African region. Ministers agreed to undertake a redefinition of the command structure within the organization in order to strengthen decision-making and the legal status of the ECOMOG force.

In July 1998 ECOWAS ministers of defence and of security adopted a draft mechanism for conflict management, peace-keeping and security, which provided for ECOWAS intervention in the internal affairs of member states, where a conflict or military uprising threatened the region's security. In October the ECOWAS Authority resolved to establish a Committee of Mediation and Security. The meeting also agreed to implement a three-year ban on the import, export or manufacture of small armaments in order to enhance the security of the sub-region. In addition, the meeting issued a declaration on the control and prevention of drug abuse and agreed to allocate US $150,000 to establish an Eco-Drug Fund to finance regional activities in countering substance abuse.

### Peace-keeping operations

In August 1990 an ECOWAS Cease-fire Monitoring Group (ECOMOG—initially comprising about 4,000 troops from The Gambia, Ghana, Guinea, Nigeria and Sierra Leone) was dispatched to Liberia in an attempt to enforce a cease-fire between conflicting factions there, to restore public order, and to establish an interim government, until elections could be held. In November a temporary cease-fire was agreed by the protagonists in Liberia, and an interim president was installed by ECOMOG. Following the signature of a new cease-fire agreement a national conference, organized by ECOWAS in March 1991, established a temporary government, pending elections to be held in early 1992. In June 1991 ECOWAS established a committee (initially comprising representatives of five member states, later expanded to nine) to co-ordinate the peace negotiations. In September, at a meeting in Yamoussoukro, Côte d'Ivoire, held under the aegis of the ECOWAS committee, two of the rival factions in Liberia agreed to encamp their troops in designated areas and to disarm under ECOMOG supervision. During the period preceding the proposed elections, ECOMOG was to occupy Liberian air and sea ports, and create a 'buffer zone' along the country's border with Sierra Leone. By September 1992, however, ECOMOG had been unable either to effect the disarmament of two of the principal military factions, the National Patriotic Front of Liberia (NPFL) and the United Liberation Movement of Liberia for Democracy (ULIMO), or to occupy positions in substantial areas of the country, as a result of resistance on the part of the NPFL. The proposed elections were consequently postponed indefinitely.

In October 1992 ECOMOG began offensive action against NPFL positions, with a campaign of aerial bombardment. In November ECOWAS imposed a land, sea and air blockade on the NPFL's territory, in response to the Front's refusal to comply with the Yamoussoukro accord of October 1991. In April 1993 ECOMOG announced that the disarmament of ULIMO had been completed, amid widespread accusations that ECOMOG had supported ULIMO against the NPFL, and was no longer a neutral force. An ECOWAS-brokered cease-fire agreement was signed in Cotonou, Benin, in July, and took effect on 1 August. In September a 300-member UN observer mission (UNOMIL) was established in Liberia to work alongside ECOMOG in monitoring the process of disarming troops, as well as to verify the impartiality of ECOMOG.

In September 1994 leaders of the country's main military factions, having negotiated with representatives of ECOWAS, the Organization of African Unity (OAU, q.v.) and the UN, signed an amendment to the Cotonou Agreement in Akosombo, Ghana. The accord provided for a new five-member Council of State, in the context of a cease-fire, as a replacement to the expired interim executive authority, and established a new timetable for democratic elections. In early 1995 negotiations to secure a peace settlement, conducted under ECOWAS auspices, collapsed, owing to disagreement on the composition of a new Council of State. In May, in an attempt to ease the political deadlock, ECOWAS heads of state and of government met leaders of the six main warring factions. Under continuing pressure from the international community, the leaders of the Liberian factions signed a new peace accord, in Abuja, Nigeria, in August. This political development led to renewed efforts on the part of ECOWAS countries to strengthen ECOMOG, and by October Burkina Faso, Nigeria, Ghana and Guinea had pledged troop contributions to increase the force strength from 7,268 to 12,000. In accordance with the peace agreement, ECOMOG forces, with UNOMIL, were to be deployed throughout Liberia and along its borders to prevent the flow of arms into the country and to monitor the disarmament of the warring parties. In December an attack on ECOMOG troops, by a dissident ULIMO faction, disrupted the deployment of the multinational forces and the disarmament process, which was scheduled to commence in mid-January 1996. At least 16 members of the peace-keeping force were killed in the fighting that ensued. Clashes between ECOMOG and the ULIMO–J forces continued in the west of the country in late December 1995 and early January 1996, during which time 130 Nigerian members of ECOMOG were held hostage. In April, following a series of violations of the cease-fire, serious hostilities erupted in the Liberian capital, Monrovia, between government forces and dissident troops. An initial agreement to end the fighting, negotiated under ECOWAS auspices, was unsuccessful; however, it secured the release of several civilians and soldiers who had been taken hostage during the civil disruption. Later in April a further cease-fire agreement was concluded, under the aegis of the US Government, the UN and ECOWAS. In May ministers of foreign affairs of the countries constituting the ECOWAS Committee of Nine advocated that all armed factions be withdrawn from Monrovia and that ECOMOG troops be deployed throughout the capital in order to re-establish the city's 'safe-haven' status. According to the Committee's demands, all property, armaments and equipment seized unlawfully from civilians, ECOMOG and other international organizations during the fighting were to be returned, while efforts to disarm the warring factions and to pursue the restoration of democracy in the country were to be resumed. At the end of May the deployment of ECOMOG troops was initiated. In August a new cease-fire accord was signed by the leaders of the principal factions in Liberia, which envisaged the completion of the disarmament process by the end of January 1997, with elections to be held in May. The disarmament process began in November 1996, and by the end of January 1997 ECOMOG confirmed that 23,000 of the targeted 30,000-35,000 soldiers had been disarmed (the original estimate of 60,000 troops having been revised, disputed by both faction leaders and ECOMOG officials once movement between factions was taken into account). The deadline for disarmament was extended by seven days, during which time a further 1,500 soldiers were reported to have been disarmed. However, vigilante attacks by remaining armed faction fighters continued and were condemned by the ECOMOG commander. In February, at the end of a meeting of the Committee of Nine, it was announced that presidential and legislative elections would be held on 30 May (later revised to 19 July). ECOMOG was to withdraw from Liberia six months after the election date, until which time it had proposed to offer security for the incoming government and to provide training for a new unified Liberian army. The Committee also agreed, in consultation with the Council of State, to replace the existing Electoral Commission with a new Commission comprising seven members, to reflect all aspects of Liberian society. The Chairman would be selected from among the seven, in consultation with ECOWAS, which along with the UN and the OAU, would act as a 'technical adviser' to the Commission. ECOMOG deployed additional troops, who were joined by other international observers in ensuring that the elections were conducted in the necessary conditions of security. In early August several ECOWAS leaders celebrated the democratic transition of power in Liberia at the inauguration of Charles Taylor (formerly leader of the NPFL) as the newly-elected President. Later in that month ECOWAS heads of state agreed that the ECOMOG force in Liberia was to be reconstituted and would henceforth assist in the process of national reconstruction, including the restructuring of the armed and security forces, and the maintenance of security; it was further envisaged that ECOMOG's mandate (officially due to expire on 2 February 1998) would be extended in agreement with the Liberian Government. A Status of Forces Agreement, which defined ECOMOG's post-conflict responsibilities (i.e. capacity-building and maintenance of security) and imposed conditions on the peace-keeping forces remaining in the country, was signed by the Liberian Government and ECOWAS in June 1998. Relations with the Taylor administration, however, deteriorated, owing to accusations that ECOMOG was providing assistance to opposition groupings. The tense political situation, therefore, and the need for greater resources in Sierra Leone, resulted in ECOMOG transferring its headquarters from Monrovia to Freetown in Sierra Leone. The transfer was reported to have been completed by October, with just two ECOMOG battalions remaining in Liberia. The ECOMOG mission in Liberia was effectively terminated in July 1999 when the final declared stocks of rebel armaments were destroyed. In August a regional meeting was convened, under ECOWAS auspices, to attempt to defuse escalating tensions between Liberia and Guinea following an incursion into northern Liberia by Guinean rebel forces earlier in that month. In September representatives of eight member countries determined to establish a monitoring body to supervise the border region between Guinea, Liberia and Sierra Leone.

In May 1997 the democratically elected Sierra Leonean leader, President Ahmed Tejan Kabbah, was overthrown by a military coup involving officers of the national army and Revolutionary United Front (RUF) rebels. Nigerian forces based in Sierra Leone as part of a bilateral defence pact attempted to restore constitutional order. Their numbers were strengthened by the arrival of more than 700 Nigerian soldiers and two naval vessels which had been serving under the ECOMOG mandate in neighbouring Liberia. At the end of June ECOWAS ministers of foreign affairs, convened in Conakry, Guinea, agreed to pursue the objective of restoring a democratic government in Sierra Leone through dialogue and the imposition of economic sanctions. In July a four-member ministerial committee, comprising Côte d'Ivoire, Ghana, Guinea and Nigeria, together with representatives of the OAU, negotiated an agreement with the so-called Armed Forces Revolutionary Council (AFRC) in Sierra Leone to establish an immediate cease-fire and to pursue efforts towards the restoration of constitutional order. In August ECOWAS heads of state reaffirmed the Community's condemnation of the removal of President Kabbah and officially endorsed a series of punitive measures against the AFRC authorities in order to accelerate the restoration of democratic government. The meeting mandated ECOMOG to maintain and monitor the cease-fire and to prevent all goods, excepting essential humanitarian supplies, from entering that country. It was also agreed that the committee on Sierra Leone include Liberia and be convened at the level of heads of state. In October the UN Security Council imposed an embargo on the sale or supply of armaments to Sierra Leone and authorized ECOWAS to ensure implementation of these measures. In September ECOMOG forces fired on container ships in the port of Freetown, which were suspected of violating the economic embargo. Clashes occurred between ECOMOG troops and AFRC/RUF soldiers, in particular around the area of Freetown's international airport which had been seized by ECOMOG; further ECOMOG air attacks against commercial and military targets were also conducted, with the aim of upholding the international sanctions and in self-defence. Despite the escalation in hostilities, the Committee of Five pursued negotiations with the military authorities, and at the end of October both sides signed a peace agreement, in Conakry, Guinea, providing for an immediate end to all fighting and the reinstatement of Kabbah's Government by April 1998; all combatants were to be disarmed and demobilized under the supervision of a disarmament committee comprising representatives of ECOMOG, the military authorities and local forces loyal to President Kabbah. In November 1997, however, the peace process was undermined by reports that ECOMOG forces had violated the cease-fire agreement following a series of air raids on Freetown, which ECOMOG claimed to have been in retaliation for attacks by AFRC/RUF-operated anti-aircraft equipment, and a demand by the AFRC authorities that the Nigerian contingent of ECOMOG leave the country. In mid-February 1998, following a series of offensive attacks against forces loyal to the military authorities, ECOMOG assumed control of Freetown and arrested several members of the AFRC/RUC regime. Some 50 AFRC officials were arrested by troops serving under ECOMOG on arrival at James Spriggs Payne Airport in Liberia, prompting protests from the Liberian Government at the Nigerian military intervention. An 11-member supervisory task force, which included the ECOMOG Commander, was established in Sierra Leone to maintain order, pending Kabbah's return from exile. ECOMOG troops subsequently also monitored the removal of the embargo against the use of the airport and port facilities in Freetown. Kabbah returned to Sierra Leone in March and installed a new administration. It was agreed that ECOMOG forces were to remain in the country in order to ensure the full restoration of peace and security, to assist in the restructuring of the armed forces and to help to resolve the problems of the substantial numbers of refugees and internally displaced persons. In early May ECOWAS Chiefs of Staff, meeting in Accra, Ghana, urged member states to provide more troops and logistical support to strengthen the ECOMOG force in Sierra Leone (at that time numbering some 10,000 troops), which was still involved in ongoing clashes with remaining rebel soldiers in eastern regions of the country. In July the UN established an Observer Mission in Sierra Leone (UNOMSIL), whose officers were to monitor the cease-fire, mainly in areas secured by ECOMOG troops. In October ECOMOG transferred its headquarters to Freetown, in order, partly, to reinforce its presence in the country. In January 1999 rebel soldiers attacked the capital and engaged in heavy fighting with ECOMOG forces, amid reports that the Liberian Government was supporting the rebels. Nigeria dispatched several thousand additional troops to counter the rebel advance and to secure the border with Liberia. In February, however, once ECOMOG had regained control of Freetown, the Nigerian Government expressed its desire to withdraw all its troops from the peace-keeping force by May, owing to financial restraints. Efforts to negotiate a peace settlement were initiated, with the current Chairman of ECOWAS, President Gnassingbe Eyadéma of Togo, actively involved in mediation between the opposing groups, despite persisting reports of fighting between ECOMOG and rebel soldiers in areas east of the capital. A cease-fire agreement was concluded in May, and a political settlement was signed, by Kabbah and the RUF leader, in Lomé, Togo, in July. ECOMOG's mandate in Sierra Leone was to be adapted to support the consolidation of peace in that country and national reconstruction.

In July 1998 ECOWAS ministers of defence and of foreign affairs met to consider the political unrest in Guinea-Bissau, following an unsuccessful attempt by rebel soldiers, in June, to overthrow the Government of President João Vieira, and urged both sides to co-operate in negotiating a settlement. An ECOWAS Committee of Seven on Guinea-Bissau (comprising the ministers of foreign affairs of Burkina Faso, Côte d'Ivoire, The Gambia, Ghana, Guinea, Nigeria and Senegal) was established and met for the first time in August. In late August, following mediation by ECOWAS representatives and a contact group of the Comunidade dos Países de Língua Portuguesa (CPLP, q.v.), which had secured an initial cease-fire, an agreement was signed by the conflicting parties providing for an end to hostilities, the reopening of the international airport to facilitate the provision of humanitarian supplies, and for independent supervision of the cease-fire agreement. ECOWAS subsequently held discussions with the CPLP in order to co-ordinate efforts to secure peace in Guinea-Bissau. In late October ECOWAS heads of state endorsed the deployment of ECOMOG forces in Guinea-Bissau. On 1 November the two sides in the dispute, meeting in Abuja, Nigeria, signed a peace accord under ECOWAS auspices, which reinforced the August cease-fire and incorporated an agreement to establish a government of national unity. ECOMOG forces were to replace all foreign troops, mainly Senegalese, currently in Guinea-Bissau, supervise the security of the border region between those two countries, and enable humanitarian organizations to have free access to those needing assistance. In addition ECOMOG was to be responsible for monitoring the conduct of presidential and legislative elections, scheduled to be held in 1999. In early February President Vieira and the rebel leader Gen. Manè signed a cease-fire accord, under ECOWAS auspices. A new Government of National Unity was established later in that month and an ECOMOG Interposition Force began to be dispatched to Guinea-Bissau. In May ECOWAS ministers of foreign affairs, meeting in Lomé, Togo, condemned the escalation of hostilities in Guinea-Bissau and the removal of President Vieira by opposition forces earlier in that month. The ministers resolved to withdraw the ECOMOG contingent, at that time numbering 600 troops from Benin, Gabon, Niger and Togo, owing to the political developments and lack of finances.

## ENVIRONMENTAL PROTECTION

ECOWAS promotes implementation of the UN Convention on Desertification Control and supports programmes initiated at national and sub-regional level within the framework of the treaty. Together with the Permanent Inter-State Committee on Drought Control in the Sahel (CILSS, q.v.). ECOWAS has been designated as a project leader for implementing the Convention in West Africa. Other environmental initiatives include a regional meteorological project to enhance meteorological activities and applications, and in particular to contribute to food security and natural resource management in the sub-region. ECOWAS pilot schemes have formed the basis of integrated control projects for the control of floating weeds in five water basins in West Africa, which had hindered the development of the local fishery sectors. A rural water supply programme aims to ensure adequate water for rural dwellers in order to improve their living standards. The first phase of the project focused on schemes to develop village and pastoral water points in Burkina Faso, Guinea, Mali, Niger and Senegal, with funds from various multilateral donors.

## AGRICULTURE AND FISHING

An Agricultural Development Strategy was adopted in 1982, aiming at sub-regional self-sufficiency by the year 2000. The strategy included plans for selecting seeds and cattle species, and called for solidarity among member states during international commodity negotiations. A transhumance certification scheme, to facilitate the monitoring of animal movement and animal health surveillance and protection in the sub-region, was under preparation in 1997.

In November 1995 an agro-industrial forum, jointly organized by ECOWAS and the European Union, was held in Dakar, Senegal. The forum aimed to facilitate co-operation between companies in the two regions, to develop the agro-industrial sector in west Africa and to promote business opportunities.

## SOCIAL PROGRAMME

Four organizations have been established within ECOWAS by the Executive Secretariat: the Organization of Trade Unions of West Africa, which held its first meeting in 1984; the West African Youth Association; the West African Universities' Association; and the West Africa Women's Association (whose statutes were approved by a meeting of ministers of social affairs in May 1987). Regional sports competitions are held annually. In 1987 ECOWAS member states agreed to establish a West African Health Organization by merger of the existing West African Health Community (q.v.) and the Organization for Co-ordination and Co-operation in the Struggle against Endemic Diseases; however, in 1999 this process was still ongoing.

## INFORMATION AND MEDIA

In March 1990 ECOWAS ministers of information formulated a policy on the dissemination of information about ECOWAS throughout the region and the appraisal of attitudes of its population towards the Community. The ministers established a new information commission. In November 1991 a conference on press communication and African integration, organized by ECOWAS, recommended the creation of an ECOWAS press card, judicial safeguards to protect journalists, training programmes for journalists and the establishment of a regional documentation centre and data bank. In November 1994 the commission of social and cultural affairs, meeting in Lagos, Nigeria, endorsed a series of measures to promote west African integration. These included special radio, television and newspaper features, sporting events and other competitions or rallies.

## Finance

ECOWAS is financed by contributions from member states, although there is a poor record of punctual payment of dues, which has hampered the work of the Secretariat. Arrears in contributions to the Secretariat were reported to total US $42m. at October 1998. Under the revised treaty, ECOWAS was to receive revenue from a community tax, based on the total value of imports from member countries. In July 1996 the summit meeting approved a protocol on a community levy, providing for the imposition of a 0.5% tax on the value of imports from a third country. Member states were requested to ratify the protocol, in order to enable its application with effect from 1 January 1997. In August 1997 the Authority of Heads of State and Government determined that the community levy should replace budgetary contributions as the organization's principal source of finance. By October 1998 only five member states had ratified the protocol.

The 1998 budget amounted to approximately US $10m.

## Publications

*Annual Report.*

*Contact.*

*ECOWAS National Accounts.*

*ECOWAS News.*

*West African Bulletin.*

# ECONOMIC CO-OPERATION ORGANIZATION—ECO

**Address:** 1 Golbou Alley, Kamranieh St, POB 14155-6176, Teheran, Iran.

**Telephone:** (21) 2831731; **fax:** (21) 2831732; **e-mail:** eco.org@neda.net.

The Economic Co-operation Organization (ECO) was established in 1985 as the successor to the Regional Co-operation for Development, founded in 1964.

**MEMBERS**

| | | |
|---|---|---|
| Afghanistan | Kyrgyzstan | Turkey |
| Azerbaijan | Pakistan | Turkmenistan |
| Iran | Tajikistan | Uzbekistan |
| Kazakhstan | | |

The 'Turkish Republic of Northern Cyprus' has been granted special guest status.

## Organization

(January 2000)

### SUMMIT MEETING

The first summit meeting of heads of state and of government of member countries was held in Teheran in February 1992. Summit meetings are held at least once every two years. The sixth summit meeting was expected to be held in Teheran in mid-2000.

### COUNCIL OF MINISTERS

The Council of Ministers, comprising ministers of foreign affairs of member states, is the principal policy- and decision-making body of ECO. It meets at least once a year.

### COUNCIL OF PERMANENT REPRESENTATIVES

Permanent representatives or Ambassadors of member countries accredited to Iran meet regularly to formulate policy for consideration by the Council of Ministers and to promote implementation of decisions reached at ministerial or summit level.

### REGIONAL PLANNING COUNCIL

The Council, comprising senior planning officials or other representatives of member states, meets annually. It is responsible for reviewing programmes of activity and evaluating results achieved, and for proposing future plans of action to the Council of Ministers.

### SECRETARIAT

The Secretariat is headed by a Secretary-General, who is supported by two Deputy Secretaries-General. The following Directorates administer and co-ordinate the main areas of ECO activities: Trade; Transport and telecommunications; Energy, minerals, environment; Industry and agriculture; Project research; and Economic research and statistics.

**Secretary-General:** ÖNDER ÖZAR (Turkey).

## Activities

The Regional Co-operation for Development (RCD) was established in 1964 as a tripartite arrangement between Iran, Pakistan and Turkey, which aimed to promote economic co-operation between member states. ECO replaced the RCD in 1985, and seven additional members were admitted to the Organization in November 1992. The main areas of co-operation are transport (including the building of road and rail links), telecommunications and post, trade and investment, energy (including the interconnection of power grids in the region), minerals, environmental issues, industry, and agriculture. ECO priorities and objectives for each sector are defined in the Quetta Plan of Action and the İstanbul Declaration; an Almaty Outline Plan, which was adopted in 1993, is specifically concerned with the development of regional transport and communication infrastructure.

A joint Chamber of Commerce and Industry was established in 1993. The third ECO summit meeting, held in Islamabad, Pakistan, in March 1995, concluded formal agreements on the establishment of several other regional institutes and agencies: an ECO Trade and Development Bank, in İstanbul, Turkey, a joint shipping company, airline, and an ECO Cultural Institute, all to be based in Iran, and an ECO Reinsurance Company and an ECO Science Foundation, with headquarters in Pakistan. In addition, heads of state and of government endorsed the establishment of an ECO eminent persons group and signed the following two agreements in order to enhance and facilitate trade throughout the region: the Transit Trade Agreement (which entered into force in December 1997) and the Agreement on the Simplification of Visa Procedures for Businessmen of ECO Countries (which came into effect in March 1998).

In September 1996, at an extraordinary meeting of the ECO Council of Ministers, held in Izmir, Turkey, member countries signed a revised Treaty of Izmir, the Organization's fundamental charter. An extraordinary summit meeting, held in Ashgabat, Turkmenistan, in May 1997, emphasized the importance of the development of the transport and communications infrastructure and the network of transnational petroleum and gas pipelines through bilateral and regional arrangements in the ECO region. In May 1998, at the fifth summit meeting, held in Almaty, Kazakhstan, ECO heads of state and of government signed a Transit Transport Framework Agreement and a memorandum of understanding to help combat the cross-border trafficking of illegal goods. The meeting also agreed to establish an ECO Educational Institute in Ankara, Turkey.

ECO has co-operation agreements with several UN agencies and other international organizations in development-related activities and has been granted observer status at the UN and the OIC.

## Finance

Member states contribute to a centralized administrative budget.

# EUROPEAN BANK FOR RECONSTRUCTION AND DEVELOPMENT—EBRD

**Address:** One Exchange Square, 175 Bishopsgate, London, EC2A 2EH, United Kingdom.

**Telephone:** (20) 7338-6000; **fax:** (20) 7338-6100; **internet:** www.ebrd.com.

The EBRD was founded in May 1990 and inaugurated in April 1991. Its object is to contribute to the progress and the economic reconstruction of the countries of central and eastern Europe which undertake to respect and put into practice the principles of multiparty democracy, pluralism, the rule of law, respect for human rights and a market economy.

### MEMBERS

Countries of Operations:

| | |
|---|---|
| Albania | Lithuania |
| Armenia | Macedonia, former Yugoslav republic |
| Azerbaijan | Moldova |
| Bosnia and Herzegovina | Poland |
| Belarus | Romania |
| Bulgaria | Russia |
| Croatia | Slovakia |
| Czech Republic | Slovenia |
| Estonia | Tajikistan |
| Georgia | Turkmenistan |
| Hungary | Ukraine |
| Kazakhstan | Uzbekistan |
| Kyrgyzstan | |
| Latvia | |

European Union members*:

| | |
|---|---|
| Austria | Italy |
| Belgium | Luxembourg |
| Denmark | Netherlands |
| Finland | Portugal |
| France | Spain |
| Germany | Sweden |
| Greece | United Kingdom |
| Ireland | |

EFTA members:

| | |
|---|---|
| Iceland | Norway |
| Liechtenstein | Switzerland |

Other countries:

| | |
|---|---|
| Australia | Malta |
| Canada | Mexico |
| Cyprus | Morocco |
| Egypt | New Zealand |
| Israel | Turkey |
| Japan | USA |
| Republic of Korea | |

* The European Community and the European Investment Bank are also shareholder members in their own right.

## Organization

(January 2000)

### BOARD OF GOVERNORS

The Board of Governors, to which each member appoints a Governor and an alternate, is the highest authority of the EBRD.

### BOARD OF DIRECTORS

The Board is responsible for the organization and operations of the EBRD. The Governors elect 23 directors for a three-year term and a President for a term of four years. Vice-Presidents are appointed by the Board on the recommendation of the President.

### ADMINISTRATION

The EBRD's operations are conducted by its Banking Department, headed by the First Vice-President. The other departments are: Finance; Personnel and Administration; Project Evaluation, Operation Support and Nuclear Safety; Internal Audit; Communications; and Offices of the Secretary-General, the General Counsel and the Chief Economist. A structure of country teams, industry teams and operations support units oversee the implementation of projects. The EBRD has 29 Resident Offices or other offices in all of its countries of operations. There were some 1,072 staff at the end of 1998.

**President:** HORST KÖHLER (Germany).

**First Vice-President:** CHARLES FRANK (USA).

## Activities

In April 1996 EBRD shareholders, meeting in Sofia, Bulgaria, agreed to increase the Bank's capital from ECU 10,000m. to ECU 20,000m., to enable the Bank to continue, and to enhance, its lending programme (the ECU was replaced by the euro, with an equivalent value, from 1 January 1999). It was agreed that 22.5% of the ECU 10,000m. of new resources, was to be paid-up, with the remainder as 'callable' shares. Contributions were to be paid over a 13-year period from April 1998. By 31 December 1998 the final stages of the capital increase were complete, with 54 of the 60 members, representing 95% of the Bank's capital, having deposited their instruments of subscription to the capital increase.

The Bank aims to assist the transition of the economies of central and eastern European countries towards a market economy system, and to encourage private enterprise. The Agreement establishing the EBRD specifies that 60% of its lending should be for the private sector. The Bank helps the beneficiaries to undertake structural and sectoral reforms, including the dismantling of monopolies, decentralization, and privatization of state enterprises, to enable these countries to become fully integrated in the international economy. To this end, the Bank promotes the establishment and improvement of activities of a productive, competitive and private nature, particularly small and medium-sized enterprises (SMEs), and works to strengthen financial institutions. It mobilizes national and foreign capital, together with experienced management teams, and helps to develop an appropriate legal framework to support a market-orientated economy. The Bank provides extensive financial services, including loans, equity and guarantees. The Bank's founding Agreement specifies that all operations are to be undertaken in the context of promoting environmentally sound and sustainable development. It undertakes environmental audits and impact assessments in areas of particular concern, which enable the Bank to incorporate environmental action plans into any project approved for funding. An Environment Advisory Council assists with the development of policy and strategy in this area.

In early 1994 the Board of Directors approved the following issues as medium-term operational priorities for the Bank: focus on private-sector development; the EBRD to be active in all countries of operations; the need to reach local private enterprises; the importance of financial intermediaries; and a more active approach towards equity investment. These guide-lines were endorsed in April and remained operational in 1998, in which year the Bank increased the equity share of its commitments to 33% of the total, from 19% in 1997. The EBRD's medium-term strategy for 1998–2001 was endorsed by the Board of Directors in September 1997. It aimed to consolidate the Bank's operational priorities and envisaged an increase in commitments from some ECU 2,300m. in 1997 to more than €2,700m. in 2001.

In the year ending 31 December 1998 the EBRD approved ECU 2,003m. for 82 projects, making a cumulative total of ECU 14,478m. since it commenced operations. Private-sector commitments amounted to 80% (by volume), increasing the total private-sector share of the committed portfolio to 68%. The Bank's share of new commitments in countries at the early or intermediate stages of transition amounted to 37% in 1998, compared with 44% in 1997.

During 1998 15% of all project financing committed was allocated to the support of the manufacturing sector, with significant projects in Poland, the former Yugoslav republic of Macedonia, and Romania. Some 39% of financing was allocated to the financial and business sector, supporting privatizations or restructuring of the sector, the development of institutions and the expansion of trade financing services. The other main area of project financing in that year was the energy and power generation sector and transport, which included assistance for railway improvements in Hungary, Latvia, Croatia and Georgia. The Bank also invests in essential municipal services; the most significant projects in this field in 1998 were in Poland and Croatia. In 1998 11 environmental projects were signed, with a total EBRD commitment of more than ECU 196m. The EBRD was also actively involved in the upgrading and privatization of national telecommunications operators; the financing of primary agriculture and related processing; and in energy efficiency programmes.

A high priority is given to attracting external finance for Bank-sponsored projects, in particular in countries at advanced stages of transition, from governments, international financial institutions, commercial banks and export credit agencies. In 1998 those sources provided co-financing funds amounting to ECU 1,933m. The EBRD's Technical Co-operation Funds Programme (TCFP) aims to facilitate access to the Bank's capital resources for countries of operations by providing support for project preparation, project implementation and institutional development. In 1998 the EBRD committed ECU 80.3m. to finance 318 consultancy assignments under the TCFP, bringing the total amount committed since 1991 to ECU 561.3m. for 2,106 assignments. Resources for technical co-operation originate from regular TCFP contributions, specific agreements and contributions to Special Funds. The Baltic Investment Programme, which is administered by Nordic countries, consists of two special funds to co-finance investment and technical assistance projects in the private sectors of Baltic states. The Funds are open to contributions from all EBRD member states. The Russia Small Business Special Funds, established in October 1993, support local SMEs through similar investment and technical co-operation activities. Other financing mechanisms that the EBRD uses to address the needs of the region include Regional Venture Funds, which invest equity in privatized companies, in particular in Russia, and provide relevant management assistance, and the Central European Agency Lines, which disburse lines of credit to small-scale projects through local intermediaries. A TurnAround Management Programme (TAM) provides practical assistance to senior managers of industrial enterprises to facilitate the expansion of businesses in a market economy.

In February 1993 the Group of Seven (G-7) industrialized countries officially proposed the establishment of a Nuclear Safety Account (NSA) to fund a multilateral programme of action for the improvement of safety in nuclear power plants of the former eastern bloc. The NSA, which is administered by the EBRD, was approved by the Bank's Board of Directors in March, and extended for further three-year periods in both April 1996 and April 1999. At 17 April 1999 14 countries and the European Community had pledged funds amounting to some €206m. to the NSA. At that time projects to improve plants in Lithuania, Russia and Ukraine were ongoing, while short-term safety improvements in Bulgaria had been completed.

In 1997 the G-7, together with the European Community and Ukraine, endorsed the creation of a supplemental multilateral funding mechanism to assist Ukraine in repairing the protective sarcophagus covering the faulty Chernobyl (Chornobyl) reactor, under the Chernobyl Unit 4 Shelter Implementation Plan (SIP). The EBRD's Board of Directors approved the participation of the Bank in September 1997. The rules of the so-called Chernobyl Shelter Fund, which the EBRD was to administer, were approved in November and the Fund became operational the following month. In 1995 the G-7 requested that the Bank fund the completion of two new nuclear reactors in Ukraine, to provide alternative energy sources to the Chernobyl power-station, which, it was agreed, was to shut down in 2000. A study questioning the financial viability of the proposed reactors threatened funding in early 1997; a second survey, carried out by the EBRD, pronounced the plan viable, although disagreement persisted. By late November 1999 funding arrangements for the two new facilities had still not been agreed, prompting the Ukrainian authorities to resume power generation at one of the Chernobyl reactors.

The economic crisis in Russia, beginning in early 1998, had an impact on the Bank's large portfolio of Russian investments. The Bank denied that it would abandon any of its investments in Russia and emphasized the necessity for continued Western support. In October the Russian central bank requested that the EBRD assist with the restructuring of the country's banking system. In January 1999 the Bank announced the creation of one large-scale programme designed to develop trade between countries in Eastern Europe and the CIS, in an attempt to remedy the severe economic situation in the region. During that year the Bank aimed to develop the private sector in Russia and the CIS and to promote a more favourable investment environment, in particular by combating corruption.

**PROJECT FINANCING COMMITTED BY SECTOR**

| | 1998 | | Cumulative to 31 Dec. 1998 | |
|---|---|---|---|---|
| | Number | Amount (ECU million) | Number | Amount (ECU million) |
| Agriculture, forestry, fishing | 3 | 36 | 21 | 260 |
| CEALs, co-financing lines and RVFs* | — | — | 2 | 38 |
| Commerce and tourism | 3 | 111 | 24 | 382 |
| Community/ social services | 5 | 96 | 20 | 265 |
| Energy/power generation | 7 | 245 | 47 | 1,571 |
| Extractive industries | 4 | 185 | 19 | 767 |
| Finance and business | 44 | 933 | 219 | 3,681 |
| Manufacturing | 16 | 351 | 94 | 1,742 |
| Telecommunications | 4 | 194 | 34 | 1,082 |
| Transport | 10 | 223 | 71 | 2,222 |
| **Total** (including others) | 96 | 2,373 | 551 | 12,010 |

* Central European Agency Lines, Regional Venture Funds.

**PROJECT FINANCING COMMITTED BY COUNTRY**

| | 1998 | | Cumulative to 31 Dec. 1998 | |
|---|---|---|---|---|
| | Number | Amount (ECU million) | Number | Amount (ECU million) |
| Albania | 1 | 7 | 8 | 68 |
| Armenia | — | — | 3 | 69 |
| Azerbaijan | 4 | 88 | 9 | 193 |
| Belarus | 1 | 3 | 7 | 151 |
| Bosnia and Herzegovina | 2 | 23 | 7 | 70 |
| Bulgaria | 2 | 33 | 20 | 296 |
| Croatia | 6 | 170 | 21 | 511 |
| Czech Republic | 2 | 87 | 24 | 525 |
| Estonia | 7 | 86 | 28 | 247 |
| Georgia | 3 | 59 | 9 | 115 |
| Hungary | 2 | 68 | 49 | 1,053 |
| Kazakhstan | 4 | 157 | 7 | 364 |
| Kyrgyzstan | 1 | 18 | 9 | 136 |
| Latvia | 3 | 38 | 17 | 213 |
| Lithuania | 3 | 39 | 13 | 173 |
| Macedonia, former Yugoslav republic | 2 | 28 | 9 | 143 |
| Moldova | 2 | 15 | 11 | 149 |
| Poland | 11 | 354 | 70 | 1,309 |
| Romania | 7 | 252 | 41 | 1,283 |
| Russia | 15 | 541 | 87 | 2,837 |
| Slovakia | 3 | 44 | 18 | 395 |
| Slovenia | 1 | 6 | 19 | 307 |
| Tajikistan | 1 | 4 | 3 | 13 |
| Turkmenistan | — | — | 4 | 126 |
| Ukraine | 6 | 133 | 24 | 605 |
| Uzbekistan | 1 | 29 | 12 | 394 |
| Regional | 6 | 91 | 22 | 266 |
| **Total** | 96 | 2,373 | 551 | 12,010 |

Note: Operations may be counted as fractional numbers if multiple sub-loans are grouped under one framework agreement.

Source: EBRD, *Annual Report 1998*.

# Publications

*Annual Report*.

*Environments in Transition* (2 a year).

*Transition Report* (annually).

# EUROPEAN SPACE AGENCY—ESA

**Address:** 8–10 rue Mario Nikis, 75738 Paris Cédex 15, France.
**Telephone:** 1-53-69-76-54; **fax:** 1-53-69-75-60; **internet:** www.esa.int.

ESA was established in 1975 to provide for, and to promote, European co-operation in space research and technology, and their applications, for exclusively peaceful purposes. It replaced the European Space Research Organisation (ESRO) and the European Launcher Development Organisation (both founded in 1962).

### MEMBERS*

| | |
|---|---|
| Austria | Italy |
| Belgium | Netherlands |
| Denmark | Norway |
| Finland | Spain |
| France | Sweden |
| Germany | Switzerland |
| Ireland | United Kingdom |

* Canada has signed an agreement for close co-operation with ESA, including representation on the ESA Council.

## Organization

(January 2000)

**Director-General:** ANTONIO RODOTÀ (Italy).

### COUNCIL

The Council is composed of representatives of all member states. It is responsible for formulating policy and meets at ministerial or delegate level.

### PROGRAMME BOARDS AND COMMITTEES

The Council is assisted in its work by six specialized Programme Boards, which oversee the management of the following ESA activities: Communication Satellite Programmes; Satellite Navigation; Earth Observation; Microgravity; Ariane Launcher; and Manned Spaceflight. The other principal bodies of the ESA administrative structure are the Committees for Long-term Space Policy, Administration and Finance, Industrial Policy, Science Programme and International Relations.

### ESA CENTRES

**European Space Research and Technology Centre—ESTEC:** Noordwijk, Netherlands. ESA's principal technical establishment, at which the majority of project teams are based, together with the space science department and the technological research and support engineers; provides the appropriate testing and laboratory facilities.

**European Space Operations Centre—ESOC:** Darmstadt, Germany. Responsible for all satellite operations and the corresponding ground facilities and communications networks.

**European Space Research Institute—ESRIN:** Frascati, Italy. Responsible for the corporate exploitation of Earth observation data from space.

**European Astronaut Centre—EAC:** Porz-Wahn, Germany. Co-ordinates all European astronaut activities, including the training of astronauts. In 1996 the Centre began to develop computer-based training courses for the ESA aspects of the International Space Station.

ESA also helps to maintain the Space Centre at Kourou, French Guiana, which is used for the Ariane launchers.

ESA had a total of some 1,700 permanent staff at November 1999.

## Activities

ESA's tasks are to define and put into effect a long-term European space policy of scientific research and technological development and to encourage all members to co-ordinate their national programmes with those of ESA to ensure that Europe maintains a competitive position in the field of space technology. ESA's basic activities cover studies on future projects, technological research, shared technical investments, information systems and training programmes. These, and the science programme, are mandatory activities to which all members must contribute; other programmes are optional and members may determine their own level of participation. In May 1999 ministers responsible for space in member states, meeting in Brussels, Belgium, endorsed a new medium-term European space strategy. It incorporated new initiatives and programmes in the fields of navigation, space multimedia, Earth observation and launchers, and was based on the following key objectives: the pursuit of highest quality science; enhancement of the quality of life; the development of an independent capability for Europe in launchers and new applications as the key to co-operation and competition; and promotion of a European industry of innovation and 'added value' services.

ESA is committed to pursuing international co-operation to achieve its objectives of developing the peaceful applications of space technology. ESA works closely with both the US National Aeronautics and Space Administration (NASA) and the Russian Space Agency. More recently it has developed a co-operative relationship with Japan, in particular in data relay satellites and the exchange of materials for the International Space Station. ESA has also concluded co-operation agreements with the Czech Republic, Greece, Hungary, Poland and Romania, providing for technical training and joint projects in the field of space science, Earth observation and telecommunications. ESA assists other developing and transitional countries to expand their space activities. It works closely with other international organizations, in particular the European Union and EUMETSAT (q.v.). ESA has observer status with the UN Committee on the Peaceful Uses of Outer Space and co-operates closely with the UN's Office of Outer Space Affairs, in particular through the organization of a training and fellowship programme.

### SCIENCE

The first European scientific space programmes were undertaken under the aegis of ESRO, which launched seven satellites during 1968–72. The science programmes are mandatory activities of the Agency and form the basis of co-operation between member states. The first astronomical satellite (COS–B) was launched by ESA in August 1975. By the end of 1998 ESA had launched 12 scientific satellites and probes, among the most successful being the Giotto probe, launched in 1985 to study the composition of Halley's comet and reactivated in 1990 to observe the Grigg-Skjellerup comet in July 1992, and Hipparcos, which, between 1989 and 1993, determined the precise astronomic positions and distances of more than 1m. stars. In November 1995 ESA launched the Infrared Space Observatory, which has successfully conducted pre-planned scientific studies providing data on galaxy and star formation and on interstellar matter. ESA is collaborating with NASA in the Ulysses space project (a solar polar mission), the Solar and Helispheric Observatory (SOHO), launched in 1995 to study the internal structure of the sun, and the Hubble Space Telescope. In October 1997 the Huygens space probe was launched under the framework of a joint NASA–ESA project (the Cassini/Huygens mission) to study the planet Saturn and its largest moon, Titan.

ESA's space missions are an integral part of its long-term science programme, Horizon 2000, which was initiated in 1984. In 1994 a new set of missions was defined, to enable the inclusion of projects using new technologies and participation in future international space activities, which formed the Horizon 2000 Plus extension covering the period 2005–16. Together they are called Horizons 2000. The revised strategy envisaged the introduction of a Small Mission for Advanced Research and Technology (SMART–1) to an asteroid or to the Moon in 2001 and a mission to the planet Mars in 2003, which may be developed in association with NASA.

The main projects being developed under the science programme in 1999 included the X-Ray Multimirror Mission (XMM, or 'Envisat'), the successor to the cluster spacecraft and satellites, which was designed to study structures in the Earth's plasma environment, the Mars Express spacecraft, scheduled to be launched in 2003, and the launch of the Far Infrared and Submilletric Space Telescope (FIRST Planck), scheduled for 2006.

### OBSERVATION OF THE EARTH AND ITS ENVIRONMENT

ESA has contributed to the understanding and monitoring of the Earth's environment through its satellite projects. Since 1977 ESA has launched seven Meteosat spacecraft into geosynchronous orbit, which have provided continuous meteorological data, mainly for the purposes of weather forecasting. The Meteosat systems are financed and owned by EUMETSAT, but were operated by ESA until December 1995. In 1998/99 ESA was developing, in collaboration with EUMETSAT, a successor to the Meteosat weather satellites (Meteosat Second Generation) to provide geostationary data coverage beyond 2000. The first satellite was to be launched in 2000. ESA and EUMETSAT have also begun development of the METOP/EPS (EUMETSAT Polar System) programme, to provide observations from polar orbit. The first METOP satellite was scheduled for launch in 2003.

In 1991 ESA launched the ERS–1 satellite, which carried sophisticated instruments to measure the Earth's surface and its atmosphere. A second ERS satellite was launched in April 1995 with the specific purpose of measuring the stratospheric and tropospheric ozone. An enhanced space mission (ENVISAT) was scheduled to assume the functions of the ERS project in 2000. It was also expected to provide greater information on the impact of human activities on the Earth's atmosphere, and land and coastal processes, and to monitor exceptional natural events, such as volcanic eruptions.

In June 1998 the ESA Council approved the initiation of activities related to the Living Planet Programme, designed to increase understanding of environmental issues. In May 1999 the Council committed funds for a research mission, Cryosat, to be undertaken, in order to study the impact of global warming on polar ice caps. The Council also approved funding for the definition phase of the Global Navigation Satellite System (GNSS-2, or 'Galileo') programme, to be developed through a public-private partnership with the European Commission, users and industry.

### TELECOMMUNICATIONS

ESA commenced the development of communications satellites in 1968. These have since become the largest markets for space use and have transformed global communications, with more than 100 satellites circling the Earth for the purposes of telecommunications. The main series of operational satellites developed by ESA are the European Communications Satellites (ECS), based on the original orbital test satellite and used by EUTELSAT, and the Maritime Communications Satellites (MARECS), which have been leased for operations to INMARSAT (q.v.).

In 1989 ESA launched an experimental civilian telecommunications satellite, Olympus, to develop and demonstrate new broadcasting services. An Advanced Relay and Technology Mission Satellite (ARTEMIS) has been developed by ESA to test and operate new telecommunications techniques, and in particular to enable the relay of information directly between satellites. ARTEMIS was scheduled to be launched in 2000. In 1998 ESA, together with the EU and EUROCONTROL (q.v.), continued to implement a satellite-based navigation system to be used for civilian aircraft and maritime services, similar to the two existing systems operational for military use. ESA was also working with the EU and representatives of the private sector to enhance the region's role in the development of electronic media infrastructure to meet the expanding global demand. In May 1999 the Council approved funding for a satellite multimedia programme, Artes 3, which aimed to support the development of satellite systems and services for delivering information through high-speed internet access.

### SPACE TRANSPORT SYSTEMS

In 1973 several European Governments adopted a programme to ensure that the future ESA had independent access to space, and determined to co-ordinate knowledge gained through national programmes to develop a space launcher. The resulting Ariane rocket was first launched in December 1979. The project, which incorporated four different launchers during the 1980s, subsequently became an essential element of ESA's programme activities and, furthermore, developed a successful commercial role in placing satellites into orbit. From 1985 ESA worked to develop Ariane–5, which was to be the prototype for future launchers. The third and final qualification flight took place in October 1998. In June the ESA Council approved funding for the first stage in the development of the more powerful Ariane-5 Plus. A future generation launcher was being researched under the framework of the Future Space Transportation Investigation Programme (FESTIP). The FESTIP studies were incorporated into a new Future Launcher Technologies Programme from January 1999.

### MANNED SPACEFLIGHT AND MICROGRAVITY

European astronauts and scientists have gained access to space through Spacelab, which ESA developed and contributed as part of the US Space Shuttle Programme, and through joint missions on the Russian space station, Mir. The Spacelab project enabled ESA to conduct research in life and material sciences under microgravity conditions. ESA has an ongoing programme of research in microgravity, and in 1997 initiated a new project to develop the facilities required for microgravity experiments to be conducted on the Columbus Laboratory module of the planned International Space Station (initiated by the US Government in 1984, and since developed as a joint project between five partners—Canada, Europe, Japan, Russia and the USA). The Laboratory was scheduled to be launched in 2002. In May 1999 the ESA Council approved funding of the initial operating phase of the Space Station and of microgravity research. ESA also envisages the development and launch of an Automated Transfer Vehicle to provide logistical support to the Space Station and, together with NASA, is pursuing studies for the possible development of a Crew Rescue Vehicle to ferry astronauts from the Station. The successful flight of an automatic capsule, the Atmosphere Re-entry Demonstrator (ARD), released during the Ariane 503 Flight in October 1998, marked significant progress towards a complete European space mission.

## Finance

All member states contribute to ESA's mandatory programme activities, on a scale based on their national income, and are free to decide on their level of commitment in optional programmes, such as telecommunications, the Ariane project and future space station and platform projects. The 1999 budget totalled about €2,600m., including €645.1m. (24.3%) for Earth observation programmes, €488.9m. (18.4%) for launchers; €435.3m. (16.4%) for manned spaceflight, and €355.2m. (13.4%) for the science programme.

## Publications

*ESA Annual Report.*
*ECSL News* (quarterly).
*ESA Bulletin* (quarterly).
*Earth Observation Quarterly.*
*Microgravity News* (3 a year).
*Preparing for the Future* (quarterly).
*Reaching for the Skies* (quarterly).
Scientific and technical reports, brochures, training manuals, conference proceedings.

# THE EUROPEAN UNION—EU

No final decision has been made on a headquarters for the Union. Meetings of the principal organs take place in Brussels, Luxembourg and Strasbourg.

The European Coal and Steel Community (ECSC) was created by a treaty signed in Paris on 18 April 1951 (effective from 25 July 1952) to pool the coal and steel production of the six original members (see below). It was seen as a first step towards a united Europe. The European Economic Community (EEC) and European Atomic Energy Community (Euratom) were established by separate treaties signed in Rome on 25 March 1957 (effective from 1 January 1958), the former to create a common market and to approximate economic policies, the latter to promote growth in nuclear industries. The common institutions of the three Communities were established by a treaty signed in Brussels on 8 April 1965 (effective from 1 July 1967).

The EEC was formally changed to the European Community (EC) under the Treaty on European Union (effective from 1 November 1993), although in practice the term EC had been used for several years to describe the three Communities together. The new Treaty established a European Union (EU), which introduced citizenship thereof and aimed to increase intergovernmental co-operation in economic and monetary affairs; to establish a common foreign and security policy; and to introduce co-operation in justice and home affairs. The EU was placed under the supervision of the European Council (comprising Heads of State or Government of member countries), while the EC continued to exist, having competence in matters relating to the Treaty of Rome and its amendments.

### MEMBERS

| | | |
|---|---|---|
| Austria | Germany* | Netherlands* |
| Belgium* | Greece | Portugal |
| Denmark | Ireland | Spain |
| Finland | Italy* | Sweden |
| France* | Luxembourg* | United Kingdom |

* Original members. Denmark, Ireland and the United Kingdom joined on 1 January 1973, and Greece on 1 January 1981. In a referendum held in February 1982, the inhabitants of Greenland voted to end their membership of the Community, entered into when under full Danish rule. Greenland's withdrawal took effect from 1 February 1985. Portugal and Spain became members on 1 January 1986. Following the reunification of Germany in October 1990, the former German Democratic Republic immediately became part of the Community, although a transitional period was to be allowed before certain Community legislation took effect there. Austria, Finland and Sweden became members on 1 January 1995.

### PERMANENT REPRESENTATIVES OF MEMBER STATES

**Austria:** 30 ave de Cortenbergh, 1040 Brussels; tel. (2) 234-51-00; fax (2) 234-53-00; e-mail austria.press@pophost.eunet.be; GREGOR WOSCHNAGG.

**Belgium:** 62 rue Belliard, 1040 Brussels; tel. (2) 233-21-11; fax (2) 233-10-75; e-mail belgoeurop@skynet.be; FRANS VAN DAELE.

**Denmark:** 73 rue d'Arlon, 1040 Brussels; tel. (2) 233-08-11; fax (2) 230-93-84; e-mail eu-rep@brubee.um.dk; POUL SKYTTE CHRISTOFFERSEN.

**Finland:** 100 rue de Trèves, 1040 Brussels; tel. (2) 287-84-11; fax (2) 287-84-00; ANTTI SATULI.

**France:** 14 place de Louvain, 1000 Brussels; tel. (2) 229-82-11; fax (2) 229-82-82; e-mail <firstname.lastname>@diplomatie.fr; internet www.rpfrance.org; PIERRE VIMONT.

**Germany:** 19–21 rue J. de Lalaing, 1040 Brussels; tel. (2) 238-18-11; fax (2) 238-19-78; Dr WILHELM SCHÖNFELDER.

**Greece:** 25 rue Montoyer, 1000 Brussels; tel. (2) 551-56-11; fax (2) 551-56-51; LOUKAS TSILAS.

**Ireland:** 89–93 rue Froissart, 1040 Brussels; tel. (2) 230-85-80; fax (2) 230-32-03; e-mail reppermirl@online.be; DENIS O'LEARY.

**Italy:** 9 rue du Marteau, 1000 Brussels; tel. (2) 220-04-11; fax (2) 219-34-49; LUIGI GUIDOBONO CAVALCHINI GAROFOLI.

**Luxembourg:** 75 ave de Cortenbergh, 1000 Brussels; tel. (2) 737-56-00; fax (2) 737-56-10; e-mail secretariat@rpue.etat.lu; NICOLAS SCHMIT.

**Netherlands:** 48 ave Herrmann Debroux, 1160 Brussels; tel. (2) 679-15-11; fax (2) 679-17-75; BERNHARD R. BOT.

**Portugal:** 12 ave de Cortenbergh, 1040 Brussels; tel. (2) 286-42-00; fax (2) 231-00-26; e-mail reper@reper.portugal.be; VASCO VALENTE.

**Spain:** 52 blvd du Régent, 1000 Brussels; tel. (2) 509-86-11; fax (2) 511-19-40; FRANCISCO JAVIER ELORZA CAVENGT.

**Sweden:** 30 square de Meeûs, 1000 Brussels; tel. (2) 289-56-11; fax (2) 289-56-00; e-mail representationen.bryssel@foreign.ministry.se; GUNNAR LUND.

**United Kingdom:** 10 ave D'Auderghem, 1040 Brussels; tel. (2) 287-82-11; fax (2) 287-83-98; internet ukrep.fco.gov.uk; Sir STEPHEN WALL.

### PERMANENT MISSIONS TO THE EUROPEAN UNION, WITH AMBASSADORS

(December 1999)

**Afghanistan:** 32 ave Raphaël, 75016 Paris, France; tel. 1-45-25-05-29; fax 1-45-24-46-87; Chargé d'affaires a.i.: MEHRABODIN MASSTAN.

**Albania:** 42 rue Alphonse Hottat, 1050 Brussels; tel. (2) 640-35-44; fax (2) 640-31-77; e-mail amba.brux@skynet.be; FERIT HOXHA.

**Algeria:** 209 ave Molière, 1050 Brussels; tel. (2) 343-50-78; fax (2) 343-51-68; MUHAMMAD LAMARI.

**Andorra:** 10 rue de la Montagne, 1000 Brussels; tel. (2) 513-28-06; fax (2) 513-07-41; e-mail meri.mateu@skynet.be; MERITXELL MATEU I PI.

**Angola:** 182 rue Franz Merjay, 1180 Brussels; tel. (2) 346-18-80; fax (2) 344-08-94; JOSÉ GUERREIRO ALVES PRIMO.

**Antigua and Barbuda:** 100 rue des Aduatiques, 1040 Brussels; tel. (2) 733-43-28; fax (2) 735-72-37; e-mail ecs.embassies@skynet.be; EDWIN P. J. LAURENT.

**Argentina:** 225 ave Louise (7e étage), Boîte 2, 1050 Brussels; tel. (2) 648-93-71; fax (2) 648-08-04; JUAN JOSÉ URANGA.

**Armenia:** 157 rue Franz Merjay, 1060 Brussels; tel. and fax (2) 346-56-67; V. CHITECHIAN.

**Australia:** 6–8 rue Guimard, 1040 Brussels; tel. (2) 286-05-00; fax (2) 230-68-02; e-mail pub.affs.brussels@dfat.gov.au; internet www.austemb.be; DONALD KENYON.

**Bahamas:** 10 Chesterfield St, London, W1X 8AH, United Kingdom; tel. (20) 7408-4488; fax (20) 7499-9937; e-mail bahamas.hicom .lon@cableinet.co.uk; BASIL G. O'BRIEN.

**Bangladesh:** 29–31 rue Jacques Jordaens, 1050 Brussels; tel. (2) 640-55-00; fax (2) 646-59-98; ASM KHAIRUL ANAM.

**Barbados:** 78 ave Gén. Lartigue, 1200 Brussels; tel. (2) 732-17-37; fax (2) 732-32-66; e-mail embar@pophost.eunet.be; internet www.foreign.barbadosgov.org; MICHAEL I. KING.

**Belize:** 100 rue des Aduatiques, 1040 Brussels; tel. (2) 732-62-04; fax (2) 732-62-46; e-mail ecs.embassies@skynet.be; EDWIN P. J. LAURENT.

**Benin:** 5 ave de l'Observatoire, 1180 Brussels; tel. (2) 375-06-74; fax (2) 375-83-26; ABOUDOU SALIOU.

**Bhutan:** 17–19 chemin du Champ d'Amier, 1209 Geneva, Switzerland; tel. (22) 7987971; fax (22) 7882593; JIGMI Y. THINLEY.

**Bolivia:** 176 ave Louise, Boîte 6, 1050 Brussels; tel. (2) 627-00-10; fax (2) 647-47-82; e-mail embolbrus@arcadis.be; ARTURO LIEBERS BALDIVIESO.

**Bosnia and Herzegovina:** 9 rue Paul Lauters, 1000 Brussels; tel. (2) 644-00-47; fax (2) 644-16-98; e-mail mission.bih.brussels@euronet.be; VITOMIR MILES RAGUZ.

**Botswana:** 169 ave de Tervueren, 1150 Brussels; tel. (2) 735-20-70; fax (2) 735-63-18; SASALA CHASALA GEORGE.

**Brazil:** 30 ave F.D. Roosevelt, 1050 Brussels; tel. (2) 640-20-40; fax (2) 648-80-40; e-mail braseuropa@compuserve.com; JORIO DAUSTER MAGALHÃES E SILVA.

**Brunei:** 238 ave F. D. Roosevelt, 1050 Brussels; tel. (2) 675-08-78; fax (2) 672-93-58; e-mail kedutaan-brunei.brussels@skynet.be; Dato' KASSIM DAUD.

**Bulgaria:** 7 ave Moscicki, 1180 Brussels; tel. (2) 374-84-68; fax (2) 374-91-88; e-mail missionlog@village.eunet.be; ANTOINETTE PRIMATAROVA.

**Burkina Faso:** 16 place Guy d'Arezzo, 1180 Brussels; tel. (2) 345-99-12; fax (2) 345-06-12; e-mail ambassade.burkina@skynet.be; YOUSSOUF OUÉDRAOGO.

**Burundi:** 46 square Marie-Louise, 1040 Brussels; tel. (2) 230-45-35; fax (2) 230-78-83; e-mail ambassade.burundi@skynet.be; internet www.burundi.gov.bi; LÉONIDAS NDORICIMPA.

**Cameroon:** 131–133 ave Brugmann, 1190 Brussels; tel. (2) 345-18-70; fax (2) 344-57-35; ISABELLE BASSONG.

**Canada:** 2 ave de Tervueren, 1040 Brussels; tel. (2) 741-06-60; fax (2) 741-06-29; internet www.dfait-maeci.gc.ca/eu-mission; JEAN-PIERRE JUNEAU.

**Cape Verde:** 29 ave Jeanne, 1050 Brussels; tel. (2) 643-62-70; fax (2) 646-33-85; José Luís Rocha.

**Central African Republic:** 416 blvd Lambermont, 1030 Brussels; tel. (2) 242-28-80; fax (2) 215-13-11; Armand Guy Zounguere-Sokambi.

**Chad:** 52 blvd Lambermont, 1030 Brussels; tel. (2) 215-19-75; fax (2) 216-35-26; Chargé d'affaires a.i.: Idriss Adjideye.

**Chile:** 13 blvd St Michel, 1040 Brussels; tel. (2) 743-36-60; fax (2) 736-49-94; e-mail misue@skynet.be; Gonzalo Arenas-Valverde.

**China, People's Republic:** 443–445 ave de Tervueren, 1150 Brussels; tel. (2) 771-33-09; fax (2) 779-28-95; Song Mingjiang.

**Colombia:** 96A ave F.D. Roosevelt, 1050 Brussels; tel. (2) 649-56-79; fax (2) 646-54-91; e-mail colombia@emcolbru.org; Robert Arenas Bonilla.

**Comoros:** 27 chemin des Pins, 1180 Brussels; tel. (2) 218-41-43; fax (2) 218-69-84; Mahamoud Soilih.

**Congo, Democratic Republic:** 30 rue Marie de Bourgogne, 1040 Brussels; tel. (2) 513-66-10; fax (2) 514-04-03; Justine M'Poyo-kasa Vubu.

**Congo, Republic:** 16–18 ave F. D. Roosevelt, 1050 Brussels: tel. (2) 648-38-56; fax (2) 648-42-13; Jacques Obia.

**Costa Rica:** 489 ave Louise (4e étage), 1050 Brussels; tel. (2) 640-55-41; fax (2) 648-31-92; e-mail embcrbel@infonie.be; Mario Fernández-Silva.

**Côte d'Ivoire:** 234 ave F. D. Roosevelt, 1050 Brussels; tel. (2) 672-95-77; fax (2) 672-04-91; Anet N'Zi Nanan Koliabo.

**Croatia:** 50 ave des Arts, Boîte 14, 1000 Brussels; tel. (2) 500-09-20; fax (2) 512-03-38; Željko Matić.

**Cuba:** 77 rue Robert Jones, 1180 Brussels; tel. (2) 343-00-20; fax (2) 344-96-91; René Mujica Cantelar.

**Cyprus:** 2 square Ambiorix, 1000 Brussels; tel. (2) 735-35-10; fax (2) 735-45-52; e-mail chypre.pio.bxl@skynet.be; internet www.pio.gov.cy; Nicos Agathocleous.

**Czech Republic:** 15 rue Caroly, 1050 Brussels; tel. (2) 213-01-10; fax (2) 213-01-85; e-mail eu.brussels@embassy.mzv.cz; Josef Kreuter.

**Djibouti:** 26 rue Emile-Menier, 75116 Paris, France; tel. 1-47-27-49-22; fax 1-45-53-52-53; Omar Mouine Robleh.

**Dominica:** 100 rue des Aduatiques, 1040 Brussels; tel. (2) 733-43-28; fax (2) 735-72-37; e-mail ecs.embassies@skynet.be; Edwin P. J. Laurent.

**Dominican Republic:** 12 ave Bel Air, 1180 Brussels; tel. (2) 346-49-35; fax (2) 346-51-52; Clara Joselyn Quiñones Rodríguez.

**Ecuador:** 363 ave Louise, 1050 Brussels; tel. (2) 644-30-50; fax (2) 644-28-13; Alfredo Pinoargote Cevallos.

**Egypt:** 44 ave Léo Errera, 1180 Brussels; tel. (2) 345-52-53; fax (2) 343-65-33; Muhammad Chabane.

**El Salvador:** 171 ave de Tervueren, 1150 Brussels; tel. (2) 733-04-85; fax (2) 735-02-11; Joaquín Rodezna Munguia.

**Equatorial Guinea:** 17 ave Jupiter, 1190 Brussels; tel. (2) 346-25-09; fax (2) 346-33-09; Aurélio Mba Olo Andeme.

**Eritrea:** 15–17 ave de Wolvendael, 1180 Brussels; tel. (2) 374-44-34; fax (2) 372-07-30; e-mail eebb@pophost.eunet.be; Andebrhan Weldegiorgis.

**Estonia:** 1–3 rue Marie-Thérèse, 1000 Brussels; tel. (2) 227-39-10; fax (2) 227-39-25; e-mail eu.all@eu.estemb.be; Priit Kolbre.

**Ethiopia:** 231 ave de Tervueren, Brussels; tel. (2) 771-32-94; fax (2) 771-49-14; Peter Gabriel Robleh.

**Fiji:** 66 ave de Cortenbergh (7e étage), Boîte 7, 1000 Brussels; tel. (2) 736-90-50; fax (2) 736-14-58; Isikeli Uluinairai Mataitoga.

**Gabon:** 112 ave Winston Churchill, 1180 Brussels; tel. (2) 340-62-10; fax (2) 346-46-69; e-mail bs.175335@skynet.be; Jean-Robert Goulongana.

**The Gambia:** 126 ave F. D. Roosevelt, 1050 Brussels; tel. (2) 640-10-49; fax (2) 646-32-77; e-mail oat.gem@skypro.be; Maudo H. N. Touray.

**Georgia:** 15 rue Vergote, 1030 Brussels; tel. (2) 732-85-50; fax (2) 732-85-47; e-mail geoemb.bru@skynet.be; Zurab Abachidze.

**Ghana:** 7 blvd Gén. Wahis, 1030 Brussels; tel. (2) 705-66-53; fax (2) 705-66-53; e-mail head@ghembassy.arc.be; Nana Oye-Mansa Yeboaa.

**Grenada:** 123 rue de Laeken, 1000 Brussels; tel. (2) 223-73-03; fax (2) 223-73-07; Fabian A. Redhead.

**Guatemala:** 185 ave Winston Churchill, 1180 Brussels; tel. (2) 345-90-58; fax (2) 344-64-99; e-mail obguab@infoboard.be; Julio Martini Herrera.

**Guinea:** 75 ave Roger Vandendriessche, 1150 Brussels; tel. (2) 771-01-26; fax (2) 762-60-36; Mamadou Bobo Camara.

**Guinea-Bissau:** 70 ave F. D. Roosevelt, 1050 Brussels; tel. (2) 647-08-90; fax (2) 640-43-12; Chargé d'affaires: José Fonseca.

**Guyana:** 12 ave du Brésil, 1000 Brussels; tel. (2) 675-62-16; fax (2) 675-55-98; e-mail embassy.guyana@skynet.be; Havelock R. H. Brewster.

**Haiti:** 160A ave Louise, Boîte 4, 1050 Brussels; tel. (2) 649-73-81; fax (2) 640-60-80; Yolette Azor-Charles.

**Holy See:** 5–9 ave des Franciscains, 1150 Brussels; tel. (2) 762-20-05; fax (2) 762-20-32; Apostolic Nuncio: Most Rev. Pier Luigi Celata, Titular Archbishop of Doclea.

**Honduras:** 3 ave des Gaulois (5e étage), 1040 Brussels; tel. (2) 734-00-00; fax (2) 735-26-26; Iván Romero Martínez.

**Hungary:** 44 ave du Vert Chasseur, 1180 Brussels; tel. (2) 372-08-00; fax (2) 372-07-84; e-mail titkarsag@humisbeu.be; Endre Juhász.

**Iceland:** 74 rue de Trèves, 1040 Brussels; tel. (2) 286-17-00; fax (2) 286-17-70; e-mail icemb.brussel@utn.stjr.is; internet www.islande.be; Gunnar Snorri Gunnarsson.

**India:** 217 chaussée de Vleurgat, 1050 Brussels; tel. (2) 640-91-40; fax (2) 648-96-38; e-mail eoibru@mail.skynet.be; C. Dasgupta.

**Indonesia:** 38 blvd de la Woluwe, 1200 Brussels; tel. (2) 779-09-15; fax (2) 772-82-10; Poedji Koentarso.

**Iran:** 415 ave de Tervueren, 1150 Brussels; tel. (2) 762-37-45; fax (2) 762-39-15; Hamid Aboutalebi.

**Iraq:** 23 ave des Aubépines, 1180 Brussels; tel. (2) 374-59-92; fax (2) 374-76-15; Chargé d'affaires a.i.: Mahdi S. Hamoudi.

**Israel:** 40 ave de l'Observatoire, 1180 Brussels; tel. (2) 373-55-00; fax (2) 373-56-17; Harry Kney-Tal.

**Jamaica:** 2 ave Palmerston, 1000 Brussels; tel. (2) 230-11-70; fax (2) 230-37-09; e-mail emb.jam.brussels@skynet.be; Douglas Anthony Clive Saunders.

**Japan:** 5–6 Sq. de Meeûs, 1000 Brussels; tel. (2) 500-77-11; fax (2) 513-32-41; internet www.jmission-eu.be; Atsushi Tokinoya.

**Jordan:** 104 ave F. D. Roosevelt, 1050 Brussels; tel. (2) 640-77-55; fax (2) 640-27-96; Dr Umayya Toukan.

**Kazakhstan:** 30 ave Van Bever, 1180 Brussels; tel. (2) 374-95-62; fax (2) 374-50-91; Akhmetzhan S. Yesimov.

**Kenya:** 208 ave Winston Churchill, 1180 Brussels; tel. (2) 340-10-40; fax (2) 340-10-50; Peter Ole Nkuraiyia.

**Kiribati:** c/o Ministry of Foreign Affairs, POB 68, Bairiki, Tarawa; tel. 21342; fax 21466.

**Korea, Republic:** 173–175 chaussée de la Hulpe, 1170 Brussels; tel. (2) 675-57-77; fax (2) 675-52-21; Lee Jai Chun.

**Kuwait:** 43 ave F. D. Roosevelt, 1050 Brussels; tel. (2) 647-79-50; fax (2) 646-12-98; Ahmad A. al-Ebrahim.

**Kyrgyzstan:** 133 rue Tenbosch, 1050 Brussels; tel. (2) 534-63-99; fax (2) 534-23-25; Chingiz Torekulovich Aitmatov.

**Laos:** 74 ave Raymond Poincaré, 75116 Paris, France; tel. 1-45-53-02-98; fax 1-47-57-27-89; Khamphan Simmalavong.

**Latvia:** 39–41 rue d'Arlon, Boîte 6, 1000 Brussels; tel. (2) 282-03-60; fax (2) 282-03-69; e-mail missioneu@mfa.gov.lv; Andris Piebalgs.

**Lebanon:** 2 rue Guillaume Stocq, 1050 Brussels; tel. (2) 649-94-60; fax (2) 649-90-02; Fawzi Fawaz.

**Lesotho:** 45 blvd Général Wahis, 1030 Brussels; tel. (2) 705-39-76; fax (2) 705-67-79; R. V. Lechesa.

**Liberia:** 50 ave du Château, 1081 Brussels; tel. (2) 414-73-17; fax (2) 411-09-12; Dr Cecil T. O. Brandy.

**Libya:** 28 ave Victoria, 1050 Brussels; tel. (2) 649-21-12; Hamed Ahmed Elhouderi.

**Liechtenstein:** 1 Place du Congrès, 1000 Brussels; tel. (2) 229-39-00; fax (2) 219-35-45; Prince Nikolaus von Liechtenstein.

**Lithuania:** 51 ave des Cinq Bonniers, 1150 Brussels; tel. (2) 771-01-40; fax (2) 771-45-97; Romualdas Kolonaitis.

**Madagascar:** 297 ave de Tervueren, 1150 Brussels; tel. (2) 770-17-26; fax (2) 772-37-31; e-mail ambassade.madagascar@skynet.be; internet www3.itu.ch/mission/Madagascar; Jean Omer Beriziky.

**Malawi:** 15 rue de la Loi, 1040 Brussels; tel. (2) 231-09-80; fax (2) 231-10-66; Julie Nanyoni Mphande.

**Malaysia:** 414A ave de Tervueren, 1150 Brussels; tel. (2) 776-03-40; fax (2) 762-67-67; e-mail embassy.malaysia@euronet.be; Dato' M. M. Sathiah.

**Maldives:** 212 East 47th St, Apt 15B, New York, NY 10017, USA; tel. (212) 688-07-76.

**Mali:** 487 ave Molière, 1050 Brussels; tel. (2) 345-74-32; fax (2) 344-57-00; Ahmed Mohamed Ag Hamani.

**Malta:** 44 rue Jules Lejeune, 1050 Brussels; tel. (2) 343-01-95; fax (2) 343-01-06; Victor Camilleri.

**Mauritania:** 6 ave de la Colombie, 1050 Brussels; tel. (2) 672-47-47; fax (2) 672-20-51; Boullah Ould Mogueye.

**Mauritius:** 68 rue des Bollandistes, 1040 Brussels; tel. (2) 733-99-88; fax (2) 734-40-21; Taye Waye Michel Wan Chat Kwong.

**Mexico:** 94 ave F.D. Roosevelt, 1050 Brussels; tel. (2) 629-07-11; fax (2) 644-08-19; e-mail mex-ue@pophost.eunet.be; JAIME ZABLUDOVSKY KUPER.

**Mongolia:** 18 ave Besme, 1190 Brussels; tel. (2) 344-69-74; fax (2) 344-32-15; e-mail embassy.mongolia@skynet.be; internet users .skynet.be/mongolia; SHUKHER ALTANGEREL.

**Morocco:** 29 blvd Saint-Michel, 1040 Brussels; tel. (2) 736-11-00; fax (2) 734-64-68; e-mail sifamabruxe@infoboard.be; Chargé d'affaires a.i.: ABDELJALIL SAUBRY.

**Mozambique:** 97 blvd Saint-Michel, 1040 Brussels; tel. (2) 736-25-64; fax (2) 735-62-07; e-mail embamoc.bru@euronet.be; ÁLVARO MANUEL TRINIDADE DA SILVA.

**Myanmar:** Schumannstrasse 112, 53113 Bonn, Germany; tel. (228) 210091; fax (228) 219316; U TUN NGWE.

**Namibia:** 454 ave de Tervueren, 1150 Brussels; tel. (2) 771-14-10; fax (2) 771-96-89; e-mail nam.emb@brutele.be; Dr ZEDEKIA JOSEF NGAVIRUE.

**Nepal:** 68 ave Winston Churchill, 1180 Brussels; tel. (2) 346-26-58; fax (2) 344-13-61; e-mail rne.bru@skynet.be; KEDAR BHAKTA SHRESTHA.

**New Zealand:** 47–48 blvd du Régent, 1000 Brussels; tel. (2) 512-10-40; fax (2) 513-48-56; e-mail nzembbru@compuserve.com; DELL HIGGIE.

**Nicaragua:** 55 ave de Wolvendael, 1180 Brussels; tel. (2) 375-64-34; fax (2) 375-71-88; ALVARO PORTA BERMÚDEZ.

**Niger:** 78 ave F. D. Roosevelt, 1050 Brussels; tel. (2) 648-61-40; fax (2) 648-27-84; HOUSSEINI ABDOU-SALEYE.

**Nigeria:** 288 ave de Tervueren, 1150 Brussels; tel. (2) 762-52-00; fax (2) 762-37-63; ALABA CORNELIUS ABIODUN ADEBOYEIO OGUNSANWO.

**Norway:** 17 rue Archimède, 1000 Brussels; tel. (2) 234-11-11; fax (2) 234-11-50; EINAR M. BULL.

**Oman:** 50 ave d'Iéna, 75116 Paris, France; tel. 1-47-23-01-63; fax 1-47-23-77-10; MUHAMMAD BIN SULTAN AL-BUSAIDI.

**Pakistan:** 57 ave Delleur, 1170 Brussels; tel. (2) 673-80-07; fax (2) 675-83-94; e-mail parepbru_econ@infoboard.be; SAIDULLA KHAN DEHLAVI.

**Panama:** 390–392 ave Louise, 1050 Brussels; tel. (2) 649-07-29; fax (2) 648-92-16; e-mail panama@antrasite.be; Chargé d'affaires a.i.: ELENA BARLETTA DE NOTTEBOHM.

**Papua New Guinea:** 430 ave de Tervueren, 1150 Brussels; tel. (2) 779-08-26; fax (2) 772-70-88; GABRIEL KOIBA PEPSON.

**Paraguay:** 475 ave Louise (12e étage), 1050 Brussels; tel. (2) 649-90-55; fax (2) 647-42-48; MANUEL MARIÁ CÁCERES.

**Peru:** 179 ave de Tervueren, 1150 Brussels; tel. (2) 733-33-19; fax (2) 733-48-19; e-mail embassy.of.peru@unicall.be; JOSÉ ANTONIO ARROSPIDE.

**Philippines:** 297 ave Molière, 1050 Brussels; tel. (2) 340-33-77; fax (2) 345-64-25; e-mail bleu.pe@skynet.be; JOSÉ U. FERNANDEZ.

**Poland:** 282–284 ave de Tervueren, 1150 Brussels; tel. (2) 777-72-00; fax (2) 777-72-97; e-mail 101642.2616@compuserve.com; JAN TRUSZCZYNSKI.

**Qatar:** 71 ave F. D. Roosevelt, 1050 Brussels; tel. (2) 640-29-00; fax (2) 648-40-78; e-mail qatar@infonie.be; Chargé d'affaires a.i.: MOHAMED AL-HAIYKI.

**Romania:** 107 rue Gabrielle, 1180 Brussels; tel. (2) 344-41-45; fax (2) 344-24-79; e-mail rommis@pophost.eunet.be; CONSTANTIN ENE.

**Russia:** 56 ave Louis Lepoutre, 1060 Brussels; tel. (2) 343-03-39; fax (2) 346-24-53; e-mail misrusce@interpac.be; VASILII LIKHACHEN.

**Rwanda:** 1 ave des Fleurs, 1150 Brussels; tel. (2) 763-07-02; fax (2) 763-07-53; e-mail rwanda.info@la.be; internet www.rwanda.net; MANZI BAKURAMURZA.

**Saint Christopher and Nevis:** 100 rue des Aduatiques, 1040 Brussels; tel. (2) 733-43-28; fax (2) 735-72-37; e-mail ecs.embassies@skynet.be; EDWIN P. J. LAURENT.

**Saint Lucia:** 100 rue des Aduatiques, 1040 Brussels; tel. (2) 733-43-28; fax (12) 735-72-37; e-mail ecs.embassies@skynet.be; EDWIN P. J. LAURENT.

**Saint Vincent and the Grenadines:** 100 rue des Aduatiques, 1040 Brussels; tel. (2) 733-43-28; fax (12) 735-72-37; e-mail ecs .embassies@skynet.be; EDWIN P. J. LAURENT.

**Samoa:** 123 ave F. D. Roosevelt, Boîte 14, 1050 Brussels; tel. (2) 660-84-54; fax (2) 675-03-36; e-mail samoa.emb.bxl@skynet.be; TAUILIILI UILI MEREDITH.

**San Marino:** 62 ave F.D. Roosevelt, 1050 Brussels; tel. (2) 644-22-24; fax (2) 644-20-57; SAVINA ZAFFERANI.

**São Tomé and Príncipe:** 175 ave de Tervueren, 1150 Brussels; tel. and fax (2) 734-88-15; e-mail ambassade.sao.tome@skynet.be; Chargé d'affaires: ARMINDO DE BRITO FERNANDES.

**Saudi Arabia:** 45 ave F. D. Roosevelt, 1050 Brussels; tel. (2) 649-20-44; fax (2) 647-24-92; NASSIR AL-ALASSAF.

**Senegal:** 196 ave F. D. Roosevelt, 1050 Brussels; tel. (2) 673-00-97; fax (2) 675-04-60; SALOUM KANDE.

**Seychelles:** 51 ave Mozart, 75016 Paris, France; tel. 1-42-30-57-47; fax 1-42-30-57-40; e-mail ambsey@aol.com; CALLIXTE FRANÇOIS-XAVIER D'OFFAY.

**Sierra Leone:** 410 ave de Tervueren, 1150 Brussels; tel. (2) 771-00-53; fax (2) 771-82-30; PETER J. KUYEMBEH.

**Singapore:** 198 ave F. D. Roosevelt, 1050 Brussels; tel. (2) 660-29-79; fax (2) 660-86-85; e-mail amb.eu@singembbru.be; A. SELVERAJAH.

**Slovakia:** 79 ave Cortenbergh, 1000 Brussels; tel. (2) 743-68-11; fax (2) 743-68-88; e-mail pmsreul@pophost.eunet.be; JURAJ MIGAS.

**Slovenia:** 30 ave Marnix, 1000 Brussels; tel. (2) 512-44-66; fax (2) 512-09-97; e-mail mission.bruxelles@mzz-dkp.sigor.si; MARKO KRANJEC.

**Solomon Islands:** 13 ave de L'Yser, Boîte 3, 1040 Brussels; tel. (2) 732-70-85; fax (2) 732-68-85; ROBERT SISILO.

**Somalia:** 26 rue Dumont d'Urville, 75116 Paris, France; tel. (1) 45-00-76-51; (vacant).

**South Africa:** 26 rue de la Loi, Boîtes 7–8, 1040 Brussels; tel. (2) 285-44-00; fax (2) 285-44-87; e-mail samission@village.uunet.be; Dr ELIAS LINKS.

**Sri Lanka:** 27 rue Jules Lejeune, 1050 Brussels; tel. (2) 344-53-94; fax (2) 344-67-37; e-mail sri.lanka@euronet.be; N. NAVARATNARAJAH.

**Sudan:** 124 ave F. D. Roosevelt, 1050 Brussels; tel. (2) 647-51-59; fax (2) 648-34-99; GALAL HASSAN ATABANI.

**Suriname:** 379 ave Louise, 1050 Brussels; tel. (2) 640-11-72; fax (2) 646-39-62; e-mail sur.amb.bru@online.be; (vacant).

**Swaziland:** 188 ave Winston Churchill, 1180 Brussels; tel. (2) 347-47-71; fax (2) 347-46-23; Dr THEMBAYENA ANNASTASIA DLAMINI.

**Switzerland:** 53 rue d'Arlon, Boîte 9, 1040 Brussels; tel. (2) 286-13-11; fax (2) 230-45-09; e-mail vertretung@brm.rep.admin.ch; ALEXIS P. LAUTENBERG.

**Syria:** 3 ave F. D. Roosevelt, 1050 Brussels; tel. (2) 648-01-35; fax (2) 646-40-18; (vacant).

**Tanzania:** 363 ave Louise (7e étage), 1050 Brussels; tel. (2) 640-65-00; fax (2) 646-80-26; ALI ABEID AMAN KARUME.

**Thailand:** 2 square du Val de la Cambre, 1050 Brussels; tel. (2) 640-68-10; fax (2) 648-30-60; e-mail thaibxl@pophost.eunet.be; internet www.waw.be/rte-be; Dr SUKHUM RASMIDATTA.

**Togo:** 264 ave de Tervueren, 1150 Brussels; tel. (2) 770-17-91; fax (2) 771-50-75; ELIOTT LATEVI-ATCHO LAWSON.

**Tonga:** 36 Molyneux St, London, W1H 6AB, United Kingdom; tel. (20) 7724-5828; fax (20) 7723-9074; e-mail tongahicommission@btinternet.com; 'AKOSITA FINEANGANOFO.

**Trinidad and Tobago:** 14 ave de la Faisanderie, 1150 Brussels; tel. (2) 762-94-15; fax (2) 772-27-83; (vacant).

**Tunisia:** 278 ave de Tervueren, 1150 Brussels; tel. (2) 771-73-95; fax (2) 771-94-33; TAHAR SIOUD.

**Turkey:** 4 rue Montoyer, 1000 Brussels; tel. (2) 513-28-36; fax (2) 511-0450; e-mail turkdelegeu@euronet.be; NIHAT AKYOL.

**Tuvalu:** c/o Prime Minister's Office, Vaiaku, Funafuti, Tuvalu.

**Uganda:** 317 ave de Tervueren, 1150 Brussels; tel. (2) 762-58-25; fax (2) 763-04-38; KAMIMA NTAMBI.

**Ukraine:** 7 rue Guimard, 1040 Brussels; tel. (2) 511-46-09; fax (2) 512-40-45; BORIS HUDYMA.

**United Arab Emirates:** 73 ave F. D. Roosevelt, 1050 Brussels; tel. (2) 640-60-00; fax (2) 646-24-73; e-mail emirates.bxl@infonie.be; ABDEL HADI ABDEL WAHID AL-KHAJA.

**USA:** 40 blvd du Régent, Boîte 3, 1000 Brussels; tel. (2) 500-27-74; fax (2) 512-57-20; e-mail useu@usinfo.be; internet www.useu.be; RICHARD L. MORNINGSTAR.

**Uruguay:** 22 ave F. D. Roosevelt, 1050 Brussels; tel (2) 640-11-69; fax (2) 648-29-09; e-mail uruemb@euronet.be; GUILLERMO VALLES.

**Vanuatu:** c/o Prime Minister's Office, POB 110, Port Vila, Vanuatu.

**Venezuela:** 10 ave F. D. Roosevelt, 1050 Brussels; tel. (2) 639-03-40; fax (2) 647-88-20; LUIS XAVIER GRISANTI.

**Viet Nam:** 130 ave de la Floride, 1180 Brussels; tel. (2) 374-91-33; fax (2) 374-93-76; HUYNH ANH DZUNG.

**Yemen:** 114 ave F. D. Roosevelt, 1050 Brussels; tel. (2) 646-52-90; fax (2) 646-29-11; GAZEM A. K. AL-AGHBARI.

**Yugoslavia:** 11 ave Emile Demot, 1000 Brussels; tel. (2) 649-83-65; fax (2) 649-08-78; DRAGOSLAV JOVANOVIĆ.

**Zambia:** 469 ave Molière, 1060 Brussels; tel. (2) 343-56-49; fax (2) 347-43-33; ISAIAH ZIMBA CHABALA.

**Zimbabwe:** 11 square Joséphine Charlotte, 1200 Brussels; tel. (2) 762-58-08; fax (2) 762-96-05; SIMBARASHE S. MUMBENGEGWI.

## Union Institutions

Originally each of the Communities had its own Commission (High Authority in the case of the ECSC) and Council, but a treaty transferring the powers of these bodies to a single Commission and a single Council came into effect in 1967.

## EUROPEAN COMMISSION

**Address:** 200 rue de la Loi, 1049 Brussels, Belgium.

**Telephone:** (2) 299-11-11; **fax:** (2) 295-01-38; **internet:** europa.eu.int/comm/index_en.htm.

### MEMBERS OF THE COMMISSION
(with their responsibilities: January 2000)

**President:** ROMANO PRODI (Italy): Secretariat General; Legal Service; Media and communication.

**Vice-Presidents:**

NEIL KINNOCK (United Kingdom): Administrative reform; Personnel and administration; Linguistic services; Protocol and security.

LOYOLA DE PALACIO (Spain): Relations with the European Parliament; Relations with the Committee of the Regions, the Economic and Social Committee, and the Ombudsman; Transport, including trans-European networks; Energy.

**Other Members:**

MARIO MONTI (Italy): Competition.

FRANZ FISCHLER (Austria): Agriculture and rural development; Fisheries.

ERKKI LIIKANEN (Finland): Enterprise; Competitiveness; Innovation; Information society.

FRITS BOLKESTEIN (Netherlands): Internal market; Financial services; Customs; Taxation.

PHILIPPE BUSQUIN (Belgium): Science, research and development; Joint Research Centre.

PEDRO SOLBES MIRA (Spain): Economic and financial affairs; Monetary matters; Statistical Office.

POUL NIELSON (Denmark): Development aid and co-operation; Humanitarian Aid Office.

GÜNTER VERHEUGEN (Germany): Enlargement process, including the pre-accession strategy.

CHRISTOPHER PATTEN (United Kingdom): External relations; Common foreign and security policy; Delegations to non-member countries; Common service for external relations.

PASCAL LAMY (France): Trade policy and instruments of trade policy.

DAVID BYRNE (Ireland): Public health; Consumer protection.

MICHEL BARNIER (France): Regional policy; Cohesion fund; Intergovernmental Conference.

VIVIANE REDING (Luxembourg): Citizens' Europe; Transparency; Education and culture; Publications office.

MICHAELE SCHREYER (Germany): Budget; Financial control; Fraud prevention.

MARGOT WALLSTRÖM (Sweden): Environment; Nuclear safety.

ANTÓNIO VITORINO (Portugal): Freedom, security and justice.

ANNA DIAMANTOPOULOU (Greece): Employment and social affairs; Equal opportunities.

The functions of the Commission are fourfold: to ensure the application of the provisions of the Treaties and of the provisions enacted by the institutions of the Communities in pursuance thereof; to formulate recommendations or opinions in matters which are the subject of the Treaties, where the latter expressly so provides or where the Commission considers it necessary; to dispose, under the conditions laid down in the Treaties, of a power of decision of its own and to participate in the preparation of acts of the Council of the European Union and of the European Parliament; and to exercise the competence conferred on it by the Council of the European Union for the implementation of the rules laid down by the latter.

The Commission may not include more than two members having the nationality of the same state; the number of members of the Commission may be amended by a unanimous vote of the Council of the European Union. In the performance of their duties, the members of the Commission are forbidden to seek or accept instructions from any Government or other body, or to engage in any other paid or unpaid professional activity.

The members of the Commission are nominated by the Governments of the member states acting in common agreement normally for a renewable term of five years. From January 1995, under the terms of the Treaty on European Union, the nominated President and other members of the Commission must be approved as a body by the European Parliament before they can take office. Once approved, the Commission may nominate one or two of its members as Vice-President. Any member of the Commission, if he or she no longer fulfils the conditions required for the performance of his or her duties, or commits a serious offence, may be declared removed from office by the Court of Justice. The Court may furthermore, on the petition of the Council of the European Union or of the Commission itself, provisionally suspend any member of the Commission from his or her duties. The European Parliament has the authority to dismiss the entire Commission.

In January 1999 Commissioners accused of mismanagement and corruption retained their positions following a vote of censure by Parliament. However, Parliament proceeded to appoint a five-member Committee of Independent Experts to investigate allegations of fraud, mismanagement and nepotism within the Commission. In early March two new codes of conduct for Commissioners were announced. On 15 March the Committee published a report that criticized the Commission's failure to control the administration and to take responsibility for the budget and other measures implemented by each department. The report also identified individual Commissioners as guilty of nepotism and mismanagement and proposed the establishment of a new independent unit to investigate fraud. As a consequence of the report the Commission agreed, collectively, to resign, although Commissioners were to retain their positions, and exercise limited duties, until their successors were appointed. In late March EU heads of state and of government nominated Romano Prodi, the former Italian Prime Minister, as the next President of the Commission. His appointment was endorsed by the outgoing Parliament in early May, but it required formal ratification by the newly-constituted Parliament, which was scheduled to convene for the first time in July, following elections in June. Prodi's appointment, and the team of Commissioners that he had appointed in the interim, were duly ratified by Parliament in September. However, Parliament made ratification subject to conditions, forming the foundation of a future inter-institutional agreement between itself and the Commission: while it did not lose any of its powers, the Commission undertook to be more open in its future dealings with the Parliament.

### ADMINISTRATION

Offices are at the address of the European Commission: 200 rue de la Loi, 1049 Brussels, Belgium; tel. (2) 299-11-11; fax (2) 295-01-38; internet europa.eu.int/comm/index_en.htm (unless otherwise stated).

**Secretariat-General of the Commission:** Sec.-Gen. CARLO TROJAN.

**Forward Studies Unit:** Dir JEAN-CLAUDE THEBAULT.

**Inspectorate-General:** Insp.-Gen. GRAHAM AVERY.

**Legal Service:** Dir-Gen. JEAN-LOUIS DEWOST.

**Joint Interpreting and Conference Service:** Head of Service ROCCO TANZILLI.

**Statistical Office (EUROSTAT):** Bâtiment Jean Monnet, rue Alcide de Gasperi, 2920 Luxembourg; tel. 4301-33-107; fax 4301-33-015; e-mail media.support@eurostat.cec.be; internet europa.eu.int/eurostat.html; Dir-Gen. YVES FRANCHET.

**Translation Service:** Dir-Gen. a.i. BRIAN MCCLUSKEY.

**Informatics Directorate:** Bâtiment Jean Monnet, rue Alcide de Gasperi, 2920 Luxembourg; tel. 4301-1; fax 4301-24; internet europa.eu.int/comm/di; Dir-Gen. COLETTE FLESCH.

**Protocol and Security Service:** Dir JACQUES DE BAENST.

**Task Force for Accession Negotiations:** Dir-Gen. NIKOLAUS VAN DER PAS.

**Press and Communications:** Dir JONATHAN FAULL.

**Directorates-General*:**

- **Agriculture:** Dir-Gen. JOSÉ MANUEL SILVA RODRÍGUEZ.
- **Budget:** Dir-Gen. JEAN-PAUL MINGASSON.
- **Common Service for External Relations:** Dir-Gen. PHILIPPE SOUBESTRE.
- **Competition:** Dir-Gen. ALEXANDER SCHAUB.
- **Development:** Dir-Gen. PHILIP LOWE.
- **Economic and Financial Affairs:** Dir-Gen. GIOVANNI RAVASIO.
- **Education and Culture:** Dir-Gen. NIKOLAUS VAN DER PAS.
- **Employment and Social Affairs:** Dir-Gen. ALLAN LARSSON.
- **Energy:** Dir-Gen. PABLO BENAVIDES SALAS.
- **Enlargement:** Dir-Gen. ENEKO LANDÁBURU ILLARRAMENDI.
- **Enterprise:** Dir-Gen. FABIO COLASANTI.
- **Environment:** Dir-Gen. JAMES CURRIE.
- **European Anti-fraud Office:** Dir-Gen. PER KNUDSEN.
- **External Relations:** Dir-Gen. GUY LEGRAS.
- **Financial Control:** Dir-Gen. ISABELLA VENTURA.
- **Fisheries:** Dir-Gen. STEFFEN SMIDT.
- **Health and Consumer Protection:** Dir-Gen. ROBERT COLEMAN.
- **Information Society:** Dir-Gen. ROBERT VERRUE.
- **Internal Market:** Dir-Gen. JOHN F. MOGG.

**Joint Research Centre:** Dir-Gen. HERBERT J. ALLGEIER.

**Justice and Home Affairs:** Dir-Gen. ADRIAN FORTESCUE.

**Personnel and Administration:** Dir-Gen. HORST REICHENBACH.

**Regional Policy:** Dir-Gen. GUY CRAUSER.

**Research:** Dir-Gen. JORMA ROUTTI.

**Taxation and Customs Union:** Dir-Gen. MICHEL VANDEN ABEELE.

**Trade:** Dir-Gen. JOHANNES-FRIEDRICH BESELER.

**Transport:** Dir-Gen. FRANÇOIS LAMOUREUX.

* In September 1999 an extensive restructuring of the Commission's administrative offices was initiated, and some of these remained in transition in January 2000. As part of the restructuring process the Directors-General responsible, respectively, for Economics and Finance, for Trade and for Budget were due to retire or otherwise relinquish their positions in 2000. It should be noted that the numerical designations formerly assigned to the Directorates-General are no longer in use.

**European Community Humanitarian Office (ECHO):** Dir ALBERTO NAVARRO GONZÁLEZ.

**Euratom Supply Agency:** Dir-Gen. MICHAEL GOPPEL.

**Office for Official Publications of the European Union (EUR-OP):** 2 rue Mercier, 2985 Luxembourg; tel. 2929-1; fax 4957-19; e-mail europ@opoce.cec.be; internet eur-op.eu.int; Dir-Gen. LUCIEN EMRINGER.

## THE EUROPEAN COUNCIL

The heads of state or of government of the member countries meet at least twice a year, in the member state which currently exercises the presidency of the Council of the European Union, or in Brussels.

Until 1975 summit meetings were held less frequently, on an *ad hoc* basis, usually to adopt major policy decisions regarding the future development of the Community. In answer to the evident need for more frequent consultation at the highest level, it was decided at the summit meeting in Paris in December 1974 to hold the meetings on a regular basis, under the rubric of the European Council. There was no provision made for the existence of the European Council in the Treaty of Rome, but its position was acknowledged and regularized in the Single European Act (1987). Its role was further strengthened in the Treaty on European Union, which entered into force on 1 November 1993. As a result of the Treaty, the European Council became directly responsible for common policies within the fields of Common Foreign and Security Policy and Justice and Home Affairs.

## COUNCIL OF THE EUROPEAN UNION

**General Secretariat:** 175 rue de la Loi, 1048 Brussels, Belgium.

**Telephone:** (2) 285-61-11; **fax:** (2) 285-73-97; **e-mail:** public.relations@consilium.eu.int; **internet:** ue.eu.int.

The Council of the European Union (until 1994 known formally as the Council of Ministers of the European Community and still frequently referred to as the Council of Ministers) is the only institution that directly represents the member states. It is the Community's principal decision-making body, acting on proposals made by the Commission, and is responsible for ensuring the co-ordination of the general economic policies of the member states and for taking the decisions necessary to implement the Treaties. The Council is composed of representatives of the member states, each Government delegating to it one of its members, according to the subject to be discussed. These meetings are generally referred to as the Agriculture Council, Telecommunications Council, etc. The Foreign Affairs, Economics and Finance ('ECOFIN') and Agriculture Councils normally meet once a month. The office of President is exercised for a term of six months by each member of the Council in rotation (January–June 2000: Portugal; July–December: France). Meetings of the Council are convened and chaired by the President, acting on his or her own initiative or at the request of a member or of the Commission.

The Treaty of Rome prescribed three types of voting: simple majority, qualified majority and unanimity. The votes of its members are weighted as follows: France, Germany, Italy and the United Kingdom 10; Spain 8; Belgium, Greece, the Netherlands and Portugal 5; Austria and Sweden 4; Denmark, Finland and Ireland 3; Luxembourg 2. Out of a total number of votes of 87, 62 are required for a qualified majority decision, making 26 votes sufficient for a blocking minority. During negotiations for enlargement of the EU, an agreement was reached, in March 1994, on new rules regulating voting procedures in the expanded Council, in response to concerns on the part of Spain and the United Kingdom that their individual influence would be diminished. Under the 'Ioannina compromise' (named after the Greek town where the agreement was concluded) 23–25 opposing votes were to be sufficient to continue debate of legislation for a 'reasonable period' until a consensus decision is reached. Amendments to the Treaty of Rome (the Single European Act), effective from July 1987, restricted the right of 'veto', and were expected to accelerate the development of a genuine common market: they allowed proposals relating to the dismantling of barriers to the free movement of goods, persons, services and capital to be approved by a majority vote in the Council, rather than by a unanimous vote. Unanimity would still be required, however, for certain areas, including harmonization of indirect taxes, legislation on health and safety, veterinary controls, and environmental protection; individual states would also retain control over immigration rules, prevention of terrorism and drugs-trafficking. The Treaty of Amsterdam, which came into force on 1 May 1999, extended the use of qualified majority voting to limited policy areas.

The Single European Act introduced a 'co-operation procedure' whereby a proposal adopted by a qualified majority in the Council must be submitted to the European Parliament for approval: if the Parliament rejects the Council's common position, unanimity shall be required for the Council to act on a second reading, and if the Parliament suggests amendments, the Commission must re-examine the proposal and forward it to the Council again. A 'co-decision procedure' was introduced in 1993 by the Treaty on European Union. The procedure allows a proposal to be submitted for a third reading by a so-called 'Conciliation Committee', composed equally of Council representatives and members of the European Parliament. The Treaty of Amsterdam was to simplify the co-decision procedure, and extend it to matters previously resolved under the co-operation procedure, although the latter was to remain in place for matters concerning economic and monetary union.

Under the Treaty of Amsterdam, the Secretary-General of the Council was also to take the role of 'High Representative', responsible for the co-ordination of common foreign and security policy. The Secretary-General was to be supported by a policy planning and early warning unit. In June 1999 Javier Solana Madariaga, at that time Secretary-General of NATO, was designated as the first Secretary-General of the Council.

### PERMANENT REPRESENTATIVES

Preparation and co-ordination of the Council's work is entrusted to a Committee of Permanent Representatives (COREPER), meeting in Brussels, consisting of the ambassadors of the member countries to the Union. A staff of national civil servants assists each ambassador.

### ADMINISTRATION

Offices are at the address of the Council of the European Union: 175 rue de la Loi, 1048 Brussels, Belgium; tel. (2) 285-61-11; fax (2) 285-73-97; e-mail public.relations@consilium.eu.int; internet ue.eu.int.

**Secretariat-General of the Council:** Sec.-Gen. JAVIER SOLANA MADARIAGA.

**Secretary-General's Private Office:** Dir and Head of Cabinet: ALBERTO NAVARRO GONZÁLEZ.

**Legal Service:** Dir-Gen. (Juriconsult of the Council) JEAN-CLAUDE PIRIS.

**Directorates-General:**

**A (Personnel and Administration; Protocol, Organization, Security, Infrastructure; Translation and Production of Documents; Finances of the Secretariat):** Dir-Gen. ULRICH WEINSTOCK.

**B (Agriculture and Fisheries):** Dir-Gen. VITTORIO GRIFFO.

**C (Internal Market; Customs Union, Industrial Policy, Approximation of Laws, Right of Establishment and Freedom to Provide Services, Company Law, Intellectual Property):** Dir-Gen. NIELS HENRIK SLIBEN.

**D (Research, Energy and Transport):** Dir-Gen. DAVID MAURICE NELIGAN.

**E (External Economic Relations and Common Foreign and Security Policy):** Dirs-Gen. BRIAN L. CROWE, CORNELIS STEKELENBURG, LEONIDAS EVANGELIDIS.

**F (Relations with the European Parliament, the Economic and Social Committee and the Committee of the Regions; Institutional Affairs; Budget and Staff Regulations; Information Policy; Public Relations):** Dir-Gen. ANGEL BOIXAREU CARRERA.

**G (Economic, Financial and Social Affairs; European Monetary Union—EMU):** Dir-Gen. SIXTEN KORKMAN.

**H (Justice and Home Affairs):** Dir-Gen. CHARLES ELSEN.

**I (Environmental and Consumer Protection; Civil Protection; Health and Food Legislation):** Dir-Gen. KERSTIN NIBLAEUS.

**J (Social Policy; Employment; Social Dialogue, Regional Policy and Economic and Social Cohesion; Education and Youth; Culture and Audio-visual Media):** Dir-Gen. MARC LEPOIVRE.

## EUROPEAN PARLIAMENT

**Address:** Centre Européen, Plateau du Kirchberg, 2929 Luxembourg.

**Telephone:** 4300-1; **fax:** 4300-7009; **internet:** www.europarl.eu.int.

### PRESIDENT AND MEMBERS
(January 2000)

**President:** NICOLE FONTAINE (France).

**Members:** 626 members, apportioned as follows: Germany 99 members; France, Italy and the United Kingdom 87 members each; Spain 64; the Netherlands 31; Belgium, Greece and Portugal 25 each; Sweden 22; Austria 21; Denmark and Finland 16 each; Ireland 15; Luxembourg 6. Members are elected for a five-year term by direct universal suffrage by the citizens of the member states. Members sit in the Chamber in political, not national, groups.

The tasks of the European Parliament are: amending legislation, scrutinizing the Union budget and exercising a measure of democratic control over the executive organs of the European Communities, the Commission and the Council. It has the power to dismiss the Commission by a vote of censure (see above). Increases in parliamentary powers have been brought about through amendments to the Treaty of Rome. The Single European Act, which entered into force on 1 July 1987, introduced, in certain circumstances where the Council normally adopts legislation through majority voting, a co-operation procedure involving a second parliamentary reading, enabling Parliament to amend legislation. Community agreements with third countries require parliamentary approval. The Treaty on European Union, which came into force in November 1993, introduced the co-decision procedure, permitting a third parliamentary reading (see Council of the European Union, above). The Treaty also gives Parliament the right to veto legislation, and allows Parliament a vote of approval for a new Commission. Parliament appoints the European Ombudsman, who investigates reports of maladministration in Community institutions. The Treaty of Amsterdam, which entered into force in May 1999, expanded and simplified Parliament's legislative role.

**Political Groupings**

| | Distribution of seats (January 2000) |
|---|---|
| Group of the European People's Party | 233 |
| Party of European Socialists | 180 |
| European Liberal Group | 51 |
| Green/European Free Alliance | 48 |
| Confederal Group of the European United Left-Nordic Green Left | 42 |
| Union for a Europe of the Nations | 30 |
| Technical Group of Independent Members | 18 |
| The Europe of Democracies and Diversities | 16 |
| Non-attached | 8 |
| **Total** | 626 |

Parliament has an annual session, divided into about 12 one-week meetings, normally held in Strasbourg, France. The session opens with the March meeting. Committees and political group meetings and additional sittings of Parliament are held in Brussels.

The budgetary powers of Parliament (which, with the Council, forms the Budgetary Authority of the Communities) were increased to their present status by a treaty of 22 July 1975. Under this treaty, it can amend non-agricultural spending and reject the draft budget, acting by a majority of its members and two-thirds of the votes cast.

The Parliament is run by a Bureau comprising the President, 14 Vice-Presidents elected from its members by secret ballot to serve for two-and-a-half years, and the four members of the College of Quaestors. Elections to the Bureau took place most recently in June 1999. Parliament has 20 specialized committees, which deliberate on proposals for legislation put forward by the Commission before Parliament's final opinion is delivered by a resolution in plenary session.

There are Standing Committees on Foreign Affairs, Security, and Defence Policies; Agriculture and Rural Development; Budgets; Budgetary Control; Economic and Monetary Affairs and Industrial Policy; Research, Technological Development and Energy; External Economic Relations; Legal Affairs and Citizens' Rights; Social Affairs and Employment; Regional Policy; Transport and Tourism; Environment, Public Health and Consumer Protection; Culture, Youth, Education and the Media; Development and Co-operation; Fisheries; Rules of Procedure, the Verification of Credentials and Immunities; Institutional Affairs; Petitions; Women's Rights; Civil Liberties and Internal Affairs.

The first direct elections to the European Parliament took place in June 1979, and Parliament met for the first time in July. The second elections were held in June 1984 (with separate elections held in Portugal and Spain in 1987, following the accession of these two countries to the Community), the third in June 1989, the fourth in June 1994. Direct elections to the European Parliament were held in Sweden in September 1995, and in Austria and Finland in October 1996. The fifth European Parliament was elected in June 1999.

## COURT OF JUSTICE OF THE EUROPEAN COMMUNITIES

**Address:** Palais de la Cour de Justice, 2925 Luxembourg.

**Telephone:** 4303-1; **fax:** 4303-2600; **internet:** www.curia.eu.int.

The task of the Court of Justice is to ensure the observance of law in the interpretation and application of the Treaties setting up the three Communities. The 15 Judges and the nine Advocates General are appointed for renewable six-year terms by the Governments of the member states. The President of the Court is elected by the Judges from among their number for a renewable term of three years. The majority of cases are dealt with by one of the six chambers, each of which consists of a President of Chamber and two or four Judges. The Court may sit in plenary session in cases of particular importance or when a member state or Community institution that is a party to the proceedings so requests. The Court has jurisdiction to award damages. It may review the legality of acts (other than recommendations or opinions) of the Council, the Commission or the European Central Bank, of acts adopted jointly by the European Parliament and the Council and of Acts adopted by Parliament and intended to produce legal effects *vis-à-vis* third parties. It is also competent to give judgment on actions by a member state, the Council or the Commission on grounds of lack of competence, of infringement of an essential procedural requirement, of infringement of a Treaty or of any legal rule relating to its application, or of misuse of power. The Court of Justice may hear appeals, on a point of law only, from the Court of First Instance.

The Court is also empowered to hear certain other cases concerning the contractual and non-contractual liability of the Communities and disputes between member states in connection with the objects of the Treaties. It also gives preliminary rulings at the request of national courts on the interpretation of the Treaties, of Union legislation, and of the Brussels Convention on Jurisdiction and the Enforcement of Judgments in Civil and Commercial Matters. During 1998 485 new cases were brought before the Court, of which 264 were cases referred to it for preliminary rulings by the national courts of the member states and 70 were appeals from the Court of First Instance. In the same period 254 judgments were delivered and 420 cases completed.

**Composition of the Court** (in order of precedence, as at January 2000):

GIL CARLOS RODRÍGUEZ IGLESIAS (Spain), President of the Court of Justice.

JOSÉ CARLOS DE CARVALHO MOITINHO DE ALMEIDA (Portugal), President of the Third and Sixth Chambers.

DAVID ALEXANDER OGILVY EDWARD (United Kingdom), President of the Fourth and Fifth Chambers.

LEIF SEVÓN (Finland), President of the First Chamber.

NIAL FENNELLY (Ireland), First Advocate General.

ROMAIN SCHINTGEN (Luxembourg), President of the Second Chamber.

FRANCIS JACOBS (United Kingdom), Advocate General.

PAUL JOAN GEORGE KAPTEYN (Netherlands), Judge.

CLAUS CHRISTIAN GULMANN (Denmark), Judge.

ANTONIO MARIO LA PERGOLA (Italy), Judge.

GEORGES COSMAS (Greece), Advocate General.

JEAN-PIERRE PUISSOCHET (France), Judge.

PHILIPPE LÉGER (France), Advocate General.

GÜNTER HIRSCH (Germany), Judge.

PETER JANN (Austria), Judge.

HANS RAGNEMALM (Sweden), Judge.

DÁMASO RUIZ-JARABO COLOMER (Spain), Advocate General.

MELCHIOR WATHELET (Belgium), Judge.

SIEGBERT ALBER (Germany), Advocate General.

JEAN MISCHO (Luxembourg), Advocate General.

ANTONIO SAGGIO (Italy), Advocate General.

VASSILIOS SKOURIS (Greece), Judge.

FIDELMA O'KELLY MACKEN (Ireland), Judge.

ROGER GRASS (France), Registrar.

### COURT OF FIRST INSTANCE OF THE EUROPEAN COMMUNITIES

**Address:** blvd Konrad Adenauer, 2925 Luxembourg.

**Telephone:** 4303-1; **fax:** 4303-2100; **internet:** www.curia.eu.int.

By a decision of 24 October 1988, as amended by decisions of 8 June 1993 and 7 March 1994, the European Council, exercising powers conferred upon it by the Single European Act, established a Court of First Instance with jurisdiction to hear and determine cases brought by natural or legal persons and which had hitherto been dealt with by the Court of Justice.

**Composition of the Court of First Instance** (in order of precedence, as at January 2000):

BO VESTERDORF (Denmark), President of the Court of First Instance.

RAFAEL GARCÍA-VALDECASAS Y FERNÁNDEZ (Spain), President of Chamber.

KOENRAAD LENAERTS (Belgium), President of Chamber.

VIRPI TIILI (Finland), President of Chamber.

JÖRG PIRRUNG (Germany), Judge.

PERNILLA LINDH (Sweden), Judge.

JOSEF AZIZI (Austria), Judge.

ANDRÉ POTOCKI (France), Judge.

RUI MOURA-RAMOS (Portugal), Judge.

JOHN D. COOKE (Ireland), Judge.

MARC JAEGER (Luxembourg), Judge.

PAOLO MENGOZZI (Italy), Judge.

ARJEN W. H. MEIJ (Netherlands), Judge.

MIHALIS VILARAS (Greece), Judge.

NICHOLAS JAMES FORWOOD (United Kingdom), Judge.

HANS JUNG (Germany), Registrar.

## COURT OF AUDITORS OF THE EUROPEAN COMMUNITIES

**Address:** 12 rue Alcide De Gasperi, 1615 Luxembourg.

**Telephone:** 4398-45410; **fax:** 4398-46430; **e-mail:** euraud@eca.eu.int; **internet:** www.eca.eu.int.

The Court of Auditors was created by the Treaty of Brussels, which was signed on 22 July 1975, and commenced its duties in late 1977. It was given the status of an institution on a par with the Commission, the Council, the Court of Justice and the Parliament by the Treaty on European Union. It is the institution responsible for the external audit of the resources managed by the three Communities and the European Union. It consists of 15 members who are appointed for six-year terms by unanimous decision of the Council of the European Union, after consultation with the European Parliament. The members elect the President from among their number for a term of three years.

The Court is organized and acts as a collegiate body. It adopts its decisions by a majority of its members. Each member, however, has a direct responsibility for the audit of certain sectors of Union activities.

The Court examines the accounts of all expenditure and revenue of the European Communities and of any body created by them in so far as the relevant constituent instrument does not preclude such examination. It examines whether all revenue has been received and all expenditure incurred in a lawful and regular manner and whether the financial management has been sound. The audit is based on records, and if necessary is performed directly in the institutions of the Communities, in the member states and in other countries. In the member states the audit is carried out in co-operation with the national audit bodies. The Court of Auditors draws up an annual report after the close of each financial year. The Court provides the Parliament and the Council with a statement of assurance as to the reliability of the accounts, and the legality and regularity of the underlying transactions. It may also, at any time, submit observations on specific questions (usually in the form of special reports) and deliver opinions at the request of one of the institutions of the Communities. It assists the European Parliament and the Council in exercising their powers of control over the implementation of the budget, in particular in the framework of the annual discharge procedure, and gives its prior opinion on the financial regulations, on the methods and procedure whereby the budgetary revenue is made available to the Commission, and on the formulation of rules concerning the responsibility of authorizing officers and accounting officers and concerning appropriate arrangements for inspection.

**President:** JAN O. KARLSSON (Sweden).

Audit Group I: BARRY DESMOND; KALLIOPI NIKOLAOU; MAARTEN ENGWIRDA.

Audit Group II: PATRICK EVERARD; ARMINDO DE JESUS DE SOUSA RIBEIRO; ANTONI CASTELLS; JØRGEN MOHR; FRANÇOIS COLLING.

Audit Group III: BERNHARD FRIEDMANN; GIORGIO CLEMENTE; AUNUS SALMI; JEAN-FRANÇOIS BERNICOT.

Audit Development and Reports (ADAR) Group: HUBERT WEBER.

Statement of Assurance (SoA) Group: JOHN WIGGINS.

**Secretary-General:** EDOUARD RUPPERT.

## EUROPEAN CENTRAL BANK

**Address:** 60066 Frankfurt am Main, Kaiserstr. 29, Postfach 160319, Germany.

**Telephone:** (69) 13440; **fax:** (69) 13446000; **internet:** www.ecb.int.

The European Central Bank (ECB) was formally established on 1 June 1998, replacing the European Monetary Institute, which had been operational since January 1994. The Bank has the authority to issue the single currency, the euro, which replaced the European Currency Unit (ECU) on 1 January 1999, at the beginning of Stage III of Economic and Monetary Union (EMU), in accordance with the provisions of the Treaty on European Union ('the Maastricht Treaty'). The Bank's leadership is provided by a six-member executive board, appointed for a non-renewable term of eight years (it should be noted that the Statute of the European System of Central Banks — ESCB — provides for a system of staggered appointments to the first executive board for members other than the President in order to ensure continuity), which is responsible for the preparation of meetings of the governing council, the implementation of monetary policy in accordance with the guide-lines and decisions laid down by the governing council and for the current business of the ECB. The ECB and the national central banks of EU member states together comprise the ESCB. The governing council of the ESCB, which consists of ECB executive board members and the governors of central banks of countries participating in EMU, meets twice a month. The general council comprises the President, the Vice-President and the governors of the central banks of all EU member states.

**President:** WILLEM (WIM) F. DUISENBERG (Netherlands).

**Vice-President:** CHRISTIAN NOYER (France).

**Executive Board:** SIRKKA HÄMÄLÄINEN (Finland), OTMAR ISSING (Germany), TOMMASO PADOA-SCHIOPPA (Italy), EUGENIO SOMINGO SOLANS (Spain).

## EUROPEAN INVESTMENT BANK

**Address:** 100 blvd Konrad Adenauer, 2950 Luxembourg.

**Telephone:** 4379-1; **fax:** 4377-04; **e-mail:** info@eib.bei.org; **internet:** www.eib.org.

The European Investment Bank (EIB) was created in 1958 by the six founder member states of the European Economic Community. At December 1998 the capital subscribed by the 15 member states totalled ECU 62,013m., of which 7.5% was paid-in or to be paid-in. In June 1998 the Board of Governors agreed to increase subscribed capital to €100,000m., from January 1999. Capital structure at 31 December 1999 was as follows: France, Germany, Italy and the United Kingdom 17.8% each; Spain 6.5%; Belgium and the Netherlands 4.9% each; Sweden 3.3%; Denmark 2.5%; Austria 2.4%; Finland 1.4%; Greece 1.3%; Portugal 0.9%; Ireland 0.6%; Luxembourg 0.1%. The bulk of the EIB's resources comes from borrowings, principally public bond issues or private placements on capital markets inside and outside the Union. In 1998 the Bank borrowed €31,463m., compared with ECU 23,071m. in 1997. Some 68% of resources raised in 1998 was in EU currencies.

The EIB's principal task, defined by the Treaty of Rome, is to work on a non-profit basis, making or guaranteeing loans for investment projects which contribute to the balanced and steady development of EU member states. Throughout the Bank's history, priority has been given to financing investment projects which further regional development within the Community. The EIB also finances projects that improve communications, protect and improve the environment, promote urban development, strengthen the competitive position of industry and encourage industrial integration within the Union, support the activities of small and medium-sized enterprises (SMEs), and help ensure the security of energy supplies. The EIB also provides finance for developing countries in Africa, the Caribbean and the Pacific, under the terms of the Lomé Convention (q.v.); for countries in the Mediterranean region, under co-operation agreements; and for countries in central and eastern Europe.

The European Investment Fund (EIF) was founded in 1994 by the EIB (which was to provide 40% of the Fund's ECU 2,000m. authorized capital), the European Communities (EC—represented by the Commission; 30%) and a group of 77 banks and financial institutions from throughout the EU (30%). The EIF's purpose is to assist SMEs and provide guarantees for the long-term financing of

European infrastructure projects, particularly for Trans-European Networks (TENs) in the fields of transport, energy transmission and telecommunications. By the end of 1998 cumulative guarantee operations signed by the EIF totalled ECU 2,259m. A European Technology Faculty (ETF) was established in November 1997 to support investment in SMEs. The EIF was to invest up to ECU 125m. in the ETF over a three-year period.

In 1998 total financing contracts signed by the EIB, both inside and outside the European Union, amounted to €29,526m., compared with ECU 26,203m. in 1997. Loans agreed for projects within member states in 1998 totalled €25,116m. Transport accounted for 26.1%, telecommunications 13.7%, industry and services 7.4% and energy 6.9%. Operations outside the Union totalled €4,410m., compared with ECU 3,244m. in 1997.

The Board of Governors of the EIB, which usually meets only once a year, lays down general directives on credit policy, approves the annual report and accounts and decides on capital increases. The Board of Directors has sole power to take decisions in respect of loans, guarantees and borrowings. Its members are appointed by the Governors for a renewable five-year term following nomination by the member states. The Bank's President presides over meetings of the Board of Directors. The day-to-day management of operations is the responsibility of the Management Committee, which is the EIB's collegiate executive body and recommends decisions to the Board of Directors. It comprises the President and seven Vice-Presidents, nominated for six-year terms by the Board of Directors and approved by the Board of Governors. The Audit Committee, which reports to the Board of Governors regarding the management of operations and the maintenance of the Bank's accounts, is an independent body comprising three members who are appointed by the Board of Governors for a renewable three-year term.

**Board of Governors:** One minister (usually the minister of finance) from each member state.

**Board of Directors:** Twenty-five directors and 13 alternates (senior officials from finance or economic ministeries, public-sector banks or credit institutions), appointed for a renewable five-year term, of whom 24 and 12 respectively are nominated by the member states; one director and one alternate are nominated by the Commission of the European Communities.

**Management Committee:**

**President:** PHILIPPE MAYSTADT.

**Vice-Presidents:** WOLFGANG ROTH, PANOGIOTIS-LOUKAS GENNIMATAS, MASSIMO PONZELLINI, LUIS MARTÍ, EWALD NOWOTNY, RUDOLF DE KORTE, FRANCIS MAYER, PETER SEDGWICK.

**FINANCE CONTRACTS SIGNED**

| Recipient | 1997 Amount (ECU million) | 1997 % | 1998 Amount (€ million) | 1998 % |
|---|---|---|---|---|
| Austria | 555 | 2.4 | 358 | 1.4 |
| Belgium | 1,140 | 5.0 | 858 | 3.4 |
| Denmark | 737 | 3.2 | 745 | 3.0 |
| Finland | 401 | 1.7 | 551 | 2.2 |
| France | 2,721 | 11.9 | 2,837 | 11.3 |
| Germany | 3,518 | 15.3 | 5,168 | 20.6 |
| Greece | 730 | 3.2 | 736 | 2.9 |
| Ireland | 207 | 0.9 | 263 | 1.0 |
| Italy | 3,517 | 15.3 | 4,387 | 17.5 |
| Luxembourg | 96 | 0.4 | 109 | 0.4 |
| Netherlands | 398 | 1.7 | 426 | 1.7 |
| Portugal | 1,350 | 5.9 | 1,505 | 6.0 |
| Spain | 2,716 | 11.8 | 3,152 | 12.6 |
| Sweden | 925 | 4.0 | 664 | 2.6 |
| United Kingdom | 3,765 | 16.4 | 3,074 | 12.2 |
| Other* | 184 | 0.8 | 282 | 1.1 |
| **EU total** | 22,958 | 100.0 | 25,116 | 100.0 |
| ACP-Overseas countries and territories | 60 | 1.8 | 560 | 12.7 |
| South Africa | 199 | 6.1 | 135 | 3.1 |
| Mediterranean | 1,122 | 34.6 | 966 | 22.0 |
| Central and Eastern Europe | 1,486 | 45.8 | 2,295 | 52.0 |
| Latin America and Asia | 378 | 11.7 | 362 | 8.2 |
| Other | — | — | 92 | 2.1 |
| **Non-EU total** | 3,244 | 100.0 | 4,410 | 100.0 |
| **Total** | 26,202 | — | 29,526 | — |

* Projects of direct benefit to the Union but located outside the member states.

# CONSULTATIVE BODIES

## ECONOMIC AND SOCIAL COMMITTEE

**Address:** 2 rue Ravenstein, 1000 Brussels.

**Telephone:** (2) 546-90-11; **fax:** (2) 513-48-93; **internet:** www.esc.eu.int.

The Committee is advisory and is consulted by the Council of the European Union or by the European Commission, particularly with regard to agriculture, free movement of workers, harmonization of laws and transport, as well as legislation adopted under the Euratom Treaty. In certain cases consultation of the Committee by the Commission or the Council is mandatory. In addition, the Committee has the power to deliver opinions on its own initiative.

The Committee has 222 members: 24 each from France, Germany, Italy and the United Kingdom, 21 from Spain, 12 each from Austria, Belgium, Greece, the Netherlands, Portugal and Sweden, nine from Denmark, Finland and Ireland, and six from Luxembourg. One-third represent employers, one-third employees, and one-third various interest groups (e.g. agriculture, small enterprises, consumers). The Committee is appointed for a renewable term of four years by the unanimous vote of the Council of the European Union. Members are nominated by their governments, but are appointed in their personal capacity and are not bound by any mandatory instructions. The Committee is served by a permanent and independent General Secretariat, headed by the Secretary-General.

**President:** BEATRICE RANGONI MACHIAVELLI (Italy).

**Vice-Presidents:** AINA MARGARETA REGNELL (Sweden), JOSLY PIETTE (Belgium).

**Secretary-General:** PATRICK VENTURINI.

## COMMITTEE OF THE REGIONS

**Address:** 79 rue Belliard, 1040 Brussels.

**Telephone:** (2) 282-22-11; **fax:** (2) 282-20-85; **internet:** www.cor.eu.int.

The Treaty on European Union provided for a committee to be established, with advisory status, comprising representatives of regional and local bodies throughout the EU. The first meeting of the Committee was held in March 1994. It may be consulted on EU proposals concerning economic and social cohesion, trans-European networks, public health, education and culture, and may issue an opinion on any issue with regional implications. The Committee meets in plenary session five times a year.

The number of members of the Committee is equal to that of the Economic and Social Committee (see above). Members are appointed for a renewable term of four years by the Council, acting unanimously on the proposals from the respective member states. The Committee elects its principal officers from among its members for a two-year term, most recently to serve 16 February 2000–25 January 2002.

**President:** JOZEF (JOS) CHABERT (Belgium).

**First Vice-President:** Prof. Dr MANFRED DAMMEYER (Germany).

## ECSC CONSULTATIVE COMMITTEE

**Address:** Bâtiment Jean Monnet, 2920 Luxembourg.

**Telephone:** 4301-32846; **fax:** 4301-34455.

The Committee is advisory and is attached to the Commission. It advises the Commission on matters relating to the coal and steel industries of the Union. Its members are appointed by the Council of the European Union for two years and are not bound by any mandate from the organizations that designated them in the first place.

There are 108 members representing, in equal proportions, producers, workers and consumers and dealers in the coal and steel industries.

**President:** GIOVANNI PEREGO (Italy).

**Vice President:** JEAN-MARC MOHR (France), (from April 2000) RUPRECHT VONDRAN (Germany).

## OTHER ADVISORY COMMITTEES

There are advisory committees dealing with all aspects of EU policy. Consultation with some committees is compulsory in the procedure for drafting EC legislation.

In addition to the consultative bodies listed above there are several hundred special interest groups representing every type of interest within the Union. All these hold unofficial talks with the Commission.

## OTHER INSTITUTIONS

**European Environment Agency (EEA):** 6 Kongens Nytorv, 1050 Copenhagen K, Denmark; tel. 33-36-71-00; fax 33-36-71-99; e-mail eea@eea.eu.int; internet www.eea.eu.int.

Became operational in 1994, having been approved in 1990, to gather and supply information to assist the implementation of Community policy on environmental protection and improvement. In 1999 the Agency's budget amounted to €18.2m. The Agency publishes a report on the state of the environment every three years.

**Chairman of the Management Board:** F. DEREK A. OSBORN (United Kingdom).

**Chairman of the Scientific Committee:** Prof. PHILIPPE BOURDEAU (Belgium).

**Executive Director:** DOMINGO JIMÉNEZ-BELTRÁN (Spain).

**European Monitoring Centre for Drugs and Drug Addiction (EMCDDA):** Palacete Mascarenhas, Rua da Cruz de Sta. Apolónia 23–25, 1149 Lisbon, Portugal; tel. (1) 21811-30-00; fax (1) 21811-17-11; e-mail info@emcdda.org; internet www.emcdda.org.

Became fully operational at the end of 1995, with the aim of providing member states with objective, reliable and comparable information on drugs and drug addiction in order to assist in combatting the problem. The Centre co-operates with other European and international organizations and non-Community countries. The Centre publishes an *Annual Report on the State of the Drugs Problem in Europe*. A newsletter, *Drugnet Europe*, is published every two months.

**President:** FRANZ-JOSEF BINDERT (Germany).

**Executive Director:** GEORGES ESTIEVENART (France).

**European Agency for the Evaluation of Medicinal Products (EMEA):** 7 Westferry Circus, Canary Wharf, London, E14 4HB, United Kingdom; tel. (20) 7418-8400; fax (20) 7418-8416; e-mail mail@emea.eudra.org; internet www.eudra.org/emea.html.

Established in 1993 for the authorization and supervision of medicinal products for human and veterinary use. In 2000 the Agency's proposed budget was €50.36m.

**Chairman of the Management Board:** STRACHAN HEPPELL (United Kingdom).

**Chairman of the Scientific Committee for Proprietary Medicinal Products (CPMP):** Prof. JEAN-MICHEL ALEXANDRE.

**Chairman of the Scientific Committee for Veterinary Medicinal Products (CVMP):** Dr REINHARD KROKER (Germany).

**Executive Director:** FERNAND SAUER (France).

**European Training Foundation (ETF):** Villa Gualino, Viale Settimio Severo 65, 10133 Turin, Italy; tel. (011) 630-22-22; fax (011) 630-22-00; e-mail info@etf.eu.int; internet www.etf.it.

Established in 1995 with the aim of contributing to the development of the vocational training systems of designated central and eastern European countries. In 1998 the Foundation's responsibilities were extended to include certain non-member Mediterranean countries.

**Director:** PETER G. M. DE ROOIJ.

**European Foundation for the Improvement of Living and Working Conditions:** Wyattville Rd, Loughlinstown, Shankill, Co Dublin, Ireland; tel. (1) 204-3100; fax (1) 282-6456; e-mail postmaster@eurofound.ie; internet www.eurofound.ie.

Established in 1975 to develop strategies for the medium- and long-term improvement of living and working conditions. The Foundation publishes a regular newsletter.

**Chairman of the Administrative Board:** J. W. VAN DEN BRAAK.

**Director:** ERIC VERBORGH (acting).

**Office for Harmonization in the Internal Market (Trade Marks and Designs) (OHIM):** Avda de Aguilera 20, 03080 Alicante, Spain; tel. (96) 513-91-00; fax (96) 513-91-73; internet www.oami.eu.int.

Established in 1993 to promote and control trade marks and designs throughout the European Union.

**Chairman of the Administrative Board:** JOSÉ MOTA MAIA (Portugal).

**Chairman of the Budget Committee:** Dr RENZO ANTONINI (Italy).

**President:** JEAN-CLAUDE COMBALDIEU.

# Activities of the Community

## AGRICULTURE

Co-operation in the Community is at its most highly-organized in the area of agriculture. The objectives of the Common Agricultural Policy (CAP) are described in the Treaty of Rome. The markets for agricultural products have been progressively organized following three basic principles: (i) unity of the market (products must be able to circulate freely within the Community and markets must be organized according to common rules); (ii) Community preference (products must be protected from low-cost imports and from fluctuations on the world market); (iii) common financial responsibility: the European Agricultural Guidance and Guarantee Fund (EAGGF) finances, through its Guarantee Section, all public expenditure intervention, storage costs, marketing subsidies and export rebates.

Agricultural prices are, in theory, fixed each year at a common level for the Community as a whole, taking into account the rate of inflation and the need to discourage surplus production of certain commodities. Export subsidies are paid to enable farmers to sell produce at the lower world market prices without loss. These subsidies account for some 50% of agricultural spending. When market prices of certain cereals, sugar, some fruits and vegetables, dairy produce and meat fall below a designated level the Community intervenes, and buys a certain quantity which is then stored until prices recover. During the 1980s expanding production led to food surpluses, costly to maintain, particularly in dairy produce, beef, cereals and wine, and to the destruction of large quantities of fruit and vegetables.

Agriculture is by far the largest item on the Community budget, accounting for about two-thirds of annual expenditure, mainly for supporting prices through the EAGGF Guarantee Section (appropriations for which amounted to €40,940m., or 48% of the total budget, in 1999). A system of 'stabilizers' was introduced in February 1988, imposing an upper limit on the production of certain products. Any over-production would result in a decrease in the guaranteed intervention price for the following year. Similar 'stabilizers' were later imposed on production of oilseeds, protein feed crops, wine, sugar, fruit and vegetables, tobacco, olive oil, cotton and mutton.

In 1990 the CAP came under attack in the 'Uruguay Round' of negotiations on the General Agreement on Tariffs and Trade (GATT, see WTO). The US Government demanded massive reductions in the EC's agricultural and export subsidies, on the grounds that they disrupted world markets. In November Community ministers of agriculture agreed to accept proposals by the Commission for a reduction of 30% in agricultural subsidies over a 10-year period. In 1990 increasing surpluses of cereals, beef and dairy products were again reported, and a decline in international wheat prices increased the cost to the Community of exporting surplus wheat. In May 1992, on the basis of proposals made by the Commission in 1991, ministers adopted a number of reforms, which aimed to transfer the Community's agricultural support from upholding prices to maintaining farmers' incomes, thereby removing the incentive to over-produce. Intervention prices were reduced by 29% for cereals, 15% for beef and poultry, and 5% for dairy products. Farmers were to be compensated for the price reductions by receiving additional grants, which, in the case of crops, took the form of a subsidy per hectare of land planted. To qualify for these subsidies, arable farmers (except for those with the smallest farms) were to be obliged to remove 15% of their land from cultivation (the 'set-aside' scheme). Incentives were to be given for alternative uses of the withdrawn land (e.g. forestry). The reform meant that prices payable for cereals would be reduced to the level of those prevailing in the international market.

In May 1992 the US Government threatened to impose a large increase in import tariffs on European products, in retaliation against subsidies paid by the EC to oilseed producers, which, the US Government claimed, led to unfair competition for US exports of soya beans. In November, however, agreement was reached between the USA and the European Commission: the USA agreed that limits should be imposed on the area of EC land on which cultivation of oilseed was permitted. The USA also agreed to accept a reduction of 21% in the volume and 36% in the value of the EC's subsidized exports of farm produce, over a six-year period (the amounts being based on average production during 1986–90). These agreements formed the basis of the GATT agricultural accord which was concluded as part of the Uruguay Round trade agreement in mid-December 1993.

The Commission estimated that between September 1992 and the end of July 1993, as a result of the turmoil in the exchange rate mechanism (see below), an extra ECU 1,500m. was spent in price support payments to farmers. In February 1995 ministers adopted a new agrimonetary regime, which limited the amount of compensation paid to farmers as a result of currency fluctuations. Further amendments, introduced in June, abandoned the existing common exchange rate, used to calculate compensation payments, and introduced two rates: one for currencies linked to the Deutsche Mark and one for all other EU currencies. Attempts by some member states to reform the system further were unsuccessful, and in October ministers agreed that national governments would be permitted to compensate farmers who had suffered loss of income as a result of currency fluctuations. In June 1997 it was reported that cereal farmers had been over-compensated by some ECU 8,500m. over the previous four years as a result of inaccurate price-reduction forecasts. In June 1995 the guaranteed intervention price for beef was decreased by 5%, and that for cereals by 7.5%. In September ministers agreed to reduce the level of compulsory 'set-aside' for 1996/97 to 10%, in response to much lower food surpluses in the EU and high world prices for cereal crops. In July 1996 agriculture ministers agreed on a further reduction in the 'set-aside' rate for cereals to 5%. Fruit and vegetable production subsidies were fixed at no more than 4% of the value of total marketed production, rising to 4.5% in 1999. The aim was to improve competitiveness in the European market and avoid the widespread destruction of surplus fruit and vegetables that had taken place in recent years. The Commission is allowed to recover from member states sums that they have paid out under the CAP without sufficient guarantees of legitimacy or without adequate regard to control and verification. In May 1998 the Commission announced that it was to recover ECU 308m. paid to member states in 1994 and in February 1999 the Commission decided to recover a further €493m., mainly relating to spending in 1995.

In July 1994 Community ministers adopted measures to prevent the spread of the disease bovine spongiform encephalopathy (BSE) by imposing strict controls on carcass beef trade, extending the time-scale for the prohibition of exports from diseased herds from two years to six years. The agreement temporarily resolved a dispute whereby Germany had attempted to impose a unilateral ban on beef exports from the United Kingdom, provoking that country to seek a judicial ruling on the action by the European Court of Justice. Despite a relaxation in the rules to allow the export of UK beef from any animal under 30 months old, three German Länder imposed a ban on UK beef imports. New fears about possible links between BSE and Creutzfeldt-Jakob disease (CJD), which affects humans, led to a collapse in consumer confidence in the European beef market in early 1996. In March the Commission accepted that member countries could unilaterally stop imports of UK beef on health grounds, pending a decision by a committee of scientific and veterinary experts from all member states. By late March 12 EU countries had banned UK beef imports, and at the end of the month the Commission agreed a ban on exports from the United Kingdom of live cattle, beef and beef products. In late May the UK Government proposed a programme of selective slaughter as a means of eradicating BSE from the national herd. At the European Council meeting held in June, the United Kingdom agreed to the slaughter of 120,000 animals born since 1989, and new legislation to ensure that meat and bonemeal were excluded from the manufacture of animal feeds. In return, the ban on UK beef exports would be gradually removed. By July European beef consumption had fallen by an average of 11%, with the largest decrease, 30%, recorded in Germany. At the end of 1996 the Commission was estimated to have spent some ECU 1,500m., including ECU 850m. as compensation paid to beef farmers, on dealing with the consequences of the BSE crisis. Meanwhile, the UK Government abandoned the planned cull, proposing instead a much smaller slaughter scheme. This provoked widespread anger in other EU member states, and in July the European Court of Justice rejected the UK Government's application for the beef export ban to be suspended.

In August 1996 evidence emerged that BSE could be transmitted from cows to their calves. In December the UK Government yielded to the European Commission's demand for an additional cull of more than 100,000 cattle. The Commission also stated that the United Kingdom was to submit plans for a certified BSE-free herd scheme, to provide computerized evidence that cattle herds had had no contact with other animals infected with BSE, before a phased removal of the embargo could begin. In June 1997 the United Kingdom's plans for monitoring and preventing BSE were judged by the Commission to be inadequate. However, in September the Scientific Veterinary Committee confirmed that a successful automated certified herd scheme had been used in Northern Ireland for nine years. In July 1997 the United Kingdom was reported by the Commission to have engaged in the illegal export of beef, while in late June the Commission commenced infringement proceedings against 10 EU countries accused of evading the full implementation of hygiene procedures for the eradication of BSE. In July agriculture ministers voted, by a narrow margin, to introduce a complete ban on the use, for any purpose, of 'specified risk materials' (SRMs), i.e. those most likely to carry BSE, from cattle, sheep and goats. In August the USA requested that US tallow manufacturers be temporarily exempted from the ban, claiming that the USA was free from BSE and that compliance with the new regulations could cause shortages within the pharmaceutical and cosmetics industries. In December the USA announced the extension of an existing ban on EU beef and lamb, in a move that was considered by some to be retaliatory. The Commission voted to postpone the introduction of the ban on SRMs from January 1998 until April (later delayed until January 1999), as a result of opposition from a number of EU member states, particularly Germany, in addition to that from the USA. In December 1997, in protest at the delay, the United Kingdom imposed a unilateral ban on imports of all beef products breaching UK meat safety regulations. In May 1998 the Commission agreed to ease the export ban on British beef, to allow the export of deboned beef from Northern-Irish herds certified as BSE-free for eight years, from June. Production and dispatch of the meat was to be carried out by approved plants. In November the Agriculture Council agreed to repeal the ban on exports of UK beef, when it endorsed the United Kingdom's Date-based Export Scheme. The Commission subsequently approved the Scheme, which permitted the export of deboned beef produced from animals born after August 1996 and tracked by an official monitoring system. In October 1998, however, Portugal was banned from exporting beef and live cattle, following a two-fold increase in reported cases of BSE, to some 69 between May and November of that year (compared with about 1,800 confirmed cases in the United Kingdom from January). The ban on beef exports was to expire after nine months, unless concerns about meat safety remained, while the ban on cattle exports was to be reviewed after 18 months. (In July 1999 the EU Veterinary Committee agreed to prolong for a further six months from 1 August the embargo on exports of Portuguese beef.)

In July 1999 the United Kingdom was deemed to have met all of the conditions pertaining to the lifting of the ban on its beef exports, and the European Commission announced that exports would be permitted to resume from 1 August. However, the French Government remained unconvinced that UK beef no longer presented any threat to consumers, citing, in support of this view, the recommendation of the French statutory Food Safety Agency on 1 October that it would be premature to resume imports of UK beef. In mid-October the UK Prime Minister warned that the United Kingdom would take legal action if France did not lift its unilateral embargo, and on 22 October the UK Minister of Agriculture, Food and Fisheries encouraged British consumers to boycott French food products in protest at France's continued failure to comply with the Commission's decision. On 29 October an EU scientific committee announced that it saw no reason, in the light of the recommendation of the French Food Safety Agency, to revise its earlier endorsement of the safety of UK beef. France did, however, continue to receive some support from Germany. On 30 October seven of the 16 German Länder announced their opposition to any hasty lifting of the ban on UK beef. By the end of 1999 France's unilateral ban remained in place (the German Government claimed that only bureaucratic reasons were preventing the resumption of UK beef exports to Germany) and, in the face of a threat of legal action by the Commission, it was reported that the French Government planned to initiate legal proceedings against the Commission for its alleged failure adequately to protect consumer health. On 4 January 2000 the Commission commenced legal action against the French Government at the European Court of Justice.

In April 1999 a dispute arose between the EU and the USA after the EU announced plans to ban all imports of US beef. The EU took this decision after traces of growth hormones were found in imported meat that was supposed to be hormone-free. In May the EU informed the World Trade Organization (WTO) that it would not be able to lift the ban it applied to imports of US hormone-treated beef by 13 May 1999, as the WTO had ordered that it should. The USA was reported to be planning to apply sanctions to some European exports as a retaliatory measure. The USA has also accused the EU of excessive caution with regard to the restrictions that it imposes on genetically-modified (GM) crops and food products derived from or containing them. In October the EU ruled that food products which were labelled as 'GM-free' could contain as much as 1% of GM material. In June the USA impounded all imports of European pork and poultry. The USA took this action because of the possibility that these imports might have been contaminated by a carcinogen, dioxin, extremely high levels of which had been discovered in some Belgian supplies of animal feedstuffs. The European Commission had already prohibited the sale of some Belgian food products.

In June 1995 the Agriculture Council agreed to new rules on the welfare of livestock during transport. The agreement, which came into effect in 1996, limited transport of livestock to a maximum of eight hours in any 24-hour period, and stipulated higher standards for their accommodation and care while in transit. In January 1996 the Commission proposed a ban on veal crates, which was to come into effect from January 1998. In June 1999 EU agriculture ministers agreed to end battery egg production within the EU by 2012.

During 1995–97 there was widespread speculation that the CAP would have to undergo dramatic reform to prevent possible economic problems, in particular following the proposed expansion of the EU into the less agriculturally-developed countries of central and eastern Europe. In March 1998 the Commission outlined firm proposals for reform of the CAP as part of its 'Agenda 2000', concerning the enlargement of the EU and the Community's budget for 2000–2006, published in July 1997. The plans envisaged imposing limits on subsidies and reductions of up to 30% in guaranteed prices, to allow compliance with WTO rules. In June 1998 the Commission adopted proposals to introduce new agrimonetary arrangements for a period of three years from January 1999, owing to the launch of the euro. The arrangements were to compensate farmers in those EU member states not participating in the process of economic and monetary union from currency fluctuations until 2002. Farmers in countries taking part in EMU were also to be compensated for reductions in prices and aid payments resulting from the abolition of currency differentials. In June 1998 the Council agreed upon reforms to the tobacco and olive oil subsidy regimes. The changes abolished guaranteed prices for olive oil and eliminated production aid for small-scale producers, despite earlier protests from Spain.

In addition, aid for hemp farmers was reduced. The 'set-aside' rate for 1999–2000 was increased to 10%, to prevent intervention stocks from rising to unacceptable levels. (In 1997 the cereals surplus amounted to 14m. metric tons.) In March 1999 EU ministers of agriculture reached a compromise agreement on reform of the CAP, which proposed reductions of up to 20% in guaranteed prices and increases in milk quotas from 2003/2004. The plans were approved by heads of state and of government later that month, although they were modified to include less dramatic reductions in the guaranteed prices for cereals and to delay reforms to the dairy sector until 2005/2006. According to the final agreement on the reforms, guaranteed prices for cereals were to be reduced by 7.5% in both 2000 and 2001, and the 'set-aside' rate was to be fixed at 10% until 2006. Guaranteed prices for beef were to be abolished and the 'basic price' offered for the meat was to decrease by a total of 20% over a three-year period from 2000. Direct annual payments to farmers were to be increased, thereby compensating farmers for the reductions in guaranteed prices and removing incentives for over-production. A proposed limit on payments made to farmers, which was to have prevented large-scale producers from receiving excessive compensation, failed to win approval. The CAP budget was expected to stabilize at some €4,500m. until 2006, although some officials expressed concern that the reforms were not sufficiently far-reaching to achieve this aim.

## FISHERIES

The Common Fisheries Policy (CFP) came into effect in January 1983 after seven years of negotiations, particularly concerning the problem of access to fishing-grounds. In 1973 a 10-year agreement had been reached, whereby member states could have exclusive access to waters up to six nautical miles (11.1 km) or, in some cases, 12 miles from their shores; 'historic rights' were reserved in certain cases for foreign fishermen who had traditionally fished within a country's waters. In 1977 the Community set up a 200-mile (370-km) fishing zone around its coastline (excluding the Mediterranean) within which all members would have access to fishing. The 1983 agreement confirmed the 200-mile zone and allowed exclusive national zones of six miles with access between six and 12 miles from the shore for other countries according to specified 'historic rights'. Rules furthering conservation (e.g. standards for fishing tackle) are imposed under the policy, with checks by a Community fisheries inspectorate. Total allowable catches are fixed annually by species, divided into national quotas under the renewable Multi-annual Guidance Programme (MAGP). In 1990 it was reported that stocks of certain species of fish in EC waters had seriously diminished, and a reduction in quotas was agreed, together with the imposition of a compulsory eight-day period in each month during which fishermen in certain areas (chiefly the North Sea) would stay in port, with exemptions for fishermen using nets with larger meshes that would allow immature fish to escape. In 1992 the compulsory non-fishing period was increased to 135 days between February and December (with similar exemptions). In December of that year EC ministers agreed to extend the CFP for a further 10-year period. In March 1998 the Commission began a review of the CFP, in preparation for a report on the development of the CFP after 2002, which was to be presented in 2001.

The proposals put forward in May 1996 by the European Commission for the fourth MAGP, covering 1997–2002, envisaged catch reductions of up to 40% for species most at risk, and set targets and detailed rules for restructuring fishing fleets in the EU. The draft MAGP IV failed to gain approval at the meeting of fisheries ministers held in November 1996. In particular, the proposed reduction in the number of fishing vessels provoked anger in many member countries. The UK Government, in October, insisted that it would not accept additional limits on catches without action to stop 'quota-hopping', in which UK-registered boats are bought by operators in other EU countries (mainly Spain and the Netherlands), which are thus able to gain part of the UK fishing quotas. (In mid-1998 the UK Government received approval from the Commission to introduce new licensing conditions from 1 January 1999 that would compel the owners of boats involved in 'quota-hopping' to establish economic links with the United Kingdom. The new restrictions require UK-registered vessels to land one-half of their catch in the United Kingdom, to employ a crew of whom the majority are resident in the United Kingdom or to incur a set level of operating expenditure in that country.) In April 1997, following a number of concessions by the Commission, ministers approved MAGP IV. The programme fixed catch reductions at 30% for species most at risk and at 20% for other over-fished species. In December 1996 ministers agreed upon the establishment of a satellite monitoring system, which was to be used to verify the fishing activities of boats greater than 20 m in length. The new system was introduced from 1 June 1998. In July it was agreed that funds of ECU 39.4m. were to be made available for monitoring activities, including the purchase of inspection boats and the provision of onshore centres for the management of satellite-monitoring activities. In June the Council had overcome long-standing objections from a number of member states and adopted a ban on the use of drift nets in the Atlantic Ocean and the Mediterranean Sea, in an attempt to prevent the unnecessary deaths of marine life such as dolphins and sharks. The ban, which was to be introduced in January 2002, would partially implement a 1992 UN resolution demanding a complete cessation of drift-net fishing. A series of compensatory measures were to be implemented to rectify any short-term detrimental impact on fishing fleets.

In December 1999 fisheries ministers agreed to implement a reduction of almost 40% in the total EU catch in 2000, with the principal objective of saving stocks in the North and Irish Seas. For some species these had been scientifically assessed as dangerously low. The Commission had demanded an even more severe reduction, including a total ban on fishing for cod in these areas.

The organization of fish marketing involves common rules on quality and packing, and a system of guide prices established annually by the Council. Fish are withdrawn from the market if prices fall too far below the guide price, and compensation may then be paid to the fishermen. Export subsidies are paid to enable the export of fish onto the lower-priced world market, and import levies are imposed to prevent competition from low-priced imports. A new import regime took effect from May 1993. The regime enabled regional fishermen's associations to increase prices to a maximum of 10% over the Community's reference price, although this was to apply to both EU and imported fish.

Agreements have been signed with other countries (Norway, Sweden, Canada and the USA) allowing reciprocal fishing rights and other advantages, and with some African countries which receive assistance in strengthening their fishing industries in return for allowing EU boats to fish in their waters. Following the withdrawal of Greenland from the Community in February 1985, Community vessels retained fishing rights in Greenland waters, in exchange for financial compensation. In 1992 fisheries agreements with Estonia, Latvia, Lithuania and Argentina were initialled; and in 1993 an agreement was reached with Mauritania to benefit Spanish fishermen in the Canary Islands. Under a four-year agreement signed with Morocco in November 1995, the size of catches by EU vessels fishing in Moroccan waters was to be reduced by 20%–40% for various species, and the EU was to provide financial compensation for Morocco amounting to ECU 355m. Morocco decided that it would not renew the fishing agreement with the EU in November 1999, but, rather, seek to renegotiate it. In 1995 relations with Canada were severely strained by a dispute concerning Spanish boats, which, Canada claimed, were breaking rules, established by the Northwest Atlantic Fisheries Organization (q.v.), to prevent overfishing of Greenland halibut. In mid-April the EU and Canada reached agreement on an increased quota for EU fishermen, and extra inspection and surveillance measures were introduced to ensure that fishing limits were observed. Following the publication of an independent scientific report in April 1996, which warned that herring stocks were in danger of being totally eradicated, the EU and Norway agreed an emergency measure to reduce by 50% catches in the North Sea and the waters around Denmark. In June 1997 the Commission voted to counteract the 'dumping' of low-cost Norwegian salmon imports on the EU market, by accepting a five-year accord, negotiated with the Norwegian Government, compelling Norway to sell its salmon at a fixed minimum price and to set its export growth to the EU at no more than 12% in the first year, and 10% per year thereafter. Norway also agreed to a voluntary increase in the export duty on Norwegian salmon imports.

In December 1994 the EU fisheries ministers concluded a final agreement on the revised CFP, allowing Spain and Portugal to be integrated into the CFP by 1 January 1996. A compromise accord was reached regarding access to waters around Ireland and off south-west Great Britain (referred to as the 'Irish box') by means of which up to 40 Spanish vessels were granted access to 80,000 sq miles of the 90,000 sq mile area. However, the accord was strongly opposed by Irish and British fishermen. In April 1995 seven Spanish vessels were seized by the Irish navy, allegedly for fishing illegally in the Irish Sea. In October fisheries ministers agreed a regime to control fishing in the 'Irish box', introducing stricter controls, and instituting new surveillance measures. In October 1999 the UK government lost a legal appeal against a decision that required it to pay compensation to Spanish trawler owners who had been illegedly prevented from exploiting UK fishing quotas by legislation enacted in 1988.

## SCIENCE AND TECHNOLOGY

In the amendments to the Treaty of Rome, effective from July 1987, a section on research and technology was included for the first time, defining the extent of Community co-operation in this area. Most of the funds allocated to research and technology are granted to companies or institutions that apply to participate in EU research programmes. The fourth framework programme (1994–98) included new areas: research into transport systems, socio-economic projects concerning the urban environment, social exclusion and education. The programme aimed to focus on important technologies of benefit to industry, and to improve dissemination of research and development findings. In January 1996 the Commission proposed that additional research funds for the programme, should be concentrated on five priority areas: aeronautics, clean cars, multimedia software, intermodal transport and environmental technologies. In December 1997 the European Parliament and the Council authorized additional funding for research on transmissible spongiform encephalopathies. The fifth framework programme, covering the period 1999–2002, was proposed by the Commission in April 1997. The programme aimed to focus on the economic and social priorities of those living in the EU and on strengthening the capacity of the EU for scientific and technological research. In January 1998 it was suggested that the new programme should concentrate on four main areas: preservation of the ecosystem, management of living resources, the information society and competitive and sustainable growth. A budget of €14,960m. was allocated to the programme. In 1998 research and development projects were allocated a total of ECU 2,999.3m. in the EU budget. In July the Commission proposed that the 11 candidate countries for EU membership should have the opportunity to contribute to the fifth framework programme.

The Community's own Joint Research Centre (JRC), following a reorganization in 1996, comprises seven institutes, based at Ispra (Italy), Geel (Belgium), Karlsruhe (Germany), Seville (Spain) and Petten (Netherlands). The institutes' work covers: nuclear measurements; transuranium elements; advanced materials; remote sensing applications; the environment; systems engineering and informatics; safety technology; and prospective technological studies. Proposed funding for the JRC under the fifth framework programme amounted to €815m.

The European Strategic Research Programme for Research and Development in Information Technology ('ESPRIT'), inaugurated in 1984, concentrates on five key areas: advanced micro-electronics; software technology; advanced information processing; office automation; and computer integrated manufacturing. The programme is financed half by the EU and half by the participating research institutes, universities and industrial companies. In November 1997 a research project to develop technology to improve the methods used to locate and deactivate landmines under the ESPRIT programme was announced by the Commission.

In February 1998 the Commission announced plans to establish a 'Year 2000' office to promote awareness and the exchange of information concerning the 'Millennium Bug' (a term used to describe possible operational problems affecting computers unable to process dates after 31 December 1999).

The Community supports biotechnological research, aiming to promote the use of modern biology in agriculture and industry. In 1998 the EU's biotechnology programme ('BRIDGE') involved 154 projects with a budget of ECU 138m. Funding for 456 biotechnology projects was approved between 1994 and mid-1998. Other programmes have focused on agro-industrial research, and food sciences and technology.

In 1985 the Council adopted a programme of basic research in industrial technologies ('BRITE'), aiming to develop new methods for the benefit of existing industries, such as aeronautics, chemicals, textiles and metalworking. A 'Euram' research programme covered raw materials and advanced materials. BRITE/Euram III, on industrial and materials technologies, covered three areas in 1997: the development of production technologies for industry in the future; materials and technologies for the design of new products; and technologies for transportation.

In March 1996 research–industry task forces established by the Commission presented a report identifying priority topics for European research: the car of tomorrow; educational software and multimedia; new generation aircraft; vaccines and viral diseases; trains and railway systems of the future; intermodal transport; maritime systems; and environment, with a particular focus on water. An action plan to encourage innovation was approved in November by the Commission. The plan aimed to create a legal, regulatory and financial framework more favourable to innovation, and to strengthen links between business and research.

In July 1997 the European Parliament approved the Life Patent Directive, a proposal aiming to harmonize European rules on gene patenting in order to promote research into genetic diseases, despite objections regarding the ethical implications.

Research in the fields of energy, the environment and telecommunications is described below under the appropriate headings.

The EU also co-operates with non-member countries (particularly EFTA states) in bilateral research projects. The Commission and 19 European countries (including the members of the EU as individuals) participate in the 'Eureka' programme of research in advanced technology. The Community research and development information service ('Cordis') disseminates findings in this field and comprises eight databases. The 'Value' programme funds the publication and dissemination of technical reports from specific research projects. From 1994 a European Technology Assessment Network (ETAN) was developed in order to improve the dissemination of technological research findings.

## ENERGY

The treaty establishing the European Atomic Energy Community ('Euratom') came into force on 1 January 1958, to encourage the growth of the nuclear energy industry in the Community by conducting research, providing access to information, supplying nuclear fuels, building reactors and establishing common laws and procedures for the nuclear industry. A common market for nuclear materials was introduced in 1959, and there is a common insurance scheme against nuclear risks. In 1977 the Commission began granting loans on behalf of Euratom to finance investment in nuclear power stations and the enrichment of fissile materials. An agreement with the International Atomic Energy Authority entered into force in 1977, to facilitate co-operation in research on nuclear safeguards and controls. The EU's Joint Research Centre (see under Science and Technology) conducts research on nuclear safety and the management of radioactive waste. The fifth framework programme for research and technological development (1999–2002) allocated €1,260m. for Euratom research projects.

The Joint European Torus (JET) is an experimental thermonuclear machine designed to pioneer new processes of nuclear fusion, using the 'Tokamak' system of magnetic confinement to heat gases to very high temperatures and bring about the fusion of tritium and deuterium nuclei. Switzerland is also a member of the JET project. Since 1974 work has been proceeding at Culham in the United Kingdom, and the project was formally inaugurated in April 1984. In 1988 work began with representatives of Japan, the former USSR and the USA on the joint design of an International Thermonuclear Experimental Reactor (ITER). Construction of a demonstration reactor was not expected to begin in the short term.

The Commission has consistently urged the formation of an effective overall energy policy. The 'Thermie' programme, initiated in 1990, fosters the development of new technologies in the energy sector; in 1997 it supported 286 energy projects at a cost of ECU 136.1m. and in 1998 the Commission was to provide funds of a further ECU 140m. The five-year 'SAVE' programme, introduced in 1991, emphasized the improvement of energy efficiency, reduction of the energy consumption of vehicles, and the use of renewable energy. A second five-year programme, SAVE II, was initiated in 1995. It was to continue the work of the first programme, and also aimed to establish energy efficiency as a criterion for all EU projects.

In 1990 Community legislation on the completion of the 'internal energy market' was adopted: it aimed to encourage the sale of electricity and gas across national borders in the Community, by opening national networks to foreign supplies, obliging suppliers to publish their prices, and co-ordinating investment in energy. Energy ministers reached agreement in June 1996 on rules for the liberalization of the electricity market, which was to be carried out progressively. Twenty-five per cent of the market was to be opened up from 19 February 1999, rising to about 33% by 2003. Belgium and Ireland were to implement the agreement in 2000, and Greece was to be exempt until 2001. In November 1999 the Commission commenced legal action against France and Luxembourg for their alleged failure to open their electricity markets by February 1999. In December 1997 the Council agreed rules to allow the gas market to be opened up in three stages, over a period of 10 years. At least 33% of the market was to be liberalized within five years, with the proportion rising to some 42% after 10 years. In the first instance those consuming 25m. cu m of gas per annum were to be eligible to benefit from liberalization, but this threshold was to decrease to 15m. cu m within five years and to 5m. cu m within 10 years. The scheme was to allow the largest gas suppliers to receive temporary exemptions from trade liberalization if the presence of competitors should cause demand for supplies to drop below the amount which the distributor was contracted to purchase in the long term.

In October 1990 the Council agreed that emissions of carbon dioxide should be stabilized at their 1990 level by 2000. It established the ALTENER programme, which aimed to increase the contribution of renewable energy sources (RES) within the Community. The programme finished at the end of 1997, having supported 278 projects since 1993, at a cost of ECU 26.9m. A replacement programme for 1998–2002, ALTENER II, was allocated a budget of ECU 22m. for the first two-year period. A green paper on ways of promoting RES in the EU was issued in November 1996. These sources (such as wind, solar, biomass and small-scale hydropower) provided less than 6% of total energy produced in the EU at that time. In May 1998 the Council committed the EU to increasing the use of RES to 12% by 2010, following the publication of a report by the Commission in late 1997. The paper also proposed a strategy which could result in a reduction in carbon dioxide emissions of 402 metric tons each year by 2010, along with significant savings on fuel costs and employment opportunities. In December 1997, in the context of the third conference of the parties to the UN Framework Convention on Climate Change (held in Kyoto, Japan), the EU adopted a target to reduce greenhouse gas emissions by 8% between 2008 and 2012, in comparison with 1990 levels.

Energy ministers from the EU member states and 12 Mediterranean countries agreed at a meeting held in June 1996 in Trieste, Italy, to develop a Euro-Mediterranean gas and electricity network. The first Euro-Mediterranean Energy Forum was held in May 1997.

In 1997 it was agreed to help a number of eastern European countries to overcome energy problems by means of the Interstate Oil and Gas to Europe programme (INOGATE), which was to receive ECU 50m. over a five-year period in order to improve energy flows in eastern Europe and increase the access of newly-independent countries to European markets. INOGATE forms part of the TACIS programme (see under External Relations). In the same year a programme for the Optimal Use of Energy Resources in Latin America (ALURE) began to undertake projects in that region.

## INDUSTRY

Industrial co-operation was the earliest activity of the Community. The treaty establishing the European Coal and Steel Community (ECSC) came into force in July 1952, and by the end of 1954 nearly all barriers to trade in coal, coke, steel, pig-iron and scrap iron had been removed. The ECSC treaty was due to expire in July 2002, and in 1991 the Council agreed that, by that date, the provisions of the ECSC treaty should be incorporated in the EEC treaty, on the grounds that it was no longer appropriate to treat the coal and steel sectors separately.

In the late 1970s and 1980s measures were adopted to restructure the steel industry in response to a dramatic reduction in world demand for steel. These included production capacity quotas and a reduction of state subsidies. In November 1992 the Commission announced a three-year emergency programme to further restructure the industry, following a reduction of 30% in steel prices over the previous two years. In December 1993 ministers approved aid totalling ECU 7,000m. to achieve a further reduction in annual capacity at a number of state-owned steel plants. The industry failed to achieve the required reduction in capacity of 19m. metric tons, and in October 1994 the Commission decided to abandon the restructuring plan, although the social measures, which allocated ECU 240m. to compensate for job losses, were to be maintained. Capital expenditure in the steel industry amounted to ECU 3,312m. in 1995, some 21.6% higher than in 1994, and it continued to increase in 1996. Output of crude steel totalled 155.8m. tons in 1995, reversing the downward trend of previous years. Coal production continued to decline in 1998. The ECSC operating budget for 1998 was set at ECU 219m. In December 1996 the Commission adopted a new code on steel aid, for the period 1997–2002, which stipulated the conditions whereby member states may grant aid to steel companies, namely for research and development, for environmental protection and for full or partial closures of capacity. In October 1997 the Commission announced plans to finance, using ECSC reserves, research of benefit to the coal and steel industries amounting to some ECU 40m. each year, after the expiry of the ECSC Treaty in 2002.

The European textile and clothing industry has been seriously affected by overseas competition over an extended period. The Community participates in the Multi-fibre Arrangement (MFA, see WTO), to limit imports from low-cost suppliers overseas. A proposal by the Commission in October 1996 to accelerate liberalization of the textiles and clothing market in the EU provoked anger among industry leaders in member states, because no reciprocal concessions, in the form of removal of trade barriers, were being obtained from the major textile-exporting countries in other parts of the world. The Commission planned to include several 'sensitive' categories in the second stage of the MFA phasing-out of trade barriers, which was to start in January 1998. These categories include woollen yarns and fabrics, gloves, and synthetic ropes. A proposal by the Commission to impose duties of between 3% and 36% on imports of unfinished cotton fabrics, to counter alleged 'dumping' by several developing countries, was opposed by a majority of EU member states. The proposal aimed to help weaving industries (mainly in France and Italy), which had been adversely affected by the developing countries' practice of sharply undercutting their prices. Duties were provisionally introduced, for a period of six months, in late 1996. In March 1998 provisional duties of between 14% and 32.5% were imposed on imports of unbleached cotton from six countries, despite opposition by nine EU member states. Ministers of foreign affairs voted to remove duties in October.

Production in EU member states' shipyards has fallen drastically since the 1970s, mainly as a result of competition from shipbuilders in the Far East. In the first half of the 1980s a Council directive allowed for subsidies to help to reorganize the shipbuilding industry and to increase efficiency, but subsequently rigorous curbs on state aid to the industry were introduced. The permitted maximum percentage of state aid for shipbuilding was reduced from 28% of the value of each vessel in 1987 to 9% in 1992. In July 1994 the EU signed an accord with Japan, the USA, the Republic of Korea and the Nordic countries to end subsidies to the shipbuilding industry from 1996, subject to ratification by member states. Subsidies available in several EU countries in 1996 were higher than the official ceiling, and state aid was also given for industrial restructuring (for example, for modernization of east German shipyards) and for rescuing state-owned yards in difficulties (as was the case in Spain). In October 1997 the Commission proposed to maintain state aid until the end of 2000.

The Commission has made a number of proposals for the development of the information technology industry in Europe, particularly in view of the superiority of Japan and the USA in the market for advanced electronic circuits. The ESPRIT research programme (see under Science and Technology) aims to build the technological foundations for a fully competitive European industry. The INFO 2000 programme (1996–1999) aims to promote development of the European multi-media industry, focusing on electronic publishing and interactive information services. In April 1998 the Commission proposed that the WTO should discuss the expanding electronic trade sector, in order to clarify international rules.

Harmonization of national company law to form a common legal structure has led to the adoption of directives concerning disclosure of information, company capital, internal mergers, the accounts of companies and of financial institutions, division of companies, the qualification of auditors, single-member private limited companies, mergers, take-over bids, and the formation of joint ventures. The Community Patent Convention was signed in 1975, subject to ratification by all member states. In June 1997 the Commission published a consultative document containing proposals that aimed to simplify the European patent system through the introduction of a unitary Community patent, thereby removing the need to file patent applications with individual member states. In 1996 EU member states filed 34,608 patents. An Office for Harmonization in the Internal Market (OHIM), based in Alicante, Spain, was established in December 1993, and is responsible for the registration of Community trade marks and ensuring that they receive uniform protection throughout the EU. Numerous directives have been adopted on the technical harmonization and standardization of products (e.g. on safety devices in motor vehicles, labelling of foodstuffs and of dangerous substances, and classification of medicines). In July 1998 the European Court of Justice ruled that the sale of 'grey imports' (often designer-label clothing), imported into the EU without the permission of the trade-mark holder, was in contravention of EU law.

The liberalization of Community public procurement formed an important part of the establishment of the internal market. A directive on public supplies contracts (effective from January 1989, or from March 1992 in Greece, Portugal and Spain) stipulated that major purchases of supplies by public authorities should be offered for tender throughout the community; while public contracts for construction or civil engineering works in excess of ECU 5m. were to be offered for tender throughout the EC from July 1990 (March 1992 for Greece, Portugal and Spain). From January 1993 the liberalization of procurement was extended to include public utilities in the previously excluded sectors of energy, transport, drinking-water and telecommunications. In mid-1998 business leaders proposed introducing independent ombudsmen to monitor the operation of public procurement throughout the EU and to verify its compliance with competition rules.

In September 1990 new regulations entered into force concerning mergers of large companies that might create unfair competition. In July 1996 the Commission proposed an extension of its authority to oversee merger operations, to include smaller mergers and joint ventures overseen by national regulators. The Commission planned to have authority over operations involving companies with combined global turnover of more than ECU 2,000m. and turnover within the EU of ECU 150m.; however, the proposal was widely opposed.

The Business Co-operation Centre, established in 1973, supplies information to businesses and introduces businesses from 70 different countries wishing to co-operate or form links. The Business Co-operation Network (BC-Net) links enterprises, both public and private, that wish to form alliances with others (e.g. licensing agreements), on a confidential basis. In September 1995 a Commission report outlined proposals to improve the business environment for small and medium-sized enterprises (SMEs) in the EU, by improving fiscal policies and access to finance, in addition to introducing measures aimed at reducing delays in payments and the costs of international transactions. The European Investment Bank (see p. 178) provides finance for small businesses by means of 'global loans' to financial intermediaries. A mechanism providing small businesses with subsidized loans was approved by ministers in April 1992. In March 1996 the Commission agreed new guide-lines for state aid to SMEs. Aid for the acquisition of patent rights, licences, expertise, etc., would now be allowed at the same level as that for tangible investment. In July 1997 the I-TEC scheme was inaugurated, with a budget of ECU 7.5m., to encourage SMEs to invest in new technology. By mid-1998 I-TEC had facilitated investments amounting to over ECU 250m. A network of 39 Euro Info Centres (EICs — aimed particularly at small businesses) began work in 1987, and a total of 227 EICs and 21 Euro Info Correspondence Centres were in operation in 1997.

A review of industry, published in early 1996, showed that EU companies were losing world market share in many areas, especially in electronics, mechanical engineering and automotive equipment. A study, published by the Commission in October, criticized the fact that, since 1960, only 10m. jobs in industry had been created in the EU (half the number created in Japan and less than one-fifth the number in the USA). The study cited high costs of labour, telecommunications and energy as being major contributory factors in the EU's declining share of export markets. Ministers of industry, meeting in November, decided to promote the use of benchmarking techniques to improve the competitiveness of European industry. They also reached political agreement on the third multiannual programme (1997–2000) for SMEs, reducing the budget from ECU 140m. to ECU 127m.

### TELECOMMUNICATIONS

In 1990 proposals were adopted by the Council on the co-ordinated introduction of a European public paging system and of cellular digital land-based mobile communications. In 1991 the Council adopted a directive requiring member states to liberalize their rules on the supply of telecommunications terminal equipment, thus ending the monopolies of national telecommunications authorities. In the same year the Council adopted a plan for the gradual introduction of a competitive market in satellite communications. In October 1995 the Commission adopted a directive liberalizing the use of cable telecommunications, requiring members states to permit a wide range of services, in addition to television broadcasts, on such networks. The EU market for mobile telephone networks was opened to full competition as a result of a directive adopted by the Commission in January 1996, according to which member states were to abolish all exclusive and special rights in this area, and establish open and fair licensing procedures for digital services. The number of subscribers to cellular networks in the EU grew from 12m. to more than 20m. during 1995. The telecommunications market was to be fully deregulated by 1998, although extensions to the deregulation schedule were agreed for a number of member states. In October 1997 the Commission announced plans to commence legal proceedings against those member states which had not yet adopted the legislation necessary to permit the liberalization of the telecommunications market. Spain agreed to bring forward the full deregulation of its telecommunications market from January 2003 to 1998, which meant that all the major EU telecommunications markets were open to competition from 1998. Greece and Ireland have until 2000 to liberalize their telecommunications markets. Portugal's market was to be open from 2003.

In July 1998 the Commission identified 14 cases of unfair pricing after commencing an investigation into the charges imposed by telecommunications companies for interconnection between fixed and mobile telephone networks. In December the Commission suspended some of its investigations, after a number of companies introduced price reductions.

In 1987 the Community began a joint programme of research and development in advanced communications technology in Europe (RACE), aiming to establish an integrated broad-band telecommunications network. The successor programme, Advanced Communications Technologies and Services (ACTS), became effective in September 1994.

### THE SCHENGEN AGREEMENT AND TRANSPORT POLICY

Measures on the abolition of customs formalities at intra-community frontiers were completed by mid-1991, and entered into force in January 1993. However, disagreements remained among member governments concerning the free movement of persons: discussions continued in 1992 on the abuse of open frontiers by organized crime, particularly for drugs-trafficking; on extradition procedures; and on rules of asylum and immigration. In June 1990 Belgium, France, Germany, Luxembourg and the Netherlands, meeting in Schengen, Luxembourg, signed a Convention to implement an earlier agreement (concluded in 1985 at the same location), abolishing frontier controls on the free movement of persons from 1993. Delay in the establishment of the Schengen Information System (SIS), providing a computer network on criminals and illegal immigrants for use by the police forces of signatory states, resulted in postponement of implementation of the new agreement. Seven countries agreed to implement the Agreement with effect from March 1995 (Belgium, France, Germany, Luxembourg, the Netherlands, Portugal and Spain). Frontier controls at airports on those travelling between the seven countries were dismantled during a three-month transition period, which ended on 1 July 1995. However, after that date the French Government announced that it would retain land-border controls for a further six months, claiming that drugs-trafficking and illegal immigration had increased as a result of the Agreement. In March 1996 France decided to lift its border controls with Spain and Germany while maintaining controls on borders with the Benelux countries, mainly because of its anxieties about drugs being brought in from the Netherlands via Belgium and Luxembourg. Italy joined the 'Schengen Group' in October 1997, and Austria was to join in December. Border controls for both countries were removed in 1998. Denmark, Finland and Sweden (and non-EU members Norway and Iceland) were admitted as observers of the accord from 1 May 1996. The latter agreement was framed in such a way as to enable the three countries to accede to the Schengen Agreement in the future without adversely affecting the border-free zone provided by the Nordic Passport Union (see Nordic Council, p. 222). In April 1998 Sweden voted to join the 'Schengen Group'. Denmark and Finland were also reported to be making preparations for membership. In March 1999 signatories of the Schengen accords on visa-free border crossings began to waive visa requirements with Estonia, Latvia and Lithuania. In June 1997 the Commission published details of an action plan to achieve a single market, which envisaged the abolition of all EU internal border controls by 1 January 1999. The Treaty of Amsterdam, which came into effect on 1 May 1999, incorporated the so-called Schengen *'acquis'* (comprising the 1985 Agreement, 1990 Convention and additional Accession Protocols and executive decisions), in order to integrate it into the framework of the EU. The Treaty permitted the United Kingdom and Ireland to maintain permanent jurisdiction over their borders and rules of asylum and immigration. Countries acceding to the EU after 2000 were automatically to adhere to the Schengen arrangements.

The establishment of a common transport policy is stipulated in the Treaty of Rome, with the aim of gradually standardizing national regulations which hinder the free movement of traffic within the Community, such as the varying safety and licensing rules, diverse restrictions on the size of lorries, and frontier-crossing formalities. In 1986 transport ministers agreed on a system of Community-wide permits for commercial vehicles, to facilitate the crossing of frontiers, and in 1993 they agreed on measures concerning road haulage. A common tax system for trucks using EC roads was to lead to full liberalization of road 'cabotage' (whereby road hauliers may provide services in the domestic market of another member state) by 1998. In 1991 directives were adopted by the Council on the compulsory use of safety belts in vehicles weighing less than 3.5 metric tons. Further regulations applying to minibuses and coaches were to be introduced, following approval by the Commission in mid-1996. In May 1998 ministers of transport approved legislation to compel member governments to clear serious obstructions, such as truck blockades, which hinder the free movement of goods, and so disrupt the operation of a single market.

In July 1998 the Commission proposed harmonizing transport costs, to link the cost of using air services, ports, railways and roads to the social costs they incur. Under the plans, vehicles weighing more than 12 metric tons were to be charged for each km travelled, and existing charges were to be removed. The new charges were to be introduced during 2001–2004.

In the late 1980s ministers of transport approved measures to contribute to the liberalization of air transport within the Community. In 1990 ministers agreed to make further reductions in guaranteed quotas for a country's airlines on routes to another country, and to liberalize air cargo services. In 1992 they approved an 'open skies' arrangement that would allow any EC airline to operate domestic flights within another member state (with effect from 1 April 1997). In June 1996 the ministers of transport approved a limited mandate for the Commission to negotiate an 'open skies' agreement with the USA, under which a common EU–US aviation area would be created. However, the USA wished to negotiate on the basis of a full mandate. In October 1998 ministers failed to award a full mandate to the Commission. In November the Commission filed a case with the European Court of Justice, accusing eight member countries that had reached bilateral 'open skies' agreements with the USA of distorting competition to the disadvantage of EU airlines. The Commission was also initiating legal action against agreements made with the USA by Iceland, Norway and Switzerland. In July 1994, despite the recommendations of a 'Committee of Wise Men' (established by the Commission in 1993) for tighter controls on subsidies awarded to airlines, as part of efforts to increase competitiveness within the industry, the Commission approved substantial subsidies that had been granted by the French and Greek governments to their respective national airlines. Subsequently the Commission specified that state assistance could be granted to airlines 'in exceptional, unforeseen circumstances, outside the control of the company'. In June 1998 the European Court of Justice declared the subsidies awarded by the French Government illegal. However, in the following month the Commission stated that the subsidies were valid, since they had been accompanied by restructuring measures and certain competition guarantees.

In 1986 progress was made towards the establishment of a common maritime transport policy, with the adoption of regulations on unfair pricing practices, safeguard of access to cargoes, application of competition rules, and the eventual elimination of unilateral cargo reservation and discriminatory cargo-sharing arrangements. In December 1990 the Council approved, in principle, the freedom for shipping companies to provide maritime transport anywhere within the Community.

In April 1998 the Commission published a report on railway policy, with the aim of achieving greater harmonization, the regulation of state subsidies and the progressive liberalization of the rail-freight market. The Commission proposed the immediate liberalization of 5% of the market, increasing to 15% after five years and to 25% after 10 years. In October 1999 EU transport ministers concluded an agreement that was regarded as a precursor to the full liberalization of the rail-freight market. The agreement provided for the extension of access to a planned Trans-European Rail Freight Network (TERFN). Officials had reportedly been instructed to devise a charging system that would ensure 'optimum competitiveness'. Ministers also approved the Commission's plan to expedite the implementation of its proposals to harmonize rail networks. Meanwhile, France, Belgium and Luxembourg were thought likely to oppose the full liberalization of the rail-freight market, even though the sector's share of the total freight market has declined from some 30% in 1970 to about 14%.

The PACT (pilot action for combined transport) scheme was instigated in 1992 and had funded 65 combined transport projects (where goods are moved by at least two forms of transport without unloading) on 22 routes by July 1996, when the Commission approved plans to extend the programme from 1997 to 2001, with an additional budget of ECU 35m.

A Commission report on growth, competitiveness and employment, issued in December 1993, proposed the establishment of trans-European networks (TENs) to improve transport, telecommunications and energy infrastructure throughout the Community. Most of the finance for the schemes is provided by individual member states, although by mid-1998 some ECU 3,000m. had been made available from the EU budget. In June 1998 the Commission revealed that three of 14 priority projects identified were expected to be complete by 2000. The projects were: a suspension bridge between Denmark and Sweden; an Irish railway, linking Cork to Larne via Dublin and Belfast; and an airport in Milan, Italy. The Commission planned to increase the TENs budget to €5,000m. during 2000–2006. In April 1997 plans to extend the TENs scheme into central and eastern Europe were disclosed. ECU 100m. was to be provided for such projects under the PHARE (Poland/Hungary Aid for Restructuring of Economies) assistance programme (see under External Relations). A project to develop a motorway providing a Berlin–Kiev link began in May, aided by a grant of ECU 68m. from the PHARE programme.

In December 1997 the Council adopted a directive on postal services defining the level of service to be provided throughout the EU and establishing a timetable for the liberalization of postal services.

## JUSTICE AND HOME AFFAIRS

Under the Treaty on European Union, EU member states undertook to co-operate in the areas of justice and home affairs, particularly in relation to the free movement of people between member states. Issues of common interest were defined as asylum policy; border controls; immigration; drug addiction; fraud; judicial co-operation in civil and criminal matters; customs co-operation; and police co-operation for the purposes of combating terrorism, drugs-trafficking and other serious forms of international crime. A European Police Office (Europol), to facilitate the exchange of information between police forces, was to be established in The Hague, the Netherlands. The special Europol unit dealing with the trafficking of illicit drugs and nuclear and radioactive materials began work in 1994. Europol later had its mandate extended to cover illegal immigrants, stolen vehicles and paedophilia. A European Council meeting in June 1996 had resolved outstanding disagreements relating to the establishment of Europol and the Europol Convention finally entered into force on 1 October 1998, after ratification by member states. Europol was allocated a budget of ECU 6.8m. and in January 1999 its mandate was further extended to include terrorist activities. The EU convention on extradition, signed by ministers of justice in September 1996 prior to ratification by national governments, simplified and accelerated procedures, reduced the number of cases where extradition can be refused, and made it easier to extradite members of criminal organizations. In November 1997 the Commission proposed an extension to European law to allow civil and commercial judgments made in the courts of member states to be enforced across the whole of the EU. In June 1998 the Council and ministers from the 11 countries applying for EU membership approved a pre-accession agreement on combating organized crime. In February 1994 the Commission issued a document concerning the formulation of a comprehensive EU policy on asylum and immigration. In September 1995, as part of a policy of achieving a common visa regime for non-EU nationals, ministers agreed a common list of 101 countries, citizens of which required visas to enter the EU. Further progress on this issue was delayed by the desire of some member states to retain existing bilateral visa agreements.

## EDUCATION, CULTURE AND BROADCASTING

The Treaty of Rome, although not covering education directly, gave the Community the role of establishing general principles for implementing a common vocational training policy. The Treaty on European Union urged greater co-operation on education policy, including the encouragement of exchanges and mobility for students and teachers, and of distance learning, and development of European studies.

The postgraduate European University Institute was founded in Florence in 1976, with departments of history, economics, law and political and social sciences, together with a European Policy Unit and a European Culture Research Centre. In 1996/97 there were 355 research students and 46 professional posts. The Commission provided ECU 4.75m. towards the Institute's budget for 1997. In April 1998 202 research and teaching projects were approved for EU universities, including the establishment of 25 Jean Monnet European Centres of Excellence. Work on the projects was to begin in October 1998.

In September 1980 an educational information network, 'Eurydice', began operations, with a central unit in Brussels and national units providing data on the widely varying systems of education within member states. In 1987 the Council adopted a European Action Scheme for the Mobility of University Students ('Erasmus'). The scheme was expanded to include EFTA member states from 1992. The 'Lingua' programme promoted the teaching of foreign languages in the Community, with a budget of ECU 200m. for 1990–94. From 1 January 1995 the Erasmus and Lingua schemes were incorporated into a new Community programme, Socrates, which was to be effective during 1995–99, with a budget of ECU 850m. The programme aims to pursue the Community's activities of promoting co-operation and the exchange of information between member states with regard to education, as well as the mobility of students, especially in higher education. In 1997 Erasmus supported educational exchanges for 180,000 students and 30,000 teachers. During 1998–99 24 countries were to take part in the Erasmus scheme, which had a budget of ECU 116m. The Trans-European Mobility Programme for University Studies (TEMPUS) was launched in 1990 to foster co-operation between institutions of higher education and their counterparts in central and eastern Europe, as part of their wider aid programme to those countries (see below). By May 1993 TEMPUS had supported 637 projects, involving more than 10,000 teachers and 6,400 students in 1,800 institutions. Under the second phase of the scheme (TEMPUS II) for 1994–98 the former Soviet republics were eligible to participate in the scheme. It also sought to provide support for the restructuring of higher education in countries of central and eastern Europe participating in the PHARE programme (see under External Relations). In 1975 a European Centre for the Development of Vocational Training (CEDEFOP) was established in Berlin, Germany. The centre relocated to Thessaloniki, Greece, in 1995. The priority areas for 1997–2000 were identified as: promoting access to skills and lifelong learning; monitoring developments in member states; and support for European mobility. From 1 January 1995 the Leonardo da Vinci programme for vocational training became effective, with a budget of ECU 620m. for 1995–99.

In December 1998 the Council agreed education, training and youth programmes for 2000–2006. Socrates was to have a budget of €1,150m. and the Leonardo da Vinci programme was to be allocated €1,550m. The TEMPUS scheme was to incorporate a third phase, TEMPUS III, which was to extend its co-operation with central and eastern European countries.

Under the Community's programme for conserving the European architectural heritage, 100 projects were approved in 1995, with a budget of ECU 4.7m. In March 1995 the Commission initiated the Raphael programme, which aimed to promote the cultural heritage of Europe, by developing links between cultural institutions and improving training. The programme had a budget of ECU 30m. for the period 1997–2000. In 1998 the Kaleidoscope programme, which encourages European cultural exchanges and other cultural projects, supported 147 projects at a total cost of ECU 8m. The programme's budget for 1996–98 was ECU 26.5m. In 1996 the Ariane programme was established to promote reading and to provide public access to books. In January 1999 the Commission selected 192 projects to receive funding under the Ariane programme in that year. In September 1998 ministers had agreed to extend its existing cultural programmes until the end of 1999, when the Culture 2000 framework programme for 2000–2004 was to replace the Raphael, Kaleidoscope and Ariane programmes. It was envisaged that the framework programme would concentrate on the following themes: legislation of benefit to cultural projects; the cultural aspects of existing support policies; and the incorporation of culture into the field of external relations.

A programme to improve awareness of information technology, promote understanding of the 'Information Society', and identify opportunities for the use of new technologies, particularly in relation to disadvantaged social groups, was proposed by the Commission in

December 1996. The ECU 45m. programme was to operate during 1997–2001. A further information technology scheme was initiated in September 1997, with a budget of ECU 13m., to examine new methods for the promotion of learning among children aged between four and eight years. The scheme formed part of the ESPRIT research programme (see under Science and Technology).

In 1989 ministers of foreign affairs adopted a directive (television without frontiers) establishing minimum standards for television programmes which could be broadcast freely throughout the Community: limits were placed on the amount of time devoted to advertisements, a majority of programmes broadcast were to be from the Community, where practicable, and governments were to be allowed to forbid the transmission of programmes considered morally harmful. The 'Media' programme was introduced in 1991 to provide financial support to the television and film industry. During 1991–95 it provided funds for some 5,000 projects, including professional training, the production of programmes and films with a European dimension and the transnational distribution of programmes. A second programme, 'Media II', was initiated in January 1996 with a planned budget of ECU 310m. for 1996–2000. In 1993 ministers approved a measure to ensure copyright protection for television programmes broadcast across borders by means of satellite and cable transmission. In March 1998 the Commission published a report suggesting that the regulatory framework of broadcasting rules might require amendment in the future, owing to the increasing convergence of the television, telecommunications and information technology industries.

## SOCIAL POLICY

The Single European Act, which entered into force in 1987, added to the original Treaty of Rome articles which emphasized the need for 'economic and social cohesion' in the Community, i.e. the reduction of disparities between the various regions, principally through the existing 'structural funds'—the European Regional Development Fund, the European Social Fund, and the Guidance Section of the European Agricultural Guidance and Guarantee Fund (for details of these funds, as well as the Cohesion Fund, which became operational in 1993, see p. 199). In 1988 the Council declared that Community operations through the structural funds, the European Investment Bank and other financial instruments should have five priority objectives: (i) promoting the development and structural adjustment of the less-developed regions (where gross domestic product per caput is less than 75% of the Community average); (ii) converting the regions, frontier regions or parts of regions seriously affected by industrial decline; (iii) combating long-term unemployment among people above the age of 25; (iv) providing employment for young people (aged under 25); (v) with a view to the reform of the common agricultural policy: speeding up the adjustment of agricultural structures and promoting the development of rural areas. 'Agenda 2000', concerning the Community's budget after 2000, which was published in July 1997, envisaged a reform of the structural funds. Political agreement on 'Agenda 2000' was reached in March 1999.

In 1989 the Commission proposed a Charter on the Fundamental Social Rights of Workers (Social Charter), covering freedom of movement, fair remuneration, improvement of working conditions, the right to social security, freedom of association and collective wage agreements, the development of participation by workers in management, and sexual equality. The Charter was approved by the heads of government of all Community member states except the United Kingdom in December. On the insistence of the United Kingdom, the chapter on social affairs of the Treaty on European Union, negotiated in December 1991, was omitted from the Treaty to form a separate protocol. In May 1997 the new UK Government approved the Social Charter, which was to be incorporated into the Treaty of Amsterdam, signed in October. The Treaty, which entered into force in May 1999, also included a new chapter on employment.

A number of Community directives have been adopted on equal rights for women in pay, access to employment and social security, and the Commission has undertaken legal proceedings against several member states before the European Court of Justice for infringements. In 1991–95 the third Community Action Programme on the Promotion of Equal Opportunities for Women was undertaken, involving action by national governments in combating unemployment among women; bringing about equal treatment for men and women in occupational social schemes (e.g. sick pay and pensions) and in self-employed occupations, including agriculture; and legislation on parental leave. The first EU meeting on female employment was held in Belfast, the United Kingdom, in May 1998. A Fourth Action Programme, with a budget of ECU 30m. for the five-year period 1996–2000, aims to ensure that the question of equality is integrated into all relevant policy issues. In 1997 Daphne, a programme to combat domestic violence, was launched. The programme's proposed budget for 2000–2004 was €25m. In December 1997 the Council adopted a directive on sex discrimination cases, whereby the plaintiff and defendant were to share the burden of proof. Legislation was to be introduced by 1 January 2000. Numerous directives on health and safety in the workplace have been adopted by the Community. The creation of a Major Accident Hazards Bureau (MAHB) was announced by the Commission in February 1996. Based at the Joint Research Centre at Ispra in Italy, its purpose is to help prevent industrial accidents in the EU. In June 1993 the Working Time directive was approved, restricting the working week to 48 hours, except where overtime arrangements are agreed with trade unions. In October ministers adopted a directive limiting the number of hours worked by young people. The United Kingdom secured a dispensation to delay implementation of these latter measures for four years. The directive, which also prescribed minimum rest periods and a minimum of four weeks' paid holiday a year, had to be implemented by 23 November 1996. Certain categories of employee were exempt from the maximum 48-hour week rule, including those in the transport sector, fishermen and junior hospital doctors, but in December 1998 the Commission proposed extending the directive to cover those groups. In September 1994 ministers adopted the first directive to be approved under the Social Charter, concerning the establishment of mandatory works councils in multinational companies. After lengthy negotiations, it was agreed that the legislation was to be applied in companies employing more than 1,000 people, of whom 150 worked in at least two EU member states. The United Kingdom was excluded from the directive; however, UK companies operating in other European countries were to participate in the scheme (although without counting UK-based employees towards the applicability thresholds). The directive came into force in September 1996. In November 1998 the Commission proposed a directive to compel companies employing more than 50 staff to consult workers about decisions likely to cause significant organizational or contractual changes. In April 1996 the Commission proposed that part-time, fixed-term and temporary employees should receive comparable treatment to permanent, full-time employees. A directive ensuring equal treatment for part-time employees was adopted by the Council in December 1997. The directive on parental leave, the second directive to be adopted under the Social Charter, provided for a statutory minimum of three months' unpaid leave to allow parents to care for young children, and was adopted in June 1996. In December 1997, following the UK Government's approval of the Social Charter in May, the Council adopted amendments extending the two directives to include the United Kingdom.

The European Confidence Pact for Employment was launched by the Commission in January 1996 as a comprehensive strategy to combat unemployment involving a common approach by public authorities, employers and employees. An employment body, EURES, launched in November 1994, operates as a network of 450 advisers who have access to two European databases listing job vacancies in the EU and in Norway and Iceland. During 1996–97 EURES assisted more than 1m. people. (Its website can be accessed at europa.eu.int/jobs/eures.) In November 1998 the Commission proposed that national public employment services should have greater involvement with EURES. The rate of unemployment across the Community averaged 9.8% of the labour force at November 1998. An employment summit was held in Luxembourg in November 1997, with the aim of promoting job creation. The conference focused on four themes: employability, entrepreneurship, equal opportunities and adaptability, and committed member governments to providing training or work placements for unemployed young people within six months, and for the long-term unemployed within 12 months. Member states also agreed to reduce taxation on labour-intensive service industries from 1 July 1998, and to produce a national action plan for employment. In April 1998 a Social Action Plan for 1998–2000 was adopted by the Commission. It concentrated on three main areas: the promotion of jobs, skills and mobility; the changing world of work; and the development of an inclusive society. In January 1999 the Commission proposed simplifying the existing social security system to ensure that the entitlements of people moving between EU countries were protected.

EU activities regarding disability include the HELIOS programme for disabled people, which focuses on the issues of mobility, integration and independence and a 'technology initiative for disabled and elderly people' (TIDE), which aims to develop technologies that improve the living conditions of the groups concerned.

The European Voluntary Service (EVS) was established in 1996 as a pilot scheme to enable young people aged 18–25 to take part in a range of projects of benefit to the community in a country other than their own. EVS was allocated a budget of ECU 47.5m. for 1998–99. In June 1998 the Council agreed to issue 'Europasses' to record vocational training carried out in other EU member states. In July 1999 the Euro-Mediterranean Youth Programme was inaugurated. The programme had initially been adopted by the Commission in October 1998 and was to receive funding of €6m. over two years, plus grants worth €3.7m. from the Youth for Europe and EVS programmes.

The European Foundation for the Improvement of Living and Working Conditions (Dublin), established in 1975, undertakes four-year research programmes. Under the Treaty on European Union, the EU assumed responsibility for addressing the problem of drug addiction, and a European Monitoring Centre for Drugs and Drug Addiction was established in Lisbon, Portugal, in 1995 (see 'Other Institutions'). A programme to promote co-operation between member states in action against drug dependency was adopted by ministers of health, meeting in November 1996. The ECU 27m. programme covers the period 1996–2000.

### CONSUMER PROTECTION

The Community's second Consumer Protection Programme was approved by the Council in 1981, based on the principles of the first programme: protection of health and safety; standardization of rules for food additives and packaging; rules for machines and equipment; and authorization procedures for new products. The programme also included measures for monitoring the quality and durability of products, improving after-sales services, legal remedies for unsatisfactory goods and services, and the encouragement of consumer associations.

In 1993 a three-year action plan was inaugurated, with the aim of strengthening consumer power in the single market. The plan's priorities were: to consolidate legislation; to improve dissemination of consumer information; to facilitate access to small claims' courts; and to increase customer security in cross-frontier payments and after-sales services. The Consumers' Consultative Council represents European consumers' organizations, and gives opinions on consumer matters. In October 1996 the Commission issued a plan for 1997–98 containing some new priorities, including the protection of consumer interests in the supply of public utilities, improving consumer confidence in foodstuffs, strengthening consumer representation and developing consumer policies in central and eastern Europe. A new framework programme was planned for 1999–2003.

In November 1996 ministers approved a Commission directive which would enable a consumer body in one member state to take action in another in connection with breaches of certain EU laws such as those on consumer credit, package holidays, and misleading advertising. In April 1998 the Council agreed to introduce two-year guarantees on consumer goods purchased in any EU country.

In February 1997 the Commission extended the function of its directorate-general on consumer policy to incorporate consumer health protection, in order to ensure that sufficient importance be given to food safety, particularly owing to consumer concerns resulting from the BSE crisis (see under Agriculture). In June the Commission announced that a Scientific Steering Committee was to be established to provide advice regarding consumer health issues. In July 1998 an Institute for Health and Consumer Protection, attached to the Commission's Joint Research Centre, was established to improve research on that subject. In January 2000, in order to improve food safety and restore consumer confidence, the Commission formally proposed the creation of an all-European, independent food safety agency in 2002.

### ENVIRONMENT POLICY

The Community's fifth environmental action programme (1993–2000), entitled 'Towards Sustainability', aims to address the root causes of environmental degradation, by raising public awareness and changing the behaviour of authorities, enterprises and the general public. The programme targets the following sectors: industry (aiming for improved resource management and production standards); energy (reducing emissions of carbon dioxide and other pollutants, by improving energy efficiency); transport (investment in public transport, cleaner fuels); agriculture (reducing pollution, encouraging tree-planting); and tourism (controls on new and existing tourist developments).

Directives have been adopted, obliging member states to introduce regulations on air and water pollution (e.g. 'acid rain', pollution by fertilizers and pesticides, and emissions from vehicles), the transport of hazardous waste across national boundaries, waste treatment, noise abatement and the protection of natural resources; and guaranteeing freedom of access to information on the environment held by public authorities. The fifth environmental action programme focuses on anticipating environmental problems, with initiatives expected on improved resource management by industry, more effective management of mass tourism, and the development of environmental policies in agriculture.

The Community's programme of research and technological development on the environment, carried out on a shared-cost basis by various scientific institutions, covers the EU's participation in global change programmes; technologies and engineering for the environment; research on economic and social aspects of environmental issues; and technological and natural hazards. The programme is open to all European countries. A separate programme covers research in marine science and technology. In 1990 the EC established a European Environment Agency (EEA, see p. 179) to monitor environmental issues. The agency became operational in November 1994.

In 1996 the LIFE programme was established as a financial instrument to promote the development and implementation of environmental policy. LIFE funds priority activities in EU member states and provides technical assistance to countries in central and eastern Europe and the Mediterranean. In 1997 LIFE supported 211 projects. In 1998 LIFE was allocated ECU 96.6m. to finance 201 projects in the EU and an additional 4.7m. ECU was provided to finance projects outside the EU. In January 1999 it was proposed to extend the LIFE programme into 2000–2004, with a budget of €613m. (The LIFE programme has a website giving details of its activities, which can be found at europa.eu.int/comm/life/home.htm.)

In 1985 the Community (and a number of individual member states) ratified the Vienna Convention for the Protection of the Ozone Layer, and in 1987 the Community signed a protocol to the treaty, controlling the production of chlorofluorocarbons. In 1990 ministers of the environment undertook to ban the production of chlorofluorocarbons by mid-1997; the introduction of the ban was brought forward to 1996. In July 1998 the Commission proposed committing EU countries to the progressive elimination of remaining ozone-depleting substances by 2001, by introducing a ban on the sale and use of CFCs and imposing production limits on HCFCs, which were originally introduced to replace CFCs. In 1990 ministers agreed to stabilize emissions of carbon dioxide, believed to be responsible for 'global warming', at 1990 levels by 2000 (2005 for the United Kingdom). In December 1997, at the third conference of parties to the UN Framework Convention on Climate Change (held in Kyoto, Japan), agreement was reached to reduce emissions of six greenhouse gases by 8% between 2008 and 2012 in member states, in comparison with 1990 levels. In June 1998 ministers of the environment agreed upon individual emission targets for each EU member state. The agreement allows a number of less industrialized countries to increase gas emissions. In May 1999 the Commission urged EU member states to redouble their efforts to reduce emissions of greenhouse gases. It was reported that while in 2000 emissions levels were expected to fall, approximately, to those prevailing in 1990, thereafter they were likely to rise again failing appropriate action.

The Eco-Management and Audit Scheme (EMAS) is a voluntary scheme, launched in April 1995, in which participating industrial companies undergo an independent audit of their environmental performance.

In June 1996 the Commission agreed a strategy, drawn up in collaboration with the European petroleum and car industries, for reducing harmful emissions from road vehicles by between 60% and 70% by 2010. In late June 1998 EU member states reached an 'auto-oil' agreement to reduce air pollution. The agreement commits member states to the progressive elimination of leaded petrol by 2000 (with limited exemptions until 2005). From 2000 petrol-powered road vehicles were to be fitted with 'on-board diagnostic' systems (OBDs) to monitor emissions. Diesel vehicles were to be installed with OBD systems by 2005. In July the Commission announced plans to decrease pollution from nuclear power stations by reducing emissions of sulphur dioxides, nitrogen oxides and dust by one-half.

An action programme for the protection and management of groundwater resources was adopted by the Commission in July 1997. Member states were to be asked to prepare national prorammes to identify, map and protect groundwater resources. In December the Council agreed upon a target to reduce the volume of waste disposed in landfill sites.

Rules governing the sale of genetically engineered foods were agreed by ministers in November 1996, despite objections from some countries, principally Germany and Austria, and strong opposition from environmental campaigners. In May 1998 measures were adopted to compel member countries to label food products containing genetically modified soya and maize. In December 1999 EU environment ministers urged the adoption of stringent global regulations to govern trade in genetically modified commodities.

A regulation revising EU laws on trade in wild animals and plants was adopted by ministers of the environment in December 1996. It was to tighten controls and improve enforcement of restrictions on trade in endangered species. In mid-1999 the EU was reported to be threatening to withhold structural fund payments from some member states if they did not implement the habitats directive and establish protected environmental areas and nature reserves.

In early 1999 a conflict arose between the EU and the USA over the introduction of new EU legislation to curb aircraft noise. Initially, the EU proposed to prevent aircraft fitted with hush kits from flying in the EU after 1 April 2002 unless they were already operating there before 1 April 1999. However, the legislation was subsequently amended in order to avert the threat of a temporary boycott of some European flights by the US authorities.

### FINANCIAL SERVICES AND CAPITAL MOVEMENTS

A directive on Community banking, adopted in 1977, laid down common prudential criteria for the establishment and operation of banks in member states. A second banking directive, adopted in 1989, aimed to create a single community licence for banking, thereby permitting a bank established in one member country to open branches in any other. The directive entered into force on 1 January 1993. Related measures were subsequently adopted with the aim of ensuring the capital adequacy of credit institutions, and the prevention of 'money-laundering' by criminals. In September 1993 ministers approved a directive on a bank deposit scheme to protect account-holders: banks were to be obliged to raise protection to 90% on the first ECU 20,000 in an account from 1 January 1995.

In 1992 the third insurance co-ordination directives, relating to life assurance and non-life insurance, were adopted, creating a framework for an integrated Community insurance market. The directives provide greater access to insurance companies and customers to the European market, guarantee greater protection for purchasers of life assurance policies and prohibit substantive control of rates. The directives came into effect on 1 July 1994.

In May 1993 ministers adopted a directive on investment services, which (with effect from 1 January 1996) allows credit institutions to offer investment services in any member state, on the basis of a licence held in one state.

In late 1999 the Commission put forward proposals to remove tax barriers and investment restrictions affecting cross-border pension schemes. At present, variations among the member states in the tax liability of contributions to supplementary pension schemes obstruct the transfer of pension rights from one state to another, contradicting the Treaty of Rome's principles of free movement of labour, capital and services.

Freedom of capital movement and the creation of a uniform financial area were regarded as vital for the completion of the internal market by 1992. In 1987, as part of the liberalization of the flow of capital, a Council directive came into force, whereby member states were obliged to remove restrictions on three categories of transactions: long-term credits related to commercial transactions; acquisition of securities; and the admission of securities to capital markets. In June 1988 the Council of Ministers approved a directive whereby all restrictions on capital movements (financial loans and credits, current and deposit account operations, transactions in securities and other instruments normally dealt in on the money market) were removed by 1 July 1990 (although a number of countries were permitted to exercise certain restrictions until the end of 1992). In September 1995 the Council adopted measures to eliminate excessive fees and delays in transfers of funds between banks in member states. In November 1997 the Commission adopted proposals to co-ordinate tax policy among member states. The measures included a code of conduct on corporate taxation and were to lead to the simplification of methods used to transfer royalty and interest payments between member countries and to prevent the withholding of taxes. In February 1999 Parliament endorsed a proposal by the Commission to harmonize taxation further, through the co-ordination of savings taxes. However, the EU's efforts in this respect were opposed by the United Kingdom on the grounds that the proposed new legislation (among other things, banks would be obliged to collect a withholding tax of at least 20% on cross-border payments of interest to individuals within the EU) would threaten the future of the international bond market, which is principally based in London. At the summit meeting of EU leaders held in Helsinki, Finland, in December 1999, it was agreed to postpone the introduction of the new tax on savings for a period of six months, in response to the United Kingdom's objections.

## ECONOMIC CO-OPERATION

A report on the economic situation is presented annually by the Commission, analysing recent developments and short- and medium-term prospects. Economic policy guide-lines for the following year are adopted annually by the Council.

The following objectives for the end of 1973 were agreed by the Council in 1971, as the first of three stages towards European economic and monetary union:

the narrowing of exchange rate margins to 2.25%; creation of a medium-term pool of reserves; co-ordination of short- and medium-term economic and budgetary policies; a joint position on international monetary issues; harmonization of taxes; creation of the European Monetary Co-operation Fund (EMCF); creation of the European Regional Development Fund.

The narrowing of exchange margins (the 'snake') came into effect in 1972; but Denmark, France, Ireland, Italy and the United Kingdom later floated their currencies, with only Denmark permanently returning to the arrangement. Sweden and Norway also linked their currencies to the 'snake'; but Sweden withdrew from the arrangement in August 1977, and Norway withdrew in December 1978.

The European Monetary System (EMS) came into force in March 1979, with the aim of creating closer monetary co-operation, leading to a zone of monetary stability in Europe, principally through an exchange rate mechanism (ERM), supervised by the ministries of finance and the central banks of member states. Not all Community members participated in the ERM: Greece did not join, Spain joined only in June 1989, the United Kingdom in October 1990 and Portugal in April 1992. To prevent wide fluctuations in the value of members' currencies against each other, the ERM fixed for each currency a central rate in European Currency Units (ECUs, see below), based on a 'basket' of national currencies; a reference rate in relation to other currencies was fixed for each currency, with established fluctuation margins (until July 1993 6% for the Portuguese escudo and the Spanish peseta, 2.25% for others). Central banks of the participating states intervened by buying or selling currencies when the agreed margin was likely to be exceeded. Each member placed 20% of its gold reserves and dollar reserves respectively into the EMCF, and received a supply of ECUs to regulate central bank interventions. Short- and medium-term credit facilities were given to support the balance of payments of member countries. The EMS was initially put under strain by the wide fluctuations in the exchange rates of non-Community currencies and by the differences in economic development among members, which led to nine realignments of currencies in 1979–83. Subsequently greater stability was achieved, with only two realignments of currencies between 1984 and 1988. In September 1992, however, the Italian and Spanish currencies were devalued, by 7% and 5% respectively, within the ERM, and Italian and British membership was suspended; in November the Portuguese and Spanish currencies were both devalued by 6% within the ERM. In May 1993 the Spanish and Portuguese currencies were further devalued (by 8% and 6.5%, respectively). In late July, as a result of intensive currency speculation on European financial markets (forcing the weaker currencies to the very edge of their permitted margins), the ERM almost collapsed. In response to the crisis, EC finance ministers decided to widen the fluctuation margins allowed for each currency to 15%, except in the cases of Germany and the Netherlands, which agreed to maintain their currencies within the original 2.25% limits. The 15% margins were regarded as allowing for so much fluctuation in exchange rates as to represent a virtual suspension of the ERM; however, some countries, notably France and Belgium, expressed determination to adhere as far as possible to the original 'bands' in order to fulfil the conditions for eventual monetary union. In practice, during 1994, most currencies remained within the former 2.25% and 6% bands. Austria became a member of the EMS in January 1995, and its currency was subject to ERM conditions. While Sweden decided to remain outside the EMS, Finland joined in October 1996. In November the Italian lira was readmitted to the ERM.

In September 1988 a committee (chaired by Jacques Delors, the President of the European Commission, and comprising the governors of member countries' central banks, representatives of the European Commission and outside experts) was established to discuss European monetary union. The resulting 'Delors plan' was presented to heads of government in June 1989, and they agreed to begin the first stage of the process of monetary union—the drafting of a treaty on the subject—in 1990. The Intergovernmental Conference on Economic and Monetary Union was initiated in December 1990, and continued to work (in parallel with the Intergovernmental Conference on Political Union) throughout 1991, with monthly meetings at ministerial level. The Intergovernmental Conference was responsible for the drafting of the economic and monetary provisions of the Treaty on European Union, which was agreed by the European Council in December 1991 and which came into force on 1 November 1993. The principal feature of the Treaty's provisions on economic and monetary union (EMU) was the gradual introduction of a single currency, to be administered by a single central bank. During the remainder of Stage I, member states were to adopt programmes for the 'convergence' of their economies and ensure the complete liberalization of capital movements. Stage II began on 1 January 1994, and included the establishment of a European Monetary Institute (EMI), replacing the EMCF and comprising governors of central banks and a president appointed by heads of government. Heads of government were to decide, not later than 31 December 1996, whether a majority of member states fulfilled the necessary conditions for the adoption of a single currency: if so, they were to establish a date for the beginning of Stage III, but if no date for this had been set by the end of 1997, Stage III was to begin on 1 January 1999, and was to be confined to those members which did fulfil the necessary conditions. After the establishment of a starting date for Stage III, the European Central Bank (ECB) and a European System of Central Banks were to be set up to replace the EMI. During Stage III, exchange rates were to be irrevocably fixed, and a single currency introduced. Member states that had not fulfilled the necessary conditions for the adoption of a single currency would be exempt from participating. The United Kingdom was to be allowed to make a later, separate decision on whether to proceed to Stage III, while Denmark reserved the right to submit its participation in Stage III to a referendum. The near-collapse of the ERM in July 1993 cast serious doubts on the agreed timetable for monetary union, although in October the EC heads of government reaffirmed their commitment to their objective.

In December 1995 the European Council, meeting in Madrid, confirmed that Stage III of Economic and Monetary Union was to begin on 1 January 1999. The economic conditions for member states wishing to enter Stage III (including an annual budget deficit of no more than 3% of annual gross domestic product—GDP—and total public debt of no more than 60% of annual GDP) were also confirmed. The meeting decided that the proposed single currency would be officially known as the 'euro'. Participants in EMU were to be selected in early 1998, on the basis of economic performance during 1997. In October 1996 the Commission issued a draft regulation on a proposed 'stability pact', intended to ensure that member countries maintained strict budgetary discipline during Stage III of monetary union. Another draft regulation formed the legal framework for the euro, confirming that it would be the single currency of participating countries from 1 January 1999. During a transitional period of up to three years, national currencies would remain in circulation, having equivalent legal status to the euro. The communication outlined the main features of a new ERM, which would act as a 'waiting room' for countries preparing to join the single currency. Member countries remaining outside the monetary system, whether or not by choice, would still be part of the single market.

Although all 15 members of the EU endorsed the principle of monetary union, with France and Germany the most ardent supporters, certain countries were known to have political doubts about joining. In October 1997 both the United Kingdom and Sweden confirmed that they would not participate in EMU from 1999. Denmark was also to remain outside the single currency.

Technical preparations for the euro were confirmed during a meeting of the European Council in Dublin in December 1996. The heads of government endorsed the new ERM and the legal framework for the euro and agreed to the proposed 'stability pact'. Controversy arose in May 1997 over plans by the German Government to revalue gold reserves in an apparent attempt to modify figures for its 1997 budget. In June the European Council, meeting in Amsterdam, reached final agreement on the content of the 'stability pact', which included a resolution on growth. In March 1998 the Commission and the EIB published reports on the progress made by member states towards the fulfilment of convergence criteria. The Commission concluded that Greece alone failed to satisfy the necessary conditions. However, the EIB warned that Italy and Belgium, with public-debt ratios of over 100% of GDP, had made insufficient progress towards the reduction of debt levels. In March Greece was admitted to the ERM, causing a 14% devaluation of its national currency. In early May 1998 heads of state and of government confirmed that Greece failed to fulfil the conditions required for the adoption of a single currency from 1999, and that 11 countries would take part in Stage III of EMU. After substantial debate, the European Council agreed to appoint Willem Duisenberg, governor of the central bank of the Netherlands, as the President of the new ECB. Duisenberg was to be succeeded by Jean-Claude Trichet, governor of the French central bank, before the end of the usual eight-year term. The Vice-President and the remaining four members of the ECB's executive board were also appointed. The meeting agreed that existing ERM central rates were to be used to determine the final rates of exchange between national currencies and the euro, which were to be adopted on 1 January 1999. The ECB, which was established on 1 June 1998 and ceremonially launched on 30 June, was to be accountable to a European Forum, comprising members of the European Parliament (MEPs) and chairmen of the finance committees of the national parliaments of EU member countries. Euro-XI, an informal grouping of the ministers of finance of member states participating in EMU, met for the first time in June 1998. The euro was to be represented at an international level by a delegation involving the Council of Ministers, the Commission and the ECB. In September Sweden and the United Kingdom came under pressure to join the successor to the ERM, ERM2, launched on 1 January 1999, as a precondition of future participation in EMU. In October 1998 ministers discussed Greece's convergence programme for 1998–2001. The programme sought to allow Greece to join the single currency from 1 January 2001. On 31 December 1998 the ECOFIN Council adopted the conversion rates for the national currencies of the countries participating in the single currency. The euro was formally launched on 1 January 1999. Both Greece and Denmark have joined ERM2. In late 1999 Greece indicated that it would apply to participate in EMU in March 2000.

### The euro

With the creation of the European Monetary System (EMS) a new monetary unit, the European Currency Unit (ECU) was adopted. Its value and composition were identical to those of the European Unit of Account (EUA) already used in the administrative fields of the Community. The ECU was a composite monetary unit, in which the relative value of each currency was determined by the gross national product and the volume of trade of each country.

The ECU, which was assigned the function of the unit of account used by the European Monetary Co-operation Fund, was also used as the denominator for the exchange rate mechanism; as the denominator for operations in both the intervention and the credit mechanisms; and as a means of settlement between monetary authorities of the European Community.

From April 1979 onwards the ECU was also used as the unit of account for the purposes of the common agricultural policy. From 1981 it replaced the EUA in the general budget of the Community; the activities of the European Development Fund under the Lomé Convention; the balance sheets and loan operations of the European Investment Bank; and the activities of the European Coal and Steel Community.

In June 1985 measures were adopted by the governors of the Community's central banks, aiming to strengthen the EMS by expanding the use of the ECU, for example by allowing international monetary institutions and the central banks of non-member countries to become 'other holders' of ECUs.

In June 1989 it was announced that, with effect from 20 September, the Portuguese and Spanish currencies were to be included in the composition of the ECU. From that date the amounts of the national currencies included in the composition of the ECU were 'weighted' as follows (in percentages): Belgian franc 7.6; Danish krone 2.45; French franc 19.0; Deutsche Mark 30.1; Greek drachma 0.8; Irish pound 1.1; Italian lira 10.15; Luxembourg franc 0.3; Netherlands guilder 9.4; Portuguese escudo 0.8; Spanish peseta 5.3; United Kingdom pound sterling 13.0. The composition of the ECU 'basket' of currencies was 'frozen' with the entry into force of the Treaty on European Union on 1 November 1993. This was not affected by the accession to the EU of Austria, Finland and Sweden; consequently those countries' currencies were not represented in the ECU 'basket'.

As part of Stage III of the process of economic and monetary union (EMU), the ECU was replaced by a single currency, the euro (€), on 1 January 1999, at a conversion rate of 1:1.

Designs for the euro bank notes, and the symbol for the single currency, were presented by the EMI in December 1996, and designs for the euro coins were presented in June 1997. The notes and coins would not be in circulation until 2002, and the euro was gradually to replace the national currencies of participating countries in the first half of that year. EU finance ministers subsequently agreed that national currencies should be replaced by the euro during the first two months of 2002. In May 1998 the French Government began minting the new euro coins. However, changes to the specifications of euro coins were proposed in July, to aid the identification of 10- and 50-cent coins by the visually impaired and vending machines.

In April 1998 ministers agreed that banks should make no charge for the conversion of accounts or payments of national currency into euros, during a transitional period. In July agreement was reached with trade and consumer groups to establish a voluntary scheme to allow retailers to display prices in euros and to accept payments made in euros without imposing any additional charges. Retailers taking part in the scheme were to display a logo to show their compliance with a code of practice on the single currency. In the same month the Commission proposed measures to combat the counterfeiting of euros. In October the ECB agreed to introduce an analysis centre for counterfeit currency, with a database accessible to national central banks. A payments settlement system, called Target (Trans-European Automated Real-time Gross Settlement Express Transfer), was introduced for countries participating in EMU on 4 January 1999. In the same month the public debt of those countries was converted into euros. A borrowing scheme worth €2,000m. was also agreed, to enable the Commission to issue euro-denominated bonds on behalf of the EU or Euratom.

The euro's value in national currencies is calculated and published daily. Its value on 1 February 1999 was US $1.1305. By mid-1999 the value of the euro had declined by some 12% against the US dollar compared with its value on introduction. The decline was attributed to the relatively high degree of economic growth taking place in the USA compared to rates in the euro-zone. In March the Commission had revised down to 2.2% its forecast of economic growth in the 11 member states participating in Stage III of EMU, compared with a forecast of 2.6% made in October 1998. Signs of economic recovery, especially in Germany, led to the strengthening of the euro against the US dollar in the second half of 1999.

## External Relations

The EU has diplomatic relations in its own right with many countries (see p. 172), and with international organizations, and participates as a body in international conferences on trade and development, such as the 'Uruguay Round' of trade negotiations, under the General Agreement on Tariffs and Trade (GATT—see WTO, p. 274). It has observer status at the United Nations. Agreements have been signed with numerous countries and groups of countries, allowing for co-operation in trade and other matters. Association agreements were initially signed between the EC and other European countries for the purpose of customs union or possible accession. After the decline of Communism in eastern Europe in 1989, it was decided that the new states, many of which expressed a desire to become full members of the EC, should be offered association status in the first instance. The resulting agreements are known as 'Europe

Agreements'. Co-operation agreements are less comprehensive, and seek to facilitate economic co-operation with both European and non-European countries. Prior to 1989 they represented the preferred form of relationship with eastern European countries. The Union is also a party to various international conventions (in some of these to the exclusion of the individual member states).

Under the Single European Act, which came into force on 1 July 1987 (amending the Treaty of Rome), it was formally stipulated for the first time that member states should inform and consult each other on foreign policy matters (as was already, in practice, often the case).

The Treaty on European Union, which came into force on 1 November 1993, provided for joint action by member governments in matters of foreign and security policy, and envisaged the eventual formation of a common defence policy, with the possibility of a common defence force. The Western European Union (WEU, q.v.), to which all EU members except Denmark, Greece and Ireland belong, was to be developed as the 'defence component' of the Union, but member states' existing commitments to NATO were to be honoured. Common foreign and security policy is the province of the EU (as opposed to the EC), and decisions in this field are made by the European Council and the Council of the European Union.

The Treaty of Amsterdam, which entered into force on 1 May 1999, aimed to strengthen the concept of a Common Foreign and Security Policy within the Union and incorporated a process of common strategies to co-ordinate external relations with a third party. Accordingly, a High Representative was to be appointed to represent the EU at international meetings. In late March representatives of the Commission and NATO held a joint meeting, for the first time, to discuss the conflict in the southern Serbian republic of Kosovo (see below). In April a meeting of NATO heads of state and of government determined that its equipment, personnel and infrastructure would be available to any future EU military operation.

## CENTRAL AND EASTERN EUROPE

### ASSOCIATION COUNCILS:

EC–POLAND (Europe Agreement entered into force 1 February 1994); EC–HUNGARY (Europe Agreement entered into force 1 February 1994); EC–CZECH REPUBLIC (Europe Agreement entered into force 1 February 1995); EC–ROMANIA (Europe Agreement entered into force 1 February 1995); EC–BULGARIA (Europe Agreement entered into force 1 February 1995); EC–SLOVAKIA (Europe Agreement entered into force 1 February 1995); EC–ESTONIA (Europe Agreement entered into force 1 February 1998); EC–LATVIA (Europe Agreement entered into force 1 February 1998); EC–LITHUANIA (Europe Agreement entered into force 1 February 1998); EC–SLOVENIA (Europe Agreement entered into force 1 February 1999).

### CO-OPERATION COUNCIL:

EC–YUGOSLAVIA (Agreement entered into force 8 April 1983—suspended in 1991).

During the late 1980s the extensive political changes and reforms in eastern European countries led to a strengthening of links with the EC. Agreements on trade and economic co-operation were concluded with Hungary (1988), Poland (1989), the USSR (1989), Czechoslovakia (1988—on trade only—and 1990), Bulgaria (1990), the German Democratic Republic (GDR—1990) and Romania (1990). In July 1989 the EC was entrusted with the co-ordination of aid from member states of the Organisation for Economic Co-operation and Development (OECD) to Hungary and Poland ('Operation PHARE'—Poland/Hungary Aid for Restructuring of Economies): this programme was subsequently extended to include Albania, Bulgaria, the Czech Republic, Slovakia, Romania and the Baltic states. Community heads of government agreed in December 1989 to establish a European Bank for Reconstruction and Development (EBRD, q.v.), with participation by member states of the OECD and the Council for Mutual Economic Assistance, to promote investment in eastern Europe; the EBRD began operations in April 1991. In June 1995 the European Council agreed to provide total funding under the PHARE programme of ECU 6,693m. to central and eastern European countries in the period 1995–99.

In August 1991 the EC formally recognized the independence of the Baltic republics (Estonia, Latvia and Lithuania), and in December the PHARE programme was extended to them. Trade and co-operation agreements with the three Baltic states were signed in May 1992. In 1991 the EC established a programme providing technical assistance to the Commonwealth of Independent States (TACIS). In 1994 Mongolia also became eligible for assistance. The programme aimed to assist in the development of successful market economies and to foster pluralism and democracy, by providing expertise and training. In 1996–99 ECU 2,224m. was to be made available under the TACIS programme. The programme's proposed budget for 2000–2006 was €4,000m.

'Europe Agreements' between the EC and Czechoslovakia, Hungary and Poland were signed in December 1991, with the aim of establishing a free-trade area within 10 years and developing political co-operation (see above). In April 1994 Hungary and Poland submitted formal applications for EU membership. In June 1991 the EC established diplomatic relations with Albania, and in May 1992 an agreement on trade and co-operation was signed. Europe Agreements were initialled with Romania in October, and with Bulgaria in March 1993 (see above). In June the European Council approved measures to accelerate the opening of EC markets to goods from central and eastern European countries, with customs duties on many industrial items to be removed by the end of 1994. In September 1993 a co-operation agreement with Slovenia came into force. A Europe Agreement was signed in 1996 (see above) and Slovenia then formally applied for EU membership. The Interim Agreement, implementing the agreement signed in June, was due to come into force on 1 January 1997 and provided for the gradual establishment of a free-trade area during a transitional period of six years. In June 1996 the Commission decided that 2002 was the earliest probable date for the Czech Republic, Poland and Hungary to become members of the EU. This decision which also applies to Estonia and Slovenia, was reaffirmed in late 1999.

In February 1994 the EU Council of Ministers agreed to pursue closer economic and political relations with Ukraine, following an agreement by that country to renounce control of nuclear weapons on its territory. A partnership and co-operation agreement was signed by the two sides in June. In December EU ministers of finance approved a loan totalling ECU 85m., conditional on Ukraine's implementation of a strategy to close the Chernobyl (Chornobyl) nuclear power plant. An Interim Trade Agreement with Ukraine came into force in February 1996. In mid-1999 Ukraine's President announced that the Chernobyl plant would be closed in 2000 if the EBRD confirmed its decision to finance the completion of alternative power-generating facilities. A partnership and co-operation agreement was successfully concluded with Russia at the European Council meeting of heads of government in June 1994. An Interim Agreement on trade concessions was initiated in July 1995, after a six-month delay, owing to EU disapproval of Russia's violent repression of an independence movement in Chechnya. This agreement came into effect in February 1996, giving EU exporters improved access to the Russian market for specific products, and at the same time abolishing quantitative restrictions on some Russian exports to the EU. A partnership and co-operation agreement with Russia came into effect in December 1997. In November 1998 the Commission prepared food aid measures for Russia amounting to ECU 400m., in response to the financial crisis there. In mid-1999 the EU expressed its deep concern at the renewed fighting between Russian and Chechen armed forces in Chechnya, and urged Russia to seek a political solution to the conflict. Partnership and co-operation agreements were signed with Kazakhstan in January 1995, with Kyrgyzstan in February 1995, with Georgia, Armenia and Azerbaijan in January 1996 and with Uzbekistan in July 1996. Free-trade agreements with the Baltic states were finalized by the EU in July 1994, and came into effect on 1 January 1995. In June 1995 the EU concluded Europe Agreements with the three Baltic states (see above). In October Latvia submitted a formal application for EU membership. In December Estonia and Lithuania also submitted membership applications. A partnership agreement with Moldova entered into force in July 1998.

In May 1994 a Conference on Stability in Europe was convened in Paris to discuss the prevention of ethnic and territorial conflicts in central and eastern Europe. In particular, the conference sought to secure bilateral 'good-neighbour' accords between nine European countries that were regarded as potential future members of the EU (Bulgaria, the Czech Republic, Estonia, Hungary, Latvia, Lithuania, Poland, Romania and Slovakia). These countries, together with EU member states and other European countries (including Belarus, Moldova, Russia and Ukraine), signed a 'Stability Pact' in Paris in March 1995.

In March 1997 the Commission agreed to extend the PHARE programme in order to provide specific assistance to applicant countries in central and eastern Europe, by helping such countries to implement the reforms required to fulfil the criteria for EU membership. In July the Commission published a report, entitled 'Agenda 2000', which proposed that accession negotiations should commence with the Czech Republic, Estonia, Hungary, Poland and Slovenia, while it was recommended that discussions with Bulgaria, Latvia, Lithuania, Romania and Slovakia be deferred, owing to the need for further economic or democratic reform in those countries. The report acknowledged that it was also necessary for the EU to be restructured in order to ensure its successful operation following expansion, after the failure of negotiations leading to the Treaty of Amsterdam, approved in June, to reach agreement upon the issue of institutional reform. An Intergovernmental Conference was expected to be convened after 2000 to formulate plans for the required reform. Ministers of foreign affairs, meeting in Luxembourg in December, endorsed the 'Agenda 2000' proposals, and membership negotiations commenced on 31 March 1998. A European Conference took place in the same month, attended by representatives of applicant countries. Also in March, the Commission approved Accession Partnerships to support preparations for accession, by identifying priority areas where progress should be made and providing financial assistance. Accession negotiations at ministerial level commenced on 10 November with the first group of applicant countries. In late 1999 it was agreed to initiate accession negotiations with Bulgaria, Latvia, Lithuania, Romania and Slovakia in 2000.

Following the introduction on 1 July 1990 of monetary, economic and social union between the Federal Republic of Germany and the GDR, and the formal integration of the two countries on 3 October, Community legislation was introduced within the former GDR over a transitional period.

A co-operation agreement was signed with Yugoslavia in 1980 (but not ratified until April 1983), allowing tariff-free imports and Community loans. New financial protocols were signed in 1987 and 1991. However, EC aid was suspended in July 1991, following the declarations of independence by the Yugoslav republics of Croatia and Slovenia, and the subsequent outbreak of civil conflict. Efforts were made in the ensuing months by EC ministers of foreign affairs to negotiate a peaceful settlement between the Croatian and Serbian factions, and a team of EC observers was maintained in Yugoslavia from July onwards, to monitor successive cease-fire agreements. In October the EC proposed a plan for an association of independent states, to replace the Yugoslav federation: this was accepted by all the Yugoslav republics except Serbia, which demanded a redefining of boundaries to accommodate within Serbia all predominantly Serbian areas. In November the application of the Community's co-operation agreements with Yugoslavia was suspended (with exemptions for the republics which co-operated in the peace negotiations). In January 1992 the Community granted diplomatic recognition to the former Yugoslav republics of Croatia and Slovenia, and in April it recognized Bosnia and Herzegovina, while withholding recognition from Macedonia (owing to pressure from the Greek Government, which feared that the existence of an independent Macedonia would imply a claim on the Greek province of the same name). In May EC ambassadors were withdrawn from Belgrade, in protest at Serbia's support for aggression by Bosnian Serbs against other ethnic groups in Bosnia and Herzegovina, and in the same month the Community imposed a trade embargo on Serbia and Montenegro.

New proposals for a settlement of the Bosnian conflict, submitted by EC and UN mediators in 1993, were accepted by the Bosnian Croats and by the Bosnian Government in March, but rejected by the Bosnian Serbs. In June the European Council pledged more rigorous enforcement of sanctions against Serbia. In July, at UN/EC talks in Geneva, all three parties to the Bosnian war agreed on a plan to divide Bosnia and Herzegovina into three separate republics; however, the Bosnian Government rejected the proposals for the share of territory to be allotted to the Muslims.

In April 1994, following a request from EU ministers of foreign affairs, a Contact Group, consisting of France, Germany, the United Kingdom, the USA and Russia, was initiated to undertake peace negotiations. The following month ministers of foreign affairs of the USA, Russia and the EU (represented by five member states) jointly endorsed a proposal to divide Bosnia and Herzegovina in proportions of 49% to the Bosnian Serbs and 51% to the newly-established Federation of Muslims and Croats. The proposal was rejected by the Bosnian Serb assembly in July and had to be abandoned after the Muslim-Croat Federation withdrew its support subsequent to the Bosnian Serb vote. In July the EU formally assumed political control of Mostar, a town in southern Bosnia and Herzegovina, in order to restore the city's administrative infrastructure and secure peace.

Negotiations towards a trade and co-operation agreement with Croatia began in June 1995, but talks were suspended in early August, following Croatia's military offensive in the Krajina region, which was strongly criticized by the EU. Despite some criticism of US policy towards the former Yugoslavia, in September the EU supported US-led negotiations in Geneva to devise a plan to end the conflict in Bosnia and Herzegovina. The plan closely resembled the previous proposals of the Contact Group: two self-governing entities were to be created within Bosnia and Herzegovina, with 51% of territory being allocated to the Muslim-Croat Federation, and 49% to Bosnian Serbs. The proposals were finally agreed after negotiations in Dayton, USA, in November 1995, and an accord was signed in Paris in December. In September EU ministers endorsed a plan to provide financial aid valued at some US $2,000m. to Bosnia and Herzegovina and other parts of the former Yugoslavia for post-war reconstruction. In January 1996 the EU announced its intention to recognize Yugoslavia (Serbia and Montenegro), despite the opposition of the USA. In September 1998 EU observers criticized the management of a general election in Bosnia and Herzegovina. In November the Commission proposed exceptional assistance of ECU 60m. to aid growth and employment in that country. During 1996–99 the EU allocated ECU 1,000m. for the repatriation of refugees, restructuring the economy and technical assistance, in addition to ECU 1,000m. in humanitarian aid provided since the beginning of the conflict in the former Yugoslavia.

In December 1993 six member states of the EU formally recognized the former Yugoslav republic of Macedonia (FYRM) as an independent state, but in February 1994 Greece imposed a commercial embargo against the FYRM, on the grounds that the use of the name and symbols (e.g. on the state flag) of 'Macedonia' was a threat to Greek national security. In March, however, ministers of foreign affairs of the EU decided that the embargo was in contravention of EU law, and in April the Commission commenced legal proceedings in the European Court of Justice against Greece. In September 1995 Greece and the FYRM began a process of normalizing relations, after the FYRM agreed to change the design of its state flag. In October Greece ended its economic blockade of the FYRM, and in November the Council of the European Union authorized the Commission to begin negotiating a trade and co-operation agreement with the FYRM, which entered into force in January 1998.

In March 1997 the EU sent two advisory delegations to Albania to help to restore order after violent unrest and political instability erupted in that country. A request by the Albanian Government for the deployment of EU peace-keeping troops was refused, but it was announced in early April that the EU was to provide humanitarian aid of some ECU 2m., to be used for emergency relief in Albania.

In 1998 the escalation of violence in Kosovo and Metohija, a southern Serbian province of Yugoslavia, between Serbs and the ethnic Albanian majority, prompted the imposition of sanctions by EU ministers of foreign affairs. In March ministers agreed to impose an arms embargo, to halt export credit guarantees to Yugoslavia and to restrict visas for Serbian officials. A ban on new investment in the region was imposed in June. In the same month military observers from the EU, Russia and the USA were deployed to Kosovo. In July an EU diplomatic delegation assessed the impact of the latest outbreak of violence in the region. In September the EU agreed to deny JAT, the Yugoslav airline, landing rights in EU countries. In October the Yugoslav Government allowed a team of international experts to investigate atrocities in the region, under an EU mandate. Several EU countries participated in the NATO military offensive against Yugoslavia, which was initiated in March 1999 owing to the continued repression of ethnic Albanians in Kosovo by Serbian forces. In early April EU ministers of foreign affairs formally endorsed NATO's objectives. Later in that month ministers approved a new series of punitive measures, including an embargo on the sale or supply of petroleum to the Yugoslav authorities and an extension of a travel ban on Serbian official and business executives. At the same time, ministers resolved to formulate a new plan to consolidate peace, security and economic stability in the countries of South-East Europe. EU humanitarian assistance was extended to provide relief for the substantial numbers of refugees who fled Kosovo amid the escalating violence, in particular to assist the Governments of Albania and the FYRM, while several countries agreed to provide asylum for those most at risk. By early May an estimated 25,000 refugees had been transported from camps in the FYRM, of whom more than 9,000 had been given shelter in Germany. In June EU foreign ministers approved the withdrawal of €150m. from unused budget resources in order to fund reconstruction in Kosovo and assist the return of refugees to the province. On 28 July the first donor conference for Kosovo was held, under the auspices of the Commission and the World Bank. It was reported that the EU had already provided aid worth €378m. through its 'Echo' humanitarian assistance programme; and that the Commission planned to implement a €500m.-aid programme for Kosovo in 2000. The Commission was to seek the approval of the member states for the provision, in the form of loans and grants, of €380m. in balance-of-payments support to Bulgaria, Romania and the FYRM, in order to alleviate economic difficulties resulting from the crisis in Kosovo.

On 31 July 1999 the USA, the EU and Russia launched a so-called 'stability pact' for the countries of South-East Europe. For its part, the EU had proposed to offer customized stabilization and association agreements to Albania, Bosnia, Croatia, Macedonia and Yugoslavia, provided that they fulfilled certain conditions. In September EU foreign ministers agreed to ease sanctions in force against Kosovo and Montenegro. In October the EU began to implement an 'Energy for Democracy' initiative, with the objective of supplying some €5m.-worth of heating oil to Serbian towns controlled by groups in opposition to the Yugoslav President Slobodan Milošević. In early December, after a lengthy delay, the first delivery of oil was made to the town of Nis, regarded as a stronghold of the Serbian opposition.

### OTHER EUROPEAN COUNTRIES

The members of the European Free Trade Association (EFTA) concluded bilateral free trade agreements with the EEC and the ECSC during the 1970s. On 1 January 1984 the last tariff barriers were eliminated, thus establishing full free trade for industrial products between the Community and EFTA members. Some EFTA members subsequently applied for membership of the EC: Austria in 1989, Sweden in 1991, and Finland, Switzerland and Norway in 1992. Formal negotiations on the creation of a 'European Economic Area' (EEA), a single market for goods, services, capital and labour among EC and EFTA members, began in June 1990, and were concluded in October 1991. The agreement was signed in May 1992 (after a delay caused by a ruling of the Court of Justice of the EC that a proposed joint EC-EFTA court, for adjudication in disputes, was incompatible with the Treaty of Rome; EFTA members then agreed to concede jurisdiction to the Court of Justice on cases of competition involving both EC and EFTA members, and to establish a special joint committee for other disputes). In a referendum in December Swiss voters rejected ratification of the agreement, and the remaining 18 countries signed an adjustment protocol in March 1993, allowing the EEA to be established without Switzerland (which was to have observer status). The EEA entered into force on 1 January 1994. Formal negotiations on the accession to the EU of Austria, Finland and Sweden began on 1 February, and those on Norway's membership started on 1 April. Negotiations were concluded with Austria, Finland and Sweden on 1 March 1994, and with Norway on 16 March, having been delayed by issues concerning the fisheries sector. Heads of government of the four countries signed treaties of accession to the EU in June, which were to come into effect from 1995, subject to approval by a national referendum in each country. Accession to the EU was endorsed by the electorates of Austria, Finland and Sweden in June, October and November respectively. Norway's accession was rejected by a referendum conducted at the end of November. Austria, Finland and Sweden became members of the EU on 1 January 1995. Liechtenstein, which became a full member of EFTA in September 1991, joined the EEA on 1 May 1995. Negotiations conducted with Switzerland since 1992 on the formulation of a new bilateral economic arrangement proceeded slowly. The main obstacles to an agreement concerned Switzerland's work permit quotas for EU citizens, and the weight limit on trucks passing through its territory. In December 1996 it was reported that Switzerland had agreed to phase out the use of work permit quotas within six years of a treaty being signed. In early December 1998 political agreement was reached with Switzerland to abolish the weight limit and instead impose road-haulage charges on trucks weighing 40 metric tons or more. Later in that month an interim trade agreement was concluded.

## THE MIDDLE EAST AND THE MEDITERRANEAN

### ASSOCIATION COUNCILS:

EC–GREECE (Agreement signed in 1961—joined the EC in 1972); EC–TURKEY (Agreement entered into force 1 December 1964); EC–MALTA (Agreement entered into force 1 April 1971); EC–CYPRUS (Agreement entered into force 1 June 1973); EC–ISRAEL (Agreement signed in November 1995); EC–MOROCCO (Agreement signed in February 1996); EC–JORDAN (Agreement signed in November 1997).

### CO-OPERATION COUNCILS:

EC–ALGERIA (Agreement entered into force 1 November 1978); EC–MOROCCO (Agreement entered into force 1 November 1978—succeeding an Association Agreement signed in March 1969); EC–TUNISIA (Agreement entered into force 1 November 1978—succeeding an Association Agreement signed in March 1969); EC–EGYPT (Agreement entered into force 1 November 1978); EC–JORDAN (Agreement entered into force 1 November 1978); EC–SYRIA (Agreement entered into force 1 November 1978); EC–LEBANON (Agreement entered into force 1 November 1978); EC–ISRAEL (Agreement entered into force 1 November 1978); EC–GULF STATES (Agreement signed in June 1988); EC–YEMEN (Agreement negotiated with the Yemen Arab Republic in 1984; extended agreement to cover the Republic of Yemen entered into force 1 February 1995; new draft agreement signed in November 1998).

The association agreements signed with Greece, Turkey, Malta and Cyprus established free access to the Community market for most industrial products and tariff reductions for most agricultural products. Annexed were financial protocols under which the Community was to provide concessional finance. Aid to Turkey was suspended, owing to human rights violations following the coup in 1980. In 1987 Turkey applied for membership of the Community. In 1989 the European Commission stated that, for formal negotiations on Turkish membership to take place it would be necessary for Turkey to restructure its economy, improve its observance of human rights, and harmonize its relations with Greece. Negotiations in early 1995 to conclude a customs union agreement with Turkey were obstructed by the opposition of Greece. In early March, however, Greece removed its veto on the customs union, having received assurance on the accession of Cyprus to the EU. Ratification of the agreement by the European Parliament was delayed until mid-December, owing to concern over issues of human rights, in particular the policies of the Turkish Government towards the Kurdish population in Turkey. Under the agreement, Turkey was to receive some ECU 1,400m. in grants and loans in 1995–99. In July 1990 Cyprus and Malta made formal applications to join the Community. In June 1993 the European Commission approved the eligibility of both countries to join the community, but in November 1996 Malta's new Government announced its intention to 'freeze' its application. In September 1998, following the return to power of a Nationalist government, Malta renewed its membership application. In February 1999 the Commission recommended the initiation of membership negotiations. In 1996 and 1997 the EU, along with the USA, took part in extensive diplomatic activity to facilitate Cyprus' accession as a single entity. In March 1997 Turkey received assurances that its application for membership would be considered on equal terms with that of any other country. However, in July the Commission published 'Agenda 2000', a report which recommended that accession negotiations should begin with the (Greek) Cypriot Government, while talks with Turkey were to be postponed indefinitely. In December ministers of foreign affairs, meeting in Luxembourg, endorsed the report's proposals. Detailed accession talks with Cyprus began on 10 November 1998. From August 1999, when a devastating earthquake struck north-western Turkey, a *rapprochement* began to take place between Greece and Turkey. Greece lifted its longstanding veto on disbursements of aid to Turkey and the EU made a loan of €600m. to the Turkish government to assist reconstruction. This improvement in relations culminated, at the Helsinki summit meeting of EU leaders in December, in a formal invitation to Turkey to present its candidacy for EU membership. A trade agreement with Andorra entered into force on 1 January 1991, establishing a customs union for industrial products, and allowing duty-free access to the EC for certain Andorran agricultural products. Negotiations on a similar agreement with San Marino were concluded in December 1991.

Co-operation agreements with Israel, the Maghreb countries (Algeria, Morocco and Tunisia) and the Mashreq countries (Egypt, Jordan, Lebanon and Syria) covered free access to the Community market for industrial products, customs preferences for certain agricultural products, and financial aid in the form of grants and loans from the European Investment Bank. The co-operation agreement negotiated with the Republic of Yemen was non-preferential. In November 1998 a new draft accord, incorporating commitments to democratic principles and a respect for human rights, was signed. In July 1987 Morocco applied to join the Community, but its application was rejected on the grounds that it is not a European country. An association agreement signed with Tunisia, which entered into force in March 1998, aimed to eliminate duties and other trade barriers on most products over a transitional 12-year period. In the short term the agreement provided for an increase in quotas for certain agricultural exports from Tunisia to the EU. In early 1998 EU delegations visited Algeria to express concern at the escalation of violence in that country. In October the EU agreed to commence negotiations with the Algerian Government, with the aim of concluding an association agreement and co-operating to combat terrorism. Preliminary negotiations towards association agreements have also taken place with Egypt and Syria, although formal authorization to conclude an agreement with Syria was only granted by EU heads of government in December 1997.

Three protocols were negotiated in 1987 on assistance to Israel for the period 1987–91; however, approval of these protocols was delayed by the European Parliament until October 1988, as a protest against Israel's response to unrest in the occupied territories of the West Bank and the Gaza Strip. In January 1989 the Community and Israel eliminated the last tariff barriers to full free trade for industrial products. An association agreement signed in 1995 established more extensive political dialogue between the two parties and provided trade concessions. In September 1993, following the signing of the Israeli-Palestine Liberation Organization (PLO) peace agreement, the EC committed ECU 33m. in immediate humanitarian assistance. In addition, a five-year assistance programme for the period 1994–98 was proposed, which was to consist of ECU 500m. in grants and loans to improve the economic and social infrastructure in the Occupied Territories. In October 1996 ministers of foreign affairs agreed to appoint a special envoy to the Middle East in order to promote a peaceful settlement. A Euro-Mediterranean Interim Association Agreement on Trade and Co-operation was signed with the PLO in January 1997 and entered into force in July. The agreement confirmed existing trade concessions offered to the Palestinians since 1986 and provided for free trade to be introduced during an initial five-year period. During 1998 diplomatic relations between Israel and the EU deteriorated. In May the Israeli Prime Minister insisted that any EU role in the Middle East peace process would be unacceptable if the European Commission proceeded with a threat to ban disputed agricultural products from being imported into the EU. Additionally, the European Commission was critical of Israel's perceived obstruction of Palestinian trade. In April 1998 the EU and the Palestinian National Authority (PNA) signed a security co-operation agreement, which provided for regular meetings to promote joint efforts on security issues, in particular in combating terrorism. In March 1999 EU heads of state and government urged Israel to fulfil within one year the 'unqualified Palestinian right' to independence. Israel was strongly critical of what it perceived as an ultimatum and stated that the EU had reduced its scope as a mediator in the Middle East peace process. In April the European Parliament demanded an investigation into the handling of Commission funds to Palestinian-controlled areas of the West Bank and Gaza. At that time the EU was reported to be the largest donor to the PNA.

Talks were held with Iran in April 1992 on the establishment of a co-operation accord. In December the Council of Ministers recommended that a 'critical dialogue' be undertaken with Iran, owing to the country's significance to regional security. In April 1997 the 'critical dialogue' was suspended and ambassadors were recalled from Iran, following a German court ruling that found the Iranian authorities responsible for ordering the murder of four Kurdish dissidents in Berlin in 1992. Later that month ministers of foreign affairs resolved to restore diplomatic relations with Iran, in order to protect the strong trading partnership. However, diplomatic relations were not resumed until November, as EU ministers reversed their decision to return diplomats to Teheran, owing to the Iranian Government's reluctance to readmit the German and Dutch ambassadors. In February 1998 EU ministers of foreign affairs removed the ban on high-level contacts with Iran, in an attempt to strengthen dialogue with that country. In August 1999 the Iranian ministry of foreign affairs acknowledged an improvement in EU-Iranian relations since the election of Muhammad Khatami as President.

In June 1995 the European Council endorsed a proposal by the Commission to reform and strengthen the Mediterranean policy of the EU. The initiative envisaged the establishment of a Euro-Mediterranean Economic Area (EMEA) by 2010, preceded by a gradual liberalization of trade within the region. The Council approved financial support amounting to ECU 4,685.5m. for the Maghreb and Mashreq agreement countries, as well as for Israel (including the Palestinian Territories), Cyprus, Malta, Turkey and Libya, for the period 1995–99. In November 1995 representatives of these countries (with the exception of Libya) and the EU finalized agreement on the EMEA at a conference held in Barcelona, Spain. In April 1997 a second Euro-Mediterranean Conference of ministers of foreign affairs was held in Malta. In September 1998 the Commission proposed measures to extend the single market to the Mediterranean countries and sought to formulate common rules on customs and taxation, free movement of goods, public procurement, intellectual property, financial services, data protection and accounting.

An agreement between the EC and the countries of the Gulf Co-operation Council (GCC) provided for co-operation in industry, energy, technology and other fields. Negotiations on a full free-trade pact began in October 1990, but it was expected that any agreement would involve transition periods of some 12 years for the reduction of European tariffs on 'sensitive products' (i.e. petrochemicals).

Contacts with the Arab world in general take place within the framework of the 'Euro-Arab Dialogue', established in 1973 to provide a forum for discussion of economic issues through working groups on specific topics. Following a decision in 1989 to reactivate the Dialogue, meetings were suspended in 1990 as a result of Iraq's invasion of Kuwait. In April 1992 senior EC and Arab officials agreed to resume the process.

### LATIN AMERICA

A non-preferential trade agreement was signed with Uruguay in 1974, and economic and commercial co-operation agreements with Mexico in 1975 and Brazil in 1980. A five-year co-operation agreement with the members of the Central American Common Market and with Panama entered into force in 1987, as did a similar agreement with the member countries of the Andean Group (now the Andean Community). Co-operation agreements were signed with Argentina and Chile in 1990, and in that year tariff preferences were approved for Bolivia, Colombia, Ecuador and Peru, in support of those countries' efforts to combat drugs-trafficking. In May 1992 an interinstitutional co-operation agreement was signed with the Southern Common Market (Mercosur); in June the EC and the member states of the Andean Group (Bolivia, Colombia, Ecuador, Peru and Venezuela) initialled a new co-operation agreement, which was to broaden the scope of economic and development co-operation and enhance trade relations, and a new co-operation agreement was signed with Brazil. In April 1997 the EU extended further trade benefits to the countries of the Andean Community. In July 1993 the EC introduced a tariff regime to limit the import of bananas from Latin America, in order to protect the banana-producing countries of the ACP group, linked to the EC by the Lomé Convention (see below). In June 1995 a Commission communication advocated greater economic co-operation with Cuba. This policy was strongly supported by a resolution of the European Parliament in January 1996, but was criticized by the US Government, which continued to maintain an economic embargo against Cuba (see Canada and the USA, below). In July 1997 the EU and Mexico concluded a co-operation agreement and an interim agreement on trade. The accords were signed in December. In November 1998 formal negotiations were commenced with Mexico, towards a more extensive free-trade agreement, which was to cover economic co-operation, drugs-trafficking and human rights issues. In November 1999 the EU and Mexico concluded a free-trade agreement which, on implementation, will lead to the removal of all tariffs on bilateral trade in industrial products by 2007.

In April 1994 ministers of foreign affairs of the EU and the Rio Group (q.v.) held their fourth meeting since formal dialogue was initiated in 1990. A final declaration issuing from the meeting, in São Paulo, Brazil, consisted of a joint commitment to protect human rights and to promote social development and the principles of free trade. The Rio Group ministers, however, rejected any imposition of social or environmental conditional terms on trading agreements.

In late December 1994 the EU and Mercosur signed a joint declaration that aimed to promote trade liberalization and greater political co-operation. In September 1995, at a meeting in Montevideo, Uruguay, a framework agreement on the establishment of a free-trade regime between the two organizations was initialled. The agreement was formally signed in December. In July 1998 the Commission voted to commence negotiations towards an inter-regional agreement with Mercosur and Chile, which would strengthen existing co-operation agreements. However, Mercosur insisted that, for a free-trade agreement to be concluded, progress would have to be made towards the elimination of EU agricultural subsidies.

### ASIA AND AUSTRALASIA

**CO-OPERATION COUNCIL:**

EC–VIET NAM (Agreement entered into force 1 June 1996).

Non-preferential co-operation agreements were signed with Bangladesh, India, Pakistan and Sri Lanka between 1973 and 1986. A trade agreement was signed with the People's Republic of China in 1978, and renewed in May 1985. A co-operation agreement was signed with the countries of the Association of South East Asian Nations (ASEAN) in 1980. In October 1992 the EC and ASEAN reached a further agreement on co-operation between the two groupings in spite of Portugal's threat to veto the agreement in protest at the killing of demonstrators in East Timor by Indonesian security forces in November 1991. (See p. 130 for the EU's relations with ASEAN.) In June 1989, following the violent repression of the Chinese pro-democracy movement by the Chinese Government, the EC imposed economic sanctions on China. In October 1990 it was decided that relations with China should be 'progressively normalized'. In November 1994 a China-Europe International Business School was initiated in Shanghai. The EU has supported China's increased involvement in the international community and, in particular, its application for membership of the WTO. In October 1997 senior EU representatives signed a memorandum of understanding with China on future co-operation. The first EU-China meeting of heads of government was convened in April 1998. In November the President of the Commission made an official visit to China and urged that country to remove trade restrictions imposed on European products. In the same month the EU and Hong Kong signed a co-operation agreement to combat drugs-trafficking and copyright piracy. The agreement was the first international accord to be signed by the territory since its reversion to Chinese sovereignty in July 1997. At the second Asia-Europe meeting (ASEM, see below) of foreign ministers in March 1999 criticism of China's human rights record was rejected by the Chinese minister of foreign affairs. In April negotiations between the EU and China regarding China's admission to the WTO were abandoned after the accidental bombing by NATO forces of the Chinese embassy in Belgrade, Yugoslavia. Negotiations resumed in January 2000. The second EU-China summit meeting was held in December 1999, in Beijing. At the meeting, among other things, EU leaders urged the Chinese Government to abandon its use of capital punishment. In October 1997 the EU and the Republic of Korea signed an agreement regarding a reciprocal opening of markets for telecommunications equipment, following a protracted dispute, which had led the EU to lodge a complaint with the WTO. In September 1997, however, the Commission submitted a further complaint to the WTO, accusing the Republic of Korea of tax discrimination against European spirits exporters. In the same month the EU joined the Korean Peninsular Energy Development Organization (KEDO), an initiative to increase nuclear safety and reduce the risk of nuclear proliferation from the energy programme of the Democratic People's Republic of Korea (DPRK). In September 1999, for the first time ever, ministerial-level discussions took place between the EU and the DPRK at the United Nations General Assembly. In June 1992 the EC signed trade and co-operation agreements with Mongolia and Macau, with respect for democracy and human rights forming the basis of envisaged co-operation. A co-operation accord was formally signed with Viet Nam in July 1995, under which the EU agreed to increase quotas for Vietnamese textile products, to support the country's efforts to join the WTO and to provide aid for environmental and public management projects. The agreement, which entered into force on 1 June 1996, incorporated a commitment by Viet Nam to guarantee human rights and a procedure for the gradual repatriation of some 40,000 Vietnamese refugees from Germany, who had lost their legal status after German reunification. A permanent EU mission to Viet Nam was established in February 1996. In July 1996 a European Business Information Centre was opened in Malaysia, with the object of promoting trade. In October the EU imposed strict limits on entry visas for Myanmar officials, because of Myanmar's refusal to allow the Commission to send a mission to investigate allegations of forced labour. In March 1997 EU ministers of foreign affairs agreed to revoke Myanmar's special trade privileges under the Generalized System of Preferences (GSP). In November a meeting of EU and ASEAN officials was postponed, owing to Myanmar's insistence (then as a full member of the ASEAN grouping) that it attend with full observer status. With no agreement having been concluded, the meeting was again postponed in July 1998 and in January 1999. In early 2000 the EU continued to impose the suspension of humanitarian aid and an arms embargo against Myanmar. Non-preferential co-operation agreements were signed with Laos and Cambodia in April 1997. The agreement with Laos entered into force on 1 December; the agreement with Cambodia was postponed owing to adverse political developments in that country. In 1998 the EU provided financial assistance to support preparations for a general election in Cambodia, and dispatched observers to monitor the election, which was held in July.

Textiles exports by Asian countries have caused concern in the EU, owing to the depressed state of its textiles industry. In 1982 bilateral negotiations were held under the Multi-fibre Arrangement (MFA, see WTO) with Asian producers, notably Hong Kong, the Republic of Korea and Macau. Agreements were eventually reached involving reductions in clothing quotas and 'anti-surge' clauses to prevent flooding of European markets. In 1986 new bilateral negotiations were held and agreements were reached with the principal Asian textile exporters, for the period 1987–91 (later extended to December 1993, when the 'Uruguay Round' of GATT negotiations was finally concluded): in most cases a slight increase in quotas was permitted. Under the conclusions of the Uruguay Round, the MFA was to be progressively eliminated over a 10-year period. In January 1995 bilateral textiles agreements, signed by the EU with India, Pakistan and the People's Republic of China, specified certain trade liberalization measures to be undertaken, including an increase of China's silk export quota to 38,000 metric tons and a removal of trade barriers on small-business and handloom textile products from India, while including commitments from the Asian countries for greater efforts to combat textile and design fraud. In October 1997 the EU agreed to increase Viet Nam's textile quotas by some 30%, in exchange for improved market access for EU exports. The agreement was ratified in September 1998. In March 1998 the European Commission, for the third time, imposed provisional six-month duties on unbleached cotton from the People's Republic of China, Egypt, India, Indonesia, Pakistan and Turkey, in response to claims by European textile manufacturers that those countries were selling products at lower prices in Europe than in their domestic markets. In July the Commission proposed that these punitive 'anti-dumping' duties be imposed for a period of at least five years (although Turkey was to be excluded from the ruling). However, the Commission's proposal was rejected by EU ministers of foreign affairs in October.

The first Asia-Europe meeting (ASEM) was held in March 1996 in Bangkok, Thailand. A wide range of political, economic and co-operation issues was discussed by representatives of the EU member countries and 10 east Asian countries. It was agreed to launch an Asia-Europe Partnership for Greater Growth, in order to expand trade, investment and technology transfer. An Asia-Business Forum was to be formed, as well as an Asia-Europe Foundation in Singapore to promote educational and cultural exchanges. The EU-Korea Framework Agreement was initialled, and Malaysia was appointed to oversee the building of an integrated Asian electric rail network to link Singapore to Europe via China. Issues of human and labour rights threatened to provoke confrontation, but this was averted by the topics being relegated to a single sentence in the final statement. The second ASEM summit, convened in the United Kingdom in April 1998, was dominated by economic and financial concerns, and both sides' declared intention to prevent a return to protectionist trading policies. A special statement, issued at the end of the meeting, identified the need for economic reform in individual countries and for a reinforcement of international financial institutions. The meeting established an ASEM Trust Fund, under the auspices of the World Bank, to alleviate the social impact of the financial crisis. Other initiatives adopted by ASEM were an Asia-Europe Co-operation Framework to co-ordinate political, economic and financial co-operation, a Trade Facilitation Action Plan, and an Investment Promotion Action Plan, which incorporated a new Investment Experts Group. The meeting resolved to promote efforts to strengthen relations in all areas, and to establish a series of working bodies to promote specific areas of co-operation; however it was decided not to establish a permanent secretariat for the ASEM arrangement. ASEM was to reconvene in the Republic of Korea in 2000.

Numerous discussions have been held since 1981 on the Community's increasing trade deficit with Japan, and on the failure of the Japanese market to accept more European exports. In July 1991 the heads of government of Japan and of the EC signed a joint declaration on closer co-operation in both economic and political matters. In the same month an agreement was reached on limiting exports of Japanese cars to the EC until the end of 1999. The agreement did not include vehicles produced in Europe by Japanese companies. In October 1995 the EU secured an agreement to establish a WTO dispute panel to consider Japan's trade restrictions on alcohol, which were subsequently judged to discriminate against European manufacturers of alcoholic spirits. Japan's restrictive trading practices in several sectors, and its treatment of foreign shipping companies using Japanese ports, was a source of disagreement between the EU and Japan during much of 1996. However, the fifth annual meeting between the EU and Japan, held in Tokyo in September, appeared to facilitate more constructive dialogue. The European office of the EU-Japan Industrial Co-operation Centre was opened in Brussels in June 1996; the Centre, which was established in 1987 as a joint venture between the Japanese Government and the European Commission, sought to boost industrial co-operation between the EU and Japan and foster business contacts between companies and universities. The Vulcanus programme, launched in June 1995 by the European Commission and the Japanese Ministry of International Trade and Industry, aims to foster links with Japan through the hosting of Japanese advanced students by European companies.

Regular consultations are held with Australia at ministerial level. In January 1996 the Commission proposed a framework agreement to formalize the EU's trade and political relationship with Australia. However, in September negotiations were suspended, following the Australian Government's objections to the human rights clause contained in all EU international agreements. In June 1997 a joint declaration was signed, committing both sides to greater political, cultural and economic co-operation. Despite intensive negotiations between the EU and the New Zealand Government in 1996, no conclusion was reached regarding import duties. In March 1997 New Zealand took the case to the WTO.

## CANADA AND THE USA

A framework agreement for commercial and economic co-operation between the Community and Canada was signed in Ottawa in 1976. It was superseded in 1990 by a Declaration on EC-Canada Relations. In 1995 relations with Canada were strained as a result of a dispute regarding fishing rights in the north-west Atlantic Ocean. An agreement on a new division of quotas between EU and Canadian fishermen was concluded in April (see above under Fisheries). In February 1996 the Commission proposed closer ties with Canada, and an action plan including early warning to avoid trade disputes, elimination of trade barriers, and promotion of business contacts. An action plan and joint political declaration were signed in December. In 1996 and 1997 negotiations took place over the use of leg-hold traps in the Canadian hunting and fur industry. In July 1997 an agreement was reached, limiting their use.

A number of specific agreements have been concluded between the Community and the USA: a co-operation agreement on the peaceful use of atomic energy entered into force in 1959, and agreements on environmental matters and on fisheries came into force in 1974 and 1984 respectively. Additional agreements provide for co-operation in other fields of scientific research and development, while bilateral contacts take place in many areas not covered by a formal agreement.

The USA has frequently criticized the Common Agricultural Policy, which it sees as creating unfair competition for American exports by its system of export refunds and preferential agreements. A similar criticism has been levelled at Community subsidies to the steel industry. In October 1985 and September 1986 agreements were reached on Community exports of steel to the USA until September 1989 (subsequently extended until March 1992). In January 1993 the USA announced the imposition of substantial duties on imports of steel from 19 countries, including seven EC member states, as an 'anti-dumping' measure. Meanwhile, a further trade dispute emerged between the EC and the USA regarding the liberalization of public procurement of services (e.g. telecommunications, transport and power). In early December the EC and the USA undertook intensive trade negotiations, which facilitated the conclusion of GATT's Uruguay Round of talks by the deadline of 15 December.

A 'Transatlantic Declaration' on EC-US relations was agreed in November 1990: the two parties agreed to consult each other on important matters of common interest, and to increase formal contacts. A new Trans-Atlantic Agenda for EU-US relations was signed by the US President and the Presidents of the European Commission and European Council at a meeting in Madrid, Spain, in December 1995. In October 1996 EU ministers of foreign affairs agreed to pursue in the WTO a complaint regarding the effects on European businesses of the USA's trade embargo against Cuba, formulated in the Helms-Burton Act. In April 1997 the EU and the USA approved a temporary resolution of the Helms-Burton dispute, whereby the US Administration was to limit the application of sanctions in return for a formal suspension of the WTO case. In mid-1996 the US Congress had adopted legislation imposing an additional trade embargo (threatening sanctions against any foreign company investing more than US $40m. in energy projects in a number of prescribed states, including Iran and Libya), the presence of which further complicated the EU-US debate in September 1997, when a French petroleum company, Total, provoked US anger, owing to its proposed investment in an Iranian natural gas project. In May 1998 an EU-USA summit meeting reached agreement on a 'Trans-Atlantic Economic Parternship' (TEP), to remove technical trade barriers, eliminate industrial tariffs, establish a free-trade area in services, and further liberalize measures relating to government procurement, intellectual property and investment. The agricultural and audio-visual sectors were to be excluded from the agreement. Initial objections from France were overcome when the EU and the USA reached a resolution to the dispute on sanctions legislation. The USA agreed to exempt European companies from the trade embargo on Iran and Libya, and to seek congressional approval for an indefinite waiver for the Helms-Burton Act, thereby removing the threat of sanctions from Total. The EU had allowed the WTO case to lapse in April, but it warned that a new WTO panel would be established if the USA took action against European companies trading with Cuba. In return, the EU agreed to increase co-operation in combating terrorism and the proliferation of weapons of mass destruction and to discourage investment in expropriated property. Following approval by the Council in November, it was agreed that implementation of the TEP would begin in advance of an EU-USA summit meeting in December.

In July 1997 the EU became involved in intensive negotiations with the US aircraft company, Boeing, over fears that its planned merger with McDonnell Douglas would harm European interests. In late July the EU approved the merger, after Boeing accepted concessions including an agreement to dispense with exclusivity clauses for 20-year supply contracts and to maintain McDonnell Douglas as a separate company for a period of 10 years. In June the EU and the USA agreed to introduce a mutual recognition agreement, which was to enable goods (including medicines, pharmaceutical products, telecommunications equipment and electrical apparatus) undergoing tests in Europe to be marketed in the USA or Canada without the need for further testing. In May 1997 the WTO upheld a US complaint against the EU's ban on imports of hormone-treated beef, which had led to a retaliatory US ban on meat imports from the EU. Negotiations took place in 1998 regarding the enforcement of European meat hygiene regulations (see under Agriculture), the reform of the EU's banana import regime (see Lomé Convention, below) and the application of a data protection law, which empowers national regulators to stop the transfer of personal information to countries judged to have inadequate data protection arrangements (including the USA). In July the Commission submitted a complaint to the WTO regarding tax exemptions granted to US companies exporting goods via subsidiaries established in tax-free countries (foreign sales corporations). Trading relations between the USA and EU deteriorated in early 1999, with regard to the disputes over the banana import regime, the EU ban on US beef imports, and new directives on acceptable levels of noise from commercial aircraft.

## GENERALIZED PREFERENCES

In July 1971 the Community introduced a system of generalized tariff preferences (GSP) in favour of developing countries, ensuring duty-free entry to the EC of all otherwise dutiable manufactured and semi-manufactured industrial products, including textiles—but subject in certain circumstances to preferential limits. Preferences, usually in the form of a tariff reduction, are also offered on some agricultural products. In 1980 the Council agreed to the extension of the scheme for a second decade (1981–90): at the same time it adopted an operational framework for industrial products, which gives individual preferential limits based on the degree of competitiveness of the developing country concerned. From the end of 1990 an interim scheme was in operation, pending the introduction of a revised scheme based on the outcome of the 'Uruguay Round' of GATT negotiations on international trade (which were finally concluded in December 1993). Since 1977 the Community has progressively liberalized GSP access for the least-developed countries by according them duty-free entry on all products and by exempting them from virtually all preferential limits. In 1992–93 the GSP was extended to Albania, the Baltic states, the CIS and Georgia; in September 1994 it was extended to South Africa.

In December 1994 the European Council adopted a revised GSP to operate during 1995–98. It provided additional trade benefits to encourage the introduction by governments of environmentally sound policies and of internationally-recognized labour standards. Conversely, a country's preferential entitlement could be withdrawn, for example, if it undertook forced labour. Under the new scheme preferential tariffs amounted to 85% of the common customs duty for very sensitive products (for example, most textile products), and 70% or 35% for products classified as sensitive (for example, chemicals, electrical goods). The common customs duty was suspended for non-sensitive products (for example, paper, books, cosmetics). In accordance with the EU's foreign policy objective of focusing on the development of the world's poorest countries, duties were eliminated in their entirety for 49 least-developed countries. Duties were also suspended for a further five Latin American countries, conditional on the implementation of campaigns against the production and trade of illegal drugs.

In September 1998 the Commission proposed a new GSP for 1999–2001, which largely extended the existing scheme unchanged.

## AID TO DEVELOPING AND NON-EU COUNTRIES

The main channels for Community aid to developing countries are the Lomé Convention (see below) and the Mediterranean Financial Protocols, but technical and financial aid, and assistance for refugees, training, trade promotion and co-operation in industry, energy, science and technology is also provided to about 30 countries in Asia and Latin America. The EC International Investment Partners facility, established in 1988, promotes private-sector investment in Asian, Latin American and Mediterranean countries, especially in the form of joint ventures. The European Community Humanitarian Office (ECHO) was established in 1991 with a mandate to co-ordinate emergency aid provided by the Community and became fully operational in early 1993. ECHO finances operations conducted by non-governmental organizations and international agencies, with which it works in partnership. In 1997 the EU provided humanitarian aid worth ECU 438m. The main areas of operation were Burundi, the Democratic Republic of the Congo, the Republic of the Congo, Rwanda and Tanzania (ECU 172m.) and the former Yugoslavia (ECU 132m., of which 84% was used for operations in Bosnia and Herzegovina). In June 1995 EU finance ministers agreed to contribute ECU 500m. during 1996–99 to fund the European Reconstruction and Development Programme for South Africa. In April 1999 ECHO signed a framework partnership agreement with the International Federation of Red Cross and Red Crescent Societies to promote effective co-operation in the provision of humanitarian assistance.

## THE LOMÉ CONVENTION

The First Lomé Convention (Lomé I), which was concluded at Lomé, Togo, in February 1975 and came into force on 1 April 1976, replaced the Yaoundé Conventions and the Arusha Agreement. Lomé I was designed to provide a new framework of co-operation, taking into account the varying needs of developing African, Caribbean and Pacific (ACP) countries. The Second Lomé Convention came into force on 1 January 1981. The Third Lomé Convention came into force on 1 March 1985 (trade provisions) and 1 May 1986 (aid). The Fourth Lomé Convention, which had a 10-year commitment period, was signed in December 1989: its trade provisions entered into force on 1 March 1990, and the remainder entered into force in September 1991. At the end of 1999 71 ACP states were parties to the Convention.

### ACP-EU Institutions

**Council of Ministers:** one minister from each signatory state; one co-chairman from each of the two groups; meets annually.

**Committee of Ambassadors:** one ambassador from each signatory state; chairmanship alternates between the two groups; meets at least every six months.

**Joint Assembly:** EU and ACP are equally represented; attended by parliamentary delegates from each of the ACP countries and an equal number of members of the European Parliament; one co-chairman from each of the two groups; meets twice a year.

**Secretariat of the ACP-EU Council of Ministers:** 175 rue de la Loi, 1048 Brussels; tel. (2) 285-61-11; fax (2) 285-84-11.

**Centre for the Development of Industry (CDI):** 52 ave Herrmann Debroux, 1160 Brussels, Belgium; tel. (2) 679-18-11; fax (2) 675-26-03; e-mail director@cdi.be; internet www.cdi.be; f. 1977 to encourage and support the creation, expansion and restructuring of industrial companies (mainly in the fields of manufacturing and agro-industry) in the ACP states by promoting co-operation between ACP and European companies, in the form of financial, technical or commercial partnership, management contracts, licensing or franchise agreements, sub-contracts, etc.; Dir SURENDRA SHARMA.

**Technical Centre for Agricultural and Rural Co-operation:** Postbus 380, 6700 AJ Wageningen, Netherlands; tel. (317) 7467100; fax (317) 460067; f. 1983 to provide ACP states with better access to information, research, training and innovations in agricultural development and extension; Dir Dr RODNEY D. COOKE.

### ACP Institutions

**ACP Council of Ministers.**

**ACP Committee of Ambassadors.**

**ACP Secretariat:** ACP House, 451 ave Georges Henri, Brussels, Belgium; tel. (2) 743-06-00; fax (2) 735-55-73; e-mail info@acpsec.org; internet www.oneworld/acpsec; Sec.-Gen. NG'ANDU PETER MAGANDE (Zambia).

### The ACP States

| | |
|---|---|
| Angola | Liberia |
| Antigua and Barbuda | Madagascar |
| Bahamas | Malawi |
| Barbados | Mali |
| Belize | Mauritania |
| Benin | Mauritius |
| Botswana | Mozambique |
| Burkina Faso | Namibia |
| Burundi | Niger |
| Cameroon | Nigeria |
| Cape Verde | Papua New Guinea |
| Central African Republic | Rwanda |
| Chad | Saint Christopher and Nevis |
| Comoros | Saint Lucia |
| Congo, Democratic Republic | Saint Vincent and the Grenadines |
| Congo, Republic | Samoa |
| Côte d'Ivoire | São Tomé and Príncipe |
| Djibouti | Senegal |
| Dominica | Seychelles |
| Dominican Republic | Sierra Leone |
| Equatorial Guinea | Solomon Islands |
| Eritrea | Somalia |
| Ethiopia | South Africa* |
| Fiji | Sudan |
| Gabon | Suriname |
| The Gambia | Swaziland |
| Ghana | Tanzania |
| Grenada | Togo |
| Guinea | Tonga |
| Guinea-Bissau | Trinidad and Tobago |
| Guyana | Tuvalu |
| Haiti | Uganda |
| Jamaica | Vanuatu |
| Kenya | Zambia |
| Kiribati | Zimbabwe |
| Lesotho | |

*Partial membership (see below).

Under Lomé I, the Community committed ECU 3,052.4m. for aid and investment in developing countries, through the European Development Fund (EDF) and the European Investment Bank (EIB). Provision was made for over 99% of ACP (mainly agricultural) exports to enter the EC market duty free, while certain products which compete directly with Community agriculture, such as sugar, were given preferential treatment but not free access. The Stabex (Stabilization of Export Earnings) scheme was designed to help developing countries to withstand fluctuations in the price of their agricultural products, by paying compensation for reduced export earnings.

The Second Lomé Convention (1981–85) envisaged Community expenditure of ECU 5,530m.: it extended some of the provisions of Lomé I, and introduced new fields of co-operation, including a scheme (Sysmin), to safeguard exports of mineral products.

Lomé III made commitments of ECU 8,500m., including loans of ECU 1,100m. from the EIB. Innovations included an emphasis on agriculture and fisheries, and measures to combat desertification; assistance for rehabilitating existing industries or sectoral improvements; improvements in the efficiency of the Stabex system (now covering a list of 48 agricultural products) and of Sysmin; simplification of the rules of origin of products; the promotion of private investment; co-operation in transport and communications; cultural and social co-operation; restructuring of emergency aid, and more efficient procedures for technical and financial assistance.

The Fourth Lomé Convention was to cover the period 1990–99. The budget for financial and technical co-operation for 1990–95 amounted to ECU 12,000m., of which ECU 10,800m. was from the EDF (including ECU 1,500m. for Stabex and ECU 480m. for Sysmin) and ECU 1,200m. from the EIB. The budget for the second five years was ECU 14,625m., of which ECU 12,967m. was from the EDF, and ECU 1,658m. from the EIB. Under Lomé IV, the obligation of most of the ACP states to contribute to the replenishment of STABEX resources, including the repayment of transfers made under the first three Conventions, was removed. In addition, special loans made to ACP member countries were to be cancelled, except in the case of profit-orientated businesses. Other innovations included the provision of assistance for structural adjustment programmes (amounting to ECU 1,150m.); increased support for the private sector, environmental protection, and control of growth in population; and measures to avoid increasing the recipient countries' indebtedness (e.g. by providing Stabex and Sysmin assistance in the form of grants, rather than loans).

**COMMITMENTS MADE UNDER THE LOMÉ CONVENTION** (ECU million)

| | 1995 | 1996* |
|---|---|---|
| Trade promotion | 57.6 | 8.7 |
| Cultural and social development | 163.8 | 69.5 |
| Education and training | 40.7 | 38.6 |
| Water engineering, urban infrastructure and housing | 65.8 | 22.7 |
| Health | 57.3 | 8.1 |
| Economic infrastructure (transport and communications) | 236.8 | 104.3 |
| Development of production | 471.2 | 122.9 |
| Rural production | 93.4 | 24.6 |
| Industrialization | 286.3 | 51.7 |
| Campaigns on specific themes[1] | 91.5 | 46.5 |
| Exceptional aid, Stabex | 334.2 | 121.3 |
| Rehabilitation | 161.0 | 47.2 |
| Disasters | 33.7 | –9.7 |
| Stabex | 131.1 | 78.8 |
| AIDS | 9.6 | 3.9 |
| Refugees and returnees | –1.2 | 1.0 |
| Other[2] | 256.5 | 170.0 |
| **Total** | 1,520.0 | 596.7 |

* Provisional figures.

[1] Including desertification and drought, natural disasters, major endemic and epidemic diseases, hygiene and basic health, endemic cattle diseases, energy-saving research, sectoral imports programmes and long-term operations.

[2] Including information and documentation, seminars, programmes and general technical co-operation, general studies, multi-sectoral programmes, delegations, public buildings and project-linked multi-sectoral technical co-operation (all projects).

Source: European Commission, *General Report* (1996).

On 1 July 1993 the EC introduced a regime covering the import of bananas into the Community. This was designed to protect the banana industries of ACP countries (mostly in the Caribbean), which were threatened by the availability of cheaper bananas, produced by countries in Latin America. The new regime guaranteed 30% of the European market to ACP producers, and established an annual quota of 2m. metric tons for bananas imported from Latin America, which would incur a uniform duty of 20%, while imports above this level were to be subject to a tariff of ECU 850 per ton. In February 1994 a dispute panel of GATT upheld a complaint, brought by five Latin American countries, that the EU banana import regime was in contravention of free-trade principles. An agreement was reached in March, under which the EU increased the annual quota for Latin American banana imports to 2.1m. tons with effect from October 1994, and to 2.2m. tons in 1995. However, in 1995 the USA, supported by Guatemala, Honduras and Mexico (and subsequently by Ecuador), filed a complaint with the WTO against the EU's banana regime. In May 1997 the WTO concluded that the EU banana import regime violated 19 free-trade regulations. The EU appealed against the ruling in July, but in September the WTO's dispute settlement body endorsed the original verdict. However, the allocation of preferential tariffs to ACP producers, covered by a waiver since late 1994, was upheld. In October 1997 the EU agreed to amend its banana import regime to comply with the WTO ruling. An arbitration report, published in January 1998, compelled the EU to implement changes by 1 January 1999. In June 1998 EU ministers of agriculture approved a reform of the import regime, providing for two separate quota systems, granting Latin American producers greater access to the European market, with a quota of 2.53m. tons (at a tariff of ECU 75 per ton), while ACP countries would have a quota of 857,000 tons (tariff-free). The quota systems, which were to apply from 1 January 1999, were approved by the Commission in October. However, in November the USA proposed the imposition of duties of 100% on a number of European imports, in protest at the reform, which it continued to regard as discriminatory and incompatible with WTO provisions. In February 1999 the EU requested that a WTO panel be established to investigate the validity of the clause of the US Trade Act that permitted the imposition of retaliatory sanctions (considered by the EU to be in breach of the WTO dispute settlement procedure). In March, however, the USA imposed provisional measures against a diverse range of EU products, prompting the EU to issue a complaint with the WTO. In April an arbitration panel of the WTO confirmed that the EU had failed to conform its banana regime with WTO rules and formally authorized the USA to impose trade sanctions, valued at US $191.4m. In November the Commission proposed a radical reform of the EU's banana regime. Subject to the approval of the member states, this would involve the gradual dismantling of the existing quota system and its replacement with a tariff system that would open the banana market to other competitors. The Commission proposed that there should be a transitional period of six years. However, US trade representatives indicated that the USA would find the reforms unacceptable and accused the Commission of ignoring US proposals to resolve the dispute.

In September 1993 the Community announced plans to revise and strengthen its relations with the ACP countries under the Lomé Convention. In May 1994 representatives of EU member states and ACP countries initiated the mid-term review of Lomé IV. The Community reiterated its intention to maintain the Convention as an aid instrument but emphasized that stricter conditions relating to the awarding of aid would be imposed, based on standards of human rights, human resource development and environmental protection. However, negotiations between EU and ACP states were adjourned in February 1995, owing to disagreements among EU states concerning reimbursement of the EDF in the period 1995–2000. In June the European Council agreed to provide ECU 14,625m. for the second phase of Lomé IV, of which ECU 12,967m. was to be allocated from the EDF and ECU 1,658m. in loans from the EIB. Agreement was also reached on revision of the 'country-of-origin' rules for manufactured goods, a new protocol on the sustainable management of forest resources and a joint declaration on support for the banana industry. The agreement was subsequently endorsed by an EU-ACP ministerial group, and the revised Convention was signed in November, in Mauritius. In March 1997 the Commission proposed granting debt relief assistance of ECU 25m. each year for the period 1997–2000 to the 11 heavily-indebted poor countries (as identified by the World Bank and the IMF) forming part of the ACP group. Funding was to be used to support international efforts to reduce debt and encourage the economic prospects of such countries.

In June 1995 negotiations opened with a view to concluding a wide-ranging trade and co-operation agreement with South Africa, including the eventual creation of a free-trade area (FTA). The accord was approved by heads of state and of government in March 1999, after agreement was reached to eliminate progressively, over a 12-year period, the use of the terms 'port' and 'sherry' to describe South African fortified wines. The accord provided for the removal of duties from about 99% of South Africa's industrial exports and some 75% of its agricultural products within 10 years, while South Africa was to liberalize its market for some 86% of EU industrial goods (with protection for the motor vehicle and textiles industries), within a 12-year period. The accord also introduced increased development assistance for South Africa after 1999. Implementation of the accord was delayed in January 2000 after some member states refused to ratify it unless South Africa also agreed to abandon the use of names such as 'ouzo' and 'grappa'. A duty-free quota for exports of South African wine was suspended pending a resolution. In March 1997 the Commission approved a Special Protocol for South Africa's accession to the Lomé Convention, and in April South Africa attained partial membership. Full membership was withheld, as South Africa was not regarded as, in all respects, a developing country, and was therefore not entitled to aid provisions. A special provision was introduced into the revised Lomé Convention to allow Somalia to accede, should constitutional government be established in that country prior to the expiry of the Convention.

Intensive debate took place from 1995 on the future of relations between the ACP states and the EU, in view of the increasingly global nature of the EU's foreign policies, and particularly the growing emphasis it is placing on relations with central and eastern Europe and countries of the Mediterranean rim. In November 1996 the Commission published a consultative document to consider the options for future ACP-EU relations. The document focused on the areas of trade, aid and politics, and included proposals to encourage competitiveness, to support private-sector investment and to enhance democracy. The report suggested abolishing or restructuring Stabex and Sysmin, and considered altering the grouping of the ACP states for the purpose of implementing economic agreements. The ultimate aim of the document was to foster conditions in which the EU and the ACP countries could co-exist as equal partners. In November 1997 the first summit of heads of state of ACP countries was held in Libreville, Gabon. The ACP council of ministers prepared a mandate for negotiations towards a renewed Lomé Convention, which was approved by the Commission in January 1998. The Joint Assembly of ACP ministers, meeting in Mauritius in April, and the ACP-EU Council of Ministers, meeting in Barbados in May, discussed proposals for future ACP-EU relations after the expiry of Lomé IV. The ACP states emphasized that they should be regarded as a single entity, with recognition for the individual requirements of each region, and that any renewed partnership should continue to support the elimination of poverty as its main objective. In late June EU ministers of foreign affairs approved preliminary directives for the negotiation of a new partnership agreement, based on proposals to replace existing trade privileges with regional free-trade areas by 2015. Additional financial support was to be made available to promote the development of the private sector in ACP states. However, any country unwilling to participate in a free-trade area arrangement would be granted trading privileges equivalent to its existing situation, and the poorest states were to be permitted to export goods to the EU tariff-free. The ministers agreed to allow Cuba to participate in the negotiations, with observer status, but emphasized that their decision would have no influence on any future accession discussions should Cuba wish to join the Lomé Convention. In November 1998 Cuba formally applied for full membership. Negotiations on the renewal of the Lomé pact, or on some new form of agreement, commenced on 30 September 1998. In October 1999 it was reported that agreement had been reached between the EU and the ACP to retain the trade arrangements contained in the Lomé pact for a period of eight years following its expiry in February 2000. Subject to the granting of a waiver by the WTO for such a prolongation, negotiations on new trading arrangements, to enter into force in January 2008, would commence in September 2002. The new partnership arrangement was reported to have been concluded in early February 2000.

## Finance

### THE COMMUNITY BUDGET

The general budget of the European Union covers all EEC and Euratom expenditure and the administrative expenditure of the ECSC. The Commission is responsible for implementing the budget. (The ECSC, like the EIB, has its own resources and conducts its own financial operations.) Under the Council decision of 24 June 1988 all revenue (except that expressly designated for supplementary research and technological development programmes) is used without distinction to finance all expenditure, and all budget expenditure must be covered in full by the revenue entered in the budget. Any amendment of this decision requires the unanimous approval of the Council and must be ratified by the member states. The Treaty of Rome requires member states to release funds to cover the appropriations entered in the budget.

Each Community institution draws up estimates of its expenditure, and sends them to the Commission before 1 July of the year preceding the financial year (1 January–31 December) in question. The Commission consolidates these estimates in a preliminary draft budget, which it sends to the Council by 1 September. Expenditure is divided into two categories: that necessarily resulting from the Treaties (compulsory expenditure) and other (non-compulsory) expenditure. The draft budget must be approved by a qualified majority in the Council, and presented to Parliament by 5 October. Parliament may propose modifications to compulsory expenditure, and may (within the limits of the 'maximum rate of increase', dependent on growth of member states' gross national product—GNP—and budgets) amend non-compulsory expenditure. The budget must normally be declared finally adopted 75 days after the draft is presented to Parliament. If the budget has not been adopted by the beginning of the financial year, monthly expenditure may amount to one-twelfth of the appropriations adopted for the previous year's budget. The Commission may (even late in the year during which the budget is being executed) revise estimates of revenue and expenditure, by presenting supplementary and/or amending budgets.

Expenditure under the general budget is financed by 'own resources', comprising agricultural duties (on imports of agricultural produce from non-member states), customs duties, application of value-added tax (VAT) on goods and services, and (since 1988) a levy based on the GNP of member states. Member states are obliged to collect 'own resources' on the Community's behalf. From May 1985 arrangements were introduced for the correction of budgetary imbalances, as a result of which the United Kingdom received compensation in the form of reductions in VAT payments. In 1988 it was decided by the Community's heads of government to set a maximum amount for 'own resources' that might be called up in any one year.

The general budget contains the expenditures of the six main Community institutions—the Commission, the Council, Parliament, the Court of Justice, the Court of Auditors, and the Economic and Social Committee and the Committee of the Regions—of which Commission expenditure (covering administrative costs and expenditure on operations) forms the largest proportion. The Common Agricultural Policy accounts for about 50% of total expenditure, principally in agricultural guarantees. In 1988 it was decided (as part of a system of budgetary discipline agreed by the Council) that the rate of increase in spending on agricultural guarantees between 1988 and a given year was not to exceed 74% of the growth

**BUDGET EXPENDITURE APPROPRIATIONS FOR THE ACTIVITIES OF THE EUROPEAN COMMISSION**
(ECU million)

| | 1998 | 1999 |
|---|---|---|
| **Administration** | | |
| Expenditure relating to persons working with the institution | 1,712.1 | 1,760.8 |
| Buildings, equipment and miscellaneous operating expenditure | 319.2 | 312.6 |
| Expenditure resulting from special functions carried out by the institution | 249.5 | 256.7 |
| Data-processing | 93.9 | 93.9 |
| Staff and administrative expenditure of EC delegations | 202.6 | 213.9 |
| Interinstitutional co-operation, services and activities | 74.5 | 73.9 |
| Decentralized expenditure | 192.5 | 211.1 |
| **Total** | 2,844.3 | 2,923.0 |
| **Operations** | | |
| EAGGF Guarantee Section | 40,437.0 | 40,940.0 |
| Structural operations, other agricultural and regional operations, transport and fisheries | 28,712.5 | 30,658.5 |
| Training, youth, culture, audiovisual media, information and other social operations | 725.4 | 741.0 |
| Energy, Euratom nuclear safeguards and environment | 182.2 | 198.4 |
| Consumer protection, internal market, industry and trans-European networks | 795.6 | 883.1 |
| Research and technological development | 3,047.6 | 2,990.2 |
| External actions | 4,666.9 | 4,275.3 |
| Common foreign and security policy | 20.3 | 23.0 |
| Repayments, guarantees and reserves | 437.0 | 346.0 |
| Other Community institutions | 1,660.3 | 1,579.3 |
| **Operations—Total** | 80,684.8 | 82,634.8 |
| **Grand total** | 83,529.2 | 85,557.7 |

Note: The funds allocated to the other Community institutions were to be supplemented by the institutions' own resources.

**REVENUE** (ECU million)

| Source of revenue | 1998 | 1999 |
|---|---|---|
| Agricultural duties | 1,101.8 | 1,054.5 |
| Sugar and isoglucose levies | 1,069.8 | 1,080.0 |
| Customs duties | 13,504.8 | 13,215.4 |
| Own resources collection costs | –1,567.8 | –1,535.0 |
| VAT own resources | 32,752.8 | 30,374.2 |
| GNP-based own resources | 34,501.6 | 39,260.0 |
| Balance of VAT and GNP own resources from previous years | 988.7 | n.a. |
| Budget balance from previous year | 960.0 | 1,400.0 |
| Other revenue | 668.1 | 708.6 |
| **Total** | 83,967.1 | 85,557.7 |

Source: European Commission, *General Report* (1998).

rate of Community GNP during the same period. In December 1992 it was agreed to increase the upper limit on Community expenditure from 1.2% of the EC's combined GNP to 1.27% in 1999. 'Agenda 2000', concerning financial arrangements for the period 2000–2006, proposed maintaining the limit at 1.27% from 2000. In December 1994, taking into account the enlargement of the EU to 15 countries (from 1 January 1995) it was agreed to set a level of maximum expenditure at ECU 75,500m. in 1995, increasing to ECU 87,000m. in 1999, at constant 1992 prices. Agenda 2000 proposed that maximum annual expenditure would increase to €104,600m. at 1999 prices, by 2006.

## STRUCTURAL FUNDS

The Community's 'structural funds' comprise the Guidance Section of the European Agricultural Guidance and Guarantee Fund, the European Regional Development Fund, the European Social Fund and the Cohesion Fund. There is also a financial instrument for fisheries guidance, commitments for which amounted to ECU 308.2m. in 1997. In accordance with the Single European Act (1987), reforms of the Community's structural funds were adopted by the Council with effect from 1 January 1989, with the aim of more accurate identification of priority targets, and greater selectivity to

**MEMBER STATES' PAYMENTS**

| Country | Contribution for 1998 (ECU million) | % of total |
|---|---|---|
| Austria | 2,067.6 | 2.5 |
| Belgium | 3,047.7 | 3.7 |
| Denmark | 1,635.4 | 2.0 |
| Finland | 1,122.1 | 1.3 |
| France | 14,064.7 | 17.0 |
| Germany | 22,668.7 | 27.3 |
| Greece | 1,324.0 | 1.6 |
| Ireland | 817.7 | 1.0 |
| Italy | 10,600.7 | 12.8 |
| Luxembourg | 183.6 | 0.2 |
| Netherlands | 4,867.2 | 5.9 |
| Portugal | 1,112.2 | 1.3 |
| Spain | 5,405.8 | 6.5 |
| Sweden | 2,296.3 | 2.8 |
| United Kingdom | 11,647.3 | 14.1 |
| **Total** | 82,861.1 | 100.0 |

enable action to be concentrated in the least-favoured regions (see Social Policy, p. 187). In December 1992 it was agreed that total 'structural' expenditure would be increased to ECU 30,000m. per year by 1999, at constant 1992 prices. Commitments in the 1998 budget totalled ECU 30,482m. 'Agenda 2000', which was approved by the Council in March 1999, provided for the reform of the structural funds to make available some €213,000m. for 2000–2006, at 1999 prices.

### Cohesion Fund

The Treaty on European Union and its protocol on economic and social cohesion provided for the establishment of a 'cohesion fund', which began operating on 1 April 1993, with a budget of ECU 1,500m. for the first year. This was to subsidize projects in the fields of the environment and trans-European energy and communications networks in member states with a per caput GNP of less than 90% of the Community average (in practice, this was to mean Greece, Ireland, Portugal and Spain). Commitments under the fund in the budget appropriations for 1998 amounted to ECU 2,871m. The fund's total budget for the period 1993–99 was ECU 15,500m.

### European Agricultural Guidance and Guarantee Fund (EAGGF)—Guidance Section

Created in 1962, the European Agricultural Guidance and Guarantee Fund is administered by the Commission. The Guidance section covers expenditure on Community aid for projects to improve farming conditions in the member states. It includes aid for poor rural areas and the structural adjustment of rural areas, particularly in the context of the reform of the common agricultural policy (CAP). This aid is usually granted in the form of financial contributions to programmes also supported by the member governments themselves. Commitments of ECU 2,578.7m. were budgeted for in 1997.

### European Regional Development Fund—ERDF

Payments began in 1975. The Fund is intended to compensate for the unequal rate of development in different regions of the Community, by encouraging investment and improving infrastructure in 'problem regions'. The 1997 budget included an allocation of ECU 10,069.9m. for the Fund's commitments.

### European Social Fund

**Internet:** europa.eu.int/comm/dgo5/esf/en/index.htm.

The Fund (established in 1960) provides resources with the aim of combating long-term unemployment and facilitating the integration into the labour market of young people and the socially disadvantaged. It also supports schemes to help workers to adapt to industrial changes. The 1997 budget allocated ECU 4,058.8m. for the Fund's commitments. The fund's total budget for the period 1994–99 was ECU 47,000m.

## Publications*

*Bulletin of the European Union* (10 a year).

*The Courier* (every 2 months, on ACP-EU affairs).

*European Economy* (every 6 months, with supplements).

*European Voice* (weekly).

*General Report on the Activities of the European Union* (annually).

*Official Journal of the European Communities.*

*Publications of the European Communities* (quarterly).

*EUR-Lex Website* (treaties, legislation and judgments, europa.eu.int/eur-lex/en/index.html).

Information sheets, background reports and statistical documents.

* Most publications are available in all the official languages of the Union. They are obtainable from the Office for Official Publications of the European Communities, 2 rue Mercier, 2985 Luxembourg; tel. 29291; fax 495719; e-mail europ@opoce.cec.be; internet eur-op.eu.int.

# THE FRANC ZONE

**Address:** Direction Générale des Services Etrangers (Service de la Zone Franc), Banque de France, 39 rue Croix-des-Petits-Champs, 75049, Paris Cédex 01, France.

**Telephone:** 1-42-92-31-46; **fax:** 1-42-92-39-88.

## MEMBERS

| | |
|---|---|
| Benin | Equatorial Guinea |
| Burkina Faso | French Republic* |
| Cameroon | Gabon |
| Central African Republic | Guinea-Bissau |
| Chad | Mali |
| The Comoros | Niger |
| Republic of the Congo | Senegal |
| Côte d'Ivoire | Togo |

* Metropolitan France, Mayotte, St Pierre and Miquelon and the Overseas Departments and Territories.

The Franc Zone embraces all those countries and groups of countries whose currencies are linked with the French franc at a fixed rate of exchange and who agree to hold their reserves mainly in the form of French francs and to effect their exchange on the Paris market. Each of these countries or groups of countries has its own central issuing bank and its currency is freely convertible into French francs. This monetary union is based on agreements concluded between France and each country or group of countries.

Apart from Guinea and Mauritania, all of the countries that formerly comprised French West and Equatorial Africa are members of the Franc Zone. The former West and Equatorial African territories are still grouped within the currency areas that existed before independence, each group having its own currency issued by a central bank.

A number of states left the Franc Zone during the period 1958–73: Guinea, Tunisia, Morocco, Algeria, Mauritania and Madagascar.

The Comoros, formerly a French Overseas Territory, did not join the Franc Zone following its unilateral declaration of independence in 1975. However, francs CFA were used as the currency of the new state and the Institut d'émission des Comores continued to function as a Franc Zone organization. In 1976 the Comoros formally assumed membership. In July 1981 the Banque centrale des Comores replaced the Institut d'émission des Comores, establishing its own currency, the Comoros franc. The island of Mayotte, however, has remained under French administration as an Overseas Collectivité Territoriale, using the French franc as its unit of currency.

Equatorial Guinea, a former Spanish possession, joined the Franc Zone in January 1985, and Guinea-Bissau, a former Portuguese territory, joined in May 1997.

During the late 1980s and early 1990s the economies of the African Franc Zone countries were adversely affected by increasing foreign debt and by a decline in the prices paid for their principal export commodities. The French Government, however, refused to devalue the franc CFA, as recommended by the IMF. In 1990 the Franc Zone governments agreed to develop economic union, with integrated public finances and common commercial legislation. In April 1992, at a meeting of Franc Zone ministers, a treaty was signed on the insurance industry whereby a regulatory body for the industry was to be established: the Conférence Intrafricaine des Marchés d'Assurances (CIMA). Under the treaty, which was to be effective from 31 December 1992, a council of Franc Zone ministers responsible for the insurance industry was also to be established with its secretariat in Libreville, Gabon. (A code of conduct for members of CIMA came into effect in early 1995.) At the meeting held in April 1992 ministers also agreed that a further council of ministers was to be created with the task of monitoring the social security systems in Franc Zone countries. A programme drawn up by Franc Zone finance ministers concerning the harmonization of commercial legislation in member states through the establishment of l'Organisation pour l'Harmonisation du Droit des Affaires en Afrique (OHADA), was approved by the Franco-African summit in October. A treaty to align corporate and investment regulations was signed by 11 member countries at the annual meeting with France in October 1993. Devaluations of the franc CFA and the Comoros franc were agreed by CFA central banks in January 1994 (see below). Following the devaluation the CFA countries embarked on programmes of economic adjustment, including restrictive fiscal and wage policies and other monetary, structural and social measures, designed to stimulate growth and to ensure eligibility for development assistance from international financial institutions. France established a special development fund of FFr 300m. to alleviate the immediate social consequences of the devaluation, and announced substantial debt cancellations. In April the French Government announced assistance amounting to FFr 10,000m. over three years to Franc Zone countries undertaking structural adjustment programmes. The IMF, which had strongly advocated a devaluation of the franc CFA, and the World Bank approved immediate soft-credit loans, technical assistance and cancellations or rescheduling of debts. In June 1994 heads of state (or representatives) of African Franc Zone countries convened in Libreville, Gabon, to review the effects of the currency realignment. The final communiqué of the meeting urged further international support for the countries' economic development efforts. In April 1995 Franc Zone finance ministers, meeting in Paris, recognized the positive impact of the devaluation on agricultural export sectors, in particular in west African countries, though central African countries, it was noted, were still afflicted by serious economic difficulties. In September the Franc Zone member countries and the French Government agreed to establish a research and training institution, Afristat, which was to support national statistical organizations in order to strengthen economic management capabilities in participating states. In April 1997 finance ministers met to review the economies of member states. Capital entries (private investment and public development aid) along with tax and wage policies and an increase in exports were found to have contributed to economic growth. Improvements were continuing within a programme supported by the IMF and the World Bank, though ministers stated that economic development efforts were not sufficiently supported by the private sector, with the average rate of investment remaining at 10% of GDP. The adoption of a charter to encourage private investors was discussed, but postponed pending an investigation into proposals made by UEMOA and CEMAC. The co-operation agreement permitting Guinea-Bissau's membership of the Franc Zone, to come into effect on 2 May, was also signed. In the same month delegates from OHADA met donors in Guinea-Bissau, aiming to raise funds worth US $50m. over a 12-year period, to allow them to train commercial court judges, provide information for businesses and cover administration costs. In April 1998 the annual meeting of finance ministers was dominated by discussions regarding the future of the Franc Zone and possible currency devaluations resulting from the introduction of a European single currency, the euro, within the framework of a European economic and monetary union, in which France was scheduled to participate when it entered into effect on 1 January 1999. In July 1998 the European Commission recommended that all convertibility arrangements concluded between France and the Franc Zone countries be preserved after the introduction of the euro, and that member countries maintain the fixed parity of the franc CFA (and of the Comoros franc). These arrangements consequently remained in effect in January 1999.

## EXCHANGE REGULATIONS

Currencies of the Franc Zone are freely convertible into the French franc at a fixed rate, through 'operations accounts' established by agreements concluded between the French Treasury and the individual issuing banks. It is backed fully by the French Treasury, which also provides the issuing banks with overdraft facilities.

The monetary reserves of the CFA countries are normally held in French francs in the French Treasury. However, the Banque centrale des états de l'Afrique de l'ouest (BCEAO) and the Banque des états de l'Afrique centrale (BEAC) are authorized to hold up to 35% of their foreign exchange holdings in currencies other than the franc. Exchange is effected on the Paris market. Part of the reserves earned by richer members can be used to offset the deficits incurred by poorer countries.

Regulations drawn up in 1967 provided for the free convertibility of currency with that of countries outside the Franc Zone. Restrictions were removed on the import and export of CFA banknotes, although some capital transfers are subject to approval by the governments concerned.

When the French Government instituted exchange control to protect the French franc in May 1968, other Franc Zone countries were obliged to take similar action in order to maintain free convertibility within the Franc Zone. The franc CFA was devalued following devaluation of the French franc in August 1969. Since March 1973 the French authorities have ceased to maintain the franc-US dollar rate within previously agreed margins, and, as a result, the value of the franc CFA has fluctuated on foreign exchange markets in line with the French franc.

In August 1993, as a result of the financial turmoil regarding the European exchange rate mechanism and the continuing weakness of the French franc, the BCEAO and the BEAC decided to suspend repurchasing of francs CFA outside the Franc Zone. Effectively this signified the withdrawal of guaranteed convertibility of the franc CFA with the French franc. In January 1994 the franc CFA was devalued by 50%, and the Comoros franc by 33.3%.

## CURRENCIES OF THE FRANC ZONE

French franc (= 100 centimes): used in Metropolitan France, in the Overseas Departments of Guadeloupe, French Guiana, Martinique, Réunion, and in the Overseas Collectivités Territoriales of Mayotte and St Pierre and Miquelon.

1 franc CFA = 1 French centime. CFA stands for Communauté financière africaine in the West African area and for Coopération financière en Afrique centrale in the Central African area. Used in the monetary areas of West and Central Africa respectively.

1 Comoros franc = 1.333 French centimes (1 French franc = 75 Comoros francs). Used in the Comoros, where it replaced the franc CFA in 1981.

1 franc CFP = 5.5 French centimes. CFP stands for Comptoirs français du Pacifique. Used in New Caledonia, French Polynesia and the Wallis and Futuna Islands.

## WEST AFRICA

**Union économique et monétaire ouest-africaine—UEMOA:** BP 543, Ouagadougou, Burkina Faso; tel. 31-88-73; fax 31-88-72; e-mail commission@uemoa.br; internet www.uemoa.bf; f. 1994; replaced the Communauté économique de l'Afrique de l'ouest–CEAO; promotes regional monetary and economic convergence, and aims to improve regional trade by facilitating the movement of labour and capital between member states. The first meeting of heads of state of UEMOA member countries, held in May 1996 in Ouagadougou, agreed to establish a customs union with effect from 1 January 1998. A preferential tariff scheme, eliminating duties on most local products and reducing by 30% import duties on many Community-produced industrial goods, became operational on 1 July 1996; in addition, from 1 July, a community solidarity tax of 0.5% was imposed on all goods from third countries sold within the Community, in order to strengthen UEMOA's capacity to promote economic integration. In June 1997 the second meeting of UEMOA heads of state and government agreed to reduce import duties on industrial products originating in the Community by a further 30%. The meeting also confirmed that Côte d'Ivoire's stock exchange was to be transformed into a regional institution serving the UEMOA sub-region, in order to further economic integration (see below). At the meeting UEMOA heads of state adopted a declaration on peace and security in the region. In November UEMOA ministers of finance, meeting in extraordinary session, agreed to postpone the establishment of a customs union until 1 January 2000, when a five-band system of tariffs of between 0% and 20% was to become effective. In March 1998 an inter-parliamentary committee, recognized as the predecessor of a UEMOA legislature, was inaugurated in Mali. In August 1999 the committee adopted a draft treaty on the establishment of a UEMOA parliament, which was scheduled to become operational in 2000 comprising 10 representatives from each member state. Mems: Benin, Burkina Faso, Côte d'Ivoire, Guinea-Bissau, Mali, Niger, Senegal and Togo. Chair. Gen. GNASSINGBE EYADÉMA (Togo).

**Union monétaire ouest-africaine—UMOA** (West African Monetary Union): established by Treaty of November 1973, entered into force 1974; in 1990 the UMOA Banking Commission was established, which is responsible for supervising the activities of banks and financial institutions in the region, with the authority to prohibit the operation of a banking institution. UMOA constitutes an integral part of UEMOA.

**Banque centrale des états de l'Afrique de l'ouest—BCEAO:** ave Abdoulaye Fadiga, BP 3108, Dakar, Senegal; tel. 839-05-00; fax 823-93-35; e-mail akangni@bceao.int; internet www.bceao.int; f. 1962; central bank of issue for the mems of UEMOA; cap. and res 806,919m. francs CFA (Dec. 1998). Mems: Benin, Burkina Faso, Côte d'Ivoire, Guinea Bissau, Mali, Niger, Senegal and Togo. Gov. CHARLES KONAN BANNY (Côte d'Ivoire); Sec.-Gen. MICHEL K. KLOUSSEH (Togo). Publs *Annual Report, Notes d'Information et Statistiques* (monthly), *Annuaire des banques, Bilan des banques et établissements financiers* (annually).

**Banque ouest-africaine de développement—BOAD:** 68 ave de la Libération, BP 1172, Lomé, Togo; tel. 21-42-44; fax 21-52-67; e-mail boadsiege@boad.org; internet www.boad.org; f. 1973 to promote the balanced development of mem. states and the economic integration of West Africa; cap. 27,435m. francs CFA (Dec. 1998). A Guarantee Fund for Private Investment in west Africa, established jtly by BOAD and the European Investment Bank, was inaugurated in Dec. 1994. The Fund, which had an initial cap. of 8,615.5m. francs CFA, aimed to guarantee medium- and long-term credits to private sector businesses in the region. Mems: Benin, Burkina Faso, Côte d'Ivoire, Guinea-Bissau, Mali, Niger, Senegal, Togo. Chair. BONI YAYI (Benin); Vice-Chair. ALPHA TOURÉ. Publs *Rapport Annuel, BOAD-INFO* (quarterly).

**Bourse Régionale des Valeurs Mobilières—BRVM:** 18 ave Joseph Anoma, BP 3802, Abidjan 01, Côte d'Ivoire; tel. 32-66-85; fax 32-66-84; f. 1998; Pres. LAMASEH ALEXIS LOOKY; Man. KOKOU GOZAN (acting).

## CENTRAL AFRICA

**Communauté économique et monétaire de l'Afrique centrale—CEMAC:** BP 969, Bangui, Central African Republic; tel. and fax 61-21-35; e-mail sgudeac@intnet.cf; internet www.socatel.intnet.cf/accueil1.html; f. 1998; formally inaugurated as the successor to the Union douanière et économique de l'Afrique centrale (UDEAC, f. 1966) at a meeting of heads of state held in Malabo, Equatorial Guinea, in June 1999; aims to promote the process of sub-regional integration within the framework of an economic union and a monetary union; CEMAC was also to comprise a parliament and sub-regional tribunal. UDEAC established a common external tariff for imports from other countries and administered a common code for investment policy and a Solidarity Fund to counteract regional disparities of wealth and economic development. Mems: Cameroon, Central African Republic, Chad, Republic of the Congo, Equatorial Guinea, Gabon. Sec.-Gen. THOMAS DAKAYI KAMGA (Cameroon).

At a summit meeting in December 1981, UDEAC leaders agreed in principle to form an economic community of Central African states (Communauté économique des états d'Afrique centrale—CEEAC), to include UDEAC members and Burundi, Rwanda, São Tomé and Príncipe and Zaire (now Democratic Republic of the Congo). CEEAC (q.v.) began operations in 1985.

**Banque de développement des états de l'Afrique centrale—BDEAC:** place du Gouvernement, BP 1177, Brazzaville, Republic of the Congo; tel. 81-18-85; fax 81-18-80; f. 1975; cap. 20,095m. francs CFA (June 1998); shareholders: Cameroon, Central African Republic, Chad, Republic of the Congo, Gabon, Equatorial Guinea, ADB, BEAC, France, Germany and Kuwait; Dir-Gen. EMMANUEL DOKOUNA.

**Banque des états de l'Afrique centrale—BEAC:** ave Mgr François Xavier Vogt, BP 1917, Yaoundé, Cameroon; tel. 23-40-30; fax 23-33-29; f. 1973 as the central bank of issue of Cameroon, the Central African Republic, Chad, Republic of the Congo, Equatorial Guinea and Gabon; a monetary market, incorporating all national financial institutions of the BEAC countries, came into effect on 1 July 1994; cap. 45,000m. francs CFA (Dec. 1998). Gov. JEAN-FÉLIX MAMALEPOT. Publs *Rapport annuel, Etudes et statistiques* (monthly).

## CENTRAL ISSUING BANKS

**Banque centrale des Comores:** place de France, BP 405, Moroni, Comoros; tel. (73) 1002; fax (73) 0349; f. 1981; cap. 1,100m. Comoros francs (Dec. 1997); Gov. SAÏD AHMED SAÏD ALI.

**Banque centrale des états de l'Afrique de l'ouest:** see above.

**Banque des états de l'Afrique centrale:** see above.

**Banque de France:** 39 rue Croix-des-Petits-Champs, BP 140-01, 75049 Paris, France; tel. 1-42-92-42-92; fax 1-42-96-04-23; f. 1800; bank of issue for Metropolitan France; Gov. JEAN-CLAUDE TRICHET; Dep. Govs DENIS FERMAN, HERVÉ HANNOUN.

**Institut d'émission des départements d'outre-mer—IEDOM:** 5 rue Roland Barthes, 75598 Paris Cédex 12, France; tel. 1-53-44-41-41; issuing authority for the French Overseas Departments and the French Overseas Collectivités Territoriales of St Pierre and Miquelon, and Mayotte; Pres. DENIS FERMAN; Dir-Gen. ANTOINE POUILLIEUTE; Dir GILLES AUDREN.

**Institut d'émission d'outre-mer—IEOM:** 5 rue Roland Barthes, 75598 Paris Cédex 12, France; tel. 1-53-44-41-41; issuing authority for the French Overseas Territories; Pres. DENIS FERMAN; Dir-Gen. ANTOINE POUILLIEUTE; Dir GILLES AUDREN.

## FRENCH ECONOMIC AID

France's connection with the African Franc Zone countries involves not only monetary arrangements, but also includes comprehensive

French assistance in the forms of budget support, foreign aid, technical assistance and subsidies on commodity exports.

Official French financial aid and technical assistance to developing countries is administered by the following agencies:

**Agence française de développement—AFD:** 5 rue Roland Barthes, 75598 Paris Cédex 12, France; tel. 1-53-44-31-31; fax 1-44-87-99-39; internet www.afd.fr/; f. 1941; fmrly the Caisse française de développement—CFD; French development bank which lends money to member states and former member states of the Franc Zone and several other states, and executes the financial operations of the FAC (see below). Following the devaluation of the franc CFA in January 1994, the French Government cancelled some 25,000m. French francs in debt arrears owed by member states to the CFD. The CFD established a Special Fund for Development and the Exceptional Facility for Short-term Financing to help alleviate the immediate difficulties resulting from the devaluation. A total of FFr 4,600m. of financial assistance was awarded to Franc Zone countries in 1994. In early 1994 the CFD made available funds totalling 2,420m. francs CFA to assist the establishment of CEMAC (see above). Serves as the secretariat for the Fonds français pour l'environnement mondial (f. 1994). Dir-Gen. ANTOINE POUILLIEUTE.

**Fonds d'aide et de coopération—FAC:** 20 rue Monsieur, 75007 Paris, France; tel. 1-53-69-00-00; fax 1-53-69-43-82; in 1959 FAC took over from FIDES (Fonds d'investissement pour le développement économique et social) the administration of subsidies and loans from the French Government to the former French African states. FAC is administered by the Ministry of Co-operation, which allocates budgetary funds to it.

# INTER-AMERICAN DEVELOPMENT BANK—IDB

**Address:** 1300 New York Ave, NW, Washington, DC 20577, USA.

**Telephone:** (202) 623-1000; **fax:** (202) 623-3096; **internet:** www.iadb.org.

The Bank was founded in 1959 to promote the individual and collective development of Latin American and Caribbean countries through the financing of economic and social development projects and the provision of technical assistance. Membership was increased in 1976 and 1977 to include countries outside the region.

### MEMBERS

| | | |
|---|---|---|
| Argentina | El Salvador | Panama |
| Austria | Finland | Paraguay |
| Bahamas | France | Peru |
| Barbados | Germany | Portugal |
| Belgium | Guatemala | Slovenia |
| Belize | Guyana | Spain |
| Bolivia | Haiti | Suriname |
| Brazil | Honduras | Sweden |
| Canada | Israel | Switzerland |
| Chile | Italy | Trinidad and Tobago |
| Colombia | Jamaica | United Kingdom |
| Costa Rica | Japan | USA |
| Croatia | Mexico | Uruguay |
| Denmark | Netherlands | Venezuela |
| Dominican Republic | Nicaragua | |
| Ecuador | Norway | |

## Organization

(January 2000)

### BOARD OF GOVERNORS

All the powers of the Bank are vested in a Board of Governors, consisting of one Governor and one alternate appointed by each member country (usually ministers of finance or presidents of central banks). The Board meets annually, with special meetings when necessary. The 40th annual meeting of the Board of Governors took place in Paris, France, in March 1999. The 41st annual meeting was to take place in New Orleans, USA, in March 2000.

### BOARD OF EXECUTIVE DIRECTORS

The Board of Executive Directors is responsible for the operations of the Bank. It establishes the Bank's policies, approves loan and technical co-operation proposals that are submitted by the President of the Bank, and authorizes the Bank's borrowings on capital markets.

There are 12 executive directors and 12 alternates. Each Director is elected by a group of two or more countries, except the Directors representing Canada and the USA. The USA holds 34.7% of votes on the Board, proportional to its contribution to the Bank's capital. The Board has four standing committees, relating to: Policy and evaluation; Organization, human resources and board matters; Budget, financial policies and audit; and Programming.

### ADMINISTRATION

In 1994 the Bank reorganized its administrative structure, in order to improve management accountability and efficiency, to strengthen country focus and regional co-operation and to address the region's priorities. The Bank now comprises the office of the Multilateral Investment Fund, three Regional Operations Departments, as well as the following departments: Finance; Strategic Planning and Budget; Integration and Regional Programmes; Private Sector; External Relations; Sustainable Development; and Human Resources and Administrative Services. In addition, there is an Office of the Chief Economist and an Evaluation Office. The Bank has country offices in each of its borrowing member states, and special offices in Paris and in Tokyo, Japan. At the end of 1998 there were 1,707 Bank staff (excluding the Board of Executive Directors and the Evaluation Office). The administrative budget for 1999 amounted to US $360.4m.

**President:** ENRIQUE V. IGLESIAS (Uruguay).

**Executive Vice-President:** K. BURKE DILLON (USA).

## Activities

Loans are made to governments, and to public and private entities for specific economic and social development projects and for sectoral reforms. These loans are repayable in the currencies lent and their terms range from 15 to 40 years. Total lending authorized by the Bank by the end of 1998 amounted to US $95,750m. During 1998 the Bank approved 110 loans totalling $10,063m., compared with 107 loans amounting to $6,048m. in 1997. Disbursements on authorized loans amounted to $6,635m., compared with $5,468m. in 1997.

The subscribed ordinary capital stock, including inter-regional capital, which was merged into it in 1987, totalled US $94,219.3m. at the end of 1998, of which $4,171.4m. was paid-in and $90,047.9m. was callable. The callable capital constitutes, in effect, a guarantee of the securities which the Bank issues in the capital markets in order to increase its resources available for lending. Replenishments are made every four years. During 1987 and 1988 agreement on a seventh replenishment of the Bank's capital was delayed by the US Government's demands for a restructuring of lending policies. Previously, a simple majority of directors' votes was sufficient to ensure the approval of a loan; developing member countries had nearly 54% of the voting power. The USA now proposed that a 65% majority should be necessary, thus giving the USA and Canada combined a virtual power of veto. In March 1989 it was agreed that authorized capital should be increased by $26,500m. to a total of some $61,000m., with effect from 17 January 1990. The proposal for loan approvals by a 65% majority was not accepted, but it was agreed that opposition by one shareholder could delay approval of a loan for two months, opposition by two for another five months, while opposition by three shareholders, holding at least 40% of the votes, could delay approval by a further five months, after which approval was to be decided by a simple majority of shareholders. In July 1995 the eighth general increase of the Bank's authorized capital was ratified by member countries: the Bank's resources were to be increased by $41,000m. to $102,000m.

In 1998 the Bank borrowed the equivalent of US $5,761m. on the international capital markets, bringing total borrowings outstanding to more than $32,511m. at the end of the year. During 1998 net earnings amounted to $393m. in ordinary capital resources and $95m. from the Fund for Special Operations (see below), and at the end of that year the Bank's total reserves were $7,291m.

The Fund for Special Operations enables the Bank to make concessional loans for economic and social projects where circumstances call for special treatment, such as lower interest rates and longer repayment terms than those applied to loans from the ordinary resources. The Board of Governors approved US $200m. in new contributions to the Fund in 1990, and in 1995 authorized $1,000m. in extra resources for the Fund. During 1998 the Fund made 25 loans totalling $686m.

In January 1993 a Multilateral Investment Fund was established to promote private investment in the region. The 21 Bank members who signed the initial draft agreement in 1992 to establish the Fund pledged to contribute US $1,200m. The Fund's activities are undertaken through three separate facilities concerned with technical co-operation, human resources development and small enterprise development. During 1998 the Fund approved $137m. for 65 projects, bringing the cumulative total approved to $413m. for 219 projects since the Fund began operations.

In 1998 the Bank agreed to participate in a joint initiative by the International Monetary Fund and the World Bank to assist heavily indebted poor countries (HIPCs) to maintain a sustainable level of debt (see p. 78). In the same year Bolivia and Guyana became eligible for assistance under the initiative. Also in 1998, following projections of reduced resources for the Fund for Special Operations, borrowing member countries agreed to convert about US $2,400m. in local currencies held by the Bank, in order to maintain a convertible concessional Fund for poorer countries, and to help to reduce the debt-servicing payments of Nicaragua and, possibly, Honduras under the HIPC initiative.

In late 1998 the Board of Governors endorsed the establishment of an Emergency Loan Programme, for a one-year period, in order to help to mitigate the effects of the global financial crisis. Funds totalling US $9,000m. were to be made available under the Programme, which was to enable the bank to make large disbursements under special terms. Two emergency loans were approved in 1998, including a loan to Argentina for $2,500m., the largest amount ever approved by the Bank. In December the Bank established an emergency Consultative Group for the Reconstruction and Transformation of Central America to co-ordinate assistance to countries that had suffered extensive damage as a result of 'Hurricane Mitch'. The Bank hosted the first meeting of the Group in the same month, which was attended by government officials, representatives of donor agencies and non-governmental organizations and academics. A total of $6,200m. was pledged in the form of emergency aid, longer-term financing and debt relief. A second meeting of the Group was held in May 1999, in Stockholm, Sweden, at which the assistance package was increased to some $9,000m., of which the Bank and World Bank committed $5,300m. In December the Bank sent an emergency mission to Venezuela to assess the needs of that country following severe floods.

An increasing number of donor countries have placed funds under the Bank's administration for assistance to Latin America, outside the framework of the Ordinary Resources and the Bank's Special Operations. These trust funds include the Social Progress Trust Fund (set up by the USA in 1961); the Venezuelan Trust Fund (set up in 1975); the Japan Special Fund (1988); and other funds administered on behalf of Austria, Belgium, Canada, Denmark, Finland, France, Israel, Italy, Japan, the Netherlands, Norway, Portugal, Spain, Sweden, Switzerland, the United Kingdom and the EU. A Program for the Development of Technical Co-operation was established in 1991, which is financed by European countries and the EU. Total cumulative lending from all these trust funds was $1,721.7m. for 205 loans approved by the end of 1997. During 1998 co-financing of projects amounted to $3,535.5m., of which $2,840.0m. was provided by several bilateral and multilateral financiers (in particular, the Japanese Government and the World Bank).

Following the capital increase approved in 1989, the Bank was to undertake sectoral lending for the first time, devoting up to 25% of its financing in 1990–93 to loans which would allow countries to make policy changes and improve their institutions. An environmental protection division was also formed in 1989. In December 1993 a task force presented a report on the Bank's operations to the Board of Executive Directors, which recommended greater responsibility for country offices throughout the project cycle; greater emphasis on development results, as opposed to lending targets; increased training for the personnel involved in implementing projects; and increased lending to social and poverty reduction programmes. A high-level Social Agenda Policy Group was created in 1993 to investigate the most effective means of supporting social reform in borrowing countries. Under the eighth general increase of the Bank's resources priority areas of operation were designated as poverty reduction and social equity; modernization of state organs; and the environment. During 1995 an inter-departmental working group on poverty was established, in order to identify policies and projects likely to be effective in reducing poverty. In 1997 an inter-departmental working group was established with the aim of helping member countries to combat corruption and to promote transparency in the Bank's own lending procedures.

The Bank provides technical co-operation to help member countries to identify and prepare new projects, to improve loan execution, to strengthen the institutional capacity of public and private agencies, to address extreme conditions of poverty and to promote small- and micro-enterprise development. The Bank has established a special co-operation programme to facilitate the transfer of experience and technology among regional programmes. In 1998 the Bank approved 407 technical co-operation operations, totalling US $105.8m., mainly financed by income from the Fund for Special Operations. The Bank supports the efforts of the countries of the region to achieve economic integration and has provided extensive technical support for the formulation of integration strategies in the Andean, Central American and Southern Cone regions. The Bank is also supporting the initiative to establish a Free Trade Area of the Americas (FTAA) by 2005 and has provided technical assistance, developed programming strategies and produced a number of studies on relevant integration and trade issues.

The IDB has created an Inter-American Institute for Social Development (INDES), which is designed to train senior officials in modern techniques for improving social policies and social services, with poverty reduction as the ultimate objective. INDES began operating in 1995 and aimed to train 4,000 officials from government and non-governmental organizations over the subsequent four years. In 1998 INDES provided training for 1,255 people.

**Distribution of loans** (US $ million)

| Sector | 1998 | % | 1961–98 | % |
|---|---|---|---|---|
| **Productive Sectors** | | | | |
| Agriculture and fisheries | 122 | 1.2 | 12,580 | 13.2 |
| Industry, mining and tourism | 1,108 | 11.0 | 7,907 | 8.3 |
| Science and technology | 14 | 0.1 | 1,339 | 1.4 |
| **Physical Infrastructure** | | | | |
| Energy | 832 | 8.2 | 16,443 | 17.2 |
| Transportation and communications | 793 | 7.8 | 12,198 | 12.7 |
| **Social Sectors** | | | | |
| Sanitation | 820 | 8.1 | 8,454 | 8.8 |
| Urban development | 672 | 6.6 | 5,758 | 6.0 |
| Education | 294 | 2.9 | 3,855 | 4.0 |
| Social investment | 1,093 | 10.8 | 4,457 | 4.7 |
| Health | 129 | 1.3 | 1,728 | 1.8 |
| Environment | 108 | 1.1 | 1,530 | 1.6 |
| Microenterprise | 215 | 2.2 | 496 | 0.5 |
| **Other** | | | | |
| Public-sector reform and modernization | 3,841 | 38.5 | 13,934 | 14.6 |
| Export financing | 22 | 0.2 | 1,518 | 1.6 |
| Other | 0 | 0.0 | 3,552 | 3.7 |
| **Total** | 10,063 | 100.0 | 95,750 | 100.0 |

## INSTITUTIONS

**Instituto para la Integración de América Latina y el Caribe** (Institute for the Integration of Latin America and the Caribbean): Esmeralda 130, 16° and 17°, 1035 Buenos Aires, Argentina; tel. (1) 320-1850; fax (1) 320-1865; e-mail int/inl@iadb.org; internet www.iadb.org/intal; f. 1965 under the auspices of the Inter-American Development Bank; forms part of the Bank's Integration and Regional Programmes Department. The Institute undertakes research on all aspects of regional integration and co-operation and issues related to international trade, hemispheric integration and relations with other regions and countries of the world. Activities come under four main headings: regional and national technical co-operation projects on integration; policy fora; integration fora; and journals and information. A Documentation Center holds 100,000 documents, 12,000 books and 400 periodical titles. Dir JUAN JOSÉ TACCONE. Publs *Integración y Comercio/Integration and Trade* (3 a year), *Carta Mensual/Monthly Newsletter, Informe Mercosur/Mercosur Report* (2 a year).

**Inter-American Investment Corporation—IIC:** 1300 New York Ave, NW, Washington, DC 20057, USA; tel. (202) 623-3900; fax (202) 623-2360; e-mail iicmail@iadb.org; f. 1986 as a legally autonomous affiliate of the Inter-American Development Bank, to promote private-sector investment in the region; commenced operations in 1989. The IIC's initial capital stock was US $200m., of which 55% was contributed by developing member nations, 25.3% by the USA, and the remainder by non-regional members. In total, the IIC has 37 shareholders (26 Latin American and Caribbean countries, eight European countries, Israel, Japan and the USA). Emphasis is placed on investment in small and medium-sized enterprises. In 1998 the IIC approved equity investments and loans totalling $223m. for 28 private-sector transactions, compared with $150m. for 25 transactions in 1997. Gen. Man. JOHN C. RAHMING (acting). Publ. *Annual Report* (in English, French, Portuguese and Spanish).

# Publications

*Annual Report* (in English, Spanish, Portuguese and French).

*Annual Report on the Environment and Natural Resources* (in English and Spanish).

*Economic and Social Progress in Latin America* (annually, in English and Spanish).

*IDB América* (monthly, English and Spanish).

*IDB Projects* (10 a year, in English).

*Proceedings of the Annual Meeting of the Boards of Governors of the IDB and IIC* (in English, Spanish, Portuguese and French).

*The IDB* (monthly, in English and Spanish).

Brochure series, occasional papers, working papers, reports.

# INTERNATIONAL CHAMBER OF COMMERCE—ICC

**Address:** 38 Cours Albert 1er, 75008 Paris, France.

**Telephone:** 1-49-53-28-28; **fax:** 1-49-53-29-42; **e-mail:** icc@iccwbo.org; **internet:** www.iccwbo.org.

The ICC was founded in 1919 to promote free trade and private enterprise, provide practical services and represent business interests at governmental and inter-governmental levels.

### MEMBERS

At the end of 1998 membership consisted of about 5,500 individual corporations and 1,700 organizations (mainly trade and industrial organizations and chambers of commerce). National Committees or Groups had been formed in more than 60 countries and territories to co-ordinate ICC objectives and functions at the national level.

| | | |
|---|---|---|
| Argentina | Hungary | Peru |
| Australia | Iceland | Philippines |
| Austria | India | Poland |
| Bangladesh | Indonesia | Portugal |
| Belgium | Iran | Saudi Arabia |
| Brazil | Ireland | Senegal |
| Burkina Faso | Israel | Singapore |
| Cameroon | Italy | South Africa |
| Canada | Japan | Spain |
| Chile | Jordan | Sri Lanka |
| China, People's Republic | Korea, Republic | Sweden |
| Colombia | Kuwait | Switzerland |
| Côte d'Ivoire | Lebanon | Syria |
| Cyprus | Lithuania | Taiwan* |
| Czech Republic | Luxembourg | Togo |
| Denmark | Madagascar | Tunisia |
| Ecuador | Mexico | Turkey |
| Egypt | Morocco | Ukraine |
| Finland | Netherlands | United Kingdom |
| France | New Zealand | USA |
| Germany | Nigeria | Uruguay |
| Greece | Norway | Venezuela |
| Hong Kong | Pakistan | Yugoslavia |

* Admitted as Chinese Taipei.

## Organization

(January 2000)

### COUNCIL

The Council is the governing body of the organization. It meets twice a year and is composed of members nominated by the National Committees. Ten direct members, from countries where no National Committee exists, may also be invited to participate. The Council elects the President and Vice-President for terms of two years.

**President:** ADNAN KASSAR (Lebanon).

### EXECUTIVE BOARD

The Executive Board consists of 15–30 members appointed by the Council on the recommendation of the President and nine *ex-officio* members. Members serve for a three-year term, one-third of the members retiring at the end of each year. It ensures close direction of ICC activities and meets at least three times each year.

### INTERNATIONAL SECRETARIAT

The ICC secretariat is based at International Headquarters in Paris, with additional offices maintained in Geneva and New York principally for liaison with the United Nations and its agencies. The Secretary-General is appointed by the Council on the recommendation of the Executive Board.

**Secretary-General:** MARIA LIVANOS CATTAUI.

### NATIONAL COMMITTEES AND GROUPS

Each affiliate is composed of leading business organizations and individual companies. It has its own secretariat, monitors issues of concern to its national constituents, and draws public and government attention to ICC policies.

### CONGRESS

The ICC's supreme assembly, to which all member companies and organizations are invited to send senior representatives. Congresses are held regulary, in a different place on each occasion, with up to 2,000 participants. The 32nd Congress was held in Shanghai, People's Republic of China, in April 1997 and the 33rd Congress was to be held in Budapest, Hungary, in May 2000, on the theme of 'The new Europe in the World Economy'.

### CONFERENCES

ICC Conferences was created in 1996 to disseminate ICC expertise in the fields of international arbitration, trade, banking and commercial practice, by means of a world-wide programme of conferences and seminars.

## Activities

The various Commissions of the ICC (listed below) are composed of some 500 practising business executives and experts from all sectors of economic life, nominated by National Committees. ICC recommendations must be adopted by a Commission following consultation with National Committees, and then approved by the Council or Executive Board, before they can be regarded as official ICC policies. Meetings of Commissions are generally held twice a year. Working Parties are frequently constituted by Commissions to undertake specific projects and report back to their parent body. Officers of Commissions, and specialized Working Parties, often meet in the intervals between Commission sessions. The Commissions produce a wide array of specific codes and guide-lines of direct use to the world business community; draw up statements and initiatives for presentation to governments and international bodies; and comment constructively and in detail on proposed actions by intergovernmental organizations that are likely to affect business.

ICC works closely with other international organizations. ICC members, the heads of UN economic organizations and the OECD convene for annual discussions on the world economy. The Commission on International Trade and Investment Policy campaigns against protectionism in world trade and in support of the World Trade Organization (WTO, q.v.). The ICC also works closely with the European Union, commenting on EU directives and making recommendations on, for example, tax harmonization and laws relating to competition.

ICC plays a part in combating international crime connected with commerce through its Commercial Crime Services, based in London, United Kingdom, and Kuala Lumpur, Malaysia. These comprise: the Commercial Crime Bureau; the International Maritime Bureau, which combats maritime fraud, including insurance fraud and the theft of cargoes; and the Counterfeiting Intelligence Bureau, established in 1985 to investigate counterfeiting in trade-marked goods, copyrights and industrial designs. Commercial disputes are submitted to the ICC International Court of Arbitration. In January 1997 the ICC opened its first regional office, in the Hong Kong Special Administrative Region. The office now also provides the secretariat for the Hong Kong, China Business Council, established in December 1998 to promote the region's business interests abroad.

In 1998 the ICC continued to develop rules and guide-lines relating to electronic transactions, including guide-lines for ethical advertising on the internet and for data protection. In September it presented model clauses for company contracts involving the electronic transfer of personal information. The Geneva Business Dialogue was held in Switzerland in September. The primary subjects discussed were the importance of globalization in business and the need to avoid protectionist reactions to recent economic upheaval. In September 1999 ICC published a fully revised and updated version of the standard commercial terms for international sales contracts, Incoterms 2000, which define the responsibilities of buyers and sellers.

**Policy and Technical Commissions:**
Commission on Air Transport
Commission on Banking Technique and Practice
Commission on Energy
Commission on Environment
Commission on Extortion and Bribery
Commission on Financial Services
Commission on Insurance
Commission on Intellectual and Industrial Property
Commission on International Arbitration
Commission on International Commercial Practice
Commission on International Trade and Investment Policy
Commission on Law and Practices Relating to Competition
Commission on Maritime and Surface Transport
Commission on Marketing, Advertising and Distribution
Commission on Taxation
Commission on Telecommunications and Information Technologies

**Bodies for the Settlement of Disputes:**
International Centre for Technical Expertise
International Court of Arbitration
International Maritime Arbitration Organization

**Other Bodies:**
ICC Centre for Maritime Co-operation
ICC Commercial Crime Bureau
ICC Corporate Security Services
ICC Counterfeiting Intelligence Bureau
ICC Institute of International Business Law and Practice
ICC International Maritime Bureau
ICC-WTO Economic Consultative Committee
Institute of World Business Law
International Bureau of Chambers of Commerce

## Finance

The International Chamber of Commerce is a private organization financed partly by contributions from National Committees and other members, according to the economic importance of the country which each represents, and partly by revenue from fees for various services and from sales of publications.

## Publications

*Annual Report.*
*Business World* (electronic magazine).
*Documentary Credits Insight* (quarterly).
*Handbook.*
*ICC Contact* (newsletter).
*ICC International Court of Arbitration Bulletin.*
*IGO Report.*
Numerous publications on general and technical business and trade-related subjects.

# INTERNATIONAL CONFEDERATION OF FREE TRADE UNIONS—ICFTU

**Address:** 5 blvd Roi Albert II, 1210 Brussels, Belgium.

**Telephone:** (2) 224-02-11; **fax:** (2) 201-58-15; **e-mail:** internetpo@icftu.org; **internet:** www.icftu.org.

ICFTU was founded in 1949 by trade union federations which had withdrawn from the World Federation of Trade Unions (see p. 272). It aims to promote the interests of working people and to secure recognition of workers' organizations as free bargaining agents; to reduce the gap between rich and poor; and to defend fundamental human and trade union rights. During 1996 it campaigned for the adoption by the World Trade Organization of a social clause, with legally-binding minimum labour standards. In 1998 it participated in negotiations on the introduction of ethical codes of conduct into global corporations in the energy sector. See also the World Confederation of Labour (p. 271).

### MEMBERS

215 organizations in 145 countries with 125m. members (Dec. 1999).

## Organization

(January 2000)

### WORLD CONGRESS

The Congress, the highest authority of ICFTU, normally meets every four years. The 16th Congress was held in Brussels, Belgium, in June 1996. The 17th Congress was to be held in Durban, South Africa, in April 2000.

Delegations from national federations vary in size according to membership. The Congress examines past activities, maps out future plans, elects the Executive Board and the General Secretary, considers the functioning of the regional machinery, examines financial reports and social, economic and political situations. It works through plenary sessions and through technical committees which report to the plenary sessions.

### EXECUTIVE BOARD

The Board meets not less than once a year, for about three days, usually at Brussels, or at the Congress venue; it comprises 53 members elected by Congress and nominated by areas of the world. The General Secretary is an *ex-officio* member. After each Congress the Board elects a President and at least seven Vice-Presidents.

The Board considers administrative questions; hears reports from field representatives, missions, regional organizations and affiliates, and makes resultant decisions; and discusses finances, applications for affiliation, and problems affecting world labour. It elects a steering committee of 19 to deal with urgent matters between Board meetings.

**President:** C. LEROY TROTMAN.

### PERMANENT COMMITTEES

**Steering Committee.** Administers the General Fund, comprising affiliation fees, and the International Solidarity Fund, constituting additional voluntary contributions.

**Economic and Social Committee.**

**Human and Trade Union Rights Committee.**

***ICFTU/ITS Working Party on Trade Union Education.**

***ICFTU/ITS Occupational Health, Safety, and the Environment Working Party.**

***ICFTU/ITS Working Party on Multinational Companies.**

**Peace, Security and Disarmament Committee.**

**Youth Committee.**

**Women's Committee.**

*A joint body of the ICFTU and International Trade Secretariats.

### SECRETARIAT

The headquarters staff numbers 75, comprising some 25 different nationalities.

The six departments are: Economic and Social Policy; Trade Union Rights; Projects, Co-ordination and Education (comprising units for Projects and Trade Union Education); Equality (including Youth); Finance and Administration; Press and Publications. There are also the Co-ordination Unit for Central and Eastern Europe, the Electronic Data Processing Unit, Personnel, Co-ordination and Regional Liaison Desks for the Americas, Africa and Asia.

**General Secretary:** WILLIAM (BILL) JORDAN (United Kingdom).

### BRANCH OFFICES

**ICFTU Geneva Office:** 46 ave Blanc, 1202 Geneva, Switzerland; tel. (22) 7384202; fax (22) 7381082; e-mail icftu-ge@geneva.icftu.org; Dir DAN CUNNIAH.

**ICFTU United Nations Office:** Room 404, 104 East 40th St, New York, NY 10016, USA; tel. (212) 986-1820; fax (212) 972-9746; e-mail icftuny@igc.org; Perm. Rep. GEMMA ADABA.

There are also Permanent Representatives accredited to FAO (Rome) to the UN, UNIDO and IAEA (Vienna) and to UNEP and UNCHS (Habitat) (Nairobi).

### REGIONAL ORGANIZATIONS

**ICFTU African Regional Organization—AFRO:** POB 67273, Ambank House, 14th Floor, University Way, Nairobi, Kenya; tel. (2) 221357; fax (2) 215072; e-mail icftuafro@form-net.com; f. 1957. Mems: 5m. workers in 36 African countries; Pres. MADIA DIOP (Senegal); Gen. Sec. ANDREW KAILEMBO (Tanzania).

**ICFTU Asian and Pacific Regional Organization—APRO:** Trade Union House, 3rd Floor, Shenton Way, Singapore 068810; tel. (65) 2226294; fax (65) 2217380; e-mail gs@icftu-apro.org.sg; f. 1951. Mems: 33m. in 38 orgs in 29 countries. Pres. KENNETH G. DOUGLAS; Gen. Sec. TAKASHI IZUMI.

**Inter-American Regional Organization of Workers—ORIT:** Edif. José Vargas, Avda Andrés Eloy Blanco No 2, 15°, Los Caobos, Caracas, Venezuela; tel. (2) 574-9313; fax (2) 592-7329; e-mail orit@ven.net; f. 1951. Mems: national unions in 28 countries and territories. Pres. A. MADARIAGA; Gen. Sec. LUIS A. ANDERSON.

There are Field Representatives in various parts of Africa. In addition, a number of Project Planners for development co-operation travel in different countries.

## Finance

Affiliated federations pay a standard fee of 6,211 Belgian francs (1998), or its equivalent in other currencies, per 1,000 members per annum, which covers the establishment and routine activities of the ICFTU headquarters in Brussels, and partly subsidizes the regional organizations.

An International Solidarity Fund was set up in 1956 to assist unions in developing countries, and workers and trade unionists victimized by repressive political measures. It provides legal assistance and supports educational activities. In cases of major natural disasters affecting workers token relief aid is granted.

## Publications

*Survey of Violations of Trade Union Rights* (annually).

*Trade Union World* (official journal, monthly).

These periodicals are issued in English, French and Spanish. In addition the Congress report is issued in English. Numerous other publications on labour, economic and trade union training have been published in various languages.

## Associated International Trade Secretariats

**Education International—EI:** 5 blvd Roi Albert II (8ème étage), 1210 Brussels, Belgium; tel. (2) 224-06-11; fax (2) 224-06-06; e-mail educint@ei-ie.org; internet www.ei-ie.org; f. 1993 by merger of the World Confederation of Organizations of the Teaching Profession (f. 1952) and the International Federation of Free Teachers' Unions (f. 1951). Mems: 294 national orgs of teachers' trade unions representing 23m. members in 152 countries and territories. Holds Congress (every three years): 2001 in Nepal. Pres. MARY HATWOOD FUTRELL (USA); Sec.-Gen. FRED VAN LEEUWEN (Netherlands). Publs *EI Monitor* (monthly), *Education International* (quarterly) (both in English, French and Spanish).

**International Federation of Building and Woodworkers—IFBWW:** 54 route des Acacias, POB 1412, 1227 Carouge, Switzerland; tel. (22) 827-37-77; fax (22) 827-37-70; e-mail info@ifbww.org; internet www.ifbww.org; f. 1934. Mems: 282 national unions with a membership of 13.0m. workers in 124 countries. Organization: Congress, Executive Committee. Pres. ROEL DE VRIES (Netherlands); Sec.-Gen. ULF ASP (Sweden). Publ. *Bulletin* (8 a year).

**International Federation of Chemical, Energy, Mine and General Workers' Unions—ICEM:** 109 ave Emile de Béco, 1050 Brussels, Belgium; tel. (2) 626-20-20; fax (2) 648-43-16; e-mail icem@geo2.poptel.org.uk; internet www.icem.org; f. 1995 by merger of the International Federation of Chemical, Energy and General Workers' Unions (f. 1907) and the Miners' International Federation (f. 1890). Mems: 403 trade unions covering approximately 20m. workers in 113 countries. Main sectors cover energy industries; chemicals; pharmaceuticals and biotechnology; mining and extraction; pulp and paper; rubber; ceramics; glass; building materials; and environmental services. Pres. HANS BERGER; Gen. Sec. VICTOR E. THORPE. Publs *ICEM Info* (quarterly), *ICEM Focus on Health, Safety and Environment* (2 a year), *ICEM Update* (Irregular).

**International Federation of Journalists—IFJ:** 266 rue Royale, 1210 Brussels, Belgium; tel. (2) 223-22-65; fax (2) 219-29-76; e-mail ifj@pophost.eunet.be; internet www.ifj.org; f. 1952 to link national unions of professional journalists dedicated to the freedom of the press, to defend the rights of journalists, and to raise professional standards; it conducts surveys, assists in trade union training programmes, organizes seminars and provides information; it arranges fact-finding missions in countries where press freedom is under pressure, and issues protests against the persecution and detention of journalists and the censorship of the mass media. Mems: 133 unions in 99 countries, comprising 450,000 individuals. Pres. CHRIS WARREN (Australia); Gen. Sec. AIDAN WHITE (UK). Publ. *IFJ Direct Line* (every two months).

**International Metalworkers' Federation—IMF:** CP 1516, Route des Acacias 54 bis, 1227 Geneva, Switzerland; tel. (22) 3085050; fax (22) 3085055; e-mail info@imfmetal.org; internet www.imfmetal.org; f. 1893. Mems: national orgs covering 22m. workers in 95 countries. Holds Congress (every four years); has six regional offices; seven industrial departments; World Company Councils for unions in multinational corporations. Pres. K. ZWICKEL (Germany); Gen. Sec. MARCELLO MALENTACCHI. Publs *IMF NewsBriefs* (weekly), *Metal World* (quarterly).

**International Textile, Garment and Leather Workers' Federation—ITGLWF:** rue Joseph Stevens 8 (Boîte 4), 1000 Brussels, Belgium; tel. (2) 512-26-06; fax (2) 511-09-04; e-mail itglwf@compuserve.com; f. 1970. Mems: 242 unions covering 9m. workers in 130 countries. Pres. PETER BOOTH (UK); Gen. Sec. NEIL KEARNEY (Ireland). Publ. *ITGLWF Newsletter* (quarterly).

**International Transport Workers' Federation—ITF:** 49-60 Borough Rd, London, SE1 1DS, United Kingdom; tel. (20) 7403-2733; fax (20) 7357-7871; e-mail mail@itf.org.uk; internet www.itf.org.uk; f. 1896. Mems: national trade unions covering 5m. workers in more than 120 countries. Holds Congress (every four years); has eight Industrial Sections. Pres. UMRAOMAL PURDIT (India); Gen. Sec. DAVID COCKROFT (UK). Publ. *ITF News* (every two months).

**International Union of Food, Agricultural, Hotel, Restaurant, Catering, Tobacco and Allied Workers' Associations—IUF:** 8 rampe du Pont-Rouge, 1213 Petit-Lancy, Switzerland; tel. (22) 7932233; fax (22) 7932238; e-mail iuf@iuf.org; f. 1920. Mems: 331 affiliated organizations covering about 2.6m workers in 112 countries. Holds Congress (every five years). Pres. FRANK HURT (USA); Gen. Sec. RON OSWALD. Publs bi-monthly bulletins.

**Public Services International—PSI:** 45 ave Voltaire, BP9, 01211 Ferney-Voltaire, France; tel. 4-50-40-64-64; fax 4-50-40-73-20; e-mail psi@world-psi.org; internet www.world-psi.org; f. 1907; Mems: 528 unions and professional associations covering 20m. workers in 144 countries. Holds Congress (every five years). Pres. WILLIAM LUCY (USA); Gen. Sec. HANS ENGELBERTS (Netherlands). Publ. *Focus* (quarterly).

**Union Network International—UNI:** 15 ave de Balexert, 1219 Châtelaine-Geneva, Switzerland; tel. (22) 9790311; fax (22) 7965321; e-mail contact@union-network.org; internet www.union-network.org; f. 2000 by merger of Communications International (CI), the International Federation of Commercial, Clerical, Professional and Technical Employees (FIET), the International Graphical Federation (IGF), and Media and Entertainment International (MEI). Mems: 900 unions in more than 140 countries, representing 15.5m. people. Activities cover the following 12 sectors: commerce; electricity; finance; graphical; hair and beauty; professional and information technology staff; media, entertainment and the arts; postal; property services; social insurance and private health care; telecommunications; and tourism. First World Congress scheduled to be convened in Berlin, Germany, in September 2001. Pres. KURT VAN HAAREN (Germany); Gen. Sec. PHILIP JENNINGS. Publs *UNIinfo* (quarterly), *UNInet News* (monthly).

**Universal Alliance of Diamond Workers—UADW:** Lange Kievitstraat 57 (Bus 3), 2018 Antwerp, Belgium; tel. (3) 232-15-57; fax (3) 226-40-09; e-mail uadw@planetinternet.be; f. 1905. Mems: 100,000 in 17 countries. Pres. DONALD WITTERWRONGEL (Belgium); Gen. Sec. JEF HOYMANS (Belgium).

# INTERNATIONAL OLYMPIC COMMITTEE

**Address:** Château de Vidy, 1007 Lausanne, Switzerland.

**Telephone:** (21) 6216111; **fax:** (21) 6216216; **internet:** www.olympic.org.

The International Olympic Committee was founded in 1894 to ensure the regular celebration of the Olympic Games.

## Organization

(January 2000)

### INTERNATIONAL OLYMPIC COMMITTEE

The International Olympic Committee (IOC) is a non-governmental international organization comprising 113 members, who are representatives of the IOC in their countries and not their countries' delegates to the IOC. The members meet in session at least once a year. In accordance with reforms adopted in December 1999, the Committee was to comprise a maximum of 115 members, including 15 active Olympic athletes, 15 National Olympic Committee presidents, 15 International Sports Federation presidents, and 70 other individuals. A nominations committee was to be established for the election to the IOC.

The IOC is the final authority on all questions concerning the Olympic Games and the Olympic movement. There are 198 recognized National Olympic Committees, which are the sole authorities responsible for the representation of their respective countries at the Olympic Games. The IOC may give recognition to International Federations which undertake to adhere to the Olympic Charter, and which govern sports that comply with the IOC's criteria.

A Supreme Council of International Sport Arbitration has been established to hear cases brought by competitors.

### EXECUTIVE BOARD

The session of the IOC delegates to the Executive Board the authority to manage the IOC's affairs. The President of the Board is elected for an eight-year term, and is eligible for re-election for successive terms of four years. The Vice-Presidents are elected for four-year terms, and may be re-elected after a minimum interval of four years. Members of the Board are elected to hold office for four years. The Executive Board generally meets four to five times per year.

**President:** Juan Antonio Samaranch (Spain).

**Vice-Presidents:** Richard Kevan Gosper (Australia); Richard W. Pound (Canada); Anita DeFrantz (USA); Kéba Mbaye (Senegal).

**Members of the Board:**

Thomas Bach (Germany)
Chiharu Igaya (Japan)
Un Yong Kim (Republic of Korea)
Marc Hodler (Switzerland)
Jacques Rogge (Belgium)
Zhenliang He (People's Republic of China)

### ETHICS COMMISSION

In March 1999 an extraordinary meeting of the IOC approved the establishment of an independent Ethics Commission to develop and monitor rules and principles to guide the selection of hosts for the Olympic Games, and the organization and execution of the Games. The eight-member Commission, which was to be responsible to the Executive Board, comprised three IOC members. The Commission aimed to strengthen the Olympic Movement by ensuring adherence to the principles of the Olympic Charter and a new IOC code of conduct, by promoting positive ethics, and by providing transparency, accountability and an effective response to ethical issues. The Commission held its first meeting in Lausanne, Switzerland, in May.

**Chairman:** Kéba Mbaye.

### ADMINISTRATION

The administration of the IOC is under the authority of the Director-General and the Secretary-General, who are appointed by the Executive Board, on the proposal of the President.

**Director-General:** François Carrard.

**Secretary-General:** Françoise Zweifel.

## Activities

The fundamental principles of the Olympic movement are:

Olympism is a philosophy of life, exalting and combining, in a balanced whole, the qualities of body, will and mind. Blending sport with culture and education, Olympism seeks to create a way of life based on the joy found in effort, the educational value of good example and respect for universal fundamental ethical principles.

Under the supreme authority of the IOC, the Olympic movement encompasses organizations, athletes and other persons who agree to be guided by the Olympic Charter. The criterion for belonging to the Olympic movement is recognition by the IOC.

The goal of the Olympic movement is to contribute to building a peaceful and better world by educating youth through sport practised without discrimination of any kind and in the Olympic spirit, which requires mutual understanding with a spirit of friendship, solidarity and fair-play.

The activity of the Olympic movement is permanent and universal. It reaches its peak with the bringing together of the athletes of the world at the great sport festival, the Olympic Games.

The Olympic Charter is the codification of the fundamental principles, rules and bye-laws adopted by the IOC. It governs the organization and operation of the Olympic movement and stipulates the conditions for the celebration of the Olympic Games.

In March 1998, at a meeting organized with other international sports governing bodies, it was agreed to form a working group to defend the principle of self-regulation in international sports organizations, against possible interference by the EU. At a meeting in August methods of containing the increase in drugs abuse in sport were discussed. In January 1999, following publication of the results of an investigation into allegations of corruption and bribery, six members of the Committee were recommended for expulsion while investigations into the conduct of other officials were to be pursued. In March an extraordinary session of the IOC was convened, at which the six Committee members were expelled for violating rules relating to Salt Lake City's bid to host the Olympic Winter Games in 2002 (four other members had already resigned, while Executive Board member Un Yong Kim had received disciplinary action). The President of the IOC retained his position after receiving a vote of confidence. The session approved far-reaching reforms, including the introduction of an interim procedure to select the host city for the Winter Games in 2006, by means of which an election college was to choose two finalists from the six cities submitting bids. Visits by IOC members to any of the bid cities were prohibited. In addition, the meeting approved the establishment of an independent Ethics Commission to oversee cities' bids to host the Olympic Games (see above) and an IOC 2000 Commission to review the bidding process after 2006 and the internal structure of the organization. A declaration on drugs and sport was also adopted by the meeting. In November 1999, an independent World Anti-Doping Agency (WADA) was established by the IOC. WADA was to hold its inaugural meeting in January 2000. In December 1999 the IOC adopted 50 reforms proposed by the IOC 2000 Commission during the Extraordinary 110th Session. The changes aimed to create a more open, responsive and accountable organization, and included the elimination of member visits to bid cities, the application of terms of office, limiting the expansion of the Summer Games, and the election of 15 active athletes to the IOC membership.

### THE GAMES OF THE OLYMPIAD

The Olympic Summer Games take place during the first year of the Olympiad (period of four years) which they are to celebrate. They are the exclusive property of the IOC, which entrusts their organization to a host city seven years in advance.

| | | | |
|---|---|---|---|
| 1896 | Athens | 1960 | Rome |
| 1900 | Paris | 1964 | Tokyo |
| 1904 | St Louis | 1968 | Mexico City |
| 1908 | London | 1972 | Munich |
| 1912 | Stockholm | 1976 | Montreal |
| 1920 | Antwerp | 1980 | Moscow |
| 1924 | Paris | 1984 | Los Angeles |
| 1928 | Amsterdam | 1988 | Seoul |
| 1932 | Los Angeles | 1992 | Barcelona |
| 1936 | Berlin | 1996 | Atlanta |
| 1948 | London | 2000 | Sydney |
| 1952 | Helsinki | 2004 | Athens |
| 1956 | Melbourne | | |

The programme of the Games must include at least 15 of the total number of Olympic sports (sports governed by recognized International Federations and admitted to the Olympic programme by decision of the IOC at least seven years before the Games). The Olympic summer sports are: archery, athletics, badminton, baseball, basketball, boxing, canoeing, cycling, equestrian sports, fencing, football, gymnastics, handball, field hockey, judo, modern pentathlon, rowing, sailing, shooting, softball, swimming (including water polo and diving), table tennis, tae kwondo, tennis, triathlon, volleyball, weight-lifting, wrestling.

### OLYMPIC WINTER GAMES

The Olympic Winter Games comprise competitions in sports practised on snow and ice. From 1994 onwards, they were to be held in the second calendar year following that in which the Games of the Olympiad take place.

| | | | |
|---|---|---|---|
| 1924 | Chamonix | 1964 | Innsbruck |
| 1928 | St Moritz | 1968 | Grenoble |
| 1932 | Lake Placid | 1972 | Sapporo |
| 1936 | Garmisch-Partenkirchen | 1976 | Innsbruck |
| 1948 | St Moritz | 1980 | Lake Placid |
| 1952 | Oslo | 1984 | Sarajevo |
| 1956 | Cortina d'Ampezzo | 1988 | Calgary |
| 1960 | Squaw Valley | 1992 | Albertville |
| 1994 | Lillehammer | 2002 | Salt Lake City |
| 1998 | Nagano | 2006 | Turin |

The Winter Games may include skiing, skating, ice hockey, bobsleigh, luge, curling and biathlon.

## Finance

The operational budget for the International Olympic Committee for 1998 was 37,240m. Swiss francs.

## Publication

*Olympic Review.*

# INTERNATIONAL ORGANIZATION FOR MIGRATION—IOM

**Address:** 17 route des Morillons, CP 71, 1211 Geneva 19, Switzerland.

**Telephone:** (22) 7179111; **fax:** (22) 7986150; **e-mail:** hq@iom.int; **internet:** www.iom.int.

The Intergovernmental Committee for Migration (ICM) was founded in 1951 as a non-political and humanitarian organization with a predominantly operational mandate, including the handling of orderly and planned migration to meet specific needs of emigration and immigration countries; and the processing and movement of refugees, displaced persons and other individuals in need of international migration services to countries offering them resettlement opportunities. In 1989 ICM's name was changed to the International Organization for Migration (IOM). IOM was admitted as an observer to the UN General Assembly in October 1992.

### MEMBERS

| | | |
|---|---|---|
| Albania | France | Panama |
| Angola | Germany | Paraguay |
| Argentina | Greece | Peru |
| Armenia | Guatemala | Philippines |
| Australia | Guinea-Bissau | Poland |
| Austria | Haiti | Portugal |
| Bangladesh | Honduras | Romania |
| Belgium | Hungary | Senegal |
| Bolivia | Israel | Slovakia |
| Bulgaria | Italy | South Africa |
| Canada | Japan | Sri Lanka |
| Chile | Jordan | Sudan |
| Colombia | Kenya | Sweden |
| Costa Rica | Korea, Republic | Switzerland |
| Croatia | Latvia | Tajikistan |
| Cyprus | Liberia | Tanzania |
| Czech Republic | Lithuania | Thailand |
| Denmark | Luxembourg | Tunisia |
| Dominican Republic | Mali | Uganda |
| | Morocco | USA |
| Ecuador | Netherlands | Uruguay |
| Egypt | Nicaragua | Venezuela |
| El Salvador | Norway | Yemen |
| Finland | Pakistan | Zambia |

Observers: Afghanistan, Algeria, Belarus, Belize, Bosnia and Herzegovina, Brazil, Cape Verde, Democratic Republic of the Congo, Republic of the Congo, Cuba, Estonia, Ethiopia, Georgia, Ghana, Guinea, Holy See, India, Indonesia, Iran, Ireland, Jamaica, Kazakhstan, Kyrgyzstan, Madagascar, Malta, Mexico, Moldova, Mozambique, Namibia, New Zealand, Papua New Guinea, Russia, Rwanda, San Marino, São Tomé and Príncipe, Slovenia, Somalia, Sovereign Military Order of Malta, Spain, Turkey, Turkmenistan, Ukraine, United Kingdom, Viet Nam, Yugoslavia, Zimbabwe. In addition, some 49 international governmental organizations hold observer status with IOM.

## Organization

(January 2000)

IOM is governed by a Council which is composed of representatives of all member governments, and has the responsibility for making final decisions on policy, programmes and financing. An Executive Committee of nine member governments elected by the Council prepares the work of the Council and makes recommendations on the basis of reports from the Sub-Committee on Budget and Finance and the Sub-Committee on the Co-ordination of Transport. IOM had a network of 80 offices in 1999.

**Director General:** BRUNSON MCKINLEY (USA).

**Deputy Director General:** NDIORO NDIAYE (Senegal).

## Activities

IOM aims to provide assistance to member governments in meeting the operational challenges of migration, to advance understanding of migration issues, to encourage social and economic development through migration and to work towards effective respect of the human dignity and well-being of migrants. It provides a full range of migration assistance to, and sometimes *de facto* protection of, migrants, refugees, displaced persons and other individuals in need of international migration services. This includes recruitment, selection, processing, medical examinations, and language and cultural orientation courses, placement, activities to facilitate reception and integration and other advisory services. IOM co-ordinates its refugee activities with the UN High Commissioner for Refugees (UNHCR, q.v.) and with governmental and non-governmental partners. In May 1997 IOM and UNHCR signed a memorandum of understanding which aimed to facilitate co-operation between the two organizations. During 1998 IOM transported and assisted some 233,166 people, of whom 213,688 were humanitarian migrants, 10,721 national migrants and 8,757 were registered as qualified human resources. Since it commenced operations in February 1952 IOM has provided assistance to an estimated 10.5m. migrants.

IOM programmes are divided into four main areas.

### HUMANITARIAN MIGRATION

Under its humanitarian migration programmes, IOM provides assistance to persons fleeing conflict situations, to refugees being resettled in third countries or repatriated, to stranded individuals and unsuccessful asylum seekers returning home, to internally and externally displaced persons, to other persons compelled to leave their homelands, to individuals seeking to reunite with other members of their families and to migrants involved in regular migration. IOM provides these individuals with secure, reliable, cost-effective services, including counselling, document processing, medical examination, transportation, language training, and cultural orientation and integration assistance. In addition, IOM organizes temporary evacuation for medical treatment where necessary.

Humanitarian migration activities also include the provision of emergency assistance to persons affected by conflict and post-conflict situations. IOM offers its services to vulnerable populations in need of evacuation, resettlement or return, both in the initial phases of an emergency and during the transition from emergency humanitarian relief, through a period of rehabilitation, to longer-term reconstruction and development efforts. Between 1996 and 1998 more than 160,000 Bosnians were assisted to return voluntarily under IOM auspices; a further 50,000 were expected to return in 1999. In late 1998 IOM mobilized all available resources in the Central American region in an attempt to provide shelter to the thousands of displaced people who lost their homes as a result of 'Hurricane Mitch'.

From April 1999 IOM co-operated with UNHCR and the OSCE to facilitate the evacuation of refugees from Kosovo and Metohija, a southern Serbian province of Yugoslavia, following an escalation of violence against the local Albanian population by Serbian forces and the initiation of a NATO military offensive. The joint Humanitarian Evacuation Programme included land transportation to move substantial numbers of refugees away from over-crowded camps in the border region of the former Yugoslav republic of Macedonia (FYRM), and the provision of charter flights to evacuate those refugees most at need to third countries. IOM was also involved in implementing a programme to register the refugees in Albania, the FYRM and Montenegro, and to reissue identification documents where necessary. Other activities being undertaken by IOM personnel included medical screening of refugees and trauma assessment and rehabilitation. Following the end of the conflict, in June, IOM co-ordinated the return movement of refugees and worked with the UN mission and UNHCR to assist returnees to move to their final destination in Kosovo. In response to the violence and humanitarian crisis which followed the popular consultation conducted in East Timor (Indonesia) in late August, IOM formulated an East Timor Assistance Programme, comprising specific projects such as the assisted return of refugees, emergency transport, and the provision of shelter materials.

In recent years IOM has increasingly assisted in the return home and reintegration of demobilized soldiers, police officials, and their dependents. In 1997 IOM provided assistance to demobilized soldiers and their families in Angola; by the end of that year IOM had helped to resettle 40,621 soldiers and 107,197 dependents. The assistance programme continued in 1998, when IOM launched a major appeal for funding of the initiative. However, at the end of March 1999 IOM ended its work in Angola, owing to a lack of resources and a deterioration of the security situation in that country. IOM was also involved in the resettlement of demobilized forces in Guatemala in 1998. In mid-1999 IOM established an Information Counselling and Referral Service to undertake the registration of former combatants in Kosovo and assist their rehabilitation.

### MIGRATION FOR DEVELOPMENT

IOM's programmes of migration for development aim to contribute towards alleviating economic and social problems through recruitment and selection of high-level workers and professionals to fill positions in priority sectors of the economy in developing countries for which qualified persons are not available locally (particularly in Latin America and Africa), taking into account national development priorities as well as the needs and concerns of receiving communities. Under the programmes for the Transfer of Qualified Human Resources IOM screens candidates, identifies employment opportunities and provides reintegration assistance. Selection Migration programmes help qualified professionals migrate to countries in need of specific expertise when the country cannot find the required skills from within or through the return of nationals. Integrated Experts programmes provide temporary expatriate expertise to states for up to six years: these experts transfer their skills to their working partners and contribute directly to productive output. Programmes of Intraregional Co-operation in the field of qualified human resources encourage collective self-reliance among developing countries by fostering the exchange of governmental experts and the transfer of professionals and technicians within a given region. IOM maintains recruitment offices throughout the world. In November 1996 IOM established a Return of Qualified Nationals programme to facilitate the employment of refugees returning to Bosnia and Herzegovina. By December 1998 more than 600 professionals had been placed in jobs in that country. In addition, IOM and the EU jointly fund a programme to support Rwandan students abroad and encourage their return to Rwanda.

### TECHNICAL CO-OPERATION

Through its technical co-operation programmes IOM offers advisory services on migration to governments, intergovernmental agencies and non-governmental organizations. They aim to assist in the formation and implementation of effective and coherent migration policy, legislation and administration. IOM technical co-operation also focuses on capacity building projects such as training courses for government migration officials, and analysis of and suggestions for solving emerging migration problems. In August 1999 IOM was responsible for organizing voting in the popular consultation in East Timor in five external areas (i.e. Indonesia, Macau, Mozambique, Portugal and the USA) under UN auspices.

### MIGRATION DEBATE, RESEARCH AND INFORMATION

IOM furthers the understanding of migration through regional and international seminars and conferences which bring together those concerned with migration issues in order to develop practical solutions on current migration problems. Recent topics have included migrant women, migrant trafficking, migration and development, undocumented migrants, the impact of migration on social structures, migration and health. In the area of healthcare, IOM is working with UNAIDS on a project aimed at improving knowledge of the impact of migration on the spread of HIV. In September 1999 IOM and UNAIDS signed a co-operation framework to promote awareness on HIV/AIDS issues relating to displaced populations, and to ensure the needs of migrants are incorporated into national and regional AIDS strategies. In October IOM and WHO signed an agreement to strengthen collaborative efforts to improve the health care of migrants.

Research on migration relates not only to the migration process but also to the specific situation and needs of the migrant as an individual human being. IOM has developed mechanisms to gather information on potential migrants' attitudes and motivations, as well as on situations which could lead to irregular migration flows. Trends in international migration point to information as an essential resource for individuals making life-changing decisions about migrating; for governments setting migration policies; for international, regional or non-governmental organizations designing migration programmes; and for researchers, the media and individuals analyzing and reporting on migration. IOM gathers information on migration to meet these growing demands. It also designs and implements information campaigns which provide potential migrants with a more accurate picture of migration realities, in order to prevent unsuccessful or unnecessary migration. In June 1998 IOM warned that the economic difficulties experienced by several South-East Asian economies could precipitate a sharp increase in migration from the region and in the risk to migrant workers presently in the region of exploitation and enforced relocation.

### INTERNATIONAL CENTRE FOR MIGRATION AND HEALTH

**Address:** 11 route du Nant-d'Avril, 1214 Geneva, Vernier, Switzerland; **tel.:** (22) 7831080; **fax:** (22) 7831087; **e-mail:** icmh@worldcom.ch.

Established in March 1995, by IOM and the University of Geneva, with the support of WHO, to respond to the growing needs for information, documentation, research, training and policy development in migration health; designated a WHO collaborating centre, in August 1996, for health-related issues among people displaced by disasters.

**Co-ordinator:** Dr Manuel Carballo.

## Finance

The approved IOM budget for 2000 amounted to US $208.4m. for operations and 34.1m. Swiss francs for administration.

## Publications

*International Migration* (quarterly).
*IOM Latin American Migration Journal* (3 a year, in English and Spanish).
*IOM News* (quarterly, in English, French and Spanish).
*IOM News—North American Supplement.*
*Migration and Health* (quarterly).
*Report by the Director General* (in English, French and Spanish).
*Trafficking in Migrants* (quarterly).
Research reports, *IOM Info Sheets,* surveys and studies.

# INTERNATIONAL RED CROSS AND RED CRESCENT MOVEMENT

The International Red Cross and Red Crescent Movement is a world-wide independent humanitarian organization, comprising three components: the International Committee of the Red Cross (ICRC), founded in 1863; the International Federation of Red Cross and Red Crescent Societies (the Federation), founded in 1919; and National Red Cross and Red Crescent Societies working mainly at national level in 175 countries.

## Organization

### INTERNATIONAL CONFERENCE

The supreme deliberative body of the Movement, the Conference comprises delegations from the ICRC, the Federation and the National Societies, and of representatives of States Parties to the Geneva Conventions (see below). The Conference's function is to determine the general policy of the Movement and to ensure unity in the work of the various bodies. It usually meets every four to five years, and is hosted by the National Society of the country in which it is held. The 26th International Conference, due to be held in November/December 1991 in Budapest, Hungary, was postponed; it was finally convened in December 1995, in Geneva, Switzerland. The 27th International Conference was held in Geneva in October/ November 1999.

### STANDING COMMISSION

The Commission meets at least twice a year in ordinary session. It promotes harmony in the work of the Movement, and examines matters which concern the Movement as a whole. It is formed of two representatives of the ICRC, two of the Federation, and five members of National Societies elected by the Conference.

### COUNCIL OF DELEGATES

The Council comprises delegations from the National Societies, from the ICRC and from the Federation. The Council is the body where the representatives of all the components of the Movement meet to discuss matters that concern the Movement as a whole.

In November 1997 the Council adopted an Agreement on the organization of the activities of the Movement's components. The Agreement aimed to promote increased co-operation and partnership between the Movement's bodies, clearly defining the distribution of tasks between agencies. In particular, the Agreement aimed to ensure continuity between international operations carried out in a crisis situation and those developed in its aftermath.

## Fundamental Principles of the Movement

**Humanity.** The International Red Cross and Red Crescent Movement, born of a desire to bring assistance without discrimination to the wounded on the battlefield, endeavours, in its international and national capacity, to prevent and alleviate human suffering wherever it may be found. Its purpose is to protect life and health and to ensure respect for the human being. It promotes mutual understanding, friendship, co-operation and lasting peace amongst all peoples.

**Impartiality.** It makes no discrimination as to nationality, race, religious beliefs, class or political opinions. It endeavours to relieve the suffering of individuals, being guided solely by their needs, and to give priority to the most urgent cases of distress.

**Neutrality.** In order to continue to enjoy the confidence of all, the Movement may not take sides in hostilities or engage in controversies of a political, racial, religious or ideological nature.

**Independence.** The Movement is independent. The National Societies, while auxiliaries in the humanitarian services of their governments and subject to national laws, must retain their autonomy so that they may always be able to act in accordance with the principles of the Movement.

**Voluntary Service.** It is a voluntary relief movement not prompted by desire for gain.

**Unity.** There can be only one Red Cross or Red Crescent Society in any one country. It must be open to all. It must carry on its humanitarian work throughout the territory.

**Universality.** The International Red Cross and Red Crescent Movement, in which all National Societies have equal status and share equal responsibilities and duties in helping each other, is world-wide.

# International Committee of the Red Cross—ICRC

**Address:** 19 avenue de la Paix, 1202 Geneva, Switzerland.

**Telephone:** (22) 7346001; **fax:** (22) 7332057; **e-mail:** press.gva@icrc.org; **internet:** www.icrc.org.

Founded in 1863, the ICRC is at the origin of the Red Cross and Red Crescent Movement, and co-ordinates all international humanitarian actvities conducted by the Movement in situations of conflict. New statutes of the ICRC, incorporating a revised institutional structure, were adopted in June 1998 and came into effect in July.

## Organization

(January 2000)

### INTERNATIONAL COMMITTEE

The ICRC is an independent institution of a private character composed exclusively of Swiss nationals. Members are co-opted, and their total number may not exceed 25. The international character of the ICRC is based on its mission and not on its composition.

**President:** JAKOB KELLENBERGER.

**Vice-Presidents:** Prof. JACQUES FORSTER; ANNE PETITPIERRE.

### ASSEMBLY

Under the new decision-making structures, approved in 1998, the Assembly was defined as the supreme governing body of the ICRC. It formulates policy, defines the Committee's general objectives and strategies, oversees its activities, and approves its budget and accounts. The Assembly is composed of the members of the ICRC, and is collegial in character. The President and Vice-Presidents of the ICRC hold the same offices in the Assembly.

### ASSEMBLY COUNCIL

The Council (formally the Executive Board) is a subsidiary body of the Assembly, to which the latter delegates certain of its responsibilities. It prepares the Assembly's activities and takes decisions on matters within its competence. The Council is composed of five members elected by the Assembly and is chaired by the President of the ICRC.

**Members:** JAKOB KELLENBERGER, ERNST A. BRUGGER, Prof. JACQUES FORSTER, LISELOTTE KRAUS-GURNY, JAKOB NÜESCH.

### DIRECTORATE

Comprising four members appointed by the Assembly, the Directorate is the executive body of the ICRC, overseeing the efficient running of the organization and responsible for the application of the general objectives and institutional strategies decided by the Assembly.

**Director-General:** PAUL GROSSRIEDER.

**Members:** JEAN-DANIEL TAUXE (Director of Operations), FRANÇOIS BUGNION (Director for International Law and Communication), JACQUES STROUN (Director of Human Resources and Finance).

## Activities

The International Committee of the Red Cross was founded in 1863 in Geneva, by Henry Dunant and four of his friends. The original purpose of the Committee was to promote the foundation, in every country, of a voluntary relief society to assist wounded soldiers on the battlefield (the origin of the National Societies of the Red Cross or Red Crescent), as well as the adoption of a treaty protecting wounded soldiers and all those who come to their rescue. The mission of the ICRC was progressively extended through the Geneva Conventions (see below). The present activities of the ICRC consist in giving legal protection and material assistance to military and civilian victims of wars (international wars, internal strife and disturbances) and in promoting and monitoring the application of international humanitarian law. The ICRC takes into account the legal standards and the specific cultural, ethical and religious features of the environment in which it operates. It aims to influence the conduct of all actual and potential perpetrators of violence by seeking direct dialogue with combatants. In 1990 the ICRC was granted the status of an observer at the United Nations General Assembly.

As well as providing medical aid and emergency food supplies in many countries, the ICRC plays an important part in monitoring prison conditions, in tracing missing persons, and in disseminating humanitarian principles in an attempt to protect non-combatants from violence. In January 1991 the World Campaign for the Protection of War Victims was initiated. This campaign aimed to draw attention to the large numbers of civilians who are killed or injured as a result of armed conflict in which they are not directly involved. At the end of August 1993 the ICRC held an international conference at which a Declaration for the Protection of War Victims was adopted to confirm adherence to the fourth Geneva Convention. In December 1995 the 26th International Conference of the Red Cross and Red Crescent was held in Geneva. It considered the following main themes: protection of the civilian population in periods of armed conflict; international humanitarian law applicable to armed conflicts at sea; principles and action in international humanitarian assistance and protection; strengthening national capacities to provide humanitarian and development assistance; and protection to the most vulnerable. At the same time the ICRC presented a new Advisory Service, which was intended to assist national authorities in their implementation of humanitarian law and to provide a basis for consultation, analysis and harmonization of legislative texts. It became fully operational in January 1996. A Documentation Centre for exchanging information on what national measures exist and what is being done to promote the law in the different states has been established. It is open to all states and National Societies, as well as interested institutions and the general public. The ICRC fully supported efforts to establish a permanent International Criminal Court, with the authority to try serious violations of international humanitarian law. A Statute on the establishment of the Court was signed in July 1998 by representatives of 120 countries, meeting in Rome, Italy, under UN auspices.

In 1996 the ICRC launched the 'Avenir' project to define the organization's future role, in recognition of significant changes in the world situation and the consequent need for changes in humanitarian action. Four main priorities were identified: improving the status of international humanitarian action and knowledge of and respect for humanitarian law; carrying out humanitarian action in closer proximity to victims, with long-term plans and identified priorities; strengthening dialogue with all parties (including launching joint appeals with other organizations if necessary, and the establishment of a combined communication and information dissemination unit); and increasing the ICRC's efficiency. The Assembly endorsed the plan of action in April 1998. In November 1999 the 27th International Conference of the Red Cross and Red Cross adopted a plan of action for the movement for the four-year period 2000–03. The plan incorporated the following three main objectives: to strengthen respect for international humanitarian law, including the conformity of weapons with legal guide-lines, in order to protect victims of armed conflict; to improve national and international preparedness to respond effectively to disaster situations, as well as to improve mechanisms of co-operation and protection of humanitarian personnel working in the field; and strategic partnerships to improve the lives of vulnerable people through health initiatives, measures to reduce discrimination and violence, and strengthening National Societies' capacities and their co-operation with other humanitarian organizations.

In April 1993 the ICRC organized a symposium in Montreux, Switzerland, to consider the use of anti-personnel mines. The ICRC has continued to convene experts to consider the issue in the context of incorporating the use of anti-personnel mines into the review of the 1980 UN Convention on prohibitions or restrictions on the use of conventional weapons. In February 1994 the ICRC issued a report for the review of the Convention. This included a recommendation for the adoption of an additional protocol on the use of laser weapons, which cause permanent blindness or irreparable damage; in October 1995 a session of the Review Conference on the Convention adopted a Protocol, which, as a binding instrument of humanitarian law, prohibits the use and transfer of these weapons. In May 1996 the Conference approved an amended protocol on prohibitions or restrictions on the use of land-mines. The ICRC subsequently resolved to continue its efforts to achieve a world-wide ban on the use of land-mines, and other anti-personnel devices. In October the ICRC supported an International Strategy Conference, organized by the Canadian Government in Ottawa, which was the first formal meeting of states committed to a comprehensive ban on land-mines. In September 1997 the ICRC participated in an international conference, held in Oslo, Norway, at which a Convention was adopted, prohibiting 'the use, stockpiling, production and transfer of anti-personnel mines' and ensuring their destruction (see below). The treaty was opened for signature in December and became legally-binding on 1 March 1999 for the 66 states that had ratified it. In November 1997 the Swiss Government announced that it was to establish a Geneva International Centre for Humanitarian Mine Clearance, in co-operation with the United Nations and the ICRC, to co-ordinate the destruction of land-mines world-wide.

In 1995 the ICRC adopted a 'Plan of Action concerning Children in Armed Conflicts', to promote the principle of non-recruitment and non-participation in armed conflict of children under the age of 18 years. A co-ordinating group was established, with representatives of the individual National Societies and the International Federation of Red Cross and Red Crescent Societies. The UN Commission of Human Rights invited the ICRC to participate in drafting an optional protocol to the Convention on the Rights of the Child, raising to 18 the minimum age for recruitment in armed conflict. The ICRC also co-operated with the UN to draw up the 'Guiding Principles on Internal Displacement', finalized in early 1998.

Examples of recent ICRC activities include the following:

**Africa:** visits to detainees; food and medical assistance, including public health services, war surgery, assistance for victims of land-mines, programmes for the rehabilitation of the disabled, food distribution; and agricultural and veterinary programmes to improve the self-sufficiency of vulnerable and displaced populations. Major operations in 1997 and 1998 covered Angola, Liberia, Mali, Rwanda, Sierra Leone, Somalia, and the Democratic Republic of the Congo (DRC). The ICRC has undertaken tracing activities to reunite Rwandan families: at December 1998 some 12,000 children had been returned to their families by the ICRC and a further 10,000 children in camps remained on an ICRC register. From October 1996 the ICRC provided assistance in the DRC (formerly Zaire) to meet the needs of the mass movement of Rwandan refugees and Zaireans after the outbreak of civil war. Work in Sudan, which was suspended in 1996, recommenced in 1998, following an agreement with the country's Government. In 1999 the ICRC assisted the repatriation of 1,300 Eritreans living in Ethiopia.

**Latin America:** protection and relief activities for civilian population, prisoners of war and detainees in the context of civil conflict, as well as in various situations of internal violence; the dissemination of the fundamental principles of international humanitarian law, in particular in the training of armed forces. In Colombia the ICRC served as a humanitarian mediator in the continuing internal conflict, securing the release of 70 army soldiers in June 1997 and working with other abductees. In 1998 the ICRC also provided assistance for those affected by adverse climatic conditions resulting from 'El Niño' and collaborated with national societies in Central America to assist victims of 'Hurricane Mitch'.

**Asia:** medical assistance to hospitals in Afghanistan; manufacture of artificial limbs and fitting of amputees in Afghanistan and Cambodia; protection of detainees and prisoners in Afghanistan, India, Bhutan, Nepal, Sri Lanka, the Philippines and Indonesia (including East Timor); tracing missing relatives among families affected by armed conflicts in Afghanistan, Sri Lanka, Cambodia; food and non-food assistance to particularly vulnerable categories of victims, and water and sanitation programmes in Afghanistan, Indonesia and Sri Lanka. Assistance was provided in Afghanistan after the earthquake near the Tajik border in February 1998, and in Bangladesh, in August, following severe floods. In the same month the ICRC assumed responsibility for evacuating foreigners from Mazar-i-Sharif, in northern Afghanistan. In February and June 1999 Afghanistan suffered more earthquakes and the ICRC returned to distribute aid and provide assistance. In August the ICRC launched an international aid appeal to assist the massive population affected by floods along China's Yangtze River basin. In October the ICRC appealed for aid for the victims of a cyclone in Orissa, India. In May ICRC personnel were permitted to inspect prisons in Myanmar, for the first time since 1995.

**Middle East:** visits to detainees in Israel, the Israeli-occupied territories and the Autonomous Territories and monitoring the implementation of the fourth Geneva Convention; visits to detainees and prisoners in Bahrain, Iraq, Jordan, Kuwait, Yemen, Morocco and the Western Sahara; sanitation and orthopaedic programmes in Iraq; acting as a neutral intermediary in the search for people missing since the 1991 Gulf War. In August 1999 the ICRC provided assistance to Turkey, following an earthquake that left some 130,000 people homeless. In October the ICRC resumed its inspection of prisons in Algeria, which had been suspended in 1992.

**Europe and Transcaucasia:** medical aid, protection of civilian population, relief assistance, support to local hospitals and visits to detainees in the former Yugoslavia, Albania, Armenia, Azerbaijan and Georgia; tracing activities in the former Yugoslavia; promoting awareness of the dangers of anti-personnel devices; assistance to persons in Chechnya and the surrounding republics affected by the outbreak of hostilities with Russian authorities in late 1994; and for victims of the crisis in Kosovo and Metohija (Serbia, Yugoslavia). In March 1998 the ICRC temporarily withdrew from Kosovo, following threats to its staff. In late March 1999 the ICRC again withdrew from Kosovo owing to the deterioriating security situation in the province. In June the ICRC was able to resume its operations. In neighbouring countries the ICRC provided emergency relief to the thousands of refugees fleeing the province (estimated at more than 500,000 by mid-April) and remained actively concerned for the safety and welfare of the civilian population throughout the region, including those displaced or affected by NATO's aerial offensive within the Federal Republic of Yugoslavia. The ICRC co-ordinated tracing procedures in order to reunite refugee families including through refugee databases on internet sites. In late 1999 the ICRC undertook humanitarian operations for refugees fleeing the renewed conflict in Chechnya.

### THE GENEVA CONVENTIONS

In 1864, one year after its foundation, the ICRC submitted to the states called to a Diplomatic Conference in Geneva a draft international treaty for 'the Amelioration of the Condition of the Wounded in Armies in the Field'. This treaty was adopted and signed by twelve states, which thereby bound themselves to respect as neutral wounded soldiers and those assisting them. This was the first Geneva Convention.

With the development of technology and weapons, the introduction of new means of waging war, and the manifestation of certain phenomena (the great number of prisoners of war during World War I; the enormous number of displaced persons and refugees during World War II; the internationalization of internal conflicts in recent years) the necessity was felt of having other international treaties to protect new categories of war victims. The ICRC, for more than 134 years, has been the leader of a movement to improve and complement international humanitarian law.

There are now four Geneva Conventions, adopted on 12 August 1949: I—to protect wounded and sick in armed forces on land, as well as medical personnel; II—to protect the same categories of people at sea, as well as the shipwrecked; III—concerning the treatment of prisoners of war; IV—for the protection of civilians in time of war; and there are two Additional Protocols of 8 June 1977, for the protection of victims in international armed conflicts (Protocol I) and in non-international armed conflicts (Protocol II).

By January 2000 188 states were parties to the Geneva Conventions; 156 were parties to Protocol I and 149 to Protocol II.

## Finance

The ICRC's work is financed by a voluntary annual grant from governments parties to the Geneva Conventions, voluntary contributions from National Red Cross and Red Crescent Societies and by gifts and legacies from private donors. The ICRC's budgets for 1999 amounted to some 911m. Swiss francs. Of the 'headquarters' budget of 140m. Swiss francs, 53.3% was allocated to field support services and 20.7% to the development, promotion and implementation of international humanitarian law. The field budget for 1999 amounted to 660m. Swiss francs. The proposed field budget for 2000 amounted to 838m. Swiss francs.

## Publications

*Annual Report* (editions in English, French and Spanish).

*The Geneva Conventions:* texts and commentaries.

*ICRC News* (weekly, French, English, Spanish and German editions).

*International Review of the Red Cross* (quarterly in French and English; annually in Russian, Arabic and Spanish).

*The Protocols Additional.*

*Yearbook of International Humanitarian Law* (annually).

Various publications on subjects of Red Cross interest (medical studies, international humanitarian law, etc.), some in electronic form.

# International Federation of Red Cross and Red Crescent Societies

**Address:** 17 chemin des Crêts, Petit-Saconnex, CP 372, 1211 Geneva 19, Switzerland.

**Telephone:** (22) 7304222; **fax:** (22) 7330395; **e-mail:** secretariat@ifrc.org; **internet:** www.ifrc.org.

The Federation was founded in 1919 (as the League of Red Cross Societies). It works on the basis of the Principles of the Red Cross and Red Crescent Movement to inspire, facilitate and promote all forms of humanitarian activities by the National Societies, with a view to the prevention and alleviation of human suffering, and thereby contribute to the maintenance and promotion of peace in the world. The Federation acts as the official representative of its member societies in the field. The Federation maintains close relations with many inter-governmental organizations, the United Nations and its Specialized Agencies, and with non-governmental organizations. It has permanent observer status with the United Nations.

### MEMBERS

National Red Cross and Red Crescent Societies in 176 countries in January 2000, with a total of 105.4m. members and volunteers.

## Organization

(January 2000)

### GENERAL ASSEMBLY

The General Assembly is the highest authority of the Federation and meets every two years in commission sessions (for development, disaster relief, health and community services, and youth) and plenary sessions. It is composed of representatives from all National Societies that are members of the Federation.

**President:** Dr Astrid Nøklebye Heiberg (Norway).

### EXECUTIVE COUNCIL

The Council, which meets every six months, is composed of the President of the Federation, nine Vice-Presidents and 16 National Societies elected by the Assembly. Its functions include the implementation of decisions of the General Assembly; it also has powers to act between meetings of the Assembly.

### ASSEMBLY AND FINANCE COMMISSIONS

Development Commission.
Disaster Relief Commission.
Finance Commission.
Health and Community Services Commission.
Youth Commision.

The Advisory Commissions meet, in principle, twice a year, just before the Executive Council. Members are elected by the Assembly under a system that ensures each Society a seat on one Commission.

### SECRETARIAT

The Secretariat assumes the statutory responsibilities of the Federation in the field of relief to victims of natural disasters, refugees and civilian populations who may be displaced or exposed to abnormal hardship. In addition, the Secretariat promotes and co-ordinates assistance to National Societies in developing their basic structure and their services to the community. In 1999 there were some 250 employees at the Secretariat from more than 50 countries.

**Secretary-General:** Didier Cherpitel (France).

## Activities

### DISASTER RESPONSE

The Federation supports the establishment of emergency response units, which aim to act effectively and independently to meet the needs of victims of natural or man-made disasters. The units cover basic health care provision, referral hospitals, water sanitation, logistics, telecommunications and information units. The Federation advises National Societies in relief health. In the event of a disaster the following areas are covered: communicable disease alleviation and vaccination; psychological support and stress management; health education; the provision of medicines; and the organization of mobile clinics and nursing care. The Societies also distribute food and clothing to those in need and assist in the provision of shelter and adequate sanitation facilities and in the management of refugee camps.

### DEVELOPMENT

The Federation undertakes capacity-building activities with the National Societies to train and develop staff and volunteers and to improve management structures and processes, in particular in the area of disaster-preparedness. Blood donor programmes are often undertaken by National Societies, sometimes in conjuction with WHO. The Federation supports the promotion of these programmes and the implementation of quality standards. Other activities in the health sector aim to strengthen existing health services and promote community-based health care and first aid; the prevention of HIV/AIDS and substance abuse; and health education and family planning initiatives. The Federation also promotes the establishment and development of education and service programmes for children and for other more vulnerable members of society, including the elderly and disabled. Education projects support the promotion of humanitarian values.

## Finance

The permanent Secretariat of the Federation is financed by the contributions of member Societies on a pro-rata basis. Each relief action is financed by separate, voluntary contributions, and development programme projects are also financed on a voluntary basis.

## Publications

*Annual Report.*

*Handbook of the International Red Cross and Red Crescent Movement* (with the ICRC).

*Red Cross, Red Crescent* (quarterly, English, French and Spanish).

*Weekly News.*

*World Disasters Report* (annually).

Newsletters on several topics; various guides and manuals for Red Cross and Red Crescent activities.

# INTERNATIONAL SEABED AUTHORITY

**Address:** 14–20 Port Royal St, Kingston, Jamaica.

**Telephone:** 922-9105; **fax:** 922-0195; **e-mail:** postmaster@isa.org.jm; **internet:** www.isa.org.jm.

The Authority was established in November 1994, upon the entry into force of the 1982 United Nations Convention on the Law of the Sea.

## Organization

(January 2000)

### ASSEMBLY

The Assembly is the supreme organ of the Authority, consisting of representatives of all member states. It formulates policies, approves the budget and elects Council members. The first session of the Assembly was initiated in November 1994 and was continued at a meeting in February/March 1995. The session was concluded in August 1995, having failed to reach agreement on the composition of the Council (see below) and to elect a Secretary-General of the Authority. In March 1996 the Assembly concluded the first part of its second session, having constituted the 36-member Council and elected, by consensus, the first Secretary-General of the Authority. Annual sessions of the Assembly are generally held in March and August. The sixth session of the Assembly was scheduled to be held in March 2000.

### COUNCIL

The Council acts as the executive organ of the Authority. It consists of 36 members, of whom 18 are elected from four 'major interest groups'—the four states who are the largest investors in sea-bed minerals, the four major importers of sea-bed minerals, the four major land-based exporters of the same minerals, and six developing countries representing special interests—while 18 are elected on the principle of equitable representation. The Council aims to reach decisions by consensus agreement, failing which a vote may be conducted, although any decision has to be approved by the majority within each of the four member groups, or chambers.

### LEGAL AND TECHNICAL COMMISSION

The 21-member Commission (originally it was to comprise 15 members) assists the Council by making recommendations concerning sea-bed activities, assessing the environmental implications of activities in the area and proposing measures to protect the marine environment. Under the terms of the agreement on the implementation of Part XI of the Convention, the Commission was to undertake the functions of a proposed economic planning commission until the Council decides otherwise or until the approval of the first work plan for mineral exploitation of the deep sea-bed. These functions include reviewing trends and factors affecting supply, demand and prices of materials that may be derived from the deep sea-bed area. The main task of the Commission between 1996 and 1998 was the elaboration of draft regulations on prospecting and exploration for polymetallic nodules in the deep sea-bed area. In 1999 the resulting draft version of the Mining Code was being assessed, before contracts could be issued to seven pioneer investors.

### FINANCE COMMITTEE

The Committee, comprising 15 members, was established to make recommendations to the Assembly and the Council on all financial and budgetary issues.

### SECRETARIAT

The Secretariat provides administrative services to all the bodies of the Authority and implements the relevant work programmes. It comprises Offices of Resources and Environmental Monitoring, Legal Affairs, and Administration and Management. Under the terms of the agreement on the implementation of Part XI of the Convention (see below), the Secretariat was to undertake the functions of the Enterprise, which was to carry out deep sea-bed mining operations, through joint ventures.

**Secretary-General:** Satya N. Nandan (Fiji).

## Activities

The Authority is the organization through which states party to the Law of the Sea Convention organize and control activities in the international sea-bed area beyond the limits of national jurisdiction, particularly with a view to administering the mineral resources of that area. It functions as an autonomous international organization in relationship with the UN. All states party to the Convention are members of the Authority.

The third UN Conference on the Law of the Sea (UNCLOS) began its work in 1973, with the aim of regulating maritime activities by defining zones and boundaries, ensuring fair exploitation of resources, and providing machinery for settlement of disputes. Negotiations, involving more than 160 countries, continued until April 1982, when the Conference finally adopted the UN Convention on the Law of the Sea: 130 states voted in its favour, while the USA, Israel, Turkey and Venezuela voted against, and there were 17 abstentions, including the then Federal Republic of Germany, the USSR and the United Kingdom. The Convention was opened for signing in December for a two-year period. By 1984 159 states had signed, but the USA, the United Kingdom and the Federal Republic of Germany refused to sign. The 60th ratification of the Convention was received in November 1993, and by December 1999 130 states had ratified, acceded or succeeded to the Convention. The main provisions of the Convention are as follows:

Coastal states are allowed sovereignty over their territorial waters of up to 12 nautical miles in breadth; foreign vessels are to be allowed 'innocent passage' through these waters.

Ships and aircraft of all states are allowed 'transit passage' through straits used for international navigation.

Archipelagic states (composed of islands) have sovereignty over a sea area enclosed by straight lines drawn between the outermost points of the islands.

Coastal states have sovereign rights in a 200-mile exclusive economic zone with respect to natural resources and jurisdiction over certain activities (such as protection and preservation of the environment), and rights over the adjacent continental shelf up to 350 miles from the shore under specified circumstances.

All states have freedom of navigation, overflight, scientific research and fishing on the high seas, but must co-operate in measures to conserve living resources.

A 'parallel system' is to be established for exploiting the international sea-bed, where all activities are to be supervised by the International Seabed Authority.

States are bound to control pollution and co-operate in forming preventive rules, and incur penalties for failing to combat pollution.

Marine scientific research in the zones under national jurisdiction is subject to the prior consent of the coastal state, but consent may be denied only under specific circumstances.

States must submit disputes on the application and interpretation of the Convention to a compulsory procedure entailing decisions binding on all parties. An International Tribunal for the Law of the Sea is to be established.

The USA and other industrialized nations witheld their support, owing to Part XI of the Convention, concerning the provisions for exploitation of the international ocean bed, and particularly the minerals to be found there (chiefly manganese, cobalt, copper and nickel), envisaged as the 'common heritage of mankind'. It was argued that those countries which possess adequate technology for deep-sea mining would be insufficiently represented in the new Authority; the operations of private mining consortia, according to the objectors, would be unacceptably limited by the stipulations that their technology should be shared with a supranational mining venture (the 'Enterprise'), and that production should be limited in order to protect land-based mineral producers. In July 1994 the UN General Assembly adopted an agreement amending the implementation of Part XI of the Convention. Under the new agreement, which aimed to counter the objections of the industrialized nations, there was to be no mandatory transfer of technology, the Enterprise was to operate according to commercial principles and there were to be no production limits, although a compensation fund was to assist land-based producers adversely affected by sea-bed mining. The agreement entered into force in July 1996. An agreement on the implementation of the provisions of the Convention relating to the conservation and management of straddling and highly migratory fish stocks was opened for signature in December 1995 and was to enter into force after ratification by 30 countries.

In August 1998 discussions began, under the auspices of the Authority, to govern the recovery of polymetallic nodules from the international sea-bed. These discussions continued in 1999; concern was expressed about the protection of the sea-bed from environmental damage.

## Finance

The Authority's budget is the responsibility of the Finance Committee. The budget for the Authority for 1999 was US $5.0m. The proposed budget for 2000 was $5.7m. The administrative expenses of the Authority are met by assessed contributions of its members.

## Publication

*Annual Report of the Secretary-General.*

## Associated Institutions

The following were also established under the terms of the Convention:

**Commission on the Limits of the Continental Shelf:** Division for Ocean Affairs and the Law of the Sea, Room DC2-0450, United Nations, New York, NY 10017, USA; tel. (212) 963-3951; fax (212) 963-5847; e-mail doalos@un.org; internet www.un.org/Depts/los; 21 members of the Commission were elected, for a five-year term, in March 1997; responsible for making recommendations regarding the establishment of the outer limits of the continental shelf of a coastal state, where the limit extends beyond 200 nautical miles (370 km).

**International Tribunal for the Law of the Sea:** Wexstrasse 4, 20355 Hamburg, Germany; tel. (40) 356070; fax (40) 35607245; e-mail itlos@itlos.hamburg.de; inaugurated in October 1996; 21 judges; responsible for interpreting the Convention and ruling on disputes brought by states party to the Convention on matters within its jurisdiction. **Registrar:** GRITAKUMAR E. CHITTY.

# INTER-PARLIAMENTARY UNION—IPU

Address: CP 438, 1211 Geneva 19, Switzerland.

**Telephone:** (22) 9194150; **fax:** (22) 9194160; **e-mail:** postbox@mail.ipu.org; **internet:** www.ipu.org.

Founded in 1889, the IPU aims to promote peace, co-operation and representative democracy by providing a forum for multilateral political debate between representatives of national parliaments.

### MEMBERS

National parliaments of 139 sovereign states; five international parliamentary associations (Associate Members).

## Organization

(January 2000)

### INTER-PARLIAMENTARY CONFERENCE

The Conference is the main statutory body of the IPU, comprising eight to 10 representatives from each member parliament. It meets twice a year to discuss current issues in world affairs and to make political recommendations. Other specialized conferences may also be held. The Conference is assisted by four plenary Study Committees on Political Questions: International Security and Disarmament; Parliamentary, Juridical and Human Rights Questions; Economic and Social Questions; and Education, Science, Culture and the Environment.

### INTER-PARLIAMENTARY COUNCIL

The Council comprises two representatives of each member parliament, usually from different political groups. It is responsible for approving membership and the annual programme and budget of the IPU, and for electing the Secretary-General. The Council may consider substantive issues and adopt resolutions and policy statements, in particular on the basis of recommendations from its subsidiary bodies.

**President:** NAJMA HEPTULLA (India).

### MEETING OF WOMEN PARLIAMENTARIANS

The Meeting is a mechanism for co-ordination between women parliamentarians. Since 1975 the Meeting has been convened twice a year, on the occasion of IPU statutory meetings, to discuss subjects of common interest, to formulate strategies to develop the IPU's women's programme, to strengthen their influence within the organization and to ensure that women are elected to key positions. The Meeting is assisted by a Co-ordinating Committee.

### SUBSIDIARY BODIES

In addition to the thematic Study Committees of the IPU Conference, various other committees and groups undertake and co-ordinate IPU activities in specific areas. All these bodies are subsidiary to the IPU Council:

Committee on the Human Rights of Parliamentarians
Committee for Sustainable Development
Committee on Middle East Questions
Group of Facilitators for Cyprus
Committee to Promote Respect for International and Humanitarian Law
CSCM Process and CSCM Co-ordinating Committee (concerned with security and co-operation in the Mediterranean)
Co-ordinating Committee of the Meeting of Women MPs
Gender Partnership Group

### EXECUTIVE COMMITTEE

The Committee, comprising 12 members and presided over by the President of the Council, oversees the administration of the IPU and advises the Council on membership, policy and programme, and any other matters referred to it.

### SECRETARIAT

**Secretary-General:** ANDERS B. JOHNSSON (Sweden).

## Activities

### PROMOTION OF REPRESENTATIVE DEMOCRACY

This is one of the IPU's core areas of activity, and covers a wide range of concerns, such as democracy, gender issues, human rights and ethnic diversity, parliamentary action to combat corruption, and links between democracy and economic growth. In September 1997 the Council adopted a Universal Declaration on Democracy. The IPU subsequently published a study entitled *Democracy: its Principles and Achievements.*

The IPU administers a Programme for the Study and Promotion of Representative Institutions, which aims to improve knowledge of the functioning of national parliaments by gathering and disseminating information on their constitutional powers and responsibilities, structure, and membership, and on the electoral systems used. The IPU also organizes international seminars and gatherings for parliamentarians, officials, academics and other experts to study the functioning of parliamentary institutions. A Technical Co-operation Programme aims to mobilize international support in order to improve the capabilities, infrastructure and technical facilities of national parliaments and enhance their effectiveness. Under the Programme, the IPU may provide expert advice on the structure of legislative bodies, staff training, and parliamentary working procedures, and provide technical equipment and other resources. In 1999 technical assistance projects were implemented in Burundi, Ethiopia, Fiji, Gabon, The Gambia, Kyrgyzstan, Laos, Malawi, Viet Nam and Yemen.

IPU teams of observers have overseen elections in Namibia, in 1989, in Cambodia, 1993, and in El Salvador, in 1994. Their duties included observing the process of voter registration, the election campaign and voting, and verifying the results. In 1993 the Council resolved that the IPU be present at all national elections organized, supervised or verified by the United Nations. The IPU has reported on the rights and responsibilities of election observers and issued guide-lines on the holding of free and fair elections. These include a *Declaration on Criteria for Free and Fair Elections,* together with a study on the subject, and Codes of Conduct for Elections.

The IPU maintains a special database (PARLINE) on parliaments of the world, giving access to information on the structure and functioning of all existing parliaments, and on national elections. It conducts regular world studies on matters regarding the structure and functioning of parliaments. It also maintains a separate database (PARLIT) comprising literature from around the world on constitutional, electoral and parliamentary matters.

### INTERNATIONAL PEACE AND SECURITY

The IPU aims to promote conflict resolution and international security through political discussion. Certain areas of conflict are monitored by the Union on an ongoing basis (for example, Cyprus and the Middle East), while others are considered as they arise. In recent years, the IPU has been particularly concerned with the situation in the former Yugoslavia, and has condemned incidents of violations of humanitarian law and supported efforts to improve the lives of those affected by the conflict. In April 1998 the Union adopted an emergency resolution on the situation in Kosovo and Metohija, southern Serbia. An extensive programme of activities is undertaken by the IPU with regard to the Mediterranean region. In June 1992 the first Conference on Security and Co-operation in the Mediterranean (CSCM) was held; the objectives outlined at the Conference have been integrated as a structured process of the IPU. A second CSCM was held in Valetta, Malta, in November 1995, and a third was scheduled to be convened in 2000. Intermediary thematic meetings are held between plenary conferences, while consultations among parties to the CSCM process take place every six months.

The IPU has worked constantly to promote international and regional efforts towards disarmament, as part of the process of enhancing peace and security. Issues that have been discussed by the Conference include nuclear non-proliferation, a ban on testing of nuclear weapons, and a global register of arms transfers.

### SUSTAINABLE DEVELOPMENT

The Committee for Sustainable Development guides the IPU's work in this area, with a broad approach of linking economic growth with social, democratic, human welfare and environmental considerations. Issues of world economic and social development on which the IPU has approved recommendations include employment in a globalizing world, the globalization of economy and liberalization of trade, Third World debt and its impact on the integration of those countries affected into the process of globalization, international mass migration and other demographic problems, and the right to food. The IPU co-operates with programmes and agencies of the UN, in particular in the preparation of major socio-economic conferences, including the World Summit for Social Development, which was held in Copenhagen, Denmark, in March 1995, the Fourth World Conference on Women, held in Beijing, People's Republic of China, in September 1995, and the World Food Summit, held in Rome, Italy, in November 1996. In September 1996 a tripartite meeting of parliamentary, governmental and inter-governmental representatives, convened at the UN headquarters in New York, considered legislative measures to pursue the objectives of the World Summit for Social Development; a follow-up meeting was held in March 1999. In November/December 1998 the IPU, in co-operation with FAO, organized an Inter-Parliamentary Conference concerned with 'Attaining the World Food Summit's Objectives through a Sustainable Development Strategy'.

Activities to protect the environment are undertaken within the framework of sustainable development. In 1984 the first Inter-Parliamentary Conference on the Environment, convened in Nairobi, Kenya, advocated the inclusion of environmental considerations into the development process. The IPU was actively involved in the preparation of the UN Conference on Environment and Development (UNCED), which was held in Rio de Janeiro, Brazil, in June 1992. Subsequently the IPU's environment programme has focused on implementing the recommendations of UNCED, and identifying measures to be taken at parliamentary level to facilitate that process. The IPU also monitors the actual measures taken by national parliaments to pursue the objective of sustainable development, as well as emerging environmental problems. In 1997 the IPU published the *World Directory of Parliamentary Bodies for Environment.*

### HUMAN RIGHTS AND HUMANITARIAN LAW

The IPU frequently considers human rights issues and makes relevant recommendations at its statutory Conferences and during specialized meetings, and aims to incorporate human rights concerns, including employment, the rights of minorities, and gender issues, in all areas of activity. A five-member Committee on the Human Rights of Parliamentarians is responsible for the consideration of complaints relating to alleged violations of the human rights of members of parliament, for example state harassment, arbitrary arrest and detention, unfair trail and violation of parliamentary immunity, based on a procedure adopted by the IPU in 1976. The Committee conducts hearings and site missions to investigate a complaint and communicates with the authorities of the country concerned. If no settlement is reached at that stage, the Committee may then publish a report for the Inter-Parliamentary Council and submit recommendations on specific measures to be adopted. By the end of 1998 1,097 cases had been declared admissible, in 87 countries, of which the majority had reached a satisfactory settlement, often through the support of IPU member parliaments.

The IPU works closely with the International Committee of the Red Cross to uphold respect for international humanitarian law. It supports the implementation of the Geneva Conventions and their Additional Protocols, and the adoption of appropriate national legislation. In 1995 the Council adopted a special resolution to establish a reporting mechanism at the parliamentary level to ensure respect for international humanitarian law. Consequently IPU initiated a world survey on legislative action regarding the application of international humanitarian law, as well as efforts to ban anti-personnel land-mines. In April and September 1998 the Council adopted special resolutions on parliamentary action to secure the entry into force and implementation of the Convention on the Prohibition of the Use, Stockpiling, Production and Transfer of Anti-personnel Mines and on their Destruction, which was signed by representatives of some 120 countries meeting in Ottawa, Canada, in December 1997. Further resolutions to that effect were adopted by the Inter-Parliamentary Conference in October 1999.

In 1998 the IPU published a *World Directory of Parliamentary Human Rights Bodies.*

### WOMEN IN POLITICS

The IPU aims to promote the participation of women in the political and parliamentary decision-making processes, and, more generally, in all aspects of society. It organizes debates and events on these issues and compiles a statistical database on women in politics, compiled by regular world surveys. The IPU also actively addresses wider issues of concern to women, such as literacy and education, women in armed conflicts, women's contribution to development, and women in the electoral process. The eradication of violence against women was the subject of a special resolution adopted by the Conference in 1991. The Meeting of Women MPs has monitored efforts by national authorities to implement the recommendations outlined in the resolution. In 1996 the IPU promoted the Framework for Model Legislation on Domestic Violence, formulated by the UN Special Rapporteur on the issue, which aimed to assist national parliaments in preparing legislation to safeguard women. At the Fourth World Conference on Women, held in Beijing, in September 1995, the IPU organized several events to bring together parliamentarians and other leading experts, diplomats and officials to promote the rights of women and of children. In February 1997 the IPU organized a Specialized Inter-Parliamentary Conference, in New Delhi, India, entitled 'Towards partnership between men and women in politics'. Following the Conference the IPU decided to establish a Gender Partnership Group, comprising two men and two women, within the Executive Committee, to ensure that IPU activities and decisions serve the interests and needs of all members of the population. The Group was authorized to report to the IPU Council.

The IPU aims to promote the importance of women's role in economic and social development and their participation in politics as a democratic necessity, and recognizes the crucial role of the media in presenting the image of women. Within the context of the 1997 New Delhi Conference, the IPU organized a second Round Table on the Image of Women Politicians in the Media (the first having been convened in November 1989). The debate urged fair and equal representation of women politicians by the media and for governments to revise their communications policies to advance the image of female parliamentarians.

**EDUCATION, SCIENCE AND CULTURE**

Activities in these sectors are often subject to consideration by statutory Conferences. Resolutions of the Conference have included the implementation of educational and cultural policies designed to foster greater respect for demographic values, adopted in April 1993, and on bioethics and its implications world-wide for human rights protection, adopted in April 1995. Specialized meetings organized by the IPU have included the Asia and Pacific Inter-Parliamentary Conference on 'Science and technology for regional sustainable development', held in Tokyo, Japan, in June 1994, and the Inter-Parliamentary Conference on 'Education, science, culture and communication on the threshold of the 21st century', organized jointly with UNESCO, and held in Paris, France, in June 1996.

## Finance

The IPU is financed by its members from public funds. The 2000 annual budget was to total 10.3m. Swiss francs.

## Publications

*Chronicle of Parliamentary Elections* (annually).

*Inter-Parliamentary Bulletin* (2 a year).

*World Directory of Parliaments* (annually).

Other reports, documents, conference proceedings.

# ISLAMIC DEVELOPMENT BANK

**Address:** POB 5925, Jeddah 21432, Saudi Arabia.

**Telephone:** (2) 6361400; **fax:** (2) 6366871; **e-mail:** archives@isdb.org.sa; **internet:** www.isdb.org.

The Bank is an international financial institution that was established following a conference of Ministers of Finance of member countries of the Organization of the Islamic Conference (OIC, q.v.), held in Jeddah in December 1973. Its aim is to encourage the economic development and social progress of member countries and of Muslim communities in non-member countries, in accordance with the principles of the Islamic *Shari'a* (sacred law). The Bank formally opened in October 1975.

**MEMBERS**

There are 53 members.

## Organization

(January 2000)

**BOARD OF GOVERNORS**

Each member country is represented by a governor, usually its Minister of Finance, and an alternate. The Board of Governors is the supreme authority of the Bank, and meets annually.

**BOARD OF EXECUTIVE DIRECTORS**

The Board consists of 11 members, five of whom are appointed by the five largest subscribers to the capital stock of the Bank; the remaining six are elected by Governors representing the other subscribers. Members of the Board of Executive Directors are elected for three-year terms. The Board is responsible for the direction of the general operations of the Bank.

**President of the Bank and Chairman of the Board of Executive Directors:** Dr Ahmed Mohamed Ali.

**Bank Secretary:** Dr Abd ar-Rahim Omrana.

**REGIONAL OFFICES**

**Kazakhstan:** c/o Director, External Aid Co-ordination Dept, 93–95 Ablay-Khan Ave, 480091 Almaty; tel. (3272) 62-18-68; fax (3272) 69-61-52; Dir Zhankyn Kakimzkanova.

**Malaysia:** Level 11, Front Wing, Bank Industri, Jalan Sultan Ismail, POB 13671, 50818 Kuala Lumpur; tel. (3) 2946627; fax (3) 2946626; Dir Dr Muhammad Siddik.

**Morocco:** 177 Ave John Kennedy, Souissi 10105, POB 5003, Rabat; tel. (7) 757191; fax (7) 775726; Dir Dr Marwan Seifuddin.

**FINANCIAL STRUCTURE**

The authorized capital of the Bank is 6,000m. Islamic Dinars (divided into 600,000 shares, having a value of 10,000 Islamic Dinars each). The Islamic Dinar (ID) is the Bank's unit of account and is equivalent to the value of one Special Drawing Right of the IMF (SDR 1 = US $1.3512 at 30 April 1999).

Subscribed capital amounts to ID 4,000m.

## Activities

The Bank adheres to the Islamic principle forbidding usury, and does not grant loans or credits for interest. Instead, its methods of project financing are: provision of interest-free loans (with a service

**SUBSCRIPTIONS** (million Islamic Dinars, as at December 1998)

| | | | |
|---|---|---|---|
| Afghanistan | 5.00 | Maldives | 2.50 |
| Albania | 2.50 | Mali | 4.92 |
| Algeria | 124.26 | Mauritania | 4.92 |
| Azerbaijan | 4.92 | Morocco | 24.81 |
| Bahrain | 7.00 | Mozambique | 2.50 |
| Bangladesh | 49.29 | Niger | 12.41 |
| Benin | 4.92 | Oman | 13.78 |
| Brunei | 12.41 | Pakistan | 124.26 |
| Burkina Faso | 12.41 | Palestine | 9.85 |
| Cameroon | 12.41 | Qatar | 49.23 |
| Chad | 4.92 | Saudi Arabia | 997.17 |
| Comoros | 2.50 | Senegal | 12.42 |
| Djibouti | 2.50 | Sierra Leone | 2.50 |
| Egypt | 49.23 | Somalia | 2.50 |
| Gabon | 14.77 | Sudan | 19.69 |
| The Gambia | 2.50 | Suriname | 2.50 |
| Guinea | 12.41 | Syria | 5.00 |
| Guinea-Bissau | 2.50 | Tajikistan | 2.50 |
| Indonesia | 124.26 | Togo | 2.50 |
| Iran | 349.97 | Tunisia | 9.85 |
| Iraq | 13.05 | Turkey | 315.47 |
| Jordan | 19.89 | Turkmenistan | 2.50 |
| Kazakhstan | 2.50 | Uganda | 12.41 |
| Kuwait | 496.64 | United Arab Emirates | 283.03 |
| Kyrgyzstan | 2.50 | Yemen | 24.81 |
| Lebanon | 4.92 | | |
| Libya | 400.00 | **Total** | 3,763.77 |
| Malaysia | 79.56 | | |

**Operations approved, Islamic year 1418 (7 May 1997–27 April 1998)**

| Type of operation | Number of operations | Total amount (million Islamic Dinars) |
|---|---|---|
| Ordinary operations | 84 | 441.89 |
| Project financing | 57 | 433.40 |
| Technical assistance | 27 | 8.49 |
| Trade financing operations* | 75 | 697.33 |
| Waqf Fund operations | 30 | 7.90 |
| **Total**† | 189 | 1,147.12 |

* Including ITFO, the EFS, and the Islamic Bank's Portfolio.

† Excluding cancelled operations.

**Project financing and technical assistance by sector, Islamic year 1418***

| Sector | Number of Operations | Amount (million Islamic Dinars) | % |
|---|---|---|---|
| Agriculture and agro-industry | 15 | 31.40 | 7.1 |
| Industry and mining . . . | 5 | 86.69 | 19.6 |
| Transport and communications . . . | 10 | 57.96 | 13.1 |
| Public utilities . . . . | 23 | 143.58 | 32.5 |
| Social sectors. . . . . | 27 | 119.69 | 27.1 |
| Other* . . . . . . | 4 | 2.57 | 0.6 |
| **Total†** . . . . . . | 84 | 441.89 | 100.0 |

* Mainly approved amounts for Islamic banks.
† Excluding cancelled operations.

fee), mainly for infrastructural projects which are expected to have a marked impact on long-term socio-economic development; provision of technical assistance (e.g. for feasibility studies); equity participation in industrial and agricultural projects; leasing operations, involving the leasing of equipment such as ships, and instalment sale financing; and profit-sharing operations. Funds not immediately needed for projects are used for foreign trade financing. Under the Import Trade Financing Operations (ITFO) scheme, funds are used for importing commodities for development purposes (i.e. raw materials and intermediate industrial goods, rather than consumer goods), with priority given to the import of goods from other member countries (see table). The Longer-term Trade Financing Scheme (LTTFS) was introduced in 1987/88 to provide financing for the export of non-traditional and capital goods. During AH 1419 the LTTFS was renamed the Export Financing Scheme (EFS). In addition, the Special Assistance Waqf Fund (which was established with effect from 7 May 1997, formerly the Special Assistance Account) provides emergency aid and other assistance, with particular emphasis on education in Islamic communities in non-member countries. A Special Account for developed member countries aims to assist these countries by providing loans on concessionary terms. Loans financed by this Account are charged an annual service fee of 0.75%, compared with 2.5% for ordinary loans, and have a repayment period of 25–30 years, compared with 15–25 years.

By 27 April 1998 the Bank had approved a total of ID 3,781.32m. for project financing and technical assistance, a total of ID 9,854.62m. for foreign trade financing, and ID 381.27m. for special assistance operations, excluding amounts for cancelled operations. During the Islamic year 1418 (7 May 1997 to 27 April 1998) the Bank approved a total of ID 1,147.12m., for 189 operations.

The Bank approved 31 loans in the year ending 27 April 1998, amounting to ID 133.90m. (compared with 33 loans, totalling ID 131.44m., in the previous year). These loans supported projects concerned with infrastructural improvements, for example of roads, canals, water-supply and rural electrification, the construction of schools and health centres, and agricultural developments.

During AH 1418 the Bank approved 12 technical assistance operations for 17 countries (as well as four regional projects) in the form of grants and loans, amounting to ID 8.49m.

Import trade financing approved during the Islamic year 1418 amounted to ID 457.39m. for 42 operations in 12 member countries. By the end of that year cumulative import trade financing amounted to ID 8,335.07m., of which 38.7% was for imports of crude petroleum, 28.7% for intermediate industrial goods, 8.0% for vegetable oil and 6.1% for refined petroleum products. Financing approved under the Export Financing Scheme amounted to ID 27.25m. for eight operations in five countries in AH 1418. In the same year the Bank's Portfolio for Investment and Development, established in AH 1407 (1986–87), approved 25 operations amounting to US $287m. (or approximately ID 212.40m.). Since its introduction, the Portfolio has approved 125 net financing operations in 18 member countries, amounting to $1,714m.

During AH 1418 the Bank approved 30 special assistance operations, amounting to ID 7.90m., providing assistance primarily in the education sector, as well as emergency relief; of the total financing, 23 operations provided for Muslim communities in 15 non-member countries.

The Bank's scholarships programme sponsored 430 students from six member and 30 non-member countries during the year to 27 April 1998. The Merit Scholarship Programme, initiated in AH 1412 (1991–92), aims to develop scientific, technological and research capacities in member countries through advanced studies and/or research. Since the beginning of the programme 134 scholars from 38 member countries have been placed in academic centres of excellence in Australia, Europe and the USA. In December 1997 the Board of Executive Directors approved a new scholarship programme designed specifically to assist scholars from least developed member countries to study for a masters degree in science and technology. An estimated 190 scholarships were expected to be awarded over a five-year period. The Bank's Programme for Technical Co-operation aims to mobilize technical capabilities among member countries and to promote the exchange of expertise, experience and skills through expert missions, training, seminars and workshops. During AH 1418 71 projects were implemented under the programme. The Bank also undertakes the distribution of meat sacrificed by Muslim pilgrims: during the year meat from approximately 500,000 animals was distributed to the needy in 26 countries.

Disbursements during the year ending 27 April 1998 totalled ID 526m., bringing the total cumulative disbursements since the Bank began operations to ID 9,604m.

The Bank's Unit Investment Fund became operational in 1990, with the aim of mobilizing additional resources and providing a profitable channel for investments conforming to *Shari'a*. The initial issue of the Fund was US $100m., which has subsequently been increased to $325m. The Fund finances mainly private-sector industrial projects in middle-income countries. In October 1998 the Bank announced the establishment of a new fund to invest in infrastructure projects in member states. The Bank committed $250m. to the fund, which was to comprise $1,000m. equity capital and a $500m. Islamic financing facility. In September 1999 the Bank's Board of Executive Directors approved the establishment of an Islamic Corporation for the Development of the Private Sector; it was scheduled to commence operations in April 2000.

## SUBSIDIARY ORGANS

**Islamic Corporation for the Insurance of Investment and Export Credit—ICIEC:** POB 15722, Jeddah 21454, Saudi Arabia; tel. (2) 6445666; fax (2) 6379504; e-mail idb.iciec@mail.oicisnet.org; internet www.isdb.org; f. 1994; aims to promote trade and the flow of investments among member countries of the OIC through the provision of export credit and investment insurance services; auth. cap. ID 100m., subscribed cap. ID 91.2m. (April 1999). Man. Dr ABDEL RAHMAN A. TAHA. Mems: 23 OIC member states.

**Islamic Research and Training Institute:** POB 9201, Jeddah 21413, Saudi Arabia; tel. (2) 6361400; fax (2) 6378927; internet www.irti.org; f. 1983 to undertake research enabling economic, financial and banking activities to conform to Islamic law, and to provide training for staff involved in development activities in the Bank's member countries. The Institute also organizes seminars and workshops, and holds training courses aimed at furthering the expertise of government and financial officials in Islamic developing countries. Dir Dr MABID ALI AL-JARHI. Publs *Annual Report*, *Islamic Economic Studies*, various research studies, monographs, reports.

## Publication

*Annual Report.*

# LEAGUE OF ARAB STATES

**Address:** POB 11642, Arab League Bldg, Tahrir Square, Cairo, Egypt.

**Telephone:** (2) 5750511; **fax:** (2) 5775626.

The League of Arab States (more generally known as the Arab League) is a voluntary association of sovereign Arab states, designed to strengthen the close ties linking them and to co-ordinate their policies and activities and direct them towards the common good of all the Arab countries. It was founded in March 1945.

### MEMBERS

| | | |
|---|---|---|
| Algeria | Lebanon | Somalia |
| Bahrain | Libya | Sudan |
| Comoros | Mauritania | Syria |
| Djibouti | Morocco | Tunisia |
| Egypt | Oman | United Arab Emirates |
| Iraq | Palestine* | Yemen |
| Jordan | Qatar | |
| Kuwait | Saudi Arabia | |

* Palestine is considered an independent state, and therefore a full member of the League.

## Organization

(January 2000)

### COUNCIL

The supreme organ of the Arab League, the Council consists of representatives of the member states, each of which has one vote, and a representative for Palestine. Unanimous decisions of the Council shall be binding upon all member states of the League; majority decisions shall be binding only on those states which have accepted them.

The Council may, if necessary, hold an extraordinary session at the request of two member states. Invitations to all sessions are extended by the Secretary-General. The ordinary sessions are presided over by representatives of the member states in turn.

The Council is supported by technical and specialized committees which advise on financial and administrative affairs, information affairs and legal affairs. In addition, specialized ministerial councils have been established to formulate common policies for the regulation and the advancement of co-operation in the following areas: information; home affairs; legal affairs; health; housing; social affairs; transport; the youth and sports sectors; environmental affairs; and telecommunications.

### GENERAL SECRETARIAT

The administrative and financial offices of the League. The Secretariat carries out the decisions of the Council, and provides financial and administrative services for the personnel of the League. General departments comprise: the Bureau of the Secretary-General, Arab Affairs, Economic Affairs, International Affairs, Palestine Affairs, Legal Affairs, Military Affairs, Social and Cultural Affairs, Information Affairs and Financial and Administrative Affairs. In addition, there are Units for Internal Auditing and Institutional Development, a Documentation and Information Centre, Arab League Centres in Tunis and, for Legal and Judicial Research, in Beirut, and a Principal Bureau for the Boycott of Israel, based in Damascus, Syria (see below).

The Secretary-General is appointed by the League Council by a two-thirds' majority of the member states, for a five-year, renewable term. He appoints the Assistant Secretaries-General and principal officials, with the approval of the Council. He has the rank of ambassador, and the Assistant Secretaries-General have the rank of ministers plenipotentiary.

**Secretary-General:** Dr AHMAD ESMAT ABD AL-MEGUID (Egypt).

### DEFENCE AND ECONOMIC CO-OPERATION

Groups established under the Treaty of Joint Defence and Economic Co-operation, concluded in 1950 to complement the Charter of the League.

**Arab Unified Military Command:** f. 1964 to co-ordinate military policies for the liberation of Palestine.

**Economic and Social Council:** to compare and co-ordinate the economic policies of the member states; supervises the activities of the Arab League's specialized agencies. The Council is composed of ministers of economic affairs or their deputies; decisions are taken by majority vote. The first meeting was held in 1953.

**Joint Defence Council:** supervises implementation of those aspects of the treaty concerned with common defence. Composed of foreign and defence ministers; decisions by a two-thirds' majority vote of members are binding on all.

**Permanent Military Commission:** established 1950; composed of representatives of army general staffs; main purpose: to draw up plans of joint defence for submission to the Joint Defence Council.

### ARAB DETERRENT FORCE

Created in June 1976 by the Arab League Council to supervise successive attempts to cease hostilities in Lebanon, and afterwards to maintain the peace. The mandate of the Force has been successively renewed. The Arab League Summit Conference in October 1976 agreed that costs were to be paid in the following percentage contributions: Saudi Arabia and Kuwait 20% each, the United Arab Emirates 15%, Qatar 10% and other Arab states 35%.

### OTHER INSTITUTIONS OF THE LEAGUE

Other bodies established by resolutions adopted by the Council of the League:

**Administrative Tribunal of the Arab League:** f. 1964; began operations 1966.

**Arab Fund for Technical Assistance to African Countries:** f. 1975 to provide technical assistance for development projects by providing African and Arab experts, grants for scholarships and training, and finance for technical studies.

**Higher Auditing Board:** comprises representatives of seven member states, elected every three years; undertakes financial and administrative auditing duties.

**Investment Arbitration Board:** examines disputes between member states relating to capital investments.

**Special Bureau for Boycotting Israel:** POB 437, Damascus, Syria; f. 1951 to prevent trade between Arab countries and Israel, and to enforce a boycott by Arab countries of companies outside the region that conduct trade with Israel.

### SPECIALIZED AGENCIES

All member states of the Arab League are also members of the Specialized Agencies, which constitute an integral part of the Arab League. (See also entries on the Arab Fund for Economic and Social Development, the Arab Monetary Fund, the Council of Arab Economic Unity and the Organization of Arab Petroleum Exporting Countries.)

**Arab Academy for Science, Technology and Maritime Transport:** POB 1029, Alexandria, Egypt; tel. (3) 5602366; fax (3) 5602144; f. 1975 as Arab Maritime Transport Academy; provides specialized training in marine transport, engineering, technology and management. Dir-Gen. Dr GAMAL ED-DIN MOUKHTAR. Publs *Maritime Research Bulletin* (monthly), *Journal of the Arab Academy for Science, Technology and Maritime Transport* (2 a year).

**Arab Administrative Development Organization—ARADO:** POB 2692 Al-Horreia, Heliopolis, Cairo, Egypt; tel. (2) 4175401; fax (2) 4175407; e-mail arado99@hotmail.com; f. 1961 (as Arab Organization of Administrative Sciences), although became operational in 1969; administration development, training, consultancy, research and studies, information, documentation; promotes Arab and international co-operation in administrative sciences; includes Arab Network of Administrative Information; 20 Arab state members; Library of 26,000 volumes, 400 periodicals. Dir-Gen. Dr MOHAMED IBRAHIM AT-TWAIJRI. Publs *Arab Journal of Administration* (biannual), *Management Newsletter* (quarterly), research series, training manuals.

**Arab Atomic Energy Agency—AAEA:** 4 rue Mouaouiya ibn Abi Soufiane, al-Menzah 8, POB 402, 1004 Tunis, Tunisia; tel. (1) 709464; fax (1) 711330; e-mail aaea@aaea.org.tn; f. 1988 to co-ordinate research into the peaceful uses of atomic energy. Dir-Gen. Prof. Dr MAHMOUD FOUAD BARAKAT (Egypt). Publs *The Atom and Development* (quarterly), other publs in the field of nuclear sciences and their applications in industry, biology, medicine, agriculture and seawater desalination.

**Arab Bank for Economic Development in Africa** (Banque arabe pour le développement économique en Afrique—BADEA): Sayed Abd ar-Rahman el-Mahdi St, POB 2640, Khartoum, Sudan; tel. (11) 773646; fax (11) 770660; e-mail badea@badea.org; internet www.badea.org; f. 1973 by Arab League; provides loans and grants to African countries to finance development projects; paid-up cap. US $1,145.8m. (Dec. 1998). In 1998 the Bank approved loans and grants totalling $109.9m. By the end of 1998 total loans and grants approved since funding activities began in 1975 amounted to $1,840.4m. Subscribing countries: all countries of Arab League, except the Comoros, Djibouti, Somalia and Yemen; recipient countries: all countries of Organization of African Unity (q.v.), except those belonging to the Arab League. Chair. AHMAD ABDALLAH AL-AKEIL (Saudi Arabia); Dir-Gen. MEDHAT SAMI LOTFY (Egypt). Publs *Annual Report, Co-operation for Development* (quarterly), Studies on Afro-Arab co-operation, periodic brochures.

**Arab Centre for the Study of Arid Zones and Dry Lands – ACSAD:** POB 2440, Damascus, Syria; tel. (11) 5323087; fax (11) 5323063; e-mail ruacsad@net.sy; f. 1971 to conduct regional research and development programmes related to water and soil resources, plant and animal production, agro-meteorology, and socio-economic studies of arid zones. The Centre holds conferences and training courses and encourages the exchange of information by Arab scientists. Dir-Gen. Dr HASSAN SEOUD.

**Arab Industrial Development and Mining Organization:** rue France, Zanagat Al Khatawat, POB 8019, Rabat, Morocco; tel. (7) 772600; fax (7) 772188; e-mail aidmo@arifonet.org.ma; internet www.arifonet.org.ma; f. 1990 by merger of Arab Industrial Development Organization, Arab Organization for Mineral Resources and Arab Organization for Standardization and Metrology. Comprises a 13-member Executive Council, a High Consultative Committee of Standardization, a High Committee of Mineral Resources and a Co-ordination Committee for Arab Industrial Research Centres; a Ministerial Council, of ministers of member states responsible for industry, meets every two years. Dir-Gen. TALA'AT AD-DAFER. Publs *Arab Industrial Development* (monthly and quarterly newsletters).

**Arab Labour Organization:** POB 814, Cairo, Egypt; f. 1965 for co-operation between member states in labour problems; unification of labour legislation and general conditions of work wherever possible; research; technical assistance; social insurance; training, etc.; the organization has a tripartite structure: governments, employers and workers. Dir-Gen. BAKR MAHMOUD RASOUL (Iraq). Publs *ALO Bulletin* (monthly), *Arab Labour Review* (quarterly), *Legislative Bulletin* (annually), series of research reports and studies concerned with economic and social development issues in the Arab world.

**Arab League Educational, Cultural and Scientific Organization—ALECSO:** POB 1120, Tunis, Tunisia; tel. (1) 784-466; fax (1) 784-965; f. 1970 to promote and co-ordinate educational, cultural and scientific activities in the Arab region. Regional units: Arab Centre for Arabization, Translation, Authorship, and Publication—Damascus, Syria; Institute of Arab Manuscript—Cairo, Egypt; Institute of Arab Research and Studies—Cairo, Egypt; Khartoum Institute for Arabic Language—Khartoum, Sudan; and the Arabization Co-ordination Bureau—Rabat, Morocco. Dir-Gen. MOHAMED ALMILI IBRAHIMI (Algeria). Publs *Arab Journal of Culture, Arab Journal of Science, Arab Bulletin of Publications, Statistical Yearbook, Journal of the Institute of Arab Manuscripts, Arab Magazine for Information Science.*

**Arab Organization for Agricultural Development:** St no. 7, Al-Amarat, POB 474, Khartoum, Sudan; tel. (11) 472176; fax (11) 471402; e-mail aoad@sudanet.net; f. 1970; began operations in 1972 to contribute to co-operation in agricultural activities, and in the development of natural and human resources for agriculture; compiles data, conducts studies, training and food security programmes; includes Arab Institute of Forestry and Range, Arab Centre for Information and Early Warning, and Arab Centre for Agricultural Documentation. Dir-Gen. Dr YAHIA BAKOUR. Publs *Agricultural Statistics Yearbook, Annual Report on Agricultural Development, the State of Arab Food Security* (annually), *Agriculture and Development in the Arab World* (quarterly), *Accession Bulletin* (every 2 months), *AOAD Newsletter* (monthly), *Arab Agricultural Research Journal.*

**Arab Satellite Communications Organization—ARABSAT:** King Fahd Express Rd (Ollaya St), POB 1038, Riyadh, 11431 Saudi Arabia; tel. (1) 464-6666; fax (1) 465-6983; e-mail albidnah@arabsat.com; internet www.arabsat.com; f. 1976; regional satellite telecommunications organization providing television, telephone and data exchange services to members and private users; operates three satellites, which cover all Arab and Mediterranean countries, controlled by a Primary Control Station in Dirab, Saudi Arabia, and a Secondary Control Facility, based in Dkhila, Tunisia. Dir-Gen. SAAD IBN ABD AL-AZIZ AL-BADNA (Saudi Arabia).

**Arab States Broadcasting Union—ASBU:** POB 250, 1080 Tunis Cedex; 6 rue des Entrepreneurs, zone industrielle Charguia 2, Ariana Aéroport, Tunisia; tel. (1) 703854; fax (1) 704203; f. 1969 to promote Arab fraternity, co-ordinate and study broadcasting subjects, to exchange expertise and technical co-operation in broadcasting; conducts training and audience research. Mems: 21 Arab radio and TV stations and eight foreign associates. Sec.-Gen. RAOUF BASTI. Publ. *ASBU Review* (quarterly).

**Inter-Arab Investment Guarantee Corporation:** POB 23568, Safat 13096, Kuwait; tel. 4844500; fax 4815741; f. 1975; insures Arab investors for non-commercial risks, and export credits for commercial and non-commercial risks; undertakes research and other activities to promote inter-Arab trade and investment; authorized capital 25m. Kuwaiti dinars (Dec. 1995). Mems: 22 Arab governments. Dir-Gen. MAMOUN I. HASSAN. Publs *News Bulletin* (monthly), *Arab Investment Climate Report* (annually).

# External Relations

### ARAB LEAGUE OFFICES AND INFORMATION CENTRES ABROAD

Established by the Arab League to co-ordinate work at all levels among Arab embassies abroad.

**Austria:** Grimmelshausengasse 12, 1030 Vienna.

**Belgium:** 89 ave de l'Uruguay, 1000 Brussels.

**China, People's Republic:** 14 Liang Male, 1-14-2 Tayuan Diplomatic Building, Beijing 100600.

**Ethiopia:** POB 5768, Addis Ababa.

**France:** 36 rue Fortuny, 75017 Paris.

**Germany:** Rheinallee 23, 53173 Bonn.

**India:** B-8/19 Vasant Vihar, New Delhi.

**Italy:** Piazzale delle Belle Arti 6, 00196 Rome.

**Russia:** 28 Koniouch Kovskaya, 132242 Moscow.

**Spain:** Paseo de la Castellana 180, 60°, 28046 Madrid.

**Switzerland:** 9 rue du Valais, 1202 Geneva.

**Tunisia:** 93 ave Louis Braille, el-Khadra, 1003 Tunis.

**United Kingdom:** 52 Green St, London, W1Y 3RH.

**USA:** 1100 17th St, NW, Suite 602, Washington, DC 20036; 17 Third Ave, 35th Floor, New York, NY 10017 (UN Office).

# Record of Events

1945 Pact of the Arab League signed, March.

1946 Cultural Treaty signed.

1950 Joint Defence and Economic Co-operation Treaty.

1952 Agreements on extradition, writs and letters of request, nationality of Arabs outside their country of origin.

1953 Formation of Economic and Social Council.
Convention on the privileges and immunities of the League.

1954 Nationality Agreement.

1956 Agreement on the adoption of a Common Tariff Nomenclature.

1962 Arab Economic Unity Agreement.

1964 First Summit Conference of Arab kings and presidents, Cairo, January.
First meeting of Arab Economic Unity Council, June. Arab Common Market Agreement endorsed by the Council, August.
Second Summit Conference welcomed establishment of Palestine Liberation Organization (PLO), September.

1965 Arab Common Market established, January.

1969 Fifth Summit Conference, Rabat. Call for mobilization of all Arab nations against Israel.

1977 Tripoli Declaration, December. Decision of Algeria, Iraq, Libya and Yemen PDR to boycott League meetings in Egypt in response to President Sadat's visit to Israel.

1979 Council meeting resolved to withdraw Arab ambassadors from Egypt; to recommend severance of political and diplomatic relations with Egypt; to suspend Egypt's membership of the League on the date of the signing of the peace treaty with Israel; to transfer the headquarters of the League to Tunis; to condemn US policy regarding its role in concluding the Camp David agreements and the peace treaty; to halt all bank loans, deposits, guarantees or facilities, as well as all financial or technical contributions and aid to Egypt; to prohibit trade exchanges with the Egyptian state and with private establishments dealing with Israel.

1981 In November the 12th Summit Conference, held in Fez, Morocco, was suspended after a few hours, following disagreement over a Saudi Arabian proposal known as the Fahd Plan, which included not only the Arab demands on behalf of the Palestinians, as approved by the UN General Assembly, but also an implied *de facto* recognition of Israel.

1982 The 12th Summit Conference was reconvened in September. It adopted a peace plan, which demanded Israel's withdrawal from territories occupied in 1967, and removal of Israeli settlements in these areas; freedom of worship for all religions in the sacred places; the right of the Palestinian people to self-determination, under the leadership of the PLO; temporary supervision for the west bank and the gaza strip; the creation of an independent Palestinian state, with Jerusalem as its capital; and a guarantee of peace for all the states of the region by the UN Security Council.

1983 The summit meeting due to be held in November was postponed owing to members' differences of opinion concerning Syria's opposition to Yasser Arafat's chairmanship of the PLO, and Syrian support of Iran in the war against Iraq.

1984 In March an emergency meeting established an Arab League committee to encourage international efforts to bring about a negotiated settlement of the Iran–Iraq war. In May ministers of foreign affairs adopted a resolution urging Iran to stop attacking non-belligerent ships and installations in the Gulf region: similar attacks by Iraq were not mentioned.

1985 In August an emergency Summit Conference was boycotted by Algeria, Lebanon, Libya, Syria and Yemen PDR, while of the other 16 members only nine were represented by their heads of state. Two commissions were set up to mediate in disagreements between Arab states (between Jordan and Syria, Iraq and Syria, Iraq and Libya, and Libya and the PLO).

1986 In July King Hassan of Morocco announced that he was resigning as chairman of the next League Summit Conference, after criticism by several Arab leaders of his meeting with the Israeli Prime Minister earlier that month. A ministerial meeting, held in October, condemned any attempt at direct negotiation with Israel.

1987 An extraordinary Summit Conference was held in November, mainly to discuss the war between Iran and Iraq. Contrary to expectations, the participants unanimously agreed on a statement expressing support for Iraq in its defence of its legitimate rights, and criticizing Iran for its procrastination in accepting the UN Security Council Resolution 598 of July, which had recommended a cease-fire and negotiations on a settlement of the conflict. The meeting also stated that the resumption of diplomatic relations with Egypt was a matter to be decided by individual states.

1988 In June a Summit Conference agreed to provide finance for the PLO to continue the Palestinian uprising in Israeli-occupied territories. It reiterated a demand for the convening of an international conference, attended by the PLO, to seek to bring about a peaceful settlement in the Middle East (thereby implicitly rejecting recent proposals by the US Government for a conference that would exclude the PLO).

1989 In January an Arab League group, comprising six ministers of foreign affairs, began discussions with the two rival Lebanese governments on the possibility of a political settlement in Lebanon. At a Summit Conference, held in May, Egypt was readmitted to the League. The Conference expressed support for the chairman of the PLO, Yasser Arafat, in his recent peace proposals made before the UN General Assembly, and reiterated the League's support for proposals that an international conference should be convened to discuss the rights of Palestinians: in so doing, it accepted UN Security Council Resolutions 242 and 338 on a peaceful settlement in the Middle East and thus gave tacit recognition to the State of Israel. The meeting also supported Arafat in rejecting Israeli proposals for elections in the Israeli-occupied territories of the West Bank and the Gaza Strip. A new mediation committee was established, with a six-month mandate to negotiate a cease-fire in Lebanon, and to reconvene the Lebanese legislature with the aim of holding a presidential election and restoring constitutional government in Lebanon. In September the principal factions in Lebanon agreed to observe a cease-fire, and the surviving members of the Lebanese legislature (originally elected in 1972) met at Ta'if, in Saudi Arabia, in October, and approved the League's proposed 'charter of national reconciliation'.

1990 In May a Summit Conference, held in Baghdad, Iraq (which was boycotted by Syria and Lebanon), criticized recent efforts by Western governments to prevent the development of advanced weapons technology in Iraq. In August an emergency Summit Conference was held to discuss the invasion and annexation of Kuwait by Iraq. Twelve members (Bahrain, Djibouti, Egypt, Kuwait, Lebanon, Morocco, Oman, Qatar, Saudi Arabia, Somalia, Syria and the United Arab Emirates) approved a resolution condemning Iraq's action, and demanding the withdrawal of Iraqi forces from Kuwait and the reinstatement of the Government. The 12 states expressed support for the Saudi Arabian Government's invitation to the USA to send forces to defend Saudi Arabia; they also agreed to impose economic sanctions on Iraq, and to provide troops for an Arab defensive force in Saudi Arabia. The remaining member states, however, condemned the presence of foreign troops in Saudi Arabia, and their ministers of foreign affairs refused to attend a meeting, held at the end of August, to discuss possible solutions to the crisis. The dissenting countries also rejected the decision, taken earlier in the year, to return the League's headquarters from Tunis to Cairo. None the less, the official transfer of the League's headquarters to Cairo took place on 31 October. In November King Hassan of Morocco urged the convening of an Arab Summit Conference, in an attempt to find an 'Arab solution' to Iraq's annexation of Kuwait. However, the divisions in the Arab world over the issue meant that conditions for such a meeting could not be agreed.

1991 The first meeting of the Arab League since August 1990 took place in March, attended by representatives of all 21 member nations, including Iraq. Discussion of the recently-ended war against Iraq was avoided, in an attempt to re-establish the unity of the League. In September, despite deep divisions between member states, it was agreed that a committee should be formed to co-ordinate Arab positions in preparation for the US-sponsored peace talks between Arab countries and Israel. (In the event, an *ad hoc* meeting, attended by Egypt, Jordan, Syria, the PLO, Saudi Arabia—representing the Gulf Co-operation Council (GCC), and Morocco—representing the Union of the Arab Maghreb, was held in October, prior to the start of the talks.) In December the League expressed solidarity with Libya, which was under international pressure to extradite two government agents who were suspected of involvement in the explosion which destroyed a US passenger aircraft over Lockerbie, United Kingdom, in December 1988.

1992 The League attempted to mediate between the warring factions in Somalia. In March the League appointed a committee to seek to resolve the disputes betwen Libya and the USA, the United Kingdom and France over the Lockerbie bomb and the explosion which destroyed a French passenger aircraft over Niger in September 1989. The League condemned the UN's decision, at the end of March, to impose sanctions against Libya, and appealed for a negotiated solution. In September the League's Council issued a condemnation of Iran's alleged occupation of three islands in the Persian (Arabian) Gulf that were claimed by the United Arab Emirates, and decided to refer the issue to the UN.

1993 In April the Council approved the creation of a committee to consider the political and security aspects of water supply in Arab countries. In the same month the League pledged its commitment to the Middle East peace talks, but warned that Israel's continued refusal to repatriate the Palestinians based in Lebanon remained a major obstacle to the process. The League sent an official observer to the independence referendum in Eritrea, held in April. In September the Council admitted the Comoros as the 22nd member of the League. Following the signing of the Israeli-PLO peace accord in September the Council convened in emergency session, at which it approved the agreement, despite opposition from some members, notably Syria. In November it was announced that the League's boycott of commercial activity with Israel was to be maintained.

1994 The League condemned a decision of the GCC, announced in late September, to end the secondary and tertiary trade embargo against Israel, by which member states refuse to trade with international companies which have investments in Israel. A statement issued by the League insisted that the embargo could be removed only on the decision of the Council. Earlier in September the Council endorsed a recommendation that the UN conduct a census of Palestinian refugees, in the absence of any such action taken by the League.

1995 In March Arab ministers of foreign affairs approved a resolution urging Israel to renew the Nuclear Non-Proliferation Treaty (NPT). The resolution stipulated that failure by Israel to do so would cause Arab states to seek to protect legitimate Arab interests by alternative means. In May an extraordinary session of the Council condemned a decision by Israel to confiscate Arab-owned land in East Jerusalem for resettlement. Arab heads of state and government were scheduled to convene in emergency session later in that month to formulate a collective response to the action. However, the meeting was postponed, following an announcement by the Israeli Government that it was suspending its expropriation plans. In September the Council discussed plans for a regional court of justice and for an Arab Code of Honour to prevent the use of force in disputes between Arab states. The Council expressed its support for the Algerian Government in its efforts to combat Muslim separatist violence. In October the League was reported to be in financial difficulties, owing to the non-payment of contributions by seven member states. At that time undisputed arrears amounted to US $80.5m. In

November the Arab League dispatched 44 observers to oversee elections in Algeria as part of an international monitoring team.

1996 In March, following protests by Syria and Iraq that extensive construction work in southern Turkey was restricting water supply in the region, the Council determined that the waters of the Euphrates and Tigris rivers be shared equitably between the three countries. In April an emergency meeting of the Council issued a further endorsement of Syria's position in the dispute with Turkey. The main objective of the meeting, which was convened at the request of Palestine, was to attract international attention to the problem of radiation from an Israeli nuclear reactor. The Council requested an immediate technical inspection of the site by the UN, and further demanded that Israel be obliged to sign the NPT to ensure the eradication of its nuclear weaponry. In June a Summit Conference was convened, the first since 1990, in order to formulate a united Arab response to the election, in May, of a new government in Israel and to the prospects for peace in the Middle East. At the Conference, which was attended by heads of state of 13 countries and senior representatives of seven others (Iraq was excluded from the meeting in order to ensure the attendance of the Gulf member states), Israel was urged to honour its undertaking to withdraw from the Occupied Territories, including Jerusalem, and to respect the establishment of an independent Palestinian state, in order to ensure the success of the peace process. A final communiqué of the meeting warned that Israeli co-operation was essential to prevent Arab states' reconsidering their participation in the peace process and the re-emergence of regional tensions. Meanwhile, there were concerns over increasing inter-Arab hostility, in particular between Syria and Jordan, owing to the latter's relations with Israel and allegations of Syrian involvement in recent terrorist attacks against Jordanian targets. In early September the League condemned US missile attacks against Iraq as an infringement of that country's sovereignty. In addition, it expressed concern at the impact on Iraqi territorial integrity of Turkish intervention in the north of Iraq. Later in September the League met in emergency session, following an escalation of civil unrest in Jerusalem and the Occupied Territories. The League urged the UN Security Council to prevent further alleged Israeli aggression against the Palestinians. In November the League criticized Israel's settlement policy, and at the beginning of December convened in emergency session to consider measures to end any expansion of the Jewish population in the West Bank and Gaza.

1997 In March the Council met in emergency session, in response to the Israeli Government's decision to proceed with construction of a new settlement at Har Homa (Jabal Abu-Ghunaim) in East Jerusalem. The Council pledged its commitment to seeking a reversal of the decision and urged the international community to support this aim. At the end of March ministers of foreign affairs of Arab League states agreed to end all efforts to secure normal diplomatic relations with Israel (although binding agreements already in force with Egypt, Jordan and Palestine were exempt) and to close diplomatic offices and missions while construction work continued in East Jerusalem. In addition, ministers recommended reactivating the economic boycott against Israel until comprehensive peace was achieved in the region and suspending Arab participation in the multilateral talks that were initiated in 1991 to further the peace process. Earlier in the year, in February, the Economic and Social Council ratified a programme to facilitate and develop inter-Arab trade through the reduction and eventual elimination of customs duties over a 10-year period, with effect from 1 January 1998. The Council agreed to supervise the process of establishing an Arab free-trade area (AFTA) and formally to review implementation of the programme twice a year. In June a 60-member delegation from the Arab League participated in an international mission to monitor legislative elections in Algeria. In the same month the League condemned Turkey's military incursion into northern Iraq and demanded a withdrawal of Turkish troops from Iraqi territory. In September ministers of foreign affairs of member states advocated a gradual removal of international sanctions against Libya, and agreed that member countries should permit international flights to leave Libya for specific humanitarian and religious purposes and when used for the purposes of transporting foreign nationals. Ministers also voted to pursue the decision, adopted in March, not to strengthen relations with Israel. Several countries urged a formal boycott of the forthcoming Middle East and North Africa economic conference, in protest at the lack of progress in the peace process (for which the League blamed Israel, which was due to participate in the conference). However, the meeting upheld a request by the Qatari Government, the host of the conference, that each member should decide individually whether to attend. In the event, only seven Arab League countries participated in the conference, which was held in Doha in mid-November, while the Secretary-General of the League decided not to attend as the organization's official representative. In November the League criticized the decision of the US Government to impose economic sanctions against Sudan. The League also expressed concern at the tensions arising from Iraq's decision not to co-operate fully with UN weapons inspectors, and held several meetings with representatives of the Iraqi administration in an effort to secure a peaceful conclusion to the impasse.

1998 In early 1998 the Secretary-General of the League condemned the use or threat of force against Iraq and continued to undertake diplomatic efforts to secure Iraq's compliance with UN Security Council resolutions. The League endorsed the agreement concluded between the UN Secretary-General and the Iraqi authorities in late February, and reaffirmed its commitment to facilitating the eventual removal of the international embargo against Iraq. A meeting of the Council in March, attended by ministers of foreign affairs of 16 member states, rejected Israel's proposal to withdraw from southern Lebanon, which was conditional on the deployment by the Lebanese Government of extra troops to secure Israeli territory from attack, and, additionally, urged international support to secure Israel's withdrawal from the Golan Heights. In April Arab League ministers of the interior and of justice signed an agreement to strengthen Arab co-operation in the prevention of terrorism, incorporating security and judicial measures, such as extradition arrangements and the exchange of evidence. The agreement was to enter into effect 30 days after being ratified by at least seven member countries. In August the League denounced terrorist bomb attacks against the US embassies in Kenya and Tanzania. Nevertheless, it condemned US retaliatory military action, a few days later, against suspected terrorist targets in Afghanistan and Sudan, and endorsed a request by the Sudanese Government that the Security Council investigate the incident. In the same month the USA and United Kingdom accepted a proposal of the Libyan Government, supported by the Arab League, that the suspects in the Lockerbie case be tried in The Hague, Netherlands, under Scottish law. In September the Council determined to remove sanctions against Libya as soon as an agreement was concluded on the terms of bringing the suspects to trial; all punitive measures were then to be cancelled on the commencement of the trial proceedings. Other items concluded by the Council were condemnation of Turkey's military co-operation with Israel, support for efforts to maintain unity in the Comoros, rejection of further Israeli construction in the Golan Heights, and a request that the UN dispatch a fact-finding mission to examine conditions in the Israeli-occupied territories and alleged violations of Palestinian property rights. In November, following an escalation of tensions between the Iraqi authorities and UN weapons inspectors, the Secretary-General reiterated the League's opposition to the use of force against Iraq, but urged Iraq to maintain a flexible approach in its relations with the UN. The League condemned the subsequent bombing of strategic targets in Iraq, conducted by US and British military aircraft in mid-December, and offered immediate medical assistance to victims of the attacks. An emergency summit meeting of the League was scheduled to be held at the end of December, further to a request by the Yemeni Government to formulate a unified Arab response to the bombings; however, it was postponed, reportedly at the request of Gulf Arab states.

1999 The postponed emergency meeting of ministers of foreign affairs was held in late January, attended by representatives of 18 member states. The meeting expressed concern at the military response to the stand-off between Iraq and the UN. However, the Iraqi delegation withdrew from the meeting in protest at the final statement, which included a request that Iraq recognize Kuwait's territorial integrity and comply with UN Security Council resolutions before sanctions may be removed. The meeting agreed to establish a seven-member *ad hoc* committee to consider the removal of punitive measures against Iraq within the framework of UN resolutions. In March the Council determined that member states would remove sanctions imposed against Libya, once arrangements for the trial of the suspects in the Lockerbie case had been finalized. (The suspects were transferred to a detention centre in the Netherlands in early April.) The meeting also expressed support for a UN resolution convening an international conference to facilitate the implementation of agreements applying to Israel and the Occupied Territories, condemned Israel's refusal to withdraw from the Occupied Territories without a majority vote in favour from its legislature, as well as its refusal to resume the peace negotiations with Lebanon and Syria that had ended in 1996, and advocated the publication of evidence of Israeli violence against Palestinians. The Council considered other issues, including the need to prevent further Israeli expansion in Jerusalem and the problem of Palestinian refugees, and reiterated demands for international support to secure Israel's withdrawal from the Golan Heights. In May the League expressed its concern at the political situation in the Comoros, following the removal of the government and establishment of a new military regime in that country at the end of April. In June the League condemned an Israeli aerial attack on Beirut and southern Lebanon. In July the League reported that it was experiencing severe financial difficulties, with member countries having contributed just US $12m. of the annual budget of $27.6m. In September Iraq chaired a meeting of the Ministerial Council for the first time since 1990. The meeting considered a range of issues, including the Middle East peace process, US military aid to Israel, and a dispute with the Walt Disney corporation regarding a forthcoming exhibition which was thought to depict Jerusalem as the capital of Israel. Later in September an extraordinary meeting of League senior media and information officials was convened to discuss the latter issue. Negotiations with representatives of Disney were pursued and the implied threat of an Arab boycott of the corporation was averted following assurances that the exhibition would be apolitical. In October the Secretary-General of the League condemned the Mauritanian authorities for concluding an agreement with Israel to establish diplomatic relations.

## Publications

*Arab Perspectives—Sh'oun Arabiyya* (monthly).

*Journal of Arab Affairs* (monthly).

Bulletins of treaties and agreements concluded among the member states, essays, regular publications circulated by regional offices.

# NORDIC COUNCIL

**Address:** Store Strandstraede 18, 1255 Copenhagen, Denmark.

**Telephone:** 33-96-04-00; **fax:** 33-11-18-70; **internet:** www.norden.org.

The Nordic Council was founded in 1952 for co-operation between the Nordic parliaments and governments. The four original members were Denmark, Iceland, Norway and Sweden; Finland joined in 1955, and the Faroe Islands and Åland Islands were granted representation in 1970 within the Danish and Finnish delegations respectively. Greenland had separate representation within the Danish delegation from 1984. Co-operation was first regulated by a Statute, and subsequently by the Helsinki Treaty of 1962. The Nordic region has a population of about 24m.

### MEMBERS

Denmark (with the autonomous territories of the Faroe Islands and Greenland)
Finland (with the autonomous territory of the Åland Islands)
Iceland
Norway
Sweden

## Organization

(January 2000)

### COUNCIL

The Nordic Council is not a supranational parliament, but a forum for co-operation between the parliaments and governments of the Nordic countries. The Nordic Council of Ministers (see below) co-ordinates the activities of the governments of the Nordic countries when decisions are to be implemented.

The Council comprises 87 members, elected annually by and from the parliaments of the respective countries (Denmark 16 members; Faroes 2; Greenland 2; Finland 18; Åland 2; Iceland 7; Norway 20; Sweden 20). The various parties are proportionately represented in accordance with their representation in the national parliaments. Sessions of the Council consider proposals submitted by Council members, by the Council of Ministers or national governments. The sessions also follow up the outcome of past decisions and the work of the various Nordic institutions. The Plenary Assembly, which convenes once a year, is the highest body of the Nordic Council. Government representatives may participate in the Assembly, but do not have the right to vote.

The Council has initiated and overseen extensive efforts to strengthen Nordic co-operation at the political, economic and social level. The intensification of co-operation among European countries, particularly since the mid-1980s, and the dissolution of the former Soviet Union created new challenges for the Nordic Council and Council of Ministers. In 1995 the Nordic Council, meeting in Reykjavík, Iceland, endorsed new guide-lines for policy and administrative reform, in response to the region's political developments. Subsequently the Council's activities have focused on the following three areas: intra-Nordic co-operation, with the emphasis on cultural, education and research co-operation; co-operation with the EU and the European Economic Area, where the aim was jointly to promote Nordic values and interests in a broader European context; and co-operation with the Adjacent Areas, i.e. the Baltic States, north-west Russia and the Arctic Area/Barents Sea, where Nordic governments are committed to furthering democracy, security and sustainable development.

### STANDING COMMITTEES

Council members are assigned to the following Standing Committees, corresponding to the Council's three pillars for co-operation: the Committee on Nordic Affairs; the Committee on the Adjacent Areas; and the Committee on European Affairs.

### PRESIDIUM

The day-to-day work of the Nordic Council is directed by a Presidium, consisting of 13 members of national legislatures. The Presidium is the Council's highest decision-making body between sessions. The Presidium secretariat is headed by a Council Director. Each delegation to the Nordic Council has a secretariat at its national legislature.

## Publications

Note: the titles listed below are joint publications of the Nordic Council and Nordic Council of Ministers.

*Norden the Top of Europe* (monthly newsletter in English, German and French).

*The Nordic Council.*

*Politik i Norden* (newsletter, in the languages of the region).

*Yearbook of Nordic Statistics* (in English and Swedish).

Books and pamphlets on Nordic co-operation; summaries of Council sessions.

# NORDIC COUNCIL OF MINISTERS

**Address:** Store Strandstraede 18, 1255 Copenhagen K, Denmark.

**Telephone:** 33-96-02-00; **fax:** 33-96-02-02; **internet:** www.norden.org.

The Governments of Denmark, Finland, Iceland, Norway and Sweden co-operate through the Nordic Council of Ministers. This co-operation is regulated by the Treaty of Co-operation between Denmark, Finland, Iceland, Norway and Sweden of 1962 (amended in 1971, 1974, 1983, 1985, 1993 and 1995) and the Treaty between Denmark, Finland, Iceland, Norway and Sweden concerning cultural co-operation of 1971 (amended in 1983 and 1985). Although the Prime Ministers do not meet formally within the Nordic Council of Ministers, they have decided to take a leading role in overall Nordic co-operation. The Ministers of Defence and Foreign Affairs do not meet within the Council of Ministers. These ministers, however, meet on an informal basis.

### MEMBERS

Denmark Finland Iceland Norway Sweden

Greenland, the Faroe Islands and the Åland Islands also participate as autonomous regions.

## Organization

(January 2000)

### COUNCIL OF MINISTERS

The Nordic Council of Ministers holds formal and informal meetings and is attended by ministers with responsibility for the subject under discussion. Each member state also appoints a minister in its own cabinet as Minister for Nordic Co-operation.

Decisions of the Council of Ministers must be unanimous, except for procedural questions, which may be decided by a simple majority of those voting. Abstention constitutes no obstacle to a decision. Decisions are binding on the individual countries, provided that no parliamentary approval is necessary under the constitution of any of the countries. If such approval is necessary, the Council of Ministers must be so informed before its decision.

Meetings are concerned with: agreements and treaties, guidelines for national legislation, recommendations from the Nordic Council, financing joint studies, setting up Nordic institutions.

The Council of Ministers reports each year to the Nordic Council on progress in all co-operation between member states, as well as on future plans.

### SECRETARIAT

The Office of the Secretary-General is responsible for co-ordination and legal matters (including co-ordination of work related to the European integration process and to the development of eastern Europe).

The work of the Secretariat is divided into the following departments:

Cultural and educational co-operation, research, advanced education, computer technology;

Budget and administration;

Environmental protection, finance and monetary policy, fisheries, industry and energy, regional policy, agriculture and forestry;

Information;

Labour market issues, social policy and health care, occupational environment, consumer affairs, equal opportunities.

**Secretary-General:** SØREN CHRISTENSEN (Denmark).

### COMMITTEES

**Nordic Co-operation Committee:** for final preparation of material for the meetings of Ministers of Nordic Co-operation.

**Senior Executives' Committees:** prepare the meetings of the Council of Ministers and conduct research at its request. There are a number of sub-committees. The Committees cover the subjects listed under the Secretariat (above).

## Activities

### ECONOMIC CO-OPERATION

Economic co-operation is undertaken in the following areas: freer markets for goods and services; measures on training and employment; elimination of trade barriers; liberalization of capital movements; research and development; export promotion; taxes and other levies; and regional policy.

**Nordic Development Fund:** f. 1989; supports activities by national administrations for overseas development with resources amounting to SDR 500m.

**Nordic Environmental Development Fund:** f. as the Nordic Environmental Financing Company (NEFCO), the Fund was to finance environmental projects during 1999–2003.

**Nordic Industrial Fund:** f. 1973 to provide grants, subsidies and loans for industrial research and development projects of interest to more than one member country.

**Nordic Investment Bank:** f. under an agreement of December 1975 to provide finance and guarantees for the implementation of investment projects and exports; authorized and subscribed capital 2,400m. IMF special drawing rights. The main sectors of the Bank's activities are energy, metal and wood-processing industries (including petroleum extraction) and manufacturing. In 1982 a separate scheme for financing investments in developing countries was established. In 1997 an Environmental Loan Facility was established to facilitate environmental investments in the Nordic Adjacent Areas.

**Nordic Project Fund:** f. 1982 to strengthen the international competitiveness of Nordic exporting companies, and to promote industrial co-operation in international projects (e.g. in environmental protection).

**NORDTEST:** f. 1973 as an inter-Nordic agency for technical testing and standardization of methods and of laboratory accreditation.

### RELATIONS WITH THE EU AND EASTERN EUROPE

In 1991 the theme 'Norden in Europe' was regarded as an area of high priority for the coming years by the Council. Nordic co-operation would be used to co-ordinate member countries' participation in the western European integration process, based on EC and EC/EFTA co-operation. Since 1995, when Finland and Sweden acceded to the European Union (joining Denmark, already a member of that organization), Europe and the EU have been an integrated part of the work of Nordic co-operation.

Since 1991 the Nordic Council of Ministers has developed its co-operation relating to the Baltic countries and north-west Russia, in order to contribute to peace, security and stability in Europe. Co-operation measures aim to promote democracy, the establishment of market economies, respect for civil rights and the responsible use of resources in these areas. The Nordic 'Working Programme of the Adjacent Areas' comprises the following three major components: Nordic Information Offices in Tallinn, Riga, Vilnius and St Petersburg, which co-ordinate Nordic projects and activities, promote regional contact at all levels and provide information about the Nordic countries in general and Nordic co-operation specifically; the Nordic-Baltic Scholarship Scheme, which awards grants to students, teachers, scientists, civil servants and parliamentarians; and the Nordic Council of Ministers Project Activities, which in 1997 was to fund 31 projects within the cultural, educational, industrial, housing, agricultural and environmental sectors.

### COMMUNICATIONS AND TRANSPORT

The main areas of co-operation have been concerned with international transport, the environment, infrastructure, road research, transport for the disabled and road safety.

### EMPLOYMENT

In 1954 an agreement entered into force on a free labour market between Denmark, Finland, Norway and Sweden. Iceland became a party to the agreement in 1982 and the Faroe Islands in 1992. In 1982 an agreement on worker training and job-oriented rehabilitation came into effect. There is a joint centre for labour market training at Övertorneå in Sweden. A convention on the working environment was signed in 1989. The Nordic Institute for Advanced Training in Occupational Health is based in Helsinki, Finland.

### GENDER EQUALITY

A Nordic co-operation programme on equality between women and men began in 1974. The main areas of co-operation have been working conditions, education, social welfare and family policy, housing and social planning, and women's participation in politics. In 1995–2000 the main areas of concern were the integration of equality aspects into all areas of society (i.e. 'mainstreaming'), the role of men, and the means of securing equal access for women and men to economic and political processes.

### ENVIRONMENT

A new Nordic Strategy for the Environment, adopted in February 1996 for the period 1996–2000, constitutes the overall guide-lines for Nordic co-operation in this field. In the Nordic region priority was to be given to nature conservation and the integration of environmental considerations into sectors such as fisheries, agriculture and forestry, finance and energy. Support for the solution of environmental problems was accorded high priority in relation to the areas adjacent to the Nordic region, with monitoring and assessment the key elements of its strategy for the Arctic region. The Nordic countries promote a high level of ambition as the basis for the environmental work conducted in the EU and at an international level.

### ENERGY AND INDUSTRY

Co-operation in the energy sector focuses on energy-saving, energy and the environment, the energy market, and the introduction of new and renewable sources of energy.

### CONSUMER AFFAIRS

The main areas of co-operation are in safety legislation, consumer education and information and consumers' economic and legal interests.

### FOOD AND NUTRITION

Co-operation in this sector began in 1982, and includes projects in food legislation, diet and nutrition, toxicology, risk evaluation and food controls.

### AGRICULTURE AND FISHERIES

In 1995 a five-year programme for Nordic co-operation in agriculture and forestry was approved for the period 1996–2000, identifying the following as areas of future co-operation activities: quality production; management of genetic resources; development of regions dependent on agriculture and forestry; and sustainable forestry. Efforts to develop co-operation in both the fisheries and agriculture and forestry sectors have been undertaken with the aim of integrating environmental aspects into the relevant policies and strategies. The four-year programme of co-operation in the Nordic fisheries sector for 1997–2000 aims to strengthen fisheries regulation, management, and research and development. It emphasizes the environmental aspects of the industry, such as the influence of land-based pollution on the sea and the integration of environmentally-compatible techniques into fishing and the on-shore industry.

### LAW

The five countries have similar legal systems and tend towards uniformity in legislation and interpretation of law. Much of the preparatory committee work within the national administrations on new legislation involves consultation with the neighbour countries.

Citizens of one Nordic country working in another are in many respects given the status of nationals. In all the Nordic countries they already have the right to vote in local elections in the country of residence. The changing of citizenship from one Nordic country to another has been simplified, and legislation on marriage and on children's rights amended to achieve the greatest possible parity.

There are special extradition facilities between the countries and further stages towards co-operation between the police and the courts have been adopted. In October 1996 justice ministers of the Nordic countries agreed to strengthen police co-operation in order to counter an increase in violent crime perpetrated by gangs. Emphasis is also placed on strengthening co-operation to combat the sexual abuse of children.

There is a permanent Council for Criminology and a Nordic Institute for Maritime Law in Oslo.

### REGIONAL POLICY

Under a joint programme, covering the period 1995–99, the Council of Ministers agreed to develop cross-border co-operation between the Nordic countries and co-operation with the EU and the Baltic countries and to give greater priority to exchanging knowledge and information.

### SOCIAL WELFARE AND HEALTH

Existing conventions and other co-operation directives ensure that Nordic citizens have the same rights, benefits and obligations in each Nordic country, with regard to sickness, parenthood, occupational injury, unemployment, disablement and old-age pension. Uniform provisions exist concerning basic pension and supplementary pension benefits when moving from one Nordic country to another. In June 1993 Nordic representatives signed an agreement providing for a common Nordic labour market for health professionals. Numerous joint initiatives have been undertaken in the social welfare and health sectors within the framework of the co-operating institutions.

**Institutions:**

Nordic Centre for the Development of Aids and Appliances for the Handicapped;
Nordic Committee on Disability;
Nordic Committee on Social Security Statistics;
Nordic Council for Alcohol and Drug Research, Helsinki, Finland;
Nordic Council on Medicines, Uppsala, Sweden;
Nordic Education Programme for Social Service Development, Gothenburg, Sweden;
Nordic Medico-statistical Committee;
Nordic School of Public Health, Gothenburg, Sweden;
Nordic Staff Training Centre for Deaf-blind Services, Dronninglund, Denmark;
Scandinavian Institute of Dental Materials.

### EDUCATIONAL AND SCIENTIFIC CO-OPERATION

**Education:** Nordic co-operation in the educational field includes the objective content and means of education, the structure of the educational system and pedagogical development work.

The Nordic Council of Ministers finances the following co-operating bodies, permanent institutions and joint programmes:

- Nordic-Baltic Scholarship Scheme
- Nordic Folk Academy
- Nordic Institute in Finland
- Nordic Language and Literature Courses
- NORDPLUS (Nordic Programme for Mobility of University Students and Teachers)
- Nordic programmes for mobility of pupils, students, and teachers at primary and secondary school level (NORDPLUS-Junior and others)
- Nordic School Data Network
- Nordic Summer University
- Programme of Action for Nordic Language Co-operation
- Steering Committee for Nordic Co-operation on General and Adult Education
- Steering Committee for Nordic Co-operation in Higher Education
- Steering Committee for Nordic Educational Co-operation (primary and secondary school)

**Research:** Nordic co-operation in research comprises information on research activities and research findings, joint research projects, joint research institutions, the methods and means in research policy, the organizational structure of research and co-ordination of the national research programmes.

Much of the research co-operation activities at the more permanent joint research institutions consists of establishing science contacts in the Nordic areas by means of grants, visiting lecturers, courses and symposia.

The research institutions and research bodies listed below receive continuous financial support via the Nordic cultural budget. In many cases, these joint Nordic institutions ensure a high international standard that would otherwise have been difficult to maintain at a purely national level.

- Nordic Academy for Advanced Study
- Nordic Committee for Bioethics
- Nordic Council for Scientific Information and Research Libraries
- Nordic Institute of Asian Studies
- Nordic Institute of Maritime Law
- Nordic Institute for Theoretical Physics
- Nordic Programme for Arctic Research
- Nordic Sami Institute
- Nordic Science Policy Council
- Nordic Vulcanological Institute
- Research Programme on the Nordic Countries and Europe

**Cultural activities:** Cultural co-operation is concerned with artistic and other cultural exchange between the Nordic countries; activities relating to libraries, museums, radio, television, and film; promotion of activities within organizations with general cultural aims, including youth and sports organizations; the improvement of conditions for the creative and performing arts; and encouragement for artists and cultural workers. Exhibitions and performances of Nordic culture are organized abroad.

Joint projects include:

- Fund for Mobility of Young Nordic Artists—SLEIPNIR
- Nordic Amateur Theatre Council
- Nordic Art Centre
- Nordic Co-operation in Athletics
- Nordic Council Literature Prize
- Nordic Council Music Prize
- Nordic Documentation Centre for Mass Communication Research
- Nordic Film and Television Fund
- Nordic House in the Faroe Islands
- Nordic House in Reykjavík
- Nordic Institute in Åland
- Nordic Institute of Contemporary Art
- Nordic Institute in Greenland
- Nordic Literature and Libraries Committee
- Nordic Music Committee
- Nordic Theatre and Dance Committee
- Nordic Visual Art Committee
- Steering Committee on Culture and Mass Media
- Steering Committee on Nordic Cultural Projects Abroad

### NORDIC CULTURAL FUND

The Nordic Cultural Fund was established through a separate agreement between the governments of the Nordic countries in 1966, and began operating in 1967, with the aim of supporting the needs of cultural life in the Nordic countries. A Board of 11 members administers and distributes the resources of the Fund and supervises its activities. Five of the members are appointed by the Nordic Council and five by the Nordic Council of Ministers (of culture and education), for a period of two years. The autonomous territories (the Åland islands, the Faroe Islands and Greenland) are represented by one member on the Board, appointed alternately by the Nordic Council and the Nordic Council of Ministers. The Fund is located within and administered by the Secretariat of the Nordic Council of Ministers. It considers applications for assistance for research, education and general cultural activities; grants may also be awarded for the dissemination of information concerning Nordic culture within and outside the region.

## Finance

Joint expenses are divided according to an agreed scale in proportion to the relative national product of the member countries. The 2000 budget of the Nordic Council of Ministers amounted to 741m. Danish kroner. Various forms of co-operation are also financed directly from the national budgets.

# NORTH AMERICAN FREE TRADE AGREEMENT—NAFTA

**Canadian section:** Royal Bank Centre, 90 Sparks St, Suite 705, Ottawa, Ontario, K1P 5B4; **tel.:** (613) 992-9388: **fax:** (613) 992-9392.

**Mexican section:** Blvd Adolfo López Mateos 3025, 2°, Col Héroes de Padierna, 10700 Mexico, DF; **tel.:** (5) 629-9630; **fax:** (5) 929-9637.

**US section:** 14th St and Constitution Ave, NW, Room 2061, Washington, DC 20230; **tel.:** (202) 482-5438; **fax:** (202) 482-0148.
**E-mail:** info@nafta.org; **internet:** www.nafta-sec-alena.org.

The North American Free Trade Agreement (NAFTA) grew out of the free-trade agreement between the USA and Canada that was signed in January 1988 and came into effect on 1 January 1989. Negotiations on the terms of NAFTA, which includes Mexico in the free-trade area, were concluded in October 1992 and the Agreement was signed in December. The accord was ratified in November 1993 and entered into force on 1 January 1994. The NAFTA Secretariat is composed of national sections in each member country.

### MEMBERS

Canada | Mexico | USA

### MAIN PROVISIONS OF THE AGREEMENT

Under NAFTA almost all restrictions on trade and investment between Canada, Mexico and the USA were to be gradually removed over a 15-year period. Most tariffs were eliminated immediately on agricultural trade between the USA and Mexico, with tariffs on 6% of agricultural products (including corn, sugar, and some fruits and vegetables) to be abolished over the 15 years. Tariffs on automobiles and textiles were to be phased out over 10 years in all three countries. Mexico was to open its financial sector to US and Canadian investment, with all restrictions to be removed by 2007. Barriers to investment were removed in most sectors, with exemptions for petroleum in Mexico, culture in Canada and airlines and radio communications in the USA. Mexico was to liberalize government procurement, removing preferential treatment for domestic companies over a 10-year period. In transport, heavy goods vehicles were to have complete freedom of movement between the three countries by 2000. An interim measure, whereby transport companies could apply for special licences to travel further within the borders of each country than the existing limit of 20 miles (32 km), was postponed in December 1995, shortly before it was scheduled to come into effect. The postponement was due to concerns, on the part of the US Government, relating to the implementation of adequate safety standards by Mexican truck-drivers. In April 1998 the fifth meeting of the three-member ministerial Free Trade Commission (see below), held in Paris, France, agreed to remove tariffs on some 600 goods, including certain chemicals, pharmaceuticals, steel and wire products, textiles, toys, and watches, from 1 August. As a result of the agreement, a number of tariffs were eliminated as much as 10 years earlier than had been originally planned.

In the case of a sudden influx of goods from one country to another that adversely affects a domestic industry, the Agreement makes provision for the imposition of short-term 'snap-back' tariffs.

Disputes are to be settled in the first instance by intergovernmental consultation. If a dispute is not resolved within 30 to 40 days, a government may call a meeting of the Free Trade Commission. In October 1944 the Commission established an Advisory Committee on Private Commercial Disputes to recommend procedures for the resolution of such disputes. If the Commission is unable to settle the issue a panel of experts in the relevant field is appointed to adjudicate. By September 1996 some 80 trade disputes had been submitted to the Free Trade Commission for adjudication, mostly by private-sector companies. In June of that year Canada and Mexico announced their decision to refer the US 'Helms-Burton' legislation on trade with Cuba to the Commission. They claimed that the legislation, which provides for punitive measures against foreign companies that engage in trade with Cuba, imposed undue restrictions on Canadian and Mexican companies and was, therefore, in contravention of NAFTA. However, at the beginning of 1997 enactment of the Helms-Burton legislation was suspended for a period of six months by the US administration. In April it was again suspended, as part of a compromise agreement with the European Union.

In December 1994 NAFTA members issued a formal invitation to Chile to seek membership of the Agreement. Formal discussions on Chile's entry began in June 1995, but were stalled in December when the US Congress failed to approve 'fast-track' negotiating authority for the US Government, which was to have allowed the latter to negotiate a trade agreement with Chile, without risk of incurring a line-by-line veto from the US Congress. In February 1996 Chile began high-level negotiations with Canada on a wide-ranging bilateral free-trade agreement. Chile, which already had extensive bilateral trade agreements with Mexico, was regarded as advancing its position with regard to NAFTA membership by means of the proposed accord with Canada. The bilateral agreement, which provided for the extensive elimination of customs duties by 2002, was signed in November 1996 and ratified by Chile in July 1997. However, in November 1997 the US Government was obliged to request the removal of the 'fast-track' proposal from the legislative agenda, owing to insufficient support within Congress.

In April 1998 heads of state of 34 countries, meeting in Santiago, Chile, agreed formally to initiate the negotiating process to establish a Free Trade Area of the Americas (FTAA). The US Government had originally proposed creating the FTAA through the gradual extension of NAFTA trading privileges on a bilateral basis. However, the framework agreed upon by ministers of trade of the 34 countries, meeting in March, provided for countries to negotiate and accept FTAA provisions on an individual basis and as part of a sub-regional economic bloc. It was envisaged that the FTAA would exist alongside the subregional associations, including NAFTA. Canada was to hold the presidency of the FTAA until 31 October 1999; the negotiating process was scheduled to be concluded in Mexico City on 31 December 2004, under the joint presidency of Brazil and the USA.

### ADDITIONAL AGREEMENTS

During 1993, as a result of domestic pressure, the new US Government negotiated two 'side agreements' with its NAFTA partners, which were to provide safeguards for workers' rights and the environment. A Commission for Labour Co-operation was established under the North American Agreement on Labour Co-operation (NAALC) to monitor implementation of labour accords and to foster co-operatiion in that area. The Commission for Environmental Co-operation (CEC) was initiated to combat pollution, to ensure that economic development was not environmentally damaging and to monitor compliance with national and NAFTA environmental regulations. Panels of experts, with representatives from each country, were established to adjudicate in cases of alleged infringement of workers' rights or environmental damage. The panels were given the power to impose fines and trade sanctions, but only with regard to the USA and Mexico; Canada, which was opposed to such measures, was to enforce compliance with NAFTA by means of its own legal system. In 1995 the North American Fund for Environmental Co-operation (NAFEC) was established. NAFEC, which is financed by the GEC, supports community environmental projects.

In February 1996 the CEC consented for the first time to investigate a complaint brought by environmentalists regarding non-compliance with domestic legislation on the environment. Mexican environmentalists claimed that a company that was planning to build a pier for tourist ships (a project that was to involve damage to a coral reef) had not been required to supply adequate environmental impact studies. The CEC was limited to presenting its findings in such a case, as it could only make a ruling in the case of complaints brought by one NAFTA government against another. The CEC allocates the bulk of its resources to research undertaken to support compliance with legislation and agreements on the environment. However, in October 1997 the council of NAFTA ministers of the environment, meeting in Montréal, Canada, approved a new structure for the CEC's activities. The CEC's main objective was to be the provision of advice concerning the environmental impact of trade issues. It was also agreed that the CEC was further to promote trade in environmentally-sound products and to encourage private-sector investment in environmental trade issues.

With regard to the NAALC, National Administration Offices have been established in each of the three NAFTA countries in order to monitor labour issues and to address complaints about non-compliance with domestic labour legislation. However, punitive measures in the form of trade sanctions or fines (up to US $20m.) may only be imposed in the specific instances of contravention of national legislation regarding child labour, a minimum wage or health and safety standards. A Commission for Labour Co-operation has been established (see below) and incorporates a council of ministers of labour of the three countries.

In August 1993 the USA and Mexico agreed to establish a Border Environmental Co-operation Commission (BECC) to assist with the co-ordination of projects for the improvement of infrastructure and to monitor the environmental impact of the Agreement on the US–Mexican border area, where industrial activity was expected to intensify. The Commission is located in Ciudad Juárez, Mexico. In 1998 the BECC authorized seven projects, bringing the total number of certified projects to 26, at a cost of some US $607m. In October 1993 the USA and Mexico concluded an agreement to establish a North American Development Bank (NADB or NADbank), which was to finance environmental and infrastructure projects along the US–Mexican border.

**Commission for Environmental Co-operation (CEC):** 393 rue St Jacques West, Montréal, Bureau 200, Montréal, Québec H2Y IN9, Canada; tel. (514) 350-4300; fax (514) 350-4314; internet www.cec.org; f. 1994; Exec. Dir JANINE FERRETI (acting); Dir GREG BLOCK. Publ. *Annual Report*.

**Commission for Labour Co-operation:** One Dallas Center, 350 N. St Paul 2424, Dallas, TX 75201-4240, USA; tel. (214) 754-1100; fax (214) 754-1199; e-mail info@naalc.org; internet www.naalc.org; f. 1994; Exec. Dir JOHN MCKENNIREY. Publ. *Annual Report*.

**North American Development Bank (NADB or NADbank):** 203 St Mary's, Suite 300, San Antonio, TX 78205, USA; tel. (210) 231-8000; fax (210) 231-6232; internet www.nadbank.org. At February 1999 the NADB had authorized capital of US $3,000m., subscribed equally by Mexico and the USA, of which $550m. was paid-up. Publ. *Annual Report*.

# NORTH ATLANTIC TREATY ORGANIZATION—NATO

**Address:** blvd Léopold III, 1110 Brussels, Belgium.

**Telephone:** (2) 707-41-11; **fax:** (2) 707-45-79; **internet:** www.nato.int.

The Atlantic Alliance was established on the basis of the 1949 North Atlantic Treaty as a defensive political and military alliance of a group of European states (then numbering 10) and the USA and Canada. The Alliance aims to provide common security for its members through co-operation and consultation in political, military and economic fields, as well as scientific and other non-military aspects. The objectives of the Alliance are implemented by NATO. Following the collapse of the communist governments in central and eastern Europe, from 1989 onwards, and the dissolution of the Warsaw Pact (which had hitherto been regarded as the Alliance's principal adversary) in 1991, NATO has undertaken a fundamental transformation of its structures and policies to meet the new security challenges in Europe.

### MEMBERS*

| | | |
|---|---|---|
| Belgium | Hungary | Poland |
| Canada | Iceland | Portugal |
| Czech Republic | Italy | Spain |
| Denmark | Luxembourg | Turkey |
| France | Netherlands | United Kingdom |
| Germany | Norway | USA |
| Greece | | |

* Greece and Turkey acceded to the Treaty in 1952, and the Federal Republic of Germany in 1955. France withdrew from the integrated military structure of NATO in 1966, although remaining a member of the Atlantic Alliance; in 1996 France resumed participation in some, but not all, of the military organs of NATO. Spain acceded to the Treaty in 1982, but remained outside the Alliance's integrated military structure until 1999. The Czech Republic, Hungary and Poland were formally admitted as members of NATO in March 1999.

## Organization

(January 2000)

### NORTH ATLANTIC COUNCIL

The Council, the highest authority of the Alliance, is composed of representatives of the 16 member states. It meets at the level of Permanent Representatives, ministers of foreign affairs, or heads of state and government, and, at all levels, has effective political and decision-making authority. Ministerial meetings are held at least twice a year. At the level of Permanent Representatives the Council meets at least once a week.

The Secretary-General of NATO is Chairman of the Council, and each year a minister of foreign affairs of a member state is nominated honorary President, following the English alphabetical order of countries.

Decisions are taken by common consent and not by majority vote. The Council is a forum for wide consultation between member governments on major issues, including political, military, economic and other subjects, and is supported by the Senior or regular Political Committee, the Military Committee and other subordinate bodies.

### PERMANENT REPRESENTATIVES

Belgium: THIERRY DE GRUBEN
Canada: DAVID WRIGHT
Denmark: NIELS EGELUND
France: PHILIPPE GUELLUY
Germany: GEBHARDT VON MOLTKE
Greece: GEORGE SAVVAIDES
Iceland: GUNNAR PÁLSSON
Italy: AMEDEO DE FRANCHIS
Luxembourg: JEAN-JACQUES KASEL
Netherlands: Dr NICOLAAS HENDRIK BIEGMANN
Norway: HANS JACOB BIØRN LIAN
Portugal: FERNANDO ANDRESEN-GUIMARÃES.
Spain: JAVIER CONDE DE SARO
Turkey: ONUR ÖYMEN
United Kingdom: Sir JOHN GOULDEN
USA: ALEXANDER R. VERSHBOW

### DEFENCE PLANNING COMMITTEE

Most defence matters are dealt with in the Defence Planning Committee, composed of representatives of all member countries except France. The Committee provides guidance to NATO's military authorities and, within the field of its responsibilities, has the same functions and authority as the Council. Like the Council, it meets regularly at ambassadorial level and assembles twice a year in ministerial sessions, when member countries are represented by their ministers of defence.

### NUCLEAR PLANNING GROUP

Defence ministers of countries participating in the Defence Planning Committee meet regularly in the Nuclear Planning Group (NPG) to discuss specific policy issues relating to nuclear forces, such as safety, deployment issues, nuclear arms control and proliferation. The NPG is supported by a Staff Group, composed of representatives of all members participating in the NPG, which meets at least once a week.

### OTHER COMMITTEES

There are also committees for political affairs, economics, military medical services, armaments, defence review, science, the environment, infrastructure, logistics, communications, civil emergency planning, information and cultural relations, and civil and military budgets. In addition, other committees consider specialized subjects such as NATO pipelines, air traffic management, etc. Since 1992 most of these committees consult on a regular basis with representatives from central and eastern European countries.

### INTERNATIONAL SECRETARIAT

The Secretary-General is Chairman of the North Atlantic Council, the Defence Planning Committee and the Nuclear Planning Group.

He is the head of the International Secretariat, with staff drawn from the member countries. He proposes items for NATO consultation and is generally responsible for promoting consultation and co-operation in accordance with the provisions of the North Atlantic Treaty. He is empowered to offer his help informally in cases of disputes between member countries, to facilitate procedures for settlement.

**Secretary-General:** Lord ROBERTSON OF PORT ELLEN (United Kingdom).

**Deputy Secretary-General:** SERGIO BALANZINO (Italy).

There is an Assistant Secretary-General for each of the operational divisions listed below.

### PRINCIPAL DIVISIONS

**Division of Political Affairs:** maintains political liaison with national delegations and international organizations. Prepares reports on political subjects for the Secretary-General and the Council, and provides the administrative structure for the management of the Alliance's political responsibilities, including disarmament and arms control. Asst Sec.-Gen. Dr KLAUS-PETER KLAIBER (Germany).

**Division of Defence Planning and Operations:** studies all matters concerning the defence of the Alliance, and co-ordinates the defence review and other force planning procedures of the Alliance. Asst Sec.-Gen. Dr EDGAR BUCKLEY (United Kingdom).

**Division of Defence Support:** promotes the most efficient use of the Allies' resources in the production of military equipment and its standardization. Asst Sec.-Gen. ROBERT BELL (USA).

**Division of Security Investment, Logistics and Civil Emergency Planning:** supervises the technical and financial aspects of the security investment programme. Provides guidance, co-ordination and support to the activities of NATO committees or bodies active in the field of consumer logistics and civil emergency planning. Asst Sec.-Gen. ØIVIND BAEKKEN (Norway).

**Division of Scientific and Environmental Affairs:** advises the Secretary-General on scientific matters of interest to NATO. Responsible for promoting and administering scientific exchange programmes between member countries, research fellowships, advanced study institutes and special programmes of support for the scientific and technological development of less-advanced member countries. Asst Sec.-Gen. YVES SILLARD (France).

## Military Organization

### MILITARY COMMITTEE

Composed of the allied Chiefs-of-Staff, or their representatives, of all member countries: the highest military body in NATO under the authority of the Council. Meets at least twice a year at Chiefs-of-Staff level and remains in permanent session with Permanent Military Representatives. It is responsible for making recommendations to the Council and Defence Planning Committee and Nuclear Planning Group on military matters and for supplying guidance on military questions to Supreme Allied Commanders and subordinate military authorities.

In December 1995 France agreed to rejoin the Military Committee, which it formally left in 1966.

**Chairman:** Adm. GUIDO VENTURONI (Italy).

### INTERNATIONAL MILITARY STAFF

**Director:** Lt-Gen. O. L. KANBORG (Norway).

### COMMANDS

**Allied Command Europe (ACE):** Casteau, Belgium—Supreme Headquarters Allied Powers Europe—SHAPE. Supreme Allied Commander Europe—SACEUR: Gen. WESLEY CLARK (USA), (from May 2000) Gen. JOSEPH W. RALSTON (USA).

**Allied Command Atlantic (ACLANT):** Norfolk, Virginia, USA. Supreme Allied Commander Atlantic—SACLANT: Adm. HAROLD W. GEHMAN, Jr (USA).

## Activities

The common security policy of the members of the North Atlantic Alliance is to safeguard peace through the maintenance of political solidarity and adequate defence at the lowest level of military forces needed to deter all possible forms of aggression. Each year, member countries take part in a Defence Review, designed to assess their contribution to the common defence in relation to their respective capabilities and constraints. Allied defence policy is reviewed periodically by ministers of defence.

Since the 1980s the Alliance has been actively involved in co-ordinating policies with regard to arms control and disarmament issues designed to bring about negotiated reductions in conventional forces, intermediate and short-range nuclear forces and strategic nuclear forces. A Verification Co-ordinating Committee was established in 1990.

Political consultations within the Alliance take place on a permanent basis, under the auspices of the North Atlantic Council (NAC), on all matters affecting the common security interests of the member countries, as well as events outside the North Atlantic Treaty area.

Co-operation in scientific and technological fields as well as co-operation on environmental challenges takes place in the NATO Science Committee and in its Committee on the Challenges of Modern Society. Both these bodies operate an expanding international programme of science fellowships, advance study institutes and research grants.

At a summit meeting of the Conference on Security and Co-operation in Europe (CSCE, now renamed as the Organization for Security and Co-operation in Europe, OSCE, see p. 237) in November 1990, the member countries of NATO and the Warsaw Pact signed an agreement limiting Conventional Armed Forces in Europe (CFE), whereby conventional arms would be reduced to within a common upper limit in each zone. The two groups also issued a Joint Declaration, stating that they were no longer adversaries and that none of their weapons would ever be used 'except in self-defence'. Following the dissolution of the USSR in December 1991, the eight former Soviet republics with territory in the area of application of the CFE Treaty committed themselves to honouring its obligations in June 1992. The Treaty entered retroactively into full force from 17 July (Armenia was unable to ratify it until the end of July, and Belarus until the end of October). In March 1992, under the auspices of the CSCE, the ministers of foreign affairs of the NATO and of the former Warsaw Pact countries (with Russia, Belarus, Ukraine and Georgia taking the place of the USSR) signed the 'Open Skies' treaty. Under this treaty, aerial reconnaissance missions by one country over another were to be permitted, subject to regulation. At the summit meeting of the OSCE in December 1996 the signatories of the CFE Treaty agreed to begin negotiations on a revised treaty governing conventional weapons in Europe. In July 1997 the CFE signatories concluded an agreement on Certain Basic Elements for Treaty Adaptation, which provided for substantial reductions in the maximum levels of conventional military equipment at national and territorial level, replacing the previous bloc-to-bloc structure of the Treaty.

In October 1991 NATO defence ministers endorsed the US decision to withdraw and destroy all its nuclear artillery shells and nuclear warheads for its short-range ballistic missiles in Europe. The ministers also agreed to reduce NATO's stock of airborne nuclear bombs by 50%. These and other measures were to reduce NATO's nuclear arsenal in Europe by 80%.

An extensive review of NATO's structures was initiated in June 1990, in response to the fundamental changes taking place in central and eastern Europe. In November 1991 NATO heads of government, convened in Rome, recommended a radical restructuring of the organization in order to meet the demands of the new security environment, which was to involve further reductions in military forces in Europe, active involvement in international peace-keeping operations, increased co-operation with other international institutions and close co-operation with its former adversaries, the USSR and the countries of eastern Europe. The basis for NATO's new force structure was incorporated into a new Strategic Concept, which was adopted in the Rome Declaration issuing from the summit meeting. The concept provided for the maintenance of a collective defence capability, with a reduced dependence on nuclear weapons. Substantial reductions in the size and levels of readiness of NATO forces were undertaken, in order to reflect the Alliance's strictly defensive nature, and forces were reorganized within a streamlined integrated command structure. Forces were categorized into immediate and rapid reaction forces (including the ACE Rapid Reaction Corps—ARRC, which was inaugurated in October 1992), main defence forces and augmentation forces, which may be used to reinforce any NATO region or maritime areas for deterrence, crisis management or defence. In December 1995 France announced that it was to resume participation in some of NATO's military organs (France had completely withdrawn from NATO's military structure in 1966), while delaying full military reintegration until certain conditions, allowing for greater European influence within the Alliance, were met. In October 1997 the French Government stated that it was not yet ready to reintegrate into the military structure, but would not obstruct any reorganization of the Alliance. In November 1996 the Spanish legislature voted to approve Spain's full integration into NATO's military structure in the light of the Alliance's proposed internal restructuring and with a reassertion of Spain's non-nuclear status. Discussions on a new command structure were hindered during 1997 by bilateral disagreements within the Alliance, notably between the United Kingdom and Spain regarding Spanish restrictions on the use of Gibraltar for military manoeuvres. In early December the United Kingdom withdrew its opposition to the establishment of a NATO command in Spain, enabling the Military

Committee to approve a new command structure. The NAC, meeting at ministerial level in mid-December, endorsed the new military structure, which envisaged a reduction in the number of NATO command headquarters from 65 to 20, and instructed the military authorities of the Alliance to formulate a plan for the transitional process. During 1998 work was undertaken on the formulation of a new Strategic Concept, reflecting the changing security environment and defining NATO's future role and objectives, which recognized a broader sphere of influence of NATO in the 21st century and confirmed NATO to be the principal generator of security in the Euro-Atlantic area. It emphasized NATO's role in crisis management and a renewed commitment to partnership and dialogue. The document was approved at a special summit meeting, convened in Washington, USA, in April 1999, to commemorate the 50th anniversary of the Alliance. A separate initiative was also approved to assist member states to adapt their defence capabilities to meet changing security requirements and to improve co-ordination on issues relating to weapons of mass destruction. A High-Level Steering Group was established to oversee implementation of the Defence Capabilities Initiative. The Washington meeting, which had been envisaged as a celebration of NATO's achievements since its foundation, was, however, dominated by consideration of the situation in the southern Serbian province of Kosovo and Metohija and the conduct of its military offensive against the Federal Republic of Yugoslavia, initiated in late March (see below).

In January 1994 NATO heads of state and government welcomed the entry into force of the Maastricht Treaty, establishing the European Union (EU, superseding the EC). The Treaty included an agreement on the development of a common foreign and security policy, which was intended to be a mechanism to strengthen the European pillar of the Alliance. In May 1995 NATO's ministers of foreign affairs supported a decision by Council of Ministers of the Western European Union (WEU) to improve the Union's operational capabilities through new mechanisms and force structures, which could be employed within the framework of NATO. In November the first memorandum of understanding between the two organizations was signed, to provide for full access to each other's communications capabilities; and in May 1996 NATO and WEU signed a security agreement concerning the safeguarding of classified material provided by either organization.

In June 1996 NATO ministers of foreign affairs reached agreement on the implementation of the 'Combined Joint Task Force (CJTF) concept', which had been adopted in January 1994. Measures were to be taken to establish the 'nuclei' of these task forces at certain NATO headquarters, which would provide the basis for missions that could be activated at short notice for specific purposes such as crisis management and peace-keeping. It was also agreed to make CJTFs available for operations undertaken by WEU. In conjunction with this, WEU was to be permitted to make use of Alliance hardware and capabilities (in practice, mostly belonging to the USA) subject to the endorsement of the NAC. This development represented the evolving construction of a European Security and Defence Identity (ESDI) within NATO. In order to support an integrated security structure in Europe, NATO also co-operates with the OSCE and has provided assistance for the development of the latter's conflict prevention and crisis management activities.

The enlargement of NATO, through the admission of new members from the former USSR and eastern and central European countries, was considered to be a progressive means of contributing to the enhanced stability and security of the Euro-Atlantic area. In December 1996 NATO ministers of foreign affairs announced that invitations to join the Alliance would be issued to some former eastern bloc countries during 1997. The NATO Secretary-General and member governments subsequently began intensive diplomatic efforts to secure Russia's tolerance of these developments. It was agreed that no nuclear weapons or large numbers of troops would be deployed on the territory of any new member country in the former Eastern bloc. In March 1997 the Presidents of the USA and Russia met to pursue negotiations on the future of Russian relations with NATO and to discuss further arms control measures. In May NATO and Russia signed the Founding Act on Mutual Relations, Co-operation and Security, which provided for enhanced Russian participation in all NATO decision-making activities, equal status in peace-keeping operations and representation at the Alliance headquarters at ambassadorial level, as part of a recognized shared political commitment to maintaining stability and security throughout the Euro-Atlantic region. A NATO-Russian Permanent Joint Council was established under the Founding Act, and met for the first time in July; the Council provided each side the opportunity for consultation and participation in the other's security decisions, but without a right of veto. A work programme for the Council in 1998 was approved in December 1997, focusing on political consultations, a programme of workshops and seminars and co-operation by military experts. In March 1999 Russia condemned NATO's military action against the Federal Republic of Yugoslavia and announced the suspension of all relations within the framework of the Founding Act, as well as negotiations on the establishment of a NATO mission in Moscow. In May 1997 NATO ministers of foreign affairs, meeting in Sintra, Portugal, concluded an agreement with Ukraine providing for enhanced co-operation between the two sides; the so-called Charter on a Distinctive Relationship was signed at the NATO summit meeting held in Madrid, Spain, in July. In May 1998 NATO agreed to appoint a permanent liaison officer in Ukraine to enhance co-operation between the two sides and assist Ukraine to formulate a programme of joint military exercises. The first NATO-Ukraine meeting at the level of heads of state took place in April 1999. The Madrid summit meeting in July 1997 endorsed the establishment of a Mediterranean Co-operation Group to enhance NATO relations with Egypt, Israel, Jordan, Mauritania, Morocco and Tunisia. The Group was to provide a forum for regular political dialogue between the two groupings and to promote co-operation in training, scientific research and information exchange. In April 1999 NATO heads of state endorsed measures to strengthen the so-called Mediterranean Dialogue.

In July 1997 heads of state and government formally invited the Czech Republic, Hungary and Poland to begin accession negotiations, with the aim of extending membership to those countries in April 1999. Romania and Slovenia were expected to be invited to join the Alliance before 2000, while the meeting also recognized the Baltic States as aspiring members. During 1997 concern was expressed on the part of some member governments with regard to the cost of expanding the Alliance; however, in November the initial cost of incorporating the Czech Republic, Hungary and Poland into NATO was officially estimated at US $1,300m. over a 10-year period, which was widely deemed to be an acceptable figure. Accession Protocols for the admission of those countries were signed in December and required ratification by all member states. The three countries formally became members of NATO in March 1999. In April the NATO summit meeting, held in Washington, DC, USA, initiated a new Membership Action Plan to extend practical support to aspirant member countries and to formalize a process of reviewing applications.

## EURO-ATLANTIC PARTNERSHIP COUNCIL—EAPC

The EAPC was inaugurated on 30 May 1997 as a successor to the North Atlantic Co-operation Council (NACC), that had been established in December 1991 as an integral part of NATO's new Strategic Concept, to provide a forum for consultation on political and security matters with the countries of central and eastern Europe, including the former Soviet republics. An EAPC Council was to meet monthly at ambassadorial level and twice a year at ministerial level. It was to be supported in its work by a steering committee and a political committee. The EAPC was to pursue the NACC Work Plan for Dialogue, Partnership and Co-operation and incorporate it into a new Work Plan, which was to include an expanded political dimension of consultation and co-operation among participating states. The Partnership for Peace (PfP) programme, which was established in January 1994 within the framework of the NACC, was to remain an integral element of the new co-operative mechanism. The PfP incorporated practical military and defence-related co-operation activities that had originally been part of the NACC Work Plan. Participation in the PfP requires an initial signature of a framework agreement, establishing the common principles and objectives of the partnership, the submission of a presentation document, indicating the political and military aspects of the partnership and the nature of future co-operation activities, and thirdly, the development of individual partnership programmes establishing country-specific objectives. In June 1994 Russia, which had previously opposed the strategy as being the basis for future enlargement of NATO, signed the PfP framework document, which included a declaration envisaging an 'enhanced dialogue' between the two sides. Despite its continuing opposition to any enlargement of NATO, in May 1995 Russia agreed to sign a PfP Individual Partnership Programme, as well as a framework document for NATO-Russian dialogue and co-operation beyond the PfP. During 1994 a Partnership Co-ordination Cell (PCC), incorporating representatives of all partnership countries, became operational in Mons, Belgium. The PCC, under the authority of the NAC, aims to co-ordinate joint military activities and planning in order to implement PfP programmes. The first joint military exercises with countries of the former Warsaw Pact were conducted in September. NATO began formulating a PfP Status of Forces Agreement (SOFA) to define the legal status of Allies' and partners' forces when they are present on each other's territory; the PfP SOFA was opened for signature in June 1995. The new EAPC was to provide a framework for the development of an enhanced PfP programme, which NATO envisaged would become an essential element of the overall European security structure. Accordingly, the military activities of the PfP were to be expanded to include all Alliance missions and incorporate all NATO committees into the PfP process, thus providing for greater co-operation in crisis management, civil emergency planning and training activities. In addition, all PfP member countries were to participate in the CJTF concept through a structure of Partners Staff Elements, working at all levels of the Alliance military structure. Defence ministers of NATO and partner countries (some 27 in late 1997) were to meet regularly to provide the political guidance for the enhanced Planning and Review Process of the PfP. During 1997 NATO provided assistance, within the framework of the PfP, to strengthen the armed forces in Albania, following a breakdown of political, economic and military infrastructures in that country. In December NATO ministers of foreign affairs endorsed an EAPC Action Plan for 1998–2000 to enhance the co-ordination and transparency of activities between participating states. The ministers also approved the establishment of a Euro-Atlantic Disaster Response Co-ordination Centre (EDRCC), and a non-permanent Euro-Atlantic Disaster Response Unit. The EDRCC was inaugurated in June 1998 and immediately commenced operations to provide relief to ethnic Albanian refugees fleeing the conflict in the Serbian province of Kosovo. In November 1998 the NAC approved the establishment of a network of PfP training centres, the first of which was inaugurated in Ankara, Turkey. The centres were a key element of a Training and Education Programme, which was endorsed at the summit meeting in April 1999.

## PEACE-KEEPING ACTIVITIES

During the 1990s NATO increasingly developed its role as a mechanism for peace-keeping and crisis management. In June 1992 NATO ministers of foreign affairs, meeting in Oslo, Norway, announced the Alliance's readiness to support peace-keeping operations under the aegis of the CSCE on a case-by-case basis: NATO would make both military resources and expertise available to such operations. In July NATO, in co-operation with WEU, undertook a maritime operation in the Adriatic Sea to monitor compliance with the UN Security Council's resolutions imposing sanctions against the Yugoslav republics of Serbia and Montenegro. In October NATO was requested to provide, staff and finance the military headquarters of the United Nations peace-keeping force in Bosnia and Herzegovina, the UN Protection Force in Yugoslavia (UNPROFOR). In November the UN Security Council gave the NATO/WEU operation in the Adriatic powers to stop and search ships suspected of flouting the blockade of Serbia and Montenegro. (The NATO/WEU maritime blockade was formally terminated in October 1996.) In December 1992 NATO ministers of foreign affairs expressed the Alliance's readiness to support peace-keeping operations under the authority of the UN Security Council; in that month NATO began formal military planning of operations designed to help bring an end to hostilities in Bosnia and Herzegovina. From April 1993 NATO fighter and reconnaissance aircraft began patrolling airspace over Bosnia and Herzegovina in order to enforce the UN prohibition of military aerial activity over the country. In addition, from July NATO aircraft provided protective cover for UNPROFOR troops operating in the 'safe areas' established by the UN Security Council. In August the NAC endorsed operational plans to conduct air attacks, at the request of the UN, to defend and deter attacks on the designated 'safe areas'. In February 1994 NATO conducted the first of several aerial strikes against artillery positions that were violating heavy-weapons exclusion zones imposed around 'safe areas' and threatening the civilian populations. Throughout the conflict the Alliance also provided transport, communications and logistics to support UN humanitarian assistance in the region.

The peace accord for the former Yugoslavia, which was initialled in Dayton, USA, in November 1995, and signed in Paris in December, provided for the establishment of a NATO-led Implementation Force (IFOR) to ensure compliance with the treaty, in accordance with a strictly defined timetable and under the authority of a UN Security Council mandate. In early December a joint meeting of allied foreign and defence ministers endorsed the military structure for the peace mission, entitled Operation Joint Endeavour, which was to involve approximately 60,000 troops from 31 NATO and non-NATO countries. The Operation was to include a Russian contingent, under an agreement that granted Russia access to the consultation and decision-making processes affecting participating troops. The mission was to be under the overall authority of the Supreme Allied Commander Europe (ACE), with the Commander of the ACE Rapid Reaction Corps providing command on the ground. The operation was to serve three separate sectors—the North, with force headquarters in Tuzla; the South-West, with forces based in Gornji Vakuf; and the South-East, based in Mostar—under immediate US, British and French command, respectively. IFOR, which constituted NATO's largest military operation ever, formally assumed responsibility for peace-keeping in Bosnia and Herzegovina from the UN on 20 December.

By mid-1996 the military aspects of the Dayton peace agreement had largely been implemented under IFOR supervision, including the withdrawal of former warring parties to behind agreed lines of separation and the release of prisoners of war. Territory was exchanged between the two Bosnian 'entities', although IFOR was criticized for failing to prevent widespread destruction in suburbs of Sarajevo that were being vacated by Bosnian Serbs on the transfer of the districts to Bosnian Federation control. Substantial progress was achieved in the demobilization of soldiers and militia and in the cantonment of heavy weaponry. However, in August and September the Bosnian Serbs obstructed IFOR weapons inspections and the force was obliged to threaten the Serbs with strong military retaliation to secure access to the arms sites. During 1996 IFOR personnel undertook many activities relating to the civilian reconstruction of Bosnia and Herzegovina, including the repair of roads, railways and bridges; reconstruction of schools and hospitals; delivery of emergency food and water supplies; and emergency medical transportation. IFOR also co-operated with, and provided logistical support for, the Office of the High Representative of the International Community in Bosnia and Herzegovina, which was charged with overseeing implementation of the civilian aspects of the Bosnian peace accord. IFOR assisted the OSCE in preparing for and overseeing the all-Bosnia legislative elections that were held in September, and provided security for displaced Bosnians who crossed the inter-entity boundary in order to vote in their towns of origin. In December NATO ministers of foreign affairs approved a follow-on operation, with an 18-month mandate, to be known as the Stabilization Force (SFOR). SFOR was to be about one-half the size of IFOR, but was to retain 'the same unity of command and robust rules of engagement' as the previous force. However, NATO failed to give SFOR an increased mandate to pursue and arrest indicted war criminals, whose prosecution at the International Criminal Tribunal for the Former Yugoslavia (ICTY, see p. 14). in The Hague, was widely regarded as essential for the success of the Bosnian peace process. SFOR became operational on 20 December. Its principal objective was to maintain a safe environment at a military level to ensure that the civil aspects of the Dayton peace accord could be fully implemented, including the completion of the de-mining process, the repatriation of refugees and preparations for municipal elections. In July 1997 NATO heads of government expressed their support for a more determined implementation of SFOR's mandate permitting the arrest of people sought by the ICTY if they were discovered within the normal course of duties. A few days later troops serving under SFOR seized two former Serb officials who had been indicted on charges of genocide. SFOR has subsequently undertaken this objective as part of its operational activities. From mid-1997 SFOR assisted efforts by the Bosnian Serb President, Biljana Plavšić, to maintain the security and territorial integrity of the Republika Srpska in the face of violent opposition from nationalist supporters of the former President, Radovan Karadžić, based in Pale. In August NATO authorized SFOR to use force to prevent the use of the local media to incite violence, following attacks on multinational forces by Serb nationalists during attempts to regain control of police buildings. In October SFOR seized radio and television transmitters, which had allegedly been exploited by Karadžić supporters. In November SFOR provided the general security framework, as well as logistical and communications assistance, in support of the OSCE's supervision of legislative elections that were conducted in the Republika Srpska. In December NATO ministers of defence confirmed that SFOR would be maintained at its current strength of some 31,000 troops, subject to the periodic six-monthly reviews. In February 1998 NATO resolved to establish within SFOR a specialized unit to respond to civil unrest and uphold public security. At the same time the NAC initiated a series of security co-operation activities to promote the development of democratic practices and defence mechanisms in Bosnia and Herzegovina. In October 1999 the NAC formally agreed to implement a reduction in SFOR's strength to some 20,000 troops, as well as a revision of its command structure, in response to the improved security situation in Bosnia and Herzegovina. The reforms were to be implemented by April 2000.

In March 1998 an emergency session of the NAC was convened at the request of the Albanian Government, which was concerned at the deteriorating security of its border region with the Serbian province of Kosovo and Metohija, following intensified action by the Kosovo Liberation Army (KLA) and retaliatory attacks by Serbian security forces. In the following month Albania appealed for the deployment of NATO troops to monitor its border with Kosovo. Diplomatic efforts were pursued to contain and resolve the conflict, at the same time as NATO undertook consideration of military options. In mid-June NATO defence ministers authorized the formulation of plans for airstrikes against Serbian targets. A few days later some 80 aircraft dispatched from 15 NATO bases flew close to Albania's border with Kosovo, in an attempt to demonstrate the Alliance's determination to prevent further reprisals agianst the ethnic Albanian population. Military exercises involving 1,700 troops from 11 NATO countries, as well as from Albania, Lithuania and Russia, were conducted in Albania in August. In September NATO defence ministers urged a diplomatic solution to the conflict, but insisted that, with an estimated 50,000 refugees living without shelter in the mountainous region bordering Albania, their main objective was to avert a humanitarian disaster. In late September the UN Security Council issued a resolution (1199) demanding an immediate cease-fire in Kosovo, the withdrawal of the majority of Serbian military and police forces, co-operation by all sides with humanitarian agencies, and the initiation of political negotiations on some form of autonomy for the province. Plans for NATO airstrikes were finalized in early October. However, the Russian Government remained strongly opposed to the use of force and there was concern among some member states whether there was sufficient legal basis for NATO action without further UN authorization. Nevertheless, in mid-October, following Security Council condemnation of the humanitarian situation in Kosovo, the NAC agreed on limited airstrikes against Serbian targets, with a 96-hour delay on the 'activation order'. At the same time the US envoy to the region, Richard Holbrooke, concluded an agreement with President Milošević to implement the conditions of UN Resolution 1199. A 2,000-member international observer force, under the auspices of the OSCE, was to be established to monitor compliance with the agreement, supported by a NATO Co-ordination Unit, based in the former Yugoslav republic of Macedonia (FYRM), to assist with aerial surveillance. At the end of October the NAC agreed to maintain the 'activation order', which had previously been extended by 10 days, although its execution would require further political approval. At that time there was evidence that Serbian security and military forces had withdrawn and that the majority of refugees living without shelter had returned home. In mid-November NATO ambassadors approved the establishment of a 1,200–1,800 strong multinational force, under French command, to assist in any necessary evacuation of OSCE monitors. A NATO Kosovo Verification Command Centre was established in Kumanovo, north-east FYRM, in late November; however, President Milošević warned that the dispatch of foreign troops into Kosovo would be treated as an act of aggression.

In mid-January 1999 NATO ambassadors convened in an emergency session following the discovery of the bodies of 45 ethnic Albanians in the Kosovan village of Racak. The meeting demanded that Serbia co-operate with an inquiry into the incident by the Prosecutor of the ICTY, guarantee the security and safety of all international personnel, withdraw security forces (which had continued to undertake offensives within Kosovo), and uphold the cease-fire. Intensive diplomatic efforts, co-ordinated by the six-country 'Contact Group' on the former Yugoslavia, succeeded in bringing both sides in the dispute to talks on the future of Kosovo. During the first stage of negotiations, held in Rambouillet, France, a provisional framework for a political settlement was formulated, based on a form of autonomy for Kosovo (to be reviewed after a three-year period), and incorporating a mandate for a NATO force of some 28,000 troops to monitor its implementation. The talks were suspended in late February with neither side having agreed to the accord. On the resumption of negotiations in mid-March representatives of the KLA confirmed that they would sign the peace settlement. President Milošević, however, continued to oppose the establishment of a NATO force in Kosovo and, despite further diplomatic efforts by Holbrooke, declined to endorse the agreement in accordance with a deadline imposed by the Contact Group. Amid reports of renewed Serbian violence against Albanian civilians in Kosovo, the NAC subsequently reconfirmed its support for NATO military intervention. On 24 March an aerial offensive against the Federal Republic of Yugoslavia was initiated by NATO, with the declared aim of reducing that country's capacity to commit attacks on the Albanian population. The first phase of the allied operation was directed against defence facilities, followed, a few days later, by the second phase which permitted direct attacks on artillery positions, command centres and other military targets in a declared exclusion zone south of the 44th parallel. The escalation of the conflict prompted thousands of Albanians to flee Kosovo, while others were reportedly forced from their homes by Serbian security personnel, creating massive refugee populations in neighbouring countries. In early April NATO ambassadors agreed to dispatch some 8,000 troops, as an ACE Mobile Force Land operation (entitled 'Operation Allied Harbour'), to provide humanitarian assistance to the estimated 300,000 refugees in Albania at that time and to provide transportation to relieve overcrowded camps, in particular in border areas. Refugees in the FYRM were to be assisted by the existing NATO contingent (numbering some 12,000 troops by early April), which was permitted by the authorities in that country to construct new camps for some 100,000 displaced Kosovans. An additional 1,000 troops were transferred from the FYRM to Albania in mid-May in order to construct a camp to provide for a further 65,000 refugees. In mid-April NATO ministers of foreign affairs, meeting in special session, expressed extreme concern at the refugee situation throughout the region. The ministers also clarified the conditions necessary to halt the offensive, which included Serbia's agreement to an international military presence in Kosovo, provision for the safe return of all refugees and an undertaking to work on the basis of the Rambouillet accord. Russia continued to pursue diplomatic efforts to secure a peaceful settlement to the conflict, however, Milošević's reported agreement to allow an unarmed international force in Kosovo, conditional on the immediate end to the NATO campaign, was dismissed by NATO governments. From early April there was increasing evidence of civilian casualties resulting from NATO's aerial bombing of transport, power and media infrastructure and suspected military targets. In mid-April NATO initiated an inquiry following the bombing of a convoy of lorries which resulted in the deaths of some 69 refugees. In the following month NATO was obliged to apologise to the authorities of the People's Republic of China after the accidental bombing of its embassy in Belgrade. At the same time there was widespread concern among governments at increasing evidence of systematic killings and ethnic violence being committed by Serbian forces within Kosovo, and at the estimated 100,000 Albanian men unaccounted for among the massive displaced population. NATO's 50th anniversary summit meeting, held in Washington, USA, in late April, was dominated by consideration of the conflict and of the future stability of the region. A joint statement declared the determination of all Alliance members to increase economic and military pressure on President Milošević to withdraw forces from Kosovo. In particular, the meeting agreed to prevent shipments of petroleum reaching Serbia through Montenegro, to complement the embargo imposed by the EU and a new focus of the bombing campaign which aimed to destroy the fuel supply within Serbia. However, there was concern on the part of several NATO governments on the legal and political aspects of implementing the embargo. The meeting failed to adopt a unified position on the use of ground forces, which many expert commentators insisted, throughout the campaign, were necessary to secure NATO's objectives. In May ministers of foreign affairs of the Group of Seven industrialized nations and Russia (the G-8) agreed on general principles for a political solution, which was to form the basis of UN Security Council resolution. Later in that month NATO estimated that a future Kosovo Peace Implementation Force (KFOR), installed to guarantee a settlement, would require at least 48,000 troops. Following further intensive diplomatic efforts to secure a cease-fire in Kosovo, on 9 June a Military Technical Agreement was signed between NATO and the Federal Republic of Yugoslavia, incorporating a timetable for the withdrawal of all Serbian security personnel. On the following day the UN Security Council adopted Resolution 1244, which authorized an international security presence in Kosovo, under NATO, and an international civilian presence, the UN Interim Administration Mission in Kosovo (UNMIK). The NAC subsequently suspended the airstrike campaign, which, by that time, had involved some 35,000 sorties. KFOR was organized into six brigades, under the leadership of France, Germany, Italy, USA and the United Kingdom (with responsibility for two brigades). An initial force of 20,000 troops entered Kosovo on 12 June. A few days later an agreement was concluded with Russia, whose troops had also entered Kosovo and taken control of Pristina airport, which provided for the joint responsibility of the airstrip with a NATO contingent and for the participation of some 3,600 Russian troops in KFOR, reporting to the country command in each sector. On 20 June the withdrawal of Yugoslav troops from Kosovo was completed, prompting the KLA to issue NATO with a voluntary undertaking to demilitarize and transform the force, as required under Resolution 1244. This was achieved in September. KFOR's immediate responsibility was to provide a secure environment to facilitate the safe return of refugees, and, pending the full deployment of UNMIK, to assist the reconstruction of infrastructure and civil and political institutions. In addition, NATO troops were to assist personnel of the international tribunal to investigate sites of alleged violations of human rights and mass graves. From August an escalation of ethnic violence and deterioration of law and order in some parts of the province was an outstanding concern. In late January 2000 NATO agreed that the Eurocorps defence force (see under WEU) would assume command of KFOR headquarters in April.

# Nato Agencies

1. Civilian production and logistics organizations responsible to the NAC:

**Central European Pipeline Management Agency—CEPMA:** BP 552, 78005 Versailles, France; tel. 1-39-24-49-00; fax 1-39-55-65-39; f. 1957 as the Central European Operating Agency; responsible for the 24-hour operation of the Central European Pipeline System and its storage and distribution facilities.

**Nato Airborne Early Warning and Control Programme Management Organisation—NAPMO:** c/o Akerstraat 7, 6445 CL Brunssum, Netherlands; fax (45) 5254373; f. 1978 to manage the procurement aspects of the NATO Airborne Early Warning and Control System.

**NATO Consultation, Command and Control Organization—NC3O:** 1110 Brussels, Belgium; tel. (2) 707-43-58; fax (2) 708-87-70; f. 1997 by restructuring of the NATO Communications and Information Systems Organization and the Tri-Service Group on Communications and Electronics; incorporates the former Allied Data Systems Interoperability Agency, the Allied Naval Communications Agency and the Allied Tactical Communications Agency; decides on policies and interoperability, supervises planning and implementation, and operates and maintains communications and information systems for tactical and strategic integrated services, including voice, data, fax, video (tele)conferencing and automated command and control capability for crisis management, consultation of the NATO nations and the command and control of NATO forces.

**NATO C3 Agency:** Responsible for planning, design, systems engineering, technical support and procurements; operates from Brussels and offices in The Hague.

**NATO CIS Operating and Support Agency—NACOSA:** Maintains NATO's communications and information system (CIS). Responsible for the NATO Communications and Information Systems School, based in Latina, Italy.

**NATO EF 2000 and Tornado Development, Production and Logistics Management Agency—NETMA:** Insel Kammerstrasse 12–14, Postfach 1302, 82008 Unterhaching, Germany; tel. (89) 666800; fax (89) 6668055; replaced the NATO Multirole Combat Aircraft (MRCA) Development and Production Management Agency (f. 1969) and the NATO European Fighter (EF) Aircraft Development, Production and Logistics Management Agency (f. 1987); responsible for the joint development and production of the European Fighter Aircraft and the MRCA (Tornado).

**NATO HAWK Management Office:** 26 rue Galliéni, 92500 Rueil-Malmaison, France; tel. 1-47-08-75-00; fax 1-47-52-10-99; f. 1959 to supervise the multinational production and upgrading programmes of the HAWK surface-to-air missile system in Europe; Gen. Man. A. BOCCHI.

**NATO Helicopter Design and Development Production and Logistics Management Agency—NAHEMA:** Le Quatuor, Bâtiment A, 42 route de Galice, 13082 Aix-en-Provence Cédex 2, France; tel. 4-42-95-92-00; fax 4-42-64-30-50.

**NATO Maintenance and Supply Agency—NAMSA:** 8302 Capellen, Luxembourg; fax 30-87-21; f. 1958; supplies spare parts and logistic support for a number of jointly-used weapon systems, missiles and electronic systems; all member nations except Iceland participate.

2. Responsible to the Military Committee:

**Allied Communications Security Agency—ACSA:** Brussels, Belgium; f. 1953.

**Military Agency for Standardization—MAS:** 1110 Brussels, Belgium; tel. (2) 707-55-76; fax (2) 707-57-18; e-mail mas@hq.nato.int; f. 1951 to foster NATO standardization in order to increase the combined operational effectiveness of the Alliance's military forces.

**NATO Defense College—NADEFCOL:** Via Giorgio Pelosi 1, 00143 Rome-Cecchiguola, Italy; tel. (06) 505259; f. 1951 to train officials for posts in NATO organizations or in national ministries.

**NATO Frequency Management Sub-Committee—FMSC:** 1100 Brussels, Belgium; tel. (2) 707-55-28; replaced the Allied Radio Frequency Agency (f. 1951); the FMSC is the frequency authority of the Alliance and establishes and co-ordinates all policy concerned with the military use of the radio frequency spectrum.

**Research and Technology Organization—RTO:** BP 25, 7 rue Ancelle, 92201 Neuilly-sur-Seine Cédex, France; tel. 1-55-61-22-00; fax 1-55-61-22-99; e-mail mailbox@rta.nato.int; f. 1998 by merger of the Advisory Group for Aerospace Research and Development and the Defence Research Group; brings together scientists and engineers from member countries for exchange of information and research co-operation (formally established 1998); provides scientific and technical advice for the Military Committee, for other NATO bodies and for member nations; comprises a Research and Technology Board and a Research and Technology Agency, responsible for implementing RTO's work programme.

3. Responsible to Supreme Allied Commander Atlantic (SACLANT):

**NATO SACLANT Undersea Research Centre—SACLANTCEN:** Viale San Bartolomeo 400, 19138 La Spezia, Italy; tel. (0187) 5271; fax (0187) 527420; e-mail library@saclantc.nato.int; internet www.saclantc.nato.int; f. 1959 to conduct research in support of NATO operational requirements in antisubmarine warfare and mine counter-measures.

4. Responsible to Supreme Allied Commander Europe (SACEUR):

**NATO (SHAPE) School:** Am Rainenbichl 54, 82487 Oberammergau, Germany; tel. (88) 224477; fax (88) 221035; e-mail postmaster@natoschool-shape.de; f. 1975; acts as a centre for training military and civilian personnel of NATO countries, and, since 1991, for officials from partner countries, in support of NATO policies, operations and objectives.

## Finance

As NATO is an international, not a supra-national, organization, its member countries themselves decide the amount to be devoted to their defence effort and the form which the latter will assume. Thus, the aim of NATO's defence planning is to develop realistic military plans for the defence of the alliance at reasonable cost. Under the annual defence planning process, political, military and economic factors are considered in relation to strategy, force requirements and available resources. The procedure for the co-ordination of military plans and defence expenditures rests on the detailed and comparative analysis of the capabilities of member countries. All installations for the use of international forces are financed under a common-funded infrastructure programme. In accordance with the terms of the Partnership for Peace strategy, partner countries undertake to make available the necessary personnel, assets, facilities and capabilities to participate in the programme. The countries also share the financial cost of military exercises in which they participate. The administrative (or 'civil') budget amounted to US $157m. in 1998. The total military budget approved for 1998 amounted to $680m. (excluding the costs of assignment of military personnel, met by the contributing countries).

## Publications

NATO publications (in English and French, with some editions in other languages) include:

*NATO Basic Fact Sheets.*

*NATO Final Communiqués.*

*NATO Handbook.*

*NATO Review* (quarterly in 11 languages; annually in Icelandic).

Economic and scientific publications.

# ORGANISATION FOR ECONOMIC CO-OPERATION AND DEVELOPMENT—OECD

**Address:** 2 rue André-Pascal, 75775 Paris Cédex 16, France.

**Telephone:** 1-45-24-82-00; **fax:** 1-45-24-85-00; **e-mail:** webmaster@oecd.org; **internet:** www.oecd.org.

OECD was founded in 1961, replacing the Organisation for European Economic Co-operation (OEEC) which had been established in 1948 in connection with the Marshall Plan. It constitutes a forum for governments to discuss, develop and attempt to co-ordinate their economic and social policies. The Organisation aims to promote policies designed to achieve the highest level of sustainable economic growth, employment and increase in the standard of living while maintaining financial stability, and to contribute to economic expansion in member and non-member states and to the expansion of world trade.

### MEMBERS

| | | |
|---|---|---|
| Australia | Hungary | Norway |
| Austria | Iceland | Poland |
| Belgium | Ireland | Portugal |
| Canada | Italy | Spain |
| Czech Republic | Japan | Sweden |
| Denmark | Republic of Korea | Switzerland |
| Finland | Luxembourg | Turkey |
| France | Mexico | United Kingdom |
| Germany | Netherlands | USA |
| Greece | New Zealand | |

The European Commission also takes part in OECD's work.

## Organization

(January 2000)

### COUNCIL

The governing body of OECD is the Council, at which each member country is represented. The Council meets from time to time (usually once a year) at the level of government ministers, the Chairmanship being rotated among member states. It also meets regularly at official level, when it comprises the Secretary-General and the Permanent Representatives of member states to OECD. It is responsible for all questions of general policy and may establish subsidiary bodies as required to achieve the aims of the Organisation. Decisions and recommendations of the Council are adopted by mutual agreement of all its members.

**Heads of Permanent Delegations** (with ambassadorial rank):

Australia: Anthony Hinton
Austria: Karl Schramek
Belgium: Pierre-Dominique Schmidt
Canada: Suzanne Hurtubise
Czech Republic: Jaromír Privratsky
Denmark: Flemming Hedegaard
Finland: Ilkka Ristimaki
France: Joëlle Bourgeois
Germany: Werner Kaufmann-Bühler
Greece: Spyros Lioukas
Hungary: Béla Kádár
Iceland: Sigridur Asdis Snaevarr
Ireland: Patrick O'Connor
Italy: Alessandro Vattani
Japan: Mutsuyoshi Nishimura
Republic of Korea: Soo-Gill Young
Luxembourg: Jean-Marc Hoscheit
Mexico: Francisco Suárez Davila
Netherlands: Egbert Jacobs
New Zealand: Richard Grant
Norway: Per Ludvig Magmus
Poland: Jan Woroniecki
Portugal: Jorge de Lemos Godinho
Spain: José Luis Feito
Sweden: Anders Ferm
Switzerland: Jean-Pierre Zehnder
Turkey: Akin Alptuna
United Kingdom: Christopher Crabbie
USA: Amy Bondurant

**Participant with Special Status:**

European Commission: Piergiorgio Mazzocchi (Italy).

### EXECUTIVE COMMITTEE

The Executive Committee prepares the work of the Council. It is also called upon to carry out specific tasks where necessary. In addition to its regular meetings, the Committee meets occasionally in special sessions attended by senior government officials.

### SECRETARIAT

The Council, the committees and other bodies in OECD are assisted by an independent international secretariat headed by the Secretary-General. An Executive Director is responsible for the management of administrative support services. Some 1,850 staff were employed in the secretariat in January 2000.

**Secretary-General:** Donald J. Johnston (Canada).

**Deputy Secretaries-General:** Thorvald Moe (Norway), Herwig Schlögl (Germany), Seiichi Kondo (Japan), Sally Shelton-Colby (USA).

**Executive Director:** Jean-Jacques Noreau (Canada).

### AUTONOMOUS AND SEMI-AUTONOMOUS BODIES

**Centre for Educational Research and Innovation–CERI:** f. 1968; includes all member countries. Dir Thomas J. Alexander (see also under Education, Employment, Labour and Social Affairs, below).

**Club du Sahel:** f. 1976; an informal forum of donor countries and member states of the Permanent Inter-State Committee on Drought Control in the Sahel (see p. 293). Dir Jacqueline Damon.

**Development Centre:** f. 1962; includes most member countries and Argentina, Brazil and Chile. Pres. Jorge Braga de Macedo (see also under Development Co-operation, below).

**European Conference of Ministers of Transport** (see p. 342).

**International Energy Agency** (see p. 235).

**Nuclear Energy Agency** (see p. 236).

## Activities

The greater part of the work of OECD, which covers all aspects of economic and social policy, is prepared and carried out in about 200 specialized bodies (Committees, Working Parties, etc.); all members are normally represented on these bodies, except on those of a restricted nature.

### ECONOMIC POLICY

The main organ for the consideration and direction of economic policy among the member countries is the Economic Policy Committee, which comprises governments' chief economic advisors and central bankers, and meets two or three times a year to review the economic and financial situation and policies of member countries. It has several working parties and groups, the most important of which are Working Party No. 1 on Macro-Economic and Structural Policy Analysis, Working Party No. 3 on Policies for the Promotion of Better International Payments Equilibrium, and the Working Group on Short-Term Economic Prospects.

The Economic and Development Review Committee, comprising all member countries, is responsible for the annual examination of the economic situation and macro economic and structural policies of each member country. A report is issued every 12 to 18 months on each country, after an examination carried out by the Committee; this process of peer review has been extended also to other branches of the Organisation's work (agriculture, environment, manpower and social affairs, scientific policy and development aid efforts).

### STATISTICS

Statistical data and related methodological information are collected from member governments and, where possible, consolidated, or converted into an internationally comparable form. The Statistics Directorate maintains data required for macroeconomic forecasting, i.e. national accounts, the labour force, foreign trade, prices, output, and monetary, financial, industrial and other short-term statistics. Specialist directorates collect and maintain other databases. In 2000 the principal concerns of the Directorate were to: improve the supply of statistical information to analysts and policy-makers within and outside the Organisation; develop international statistical standards, systems and classifications, in collaboration with other international agencies; and provide a mechanism for the improved co-ordination of statistical activities within the Organisation and with other agencies.

## DEVELOPMENT CO-OPERATION

The Development Assistance Committee (DAC) is the principal body through which the Organisation deals with issues relating to co-operation with developing countries and is one of the key forums in which the major bilateral donors work together to increase their effectiveness in support of sustainable development. Guided by the Development Partnerships Strategy formulated in 1996, the DAC's mission is to foster co-ordinated, integrated, effective and adequately financed international efforts in support of sustainable economic and social development. Recognizing that developing countries themselves are ultimately responsible for their own development, the DAC concentrates on how international co-operation can contribute to the population's ability to overcome poverty and participate fully in society. Principal activities include: adopting authoritative policy guide-lines; conducting periodic critical reviews of members' programmes of development co-operation; providing a forum for dialogue, exchange of experience and the building of international consensus on policy and management issues; and publishing statistics and reports on aid and other resource flows to developing countries and countries in transition. A working set of indicators of development progress has been established by the DAC, in collaboration with experts from the UN agencies, the World Bank and developing countries.

The OECD Development Centre was established in 1962 to provide a focal point within the Organisation for analysis and policy dialogue on economic and social aspects of development in Africa, Asia, Latin America, the Caribbean and the Middle East. The Centre informs member countries of emerging issues and offers developing countries objective, in-depth analyses, with a view to promoting constructive policy reform. It serves as an intermediary between OECD and the developing countries by promoting the exchange of ideas and information. Research and dialogue activities are orientated towards topics with a high priority on the agenda of policy-makers. The Centre's work programme for 1999–2000, entitled 'The Sustainability of Economic Policy Reform', focused on four main themes: Financial Crises and Structural Implications; Implementation of the Development Partnerships Strategy; Sustainable Development; Globalization, Social Cohesion and Demography.

The Club du Sahel provides an informal framework for dialogue and co-operation between Sahelian countries, donor governments, and concerned organizations. Its work programme has evolved since its establishment to reflect the most pressing needs and concerns of the sub-region. In the late 1990s the principal issues under consideration were demographic change; regional economic development; environmental restoration; food crisis prevention; globalization; and the emergence of civil society.

In a report to the Secretary-General in late 1997 an advisory group on the environment, comprising non-governmental experts, recommended that OECD should evolve into the principal intergovernmental organization providing the analytical and comparative framework of policy necessary for industrialized countries to make the transition to sustainable development. At a meeting in April 1998 ministers from member countries reiterated that the achievement of sustainable development was a priority, and recommended wide-ranging projects over the forthcoming three years in areas relating to technology, the effects of climate change, the environmental impact of subsidies, and the creation of indicators of sustainability, in order comprehensively to address the economic, social and environmental dimensions of sustainable development.

In May 1999 the Executive Committee in Special Session considered OECD's role in South-East Europe once a peace settlement had been agreed on the future of Kosovo and Metohija, in southern Serbia. The Committee determined that OECD should collaborate with the World Bank, IMF and other agencies to promote economic and social development in countries bordering the Federal Republic of Yugoslavia, in order to strengthen political stability throughout the region.

## PUBLIC MANAGEMENT

The Public Management Committee, and its secretariat, the Public Management Service (PUMA) are concerned with issues of governance, including: the formulation of policies and their implementation; the allocation of resources; the renewal of the institutions of state; and questions of accountability, consultation and transparency. PUMA serves as a forum for senior officials responsible for the central management systems of government, providing information, analysis and recommendations on public management and governing capacity. A joint initiative of OECD and the EU, operating within PUMA, supports good governance in countries of Central and Eastern Europe. The so-called Support for Improvement in Governance and Management (SIGMA) programme advises countries on improving their administrative efficiency and promotes the adherence of public sector staff to democratic values and ethics and respect for the rule of law. SIGMA also helps to strengthen capacities at the level of central government to address the challenges of EU integration, and greater global interdependence.

## CO-OPERATION WITH NON-MEMBER ECONOMIES

The Centre for Co-operation with Non-Members (CCNM) was established in January 1998, by merger of the Centre for Co-operation with Economies in Transition (founded in 1990) and the Liaison and Co-ordination Unit. It serves as the focal point for the development of policy dialogue with non-member economies, managing multi-country, thematic, regional and country programmes. An Emerging Market Economy Forum brings together non-member economies engaged in market-oriented policy reform of interest to members. Recent topics discussed included tax evasion, the regulation of securities markets and foreign direct investment policy. In 1998 a programme addressing issues arising from financial instability in East Asia was instituted within the Centre. There is also a Transition Economy Programme, which covers a broad range of economic and social policy issues, as well as structural adjustment, and aims to provide insights into policy design and implementation. Country and regional programmes were in place for Bulgaria, China, Romania, Russia, Slovakia, Slovenia, South America and the Baltic States at early 1999.

Non-member economies are invited, on a selective basis by the CCNM, to participate in or observe the work of certain OECD committees and working parties. The Centre also provides a limited range of training activities in support of policy implementation and institution building. Five multilateral tax centres provide workshops and seminars for senior officials in tax administration and policy. OECD, through the CCNM, co-sponsors the Centre for Private Sector Development in İstanbul, Turkey, with the Turkish and German Governments. This assists various countries to develop the necessary framework and policies for a market economy and integration into the world economy. The CCNM also sponsors the Joint Vienna Institute (see IMF, p. 94), which offers a variety of administrative, economic and financial management courses to participants from transition economies. The Centre co-operates with a number of other international organizations.

## INTERNATIONAL TRADE

OECD's Trade Committee supports the continued liberalization and efficient operation of the multilateral trading system, with the aim of contributing to the expansion of world trade on a non-discriminatory basis. Its activities include examination of issues concerning trade relations among member countries as well as relations with non-member countries, and consideration and discussion of trade measures taken by a member country which adversely affect another's interests. The Committee also considers the challenges that are presented to the existing international trading system by financial or economic instability, the process of globalization of production and markets and the ensuing deeper integration of national economies. OECD provided support to the multilateral trade negotiations conducted under the General Agreement on Tariffs and Trade (GATT), assisting member countries to analyse the effects of the trade accords and promoting its global benefits. Following the conclusion of the negotiations in December 1993, and the entry into force of the World Trade Organization (WTO) agreements in 1995, OECD has continued to study and assess aspects of the international trade agenda, such as integrating emerging market economies into the international trading system, trade and environment, trade and competition policy, trade and investment and trade and industry. In November 1999 OECD published a report on the impact of further trade liberalization on developing countries, in preparation for the next round of multilateral trade negotiations, scheduled to be initiated by WTO later in that month.

## FINANCIAL, FISCAL AND ENTERPRISE AFFAIRS

Promoting the efficient functioning of markets and enterprises and strengthening the multilateral framework for trade and investment is the responsibility of a number of OECD Committees under the Directorate for Financial, Fiscal and Enterprise Affairs. The Committee on Capital Movements and Invisible Transactions monitors the implementation of the Codes of Liberalization of Invisible Transactions and of Capital Movements as legally binding norms for all member countries. The Committee on International Investment and Multinational Enterprises is reviewing the OECD Guide-lines for Multinational Enterprises, a corporate Code of Conduct recommended by OECD member governments, business and labour units. A Declaration on International Investment and Multinational Enterprises, while non-binding, contains commitments on the conduct and treatment of foreign-owned enterprises established in member countries. Negotiations on a Multilateral Agreement on Investment (MAI), initiated by OECD ministers in 1995 to provide a legal framework for international investment, broke down in October 1998, although 'informal consultation' on the issue was to continue. OECD has initiated an extensive work programme on investment policy issues for the 21st century.

The Committee on Competition Law and Policy promotes the harmonization of national competition policies, co-operation in competition law enforcement, common merger reporting rules and pro-competitive regulatory reform. The Committee on Financial Markets exercises surveillance over recent developments, reform measures and structural and regulatory conditions in financial markets. It aims to promote international trade in financial services, to encourage the integration of non-member countries into the global financial system, and to improve financial statistics. The Committee on Fiscal Affairs has recently focused its efforts on the tax implications of the globalization of national economies. Its activities include promoting the removal of tax barriers and monitoring the implementation and impact of major tax reforms, as well as developing a neutral tax framework for electronic commerce. The Insurance Committee monitors and surveys structural changes and reform measures in insurance markets.

In May 1997 the OECD Council endorsed plans to introduce a global ban on the corporate bribery of public officials. In December ministers from 33 member and non-member countries signed the OECD Convention on Bribery. The Convention entered into force in February 1999. By the end of that year the Convention had been ratified by 19 countries. A monitoring framework was established to ensure conformity. In May ministers endorsed a set of OECD Principles for Corporate Governance, which covered of ownership and control of corporate entities, the rights of shareholders, the role of stakeholders, transparency, disclosure and the responsibilities of boards. OECD was collaborating with the World Bank and other organizations to promote good governance world-wide, for example through regional meetings. OECD provides the secretariat for the Financial Action Task Force on Money Laundering (q.v.).

## FOOD, AGRICULTURE AND FISHERIES

The Committee for Agriculture reviews major developments in agricultural policies, deals with the adaptation of agriculture to changing economic conditions, elaborates forecasts of production and market prospects for the major commodities, promotes the use of sustainable practices in the sector, assesses implications of world developments in food and agriculture for member countries' policies and evaluates progress towards the integration of the agro-food sector into the multilateral trading system. A separate Fisheries Committee carries out similar tasks in its own sector, and, in particular, analyses the consequences of policy measures with a view to promoting responsible and sustainable fisheries.

## TERRITORIAL DEVELOPMENT

The Territorial Development Service assists central governments with the design and implementation of more effective, area-based strategies, encourages the emergence of locally driven initiatives for economic development, and promotes better integration of local and national approaches. Territorial policies have recently emphasized the need to mobilize local resources to enhance regional competitiveness and to create employment. The Service comprises two intergovernmental bodies—the Local Economic and Employment Development Committee and the Territorial Development Policy Committee—which share an overall work programme emphasizing the need for innovative policy initiatives and exchange of knowledge in a wide range of policies, such as entrepreneurship and technology diffusion and issues of social exclusion and urban deprivation.

## ENVIRONMENT

The OECD Environment Directorate works in support of the Environment Policy Committee (EPOC) on environmental issues. In April 1998 environment ministers of member countries agreed upon a set of 'Shared Goals for Action', with four principal aims: to promote strong national policies and effective regulatory structures for the protection of the natural environment and human health; to promote an integrated policy approach, encouraging coherence among economic, environmental and social policies; to strengthen international co-operation in meeting global and regional environmental commitments; and to support participation, transparency, the provision of information and accountability in environmental policy-making at all levels. The Environment Directorate's work programme for the two year period 1999–2000 outlined 12 main activities consistent with these goals and the Organisation's priorities. There were three new activities: the Environmental Outlook and Strategy aspect, which aimed to establish a conceptual and quantitative foundation for the programme on sustainable development; the work on Sustainable Consumption Patterns, to support member countries in efforts to achieve more sustainable patterns of consumption; and the project on Increasing Resource Efficiency, to assist members and non-members in developing approaches to managing resources more efficiently. Other aspects of the work programme address issues such as climate change, the promotion of environmentally sustainable transport, and the management of transborder movements of waste. An important element of the programme concentrates on chemicals and biotechnology, specifically, on the risks to health and the environment from chemicals. The Environment Directorate also provides the secretariat for the Environmental Action Programme Task Force of the Environment for Europe process, which encourages countries in Eastern Europe and the CIS to take environmental issues into consideration in the process of economic restructuring. A further part of the environment programme considers environmental data, indicators and measurement of performance. The first cycle of a programme of Environmental Performance Reviews of all OECD countries was completed in 1999. By December 28 OECD member countries had been assessed.

## SCIENCE, TECHNOLOGY AND INDUSTRY

The principal objective of the Directorate for Science, Technology and Industry is to assist member countries in formulating and implementing policies that optimize the contribution of science, technology, industrial development and structural change to economic growth, employment and social development. The Committee for Scientific and Technological Policy reviews national and international policy issues relating to science and technology. It provides indicators and analysis on emerging trends in these fields, identifies and promotes best practices, and offers a forum for dialogue. Important themes include: the management and reform of science systems; the development of policies to promote the innovative capacity of members' economies; and policy responses to the globalization of science and technology.

A Working Party on Biotechnology was established in 1993 and its mandate was renewed in 1998. Among the priority topics in its most recent work programme were scientific and technological infrastructure, and the relation of biotechnology to sustainable industrial development. In June 1999 it was requested to undertake a study of aspects of biotechnology with respect to food safety. In 1992 a Megascience Forum was established to bring together senior science policy-makers for consultations regarding large scientific projects and programmes. It was succeeded, in 1999, by a Global Science Forum. In 1999 work was proceeding on the establishment of a Global Biodiversity Information Forum to collate, co-ordinate and disseminate data on biodiversity.

The Committee for Information, Computer and Communications Policy monitors developments in telecommunications and information technology and their impact on competitiveness and productivity, with a new emphasis on technological and regulatory convergence. It also promotes the development of new rules (e.g. guide-lines on information security) and analyses trade and liberalization issues. In 1998 the Committee concentrated on issues related to electronic commerce, and played a leading role in the preparation of the Ministerial Conference on this subject in October. In December 1999 the OECD Council approved a set of Guide-lines for Consumer Protection in the Context of Electronic Commerce, which had been prepared by the Committee on Consumer Policy.

The Industry Committee regularly reviews issues of competitiveness in industry and policies for private sector development in member and selected non-member economies. The Committee is particularly concerned with the issues of globalization, regulatory reform, intangible investments and business services, corporate governance, small and medium-sized enterprises (SMEs) and the role of industry in sustainable development. A business and industry policy forum exists for senior policy-makers and representatives of the business sector to address topical issues. A working party on SMEs conducts an ongoing review of the contribution of SMEs to growth and employment and a comparative assement of best practice policies. Databases enabling internationally comparable monitoring of structural change in areas of science and technology, investment, production, employment and trade were being prepared by a working party on statistics in 1998/99.

A Programme of Co-operation in the Field of Research on Road Transport and its Intermodal Linkages examines a range of issues related primarily to the institutional and economic aspects of advanced logistics, freight transport, intelligent transport systems and asset management. The programme also maintains two databases on road transport research and road safety. The Maritime Transport and Steel Committees aim to promote multilateral solutions to sectoral friction and instability based on the definition and monitoring of rules. In June 1994 negotiations between leading shipbulding nations, conducted under OECD auspices, concluded a multilateral agreement to end state subsidies to the industry. However, continued failure by the US Congress to ratify the agreement disrupted its entry into force.

## EDUCATION, EMPLOYMENT, LABOUR AND SOCIAL AFFAIRS

The Employment, Labour and Social Affairs Committee is concerned with the development of labour market and selective employment policies to ensure the utilization of human capital at the highest possible level and to improve the quality and flexibility of working life, as well as the effectiveness of social policies; it plays a central role in addressing OECD's concern to reduce high and persistent unemployment through the creation of high-quality jobs. The Committee's work covers such issues as the role of women in the economy, industrial relations, international migration and the development of an extensive social data base. The Committee also carries out single-country and thematic reviews of labour-market policies and social assistance systems. In addition, it has assigned a high priority to work on the policy implications of an ageing population and on indicators of human capital investment. The Education Committee analyses policies for education and training at all levels, carries out education and training policy reviews, conducts an international adult literacy survey, and produces education data and indicators. Together, the Employment, Labour and Social Affairs and Education Committees seek to provide for the greater integration of labour market and educational policies and the prevention of social exclusion.

OECD's Centre for Educational Research and Innovation (CERI) promotes the development of research activities in education together with experiments of an advanced nature designed to test innovations in educational systems and to stimulate research and development. A programme for the production of policy-oriented and comparable indicators of student achievement on a regular basis was established in 1998, in order to provide a profile of the knowledge, skills and competencies of students towards the end of compulsory schooling and information on how such skills relate to important social, economic and educational variables. A Programme on Educational Building provides analysis and advice on the management of educational facilities and infrastructure, while the Programme on Institutional Management in Higher Education focuses on the relation between higher education policy and the management of institutions in the sector.

### RELATIONS WITH OTHER INTERNATIONAL ORGANIZATIONS

Under a Protocol signed at the same time as the OECD Convention, the European Commission generally takes part in the work of OECD. EFTA may also send representatives to OECD meetings. Formal relations exist with a number of other international organizations, including the ILO, FAO, IMF, IBRD, UNCTAD, IAEA and the Council of Europe. A few non-governmental organizations have been granted consultative status, notably the Business and Industry Advisory Committee to OECD (BIAC) and the Trade Union Advisory Committee to OECD (TUAC).

## Finance

In 1998 OECD's total budget amounted to 1,300m. French francs, of which some 75% was funded by regular contributions from member states and the remainder by special income or project participants.

## Publications

*Activities of OECD* (Secretary-General's Annual Report).

*Agricultural Outlook* (annually).

*Energy Balances* (quarterly).

*Energy Prices and Taxes* (quarterly).

*Financial Market Trends* (3 a year).

*Financial Statistics* (Part 1 (domestic markets): monthly; Part 2 (international markets): monthly; Part 3 (OECD member countries): 25 a year).

*Foreign Trade Statistics* (monthly).

*Higher Education Management* (3 a year).

*Indicators of Industrial Activity* (quarterly).

*Joint BIS-IMF-OECD-World Bank Statistics on External Debt* (quarterly).

*Main Developments in Trade* (annually).

*Main Economic Indicators* (monthly).

*National Accounts Quarterly*.

*OECD Economic Outlook* (2 a year).

*OECD Economic Studies* (2 a year).

*OECD Economic Surveys* (every 12 to 18 months for each country).

*OECD Employment Outlook* (annually).

*The OECD Observer* (every 2 months).

*Oil and Gas Statistics* (quarterly).

*PEB Exchange* (newsletter of the Programme on Educational Building, 3 a year).

*Quarterly Labour Force Statistics*.

*Science, Technology, Industry Review* (2 a year).

*Short-term Economic Indicators: Transition Economies* (quarterly).

Numerous specialized reports, working papers, books and statistics on economic and social subjects (about 130 titles a year, both in English and French) are also published.

# International Energy Agency—IEA

**Address:** 9 rue de la Fédération, 75739 Paris Cédex 15, France.

**Telephone:** 1-40-57-65-00; **fax:** 1-40-57-65-09; **e-mail:** info@iea.org; **internet:** www.iea.org.

The Agency was established by the OECD Council in 1974 to develop co-operation on energy questions among participating countries.

### MEMBERS

| | | |
|---|---|---|
| Australia | Greece | Norway |
| Austria | Hungary | Portugal |
| Belgium | Ireland | Spain |
| Canada | Italy | Sweden |
| Denmark | Japan | Switzerland |
| Finland | Luxembourg | Turkey |
| France | Netherlands | United Kingdom |
| Germany | New Zealand | USA |

The European Commission is also represented.

## Organization

(January 2000)

### GOVERNING BOARD

Composed of ministers or senior officials of the member governments. Decisions may be taken by a weighted majority on a number of specified subjects, particularly concerning emergency measures and the emergency reserve commitment; a simple weighted majority is required for procedural decisions and decisions implementing specific obligations in the agreement. Unanimity is required only if new obligations, not already specified in the agreement, are to be undertaken.

The Governing Board is assisted by a Coal and an Oil Industry Advisory Board, composed of industrial executives.

### SECRETARIAT

The Secretariat comprises the following four Offices: Long-Term Co-operation and Policy Analysis; Non-member Countries; Oil Markets and Emergency Preparedness; and Energy Efficiency, Technology and Research and Development.

**Executive Director:** Robert Priddle (United Kingdom).

## Activities

The Agreement on an International Energy Programme was signed in November 1974 and formally entered into force in January 1976. The Programme commits the participating countries of the International Energy Agency to share petroleum in emergencies, to strengthen their long-term co-operation in order to reduce dependence on petroleum imports, to increase the availability of information on the petroleum market and to develop relations with the petroleum-producing and other petroleum-consuming countries.

An emergency petroleum-sharing plan has been established, and the IEA ensures that the necessary technical information and facilities are in place so that it can be readily used in the event of a reduction in petroleum supplies. The IEA undertakes emergency response reviews and workshops, and publishes an Emergency Management Manual to facilitate a co-ordinated response to a severe disruption in petroleum supplies. A separate division monitors and reports on short-term developments in the petroleum market. It also considers other related issues, including international crude petroleum pricing, petroleum trade and stock developments and investments by major petroleum-producing countries.

The IEA Long-Term Co-operation Programme is designed to strengthen the security of energy supplies and promote stability in world energy markets. It provides for co-operative efforts to conserve energy, to accelerate the development of alternative energy sources by means of both specific and general measures, to strengthen research and development of new energy technologies and to remove legislative and administrative obstacles to increased energy supplies. Regular reviews of member countries' efforts in the fields of energy conservation and accelerated development of alternative energy sources assess the effectiveness of national programmes in relation to the objectives of the Agency.

The IEA also reviews the energy situation in non-member countries, in particular the petroleum-producing countries of the Middle East and central and eastern European countries. In the latter states the IEA has provided technical assistance for the development of national energy legislation and energy efficiency projects. The IEA has entered into co-operation agreements with Russia, the People's Republic of China and India.

The IEA aims to contribute to the energy security of member countries through energy technology and research and development projects, in particular those concerned with energy efficiency, conservation and protection of the environment. The IEA promotes international collaboration in this field and the participation of energy industries to facilitate the application of new technologies, through effective transfer of knowledge, technology innovation and training. Member states adopt Implementing Agreements, which provide mechanisms for collaboration and information exchange in specific areas, for example electric vehicle technologies, electric demand-side management and photovoltaic power systems. Non-member states are encouraged to participate in these Agreements. The Agency sponsors conferences, symposia and workshops to further enhance international co-operation among member and non-member countries.

## Publications

*Coal Information* (annually).
*Electricity Information* (annually).
*Natural Gas Information* (annually).
*Oil Information* (annually).
*Oil Market Report* (monthly).
*World Energy Outlook* (annually).
Reports, studies, statistics, country reviews.

# OECD Nuclear Energy Agency—NEA

**Address:** Le Seine Saint-Germain, 12 blvd des Îles, 92130 Issy-les-Moulineaux, France.

**Telephone:** 1-45-24-82-00; **fax:** 1-45-24-11-10; **e-mail:** nea@nea.fr; **internet:** www.nea.fr.

The NEA was established in 1958 to further the peaceful uses of nuclear energy. Originally a European agency, it has since admitted OECD members outside Europe.

### MEMBERS

All members of OECD (except New Zealand and Poland).

## Organization

(January 2000)

### STEERING COMMITTEE FOR NUCLEAR ENERGY

**Chairman:** Dr LARS HØGBERG.

### SECRETARIAT

**Director-General:** LUIS ENRIQUE ECHAVARRI (Spain).
**Deputy Director-General:** SAMUEL THOMPSON (USA).

### MAIN COMMITTEES

Committee on Nuclear Regulatory Activities;
Committee on Radiation Protection and Public Health;
Committee on the Safety of Nuclear Installations;
Committee for Technical and Economic Studies on Nuclear Energy Development and the Fuel Cycle;
Group of Governmental Experts on Third Party Liability in the Field of Nuclear Energy;
Nuclear Science Committee;
Radioactive Waste Management Committee.

### NEA DATA BANK

The Data Bank was established in 1978, as a successor to the Computer Programme Library and the Neutron Data Compilation Centre. The Data Bank develops and supplies data and computer programmes for nuclear technology applications to users in laboratories, industry, universities and other areas of interest. Under the supervision of the Nuclear Science Committee, the Data Bank collates integral experimental data, and functions as part of a network of data centres to provide direct data services. It was responsible for co-ordinating the development of the Joint Evaluation Fission and Fusion (JEFF) data reference library, and works with the Radioactive Waste Management Division of the NEA to develop the Thermochemical Database project.

## Activities

The main purpose of the Agency is to promote international co-operation and develop consensus opinions within the OECD area for the development and application of nuclear power for peaceful purposes through international research and development projects and exchange of scientific and technical experience and information. It aims to contribute to the development of nuclear energy as a safe, economical and environmentally acceptable energy source. The Agency maintains a continual survey with the co-operation of other organizations, notably the International Atomic Energy Agency (IAEA, see p. 74), of world uranium resources, production and demand, and of economic and technical aspects of the nuclear fuel cycle.

A major part of the Agency's work is devoted to the safety and regulation of nuclear power, including co-operative studies and projects related to the prevention of nuclear accidents and the long-term safety of radioactive waste disposal systems. It is also concerned with the harmonization of nuclear legislation and the dissemination of information on nuclear law issues. In 1997 two new legal instruments were adopted, under the auspices of the IAEA: the Protocol to Amend the Vienna Convention on Civil Liability for Nuclear Damage and the Convention on Supplementary Compensation for Nuclear Damage. A Nuclear Development Committee provides members with statistics and analysis on nuclear resources, economics, technology and prospects. The NEA also co-operates with non-member countries of central and eastern Europe and the CIS in areas such as nuclear safety, radiation protection and nuclear law.

### JOINT PROJECTS

**Decommissioning of Nuclear Installations:** this co-operative programme, set up in 1985, provides for an exchange of scientific and technical information to develop the operational experience and data base needed for the future decommissioning of large nuclear power plants and other nuclear fuel cycle facilities. The Programme is administered by a Liaison Committee, while technical discussions and exchanges are undertaken in the context of a Technical Advisory Group. In 2000 the Programme comprised 31 projects in 13 countries.

**Halden Reactor Project:** Halden, Norway; experimental boiling heavy water reactor, which became an OECD project in 1958. From 1964, under successive agreements with participating countries, the reactor has been used for long-term testing of water reactor fuels and for research into automatic computer-based control of nuclear power stations. Some 100 nuclear energy research institutions and authorities in 20 countries support the project.

**Incident Reporting System—IRS:** introduced in 1980 to exchange experience in operating nuclear power plants in OECD member countries and to improve nuclear safety by facilitating feedback of this experience to nuclear regulatory authorities, utilities and manufacturers. Since 1995 the IRS has operated in conjunction with the IAEA.

**Information System on Occupational Exposure—ISOE:** initiated in 1992; ISOE databases contain annual collective dose information on 383 reactors in some 26 countries; the system also contains information from 39 nuclear reactors which are either defunct or actively decommissioning.

**Lower Head Failure Project:** initiated in 1999; aims to provide experimental data on lower head deformation and failure phenomena; uses prototypic material and geometry to simulate conditions.

Several OECD countries are participating in this project, which was to last for three years.

**Rasplav Project:** initiated in 1994, in Moscow, Russia, to study the behaviour of molten core material in a reactor pressure vessel during a severe accident. Seventeen countries participate in the project. The second three-year phase of the project began in July 1997. There was to be a final presentation in November 2000.

**Scorpio Project:** initiated in 1996, in agreement with the Japanese Science and Technology Agency and in co-operation with the Halden Reactor Project, the Scorpio Project aims to improve the surveillance capabilities for WER reactor cores in various operational conditions. The surveillance system is installed at the Dukovang Nuclear Power Plant in the Czech Republic, for the purpose of developing a general framework for WER-type reactors.

## Finance

The Agency's annual budget amounts to 78m. French francs.

## Publications

*Annual Report.*

*NEA Newsletter* (2 a year).

*Newsletter on International Nuclear Data Measurement Activities* (annually).

*Nuclear Law Bulletin* (2 a year).

Publications on a range of issues relating to nuclear energy, reports and proceedings.

# ORGANIZATION FOR SECURITY AND CO-OPERATION IN EUROPE—OSCE

**Address:** 1010 Vienna, Kärntner Ring 5–7, Austria.

**Telephone:** (1) 514-36-0; **fax:** (1) 514-36-105; **e-mail:** info@osce.org; **internet:** www.osce.org.

The OSCE was established in 1972 as the Conference on Security and Co-operation in Europe (CSCE), providing a multilateral forum for dialogue and negotiation. It produced the Helsinki Final Act of 1975 on East–West relations (see below). The areas of competence of the CSCE were expanded by the Charter of Paris for a New Europe (1990), which transformed the CSCE from an *ad hoc* forum to an organization with permanent institutions, and the Helsinki Document 1992 (see 'Activities'). In December 1994 the summit conference adopted the new name of OSCE, in order to reflect the Organization's changing political role and strengthened secretariat. The OSCE has 55 participating states and comprises all the recognized countries of Europe, and Canada, the USA and all the former republics of the USSR.

### PARTICIPATING STATES

| | | |
|---|---|---|
| Albania | Greece | Portugal |
| Andorra | Hungary | Romania |
| Armenia | Iceland | Russia |
| Austria | Ireland | San Marino |
| Azerbaijan | Italy | Slovakia |
| Belarus | Kazakhstan | Slovenia |
| Belgium | Kyrgyzstan | Spain |
| Bosnia and Herzegovina | Latvia | Sweden |
| Bulgaria | Liechtenstein | Switzerland |
| Canada | Lithuania | Tajikistan |
| Croatia | Luxembourg | Turkey |
| Cyprus | Macedonia, former Yugoslav republic | Turkmenistan |
| Czech Republic | Malta | Ukraine |
| Denmark | Moldova | United Kingdom |
| Estonia | Monaco | USA |
| Finland | Netherlands | Uzbekistan |
| France | Norway | Vatican City (Holy See) |
| Georgia | Poland | Yugoslavia* |
| Germany | | |

* The Federal Republic of Yugoslavia was suspended from the CSCE in July 1992.

## Organization

(January 2000)

### SUMMIT CONFERENCES

Heads of state or government of OSCE participating states normally meet every two years to set priorities and political orientation of the Organization. The most recent conference was held in İstanbul, Turkey, in November 1999.

### MINISTERIAL COUNCIL

The Ministerial Council (formerly the Council of Foreign Ministers) comprises ministers of foreign affairs of member states. It is the central decision-making and governing body of the OSCE and meets at least once a year.

### SENIOR COUNCIL

The Senior Council (formerly the Council of Senior Officials—CSO) is responsible for the supervision, management and co-ordination of OSCE activities. Member states are represented by senior political officers, who convene at least twice a year in Prague, Czech Republic, and once a year as the Economic Forum.

### PERMANENT COUNCIL

The Council, which is based in Vienna, is responsible for day-to-day operational tasks. Members of the Council, comprising the permanent representatives of member states to the OSCE, convene weekly. The Council is the regular body for political consultation and decision-making, and may be convened for emergency purposes.

### FORUM FOR SECURITY CO-OPERATION—FSC

The FSC, comprising representatives of delegations of member states, meets weekly in Vienna to negotiate and consult on measures aimed at strengthening security and stability throughout Europe. Its main objectives are negotiations on arms control, disarmament, and confidence- and security-building; regular consultations and intensive co-operation on matters related to security; and the further reduction of the risks of conflict. The FSC is also responsible for the implementation of confidence- and security-building measures (CSBMs); the preparation of seminars on military doctrine; the holding of annual implementation assessment meetings; and the provision of a forum for the discussion and clarification of information exchanged under agreed CSBMs.

### CHAIRMAN-IN-OFFICE—CIO

The CIO is vested with overall responsibility for executive action. The position is held by a minister of foreign affairs of a member state for a one-year term. The CIO may be assisted by a troika, consisting of the preceding, current and succeeding chairpeople; *ad hoc* steering groups; or personal representatives, who are appointed by the CIO with a clear and precise mandate to assist the CIO in dealing with a crisis or conflict.

**Chairman-in-Office:** BENITA FERRERO-WALDNER (Austria).

### SECRETARIAT

In 1998 the Secretariat was restructured on the basis of two departments: the Conflict Prevention Centre, which focuses on the support of the CIO in the implementation of OSCE policies, in particular the monitoring of field activities and co-operation with other international bodies; and the Department for Administration and Operations, responsible for technical, administrative and operational support activities. The OSCE maintains an office in Prague, Czech Republic, which assists with documentation and information activities, and a liaison office in Central Asia, based in Tashkent, Uzbekistan.

The position of Secretary-General was established in December 1992 and the first appointment to the position was made in June 1993. The Secretary-General is the representative of the CIO and is responsible for the management of OSCE structures and operations.

**Secretary-General:** JÁN KUBIŠ (Slovakia).

### HIGH COMMISSIONER ON NATIONAL MINORITIES

**Address:** POB 20062, 2500 EB The Hague, Netherlands.

**Telephone:** (70) 3125500; **fax:** (70) 3635910; **e-mail:** hcnm@hcnm.org.

The establishment of the office of High Commissioner on National Minorities was proposed in the 1992 Helsinki Document, and endorsed by the Council of Foreign Ministers in Stockholm in December 1992. The role of the High Commissioner is to identify ethnic tensions that might endanger peace, stability or relations between OSCE participating states, and to promote their early resolution. The High Commissioner may issue an 'early warning' for the attention of the Senior Council of an area of tension likely to degenerate into conflict. The High Commissioner is appointed by the Ministerial Council, on the recommendation of the Senior Council, for a three-year term.

**High Commissioner:** MAX VAN DER STOEL (Netherlands).

### OFFICE FOR DEMOCRATIC INSTITUTIONS AND HUMAN RIGHTS—ODIHR

**Address:** Aleje Ujazdowskie 19, 00-517 Warsaw, Poland.

**Telephone:** (22) 520-06-00; **fax:** (22) 520-06-05; **e-mail:** office@odihr.osce.waw.pl; **internet:** www.osce.odihr.org.

The ODIHR, which was originally called the Office for Free Elections with a mandate to promote multiparty democracy, was assigned major new tasks under the Helsinki Document 1992, including responsibility for promoting human rights, democracy and the rule of law. The Office provides a framework for the exchange of information on and the promotion of democracy-building, respect for human rights and elections within OSCE states. In addition, it co-ordinates the monitoring of elections and provides expertise and training on constitutional and legal matters.

**Director:** GÉRARD STOUDMANN (Switzerland).

### OFFICE OF THE REPRESENTATIVE ON FREEDOM OF THE MEDIA

**Address:** 1010 Vienna, Kärntner Ring 5–7, Austria.

**Telephone:** (1) 512-21-450; **fax:** (1) 512-21-459; **e-mail:** pm-fom@osce.org; **internet:** www.osce.org/inst/fom.

The office was founded in 1998 to strengthen the implementation of OSCE commitments regarding free, independent and pluralistic media.

**Representative:** FREIMUT DUVE (Germany).

### PARLIAMENTARY ASSEMBLY

**Address:** Radhusstraede 1, 1466 Copenhagen K, Denmark.

**Telephone:** 33-37-80-40; **fax:** 33-37-80-30; **e-mail:** osce@oscepa.dk; **internet:** www.oscepa.com.

The OSCE Parliamentary Assembly, which is composed of 317 parliamentarians from 55 participating countries, was inaugurated in July 1992, and meets annually. The Assembly comprises a Standing Committee, a Bureau and three General Committees and is supported by a Secretariat in Copenhagen, Denmark.

**President:** HELLE DEGN (Denmark).

**Secretary-General:** R. SPENCER OLIVER.

## OSCE Related Bodies

### COURT OF CONCILIATION AND ARBITRATION

**Address:** 266 route de Lausanne, 1292 Chambesy, Geneva, Switzerland.

**Telephone:** (22) 7580025; **fax:** (22) 7582510.

The establishment of the Court of Conciliation and Arbitration was agreed in 1992 and effected in 1994. OSCE states that have ratified the OSCE Convention on Conciliation and Arbitration may submit a dispute to the Court for settlement by the Arbitral Tribunal or the Conciliation Commission.

### JOINT CONSULTATIVE GROUP (JCG)

The states that are party to the Treaty on Conventional Armed Forces in Europe (CFE), which was concluded within the CSCE framework in 1990, established the Joint Consultative Group (JCG). The JCG, which meets in Vienna, addresses questions relating to compliance with the Treaty; enhancement of the effectiveness of the Treaty; technical aspects of the Treaty's implementation; and disputes arising out of its implementation. There are currently 30 states participating in the JCG.

### OPEN SKIES CONSULTATIVE COMMISSION

The Commission represents all states parties to the 1992 Treaty on Open Skies, and promotes its implementation. Its regular meetings are serviced by the OSCE secretariat.

## Activities

In July 1990 heads of government of the NATO member countries proposed to increase the role of the CSCE 'to provide a forum for wider political dialogue in a more united Europe'. In November heads of government of the participating states signed the Charter of Paris for a New Europe, which undertook to strengthen pluralist democracy and observance of human rights, and to settle disputes between participating states by peaceful means. At the summit meeting the Treaty on Conventional Armed Forces in Europe (CFE), which had been negotiated within the framework of the CSCE, was signed by the member states of NATO (q.v.) and of the Warsaw Pact. The Treaty limits non-nuclear air and ground armaments in the signatory countries. It was decided at the same meeting to establish a secretariat in Prague, Czechoslovakia, which was opened in February 1991. (The secretariat was moved to Vienna, Austria, in 1993.) It was also decided to create a Conflict Prevention Centre, which was established in Vienna, Austria, in March 1991, and an Office for Free Elections (later renamed the Office for Democratic Institutions and Human Rights), which was established in Warsaw, Poland, in July. In April parliamentarians from the CSCE countries agreed on the creation of a pan-European parliamentary assembly. Its first session was held in Budapest, Hungary, in July 1992.

The Council of Foreign Ministers met for the first time in Berlin, Germany, in June 1991. The meeting adopted a mechanism for consultation and co-operation in the case of emergency situations, to be implemented by the Council of Senior Officials (CSO, which was subsequently renamed the Senior Council). A separate mechanism regarding the prevention of the outbreak of conflict was also adopted, whereby a country can demand an explanation of 'unusual military activity' in a neighbouring country. These mechanisms were utilized in July in relation to the armed conflict in Yugoslavia between the Republic of Croatia and the Yugoslav Government. The CSCE appealed to all parties involved in the conflict to uphold a cease-fire. In mid-August a meeting of the CSO resolved to reinforce the CSCE's mission in Yugoslavia considerably and requested all the parties involved in the conflict to begin negotiations as a matter of urgency. In September the CSO agreed to impose an embargo on the export of armaments to Yugoslavia. In October the CSO resolved to establish an observer mission to monitor the observance of human rights in Yugoslavia.

The third CSCE Conference on Human Dimensions (the CSCE term used with regard to issues concerning human rights and welfare) was held in Moscow in September 1991. The Conference formulated an accord which empowers CSCE envoys to investigate reported abuses of human rights in any CSCE country, either at the request of the country concerned, or if six participating states deem such an investigation necessary. In 1993 the First Implementation Meeting on Human Dimension Issues took place; meetings were subsequently held biannually. The Meeting, for which the ODIHR serves as a secretariat, provides a forum for the exchange of news regarding OSCE commitments in the fields of human rights and democracy. The Fourth Meeting took place in Warsaw, Poland in October–November 1998.

In January 1992 the Council of Foreign Ministers agreed that the Conference's rule of decision-making by consensus was to be altered to allow the CSO to take appropriate action against a participating state 'in cases of clear and gross violation of CSCE commitments'. This development was precipitated by the conflict in Yugoslavia, where the Yugoslav Government was held responsible by the majority of CSCE states for the continuation of hostilities. It was also agreed at the meeting that the CSCE should undertake fact-finding and conciliation missions to areas of tension, with the first such mission to be sent to Nagornyi Karabakh, the largely Armenian-populated enclave in Azerbaijan.

In March 1992 CSCE participating states reached agreement on a number of confidence-building measures, including commitments to exchange technical data on new weapons systems; to report activation of military units; and to prohibit military activity involving very large numbers of troops or tanks. Later in that month at a meeting of the Council of Foreign Ministers, which opened the Helsinki Follow-up Conference, the members of NATO and the former members of the Warsaw Pact (with Russia, Belarus, Ukraine and Georgia taking the place of the USSR) signed the Open Skies Treaty. Under the treaty, aerial reconnaissance missions by one country over another were permitted, subject to regulation. An Open Skies Consultative Commission was subsequently established (see above).

The Federal Republic of Yugoslavia (Serbia and Montenegro) was suspended from the CSCE immediately prior to the summit meeting of heads of state and government that took place in Helsinki, Finland, in July 1992. The meeting adopted the Helsinki Document 1992, in which participating states defined the terms of future CSCE peace-keeping activities. Conforming broadly to UN practice, peace-keeping operations would be undertaken only with the full consent of the parties involved in any conflict and only if an effective cease-fire were in place. The CSCE may request the use of the military resources of NATO, WEU, the EU, the CIS or other international bodies. (NATO and WEU had recently changed their constitutions to permit the use of their forces for CSCE purposes.) The Helsinki Document declared the CSCE a 'regional arrangement' in the sense of Chapter VIII of the UN's Charter, which states that such a regional grouping should attempt to resolve a conflict in the region before referring it to the Security Council. In December 1993 a Permanent Committee (now renamed the Permanent Council) was established in Vienna, providing for greater political consultation and dialogue through its weekly meetings. In December 1994 the summit conference endorsed the organization's role as the primary instrument for early warning, conflict prevention and crisis management in the region, and adopted a 'Code of Conduct on Politico-Military Aspects of Security', which set out principles to guide the role of the armed forces in democratic societies. The summit conference that was held in Lisbon, Portugal, in December 1996 agreed to adapt the CFE Treaty, in order to further arms reduction negotiations on a national and territorial basis. The conference also adopted the 'Lisbon Declaration on a Common and Comprehensive Security Model for Europe for the 21st Century' (see below), committing all parties to pursuing measures to ensure regional security. A Security Model Committee was established and began to meet regularly during 1997 to consider aspects of the Declaration, including the identification of risks and challenges to future European security; enhancing means of joint co-operative action within the OSCE framework in the event of non-compliance with OSCE commitments by participating states; considering other new arrangements within the OSCE framework that could reinforce security and stability in Europe; and defining a basis of co-operation between the OSCE and other relevant organizations to co-ordinate security enforcement. In November 1997 the Office of the Representative on Freedom of the Media was established in Vienna, to support the OSCE's activities in this field.

In November 1999 OSCE heads of state and of government, convened in İstanbul, Turkey, signed a new Charter for European Security, which aimed to formalize existing norms regarding the observance of human rights and to strengthen co-operation with other organizations and institutions concerned with international security. The Charter focused on measures to improve the operational capabilities of the OSCE in early warning, conflict prevention, crisis management and post-conflict rehabilitation. Accordingly, Rapid Expert Assistance and Co-operation (REACT) teams were to be established to enable the organization to respond rapidly to requests from participating states for assistance in crisis situations. At the meeting a revised CFE Treaty was also signed, providing for a stricter system of limitations and increased transparency, which was to be open to other OSCE states not currently signatories. The US and EU governments determined to delay ratification of the Agreement of the Adaptation of the Treaty until Russian troop levels in the Caucasus had been reduced.

## OSCE MISSIONS AND FIELD ACTIVITIES

In December 1994 OSCE heads of state and government authorized the establishment of a 3,000-strong peace-keeping force for the Nagornyi Karabakh region, which was the focus of a conflict between Armenia and Azerbaijan. However, in the absence of a formal cease-fire and the start of peace negotiations, the proposed force was not dispatched. The OSCE continued to provide a framework for discussions between the two countries through its 11-nation Minsk Group, which from early 1997 was co-chaired by France, Russia and the USA. In October 1997 Armenia and Azerbaijan reached agreement on OSCE proposals for a political settlement; however, the concessions granted by the Armenian President, Levon Ter-Petrossian, which included the withdrawal of troops from certain strategic areas of Nagornyi Karabakh precipitated his resignation in February 1998. The proposals were rejected by his successor, Robert Kocharian. Nevertheless, meetings of the Minsk Group continued in 1998 and both countries expressed their willingness to recommence negotiations. The then CIO, Bronisław Geremek, met with the leaders of both countries in November and persuaded them to exchange prisoners of war. The Azeri President, however, rejected a new proposal to settle the dispute.

In January 1995 Russia agreed to an OSCE proposal to send a fact-finding mission to assist in the conflict between the Russian authorities and an independence movement in Chechnya. The mission criticized the Russian army for using excessive force against Chechen rebels and civilians; reported that violations of human rights had been perpetrated by both sides in the conflict; and urged Russia to enforce a cease-fire in Groznyi to allow the delivery of humanitarian supplies by international aid agencies to the population of the city. An OSCE Assistance Group mediated between the two sides, and, in July, brokered a cease-fire agreement between the Russian military authorities in Chechnya and the Chechen rebels. A further peace accord was signed, under the auspices of the OSCE, in May 1996, but the truce was broken in July. A more conclusive cease-fire agreement was signed by the two parties to the conflict in August. In January 1997 the OSCE assisted in the preparation and monitoring of general elections conducted in Chechnya. The Assistance Group remained in the territory to help with post-conflict rehabilitation, including the promotion of democratic institutions and respect for human rights. In September 1999, following a resurgence of separatist activity, Russian launched a military offensive against Chechnya. In early November an OSCE mission arrived in the neighbouring republic of Ingushetia to assess the condition and needs of the estimated 200,000 refugees who had fled the hostilities; however, the officials were prevented by the Russian authorites from travelling into Chechnya. The issue dominated the OSCE summit meeting, held in İstanbul, Turkey, later in that month. The meeting insisted upon a political solution to the conflict and called for an immediate cease-fire. An agreement was reached with the Russian President to allow the CIO to visit the region, and to an OSCE role in initiating political dialogue.

In late 1996 the OSCE declared the constitutional referendum held in Belarus in November to be illegal and urged that country's Government to ensure political freedoms and respect for human rights. An OSCE fact-finding mission visited Belarus in April 1997 and recommended the establishment of a permanent presence in the country, to assist with the process of democratization. This was established in February 1998. In October the OSCE Parliamentary Assembly formed an *ad hoc* Committee on Belarus, to act as a working group to support and intensify the organization's work in the country.

In March 1997 the OSCE dispatched a fact-finding mission to Albania to help restore political and civil stability, which had been undermined by the collapse of national pyramid saving schemes at the start of the year. An agreement was negotiated between Albania's President Sali Berisha and opposition parties to hold elections in mid-1997 and to establish a government of national reconciliation. At the end of March the Permanent Council agreed to establish an OSCE Presence in Albania, and confirmed that the organization should provide the framework for co-ordinating other international efforts in the country. OSCE efforts focused on reaching a political consensus on new legislation for the conduct of the forthcoming elections. Voting took place in June/July, with 500 OSCE observers providing technical electoral assistance and helping to monitor the voting. In March 1998 the OSCE Presence was mandated to monitor the country's borders with the Kosovan region of southern Serbia and to prevent any spillover effects from the escalating crisis. This role was reduced following the political setlement for Kosovo and Metohija concluded in mid-1999. In June 1998 the OSCE observed local elections in Albania. It became the Co-Chair, with the EU, of the Friends of Albania group, which then brought together countries and international bodies concerned with the situation in Albania for the first time in September. In October a decision was taken by the Permanent Council to enhance the Presence's role in border-monitoring activities. With other organizations, the OSCE was involved in the preparation of the country's draft constitution, finalized in October, and an ODIHR Election Observation Mission was established to observe the referendum on the constitution held in November.

Under the Dayton peace accords for the former Yugoslavia, which were concluded in late 1995, the OSCE was assigned the tasks of supervising post-war Bosnian elections; drafting arms-control agreements for the former Yugoslavia; and monitoring the observance of human rights in Bosnia and Herzegovina. The OSCE mission to organize and oversee the Bosnian national elections, which were held on 14 September 1996, was the largest-ever operation undertaken by the organization, with some 1,200 electoral observers deployed. The OSCE subsequently monitored Bosnian municipal elections, twice rescheduled by the organization and eventually held in September 1997, and the elections to the National Assembly of the Serb Republic and to the Bosnian Serb presidency in November. In 1998 the mission was charged with organizing the second post-war general elections in Bosnia and Herzegovina (comprising elections to the legislature of Bosnia and Herzegovina, the Federation and the Serb Republic, and to the presidencies of Bosnia and Herzegovina and the Serb Republic). The mission assisted with the registration of voters and, in September, was responsible for the supervision of the elections at polling stations within and outside the country. The final results of the election to the Bosnian Serb presidency were delayed, owing to the unexpected victory of an extreme nationalist, Nikola Poplasen, which, it was feared, could jeopardize the peace process. The OSCE immediately emphasized the necessity of maintaining the process. It also insisted on the need to transfer responsibility for the electoral process to the national authorities for future elections. In March 1999 the OSCE initiated an educational campaign relating to new election laws. Progress was made from 1995 in the area of arms control, under the Agreement on Regional Arms Control, with confidence- and security-building measures implemented and excess armaments reduced.

In April 1997 the OSCE monitored legislative and municipal elections in Croatia, including the Eastern Slavonia, Baranja and Western Srem (Sirmium) region under UN administration. In June the Permanent Council agreed to increase the OSCE Presence in Croatia, and to enhance the mission's capacity to protect human rights, in particular the rights of minorities, and to monitor the implementation of legislation and other commitments concerning the return and treatment of refugees and displaced persons, under a new mandate extending until 31 December 1998. In March 1998, following the integration of the disputed region into Croatia, the OSCE criticized the conditions imposed by the Croatian Government for the return of Serb refugees, stating that the right to return to one's own country was inalienable and must not depend on the fulfilment of conditions. In October the mission to Croatia assumed the responsibilities of the United Nations Police Support Group (UNPSG). A maximum of 120 unarmed OSCE civilian police monitors were deployed in the region in the OSCE's first police-monitoring role. The OSCE was also to be responsible for monitoring the border regions, with particular concern for customs activities.

In Yugoslavia the OSCE was invited to verify the results of elections held in Serbia in November 1996; it also monitored the presidential poll in Montenegro in October 1997. In mid-1998 the OSCE was involved in the mediation effort to resolve the conflict between the Serbian authorities and ethnic Albanian separatists in the formerly autonomous province of Kosovo and Metohija. In October, following months of diplomatic effort and the threat of NATO air strikes, Yugoslav President Slobodan Milošević agreed to comply with UN Security Council Resolution 1199, which required an immediate cease-fire, Serbian troop withdrawals, the commencement of meaningful peace negotiations, and unrestricted access for humanitarian aid. Under a peace plan proposed by the US special envoy, Richard Holbrooke, President Milošević agreed to the formation of a 2,000-member OSCE Kosovo Verification Mission (KVM) to monitor compliance, in addition to surveillance flights by unarmed NATO aircraft. The KVM was to patrol the region to ensure the withdrawal of Serbian military and police units, and to oversee the safe return of refugees and the non-harassment of ethnic Albanian inhabitants. It was also to monitor border control activities and accompany police units in Kosovo, when necessary, to assist them to perform their normal policing roles. The mission was guaranteed free access through the area and aimed to open offices in all of Kosovo's 29 regions. Examples of progress and non-compliance were to be reported to the OSCE Permanent Council, the UN Security Council and other organizations. The mission's mandate was formally established on 25 October 1998 for a period of one year. Upon achievement of a political settlement defining the area's self-government, and its subsequent implementation, the KVM was to be responsible for supervising elections in Kosovo, assisting in the establishment of democratic institutions and developing a Kosovo police force. The long-term mission was accepted in return for the eventual removal of Yugoslavia's suspension from the OSCE. However, sporadic fighting continued in the province, and the monitoring force began unofficially to assume a peace-keeping role. In January 1999 the KVM successfully negotiated for the release of eight Yugoslav soldiers held hostage by the separatist forces. Later in that month following the KVM's denunciation of the killing of some 45 ethnic Albanians by Serbian security forces in the village of Racak, President Milošević ordered the head of the mission, William Walker, to leave the region. This was later revoked. Meanwhile, OSCE monitors were forced to withdraw from Racak under fire from Serbian troops. An emergency meeting of the OSCE in Vienna agreed to maintain the mission. However, on 19 March, following the failure of negotiations to resolve the crisis, the CIO decided to evacuate the 1,380 unarmed monitors to the former Yugoslav republic of Macedonia, owing to the deteriorating security situation in Kosovo. NATO commenced an aerial offensive against Yugoslavia in late March. In early April the CIO condemned the mass expulsion of ethnic Albanians from Kosovo and other violations of human rights committed by Serbian forces. Later in the same month the CIO, at a meeting of a ministerial troika attended by the Secretary-General, announced that the OSCE was willing to assist in the implementation of a political settlement in Kosovo. The OSCE was also concerned with measures to prevent the crisis affecting the other Balkan states. Within the framework of a political settlement for Kosovo, which was formally concluded in June, the OSCE was responsible for democracy- and institution-building under the auspices of the UN Interim Administration Mission for Kosovo (UNMIK). OSCE monitors were deployed to assess the human rights situation throughout the region, and in August a new OSCE-administered police training school was inaugurated. Later in the year the OSCE commenced the training of judicial and administrative officers. At that time the OSCE mission consisted of 1,400 personnel. In December the OSCE published a report on the situation in Kosovo, which confirmed that Serbian forces had conducted systematic abuses of human rights but also raised suspicion against the KLA for organizing retribution attacks against Serbian civilians later in the year. The OSCE was actively involved in co-ordinating the Stability Pact for South-Eastern Europe, which was initiated, in June, as a collaborative plan of action by the EU, Group of Seven industrialized nations and Russia (the G-8), regional governments and other organizations concerned with the stability of the region. A meeting of participants in the Pact was convened to coincide with the OSCE summit meeting, held in November.

During 1998 the High Commissioner on National Minorities, Max van der Stoel, advised Latvia on the development of liberal amendments to its citizenship law, which were presented to parliament in June. The OSCE closely observed the referendum on these amendments, which took place in October, and continued to monitor the implementation of the amendments, following their approval by the electorate. In January 1999, for the first time, the OSCE refused to dispatch official observers to monitor presidential elections in a member state, owing to concerns about the legitimacy of elections held in Kazakhstan. In December the OSCE and ODIHR decided not to deploy a mission to observe parliamentary elections in Turkmenistan owing to an inadequate legislative framework.

At the end of 1999 there were long-term OSCE missions, with the objectives of conflict prevention and crisis management, in Bosnia and Herzegovina, Croatia, Estonia, Georgia, Latvia, the former Yugoslav republic of Macedonia, Moldova, Tajikistan, Kosovo, Sandjak and Vojvodina (Federal Republic of Yugoslavia), and Kosovo. The OSCE also operated field activities in Albania, Belarus, Chechenya and Ukraine, and maintained offices in Yerevan (Armenia) and Baku (Azerbaijan), and Centres in Almaty (Kazakhstan), Ashgabad (Turkmenistan) and Bishkek (Kyrgyzstan), which opened in 1998. The OSCE also has institutionalized structures to assist in the implementation of certain bilateral agreements. At the end of 1999 there were OSCE representatives to the Russian-Latvian Joint Commission on Military Pensioners; the Estonian Government Commission on Military Pensioners; and the Joint Committee on the Skrunda Radar Station.

Japan and the Republic of Korea have the status of 'partners for co-operation' with the OSCE, while Algeria, Egypt, Israel, Jordan, Morocco and Tunisia are 'Mediterranean partners for co-operation'. Consultations are held with these countries in order to discuss security issues of common concern.

## Finance

All activities of the institutions, negotiations, *ad hoc* meetings and missions are financed by contributions from member states. The budget for 2000 amounted to €191m., of which some 86% was allocated to OSCE missions and field activities.

## Publications

*Decision Manual* (annually).

*OSCE Handbook* (annually).

*OSCE Newsletter* (monthly).

# ORGANIZATION OF AFRICAN UNITY—OAU

**Address:** POB 3243, Addis Ababa, Ethiopia.

**Telephone:** (1) 517700; **fax:** (1) 513036.

The Organization was founded in 1963 to promote unity and solidarity among African states.

### FORMATION

There were various attempts at establishing an inter-African organization before the OAU Charter was drawn up. In November 1958 Ghana and Guinea (later joined by Mali) drafted a Charter which was to form the basis of a Union of African States. In January 1961 a conference was held at Casablanca, attended by the heads of state of Ghana, Guinea, Mali, Morocco, and representatives of Libya and of the provisional government of the Algerian Republic (GPRA). Tunisia, Nigeria, Liberia and Togo declined the invitation to attend. An African Charter was adopted and it was decided to set up an African Military Command and an African Common Market.

Between October 1960 and March 1961 three conferences were held by French-speaking African countries, at Abidjan, Brazzaville and Yaoundé. None of the 12 countries which attended these meetings had been present at the Casablanca Conference. These conferences led eventually to the signing in September 1961, at Tananarive, of a charter establishing the Union africaine et malgache, later the Organisation commune africaine et mauricienne (OCAM).

In May 1961 a conference was held at Monrovia, Liberia, attended by the heads of state or representatives of 19 countries: Cameroon, Central African Republic, Chad, Congo Republic (ex-French), Côte d'Ivoire, Dahomey, Ethiopia, Gabon, Liberia, Madagascar, Mauritania, Niger, Nigeria, Senegal, Sierra Leone, Somalia, Togo, Tunisia and Upper Volta. They met again (with the exception of Tunisia and with the addition of the ex-Belgian Congo Republic) in January 1962 at Lagos, Nigeria, and set up a permanent secretariat and a standing committee of finance ministers, and accepted a draft charter for an Organization of Inter-African and Malagasy States.

It was the Conference of Addis Ababa, held in 1963, which finally brought together African states despite the regional, political and linguistic differences which divided them. The foreign ministers of 32 African states attended the Preparatory Meeting held in May: Algeria, Burundi, Cameroon, Central African Republic, Chad, Congo (Brazzaville) (now Republic of the Congo), Congo (Léopoldville) (now Democratic Republic of the Congo), Côte d'Ivoire, Dahomey (now Benin), Ethiopia, Gabon, Ghana, Guinea, Liberia, Libya, Madagascar, Mali, Mauritania, Morocco, Niger, Nigeria, Rwanda, Senegal, Sierra Leone, Somalia, Sudan, Tanganyika (now Tanzania), Togo, Tunisia, Uganda, the United Arab Republic (Egypt) and Upper Volta (now Burkina Faso).

The topics discussed by the meeting were: (i) creation of the Organization of African States; (ii) co-operation among African states in the following fields: economic and social; education, culture and science; collective defence; (iii) decolonization; (iv) apartheid and racial discrimination; (v) effects of economic grouping on the economic development of Africa; (vi) disarmament; (vii) creation of a Permanent Conciliation Commission; and (viii) Africa and the United Nations.

The Heads of State Conference which opened on 23 May drew up the Charter of the Organization of African Unity, which was then signed by the heads of 30 states on 25 May 1963. The Charter was essentially functional and reflected a compromise between the concept of a loose association of states favoured by the Monrovia Group and the federal idea supported by the Casablanca Group, and in particular by Ghana.

**MEMBERS***

| | | |
|---|---|---|
| Algeria | Eritrea | Nigeria |
| Angola | Ethiopia | Rwanda |
| Benin | Gabon | São Tomé and Príncipe |
| Botswana | The Gambia | Senegal |
| Burkina Faso | Ghana | Seychelles |
| Burundi | Guinea | Sierra Leone |
| Cameroon | Guinea-Bissau | Somalia |
| Cape Verde | Kenya | South Africa |
| Central African Republic | Lesotho | Sudan |
| Chad | Liberia | Swaziland |
| The Comoros | Libya | Tanzania |
| Congo, Democratic Republic† | Madagascar | Togo |
| Congo, Republic | Malawi | Tunisia |
| Côte d'Ivoire | Mali | Uganda |
| Djibouti | Mauritania | Zambia |
| Egypt | Mauritius | Zimbabwe |
| Equatorial Guinea | Mozambique | |
| | Namibia | |
| | Niger | |

* The Sahrawi Arab Democratic Republic (SADR–Western Sahara) was admitted to the OAU in February 1982, following recognition by 26 of the 50 members, but its membership was disputed by Morocco and other states which claimed that a two-thirds majority was needed to admit a state whose existence was in question. Morocco withdrew from the OAU with effect from November 1985.

† Known as Zaire between 1971 and 1997.

# Organization

(January 2000)

### ASSEMBLY OF HEADS OF STATE

The Assembly of Heads of State and Government meets annually to co-ordinate policies of African states. Resolutions are passed by a two-thirds majority, procedural matters by a simple majority. A chairman is elected at each meeting from among the members, to hold office for one year.

**Chairman** (1999/2000): ABDELAZIZ BOUTEFLIKA (Algeria).

### COUNCIL OF MINISTERS

Consists of ministers of foreign affairs and others and meets twice a year, with provision for extraordinary sessions. Each session elects its own Chairman. Prepares meetings of, and is responsible to, the Assembly of Heads of State.

### GENERAL SECRETARIAT

The permanent headquarters of the organization. It carries out functions assigned to it in the Charter of the OAU and by other agreements and treaties made between member states. Departments: Political; Finance; Education, Science, Culture and Social Affairs; Economic Development and Co-operation; Administration and Conferences. The Secretary-General is elected for a four-year term by the Assembly of Heads of State.

**Secretary-General:** SALIM AHMED SALIM (Tanzania).

### ARBITRATION COMMISSION

**Commission of Mediation, Conciliation and Arbitration:** Addis Ababa; f. 1964; consists of 21 members elected by the Assembly of Heads of State for a five-year term; no state may have more than one member; has a Bureau consisting of a President and two Vice-Presidents, who shall not be eligible for re-election. Its task is to hear and settle disputes between member states by peaceful means.

### SPECIALIZED COMMISSIONS

There are specialized commissions for economic, social, transport and communications affairs; education, science, culture and health; defence; human rights; and labour.

# Finance

Member states contribute in accordance with their United Nations assessment. No member state is assessed for an amount exceeding 20% of the yearly regular budget of the Organization. The biennial budget for 1996-98 was US $61.45m. At March 1999 member states owed some $45m. in outstanding contributions. By July the following countries had had their voting rights in the Organization suspended owing to outstanding arrears: Cape Verde, Central African Republic, Comoros, Equatorial Guinea, Guinea-Bissau, Liberia, Niger, São Tomé and Príncipe, and the Seychelles.

# Principal Events, 1989–99

1989

Jan. A meeting on apartheid, organized by the OAU, resulted in the formation of an African Anti-Apartheid Committee.

May The OAU Chairman undertook a mission of mediation between the governments of Mauritania and Senegal, following ethnic conflict between the citizens of the two countries.

July The Assembly of Heads of State discussed the Namibian independence process, and urged that the UN should ensure that the forthcoming elections there would be fairly conducted. They reiterated requests that an international conference on Africa's substantial external debt should be held.

Sept.–Dec. The newly-elected OAU Secretary-General, Salim Ahmed Salim, attempted to mediate in the dispute between Mauritania and Senegal. In November a mediation committee, comprising representatives of six countries, visited Mauritania and Senegal.

1990

March A monitoring group was formed by the OAU to report on events in South Africa. The OAU urged the international community to continue imposing economic sanctions on South Africa.

July The Assembly of Heads of State reviewed the implications for Africa of recent socio-economic and political changes in Eastern Europe, and of the European Community's progress towards monetary and political union.

1991

June The Assembly of Heads of State signed the treaty on the creation of an African Economic Community (AEC). The treaty was to enter into force after ratification by two-thirds of OAU member states. The Community was to be established by 2025, beginning with a five-year stage during which measures would be taken to strengthen existing economic groupings. The meeting also established a committee of heads of state to assist national reconciliation in Ethiopia; and gave a mandate to the OAU Secretary-General to undertake a mission to assist in restoring political stability in Somalia.

1992

Feb.–March The OAU was involved, together with the UN and the Organization of the Islamic Conference (OIC, q.v.), in mediation between the warring factions in Mogadishu, Somalia. The OAU subsequently continued to assist in efforts to achieve a peace settlement in Somalia.

May An OAU mission was dispatched to South Africa to monitor the continued violence in that country.

June–July Proposals were advanced at the Assembly of Heads of State, held in Dakar, Senegal, for a mechanism to be established within the OAU for 'conflict management, prevention and resolution'. These proposals were accepted in principle, but operational details were to be elaborated at a later stage.

Oct. The *Ad Hoc* Committee on Southern Africa met in Gaborone, Botswana, to discuss a report compiled by a team of OAU experts on practical steps to be taken towards the democratization of South Africa. Plans to send a mission to monitor the Mozambican peace accord were announced.

1993

Feb. A session of the Council of Ministers discussed the OAU's serious financial crisis. The meeting agreed to allocate US $250,000 to the creation of a conflict prevention bureau, and a further $250,000 for the purposes of monitoring elections.

May A Pan-African Conference on Reparations for the suffering caused by colonialism in Africa, organized by the OAU together with the Nigerian Government, was held in Abuja. The Conference appealed to those countries which had benefited from the colonization of Africa and the use of Africans as slaves (particularly European countries and the USA) to make reparations to Africans and their descendants, either in the form of capital transfers, or cancellation of debt.

June Eritrea was admitted as the 52nd member of the OAU. The 29th Assembly of Heads of State resolved to establish a mechanism for conflict prevention and resolution. The mechanism's primary objective was to be anticipation and prevention of conflict. In cases where conflicts had already occurred, the OAU was to undertake peace-making and peace-building activities, including the deployment of civilian or military monitoring missions. However, in the case of a conflict seriously degenerating, assistance would be sought from the United Nations.

July A seminar on the AEC was held in Addis Ababa, Ethiopia, concerned with the popularization of the treaty establishing the Community. Lack of resources emerged as one of the main barriers to the actual creation of the Community.

Sept. The OAU announced the immediate removal of economic sanctions against South Africa, following the approval by that country's Parliament of a bill to establish a transitional executive council prior to the democratic elections, scheduled to be conducted in April 1994.

Oct. The OAU Secretary-General condemned an attempted military coup in Burundi, in which the President and six Cabinet ministers were killed, and the subsequent civil unrest.

Nov. A summit conference of African ministers of foreign affairs, conducted in Addis Ababa, resolved to establish a 200-member OAU protection and observation mission to Burundi, and appealed for international financial and material support to assist the mission. The ministers approved the principles for the establishment of a mechanism for conflict prevention, management and resolution. The meeting suggested that 5% of the OAU budget, but not less than US $1m., be allocated for an OAU Peace Fund to finance the mechanism, and that $0.5m. be made available for 1993.

Dec. A meeting of 11 African Heads of State approved the establishment of the Peace Fund and called for contributions from the international community. A draft statement of the mechanism for conflict prevention, management and resolution, issued by the OAU Secretary-General, expressed support for the efforts to resolve the conflict in Somalia and emphasized the need to promote national reconciliation.

1994

Feb. The Council of Ministers reaffirmed its support for the results of elections in Burundi, which were conducted in 1993, and endorsed the establishment of an OAU mission to promote dialogue and national reconciliation in that country. The Council condemned anti-government forces for the escalation of violence in Angola.

April The OAU mission to South Africa participated as observers of the electoral process. An OAU delegation visited Nigeria and Cameroon to investigate the border dispute between the two countries.

May South Africa was admitted as the 53rd member of the OAU.

June Consultations with each of the conflicting parties in Rwanda were conducted by the OAU. The Assembly of Heads of State, meeting in Tunis, approved a code of conduct for inter-African relations, in order to strengthen political consultation and co-operation for the promotion of security and stability in the region. Nine countries were nominated to serve on the central committee (organ) of the mechanism for conflict prevention, management and resolution. The military component of the OAU mission in Burundi was now deployed in that country, and its mandate was extended until mid-September. (The mission was subsequently granted three-monthly extensions of its mandate.)

Nov. The Secretary-General, noting the Organization's serious financial situation, warned that most activities of the regular budget for 1994/95 would have to be suspended. Certain sanctions were to be imposed on any country that had not paid its contribution in full by 1 June 1995.

1995

March An extraordinary session of the Council of Ministers, held in Cairo, Egypt, adopted an Agenda for Action, which aimed to stimulate African economic and social development. The document emphasized the importance of peace, democratic government and stability in achieving development targets. It also assessed Africa's role in the world economy and the need for structural reforms of countries' economies, in particular in view of agreements reached under the GATT Uruguay Round of trade negotiations. The OAU, together with representatives of the UN and the Commonwealth Secretariat, dispatched a special mission to Sierra Leone, in order to assess means of facilitating the peace process in that country.

April A meeting of the conflict mechanism's central organ, held in Tunis, Tunisia, reviewed OAU peace initiatives. The meeting urged OAU member states to offer humanitarian aid to consolidate the peace process in Angola and for further OAU assistance for the rehabilitation and reconstruction of Somalia. A seminar, organized jointly by the OAU and the International Committee of the Red Cross, assembled military and civil experts in Yaoundé, Cameroon, to discuss the issue of land-mines.

May An 81-member OAU observer group was deployed to monitor a general election in Ethiopia. The group confirmed that the electoral process had been 'free and fair'.

June At the 31st Assembly of Heads of State, held in Addis Ababa, Ethiopia, the Secretary-General observed that the OAU's peace-keeping role had been severely affected by the failure of member states to pay their contributions. Sanctions were to be imposed on those countries which had failed to pay 25% of their arrears by the end of June. (Liberia and Somalia were exempted from this deadline.) The meeting endorsed a proposal to establish a conflict management centre, provisionally in Cairo, Egypt, to strengthen the OAU's role in conflict prevention. The situation in warring African countries was discussed, as well as the problem of large-scale refugee and displaced populations in the region. In addition, member states urged the international community to end the application of sanctions against Libya.

Sept. An extraordinary meeting of the conflict mechanism's central organ condemned the attempted assassination of Egypt's President Mubarak prior to the Heads of State meeting in June. The committee censured Sudan for protecting the alleged perpetrators of the attack and for supporting other terrorist elements in the country.

Oct. OAU observers monitored the conduct of elections in Zanzibar and attempted to mediate between the parties when the vote failed to secure a decisive result.

Nov. A 50-member OAU observer group was deployed to monitor elections in Algeria, as part of an international team.

1996

Feb. The Council of Ministers reiterated the OAU's readiness to promote and support dialogue and reconciliation in Burundi. However, the meeting did not support military intervention in that country, despite a UN report proposing international co-operation with the OAU to establish a stand-by force for Burundi.

March The UN Secretary-General launched a system-wide Special Initiative on Africa, which was based on the development objectives outlined in the OAU Agenda for Action (see above). Funds were to be allocated under the Initiative to strengthen the OAU's capacity for conflict prevention, management and resolution.

May-June The OAU assisted the International Peace Academy to conduct a meeting of international organizations, in Cape Town, South Africa, to promote the OAU's conflict mechanism, under the theme of 'Civil Society and Conflict Management in Africa'.

July The 32nd Assembly of Heads of State agreed to support a plan, formulated earlier that month by the Governments of Tanzania, Uganda and Ethiopia, to send troops to Burundi in a peace-keeping capacity. The Assembly requested logistical and financial support from the international community for the initiative. In a separate declaration OAU leaders expressed their support for Boutros Boutros-Ghali's candidacy for a second term as the UN Secretary-General. The endorsement was opposed by the President of Rwanda, Pasteur Bizimungu, who condemned the lack of UN protection afforded to his country during the civil unrest in 1994. At the end of July, following a military coup in Burundi, the OAU endorsed a decision of seven east and central African states to impose economic sanctions against the new regime.

Oct. The OAU Secretary-General cautiously endorsed a US proposal to establish an African military force for the protection of civilian populations in areas of conflict. A regional committee of the OAU declared its support for the continuation of the economic embargo against Burundi.

Nov. An OAU delegation, meeting with the heads of state of eight African countries in Nairobi, Kenya, supported the establishment of an international humanitarian force, to be sent to Zaire (although this was never deployed).

Dec. The OAU President, in an attempt to overcome the impasse reached regarding the election of a new UN Secretary-General (owing to US opposition to Boutros-Ghali), confirmed that African nations should propose alternative candidates for the position.

1997

Jan. The UN and the OAU appointed Muhamed Sahnoun as a joint Special Representative for the Great Lakes Region.

Feb. The 65th session of the Council of Ministers, meeting in Libya, expressed its support of that country in the face of sanctions imposed upon it by the international community. The OAU welcomed the newly-elected Secretary-General of the UN, the Ghanaian, Kofi Annan. The situation in Zaire was discussed and an extraordinary summit of the OAU's conflict management mechanism was scheduled for March. Further donations to the OAU Peace Fund were requested.

March A special summit of the OAU Organ on conflict prevention, management and resolution, which was attended by delegations from both the Zairean Government and the rebel AFDL forces, called for an immediate cease-fire and concluded a provisional agreement for negotiations between the two sides based on a five-point plan that had been formulated by Sahnoun and approved by the UN Security Council in February.

June The Assembly of Heads of State, meeting in Harare, Zimbabwe, condemned the military coup in Sierra Leone, which took place in May, and endorsed the intervention of ECOMOG troops in order to restore a democratic government in that country. The OAU stated that future coups in the continent would not be tolerated, and the importance of universal human rights to be established across Africa was reiterated throughout the meeting. The first meeting between ministers of the OAU and the European Union was held in New York, USA. The inaugural meeting of the African Economic Community took place.

July The UNDP donated US $3m. to the OAU conflict management mechanism. An OAU observer group was deployed to monitor elections in Liberia.

Aug. The OAU appointed a special envoy to the Comoros, Pierre Yere, following a declaration of independence by separatists on the islands of Anjouan and Mohéli.

Oct. Chiefs of Defence Staff, meeting in Harare, Zimbabwe, proposed a series of measures to strengthen the capacity of African countries to lead peace-keeping missions in the region, which included the establishment of operations, training and early-warning units.

Nov. A group of OAU military observers was reported to have been dispatched to the Comoros.

Dec. The OAU organized an international conference, held in Addis Ababa, Ethiopia, which aimed to resolve the dispute between the Comoran Government and the secessionists and to initiate a process of political dialogue. In a separate meeting OAU ministers of justice adopted a protocol approving the creation of a permanent African court of human rights (based on the African Charter of Human and People's Rights, signed in 1981).

1998

Feb. The OAU concluded an agreement with La Francophonie (q.v.) to co-operate in economic and cultural areas.

March The OAU declared its support for ECOWAS efforts in restoring President Ahmed Tejan Kabbah to power in Sierra Leone. A nine-member OAU ministerial mission visited the Comoros in an attempt to further a peaceful solution to the dispute; however, it was prevented from conducting discussions with the separatist leaders in Anjouan.

June Fighting between Eritrea and Ethiopia dominated discussions at the 34th Assembly of Heads of State, held in Burkina Faso. It was agreed to send a delegation to attempt to resolve the dispute. The Assembly also considered economic issues affecting the region, and resolved to disregard certain economic and humanitarian sanctions imposed against Libya, owing to that country's refusal to release two people suspected of the bombing of a US aircraft over the United Kingdom in 1988. The OAU leaders reiterated their support for the proposal of the Libyan authorities that the suspects be tried in a neutral venue. The OAU agreed to establish a seven-member International Panel of Eminent Personalities to examine all aspects of the genocide that occurred in Rwanda in 1994; a special trust fund was to be established to finance its activities. (The Panel met for the first time in October.)

July An OAU delegation conducted discussions with the Eritrean and Ethiopian authorities in an attempt to conclude a peace settlement. The OAU Secretary-General also expressed support for efforts to negotiate a settlement between the conflicting parties in Guinea-Bissau.

Aug. The OAU expressed its concern at the escalating violence in the Democratic Republic of the Congo (DRC), in particular the involvement of armed forces from other countries in the region, and resolved to send a mission to negotiate a cease-fire. An OAU ministerial committee (comprising representatives of Burkina Faso, Djibouti and Zimbabwe) pursued efforts to negotiate an accord between Eritrea and Ethiopia. The proposed OAU framework agreement was based on a US-Rwandan peace plan, presented to both sides in June, and included implementation of an immediate cease-fire, the initiation of peace discussions and recognition of the positions prior to the start of hostilities in May. At the end of August delegates of the SADC held talks at OAU headquarters, and urged an immediate cease-fire by all sides in the Congolese conflict.

Sept. The OAU Secretary-General supported a request of the Sudanese Government for an international commission of inquiry to be established to examine the US airstrike on a pharmaceutical plant in Khartoum, in retaliation to terrorist bombing incidents in August.

Nov. A meeting of the OAU mediation committee on the Eritrean/Ethiopian dispute was held in Ouagadougou.

Dec. A special meeting of the conflict resolution mechanism, at the level of heads of state, was held to pursue a peace settlement in the DRC. The ongoing Eritrean-Ethiopian dispute and the unstable security situation in Angola were also considered. A Special OAU Ministerial Meeting on Refugees, Returnees and Internally Displaced Persons was convened, in Khartoum; the meeting urged member states to implement efforts to mitigate problems associated with the mass movement of populations, and to promote humanitarian assistance efforts.

1999

Feb. A high-level OAU delegation, including the Chairman and Secretary-General, replaced the previous ministerial committee on a visit to Eritrea, following that country's refusal to negotiate with a representative of Djibouti. In early February an OAU delegation conducted talks with representatives of the Anjouan separatist factions and the Government of the Comoros; however, the negotiations failed to conclude an agreement on a political settlement to the conflict or on the establishment of an OAU peace-keeping mission.

March An OAU mission visited the authorities in Ethiopia and Eritrea to pursue efforts towards settling the conflict. The Chairman of the OAU cancelled a special summit meeting on African conflict scheduled to take place at the end of March, owing to controversy over the extension of invitations to rebel leaders from those countries affected by civil conflict. A meeting of the Council of Ministers appointed the President of Zambia, Frederick Chiluba, to co-ordinate efforts to resolve the conflict in the DRC. The meeting also imposed sanctions against eight countries that had failed to pay their annual contributions to the Organization for two years. The sanctions denied nationals from those countries the right to vote or to work at the OAU offices, which resulted in a substantial reduction in personnel at OAU headquarters.

April The first OAU conference on human rights, at ministerial level, was convened in Mauritius.

An inter-island conference was held, under OAU auspices, in Antananarivo, Madagascar, to conclude arrangements for a new political union in the Comoros. At the end of the month, however, the Government of the Comoros was removed by army officers following renewed unrest. The OAU condemned the coup, but urged the Anjouan representatives to sign the agreed framework.

May The OAU announced the withdrawal of the military component of its observer mission in the Comoros. A new round of talks with the heads of government of Eritrea and Ethiopia was initiated to provide for a cessation of hostilities.

July The summit meeting, held in Algiers, was concerned with the economic development of Africa and prospects for greater integration, as well as ongoing conflicts in the region. The meeting requested the Secretary-General to send a fact-finding mission to Somalia to assess its post-conflict needs. The OAU also appointed a senior Algerian army general to chair a Joint Military Commission in the DRC, which was to be established according to the terms of a peace accord signed earlier in July. Heads of state declared that the Organization would not recognize any authority in a member state which assumed power illegally. An African convention for the prevention and combating of terrorism was signed, which included provisions for the exchange of information to help counter terrorism and for signatory states to refrain from granting asylum to terrorists. The meeting also declared that 2000 was to be the Year of Peace, Security and Solidarity in Africa.

Sept. An extraordinary summit meeting was convened in Sirte, Libya, at the request of the Libyan leader Col al-Qaddafi, in order to promote African unity and to demonstrate African solidarity with Libya. The meeting determined to establish an African Union, based on the principles and objectives of the OAU. A new charter was to be adopted by 2001. In addition, heads of state declared their commitment to accelerating the establishment of regional institutions, including an African parliament, court of justice, and central bank, as well as the implementation of an economic and monetary union. The Ethiopian Government reportedly rejected the final technical arrangements for implementation of the framework peace plan, which had been approved by Eritrea in August.

Oct. A conference on Industrial Partnerships and Investment in Africa was held in Dakar, Senegal, jointly organized by OAU with UNIDO, the ECA, the African Development Bank, and the Alliance for Africa's Industrialization.

Dec. The OAU Chairman, President Bouteflika of Algeria, urged the removal of UN sanctions against Libya. The OAU condemned the military's seizure of power in Côte d'Ivoire.

# Specialized Agencies

**African Accounting Council:** POB 11223, Kinshasa, Democratic Republic of the Congo; tel. (12) 33567; f. 1979; provides assistance to institutions in member countries on standardization of accounting; promotes education, further training and research in accountancy and related areas of study. Publ. *Information and Liaison Bulletin* (every two months).

**African Bureau for Educational Sciences:** 29 ave de la Justice, BP 1764, Kinshasa I, Democratic Republic of the Congo; tel. (12) 22006; f. 1973 to conduct educational research. Publs *Bulletin d'Information* (quarterly), *Revue africaine des sciences de l'éducation* (2 a year), *Répertoire africain des institutions de recherche* (annually).

**African Civil Aviation Commission—AFCAC:** 15 blvd de la République, BP 2356, Dakar, Senegal; tel. 839-93-93; fax 823-26-61; f. 1969 to encourage co-operation in all civil aviation activities; promotes co-ordination and better utilization and development of African air transport systems and the standardization of aircraft, flight equipment and training programmes for pilots and mechanics; organizes working groups and seminars, and compiles statistics. Pres. Capt. SHETTIMA ABBA-GANA (Nigeria); Sec. A. CHEIFFOU (acting).

**Pan-African News Agency—PANA:** BP 4650, Dakar, Senegal; tel. 824-14-10; fax 824-13-90; internet www.africanews.org/PANA; regional headquarters in Khartoum, Sudan; Lusaka, Zambia; Kinshasa, Democratic Republic of the Congo; Lagos, Nigeria; Tripoli, Libya; began operations in May 1983; receives information from national news agencies and circulates news in English and French. Following financial problems, plans to restructure the agency at a cost of US $4.7m., in order to allow shares to be held by the private sector, were announced in June 1997. Capital was to be increased by 25,000 shares, while the agency was to be renamed PANA Presse. Co-ordinator BABACAR FALL. Publ. *PANA Review*.

**Pan-African Postal Union—PAPU:** POB 6026, Arusha, Tanzania; tel. (57) 8603; fax (57) 8606; f. 1980 to extend members' co-operation in the improvement of postal services. Sec.-Gen. GEZAHEGNE GEBREWOLD (Ethiopia). Publ. *PAPU Bulletin*.

**Pan-African Railways Union:** BP 687, Kinshasa, Democratic Republic of the Congo; tel. (12) 23861; f. 1972 to standardize, expand, co-ordinate and improve members' railway services; the ultimate aim is to link all systems; main organs: Gen. Assembly, Exec. Bd, Gen. Secr., five tech. cttees. Mems in 30 African countries.

**Pan-African Telecommunications Union:** POB 7248, Kinshasa, Democratic Republic of the Congo; f. 1977; co-ordinates devt of telecommunications networks and services in Africa.

**Supreme Council for Sports in Africa:** BP 1363, Yaoundé, Cameroon; tel. and fax 23-95-80; Sec.-Gen. Dr AWOTURE ELEYAE (Nigeria). Publs *SCSA News* (6 a year), *African Sports Movement Directory* (annually).

# ORGANIZATION OF AMERICAN STATES—OAS

## (ORGANIZACIÓN DE LOS ESTADOS AMERICANOS—OEA)

**Address:** 17th St and Constitution Ave, NW, Washington, DC 20006, USA.

**Telephone:** (202) 458-3000; **fax:** (202) 458-3967; **e-mail:** pi@oas.org; **internet:** www.oas.org.

The OAS was founded at Bogotá, Colombia, in 1948 (succeeding the International Union of American Republics, founded in 1890) to foster peace, security, mutual understanding and co-operation among the nations of the Western Hemisphere.

### MEMBERS

| | |
|---|---|
| Antigua and Barbuda | Guyana |
| Argentina | Haiti |
| Bahamas | Honduras |
| Barbados | Jamaica |
| Belize | Mexico |
| Bolivia | Nicaragua |
| Brazil | Panama |
| Canada | Paraguay |
| Chile | Peru |
| Colombia | Saint Christopher and Nevis |
| Costa Rica | Saint Lucia |
| Cuba* | Saint Vincent and the Grenadines |
| Dominica | Suriname |
| Dominican Republic | Trinidad and Tobago |
| Ecuador | USA |
| El Salvador | Uruguay |
| Grenada | Venezuela |
| Guatemala | |

* The Cuban Government was suspended from OAS activities in 1962.

**Permanent Observers:** Algeria, Angola, Austria, Belgium, Bosnia and Herzegovina, Bulgaria, Croatia, Cyprus, Czech Republic, Egypt, Equatorial Guinea, Finland, France, Germany, Ghana, Greece, the Holy See, Hungary, India, Israel, Italy, Japan, Kazakhstan, the Republic of Korea, Latvia, Lebanon, Morocco, the Netherlands, Pakistan, Poland, Portugal, Romania, Russia, Saudi Arabia, Spain, Sri Lanka, Sweden, Switzerland, Thailand, Tunisia, Turkey, Ukraine, the United Kingdom, Yemen and the European Union.

## Organization

(January 2000)

### GENERAL ASSEMBLY

The Assembly meets annually and may also hold special sessions when convoked by the Permanent Council. As the supreme organ of the OAS, it decides general action and policy.

### MEETINGS OF CONSULTATION OF MINISTERS OF FOREIGN AFFAIRS

Meetings are held to consider problems of an urgent nature and of common interest to member states; they may be held at the request of any member state.

### PERMANENT COUNCIL

The Council meets regularly throughout the year at OAS headquarters. It is composed of one representative of each member state with the rank of ambassador; each government may accredit alternate representatives and advisers and when necessary appoint an interim representative. The office of Chairman is held in turn by each of the representatives, following alphabetical order according to the names of the countries in Spanish. The Vice-Chairman is determined in the same way, following reverse alphabetical order. Their terms of office are three months.

The Council acts as an organ of consultation and oversees the maintenance of friendly relations between members. It supervises the work of the OAS and promotes co-operation with a variety of other international bodies including the United Nations. The official languages are English, French, Portuguese and Spanish.

### INTER-AMERICAN COUNCIL FOR INTEGRAL DEVELOPMENT—CIDI

The Council was established in 1996, replacing the Inter-American Economic and Social Council and the Inter-American Council for Education, Science and Culture. Its aim is to promote co-operation among the countries of the region, in order to accelerate economic and social development. CIDI's work focuses on eight areas: social development and education; cultural development; the generation of productive employment; economic diversification, integration and trade liberalization; strengthening democratic institutions; the exchange of scientific and technological information; the development of tourism; and sustainable environmental development. CIDI comprises three committees: a special committee on trade, a social development committee and an inter-American committee for sustainable development.

**Executive Secretary:** LEONEL ZÚÑIGA (Mexico).

### INTER-AMERICAN JURIDICAL COMMITTEE

**Address:** Rua Senador Vergueiro 81, Rio de Janeiro, RJ 22230-000, Brazil.

**Telephone:** (21) 558-3204; **fax:** (21) 558-4600; **e-mail:** cjioea@trip.com.br.

The Committee is composed of 11 jurists, nationals of different member states, elected for a period of four years, with the possibility of re-election. The Committee's purposes are: to serve as an advisory body to the Organization on juridical matters; to promote the progressive development and codification of international law; and to study juridical problems relating to the integration of the developing countries in the hemisphere, and, in so far as may appear desirable, the possibility of attaining uniformity in legislation.

**Secretary:** MANOEL TOLOMEI MOLETTA.

### INTER-AMERICAN COMMISSION ON HUMAN RIGHTS

**Address:** 1889 F St, NW, Washington, DC 20006, USA.

**Telephone:** (202) 458-6002; **fax:** (202) 458-3992; **e-mail:** cidhoea@oas.org; **internet:** www.cidh.oas.org.

The Commission was established in 1960 and comprises seven members. It promotes the observance and protection of human rights in the member states of the OAS; it examines and reports on the human rights situation in member countries, and provides consultative services.

**President:** ALVARO TIRADO.

### INTER-AMERICAN COURT OF HUMAN RIGHTS

**Address:** Apdo Postal 6906-1000, San José, Costa Rica.

**Telephone:** 234-0581; **fax:** 234-0584; **e-mail:** corteidh@racsa.co.cr; **internet:** www.corteidh-oea.nu.or.cr/ci.

The Court was formally established in 1978, as an autonomous judicial institution whose purpose is to apply and interpret the American Convention on Human Rights (which entered into force in 1978: at November 1998 the Convention had been ratified by 25 OAS member states, of which 18 had accepted the competence of the Court). The Court comprises seven jurists from OAS member states.

**President:** ANTÔNIO CANÇADO TRINDADE.

**Secretary:** MANUEL E. VENTURA-ROBLES.

### GENERAL SECRETARIAT

The Secretariat, the central and permanent organ of the Organization, performs the duties entrusted to it by the General Assembly, Meetings of Consultation of Ministers of Foreign Affairs and the Councils.

**Secretary-General:** CÉSAR GAVIRIA TRUJILLO (Colombia).

**Assistant Secretary-General:** CHRISTOPHER THOMAS (Trinidad and Tobago).

## Activities

In December 1994 the first Summit of the Americas was convened in Miami, USA. The meeting endorsed the concept of a Free Trade Area of the Americas (FTAA), and also approved a Plan of Action to strengthen democracy, eradicate poverty and promote sustainable development throughout the region. The OAS subsequently embarked on an extensive process of reform and modernization to strengthen its capacity to undertake a lead role in implementing the Plan. The Organization realigned its priorities in order to respond to the mandates emerging from the Summit and developed a new institutional framework for technical assistance and co-operation, although many activities continued to be undertaken by the specialized or associated organizations of the OAS (see below). In 1998, following the second Summit of the Americas, held in April, in Santiago, Chile, the OAS established an Office of Summit Follow-Up, in order to strengthen its servicing of the meetings, and to co-ordinate tasks assigned to the Organization.

## TRADE AND ECONOMIC INTEGRATION

A trade unit was established in 1995 in order to strengthen the Organization's involvement in trade issues and the process of economic integration, which became a priority area following the first Summit of the Americas. The unit was to provide technical assistance in support of the establishment of the FTAA, and to co-ordinate activities between regional and sub-regional integration organizations. In 1999 the unit was providing technical support to six of the nine FTAA negotiating groups, relating to the following areas: investment; services; dispute settlement; intellectual property rights; subsidies; anti-dumping and countervailing duties; and competition policy.

The unit operates in consultation with a Special Committee on Trade, which was established in 1993 comprising high-level officials representing each member state. The Committee studies trade issues, provides technical analyses of the economic situation in member countries and the region, and prepares reports for ministerial meetings of the FTAA. The OAS also administers an Inter-American Foreign Trade Information System which facilitates the exchange of information.

## DEMOCRACY AND CIVIL SOCIETY

Two principal organs of the OAS, the Inter-American Commission on Human Rights and the Inter-American Court of Human Rights, work to secure respect for human rights in all member countries. The OAS aims to encourage more member governments to accept jurisdiction of the Court. The OAS also collaborates with member states in the strengthening of representative institutions within government and as part of a democratic civil society.

Through its unit for the promotion of democracy, established in 1990, the OAS provides electoral technical assistance to member states and undertakes missions to observe the conduct of elections. In 1999, for example, OAS observers monitored general elections in Grenada, in January, and in Panama, in April, and supervised a constitutional referendum and a presidential election held in Guatemala, in May and in November/December respectively. The OAS also supports societies in post-conflict situations and recently-installed governments to promote democratic practices. In 1993 the OAS participated in a joint civil mission with the UN in Haiti in order to promote respect for human rights and the re-establishment of a democratically-elected government.

In June 1991 the OAS General Assembly approved a resolution on representative democracy, which authorized the Secretary-General to summon a session of the Permanent Council in cases where a democratically-elected government had been overthrown or democratic procedures abandoned in member states. The Council could then convene an *ad hoc* meeting of ministers of foreign affairs to consider the situation. The procedure was invoked following political developments in Haiti, in September 1991, and Peru, in April 1992. Ministers determined to impose trade and diplomatic sanctions against Haiti and sent missions to both countries. The resolution was incorporated into the Protocol of Washington, amending the OAS charter, which was adopted in December 1992 and entered into force in September 1997.

An OAS Assistance Programme for Demining in Central America was established in 1992, as part of efforts to facilitate the social and economic rehabilitation of the region. By 1999 the programme had provided training for 250 de-mining experts and assisted countries in the clearance of some 28,000 anti-personnel devices. Technical support was provided by the Inter-American Defense Board (see below).

The OAS has adopted an Inter-American Programme of Co-operation to Combat Corruption and a Convention against Corruption, in order to address the problem at national level. A working group on transparency aims to promote accountability throughout the public sector and supports national institutions responsible for combating corruption. In 1997 the OAS organized a meeting of experts to consider measures for the prevention of crime. The meeting adopted a work programme which included commitments to undertake police training in criminology and crime investigation, to exchange legal and practical knowledge, and to measure crime and violence in member countries.

## REGIONAL SECURITY

In 1991 the General Assembly established a working group to consider issues relating to the promotion of co-operation in regional security. A Special Commission on Hemispheric Security was subsequently established, while two regional conferences have been held on security and confidence-building measures. Voluntary practices agreed by member states include the holding of border meetings to co-ordinate activities, co-operation in natural disaster management, and the exchange of information on military exercises and expenditure. From 1995 meetings of ministers of defence have been convened regularly, which provide a forum for discussion of security matters.

The OAS is actively involved in efforts to combat the abuse and trafficking of illegal drugs. In 1996 members approved a Hemispheric Anti-drug Strategy, reiterating their commitment to combating the problem. Negotiations to design and implement a mechanism to ensure compliance with the Strategy were initiated in May 1998. Also under consideration were measures to support national anti-drugs institutions and the formulation of national plans of action to combat drugs-trafficking. The training of police and customs officers was to be enhanced. Since 1996 an OAS group of experts has undertaken efforts to assist countries in reducing the demand for illegal substances. Activities include the implementation of prevention programmes for street children; the development of communication strategies; and education and community projects relating to the prevention of drug dependence.

The first Specialized Inter-American Conference on Terrorism was held in Lima, Peru, in April 1996. A Declaration and Plan of Action were adopted, according to which member states agreed to co-operate and implement measures to combat terrorism and organized crime. A second conference was held in Mar del Plata, Argentina, in 1998. Member states recommended the establishment of an Inter-American Committee against Terrorism to implement decisions relating to judicial, police and intelligence co-operation.

## SOCIAL DEVELOPMENT AND EDUCATION

In June 1996 the OAS established a specialized unit for social development and education to assist governments and social institutions of member states to formulate public policies and implement initiatives relating to employment and labour issues, education development, social integration and poverty elimination. It was also to provide technical and operational support for the implementation of inter-American programmes in those sectors, and to promote the exchange of information among experts and professionals working in those fields. In June 1997 the OAS approved an Inter-American Programme to Combat Poverty. The unit serves as the technical secretariat for annual meetings on social development that were to be convened within the framework of the Programme. The unit also administers the Social Networks of Latin America and the Caribbean project, and its co-ordinating committee, which promotes sub-regional co-operation to combat poverty and discrimination. In 1999 the unit was to implement a project funded by the Inter-American Development Bank to place interns and trainees within the Social Network institutions and to promote exchanges between the institutions.

The first meeting of ministers of education of the Americas was held in Brasilia, Brazil, in July 1998, based on the mandate of the second Summit of the Americas. The meeting approved an Inter-American Education Programme, which had been formulated by the unit for social development and education, which incorporated the following six priority initiatives: education for priority social sectors; strengthening educational management and institutional development; education for work and youth development; education for citizenship and sustainability in multicultural societies; training in the use of new technologies in teaching the official languages of the OAS; and training of teachers and education administrators. Other programmes in the education sector are undertaken with international agencies and non-governmental organizations.

The OAS supports member states to formulate and implement programmes to promote productive employment and vocational training, to develop small businesses and other employment generation initiatives, and to regulate labour migration. In 1998 the OAS initiated the Labour Market Information System project, which aimed to provide reliable and up-to-date indicators of the labour situation in member countries, to determine the impact of economic policy on the labour situation, and to promote the exchange of information among relevant national and regional institutions. Labour issues were addressed by the second Summit of the Americas, and, following an Inter-American Conference of Labour Ministers, held in Viña del Mar, Chile, in October 1998, two working groups were established to consider the globalization of the economy and its social and labour dimension and the modernization of the state and labour administration.

## SUSTAINABLE DEVELOPMENT AND THE ENVIRONMENT

In 1996 a summit meeting on social development adopted a plan of action, based on the objectives of the UN Conference on the Environment and Development, which was held in Rio de Janeiro, Brazil, in June 1992. The OAS was to participate in an inter-agency group to monitor implementation of the action plan. The OAS has subsequently established new financing mechanisms and networks of experts relating to aspects of sustainable development. Technical co-operation activities include multinational basin management; a strategic plan for the Amazon; natural disaster management; and the sustainable development of border areas in Central America and South America.

The following initiatives have also been undertaken: a Caribbean Disaster Mitigation Project, to help those countries to counter and manage the affects of natural disasters; a Natural Hazards Project to provide a general programme of support to assess member states' vulnerability, to provide technical assistance and training to mitigate the effects of a disaster, and to assist in the planning and formulation of development and preparedness policies; the Renewable Energy in the Americas initiative to promote co-operation and strengthen renewable energy and energy efficiency; and the Inter-American Water Resources Network, which aims to promote collaboration, training and the exchange of information within the sector.

### SCIENCE AND TECHNOLOGY

The OAS supports and develops activities to contribute to the advancement of science and technology throughout the Americas, and to promote its contribution to social and sustainable development. In particular, it promotes collaboration, dissemination of information and improved communication between experts and institutions working in the sector. Specialized bodies and projects have been established to promote activities in different fields, for example metrology; co-operation between institutions of accreditation, certification and inspection; the development of instruments of measurements and analysis of science and technology; chemistry; the development of technical standardization and related activities; and collaboration between experts and institutions involved in biotechnology and food technology. The OAS also maintains an information system to facilitate access to databases on science and technology throughout the region.

### TOURISM AND CULTURE

A specialized unit for tourism was established in 1996 in order to strengthen and co-ordinate activities for the sustainable development of the tourism industry in the Americas. The unit supports regional and sub-regional conferences and workshops, as well as the Inter-American Travel Congress, which was convened for the first time in 1993 to serve as a forum to formulate region-wide tourism policies. The unit also undertakes research and analysis of the industry.

In 1998 the OAS approved an Inter-American Programme of Culture to support efforts being undertaken by member states and to promote co-operation in areas such as cultural diversity; protection of cultural heritage; training and dissemination of information; and the promotion of cultural tourism. The OAS also assists with the preparation of national and multilateral cultural projects, and co-operates with the private sector to protect and promote cultural assets and events in the region.

### COMMUNICATIONS

In June 1993 the OAS General Assembly approved the establishment of an Inter-American Telecommunication Commission. The body has technical autonomy, within the statute and mandate agreed by the Assembly. It aims to facilitate and promote the development of communications in all member countries, in collaboration with the private sector and other organizations, and serves as the principal advisory body of the OAS on matters related to telecommunications.

A Special Inter-American Ports Commission was established by the General Assembly in 1998. It comprises seven standing committees to co-ordinate and develop activities in the following areas: port management; port operations; port training; port policy; inland ports and waterways; labour issues; and the privatization of ports.

## Finance

The OAS budget for 2000, approved by the General Assembly in mid-1999, amounted to US $88m.

## Publications

(in English and Spanish)

*Américas* (6 a year).

*Annual Report*.

*Catalog of Publications* (annually).

*Ciencia Interamericana* (quarterly).

*La Educación* (quarterly).

*Statistical Bulletin* (quarterly).

Numerous cultural, legal and scientific reports and studies.

## Specialized and Associated Organizations

**Inter-American Children's Institute:** Avda 8 de Octubre 2904, Montevideo, Uruguay; tel. (2) 4872150; fax (2) 4873242; e-mail iin@redfacil.com.uy; internet www.iin.org.uy; f. 1927; promotes the implementation of the Convention on the Rights of the Child in the region; assists in the development of child-oriented public policies; promotes co-operation between states; and aims to develop awareness of problems affecting children and young people in the region. The Institute organizes workshops, seminars, courses, training programmes and conferences on issues relating to children, including, for example, the rights of children, children with disabilities, and the child welfare system. It also provides advisory services, statistical data and other relevant information to authorities and experts throughout the region. Dir-Gen. Rodrigo Quintana (Chile). Publs *Boletín* (quarterly), *IINfancia* (2 a year).

**Inter-American Commission of Women:** 1889 F St, NW, Suite 880 Washington, DC 20006, USA; tel. (202) 458-6084; fax (202) 458-6094; f. 1928 for the extension of civil, political, economic, social and cultural rights for women. In 1991 a Seed Fund was established to provide financing for grass-roots projects consistent with the Commission's objectives. Pres. Dulce Maria Sauri Riancho (Mexcio); Exec. Sec. Carmen Lomellin.

**Inter-American Defense Board:** 2600 16th St, NW, Washington, DC 20441, USA; tel. (202) 939-6600; works in liaison with member governments to plan and train for the common defence of the western hemisphere; operates the Inter-American Defense College. Chair. Maj.-Gen. John C. Thompson (USA).

**Inter-American Drug Abuse Control Commission—CICAD:** c/o OAS Secretariat; tel. (202) 458-3178; fax (202) 458-3658; e-mail cicad@oas.org; internet www.cicad.oas.org; f. 1986 by the OAS to promote and facilitate multilateral co-operation in the control and prevention of the trafficking, production and use of illegal drugs. Mems 34 countries. Exec. Sec. David R. Beall. Publ. *Statistical Survey* (annually).

**Inter-American Indian Institute:** Av. de las Fuentes 106, Col. Jardines del Pedregal 01900 México, DF, Mexico; tel. (5) 595-8410; fax (5) 652-0089; f. 1940; conducts research on the situation of the indigenous peoples of America; assists the exchange of information; promotes indigenist policies in member states aimed at the elimination of poverty and development within Indian communities, and to secure their position as ethnic groups within a democratic society. Dir Dr José Manuel del Val (Mexico); Exec. Co-ordinator Evangelina Mendizabal. Publs *América Indígena* (quarterly), *Anuario Indigenista*.

**Inter-American Institute for Co-operation on Agriculture:** Apdo 55–2200 Coronado, San José, Costa Rica; tel. 229-0222; fax 229-4741; f. 1942 (as the Inter-American Institute of Agricultural Sciences: new name 1980); supports the efforts of member states to improve agricultural development and rural well-being; encourages co-operation between regional organizations, and provides a forum for the exchange of experience. Dir-Gen. Carlos Aquino González (Dominican Republic). Publ. *Comuniica* (quarterly).

**Inter-American Telecommunication Commission:** 1889 F St, NW, Washington, DC 20006, USA; tel. (202) 458-3004; fax (202) 458-6854; e-mail citel@oas.org; f. 1993.

**Pan American Health Organization:** 525 23rd St, NW, Washington, DC 20037, USA; tel. (202) 974-3000; fax (202) 974-3663; e-mail webmaster@paho.org; internet www.paho.org; f. 1902; co-ordinates regional efforts to improve health; maintains close relations with national health organizations and serves as the Regional Office for the Americas of the World Health Organization. Dir Sir George Alleyne (Barbados).

**Pan-American Institute of Geography and History:** Ex-Arzobispado 29, 11869 México, DF, Mexico; tel. (5) 277-5888; fax (5) 271-6172; e-mail ipgh@laneta.apc.org; internet www.spin.com.mx/~ipgh; f. 1928; co-ordinates and promotes the study of cartography, geophysics, geography, history, anthropology, archaeology, folklore, and other related scientific studies. Pres. Dr Noé Pineda Portillo (Honduras); Sec.-Gen. Carlos Carvallo Yáñez (Chile). Publs *Boletín Aéreo* (quarterly), *Revista Cartográfica* (2 a year), *Revista Geográfica* (2 a year), *Revista Historia de América* (2 a year), *Revista de Arqueología Americana* (2 a year), *Revista Geofísica* (2 a year), *Folklore Americano* (2 a year), *Boletín de Antropología Americana* (2 a year).

# ORGANIZATION OF ARAB PETROLEUM EXPORTING COUNTRIES—OAPEC

**Address:** POB 20501, Safat 13066, Kuwait.

**Telephone:** 4844500; **fax:** 4815747; **e-mail:** oapec@kuwait.net; **internet:** www.kuwait.net/~oapec.

OAPEC was established in 1968 to safeguard the interests of members and to determine ways and means for their co-operation in various forms of economic activity in the petroleum industry. In 1997 member states accounted for 25.95% of total world petroleum production.

### MEMBERS

| | | |
|---|---|---|
| Algeria | Kuwait | Saudi Arabia |
| Bahrain | Libya | Syria |
| Egypt | Qatar | United Arab Emirates |
| Iraq | | |

## Organization

(January 2000)

### MINISTERIAL COUNCIL

The Council consists normally of the ministers of petroleum of the member states, and forms the supreme authority of the Organization, responsible for drawing up its general policy, directing its activities and laying down its governing rules. It meets twice yearly, and may hold extraordinary sessions. Chairmanship is on an annual rotation basis.

### EXECUTIVE BUREAU

Assists the Council to direct the management of the Organization, approves staff regulations, reviews the budget, and refers it to the Council, considers matters relating to the Organization's agreements and activities and draws up the agenda for the Council. The Bureau comprises one senior official from each member state. Chairmanship is by rotation. The Bureau convenes at least three times a year.

### GENERAL SECRETARIAT

**Secretary-General:** ABD AL-AZIZ AT-TURKI (Saudi Arabia).

Besides the Office of the Secretary-General, there are four departments: Finance and Administrative Affairs, Information and Library, Technical Affairs and Economics. The last two form the Arab Centre for Energy Studies (which was established in 1983). At the end of 1997 there were 21 professional staff members and 30 general personnel at the General Secretariat.

### JUDICIAL TRIBUNAL

The Tribunal comprises seven judges from Arab countries. Its task is to settle differences in interpretation and application of the OAPEC Agreement, arising between members and also between OAPEC and its affiliates; disputes among member countries on petroleum activities falling within OAPEC's jurisdiction and not under the sovereignty of member countries; and disputes that the Ministerial Council decides to submit to the Tribunal.

**President:** FARIS AL-WAGAYAN.

**Registrar:** Dr RIAD AD-DAOUDI.

## Activities

OAPEC co-ordinates different aspects of the Arab petroleum industry through the joint undertakings described below. It co-operates with the League of Arab States and other Arab organizations, and attempts to link petroleum research institutes in the Arab states. It organizes or participates in conferences and seminars, many of which are held jointly with non-Arab organizations in order to enhance Arab and international co-operation.

OAPEC provides training in technical matters and in documentation and information. The General Secretariat also conducts technical and feasibility studies and carries out market reviews. It provides information through a library, 'databank' and the publications listed below.

The invasion of Kuwait by Iraq in August 1990, and the subsequent international embargo on petroleum exports from Iraq and Kuwait, severely disrupted OAPEC's activities. In December the OAPEC Council decided to establish temporary headquarters in Cairo while Kuwait was under occupation. The Council resolved to reschedule overdue payments by Iraq and Syria over a 15-year period, and to postpone the Fifth Arab Energy Conference from mid-1992 to mid-1994. The Conference was held in Cairo, Egypt, in May 1994, attended by OAPEC ministers of petroleum and energy, senior officials from nine other Arab states and representatives of regional and international organizations. In June OAPEC returned to its permanent headquarters in Kuwait. The Sixth Conference was held in Damascus, Syria, in May 1998, with the theme of 'Energy and Arab Co-operation'.

## Finance

The 2000 budget amounted to 1,450,000 Kuwaiti dinars (KD). In addition, a budget of 120,600 KD was approved for the Judicial Tribunal.

## Publications

*Annual Statistical Report.*

*Energy Resources Monitor* (quarterly, Arabic).

*OAPEC Monthly Bulletin* (Arabic and English editions).

*OAPEC Statistical Bulletin* (Arabic and English editions).

*Oil and Arab Co-operation* (quarterly, Arabic).

*Secretary-General's Annual Report* (Arabic and English editions).

Papers, studies, conference proceedings.

## OAPEC-Sponsored Ventures

**Arab Maritime Petroleum Transport Company—AMPTC:** POB 22525, Safat 13086, Kuwait; tel. 4844500; fax 4842996; f. 1973 to undertake transport of crude petroleum, gas, refined products and petro-chemicals, and thus to increase Arab participation in the tanker transport industry; auth. cap. US $200m. Gen. Man. SULAYMAN AL-BASSAM.

**Arab Petroleum Investments Corporation—APICORP:** POB 448, Dhahran Airport 31932, Saudi Arabia; tel. (3) 864-7400; fax (3) 898-1883; e-mail info@apicorp-arabia.com; f. 1975 to finance investments in petroleum and petrochemicals projects and related industries in the Arab world and in developing countries, with priority being given to Arab joint ventures. Projects financed include gas liquefaction plants, petrochemicals, tankers, oil refineries, pipelines, exploration, detergents, fertilizers and process control instrumentation; auth. cap. US $1,200m.; subs. cap. $460m. (31 Dec. 1996). Shareholders: Kuwait, Saudi Arabia and United Arab Emirates (17% each), Libya (15%), Iraq and Qatar (10% each), Algeria (5%), Bahrain, Egypt and Syria (3% each). Chair. ABDULLAH A. AZ-ZAID; Gen. Man. Dr NUREDDIN FARRAG.

**Arab Company for Detergent Chemicals—ARADET:** POB 27864, el-Monsour, Baghdad, Iraq; tel. (1) 541-9893; f. 1981 to implement two projects in Iraq; APICORP and the Iraqi Government each hold 32% of shares in the co; auth. cap. 72m. Iraqi dinars.

**Arab Petroleum Services Company—APSCO:** POB 12925, Tripoli, Libya; tel. (21) 45861; fax (21) 3331930; f. 1977 to provide petroleum services through the establishment of companies specializing in various activities, and to train specialized personnel; auth. cap. 100m. Libyan dinars; subs. cap. 15m. Libyan dinars. Chair. AYAD HUSSEIN AD-DALI; Gen. Man. ISMAIL AL-KORAITLI.

**Arab Drilling and Workover Company:** POB 680, Suani Rd, km 3.5, Tripoli, Libya; tel. (21) 800064; fax (21) 805945; f. 1980; auth. cap. 12m. Libyan dinars; Gen. Man. MUHAMMAD AHMAD ATTIGA.

**Arab Geophysical Exploration Services Company—AGESCO:** POB 84224, Airport Rd, Tripoli, Libya; tel. (21) 4804863; fax (21) 4803199; f. 1985; auth. cap. 12m. Libyan dinars; Gen. Man. AYAD HUSSEIN AD-DALI.

**Arab Well Logging Company—AWLCO:** POB 6225, Baghdad, Iraq; tel. (1) 541-8259; f. 1983; provides well-logging services and data interpretation; auth. cap. 7m. Iraqi dinars.

**Arab Petroleum Training Institute—APTI:** POB 6037, Al-Tajeyat, Baghdad, Iraq; tel. (1) 523-4100; fax (1) 521-0526; f. 1978 to provide instruction in many technical and managerial aspects of the oil industry. Since Dec. 1994 the Institute has been place under the trusteeship of the Iraqi Government; the arrangement was scheduled to come to an end in Dec. 1998. Dir HAZIM A. AS-SULTAN.

**Arab Shipbuilding and Repair Yard Company—ASRY:** POB 50110, Hidd, Bahrain; tel. 671111; fax 670236; e-mail asry@batelco.com.bh; internet www.asry.net; f. 1974 to undertake repairs and servicing of vessels; operates a 500,000 dwt dry dock in Bahrain; two floating docks operational since 1992. Cap. (auth. and subs.) US $340m. Chair. Sheikh DAIJ BIN KHALIFA AL-KHALIFA; Chief Exec. MUHAMMAD M. AL-KHATEEB.

# ORGANIZATION OF THE ISLAMIC CONFERENCE—OIC

**Address:** Kilo 6, Mecca Rd, POB 178, Jeddah 21411, Saudi Arabia.

**Telephone:** (2) 680-0800; **fax:** (2) 687-3568.

The Organization was formally established in May 1971, when its Secretariat became operational, following a summit meeting of Muslim heads of state at Rabat, Morocco, in September 1969, and the Islamic Foreign Ministers' Conference in Jeddah in March 1970, and in Karachi, Pakistan, in December 1970.

### MEMBERS

| | | |
|---|---|---|
| Afghanistan | Indonesia | Palestine |
| Albania | Iran | Qatar |
| Algeria | Iraq | Saudi Arabia |
| Azerbaijan | Jordan | Senegal |
| Bahrain | Kazakhstan | Sierra Leone |
| Bangladesh | Kuwait | Somalia |
| Benin | Kyrgyzstan | Sudan |
| Brunei | Lebanon | Suriname |
| Burkina Faso | Libya | Syria |
| Cameroon | Malaysia | Tajikistan |
| Chad | Maldives | Togo |
| The Comoros | Mali | Tunisia |
| Djibouti | Mauritania | Turkey |
| Egypt | Morocco | Turkmenistan |
| Gabon | Mozambique | Uganda |
| The Gambia | Niger | United Arab Emirates |
| Guinea | Nigeria* | |
| Guinea-Bissau | Oman | Uzbekistan |
| Guyana | Pakistan | Yemen |

* Nigeria renounced its membership of the OIC in May 1991; however, the OIC has not formally recognized this decision.

Note: Observer status has been granted to Bosnia and Herzegovina, the Central African Republic, Côte d'Ivoire, Thailand, the Muslim community of the 'Turkish Republic of Northern Cyprus', the Moro National Liberation Front (MNLF) of the southern Philippines, the United Nations, the Non-Aligned Movement, the League of Arab States, the Organization of African Unity, the Economic Co-operation Organization, the Union of the Arab Maghreb and the Co-operation Council for the Arab States of the Gulf.

## Organization

(January 2000)

### SUMMIT CONFERENCES

The supreme body of the Organization is the Conference of Heads of State, which met in 1969 at Rabat, Morocco, in 1974 at Lahore, Pakistan, and in January 1981 at Mecca, Saudi Arabia, when it was decided that summit conferences would be held every three years in future. Eighth Conference: Teheran, Iran, December 1997. The ninth Conference was to be held in Doha, Qatar, in 2000.

### CONFERENCE OF MINISTERS OF FOREIGN AFFAIRS

Conferences take place annually, to consider the means for implementing the general policy of the Organization, although they may also be convened for extraordinary sessions.

### SECRETARIAT

The executive organ of the Organization, headed by a Secretary-General (who is elected by the Conference of Ministers of Foreign Affairs for a four-year term, renewable only once) and four Assistant Secretaries-General (similarly appointed).

**Secretary-General:** AZEDDINE LARAKI (Morocco).

At the summit conference in January 1981 it was decided that an International Islamic Court of Justice should be established to adjudicate in disputes between Muslim countries. Experts met in January 1983 to draw up a constitution for the court; however, by 1999 it was not yet in operation.

### SPECIALIZED COMMITTEES

**Al-Quds Committee:** f. 1975 to implement the resolutions of the Islamic Conference on the status of Jerusalem (Al-Quds); it meets at the level of foreign ministers; maintains the Al-Quds Fund; Chair. King MUHAMMAD VI of Morocco.

**Standing Committee for Economic and Commercial Co-operation (COMCEC):** f. 1981; Chair. SÜLEYMAN DEMIREL (Pres. of Turkey).

**Standing Committee for Information and Cultural Affairs (COMIAC):** f. 1981; Chair. ABDOU DIOUF (Pres. of Senegal).

**Standing Committee for Scientific and Technological Co-operation (COMSTECH):** f. 1981; Chair. MOHAMMAD RAFIQ TARAR (Pres. of Pakistan).

**Islamic Commission for Economic, Cultural and Social Affairs:** f. 1976.

**Permanent Finance Committee.**

Other committees comprise the Committee of Islamic Solidarity with the Peoples of the Sahel, the Six-Member Committee on the Situation of Muslims in the Philippines, the Six-Member Committee on Palestine, the *ad hoc* Committee on Afghanistan, the OIC contact group on Bosnia and Herzegovina (with an expanded mandate to include Kosovo and Metohija, Yugoslavia), and the OIC contact group on Jammu and Kashmir.

## Activities

The Organization's aims, as proclaimed in the Charter that was adopted in 1972, are:

(i) To promote Islamic solidarity among member states;

(ii) To consolidate co-operation among member states in the economic, social, cultural, scientific and other vital fields, and to arrange consultations among member states belonging to international organizations;

(iii) To endeavour to eliminate racial segregation and discrimination and to eradicate colonialism in all its forms;

(iv) To take necessary measures to support international peace and security founded on justice;

(v) To co-ordinate all efforts for the safeguard of the Holy Places and support of the struggle of the people of Palestine, and help them to regain their rights and liberate their land;

(vi) To strengthen the struggle of all Muslim people with a view to safeguarding their dignity, independence and national rights; and

(vii) To create a suitable atmosphere for the promotion of co-operation and understanding among member states and other countries.

The first summit conference of Islamic leaders (representing 24 states) took place in 1969 following the burning of the Al Aqsa Mosque in Jerusalem. At this conference it was decided that Islamic governments should 'consult together with a view to promoting close co-operation and mutual assistance in the economic, scientific, cultural and spiritual fields, inspired by the immortal teachings of Islam'. Thereafter the foreign ministers of the countries concerned met annually, and adopted the Charter of the Organization of the Islamic Conference in 1972.

At the second Islamic summit conference (Lahore, Pakistan, 1974), the Islamic Solidarity Fund was established, together with a committee of representatives which later evolved into the Islamic Commission for Economic, Cultural and Social Affairs. Subsequently, numerous other subsidiary bodies have been set up (see below).

### ECONOMIC CO-OPERATION

A general agreement for economic, technical and commercial co-operation came into force in 1981, providing for the establishment of joint investment projects and trade co-ordination. This was followed by an agreement on promotion, protection and guarantee of investments among member states. A plan of action to strengthen economic co-operation was adopted at the third Islamic summit conference in 1981, aiming to promote collective self-reliance and the development of joint ventures in all sectors. In May 1993 the OIC committee for economic and commercial co-operation, meeting in İstanbul, agreed to review and update the 1981 plan of action.

A meeting of ministers of industry was held in February 1982, and agreed to promote industrial co-operation, including joint ventures in agricultural machinery, engineering and other basic industries. The fifth summit conference, held in 1987, approved proposals for joint development of modern technology, and for improving scientific and technical skills in the less developed Islamic countries. In December 1988 it was announced that a committee of experts, established by the OIC, was to draw up a 10-year programme of assistance to developing countries (mainly in Africa) in science and technology.

## CULTURAL CO-OPERATION

The Organization supports education in Muslim communities throughout the world, and was instrumental in the establishment of Islamic universities in Niger and Uganda (see below). It organizes seminars on various aspects of Islam, and encourages dialogue with the other monotheistic religions. Support is given to publications on Islam both in Muslim and Western countries.

## HUMANITARIAN ASSISTANCE

Assistance is given to Muslim communities affected by wars and natural disasters, in co-operation with UN organizations, particularly UNHCR. The countries of the Sahel region (Burkina Faso, Cape Verde, Chad, The Gambia, Guinea, Guinea-Bissau, Mali, Mauritania, Niger and Senegal) receive particular attention as victims of drought. In April 1993 member states pledged US $80m. in emergency assistance for Muslims affected by the war in Bosnia and Herzegovina (see below for details of subsequent assistance). In April 1999 the OIC resolved to send humanitarian aid to assist the displaced ethnic Albanian population of Kosovo and Metohija, in southern Serbia.

## POLITICAL CO-OPERATION

Since its inception the OIC has called for vacation of Arab territories by Israel, recognition of the rights of Palestinians and of the Palestine Liberation Organization (PLO) as their sole legitimate representative, and the restoration of Jerusalem to Arab rule. The 1981 summit conference called for a *jihad* (holy war—though not necessarily in a military sense) 'for the liberation of Jerusalem and the occupied territories'; this was to include an Islamic economic boycott of Israel. In 1982 Islamic ministers of foreign affairs decided to establish Islamic offices for boycotting Israel and for military co-operation with the PLO. The 1984 summit conference agreed to reinstate Egypt (suspended following the peace treaty signed with Israel in 1979) as a member of the OIC, although the resolution was opposed by seven states.

The fifth summit conference, held in January 1987, discussed the continuing Iran–Iraq war, and agreed that the Islamic Peace Committee should attempt to prevent the sale of military equipment to the parties in the conflict. The conference also discussed the conflicts in Chad and Lebanon, and requested the holding of a United Nations conference to define international terrorism, as opposed to legitimate fighting for freedom.

In August 1990 a majority of ministers of foreign affairs condemned Iraq's recent invasion of Kuwait, and demanded the withdrawal of Iraqi forces. In August 1991 the Conference of Ministers of Foreign Affairs obstructed Iraq's attempt to propose a resolution demanding the repeal of economic sanctions against the country. The sixth summit conference, held in Senegal in December 1991, reflected the divisions in the Arab world that resulted from Iraq's invasion of Kuwait and the ensuing war. Twelve heads of state did not attend, reportedly to register protest at the presence of Jordan and the PLO at the conference, both of which had given support to Iraq. Disagreement also arose between the PLO and the majority of other OIC members when a proposal was adopted to cease the OIC's support for the PLO's *jihad* in the Arab territories occupied by Israel, in an attempt to further the Middle East peace negotiations.

In August 1992 the UN General Assembly approved a non-binding resolution, introduced by the OIC, that requested the UN Security Council to take increased action, including the use of force, in order to defend the non-Serbian population of Bosnia and Herzegovina (some 43% of Bosnians being Muslims) from Serbian aggression, and to restore its 'territorial integrity'. The OIC Conference of Ministers of Foreign Affairs, which was held in Jeddah, Saudi Arabia, in December, demanded anew that the UN Security Council take all necessary measures against Serbia and Montenegro, including military intervention, in accordance with Article 42 of the UN Charter, in order to protect the Bosnian Muslims. In February 1993 the OIC appealed to the Security Council to remove the embargo on armaments to Bosnia and Herzegovina with regard to the Bosnian Muslims, to allow them to defend themselves from the Bosnian Serbs, who were far better armed.

A report by an OIC fact-finding mission, which in February 1993 visited Azad Kashmir while investigating allegations of repression of the largely Muslim population of the Indian state of Jammu and Kashmir by the Indian armed forces, was presented to the 1993 Conference. The meeting urged member states to take the necessary measures to persuade India to cease the 'massive human rights violations' in Jammu and Kashmir and to allow the Indian Kashmiris to 'exercise their inalienable right to self-determination'. In September 1994 ministers of foreign affairs, meeting in Islamabad, Pakistan, urged the Indian Government to grant permission for an OIC fact-finding mission, and for other human rights groups, to visit Jammu and Kashmir (which it had continually refused to do) and to refrain from human rights violations of the Kashmiri people. The ministers agreed to establish a contact group on Jammu and Kashmir, which was to provide a mechanism for promoting international awareness of the situation in that region and for seeking a peaceful solution to the dispute. In December OIC heads of state approved a resolution condemning reported human rights abuses by Indian security forces in Kashmir.

In July 1994 the OIC Secretary-General visited Afghanistan and proposed the establishment of a preparatory mechanism to promote national reconciliation in that country. In mid-1995 Saudi Arabia, acting as a representative of the OIC, pursued a peace initiative for Afghanistan and issued an invitation for leaders of the different factions to hold negotiations in Jeddah.

A special ministerial meeting on Bosnia and Herzegovina was held in July 1993, at which seven OIC countries committed themselves to making available up to 17,000 troops to serve in the UN Protection Force in the former Yugoslavia (UNPROFOR). The meeting also decided to dispatch immediately a ministerial mission to persuade influential governments to support the OIC's demands for the removal of the arms embargo on Bosnian Muslims and the convening of a restructured international conference to bring about a political solution to the conflict. At the end of September 1994 ministers of foreign affairs of nine countries constituting the OIC contact group on Bosnia and Herzegovina, meeting in New York, resolved to prepare an assessment document on the issue, and to establish an alliance with its Western counterpart (comprising France, Germany, Russia, the United Kingdom and the USA). The two groups met in Geneva, Switzerland, in January 1995. In December 1994 OIC heads of state, convened in Morocco, proclaimed that the UN arms embargo on Bosnia and Herzegovina could not be applied to the Muslim authorities of that Republic. The Conference also resolved to review economic relations between OIC member states and any country that supported Serbian activities. An aid fund was established, to which member states were requested to contribute between US $500,000 and US $5m., in order to provide further humanitarian and economic assistance to Bosnian Muslims. In relation to wider concerns the conference adopted a Code of Conduct for Combating International Terrorism, in an attempt to control Muslim extremist groups. The code commits states to ensuring that militant groups do not use their territory for planning or executing terrorist activity against other states, in addition to states refraining from direct support or participation in acts of terrorism. In a further resolution the OIC supported the decision by Iraq to recognize Kuwait, but advocated that Iraq comply with all UN Security Council decisions.

In July 1995 the OIC contact group on Bosnia and Herzegovina (at that time comprising Egypt, Iran, Malaysia, Morocco, Pakistan, Saudi Arabia, Senegal and Turkey), meeting in Geneva, declared the UN arms embargo against Bosnia and Herzegovina to be 'invalid'. Several Governments subsequently announced their willingness officially to supply weapons and other military assistance to the Bosnian Muslim forces. In September a meeting of all OIC ministers of defence and foreign affairs endorsed the establishment of an 'assistance mobilization group' which was to supply military, economic, legal and other assistance to Bosnia and Herzegovina. In a joint declaration the ministers also demanded the return of all territory seized by Bosnian Serb forces, the continued NATO bombing of Serb military targets, and that the city of Sarajevo be preserved under a Muslim-led Bosnian Government. In November the OIC Secretary-General endorsed the peace accord for the former Yugoslavia, which was concluded, in Dayton, USA, by leaders of all the conflicting factions, and reaffirmed the commitment of Islamic states to participate in efforts to implement the accord. In the following month the OIC Conference of Ministers of Foreign Affairs, convened in Conakry, Guinea, requested the full support of the international community to reconstruct Bosnia and Herzegovina through humanitarian aid as well as economic and technical co-operation. Ministers declared that Palestine and the establishment of fully-autonomous Palestinian control of Jerusalem were issues of central importance for the Muslim world. The Conference urged the removal of all aspects of occupation and the cessation of the construction of Israeli settlements in the occupied territories. In addition, the final statement of the meeting condemned Armenian aggression against Azerbaijan, registered concern at the persisting civil conflict in Afghanistan, demanded the elimination of all weapons of mass destruction and pledged support for Libya (affected by the US trade embargo).

In December 1996 OIC ministers of foreign affairs, meeting in Jakarta, Indonesia, urged the international community to apply pressure on Israel in order to ensure its implementation of the terms of the Middle East peace process. The ministers reaffirmed the importance of ensuring that the provisions of the Dayton Peace Agreement for the former Yugoslavia were fully implemented, called for a peaceful settlement of the Kashmir issue, demanded that Iraq fulfil its obligations for the establishment of security, peace and stability in the region and proposed that an international conference on peace and national reconciliation in Somalia be convened. The ministers elected a new Secretary-General, Azeddine Laraki, who confirmed that the organization would continue to develop its role as an international mediator. In March 1997, at an extraordinary summit held in Pakistan, OIC heads of state and of government reiterated the organization's objective of increasing international pressure on Israel to ensure the full implementation of the terms of the Middle East peace process. An 'Islamabad Declaration' was also adopted, which pledged to increase co-operation between members of the OIC. In June the OIC condemned the decision by the US House of Representatives to recognize Jerusalem as the Israeli capital. The Secretary-General of the OIC issued a statement rejecting the US decision as counter to the role of the USA as sponsor of the Middle East peace plan. In December OIC heads of state attended the eighth summit conference, held in Iran. The Teheran Declaration, issued at the end of the conference, demanded the 'liberation' of the Israeli-occupied territories and the creation of an autonomous Palestinian state. The conference also appealed for a cessation of the conflicts in Afghanistan, and between Armenia and Azerbaijan. It was requested that the UN sanctions against Libya be removed and that the US legislation threatening sanctions against foreign companies investing in certain countries (including Iran and Libya), introduced in July 1996, be dismissed as invalid. In addition, the Declaration encouraged the increased participation of women in OIC activities.

In early 1998 the OIC appealed for an end to the threat of US-led military action against Iraq arising from a dispute regarding access granted to international weapons inspectors. The crisis was averted by an agreement concluded between the Iraqi authorities and the UN Secretary-General in February. In March OIC ministers of foreign affairs, meeting in Doha, Qatar, requested an end to the international sanctions against Iraq. Additionally, the ministers urged all states to end the process of restoring normal trading and diplomatic relations with Israel until that country withdraws from the occupied territories and permits the establishment of an independent Palestinian state.

In April 1998 the OIC, jointly with the UN, sponsored new peace negotiations between the main disputing factions in Afghanistan, which were conducted in Islamabad, Pakistan. In early May, however, the talks collapsed and were postponed indefinitely. In September the Secretaries-General of the OIC and UN agreed to establish a joint mission to counter the deteriorating security situation along the Afghan-Iranian border, following the large-scale deployment of Taliban troops in the region and consequent military manoeuvres by the Iranian authorities. They also reiterated the need to proceed with negotiations to conclude a peaceful settlement in Afghanistan.

In December 1998 the OIC appealed for a diplomatic solution to the tensions arising from Iraq's withdrawal of co-operation with UN weapons inspectors, and criticized subsequent military airstrikes, led by the USA, as having been conducted without renewed UN authority.

In early April 1999 ministers of foreign affairs of the countries comprising OIC's Contact Group met to consider the crisis in Kosovo. The meeting condemned Serbian atrocities being committed against the local Albanian population and urged the provision of international assistance for the thousands of people displaced by the conflict. The Group resolved to establish a committee to co-ordinate relief aid provided by member states. The ministers also expressed their willingness to help to formulate a peaceful settlement and to participate in any subsequent implementation force.

## SUBSIDIARY ORGANS

**International Commission for the Preservation of Islamic Cultural Heritage (ICPICH):** POB 24, 80692 Beşiktaş, İstanbul, Turkey; tel. (212) 2591742; fax (212) 2584365; e-mail ircica@superonline.com; internet www.ircica.hypermart.net/ircica.html; f. 1982. Sec. Prof. Dr Ekmeleddin İhsanoğlu (Turkey). Publ. *Newsletter* (3 a year).

**Islamic Centre for the Development of Trade:** Complexe Commercial des Habous, ave des FAR, BP 13545, Casablanca, Morocco; tel. (2) 314974; fax (2) 310110; e-mail icdt@icdt.org; internet www.icdt.org; f. 1983 to encourage regular commercial contacts, harmonize policies and promote investments among OIC mems. Dir Badre Eddine Allali. Publs *Tijaris: International and Inter-Islamic Trade Magazine* (quarterly), *Inter-Islamic Trade Report* (annually).

**Islamic Institute of Technology (IIT):** GPO Box 3003, Board Bazar, Gazipur 1704, Dhaka, Bangladesh; tel. (2) 980-0960; fax (2) 980-0970; e-mail dg@iit.bangla.net; internet www.iitoic-dhaka.edu; f. 1981 to develop human resources in OIC mem. states, with special reference to engineering, technology, tech. and vocational education and research; 224 staff and 1,000 students; library of 23,000 vols. Dir-Gen. Prof. Dr M. Anwar Hossain. Publs *News Bulletin* (annually), annual calendar and announcement for admission, reports, human resources development series.

**Islamic Jurisprudence Academy:** Jeddah, Saudi Arabia; f. 1982. Sec.-Gen. Sheikh Mohamed Habib Belkhojah.

**Islamic Solidarity Fund:** c/o OIC Secretariat, POB 178, Jeddah 21411, Saudi Arabia; tel. (2) 680-0800; fax (2) 687-3568; f. 1974 to meet the needs of Islamic communities by providing emergency aid and the finance to build mosques, Islamic centres, hospitals, schools and universities. Chair. Sheikh Nasir Abdullah bin Hamdan; Exec. Dir Abdullah Hersi.

**Islamic University of Niger:** BP 11507, Niamey, Niger; tel. 723903; fax 733796; f. 1984; provides courses of study in *Shari'a* (Islamic law) and Arabic language and literature; also offers courses in pedagogy and teacher training; receives grants from Islamic Solidarity Fund and contributions from OIC member states. Rector Prof. Abdelali Oudhriri.

**Islamic University in Uganda:** POB 2555, Mbale, Uganda; tel. (45) 33502; fax (45) 34452; e-mail iuiu@info.com.co.ug; Kampala Liaison Office: POB 7689, Kampala; tel. (41) 236874; fax (41) 254576; f. 1988 to meet the educational needs of Muslim populations in English-speaking African countries; mainly financed by OIC. Principal Officer Prof. Mahdi Adamu.

**Research Centre for Islamic History, Art and Culture (IRCICA):** POB 24, Beşiktaş 80692, İstanbul, Turkey; tel. (212) 2591742; fax (212) 2584365; e-mail ircica@superonline.com; internet www.ircica.hypermart.net/ircica.html; f. 1980; library of 50,000 vols. Dir-Gen. Prof. Dr Ekmeleddin İhsanoğlu. Publs *Newsletter* (3 a year), monographical studies.

**Statistical, Economic and Social Research and Training Centre for the Islamic Countries:** Attar Sok 4, GOP 06700, Ankara, Turkey; tel. (312) 4686172; fax (312) 4673458; e-mail sesrtcic@tr-net.net.tr; f. 1978. Dir-Gen. Erdinç Erdün.

## SPECIALIZED INSTITUTIONS

**International Islamic News Agency (IINA):** King Khalid Palace, Madinah Rd, POB 5054, Jeddah, Saudi Arabia; tel. (2) 665-8561; fax (2) 665-9358; e-mail iina@mail.gcc.com.bh; internet www.islamicnews.org; f. 1972. Dir-Gen. Abdulwahab Kashif.

**Islamic Educational, Scientific and Cultural Organization (ISESCO):** Ave Attine, Hay Ryad, BP 2275, Rabat 10104, Morocco; tel. (7) 772433; fax (7) 777459; e-mail cid@isesco.org.ma; internet www.isesco.org.ma; f. 1982. Dir-Gen. Dr Abdulaziz bin Othman al-Twaijri. Publs *ISESCO Newsletter* (quarterly), *Islam Today* (2 a year), *ISESCO Triennial*.

**Islamic States Broadcasting Organization (ISBO):** POB 6351, Jeddah 21442, Saudi Arabia; tel. (2) 672-1121; fax (2) 672-2600; f. 1975. Sec.-Gen. Hussein al-Askary.

## AFFILIATED INSTITUTIONS

**International Association of Islamic Banks (IAIB):** King Abdulaziz St, Queen's Bldg, 23rd Floor, Al-Balad Dist, POB 23425, Jeddah 21426, Saudi Arabia; tel. (2) 643-1276; fax (2) 644-7239; f. 1977 to link financial institutions operating on Islamic banking principles; activities include training and research; mems: 192 banks and other financial institutions in 34 countries. Sec.-Gen. Samir A. Shaikh.

**Islamic Chamber of Commerce and Industry:** POB 3831, Clifton, Karachi 75600, Pakistan; tel. (21) 5874756; fax (21) 5870765; e-mail icci@icci-oic.org; internet www.icci.org.pk/islamic/main.html; f. 1979 to promote trade and industry among member states; comprises nat. chambers or feds of chambers of commerce and industry. Sec.-Gen. Aqeel Ahmad al-Jassem.

**Islamic Committee for the International Crescent:** c/o OIC, Kilo 6, Mecca Rd, POB 178, Jeddah 21411, Saudi Arabia; tel. (2) 680-0800; fax (2) 687-3568; f. 1979 to attempt to alleviate the suffering caused by natural disasters and war. Sec.-Gen. Dr Ahmad Abdallah Cherif.

**Islamic Solidarity Sports Federation:** POB 6040, Riyadh 11442, Saudi Arabia; tel. and fax (1) 482-2145; f. 1981. Sec.-Gen. Dr Mohammad Saleh Gazdar.

**Organization of Islamic Capitals and Cities—OICC:** POB 13621, Jeddah 21414, Saudi Arabia; tel. (2) 698-1953; fax (2) 698-1053; e-mail oicc@compuserve.com; f. 1980 to promote and develop co-operation among OICC mems, to preserve their character and heritage, to implement planning guide-lines for the growth of Islamic cities and to upgrade standards of public services and utilities in those cities. Sec.-Gen. OMAR ABDULLAH KADI.

**Organization of the Islamic Shipowners' Association:** POB 14900, Jeddah 21434, Saudi Arabia; tel. (2) 663-7882; fax (2) 660-4920; internet www.icdt.org/oisa.htm; f. 1981 to promote co-operation among maritime cos in Islamic countries. In 1998 mems approved the establishment of a new commercial venture, the Bakkah Shipping Company, to enhance sea transport in the region. Sec.-Gen. Dr ABDULLATIF A. SULTAN.

# ORGANIZATION OF THE PETROLEUM EXPORTING COUNTRIES—OPEC

**Address:** Obere Donaustrasse 93, 1020 Vienna, Austria.

**Telephone:** (1) 211-12; **fax:** (1) 214-98-27; **e-mail:** prid@opec.org; **internet:** www.opec.org.

OPEC was established in 1960 to link countries whose main source of export earnings is petroleum; it aims to unify and co-ordinate members' petroleum policies and to safeguard their interests generally. The OPEC Fund for International Development is described on p. 000.

OPEC's share of world petroleum production was 42.6% in 1998 (compared with 44.7% in 1980 and 54.7% in 1974). It is estimated that OPEC members possess more than 75% of the world's known reserves of crude petroleum, of which about two-thirds are in the Middle East. In 1998 OPEC members possessed about 43.5% of known reserves of natural gas.

### MEMBERS

| | | |
|---|---|---|
| Algeria | Kuwait | Saudi Arabia |
| Indonesia | Libya | United Arab Emirates |
| Iran | Nigeria | Venezuela |
| Iraq | Qatar | |

## Organization

(January 2000)

### CONFERENCE

The Conference is the supreme authority of the Organization, responsible for the formulation of its general policy. It consists of representatives of member countries, who examine reports and recommendations submitted by the Board of Governors. It approves the appointment of Governors from each country and elects the Chairman of the Board of Governors. It works on the unanimity principle, and meets at least twice a year.

### BOARD OF GOVERNORS

The Board directs the management of the Organization; it implements resolutions of the Conference and draws up an annual budget. It consists of one governor for each member country, and meets at least twice a year.

### MINISTERIAL MONITORING COMMITTEE

The Committee (f. 1988) is responsible for monitoring price evolution and ensuring the stability of the world petroleum market. As such, it is charged with the preparation of long-term strategies, including the allocation of quotas to be presented to the Conference. The Committee consists of all national representatives, and is normally convened four times a year. A Ministerial Monitoring Sub-committee, reporting to the Committee on production and supply figures, was established in 1993.

### ECONOMIC COMMISSION

A specialized body operating within the framework of the Secretariat, with a view to assisting the Organization in promoting stability in international prices for petroleum at equitable levels; consists of a Board, national representatives and a commission staff; meets at least twice a year.

### SECRETARIAT

**Secretary-General:** (until March 2000) Dr RILWANU LUKMAN (Nigeria).

**Research Division:** comprises three departments:

**Data Services Department:** Maintains and expands information services to support the research activities of the Secretariat and those of member countries; collects, collates and analyses statistical information and provides essential data for forecasts and estimates necessary for OPEC medium- and long-term strategies.

**Energy Studies Department:** Energy Section monitors, forecasts and analyses developments in the energy and petrochemical industries and their implications for OPEC, and prepares forecasts of demands for OPEC petroleum and gas. Petroleum Section assists the Board of the Economic Commission in determining the relative values of OPEC crude petroleum and gases and in developing alternative methodologies for this purpose.

**Economics and Finance Department:** Comprises the Economics Section and a Finance Section. Analyses and reports on economic and financial developments relevant to the world energy market and the deliberations of the Economic Commission Board and the Conference, including world trade, international monetary movements, Third World debt, the financial performance of petroleum companies and oil revenues of member states.

**Division Director:** Dr SHOKRI M. GHANEM (Libya).

**Administration and Human Resources Department:** Responsible for all organization methods, provision of administrative services for all meetings, personnel matters, budgets, accounting and internal control; reviews general administrative policies and industrial relations practised throughout the oil industry; **Head:** Dr TALAL DEHRAB (Kuwait).

**Public Relations and Information Department:** Concerned with communicating OPEC objectives, decisions and actions; produces and distributes a number of publications, films, slides and tapes; and disseminates news of general interest regarding the Organization and member countries on energy and other related issues. Operates a daily on-line news service, the OPEC News Agency (OPECNA). An OPEC Library contains an extensive collection of energy-related publications; **Head:** FAROUK U. MUHAMMED (Nigeria).

**Legal Office:** Provides legal advice, supervises the Secretariat's legal commitments, evaluates legal issues of concern to the Organization and member countries, and recommends appropriate action; **Legal Officer:** DOLORES DOBARRO DE TORRES (Venezuela).

**Office of the Secretary-General:** Provides the Secretary-General with executive assistance in maintaining contacts with governments, organizations and delegations, in matters of protocol and in the preparation for and co-ordination of meetings; **Officer-in-Charge:** Dr DEYAA L. ALKHATEEB.

## Record of Events

1960 The first OPEC Conference was held in Baghdad in September, attended by representatives from Iran, Iraq, Kuwait, Saudi Arabia and Venezuela.

1961 Second Conference, Caracas, January. Qatar was admitted to membership; a Board of Governors was formed and statutes agreed.

1962 Fourth Conference, Geneva, April and June. Protests were addressed to petroleum companies against price cuts introduced in August 1960. Indonesia and Libya were admitted to membership.

1965 In July the Conference reached agreement on a two-year joint production programme, implemented from 1965 to 1967, to limit annual growth in output to secure adequate prices.

1967 Abu Dhabi was admitted to membership.

1969 Algeria was admitted to membership.

1970 Twenty-first Conference, Caracas, December. Tax on income of petroleum companies was raised to 55%.

1971 A five-year agreement was concluded in February between the six producing countries in the Gulf and 23 international petroleum companies (Teheran Agreement). Nigeria was admitted to membership.

1972 In January petroleum companies agreed to adjust petroleum revenues of the largest producers after changes in currency exchange rates (Geneva Agreement).

1973 OPEC and petroleum companies concluded an agreement whereby posted prices of crude petroleum were raised by 11.9% and a mechanism was installed to make monthly adjustments to prices in future (Second Geneva Agreement). Negotiations with petroleum companies on revision of the Teheran Agreement collapsed in October, and the Gulf states unilaterally declared 70% increases in posted prices, from US $3.01 to $5.11 per barrel. In December the Conference resolved to increase the posted price by nearly 130%, to $11.65 per barrel, from 1 January 1974. Ecuador was admitted to full membership and Gabon became an associate member.

1974 As a result of Saudi opposition to the December price increase, prices were held at current level for first quarter (and subsequently for the remainder of 1974). Abu Dhabi's membership was transferred to the United Arab Emirates (UAE). A meeting in June increased royalties charged to petroleum companies from 12.5% to 14.5% in all member states except Saudi Arabia. A meeting in September increased governmental take by about 3.5% through further increases in royalties on equity crude to 16.67% and in taxes to 65.65%, except in Saudi Arabia.

1975 OPEC's first summit conference was held in Algiers in March. Gabon was admitted to full membership. A ministerial meeting in September agreed to raise prices by 10% for the period until June 1976.

1976 The OPEC Fund for International Development was created in May. In December 11 member states endorsed a rise in basic prices of 10% as of 1 January 1977, and a further 5% rise as of 1 July 1977. However, Saudi Arabia and the UAE decided to raise their prices by 5% only.

1977 Following an earlier waiver by nine members of the 5% second stage of the price increase, Saudi Arabia and the UAE announced in July that they would both raise their prices by 5%. As a result, a single level of prices throughout the organization was restored. Because of continued disagreements between the 'moderates', led by Saudi Arabia and Iran, and the 'radicals', led by Algeria, Libya and Iraq, the Conference, held in December, was unable to settle on an increase in prices.

1978 The June Conference agreed that price levels should remain stable until the end of the year. In December it was decided to raise prices in four instalments, in order to compensate for the effects of the depreciation of the US dollar. These would bring a rise of 14.5% over nine months, but an average increase of 10% for 1979.

1979 At an extraordinary meeting in March members decided to raise prices by 9%. In June the Conference agreed minimum and maximum prices which seemed likely to add between 15% and 20% to import bills of consumer countries. The December Conference agreed in principle to convert the OPEC Fund into a development agency with its own legal personality.

1980 In June the Conference decided to set the price for a marker crude at US $32 per barrel, and that the value differentials which could be added above this ceiling (on account of quality and geographical location) should not exceed $5 per barrel. The planned OPEC summit meeting in Baghdad in November was postponed indefinitely because of the Iran–Iraq war, but the scheduled ministerial meeting went ahead in Bali in December, with both Iranians and Iraqis present. A ceiling price of $41 per barrel was fixed for premium crudes.

1981 In May attempts to achieve price reunification were made, but Saudi Arabia refused to increase its US $32 per barrel price unless the higher prices charged by other countries were lowered. Most of the other OPEC countries agreed to cut production by 10% so as to reduce the surplus. An emergency meeting in Geneva in August again failed to unify prices, although Saudi Arabia agreed to reduce production by 1m. barrels per day (b/d). In October OPEC countries agreed to increase the Saudi marker price to $34 per barrel, with a ceiling price of $38 per barrel.

1982 In March an emergency meeting of petroleum ministers was held in Vienna and agreed (for the first time in OPEC's history) to defend the Organization's price structure by imposing an overall production ceiling of 18m. b/d. At the same time Saudi Arabia announced a reduction in its own production to 7m. b/d. In December the Conference agreed to limit OPEC production to 18.5m. b/d in 1983 but postponed the allocation of national quotas pending consultations among the respective governments.

1983 In January an emergency meeting of petroleum ministers, fearing a collapse in world petroleum prices, decided to reduce the production ceiling to 17.5m. b/d, but failed to agree on individual production quotas or on adjustments to the differentials in prices charged for the high-quality crude petroleum produced by Algeria, Libya and Nigeria compared with that produced by the Gulf States. In February Nigeria cut its prices to US $30 per barrel, following a collapse in its production. To avoid a 'price war' OPEC set the official price of marker crude at $29 per barrel, and agreed to maintain existing price differentials at the level agreed on in March 1982, with the temporary exception that the differentials for Nigerian crudes should be $1 more than the price of the marker crude. It also agreed to maintain the production ceiling of 17.5m. b/d and allocated quotas for each member country except Saudi Arabia, which was to act as a 'swing producer' to supply the balancing quantities to meet market requirements.

1984 In October the production ceiling was lowered to 16m. b/d. In December price differentials for light (more expensive) and heavy (cheaper) crudes were slightly altered in an attempt to counteract price-cutting by non-OPEC producers, particularly Norway and the United Kingdom.

1985 In January members (except Algeria, Iran and Libya) effectively abandoned the marker price system. During the year production in excess of quotas by OPEC members, unofficial discounts and barter deals by members, and price cuts by non-members (such as Mexico, which had hitherto kept its prices in line with those of OPEC) contributed to a weakening of the market.

1986 During the first half of the year petroleum prices dropped to below US $10 per barrel. In April ministers agreed to set OPEC production at 16.7m. b/d for the third quarter of 1986 and at 17.3m. b/d for the fourth quarter. Algeria, Iran and Libya dissented. Discussions were also held with non-member countries (Angola, Egypt, Malaysia, Mexico and Oman), which agreed to co-operate in limiting production, although the United Kingdom declined. In August all members, with the exception of Iraq (which demanded to be allowed the same quota as Iran and, when this was denied it, refused to be a party to the agreement), agreed upon a return to production quotas, with the aim of cutting production to 14.8m. b/d (about 16.8m. b/d including Iraq's production) for the ensuing two months. This measure resulted in an increase in prices to about $15 per barrel, and was extended until the end of the year. In December members (with the exception of Iraq) agreed to return to a fixed pricing system at a level of $18 per barrel as the OPEC reference price, with effect from 1 February 1987. OPEC's total production for the first half 1987 was not to exceed 15.8m. b/d.

1987 In June, with prices having stabilized, the Conference decided that production during the third and fourth quarters of the year should be limited to 16.6m. b/d (including Iraq's production). However, total production continued to exceed the agreed levels. In December ministers decided to extend the existing agreement for the first half of 1988, although Iraq, once more, refused to participate.

1988 By March prices had fallen below US $15 per barrel. In April non-OPEC producers offered to reduce the volume of their petroleum exports by 5% if OPEC members would do the same. Saudi Arabia, however, refused to accept further reductions in production, insisting that existing quotas should first be more strictly enforced. In June the previous production limit (15.06m. b/d, excluding Iraq's production) was again renewed for six months, in the hope that increasing demand would be sufficient to raise prices. By October, however, petroleum prices were below $12 per barrel. In November a new agreement was reached, limiting total production (including that of Iraq) to 18.5m. b/d, with effect from 1 January 1989. Iran and Iraq finally agreed to accept identical quotas.

1989 In June (when prices had returned to about US $18 per barrel) ministers agreed to increase the production limit to 19.5m. b/d for the second half of 1989. However, Kuwait and the UAE indicated that they would not feel bound to observe this limit. In September the production limit was again increased, to 20.5m. b/d, and in November the limit for the first half of 1990 was increased to 22m. b/d.

1990 In May members resolved to adhere more strictly to the agreed production quotas, in response to a sharp decline in prices. By late June, however, it was reported that total production had decreased by only 400,000 b/d, and prices remained at about US $14 per barrel. In July Iraq threatened to take military action against Kuwait unless it reduced its petroleum production. In the same month OPEC members agreed to limit output to 22.5m. b/d. In August Iraq invaded Kuwait, and petroleum exports by the two countries were halted by an international embargo. Petroleum prices immediately increased to exceed $25 per barrel. Later in the month an informal consultative meeting of OPEC ministers placed the July agreement in abeyance, and permitted a temporary increase in production of petroleum, of between 3m. and 3.5m. b/d (mostly by Saudi Arabia, the UAE and Venezuela). In September and October prices fluctuated in response to political developments in the Gulf region, reaching a point in excess of $40 per barrel in early October, but falling to about $25 per barrel by the end of the month. In December a meeting of OPEC members voted to maintain the high levels of production and to reinstate the quotas that had been agreed in July, once the Gulf crisis was over. During the period August 1990–February 1991 Saudi Arabia increased its petroleum output from 5.4m. to 8.5m. b/d. Seven of the other OPEC states also produced in excess of their agreed quotas.

1991 In March, in an attempt to reach the target of a minimum reference price of US $21 per barrel, ministers agreed to reduce production from 23m. b/d to 22.3m. b/d, although Saudi Arabia refused to return to its pre-August 1990 quota. In June ministers decided to maintain the ceiling of 22.3m. b/d into the third quarter of the year, since Iraq and Kuwait were still unable to export their petroleum. In September it was agreed that OPEC members' production for the last quarter of 1991 should be raised to 23.65m. b/d, and in November the OPEC Conference decided to maintain the increased production ceiling during the first quarter of 1992. From early November, however, the price of petroleum declined sharply, with demand less than anticipated as a result of continuing world recession and a mild winter in the northern hemisphere.

1992 The Ministerial Monitoring Committee, meeting in February, decided to impose a production ceiling of 22.98m. b/d with immediate effect. The agreement was, however, repudiated by both Saudi Arabia, which stated that it would not abide by its allocated quota of 7.9m. b/d, and Iran, unhappy that the production ceiling had not been set lower. In May it was agreed to continue the production restriction of 22.98m. b/d during the third quarter of 1992. Kuwait, which was resuming production in the wake of the extensive damage inflicted on its oil-wells by Iraq during the Gulf War, was granted a special dispensation to produce without a fixed quota. During the first half of 1992 member states' petroleum output consistently exceeded agreed levels, with Saudi Arabia and Iran (despite its stance on reducing production) the principal over-producers. In June, at the UN Conference on Environment and Development, OPEC's Secretary-General expressed its member countries' strong objections to the tax on fossil fuels (designed to reduce pollution) proposed by the EC. In September negotiations between OPEC ministers in Geneva were complicated by Iran's alleged annexation of Abu Musa and two other islands in the territorial waters of the UAE. However, agreement was reached on a production ceiling of 24.2m. b/d for the final quarter of 1992, in an attempt to raise the price of crude petroleum to the OPEC target of US $21 per barrel. At the Conference, held in late November, Ecuador formally resigned from OPEC, the first country ever to do so, citing as reasons the high membership fee and OPEC's refusal to increase Ecuador's quota. The meeting agreed to restrict production to 24.58m. b/d for the first quarter of 1993 (24.46m. b/d, excluding Ecuador).

1993 In mid-February a quota was set for Kuwait for the first time since the onset of the Gulf crisis. Kuwait agreed to produce 1.6m. b/d (400,000 less than current output) from 1 March, on the understanding that this would be substantially increased in the third quarter of the year. The quota for overall production from 1 March was set at 23.58m. b/d. A Ministerial Monitoring Sub-committee was established to supervise compliance with quotas. In June OPEC ministers decided to 'roll over' the overall quota of 23.58m. b/d into the third quarter of the year. However, Kuwait rejected its new allocation of 1.76m. b/d, demanding a quota of at least 2m. In July discussions between Iraq and the UN on the possible supervised sale of Iraqi petroleum depressed petroleum prices to below US $16 per barrel. The Monitoring Sub-committee urged member states to adhere to their production quotas (which were exceeded by a total of 1m. b/d in July). At the end of September an extraordinary meeting of the Conference agreed on a raised production ceiling of 24.52m. b/d, to be effective for six months from 1 October. Kuwait accepted a quota of 2m. b/d, which brought the country back into the production ceiling mechanism. Iran agreed on an allocation of 3.6m. b/d, while Saudi Arabia consented to freeze production at current levels, in order to support petroleum prices which remained persistently low. In November the Conference rejected any further reduction in production. Prices subsequently fell below $14, owing partly to a decision by Iraq to allow the UN to monitor its weapons programme (a move that would consequently lead to a repeal of the UN embargo on Iraqi petroleum exports).

1994 In March ministers opted to maintain the output quotas, agreed in September 1993, until the end of the year, and urged non-OPEC producers to freeze their production levels. (Iraq failed to endorse the agreement, since it recognizes only the production agreement adopted in July 1990.) At the meeting Saudi Arabia resisted a proposal from Iran and Nigeria, both severely affected by declines in petroleum revenue, to reduce its production by 1m. b/d in order to boost prices. In June the Conference endorsed the decision to maintain the existing production ceiling, and attempted to reassure commodity markets by implying that the production agreement would remain in effect until the end of 1994. Ministers acknowledged that there had been a gradual increase in petroleum prices in the second quarter of the year, with an average basket price of US $15.6 per barrel for that period. Political disruption in Nigeria, including a strike by petroleum workers, was considered to be the principal factor contributing to the price per barrel rising above $19 in August. In November OPEC ministers endorsed a proposal by Saudi Arabia to maintain the existing production quota, of 24.52m. b/d, until the end of 1995.

1995 In January it was reported that Gabon was reconsidering its membership of OPEC, owing to difficulties in meeting its budget contribution. During the first half of the year Gabon consistently exceeded its quota of 287,000 b/d, by 48,000 b/d, and the country failed to send a delegate to the ministerial Conference in June. At the Conference ministers expressed concern at OPEC's falling share of the world petroleum market. The Conference criticized the high level of North Sea production, by Norway and the United Kingdom, and urged collective production restraint in order to stimulate prices. In November the Conference agreed to extend the existing production quota, of 24.52m. b/d, for a further six months, in order to stabilize prices. During the year, however, output remained in excess of the production quotas, some 25.58m. b/d.

1996 The possibility of a UN-Iraqi agreement permitting limited petroleum sales dominated OPEC concerns in the first half of the year and contributed to price fluctuations in the world markets. By early 1996 output by OPEC countries was estimated to be substantially in excess of quota levels; however, the price per barrel remained relatively buoyant (the average basket price reaching US $21 in March), owing largely to unseasonal cold weather in the northern hemisphere. In May a memorandum of understanding was signed between Iraq and the UN to allow the export of petroleum, up to a value of $2,000m. over a six-month period, in order to fund humanitarian relief efforts within that country. In June the Conference agreed to increase the overall output ceiling by 800,000 b/d, i.e. the anticipated level of exports from Iraq in the first six months of the agreement. A proposal, endorsed by Iran, to raise the individual country quotas failed to win support, while a comprehensive reduction in output, in order to accommodate the Iraqi quota without adjusting the existing production ceiling, was also rejected, notably by Saudi Arabia and Venezuela. At the meeting Gabon's withdrawal from the Organization was confirmed. As a result of these developments, the new ceiling was set at 25.03m. b/d. Independent market observers expressed concern that, without any formal agreement to reduce overall production and given the actual widespread violation of the quota system, the renewed export of Iraqi petroleum would substantially depress petroleum prices. However, the markets remained stable as implementation of the UN-Iraqi agreement was delayed. In September the monitoring group acknowledged that members were exceeding their production quotas, but declined to impose any punitive measures (owing to the steady increase in petroleum prices). In late November the Conference agreed to maintain the existing production quota for a further six months. Also in November, Iraq accepted certain disputed technical terms of the UN agreement, enabling the export of petroleum to commence in December.

1997 During the first half of the year petroleum prices declined, reaching a low of US $16.7 per barrel in early April, owing to the Iraqi exports, depressed world demand and persistent overproduction. In June the Conference agreed to extend the existing production ceiling, of 25.03m. b/d, for a further six-month period. Member states resolved to adhere to their individual quotas in order to reduce the cumulative excess production of an estimated 2m. b/d; however, Venezuela, which (some sources claimed) was producing almost 800,000 b/d over its quota of 2.4m. b/d, declined to co-operate. An escalation in political tensions in the Gulf region in October, in particular Iraq's reluctance to co-operate with UN inspectors, prompted an increase in the price of crude petroleum to some $21.2 per barrel. Price fluctuations ensued, although there was a general downward trend. In November the OPEC Conference, meeting in Jakarta, approved a proposal by Saudi Arabia, to increase the overall production ceiling by some 10%, with effect from 1 January 1998, in order to meet the perceived stable world demand and to reflect more accurately current output levels. At the same time the Iranian Government announced its intention to increase its production capacity and maintain its share of the quota by permitting foreign companies to conduct petroleum exploration in Iran.

1998 A decline in petroleum prices at the start of the year caused widespread concern, and speculation that this had resulted from the decision to increase production to 27.5m. b/d, coinciding with the prospect of a decline in demand from Asian economies that had been undermined by extreme financial difficulties and of a new Iraqi agreement with the UN with provision for increased petroleum exports. A meeting of the Monitoring Sub-committee, in late January, urged members to implement production restraint and resolved to send a monitoring team to member states to encourage compliance with the agreed quotas. In February the UN Security Council approved a new agreement permitting Iraq to export petroleum valued at up to US $5,200m. over a six-month period, although the Iraqi Government insisted that its production and export capacity was limited to $4,000m. Indonesia requested an emergency meeting of ministers to discuss this development and the ongoing decline in petroleum prices. Saudi Arabia rejected the proposal unless member states agreed to adhere to their quotas, with particular reference to Venezuela, which was still OPEC's largest over-producer. In March Saudi Arabia, Venezuela and Mexico announced a joint agreement to reduce domestic production by 300,000 b/d, 200,000 b/d and 100,000 b/d respectively, with effect from 1 April, and agreed to co-operate in persuading other petroleum producing countries to commit to similar reductions. At the end of March an emergency ministerial meeting ratified the reduction proposals (the so-called 'Riyadh Pact'), which amounted to 1.245m. b/d pledged by OPEC members and 270,000 b/d by non-member states. Nevertheless, prices remained low, with over-production, together with lack of market confidence in member states' willingness to comply with the restricted quotas, an outstanding concern. In June Saudi Arabia, Venezuela and Mexico reached agreement on further reductions in output of some 450,000 b/d. Later in that month the Conference, having reviewed the market situation, agreed to implement a new reduction in total output of some 1.36m b/d, with effect from 1 July, reducing the total production target for OPEC members to 24.387m. b/d. Iran, which had been criticized for not adhering to the reductions agreed in March, confirmed that it would reduce output by 305,000 b/d. At the meeting, which was also attended by senior officials from Mexico, Oman and Russia, Saudi Arabia proposed the establishment of a new *ad hoc* grouping of the world's largest petroleum producers, in order to monitor output and support price initiatives. In early August petroleum prices fell below $12 per barrel. In September the Kuwaiti authorities, which advocated further production cuts, arranged meetings with Saudi Arabia and Qatar, and later with the petroleum ministers of Algeria, Iran, Oman and the UAE, to discuss the situation in the petroleum markets, and to co-ordinate efforts to stabilize and uphold petroleum prices. In that month Iraq's petroleum production reached an estimated 2.4m. b/d, contributing to concerns of over-supply in the world market. In early November OPEC members attending a conference of the parties to the UN Framework Convention on Climate Change, held in Buenos Aires, Argentina, warned that they would claim compensation for any lost revenue resulting from initiatives to limit the emission of 'greenhouse gases' and reduce the consumption of petroleum. Later in November OPEC ministers, meeting in Vienna, resolved to maintain the existing production levels, but improve compliance. Subsequently, despite the escalation of tensions between the UN and Iraqi authorities, prices remained consistently around the level of $11 per barrel. Air strikes conducted by the USA and United Kingdom against strategic targets in Iraq in mid-December were not considered to have interrupted petroleum supplies and therefore had little impact on prices. Lost export earnings by OPEC member states as a result of the depressed oil prices amounted to some $50,000m. in 1998.

1999 In March ministers from Algeria, Iran, Mexico, Saudi Arabia and Venezuela, meeting in The Hague, the Netherlands, agreed further to reduce petroleum production, owing to the continued weakness of the global market. Subsequently, petroleum prices rose by nearly 40%, after reaching the lowest price of US $9.9 per barrel in mid-February. Later in March OPEC confirmed a new reduction in output of 2.104m. b/d from 1 April, including commitments from non-OPEC members Mexico, Norway, Oman and Russia to decrease production by a total of 388,000 b/d. The agreement envisaged a total production target for OPEC member countries of 22.976m. b/d. Actual output in April was estimated at 26.38m. b/d (compared with 27.72m. in March), which contributed to prices reaching $17 per barrel. Prices continued to fluctuate, however, owing to concern at Iraq's potential production capacity. By June total production by OPEC member states (excluding Iraq) had declined to a reported 23.25m. b/d. The evidence of almost 90% compliance with the new production quotas contributed to market confidence that stockpiles of petroleum would be reduced, and resulted in sustained price increases. At the end of July a meeting of the Ministerial Monitoring Sub-committee confirmed that adherence to the production quotas in the period April to June had been strong, but reiterated the need to maintain the total production level at least until March 2000 given that the year's average basket price was under $14 per barrel and markets remained volatile. In late August 1999 Saudi Arabia, Mexico and Venezuela agreed to extend production reductions until March 2000. In September 1999 OPEC ministers confirmed that the existing quotas would be maintained for a further six-month period. At the end of September the reference price for petroleum rose above $24, its highest level since January 1997. Prices remained buoyant during the rest of the year; however, there was increasing speculation at whether the situation was sustainable. At the end of November Iraq temporarily suspended its petroleum exports, totalling some 2.2m. b/d, pending agreement on a new phase of the oil-for-food arrangement and concern at the lack of progress on the removal of international sanctions.

## Finance

The budget for 2000 amounted to 196.1m. Austrian Schilling, of which 31.1m. Schilling was to be financed by transfer from the Reserve Fund and the balance was to be contributed by member states.

## Publications

*Annual Report.*
*Annual Statistical Bulletin.*
*Monthly Oil Market Report.*
*OPEC Bulletin* (monthly).
*OPEC Review* (quarterly).
Reports, information papers, press releases.

# OPEC FUND FOR INTERNATIONAL DEVELOPMENT

**Address:** POB 995, 1011 Vienna, Austria.
**Telephone:** (1) 515-64-0; **fax:** (1) 513-92-38.

The Fund was established by OPEC member countries in 1976.

### MEMBERS

Member countries of OPEC (q.v.).

## Organization

(January 2000)

### ADMINISTRATION

The Fund is administered by a Ministerial Council and a Governing Board. Each member country is represented on the Council by its minister of finance. The Board consists of one representative and one alternate for each member country.

**Chairman, Ministerial Council:** Dr BAMBANG SUBIANTO (Indonesia).

**Chairman, Governing Board:** Dr SALEH AL-OMAIR (Saudi Arabia).

**Director-General of the Fund:** Dr YESUFU SEYYID ABDULAI (Nigeria).

### FINANCIAL STRUCTURE

The resources of the Fund, whose unit of account is the US dollar, consist of contributions by OPEC member countries, and income received from operations or otherwise accruing to the Fund.

The initial endowment of the Fund amounted to US $800m. Its resources have been replenished three times, and have been further increased by the profits accruing to seven OPEC member countries through the sales of gold held by the International Monetary Fund. The pledged contributions to the OPEC Fund amounted to $3,435.0m. at the end of 1998, and paid-in contributions totalled $2,870.1m.

## Activities

The OPEC Fund for International Development is a multilateral agency for financial co-operation and assistance. Its objective is to reinforce financial co-operation between OPEC member countries and other developing countries through the provision of financial support to the latter on appropriate terms, to assist them in their economic and social development. The Fund was conceived as a collective financial facility which would consolidate the assistance extended by its member countries; its resources are additional to those already made available through other bilateral and multilateral aid agencies of OPEC members. It is empowered to:

(*i*) Provide concessional loans for balance-of-payments support;

(*ii*) Provide concessional loans for the implementation of development projects and programmes;

(*iii*) Make contributions and/or provide loans to eligible international agencies; and

(*iv*) Finance technical assistance and research through grants.

The eligible beneficiaries of the Fund's assistance are the governments of developing countries other than OPEC member countries, and international development agencies whose beneficiaries are developing countries. The Fund gives priority to the countries with the lowest income.

**OPEC FUND COMMITMENTS AND DISBURSEMENTS IN 1998** (US $ million)

| | Commitments | Disbursements |
|---|---|---|
| **Lending operations:** | 155.65 | 129.23 |
| Project financing | 143.65 | 111.01 |
| Programme financing | 12.00 | 18.23 |
| **Grant Programme:** | 4.48 | 4.13 |
| Technical assistance | 2.71 | 2.30 |
| Research and other activities | 0.22 | 0.11 |
| Emergency aid | 1.55 | 1.59 |
| Common Fund for Commodities | – | 0.14 |
| **Total** | 160.12 | 133.37 |

**Project loans approved in 1998** (US $ million)

| Region and country | Sector | Loans approved |
|---|---|---|
| **Africa** | | 60.15 |
| Benin | Transportation | 4.38 |
| Burkina Faso | Transportation | 7.00 |
| Chad | Transportation | 7.10 |
| The Gambia | Transportation | 1.93 |
| Guinea | Agriculture and agro-industry | 4.50 |
| Madagascar | Education | 10.00 |
| Malawi | Transportation | 7.00 |
| Mali | Transportation | 5.50 |
| | Agriculture and agro-industry | 3.84 |
| Mauritania | Transportation | 4.00 |
| Tanzania | Transportation | 5.00 |
| **Asia** | | 63.50 |
| Bangladesh | Transportation | 10.00 |
| Cambodia | Transportation | 6.00 |
| India | Education | 10.00 |
| Kyrgyzstan | Other (rural health and education services) | 3.58 |
| Laos | Transportation | 4.42 |
| Maldives | Transportation | 1.50 |
| Palestine | Other (rehabilitation of basic infrastructure) | 8.00 |
| Philippines | Other (rehabilitation of essential services and facilities) | 10.00 |
| Viet Nam | National development bank | 10.00 |
| **Latin America and the Caribbean** | | 20.00 |
| Bolivia | Other (rural development project) | 5.00 |
| Haiti | Education | 5.00 |
| Honduras | Other (infrastructure development) | 5.00 |
| Nicaragua | Agriculture and agro-industry | 5.00 |
| **Total** | | 143.65 |

The Fund may undertake technical, economic and financial appraisal of a project submitted to it, or entrust such an appraisal to an appropriate international development agency, the executing national agency of a member country, or any other qualified agency. Most projects financed by the Fund have been co-financed by other development finance agencies. In each such case, one of the co-financing agencies may be appointed to administer the Fund's loan in association with its own. This practice has enabled the Fund to extend its lending activities to 105 countries over a short period of time and in a simple way, with the aim of avoiding duplication and complications. As its experience grew, the Fund increasingly resorted to parallel, rather than joint financing, taking up separate project components to be financed according to its rules and policies. In addition, it started to finance some projects completely on its own. These trends necessitated the issuance in 1982 of guide-lines for the procurement of goods and services under the Fund's loans, allowing for a margin of preference for goods and services of local origin or originating in other developing countries: the general principle of competitive bidding is, however, followed by the Fund. The loans are not tied to procurement from Fund member countries or from any other countries. The margin of preference for goods and services obtainable in developing countries is allowed on the request of the borrower and within defined limits. Fund assistance in the form of programme loans has a broader coverage than project lending. Programme loans are used to stimulate an economic sector or sub-sector, and assist recipient countries in obtaining inputs, equipment and spare parts. Besides extending loans for project and programme financing and balance of payments support, the Fund also undertakes other operations, including grants in support of technical assistance and other activities (mainly research), and financial contributions to other international institutions.

The Fund's thirteenth lending programme, covering a two-year period effective from 1 January 1998, aimed, in particular, to target 71 developing countries. By the end of December 1998 the Fund had extended 778 loans since operations began in 1976, totalling US $3,982.7m., of which $2,953.1m. (or 74.1%) was for project financing, $724.2m. (18.2%) was for balance-of-payments support and $305.3m. (7.7%) was for programme financing.

Direct loans are supplemented by grants to support technical assistance, food aid and research. By the end of December 1998 478 grants, amounting to US $240.9m., had been extended, including $83.6m. to the Common Fund for Commodities (established by UNCTAD), $40.9m. in support of emergency relief operations and a special contribution of $20m. to the International Fund for Agricultural Development (IFAD). In addition, the OPEC Fund had committed $971.9m. to other international institutions by the end of 1998, comprising OPEC members' contributions to the resources of IFAD, and irrevocable transfers in the name of its members to the IMF Trust Fund. By the end of 1998 69.7% of total commitments had been disbursed.

During the year ending 31 December 1998 the Fund's total commitments amounted to US $160.1m. (compared with $240.4m. in 1997). These commitments included 24 project loans, amounting to $143.6m., and two loans to finance commodity import programmes in Burundi and Rwanda, totalling $12.0m. The largest proportion of project loans (44.4%) was to support improvements in the transportation sector in 12 countries and included rural road improvements in Bangladesh, the restoration of primary roads in Cambodia, improvements to the international airport in the Maldives, and construction of a highway in Mali and Mauritania. The education sector received 17.4% of loans, financing improved teaching programmes and access to basic education in Haiti, improvements at late primary and secondary school levels in Tripura State, India, and the rehabilitation of schools damaged by cyclones in Madagascar. Agriculture and agro-industry loans, amounting to 9.3%, supported intensified crop production in Guinea, an irrigation scheme in Mali and smallholder farmers in Nicaragua. A loan of US $10m. (7.0%) was awarded to Viet Nam, under the national development banks sector, to provide income-generating activities among the rural poor. Other loans, including multisector loans, amounting to 22.0% of the total, supported a range of projects in Bolivia, Honduras, Kyrgyzstan, the Philippines and the West Bank and Gaza.

During 1998 the Fund approved US $4.48m. for 32 grants, of which $2.7m. was for technical assistance activities, $215,000 for research, and $1.6m. to provide emergency assistance to Afghanistan, Bangladesh, Bolivia, Guatemala, Honduras, Nicaragua, Papua New Guinea and Sudan (for victims of natural disasters), to Tanzania (urgent sanitation and drainage improvements in Zanzibar) and to refugees and other people displaced by the conflict in Kosovo and Metohija, the Federal Republic of Yugoslavia.

## Publications

*Annual Report* (in Arabic, English, French and Spanish).

*OPEC Aid and OPEC Aid Institutions—A Profile* (annually).

*OPEC Fund Newsletter* (3 a year).

Occasional books and papers.

# PACIFIC COMMUNITY

**Address:** BP D5, 98848 Nouméa Cédex, New Caledonia.

**Telephone:** 26-20-00; **fax:** 26-38-18; **e-mail:** spc@spc.org.nc; **internet:** www.spc.org.nc/.

In February 1947 the Governments of Australia, France, the Netherlands, New Zealand, the United Kingdom, and the USA signed an agreement to establish the South Pacific Commission, which came into effect in July 1948. (The Netherlands withdrew from the Commission in 1962, when it ceased to administer the former colony of Dutch New Guinea, now Irian Jaya, part of Indonesia.) In October 1997 the 37th South Pacific Conference, convened in Canberra, Australia, agreed to rename the organization the Pacific Community, with effect from 6 February 1998. The Secretariat of the Pacific Community (SPC) services the Community, and provides technical advice, training and assistance in economic, social and cultural development to 22 countries and territories of the Pacific region. It serves a population of about 6.8m., scattered over some 30m. sq km, more than 98% of which is sea.

### MEMBERS

American Samoa
Australia
Cook Islands
Fiji
France
French Polynesia
Guam
Kiribati
Marshall Islands
Federated States of Micronesia
Nauru
New Caledonia
New Zealand
Niue
Northern Mariana Islands
Palau
Papua New Guinea
Pitcairn Islands
Samoa
Solomon Islands
Tokelau
Tonga
Tuvalu
United Kingdom
USA
Vanuatu
Wallis and Futuna Islands

## Organization

(January 2000)

### CONFERENCE OF THE PACIFIC COMMUNITY

The Conference is the governing body of the Community (replacing the former South Pacific Conference) and is composed of representatives of all member countries and territories. The main responsibilities of the Conference, which meets annualy, are to appoint the Director-General, to determine major national or regional policy issues in the areas of competence of the organization and to note changes to the Financial and Staff Regulations approved by the Committee of Representatives of Governments and Administrations (CRGA).

### COMMITTEE OF REPRESENTATIVES OF GOVERNMENTS AND ADMINISTRATIONS (CRGA)

This Committee comprises representatives of all member states and territories, having equal voting rights. It meets annually to consider the work programme evaluation conducted by the Secretariat and to discuss any changes proposed by the Secretariat in the context of regional priorities; to consider and approve any policy issues for the organization presented by the Secretariat or by member countries and territories; to consider applicants and make recommendations for the post of Director-General; to approve the administrative and work programme budgets; to approve amendments to the Financial and Staff Regulations; and to conduct annual performance evaluations of the Director-General.

### SECRETARIAT

The Secretariat is headed by a Director-General and two Deputy Directors-General, based in Suva and Nouméa. Three administrative Divisions cover Land Resources, Marine Resources and Social Resources. The Secretariat also provides information services, including library facilities, publications, translation and computer services. The organization has more than 200 staff members.

**Director-General:** LOURDES PANGELINAN (Guam).

**Deputy Directors-General:** Dr JIMMIE RODGERS (Solomon Islands), (vacant).

**Regional Office:** Private Mail Bag, Suva, Fiji; tel. 370733; fax 370021; e-mail spcsuva@spc.org.fj.

## Activities

The SPC provides, on request of its member countries, technical assistance, advisory services, information and clearing-house services. The organization also conducts regional conferences and technical meetings, as well as training courses, workshops and seminars at the regional or country level. It provides small grants-in-aid and awards to meet specific requests and needs of members. In November 1996 the Conference agreed to establish a specific Small Islands States fund to provide technical services, training and other relevant activities. The Conference also endorsed a series of organizational reforms, on the basis of a review conducted earlier in the year. The reforms were implemented during 1997. From

1 January 1997 the Commission assumed responsibility for the maritime programme and telecommunications policy activities of the South Pacific Forum Secretariat (q.v.).

### LAND RESOURCES

The SPC's agriculture programme, which is based in Suva, Fiji, aims to promote land and agricultural management practices that are both economically and environmentally sustainable; to strengthen national capabilities to reduce losses owing to crop pests (insects, pathogens and weeds) and animal diseases already present and to prevent the introduction of new pests and diseases; to facilitate trade through improved quarantine procedures; and to improve access to, and use of, sustainable development information for all. The programme incorporates the following five main policy units: agriculture programme management, to ensure overall management and co-ordination; general agriculture, including advice on general agriculture and specific activities in crop diversification, such as coconut technology development, and the provision of agricultural training; plant protection, through the implementation of regional research and technical support projects; animal health and animal production; and the provision of advice and information on agricultural concerns and sustainable development. A new Pacific Regional Agricultural Programme (PRAP) was to be implemented by the Land Resources Division. The SPC administers a Pacific Islands Forests and Trees Support Project, which is concerned with natural forest management and conservation, agroforestry and development and the use of tree and plant resources, and a regional project relating to the sustainable management of forests and agroforesty. Maritime activities are also covered by the Land Resources Division.

The SPC office in Suva, Fiji, administers a Community Education Training Centre (CETC), which conducts a seven-month training course for up to 36 women community workers annually, with the objective of training women in methods of community development so that they can help others to achieve better living conditions for island families and communities. A Regional Media Centre provides training, technical assistance and production materials in all areas of the media for member countries and territories, Community work programmes, donor projects and regional non-governmental organizations. The Centre comprises a radio broadcast unit, a graphic design and publication unit and a TV and video unit.

### MARINE RESOURCES

The SPC aims to support and co-ordinate the sustainable development and management of inshore fisheries resources in the region, to undertake scientific research in order to provide member governments with relevant information for the sustainable development and management of tuna and billfish resources in and adjacent to the South Pacific region, and to provide data and analytical services to national fisheries departments. The main components of the Community's fisheries activities are the Coastal Fisheries Programme (CFP) and the Oceanic Fisheries Programme (OFP). The CFP is divided into the following sections: capture—to provide practical, field-based training, through the services of experts in support of captive fisheries development activities; post-harvest—to offer advice and training in order to improve handling practices, storage, seafood product development, quality control and marketing; training—to improve manpower development and assist in the co-ordination of fisheries training; resource assessment and management—to assist with the design and implementation of inshore resources surveys, programmes for the collection, analysis and interpretation of fishery statistics, and other activities directed towards the acquisition of information necessary for sound management of national fishery resources; and an information section. The SPC also implements a Women's Fisheries Development Project, which assists women from coastal fishing communities to participate more effectively in, and benefit from, fisheries activities, particularly in the post-harvest, processing industry. The OFP consists of the Tuna and Billfish Research Section Project, the South Pacific Regional Tuna Resource Assessment and Monitoring Project, which was to promote the sustainable management of tuna fisheries in the region through continuous scientific monitoring, and a Fisheries Statistics Section, which maintains a database of industrial tuna fisheries in the region. The OFP contributed research and statistical information to a multilateral high-level conference that was convened in Majuro, the Marshall Islands, in June 1997, to formulate a framework for the conservation and management of highly migratory fish stocks in the Western and Central Pacific.

### SOCIAL RESOURCES

A Community Health Programme aims to implement health promotion programmes; to assist regional authorities to strengthen health information systems and to promote the use of new technology for health information development and disease control (for example, through the Public Health Surveillance and Disease Control Programme); to promote efficient health services management; and to help all Pacific Islanders to attain a level of health and quality of life that will enable them to contribute to the development of their communities. The Community Health Services also work in the areas of non-communicable diseases and nutrition, in particular the high levels of diabetes and heart disease in parts of the region, environmental health, through the improvement of water and sanitation facilities, and to reduce the incidence of HIV/AIDS and other sexually-transmitted diseases (STDs). The SPC has initiated, with funding from the European Union, a project to prevent AIDS and STDs among young people based on peer education and awareness. The Division is responsible for implementing a Pacific Regional Vector-Borne Diseases Project that was established in 1996, with particular emphasis on Fiji, Vanuatu and the Solomon Islands.

A Statistics Programme assists governments and administrations in the region to provide effective and efficient national statistical services through the provision of training activities, a statistical information service and other advisory services. A Regional Conference of Statisticians facilitates the integration and co-ordination of statistical services throughout the region.

The Population and Demography Programme aims to assist governments effectively to utilize and incorporate data into the formulation of development policies and programmes and to provide technical support in population, demographic and development issues to member governments, other SPC programmes and organizations active in the region. The Programme organizes national workshops in population and development planning, provides short-term professional attachments, undertakes demographic research and analysis and disseminates information.

The Rural Development Programme promotes active participation of the rural population and encourages the use of traditional practices and knowledge in the formulation of rural development projects and income-generating activities. The Rural Technology Programme aims to provide technical assistance, advice and monitoring of pilot regional programmes, with emphasis on technologies to generate renewable energy in rural areas, to help achieve environmentally-sustainable development.

The Youth and Community Development Programme provides non-formal education and support for youth, community workers and young adults in community development subjects. It also advises and assists the Pacific Youth Council in promoting a regional youth identity. The SPC implements its cultural affairs and conservation programme mainly through the Council of Pacific Arts. A Pacific Women's Resource Bureau aims to promote the social, economic and cultural advancement of women in the region by assisting governments and regional organizations to include women in the development planning process. The Bureau also provides technical and advisory services, advocacy and management support training to groups concerned with women in development and gender and development, and supports the production and exchange of information regarding women.

## Finance

The organization's budget is divided into administrative and work programme budgets. The administrative budget is funded by assessed contributions from member states, while the work programme is financed in part by assessed contributions, but in the main by voluntary contributions from industrialized member governments, other governments, aid agencies and other sources. The approved administrative budget for 2000 amounted to US $2.5m.

## Publications

*Annual Report.*
*Fisheries Newsletter* (quarterly).
*Pacific Aids Alert Bulletin* (quarterly).
*Pacific Island Nutrition* (quarterly).
*Regional Tuna Bulletin* (quarterly).
*Report of the Conference of the Pacific Community.*
*Women's Newsletter* (quarterly).
Technical publications, statistical bulletins, advisory leaflets and reports.

# SOUTH ASIAN ASSOCIATION FOR REGIONAL CO-OPERATION—SAARC

**Address:** POB 4222, Kathmandu, Nepal.

**Telephone:** (1) 221785; **fax:** (1) 227033; **e-mail:** saarc@mos.com.np; **internet:** www.south-asia.com/saarc.

The South Asian Association for Regional Co-operation (SAARC) was formally established in 1985 in order to strengthen and accelerate regional co-operation, particularly in economic development.

### MEMBERS

| | |
|---|---|
| Bangladesh | Nepal |
| Bhutan | Pakistan |
| India | Sri Lanka |
| Maldives | |

## Organization

(January 2000)

### SUMMIT MEETING

Heads of state and of government of member states represent the body's highest authority, and a summit meeting is normally held annually.

### COUNCIL OF MINISTERS

The Council of Ministers comprises the ministers of foreign affairs of member countries, who meet twice a year. The Council may also meet in extraordinary session at the request of member states. The responsibilities of the Council include formulating of policies, assessing progress and confirming new areas of co-operation.

### STANDING COMMITTEE

The Committee consists of the secretaries of foreign affairs of member states. It has overall responsibility for the monitoring and co-ordination of programmes and financing, and determines priorities, mobilizes resources and identifies areas of co-operation. It usually meets twice a year, and submits its reports to the Council of Ministers. The Committee is supported by an *ad hoc* Programming Committee made up of senior officials, who meet to examine the budget of the Secretariat, confirm the Calendar of Activities and resolve matters assigned to it by the Standing Committee.

### TECHNICAL COMMITTEES

SAARC comprises 11 technical committees covering: agriculture and forestry; education, culture and sports; health, population and child welfare; environment and meteorology; rural development (including the SAARC Youth Volunteers Programme—SYVOP); tourism; transport; science and technology; communications; women in development; and the prevention of drugs-trafficking and drug abuse. Each committee is headed by a representative of a member state.

### SECRETARIAT

The Secretariat was established in January 1987 to co-ordinate and oversee SAARC activities. It comprises the Secretary-General and a Director from each member country. The Secretary-General is appointed by the Council of Ministers, after being nominated by a member state. The ninth summit meeting of heads of state and of government, held in Malé, Maldives, in 1997, extended the Secretary-General's term of office from two to three years. The Director is nominated by member states and appointed by the Secretary-General for a term of three years, although this may be increased in special circumstances.

**Secretary-General:** NIHAL RODRIGO (Sri Lanka).

## Activities

In August 1993 ministers of foreign affairs of seven countries, meeting in New Delhi, India, adopted a Declaration on South Asian Regional Co-operation and launched an Integrated Programme of Action, which identified the main areas for regional co-operation. The first summit meeting of heads of state and of government, held in Dhaka, Bangladesh, in December 1985, resulted in the signing of the Charter of the South Asian Association for Regional Co-operation (SAARC).

SAARC is committed to improving quality of life in the region by accelerating economic growth, social progress and cultural development; promoting self-reliance; encouraging mutual assistance; increasing co-operation with other developing countries; and co-operating with other regional and international organizations. The SAARC Charter stipulates that decisions should be made unanimously, and that 'bilateral and contentious issues' should not be discussed. Regular meetings, at all levels, are held to further co-operation in areas covered by the Technical Committees (see above). A priority objective is the eradication of poverty in the region, and in 1993 SAARC endorsed an Agenda of Action to help achieve this by 2002. A framework for exchanging information on poverty eradication has also, since, been established.

A Committee on Economic Co-operation (CEC), comprising senior trade officials of member states, was established in July 1991 to monitor progress concerning trade and economic co-operation issues. In the same year the summit meeting approved the creation of an inter-governmental group to establish a framework for the promotion of specific trade liberalization measures. A SAARC Chamber of Commerce (SCCI) became operational in 1992, with headquarters in Karachi, Pakistan. In April 1993 ministers signed a SAARC Preferential Trading Arrangement (SAPTA) which came into effect in December 1995. By the end of 1996 more than 2,000 products had been identified as eligible for preferential trade tariffs. In December 1995 the Council resolved that the ultimate objective for member states should be the establishment of a South Asian Free Trade Area (SAFTA), superseding SAPTA. An *ad hoc* inter-governmental expert group was constituted to formulate a framework to realize SAFTA. In January 1996 the first SAARC Trade Fair was held, in New Delhi, India, to promote intra-SAARC commerce.

An Agricultural Information Centre was founded in 1988, in Dhaka, Bangladesh, to serve as a central institution for the dissemination of knowledge and information in the agricultural sector. It maintains a network of centres in each member state, which provide for the efficient exchange of technical information and for strengthening agricultural research. An agreement establishing a Food Security Reserve to meet emergency food requirements was signed in November 1987, and entered into force in August 1988. The Board of the Reserve meets annually to assess the food security of the region. At mid-1998 the Reserve contained some 241,580 metric tons of grain. Other regional institutions are the SAARC Tuberculosis Centre in Thimi, Nepal, which opened in July 1992 with the aim of preventing and reducing the prevalence of the disease in the region through the co-ordination of tuberculosis control programmes, research and training. A SAARC Documentation Centre opened in New Delhi in May 1994. A SAARC Meteorological Research Centre was established in Dhaka in January 1995. A Human Resource Development Centre is being established in Islamabad, Pakistan. Regional funds include a SAARC—Japan Special Fund established in September 1993. One-half of the fund's resources, which were provided by the Japanese Government, was to be used to finance projects identified by the Japanese Government, and one-half was to be used to finance projects identified by SAARC member states. The eighth SAARC summit meeting, held in New Delhi in May 1996, established a South Asian Development Fund, comprising a Fund for Regional Projects, a Regional Fund and a fund for social development and infrastructure building.

A SAARC Youth Volunteers Programme (SYVOP) enables young people to work in other member countries in the agriculture and forestry sectors. By early 1997 seven such projects had been organized. The Programme is part of a series of initiatives designed to promote intra-regional exchanges and contact. A Youth Awards Scheme to reward outstanding achievements by young people was inaugurated in 1996. The theme selected for recognition in 1999 was 'Creative Skills'. Founded in 1987, the SAARC Audio-visual Exchange Programme (SAVE) broadcasts radio and television programmes on social and cultural affairs to all member countries, twice a month, in order to disseminate information about SAARC and its members. The first South Asian festival was held in India in 1992. A Visa Exemption Scheme, exempting 21 specified categories of person from visa requirements, with the aim of promoting closer regional contact, became operational in March 1992. A SAARC citizens forum promotes interaction among the people of South Asia. In addition, SAARC operates a fellowships, scholarships and chairs scheme and a scheme for the promotion of organized tourism.

At the third SAARC summit, held in Kathmandu in November 1987, member states signed a regional convention on measures to counteract terrorism. The convention, which entered into force in August 1988, commits signatory countries to the extradition or prosecution of alleged terrorists and to the implementation of preventative measures to combat terrorism. Monitoring desks for terrorist and drugs offences have been established to process information relating to those activities. The first SAARC conference on co-operation in police affairs, attended by the heads of the police forces of member states, was held in Colombo in July 1996. The conference discussed the issues of terrorism, organized crime, the extradition of criminals, drugs-trafficking and drug abuse. A convention on narcotic drugs and psychotropic substances was signed during the fifth SAARC summit meeting, held in Malé in 1990. The convention entered into force in September 1993, following its ratification by member states.

SAARC co-operates with other regional and international organizations. In February 1993 SAARC signed a memorandum of understanding with UNCTAD, whereby both parties agreed to exchange information on trade control measures regionally and in 50 developed and developing countries, respectively, in order to increase transparency and thereby facilitate trade. SAARC has also signed co-operation agreements with UNICEF, UNDP, UNDCP, the European Union, ESCAP, the International Telecommunication Union, the Asia Pacific Telecommunity, the Colombo Plan and the Canadian International Development Agency.

## Finance

The national budgets of member countries provide the resources to finance SAARC activities. The Secretariat's annual budget is shared among member states according to a specified formula.

## Publications

*SAARC Newsletter* (monthly).

*SPECTRUM* (irregular).

## Regional Apex Bodies

**Association of Persons of the Legal Communities of the SAARC Countries—SAARCLAW:** 129 Hulftsdorp St, Colombo 12, Sri Lanka; tel. (1) 323979; fax (1) 445447; f. 1991; recognized as a SAARC regional apex body in July 1994; aims to enhance exchanges and co-operation amongst the legal communities of the sub-region and to promote the development of law.

**SAARC Chamber of Commerce:** Federation House, Main Clifton, Karachi 75600, Pakistan; tel. (21) 5871552; fax (21) 5871554; e-mail sc-cihq@biruni.erum.com.pk; f. 1992; promotes economic and trade co-operation throughout the sub-region and greater interaction between the business communities of member countries; organizes SAARC Economic Co-operation Conferences and Trade Fairs. Pres. KANTIKUMAR R. PODAR; Sec.-Gen. SYED ABUL HASAN.

Other recognized regional bodies include the South Asian Association for Regional Co-operation of Architects, the Association of Management Development Institutions, the SAARC Federation of University Women, the South Asian Federation of Accountants and the Association of SAARC Speakers and Parliamentarians.

# SOUTH PACIFIC FORUM*

**MEMBERS**

| | |
|---|---|
| Australia | Niue |
| Cook Islands | Palau |
| Fiji | Papua New Guinea |
| Kiribati | Samoa |
| Marshall Islands | Solomon Islands |
| Federated States of Micronesia | Tonga |
| Nauru | Tuvalu |
| New Zealand | Vanuatu |

Note: New Caledonia was admitted as an observer at the Forum in 1999.

The South Pacific Forum is the gathering of Heads of Government of the independent and self-governing states of the South Pacific. Its first meeting was held on 5 August 1971, in Wellington, New Zealand. It provides an opportunity for informal discussions to be held on a wide range of common issues and problems and meets annually or when issues require urgent attention. The Forum has no written constitution or international agreement governing its activities nor any formal rules relating to its purpose, membership or conduct of meeting. Decisions are always reached by consensus, it never having been found necessary or desirable to vote formally on issues. In October 1994 the Forum was granted observer status by the General Assembly of the United Nations.

Since 1989 each Forum has been followed by 'dialogues' with representatives of other countries with a long-term interest in and commitment to the region. In October 1995 the Forum Governments suspended France's 'dialogue' status, following that country's resumption of the testing of nuclear weapons in French Polynesia. France was reinstated as a 'dialogue partner' in September 1996. In 1998 'dialogue partners' comprised Canada, the People's Republic of China, France, Japan, Malaysia, the United Kingdom, the USA, the Republic of Korea and the European Union. In 1999 the Forum agreed to admit the Philippines as a 'dialogue partner', with effect from 2000.

The South Pacific Nuclear-Free Zone Treaty (Treaty of Rarotonga), prohibiting the acquisition, stationing or testing of nuclear weapons in the region, came into effect in December 1986, following ratification by eight states. The USSR signed the protocols to the treaty (whereby states possessing nuclear weapons agree not to use or threaten to use nuclear explosive devices against any non-nuclear party to the Treaty) in December 1987 and ratified them in April 1988; the People's Republic of China did likewise in December 1987 and October 1988 respectively. The other three major nuclear powers, however, intimated that they did not intend to adhere to the Treaty. In July 1993 the Forum petitioned the USA, the United Kingdom and France, asking them to reconsider their past refusal to sign the Treaty in the light of the end of the 'Cold War'. In July 1995, following the decision of the French Government to resume testing of nuclear weapons in French Polynesia, members of the Forum resolved to increase diplomatic pressure on the three Governments to sign the Treaty. In October the United Kingdom, the USA and France announced their intention to accede to the Treaty, by mid-1996. While the decision was approved by the Forum, it urged the Governments to sign with immediate effect, thus accelerating the termination of France's testing programme. Following France's decision, announced in January 1996, to end the programme four months earlier than scheduled, representatives of the Governments of the three countries signed the Treaty in March.

In 1990 five of the Forum's smallest island member states formed an economic sub-group to address their specific concerns, in particular economic disadvantages resulting from a poor resource base, absence of a skilled work-force and lack of involvement in world markets. In September 1997 the 28th Forum, convened in Rarotonga, the Cook Islands, endorsed the inclusion of the Marshall Islands as the sixth member of the Smaller Island States sub-group. Representatives of the grouping, which also includes Kiribati, the Cook Islands, Nauru, Niue and Tuvalu, meet regularly. In February 1998 senior Forum officials, for the first time, met with representatives of the Caribbean Community and the Indian Ocean Commission, as well as other major international organizations, to discuss means to enhance consideration and promotion of the interests of small island states.

The 21st Forum, held in August 1990 in Vanuatu, criticized the US Government's proposal to use the US external territory of Johnston Atoll for the destruction of chemical weapons. The meeting urged industrialized countries to reduce the emission of gases that contribute to the so-called 'greenhouse effect', or warming of the earth's atmosphere. A ministerial committee was established to monitor political developments in New Caledonia, in co-operation with the French authorities.

The 22nd Forum took place in Pohnpei, Federated States of Micronesia, in July 1991. It issued a strong condemnation of French testing of nuclear weapons in the region. The Forum examined the report of the ministerial committee on New Caledonia, and instructed the committee to visit New Caledonia annually. However, this proposal was rejected by the French Government.

The 23rd Forum, held in Honiara, Solomon Islands, in July 1992, welcomed France's suspension of its nuclear-testing programme until the end of the year, but urged the French Government to make the moratorium permanent. Forum members discussed the decisions made at the UN Conference on Environment and Development held in June, and approved the Cook Islands' proposal to host a 'global conference for small islands'. The Niue Fisheries Surveillance and Law Enforcement Co-operation Treaty was signed by members, with

* The 30th Forum, held in October 1999, determined to rename the grouping the Pacific Islands' Forum, to take effect after a transitional period of one year.

the exception of Fiji, Kiribati and Tokelau, which were awaiting endorsement from their legislatures. The treaty provides for co-operation in the surveillance of fisheries resources and in defeating drugs-trafficking and other organized crime. Forum leaders also adopted a separate declaration on future priorities in law enforcement co-operation.

At the 24th Forum, held in Yaren, Nauru, in August 1993 it was agreed that effective links needed to be established with the broader Asia-Pacific region, with participation in Asia-Pacific Economic Co-operation (APEC), where the Forum has observer status, to be utilized to the full. The Forum urged an increase in intra-regional trade and asked for improved opportunities for Pacific island countries exporting to Australia and New Zealand. New Caledonia's right to self-determination was supported. Environmental protection measures and the rapid growth in population in the region, which was posing a threat to economic and social development, were also discussed by the Forum delegates.

The 25th Forum was convened in Brisbane, Australia, in August 1994 under the theme of 'Managing Our Resources'. In response to the loss of natural resources as well as of income-earning potential resulting from unlawful logging of timber by foreign companies, Forum members agreed to impose stricter controls on the exploitation of forestry resources and to begin negotiations to standardize monitoring of the region's resources. The Forum also agreed to strengthen its promotion of sustainable exploitation of fishing stocks, reviewed preparations of a convention to control the movement and management of radioactive waste within the South Pacific and discussed the rationalization of national airlines, on a regional or sub-regional basis, to reduce operational losses.

The 26th Forum, held in Madang, Papua New Guinea, in September 1995, was dominated by extreme hostility on the part of Forum Governments to the resumption of testing of nuclear weapons by France in the South Pacific region. The decision to recommence testing, announced by the French Government in June, had been instantly criticized by Forum Governments. The 26th Forum reiterated their demand that France stop any further testing, and also condemned the People's Republic of China for conducting nuclear tests in the region. The meeting endorsed a draft Code of Conduct on the management and monitoring of indigenous forest resources in selected South Pacific countries, which had been initiated at the 25th Forum; however, while the six countries concerned committed themselves to implementing the Code through national legislation, its signing was deferred, owing to an initial unwillingness on the part of Papua New Guinea and Solomon Islands. The Forum did adopt a treaty to ban the import into the region of all radioactive and other hazardous wastes, and to control the transboundary movement and management of these wastes (the so-called Waigani Convention). The Forum agreed to reactivate the ministerial committee on New Caledonia, comprising Fiji, Nauru and Solomon Islands, which was to monitor political developments in that territory prior to its referendum on independence, scheduled to be held in 1998. In addition, the Forum resolved to implement and pursue means of promoting economic co-operation and long-term development in the region. In December 1995 Forum finance ministers, meeting in Port Moresby, Papua New Guinea, discussed the issues involved in the concept of 'Securing Development Beyond 2000' and initiated an assessment project to further trade liberalization efforts in the region.

The 27th Forum, held in Majuro, the Marshall Islands, in September 1996, supported the efforts of the French Government to improve relations with countries in the South Pacific and agreed to readmit France to the post-Forum dialogue. The Forum meeting recognized the importance of responding to the liberalization of the global trading system by reviewing the region's economic tariff policies, and of assisting members in attracting investment for the development of the private sector. The Forum advocated that a meeting of economy ministers of member countries be held each year. The Forum was also concerned with environmental issues: in particular, it urged the ratification and implementation of the Waigani Convention by all member states, the formulation of an international, legally-binding agreement to reduce gas emissions, and the promotion of regional efforts to conserve marine resources and to protect the coastal environment. The Forum requested the ministerial committee on New Caledonia, which had visited the territory in July, to pursue contacts with all parties and to continue to monitor preparations for the 1998 referendum.

In July 1997 the inaugural meeting of Forum economy ministers was convened in Cairns, Australia. It formulated an Action Plan to encourage the flow of foreign investment into the region by committing members to economic reforms, good governance and the implementation of multilateral trade and tariff policies. The meeting also commissioned a formal study of the establishment of a free-trade agreement between Forum island states. The 28th Forum, held in Rarotonga, the Cook Islands, in September, considered the economic challenges confronting the region. However, it was marked by a failure to conclude a common policy position on mandatory targets for the emission of so-called 'greenhouse gases', which some members considered to be a threat to low-lying islands in the region, owing to an ongoing dispute between Australia and other Forum Governments.

The 29th Forum, held in Pohnpei, Federated States of Micronesia, in August 1998, considered the need to pursue economic reforms and to stimulate the private sector and foreign investment in order to ensure economic growth. Leaders reiterated their support for efforts to implement the economic Action Plan and to develop a framework for a free-trade agreement, and endorsed specific recommendations of the second Forum Economic Ministers Meeting, which was held in Fiji, in July, including the promotion of competitive telecommunications markets, the development of information infrastructures and support for a new economic vulnerability index at the UN to help determine least developed country status. The Forum was also concerned with environmental issues, notably the shipment of radioactive wastes, the impact of a multinational venture to launch satellites from the Pacific, the need for ongoing radiological monitoring of the Mururoa and Fangataufa atolls, and the development of a South Pacific Whale Sanctuary. The Forum adopted a Statement on Climate Change, which urged all countries to ratify and implement the gas emission reductions agreed upon in December 1997 (the so-called Kyoto Protocol of the UN Framework Convention on Climate Change), and emphasized the Forum's commitment to further measures for verifying and enforcing emission limitation.

In October 1999 the 30th Forum, held in Koror, Palau, endorsed in principle the establishment of a regional free-trade area (FTA), which had been approved at a special ministerial meeting held in June. The FTA was to be implemented from 2001 over a period of eight years for developing member countries and 10 years for smaller island states and least developed countries. The Forum requested officials from member countries to negotiate the details of a draft agreement on the FTA, including possible extensions of the arrangements to Australia and New Zealand. The heads of government adopted a Forum Vision for the Pacific Information Economy, which recognized the importance of information technology infrastructure for the region's economic and social development and the possibilities for enhanced co-operation in investment, job creation, education, training and cultural exchange. Forum Governments also expressed concern at the shipment of radioactive waste through the Pacific and determined to pursue negotiations with France, Japan and the United Kingdom regarding liability and compensation arrangements; confirmed their continued support for the multinational force and UN operations in East Timor; and urged more countries to adopt and implement the Kyoto Protocol to limit the emission of 'greenhouse gases'. In addition, the Forum agreed to rename the grouping the Pacific Islands' Forum, which was to take effect after a transitional period of one year.

# South Pacific Forum Secretariat

**Address:** Private Mail Bag, Suva, Fiji.

**Telephone:** 312600; **fax:** 301102; **e-mail:** info@forumsec.org.fj; **internet:** www.forumsec.org.fj.

The South Pacific Bureau for Economic Co-operation (SPEC) was established by an agreement signed on 17 April 1973, at the third meeting of the South Pacific Forum in Apia, Western Samoa (now Samoa). SPEC was renamed the South Pacific Forum Secretariat in 1988.

## Organization

(January 2000)

### COMMITTEE

The Committee is the Secretariat's executive board. It comprises representatives and senior officials from all member countries. It meets twice a year, immediately before the meetings of the South

Pacific Forum and at the end of the year, to discuss in detail the Secretariat's work programme and annual budget.

### SECRETARIAT

The Secretariat undertakes the day-to-day activities of the Forum. It is headed by a Secretary-General, with a staff of some 70 people drawn from the member countries. The Secretariat comprises the following four Divisions: Corporate Services; Development and Economic Policy; Trade and Investment; and Political and International Affairs.

**Secretary-General:** NOEL LEVI (Papua New Guinea).

**Deputy Secretary-General:** IOSEFA MAIAVA (Samoa).

## Activities

The Secretariat's aim is to enhance the economic and social well-being of the people of the South Pacific, in support of the efforts of national governments.

The Secretariat's trade and investment services extend advice and technical assistance to member countries in policy, development, export marketing, and information dissemination. Trade policy activities are mainly concerned with improving private sector policies, for example investment promotion, assisting integration into the world economy, and the development of businesses. The Secretariat aims to assist both island governments and private sector companies to enhance their capacity in the development and exploitation of export markets, product identification and product development. A trade exhibition was held in French Polynesia in 1997, and support was granted to provide for visits to overseas trade fairs and the development of promotional materials. Other trade activities in 1997 included capacity-building in new technologies, business marketing workshops, and technical assistance to improve the cost and efficiency of petroleum management by member countries. Two trade missions, to the Republic of Korea and Taiwan, were undertaken to generate mutual awareness of business opportunities. The Trade and Investment Division of the Secretariat also co-ordinates the activities of the regional trade offices located in Australia, New Zealand and Japan (see below). The establishment of an economic exchange support centre in the People's Republic of China was under consideration in 1998.

The South Pacific Regional Trade and Economic Co-operation Agreement (SPARTECA), which came into force in 1981, aims to redress the trade deficit of the South Pacific countries with Australia and New Zealand. It is a non-reciprocal trade agreement under which Australia and New Zealand offer duty-free and unrestricted access or concessional access for specified products originating from the developing island member countries of the Forum. In 1985 Australia agreed to further liberalization of trade by abolishing (from the beginning of 1987) duties and quotas on all Pacific products except steel, cars, sugar, footwear and garments. In August 1994 New Zealand expanded its import criteria under the agreement by reducing the rule of origin requirement for garment products from 50% to 45% of local content. In response to requests from Fiji, Australia agreed to widen its interpretation of the agreement by accepting as being of local content manufactured products that consist of goods and components of 50% Australian content. A new Fiji/Australia Trade and Economic Relations Agreement (FATERA) was concluded in March 1999 to complement SPARTECA and compensate for certain trade benefits that were in the process of being withdrawn.

The Political and International Affairs Division of the Secretariat organizes and services the meetings of the Forum, disseminates its views, administers the Forum's observer office at the United Nations, and aims to strengthen relations with other regional and international organizations, in particular APEC and ASEAN. The Division's other main concern is to promote regional co-operation in law enforcement and legal affairs, and it provides technical support for the drafting of legal documents and for law enforcement capacity-building. In 1997 the Secretariat undertook an assessment to survey the need for specialist training in dealing with money laundering in member countries. In September 1998 the Forum Secretariat was concerned with assessing the legislative reforms and other commitments needed to ensure implementation of the 1992 Honiara Declaration on Law Enforcement Co-operation, which was scheduled to enter into effect in 2000. The Division administers a South Pacific Police Customs Drug Enforcement Project and assists member countries to ratify and implement the 1988 UN Convention against Illicit Trafficking in Narcotic Drugs and Psychotropic Substances. In December 1998 the Secretariat initiated a five-year programme to strengthen regional law enforcement capabilities, in particular to counter cross-border crimes such as money-laundering, drugs-trafficking and smuggling. All member states, apart from Australia and New Zealand, were to participate in the initiative.

The Secretariat helps to co-ordinate environmental policy. With support from the Australian Government, it administers a network of stations to monitor sea-levels and climate change throughout the Pacific region. In 1998 the Secretariat hosted a preparatory meeting for Forum delegates to help establish a common position on climate change issues prior to the fourth Conference of the Parties to the Framework Convention on Climate Change, which was held in Buenos Aires, Argentina, in November.

The Development and Economic Policy Division of the Secretariat aims to co-ordinate and promote co-operation in development activities and programmes throughout the region. The Division administers a Short Term Advisory Service, which provides consultancy services to help member countries meet economic development priorities, and a Fellowship Scheme to provide practical training in a range of technical and income-generating activities. A Small Island Development Fund aims to assist the economic development of this sub-group of member countries (i.e. the Cook Islands, Kiribati, the Marshall Islands, Nauru, Niue and Tuvalu) through project financing. A separate fellowship has also been established to provide training to the Kanak population of New Caledonia, to assist in their social, economic and political development. The Division aims to assist regional organizations to identify development priorities and to provide advice to national governments on economic analysis, planning and structural reforms.

The Secretariat services the Pacific Group Council of ACP states receiving assistance from the EU under the Lomé Convention (q.v.), and in early 1993 a joint unit was established within the Secretariat headquarters to assist Pacific ACP countries and regional organizations in submitting projects to the EU for funding. In October 1994 the Secretariat signed an agreement with representatives of the EU for the establishment of a Pacific Regional Agricultural Programme. The four-year programme was to be funded under the Lomé IV Pacific Regional Programme, with the aim of improving agricultural productivity in the region.

The South Pacific Forum established the Pacific Forum Line and the Association of South Pacific Airlines (see below), as part of its efforts to promote co-operation in regional transport. On 1 January 1997 the work of the Forum Maritime Programme, which included assistance for regional maritime training and for the development of regional maritime administrations and legislation, was transferred to the regional office of the South Pacific Commission (renamed the Pacific Community from February 1998) at Suva. At the same time responsibility for the Secretariat's civil aviation activities was transferred to individual countries, to be managed at a bilateral level. Telecommunications policy activities were also transferred to the then South Pacific Commission at the start of 1997. In May 1998 ministers responsible for aviation in member states approved a new regional civil aviation policy, which envisaged liberalization of air services, common safety and security standards and provisions for shared revenue.

## Finance

The Governments of Australia and New Zealand each contribute some 37% of the annual budget and the remaining amount is shared by the other member Governments. Extra-budgetary funding is contributed mainly by Australia, New Zealand, Japan, the EU and France. In December 1996 Forum officials approved a budget of $F 14.1m. for the Secretariat's 1997 work programme.

## Publications

*Annual Report.*

*Forum News* (quarterly).

*Forum Trends.*

*Forum Secretariat Directory of Aid Agencies.*

*South Pacific Trade Directory.*

*SPARTECA* (guide for Pacific island exporters).

Reports of meetings; profiles of Forum member countries.

## Associated and Affiliated Organizations

**Association of South Pacific Airlines—ASPA:** POB 9817, Nadi Airport, Nadi, Fiji; tel. 723526; fax 720196; f. 1979 at a meeting of airlines in the South Pacific, convened to promote co-operation among the member airlines for the development of regular, safe and economical commercial aviation within, to and from the South Pacific. Mems: 14 regional airlines, three associates. Pres. RICHARD GATES; Sec.-Gen. GEORGE E. FAKTAUFON.

**Pacific Forum Line:** POB 796, Auckland, New Zealand; tel. (9) 356-2333; fax (9) 356-2330; e-mail info@pflnz.co.nz; f. 1977 as a joint venture by South Pacific countries, to provide shipping services to meet the special requirements of the region; operates three container vessels; conducts shipping agency services in Australia, Fiji, New

Zealand and Samoa, and stevedoring in Samoa. Chair. T. TUFUI; CEO W. J. MACLENNAN.

**Pacific Islands' Centre—PIC:** Akasaka Twin Tower, Main Bldg, 1st Floor, 2-17-22 Akasaka, Minato-ku, Tokyo 107-0052, Japan; tel. (3) 3585-8419; fax (3) 3585-8637; f. 1996 to promote and to facilitate trade, investment and tourism among Forum members and Japan. Dir HIDEO FUJITA.

**South Pacific Forum Fisheries Agency—FFA:** POB 629, Honiara, Solomon Islands; tel. (677) 21124; fax (677) 23995; e-mail info@ffa.int; internet www.ffa.int; f. 1979 to promote co-operation in fisheries among coastal states in the region; collects and disseminates information and advice on the living marine resources of the region, including the management, exploitation and development of these resources; provides assistance in the areas of law (treaty negotiations, drafting legislation, and co-ordinating surveillance and enforcement), fisheries development, research, economics, computers, and information management. A Vessel Monitoring System, to provide automated data collection and analysis of fishing vessel activities throughout the region, was inaugurated by the FFA in 1998. On behalf of its member countries, the FFA administers a multilateral fisheries treaty, under which vessels from the USA operate in the region, in exchange for an annual payment. Dir VICTORIO UHERBELAU. Publs *FFA News Digest* (every two months), *FFA Reports*.

**South Pacific Trade Commission:** Suite 3003, Piccadilly Tower, 133 Castlereagh St, Sydney, NSW 2000, Australia; tel. (2) 9283-5933; fax (2) 9283-5948; e-mail info@sptc.gov.au; internet www.sptc.gov.au; f. 1979; assists Pacific Island Governments and business communities to identify market opportunities in Australia and promotes investment in the Pacific Island countries. Senior Trade Commr AIVU TAUVASA (Papua New Guinea).

**New Zealand Office:** 48 Emily Pl., Auckland; tel. (9) 3020465; fax (9) 3776642; e-mail parmeshc@sptc.org.nz; internet www.sptc.org.nz.

# SOUTHERN AFRICAN DEVELOPMENT COMMUNITY—SADC

**Address:** SADC Bldg, Private Bag 0095, Gaborone, Botswana.

**Telephone:** 351863; **fax:** 372848; **e-mail:** sadcsec@sadc.int; **internet:** www.sadc.int.

The first Southern African Development Co-ordination Conference (SADCC) was held at Arusha, Tanzania, in July 1979, to harmonize development plans and to reduce the region's economic dependence on South Africa. On 17 August 1992 the 10 member countries of the SADCC signed a treaty establishing the Southern African Development Community (SADC), which replaced the SADCC. The treaty places binding obligations on member countries, with the aim of promoting economic integration towards a fully developed common market. A tribunal was to be established to arbitrate in the case of disputes between member states arising from the treaty. By September 1993 all of the member states had ratified the treaty; it came into effect on 5 October.

### MEMBERS

| | | |
|---|---|---|
| Angola | Malawi | South Africa |
| Botswana | Mauritius | Swaziland |
| Congo, Democratic Republic | Mozambique | Tanzania |
| Lesotho | Namibia | Zambia |
| | Seychelles | Zimbabwe |

## Organization

(January 2000)

### SUMMIT MEETING

The meeting is held at least once a year and is attended by heads of state and government or their representatives. It is the supreme policy-making organ of the SADC and is responsible for the appointment of the Executive Secretary.

### COUNCIL OF MINISTERS

Representatives of SADC member countries at ministerial level meet at least once a year. In addition, special meetings of sectoral committees of ministers are held to co-ordinate regional policy in a particular field by, for example, ministers of energy and ministers of transport.

### STANDING COMMITTEE OF OFFICIALS

The Committee, comprising senior officials, usually from the ministry responsible for economic planning or finance, acts as the technical advisory body to the Council. It meets at least once a year. Members of the Committee also act as a national contact point for matters relating to SADC.

### SECRETARIAT

**Executive Secretary a.i.:** PAKEREESAMY ('PREGA') RAMSAMY (Mauritius).

### SECTORAL CO-ORDINATION OFFICES

Each member state has a responsibility to promote and co-ordinate regional policies and programmes in specific areas on behalf of the organization as a whole. Accordingly, the Sectoral Co-ordinating Units are part of national governments and administered by the civil service of that country. Sectoral Commissions and Centres are regional institutions, which are established and supported by all member states.

**Agricultural Research and Training:** Private Bag 0033, Gaborone, Botswana; tel. 328780; fax 328965; e-mail dar@info.bw; Dir Dr L. M. MAZHANI.

**Culture, Information and Sport:** Avda Francisco Orlando Magumbwe 780, 10th Floor, POB 1154, Maputo, Mozambique; tel. (1) 497944; fax (1) 497943; e-mail sacis@sadc.uem.mz; Dir RENATO MATUSSE.

**Employment and Labour:** POB 31969, Lusaka, Zambia; tel. (1) 251719; fax (1) 252095; Dir C. J. CHANDA.

**Energy:** rua Gil Vicente No. 2, CP 2876, Luanda, Angola; tel. (2) 345288; fax (2) 343003; e-mail sadc_elec@ebonet.net; internet www.ebonet.net/sadc; Dir ANTONIO HENRIQUE DA SILVA.

**Environment and Land Management:** Ministry of Agriculture and Co-operatives, POB 24, Maseru 100, Lesotho; tel. 323561; fax 310349; Dir BATAUNG LELEKA.

**Finance and Investment:** Private Bag X115, Pretoria, 0001, South Africa; tel. (12) 3155653; fax (12) 3219580; Dir SECHOCHA MAKHOALIBE.

**Food, Agriculture and Natural Resources:** 43 Robson Manyika Ave, POB 4046, Harare, Zimbabwe; tel. (4) 736051; telex 22440; fax (4) 795345; e-mail fstau@fanr-sadc.org.zw; Dir REGINALD MUGWARA.

**Human Resources Development:** Ministry of Public Service and Information, POB 5873, Mbabane, Swaziland; tel. 4046344; fax 4046407; e-mail sadchrd@realnet.co.sz; Dir ENNET NKAMBULE.

**Industry and Trade:** POB 9491, Dar es Salaam, Tanzania; tel. (51) 31455; fax (51) 46919; Dir ABRAHIM PALLANGYO.

**Inland Fisheries, Wildlife and Forestry:** Ministry of Forestry, Fisheries and Environmental Affairs, Private Bag 350, Lilongwe 3, Malawi; tel. 782600; fax 780260; Dir D. KAMBAUWA.

**Livestock Production and Animal Disease Control:** Private Bag 0032, Gaborone, Botswana; tel. 350620; fax 303744; Dir M. FANIKISO.

**Marine Fisheries and Resources:** Private Bag 13355, Windhoek, Namibia; tel. (61) 2053911; fax (61) 235269; Dir Z. A. ISHITILE.

**Mining:** Ministry of Mines and Mineral Development, Chilufya Mulenga Rd, POB 31969, 10101 Lusaka, Zambia; tel. (1) 254043; fax (1) 252095; e-mail sadc-mcu@zamnet.zm; internet www.sadcmining.org.zm; Dir C. J. CHANDA.

**Southern African Centre for Co-operation in Agricultural Research (SACCAR):** Private Bag 00108, Gaborone, Botswana; tel. 328847; fax 328806; Dir K. MOLAPONG.

**Southern African Transport and Communications Commission (SATCC):** CP 2677, Maputo, Mozambique; tel. (1) 427202; fax (1) 420213; e-mail director@satcc.org; internet www.satcc.org; Dir E. H. MSOLOMBA.

**Tourism:** c/o Ministry of Tourism and Leisure, Air Mauritius Centre, Level 12, Pres. J. F. Kennedy St, Port Louis, Mauritius; tel. 210-1329; fax 208-6776; e-mail mot@intnet.mu; Dir SUSY EDUARD.

**Water:** c/o Ministry of Natural Resources, POB 426, Maseru 100, Lesotho; tel. 323163; fax 310250.

## Activities

In July 1979 the first Southern African Development Co-ordination Conference was attended by delegations from Angola, Botswana, Mozambique, Tanzania and Zambia, with representatives from donor governments and international agencies. In April 1980 a regional economic summit conference was held in Lusaka, Zambia, and the Lusaka Declaration, a statement of strategy entitled 'Southern Africa: Towards Economic Liberation', was approved, together with a programme of action allotting specific studies and tasks to member governments (see list of co-ordinating offices, above). The members aimed to reduce their dependence on South Africa for rail and air links and port facilities, imports of raw materials and manufactured goods, and the supply of electric power. In 1985, however, an SADCC report noted that since 1980 the region had become still more dependent on South Africa for its trade outlets, and the 1986 summit meeting, although it recommended the adoption of economic sanctions against South Africa, failed to establish a timetable for doing so.

In January 1992 a meeting of the SADCC Council of Ministers approved proposals to transform the organization (by then expanded to include Lesotho, Malawi, Namibia and Swaziland) into a fully integrated economic community, and in mid-August the treaty establishing the SADC (see above) was signed. South Africa became a member of the SADC in August 1994, thus strengthening the objective of regional co-operation and economic integration. Mauritius became a member in August 1995. In September 1997 SADC heads of state agreed to admit the Democratic Republic of the Congo and Seychelles as members of the Community.

A possible merger between the SADC and the Preferential Trade Area for Eastern and Southern African States (PTA), which consisted of all the members of the SADC apart from Botswana and had similar aims of enhancing economic co-operation, was rejected by the SADC's Executive Secretary in January 1993. He denied that the two organizations were duplicating each other's work, as had been suggested. In August 1994 SADC heads of state, meeting in Gaborone, Botswana, advocated that, in order to minimize any duplication of activities, the PTA be divided into two sections: a southern region, incorporating all SADC members, and a northern region. It was emphasized that there would not be a merger between the two groupings. However, concerns of regional rivalry with the PTA's successor, the Common Market for Eastern and Southern Africa (COMESA, q.v.), persisted. In August 1996 an SADC–COMESA ministerial meeting advocated the continued separate functioning of the two organizations.

In September 1994 the first meeting of ministers of foreign affairs of the SADC and the European Union (EU) was held in Berlin, Germany. The two sides agreed to establish working groups to promote closer trade, political, regional and economic co-operation. In particular, a declaration issued from the meeting specified joint objectives, including a reduction of exports of weapons to southern Africa and of the arms trade within the region, promotion of investment in the region's manufacturing sector and support for democracy at all levels. A consultative meeting between representatives of the SADC and EU was held in February 1995, in Lilongwe, Malawi, at which both groupings resolved to strengthen security in the southern African region. The meeting proposed initiating mechanisms to prevent conflicts and to maintain peace, and agreed to organize a conference to address the problems of drugs-trafficking and cross-border crime in the region. A second SADC–EU ministerial meeting, held in Namibia in October 1996, endorsed a Regional Indicative Programme to enhance co-operation between the two organizations over the next five years. The third ministerial meeting took place in Vienna, Austria, in November 1998. In September 1999 the SADC signed a co-operation agreement with the US Government, which incorporated measures to promote US investment in the region, and commitments to support HIV/AIDS assessment and prevention programmes, and to assist member states to develop environmental protection capabilities.

In April 1997 the SADC announced the establishment of a Parliamentary Forum to promote democracy, human rights and good governance throughout the region. Membership was to be open to national parliaments of all SADC countries, and was to offer fair representation for women. Representatives were to serve for a period of five years. The Parliamentary Forum, with its headquarters in Windhoek, Namibia, was to receive funds from member parliaments, governments and charitable and international organizations. In September SADC heads of state endorsed the establishment of the Forum as an autonomous institution.

## REGIONAL SECURITY

In November 1994 SADC ministers of defence, meeting in Arusha, Tanzania, approved the establishment of a regional rapid-deployment peace-keeping force, which could be used to contain regional conflicts or civil unrest in member states. In April 1997 a training programme was held, which aimed to inform troops from nine SADC countries of UN peace-keeping doctrines, procedures and strategies. The exercise took place in Zimbabwe at a cost of US $900,000, provided by the British Government and the Zimbabwe National Army. A peace-keeping exercise involving 4,000 troops was held in South Africa, in April 1999. An SADC Mine Action Committee has been established to monitor and co-ordinate the process of removing anti-personnel land devices from countries in the region.

In June 1996 SADC heads of state and government, meeting in Gaborone, Botswana, inaugurated a new Organ on Politics, Defence and Security, which was expected to enhance co-ordination of national policies and activities in these areas. The objectives of the body were, *inter alia,* to safeguard the people and development of the region against instability arising from civil disorder, inter-state conflict and external aggression; to undertake conflict prevention, management and resolution activities, by mediating in inter-state and intra-state disputes and conflicts, pre-empting conflicts through an early-warning system and using diplomacy and peace-keeping to achieve sustainable peace; to promote the development of a common foreign policy, in areas of mutual interest, and the evolution of common political institutions; to develop close co-operation between the police and security services of the region; and to encourage the observance of universal human rights, as provided for in the charters of the UN and OAU. The summit meeting elected the Zimbabwean President, Robert Mugabe, to chair the Organ. The Zambian President, Frederick Chiluba, failed to attend the meeting, owing to his Government's concern that the new body was empowered to interfere in the country's internal affairs. In October the Organ convened, at summit level, to consider measures to promote the peace process in Angola; however, there were disagreements within SADC regarding the future status of the security Organ either as an integrated part of the community (favoured by South Africa) or as a more autonomous body (supported by Zimbabwe). In March 1998 the Presidents of Malawi, Mozambique and Namibia were charged by SADC leaders to undertake a review of the issue.

In August 1998 the Zimbabwean Government convened a meeting of the heads of state of seven SADC member states to discuss the escalation of civil conflict in the Democratic Republic of the Congo (DRC) and the threat to regional security, with Rwanda and Uganda reportedly having sent troops to assist anti-government forces. Later in that month ministers of defence and defence officials of several SADC countries declared their support for an initiative of the Zimbabwean Government to send military assistance to the forces loyal to President Kabila in the DRC. South Africa, which did not attend the meeting, rejected any military intervention under SADC auspices and insisted that the organization would pursue a diplomatic initiative. Zimbabwe, Angola and Namibia proceeded to send troops and logistical support to counter rebel Congolese forces. The Presidents of those countries failed to attend an emergency meeting of heads of state, convened by President Mandela of South Africa, which called for an immediate cease-fire and presented a 10-point-peace plan. A further emergency meeting, held in early September and attended by all SADC leaders, agreed to pursue negotiations for a peaceful settlement of the conflict. Some unity within the grouping was restored by Mandela's endorsement of the objective of supporting Kabila as the legitimate leader in the DRC. Furthermore, at the annual SADC summit meeting, held in Mauritius, it was agreed that discussion of the report on the security Organ, scheduled to have been presented to the conference, would be deferred to a specially convened summit meeting (although no date was agreed). Talks attended by Angola, the DRC, Namibia, Rwanda, Uganda, Zambia and Zimbabwe, conducted in mid-September, in Victoria Falls, agreed in principle on a cease-fire in the DRC but failed to conclude a detailed peace accord. Fighting continued to escalate, and in October Zimbabwe, Angola and Namibia resolved to send reinforcements to counter the advancing rebel forces. Meanwhile, in September representatives of the SADC attempted to mediate between government and opposition parties in Lesotho amidst a deteriorating security situation in that country. At the end of the month, following an attempt by the Lesotho military to seize power, South Africa, together with Botswana, sent troops into Lesotho to restore civil order. The operation was declared to have been conducted under SADC auspices, however it prompted widespread criticism owing to the troops' involvement in heavy fighting with opposition forces. A committee was established by SADC to secure a cease-fire in Lesotho. Also at the end of September SADC chiefs of staff agreed that the Community would assist the Angolan Government to eliminate the UNITA movement, owing to its adverse impact on the region's security. In mid-October an SADC ministerial team, comprising representatives of South Africa, Botswana, Mozambique and Zimbabwe, negotiated an accord between the opposing sides in Lesotho providing for the conduct of democratic elections. The withdrawal of foreign troops from Lesotho was initiated at the end of April 1999, and was reported to have been completed by mid-May.

During the first half of 1999 Zambia's President Chiluba pursued efforts, under SADC auspices, to negotiate a political solution to the conflict in the DRC. Troops from the region, in particular from Angola and Zimbabwe, remained actively involved in the struggle to uphold Kabila's administration. SADC ministers of defence and of foreign affairs convened in Lusaka, in late June, in order to secure a cease-fire agreement. An accord was finally signed in July between Kabila, leaders of the rebel forces and foreign allies of both sides. All foreign troops were to be withdrawn within nine months according to a schedule to be drawn up by the UN, OAU and a Joint Military Commission. By late 1999, however, there were reports of frequent outbreaks of fighting in the DRC.

## TRANSPORT AND COMMUNICATIONS

At the SADC's inception transport was seen as the most important area to be developed, on the grounds that, as the Lusaka Declaration noted, without the establishment of an adequate regional transport and communications system, other areas of co-operation become impractical. Priority was to be given to the improvement of road and railway services into Mozambique, so that the landlocked countries of the region could transport their goods through Mozambican ports instead of South African ones. The Southern African Transport and Communications Commission (SATCC) was established, in Maputo, Mozambique, in order to undertake SADC's activities in this sector. The successful distribution of emergency supplies in 1992/93, following a severe drought in the region, was reliant on improvements made to the region's infrastructure. The facilities of 12 ports in southern Africa, including South Africa, were used to import some 11.5m. metric tons of drought-related commodities, and the SADC co-ordinated six transport corridors to ensure unobstructed movement of food and other supplies. During 1995 the SATCC undertook a study of regional transport and communications to provide a comprehensive framework and strategy for future courses of action. A task force was also established to identify measures to simplify procedures at border crossings throughout southern Africa. In 1996 the SATCC Road Network Management and Financing Task Force was established.

In 1996/97 174 of the SADC's 407 development projects were in the transport and communications sector, amounting to US $ 6,474.4m., or 80% of total project financing. These projects aimed to address missing links and over-stretched sections of the regional network, as well as to improve efficiency, operational co-ordination and human resource development, such as management training projects. Other sectoral objectives were to ensure the compatibility of technical systems within the region and to promote the harmonization of regulations relating to intra-regional traffic and trade. In 1997 Namibia announced plans, supported by the SADC, to establish a rail link with Angola in order to form a trade route similar to that created in Mozambique, on the western side of southern Africa. In March 1998 the final stage of the trans-Kalahari highway, linking ports on the east and west coasts of southern Africa, was officially opened. In July 1999 a 317-km rail link between Bulawayo, Zimbabwe, and the border town of Beitbridge, administered by the SADC as its first build-operate-transfer project, was opened.

The SADC promotes greater co-operation in the civil aviation sector, in order to improve efficiency and to reverse a steady decline in the region's airline industries. Within the telecommunications sector efforts have been made to increase the capacity of direct exchange lines and international subscriber dialling (ISD) services. In January 1997 the Southern African Telecommunications Regional Authority (SATRA), a regulatory authority, was established. An SADC Expedited Mail Service operates in the postal services sector. The SATCC's Technical Unit oversees the region's meteorological services and issues a regular *Drought-Watch for Southern Africa* bulletin, a monthly *Drought Overview* bulletin and forewarnings of impending natural disasters.

## FOOD, AGRICULTURE AND NATURAL RESOURCES

The food, agriculture and natural resources sector covers eight subsectors: agricultural research and training; inland fisheries; forestry; wildlife; marine fisheries and resources; food security; livestock production and animal disease control; and environment and land management. The importance of this sector is evident in the fact that, according to SADC figures, agriculture contributes one-third of the region's GNP, accounts for 26% of total earnings of foreign exchange and employs some 80% of the labour force. The sector's principal objectives are regional food security, agricultural development and natural resource development.

The Southern African Centre for Co-operation in Agricultural Research (SACCAR), was established in Gaborone, Botswana, in 1985. It aims to strengthen national agricultural research systems, in order to improve management, increase productivity, promote the development and transfer of technology to assist local farmers, and improve training. Examples of activity include: a sorghum and millet improvement programme; a land and water management research programme; a root crop research network; agroforestry research, implemented in Malawi, Tanzania, Zambia and Zimbabwe; and a grain legume improvement programme, comprising separate research units for groundnuts, beans and cowpeas. The SADC's Plant Genetic Resources Centre was established in 1988, near Lusaka, Zambia, to collect, conserve and utilize indigenous and exotic plant genetic resources and to develop appropriate management practices.

The sub-sector for livestock production and animal disease control aims to improve breeding methods in the region through the Management of Farm Animal Genetic Research Programme. It also seeks to control diseases such as contagious bovine pleuropneumonia, foot and mouth disease and heartwater through diagnosis, monitoring and vaccination programmes. An *Animal Health Mortality Bulletin* is published, as is a monthly *Animal Disease Situation Bulletin*, which alerts member states to outbreaks of disease in the region.

The sector aims to promote inland and marine fisheries as an important, sustainable source of animal protein. Marine fisheries are also considered to be a potential source of income of foreign exchange. In May 1993 the first formal meeting of SADC ministers of marine fisheries convened in Namibia, and it was agreed to hold annual meetings. In April 1997 it was agreed that Namibia would co-ordinate the establishment of inspectorates to monitor and control marine fisheries in the region for a period of five years. The development of fresh water fisheries is focused on aquaculture projects, and their integration into rural community activities. The environment and land management sub-sector is concerned with sustainability as an essential quality of development. It aims to protect and improve the health, environment and livelihoods of people living in the southern African region; to preserve the natural heritage and biodiversity of the region; and to support regional economic development on a sustainable basis. The sector also focuses on capacity-building, training, regional co-operation and the exchange of information in all areas related to the environment and land management. It administers an SADC Environmental Exchange Network, which was established in 1995, and the Community's Land Degradation and Desertification Control Programme. The sector also undertakes projects for the conservation and sustainable development of forestry and wildlife.

Under the food security programme, the Harare-based Regional Early Warning System aims to anticipate and prevent food shortages through the provision of information relating to the food security situation in member states. As a result of the drought crisis experience, SADC member states have agreed to inform the food security sector of their food and non-food requirements on a regular basis, in order to assess the needs of the region as a whole. A regional food reserve project was also to be developed.

## WATER

Following the severe drought in the region in 1991/92, the need for water resource development became a priority. The water sector was established as a separate administrative unit in August 1996, although the terms of reference of the sector were only formally approved by the Council, meeting in Windhoek, Namibia, in February 1997. The sector aims to promote the equitable distribution and effective management of water resources, in order to address the concern that many SADC member countries may be affected by future droughts and water scarcity. In April a workshop was held in Swaziland concerning the implementation of a new SADC Protocol on Shared Watercourse Systems. The involvement of the private sector in the region's water policies was under consideration at the Round Table Conference on Integrated Water Resources Development in October 1998.

## ENERGY

Areas of activity in the energy sector include: joint petroleum exploration, training programmes for the petroleum sector and studies for strategic fuel storage facilities; promotion of the use of coal; development of hydroelectric power and the co-ordination of SADC generation and transmission capacities; new and renewable sources of energy, including pilot projects in solar energy; assessment of the environmental and socio-economic impact of wood-fuel scarcity and relevant education programmes; and energy conservation. In July 1995 SADC energy ministers approved the establishment of a Southern African Power Pool, whereby all member states were to be linked into a single electricity grid. (Several grids are already integrated and others are being rehabilitated.) At the same time, ministers endorsed a Protocol to promote greater co-operation in energy development within the SADC. On receiving final approval and signature by member states, the Protocol was to replace the energy sector with an Energy Commission, responsible for 'demand-side' management, pricing, ensuring private-sector involvement and competition, training and research, collecting information, etc. The sector administers a joint SADC Petroleum Exploration Programme. In September 1997 heads of state endorsed an Energy Action Plan to proceed with the implementation of co-operative policies and strategies in four key areas of energy: trade, information exchange, training and organizational capacity-building, and investment and financing. A technical unit of the Energy Commission was to be responsible for implementation of the Action Plan.

## TRADE, INDUSTRY AND MINING

Under the treaty establishing the SADC, efforts were to be undertaken to achieve regional economic integration. The trade and industry sector aims to facilitate this by the creation of an enabling investment and trade environment in SADC countries, the establishment of a single regional market, by progressively removing barriers to the movement of goods, services and people, and the promotion of cross-border investment. The sector supports programmes for industrial research and development and standardization and quality assurance. A sector of finance and investment has been established to mobilize industrial investment resources and to co-ordinate economic policies and the development of the financial sector. During 1995 work continued on the preparation of two Protocols on trade co-operation and finance and investment, which were to provide the legal framework for integration. In August 1996 SADC member states (except Angola) signed a Protocol providing for the establishment of a free-trade area, through the gradual elimination of tariff barriers over an eight-year period, at a summit meeting held in Lesotho. The Protocol was to come into effect following its ratification by two-thirds of member states. By September 1999 the Protocol had been ratified by seven member countries. In that month representatives of the private sector in SADC member states, meeting in Mauritius, agreed to establish an Association of SADC Chambers of Commerce.

In January 1992 a five-year strategy for the promotion of mining in the region was approved, with the principal objective of stimulating local and foreign investment in the sector to maximize benefits from the region's mineral resources. In December 1994 the SADC held a mining forum, jointly with the EU, in Lusaka, Zambia, with the aim of demonstrating to potential investors and promoters the possibilities of mining exploration in the region. A second mining investment forum was held in Lusaka in December 1998. Other objectives of the mining sector are the improvement of industry training, increasing the contribution of small-scale mining, reducing the illicit trade in gemstones and gold, increasing co-operation in mineral exploration and processing, and minimizing the adverse impact of mining operations on the environment. At the summit meeting, held in September 1997, SADC heads of state signed a Protocol providing for the harmonization of policies and programmes relating to the development and exploitation of mineral resources in the region.

### HUMAN RESOURCES DEVELOPMENT

The SADC helps to supply the region's requirements in skilled manpower by providing training in the following categories: high-level managerial personnel; agricultural managers; high- and medium-level technicians; artisans; and instructors. The Technical Committee on Accreditation and Certification aims to harmonize and strengthen the education and training systems in the SADC through initiatives such as the standardization of curricula and examinations. The sector also aims to determine active labour market information systems and institutions in the region, improve education policy analysis and formulation, and address issues of teaching and learning materials in the region. It administers an Intra-regional Skills Development Programme. The sector has initiated a programme of distance education to enable greater access to education, and operates the SADC's scholarship and training awards programme. In September 1997 heads of state, meeting in Blantyre, Malawi, endorsed the establishment of a Gender Department within the Secretariat to promote the advancement and education of women. At the same time representatives of all member countries (except Angola) signed a Protocol on Education and Training, which was to provide a legal framework for co-operation in this sector.

### EMPLOYMENT AND LABOUR

The sector was founded in 1996, and is co-ordinated by Zambia. It seeks to promote employment and harmonize legislation concerning labour and social protection. Its activities include: the implementation of International Labour Standards, the improvement of health and safety standards in the workplace, combating child labour and the establishment of a statistical database for employment and labour issues.

### CULTURE, SPORT AND INFORMATION

A culture and information sector was established in 1990, and is co-ordinated by Mozambique. Following the ratification of the treaty establishing the Community, the sector was expected to emphasize regional socio-cultural development as part of the process of greater integration. The SADC Press Trust was established, in Harare, Zimbabwe, to disseminate information about the SADC and to articulate the concerns and priorities of the region. Public education initiatives have commenced to encourage the involvement of people in the process of regional integration and development, as well as to promote democratic and human rights' values. In 1998 a new project—'Information 21'—was to be implemented under the sector, in collaboration with the SADC secretariat and the Southern African Research and Documentation Centre (q.v.), which aimed to promote community-building and greater participation in decision-making at all levels of government. Efforts to harmonize legislation in order to prevent breaches of copyright were underway in early 1999. A four-year programme, entitled the SADC Festival on Arts and Culture, was initiated in 1994. Events included a theatre festival, held in Maputo, Mozambique, in June 1997, a visual arts and crafts regional exposition, in Namibia, in April 1998, and a dance festival in Mauritius in 1999.

### TOURISM

The sector aims to promote tourism within the context of national and regional socio-economic development objectives. It comprises four components: tourism product development; tourism marketing and research; tourism services; and human resources development and training. The SADC has promoted tourism for the region at trade fairs in Europe, and has initiated a project to provide a range of promotional material and a regional tourism directory. By September 1993 a project to design a standard grading classification system for tourist accommodation in the region was completed, with the assistance of the World Tourism Organization, and the Council approved its implementation. A new five-year development strategy for tourism in the region was initiated in 1995, the key element of which was the establishment of a new tourism body, to be administered jointly by SADC officials and private-sector operators. The Regional Tourism Organization for Southern Africa (RETOSA) was to assist member states to formulate tourism promotion policies and strategies. A legal charter for the establishment of RETOSA was signed by ministers of tourism in September 1997. During 1999 a feasibility study on the development of the Upper Zambezi basin as a site for eco-tourism was initiated.

### FINANCE AND INVESTMENT

In July 1998 a Banking Association was officially constituted by representatives of SADC member states. The Association was to establish international banking standards and regional payments systems, organize training and harmonize banking legislation in the region. In April 1999 governors of SADC central banks determined to strengthen and harmonize banking procedures and technology in order to facilitate the financial integration of the region. Efforts to harmonize stock exchanges in the region were also initiated in 1999.

## Finance

The SADC's administrative budget for 1998, approved by the Council in February, amounted to US $12.5m., financed mainly by contributions from member states. At February 1998 members owed some $4.5m. in unpaid arrears.

**SADC PROJECT FINANCING BY SECTOR** (July 1996/97)

| Sector | Number of projects | Total cost (US $ million) | Funding secured (US $ million)* |
|---|---|---|---|
| Culture and information | 7 | 15.90 | 4.95 |
| Energy | 48 | 924.67 | 627.14 |
| Food, agriculture and natural resources | 83 | 573.91 | 320.21 |
| Agricultural research and training | 14 | 120.44 | 77.16 |
| Inland fisheries | 8 | 44.91 | 26.12 |
| Food security | 11 | 71.21 | 22.35 |
| Forestry | 15 | 125.94 | 46.71 |
| Wildlife | 11 | 94.30 | 81.99 |
| Livestock production and animal disease control | 11 | 96.27 | 59.24 |
| Environment and land management | 7 | 18.99 | 5.93 |
| Marine fisheries and resources | 6 | 1.85 | 0.71 |
| Finance and investment | 10 | 1.92 | 0.37 |
| Human resources development | 16 | 44.76 | 16.27 |
| Industry and trade | 19 | 20.01 | 10.45 |
| Mining | 36 | 18.51 | 10.15 |
| Tourism | 11 | 4.96 | 2.95 |
| Transport and communications | 174 | 6,474.40 | 2,991.70 |
| Water | 3 | 11.05 | 9.75 |
| **Total** | 407 | 8,090.09 | 3,993.95 |

* Includes both local and foreign resources.

## Publications

*SACCAR Newsletter* (quarterly).

*SADC Annual Report.*

*SADC Energy Bulletin.*

*SADC Today* (six a year)

*SATCC Bulletin* (quarterly).

*SKILLS.*

*SPLASH.*

# SOUTHERN COMMON MARKET—MERCOSUR/MERCOSUL

## (MERCADO COMÚN DEL SUR/MERCADO COMUM DO SUL)

**Address:** Edificio Mercosur, Dr Luis Piera 1992, 1°, Montevideo, Uruguay.

**Telephone:** (2) 4029024; **fax:** (2) 4080557; **e-mail:** sam@netgate.com.uy; **internet:** algarbull.com.uy/secretariamercosur/1.HTM.

Mercosur (known as Mercosul in Portuguese) was established in March 1991 by the heads of state of Argentina, Brazil, Paraguay and Uruguay with the signature of the Treaty of Asunción. The primary objective of the Treaty is to achieve the economic integration of member states by means of a free flow of goods and services between member states, the establishment of a common external tariff, the adoption of common commercial policy, and the co-ordination of macroeconomic and sectoral policies. The Ouro Preto Protocol, which was signed in December 1994, conferred on Mercosur the status of an international legal entity with the authority to sign agreements with third countries, group of countries and international organizations.

### MEMBERS

Argentina  Brazil  Paraguay  Uruguay

Chile and Bolivia are associate members.

## Organization

(January 2000)

### COMMON MARKET COUNCIL

The Common Market Council (Consejo Mercado Común) is the highest organ of Mercosur and is responsible for leading the integration process and for taking decisions in order to achieve the objectives of the Asunción Treaty.

### COMMON MARKET GROUP

The Common Market Group (Grupo Mercado Común) is the executive body of Mercosur and is responsible for implementing concrete measures to further the integration process. The Group is assisted by an Administrative Secretariat.

**Administrative Secretary:** MANUEL OLARREAGA.

### TRADE COMMISSION

The Trade Commission has competence for the area of joint commercial policy and, in particular, is responsible for monitoring the operation of the common external tariff (see below). The Brasília Protocol may be referred to for the resolution of trade disputes between member states.

### JOINT PARLIAMENTARY COMMISSION

The Joint Parliamentary Commission (Comisión Parliamentaria Conjunto) is made up of parliamentarians from the member states and is charged with accelerating internal national procedures to implement Mercosur decisions, including the harmonization of country legislation.

### CONSULTATIVE ECONOMIC AND SOCIAL FORUM

The Consultative Economic and Social Forum is made up of representatives from the business community and trade unions in the member countries and has a consultative role in relation to Mercosur.

### ADMINISTRATIVE SECRETARIAT

**Director:** Dr RAMÓN DÍAZ PEREIRA.

## Activities

Mercosur's free trade zone entered into effect on 1 January 1995, with tariffs removed from 85% of intra-regional trade. A regime of gradual removal of duties on a list of special products was agreed, with Argentina and Brazil given four years to complete this process while Paraguay and Uruguay were allowed five years. Regimes governing intra-zonal trade in the automobile and sugar sectors remained to be negotiated. Mercosur's customs union also came into force at the start of 1995, comprising a common external tariff of 0–20%. A list of exceptions from the common external tariff was also agreed; these products were to lose their special status and be subject to the general tarification concerning foreign goods by 2006. The value of intra-Mercosur trade was estimated to have tripled during the period 1991–95 and was reported to have amounted to US $20,300m. in 1998.

In June 1995 Mercosur ministers responsible for the environment held a meeting at which they agreed to harmonize environmental legislation and to form a permanent sub-group of Mercosur. In December Mercosur and the EU signed a framework agreement for commercial and economic co-operation, which provides for co-operation in the economic, trade, industrial, scientific, institutional and cultural fields and the promotion of wider political dialogue on issues of mutual interest.

At the summit meeting in December 1995 the presidents affirmed the consolidation of free trade as Mercosur's 'permanent and most urgent goal'. To this end they agreed to prepare norms of application for Mercosur's customs code, accelerate paper procedures and increase the connections between national computerized systems. It was also agreed to increase co-operation in the areas of agriculture, industry, mining, energy, communications, transport and tourism, and finance. At this meeting Argentina and Brazil reached an agreement aimed at overcoming their dispute regarding the trade in automobiles between the two countries. They agreed that cars should have a minimum of 60% domestic components and that Argentina should be allowed to complete its balance of exports of cars to Brazil, which had earlier imposed a unilateral quota on the import of Argentine cars. In December 1998 a framework agreement implementing a common manufacturing policy for the free trade of motor vehicles was signed. The agreement was to take effect within four years, from 1 January 2000.

In May 1996 Mercosur parliamentarians met with the aim of harmonizing legislation on patents in member countries. In December Mercosur heads of state, meeting in Fortaleza, Brazil, approved agreements on harmonizing competition practices (by 2001), on the integration of educational opportunities for post-graduates and human resources training, on the standardization of trading safeguards applied against third-country products (by 2001) and for intra-regional cultural exchanges. An Accord on Sub-regional Air Services was signed at the meeting (including by the heads of state of Bolivia and Chile) to liberalize civil transport throughout the region. In addition, the heads of state endorsed texts on consumer rights that were to be incorporated into a Mercosur Consumers' Defence Code and agreed to consider the establishment of a bank to finance the integration and development of the region.

In June 1996 the Joint Parliamentary Commission agreed that Mercosur should endorse a 'Democratic Guarantee Clause', whereby a country would be prevented from participation in Mercosur unless democratic, accountable institutions were in place. The clause was adopted by Mercosur heads of state at the summit meeting that was held in San Luis de Mendoza, in Argentina, later in the month. The presidents approved the entry into Mercosur of Bolivia and Chile as associate members. An Economic Complementation Accord with Bolivia, which includes Bolivia in Mercosur's free-trade zone, but not in the customs union, was signed in December 1995 and was to come into force on 1 January 1997. In December 1996 the Accord was extended until 30 April 1997, when a free-trade zone between Bolivia and Mercosur was to become operational. Measures of the free-trade agreement, which was signed in October 1996, were to be implemented over a transitional period commencing on 28 February 1997 (revised from 1 January). Chile's Economic Complementation Accord with Mercosur entered into effect on 1 October 1996, with duties on most products to be removed over a 10-year period (Chile's most sensitive products were given 18 years for complete tariff elimination). Chile was also to remain outside the customs union, but was to be involved in other integration projects, in particular infrastructure projects designed to give Mercosur countries access to both the Atlantic and Pacific Oceans (Chile's Pacific coast was regarded as Mercosur's potential link to the economies of the Far East).

In June 1997 the first meeting of tax administrators and customs officials of Mercosur member countries was held, with the aim of enhancing information exchange and promoting joint customs inspections. Later in that month Mercosur heads of state convened in Asunción, Paraguay. The meeting reaffirmed the group's intention to pursue trade negotiations with the EU, Mexico and the Andean Community, as well as to negotiate as a single economic bloc in discussions with regard to the establishment of a Free Trade Area of the Americas (FTAA). Chile and Bolivia were to be incorporated into these negotiations. During 1997 Mercosur's efforts towards regional economic integration were threatened by Brazil's adverse external trade balance and its Government's measures to counter the deficit, which included the imposition of import duties on certain products. In November the Brazilian Government announced that it was to increase its import tariff by 3%, in a further effort to improve its external balance. The measure was endorsed by Argentina as a means of maintaining regional fiscal stability. The new external tariff, which was to remain in effect until 31 December 2000, was formally adopted by Mercosur heads of state at a meeting held in Montevideo, Uruguay, in December 1997. At the summit meeting a separate Protocol was signed providing for the liberalization of trade in services and government purchases over a 10-year period. In order to strengthen economic integration throughout the region, Mercosur leaders agreed that Chile, while still not a full member of the organization, be integrated into the Mercosur political structure, with equal voting rights. In December 1998 Mercosur heads of states agreed on the establishment of an arbitration mechanism for disputes between members, and on measures to standardize human, animal and plant health and safety regulations throughout the grouping.

In January 1999 economic instability in Brazil, and the Government's decision effectively to devalue the national currency, the real, added pressures to relations within Mercosur. Measures to combat major adverse effects on trade throughout the region caused by the devaluation of the Brazilian currency were to be considered by the Common Market Council. Further trade liberalization was expected to be delayed until the region's economy registered a recovery. Mercosur's efforts at integration were further undermined, in March, by political instability within Paraguay. In April Argentina imposed tariffs on imports of Brazilian steel. In July the Argentine authorities approved a decree permitting restrictions on all imports from neighbouring countries, in order to protect local industries, prompting Brazil to suspend negotiations to resolve the trading differences between the two countries. Argentina withdrew the decree a few days later, but reiterated its demand for some form of temporary safeguards on certain products as compensation for their perceived loss of competitiveness resulting from the devalued real. An extraordinary meeting of the Common Market Council was convened, at Brazil's request, in early August, in order to discuss the dispute, as well as measures to mitigate the effects of economic recession throughout the sub-region. However, little progress was achieved and the bilateral trade dispute continued to undermine Mercosur. Argentina imposed new restrictions on textiles and footwear, while, in September, Brazil withdrew all automatic import licences for Argentine products, which were consequently to be subject to the same quality control, sanitary measures and accounting checks applied to imports from non-Mercosur countries.

During 1997 negotiations to establish a free-trade accord with the Andean Community were hindered by differences regarding schedules for tariff elimination and Mercosur's insistence on a local content of 60% to qualify for rules of origin preferences. However, in April 1998 the two groupings signed an accord which committed them to the establishment of a free-trade area by 1 January 2000. It was agreed that negotiations would commence later in 1998 on the elimination of tariffs and otheer restrictions to trade, measures to expand and diversify commercial activity between countries of the two groups and on the formulation of a legal and institutional framework for co-operation and economic and physical integration. In October it was reported that Mercosur was to extend existing bilateral trade agreements with the Andean Community until 31 March 1999. Negotiations in early 1999 failed to conclude an agreement on preferential tariffs between the two blocs (intended to be a basis for the establishment of a free-trade area) and the existing arrangements were again extended on a bilateral basis. At the end of March the Andean Community agreed to initiate free-trade negotiations with Brazil. In December 1997 the Mercosur summit meeting failed to conclude a single trading policy with Mexico, although Argentina, Paraguay and Uruguay resolved to extend the existing bilateral trade preferences with that country beyond their expiry at the end of the year. In January 1998 Brazil and Mexico agreed to pursue regular dialogue on bilateral and regional trade issues.

In March 1998 ministers of trade of 34 countries agreed a detailed framework for negotiations to establish the FTAA by 2005. Mercosur secured support for its request that a separate negotiating group be established to consider issues relating to agriculture, as one of nine key sectors to be discussed. The FTAA negotiating process was formally initiated by heads of state of the 34 countries meeting in Santiago, Chile in April 1998. In June Mercosur and Canada signed a Trade and Investment Co-operation Arrangement, which aimed to remove obstacles to trade and to increase economic co-operation between the two signatories. In July the European Commission proposed obtaining a mandate to commence negotiations with Mercosur and Chile towards a free-trade agreement, which, it was envisaged,would provide for the elimination of tariffs over a period of 10 years. However, Mercosur requested that the EU abolish agricultural subsidies as part of any accord. In June 1999 it was agreed that trade negotiations between Mercosur, Chile and the EU would commence later in that year.

In March 1998 the ministers of the interior of Mercosur countries, together with representatives of the Governments of Chile and Bolivia, agreed to implement a joint security arrangement for the border region linking Argentina, Paraguay and Brazil. In particular, the initiative aimed to counter drugs-trafficking, money-laundering and other illegal activities in the area.

## Finance

In December 1996 the Mercosur summit meeting approved an annual budget of US $1.2m. for the Mercosur secretariat, to be contributed by the four full member countries.

## Publication

*Boletín Oficial del Mercosur* (quarterly).

# WESTERN EUROPEAN UNION—WEU

**Address:** 4 rue de la Régence, 1000 Brussels, Belgium

**Telephone:** (2) 500-44-11; **fax:** (2) 511-35-19; **e-mail:** ueo .presse@skynet.be; **internet:** www.weu.int.

Based on the Brussels Treaty of 1948, the Western European Union (WEU) was set up in 1955. WEU is an intergovernmental organization for European co-operation in the field of security and defence. It seeks to define common positions and harmonize the policies of its member states. WEU now has a dual objective: being developed as the defence component of the European Union, and as the means of strengthening the European pillar of the Atlantic Alliance under NATO.

**MEMBERS***

| | |
|---|---|
| Belgium | Luxembourg |
| France | Netherlands |
| Germany | Portugal |
| Greece | Spain |
| Italy | United Kingdom |

* WEU has invited the other members of the EU to join the organization and has invited other European members of NATO to become Associate Members to enable them to participate fully in WEU activities. In November 1992 Denmark and Ireland took up observer status and on 1 January 1995 Austria, Finland and Sweden became Observers following their accession to the EU. Associate membership has been granted to Iceland, Norway and Turkey in November 1992, to Bulgaria, the Czech Republic, Estonia, Hungary, Latvia, Lithuania, Poland, Romania and Slovakia in May 1994, to Slovenia in June 1996, and to the Czech Republic, Hungary and Poland in March 1999.

## Organization

(January 2000)

WEU comprises an intergovernmental policy-making Council and an Assembly of parliamentary representatives, together with a number of subsidiary bodies established by the Council to facilitate its work. The subsidiary bodies act according to the decisions of the Council and are subject to its supervision and control.

### COUNCIL

The Council is the WEU's main body, responsible for addressing all security and defence matters within WEU's remit. It is organized so as to be able to function on a permanent basis and may be convened at any time at the request of a member state. The Council of Ministers, comprising ministers of defence and of foreign affairs, meets usually once every six months in the country holding the WEU presidency. The Permanent Council, chaired by the WEU Secretary-General, is the central body responsible for day-to-day management of the organization and for assigning tasks to and co-ordinating the activities of the various working groups. It is composed of permanent representatives, supported by military delegates, and meets as often as required (normally once a week). The presidency of the Council is rotated between member states on a six-monthly basis.

### MILITARY COMMITTEE

In May 1997 WEU ministers agreed to establish a WEU Military Committee. The necessary implementing measures were taken at a ministerial meeting in Erfurt, Germany, in November and came into effect in 1998. The new Military Committee is the senior authority in WEU, operating under the authority of the Council. The Committee consists of Chiefs of Defence Staff who are represented in permanent session by a Military Delegates Committee, under a permanent chairman, who is also the director of the WEU military staff.

### SECRETARIAT-GENERAL

**Secretary-General:** Dr JAVIER SOLANA MADARIAGA (Spain).

### SUBSIDIARY BODIES

**WEU Institute for Security Studies:** 43 ave du Président Wilson, 75775 Paris Cédex 16, France; tel. 1-53-67-22-00; fax 1-47-20-81-78; e-mail weu_iss@compuserve.com; internet www.weu.int; f. 1990; Dir NICOLE GNESSOTO (France).

**WEU Satellite Centre:** Avda de Cádiz, Edif. 457, Base Aérea de Torrejón, 28850 Torrejón de Ardoz, Madrid, Spain; tel. (91) 6786000; fax (91) 6786006; e-mail info@weusc.es; internet www.weu.int/satellite/en; imagery for the general surveillance of areas of interest to WEU, used, for example, in support of treaty verification, arms control, maritime surveillance and environmental monitoring; Dir FERNANDO DAVARA (Spain).

### ASSEMBLY

**Address:** 43 ave du Président Wilson, 75775 Paris Cédex 16, France; tel. 1-53-67-22-00; fax 1-53-67-22-01; e-mail assembly@weu.int; internet www.weu.int/assembly/welcome.html.

The Assembly of Western European Union is composed of the representatives of the Brussels Treaty powers to the Parliamentary Assembly of the Council of Europe. It meets at least twice a year, usually in Paris. The Assembly may proceed on any matter regarding the application of the Brussels Treaty and on any matter submitted to the Assembly for an opinion by the Council. Resolutions may be adopted in cases where this form is considered appropriate. When so directed by the Assembly, the President transmits such resolutions to international organizations, governments and national parliaments. An annual report is presented to the Assembly by the Council.

**President:** KLAUS BUEHLER (Germany).

**Clerk:** COLIN CAMERON (United Kingdom).

### PERMANENT COMMITTEES OF THE ASSEMBLY

There are permanent committees on: Defence Questions and Armaments; General Affairs; Scientific Questions; Budgetary Affairs and Administration; Rules of Procedure and Privileges; and Parliamentary and Public Relations.

## Activities

The Brussels Treaty (see below) was signed in 1948 by Belgium, France, Luxembourg, the Netherlands and the United Kingdom. It foresaw the potential for international co-operation in Western Europe and provided for collective defence and collaboration in economic, social and cultural activities. Within this framework, NATO and the Council of Europe (see chapters) were formed in 1949.

On the collapse in 1954 of plans for a European Defence Community, a nine-power conference was convened in London to try to reach a new agreement. This conference's decisions were embodied in a series of formal agreements drawn up by a ministerial conference held in Paris in October. The agreements entailed: arrangements for the Brussels Treaty to be strengthened and modified to include the Federal Republic of Germany and Italy, the ending of the occupation regime in the Federal Republic of Germany, and the invitation to the latter to join NATO. These agreements were ratified on 6 May 1955, on which date the seven-power Western European Union came into being.

A meeting of ministers of defence and of foreign affairs, held in Rome in October 1984, agreed to 'reactivate' WEU by restructuring its organization and by holding more frequent ministerial meetings, in order to harmonize members' views on defence questions, arms control and disarmament, developments in East-West relations, Europe's contribution to the Atlantic alliance, and European armaments co-operation.

In October 1987 the Council adopted a 'Platform on European Security Interests', declaring its intention to develop a 'more cohesive European defence identity', while affirming that 'the substantial presence of US conventional and nuclear forces plays an irreplaceable part in the defence of Europe'. The document also resolved to improve consultations and extend co-ordination in defence and security matters, and to use existing resources more effectively by expanding bilateral and regional military co-operation.

In April 1990 ministers of foreign affairs and defence discussed the implications of recent political changes in central and eastern Europe, and mandated WEU to develop contacts with democratically elected governments there. WEU dispatched fact-finding missions to Hungary, Czechoslovakia, Poland, Romania, Bulgaria, Estonia, Latvia and Lithuania in late 1990 and early 1991. An extraordinary meeting of WEU's Ministerial Council with the ministers of defence and foreign affairs of those countries, held in Bonn, Germany, in June 1992, agreed on measures to enhance co-operation. The ministers were to meet annually, while a forum of consultation was to be established between the WEU Council and the ambassadors of the countries concerned, which was to meet at least twice a year. The focus of consultations was to be the security structure and political stability of Europe; the future development of the CSCE (now the OSCE); and arms control and disarmament, in particular the implementation of the Treaty on Conventional Armed Forces in Europe (the CFE Treaty) and the 'Open Skies' Treaty (see NATO for both). In May 1994 the Council of Ministers, meeting in Luxembourg, issued the Kirchberg Declaration, according the nine eastern and central European countries concerned (including the Czech Republic and Slovakia, which were the legal successors to Czechoslovakia) the status of Associate Members of WEU, thereby suspending the forum of consultation.

The EC Treaty on European Union, which was agreed at Maastricht, in the Netherlands, in December 1991, and entered into force on 1 November 1993, referred to WEU as an 'integral part of the development of European Union' and requests WEU 'to elaborate and implement decisions and actions of the Union which have defence implications'. The Treaty also committed EU member countries to the 'eventual framing of a common defence policy which might in time lead to a common defence'. A separate declaration, adopted by WEU member states in Maastricht, defined WEU's role as being the defence component of the European Union but also as the instrument for strengthening the European pillar of the Atlantic Alliance, thus maintaining a role for NATO in Europe's defence and retaining WEU's identity as distinct from that of the EU. In January 1993 WEU's Council and Secretariat-General moved to Brussels (from Paris and London, respectively), in order to promote closer co-operation with both the EU and NATO, which have their headquarters there.

In June 1992 WEU ministers of defence and foreign affairs convened in Petersberg, Germany, to consider the implementation of the Maastricht decisions. The resulting Declaration was significant in defining WEU's operational role. Member states declared that they were prepared to make available military units from the whole spectrum of their conventional armed forces for military tasks conducted under the authority of WEU. In addition to contributing to the common defence in accordance with Article V of the modified Brussels Treaty, three categories of missions have been identified for the possible employment of military units under the aegis of WEU: humanitarian and rescue tasks; peace-keeping tasks; and crisis management, including peace-making. Missions of this kind are often described as 'Petersberg tasks'. The Petersberg Declaration stated that the WEU was prepared to support peace-keeping activities of the CSCE and UN Security Council on a case-by-case basis. A WEU planning cell was established in Brussels in October, which was to be responsible for preparing contingency plans for the employment of forces under WEU auspices for humanitarian operations, peace-keeping and crisis-management activities. It was expected that the same military units identified by member states for deployment under NATO would be used for military operations under WEU: this arrangement was referred to as 'double-hatting'. In May 1995 WEU ministers, convened in Lisbon, Portugal, agreed to strengthen WEU's operational capabilities through new structures and mechanisms, including the establishment of a politico-military group to advise on crises and crisis management, a Situation Centre able to monitor WEU operations and support decisions taken by the Council, and an Intelligence Section within the planning cell. WEU rules of engagement, with a view to implementing the missions identified in the Petersberg Declaration, were to be formulated.

In November 1994 a WEU ministerial meeting in Noordwijk, the Netherlands, adopted a set of preliminary conclusions on the formulation of a common European defence policy. The role and place of WEU in further European institutional arrangements were addressed by the EU's Intergovernmental Conference, which commenced in March 1996. The process was concluded in June 1997 with agreement having been reached on the Treaty of Amsterdam (see EU chapter). The Treaty, which was signed in October and entered into force on 1 May 1999, confirmed WEU as providing the EU with access to operational capability for undertaking the Petersberg tasks, which were incorporated into the revised Treaty. It advocated enhanced EU-WEU co-operation and referred to the possible integration of the WEU into the EU, should the European Council so decide (the United Kingdom being the main opponent). Following the entry into force of the Treaty of Amsterdam WEU and the EU approved a set of arrangements for enhanced co-operation. In mid-1999 WEU undertook an audit of assets available for European operations. In November WEU ministers adopted a series of recommendations, based on the results of the audit, to enable European countries to respond rapidly to conduct crisis management operations. In particular, ministers urged greater efforts to establish collective capabilities in strategic intelligence and planning and to strengthen military air, sea and transport equipment and capabilities for use in humanitarian and peace-keeping operations. The meeting confirmed that the EU would have access to WEU military expertise and intelligence through the new WEU Secretary-General, Javier Solana, who had been appointed as the EU's first high representative for common foreign and security policy in June.

In January 1994 NATO heads of state gave their full support to the development of a European Security and Defence Identity (ESDI) and to the strengthening of WEU. They declared their readiness to make collective assets of the Alliance available for WEU operations, on the basis of consultations in the North Atlantic Council. The Alliance leaders also endorsed the concept of Combined Joint Task Forces (CJTFs), which was to provide separable, but not separate, military capabilities that could be employed by either organization. In May 1996 NATO and WEU signed a security agreement, which provided for the protection and shared use of classified information. In June NATO ministers, meeting in Berlin, Germany, agreed on a framework of measures to enable the implementation of the CJTF concept and the development of an ESDI within the Alliance. WEU was to be permitted to request the use of a CJTF headquarters for an operation under its command and to use Alliance planning capabilities and military infrastructure. In May 1998 the Council of both organizations approved a set of consultation arrangements as a guide to co-operation in a crisis situation. A framework document on principles and guide-lines for detailed practicalities of cases where NATO assets and/or capabilities were loaned to WEU was subsequently prepared. By April 1999, when NATO heads of state convened in Washington, DC, USA, the key elements of the Berlin decisions had been implemented. The meeting confirmed NATO's willingness to enhance existing WEU-NATO joint mechanisms and to establish a direct NATO-EU relationship.

From mid-July 1992 warships and aircraft of WEU members undertook a monitoring operation in the Adriatic Sea, in co-ordination with NATO, to ensure compliance with the UN Security Council's resolutions imposing a trade and armaments embargo on Serbia and Montenegro. In mid-November the UN Security Council gave the NATO/WEU operation the power to search vessels suspected of attempting to flout the embargo. In June 1993 the Councils of WEU and NATO agreed to establish a unified command for the operation, which was to implement a Security Council resolution to strengthen the embargo against Serbia and Montenegro. Under the agreement, the Councils were to exert joint political control, and military instructions were to be co-ordinated within a joint *ad hoc* headquarters. In April WEU ministers offered civil assistance to Bulgaria, Hungary and Romania in enforcing the UN embargo on the Danube. A monitoring mission, consisting of some 270 experts and 10 patrol boats, began operations in June. In June 1996 the NATO/WEU naval monitoring mission in the Adriatic Sea was suspended, following the decision of the UN Security Council to remove the embargo on the delivery of armaments to the former Yugoslavia. At that time more than 73,000 ships had been challenged, and 5,800 inspected, under the operation. WEU provides assistance for the administration of Mostar, Bosnia and Herzegovina, for which the EU assumed responsibility in July 1994.

In May 1997 WEU dispatched a Multinational Advisory Police Element (MAPE) to Albania to provide training and advice on restructuring the police force in that country. By mid-1999 a new State Police Law had been formulated, with MAPE's support, while some 3,000 police officers had been trained at centres in Tirana and Dürres and through field programmes. In February the WEU Council approved plans for an enhanced MAPE, with greater geographical coverage and operational mobility, with a mandate until April 2000. The mission was being conducted by WEU at the request of the EU, enabling a large part of the costs to be met from the EU budget. In response to the escalation of conflict in the Serbian province of Kosovo and Metohija, MAPE assisted the Albanian authorities to establish an Emergency Crisis Group to help to administer and to assist the massive refugee population which entered Albania in March and April. In November 1998, in response to a request by the EU, the WEU Satellite Centre initiated a mission of 'general security surveillance' of the Kosovo region. Since July 1999 the Centre has focused on the completion of a digital map, or geographic information system (GIS), of the entire region, which may be used to assist aspects of the reconstruction and de-mining efforts being undertaken in Kosovo.

In April 1999 WEU and Croatia signed an agreement to establish a WEU De-mining Assistance Mission (WEUDAM) in that country, upon a request by the Council of the EU. WEUDAM, which commenced work in May, was to provide advice, technical expertise and training to the Croatian Mine Action Centre, for a period of one year.

In May 1992 France and Germany announced their intention to establish a joint defence force, the 'Eurocorps', which was to be based in Strasbourg, France, and which was intended to provide a basis for a European army under the aegis of WEU. This development caused concern among some NATO member countries, particularly the USA and United Kingdom, which feared that it represented a fresh attempt (notably on the part of France, which is outside NATO's military structure) to undermine the Alliance's role in Europe. In November, however, France and Germany stated that troops from the joint force could serve under NATO military command. This principle was recognized in an agreement signed in January 1993, which established links between the proposed joint force and NATO's military structure. In June Belgium opted to participate in the Eurocorps. In December Spain agreed to provide troops for the force. Luxembourg agreed to participate in May 1994. Eurocorps formally became operational on 30 November 1995. In May France, Italy, Spain and Portugal announced the establishment of two new forces, which were to be at the disposal of WEU as well as NATO and the UN: EUROFOR, consisting of up to 14,000 ground troops, to be based in Florence, Italy; and EUROMARFOR, a maritime force serving the Mediterranean. A number of other multinational forces are also designated as forces answerable to WEU (FAWEU) or that were to be available to WEU: the Multinational Division (Central—comprising Belgium, Germany, the Netherlands and the United Kingdom, the Headquarters of the First German-Netherlands Corps, the United Kingdom-Netherlands Amphibious Force, the Spanish-Italian Amphibious Force, and the European Air Group (EAG), comprising Belgium, France, Germany, Italy, Netherlands, Spain and the United Kingdom.

# Publications

*Account of the Session* (WEU Assembly, 2 a year).

*Annual Report of the Council.*

*Assembly of Western European Union: Texts adopted and Brief Account of the Session* (2 a year).

*Chaillot Papers* (WEU Institute for Security Studies).

Assembly documents and reports.

# WORLD CONFEDERATION OF LABOUR—WCL

**Address:** 33 rue de Trèves, 1040 Brussels, Belgium.

**Telephone:** (2) 285-47-00; **fax:** (2) 230-87-22; **e-mail:** info@cmt_wcl.org; **internet:** www.cmt-wcl.org.

Founded in 1920 as the International Federation of Christian Trade Unions (IFCTU); reconstituted under present title in 1968. (See also the International Confederation of Free Trade Unions and the World Federation of Trade Unions.)

### MEMBERS

Affiliated national federations and trade union internationals; about 26m. members in 113 countries.

## Organization

(January 2000)

### CONGRESS

The supreme and legislative authority. The most recent meeting was held in December 1997 in Bangkok, Thailand. Congress consists of delegates from national confederations and trade internationals. Delegates have votes according to the size of their organization. Congress receives official reports, elects the Executive Board, considers the future programme and any proposals.

### CONFEDERAL BOARD

The Board meets annually, and consists of 38 members (including 18 representatives of national confederations and 11 representatives of trade internationals) elected by Congress from among its members for four-year terms. It issues executive directions and instructions to the Secretariat.

### SECRETARIAT-GENERAL

**Secretary-General:** WILLY THYS (Belgium).

### REGIONAL OFFICES

**Africa:** Democratic Organization of African Workers' Trade Unions (ODSTA), BP 4401, Route International d'Atakpamé, Lomé, Togo; tel. 250710; fax 256113. Pres. F. KIKONGI.

**Asia:** Brotherhood of Asian Trade Unionists (BATU), 1943 Taft Avenue, 1004 Malate, Manila, Philippines; tel. (2) 500709; fax (2) 5218335; e-mail batunorm@iconn.con.ph. Pres. J. TAN.

**Latin America:** Latin-American Confederation of Workers (CLAT), Apdo 6681, Caracas 1010, Venezuela; tel. (32) 720794; fax (32) 720463; e-mail clat@telcel.net.ve. Sec.-Gen. EMILIO MASPERO.

**North America:** c/o National Alliance of Postal and Federal Employees, 1628 11th St, NW, Washington, DC 20001, USA.

### INTERNATIONAL INSTITUTES OF TRADE UNION STUDIES

**Africa:** Fondation panafricaine pour le développement économique, social et culturel (Fopadesc), Lomé, Togo.

**Asia:** BATU Social Institute, Manila, Philippines.

**Latin America:**
Instituto Andino de Estudios Sociales, Lima, Peru.
Instituto Centro-Americano de Estudios Sociales (ICAES), San José, Costa Rica.
Instituto del Cono Sur (INCASUR), Buenos Aires, Argentina.
Instituto de Formación del Caribe, Willemstad, Curaçao, Netherlands Antilles.
Universidad de Trabajadores de América Latina (UTAL).

## Finance

Income is derived from affiliation dues, contributions, donations and capital interest.

## Publications

*Tele-flash* (every 2 weeks).
*Labor magazine* (quarterly).
Reports of Congresses; Study Documents.

## International Trade Union Federations

**International Federation of Textile and Clothing Workers—IFTC:** 27 Koning Albertlaan, 9000 Ghent, Belgium; tel. (9) 222-57-01; fax (9) 220-45-59; e-mail piet.nelissen@cmt-wcl.org; f. 1901. Mems: unions covering 800,000 workers in 39 countries. Organization: Congress (every three years), Board, Exec. Committee, Pres. JACQUES JOURET (Belgium); Gen. Sec. BART BRUGGEMAN (Netherlands).

**International Federation of Trade Unions of Employees in Public Service—INFEDOP:** 33 rue de Trèves, 1040 Brussels, Belgium; tel. (2) 230-38-65; fax (2) 231-14-72; e-mail info@infedop_eurofedop.com; f. 1922. Mems: national federations of workers in public service, covering 4m. workers. Organization: World Congress (at least every five years), World Confederal Board (meets every year), 10 Trade Groups, Secretariat. Pres. GUY RASNEUR (Belgium); Sec.-Gen. BERT VAN CAELENBERG (Belgium). Publ. *Servus* (monthly).

**European Federation of Employees in Public Services—EUROFEDOP:** 33 rue de Trèves, 1040 Brussels, Belgium; tel. (2) 230-38-65; fax (2) 231-14-72; e-mail info@infedop-eurofedop.com; Chair. GUY RASNEUR (Belgium); Sec.-Gen. BERT VAN CAELENBERG (Belgium).

**International Federation of Trade Unions of Transport Workers—FIOST:** Galerie Agora, 105 rue du Marché aux Herbes, bte 40, 1000 Brussels, Belgium; tel. (2) 549-07-62; fax (2) 512-85-91; e-mail freddy.pools@cmt-wcl.org; f. 1921. Mems: national federations in 28 countries covering 600,000 workers. Organization: Congress (every four years), Committee (meets twice a year), Executive Board. Pres. MICHEL BOVY (Belgium); Exec. Sec. FREDDY POOLS (Belgium). Publ. *Labor* (6 a year).

**World Confederation of Teachers—WCL:** 33 rue de Trèves, 1040 Brussels, Belgium; tel. (2) 285-47-29; fax (2) 230-87-22; e-mail wct@cmt-wcl.org; internet www.wctcsme.org; f. 1963. Mems: national federations of unions concerned with teaching. Organization: Congress (every four years), Council (at least once a year), Steering Committee. Pres. LOUIS VAN BENEDEN; Sec.-Gen. GASTON DE LA HAYE.

**World Federation of Agriculture and Food Workers—WFAFW:** 33 rue de Trèves, 1040 Brussels, Belgium; tel. (2) 230-60-90; fax (2) 230-87-22; f. 1982 (merger of former World Federation of Agricultural Workers and World Federation of Workers in the Food, Drink, Tobacco and Hotel Industries). Mems: national federations covering 2,800,000 workers in 38 countries. Organization: Congress (every five years), World Board, Daily Management Board. Pres. GUY DRILLEAUD (France); Exec. Sec. JOSÉ GÓMEZ CERDA (Dominican Republic).

**World Federation of Building and Woodworkers Unions—WFBW:** 33 rue de Trèves, 1040 Brussels, Belgium; tel. (2) 285-47-33; fax (2) 230-87-22; e-mail piet.nelissen@cmt-wcl.org; f. 1936. Mems: national federations covering 2,438,000 workers in several countries. Organization: Congress, Bureau, Permanent Secretariat. Pres. JACKY JACKERS; Sec.-Gen. DICK VAN DE KAMP (Netherlands). Publ. *Bulletin*.

**World Federation of Clerical Workers—WFCW:** 33 rue de Trèves, 1040 Brussels, Belgium; tel. (2) 285-47-00; fax (2) 230-87-22; e-mail piet.nelissen@cmt-wcl.org; f. 1921. Mems: national federations of unions and professional associations covering 600,000 workers in 38 countries. Organization: Congress (every four years), Council, Executive Board, Secretariat. Pres. ROEL ROTSHUIZEN (Netherlands); Sec. PIET NELISSEN. Publ. *Labor*.

**World Federation of Industry Workers—WFIW:** 33 rue de Trèves, 1040 Brussels, Belgium; e-mail piet.nelissen@cmt-wcl.org; f. 1985. Mems: regional and national federations covering about 500,000 workers in 30 countries. Organization: Congress (every five years), World Board (every year), Executive Committee, six World Trade Councils. Pres. JAAP WIENEN; Gen. Sec. ALFONS VAN GENECHTEN. Publ. *Labor*.

**World Federation of Professional Sportsmen:** Chaussée de Haecht 579, 1031 Brussels, Belgium; tel. (2) 246-35-41; fax (2) 246-35-42. Sec. MARCEL VAN MOL.

# WORLD COUNCIL OF CHURCHES—WCC

**Address:** 150 route de Ferney, POB 2100, 1211 Geneva 2, Switzerland.

**Telephone:** (22) 7916111; **fax:** (22) 7910361; **e-mail:** info@wcc-coe.org; **internet:** www.wcc-coe.org.

The Council was founded in 1948 to promote co-operation between Christian Churches and to prepare for a clearer manifestation of the unity of the Church.

### MEMBERS

There are 337 member Churches in more than 120 countries. Chief denominations: Anglican, Baptist, Congregational, Lutheran, Methodist, Moravian, Old Catholic, Orthodox, Presbyterian, Reformed and Society of Friends. The Roman Catholic Church is not a member but sends official observers to meetings.

## Organization

(January 2000)

### ASSEMBLY

The governing body of the World Council, consisting of delegates of the member Churches, it meets every seven or eight years to frame policy and consider some main themes. It elects the Presidents of the Council, who serve as members of the Central Committee. The eighth Assembly was held at Harare, Zimbabwe, in December 1998.

**Presidium:** Dr AGNES ABOUM (Kenya), Rev KATHRYN K. BANNISTER (USA), Bishop JABEZ L. BRYCE (Fiji), His Eminence CHRYSOSTOMOS OF EPHESUS (Greece), Dr MOON-KYU KANG (Republic of Korea), Bishop FEDERICO J. PAGURA (Argentina), Bishop EBERHARDT RENZ (Germany), His Holiness IGNATIUS ZAKKA I (Syria).

### CENTRAL COMMITTEE

Appointed by the Assembly to carry out its policies and decisions, the Committee consists of 150 members chosen from Assembly delegates. It meets every 12 to 18 months.

**Moderator:** His Holiness ARAM I, Catholicos of Cilicia (Armenian Apostolic Church, Lebanon).

**Vice-Moderators:** Justice SOPHIA O. A. ADINYIRA (Ghana), Dr MARION S. BEST (Canada).

### EXECUTIVE COMMITTEE

Consists of the Presidents, the Officers and 20 members chosen by the Central Committee from its membership to prepare its agenda, expedite its decisions and supervise the work of the Council between meetings of the Central Committee. Meets every six months.

### GENERAL SECRETARIAT

The General Secretariat implements the policies laid down by the WCC, and co-ordinates the work of the programme units described below. The General Secretariat is also responsible for the Ecumenical Centre Library and an Ecumenical Institute, at Bossey, which provides training in ecumenical leadership.

**General Secretary:** Rev. Dr KONRAD RAISER (Germany).

## Activities

The Central Committee comprises the Programme Committee and the Finance Committee. Within the Programme Committee there are advisory groups on issues relating to communication, women, justice, peace and creation, youth, ecumenical relations, and inter-religious relations. There are also five commissions and boards.

Following the Assembly in Harare in December 1998 the work of the WCC was restructured. Activities were grouped into four 'clusters':

### RELATIONSHIPS

The cluster group on relationships carries out the Council's work in promoting unity and community. It concentrates on issues relating to ecumenical, regional, international and inter-religious relations. Two programmes—Action by Churches Together (ACT) and the Ecumenical Church Loan Fund (ECLOF) are included in this grouping.

### ISSUES AND THEMES

This grouping, dealing with issues and themes encompassed by the aims of the Council, comprises four teams: Faith and Order; Mission and Evangelism; Justice, Peace, Creation; and Education and Ecumenical Formation.

### COMMUNICATION

The Communication cluster unites those parts of the Council involved in the provision of public information, documentation, and the production of publications.

### FINANCE, SERVICES AND ADMINISTRATION

This grouping comprises the following teams: Finance, Personnel, Income Development, Information Services, and Building Services.

## Finance

The WCC's total budget for 1999 amounted to 53.9m. Swiss francs. The main contributors are the churches and their agencies, with funds for certain projects contributed by other organizations.

## Publications

Catalogue of periodicals, books and audio-visuals.

*Ecumenical News International* (weekly).

*Ecumenical Review* (quarterly).

*International Review of Mission* (quarterly).

*WCC Yearbook*.

# WORLD FEDERATION OF TRADE UNIONS—WFTU

**Address:** Branická 112, 14701 Prague 4, Czech Republic.

**Telephone:** (2) 44462140; **fax:** (2) 44461378; **e-mail:** wftu@login.cz.

The Federation was founded in 1945, on a world-wide basis. A number of members withdrew from the Federation in 1949 to establish the International Confederation of Free Trade Unions (see p. 205). (See also the World Confederation of Labour, p. 271.)

### MEMBERS

In 1996 there were 132m. members, organized in 93 affiliated or associated national federations and six Trade Unions Internationals, in 121 countries.

## Organization

(January 2000)

### WORLD TRADE UNION CONGRESS

The Congress meets every five years. It reviews WFTU's work, endorses reports from the executives, and elects the General Council. The size of the delegations is based on the total membership of national federations. The Congress is also open to participation by non-affiliated organizations. The 14th Congress was held in New Delhi, India, in November 1999.

### GENERAL COUNCIL

The General Council meets three times between Congresses, and comprises members and deputies elected by Congress from nominees of national federations. Every affiliated or associated organization and Trade Unions International has one member and one deputy member.

The Council receives reports from the Presidential Council, approves the plan and budget and elects officers.

### PRESIDENTIAL COUNCIL

The Presidential Council meets twice a year and conducts most of the executive work of WFTU. It elects the President each year from among its members.

### SECRETARIAT

The Secretariat consists of the General Secretary, the Deputy General Secretary and five secretaries. It is appointed by the General Council and is responsible for general co-ordination, regional activities, national trade union liaison, press and information, administration and finance.

WFTU has regional offices in New Delhi, India (for the Asia-Pacific region), Havana, Cuba (covering the Americas), Dakar, Senegal, (for Africa), Damascus, Syria (for the Middle East) and in Moscow, Russia (covering the CIS countries).

**General Secretary:** ALEKSANDR ZHARIKOV (Russia).

## Finance

Income is derived from affiliation dues, which are based on the number of members in each trade union federation.

## Publication

*Flashes from the Trade Unions* (fortnightly, in English, French and Spanish; monthly in Arabic and Russian).

# Trade Unions Internationals

The following autonomous Trade Unions Internationals (TUIs) are associated with WFTU:

**Trade Unions International of Agriculture, Food, Commerce, Textile and Allied Workers:** c/o POB 50, Central International Post, Moscow, Russia; tel. and fax (95) 938-82-63; f. 1997 by merger of the TUI of Agricultural, Forestry and Plantation Workers (f. 1949), the TUI of Food, Tobacco, Hotel and Allied Industries Workers (f. 1949), the TUI of Workers in Commerce (f. 1959) and the TUI of Textile, Clothing, Leather and Fur Workers (f. 1949). Pres. FREDDY HUCK (France); Gen. Sec. DMITRII DOZORIN (Russia).

**Trade Unions International of Public and Allied Employees:** 4 Windsor Pl., New Delhi 110 001, India; tel. (11) 3311829; fax (11) 3311849; f. 1949. Mems: 34m. in 152 unions in 54 countries. Branch Commissions: State, Municipal, Postal and Telecommunications, Health, Banks and Insurance. Gen. Sec. SUKOMAL SEN (India) (acting). Publ. *Information Bulletin* (in three languages).

**Trade Unions International of Transport Workers:** Tengerszem U. 21/B, 1142 Budapest, Hungary; tel. (1) 2511282; fax (1) 2524921; f. 1949. Mems: 160 unions from 67 countries. Pres. NASR ZARIF MOUHREZ (Syria); Gen. Sec. JÓZSEF TÓTH. Publ. *TUI Reporter* (every 2 months, in English and Spanish).

**Trade Unions International of Workers of the Building, Wood and Building Materials Industries** (Union Internationale des Syndicats des Travailleurs du Bâtiment, du Bois et des Matériaux de Construction—UITBB): Box 281, 00101 Helsinki, Finland; tel. (9) 6931130; fax (9) 6931020; e-mail rguitbb@kaapeli.fi; f. 1949. Mems: 78 unions in 60 countries, grouping 17m. workers. Sec.-Gen. J. DINIS. Publ. *Bulletin*.

**Trade Unions International of Workers in the Chemical, Energy, Oil, Metal and Allied Industries:** c/o Kopernika 36/40, 00924 Warsaw, Poland; tel. (22) 268049; fax (22) 6358688; f. 1998 by merger of the TUI of Chemical, Oil and Allied Workers (f. 1950), the TUI of Energy Workers (f. 1949) and the TUI of Workers in the Metal Industry (f. 1949). Gen. Sec. EUGENIUSZ MIELNICKI (Poland).

**World Federation of Teachers' Unions:** 4 Windsor Pl., New Delhi 110 001, India; tel. (11) 3311829; fax (11) 3311849; f. 1946. Mems: 132 national unions of teachers and educational and scientific workers in 85 countries, representing over 25m. individuals. Pres. LESTURUGE ARIYAWANSA (Sri Lanka); Gen. Sec. MRINMOY BHATTACHARYYA (India). Publ. *FISE-Infos* (quarterly, in English, French and Spanish).

# WORLD TRADE ORGANIZATION—WTO

**Address:** Centre William Rappard, rue de Lausanne 154, 1211 Geneva, Switzerland.

**Telephone:** (22) 7395111; **fax:** (22) 7314206; **e-mail:** enquiries@wto.org; **internet:** www.wto.org.

The WTO is the legal and institutional foundation of the multilateral trading system. It was established on 1 January 1995, as the successor to the General Agreement on Tariffs and Trade (GATT).

### MEMBERS*

Angola
Antigua and Barbuda
Argentina
Australia
Austria
Bahrain
Bangladesh
Barbados
Belgium
Belize
Benin
Bolivia
Botswana
Brazil
Brunei
Bulgaria
Burkina Faso
Burundi
Cameroon
Canada
Central African Republic
Chad
Chile
Colombia
Congo, Democratic Republic
Congo, Republic
Costa Rica
Côte d'Ivoire
Cuba
Cyprus
Czech Republic
Denmark
Djibouti
Dominica
Dominican Republic
Ecuador
Egypt
El Salvador
Estonia
Fiji
Finland
France
Gabon
The Gambia
Germany
Ghana
Greece
Grenada
Guatemala
Guinea
Guinea-Bissau
Guyana
Haiti
Honduras
Hong Kong
Hungary
Iceland
India
Indonesia
Ireland
Israel
Italy
Jamaica
Japan
Jordan
Kenya
Korea, Republic
Kuwait
Kyrgyzstan
Latvia
Lesotho
Liechtenstein
Luxembourg
Macau
Madagascar
Malawi
Malaysia
Maldives
Mali
Malta
Mauritania
Mauritius
Mexico
Mongolia
Morocco
Mozambique
Myanmar
Namibia
Netherlands
New Zealand
Nicaragua
Niger
Nigeria
Norway
Pakistan
Panama
Papua New Guinea
Paraguay
Peru
Philippines
Poland
Portugal
Qatar
Romania
Rwanda
Saint Christopher and Nevis
Saint Lucia
Saint Vincent and the Grenadines
Senegal
Sierra Leone
Singapore
Slovakia
Slovenia
Solomon Islands
South Africa
Spain
Sri Lanka
Suriname
Swaziland
Sweden
Switzerland
Tanzania
Thailand
Togo
Trinidad and Tobago
Tunisia
Turkey
Uganda
United Arab Emirates
United Kingdom
USA
Uruguay
Venezuela
Zambia
Zimbabwe

* The European Community also has membership status.

Note: In early 2000 a further 30 governments had requested to join the WTO, and their applications were under consideration by accession working parties.

## Organization

(February 2000)

### MINISTERIAL CONFERENCE

The Ministerial Conference is the highest authority of the WTO. It is composed of representatives of all WTO members at ministerial level, and may take decisions on all matters under any of the multilateral trade agreements. The Conference is required to meet at least every two years, and was convened most recently in Seattle, USA, in November/December 1999.

### GENERAL COUNCIL

The General Council, which is also composed of representatives of all WTO members, is required to report to the Ministerial Conference and conducts much of the day-to-day work of the WTO. The Council convenes as the Dispute Settlement Body, to oversee the trade dispute settlement procedures, and as the Trade Policy Review Body, to conduct regular reviews of the trade policies of WTO members. The Council delegates responsibility to three other major Councils: for trade-related aspects of intellectual property rights, for trade in goods and for trade in services.

### SECRETARIAT

The WTO Secretariat comprises some 500 staff. Its responsibilities include the servicing of WTO delegate bodies, with respect to negotiations and the implementation of agreements, undertaking accession negotiations for new members and providing technical support and expertise to developing countries. In July 1999 member states reached a compromise agreement on the appointment of a new Director-General, having postponed the decision several times after failing to achieve the required consensus. Two candidates were appointed to serve consecutive three-year terms-in-office. New procedures for the appointment of officers were expected to be negotiated.

**Director-General:** MICHAEL MOORE (New Zealand); (from Sept. 2002) SUPACHAI PANITCHPAKDI (Thailand).

**Deputy Directors-General:** (until Aug. 2002) ANDREW STOLER (USA), ABLASSE OUÉDRAOGO (Burkina Faso), PAUL-HENRI RAVIER (France), MIGUEL RODRÍGUEZ MENDOZA (Venezuela).

## Activities

The Final Act of the Uruguay Round of GATT multilateral trade negotiations, which were concluded in December 1993, provided for extensive trade liberalization measures and for the establishment of a permanent structure to oversee international trading procedures. The Final Act was signed in April 1994, in Marrakesh, Morocco. At the same time a separate accord, the Marrakesh Declaration, was signed by the majority of GATT contracting states, endorsing the establishment of the WTO. The essential functions of the WTO are: to administer and facilitate the implementation of the results of the Uruguay Round; to provide a forum for multilateral trade negotiations; to administer the trade dispute settlement procedures; to review national trade policies; and to co-operate with other international institutions, in particular the IMF and World Bank, in order to achieve greater coherence in global economic policy-making.

The WTO Agreement contains some 29 individual legal texts and more than 25 additional Ministerial declarations, decisions and understandings, which cover obligations and commitments for member states. All these instruments are based on a few fundamental principles, which form the basis of the WTO Agreement. An integral part of the Agreement is 'GATT 1994', an amended and updated version of the original GATT Agreement of 1947, which was formally concluded at the end of 1995. Under the 'most-favoured nation' (MFN) clause, members are bound to grant to each other's products treatment no less favourable than that accorded to the products of any third parties. A number of exceptions apply, principally for customs unions and free-trade areas and for measures in favour of and among developing countries. The principle of 'national treatment' requires goods, having entered a market, to be treated no less favourably than the equivalent domestically-produced goods. Secure and predictable market access, to encourage trade, investment and job creation, may be determined by 'binding' tariffs, or customs duties. This process means that a tariff level for a particular product becomes a commitment by a member state, and cannot be increased without compensation negotiations with its main trading partners. Other WTO agreements also contribute to predictable trading conditions by demanding commitments from member countries and greater transparency of domestic laws and national trade policies. By permitting tariffs, whilst adhering to the guide-lines of being non-discriminatory, the WTO aims to promote open, fair and undistorted competition.

The WTO aims to encourage development and economic reform among the increasing number of developing countries and countries with economies in transition participating in the international trading system. These countries, particularly the least-developed states, have been granted transition periods and greater flexibility to implement certain WTO provisions. Industrial member countries are encouraged to assist developing nations by their trading conditions and by not expecting reciprocity in trade concession negotiations. In addition, the WTO operates a limited number of technical assistance programmes, mostly relating to training and the provision of information technology.

Finally, the WTO Agreement recognizes the need to protect the environment and to promote sustainable development. A new Committee on Trade and Environment was established to identify the relationship between trade policies, environmental measures and sustainable development and to recommend any appropriate modifications of the multilateral trading provisions. There was much contention over the compatibility of environmental and free-trade concerns in 1998, which was highlighted by a dispute settlement relating to shrimp-fishing in Asia (see below).

At the end of the Uruguay Round a 'built-in' programme of work for the WTO was developed. In addition, the Ministerial Conferences in December 1996 and May 1998 addressed a range of issues. The final declaration issued from the Ministerial Conference in December 1996 incorporated a text on the contentious issue of core labour standards, although it was emphasized that the relationship between trade and labour standards was not part of the WTO agenda. The text recognized the International Labour Organization's competence in establishing and dealing with core labour standards and endorsed future WTO/ILO co-operation. The declaration also included a plan of action on measures in favour of the world's least-developed countries, to assist these countries in enhancing their trading opportunities. The second Conference, convened in May 1998, decided against imposing customs duties on international electronic transactions, and agreed to establish a comprehensive work programme to address the issues of electronic commerce. The Conference also supported the creation of a framework of international rules to protect intellectual property rights and provide security and privacy in transactions. Developing countries were assured that their needs in this area would be taken into account. Members agreed to begin preparations for the launch of comprehensive talks on global trade liberalization. In addition, following repeated mass public demonstrations against free trade, it was agreed to try to increase the transparency of the WTO and improve public understanding of the benefits of open global markets.

Formal negotiations on the agenda of a new multilateral trade 'round', which was scheduled to be launched at the third Ministerial Conference, to be held in Seattle, USA, in late November/December 1999, commenced in September. While it was confirmed that further liberalization of agriculture and services was to be considered, no consensus was reached (in particular between the Cairns Group of countries and the USA, and the EU, supported by Japan) on the terms of reference or procedures for these negotiations prior to the start of the Conference. In addition, developing countries criticized renewed efforts, mainly by the USA, to link trade and labour standards and to incorporate environmental considerations into the discussions. Efforts by the EU to broaden the talks to include investment and competition policy were also resisted by the USA. The conduct of the Ministerial Conference was severely disrupted by public demonstrations by a diverse range of interest groups concerned with the impact of WTO accords on the environment, workers' rights and developing countries. The differences between member states with regard to a formal agenda failed to be resolved during extensive negotiations, and the Conference was suspended. At a meeting of the General Council, convened later in December, member countries reached an informal understanding that any agreements concluding on 31 December would be extended. Meanwhile, the Director-General attempted to maintain a momentum for proceeding with a new round of trade negotiations, although it was considered unlikely to be initiated before 2001. In February 2000 the General Council agreed to resume talks with regard to agriculture and services, and to consider difficulties in implementing the Uruguay Accord, which was a main concern of developing member states. The Council also urged industrialized nations to pursue an earlier initiative to grant duty-free access to the exports of least developed countries.

At the 1996 Conference representatives of some 28 countries signed a draft Information Technology Agreement (ITA), which aimed to eliminate tariffs on the significant global trade in IT products by 2000. By late February 1997 some 39 countries, representing the required 90% share of the world's IT trade, had consented to implement the ITA. It was signed in March, and was to cover the following main product categories: computers; telecommunications products; semiconductors or manufacturing equipment; software; and scientific instruments. Tariff reductions in these sectors were to be undertaken in four stages, commencing in July, and subsequently on 1 January each year, providing for the elimination of all tariffs by the start of 2000. In February 1999 the WTO announced plans to investigate methods of removing non-tariff barriers to trade in IT products, such as those resulting from non-standardization of technical regulations.

## AGRICULTURE

The Final Act of the Uruguay Round extended previous GATT arrangements for trade in agricultural products through new rules and commitments to ensure more predictable and fair competition in the sector. All quantitive measures limiting market access for agricultural products were to be replaced by tariffs (i.e. a process of 'tariffication'), enabling more equal protection and access opportunities. All tariffs on agricultural items were to be reduced by 36% by developed countries, over a period of six years, and by 24% by developing countries (excluding least-developed member states) over 10 years. A special treatment clause applied to 'sensitive' products (mainly rice) in four countries, for which limited import restrictions could be maintained. Efforts to reduce domestic support measures for agricultural products were to be based on calculations of total aggregate measurements of support (Total AMS) by each member state. A 20% reduction in Total AMS was required by developed countries over six years, and 13% over 10 years by developing countries. No reduction was required of least-developed countries. Developed member countries were required to reduce the value and quantity of direct export subsidies by 36% and 21% respectively (on 1986–90 levels) over six years. For developing countries these reductions were to be two-thirds those of developed nations, over 10 years. A specific concern of least-developed and net-food importing developing countries, which had previously relied on subsidized food products, was to be addressed through other food aid mechanisms and assistance for agricultural development. The situation was to be monitored by WTO's Committee on Agriculture. Negotiations on the further liberalization of agricultural markets were part of the WTO 'built-in' programme for 2000 or earlier, but remained a major area of contention.

The Agreement on the Application of Sanitary and Phytosanitary Measures aims to regulate world-wide standards of food safety and animal and plant health in order to encourage the mutual recognition of standards and conformity, so as to facilitate trade in these products. The Agreement includes provisions on control inspection and approval procedures. In September 1997, in the first case to be brought under the Agreement, a dispute panel of the WTO ruled that the EU's ban on imports of hormone-treated beef and beef products from the USA and Canada was in breach of international trading rules. In January 1998 the Appellate Body upheld the panel's ruling, but expressed its support for restrictions to ensure food standards if there was adequate scientific evidence of risks to human health. The EU maintained the ban, against resistance from the USA, while it carried out scientific risk assessments. In early 1999 the USA proposed a labelling scheme to resolve the dispute, while the WTO reaffirmed its decision that the EU was obliged to remove all restrictions by mid-May unless there was scientific evidence to justify the action. In early May the European Commission published a study which supported its concerns of the existence of hormone residues in meat declared to be clear of those products, and resolved not to remove the ban. At the same time the USA issued a provisional list of EU products that were to be subject to retaliatory measures.

## TEXTILES AND CLOTHING

From 1974 the Multi-fibre Arrangement (MFA) provided the basis of international trade concerning textiles and clothing, enabling the major importers to establish quotas and protect their domestic industries, through bilateral agreements, against more competitive low-cost goods from developing countries. MFA restrictions that were in place on 31 December 1994 were carried over into the new agreement and were to be phased out through integration into GATT 1994, under which they would be subject to the same rules applying to other industrial products. This was to be achieved in four stages: products accounting for 16% of the total volume of textiles and clothing imports (at 1990 levels) were to be integrated from 1 January 1995; a further 17% on 1 January 1998; and not less than a further 18% on 1 January 2002, with all remaining products to be integrated by 1 January 2005.

## TRADE IN SERVICES

The General Agreement on Trade in Services (GATS), which was negotiated during the GATT Uruguay Round, is the first set of multilaterally-agreed and legally-enforceable rules and disciplines ever negotiated to cover international trade in services. The GATS comprises a framework of general rules and disciplines, annexes addressing special conditions relating to individual sectors and national schedules of market access commitments. A Council for Trade in Services oversees the operation of the agreement.

The GATS framework consists of 29 articles, including the following set of basic obligations: total coverage of all internationally-traded services; national treatment, i.e. according services and service suppliers of other members no less favourable treatment than that accorded to domestic services and suppliers; MFN treatment (see above), with any specific exemptions to be recorded prior to the implementation of the GATS, with a limit of 10 years duration; transparency, requiring publication of all relevant national laws and legislations; bilateral agreements on recognition of standards and qualifications to be open to other members who wish to negotiate accession; no restrictions on international payments and transfers; progressive liberalization to be pursued; and market access and national treatment commitments to be bound and recorded in national schedules. These schedules, which include exemptions to the MFN principles, contain the negotiated and guaranteed conditions under which trade in services is conducted and are an integral part of the GATS.

Annexes to the GATS cover the movement of natural persons, permitting governments to negotiate specific commitments regarding the temporary stay of people for the purpose of providing a service; the right of governments to take measures in order to ensure the integrity and stability of the financial system; the role of telecommunications as a distinct sector of economic activity and as a means of supplying other economic activities; and air transport services, excluding certain activities relating to traffic rights.

At the end of the Uruguay Round governments agreed to continue negotiations in the following areas: basic telecommunications, maritime transport, movement of natural persons and financial services. The Protocol to the GATS relating to movement of natural persons was concluded in July 1995. In May 1996 the USA withdrew from negotiations to conclude an agreement on maritime transport services. At the end of June the participating countries agreed to suspend the discussions and to recommence negotiations in 2000. At the end of July 1995 some 29 members signed an interim agreement to grant greater access to the banking, insurance, investment and securities sectors from August 1996. Negotiations to strengthen the agreement and to extend it to new signatories (including the USA, which had declined to sign the agreement, claiming lack of reciprocity by some Asian countries) commenced in April 1997. A final agreement was successfully concluded in mid-December: 102 countries endorsed the elimination of restrictions on access to the financial services sectors from 1 March 1999, and agreed to subject those services to legally-binding rules and disciplines. Further negotiations were scheduled to commence in 2000. In late January 1999 some 35 signatory states had yet to ratify the financial services agreement, and its entry into force was postponed. Negotiations on trade in basic telecommunications began in May 1994 and were scheduled to conclude in April 1996. Before the final deadline, however, the negotiations were suspended, owing to US concerns, which included greater access to satellite telecommunications markets in Asia and greater control over foreign companies operating from the domestic markets. An agreement was finally concluded by the new deadline of 15 February 1997. Accordingly the largest telecommunications markets, i.e. the USA, the EU and Japan, were to eliminate all remaining restrictions on domestic and foreign competition in the industry by 1 January 1998 (although delays were granted to Spain, until December 1998, Ireland, until 2000, and Greece and Portugal, until 2003). The majority of the 69 signatories to the accord also agreed on common rules to ensure that fair competition could be enforced by the WTO disputes settlement mechanism, and pledged their commitment to establishing a regulatory system for the telecommunications sector and guaranteeing transparency in government licensing. The agreement entered into force on 5 February 1998, having been rescheduled, owing to the delay on the part of some signatory countries (then totalling 72 states) in ratifying the accord and incorporating the principles of industry regulation into national legislation.

## INTELLECTUAL PROPERTY RIGHTS

The WTO Agreement on Trade-Related Aspects of Intellectual Property Rights (TRIPS) recognizes that widely varying standards in the protection and enforcement of intellectual property rights and the lack of multilateral disciplines dealing with international trade in counterfeit goods have been a growing source of tension in international economic relations. The TRIPS agreement aims to ensure that nationals of member states receive equally favourable treatment with regard to the protection of intellectual property and that adequate standards of intellectual property protection exist in all WTO member countries. These standards are largely based on the obligations of the Paris and Berne Conventions of WIPO (see p. 109), however, the agreement aims to expand and enhance these where necessary, for example: computer programmes, to be protected as literary works for copyright purposes; definition of trade marks eligible for protection; stricter rules of geographical indications of consumer products; a 10-year protection period for industrial designs; a 20-year patent protection available for all inventions; tighter protection of layout design of integrated circuits; and protection for trade secrets and 'know-how' with a commercial value.

Under the agreement member governments are obliged to provide procedures and remedies to ensure the effective enforcement of intellectual property rights. Civil and administrative procedures outlined in the TRIPS include provisions on evidence, injunctions, judicial authority to order the disposal of infringing goods, and criminal procedures and penalties, in particular for trade-mark counterfeiting and copyright piracy. A one-year period was envisaged for developed countries to bring their legislation and practices into conformity with the agreement. Developing countries were to do so in five years (or 10 years if an area of technology did not already have patent protection) and least-developed countries in 11 years. A Council for Trade-Related Property Rights monitors the compliance of governments with the agreement and its operation.

## LEGAL FRAMEWORK

In addition to the binding agreements mentioned above, WTO aims to provide a comprehensive legal framework for the international trading system. Under GATT 1994 'anti-dumping' measures were permitted against imports of a product with an export price below its normal value, if these imports were are likely to cause damage to a domestic industry. The WTO agreement provides for greater clarity and more-detailed rules determining the application of these measures and determines settlement procedures in disputes relating to anti-dumping actions taken by WTO members. In general, anti-dumping measures were to be limited to five years. WTO's Agreement on Subsidies and Countervailing Measures is intended to expand on existing GATT agreements. It classifies subsidies into three categories: prohibited, which may be determined by the Dispute Settlement Body and must be immediately withdrawn; actionable, which must be withdrawn or altered if the subsidy is found to cause adverse effects on the interests of other members; and non-actionable, for example subsidies involving assistance to industrial research, assistance to disadvantaged regions or adaptation of facilities to meet new environmental requirements. The Agreement also contains provisions on the use of duties to offset the effect of a subsidy (so-called countervailing measures) and establishes procedures for the initiation and conduct of investigations into this action. Countervailing measures must generally be terminated within five years of their imposition. Least-developed countries, and developing countries with gross national product per capita of less than US $1,000, are exempt from disciplines on prohibited export subsidies; however, these were to be eliminated by 2003 in all other developing countries and by 2002 in countries with economies in transition.

WTO members may take safeguard actions to protect a specific domestic industry from a damaging increase of imported products. However, the WTO agreement aims to clarify criteria for imposing safeguards, their duration (normally to be no longer than four years, which may be extended to eight years) and consultations on trade compensation for the exporting countries. At 1 December 1995 50 member states had notified the Committee on Safeguards of the WTO Secretariat of their existing domestic safeguard legislations, as required under the agreement. Any measures to protect domestic industries through voluntary export restraints or other market-sharing devices were to be phased out by the end of 1998, or a year later for one specific safeguard measure, subject to mutual agreement of the members directly concerned. Safeguard measures are not applicable to products from developing countries as long as their share of imports of the product concerned does not exceed 3%.

Further legal arrangements act to ensure the following: that technical regulations and standards (including testing and certification procedures) do not create unnecessary obstacles to trade; that import licensing procedures are transparent and predictable; that the valuation of goods for customs purposes are fair and uniform; that GATT principles and obligations apply to import preshipment inspection activities; the fair and transparent administration of rules of origin; and that no investment measures which may restrict or distort trade may be applied. A Working Group on Notification Obligations and Procedures aims to ensure that members fulfil their notification requirements, which facilitate the transparency and surveillance of the trading rules.

## PLURILATERAL AGREEMENTS

The majority of GATT agreements became multilateral obligations when the WTO became operational in 1995; however, four agreements, which have a selective group of signatories, remained in effect. These so-called plurilateral agreements, the Agreement on Trade in Civil Aircraft, the Agreement on Government Procurement, the International Dairy Agreement and the International Bovine Meat Agreement, aim to increase international co-operation and fair and open trade and competition in these areas. Each of the agreements establish their own management bodies, which are required to report to the General Council.

## TRADE POLICY REVIEW MECHANISM

The mechanism, which was established provisionally in 1989, was given a permanent role in the WTO. Through regular monitoring and surveillance of national trade policies the mechanism aims to increase the transparency and understanding of trade policies and practices and to enable assessment of the effects of policies on the world trading system. In addition, it records efforts made by governments to bring domestic trade legislation into conformity with WTO provisions and to implement WTO commitments. Reviews are conducted in the Trade Policy Review Body on the basis of a policy statement of the government under review and an independent report prepared by the WTO Secretariat. Under the mechanism the world's four largest traders, the European Union, the USA, Japan and Canada, were to be reviewed every two years. Special groups were established to examine new regional free-trade arrangements and the trade policies of acceding countries. In February 1996 a single Committee on Regional Trade Agreements was established, superseding these separate working parties. The Committee aimed to ensure that these groupings contributed to the process of global trade liberalization and to study the implications of these arrangements on the multilateral system. At the Ministerial Conference held in December 1996 it was agreed to establish a new working group to conduct a study of transparency in government procurement practices.

### SETTLEMENT OF DISPUTES

A separate annex to the WTO agreement determines a unified set of rules and procedures to govern the settlement of all WTO disputes, substantially reinforcing the GATT procedures. WTO members are committed not to undertake unilateral action against perceived violations of the trade rules, but to seek recourse in the dispute settlement mechanism and abide by its findings.

The first stage of the process requires bilateral consultations between the members concerned in an attempt to conclude a mutually-acceptable solution to the issue. These may be undertaken through the good offices and mediation efforts of the Director-General. Only after a consultation period of 60 days may the complainant ask the General Council, convened as the Dispute Settlement Body (DSB), to establish an independent panel to examine the case, which then does so within the terms of reference of the agreement cited. Each party to the dispute submits its arguments and then presents its case before the panel. Third parties which notify their interest in the dispute may also present views at the first substantive meeting of the panel. At this stage an expert review group may be appointed to provide specific scientific or technical advice. The panel submits sections and then a full interim report of its findings to the parties, who may then request a further review involving additional meetings. A final report should be submitted to the parties by the panel within six months of its establishment, or within three months in cases of urgency, including those related to perishable goods. Final reports are normally adopted by the DSB within 60 days of issuance. In the case of a measure being found to be inconsistent with the relevant WTO agreement, the panel recommends ways in which the member may bring the measure into conformity with the agreement. However, under the WTO mechanism either party has the right to appeal against the decision and must notify the DSB of its intentions before adoption of the final report. Appeal proceedings, which are limited to issues of law and the legal interpretation covered by the panel report, are undertaken by three members of the Appellate Body within a maximum period of 90 days. The report of the Appellate Body must be unconditionally accepted by the parties to the dispute (unless there is a consensus within the DSB against its adoption). If the recommendations of the panel or appeal report are not implemented immediately, or within a 'reasonable period' as determined by the DSB, the parties are obliged to negotiate mutually-acceptable compensation pending full implementation. Failure to agree compensation may result in the DSB authorizing the complainant to suspend concessions or obligations against the other party. In any case the DSB monitors the implementation of adopted recommendations or rulings, while any outstanding cases remain on its agenda until the issue is resolved. In 1997 and 1998 panel and Appellate Body investigations included: consideration of access to the Japanese domestic market for imports of photographic film (a complaint brought by the USA, with the panel ruling in favour of Japan in December 1997); a complaint brought by the USA against the EU, relating to the latter's re-categorization of computer-networking equipment, in order to retain tariffs (the panel supported the USA in a ruling in February 1998, but upheld an appeal by the EU in June); and the USA's import prohibition on certain shrimp and shrimp products from countries without safeguards to prevent the deaths of turtles during the fishing process. The complainants in the latter case, India, Malaysia, Pakistan and Thailand, were supported by the panel in May 1998, which ruled that the USA could not unilaterally impose its environmental standards on others. An appeal in October by the USA was defeated, leading to protests by environmental groups. In May 1997 a WTO dispute panel upheld a complaint against the EU's banana import regime (brought by Ecuador, Guatemala, Honduras, Mexico and the USA in 1996), which granted preferential market access to Caribbean-produced goods. An appeal was rejected. In late 1998 the USA alleged that the EU had failed to comply with the panel's ruling and announced its intention to impose punitive measures against a series of European products. The legality of the action, in the absence of any panel ruling on the modified import arrangements (which entered into force on 1 January 1999), was disputed by several member governments and generated intensive consideration of the dispute procedures. In March, at the request of the EU, the WTO authorized the establishment of a panel to investigate the validity of a section of US trade legislation that permitted the imposition of duties, on the basis that it was incompatible with existing procedures authorized by the WTO. The EU also brought a complaint against the imposition of 100% tariffs on 15 products, of which the US Government issued formal notification earlier in that month. In early April a WTO panel upheld US claims that the modified banana regime was discriminatory and permitted trade measures to compensate for losses incurred by US companies, the first time punitive measures had been approved by the WTO, although that figure was set at US $191.4m. annually, compared with $520m. originally claimed. Other disputes considered in 1999 included Canadian subsidies to dairy exporters, Australia's ban on salmon imports, restrictive bidding procedures for airport contracts in the Republic of Korea (dispute panels established at the request of the USA), and lamb import tariffs (a complaint brought by Australia against the USA). By January 2000 188 trade complaints had been notified to the WTO (on some 147 different issues) since 1995; 31 Appellate Body or panel reports had been adopted, while 23 cases remained active at that time. An Advisory Centre on WTO Law, to assist poorer countries with the dispute procedures, was to be established, in Geneva, in 2000.

### CO-OPERATION WITH OTHER ORGANIZATIONS

WTO is mandated to pursue co-operation with the IMF and the World Bank, as well as with other multilateral organizations, in order to achieve greater coherence in global economic policy-making. In November 1994 the preparatory committee of the WTO resolved not to incorporate the new organization into the UN structure as a specialized agency. Instead, co-operation arrangements with the IMF and World Bank were to be developed. In addition, efforts were pursued to enhance co-operation with UNCTAD in research, trade and technical issues. The Directors-General of the two organizations agreed to meet at least twice a year in order to develop the working relationship. In particular, co-operation was to be undertaken in WTO's special programme of activities for Africa, which aimed to help African countries expand and diversify their trade and benefit from the global trading system.

**International Trade Centre UNCTAD/WTO:** Palais des Nations, 1211 Geneva 10, Switzerland; tel. (22) 7300111; fax (22) 7334439; e-mail itcreg@intracen.org; internet www.intracen.org; f. 1964 by GATT; jointly operated with the UN (through UNCTAD) since 1968; ITC works with developing countries in product and market development, the development of trade support services, trade information, human resource development, international purchasing and supply management, and needs assessment and programme design for trade promotion. Publs *International Trade Forum* (quarterly), market studies, handbooks etc.

**Executive Director:** J. DENIS BÉLISLE.

## Finance

The WTO's 1999 budget amounted to 122m. Swiss francs, financed by contributions from members in proportion to their share of total trading conducted by WTO members.

## Publications

*Annual Report* (2 volumes).

*WTO Focus* (monthly).

# OTHER INTERNATIONAL ORGANIZATIONS

# OTHER INTERNATIONAL ORGANIZATIONS

## Agriculture, Food, Forestry and Fisheries

(For organizations concerned with agricultural commodities, see Commodities, p. 286)

**African Timber Organization—ATO:** BP 1077, Libreville, Gabon; tel. 732928; fax 734030; f. 1976 to enable members to study and co-ordinate ways of ensuring the optimum utilization and conservation of their forests. Mems: Angola, Cameroon, Central African Republic, Democratic Republic of the Congo, Republic of the Congo, Côte d'Ivoire, Equatorial Guinea, Gabon, Ghana, Liberia, Nigeria, São Tomé and Príncipe, Tanzania. Sec.-Gen. MOHAMMED LAWAL GARBA. Publs *ATO Information Bulletin* (quarterly), *International Magazine of African Timber* (2 a year).

**Asian Vegetable Research and Development Center:** POB 42, Shanhua, Tainan 741, Taiwan; tel. (6) 5837801; fax (6) 5830009; e-mail avrdcbox@netra.avrdc.org.tw; internet www.avrdc.org.tw; f. 1971; aims to enhance the nutritional well-being and raise the incomes of the poor in rural and urban areas of developing countries, through improved varieties and methods of vegetable production, marketing and distribution, taking into account the need to preserve the quality of the environment; the Centre has an experimental farm, laboratories, gene-bank, greenhouses, quarantine house, insectarium, library and weather station and provides training for research and production specialists in tropical vegetables; exchanges and disseminates vegetable germplasm through regional centres in the developing world; serves as a clearing-house for vegetable research information and undertakes scientific publishing. Mems: Australia, France, Germany, Japan, Republic of Korea, Philippines, Taiwan, Thailand, USA. Dir-Gen. Dr SAMSON C. S. TSOU. Publs *Progress Report, Newsletter, Technical Bulletin, Proceedings, Centerpoint* (3 a year).

**CAB International (CABI):** Wallingford, Oxon, OX10 8DE, United Kingdom; tel. (1491) 832111; fax (1491) 833508; e-mail cabi@cabi.org; internet www.cabi.org; f. 1929 as the Imperial Agricultural Bureaux (later Commonwealth Agricultural Bureaux); current name adopted in 1985; inter-governmental organization which aims to improve human welfare world-wide through the generation, dissemination and application of scientific knowledge in support of sustainable development. It places particular emphasis on forestry, human health and the management of natural resources, with priority given to the needs of developing countries. CABI compiles and publishes extensive information (in a variety of print and electronic forms) on aspects of agriculture, forestry, veterinary medicine, the environment and natural resources, Third World rural development, leisure, recreation and tourism, human nutrition, and human health. Maintains regional centres in Kenya, Malaysia, Pakistan, Switzerland and Trinidad and Tobago. Mems: 40 countries. Dir-Gen. DENIS BLIGHT.

**CABI Bioscience:** Bakeham Lane, Egham, Surrey, TW20 9TY, United Kingdom; tel. (1784) 470111; fax (1784) 470909; e-mail bioscience@cabi.org; f. 1998 by integration of the capabilities and resources of the following four CABI scientific institutions: International Institute of Biological Control; International Institute of Entomology; International Institute of Parasitology; International Mycological Institute; undertakes research, training, capacity-building and institutional development in the three general sectors of biological pest management, biodiversity and biosystematics, and environment.

**Caribbean Food and Nutrition Institute:** UWI Campus, St Augustine, Trinidad and Tobago; tel. 662-7025; fax 662-5511; e-mail mail@cfni.paho.org; f. 1967 to serve the governments and people of the region and to act as a catalyst among persons and organizations concerned with food and nutrition through research and field investigations, training in nutrition, dissemination of information, advisory services and production of educational material. Mems: all English-speaking Caribbean territories including Belize and Guyana. Dir Dr FITZROY HENRY. Publs *Cajanus* (quarterly), *Nyam News* (2 a month), *Nutrient-Cost Tables* (quarterly), educational material.

**Collaborative International Pesticides Analytical Council Ltd—CIPAC:** c/o Dr A. Martijn, 't Gotink 7, 7261 VE Ruurlo, Netherlands; tel. and fax (573) 452851; f. 1957 to organize international collaborative work on methods of analysis for pesticides used in crop protection. Mems: in 46 countries. Chair. Dr F. SÁNCHEZ RASERO (Spain); Sec. Dr A. MARTIJN (Netherlands).

**Dairy Society International—DSI:** 7185 Ruritan Drive, Chambersburg, PA 17201, USA; tel. (717) 375-4392; f. 1946 to foster the extension of dairy and dairy industrial enterprise internationally through an interchange and dissemination of scientific, technological, economic, dietary and other relevant information; organizer and sponsor of the first World Congress for Milk Utilization. Mems: in 50 countries. Pres. JAMES E. CLICK (USA); Man. Dir G. W. WEIGOLD (USA). Publs *DSI Report to Members, DSI Bulletin, Market Frontier News, Dairy Situation Review*.

**Desert Locust Control Organization for Eastern Africa:** POB 30023, Nairobi, Kenya; tel. (2) 501704; fax (2) 505137; f. 1962 to promote effective control of desert locust in the region and to conduct research into the locust's environment and behaviour; conducts pesticides residue analysis; assists member states in the monitoring and extermination of other migratory pests such as the quelea-quelea (grain-eating birds), the army worm and the tsetse fly; bases at Asmara (Eritrea), Dire Dawa (Ethiopia), Mogadishu and Hargeisa (Somalia), Nairobi (Kenya), Khartoum (Sudan), Arusha (Tanzania), Kampala (Uganda) and Djibouti. Mems: Djibouti, Eritrea, Ethiopia, Kenya, Somalia, Sudan, Tanzania, Uganda. Dir Dr A. H. M. KARRAR; Co-ordinator C. K. MUINAMIA. Publs *Desert Locust Situation Reports* (monthly), *Annual Report*, technical reports.

**European and Mediterranean Plant Protection Organization:** 1 rue Le Nôtre, 75016 Paris, France; tel. 1-45-20-77-94; fax 1-42-24-89-43; e-mail hq@eppo.fr; internet www.eppo.org; f. 1951, present name adopted in 1955; aims to promote international co-operation between government plant protection services and in preventing the introduction and spread of pests and diseases of plants and plant products. Mems: governments of 41 countries and territories. Chair. R. PETZOLD; Dir-Gen. I. M. SMITH. Publs *EPPO Bulletin, Data Sheets on Quarantine Organisms, Guidelines for the Efficacy Evaluation of Pesticides, Crop Growth Stage Keys, Summary of the Phytosanitary Regulations of EPPO Member Countries, Reporting Service*.

**European Association for Animal Production** (Fédération européenne de zootechnie): Via A. Torlonia 15A, 00161 Rome, Italy; tel. (06) 44238013; fax (06) 44241466; e-mail zoorec@mnet.it; f. 1949 to help improve the conditions of animal production and meet consumer demand; holds annual meetings. Mems: associations in 37 member countries. Pres. Prince P. ZU SOLMS-LICH (Germany). Publ. *Livestock Production Science* (16 a year).

**European Association for Research on Plant Breeding—EUCARPIA:** c/o POB 315, 6700 AH Wageningen, Netherlands; e-mail marjo.dejeu@users.pv.wau.nl; f. 1956 to promote scientific and technical co-operation in the plant breeding field. Mems: 1,000 individuals, 64 corporate mems; 12 sections and several working groups. Pres. Dr G. R. MACKAY (UK); Sec. Dr Ir M. J. DE JEU (Netherlands). Publ. *Bulletin*.

**European Confederation of Agriculture:** 23 rue de la Science, 1040 Brussels, Belgium; tel. (2) 230-43-80; fax (2) 230-46-77; e-mail cea@pophost.eunet.be; f. 1889 as International Confederation, reformed in 1948 as European Confederation; represents the interests of European agriculture in the international field; social security for independent farmers and foresters in the member countries; currently giving priority to developing relations with the countries of central and eastern Europe. Mems: 300 mems. from 30 countries. Pres. HANS JONSSON (Sweden); Gen. Sec. CHRISTOPHE HÉMARD (France). Publs *CEA Dialog, Annual Report*.

**European Grassland Federation:** c/o Dr W. H. Prins, Hollandseweg 382, 6705 BE Wageningen, Netherlands; tel. (317) 416386; fax (317) 416386; e-mail egf-secr@pckassa.com; internet www.pckassa.com/egf/; f. 1963 to facilitate and maintain liaison between European grassland organizations and to promote the interchange of scientific and practical knowledge and experience; general meeting is held every two years and symposia at other times. Mems: 28 full and eight corresponding member countries in Europe. Pres. V. JORGENSEN; Sec. Dr W. H. PRINS. Publ. *Proceedings (Grassland Science in Europe)*.

**European Livestock and Meat Trading Union:** 81A rue de la Loi, 1040 Brussels, Belgium; tel. (2) 230-46-03; fax (2) 230-94-00; e-mail uecbv@pophost.eunet.be; internet uecbv.eunet.be; f. 1952 to study problems of the European livestock and meat trade and inform members of all legislation affecting it, and to act as an international arbitration commission; conducts research on agricultural markets, quality of livestock, and veterinary regulations. Mems: national organizations in Austria, Belgium, Czech Republic, Denmark, Finland, France, Germany, Greece, Hungary, Ireland, Italy, Luxembourg, Netherlands, Norway, Poland, Portugal, Spain, Sweden, Switzerland, United Kingdom; corresponding mems in Estonia, Slovenia and Federal Republic of Yugoslavia; and the European Association of Livestock Markets. Pres. A. ANORO; Sec.-Gen. J.-L. MERIAUX.

**Inter-American Association of Agricultural Librarians, Documentalists and Information Specialists** (Asociación Interamericana de Bibliotecarios, Documentalistas y Especialistas en Información Agrícolas—AIBDA): c/o IICA-CIDIA, Apdo 55-2200 Coronado, Costa Rica; tel. 216-0290; fax 216-0291; e-mail cmolesti@iica.ac.cr; internet www.iica.ac.cr; f. 1953 to promote professional improvement of its members through technical publications and meetings, and to promote improvement of library services in agricultural sciences. Mems: about 400 in 29 countries and territories. Pres. MAGDA SAUDÍ; Exec. Sec. CARLOS J. MOLESTINA; Publs *Boletín Informativo* (3 a year), *Boletín Especial* (irregular), *Revista AIBDA* (2 a year), *AIBDA Actualidades* (4 or 5 a year).

**Inter-American Tropical Tuna Commission—IATTC:** Scripps Institution of Oceanography, 8604 La Jolla Shores Drive, La Jolla, CA 92037-1508, USA; tel. (858) 546-7100; fax (858) 546-7133; e-mail rallen@iattc.ucsd.edu; f. 1950; two programmes, the Tuna-Billfish Programme and the Tuna-Dolphin Programme. The Tuna-Billfish Programme investigates the biology of the tunas and related species of the eastern Pacific Ocean to determine the effects of fishing and natural factors on the stocks of tunas and billfish, and recommends appropriate conservation measures to maintain stocks at levels which will afford maximum sustainable catches; the Tuna-Dolphin Programme monitors dolphin levels and the number of deaths caused to dolphins by tuna-fishers, in order to recommend measures to maintain dolphin stocks; promotes fishing methods that avoid the needless killing of dolphins; investigates the effect of various fishing methods on different species of fish and other aquatic animals. Mems: Costa Rica, Ecuador, El Salvador, France, Japan, Mexico, Nicaragua, Panama, USA, Vanuatu, Venezuela. Dir ROBIN L. ALLEN; Publs *Bulletin* (irregular), *Annual Report*.

**International Association for Cereal Science and Technology—ICC:** Wiener Strasse 22A, POB 77, 2320 Schwechat, Austria; tel. (1) 707-72-02; fax (1) 707-72-04; e-mail gen.sec@icc.or.at; internet www.icc.or.at/icc/; f. 1955 (as the International Association for Cereal Chemistry; name changed 1986); aims to promote international co-operation in the field of cereal science and technology through the dissemination of information and the development of standard methods of testing and analysing products. Mems: 50 mem. states. Sec.-Gen. Dr HELMUT GLATTES (Austria).

**International Association for Vegetation Science:** IBN-DLO, POB 23, 6700 AA Wageningen, Netherlands; tel. (317) 477914; fax (317) 424988; e-mail j.h.j.schaminee@ibn.dlo.nl; f. 1938. Mems: 1,330 from 70 countries. Chair. Prof. Dr E. O. BOX; Sec.-Gen. Dr J. H. J. SCHAMINÉE; Publs *Phytocoenologia, Journal of Vegetation Science, Applied Vegetation Science*.

**International Association of Agricultural Economists:** 1211 West 22nd St, Suite 216, Oak Brook, IL 60523-2197, USA; tel. (708) 571-9393; fax (708) 571-9580; e-mail iaae@interaccess.com; f. 1929 to foster development of the sciences of agricultural economics and further the application of the results of economic investigation in agricultural processes and the improvement of economic and social conditions relating to agricultural and rural life. Mems: in 96 countries. Pres. DOUGLAS HEDLEY; Sec. and Treas. WALTER J. ARMBRUSTER (USA). Publs *Agricultural Economics* (8 a year), *IAAE Newsletter* (2 a year).

**International Association of Agricultural Information Specialists:** c/o Margot Bellamy, CAB International, Wallingford, Oxon OX10 8DE, United Kingdom; tel. (1491) 829346; fax (1491) 833508; e-mail m.bellamy@cabi.org; f. 1955 to promote agricultural library science and documentation, and the professional interests of agricultural librarians and documentalists; affiliated to the International Federation of Library Associations and to the Fédération Internationale de Documentation. Mems: 600 in 84 countries. Pres. Dr J. VAN DER BURG (Netherlands); Sec.-Treas. MARGOT BELLAMY (UK). Publs *Quarterly Bulletin, IAALD News, World Directory of Agricultural Information Resource Centres*.

**International Association of Horticultural Producers:** Postbus 200, 2700 AG Zoetermeen, Netherlands; tel. (79) 3470707; fax (79) 3470404; e-mail e.clemens@tuinbouw.nl; f. 1948; represents the common interests of commercial horticultural producers in the international field by frequent meetings, regular publications, press-notices, resolutions and addresses to governments and international authorities; authorizes international horticultural exhibitions. Mems: national associations in 25 countries. Pres. B. WERNER; Gen. Sec. Dr J. B. M. ROTTEVEEL. Publ. *Yearbook of International Horticultural Statistics*.

**International Bee Research Association:** 18 North Rd, Cardiff, CF10 3DT, United Kingdom; tel. (29) 2037-2409; fax (29) 2066-5522; e-mail ibra@cardiff.ac.uk; f. 1949 to further bee research and provide an information service for bee scientists and bee-keepers worldwide. Mems: 1,200 in 130 countries. Dir RICHARD JONES; Asst Dir Dr PAMELA MUNN. Publs *Bee World* (quarterly), *Apicultural Abstracts* (quarterly), *Journal of Apicultural Research* (quarterly).

**International Centre for Integrated Mountain Development:** POB 3226, Kathmandu, Nepal; tel. (1) 525313; fax (1) 524509; e-mail dits@icimod.org.np; internet www.icimod.org.sg; f. 1983 with the primary objective of promoting the sustained well-being of mountain communities through effective socioeconomic development policies and programmes, and through the sound management of fragile mountain habitats, especially in the Hindu Kush-Himalayan region, covering all or parts of Afghanistan, Bangladesh, Bhutan, China, India, Myanmar, Nepal and Pakistan; international staff of 30; Dir-Gen. EGBERT PELINCK.

**International Centre for Tropical Agriculture** (Centro Internacional de Agricultura Tropical—CIAT): Apdo Aéreo 6713, Cali, Colombia; tel. (2) 445-0000; fax (2) 445-0073; e-mail ciat@cgiar.org; internet www.ciat.cgiar.org; f. 1967 to contribute to the alleviation of hunger and poverty in tropical developing countries by using new techniques in agriculture research and training; focuses on production problems of the tropics concentrating on field beans, cassava, rice and tropical pastures. Dir-Gen. Dr JOACHIM VOSS. Publs *Annual Report, Growing Affinities* (2 a year), *Pasturas Tropicales* (3 a year), catalogue of publications.

**International Commission for the Conservation of Atlantic Tunas—ICCAT:** Calle Corazón de Maria 8, 28020 Madrid, Spain; tel. (91) 4165600; fax (91) 4152612; internet www.iccat.es; f. 1969 under the provisions of the International Convention for the Conservation of Atlantic Tunas (1966) to maintain the populations of tuna and tuna-like species in the Atlantic Ocean and adjacent seas at levels that will permit the maximum sustainable catch; collects statistics, conducts studies. Mems: 24 contracting parties. Pres. Dr A. RIBEIRO LIMA (Portugal); Exec. Sec. Dr ANTONIO FERNANDEZ. Publs *ICCAT Newsletter, Statistical Bulletin* (annually), *Data Record* (annually).

**International Commission of Sugar Technology:** c/o Dr H. van Malland, 97199 Ochsenfurt, Marktbreiter Str. 74, Germany; tel. (9331) 91450; fax (9331) 91462; f. 1949 to discuss investigations and promote scientific and technical research work. Pres. of Scientific Cttee. Dr JAN MAARTEN DE BRUIJN (Netherlands); Sec.-Gen. Dr HENK VAN MALLAND.

**International Committee for Animal Recording:** Via Nomentana 134, 00161 Rome, Italy; tel. (06) 86329141; fax (06) 86329263; e-mail zoorec@rmnet.it; f. 1951 to extend and improve the work of recording and to standardize methods. Mems: in 40 countries. Pres. Dr JOSEPH CRETTENAND (Switzerland).

**International Crops Research Institute for the Semi-Arid Tropics—ICRISAT:** Patancheru, Andhra Pradesh, India; tel. (40) 596161; fax (40) 241239; e-mail icrisat@cgnet.com; internet www.cgiar.org/icrisat; f. 1972 as world centre for genetic improvement of sorghum, millet, pigeonpea, chickpea and groundnut, and for research on the management of resources in the world's semi-arid tropics with the aim of reducing poverty and protecting the environment; research covers all physical and socio-economic aspects of improving farming systems on unirrigated land. Dir SHAUKI M. BARGHOUTI (Jordan). Publs *ICRISAT Report* (annually), *SAT News* (2 a year), *International Chickpea and Pigeonpea Newsletter, International Arachis Newsletter, International Sorghum and Millet Newsletter* (annually), information and research bulletins.

**International Dairy Federation:** 41 Square Vergote, 1030 Brussels, Belgium; tel. (2) 733-98-88; fax (2) 733-04-13; e-mail info@fil-idf.org; internet www.fil-idf.org; f. 1903 to link all dairy associations in order to encourage the solution of scientific, technical and economic problems affecting the dairy industry. Mems: national committees in 34 countries. Dir. Gen. E. HOPKIN (UK). Publs *Bulletin of IDF, IDF Standards*.

**International Federation of Agricultural Producers—IFAP:** 60 rue St Lazare, 75009 Paris, France; tel. 1-45-26-05-53; fax 1-48-74-72-12; e-mail ifap@club-internet.fr; internet www.ifap.org; f. 1946 to represent, in the international field, the interests of agricultural producers; to exchange information and ideas and help develop understanding of world problems and their effects upon agricultural producers; to encourage efficiency of production, processing, and marketing of agricultural commodities; holds conference every two years. National farmers' organizations and agricultural co-operatives of 55 countries are represented in the Federation. Pres. GERARD DOORNBOS (Netherlands); Sec.-Gen. DAVID KING. Publs *The World Farmer* (bimonthly), *Proceedings of General Conferences*.

**International Federation of Beekeepers' Associations—APIMONDIA:** Corso Vittorio Emanuele 101, 00186 Rome, Italy; tel. and fax (06) 6852286; e-mail apimondia@mclink.it; f. 1949; collects and brings up to date documentation concerning international beekeeping; studies the particular problems of beekeeping through its permanent committees; organizes international congresses, seminars, symposia and meetings; stimulates research into new techniques for more economical results; co-operates with other international organizations interested in beekeeping, in particular with FAO. Mems: 56 associations from 52 countries. Pres. RAYMOND BORNECK; Sec.-Gen. RICCARDO JANNONI-SEBASTIANINI. Publs *Apiacta* (quarterly, in English, French, German and Spanish), *Dictionary of Beekeeping Terms,* AGROVOC (thesaurus of agricultural terms), studies.

**International Hop Growers' Convention:** c/o Inštitut za hmeljarstvo in pivovarstvo, POB 51, 3310 Žalec, Slovenia; tel. (63) 715214; fax (63) 717163; e-mail martin.pavlovic@uni-lj.si; internet www.hmelj-giz.si/ihgc/; f. 1950 to act as a centre for the collection of data on hop production, and to conduct scientific, technical and economic commissions. Mems: national associations in Australia, Belgium, Bulgaria, the People's Republic of China, Czech Republic, France, Germany, New Zealand, Poland, Portugal, Russia, Slovakia, Slovenia, Spain, Ukraine, United Kingdom, USA, Federal Republic of Yugoslavia. Pres. GREGORIO GARCIA ALONSO (Spain); Gen. Sec. Dr MARTIN PAVLOVIČ. Publ. *Hopfen-Rundschau* (fortnightly).

**International Institute for Beet Research:** 195 ave de Tervueren, 1150 Brussels, Belgium; tel. (2) 737-70-91; fax (2) 737-70-99; e-mail mail@iirb.org; f. 1932 to promote research and exchange of information, by organizing meetings and study groups. Mems: 600 in 33 countries. Pres. of the Admin. Council C. SPERLINGSSON; Sec.-Gen. R. BECKERS.

**International Institute of Tropical Agriculture—IITA:** Oyo Rd, PMB 5320, Ibadan, Nigeria; tel. (2) 241-2626; fax (2) 241-2221; e-mail iita@cgiar.org; internet www.cgiar.org/iita; f. 1967; principal financing arranged by the Consultative Group on International Agricultural Research (CGIAR), co-sponsored by the FAO, the IBRD and the UNDP. The research programmes comprise crop management, improvement of crops (cereals, legumes and root crops) and plant protection and health; training programme for researchers in tropical agriculture; library of 75,000 vols and data base of 115,180 records; also administers six agro-ecological research stations. Dir-Gen. Dr LUKAS BRADER. Publs *Annual Report, IITA Research* (quarterly), technical bulletins, research reports.

**International Livestock Research Institute—ILRI:** POB 30709, Nairobi, Kenya; tel. (2) 632311; fax (2) 631499; e-mail ilri-kenya@cgiar.org; internet www.cgiar.org/ilri; f. 1995, to supersede the International Laboratory for Research on Animal Diseases and the International Livestock Centre for Africa; conducts laboratory and field research on animal health (in particular, animal trypanosomiasis and theileriosis), the conservation of genetic resources, production systems analysis, natural resource management, livestock policy analysis and strengthening national research capacities; undertakes training programmes for scientists and technicians; specialized science library. Dir Dr HANK FITZHUGH. Publs *Annual Report, Livestock Research for Development* (newsletter, 2 a year).

**International Maize and Wheat Improvement Centre—CIMMYT:** Lisboa 27—Col Juarez, Apdo Postal 6-641, 06600 México, DF, Mexico; tel. (5) 7269091; fax (5) 7267558; e-mail cimmyt@cgiar.org; internet www.cimmyt.mx; conducts world-wide research programme for sustainable increase in production of maize, wheat and triticale in developing countries. Dir-Gen. Prof. TIMOTHY REEVES.

**International Organization for Biological Control of Noxious Animals and Plants:** IOBC Permanent Secretariat, AGROPOLIS, Ave Agropolis, 34394 Montpellier Cédex 5, France; e-mail iobc@agropolis.fr; f. 1955 to promote and co-ordinate research on the more effective biological control of harmful organisms; re-organized in 1971 as a central council with world-wide affiliations and largely autonomous regional sections in different parts of the world: the West Palaearctic (Europe, North Africa, the Middle East), the Western Hemisphere, South-East Asia, Pacific Region and Tropical Africa. Pres. Dr J. WAAGE (UK); Sec.-Gen. Dr E. WAJNBERG (France). Publs *Entomophaga* (quarterly), *Newsletter*.

**International Organization of Citrus Virologists:** c/o C. N. Roistacher, Dept of Plant Pathology, Univ. of California, Riverside, CA 92521, USA; tel. (909) 684-0934; fax (909) 684-4324; f. 1957 to promote research on citrus virus diseases at international level by standardizing diagnostic techniques and exchanging information. Mems: 250. Chair. R. F. LEE; Sec. C. N. ROISTACHER.

**International Red Locust Control Organization for Central and Southern Africa:** POB 240252, Ndola, Zambia; tel. (2) 615684; fax (2) 614285; e-mail locust@zamnet.zm; f. 1971 to control locusts in eastern, central and southern Africa, and assists in the control of African army-worm and quelea-quelea. Mems: eight countries. Dir E. K. BYARUHANGA. Publs *Annual Report, Monthly Report* and scientific reports.

**International Regional Organization of Plant Protection and Animal Health** (Organismo Internacional Regional de Sanidad Agropecuaria—OIRSA): Apdo 0161, Calle Ramón Belloso, Final Pasaje Isolde, Col. Escalón, San Salvador, El Salvador; tel. 263-1123; fax 263-1128; e-mail oirsa@ns1.oirsa.org.sv; internet www.oirsa.org.sv; f. 1953 for the prevention of the introduction of animal and plant pests and diseases unknown in the region; research, control and eradication programmes of the principal pests present in agriculture; technical assistance and advice to the ministries of agriculture and livestock of member countries; education and qualification of personnel. Mems: Belize, Costa Rica, El Salvador, Guatemala, Honduras, Mexico, Nicaragua, Panama. Exec. Dir Dr CELIO HUMBERTO BARRETO.

**International Rice Research Institute—IRRI:** MCPO Box 3127, 1271 Makati City, Philippines; tel. (2) 8450563; fax (2) 8911292; e-mail irri@cgnet.com; internet www.cgiar.org/irri; f. 1960; conducts research on rice, aiming to develop technology that is of environmental, social and economic benefit, and to enhance national rice research systems; maintains a library to collect and provide access to the world's technical rice literature; publishes and disseminates research results; conducts regional rice research projects in co-operation with scientists in rice-producing countries; offers training in rice research methods and techniques; organizes international conferences and workshops and operates Riceworld, a museum and learning centre about rice and rice-related culture and research. Dir-Gen. Dr RONALD CANTRELL. Publs *Annual Report, Annual Corporate Report, Rice Literature Update, Hotline, Facts about IRRI, News about Rice and People, IRRI Information Series.*

**International Scientific Council for Trypanosomiasis Research and Control:** c/o OAU Interafrican Bureau for Animal Resources, POB 30786, Nairobi, Kenya; tel. (2) 338544; fax (2) 332046; e-mail parcibar@africaonline.co.ke; f. 1949 to review the work on tsetse and trypanosomiasis problems carried out by organizations and workers concerned in laboratories and in the field; to stimulate further research and discussion and to promote co-ordination between research workers and organizations in the different countries in Africa, and to provide a regular opportunity for the discussion of particular problems and for the exposition of new experiments and discoveries. Sec. Dr SOLOMON H. MARIAM.

**International Seed Testing Association—ISTA:** Reckenholz-str 191, POB 412, 8046 Zürich, Switzerland; tel. (1) 3713133; fax (1) 3713427; e-mail istach@iprolink.ch; f. 1906 (reconstituted 1924) to promote uniformity and accurate methods of seed testing and evaluation in order to facilitate efficiency in production, processing, distribution and utilization of seeds; organizes triennial congresses, meetings, workshops, symposia and training courses. Mems: 67 countries. Exec. Officer H. SCHMID; Hon. Sec. Treas. Prof. A. LOVATO (Italy). Publs *Seed Science and Technology* (3 a year), *ISTA News Bulletin* (3 a year).

**International Sericultural Commission:** 25 quai JeanJacques Rousseau, 69350 La Mulatière, France; tel. 4-78-50-41-98; fax 4-78-86-09-57; f. 1948 to encourage the development of silk production. Library of 1,215 vols. Mems: governments of Brazil, Egypt, France, India, Indonesia, Japan, Lebanon, Madagascar, Romania, Thailand, Tunisia, Turkey. Sec.-Gen. Dr GÉRARD CHAVANCY (France). Publ. *Sericologia* (quarterly).

**International Service for National Agricultural Research—ISNAR:** POB 93375, 2509 AJ The Hague, Netherlands; tel. (70) 349-61-00; fax (70) 381-96-77; e-mail isnar@cgiar.org; internet www.cgiar.org/isnar; f. 1980 by the Consultative Group on International Agricultural Research (q.v.) to strengthen national agricultural research systems in developing countries by promoting appropriate research policies, sustainable research institutions, and improved research management; provides advisory service, training, research services and information. Chair. MOÏSE MENSAH; Dir-Gen. STEIN BIE.

**International Society for Horticultural Science:** Kardinaal Mercierlaan 92, 3001 Leuven, Belgium; tel. (16) 22-94-27; fax (16) 22-94-50; e-mail info@ishs.org; internet www.ishs.org; f. 1959 to co-operate in the research field. Mems: 54 member countries, 265 organizations, 3,050 individuals. Pres. Prof. Dr C. D. BRICKELL (UK); Exec. Dir Ir J. VAN ASSCHE (Belgium). Publs *Chronica Horticulturae* (quarterly), *Acta Horticulturae, Scientia Horticulturae* (monthly), *Horticultural Research International.*

**International Society for Soilless Culture—ISOSC:** POB 52, 6700 AB Wageningen, Netherlands; tel. (317) 413809; fax (317) 423457; f. 1955 as International Working Group on Soilless Culture, to promote world-wide distribution and co-ordination of research, advisory services, and practical application of soilless culture (hydroponics); international congress held every four years (9th congress: Jersey, Channel Islands, April 1996). Mems: 450 from 69 countries. Pres. RICK S. DONNAN (Australia); Sec.-Gen. Ing. Agr. ABRAM A.STEINER. Publ. *ISOSC Proceedings* (every 4 years).

**International Union of Forestry Research Organizations—IUFRO:** 1131 Vienna, Seckendorff-Gudent-Weg 8, Austria; tel. (1) 877-01-51; fax (1) 877-93-55; e-mail iufro@forvie.ac.at; f. 1892. Mems: 700 organizations in 115 countries, involving more than 15,000 scientists. Pres. Dr JEFFREY BURLEY (UK); Sec. HEINRICH SCHMUTZENHOFER (Austria). Publs *Annual Report, IUFRO News* (quarterly), *IUFRO World Series, IUFRO Paper Series* (occasional).

**International Union for the Protection of New Plant Varieties—UPOV:** c/o 34 chemin des Colombettes, 1211 Geneva 20,

Switzerland; tel. (22) 3389153; fax (22) 7330336; e-mail upov.mail@wipo.org; internet www.upov.int/; f. 1961 by the International Convention for the Protection of New Varieties of Plants (entered into force 1968, revised in 1972, 1978 and 1991). Aims to protect intellectual property rights of plant breeders and to harmonize legislation in the field. Admin. support provided by WIPO (q.v.). Signatory states: 44 (June 1999). Sec.-Gen. Dr KAMIL IDRIS.

**International Union of Soil Sciences:** c/o Institute of Soil Science, University of Agriculture, Gregor-Mendel-Strasse 33, 1180 Vienna, Austria; tel. (1) 310-60-26; fax (1) 310-60-27; e-mail iusss@edv1.boku.ac.at; internet www.cirad.fr/iusss/aiss.html; f. 1924. Mems: 8,000 individuals and associations in 163 countries. Pres. Dr SOMPONG THEERAWONG; Sec.-Gen. Prof. Dr W. E. H. BLUM (Austria). Publ. *Bulletin* (2 a year).

**International Whaling Commission—IWC:** The Red House, Station Rd, Impington, Cambridge, CB4 9NP, United Kingdom; tel. (1223) 233971; fax (1223) 232876; e-mail iwcoffice@compuserve.com; internet ourworld.compuserve.com.homepages/iwcoffice; f. 1946 under the International Convention for the Regulation of Whaling, for the conservation of the world whale stocks; aims to review the regulations covering the operations of whaling, to encourage research relating to whales and whaling, to collect and analyse statistical information and to study and disseminate information concerning methods of increasing whale stocks; a ban on commercial whaling was passed by the Commission in July 1982, to take effect three years subsequently (although, in some cases, a phased reduction of commercial operations was not completed until 1988). An assessment of the effects on whale stocks of this ban was under way in the early 1990s, and a revised whale-management procedure was adopted in 1992, to be implemented only after the development of a complete whale management scheme, including arrangements for data collection and an inspection and monitoring scheme; Iceland left the IWC in June 1992 and Norway resumed commercial whaling in 1993. Mems: governments of 40 countries. Chair. MICHAEL CANNY (Ireland); Sec. Dr R. GAMBELL. Publ. *Annual Report*.

**Joint Organization for the Control of Desert Locust and Bird Pests** (Organisation commune de lutte anti-acridienne et de lutte antiaviaire—OCLALAV): BP 1066, route des Pères Maristes, Dakar, Senegal; tel. 832-32-80; fax 832-04-87; f. 1965 to destroy insect pests, in particular the desert locust, and grain-eating birds, in particular the quelea-quelea, and to sponsor related research projects. Mems: Benin, Burkina Faso, Cameroon, Chad, Côte d'Ivoire, The Gambia, Mali, Mauritania, Niger, Senegal. Dir-Gen. ABDULLAHI OULD SOUEÏD AHMED. Publ. *Bulletin* (monthly).

**North Pacific Anadromous Fish Commission:** 889 W. Pender St, Suite 502, Vancouver, BC V6C 3B2, Canada; tel. (604) 775-5550; fax (604) 775-5577; e-mail secretariat@npafc.org; f. 1993. Mems: Canada, Japan, Russia, USA. Exec. Dir VLADIMIR FEDORENKO. Publs *Annual Report, Newsletter* (2 a year), *Statistical Yearbook, Scientific Bulletin*.

**Northwest Atlantic Fisheries Organization:** POB 638, Dartmouth, NS B2Y 3Y9, Canada; tel. (902) 468-5590; fax (902) 468-5538; e-mail nafo@fox.nstn.ca; f. 1979 (formerly International Commission for the Northwest Atlantic Fisheries); aims at optimum use, management and conservation of resources, promotes research and compiles statistics. Pres. E. OLTUSKI (Cuba); Exec. Sec. Dr L. I. CHEPEL. Publs *Annual Report, Statistical Bulletin, Journal of Northwest Atlantic Fishery Science, Scientific Council Reports, Scientific Council Studies, Sampling Yearbook, Proceedings*.

**World Association for Animal Production:** Via A. Torlonia 15A, 00161 Rome, Italy; tel. (06) 44238013; fax (06) 44241466; e-mail zoorec@rmnet.it; f. 1965; holds world conference on animal production every five years; encourages, sponsors and participates in regional meetings, seminars and symposia. Pres. Prof. Ing. K. HAN (Republic of Korea); Sec.-Gen. J. BOYAZOGLU (Greece). Publ. *News Items* (2 a year).

**World Association of Veterinary Food-Hygienists:** Federal Institute for Health Protection of Consumers and Veterinary Medicine (BgVV), Diedersdorfer Weg 1, 12277 Berlin, Germany; tel. (30) 8412-2101; fax (30) 8412-2951; e-mail p.teufel@bgvv.de; f. 1955 to promote hygienic food control and discuss research. Mems: national asscns in 40 countries. Pres. Prof. PAUL TEUFEL; Sec. Treas. Dr L. ELLERBROEK.

**World Association of Veterinary Microbiologists, Immunologists and Specialists in Infectious Diseases:** Ecole Nationale Vétérinaire d'Alfort, 7 ave du Général de Gaulle, 94704 Maisons-Alfort Cédex, France; tel. 1-43-96-70-21; fax 1-43-96-70-22; f. 1967 to facilitate international contacts in the fields of microbiology, immunology and animal infectious diseases. Pres. Prof. CH. PILET (France). Publs *Comparative Immunology, Microbiology and Infectious Diseases*.

**World Ploughing Organization—WPO:** Søkildevej 17, 5270 Odense N, Denmark; tel. 65-97-80-06; fax 65-93-24-40; f. 1952 to promote World Ploughing Contest in a different country each year, to improve techniques and promote better understanding of soil cultivation practices through research and practical demonstrations; arranges tillage clinics world-wide to improve the use of new techniques. Affiliates in 28 countries. Gen. Sec. CARL ALLESO. Publs *WPO Handbook* (annual), *WPO Bulletin of News and Information* (irregular).

**World's Poultry Science Association:** c/o Dr P. C. M. Simons, Centre for Applied Poultry Research, 'Het Spelderholt', POB 31, 7360 AA Beekbergen, Netherlands; tel. (55) 506-6534; fax (55) 506-4858; e-mail p.c.m.simons@pp.agro.nl; internet www.wpsa.com; f. 1912 to exchange knowledge in the industry, to encourage research and teaching, to publish information relating to production and marketing problems; to promote World Poultry Congresses and co-operate with governments. Mems: individuals in 95 countries, branches in 55 countries. Pres. ANURADHA DESAI (India); Sec. Dr P. C. M. SIMONS (Netherlands). Publ. *The World Poultry Science Journal* (quarterly).

**World Veterinary Association:** Rosenlunds Allé 8, 2720 Vanlose, Denmark; tel. 38-71-01-56; fax 38-71-03-22; e-mail wva@ddd.dk; internet www.worldvet.org; f. 1959 as a continuation of the International Veterinary Congresses; organizes quadrennial congress. Mems: organizations in 76 countries and 19 organizations of veterinary specialists as associate members. Pres. Dr JIM EDWARDS (New Zealand); Exec. Sec. Dr LARS HOLSAAE. Publs *WVA Bulletin, World Veterinary Directory*.

# Arts and Culture

**Europa Nostra—Federation of Non-Governmental Organizations for the Protection of Pan-European Heritage:** Lange Voorhout 35, 2514 EC The Hague, Netherlands; tel. (70) 3560333; fax (70) 3617865; e-mail office@europanostra.org; f. 1963; a large grouping of organizations and individuals concerned with the protection and enhancement of the European architectural and natural heritage and of the European environment; has consultative status with the Council of Europe. Mems: more than 200 mem. organizations, more than 100 allied mems, more than 40 supporting bodies, more than 1,000 individual mems. Pres. HRH The Prince Consort of Denmark; Exec. Pres. DANIEL CARDON DE LICHTBUER (Belgium); Sec.-Gen. ANTONIO MARCHINI CAMIA (Italy).

**European Association of Conservatoires, Music Academies and Music High Schools:** c/o Conservatoire de Paris, 209 ave Jean-Jaurès, 75019 Paris, France; tel. 1-40-40-46-03; fax 1-40-40-46-09; e-mail accinfo@accinfo.org; internet www.accinfo.org; f. 1953 to establish and foster contacts and exchanges between members. Mems: 120; eight associate mems. Pres. IAN HORSBRUGH; Gen. Sec. MARC-OLIVIER DUPIN.

**European Centre for Culture** (Centre Européen de la Culture): Maison de l'Europe, 120B rue de Lausanne, 1202 Geneva, Switzerland; tel. (22) 7322803; fax (22) 7384012; e-mail cecge@vtx.ch; internet www.europeans.ch; f. 1950 to contribute to the union of Europe by encouraging cultural pursuits, providing a meeting place, and conducting research in the various fields of European Studies; holds conferences and training on European subjects, European documentation and archives. Pres. JEAN-FRED BOURQUIN (Switzerland). Publ. *Newsletter* (3 a year).

**European Society of Culture:** Guidecca 54P (Calle Michelangelo, Villa Hériot), 30133 Venice, Italy; tel. (041) 5230210; fax (041) 5231033; e-mail soceurcultur@flashnet.it; f. 1950 to unite artists, poets, scientists, philosophers and others through mutual interests and friendship in order to safeguard and improve the conditions required for creative activity; library of 10,000 volumes. Mems: national and local centres, and 2,000 individuals, in 60 countries. Pres. Prof. VINCENZO CAPPELLETTI (Italy); Gen. Sec. Dott. MICHELLE CAMPAGNOLO-BOUVIER.

**Inter-American Music Council** (Consejo Interamericano de Música—CIDEM): 2511 P St NW, Washington, DC 20007, USA; f. 1956 to promote the exchange of works, performances and information in all fields of music, to study problems relative to music education, to encourage activity in the field of musicology, to promote folklore research and music creation, to establish distribution centres for music material of the composers of the Americas, etc. Mems: national music societies of 33 American countries. Sec.-Gen. EFRAÍN PAESKY.

**International Association of Art:** Maison de l'UNESCO, 1 rue Miollis, 75732 Paris Cédex 15, France; tel. 1-45-68-26-55; fax 1-45-67-22-87; f. 1954. Mems: 104 national committees. Pres. UNA WALKER; Sec.-Gen. J. C. DE SALINS. Publ. *IAA Newsletter* (quarterly).

**International Association of Art Critics:** 11 rue Berryer, 75008 Paris, France; tel. 1-42-56-17-53; fax 1-42-56-08-42; internet www.aagif.fr.sermadiras; f. 1949 to increase co-operation in plastic arts, promote international cultural exchanges and protect the interests of members. Mems: 4,062 in 77 countries. Pres. KIM LEVIN (USA); Sec.-Gen. RAMON TIO BELLIDO (France). Publs *Annuaire, Newsletter* (quarterly).

**International Association of Bibliophiles:** Bibliothèque nationale de France, réserve des livres rares, quai François-Mauriac,

75706 Paris Cédex 13, France; fax 1-53-79-54-60; f. 1963 to create contacts between bibliophiles and to encourage book-collecting in different countries; to organize or encourage congresses, meetings, exhibitions, the award of scholarships, the publication of a bulletin, yearbooks, and works of reference or bibliography. Mems: 450. Pres. CONDE DE ORGAZ (Spain); Sec.-Gen. JEAN-MARC CHATELAIN (France). Publ. *Le Bulletin du Bibliophile*.

**International Association of Literary Critics:** 38 rue du Faubourg St-Jacques, 75014 Paris, France; tel. 1-53-10-12-13; fax 1-53-10-12-12; f. 1969; national centres in 34 countries; organizes congresses. Pres. ROBERT ANDRÉ. Publ. *Revue* (2 a year).

**International Association of Museums of Arms and Military History—IAMAM:** c/o Dr C. Gaier, Musée d'Armes de Liège, Quai de Maastricht 8, 4000 Liège, Belgium; tel. (4) 221-94-16; fax (4) 221-94-01; f. 1957; links museums and other scientific institutions with public collections of arms and armour and military equipment, uniforms, etc.; triennial conferences and occasional specialist symposia. Mems: 252 institutions in 50 countries. Pres. CLAUDE GAIER (Belgium); Sec.-Gen. JAN PIET PUYPE (Netherlands). Publ. *The Mohonk Courier*.

**International Board on Books for Young People—IBBY:** Nonnenweg 12, Postfach, 4003 Basel, Switzerland; tel. (61) 2722917; fax (61) 2722757; e-mail ibby@eye.ch; internet www.ibby.org; f. 1953 to support and link bodies in all countries connected with children's book work; to encourage the distribution of good children's books; to promote scientific investigation into problems of juvenile books; presents the Hans Christian Andersen Award every two years to a living author and a living illustrator whose work is an outstanding contribution to juvenile literature, and the IBBY-Asahi Reading Promotion Award annually to an organization that has made a significant contribution towards the encouragement of reading; sponsors International Children's Book Day (2 April). Mems: national sections and individuals in more than 60 countries. Pres. TAYO SHIMA (Japan); Sec. LEENA MAISSEN. Publs *Bookbird* (quarterly, in English), *Congress Papers, IBBY Honour List* (every 2 years); special bibliographies.

**International Centre for the Study of the Preservation and Restoration of Cultural Property—ICCROM:** Via di San Michele 13, 00153 Rome, Italy; tel. (06) 585-531; fax (06) 5855-3349; e-mail iccrom@iccrom.org; internet www.iccrom.org; f. 1959; assembles documents on preservation and restoration of cultural property; stimulates research and proffers advice; organizes missions of experts; undertakes training of specialists and heritage conservation worldwide. Mems: 96 countries. Dir-Gen. MARC LAENEN. Publ. *Newsletter* (annually, English and French).

**International Centre of Films for Children and Young People—Centre international des films pour les enfants et les jeunes—CIFEJ:** 3774 rue Saint-Denis, Bureau 200, Montréal, PQ H2W 2M1, Canada; tel. (514) 284-9388; fax (514) 284-0168; e-mail cifej@odyssee.net; internet www.odyssee.net/cifej; f. 1955; a clearing house for information about: entertainment films (cinema and television) for children and young people, influence of films on the young, and regulations in force for the protection and education of young people; promotes production and distribution of suitable films and their appreciation. The CIFEJ prize is awarded at selected film festivals. Mems: 163 mems from 53 countries. Exec. Dir JO-ANNE BLOUIN. Publ. *CIFEJ Info* (monthly).

**International Committee for the Diffusion of Arts and Literature through the Cinema** (Comité international pour la diffusion des arts et des lettres par le cinéma—CIDALC): 24 blvd Poissonnière, 75009 Paris, France; tel. 1-42-46-13-60; f. 1930 to promote the creation and release of educational, cultural and documentary films and other films of educational value in order to contribute to closer understanding between peoples; awards medals and prizes for films of exceptional merit. Mems: national committees in 19 countries. Pres. JEAN-PIERRE FOUCAULT (France); Sec.-Gen. MARIO VERDONE (Italy). Publs *Annuaire CIDALC, Cinéma éducatif et culturel*.

**International Comparative Literature Association:** c/o Paola Mildonian, Letterature Comparate, Dipartim. di Studi Anglo-Americani e Ibero-Americani, Università Ca' Foscari-Venezia, Ca' Garzoni, S. Marco 3417, 30124 Venice, Italy; tel. (041) 257-8427; fax (041) 257-8476; e-mail pamildo@unive.it; f. 1954 to work for the development of the comparative study of literature in modern languages. Member societies and individuals in 78 countries. Sec. PAOLA MILDONIAN. Publ. *ICLA Bulletin* (2 a year).

**International Confederation of Societies of Authors and Composers—World Congress of Authors and Composers:** 11 rue Kepler, 75116 Paris, France; tel. 1-53-57-34-00; fax 1-53-57-34-10; e-mail cisac@cisac.org; internet www.cisac.org; f. 1926 to protect the rights of authors and composers; organizes biennial congress. Mems: 173 member societies from 91 countries. Sec.-Gen. ERIC BAPTISTE.

**International Council of Graphic Design Associations—ICOGRADA:** POB 398, London, W11 4UG, United Kingdom; tel. (20) 7603-8494; fax (20) 7371-6040; e-mail 106065.2235@compuserve.com; internet www.icograda.org; f. 1963; aims to raise standards of graphic design, to exchange information, and to organize exhibitions and congresses; maintains library, slide collection and archive. Mems: 62 associations in 38 countries. Pres. DAVID GROSSMAN; Sec.-Gen. MARY V. MULLIN. Publs *Newsletter* (quarterly), *Regulations and Guidelines governing International Design Competitions, Model Code of Professional Conduct* and other professional documents.

**International Council of Museums—ICOM:** Maison de l'UNESCO, 1 rue Miollis, 75732 Paris Cédex 15, France; tel. 1-47-34-05-00; fax 1-43-06-78-62; e-mail secretariat@icom.org; internet www.icom.org; f. 1946 to further international co-operation among museums and to advance museum interests; maintains with UNESCO the organization's documentation centre. Mems: 15,000 individuals and institutions from 147 countries. Pres. JACQUES PEROT (France); Sec.-Gen. MANUS BRINKMAN (Netherlands). Publ. *ICOM News—Nouvelles de l'ICOM—Noticias del ICOM* (quarterly).

**International Council on Monuments and Sites—ICOMOS:** 49–51 rue de la Fédération, 75015 Paris, France; tel. 1-45-67-67-70; fax 1-45-66-06-22; e-mail icomos@ciap.jussieu.fr; internet www.icomos.org; f. 1965 to promote the study and preservation of monuments and sites; to arouse and cultivate the interest of public authorities, and people of every country in their monuments and sites and in their cultural heritage; to liaise between public authorities, departments, institutions and individuals interested in the preservation and study of monuments and sites; to disseminate the results of research into the problems, technical, social and administrative, connected with the conservation of the architectural heritage, and of centres of historic interest; holds triennial General Assembly and Symposium. Mems: c. 6,000; 18 international committees, 90 national committees. Pres. ROLAND SILVA (Sri Lanka); Sec.-Gen. JEAN-LOUIS LUXEN (Belgium). Publs *ICOMOS Newsletter* (quarterly), *Scientific Journal* (quarterly).

**International Federation for Theatre Research:** c/o Flat 9, 118 Avenue Rd, London, W3 8QG, United Kingdom; tel. (20) 8608-1550; fax (20) 8679-3488; e-mail bsnglton@tcd.ie; internet www.tcd.ie/iftr; f. 1955 by 21 countries at the International Conference on Theatre History, London. Pres. Prof. JOSETTE FÉRAL; Joint Secs-Gen. Prof. BRIAN SINGLETON, Prof. CHRISTIANE PAGE. Publs *Theatre Research International* (in association with Oxford University Press) (3 a year), *Bulletin* (2 a year).

**International Federation of Film Archives—FIAF:** c/o Christian Dimitriu, rue Defacqz 1, 1000 Brussels, Belgium; tel. (2) 538-30-65; fax (2) 534-47-74; e-mail info@fiafnet.org; internet www.fiafnet.org; f. 1938 to encourage the creation of audio-visual archives in all countries for the collection and conservation of the moving image heritage of each land; to facilitate co-operation and exchanges between these film archives; to promote public interest in the art of the cinema; to aid research in this field and to compile new documentation; conducts research; publishes manuals, etc.; holds annual congresses. Mems in 60 countries. Pres. IVAN TRUJILLO BOLIO (Mexico); Sec.-Gen. ROGER SMITHER (UK). Publ. *Journal of Film Preservation* (2 a year).

**International Federation of Film Producers' Associations:** 33 ave des Champs-Elysées, 75008 Paris, France; tel. 1-42-25-62-14; fax 1-42-56-16-52; f. 1933 to represent film production internationally, to defend its general interests and promote its development, to study all cultural, legal, economic, technical and social problems of interest to the activity of film production. Mems: national associations in 23 countries. Pres. AURELIO DE LAURENTIIS (Italy); Dir-Gen. ANDRÉ CHAUBEAU (France).

**International Institute for Children's Literature and Reading Research** (Internationales Institut für Jugendliteratur und Leseforschung): 1040 Vienna, Mayerhofgasse 6, Austria; tel. (1) 50503-59; fax (1) 50503-5917; e-mail kidlit@netway.at; internet www.netway.at/kidlit; f. 1965 as an international documentation, research and advisory centre of juvenile literature and reading; maintains specialized library; arranges conferences and exhibitions; compiles recommendation lists. Mems: individual and group members in 28 countries. Pres. Dr HILDE HAWLICEK; Dir KARIN SOLLAT. Publs *1000 & 1 Buch* (quarterly and 1 special issue).

**International Institute for Conservation of Historic and Artistic Works:** 6 Buckingham St, London, WC2N 6BA, United Kingdom; tel. (20) 7839-5975; fax (20) 7976-1564; e-mail iicon@compuserve.com; internet www.iiconservation.org; f. 1950. Mems: 3,350 individual, 450 institutional members. Pres. JOHN WINTER; Sec.-Gen. DAVID BOMFORD. Publ. *Studies in Conservation* (quarterly).

**International Liaison Centre for Cinema and Television Schools** (Centre international de liaison des écoles de cinéma et de télévision): 8 rue Thérésienne, 1000 Brussels, Belgium; tel. (2) 511-98-39; fax (2) 511-98-39; e-mail hverh.cilect@skynet.be; internet www.cilect.org; f. 1955 to link higher teaching and research institutes and to improve education of makers of films and television programmes; organizes conferences, student film festivals, training programme for developing countries. Mems: 103 institutions in 52 countries. Pres. GUSTAVO MONTIEL (Mexico); Exec. Sec. HENRY VERHASSELT (Belgium). Publ. *Newsletter*.

**International Music Council—IMC:** Maison de l'UNESCO, 1 rue Miollis, 75732 Paris Cédex 15, France; tel. 1-45-68-25-50; fax 1-43-

06-87-98; e-mail imc_cim@compuserve.com; internet www.unesco.org/imc; f. 1949 to foster the exchange of musicians, music (written and recorded), and information between countries and cultures; to support traditional music, contemporary composers and young professional musicians. Mems: 30 international non-governmental organizations, national committees in 65 countries. Pres. FRANS DE RUITER (Netherlands); Sec.-Gen. GUY HUOT.

Members of IMC include:

**European Festivals Association:** 120B rue de Lausanne, 1202 Geneva, Switzerland; tel. (22) 7386873; fax (22) 7384012; e-mail geneva@eurofestivals.efa.ch; internet www.eurofestivals.efa.ch; f. 1952; aims to maintain high artistic standards and the representative character of art festivals; holds annual General Assembly. Mems: 75 regularly-held music festivals in 26 European countries, Israel, Japan and Mexico. Pres. FRANS DE RUITER. Publ. *Festivals* (annually).

**International Association of Music Libraries, Archives and Documentation Centres—IAML:** c/o Cataloguing Dept, Carleton Univ. Library, 1125 Colonel By Drive, Ottawa, ON K1S 5B6, Canada; tel. (613) 520-2600; fax (613) 520-3583; e-mail alisonhall@carleton.ca; internet www.cilea.it/music/iame/iamchome.htm; f. 1951. Mems: 2,003 institutions and individuals in 58 countries. Pres. PAMELA THOMPSON (UK); Sec.-Gen. ALISON HALL (Canada). Publ. *Fontes artis musicae* (quarterly).

**International Council for Traditional Music:** Dept of Music–MC 1815, Columbia University, 2960 Broadway, New York, NY 10027, USA; tel. (212) 678-0332; fax (212) 678-2513; e-mail ictm@compuserve.com; internet www.music.columbia.edu/~ictm; f. 1947 (as International Folk Music Council) to further the study, practice, documentation, preservation and dissemination of traditional music of all countries; conferences held every two years. Mems: 1,350. Pres. Dr KRISTER MALM (Sweden); Sec.-Gen. Prof. DIETER CHRISTENSEN (USA). Publs *Yearbook for Traditional Music, Bulletin* (2 a year), *Directory of Traditional Music* (every 2 years).

**International Federation of Musicians:** 21 bis rue Victor Massé, 75009 Paris, France; tel. 1-45-26-31-23; fax 1-45-26-31-57; e-mail fiiyparis2@compuserve.com; f. 1948 to promote and protect the interests of musicians in affiliated unions; promotes international exchange of musicians. Mems: 50 unions totalling 200,000 individuals in 43 countries. Pres. JOHN MORTON (UK); Gen. Sec. JEAN VINCENT (France).

**International Institute for Traditional Music:** Winkler Str. 20, 14193 Berlin, Germany; tel. (30) 826-28-53; fax (30) 825-99-91; e-mail iitm@netmbx.netmbx.de; f. 1963 to promote traditional folk music and non-European traditional music; annual festival. Mems from 20 countries. Dir Prof. MAX PETER BAUMANN. Publs *The World of Music* (3 a year), *Intercultural Music Studies* (book series), *Traditional Music of the World* (CD/MC series), *Musikbogen*.

**International Jazz Federation:** c/o Jan A. Byrczek, 117 W 58th St, Ste 12G, New York, NY 10019, USA; tel. (212) 581-7188; f. 1969 to promote the knowledge and appreciation of jazz throughout the world; arranges jazz education conferences and competitions for young jazz groups; encourages co-operation among national societies. Mems: national organizations and individuals in 24 countries. Pres. ARNVID MEYER (Denmark); Exec. Dir JAN A. BYRCZEK. Publ. *Jazz Forum* (6 a year).

**International Music Centre** (Internationales Musikzentrum—IMZ): 1230 Vienna, Speisinger Str. 121–127, Austria; tel. (1) 889-03-15; fax (1) 889-03-15-77; e-mail office@imz.at; internet www.imz.at; f. 1961 for the study and dissemination of music through the technical media (film, television, radio, gramophone); organizes congresses, seminars and screenings on music in the audio-visual media; courses and competitions to strengthen the relationship between performing artists and the audio-visual media. Mems: 110 ordinary mems and 30 associate mems in 33 countries, including 50 broadcasting organizations. Pres. AVRIL MACRORY (UK); Sec.-Gen. FRANZ A. PATAY (Austria). Publ. *IMZ-Bulletin* (6 a year in English, French and German).

**International Society for Contemporary Music:** c/o Gaudeamus, Swammerdamstraat 38, 1091 RV Amsterdam, Netherlands; tel. (20) 6947349; fax (20) 6947258; f. 1922 to promote the development of contemporary music and to organize annual World Music Days. Member organizations in 48 countries. Pres. ARNE MELLNAS; Sec.-Gen. HENK HEUVELMANS.

**Jeunesses Musicales International:** Palais des Beaux-Arts, 10 rue Royale, 1000 Brussels, Belgium; tel. (2) 513-97-74; fax (2) 514-47-55; e-mail mail@jmi.net; internet www.jmi.net; f. 1945 to enable young people to develop, through music, across all boundaries and to stimulate contacts between member countries. Mems: organizations in 40 countries. Sec.-Gen. DAG FRANZÉN.

**World Federation of International Music Competitions:** 104 rue de Carouge, 1205 Geneva, Switzerland; tel. (22) 3213620; fax (22) 7811418; e-mail fmcim@iprolink.ch; internet www.wfimc.org; f. 1957 to co-ordinate the arrangements for affiliated competitions, to exchange experience, etc.; a General Assembly is held every May. Mems: 107. Pres. RENATE RONNEFELD; Sec.-Gen. JACQUES HALDENWANG.

**International PEN** (A World Association of Writers): 9–10 Charterhouse Bldgs, Goswell Rd, London, EC1M 7AT, United Kingdom; tel. (20) 7253-4308; fax (20) 7253-5711; e-mail intpen@gn.apc.org; internet www.oneworld.org/internatpen; f. 1921 to promote co-operation between writers. There are 133 centres throughout the world, with total membership about 13,500. International Pres. HOMERO ARIDJIS; International Sec. TERRY CARLBOM. Publ. *PEN International* (2 a year in English, French and Spanish, with the assistance of UNESCO).

**International Theatre Institute—ITI:** Maison de l'UNESCO, 1 rue Miollis, 75732 Paris Cédex 15, France; tel. 1-45-68-26-50; fax 1-45-66-50-40; e-mail iti@unesco.org; internet iti-worldwide.org; f. 1948 to facilitate cultural exchanges and international understanding in the domain of the theatre; conferences, publications, etc. Mems: 87 member nations, each with an ITI national centre. Pres. KIM JEONG-OK (Republic of Korea); Sec.-Gen. ANDRÉ-LOUIS PERINETTI.

**International Typographic Association:** c/o Nordic Trade Centre, Eggerstedstrasse 13, 24103 Kiel, Germany; tel. (431) 97-406-23; fax (431) 97-83-67; f. 1957 to co-ordinate the ideas of those whose profession or interests are concerned with the art of typography and to obtain effective international legislation to protect type designs. Mems: 400 in 25 countries. Pres. ERNST-ERICH MARHENCKE. Publs *TypoGraphic News* (quarterly), *Letter Letter* (2 or 3 times a year), *Journal of Typographic Metaphysics*.

**Organization of World Heritage Cities:** 56 Saint-Pierre St, Suite 401, Quebec City, Quebec, G1K 4AI, Canada; tel. (418) 692-0000; fax (418) 692-5558; e-mail secretariat@ovpm.org; internet www.ovpm.org; f. 1993; aims to assist cities inscribed on the UNESCO World Heritage List to implement the Convention concerning the Protection of the World Cultural and Natural Heritage (1972); promotes co-operation between city authorities, in particular in the management and sustainable development of historic sites. A General Assembly, comprising the mayors of member cities, meets at least every two years. Mems: 140 cities world-wide. Sec.-Gen. DENIS RICARD.

**Pan-African Writers' Association:** POB C450, Cantonments, Accra, Ghana; tel. (21) 773062; fax (21) 773042; f. 1989 to link African creative writers, defend the rights of authors and promote awareness of literature. Sec.-Gen. ATUKWEI OKAI (Ghana); Dep. Sec.-Gen. MAHAMADU TRAORÉ DIOP (Senegal).

**Royal Asiatic Society of Great Britain and Ireland:** 60 Queen's Gardens, London, W2 3AF, United Kingdom; tel. (20) 7724-4742; e-mail royalasiaticsociety@btinternet.com; internet www.royalasiaticsociety.co.uk; f. 1823 for the study of history and cultures of the East. Mems: c. 1,000, branch societies in Asia. Dir Dr G. TILLOTSON; Sec. T. N. GUINA. Publ. *Journal* (3 a year).

**Society of African Culture:** 25 bis rue des Ecoles, 75005 Paris, France; tel. 1-43-54-15-88; fax 1-43-25-96-67; f. 1956 to create unity and friendship among scholars in Africa for the encouragement of their own cultures. Mems: national asscns and individuals in 44 countries and territories. Pres. AIMÉ CÉSAIRE; Sec.-Gen. CHRISTIANE YANDÉ DIOP. Publ. *La Revue Présence Africaine* (2 a year).

**United Towns Organization:** 60 rue de la Boétie, 75008 Paris, France; tel. 1-53-96-05-80; fax 1-53-96-05-81; e-mail cites.unies@wanadoo.fr; f. 1957 by Le Monde Bilingue (f. 1951); aims to set up permanent links between towns throughout the world, leading to social, cultural, economic and other exchanges favouring world peace, understanding and development; involved in sustainable development and environmental activities at municipal level; mem. of the Habitat II follow-up group. Mems: 4,000 local and regional authorities throughout the world. World Pres. DABY DIAGNE; Dir-Gen. MICHEL BESCOND. Publs *Cités Unies* (quarterly, French, English and Spanish), *Newsletter* (3 a year in English, French, Italian and Spanish).

**World Crafts Council:** 19 Race Course Ave, Colombo 7, Sri Lanka; tel. (1) 695831; fax (1) 692554; f. 1964; aims to strengthen the status of crafts as a vital part of cultural life, to link crafts people around the world, and to foster wider recognition of their work. Mems: national organizations in more than 80 countries. Pres. SIVA OBEYESEKERE. Publs *Annual Report, Newsletter* (2 a year).

# Commodities

**African Groundnut Council:** Trade Fair Complex, Badagry Expressway Km 15, POB 3025, Lagos, Nigeria; tel. (1) 880982; fax (1) 887811; f. 1964 to advise producing countries on marketing policies. Mems: The Gambia, Mali, Niger, Nigeria, Senegal, Sudan. Chair. MUSTAFA BELLO; Exec. Sec. Elhadj MOUR MAMADOU SAMB (Senegal). Publ. *Groundnut Review*.

**African Oil Palm Development Association—AFOPDA:** 15 BP 341, Abidjan 15, Côte d'Ivoire; tel. 25-15-18; f. 1985; seeks to increase production of, and investment in, palm oil. Mems: Benin, Cameroon, Democratic Republic of the Congo, Côte d'Ivoire, Ghana, Guinea, Nigeria, Togo. Exec. Sec. BAUDELAIRE SOUROU.

**African Petroleum Producers' Association—APPA:** POB 1097, Brazzaville, Republic of the Congo; tel. 83-64-38; fax 83-67-99; f. 1987 by African petroleum-producing countries to reinforce co-operation among regional producers and to stabilize prices; council of ministers responsible for the hydrocarbons sector meets twice a year. Mems: Algeria, Angola, Benin, Cameroon, Democratic Republic of the Congo, Republic of the Congo, Côte d'Ivoire, Egypt, Equatorial Guinea, Gabon, Nigeria. Publ. *APPA Bulletin* (2 a year).

**Asian and Pacific Coconut Community:** POB 1343, 3rd Floor, Lina Bldg, Jalan H. R. Rasuna Said Kav. B7, Kuningan, Jakarta 10002, Indonesia; tel. (21) 5221712; fax (21) 5221714; e-mail apcc@indo.net.id; internet www.apcc.org.sg; f. 1969 to promote, co-ordinate, and harmonize all activities of the coconut industry towards better production, processing, marketing and research. Mems: Fiji, India, Indonesia, Malaysia, Federated States of Micronesia, Papua New Guinea, Philippines, Samoa, Solomon Islands, Sri Lanka, Thailand, Vanuatu, Viet Nam; assoc. mem.: Palau. Exec. Dir P. G. PUNCHIHEWA. Publs *Cocomunity* (2 a month), *CORD* (2 a year), *Statistical Yearbook, Cocoinfo International* (2 a year).

**Association of Coffee Producing Countries:** Suite B, 5th Floor, 7/10 Old Park Lane, London, W1Y 3LJ, United Kingdom; tel. (20) 7493-4790; fax (20) 7355-1690; f. 1993; aims to co-ordinate policies of coffee production and to co-ordinate the efforts of producer countries to secure a stable situation in the world coffee market. Mems 29 African, Asian and Latin American countries. Pres. Ambassador RUBENS ANTÔNIO BARBOSA (Brazil); Sec.-Gen. ROBÉRIO OLIVEIRA SILVA.

**Association of Natural Rubber Producing Countries—ANRPC:** Bangunan Getah Asli, 148 Jalan Ampang, 7th Floor, 50450 Kuala Lumpur, Malaysia; tel. (3) 2611900; fax (3) 2613014; f. 1970 to co-ordinate the production and marketing of natural rubber, to promote technical co-operation amongst members and to bring about fair and stable prices for natural rubber. A joint regional marketing system has been agreed in principle. Seminars, meetings and training courses on technical and statistical subjects are held. Mems: India, Indonesia, Malaysia, Papua New Guinea, Singapore, Sri Lanka, Thailand. Sec.-Gen. GNOH CHONG HOCK. Publs *ANRPC Statistical Bulletin* (quarterly), *ANRPC Newsletter*.

**Association of Tin Producing Countries—ATPC:** Menara Dayabumi, 4th Floor, Jalan Sultan Hishamuddin, 50050 Kuala Lumpur, Malaysia; tel. (3) 2747620; fax (3) 2740669; e-mail atpc@tm.net.my; f. 1983; promotes co-operation in marketing of tin, supports research, compiles and analyses data. The headquarters were scheduled to be moved to Rio de Janeiro, Brazil, in 1999. Mems: Bolivia, Brazil, People's Republic of China, Democratic Republic of the Congo, Malaysia, Nigeria; observers: Peru, Viet Nam. Exec. Sec. MOHAMED ZARIF MOHAMED ZAMAN (Malaysia).

**Cocoa Producers' Alliance:** POB 1718, Western House, 8–10 Broad St, Lagos, Nigeria; tel. (1) 2635506; fax (1) 2635684; f. 1962 to exchange technical and scientific information; to discuss problems of mutual concern to producers; to ensure adequate supplies at remunerative prices; to promote consumption. Mems: Brazil, Cameroon, Côte d'Ivoire, Dominican Republic, Ecuador, Gabon, Ghana, Malaysia, Nigeria, São Tomé and Príncipe, Togo, Trinidad and Tobago. Sec.-Gen. DJEUMO SILAS KAMGA.

**Common Fund for Commodities:** Postbus 74656, 1070 BR, Amsterdam, Netherlands; tel. (20) 575-4949; fax (20) 676-0231; e-mail managingdirector@common-fund.org; f. 1989 as the result of an UNCTAD agreement; finances commodity development measures such as research, marketing, productivity improvements and vertical diversification, with the aim of increasing the long-term competitiveness of particular commodities; paid-in capital US $165m. Mems 104 countries and the EC, OAU and COMESA, Man. Dir (also Chief Exec. and Chair.) ROLF BOEHNKE.

**European Aluminium Association:** 12 ave de Broqueville, 1150 Brussels, Belgium; tel. (2) 755-63-11; fax (2) 779-05-31; f. 1981 to encourage studies, research and technical co-operation, to make representations to international bodies and to assist national associations in dealing with national authorities. Mems: individual producers of primary aluminium, 16 national groups for wrought producers, the Organization of European Aluminium Smelters, representing producers of secondary aluminium, and the European Aluminium Foil Association, representing foil rollers and converters. Chair. KURT WOLFENSBERGER; Sec.-Gen. DICK DERMER. Publs *Annual Report, EAA Quarterly Report*.

**European Association for the Trade in Jute and Related Products:** Adriaan Goekooplaan 5, 2517 JX The Hague, Netherlands; tel. (70) 354-68-11; fax (70) 351-27-77; e-mail jute@verbondgroothandel.nl; f. 1970 to maintain contacts between national associations and carry out scientific research; to exchange information and to represent the interests of the trade. Mems: enterprises in Belgium, Denmark, France, Germany, Italy, Netherlands, Spain, Sweden, Switzerland, United Kingdom. Sec.-Gen. H. J. J. KRUIPER.

**European Committee of Sugar Manufacturers:** 182 ave de Tervueren, 1150 Brussels, Belgium; tel. (2) 762-07-60; fax (2) 771-00-26; e-mail cefs@euronet.be; internet www.ib.be.cefs; f. 1954 to collect statistics and information, conduct research and promote co-operation between national organizations. Mems: national associations in Austria, Belgium, Denmark, Finland, France, Germany, Greece, Ireland, Italy, Netherlands, Portugal, Spain, Sweden, Switzerland, United Kingdom. Pres. RENATO PICCO; Dir-Gen. JULES BEAUDUIN.

**Group of Latin American and Caribbean Sugar Exporting Countries—GEPLACEA:** Ejército Nacional 373, 1°, 11520 México DF, Mexico; tel. (5) 250-7566; fax (5) 250-7591; f. 1974 to serve as a forum of consultation on the production and sale of sugar; to contribute to the adoption of agreed positions at international meetings on sugar; to provide training and the transfer of technology; to exchange scientific and technical knowledge on agriculture and the sugar industry; to co-ordinate the various branches of sugar processing; to co-ordinate policies of action in order to achieve fair and remunerative prices. Mems: 23 Latin American and Caribbean countries (accounting for about 45% of world sugar exports and 66% of world cane sugar production). Exec. Sec. LUIS CUSTODIO COTTA.

**Inter-African Coffee Organization—IACO:** BP V210, Abidjan, Côte d'Ivoire; tel. 21-61-31; fax 21-62-12; e-mail oiac-iaco@netafric.ci; f. 1960 to adopt a common policy on the marketing of coffee; aims to collaborate on research, in particular through the establishment of the African Coffee Research Network, and improvement in the quality of exports. Mems: 25 coffee-producing countries in Africa. Pres. GUY ALAIN EMMANUEL GAUZE (Côte d'Ivoire); Sec.-Gen. G. MELEDJE ENOCK (Côte d'Ivoire) (acting).

**International Cadmium Association:** 42 Weymouth St, London, W1N 3LQ, United Kingdom; tel. (20) 7499-8425; fax (20) 7486-4007; f. 1976; covers all aspects of the production and use of cadmium and its compounds; includes almost all producers and users of cadmium outside the USA. Chair. JEAN FEUILLAT (Belgium); Dir J. K. ATHERTON (UK).

**International Cocoa Organization—ICCO:** 22 Berners St, London, W1P 3DB, United Kingdom; tel. (20) 7637-3211; fax (20) 7631-0114; e-mail exec.dir@icco.org; internet www.icco.org; f. 1973 under the first International Cocoa Agreement, 1972 (renewed in 1975 and 1980; the fourth agreement entered into force in January 1987; it was extended, without its economic clauses, for two years from October 1990, and again to 30 September 1993). ICCO supervises the implementation of the agreement, and provides member governments with conference facilities and up-to-date information on the world cocoa economy and the operation of the agreement (price-stabilizing activities were suspended in March 1990). Negotiations on a fifth agreement were concluded in July 1993, under the auspices of UNCTAD, which came into force in February 1994 (the agreement was extended for a further 2 years from 1 October 1999). Mems: 18 exporting countries and 21 importing countries; and the European Union. Exec. Dir EDOUARD KOUAMÉ (Côte d'Ivoire); Council Chair. 1999-2000 D. P. VAN RAPPARD (Netherlands). Publs *Quarterly Bulletin of Cocoa Statistics, Annual Report, World Cocoa Directory, Cocoa Newsletter*, studies on the world cocoa economy.

**International Coffee Organization:** 22 Berners St, London, W1P 4DD, United Kingdom; tel. (20) 7580-8591; fax (20) 7580-6129; e-mail info@ico.org; internet www.icoffee.com; f. 1963 under the International Coffee Agreement, 1962, which was renegotiated in 1968, 1976, 1983 and 1994. The objectives of the 1994 Agreement are to improve international co-operation and provide a forum for intergovernmental consultations on coffee matters; to facilitate international trade in coffee by the collection, analysis and dissemination of statistics; to act as a centre for the collection, exchange and publication of coffee information; to promote studies in the field of coffee; and to encourage an increase in coffee consumption. Mems: 44 exporting and 18 importing countries. Chair. of Council WALTER BASTIAAUSE (Honduras); Exec. Dir CELSIUS A. LODDER (Brazil).

**International Confederation of European Sugar Beet Growers:** 29 rue du Général Foy, 75008 Paris, France; tel. 1-44-69-41-80; fax 1-42-93-28-93; f. 1925 to act as a centre for the co-ordination and dissemination of information about beet sugar production and the industry; to represent the interests of sugar beet growers at an international level. Member associations in Austria, Belgium, Czech Republic, Denmark, Finland, France, Germany, Greece, Hungary, Ireland, Italy, Netherlands, Poland, Portugal, Slovakia, Spain, Sweden, Switzerland, United Kingdom. Pres. J. KIRSCH (Germany); Sec.-Gen. H. CHAVANES (France).

**International Cotton Advisory Committee:** 1629 K St, NW, Suite 702, Washington, DC 20006, USA; tel. (202) 463-6660; fax (202) 463-6950; e-mail secretariat@icac.org; internet www.icac.org; f. 1939 to observe developments affecting the world cotton situation; to collect and disseminate statistics; to suggest to the governments represented any measures for the furtherance of international collaboration in maintaining and developing a sound world cotton economy; and to provide a forum for international discussions on cotton prices. Mems: 40 countries. Exec. Dir Dr TERRY TOWNSEND.

Publs *Cotton: Review of the World Situation, Cotton: World Statistics, The ICAC Recorder*.

**International Grains Council:** 1 Canada Sq., Canary Wharf, London, E14 5AE, United Kingdom; tel. (20) 7513-1122; fax (20) 7513-0630; e-mail igc@igc.org.uk; internet www.igc.org.uk; f. 1949 as International Wheat Council, present name adopted in 1995; responsible for the administration of the Grains Trade Convention of the International Grains Agreement, 1995; aims to further international co-operation in all aspects of trade in grains, to promote international trade in grains, and to secure the freest possible flow of this trade in the interests of members, particularly developing member countries; and to contribute to the stability of the international grain market; acts as forum for consultations between members, and provides comprehensive information on the international grain market and factors affecting it. Mems: 30 countries and the EU. Exec. Dir. G. DENIS. Publs *World Grain Statistics* (annually), *Wheat and Coarse Grain Shipments* (annually), *Report for the Fiscal Year* (annually), *Grain Market Report* (monthly).

**International Jute Organization—IJO:** 145 Monipuriparu, Old Airport Rd, Dhaka 1215, Bangladesh; tel. (2) 9125581; fax (2) 9125248; e-mail ijoinf@bdmail.net; f. 1984 in accordance with an agreement made by 48 producing and consuming countries in 1982, under the auspices of UNCTAD (new agreement negotiated in 1989, to expire in April 2000); aims to improve the jute economy and the quality of jute and jute products through research and development projects and market promotion. Mems: three exporting and 20 importing countries, as well as the European Union. Dir HENRI L. JASON (France). Publs *Jute* (quarterly), *Annual Report*.

**International Lead and Zinc Study Group:** 2 King St, London, SW1Y 6OP, United Kingdom; tel. (20) 7839-8550; fax (20) 7930-4635; e-mail root@ilzsg.org; internet www.ilzsg.org; f. 1959, for intergovernmental consultation on world trade in lead and zinc; conducts studies and provides information on trends in supply and demand. Mems: 27 countries. Chair. A. IGNATOW (Canada); Sec.-Gen. F. LABRO. Publ. *Lead and Zinc Statistics* (monthly).

**International Molybdenum Association:** Unit 7, Hackford Walk, 119–123 Hackford Rd, London, SW9 0QT, United Kingdom; tel. (20) 7582-2777; fax (20) 7582-0556; e-mail itia_imoa@compuserve.com; internet www.imoa.org.uk/; f. 1989; collates statistics, promotes the use of molybdenum, monitors health and environmental issues. Mems: 49. Pres. R. S. DE CESARE; Sec.-Gen. MICHAEL MABY.

**International Natural Rubber Organization—INRO:** POB 10374, 50712 Kuala Lumpur, Malaysia; tel. (3) 2486466; fax (3) 2486485; e-mail inro@po.jaring.my; internet www.inro.com.my/inro; f. 1980 to stabilize natural rubber prices by operating a buffer stock, and to seek to ensure an adequate supply, under the International Natural Rubber Agreement (1979), which entered into force in April 1982, and was extended for two years in 1985; a second agreement came into effect in 1988, to expire in Dec. 1993 but was extended to Dec. 1995; a third agreement was adopted in Feb. 1995 and entered into effect in 1997. By October 1999 Malaysia, Thailand and Sri Lanka had confirmed their intention to withdraw from the organization owing to its failure to support market prices, and a decision was taken to terminate the International Natural Rubber Agreement and to disband the organization. A special session of INRO was held in December to discuss the disposal of existing buffer stocks. Mems: 17 importing countries (including the European Union) and six exporting countries (Côte d'Ivoire, Indonesia, Malaysia, Nigeria, Sri Lanka and Thailand).

**International Olive Oil Council:** Príncipe de Vergara 154, 28002 Madrid, Spain; tel. (91) 5903638; fax (91) 5631263; e-mail iooc@mad.servicom.es; f. 1959 to administer the International Agreement on Olive Oil and Table Olives, which aims to promote international co-operation in connection with problems of the world economy for olive products; to prevent unfair competition; to encourage the production and consumption of, and international trade in, olive products, and to reduce the disadvantages due to fluctuations of supplies on the market. Mems: of the 1986 Agreement (Fourth Agreement, amended and extended in 1993): eight mainly producing countries, one mainly importing country, and the European Commission. Dir FAUSTO LUCHETTI. Publs *Information Sheet of the IOOC* (fortnightly, French and Spanish), *OLIVAE* (5 a year, in English, French, Italian and Spanish), *National Policies for Olive Products* (annually).

**International Pepper Community:** 4th Floor, Lina Bldg, Jalan H. R. Rasuna Said, Kav. B7, Kuningan, Jakarta 12920, Indonesia; tel. (21) 5224902; fax (21) 5224905; e-mail ipc@indo.net.id; f. 1972 for promoting, co-ordinating and harmonizing all activities relating to the pepper economy. Mems: six exporting countries (Brazil, India, Indonesia, Malaysia, Sri Lanka, Thailand), 30 importing countries; assoc. mem. Federated States of Micronesia. Exec. Dir Dr K. P. G. MENON. Publs *Pepper Statistical Yearbook, International Pepper News Bulletin* (quarterly), *Directory of Pepper Exporters, Directory of Pepper Importers, Weekly Prices Bulletin, Pepper Market Review*.

**International Platinum Association:** 60313 Frankfurt-am-Main, Kroegerstr. 5, Germany; tel. (69) 287941; fax (69) 283601; links principal producers and fabricators of platinum. Pres. EDWARD HASLAM; Man. Dir MARCUS NURDIN.

**International Rubber Study Group:** Heron House, 109–115 Wembley Hill Rd, Wembley, HA9 8DA, United Kingdom; tel. (20) 8903-7727; fax (20) 8903-2848; e-mail irsg@compuserve.com; internet www.rubberstudy.org; f. 1944 to provide a forum for the discussion of problems affecting synthetic and natural rubber and to provide statistical and other general information on rubber. Mems: 19 governments. Sec.-Gen. Dr A. F. S. BUDIMAN (Indonesia). Publs *Rubber Statistical Bulletin* (monthly), *International Rubber Digest* (monthly), *Proceedings of International Rubber Forums* (annually), *World Rubber Statistics Handbook, Key Rubber Indicators, Rubber Statistics Yearbook* (annually), *Rubber Economics Yearbook* (annually), *Outlook for Elastomers* (annually).

**International Silk Association:** 34 rue de la Charité, 69002 Lyon, France; tel. 4-78-42-10-79; fax 4-78-37-56-72; e-mail isa-silk.ais-sole@wanadoo.fr; f. 1949 to promote closer collaboration between all branches of the silk industry and trade, develop the consumption of silk and foster scientific research; collects and disseminates information and statistics relating to the trade and industry; organizes biennial Congresses. Mems: employers' and technical organizations in 40 countries. Pres. MICHELE CANEPA (Italy); Gen. Sec. R. CURRIE. Publs *ISA Newsletter* (monthly), congress reports, standards, trade rules, etc.

**International Spice Group:** c/o Commonwealth Secretariat, Marlborough House, Pall Mall, London, SW1Y 5HX, United Kingdom; tel. (20) 7839-3411; fax (20) 7930-0827; f. 1983 to provide forum for producers and consumers of spices, and to attempt to increase the consumption of spices; under arrangement adopted in 1991 (subject to acceptance by member govts), secretariat services were to be transferred to the International Trade Centre (UNCTAD/WTO). Mems: 33 producer countries, 15 importing countries. Chair. HERNAL HAMILTON (Jamaica).

**International Sugar Organization:** 1 Canada Sq., Canary Wharf, London, E14 5AA, United Kingdom; tel. (20) 7513-1144; fax (20) 7513-1146; e-mail exdir@isolondon.demon.co.uk; internet www.isugar.com; administers the International Sugar Agreement (1992); the agreement does not include measures for stabilizing markets. Mems: 54 countries. Exec. Dir Dr P. BARON. Publs *Sugar Year Book, Monthly Statistical Bulletin, Market Report and Press Summary, Quarterly Market Review*, seminar proceedings.

**International Tea Committee Ltd:** Sir John Lyon House, 5 High Timber St, London, EC4V 3NH, United Kingdom; tel. (20) 7248-4672; fax (20) 7329-6955; e-mail inteacom@globalnet.co.uk; internet www.intteacomm.co.uk; f. 1933 to administer the International Tea Agreement; now serves as a statistical and information centre; in 1979 membership was extended to include consuming countries. Producer Mems: national tea boards or associations of Bangladesh, India, Indonesia, Japan, Kenya, Malawi, Sri Lanka, Zimbabwe; Consumer Mems: United Kingdom Tea Assn, Tea Assn of the USA Inc., Comité Européen du Thé and the Tea Council of Canada; Assoc. Mems: Netherlands and UK ministries of agriculture, Cameroon Development Corpn. Chair. M. J. BUNSTON; Consultant and Sec. PETER ABEL. Publs *Annual Bulletin of Statistics, Monthly Statistical Summary*.

**International Tea Promotion Association:** POB 20064, Tea Board of Kenya, Nairobi, Kenya; tel. (2) 220241; fax (2) 331650; f. 1979. Mems: Bangladesh, Indonesia, Kenya, Malawi, Mauritius, Mozambique, Tanzania, Uganda. Chair. GEORGE M. KIMANI; Liaison Officer NGOIMA WA MWAURA. Publ. *International Tea Journal* (2 a year).

**International Tobacco Growers' Association:** Apdo 5, 6001 Castelo Branco, Portugal; tel. (72) 325901; fax (72) 325906; e-mail itga@mail.telepac.pt; internet www.tobaccoleaf.org; f. 1984 to provide forum for the exchange of views and information of interest to tobacco producers. Mems: 23 countries producing over 80% of the world's internationally traded tobacco. Pres. RICHARD TATE (Zimbabwe); Exec. Dir Dr ANTONIO ABRUNHOSA (Portugal). Publs *Tobacco Courier* (quarterly), *Tobacco Briefing*.

**International Tropical Timber Organization—ITTO:** International Organizations Center, 5th Floor, Pacifico-Yokohama, 1-1-1, Minato-Mirai, Nishi-ku, Yokohama 220, Japan; tel. (45) 223-1110; fax (45) 223-1111; e-mail itto@mail.itto-unet.ocn.ne.jp; internet www.itto.or.jp; f. 1985 under the International Tropical Timber Agreement (1983); a new treaty, ITTA 1994, came into force in 1997; provides a forum for consultation and co-operation between countries that produce and consume tropical timber; facilitates progress towards 'the objective for the year 2000' (all trade in tropical timber to be derived from sustainably managed resources by 2000) financed by a special Bali Partnership Fund; conducts research and development, reafforestation and forest management, further processing of tropical timber in producing countries, and establishment of market intelligence and economic information; no economic provision is made for price stabilization. Mems: 26 producing and 26 consuming countries and the EU. Exec. Dir Dr FREEZAILAH BIN CHE YEOM (Malaysia). Publs *Annual Review*, *Market Information Service* (every 2 weeks), *Tropical Forest Update* (quarterly).

**International Tungsten Industry Association:** Unit 7, Hackford Walk, 119–123 Hackford Rd, London, SW9 0QT, United Kingdom; tel. (20) 7582-2777; fax (20) 7582-0556; e-mail itia_imoa@compuserve.com; internet www.itia.org.uk/; f. 1988 (fmrly Primary Tungsten Asscn, f. 1975); promotes use of tungsten, collates statistics, prepares market reports, monitors health and environmental issues. Mems: 51. Pres. S. OGURA; Sec.-Gen. MICHAEL MABY.

**International Vine and Wine Office:** 18 rue d'Aguesseau, 75008 Paris, France; tel. 1-44-94-80-80; fax 1-42-66-90-63; e-mail 101675.2013@compuserve.com; f. 1924 to study all the scientific, technical, economic and human problems concerning the vine and its products; to spread knowledge by means of its publications; to assist contacts between researchers and establish international research programmes. Mems: 45 countries. Dir-Gen. GEORGES DUTRUC-ROSSET. Publs *Bulletin de l'OIV* (every 2 months), *Lettre de l'OIV* (monthly), *Lexique de la Vigne et du Vin*, *Recueil des méthodes internationales d'analyse des vins*, *Code international des Pratiques oenologiques*, *Codex oenologique international*, numerous scientific publications.

**Lead Development Association International:** 42 Weymouth St, London, W1N 3LQ, United Kingdom; tel. (20) 7499-8422; fax (20) 7493-1555; e-mail eng@ldaint.org; internet www.ldaint.org; f. 1956; provides authoritative information on the use of lead and its compounds; maintains a library and abstracting service in collaboration with the Zinc Development Association (see below). Financed by lead producers and users in the United Kingdom, Europe and elsewhere. Dir Dr D. N. WILSON (UK).

**Regional Association of Oil and Natural Gas Companies in Latin America and the Caribbean** (Asociación Regional de Empresas de Petróleo y Gas Natural en América Latina y el Caribe—ARPEL): Javier de Viana 2345, Casilla de correo 1006, 11200 Montevideo, Uruguay; tel. (2) 4006993; fax (2) 4009207; e-mail arpel@adinet.com.uy; f. 1965 as the Mutual Assistance of the Latin American Oil Companies; aims to initiate and implement activities for the development of the oil and natural gas industry in Latin America and the Caribbean; promotes the expansion of business opportunities and the improvement of the competitive advantages of its members; promotes guide-lines in support of competition in the sector; and supports the efficient and sustainable exploitation of hydrocarbon resources and the supply of products and services. Works in co-operation with international organizations, governments, regulatory agencies, technical institutions, universities and non-governmental organizations. Mems: state enterprises in Argentina, Bolivia, Brazil, Canada, Chile, Colombia, Costa Rica, Cuba, Ecuador, Jamaica, Mexico, Nicaragua, Paraguay, Peru, Suriname, Trinidad and Tobago, Uruguay, Venezuela. Sec.-Gen. ANDRÉS TIERNO ABREU. Publ. *Boletín Técnico*.

**Sugar Association of the Caribbean (Inc.):** c/o Caroni (1975) Ltd, Brechin Castle, Conva, Trinidad; tel. 636-2449; fax 636-2847; f. 1942. Mems: national sugar cos of Barbados, Belize, Guyana, Jamaica and Trinidad and Tobago, and Sugar Asscn of St Kitts–Nevis–Anguilla. Sec. AZIZ MOHAMMED. Publs *SAC Handbook*, *SAC Annual Report*, *Proceedings of Meetings of WI Sugar Technologists*.

**Union of Banana-Exporting Countries—UPEB:** Apdo 4273, Bank of America, piso 7, Panamá 5, Panama; tel. 263-6266; fax 264-8355; e-mail iicapan@pan.gbm.net; f. 1974 as an intergovernmental agency to assist the cultivation and marketing of bananas and secure prices; collects statistics and compiles bibliographies. Mems: Colombia, Costa Rica, Guatemala, Honduras, Nicaragua, Panama, Venezuela. Exec. Dir J. ENRIQUE BETANCOURT. Publs *Informe UPEB*, *Fax UPEB*, *Anuario de Estadísticas*, bibliographies.

**West Africa Rice Development Association—WARDA:** 01 BP 2551 Bouaké 01, Côte d'Ivoire; tel. 63-45-14; fax 63-47-14; e-mail warda@cgiar.org; internet www.cgiar.org/warda; f. 1971; aims to contribute to food security and poverty eradication in poor rural and urban populations, particularly in West and Central Africa, through research, partnerships, capacity strengthening and policy support on rice-based systems, and in ways that promote sustainable agricultural development based on environmentally-sound management of natural resources; maintains research stations in Côte d'Ivoire, Nigeria and Senegal; four research programmes—Rainfed rice, Irrigated rice, Policy support, and Systems development and technology transfer; provides training and consulting services; revenue: US $9.1m. in 1998. WARDA is a member of the network of agricultural research centres supported by the Consultative Group on International Agricultural Research (CGIAR, q.v.). Mems: Benin, Burkina Faso, Cameroon, Chad, Côte d'Ivoire, The Gambia, Ghana, Guinea, Guinea-Bissau, Liberia, Mali, Mauritania, Niger, Nigeria, Senegal, Sierra Leone, Togo. Dir-Gen. Dr KANAYO F. NWANZE (Nigeria). Publs *Annual Report*, *Current Contents at WARDA* (monthly), *Programme Report*, *Advances in Rice Research*, proceedings, leaflets, brochures.

**West Indian Sea Island Cotton Association (Inc.):** c/o Barbados Agricultural Development Corporation, Fairy Valley, Christ Church, Barbados. Mems: organizations in Antigua-Barbuda, Barbados, Jamaica, Montserrat, St Christopher and Nevis, St Vincent and the Grenadines. Pres. E. LEROY WARD; Sec. MICHAEL I. EDGHILL.

**World Federation of Diamond Bourses:** 62 Pelikaanstraat, 2018 Antwerp, Belgium; tel. (3) 234-07-78; fax (3) 226-40-73; e-mail wfdb@iway.be; f. 1947 to protect the interests of affiliated organizations and their individual members and to settle or arbitrate in disputes. Mems: 22 bourses in 13 countries. Pres. I. FOREM (Israel); Sec.-Gen. G. GOLDSCHMIDT (Belgium).

**World Gold Council:** King's House, 10 Haymarket, London, SW1Y 4BP, United Kingdom; tel. (20) 7930-5171; fax (20) 7839-6561; internet www.gold.org; f. 1987 as world-wide international association of gold producers, to promote the demand for gold. Chair. D. M. MORLEY; Chief Exec. HARUKO FUKUDA (Japan).

**Zinc Development Association:** 42 Weymouth St, London, W1N 3LQ, United Kingdom; tel. (20) 7499-6636; fax (20) 7493-1555; e-mail enq@zda.org; provides authoritative advice on the uses of zinc, its alloys and its compounds; maintains a library in collaboration with the Lead Development Association (q.v.). Affiliate: Zinc Pigment Development Association. Financed by zinc producers and users in Europe and North America. Chair. P. NEATBY (UK).

# Development and Economic Co-operation

**African Capacity Building Foundation:** Southampton Life Centre, 7th Floor, Jason Moyo Ave/Second St, POB 1562, Harare, Zimbabwe; tel. (4) 738520; fax (4) 702915; e-mail root@acbf.co.zw; f. 1991 by the World Bank, UNDP, the African Development Bank, African and non-African governments; assists African countries to strengthen and build local capacity in economic policy analysis and development management. Exec. Sec. ABEL L. THOAHLANE.

**African Training and Research Centre in Administration for Development** (Centre africain de formation et de recherche administratives pour le développement—CAFRAD): ave Mohamed V, BP 310, Tangier, 90001 Morocco; tel. 942652; fax 941415; e-mail cafradt@pchalle.net.ma; internet www.cafrad.com/; f. 1964 by agreement between Morocco and UNESCO; undertakes research into administrative problems in Africa, documentation of results, provision of a consultation service for governments and organizations; holds frequent seminars. Mems: 26 African countries. Pres. M. EL HOUSSINE AZIZ; Dir-Gen. Dr MOHAMED AHMED WALI. Publs *African Administrative Studies* (2 a year), *Directory of African Consultants*, *CAFRAD News* (2 a year, in English, French and Arabic).

**Afro-Asian Rural Reconstruction Organization—AARRO:** No. 2, State Guest Houses Complex, Chanakyapuri, New Delhi 110 021, India; tel. (11) 6877783; fax (11) 6115937; e-mail aarrohq@nde.vsnl.net.in; internet www.aarro.org; f. 1962 to act as a catalyst for co-operative restructuring of rural life in Africa and Asia; and to explore collectively opportunities for co-ordination of efforts for promoting welfare and eradicating hunger, thirst, disease, illiteracy and poverty among the rural people. Activities include collaborative research on development issues; training; the exchange of information; international conferences and seminars; and awarding 100 individual training fellowships at nine institutes in Egypt, India, Japan, the Republic of Korea and Taiwan. Mems: 12 African, 14 Asian countries, and one African associate. Sec.-Gen. Dr BAHAR MUNIP. Publs *Annual Report*, *Journal of Rural Reconstruction* (2 a year), *AARRO Newsletter* (quarterly).

**Agence de la Francophonie:** 13 quai André Citroën, 75015 Paris, France; tel. 1-44-37-33-00; fax 1-45-79-14-98; internet www.francophonie.org; f. 1970 as l'Agence de coopération culturelle et technique; promotes co-operation among French-speaking countries in the areas of education, culture, science and technology; implements decisions of the Sommet francophone (q.v.); technical and financial assistance has been given to projects in every member country, mainly to aid rural people. Mems: 47 countries and territories. Gen. Dir ROGER DEHAYBE (Belgium). Publs *Journal de l'Agence de la Francophonie* (monthly).

**Amazonian Co-operation Council:** f. 1978 by signature of the Amazon Region Co-operation Treaty; aims to promote the harmonious development of the Amazon territories of signatory countries; Lima Declaration on Sustainable Development signed by ministers of foreign affairs in December 1995. Mems: Bolivia, Brazil, Colombia, Ecuador, Guyana, Peru, Suriname, Venezuela.

**Arab Authority for Agricultural Investment and Development—AAAID:** POB 2102, Khartoum, Sudan; tel. 773752; fax 772600; f. 1976 to accelerate agricultural development in the Arab world and to ensure food security; acts principally by equity participation in agricultural projects in Iraq, Sudan and Tunisia; authorized capital US $ 501.8m., paid-in capital $ 334.6m. (Dec. 1995). Mems: Algeria, Egypt, Iraq, Jordan, Kuwait, Mauritania, Morocco, Oman, Qatar, Saudi Arabia, Somalia, Sudan, Syria, Tunisia, United Arab Emirates. Pres. YOUSIF ABDAL LATIF ALSERKAL. Publ. *Annual Report.*

**Arab Co-operation Council:** Amman, Jordan; f. 1989 to promote economic co-operation between member states, including free movement of workers, joint projects in transport, communications and agriculture, and eventual integration of trade and monetary policies. Mems: Egypt, Iraq, Jordan, Yemen. Sec.-Gen. HELMI NAMRAR (Egypt).

**Arab Fund for Economic and Social Development—AFESD:** POB 21923, Safat, 13080 Kuwait; tel. 4844500; fax 4815750; internet www.arabfund.org; f. 1968; participates in the financing of economic and social development projects in Arab states by issuing loans on concessional terms to governments and public or private institutions; by encouraging directly or indirectly the investment of public and private capital in projects consistent with development; and by providing technical assistance in the various fields of economic development. The Fund's authorized capital amounts to 800m. Kuwaiti dinars (KD); at the end of 1997 paid-up capital was KD 663.04m.; loans approved during 1997 totalled KD 244.1m. Mems: 21 Arab countries. Dir-Gen. and Chair. of Bd of Dirs ABDLATIF YOUSOUF AL-HAMAD.

**Arab Gulf Programme for the United Nations Development Organizations—AGFUND:** POB 18371, Riyadh 11415, Saudi Arabia; tel. (1) 4416240; fax (1) 4412963; e-mail agfund@khaleej.net.bh; f. 1981 to provide grants for projects in mother and child care carried out by United Nations organizations, Arab non-governmental organizations and other international bodies, and co-ordinate assistance by the nations of the Gulf; financing comes mainly from member states, all of which are members of OPEC. Mems: Bahrain, Iraq, Kuwait, Oman, Qatar, Saudi Arabia, UAE. Pres. HRH Prince TALAL IBN ABD AL-AZIZ AL-SAUD.

**Arab Monetary Fund:** POB 2818, Abu Dhabi, United Arab Emirates; tel. (2) 215000; fax (2) 326454; f. 1977 to encourage Arab economic integration and development, by assisting member states' balance of payments, co-ordinating their monetary policies, and promoting stability of exchange rates. The Fund provides loans, loan guarantees and technical assistance; its unit of account is the Arab Accounting Dinar (AAD), equivalent to three IMF Special Drawing Rights. Authorized capital AAD 600m., paid-up capital AAD 324.1m. (Dec. 1998); loans in 1998 amounted to AAD 15.0m. Mems: 20 Arab countries. Dir-Gen Dr JASSIM A. AL-MANNAI.

**Arab Trade Financing Program (ATFP):** POB 26799, Abu Dhabi, United Arab Emirates; tel. (2) 316999; fax (2) 316793; e-mail iatinhq@emirates.net.ae; internet www.atfp.ae; f. 1989 to develop and promote trade among Arab countries and to enhance the competitive ability of Arab exporters; operates by extending lines of credit to Arab exporters and importers through national agencies (some 105 agencies designated by the monetary authorities of 18 Arab countries at late 1999); also provides information on Arab goods and trade opportunities through the Inter-Arab Trade Information Network. The ATFP's authorized capital is US $500m. Chief Exec. and Chair. Dr JASSIM A. AL-MANNAI.

**Arctic Council:** Place Vanier, Tower A, 18th Floor, 333 River Rd, Ottawa, K1A DG2, Canada; internet www.nrc.ca/arctic/; f. 1996 to promote co-ordination of activities in the Arctic region, in particular in the areas of education, development and environmental protection. Mems: govts of eight circumpolar countries.

**Association of Caribbean States—ACS:** 11–13 Victoria Ave, POB 660, Port of Spain, Trinidad and Tobago; tel. 623-2783; fax 623-2679; e-mail mail@acs-aec.org; internet www.acs-aec.org; f. 1994 by the Governments of the 13 CARICOM countries (q.v.) and Colombia, Costa Rica, Cuba, the Dominican Republic, El Salvador, Guatemala, Haiti, Honduras, Mexico, Nicaragua, Suriname and Venezuela. Aims to promote economic integration and co-operation in the region; to co-ordinate participation in multilateral forums; to undertake concerted action to protect the environment, particularly the Caribbean Sea; and to co-operate in the areas of science and technology, health, transport, education and culture. Policy is determined by a Ministerial Council and implemented by a Secretariat based in Port of Spain, Trinidad and Tobago. The Fourth Ordinary Meeting of the Ministerial Council was held in Bridgetown, Barbados in December 1998. The Ministers urged States to study the Draft Regional Co-operation Agreement on Natural Disasters in preparation for the 1999 Summit. In April 1999 a second Summit of Heads of State and Government was convened in Santo Domingo, Dominican Republic; a Declaration of Santo Domingo, a Plan of Action and a Declaration of the Caribbean Zone of Sustainable Tourism were signed. The Fifth Ordinary Meeting of the Council was held in Panama City, Panama, in December 1999. Mems: 25 signatory states, three associate members, and a further 14 countries have observer status. Sec.-Gen. SIMÓN MOLINA DUARTE.

**Association of Development Financing Institutions in Asia and the Pacific—ADFIAP:** Skyland Plaza, 2nd Floor, Sen. Gil J. Puyat Ave, City of Makati 1200, Metro Manila, Philippines; tel. (2) 816-1672; fax (2) 817-6498; e-mail inquire@adfiap.org; internet www.adfiap.org; f. 1976 to promote the interests and economic development of the respective countries of its member institutions, through development financing. Mems: 81 institutions in 35 countries. Chair. ASWIN KONGSIRI (Thailand); Sec.-Gen. ORLANDO P. PEÑA (Philippines). Publs *Asian Banking Digest, Journal of Development Finance* (2 a year), *ADFIAP Newsletter,* surveys.

**Benelux Economic Union:** 39 rue de la Régence, 1000 Brussels, Belgium; tel. (2) 519-38-11; fax (2) 513-42-06; f. 1960 to bring about the economic union of Belgium, Luxembourg and the Netherlands; aims to introduce common policies in the field of cross-border co-operation and establish co-operation in the harmonization of standards and intellectual-property legislation; structure comprises: Committee of Ministers; Council; Court of Justice; Consultative Inter-Parliamentary Council; the Economic and Social Advisory Council; and the General Secretariat; Secs-Gen. B. M. J. HENNEKAM (Netherlands), MARIE-ROSE BERNA (Luxembourg). Publs *Benelux Newsletter, Bulletin Benelux.*

**Caritas Internationalis** (International Confederation of Catholic Organizations for charitable and social action): Palazzo San Calisto, 00120 Città del Vaticano; tel. (06) 69887197; fax (06) 69887237; e-mail ci.comm@caritas.va; f. 1950 to study problems arising from poverty, their causes and possible solutions; national member organizations undertake assistance and development activities. The Confederation co-ordinates emergency relief and development projects, and represents members at international level. Mems: 135 national orgs. Pres. Mgr AFFONSO GREGORY, Bishop of Imperatriz (Brazil); Sec.-Gen. LUC TROUILLARD. Publs *Caritas Matters* (quarterly), *Emergency Calling* (2 a year).

**Caribbean Council for Europe:** Nelson House, 8/9 Northumberland St, London, WC2N 5RA, United Kingdom; tel. (20) 7976-1493; fax (20) 7976-1541; e-mail caribbean@compuserve.com; f. 1992 by the Caribbean Association of Industry and Commerce and other regional organizations, to represent the interests of the Caribbean private sector in the European Union; organizes regular Europe/Caribbean Conference. Chair. YESU PERSAUD; Exec. Dir DAVID JESSOP.

**Central European Free Trade Association:** f. 1992, entered into force 1993; free-trade agreement covering a number of sectors. Mems: Bulgaria, Czech Republic, Hungary, Poland, Romania, Slovakia, Slovenia.

**Colombo Plan:** POB 596, 12 Melbourne Ave, Colombo 4, Sri Lanka; tel. (1) 581853; fax (1) 581754; e-mail cplan@slt.lk; internet www.colombo-plan.org; f. 1950 by seven Commonwealth countries, to encourage economic and social development in Asia and the Pacific. The Plan comprises the Programme for Public Administration, to provide training for officials in the context of a market-orientated economy; the Programme for Private Sector Development, which organizes training programmes to stimulate the economic benefits of development of the private sector; a Drug Advisory Programme, to encourage regional co-operation in efforts to control drug-related problems, in particular through human resources development; a programme to establish a South-South Technical Co-operation Data Bank, to collate, analyse and publish information in order to facilitate south-south co-operation; and a Staff College for Technician Education (see below). All programmes are voluntarily funded; developing countries are encouraged to become donors and to participate in economic and technical co-operation activities among developing members. Mems: 24 countries. Sec.-Gen. U. SARAT CHANDRAN (India). Publs *Annual Report, Colombo Plan Focus* (quarterly), Consultative Committee proceedings (every 2 years).

**Colombo Plan Staff College for Technician Education:** POB 7500, Domestic Airport Post Office, NAIA, Pasay City 1300, Metro Manila, Philippines; tel. (2) 6310991; fax (2) 6310996; e-mail cpsc@skyinet.net; internet www.skyinet.net/users/cpsc; f. 1973 with the support of member Governments of the Colombo Plan; aims to enhance the development of technician education systems in developing member countries. Dir Dr BERNARDO F. ADIVISO. Publ. *CPSC Quarterly.*

**Communauté économique des états de l'Afrique centrale—CEEAC** (Economic Community of Central African States): BP 2112, Libreville, Gabon; tel. 73-35-48; f. 1983; operational 1 January 1985; aims to promote co-operation between member states by abolishing trade restrictions, establishing a common external customs tariff, linking commercial banks, and setting up a development fund, over a period of 12 years; combat drug abuse; and to promote regional security. Budget (1998): US $1.82m. Mems: Angola, Burundi, Central African Repub., Chad, the Democratic Repub. of the Congo, the Repub. of the Congo, Equatorial Guinea, Gabon, Rwanda and São Tomé and Príncipe. Sec.-Gen. LOUIS-SYLVAIN GOMA (Republic of the Congo).

**Community of the Sahel-Saharan States** (Communauté des Etats du Sahel et du Sahara—COMESSA): Tripoli, Libya; f. 1997; aims to strengthen co-operation between signatory states; established a joint commission with the OAU, in 1998, to support mediation in the conflicts between Eritrea and Ethiopia; mems. Burkina Faso, Central African Republic, Chad, Djibouti, Egypt, Eritrea, The Gambia, Libya, Mali, Niger, Senegal, Sudan, Tunisia. Sec.-Gen. ALMADANI AL-AZHARI (Libya).

**Conseil de l'Entente** (Entente Council): 01 BP 3734, Abidjan 01, Côte d'Ivoire; tel. 33-28-35; fax 33-11-49; f. 1959 to promote economic development in the region. The Council's Mutual Aid and Loan Guarantee Fund (Fonds d'Entraide et de Garantie des Emprunts) finances development projects, including agricultural projects, support for small and medium-sized enterprises, vocational training centres, research into new sources of energy and building of hotels to encourage tourism. A Convention of Assistance and Co-operation was signed in February 1996. Holds annual summit: 1999 in Yamoussoukro, Côte d'Ivoire, in May. Fund budget (1999): 2,074m. francs CFA. Mems: Benin, Burkina Faso, Côte d'Ivoire, Niger, Togo. Sec.-Gen. PAUL KOUAMÉ. Publ. *Rapport d'activité* (annually).

**Communauté économique du bétail et de la viande (CEBV) du Conseil de l'Entente** (Livestock and Meat Economic Community of the Entente Council): 01 BP 638 Ouagadougou, Burkina Faso; tel. 30-62-67; fax 30-62-68; f. 1970 to promote the production, processing and marketing of livestock and meat; negotiates between members and with third countries on technical and financial co-operation and co-ordinated legislation; attempts to co-ordinate measures to combat drought and cattle diseases. Mems: states belonging to the Conseil de l'Entente. Exec. Sec. Dr ELIE LADIKPO.

**Council of American Development Foundations—SOLIDARIOS:** Calle 6 No. 10 Paraiso, Apdo Postal 620, Santo Domingo, Dominican Republic; tel. (809) 549-5111; fax (809) 544-0550; e-mail solidarios@codetel.net.do; f. 1972; exchanges information and experience, arranges technical assistance, raises funds to organize training programmes and scholarships; administers development fund to finance programmes carried out by members through a loan guarantee programme; provides consultancy services. Member foundations provide technical and financial assistance to low-income groups for rural, housing and microenterprise development projects. Mems: 18 institutional mems in 14 Latin American and Caribbean countries. Pres. MERCEDES P. DE CANALDA; Sec.-Gen. ISABEL C. ARANGO. Publs *Solidarios* (quarterly), *Annual Report*.

**Developing Eight – D-8:** Atikali Paşa Yalısı, Çırağan Cad. 80, Beşiktaş, İstanbul, Turkey; tel. (212) 2275610; fax (212) 2275613; inaugurated at a meeting of heads of state in June 1997; aims to foster economic co-operation between member states and to strengthen the role of developing countries in the global economy; project areas include trade and industry, agriculture, poverty alleviation, human resources development, telecommunications, rural development, finance (including banking and privatization), energy, environment, and health. Second Summit meeting, convened in Dhaka, Bangladesh, in March 1999, agreed to enhance co-operation and to promote the development of the private sector in each member economy. Mems: Bangladesh, Egypt, Indonesia, Iran, Malaysia, Nigeria, Pakistan, Turkey. Exec. Dir AYHAN KAMEL.

**Economic Community of the Great Lakes Countries** (Communauté économique des pays des Grands Lacs—CEPGL): POB 58, Gisenyi, Rwanda; tel. 61309; fax 61319; f. 1976; main organs: annual Conference of Heads of State, Council of Ministers of Foreign Affairs, Permanent Executive Secretariat, Consultative Commission, Security Commission, three Specialized Technical Commissions. There are four specialized agencies: a development bank, the Banque de Développement des Etats des Grands Lacs (BDEGL) at Goma, Democratic Republic of the Congo; an energy centre at Bujumbura, Burundi; the Institute of Agronomic and Zootechnical Research, Gitega, Burundi; and a regional electricity company (SINELAC) at Bukavu, Democratic Republic of the Congo. Two extraordinary summit meetings were held in 1994 to discuss security concerns in the region and efforts to revive economic co-operation activities. Mems: Burundi, the Democratic Republic of the Congo, Rwanda. Publs *Grands Lacs* (quarterly review), *Journal* (annually).

**European Free Trade Association—EFTA:** 9–11 rue de Varembé, 1211 Geneva 20, Switzerland; tel. (22) 7491111; fax (22) 7339291; e-mail efta-mailbox@secrbru.efta.be; internet www.efta.int; f. 1960 to bring about free trade in industrial goods and to contribute to the liberalization and expansion of world trade; EFTA states (except Switzerland) now participate in the European Economic Area (EEA) with the 15 member countries of the European Union; has concluded 15 free-trade agreements with countries in central, eastern and southern Europe. Mems: Iceland, Liechtenstein, Norway, Switzerland. Sec.-Gen. KJARTAN JÓHANNSSON (Iceland). Publs *EFTA Annual Report, EFTA Traders' ABC*.

**Food Aid Committee:** c/o International Grains Council, 1 Canada Square, Canary Wharf, London, E14 5AE, United Kingdom; tel. (20) 7513-1122; fax (20) 7513-0630; e-mail igc-fac@igc.org.uk; internet www.igc.org.uk; f. 1967; responsible for administration of the Food Aid Convention (1995), a constituent element of the International Grains Agreement (1995); monitors execution of members' obligations and provides forum for discussion on food aid issues. The 23 donor members are pledged to supply 5.3m. metric tons of grain suitable for human consumption annually to developing countries, mostly as gifts: in practice aid has usually exceeded 10m. tons annually. Exec. Dir G. DENIS. Publ. *Report on shipments* (annually).

**Gambia River Basin Development Organization** (Organisation de mise en valeur du fleuve Gambie—OMVG): BP 2353, 13 passage Leblanc, Dakar, Senegal; tel. 822-31-59; fax 822-59-26; e-mail omvg@telecomplus.sn; f. 1978 by Senegal and The Gambia; Guinea joined in 1981 and Guinea-Bissau in 1983. An agricultural plan for the integrated development of the Kayanga/Geba and Koliba/Corubal river basins commenced in 1993 and was extended to encompass an agro-sylvo-pastoral project (to commence in the near future); work on a hydraulic development plan for the Gambia river commenced in late 1996 and was to be completed by mid-1998; a study to connect the national electric grids of the four member states, and a feasibility study for the construction of four hydroelectric dams was also to be undertaken; maintains documentation centre. Exec. Sec. MAMADOU NASSIROU DIALLO.

**Group of Three—G3:** f. 1993 by Colombia, Mexico and Venezuela to remove restrictions on trade between the three countries. The trade agreement covers market access, rules of origin, intellectual property, trade in services, and government purchases, and entered into force in early 1994. Tariffs on trade between member states were to be removed on a phased basis. Co-operation was also envisaged in employment creation, the energy sector and the fight against cholera.

**Indian Ocean Commission—IOC:** Q4, Ave Sir Guy Forget, BP 7, Quatre Bornes, Mauritius; tel. 425-9564; fax 425-1209; e-mail coi7@intnet.mu; internet www.coi.intnet.mu; f. 1982 to promote regional co-operation, particularly in economic development; principal projects under way in the early 1990s (at a cost of 11.6m. francs CFA) comprised tuna-fishing development, protection and management of environmental resources and strengthening of meteorological services, with assistance principally from the EU; tariff reduction is also envisaged. Permanent technical committees cover: tuna-fishing; regional industrial co-operation; regional commerce; tourism; environment; maritime transport; handicrafts; labour; sports. The IOC organizes an annual regional trade fair. Mems: Comoros, France (representing the French Overseas Department of Réunion), Madagascar, Mauritius, Seychelles. Sec.-Gen. (vacant). Publ. *La Gazette de la Commission de l'Océan Indien*.

**Indian Ocean Rim Association for Regional Co-operation—IOR–ARC:** Sorèce House, 14 Angus Rd, Vacoas, Mauritius; tel. 698-3979; fax 697-5390; e-mail iorarchq@intnet.mu; the first intergovernmental meeting of countries in the region to promote an Indian Ocean Rim initiative was convened in March 1995; charter to establish the Asscn signed at a ministerial meeting in March 1997; aims to promote regional economic co-operation through trade, investment, infrastructure, tourism, science and technology. Mems: Australia, India, Indonesia, Kenya, Madagascar, Malaysia, Mauritius, Mozambique, Oman, Singapore, South Africa, Sri Lanka, Tanzania and Yemen. Chair. Dr LEONARDO SIMÃO (Mozambique); Sec.-Gen. KAILASH RUHEE (Mauritius).

**Inter-American Planning Society** (Sociedad Interamericana de Planificación—SIAP): c/o Revista Interamericana de Planificación, Casilla 01-05-1978, Cuenca, Ecuador; tel. (7) 823-860; fax (7) 823-949; f. 1956 to promote development of comprehensive planning as a continuous and co-ordinated process at all levels. Mems: institutions and individuals in 46 countries. Pres. Arq. HERMES MARROQUÍN (Guatemala); Exec. Sec. LUIS E. CAMACHO (Colombia). Publs *Correo Informativo* (quarterly), *Inter-American Journal of Planning* (quarterly).

**Intergovernmental Authority on Development—IGAD:** BP 2653, Djibouti; tel. 354050; fax 356994; e-mail igad@itnet.dj; internet www.igad.org; f. 1966 (as Intergovernmental Authority on Drought and Development—present name adopted in March 1996) to co-ordinate measures to combat the effects of drought and desertification control, environmental protection, agricultural research, water resources management, fisheries, early warning and remote-sensing for food security and manpower devt. In March 1996 heads of state and government of mem. states agreed to amend the Authority's charter and expand its mandate to cover issues of economic co-operation, regional integration and other political and social concerns, including conflict prevention and resolution; during 1997 and 1998 led initiatives to negotiate a peaceful settlement to internal conflict in Sudan. Mems: Djibouti, Eritrea, Ethiopia, Kenya, Somalia, Sudan, Uganda. Exec. Sec. Dr TEKESTE GHEBRAY (Eritrea). Publs *IGAD News* (2 a year), *Annual Report, Food Situation Report* (quarterly), *Agromet Bulletin* (quarterly).

**International Bank for Economic Co-operation—IBEC:** 107815 GSP Moscow B-78, 11 Masha Poryvaeva St, Russia; tel. (95) 975-38-61; fax (95) 975-22-02; f. 1963 by members of the Council for Mutual Economic Assistance (dissolved in 1991), as a central institution for credit and settlements; following the decision in

1989–91 of most member states to adopt a market economy, the IBEC abandoned its system of multilateral settlements in transferable roubles, and (from 1 January 1991) began to conduct all transactions in convertible currencies. The Bank provides credit and settlement facilities for member states, and also acts as an international commercial bank, offering services to commercial banks and enterprises. Authorized capital ECU 400m., paid-up capital ECU 143.5m., reserves ECU 164.8m. (Dec. 1997). Mems: Bulgaria, Cuba, Czech Republic, Hungary, Mongolia, Poland, Romania, Russia, Slovakia, Viet Nam. Chair. VITALI S. KHOKHLOV; Man. Dirs V. SYTNIKOV, S. CONSTANTINESCU.

**International Co-operation for Development and Solidarity—CIDSE:** 16 rue Stévin, 1000 Brussels, Belgium; tel. (2) 230-77-22; fax (2) 230-70-82; e-mail postmaster@cidse.be; internet www.cidse.be; f. 1967 to link Catholic development organizations and assist in co-ordination of projects, co-ordinating advocacy and lobbying and providing information. Mems: 15 Catholic agencies in 12 countries and territories. Pres. JUSTIN KILCULLEN; Sec.-Gen. JEF FELIX.

**International Investment Bank:** 107078 Moscow, 7 Masha Poryvaeva St, Russia; tel. (95) 975-40-08; fax (95) 975-20-70; f. 1970 by members of the CMEA (q.v.) to grant credits for joint investment projects and the development of enterprises; following the decision in 1989–91 of most member states to adopt a market economy, the Bank conducted its transactions (from 1 January 1991) in convertible currencies, rather than in transferable roubles. The Bank focuses on production and scientific and technical progress. By the end of 1996 the Bank had approved financing of some ECU 7,000m. for 159 projects. Authorized capital ECU 1,300m., paid-up capital ECU 214.5m., reserves ECU 835.4m. (Dec. 1997). Mems: Bulgaria, Cuba, Czech Republic, Hungary, Mongolia, Poland, Romania, Russia, Slovakia, Viet Nam.

**Lake Chad Basin Commission:** BP 727, N'Djamena, Chad; tel. 52-41-45; fax 52-41-37; e-mail lcbc@intnet.td; f. 1964 to encourage co-operation in developing the Lake Chad region and to promote the settlement of regional disputes. Work programmes emphasize the regulation of the utilization of water and other natural resources in the basin; the co-ordination of natural resources development projects and research; in 1988–92 a border demarcation exercise concerning all five member states was conducted. Annual summit of heads of state. Budget 400m. francs CFA. Mems: Cameroon, Central African Republic, Chad, Niger, Nigeria. Exec. Sec. BOBBOÏ JAURO ABUBAKAR.

**Latin American Association of Development Financing Institutions** (Asociación Latinoamericana de Instituciones Financieras de Desarrollo—ALIDE): Apdo Postal 3988, Paseo de la República 3211, Lima 100, Peru; tel. (1) 442-2400; fax (1) 442-8105; e-mail sg@mail.alide.org.pe; internet www.alide.org.com; f. 1968 to promote co-operation among regional development financing bodies. Mems: 67 active, 12 associate and 12 collaborating (banks and financing institutions and development organizations in 22 Latin American countries, Canada, Slovenia, Spain and Portugal). Pres. Dr CÉSAR RODRIGUEZ; Sec.-Gen. CARLOS GARATEA YORI. Publs *ALIDE Bulletin* (6 a year), *ALIDE NOTICIAS Newsletter* (monthly), *Annual Report, Latin American Directory of Development Financing Institutions*.

**Latin American Economic System** (Sistema Económico Latinoamericano—SELA): Apdo 17035, Avda Francisco de Miranda, Centro Empresarial Parque del Este, 1°, La Carlota, Caracas 1017, Venezuela; tel. (2) 202-5111; fax (2) 238-8923; e-mail difusion@sela.org; internet www.sela.org; f. 1975 by the Panama Convention; aims to accelerate the economic and social development of its members through intra-regional co-operation, and to provide a permanent system of consultation and co-ordination in economic and social matters; conducts studies; provides library, information service and data bases on regional co-operation. The Latin American Council meets annually at ministerial level and high-level regional consultation and co-ordination meetings are held; there is also a Permanent Secretariat. Mems: 28 countries. The following organizations have also been created within SELA:

Latin American and Caribbean Trade Information and Foreign Trade Support Programme (PLACIEX): Lima, Peru.

Latin American Fisheries Development Organization (OLDEPESCA): Lima, Peru.

Latin American Handicraft Co-operation Programme (PLACART): Caracas, Venezuela.

Latin American Technological Information Network (RITLA): Brasilia, Brazil.

Perm. Sec. CARLOS J. MONETA (Argentina). Publs *Capítulos del SELA* (quarterly), *SELA Newsletter* (monthly), *Strategic Issues* (monthly).

**Latin American Integration Association—LAIA** (Asociación Latinoamericana de Integración—ALADI): Cebollatí 1461, Casilla 577, 11000 Montevideo, Uruguay; tel. (2) 4001121; fax (2) 4090649; e-mail aladi@chasque.apc.org; internet www.aladi.org; f. 1980 as successor to the Latin American Free Trade Association (f. 1960); aims to establish an area of economic preferences, in order to promote trade throughout Latin America, with the eventual objective of establishing a regional common market. Mems divided into three categories: most developed (Argentina, Brazil, Mexico); intermediate (Chile, Colombia, Cuba, Peru, Uruguay, Venezuela); least developed (Bolivia, Ecuador, Paraguay). Sec.-Gen. JUAN FRANCISCO ROJAS PENSO (Venezuela). Publs *ALADI News* (monthly), other reports, studies, texts and agreements.

**Liptako-Gourma Integrated Development Authority:** POB 619, ave M. Thevenond, Ouagadougou, Burkina Faso; tel. (3) 30-61-48; f. 1972; scope of activities includes water infrastructure, telecommunications and construction of roads and railways; in 1986 undertook study on development of water resources in the basin of the Niger river (for hydroelectricity and irrigation). Mems: Burkina Faso, Mali, Niger. Dir-Gen. GISANGA DEMBÉLÉ (Mali).

**Mano River Union:** Private Mail Bag 133, Delco House, Lightfoot Boston St, Freetown, Sierra Leone; tel. (22) 226883; f. 1973 to establish a customs and economic union between member states to accelerate development via integration. A common external tariff was instituted in October 1977. Intra-union free trade was officially introduced in May 1981, as the first stage in progress towards a customs union. An industrial development unit was set up in 1980 to identify projects and encourage investment. Construction of the Monrovia-Freetown-Conakry highway was partially completed by 1990. The Union was inactive for three years until mid-1994, owing to disagreements regarding funding. In January 1995 a Mano River Centre for Peace and Development was established, which was to be temporarily based in London. The Centre aims to provide a permanent mechanism for conflict prevention and resolution, and monitoring of human rights violations, and to promote sustainable peace and development following a peaceful resolution of the conflicts currently under way in the region. Decisions are taken at meetings of a joint ministerial council formed by the ministers of member states. Mems: Guinea, Liberia, Sierra Leone. Dir Dr KABINEH KOROMAH (Sierra Leone).

**Mekong River Commission:** 364 M. V. Preah Monivong, Sangkat Phsar Doerm Thkouv, Khan Chamkar Mon, POB 1112, Phnom Penh, Cambodia; tel. (23) 720979; fax (23) 720972; e-mail mrcs@bigpond.com.kh; f. 1995, as successor to the Committee for Co-ordination of Investigations of the Lower Mekong Basin (f. 1957); aims to promote and co-ordinate the sustainable development, utilization and conservation of the resources of the Mekong River Basin for navigational and non-navigational purposes, in order to assist the social and economic development of member states, while at the same time preserving the ecological balance of the basin. Provides scientific information and policy advice; supports the implementation of strategic programmes and activities; organizes an annual donor consultative group meeting; maintains regular dialogue with Myanmar and the People's Republic of China. Mems: Cambodia, Laos, Thailand, Viet Nam. CEO JOERN KRISTENSEN.

**Niger Basin Authority** (Autorité du bassin du Niger): BP 729, Niamey, Niger; tel. 723102; fax 735310; f. 1964 (as River Niger Commission; name changed 1980) to harmonize national programmes concerned with the River Niger Basin and to execute an integrated development plan; activities comprise: statistics; navigation regulation; hydrological forecasting; environmental control; infrastructure and agro-pastoral development; and arranging assistance for these projects. Mems: Benin, Burkina Faso, Cameroon, Chad, Côte d'Ivoire, Guinea, Mali, Niger, Nigeria. Exec. Sec. OTHMAN MUSTAPHA (Nigeria). Publ. *Bulletin*.

**Organisation of Eastern Caribbean States—OECS:** POB 179, Morne Fortune, Castries, Saint Lucia; tel. 452-2537; fax 453-1628; e-mail oesec@oecs.org; internet www.oecs.org; f. 1981 by the seven states which formerly belonged to the West Indies Associated States (f. 1966). Aims to promote the harmonized development of trade and industry in member states; single market created on 1 January 1988. Principal institutions are: the Authority of Heads of Government (the supreme policy-making body), the Foreign Affairs Committee, the Defence and Security Committee, and the Economic Affairs Committee. There is also an Export Development and Agricultural Diversification Unit—EDADU (based in Dominica). Mems: Antigua and Barbuda, Dominica, Grenada, Montserrat, Saint Christopher and Nevis, Saint Lucia, Saint Vincent and the Grenadines; assoc. mems: Anguilla, British Virgin Islands. Dir-Gen. SWINBURNE LESTRADE.

**Organization for the Development of the Senegal River** (Organisation pour la mise en valeur du fleuve Sénégal—OMVS): 46 rue Carnot, BP 3152, Dakar, Senegal; tel. 823-45-30; fax 823-47-62; e-mail omvs.sphc@telecomplus.sn; f. 1972 to use the Senegal river for hydroelectricity, irrigation and navigation. The Djama dam in Senegal provides a barrage to prevent salt water from moving upstream, and the Manantali dam in Mali is intended to provide a reservoir for irrigation of about 375,000 ha of land and for production of hydroelectricity and provision of year-round navigation for ocean-going vessels. In 1997 two companies were formed to manage the dams: Société de Gestion de l'Energie de Manantali (SOGEM) and Société de Gestion et d'Exploitation du Barrage de Djama (SOGED). Work began in 1997 on a hydro-electric power station on the Senegal River: international donors provided US $440m. for the project which was due for completion in 2001. Mems: Mali, Mauritania, Senegal; Guinea has held observer status since 1987. Chair. MAAOUYA OULD SID'AHMED TAYA.

**Organization for the Management and Development of the Kagera River Basin** (Organisation pour l'aménagement et le développement du bassin de la rivière Kagera): BP 297, Kigali, Rwanda; tel. (7) 84665; fax (7) 82172; f. 1978; envisages joint development and management of resources, including the construction of an 80-MW hydroelectric dam at Rusumo Falls, on the Rwanda-Tanzania border, a 2,000-km railway network between the four member countries, road construction (914 km), and a telecommunications network between member states (financed by US $16m. from the African Development Bank). A tsetse-fly control project began in 1990. Budget (1992) $2m. Mems: Burundi, Rwanda, Tanzania, Uganda. Exec. Sec. JEAN-BOSCO BALINDA.

**Pacific Basin Economic Council—PBEC:** 900 Fort St, Suite 1080, Honolulu, HI 96813, USA; tel. (808) 521-9044; fax (808) 521-8530; e-mail info@pbec.org; internet www.pbec.org; f. 1967; an association of business representatives which aims to promote business opportunities in the region in order to enhance overall economic development; to advise governments and to serve as a liaison between business leaders and government officials; encourages business relationships and co-operation among members; holds business symposia. Mems: 20 country committees (Australia, Canada, Chile, People's Republic of China, Colombia, Ecuador, Fiji, Hong Kong, Indonesia, Japan, Republic of Korea, Malaysia, Mexico, New Zealand, Peru, Philippines, Russia, Taiwan, Thailand, USA). Chair. HELMUT SOHMEN; Sec.-Gen. ROBERT G. LEES.

**Pacific Economic Co-operation Council—PECC:** 4 Nassim Rd, Singapore 258372; tel. 7379823; fax 7379824; e-mail peccsec@pacific.net.sg; f. 1980; an independent, policy-orientated organization of senior research, government and business representatives from 23 economies in the Asia-Pacific region; aims to foster economic development in the region by providing a forum for discussion and co-operation in a wide range of economic areas; general meeting every 2 years. Mems: Australia, Brunei, Canada, Chile, the People's Republic of China, Colombia, Hong Kong, Indonesia, Japan, the Republic of Korea, Malaysia, Mexico, New Zealand, Peru, Philippines, Russia, Singapore, Taiwan, Thailand, USA, Viet Nam and the South Pacific Forum; French Pacific Territories (assoc. mem.); Dir-Gen. MIGNON CHAN MAN-JUNG. Publs *PECC Link* (quarterly), *Pacific Economic Outlook* (annually).

**Pan-African Institute for Development—PAID:** BP 4056, Douala, Cameroon; tel. 42-10-61; fax 42-43-35; f. 1964; gives training to people involved with development at grassroots, intermediate and senior levels coming from African countries (48 countries in 1998); emphasis in education is given to: development management and financing; agriculture and rural development; gender and development; promotion of small and medium-sized enterprises; training policies and systems; environment, health and community development; research, support and consultancy services; and specialized training. There are four regional institutes: Central Africa (Douala), Sahel (Ouagadougou, Burkina Faso) (French-speaking), West Africa (Buéa, Cameroon), Eastern and Southern Africa (Kabwe, Zambia) (English-speaking), and a European office in Geneva. Sec.-Gen. FAYA KONDIANO. Publs *Newsletter* (2 a year), *Annual Progress Report*, *PAID Report* (quarterly).

**Pan American Development Foundation—PADF:** 2600 16th St, NW, Washington, DC 20009-4202, USA; tel. (202) 458-3969; fax (202) 458-6316; f. 1962 to improve economic and social conditions in Latin America and the Caribbean through providing low-interest credit for small-scale entrepreneurs, vocational training, improved health care, agricultural development and reafforestation, and strengthening local non-governmental organizations; provides emergency disaster relief and reconstruction assistance. Mems: foundations and institutes in 35 countries. Pres. JACK HELLER; Exec. Dir BOB MOORE. Publ. *PADF Newsletter* (2 a year).

**Permanent Inter-State Committee on Drought Control in the Sahel—CILSS:** POB 7049, Ouagadougou, Burkina Faso; tel. 306758; fax 306757; e-mail cilss@fasonet.bf; f. 1973; works in co-operation with UN Sudano-Sahelian Office (UNSO, q.v.); aims to combat the effects of chronic drought in the Sahel region (where the deficit in grain production was estimated at 1.7m. metric tons for 1988), by improving irrigation and food production, halting deforestation and creating food reserves; maintains Institut du Sahel at Bamako (Mali) and centre at Niamey (Niger). Budget (2000): 9,506.1m. francs CFA, of which 318.5m. francs CFA was to be provided by mems. Mems: Burkina Faso, Cape Verde, Chad, The Gambia, Guinea-Bissau, Mali, Mauritania, Niger, Senegal. Chair. (1997–2000) Pres. YAHYA A. J. J. JAMMEH (The Gambia); Exec. Sec. CISSÉ MARIAM K. SIDIBE. Publ. *Reflets Sahéliens* (quarterly).

**Permanent Tripartite Commission for East African Co-operation:** Arusha International Conference Centre, Arusha, Tanzania; tel. (57) 4253; fax (57) 4255; e-mail eac@cybernet.co.tz; internet home.twiga.com/eac; f. 1993, by agreement between the heads of state of Kenya, Tanzania and Uganda, to promote greater regional co-operation (previously pursued under the East African Community, f. 1967; dissolved 1977); agreement to establish a secretariat was signed in Nov. 1994; initial areas for co-operation were to be trade and industry, security, immigration, transport and communications, and promotion of investment; further objectives were the elimination of trade barriers and ensuring the free movement of people and capital within the grouping; secretariat inaugurated in March 1996. A draft treaty on political and economic integration, providing for the formal establishment of the Community, was signed on 30 November 1999. Exec. Sec. FRANCIS KIRIMI MUTHAURA.

**Population Council:** 1 Dag Hammarskjöld Plaza, New York, NY 10017, USA; tel. (212) 339-0500; fax (212) 755-6052; e-mail pubinfo@popcouncil.org; internet www.popcouncil.org; f. 1952; aims to improve reproductive health and achieve a balance between people and resources; analyses demographic trends; conducts biomedical research to develop new contraceptives; works with private and public agencies to improve the quality and scope of family planning and reproductive health services; helps governments to design and implement population policies; communicates results of research. Five regional offices, in India, Mexico, Egypt, Kenya and Senegal, and 13 country offices. Additional office in Washington, DC, USA, carries out world-wide operational research and activities for the prevention of HIV and AIDS. Chair. ELIZABETH J. MCCORMACK; Pres. MARGARET CATLEY-CARLSON. Publs *Studies in Family Planning* (quarterly), *Population and Development Review* (quarterly), *Population Briefs* (quarterly).

**Society for International Development:** Via Panisperna 207, 00184 Rome, Italy; tel. (06) 4872172; fax (06) 4872170; e-mail info@sidint.org; internet www.sidint.org; f. 1957; a global network of individuals and institutions concerned with development that is participative, pluralistic and sustainable; mobilizes and strengthens civil society groups by actively building partnerships among them and with other sectors; fosters local initiatives and new forms of social experimentation. Mems: over 3,000 in 115 countries and 60 local chapters. Pres. BOUTROS BOUTROS-GHALI (Egypt); Sec.-Gen. ROBERTO SAVIO. Publs *Development* (quarterly), *Bridges* (bimonthly newsletter).

**South Centre:** Chemin du Champ-d'Anier 17–19, BP 228, 1211 Geneva 19, Switzerland; tel. (22) 7918050; fax (22) 7988531; e-mail south@southcentre.org; internet www.southcentre.org; f. 1990 as a follow-up mechanism of the South Commission (f. 1987); 1995 established as an intergovernmental body that aims to promote South–South solidarity and co-operation by generating ideas and action-oriented proposals on major policy issues for consideration by collective institutions and intergovernmental organizations of the South and individual governments. Chair. (vacant). Publ. *South Letter* (quarterly).

**Union of the Arab Maghreb** (Union du Maghreb arabe—UMA): 26–27 rue Okba, Agdal, Rabat, Morocco; tel. (7) 772668; fax (7) 772693; e-mail uma@mtds.com; internet www.maghrebarabe.org; f. 1989; aims to encourage joint ventures and to create a single market; structure comprises a council of heads of state (meeting annually), a council of ministers of foreign affairs, a consultative council of 30 delegates from each country, a UMA judicial court, and four specialized ministerial commissions. Chairmanship rotates annually between heads of state. By 1995 joint projects that had been approved or were under consideration included: free movement of citizens within the region; joint transport undertakings, including road and railway improvements; establishment of the Maghreb Investment and Foreign Trade Bank to fund joint agricultural and industrial projects (with a capital of US $500m.); and the creation of a customs union. In April 1994 the Supreme Council agreed to undertake measures to establish a free trade zone, and to set up a Maghrebian Agency for Youth Tourism and a Maghrebian Union of Sport. In 1992 UMA adopted the Maghrebian Charter for Environment Protection and Sustainable Development. In September 1999 the Sub-regional Action Programme to Combat Desertification in the Maghreb was inaugurated. Sec.-Gen. MOHAMED AMAMOU (Tunisia). Mems: Algeria, Libya, Mauritania, Morocco, Tunisia.

**Vienna Institute for Development and Co-operation** (Wiener Institut für Entwicklungsfragen und Zusammenarbeit): Weyrgasse 5, 1030 Vienna, Austria; tel. (1) 713-35-94; fax (1) 713-35-94-73; e-mail vidc@magnet.at; internet www.oneworld.at; f. 1987 (fmrly Vienna Institute for Development, f. 1964); disseminates information on the problems and achievements of developing countries; encourages increased aid-giving and international co-operation; conducts research. Pres. FRANZ VRANITZKY; Dir ERICH ANDLIK. Publs *Report Series*, *Echo*.

## Economics and Finance

**African Centre for Monetary Studies:** 15 blvd Franklin Roosevelt, BP 4128, Dakar, Senegal; tel. 821-93-80; fax 822-73-43; e-mail caem@syfed.refer.sn; began operations 1978; aims to promote better understanding of banking and monetary matters; to study monetary problems of African countries and the effect on them of international monetary developments; seeks to enable African countries to co-ordinate strategies in international monetary affairs. Established as an organ of the Association of African Central Banks (AACB) as a result of a decision by the OAU Heads of State and Government. Mems: all mems of AACB (q.v.). Chair. Dr PAUL A. OGWUMA (Nigeria); Dir MAMADOU SIDIBE (acting).

**African Insurance Organization:** BP 5860, Douala, Cameroon; tel. 42-47-58; fax 43-20-08; e-mail aio@sprynet.com; internet www.africaninsurance.org; f. 1972 to promote the expansion of the insurance and reinsurance industry in Africa, and to increase regional co-operation; holds annual conference, (2000: Abuja, Nigeria), periodic seminars and workshops, and arranges meetings for reinsurers, brokers, consultant and regulators in Africa; has established African insurance 'pools' for aviation, petroleum and fire risks, and has created associations of African insurance educators, supervisory authorities and insurance brokers and consultants. Sec.-Gen. YOSEPH ASEFFA.

**Asian Clearing Union—ACU:** c/o Central Bank of the Islamic Republic of Iran, POB 11365/8531, Teheran, Iran; tel. (21) 2842076; fax (21) 2847677; e-mail acusecret@neda.net; f. 1974 to provide clearing arrangements, whereby members settle payments for intra-regional transactions among the participating central banks, on a multilateral basis, in order to economize on the use of foreign exchange and promote the use of domestic currencies in trade transactions among developing countries; part of ESCAP's Asian trade expansion programme; the Central Bank of Iran is the Union's agent; in September 1995 the ACU unit of account was changed from SDR to US dollars, with effect from 1 January 1996. Mems: central banks of Bangladesh, India, Iran, Myanmar, Nepal, Pakistan, Sri Lanka. Sec.-Gen. MOHAMMAD FIROUZDOR. Publs *Annual Report, Newsletter* (monthly).

**Asian Reinsurance Corporation:** 17th Floor, Tower B, Chamnan Phenjati Business Center, 65 Rama 9 Rd, Huaykwang, Bangkok 10320, Thailand; tel. (2) 245-2169; fax (2) 248-1377; e-mail asianre@loxinfo.co.th; f. 1979 by ESCAP with UNCTAD, to operate as a professional reinsurer, giving priority in retrocessions to national insurance and reinsurance markets of member countries, and as a development organization providing technical assistance to countries in the Asia-Pacific region; cap. (auth.) US $15m., (p.u.) $5m. Mems: Afghanistan, Bangladesh, Bhutan, People's Republic of China, India, Iran, Republic of Korea, Philippines, Sri Lanka, Thailand. Gen. Man. A. S. MALABANAN.

**Association of African Central Banks:** 15 blvd Franklin Roosevelt, BP 4128, Dakar, Senegal; tel. 821-93-80; fax 822-73-43; f. 1968 to promote contacts in the monetary and financial sphere in order to increase co-operation and trade among member states; to strengthen monetary and financial stability on the African continent. Mems: 36 African central banks representing 47 states. Chair. Dr PAUL A. OGWUMA (Nigeria).

**Association of African Tax Administrators:** POB 13255, Yaoundé, Cameroon; tel. 22-41-57; fax 23-18-55; f. 1980 to promote co-operation in the field of taxation policy, legislation and administration among African countries. Mems: 20 states. Exec. Sec. OWONA PASCAL-BAYLON.

**Association of Asian Confederation of Credit Unions:** POB 24-171, Bangkok 10240, Thailand; tel. (2) 374-3170; fax (2) 374-5321; e-mail accuran@ksc.th.com; internet www.aaccu.net; links and promotes credit unions in Asia, provides research facilities and training programmes. Mems in Bangladesh, Hong Kong, Indonesia, Japan, Republic of Korea, Malaysia, Philippines, Sri Lanka, Taiwan, Thailand. Gen. Man. RANJITH HETTIARACHICHI. Publs *ACCU News* (every 2 months), *Annual Report and Directory*.

**Association of European Institutes of Economic Research** (Association d'instituts européens de conjoncture économique): 3 place Montesquieu, BP 4, 1348 Louvain-la-Neuve, Belgium; tel. (10) 47-41-52; fax (10) 47-39-45; f. 1955; provides a means of contact between member institutes; organizes two meetings yearly, at which discussions are held on the economic situation and on a special theoretical subject. Mems: 40 institutes in 20 European countries. Admin. Sec. PAUL OLBRECHTS.

**Central Asian Bank for Co-operation and Development:** 115a Abay, Almaty, Kazakhstan; tel. (2) 422737; fax (2) 428627; f. 1994; to support trade and development in the sub-region. Auth. cap. US $9m. Mems: Kazakhstan, Kyrgyzstan, Uzbekistan.

**Centre for Latin American Monetary Studies** (Centro de Estudios Monetarios Latinoamericanos): Durango 54, Col. Roma, Del. Cuauhtémoc, 06700 México, DF, Mexico; tel. and fax (5) 533-03-00; e-mail cemlainf@mail.internet.com.mx.; f. 1952; organizes technical training programmes on monetary policy, development finance, etc., applied research programmes on monetary and central banking policies and procedures, regional meetings of banking officials. Mems: 31 associated members (Central Banks of Latin America and the Caribbean), 28 co-operating members (supervisory institutions of the region and non-Latin American Central Banks). Dir SERGIO GHIGLIAZZA. Publs *Bulletin* (every 2 months), *Monetaria* (quarterly), *Money Affairs* (2 a year).

**Comité Européen des Assurances:** 3 bis rue de la Chaussée d'Antin, 75009 Paris, France; tel. 1-44-83-11-83; fax 1-47-70-03-75; internet www.cea.assur.org; f. 1953 to represent the interests of European insurers, to encourage co-operation between members, to allow the exchange of information and to conduct studies. Mems: national insurance associations of 29 countries. Pres. PETER ECKERT (Switzerland); Sec.-Gen. FRANCIS LOHEAC (France). Publs *CEA INFO—Euro Brief* (every 2 months), *European Insurance in Figures* (annually), *The European Life Insurance Market* (annually).

**Eastern Caribbean Central Bank:** POB 89, Basseterre, St Christopher and Nevis; tel. 465-2537; fax 466-8954; e-mail eccberu@caribsurf.com; f. 1983 by OECS governments; maintains regional currency (Eastern Caribbean dollar) and advises on the economic development of member states. Mems: Anguilla, Antigua and Barbuda, Dominica, Grenada, Montserrat, Saint Christopher and Nevis, Saint Lucia, Saint Vincent and the Grenadines. Gov. DWIGHT VENNER.

**Econometric Society:** Dept of Economics, Northwestern University, Evanston, IL 60208, USA; tel. (847) 491-3615; internet www.econometricsociety.org; f. 1930 to promote studies that aim at a unification of the theoretical-quantitative and the empirical-quantitative approach to economic problems. Mems: 7,000. Exec. Dir and Sec. JULIE P. GORDON. Publ. *Econometrica* (6 a year).

**European Federation of Finance House Associations—Eurofinas:** 267 ave de Tervueren, 1150 Brussels, Belgium; tel. (2) 778-05-60; fax (2) 778-05-79; f. 1959 to study the development of instalment credit financing in Europe, to collate and publish instalment credit statistics, to promote research into instalment credit practice; mems: finance houses and professional associations in Austria, Belgium, Finland, France, Germany, Ireland, Italy, Netherlands, Norway, Portugal, Spain, Sweden, Switzerland, United Kingdom. Chair. GREGORIO D'OTTAVIANO (Italy); Sec.-Gen. MARC BAERT. Publs *Eurofinas Newsletter* (monthly), *Annual Report, Study Reports*.

**European Federation of Financial Analysts Societies:** 3 rue d'Antin, 75002 Paris, France; tel. 1-42-98-02-00; fax 1-42-98-02-02; f. 1962 to co-ordinate the activities of all European associations of financial analysts. Biennial congress: Barcelona, Spain, 1996. Mems: 10,700 in 17 societies. Chair. J.-G. DE WAEL.

**European Financial Management and Marketing Association:** 16 rue d'Aguesseau, 75008 Paris, France; tel. 1-47-42-52-72; fax 1-47-42-56-76; f. 1971 to link financial institutions by organizing seminars, conferences and training sessions and an annual World Convention, and by providing documentation services. Mems: 145 European financial institutions. Pres. BERNARD THIOLON; Sec.-Gen. MICHEL BARNICH (acting). Publ. *Newsletter*.

**European Private Equity and Venture Capital Association:** Minervastraat 6, Box 6, 1930 Zaventem, Belgium; tel. (2) 715-00-20; fax (2) 725-07-04; e-mail evca@evca.com; internet www.evca.com; f. 1983 to link venture capital companies within Europe and to encourage joint investment projects, particularly in support of small and medium-sized businesses; holds annual symposium, seminars and training courses. Mems: over 550 in more than 30 countries. Chair. EMILE VAN DER BURG; Sec.-Gen. SERGE RAICHER.

**Fédération Internationale des Bourses de Valeurs—FIBV** (International Federation of Stock Exchanges): 22 boulevard de Courcelles, 75017 Paris, France; tel. 1-44-01-05-45; fax 1-47-54-94-22; f. 1961; assumes a leadership role in advocating the benefits of self-regulation in the regulatory process, offers a platform for closer collaboration between member exchanges, promotes enhanced ethical and professional behaviour in the securities industry. Mems: 51 and 42 corresponding exchanges. Pres. MANUEL ROBLEDA; Sec-Gen. GERRIT H. DE MAREZ OYENS.

**Financial Action Task Force on Money Laundering—FATF:** 37 bis blvd Suchet, 75016 Paris, France; tel. 1-45-24-79-45; fax 1-45-24-17-60; f. 1989 to develop and promote policies to combat money laundering; formulated a set of Recommendations for member countries to implement; established regional task forces in the Caribbean and Asia-Pacific. Mems: 26 countries, the European Commission, and the Co-operation Council for the Arab States of the Gulf. Exec. Sec. PATRICK MOULETTE.

**Fonds Africain de Garantie et de Co-opération Economique—FAGACE** (African Guarantee and Economic Co-operation Fund): BP 2045, Cotonou, Benin; tel. 300376; fax 300284; commenced operations in 1981; guarantees loans for development projects, provides loans and grants for specific operations and supports national and regional enterprises. Cap. 7,750m. francs CFA. Mems: Benin,

Burkina Faso, Central African Republic, Côte d'Ivoire, Mali, Niger, Rwanda, Senegal, Togo. Dir-Gen. SOULEYMANE GADO.

**International Accounting Standards Committee—IASC:** 166 Fleet St, London, EC4A 2DY, United Kingdom; tel. (20) 7353-0565; fax (20) 7353-0562; f. 1973 to formulate and publish in the public interest accounting standards to be observed in the presentation of financial statements and to promote worldwide acceptance and observance, and to work for the improvement and harmonization of regulations, accounting standards and procedures relating to the presentation of financial statements. Mems: 118 accounting bodies representing more than 1.7m. accountants in 104 countries. Chair. STIG ENEVOLDSEN; Sec.-Gen. Sir BRYAN CARSBERG. Publs *International Accounting Standards, Exposure Drafts, IASC Insight* (quarterly), *IASC Update* (3 a year), *Bound Volume of International Accounting Standards* (annually), *Annual Review*.

**International Association for Research in Income and Wealth:** Dept of Economics, New York University, 269 Mercer St, Room 700, New York, NY 10003, USA; tel. (212) 924-4386; fax (212) 366-5067; e-mail iariw@fasecon.econ.nyu.edu; internet www.econ.nyu.edu/dept/iariw; f. 1947 to further research in the general field of national income and wealth and related topics by the organization of biennial conferences and by other means. Mems: approx. 425. Chair. ANNE HARRISON; Exec. Sec. JANE FORMAN (USA). Publ. *Review of Income and Wealth* (quarterly).

**International Association of Islamic Banks:** Queen's Bldg, 23rd Floor, Al Balad Dist., POB 9707, Jeddah 21423, Saudi Arabia; tel. (2) 643-1276; fax (2) 644-7239; f. 1977 to link Islamic banks, which do not deal at interest but operate on a profit-/loss-sharing basis; activities include training and research. Mems: 42 banks and financial institutions in 18 countries. Chair. Prince MOHAMED AL-FAISAL AL-SAUD; Sec.-Gen. SAMIR ABID SHAIKH.

**International Bureau of Fiscal Documentation:** Sarphatistraat 600, POB 20237, 1018 AV Amsterdam, Netherlands; tel. (20) 5540100; fax (20) 6228658; e-mail info@ibfd.nl; internet www.ibfd.nl; f. 1938 to supply information on fiscal law and its application; library on international taxation. Pres. J. F. AVERY JONES; Man. Dir H. M. A. L. HAMAEKERS. Publs *Bulletin for International Fiscal Documentation, European Taxation, International VAT Monitor, Supplementary Service to European Taxation* (all monthly), *Tax News Service* (fortnightly); studies, data bases, regional tax guides.

**International Centre for Local Credit:** Koninginnegracht 2, 2514 AA The Hague, Netherlands; tel. (70) 3750850; fax (70) 3454743; e-mail centre@bng.nl; f. 1958 to promote local authority credit by gathering, exchanging and distributing information and advice on member institutions and on local authority credit and related subjects; studies important subjects in the field of local authority credit. Mems: 22 financial institutions in 14 countries. Pres. F. NARMON (Belgium); Sec.-Gen. P. P. VAN BESOUW (Netherlands). Publs *Bulletin, Newsletter* (quarterly).

**International Economic Association:** 23 rue Campagne Première, 75014 Paris, France; tel. 1-43-27-91-44; fax 1-42-79-92-16; e-mail iea23aise@hol.fr; f. 1949 to promote international collaboration for the advancement of economic knowledge and develop personal contacts between economists, and to encourage provision of means for the dissemination of economic knowledge. Member associations in 59 countries. Pres. Prof. ROBERT SOLOW; Sec.-Gen. Prof. JEAN-PAUL FITOUSSI (France).

**International Federation of Accountants:** 535 Fifth Ave, 26th Floor, New York, NY 10017, USA; tel. (212) 286-9344; fax (212) 286-9570; internet www.ifac.org; f. 1977 to develop a co-ordinated world-wide accounting profession with harmonized standards. Mems: 143 accountancy bodies in 104 countries. Pres. FRANK HARDING; Gen. Dir JOHN GRUNER (USA). Publ. *Codification of International Standards on Auditing*.

**International Fiscal Association:** World Trade Center, POB 30215, 3001 DE Rotterdam, Netherlands; tel. (10) 4052990; fax (10) 4055031; e-mail n.gensecr@ifa.nl; internet www.ifa.nl; f. 1938 to study international and comparative public finance and fiscal law, especially taxation; holds annual congresses. Mems in 90 countries and national branches in 45 countries. Pres. S. O. LODIN (Sweden); Sec.-Gen. J. FRANS SPIERDIJK (Netherlands). Publs *Cahiers de Droit Fiscal International, Yearbook of the International Fiscal Association, IFA Congress Seminar Series*.

**International Institute of Public Finance:** University of the Saar, PO Box 151150, 66041 Saarbrücken, Germany; fax (681) 302-4369; e-mail iipf@rz.uni-sb.de; internet www.wiwi.unisb/iipf/; f. 1937; a private scientific organization aiming to establish contacts between people of every nationality, whose main or supplementary activity consists in the study of public finance; holds one meeting a year devoted to a certain scientific subject. Pres. ROBERT HAVEMAN (USA).

**International Organization of Securities Commissions—IOSCO;** CP 171, Tour de la Bourse, 800 Square Victoria, Suite 4210, Montréal H4Z 1C8, Canada; tel. (514) 875-8278; fax (514) 875-2669; e-mail mail@oicv.iosco.org; internet www.iosco.org; f. 1983 to facilitate co-operation between securities and futures regulatory bodies at the international level. Mems: 163 agencies. Sec.-Gen. PETER CLARK. Publ. *IOSCO News* (3 a year).

**International Securities Market Association:** Rigistr. 60, PO Box, 8033 Zürich, Switzerland; tel. (1) 3634222; fax (1) 3637772; f. 1969 for discussion of questions relating to the international securities market, to issue rules governing their functions, and to maintain a close liaison between the primary and secondary markets in international securities. Mems: 838 banks and major financial institutions in 48 countries. Chair. RIJNHARD W. F. VAN TETS (Netherlands); Chief Exec. and Sec.-Gen. JOHN L. LANGTON (Switzerland). Publs *International Bond Manual*, daily Eurobond listing, electronic price information, weekly Eurobond guide, ISMA formulae for yield, members' register, ISMA quarterly comment, reports, etc.

**International Union for Housing Finance:** Suite 400, 111 East Wacker Drive, Chicago, IL 60601-4389, USA; tel. (312) 946-8200; fax (312) 946-8202; e-mail iuhf@wwa.com; internet www.housingfinance.org; f. 1914 to foster world-wide interest in savings and home-ownership and co-operation among members; to encourage comparative study of methods and practice in housing finance; to encourage appropriate legislation on housing finance. Mems: 350 in 71 countries, 8 regional affiliates. Sec.-Gen. DONALD R. HOLTON. Publs *Housing Finance International* (quarterly), *Directory, International Housing Finance Factbook* (every 2 years), *IUHFI Newsletter* (3 a year).

**Latin American Banking Federation** (Federación Latinoamericana de Bancos—FELABAN): Apdo Aéreo 091959, Santafé de Bogotá, DE8, Colombia; tel. (1) 621-8617; fax (1) 621-8021; f. 1965 to co-ordinate efforts towards a wide and accelerated economic development in Latin American countries. Mems: 19 Latin American national banking associations. Pres. of Board MILTON AYON WONG; Sec.-Gen. Dra MARICIELO GLEN DE TOBÓN (Colombia).

**West African Monetary Agency:** 11–13 ECOWAS St, PMB 218, Freetown, Sierra Leone; tel. 224485; fax 223943; e-mail wama@sierratel.sl; f. 1975 as West African Clearing House; administers transactions between its 10 member central banks in order to promote sub-regional trade and monetary co-operation; administers ECOWAS travellers' cheques scheme. Mems: Banque Centrale des Etats de l'Afrique de l'Ouest (serving Benin, Burkina Faso, Côte d'Ivoire, Guinea-Bissau, Mali, Niger, Senegal, Togo) and the central banks of Cape Verde, The Gambia, Ghana, Guinea, Liberia, Mauritania, Nigeria and Sierra Leone. Dir-Gen. ANTOINE M. F. NDIAYE (Senegal). Publ. *Annual Report*.

**World Council of Credit Unions—WOCCU:** POB 2982, 5710 Mineral Point Rd, Madison, WI 53705, USA; tel. (608) 231-7130; fax (608) 238-8020; e-mail mail@woccu.org; internet www.woccu.org; f. 1970 to link credit unions and similar co-operative financial institutions and assist them in expanding and improving their services; provides technical and financial assistance to credit union associations in developing countries. Mems: 35,000 credit unions in 86 countries. CEO CHRISTOPHER BAKER. Publs *WOCCU Annual Report, Perspectives* (quarterly).

**World Savings Banks Institute:** 11 rue Marie Thérèse, 1000 Brussels, Belgium; tel. (2) 211-11-11; fax (2) 211-11-99; internet www.savings-banks.com/wsbi; f. 1924 as International Savings Banks Institute, present name and structure adopted in 1994; promotes co-operation among members and the development of savings banks world-wide. Mems: 107 banks and asscns in 88 countries. Pres. MANUEL PIZARRO (Spain). Publs *Annual Report, International Savings Banks Directory, Perspectives* (8–10 a year).

# Education

**African Association for Literacy and Adult Education:** POB 50768, Finance House, 6th Floor, Loita St, Nairobi, Kenya; tel. (2) 222391; fax (2) 340849; f. 1984, combining the former African Adult Education Association and the AFROLIT Society (both f. 1968); aims to promote adult education and literacy in Africa, to study the problems involved, and to allow the exchange of information; programmes are developed and implemented by 'networks' of educators; holds Conference every three years. Mems: 28 national education associations and 300 institutions in 33 countries. Chair. (vacant). Publs *The Spider Newsletter* (quarterly, French and English), *Journal* (2 a year).

**Agence Universitaire de la Francophonie (AUPELF–UREF):** BP 400, succ. Côte-des-Neiges, Montréal, Canada H3S 2S7; tel. (514) 343-6630; fax (514) 343-2107; e-mail rectorat@aupelf.refer.org; internet www.aupelf-uref.org; f. 1961; aims: documentation, co-ordination, co-operation, exchange. Mems: 391 institutions. Pres. ARTHUR BODSON (Canada); Dir-Gen. and Rector MICHEL GUILLOU (France). Publs *Universités* (quarterly), *UREF Actualités* (every 2 months), directories (Francophone universities, Professors from francophone universities, Departments of French studies world-wide).

**Asian Confederation of Teachers:** 2nd Floor, Wisma DTC, 3455-B Jalan Sultansh Zainab, 15050 Kota Bharu, Kelatan, Malaysia; f. 1990. Pres. MUHAMMAD MUSTAPHA; Sec.-Gen. LAM WAH-HUI.

**Association for Childhood Education International:** 11501 Georgia Ave, Suite 315, Wheaton, MD 20902, USA; tel. (301) 942-2443; fax (301) 942-3012; f. 1892 to work for the education of children (from infancy through early adolescence) by promoting desirable conditions in schools, raising the standard of teaching, co-operating with all groups concerned with children, informing the public of the needs of children. Mems: 12,000. Pres. SUE WORTHAM; Exec. Dir GERALD C. ODLAND. Publs *Childhood Education* (6 a year), *ACEI Exchange Newsletter* (6 a year), *Journal of Research in Childhood Education* (2 a year), books on current educational subjects (3 a year).

**Association Montessori Internationale:** Koninginneweg 161, 1075 CN Amsterdam, Netherlands; tel. (20) 6798932; e-mail ami@xs4all.nl; f. 1929 to propagate the ideals and educational methods of Dr Maria Montessori on child development, without racial, religious or political prejudice; organizes training courses for teachers in 15 countries. Pres. G. J. PORTIELJE; Sec. RENILDE MONTESSORI. Publ. *Communications* (quarterly).

**Association of African Universities:** POB 5744, Accra North, Ghana; tel. (21) 774495; fax (21) 774821; f. 1967 to promote exchanges, contact and co-operation among African university institutions and to collect and disseminate information on research and higher education in Africa. Mems: 132 university institutions. Sec.-Gen. Prof. NARCISO MATOS (Mozambique). Publs *AAU Newsletter* (3 a year), *Directory of African Universities* (every 2 years).

**Association of Arab Universities:** POB 401, Jubeyha, Amman, Jordan; tel. (6) 5345131; fax (6) 5332994; e-mail secgen@aaru.edu.jo; internet www.aaru.edu.jo; f. 1964. Mems: 137 universities. Sec.-Gen. Dr MARWAN RASIM KAMAL. Publ. *AARU Bulletin* (annually and quarterly, in Arabic).

**Association of Caribbean University and Research Institutional Libraries—ACURIL:** Apdo postal 23317, San Juan 00931, Puerto Rico; tel. 764-0000; fax 763-5685; e-mail vtorres@upracd.upr.clu.edu; f. 1968 to foster contact and collaboration between member universities and institutes; conferences, meetings, seminars, etc.; circulation of information through newsletters, bulletins; facilitates co-operation and the pooling of resources in research; encourages exchange of staff and students. Mems: 250. Exec.-Sec. ONEIDA R. ORTIZ. Publ. *Newsletter* (2 a year).

**Association of European Universities** (Association des Universités Européennes; formerly the Conférence permanente des recteurs, présidents et vice-chanceliers des universités européennes—CRE): 10 rue du Conseil Général, 1211 Geneva 4, Switzerland; tel. (22) 3292644; fax (22) 3292821; e-mail cre@uni2a.unige.ch; internet www.unige.ch/cre/; f. 1959; holds two conferences a year, a General Assembly every four years, and training seminars for university executive heads; also involved in various programmes: new technologies to help universities face new teaching methods; an Academic Task Force to mobilize the support needed by war-damaged universities; institutional evaluation of quality management strategies; transatlantic dialogue between leaders of European and North American universities; a history of the university in Europe in four volumes; a joint university programme on institutional development with Latin American universities (*Columbus*). Mems: 530 universities and associate members in 41 countries. Pres. Dr KENNETH EDWARDS; Sec.-Gen. Dr ANDRIS BARBLAN. Publs *CRE-Info* (quarterly), *CREdoc, CREguide, Directory*.

**Association of South-East Asian Institutions of Higher Learning—ASAIHL:** Secretariat, Ratasastra Bldg 2, Chulalongkorn University, Henri Dunant Rd, Bangkok 10330, Thailand; tel. (2) 251-6966; fax (2) 253-7909; f. 1956 to promote the economic, cultural and social welfare of the people of South-East Asia by means of educational co-operation and research programmes; and to cultivate a sense of regional identity and interdependence; collects and disseminates information, organizes discussions. Mems: 160 university institutions in 14 countries. Pres. Prof. Tan Sri Dr SYED JALALUDIN SYED SALIM; Sec.-Gen. Dr NINNAT OLANVORAVUTH. Publs *Newsletter, Handbook* (every 3 years).

**Caribbean Council of Legal Education:** Mona Campus, Kingston 7, Jamaica; tel. 92-71899; fax 92-73927; f. 1971; responsible for the training of members of the legal profession. Mems: govts of 15 countries and territories.

**Caribbean Examinations Council:** The Garrison, St Michael 20, Barbados; tel. 436-6261; fax 429-5421; f. 1972; develops syllabuses and conducts examinations. Mems: govts of 16 English-speaking countries and territories.

**Catholic International Education Office:** 60 rue des Eburons, 1000 Brussels, Belgium; tel. (2) 230-72-52; fax (2) 230-97-45; e-mail oiec@pophost.eunet.be; internet www.ciateq.mx/~maria/oiec; f. 1952 for the study of the problems of Catholic education throughout the world; co-ordination of the activities of members; and representation of Catholic education at international bodies. Mems: 98 countries, 16 assoc. mems, 13 collaborating mems, 5 corresponding mems. Pres. Mgr CESARE NOSIGLIA; Sec.-Gen. ANDRÉS DELGADO HERNÁNDEZ. Publs *OIEC Bulletin* (every 3 months in English, French and Spanish), *OIEC Tracts on Education*.

**Catholic International Federation for Physical and Sports Education:** 22 rue Oberkampf, 75011 Paris, France; tel. 1-43-38-50-57; f. 1911 to group Catholic associations for physical education and sport of different countries and to develop the principles and precepts of Christian morality by fostering meetings, study and international co-operation. Mems: 14 affiliated national federations representing about 3.5m. members. Pres. ACHILLE DIEGENANT (Belgium); Sec.-Gen. CLÉMENT SCHERTZINGER (France).

**Comparative Education Society in Europe:** Institut für Augemeine Pädagogik, Humboldt-Universität zu Berlin, Unter den Linden 6, 10099 Berlin, Germany; tel. (30) 20934094; fax (30) 20931006; e-mail juergen.schriewer@educat.hu-berlin.de; f. 1961 to promote teaching and research in comparative and international education; the Society organizes conferences and promotes literature. Mems in 49 countries. Pres. Prof. J. SCHRIEWER (Belgium); Sec. and Treasurer Prof. M. A. PEREYRA (Spain). Publ. *Newsletter* (quarterly).

**European Association for the Education of Adults:** Pere Vergés 1, 08020 Barcelona, Spain; tel. (93) 2780294; fax (93) 2780174; e-mail eaea@mx3.redestb.es; internet www.vsy.fi/eaea; f. 1953 as a clearing-house and centre of co-operation for all groups concerned with adult education in Europe. Mems: 150 in 18 countries. Pres. P. FEDERIGHI (Italy); Publs *Conference Reports, Directory of Adult Education Organisations in Europe, Newsletter, Survey of Adult Education Legislation, Glossary of Terms*.

**European Cultural Foundation:** Jan van Goyenkade 5, 1075 HN Amsterdam, Netherlands; tel. (20) 6760222; fax (20) 6752231;e-mail eurocult@eurocult.org; internet www.eurocult.org; f. 1954 as a non-governmental organization, supported by private sources, to promote activities of mutual interest to European countries, concerning culture, education, environment, East-West cultural relations, media, cultural relations with the countries of the Mediterranean, issues regarding cultural pluralism; national committees in 23 countries; transnational network of institutes and centres: European Institute of Education and Social Policy, Paris; Institute for European Environmental Policy, London, Madrid and Berlin; Association for Innovative Co-operation in Europe (AICE), Brussels; EURYDICE Central Unit (the Education Information Network of the European Community), Brussels; European Institute for the Media, Düsseldorf; European Foundation Centre, Brussels; Fund for Central and East European Book Projects, Amsterdam; Institute for Human Sciences, Vienna; East West Parliamentary Practice Project, Amsterdam; Centre Européen de la Culture, Geneva. A grants programme, for European co-operation projects is also conducted. Pres. HRH Princess MARGRIET of the Netherlands; Sec.-Gen. Dr R. STEPHAN. Publs *Annual Report, Newsletter* (3 a year).

**European Federation for Catholic Adult Education:** Bildungshaus Mariatrost, Kirchbergstrasse 18, A-8044 Graz, Austria; tel. (316) 39-11-31-35; fax (316) 39-11-31-30; f. 1963 to strengthen international contact between members, to assist international research and practical projects in adult education; to help communications between its members and other international bodies; holds conference every two years. Pres. Prof. Mag. KARL KALCSICS (Austria).

**European Foundation for Management Development:** 88 rue Gachard, 1050 Brussels, Belgium; tel. (2) 648-03-85; fax (2) 646-07-68; e-mail info@efmd.be; internet www.efmd.be; f. 1971 through merger of European Association of Management Training Centres and International University Contact for Management Education; aims to help improve the quality of management development and disseminate information within the economic, social and cultural context of Europe and promote international co-operation. Mems: more than 390 institutions in 41 countries world-wide (26 in Europe). Dir-Gen. ERIC CORNUEL. Publs *Forum* (3 a year), *Guide to European Business Schools and Management Centres* (annually).

**European Union of Arabic and Islamic Scholars:** c/o Dipartimento di studi e ricerche su Africa e Paesi arabi, Istituto universitario orientale, Piazza S. Domenico Maggiore 12, 80134 Naples, Italy; tel. (081) 5517840; fax (081) 5515386; f. 1964 to organize congresses of Arabic and Islamic Studies; congresses are held every two years. Mems: 300 in 28 countries. Pres. Prof. URBAIN VERMEULEN (Belgium); Sec. Prof. CARMELA BAFFIONI (Italy).

**Graduate Institute of International Studies** (Institut universitaire de hautes études internationales): POB 36, 132 rue de Lausanne, Geneva, Switzerland; tel. (22) 7311730; fax (22) 7384306; e-mail info@hei.unige.ch; internet heiwww.unige.ch; f. 1927 to establish a centre for advanced studies in international relations of the present day, juridical, historical, political and economic. Library of 147,000 vols. Dir Prof. PETER TSCHOPP; Sec.-Gen. L. HEIMENDINGER.

**Inter-American Centre for Research and Documentation on Vocational Training** (Centro Interamericano de Investigación y Documentación sobre Formación Profesional—CINTERFOR): Avda Uruguay 1238, Casilla de correo 1761, Montevideo, Uruguay; tel. (2) 920557; fax (2) 921305; e-mail dirmvd@cinterfor.org.uy; internet www.cinterfor.org.uy; f. 1964 by the International Labour Organization (q.v.) for mutual help among the Latin American and Caribbean countries in planning vocational training; services are provided in documentation, research, exchange of experience; holds seminars and courses. Dir PEDRO DANIEL WEINBERG. Publs *Bulletin* (quarterly), *Documentation* (2 a year), *Herramientas para la transformación, Trazos de la formación*, studies, monographs and technical office papers.

**Inter-American Confederation for Catholic Education** (Confederación Interamericana de Educación Católica—CIEC): Calle 78 No 12–16 (ofna 101), Apdo Aéreo 90036, Santafé de Bogotá 8 DE, Colombia; tel. (1) 255-3676; fax (1) 255-0513; e-mail ciec@latino.net.co; internet www.ciec.to; f. 1945 to defend and extend the principles and rules of Catholic education, freedom of education, and human rights; organizes congress every three years. Pres. ADRIANO PACIFICO TOMASI; Sec. Gen. MARIA CONSTANZA ARANGO. Publ. *Educación Hoy*.

**International Association for Educational and Vocational Guidance—IAEVG:** c/o Linda Taylor, Kent Careers Services, 2nd Floor, 35 Earl St, Maidstone, Kent, ME14 1LG, United Kingdom; tel. (1622) 200711; fax (1622) 751157; e-mail linda.taylor@kentcareers.co.uk; f. 1951 to contribute to the development of vocational guidance and promote contact between persons associated with it. Mems: 40,000 from 60 countries. Pres. Dr BERNHARD JENSCHKE (Germany); Sec.-Gen. LINDA TAYLOR (UK). Publs *Bulletin* (2 a year), *Newsletter* (3 a year).

**International Association for the Development of Documentation, Libraries and Archives in Africa:** Villa 2547 Dieuppeul II, BP 375, Dakar, Senegal; tel. 824-09-54; f. 1957 to organize and develop documentation and archives in all African countries. Mems: national asscns, institutions and individuals in 48 countries. Sec.-Gen. ZACHEUS SUNDAY ALI (Nigeria).

**International Association of Educators for World Peace:** POB 3282, Mastin Lake Station, Huntsville, AL 35810, USA; tel. (256) 534-5501; fax (256) 536-1018; e-mail mercieca@hiwaay.net; internet www.earthportals.com/portal_messenger/mercieca.html; f. 1969 to develop the kind of education which will contribute to the promotion of peaceful relations at personal, community and international levels, to communicate and clarify controversial views in order to achieve maximum understanding and to help put into practice the Universal Declaration of Human Rights. Mems: 35,000 in 102 countries. Pres. Dr CHARLES MERCIECA (USA); Exec. Vice-Pres. RAJWANT SINGH SIDHU (UK); Sec.-Gen. Dr SURYA NATH PRASAD (India). Publs *Peace Progress* (annually), *IAEWP Newsletter* (6 a year), *Peace Education* (2 a year), *UN News*(monthly).

**International Association of Papyrologists:** Fondation Egyptologique Reine Elisabeth, Parc du Cinquantenaire 10, 1000 Brussels, Belgium; tel. (2) 741-73-64; e-mail amartin@ulb.ac.be; internet www.ulb.ac.be/assoc/aip; f. 1947; Mems: about 400. Pres. Prof. LUDWIG KOENEN (USA); Sec. Prof. ALAIN MARTIN (Belgium).

**International Association of Physical Education in Higher Education:** Institut Supérieur d'Education Physique, Bâtiment B21, Université de Liège au Sart Tilman, 4000 Liège, Belgium; tel. (4) 366-38-90; fax (4) 366-29-01; e-mail mpieron@ulg.ac.be; f. 1962; organizes congresses, exchanges, and research in physical education. Mems: institutions in 51 countries. Sec.-Gen. Dr MAURICE PIERON.

**International Association of Universities—IAU/International Universities Bureau—IUB:** 1 rue Miollis, 75732 Paris Cédex 15, France; tel. 1-45-68-25-45; fax 1-47-34-76-05; e-mail iau@unesco.org; internet www.unesco.org/iau; f. 1950 to allow co-operation at the international level among universities and other institutions of higher education; provides clearing-house services and operates the joint IAU/UNESCO Information Centre on Higher Education; conducts meetings and research on issues concerning higher education. Mems: more than 600 universities and institutions of higher education in some 150 countries; assoc. mems: 26 international and national university organizations. Pres. WATARU MORI; Sec.-Gen. FRANZ EBERHARD. Publs *Higher Education Policy* (quarterly), *IAU Newsletter* (every 2 months), *International Handbook of Universities* (every 2 years), *Issues in Higher Education* (monographs), *World Academic Database* (CD-ROM, annually), *World List of Universities* (every 2 years).

**International Association of University Professors and Lecturers—IAUPL:** c/o F. Mauro, 18 rue du Docteur Roux, 75015 Paris, France; f. 1945 for the development of academic fraternity amongst university teachers and research workers; the protection of independence and freedom of teaching and research; the furtherance of the interests of all university teachers; and the consideration of academic problems. Mems: federations in 17 countries. Sec.-Gen. F. MAURO.

**International Baccalaureate Organization—IBO:** Route des Morillons 15, Grand-Saconnex 1218, Geneva, Switzerland; tel. (22) 7917740; fax (22) 7910277; e-mail ibhq@ibo.org; f. 1967 to plan curricula and an international university entrance examination, the International Baccalaureate, recognized by major universities world-wide; offers the Primary Years Programme for children aged between 3 and 12, the Middle Years Programme for students in the 11–16 age range, and the Diploma Programme for 17–18 year olds; Mems: over 1,000 participating schools in 95 countries. Pres. of Council GREG CRAFTER (Australia); Dir-Gen. GEORGE WALKER.

**International Council for Adult Education:** 720 Bathurst St, Suite 500, Toronto, Canada M5S 2R4; tel. (416) 588-1211; fax (416) 588-5725; e-mail icae@web.net; internet www.web.net/icae; f. 1973 to promote the education of adults in relation to the need for healthy growth and development of individuals and communities; undertakes research and training; organizes seminars, the exchange of information, and co-operative publishing; maintains resource centre with extensive material on literacy, adult education and development education; General Assembly meets every four years. Mems: seven regional organizations and 95 national associations in 80 countries. Pres. PAUL BÉLANGER. Publs *Convergence, ICAE News*.

**International Council for Open and Distance Education—ICDE:** Gjerdrums Vei 12, 0486 Oslo, Norway; tel. 22-02-81-70; fax 22-02-81-61; e-mail icde@icde.no; internet www.icde.org; f. 1938 (name changed 1982); furthers distance (correspondence) education by promoting research, encouraging regional links, providing information and organizing conferences. Mems: institutions,corporations and individuals in 120 countries. Pres. A. ROCHA TRINDADE (Portugal); Sec.-Gen. REIDAR ROLL (Norway). Publ. *Open Praxis* (2 a year).

**International Federation for Parent Education:** 1 ave Léon Journault, 92311 Sèvres Cédex, France; tel. 1-45-07-21-64; fax 1-46-26-69-27; f. 1964 to gather in congresses and colloquia experts from different scientific fields and those responsible for family education in their own countries and to encourage the establishment of family education where it does not exist. Mems: 120. Pres. MONEEF GUITOUNI (Canada). Publ. *Lettre de la FIEP* (2 a year).

**International Federation of Catholic Universities** (Fédération internationale d'universités catholiques—FIUC): 21 rue d'Assas, 75270 Paris Cédex 06, France; tel. 1-44-39-52-26; fax 1-44-39-52-28; e-mail sgfiuc@club-internet.fr; internet www.fiuc.org/; f. 1948; to ensure a strong bond of mutual assistance among all Catholic universities in the search for truth; to help to solve problems of growth and development, and to co-operate with other international organizations. Mems: 191 in 41 countries. Pres. ANDREW GONZALEZ (Philippines); Sec.-Gen. VINCENT HANSSENS (Belgium). Publ. *Quarterly Newsletter*.

**International Federation of Library Associations and Institutions—IFLA:** POB 95312, 2509 CH The Hague, Netherlands; tel. (70) 3140884; fax (70) 3834827; e-mail ifla@ifla.org; internet www.ifla.org; f. 1927 to promote international co-operation in librarianship and bibliography. Mems: 155 associations, 1,082 institutions and 318 individual members in 143 countries. Pres. CHRISTINE DESCHAMPS; Sec.-Gen. ROSS SHIMMON. Publs *IFLA Council Report* (every 2 years), *IFLA Directory, IFLA Journal, International Cataloguing and Bibliographic Control* (quarterly), *IFLA Professional Reports*.

**International Federation of Organizations for School Correspondence and Exchange:** Via Torino 256, 10015 Ivrea, Italy; tel. (0125) 234433; fax (0125) 234761; e-mail fioces@ipfs.org; internet ipfs.org/fioces.htm; f. 1929; aims to contribute to the knowledge of foreign languages and civilizations and to bring together young people of all nations by furthering international scholastic correspondence. Mems: comprises 78 national bureaux of scholastic correspondence and exchange in 21 countries. Pres. ALBERT V. RUTTER (Malta); Gen. Sec. LIVIO TONSO (Italy).

**International Federation of Physical Education** (Fédération internationale d'éducation physique—FIEP): c/o Prof. Robert Decker, 76 rue du 10 Octobre, 7243 Bereldange, Luxembourg; f. 1923; studies physical education on scientific, pedagogic and aesthetic bases in order to stimulate health, harmonious development or preservation, healthy recreation, and the best adaptation of the individual to the general needs of social life; organizes international congresses and courses, and awards research prize. Mems: from 112 countries. Vice-Pres. (Europe) Prof. ROBERT DECKER. Publ. *FIEP Bulletin* (trilingual edition in French, English and Spanish, 3 a year).

**International Federation of Teachers of Modern Languages:** Seestrasse 247, 8038 Zürich, Switzerland; tel. (1) 4855251; fax (1) 4825054; f. 1931; holds meetings on every aspect of foreign-language teaching; has consultative status with UNESCO. Mems: 33 national and regional language associations and six international unilingual associations (teachers of English, French, German, Italian and Spanish). Pres. MICHAEL CANDELIER; Sec.-Gen. DENIS CUNNINGHAM. Publ. *FIPLV World News* (quarterly in English, French and Spanish).

**International Federation of University Women:** 8 rue de l'Ancien Port, 1201 Geneva, Switzerland; tel. (22) 7312380; fax (22) 7380440; e-mail ifuw@ifuw.org; internet www.ifuw.org; f. 1919 to promote understanding and friendship among university women of the world; to encourage international co-operation; to further the development of education; to represent university women in international organizations; to encourage the full application of members' skills to the problems which arise at all levels of public life. Affiliates: 66 national associations with over 180,000 mems. Pres. Linda F. Souter (Canada). Publs *IFUW News* (6 a year), triennial report.

**International Federation of Workers' Education Associations:** c/o AOF Postboks 8703, Youngstorget, 0028 Oslo 1, Norway; tel. 23-06-12-88; fax 23-06-12-70; e-mail jmehlum@online.no; internet www.ifwea.org; f. 1947 to promote co-operation between non-governmental bodies concerned with workers' education, through clearing-house services, exchange of information, publications, international seminars, conferences, summer schools, etc. Pres. Dan Gallin (Switzerland); Gen. Sec. Jan Mehlum (Norway).

**International Institute for Adult Literacy Methods:** POB 19395/6194, 5th Floor, Golfam St, 19156 Teheran, Iran; tel. (21) 2220313; f. 1968 by UNESCO and the Government of Iran, to collect, analyse and distribute information on activities concerning methods of literacy training and adult education; sponsors seminars; maintains documentation service and library on literacy and adult education. Dir Dr Mohammad Reza Hamidizade. Publs *Selection of Adult Education Issues* (monthly), *Adult Education and Development* (quarterly), *New Library Holdings* (quarterly).

**International Institute of Philosophy—IIP** (Institut international de philosophie—IIP): 8 rue Jean-Calvin, 75005 Paris, France; tel. 1-43-36-39-11; e-mail inst.intern.philo@wanadoo.fr; f. 1937 to clarify fundamental issues of contemporary philosophy in annual meetings and to promote mutual understanding among thinkers of different backgrounds and traditions; a maximum of 115 members are elected, chosen from all countries and representing different tendencies. Mems: 93 in 35 countries. Pres. Jaakko Hintikka (Finland); Sec.-Gen. P. Aubenque (France). Publs *Bibliography of Philosophy* (quarterly), *Proceedings* of annual meetings, *Chroniques, Philosophy and World Community* (series), *Philosophical Problems Today, Controverses philosophiques*.

**International Institute of Public Administration:** 2 ave de l'Observatoire, 75272 Paris Cédex 06; tel. 1-44-41-85-00; fax 1-44-41-86-19; e-mail iiap.bib@wanadoo.fr; f. 1966; trains high-ranking civil servants from abroad; administrative, economic, financial and diplomatic programmes; Africa, Latin America, Asia, Europe and Near East departments; research department, library of 80,000 vols; Documentation Centre. Dir M. Maus. Publs *Revue française d'administration publique* (quarterly).

**International Reading Association:** 800 Barksdale Rd, POB 8139, Newark, DE 19714-8139, USA; tel. (302) 731-1600; fax (302) 731-1057; internet www.reading.org; f. 1956 to improve the quality of reading instruction at all levels, to promote the habit of lifelong reading, and to develop every reader's proficiency. Mems: 90,000 in 99 countries. Pres. Carol M. Santa; Publs *The Reading Teacher* (8 a year), *Journal of Adolescent and Adult Literacy* (8 a year), *Reading Research Quarterly, Lectura y Vida* (quarterly in Spanish), *Reading Today* (6 a year).

**International Schools Association—ISA:** CIC CASE 20, 1211 Geneva 20, Switzerland; tel. (22) 7336717; f. 1951 to co-ordinate work in international schools and promote their development; member schools maintain the highest standards and accept pupils of all nationalities, irrespective of race and creed. ISA carries out curriculum research; convenes annual conferences on problems of curriculum and educational reform; organizes occasional teachers' training workshops and specialist seminars. Mems: 85 schools throughout the world. Pres. James McLellan. Publs *Education Bulletin* (2 a year), *ISA Magazine* (annually), *Conference Report* (annually), curriculum studies (occasional).

**International Society for Business Education:** 3550 Anderson St, Madison, WI 53704-2599, USA; tel. (608) 837-7518; fax (608) 834-1301; e-mail lkantine@prodigy.net; internet www.bminet.com/siec; f. 1901 to encourage international exchange of information and organize international courses and congresses on business education; 2,200 mems, national organizations and individuals in 20 countries. Pres. Michaela Fever Stein (Germany); Gen. Sec. G. Lee Kantin (USA). Publ. *International Review for Business Education*.

**International Society for Education through Art:** c/o Diederik Schönau, CITO, POB 1109, 6801 BC Arnhem, Netherlands; fax (26) 3521202; e-mail insea@cito.nl; f. 1951 to unite art teachers throughout the world, to exchange information and to co-ordinate research into art education; organizes international congresses and exhibitions of children's art. Pres. Kit Grauer (Canada). Publ. *INSEA News* (3 a year).

**International Society for Music Education:** ICRME, University of Reading, Bulmershe Court, Reading, RG6 1HY, United Kingdom; tel. (118) 9318846; fax (118) 9318846; e-mail e.smith@reading.ac.uk; internet www.isme.org; f. 1953 to organize international conferences, seminars and publications on matters pertaining to music education; acts as advisory body to UNESCO in matters of music education. Mems: national committees and individuals in 60 countries. Pres. Einar Solbu (Norway); Sec.-Gen. Joan Therens (Canada). Publs *ISME Newsletter, Journal*.

**International Society for the Study of Medieval Philosophy:** Collège Mercier, place du Cardinal Mercier 14, 1348 Louvain-la-Neuve, Belgium; tel. (10) 47-48-07; fax (10) 47-82-85; e-mail accademia.belgio@hella.stm.it; internet www.isp.ucl.ac.be/isp/siepm/siepm.html; f. 1958 to promote the study of medieval thought and the collaboration between individuals and institutions concerned in this field; organizes international congresses. Mems: 576. Pres. Prof. David Luscombe (United Kingdom); Sec. Prof. Jacqueline Hamesse (Belgium). Publ. *Bulletin de Philosophie Médiévale* (annually).

**International Youth Library** (Internationale Jugendbibliothek): 81247 Munich, Schloss Blutenburg, Germany; tel. (89) 8912110; fax (89) 8117553; e-mail bib@ijb.de; f. 1948, since 1953 an associated project of UNESCO, to promote the international exchange of children's literature and to provide study opportunities for specialists in children's books; maintains a library of 460,000 volumes in about 120 languages. Dir Dr Barbara Scharioth. Publs *The White Ravens, IJB Report*, catalogues.

**League of European Research Libraries—LIBER:** c/o Prof. Elmar Mittler, Göttingen Univ. Library, 37070 Göttingen, Germany; tel. (551) 395212; fax (551) 395222; f. 1971 to establish close collaboration between the general research libraries of Europe, and national and university libraries in particular; and to help in finding practical ways of improving the quality of the services these libraries provide. Mems: 310 libraries and individuals in 33 countries. Pres. Prof. Elmar Mittler; Sec. Dr Ann Matheson (UK). Publ. *LIBER Quarterly*.

**Organization of Ibero-American States for Education, Science and Culture** (Organización de Estados Iberoamericanos para la Educación, la Ciencia y la Cultura): Centro de Recursos Documentales e Informáticos, Calle Bravo Murillo, No 38, 28015 Madrid, Spain; tel. (91) 594-44-42; fax (91) 594-32-86; e-mail oeimad@oei.es; internet www.oei.es; f. 1949 (as the Ibero-American Bureau of Education); promotes peace and solidarity between member countries, through education, science, technology and culture; provides information, encourages exchanges and organizes training courses; the General Assembly (at ministerial level) meets every four years. Mems: governments of 20 countries. Sec.-Gen. Francisco José Piñón. Publ. *Revista Iberoamericana de Educacion* (quarterly).

**Organization of the Catholic Universities of Latin America** (Organización de Universidades Católicas de América Latina—ODUCAL): c/o Dr J. A. Tobías, Universidad del Salvador, Viamonte 1856, CP 1056, Buenos Aires, Argentina; tel. (1) 813-1408; fax (1) 812-4625; f. 1953 to assist the social, economic and cultural development of Latin America through the promotion of Catholic higher education in the continent. Mems: 43 Catholic universities in Argentina, Bolivia, Brazil, Chile, Colombia, Dominican Republic, Ecuador, Guatemala, Mexico, Panama, Paraguay, Peru, Puerto Rico, Uruguay, Venezuela. Pres. Dr Juan Alejandro Tobías (Argentina); Publs *Anuario, Sapientia, Universitas*.

**Southeast Asian Ministers of Education Organization—SEAMEO:** Darakarn Bldg, 920 Sukhumvit Rd, Bangkok 10110, Thailand; tel. (2) 391-0144; fax (2) 381-2587; e-mail secretariat@seameo.org; internet www.seameo.org; f. 1965 to promote co-operation among the Southeast Asian nations through projects in education, science and culture; SEAMEO has 14 regional centres including: BIOTROP for tropical biology, in Bogor, Indonesia; INNOTECH for educational innovation and technology; an Open-Learning Centre in Indonesia; RECSAM for education in science and mathematics, in Penang, Malaysia; RELC for languages, in Singapore; RIHED for higher education development in Bangkok, Thailand; SEARCA for graduate study and research in agriculture, in Los Baños, Philippines; SPAFA for archaeology and fine arts in Bangkok, Thailand; TROPMED for tropical medicine and public health with regional centres in Indonesia, Malaysia, Philippines and Thailand and a central office in Bangkok; VOCTECH for vocational and technical education; and the SEAMO Training Centre in Ho Chi Minh City, Viet Nam. Mems: Brunei, Cambodia, Indonesia, Laos, Malaysia, Philippines, Singapore, Thailand, Viet Nam. Assoc. mems: Australia, Canada, France, Germany, Netherlands, New Zealand. Pres. Teo Chee Hean (Singapore); Dir Dr Suparak Rachaintra. Publs *Annual Report, SEAMEO Horizon*.

**Union of Latin American Universities** (Unión de Universidades de América Latina—UDUAL): Edificio UDUAL, Apdo postal 70-232, Ciudad Universitaria, Del. Coyoacán, 04510 México, DF, Mexico; tel. (5) 622-0991; fax (5) 616-1414; f. 1949 to organize the interchange of professors, students, research fellows and graduates and generally encourage good relations between the Latin American universities; arranges conferences, conducts statistical research; centre for university documentation. Mems: 165 universities. Pres. Dr Jorge Bro-

VETO (Uruguay); Sec.-Gen. Dr ABELARDO VILLEGAS (Mexico). Publs *Universidades* (2 a year), *Gaceta UDUAL* (quarterly), *Censo* (every 2 years).

**Universal Esperanto Association:** Nieuwe Binnenweg 176, 3015 BJ Rotterdam, Netherlands; tel. (10) 4361044; fax (10) 4361751; e-mail uea@inter.nl.net; f. 1908 to assist the spread of the international language, Esperanto, and to facilitate the practical use of the language. Mems: 60 affiliated national associations and 20,171 individuals in 120 countries. Pres. KEPPEL E. ENDERBY (Australia); Gen. Sec. MICHELA LIPARI (Italy). Publs *Esperanto* (monthly), *Kontakto* (every 2 months), *Jarlibro* (yearbook), *Esperanto Documents*.

**World Association for Educational Research:** Schloss-strasse 29, 60486 Frankfurt-am-Main, Germany; f. 1953, present title adopted 1977; aims to encourage research in educational sciences by organizing congresses, issuing publications, the exchange of information, etc. Member societies and individual members in 50 countries. Pres. Prof. Dr W. MITTER; Sec.-Gen. Prof. A. HOURDAKIS.

**World Education Fellowship:** 22A Kew Gardens, Kew, Richmond, TW9 3HD, United Kingdom; tel. (20) 8940-0131; f. 1921 to promote education for international understanding, and the exchange and practice of ideas together with research into progressive educational theories and methods. Sections and groups in 20 countries. Chair. CHRISTINE WYKES; Sec. ROSEMARY CROMMELIN. Publ. *The New Era in Education* (3 a year).

**World Union of Catholic Teachers** (Union Mondiale des Enseignants Catholiques—UMEC): Piazza San Calisto 16, 00120 Città del Vaticano; tel. 698-87286; f. 1951; encourages the grouping of Catholic teachers for the greater effectiveness of the Catholic school, distributes documentation on Catholic doctrine with regard to education, and facilitates personal contacts through congresses, seminars, etc., nationally and internationally. Mems: 32 organizations in 29 countries. Pres. ARNOLD BACKX; Sec.-Gen. MICHAEL EMM. Publ. *Nouvelles de l'UMEC*.

**World University Service—WUS:** 383 Los Jardines, Nuñoa, Santiago de Chile, Chile; tel. (2) 272375; fax (2) 2724002; f. 1920; links students, faculty and administrators in post-secondary institutions concerned with economic and social development, and seeks to protect their academic freedom and autonomy; seeks to extend technical, personal and financial resources of post-secondary institutions to under-developed areas and communities; provides scholarships at university level for refugees, displaced people, and returnees, and supports informal education projects for women; the principle is to assist people to improve and develop their own communities. WUS is independent and is governed by an assembly of national committees. Pres. CALEB FUNDANGA (Zambia); Sec.-Gen. XIMENA ERAZO. Publs *WUS News, WUS and Human Rights* (quarterly).

# Environmental Conservation

**BirdLife International:** Wellbrook Ct, Girton Rd, Cambridge, CB3 0NA, United Kingdom; tel. (1223) 277318; fax (1223) 277200; e-mail birdlife@birdlife.org.uk; internet www.birdlife.net; f. 1922 as the International Council for Bird Preservation; a global partnership of organizations that determines status of bird species throughout the world and compiles data on all endangered species; identifies conservation problems and priorities; initiates and co-ordinates conservation projects and international conventions. Partners in 60 countries; representatives in around 31 more. Chair. GERARD A. BERTRAND; Dir Dr MICHAEL RANDS (UK). Publs *Bird Red Data Book, World Birdwatch* (quarterly), *Bird Conservation Series* and study reports.

**Friends of the Earth International:** Prins Hendrikkade 48, POB 19199, 1000 GD Amsterdam, Netherlands; tel. (20) 6221369; fax (20) 6392181; e-mail foeint@antenna.nl; internet www.xs4all-nl/~foeint; f. 1971 to promote the conservation, restoration and rational use of the environment and natural resources through public education and campaigning. Mems: 56 national groups. Publ. *FoE Link* (6 a year).

**Greenpeace International:** Keizersgracht 176, 1016 DW Amsterdam, Netherlands; tel. (20) 5236222; fax (20) 5236200; e-mail greenpeaceinternational@green2.greenpeace.org; internet www.greenpeace.org; f. 1971 to campaign for the protection of the environment; aims to bear witness to environmental destruction, and to demonstrate solutions for positive change. Mems: offices in 34 countries. Chair. CORNELIA DURRANT; Exec. Dir THILO BODE.

**Independent World Commission on the Oceans—IWCO:** c/o Palácio de Belém, 1300 Lisbon, Portugal; tel. (1) 3637141; fax (1) 3636603; e-mail secretariat@world-oceans.org; internet www.world-oceans.org; f. 1995 to study ways of protecting maritime resources and coastal areas. Chair. MÁRIO SOARES.

**International Commission for the Protection of the Rhine against Pollution:** 56002 Koblenz, Hohenzollernstrasse 18, POB 200253, Germany; tel. (261) 12495; fax (261) 36572; e-mail iksr@rz-online.de; internet www.iksr.org; f. 1950 to prepare and commission research to establish the nature of the pollution of the Rhine; to propose measures of protection, ecological rehabilitation and flood prevention of the Rhine to the signatory governments. Mems: 23 delegates from France, Germany, Luxembourg, Netherlands, Switzerland and the EU. Pres. A. JACOBOVITZ DE SZEGED; Sec. J. P. WIERIKS. Publ. *Annual Report*.

**International Council on Metals and the Environment:** 294 Albert St, Suite 506, Ottawa, ON K1P 6E6, Canada; tel. (613) 235-4263; fax (613) 235-2865; e-mail info@icme.com; internet www.icme.com; f. 1991 by metal-producing and mining companies to promote responsible environmental practices and policies in the mining, use, recycling and disposal of metals. Mems: companies from six continents. Chair. HUGH M. MORGAN (Australia); Sec.-Gen. GARY NASH (Canada). Publ. *ICME Newsletter* (quarterly).

**South Pacific Regional Environment Programme—SPREP:** POB 240, Apia, Samoa; tel. 21929; fax 20231; e-mail sprep@sprep.org.ws; internet www.sprep.org.ws; f. 1978 by the South Pacific Commission (where it was based), the South Pacific Forum, ESCAP and UNEP; formally established as an independent institution in June 1993 when members signed the *Agreement Establishing SPREP*; aims to promote regional co-operation in environmental matters, to assist members to protect and improve their shared environment, and to help members to work towards sustainable development; adopted the Action Plan for Managing the Environment of the South Pacific Region 1997–2000, in November 1996; responsible for implementation of the South Pacific Biodiversity Conservation Programme, a five-year project funded by the UN's Global Environment Facility. Mems: 22 Pacific islands, Australia, France, New Zealand, USA. Dir TAMARI'I P. TUTANGATA (Cook Islands). Publs *SPREP Newsletter* (quarterly), *CASOLink* (quarterly), *La letter de l'environnement* (quarterly), *South Pacific Sea Level and Climate Change Newsletter* (quarterly).

**Wetlands International – Africa, Europe, Middle East (AEME):** Droevendaalsteeg 3A, POB 7002, 6700 CA Wageningen, Netherlands; tel. (317) 478884; fax (317) 478885; e-mail post@wetlands.agro.nl; internet www.wetlands.agro.nl; f. 1995 by merger of several regional wetlands organizations; aims to sustain and restore wetlands, their resources and biodiversity through research, information exchange and conservation activities; promotes implementation of the 1971 Ramsar Convention on Wetlands. Exec. Dir JAMES MCCUAIG. Publs *Wetlands* (2 a year), other studies, technical publications, manuals, proceedings of meetings.

**World Conservation Union—IUCN:** rue Mauverney 28, 1196 Gland, Switzerland; tel. (22) 9990001; fax (22) 9990002; e-mail mail@iucn.org; internet www.iucn.org; f. 1948, as the International Union for Conservation of Nature and Natural Resources; supports partnerships and practical field activities to promote the conservation of natural resources, to secure the conservation of nature, and especially of biological diversity, as an essential foundation for the future; to ensure wise use of the earth's natural resources in an equitable and sustainable way; to guide the development of human communities towards ways of life in enduring harmony with other components of the biosphere, developing programmes to protect and sustain the most important and threatened species and eco-systems and assisting governments to devise and carry out national conservation strategies; maintains a conservation library and documentation centre and units for monitoring traffic in wildlife. Membership of governments, government agencies and non-governmental organizations represent 140 countries. Pres. YOLANDA KAKABADSE (Ecuador); Dir-Gen. MARITTA R. VON BIEBERSTEIN KOCH-WESER (Brazil). Publs *World Conservation Strategy, Caring for the Earth, Red List of Threatened Plants, Red List of Threatened Animals, United Nations List of National Parks and Protected Areas, World Conservation* (quarterly).

**World Society for the Protection of Animals:** 2 Langley Lane, London, SW8 1TJ, United Kingdom; tel. (20) 7793-0540; fax (20) 7793-0208; f. 1981, incorporating the World Federation for the Protection of Animals (f. 1950) and the International Society for the Protection of Animals (f. 1959); promotes animal welfare and conservation by humane education, practical field projects, international lobbying and legislative work. Chief Exec. ANDREW DICKSON.

**World Wide Fund for Nature—WWF:** ave de Mont-Blanc, 1196 Gland, Switzerland; tel. (22) 3649111; fax (22) 3643239; e-mail userid@wwfnet.org; internet www.panda.org; f. 1961 (as World Wildlife Fund); aims to conserve nature and ecological processes by preserving genetic, species and ecosystem diversity; to ensure the sustainable use of resources; to reduce pollution and wasteful consumption of resources and energy. Mems: 27 national organizations, and five associates. Pres. Prof. RUUD LUBBERS (Netherlands); Dir-Gen. Dr CLAUDE MARTIN. Publs *Annual Report, WWF News* (quarterly).

# Government and Politics

**African Association for Public Administration and Management:** POB 48677, Nairobi, Kenya; tel. (2) 52-19-44; fax (2) 52-18-45; e-mail aapam@africaonline.co.ke; f. 1971 to provide senior officials with a forum for the exchange of ideas and experience, to promote the study of professional techniques and encourage research in particular African administrative problems. Mems: over 500 corporate and individual. Pres Dr ROBERT DODOO; Sec.-Gen. Dr IJUKA KABUMBA. Publs *Newsletter* (quarterly), *Annual Seminar Report, African Journal of Public Administration and Management,* studies.

**Afro-Asian Peoples' Solidarity Organization—AAPSO:** 89 Abdel Aziz Al-Saoud St, POB 11559-61 Manial El-Roda, Cairo, Egypt; tel. (2) 3636081; fax (2) 3637361; e-mail aapso@idsc.gov.eg; f. 1958; acts among and for the peoples of Africa and Asia in their struggle for genuine independence, sovereignty, socio-economic development, peace and disarmament. Mems: national committees and affiliated organizations in 66 countries and territories, assoc. mems in 15 European countries. Pres. Dr MOURAD GHALEB; Sec.-Gen. NOURI ABD AR-RAZZAK HUSSEIN (Iraq). Publs *Solidarity Bulletin* (monthly), *Development and Socio-Economic Progress* (quarterly), *Human Rights Newsletter* (6 a year).

**Agency for the Prohibition of Nuclear Weapons in Latin America and the Caribbean** (Organismo para la Proscripción de las Armas Nucleares en la América Latina y el Caribe—OPANAL): Temístocles 78, Col. Polanco, CP 11560, México, DF, Mexico; tel. (5) 280-4923; fax (5) 280-2965; f. 1969 to ensure compliance with the Treaty for the Prohibition of Nuclear Weapons in Latin America (Treaty of Tlatelolco), 1967; to ensure the absence of all nuclear weapons in the application zone of the Treaty; to contribute to the movement against proliferation of nuclear weapons; to promote general and complete disarmament; to prohibit all testing, use, manufacture, acquisition, storage, installation and any form of possession, by any means, of nuclear weapons. The organs of the Agency comprise the General Conference, meeting every two years, the Council, meeting every two months, and the secretariat. Holds General Conference every two years. Mems: 30 states which have fully ratified the Treaty: Antigua and Barbuda, Argentina, Bahamas, Barbados, Belize, Bolivia, Brazil, Chile, Colombia, Costa Rica, Dominica, Dominican Republic, Ecuador, El Salvador, Grenada, Guatemala, Haiti, Honduras, Jamaica, Mexico, Nicaragua, Panama, Paraguay, Peru, Saint Vincent and the Grenadines, Suriname, Trinidad and Tobago, Uruguay and Venezuela. The Treaty has two additional Protocols: the first signed and ratified by France, the Netherlands, the United Kingdom and the USA; the second signed and ratified by China, the USA, France, the United Kingdom and Russia. Sec.-Gen. ENRIQUE ROMÁN-MOREY (Peru).

**Alliance of Small Island States—AOSIS:** c/o 800 Second Ave, Suite 400D New York, NY 10017, USA; tel. (212) 599-6196; fax (212) 599-0797; f. 1990 as an *ad hoc* intergovernmental grouping to focus on the special problems of small islands and low-lying coastal developing states. Mems: 43 island nations. Chair. TUILOMA NERONI SLADE (Samoa). Publ. *Small Islands, Big Issues.*

**ANZUS:** c/o Dept of Foreign Affairs and Trade, Locked Bag 40, Queen Victoria Terrace, Canberra, ACT 2600, Australia; tel. (2) 6261-9111; fax (2) 6273-3577; internet www.dfat.gov.au; the ANZUS Security Treaty was signed in 1951 by Australia, New Zealand and the USA, and ratified in 1952 to co-ordinate partners' efforts for collective defence for the preservation of peace and security in the Pacific area, through the exchange of technical information and strategic intelligence, and a programme of exercises, exchanges and visits. In 1984 New Zealand refused to allow visits by US naval vessels that were either nuclear-propelled or potentially nuclear-armed, and this led to the cancellation of joint ANZUS military exercises: in 1986 the USA formally announced the suspension of its security commitment to New Zealand under ANZUS. Instead of the annual ANZUS Council meetings, bilateral talks were subsequently held every year between Australia and the USA. ANZUS continued to govern security relations between Australia and the USA, and between Australia and New Zealand; security relations between New Zealand and the USA were the only aspect of the treaty to be suspended. Senior-level contacts between New Zealand and the USA resumed in 1994.

**Association of Secretaries General of Parliaments:** c/o Committee Office, House of Commons, London, SW1, United Kingdom; tel. (20) 7219-3259; f. 1938; studies the law, practice and working methods of different Parliaments and proposes measures for improving those methods and for securing co-operation between the services of different Parliaments; operates as a consultative body to the Inter-Parliamentary Union (q.v.), and assists the Union on subjects within the scope of the Association. Mems: about 200 representing about 90 countries. Pres. JACQUES OLLÉ-LAPRUNE (France); Joint Sec. Y. AZAD (UK). Publ. *Constitutional and Parliamentary Information* (2 a year).

**Atlantic Treaty Association:** 10 rue Crevaux, 75116 Paris, France; tel. 1-45-53-28-80; fax 1-47-55-49-63; e-mail ata_sg@wanadoo.fr; f. 1954 to inform public opinion on the North Atlantic Alliance and to promote the solidarity of the peoples of the North Atlantic; holds annual assemblies, seminars, study conferences for teachers and young politicians. Mems: national associations in the 19 member countries of NATO (q.v.); 13 assoc. mems from central and eastern Europe. Chair. THEODOSSIS GEORGIOU (Greece); Sec.-Gen. ALFRED CAHEN (Belgium).

**Baltic Council:** f. 1993 by the Baltic Assembly comprising 60 parliamentarians from Estonia, Latvia and Lithuania; Council of Ministers of the three Baltic countries to co-ordinate policy in the areas of foreign policy, justice, the environment, education and science.

**Celtic League:** 11 Hilltop View, Farmhill, Braddan, Isle of Man; tel. (1624) 627128; e-mail b.moffatt@advsys.co.im; internet www.manxman.co.im/cleague/index.html; f. 1961 to foster co-operation between the six Celtic nations (Ireland, Scotland, Man, Wales, Cornwall and Brittany), especially those who are actively working for political autonomy by non-violent means; campaigns politically on issues affecting the Celtic countries; monitors military activity in the Celtic countries; co-operates with national cultural organizations to promote the languages and culture of the Celts. Mems: approx. 1,400 individuals in the Celtic communities and elsewhere. Chair. CATHAL Ó LUAIN; Gen. Sec. J. B. MOFFAT. Publ. *Carn* (quarterly).

**Central European Initiative—CEI:** c/o Ambassador Paul Hartig, CEI Executive Secretariat, Via Genova 9, 34132 Trieste, Italy; tel. (040) 7786777; fax (040) 360640; internet ceinet.org; f. 1989 as 'Pentagonal' group of central European countries (Austria, Czechoslovakia, Italy, Hungary, Yugoslavia); became 'Hexagonal' with the admission of Poland in July 1991; present name adopted in March 1992, when Croatia and Slovenia replaced Yugoslavia as members (Bosnia and Herzegovina and the former Yugoslav republic of Macedonia subsequently became members); the Czech Republic and Slovakia became separate mems in January 1993; Albania, Belarus, Bulgaria, Romania and Ukraine joined the CEI in June 1996 and Moldova in November; aims to encourage regional and bilateral co-operation, working within the OSCE (q.v.).

**Christian Democrat International:** 16 rue de la Victoire, Boîte 1, 1060 Brussels, Belgium; tel. (2) 537-13-22; fax (2) 537-93-48; f. 1961 to serve as a platform for the co-operation of political parties of Christian Social inspiration. Mems: parties in 64 countries (of which 47 in Europe). Pres. JAVIER RUPÉREZ. Publs *DC-Info* (quarterly), *Human Rights* (5 a year), *Documents* (quarterly).

**Comunidade dos Países de Língua Portuguesa** (Community of Portuguese-Speaking Countries): rua S. Caetano 32, 1200 Lisbon, Portugal; tel. (1) 392-8560; fax (1) 392-8588; f. 1996; aims to produce close political, economic, diplomatic and cultural links between Portuguese-speaking countries and to strengthen the influence of the Lusophone commonwealth within the international community. Undertook efforts to negotiate a cease-fire agreement in Guinea-Bissau in mid-1998. Mems: Angola, Brazil, Cape Verde, Guinea-Bissau, Mozambique, Portugal, São Tomé e Príncipe; East Timor has observer status. Exec. Sec. MARCOLINO MOCO (Angola).

**Eastern Regional Organization for Public Administration—EROPA:** POB 198, National College of Public Administration and Governance, University of the Philippines, Diliman, Quezon City, Metro Manila, Philippines; tel. (2) 9285411; fax (2) 9283861; f. 1960 to promote regional co-operation in improving knowledge, systems and practices of governmental administration to help accelerate economic and social development; organizes regional conferences, seminars, special studies, surveys and training programmes. There are three regional centres: Training Centre (New Delhi), Local Government Centre (Tokyo), Development Management Centre (Seoul). Mems: 12 countries, 102 organizations/groups, 418 individuals. Chair. CORAZON ALMA G. DE LEON (Philippines); Sec.-Gen. PATRICIA A. STO TOMAS (Philippines). Publs *EROPA Bulletin* (quarterly), *Asian Review of Public Administration* (2 a year).

**European Movement:** European Action Centre, place du Luxembourg 1, 1040 Brussels, Belgium; tel. (2) 512-44-44; fax (2) 512-66-73; f. 1947 by a liaison committee of representatives from European organizations, to study the political, economic and technical problems of a European Union and suggest how they can be solved; to inform and lead public opinion in the promotion of integration. Conferences have led to the creation of the Council of Europe, College of Europe, etc. Mems: national councils and committees in Austria, Belgium, Croatia, Cyprus, Czech Republic, Denmark, France, Germany, Greece, Hungary, Ireland, Italy, Luxembourg, former Yugoslav republic of Macedonia, Malta, Netherlands, Norway, Poland, Portugal, Romania, Slovakia, Slovenia, Spain, Switzerland, Turkey, United Kingdom, Yugoslavia; and several international social and economic organizations. Sec.-Gen. PIER VIRGILIO DASTOLI (Italy). Publ. *Lettre du Mouvement Européen* (6 a year).

**European Union of Women—EUW:** Auklands, Gloucester Rd, Thornbury, Bristol, BS35 1JH, United Kingdom; tel. (1454) 413865; fax (1454) 412490; e-mail euwinternat@aol.com; f. 1955 to increase the influence of women in the political and civic life of their country and of Europe. Mems: national organizations in 21 countries. Pres. ANGELA GUILLAUME; Sec.-Gen. PAM RICKARDS.

**European Young Christian Democrats—EYCD:** 16 rue de la Victoire, 1060 Brussels, Belgium; tel. (2) 537-41-47; fax (2) 534-50-28; f. 1947; holds monthly seminars and meetings for young political leaders; conducts training in international political matters. Mems: 28 national organizations in 25 European countries. Pres. ENRICO LETTA (Italy); Sec.-Gen. MARC BERTRAND (Belgium). Publ. *EYCD File* (6 a year).

**La Francophonie:** c/o Agence de la Francophonie, 13 quai André-Citroën, 75015 Paris, France; tel. 1-44-37-33-00; fax 1-45-79-14-98; political grouping of French-speaking countries; conference of heads of state convened every two years to promote co-operation throughout the French-speaking world (1997: Hanoi, Viet Nam). Mems: Governments of 49 countries. Sec.-Gen. BOUTROS BOUTROS-GHALI (Egypt).

**Gulf of Guinea Commission** (Commission du Golfe de Guinée—CGG): f. Nov. 1999 to promote co-operation among member countries and the peaceful and sustainable development of natural resources in the sub-region. Mems: Angola, Cameroon, the Repub. of the Congo, Equatorial Guinea, Gabon, Nigeria, Sao Tomé e Principe.

**Hansard Society:** St Philips Bldg North, LSE, Sheffield St, London, WC2A 2EX, United Kingdom; tel. (20) 7955-7459; fax (20) 7955-7492; e-mail hansardsociety@lse.ac.uk; internet www.hansardsociety.org.uk; f. 1944 as Hansard Society for Parliamentary Government; aims to promote political education and research and the informed discussion of all aspects of modern parliamentary government. Dir SHELAGH DIPLOCK. Publ. *Parliamentary Affairs—A Journal of Comparative Politics* (quarterly).

**Inter-African Socialists and Democrats:** 6 rue al-Waquidi 1004, al-Menzah IV, Tunis, Tunisia; tel. 231-138; f. 1981 (as Inter-African Socialist Organization; name changed 1988). Sec.-Gen. SADOK FAYALA (Tunisia).

**International Alliance of Women:** 9/10 Queen St, Melbourne, Vic 3000, Australia; tel. (3) 9629-3653; fax (3) 9629-2904; e-mail toddsec@surfnetcity.com.au; f. 1904 to obtain equality for women in all fields and to encourage women to take up their responsibilities; to join in international activities. Mems: 78 national affiliates in 67 countries. Pres. PATRICIA GILES. Publ. *International Women's News* (quarterly).

**International Association for Community Development:** 179 rue du Débarcadère, 6001 Marcinelle, Belgium; tel. (71) 44-72-78; fax (71) 47-11-04; organizes annual international colloquium for community-based organizations. Sec.-Gen. PIERRE ROZEN. Publ. *IACD Newsletter* (2 a year).

**International Commission for the History of Representative and Parliamentary Institutions:** c/o John Rogister, Dept of History, 43–46 North Bailey, Durham DH1 3EX, United Kingdom; fax (191) 374-4754; f. 1936. Mems: 300 individuals in 31 countries. Pres. JOHN ROGISTER (UK); Sec. JOHN H. GREVER (USA). Publs *Parliaments, Estates and Representation* (annually), studies.

**International Democrat Union:** 32 Smith Sq., London, SW1P 3HH, United Kingdom; tel. (20) 7984-8052; fax (20) 7976-0486; e-mail idu@compuserve.com; internet www.idu.org; f. 1983; group of centre-right political parties; holds conference every six months. Mems: political parties in 35 countries, four assoc. mems. Exec. Sec. RICHARD NORMINGTON.

**International Federation of Resistance Movements:** c/o R. Maria, 5 rue Rollin, 75005 Paris, France; tel. 1-43-26-84-29; f. 1951; supports the medical and social welfare of former victims of fascism; works for peace, disarmament and human rights, against fascism and neo-fascism. Mems: 82 national organizations in 29 countries. Pres. ALIX LHOTE (France); Sec.-Gen. Prof. ILYA KREMER (Russia). Publs *Feuille d'information* (in French and German), *Cahier d'informations médicales, sociales et juridiques* (in French and German).

**International Institute for Peace:** Möllwaldplatz 5, 1040 Vienna, Austria; tel. (1) 504-43-76; fax (1) 505-32-36; f. 1957; non-governmental organization with consultative status at ECOSOC (see UN) and UNESCO; studies interdependence as a strategy for peace, conflict prevention and the transformation of central and eastern Europe. Mems: individuals and corporate bodies invited by the executive board. Pres. ERWIN LANC (Austria); Dir Prof. LEV VORONKOV (Russia). Publs *Peace and the Sciences* (quarterly, in English), occasional papers (2 or 3 a year, in English and German).

**International Institute for Strategic Studies:** 23 Tavistock St, London, WC2E 7NQ, United Kingdom; tel. (20) 7379-7676; fax (20) 7836-3108; e-mail iiss@iiss.org.uk; internet www.isn.eth3.ch/iiss/; f. 1958; concerned with the study of the role of force in international relations, including problems of international strategy, the ethnic, political and social sources of conflict, disarmament and arms control, peace-keeping and intervention, defence economics, etc.; independent of any government. Mems: 3,000. Dir Dr JOHN M. W. CHIPMAN. Publs *Survival* (quarterly), *The Military Balance* (annually), *Strategic Survey* (annually), *Adelphi Papers* (10 a year), *Strategic Comments* (10 a year).

**International Lesbian and Gay Association—ILGA:** 81 rue Marché-au-charbon, 1000 Brussels 1, Belgium; tel. and fax (2) 502-24-71; e-mail ilga@ilga.org; f. 1978; works to remove legal, social and economic discrimination against homosexual and bisexual women and men, and transexuals, throughout the world; co-ordinates political action at an international level; co-operates with other supportive movements. 1997 world conference: Cologne, Germany. Mems: 300 national and regional associations in 75 countries. Secs-Gen. JENNIFER WILSON, JORDI PETIT. Publ. *ILGA Bulletin* (quarterly).

**International Peace Bureau:** 41 rue de Zürich, 1201 Geneva, Switzerland; tel. (22) 7316429; fax (22) 7389419; e-mail ipb@gn.apc.org; internet www.ial.ch/ipb; f. 1892; promotes international co-operation for general and complete disarmament and the non-violent solution of international conflicts; co-ordinates and represents peace movements at the UN; conducts projects on the abolition of nuclear weapons and the role of non-governmental organizations in conflict prevention/resolution. Mems: 158 peace organizations in 40 countries. Pres. Maj. BRITT THEORIN; Sec.-Gen. COLIN ARCHER. Publs *Geneva Monitor* (every 2 months), *IPB Geneva News*.

**International Political Science Association:** c/o Prof. John Coakley, Dept. of Politics, Univ. College Dublin, Belfield, Dublin 4, Ireland; tel. (1) 706-8182; fax (1) 706-1171; e-mail ipsa@ucd.ie; internet www.ucd.ie/~ipsa/index.html; f. 1949; aims to promote the development of political science. Mems: 41 national associations, 100 institutions, 1,350 individual mems. Pres. Prof. THEODORE J. LOWI (USA); Sec.-Gen. JOHN COAKLEY. Publs *Participation* (3 a year), *International Political Science Abstracts* (6 a year), *International Political Science Review* (quarterly).

**International Union of Local Authorities:** POB 90646, 2509 LP, The Hague, Netherlands; tel. (70) 3066066; fax (70) 3500496; e-mail iula@iula-hq.nl; internet www.iula.org; f. 1913 to promote local government, improve local administration and encourage popular participation in public affairs. Activities include organization of a biennial international congress; operation of specific 'task forces' (Association Capacity–Building, Women in Local Government, Information Technology); development of intermunicipal relations to provide a link between local authorities of countries; maintenance of a permanent office for the collection and distribution of information on municipal affairs. Mems in over 110 countries; seven regional sections. Pres. MAX NG'ANDWE (Zambia); Sec.-Gen. JACQUES JOBIN.

**International Union of Young Christian Democrats—IUYCD:** 16 rue de la Victoire, 1060 Brussels, Belgium; tel. (2) 537-77-51; fax (2) 534-50-28; f. 1962. Mems: national organizations in 59 countries and territories. Sec.-Gen. MARCOS VILLASMIL (Venezuela). Publs *IUYCD Newsletter* (fortnightly), *Debate* (quarterly).

**Inuit Circumpolar Conference:** 170 Laurier Ave West, Suite 504, Ottawa, ON K1P 5V5, Canada; tel. (613) 563-2642; fax (613) 565-3089; f. 1977 to protect the indigenous culture, environment and rights of the Inuit people (Eskimoes), and to encourage co-operation among the Inuit; conferences held every three years. Mems: Inuit communities in Canada, Greenland, Alaska and Russia. Pres. ROSEMARIE KUPTANA. Publ. *ICC Arctic Policy Review*.

**Jewish Agency for Israel:** POB 92, 48 King George St, Jerusalem, Israel; tel. (2) 6202297; fax (2) 6202412; e-mail elibir@jazo.org.il; internet www.jafi.org.il; f. 1929; reconstituted 1971 as an instrument through which world Jewry could develop a national home. Constituents are: World Zionist Organization, United Israel Appeal, Inc. (USA), and Keren Hayesod. Chair. Exec. SALLAI MERIDOR; Chair. Bd. ALEX GRASS.

**Latin American Parliament** (Parlamento Latinoamericano): Avda Auro Soares de Moura Andrade 564, São Paulo, Brazil; tel. (11) 38246325; fax (11) 38246324; internet www.parlatino.org; f. 1965; permanent democratic institution, representative of all existing political trends within the national legislative bodies of Latin America; aims to promote the movement towards economic, political and cultural integration of the Latin American republics, and to uphold human rights, peace and security. Publs *Acuerdos, Resoluciones de las Asambleas Ordinarias* (annually), *Revista del Parlamento Latinoamericano* (annually); statements and agreements.

**Liberal International:** 1 Whitehall Place, London, SW1A 2HD, United Kingdom; tel. (20) 7839-5905; fax (20) 7925-2685; e-mail li@worldlib.org; internet www.worldlib.org/li/; f. 1947; world union of 83 liberal parties in 58 countries; co-ordinates foreign policy work of member parties, and promotes freedom, tolerance, democracy, international understanding, protection of human rights and market-based economics; has consultative status at ECOSOC of United Nations and the Council of Europe. Pres. ANNEMIE NEYTS-UYTTEBROECK; Sec.-Gen. JAN WEIJERS. Publ. *London Aerogramme* (monthly).

**Nato Parliamentary Assembly:** 3 place du Petit Sablon, 1000 Brussels, Belgium; tel. (2) 513-28-65; fax (2) 514-18-47; internet www.nna.be; f. 1955 as the NATO Parliamentarians' Conference; name changed 1966 to North Atlantic Assembly; renamed as above 1999; the inter-parliamentary assembly of the North Atlantic Alliance; holds two plenary sessions a year and meetings of committees (Political, Defence and Security, Economic, Scientific and Technical, Civilian Affairs) where parliamentarians from North America, western Europe and eastern Europe (associate delegates) examine the problems confronting the Alliance and European security issues in general. Pres. JAVIER RUPEREZ; Sec.-Gen. SIMON LUNN.

**Non-aligned Movement:** c/o Permanent Representative of South Africa to the UN, 333 East 38th St, 9th Floor, New York, NY 10016, USA (no permanent secretariat); tel. (212) 213-5583; fax (212) 692-2498; f. 1961 by a meeting of 25 Heads of State, aiming to link countries which refused to adhere to the main East-West military and political blocs; co-ordination bureau established in 1973; works for the establishment of a new international economic order, and especially for better terms for countries producing raw materials; maintains special funds for agricultural development, improvement of food production and the financing of buffer stocks; 'South Commission' (q.v.) promotes co-operation between developing countries; seeks changes in the United Nations to give developing countries greater decision-making power; in October 1995 member states urged the USA to lift its economic embargo against Cuba; summit conference held every three years, 12th conference of heads of state and government was held in Durban, South Africa, in 1998. Mems: 113 countries (at Sept. 1998).

**Open Door International** (for the Economic Emancipation of the Woman Worker): 16 rue Américaine, 1060 Brussels, Belgium; tel. (2) 537-67-61; f. 1929 to obtain equal rights and opportunities for women in the whole field of work. Mems in 10 countries. Hon. Sec. ADÈLE HAUWEL (Belgium).

**Organization for the Prohibition of Chemical Weapons—OPCW:** Johan de Wittlaan 32, 2517JR The Hague, Netherlands; tel. (70) 4163300; fax (70) 3063535; e-mail mediabr@opcw.org; internet www.opcw.org; f. 1997 to oversee implementation of the Chemical Weapons Convention, which aims to ban the development, production, stockpiling and use of chemical weapons. The Convention was negotiated under the auspices of the UN Conference on Disarmament and opened for signature in January 1993; it entered into force in April 1997, at which time the OPCW was inaugurated. Governed by an Executive Council, comprising representatives of 41 States Parties, elected on a regional basis; undertakes mandatory inspections of member states party to the Convention. Provisional 1999 budget: US $69m. Dir-Gen. JOSÉ MAURICIO BUSTANI (Brazil).

**Organization of Solidarity of the Peoples of Africa, Asia and Latin America** (Organización de Solidaridad de los Pueblos de Africa, Asia y América Latina—OSPAAAL): Apdo 4224 y 6130, Calle C No 670 esq. 29, Vedado, Havana 10400, Cuba; tel. (7) 30-5136; fax (7) 33-3985; f. 1966 at the first Conference of Solidarity of the Peoples of Africa, Asia and Latin America, to unite, co-ordinate and encourage national liberation movements in the three continents, to oppose foreign intervention in the affairs of sovereign states, colonial and neo-colonial practices, and to fight against racialism and all forms of racial discrimination; favours the establishment of a new international economic order. Mems: organizations in Angola, Republic of the Congo, Guatemala, Guinea, Democratic People's Republic of Korea, Palestine, Puerto Rico, South Africa, Syria and Viet Nam. Sec.-Gen. Dr RAMÓN PEZ FERRO. Publ. *Tricontinental* (quarterly).

**Organization of the Cooperatives of America** (Organización de las Cooperativas de América): Apdo postal 241263, Carrera 11, No. 86-32 Of. 101, Santafé de Bogotá, DC, Colombia; tel. (1) 610-3296; fax (1) 610-1912; f. 1963 for improving socio-economic, cultural and moral conditions through the use of the co-operative system; works in every country of the continent; regional offices sponsor plans of activities based on the most pressing needs and special conditions of individual countries. Mems: organizations in 23 countries and territories. Pres. Dr ARMANDO TOVAR PARADA; Exec. Sec. Dr CARLOS JULIO PINEDA. Publs *OCA News* (monthly), *América Cooperativa* (3 a year).

**Parliamentary Association for Euro-Arab Co-operation:** 21 rue de la Tourelle, 1040 Brussels, Belgium; tel. (2) 231-13-00; fax (2) 231-06-46; e-mail paeac@medea.be; internet www.medea.be; f. 1974 as an association of 650 parliamentarians of all parties from the national parliaments of the Council of Europe countries and from the European Parliament, to promote friendship and co-operation between Europe and the Arab world; Executive Committee holds annual joint meetings with Arab Inter-Parliamentary Union; represented in Council of Europe, Western European Union and European Parliament; works for the progress of the Euro-Arab Dialogue and a settlement in the Middle East which takes into account the national rights of the Palestinian people. Joint Chair. ROSELYNE BACHELOT (France), HENNING GJELLEROD (Denmark); Sec.-Gen. JEAN-MICHEL DUMONT (Belgium). Publs *Information Bulletin* (quarterly), *Euro-Arab and Mediterranean Political Fact Sheets* (2 a year).

**Party of European Socialists:** 60 rue Wiertz, 1047 Brussels, Belgium; tel. (2) 284-29-78; fax (2) 230-17-66; e-mail pes@pes.org; internet www.pes.org; f. 1974 as the Confederation of the Socialist Parties of the EC; affiliated to the Socialist International (q.v.). Mems: 21 full member parties, two associate, 17 with observer status. Chair. RUDOLF SCHARPING (Germany); Sec.-Gen. JEAN FRANÇOIS VALLIN (France).

**Rio Group:** f. 1987 at a meeting in Acapulco, Mexico, of eight Latin American government leaders, who agreed to establish a 'permanent mechanism for joint political action'; additional countries subsequently joined the Group (see below); holds annual summit meetings at presidential level. At the ninth presidential summit (Quito, Ecuador, September 1995) a 'Declaration of Quito' was adopted, which set out joint political objectives, including the strengthening of democracy; combating corruption, drugs-production and -trafficking and 'money laundering'; and the creation of a Latin American and Caribbean free trade area by 2005 (supporting the efforts of the various regional groupings). Opposes US legislation (the 'Helms-Burton' Act), which provides for sanctions against foreign companies that trade with Cuba; also concerned with promoting sustainable development in the region, the elimination of poverty, and economic and financial stability. The Rio Group holds annual ministerial conferences with the European Union. Mems: Argentina, Bolivia, Brazil, Chile, Colombia, Ecuador, Mexico, Panama, Paraguay, Peru, Uruguay, Venezuela.

**Socialist International:** Maritime House, Clapham, London, SW4 0JW, United Kingdom; tel. (20) 7627-4449; fax (20) 7720-4448; e-mail socint@gn.apc.org; internet www.gn.apc.org/socint; f. 1864; the world's oldest and largest association of political parties, grouping democratic socialist, labour and social democratic parties from every continent; provides a forum for political action, policy discussion and the exchange of ideas; works with many international organizations and trades unions (particularly members of ICFTU, q.v.); holds Congress every three years; the Council meets twice a year, and regular conferences and meetings of party leaders are also held; committees and councils on a variety of subjects and in different regions meet frequently. Mems: 66 full member parties, 25 consultative and 8 observer parties in 85 countries. There are three fraternal organizations and nine associated organizations, including: the Party of European Socialists (PES), the Group of the PES at the European Parliament and the International Federation of the Socialist and Democratic Press (q.v.). Pres. ANTONIO GUTTERES (Portugal); Gen. Sec. LUIS AYALA (Chile); Publ. *Socialist Affairs* (quarterly).

**International Falcon Movement—Socialist Educational International:** 3 rue Quinaux, 1030 Brussels, Belgium; tel. (2) 215-79-27; fax (2) 245-00-83; e-mail ifm-sei@infonie.be; f. 1924 to promote international understanding, develop a sense of social responsibility and to prepare children and adolescents for democratic life; co-operates with several institutions concerned with children, youth and education. Mems: about 1m.; 62 co-operating organizations in all countries. Pres. JESSI SÖRENSEN (Denmark); Sec.-Gen. ODETTE LAMBERT (Belgium). Publs *IFM-SEI Bulletin* (quarterly), *IFM-SEI Documents, Flash Infos* (6 a year), *Asian Regional Bulletin, Latin American Regional Bulletin*.

**International Union of Socialist Youth:** 1070 Vienna, Neustiftgasse 3/13, Austria; tel. (1) 523-12-67; fax (1) 523-12-679; e-mail iusy@isuy.org; internet www.iusy.org; f. 1907 as Socialist Youth International (present name from 1946) to educate young people in the principles of free and democratic socialism and further the co-operation of democratic socialist youth organizations; conducts international meetings, symposia, etc. Mems: 132 youth and student organizations in 100 countries. Pres. UMBERTO GENTILONI; Gen. Sec. LISA PELLING. Publs *IUSY Newsletter, FWG News, IUSY—You see us in Action*.

**Socialist International Women:** Maritime House, Old Town, Clapham, London, SW4 0JW, United Kingdom; tel. (20) 7627-4449; fax (20) 7720-4448; e-mail socintwomen@gn.apc.org; f. 1907 to strengthen relations between its members, to exchange experience and views, to promote the understanding among women of the aims of democratic socialism, to promote programmes to oppose any discrimination in society and to work for human rights in general and for development and peace. Mems: 131 organizations. Pres. DOLORS RENAU; Gen. Sec. MARLÈNE HAAS. Publ. *Women and Politics* (quarterly).

**Stockholm International Peace Research Institute—SIPRI:** Signalistgatan 9, 169 70 Solna, Sweden; tel. (8) 655-97-00; fax (8) 655-97-33; e-mail sipri@sipri.se; internet www.sipri.se; f. 1966; studies relate to international security and arms control, e.g. peacekeeping and regional security, chemical and biological warfare, production and transfer of arms, military expenditure, etc. About 50 staff mems, half of whom are researchers. Dir Dr ADAM DANIEL ROTFELD (Poland); Chair. Prof. DANIEL TARSCHYS (Sweden). Publs

*SIPRI Yearbook: Armaments, Disarmament and International Security*, monographs and research reports.

**Transparency International:** Otto-Suhr-Allee 97-99, 10585 Berlin, Germany; tel. (30) 3438200; fax (30) 34703912; e-mail ti@transparency.de; internet www.transparency.de; f. 1993; aims to promote governmental adoption of anti-corruption practices and accountability at all levels of the public sector; aims to ensure international business transactions conducted with integrity and without resort to corrupt practices. Formulates an annual Corruption Perception Index and a Bribe Payers Index. An International Anti-Corruption Conference is held every two years. Chair. Dr PETER EIGEN.

**Trilateral Commission:** 345 East 46th St, New York, NY 10017, USA; tel. (212) 661-1180; fax (212) 949-7268; e-mail admin@trilateral.org; internet www.trilateral.org; (also offices in Paris and Tokyo); f. 1973 by private citizens of western Europe, Japan and North America, to encourage closer co-operation among these regions on matters of common concern; by analysis of major issues the Commission seeks to improve public understanding of such problems, to develop and support proposals for handling them jointly, and to nurture the habit of working together in the 'trilateral' area. The Commission issues 'task force' reports on such subjects as monetary affairs, political co-operation, trade issues, the energy crisis and reform of international institutions. Mems: about 335 individuals eminent in academic life, industry, finance, labour, etc.; those currently engaged as senior government officials are excluded. Chairmen PAUL A. VOLCKER, OTTO Graf LAMBSDORFF, YOTANO KOBAYASHI; Dirs CHARLES B. HECK, PAUL REVAY, TADASHI YAMAMOTO. Publs *Task Force Reports, Triangle Papers.*

**Unrepresented Nations' and Peoples' Organization—UNPO:** Javastraat, 40A, 2585 AP, Netherlands; tel. (70) 360-3318; fax (70) 360-3346; e-mail unpo@unpo.nl; internet www.unpo.org; f. 1991 to provide an international forum for indigenous and other unrepresented peoples and minorities; provides training in human rights, law, diplomacy and public relations to UNPO members; provides conflict resolution services. Mems: 50 peoples and minorities. Gen.-Sec. HELEN CORBETT. Publs *UNPO News, UNPO Yearbook.*

**War Resisters' International:** 5 Caledonian Rd, London, N1 9DX, United Kingdom; tel. (20) 7278-4040; fax (20) 7278-0444; e-mail warresisters@gn.apc.org; internet www.gn.apc.org/warresisters; f. 1921; encourages refusal to participate in or support wars or military service, collaborates with movements that work for peace and non-violent social change. Mems: approx. 150,000. Chair. JOANNE SHEEHAN; Secs ROBERTA BACIC, LUCIA BRANDI. Publ. *Peace News* (quarterly).

**Women's International Democratic Federation:** c/o 'Femmes solidaires', 25 rue du Charolais, 75012 Paris, France; tel. 1-40-01-90-90; fax 1-40-01-90-81; e-mail fdif@fdif.eu.org; internet www.fdif.eu.org; f. 1945 to unite women regardless of nationality, race, religion and political opinion, so that they may work together to win and defend their rights as citizens, mothers and workers, to protect children and to ensure peace and progress, democracy and national independence. Structure: Congress, Secretariat and Executive Committee. Mems: 180 organizations in 101 countries as well as individual mems. Pres. SYLVIE JAN (France); Vice-Pres. MAYADA ABBASSI (Palestine). Publs *Women of the Whole World* (6 a year), *Newsletter.*

**World Council of Indigenous Peoples:** 100 Argyle Ave, 2nd Floor, Ottawa, K2P 1B6, Canada; tel. (613) 230-9030; fax (613) 230-9340; f. 1975 to promote the rights of indigenous peoples and to support their cultural, social and economic development. The Council comprises representatives of indigenous organizations from five regions: North, South and Central America, Pacific-Asia and Scandinavia; a general assembly is held every three years. Pres. CONRADO JORGE VALIENTE. Publ. *WCIP Newsletter* (4–6 a year).

**World Disarmament Campaign:** 45–47 Blythe St, London, E2 6LN, United Kingdom; tel. (20) 7729-2523; f. 1980 to encourage governments to take positive and decisive action to end the arms race, acting on the four main commitments called for in the Final Document of the UN's First Special Session on Disarmament; aims to mobilize people of every country in a demand for multilateral disarmament, to encourage consideration of alternatives to the nuclear deterrent for ensuring world security, and to campaign for a strengthened role for the UN in these matters. Chair. Dr FRANK BARNABY, Dr TONY HART. Publ. *World Disarm!* (6 a year).

**World Federalist Movement:** 777 UN Plaza, New York, NY 10017, USA; tel. (212) 599-1320; fax (212) 599-1332; e-mail wfm@igc.apc.org; f. 1947 to achieve a just world order through a strengthened United Nations; to acquire for the UN the authority to make and enforce laws for peaceful settlement of disputes, and to raise revenue under limited taxing powers; to establish better international co-operation in areas of environment, development and disarmament and to promote federalism throughout the world. Mems: 25,000 in 41 countries. Pres. Sir PETER USTINOV; Exec. Dir WILLIAM R. PACE. Publ. *World Federalist News* (quarterly).

**World Federation of United Nations Associations—WFUNA:** c/o Palais des Nations, 1211 Geneva 10, Switzerland; tel. (22) 7330730; fax (22) 7334838; f. 1946 to encourage popular interest and participation in United Nations programmes, discussion of the role and future of the UN, and education for international understanding. Plenary Assembly meets every two years; WFUNA founded International Youth and Student Movement for the United Nations (q.v.). Mems: national associations in 80 countries. Pres. HASHIM ABDUL HALIM (India); Sec.-Gen. L. H. HORACE PERERA (Sri Lanka) (acting). Publ. *WFUNA News.*

**World Peace Council:** 94 rue Jean-Pierre Timbaud, 75011 Paris, France; tel. 1-40-12-09-12; fax 1-40-11-57-87; e-mail 100144.1501@compuserve.com; f. 1950 at the Second World Peace Congress, Warsaw. Principles: the prevention of nuclear war; the peaceful co-existence of the various socio-economic systems in the world; settlement of differences between nations by negotiation and agreement; complete disarmament; elimination of colonialism and racial discrimination; respect for the right of peoples to sovereignty and independence. Mems: Representatives of national organizations, groups and individuals from 140 countries, and of 30 international organizations; Executive Committee of 40 mems elected by world assembly held every 3 years. Pres. ALBERTINA SISULU; Exec. Sec. LYSIANE ALEZARD. Publ. *Peace Courier* (monthly).

# Industrial and Professional Relations

See also the chapters on ICFTU, WCL and WFTU.

**Arab Federation of Petroleum, Mining and Chemicals Workers:** POB 5339, Tripoli, Libya; tel. (2) 608501; fax (2) 608989; f. 1961 to establish industrial relations policies and procedures for the guidance of affiliated unions; promotes establishment of trade unions in the relevant industries in countries where they do not exist. Publs *Arab Petroleum* (monthly), specialized publications and statistics.

**Association for Systems Management:** POB 38370, Cleveland, OH 44138-0370, USA; tel. (216) 243-6900; fax (216) 234-2930; f. 1947; an international professional organization for the advancement and self-renewal of information systems professionals throughout business and industry. Mems: 6,500 in 35 countries. Pres. WILLIAM MUNCH; Dir BOB LA PRAD. Publ. *Journal of Systems Management.*

**European Association for Personnel Management:** c/o ANDCP, 29 ave Hoche, 75008 Paris, France; tel. 1-45-63-03-65; fax 1-42-56-41-15; e-mail eamp@eamp.org; f. 1962 to disseminate knowledge and information concerning the personnel function of management, to establish and maintain professional standards, to define the specific nature of personnel management within industry, commerce and the public services, and to assist in the development of national associations. Mems: 22 national associations. Sec.-Gen. ARMAND NELLA (France); Pres. PEDRO NEUDES (Portugal).

**European Civil Service Federation:** Ave d'Aderghem, 1040 Brussels, Belgium; tel. (2) 230-84-33; fax (2) 230-69-05; f. 1962 to foster the idea of a European civil service of staff of international organizations operating in western Europe or pursuing regional objectives; upholds the interests of civil service members. Mems: local cttees in 12 European countries and individuals in 66 countries. Sec.-Gen. L. RIJNOUDT. Publ. *Eurechos.*

**European Construction Industry Federation:** 66 ave Louise, 1050 Brussels, Belgium; tel. (2) 514-55-35; fax (2) 511-02-76; e-mail fiec_bru@enter.org; internet www.fiec.be; f. 1905 as International European Construction Federation; present name 1999; Mems: 25 national employers' organizations in 18 countries. Pres. PAUL WILLEMEN (Belgium); Sec.-Gen. ERIC LEPAGE (France). Publ. *L'Entreprise Européenne.*

**European Federation of Conference Towns:** POB 182, 1040 Brussels, Belgium; tel. (2) 732-69-54; fax (2) 732-58-62; lays down standards for conference towns; provides advice and assistance to its members and other organizations holding conferences in Europe; undertakes publicity and propaganda for promotional purposes; helps conference towns to set up national centres. Exec. Dir ALINE LEGRAND.

**European Federation of Lobbying and Public Affairs** (Fédération Européenne du Lobbying et Public Affairs—FELPA): rue du Trône 61, 1050 Brussels, Belgium; tel. (2) 511-74-30; fax (2) 511-12-84; aims to enhance the development and reputation of the industry; encourages professionals active in the industry to sign a code of conduct outlining the ethics and responsibilities of people involved in lobbying or public relations work with the institutions of the EU. Pres. Y. DE LESPINAY.

**European Industrial Research Management Association—EIRMA:** 34 rue de Bassano, 75008 Paris, France; tel. 1-53-23-83-

10; fax 1-47-20-05-30; e-mail info@eirma.asso.fr; internet www.eirma.asso.fr; f. 1966 under auspices of the OECD (q.v.); a permanent body in which European science-based firms meet to discuss and study industrial research policy and management and take joint action in trying to solve problems in this field. Mems: 170 in 21 countries. Pres. Dr G. HAEMERS. Gen. Sec. B. A. WATKINSON. Publs *Annual Report, Conference Reports, Working Group Reports.*

**European Trade Union Confederation** (Confédération Européenne des Syndicats): 5 blvd du Roi Albert II, 1210 Brussels, Belgium; tel. (2) 224-04-11; fax (2) 224-04-54; e-mail etuc@etuc.org; internet www.etuc.org; f. 1973; comprises 74 national trade union confederations and 15 European industrial federations in 33 European countries, representing 60m. workers; holds congress every four years (1999—Helsinki, Finland). Gen. Sec. EMILIO GABAGLIO.

**Federation of International Civil Servants' Associations:** Palais des Nations, 1211 Geneva 10, Switzerland; tel. (22) 7988400; fax (22) 7330096; e-mail 100306.3212@compuserve.com; f. 1952 to co-ordinate policies and activities of member associations and unions, to represent staff interests before inter-agency and legislative organs of the UN and to promote the development of an international civil service. Mems: 27 associations and unions consisting of staff of UN organizations, 23 consultative associations and 13 inter-organizational federations with observer status. Pres. MARGARET ELDON. Publs *Annual Report, FICSA Newsletter, FICSA Update, FICSA circulars.*

**Graphical International Federation:** Valeriusplein 30, 1075 BJ Amsterdam, Netherlands; tel. (20) 671-32-79; fax (20) 675-13-31; f. 1925. Mems: national federations in 15 countries, covering 100,000 workers. Pres. L. VAN HAUDT (Belgium); Sec.-Gen. R. E. VAN KESTEREN (Netherlands).

**International Association of Conference Interpreters:** 10 ave de Sécheron, 1202 Geneva, Switzerland; tel. (22) 9081540; fax (22) 7324151; e-mail 100665.2456@compuserve.com; f. 1953 to represent professional conference interpreters, ensure the highest possible standards and protect the legitimate interests of members. Establishes criteria designed to improve the standards of training and recognizes schools meeting the required standards. Has consultative status with the UN and several of its agencies. Mems: 2,300 in 53 countries. Pres. MALICK SY (Switzerland); Exec. Sec. JOSYANE CRISTINA. Publs *Code of Professional Conduct, Yearbook* (listing interpreters), etc.

**International Association of Conference Translators:** 15 route des Morillons, 1218 Le Grand-Saconnex, Geneva, Switzerland; tel. (22) 7910666; fax (22) 7885644; e-mail secretariat@aitc.ch; f. 1962; represents revisers, translators, précis writers and editors working for international conferences and organizations, to protect the interests of those in the profession and help maintain high standards; establishes links with international organizations and conference organizers. Mems: 419 in 33 countries. Pres. GENEVIÈVE SÉRIOT (Switzerland); Exec. Sec. MICHEL BOUSSOMMIER (France). Publs *Directory, Bulletin.*

**International Association of Crafts and Small and Medium-Sized Enterprises—IACME:** c/o Centre patronal, 2 ave Agassi, CP 1215, 1001 Lausanne, Switzerland; tel. (21) 3197111; fax (21) 3197910; f. 1947 to defend undertakings and the freedom of enterprise within private economy, to develop training, to encourage the creation of national organizations of independent enterprises and promote international collaboration, to represent the common interests of members and to institute exchange of ideas and information. Mems: organizations in 26 countries. Chair. MARIO SECCA; Gen. Sec. JACQUES DESGRAZ.

**International Association of Medical Laboratory Technologists:** Adolf Fredriks Kyrkogata 11, 111 37 Stockholm, Sweden; tel. (8) 10-30-31; fax (8) 10-90-61; e-mail m.haag@iamlt.se; internet www.iamlt.se; f. 1954 to allow discussion of matters of common professional interest; to promote national organizations of medical laboratory technologists; to raise training standards and to standardize training in different countries in order to facilitate free exchange of labour; holds international congress every second year. Mems: 180,000 in 39 countries. Pres. WILLIAM R. YOUNGER; Exec. Dir MARGARETA HAAG. Publs *MedTecInternational* (2 a year), *Newsletter* (6 a year).

**International Association of Mutual Insurance Companies:** 114 rue La Boëtie, 75008 Paris, France; tel. 1-42-25-84-86; fax 1-42-56-04-49; f. 1963 for the establishment of good relations between its members and the protection of the general interests of private insurance based on the principle of mutuality. Mems: over 250 in 25 countries. Pres. E. J. ALDEWEIRELDT (Belgium); Sec.-Gen. A. TEMPELAERE (France). Publs *Mutuality* (2 a year), *AISAM Dictionary, Newsletter* (3 a year).

**International Confederation of Executive and Professional Staffs** (Confédération internationale des cadres): 30 rue de Gramont, 75002 Paris, France; f. 1950 to represent the interests of managerial and professional staff and to improve their material and moral status. Mems: national organizations in Austria, Belgium, Denmark, France, Germany, Italy, Luxembourg, Netherlands, Norway, Portugal, Spain, Sweden, UK, and international professional federations for chemistry and allied industries (FICCIA), mines (FICM), transport (FICT), metallurgical industries (FIEM), agriculture (FIDCA) and insurance (AECA). There are affiliated members in Hungary and Slovenia. Pres. HENRY BORDES-PAGES (France); Sec.-Gen. FLEMING FRIIS LARSEN (Denmark). Publ. *Cadres.*

**International Federation of Actors:** Guild House, Upper St Martin's Lane, London, WC2H 9EG, United Kingdom; tel. (20) 7379-0900; fax (20) 7379-8260; e-mail office@fia-actors.com; internet www.fia-actors.com; f. 1952. Mems: 92 performers' unions in 63 countries. Pres. TOMAS BOLME (Sweden); Gen. Sec. KATHERINE SAND.

**International Federation of Air Line Pilots' Associations:** Interpilot House, Gogmore Lane, Chertsey, Surrey, KT16 9AP, United Kingdom; tel. (1932) 571711; fax (1932) 570920; e-mail admin@ifalpa.org; f. 1948 to aid in the establishment of fair conditions of employment; to contribute towards safety within the industry; to provide an international basis for rapid and accurate evaluation of technical and industrial aspects of the profession. Mems: 93 associations, over 100,000 pilots. Pres. Capt. R. J. MCINNIS; Exec. Dir CATHY BILL.

**International Federation of Business and Professional Women:** Studio 16, Cloisters Business Centre, 8 Battersea Park Rd, London, SW8 4BG, United Kingdom; tel. (20) 7738-8323; fax (20) 7622-8528; e-mail bpwi_hq@compuserve.com; internet www.bpwintl.com; f. 1930 to promote interests of business and professional women and secure combined action by them. Mems: national federations, associate clubs and individual associates, totalling more than 200,000 mems in over 100 countries. Pres. SYLVIA G. PERRY; Dir TAMARA MARTINEZ. Publ. *BPW News International* (monthly).

**International Industrial Relations Association:** c/o International Labour Office, 1211 Geneva 22, Switzerland; tel. (22) 7996841; fax (22) 7998541; e-mail mennie@ilo.org; f. 1966 to encourage development of national associations of specialists, facilitate the spread of information, organize conferences, and to promote internationally planned research, through study groups and regional meetings; a World Congress is held every three years. Mems: 38 associations, 45 institutions and 1,100 individuals. Pres. Prof. TADASHI HANAMI; Sec. HONG-TRANG PERRET-NGUYÊN. Publs *IIRA Bulletin* (3 a year), *IIRA Membership Directory, IIRA Congress proceedings.*

**International Organisation of Employers—IOE:** 26 chemin de Joinville, BP 68, 1216 Cointrin/Geneva, Switzerland; tel. (22) 7981616; fax (22) 7988862; f. 1920, reorganized 1948; aims to establish and maintain contacts between members and to represent their interests at the international level; to promote free enterprise; and to assist the development of employers' organizations. General Council meets annually; there is an Executive Committee and a General Secretariat. Mems: 122 federations in 119 countries. Chair. JEAN-JACQUES OECHSLIN (France); Sec.-Gen. COSTAS KAPARTIS (Cyprus). Publ. *The Free Employer*.

**International Organization of Experts—ORDINEX:** 19 blvd Sébastopol, 75001 Paris, France; tel. 1-40-28-06-06; fax 1-40-28-03-13; e-mail contact@ordinex.net; internet www.ordinex.net; f. 1961 to establish co-operation between experts on an international level. Mems: 600. Pres. ALI EL KAÏBI (Tunisia); Sec.-Gen. PIERRE ROYER (France). Publ. *General Yearbook*.

**International Public Relations Association—IPRA:** Cardinal House, 7 Wolsey Rd, KT8 9EL, United Kingdom; tel. (20) 8481-7634; fax (20) 8481-7648; e-mail iprasec@compuserve.com; internet www.ipranet.org; f. 1955 to provide for an exchange of ideas, technical knowledge and professional experience among those engaged in international public relations, and to foster the highest standards of professional competence. Mems: 750 in 73 countries. Sec.-Gen. FRANS VOORHOEVE. Publs *Newsletter* (6 a year), *Frontline 21* (quarterly), *Members' Manual* (annually).

**International Society of City and Regional Planners—ISoCaRP:** Mauritskade 23, 2514 HD The Hague, Netherlands; tel. (70) 3462654; fax (70) 3617909; e-mail isocarp@bart.nl; internet www.soc.titech.ac.jp/isocarp; f. 1965 to promote better planning practice through the exchange of knowledge. Holds annual international congress (2000-Mexico). Mems: 450 in 64 countries. Pres. Prof. IR MAX VAN DEN BERG (Netherlands); Sec.-Gen. PETER JONQUIÈRE (Netherlands). Publs *News Bulletin* (4 a year), *Bulletin* (2 a year); seminar and congress reports.

**International Union of Architects:** 51 rue Raynouard, 75016 Paris, France; tel. 1-45-24-36-88; fax 1-45-24-02-78; e-mail uia@uia.architects.org; internet www.uia-architects.org; f. 1948; holds triennial congress. Mems: 106 countries. Pres. VASSILIS SGOUTAS (Greece); Sec.-Gen JEAN-CLAUDE RIGUET (France). Publ. *Lettre d'informations* (monthly).

**Latin American Federation of Agricultural and Food Industry Workers** (Federación Latinoamericana de Trabajadores Campesinos y de la Alimentación): Avda Baralt esq. Conde a Padre Cierra,

Edificio Bapgel, 4°, Oficina 42, Apdo 1422, Caracas 1010A, Venezuela; tel. (2) 863-2447; fax (2) 720463; e-mail lassofeltaca@cantv.net; f. 1961 to represent the interests of agricultural workers and workers in the food and hotel industries in Latin America. Mems: national unions in 28 countries and territories. Sec.-Gen. JOSÉ LASSO. Publ. *Boletín Luchemos* (quarterly).

**Nordic Industry Workers' Federation** (Nordiska Industriarbetare Federationen): Vasagatan 11, 9 tr, Box 1127, 111 81 Stockholm, Sweden; tel. (8) 7966100; fax (8) 114179; f. 1901 to promote collaboration between affiliates in Denmark, Finland, Iceland, Norway and Sweden; supports sister unions economically and in other ways in labour market conflicts. Mems: 408,000 in 17 unions. Pres. SUNE EKBÅGE (Sweden); Sec. ARNE LÖKKEN (Sweden).

**Organisation of African Trade Union Unity—OATUU:** POB M386, Accra, Ghana; tel. (21) 772574; fax (21) 772621; f. 1973 as a single continental trade union org, independent of international trade union organizations; has affiliates from all African trade unions. Congress, composed of four delegates from all affiliated trade union centres, meets at least every four years as supreme policy-making body; General Council, composed of one representative from all affiliated trade unions, meets annually to implement Congress decisions and to approve annual budget. Mems: trade union movements in 52 independent African countries. Sec.-Gen. HASSAN SUNMONU (Nigeria). Publ. *Voices of African Workers*.

**Pan-African Employers' Confederation:** c/o Federation of Kenya Employers, POB 48311, Nairobi, Kenya; tel. (2) 721929; fax (2) 721990; f. 1986 to link African employers' organizations and to represent them at the UN, the International Labour Organization and the OAU. Pres. HEDI JILIANI (Tunisia); Sec.-Gen. TOM DIJU OWUOR (Kenya).

**World Federation of Scientific Workers:** 1–7 Great George St, London, SW1P 3AA, United Kingdom; tel. (20) 7222-7722; e-mail 100764.1427@compuserve.com; f. 1946 to improve the position of science and scientists, to assist in promoting international scientific co-operation and to promote the use of science for beneficial ends; studies and publicizes problems of general, nuclear, biological and chemical disarmament; surveys the position and activities of scientists. Member organizations in 37 countries, totalling over 500,000 mems. Sec.-Gen. S. DAVISON (UK). Publ. *Scientific World* (quarterly in English, Esperanto, German and Russian).

**World Movement of Christian Workers—WMCW:** 124 blvd du Jubilé, 1080 Brussels, Belgium; tel. (2) 421-58-40; fax (2) 421-58-49; e-mail mmtc@skynet.be; f. 1961 to unite national movements that advance the spiritual and collective well-being of workers; general assembly every four years. Mems: 47 affiliated movements in 39 countries. Sec.-Gen. NORBERT KLEIN. Publ. *Infor-WMCW*.

**World Union of Professions** (Union mondiale des professions libérales): 38 rue Boissière, 75116 Paris, France; tel. 1-44-05-90-15; fax 1-44-05-90-17; e-mail info@umpl.com; internet www.umpl.com; f. 1987 to represent and link members of the liberal professions. Mems: 27 national inter-professional organizations, two regional groups and 12 international federations. Pres. LUIS EDUARDO GAUTERIO GALLO; Sec.-Gen. HENRY SALMON.

# Law

**African Bar Association:** POB 3451, 29 La Tebu St, East Cantonments, Accra, Ghana; f. 1971; aims to uphold the rule of law, to maintain the independence of the judiciary, and to improve legal services. Pres. CHARLES IDEHEN (Nigeria).

**African Society of International and Comparative Law:** Private Bag 520, Kairaba ave KSMD, Banjul, The Gambia; tel. 375476; fax 375469; f. 1986; promotes public education on law and civil liberties; aims to provide a legal aid and advice system in each African country, and to facilitate the exchange of information on civil liberties in Africa. Ninth annual conference: Abidjan, Côte d'Ivoire, 1997. Pres. MOHAMED BEDJAOUI; Sec. EMILE YAKPO (Ghana). Publs *Newsletter* (every 2 months), *African Journal of International and Comparative Law* (quarterly).

**Asian-African Legal Consultative Committee:** E-66, Vasant Marc, Vasant Vihar, New Delhi 110057, India; tel. (11) 6152251; fax (11) 6152041; f. 1956 to consider legal problems referred to it by member countries and to be a forum for Afro-Asian co-operation in international law and economic relations; provides background material for conferences, prepares standard/model contract forms suited to the needs of the region; promotes arbitration as a means of settling international commercial disputes; trains officers of member states; has permanent UN observer status. Mems: 44 states. Pres. A. B. K. AMIDU (Ghana); Sec.-Gen. TANG CHENG YUAN (China).

**Council of the Bars and Law Societies of the European Union—CCBE:** 45 rue de Trèves, 1040 Brussels, Belgium; tel. (2) 234-65-10; fax (2) 234-65-11; e-mail ccbe@ccbe.org; internet www.ccbe.org; f. 1960; the officially recognized organization in the European Union for the legal profession; liaises both among the bars and law societies themselves and between them and the Community institutions and the European Economic Area; also maintains contact with other international organizations of lawyers. The CCBE's principal objective is to study all questions affecting the legal profession in member states and to harmonize professional practice. Mems: 18 delegations from EU and EEA countries, and observers from Cyprus, the Czech Republic, Hungary, Poland, Slovakia, Slovenia, Switzerland and Turkey. Pres. DAG WERSEN; Sec.-Gen. VALÉRIE BAUER.

**Hague Conference on Private International Law:** Scheveningseweg 6, 2517 KT The Hague, Netherlands; tel (70) 3633303; fax (70) 3604867; e-mail secretariat@hcch.net; internet www.hcch.net; f. 1893 to work for the unification of the rules of private international law, Permanent Bureau f. 1955. Mems: 32 European and 15 other countries. Sec.-Gen. J. H. A. VAN LOON.

**Institute of International Law** (Institut de Droit international): c/o IUHEI, 132 rue de Lausanne, CP 36, 1211 Geneva 21, Switzerland; tel. (22) 7311730; e-mail gerardi@hei.unige.ch; f. 1873 to promote the development of international law by endeavouring to formulate general principles in accordance with civilized ethical standards, and by giving assistance to genuine attempts at the gradual and progressive codification of international law. Mems: limited to 132 members and associates from all over the world. Sec.-Gen. CHRISTIAN DOMINICÉ (Switzerland). Publ. *Annuaire de l'Institut de Droit international*.

**Inter-African Union of Lawyers:** 12 rue du Prince Moulay Abdullah, Casablanca, Morocco; tel. (2) 271017; fax (2) 204686; f. 1980; holds congress every three years. Pres. ABDELAZIZ BENZAKOUR (Morocco); Sec.-Gen. FRANÇOIS XAVIER AGONDJO-OKAWE (Gabon). Publ. *L'avocat africain* (2 a year).

**Inter-American Bar Association:** 815 15th St, NW, Suite 921, Washington, DC 20005-2201, USA; tel. (202) 393-1217; fax (202) 393-1241; f. 1940 to promote the rule of law and to establish and maintain relations between associations and organizations of lawyers in the Americas. Mems: 90 associations and 3,500 individuals in 27 countries. Sec.-Gen. LOUIS G. FERRANT (USA). Publs *Newsletter* (quarterly), *Conference Proceedings*.

**Intergovernmental Committee of the Universal Copyright Convention:** Division of Creativity, Cultural Industries and Copyright, UNESCO, 7 place de Fontenoy, 75700 Paris, France; tel. 1-45-68-47-05; fax 1-45-68-55-89; e-mail m.bastide@unesco.org; established to study the application and operation of the Universal Copyright Convention and to make preparations for periodic revisions of this Convention; and to study any other problems concerning the international protection of copyright, in co-operation with various international organizations. Mems: 18 states. Chair. 1997–99 MAYER GABAY (Israel). Publ. *Copyright Bulletin* (quarterly).

**International Association for the Protection of Industrial Property (AIPPI):** Bleicherweg 58, Postfach, 8027 Zürich 27, Switzerland; tel. (1) 2041260; fax (1) 2041261; e-mail general_secretariat@aippi.org; internet www.aippi.org; f. 1897 to encourage legislation regarding the international protection of industrial property and the development and extension of international conventions, and to make comparative studies of existing legislation with a view to its improvement and unification; holds triennial congress. Mems: 7,900 (national and regional groups and individual mems) in 108 countries. Exec. Pres. J. MICHAEL DOWLING (Australia); Sec.-Gen. VINCENZO M. PEDRAZZINI (Switzerland). Publs *Yearbook*, reports.

**International Association of Democratic Lawyers:** 21 rue Brialmont, 1210 Brussels, Belgium; tel. and fax (2) 223-33-10; e-mail iadl@ist.cerist.dz; f. 1946 to facilitate contacts and exchange between lawyers, to encourage study of legal science and international law and support the democratic principles favourable to maintenance of peace and co-operation between nations; promotes the preservation of the environment; conducts research on labour law, private international law, agrarian law, etc.; consultative status with UN. Mems: in 96 countries. Pres. AMAR BENTOUMI (Algeria); Sec.-Gen. JITENDRA SHARMA (India). Publ. *International Review of Contemporary Law*, in French, English and Spanish (2 a year).

**International Association of Juvenile and Family Court Magistrates:** Molenstraat 15, 4851 SG Ulvenhout, Netherlands; tel. (76) 561240; fax (76) 5311169; e-mail j.vandergoes@tip.nl; f. 1928 to consider questions concerning child welfare legislation and to encourage research in the field of juvenile courts and delinquency. Activities: international congress, study groups and regional meetings. Mems: 23 national associations. Pres. J. ZERMATTEN (Switzerland); Gen.-Sec. J. VAN DER GOES (Netherlands).

**International Association of Law Libraries:** POB 5709, Washington, DC 20016-1309, USA; tel. (804) 924-3384; fax (804) 982-2232; e-mail mber@loc.gov; internet www.iall.org; f. 1959 to encourage and facilitate the work of librarians and others concerned with the bibliographic processing and administration of legal materials. Mems: 600 from more than 50 countries (personal and institutional). Pres. LARRY B. WENGER (USA); Sec. MARIE-LOUISE H. BERNAL (USA). Publs *International Journal of Legal Information* (3 a year).

**International Association of Lawyers:** 25 rue du Jour, 75001 Paris, France; tel. 1-44-88-55-66; fax 1-44-83-55-77; e-mail uiacentre@wanandoo.fr; internet www.uianet.org; f. 1927 to promote the independence and freedom of lawyers, and defend their ethical and material interests on an international level; to contribute to the development of international order based on law. Mems: 250 asscns and 3,000 lawyers in over 120 countries. Pres. LUIS DELGADO DE MOLINA.

**International Association of Legal Sciences** (Association internationale des sciences juridiques): c/o CISS, 1 rue Miollis, 75015 Paris, France; tel. 1-45-68-25-59; fax 1-43-06-87-98; f. 1950 to promote the mutual knowledge and understanding of nations and the increase of learning by encouraging throughout the world the study of foreign legal systems and the use of the comparative method in legal science. Governed by a president and an executive committee of 11 members known as the International Committee of Comparative Law. National committees in 47 countries. Sponsored by UNESCO. Pres. Prof. WLADIMIR TOUMANOV (Russia); Sec.-Gen. M. LEKER (Israel).

**International Association of Penal Law:** BP 1146, 64013 Pau, Université Cédex, France; tel. 5-59-80-75-56; fax 5-59-80-75-59; e-mail aidp-pau@univ_pau.fr; f. 1924 to establish collaboration between those from different countries who are working in penal law, studying criminology, and promoting the theoretical and practical development of an international penal law. Mems: 1,800. Pres. Prof. M. C. BASSIOUNI; Sec.-Gen. Dr H. EPP. Publ. *Revue Internationale de Droit Pénal* (2 a year).

**International Bar Association:** 271 Regent St, London, W1R 7PA, United Kingdom; tel. (20) 7629-1206; fax (20) 7409-0456; internet www.ibanet.org; f. 1947; a non-political federation of national bar associations and law societies; aims to discuss problems of professional organization and status; to advance the science of jurisprudence; to promote uniformity and definition in appropriate fields of law; to promote administration of justice under law among peoples of the world; to promote in their legal aspects the principles and aims of the United Nations. Mems: 154 member organizations in 164 countries, 17,500 individual members in 173 countries. Pres. KLAUS BÖHLHOFF (Germany); Exec. Dir PAUL HODDINOTT (UK). Publs *International Business Lawyer* (11 a year), *International Bar News* (3 a year), *International Legal Practitioner* (quarterly), *Journal of Energy and Natural Resources Law* (quarterly).

**International Commission of Jurists:** POB 216, 81A ave de Châtelaine, 1219 Châtelaine/Geneva, Switzerland; tel. (22) 9793805; fax (22) 9793801; e-mail bovay@icj.org; f. 1952 to promote the understanding and observance of the rule of law and the protection of human rights throughout the world; maintains Centre for the Independence of Judges and Lawyers (f. 1978); contributes to the elaboration of international human rights instruments and their adoption and implementation by governments. Mems: 81 sections and affiliates. Pres. MICHAEL D. KIRBY (Australia); Sec.-Gen. ADAMA DIENG. Publs *CIJL Yearbook, The Review, ICJ Newsletter,* special reports.

**International Commission on Civil Status:** 3 place Arnold, 67000 Strasbourg, France; f. 1950 for the establishment and presentation of legislative documentation relating to the rights of individuals, and research on means of simplifying the judicial and technical administration concerning civil status. Mems: governments of Austria, Belgium, Croatia, France, Germany, Greece, Hungary, Italy, Luxembourg, Netherlands, Poland, Portugal, Spain, Switzerland, Turkey, United Kingdom. Pres. R. FRANK (Germany); Sec.-Gen. J. MASSIP (France).

**International Copyright Society:** 81667 Munich, Rosenheimer Strasse 11, Germany; tel. (89) 480-03-00; fax (89) 480-03-969; f. 1954 to enquire scientifically into the natural rights of the author and to put the knowledge obtained to practical application all over the world, in particular in the field of legislation. Mems: 393 individuals and corresponding organizations in 52 countries. Pres. Prof. Dr REINHOLD KREILE; Gen. Sec. Dr MARTIN VOGEL. Publs *Schriftenreihe* (61 vols), *Yearbook.*

**International Council of Environmental Law:** 53113 Bonn, Adenauerallee 214, Germany; tel. (228) 2692-240; fax (228) 2692-250; e-mail 100651.317@compuserve.com; f. 1969 to exchange information and expertise on legal, administrative and policy aspects of environmental questions. Exec. Governors Dr WOLFGANG BURHENNE, Dr ABDULBAR AL-GAIN. Publs *Directory, References, Environmental Policy and Law, International Environmental Law—Multilateral Treaties,* etc.

**International Criminal Police Organization—INTERPOL:** BP 6041, 69411 Lyon Cédex 06, France; tel. 4-72-44-70-00; fax 4-72-44-71-63; internet www.interpol.int; f. 1923, reconstituted 1946; aims to promote and ensure the widest possible mutual assistance between police forces within the limits of laws existing in different countries, to establish and develop all institutions likely to contribute to the prevention and suppression of ordinary law crimes; co-ordinates activities of police authorities of member states in international affairs, centralizes records and information regarding international criminals; operates a telecommunications network of 176 stations. The General Assembly is held annually. Mems: official bodies of 177 countries. Sec.-Gen. RAYMOND E. KENDALL (United Kingdom). Publs *International Criminal Police Review* (6 a year), *International Crime Statistics, Stolen Works of Art* (CD rom), *Interpol Guide to Vehicle Registration Documents* (annually).

**International Customs Tariffs Bureau:** 38 rue de l'Association, 1000 Brussels, Belgium; tel. (2) 501-87-74; fax (2) 218-30-25; e-mail bitd@euronet.be; internet www.bitd.org; the executive instrument of the International Union for the Publication of Customs Tariffs; f. 1890, to translate and publish all customs tariffs in five languages—English, French, German, Italian, Spanish. Mems: 71. Pres. JAN DE BOCK (Belgium); Dir MARTIN WERNER. Publs *International Customs Journal, Annual Report.*

**International Development Law Institute:** Via di San Sebastianello 16, 00187 Rome, Italy; tel. (06) 697-9261; fax (06) 678-1946; e-mail idli@idli.org; internet www.idli.org; f. 1983; designs and conducts courses and seminars for lawyers, legal advisors and judges from developing countries, central and eastern Europe and the former USSR; also provides in-country training workshops; training programme addresses legal skills, international commercial law, economic law reform, governance and the role of the judiciary. Dir L. MICHAEL HAGER.

**International Federation for European Law—FIDE:** Via Nicolò Tartaglia 5, 00197 Rome, Italy; fax (06) 8080731; f. 1961 to advance studies on European law among members of the European Community by co-ordinating activities of member societies and by organizing conferences every two years. Mems: 12 national associations. Pres. FRANCESCO CAPOTORIL; Sec.-Gen. Prof. P.-C. MÜLLER-GRAFF.

**International Federation of Senior Police Officers:** 26 rue Cambacères, 75008 Paris, France; tel. 1-49-27-40-67; fax 1-49-24-01-13; f. 1950 to unite policemen of different nationalities, adopting the general principle that prevention should prevail over repression, and that the citizen should be convinced of the protective role of the police; seeks to develop methods, and studies problems of traffic police. Set up International Centre of Crime and Accident Prevention, 1976. Established International Association against Counterfeiting, 1994. Mems: 34 national organizations. Sec.-Gen. JEAN-PIERRE HAVRIN (France). Publ. *International Police Information* (every 3 months, French, German and English).

**International Institute for the Unification of Private Law—UNIDROIT:** Via Panisperna 28, 00184 Rome, Italy; tel. (06) 696211; fax (06) 69941394; e-mail unidroit.rome@unidroit.org; internet www.unidroit.org; f. 1926 to undertake studies of comparative law, to prepare for the establishment of uniform legislation, to prepare drafts of international agreements on private law and to organize conferences and publish works on such subjects; holds international congresses on private law and meetings of organizations concerned with the unification of law; library of 215,000 vols. Mems: governments of 58 countries. Pres. LUIGI FERRARI BRAVO (Italy); Sec.-Gen. Prof. Dr HERBERT KRONKE (Germany). Publs *Uniform Law Review* (quarterly), *Digest of Legal Activities of International Organizations,* etc.

**International Institute of Space Law—IISL:** 3–5 rue Mario Nikis, 75015 Paris, France; tel. 1-45-67-42-60; fax 1-42-73-21-20; e-mail rtmasson@cyberway.com.sg; internet www.iafastro.com; f. 1959 at the XI Congress of the International Astronautical Federation; organizes annual Space Law colloquium; studies juridical and sociological aspects of astronautics and makes awards. Mems: individuals from many countries. Pres. NANDARI JASENTULYIANA (acting). Publs *Proceedings of Annual Colloquium on Space Law, Survey of Teaching of Space Law in the World.*

**International Juridical Institute:** Permanent Office for the Supply of International Legal Information, Spui 186, 2511 BW, The Hague, Netherlands; tel. (70) 3460974; fax (70) 3625235; e-mail iji@worldonline.nl; f.1918 to supply information on any matter of international interest, not being of a secret nature, respecting international, municipal and foreign law and the application thereof. Pres. A. V. M. STRUYCKEN; Dir A. L. G. A. STILLE.

**International Law Association:** Charles Clore House, 17 Russell Sq., London, WC1B 5DR, United Kingdom; tel. (20) 7323-2978; fax (20) 7323-3580; e-mail secretariat@ila-hq.org; internet www .ila-hq.org; f. 1873 for the study and advancement of international law, public and private; the promotion of international understanding and goodwill. Mems: 4,000 in 51 regional branches; 25 international cttees. Pres. Prof. HUNGDAH CHIU (Taiwan); Chair. Exec. Council Lord SLYNN OF HADLEY (UK); Sec.-Gen. DAVID J. C. WYLD (UK).

**International Maritime Committee** (Comité Maritime International): Markgravestraat 9, 2000 Antwerp, Belgium; tel. (3) 227-35-26; fax (3) 227-35-28; e-mail admin@cmi-imc.org; f. 1897 to contribute to the unification of maritime law by means of conferences, publications, etc. and to encourage the creation of national associations; work includes drafting of conventions on collisions at sea, salvage and assistance at sea, limitation of shipowners' liability, maritime mortgages, etc. Mems: national associations in 50 countries. Pres. PATRICK GRIGGS (UK); Administrator LEO DELWAIDE. Publs *CMI Newsletter, Year Book*.

**International Nuclear Law Association:** 29 sq. de Meeûs, 1000 Brussels, Belgium; tel. (2) 547-58-41; fax (2) 503-04-40; e-mail aidn.inla@skynet.be; f. 1972 to promote international studies of legal problems related to the peaceful use of nuclear energy, particularly the protection of man and the environment; holds conference every two years. Mems: 500 in 30 countries. Sec.-Gen. V. VERBRAEKEN.

**International Penal and Penitentiary Foundation:** c/o Dr K. Hobe, Bundesministerium der Justiz, 10104 Berlin, Germany; tel. (30) 20259226; fax (30) 20259525; f. 1951 to encourage studies in the field of prevention of crime and treatment of delinquents. Mems in 23 countries (membership limited to three people from each country) and corresponding mems. Pres. JORGE DE FIGUEIREDO DIAS (Portugal); Sec.-Gen. KONRAD HOBE (Germany).

**International Police Association—IPA:** 1 Fox Rd, West Bridgford, Nottingham, NG2 6AJ, United Kingdom; tel. (115) 945-5985; fax (115) 982-2578; e-mail wendy@ipa-iac.demon.co.uk; internet www.ipa-iac.org; f. 1950 to exchange professional information, create ties of friendship between all sections of police service, organize group travel, studies, etc. Mems: 273,000 in over 62 countries. International Sec.-Gen. A. F. CARTER.

**International Society for Labour Law and Social Security:** CP 500, 1211 Geneva 22, Switzerland; tel. (22) 7996343; fax (22) 7998542; e-mail servaisjm@ilo.org; f. 1958 to encourage collaboration between specialists; holds World Congress every three years as well as irregular regional congresses (Europe, Africa, Asia and Americas). Mems: 66 national associations of labour law officers. Pres. Prof. AMÉRICO PLÁ RODRÍGUEZ (Argentina); Sec.-Gen. J.-M. SERVAIS (Belgium).

**International Union of Latin Notaries** (Unión Internacional del Notariado Latino): Via Locatelli 5, 20124 Milan, Italy; f. 1948 to study and standardize notarial legislation and promote the progress, stability and advancement of the Latin notarial system. Mems: organizations and individuals in 68 countries. Sec. EMANUELE FERRARI. Publ. *Revista Internacional del Notariado* (quarterly), *Notarius International*.

**Law Association for Asia and the Pacific—LAWASIA:** GPO Box 3275, NT House, 11th Floor, 22 Mitchell St, Darwin, Northern Territory 0800, Australia; tel. (8) 8946-9500; fax (8) 8946-9505; e-mail lawasia@lawasia.asn.au; internet lawasia.asn.au; f. 1966; provides an international, professional network for lawyers to update, reform and develop law within the region; comprises five Sections and 21 Standing Committees in Business Law and General Practice areas which organize speciality conferences. Also holds a biennial conference (2001–Christchurch, New Zealand). Mems: national orgs in 23 countries; 2,500 mems in 55 countries. Sec.-Gen. ROSLYN WEST (Australia). Publs *Directory* (annually), *LAWASIA Update* (quarterly), *Directory* (annually), *Journal* (annually).

**Permanent Court of Arbitration:** Peace Palace, Carnegieplein 2, 2517 KJ The Hague, Netherlands; tel. (70) 3024165; fax (70) 3024167; e-mail bureau@pca-cpa.org; internet www.pca-cpa.org; f. by the Convention for the Pacific Settlement of International Disputes (1899, 1907) to enable immediate recourse to be made to arbitration for international disputes which cannot be settled by diplomacy, to facilitate the solution of disputes by international inquiry and conciliation commissions. Mems: governments of 89 countries. Sec.-Gen. TJACO VAN DEN HOUT (Netherlands).

**Society of Comparative Legislation:** 28 rue Saint-Guillaume, 75007 Paris, France; tel. 1-44-39-86-23; fax 1-44-39-86-28; e-mail slc@sky.fr; f. 1869 to study and compare laws of different countries, and to investigate practical means of improving the various branches of legislation. Mems: 600 in 48 countries. Pres. XAVIER BLANC-JOUVAN (France); Sec.-Gen. MARIE-ANNE GALLOT LE LORIER (France). Publs *Revue Internationale de Droit Comparé* (quarterly).

**Union of Arab Jurists:** POB 6026, Al-Mansour, Baghdad, Iraq; tel. (1) 8840051; fax (1) 8849973; f. 1975 to facilitate contacts between Arab lawyers, to safeguard the Arab legislative and judicial heritage; to encourage the study of Islamic jurisprudence; and to defend human rights. Mems: national jurists asscns in 15 countries. Sec.-Gen. SHIBIB LAZIM AL-MALIKI. Publ. *Al-Hukuki al-Arabi* (Arab Jurist).

**Union of International Associations:** 40 rue Washington, 1050 Brussels, Belgium; tel. (2) 640-41-09; fax (2) 643-61-99; e-mail uia@uia.be; internet www.uia.org/; f. 1907, present title adopted 1910; aims to facilitate the evolution of the activities of the world-wide network of non-profit organizations, especially non-governmental and voluntary associations; collects information on such organizations and makes this information available; promotes research on the legal, administrative and other problems common to these associations. Mems: 200 in 54 countries. Sec.-Gen. JACQUES RAEYMAECKERS (Belgium). Publs *Transnational Associations* (6 a year), *International Congress Calendar* (quarterly), *Yearbook of International Organizations, International Organization Participation* (annually), *Global Action Network* (annually), *Encyclopedia of World Problems and Human Potential, Documents for the Study of International Non-Governmental Relations, International Congress Science* series, *International Association Statutes* series, *Who's Who in International Organizations*.

**World Jurist Association—WJA:** 1000 Connecticut Ave, NW, Suite 202, Washington, DC 20036, USA; tel. (202) 466-5428; fax (202) 452-8540; e-mail wja@geocities.com; internet www.geocities.com/capitolhill/4165; f. 1963; promotes the continued development of international law and legal maintenance of world order; holds biennial world conferences, World Law Day, demonstration trials; organizes research programmes. Mems: lawyers, jurists and legal scholars in 155 countries. Pres. VED P. NANDA (USA); Exec. Vice-Pres. MARGARETHA M. HENNEBERRY (USA). Publs *The World Jurist* (English, every 2 months), Research Reports, *Law and Judicial Systems of Nations*, 3rd revised edn (directory), *World Legal Directory, Law/Technology* (quarterly), *World Law Review* Vols I–V (World Conference Proceedings), *The Chief Justices and Judges of the Supreme Courts of Nations* (directory), etc.

**World Association of Judges—WAJ:** 1000 Connecticut Ave, NW, Suite 202, Washington, DC 20036, USA; tel. (202) 466-5428; fax (202) 452-8540; f. 1966 to advance the administration of judicial justice through co-operation and communication among ranking jurists of all countries. Pres. Prince BOLA AJIBOLA (Nigeria).

**World Association of Law Professors—WALP:** 1000 Connecticut Ave, NW, Suite 202, Washington, DC 20036, USA; tel. (202) 466-5428; fax (202) 452-8540; f. 1975 to improve scholarship and education in dealing with matters related to international law. Pres. SERAFIN V. C. GUINGONA (Philippines).

**World Association of Lawyers—WAL:** 1000 Connecticut Ave, NW, Suite 202, Washington, DC 20036, USA; tel. (202) 466-5428; fax (202) 452-8540; f. 1975 to develop international law and improve lawyers' effectiveness in dealing with it. Pres. JACK STREETER (USA).

# Medicine and Health

**Council for International Organisations of Medical Sciences—CIOMS:** c/o WHO, ave Appia, 1211 Geneva 27, Switzerland; tel. (22) 7913406; fax (22) 7910746; f. 1949; general assembly every three years. Mems: 104 organizations. Pres. Prof. JOHN H. BRYANT; Sec.-Gen. Dr Z. BANKOWSKI. Publs *Calendar of International and Regional Congresses* (annually), *Proceedings of CIOMS, Round Table Conferences, International Nomenclature of Diseases*.

## MEMBERS OF CIOMS

Members of CIOMS include the following:

**FDI World Dental Federation:** 7 Carlisle St, London, W1V 5RG, United Kingdom; tel. (20) 7935-7852; fax (20) 7486-0183; internet www.fdi.org.uk\worldental; f. 1900. Mems: 129 national dental associations and 29 affiliates. Pres. Dr KATSUO TSURUMAKI (Japan); Exec. Dir Dr P. Å. ZILLÉN (Sweden). Publs *International Dental Journal* (every 2 months) and *FDI World* (every 2 months).

**International Academy of Legal and Social Medicine:** c/o 49A ave Nicolai, BP 8, 4802 Verviers, Belgium; tel. and fax (87) 22-98-21; f. 1938; holds an international Congress and General Assembly every three years, and interim meetings. Mems in 50 countries. Perm. Sec. and Treas. ELISABETH FRANCSON. Publs *Acta Medicinae Legalis et Socialis* (annually), *Newsletter* (3 a year).

**International Association for the Study of the Liver:** c/o Prof. June W. Halliday, Queensland Institute of Medical Research, The Bancroft Centre, PO Royal Brisbane Hospital, Brisbane, Australia 4029; tel. (7) 3362-0373; fax (7) 3362-0191; e-mail jhallid@tpgi.com.au; internet www.powerup.com.au/~iasl; Pres. Dr JOHN L. GOLLAN; Sec. Prof. JUNE W. HALLIDAY.

**International Association of Allergology and Clinical Immunology:** Health Science Center, State Univ. of New York at Stony Brook, Stony Brook, NY 11794, USA; tel. (414) 276-6445; fax (414) 276-3349; f. 1945 to further work in the educational, research and practical medical aspects of allergic and immunological diseases; 1997 Congress: Cancun, Mexico. Mems: 42 national societies. Pres. ALBERT OEHLING (Spain); Sec.-Gen. ALLEN KAPLAN (USA); Exec. Sec. R. IBER (USA). Publ. *Allergy and Clinical Immunology News* (6 a year).

**International College of Surgeons:** 1516 N. Lake Shore Drive, Chicago, IL 60610, USA; tel. (312) 642-3555; fax (312) 787-1624; e-mail info@icsglobal.org; internet www.icsglobal.org; f. 1935, as a world-wide federation of surgeons and surgical specialists for the advancement of the art and science of surgery, to create a common bond among the surgeons of all nations and promote the highest standards of surgery without regard to nationality, creed, or colour; sends teams of surgeons to developing countries to teach local surgeons; provides research and scholarship grants, organizes surgical congresses around the world; manages the International Museum of Surgical Science in Chicago. Mems: about 14,000 in 111 countries. Pres. Prof. WILSON POLLARA (USA); Exec. Dir MAX DOWNHAM (USA). Publ. *International Surgery* (quarterly).

**International Diabetes Federation:** 1 rue Defacqz, 1000 Brussels, Belgium; tel. (2) 538-55-11; fax (2) 538-51-14; e-mail idf@idf.org; internet www.idf.org; f. 1949 to help in the collection and dissemination of information regarding diabetes and to improve the welfare of people suffering from that disease. Mems: 161 associations in 129 countries. Pres. MARIA L. DEALVA; Exec. Dir MARTA LEVY. Publs *Diabetes Voice, Bulletin of the IDF* (quarterly).

**International Federation of Clinical Neurophysiology:** c/o Prof. G. Caruso, Clinica Neurologica, Univ. di Napoli 'Federico II', Via S. Panini 5, 80131 Naples, Italy; tel. (081) 746-3793; fax (081) 546-9861; f. 1949 to attain the highest level of knowledge in the field of electro-encephalography and clinical neurophysiology in all the countries of the world. Mems: 48 organizations. Pres. Prof. MARC NUWER; Sec. Prof. HIROSHI SHIBASAKI. Publs *The EEG Journal* (monthly), *Evoked Potentials* (every 2 months), *EMG and Motor Control* (every 2 months).

**International Federation of Oto-Rhino-Laryngological Societies:** Oosterveldlaan 24, 2610 Wilrijk, Belgium; tel. and fax (3) 443-36-11; e-mail ifos@uia.ua.ac.be; internet www.ifosworld.org; f. 1965 to initiate and support programmes to protect hearing and prevent hearing impairment; Congresses every four years. Pres. G. J. MCCAFFERTY (Australia); Sec.-Gen. P. W. ALBERTI. Publ. *IFOS Newsletter* (quarterly).

**International Federation of Surgical Colleges:** c/o Prof. S. W. A. Gunn, La Panetiere, 1279 Bogis-Bossey, Switzerland; tel. (22) 7762161; fax (22) 7766417; e-mail muldoon@mail.med.upenn.edu; f. 1958 to encourage high standards in surgical training; co-operates with the World Health Organization in developing countries; conducts international symposia; receives volunteers to serve as surgical teachers in developing countries; provides journals and text books for needy medical schools; offers travel grants. Mems: colleges or associations in 55 countries, and 420 individual associates. Pres. Prof. JONATHAN MEAKINS (Canada); Hon. Sec. Prof. S. W. A. GUNN. Publ. *World Journal of Surgery*.

**International League of Associations for Rheumatoloy:** c/o Dr J. Sergent, Chief Medical Officer, Vanderbilt Univ., 3810 Nashville, TN 37232-5545, USA; tel. (615) 343-9324; fax (615) 343-6478; f. 1927 to promote international co-operation for the study and control of rheumatic diseases; to encourage the foundation of national leagues against rheumatism; to organize regular international congresses and to act as a connecting link between national leagues and international organizations. Mems: 13,000. Pres. Dr ROBERTO ARINOVICHE (Chile); Sec.-Gen. Dr JOHN SERGENT (USA). Publs *Annals of the Rheumatic Diseases* (in the UK), *Revue du Rhumatisme* (in France), *Reumatismo* (in Italy), *Arthritis and Rheumatism* (in the USA), etc.

**International Leprosy Association (ILA):** c/o ALM, 1 ALM Way, Greenville, SC 29601, USA; tel. (864) 271-7040; fax (864) 271-7062; e-mail amlep@leprosy.org; f. 1931 to promote international co-operation in work on leprosy, from which some 1m. people still suffer; holds congress every five years (2002—Brazil). Pres. Dr YO YUASA (Japan); Sec. Dr PIETER FEENSTRA (Netherlands). Publ. *International Journal of Leprosy and Other Mycobacterial Diseases* (quarterly).

**International Pediatric Association:** c/o Univ. of Rochester School of Medicine and Dentistry, Dept. of Pediatrics (Rm 4-8104), 601 Elmwood, Rochester NY 14642-8777, USA; tel. (716) 275-0225; fax (716) 273-1038; f. 1912; holds triennial congresses and regional and national workshops. Mems: 135 national paediatric societies in 131 countries, 9 regional affiliate societies, 9 paediatric specialty societies. Pres. Prof. GAVIN C. ARNEIL (United Kingdom); Exec. Dir Dr ROBERT J. HAGGERTY. Publ. *International Child Health* (quarterly).

**International Rhinologic Society:** c/o Prof. Clement, ENT-Dept, AZ-VUB, Laarbeeklaan 101, 1090 Brussels, Belgium; tel. (2) 477-60-02; fax (2) 477-64-23; e-mail knoctp@az.vub.ac.be; f. 1965; holds congress every four years. Pres. EUGENE B. KERN (USA); Sec. Prof. P. A. R. CLEMENT (Belgium). Publ. *Rhinology*.

**International Society of Audiology:** University Hospital Rotterdam, Audiological Centre, Molewaterplein 40, 3015 GD Rotterdam, Netherlands; tel. (10) 463-4586; fax (10) 463-3102; e-mail verschuure@kno.fgg.eur.nl; f. 1952. Mems: 300 individuals. Pres. Prof. G. MENCHER; Gen. Sec. Dr J. VERSCHUURE. Publ. *Audiology* (every 2 months).

**International Society of Dermatopathology:** 1398 Semoran Blvd, Suite 102, Casselberry, FL 32707, USA; tel. (407) 678-5563; e-mail isdpoffice@aol.com; f. 1958; holds quinquennial congress. Pres. Dr JORGE SANCHEZ; Sec. Dr LORENZO CERRONI.

**International Society of Internal Medicine:** Dept. of Medicine, Regionalspital, 4900 Langenthal, Switzerland; tel. (62) 9163102; fax (62) 9164155; e-mail r.streuli@sro.ch; internet www.acponline.org/isim; f. 1948 to encourage research and education in internal medicine. Mems: 51 national societies, 3,000 individuals in 54 countries. Congresses: Manila, Philippines 1996; Lima, Peru 1998. Pres. Prof. AKIHIRO IGATA (Japan); Sec. Prof. ROLF A. STREULI (Switzerland).

**International Society of Physical and Rehabilitation Medicine:** c/o Dr J. Jimenez, 600 University Ave, Rm 215, Toronto, M5G 1XJ, Canada; f. 1999 by merger of International Federation of Physical Medicine and Rehabilitation (f. 1952) and International Rehabilitation Medicine Association (f. 1968); World Congress to be held in Amsterdam, the Netherlands, in 2001. Mems in 68 countries.

**International Union against Cancer:** 3 rue du Conseil Général, 1205 Geneva, Switzerland; tel. (22) 8091811; fax (22) 8091810; e-mail info@uicc.org; internet www.uicc.org; f. 1933 to promote on an international level the campaign against cancer in its research, therapeutic and preventive aspects; organizes International Cancer Congress every four years; administers the American Cancer Society International Cancer Research Fellowships, the International Cancer Research Technology Transfer Fellowships, the Yamagiwa-Yoshida Memorial International Cancer Study Grants and the International Oncology Nursing Fellowships; conducts worldwide programmes of campaign organization, public education and patient support, detection and diagnosis, epidemiology and prevention, professional education, tobacco and cancer, treatment of cancer and tumour biology. Mems: voluntary national organizations, private or public cancer research and treatment organizations and institutes and governmental agencies in more than 80 countries. Pres. Dr E. ROBINSON (Israel); Sec.-Gen. Dr G. P. MURPHY (USA); Exec. Dir A. J. TURNBULL. Publs *UICC International Directory of Cancer Institutes and Organizations* (every 4 years), *International Journal of Cancer* (18 a year), *UICC News* (quarterly), *International Calendar of Meetings on Cancer* (2 a year).

**Latin American Association of National Academies of Medicine:** Col 7 No 60–15, Santafé de Bogotà, Colombia; tel. (1) 2493122; fax (1) 2128670; f. 1967. Mems: nine national Academies. Pres. Dr PLUTARCO NARANJO (Peru); Sec. Dr ALBERTO CÁRDENAS-ESCOVAR (Colombia).

**Medical Women's International Association:** 50931 Cologne, Herbert-Lewin-Str. 1, Germany; tel. (221) 4004558; fax (221) 4004557; e-mail mwia@aol.com; internet members.aol.com/mwia/index.htm; f. 1919 to facilitate contacts between medical women and to encourage their co-operation in matters connected with international health problems. Mems: national associations in 43 countries, and individuals. Pres. Dr LILA S. KROSER (USA); Sec.-Gen. Dr WALTRAUD DIEKHAUS (Germany). Publ. *MWIA UPDATE* (3 a year).

**Organisation panafricaine de lutte contre le SIDA—OPALS:** 15/21 rue de L'Ecole de Médecine, 75006 Paris, France; tel. 1-43-26-72-28; fax 1-43-29-70-93; f. 1988; disseminates information relating to the treatment and prevention of AIDS; provides training of medical personnel; promotes co-operation between African medical centres and specialized centres in the USA and Europe. Publ. *OPALS Liaison*.

**World Federation for Medical Education:** University of Edinburgh Centre for Medical Education, 11 Hill Square, Edinburgh, EH8 9DR, United Kingdom; tel. (131) 650-6209; fax (131) 650-6537; f. 1972; promotes and integrates medical education world-wide; links regional and international associations, and has official relations with WHO, UNICEF, UNESCO, UNDP and the World Bank. Pres. Prof. H. J. WALTON.

**World Federation of Associations of Paediatric Surgeons:** c/o Prof. J. Boix-Ochoa, Clinica Infantil 'Vall d'Hebrón', Departamento de Cirugía Pediátrica, Valle de Hebrón, s/n, Barcelona 08035, Spain; f. 1974. Mems: 50 associations. Pres. Prof. W. MAIER; Sec. Prof. J. BOIX-OCHOA.

**World Federation of Neurology:** 12 Chandos St, London, W1M 9DE, United Kingdom; tel. (20) 7323-4011; fax (20) 7323-4012; e-mail wfnlondon@aol.com; f. 1955 as International Neurological Congress, present title adopted 1957. Aims to assemble members of various congresses associated with neurology, and organize co-operation of neurological researchers. Organizes Congress every four years. Mems: 23,000 in 70 countries. Pres. Dr J. F. TOOLE (USA); Sec.-Treas. Dr R. GODWIN-AUSTEN (UK); Administrator K. M. NEWTON (UK). Publs *Journal of the Neurological Sciences, World Neurology* (quarterly).

**World Heart Federation:** 34 rue de l'Athénée, CP 117, 1211 Geneva 12, Switzerland; tel. (22) 3476755; fax (22) 3471028; e-mail worldheart@compuserve.com; internet www.worldheart.org; f. 1978 as International Society and Federation of Cardiology, through merger of the International Society of Cardiology and the International Cardiology Federation; name changed as above 1998; aims to promote the study, prevention and relief of cardiovascular diseases through scientific and public education programmes and the exchange of materials between its affiliated societies and foundations and with other agencies having related interests. Organizes world congresses every four years. Mems: national cardiac societies and heart foundations in 84 countries. Pres. Dr T.-F. TSE (Hong Kong);

Sec. Dr J. G. PAPP (Hungary); Exec. Dir M. B. DE FIGUEIREDO. Publs *CVD Prevention, Heartbeat* (quarterly).

**World Medical Association:** 28 ave des Alpes, 01210 Ferney-Voltaire, France; tel. 4-50-40-75-75; fax 4-50-40-59-37; e-mail wma@iprolink.fr; internet www.wma.net; f. 1947 to achieve the highest international standards in all aspects of medical education and practice, to promote closer ties among doctors and national medical associations by personal contact and all other means, to study problems confronting the medical profession and to present its views to appropriate bodies. Structure: annual General Assembly and Council (meets twice a year). Mems: 65 national medical associations. Pres. Dr D. H. JOHNSON (USA); Sec.-Gen. Dr DELON HUMAN (South Africa). Publ. *The World Medical Journal* (6 a year).

**World Organization of Gastroenterology:** II Medizinische Klinik und Poliklinik der Technischen Universität München, Ismaninger Str. 22, 81675 Munich, Germany; tel. (89) 41402250; fax (89) 41404871; f. 1958 to promote clinical and academic gastroenterological practice throughout the world, and to ensure high ethical standards. Mems in 80 countries. Sec.-Gen. MEINHARD CLASSEN.

**World Psychiatric Association:** Mt Sinai School of Medicine, Fifth Ave and 100th St, POB 1093, New York, NY 10029-6574, USA; tel. (212) 241-6133; fax (212) 426-0437; e-mail wpa@dti.net; internet www.wpanet.org; f. 1961 for the exchange of information concerning the problems of mental illness and the strengthening of relations between psychiatrists in all countries; organizes World Psychiatric Congresses and regional and inter-regional scientific meetings. Mems: 140,000 psychiatrists in 93 countries. Pres. NORMAN SARTORIUS (Switzerland); Sec.-Gen. Dr JUAN ENRIQUE MEZZICH (USA).

## ASSOCIATE MEMBERS OF CIOMS

Associate members of CIOMS include the following:

**Asia Pacific Academy of Ophthalmology:** c/o Prof. Arthur S. M. Lim, Eye Clinic Singapura, 6A Napier Rd, 02-38 Gleneagles Annexe Block Gleneagles Hospital, Singapore 258500; tel. 466-6666; fax 733-3360; f. 1956; holds congress every two years. Pres. S. SELVARAJAH (Malaysia); Sec.-Gen. Prof. ARTHUR S. M. LIM (Singapore).

**International Association of Medicine and Biology of the Environment:** c/o 115 rue de la Pompe, 75116 Paris, France; tel. 1-45-53-45-04; fax 1-45-53-41-75; e-mail celine.abbou@free.fr; f. 1971 with assistance from the UN Environment Programme; aims to contribute to the solution of problems caused by human influence on the environment; structure includes 13 technical commissions. Mems: individuals and organizations in 73 countries. Hon. Pres. Prof. R. DUBOS; Pres. Dr R. ABBOU.

**International Committee of Military Medicine:** Hôpital Militaire Reine Astrid, rue Bruyn, 1120 Brussels, Belgium; tel. (2) 264-43-48; fax (2) 264-43-67; f. 1921. Mems: official delegates from 94 countries. Pres. Dr R. SCHLÖGEL (Austria); Sec.-Gen. Col Dr J. SANABRIA (Belgium). Publ. *Revue Internationale des Services de Santé des Forces Armées* (quarterly).

**International Congress on Tropical Medicine and Malaria:** congress held every four years to work towards the solution of the problems concerning malaria and tropical diseases; 1996 congress: Japan. Pres. Dr S. SORNMANI.

**International Council for Laboratory Animal Science—ICLAS:** Canadian Council on Animal Care, 315-350 Albert Street, Ottawa, Ontario, K1R 1B1, Canada; tel. (613) 238-4031 ext. 28; fax (613) 238-2837; e-mail gdemers@bart.ccac.ca; internet www.iclas.org; f. 1956. Pres. Prof. STEVEN PAKES (USA); Sec.-Gen. Dr GILLES DEMERS (Canada).

**International Federation of Clinical Chemistry and Laboratory Medicine:** 30 rue Lionnois, 54000 Nancy, France; tel. (2) 3-83-35-26-16; fax 3-83-32-13-22; e-mail thirion@ifccts.u-nancy.fr; f. 1952. Mems: 76 national societies (about 33,000 individuals). Pres. Prof. M. MÜLLER (Austria); Sec. Dr R. BAIS (Australia). Publs *Journal* (quarterly), *Annual Report*.

**International Medical Society of Paraplegia:** National Spinal Injuries Centre, Stoke Mandeville Hospital, Aylesbury, Bucks, HP21 8AL, United Kingdom; tel. (1296) 315866; fax (1296) 315870; e-mail imsop@bucks.net; Pres. Dr HANS L. FRANKEL; Hon. Sec. Prof. J. J. WYNDALE. Publ. *Spinal Cord*.

**International Society of Blood Transfusion:** Gateway House, Picadilly South, Manchester M60 7LP, United Kingdom; tel. (161) 236-2263; fax (161) 236-0519; f. 1937. Mems: about 1,300 in 100 countries. Pres. S. LEONG (Hong Kong); Sec.-Gen. H. GUNSON (UK). Publ. *Transfusion Today* (quarterly).

**Rehabilitation International:** 25 East 21st St, New York, NY 10010, USA; tel. (212) 420-1500; fax (212) 505-0871; f. 1922 to improve the lives of disabled people through the exchange of information and research on equipment and methods of assistance; organizes international conferences and co-operates with UN agencies and other international organizations. Mems: organizations in 92 countries. Pres. Dr ARTHUR O'REILLY; Sec.-Gen. SUSAN PARKER. Publs *International Rehabilitation Review, Rehabilitación* (2 a year).

**Transplantation Society:** c/o Dr Felix Rapaport, PR Transplant Program, University Hospital, Health Science Centre, State Univ. of New York at Stony Brook, Stony Brook, NY 11794-8192, USA; tel. (516) 444-2209; fax (516) 444-3831; e-mail rapaport@surg.som.sunysb.edu; Sec. EDUARDO A. SANTIAGO-DELPÍN.

**World Federation of Associations of Clinical Toxicology Centres and Poison Control Centres:** c/o Prof. Jacques Descotes, Centre anti-poisons, Pavilion N, Hôpital Edouard Herriot, 69009 Lyon, France. Pres. Prof. A. FURTADO RAHDE; Sec. Prof. JACQUES DESCOTES.

## OTHER ORGANIZATIONS

**Aerospace Medical Association:** 320 So. Henry St, Alexandria, VA 22314, USA; tel. (703) 739-2240; fax (703) 739-9652; e-mail rrayman@asma.org; f. 1929 as Aero Medical Association; to advance the science and art of aviation and space medicine; to establish and maintain co-operation between medical and allied sciences concerned with aerospace medicine; to promote, protect, and maintain safety in aviation and astronautics. Mems: individual, constituent and corporate in 75 countries. Pres. ROGER F. LANDRY (USA); Exec. Dir RUSSELL B. RAYMAN (USA). Publ. *Aviation Space and Environmental Medicine* (monthly).

**Asian-Pacific Dental Federation:** 242 Tanjong Katong Rd, Singapore 437030; tel. 3453125; fax 3442116; e-mail bibi@pacific.net.sg; f. 1955 to establish closer relationship among dental associations in Asian and Pacific countries and to encourage research on dental health in the region; holds congress every year. Mems: 19 national associations. Sec.-Gen. Dr OLIVER HENNEDIGE. Publ. *Asian Dentist* (every 2 months).

**Association for Paediatric Education in Europe:** c/o Dr Claude Billeaud, Dept. Néonatal Médicine, Maternité-CHU Pellegrin, 33076 Bordeaux Cédex, France; fax 5-56-79-60-38; e-mail claude.billeaud@neonata.u-bordeaux2.fr; internet www.atinternet.com/apee; f. 1970 to promote research and practice in educational methodology in paediatrics. Mems: 80 in 20 European countries. Pres. Dr JUAN BRINES (Spain); Sec.-Gen. Dr CLAUDE BILLEAUD (France).

**Association of National European and Mediterranean Societies of Gastroenterology—ASNEMGE:** c/o Mrs A. C. M. van Dijk-Meijer, Wolkendek 5, 3454 TG De Meern, Netherlands; tel. (30) 6667400; fax (30) 6622808; e-mail info@asnemge.org; internet www.asnemge.org; f. 1947 to facilitate the exchange of ideas between gastroenterologists and disseminate knowledge; organizes International Congress of Gastroenterology every four years. Mems in 37 countries, national societies and sections of national medical societies. Pres. Prof. COLM D'MORAÍN (Ireland); Sec. Prof. JØRGEN RASK-MADSEN (Denmark).

**Balkan Medical Union:** 1 rue G. Clémenceau, 70148 Bucharest, Romania; tel. (1) 6137857; fax (1) 3121570; f. 1932; studies medical problems, particularly ailments specific to the Balkan region, to promote a regional programme of public health; enables exchange of information between doctors in the region; organizes research programmes and congresses. Mems: doctors and specialists from Albania, Bulgaria, Cyprus, Greece, Moldova, Romania, Turkey and the former Yugoslav republics. Pres. Prof. NIKI AGNANTIS (Greece); Sec.-Gen. (1997–2000) Prof. Dr VASILE CÂNDEA (Romania). Publs *Archives de l'union médicale Balkanique* (quarterly), *Bulletin de l'union médicale Balkanique* (6 a year), *Annuaire*.

**European Association for Cancer Research:** c/o P. Saunders, Cancer Research Laboratories, University of Nottingham, University Park, Nottingham, NG7 2RD, United Kingdom; tel. and fax (115) 9515114; e-mail paul.saunders@nottingham.ac.uk; internet www.oncoweb.com/EACR; f. 1968 to facilitate contact between cancer research workers and to organize scientific meetings in Europe. Mems: over 3,000 in more than 40 countries in and outside Europe. Pres. E. OLAH; Sec. Dr HELGA ÖGMUNDSDÓTTIR (Iceland).

**European Association for Health Information and Libraries—EAHIL:** c/o ICP-NTI, POB 23213, 1100 DS Amsterdam, Netherlands; tel. (20) 566-2095; fax (20) 696-3228; e-mail eahil@amc.uva.nl; f. 1987; serves professionals in health information and biomedical libraries in Europe; holds biennial conferences of medical and health librarians. Pres. MANVELA COLOMBI (Italy); Sec. S. LAEVEN. Publs *Newsletter to European Health Librarians* (quarterly), conference proceedings.

**European Association for the Study of Diabetes:** 40223 Düsseldorf, Merowingerstr. 29, Germany; tel. (211) 316738; fax (211) 3190987; e-mail easd@uni-duesseldorf.de; internet www.easd.org; f. 1965 to support research in the field of diabetes, to promote the rapid diffusion of acquired knowledge and its application; holds annual scientific meetings within Europe. Mems: 6,000 in 101 countries, not confined to Europe. Pres. Prof. J. NERUP (Denmark); Exec. Dir Dr VIKTOR JOERGENS. Publ. *Diabetologia* (13 a year).

**European Association of Radiology:** c/o Prof. Dr P. Vock, Institut für Diagnostische Radiologie der Universität Bern, Inselspital, 3010 Bern, Switzerland; tel. (31) 632-24-35; fax (31) 632-48-74; e-mail p.vock@insel.unibe.ch; f. 1962 to develop and co-ordinate the efforts of radiologists in Europe by promoting radiology in both biology and medicine, studying its problems, developing professional training and establishing contact between radiologists and professional, scientific and industrial organizations. Mems: national associations in 38 countries. Sec.-Gen. Prof. Dr PETER VOCK.

**European Association of Social Medicine:** Corso Vittorio Emanuele 92, 10121 Turin, Italy; f. 1953 to provide co-operation between national associations of preventive medicine and public health. Mems: associations in 10 countries. Pres. Dr JEAN-PAUL FOURNIER (France); Sec.-Gen. Prof. Dr ENRICO BELLI (Italy).

**European Brain and Behaviour Society:** c/o Dr S. J. Sara, UPMC, Institut des Neurosciences, 9 quai St Bernard, 75005 Paris, France; fax 1-44-27-32-51; e-mail ebbs@snv.jussieu.fr; internet www.uio.no/~terjesa/ebbs/; f. 1969; holds two conferences a year. Pres. B. J. EVERITT; Sec.-Gen. Dr SUSAN J. SARA. Publ. *Newsletter*.

**European Federation of Internal Medicine:** c/o Dr Davidson, Royal Sussex County Hospital, Eastern Rd, Brighton, United Kingdom; tel. (1273) 696955; fax (1273) 684554; internet www.efim.org; f. 1969 as European Assen of Internal Medicine (present name adopted 1996); aims to promote internal medicine on the ethical, scientific and professional level; to bring together European specialists and establish communication between them; to organize congresses and meetings; and to provide information. Mems: 400 in 20 European countries. Sec. Dr CHRISTOPHER DAVIDSON. Publ. *European Journal of Internal Medicine* (quarterly).

**European Health Management Association:** Vergemount Hall, Clonskeagh, Dublin 6, Ireland; tel. (1) 2839299; fax (1) 2838653; e-mail pcberman@ehma.org; internet www.ehma.org; f. 1966; aims to improve health care in Europe by raising standards of managerial performance in the health sector; fosters co-operation between health service organizations and institutions in the field of healthcare management education and training. Mems: 225 in 30 countries. Pres. Dr PETER BAECKSTRÖM; Dir PHILIP C. BERMAN. Publs *Newsletter*, *Eurobriefing* (quarterly).

**European League against Rheumatism:** Witikonerstr. 15, 8032 Zürich, Switzerland; tel. (1) 3839690; fax (1) 3839810; f. 1947 to co-ordinate research and treatment of rheumatic complaints, conducted by national societies; holds an annual congress. Mems in 41 countries. Exec. Sec. F. WYSS. Publ. *Annals of the Rheumatic Diseases*.

**European Organization for Caries Research—ORCA:** c/o Lutz Stösser, Dept of Preventive Dentistry, Dental School of Erfurt, Univ. of Jena, Nordhauser Str. 78, 99089 Erfurt, Germany; tel. (361) 7411205; e-mail stoesser@zmkh.ef.uni-jena.de; f. 1953 to promote and undertake research on dental health, encourage international contacts, and make the public aware of the importance of care of the teeth. Mems: research workers in 23 countries. Pres. Prof. C. ROBINSON (UK); Sec.-Gen. Prof. L. STÖSSER (Germany).

**European Orthodontic Society:** Flat 31, 49 Hallam St, London, W1N 5LL, United Kingdom; tel. (20) 7935-2795; fax (20) 7323-0410; e-mail eoslondon@compuserve.com; f. 1907 (name changed in 1935) to advance the science of orthodontics and its relations with the collateral arts and sciences. Mems: 2,437 in 77 countries. Sec. Prof. J. MOSS. Publ. *European Journal of Orthodontics* (6 a year).

**European Union of Medical Specialists:** 20 ave de la Couronne, Brussels 1050, Belgium; tel. (2) 649-51-64; fax (2) 640-37-30; e-mail uems@skynet.be; internet www.uems.be; f. 1958 to safeguard the interests of medical specialists. Mems: two representatives each from Austria, Belgium, Denmark, Finland, France, Germany, Greece, Iceland, Ireland, Italy, Luxembourg, Netherlands, Norway, Portugal, Spain, Sweden, Switzerland, United Kingdom. Pres. Dr C. TWOMEY (Ireland); Sec.-Gen. Dr C. LEIBBRANDT (Netherlands).

**Eurotransplant International Foundation:** POB 2304, 2301 CH Leiden, Netherlands; tel. (71) 5795795; fax (71) 5790057; internet www.eurotransplant.nl; f. 1967; co-ordinates the exchange of organs for transplants in Austria, Belgium, Germany, Luxembourg, Netherlands and Slovenia; keeps register of almost 15,000 patients with all necessary information for matching with suitable donors in the shortest possible time; organizes transport of the organ and the transplantation; collaboration with similar organizations in western and eastern Europe. Dirs Dr B. COHEN, Dr G. G. PERSIJN.

**Federation of French-Language Obstetricians and Gynaecologists** (Fedération des gynécologues et obstetriciens de langue française): Clinique Baudelocque, 123 blvd de Port-Royal, 75674 Paris Cédex 14, France; tel. 1-42-34-11-43; fax 1-42-34-12-31; f. 1920 for the scientific study of phenomena having reference to obstetrics, gynaecology and reproduction in general. Mems: 1,500 in 50 countries. Pres. Prof. H. RUF (France); Gen. Sec. Prof. J. R. ZORN (France). Publ. *Journal de Gynécologie Obstétrique et Biologie de la Reproduction* (8 a year).

**Federation of the European Dental Industry:** 50858 Cologne, Kirchweg 2, Germany; tel. (221) 9486280; fax (221) 483428; f. 1957 to promote the interests of the dental industry. Mems: national associations in Austria, Belgium, Denmark, Germany, Italy, Netherlands, Spain, Sweden, Switzerland, United Kingdom. Pres. and Chair. Dr J. EBERLEIN (Germany); Sec. HARALD RUSSEGGER (Germany).

**General Association of Municipal Health and Technical Experts:** 83 ave Foch, BP 3916, 75761 Paris Cédex 16, France; tel. 1-53-70-13-53; fax 1-53-70-13-40; e-mail aghtm@aghtm.org; internet www.aghtm.org; f. 1905 to study all questions related to urban and rural health—the control of preventable diseases, disinfection, distribution and purification of drinking water, construction of drains, sewage, collection and disposal of household refuse, etc. Mems in 35 countries. Dir.-Gen. ALAIN LASALMONIE (France). Publ. *TSM-Techniques, Sciences, Méthodes* (monthly).

**Inter-American Association of Sanitary and Environmental Engineering:** Rua Nicolau Gagliardi 354, 05429-010 São Paulo, SP, Brazil; tel. (11) 212-4080; fax (11) 814-2441; e-mail aidis@unisys.com.br; internet www.aidis.org.br; f. 1948 to assist the development of water supply and sanitation. Mems: 32 countries. Exec. Dir LUIZ AUGUSTO DE LIMA PONTES. Publs *Revista Ingeniería Sanitaria* (quarterly), *Desafío* (quarterly).

**International Academy of Aviation and Space Medicine:** 21 Antares Dr., Suite 112, Nepean, ON K2E 7T8, Canada; tel. (613) 228-9345; fax (613) 228-0242; e-mail g.takahashi@sympatico.ca; f. 1955 to facilitate international co-operation in research and teaching in the fields of aviation and space medicine. Mems: in 41 countries. Sec.-Gen. Dr GEORGE TAKAHASHI.

**International Academy of Cytology:** 79104 Freiburg, Burgunderstr. 1, Germany; tel. (761) 292-3801; fax (761) 292-3802; internet www.cytology-iac.org; f. 1957 to facilitate international exchange of information on specialized problems of clinical cytology, to stimulate research and to standardize terminology. Mems: 2,400. Pres. HARUBUMI KATO; Sec. VOLKER SCHNEIDER. Publs *Acta Cytologica*, *Analytical and Quantitative Cytology and Histology* (both every 2 months).

**International Agency for the Prevention of Blindness:** L. V. Prasad Eye Institute, L. V. Prasad Marg, Banjara Hills, Hyderabad 500 034, India; tel. (40) 3545389; fax (40) 3548271; e-mail IAPB_SECT/eye@lvp.lvpeye.stph.net; f. 1975; overarching organization whose objectives include advocacy and information sharing on prevention of blindness; aims to encourage the formation of national prevention of blindness committees and programmes; in official relationship with WHO. Pres. Dr HANNAH FAAL; Sec.-Gen. Dr GULLAPALLI N. RAO. Publ. *IAPB News*.

**International Anatomical Congress:** c/o Prof. Dr Wolfgang Kühnel, Institut für Anatomie, Medizinische Universität zu Lübeck, Ratzeburger Allee 160, 23538 Lübeck, Germany; tel. (451) 500-4030; fax (451) 500-4034; e-mail buchuel@anet.mu-luebeck.de; internet www.anet.mu-luebeck.de/anetpes.html; f. 1903; runs congresses for anatomists from all over the world to discuss research, teaching methods and terminology in the fields of gross and microscopical anatomy, histology, cytology, etc. Pres. J. ESPERENCA-PINE (Portugal); Sec.-Gen. Prof. Dr WOLFGANG KÜHNEL (Germany). Publ. *Annals of Anatomy*.

**International Association for Child and Adolescent Psychiatry and Allied Professions:** c/o Prof. Kosuke Yamazaki, Tokai Univ. School of Medicine, Dept of Psychiatry, Bohseidai, Isehara, Kanagawaken 259 11, Japan; tel. (463) 93-11-21; fax (463) 94-55-32; f. 1937 to promote scientific research in the field of child psychiatry by collaboration with allied professions. Mems: national associations and individuals in 44 countries. Sec.-Gen. Prof. KOSUKE YAMAZAKI. Publs *The Child in the Family (Yearbook of the IACAPP)*, *Newsletter*.

**International Association for Dental Research:** 1619 Duke St, Alexandria, VA 22314, USA; tel. (703) 548-0066; fax (703) 548-1883; e-mail research@iadr.com; internet www.iadr.com; f. 1920 to encourage research in dentistry and related fields, and to publish the results; holds annual meetings, triennial conferences and divisional meetings. Pres. Dr SALLY MARSHALL; Exec. Dir Dr ELI SCHWARZ.

**International Association of Agricultural Medicine and Rural Health:** Saku Central Hospital, 197 Usuda-machi, Minamisaku-Gun, Nagano 384-0301, Japan; tel. (267) 82-3131; fax (267) 82-7533; e-mail sakuchp@valley.or.jp; internet www.valley.ne.jp/-sakuchp/; f. 1961 to study the problems of medicine in agriculture in all countries and to prevent the diseases caused by the conditions of work in agriculture. Mems: 405. Pres. Prof. J. TÉNYI (Hungary); Sec.-Gen. Dr SHOSUI MATSUSHIMA (Japan) (acting).

**International Association of Applied Psychology:** c/o Prof. J. M. Prieto, Colegio Oficial de Psicólogos, Cuesta de San Vicente 4, 5-28008 Madrid, Spain; e-mail iaap@cop.es; internet www.iaapsy.org; f. 1920, present title adopted in 1955; aims to establish contacts between those carrying out scientific work on applied psychology, to promote research and the adoption of measures contributing to this work. Mems: 2,200 in 94 countries. Pres. Prof. C. D. SPIELBERGER (USA); Sec.-Gen. Prof. J. M. PRIETO (Spain). Publ. *Applied Psychology: An International Review* (quarterly).

**International Association of Asthmology—INTERASMA:** c/o Prof. Hugo Neffen, Irigoyen Freyre 2670, 3000 Santa Fé, Argentina; tel. (42) 453-7638; fax (42) 456-9773; e-mail interasm@neffen.satlink .net; f. 1954 to advance medical knowledge of bronchial asthma and allied disorders. Mems: 1,100 in 54 countries. Pres. Prof. GAETANO MELILLO (Italy); Sec./Treas. Prof. H. NEFFEN. Publs *Journal of Investigative Allergology and Clinical Immunology* (every 2 months), *Allergy and Clinical Immunology International* (every 2 months).

**International Association of Gerontology:** Centre for Ageing Studies, Flinders Univ. of S. Australia, Lafter Dr., Science Park, Bedford Park, S. Australia; tel. (618) 8201-7552; fax (618) 8201-7551; e-mail iag@flinders.edu.au; internet www.cas.flinders.edu.au /iag; f. 1950 to promote research and training in all fields of gerontology and to protect interests of gerontologic societies and institutions. Holds World Congress every four years. Mems: 60 national societies in 51 countries. Pres. Prof. GARY ANDREWS; Sec.-Gen. Prof. MARY LUSZCZ. Publ. *International Newsletter* (2 a year).

**International Association of Group Psychotherapy:** c/o Dr E. Hopper, 11 Heath Mansions, The Mount, London NW3 6SN, United Kingdom; f. 1954; holds congresses every three years. Mems: in 35 countries. Pres. Dr E. HOPPER; Sec. Dr C. SANDAHL (Sweden). Publs *Newsletter, Yearbook of Group Psychotherapies*.

**International Association of Hydatidology:** Florida 460, Piso 3, 1005 Buenos Aires, Argentina; tel. (1) 4324-4700; fax (1) 4325-8231; f. 1941. Mems: 1,200 in more than 40 countries. Pres. Dr RAÚL UGARTE ARTOLA (Uruguay); Sec.-Gen. Prof. Dr JORGE ALFREDO (Argentina). Publs *Archivos Internacionales de la Hidatidosis* (every 2 years), *Boletín de Hidatidosis* (quarterly).

**International Association of Logopedics and Phoniatrics:** 43 Louis de Savoie, 1110 Morges, Switzerland; fax (21) 3209300; f. 1924 to promote standards of training and research in human communication disorders in all countries, to establish information centres and communicate with kindred organizations. Mems: 125,000 in 60 societies from 54 countries. Pres. Dr EWA SÖDERPALM. Publ. *Folia Phoniatrica et Logopedica* (6 a year).

**International Association of Oral and Maxillofacial Surgeons:** 9700 W. Bryn Mawr, Suite 210, Rosemont, ILL 60018-5701, USA; tel. (847) 678-9370; fax (847) 678-9380; e-mail lsavler@iaoms .org; f. 1963 to advance the science and art of oral and maxillofacial surgery; organizes biennial international conference. Mems: over 3,000. Pres. JOHN HELFRICK (USA); Exec. Dir VICTOR MONCARZ (Canada). Publs *International Journal of Oral and Maxillofacial Surgery* (every 2 months), *Newsletter* (every 6 months).

**International Brain Research Organization—IBRO:** 51 blvd de Montmorency, 75016 Paris, France; tel. 1-46-47-92-92; fax 1-45-20-60-06; e-mail ibro@wanadoo.fr; internet www.ibro.org; f. 1958 to further all aspects of brain research. Mems: 45 corporate, 15 academic and 51,000 individual. Pres. Prof. T. N. WIESEL (USA); Sec.-Gen. Prof. C. BELMONTE (Spain). Publs *IBRO News, Neuroscience* (bi-monthly), *IBRO Membership Directory*.

**International Bronchoesophagological Society:** Mayo Clinic, 13400 E. Shea Blvd, Scottsdale, AZ 85259, USA; f. 1951 to promote by all means the progress of bronchoesophagology and to provide a forum for discussion among broncho-esophagologists of various specialities; holds congress every three years. Mems: 500 in 37 countries. Exec. Sec. Dr DAVID SANDERSON.

**International Bureau for Epilepsy:** POB 21, 2100 AA Heemstede, Netherlands; tel. (23) 5237411; fax (23) 5470119; e-mail ibe@xs4all.nl; internet www.epilepsy.org; f. 1961 to collect and disseminate information about social and medical care for people with epilepsy; to organize international and regional meetings; to advise and answer questions on social aspects of epilepsy. Mems: 55 national epilepsy organizations. Sec.-Gen. MICHAEL D. HILLS. Publ. *International Epilepsy News* (quarterly).

**International Cell Research Organization:** c/o UNESCO, SC/LSC, 1 rue Miollis, 75015 Paris, France; e-mail icro@unesco.org; internet www.unesco.org/icro; f. 1962 to create, encourage and promote co-operation between scientists of different disciplines throughout the world for the advancement of fundamental knowledge of the cell, normal and abnormal; organizes every year 10 to 12 international laboratory courses on modern topics of cell and molecular biology and biotechnology for young research scientists in important research centres all over the world. Mems: 400. Pres. Prof. J. E. ALLENDE (Chile); Exec. Sec. Prof. G. N. COHEN (France).

**International Centre for Diarrhoeal Disease Research, Bangladesh:** GPO Box 128, Dhaka 1000, Bangladesh; tel. (2) 871751; fax (2) 871686; e-mail info@icddrb.org; internet www.icddrb.org; f. 1960; undertakes research, training and information dissemination on diarrhoeal diseases, with particular reference to developing countries; supported by 45 governments and international organizations. Dir (from Oct. 1999) Dr DAVID PACK. Publs *Annual Report, ICDDR, B News* (quarterly), *Journal of Diarrhoeal Diseases Research* (quarterly), *Glimpse* (quarterly), *Shasthya Sanglap* (3 a year), *DISC Bulletin* (2 a month), scientific reports, working papers, monographs.

**International Chiropractors' Association:** 1110 North Glebe Rd, Suite 1000, Arlington, VA 22201, USA; tel. (703) 528-5000; f. 1926 to promote advancement of the art and science of chiropractic. Mems: 7,000 individuals in addition to affiliated associations. Pres. FRED BARGE; Exec. Vice-Pres. RON HENRIKSON. Publs *International Review of Chiropractic* (every 2 months), *ICA Today* (every 2 months).

**International Commission on Occupational Health:** Dept of Community, Occupational and Family Medicine, MD3, National University of Singapore, 16 Medical Drive, Singapore 117597; tel. (65) 8744985; fax (65) 7791489; e-mail icohsg@singnet.com.sg; internet www.icoh.org.sg; f. 1906 (present name 1985) to study and prevent pathological conditions arising from industrial work; arranges congresses on occupational medicine and the protection of workers' health; provides information for public authorities and learned societies. Mems: 2,060 from 94 countries. Pres. Prof. J.-F. CAILLARD (France); Sec.-Gen. Prof. J. JEYARATNAM (Singapore). Publ. *Newsletter* (quarterly).

**International Commission on Radiological Protection—ICRP:** 17116 Stockholm, Sweden; tel. (8) 729-72-75; fax (8) 729-72-98; e-mail jack.valentin@ssi.se; internet www.icrp.org; f. 1928 to provide technical guidance and promote international co-operation in the field of radiation protection; committees on Radiation Effects, Doses from Radiation Exposure, Protection in Medicine, and the Application of Recommendations. Mems: about 70. Chair. Prof. R. H. CLARKE (UK); Scientific Sec. Dr J. VALENTIN (Sweden). Publ. *Annals of the ICRP*.

**International Committee of Catholic Nurses:** 43 Square Vergote, 1040 Brussels, Belgium; tel. (2) 732-10-50; fax (2) 734-84-60; f. 1933 to group professional Catholic nursing associations; to represent Christian thought in the general professional field at international level; to co-operate in the general development of the profession and to promote social welfare. Mems: 49 full, 20 corresponding mems. Pres. R. LAI; Gen. Sec. AN VERLINDE. Publ. *Nouvelles / News / Nachrichten* (3 a year).

**International Council for Physical Activity and Fitness Research—ICPAFR:** Faculty of Physical Education and Physiotherapy, Catholic Univ. of Leuven, 3001 Heverlee (Leuven), Belgium; tel. (16) 32-90-83; fax (16) 32-91-97; e-mail albrecht .claessens@flok.kuleuven.ac.be; f. 1964 to construct international standardized physical fitness tests, to encourage research based upon the standardized tests and to encourage research to enhance participation in physical activity. Mems: some 35 countries. Pres. Prof. ALBRECHT L. CLAESSENS (Belgium); Sec. Treas. Prof. ANDREW HILLS (Australia).

**International Council of Nurses—ICN:** 3 place Jean-Marteau, 1201 Geneva, Switzerland; tel. (22) 8090100; fax (22) 8090101; f. 1899 to allow national associations of nurses to share their common interests, working together to develop the contribution of nursing to the promotion of health. Quadrennial congresses are held. Mems: 112 national nurses' associations. Pres. Dr MARGRETTA MADDEN STYLES (USA); Exec. Dir JUDITH OULTON. Publ. *The International Nursing Review* (6 a year, in English).

**International Cystic Fibrosis (Mucoviscidosis) Association:** Avda Campanar 106-3a-6a, 46015 Valencia, Spain; tel. (96) 346-1414; fax (96) 349-4047; e-mail fq@vlc.servicom.es; f. 1964 to disseminate current information on cystic fibrosis in those areas of the world where the disease occurs and to stimulate the work of scientific and medical researchers attempting to discover its cure. Conducts annual medical symposia. Mems: 54 national organizations; 14 associate mems. Pres. IAN THOMPSON (Canada); Sec. AISHA RAMOS (Spain).

**International Epidemiological Association—IEA:** Suite 840, 111 Market Place, Baltimore, MD 21202-6709, USA; tel. (410) 223-1600; fax (410) 223-1620; e-mail harmenia@jhsph.edu; f. 1954. Mems: 2,237. Pres. and Chair. Dr RODOLFO SARACCI; Sec. Prof. HAROUTUNE ARMENIAN. Publ. *International Journal of Epidemiology* (6 a year).

**International Federation for Medical and Biological Engineering:** c/o Prof. Jos A. E. Spaan, Faculty of Medicine, Meibergdreef 15, 1105 AZ Amsterdam, Netherlands; tel. (20) 566-5200; fax (20) 691-7233; e-mail ifmbe@amc.uva.nl; internet www.vub.vub.oc.be/ ~ifmbe/ifmbe-html; f. 1959. Mems: organizations in 40 countries. Sec.-Gen. Prof. JOS A. E. SPAAN (Netherlands).

**International Federation for Medical Psychotherapy:** c/o Prof. E. Heim, Tannackstr. 3, 3653 Oberhofen, Switzerland; tel. and fax (33) 2431141; e-mail senf-blum@t-online.de; f. 1946 to further research and teaching of psychotherapy and to organize international congresses. Mems: some 6,000 psychotherapists from around 40 countries, 36 societies. Pres. Dr EDGAR HEIM (Switzerland); Sec.-Gen. Prof. Dr WOLFGANG SENE (Germany).

**International Federation of Fertility Societies—IFSS:** c/o CSI, 337 rue de la Combe Caude, 34090 Montpellier, France; tel. 4-67-63-53-40; fax 4-67-41-94-27; e-mail algcsi@mnet.fr; internet www.mnet.fr/iffs; f. 1951 to study problems of fertility and sterility. Sec.-Gen. Prof. BERNARD HEDON.

**International Federation of Gynecology and Obstetrics—FIGO:** 27 Sussex Place, Regent's Park, London, NW1 4RG, United Kingdom; tel. (20) 7723-2951; fax (20) 7258-0737; e-mail secret@figo.win-uk.net; internet www.figo.org; f. 1954; aims to improve standards in gynaecology and obstetrics, to promote better health care for women, and to facilitate the exchange of information and perfect methods of teaching. Membership: national societies in 100 countries. Pres. Prof. M. SEPPÄLÄ (Finland); Sec.-Gen. Prof. G. BENAGIANO (Italy). Publ. *International Journal of Obstetrics and Gynecology*.

**International Federation of Multiple Sclerosis Societies:** 10 Heddon St, London, W1R 7LJ, United Kingdom; tel. (20) 7734-9120; fax (20) 7287-2587; e-mail info@ifmss.org.uk; internet www.ifmss.org.uk; f. 1965 to co-ordinate the work of 38 national multiple sclerosis organizations throughout the world, to encourage scientific research in this and related neurological diseases, to aid member societies in helping individuals who are in any way affected as a result of these diseases, to collect and disseminate information and to provide counsel and active help in furthering the development of voluntary national multiple sclerosis organizations. Pres. PETER SCHWEITZER; Chief Exec. CHRISTINE PURDY. Publs *Making Connections* (annually), *MS Research in Progress* (every 2 years), *MS Management* (2 a year), *Therapeutic Claims in MS* (annually).

**International Federation of Ophthalmological Societies:** c/o Dr Bruce E. Spivey, Northwestern Healthcare, 980 North Michigan Ave, Suite 1500, Chicago, IL 60611, USA; tel. (312) 335-6035; fax (312) 335-6030; f. 1953; holds international congress every four years. Pres. Prof. A. NAKAJIMA (Japan); Sec. Dr BRUCE E. SPIVEY.

**International Hospital Federation:** 46–48 Grosvenor Gdns, London, SW1W 0EB, United Kingdom; tel. (20) 7881-9222; fax (20) 7881-9223; e-mail 101662.1262@compuserve.com; f. 1947 for information exchange and education in hospital and health service matters; represents institutional health care in discussions with WHO; conducts conferences and courses on management and policy issues.Mems in five categories: national hospital and health service organizations; professional associations, regional organizations and individual hospitals; individual mems; professional and industrial mems; honorary mems. Dir-Gen. Prof. PER-GUNNAR SVENSSON. Publs *Yearbook, Journal, Newsletter*.

**International League against Epilepsy:** c/o Prof. Peter Wolf, Klinik Mara I, Epilepsie-Zentrum Bethel, Maraweg 21, 33617 Bielefeld, Germany; tel. (521) 144-4897; fax (521) 144-4637; e-mail ilae-secretariat@mara.de; f. 1909 to link national professional associations and to encourage research, including classification and anti-epileptic drugs; collaborates with the International Bureau for Epilepsy (q.v.) and with WHO. Mems: 72 associations. Pres. JEROME ENGEL, Jr (USA); Sec.-Gen. P. WOLF.

**International Narcotics Control Board—INCB:** 1400 Vienna, POB 500, Austria; tel. (1) 260-60-42-77; fax (1) 260-60-58-67; e-mail secretariat@incb.org; f. 1961 by the Single Convention on Narcotic Drugs to supervise the implementation of the drug control treaties by governments. Mems: 13 individuals. Pres. ANTONIO G. LOURENÇO MARTINS (Portugal); Sec. HERBERT SCHAEPE (Germany). Publ. *Annual Report* (with three technical supplements).

**International Opticians' Association:** 6 Hurlingham Business Park, Sulivan Rd, London SW6 3DU, United Kingdom; tel. (20) 7736-0088; fax (20) 7731-5531; f. 1951 to promote the science of, and to maintain and advance standards and effect co-operation in optical dispensing.

**International Organization for Medical Physics:** c/o Prof. Hans Svensson, Radiation Physics Dept, Univ. Hospital, 90185 Umea, Sweden; tel. (90) 785-3891; fax (90) 785-1588; f. 1963 to organize international co-operation in medical physics, to promote communication between the various branches of medical physics and allied subjects, to contribute to the advancement of medical physics in all its aspects and to advise on the formation of national organizations. Mems: national organizations of medical physics in 56 countries. Pres. Prof. KEITH BODDY (UK); Sec.-Gen. Prof. HANS SVENSSON. Publ. *Medical Physics World*.

**International Pharmaceutical Federation:** POB 84200, 2508 AE The Hague, Netherlands; tel. (70) 3021970; fax (70) 3021999; e-mail int.pharm.fed@fip.nl; f. 1912; aims to represent and serve pharmacy and pharmaceutical sciences world-wide; holds Assembly of Pharmacists every two years, International Congress every year. Mems: 86 national pharmaceutical organizations in 62 countries, 55 associate, supportive and collective mems, 4,000 individuals. Dir A. H. M (TON) HOEK (Netherlands). Publ. *International Pharmacy Journal* (every 2 months).

**International Psycho-Analytical Association:** Broomhills, Woodside Lane, London, N12 8UD, United Kingdom; tel. (20) 8446-8324; fax (20) 8445-4729; e-mail ipa@ipa.org.uk; internet www.ipa@ipa.org.uk; f. 1908 to hold meetings to define and promulgate the theory and teaching of psychoanalysis, to act as a forum for scientific discussions, to control and regulate training and to contribute to the interdisciplinary area which is common to the behavioural sciences. Mems: 10,000. Pres. Dr OTTO KERNBERG; Sec. Dr ROBERT TYSON. Publs *Bulletin, Newsletter*.

**International Society for Cardiovascular Surgery:** 13 Elm St, Manchester, MA 01944-0865, USA; tel. (978) 526-8330; fax (978) 526-4018; e-mail iscvs@prri.com; f. 1950 to stimulate research in the diagnosis and therapy of cardiovascular diseases and to exchange ideas on an international basis. Sec.-Gen. Dr LAZAR J. SHEENFIELD (USA). Publ. *Cardiovascular Surgery*.

**International Society for Oneiric Mental Imagery Techniques:** c/o André Virel, 69 rue Sasco de Gamma, 75015 Paris, France; tel. 1-48-28-46-81; a group of research workers, technicians and psychotherapists using oneirism techniques under waking conditions, with the belief that a healing action cannot be dissociated from the restoration of creativity. Mems: in 17 countries. Pres. Dr ANDRÉ VIREL (France); Vice-Pres. ODILE DORKEL (France).

**International Society of Art and Psychopathology:** c/o Dr G. Roux, 27 rue du mal Joffre, 64000 Pau, France; tel. and fax 1-59-27-69-74; e-mail sipearther@aol.com; f. 1959 to bring together the various specialists interested in the problems of expression and artistic activities in connection with psychiatric, sociological and psychological research, as well as in the use of methods applied to other fields than that of mental illness. Mems: 625. Pres. Dr G. ROUX (France); Sec.-Gen. Dr J. VERDEAU-PAILLÈS (France).

**International Society of Developmental Biologists:** c/o Dr Paul T. van der Saag, Hubrecht Laboratorium/Netherlands Institute for Developmental Biology, Uppsalalaan 8, 3584 CT, Utrecht, Netherlands; tel. (30) 2510-211; e-mail directie@niob.knaw.nl; f. 1911 as International Institute of Embryology. Objects: to promote the study of developmental biology and to promote international co-operation among the investigators in this field. Mems: 850 in 33 countries. Pres. Prof. WALTER GEHRING (Switzerland); Sec.-Treas. Prof. SIEGFRIED DE LAAT (Netherlands). Publ. *Mechanisms of Development*.

**International Society of Lymphology:** POB 245063, University of Arizona, 1501 North Campbell Ave, Room 4406, Tucson, AZ 85724-5063, USA; tel. (520) 626-6118; fax (520) 626-0822; e-mail lymph@u.arizona.edu; f. 1966 to further progress in lymphology through personal contact and exchange of ideas among members. Mems: 400 in 43 countries. Pres. C. PAPENDIECK (Argentina); Sec.-Gen. M. H. WITTE (USA). Publ. *Lymphology* (quarterly).

**International Society of Neuropathology:** c/o Dr Janice Anderson, Dept of Histopathology, Addenbrooke's Hospital, Hills Rd, Cambridge CB2 2OO, United Kingdom; tel. (1223) 217170; fax (1223) 216980; e-mail jra20@cam.ac.uk. Pres. Prof. YNGVE OLSSON; Sec.-Gen. Dr JANICE R. ANDERSON.

**International Society of Orthopaedic Surgery and Traumatology:** 40 rue Washington, 1050 Brussels, Belgium; tel. (2) 648-68-23; fax (2) 649-86-01; f. 1929; world congresses are convened every three years. Mems: 102 countries, 3,000 individuals. Pres. RAINER KOTZ (Austria); Sec.-Gen. ANTHONY J. HALL (UK). Publ. *International Orthopaedics* (every 2 months).

**International Society of Radiology:** Dept of Radiology, Helsinki University Central Hospital, Meilahti Clinics, 00290 Helsinki, Finland; tel. 471-24-80; fax 471-44-04; f. 1953 to promote radiology world-wide. International Commissions on Radiation Units and Measurements, on Radiation Protection, on Radiological Education and on Rules and Regulations; organizes biannual International Congress of Radiology; collaborates with WHO. Mems: 68 national radiological societies. Sec. C. G. STANDERTSKJÖLD-NORDENSTAM.

**International Society of Surgery:** Netzibodenstr. 34, POB 1527, 4133 Pratteln, Switzerland; tel. (61) 8159666; fax (61) 8114775; e-mail surgery@nbs.ch; internet www.surgery.nbs.ch; f. 1902; organizes congresses: 39th World Congress of Surgery (Centennial Congress), Brussels, Belgium, August 2001. Mems: 4,000. Admin. Dir. VICTOR BERTSCHI; Sec.-Gen. Prof. J. RÜDIGER SIEWERT. Publ. *World Journal of Surgery* (monthly).

**International Union against Tuberculosis and Lung Disease:** 68 blvd St Michel, 75006 Paris, France; tel. 1-44-32-03-60; fax 1-43-29-90-87; e-mail iuatldparis@compuserve.com; f. 1920 to co-ordinate the efforts of anti-tuberculosis and respiratory disease associations, to mobilize public interest, to assist control programmes and research around the world, to collaborate with governments and WHO and to promote conferences. Mems: associations in 165 countries, 3,000 individual mems. Pres. Prof. S. SUPCHAROEN; Exec. Dir Dr NILS BILLO. Publs *The International Journal of Tuberculosis and Lung Disease* (in English with summaries in French and Spanish; incl. conference proceedings), *Newsletter*.

**International Union for Health Promotion and Education:** Immeuble le Berry, 2 rue Auguste Comte, 92170 Vanves, France; tel. 1-46-45-00-59; fax 1-46-45-00-45; e-mail iuhpemcl@worldnet.fr; internet www.iuhpe.org; f. 1951; provides an international network for the exchange of practical information on developments in health promotion and education; promotes research into effective methods and techniques in health promotion and education and encourages professional training in health promotion and education for health workers, teachers, social workers and others; holds a World Conference on Health Promotion and Health Education every three years, and also holds regional conferences and seminars. Mems: in more than 90 countries. Pres. Dr SPENCER HAGARD (UK). Publ. *International Journal of Health Promotion and Education* (quarterly, in English, French and Spanish).

**International Union of Therapeutics:** c/o Prof. A. Pradalier, Hôpital Louis Mourier, 178 rue des Renouillers, 92700 Colombes, France; tel. 1-47-60-67-05; f. 1934; international congress held every other year. Mems: 500 from 22 countries. Pres. Prof. A. PRADALIER; Gen. Sec. Prof. P. LECHAT.

**Middle East Neurosurgical Society:** c/o Dr Fuad S. Haddad, Neurosurgical Department, American University Medical Centre, POB 113-6044, Beirut, Lebanon; tel. (1) 347348; fax (1) 342517; e-mail gfhaddad@aub.edu.lb; f. 1958 to promote clinical advances and scientific research among its members and to spread knowledge of neurosurgery and related fields among all members of the medical profession in the Middle East. Mems: 684 in nine countries. Pres. Dr FUAD S. HADDAD; Hon. Sec. Dr GEDEON MOHASSEB.

**Organization for Co-ordination and Co-operation in the Struggle against Endemic Diseases** (Organisation de coordination et de coopération pour la lutte contre les grandes endémies—OCCGE): 01 BP 153, Bobo-Dioulasso 01, Burkina Faso; tel. 97-01-55; fax 97-00-99; e-mail sq@pegase.occge.bf; f. 1960; conducts research, provides training and maintains a documentation centre and computer information system. Mems: governments of Benin, Burkina Faso, Côte d'Ivoire, Mali, Mauritania, Niger, Senegal, Togo. Sec.-Gen. Prof. ABDOULAYE RHALY. Publs *Rapport annuel, OCCGE Info* (3 a year), *Bulletin Bibliographique* (quarterly).

Research centres:

**Centre de Recherches sur les Méningites et les Schistosomiases:** BP 10 887, Niamey, Niger; tel. 75-20-45; fax 75-31-80; e-mail chippaux@ird.ne; internet www.mpl.ird.fr.cermes; f. 1978; Dir J. P. CHIPPAUX.

**Centre Muraz:** 01 BP 153, Bobo-Dioulasso 01, Burkina Faso; tel. 97-01-02; fax 97-04-57; e-mail direction.muraz@fasonet.bf; f. 1939; multi-disciplinary research centre with special interest in biology and epidemiology of tropical diseases and training of health workers. Dir Prof. PHILIPPE VAN DE PERRE.

**Centre Régional de Recherches entomologiques:** Cotonou, Benin.

**Institut de Recherche sur la Tuberculose et les Infections respiratoires aigües:** Nouakchott, Mauritania.

**Institut d'ophtalmologie tropicale africaine—IOTA:** BP 248, Bamako, Mali; tel. 22-34-21; fax 22-51-86; e-mail iota@iotaoecge.org; f. 1953; eye care, clinical, operational and epidemiological research, training; Dir Dr AUZEMERY.

**Institut Marchoux:** BP 251, Bamako, Mali; tel. 22-51-31; fax 22-28-45; research, epidemiology and training on leprosy, dermatology, surgery. Dir Prof. MAMADOU HAMET CISSÉ.

**Institut Pierre Richet:** BP 1500, Bouaké 01, Côte d'Ivoire; tel. 63-37-46; fax 63-27-38; e-mail carneval@bouake2.orsrom.ci; f. 1974; research on trypanosomiasis, onchocerciasis, malaria and vector control; maintains a geographical information system; Dir Dr PIERRE CARNEVALE.

**Office de Recherches sur l'Alimentation et la Nutrition africaine:** BP 2089, Dakar, Senegal; tel. 822-58-92; Dir Dr MAKHTAR N'DIAYE.

In 1990 it was announced that the West African Health Community was to be amalgamated with the Organization for Co-ordination and Co-operation in the Struggle against Endemic Diseases to form the West African Health Organization, covering all the member states of ECOWAS (subject to ratification by member states).

**Organization for Co-ordination in the Struggle against Endemic Diseases in Central Africa** (Organisation de coordination pour la lutte contre les endémies en Afrique Centrale—OCEAC): BP 288, Yaoundé, Cameroon; tel. 23-22-32; fax 23-00-61; f. 1965 to standardize methods of controlling endemic diseases, to co-ordinate national action, and to negotiate programmes of assistance and training on a regional scale. Mems: Cameroon, Central African Republic, Chad, Republic of the Congo, Equatorial Guinea, Gabon. Pres. JEAN RÉMY PENDY BOUYIKI; Sec.-Gen. Dr AUGUSTE BILONGO MANENE. Publ. *Bulletin de Liaison et de Documentation* (quarterly).

**Pan-American Association of Ophthalmology:** 1301 South Bowen Rd, Suite 365, Arlington, TX 76013, USA; tel. (817) 265-2831; fax (817) 275-3961; e-mail paao@flash.net; f. 1939 to promote friendship and dissemination of scientific information among the profession throughout the Western Hemisphere; holds biennial congress (1999—Florida, USA) meetings. Mems: national ophthalmological societies and other bodies in 39 countries. Pres. Dr PAUL R. LICHTER (Chile); Exec. Dir Dr FRANCISCO MARTINEZ CASTRO (Mexico). Publs *The Pan American* (2 a year), *El Noticiero* (quarterly).

**Pan-Pacific Surgical Association:** 2000 L. St, NW, Suite 200, Washington, DC 20036, USA; tel. (202) 416-1866; fax (202) 416-1867; e-mail ppsa@slackinc.com; f. 1929 to bring together surgeons to exchange scientific knowledge relating to surgery and medicine, and to promote the improvement and standardization of hospitals and their services and facilities; congresses are held every two years. Mems: 2,716 regular, associate and senior mems from 44 countries. Chair. ALLAN KUNIMOTO.

**Society of French-speaking Neuro-Surgeons** (Société de neurochirurgie de langue française): Hôpital d'Enfants de la Timone, 13385 Marseille, France; f. 1949; holds annual convention and congress. Mems: 700 in numerous countries. Pres. M. CHOUX (France); Sec. J. LAGARRIGUE (France). Publ. *Neuro-Chirurgie* (6 a year).

**World Association for Disaster and Emergency Medicine—WADEM:** c/o Marvin L. Birnbaum, E5/615 CSC, 600 Highland Avenue, Madison, WI 53791-9744, USA; tel. (608) 263-2069; fax (608) 265-3037; e-mail mlb@medicine.wisc.edu; internet www.pdm.medicine.wisc.edu; f. 1976 to improve the world-wide delivery of emergency and humanitarian care in mass casualty and disaster situations through training, symposia, publications and emergency missions. Mems: 600 in 62 countries. Pres. STEVEN ROTTMAN (USA); Hon. Sec. Prof. W. DICK (Germany). Publ. *Prehospital and Disaster Medicine*.

**World Association of Societies of (Anatomic and Clinical) Pathology—WASP:** c/o Japan Clinical Pathology Foundation for International Exchange, Sakura-Sugamo Bldg 7F, Sugamo 2-11-1, Toshima-ku, Tokyo 170, Japan; tel. (3) 3918-8161; fax (3) 3949-6168; f. 1947 to link national societies and to co-ordinate their scientific and technical means of action; and to promote the development of anatomic and clinical pathology, especially by convening conferences, congresses and meetings, and by the interchange of publications and personnel. Membership: 54 national associations. Pres. PETER B. HERDSON; Sec. WALTER TIMPERLEY. Publ. *Newsletter* (quarterly).

**World Confederation for Physical Therapy:** 4A Abbots Pl., London, NW6 4NP, United Kingdom; tel. (20) 7328-5448; fax (20) 7624-7579; f. 1951; represents physical therapy internationally; encourages high standards of physical therapy education and practice; promotes exchange of information among members, and the development of a scientific professional base through research; aims to contribute to the development of informed public opinion regarding physical therapy. Mems: 67 organizations. Pres. Prof. D. P. G. TEAGER; Sec.-Gen. B. J. MYERS. Publ. *Newsletter* (2 a year).

**World Council of Optometry—WCO:** 10 Knaresborough Pl., London, SW5 0TG, United Kingdom; tel. (20) 7370-4765; fax (20) 7373-1143; f. 1927 to co-ordinate efforts to provide a good standard of ophthalmic optical (optometric) care throughout the world; enables exchange of ideas between different countries; a large part of its work is concerned with optometric education, and advice upon standards of qualification. The WCO also interests itself in legislation in relation to optometry throughout the world. Mems: 70 optometric organizations in 47 countries and four regional groups. Pres. ROLAND DES GROSEILLIERS; Sec. D. A. LEASON. Publ. *Interoptics* (quarterly).

**World Federation for Mental Health:** 1021 Prince St, Alexandria, VA 22314, USA; tel. (703) 838-7543; fax (703) 519-7648; e-mail wfmh@erols.com; internet www.wfmh.org; f. 1948 to promote among all nations the highest possible standard of mental health; to work with agencies of the United Nations in promoting mental health; to help other voluntary associations in the improvement of mental health services. Mems: 250 national or international associations in 115 countries. Pres. Dr AHMED EL-AZAYEM; Sec.-Gen. Prof. Dr MARTEN DE VRIES. Publs *Newsletter* (quarterly), *Annual Report*.

**World Federation of Hydrotherapy and Climatotherapy:** Centre thermal, ave des Bains, 1400 Yverdon-les-Bains, Switzerland; tel. (24) 4230232; fax (24) 4230252; e-mail info@thermes-yverdon.ch; internet www.thermes-yverdon.ch; f. 1947 as International Federation of Thermalism and Climatism; present name adopted 1999. Mems in 36 countries. Pres. M. NIKOLAI A. STOROJENKO; Gen. Sec. M. CLAUDE OGAY.

**World Federation of Neurosurgical Societies:** c/o Prof. Edward R. Laws, Dept. of Neurological Surgery, Univ. of Virginia, Box 212, Health Science Center, Charlottesville, VA 22908, USA; tel. (804) 924-2650; fax (804) 924-5894; f. 1957 to assist the development of neurosurgery and to help the formation of associations; to assist the exchange of information and to encourage research. Mems: 57 societies representing 56 countries. Pres. Prof. ARMANDO BASSO; Sec. Prof. EDWARD R. LAWS, Jr.

**World Federation of Occupational Therapists:** c/o Carolyn Webster, Disabilities Services Comm., PO Box 441, West Perth, 6872 Western Australia, Australia; tel. (8) 9426-9200; fax (8) 9490-5223; e-mail wfot@multiline.com.au; internet wfot.org.au; f. 1952 to further the rehabilitation of the physically and mentally disabled by promoting the development of occupational therapy in all countries; to facilitate the exchange of information and publications; to promote research in occupational therapy; international congresses are held every four years. Mems: national professional associations in 50 countries, with total membership of approximately 100,000. Pres. CAROLYN WEBSTER (Australia); Hon. Sec. CLEPHANE HUME (UK). Publ. *Bulletin* (2 a year).

**World Federation of Public Health Associations:** c/o Allen Jones, APHA, 800 I St, NW, Washington, DC 20001-3710, USA; tel. (202) 777-2487; fax (202) 777-2534; e-mail allen.jones@apha.org; internet www.apha.org; f. 1967. Triennial Congress: Beijing, People's Republic of China, 2000. Mems: 61 national public health associations. Exec. Sec. ALLEN JONES (USA). Publs *WFPHA News* (in English), and occasional technical papers.

**World Federation of Societies of Anaesthesiologists—WFSA:** Imperial House, 8th Floor, 15–19 Kingsway, London, WC2B 6TH, United Kingdom; tel. (20) 7836-5652; fax (20) 7836-5616; e-mail wfsa@compuserve.com; internet www.nda.ox.ac.uk/wfsa; f. 1955 to make available the highest standards of anaesthesia to all peoples of the world. Mems: 106 national societies. Pres. Prof. M. D. VICKERS (UK); Sec. Dr A. E. E. MEURSING; Publs *World Anaesthesia Newsletter* (2 a year), *Annual Report*.

# Posts and Telecommunications

**African Posts and Telecommunications Union:** ave Patrice Lumumba, BP 44, Brazzaville, Republic of the Congo; tel. 83-27-78; fax 83-27-79; f. 1961 to improve postal and telecommunication services between member administrations. Mems: 11 countries. Sec.-Gen. MAHMOUDOU SAMOURA.

**Arab Permanent Postal Commission:** c/o Arab League Bldg, Tahrir Sq., Cairo, Egypt; tel. (2) 5750511; fax (2) 5775626; f. 1952; aims to establish stricter postal relations between the Arab countries than those laid down by the Universal Postal Union, and to pursue the development and modernization of postal services in member countries. Publs *APU Bulletin* (monthly), *APU Review* (quarterly), *APU News* (annually).

**Arab Telecommunications Union:** POB 2397, Baghdad, Iraq; tel. (1) 555-0642; f. 1953 to co-ordinate and develop telecommunications between member countries; to exhange technical aid and encourage research; promotes establishment of new cable telecommunications networks in the region. Sec.-Gen. ABDUL JAFFAR HASSAN KHALAF IBRAHIM AL-ANI. Publs. *Arab Telecommunications Union Journal* (2 a year), *Economic and Technical Studies*.

**Asia-Pacific Telecommunity:** No. 12/49, Soi 5, Chaengwattana Rd, Thungsonghong, Bangkok 10210, Thailand; tel. (2) 573-0044; fax (2) 573-7479; e-mail apthq@mozart.inet.co.th; f. 1979 to cover all matters relating to telecommunications in the region. Mems: Afghanistan, Australia, Bangladesh, Brunei, the People's Republic of China, India, Indonesia, Iran, Japan, the Republic of Korea, Laos, Malaysia, Maldives, Myanmar, Nauru, Nepal, Pakistan, the Philippines, Singapore, Sri Lanka, Thailand, Viet Nam; assoc. mems: Cook Islands, Hong Kong; two affiliated mems each in Indonesia, Japan and Thailand, three in the Republic of Korea, four in Hong Kong, one in Maldives and six in the Philippines. Exec. Sec. HIROYASU SONAKI.

**Asian-Pacific Postal Union:** Post Office Bldg, 1000 Manila, Philippines; tel. (2) 470760; fax (2) 407448; f. 1962 to extend, facilitate and improve the postal relations between the member countries and to promote co-operation in the field of postal services. Mems: 23 countries. Dir JORGE SARMIENTO. Publs *Annual Report, Exchange Program of Postal Officials, APPU Newsletter*.

**European Conference of Postal and Telecommunications Administrations:** Ministry of Transport and Communications, Odos Xenofontos 13, 10191 Athens, Greece; tel. (1) 9236494; fax (1) 9237133; f. 1959 to strengthen relations between member administrations and to harmonize and improve their technical services; set up Eurodata Foundation, for research and publishing. Mems: 26 countries. Sec. Z. PROTOPSALTI. Publ. *Bulletin*.

**European Telecommunications Satellite Organization—EUTELSAT:** 70 rue Balard, 75502, Paris Cédex 15, France; tel. 1-53-98-47-47; fax 1-53-98-37-00; internet www.eutelsat.com/; f. 1977 to operate satellites for fixed and mobile communications in Europe; operates an eight-satellite system, incorporating four EUTELSAT I and four EUTELSAT II satellites. Mems: public and private telecommunications operations in 47 countries. Dir-Gen. GIULIANO BERRETTA.

**INMARSAT—International Mobile Satellite Organization:** 99 City Rd, London, EC1Y 1AX, United Kingdom; tel. (20) 7728-1000; fax (20) 7728-1044; internet www.inmarsat.org; f. 1979, as International Maritime Satellite Organization, to provide (from February 1982) global communications for shipping via satellites on a commercial basis; satellites in geo-stationary orbit over the Atlantic, Indian and Pacific Oceans provide telephone, telex, facsimile, telegram, low to high speed data services and distress and safety communications for ships of all nations and structures such as oil rigs; in 1985 the operating agreement was amended to include aeronautical communications, and in 1988 amendments were approved which allow provision of global land-mobile communications. In April 1999 INMARSAT was transferred to the private sector and became a limited company; an intergovernmental secretariat was to be maintained to monitor INMARSAT's public service obligations. Mems: 86 countries. Chair. RICHARD VOS; Dir of Secretariat JERZY VONAU (Poland).

**International Telecommunications Satellite Organization—INTELSAT:** 3400 International Drive, NW, Washington, DC 20008-3098, USA; tel. (202) 944-6800; fax (202) 944-7860; f. 1964 to establish a global commercial satellite communications system. Assembly of Parties attended by representatives of member governments, meets every two years to consider policy and long-term aims and matters of interest to members as sovereign states. Meeting of Signatories to the Operating Agreement held annually. Twenty-four INTELSAT satellites in geosynchronous orbit provide a global communications service; INTELSAT provides most of the world's overseas traffic. In 1998 INTELSAT agreed to establish a private enterprise, incorporated in the Netherlands, to administer six satellite services. Mems: 143 governments. Dir-Gen. and Chief Exec. CONNY KULLMAN (Sweden).

**Pacific Telecommunications Council:** 2454 S. Beretania St, 302 Honolulu, HI 96826, USA; tel. (808) 941-3789; fax (808) 944-4874; e-mail info@ptc.org; f. 1980 to promote the development, understanding and beneficial use of telecommunications and information systems/services throughout the Pacific region; provides forum for users and providers of communications services; sponsors annual conference and seminars. Mems: 650 (corporate, government, academic and individual). Pres. JANE HURD; Exec. Dir HOYT ZIA. Publ. *Pacific Telecommunications Review* (quarterly).

**Postal Union of the Americas, Spain and Portugal** (Unión Postal de las Américas, España y Portugal): Calle Cebollatí 1468/70, 1°, Casilla de Correos 20.042, Montevideo, Uruguay; tel. (2) 4000070; fax (2) 405046; internet www.upaepadinet.com.uy; f. 1911 to extend, facilitate and study the postal relationships of member countries. Mems: 27 countries. Sec.-Gen. MARIO FELMER KLENNER (Chile).

# Press, Radio and Television

**Asia-Pacific Broadcasting Union—ABU:** POB 1164, 59700 Kuala Lumpur, Malaysia; tel. (3) 2823592; fax (3) 2825292; e-mail sg@abu.org.my; internet www.abu.org.my; f. 1964 to foster and co-ordinate the development of broadcasting in the Asia-Pacific area, to promote greater collaboration and co-operation among broadcasting orgs and to serve the professional needs of broadcasters in Asia and the Pacific; holds annual General Assembly. Mems: 47 full, 29 additional and 26 associates in 51 countries and territories. Pres. KATSUJI EBISAWA (Japan); Sec.-Gen. HUGH LEONARD. Publs *ABU News* (every 2 months), *ABU Technical Review* (every 2 months).

**Association for the Promotion of the International Circulation of the Press—DISTRIPRESS:** 8002 Zürich, Beethovenstrasse 20, Switzerland; tel. (1) 2024121; fax (1) 2021025; f. 1955 to assist in the promotion of the freedom of the press throughout the world, supporting and aiding UNESCO in promoting the free flow of ideas. Organizes meetings of publishers and distributors of newspapers, periodicals and paperback books, to promote the exchange of information and experience among members. Mems: 458. Pres. CHRIS HADZOPOULOS (Greece); Man. HEINZ E. GRAF (Switzerland). Publs *Distripress Gazette, Who's Who*.

**Association of European Journalists:** 5300 Bonn 2, Kastanienweg 26, Germany; tel. and fax (228) 321712; f. 1963 to participate actively in the development of a European consciousness; to promote deeper knowledge of European problems and secure appreciation by the general public of the work of European institutions; and to facilitate members' access to sources of European information. Mems: 1,500 individuals and national associations in 15 countries. Sec.-Gen. GUENTHER WAGENLEHNER.

**Association of Private European Cable Operators:** 1 blvd Anspach, boîte 25, 1000 Brussels, Belgium; tel. (2) 223-25-91; fax (2) 223-06-96; f. 1995 aims to promote the interests of independent cable operators and to ensure exchange of information on cable and telecommunications; carries out research on relevant technical and legal questions. Mems: 27 organizations in 19 countries. Pres. M. DE SUTTER.

**Broadcasting Organization of Non-aligned Countries—BONAC:** c/o Cyprus Broadcasting Corpn, POB 4824, 1397 Nicosia, Cyprus; tel. (2) 422231; fax (2) 314050; e-mail rik@cybc.com.cy; f. 1977 to ensure an equitable, objective and comprehensive flow of information through broadcasting; Secretariat moves to the broadcasting organization of host country. Mems: in 102 countries.

**European Alliance of Press Agencies:** c/o Agence Belga, rue F. Pelletier 8B, 1030 Brussels, Belgium; tel. (2) 743-13-11; fax (2) 735-18-74; e-mail dir@belganews.be; f. 1957 to assist co-operation among members and to study and protect their common interests; annual assembly. Mems in 30 countries. Sec.-Gen. RUDI DE CEUSTER.

**European Broadcasting Union—EBU:** Ancienne-Route 17A, 1218 Grand-Saconnex, Geneva, Switzerland; tel. (22) 7172111; fax (22) 7472200; e-mail ebu@ebu.ch; internet www.ebu.ch; f. 1950 in succession to the International Broadcasting Union; a professional association of broadcasting organizations, supporting the interests of members and assisting the development of broadcasting in all its forms; activities include the Eurovision news and programme exchanges and the Euroradio music exchanges. Mems: 69 active (European) in 50 countries, and 49 associate in 30 countries. Pres. Prof. ALBERT SCHARF (Germany); Sec.-Gen. JEAN BERNARD MÜNCH (Switzerland). Publs *EBU Technical Review* (annually), *Diffusion* (quarterly).

**IFRA:** Washingtonplatz 1, 64287 Darmstadt, Germany; tel. (6151) 7336; fax (6151) 733800; e-mail info@ifra.com; internet www.ifra.com; f. 1961 as Inca-Fiej Research Asscn to develop methods and techniques for the newspaper industry; to evaluate standard specifications for raw materials for use in newspaper production; to investigate economy and quality improvements for newspaper printing and publishing. Mems: more than 1,300 newspapers, 400 suppliers. Pres. MURDOCH MACLENNAN; Man. Dir G. W. BOETTCHER. Publ. *Newspaper Techniques* (monthly in English, French and German).

**Inter-American Press Association** (Sociedad Interamericana de Prensa): 2911 NW 39th St, Miami, FL 33142, USA; tel. (305) 634-2465; fax (305) 635-2272; e-mail siptroti@aol.com; f. 1942 to guard the freedom of the press in the Americas; to promote and maintain the dignity, rights and responsibilities of the profession of journalism; to foster a wider knowledge and greater interchange among the peoples of the Americas. Mems: 1,400. Exec. Dir JULIO E. MUÑOZ. Publ. *IAPA News*.

**International Association of Broadcasting** (Asociación Internacional de Radiodifusión—AIR): Cnel Brandzen 1961, Office 402, 11200 Montevideo, Uruguay; tel. (2) 408-81-29; fax (2) 408-81-21; e-mail airiab@distrinet.com.uy; f. 1946 to preserve free and private broadcasting; to promote co-operation between the corporations and public authorities; to defend freedom of expression. Mems: national associations of broadcasters. Pres. Dr LUIS H. TARSITANO; Dir-Gen. Dr HÉCTOR OSCAR AMENGUAL. Publ. *La Gaceta de AIR* (every 2 months).

**International Association of Sound and Audio-visual Archives:** c/o Albrecht Häfner, Südwestrundfunk, Documentation and Archives Dept, 76522 Baden-Baden, Germany; tel. (7221) 9293487; fax (7221) 9292094; e-mail albrecht.haefner@swr-online.de; internet www.llgc.org.uk/iasa; f. 1969; involved in the preservation and exchange of sound and audio-visual recordings, and in developing recording techniques; holds annual conference. Mems: 380 individuals and institutions in 48 countries. Sec.-Gen. ALBRECHT HÄFNER. Publs. *IASA Journal* (2 a year), *IASA Information Bulletin* (quarterly).

**International Catholic Union of the Press** (Union catholique internationale de la presse—UCIP): 37–39 rue de Vermont, Case Postale 197, 1211 Geneva 20, Switzerland; tel. (22) 7340017; fax (22) 7340053; f. 1927 to link all Catholics who influence public opinion through the press, to inspire a high standard of professional conscience and to represent the interest of the Catholic press at international organizations. Mems: Federation of Catholic Press Agencies, Federation of Catholic Journalists, Federation of Catholic Dailies, Federation of Catholic Periodicals, Federation of Teachers in the Science and Technics of Information, Federation of Church Press Associations, Federation of Book Publishers, seven regional asscns. Pres. GÜNTHER MEES; Sec.-Gen. JOSEPH CHITTILAPPILLY (India). Publ. *UCIP-Information*.

**International Council for Film, Television and Audiovisual Communication:** 1 rue Miollis, 75732 Paris Cédex 15, France; tel. 1-45-68-48-55; fax 1-45-67-28-40; f. 1958 to arrange meetings and co-operation generally. Mems: 36 international film and television organizations. Pres. JEAN ROHCH; Sec.-Gen. Dr ROBERT E. KALMAN. Publ. *Letter of Information* (monthly).

**International Council of French-speaking Radio and Television Organizations** (Conseil international des radios-télévisions d'expression française): 52 blvd Auguste-Reyers, 1044 Brussels, Belgium; tel. (2) 732-45-85; fax (2) 732-62-40; f. 1978 to establish links between French-speaking radio and television organizations. Mems: 46 organizations. Pres. GERVAIS MENDO; Sec.-Gen. ABDELKADER MARZOUKI (Tunisia).

**International Federation of Press Cutting Agencies:** Streulistr. 19, POB 8030 Zürich, Switzerland; tel. (1) 3888200; fax (1) 3888201; e-mail fibep@swissline.ch; f. 1953 to improve the standing of the profession, prevent infringements, illegal practices and unfair competition; and to develop business and friendly relations among press cuttings agencies throughout the world. Annual meeting, 1999: Malta. Mems: 71 agencies. Pres. XAVIER DE MONREDON (France); Gen. Sec. Dr DIETER HENNE (Switzerland).

**International Federation of the Cinematographic Press—FIPRESCI:** Schleissheimerstr. 83, 80797 Munich, Germany; tel. (89) 182303; fax (89) 184766; e-mail keder@fipresci.org; f. 1930 to develop the cinematographic press and promote cinema as an art; organizes international meetings and juries in film festivals. Mems: national organizations or corresponding members in 68 countries. Pres. DEREK MALCOLM (UK); Sec.-Gen. KLAUS EDER (Germany).

**International Federation of the Periodical Press—FIPP:** Queen's House, 55/56 Lincoln's Inn Fields, London, WC2A 3LJ, United Kingdom; tel. (20) 7404-4169; fax (20) 7404-4170; e-mail info@fipp.com; internet www.fipp.com; f. 1925; works through national associations to promote optimum conditions for the development of periodical publishing; fosters formal and informal alliances between magazine publishers. Mems: 35 national asscns representing 2,500 publishing cos and 75 international publishing cos and assoc. mems. Pres. and CEO PER R. MORTENSEN; Chair. AXEL GANZ (Germany). Publ. *Magazine World* (6 a year).

**International Federation of the Socialist and Democratic Press:** CP 737, 20101 Milan, Italy; tel. (02) 8050105; f. 1953 to promote co-operation between editors and publishers of socialist newspapers; affiliated to the Socialist International (q.v.). Mems: about 100. Sec. UMBERTO GIOVINE.

**International Institute of Communications:** Tavistock House South, Tavistock Sq., London, WC1H 9LF, United Kingdom; tel. (20) 7388-0671; fax (20) 7380-0623; f. 1969 (as the International Broadcast Institute) to link all working in the field of communications, including policy makers, broadcasters, industrialists and engineers; holds local, regional and international meetings, undertakes research and publishes journal. Mems: over 1,000 corporate, institutional and individual. Pres. HENRI PIGEAT; Exec. Dir VICKI MACLEOD.

**International Maritime Radio Association:** South Bank House, Black Prince Rd, London, SE1 7SJ, United Kingdom; tel. (20) 7587-1245; fax (20) 7587-1436; e-mail secgen@cirm.org; internet www.cirm.org; f. 1928 to study and develop means of improving marine radio communications and radio aids to marine navigation. Mems: over 70 organizations and companies are involved in marine electronics in the areas of radio communications and navigation. The member companies are located in the major maritime nations of the world. Pres. G. SEUTIN (Belgium); Sec.-Gen. and Chair. of Technical Cttee Capt. C. K. D. COBLEY.

**International Organization of Journalists:** Calle Mayor 81, Madrid 28013, Spain; tel. (91) 24224243; fax (91) 24223853; f. 1946 to defend the freedom of the press and of journalists and to promote their material welfare. Activities include the maintenance of international training centres and international recreation centres for journalists. Mems: national organizations and individuals in 120 countries. Pres. ARMANDO S. ROLLEMBERG; Sec.-Gen. GERARD GATINOT. Publs *The World of Journalists* (quarterly, in English, French and Spanish), *IOJ Newsletter* (2 a month, in Arabic, English, French, Russian and Spanish).

**International Press Institute—IPI:** Spiegelgasse 2/29, 1010 Vienna, Austria; tel. (1) 5129011; fax (1) 5129014; e-mail ipi.vienna@xpoint.at; f. 1951 as a non-governmental organization of editors, publishers and news broadcasters who support the principles of a free and responsible press; activities: defence of press freedom, regional meetings of members, training programmes, research and library; annual World Congress. Mems: about 2,000 from 100 countries. Pres. MOEGSTEN WILLIAMS (South Africa); Dir JOHANN FRITZ (Austria). Publs *IPI Report* (quarterly), *World Press Freedom Review* (annually).

**International Press Telecommunications Council:** Royal Albert House, Sheet St, Windsor, Berks, SL4 1BE, United Kingdom; tel. (1753) 705051; fax (1753) 831541; e-mail m_director_iptc@dial.pipex.com; internet www.iptc.org/iptc; f. 1965 to safeguard and promote the interests of the Press on all matters relating to telecommunications; keeps its members informed of current and future telecommunications developments; to act as the news information formal standards body. The Council meets three times a year and maintains four committees and 10 working parties. Mems: 44 press associations, newspapers, news agencies and industry vendors. Chair. PETER MÜLLER; Man. Dir DAVID ALLEN. Publs *IPTC Spectrum* (annually), *IPTC Mirror* (monthly).

**Latin-American Catholic Press Union:** Apdo Postal 17-21-178, Quito, Ecuador; tel. (2) 548046; fax (2) 501658; f. 1959 to co-ordinate, promote and improve the Catholic press in Latin America. Mems: national asscns and local groups in most Latin American countries. Pres. ISMAR DE OLIVEIRA SOARES (Brazil); Sec. CARLOS EDUARDO CORTÉS (Colombia).

**Organization of Asia-Pacific News Agencies—OANA:** c/o Xinhua News Agency, 57 Xuanwumen Xidajie, Beijing 100803, People's Republic of China; tel. (10) 3074762; fax (10) 3072707; f. 1961 to promote co-operation in professional matters and mutual exchange of news, features, etc. among the news agencies of Asia and the Pacific via the Asia-Pacific News Network (ANN). Mems: Anadolu Ajansi (Turkey), Antara (Indonesia), APP (Pakistan), Bakhtar (Afghanistan), BERNAMA (Malaysia), BSS (Bangladesh), ENA (Bangladesh), Hindustan Samachar (India), IRNA (Iran), ITAR-TASS (Russia), Kaz-TAG (Kazakhstan), KABAR (Kyrgyzstan), KCNA (Korea, Democratic People's Republic), KPL (Laos), Kyodo (Japan), Lankapuvath (Sri Lanka), Montsame (Mongolia), PNA (Philippines), PPI (Pakistan), PTI (India), RSS (Nepal), Samachar Bharati (India), TNA (Thailand), UNB (Bangladesh), UNI (India), Viet Nam News Agency, Xinhua (People's Republic of China), Yonhap (Republic of Korea). Pres. GUO CHAOREN; Sec.-Gen. YU JIAFU.

**Press Foundation of Asia:** POB 1843, 1500 Roxas Blvd, Manila, Philippines; tel. (2) 598633; fax (2) 5224365; f. 1967; an independent, non-profit making organization governed by its newspaper members; acts as a professional forum for about 200 newspapers in Asia; aims to reduce cost of newspapers to potential readers, to improve editorial and management techniques through research and training programmes and to encourage the growth of the Asian press; operates *Depthnews* feature service. Mems: 200 newspapers. Exec. Chair. EUGENIO LOPEZ (Philippines); Dir-Gen. MOCHTAR LUBIS (Indonesia). Publs *Pressasia* (quarterly), *Asian Women* (quarterly).

**Reporters sans Frontières:** 5 rue Geoffroy Marie, 75009 Paris, France; tel. 1-44-83-84-84; fax 1-45-23-11-51; e-mail rsf@cavanet.calvacom.fr/rsf/; internet www.rsf.fr; f. 1985 to defend press freedoms throughout the world; generates awareness of violations of press freedoms and supports journalists under threat or imprisoned as a result of their work. Mems in 77 countries. Dir ROBERT MÉNARD. Publs *Quarterly Digest, La Lettre de Reporters sans Frontières* (2 a month).

**Union of National Radio and Television Organizations of Africa—URTNA:** 101 rue Carnot, BP 3237, Dakar, Senegal; tel. 821-16-25; fax 822-51-13; e-mail urtnadkr@telecomplus.sn; f. 1962; co-ordinates radio and television services, including monitoring and frequency allocation, the exchange of information and coverage of national and international events among African countries; maintains programme exchange centre (Nairobi, Kenya), technical centre (Bamako, Mali), a centre for rural radio studies (Ouagadougou, Burkina Faso) and a centre for the exchange of television news in Algiers, Algeria. Mems: 48 organizations and six associate members. Sec.-Gen. ABDELHAMID BOUKSANI. Publ. *URTNA Review* (English and French, 2 a year).

**World Association for Christian Communication—WACC:** 357 Kennington Lane, London, SE11 5QY, United Kingdom; tel. (20) 7582-9139; fax (20) 7735-0340; e-mail wacc@wacc.org.uk; internet www.wacc.org.uk; f. 1975; WACC seeks to promote human dignity, justice and peace through freedom of expression and the democratization of communication. It offers professional guidance on communication policies and interprets developments in and consequences of global communication methods. WACC works towards the empowerment of women and assists the training of Christian communicators. Mems: more than 800 corporate and personal mems in 115 countries, organized in eight regional assocs. Pres. ALBERT VAN DEN HEUVEL; Gen.-Sec. CARLOS A. VALLE. Publs *Action* newsletter (10 a year), *Media Development* (quarterly), *Communication Resource, Media and Gender Monitor* (both occasional).

**World Association of Newspapers:** 25 rue d'Astorg, 75008 Paris, France; tel. 1-47-42-85-00; fax 1-47-42-49-48; e-mail tbalding@wan.asso.fr; internet www.wan-press.org; f. 1948 to defend the freedom of the press, to safeguard the ethical and economic interests of newspapers and to study all questions of interest to newspapers at international level. Mems: 57 national organizations in 53 countries, individual publishers in 90 others, and 17 news agencies. Pres. BENGT BRAUN (Sweden); Dir-Gen. TIMOTHY BALDING. Publ. *Newsletter*.

# Religion

**Agudath Israel World Organisation:** Hacherut Sq., POB 326, Jerusalem 91002, Israel; tel. (2) 5384357; fax (2) 5383634; f. 1912 to help solve the problems facing Jewish people all over the world in the spirit of the Jewish tradition; holds World Rabbinical Council (every five years), and an annual Central Council comprising 100 mems nominated by affiliated organizations. Mems: over 500,000 in 25 countries. Chair. J. M. ABRAMOWITZ (Jerusalem). Publs *Hamodia* (Jerusalem weekly newspaper), *Jewish Tribune* (London, weekly), *Jewish Observer* (New York, monthly), *Dos Yiddishe Vort* (New York, monthly), *Coalition* (New York), *Perspectives* (Toronto, monthly), *La Voz Judia* (Buenos Aires, monthly), *Jüdische Stimme* (Zürich, monthly).

**All Africa Conference of Churches—AACC:** POB 14205, Waiyaki Way, Nairobi, Kenya; tel. (2) 441483; fax (2) 443241; e-mail aacc-secretariat@maf.org; f. 1958; an organ of co-operation and continuing fellowship among Protestant, Orthodox and independent churches and Christian Councils in Africa. 1997 Assembly: Addis Ababa, Ethiopia. Mems: 147 churches and affiliated Christian councils in 39 African countries. Pres. The Very Rev. Prof. KWESI DICKSON (Ghana); Gen. Sec. Canon CLEMENT JANDA (Uganda). Publs *ACIS/APS Bulletin, ACLCA News, Tam Tam*.

**Alliance Israélite Universelle;** 45 rue La Bruyère, 75425 Paris Cédex 09, France; tel. 1-53-32-88-55; fax 1-48-74-51-33; e-mail aiu@imaginet.fr; internet www.aiu.org; f. 1860 to work for the emancipation and moral progress of the Jews; maintains 40 schools in eight countries; library of 120,000 vols. Mems: 8,000 in 16 countries. Pres. ADY STEG; Dir JEAN-JACQUES WAHL (France). Publs *Cahiers de l'Alliance Israélite Universelle* (3 a year, in French), *Cahiers du Judaïsme, The Alliance Review* (in English).

**Bahá'í International Community:** Bahá'í World Centre, POB 155, 31 001 Haifa, Israel; tel. (4) 8358394; fax (4) 8358522; f. 1844 in Persia to promote the unity of mankind and world peace through the teachings of the Bahá'í religion, including the equality of men and women and the elimination of all forms of prejudice; maintains schools for children and adults worldwide, and maintains educational and cultural radio stations in the USA, Asia and Latin America; has 31 publishing trusts throughout the world. Governing body: Universal House of Justice (nine mems elected by 181 National Spiritual Assemblies). Mems: in 127,683 centres (190 countries and 45 dependent territories or overseas departments). Sec.-Gen. ALBERT LINCOLN (USA). Publs *Bahá'í World* (annually), *One Country* (quarterly, in 6 languages).

**Baptist World Alliance:** 6733 Curran St, McLean, VA 22101-6005, USA; tel. (703) 790-8980; fax (703) 893-5160; e-mail bwa@bwanet.org; f. 1905; aims to unite Baptists, lead in evangelism, respond to people in need and defend human rights. Mems: 191 Baptist unions and conventions comprising 42m. people in 200 countries and territories. Pres. Dr NILSON DO AMARAL FANINI (Brazil); Gen. Sec. Dr DENTON LOTZ. Publ. *The Baptist World* (quarterly).

**Caribbean Conference of Churches:** POB 616, Bridgetown, Barbados; tel. (246) 427-2681; fax (246) 429-2075; e-mail cccbdos@cariaccess.com; f. 1973; holds Assembly every five years; conducts study and research programmes and supports education and community projects. Mems: 34 churches. Gen. Sec. GERARD GRANADO.

**Christian Conference of Asia:** Pak Tin Village, Mei Tin Rd, Shatin, NT, Hong Kong; tel. 26911068; fax 26924378; e-mail cca@hk.super.net; f. 1957 (present name adopted 1973) to promote co-operation and joint study in matters of common concern among the Churches of the region and to encourage interaction with other regional Conferences and the World Council of Churches. Mems: 119 churches and 16 national councils of churches. Gen. Sec. Dr FELICIANO V. CARIÑO. Publ. *CCA News* (quarterly).

**Christian Peace Conference:** 130 11, Prague 3, POB 136, Prokopova 4, Czech Republic; tel. (2) 22781800; fax (2) 22781801; e-mail cpc.off@iol.cz; f. 1958 as an international movement of theologians, clergy and lay-people, aiming to bring Christendom to recognize its share of guilt in both world wars and to dedicate itself to the service of friendship, reconciliation and peaceful co-operation of nations, to concentrate on united action for peace and justice, and to co-ordinate peace groups in individual churches and facilitate their effective participation in the peaceful development of society. It works through five continental associations, regional groups and member churches in many countries. Moderator Dr SERGIO ARCE MARTÍNEZ; Co-ordinator Rev. BRIAN G. COOPER. Publs *CPC INFORMATION* (8 a year in English and German), occasional *Study Volume*.

**Conference of European Churches—CEC:** POB 2100, 150 route de Ferney, 1211 Geneva 2, Switzerland; tel. (22) 7916111; fax (22) 7916227; e-mail reg@wcc-coe.org; internet www.cec-kek.org; f. 1959 as a regional ecumenical organization for Europe and a meeting-place for European churches, including members and non-members of the World Council of Churches; assemblies every few years. Mems: 126 Protestant, Anglican, Orthodox and Old Catholic churches in all European countries. Gen. Sec. Rev. Dr KEITH CLEMENTS. Publs *Monitor*, CEC communiqués.

**Conference of International Catholic Organizations:** 37–39 rue de Vermont, 1202 Geneva, Switzerland; tel. (22) 7338392; f. 1927 to encourage collaboration and agreement between the different Catholic international organizations in their common interests, and to contribute to international understanding; organizes international assemblies and meetings to study specific problems. Permanent commissions deal with human rights, the new international economic order, social problems, the family health, education, etc. Mems: 36 Catholic international organizations. Administrator PAUL MORAND (Switzerland).

**Consultative Council of Jewish Organizations—CCJO:** 420 Lexington Ave, New York, NY 10170, USA; tel. (212) 808-5437; f. 1946 to co-operate and consult with the UN and other international bodies directly concerned with human rights and to defend the cultural, political and religious rights of Jews throughout the world. Sec.-Gen. WARREN GREEN (USA).

**European Baptist Federation:** Postfach 610340, 22423 Hamburg, Germany; tel. (40) 5509723; fax (40) 5509725; e-mail office@ebf.org; f. 1949 to promote fellowship and co-operation among Baptists in Europe; to further the aims and objects of the Baptist World Alliance; to stimulate and co-ordinate evangelism in Europe; to provide for consultation and planning of missionary work in Europe and elsewhere in the world. Mems: 49 Baptist Unions in European countries and the Middle East. Pres. DAVID COFFEY; Sec.-Treas. Rev. KARL-HEINZ WALTER (Germany).

**European Evangelical Alliance:** Wilhelmshoeher Allee 258, 34131 Kassel, Germany; tel. (561) 3149711; fax (561) 9387520; e-mail 100341.550@compuserve.com; internet www.hfe.org; f. 1953 to promote understanding and co-operation among evangelical Christians in Europe and to stimulate evangelism. Mems: 25 national alliances from 24 countries, 6 pan-European asscns. Pres. DEREK COPLEY (UK); Sec. GORDON SHOWELL-ROGERS.

**Friends World Committee for Consultation:** 4 Byng Pl., London, WC1E 7JH, United Kingdom; tel. (20) 7388-0497; fax (20) 7383-4644; e-mail fwccworldofficelondon@compuserve.com; internet www.quaker.org/fwcc/; f. 1937 to encourage and strengthen the spiritual life within the Religious Society of Friends (Quakers); to help Friends to a better understanding of their vocation in the world; to promote consultation among Friends of all countries; representation at the United Nations as a non-governmental organization. Mems: appointed representatives and individuals from 70 countries. Gen. Sec. ELIZABETH DUKE. Publs *Friends World News* (2 a year), *Calendar of Yearly Meetings* (annually), *Quakers around the World* (handbook).

**International Association for Religious Freedom—IARF:** 2 Market St, Oxford OX1 3EF, United Kingdom; tel. (1865) 202-744; fax (1865) 202-746; e-mail iarf@interfaith-center.org; internet www.iarf-religiousfreedom.net; f. 1900 as a world community of religions, subscribing to the principle of openness and to respect for fundamental human rights; conducts intercultural encounters, inter-religious dialogues, a social service network and development programme. Regional conferences and triennial congress. Mems: 70 groups in 25 countries. Pres. YUKITAKA YAMAMOTO (Japan); Gen. Sec. Rev. Dr ROBERT TRAER (UK). Publ. *IARF World* (2 a year).

**International Association of Buddhist Studies:** c/o Prof. Oskar von Hinüber, Orientalisches Seminar, Indologie, Humboldtstr. 5, Freiburg 79085, Germany; tel. (761) 203-3158; fax (761) 203-3152; f. 1976; holds international conference every three or four years; supports studies of Buddhist life and literature. Gen. Sec. OSKAR VON HINÜBER. Publ. *Journal* (2 a year).

**International Council of Christians and Jews:** 64629 Heppenheim, Werlestrasse 2, Postfach 1129, Germany; tel. (6252) 5041; fax (6252) 68331; e-mail iccj_buberhouse@t-online.de; f. 1955 to promote mutual respect and co-operation; holds annual international colloquium, seminars, meetings for young people and for women; forum for Jewish–Christian–Muslim relations established. Mems: national councils in 29 countries. Pres. Rabbi Prof. DAVID ROSEN; Sec.-Gen. Rev. FRIEDHELM PIEPER.

**International Council of Jewish Women:** 24–32 Stephenson Way, London, NW1 2JW, United Kingdom; tel. (20) 7388-8311; fax (20) 7387-2110; e-mail hq@icjw.demon.co.uk; internet www.icjw.org.uk; f. 1912 to promote friendly relations and understanding among Jewish women throughout the world; campaigns for human and women's rights, exchanges information on community welfare activities, promotes volunteer leadership, sponsors field work in social welfare, co-sponsors the International Jewish Women's Human Rights Watch and fosters Jewish education. Mems: affiliates totalling over 1.5m. members in 46 countries. Pres. JUNE JACOBS. Publs *Newsletter, Links around the World* (2 a year, English and Spanish), *International Jewish Women's Human Rights Watch* (2 a year).

**International Fellowship of Reconciliation:** Spoorstraat 38, 1815 BK Alkmaar, Netherlands; tel. (72) 512-30-14; fax (72) 515-11-02; e-mail office@ifor.org; internet www.ifor.org; f. 1919; international, spiritually-based movement committed to active non-violence as a way of life and as a means of transformation, to build a culture of peace and non-violence. Branches, affiliates and groups in more than 50 countries. Gen. Sec. JOHANNA S. M. KOOKE. Publs *Reconciliation International* (every 2 months), *Patterns in Reconciliation* (2 a year), *Non-violence Training in Africa* (3 a year, in English and French), *Cross the Lines* (3 a year, in English, French and Spanish).

**International Humanist and Ethical Union:** 47 Theobald's Rd, London, WC1X 8SP, United Kingdom; tel. (20) 7831-4817; fax (20) 7404-8641; internet www.iheu.org; f. 1952 to bring into association all those interested in promoting ethical and scientific humanism. Mems: national organizations and individuals in more than 51 countries. Exec. Dir BABU R. R. GOGINENI. Publ. *International Humanist News* (quarterly).

**International Organization for the Study of the Old Testament:** Faculteit der Godgeleerdheid, POB 9515, 2300 RA Leiden, Netherlands; tel. (71) 5272577; fax (71) 5272571; f. 1950. Holds triennial congresses. Pres. Prof. E. JENNI (Switzerland); Sec. Prof. A. VAN DER KOOIJ (Netherlands). Publ. *Vetus Testamentum* (quarterly).

**Latin American Council of Churches** (Consejo Latinoamericano de Iglesias—CLAI): Casilla 17-08-8522, Calle Inglaterra 943 y Mariana de Jesús, Quito, Ecuador; tel. and fax (2) 553996; e-mail israel@clai.ecuanex.net.ec; f. 1982. Mems: 147 churches in 19 countries. Gen. Sec. Rev. ISRAEL BATISTA.

**Latin American Episcopal Council:** Apartado Aéreos 5278 y 51086, Santafé de Bogotá, Colombia; tel. (1) 612-1620; fax (1) 612-1929; f. 1955 to study the problems of the Roman Catholic Church in Latin America and to co-ordinate Church activities. Mems: the Episcopal Conferences of Central and South America and the Caribbean. Pres. Archbishop OSCAR ANDRÉS RODRÍGUEZ MARADIAGA (Honduras). Publ. *CELAM* (6 a year).

**Lutheran World Federation:** 150 route de Ferney, POB 2100, 1211 Geneva 2, Switzerland; tel. (22) 7916111; fax (22) 7988616; e-mail info@lutheranworld.org; internet www.lutheranworld.org; f. 1947; communion of 128 Lutheran Churches of 70 countries. Current activities: inter-church aid; relief work in various areas of the globe; service to refugees including resettlement; aid to missions; theological research, conferences and exchanges; scholarship aid in various fields of church life; inter-confessional dialogue with Roman Catholic, Seventh-day Adventist, Anglican and Orthodox churches; Christian communications projects and international news and information services; Ninth Assembly: Hong Kong, 1997. Pres. Rt Rev. Dr CHRISTIAN KRAUSE (Germany); Gen. Sec. Rev. Dr ISHMAEL NOKO (Zimbabwe). Publs *Lutheran World Information* (English and German, every 2 weeks), *LWF Today* and *LWF Documentation* (both irregular).

**Middle East Council of Churches:** Makhoul St, Deep Bldg, POB 5376, Beirut, Lebanon; tel. and fax (1) 344894; f. 1974. Mems: 28 churches. Pres Pope SHENOUDAH III, Patriarch PETROS VII PAPAPETRO, Rev. Dr SELIM SAHYOUNI, Archbishop KYRILLOS BUSTROS; Gen. Sec. Rev. Dr RIAD JARJOUR. Publs *MECC News Report* (monthly), *Al Montada News Bulletin* (quarterly, in Arabic), *Courrier oecuménique du Moyen-Orient* (quarterly), *MECC Perspectives* (3 a year).

**Moral Re-Armament:** POB 3, 1211 Geneva 20, Switzerland; tel. (22) 7330920; fax (22) 7330267; e-mail media@caux.ch; internet www.caux.ch; other international centres at Panchgani, India, Petropolis, Brazil, London and Tirley Garth, UK, and Gweru, Zimbabwe; f. 1921; aims: a new social order for better human relations and the elimination of political, industrial and racial antagonism. Legally incorporated bodies in 20 countries. Pres. of Swiss foundation MARCEL GRANDY. Publs *Changer* (French, 6 a year), *For a Change* (English, 6 a year), *Caux Information* (German, monthly).

**Muslim World League** (Rabitat al-Alam al-Islami): POB 537–538, Makkah, Saudi Arabia; tel. (2) 5422733; fax (2) 5436619; e-mail mwlhq@aol.com; internet www.arab.net/mwl; f. 1962; aims to advance Islamic unity and solidarity, and to promote world peace and respect for human rights; provides financial assistance for education, medical care and relief work; has 30 offices throughout the world. Sec.-Gen. Sheikh Prof. Dr ABD' ALLAH BIN SALEH EL-OBEID. Publs *Majalla al-Rabita* (monthly, Arabic), *Akhbar al-Alam al Islami* (weekly, Arabic), *Journal* (monthly, English).

**Opus Dei** (Prelature of the Holy Cross and Opus Dei): Viale Bruno Buozzi 73, 00197 Rome, Italy; tel. (06) 808961; f. 1928 by Blessed Josemaría Escrivá de Balaguer to spread, at every level of society, a profound awakening of consciences to the universal calling to sanctity and apostolate in the course of members' own professional work. Mems: 81,123 Catholic laypeople and 1,697 priests. Bishop Prelate Most Rev. JAVIER ECHEVARRÍA. Publ. *Romana, Bulletin of the Prelature* (every six months).

**Pacific Conference of Churches:** POB 208, 4 Thurston St, Suva, Fiji; tel. 311277; fax 303205; f. 1961; organizes assembly every five years, as well as regular workshops, meetings and training seminars throughout the region. Mems: 36 churches and councils. Moderator Pastor REUBEN MAGEKON; Gen. Sec. Rev. VALAMOTU PALU.

**Pax Romana International Catholic Movement for Intellectual and Cultural Affairs—ICMICA; and International Movement of Catholic Students—IMCS:** 15 rue du Grand-Bureau, POB 315, 1211 Geneva 24, Switzerland; tel. (22) 8230707; fax (22) 8230708; e-mail miicmica@paxromana.int.ch; internet www.pax-romana.org; f. 1921 (IMCS), 1947 (ICMICA), to encourage in members an awareness of their responsibilities as people and Christians in the student and intellectual milieux; to promote contacts between students and graduates throughout the world and co-ordinate the contribution of Catholic intellectual circles to international life. Mems: 80 student and 60 intellectual organizations in 80 countries. ICMICA—Pres. MARY J. MWINGIRA (Tanzania); Gen. Sec. ANSELMO LEE SEONG-HOON (Republic of Korea); IMCS—Gen. Secs WALTER PRYSTHON (Brazil), ROLAND RANAIVOARISON (Madagascar). Publ. *Convergence* (3 a year).

**Salvation Army:** International HQ, 101 Queen Victoria St, London, EC4P 4EP, United Kingdom; tel. (20) 7332-0022; fax (20) 7236-

4981; e-mail er@salvationarmy.org.uk; internet www.salvationarmy.org.uk; f. 1865 to spread the Christian gospel and relieve poverty; emphasis is placed on the need for personal discipleship, and to make its evangelism effective it adopts a quasi-military form of organization. Social, medical and educational work is also performed in the 99 countries where the Army operates. Pres. Gen. PAUL RADER; Chief of Staff Commissioner EARLE MAXWELL. Publs 132 periodicals in 31 languages.

**Soroptimist International:** 87 Glisson Rd, Cambridge, CB1 2HG, United Kingdom; tel. (1223) 311833; fax (1223) 467951; e-mail sorophq@dial.pipex.com; internet www.sorop.org/; f. 1921 to maintain high ethical standards in business, the professions, and other aspects of life; to strive for human rights for all people and, in particular, to advance the status of women; to develop friendship and unity among Soroptimists of all countries; to contribute to international understanding and universal friendship. Convention held every 4 years, 2003: Sydney, Australia. Mems: 95,000 in 3,000 clubs in 119 countries and territories. International Pres. JANE ZIMMERMAN (Australia); Exec. Officer JANET BILTON. Publ. *International Soroptimist* (quarterly).

**Theosophical Society:** Adyar, Chennai 600 020, India; tel. (44) 4915552; fax (44) 4902706; e-mail para.vidya@gems.vsnl.net.in; f. 1875; aims at universal brotherhood, without distinction of race, creed, sex, caste or colour; study of comparative religion, philosophy and science; investigation of unexplained laws of nature and powers latent in man. Mems: 35,000 in 70 countries. Pres. RADHA S. BURNIER; Int. Sec. DOLORES GAGO. Publs *The Theosophist* (monthly), *Adyar News Letter* (quarterly), *Brahmavidya* (annually).

**United Bible Societies:** 7th Floor, Reading Bridge House, Reading, RG1 8PJ, United Kingdom; tel. (118) 950-0200; fax (118) 950-0857; e-mail jphillips@ubs-wsc.org; internet www.biblesociety.org; f. 1946. Mems: 135 Bible Societies in more than 200 countries. Pres. Dr SAMUEL ESCOBAR (Peru/USA); Gen. Sec. Rev. FERGUS MACDONALD (UK). Publs *United Bible Societies Bulletin, The Bible Translator* (quarterly), *Publishing World* (3 a year), *Prayer Booklet* (annually), *World Report* (monthly).

**Watch Tower Bible and Tract Society:** The Ridgeway, London NW7 1RN, United Kingdom; tel. (20) 8906-2211; fax (20) 8959-3855; e-mail pgillies@wtbts.org.uk; internet www.watchtower.org; f. 1881; 109 branches; serves as legal agency for Jehovah's Witnesses, whose membership is 5.9m. Pres. MILTON G. HENSCHEL; Sec. and Treas. LYMAN SWINGLE. Publs *The Watchtower* (2 a month, in 132 languages), *Awake!* (2 a month, in 83 languages).

**World Alliance of Reformed Churches (Presbyterian and Congregational):** Box 2100, 150 route de Ferney, 1211 Geneva 2, Switzerland; tel. (22) 7916238; fax (22) 7916505; e-mail mil@wcc-coe.org; f. 1970 by merger of WARC (Presbyterian) (f. 1875) with International Congregational Council (f. 1891) to promote fellowship among Reformed, Presbyterian and Congregational churches. Mems: 216 churches in 106 countries. Pres. Prof. CHOAN-SENG SONG; Gen. Sec. Prof. MILAN OPOCENSKY (Czech Republic). Publs *Reformed World* (quarterly), *Up-Date*.

**World Christian Life Community:** Borgo S. Spirito 8, Casella Postale 6139, 00195 Rome, Italy; tel. (06) 6868079; e-mail mcvx.wclc@agora.stm.it; f. 1953 as World Federation of the Sodalities of our Lady (first group founded 1563) as a lay movement (based on the teachings of Ignatius Loyola) to integrate Christian faith and daily living. Mems: groups in 55 countries representing about 100,000 individuals. Pres. JOSÉ MARÍA RIERA; Exec. Sec. GILLES MICHAUD. Publ. *Progressio* (in English, French, Spanish).

**World Conference on Religion and Peace:** 777 United Nations Plaza, New York, NY 10017, USA; tel. (212) 687-2163; fax (212) 983-0566; f. 1970 to co-ordinate education and action of various world religions for world peace and justice. Mems: religious organizations and individuals in 100 countries. Sec.-Gen. Dr WILLIAM VENDLEY. Publ. *Religion for Peace*.

**World Congress of Faiths:** 2 Market St, Oxford OX1 3EF, United Kingdom; tel. (1865) 202751; fax (1865) 202746; f. 1936 to promote a spirit of fellowship among mankind through an understanding of each other's religion, to bring together people of all nationalities, backgrounds and creeds in mutual respect and tolerance, to encourage the study and understanding of issues arising out of multi-faith societies, and to promote welfare and peace. Mems: about 800. Vice-Pres Rev. Dr EDWARD CARPENTER, Prof. KEITH WARD; Chair. MARCUS BRAYBROOKE. Publ. *World Faiths Encounter* (3 a year).

**World Evangelical Fellowship:** 141 Middle Rd 05-05, GSM Bldg, Singapore 188976, Singapore; tel. 3397900; fax 3383756; e-mail 100012.345@compuserve.com; f. 1951, on reorganization of World Evangelical Alliance (f. 1846); an int. grouping of national and regional bodies of evangelical Christians; encourages the organization of national fellowships and assists national mems in planning their activities. Mems: national evangelical asscns in 110 countries. International Dir AUGUSTIN B. VENCER, Jr. Publs *Evangelical World* (monthly), *Evangelical Review of Theology* (quarterly).

**World Fellowship of Buddhists:** 616 Benjasiri Pk, Soi Medhinivet off Soi Sukhumvit 24, Bangkok 10110, Thailand; tel. (2) 661-1284; fax (2) 661-0555; e-mail wfb_hq@asianet.co.th; internet www.wfb_hq.org; f. 1950 to promote strict observance and practice of the teachings of the Buddha; holds General Conference every 2 years; 135 regional centres in 37 countries. Pres. PHAN WANNAMETHEE; Hon. Sec.Gen. Dr NANTASARN SEESALAB. Publs *WFB Journal* (6 a year), *WFB Review* (quarterly), *WFB Newsletter* (monthly), documents, booklets.

**World Hindu Federation:** c/o Dr Jogendra Jha, Pashupati Kshetra, Kathmandu, Nepal; tel. (1) 470182; fax (1) 470131; e-mail jhas@ecsl.com.np; f. 1981 to promote and preserve Hindu philosophy and culture; to protect the rights of Hindus, particularly the right to worship. Executive Board meets annually. Mems: in 45 countries and territories. Sec.-Gen. Dr JOGENDRA JHA. Publ. *Vishwa Hindu* (monthly).

**World Jewish Congress:** 501 Madison Ave, New York, NY 10022, USA; tel. (212) 755-5770; fax (212) 755-5883; f. 1936; a voluntary association of representative Jewish communities and organizations throughout the world, aiming to foster the unity of the Jewish people and to ensure the continuity and development of their heritage. Mems: Jewish communities in 84 countries. Pres. EDGAR M. BRONFMAN; Sec.-Gen. ISRAEL SINGER. Publs *Gesher* (Hebrew quarterly, Israel), *Boletín Informativo OJI* (fortnightly, Buenos Aires).

**World Methodist Council:** International Headquarters, POB 518, Lake Junaluska, NC 28745, USA; tel. (704) 456-9432; fax (704) 456-9433; e-mail wmc6@juno.com; internet www.worldmethodistcouncil.org; f. 1881 to deepen the fellowship of the Methodist peoples, to encourage evangelism, to foster Methodist participation in the ecumenical movement, and to promote the unity of Methodist witness and service. Mems: 75 churches in 130 countries, comprising 32m. individuals. Gen. Sec. JOE HALE (USA). Publ. *World Parish* (6 a year).

**World Sephardi Federation:** 13 rue Marignac, 1206 Geneva, Switzerland; tel. (22) 3473313; fax (22) 3472839; f. 1951 to strengthen the unity of Jewry and Judaism among Sephardi and Oriental Jews, to defend and foster religious and cultural activities of all Sephardi and Oriental Jewish communities and preserve their spiritual heritage, to provide moral and material assistance where necessary and to co-operate with other similar organizations. Mems: 50 communities and organizations in 33 countries. Pres. NESSIM D. GAON; Sec.-Gen. SHIMON DERY.

**World Student Christian Federation:** 5 route des Morillons, Grand-Saconnex, 1218 Geneva, Switzerland; tel. (22) 7988953; fax (22) 7982370; e-mail wscf@worldcom.ch; f. 1895 to proclaim Jesus Christ as Lord and Saviour in the academic community, and to present students with the claims of the Christian faith over their whole life. Gen. Assembly every four years. Mems: 67 national Student Christian Movements, and 34 national correspondents. Chair. Rev. EJIKE OKORD (Nigeria); Secs-Gen. BEATE FAGERLI (Norway), LAWRENCE BREW (Ghana).

**World Union for Progressive Judaism:** 633 Third Ave, New York, NY 10017, USA; tel. (212) 249-0100; fax (212) 650-4099; f. 1926; promotes and co-ordinates efforts of Reform, Liberal, Progressive and Reconstructionist congregations throughout the world; supports new congregations; assigns and employs rabbis; sponsors seminaries and schools; organizes international conferences; maintains a youth section. Mems: organizations and individuals in 30 countries. Pres. AUSTIN BEUTEL; Exec. Dir Rabbi RICHARD G. HIRSCH (Israel). Publs *News Updates, International Conference Reports, European Judaism* (bi-annual).

**World Union of Catholic Women's Organisations:** 18 rue Notre-Dame-des-Champs, 75006 Paris, France; tel. 1-45-44-27-65; fax 1-42-84-04-80; e-mail wucwoparis@wanadoo.fr; f. 1910 to promote and co-ordinate the contribution of Catholic women in international life, in social, civic, cultural and religious matters. Mems: 20m. Pres.-Gen. MARÍA EUGENIA DÍAZ DE PFENNICH (Mexico); Sec.-Gen. GILLIAN BADCOCK (UK). Publ. *Newsletter* (quarterly in four languages).

## Science

**International Council for Science—ICSU:** 51 blvd de Montmorency, 75016 Paris, France; tel. 1-45-25-03-29; fax 1-42-88-94-31; e-mail secretariat@icsu.org; f. 1919 as International Research Council; present name adopted 1931; new statutes adopted 1996; to co-ordinate international co-operation in theoretical and applied sciences and to promote national scientific research through the intermediary of affiliated national organizations; General Assembly of representatives of national and scientific members meets every three years to formulate policy. The following committees have been established: Cttee on Science for Food Security, Scientific Cttee on Antarctic Research, Scientific Cttee on Oceanic Research, Cttee on Space Research, Scientific Cttee on Water Research, Scientific Cttee on Solar-Terrestrial Physics, Cttee on Science and Technology in Developing Countries, Cttee on Data for Science and Technology,

Programme on Capacity Building in Science, Scientific Cttee on Problems of the Environment, Steering Cttee on Genetics and Biotechnology and Scientific Cttee on International Geosphere-Biosphere Programme. The following services and Inter-Union Committees and Commissions have been established: Federation of Astronomical and Geophysical Data Analysis Services, Inter-Union Commission on Frequency Allocations for Radio Astronomy and Space Science, Inter-Union Commission on Radio Meteorology, Inter-Union Commission on Spectroscopy, Inter-Union Commission on Lithosphere. National mems: academies or research councils in 95 countries; Scientific mems and assocs: 25 international unions (see below) and 28 scientific associates. Pres. W. ARBER; Sec.-Gen. H. A. MOONEY. Publs *ICSU Yearbook, Science International* (quarterly), *Annual Report*.

## UNIONS FEDERATED TO THE ICSU

**International Astronomical Union:** 98 bis blvd d'Arago, 75014 Paris, France; tel. 1-43-25-83-58; fax 1-43-25-26-16; e-mail iau@iap.fr; internet www.iau.org; f. 1919 to facilitate co-operation between the astronomers of various countries and to further the study of astronomy in all its branches. Mems: organizations in 61 countries, and 8,000 individual mems. Pres. ROBERT KRAFT (USA); Gen. Sec. JOHANNES ANDERSEN (Denmark). Publ. *IAU Information Bulletin* (2 a year).

**International Geographical Union—IGU:** Dept of Geography, University of Bonn, 53115 Bonn, Meckenheimer Allee 166, Germany; tel. (228) 739287; fax (228) 739272; e-mail secretariat@igu.bn.eunet.be; internet www.helsinki.fi/science/igu; f. 1922 to encourage the study of problems relating to geography, to promote and co-ordinate research requiring international co-operation, and to organize international congresses and commissions. Mem. countries: 83, and 11 associates. Pres. Prof. BRUNO MESSERLI (Switzerland); Sec.-Gen. Prof. ECKART EHLERS (Germany). Publ. *IGU Bulletin* (2 a year).

**International Mathematical Union:** c/o Institute for Advanced Study (IAS), Olden Lane, Princeton, NJ 08540, USA; e-mail imu@ias.edu; f. 1952 to support and assist the International Congress of Mathematicians and other international scientific meetings or conferences; to encourage and support other international mathematical activities considered likely to contribute to the development of mathematical science—pure, applied or educational. Mems: 63 countries. Pres. Prof. JACOB PALIS; Sec.-Gen. Prof. PHILLIP GRIFFITHS.

**International Union for Pure and Applied Biophysics:** School of Biochemistry and Molecular Biology, University of Leeds, Leeds, LS2 9JT, United Kingdom; tel. (113) 2333023; fax (113) 2333167; e-mail a.c.t.north@leeds.ac.uk; internet www.iupab.leeds.ac.uk/iupab; f. 1961 to organize international co-operation in biophysics and promote communication between biophysics and allied subjects, to encourage national co-operation between biophysical societies, and to contribute to the advancement of biophysical knowledge. Mems: 45 adhering bodies. Pres. D. A. D. PARRY (New Zealand); Sec.-Gen. Prof. A. C. T. NORTH (UK). Publ. *Quarterly Reviews of Biophysics*.

**International Union of Biochemistry and Molecular Biology:** Institute for Biophysical Chemistry and Biochemistry, Technical University Berlin, Franklinstr. 29, 10587 Berlin, Germany; tel. (30) 31424205; fax (30) 31424783; e-mail kleinkauf@chem.tu-berlin.de; f. 1955 to sponsor the International Congresses of Biochemistry, to co-ordinate research and discussion, to organize co-operation between the societies of biochemistry and molecular biology, to promote high standards of biochemistry and molecular biology throughout the world and to contribute to the advancement of biochemistry and molecular biology in all its international aspects. Mems: 65 bodies. Pres. W. WHELAN (USA); Gen. Sec. Prof. Dr H. KLEINKAUF (Germany).

**International Union of Biological Sciences:** 51 blvd de Montmorency, 75016 Paris, France; tel. 1-45-25-00-09; fax 1-45-25-20-29; e-mail iubs@paris7.jussieu.fr; f. 1919. Mems: 41 national bodies, 80 scientific bodies. Exec. Dir Dr T. YOUNES. Publs *Biology International* (2 a year, plus special issues), *IUBS Monographs, IUBS Methodology, Manual Series*.

**International Union of Crystallography:** c/o M. H. Dacombe, 2 Abbey Sq., Chester, CH1 2HU, United Kingdom; tel. (1244) 345431; fax (1244) 344843; f. 1947 to facilitate international standardization of methods, of units, of nomenclature and of symbols used in crystallography; and to form a focus for the relations of crystallography to other sciences. Mems in 40 countries. Pres. Prof. H. SCHENK (Netherlands); Gen. Sec. S. LARSEN (Denmark); Exec. Sec. M. H. DACOMBE. Publs *Acta Crystallographica, Journal of Applied Crystallography, Journal of Synchroton Radiation, International Tables for Crystallography, World Directory of Crystallographers, IUCr/OUP Crystallographic Symposia, IUCr/OUP Monographs on Crystallography, IUCr/OUP Texts on Crystallography*.

**International Union of Geodesy and Geophysics—IUGG:** Cires Campus Box 216, University of Colorado, Boulder, CO 80309, USA; tel. (303) 497-51-47; fax (303) 497-36-45; e-mail jjoselyn@cisnes.colorado.edu; internet www.obs-mip.fr/uggi/; f. 1919; federation of seven associations representing Geodesy, Seismology and Physics of the Earth's Interior, Physical Sciences of the Ocean, Volcanology and Chemistry of the Earth's Interior, Hydrological Sciences, Meteorology and Atmospheric Physics, Geomagnetism and Aeronomy, which meet at the General Assemblies of the Union. In addition, there are Joint Committees of the various associations either among themselves or with other unions. The Union organizes scientific meetings and also sponsors various permanent services, to collect, analyse and publish geophysical data. Mems: in 75 countries. Pres. Prof. MASARU KONO (Japan); Sec.-Gen. Dr JOANN JOSELYN (USA). Publs *IUGG Yearbook, Journal of Geodesy* (quarterly), *IASPEI Newsletter* (iregular), *Bulletin Volcanologique* (2 a year), *Hydrological Sciences Journal* (quarterly), *Bulletin de l'Association Internationale d'Hydrologie Scientifique* (quarterly), *IAMAP News Bulletin* (iregular).

**International Union of Geological Sciences—IUGS:** c/o Norges Geologiske Undersøkelse, N-7491 Trondheim, Norway; tel. (73) 90-40-40; fax (73) 92-16-20; e-mail iugs.secretariat.ngu.no; internet www.iugs.org/; f. 1961 to encourage the study of geoscientific problems, facilitate international and inter-disciplinary co-operation in geology and related sciences, and support the quadrennial International Geological Congress. IUGS organizes international meetings and co-sponsors joint programmes, including the International Geological Correlation Programme (with UNESCO). Mems from 105 countries. Pres. Dr ROBIN BRETT (USA); Sec.-Gen. Prof. A. BORIANI (Italy).

**International Union of Immunological Societies:** Dept of Surgery, University of Edinburgh Medical School, Teviot Place, Edinburgh, EH8 9AG, United Kingdom; tel. (131) 650-3557; fax (131) 667-6190; f. 1969; holds triennial international congress. Mems: national societies in 50 countries and territories. Pres. TOMIO TADA; Sec.-Gen. KEITH JAMES.

**International Union of Microbiological Societies—IUMS:** c/o Prof. John S. Mackenzie, Dept. of Microbiology, University of Queensland, Brisbane QLD 4072, Australia; tel. (7) 3365-4648; fax (7) 3365-6265; e-mail jmac@biosci.uq.edu.au; f. 1930. Mems: 106 national microbiological societies. Pres. P. HELENA MÄKELÄ (Finland); Sec.-Gen. Prof. JOHN S. MACKENZIE. Publs *International Journal of Systematic Bacteriology* (quarterly), *International Journal of Food Microbiology* (every 2 months), *Advances in Microbial Ecology* (annually), Archives of Virology.

**International Union of Nutritional Sciences:** c/o Prof. Galal, UCLA School of Public Health, International Health Program, 10833 Le Conte Ave, POB 951772, Los Angeles, CA 90095-1772, USA; tel. (310) 2069639; fax (310) 7941805; e-mail ogalal@ucla.edu; f. 1946 to promote international co-operation in the scientific study of nutrition and its applications, to encourage research and exchange of scientific information by holding international congresses and issuing publications. Mems: 67 organizations. Pres. Dr B. A. UNDERWOOD (USA); Sec.-Gen. Prof. OSMAN M. GALAL. Publs *Annual Report, IUNS Directory, Newsletter*.

**International Union of Pharmacology:** Dept of Physiology and Pharmacology, Univ. of Strathclyde, 204 George St, Glasgow, G1 1XW, United Kingdom; tel. (141) 552-4400; fax (141) 552-2562; f. 1963 to promote international co-ordination of research, discussion and publication in the field of pharmacology, including clinical pharmacology, drug metabolism and toxicology; co-operates with WHO in all matters concerning drugs and drug research; holds international congresses. Mems: 52 national and four regional societies. Pres. T. GODFRAIND (Belgium); Sec.-Gen. W. C. BOWMAN (UK). Publ. *TIPS (Trends in Pharmacological Sciences)*.

**International Union of Physiological Sciences:** IUPS Secretariat, LGN, Bâtiment CERVI, Hôpital de la Pitié-Salpêtrière, 83 blvd de l'Hôpital, 75013 Paris, France; tel. 1-42-17-75-37; fax 1-42-17-75-75; e-mail svorsoni@infobiogen.fr; f. 1955. Mems: 50 national, six assoc., four regional, two affiliated and 14 special mems. Pres. Prof. EWALD WEIBEL (Switzerland); Sec. Prof. DENIS NOBLE.

**International Union of Psychological Science:** c/o Prof. P. L.-J. Ritchie, Ecole de psychologie, Université d'Ottawa, 145 Jean-Jacques-Lussier, CP 450, Succ. A, Ottawa, ON KIN 6N5, Canada; tel (613) 562-5289; fax (613) 562-5169; e-mail pritchie@uottawa.ca; internet www.aixl.uottawa.ca~pritchie; f. 1951 to contribute to the development of intellectual exchange and scientific relations between psychologists of different countries. Mems: 64 national and 10 affiliate organizations. Pres. Prof. GÉRY D'YDEWALLE (Belgium); Sec.-Gen. Prof. P. L.-J. RITCHIE (Canada). Publs *International Journal of Psychology* (quarterly), *The IUPsyS Directory* (irregular).

**International Union of Pure and Applied Chemistry—IUPAC:** Bldg 19, 104 T. W. Alexander Dr., Research Triangle Park, POB 13757, NC 27709-3757, USA; tel. (919) 485-8700; fax (919) 485-8706; e-mail secretariat@iupac.org; internet www.iupac.org; f. 1919 to organize permanent co-operation between chemical associations in the member countries, to study topics of international importance requiring standardization or codification, to co-operate with other international organizations in the field of chemistry and to contribute to the advancement of all aspects of chemistry. Biennial General Assembly. Mems: in 44 countries. Pres. Dr A. HAYES (UK); Sec.-Gen. Dr E. D. BECKER (USA). Publs *Chemistry International* (bi-monthly), *Pure and Applied Chemistry* (monthly).

**International Union of Pure and Applied Physics:** CEN Saclay, 91191 Gif-sur-Yvette Cédex, France; tel. 1-69-08-84-18; fax 1-69-08-76-36; e-mail turlay@hep.saclay.cea.fr; f. 1922 to promote and encourage international co-operation in physics. Mems: in 46 countries. Pres. B. RICHTER (USA); Sec.-Gen. Dr RENÉ TURLAY (France).

**International Union of Radio Science:** c/o University of Ghent (INTEC), Sint-Pietersnieuwstraat 41, 9000 Ghent, Belgium; tel. (9) 264-33-20; fax (9) 264-42-88; e-mail inge.heleu@intec.rug.ac.be; internet www.intec.rug.ac.be/ursi; f. 1919 to stimulate and co-ordinate, on an international basis, studies in radio, telecommunications and electronics; to promote research and disseminate the results; to encourage the adoption of common methods of measurement, and the standardization of measuring instruments; and to stimulate studies of the scientific aspects of telecommunications using electromagnetic waves. There are 47 national committees. Pres. Prof. T. B. A. SENIOR (USA); Sec.-Gen. Prof. P. LAGASSE (Belgium). Publs *The Radio Science Bulletin* (quarterly), *Proceedings of General Assemblies* (every 3 years), *Modern Radio Science* (every 3 years), *Review of Radio Science* (every 3 years).

**International Union of the History and Philosophy of Science:** Division of the History of Science (DHS): Centre d'Histoire des Sciences et des Techniques, 15 ave des Tilleuls, 4000 Liège, Belgium; tel. (4) 366-94-79; fax (4) 366-94-47; e-mail chst@ulg.ac.be; Division of the History of Logic, Methodology and Philosophy of Science (DLMPS): 161 rue Ada, 34392 Montpellier, France; f. 1956 to promote research into the history and philosophy of science. DHS has 44 national committees and DLMPS has 35 committees. DHS Council: Pres. Prof. B. V. SUBBARAYAPPA (India); Sec. Prof. R. HALLEUX (Belgium). DLMPS Council: Pres. Prof. M. RABIN (Israel); Sec.-Gen. Prof. D. WESTERSTAHL (Sweden).

**International Union of Theoretical and Applied Mechanics:** c/o Prof. Michael A. Hayes, Mathematical Physics Dept, University College Dublin, Belfield, Dublin 4, Ireland; tel. and fax (1) 706-1172; e-mail iutam@ucd.ie; internet www.iutam.org; f. 1947 to form a link beween persons and organizations engaged in scientific work (theoretical or experimental) in mechanics or in related sciences; to organize international congresses of theoretical and applied mechanics, through a standing Congress Committee, and to organize other international meetings for subjects falling within this field; and to engage in other activities meant to promote the development of mechanics as a science. Mems: from 49 countries. Pres. Prof. W. SCHIEHLEN (Germany); Sec.-Gen. Prof. M. HAYES (Ireland); Publs *Annual Report, Newsletter.*

## OTHER ORGANIZATIONS

**Association for the Taxonomic Study of the Flora of Tropical Africa:** National Botanic Garden of Belgium, Domein van Bouchout, 1860 Meise, Belgium; tel. (2) 269-39-05; fax (2) 270-15-67; e-mail rammeloo@br.fgov.be; f. 1950 to facilitate co-operation and liaison between botanists engaged in the study of the flora of tropical Africa south of the Sahara including Madagascar; maintains a library. Mems: about 800 botanists in 63 countries. Sec.-Gen. Prof. J. RAMMELOO. Publs *AETFAT Bulletin* (annually), *Proceedings.*

**Association of European Atomic Forums—FORATOM:** 15–17 rue Belliard, 1040 Brussels, Belgium; tel. (2) 502-45-95; fax (2) 502-39-02; e-mail foratom@skynet.be; internet www.foratom.org; f. 1960; holds periodical conferences. Mems: atomic 'forums' in Austria, Belgium, Czech Republic, Finland, France, Germany, Italy, Netherlands, Spain, Sweden, Switzerland and the United Kingdom. Pres. JEAN-PIERRE ROUGEAU; Sec.-Gen. Dr W.-J. SCHMIDT-KÜSTER. Publ. *Almanac* (annually).

**Association of Geoscientists for International Development—AGID:** Institute of Geoscience, University of São Paulo, 11348 São Paulo, 05422-970 Brazil; tel. (11) 818-4232; fax (11) 818-4207; e-mail abmacedo@usp.br; internet agid.igc.usp.br; f. 1974 to encourage communication between those interested in the application of the geosciences to international development; to give priority to the developing countries in these matters; to organize meetings and publish information; affiliated to the International Union of Geological Sciences (q.v.) and the Economic and Social Council of the United Nations. Mems: in 149 countries (2,000 individuals, and 57 institutions). Pres. S. D. LIMAYE; Sec. A. J. REEDMAN; Exec. Dir A. B. MACEDO. Publs *AGID Update Newsletter* (2 a year), *Geoscience and Development* (annually).

**Council for the International Congresses of Entomology:** c/o FAO, POB 3700 MCPO, 1277 Makati, Philippines; tel. (2) 8134229; fax (2) 8127725; f. 1910 to act as a link between quadrennial congresses and to arrange the venue for each congress; the committee is also the entomology section of the International Union of Biological Sciences (q.v.). Chair. Dr M. J. WHITTAM (Australia); Sec. Dr J. OLIVER (USA).

**European Association of Geoscientists and Engineers—EAGE:** c/o EAGE Business Office, 3990 DB Houten, Netherlands; tel. (30) 6354055; fax (30) 6343524; e-mail eage@eage.nl; internet www.eage.nl; f. 1997 by merger of European Asscn of Exploration Geophysicists and Engineers (f. 1951) and the European Asscn of Petroleum Geoscientists and Engineers (f. 1988); these two organizations have become, respectively, the Geophysical and the Petroleum Divisions of the EAGE; aims to promote the applications of geoscience and related subjects, to foster communication, fellowship and co-operation between those working or studying in the fields; organizes conferences, workshops, education programmes and exhibitions and seeks global co-operation with other organizations having similar objectives. Mems approx. 5,400 in 95 countries throughout the world. Pres. M. PELTONIEMI; Sec. J.-C. GROSSET. Publs *Geophysical Prospecting* (6 a year), *First Break* (monthly), *Petroleum Geoscience* (quarterly).

**European Molecular Biology Organization—EMBO:** Meyerhofstr. 1, Postfach 1022.40, 69012 Heidelberg, Germany; tel. (6221) 383031; fax (6221) 384879; e-mail embo@embl-heidelberg.de; internet www.embo.org; f. 1962 to promote collaboration in the field of molecular biology; to establish fellowships for training and research; established a European Molecular Biology Laboratory where a majority of the disciplines comprising the subject are represented. Mems: 965. Exec. Dir Prof. FRANK GANNON. Publ. *EMBO Journal* (24 a year).

**European Organization for Nuclear Research—CERN:** European Laboratory for Particle Physics, 1211 Geneva 23, Switzerland; tel. (22) 7676111; fax (22) 7676555; internet www.cern.ch/; f. 1954 to provide for collaboration among European states in nuclear research of a pure scientific and fundamental character; the work of CERN is for peaceful purposes only and concerns subnuclear, high-energy and elementary particle physics; it is not concerned with the development of nuclear reactors or fusion devices. Council comprises two representatives of each member state. Major experimental facilities: Proton Synchrotron (of 25–28 GeV), Super Proton Synchrotron (of 450 GeV), and a Large Electron-Positron Collider (LEP) of 27 km circumference (of 94 GeV per beam). Budget (1998) 875m. Swiss francs. Mems: Austria, Belgium, Bulgaria, Czech Republic, Denmark, Finland, France, Germany, Greece, Hungary, Italy, Netherlands, Norway, Poland, Portugal, Slovakia, Spain, Sweden, Switzerland, United Kingdom; Observers: Israel, Japan, Russia, Turkey, USA, European Commission, UNESCO. Dir-Gen. LUCIANO MAIANI (Italy). Publs *CERN Courier* (monthly), *Annual Report, Scientific Reports.*

**European-Mediterranean Seismological Centre:** c/o LDG, BP 12, 91680 Bruyères-le-Châtel, France; tel. 1-69-26-78-14; fax 1-69-26-70-00; e-mail csem@mail.csem.fr; f. 1976 for rapid determination of seismic hypocentres in the region; maintains data base. Mems: institutions in 21 countries. Pres. C. BROWITT; Sec.-Gen. F. RIVIERE. Publ. *Newsletter* (two a year).

**Federation of Arab Scientific Research Councils:** POB 13027, Al Karkh/Karadat Mariam, Baghdad, Iraq; tel. (1) 8881709; fax (1) 8866346; f. 1976 to encourage co-operation in scientific research, to promote the establishment of new institutions and plan joint regional research projects. Mems: national science bodies in 15 countries. Sec.-Gen. Dr TAHA AL-NUEIMI. Publs *Journal of Computer Research, Journal of Environmental and Sustained Development, Journal of Biotechnology.*

**Federation of Asian Scientific Academies and Societies—FASAS:** c/o Indian National Science Academy, Bahadur Shah Zafar Marg, New Delhi 110 002, India; tel. (11) 3232066; fax (11) 3235648; e-mail insa@giasdl01.vsnl.net.in; f. 1984 to stimulate regional co-operation and promote national and regional self-reliance in science and technology, by organizing meetings, training and research programmes and encouraging the exchange of scientists and of scientific information. Mems: national scientific academies and societies from Afghanistan, Australia, Bangladesh, People's Republic of China, India, Republic of Korea, Malaysia, Nepal, New Zealand, Pakistan, Philippines, Singapore, Sri Lanka, Thailand. Pres. Prof. C. S. DAYRIT (Philippines); Sec. Prof. INDIRA NATH (India).

**Federation of European Biochemical Societies:** c/o Dept of Medical Biochemistry and Danish Centre for Human Genome Research, Bldg 170, Ole Worms Allé, 8000 Arhus C, Denmark; tel. 8942-2880; fax 8613-1160; e-mail jec@biokemi.an.dk; f. 1964 to promote the science of biochemistry through meetings of European biochemists, provision of fellowships and advanced courses and issuing publications. Mems: 40,000 in 34 societies. Chair. Prof. G. DIRHEIMER; Sec.-Gen. Prof. JULIO E. CELIS. Publs *European Journal of Biochemistry, FEBS Letters, FEBS Bulletin.*

**Foundation for International Scientific Co-ordination** (Fondation 'Pour la science', Centre international de synthèse): 12 rue Colbert, 75002 Paris, France; tel. 1-42-97-50-68; fax 1-42-97-46-46; e-mail synthese@filnet.fr; f. 1925. Dirs MICHEL BLAY, ERIC BRIAN;

Publs *Revue de Synthèse, Revue d'Histoire des Sciences, Semaines de Synthèse, L'Evolution de l'Humanité.*

**Intergovernmental Oceanographic Commission:** UNESCO, 1 rue Miollis, 75732 Paris Cédex 15, France; tel. 1-45-68-39-83; fax 1-45-68-58-10; f. 1960 to promote scientific investigation of the nature and resources of the oceans through the concerted action of its members. Mems: 127 governments. Chair. SU JILAN (China); Exec. Sec. Dr PATRICIO BERNAL. Publs *IOC Technical Series* (irregular), IOC *Manuals* and *Guides* (irregular), *IOC Workshop Reports* (irregular) and *IOC Training Course Reports* (irregular), annual reports.

**International Academy of Astronautics—IAA:** 6 rue Galilee, POB 1268–16, 75766 Paris Cédex 16, France; tel. 1-47-23-82-15; fax 1-47-23-82-16; f. 1960; fosters the development of astronautics for peaceful purposes, holds scientific meetings and makes scientific studies, reports, awards and book awards; maintains 19 scientific cttees and a multilingual terminology data base (20 languages). Mems: 681, and 382 corresponding mems, in basic sciences, engineering sciences, life sciences and social sciences, from 57 countries. Sec.-Gen. Dr JEAN-MICHEL CONTANT. Publ. *Acta Astronautica* (monthly).

**International Association for Biologicals:** CP 456, 1211 Geneva 4, Switzerland; fax (22) 702-93-55; internet www.iabs.org; f. 1955 to connect producers and controllers of immunological products (sera, vaccines, etc.) for the study and the development of methods of standardization; supports international organizations in their efforts to solve problems of standardization. Mems: 500. Pres. F. HORAUD (France); Sec.-Gen. D. GAUDRY (France). Publs *Newsletter* (quarterly), *Biologicals* (quarterly).

**International Association for Earthquake Engineering:** Kenchiku Kaikan, 3rd Floor, 5-26-20, Shiba, Minato-ku, Tokyo 108, Japan; tel. (3) 453-1281; fax (3) 453-0428; f. 1963 to promote international co-operation among scientists and engineers in the field of earthquake engineering through exchange of knowledge, ideas and results of research and practical experience. Mems: national cttees in 49 countries. Pres. SHELDON CHERRY (Canada); Sec.-Gen. Dr TSUNEO KATAYAMA.

**International Association for Ecology—INTECOL:** Lunigiana Museum of Natural History, 54011 Aulla, Italy; tel. (0187) 400252; fax (0187) 420727; e-mail afarina@tamnet.it; f. 1967 to provide opportunities for communication between ecologists world-wide; to co-operate with organizations and individuals having related aims and interests; to encourage studies in the different fields of ecology; affiliated to the International Union of Biological Sciences (q.v.). Mems: 35 national and international ecological societies, and 1,000 individuals. Pres. J. A. LEE (UK); Sec.-Gen. A. FARINA (Italy).

**International Association for Mathematical Geology:** c/o T. A. Jones, POB 2189, Houston, TX 77252-2189, USA; tel. (713) 431-6546; fax (713) 431-6336; internet www.iamg.org; f. 1968 for the preparation and elaboration of mathematical models of geological processes; the introduction of mathematical methods in geological sciences and technology; assistance in the development of mathematical investigation in geological sciences; the organization of international collaboration in mathematical geology through various forums and publications; educational programmes for mathematical geology; affiliated to the International Union of Geological Sciences (q.v.). Mems: c. 600. Pres. Dr R. A. OLEA (USA); Sec.-Gen. Dr T. A. JONES (USA). Publs *Mathematical Geology* (8 a year), *Computers and Geosciences* (10 a year), *Natural Resources Research* (quarterly), *Newsletter* (2 a year).

**International Association for Mathematics and Computers in Simulation:** c/o Free University of Brussels, Automatic Control, CP 165, 50 ave, F. D. Roosevelt, 1050 Brussels, Belgium; tel. (2) 650-20-97; fax (2) 650-35-64; f. 1955 to further the study of mathematical tools and computer software and hardware, analogue, digital or hybrid computers for simulation of soft or hard systems. Mems: 1,100 and 27 assoc. mems. Pres. R. VICHNEVETSKY (USA); Sec. Prof. RAYMOND HANUS. Publs *Mathematics and Computers in Simulation* (6 a year), *Applied Numerical Mathematics* (6 a year), *Journal of Computational Acoustics.*

**International Association for the Physical Sciences of the Ocean—IAPSO:** POB 820440, Vicksburg, MS 39182-0440, USA; tel. (601) 636-1363; fax (601) 629-9640; e-mail camfield@vicksburg.com; f. 1919 to promote the study of scientific problems relating to the oceans and interactions occurring at its boundaries, chiefly in so far as such study may be carried out by the aid of mathematics, physics and chemistry; to initiate, facilitate and co-ordinate research; to provide for discussion, comparison and publication; affiliated to the International Union of Geodesy and Geophysics (q.v.). Mems: 81 member states. Pres. Dr ROBIN D. MUENCH (USA); Sec.-Gen. Dr FRED E. CAMFIELD (USA). Publ. *Publications Scientifiques* (irregular).

**International Association for Plant Physiology—IAPP:** c/o Dr D. Graham, Div. of Food Science and Technology, CSIRO, POB 52, North Ryde, NSW, Australia 2113; tel. (2) 9490-8333; fax (2) 9490-3107; e-mail douglasgraham@dfst.csiro.au; f. 1955 to promote the development of plant physiology at the international level through congresses, symposia and workshops, by maintaining communication with national societies and by encouraging interaction between plant physiologists in developing and developed countries; affiliated to the International Union of Biological Sciences (q.v.). Pres. Prof. S. MIYACHI; Sec.-Treas. Dr D. GRAHAM.

**International Association for Plant Taxonomy:** c/o Prof. Tod F. Stuessy, Institut für Botanik und Botanischer Garten, Universität Wien, Rennweg 14, A-1030 Wien, Austria; f. 1950 to promote the development of plant taxonomy and encourage contacts between people and institutes interested in this work; affiliated to the International Union of Biological Sciences (q.v.). Mems: institutes and individuals in 85 countries. Publs *Taxon* (quarterly), *Regnum vegetabile* (irregular).

**International Association of Botanic Gardens:** c/o Prof. J. E. Hernández-Bermejo, Córdoba Botanic Garden, Avda de Linneo, s/n, 14004 Córdoba, Spain; tel. (957) 200077; fax (957) 295333; f. 1954 to promote co-operation between scientific collections of living plants, including the exchange of information and specimens; to promote the study of the taxonomy of cultivated plants; and to encourage the conservation of rare plants and their habitats; affiliated to the International Union of Biological Sciences (q.v.). Pres. Prof. KUNIO IWATSUKI (Japan); Sec. Prof. J. ESTEBAN HERNÁNDEZ-BERMEJO (Spain).

**International Association of Geodesy:** Dept of Geophysics, Juliane Maries Vej 30, 2100 Copenhagen Oe, Denmark; tel. (45) 3532-0582; fax (45) 3536-5357; internet www.gfy.ku.dk/~iag/~iag; f. 1922 to promote the study of all scientific problems of geodesy and encourage geodetic research; to promote and co-ordinate international co-operation in this field; to publish results; affiliated to the International Union of Geodesy and Geophysics (q.v.). Mems: national committees in 73 countries. Pres. F. SANSÒ (Italy); Sec.-Gen. C. C. TSCHERNING (Denmark). Publs *Journal of Geodesy, Travaux de l'AIG.*

**International Association of Geomagnetism and Aeronomy—IAGA:** c/o Dr JoAnn Joselyn, NOAA Space Environment Center, 325 Broadway, Boulder, CO 80303, USA; tel. (303) 497-5147; fax (303) 494-0980; e-mail jjoselyn@sec.noaa.gov; f. 1919 for the study of questions relating to geomagnetism and aeronomy and the encouragement of research; holds General and Scientific Assemblies every two years; affiliated to the International Union of Geodesy and Geophysics (IUGG, q.v.). Mems: the countries which adhere to the IUGG. Pres. M. KONO (Japan); Sec.-Gen. Dr JOANN JOSELYN. Publs *IAGA Bulletin* (including annual *Geomagnetic Data), IAGA News* (annually).

**International Association of Hydrological Sciences:** Dept of Geography, Wilfrid Laurier Univ., Waterloo, ON N2L 3C5, Canada; tel. (519) 884-1970; fax (519) 846-0968; e-mail 44iahs@mach1.wlu.ca; internet www.wlu.ca/~wwwiahs/index.html; f. 1922 to promote co-operation in the study of hydrology and water resources. Pres. Dr J. C. RODDA (UK); Sec.-Gen. Dr GORDON J. YOUNG (Canada). Publs *Journal* (every 2 months), *Newsletter* (3 a year).

**International Association of Meteorology and Atmospheric Sciences—IAMAS:** Dept of Physics, Univ. of Toronto, Toronto, ON M5S 1A7, Canada; f. 1919; permanent commissions on atmospheric ozone, radiation, atmospheric chemistry and global pollution, dynamic meteorology, polar meteorology, clouds and precipitation, climate, atmospheric electricity, planetary atmospheres and their evolution, and meteorology of the upper atmosphere; general assemblies held once every four years; special assemblies held once between general assemblies; affiliated to the International Union of Geodesy and Geophysics (q.v.). Pres. Prof. R. DUCE (USA); Sec.-Gen. Prof. R. LIST (Canada).

**International Association of Sedimentologists:** c/o Prof. A. Strasser, Institut de Géologie, Pérolles, 1700 Fribourg, Switzerland; tel. (26) 3008978; fax (26) 3009742; e-mail andreas.strasser@unifr.ch; internet www.blackwell-science.com/uk/society/ias; f. 1952; affiliated to the International Union of Geological Sciences (q.v.). Mems: 2,200. Pres. Prof. M. E. TUCKER (UK); Gen. Sec. Prof. A. STRASSER (Switzerland). Publ. *Sedimentology* (every 2 months).

**International Association of Theoretical and Applied Limnology** (Societas Internationalis Limnologiae): Dept of Biology, University of Alabama, Tuscaloosa, AL 35487-0206, USA; tel. (205) 348-1793; fax (205) 348-1403; e-mail rwetzel@biology.as.ua.edu; internet www.limnology.org; f. 1922; study of physical, chemical and biological phenomena of lakes and rivers; affiliated to the International Union of Biological Sciences (q.v.). Mems: about 3,200. Pres. C. W. BURNS (New Zealand); Gen. Sec. and Treas. ROBERT G. WETZEL (USA).

**International Association of Volcanology and Chemistry of the Earth's Interior—IAVCEI:** Geophysical Institute, University of Alaska Fairbanks, POB 757320, Fairbanks, AK 99775, USA; tel. (907) 474-7131; fax (907) 474-5618; f. 1919 to examine scientifically all aspects of volcanology; affiliated to the International Union of Geodesy and Geophysics (q.v.). Pres. R. S. J. SPARKS (UK); Sec.-Gen.

S. R. McNutt (USA). Publs *Bulletin of Volcanology, Catalogue of the Active Volcanoes of the World, Proceedings in Volcanology.*

**International Association of Wood Anatomists:** Herbarium Division, University of Utrecht, Netherlands; tel. (30) 532643; f. 1931 for the purpose of study, documentation and exchange of information on the structure of wood. Mems: 500 in 61 countries. Exec. Sec. Regis B. Miller. Publ. *IAWA Journal.*

**International Astronautical Federation—IAF:** 3–5 rue Mario-Nikis, 75015 Paris, France; tel. 1-45-67-42-60; fax 1-42-73-21-20; e-mail iaf@wanadoo.fr; internet www.iafastro.com; f. 1950 to foster the development of astronautics for peaceful purposes at national and international levels. The IAF has created the International Academy of Astronautics (IAA) and the International Institute of Space Law (IISL). Mems: 153 national astronautical societies in 45 countries. Pres. Dr Tomifumi Godai (Japan); Exec. Sec. Claude Gourdet.

**International Biometric Society:** c/o Prof. E. Baráth, Chair. of Statistics, 2103 Gödöllö, Hungary; tel. (28) 410-694; fax (28) 430-336; f. 1947 for the advancement of quantitative biological science through the development of quantitative theories and the application, development and dissemination of effective mathematical and statistical techniques; the Society has 16 regional organizations and 17 national groups, is affiliated with the International Statistical Institute and the World Health Organization, and constitutes the Section of Biometry of the International Union of Biological Sciences (q.v.). Mems: over 6,000 in more than 70 countries. Pres. Prof. Sue Wilson (Australia); Sec. Prof. E. Baráth (Hungary). Publs *Biometrics* (quarterly), *Biometric Bulletin* (quarterly), *Journal of Agricultural, Biological and Environmental Statistics* (quarterly).

**International Botanical Congress:** c/o Dr Peter Hoch, Missouri Botanical Garden, PO Box 299, St Louis, MO 63166-0299, USA; tel. (314) 577-5175; fax (314) 577-9589; e-mail ibc16@mobot.org; f. 1864 to inform botanists of recent progress in the plant sciences; the Nomenclature Section of the Congress attempts to provide a uniform terminology and methodology for the naming of plants; other Divisions deal with developmental, metabolic, structural, systematic and evolutionary, ecological botany; genetics and plant breeding; next Congress: St Louis, 1999; affiliated to the International Union of Biological Sciences (q.v.). Sec. Dr Peter Hoch.

**International Bureau of Weights and Measures:** Pavillon de Breteuil, 92312 Sèvres Cédex, France; tel. 1-45-07-70-70; fax 1-45-34-20-21; e-mail info@bipm.fr; internet www.bipm.fr; f. 1875 for the international unification of physical measures; establishment of fundamental standards and of scales of the principal physical dimensions; preservation of the international prototypes; determination of national standards; precision measurements in physics. Mems: 48 states. Pres. J. Kovalevsky (France); Sec. W. R. Blevin (Austria).

**International Cartographic Association:** 136 bis rue de Grenelle, 75700 Paris 07 SP, France; tel. 1-43-98-82-95; fax 1-43-98-84-00; f. 1959 for the advancement, instigation and co-ordination of cartographic research involving co-operation between different nations. Particularly concerned with furtherance of training in cartography, study of source material, compilation, graphic design, drawing, scribing and reproduction techniques of maps; organizes international conferences, symposia, meetings, exhibitions. Mems: 80 nations. Pres. Michael Wood. Publ. *ICA Newsletter* (2 a year).

**International Centre of Insect Physiology and Ecology:** POB 30772, Nairobi, Kenya; tel. (2) 861680; fax (2) 803360; e-mail icipe@africaonline.co.ke; f. 1970; specializes in research and development of environmentally sustainable and affordable methods of managing tropical arthropod plant pests and disease vectors, and in the conservation and utilisation of biodiversity of insects of commercial and ecological importance; organizes training programmes. Dir-Gen. Dr Hans Rudolph Herren. Publs *Insect Science and its Application* (quarterly), *Annual Report*, training manuals, technical bulletins, newsletter.

**International Commission for Optics:** Institut d'Optique/CNRS, POB 147, 91403 Orsay Cédex, France; tel. 1-69-35-87-41; fax 1-69-35-87-00; internet www.ico-optics.org; f. 1948 to contribute to the progress of theoretical and instrumental optics, to assist in research and to promote international agreement on specifications; Gen. Assembly every three years. Mems: committees in 44 territories. Pres. Prof. T. Asakura (Japan); Sec.-Gen. Dr P. Chavel (France). Publ. *ICO Newsletter.*

**International Commission for Plant-Bee Relationships:** c/o Prof. I. Williams, Entomology-Nematology Dept, Rothamsted Experimental Station, Harpenden, Herts, AL5 2JQ, United Kingdom; f. 1950 to promote research and its application in the field of bee botany, and collect and spread information; to organize meetings, etc., and collaborate with scientific organizations; affiliated to the International Union of Biological Sciences (q.v.). Mems: 175 in 34 countries. Pres. Prof. Ingrid Williams; Sec. Dr J. N. Tasei.

**International Commission for the Scientific Exploration of the Mediterranean Sea** (Commission internationale pour l'exploration scientifique de la mer Méditerranée—CIESM): 16 blvd de Suisse, 98000 Monaco; tel. 93-30-38-79; fax 92-16-11-95; internet www.ciesm.org; f. 1919 for scientific exploration and sustainable management of the Mediterranean Sea; includes 6 scientific committees. Mems: 23 member countries, 2,500 scientists. Pres. SAS The Prince Rainier III of Monaco; Sec.-Gen. Prof. F. Doumenge; Dir-Gen. Prof. F. Briand.

**International Commission on Physics Education:** c/o Prof. J. Barojas, POB 55534, 09340 México DF, Mexico; tel. (5) 686-35-19; f. 1960 to encourage and develop international collaboration in the improvement and extension of the methods and scope of physics education at all levels; collaborates with UNESCO and organizes international conferences. Mems: appointed triennially by the International Union of Pure and Applied Physics. Sec. Prof. J. Barojas.

**International Commission on Radiation Units and Measurements—ICRU:** 7910 Woodmont Ave, Suite 800, Bethesda, MD 20814, USA; tel. (301) 657-2652; fax (301) 907-8768; e-mail icru@icru.org; f. 1925 to develop internationally acceptable recommendations regarding: (1) quantities and units of radiation and radioactivity, (2) procedures suitable for the measurement and application of these quantities in clinical radiology and radiobiology, (3) physical data needed in the application of these procedures. Makes recommendations on quantities and units for radiation protection (see below, International Radiation Protection Association). Mems: from about 18 countries. Chair. A. Allisy; Sec. R. S. Caswell. Publs *Reports.*

**International Commission on Zoological Nomenclature:** c/o The Natural History Museum, Cromwell Rd, London, SW7 5BD, United Kingdom; tel. (20) 7942-5653; e-mail iczn@nhm.ac.uk; f. 1895; has judicial powers to determine all matters relating to the interpretation of the International Code of Zoological Nomenclature and also plenary powers to suspend the operation of the Code where the strict application of the Code would lead to confusion and instability of nomenclature; the Commission is responsible also for maintaining and developing the Official Lists and Official Indexes of Names in Zoology; affiliated to the International Union of Biological Sciences (q.v.). Pres. Prof. A. Minelli (Italy); Exec. Sec. Dr P. K. Tubbs (UK). Publs *International Code of Zoological Nomenclature, Bulletin of Zoological Nomenclature, Official Lists and Indexes of Names and Works in Zoology, Towards Stability in the Names of Animals.*

**International Council for Scientific and Technical Information:** 51 blvd de Montmorency, 75016 Paris, France; tel. 1-45-25-65-92; fax 1-42-15-12-62; e-mail icsti@dial.oleane.com; internet www.icsti.org; f. 1984 as the successor to the International Council of Scientific Unions Abstracting Board (f. 1952); aims to increase accessibility to scientific and technical information; fosters communication and interaction among all participants in the information transfer chain. Mems: 50 organizations. Pres. David Russon (UK); Gen. Sec. Marie Wallin (Sweden).

**International Council for the Exploration of the Sea—ICES:** Palægade 2–4, 1261 Copenhagen K, Denmark; tel. 33-15-42-25; fax 33-93-42-15; e-mail ices.info@ices.dk; internet www.ices.dk; f. 1902 to encourage and facilitate marine research on the utilization and conservation of living resources and the environment in the North Atlantic Ocean and its adjacent seas; to publish and disseminate results of research; to advise member countries and regulatory commissions. Gen. Sec. D. de G. Griffith. Publs *ICES Journal of Marine Science, ICES Marine Science Symposia, ICES Fisheries Statistics, ICES Cooperative Research Reports, ICES Oceanographic Data Lists and Inventories, ICES Techniques in Marine Environmental Sciences, ICES Identification Leaflets for Plankton, ICES Identification Leaflets for Diseases and Parasites of Fish and Shellfish, ICES/CIEM Information.*

**International Council of Psychologists:** Dept. of Psychology, Southwest Texas State University, San Marcos, TX 78666, USA; tel. (512) 245-7605; fax (512) 245-3153; f. 1941 to advance psychology and the application of its scientific findings throughout the world; holds annual conventions. Mems: 1,200 qualified psychologists. Sec.-Gen. Dr John M. Davis. Publs *International Psychologist* (quarterly), *World Psychology* (quarterly).

**International Council of the Aeronautical Sciences:** 66 route de Verneuil, BP 3002, 78133 Les Mureaux Cédex, France; tel. 1-39-06-34-23; fax 1-39-06-36-15; e-mail secr.exec@icas.org; internet www.icas.org; f. 1957 to encourage free interchange of information on all phases of mechanical flight; holds biennial Congresses. Mems: national associations in 27 countries. Pres. Jean-Pierre Marec (France); Exec. Sec. Clement Dousset (France).

**International Earth Rotation Service:** Central Bureau, Paris Observatory, 61 ave de l'Observatoire, 75014 Paris, France; tel. 1-40-51-22-26; fax 1-40-51-22-91; e-mail iers@obspm.fr; f. 1988 (fmrly International Polar Motion Service and Bureau International de l'Heure); maintained by the International Astronomical Union and the International Union of Geodesy and Geophysics; defines and maintains the international terrestrial and celestial reference systems; determines earth orientation parameters (terrestrial and celestial co-ordinates of the pole and universal time) connecting these systems; monitors global geophysical fluids; organizes collection, analysis and dissemination of data. Pres. Directing Bd Prof. C. REIGBER.

**International Federation for Cell Biology:** c/o Dr Ivan Cameron, Dept of Cellular and Structural Biology, Univ. of Texas Health Science Center, 7703 Floyd Curl Drive, San Antonio, Texas 78229, USA; f. 1972 to foster international co-operation, and organize conferences. Pres. Dr JUDIE WALTON; Sec.-Gen. Dr IVAN CAMERON. Publs *Cell Biology International* (monthly), reports.

**International Federation of Operational Research Societies:** c/o Loretta Peregrina, Richard Ivey School of Business, University of Western Ontario, London N6A 3K7, Canada; tel. (519) 661-4220; fax (519) 661-3485; e-mail ifors@ivey.uwo.ca; f. 1959 for development of operational research as a unified science and its advancement in all nations of the world. Mems: about 30,000 individuals, 44 national societies, four kindred societies. Pres. Prof. PETER BELL (Canada); Sec. LORETTA PEREGRINA. Publs *International Abstracts in Operational Research, IFORS Bulletin, International Transactions in Operational Research.*

**International Federation of Science Editors:** School for Scientific Communication, Abruzzo Science Park, Via Antica Arischia 1, 67100 L'Aquila, Italy; tel. (0862) 3475308; fax (0862) 3475213; e-mail miriam.balaban@aquila.infn.it; f. 1978; links editors in different branches of science with the aim of improving scientific writing, editing, ethics and communication internationally. Pres. MIRIAM BALABAN (Italy).

**International Federation of Societies for Electron Microscopy:** Electron Microscope Unit, University of Sydney, Sydney, NSW 2006, Australia; tel. (2) 9351-2351; fax (2) 9351-7682; e-mail djhc@emu.usyd.edu.au; f. 1955. Mems: representative organizations of 40 countries. Pres. Prof. A. HOWIE (UK); Gen.-Sec. D. J. H. COCKAYNE (Australia).

**International Food Information Service—IFIS:** UK Office (IFIS Publishing), Lane End House, Shinfield, Reading, RG2 9BB, United Kingdom; tel. (118) 988-3895; fax (118) 988-5065; e-mail ifis@ifis.org; internet www.ifis.org; f. 1968; board of governors comprises two members each from CAB-International (UK), Bundesministerium für Landwirtschaft, Ernährung und Forsten (represented by Deutsche Landwirtschafts-Gesellschaft e.V.) (Germany), the Institute of Food Technologists (USA), and the Centrum voor Landbouwpublikaties en Landbouwdocumentaties (Netherlands); collects and disseminates information on all disciplines relevant to food science, food technology and human nutrition. Man. Dir Prof. J. D. SELMAN. Publ. *Food Science and Technology Abstracts* (monthly, also available via the internet and on CD-ROM).

**International Foundation of the High-Altitude Research Stations Jungfraujoch and Gornergrat:** Sidlerstrasse 5, 3012 Berne, Switzerland; tel. (31) 6314052; fax (31) 6314405; e-mail debrunner@phim.unibe.ch; f. 1931; international research centre which enables scientists from many scientific fields to carry out experiments at high altitudes. Six countries contribute to support the station: Austria, Belgium, Germany, Italy, Switzerland, United Kingdom. Pres. Prof. H. DEBRUNNER.

**International Glaciological Society:** Lensfield Rd, Cambridge, CB2 1ER, United Kingdom; tel. (1223) 355974; e-mail int_glaciol_soc@compuserve.com; internet www.spri.cam.ac.uk/igs/home.htm; f. 1936 to stimulate interest in and encourage research into the scientific and technical problems of snow and ice in all countries. Mems: 850 in 29 countries. Pres. Dr R. A. BINDSCHADLER; Sec.-Gen. C. S. L. OMMANNEY. Publs *Journal of Glaciology* (quarterly), *Ice* (News Bulletin—4 a year), *Annals of Glaciology.*

**International Hydrographic Organization:** 4 quai Antoine 1er, BP 445, Monte Carlo, 98011 Monaco; tel. 93-10-81-00; fax 93-10-81-40; e-mail info@ihb.mc; f. 1921 to link the hydrographic offices of its member governments and co-ordinate their work with a view to rendering navigation easier and safer on all the seas of the world; to obtain as far as possible uniformity in charts and hydrographic documents; to foster the development of electronic chart navigation; to encourage the adoption of the best methods of conducting hydrographic surveys and improvements in the theory and practice of the science of hydrography, and to encourage surveying in those parts of the world where accurate charts are lacking; to extend and facilitate the application of oceanographic knowledge for the benefit of navigators and specialists in marine sciences; to render advice and assistance to developing countries upon request, facilitating their application for financial aid from the UNDP and other aid organizations for creation or extension of their hydrographic capabilities; to fulfil the role of world data centre for bathymetry; provides computerized Tidal Constituent Data Bank and IHO Data Centre for Digital Bathymetry; organizes quinquennial conference. Mems: 66 states. Directing Committee: Pres. Rear-Adm. GIUSEPPE ANGRISANO (Italy); Dirs Commodore N. GUY (South Africa), Commodore J. LEECH (Australia). Publs *International Hydrographic Review* (2 a year), *International Hydrographic Bulletin* (monthly), *IHO Yearbook.*

**International Institute of Refrigeration:** 177 blvd Malesherbes, 75017 Paris, France; tel. 1-42-27-32-35; fax 1-47-63-17-98; e-mail iifiir@ibm.net; internet www.iifiir.org; f. 1908 to further the development of the science of refrigeration and its applications on a world-wide scale; to investigate, discuss and recommend any aspects leading to improvements in the field of refrigeration; maintains FRIDOC data-base (available on CD-ROM). Mems: 61 national, 1,500 associates. Dir FRANÇOIS BILLIARD (France). Publs *Bulletin* (every 2 months), *International Journal of Refrigeration* (8 a year), books, proceedings, recommendations.

**International Mineralogical Association:** Institute of Mineralogy, University of Marburg, 3550 Marburg, Germany; tel. 28-5617; fax 285831; f. 1958 to further international co-operation in the science of mineralogy; affiliated to the International Union of Geological Sciences (q.v.). Mems: national societies in 31 countries. Sec. Prof. S. S. HAFNER.

**International Organization of Legal Metrology:** 11 rue Turgot, 75009 Paris, France; tel. 1-48-78-12-82; fax 1-42-82-17-27; f. 1955 to serve as documentation and information centre on the verification, checking, construction and use of measuring instruments, to determine characteristics and standards to which measuring instruments must conform for their use to be recommended internationally, and to determine the general principles of legal metrology. Mems: governments of 50 countries. Dir B. ATHANÉ (France). Publ. *Bulletin* (quarterly).

**International Palaeontological Association:** c/o Prof. D. L. Bruton, Palentologisk Museum, Sars Gate 1, 0562 Oslo, Norway; tel. 2285-1668; fax 2285-1810; e-mail d.l.bruton@toyen.uio.no; f. 1933; affiliated to the International Union of Geological Sciences and the International Union of Biological Sciences (q.v.). Pres. Dr J. TALENT (Australia); Sec.-Gen. D. L. BRUTON (Norway). Publs *Lethaia* (quarterly), *Directory.*

**International Peat Society:** Kuokkalantie 4, 40520 Jyväskylä, Finland; tel. (14) 674042; fax (14) 677405; e-mail ips@peatsociety.fi; internet www.peatsociety.fi; f. 1968 to encourage co-operation in the study and use of mires, peatlands, peat and related material, through international meetings, research groups and the exchange of information. Mems: 18 Nat. Cttees, research institutes and other organizations, and individuals from 35 countries. Pres. Dr JENS DIETER BECKER-PLATEN (Germany); Sec.-Gen. RAIMO SOPO (Finland). Publs *Peatlands International* (2 a year), *International Peat Journal* (annually).

**International Phonetic Association—IPA:** Dept of Linguistics, University of Victoria, POB 3045, Victoria, V8W 3P4, Canada; e-mail esling@uvic.ca; internet www.arts.gla.ac.uk/ipa/ipa.html; f. 1886 to promote the scientific study of phonetics and its applications. Mems: 1,000. Pres. K. KOHLER (Germany). Publ. *Journal* (2 a year).

**International Photobiology Association:** c/o Dr Tom Dubbelman, POB 9503, 2300 RA Leiden, Netherlands; tel. (71) 5276053; fax (71) 5276125; e-mail t.m.a.r.dubbelman@mcb.medfac.leidenuniv.nl; f. 1928; stimulation of scientific research concerning the physics, chemistry and climatology of non-ionizing radiations (ultra-violet, visible and infra-red) in relation to their biological efffects and their applications in biology and medicine; 18 national committees represented; affiliated to the International Union of Biological Sciences (q.v.). International Congresses held every four years. Pres. Prof. PILL SOON SONG; Sec.-Gen. Dr TOM DUBBELMAN.

**International Phycological Society:** c/o Harbor Branch Oceanographic Institution, 5600 Old Dixie Highway, Fort Pierce, FL 34946, USA; fax (561) 468-0757; e-mail hanisak@hboi.edu; f. 1961 to promote the study of algae, the distribution of information, and international co-operation in this field. Mems: about 1,000. Pres. C. J. BIRD; Sec. M. D. HANISAK. Publ. *Phycologia* (every 2 months).

**International Primatological Society:** c/o Dr D. Fragaszy, Dept of Psychology, Univ. of Georgia, Athens, GA 30602, USA; tel. (706) 542-3036; fax (706) 542-3275; e-mail doree@arches.uga.edu; f. 1964 to promote primatological science in all fields. Mems: about 1,500. Pres. Dr T. NISHIDA; Sec.-Gen. Dr D. FRAGASZY.

**International Radiation Protection Association—IRPA:** POB 662, 5600 AR Eindhoven, Netherlands; tel. (40) 247-33-55; fax (40) 243-50-20; e-mail irpa.exof@sbd.tue.nl; f. 1966 to link individuals and societies throughout the world concerned with protection against ionizing radiations and allied effects, and to represent doctors, health physicists, radiological protection officers and others engaged in radiological protection, radiation safety, nuclear safety, legal, medical and veterinary aspects and in radiation research and other allied activities. Mems: 16,000 in 42 societies. Pres. Prof. K. DUFTSCMID (Austria); Sec.-Gen. C. J. HUYSKENS (Netherlands). Publ. *IRPA Bulletin.*

**International Society for General Semantics:** POB 728, Concord, CA 94522, USA; tel. (925) 798-0311; e-mail isgs@a.crl.com; internet www.generalsemantics.org; f. 1943 to advance knowledge of and inquiry into non-Aristotelian systems and general semantics. Mems: 2,000 individuals in 40 countries. Pres. D. DAVID BOURLAND, Jr (USA); Exec. Dir PAUL D. JOHNSTON (USA).

**International Society for Human and Animal Mycology—ISHAM:** Mycology Unit, Women's and Children's Hospital, N. Adelaide 5006, Australia; tel. (8) 8204-7365; fax (8) 8204-7589; e-mail dellis@mad.adelaide.edu.au; f. 1954 to pursue the study of fungi pathogenic for man and animals; holds congresses (2000 Congress: Buenos Aires, Argentina). Mems: 1,100 from 70 countries. Pres. Prof. E. G. V. EVANS; Gen. Sec. Dr D. H. ELLIS. Publ. *Medical Mycology* (6 a year).

**International Society for Rock Mechanics:** c/o Laboratório Nacional de Engenharia Civil, 101 Av. do Brasil, 1799 Lisboa Codex, Portugal; tel. (21) 8482131; fax (21) 8497660; e-mail isrm@lnec.pt; internet www.lnec.pt/isrm; f. 1962 to encourage and co-ordinate international co-operation in the science of rock mechanics; to assist individuals and local organizations to form national bodies; to maintain liaison with organizations that represent related sciences, including geology, geophysics, soil mechanics, mining engineering, petroleum engineering and civil engineering. The Society organizes international meetings and encourages the publication of the results of research in rock mechanics. Mems: c. 6,000. Pres. Prof. SHUNSUKE SAKURAI; Sec.-Gen. JOSÉ DELGADO RODRIGUES. Publ. *News Journal* (3 a year).

**International Society for Stereology:** c/o Dr Jens R. Nyengaard, Stereological Research Laboratory, Bartholin Bldg, Aarhus Univ., 8000 Århus C, Denmark; tel. 89-49-36-54; fax 89-49-36-50; e-mail stereo@svfcd.aau.dk; internet www.health.aau.dk/stereology/iss; f. 1962; an interdisciplinary society gathering scientists from metallurgy, geology, mineralogy and biology to exchange ideas on three-dimensional interpretation of two-dimensional samples (sections, projections) of their material by means of stereological principles; tenth Congress: Melbourne, Australia, 1999. Mems: 300. Pres. BENTE PAKKENBERG; Treas. JENS R. NYENGAARD.

**International Society for Tropical Ecology:** c/o Botany Dept, Banaras Hindu University, Varanasi, 221 005 India; tel. (542) 317099; fax (542) 317074; f. 1956 to promote and develop the science of ecology in the tropics in the service of humanity; to publish a journal to aid ecologists in the tropics in communication of their findings; and to hold symposia from time to time to summarize the state of knowledge in particular or general fields of tropical ecology. Mems: 500. Sec. Prof. J. S. SINGH (India); Editor Prof. K. P. SINGH. Publ. *Tropical Ecology* (2 a year).

**International Society of Biometeorology:** Dept of Physical Geography, Div. of Environmental and Life Sciences, Macquarie Univ., Sydney, NSW 2109, Australia; tel. (2) 9850-8399; fax (2) 9850-8420; e-mail pbeggs@ocs1.ocs.mq.edu.au; internet www.es.mq.edu.au/isb; f. 1956 to unite all biometeorologists working in the fields of agricultural, botanical, cosmic, entomological, forest, human, medical, veterinarian, zoological and other branches of biometeorology. Mems: 350 individuals, nationals of 46 countries. Pres. Dr PETER HÖPPE (Germany); Sec. Dr PAUL J. BEGGS (Australia). Publs *Biometeorology* (Proceedings of the Congress of ISB), *International Journal of Biometeorology* (quarterly), *Biometeorology Bulletin*.

**International Society of Criminology:** 4–14 rue Ferrus, 75014 Paris, France; tel. 1-45-88-00-23; f. 1934 to promote the development of the sciences in their application to the criminal phenomenon. Mems: in 63 countries. Sec.-Gen. GEORGES PICCA. Publ. *Annales internationales de Criminologie* (2 a year).

**International Union for Quaternary Research—INQUA:** c/o G. Kroon, Netherlands Institute of Applied Geoscience, National Geological Survey, Secretariat Dept Geo-mapping, POB 157, 2000 Haarlem, Netherlands; tel. (23) 5300261; fax (23) 5367064; e-mail g.kroon@nitg.tno.nl; f. 1928 to co-ordinate research on the Quaternary geological era throughout the world. Pres. Prof. NICHOLAS J. SHACKLETON (UK); Sec. Prof. S. HALDORSEN (Norway); Administrative Sec. GERRY KROON (Netherlands).

**International Union of Food Science and Technology:** 522 Maple Ave, Oakville, Ontario, L6J 2J4, Canada; tel. (905) 815-1926; fax (905) 815-1574; e-mail iufost@inforamp-net; internet home.inforamp.net/-iufost; f. 1970; sponsors international symposia and congresses. Mems: 60 national groups. Pres. Prof. WALTER SPIESS (Germany); Sec.-Gen. JUDITH MEECH (Canada). Publ. *IUFOST Newsline* (3 a year).

**International Water Association:** Alliance House, 12 Caxton Street, London SW1H 0QS, United Kingdom; tel. (20) 7654-5500; fax (20) 7654-5555; e-mail water@iwahq.org.uk; internet www.iwahq.org.uk; f. 1999 by merger of the International Water Services Association and the International Association on Water Quality; aims to encourage international communication, co-operative effort, and a maximum exchange of information on water quality management through conferences, electronic media, and publication of research reports. Mems: approx. 9,000. Co-Pres. VINCENT BATH (South Africa), PIET ODENDAAL (South Africa); Exec. Dir ANTHONY MILBURN (UK). Publs *Water Research* (monthly), *Water Science and Technology* (24 a year), *Water Quality International* (6 a year), *Yearbook*, *Scientific and Technical Reports*.

**Nordic Molecular Biology Association:** c/o Prof. Bjursell, Institute of Molecular Biology, Univ. of Göteborg, Göteborg, Sweden; organizes congress every two years, symposia. Mems: 1,000 in Denmark, Finland, Iceland, Norway, Sweden. Chair. Prof. GUNNAR BJURSELL; Sec. LENE SVITH. Publ. *NOMBA Bulletin* (2 a year).

**Pacific Science Association:** 1525 Bernice St, POB 17801, Honolulu, HI 96817; tel. (808) 848-4139; fax (808) 847-8252; e-mail psa@bishop.bishop.hawaii.org; f. 1920 to promote co-operation in the study of scientific problems relating to the Pacific region, more particularly those affecting the prosperity and well-being of Pacific peoples; sponsors Pacific Science Congresses and Inter-Congresses. Mems: institutional representatives from 35 areas, scientific societies, individual scientists. Ninth Inter-Congress: Taipei, Taiwan, Nov. 1998; 19th Congress: Sydney, Australia, 1997. Pres. Dr AKITA ARIMA (Japan); Exec. Sec. Dr LUCIUS G. ELDREDGE. Publ. *Information Bulletin* (2 a year).

**Pan-African Union of Science and Technology:** POB 2339, Brazzaville, Republic of the Congo; tel. 832265; fax 832185; f. 1987 to promote the use of science and technology in furthering the development of Africa; organizes triennial congress. Pres. Prof. EDWARD AYENSU; Sec.-Gen. Prof. LÉVY MAKANY.

**Pugwash Conferences on Science and World Affairs:** 63A Great Russell St, London, WC1B 3BJ, United Kingdom; tel. (20) 7405-6661; fax (20) 7831-5651; f. 1957 to organize international conferences of scientists to discuss problems arising from development of science, particularly the dangers to mankind from weapons of mass destruction. Mems: national Pugwash groups in 38 countries. Pres. Prof. JOSEPH ROTBLAT; Sec.-Gen. Prof. FRANCESCO CALOGERO. Publs *Pugwash Newsletter* (quarterly), *Annals of Pugwash*, proceedings of Pugwash conferences, monographs.

**Scientific, Technical and Research Commission—STRC:** Nigerian Ports Authority Bldg, PMB 2359, Marina, Lagos, Nigeria; tel. (1) 2633430; fax (1) 2636093; e-mail oaustrc@rcl.nig.com; f. 1965 to succeed the Commission for Technical Co-operation in Africa (f. 1954). Supervises the Inter-African Bureau for Animal Resources (Nairobi, Kenya), the Inter-African Bureau for Soils (Lagos, Nigeria) and the Inter-African Phytosanitary Commission (Yaoundé, Cameroon) and several joint research projects. The Commission provides training in agricultural man., and conducts pest control programmes. Exec. Sec. Dr ROBERT N. MSHANA.

**Unitas Malacologica** (Malacological Union): Dr E. Gittenberger, Nationaal Natuurhistorisch Museum, POB 9517, 2300 RA Leiden, Netherlands; tel. (71) 5687614; fax (71) 5687666; f. 1962 to further the study of molluscs; affiliated to the International Union of Biological Sciences (q.v.); holds triennial congress. Mems: 400 in over 30 countries. Pres. Prof. L. VON SALVINI-PLAWEN (Austria); Sec. Dr PETER B. MORDAN (UK). Publ. *UM Newsletter* (2 a year).

**World Organisation of Systems and Cybernetics—WOSC:** c/o Prof. R. Vallée, 2 rue de Vouillé, 75015 Paris, France; tel. and fax 1-45-33-62-46; f. 1969 to act as clearing-house for all societies concerned with cybernetics and systems, to aim for the recognition of cybernetics as fundamental science, to organize and sponsor international exhibitions of automation and computer equipment, congresses and symposia, and to promote and co-ordinate research in systems and cybernetics; sponsors an honorary fellowship and awards a Norbert Wiener memorial gold medal. Mems: national and international societies in 30 countries. Pres. Prof. S. BEER (UK); Dir-Gen. Prof. R. VALLÉE (France). Publs *Kybernetes, the International Journal of Cybernetics and Systems*.

## Social Sciences

**International Council for Philosophy and Humanistic Studies—ICPHS:** Maison de l'UNESCO, 1 rue Miollis, 75732 Paris Cédex 15, France; tel. 1-45-68-26-85; fax 1-40-65-94-80; f. 1949 under the auspices of UNESCO to encourage respect for cultural autonomy by the comparative study of civilization and to contribute towards international understanding through a better knowledge of humanity; to develop international co-operation in philosophy, humanistic and kindred studies and to encourage the setting up of international organizations; to promote the dissemination of information in these fields; to sponsor works of learning, etc. Mems: organizations (see below) representing 145 countries. Pres. JEAN D'ORMESSON (France); Sec.-Gen. TILO SCHABERT (Germany). Publs *Bulletin of Information* (biennially), *Diogenes* (quarterly).

### UNIONS FEDERATED TO THE ICPHS

**International Academic Union:** Palais des Académies, 1 rue Ducale, 1000 Brussels, Belgium; tel. (2) 550-22-00; fax (2) 550-22-05; f. 1919 to promote international co-operation through collective research in philology, archaeology, art history, history and social sciences. Mems: academic institutions in 47 countries. Pres. M. CAVINESS (USA); Sec. J.-L. DE PAEPE.

**International Association for the History of Religions:** c/o Prof. Michael Pye, FG Religionswissenschaft, Philipps-Universität, Landgraf-Philipp-Strasse 4, 35032 Marburg, Germany; tel. (6421) 2823662; fax (6421) 2823944; e-mail pye@mailer.uni-marburg.de; f. 1950 to promote international collaboration of scholars, to organize congresses and to stimulate research. Mems: 24 countries. Pres. MICHAEL PYE; Sec.-Gen. Prof. ARMIN W. GEERTZ.

**International Committee for the History of Art:** 13 rue de Seine, 75006 Paris, France; e-mail senechal@num-inha.edu; internet www.esteticas.unam.mx/ciha; f. 1930 by the 12th International Congress on the History of Art, for collaboration in the scientific study of the history of art. International congress every four years, and at least two colloquia between congresses. Mems: National Committees in 34 countries. Pres. Prof. RONALD DE LEEUW (Netherlands); Sec. PHILIPPE SENECHAL (France). Publ. *Bibliographie d'histoire de l'Art* (quarterly).

**International Committee of Historical Sciences:** Bâtiment Laplace, École Normale Supérieure de Cachan, 94235 Cachan Cédex, France; e-mail cish@ihtp-cnrs.ens-cachan.fr; f. 1926 to work for the advancement of historical sciences by means of international co-ordination; an international congress is held every five years. Mems: 53 national committees, 22 affiliated international organizations and 18 internal commissions. Pres. IVAN T. BEREND (USA); Sec.-Gen. FRANÇOIS BÉDARIDA (France). Publ. *Bulletin d'Information du CISH*.

**International Congress of African Studies:** c/o School of Oriental and African Studies, Thornhaugh St, London, WC1H 0XG, United Kingdom; tel. (20) 7323-6035; fax (20) 7323-6118; f. 1962.

**International Federation for Modern Languages and Literatures:** c/o D. A. Wells, Dept of German, Birkbeck College, Malet St, London, WC1E 7HX, United Kingdom; tel. (20) 7631-6103; fax (20) 7383-3729; f. 1928 to establish permanent contact between historians of literature, to develop or perfect facilities for their work and to promote the study of modern languages and literature. Congress every three years. Mems: 19 associations, with individual mems in 98 countries. Sec.-Gen. D. A. WELLS (UK).

**International Federation of Philosophical Societies:** c/o I. Kuçuradi, Ahmet Rasim Sok. 8/4, Çankaya, 06550 Ankara, Turkey; tel. (312) 2351219; fax (312) 4410297; f. 1948 under the auspices of UNESCO, to encourage international co-operation in the field of philosophy; holds World Congress of Philosophy every five years. Mems: 120 societies from 50 countries; 27 international societies. Pres. F. MIRÓ QUESADA (Peru); Sec.-Gen. IOANNA KUÇURADI (Turkey). Publs *International Bibliography of Philosophy, Chroniques de Philosophie, Contemporary Philosophy, Philosophical Problems Today, Philosophy and Cultural Development*.

**International Federation of Societies of Classical Studies:** c/o Prof. F. Paschoud, 6 chemin aux Folies, 1293 Bellevue, Switzerland; tel. (22) 7742656; fax (22) 7742734; e-mail josime@isuisse.com; f. 1948 under the auspices of UNESCO. Mems: 79 societies in 44 countries. Pres. C. J. CLASSEN; Sec. Prof. F. PASCHOUD (Switzerland). Publs *L'Année Philologique, Thesaurus linguae Latinae*.

**International Musicological Society:** CP 1561, 4001 Basel, Switzerland; fax (1) 9231027; e-mail imsba@swissonline.ch; internet www.ims-online.ch; f. 1927; international congresses every five years. Pres. LÁSZLÓ SOMFAI; Sec.-Gen. DOROTHEA BAUMANN (Switzerland). Publ. *Acta Musicologica* (2 a year, available on the internet at www.music.indiana.edu/acta).

**International Union for Oriental and Asian Studies:** Közraktar u. 12A 11/2, 1093 Budapest, Hungary; f. 1951 by the 22nd International Congress of Orientalists under the auspices of UNESCO, to promote contacts between orientalists throughout the world, and to organize congresses, research and publications. Mems: in 24 countries. Sec.-Gen. Prof. GEORG HAZAI. Publs *Philologiae Turcicae Fundamenta, Materialien zum Sumerischen Lexikon, Sanskrit Dictionary, Corpus Inscriptionum Iranicarum, Linguistic Atlas of Iran, Matériels des parlers iraniens, Turcology Annual, Bibliographie égyptologique*.

**International Union of Anthropological and Ethnological Sciences:** c/o Dr P. J. M. Nas, Faculty of Social Sciences, Univ. of Leiden, Wassenaarseweg 52, POB 9555, 2300 RB Leiden, Netherlands; tel. (71) 5273992; fax (71) 5273619; e-mail nas@rulfsw.leidenuniv.nl; f. 1948 under the auspices of UNESCO; has 19 international research commissions. Mems: institutions and individuals in 100 countries. Pres. Prof. ERIC SUNDERLAND (UK); Sec.-Gen. Dr P. J. M. NAS (Netherlands). Publ. *IUAES Newsletter* (3 a year).

**International Union of Prehistoric and Protohistoric Sciences:** c/o Prof. J. Bourgeois, Dept of Archaeology and Ancient History of Europe, University of Ghent, Blandijnberg 2, 9000 Ghent, Belgium; tel. (9) 264-41-06; fax (9) 264-41-73; e-mail jbourbeo@allserv.rug.ac.be; f. 1931 to promote congresses and scientific work in the fields of pre- and proto-history. Mems: 120 countries. Pres. Prof. A. M. RADMILLI (Italy); Sec.-Gen. Prof. J. BOURGEOIS (Belgium).

**Permanent International Committee of Linguists:** Instituut voor Nederlandse Lexicologie, Matthias de Vrieshof 2, 2311 BZ Leiden, Netherlands; tel. (71) 5141648; fax (71) 5272115; e-mail secretariaat@inl.nl; f. 1928; to further linguistic research, to co-ordinate activities undertaken for the advancement of linguistics, and to make the results of linguistic research known internationally; holds Congress every five years. Mems: 48 countries and two international linguistic organizations. Pres. S. A. WURM (Australia); Sec.-Gen. P. G. J. VAN STERKENBURG (Netherlands). Publ. *Linguistic Bibliography* (annually).

## OTHER ORGANIZATIONS

**African Social and Environmental Studies Programme:** Box 44777, Nairobi, Kenya; tel. (2) 747960; fax (2) 740817; f. 1968; develops and disseminates educational material on social and environmental studies, and education for all in eastern and southern Africa. Mems: 18 African countries. Chair. Prof. WILLIAM SENTEZA-KAJUBI; Exec. Dir Prof. PETER MUYANDA MUTEBI. Publs *African Social Studies Forum* (2 a year), teaching guides.

**Arab Towns Organization—ATO:** POB 68160, Kaifan 71962, Kuwait; tel. 4849705; fax 4849322; e-mail ato@ato.net; f. 1967; aims to promote co-operation and the exchange of expertise with regard to urban administration; to improve the standard of municipal services and utilities in Arab towns; and to preserve the character and heritage of Arab towns. Administers an Institute for Urban Development (AUDI), based in Riyadh, Saudi Arabia, which provides training and research for municipal officers; the Arab Towns Development Fund, to provide financial assistance to help member towns implement projects; and the ATO Award, to encourage the preservation of Arab architecture. Mems: 413 towns. Dir-Gen. MOHAMMED ABDUL HAMID AL-SAQR; Sec.-Gen. ABD AL-AZIZ Y. AL-ADASANI. Publ. *Al-Madinah Al-Arabiyah* (every 2 months).

**Association for the Study of the World Refugee Problem—AWR:** Piazzale di Porta Pia 121, 00198 Rome, Italy; tel. (06) 44250159; f. 1951 to promote and co-ordinate scholarly research on refugee problems. Mems: 475 in 19 countries. Pres. FRANCO FOSCHI (Italy); Sec.-Gen. ALDO CLEMENTE (Italy). Publs *AWR Bulletin* (quarterly, in English, French, Italian and German), treatises on refugee problems (17 vols).

**Council for the Development of Social Science Research in Africa—CODESRIA:** BP 3304, Dakar, Senegal; tel. 825-98-22; fax 824-12-89; e-mail codesria@sonatel.senet.net; f. 1973; promotes research, provides conferences, working groups and information services. Mems: research institutes and university faculties in African countries. Exec. Sec. ACHILLE MBEMBE. Publs *Africa Development* (quarterly), *CODESRIA Bulletin* (quarterly), *Index of African Social Science Periodical Articles* (annually), directories of research.

**Council for Research in Values and Philosophy:** c/o Prof. G. F. McLean, School of Philosophy, Catholic University of America, Washington, DC 20064, USA; tel. (202) 319-5636; fax (202) 319-6089; e-mail cua-rvp@cua.edu; internet www.campus.cua.edu~mclean/home.htm; f. 1948. Mems: 33 teams from 24 countries. Pres. Prof. KENNETH L. SCHMITZ (Canada); Sec.-Gen. Prof. GEORGE F. MCLEAN (USA).

**Eastern Regional Organisation for Planning and Housing:** POB 10867, 50726 Kuala Lumpur, Malaysia; tel. (3) 718-7068; fax (3) 718-3931; f. 1958 to promote and co-ordinate the study and practice of housing and regional town and country planning. Offices in Japan, India and Indonesia. Mems: 57 organizations and 213 individuals in 28 countries. Sec.-Gen. JOHN KOH SENG SIEW. Publs *EAROPH News and Notes* (monthly), *Town and Country Planning* (bibliography).

**English-Speaking Union of the Commonwealth:** Dartmouth House, 37 Charles St, Berkeley Sq., London, W1X 8AB, United Kingdom; tel. (20) 7493-3328; fax (20) 7495-6108; e-mail esu@esu.org; internet www.esu.org; f. 1918 to promote international understanding between Britain, the Commonwealth, the United States and Europe, in conjunction with the ESU of the USA. Mems: 70,000 (incl. USA). Chair. Baroness BRIGSTOCKE; Dir-Gen. VALERIE MITCHELL. Publ. *Concord*.

**European Association for Population Studies:** POB 11676, 2502 AR The Hague, Netherlands; tel. (70) 3565200; fax (70) 3647187; e-mail eaps@nidi.nl; internet www.nidi.nl/eaps; f. 1983 to foster research and provide information on European population problems; organizes conferences, seminars and workshops. Mems: demographers from 40 countries. Exec. Sec. VERA HOLMAN. Publ. *European Journal of Population / Revue Européenne de Démographie* (quarterly).

**European Co-ordination Centre for Research and Documentation in Social Sciences:** 1010 Vienna, Grünangergasse 2, Austria; tel. (1) 512-43-33-0; fax (1) 512-53-66-16; f. 1963 for promotion of contacts between East and West European countries in all areas of social sciences. Activities include co-ordination of international comparative research projects; training of social scientists in problems of international research; organization of conferences; exchange of information and documentation; administered by a Board of Directors (23 social scientists from East and West) and a permanent secretariat in Vienna. Pres. ØRJAR ØYEN (Norway); Dir L. KIUZADJAN. Publs *Vienna Centre Newsletter, ECSSID Bulletin*, and books.

**European Society for Rural Sociology:** c/o C. Ray, Centre for Rural Economy, Univ. of Newcastle upon Tyne, NE1 7RU, United Kingdom; tel. (191) 2226460; fax (191) 2226720; e-mail christopher.ray@newcastle.ac.uk; f. 1957 to further research in, and co-ordination of, rural sociology and provide a centre for documentation of information. Mems: 300 individuals, institutions and associations in 29 European countries and nine countries outside Europe. Pres. Dr HILARY TOVEY (Ireland); Sec. CHRISTOPHER RAY (United Kingdom). Publ. *Sociologia Ruralis* (quarterly).

**Experiment in International Living:** POB 595, Main St, Putney, VT 05346, USA; tel. (802) 387-4210; fax (802) 387-5783; f. 1932 as an international federation of non-profit educational and cultural exchange institutions, to create mutual understanding and respect among people of different nations, as a means of furthering peace. Mems: organizations in 25 countries. Dir ROBIN BITTERS.

**Institute for International Sociological Research:** POB 50858, Cologne 40, Wiener Weg 6, Germany; tel. (221) 486019; f. 1964; diplomatic and international affairs, social and political sciences, moral and behavioural sciences, arts and literature. Mems: 132 Life Fellows, 44 Assoc. Fellows; 14 research centres; affiliated institutes: Academy of Diplomacy and International Affairs, International Academy of Social and Moral Sciences, Arts and Letters. Pres., Chair. Exec. Cttee and Dir-Gen. Consul Dr EDWARD S. ELLENBERG. Publs *Diplomatic Observer* (monthly), *Newsletter, Bulletin* (quarterly), *Annual Report*, etc.

**International African Institute:** School of Oriental and African Studies, Thornhaugh St, Russell Sq., London, WC1H 0XG, United Kingdom; tel. (20) 7323-6035; fax (20) 7323-6118; e-mail iai@soas.ac.uk; internet www.oneworld.org/iai; f. 1926 to promote the study of African peoples, their languages, cultures and social life in their traditional and modern settings; international seminar programme brings together scholars from Africa and elsewhere; links scholars so as to facilitate research projects, especially in the social sciences. Mems: 1,500 in 97 countries. Chair. Prof. GEORGE C. BOND; Dir Prof. PAUL SPENCER. Publs *Africa* (quarterly), *Africa Bibliography* (annually).

**International Association for Mass Communication Research:** c/o Prof. Dr Cees J. Hamelink, IAMCR Administrative Office, Baden Powellweg 109-111, 1069 LD Amsterdam, Netherlands; tel. (20) 6101581; fax (20) 6104821; f. 1957 to stimulate interest in mass communication research and the dissemination of information about research and research needs, to improve communication practice, policy and research and training for journalism, to provide a forum for researchers and others involved in mass communication to meet and exchange information. Mems: over 2,000 in 65 countries. Pres. Prof. Dr CEES J. HAMELINK (Netherlands); Sec.-Gen. Dr ROBIN CHEESMAN (Denmark).

**International Association of Applied Linguistics:** c/o Prof. Andrew D. Cohen, ESL, 130 Klaeber Court, University of Minnesota, 320 16th Ave SE, Minneapolis, MN 55455, USA; tel. (612) 624-3806; fax (612) 624-4579; e-mail adcohen@tc.umn.edu; internet www.brad.ac.uk/acad/aila/; f. 1964; organizes seminars on applied linguistics, and a World Congress every three years. Mems: associations in 38 countries. Pres. Prof. CHRISTOPHER CANDLIN (Hong Kong); Sec.-Gen. Prof. ANDREW D. COHEN (USA). Publs. *AILA Review* (annually), *AILA News* (2 a year).

**International Association of Metropolitan City Libraries—INTAMEL:** c/o Frances Schwenger, Metropolitan Toronto Reference Library, 789 Yonge St, Toronto, Ontario, Canada M4W 2G8; tel. (416) 393-7215; fax (416) 393-7229; f. 1967. Mems: 93 libraries in 28 countries. Sec. and Treas. FRANCES SCHWENGER.

**International Committee for Social Sciences Information and Documentation:** c/o Dr A. F. Marks, Herengracht 410 (Swidoc), 1017BX Amsterdam, Netherlands; tel. (20) 6225061; fax (20) 6238374; f. 1950 to collect and disseminate information on documentation services in social sciences, to help improve documentation, to advise societies on problems of documentation and to draw up rules likely to improve the presentation of all documents. Members from international associations specializing in social sciences or in documentation, and from other specialized fields. Sec.-Gen. ARNAUD F. MARKS (Netherlands). Publs *International Bibliography of the Social Sciences* (annually), *Newsletter* (2 a year).

**International Council on Archives:** 60 rue des Francs-Bourgeois, 75003 Paris, France; tel. 1-40-27-63-06; fax 1-42-72-20-65; e-mail secretariat@ica.cia.org; internet www.archives.ca/ica; f. 1948. Mems: 1,574 in 176 countries and territories; work includes conservation, training, automation, development of standards for description of archives; 10 regional branches. Pres. WANG GANG; Sec.-Gen. JOAN VAN ALBADA (Netherlands). Publs *Archivum* (annually), *Janus* (2 a year), *ICA Bulletin* (2 a year), *Directory*.

**International Ergonomics Association:** BP 2025, 3500 HA Utrecht, Netherlands; tel. (30) 35-44-55; fax (30) 35-76-39; f. 1957 to bring together organizations and persons interested in the scientific study of human work and its environment; to establish international contacts among those specializing in this field, co-operate with employers' associations and trade unions in order to encourage the practical application of ergonomic sciences in industries, and promote scientific research in this field. Mems: 17 federated societies. Pres. ILKKA KUORINKA (Finland); Sec.-Gen. Prof. D. P. ROOKMAAKER. Publ. *Ergonomics* (monthly).

**International Federation for Housing and Planning:** Wassenaarseweg 43, 2596 CG The Hague, Netherlands; tel. (70) 3244557; fax (70) 3282085; e-mail ifhp.nl@inter.nl.net; internet www.ifhp.org; f. 1913 to study and promote the improvement of housing, the theory and practice of town planning inclusive of the creation of new agglomerations and the planning of territories at regional, national and international levels; world congress and international conference held every 2 years. Mems: 200 organizations and 300 individuals in 65 countries. Pres. IRENE WIESE-VON OFEN (Germany); Sec.-Gen. E. E. VAN HYLCKAMA VLIEG (Netherlands). Publ. *Newsletter* (quarterly).

**International Federation of Institutes for Socio-religious Research:** 1 place Montesquieu, Bte 13, 1348 Louvain-la-neuve, Belgium; e-mail gendebien@anso.ucl.ac.be; f. 1958; federates centres engaged in undertaking scientific research in order to analyse and discover the social and religious phenomena at work in contemporary society. Mems: institutes in 26 countries. Pres. Canon Fr. HOUTART (Belgium); Sec. F. GENDEBIEN. Publ. *Social Compass (International Review of Sociology of Religion)* (quarterly, in English and French).

**International Federation of Social Science Organizations:** Via dei Laghi 14, 00198 Rome, Italy; tel. and fax (06) 884-8943; f. 1979 to assist research and teaching in the social sciences, and to facilitate co-operation and enlist mutual assistance in the planning and evaluation of programmes of major importance to members. Mems: 23 organizations. Pres. Prof. CARMENCITA T. AGUILAR; Sec.-Gen. Prof. J. BLAHOZ. Publs *Newsletter, International Directory of Social Science Organizations*.

**International Federation of Vexillological Associations:** Box 580, Winchester, MA 01890, USA; tel. (781) 729-9410; fax (781) 721-4817; f. 1967 to promote through its member organizations the scientific study of the history and symbolism of flags, and especially to hold International Congresses every two years and sanction international standards for scientific flag study. Mems: 39 institutions and associations in 27 countries. Pres. Prof. MICHEL LUPANT (Belgium); Liaison Officer WHITNEY SMITH. Publs *Recueil* (every 2 years), *The Flag Bulletin* (every 2 months), *Info FIAV* (every 4 months).

**International Institute for Ligurian Studies:** Museo Bicknell, Via Romana 39, 18012 Bordighera, Italy; tel. (0184) 263601; fax (0184) 266421; f. 1947 to conduct research on ancient monuments and regional traditions in the north-west arc of the Mediterranean (France and Italy). Library of 80,000 vols. Mems: in France, Italy, Spain, Switzerland. Dir Prof. CARLO VARALDO (Italy).

**International Institute of Administrative Sciences:** 1 rue Defacqz, 1000 Brussels, Belgium; tel. (2) 538-91-65; fax (2) 537-97-02; e-mail iias@iiasiisa.be; internet www.iiasiisa.be; f. 1930 for comparative examination of administrative experience in the various countries; research and programmes for improving administrative law and practices and for technical assistance; library of 15,000 vols; consultative status with UN, UNESCO and ILO; international congresses. Mems: 46 mem. states, 55 national sections, 9 international governmental organizations, 51 corporate mems, 13 individual members. Pres. IGNACIO PICHARDO PAGAZA (Mexico); Dir-Gen. GIANCARLO VILELLA (Italy). Publs *International Review of Administrative Sciences* (quarterly), *Newsletter* (3 a year).

**International Institute of Sociology:** c/o Facoltà di Scienze Politiche, Università di Roma 'La Sapienza', Piazzale A. Moro 5, 00185 Rome, Italy; tel. (06) 3451017; fax (06) 3451017; f. 1893 to enable sociologists to meet and study sociological questions. Mems: 300, representing 45 countries. Pres. PAOLO AMMASSARI (Italy); Gen. Sec. ALAN HEDLEY. Publ. *The Annals of the IIS*.

**International Numismatic Commission:** Coins and Medals Dept, British Museum, London, WC1B 3DG, United Kingdom; tel. (20) 7323-8227; fax (20) 7323-8171; f. 1936; enables co-operation between scholars studying coins and medals. Mems: numismatic organizations in 35 countries. Pres. A. BURNETT; Sec. M. AMANDRY.

**International Peace Academy:** 777 United Nations Plaza, New York, NY 10017, USA; tel. (212) 949-8480; fax (212) 983-8246; e-mail ipa@ipapost.ipacademy.org; internet www.ipacademy.org/; f. 1967 to educate government officials in the procedures needed for conflict resolution, peace-keeping, mediation and negotiation, through international training seminars and publications; off-the-record meetings are also conducted to gain complete understanding of a specific conflict. Chair. RITA E. HAUSER; Pres. OLARA A. OTUNNU. Publs *Annual Report, Newsletter* (2 a year).

**International Peace Research Association:** c/o Copenhagen Peace Research Institute, University of Copenhagen, Fredericiagade 18, 1310 Copenhagen, Denmark; tel. 3345-5052; fax 3345-5060; e-mail bmoeller@copn.dk; internet www.copn.dk/ipra/ipra.html; f. 1964 to encourage interdisciplinary research on the conditions of peace and the causes of war. Mems: 150 corporate, five regional branches, 1,000 individuals, in 93 countries. Pres. URSULA OSWALD (Mexico); Sec.-Gen. BJOERN MOELLER (Denmark). Publ. *IPRA Newsletter* (quarterly).

**International Social Science Council—ISSC:** Maison de l'UNESCO, 1 rue Miollis, 75732 Paris Cédex 15, France; tel. 1-45-68-25-58; fax 1-45-66-76-03; e-mail issclak@unesco.org; internet www.unesco.org/ngo/issc; f. 1952; since 1973 a federation of the organizations listed below. Aims: the advancement of the social sciences throughout the world and their application to the major problems of the world; the spread of co-operation at an international level between specialists in the social sciences. ISSC has a Senior Board; and programmes on International Human Dimensions of Global Environmental Change (IHDP), co-sponsored by the International Council of Scientific Unions (q.v.), and Comparative Research on Poverty (CROP). Pres. KURT PAWLIK (Germany); Sec.-Gen. LESZEK A. KOSINSKI (Canada).

**Associations Federated to the ISSC**

(details of these organizations will be found under their appropriate category elsewhere in the International Organizations section)

International Association of Legal Sciences (p. 306).
International Economic Association (p. 295).
International Federation of Social Science Organizations (p. 326).
International Geographical Union (p. 319).
International Institute of Administrative Sciences (p. 326).
International Law Association (p. 306).
International Peace Research Association (p. 327).
International Political Science Association (p. 301).
International Sociological Association (p. 327).
International Union for the Scientific Study of Population (p. 327).
International Union of Anthropological and Ethnological Sciences (p. 325).
International Union of Psychological Science (p. 319).
World Association for Public Opinion Research (p. 327).
World Federation for Mental Health (p. 313).

**International Society of Social Defence and Humane Criminal Policy:** c/o Centro nazionale di prevenzione e difesa sociale, Piazza Castello 3, 20121 Milan, Italy; tel. (02) 86460714; fax (02) 72008431; e-mail cnpds.ispac@iol.it; f. 1945 to combat crime, to protect society and to prevent citizens from being tempted to commit criminal actions. Mems: in 34 countries. Pres. SIMONE ROZES (France); Sec.-Gen. EDMONDO BRUTI LIBERATI (Italy). Publ. *Cahiers de défense sociale* (annually).

**International Sociological Association:** c/o Faculty of Political Sciences and Sociology, Universidad Complutense, 28223 Madrid, Spain; tel. (91) 3527650; fax (91) 3524945; e-mail isa@sis.ucm.es; internet www.ucm.es/info/isa; f. 1949 to promote sociological knowledge, facilitate contacts between sociologists, encourage the dissemination and exchange of information and facilities and stimulate research; has 53 research committees on various aspects of sociology; holds World Congresses every four years (15th Congress: Brisbane, Australia, 2002). Pres. A. MARTINELLI (Italy); Exec. Sec. IZABELA BARLINSKA. Publs *Current Sociology* (3 a year), *International Sociology* (quarterly), *Sage Studies in International Sociology* (based on World Congress).

**International Statistical Institute:** POB 950, Prinses Beatrixlaan 428, 2270 AZ Voorburg, Netherlands; tel. (70) 3375737; fax (70) 3860025; e-mail isi@cbs.nl; internet www.cbs.nl/isi; f. 1885; devoted to the development and improvement of statistical methods and their application throughout the world; administers among others a statistical education centre in Calcutta in co-operation with the Indian Statistical Institute; executes international research programmes. Mems: 2,000 ordinary mems; 10 hon. mems; 110 ex-officio mems; 75 corporate mems; 45 affiliated organizations; 32 national statistical societies. Pres. J.-L. BODIN; Dir Permanent Office M. P. R. VAN DEN BROECKE. Publs *Bulletin of the International Statistical Institute* (proceedings of biennial sessions), *International Statistical Review* (3 a year), *Short Book Reviews* (3 a year), *Statistical Theory and Method Abstracts* (quarterly), *ISI Newsletter* (3 a year), *Directories* (every 2 years).

**International Studies Association:** Social Science 324, Univ. of Arizona, Tucson, AZ 85721, USA; tel. (520) 621-7715; fax (520) 621-5780; e-mail isa@u.arizona.edu; internet www.isanet.org; f. 1959; links those whose professional concerns extend beyond their own national boundaries (government officials, representatives of business and industry, and scholars). Mems: 3,500 in 60 countries. Pres. MICHAEL BRECHER; Exec. Dir THOMAS J. VOLGY. Publs *International Studies Quarterly, International Studies Perspectives, International Studies Review, ISA Newsletter.*

**International Union for the Scientific Study of Population:** 34 rue des Augustins, 4000 Liège, Belgium; tel. (4) 222-40-80; fax (4) 222-38-47; e-mail iussp@iussp.org; internet www.iussp.org; f. 1928 to advance the progress of quantitative and qualitative demography as a science. Mems: 1,917 in 121 countries. Pres. JOSÉ ALBERTO M. DE CARVALHO. Publs *IUSSP Bulletin* and books on population.

**Mensa International:** 15 The Ivories, 6–8 Northampton St, London, N1 2HY, United Kingdom; tel. (20) 7226-6891; fax (20) 7226-7059; internet www.mensa.org/mensa-international; f. 1946 to identify and foster intelligence for the benefit of humanity. Members are individuals who score in a recognized intelligence test higher than 98% of people in general: there are 100,000 mems world-wide. Exec. Dir E. J. VINCENT (UK). Publ. *Mensa International Journal* (monthly).

**Third World Forum:** 39 Dokki St, POB 43, Orman, Cairo, Egypt; tel. (2) 3488092; fax (2) 3480668; e-mail isabry@idsc1.gov.eg; f. 1973 to link social scientists and others from the developing countries, to discuss alternative development policies and encourage research; undertaking Egypt 2020 research project. Regional offices in Egypt, Mexico, Senegal and Sri Lanka. Mems: individuals in more than 50 countries. Chair. ISMAIL-SABRI ABDALLA.

**World Association for Public Opinion Research:** c/o The School of Journalism and Mass Communication, University of North Carolina, CB 3365, Carroll Hall, Chapel Hill, NC 27599-3365, USA; tel. (919) 962-6396; fax (919) 962-4079; e-mail wapor@unc.edu; internet www.wapor.org; f. 1947 to establish and promote contacts between persons in the field of survey research on opinions, attitudes and behaviour of people in the various countries of the world; to further the use of objective, scientific survey research in national and international affairs. Mems: 450 from 72 countries. Man. Dir JANE SHEALY. Publs *WAPOR Newsletter* (quarterly), *International Journal of Public Opinion* (quarterly).

**World Society for Ekistics:** c/o Athens Centre of Ekistics, 24 Strat. Syndesmou St, 106 73 Athens, Greece; tel. (1) 3623216; fax (1) 3629337; f. 1965; aims to promote knowledge and ideas concerning human settlements through research, publications and conferences; to recognize the benefits and necessity of an inter-disciplinary approach to the needs of human settlements. Pres. Prof. WESLEY W. POSVAR; Sec.-Gen. P. PSOMOPOULOS.

# Social Welfare and Human Rights

**African Commission on Human and People's Rights:** Kairaba Ave, POB 673, Banjul, The Gambia; tel. 392962; fax 390764; f. 1987; meets twice a year for 10 days in March and Oct.; the Commission comprises 11 members. Its mandate is to monitor compliance with the African Charter on Human and People's Rights (ratified in 1986), and it investigates claims of human rights abuses perpetrated by govts that have ratified the Charter. Claims may be brought by other African govts, the victims themselves, or by a third party. Sec. GERMAIN BARICAKO (Burundi).

**Aid to Displaced Persons and its European Villages:** 35 rue du Marché, 4500 Huy, Belgium; tel. (85) 21-34-81; f. 1957 to carry on and develop work begun by the Belgian association Aid to Displaced Persons; aims to provide material and moral aid for refugees; European Villages established at Aachen, Bregenz, Augsburg, Berchem-Ste-Agathe, Spiesen, Euskirchen, Wuppertal as centres for refugees. Pres. LUC DENYS (Belgium).

**Amnesty International:** 1 Easton St, London, WC1X 8DJ, United Kingdom; tel. (20) 7413-5500; fax (20) 7956-1157; e-mail amnestyis@amnesty.org; internet www.amnesty.org/; f. 1961; an independent worldwide movement, campaigning impartially for the release of all prisoners of conscience, fair and prompt trials for all political prisoners, the abolition of torture and the death penalty and the end of extrajudicial executions and 'disappearances'; also opposes abuses by opposition groups (hostage-taking, torture and arbitrary killings); financed by donations. Mems: 1m. in over 160 countries; 4,500 locally organized groups in over 70 countries; nationally organized sections in 55 countries. Sec.-Gen. PIERRE SANÉ (Senegal). Publs *International Newsletter* (every 2 months), *Annual Report*, other country reports.

**Anti-Slavery International:** Thomas Clarkson House, The Stableyard, Broomgrove Rd, London, SW9 9TL, United Kingdom; tel. (20)

7501-8920; fax (20) 7738-4110; e-mail antislavery@antislavery.org; internet www.antislavery.org; f. 1839 to eradicate slavery and forced labour in all their forms, to generate awareness of such abuses, to promote the well-being of indigenous peoples, and to protect human rights in accordance with the Universal Declaration of Human Rights, 1948. Mems: 1,800 members in 30 countries. Chair. Reggie Norton; Dir Mike Dottridge. Publs *Annual Report, Anti-Slavery Reporter* (quarterly), special reports on research.

**Associated Country Women of the World:** Clutha House, 10 Storey's Gate, London, SW1P 3AY, United Kingdom; tel. (20) 7834-8635; f. 1933; aims to aid the economic and social development of countrywomen and home-makers of all nations; to promote international goodwill and understanding; and to work to alleviate poverty, and promote good health and education. Mems: several million. Gen. Sec. Anna Frost. Publ. *The Countrywoman* (quarterly).

**Association Internationale de la Mutualité** (International Association for Mutual Benefit Societies): 50 rue d'Arlon, 1000 Brussels, Belgium; tel. (2) 234-57-00; fax (2) 234-57-08; e-mail aim .secretariat@skynet.be; internet www.hurisc.org/aim; f. 1950; aims to promote and reinforce access to health care by developing the sound management of mutualities. Mems: 44 federatons of mutualities in 28 countries. Pres. Michel Schmite (Luxembourg); Dir Willy Palm (Belgium).

**Aviation sans frontières—ASF:** Brussels National Airport, Brucargo 706, POB 7513/14, 1931 Brucargo, Belgium; tel. (2) 751-24-70; fax (2) 751-24-71; e-mail alain.peeters@msf.be; f. 1980 to make available the resources of the aviation industry to humanitarian organizations, for carrying supplies and equipment at minimum cost, both on long-distance flights and locally. Pres. Philippe Dehenniu; Gen. Man. Alain Peeters.

**Catholic International Union for Social Service:** 31 rue de la Citronelle, 1348 Louvaine-la-Neuve, Belgium; tel. (10) 45-25-13; f. 1925 to develop social service on the basis of Christian doctrine; to unite Catholic social schools and social workers' associations in all countries to promote their foundation; to represent at the international level the Catholic viewpoint as it affects social service. Mems: 172 schools of social service, 26 associations of social workers, 52 individual members. Exec. Sec. Alexandre Carlson. Publs *Service Social dans le monde* (quarterly), *News Bulletin, Bulletin de Liaison, Boletín de Noticias* (quarterly).

**Co-ordinating Committee for International Voluntary Service—CCIVS:** Maison de l'UNESCO, 1 rue Miollis, 75732 Paris Cédex 15, France; tel. 1-45-68-49-36; fax 1-42-73-05-21; e-mail ccivs@zcc.net; internet www.unesco.org/ccivs; f. 1948; acts as an information centre and co-ordinating body for youth voluntary service organizations all over the world. Affiliated mems: 142 organizations. Pres. G. Orsini; Dir P. Duong . Publs *News from CCIVS* (3 a year), handbook, directories.

**EIRENE—International Christian Service for Peace:** 56503 Neuwied, Postfach 1322, Germany; tel. (2631) 83790; fax (2631) 31160; e-mail eirene-int@eirene.org; internet www.eirene.org; f. 1957; works in Africa and Latin America (professional training, apprenticeship programmes, agricultural work and co-operatives), Europe and the USA (volunteer programmes in co-operation with peace groups). Gen. Sec. Eckehard Fricke.

**European Federation for the Welfare of the Elderly—EURAG:** Wielandgasse 9, 1 Stock, 8010 Graz, Austria; tel. (316) 81-46-08; fax (316) 81-47-67; e-mail eurag.europe@aon.at; internet www .eurag.org; f. 1962 for the exchange of experience among member associations; practical co-operation among member organizations to achieve their objectives in the field of ageing; representation of the interests of members before international organizations; promotion of understanding and co-operation in matters of social welfare; to draw attention to the problems of old age. Mems: organizations in 33 countries. Pres. Edmée Mangers-Anen (Luxembourg); Sec.-Gen. Gregor Hammerl (Austria). Publs (in English, French, German and Italian) *EURAG Newsletter* (quarterly), *EURAG Information* (monthly).

**Federation of Asian Women's Associations—FAWA:** Centro Escolar University, 9 Mendiola St, San Miguel, Manila, Philippines; tel. (2) 741-04-46; f. 1959 to provide closer relations, and bring about joint efforts among Asians, particularly among the women, through mutual appreciation of cultural, moral and socio-economic values. Mems: 415,000. Pres. Madeleine Bordallo (Guam); Sec. Evelina McDonald (Guam). Publ. *FAWA News Bulletin* (quarterly).

**Interamerican Conference on Social Security** (Conferencia Interamericano de Seguridad Social—CISS): Calle San Ramon s/n Unidad Independencia, Apdo 99089, San Jerónimo Lidice, 10100 México DF, Mexico; tel. (5) 595-01-77; fax (5) 683-85-24; e-mail ciss@data.net.mx; internet www.ciss.org.mx; f. 1942 to contribute to the development of social security in the countries of the Americas and to co-operate with social security institutions. CISS bodies are: the General Assembly, the Permanent Interamerican Committee on Social Security, the Secretariat General, the American Commissions of Social Security and the Interamerican Center for Social Security Studies. Mems: social security institutions in 38 countries. Pres. Genaro Borrego Estrada (Mexico); Sec.-Gen. Maria Elvira Contreras Saucedo (Mexico). Publs *Social Security Journal*, monographs, study series.

**International Abolitionist Federation:** 16 rue Cassette, 75006 Paris, France; f. 1875 for the abolition of the organization and exploitation of prostitution by public authorities, sex discrimination, and for the rehabilitation of the victims of traffic and prostitution; holds international congress every three years and organizes regional conferences to raise awareness regarding the cultural, religious and traditional practices which affect adversely the lives of women and children. Affiliated organizations in 17 countries. Corresponding mems in 40 countries. Pres. Brigitte Polonovski (Switzerland); Exec. Sec. Hélène Sackstein (France). Publ. *IAF Information* (3 a year).

**International Association against Noise:** Hirschenplatz 7, 6004 Lucerne, Switzerland; tel. (41) 513013; fax (41) 529093; f. 1959 to promote noise-control at an international level; to promote co-operation and the exchange of experience and prepare supranational measures; issues information, carries out research, organizes conferences, and assists national anti-noise associations. Mems: 17, and three associate mems. Pres. Karel Novotný (Czech Republic); Sec. Dr Willy Aecherli (Switzerland).

**International Association of Children's International Summer Villages—CISV International:** Mea House, Ellison Place, Newcastle upon Tyne, NE1 8XS, United Kingdom; tel. (191) 232-4998; fax (191) 261-4710; e-mail cisvio@dial.pipex .com; f. 1950 to conduct International Camps for children and young people between the ages of 11 and 18. Mems: 40,268. International Pres. David Lister; Sec.-Gen. Joseph G. Banks. Publs *CISV News* (2 a year), *Annual Report, Local Work Magazine* (2 a year), *Interspectives* (annually).

**International Association for Education to a Life without Drugs** (Internationaler Verband für Erziehung zu suchtmittelfreiem Leben—IVES): c/o W. Stuber, Lerchenweg 13, 4912 Aarwangen, Switzerland; tel. and fax (62) 9222673; f. 1954 (as the International Association for Temperance Education) to promote international co-operation in education on the dangers of alcohol and drugs; collection and distribution of information on drugs; maintains regular contact with national and international organizations active in these fields; holds conferences. Mems: 77,000 in 10 countries. Pres. Willy Stuber; Sec. Uljas Syväniemi.

**International Association for Suicide Prevention:** c/o Ms M. Campos, IASP Central Administrative Office, 1725 West Harrison St, Suite 955, Chicago, IL 60612, USA; tel. (312) 942-7208; fax (312) 942-2177; f. 1960 to establish an organization where individuals and agencies of various disciplines and professions from different countries can find a common platform for interchange of acquired experience, literature and information about suicide; disseminates information; arranges special training; encourages and carries out research; organizes the Biennial International Congress for Suicide Prevention. Mems: 340 individuals and societies, in 55 countries of all continents. Pres. Dr Diego de Leo. Publ. *Crisis* (quarterly).

**International Association of Schools of Social Work:** 1010 Vienna, Palais Palfy, Josefplatz 6, Austria; tel. (1) 513-4297; fax (1) 513-8468; f. 1928 to provide international leadership and encourage high standards in social work education. Mems: 1,600 schools of social work in 70 countries, and 25 national associations of schools. Pres. Dr Ralph Garber (Canada); Sec.-Gen. Vera Mehta (India). Publs *International Social Work* (quarterly), *Directory of Members, IASSW News*.

**International Association of Workers for Troubled Children and Youth:** 22 rue Halévy, 59000 Lille, France; tel. 3-20-93-70-16; fax 3-20-09-18-39; e-mail aieji@nordnet.fr; f. 1951 to promote the profession of specialized social workers for troubled children and youth; to provide a centre of information about child welfare and encourage co-operation between the members; 1997 Congress: Brescia, Italy. Mems: national and regional public or private associations from 22 countries and individual members in many other countries. Pres. Gustavo Velastegui (France); Sec.-Gen. Isabelle Persoons (Belgium).

**International Catholic Migration Commission:** CP 96, 37–39 rue de Vermont, POB 96, 1211 Geneva 20, Switzerland; tel. (22) 9191020; fax (22) 9191048; e-mail secretariat@icmc.dpn.ch; f. 1951; offers migration aid programmes to those who are not in a position to secure by themselves their resettlement elsewhere; grants interest-free travel loans; assists refugees on a worldwide basis, helping with all social and technical problems. Sub-committees dealing with Europe and Latin America. Mems: in 85 countries. Pres. Prof. Stefano Zamagni (Italy); Sec.-Gen. William Canny (USA). Publ. *Annual Report*.

**International Christian Federation for the Prevention of Alcoholism and Drug Addiction:** 20a Ancienne Route, Apt. No 42, 1218 Grand-Saconnex, Geneva, Switzerland; tel. (22) 7888158; fax (22) 7888136; e-mail jonathan@iprolink.ch; f. 1960, reconstituted

1980 to promote worldwide education and remedial work through the churches, to co-ordinate Christian concern about alcohol and drug abuse, in co-operation with the World Council of Churches and WHO. Chair. Karin Israelsson (Sweden); Gen. Sec. Jonathan N. Gnanadason.

**International Civil Defence Organization:** POB 172, 10–12 chemin de Surville, 1213 Petit-Lancy 2, Geneva, Switzerland; tel. (22) 8796969; fax (22) 8796979; e-mail icdo@icdo.org; internet www.icdo.org; f. 1931, present statutes in force 1972; aims to intensify and co-ordinate on a world-wide scale the development and improvement of organization, means and techniques for preventing and reducing the consequences of natural disasters in peacetime or of the use of weapons in time of conflict. Sec.-Gen. Sadok Znaïdi (Tunisia). Publs *International Civil Defence Journal* (quarterly, in English, French, Spanish, Russian and Arabic).

**International Commission for the Prevention of Alcoholism and Drug Dependency:** 12501 Old Columbia Pike, Silver Spring, MD 20904-6600 USA; tel. (301) 680-6719; fax (301) 680-6090; f. 1952 to encourage scientific research on intoxication by alcohol, its physiological, mental and moral effects on the individual, and its effect on the community; ninth World Congress, Hamburg, Germany, 1994. Mems: individuals in 90 countries. Exec. Dir Thomas R. Neslund. Publ. *ICPA Quarterly*.

**International Council of Voluntary Agencies—ICVA:** 48 Chemin du Grand-Montfleury, 1290 Versoix, Switzerland; tel. (22) 9509600; fax (22) 9509609; e-mail secretariat@icva.ch; internet www.icva.ch; f. 1962 to provide a forum for voluntary humanitarian and development agencies. Mems: 78 non-governmental organizations. Chair. Anders Ladekarl; Co-ordinator Ed Schenkenberg van Mierop; Publ. *Newsletter* (available on website).

**International Council of Women:** c/o 13 rue Caumartin, 75009 Paris, France; tel. 1-47-42-19-40; fax 1-42-66-26-23; e-mail icw-cif@wanadoo.fr; f. 1888 to bring together in international affiliation Nat. Councils of Women from all continents for consultation and joint action in order to promote equal rights for men and women and the integration of women in development and in decision-making; five standing committees. Mems: 78 national councils. Pres. Pnina Herzog; Sec.-Gen. Marie-Christine Lafargue.

**International Council on Alcohol and Addictions:** CP 189, 1001 Lausanne, Switzerland; tel. (21) 3209865; fax (21) 3209817; e-mail icaa@pingnet.ch; f. 1907; organizes training courses, congresses, symposia and seminars in different countries. Mems: affiliated organizations in 74 countries, as well as individual members. Pres. Dr Ibrahim al-Awaji (Saudi Arabia); Exec. Dir Dr Eva Tongue (UK). Publs *ICAA News* (quarterly), *Alcoholism* (2 a year).

**International Council on Disability:** c/o Rehabilitation International, 25 East 21st St, New York, NY 10010, USA; tel. (212) 420-1500; f. 1953 to assist the UN and its specialized agencies to develop a well co-ordinated international programme for rehabilitation of the handicapped. Mems: 66 organizations. Pres. Sheikh al-Ghanim; Sec.-Gen. Susan Hammerman.

**International Council on Jewish Social and Welfare Services:** 75 rue de Lyon, 1211 Geneva 13, Switzerland; tel. (22) 3449000; fax (22) 3457013; f. 1961; functions include the exchange of views and information among member agencies concerning the problems of Jewish social and welfare services including medical care, old age, welfare, child care, rehabilitation, technical assistance, vocational training, agricultural and other resettlement, economic assistance, refugees, migration, integration and related problems; representation of views to governments and international organizations. Mems: six national and international organizations. Exec. Sec. Cheryl Mariner.

**International Council on Social Welfare:** 380 St Antoine St West, Suite 3200, Montreal H2Y 3X7, Canada; tel. (514) 287-3280; fax (514) 287-9702; e-mail icsw@icsw.org; internet www.icsw.org; f. 1928 to provide an international forum for the discussion of social work and related issues; to promote interest in social welfare; holds international conference every two years; provides documentation and information services. Mems: 45 national committees, 12 international organizations and 33 other organizations. Pres. Julian Disney (Australia); Exec. Dir Stephen King (UK). Publ. *Social Development Review* (quarterly).

**International Dachau Committee:** 95 ave des Ortolans, 1170 Brussels, Belgium; f. 1958 to perpetuate the memory of the political prisoners of Dachau; to manifest the friendship and solidarity of former prisoners whatever their beliefs or nationality; to maintain the ideals of their resistance, liberty, tolerance and respect for persons and nations; and to maintain the former concentration camp at Dachau as a museum and international memorial. Pres. Gen. André Delpech; Sec.-Gen. Jean Samuel. Publ. *Bulletin Officiel du Comité International de Dachau* (2 a year).

**International Federation of the Blue Cross:** CP 6813, 3001 Bern, Switzerland; tel. (31) 3005860; fax (31) 3005869; e-mail ifbc.bern@bluewin.ch; internet www.eurocare.org/bluecross; f. 1877 to aid the victims of intemperance and drug addicts, and to take part in the general movement against alcoholism. Pres. Pastor Raymond Bassin (Switzerland); Gen. Sec. Hans Rüttiman.

**International Federation of Disabled Workers and Civilian Handicapped—FIMITIC:** 53173 Bonn, Beethovenallee 56–58, Germany; tel. (228) 95640; fax (228) 9564132; e-mail fimitic@tonline.de; internet www.193.189.189.10/fimitic/default.htm; f. 1953 to bring together representatives of the disabled and handicapped into an international non-political organization under the guidance of the disabled themselves; to promote greater opportunities for the disabled; to create rehabilitation centres; to act as a co-ordinating body for all similar national organizations. Mems: national groups from 27 European countries, and corresponding mems from eight countries. Pres. Marcel Royez (France); Gen. Sec. Marija Štiglic (Germany). Publs *Bulletin, Nouvelles*.

**International Federation of Educative Communities:** Piazza S.S. Annunziale 12, 50122 Florence, Italy; tel. (055) 2469162; fax (055) 2347041; e-mail lice@lycosmail.com; f. 1948 under the auspices of UNESCO to co-ordinate the work of national associations, and to promote the international exchange of knowledge and experience in the field of childcare. Mems: national associations from 20 European countries, Israel, Canada, the USA and South Africa. Pres. Robert Soisson (Luxembourg); Gen. Sec. Gianluca Barbonotti (Italy). Publ. *Bulletin* (2 a year).

**International Federation of Human Rights Leagues—FIDH:** 17 passage de la Main d'Or, 75011 Paris, France; tel. 1-43-55-25-28; fax 1-43-55-18-80; e-mail fidh@csi.com; internet www.fidh.imaginet.fr; f. 1922; promotes the implementation of the Universal Declaration of Human Rights and other instruments of human rights protection; aims to raise awareness and alert public opinion to issues of human rights violations and undertakes investigation and observation missions, training and uses its consultative and observer status to lobby international authorities. Mems 105 national leagues in more than 86 countries. Pres. Patrick Baudouin. Publs *Lettre* (2 a month), mission reports.

**International Federation of Social Workers—IFSW:** POB 6875, Schwarztorstrasse 20, 3000 Bern, Switzerland; tel. (31) 3826015; fax (31) 3826017; e-mail secr.gen@ifsw.org; internet www.ifsw.org; f. 1928 as International Permanent Secretariat of Social Workers; present name adopted 1950; aims to promote social work as a profession through international co-operation concerning standards, training, ethics and working conditions; organizes international conferences; represents the profession at the UN and other international bodies; supports national associations of social workers. Mems: national associations in 70 countries. Pres. Elis Envall (Sweden); Sec.-Gen. Tom Johannesen (Switzerland).

**International League against Racism and Antisemitism:** CP 1754, 1211 Geneva 1, Switzerland; tel. (22) 7310633; fax (22) 7370634; e-mail licra@mnet.ch; f. 1927; mems in 17 countries. Pres. Pierre Aidenbaum (France).

**International League for Human Rights:** 432 Park Avenue South, 11th Floor, New York, NY 10016, USA; tel. (212) 684-1221; fax (212) 684-1696; e-mail info@ilhr.org; internet www.ilhr.org; f. 1942 to implement political, civil, social, economic and cultural rights contained in the Universal Declaration of Human Rights adopted by the United Nations and to support and protect defenders of human rights world-wide. Mems: individuals, national affiliates and correspondents throughout the world. Exec. Dir Catherine A. Fitzpatrick. Publs various human rights reports.

**International League of Societies for Persons with Mental Handicap** (European Association): Galeries de la Toison d'Or, 29 chaussée d'Ixelles, Ste 393/35, 1050 Brussels, Belgium; tel. (2) 502-28-15; fax (2) 502-80-10; e-mail secretariat@ilsmh-ea.be; internet www.ilsmh-ea.be; f. 1988 to promote the interests of people with a mental handicap without regard to nationality, race or creed; furthers co-operation between national bodies; organizes congresses, meetings and seminars. Mems: 20 societies in the 15 EU member states.

**International Planned Parenthood Federation—IPPF:** Regent's College, Inner Circle, Regent's Park, London, NW1 4NS, United Kingdom; tel. (20) 7487-7900; fax (20) 7487-7950; e-mail info@ippf.org; internet www.ippf.org; f. 1952; aims to promote and support sexual and reproductive health and family planning services throughout the world, and to increase understanding of population problems; offers technical assistance and training; collaborates with other international organizations and provides information. Mems: independent family planning associations in over 150 countries. Pres. Dr Attiya Inayatullah; Dir-Gen. Ingar Brueggemann.

**International Prisoners Aid Association:** c/o Dr Ali, Department of Sociology, University of Louisville, Louisville, KY 40292, USA; tel. (502) 588-6836; fax (502) 852-7042; f. 1950; to improve prisoners' aid services for rehabilitation of the individual and protection of society. Mems: national federations in 29 countries. Pres. Dr Wolfgang Doleisch (Austria); Exec. Dir Dr Badr-el-Din Ali. Publ. *Newsletter* (3 a year).

**International Scout and Guide Fellowship—ISGF:** 9 rue du Champ de Mars, bte 14, 1050 Brussels, Belgium; tel. (2) 511-46-95; fax (2) 511-84-36; e-mail isgf_aisg@euronet.be; f. 1953 to help adult scouts and guides to keep alive the spirit of the Scout and Guide Promise and Laws in their own lives; to bring that spirit into the communities in which they live and work; to establish liaison and co-operation between national organizations for adult scouts and guides; to encourage the founding of an organization in any country where no such organization exists; to promote friendship amongst adult scouts and guides throughout the world. Mems: 90,000 in 45 member states. Chair. of Cttee NIELS ROSENBOM; Sec.-Gen. NAÏC PIRARD. Publ. *World Gazette Mondiale* (quarterly).

**International Social Security Association:** CP 1, 1211 Geneva 22, Switzerland; tel. (22) 7996617; fax (22) 7998509; internet www.aiss.org; f. 1927 to promote the development of social security throughout the world, mainly through the improvement of techniques and administration, in order to advance social and economic conditions on the basis of social equality. Mems: 364 institutions in 143 countries. Pres. JOHAN VERSTRAETEN (Belgium); Sec.-Gen. DALMER HOSKINS (USA). Publs *International Social Security Review* (quarterly in English, French, German, Spanish), *Trends in Social Security* (quarterly in English, French, German, Spanish), *African News Sheet, ISSA Bulletin, EuropInform, Asia and Pacific Link, Contacto, Reforma de los Sistemas de Pensiones en América Latina, Social Security Documentation* (African, Asian-Pacific, European and American series).

**International Social Service:** 32 quai du Seujet, 1201 Geneva, Switzerland; tel. (22) 9067700; fax (22) 9067701; e-mail iss.gs@span.ch; internet www.childhub.ch/iss/eng; f. 1921 to aid families and individuals whose problems require services beyond the boundaries of the country in which they live and where the solution of these problems depends upon co-ordinated action on the part of social workers in two or more countries; to study from an international standpoint the conditions and consequences of emigration in their effect on individual, family, and social life. Operates on a non-sectarian and non-political basis. Mems: branches in 14 countries, six affiliated offices, and correspondents in some 100 other countries. Pres. Prof. Dr RAINER FRANK (Germany); Sec.-Gen. DAMIEN NGABONZIZA.

**International Union of Family Organisations:** 28 place Saint-Georges, 75009 Paris, France; tel. 1-48-78-07-59; fax 1-42-82-95-24; f. 1947 to bring together all organizations throughout the world which are working for family welfare; conducts permanent commissions on standards of living, housing, marriage guidance, work groups on family movements, rural families, etc.; there are six regional organizations: the Pan-African Family Organisation (Rabat, Morocco), the North America organization (Montreal, Canada), the Arab Family Organisation (Tunis, Tunisia), the Asian Union of Family Organisations (New Delhi, India), the European regional organization (Berne, Switzerland) and the Latin American Secretariat (Curitiba, Brazil). Mems: national associations, groups and governmental departments in more than 55 countries. Pres. MARIA TERESA DA COSTA MACEDO (Portugal).

**International Union of Societies for the Aid of Mental Health:** CSM, BP 323, 40107 Dax Cédex, France; tel. 5-58-91-48-38; fax 5-58-91-46-84; f. 1964 to group national societies and committees whose aim is to help mentally handicapped or maladjusted people. Gen. Pres Dr DEMANGEAT; Gen. Sec. Dr MINARD.

**International Union of Tenants:** Box 7514, 10392 Stockholm, Sweden; tel. (8) 791-02-00; fax (8) 20-88-46; e-mail magnus.hammar@hyresgasterna.se; internet www.iut.nu; f. 1955 to collaborate in safeguarding the interests of tenants; participates in activities of UNCHS (Habitat); has working groups for EC matters, eastern Europe, developing countries and for future development; holds annual council meeting and triennial congress. Mems: national tenant organizations in 24 European countries, Australia, Benin, Canada, Ecuador, India, Kenya, New Zealand, Tanzania and Uganda. Chair. JAN DANNEMANN; Sec. Gen. MAGNUS HAMMAR. Publ. *The Global Tenant* (quarterly).

**Inter-University European Institute on Social Welfare—IEISW:** 179 rue du Débarcadère, 6001 Marcinelle, Belgium; tel. (71) 36-62-73; f. 1970 to promote, carry out and publicize scientific research on social welfare and community work. Chair. Board of Dirs JACQUES HOCHEPIED (Belgium); Gen. Sec. P. ROZEN (Belgium). Publ. *COMM*.

**Lions Clubs International:** 300 West 22nd St, Oak Brook, IL 60523-8842, USA; tel. (630) 571-5466; fax (630) 571-8890; e-mail lions@lionsclubs.org; internet www.lionsclubs.org; f. 1917 to foster understanding among people of the world; to promote principles of good government and citizenship; and an interest in civic, cultural, social and moral welfare; to encourage service-minded people to serve their community without financial reward. Mems: 1.4m. with over 44,500 clubs in 185 countries and geographic areas. Exec. Admin. WIN HAMILTON. Publ. *The Lion* (10 a year, in 20 languages).

**Médecins sans frontières—MSF:** 39 rue de la Tourelle, 1040 Brussels, Belgium; tel. (2) 280-18-81; fax (2) 280-01-73; f. 1971; composed of physicians and other members of the medical profession; aims to provide medical assistance to victims of war and natural disasters, and medium-term programmes of nutrition, immunization, sanitation, public health, and rehabilitation of hospitals and dispensaries. Awarded the Nobel peace prize in Oct. 1999. Centres in France, Luxembourg, the Netherlands, Spain and Switzerland; delegate offices in other European countries, North America and Asia. Dir.-Gen. Dr ERIC GOEMAERE.

**Pan Pacific and South East Asia Women's Association—PPSEAWA:** 707 Kent Rd, Kenilworth, IL 60043, USA; tel. (847) 251-3227; fax (847) 256-3862; f. 1928 to strengthen the bonds of peace by fostering better understanding and friendship among women in this region, and to promote co-operation among women for the study and improvement of social conditions; holds international conference every three years. Pres. Dr ELIZABETH-LOUISE GIRARDI. Publ. *PPSEAWA Bulletin*.

**Rotary International:** 1560 Sherman Ave, Evanston, IL 60201, USA; tel. (847) 866-3000; fax (847) 328-8554; f. 1905 to carry out activities for the service of humanity, to promote high ethical standards in business and professions and to further international understanding, goodwill and peace. Mems: over 1,195,000 in 28,200 Rotary Clubs in 154 countries and 35 regions. Pres. LUIS VICENTE GIAY; Gen. Sec. GEOFFREY LARGE (USA). Publs *The Rotarian* (monthly, English), *Revista Rotaria* (bi-monthly, Spanish).

**Service Civil International—SCI:** St-Jacobsmarket 82, 2000 Antwerp, Belgium; tel. (3) 266-57-27; fax (3) 232-03-44; e-mail sciint@xs4all.be; internet www.ines.org/sci; f. 1920 to promote peace and understanding through voluntary service projects (work-camps, local groups, long-term community development projects and education). Mems: 14,000 in 36 countries; projects in 20 countries. Pres. HELEN HONEYMAN. Publ. *Action* (quarterly).

**Society of Saint Vincent de Paul:** 5 rue du Pré-aux-Clercs, 75007 Paris, France; tel. 1-44-55-36-55; fax 1-42-61-72-56; e-mail stvincent.cgi@wanadoo.fr; internet www.cef.fr/vincenpaul; f. 1833 to conduct charitable activities such as child care, youth work, work with immigrants, adult literacy programmes, residential care for the sick, handicapped and elderly, social counselling and work with prisoners and the unemployed—all conducted through personal contact. Mems: over 800,000 in 132 countries. Pres. JOSÉ RAMÓN DÍAZ TORREMOCHA; Sec.-Gen. PIERRE BONNASSIES. Publ. *Vincenpaul* (quarterly, in French, English and Spanish).

**SOLIDAR:** 22 rue de Commerce, 1000 Brussels, Belgium; tel. (2) 500-10-20; fax (2) 500-10-30; e-mail solidar@compuserve.com; internet www.solidar.org; frmly International Workers' Aid f. 1951; an association of independent development and social welfare agencies based in Europe, which are linked to the labour and democratic socialist movements; aims to contribute to the creation of radical models of economic and social development, and to advance practical solutions that enable people in all parts of the world to have increased control over their own future. Mems: agencies in 90 countries. Sec.-Gen. GIAMPI ALPHADEFF.

**World Blind Union:** c/o CBC ONCE, 18 La Coruña, 28020 Madrid, Spain; tel. (91) 5713675; fax (91) 5715777; e-mail umc@once.es; internet www.once.es/wbu; f. 1984 (amalgamating the World Council for the Welfare of the Blind and the International Federation of the Blind) to work for the prevention of blindness and the welfare of blind and visually-impaired people; encourages development of braille, talking book programmes and other media for the blind; rehabilitation, training and employment; prevention and cure of blindness in co-operation with the International Agency for the Prevention of Blindness; co-ordinates aid to the blind in developing countries; conducts studies on technical, social and educational matters, maintains the Louis Braille birth-place as an international museum. Mems in 146 countries. Pres. EUCLID HERIE (Canada); Sec.-Gen. PEDRO ZURITA (Spain). Publs *World Blind* (2 a year, in English, English Braille and on cassette, in Spanish and Spanish Braille and on cassette and in French).

**World Federation of the Deaf—WFD:** Magnus Ladulåsgaten 63, 4tr, 118 27 Stockholm, Sweden; e-mail carol-lee.aquiline@wfdnews.org; internet www.wfdnews.org; f. 1951 aims to serve deaf people and their national organizations, and to represent the interests of deaf people in international forums, such as the UN system; to achieve the goal of full participation by deaf people in society; encourages deaf people to set up and run their own organizations. Priority is given to the promotion of the recognition and use of national sign languages; human rights; the education of deaf people; and deaf people in the developing world. Mems: 120 member countries. Pres. LIISA KAUPPINEN; Gen. Sec. CAROL-LEE AQUILINE. Publ. *WFD News* (3 a year).

**World ORT Union:** ORT House, 126 Albert St, London, NW1 7NE, United Kingdom; tel. (20) 7446-8500; fax (20) 7446-8650; e-mail wou@ort.org; f. 1880 for the development of industrial, agricultural and artisan skills among Jews; now, a highly developed educational and training organization active in over 60 countries throughout the world; conducts vocational training programmes for adolescents and adults, including instructors' and teachers' education and apprenticeship training in more than 40 countries, including technical assistance programmes in co-operation with interested governments. Mems: committees in over 40 countries. Dir-Gen. ROBERT SINGER. Publs *Annual Report, Frontline News, What in the World is ORT?*

**World Veterans Federation:** 17 rue Nicolo, 75116 Paris, France; tel. 1-40-72-61-00; fax 1-40-72-80-58; e-mail 101727.1446@compuserve.com; f. 1950 to maintain international peace and security by the application of the San Francisco Charter and helping to implement the Universal Declaration of Human Rights and related international conventions, to defend the spiritual and material interests of war veterans and war victims. It promotes practical international co-operation in disarmament, human rights problems, economic development, rehabilitation of the handicapped, accessibility of the man-made environment, legislation concerning war veterans and war victims, and development of international humanitarian law; in 1986 established International Socio-Medical Information Centre (United Kingdom) for psycho-medical problems resulting from stress. Regional committees for Africa, Asia and the Pacific, and Europe and Standing Committee on Women. Mems: national organizations in 77 countries, representing about 27m. war veterans and war victims. Pres. SERGE WOURGAFT (France); Sec.-Gen. MAREK HAGMAJER (Poland). Publs special studies (disarmament, human rights, rehabilitation).

**Zonta International:** 557 W. Randolph St, Chicago, IL 60661-2206, USA; tel. (312) 930-5848; fax (312) 930-0951; f. 1919; executive service organization; international and community service projects to promote the status of women. Mems: 36,000 in 67 countries. Pres. JOSEPHINE G. COOKE; Exec. Dir JANET HALSTEAD. Publ. *The Zontian* (quarterly).

# Sport and Recreations

**Arab Sports Confederation:** POB 62997, Riyadh 11442, Saudi Arabia; tel. (1) 482-9427; fax (1) 482-3196; f. 1976 to encourage regional co-operation in sport. Mems: 20 national Olympic Committees, 36 Arab sports federations. Sec.-Gen. OTHMAN M. AL-SAAD. Publ. *Annual Report.*

**Fédération Aéronautique Internationale** (International Aeronautical Federation): 24 ave Mon Repos, 1005 Lausanne, Switzerland; e-mail sec@fai.org; internet www.fai.org; f. 1905 to encourage all aeronautical sports; organizes world championships and makes rules through Air Sports Commissions; endorses world aeronautical and astronautical records. Mems: in 93 countries and territories. Pres. EILIF NESS; Sec.-Gen. MAX BISHOP. Publ. *Air Sports International.*

**General Association of International Sports Federations—GAISF:** 4 blvd du Jardin Exotique, Monte Carlo, Monaco; tel. 93-50-74-13; fax 93-25-28-73; e-mail gaist@mcn.mc; f. 1967 to act as a forum for the exchange of ideas and discussion of common problems in sport; to collect and circulate information; to provide secretarial and translation services for members, organize meetings and provide technical documentation and consultancy services. Mems: 88 international sports organizations; Pres. Dr UN YONG KIM; Sec.-Gen. PETER TALLBERG (Finland). Publs *Calendar of International Sports Competitions* (2 a year), *Sportime Magazine* (quarterly, in English and French), *GAISF Calendar, Sport and Education* and *Sport and Media.*

**International Amateur Athletic Federation:** 17 rue Princesse Florestine, BP 359, 98007 Monte Carlo Cédex, Monaco; tel. 93-10-88-88; fax 93-15-95-15; e-mail headquarters@iaaf.org; f. 1912 to ensure co-operation and fairness among members, and to combat discrimination in athletics; to affiliate national governing bodies, to compile athletic competition rules and to organize championships at all levels; to settle disputes between members, and to conduct a programme of development for members who need coaching, judging courses, etc., and to frame regulations for the establishment of World, Olympic and other athletic records. Mems: national asscns in 210 countries and territories. Gen. Sec. ISTVÁN GYULAI (Hungary). Publs *IAAF Handbook* (every 2 years), *IAAF Review* (quarterly), *IAAF Directory* (annually), *New Studies in Athletics* (quarterly).

**International Amateur Boxing Association—AIBA:** POB 76343, Atlanta, GA 30358, USA; tel. (770) 455-8350; fax (770) 454-6467; e-mail lbaker27@mindspring.com; internet www.aiba.net; f. 1946 as the world body controlling amateur boxing for the Olympic Games, continental, regional and inter-nation championships and tournaments in every part of the world. Mems: 190 national asscns. Pres. Prof. A. CHOWDHRY (Pakistan); Sec.-Gen. LORING K. BAKER (USA). Publ. *World Amateur Boxing Magazine* (quarterly).

**International Amateur Radio Union:** POB 310905, Newington, CT 06131-0905, USA; tel. (860) 594-0200; fax (860) 594-0259; internet www.iaru.org; f. 1925 to link national amateur radio societies and represent the interests of two-way amateur radio communication. Mems: 150 national amateur radio societies. Pres. LARRY E. PRICE; Sec. DAVID SUMNER.

**International Amateur Swimming Federation** (Fédération Internationale de Natation Amateur—FINA): 9 ave de Beaumont, 1012 Lausanne, Switzerland; tel. (21) 3126602; fax (21) 3126610; internet www.fina.org; f. 1908 to promote amateur swimming and swimming sports internationally; to administer rules for swimming sports, for competitions and for establishing records; to organize world championships and FINA events; development programme to increase the popularity and quality of aquatic sports. Mems: 139 federations. Pres. MUSTAPHA LARFAOUI (Algeria); Dir CORNEL MARCULESCU. Publs *Handbook* (every 2 years), *FINA News* (monthly), *World of Swimming* (quarterly).

**International Archery Federation** (Fédération internationale de tir à l'arc—FITA): 135 ave de Cour, 1007 Lausanne, Switzerland; tel. (21) 6143050; fax (21) 6143055; e-mail fita@worldcom.ch; internet www.archery.org; f. 1931 to promote international archery; organizes world championships and Olympic tournaments; Biennial Congress: France, 1999. Mems: national amateur associations in 118 countries. Pres. JAMES L. EASTON (USA); Sec.-Gen. GIUSEPPE CINNIRELLA (Italy). Publs *Information FITA* (monthly), *The Arrow* (bulletin, quarterly), *The Target* (annually).

**International Automobile Federation** (Fédération Internationale de l'Automobile—FIA): 2 chemin de Blandonnet, CP 296, 1215 Geneva, Switzerland; tel. (22) 5444400; fax (22) 5444450; internet www.fia.com; f. 1904; manages world motor sport and organizes international championships. Mems: 157 national automobile clubs or asscns in 119 countries. Pres. MAX MOSLEY; Sec.-Gen. (Sport) PIERRE DE CONINCK; Sec.-Gen. (Tourism) PETER DOGGWILER.

**International Badminton Federation—IBF:** Manor Park Place, Rutherford Way, Cheltenham, Gloucestershire, GL51 9TU, United Kingdom; tel. (1242) 234904; fax (1242) 221030; e-mail info@intbadfed.org; internet www.intbadfed.org; f. 1934 to oversee the sport of badminton world-wide. Mems: affiliated national organizations in 141 countries and territories. Pres. LU SHENGRONG; Chief Exec. NEIL CAMERON (UK). Publs *World Badminton* (available on internet), *Statute Book* (annually).

**International Basketball Federation** (Fédération Internationale de Basketball): PO Box 700607, 81306 Munich, Germany; tel. (89) 7481580; fax (89) 74815833; e-mail secretariat@office.fiba.com; internet www.fiba.com; f. 1932 as International Amateur Basketball Federation (present name adopted 1989); aims to promote, supervise and direct international basketball; organizes quadrennial congress. Mems: affiliated national federations in 208 countries. Sec.-Gen. BORISLAV STANKOVIC. Publs *FIBA Bulletin* (2 a year), *FIBA Media Guide.*

**International Canoe Federation:** Dozsa György ut. 1-3, 1143 Budapest, Hungary; tel. (1) 363-4832; fax (1) 221-4130; e-mail icf-hq-budapest@mail.datanet.hu; internet www.datanet.hu/icf-hq; f. 1924; administers canoeing at the Olympic Games; promotes canoe/kayak activity in general. Mems: 108 national federations. Pres. ULRICH FELDHOFF; Sec.-Gen. OTTO BONN.

**International Council for Health, Physical Education, Recreation, Sport and Dance:** 1900 Association Drive, Reston, VA 20191, USA; tel. (800) 213-7193; f. 1958 to encourage the development of programmes in health, physical education, recreation, sport and dance throughout the world, by linking teaching professionals in these fields.

**International Cricket Council:** Lord's Cricket Ground, London, NW8 8QN, United Kingdom; tel. (20) 7266-1818; fax (20) 7266-1777; f. 1909; governing body for international cricket. Annual conference. Mems: Australia, England, India, New Zealand, Pakistan, South Africa, Sri Lanka, West Indies, Zimbabwe; and 23 associate and 13 affiliate mems. Chief Exec. D. L. RICHARDS.

**International Cycling Union:** 37 route de Chavannes, 1007 Lausanne, Switzerland; tel. (21) 6220580; fax (21) 6220588; e-mail admin@uci.ch; internet www.uci.ch; f. 1900 to develop, regulate and control all forms of cycling as a sport. Mems: 168 federations. Pres. HEIN VERBRUGGEN (Netherlands). Publs *International Calendar* (annually), *Velo World* (6 a year).

**International Equestrian Federation:** CP 157, ave Mon-Repos 24, 1000 Lausanne 5, Switzerland; tel. (21) 3104747; fax (21) 3104760; e-mail info@horsesport.org; internet www.horsesport.org; f. 1921; administers equestrian events at the Olympic Games. Sec.-Gen. Dr BO HELANDER.

**International Federation of Associated Wrestling Styles:** 17 ave Juste-Olivier, 1006 Lausanne, Switzerland; tel. (21) 3128426; fax (21) 3236073; e-mail filalausanne@bluewin.ch; internet www.fila_wrestling.org; f. 1912 to encourage the development of amateur wrestling and promote the sport in countries where it is not yet practised; to further friendly relations between all members; to oppose any form of political, racial or religious discrimination.

Mems: 142 federations. Pres. MILAN ERCEGAN; Sec.-Gen. MICHEL DUSSON. Publs *News Bulletin, Wrestling Revue.*

**International Federation of Association Football** (Fédération Internationale de Football Association—FIFA): Hitzigweg 11, POB 85, 8030 Zürich, Switzerland; tel. (1) 3849595; fax (1) 3849696; internet www.fifa.com; f. 1904 to promote the game of association football and foster friendly relations among players and national associations; to control football and uphold the laws of the game as laid down by the International Football Association Board; to prevent discrimination of any kind between players; and to provide arbitration in any disputes between national associations; organizes World Cup competition every four years. Mems: 203 national associations, six regional confederations. Pres. JOSEPH S. BLATTER (Switzerland). Publs *FIFA News* (monthly), *FIFA Magazine* (every 2 months) (both in English, French, Spanish and German).

**International Federation of Park and Recreation Administration—IFPRA:** The Grotto, Lower Basildon, Reading, Berkshire, RG8 9NE, United Kingdom; tel. (1491) 874800; fax (1491) 874801; e-mail alansmith@ilam.co.uk; f. 1957 to provide a world centre where members of government departments, local authorities, and all organizations concerned with recreational services can discuss relevant matters. Mems: 550 in over 50 countries. Gen. Sec. ALAN SMITH (UK).

**International Fencing Federation:** ave Mon-Repos 24, CP 128, 1000 Lausanne 5, Switzerland; tel. (21) 3203115; fax (21) 3203116; e-mail contact@fie.ch; internet www.fie.ch; f. 1913; administers fencing at the Olympic Games. Mems: 96 national federations. Pres. RENÉ ROCH.

**International Gymnastic Federation:** rue des Oeuches 10, CP 359, 2740 Moutier 1, Switzerland; tel. (32) 4946410; fax (32) 4946419; f. 1881 to promote the exchange of official documents and publications on gymnastics. Mems: 124 affiliated federations. Pres. BRUNO GRANDI; Gen. Sec. NORBERT BUECHE (Switzerland). Publs *Bulletin* (3 a year), *World of Gymnastics Magazine* (3 a year).

**International Hockey Federation:** 1 ave des Arts, Boîte 5, 1210 Brussels, Belgium; tel. (2) 219-45-37; fax (2) 219-27-61; e-mail fih@fihockey.org; internet www.fihockey.org; f. 1924 to fix the rules of outdoor and indoor hockey for all affiliated national associations; to control the game of hockey and indoor hockey; to control the organization of international tournaments, such as the Olympic Games and the World Cup. Mems: 120 national associations. Pres. JUAN ANGEL CALZADO; Sec.-Gen. ELS VAN BREDA-VRIESMAN. Publ. *World Hockey* (quarterly).

**International Judo Federation:** 12 rue Maamoun, 1082 Tunis, Tunisia; tel. (1) 781-057; fax (1) 801-517; e-mail dhouib@gnet.tn; internet www.ijf.org; f. 1951 to promote cordial and friendly relations between members; to protect the interests of judo throughout the world; to organize World Championships and the judo events of the Olympic Games; to develop and spread the techniques and spirit of judo throughout the world and to establish international judo regulations. Pres. YONG SUNG PARK (Republic of Korea); Gen. Sec. Dr HEDI DHOUIB (Tunisia).

**International Paralympic Committee:** Adenauerallee 212–214, 53113 Bonn, Germany; f. 1989; responsible for organizing the paralympic games for sportspeople with disabilities, which are held alongside the Olympic Games; Pres. Dr ROBERT STEADWARD (Canada); Sec.-Gen. MIGUEL SAGARRA (Spain).

**International Philatelic Federation:** Zollikerstrasse 128, 8008 Zürich, Switzerland; tel. (1) 4223839; fax (1) 3831446; f. 1926 to promote philately internationally. Pres. D. N. JATIA; Sec.-Gen. M. L. HEIRI.

**International Rowing Federation** (Fédération internationale des Sociétés d'Aviron—FISA): 135 ave de Cour, CP 18, 1000 Lausanne 3, Switzerland; tel. (21) 6178373; fax (21) 6178375; e-mail info@fisa.org; internet www.fisa.org; f. 1892 to establish contacts between rowers in all countries and to draw up racing rules; world controlling body of the sport of rowing. Mems: national federations in 106 countries. Pres. DENIS OSWALD; Sec.-Gen. and Exec. Dir MATTHEW SMITH. Publs *FISA Directory* (annually), *FISA Info* (quarterly), *FISA Coach* (quarterly).

**International Shooting Sport Federation:** 80336 Munich, Bavariaring 21, Germany; tel. (89) 5443550; fax (89) 54435544; e-mail issfmunich@compuserve.com; internet www.issf-shooting.org; f. 1907 to promote and guide the development of the amateur shooting sports; to organize World Championships; to control the organization of continental and regional championships; to supervise the shooting events of the Olympic and Continental Games under the auspices of the International Olympic Committee. Mems: 151 federations in 146 countries. Pres. OLEGARIO VÁZQUEZ-RAÑA (Mexico); Sec.-Gen. HORST G. SCHREIBER (Germany). Publs *ISSF News, International Shooting Sport* (6 a year).

**International Skating Union—ISU:** chemin de Primerose 2, 1007 Lausanne, Switzerland; tel. (21) 6126666; fax (21) 6126677; e-mail info@isu.ch; internet www.isu.org; f. 1892; holds regular conferences. Mems: 70 national federations in 55 countries. Pres. OTTAVIA CINQUANTA; Gen.-Sec. FREDI SCHMID.

**International Ski Federation:** 3653 Oberhofen am Thunersee, Switzerland; tel. (33) 2446161; fax (33) 2435353; internet www.fis_ski.org; f. 1924 to further the sport of skiing; to prevent discrimination in skiing matters on racial, religious or political grounds; to organize World Ski Championships and regional championships and, as supreme international skiing authority, to establish the international competition calendar and rules for all ski competitions approved by the FIS, and to arbitrate in any disputes. Mems: 100 national ski associations. Pres. GIAN-FRANCO KASPER (Switzerland); Dir SARAH LEWIS (UK). Publ. *FIS Bulletin* (quarterly).

**International Table Tennis Federation:** 53 London Rd, St Leonards-on-Sea, East Sussex, TN37 6AY, United Kingdom; tel. (1424) 721414; fax (1424) 431871; e-mail hq@ittf.cablenet.co.uk; internet www.ittf.com; f. 1926. Pres. ADHAM SHARARA.

**International Tennis Federation:** Bank Lane, Roehampton, London, SW15 5XZ, United Kingdom; tel. (20) 8878-6464; fax (20) 8878-7799; e-mail communications@itftennis.com; internet www.itftennis.com; f. 1913 to govern the game of tennis throughout the world and promote its teaching; to preserve its independence of outside authority; to produce the Rules of Tennis, to promote the Davis Cup Competition for men, the Fed. Cup for women, Olympic Games Tennis Event, wheelchair tennis, 16 cups for veterans, the ITF Sunshine Cup and ITF Continental Connelly Cup for players of 18 years old and under, the World Youth Cup for players of 16 years old and under, and the World Junior Tennis Tournament for players of 14 years old and under; to organize tournaments. Mems: 132 full and 68 associate. Pres. FRANCESCO RICCI BITTI. Publs *World of Tennis* (annually), *Davis Cup Yearbook, ITF World* (quarterly), *ITF This Week* (weekly).

**International Volleyball Federation** (Fédération Internationale de Volleyball—FIVB): ave de la Gare 12, 1001 Lausanne, Switzerland; tel. (21) 345-35-35; fax (21) 345-35-45; e-mail info@mail.fivb.ch; internet www.fivb.org; f. 1947 to encourage, organize and supervise the playing of volleyball, beach volleyball, and park volley; organizes biennial congress. Mems: 217 national federations. Pres. Dr RUBÉN ACOSTA HERNÁNDEZ; Dir ALAIN COUPAT. Publs *VolleyWorld* (every 2 months), *X-Press* (monthly).

**International Weightlifting Federation:** PF 614, 1374 Budapest, Hungary; tel. (1) 3530530; fax (1) 3530199; e-mail iwf@iwf.net; internet www.iwf.net; f. 1905 to control international weightlifting; to set up technical rules and to train referees; to supervise World Championships, Olympic Games, regional games and international contests of all kinds; to supervise the activities of national and continental federations; to register world records. Mems: 167 national organizations. Pres. GOTTFRIED SCHÖDL (Austria); Gen. Sec. TAMÁS AJAN (Hungary). Publs *IWF Constitution and Rules* (every 4 years), *World Weightlifting* (quarterly).

**International World Games Association:** Ekeby House, Luiksestraat 23, 2587 The Hague, Netherlands; tel. (70) 3512774; fax (70) 3509911; e-mail iwga@hetnet.nl; f. 1980; organizes World Games every four years, comprising 25 sports that are not included in the Olympic Games. Sec.-Gen. J. A. P. KOREN.

**International Yacht Racing Union:** 27 Broadwall, London, SE1 9PL, United Kingdom; tel. (20) 7928-6611; fax (20) 7401-8304; f. 1907; controlling authority of sailing in all its forms throughout the world; establishes and amends international yacht racing rules, organizes the Olympic Yachting Regatta and other championships. Mems: 117 national yachting federations. Pres. PAUL HENDERSON; Sec.-Gen. ARVE SUNDHEIM.

**Union of European Football Associations—UEFA:** chemin de la Redoute 54, 1260 Nyon, Switzerland; tel. (22) 9944444; fax (22) 9944488; internet www.uefa.com; f. 1954. Mems: 51 national associations. Pres. LENNART JOHANSSON; Sec.-Gen. GERHARD AIGNER.

**World Boxing Organization:** c/o 100 West Randolph St, 9th Floor, Chicago, IL 60601, USA; tel. (312) 814-3145; fax (312) 814-2719; f. 1962; regulates professional boxing.

**World Bridge Federation:** 56 route de Vandoeuvres, 1253 Geneva, Switzerland; tel. (22) 7501541; fax (22) 7501620; f. 1958 to promote the game of contract bridge throughout the world, federate national bridge associations in all countries, conduct bridge associations in all countries, conduct world championships competitions, establish standard bridge laws. Mems: 89 countries. Pres. ERNESTO D'ORSI (Brazil). Publ. *World Bridge News* (quarterly).

**World Chess Federation** (Fédération Internationale des Echecs—FIDE): POB 166, 1000 Lausanne 4, Switzerland; tel. (21) 3103900; e-mail fide@fide.ch; internet www.fide@chessweb.com; f. 1924; controls chess competitions of world importance and awards international chess titles. Mems: national orgs in more than 150 countries. Pres. KIRSAN ILYUMZHINOV. Publs *President's Circular Letter* (5 a year), *FIDE Forum* (every 2 months), *International Rating List.*

**World Squash Federation Ltd:** 6 Havelock Rd, Hastings, East Sussex, TN43 1BP, United Kingdom; tel. (1424) 429245; fax (1424)

429250; e-mail squash@wsf.cablenet.co.uk; internet www.squash.org; f. 1966. Mems: 115 national organizations. Exec. Dir EDWARD J. WALLBUTTON.

**World Underwater Federation:** Viale Tiziano 74, 00196 Rome, Italy; tel. (06) 36858480; fax (06) 36858490; e-mail amasmond@tin.it; internet www.cmas.org; f. 1959 to develop underwater activities; to form bodies to instruct in the techniques of underwater diving; to perfect existing equipment and encourage inventions and to experiment with newly marketed products, suggesting possible improvements; to organize international competitions. Mems: organizations in 90 countries. Pres. ACHILLE FERRERO (Italy); Sec. PIERRE DERNIER (Belgium). Publs *International Year Book of CMAS, Scientific Diving: A Code of Practice,* manuals.

# Technology

**International Union of Technical Associations and Organizations** (Union Internationale des Associations et Organismes Techniques—UATI): UNESCO House, 1 rue Miollis, 75015 Paris Cédex 15, France; tel. 1-45-68-27-70; fax 1-43-06-29-27;e-mail uati@unesco.org; f. 1951 (fmrly Union of International Technical Associations) under the auspices of UNESCO; aims to promote and co-ordinate activities of member organizations and represent their interests; facilitates relations with international organizations, notably UN agencies, receives proposals and makes recommendations on the establishment of new international technical associations. Mems: 25 organizations. Chair. MICHEL SAILLARD (France). Publ. *UATI Magazine* (2 a year).

### MEMBER ORGANIZATIONS

Members of UATI include the following:

**International Association of Hydraulic Engineering and Research—IAHR:** c/o Delft Hydraulics, Rotterdamseweg 185, 2629 HD Delft, Netherlands; tel. (15) 285-88-79; fax (15) 285-84-17; e-mail iahr@iahr.nl; internet www.iahr.org; f. 1935; holds biennial congresses. Mems: 2,150 individual, 200 corporate. Sec.-Gen. H. J. OVERBEEK (Netherlands). Publs *AHR Bulletin, Journal of Hydraulic Research, Proceedings of Biennial Conferences.*

**International Association of Lighthouse Authorities:** 20 ter rue Schnapper, 78100 St Germain en Laye, France; tel. 1-34-51-70-01; fax 1-34-51-82-05; e-mail aismiala@easynet.fr; f. 1957; holds technical conference every four years; working groups study special problems and formulate technical recommendations, guide-lines and manuals. Mems in 80 countries. Sec.-Gen. TORSTEN KRUUSE. Publ. *Bulletin* (quarterly).

**International Bridge, Tunnel and Turnpike Association:** 2120 L St, NW, Suite 305, Washington, DC 20037, USA; tel. (202) 659-4620; fax (202) 659-0500; e-mail ibtta@ibtta.org; internet www.ibtta.org; f. 1932. Pres. LUIS FERREIRO; Exec. Dir. NEIL D. SCHUSTER. Publ. *Tollways* (monthly).

**International Commission of Agricultural Engineering—CIGR:** Institut für Landtechnik, Universität Bonn, Nassallee 5, 53 115 Bonn, Germany; tel. (228) 732389; fax (228) 739644; e-mail cigr@uni-bonn.de; internet www.ucd.ie/cigr; f. 1930. Mems: associations from 40 countries, individual mems from six countries. Pres. Prof. B. STOUT (USA); Sec.-Gen. P. SCHULZE LAMMERS (Germany). Publs *Bulletin de la CIGR, Newsletter* (quarterly), technical reports.

**International Commission on Glass:** Stazione Sperimentale del Vetro, Via Briati 10, 30141 Murano, Venice, Italy; tel. (041) 739422; fax (041) 739420; e-mail spevetro@ve-nettuno.it; internet www.nettuno.it/fiera/spevetro; f. 1933 to co-ordinate research in glass and allied products, exchange information and organize conferences. Mems: 30 organizations. Pres. D. PYE; Sec.-Gen. F. NICOLETTI.

**International Commission on Irrigation and Drainage:** 48 Nyaya Marg, Chanakyapuri, New Delhi 110 021, India; tel. (11) 6115679; fax (11) 6115962; e-mail icoiad@giasdlo1.vsnl.net.in; f. 1950; holds triennial congresses. Mems: 66 national committees. Pres. ALY M. SHADY (Canada); Sec.-Gen. C. D. THATTE (India). Publs *Journal* (2 a year), *Bibliography* (annually), *World Irrigation, Multilingual Technical Dictionary, World Flood Control,* technical books.

**International Committee of Foundry Technical Associations:** Konradstr. 9, POB 7190, 8023 Zürich, Switzerland; tel. (1) 2719090; fax (1) 2719292; e-mail gerster@jgp.ch; Pres. Prof. J. SUCHY; Gen. Sec. Dr J. GERSTER.

**International Federation for the Theory of Machines and Mechanisms:** PO Box 4200, Univ. of Oulu, 90014 Oulu, Finland; tel. (8) 553-2050; fax 8) 553-2026; e-mail tatu@me.oulu.fi; internet www.cim.mcgill.ca/niftomm; f. 1969; study of robots, man-machine systems, etc. Pres. K. WALDRON; Sec.-Gen. T. LEINONEN. Publ. *Mechanism and Machine Theory.*

**International Federation of Automatic Control—IFAC:** 2361 Laxenburg, Schlossplatz 12, Austria; tel. (2236) 71447; fax (2236) 72859; e-mail secr@ifac.co.at; internet www.ifac-control.org; f. 1957 to serve those concerned with the theory and application of automatic control and systems engineering. Mems: 48 national associations. Pres. Prof. YONG ZAI LU (China); Sec. G. HENCSEY. Publs *Automatica and Control Engineering Practice* (bi-monthly), *Newsletter* and affiliated journals.

**International Gas Union:** c/o N.V. Nederlandse Gasunie, POB 19, 9700 MA Groningen, Netherlands; tel. (50) 5212999; fax (50) 5255951; e-mail secr.igu@gasnie.nl; internet www.igu.org; f. 1931 to study all aspects and problems of the gas industry with a view to promoting international co-operation and the general improvement of the industry. Mems: national organizations in 59 countries. Pres. C. DÉTOURNÉ (France); Sec.-Gen. J. F. MEEDER (Netherlands).

**International Institute of Welding:** 90 rue des Vanesses, Z1 Paris Nord II, 93420 Villepinte, France; tel. 1-49-90-36-08; fax 1-49-90-36-80; e-mail iiw@wanadoo.fr; f. 1948. Mems: 52 societies in 40 countries. Pres. Y. FUJITA (Japan); Chief Exec. M. BRAMAT (France). Publ. *Welding in the World* (7 a year).

**International Measurement Confederation:** POB 457, 1371 Budapest 5, Hungary; tel. (1) 153-1562; fax (1) 156-1215; e-mail imeko.ime@mtesz.hu; internet mit.tut.fi/imeko; f. 1961; holds Congress every 3 years. Sec.-Gen. Dr TAMÁS KEMÉNY (Hungary).

**International Navigation Association:** Graaf de Ferraris, 11e étage, Bte 3, 156 blvd Roi Albert II, 1000 Brussels, Belgium; tel. (2) 553-71-60; fax (2) 553-71-55; e-mail navigation-aipcn-pianc@tornado.be; internet www.tornado.be/~navigation-aipcn-pianc/; f. 1885; fmrly Permanent International Assoc. of Navigation Congresses (PIANC); fosters progress in the construction, maintenance and operation of inland and maritime waterways, of inland and maritime ports and of coastal areas; publishes information in this field, undertakes studies, organizes international and national meetings. Congresses are held every four years. Mems: 40 governments, 2,780 others. Pres. Ir. R. DE PAEPE; Sec.-Gen. C. VAN BEGIN. Publs *Bulletin* (quarterly), *Illustrated Technical Dictionary* (in 6 languages), technical reports, Congress papers.

**International Union for Electricity Applications:** Espace Elec. CNIT, BP 10, 92053 Paris-la-Défense, France; tel. 1-41-26-56-48; fax 1-41-26-56-49; e-mail uie@uie.org; internet www.uie.org; f. 1953, present title adopted 1994. Aims to study all questions relative to electricity applications, except commercial questions; links national groups and organizes international congresses on electricity applications. Mems: national committees and corporate members in 18 countries. Pres. RONNIE BELMANS (Belgium); Gen. Sec. G. VANDERSCHUEREN (Belgium).

**International Union of Air Pollution Prevention and Environmental Protection Associations:** 136 North St, Brighton, BN1 1RG, United Kingdom; tel. (1273) 326313; fax (1273) 735802; e-mail iuappa@nsca.org; f. 1963; organizes triennial World Clean Air Congress and regional conferences for developing countries (several a year). Pres. Dr W. H. PARK (Korea); Dir-Gen. R. MILLS. Publs *IUAPPA Newsletter* (quarterly), *Clean Air around the World.*

**International Union of Producers and Distributors of Electrical Energy (UNIPEDE), and European Grouping of the Electricity Industry:** Blvd de l'Impératrice 66, Box 2, 1000 Brussels, Belgium; tel. (2) 515-1000; fax (2) 510-1010; e-mail unipede@unipede.org, or eurelectric@eurelectric.org; f. 1925, joined with EEIG in 1999; aims to study all questions relating to the production, transmission and distribution of electrical energy, to promote the image of and defend the interests of the electricity supply industry. Pres. ROLF BIERHOFF (Eurelectric), and FRANÇOIS AILLERET (Unipede); Sec.-Gen. PAUL BULTEEL. Publ. *Watt's New* (newsletter).

**International Union of Testing and Research Laboratories for Materials and Structures:** Ecole Normale Supérieure, 61 ave du Président Wilson, 94235 Cachan Cédex, France; tel. 1-47-40-23-97; fax 1-47-40-01-13; e-mail sg@rilem.ens-cachan.fr; f. 1947 for the exchange of information and the promotion of co-operation on experimental research concerning structures and materials, for the study of research methods with a view to improvement and standardization. Mems: laboratories and individuals in 73 countries. Pres. Dr JACQUES BRESSON (France); Sec.-Gen. M. BRUSIN (France). Publ. *Materials and Structures—Testing and Research* (10 a year).

**World Energy Council:** 34 St James's St, London, SW1A 1HD, United Kingdom; tel. (20) 7930-3966; fax (20) 7925-0452; f. 1924 to link all branches of energy and resources technology and maintain liaison between world experts; holds congresses every three years. Mems: 99 committees. Pres. M. GÓMEZ DE PABLOS (Spain); Sec.-Gen. GERALD DOUCET (Canada). Publs energy supply and demand projections, resources surveys, technical assessments, reports.

**World Road Association (PIARC):** La Grande Arche, Paroi Nord, Niveau 8, 92055 La Défense Cédex, France; tel. 1-47-96-81-21; fax 1-49-00-02-02; e-mail piarc@wanadoo.fr; internet www.piarc.org; f. 1909 as the Permanent International Association of Road Congresses; aims to promote the construction, improvement, maintenance, use and economic development of roads; organizes technical committees and study sessions. Mems: governments, public bodies, organizations and private individuals in 100 countries. Pres. H. Mitani (Japan); Sec.-Gen. J. F. Coste (France). Publs *Bulletin, Technical Dictionary, Lexicon,* technical reports.

## OTHER ORGANIZATIONS

**African Organization of Cartography and Remote Sensing:** 5 Route de Bedjarah, BP 102, Hussein Dey, Algiers, Algeria; tel. (2) 77-79-34; fax (2) 77-79-34; f. 1988 by amalgamation of African Association of Cartography and African Council for Remote Sensing; aims to encourage the development of cartography and of remote sensing by satellites; organizes conferences and other meetings, promotes establishment of training institutions; four regional training centres (in Burkina Faso, Kenya, Nigeria and Tunisia). Mems: national cartographic institutions of 24 African countries. Sec.-Gen. Unis Muftah.

**African Regional Centre for Technology:** Imm. Fahd, 17th Floor, blvd Djilly Mbaye, BP 2435, Dakar, Senegal; tel. 823-77-12; fax 823-77-13; f. 1980 to encourage the development of indigenous technology and to improve the terms of access to imported technology; assists the establishment of national centres. Dep. Exec. Dir Dr Ousmane Kane. Publs *African Technodevelopment, Alert Africa.*

**Bureau International de la Recupération et du Recyclage** (Bureau of International Recycling): 24 ave Franklin Roosevelt, 1050 Brussels, Belgium; tel. (2) 627-57-70; fax (2) 627-57-73; e-mail bir@bir.org; internet www.bir.org; f. 1948 as the world federation of the reclamation and recycling industries, to promote international trade in scrap iron and steel, non-ferrous metals, paper, textiles, plastics and glass. Mems: associations and individuals in 53 countries. Dir-Gen. Francis Veys.

**ECMA—Standardizing Information and Communication Systems:** 114 rue de Rhône, 1204 Geneva, Switzerland; tel. (22) 8496000; fax (22) 8496001; e-mail helpdesk@ecma.ch; f. 1961 to develop, in co-operation with the appropriate national, European and international organizations, as a scientific endeavour and in the general interest, standards and technical reports in order to facilitate and standardize the use of information processing and telecommunications systems; and to promulgate various standards applicable to the functional design and use of these systems. Mems: 28 ordinary and 18 associate. Sec.-Gen. Jan van den Beld. Publs *ECMA Standards, ECMA Memento.*

**EUREKA:** 107 rue Neerveld, Bte 5, 1200 Brussels, Belgium; tel. (2) 777-09-50; fax (2) 777-74-95; e-mail eureka.secretariat@es.eureka.be; f. 1985; aims to promote collaboration between member countries of non-military research and development activities; enables joint development of technology and supports systematic use of standardization in new technology sectors. Mems: 26 in 25 countries. Sec.-Gen. L. J. A. M. van den Bergen.

**European Convention for Constructional Steelwork—ECCS:** 32/36 ave des Ombrages, bte 20, 1200 Brussels, Belgium; tel. (2) 762-04-29; fax (2) 762-09-35; e-mail eccs@steelconstruct.com; internet www.steelconstruct.com; f. 1955 for the consideration of problems involved in metallic construction. Member organizations in Austria, Belgium, Denmark, Croatia, Czech Republic, Finland, France, Germany, Italy, Japan, Republic of Korea, Luxembourg, Netherlands, Norway, Portugal, Romania, Slovenia, Spain, Sweden, Switzerland, Turkey, United Kingdom, USA. Gen. Sec. R. V. Salkin.

**European Federation of Chemical Engineering:** c/o Institution of Chemical Engineers, Davis Bldg, 165–189 Railway Terrace, Rugby, Warwickshire, CV21 3HQ, United Kingdom; tel. (1788) 578214; fax (1788) 560833; internet www.icheme.org; f. 1953 to encourage co-operation in Europe between non-profit-making scientific and technical societies for the advancement of chemical engineering and its application in the process industries. Mems: 65 societies in 25 European countries; 15 corresponding societies in other countries. Chief Exec. Dr T. J. Evans.

**European Federation of Corrosion:** 1 Carlton House Terrace, London, SW1Y 5DB, United Kingdom; tel. (20) 7839-4071; fax (20) 7839-1702; internet www.materials.org; f. 1955 to encourage co-operation in research on corrosion and methods of combating it. Member societies in 20 countries. Hon. Secs G. Mattioda (France), G. Kreysa (Germany), B. A. Rickinson (UK); Scientific Sec. P. McIntyre (UK).

**European Federation of National Engineering Associations—FEANI:** 21 rue du Beau Site, 1000 Brussels, Belgium; tel (2) 639-03-90; fax (2) 639-03-99; e-mail barbel.hokimi@feani.org; internet www.feani.org; f. 1951 to affirm the professional identity of the engineers of Europe; to strive for the unity of the engineering profession in Europe. Mems: 27 mem. countries. Pres. K. Alexopoulos (Greece); Sec.-Gen. Sirkka Pöyry. Publs *FEANI News, FEANI Handbook, Engineering Development International.*

**European Metal Union:** Einsteinbaan 1, POB 2600, 3430 GA Nieuwegein, Netherlands; tel. (30) 605-33-44; fax (30) 605-31-15; e-mail info@metaalunie.nl; f. 1954 as International Union of Metal; aims to provide liaison between national craft organizations and small and medium-sized enterprises in the metal industry; to represent members' interests at a European level; to exchange information and ideas on related subjects, such as vocational training, quality assurance, European legislation, and normalization and standardization. Mems: national federations from Austria, Belgium, Germany, Luxembourg, Netherlands and Switzerland. Pres. Willemien van Gardingen (Netherlands); Sec. Harm-Jan Keijer (Netherlands).

**European Organisation for the Exploitation of Meteorological Satellites—EUMETSAT:** 64295 Darmstadt, Am Kavalleriesand 31, Germany; tel. (6151) 8077; fax (6151) 807555; internet www.eumetsat.de; f. 1986; maintains and exploits European systems of meteorological satellites, including the Meteosat programme for gathering weather data. Mems: 17 European countries and two co-operating states. Chair. Dr Henri Malcorps (Belgium); Dir Dr Tillmann Mohr.

**European Organization for Civil Aviation Equipment—EUROCAE:** 17 rue Hamelin, 75783 Paris Cédex 16, France; tel. 1-45-05-71-88; fax 1-45-05-72-30; e-mail eurocae@compuserve.com; internet www.eurocae.org; f. 1963; studies and advises on problems related to the equipment used in aeronautics and assists international bodies in the establishment of international standards. Mems: 92 manufacturers, organizations and research bodies. Pres. Alan Garcia; Sec.-Gen. Francis Grimal.

**Eurospace:** 16 rue Hamelin, 75116 Paris, France; tel. (1) 47-55-83-00; fax (1) 47-55-63-30; e-mail letterbox@eurospace.org; internet www.eurospace.org; f. 1961; an association of European aerospace industrial companies, it is responsible for promotion of European Space activity. The Association carries out studies on the legal, economic, technical and financial aspects. It acts as an industrial adviser to the European Space Agency, in particular with regard to future space programmes and industrial policy matters. Mems: 60 in Austria, Belgium, Denmark, Finland, France, Germany, Italy, Netherlands, Norway, Spain, Sweden, Switzerland, United Kingdom. Pres. Ivan Öfverholm (Sweden); Sec.-Gen. Alain Gaubert.

**Inter-African Committee for Hydraulic Studies—CIEH:** 01 BP 369, Ouagadougou, Burkina Faso; tel. 30-71-12; f. 1960 to ensure co-operation in hydrology, hydrogeology, climatology, urban sanitation and other water sciences, through exchange of information and co-ordination of research and other projects; administrative budget (1988/89): 110m. francs CFA; investment budget 400m. francs CFA. Mems: 13 African countries. Sec.-Gen. Amadou Diaw. Publs *Bulletin de Liaison technique* (quarterly), research studies.

**International Association for Bridge and Structural Engineering:** ETH—Hönggerberg, 8093 Zürich, Switzerland; tel. (1) 6332647; fax (1) 6331241; e-mail secretariat@iabse.ethz.ch; internet www.iabse.ethz.ch; f. 1929 to exchange knowledge and advance the practice of structural engineering world-wide. Mems: 4,300 government departments, local authorities, universities, institutes, firms and individuals in 101 countries. Pres. Klaus Ostenfeld (Denmark); Exec. Dir A. Golay. Publs *Structural Engineering International* (quarterly), *Congress Report, IABSE Report, Structural Engineering Documents.*

**International Association for Cybernetics** (Association Internationale de Cybernétique): Palais des Expositions, ave Sergent Vrithoff 2, 5000 Namur, Belgium; tel. (81) 71-71-71; fax (81) 71-71-00; e-mail cyb@info.fundp.ac.be; f. 1957 to ensure liaison between research workers engaged in various sectors of cybernetics, to promote the development of the science and of its applications and to disseminate information about it. Mems: firms and individuals in 42 countries. Chair. J. Ramaekers; Gen. Sec. Carine Aigret. Publ. *Cybernetica* (quarterly).

**International Association of Technological University Libraries:** c/o Helsinki University of Technology Library, POB 7000, 02015 HUT, Finland; tel. (9) 4514112; fax (9) 4514132; e-mail sinikka.koskiala@hut.fi; internet educate.lib.chalmers.se/iatul/; f. 1955 to promote co-operation between member libraries and stimulate research on library problems. Mems: 202 university libraries in 41 countries. Pres. Dr Nancy Fjällbrant (Sweden); Sec. Dr Sinikka Koskiala (Finland). Publs *IATUL Proceedings, IATUL Newsletter.*

**International Cargo Handling Co-ordination Association—ICHCA:** 71 Bondway, London, SW8 1SH, United Kingdom; tel. (20) 7793-1022; fax (20) 7820-1703; e-mail postmaster@ichca.org.uk; internet www.ichca.org.uk; f. 1952 to foster economy and efficiency in the movement of goods from origin to destination. Mems: 2,000 in 90 countries. Pres. Ken Hoggat; Chief Exec. Gerry Askham. Publs *Cargo Today* (bimonthly), *World of Cargo Handling* (annually), *Who's Who in Cargo Handling* (annually), *Buyers' Guide to Manufacturers* (annually), safety panel briefing pamphlets.

**International Colour Association:** Philips Lighting, POB 80020, 5600 JM, Eindhoven, Netherlands; tel. (40) 2262788; fax (40) 22755861; f. 1967 to encourage research in colour in all its aspects, disseminate the knowledge gained from this research and promote its application to the solution of problems in the fields of science, art and industry; holds international congresses and symposia.

Mems: organizations in 21 countries. Pres. Dr L. RONCHI (Italy); Sec. Dr C. VAN TRIGT (Netherlands).

**International Commission on Illumination—CIE:** Kegelgasse 27, 1030 Vienna, Austria; tel. (1) 714-31-87-0; fax (1) 713-08-38-18; e-mail ciecb@ping.at; f. 1900 as International Commission on Photometry, present name 1913; aims to provide an international forum for all matters relating to the science and art of light and lighting; to exchange information; to develop and publish international standards, and to provide guidance in their application. Mems: 40 national committees and 12 individuals. Gen. Sec. C. HERMANN. Publs standards, technical reports.

**International Commission on Large Dams:** 151 blvd Haussmann, 75008 Paris, France; tel. 1-40-42-68-24; fax 1-40-42-60-71; e-mail secretaire.general@icold-cigb.org; internet www.icold-cigb.org./; f. 1928; holds triennial congresses; 2000 congress: Beijing, People's Republic of China. Mems in 81 countries. Pres. K. HOËG (Norway); Sec.-Gen. JACQUES LECORNU. Publs *Technical Bulletin* (3/4 a year), *World Register of Dams, World Register of Mine and Industrial Wastes, Technical Dictionary on Dams,* studies.

**International Committee on Aeronautical Fatigue—ICAF:** c/o Prof. O. Buxbaum, Fraunhofer-Institut für Betriebsfestigkeit LBF, 64289 Darmstadt, Bartningstrasse 47, Germany; tel. (6151) 7051; fax (6151) 705214; f. 1951 for collaboration on fatigue of aeronautical structures among aeronautical bodies and laboratories by means of exchange of documents and by organizing periodical conferences. Mems: national centres in 13 countries. Sec. Prof. O. BUXBAUM (Germany).

**International Conference on Large High-Voltage Electric Systems—CIGRE:** 21 rue d'Artois, 75008 Paris, France; tel. 1-53-89-12-90; fax 1-53-89-12-99; e-mail cigre@world-net.sct.fr; internet www.worldnet.net/~cigre; f. 1921 to facilitate and promote the exchange of technical knowledge and information between all countries in the general field of electrical generation and transmission at high voltages; holds general sessions (every 2 years), symposia. Mems: 5,000 in 79 countries. Pres. M. CHAMIA; Sec.-Gen. Y. THOMAS (France). Publ. *Electra* (every 2 months).

**International Council for Research and Innovation in Building and Construction:** Postbox 1837, 3000 BV Rotterdam, Netherlands; tel. (10) 411-02-40; fax (10) 433-43-72; e-mail secretariat@cibworld.nl; internet www.cibworld.nl; f. 1953 to encourage and facilitate co-operation in building research, studies and documentation in all aspects. Mems: governmental and industrial organizations and qualified individuals in 70 countries. Pres. Dr J. R. DUNCAN (New Zealand); Sec.-Gen. W. J. P. BAKENS. Publs *Information Bulletin* (bi-monthly), conference proceedings and technical, best practice and other reports.

**International Electrotechnical Commission—IEC:** 3 rue de Varembé, POB 131, 1211 Geneva 20, Switzerland; tel. (22) 9190211; fax (22) 9190300; e-mail info@iec.ch; internet www.iec.ch; f. 1906 as the authority for world standards for electrical and electronic engineering: its standards are used as the basis for regional and national standards, and are used in preparing specifications for international trade. Mems: national committees representing all branches of electrical and electronic activities in some 60 countries. Gen.-Sec. A. AMIT. Publs *International Standards and Reports, IEC Bulletin, Annual Report, Catalogue of Publications.*

**International Special Committee on Radio Interference:** British Electrotechnical Committee, British Standards Institution, 389 Chiswick High Rd, London, W4 4AL, United Kingdom; tel. (20) 8996-9000; fax (20) 8996-7400; f. 1934; special committee of the IEC to promote international agreement on the protection of radio reception from interference by equipment other than authorized transmitters; recommends limits of such interference and specifies equipment and methods of measurement; determines requirements for immunity of sound and TV broadcasting receivers from interference and the impact of safety regulations on interference suppression. Mems: national committees of IEC and seven other international organizations. Sec. C. BECKLEY.

**International Federation for Information and Documentation:** POB 90402, 2509 LK The Hague, Netherlands; tel. (70) 314-06-71; fax (70) 314-06-67; e-mail fid@fid.nl; internet www.fid.nl; f. 1895; aims to promote, through international co-operation, research in and development of information science; information management and documentation; and improvement of all the processes involved in the entire life-cycle of data, information and knowledge in all fields; regional commissions for Latin America, North America and the Caribbean, Asia and Oceania, Western, Eastern and Southern Africa, North Africa and the Near East, and for Europe. Mems: 62 national, five international, 330 institutional or individual. Pres. MARTHA STONE; Exec. Dir J. STEPHEN PARKER. Publs *FID Review* (every 2 months), *FID Directory* (every 2 years).

**International Federation for Information Processing:** Hofstrasse 3, 2361 Laxenburg, Austria; tel. (2236) 73616; fax (2236) 736169; e-mail ifip@ifip.or.at; internet www.ifip.or.at; f. 1960 to promote information science and technology; to stimulate research, development and application of information processing in science and human activities; to further the dissemination and exchange of information on information processing; to encourage education in information processing; to advance international co-operation in the field of information processing. Mems: 45 organizations, 3 corresponding mems, 1 assoc. mem. and 11 affiliate mems. Pres. P. BOLLERSLEV (Denmark); Exec. Dir PLAMEN NEDKOV.

**International Federation of Airworthiness—IFA:** Suite 1A, Dralda House, Crendon Street, High Wycombe, Bucks HP13 6LS, United Kingdom; tel. (1494) 530404; fax (1494) 439984; e-mail mail@aviation-training.org; internet www.ifairworthy.org; f. 1964 to provide a forum for the exchange of international experience in maintenance, design and operations; holds annual conference; awards international aviation scholarship annually. Mems: 120, comprising 50 airlines, 17 airworthiness authorities, 23 aerospace manufacturing companies, 17 service and repair organizations, three consultancies, six professional societies, two aviation insurance companies, one aircraft leasing company, and the Flight Safety Foundation (USA). Pres. (1998–2000) ROBERT A. DAVIS (USA); Exec. Dir J. W. SAULL (UK). Publ. *IFA News* (quarterly).

**International Federation of Automotive Engineering Societies—FISITA:** 1 Birdcage Walk, London SW1H 9JJ, United Kingdom; tel. (20) 7973-1275; fax (20) 7973-1285; e-mail i_dickie@imeche.org.uk; internet www.fisita.com; f. 1947 to promote the technical and sustainable development of all forms of automotive transportation; congresses every two years. Mems: national organizations in 32 countries. Chief Exec. IAN DICKIE. Publ. *Global Automotive Network*.

**International Federation of Consulting Engineers:** 13C ave du Temple, POB 86, 1000 Lausanne 12, Switzerland; tel. (21) 6544411; fax (21) 6535432; e-mail fidic@pobox.com; f. 1913 to encourage international co-operation and the setting up of standards for consulting engineers. Mems: national associations in 68 countries, comprising some 500,000 design professionals. Pres. R. WAYNE BOWES.

**International Federation of Hospital Engineering:** Via Michelino 69, 40127 Bologna, Italy; tel. and fax (051) 6332288; f. 1970 to promote internationally the standards of hospital engineering and to provide for the interchange of knowledge and ideas. Mems: 106. Pres. PAUL ERIK REE (Denmark); Gen. Sec. COSIMO PIPOLI (Italy).

**International Information Management Congress:** 1650 38th St, Suite 205W, Boulder, CO 80301, USA; tel. (303) 440-7085; fax (303) 440-7234; internet www.iimc.org; f. 1962 to promote co-operation in document-based information management; to provide an international clearing-house for information, exchange publications and encourage the establishment of international standards; to promote international product exhibitions, seminars and conventions. Mems: 30 associations, 80 regular and 350 affiliate mems from 64 countries. Exec. Dir PAUL CARMEN (USA). Publ. *Document World* (every 2 months).

**International Institute of Seismology and Earthquake Engineering:** Building Research Institute, Ministry of Construction, 1 Tatehara, Tsukuba City, Ibaraki Pref., Japan; tel. (298) 79-0677; fax (298) 64-6777; e-mail iisee@kenken.go.jp; internet www.iisee.kenken.go.jp; f. 1962 to work on seismology and earthquake engineering for the purpose of reducing earthquake damage in the world; trains seismologists and earthquake engineers from the earthquake-prone countries and undertakes surveys, research, guidance and analysis of information on earthquakes and related matters. Mems: 75 countries. Dir M. MIZUNO.

**International Institution for Production Engineering Research:** 10 rue Mansart, 75009 Paris, France; tel. 1-45-26-21-80; fax 1-40-16-40-75; internet www.lurpa.ens-cachan.fr/cirp.html; f. 1951 to promote by scientific research the study of the mechanical processing of all solid materials including checks on efficiency and quality of work. Mems: 510 in 40 countries. Pres. M. F. DE VRIES (USA); Sec.-Gen. M. VÉRON (France). Publ. *Annals* (2 a year).

**International Iron and Steel Institute—IISI:** 120 rue Col Bourg, 1140 Brussels, Belgium; tel. (2) 702-89-00; fax (2) 702-88-99; e-mail steel@iisi.be; internet www.worldsteel.org; f. 1967 to promote the welfare and interest of the world's steel industries; to undertake research in all aspects of steel industries; to serve as a forum for exchange of knowledge and discussion of problems relating to steel industries; to collect, disseminate and maintain statistics and information; to serve as a liaison body between international and national steel organizations. Mems: in over 50 countries. Sec.-Gen. IAN CHRISTMAS.

**International Organization for Standardization:** POB 56, 1 rue de Varembé, 1211 Geneva 20, Switzerland; tel. (22) 7490111; fax (22) 7333430; e-mail central@iso.ch; internet www.iso.ch/; f. 1947 to reach international agreement on industrial and commercial standards. Mems: national standards bodies of 90 countries. Pres. Prof. GIACOMO ELIAS; Sec.-Gen. LAWRENCE D. EICHER. Publs *ISO International Standards, ISO Memento* (annually), *ISO 9000 News* (6 a year), *ISO Bulletin* (monthly).

**International Research Group on Wood Preservation:** Box 5607, 114 86 Stockholm, Sweden; tel. (8) 10-14-53; fax (8) 10-80-81; f. 1965 as Wood Preservation Group by OECD; independent since 1969; consists of five sections; holds plenary annual meeting. Mems: 315 in 51 countries. Pres. Prof. JOHN N. R. RUDDICK (Canada); Sec.-Gen. JÖRAN JERMER (Sweden). Publs technical documents and books, *Annual Report*.

**International Rubber Research and Development Board—IRRDB:** Brickendonbury, Hertford, SG13 8NP, United Kingdom; tel. (1992) 584966; fax (1992) 504267; e-mail irrdb@aol.com; internet www.irrdb.org; f. 1937. Mems: 15 research institutes. Sec. KEVIN P. JONES.

**International Society for Photogrammetry and Remote Sensing:** Martin Marietta Corporation, POB 8048-13A24, Philadelphia, PA 19101, USA; tel. (610) 531-3205; fax (510) 889-3296; f. 1910; holds congress every four years, and technical symposia. Mems: 81 countries. Pres. SHUNJI MURAI (Japan); Sec.-Gen. LAWRENCE W. FRITZ (USA). Publs *International Archives of Photogrammetry and Remote Sensing, Photogrammetria*.

**International Society for Soil Mechanics and Geotechnical Engineering:** City University, Northampton Sq., London, EC1V 0HB, United Kingdom; tel. (20) 7477-8154; fax (20) 7477-8832; e-mail secretariat@issmge.org; internet www.issmge.org/; f. 1936 to promote international co-operation among scientists and engineers in the field of geotechnics and its engineering applications; maintains 30 technical committees; holds quadrennial international conference, regional conferences and specialist conferences. Mems: 17,000 individuals, 71 national societies, 23 corporate members. Pres. Prof. KENJI ISHIHARA; Sec.-Gen. Prof. R. NEIL TAYLOR. Publs *ISSMGE News* (quarterly), *Lexicon of Soil Mechanics Terms* (in eight languages).

**International Solar Energy Society:** Wiesentalstrasse 50, 79115 Freiburg, Germany; tel. (761) 459060; fax (761) 4590699; e-mail hq@ises.org; internet www.ises.org; f. 1954 to foster science and technology relating to the applications of solar energy, to encourage research and development, to promote education and to gather, compile and disseminate information in this field; holds international conferences. Mems: approximately 4,000 in some 100 countries. Pres. Dr CESARE SILVI (Italy); Exec. Dir. BURKHARD HOLDER (Germany). Publs *Solar Energy Journal* (monthly), *Sunworld* (quarterly).

**International Solid Wastes Association—ISWA:** Overgaden Oven Vandet 48E, 1415 Copenhagen K, Denmark; tel. 32-96-15-88; fax 32-96-15-84; e-mail iswa@inet.uni2.dk; internet www.iswa.org; f. 1970; organizes conferences and establishes technical working groups. Pres. JOHN FERGUSON (UK); Man. Dir SUZANNE ARUP VELTZÉ (Denmark) (acting).

**International Tin Research Institute Ltd:** Kingston Lane, Uxbridge, Middx, UB8 3PJ, United Kingdom; tel. (1895) 272406; fax (1895) 251841; internet www.itri.co.uk; f. 1932, privatized in 1995; provides technological support for the tin-producing and -consuming industries world-wide. Facilities include: soldering, electroplating, metallography, and chemical and analytical laboratories; a technical enquiry and information service; research is conducted to support existing uses of tin and to develop new applications. Dir ALAN DIBBO. Publs *Soldering Bits* (quarterly), *Tin International* (monthly).

**International Union for Vacuum Science, Technique and Applications—IUVSTA:** 7 Mohawk Cres., Nepean, Ontario K2H 7G7, Canada; tel. (613) 829-5790; fax (613) 829-3061; e-mail westwood@istar.ca; internet www.vacuum.org/iuvsta.html; f. 1958; collaborates with the International Standards Organization in defining and adopting technical standards; holds triennial International Vacuum Congress, European Vacuum Conference, triennial International Conference on Thin Films, and International Conference on Solid Surfaces; administers the Welch Foundation scholarship for postgraduate research in vacuum science and technology; scientific divisions for surface science, applied surface science, thin film, vacuum science, electronic materials, nanometer structures, plasma science and technique and vacuum metallurgy. Mems: organizations in 30 countries. Pres. Prof. D. P. WOODRUFF (UK); Sec.-Gen. Dr W. D. WESTWOOD (Canada). Publ. *News Bulletin* (quarterly).

**International Water Resources Association:** University of New Mexico, 1915 Roma NE, Albuquerque, NM 87131-1436, USA; tel. (505) 277-9400; fax (505) 277-9405; e-mail iwra@unm.edu; f. 1972 to promote collaboration in and support for international water resources programmes; holds conferences; conducts training in water resources management. Pres. GLENN E. STOUT (USA); Sec.-Gen. VICTOR DE KOSINSKY (Belgium). Publ. *Water International* (quarterly).

**International Water Services Association:** 1 Queen Anne's Gate, London, SW1H 9BT, United Kingdom; tel. (20) 7957-4567; fax (20) 7222-7243; e-mail iwsa@dial.pipex.com; internet www.iwsa.org.uk; f. 1947 to co-ordinate technical, legal and administrative aspects of public water supply; congresses held every two years, workshops and conferences held throughout the year. Mems: national organizations, water authorities and individuals in 95 countries. Pres. NICHOLAS HOOD; Exec. Dir M. J. SLIPPER (UK). Publs *Aqua* (6 a year), *Water Supply* (quarterly), *Yearbook*.

**Latin-American Energy Organization** (Organización Latinoamericana de Energía—OLADE): Avda Mariscal Antonio José de Sucre, No N58–63 y Fernándes Salvador, Fdif. OLADE, Sector San Carlos, POB 17-11-6413 CCI, Quito, Ecuador; tel. (2) 598-122; fax (2) 539-684; e-mail oladel@olade.org.ec; internet www.olade.org.ec; f. 1973 to act as an instrument of co-operation in using and conserving the energy resources of the region. Mems: 26 Latin-American and Caribbean countries. Exec. Sec. LUIZ AUGUSTO DA FONSECA. Publs *Energy Magazine, Energy Update*.

**Latin-American Iron and Steel Institute:** Benjamín 2944, 5°, Las Condes, Santiago, Chile; tel. (2) 233-0545; fax (2) 233-0768; e-mail ilafa@entelchile.net; f. 1959 to help achieve the harmonious development of iron and steel production, manufacture and marketing in Latin America; conducts economic surveys on the steel sector; organizes technical conventions and meetings; disseminates industrial processes suited to regional conditions; prepares and maintains statistics on production, end uses, prices, etc., of raw materials and steel products within this area. Hon. mems 31; mems 69; assoc. mems 64; Chair. JAVIER O. TIZADO; Sec.-Gen. ANÍBAL GÓMEZ. Publs *Acero Latinoamericano* (every 2 months), *Siderurgia Latinoamericana* (monthly), *Statistical Year Book, Directory of Latin American Iron and Steel Companies* (every 2 years).

**Regional Centre for Services in Surveying, Mapping and Remote Sensing:** POB 18118, Nairobi, Kenya; tel. (2) 803320; fax (2) 802767; e-mail rcssmrs@unep.org; f. 1975 to provide services in the professional techniques of map-making, and the application of satellite and remote sensing data in resource analysis and development planning; undertakes research and provides advisory services to African governments. Mems: 14 signatory and 10 non-signatory governments. Dir-Gen. Prof. SIMON NDYETABULA.

**Regional Centre for Training in Aerospace Surveys:** PMB 5545, Ile-Ife, Nigeria; tel. (36) 230050; fax (36) 230481; f. 1972 for training, research and advisory services; administered by the ECA. Mems: eight governments. Dir J. A. OGUNLAMI.

**Regional Council of Co-ordination of Central and East European Engineering Organizations:** c/o MTESZ, 1055 Budapest, Kossuth Lajos tér 6–8, Hungary; tel. (361) 353-4795; fax (361) 353-0317; e-mail mtesz@mtesz.hu; f. 1992. Hon. Pres. JÁNOS TÓTH.

**World Association of Industrial and Technological Research Organizations—WAITRO:** c/o Danish Technological Institute, POB 141, 2630 Taastrup, Denmark; tel. 43-50-43-50; fax 43-50-72-50; e-mail waitro@dti.dk; internet www.waitro.dti.dk; f. 1970 by the UN Industrial Development Organization to encourage co-operation in industrial and technological research, through financial assistance for training and joint activities, arranging international seminars, and allowing the exchange of information. Mems: 200 research institutes in 80 countries. Pres. ÖMER KAYMAKCALAN (Turkey); Contact MOSES MENGU. Publs *WAITRO News* (quarterly), *WAITRO Outline*.

**World Association of Nuclear Operators—WANO-CC:** Kings Bldgs, 16 Smith Sq., London, SW1P 3JG, United Kingdom; tel. (20) 7828-2111; fax (20) 7828-6691; f. 1989 by operators of nuclear power plants; aims to improve the safety and operability of nuclear power plants by exchange of operating experience; four regional centres (in France, Japan, Russia and the USA) and a co-ordinating centre in the UK. Mems in 34 countries. Dir (Co-ordinating Centre) V. J. MADDEN.

**World Bureau of Metal Statistics:** 27A High St, Ware, Herts, SG12 9BA, United Kingdom; tel. (1920) 461274; fax (1920) 464258; f. 1949; statistics of production, consumption, stocks, prices and international trade in copper, lead, zinc, tin, nickel, aluminium and several other minor metals. Gen. Man. J. L. T. DAVIES. Publs *World Metal Statistics* (monthly), *World Tin Statistics* (monthly), *World Nickel Statistics* (monthly), *World Metal Statistics Yearbook, World Metal Statistics Quarterly Summary, World Stainless Steel Statistics* (annually), *World Wrought Copper Statistics* (annually).

**World Federation of Engineering Organizations—WFEO:** Maison de l'UNESCO, 1 rue Miollis, 75015 Paris, France; tel. 1-45-68-31-92; fax 1-45-68-31-14; e-mail pdeboigne@fmoi.org; internet www.unesco.org/ngo/fmoi/; f. 1968 to advance engineering as a profession in the interests of the world community; to foster co-operation between engineering organizations throughout the world; to undertake special projects through co-operation between members and in co-operation with other international bodies. Mems: 80 national, nine international. Pres. JOSÉ MEDEM SANJUAN (Spain); Exec. Dir PIERRE EDOUARD DE BOIGNE (France). Publ. *WFEO Newsletter* (2 a year).

**World Petroleum Congresses:** 61 New Cavendish St, London, W1M 8AR, United Kingdom; tel. (20) 7467-7100; fax (20) 7255-1472; f. 1933 to provide an international congress as a forum for petroleum science, technology, economics and management; to publish the proceedings, and to undertake related information and liaison activities; Permanent Council includes 56 member countries; 16th Congress: Calgary, Canada, June 2000. Pres. Ir D. VAN DER MEER (Netherlands); Dir-Gen. Dr PIERCE W. F. RIEMER (UK).

## Tourism

**Alliance Internationale de Tourisme:** 2 Chemin de Blandonnet, CP 111, 1215 Geneva 15, Switzerland; tel. (22) 7352727; fax (22) 7352326; e-mail ait@aitgva.ch; internet www.aitgva.ch; f. 1898, present title adopted 1919; represents motoring organizations and touring clubs around the world; aims to study all questions relating to international touring and to suggest reforms, to encourage the development of tourism and all matters concerning the motorist, traffic management, the environment, road safety, consumer protection and to defend the interests of touring associations. Mems: 132 associations totalling 100m. members in 98 countries. Pres. F. FALCÓ (Spain); Dir Gen. P. DOGGWILER (Switzerland).

**Caribbean Tourism Organization:** Sir Frank Walcott Bldg, 2nd Floor, Culloden Farm Complex, St Michael, Barbados; tel. 427-5242; fax 429-3065; e-mail ctobar@caribsurf.com; offices in New York (tel. (212) 635-9530), Canada (tel. (6) 485-7827) and London (tel. (20) 7222-4335); f. 1989, by merger Caribbean Tourism Association (f. 1951) and Caribbean Tourism Research and Development Centre (f. 1974); aims to encourage tourism in the Caribbean region. Mems: 33 Caribbean governments and 400 allied mems. Sec.-Gen. JEAN HOLDER. Publs *Caribbean Tourism Statistical News* (quarterly), *Caribbean Tourism Statistical Report* (annually).

**East Asia Travel Association:** c/o Japan National Tourist Organization, 2-10-1 Yurakucho, Chiyoda-ku, Tokyo, Japan; tel. (3) 3216-2910; fax (3) 3214-7680; f. 1966 to promote tourism in the East Asian region, encourage and facilitate the flow of tourists to that region from other parts of the world, and to develop regional tourist industries by close collaboration among members. Mems: six national tourist organizations and one travel association. Pres. ICHIRO TANAKA; Sec.-Gen. JOÃO MANUEL COSTA ANTUNES.

**European Travel Commission:** 61 rue du Marché aux Herbes, 1000 Brussels, Belgium; tel. (2) 504-03-03; fax (2) 514-18-43; e-mail etc@planetinternet.be; f. 1948 to promote tourism in and to Europe, to foster co-operation and the exchange of information, to organize research. Mems: national tourist organizations of 29 European countries. Exec. Dir WALTER LEU (Switzerland).

**International Association of Scientific Experts in Tourism:** Varnbüelstrasse 19, 9000 St Gallen, Switzerland; tel. (71) 2242530; fax (71) 2242536; e-mail aiest@unisg.ch; f. 1949 to encourage scientific activity by its members; to support tourist institutions of a scientific nature; to organize conventions. Mems: 400 from 40 countries. Pres. Prof. Dr PETER KELLER (Switzerland); Gen. Sec. Prof. Dr THOMAS BIEGER (Switzerland). Publ. *The Tourist Review* (quarterly).

**International Congress and Convention Association:** Entrada 121, 1096 EB Amsterdam, Netherlands; tel. (20) 398-19-19; fax (20) 699-07-81; e-mail icca@icca.nl; internet www.icca.nl; f. 1963 to establish worldwide co-operation between all involved in organizing congresses, conventions and exhibitions (including travel agents, airlines, hotels, congress centres, professional congress organizers, tourist and convention bureaux and ancillary congress services). Mems: more than 500 meeting experts from 71 countries. Pres. TUUIA LINDBERG; Exec. Dir. TOM HULTON. Publ. *International Meetings News* (6 a year).

**International Hotel and Restaurant Association:** 251 rue du Faubourg St Martin, 75010 Paris, France; tel. 1-44-89-94-00; fax 1-40-36-73-30; e-mail members@ih-ra.com; internet www.ih-ra.com; f. 1946 to act as the leader and authority on matters affecting the international hotel industry, to promote its interests and to contribute to its growth, profitability and quality of the industry worldwide; membership extended to restaurants in 1996. Mems: 120 national hospitality associations, 100 national and international hotel and restaurant chains; also independent hotels and restaurant and allied members. Dir-Gen. MICHAEL NOWLIS; Sec.-Gen. CHRISTIANE CLECH. Publs *Hotels* (monthly), *International Hotel Guide* (annually).

**Latin-American Confederation of Tourist Organizations—COTAL:** Viamonte 640, 8°, 1053 Buenos Aires, Argentina; tel. (11) 4322-4003; fax (11) 4393-5696; e-mail cotal@cscom.com.ar; f. 1957 to link Latin American national associations of travel agents and their members with other tourist bodies around the world. Mems: in 21 countries and affiliate mems in 55 countries. Pres. FERNANDO SOLER. Publ. *Revista COTAL* (every 2 months).

**Pacific Asia Travel Association—PATA:** Unit B1, 28th floor, Siam Tower, 989 Rama 1 Rd, Pratumwan, Bangkok 10330, Thailand; tel. (2) 658-2000; fax (2) 658-2010; e-mail patabkk@pata.th.com; internet www.pata.org; f. 1951; aims to enhance the growth, value and quality of Pacific Asia travel and tourism for the benefit of PATA members. Annual Conference held in April. Divisional offices in Monaco, Sydney, Singapore, USA; representative office in Japan. Mems: more than 2,200 governments, carriers, tour operators, travel agents and hotels. Publs *PATA Compass* (every 2 months), *Statistical Report* (quarterly), research reports, directories, newsletters.

**South Pacific Tourism Organization:** POB 13119, Suva, Fiji; tel. 304177; fax 301995; e-mail info@spto.org; internet www.tcsp.com; formerly the Tourism Council of the South Pacific; aims to foster regional co-operation in the development, marketing and promotion of tourism in the island nations of the South Pacific; receives EU funding and undertakes sustainable activities. Mems: American Samoa, Cook Islands, Fiji, French Polynesia, Kiribati, New Caledonia, Niue, Papua New Guinea, Samoa, Solomon Islands, Tonga, Tuvalu, Vanuatu; Chief Exec. LEVANI TUINABUA.

**Universal Federation of Travel Agents' Associations—UFTAA:** 1 ave des Castelans, Stade Louis II-Entrée H, 98000 Monaco; tel. 92-05-28-29; fax 92-05-29-87; e-mail uftaamc@tekworld.mc; internet www.uftaa.com; f. 1966 to unite travel agents' associations, to represent the interests of travel agents at the international level, to help in international legal differences; issues literature on travel, etc. Mems: national associations of travel agencies in 112 countries. Sec.-Gen. BIRGER BÄCKMAN.

**World Association of Travel Agencies:** 14 rue Ferrier,1202 Geneva, Switzerland; tel. (22) 7314760; fax (22) 7328161; e-mail wata@wata.net; internet www.wata.net; f. 1949 to foster the development of tourism, to help the rational organization of tourism in all countries, to collect and disseminate information and to participate in all commercial and financial operations which will foster the development of tourism. Individual travel agencies may use the services of the world-wide network of 200 members. Pres. ADEL ZAKI (Egypt); Sec.-Gen. MARCO AGUSTONI (Switzerland). Publ. *WATA Gazette* (quarterly).

**World Tourism Organization:** Calle Capitán Haya 42, 28020 Madrid, Spain; tel. (91) 5678100; fax (91) 5713733; e-mail comm@world-tourism.org; internet www.world-tourism.org; f. 1975 to promote travel and tourism; co-operates with member governments; secures financing for and carries out tourism development projects; provides training in tourism-related issues; works for sustainable and environmentally-friendly tourism development; encourages the liberalization of trade in tourism services; considers health and safety issues related to tourism; collects, analyses and disseminates data and operates a Documentation Centre. Mems: governments of 138 countries and territories, also associate members, observers and over 300 affiliated mems. Sec.-Gen. FRANCESCO FRANGIALLI. Publs *Yearbook of Tourism Statistics, Compendium of Tourism Statistics, Travel and Tourism Barometer, WTO News, Tourism Market Trends, Directory of Multilateral and Bilateral Sources of Financing for Tourism Development*, guide-lines and studies.

**World Travel and Tourism Council—WTTC:** 20 Grosvenor Pl., London, SW1X 7TT, United Kingdom; tel. (20) 7838-9400; fax (20) 7838-9050; e-mail enquiries@wttc.org; internet www.wttc.org; f. 1989; promotes the development of the travel/tourism industry; analyses impact of tourism on employment levels and local economies and promotes greater expenditure on tourism infrastructure; administers a 'Green Globe' certification programme to enhance environmental management throughout the industry. Pres. JEAN-CLAUDE BAUMGARTEN.

## Trade and Industry

**African Regional Organization for Standardization:** POB 57363, Nairobi, Kenya; tel. (2) 224561; fax (2) 218792; e-mail arso@nbnet.co.ke; internet www.nbnet.co.ke/test/arso; f. 1977 to promote standardization, quality control, certification and metrology in the African region, formulate regional standards, and co-ordinate participation in international standardization activities. Mems: 24 states. Sec.-Gen. Dr ADEBAYO O. OYEJOLA. Publs *ARSO Bulletin* (2 a year), *ARSO Catalogue of Regional Standards* (annually), *ARSO Annual Report*.

**Arab Iron and Steel Union—AISU:** BP 4, Chéraga, Algiers, Algeria; tel. (2) 371579; fax (2) 371975; f. 1972 to develop commercial and technical aspects of Arab steel production by helping member associations to commercialize their production in Arab markets, guaranteeing them high quality materials and intermediary products, informing them of recent developments in the industry and organizing training sessions. Mems: 73 companies in 13 Arab countries. Gen. Sec. MUHAMMAD LAID LACHGAR. Publs *Arab Steel Review* (monthly), *Information Bulletin* (2 a month), *Directory* (annually).

**Asian Productivity Organization:** 2/F Hirakawa-cho Dai-ichi Seimei Bldg, 1-2-10, Hirakawa-cho, Chiyoda-ku, Tokyo 102–0093, Japan; tel. (3) 3408-7221; fax (3) 3408-7220; e-mail apo@gol.com; internet www.apo-tokyo.com; f. 1961 to strengthen the productivity movement in the Asian and Pacific region and disseminate technical knowledge on productivity. Mems: 18 countries. Sec.-Gen. TAKASHI TAJIMA. Publs *APO News* (monthly), *Annual Report, APO Productivity Journal* (2 a year), *Directory of National Productivity Organizations in APO member countries* (irregular) and other related studies.

**Association of African Trade Promotion Organizations—AATPO:** Pavillion International, BP 23, Tangier, Morocco; tel. (9) 324465; fax (9) 943779; e-mail aoapc@mtds.com; f. 1975 under the auspices of the OAU and the ECA to foster regular contact between African states in trade matters and to assist in the harmonization of their commercial policies in order to promote intra-African trade; conducts research and training; organizes meetings and trade information missions. Mems: 26 states. Sec.-Gen. Prof. ADEYINKA W. ORIMALADE. Publs *FLASH: African Trade* (monthly), *Directory of African Consultants and Experts in Trade Promotion, Directory of Trade Information Contacts in Africa, Directory of Trade Information Sources in Africa, Directory of State Trading Organizations, Directory of Importers and Exporters of Food Products in Africa, Basic Information on Africa*, studies.

**Association of European Chambers of Commerce and Industry (EUROCHAMBRES):** 5 rue d'Archimède, 1000 Brussels, Belgium; tel. (2) 282-08-50; fax (2) 230-00-38; e-mail eurochambres@eurochambres.be; internet www.eurochambres.be; f. 1958 to promote the exchange of experience and information among its members and to bring their joint opinions to the attention of the institutions of the European Union; conducts studies and seminars; co-ordinates EU projects. Mems: 15 full and 18 affiliated mems. Pres. JÖRG MITTELSTEN SCHEID (Germany); Sec.-Gen. ARNALDO ABRUZZINI (Italy).

**Cairns Group:** c/o Department of Foreign Affairs and Trade, Locked Bag 40, QVT, Canberra, ACT 2600, Australia; tel. (2) 6263-2222; fax (2) 6261-3111; internet www.dfat.gov.au/trade/negotiations/cairns_group/index.html; f. 1986 by major agricultural exporting countries, aiming to bring about reforms in international agricultural trade, including reductions in export subsidies, in barriers to access and in internal support measures; represents members' interests in WTO negotiations. Mems: Argentina, Australia, Brazil, Canada, Chile, Colombia, Fiji, Indonesia, Malaysia, New Zealand, Paraguay, Philippines, South Africa, Thailand, Uruguay. Chair. MARK VAILE (Australia).

**Caribbean Association of Industry and Commerce—CAIC:** Musson Bldg, Hincks St, POB 259, Bridgetown, Barbados; tel. (809) 436-6385; fax (809) 436-9937; f. 1955; aims to encourage economic development through the private sector; undertakes research, training, assistance for small enterprises, and export promotion. Mems: chambers of commerce and enterprises in 17 countries and territories. Exec. Dir FELIPE NAGUERA. Publ. *CAIC News* (2 a month), *Business Wave* (6 a year).

**Committee for European Construction Equipment—CECE:** 101 rue de Stassart, 1050 Brussels, Belgium; tel. (2) 512-72-02; fax (2) 502-54-42; f. 1959 to further contact between manufacturers, to improve market conditions and productivity and to conduct research into techniques. Mems: representatives from Belgium, Finland, France, Germany, Italy, Netherlands, Spain, Sweden, United Kingdom. Pres. J. GUIGNABODET (France); Sec.-Gen. D. BARRELL (UK).

**Committee of European Foundry Associations:** 2 rue de Bassano, 75783 Paris Cédex 16, France; tel. 1-47-23-55-50; fax 1-47-20-44-15; f. 1953 to safeguard the common interests of European foundry industries; to collect and exchange information. Mems: associations in 14 countries. Sec.-Gen. H. CHAPOTOT.

**Confederation of Asia-Pacific Chambers of Commerce and Industry:** 7th Floor, 3 Sungshou Rd, Taipei 110, Taiwan; tel. (2) 27255663; fax (2) 27255665; e-mail cacci@ficnet.net; f. 1966; holds biennial conferences to examine regional co-operation; undertakes liaison with governments in the promotion of laws conducive to regional co-operation; serves as a centre for compiling and disseminating trade and business information; encourages contacts between businesses; conducts training and research. Mems: national chambers of commerce and industry of Australia, Bangladesh, Brunei, Cambodia, Hong Kong, India, Indonesia, Japan, Republic of Korea, Malaysia, Mongolia, Nepal, New Zealand, Pakistan, Papua New Guinea, Philippines, Russia, Singapore, Sri Lanka, Taiwan, Thailand, Viet Nam; also affiliate and special mems. Dir-Gen. LAWRENCE T. LIU. Publs *CACCI Profile* (monthly), *CACCI Journal of Commerce and Industry* (2 a year).

**Confederation of International Soft Drinks Associations—CISDA:** 79 blvd St Michel, 1040 Brussels, Belgium; tel. (2) 743-40-50; fax (2) 732-51-02; e-mail mail@unesda-cisda.org; internet www.unesda-cisda.org; f. 1961 to promote co-operation among the national associations of soft drinks manufacturers on all industrial and commercial matters, to stimulate the sales and consumption of soft drinks, to deal with matters of interest to all member associations and to represent the common interests of member associations; holds a congress every year. Gen. Sec. ALAIN BEAUMONT.

**Consumers International:** 24 Highbury Crescent, London, N5 1RX, United Kingdom; tel. (20) 7226-6663; fax (20) 7354-0607; f. 1960 as International Organization of Consumers' Unions—IOCU; links consumer groups worldwide through information networks and international seminars; supports new consumer groups and represents consumers' interests at the international level; five regional offices. Mems: 215 associations in 93 countries. Dir-Gen. JULIAN EDWARDS. Publs *Consumer Currents* (10 a year), *World Consumer* (quarterly), *Consumidores y Desarollo* (10 a year), *Consommation-Developpement* (quarterly).

**Energy Charter Secretariat:** blvd de la Woluwe 56, 1200 Brussels, Belgium; tel. (2) 775-98-00; fax (2) 775-98-01; e-mail info@encharter.org; internet www.encharter.org; f. 1995 under the provisions of the Energy Charter Treaty (1991); aims to promote trade and investment in the petroleum and gas industries. Mems: 50 signatory states. Sec.-Gen. RIA KEMPER (Germany).

**European Association of Advertising Agencies:** 5 rue St Quentin, 1000 Brussels, Belgium; tel. (2) 280-16-03; fax (2) 230-09-66; f. 1960 to maintain and to raise the standards of service to advertisers of all European advertising agencies, and to strive towards uniformity in fields where this would be of benefit; to serve the interests of all agency members in Europe. Mems: 16 national advertising agency associations and 24 multinational agency groups. Pres. ALBERT WINNINGHOFF (Netherlands); Sec.-Gen. STIG CARLSON (Sweden). Publ. *Next Steps* (monthly).

**European Association of Manufacturers of Radiators—EURORAD:** Konradstr. 9, 8023 Zürich, Switzerland; tel. (1) 2719090; fax (1) 2719292; f. 1966 to represent the national associations of manufacturers of radiators made of steel and cast iron, intended to be attached to central heating plants and which convey heat by natural convection and radiation without the need for casing. Mems: in 12 countries. Pres. G. VANDENSCHRIECK (Belgium); Gen. Sec. K. EGLI (Switzerland).

**European Association of National Productivity Centres:** 60 rue de la Concorde, 1050 Brussels, Belgium; tel. (2) 511-71-00; fax (2) 511-02-97; e-mail eanpc@skynet.be; f. 1966 to enable members to pool knowledge about their policies and activities, specifically as regards the relative importance of various productivity factors, and the ensuing economic and social consequences. Mems: 19 European centres. Pres. PETER REHNSTRÖM; Sec.-Gen. A. C. HUBERT. Publs *EPI* (quarterly), *EUROproductivity* (monthly), *Annual Report*.

**European Brewery Convention:** POB 510, 2380 BB Zoeterwoude, Netherlands; tel. (71) 545-60-47; fax (71) 541-00-13; e-mail secretariat@ebc_nl.com; internet www.ebc-nl.com; f. 1947, present name adopted 1948; aims to promote scientific co-ordination in malting and brewing. Mems: national associations in Austria, Belgium, Bulgaria, Czech Republic, Denmark, Finland, France, Germany, Hungary, Ireland, Italy, Latvia, Netherlands, Norway, Portugal, Slovakia, Slovenia, Spain, Sweden, Switzerland, United Kingdom. Pres. E. PAJUNEN (Finland); Sec.-Gen. M. VAN WIJNGAARDEN (Netherlands).

**European Chemical Industry Council:** ave E. van Nieuwenhuyse 4, 1160 Brussels, Belgium; tel. (2) 676-72-11; fax (2) 676-73-00; e-mail mail@cefic.be; internet www.cefic.org; f. 1972; represents and defends the interests of the chemical industry relating to legal and trade policy, internal market, environmental and technical matters; liaises with intergovernmental organizations; provides secretariat for some 100 product sector groups. Mems: 16 national federations; Dir.-Gen. Dr HUGO LEVER; Sec.-Gen. JEAN-MARIE DEVOS.

**European Committee for Standardization** (Comité européen de normalisation—CEN): 36 rue de Stassart, 1050 Brussels, Belgium; tel. (2) 550-08-11; fax (2) 550-08-19; e-mail infodesk@cenorm.be; internet www.cenorm.be; f. 1961 to promote European standardization so as to eliminate obstacles caused by technical requirements in order to facilitate the exchange of goods and services. Mems: 19 national standards bodies, 6 associated and 14 affiliated bodies in central and eastern Europe and 4 corresponding organizations. Sec.-Gen. GEORG HONGLER.

**European Committee of Associations of Manufacturers of Agricultural Machinery:** 19 rue Jacques Bingen, 75017 Paris, France; tel. 1-42-12-85-90; fax 1-40-54-95-60; f. 1959 to study economic and technical problems, to protect members' interests and to disseminate information. Mems: Austria, Belgium, Denmark, Finland, France, Germany, Italy, Netherlands, Norway, Spain, Sweden, Switzerland, United Kingdom. Pres. N. RAHBEK (Denmark); Sec.-Gen. J. DEHOLLAIN (France).

**European Committee of Textile Machinery Manufacturers:** POB 190, 2700-AD Zoetermeer, Netherlands; tel. (79) 531-100; fax (79) 531-365; f. 1952; promotes general interests of the industry. Mems: organizations in Belgium, France, Germany, Italy, Netherlands, Spain, Switzerland, United Kingdom. Pres. Dr F. PAETZOLD (Germany); Gen. Sec. R. BICKER CAARTEN.

**European Confederation of Iron and Steel Industries—EUROFER:** 211 rue du Noyer, 1000 Brussels, Belgium; tel. (2) 738-79-20; fax (2) 736-30-01; e-mail mail@eurofer.be; f. 1976; a confederation of national federations and companies in the European steel industry which aims to foster co-operation between the member federations and companies and to represent their common interests to the EU and other international organizations. Mems: Austria, Belgium, Finland, France, Germany, Ireland, Italy, Luxembourg, Netherlands, Portugal, Spain, Sweden, United Kingdom; assoc.

mems from countries of central and eastern European countries. Dir-Gen. D. von Hülsen.

**European Council of Paint, Printing Ink and Artists' Colours Industry:** ave E. van Nieuwenhuyse 4, 1160 Brussels, Belgium; tel. (2) 676-7480; fax (2) 676-7490; e-mail secretariat@cepe.org; internet www.cepe.org; f. 1951 to study questions relating to paint and printing ink industries, to take or recommend measures for their development and interests, to exchange information. Mems: national associations in 17 European countries and 13 company members. Pres. F. J. Rankl; Gen. Sec. J. Schoder.

**European Confederation of Woodworking Industries:** Allee Hof-Ter-Vleest 5, Boîte 4, 1070 Brussels, Belgium; tel. (2) 556-25-85; fax (2) 556-25-95; e-mail euro.wood.fed@skynet.be; f. 1952 to act as a liaison between national organizations, to undertake research and to defend the interests of the industry. Mems: national federations in 18 European countries and European sectoral organizations in woodworking. Pres. B. Castellini (Italy); Sec.-Gen. Dr G. Van Steertegem.

**European Federation of Associations of Insulation Enterprises:** Karl Liebknecht Str. 33, 10178 Berlin, Germany; tel. (30) 242-68-63; fax (30) 242-55-97; f. 1970; groups the organizations in Europe representing insulation firms including thermal insulation, sound-proofing and fire-proofing insulation; aims to facilitate contacts between member associations, to study any problems of interest to the profession, to safeguard the interests of the profession and represent it in international forums. Mems: professional organizations in 15 European countries. Chair. T. Wrede.

**European Federation of Handling Industries:** POB 179, Kirchenweg 4, 8032 Zürich, Switzerland; tel. (1) 3844844; fax (1) 3844848; f. 1953 to facilitate contact between members of the profession, conduct research, standardize methods of calculation and construction and promote standardized safety regulations. Mems: organizations in 14 European countries. Pres. Paolo Cavandoli; Sec. Dr K. Meier (Switzerland).

**European Federation of Management Consultants' Associations:** 3–5 Ave des Arts, 1210 Brussels, Belgium; tel. (2) 250-06-50; fax (2) 250-06-51; e-mail feaco@feaco.org; internet www.feaco.org; f. 1960 to bring management consultants together and promote a high standard of professional competence in all European countries concerned, by encouraging discussions of, and research into, problems of common professional interest. Mems: 23 associations. Pres. and Chair. Gil Gidron; Exec. Man. Else Groen. Publs *Newsletter* (3 a year), *Annual Survey of the European Management Consultancy Market*.

**European Federation of Plywood Industry:** 33 rue de Naples, 75008 Paris, France; tel. (1) 53-42-15-57; fax (1) 53-42-15-51; f. 1957 to organize joint research between members of the industry at international level. Mems: associations in 14 European countries. Pres. Pierre Lapeyre.

**European Federation of Tile and Brick Manufacturers:** Obstgartenstrasse 28, 8035 Zürich, Switzerland; tel. (1) 3619650; fax (1) 3610205; e-mail office@tbe-euro.ch; internet www.tbe-euro.com; f. 1952 to co-ordinate research between members of the industry, improve technical knowledge, encourage professional training. Mems: associations in Austria, Belgium, Czech Republic, Denmark, Finland, France, Germany, Greece, Hungary, Ireland, Italy, Netherlands, Norway, Poland, Portugal, Serbia, Slovakia, Spain, Sweden, Switzerland, Tunisia, United Kingdom. Chair. Peter Keller; Dir Dr W. P. Weller.

**European Furniture Manufacturers Federation:** 35 chaussé de Haecht, 1210 Brussels; tel. (2) 223-39-64; e-mail u.e.a.@euronet.be; internet www.u-e-a.com; f. 1950 to determine and support general interests of the European furniture industry and to facilitate contacts between members of the industry. Mems: organizations in Belgium, Denmark, Finland, France, Germany, Italy, Netherlands, Norway, Portugal, Slovenia, Spain, Sweden, Switzerland, United Kingdom. Pres. J. Engels; Sec.-Gen. B. de Turck.

**European General Galvanizers Association:** Croudace House, Godstone Rd, Caterham, Surrey, CR3 6RE, United Kingdom; tel. (1883) 331277; fax (1883) 331287; e-mail mail@egga.com; internet www.egga.com; f. 1955 to promote co-operation between members of the industry, especially in improving processes and finding new uses for galvanized products. Mems: associations in Austria, Belgium, Czech Republic, Denmark, Finland, France, Germany, Hungary, Iceland, Italy, Netherlands, Norway, Portugal, Spain, Sweden, Switzerland, United Kingdom. Pres. E. Hoffmann (Germany).

**European Glass Container Manufacturers' Committee:** Northumberland Rd, Sheffield, S10 2UA, United Kingdom; tel. (114) 268-6201; fax (114) 268-1073; e-mail l.roe@britglass.co.uk; internet www.britglass.co.uk; f. 1951 to facilitate contacts between members of the industry, inform them of legislation regarding it. Mems: representatives from 15 European countries. Sec. Dr W. G. A. Cook.

**European Organization for Quality—EOQ:** 3 rue de Luxembourg, 1000 Brussels, Belgium; tel. (2) 501-07-35; fax (31) 501-07-36; e-mail bjouslin@compuserve.com; internet www.eoq.org; f. 1956 to encourage the use and application of quality management with the intent to improve quality, reduce costs and increase productivity; organizes the exchange of information, documentation, etc. Member organizations in 31 European countries. Sec.-Gen. Bertrand Jouslin de Noray. Publs *European Quality* (6 a year), *Annual Report*.

**European Packaging Federation:** c/o Institut Français de l'Emballage et du Conditionnement IFEC, 33 rue Louis Blanc, 93582 St-Ouen Cédex, France; tel. 1-40-11-22-12; fax 1-40-11-01-06; f. 1953 to encourage the exchange of information between national packaging institutes and to promote technical and economic progress. Mems: organizations in Austria, Belgium, Denmark, Finland, France, Germany, Hungary, Italy, Netherlands, Poland, Spain, Switzerland, United Kingdom. Pres. J. P. Pothet (France); Sec.-Gen. A. Freidinger-Legay (France).

**European Panel Federation:** Hof-ter-Vleestdreef 5, 1070 Brussels, Belgium; tel. (2) 556-25-89; fax (2) 556-25-94; e-mail euro.wood.fed@skynet.be; f. 1958 as European Federation of Associations of Particle Board Manufacturers; present name adopted 1999; to develop and encourage international co-operation in the particle board and MDF industry. Pres. F. de Cock; Sec.-Gen. G. van Steertegem (Belgium). Publ. *Annual Report*.

**European Patent Office—EPO:** 80331 Munich, Erhardtstrasse 27, Germany; tel. (89) 2399-0; fax (89) 23994560; internet www.european-patent-office.org; f. 1977 to grant European patents according to the Munich convention of 1973; conducts searches and examination of patent applications. Mems: Austria, Belgium, Cyprus, Denmark, Finland, France, Germany, Greece, Ireland, Italy, Liechtenstein, Luxembourg, Monaco, Netherlands, Portugal, Spain, Sweden, Switzerland, United Kingdom. Pres. Ingo Kober (Germany); Chair. Admin. Council Sean Fitzpatrick. Publs *Annual Report, Official Journal* (monthly), *European Patent Bulletin, European Patent Applications, Granted Patents*.

**European Society for Opinion and Marketing Research—ESOMAR:** Vondelstraat 172, 1054 GV Amsterdam, Netherlands; tel. (20) 664-21-41; fax (20) 664-29-22; e-mail email@esomar.nl; internet www.esomar.nl; f. 1948 to further professional interests and encourage high technical standards. Mems: about 3,750 in 100 countries. Pres. Daniel Leconte (Portugal); Dir-Gen. Juergen Schwoerer. Publs *Marketing and Research Today, Newsbrief* (monthly), *ESOMAR Directory* (annually).

**European Union of Coachbuilders:** 46 Woluwedal, bte 14, 1200 Brussels, Belgium; tel. (2) 778-62-00; fax (2) 778-62-22; e-mail mail@federauto.be; f. 1948 to promote research on questions affecting the industry, exchange information, and establish a common policy for the industry. Mems: national federations in Belgium, France, Germany, Italy, Luxembourg, Netherlands, Switzerland, United Kingdom. Pres. J. Blyweert (Belgium); Sec.-Gen. Hilde Vander Stichele (Belgium).

**European Union of the Natural Gas Industry—EUROGAS:** 4 ave Palmerston, 1000 Brussels, Belgium; tel. (2) 237-11-11; fax (2) 230-62-91; e-mail eurogas@arcadis.be. Mem. organizations in Austria, Belgium, Denmark, Finland, France, Germany, Ireland, Italy, Netherlands, Spain, Sweden, Switzerland, United Kingdom. Pres. B. Bergmann (Germany); Gen. Sec. P. Claus (Belgium).

**Federación de Cámaras de Comercio del Istmo Centroamericano** (Federation of Central American Chambers of Commerce): Avda Cuba y Calle 33, Apdo 74, Panamá 1, Panama; tel. 227-1233; fax 227-4186; e-mail cciap@panama.phoenix.net; internet www.panacamara.com; f. 1961; for planning and co-ordinating industrial and commercial exchanges and exhibitions. Pres. Edgardo R. Carles; Exec. Dir José Ramón Varela C.

**Federation of European Marketing Research Associations—FEMRA:** Studio 38, Wimbledon Business Centre, Riverside Road, London, SW17 0BA, United Kingdom; tel. (20) 8879-0709; fax (20) 8947-2637; f. 1965 to facilitate contacts between researchers; main specialist divisions: European chemical marketing research; European technological forecasting; paper and related industries; industrial materials; automotive; textiles; methodology; information technology. Mems: 500. Pres. David A. Clark (Belgium).

**General Union of Chambers of Commerce, Industry and Agriculture for Arab Countries:** POB 11-2837, Beirut, Lebanon; tel. (1) 814269; fax (1) 862841; e-mail gucciaac@destination.com.lb; internet www.gucciaac.org.lb; f. 1951 to foster Arab economic collaboration, to increase and improve production and to facilitate the exchange of technical information in Arab countries. Mems: chambers of commerce, industry and agriculture in 22 Arab countries. Gen. Sec. Burhan Dajani. Publs *Arab Economic Report, Al-Omran Al-Arabi* (every 2 months), economic papers, proceedings.

**Global Crop Protection Federation—GCPF:** ave Louise 143, 1050 Brussels, Belgium; tel. (2) 542-04-10; fax (2) 542-04-19; e-mail gcpf@pophost.eunet.be/; internet www.gcpf.org; f. 1960 as European Group of National Asscns of Pesticide Manufacturers; international body since 1967; present name adopted in 1996. Aims to harmonize national and international regulations concerning crop protection products, to support the development of the industry and to promote observation of the FAO Code of Conduct on the Distribution and Use of Pesticides. Mems: 6 regional asscns covering Africa/Middle East, Asia-Pacific, Europe, Latin America, North America and Japan. Dir-Gen. K. P. VLAHODIMOS.

**Gulf Organization for Industrial Consulting:** POB 5114, Doha, Qatar; tel. 858888; fax 831465; f. 1976 by the Gulf Arab states to encourage industrial co-operation among Gulf Arab states, and to pool industrial expertise and encourage joint development of projects; undertakes feasibility studies, market diagnosis, assistance in policy-making, legal consultancies, project promotion, promotion of small and medium industrial investment profiles and technical training; maintains industrial data bank. Mems: member states of Gulf Co-operation Council (q.v.). Sec.-Gen. Dr IHSAN ALI BU-HULAIGA (Saudi Arabia). Publs *GOIC Monthly Bulletin* (in Arabic), *Al Ta'awon al Sina'e* (quarterly, in Arabic and English).

**Instituto Centroamericano de Administración de Empresas—INCDE** (Central American Institute for Business Administration): Apdo 960, 4050 Alajuela, Costa Rica; tel. 443-0506; fax 433-9101; f. 1964; provides postgraduate programme in business administration; executive training programmes; management research and consulting; second campus in Nicaragua, libraries of 85,000 vols. Rector Dr BRIZZIO BIONDI-MORRA.

**Inter-American Commercial Arbitration Commission:** OAS Administrative Bldg, Rm 211, 19th and Constitution Ave, NW, Washington, DC 20006, USA; tel. (202) 458-3249; fax (202) 458-3293; f. 1934 to establish an inter-American system of arbitration for the settlement of commercial disputes by means of tribunals. Mems: national committees, commercial firms and individuals in 22 countries. Dir-Gen. Dr ADRIANA POLANIA POLANIA.

**International Advertising Association Inc:** 521 Fifth Ave, Suite 1807, New York, NY 10175, USA; tel. (212) 557-1133; fax (212) 983-0455; e-mail iaaglobal@worldnet.att.net; internet www.iaaglobal.org; f. 1938; a global partnership of advertisers, agencies, the media and other marketing communications professionals; aims to protect freedom of commercial speech and consumer choice. Mems: more than 3,600 in 95 countries. World Congress held every 2 years, 1998: Cairo, Egypt. Pres. JOE CAPPO (USA); Dir-Gen. NORMAN VALE (USA). Publs *IAA Membership Directory and Annual Report, IAA World News*.

**International Association of Buying Groups:** 5300 Bonn 1, Vongelsingsstr. 43, Germany; tel. (228) 985840; fax (228) 9858410; f. 1951 for research, documentation and compilation of statistics; holds congress every three years. Mems: 80 buying groups in 12 countries. Sec.-Gen. Dr GÜNTER OLESCH.

**International Association of Congress Centres** (Association internationale des palais de Congrès—AIPC): c/o Muzejski prostor, Jezuitski trg 4, POB 19, 41000 Zagreb, Croatia; tel. (41) 433-722; f. 1958 to unite conference centres fulfilling certain criteria, to study the administration and technical problems of international conferences, to promote a common commercial policy and co-ordinate all elements of conferences. Mems: 73 from 29 countries. Pres. MATTHIAS FUCHS; Sec.-Gen. RADOVAN VOLMUT (Yugoslavia). Publ. list of principal conferences of the world (3 a year).

**International Association of Department Stores:** 4 rue de Rome, 75008 Paris, France; tel. 1-42-94-02-02; fax 1-42-94-02-04; e-mail iads@iads.org; internet www.iads.org; f. 1928 to conduct research, exchange information and statistics on management, organization and technical problems; centre of documentation. Mems: large-scale retail enterprises in Andorra, Belgium, Czech Republic, Denmark, Finland, France, Germany, Italy, Lebanon, Netherlands, Singapore, Spain, Switzerland, United Kingdom. Pres. L. MANDAC (Germany); Gen. Sec. M. DE GROOT VAN EMBDEN (Netherlands). Publ. *Retail News Letter* (monthly).

**International Association of Electrical Contractors:** 5 rue Hamelin, 75116 Paris, France; tel. 1-44-05-84-20; fax 1-44-05-84-05; e-mail aie@wanadoo.fr; Pres. AAGE KJAERGAARD; Gen. Sec. DENIS HANNOTIN.

**International Association of Scholarly Publishers:** c/o Tønnes Bekker-Nielsen, Aarhus Universitetsforlag, 8000 Århus C, Denmark; tel. 86-19-70-33; fax 86-19-84-33; f. 1972 for the exchange of information and experience on scholarly and academic publishing by universities and others; assists in the transfer of publishing skills to developing countries. Mems: 139 in 40 countries. Pres. TØNNES BEKKER-NIELSEN (Denmark); Sec.-Gen. CHRISTOPHER HUDSON (USA). Publs *IASP Newsletter* (every 2 months), *International Directory of Scholarly Publishers*.

**International Association of the Soap, Detergent and Maintenance Products Industry:** 49 sq. Marie-Louise, 1000 Brussels, Belgium; tel. (2) 230-83-71; fax (2) 230-82-88; e-mail a.i.s.e@euronet.be; f. 1967 to promote in all fields the manufacture and use of a wide range of cleaning products, polishes, bleaches, disinfectants and insecticides, to develop the exchange of statistical information and to study technical, scientific, economic and social problems of interest to its members. Mems: 31 national asscns in 25 countries. Pres. H. R. BIRCHER; Sec. P. COSTA (Belgium).

**International Association of Textile Dyers and Printers:** POB 518, 3900 AM Veenendaal, Netherlands; tel. (318) 564-488; fax (318) 564-487; e-mail krl@wxs.nl; f. 1967 to defend and promote the interests of members in international affairs and to provide a forum for discussion of matters of mutual interest. Mems: national trade associations representing dyers and printers in nine countries. Pres. M. TRONCONI (Italy); Sec.-Gen. C. LODIERS (Netherlands).

**International Booksellers Federation—IBF:** rue du Grand Hospice 34a, 1000 Belgium; tel. (2) 223-49-40; fax (2) 223-49-41; e-mail eurobooks@skynet.be; f. 1956 to promote the booktrade and the exchange of information and to protect the interests of booksellers when dealing with other international organizations; special committees deal with questions of postage, resale price maintenance, book market research, advertising, customs and tariffs, the problems of young booksellers, etc. Mems: 200 in 22 countries. Pres. YVONNE STEINBERGER; Sec.-Gen. CHRISTIANE VUIDAR. Publs *IBF-bulletin* (2 a year), *Booksellers International*.

**International Bureau for the Standardization of Man-Made Fibres (BISFA):** 4 ave van Nieuwenhuyse, 1160 Brussels, Belgium; tel. (2) 676-74-55; fax (2) 676-74-54; e-mail van@cirfs.org; internet www.bisfa.org; f. 1928 to examine and establish rules for the standardization, classification and naming of various categories of man-made fibres. Mems: 49. Sec.-Gen. A. KRIEGER.

**International Butchers' Confederation:** 10 Bte, 4 rue Jacques de Lalaing, 1040 Brussels, Belgium; tel. (2) 230-38-76; fax (2) 230-34-51; e-mail info@cibc.be; f. 1907; aims to defend the interests of small and medium-sized enterprises in the meat trading and catering industry. Pres. ANTON KARL; Sec.-Gen. THEO WERSHOVEN.

**International Confederation for Printing and Allied Industries—INTERGRAF:** 18 sq. Marie-Louise, bte 25, 1040 Brussels, Belgium; tel. (2) 230-86-46; fax (2) 231-14-64; f. 1983 (formerly EUROGRAF, f. 1975) to defend the common interests of the printing and allied interests in member countries. Mems: federations in 20 countries. Pres. MARTIN HANDGRAAF; Sec.-Gen. GEOFFREY WILSON.

**International Confederation of Art Dealers:** Freustrasse 116, 8032 Zurich, Switzerland; f. 1936 to co-ordinate the work of associations of dealers in works of art and paintings and to contribute to artistic and economic expansion. Mems: associations in 24 countries. Pres. R. OTTO (Austria).

**International Co-operative Alliance—ICA:** 15 route des Morillons, 1218 Grand-Saconnex, Geneva, Switzerland; tel. (22) 929-88-88; fax (22) 798-41-22; e-mail ica@coop.org; internet www.coop.org; f. 1895 for the pursuit of co-operative aims. A General Assembly and four Regional Assemblies meet every two years, on an alternating basis; a 20-member ICA Board controls the affairs of the organization between meetings of the General Assembly. Specialized bodies have been established to promote co-operative activities in the following fields: agriculture, banking, fisheries, consumer affairs, energy, tourism, communications, co-operative research, health, human resources, wholesale distribution, housing, insurance, women's participation and industrial and artisanal and service producers' co-operatives. Mems: 242 affiliated national orgs, with a total membership of more than 760m. individuals in 100 countries and four int. orgs. Pres. ROBERTO RODRIGUES (Brazil); Dir-Gen. BRUCE THORDARSON (Canada). Publs *Review of International Co-operation* (quarterly), *ICA News* (every 2 months), *Co-op Dialogue* (2 a year).

**International Council of Societies of Industrial Design—ICSID:** Erottajankatu 11A, 00130 Helsinki, Finland; tel. (9) 6962290; fax (9) 69622910; e-mail icsidsec@icsid.org; internet www.icsid.org; f. 1957 to encourage the development of high standards in the practice of industrial design; to improve and expand the contribution of industrial design throughout the world. Mems: 150 in 53 countries. Pres. AUGUSTO MORELLO (Italy); Sec.-Gen. KAARINA POHTO. Publs *ICSID News, World Directory of Design Schools*.

**International Council of Tanners:** Leather Trade House, Kings Park Rd, Moulton Park, Northampton, NN3 6JD, United Kingdom; tel. (1604) 679917; fax (1604) 679998; e-mail sec@tannerscounciliat.com; internet www.tannerscounciliat.org; f. 1926 to study all questions relating to the leather industry and maintain contact with national associations. Mems: national tanners' organizations in 33 countries. Pres. Dr FOLKART SCHWEIZER (Germany); Sec. PAUL PEARSON (UK).

**International Exhibitions Bureau:** 56 ave Victor Hugo, Paris 16e, France; tel. 1-45-00-38-63; fax 1-45-00-96-15; e-mail bie@wanadoo.fr; f. 1928, revised by Protocol 1972, for the authorization and registration of international exhibitions falling under the 1928 Convention. Mems: 84 states. Pres. OLE PHILIPSON; Sec.-Gen. VICENTE GONZALES LOSCERTALES.

**International Federation of Associations of Textile Chemists and Colourists—IFATCC:** Postfach 403, 4153 Reinach 1, Switzerland; e-mail markus.krayer@cibas.com; f. 1930 for liaison on professional matters between members; and the furtherance of scientific and technical collaboration in the development of the textile finishing industry and the colouring of materials. Mems: in 22 countries. Pres. JOHN HANSEN (Denmark); Sec. MARKUS KRAYER (Switzerland).

**International Federation of Grocers' Associations—IFGA:** Falkenplatz 1, 3001 Berne, Switzerland; tel. (31) 3024249; fax (31) 3017646; f. 1927; initiates special studies and works to further the interests of members having special regard to new conditions resulting from European integration and developments in consuming and distribution. Mems: 500,000. Sec.-Gen. PETER SCHUETZ (Switzerland).

**International Federation of Insurance Intermediaries** (Bureau International des Producteurs d'Assurances et de Réassurances—BIPAR): 40 ave Albert-Elisabeth, 1200 Brussels, Belgium; tel. (2) 735-60-48; fax (2) 732-14-18; e-mail bipar@skynet.be; f. 1937. Mems: 47 associations from 29 countries, representing approx. 250,000 brokers and agents. Pres. KURT SEDLER; Dir HARALD KRAUSS. Publ. *BIPAR Intern* (quarterly).

**International Federation of Pharmaceutical Manufacturers Associations—IFPMA:** 30 rue de St Jean, POB 758, 1211 Geneva 13, Switzerland; tel. (22) 3383200; fax (22) 3383299; internet www.ifpma.org; f. 1968 for the exchange of information and international co-operation in all questions of interest to the pharmaceutical industry, particularly in the field of health legislation, science and research; development of ethical principles and practices and co-operation with national and international organizations, governmental and non-governmental. Mems: the national pharmaceutical associations of 56 countries and one regional association (representing Latin America). Pres. LODEWIJK DE VINK (USA); Vice-Pres KUNIO TAKEDA (Japan), Prof. ROLF KREBS. Publ. *Health Horizons* (3 a year).

**International Federation of the Phonographic Industry—IFPI:** 54 Regent St, London, W1R 5PJ, United Kingdom; tel. (20) 7878-7900; fax (20) 7878-7950; e-mail info@ifpi.org; f. 1933; represents the interests of record producers by campaigning for the introduction, improvement and enforcement of copyright and related rights legislation and co-ordinating the recording industry's anti-piracy activities. Mems: 1,419 in 76 countries. Chair. and Chief Exec. JASON BURMAN.

**International Fertilizer Industry Association:** 28 rue Marbeuf, 75008 Paris, France; tel. 1-53-93-05-00; fax 1-53-93-05-45; e-mail ifa@fertilizer.org; internet www.fertilizer.org; Pres. C. E. CHILDERS; Sec.-Gen. L. M. MAENE.

**International Fragrance Association—IFRA:** 8 rue Charles-Humbert, 1205 Geneva, Switzerland; tel. (22) 3213548; fax (22) 7811860; e-mail ifra@dial.eunet.ch; f. 1973 to collect and study scientific data on fragrance materials and to make recommendations on their safe use. Mems: national associations in 14 countries. Pres. Dr J. ADAMS; Sec.-Gen. Dr F. GRUNDSCHOBER.

**International Fur Trade Federation:** POB 318, Walton, KT12 2WH, United Kingdom; fax (1932) 232656; internet www.iftf.com; f. 1949 to promote and organize joint action by fur trade organizations for promoting, developing and protecting trade in fur skins and/or processing thereof. Mems: 33 organizations in 27 countries. Exec. Dir J. BAILEY.

**International Group of National Associations of Manufacturers of Agrochemical Products:** 79A ave Albert Lancaster, 1180 Brussels, Belgium; tel. (2) 375-68-60; f. 1967 to encourage the rational use of chemicals in agriculture, the harmonization of national and international legislation, and the respect of industrial property rights; encourages research on chemical residues and toxicology. Mems: associations in 50 countries. Dir-Gen. HANS G. VAN LOEPER.

**International Meat Secretariat** (Office International de la Viande): 64 rue Taitbout, 75009 Paris, France; tel. 1-42-80-04-72; fax 1-42-80-67-45; e-mail ims@wanadoo.fr; internet www.meat-ims.org. Pres. PHILIP M. SENG; Sec.-Gen. LAURENCE WRIXON.

**International Organization of Motor Manufacturers:** 4 rue de Berri, 75008 Paris; tel. 1-43-59-00-13; fax 1-45-63-84-41; e-mail oica@club-internet.fr; f. 1919 to co-ordinate and further the interests of the automobile industry, to promote the study of economic and other matters affecting automobile construction; to control automobile manufacturers' participation in international exhibitions in Europe. Mems: manufacturers' associations of 16 European countries, China, Japan, the Republic of Korea and the USA; 38 assoc. mems. Gen. Sec. J. M. MULLER. Publ. *Yearbook of the World's Motor Industry*.

**International Organization of the Flavour Industry—IOFI:** 8 rue Charles-Humbert, 1205 Geneva, Switzerland; tel. (22) 3213548; fax (22) 7811860; e-mail iofi@dial.eunet.ch; f. 1969 to support and promote the flavour industry; active in the fields of safety evaluation and regulation of flavouring substances. Mems: national associations in 21 countries. Pres. Dr S. M. A. LECCHINI; Sec.-Gen. F. GRUNDSCHOBER. Publs *Documentation Bulletin* (monthly), *Information Letters, Code of Practice*.

**International Publishers' Association:** 3 ave de Miremont, 1206 Geneva, Switzerland; tel. (22) 3463018; fax (22) 3475717; e-mail secretariat@ipa-uie.org; internet www.ipa-uie.org; f. 1896 to defend the freedom of publishers, promote their interests and foster international co-operation; helps the international trade in books and music, works on international copyright, and translation rights. Mems: 74 professional book publishers' organizations in 65 countries and music publishers' associations in 20 countries. Pres. ALAIN GRÜND; Sec.-Gen. J. ALEXIS KOUTCHOUMOW.

**International Rayon and Synthetic Fibres Committee—CIRFS:** 4 ave E. van Nieuwenhuyse, 1160 Brussels, Belgium; tel. (2) 676-74-55; fax (2) 676-74-54; e-mail pur@cisfs.org; f. 1950 to improve the quality and use of man-made fibres and of products made from fibres. Mems: individual producers in 24 countries. Pres. FOLKERT BLAISSE; Dir-Gen. C. PURVIS (UK). Publs *Statistical Booklet* (annually), market reports, technical test methods.

**International Shopfitting Organisation:** Schmelzbergstr. 56, 8044 Zürich, Switzerland; tel. (1) 2678100; fax (1) 2678150; f. 1959 to promote interchange of ideas between individuals and firms concerned with the common interests of shopfitting. Mems: companies in 16 countries. Pres. U. FAETCH; Sec. PETRA ISENBERG.

**International Textile Manufacturers Federation—ITMF:** Am Schanzengraben 29, Postfach, 8039 Zürich, Switzerland; tel. (1) 2017080; fax (1) 2017134; e-mail secretariat@itmf.org; internet www.itmf.org; f. 1904, present title adopted 1978. Aims to protect and promote the interests of its members, to disseminate information, and encourage co-operation. Mems: national textile trade associations in about 50 countries. Pres. MIN-SOK SUH (Republic of Korea); Dir-Gen. Dr HERWIG STROLZ (Austria). Publs *State of Trade Report* (quarterly), various statistics.

**International Union of Marine Insurance:** Löwenstr. 19, POB 6333, 8023 Zürich, Switzerland; tel. (1) 2155275; fax (1) 2122072; e-mail mail@iumi.com; internet www.iumi.com; f. 1873 to collect and distribute information on marine insurance on a world-wide basis. Mems: 54 associations. Pres. GEORG MEHL (Germany); Gen. Sec. STEFAN PELLER.

**International Wool Textile Organisation:** 63 Albert Drive, London, SW19 6LB, United Kingdom; tel. (20) 8788-8876; fax (20) 8788-5171; f. 1929 to link wool textile organizations in member-countries and represent their interests; holds annual International Wool Conference. Mems: in 28 countries. Pres. H. GRUNZKE (Germany); Sec.-Gen. W. H. LAKIN (UK).

**International Wrought Copper Council:** 6 Bathurst St, Sussex Sq., London, W2 2SD, United Kingdom; tel. (20) 7724-7465; fax (20) 7724-0308; f. 1953 to link and represent copper fabricating industries, and to represent the views of copper consumers to raw material producers; organizes specialist activities on technical work and the development of copper. Mems: 18 national groups in Europe, Australia, Japan and Malaysia, 4 assoc. mems. Chair. TETSURO KAWAKAMI; Sec.-Gen. SIMON PAYTON.

**Liaison Group of the European Mechanical, Electrical, Electronic and Metalworking Industries:** Diamant Bldg, 80 blvd Reyers, 1030 Brussels, Belgium; tel. (2) 511-34-84; fax (2) 512-99-70; e-mail secretariat@orgalime.be; f. 1954 to provide a permanent liaison between the mechanical, electrical and electronic engineering, and metalworking industries of member countries. Mems: 25 trade associations in 16 European countries. Pres. ENRICO MASSIMO CARLE (Italy); Sec.-Gen. PATRICK KNOX-PEEBLES.

**Union of Industrial and Employers' Confederations of Europe—UNICE:** 40 rue Joseph II, 1000 Brussels, Belgium; tel. (2) 237-65-11; fax (2) 231-14-45; e-mail main@unice.be; f. 1958; aims to ensure that European Community policy-making takes account of the views of European business; committees and working groups work out joint positions in the various fields of interest to business and submit them to the Community institutions concerned. The Council of Presidents (of member federations) lays down general policy; the Executive Committee (of Directors-General of member federations) is the managing body; and the Committee of Permanent Delegates, consisting of federation representatives in Brussels, ensures permanent liaison with members. Mems: 20 industrial and employers' federations from the EU member states, and 13 federations from non-EU countries. Pres. GEORGES JACOBS; Sec.-Gen. DICK HUDIG. Publs *UNICE Information* (every 2 months), *Compendium of Position Papers* (2 a year).

**Union of International Fairs:** 35 bis, rue Jouffroy d'Abbans, 75017 Paris, France; tel. 1-42-67-99-12; fax 1-42-27-19-29; e-mail info@ufinet.org; internet www.ufinet.org; f. 1925 to increase co-operation between international fairs, safeguard their interests and extend their operations; holds annual congress and educational seminars. The Union has defined the conditions to be fulfilled to qualify as an international fair, and is concerned with the standards of the fairs. It studies improvements which could be made in the conditions of the fairs and organizes educational seminars. Mems: 167 organizers with 579 approved events, 30 assoc. mems in 67 countries. Pres. Prof. MANFRED BUSCHE (Germany); Sec.-Gen. GERDA MARQUARDT (France).

**World Council of Management—CIOS:** c/o RKW, 6236 Eschborn, Düsseldorfstr. 40, POB 5867, Germany; tel. (6196) 495366; fax (6196) 495304; f. 1926 to promote the understanding of the principles and the practice of the methods of modern management; to organize conferences, congresses and seminars on management; to exchange information on management techniques; to promote training programmes. Mems: national organizations in 45 countries. Pres. JOHN DIEBOLU (USA); Sec. HERBERT MÜLLER (Germany). Publ. *Newsletter*.

**World Customs Organization—WCO:** 30 rue du Marché, 1210 Brussels, Belgium; tel. (2) 209-92-11; fax (2) 209-92-92; e-mail info@wcoomd.org; internet www.wcoomd.org; f. 1952 as Customs Co-operation Council; an independent intergovernmental body that aims to enhance the effectiveness and efficiency of customs administrations in the areas of compliance with trade regulations; the protection of society; and revenue collection. Mems: governments of 150 countries or territories. Chair. ENRIQUE FANTA IVANOVIC (Chile); Sec.-Gen. MICHEL DANET (France). Publ. *WCO News* (2 a year).

**World Federation of Advertisers:** 18–24 rue des Colonies, Bte 6, 1000 Brussels; tel. (2) 5025740; fax (2) 5025666; e-mail info@wfa.be; internet www.wfa.be/; f. 1953; promotes and studies advertising and its related problems. Mems: associations in 42 countries and 24 international companies. Pres. HANS MERKLE; Dir-Gen. BERNHARD ADRIAENSENS. Publ. *E-Monitor* (monthly).

**World Packaging Organisation:** 481 Carlisle Dr., Herndon, VA 20170-4823, USA; tel. (703) 318-5512; fax (703) 814-4961; e-mail wpo@pkgmatters.com; internet www.packinfo-world.org/; f. 1967 to provide a forum for the exchange of knowledge of packaging technology and, in general, to create conditions for the conservation, preservation and distribution of world food production; holds annual congress and competition. Mems: Asian, North American, Latin American, European and South African packaging federations. Pres. SERGIO HABERFELD (Brazil); Gen. Sec. WILLIAM C. PFLAUM (USA).

**World Trade Centers Association:** One World Trade Center, Suite 7701, New York, NY 10048, USA; tel. (212) 432-2626; fax (212) 488-0064; internet www.wtca.org/; f. 1968 to promote trade through the establishment of world trade centres, including education facilities, information services and exhibition facilities; operates an electronic trading and communication system (WTC On-Line). Mems: trade centres, chambers of commerce and other organizations in 101 countries. Pres. GUY F. TOZZOLI; Chair. ANTONIO TRUEBA. Publ. *WTCA News* (monthly).

# Transport

**African Airlines Association:** POB 20116, Nairobi, Kenya; tel. (2) 502645; fax (2) 502650; e-mail afraa@africaonline.co.ke; f. 1968 to give African air companies expert advice in technical, financial, juridical and market matters; to improve air transport in Africa through inter-carrier co-operation; and to develop manpower resources. Mems: 34 national carriers.

**Airports Council International—ACI:** POB 16, 1215 Geneva 15-Airport, Switzerland; tel. (22) 7984141; fax (22) 7880909; f. 1991, following merger of Airport Operators Council International and International Civil Airports Association; aims to represent and develop co-operation among airports of the world. Mems: 530 operating more than 1,400 airports in 163 countries and territories. Chair. JEAN FLEURY; Dir-Gen. JONATHAN HOWE; Sec.-Gen. ALEXANDER STRAHL.

**Arab Air Carriers' Organization—AACO:** PO Box 13-5468, Beirut, Lebanon; tel. (1) 861297; fax (1) 863168; e-mail info@aaco.org; f. 1965 to co-ordinate and promote co-operation in the activities of Arab airline companies. Mems: 19 Arab air carriers. Pres.-Gen. MOHAMED FAHIM RAYAN (Egypt); Sec.-Gen. ABDUL WAHAB TEFFAHA.

**Arab Union of Railways:** POB 6599, Aleppo, Syria; tel. 220302; f. 1979 to stimulate co-operation between railways in Arab countries, to co-ordinate their activities and to ensure the interconnection of Arab railways with each other and with international railways; holds symposium every two years. Mems: 19 railways companies, railway infrastructure companies and associated organizations. Chair. TAHAR AZAIEZ; Gen. Sec. MOURHAF SABOUNI. Publs *Al Sikak Al Arabiye* (Arab Railways, quarterly), *Statistics of Arab Railways* (annually), *Glossary of Railway Terms* (Arabic, English, French and German).

**Association of Asia Pacific Airlines:** 5/F Corporate Business Centre, 151 Paseo de Roxas, 1226 Makati, Philippines; tel. (2) 8403191; fax (2) 8103518; e-mail aapahdq@aapa.org.ph; f. 1966 as Orient Airlines Asscn; present name adopted in April 1997; member carriers exchange information and plan the development of the industry within the region by means of commercial, technical and management information committees. Mems: Air New Zealand, Air Niugini, All Nippon Airways, Ansett Australia, Asiana Airlines, Cathay Pacific Airways, China Airlines, Dragonair, EVA Airways, Garuda Indonesia, Japan Airlines, Korean Air, Malaysia Airlines, Philippine Airlines, Qantas Airways, Royal Brunei Airlines, Singapore Airlines, Thai Airways International and Viet Nam Airlines. Dir.-Gen. RICHARD T. STIRLAND. Publs *AAPA Annual and Statistical Report, Orient Aviation*.

**Association of European Airlines:** 350 ave Louise, Bte 4, 1050 Brussels, Belgium; tel. (2) 627-06-00; fax (2) 648-40-17; f. 1954 to carry out research on political, commercial, economic and technical aspects of air transport; maintains statistical data bank. Mems: 27 airlines. Pres. XABIER DE IRALA (Spain); Sec.-Gen. KARL-HEINZ NEUMEISTER.

**Baltic and International Maritime Council—BIMCO:** Bagsvaerdvej 161, 2880 Bagsvaerd, Denmark; tel. 44-44-45-00; fax 44-44-44-50; e-mail mailbox@bimco.dk; internet www.bimco.dk; f. 1905 to unite shipowners and other persons and organizations connected with the shipping industry. Mems: in 115 countries, representing over 60% of world merchant tonnage. Pres. PHILIPPE POIRIER D'ANGE D'ORSAY (France); Sec.-Gen. FINN FRANDSEN.

**Central Commission for the Navigation of the Rhine:** Palais du Rhin, Place de la République, 67000 Strasbourg, France; tel. 3-88-52-20-10; fax 3-88-32-10-72; e-mail ccmn@wanadoo.fr; f. 1815 to ensure free movement of traffic and standard river facilities to ships of all nations; draws up navigational rules, standardizes customs regulations, arbitrates in disputes involving river traffic, approves plans for river maintenance work; there is an administrative centre for social security for boatmen, and a tripartite commission for labour conditions. Mems: Belgium, France, Germany, Netherlands, Switzerland. Pres. GERHARD FULDA (Germany); Sec.-Gen. JEAN-MARIE WOEHRLING (France).

**Danube Commission:** Benczúr utca 25, 1068 Budapest, Hungary; tel. (1) 352-1835; fax (1) 352-1839; e-mail dunacom@mail.matav.hu; internet www.dunacom.matav.hu; f. 1948; supervises implementation of the convention on the regime of navigation on the Danube; holds annual sessions; approves projects for river maintenance, supervises a uniform system of traffic regulations on the whole navigable portion of the Danube and on river inspection. Mems: Austria, Bulgaria, Croatia, Germany, Hungary, Moldova, Romania, Russia, Slovakia, Ukraine, Yugoslavia. Pres. Dr H. STRASSER; Dir-Gen. Capt. D. NEDIALKOV. Publs *Basic Regulations for Navigation on the Danube, Hydrological Yearbook, Statistical Yearbook*, proceedings of sessions.

**European Civil Aviation Conference—ECAC:** 3 bis Villa Emile-Bergerat, 92522 Neuilly-sur-Seine Cédex, France; tel. 1-46-41-85-44; fax 1-46-24-18-18; e-mail 101575.1313@compuserve.com; internet www.ecac-ceac.org; f. 1955; aims to promote the continued development of a safe, efficient and sustainable European air transport system. Mems: 37 European states. Pres. ANDRÉ AUER; Exec. Sec. RAYMOND BENJAMIN.

**European Conference of Ministers of Transport—ECMT:** 2 rue André Pascal, 75775 Paris Cédex 16, France; tel. 1-45-24-82-00; fax 1-45-24-97-42; e-mail ecmt.contact@oecd.org; internet www.oecd.org/cem; f. 1953 to achieve the maximum use and most rational development of European inland transport. Council of Ministers of Transport meets annually; Committee of Deputy Ministers meets three times a year and is assisted by Subsidiary Bodies concerned with: General Transport Policy, Railways, Roads, Inland Waterways, Investment, Road and Traffic Signs and Signals, Urban Safety, Economic Research, and other matters. Shares Secretariat staff with OECD (q.v.). Mems: 39 European countries; Associate Mems: Australia, Canada, Japan, New Zealand, USA. Sec.-Gen. G. AURBACH.

**European Organisation for the Safety of Air Navigation—EUROCONTROL:** 96 rue de la Fusée, 1130 Brussels, Belgium; tel. (2) 729-90-11; fax (2) 729-90-44; internet www.eurocontrol.be; f. 1963 principal objective is the development of a coherent and co-ordinated air traffic control system in Europe. A revised Convention was signed in June 1997, incorporating the following institutional structure: a General Assembly (known as the Commission in the transitional period), a Council (known as the Provisional Council) and an Agency under the supervision of the Director General; there are directorates, covering human resources and finance matters and a general secretariat. A special organizational structure covers the management of the European Air Traffic Management Programme. EUROCONTROL also operates the Experimental Centre (at Brétigny-sur-Orge, France), the Institute of Air Navigation Services (in Luxembourg), the Central Route Charges Office, the Central Flow Management Unit (both in Brussels) and the Upper Area Control Centre (in Maastricht, Netherlands). Budget (1999) €515m. Mems: Austria, Belgium, Bulgaria, Croatia, Cyprus, Czech Republic, Denmark, France, Germany, Greece, Hungary, Ireland, Italy, Luxembourg, the former Yugoslav republic of Macedonia, Malta, Monaco, Netherlands, Norway, Portugal, Romania, Slovakia, Slovenia, Spain,

Sweden, Switzerland, Turkey, United Kingdom. Dir-Gen. YVES LAMBERT (France).

**European Railway Wagon Pool—EUROP:** SNCB/NMBS, B-Cargo 407, Section 2014, 60 rue du Trône, 1050 Brussels, Belgium; tel. (2) 525-88-55; fax (2) 525-86-91; f. 1953 for the common use of wagons put into the pool by member railways. Mems: national railway administrations of Austria, Belgium, Denmark, France, Germany, Italy, Luxembourg, Netherlands, Switzerland. Managing railway: Belgian Railways. Pres. A. MARTENS.

**Forum Train Europe—FTE:** Direction générale des chemins de fer fédéraux suisses, Hochschulstrasse 6, 3030 Berne, Switzerland; f. 1923 as the European Passenger Train Time-Table Conference to arrange international passenger connections by rail and water; since 1997 concerned also with rail freight. Mems: rail and steamship companies and administrations. Administered by the Directorate of the Swiss Federal Railways. Pres. P. A. URECH.

**Institute of Air Transport:** 103 rue la Boétie, 75008 Paris, France; tel. 1-43-59-38-68; fax 1-43-59-47-37; f. 1945 as an international centre of research on economic, technical and policy aspects of air transport, and on the economy and sociology of transport and tourism; acts as economic and technical consultant in carrying out research requested by members on specific subjects; maintains a data bank, a library and a consultation and advice service; organizes training courses on air transport economics. Mems: organizations involved in air transport, production and equipment, universities, banks, insurance companies, private individuals and government agencies in 79 countries. Dir-Gen. JACQUES PAVAUX. Publs (in French and English), *ITA Press* (2 a month), *ITA Studies and Reports* (quarterly), *Aviation Industry Barometer* (quarterly).

**Intergovernmental Organization for International Carriage by Rail:** Gryphenhübeliweg 30, 3006 Berne, Switzerland; tel. (31) 3591010; fax (31) 3591011; e-mail otif@otif.ch; f. 1893 as Central Office for International Carriage by Rail, present name adopted 1985; aims to establish and develop a uniform system of law governing the international carriage of passengers, luggage and goods by rail in member states, which between them have a total of 240,000 km of railway lines. Mems: 39 states. Dir-Gen. M. BURGMANN. Publ. *Bulletin des Transports Internationaux ferroviaires* (every 2 months, in French and German).

**International Air Transport Association—IATA:** 33 route de l'Aéroport, CP 416, 1215 Geneva 15, Switzerland; tel. (22) 7992525; fax (22) 7983553; e-mail information@iata.org; internet www.iata.org; f. 1945 to represent and serve the airline industry. Aims to promote safe, reliable and secure air services; to assist the industry to attain adequate levels of profitability while developing cost-effective operational standards; to promote the importance of the industry to global social and economic development; and to identify common concerns and represent the industry in addressing these at regional and international level. Maintains regional offices in Amman, Brussels, Dakar, London, Nairobi, Santiago, Singapore and Washington, DC. Mems: 258 airline cos. Dir-Gen. PIERRE JEANNIOT; Corporate Sec. LORNE CLARK. Publ. *Airlines International* (every 2 months).

**International Association for the Rhine Vessels Register—IVR:** Vasteland 12E, 3011 BL Rotterdam (POB 23210, 3001 KE Rotterdam), Netherlands; tel. (10) 4116070; fax (10) 4129091; e-mail info@ivr.ne; internet www.ivr.ne; f. 1947 for the classification of Rhine ships, the organization and publication of a Rhine ships register and for the unification of general average rules, etc. Mems: shipowners and associations, insurers and associations, shipbuilding engineers, average adjusters and others interested in Rhine traffic. Gen. Sec. T. K. HACKSTEINER.

**International Association of Ports and Harbors:** Kono Bldg, 1-23-9 Nishi-Shimbashi, Minato-ku, Tokyo 105, Japan; tel. (3) 3591-4261; fax (3) 3580-0364; e-mail iaph@msn.com; internet www.iaph.or.jp; f. 1955 to increase the efficiency of ports and harbours through the dissemination of information relative to the fields of port organization, management, administration, operation, development and promotion; to encourage the growth of water-borne commerce; holds conference every two years. Mems: 350 in 85 states. Pres. DOMINIC J. TADDEO (Canada); Sec.-Gen. SATOSHI INOUE (Japan). Publs *Ports and Harbors* (10 a year), *Membership Directory* (annually).

**International Chamber of Shipping:** Carthusian Court, 12 Carthusian St, London, EC1M 6EZ, United Kingdom; tel. (20) 7417-8844; fax (20) 7417-8877; e-mail ics@marisec.org; internet www.marisec.org; f. 1921 to co-ordinate the views of the international shipping industry on matters of common interest, in the policy-making, technical and legal fields of shipping operations. Mems: national associations representative of free-enterprise shipowners and operators in 39 countries, covering 50% of world merchant shipping. Sec.-Gen. J. C. S. HORROCKS.

**International Container Bureau:** 167 rue de Courcelles, 75017 Paris, France; tel. 1-47-66-03-90; fax 1-47-66-08-91; f. 1933 to group representatives of all means of transport and activities concerning containers, to promote combined door-to-door transport by the successive use of several means of transport; to examine and bring into effect administrative, technical and customs advances and to centralize data on behalf of its members. Mems: 800. Sec.-Gen. JEAN REY. Publ. *Container Bulletin*.

**International Federation of Freight Forwarders' Associations:** Baumackerstr. 24, POB 8050 Zürich, Switzerland; tel. (1) 3116511; fax (1) 3119044; e-mail info@fiata.com; internet www.fiata.com; f. 1926 to protect and represent its members at international level. Mems: 95 organizations and more than 2,500 associate members in 150 countries. Pres. CHRISTOPHER GILLESPIE; Dir MARCO A. SANGALETTI. Publ. *FIATA Review* (every 2 months).

**International Rail Transport Committee** (Comité international des transports ferroviaires—CIT): Chemins de fer fédéraux suisses, 6 Hochschulstrasse, 3000 Berne 65, Switzerland; tel. (512) 202806; fax (512) 203457; e-mail henri.troiliet@sbb.ch; f. 1902 for the development of international law relating to railway transport on the basis of the Convention concerning International Carriage by Rail (COTIF) and its Appendices (CIV, CIM), and for the adoption of standard rules on other questions relating to international transport law. Mems: 300 transport undertakings in 37 countries. Pres. M. WEIBEL (Switzerland); Sec. M. LEIMGRUBER (Switzerland).

**International Railway Congress Association:** Section 10, 85 rue de France, 1060 Brussels, Belgium; tel. (2) 520-78-31; fax (2) 525-40-84; f. 1885 to facilitate the progress and development of railways by holding periodical congresses and by issuing publications. Mems: governments, railway administrations and national or international organizations. Pres. E. SCHOUPPE; Sec.-Gen. A. MARTENS. Publ. *Rail International* (monthly).

**International Road Federation—IRF:** Washington office: 1010 Massachusetts Ave, NW, Suite 410, Washington, DC 20037, USA; tel. (202) 371-5544; fax (202) 371-5565; e-mail info@irfnet.org; internet www.irfnet.org; Geneva Office: 2 chemin de Blandonnet 1214, Vernier, Geneva, Switzerland; tel. (22) 3060260; fax (22) 3060270; f. 1948 to encourage the development and improvement of highways and highway transportation; organizes IRF world and regional meetings. Mems: 70 national road associations and 500 individual firms and industrial associations. Dir-Gen. (Washington) GERALD P. SHEA; Dir-Gen. (Geneva) M. W. WESTERHUIS. Publs *World Road Statistics* (annually), *World Highways* (8 a year).

**International Road Safety (La Prevention Routière Internationale—PRI:** POB 40, 8005 Luxembourg-Bertrange; tel. 31-83-41; fax 31-14-60; e-mail int.road.safety@pri.lu; internet www.pri.lu; f. 1959 for exchange of ideas and material on road safety; organizes international action and congresses; assists non-member countries. Mems: 60 national organizations. Sec.-Gen. MARTINE PETERS. Publ. *Revue-Pri* (3 a year).

**International Road Transport Union—IRU:** Centre International, 3 rue de Varembé, BP 44, 1211 Geneva, Switzerland; tel. (22) 9182700; fax (22) 9182741; e-mail iru@iru.org; internet www.itu.org; f. 1948 to study all problems of road transport, to promote unification and simplification of regulations relating to road transport, and to develop the use of road transport for passengers and goods. Represents and promotes the industry at an international level. Mems: 160 national assocns in 65 countries. Dir MARTIN MARMY.

**International Shipping Federation:** Carthusian Court, 12 Carthusian St, London, EC1M 6EZ, United Kingdom; tel. (20) 7417-8844; fax (20) 7417-8877; e-mail isf@marisec.org; internet www.marisec.org; f. 1909 to consider all personnel questions affecting the interests of shipowners; responsible for Shipowners' Group at conferences of the International Labour Organisation. Mems: national shipowners' organizations in 34 countries. Pres. R. WESTFAL-LARSON (Germany); Sec.-Gen. J. C. S. HORROCKS.

**International Union Assocation of Public Transport:** 17 ave Herrmann-Debroux, 1160 Brussels, Belgium; tel. (2) 673-61-00; fax (2) 660-10-72; e-mail administration@uitp.com; internet www.uitp.com; f. 1885 to study all problems connected with the urban and regional public passenger transport industry. Mems: 1,700 in 70 countries. Pres. JEAN-PAUL BAILLY (France); Sec.-Gen. HANS RAT. Publs *Public Transport International* (every 2 months), *EUExpress, UITP Express*, Statistics reports.

**International Union for Inland Navigation:** 7 quai du Général Koenig, 67085 Strasbourg Cédex, France; tel. 3-88-36-28-44; fax 3-88-37-04-82; f. 1952 to promote the interests of inland waterways carriers. Mems: national waterways organizations of Austria, Belgium, France, Germany, Italy, Luxembourg, Netherlands, Switzerland. Pres. PH. GRULOIS (Belgium); Sec. M. RUSCHER. Publs annual and occasional reports.

**International Union of Railways—UIC:** 16 rue Jean-Rey, 75015 Paris, France; tel. 1-44-49-20-20; fax 1-44-49-20-29; e-mail communication@uic.asso.fr; internet www.uic.asso.fr; f. 1922 for the harmonization of railway operations and the development of international rail transport; aims to ensure international interoperability of the rail system; compiles information concerning economic, management and technical aspects of railways; co-ordinates research and collaborates with industry and the EU; organizes international conferences. Mems: 142 railways in 82 countries. Pres. ADAM WIELADEK; Chief Exec. PHILIPPE ROUMEGUÈRE. Publs *Rail International*, jointly with the International Railway Congress Association (IRCA) (monthly, in English, French and German), *International Railway Statistics* (annually), *Activities Reports, UIC Panorama* (newsletter).

**Northern Shipowners' Defence Club** (Nordisk Skibsrederforening): Kristinelundv. 22, POB 3033 El., 0207 Oslo, Norway; tel. 22-13-56-00; fax 22-43-00-35; e-mail post@nordiskskibsrederforening.no; f. 1889 to assist members in disputes over charter parties, contracts, sale and purchase, taking the necessary legal steps on behalf of members and bearing the cost of such claims. Members are mainly Finnish, Swedish and Norwegian and some non-Scandinavian shipowners, representing about 1,800 ships and drilling rigs with gross tonnage of about 50 million. Man. Dir NICHOLAS HAMBRO; Chair. MORTEN WERRING. Publ. *A Law Report of Scandinavian Maritime Cases* (annually).

**Organisation for the Collaboration of Railways:** Hozà 63–67, 00681 Warsaw, Poland; tel. (22) 6573600; fax (22) 6573654; e-mail osjd@osjd.org.pl; f. 1956; aims to improve standards and co-operation in railway traffic between countries of Europe and Asia; promotes co-operation on issues relating to traffic policy and economic and environmental aspects of railway traffic; ensures enforcement of the following agreements: Convention concerning international passenger traffic by railway; Regulation concerning the use of wagons in international traffic; International passenger tariff; Standard transit tariff to the convention concerning international goods traffic by rail; and contracts referring to the international transport of passengers and goods. Aims to elaborate and standardize general principles for international transport law. Conference of Ministers of member countries meets annually; Conference of Gen. Dirs of Railways meets at least once a year. Mems: ministries of transport of Albania, Azerbaijan, Belarus, Bulgaria, People's Republic of China, Cuba, Czech Republic, Estonia, Georgia, Hungary, Iran, Kazakhstan, Democratic People's Republic of Korea, Kyrgyzstan, Latvia, Lithuania, Moldova, Mongolia, Poland, Romania, Russia, Slovakia, Tajikistan, Turkmenistan, Ukraine, Uzbekistan, Viet Nam. Chair. TADEUSZ SZOZDA. Publ. *OSShD Journal* (every 2 months, in Chinese, German and Russian).

**Pan American Railway Congress Association** (Asociación del Congreso Panamericano de Ferrocarriles): Av. 9 de Julio 1925, 13°, 1332 Buenos Aires, Argentina; tel. (11) 4381-4625; fax (11) 4814-1823; f. 1907; present title adopted 1941; aims to promote the development and progress of railways in the American continent; holds Congresses every three years. Mems: government representatives, railway enterprises and individuals in 21 countries. Pres. JUAN CARLOS DE MARCHI (Argentina); Gen. Sec. CAYETANO MARLETTA RAINIERI (Argentina). Publ. *Technical Bulletin* (every 2 months).

**Union of European Railway Industries—UNIFE:** 221 ave Louise, 1050 Brussels, Belgium; tel. (2) 626-12-60; fax (2) 626-12-61; e-mail mail@unife.org; f. 1975 to represent companies concerned in the manufacture of railway equipment in Europe, in order to represent their collective interests towards all European and international organizations concerned. Mems: 140 companies in 14 countries; Chair. ROLF ECKRODT; Dir Gen. DREWIN NIEUWENHUIS.

**World Airlines Clubs Association:** c/o IATA, 800 Pl. Victoria, POB 113, Montréal, Québec, Canada H3A 2R4; tel. (514) 874-0202; fax (514) 874-1753; internet www.waca.org/; f. 1966; holds a General Assembly annually, regional meetings, international events and sports tournaments. Mems: clubs in 38 countries. Man. AUBREY WINTERBOTHAM. Publs *WACA World, WACA Contact, WACA World News*, annual report.

# Youth and Students

**AIESEC International:** Teilingerstraat 126–128, 3032 Rotterdam, Netherlands; tel. (10) 243-06-03; fax (10) 265-13-86; e-mail info@ai.aiesec.org; internet www.aiesec.org; f. 1948 as International Association of Students in Economics and Management; develops leadership skills, and socio-economic and international understanding among young people through exchange programmes and related educational activities. Mems: 50,000 students in more than 750 higher education institutions in 87 countries and territories. Pres. MURATCAN USTUNKAYA; Vice-Pres. DAVID WHERRY. Publs *Annual Report, International Link* (magazine).

**Asian Students' Association:** 511 Nathan Rd, 1/F, Kowloon, Hong Kong; tel. 23880515; fax 27825535; f. 1969; aims to promote students' solidarity in struggling for democracy, self-determination, peace, justice and liberation; conducts campaigns, training of activists, and workshops on human rights and other issues of importance.There are Student Commissions for Peace, Education and Human Rights. Mems: 34 national or regional student unions, four observers. Secretariat: LINA CABAERO (Philippines), STEVEN GAN (Malaysia), CHOW WING-HANG (Hong Kong). Publs *Movement News* (monthly), *ASA News* (quarterly).

**Council of European National Youth Committees—CENYC:** 517–519 Chaussée de Wavre, 1040 Brussels, Belgium; tel. (2) 648-91-01; fax (2) 648-96-40; f. 1963 to further the consciousness of European youth and to represent the National Co-ordinating Committees of youth work vis-à-vis European and international institutions. Activities include research on youth problems in Europe; projects, seminars, study groups, study tours; the Council provides a forum for the exchange of information, experiences and ideas between members, and represents European youth organizations in relations with other regions; furthers contact between young people in eastern and western Europe. Mems: 32 national councils in 30 countries. Sec.-Gen. WILLY BORSUS (Belgium). Publ. *CENYC Scene* (quarterly).

**Council on International Educational Exchange:** 205 East 42nd St, New York, NY 10017, USA; tel. (212) 661-1414; fax (212) 972-3231; e-mail strooboff@ciee.org; f. 1947; issues International Student Identity Card entitling holders to discounts and basic insurance; arranges overseas work and study programmes for students; co-ordinates summer work programme in the USA for foreign students; administers programmes for teachers and other professionals, sponsors conferences on educational exchange; operates a voluntary service programme. Mems: 307 colleges, universities and international educational organizations. Pres. and CEO STEVAN TROOBOFF. Publs include *Work, Study, Travel Abroad: The Whole World Handbook, Update, Volunteer!, High-School Student's Guide to Study, Travel and Adventure Abroad.*

**European Law Students' Association—ELSA:** 1 rue Defacqz, 1050 Brussels, Belgium; tel. (2) 534-56-79; fax (2) 534-65-86; f. 1981 to foster mutual understanding and promote social responsibility of law students and young laywers. Publs *ELSA Law Review, Legal Studies in Europe.*

**International Association for the Exchange of Students for Technical Experience—IAESTE:** e-mail webmaster@iaeste.org; internet www.iaeste.org; f. 1948. Mems: 63 national committees. Publs *Activity Report, Annual Report.*

**International Association of Dental Students:** c/o FDI World Dental Federation, 7 Carlisle St, London, W1V 5RG, United Kingdom; tel. (20) 7935-7852; fax (20) 7486-0183; f. 1951 to represent dental students and their opinions internationally, to promote dental student exchanges and international congresses. Mems: 60,000 students in 45 countries (and 15,000 corresponding mems). Pres. VALENTINA STERJOVA (UK). Publ. *IADS Newsletter* (3 a year).

**International Federation of Medical Students' Associations:** Institute of Social Medicine, Academisch Medisch Centrum, Meibergdreef 15, 1105 Amsterdam, Netherlands; tel. (20) 5665366; fax (20) 6972316; e-mail f.w.hilhorst@amc.uva.nl; f. 1951 to promote international co-operation in professional treatment and the achievement of humanitarian ideals; provides forum for medical students; standing committees on professional exchange, electives exchange, medical education, public health, refugees and AIDS; organizes annual General Assembly. Mems: 57 associations. Sec.-Gen. MIA HILHORST. Publ. *IFMSA Newsletter* (quarterly).

**International Pharmaceutical Students' Federation:** POB 84200, 2508 AE The Hague, Netherlands; tel. (70) 302-19-92; fax (70) 302-19-99; e-mail ipsf@fip.nl; internet www.pharmweb.net/ipsf.html; f. 1949 to study and promote the interests of pharmaceutical students and to encourage international co-operation. Mems: 31 full mems from national organizations and 23 mems in assoc. from national or local organizations. Pres. GONÇALO SOUSA PINTO; Sec.-Gen. HELENA WESTERMARK. Publ. *IPSF News Bulletin* (3 a year).

**International Union of Students:** POB 58, 17th November St, 110 01 Prague 01, Czech Republic; tel. (2) 312812; fax (2) 316100; f. 1946 to defend the rights and interests of students and strive for peace, disarmament, the eradication of illiteracy and of all forms of discrimination; operates research centre, sports and cultural centre and student travel bureau; activities include conferences, meetings, solidarity campaigns, relief projects, award of 30–40 scholarships annually, travel and exchange, sports events, cultural projects. Mems: 140 organizations from 115 countries. Pres. JOSEF SKALA; Vice-Pres. MARTA HUBIČKOVÁ; Gen. Sec. GIORGOS MICHAELIDES (Cyprus). Publs *World Student News* (quarterly), *IUS Newsletter, Student Life* (quarterly), *DE—Democratization of Education* (quarterly).

**International Young Christian Workers:** 11 rue Plantin, 1070 Brussels, Belgium; tel. (2) 521-69-83; fax (2) 521-69-44; e-mail jociycw@skynet.be; internet www.skynet.be/sky34197; f. 1925, on the inspiration of the Priest-Cardinal Joseph Cardijn; aims to educate young workers to take on present and future responsibilities in their commitment to the working class, and to confront all the situations which prevent them from fulfilling themselves. Pres. HELIO ALVES (Brazil); Sec.-Gen. DOMINADOR OLAVERE (Philippines). Publs *International INFO* (3 a year), *IYCW Bulletin* (quarterly).

**International Youth and Student Movement for the United Nations—ISMUN:** c/o Palais des Nations, 16 ave Jean-Tremblay, 1211 Geneva 10, Switzerland; tel. (22) 7985850; fax (22) 7334838;

f. 1948 by the World Federation of United Nations Associations, independent since 1949; an international non-governmental organization of students and young people dedicated especially to supporting the principles embodied in the United Nations Charter and Universal Declaration of Human Rights; encourages constructive action in building economic, social and cultural equality and in working for national independence, social justice and human rights on a worldwide scale; regional offices in Austria, France, Ghana, Panama and the USA. Mems: associations in 53 countries. Sec.-Gen. JAN LÖNN. Publs *ISMUN Newsletter* (monthly).

**International Youth Hostel Federation:** 1st floor, Fountain House, Parkway, Welwyn Garden City, Herts., AL8 6QW, United Kingdom; tel. (1707) 324170; fax (1707) 323980; e-mail iyhf@iyhf.demon.co.uk; f. 1932; facilitates international travel by members of the various youth hostel associations and advises and helps in the formation of youth hostel associations in all countries where no such organizations exist; records over 32m. overnight stays annually in over 4,500 youth hostels. Mems: 60 national associations with 3.7m. individual members; 17 associated national organizations. Pres. FRIEDRICH MUTH (Germany); Sec.-Gen. RAWDON LAU (Hong Kong). Publs *Annual Report, Guidebook on World Hostels* (annually), *Manual, News Bulletin*.

**Junior Chamber International (JCI), Inc.:** 400 University Drive (POB 140-577), Coral Gables, FL 33114-0577, USA; tel. (305) 446-7608; fax (305) 442-0041; e-mail jciwhq@ix.netcom.com; f. 1944 to encourage and advance international understanding and goodwill. Junior Chamber organizations throughout the world provide young people with opportunities for leadership training, promoting goodwill through international fellowship, solving civic problems by arousing civic consciousness and discussing social, economic and cultural questions. Mems: 400,000 in 90 countries. Pres. PETRI NISKANEN (1998); Sec.-Gen. BENNY ELLERBE. Publ. *JCI News* (quarterly, in English and more than six other languages).

**Latin American and Caribbean Confederation of Young Men's Christian Associations** (Confederación Latinoamericana y del Caribe de Asociaciones Cristianas de Jóvenes): Culpina 272, 1406 Buenos Aires, Argentina; tel. (11) 4637-4727; fax (11) 4637-4867; e-mail clacj@wamani.apc.org; f. 1914; aims to encourage the moral, spiritual, intellectual, social and physical development of young men; to strengthen the work of national Associations and to sponsor the establishment of new Associations. Mems: affiliated YMCAs in 25 countries (comprising 350,000 individuals). Pres. GERARDO VITUREIRA (Uruguay); Gen. Sec. MARCO ANTONIO HOCHSCHEIT (Brazil). Publs *Diecisiete/21* (bulletin), *Carta Abierta, Brief*, technical articles and other studies.

**Pan-African Youth Movement** (Mouvement pan-africain de la jeunesse): 19 rue Debbih Chérif, BP 72, Didouch Mourad, 16000 Algiers, Algeria; tel. and fax (2) 71-64-71; f. 1962; aims to mobilize and sensitize African youth to participate in socio-economic and political development and democratization; organizes conferences and seminars, youth exchanges, youth festivals. Mems: youth groups in 52 African countries and liberation movements. Publ. *MPJ News* (quarterly).

**World Alliance of Young Men's Christian Associations:** 12 clos Belmont, 1208 Geneva; tel. (22) 8495100; fax (22) 8495110; e-mail office@ymca.int; internet www.ymca.int; f. 1855 to unite the National Alliances of Young Men's Christian Associations throughout the world. Mems: national alliances and related associations in 128 countries. Pres. MARTIN VÖGLER (Switzerland); Sec.-Gen. NICK NIGHTINGALE (UK). Publ. *YMCA World* (quarterly).

**World Assembly of Youth:** International Youth Centre, Jalan Tenteram, Bandar Tun Razak, 56000 Kuala Lumpur, Malaysia; tel. 9732722; fax 9736011; internet www.jaring.my/way; f. 1949 as co-ordinating body for youth councils and organizations; organizes conferences, training courses and practical development projects. Pres. Datuk ALI RUSTAM; Sec.-Gen. HEIKKI PAKARINEN. Publs *WAY Information* (every 2 months), *Youth Roundup* (monthly), *WAY Forum* (quarterly).

**World Association of Girl Guides and Girl Scouts:** World Bureau, Olave Centre, 12c Lyndhurst Rd, London, NW3 5PQ, United Kingdom; tel. (20) 7794-1181; fax (20) 7431-3764; e-mail wagggs@wagggsworld.org; f. 1928 to promote unity of purpose and common understanding in the fundamental principles of the Girl Guide and Girl Scout Movement throughout the world and to encourage friendship and mutual understanding among girls and young women world-wide; World Conference meets every three years. Mems: about 9m. individuals in 136 organizations. Chair. World Board HEATHER BRANDON; Dir World Bureau LESLEY BULMAN. Publs *Triennial Report, Trefoil Round the World, Our World News*.

**World Council of Service Clubs:** POB 148, Wallaroo, South Australia 5556, Australia; e-mail kelly@kadina.mtx.net.au; f. 1946 to provide a means of exchange of information and news for furthering international understanding and co-operation, to facilitate the extension of service clubs, and to create in young people a sense of civic responsibility. Mems: more than 3,000 clubs in 83 countries. Sec.-Gen. SHANE KELLY.

**World Federation of Democratic Youth—WFDY:** POB 147, 1389 Budapest, Hungary; tel. (1) 3502202; fax (1) 3501204; e-mail wfdy@mail.matav.hu; f. 1945 to strive for peace and disarmament and joint action by democratic and progressive youth movements in support of national independence, democracy, social progress and youth rights; to support liberation struggles in Asia, Africa and Latin America; and to work for a new and more just international economic order. Mems: 152 members in 102 countries. Pres. IRAKLIS TSAVDARIDIS (Greece). Publ. *WFDY News* (every 3 months, in English, French and Spanish).

**World Organization of the Scout Movement:** Case Postale 241, 1211 Geneva 4, Switzerland; tel. (22) 7051010; fax (22) 7051020; e-mail worldbureau@world.scout.org; f. 1922 to promote unity and understanding of scouting throughout the world; to develop good citizenship among young people by forming their characters for service, co-operation and leadership; to provide aid and advice to members and potential member associations. The World Scout Bureau (Geneva) has regional offices in Chile, Egypt, Kenya and the Philippines (the European Region has its offices in Brussels and Geneva). Mems: over 25m. in 215 countries and territories. Sec.-Gen. Dr JACQUES MOREILLON (Switzerland). Publs *World Scouting News* (every 2 months), *Triennial Report*.

**World Union of Jewish Students:** Terra Sancta Compound, POB 7914, Rechavia, 91077 Jerusalem, Israel; tel. (2) 610133; fax (2) 610741; e-mail wujs@netvision.net.il; internet www.wujs.org.il; f. 1924 (by Albert Einstein); organization for national student bodies concerned with educational and political matters, where possible in co-operation with non-Jewish student organizations, UNESCO, etc.; divided into six regions; organizes Congress every two years. Mems: 52 national unions representing over 1,500,000 students. Chair. ILANIT SASSON MELCHIDE. Publs *The Student Activist Yearbook, Heritage and History, Forum, WUJS Report*.

**World Young Women's Christian Association—World YWCA:** 16 Ancienne Route, 1218 Grand-Saconnex, Geneva, Switzerland; tel. (22) 9296040; fax (22) 9296044; e-mail worldoffice@worldywca.org; internet www.worldywca.org; f. 1894 for the linking together of national YWCAs (now in 98 countries) for their mutual help and development and the initiation of work in countries where the Association does not yet exist; works for international understanding, for improved social and economic conditions and for basic human rights for all people. Pres. JANE WOLFE; Gen. Sec. MUSIMBI KANYORO. Publs *Annual Report, Common Concern*.

**Youth for Development and Co-operation—YDC:** Rijswijkstrasse 141, 1062 HN Amsterdam, Netherlands; tel. (20) 614-25-10; fax (20) 617-55-45; e-mail ydc@geo2.geonet.de; aims to strengthen youth structures that promote new co-operation between young people in the industrialized and developing worlds, in order to achieve development that is environmentally sustainable and socially just; seminars, conferences and campaigns on issues related to youth and development (employment, young women, structural adjustment programmes etc.) Mems: 51 organizations. Sec.-Gen. B. AUER. Publ. *FLASH Newsletter* (irregular).

# PART TWO

# Afghanistan–Jordan

# AFGHANISTAN

## Introductory Survey

### Location, Climate, Language, Religion, Flag, Capital

The Islamic State of Afghanistan (or Islamic Emirate of Afghanistan, as it was unilaterally renamed by Taliban in late 1997) is a land-locked country in south-western Asia. Its neighbours are Turkmenistan, Uzbekistan and Tajikistan to the north, Iran to the west, the People's Republic of China to the north-east and Pakistan to the east and south. The climate varies sharply between the highlands and lowlands; the temperature in the south-west in summer reaches 48.8°C (120°F), but in the winter, in the Hindu Kush mountains of the north-east, it falls to −26°C (−15°F). Of the many languages spoken in Afghanistan, the principal two are Pashtu and Dari (a dialect of Farsi or Iranian). The majority of Afghans are Muslims of the Sunni sect; there are also minority groups of Shi'ite Muslims, Hindus, Sikhs and Jews. The state flag (proportions 2 by 1) has three equal horizontal stripes from top to bottom of green, white and black, bearing in the centre in gold the state arms overlapping the three stripes. In October 1997 the Taliban administration in Kabul unilaterally decided to change the state flag: henceforth, it was to be plain white (proportions approximately 3 by 2) with, in the centre, an Arabic inscription in green lettering reading 'There is no God but Allah, and Muhammad is the Prophet of Allah'. The capital is Kabul.

### Recent History

The last King of Afghanistan, Mohammad Zahir Shah, reigned from 1933 to 1973. His country was neutral during both World Wars and became a staunch advocate of non-alignment. In 1953 the King's cousin, Lt-Gen. Sardar Mohammad Daud Khan, was appointed Prime Minister and, securing aid from the USSR, initiated a series of economic plans for the modernization of the country. In 1963 Gen. Daud resigned and Dr Mohammad Yusuf became the first Prime Minister not of royal birth. Dr Yusuf introduced a new democratic Constitution in the following year, which combined Western ideas with Islamic religious and political beliefs; the King, however, did not permit political parties to operate. Afghanistan made little progress under the succeeding Prime Ministers.

In July 1973, while King Zahir was in Italy, the monarchy was overthrown by a coup, in which the main figure was the former Prime Minister, Gen. Daud. The 1964 Constitution was abolished and Afghanistan was declared a republic. Daud renounced his royal titles and took office as Head of State, Prime Minister and Minister of Foreign Affairs and Defence.

A Loya Jirgah (Supreme National Tribal Assembly), appointed from among tribal elders by provincial governors, was convened in January 1977 and adopted a new Constitution, providing for presidential government and a one-party state. Daud was elected to continue as President for six years and the Loya Jirgah was then dissolved. In March President Daud formed a new civilian Government, nominally ending military rule. However, during 1977 there was growing discontent with Daud, especially within the armed forces, and in April 1978 a coup, known (from the month) as the 'Saur Revolution', ousted the President, who was killed with several members of his family. Nur Mohammad Taraki, the imprisoned leader of the formerly banned People's Democratic Party of Afghanistan (PDPA), was released and installed as President of the Revolutionary Council and Prime Minister. The country was renamed the Democratic Republic of Afghanistan, the year-old Constitution was abolished and no political parties other than the communist PDPA were allowed to function. Afghanistan's already close relations with the USSR were further strengthened. However, opposition to the new regime led to armed insurrection, particularly by fiercely traditionalist Islamist rebel tribesmen (known, collectively, as the *mujahidin*), in almost all provinces, and the flight of thousands of refugees to Pakistan and Iran. In spite of purges of the army and civil service, Taraki's position became increasingly insecure, and in September 1979 he was ousted by Hafizullah Amin, an erstwhile Deputy Prime Minister and Minister of Foreign Affairs. Amin's imposition of rigorous communist policies proved unsuccessful and unpopular. In December he was killed in a coup, which was supported by the entry into Afghanistan of about 80,000 combat troops from the USSR. This incursion by Soviet armed forces into a traditionally non-aligned neighbouring country aroused world-wide condemnation. Babrak Karmal, a former Deputy Prime Minister under Taraki, was installed as the new Head of State, having been flown into Kabul by a Soviet aircraft from virtual exile in eastern Europe.

Riots, strikes and inter-factional strife and purges continued into 1980 and 1981. Sultan Ali Keshtmand, hitherto a Deputy Prime Minister, replaced Karmal as Prime Minister in June 1981. In the same month the regime launched the National Fatherland Front (NFF), incorporating the PDPA and other organizations, with the aim of promoting national unity. Despite a series of government reshuffles carried out in the early 1980s, the PDPA regime continued to fail to win widespread popular support. Consequently, the Government attempted to broaden the base of its support: in April 1985 it summoned a Loya Jirgah, which ratified a new Constitution for Afghanistan, and during the second half of 1985 and the first half of 1986 elections were held for new local government organs (it was claimed that 60% of those elected were non-party members) and several non-party members were appointed to high-ranking government posts (including the chairmanship of the NFF).

In May 1986 Dr Najibullah (the former head of the state security service, KHAD) succeeded Karmal as General Secretary of the PDPA. Karmal retained the lesser post of President of the Revolutionary Council. In the same month Najibullah announced the formation of a collective leadership comprising himself, Karmal and Prime Minister Keshtmand. In November, however, Karmal was relieved of all party and government posts. Haji Muhammad Chamkani, formerly First Vice-President (and a non-PDPA member), became Acting President of the Revolutionary Council, pending the introduction of a new constitution and the establishment of a permanent legislature.

In December 1986 an extraordinary plenum of the PDPA Central Committee approved a policy of national reconciliation, involving negotiations with opposition groups, and the proposed formation of a coalition government of national unity. In early January 1987 a Supreme Extraordinary Commission for National Reconciliation, led by Abd ar-Rahim Hatif (the Chairman of the National Committee of the NFF), was formed to conduct the negotiations. The NFF was renamed the National Front (NF), and became a separate organization from the PDPA. The new policy of reconciliation won some support from former opponents, but the seven-party *mujahidin* alliance (Ittehad-i-Islami Afghan Mujahidin, Islamic Union of Afghan Mujahidin—IUAM), which was based in Peshawar, Pakistan, refused to observe the cease-fire or to participate in negotiations, while continuing to demand a complete and unconditional Soviet withdrawal from Afghanistan.

In July 1987, as part of the process of national reconciliation, several important developments occurred: a law permitting the formation of other political parties (according to certain provisions) was introduced; Najibullah announced that the PDPA would be prepared to share power with representatives of opposition groups in the event of the formation of a coalition government of national unity; and the draft of a new Constitution was approved by the Presidium of the Revolutionary Council. The main innovations incorporated in the draft Constitution were: the formation of a multi-party political system, under the auspices of the NF; the formation of a bicameral legislature, called the Meli Shura (National Assembly), composed of a Sena (Senate) and a Wolasi Jirgah (House of Representatives); the granting of a permanent constitutional status to the PDPA; the bestowal of unlimited power on the President, who was to hold office for seven years; and the reversion of the name of the country from the Democratic Republic to the Republic of Afghanistan. A Loya Jirgah ratified the new Constitution in November.

Meanwhile, a considerable proportion of the successful candidates in local elections held throughout the country in August 1987 were reported to be non-PDPA members. On 30 September Najibullah was unanimously elected as President of the Revolutionary Council, and Haji Muhammad Chamkani resumed his former post as First Vice-President. In order to strengthen his position, Najibullah ousted all the remaining supporters of former President Karmal from the Central Committee and Politburo of the PDPA in October. In the following month a Loya Jirgah unanimously elected Najibullah as President of the State.

In April 1988 elections were held to both houses of the new National Assembly, which replaced the Revolutionary Council. Although the elections were boycotted by the *mujahidin*, the Government left vacant 50 of the 234 seats in the House of Representatives, and a small number of seats in the Senate, in the hope that the guerrillas would abandon their armed struggle and present their own representatives to participate in the new administration. The PDPA itself won only 46 seats in the House of Representatives, but was guaranteed support from the NF, which gained 45, and from the various newly-recognized left-wing parties, which won a total of 24 seats. In May Dr Muhammad Hasan Sharq (a non-PDPA member and a Deputy Prime Minister since June 1987) replaced Keshtmand as Prime Minister, and in June a new Council of Ministers was appointed.

On 18 February 1989, following the completion of the withdrawal of Soviet troops from Afghanistan (see below), Najibullah implemented a government reshuffle, involving the replacement of non-communist ministers with loyal PDPA members. On the same day, Prime Minister Sharq (who had been one of the main promoters of the policy of national reconciliation) resigned from his post and was replaced by Keshtmand. Following the declaration of a state of emergency by Najibullah (citing allegations of repeated violations of the Geneva accords by Pakistan and the USA—see below) on 19 February, a PDPA-dominated 20-member Supreme Council for the Defence of the Homeland was established. The Council, which was headed by President Najibullah and was composed of ministers, members of the PDPA Politburo and high-ranking military figures, assumed full responsibility for the country's economic, political and military policies (although the Council of Ministers continued to function).

In early March 1990 the Minister of Defence, Lt-Gen. Shahnawaz Tanay, with the alleged support of the air force and some divisions of the army, led an unsuccessful coup attempt against Najibullah's Government. Najibullah subsequently enacted thorough purges of PDPA and army leaders and decided to revert rapidly to some form of constitutional civilian government. On 20 May the state of emergency was lifted; the Supreme Council for the Defence of the Homeland was disbanded; and a new Council of Ministers, under the premiership of Fazle Haq Khalikyar, was appointed. At the end of the month a Loya Jirgah was convened in Kabul, which ratified constitutional amendments, greatly reducing Afghanistan's socialist orientation; ending the PDPA's and the NF's monopoly over executive power and paving the way for fully democratic elections; introducing greater political and press freedom; encouraging the development of the private sector and further foreign investment; lessening the role of the State and affording greater prominence to Islam. The extensive powers of the presidency were, however, retained. In addition, in late June the PDPA changed its name to the Homeland Party (HP—Hizb-i Watan), and dissolved the Politburo and the Central Committee, replacing them with an Executive Board and a Central Council, respectively. The party adopted a new programme, of which the hallmark was hostility to ideology. Najibullah was unanimously elected as Chairman of the HP. An important factor in Najibullah's decision to continue with, and to extend, the process of national reconciliation was the fact that the USSR's own internal problems meant that the Soviet administration was unwilling to sustain, for much longer, the supplies of arms, goods and credits that were helping to uphold the Kabul regime.

Fighting between the *mujahidin* and Afghan army units had begun in the eastern provinces after the 1978 coup and was aggravated by the implementation of unpopular social and economic reforms by the new administrations. The Afghan army relied heavily upon Soviet military aid in the form of weapons, equipment and expertise, but morale and resources were severely affected by defections to the rebels' ranks: numbers fell from around 80,000 men in 1978 to about 40,000 in 1985. During 1984–89 the guerrilla groups, which had been poorly armed at first, received ever-increasing support (both military and financial) from abroad, notably from the USA (which began to supply them with sophisticated anti-aircraft weapons in 1986), the United Kingdom and the People's Republic of China. Despite the Government's decision to seal the border with Pakistan, announced in September 1985, and the strong presence of Soviet forces there, foreign weapons continued to reach the guerrillas via Pakistan. Many of the guerrillas established bases in the North-West Frontier Province of Pakistan (notably in the provincial capital, Peshawar). From 1985 the fighting intensified, especially in areas close to the border between Afghanistan and Pakistan. There were many violations of the border, involving shelling, bombing and incursions into neighbouring airspace. The general pattern of the war, however, remained the same: the regime held the main towns and a few strategic bases, and relied on bombing of both military and civilian targets, and occasional attacks in force, together with conciliatory measures such as the provision of funds for local development, while the rebel forces dominated rural areas and were able to cause serious disruption.

With the civil war came famine in parts of Afghanistan, and there was a mass movement of population from the countryside to Kabul, and of refugees to Pakistan and Iran. In mid-1988 a UNHCR estimate assessed the number of Afghan refugees in Pakistan at 3.15m., and the number in Iran at 2.35m. Supply convoys were often prevented from reaching the cities, owing to the repeated severing of major road links by the guerrillas. Kabul, in particular, began to suffer from severe shortages of food and fuel, which were only partially alleviated by airlifts of emergency aid supplies. As a result of the increasing danger and hardship, a number of countries temporarily closed their embassies in the capital.

From 1980 extensive international negotiations took place to try to achieve the complete withdrawal of Soviet forces from Afghanistan. Between June 1982 and September 1987 seven rounds of indirect talks took place between the Afghan and Pakistani Ministers of Foreign Affairs in Geneva, under the auspices of the UN. In October 1986 the USSR made a token withdrawal of six regiments (6,000–8,000 men) from Afghanistan. As a result of the discussions in Geneva, an agreement was finally signed on 14 April 1988. The Geneva accords consisted of five documents: detailed undertakings by Afghanistan and Pakistan, relating to non-intervention and non-interference in each other's affairs; international guarantees of Afghan neutrality (with the USA and the USSR as the principal guarantors); arrangements for the voluntary and safe return of Afghan refugees; a document linking the preceding documents with a timetable for a Soviet withdrawal; and the establishment of a UN monitoring force, which was to oversee both the Soviet troop departures and the return of the refugees. The withdrawal of Soviet troops (numbering 100,000, according to Soviet figures, or 115,000, according to Western sources) commenced on 15 May.

Neither the *mujahidin* nor Iran played any role in the formulation of the Geneva accords, and, in spite of protests by Pakistan, no agreement was incorporated regarding the composition of an interim coalition government in Afghanistan, or the 'symmetrical' cessation of Soviet aid to Najibullah's regime and US aid to the *mujahidin*. Therefore, despite the withdrawal of the Soviet troops, the supply of weapons to both sides was not halted, and the fighting continued. Pakistan repeatedly denied accusations, made by the Afghan and Soviet Governments, that it had violated the accords by continuing to harbour Afghan guerrillas and to act as a conduit for arms supplies to the latter from various sympathizers. At the end of November 1988 Soviet officials held direct talks with representatives of the *mujahidin* in Peshawar, Pakistan, the first such meeting since the start of the 10-year conflict. High-level discussions were held in early December in Saudi Arabia between Prof. Burhanuddin Rabbani, the Chairman of the IUAM, and the Soviet ambassador to Afghanistan. These discussions collapsed, however, when the *mujahidin* leaders reiterated their demand that no members of Najibullah's regime should be incorporated in any future Afghan government, while the Soviet officials continued to insist on a government role for the PDPA. In spite of the unabated violence, the USSR, adhering to the condition specified in the Geneva accords, had withdrawn all of its troops from Afghanistan by mid-February 1989.

In mid-1988 the *mujahidin* had intensified their military activities, attacking small provincial centres and launching missiles against major cities, several of which were unsuccessfully besieged. By the end of 1990, owing mainly to their lack of organization and limited experience of modern strategic warfare, the *mujahidin* had failed to achieve any significant military successes and their limited control was confined to rural areas (including several small provincial capitals). The guerrillas also failed to make any important advances on the political front. Talks between the IUAM and the Iranian-based Hizb-i Wahadati-i Islami (Islamic Unity Party), an alliance of eight Shi'ite Afghan resistance groups, repeatedly failed to reach any agreement as to the composition of a broadly-based interim government. Consequently, in February 1989 the IUAM convened its own Shura (Assembly) in Rawalpindi, Pakistan, at which an interim government-in-exile (known as the Afghan Interim Government, AIG) was elected. The AIG, however, was officially recognized by only four countries. It also failed to gain any substantial support or recognition from the guerrilla commanders, who were beginning to establish their own unofficial alliances inside the country. In March, however, the AIG received a form of diplomatic recognition, when it was granted membership of the Organization of the Islamic Conference (OIC). In addition, in June the US Government appointed a special envoy to the *mujahidin*, with the rank of personal ambassador. In mid-1989 the unity of the *mujahidin* forces was seriously weakened by an increase in internecine violence between the various guerrilla groups, while the AIG was riven by disputes between the moderates and the fundamentalists. The USA, Saudi Arabia and Pakistan began to reduce financial aid and military supplies to the IUAM in Peshawar, and to undertake the difficult task of delivering weapons and money directly to guerrilla commanders and tribal leaders inside Afghanistan.

Following extensive negotiations with the regional powers involved in the crisis, the UN Secretary-General made a declaration in May 1991, setting out five principles for a settlement, the main points of which were: recognition of the national sovereignty of Afghanistan; the right of the Afghan people to choose their own government and political system; the establishment of an independent and authorized mechanism to oversee free and fair elections to a broadly-based government; a UN-monitored cease-fire; and the donation of sufficient financial aid to facilitate the return of the refugees and internal reconstruction. The declaration received the approval of the Afghan and Pakistani Governments, but was rejected by the AIG.

Reflecting its disenchantment with the guerrilla cause, the US Government substantially reduced its aid to the *mujahidin* in 1991. New military campaigns had been launched by the *mujahidin* in the second half of 1990 in an attempt to impress their international supporters, disrupt the return of refugees and obstruct contacts between the Government and moderate guerillas. At the end of March 1991, following more than two weeks of heavy fighting, the south-eastern city of Khost was captured by the *mujahidin*, representing the most severe reversal sustained by the Government since the Soviet withdrawal. The *mujahidin* also carried out attacks on Gardez, Jalalabad, Ghazni, Qandahar and Herat in 1991, and communications between cities and with the Soviet border were severed.

An unexpected breakthrough towards resolving the Afghan crisis occurred in mid-September 1991, when the USA and the USSR announced that they would stop supplying arms to the warring factions, and would encourage other countries (namely Pakistan, Saudi Arabia and Iran) to do likewise. Although both the Afghan Government and the *mujahidin* welcomed this pledge, neither side showed any sign of implementing the proposed cease-fire, and, indeed, the fighting intensified around Kabul. In February 1992, however, the peace process was given a major boost when Pakistan made it clear that, rather than continuing actively to encourage the *mujahidin*, through arms supplies and training, it was urging all the guerrilla factions to support the five-point UN peace plan (see above). In doing so, Pakistan was effectively abandoning its insistence on the installation of a fundamentalist government in Kabul. There were growing fears, none the less, that the peace process might be placed in jeopardy by an increase in ethnic divisions within both the government forces and a number of *mujahidin* groups, between the majority Pashtuns and minority groups such as the Tajiks and Uzbeks. As a result of a mutiny staged by Uzbek militia forces in the Afghan army, under the command of Gen. Abdul Rashid Dostam, the northern town of Mazar-i-Sharif was captured by the *mujahidin* in March.

On 16 April 1992 events took an unexpected turn when Najibullah was forced to resign by his own ruling party, following the capture of the strategically-important Bagram air base and the nearby town of Charikar, only about 50 km north of Kabul, by the Jamiat-i Islami guerrilla group under the command of the Tajik general, Ahmad Shah Masoud. Najibullah went into hiding in the capital, under UN protection, while one of the Vice-Presidents, Abd ar-Rahim Hatif, assumed the post of acting President. Within a few days of Najibullah's downfall, every major town in Afghanistan was under the control of different coalitions of *mujahidin* groups co-operating with disaffected army commanders. Masoud was given orders by the guerrilla leaders in Peshawar to secure Kabul. On 25 April the forces of both Masoud and of Gulbuddin Hekmatyar, the leader of a rival guerrilla group, the Pashtun-dominated Hizb-i Islami (Islamic Party), whose men were massed to the south of the capital, entered Kabul. The army surrendered its key positions, and immediately the city was riven by *mujahidin* faction-fighting. The military council that had, a few days earlier, replaced the Government handed over power to the *mujahidin*. Having discarded the UN's proposal to form a neutral body, the guerrilla leaders in Peshawar agreed to establish a 51-member interim Islamic Jihad Council, composed of military and religious leaders, which was to assume power in Kabul. The leader of the small, moderate Jebha-i-Nejat-i-Melli (National Liberation Front), Prof. Sibghatullah Mojaddedi, was to chair the Islamic Jihad Council for two months, after which period a 10-member Leadership Council, comprising *mujahidin* chiefs and presided over by the head of the Jamiat-i Islami, Prof. Burhanuddin Rabbani, would be set up for a period of four months. Within the six months a special council was to meet to designate an interim administration which was to hold power for up to a year pending elections.

Mojaddedi arrived in Kabul on 28 April 1992 as the President of the new interim administration. The Islamic Jihad Council was not, however, supported by Hekmatyar, whose radical stance differed substantially from Mojaddedi's more tolerant outlook. At the end of the month Hekmatyar's forces lost control of their last stronghold in the centre of Kabul. Within a few weeks the Government of the newly-proclaimed Islamic State of Afghanistan had won almost universal diplomatic recognition, and by early May about one-half of the Islamic Jihad Council had arrived in the capital. An acting Council of Ministers was formed, in which Masoud was given the post of Minister of Defence and the premiership was set aside for Ustad Abdol Sabur Farid, a Tajik commander from the Hizb-i Islami (Hekmatyar declined to accept the post). As part of the process of 'Islamization', the death penalty was introduced, alcohol and narcotics were banned and the wearing of strict Islamic dress by all women was enforced. Despite Mojaddedi's repeated pleas to Hekmatyar and his followers to lay down their arms, Hekmatyar, who was particularly angered by the presence of Gen. Dostam's Uzbek forces in the capital, continued to bombard Kabul with artillery and indiscriminate rocket launches from various strongholds around the city, killing and wounding scores of citizens.

On 28 June 1992 Mojaddedi surrendered power to the Leadership Council, which immediately offered Burhanuddin Rabbani the presidency of the country and the concomitant responsibility for the interim Council of Ministers for four months, as set forth in the Peshawar Agreement (see above). In early July Farid assumed the premiership, which had been held open for him since late April. On assuming the presidency Rabbani announced the adoption of a new Islamic flag, the establishment of an economic council, which was to tackle the country's severe economic problems, and the appointment of a commission to draw up a new Constitution. A Deputy President was appointed in late July. In early August the withdrawal of the members of the Hizb-i Islami faction led by Maulvi Muhammad Yunus Khalis from the Leadership Council revealed serious rifts within the Government. A further problem was the continuing inter-*mujahidin* violence in Kabul. Within days the violence had escalated into a full-scale ground offensive, launched by Hekmatyar's forces against the capital. The airport was closed down, hundreds of people were killed or wounded, and tens of thousands of civilians fled Kabul in fear of their lives. In response President Rabbani expelled Hekmatyar from the Leadership Council and dismissed Prime Minister Farid. Hekmatyar demanded the expulsion of the 75,000 Uzbek militia from Kabul as a precondition to peace talks, alleging that Gen. Dostam was still closely allied to former members of the communist regime. At the end of the month a cease-fire agreement was reached between Rabbani and Hekmatyar and, after a few days of relative peacefulness the airport was reopened. Sporadic fighting involving various *mujahidin* and militia groups (notably Gen. Dostam's Uzbek forces) continued, however, in Kabul itself and in the provinces throughout the remainder of the year. At the end of October the Leadership Council agreed to extend Rabbani's tenure of the presidency by two months. On 30

December a special advisory council, known as the Resolution and Settlement Council (Shura-e Ahl-e Hal wa Aqd), which was composed of 1,335 tribal leaders, was convened in Kabul. The Council elected Rabbani, who was the sole candidate, as President of the country for a period of a further two years. In early January 1993 200 members of the advisory council were selected to constitute the future membership of the country's legislature.

The establishment of the advisory council and the re-election of President Rabbani provoked yet further heavy fighting in Kabul and other provinces in early 1993. Owing to the worsening violence, all of the Western diplomats had left the capital by the end of January. In early March, however, President Rabbani, Hekmatyar, Mojaddedi and leaders of other major *mujahidin* factions held negotiations in Islamabad, at the end of which a peace accord was signed. Under the terms of the accord, an interim Government was to be established, which would hold power for 18 months; President Rabbani was to remain as Head of State, and Hekmatyar (or his nominee) was to assume the premiership of the acting Council of Ministers; a cease-fire was to be imposed with immediate effect; legislative elections were to be held within six months; a 16-member defence commission was to be formed, which would be responsible for the establishment of a national army; and all weaponry was to be seized from the warring factions in an attempt to restore peace and order. The peace accord was officially approved and signed by the Governments of Pakistan, Saudi Arabia and Iran.

Confronted with the difficult task of satisfying the demands of all the *mujahidin* groups, Hekmatyar was not able to present a new Council of Ministers until late May 1993 (it was sworn in the following month). Each *mujahidin* faction was allocated two ministerial posts, with further positions left vacant for other representatives (representatives from Gen. Dostam's group of predominantly Uzbek militiamen—known collectively as the National Islamic Movement (NIM) (Jonbesh-e Melli-e Eslami)—were offered two posts in July). One of Hekmatyar's most noteworthy decisions in the formation of the new Council of Ministers was to remove one of his most powerful rivals, Ahmad Shah Masoud, from the crucial post of Minister of Defence. The new Prime Minister promised to hold a general election by October. The temporary headquarters of the Government were situated in Charasiab, Hekmatyar's military base, about 25 km south of Kabul.

Despite the signing of the Islamabad peace accord in March 1993, the violence between the various *mujahidin* groups did not cease, and hundreds of people continued to be killed and wounded. The interim Government was beset by internal dissension and proved rather ineffectual in the administration of the war-torn country. Hekmatyar refused to co-operate with Rabbani, and frequently demanded the President's immediate and unconditional resignation. In September, however, it was reported that a new draft Constitution (known as the Basic Law) had been drawn up and approved by a special commission, in preparation for the holding of a general election. The fighting intensified in late December, when Gen. Dostam transferred his allegiance to his hitherto arch-enemy, Hekmatyar, and the supporters of the two combined to confront the forces of Rabbani and Masoud. The violence spread throughout the provinces, resulting in large numbers of military and civilian casualties and the internal displacement of thousands of people. Various unsuccessful attempts were made in 1994 by neighbouring countries and by international organizations, such as the UN and the OIC, to achieve a negotiated settlement between the main warring factions. In late June the Supreme Court ruled that Rabbani could retain the presidency for a further six months, but failed to grant a similar extension to Hekmatyar's premiership. President Rabbani's extended term in office expired at the end of December. However, he did not resign, owing to, according to various sources, the continuation of the civil war and the lack of a suitable replacement for the post.

In the latter half of 1994, a new, hitherto unknown, militant grouping emerged in Afghanistan, known as Taliban (the plural form of 'Talib', meaning 'seeker of religious knowledge'). The movement, which at the outset comprised an estimated 25,000 fighters (the majority of whom were reported to be young Pashtun graduates of fundamentalist Islamic schools established by Afghan refugees in Pakistan), advocated the adoption of extremist practices, including the complete seclusion of women from society. Although initially claiming that it had no interest in actually assuming power in Afghanistan, Taliban, which was led by Mola Mohammad Omar, won a major victory in October, when it captured the city of Qandahar from the forces of Hekmatyar, which had hitherto dominated the southern provinces of the country. In February 1995 Taliban routed Hekmatyar's men from their headquarters in Charasiab, and within a month it controlled 10 provinces, mostly in southern and south-eastern Afghanistan. However, Taliban retreated from its advance on Kabul when Rabbani's troops launched a massive counter-offensive. By mid-1995, with both Taliban and Hekmatyar's men held in check, President Rabbani and his supporters were enjoying an unprecedented level of authority and confidence in Kabul and its environs. This was reflected in Rabbani's reneging on his earlier promise of standing down from the presidency in late March and in the growing number of countries that were considering reopening their embassies in the Afghan capital (the Indian embassy reopened in May). In mid-1995 talks were held between Rabbani and Taliban, but relations between the two sides remained extremely strained. In early September Taliban achieved a notable gain when it captured the key north-western city of Herat and the surrounding province from government forces. Taliban's resurgence apparently provoked an attack on the Pakistani embassy in Kabul by hundreds of pro-Government demonstrators protesting against Pakistan's alleged support for the student militia; the embassy was destroyed by fire, one employee was killed and a number wounded (including the ambassador himself). In response, the Afghan ambassador to Pakistan and six other Afghan diplomats were expelled from Islamabad. In October Taliban launched a massive ground and air assault on Kabul, but by early January 1996 had failed to breach the capital's defences. The constant bombardment of the besieged city, however, resulted in hundreds of civilian deaths, and the road blockades around the capital caused serious shortages of vital supplies.

Despite the holding of exploratory negotiations between the Rabbani Government and major opposition parties in the first quarter of 1996, the fighting in and around Kabul intensified. The President's attempts at conciliation finally proved successful, however, in late May when, in a critical development (known as the Mahipar Agreement), he persuaded Hekmatyar to rejoin the Government. Hekmatyar's forces arrived in the capital during May to defend the city against Taliban. In late June Hekmatyar resumed the post of Prime Minister and President Rabbani appointed a new Council of Ministers in early July, which was to hold power for a period of six–12 months pending the staging of a general election. In addition, under the terms of the Mahipar Agreement, a Constitution to cover the interim period was drawn up and published.

The political situation was radically altered in late September 1996 when, as a culmination of two weeks of sweeping military advances (including the capture of the crucial eastern city of Jalalabad), Taliban seized control of Kabul following fierce clashes with government troops, who fled northwards together with the deposed Government. One of Taliban's first actions in the captured capital was the summary execution of former President Najibullah and his brother. On assuming power, Taliban declared Afghanistan a 'complete' Islamic state and appointed an interim Council of Ministers, led by Mola Mohammad Rabbani, to administer the country (of which it now controlled about two-thirds). Pakistan, which was widely suspected of actively aiding the Islamic militia, was the first country officially to recognize the new regime. (By mid-November, however, few other countries or international organizations had followed suit—neither the UN, India, Russia nor Iran had given official recognition to the Taliban administration.) Taliban imposed a strict and intimidatory Islamic code—women were not permitted to enter employment or be formally educated beyond the age of eight; television, non-religious music, gambling and alcohol were all banned; amputations and public stonings were enforced as forms of punishment; compulsory attendance at mosques by all men was introduced; and women were ordered into purdah.

Taliban's hopes that the opposition would remain divided were thwarted following the formation in October 1996 of a powerful military and logistical alliance by Gen. Dostam, the former Minister of Defence, Ahmad Shah Masoud, and the leader of the Shi'ite Hizb-i Wahadat-i Islami, Gen. Abdol Karim Khalili. Gen. Dostam, who controlled six northern provinces, apparently decided to establish this unlikely alliance after cease-fire talks between himself and Taliban broke down. By late October the anti-Taliban forces, whose leaders were now collectively known as the Supreme Council for the Defence of Afghanistan (the headquarters of which were situated in Gen. Dostam's stronghold of Mazar-i-Sharif), had launched a concerted offensive against Kabul in the hope of ousting the Islamic militia. Despite repeated calls for a cease-fire from various foreign governments and the UN and despite complaints by Amnesty International regarding civilian casualties and abuses of human rights, the fighting between Taliban and the allied opposition continued into January 1997. In mid-January, following the rapid collapse of UN-sponsored talks in Islamabad, Taliban launched an unexpected offensive, advancing north and capturing Bagram air base and the provincial capital of Charikar. By late January Taliban had made significant military gains and had pushed the front line to about 100 km north of Kabul. The situation underwent a dramatic development in mid-May when, following the defection of the Uzbek Gen. Abdul Malik and his men to Taliban, the latter was able to capture the strategically-important northern town of Mazar-i-Sharif with relatively little bloodshed. Gen. Dostam was reported to have fled to Turkey, and his position as leader of the NIM was assumed by Gen. Malik. Taliban now controlled about 90% of the country, including all of the major towns and cities. Its position was also strengthened around this time by Pakistan's decision to be the first country to accord formal recognition to the Taliban Government (closely followed by Saudi Arabia and the United Arab Emirates). Taliban's control of Mazar-i-Sharif, however, was extremely short-lived, and within only three days of entering the town it was in full retreat. It appeared that Gen. Malik's tenuous alliance with Taliban had collapsed almost immediately and his troops, together with Shi'ite militia, forced the newcomers out after ferocious fighting. Taliban was soundly routed and by early June its forces had retreated almost 200 km south of Mazar-i-Sharif. Taliban officials later alleged that, following the recapture of Mazar-i-Sharif, about 3,000 Taliban prisoners-of-war were summarily executed by their captors. The regional aspect of the Afghan conflict was highlighted at the beginning of June by Taliban's decision to close down the Iranian embassy in Kabul; the Iranian Government was widely suspected of actively aiding the anti-Taliban northern alliance. The alliance was reported to have been expanded and strengthened in early June by the inclusion of the forces of Hekmatyar and of the Mahaz-i-Melli-i-Islami (National Islamic Front), led by Pir Sayed Ahmad Gailani. This new coalition, which superseded the Supreme Council for the Defence of Afghanistan, was known as the United Islamic Front for the Salvation of Afghanistan (UIFSA). Despite the arrival of thousands of reinforcements from training camps in Pakistan (many of whom were, however, inexperienced teenagers), Taliban suffered a series of military defeats in northern Afghanistan, and by late July the UIFSA forces were within firing range of Kabul, having recaptured Charikar and the air base at Bagram. In the same month the UN Security Council demanded a cease-fire and an end to all foreign intervention in Afghanistan. In mid-1997 it was widely believed that Taliban was supported by Pakistan and Saudi Arabia; on the opposing side, to various degrees, were ranged Iran, India, the Central Asian states (which feared the encroachment of Taliban's fundamentalism) and Russia.

In mid-August 1997 it was reported that the UIFSA had appointed a new Government, based in Mazar-i-Sharif, with Rabbani continuing as President, Abdorrahim Ghafurzai as Prime Minister, Masoud as Minister of Defence and Gen. Malik as Minister of Foreign Affairs. The former Prime Minister in the anti-Taliban administration, Gulbuddin Hekmatyar, refused to recognize the new Government. Within a few days of its appointment, however, seven members of the new Government, including Prime Minister Ghafurzai, were killed in an aeroplane crash. In late August the anti-Taliban opposition alliance appointed Abdolghaffur Rawanfarhadi as new Prime Minister.

In September 1997 Gen. Dostam was reported to have returned to Mazar-i-Sharif from Turkey, and in the following month the member parties of the UIFSA re-elected him as commander of the forces of the alliance and appointed him as Vice-President of the anti-Taliban administration. However, there were reports of a bitter rivalry between Gen. Dostam and Gen. Malik and skirmishes between their respective forces. Dostam's battle for supremacy with his rival led him to make overtures to Taliban, including offers of exchanges of prisoners of war. Gen. Dostam also accused Gen. Malik of having massacred about 3,000 Taliban prisoners earlier in the year. By late November Gen. Dostam had resumed the leadership of the NIM, ousting Gen. Malik. In late October Taliban unilaterally decided to change the country's name to the Islamic Emirate of Afghanistan and altered the state flag, moves that were condemned by the opposition alliance and all of Afghanistan's neighbours (with the exception of Pakistan). In late 1997 the World Food Programme launched an emergency operation to help people facing starvation in the impoverished central region of Hazarajat (held by the Shi'ite Hizb-i Wahadat-i Islami), which had been blockaded by Taliban since August. In January 1998, however, the UN was forced to suspend its airlifts of emergency supplies when Taliban aircraft bombed the area. Meanwhile, in mid-December 1997 the UN Security Council issued a communiqué expressing its concern at the alleged massacres of civilians and prisoners of war being perpetrated by various factions in Afghanistan. In May 1998 a UN exploratory mission visited the sites of alleged atrocities to assess the feasibility of a full-scale war-crimes investigation being carried out.

In early February 1998 the political crisis in Afghanistan was temporarily overshadowed by a devastating earthquake in the northern province of Takhar, which resulted in the deaths of more than 4,500 people and left about 30,000 homeless. The international relief campaign was hampered both by poor weather conditions and by the continuing fighting. Unused aid supplies proved invaluable in late May when a second severe earthquake struck north-eastern Afghanistan, killing more than 5,000 people.

In late March 1998 the UN ceased operating aid programmes in the southern province of Qandahar (where the headquarters of Taliban were located) following attacks on staff and constant harassment by Taliban. In the same month there were reports of factional fighting between rival members of the UIFSA in and around Mazar-i-Sharif, highlighting the fragile nature of the anti-Taliban alliance. In late April, following the launch of a major diplomatic initiative by the USA, Taliban and the UIFSA held talks, sponsored by the UN and the OIC, in Islamabad, the first formal peace negotiations between the two opposing sides for more than a year. In early May, however, the talks broke down and fighting resumed to the north of Kabul. One of the main reasons cited for the failure of the negotiations was Taliban's refusal to lift the blockade on Hazarajat, where thousands of people were reported to be at risk of imminent starvation.

Relations between the Taliban Government and the UN deteriorated in June 1998, as a result of the former's decision to close more than 100 private schools and numerous small, home-based vocational courses in Kabul, many of which were educating girls. In the following month the living conditions of the 1.2m. inhabitants of the capital were expected to worsen considerably as a result of the expulsion of almost all international aid agencies by Taliban (amongst the most vital areas affected were hospitals and supplies of safe drinking water).

On 1 August 1998 Taliban captured the northern city of Shiberghan, Gen. Dostam's new headquarters, after a number of his Uzbek commanders allegedly accepted bribes from Taliban and switched allegiance. Gen. Dostam was reported to have fled to the Uzbek border and thence to Turkey. Following the recapture of Mazar-i-Sharif by Taliban (which allegedly now included considerable numbers of extremist volunteers from various other Islamic countries, including Pakistan, Saudi Arabia, Algeria and Egypt) in early August 1998, 10 Iranian diplomats and one Iranian journalist who were based in the city were reported to have been captured and killed by Taliban militia. Taliban, however, initially denied any knowledge of the whereabouts of the Iranian nationals. In early September Afghanistan and Iran appeared to be on the verge of open warfare, as 70,000 Iranian troops were deployed on the mutual border. The situation became more serious when it emerged that nine of the missing Iranian nationals were, in fact, murdered by members of Taliban as they stormed Mazar-i-Sharif (it was later reported that 2,000–6,000 Shi'ite Hazara civilians were systematically massacred by the guerrillas after recapturing the city). Both Iran and Afghanistan massed more troops on the border; by mid-September 500,000 Iranian troops had reportedly been placed on full military alert in readiness for conflict with their neighbour. Tension was further heightened in early October as Iran accused Taliban of opening fire on its troops as they continued their military exercises in the border region; Taliban responded with similar counter-accusations. In mid-October, in an attempt to defuse the tension, Taliban agreed to free all Iranian prisoners being held in Afghanistan and to punish those responsible for the killing of the nine Iranian diplomats (or military advisers, according to Taliban). By the end of the year the situation appeared much calmer, with Taliban having expressed regret for the deaths of the Iranian

nationals and Iran having scaled down its border forces and announced that it had no intention of invading Afghanistan.

Meanwhile, on 20 August 1998 the USA launched simultaneous air-strikes against alleged terrorist bases in eastern Afghanistan and Sudan, reportedly operated by an exiled Saudi Arabian militant leader, Osama bin Laden (who was supported by Taliban), in retaliation for the bombing of two US embassies in East Africa earlier that month. Following this action, many aid agencies (including UN agencies) withdrew their remaining expatriate staff from Afghanistan, fearing terrorist acts of vengeance. In September Taliban suffered a considerable set-back when Saudi Arabia (one of only three countries officially to recognize the regime) withdrew its funding and political support and recalled its envoy from Kabul. The decision by the Saudi Government substantially to downgrade its relations with Taliban appeared to have been prompted by its opposition to the reported brutality of the guerrilla authorities and to their sheltering of bin Laden. In the following month Taliban stated that, although it was not willing to extradite the Saudi dissident, in the event of a law suit being filed against him, it would be prepared to place him on trial in Afghanistan. Taliban also insisted that bin Laden (who had reportedly been resident in Afghanistan for at least two years) was under close supervision, with his activities and media access suitably restricted. In late November evidence submitted by the US Government to the Afghan Supreme Court was deemed by the latter as inadequate grounds for bin Laden's arrest.

In mid-September 1998 Taliban captured Bamian, a Shi'ite stronghold and the last major town outside its control; this victory meant that any substantial anti-Taliban opposition was effectively restricted to Masoud's stronghold in the Panjshir Valley to the north of Kabul. Taliban's advances in the north of Afghanistan alarmed Russia and the Central Asian states, which feared the unsettling potential of an extremist Islamic army along their southern borders. In December the UN Security Council threatened Taliban with the imposition of sanctions and called on the regime to commence negotiations with the opposition. Pakistan, on the other hand, demonstrated its diplomatic isolation with regard to the Afghan situation, by defending Taliban and urging the other members of the UN to recognize its government. In December 1998–January 1999, despite threats from local Taliban commanders, the World Food Programme delivered emergency food aid to more than 120,000 people in the beleaguered region of Hazarajat.

In January 1999 it was reported that the UIFSA had established a multi-ethnic Supreme Military Council, under the command of Masoud, the aim of which was to give fresh impetus to the anti-Taliban movement and to co-ordinate manoeuvres against Taliban forces in northern Afghanistan. Despite a certain degree of optimism being raised by the holding of UN-monitored direct peace talks between representatives of Taliban and the UIFSA in Ashgabat, Turkmenistan, in February and mid-March, and in Tashkent, Uzbekistan, in July, ultimately very little was actually achieved as a result of the negotiations. On a more positive note, however, in March the first UN personnel returned to Afghanistan since their evacuation in August 1998 (following the murder of three UN employees); this represented the beginning of a phased return of UN international staff to Afghanistan. In June 1999, however, the International Red Cross temporarily withdrew non-essential foreign staff from Afghanistan, following an attack on a group of the aid organization's employees by suspected Taliban guerrillas; the Red Cross demanded security guarantees for its workers before it resumed operations.

In early July 1999, following reports that bin Laden was being sheltered in eastern Afghanistan, the USA imposed financial and economic sanctions on the Taliban regime in a further attempt to persuade it to hand over the terrorist leader (who the US authorities suspected of planning more atrocities) to stand trial in the USA. In response, Taliban claimed that the sanctions would have very little impact, since the volume of direct trade between Afghanistan and the USA was minimal, and again refused to extradite bin Laden. In the following month 10 people were killed when a large bomb exploded outside the residence of the Taliban leader, Mola Mohammad Omar, in Qandahar. Taliban initially suspected foreign involvement in the attack (which was generally believed to have been an assassination attempt), while other commentators alleged that the incident illustrated growing divisions within Taliban itself and increasing opposition to Omar's perceived autocracy. In late October the Taliban leader announced an extensive reorganization of key civilian, military and diplomatic posts, including changes in the Council of Ministers. Of especial note was the appointment of an English-speaking moderate, Wakil Ahmad Motawakkil, to the post of Minister of Foreign Affairs, in an apparent attempt to improve Taliban's image with the outside world.

Meanwhile, following the collapse of the peace talks in Tashkent in July 1999, Taliban launched a massive offensive against the UIFSA in the Panjshir Valley in early August; tens of thousands of (mainly Tajik) civilians were displaced in the fighting. Masoud rapidly instigated a devastating counter-attack, and Taliban was forced into a high-speed retreat back towards Kabul.

In October 1999 the UN Secretary-General's Special Envoy to Afghanistan, Lakhdar Brahimi, announced his withdrawal from his mission, owing to his frustration and disappointment at the lack of progress (and particularly at the allegedly negative and unco-operative attitude of Taliban) regarding the Afghan crisis. In mid-November the UN Security Council imposed an embargo on all Taliban-controlled overseas assets and a ban on the international flights of the national airline, Ariana Afghan Airlines, as a result of the Afghan regime's continuing refusal to hand over the suspected terrorist leader bin Laden to stand trial in the USA or in a third (possibly Islamic) country. Following the imposition of the sanctions (which, although limited and largely irrelevant in economic terms, were, nonetheless, deeply demoralizing for the already beleaguered Afghan people), there were reports of large-scale demonstrations throughout Afghanistan, and international aid organizations once again came under attack. The impact of the sanctions was expected to be alleviated, however, by the reopening of key trade routes along the Afghan–Iranian border (which had been closed for 18 months) in late November. The Taliban Government expressed its hopes that the trade with Iran would compensate for the significant decrease in imports of wheat and flour from Pakistan caused by the recent imposition of stricter border controls by the new military regime in Pakistan. Following the coup in Pakistan, which took place in October, there were indications that relations between Taliban and the new Pakistani administration, headed by Gen. Pervez Musharraf, might not prove as amicable as they had been since 1996. In his first major address to the Pakistani nation shortly after assuming power, Gen. Musharraf pledged to work for a 'truly representative government' in Afghanistan, and in the following month the State Bank of Pakistan complied with the UN sanctions in ordering a 'freeze' on all Taliban financial assets in Pakistan.

In the latter half of 1999 it was reported that Taliban had moderated its original policy regarding female education by officially sanctioning the opening of about 13 schools for girls (up to the age of 12) in Kabul and its environs; the majority of the new schools were funded by international organizations.

In 1998–99 the Taliban regime, which remained almost completely isolated in diplomatic and political terms world-wide, cultivated relations with the People's Republic of China; a defence co-operation agreement was signed by the two parties and oil and gas contracts in Afghanistan (previously given to Turkmenistan) were awarded to China. China's investment in Afghanistan over this period (including the proposed construction of a new cement factory in Qandahar) was the highest among the country's limited foreign investors.

**Government**

Following the collapse of Najibullah's regime in April 1992, a provisional *mujahidin* Government was established in Kabul. For the first two months, Prof. Sibghatullah Mojaddedi held the post of acting President and headed a 51-member executive body, known as the Islamic Jihad Council, which appointed an interim Council of Ministers in early May. On 28 June Mojaddedi, in line with the proposals set out in the Peshawar Agreement (see History), surrendered the presidency to Prof. Burhanuddin Rabbani, who presided over another executive body, called the Leadership Council. Rabbani was granted power until October, when his tenure of the presidency was extended for a further two months. In December he was elected as President of the country for a two-year term. Following the signing of a peace accord by the majority of *mujahidin* groups in Islamabad in March 1993, an interim multi-faction Government, which was to hold power for 18 months, was established just south of Kabul in June. In January 1996 Rabbani remained in the presidency, despite the official expiry of his tenure of office, and there seemed no prospect of any elections being held in the near future, owing to the continuing civil war.

In September 1996, however, the extremist Islamic militia Taliban seized control of Kabul and Rabbani's Government fled north. On assuming power, Taliban declared Afghanistan a 'complete' Islamic state and appointed an interim Council of Ministers to administer the country (of which they now controlled about two-thirds). Pakistan was the first country officially to recognize the new regime, but by the end of 1999 few other countries or international organizations—including the UN, India, Russia and Iran—had followed suit.

The 31 provinces of Afghanistan are each administered by an appointed governor.

## Defence

Following the installation of a *mujahidin* Government in Kabul in April 1992, it was announced that all the military bodies of the former communist regime, including the army (which was estimated to number 40,000 men in June 1991), the gendarmerie (Sarandoy), the state security service (KHAD), the border guard and all the regional militias, were to be dissolved and combined with the *mujahidin* to form a new national Islamic military force. In mid-1993, as part of the Islamabad Peace Accord of March 1993, a 16-member defence commission was formed with the responsibility of establishing a national army.

According to Russian estimates, Taliban, which captured Kabul in September 1996, commanded an army of about 40,000 men in late 1996. In March 1998 it was reported that Taliban, which controlled about two-thirds of the country, had started preliminary work to establish a national army, involving the dispatch of young men to military centres for training. Defence expenditure in 1998 was estimated at US $250m., compared with an estimated $200m. in 1997.

## Economic Affairs

According to the latest figures published by the US Central Intelligence Agency (CIA) on Afghanistan, the country's gross domestic product (GDP) has fallen substantially over the past 20 years, primarily owing to the loss of labour and capital, the devastation caused to the infrastructure, and the disruption in the trade and transport sectors. It was estimated that in 1997 GDP in terms of purchasing power parity totalled US $19,300m. (equivalent to $800 per head).

Agriculture (including hunting, forestry and fishing), according to UN estimates, contributed 64.4% of GDP in 1993. According to the FAO, 67.7% of the economically active population were employed in the agricultural sector in 1998. Livestock plays an important role in the traditional Afghan economy and is a major source of income for the country's numerous nomadic groups. In 1998 wheat production was estimated at 2.8m. metric tons. The principal commercial products of the sector are fruit and nuts (which accounted for around 39.7% of total export earnings, according to the IMF, in 1990/91), wool and cotton, and processed hides and skins. With the return of a certain degree of normality to most parts of the country in the late 1990s, agricultural production increased. Total cereal output rose by 5% in 1998 to reach an estimated 3.85m. tons, although production was expected to decline to around 3.24m. tons in 1999, owing to a shortage of irrigation water. Afghanistan continues to depend on food imports from abroad or in the form of aid. The total cereal import requirement for the period June 1998–July 1999 was estimated by the FAO at 740,000 tons, of which about 140,000 tons was to be wheat provided by the international aid community.

According to UN estimates, the industrial sector (including mining, manufacturing, construction and power) contributed 20% of GDP in 1993, while the value of industrial output in that year decreased by 11.4%, compared with the previous year.

Mining and quarrying employed about 1.5% of the settled labour force in 1979. Natural gas is the major mineral export (accounting for about 23.6% of total export earnings, according to the IMF, in 1988/89). Salt, hard coal, copper, lapis lazuli, barytes and talc are also mined. In addition, Afghanistan has small reserves of petroleum and iron ore. In November 1998 the Taliban Government announced its intention to resume operating ruby mines in Nangarhar province. Earlier in the year Taliban had claimed that monthly revenue from the allegedly renascent mining sector in Afghanistan totalled US $3.5m. (including revenue from the recently revived steel-smelting plant in Baghlan province).

Manufacturing employed about 10.9% of the settled labour force in 1979. Afghanistan's major manufacturing industries include food products, cotton textiles, chemical fertilizers, cement, leather and plastic goods. In 1999 only one of the four existing cement plants in Afghanistan and about 10% of the textile mills remained in operation (prior to the Soviet invasion in 1979 there were about 220 state-owned factories operating in Afghanistan). The traditional handicraft sector has better survived the devastating effects of war, however, and carpets, leather, embroidery and fur products continued to be produced.

Energy is derived principally from petroleum (which is imported from Iran and republics of the former USSR, notably Turkmenistan) and coal. The Government plans to increase internal sources of energy by establishing hydro- and thermal electric power stations. In early 1996 Afghanistan signed an agreement that could eventually lead to the construction of a high-pressure natural gas pipeline across the country, which would transport gas from Turkmenistan to Pakistan. In October 1997 the US petroleum company Unocal established a consortium which proposed to build a US $2,000m.-pipeline across Afghanistan. In March 1998, however, Unocal announced that the project was to be indefinitely postponed, owing to the continuing civil war; the project looked unlikely ever to be carried out, following Unocal's withdrawal from the consortium in December.

The negative trend in trade was apparent throughout the 1990s. The sharpest declines in both exports and imports occurred in 1992 and 1993. During these two years the total value of exports fell to US $60m. and $62m., respectively, compared with $284m. in 1991. Similarly, the cost of imports decreased from $765m. in 1991 to $237m. in 1992 and $200m. in 1993 and continued to decline thenceforth. In 1996, following Taliban's accession to power, trade showed little sign of revival. In that year total exports were estimated at $80m. and the major export commodities included fruits and nuts, hand-woven carpets, wool, cotton, hides and pelts, and precious and semi-precious gems. The most important export markets were the territories constituting the former USSR, Pakistan, Iran, Germany, the United Kingdom, Belgium, Luxembourg and the Czech Republic. Total imports were estimated at $150m. and consisted mainly of food, petroleum products and other consumer goods. The principal sources of imports were the territories constituting the former USSR, Pakistan, Iran, Japan, Singapore, India, the Republic of Korea and Germany. These official statistics do not, however, include illegal trade and smuggling. The trade deficit would be much lower if the illegal revenue from the export of opium were included. A recent World Bank study estimated that $2,500m. worth of goods are smuggled between Afghanistan and Pakistan each year. In late 1995 it was announced that trade tariffs were to be reduced between the member states of the Economic Co-operation Organization (ECO, see p. 167), which Afghanistan joined in late 1992.

In 1995, according to UN figures, Afghanistan received US $105.5m. in bilateral official development assistance and $109.1m. in multilateral official development assistance. In 1997 the European Union (EU) was the largest single aid donor to Afghanistan.

It is extremely difficult to provide an accurate economic profile of Afghanistan, owing to the continuing civil war, population movements, communication problems and lack of reliable official statistics. Over the past 20 years the traditional economy has been largely replaced by a criminal economy based on drugs and smuggling. The *mujahidin* Government, which came to power in April 1992, was faced with immense economic problems, including serious food and fuel shortages, a collapsed industrial sector, a severely-damaged infrastructure, the difficulties of thousands of refugees returning to their ravaged farms and fields studded with mines, and high inflation (according to one source, inflation reached an estimated 56.7% in 1991). Urgent requests for foreign aid, however, were jeopardized to some extent by the continuing bitter infighting between rival guerrilla and militia groups and by the fact that in 1994 Afghanistan overtook Myanmar in becoming the world's leading producer of opium. According to certain Western sources, the area of land in Afghanistan under poppy cultivation increased by more than 50% in the first half of the 1990s (mainly at the expense of the traditional wheat crop). There appeared little prospect of an improvement in Afghanistan's economic situation following Taliban's seizure of power in Kabul in September 1996, particularly taking into account the subsequent introduction of a decree banning women from working (with the exception of a small number of medical staff). Levels of aid to Afghanistan fell markedly in 1997, partly in response to Taliban's harsh treatment of women and other abuses of human rights. In late 1997 the World Food Programme launched an emergency operation to help people facing starvation in the impoverished central province of Bamian. In late 1998 the UN launched an appeal for humanitarian assistance of US $113m. for Afghanistan.

In 1997, according to UN estimates, about 1m. Afghans were involved in the opium trade and UN field surveys indicated that around 165,000 acres of arable land were under poppy cultivation. Despite its strict opposition to drug abuse, the main source of unofficial revenue for Taliban is undoubtedly the drugs trade. Taliban is reported to be levying a 20% *zakat* (a type of wealth tax) from drugs-dealers on the transport of opium out of the country. In spite of Taliban's promise to ban the crop, new areas have recently been opened up to poppy cultivation, and Afghanistan's output of raw opium increased by 117% in 1999, compared with the previous year, to reach 4,581 metric tons (most of which was exported to Pakistan, Russia and Europe). A UN-sponsored drugs control programme, which is attempting to encourage Afghanistan's estimated 200,000 opium farmers to plant vegetables and cereals rather than poppies, has met with only very limited success.

The Taliban administration's lack of state funds was clearly illustrated by the fact that the budget for 1997/98 (excluding military expenditure) totalled a mere US $100,000. In a highly optimistic attempt to attract foreign investment, Taliban has offered free land to anyone who wants to build a new factory in Afghanistan; not surprisingly, very few serious foreign investors showed any interest in this scheme. In September 1998, however, a US company, Telephone Systems International, agreed a US $415m.-contract with Taliban to provide a telecommunications system in Kabul.

At the end of 1998 UNHCR estimated that about 4m. Afghan refugees had been repatriated since 1988, with around 2.6m. remaining in exile abroad (mainly in Pakistand and Iran). In addition to the refugees living abroad, it was estimated that about 1m. people were internally displaced within Afghanistan itself.

## Social Welfare

Health services available to the people of Afghanistan were scarce even before the outbreak of civil war, but have rapidly deteriorated over the past 20 years. There is an immense shortage of drugs and medical supplies. Qualified health personnel and medicines are provided by the international organizations and NGOs and whatever health facilities exist now are also operated by these bodies. In view of the fact that only 29% of the population has access to health services, it is not surprising that diseases of various sorts are on the increase. The estimated average life expectancy at birth in 1998 stood at only 46 years for males and 45 for females, by far the lowest in Asia. In that year there were 150 deaths of children under 12 months old for every 1,000 live births, the highest infant mortality rate in Asia. In 1987, according to UN figures, there were 2,957 physicians (2 per 10,000 population), 329 dentists and 2,135 nursing personnel in Afghanistan. In 1988 government officials assessed the combined total of medical centres and hospitals at 196. In mid-1996 only four regional hospitals were functioning in Afghanistan.

## Education

The prolonged war has resulted in a large-scale exodus of teachers, and nearly 2,000 school buildings have been destroyed. In 1996/97 it was estimated that only about 600–650 primary and secondary schools were functioning.

Primary education, which is officially compulsory, begins at seven years of age and lasts for six years. Secondary education, beginning at 13 years of age, lasts for a further six years. As a proportion of the school-age population, the total enrolment at primary and secondary schools was equivalent to 36% (males 49%; females 22%) in 1995. Primary enrolment in that year was equivalent to an estimated 49% of children in the relevant age-group (boys 64%; girls 32%), while the enrolment ratio at general secondary schools was equivalent to 22% (boys 32%; girls 11%).

Afghanistan has one of the highest levels of adult illiteracy in Asia, with an average rate (excluding the nomadic population) of 68.5% (males 52.8%; females 85.0%) in 1995, according to estimates by UNESCO.

Since 1979 higher education has been disrupted by the departure of many teaching staff from Afghanistan. In 1980 it was reported that up to 80% of university staff had fled their posts. In 1991 there were six institutions of higher education (including Kabul University, which was founded in 1932) in Afghanistan; a total of 17,000 students were enrolled in these institutions in that year.

Following its seizure of power in late September 1996, Taliban banned education for girls over the age of eight, closed all the women's institutes of higher education and planned to draw up a new Islamic curriculum for boys' schools. In early 1998, however, there were still two co-educational universities functioning in Afghanistan (in areas not under Taliban control), one of which was situated in Bamian (with 300 students and 16 teachers). In mid-1998 the UN was angered by Taliban's decision to close more than 100 private schools and numerous small, home-based vocational courses in Kabul, many of which were educating girls. In 1999, however, Taliban officially sanctioned the establishment of 13 schools for girls (up to the age of 12) in Kabul and its environs. According to Taliban figures, in September of that year 1,586,026 pupils were being educated by 59,792 teachers in 3,836 *madrassas* (mosque schools).

## Public Holidays

According to the Hejri solar calendar, the Afghan year 1378 runs from 21 March 1999 to 20 March 2000, and the year 1379 runs from 21 March 2000 to 20 March 2001.

In March 1998 the Taliban authorities in Kabul ordered the replacement of the Hejri solar calendar with the Hejri lunar calendar.

**2000:** 8 January*† (Id al-Fitr, end of Ramadan), 16 March* (Id al-Adha, Feast of the Sacrifice), 21 March (Nau-roz: New Year's Day, Iranian calendar), 15 April* (Ashura, Martyrdom of Imam Husayn), 18 April (Liberation Day), 27 April (Revolution Day), 1 May (Workers' Day), 15 June* (Roze-Maulud, Birth of Prophet Muhammad), 18 August (Independence Day), 28 November* (first day of Ramadan), 28 December*† (Id al-Fitr, end of Ramadan).

**2001:** 6 March* (Id al-Adha, Feast of the Sacrifice), 21 March (Nau-roz: New Year's Day, Iranian calendar), 4 April* (Ashura, Martyrdom of Imam Husayn), 18 April (Liberation Day), 27 April (Revolution Day), 1 May (Workers' Day), 4 June * (Roze-Maulud, Birth of Prophet Muhammad), 18 August (Independence Day), 17 November* (first day of Ramadan), 17 December* (Id al-Fitr, end of Ramadan).

* These holidays are dependent on the Islamic lunar calendar and may vary by one or two days from the dates given.

† This festival will occur twice (in the Islamic years AH 1420 and 1421) within the same Gregorian year.

## Weights and Measures

The metric system has been officially adopted but traditional weights are still used. One 'seer' equals 16 lb (7.3 kg).

# Statistical Survey

Source (unless otherwise stated): Central Statistics Authority, Block 4, Macroraion, Kabul; tel. (93) 24883.

## Area and Population

### AREA, POPULATION AND DENSITY

| | |
|---|---|
| Area (sq km) | 652,225* |
| Population (census results) | |
| 23 June 1979† | |
| Males | 6,712,377 |
| Females | 6,338,981 |
| Total | 13,051,358 |
| Population (official estimates at mid-year)‡ | |
| 1984 | 17,672,000 |
| 1985 | 18,136,000 |
| 1986 | 18,614,000 |
| Density (per sq km) at mid-1986 | 28.5 |

* 251,773 sq miles.

† Figures exclude nomadic population, estimated to total 2,500,000. The census data also exclude an adjustment for underenumeration, estimated to have been 5% for the urban population and 10% for the rural population.

‡ These data include estimates for nomadic population (2,734,000 in 1983), but take no account of emigration by refugees. Assuming an average net outflow of 703,000 persons per year in 1980–85, the UN Population Division has estimated Afghanistan's total mid-year population (in '000) as: 14,519 in 1985; 14,529 in 1986; 14,709 in 1987 (Source: UN, *World Population Prospects: 1988*). In 1988, according to UNHCR estimates, the total Afghan refugee population numbered 5.5m., of whom 3.15m. were living in Pakistan and 2.35m. in Iran.

**Population** (official estimates, excluding nomads, at mid-year): 15,219,000 in 1987; 15,513,000 in 1988; 15,814,000 in 1989; 16,121,000 in 1990; 16,433,000 in 1991; 16,750,000 in 1992; 17,080,000 in 1993; 17,420,000 in 1994; 19,663,000* in 1995; 20,368,000* in 1996; 20,893,000* in 1997; 18,800,000 in 1998.

* UN estimates, including nomadic population, at mid-year.

### PROVINCES (estimates, March 1982)*

| | Area (sq km) | Population | Density (per sq km) | Capital (with population) |
|---|---|---|---|---|
| Kabul | 4,585 | 1,517,909 | 331.1 | Kabul (1,036,407) |
| Kapesa† | 1,871 | 262,039 | 140.1 | Mahmudraki (1,262) |
| Parwan | 9,399 | 527,987 | 56.2 | Sharikar (25,117) |
| Wardag† | 9,023 | 300,796 | 33.3 | Maidanshar (2,153) |
| Loghar† | 4,652 | 226,234 | 48.6 | Baraiki Barak (1,164)‡ |
| Ghazni | 23,378 | 676,416 | 28.9 | Ghazni (31,985) |
| Paktia | 9,581 | 506,264 | 52.8 | Gardiz (10,040) |
| Nangarhar | 7,616 | 781,619 | 102.6 | Jalalabad (57,824) |
| Laghman | 7,210 | 325,010 | 45.0 | Mehterlam (4,191) |
| Kunar | 10,479 | 261,604 | 25.0 | Asadabad (2,196) |
| Badakhshan | 47,403 | 520,620 | 10.9 | Faizabad (9,564) |
| Takhar | 12,376 | 543,818 | 43.9 | Talukan (20,947) |
| Baghlan | 17,109 | 516,921 | 30.2 | Baghlan (41,240) |
| Kunduz | 7,827 | 582,600 | 74.4 | Kunduz (57,112) |
| Samangan | 15,465 | 273,864 | 17.7 | Aibak (5,191) |
| Balkh | 12,593 | 609,590 | 48.4 | Mazar-i-Sharif (110,367) |
| Jawzjan | 25,553 | 615,877 | 24.1 | Shiberghan (19,969) |
| Fariab | 22,279 | 609,703 | 27.3 | Maymana (40,212) |
| Badghis | 21,858 | 244,346 | 11.2 | Kalainow (5,614) |
| Herat | 61,315 | 808,224 | 13.2 | Herat (150,497) |
| Farah | 47,788 | 245,474 | 5.1 | Farah (19,761) |
| Neemroze | 41,356 | 108,418 | 2.6 | Zarang (6,809) |
| Helmand | 61,829 | 541,508 | 8.8 | Lashkargha (22,707) |
| Qandahar | 47,676 | 597,954 | 12.5 | Qandahar (191,345) |
| Zabul | 17,293 | 187,612 | 10.8 | Qalat (6,251) |
| Uruzgan | 29,295 | 464,556 | 15.5 | Terincot (3,534) |
| Ghor | 38,666 | 353,494 | 9.1 | Cheghcheran (3,126) |
| Bamian | 17,414 | 280,859 | 16.1 | Bamian (7,732) |
| Paktika | 19,336 | 256,470 | 13.3 | Sheran (1,469) |
| **Total** | 652,225 | 13,747,786 | 21.1 | |

* Population figures refer to settled inhabitants only, excluding kuchies (nomads), estimated at 2,600,000 for the whole country.

† Formed in 1981.

‡ The capital of Loghar Province was later changed to Pul-i-Alam.

### PRINCIPAL TOWNS (estimated population at March 1982)

| | | | |
|---|---|---|---|
| Kabul (capital) | 1,036,407 | Kunduz | 57,112 |
| Qandahar | 191,345 | Baghlan | 41,240 |
| Herat | 150,497 | Maymana | 40,212 |
| Mazar-i-Sharif | 110,367 | Pul-i-Khomri | 32,695 |
| Jalalabad | 57,824 | Ghazni | 31,985 |

Estimated population at July 1988: Kabul 1,424,400; Qandahar 225,500; Herat 177,300; Mazar-i-Sharif 130,600 (Source: UN, *Demographic Yearbook 1997*).

### BIRTHS AND DEATHS (UN estimates, annual averages)

| | 1980–85 | 1985–90 | 1990–95 |
|---|---|---|---|
| Birth rate (per 1,000) | 48.9 | 47.1 | 49.7 |
| Death rate (per 1,000) | 23.0 | 22.7 | 21.7 |

**Expectation of life** (UN estimates, years at birth, 1990–95): 43.5 (males 43.0; females 44.0).

Source: UN, *World Population Prospects: The 1998 Revision*.

### ECONOMICALLY ACTIVE POPULATION*
(ISIC Major Divisions, persons aged 8 years and over, 1979 census)

| | Males | Females | Total |
|---|---|---|---|
| Agriculture, hunting, forestry and fishing | 2,358,821 | 10,660 | 2,369,481 |
| Mining and quarrying | 57,492 | 1,847 | 59,339 |
| Manufacturing | 170,908 | 252,465 | 423,373 |
| Electricity, gas and water | 11,078 | 276 | 11,354 |
| Construction | 50,670 | 416 | 51,086 |
| Wholesale and retail trade | 135,242 | 2,618 | 137,860 |
| Transport, storage and communications | 65,376 | 867 | 66,243 |
| Other services | 716,511 | 32,834 | 749,345 |
| **Total** | 3,566,098 | 301,983 | 3,868,081 |

* Figures refer to settled population only and exclude 77,510 persons seeking work for the first time (66,057 males; 11,453 females).

# Agriculture

**PRINCIPAL CROPS** ('000 metric tons)

| | 1996* | 1997 | 1998 |
|---|---|---|---|
| Wheat | 2,650 | 2,711 | 2,834 |
| Rice (paddy) | 350 | 400† | 450 |
| Barley | 220 | 300 | 330 |
| Maize | 280 | 250 | 240 |
| Millet | 22 | 22* | 22* |
| Potatoes | 235 | 235* | 235* |
| Pulses | 35 | 35* | 35* |
| Sesame seed | 24 | 24* | 24* |
| Cottonseed | 44 | 44* | 44* |
| Cotton (lint) | 22 | 22* | 22* |
| Vegetables | 380 | 380* | 380* |
| Watermelons | 90 | 90* | 90* |
| Cantaloupes and other melons | 22 | 22* | 22* |
| Grapes | 330 | 330* | 330* |
| Sugar cane | 38 | 38* | 38* |
| Sugar beets | 1 | 1* | 1* |
| Apples | 18 | 18* | 18* |
| Peaches and nectarines | 14 | 14* | 14* |
| Plums | 35 | 35* | 35* |
| Oranges | 12 | 12* | 12* |
| Apricots | 38 | 38* | 38* |
| Other fruit | 168 | 168* | 168* |

* FAO estimate(s). † Unofficial figure.

Source: FAO, *Production Yearbook*.

**LIVESTOCK** (FAO estimates, '000 head, year ending 30 September)

| | 1996 | 1997 | 1998 |
|---|---|---|---|
| Horses | 300 | 300 | 300 |
| Mules | 23 | 23 | 23 |
| Asses | 1,160 | 1,160 | 1,160 |
| Cattle | 1,500 | 1,500 | 1,500 |
| Camels | 265 | 265 | 265 |
| Sheep | 14,300 | 14,300 | 14,300 |
| Goats | 2,200 | 2,200 | 2,200 |

Poultry (FAO estimates, million): 7 in 1996; 7 in 1997; 7 in 1998.

Source: FAO, *Production Yearbook*.

**LIVESTOCK PRODUCTS** (FAO estimates, '000 metric tons)

| | 1996 | 1997 | 1998 |
|---|---|---|---|
| Beef and veal | 65 | 65 | 65 |
| Mutton and lamb | 117 | 117 | 117 |
| Goat meat | 24 | 24 | 24 |
| Poultry meat | 14 | 14 | 14 |
| Other meat | 11 | 11 | 11 |
| Cows' milk | 300 | 300 | 300 |
| Sheep's milk | 201 | 201 | 201 |
| Goats' milk | 41 | 41 | 41 |
| Cheese | 16 | 16 | 16 |
| Butter and ghee | 11 | 11 | 11 |
| Hen eggs | 18 | 18 | 18 |
| Honey | 3 | 3 | 3 |
| Wool: | | | |
| greasy | 16 | 16 | 16 |
| clean | 9 | 9 | 9 |
| Cattle hides | 11 | 11 | 11 |
| Sheepskins | 18 | 18 | 18 |
| Goatskins | 4 | 4 | 4 |

Source: FAO, *Production Yearbook*.

# Forestry

**ROUNDWOOD REMOVALS**
('000 cu m, excluding bark)

| | 1995 | 1996 | 1997 |
|---|---|---|---|
| Sawlogs, veneer logs and logs for sleepers* | 856 | 856 | 856 |
| Other industrial wood | 811 | 862 | 913 |
| Fuel wood | 5,850 | 6,213 | 6,586 |
| **Total** | 7,517 | 7,931 | 8,355 |

* Assumed to be unchanged from 1976.

Source: FAO, *Yearbook of Forest Products*.

**SAWNWOOD PRODUCTION** (FAO estimates, '000 cu m)

| | 1974 | 1975 | 1976 |
|---|---|---|---|
| Coniferous (softwood) | 360 | 310 | 380 |
| Broadleaved (hardwood) | 50 | 20 | 20 |
| **Total** | 410 | 330 | 400 |

**1977–97:** Annual production as in 1976 (FAO estimates).

Source: FAO, *Yearbook of Forest Products*.

# Fishing

(FAO estimates, '000 metric tons, live weight)

| | 1995 | 1996 | 1997 |
|---|---|---|---|
| Total catch | 1.3 | 1.3 | 1.3 |

Source: FAO, *Yearbook of Fishery Statistics*.

# Mining

('000 metric tons, unless otherwise indicated)

| | 1993 | 1994 | 1995 |
|---|---|---|---|
| Hard coal* | 7† | 6† | 5† |
| Gypsum (crude)‡ | 3 | 3 | 3 |
| Natural gas (petajoules)*† | 7 | 7 | 7 |

**1996** ('000 metric tons): Gypsum (crude) 3†‡.

* Twelve months beginning 21 March of year stated.

† Estimate.

‡ Data from the US Bureau of Mines.

Source: UN, *Industrial Commodity Statistics Yearbook*.

# Industry

### SELECTED PRODUCTS

(year ending 20 March, '000 metric tons, unless otherwise indicated)

| | 1986/87 | 1987/88 | 1988/89 |
|---|---|---|---|
| Margarine | 3.5 | 3.3 | 1.8 |
| Vegetable oil | 4 | n.a. | n.a. |
| Wheat flour* | 187 | 203 | 166 |
| Wine ('000 hectolitres)* | 289 | 304 | 194 |
| Soft drinks ('000 hectolitres) | 8,500 | 10,300 | 4,700 |
| Woven cotton fabrics (million sq metres) | 58.1 | 52.6 | 32.1 |
| Woven woollen fabrics (million sq metres) | 0.4 | 0.3 | 0.3 |
| Footwear—excl. rubber ('000 pairs)* | 613 | 701 | 607 |
| Rubber footwear ('000 pairs)* | 2,200 | 3,200 | 2,200 |
| Nitrogenous fertilizers† | 56 | 57 | 55 |
| Cement | 103 | 104 | 70 |
| Electric energy (million kWh)*‡ | 1,171 | 1,257 | 1,109 |

* Production in calendar years 1986, 1987 and 1988.

† Production in year ending 30 June.

‡ Provisional.

**Wheat flour** ('000 metric tons): 1,832 in 1994; 2,029 in 1995; 2,145 in 1996.
**Nitrogenous fertilizers** (provisional, year ending 30 June, '000 metric tons): 42 in 1992/93; 40 in 1993/94; 49 in 1994/95.
**Cement** (provisional, '000 metric tons): 115 in 1993; 115 in 1994; 115 in 1995.
**Electric energy** (provisional, year ending 20 March, million kWh): 695 in 1993/94; 687 in 1994/95; 625 in 1995/96.

Sources: UN, *Industrial Commodity Statistics Yearbook* and *Statistical Yearbook for Asia and the Pacific*, FAO (Rome) and US Bureau of Mines.

# Finance

### CURRENCY AND EXCHANGE RATES

**Monetary Units**

100 puls (puli) = 2 krans = 1 afghani (Af).

**Sterling, Dollar and Euro Equivalents** (30 September 1999)

£1 sterling = 4,939.5 afghanis;
US $1 = 3,000.0 afghanis;
€1 = 3,199.5 afghanis;
10,000 afghanis = £2.024 = $3.333 = €3.125.

**Exchange Rate**

The foregoing information refers to the official exchange rate. The official rate was maintained at US $1 = 1,000 afghanis between 1 May 1995 and 30 April 1996. From 1 May 1996 a rate of US $1 = 3,000 afghanis has been in operation. However, this rate is applicable to only a limited range of transactions. There is also a market-determined rate, which was US $1 = 28,700 afghanis in March 1998.

### BUDGET (million afghanis, year ending 20 March)

| | 1983/84 | 1984/85 |
|---|---|---|
| Current revenue | 34,744 | 37,615 |
| Taxes | 13,952 | 17,081 |
| Non-taxes | 20,792 | 20,534 |
| Current expenditure | 37,760 | 43,177 |
| Capital expenditure | 5,433 | 8,000 |

Source: UN, *Statistical Yearbook for Asia and the Pacific*.

### BANK OF AFGHANISTAN RESERVES* (US $ million at December)

| | 1989 | 1990 | 1991 |
|---|---|---|---|
| IMF special drawing rights | 10.63 | 9.02 | 6.67 |
| Reserve position in IMF | 6.41 | 6.97 | 7.01 |
| Foreign exchange | 226.65 | 250.41 | 221.22 |
| **Total** | 243.69 | 266.40 | 234.89 |

* Figures exclude gold reserves, totalling 965,000 troy ounces since 1980. Assuming a gold price of 12,850 afghanis per ounce, these reserves were officially valued at US $245.06 million in December of each year 1985–91.

**1992** (US $ million at December): IMF special drawing rights 4.37; Reserve position in IMF 6.78.

**1993** (US $ million at December): IMF special drawing rights 2.76; Reserve position in IMF 6.77.

**1994** (US $ million at December): IMF special drawing rights 1.40; Reserve position in IMF 7.19.

**1995** (US $ million at December): Reserve position in IMF 7.33.

**1996** (US $ million at December): Reserve position in IMF 7.09.

**1997** (US $ million at December): Reserve position in IMF 6.65.

**1998** (US $ million at December): Reserve position in IMF 6.94.

Source: IMF, *International Financial Statistics*.

### MONEY SUPPLY (million afghanis at 21 December)

| | 1989 | 1990 | 1991 |
|---|---|---|---|
| Currency outside banks | 222,720 | 311,929 | 454,750 |
| Private-sector deposits at Bank of Afghanistan | 12,838 | 13,928 | 19,368 |
| Demand deposits at commercial banks | 11,699 | 18,217 | n.a. |

Source: IMF, *International Financial Statistics*.

### COST OF LIVING

(retail price index, excluding rent; base: 1990 = 100)

| | 1989 | 1990 | 1991 |
|---|---|---|---|
| All items | 67.9 | 100.0 | 143.8 |

Source: UN, *Statistical Yearbook for Asia and the Pacific*.

### NATIONAL ACCOUNTS

('000 million afghanis at constant 1978 prices)

**Gross Domestic Product by Economic Activity**

| | 1991 | 1992 | 1993 |
|---|---|---|---|
| Agriculture, hunting, forestry and fishing | 59.9 | 62.7 | 57.3 |
| Mining and quarrying; Manufacturing; Electricity, gas and water | 29.2 | 14.3 | 12.3 |
| Construction | 7.0 | 5.8 | 5.5 |
| Wholesale and retail trade, restaurants and hotels | 11.1 | 10.5 | 10.1 |
| Transport, storage and communications | 4.8 | 4.5 | 2.0 |
| Finance, insurance, real estate and business services | 2.1 | 2.0 | 1.8 |
| **GDP in purchasers' values** | 114.1 | 99.8 | 89.0 |

Source: UN, *Statistical Yearbook for Asia and the Pacific*.

**BALANCE OF PAYMENTS** (US $ million)

| | 1987 | 1988 | 1989 |
|---|---|---|---|
| Exports of goods f.o.b. | 538.7 | 453.8 | 252.3 |
| Imports of goods f.o.b. | −904.5 | −731.8 | −623.5 |
| **Trade balance** | −365.8 | −278.0 | −371.2 |
| Exports of services | 35.6 | 69.6 | 8.2 |
| Imports of services | −156.3 | −120.0 | −103.4 |
| **Balance on goods and services** | −486.5 | −328.4 | −466.4 |
| Other income received | 19.2 | 23.3 | 20.1 |
| Other income paid | −11.3 | −11.5 | −7.9 |
| **Balance on goods, services and income** | −478.6 | −316.6 | −454.2 |
| Current transfers received | 311.7 | 342.8 | 312.1 |
| Current transfers paid | — | — | −1.2 |
| **Current balance** | −166.9 | 26.2 | −143.3 |
| Investment liabilities | −33.9 | −4.1 | −59.6 |
| Net errors and omissions | 211.6 | −47.7 | 182.8 |
| **Overall balance** | 10.8 | −25.6 | −20.1 |

Source: IMF, *International Financial Statistics*.

**OFFICIAL DEVELOPMENT ASSISTANCE** (US $ million)

| | 1993 | 1994 | 1995 |
|---|---|---|---|
| Bilateral | 110.7 | 141.2 | 105.5 |
| Multilateral | 116.6 | 88.8 | 109.1 |
| Total | 227.2 | 230.0 | 214.6 |
| Grants | 222.6 | 230.1 | 214.7 |
| Loans | 4.6 | −0.1 | −0.1 |
| Per caput assistance (US $) | 13.3 | 13.2 | 10.9 |

Source: UN, *Statistical Yearbook for Asia and the Pacific*.

# External Trade

**PRINCIPAL COMMODITIES** (US $ '000, year ending 20 March)

| Imports c.i.f. | 1980/81 | 1981/82 | 1983/84* |
|---|---|---|---|
| Wheat | 798 | 18,100 | 38,251 |
| Sugar | 40,833 | 50,328 | 25,200 |
| Tea | 28,369 | n.a. | 23,855 |
| Cigarettes | 5,114 | 7,219 | 12,755 |
| Vegetable oil | 17,320 | 26,332 | 30,481 |
| Drugs | 4,497 | 4,195 | 3,768 |
| Soaps | 9,991 | 17,256 | 8,039 |
| Tyres and tubes | 16,766 | 12,764 | 28,823 |
| Textile yarn and thread | 16,800 | 24,586 | n.a. |
| Cotton fabrics | 873 | 6,319 | n.a. |
| Rayon fabrics | 6,879 | 9,498 | n.a. |
| Other textile goods | 52,546 | 49,036 | n.a. |
| Vehicles and spare parts | 89,852 | 141,062 | n.a. |
| Petroleum products | 124,000 | 112,093 | n.a. |
| Footwear (new) | 2,058 | 5,275 | 5,317 |
| Bicycles | 2,042 | 488 | 1,952 |
| Matches | 1,171 | 1,542 | 1,793 |
| Sewing machines | 140 | 285 | 266 |
| Electric and non-electric machines | 2,333 | 765 | n.a. |
| Chemical materials | 7,464 | 6,636 | n.a. |
| Agricultural tractors | 1 | 8,280 | n.a. |
| Fertilizers | 8,325 | 3,300 | 3,904 |
| Used clothes | 2,523 | 1,875 | 5,334 |
| Television receivers | 5,391 | 3,241 | 10,139 |
| Other items | 106,662 | 92,307 | n.a. |
| **Total** | 551,748 | 622,416 | 846,022 |

* Figures for 1982/83 are not available.

**Total imports c.i.f.** (US $ million, year ending 20 March): 740 in 1993/94; 142 in 1994/95; 50 in 1995/96. Source: UN, *Statistical Yearbook for Asia and the Pacific.*

| Exports f.o.b. | 1988/89 | 1989/90 | 1990/91 |
|---|---|---|---|
| Fruit and nuts | 103,400 | 110,200 | 93,300 |
| Karakul fur skins | 6,100 | 3,600 | 3,000 |
| Natural gas | 93,200 | n.a. | n.a. |
| Wool | 30,900 | 5,500 | 9,600 |
| Carpets | 39,100 | 38,000 | 44,000 |
| Cotton | 8,000 | 5,300 | 2,500 |
| **Total** (incl. others) | 394,700 | 235,900 | 235,100 |

Source: IMF, *International Financial Statistics*.

**1991/92** (million afghanis, year ending 20 March): Dried fruit and nuts 165,770; Karakul skins 4,303; Wool 19,953; Carpets and rugs 52,887.

**1992/93** (million afghanis, year ending 20 March): Dried fruit and nuts 33,259; Wool 7,585; Carpets and rugs 21,920.

**1995/96** (million afghanis, year ending 20 March): Dried fruit and nuts 19,282; Karakul skins 27; Wool 122; Carpets and rugs 67,083.

**Total exports f.o.b.** (US $ million, year ending 20 March): 180 in 1993/94; 24 in 1994/95; 26 in 1995/96.

Source: UN, *Statistical Yearbook for Asia and the Pacific*.

**PRINCIPAL TRADING PARTNERS** (estimates, US $ million)

| Imports | 1993 | 1994 | 1995 |
|---|---|---|---|
| ASEAN members | 59 | 48 | 50 |
| Singapore | 37 | 20 | 19 |
| Malaysia | 11 | 7 | 15 |
| Thailand | 8 | 19 | 13 |
| SAARC members | 50 | 50 | 41 |
| India | 32 | 16 | 16 |
| Pakistan | 17 | 28 | 22 |
| Bangladesh | — | 5 | 1 |
| Other Asian countries | | | |
| China, People's Republic | 36 | 30 | 35 |
| Hong Kong | 30 | 26 | 12 |
| Japan | 101 | 89 | 92 |
| Turkey | — | 2 | 6 |
| Western Europe | 69 | 67 | 62 |
| Russia | 55 | 17 | 19 |
| USA | 10 | 6 | 4 |
| **Total** (incl. others) | 421 | 345 | 341 |

| Exports | 1993 | 1994 | 1995 |
|---|---|---|---|
| ASEAN members | 3 | 5 | 3 |
| Malaysia | 1 | 1 | 1 |
| Thailand | 1 | 4 | 2 |
| SAARC members | 11 | 12 | 22 |
| India | 2 | 2 | 7 |
| Pakistan | 9 | 10 | 14 |
| Other Asian countries | | | |
| China, People's Republic | 2 | 11 | 15 |
| Japan | 1 | 1 | 1 |
| Western Europe | 37 | 31 | 29 |
| Russia | 618 | 7 | 12 |
| Azerbaijan | 2 | 1 | — |
| Kyrgyzstan | — | — | 62 |
| USA | 3 | 6 | 5 |
| **Total** (incl. others) | 680 | 79 | 153 |

Source: UN, *Statistical Yearbook for Asia and the Pacific*.

## Transport

**ROAD TRAFFIC** (estimates, '000 motor vehicles in use)

| | 1994 | 1995 | 1996 |
|---|---|---|---|
| Passenger cars | 31.0 | 31.0 | 31.0 |
| Commercial vehicles | 25.0 | 25.0 | 25.0 |

Source: International Road Federation, *World Road Statistics*.

**CIVIL AVIATION** ('000)

| | 1993 | 1994 | 1995 |
|---|---|---|---|
| Kilometres flown | 4,000 | 5,000 | 6,000 |
| Passengers carried | 197 | 238 | 250 |
| Passenger-km | 197,000 | 263,000 | 276,000 |
| Freight ton-km | 25,000 | 36,000 | 38,000 |

Source: UN, *Statistical Yearbook*.

## Tourism

| | 1994 | 1995 | 1996 |
|---|---|---|---|
| Tourist arrivals ('000) | 5 | 4 | 4 |
| Tourism receipts (US $ million) | 1 | 1 | 1 |

Source: World Tourism Organization, *Yearbook of Tourism Statistics*.

## Communications Media

| | 1994 | 1995 | 1996 |
|---|---|---|---|
| Radio receivers ('000 in use) | 2,230 | 2,400 | 2,550 |
| Television receivers ('000 in use) | 185 | 200 | 250 |
| Daily newspapers | 15 | 15* | 12 |

* Estimate.

Source: UNESCO, *Statistical Yearbook*.

**Telephones** ('000 main lines in use): 29 in 1995.
Source: UN, *Statistical Yearbook*.

## Education

(1995/96)

| | Institutions | Teachers | Pupils |
|---|---|---|---|
| Pre-primary | 88 | 2,110 | n.a. |
| Primary | 2,146 | 21,869 | 1,312,200 |
| Secondary* | n.a. | 19,085 | 512,900 |
| Higher | n.a. | n.a. | 12,800 |

* Figures refer to general secondary education only, excluding vocational and teacher training.

Source: UN, *Statistical Yearbook for Asia and the Pacific*.

# Directory

## The Constitution

Immediately after the coup of 27 April 1978 (the Saur Revolution), the 1977 Constitution was abolished. Both Nur Muhammad Taraki (Head of State from April 1978 to September 1979) and his successor, Hafizullah Amin (September–December 1979), promised to introduce new constitutions, but these leaders were removed from power before any drafts had been prepared by special commissions which they had appointed. On 21 April 1980 the Revolutionary Council ratified the Basic Principles of the Democratic Republic of Afghanistan. These were superseded by a new Constitution ratified in April 1985. Another new Constitution was ratified during a meeting of a Loya Jirgah (Supreme National Tribal Assembly), held on 29–30 November 1987. This Constitution was amended in May 1990. The following is a summary of the Constitution as it stood in May 1990.

### GENERAL PROVISIONS

The fundamental duty of the State is to defend the independence, national sovereignty and territorial integrity of the Republic of Afghanistan. National sovereignty belongs to the people. The people exercise national sovereignty through the Loya Jirgah and the Meli Shura.

Foreign policy is based on the principle of peaceful co-existence and active and positive non-alignment. Friendship and co-operation are to be strengthened with all countries, particularly neighbouring and Islamic ones. Afghanistan abides by the UN Charter and the Universal Declaration of Human Rights and supports the struggle against colonialism, imperialism, Zionism, racism and fascism. Afghanistan favours disarmament and the prevention of the proliferation of nuclear and chemical weapons. War propaganda is prohibited.

Islam is the religion of Afghanistan and no law shall run counter to the principles of Islam.

Political parties are allowed to be formed, providing that their policies and activities are in accordance with the provisions of the Constitution and the laws of the country. A party that is legally formed cannot be dissolved without legal grounds. Judges and prosecutors cannot be members of a political party during their term of office.

Pashtu and Dari are the official languages.

The capital is Kabul.

The State shall follow the policy of understanding and co-operation between all nationalities, clans and tribes within the country to ensure equality and the rapid development of backward regions.

The family constitutes the basic unit of society. The State shall adopt necessary measures to ensure the health of mothers and children.

The State protects all forms of legal property, including private property. The hereditary right to property shall be guaranteed according to Islamic law.

For the growth of the national economy, the State encourages foreign investment in the Republic of Afghanistan and regulates it in accordance with the law.

### RIGHTS AND DUTIES OF THE PEOPLE

All subjects of Afghanistan are equal before the law. The following rights are guaranteed: the right to life and security, to complain to the appropriate government organs, to participate in the political sphere, to freedom of speech and thought, to hold peaceful demonstrations and strikes, to work, to free education, to protection of health and social welfare, to scientific, technical and cultural activities, to freedom of movement both within Afghanistan and abroad, to observe the religious rites of Islam and of other religions, to security of residence and privacy of communication and correspondence, and to liberty and human dignity.

In criminal cases, an accused person is considered innocent until guilt is recognized by the court. Nobody may be arrested, detained or punished except in accordance with the law.

Every citizen is bound to observe the Constitution and the laws of the Republic of Afghanistan, to pay taxes and duties to the State in accordance with the provisions of the law, and to undertake military service, when and as required.

### LOYA JIRGAH

This is the highest manifestation of the will of the people of Afghanistan. It is composed of: the President and Vice-Presidents, members of the Meli Shura (National Assembly), the General Prosecutor, the Council of Ministers, the Attorney-General, his deputies and members of the Attorney-General's Office, the chairman of the Constitution Council, the heads of the provincial councils, representatives from each province, according to the number of their representatives in the Wolasi Jirgah (House of Representatives), elected by the people by a general secret ballot, and a minimum of 50 people, from among prominent political, scientific, social and religious figures, appointed by the President.

The Loya Jirgah is empowered: to approve and amend the Constitution; to elect the President and to accept the resignation of the President; to consent to the declaration of war and armistice; and to adopt decisions on major questions regarding the destiny of the country. The Loya Jirgah shall be summoned, opened and chaired by the President. Sessions of the Loya Jirgah require a minimum attendance of two-thirds of the members. Decisions shall be adopted by a majority vote. In the event of the dissolution of the Wolasi Jirgah (House of Representatives), its members shall retain their membership of the Loya Jirgah until a new Wolasi Jirgah is elected. Elections to the Loya Jirgah shall be regulated by law and the procedure laid down by the Loya Jirgah itself.

### THE PRESIDENT

The President is the Head of State and shall be elected by a majority vote of the Loya Jirgah for a term of seven years. No person can be elected as President for more than two terms. The President is accountable, and shall report, to the Loya Jirgah. The Loya Jirgah shall be convened to elect a new President 30 days before the end of the term of office of the outgoing President. Any Muslim citizen of the Republic of Afghanistan who is more than 40 years of age can be elected as President.

The President shall exercise the following executive powers: the supreme command of the armed forces; the ratification of the resolutions of the Meli Shura; the appointment of the Prime Minister; the approval of the appointment of ministers, judges and army officials; the granting of citizenship and the commuting of punishment; the power to call a referendum, to proclaim a state of emergency, and to declare war (with the consent of the Loya Jirgah). Should a state of emergency continue for more than three months, the consent of the Loya Jirgah is imperative for its extension.

In the event of the President being unable to perform his duties, the presidential functions and powers shall be entrusted to the first Vice-President. In the event of the death or resignation of the President, the first Vice-President shall ask the Loya Jirgah to elect a new President within one month. In the event of resignation, the President shall submit his resignation directly to the Loya Jirgah.

### MELI SHURA

The Meli Shura (National Assembly) is the highest legislative organ of the Republic of Afghanistan. It consists of two houses: the Wolasi Jirgah (House of Representatives) and the Sena (Senate). Members of the Wolasi Jirgah (representatives) are elected by general secret ballot for a legislative term of five years. Members of the Sena (senators) are elected and appointed in the following manner: two people from each province are elected for a period of five years; two people from each provincial council are elected by the council for a period of three years; and the remaining one-third of senators are appointed by the President for a period of four years.

The Meli Shura is vested with the authority: to approve, amend and repeal laws and legislative decrees, and to present them to the President for his signature; to interpret laws; to ratify and annul international treaties; to approve socio-economic development plans and to endorse the Government's reports on their execution; to approve the state budget and to evaluate the Government's report on its execution; to establish and make changes to administrative units; to establish and abolish ministries; to appoint and remove Vice-Presidents, on the recommendation of the President; and to endorse the establishment of relations with foreign countries and international organizations. The Wolasi Jirgah also has the power to approve a vote of confidence or no confidence in the Council of Ministers or one of its members.

At its first session, the Wolasi Jirgah elects, from among its members, an executive committee, composed of a chairman, two deputy chairmen and two secretaries, for the whole term of the legislature. The Sena elects, from among its members, an executive committee, composed of a chairman for a term of five years, and two deputy chairmen and two secretaries for a term of one year.

Ordinary sessions of the Meli Shura are held twice a year and do not normally last longer than three months. An extraordinary session can be held at the request of the President, the chairman of either house, or one-fifth of the members of each house. The houses of the Meli Shura can hold separate or joint sessions. Sessions require a minimum attendance of two-thirds of the members of each house and decisions shall be adopted by a majority vote. Sessions are open, unless the houses decide to meet in closed sessions.

The following authorities have the right to propose the introduction, amendment or repeal of a law in either house of the Meli Shura: the President, the standing commissions of the Meli Shura, at least one-tenth of the membership of each house, the Council of Ministers, the Supreme Court, and the office of the Attorney-General.

If the decision of one house is rejected by the other, a joint committee, consisting of an equal number of members from both houses, shall be formed. A decision by the joint committee, which will be agreed by a two-thirds majority, will be considered valid after approval by the President. If the joint committee fails to resolve differences, the matter shall be discussed in a joint session of the Meli Shura, and a decision reached by a majority vote. The decisions that are made by the Meli Shura are enforced after being signed by the President.

After consulting the chairman of the Wolasi Jirgah, the chairman of the Sena, the Prime Minister, the Attorney-General and the chairman of the Constitution Council, the President can declare the dissolution of the Wolasi Jirgah, stating his justification for doing so. Re-elections shall be held within 3 months of the dissolution.

### COUNCIL OF MINISTERS

The Council of Ministers is composed of: a Prime Minister, deputy Prime Ministers and Ministers. The Council of Ministers is appointed by the Prime Minister. It is empowered: to formulate and implement domestic and foreign policies; to formulate economic development plans and state budgets; and to ensure public order.

The Council of Ministers is dissolved under the following conditions: the resignation of the Prime Minister, chronic illness of the Prime Minister, the withdrawal of confidence in the Council of Ministers by the Meli Shura, the end of the legislative term, or the dissolution of the Wolasi Jirgah or the Meli Shura.

### THE JUDICIARY

(See section on the Judicial System.)

### THE CONSTITUTION COUNCIL

The responsibilities of this body are: to evaluate and ensure the conformity of laws, legislative decrees and international treaties with the Constitution; and to give legal advice to the President on constitutional matters. The Constitution Council is composed of a chairman, a vice-chairman and eight members, who are appointed by the President.

### LOCAL ADMINISTRATIVE ORGANS

For the purposes of local administration, the Republic of Afghanistan is divided into provinces, districts, cities and wards. These administrative units are led, respectively, by governors, district administrators, mayors and heads of wards. In each province a provincial council and district councils are formed in accordance with the law. Provincial councils and district councils each elect a chairman and a secretary from among their members. The term of office of a provincial council and a district council is three years.

### FINAL PROVISIONS

Amendments to the Constitution shall be made by the Loya Jirgah. Any amendment shall be on the proposal of the President, or on the proposal of one-third and the approval of two-thirds of the members of the Meli Shura. Amendment to the Constitution during a state of emergency is not allowed.

Note: Following the downfall of Najibullah's regime in April 1992, a provisional *mujahidin* Government assumed power in Kabul. In July an acting executive body, known as the Leadership Council, appointed a special commission to draw up a new and more strictly Islamic Constitution. In September 1993 it was reported that a draft Constitution had been approved by the commission, in preparation for the holding of a general election.

In May 1996, following the signing of the Mahipar Agreement between President Burhanuddin Rabbani and Gulbuddin Hekmatyar, a Constitution to cover the interim period pending the holding of a general election was drawn up and published. The main provisions of the **Constitution of the Interim Period** are as follows:

**General provision:** Afghanistan is an Islamic country where all aspects of the life of the people shall be conducted according to the tenets of Shari'a.

**President:** The President is the Head of State and exercises the highest executive power; the President is the supreme commander of the armed forces and his approval is required for the appointment of all civil and military officials; the President is authorized to declare war or peace (on the advice of the Council of Ministers or an Islamic Shura), to approve death sentences or grant pardons, to summon and dismiss a Shura, and to sign international treaties. In the event of the President's death, the presidential functions and powers shall be entrusted to the President of the Supreme Court until a new Head of State can be appointed.

**Council of Ministers:** The Council of Ministers, under the leadership of the Prime Minister, shall discuss and make decisions regarding government policy (both internal and external), the annual budget and administrative regulations, all of which shall be referred to the President for his assent.

According to the Iranian news agency, IRNA, in early October 1996 the Pakistani political party, Jamiat-e-Ulema-e-Islam, had prepared a draft Constitution for Afghanistan at the request of Taliban, which had seized control of the capital in late September.

# The Government

Following the collapse of Najibullah's regime in April 1992, a provisional *mujahidin* Government was established in Kabul. For the first two months, Prof. Sibghatullah Mojaddedi held the post of acting President and headed a 51-member executive body, known as the Islamic Jihad Council, which appointed an interim Council of Ministers in early May. On 28 June Mojaddedi, in accordance with the proposals formulated in the Peshawar Agreement (see History), surrendered the presidency to Prof. Burhanuddin Rabbani, who presided over another executive body, called the Leadership Council. Rabbani held power until the end of October, when his tenure of the presidency was extended for a further two months. On 30 December a special advisory council elected Rabbani, unopposed, as President of the country for a period of a further two years. Following the signing of a peace accord by the majority of *mujahidin* groups in Islamabad in March 1993, an interim multi-faction Government was established, about 25 km south of Kabul, in June. In June 1994 the Supreme Court extended Rabbani's presidency for a further six months. When this six-month period ended in early 1995, Rabbani continued to exercise power.

In late September 1996 Rabbani's Government was ousted from power by Taliban, which captured the capital and installed a strict Islamic regime. An interim Council of Ministers was appointed, but Taliban gave no indication of when elections would be held. The Taliban Government won little international recognition (the UN refused to recognize it) and former President Rabbani continued to be acknowledged by many as the rightful leader of Afghanistan.

### HEAD OF STATE
(January 2000)

**President:** Prof. BURHANUDDIN RABBANI.

**Vice-Presidents:** Gen. ABDUL RASHID DOSTAM, SAYD MANSUR NADIRI.

### INTERIM COUNCIL OF MINISTERS
(January 2000)

**Prime Minister and Minister of Planning:** Hojjat-ol Islam SAYD MOHAMMAD ALI JAWID.

**First Deputy Prime Minister:** Eng. QOTBODDIN HELAL.

**Deputy Prime Minister:** ABDOL MANAN MAKHDUM.

**Minister of Defence:** AHMAD SHAH MASOUD

**Minister of Internal Affairs:** MOHAMMAD MOHAQQEQ.

**Minister of Foreign Affairs:** Dr ABDOLLAH.

**Minister of Security:** Maj.-Gen. FAHIM.

**Minister of Water and Power:** Eng. AL-SAYED AHMAD MUSAVI.

**Minister of Information and Culture:** HEDAYATOLLAH HEDAYAT.

**Minister of Agriculture:** Eng. GARDIZI.

**Minister of Construction Affairs:** Eng. MOHAMMAD IBRAHIM ADIL.

**Minister of Education:** ABDOLWAKIL ABDOLWAHAB.

**Minister of Finance:** Eng. WAHIDOLLAH SABA'UN.

**Minister of Civil Aviation:** Gen. HELALODDIN.

**Minister of Martyrs and the Disabled:** Mawlawi SAMIOLLAH NAJEBI.

**Minister of Commerce:** Hojjat-ol Islam SAYD HOSAYN ALEMI BALKHI.

**Minister of Labour and Social Affairs:** GHULAM HUSAYN SHAHAQ.

**Minister of State for Foreign Affairs:** Dr NAJIBULLAH LAFRA'I.

**Minister without Portfolio and Co-ordinator of International Aid:** ABDOLHAI ILAHI.

**Deputy Minister of Trade:** MUHAMMAD AWAZ FIKRAT.

**Deputy Minister of Higher Education:** Mr MA'SUMYAR.

**Government Adviser:** SAYED ABDULHADI BALKHI.

### TALIBAN INTERIM COUNCIL OF MINISTERS
(January 2000)

**Chairman:** Haji Mola MOHAMMAD RABBANI.

**Deputy Chairmen:** Mawlawi ABDOL KABIR, Alhaj Mola MOHAMMAD HASAN AKHOND.

**Minister of Foreign Affairs:** Mawlawi WAKIL AHMAD MOTAWAKKIL.

**Minister of Finance:** Haji Mola AKHOND.

**Minister of Civil Aviation and Tourism:** Mola AKHTAR MOHAMMAD MANSUR.

**Minister of Telecommunications and of Labour:** Mawlawi AHMADOLLAH MOTEE.

**Minister of Water and Power:** Mawlawi AHMAD JAN.

**Minister of Internal Affairs:** Mola ABDOL RAZZAQ AKHOND.

**Minister of Public Works:** Mola ALAHDAD AKHOND.

**Minister of Justice:** Alhaj Mola NORUDDIN TORABI.

**Minister of Light Industries and Food:** Mawlawi HAMDOLLAH ZAHED.

**Minister of Agriculture and Animal Husbandry:** Mawlawi ABDOL LATIF MANSUR.

**Minister of Pilgrimage and Endowment:** Alhaj Mawlawi MOHAMMAD MOSLEM HAQQANI.

**Minister of Education:** Alhaj Mawlawi ABDUL SALAAM HANIFI.

**Minister of Information and Culture:** Mawlawi QODRATOLLAH JAMAL.

**Minister of Rural Development:** Mawlawi SEDIQOLLAH.

**Minister of Planning:** Qari DIN MOHAMMAD HANIF.

**Minister of Trade:** ABDUL RAZAQ.

**Minister of Martyrs and Refugee Affairs:** Mawlawi ABDOL RAQIB.

**Minister of Mines and Industries:** Mola MOHAMMAD ISA AKHUND.

**Minister of Borders:** Mawlawi JALALODDIN HAQQANI.

**Minister of Logistics:** Mawlawi YAR MOHAMMAD.

**Minister of National Defence:** Alhaj Mola OBAIDOLLAH AKHOND.

**Minister of Security:** Mola MOHAMMAD FAZEL.

**Minister of Public Health:** MOHAMMAD STANAKZAI.

**Minister of Higher Education:** Mawlawi HAMDOLLAH NOMANI.

**Minister for the Promotion of Virtue and the Prevention of Vice:** MOHAMMAD WALI.

**Minister without Portfolio:** Mawlawi GHIASODDIN.

### MINISTRIES

**Office of the Council of Ministers:** Shar Rahi Sedarat, Kabul; tel. (93) 26926.

**Office of the Prime Minister:** Shar Rahi Sedarat, Kabul; tel. (93) 26926.

**Ministry of Agriculture and Land Reform:** Jamal Mina, Kabul; tel. (93) 41151.

**Ministry of Border Affairs:** Shah Mahmud Ghazi Ave, Kabul; tel. (93) 21793.

**Ministry of Civil Aviation and Tourism:** POB 165, Ansari Wat, Kabul; tel. (93) 21015.

**Ministry of Commerce:** Darulaman Wat, Kabul; tel. (93) 41041.

**Ministry of Construction Affairs:** Micro-Rayon, Kabul; tel. (93) 63701.

**Ministry of Defence:** Darulaman Wat, Kabul; tel. (93) 41232.

**Ministry of Education and Training:** Mohd Jan Khan Wat, Kabul; tel. (93) 20666.

**Ministry of Energy:** Micro-Rayon, Kabul; tel. (93) 25109.

**Ministry of Finance:** Shar Rahi Pashtunistan, Kabul; tel. (93) 26041.

**Ministry of Foreign Affairs:** Shah Mahmud Ghazi St, Shar-i-Nau, Kabul; tel. (93) 25441.

**Ministry of Higher and Vocational Education:** Jamal Mina, Kabul; tel. (93) 40041; f. 1978.

**Ministry of Information and Culture:** Mohd Jan Khan Wat, Kabul.

**Ministry of Internal Affairs:** Shar-i-Nau, Kabul; tel. (93) 32441.

**Ministry of Islamic Affairs:** Kabul.

**Ministry of Justice:** Shar Rahi Pashtunistan, Kabul; tel. (93) 23404.

**Ministry of Light Industries and Foodstuffs:** Ansari Wat, Kabul; tel. (93) 41551.

**Ministry of Mines and Industries:** Shar Rahi Pashtunistan, Kabul; tel. (93) 25841.

**Ministry of Planning:** Shar-i-Nau, Kabul; tel. (93) 21273.

**Ministry for the Promotion of Virtue and Prevention of Vice:** Kabul.

**Ministry of Public Health:** Micro-Rayon, Kabul; tel. (93) 40851.

**Ministry of Telecommunications:** Puli Bagh-i-Omomi, Kabul; tel. (93) 21341.

**Ministry of Transport:** Ansari Wat, Kabul; tel. (93) 25541.

**Ministry of Water Resources Development and Irrigation:** Darulaman Wat, Kabul; tel. (93) 40743.

# Legislature

### MELI SHURA*
(National Assembly)

The Meli Shura, which was established in 1987 and replaced the Revolutionary Council, was composed of two houses: the Wolasi

Jirgah (House of Representatives) and the Sena (Senate). Elections were held to both houses in April 1988.

### Wolasi Jirgah

Representatives were elected for five years. Of the total 234 seats, 184 were contested in the general election in April 1988. The remaining 50 seats were reserved for members of the opposition.

### Sena

The Sena comprised 192 members. One-third of its members were elected for five years, one-third were elected for three years, and one-third were appointed for three years. At the general election in 1988, 115 senators were elected, while the majority of the remaining 77 seats were filled by senators appointed by the President. A small number of seats were reserved for members of the opposition.

* Following the downfall of Najibullah's regime in April 1992, an interim *mujahidin* Government took power in Kabul and both houses of the Meli Shura were dissolved. A High State Council (HSC) was formed, which was to meet regularly, under the chairmanship of the President, to discuss and make decisions regarding matters of national importance.

## Political Organizations

The following were the principal *mujahidin* and militia groups operating in 1999:

The seven below were formerly members of a grand alliance, formed in 1985 and called the Ittehad-i-Islami Afghan Mujahidin (Islamic Union of Afghan Mujahidin—IUAM), based in Peshawar, Pakistan:

Three moderate/traditionalist groups:

**Harakat-i-Inqilab-i-Islami** (Islamic Revolutionary Movement): Pashtun; supports Taliban; Leader Mawlawi MOHAMMAD NABI MOHAMMADI; c. 25,000 supporters (estimate). In late 1999 there were reports that the Harakat-i-Inqilab-i-Islami had been dissolved and that its former leader had joined Taliban.

**Jebha-i-Nejat-i-Melli** (National Liberation Front): Pashtun; Leader Prof. Hazrat SIBGHATULLAH MOJADDEDI; Sec.-Gen. ZABIHOLLAH MOJADDEDI; c. 15,000 supporters (estimate).

**Mahaz-i-Melli-i-Islami** (National Islamic Front): Pashtun; Leader Pir SAYED AHMAD GAILANI; Dep. Leader HAMED GAILANI; c. 15,000 supporters (estimate).

Four Islamic fundamentalist groups:

**Hizb-i Islami Gulbuddin** (Islamic Party Gulbuddin): Pashtun/Turkmen/Tajik; Leader GULBUDDIN HEKMATYAR; c. 50,000 supporters (estimate); based in Iran in 1998–99.

**Hizb-i Islami Khalis** (Islamic Party Khalis): Pashtun; Leader Maulvi MUHAMMAD YUNUS KHALIS; c. 40,000 supporters (estimate).

**Ittehad-i-Islami** (Islamic Union): Pashtun; Leader Prof. ABD AR-RASUL SAYEF; Dep. Leader AHMAD SHAH AHMADZAY; c. 18,000 supporters (estimate).

**Jamiat-i Islami** (Islamic Society): internet www.jamiat.com; Turkmen/Uzbek/Tajik; Leaders Prof. BURHANUDDIN RABBANI, Gen. AHMAD SHAH MASOUD; Sec.-Gen. ENAYATOLLAH SHADAB; c. 60,000 supporters (estimate).

In June 1987 eight Afghan Islamic (Shi'ite) factions (based in Teheran, Iran) formed the **Hizb-i Wahadat-i Islami** (Islamic Unity Party; Hazara; Chair. of Supreme Council ALEMI BALKHI; Sec.-Gen. ABDOL KARIM KHALILI), comprising: the **Afghan Nasr Organization** (Hazara; c. 50,000 supporters), the **Guardians of Islamic Jihad of Afghanistan,** the **United Islamic Front of Afghanistan,** the **Islamic Force of Afghanistan,** the **Dawa Party of Islamic Unity of Afghanistan,** the **Harakat-e Eslami Afghanistan** (the Islamic Movement of Afghanistan; Pashtun/Tajik/Uzbek; Leader: Ayatollah MOHAMMAD ASEF MOHSENI; Chair. of Central Council Hojjat-ol Islam SAYD MOHAMMAD ALI JAWID; c. 20,000 supporters), the **Hezbollah** (c. 4,000 supporters), and the **Islamic Struggle for Afghanistan.**

**National Islamic Movement** (Jonbesh-e Melli-e Eslami): f. 1992; formed mainly from troops of former Northern Command of the Afghan army; predominantly Uzbek/Tajik/Turkmen/Ismaili and Hazara Shi'ite; Leader Gen. ABDUL RASHID DOSTAM; 65,000–150,000 supporters.

**Taliban:** headquarters in Qandahar; emerged in 1994; Islamic fundamentalist; mainly Sunni Pashtuns; Leader Mola MOHAMMAD OMAR; Dep. Leader Mola WAKIL AHMAD; c. 40,000 armed supporters.

## Diplomatic Representation

By the end of 1992 many of the embassies listed below had been temporarily closed down and the diplomatic staff had left Kabul, owing to the continuing unrest in the capital.

### EMBASSIES IN AFGHANISTAN

**Austria:** POB 24, Zarghouna Wat, Kabul; tel. (93) 32720; Ambassador: (vacant).

**Bangladesh:** Kabul; tel. (93) 25783; Chargé d'affaires a.i.: MAHMOOD HASAN.

**Bulgaria:** Wazir Akbar Khan Mena, Kabul; tel. (93) 20683; Ambassador: VALENTIN PETKOV GATSINSKI.

**China, People's Republic:** Shah Mahmud Wat, Shar-i-Nau, Kabul; tel. (93) 20446; Chargé d'affaires a.i.: ZHANG DELIANG.

**Cuba:** Shar Rahi Haji Yaqub, opp. Shar-i-Nau Park, Kabul; tel. (93) 30863; Ambassador: REGINO FARINAS CANTERO.

**Czech Republic:** Taimani Wat, Kala-i-Fatullah, Kabul; tel. (93) 32082.

**France:** POB 62, Shar-i-Nau, Kabul; tel. (93) 23631; Ambassador-at-large: JEAN SAINT-BACAL.

**Germany:** Wazir Akbar Khan Mena, POB 83, Kabul; tel. (93) 22432; Ambassador: (vacant).

**Hungary:** POB 830, Sin 306–308, Wazir Akbar Khan Mena, Kabul; tel. (93) 24281; Ambassador: MIHÁLY GOLUB.

**India:** Malalai Wat, Shar-i-Nau, Kabul; tel. (93) 30556; Chargé d'affaires a.i.: A. S. TOOR.

**Indonesia:** POB 532, Wazir Akbar Khan Mena, District 10, Zone 14, Road Mark Jeem House 93, Kabul; tel. (93) 20586; Ambassador: HAVID ABDUL GHANI.

**Iran:** Shar-i-Nau, Kabul; tel. (93) 26255; Ambassador: GHOLAMREZA HADDADI. (Closed down by Taliban administration in June 1997.)

**Iraq:** POB 523, Wazir Akbar Khan Mena, Kabul; tel. (93) 24797; Ambassador: BURHAN KHALIL GHAZAL.

**Italy:** POB 606, Khoja Abdullah Ansari Wat, Kabul; tel. (93) 24624; Chargé d'affaires a.i.: Mr CALAMAI.

**Japan:** POB 80, Wazir Akbar Khan Mena, Kabul; tel. (93) 26844; Chargé d'affaires a.i.: KEIKI HIRAGA.

**Korea, Democratic People's Republic:** Wazir Akbar Khan Mena, House 28, Sarak 'H' House 103, Kabul; tel. (93) 22161; Ambassador: OH IN YONG.

**Libya:** 103 Wazir Akbar Khan Mena, Kabul; tel. (93) 25947; Ambassador: ALI AL-BARUQ AL-SHARIFI.

**Mongolia:** Wazir Akbar Khan Mena, Sarak 'T' House 8714, Kabul; tel. (93) 22138; Ambassador: (vacant).

**Pakistan:** Kabul; Ambassador: AZIZ AHMAD KHAN.

**Poland:** Gozargah St, POB 78, Kabul; tel. (93) 42461; Chargé d'affaires: Prof. ANDRZEJ WAWRZYNIAK.

**Russia:** Darulaman Wat, Kabul; tel. (93) 41541; Ambassador: BORIS NIKOLAYEVICH PASTUKHOV.

**Saudi Arabia:** Kabul; Chargé d'affaires: (vacant).

**Slovakia:** Taimani Wat, Kala-i-Fatullah, Kabul; tel. (93) 32082.

**Sudan:** Kabul.

**Turkey:** Shar-i-Nau, Kabul; tel. (93) 20072; Chargé d'affaires a.i.: SALEH AHSAN.

**United Kingdom:** Karte Parwan, Kabul; tel. (93) 30512; Ambassador: (vacant).

**USA:** Wazir Akbar Khan Mena, Kabul; tel. (93) 62230; Chargé d'affaires a.i.: JON D. GLASSMANN (embassy closed January 1989).

**Viet Nam:** 3 Nijat St, Wazir Akbar Khan Mena, Kabul; tel. (93) 26596; Ambassador: NGUYEN NGOC SINH.

**Yugoslavia:** POB 53, 923 Main Rd, Wazir Akbar Khan Mena, Kabul; tel. (93) 61671; Chargé d'affaires a.i.: VELIBOR DULOVIĆ.

## Judicial System

The functions and structure of the judiciary are established in Articles 107–121 of the Constitution ratified by the Loya Jirgah in November 1987 and amended in May 1990.

The courts apply the provisions of the Constitution and the laws of Afghanistan, and, in cases of ambivalence, will judge in accordance with the rules of Shari'a (Islamic religious law). Trials are held in open session except when circumstances defined by law deem the trial to be held in closed session. Trials are conducted in Pashtu and Dari or in the language of the majority of the inhabitants of the locality. The right to speak in court in one's mother tongue is guaranteed to the two sides of the lawsuit.

The judiciary comprises the Supreme Court and those courts which are formed in accordance with the directives of the law. The State may establish specialized courts within the unified system of the judiciary.

The highest judicial organ is the Supreme Court, which consists of a President, Vice-President and judges, all of whom are appointed by the Head of State in accordance with the law. It supervises the judicial activities of the courts and ensures the uniformity of law enforcement and interpretation by those courts.

Death sentences are carried out after ratification by the Head of State.

**President of the Supreme Court:** MOHAMMAD SHAH FAZLI.

The public prosecutor's office consists of the Attorney-General's office and those other attorneys' offices which are formed in accordance with the directives of the law. The Attorney-General supervises the activities of all the attorney offices, which are independent of local organs and answerable only to the Attorney-General himself. The Attorney-General and his deputies, who are appointed by the Head of State in accordance with the law, supervise the implementation and observance of all laws.

**Attorney-General:** SAYED ABDORRAZAQ MOSAMEM (acting).

**Deputy Attorney-General:** ABDUL HADY KHALILZIA.

Following the collapse of Najibullah's regime and the installation of a *mujahidin* Government in Kabul in April 1992, a judicial system fully based on the rules of Shari'a was expected to be incorporated in the *mujahidin's* new Constitution. In an apparent attempt to improve security in Kabul, special courts were established by the *mujahidin* administration to prosecute 'people who violate homes, honour, children and property'.

Following its seizure of power in the capital in September 1996, Taliban imposed a strict Islamic code of conduct on Kabul, including the introduction of stonings, lashings, amputations and the death penalty as punishment for various crimes.

**Taliban Prosecutor-General and President of the Supreme Court:** Alhaj Mawlawi NUR MOHAMMAD SAQEB.

**Taliban Vice-Presidents of the Supreme Court:** Mawlawi SULAYMAN, Mawlawi ABDOL SATAR SEDIQI, Mawlawi RAFIOLLAH MO'AZEN, Mawlawi SHAHABODDIN DELAWAR.

# Religion

The official religion of Afghanistan is Islam. Muslims comprise 99% of the population, approximately 84% of them of the Sunni and the remainder of the Shi'ite sect. There are small minority groups of Hindus, Sikhs and Jews.

### ISLAM

**The High Council of Ulema and Clergy of Afghanistan:** Kabul; f. 1980; 7,000 mems; Chair. Mawlawi ABDOL GHAFUR SENANI.

# The Press

Some of the following newspapers and periodicals have not always appeared on a regular basis or, in a number of cases, may have ceased publication.

### PRINCIPAL DAILIES

**Anis:** (Friendship): Kabul; f. 1927; revived by Taliban in 1998; evening; independent; Dari, Uzbek and Pashtu; state-owned; news and literary articles; Chief Editor MOHAMMAD S. KHARNIKASH; circ. 25,000.

**Badakhshan:** Faizabad; f. 1945; Dari and Pashtu; Chief Editor HADI ROSTAQI; circ. 3,000.

**Dariz:** Kabul.

**Ettehadi-Baghlan:** Baghlan; f. 1930; Dari and Pashtu; Chief Editor SHAFIQULLAH MOSHFEQ; circ. 1,200.

**Hewad** (Homeland): Kabul; tel. (93) 26851; f. 1959; revived by Taliban in 1998; Pashtu; state-owned; Editor-in-Chief AMIR AFGHANPUR; circ. 12,200.

**Jawzjan:** Jawzjan; f. 1942; Dari and Pashtu; Chief Editor A. RAHEM HAMRO; circ. 1,500.

**Kabul New Times:** POB 983, Ansari Wat, Kabul; tel. (93) 61847; f. 1962 as Kabul Times, renamed 1980; English; state-owned; Editor-in-Chief M. SEDDIQ RAHPOE; circ. 5,000.

**Nangarhar:** Jalalabad; f. 1919; revived by Taliban in 1998; Pashtu; state-owned; Chief Editor MORAD SANGARMAL; circ. 1,500.

**Sanae:** Parwan; f. 1953; Dari and Pashtu; Chief Editor G. SAKHI ESHANZADA; circ. 1,700.

**Seistan:** Farah; f. 1947; Dari and Pashtu; Editor-in-Chief M. ANWAR MAHAL; circ. 1,800.

**Shahadat:** organ of the Hizb-i Islami Gulbuddin.

**Times:** Kabul; English; state-owned.

**Tulu-i-Afghan:** Qandahar; f. 1924; Pashtu; Chief Editor TAHER SHAFEQ; circ. 1,500.

**Wolanga:** Paktia; f. 1943; Pashtu; Chief Editor M. ANWAR; circ. 1,500.

### PERIODICALS

**Afghanistan:** Historical Society of Afghanistan, Kabul; tel. (93) 30370; f. 1948; quarterly; English and French; historical and cultural; Editor MALIHA ZAFAR.

**Afghanistan Today:** Block 106, Ansari Wat, Kabul; tel. (93) 61868; f. 1985; every 2 months; state-owned; socio-political, economics and cultural; CEO KARIM HOQOUQ; circ. 10,500.

**Ahbar:** Baihaki Book Publishing and Import Institute, Kabul; illustrated monthly; Dari and Pashtu; publ. by Rossiiskoye Informatsionnoye Agentstvo-Vesti.

**Akhbar-e-Hafta:** Kabul; f. 1989; weekly; Editor ZAHER TANIN.

**Aryana:** ISA Academy of Sciences, Kabul; tel. (93) 25106; f. 1943; quarterly; Pashtu and Dari; culture, history, ethnography, socio-economics; Editor SAYED AMIN MUJAHED.

**Awaz:** Kabul; f. 1940; monthly; Pashtu and Dari; radio and television programmes; Editor NASIR TOHORI; circ. 20,000.

**Bedar:** Mazar-i-Sharif; f. 1920; weekly; Dari and Pashtu; Chief Editor ROZEQ FANI; circ, 2,500.

**Erfan:** Ministry of Education and Training, Mohd Jan Khan Wat, Kabul; tel. (93) 21612; f. 1923; every two months; Dari and Pashtu; education, psychology, mathematics, religion, literature and technology; Chief Editor MOHAMMAD QASEM HILAMAN; circ. 7,500.

**Ershad-e-Islam** (Islamic Precepts): Kabul; f. 1987; publ. by the Ministry of Islamic Affairs; Editor MUHAMMAD SALEM KHARES.

**Gharjestan:** Kabul; f. 1988; every two months; political and cultural; for the people of Hazara.

**Gorash:** Ministry of Information and Culture, Mohd Jan Khan Wat, Kabul; f. 1979; weekly; Turkmen; Chief Editor S. MISEDIQ AMINI; circ, 1,000.

**Haqiqat-e-Sarbaz:** Ministry of Defence, Kabul; f. 1980; 3 a week; Dari and Pashtu; Chief Editor MER JAMALUDDIN FAKHR; circ. 18,370.

**Helmand:** Bost; f. 1954; 2 a week; Pashtu; Editor-in-Chief M. OMER FARHAT BALEGH; circ. 1,700.

**Herat:** Ministry of Information and Culture, Mohd Jan Khan Wat, Kabul; f. 1923; monthly; Dari and Pashtu; Chief Editor JALIL SHABGER FOLADYON.

**Ittifak Islam:** Herat; f. 1921; weekly; Dari and Pashtu; organ of Taliban; Chief Editor ABDULLAH HERAWEE.

**Kabul:** Afghanistan Academy of Sciences, Research Centre for Languages and Literature, Akbar Khan Mena, Kabul; f. 1931; monthly; Pashtu; literature and language research; Editor N. M. SAHEEM.

**Kar:** POB 756, Kabul; tel. (93) 25629; monthly; publ. by the Central Council of the National Union of Afghanistan Employees; Editor-in-Chief AZIZ AHMAD NASIR; circ. 2,500.

**Kunar Periodical Journal:** Asadabad; f. 1987; Pashtu; news and socio-economic issues; circ. 5,000.

**Meli Jabha:** Kabul; weekly.

**Mojahed:** Kabul; weekly; organ of the Jamiat-i Islami.

**Mojala-e-Ariana** (Light): Kabul; f. 1978; monthly; Dari and Pashtu; Editor-in-Chief RASHID ASHTI; circ. 1,000.

**Muhasel-e-Emroz** (Today's Student): Kabul; f. 1986; monthly; state-owned; juvenile; circ. 5,000.

**Nengarhar:** Kabul; f. 1919; weekly; Pashtu; Editor-in-Chief KARIM HASHIMI; circ. 1,500.

**Palwasha:** Kabul; f. 1988; fortnightly; Editor-in-Chief SHAH ZAMAN BREED.

**Pamir:** Micro-Rayon, Kabul; tel. (93) 20585; f. 1952; fortnightly; Dari and Pashtu; combined organ of the Kabul Cttee and Municipality; Chief Editor ENAYET POZHOHAN GURDANI; circ. 30,000.

**Payam-e-Haq:** Kabul; f. 1953; monthly; Dari and Pashtu; Editor-in-Chief FARAH SHAH MOHIBI; circ. 1,000.

**Payam-e-Mojahed:** Panjshir; weekly; organ of UIFSA.

**Samangon:** Aibak; f. 1978; weekly; Dari; Editor-in-Chief M. MOHSEN HASSAN; circ. 1,500.

**Sawad** (Literacy): Kabul; f. 1954; monthly; Dari and Pashtu; Editor-in-Chief MALEM GOL ZADRON; circ. 1,000.

**Seramiasht:** POB 3066, Afghan Red Crescent Society, Puli Artal, Kabul; tel. (93) 30969; f. 1958; quarterly; Dari, Pashtu and English; Editor-in-Chief SAYED ASSADULLAH STOMAN; circ. 1,000.

**Shari'at:** Kabul; weekly; Pashtu; central organ of Taliban.

**Sob:** Kabul; tel. (93) 25240; f. 1979; weekly; Balochi; Editor-in-Chief WALIMUHAMMAD ROKHSHONI; circ. 1,000.

**Talim wa Tarbia** (Education): Kabul; f. 1954; monthly; publ. by Institute of Education.

**Urdu** (Military): Kabul; f. 1922; quarterly; Dari and Pashtu; military journal; issued by the Ministry of Defence; Chief Editor KHALILULAH AKBARI; circ. 500.

**Yulduz** (Star): Ministry of Information and Culture, Mohd Jan Khan Wat, Kabul; f. 1979; weekly; Uzbek and Turkmen; Chief Editor EKHAN BAYONI; circ. 2,000.

**Zeray:** Afghanistan Academy of Sciences, Research Centre for Languages and Literature, Akbar Khan Mena, Kabul; f. 1938; weekly; Pashtu; Pashtu folklore, literature and language; Editor MUHAMMAD NASSER; circ. 1,000.

**Zhwandoon** (Life): Kabul; tel. (93) 26849; f. 1944; weekly; Pashtu and Dari; illustrated; Editor ROHELA ROSEKH KHORAMI; circ. 1,400.

### NEWS AGENCIES

**Afghan Islamic Press:** Peshawar, North-West Frontier Province, Pakistan.

**Bakhtar Information Agency (BIA):** Ministry of Information and Culture, Mohd Jan Khan Wat, Kabul; tel. (93) 24089; f. 1939; Man. Dir Mawlawi MOHAMMAD YAQUB QANI.

#### Foreign Bureaux

**Česká tisková kancelář (ČTK)** (Czech Republic): POB 673, Kabul; tel. (93) 23419.

The following foreign agencies are also represented in Kabul: Rossiiskoye Informatsionnoye Agentstvo—Novosti (RIA—Novosti) (Russia) and Tanjug (Yugoslavia).

### PRESS ASSOCIATIONS

**Journalists' Association:** Kabul; f. 1991; Chair. AMIR AFGHANPUR; Dep. Chair. HABIB SHAMS, LT FARUQ.

**Union of Journalists of Afghanistan:** Wazir Akbar Khan Mena, St 13, Kabul; f. 1980; Pres. MOHAMMAD YUSUF AYINA.

## Publishers

**Afghan Book:** POB 206, Kabul; f. 1969; books on various subjects, translations of foreign works on Afghanistan, books in English on Afghanistan and Dari language textbooks for foreigners; Man. Dir JAMILA AHANG.

**Afghanistan Today Publishers:** POB 983, c/o The Kabul New Times, Ansari Wat, Kabul; tel. (93) 61847; publicity materials; answers enquiries about Afghanistan.

**Balhaqi Book Publishing and Importing Institute:** POB 2025, Kabul; tel. (93) 26818; f. 1971 by co-operation of the Government Printing House, Bakhtar News Agency and leading newspapers; publishers and importers of books; Pres. MUHAMMAD ANWAR NUMYALAI.

**Book Publishing Institute:** Herat; f. 1970 by co-operation of Government Printing House and citizens of Herat; books on literature, history and religion.

**Book Publishing Institute:** Qandahar; f. 1970; supervised by Government Printing House; mainly books in Pashtu language.

**Educational Publications:** Ministry of Education and Training, Mohd Jan Khan Wat, Kabul; tel. (93) 21716; textbooks for primary and secondary schools in the Pashtu and Dari languages; also three monthly magazines in Pashtu and in Dari.

**Franklin Book Programs Inc:** POB 332, Kabul.

**Historical Society of Afghanistan:** Kabul; tel. (93) 30370; f. 1931; mainly historical and cultural works and two quarterly magazines: *Afghanistan* (English and French), *Aryana* (Dari and Pashtu); Pres. AHMAD ALI MOTAMEDI.

**Institute of Geography:** Kabul University, Kabul; geographical and related works.

**International Center for Pashtu Studies:** Kabul; f. 1975 by the Afghan Govt with the assistance of UNESCO; research work on the Pashtu language and literature and on the history and culture of the Pashtu people; Pres. and Assoc. Chief Researcher J. K. HEKMATY; publs *Pashtu* (quarterly).

**Kabul University Press:** Kabul; tel. (93) 42433; f. 1950; textbooks; two quarterly scientific journals in Dari and in English, etc.

**Research Center for Linguistics and Literary Studies:** Afghanistan Academy of Sciences, Akbar Khan Mena, Kabul; tel. (93) 26912; f. 1978; research on Afghan languages (incl. Pashtu, Dari, Balochi and Uzbek) and Afghan folklore; Pres. Prof. MOHAMMED R. ELHAM; publs *Kabul* (Pashtu), *Zeray* (Pashtu weekly) and *Khurasan* (Dari).

#### Government Publishing House

**Government Printing House:** Kabul; tel. (93) 26851; f. 1870 under supervision of the Ministry of Information and Culture; four daily newspapers in Kabul, one in English; weekly, fortnightly and monthly magazines, one of them in English; books on Afghan history and literature, as well as textbooks for the Ministry of Education; 13 daily newspapers in 13 provincial centres and one journal and also magazines in three provincial centres; Dir MUHAMMAD AYAN AYAN.

## Broadcasting and Communications

Following its capture of Kabul in September 1996, Taliban banned television and closed down the station. Radio Afghanistan was renamed Radio Voice of Shari'a; this Kabul-based station also operates Balkh Radio in Mazar-i-Sharif and Takhar Radio in Talukan.

**Radio Voice of Shari'a:** POB 544, Ansari Wat, Kabul; tel. (93) 20355; under the supervision of the Ministry of Information and Culture; home service in Dari and Pashtu (10 hours daily); home service in Uzbek, Turkmen, Nurestani and Pashai (50 minutes daily); foreign service in Urdu and English (30 minutes daily); Gen. Pres. Ustad Mawlawi MOHAMMED ESAQ NIZAMI; Gen. Dir of Planning and Foreign Relations Eng. ABDUL RAHMAN NASERI.

**Badakhshan TV:** Faizabad; operated by anti-Taliban UIFSA; broadcasts three hrs daily; Dir MOHAMMAD DIN.

## Finance

(cap. = capital; auth. = authorized; p.u. = paid up; res = reserves; m. = million; brs = branches; amounts in afghanis unless otherwise stated)

### BANKING

In June 1975 all banks were nationalized. There are no foreign banks operating in Afghanistan.

**Da Afghanistan Bank** (Central Bank of Afghanistan): Ibne Sina Wat, Kabul; tel. (93) 24075; f. 1939; main functions: banknote issue, foreign exchange regulation, credit extensions to banks and leading enterprises and companies, govt and private depository, govt fiscal agency; cap. 4,000m., res 5,299m., dep. 15,008m. (1985); Pres. Mawlawi ABDORRAHMAN ZAHED; Vice-Pres. Mawlawi ABDORRAB; 65 brs.

**Agricultural Development Bank of Afghanistan:** POB 414, Cineme Pamir Bldg, Jade Maiwand, Kabul; tel. (93) 24459; f. 1959; makes available credits for farmers, co-operatives and agro-business; aid provided by IBRD and UNDP; cap. 666.8m., res 498.7m., total resources 3,188.3m. (March 1987); Chair. Dr M. KABIAR; Pres. Dr ABDULLAH NAQSHBANDI.

**Banke Milli Afghan** (Afghan National Bank): Jana Ibn Sina, Kabul; tel. (93) 25451; f. 1932; cap. p.u. 1,000m., res 100.7m., total resources 6,954.8m. (1986); Chair. ABDUL WAHAB ASSEFI; Pres. ELHAMUDDIN QIAM; 16 brs.

**Export Promotion Bank of Afghanistan:** 24 Mohd Jan Khan Wat, Kabul; tel. (93) 24447; f. 1976; provides financing for exports and export-orientated investments; total assets 12,904.1m. (March 1988); Pres. MOHAMMAD YAQUB NEDA; Vice-Pres. BURHANUDDIN SHAHIM.

**Industrial Development Bank of Afghanistan:** POB 14, Shar-i-Nau, Kabul; tel. (93) 33336; f. 1973; provides financing for industrial development; cap. 10,500m. (1996); Pres. Haji RAHMATULLAH.

**Mortgage and Construction Bank:** Bldg No. 2, First Part Jade Maiwand, Kabul; tel. (93) 23341; f. 1955 to provide short- and long-term building loans; auth. cap. 200m.; cap. p.u. 100m. (1987); Pres. FAIZ MUHAMMAD ALOKOZI.

**Pashtany Tejaraty Bank** (Afghan Commercial Bank): Mohd Jan Khan Wat, Kabul; tel. (93) 26551; f. 1954 to provide short-term credits, forwarding facilities, opening letters of credit, purchase and sale of foreign exchange; cap. p.u. 1,000m., dep. 7,085.7m., total assets 19,826.4m. (1987); Chair. Dr BASIR RANJBAR; Pres. and CEO ZIR GUL WARDAK; 14 brs.

### INSURANCE

There is one national insurance company:

**Afghan National Insurance Co:** National Insurance Bldg, Park, Shar-i-Nau, POB 329, Kabul; tel. (93) 33531; f. 1964; mem. of Asian Reinsurance Corpn; marine, aviation, fire, motor and accident insurance; cap. 750m.; Pres. M. ABDULLAH MUDASIR; Claims Man. Eng. A. S. ALIZAI.

No foreign insurance companies are permitted to operate in Afghanistan.

## Trade and Industry

### GOVERNMENT AGENCY

**Board for the Promotion of Private Investments:** Kabul; Head of Bd Mawlawi SHOJA'ODDIN QADAH.

### CHAMBERS OF COMMERCE AND INDUSTRY

**Afghan Chamber of Commerce and Industry:** Mohd Jan Khan Wat, Kabul; tel. (93) 26772; fax (93) 26796; Dir-Gen. MOHAMMAD DAWOOD SAFI.

**Federation of Afghan Chambers of Commerce and Industry:** Darulaman Wat, Kabul; f. 1923; includes chambers of commerce and industry in Ghazni, Qandahar, Kabul, Herat, Mazar-i-Sharif, Fariab, Jawzjan, Kunduz, Jalalabad and Andkhoy.

### INDUSTRIAL AND TRADE ASSOCIATIONS

**Afghan Carpet Exporters' Guild:** POB 3159, Darulaman Wat, Kabul; tel. (93) 41765; f. 1967; a non-profit-making, independent organization of carpet manufacturers and exporters; Pres. Ziauddin Zia; c. 1,000 mems.

**Afghan Cart Company:** POB 61, Zerghona Maidan, Kabul; tel. (93) 31068; f. 1988; the largest export/import company in Afghanistan; imports electrical goods, machinery, metal, cars, etc.; exports raisins, carpets, medical herbs, wood, animal hides, etc.

**Afghan Fruit Processing Co:** POB 261, Industrial Estate, Puli Charkhi, Kabul; tel. (93) 65186; f. 1960; exports raisins, other dried fruits and nuts.

**Afghan Raisin and Other Dried Fruits Institute:** POB 3034, Sharara Wat, Kabul; tel. (93) 30463; exporters of dried fruits and nuts; Pres. Najmuddin Musleh.

**Afghan Wool Enterprises:** Shar-i-Nau, Kabul; tel. (93) 31963.

**Afghanistan Karakul Institute:** POB 506, Puli Charkhi, Kabul; tel. (93) 61852; f. 1967; exporters of furs; Pres. G. M. Baheer.

**Afghanistan Plants Enterprise:** POB 122, Puli Charkhi, Kabul; tel. (93) 31962; exports medicines, plants and spices.

**Handicraft Promotion and Export Centre:** POB 3089, Sharara Wat, Kabul; tel. (93) 32935; Momena Ranjbar.

**Parapamizad Co Ltd:** Jadai Nader Pashtoon, Sidiq Omar Market, POB 1911, Kabul; tel. (93) 22116; export/import co; Propr Padshah Sarbaz.

### TRADE UNIONS

**National Union of Afghanistan Employees (NUAE):** POB 756, Kabul; tel. (93) 23040; f. 1978, as Central Council of Afghanistan Trade Unions, to establish and develop the trade union movement, including the formation of councils and organizational cttees in the provinces; name changed in 1990; composed of seven vocational unions; 300,000 mems; Pres. A. Habib Hardamshaid; Vice-Pres. Asadollah Poya.

**Artists' Union:** Kabul; tel. (93) 23195; Chair. Nasim Khushgawar.

**Balkh Council of Trade Unions:** Mazar-i-Sharif; Pres. Muhammad Kabir Kargar.

**Central Council of the Union of Craftsmen:** Kabul; f. 1987; c. 58,000 mems.

**Commerce and Transport Employees' Union:** Kabul; Gen. Sec. Ahmad Zia Siddiqi.

**Construction Employees' Union:** Kabul; Gen. Sec. Aminullah.

**Kabul Union of Furriers:** Kabul; Leader Abd al-Khaliq.

**Mines and Industries Employees' Union:** Kabul; Gen. Sec. Mohammed Amin.

**Nangarhar Council of Trade Unions:** Jalalabad; Deputy Chair. Muqrebuddin Kargar.

**Public Health Employees' Union:** Kabul; Pres. Prof. M. Rahim Khushdel.

**Public Services Employees' Union:** Kabul; Gen. Sec. Abdul Mejjer Temory.

**Science and Culture Employees' Union:** Kabul; Gen. Sec. T. Habibzai.

**Traders' Union of Afghanistan:** Kabul; Chair. Rezwanqol Tamana.

**Union of Peasant Co-operatives of the Republic of Afghanistan (UPCRA):** POB 3272, Dehmazang, Kabul; tel. (93) 42683; 1,370,000 mems; Chair. Fazullah Alburz.

**Weaving and Sewing Employees' Union:** Kabul; Gen. Sec. A. W. Kargar.

**Writers' Union of Afghanistan:** Kabul; Chair. Mohammad Azam Rahnaward Zaryab; Vice-Chair. Abdollah Bakhtiani, Akbar Karkar.

## Transport

### RAILWAYS

In 1977 the Government approved plans for the creation of a railway system. The proposed line (of 1,815 km) was to connect Kabul to Qandahar and Herat, linking with the Iranian State Railways at Islam Quala and Tarakun, and with Pakistan Railways at Chaman. By 1999, however, work had not yet begun on the proposed railway.

A combined road and rail bridge was completed across the Amu-Dar'ya (Oxus) river in 1982, linking the Afghan port of Hairatan with the Soviet port of Termez. There were also plans for a 200-km railway line from Hairatan to Pul-i-Khomri, 160 km north of Kabul, but work had not begun by 1999.

### ROADS

In 1996 there were an estimated 21,000 km of roads, of which more than 18,000 km were unpaved. All-weather highways now link Kabul with Qandahar and Herat in the south and west, Jalalabad in the east and Mazar-i-Sharif and the Amu-Dar'ya river in the north.

**Afghan International Transport Company:** Kabul.

**Afghan Container Transport Company Ltd:** POB 3234, Shar-i-Nau, Kabul; tel. (93) 23088.

**Afghan Transit Company:** POB 530, Ghousy Market, Mohd Jan Khan Wat, Kabul; tel. (93) 22654.

**AFSOTR:** Kabul; resumed operations in 1998; transport co; 90 vehicles.

**Land Transport Company:** Khoshal Mena, Kabul; tel. (93) 20345; f. 1943; commercial transport within Afghanistan.

**The Milli Bus Enterprise:** Ministry of Transport, Ansari Wat, Kabul; tel. (93) 25541; state-owned and -administered; 721 buses; Pres. Eng. Aziz Naghaban.

**Salang-Europe International Transport and Transit:** Kabul; f. 1991 as joint Afghan/Soviet co; 500 vehicles.

### INLAND WATERWAYS

There are 1,200 km of navigable inland waterways, including the Amu-Dar'ya (Oxus) river, which handles vessels of up to about 500 dwt. River ports on the Amu-Dar'ya are linked by road to Kabul.

### CIVIL AVIATION

There are international airports at Kabul and Qandahar, and about 40 local airports are located throughout the country.

**Ministry of Civil Aviation and Tourism:** POB 165, Ansari Wat, Kabul; tel. (93) 21015; Deputy Dir-Gen. of Civil Aviation Raz Mohammad Alami.

**Ariana Afghan Airlines:** POB 76, Afghan Air Authority Bldg, Ansari Wat, Kabul; tel. (93) 25541; f. 1955; merged with Bakhtar Afghan Airlines Co Ltd in 1985; govt-owned; internal services between Kabul and three provincial capitals; external services to India, Pakistan, the United Arab Emirates and Saudi Arabia; Pres. Mola Hamidullah Akhund; Operations Man. F. M. Fedawi.

**Balkh Airlines:** Mazar-i-Sharif; f. 1996; passenger and cargo flights to Pakistan, Iran and Central Asian republics; Owner Gen. Abdul Rashid Dostam.

**Khyber Afghan Airlines:** Jalalabad; Owner Haji Abdul Qadeer.

**Pameer Airlines:** Bagram; flights to Iran, India, Russia, Albania, Bulgaria and the UAE.

**Taliban Airways Co.**

## Tourism

Afghanistan's potential attractions for the foreign visitor include: Bamian, with its high statue of Buddha and thousands of painted caves; Bandi Amir, with its suspended lakes; the Blue Mosque of Mazar; Herat, with its Grand Mosque and minarets; the towns of Qandahar and Girishk; Balkh (ancient Bactria), 'Mother of Cities', in the north; Bagram, Hadda and Surkh Kotal (of interest to archaeologists); and the high mountains of the Hindu Kush. In 1996 there were an estimated 4,000 foreign visitors and tourist receipts amounted to around US $1m.

**Afghan Tour:** Ansari Wat, Shar-i-Nau, Kabul; tel. (93) 30152; official travel agency supervised by ATO; Pres. Mohd Kazim Wardak (acting).

**Afghan Tourist Organization (ATO):** Ansari Wat, Shar-i-Nau, Kabul; tel. (93) 30323; f. 1958; Pres. Mohd Kazim Wardak (acting).

# ALBANIA

## Introductory Survey

### Location, Climate, Language, Religion, Flag, Capital

The Republic of Albania lies in south-eastern Europe. It is bordered by Yugoslavia to the north and north-east, by the former Yugoslav republic of Macedonia to the east, by Greece to the south and by the Adriatic and Ionian Seas (parts of the Mediterranean Sea) to the west. The climate is Mediterranean throughout most of the country. The sea plays a moderating role, although frequent cyclones in the winter months make the weather unstable. The average temperature is 14°C (57°F) in the north-east and 18°C (64°F) in the south-west. The language is Albanian, the principal dialects being Gheg (north of the Shkumbini river) and Tosk (in the south). The literary language is being formed on the basis of a strong fusion of the two dialects, with the phonetic and morphological structure of Tosk prevailing. An official ban on religious worship was in effect between 1967 and 1990. Before 1946 Islam was the predominant faith, and there were small groups of Christians (mainly Roman Catholic in the north and Eastern Orthodox in the south). The national flag (proportions 7 by 5) is red, with a two-headed black eagle in the centre. The capital is Tirana (Tiranë).

### Recent History

On 28 November 1912, after more than 400 years of Turkish rule, Albania declared its independence under a provisional Government. The country was occupied by Italy in 1914 but its independence was re-established in 1920. Albania was declared a republic in 1925 and Ahmet Beg Zogu was elected President. He was proclaimed King Zog in 1928 and reigned until the occupation of Albania by Italy in April 1939. Albania was united with Italy for four years, before being occupied by German forces in 1943; the Germans withdrew one year later.

The communist-led National Liberation Front (NLF), established with help from Yugoslav communists in 1941, was the most successful wartime resistance group and took power on 29 November 1944. Elections in December 1945 were based on a single list of candidates, sponsored by the communists. The new regime was led by Enver Hoxha, who had been the head of the Albanian Communist Party (ACP) since 1943. King Zog was deposed and the People's Republic of Albania was proclaimed on 11 January 1946. The ACP was renamed the Party of Labour of Albania (PLA) in 1948, the NLF having been succeeded by the Democratic Front of Albania (DFA) in 1945.

The communist regime developed close relations with Yugoslavia, including a monetary and customs union, until the latter's expulsion from the Cominform (a Soviet-sponsored body co-ordinating the activities of European communist parties) in 1948. Albania, fearing Yugoslav expansionism, became a close ally of the USSR and joined the Moscow-based Council for Mutual Economic Assistance (CMEA) in 1949. Hoxha resigned as Head of Government in 1954 but retained effective national leadership as First Secretary of the PLA. Albania joined the Warsaw Treaty Organization (Warsaw Pact) in 1955, but relations with the USSR deteriorated when Soviet leaders attempted a *rapprochement* with Yugoslavia. The Albanian leadership declared its support for the People's Republic of China in the Sino-Soviet ideological dispute, prompting the USSR to suspend relations with Albania in 1961. Albania established increasingly close relations with China, ended participation in the CMEA in 1962 and withdrew from the Warsaw Pact in 1968. However, following the improvement of relations between China and the USA after 1972, and the death of Mao Zedong, the Chinese leader, in 1976, Sino-Albanian relations progressively deteriorated. In 1978 Albania declared its support for Viet Nam in its dispute with China, prompting the Chinese Government to suspend all economic and military co-operation with Albania.

A new Constitution was adopted in December 1976, and the country was renamed the People's Socialist Republic of Albania. In December 1981 Mehmet Shehu, Chairman of the Council of Ministers (Prime Minister) since 1954, died as a result of a shooting incident. It was officially reported that he had committed suicide, but other sources suggested his involvement in a leadership struggle with Hoxha, and there were subsequent allegations that he had been executed. Following the death of Shehu, a new Government was formed under Adil Çarçani, hitherto the First Deputy Chairman. Feçor Shehu, the Minister of the Interior and a nephew of Mehmet Shehu, was not reappointed. In November 1982 Ramiz Alia replaced Haxhi Lleshi as President of the Presidium of the People's Assembly (Head of State). A number of former state and PLA officials, including Feçor Shehu and two other former ministers, were reportedly executed in September 1983.

Enver Hoxha died in April 1985, and was succeeded as First Secretary of the PLA by Alia. In March 1986 Nexhmije Hoxha, widow of Enver Hoxha, was elected to the chairmanship of the General Council of the DFA. Alia was re-elected as First Secretary of the PLA and as President of the Presidium of the People's Assembly in November 1986 and February 1987, respectively. In the latter month Adil Çarçani was reappointed Chairman of the Council of Ministers.

In November 1989, on the 45th anniversary of Albania's liberation from Nazi occupation, an amnesty for certain prisoners (including some political prisoners) was declared. In December 1989 and January 1990 a number of anti-Government demonstrations were reported to have taken place, particularly in the northern town of Shkodër. In late January, while continuing to deny the reports of internal unrest, Alia announced proposals for limited political and economic reforms, including the introduction of a system of multi-candidate elections (although the leading role of the PLA was to be maintained). Extensive reforms of the judicial system were approved by the People's Assembly in May, shortly before a visit to Tirana by the UN Secretary-General, Javier Pérez de Cuéllar. The Ministry of Justice was re-established, and the number of capital offences was considerably reduced. Although Albania was to remain a secular state, the practice of religion was henceforth to be tolerated. Furthermore, Albanians were to be granted the right to a passport for the purposes of foreign travel, while the penalty for attempting to flee the country illegally was reduced. In July there was renewed unrest, when anti-Government demonstrators occupied the streets of Tirana and were violently dispersed by the security forces. More than 5,000 Albanians took refuge in foreign embassies, and were subsequently granted permission to leave the country. Meanwhile, the membership of both the Council of Ministers and the Political Bureau of the PLA had been reorganized; a number of prominent anti-reformists were among those replaced.

In November 1990, in response to increasing domestic pressure, Alia announced proposals for more radical political reforms, urging that the leading role of the PLA be redefined. In December it was announced that the establishment of independent political parties was to be permitted, in preparation for elections to the People's Assembly (scheduled to take place in February 1991). In mid-December 1990, however, anti-Government demonstrators clashed with the security forces in several cities. Nexhmije Hoxha resigned from the chairmanship of the General Council of the DFA, and was replaced by Çarçani (who was, in turn, replaced in mid-1991).

On 20 February 1991, following widespread anti-Government demonstrations, Alia declared presidential rule. An eight-member Presidential Council was established, and a provisional Council of Ministers was appointed. Çarçani was replaced as Chairman of the Council of Ministers by Fatos Nano, a progressive economist, who had been appointed Deputy Chairman at the end of January. In late February the unrest finally ended, owing, in part, to an increased use of force by the authorities to quell the protests.

Meanwhile, following pressure from the newly-established opposition parties, the elections had been postponed until the end of March 1991 to allow political organizations more time to prepare. Despite these concessions, an increasing number of ethnic Greek Albanians attempted to leave the country; by mid-January more than 5,000 had crossed the border into Greece. Furthermore, by early March it was estimated that as many as 20,000 Albanians had sailed to Italy, after seizing vessels in Albanian ports.

In mid-March 1991 a general amnesty for all political prisoners was declared. The first stage of the multi-party elections to the People's Assembly duly took place on 31 March, and the second and third rounds of voting were held on 7 and 14 April. The PLA and affiliated organizations won 169 of the 250 seats, while the Democratic Party of Albania (DPA) secured 75 seats, and the Democratic Union of the Greek Minority (OMONIA) obtained five seats. The victory of the PLA, amid allegations of electoral malpractice, prompted dismay in some urban areas, where support for the DPA had been strong. Widespread protests ensued, and in Shkodër four people, including a local DPA leader, were killed when the security forces opened fire on demonstrators.

In late April 1991 an interim Constitution replaced that of 1976, pending the drafting of a new constitution. The country was renamed the Republic of Albania, and the post of executive President, who was to be elected by two-thirds of votes cast in the People's Assembly, was created. Alia was subsequently elected to the new post, defeating the only other candidate, Namik Dokle, also of the PLA; all the opposition deputies abstained from voting. In early May Nano was reappointed Chairman of the Council of Ministers, and the Government was again reorganized. In accordance with the provisions of the interim Constitution, President Alia resigned from the leadership of the PLA. In mid-May, however, the newly-established Union of Independent Trade Unions of Albania (UITUA) initiated a general strike in support of demands for substantial pay increases and for the resignation of the Government.

In early June 1991 the continuing general strike forced the resignation of Nano's Government. A Government of National Stability was subsequently formed, with Ylli Bufi (hitherto Minister of Food) as Chairman of the Council of Ministers. The coalition included representatives of the PLA, the DPA, the Albanian Republican Party (ARP), the Social Democratic Party (SDP) and the Agrarian Party (AP). Gramoz Pashko, a prominent member of the DPA, was appointed Deputy Chairman of the Council of Ministers and Minister of the Economy. At its 10th Congress, which took place later in June, the PLA was renamed the Socialist Party of Albania (SPA).

In August 1991, following a further seaborne exodus of migrants to Italy, the ports of Albania were placed under military control. Several vessels were refused entry by the Italian authorities, while many of the Albanians who had succeeded in disembarking were subsequently repatriated. Further opposition strikes and demonstrations were staged in subsequent weeks. In early December the Chairman of the DPA, Dr Sali Berisha, announced the withdrawal of party members from the coalition Government, despite opposition from other prominent DPA officials. The withdrawal of the seven DPA representatives, following the expulsion of three ARP ministers who had criticized the administration, forced Bufi's Government to resign. President Alia subsequently appointed an interim Government, principally composed of non-party specialists, under a new Prime Minister, Vilson Ahmeti (hitherto Minister of Food); new elections were to take place in March 1992.

A new electoral law, which was approved by the People's Assembly in early February 1992, reduced the number of deputies in the Assembly from 250 to 140, of whom 100 were to be elected by majority vote from single-member constituencies, while the remaining deputies were to be elected according to a system of proportional representation. Under provisions that defined legitimate political parties, OMONIA, as an organization representing an ethnic minority, was prohibited from contesting the forthcoming general election, prompting widespread protest from the Greek minority. At the general election, which was conducted in two rounds on 22 and 29 March, the DPA secured 92 of the 140 contested seats, while the SPA obtained 38 seats, the SDP seven seats, the Union for Human Rights Party (UHRP—supported by the minority Greek and Macedonian communities) two seats and the ARP one seat. According to official figures, 90% of the electorate participated. Following the defeat of the SPA, Alia resigned as President on 3 April. A few days later the new People's Assembly elected Berisha to the presidency. Berisha subsequently appointed a coalition Government, headed by Aleksander Meksi, a member of the DPA. In addition to the premiership, the DPA held 14 ministerial portfolios, while the SDP and ARP were allocated one portfolio each.

In July 1992 an amendment to the law on political organizations effectively banned the Albanian Communist Party. At the end of that month the DPA secured 43% of the total votes cast in the country's first multi-party local elections since the Second World War, while the SPA recovered some of the support that it had lost in the March general election, with 41% of the votes. In September divisions within the DPA resulted in the defection of a number of prominent party members, who had accused the Berisha administration of becoming increasingly right-wing and authoritarian, to form a new political grouping, the Democratic Alliance Party (DAP).

In 1992 a number of former communist officials were detained, including Nexhmije Hoxha, who had been arrested on charges of corruption. In February 1993 the former Prime Minister, Vilson Ahmeti, was placed under house arrest, following charges of corruption; further allegations concerning abuse of power resulted in the arrest of another former Prime Minister, Fatos Nano (who was now President of the SPA), in July. Nexhmije Hoxha was imprisoned for nine years in January 1993, having been convicted of embezzling state funds. (She was released in January 1997, after her term of imprisonment was twice reduced.) In August 1993 Alia was arrested on charges of abuse of power. Later that month Ahmeti was sentenced to two years' imprisonment. The trial of Nano commenced in April 1994, despite an international campaign on his behalf, organized by the SPA, and a European Parliament resolution appealing for his release. Nano was convicted of misappropriation of state funds during his premiership in 1991, and was sentenced to 12 years' imprisonment. In July 1994 Alia, who had denied the charges against him, was sentenced to nine years' imprisonment for abuse of power and violating the rights of citizens. (In July 1995, however, under the terms of a general amnesty, Alia, and a further 30 political prisoners, were released.)

In late July 1994 the SPA deputies unsuccessfully proposed a motion of 'no confidence' in the People's Assembly against the Government. In October the draft Constitution was finally presented to Berisha, but failed to obtain the requisite two-thirds' majority approval in the People's Assembly, and was consequently submitted for endorsement at a national referendum. As a result of Berisha's personal campaign in support of the draft Constitution (which was to vest additional powers in the President, and reduce those of the legislature), the referendum was widely perceived as a vote of confidence in his leadership. At the referendum, which took place on 6 November with the participation of 84.4% of the electorate, the draft Constitution was rejected by 53.9% of the voters, prompting demands for a general election (on the grounds that the administration lacked a popular mandate). Later that month the Minister of Culture, Youth and Sport resigned, citing his personal opposition to Prime Minister Meksi. In early December Berisha effected an extensive reorganization of the Council of Ministers. On the following day the ARP, which held only one seat in the People's Assembly, withdrew from the governing coalition. The SDP split into two factions; a new grouping, known as the Union of Social Democrats (USD—led by the new Minister of Culture, Youth and Sport, Teodor Laco), remained in the coalition, while the SDP withdrew.

In March 1995 the Chairman of the DPA, Eduard Selami, was removed from his post at an extraordinary party congress for opposing Berisha's efforts to organize a further referendum on the draft Constitution. Selami's accusations concerning Berisha's abuse of his position reinforced widespread discontent at the perceived corruption in the latter's administration. Public discontent at the slow pace of economic recovery in Albania was demonstrated by the continued flow of illegal immigrants to Italy, which, in May, deployed troops along its coast in an attempt to stem the influx. In that month the Albanian Government also assigned 300 troops to prevent people from leaving the country by sea.

In June 1995 Ilir Hoxha, the son of Enver Hoxha, was convicted on charges of inciting national hatred, after condemning leaders of the DPA in a newspaper interview. In September the People's Assembly adopted a 'Genocide Law' prohibiting those in power under the former communist regime from holding public office until the year 2002 (thereby banning a large number of prospective candidates, including incumbent SPA deputies, from contesting legislative elections in 1996). In the same month the Minister of Justice dismissed three Supreme Court judges, owing to their alleged activities under the communist regime. The Chairman of the Supreme Court, Zef Brozi (who had previously accused the Government of exerting undue pressure on the judiciary), challenged the Minister's authority to dismiss employees of the court and refused to accept the decision. Brozi had aroused the disapproval of the Government earlier in the year, when he recommended a review of Fatos Nano's case and advocated his release. However, as a result of an amendment to the penal code, which was subsequently adopted by the Government, the Supreme Court was forced to reject Nano's appeal. Following an ensuing ruling against Brozi by the Constitutional Court, which declared his previous suspension of lower court verdicts to be illegal, he was dismissed as Chairman of the Supreme Court by the People's Assembly, and replaced by his deputy. The SPA deputies boycotted the People's Assembly, in protest at Brozi's dismissal and the Government's alleged infringement of the independence of the judiciary.

In November 1995 a parliamentary commission initiated an inquiry following the discovery of a mass grave near the border town of Shkodër. Families of the deceased urged the prosecution service to initiate charges against former members of the communist regime, including Alia, who had allegedly been responsible for the killing by border guards of nationals attempting to flee the country in 1990–92. Also in November 1995 the People's Assembly approved legislation requiring senior civil servants to be investigated for their activities under the communist regime. In December 14 prominent former members of the communist regime were arrested on charges of involvement in the execution, internment and deportation of citizens for political reasons. (In May 1996 three of the former officials received death sentences, which were later commuted to terms of imprisonment, while the remaining defendants also received custodial terms in August and September of that year.) In February 1996 Alia was detained in connection with the killing of demonstrators in Shkodër in April 1991 and the border incidents.

Following increasing division within the SPA, in March 1996 a liberal faction left the organization to form the Albanian New Socialist Party. Later that month the Government invited international representatives to observe the legislative elections, which were scheduled to take place in late May. The first round of the elections (which was preceded by SPA allegations of intimidation by the security forces) took place on 26 May; following alleged incidents of electoral irregularities, however, the principal opposition parties, including the SPA, the SDP and the DAP, withdrew from the poll and issued a statement rejecting the election results. A subsequent SPA demonstration held in protest at the alleged malpractices was violently dispersed by the security forces. The second round of the elections took place on 2 June; as a result of opposition demands for a boycott, only 59.4% of the electorate participated in the poll (compared with 89% in the first round). According to official results, the DPA secured 101 of the 115 directly-elected seats (25 seats were to be allocated proportionately). However, international observers, who included representatives of the Organization for Security and Co-operation in Europe (OSCE, formerly the Conference on Security and Co-operation in Europe—CSCE, see p. 237), claimed that widespread malpractice and intimidation of voters had been perpetrated and urged the Government to conduct fresh elections, while SPA deputies initiated a hunger strike in an attempt to oblige Berisha to annul the results. Berisha rejected the allegations of government malpractice, and agreed to conduct further elections in only 17 constituencies. The principal opposition parties (which demanded that fresh elections be held, under international supervision, in all constituencies) continued their electoral boycott. Consequently, the DPA won all the seats contested in the partial elections, which took place on 16 June, thereby securing a total of 122 of the 140 seats in the People's Assembly. The SPA won 10 of the remaining seats, while the UHRP and the ARP each acquired three and the National Front two. (The SPA, however, refused to recognize the new legislature and boycotted the inaugural session of the People's Assembly.) The OSCE subsequently issued a report, stating that the elections had failed to meet international legal standards. In early July Aleksander Meksi, who had been reappointed to the office of Prime Minister, formed a new Council of Ministers, principally comprising members of the DPA; the ARP, the Christian Democratic Party and the USD were also represented. Later that month a parliamentary commission was established to investigate the reported electoral violations.

In August 1996 the Government established a permanent Central Election Commission, prior to local government elections, which were scheduled to take place in October; the main opposition parties subsequently nominated a number of representatives to the Commission. Despite continued division within the SPA, Nano (who remained in prison) was re-elected as Chairman at a party congress in late August. In the local government elections, which took place in two rounds in late October, the DPA secured the highest number of votes in 58 of the 64 municipalities and in 267 of the 309 communes. Shortly before the elections the OSCE had withdrawn its observers, after Berisha objected to one of its members, who, he claimed, was biased against the DPA. Nevertheless, observers from the Council of Europe (see p. 158) declared that, despite some irregularities, the elections had been conducted fairly.

In January 1997 the collapse of several widely-popular 'pyramid' financial investment schemes (which had offered high rates of interest), resulting in huge losses of individual savings, prompted violent anti-Government demonstrations, particularly in Tirana and the southern town of Vlorë. It was widely believed that members of the Government were associated with the 'pyramid' schemes, which had allegedly financed widespread illegal activities. The People's Assembly subsequently adopted legislation prohibiting the 'pyramid' schemes. However, the Government increased efforts to suppress the protests (which were supported by a newly-established opposition alliance, Forum for Democracy): large numbers of demonstrators were arrested, while prominent opposition members were publicly assaulted by the security forces. At the end of January the People's Assembly granted Berisha emergency powers to mobilize special army units to restore order. It was reported that several people were killed in ensuing violent clashes between security forces and protesters (who continued to demand the resignation of Berisha and state reimbursement for the financial losses that they had incurred). At the end of February, however, Berisha (whose mandate was due to expire in April) was nominated as the presidential candidate for the DPA. On 3 March he was re-elected unopposed for a second five-year term (with the SPA continuing to boycott the People's Assembly).

Following an escalation in hostilities between insurgents (who seized armaments from military depots) and government troops in the south of the country, Berisha declared a national state of emergency at the beginning of March 1997, empowering security forces to shoot demonstrators and imposing total official censorship. However, insurgent groups gained control of the southern towns of Vlorë, Sarandë and Gjirokastër, while it was reported that large numbers of government forces had deserted or defected to join the rebels. Following negotiations with representatives of nine principal opposition parties, Berisha signed an agreement whereby an interim coalition government was to be installed, pending elections in June, and offered an amnesty to rebels who surrendered to the authorities. A former SPA mayor of Gjirokastër, Bashkim Fino, was appointed to the office of Prime Minister. Berisha subsequently approved the formation of a Government of National Reconciliation, which included representatives of eight opposition parties. (The DAP had withdrawn from the negotiations, after its proposal that the interior portfolio be allocated to an opposition member was rejected.) Despite these concessions, the insurgency continued, reaching the northern town of Tropojë and Tirana (where rebels seized the airport). All those detained in Tirana central prison, including Nano and Alia, were released; Nano was subsequently granted an official pardon by Berisha. The evacuation of western European and US nationals from Tirana and Durrës was impeded by the rebels, who exchanged fire with foreign troops effecting the evacuation. Extreme hardship and concern that the fighting would escalate into widespread civil conflict prompted thousands of Albanians to flee to Italy (where the Italian authorities announced they would be permitted to remain for a maximum of three months). Later in March, however, Italian naval authorities were ordered to intercept boats transporting Albanian refugees, in an effort to halt the exodus.

In late March 1997 it was reported that government forces had regained control of Tirana; the south of the country was controlled by insurgent groups opposed to the Government, while the north was largely held by paramilitary units loyal to Berisha. Following mediation by the Italian Government and an OSCE special envoy, Franz Vranitzky, southern rebel leaders, grouped in a self-designated 'national committee for public salvation', agreed to abandon hostilities in return for guarantees of amnesty. However, the rebels subsequently refused to surrender their armaments, and demanded that further legislative elections take place. The Government of National Reconciliation requested military assistance in the restoration of civil order, and in late March Fino attended a meeting of European Union (EU, see p. 172) foreign ministers in Rome to appeal for the establishment of a multinational force which would supervise humanitarian aid operations in Albania. At the end of March the UN Security Council endorsed an OSCE proposal that member states be authorized to contribute troops to the force. The 5,915-member Multinational Protection Force for Albania was established in April, with an official mission (known as Operation Alba) to facilitate the distribution of humanitarian assistance; the Italian contingent numbered 2,500, and the French 1,000, while Turkey, Greece, Spain, Romania, Austria and Denmark also contributed troops. The Multinational Protection Force (which had a mandate to remain in the country for three months) began to arrive in mid-April, and was subsequently deployed in regions under government control in northern and central Albania. After negotiations between Italian forces and insurgents at Vlorë, the leader of the 'national committee for public salvation', Ekeren Osmani, announced that he would co-operate with the Italian troops.

At the beginning of April 1997 the SPA ended its boycott of the People's Assembly, which subsequently voted to end press restrictions that had been imposed under the state of emergency in March. Later in April the National Council of the DPA endorsed Berisha's leadership of the party and removed a number of dissident members who had demanded his resignation. In the same month Berisha rejected a decision by the Government of National Reconciliation to remove the Deputy Minister of the Interior, Gen. Agim Shehu (who was an ally of Berisha) from his post. The son of King Zog and claimant to the throne, Leka Zogu, who returned to Albania in April, with the support of the pro-monarchist Legality Movement Party, urged that a referendum on the restoration of the monarchy take place; the principal political parties had already agreed that such a referendum be conducted. In early May the People's Assembly adopted legislation regulating the operation of the 'pyramid' investment schemes. Following mediation by Vranitzky, the leaders of 10 major political parties agreed that further elections would take place by the end of June. However, negotiations between the parties regarding the drafting of a new electoral code ended in failure, owing to disagreement over the number of parliamentary deputies who would be elected by proportional representation. Later in May the DPA submitted to the People's Assembly legislation on a new electoral system, which was approved, despite a further parliamentary boycott by SPA deputies; under the new legislation, the number of deputies in the People's Assembly was to be increased from 140 to 155, of whom 115 were to be directly elected and 40 elected on the basis of proportional representation. After Vranitzky mediated further discussions between the parties, he announced that the elections would take place on 29 June; the percentage of the total vote required for representation in the People's Assembly was reduced from 4% to 3%. The SPA and its allied parties agreed to participate in the elections, after Berisha complied with the stipulation that the central electoral commission be appointed by the interim Government (rather than by himself).

Election campaigning was marred by a number of violent incidents, including a number of bomb explosions in Tirana. In June 1997 the UN Security Council voted to extend the mandate of the Multinational Protection Force to mid-August. Leaders of the DPA and SPA signed an agreement in Rome pledging to abide by the results of the elections. On 29 June the first round of voting in the elections to the People's Assembly took place; a referendum on the restoration of the monarchy was conducted on the same day. Despite the presence of the Multinational Protection Force, some three people were killed in violent incidents during the voting. A further electoral ballot took place in 32 constituencies on 6 July. OSCE observers, who had monitored the voting, subsequently declared the electoral process to have been conducted satisfactorily. Later in July the central electoral commission announced that the SPA had secured 101 seats in the People's Assembly, while the DPA had won 29 seats; the SPA and its allied parties (the SDP, the Democratic Alliance Party, the AP and the UHRP) thereby secured the requisite two-thirds majority for the approval of constitutional amendments that they had proposed earlier in the month. At the referendum, 66.7% of the electorate voted in favour of retaining a republic, while only 33.3% voted in favour of the restoration of the monarchy. On 24 July, following Berisha's resignation, the Secretary-General of the SPA, Dr Rexhep Mejdani, was elected President by the People's Assembly. Parliamentary deputies also voted to end the state of emergency, which had been imposed in March. The SPA proposed Nano to the office of Prime Minister, and a new Council of Ministers was appointed, which comprised representatives of the SPA and its allied parties, and retained Fino in the post of Deputy Prime Minister. At the end of July the new Government submitted a programme for the restoration of civil order and economic reconstruction, which received a vote of confidence in the People's Assembly. The legislature also voted in favour of auditing the existing 'pyramid' schemes and investigating those that had been dissolved, in an effort to reimburse lost savings.

In August 1997 the Government dispatched troops to the south of the country, in an effort to restore order in major towns that were under the control of rebel forces. It was subsequently announced that Vlorë had been recaptured and a number of rebel forces arrested; the Minister of the Interior ordered that all the armaments that had been looted during the unrest be surrendered to the authorities. By mid-August the mandate of the Multinational Protection Force had officially ended and the contingent had left Albania. Foreign advisers subsequently returned to the country to assist the Government in the reorganization of the military and security services, under the terms of existing bilateral treaties. In late August a number of prominent officials and members of the armed forces, including the army Chief of Staff, the head of the security services and the Governor of the Central Bank, were replaced as part of an extensive reorganization of public services.

At the end of August 1997 the Constitutional Court upheld the results of the referendum in which voters had rejected the restoration of the monarchy, following a legal challenge by monarchists (who had accused the central electoral commission of malpractice). In early September the People's Assembly established a parliamentary commission which was to draft a new constitution in accordance with the amendments proposed by the SPA. Later in September an SPA member, Gafur Mazreku, shot and wounded an opposition deputy, following an acrimonious parliamentary session. Mazreku was subsequently charged with attempted murder, and the incident further exacerbated relations between the SPA and the DPA, which initiated a boycott of the People's Assembly. In October Berisha was re-elected Chairman of the DPA. In the same month Alia and a further three former senior officials were acquitted of genocide by a Tirana court (upholding a ruling of the Supreme Court), on the grounds that the charge did not exist under the penal legislation of the former communist Government.

Violent unrest continued in early 1998, with numerous minor bomb attacks, one of which, in January, destroyed SPA offices in Gjirokastër. In February tensions in Shkodër precipitated an armed revolt by civilians and rebel members of the local security forces, who seized the town's police station and released a number of prisoners from custody. Government troops subsequently restored order in Shkodër; Berisha, however, attributed responsibility for the uprising to the Nano administration, and reiterated demands that further elections be organized.

In March 1998 the DPA announced that it was to end its boycott of the People's Assembly in order to demonstrate support for ethnic Albanians in Kosovo, Yugoslavia (see below). Partial local government elections took place on 21 June: a government electoral coalition, Alliance for the State, secured five of the seven contested municipalities and six of the nine contested communes, while an opposition grouping, led by the DPA, known as the Union for Democracy, won the remaining polls. Despite opposition claims of irregularities, OSCE observers declared that the elections had been conducted fairly. In early July a parliamentary commission, which had been established in October 1997 to investigate the unrest earlier that year, submitted a report recommending that several senior DPA officials, including Berisha, be charged in connection with the deployment of the armed forces to suppress the protests. Later in July 1998 Nano announced that the constitutional commission had presented draft legislation, which would be submitted for approval by the People's Assembly in October; the new Constitution was subsequently to be referred for endorsement at a national referendum. In August six prominent DPA officials who had served in the previous Government were arrested in connection with alleged human rights' violations committed during the civil unrest in 1997. The DPA subsequently staged an unauthorized demonstration in Tirana to demand their release. (In November the Supreme Court rejected an appeal against the arrest of four of the six officials.)

In early September 1998 Azem Hajdari, a prominent DPA official and close associate of Berisha, was assassinated outside the party headquarters in Tirana; Berisha accused Nano of involvement in the killing, and demanded the resignation of the Government. The incident prompted violent protests by DPA supporters, who seized government offices and occupied the state television and radio buildings. Government security forces subsequently regained control of the capital, after clashes with protesters in which about seven people were reported to have been killed. Berisha denied government claims that the uprising constituted a coup attempt, and DPA supporters staged a demonstration in his support in Tirana. Later in September the People's Assembly voted in favour of ending Berisha's parliamentary exemption from prosecution, thereby allowing him to be charged with attempting to overthow the Government. An OSCE delegation, which mediated subsequent discussions between the political parties, condemned Berisha for inciting unrest, but also criticized Nano owing to continued corruption within his administration. At the end of September the Minister of Public Order resigned, amid widespread criticism of the Government's failure to improve public security. Shortly afterwards Nano tended his resignation, following a meeting of the SPA leadership, having failed to reach agreement with the government coalition on the composition of a new Council of Ministers. Mejadni subsequently requested that the Secretary-General of the SPA, Pandeli Majko, who had been nominated by the party to the office of Prime Minister, form a new government. In early October a new coalition Council of Ministers, headed by Majko, was installed. Later that month the People's Assembly approved the draft Constitution; DPA members and other deputies belonging to the Union for Democracy initiated a legislative boycott. The new Constitution, which provided for the post-communist system of government, was submitted for endorsement at a national referendum, which was monitored by OSCE observers, on 22 November. The Government subsequently announced that 50.1% of the registered electorate had participated in the referendum, of whom 93.1% had voted in favour of adopting the draft Constitution. However, Berisha claimed that only 17% of the votes cast by a total of 35% of the electorate had been in favour of the new Constitution, and urged his supporters to stage further protests against the preliminary results of the referendum. The Government deployed additional security forces in Tirana in an effort to maintain public order. On 28 November Mejdani officially adopted the new Constitution. However, Berisha subsequently announced that the DPA would continue to refuse to recognize the Constitution. In February 1999 Leka Zogu was arrested in the South African capital, Johannesburg, and charged with illegal possession of armaments. In the same month the trial commenced of a prominent member of the Legality Movement Party, Ekrem Spahia, on charges of involvement with the alleged coup attempt of September 1998. In July a DPA congress voted in favour of ending the boycott of the legislature, which had been initiated following the killing of Hajdari.

At an SPA party congress in September 1999 Nano (who had resigned from the party chairmanship in January) was re-elected to the post, narrowly defeating Majko. In October Majko (who consequently no longer had the support of the SPA deputies in the People's Assembly) resigned from the office of Prime Minister. Mejdani subsequently nominated Ilir Meta (hitherto Deputy Prime Minister), whom Nano supported, as Prime Minister. Berisha announced that the DPA would boycott a parliamentary motion to approve the new Council of Ministers formed by Meta, and that his supporters would stage mass protests following the return of Nano to the SPA leadership. In early November the new Government was formally approved in the People's Assembly (despite the opposition boycott).

The gradual relaxation of Albania's isolationist policies culminated in 1990, in a declaration of its intention to establish good relations with all countries, irrespective of their social system. Until 1990 Albania remained hostile to the USSR; in July of that year, however, Albania and the USSR formally agreed to restore diplomatic relations. Diplomatic relations between Albania and the USA were re-established in March 1991 (they had been suspended since 1946), while diplomatic links between Albania and the United Kingdom were restored in May. Albania was granted observer status at the 1990 CSCE summit meeting, and became a full member of the organization in June 1991. In May 1992 the newly-elected President Berisha made a tour of Europe. In the same month, Albania and the EC signed a 10-year agreement on trade and co-operation. In June Albania, together with 10 other countries (including six of the former Soviet republics), signed a pact to establish the Black Sea Economic Co-operation group (see p. 135), envisaging the creation of a Black Sea economic zone that would complement the EC. In December Albania was granted membership of the Organization of the Islamic Conference (OIC, see p. 249), and in the same month applied to join NATO (see p. 226), thus becoming the first former Warsaw Pact country formally to seek membership of the Western alliance. Albania joined NATO's 'partnership for peace' programme of military co-operation in April 1994. Albania was admitted to the Council of Europe in July 1995, having agreed to adopt a new Constitution and to take measures to fulfil the Council's requirements concerning human rights.

Albania's relations with neighbouring Greece and Yugoslavia have been strained. In August 1987 Greece formally ended the technical state of war with Albania that had been in existence since 1945. However, the status of the Greek minority in Albania, unofficially estimated to number between 200,000 and 400,000, remained a sensitive issue. Relations between Albania and Greece deteriorated in 1993, owing to Greece's deportation of some 20,000 Albanian immigrants and to the alleged mistreatment of the Greek minority in southern Albania. Relations between the two states were exacerbated further in April 1994, following a violent border incident in which two Albanian guards were killed by unidentified opponents; a series of diplomatic expulsions ensued on both sides, and the border situation remained tense, with a number of reports of minor skirmishes. In May six prominent members of the ethnic Greek organization, OMONIA, were arrested, following the alleged seizure by Albanian police of weapons and 'anti-constitutional' documents. Greece subsequently protested at the actions of the Albanian authorities by vetoing the provision of funds from the EU to Albania and by increasing the deportations of illegal Albanian immigrants. In September five of the OMONIA detainees were convicted on a number of charges, including espionage and the illegal possession of weapons, and received custodial sentences. Following the verdict, Greece and Albania recalled their mutual ambassadors. In addition, the Greek Government submitted formal protests to the UN and the EU regarding Albania's perceived maltreatment of its ethnic Greek population and closed the important Kakavija border crossing, which had hitherto been used by Albanian migrant workers. One of the OMONIA defendants was pardoned in December, following a reduction in tension between the two countries (in November Greece had withdrawn its veto on EU aid to Albania). In early February 1995 the four remaining OMONIA prisoners were released. Later that month the OSCE suspended its inquiries into the alleged persecution of the Greek minority in Albania, on the grounds that there was no case to answer. In March relations between Albania and Greece improved dramatically, following a two-day official visit to Albania by the Greek Minister of Foreign Affairs. In June the Albanian Government approved a new education bill, which recognized the right of ethnic minorities to their own language and culture. In March 1996 the Greek President, Konstantinos Stefanopoulos, visited Albania for discussions, during which a co-operation agreement was signed, apparently resolving outstanding issues of concern between the two nations. In August 1997 Albania and Greece signed an agreement whereby Albanian migrant workers in Greece would receive temporary work permits. In July 1999 the Albanian Minister of Foreign Affairs visited Greece to discuss the increasing number of expulsions of Albanian migrants by the Greek authorities.

Relations with Yugoslavia deteriorated sharply in early 1989, when many ethnic Albanian demonstrators were killed during renewed unrest in the Yugoslav province of Kosovo and Metohija (where the population was principally composed of ethnic Albanian Muslims). In April 1993 it was reported that 10 Albanians had been killed by Yugoslav guards while unwittingly crossing the border. As a result of increasing tension in this area, in the following month the Albanian Government requested the establishment of a UN peace-keeping mission in Kosovo to protect Albanians there. This was refused, however, and Kosovo remained a focus of political and ethnic tension. The insurgency in southern Albania in early 1997 (see above) prompted concern among western European Governments that armaments seized by the rebels might also be used to support an insurrection by ethnic Albanians in Kosovo. In November 1997, following a meeting between Prime Minister Nano and the Yugoslav President, Slobodan Milošević, it was announced that relations between Albania and Yugoslavia were to be normalized (although Milošević emphasized during the discussions that the unrest in Kosovo remained an internal issue of Yugoslavia). However, increased Serbian military activity against the ethnic Albanian majority in Kosovo in early 1998 (see chapter on Yugoslavia) was condemned by the Albanian Government; Nano urged international intervention to prevent widespread conflict in the region. In March large demonstrations were staged in Tirana in protest at Serbian violence against ethnic Albanian civilians in Kosovo. In April clashes were reported on the Albanian border with Kosovo between Serbian troops and suspected members of the paramilitary Kosovo Liberation Army (KLA, Ushtria Çlirimtare e Kosovës). The Albanian administration initiated measures to prevent the illicit transportation of armaments from northern Albania to KLA forces in Kosovo. By June, according to official figures, some 10,000 ethnic Albanian refugees had fled to northern Albania (particularly to the region of Tropojë), following continued Serbian military reprisals against the ethnic Albanian population in Kosovo. The Albanian Government adopted a programme for the resettlement of the Kosovan refugees. In mid-1998 NATO conducted a number of military exercises in Albania, in conjunction with the Albanian armed forces, in an attempt to increase pressure on the Serbian Government to end military action in Kosovo.

In late March 1999, following the failure of diplomatic efforts to persuade Milošević to accede to NATO demands (see chapter on Yugoslavia), NATO forces commenced an intensive aerial bombardment of Yugoslavia. The Albanian Government expressed support for NATO military action (and allowed Albania's air and sea facilities to be used for NATO operations), but urged the introduction of ground troops in Kosovo to prevent increasing large-scale massacres of the ethnic Albanian civilian population by Serbian forces. Further Albanian troops were deployed on the northern border with Serbia in preparation for a possible Serbian retaliatory offensive. The atrocities committed by Serbian forces in Kosovo precipitated a mass exodus of ethnic Albanian refugees from the province; by early April some 300,000 had fled to Albania. NATO troops (which later numbered about 8,000, and became known as AFOR) were dispatched to Albania to provide logistic support for humanitarian aid operations. The Government appealed for international financial assistance in providing for the Kosovo refugee population, and urged NATO to expedite Albania's admission to the organization. It was reported that a number of ethnic Albanians had returned from abroad to join the KLA (which operated training camps in northern Albania). In early April Serbian forces bombarded Albanian border villages during heavy fighting with the KLA in Kosovo, increasing international concern that a broader regional conflict might develop. Later that month Serbian troops advanced into Albanian territory, but were repelled by members of the Albanian armed forces. By May the KLA had succeeded in establishing a supply route for the transportation of armaments from bases in northern Albania to Kosovo. Despite the further reinforcement of Albanian troops at the border with Kosovo, Serbian forces launched further attacks on KLA positions in northern Albania. Also in May Prime Minister Majko met ethnic Albanian representatives from Kosovo, in an effort to resolve differences between factions of the Kosovo Albanian leadership. In early June Milošević finally accepted a peace plan for Kosovo (see chapter on Yugoslavia). Following the subsequent withdrawal of Serbian forces from Kosovo and the deployment of an international peace-keeping force (known as KFOR) in the province, under the terms of the peace agreement, about one-half of the ethnic Albanian refugees returned to Kosovo from Albania and the former Yugoslav republic of Macedonia (FYRM) later that month. According to the UN High Commissioner for Refugees, only 209,000 of the 444,600 refugees who had fled to Albania remained in the country at the end of June. In September NATO announced that AFOR, which had been gradually withdrawing from the country, was to be replaced by a 2,400-member contingent, to be known as Communications Zone West (COMMZ-W), of which Italy was to contribute 1,400 personnel; the new force was to be mandated to maintain civil order in Albania and to assist KFOR troops in Kosovo.

In February 1993 Albania refused to accept an application by the FYRM for membership of the CSCE, and it was only in April that Albania officially recognized the existence of the republic as an independent state. Albania was concerned at the oppression of the large ethnic Albanian minority in the FYRM, who constituted about 21% of the population and the majority of whom were Muslims. Relations between the two countries deteriorated in the course of the year, owing to a number of shooting incidents on the border. In March 1994, however, Albania urged Greece to end its economic embargo on the FYRM. Following the civil unrest in Albania in early 1997 (see above), a number of incursions into FYRM territory by armed groups of Albanian rebels were reported; in September of that year two members of the FYRM's security forces were killed in a clash with Albanians who had entered the country illegally. In October the Ministers of Defence of Albania and the FYRM signed an agreement providing for increased security at the joint border between the two countries.

## Government

Under the Constitution adopted in November 1998, legislative power is vested in the unicameral People's Assembly. The People's Assembly, which is elected for a term of four years, comprises at least 140 deputies, of whom 100 are directly elected by a simple majority and the remainder on the basis of proportional representation. The President of the Republic is Head of State, and is elected by the People's Assembly for a term of five years. Executive authority is held by the Council of Ministers, which is led by the Prime Minister as Head of Government. The Prime Minister is appointed by the President. The Prime Minister appoints a Council of Ministers, which is then presented for approval to the People's Assembly. For the purposes of local government, Albania is divided into 36 districts *(rrethe),* which comprise 309 communes. The representative organs of the basic units of local government are councils, which are elected by general direct elections for a period of three years. The Council of Ministers appoints a Prefect in every region as its representative.

## Defence

In August 1996 the total strength of the armed forces was 54,000 (including 22,050 conscripts): army 45,000, air force 6,500 and navy 2,500. The paramilitary forces numbered 13,500 (including an internal security force of 5,000 and a people's militia of 3,500). Budgetary expenditure on defence in 1998 was estimated at 10,500m. lekë. The budget proposals for 1999 allocated about 1.0% of total projected government expenditure to defence. Military service is compulsory and lasts for 12 months. In 1999 the armed forces were in the process of being reconstructed, with assistance from European Governments (particularly those of Greece and Italy). From April of that year a NATO contingent (known as AFOR), numbering about 8,000, was deployed in Albania, to assist in humanitarian aid operations, following a mass influx of refugees from Kosovo (see Recent History). In September it was announced that AFOR was to be reconstituted as a 2,400-strong contingent, to be known as Communications Zone West (COMMZ-W), which was to maintain civil order in Albania and support NATO forces in Kosovo.

## Economic Affairs

In 1997, according to World Bank estimates, Albania's gross national product (GNP), measured at average 1995–97 prices, was US $2,540m., equivalent to $760 per head. During 1990–97, it was estimated, GNP per head increased, in real terms, at an average annual rate of 2.2%. In 1998 GNP was estimated at $2,700m. ($810 per head). In 1990–97 the population increased at an average annual rate of 0.2%, according to the World Bank. Albania's gross domestic product (GDP) declined, in real terms, by an average of 0.2% per year in 1990–98, according to the IMF; it increased by 8.0% in 1998.

Agriculture (including forestry and fishing) contributed an estimated 54.4% of GDP in 1998. Some 49.5% of the labour force were engaged in the sector in 1998. In 1988 co-operatives accounted for almost 75% of agricultural output; from 1990, however, an increasing degree of private enterprise was permitted, and agricultural land was subsequently redistributed to private ownership. The principal crops are wheat, sugar beet, maize, potatoes, barley and sorghum. Agricultural GDP increased at an average annual rate of 4.7% in 1990–98, rising by 5.0% in 1998.

Industry (comprising mining, manufacturing, construction and utilities) accounted for an estimated 24.5% of GDP in 1998 and employed 22.5% of the labour force in 1989. Principal contributors to industrial output include mining, energy generation and food-processing. Construction was the fastest-growing sector in recent years, with GDP increasing at an average annual rate of 7.8% in 1990–98 (declining by 6.3% in 1997, but rising by 21.0% in 1998). Industrial GDP declined at an average rate of 7.9% per year during 1990–98 (increasing by 12.2% in 1998).

Albania is one of the world's largest producers of chromite (chromium ore), possessing Europe's only significant reserves (an estimated 37m. metric tons of recoverable ore, constituting about 5% of total world deposits). The mining sector has been centred on chromite and copper since the closure of nickel and iron ore operations, together with more than one-half of the country's coal mines, in 1990. Albania has petroleum resources and its own refining facilities, and there has been considerable foreign interest in the exploration of both onshore and offshore reserves since 1991. (The acceptance of foreign capital in order to establish joint ventures was authorized in 1990.)

As in the mining sector, output in manufacturing has declined sharply since 1990. The manufacturing sector is based largely on the processing of agricultural products, minerals, chemicals and building materials.

Hydroelectric generation accounted for more than 80% of total electricity production in 1988. A serious drought in 1988–90, however, led to problems in the hydroelectric sector.

Services employed 21.5% of the labour force in 1989 and provided an estimated 21.0% of GDP in 1998. In real terms, the combined GDP of the service sectors increased by an average of 2.9% per year during 1990–98 (rising by 11.3% in 1998).

In 1998 Albania recorded a visible trade deficit of US $603.6m., and there was a deficit of $65.1m. on the current account of the balance of payments. In 1998 the principal source of imports (an estimated 44.1%) was Italy; the other major supplier was Greece. Italy was also the principal market for exports (taking an estimated 60.1% of the total); Greece and Germany were also important purchasers. The principal exports in 1998 were miscellaneous manufactured articles, crude materials, basic manufactures, and food, beverages and tobacco. The main imports in that year were food, beverages and tobacco, basic manufactures, machinery and transport equipment and miscellaneous manufactured articles.

Albania's overall budget deficit in 1998 was 47,745m. lekë (10.4% of GDP). At the end of 1997 Albania's total external debt was US $706.0m., of which $603.3m. was long-term public debt. In that year the cost of servicing the debt was equivalent to 7.1% of the value of exports of goods and services. Remittances from Albanians working abroad totalled $266m. in 1994. Foreign aid and remittances together contributed 40% of GDP in 1993. In 1992–98 the average annual rate of inflation was 28.1%; consumer prices increased by an average of 20.6% in 1998, but declined by 0.6% in the year to August 1999. In 1997 the average rate of unemployment was 14.9% of the domestic labour force; the rate of unemployment was estimated at 17.1% in mid-1998. An estimated 25.1% of the Albanian labour force were working abroad in 1996.

Having reversed its long-standing policy of economic self-sufficiency, in 1991 Albania became a member of the World Bank, the IMF and the newly-established European Bank for Reconstruction and Development (EBRD, see p. 168). In 1992 Albania became a founder member of the Black Sea Economic Co-operation group (see p. 135).

In late 1991, despite reforms to the centralized economy implemented in that year (permitting limited free enterprise and beginning a programme of comprehensive land redistribution), Albania was experiencing a serious economic crisis. In 1992 the newly-elected Government introduced an extensive programme of economic reforms, providing for the transfer to private ownership of farm land, state-owned companies and housing, and the abolition of trade restrictions and price controls. A strict programme of high interest rates, reduced subsidies, banking reforms and trade liberalization, supported by the IMF, was successful in reducing the massive budget deficit, controlling inflation and stabilizing the currency. Nevertheless, illicit trade was believed to account for a high proportion of total revenue, while the country remained dependent on remittances from Albanian emigrants and foreign aid to support the current account of the balance of payments. In early 1997 the collapse of the 'pyramid' investment schemes, resulting in huge losses of individual savings, precipitated widespread civil unrest. In 1998 the economic situation stabilized, as a result of the Government's adherence to policies of fiscal restraint. In early 1999, however, a mass influx of refugees (see Recent History), which reached 430,000 (equivalent to 13% of the population) by mid-May, placed considerable pressure on social and economic infrastructure, as well as on government finances. The arrival of large amounts of humanitarian and military supplies at Albanian ports impeded commercial trade. Following an appeal from the Government, the international community provided emergency relief aid. In June the IMF approved a second annual loan under its enhanced structural adjustment facility for Albania, with an 'augmentation' to compensate for the increased fiscal requirements resulting from the refugee crisis. Credit from the World Bank was expected to finance the Government's privatization programme, the rehabilitation of essential infrastructure and the development of small enterprises. Although about half of the refugees had left Albania by the end of June, the internal situation remained unstable, and organized crime endemic. In October the new Government announced its aim of continuing structural reforms and measures to combat corruption; main priorities included the restructuring of the banking system, the extension of privatization, the strengthening of tax administration, and the further reduction of trade tariffs.

### Social Welfare

All medical services are provided free of charge, and medicines are supplied free to infants of up to one year of age. In 1993 the number of hospitals totalled 40, and there were 10,500 beds available. In the same year there was one doctor for every 735 persons. Kindergartens and nursery schools receive large subsidies. Women are entitled to 180 to 360 days' maternity leave, receiving 80% of their salary. There is a non-contributory state social insurance system for all workers, with 70%–100% of salary being paid during sick leave, and a pension system for the old and disabled. Retirement pensions represent 70% of the average monthly salary. Men retire between the ages of 55 and 65 years, and women between 50 and 60. Legislation relating to social assistance for the unemployed entered into force in November 1991. Municipalities and communes became responsible for social assistance in mid-1993. Of total current expenditure in the 1998 state budget, 24,329m. lekë (20.7%) was for social security, 1,621m. lekë (1.4%) for unemployment insurance, and 6,168m. lekë (5.2%) for social assistance.

### Education

Education in Albania is provided free at primary and secondary level. Approximately 38% of children aged three to six years attended nursery school in 1995, compared with 59% in 1990. Children between the ages of six and 14 years attend an 'eight-year school', which is compulsory. In 1995 96% of children in the relevant age-group (boys 95%; girls 97%) were enrolled at primary schools. In 1990/91 about 75% of pupils leaving the 'eight-year school' proceeded to secondary education. In 1995 secondary education was undergoing restructuring to a system comprising two alternative levels. The second level lasts for five years and qualifies students for management-level employment or higher studies. In 1995 enrolment at secondary schools was equivalent to only 35% of children in the relevant age-group, compared with 78% in 1990. In the same year there were eight universities and two institutes of higher education. In 1994/95 about 2.4% of secondary school-leavers continued into higher education. Government expenditure on education amounted to 5,893m. lekë in 1994 (equivalent to 3.4% of GNP). The budget for 1999 allocated about 2.5% of projected government expenditure to education.

### Public Holidays

**2000:** 1 January (New Year's Day), 8 January*† (Small Bayram, end of Ramadan), 8 March (International Women's Day), 16 March* (Great Bayram, Feast of the Sacrifice), 21–24 April (Catholic Easter), 1 May (Orthodox Easter), 28 November (Independence and Liberation Day), 25 December (Christmas Day), 28 December*† (Small Bayram, end of Ramadan).

**2001:** 1 January (New Year's Day), 6 March* (Great Bayram, Feast of the Sacrifice), 8 March (International Women's Day), 13–16 April (Catholic Easter), 16 April (Orthodox Easter), 28 November (Independence and Liberation Day), 17 December* (Small Bayram, end of Ramadan), 25 December (Christmas Day).

* These holidays are dependent on the Islamic lunar calendar and may vary by one or two days from the dates given.

† This festival will occur twice (in the Islamic years AH 1420 and AH 1421) within the same Gregorian year.

### Weights and Measures

The metric system is in force.

# Statistical Survey

Source (unless otherwise stated): Institute of Statistics (Drejtoria e Statistikës), Tirana.

## Area and Population

**AREA, POPULATION AND DENSITY**

| | |
|---|---|
| Area (sq km) | |
| Land | 27,398 |
| Inland water | 1,350 |
| Total | 28,748* |
| Population (census results) | |
| January 1979 | 2,591,000 |
| 2 April 1989 | |
| Males | 1,638,900† |
| Females | 1,543,500† |
| Total | 3,182,417 |
| Population (official estimates at mid-year) | |
| 1995 | 3,609,000 |
| 1996 | 3,670,000 |
| 1997 | 3,731,000 |
| Density (per sq km) at mid-1997 | 129.8 |

* 11,100 sq miles. † Provisional.

**Ethnic Groups** (census of 2 April 1989): Albanian 3,117,601; Greek 58,758; Macedonian 4,697; Montenegrin, Serb, Croat, etc. 100; others 1,261.

**DISTRICTS** (estimated population at 1 January 1993)

| | Population |
|---|---|
| Berat | 136,939 |
| Bulqizë | 43,363 |
| Delvinë | 29,926 |
| Devoll | 37,744 |
| Dibër | 91,916 |
| Durrës | 162,846 |
| Elbasan | 215,240 |
| Fier | 208,646 |
| Gjirokastër | 60,547 |
| Gramsh | 42,087 |
| Has | 21,271 |
| Kavajë | 85,120 |
| Kolonjë | 25,089 |
| Korçë | 171,205 |
| Krujë | 59,997 |
| Kuçovë | 40,035 |
| Kukës | 78,061 |
| Laç | 50,712 |
| Lezhë | 65,075 |
| Librazhd | 75,300 |
| Lushnjë | 136,865 |
| Malësi e Madhe | 43,924 |
| Mallakastër | 36,287 |
| Mat | 75,436 |
| Mirditë | 49,900 |
| Peqin | 29,831 |
| Përmet | 36,979 |
| Pogradec | 72,203 |
| Pukë | 47,621 |
| Sarandë | 53,730 |
| Shkodër | 195,424 |
| Skrapar | 44,339 |
| Tepelenë | 42,365 |
| Tiranë | 384,010 |
| Tropojë | 44,761 |
| Vlorë | 171,131 |
| **Total** | 3,165,925 |

**PRINCIPAL TOWNS** (population at mid-1990)

| | |
|---|---|
| Tiranë (Tirana, the capital) | 244,200 |
| Durrës (Durazzo) | 85,400 |
| Elbasan | 83,300 |
| Shkodër (Scutari) | 81,900 |
| Vlorë (Vlonë or Valona) | 73,800 |
| Korçë (Koritsa) | 65,400 |
| Fier | 45,200 |
| Berat | 43,800 |
| Lushnjë | 31,500 |
| Kavajë | 25,700 |
| Gjirokastër | 24,900 |
| Kuçovë* | 22,300 |

* This town was known as Qyteti Stalin during the period of Communist rule, but has since reverted to its former name.

Source: *Statistical Directory of Albania.*

**BIRTHS, MARRIAGES AND DEATHS***

| | Registered live births | | Registered marriages | | Registered deaths | |
|---|---|---|---|---|---|---|
| | Number | Rate (per 1,000) | Number | Rate (per 1,000) | Number | Rate (per 1,000) |
| 1986 | 76,435 | 25.3 | 25,718 | 8.5 | 17,369 | 5.7 |
| 1987 | 79,696 | 25.9 | 27,370 | 8.9 | 17,119 | 5.6 |
| 1988 | 80,241 | 25.5 | 28,174 | 9.0 | 17,027 | 5.4 |
| 1989 | 78,862 | 24.7 | 27,655 | 8.6 | 18,168 | 5.7 |
| 1990 | 82,125 | 25.2 | 28,992 | 8.9 | 18,193 | 5.6 |
| 1991 | 77,361 | 23.8 | 24,853 | 7.6 | 17,743 | 5.4 |

**Registered births:** 60,696 (16.6 per 1,000) in 1996.

**Registered marriages** (provisional): 25,260 (6.8 per 1,000) in 1997.

**Registered deaths:** 17,238 (5.1 per 1,000) in 1992; 16,639 (4.8 per 1,000) in 1993; 17,027 (4.7 per 1,000) in 1996.

* For 1990–92 rates are based on unrevised estimates of mid-year population.

**Expectation of life** (years at birth, 1989/90): 72.2 (Males 69.3; Females 75.4).

Source: *Statistical Yearbook of the PSR of Albania*, *Statistical Yearbook of Albania* and UN, *Demographic Yearbook.*

**ECONOMICALLY ACTIVE POPULATION**
(ISIC Major Divisions, 1989 census)

| | Males | Females | Total |
|---|---|---|---|
| Agriculture, hunting, forestry and fishing | 399,810 | 399,249 | 799,059 |
| Mining and quarrying; Manufacturing; Electricity, gas and water | 160,833 | 118,155 | 278,988 |
| Construction | 41,979 | 7,312 | 49,291 |
| Trade, restaurants and hotels | 22,171 | 26,447 | 48,618 |
| Transport, storage and communications | 36,324 | 8,109 | 44,433 |
| Financing, insurance, real estate and business services; Community, social and personal services | 119,279 | 100,905 | 220,184 |
| Activities not adequately defined | 10,293 | 6,798 | 17,091 |
| **Total employed** | 790,689 | 666,975 | 1,457,664 |

Source: ILO, *Yearbook of Labour Statistics.*

**1997** (annual averages, '000 persons): Total domestic employment 1,107 (Agricultural sector 761); Unemployed 194; Domestic labour force 1,301 (males 794, females 507). Source: IMF, *Albania: Recent Economic Development and Statistical Appendix* (July 1999).

# Agriculture

**PRINCIPAL CROPS** ('000 metric tons)

| | 1996 | 1997 | 1998 |
|---|---|---|---|
| Wheat and spelt | 271 | 388 | 403 |
| Barley | 4 | 4 | 4 |
| Maize | 214 | 195 | 200 |
| Rye | 4 | 3 | 3 |
| Oats | 15 | 12 | 13 |
| Sorghum* | 15 | 14 | 14 |
| Potatoes | 137 | 127 | 130 |
| Dry beans | 23 | 20 | 24 |
| Sunflower seed | 2 | 2 | 2 |
| Olives | 28 | 33 | 40 |
| Tomatoes | 180 | 150 | 156 |
| Other vegetables | 250 | 250 | 250 |
| Watermelons | 250 | 200 | 210 |
| Grapes | 59 | 68 | 68 |
| Sugar beet | 74 | 51 | 62 |
| Apples | 10 | 11 | 12 |
| Pears | 2 | 2 | 2 |
| Peaches and nectarines | 2 | 2 | 2 |
| Plums | 15 | 11 | 12 |
| Oranges | 2 | 3 | 3 |
| Other fruits and berries | 27 | 26 | 27 |
| Tree-nuts* | 4 | 4 | 4 |
| Tobacco (leaves) | 6 | 8 | 9 |

* FAO estimates.

Source: FAO, *Production Yearbook*.

**LIVESTOCK** ('000 head, year ending September)

| | 1996 | 1997 | 1998 |
|---|---|---|---|
| Horses* | 58 | 58 | 58 |
| Mules* | 25 | 25 | 25 |
| Asses* | 113 | 113 | 113 |
| Cattle | 806 | 771 | 780 |
| Pigs | 98 | 97 | 98 |
| Sheep | 1,982 | 1,858 | 1,890 |
| Goats | 1,250 | 1,148 | 1,300 |

* FAO estimates.

Source: FAO, *Production Yearbook*.

**Poultry** ('000 head): 4,108 in 1996; 4,566 in 1997; 4,600 in 1998 (estimate) (Source: IMF, *Albania: Recent Economic Developments and Statistical Appendix*, July 1999).

**LIVESTOCK PRODUCTS** ('000 metric tons)

| | 1996 | 1997 | 1998 |
|---|---|---|---|
| Beef and veal* | 33 | 32 | 32 |
| Mutton and lamb* | 12 | 11 | 11 |
| Goat meat | 8* | 9* | 9† |
| Pig meat† | 5 | 5 | 5 |
| Poultry meat | 4 | 4* | 5 |
| Cows' milk | 895 | 707 | 720 |
| Sheep's milk | 70 | 68 | 69 |
| Goats' milk | 80 | 85 | 81 |
| Cheese† | 15 | 11 | 11 |
| Butter† | 2 | 2 | 2 |
| Poultry eggs | 17 | 19 | 20 |
| Wool: | | | |
| greasy | 3 | 3 | 3 |
| scoured (clean) | 2 | 1 | 1 |
| Cattle hides† | 7 | 7 | 7 |
| Sheep and lamb skins† | 3 | 3 | 3 |
| Goat and kid skins† | 2 | 1 | 1 |

* Unofficial figure(s). † FAO estimate(s).

Source: FAO, *Production Yearbook*.

# Forestry

**ROUNDWOOD REMOVALS** ('000 cubic metres, excl. bark)

| | 1995 | 1996 | 1997 |
|---|---|---|---|
| Industrial wood | 64 | 64 | 64 |
| Fuel wood | 346 | 346 | 346 |
| **Total** | 409 | 409 | 409 |

Source: FAO, *Yearbook of Forest Products*.

**SAWNWOOD PRODUCTION** ('000 cubic metres, incl. railway sleepers)

| | 1995 | 1996 | 1997 |
|---|---|---|---|
| Coniferous (softwood) | 2 | 2 | 2 |
| Broadleaved (hardwood) | 3 | 3 | 3 |
| **Total** | 5 | 5 | 5 |

Source: FAO, *Yearbook of Forest Products*.

# Fishing

(metric tons, live weight)

| | 1995 | 1996 | 1997 |
|---|---|---|---|
| Inland waters | 219 | 317 | 180 |
| Mediterranean Sea | 1,160 | 1,808 | 833 |
| **Total catch** | 1,379 | 2,125 | 1,013 |

Source: FAO, *Yearbook of Fishery Statistics*.

# Mining

('000 metric tons, unless otherwise indicated)

| | 1993 | 1994 | 1995 |
|---|---|---|---|
| Lignite (brown coal) | 215 | 169 | 120 |
| Crude petroleum | 568 | 535 | 521 |
| Natural gas (million cu metres) | 82 | 52 | 28 |
| Copper ore†‡ | 8.0 | 2.2 | 4.2 |
| Nickel ore (metric tons)†§ | 75 | — | — |
| Chromium ore† | 24 | 31 | 75§ |
| Cobalt ore (metric tons)*†§ | 10 | 10 | — |

* Provisional or estimated production.

† Figures refer to the metal content of ores.

‡ Data from *World Metal Statistics* (London).

§ Data from the US Bureau of Mines.

Source: mainly UN, *Industrial Commodity Statistics Yearbook*.

**1996:** Chromium ore ('000 metric tons) 236 (gross weight); Copper ('000 metric tons) 188 (gross weight); Lignite ('000 metric tons) 113; Crude petroleum ('000 metric tons) 488; Natural gas (million cu metres) 23.

**1997:** Chromium ore ('000 metric tons) 157 (gross weight); Copper ('000 metric tons) 25 (gross weight); Lignite ('000 metric tons) 40; Crude petroleum ('000 metric tons) 360; Natural gas (million cu metres) 18.

**1998:** Chromium ore ('000 metric tons) 150 (gross weight); Copper ('000 metric tons) 55 (gross weight); Lignite ('000 metric tons) 49; Crude petroleum ('000 metric tons) 365; Natural gas (million cu metres) 17.

Source: IMF, *Albania: Recent Economic Developments and Statistical Appendix* (July 1999).

# Industry

## SELECTED PRODUCTS

('000 metric tons, unless otherwise indicated)

| | 1994 | 1995 | 1996 |
|---|---|---|---|
| Wheat flour | 44 | 282† | 100† |
| Raw sugar | — | 3* | 7* |
| Wine ('000 hectolitres) | 50 | 170 | 290 |
| Cigarettes (million) | 929 | n.a. | n.a. |
| Veneer sheets ('000 cubic metres)† | 10 | 10 | 10 |
| Plywood ('000 cubic metres)† | 6 | 6 | 6 |
| Mechanical wood pulp† | 2 | 2 | 2 |
| Chemical wood pulp† | 14 | 14 | 14 |
| Paper and paperboard† | 44 | 44 | 44 |
| Sulphuric acid | 4 | — | — |
| Nitrogenous fertilizers (a)‡ | 9 | 4 | n.a. |
| Phosphatic fertilizers (b)‡ | 11 | 14 | — |
| Soap | 3 | 2 | 2 |
| Motor spirit (petrol) | 39 | 43 | 37 |
| Kerosene | 29 | 29 | 26 |
| Gas-diesel (distillate fuel) oil | 111 | 106 | 95 |
| Residual fuel oils | 82 | 123 | n.a. |
| Petroleum bitumen (asphalt)* | 34 | 33 | n.a. |
| Cement | 240 | 238 | 203 |
| Ferro-chromium | 34 | 43 | 32 |
| Crude steel | 19 | 22 | 23 |
| Copper (unrefined)§ | 1.5 | 2.9 | 1.4 |
| Electric energy (million kWh) | 3,903 | 4,414 | 5,926 |

* Provisional or estimated production.

† FAO estimate(s).

‡ Production in terms of (a) nitrogen or (b) phosphoric acid.

§ Data from *World Metal Statistics* (London).

Source: mainly UN, *Industrial Commodity Statistics Yearbook*.

**1997** ('000 metric tons): Wine 17; Phosphatic fertilizers 27; Raw sugar 5 (unofficial figure); Soap 2; Motor spirit 15; Kerosene 11; Gas-diesel oil 57; Cement 100; Ferro-chromium 31; Electric energy (million kWh) 5,184.

**1998** ('000 metric tons): Wine 17; Phosphatic fertilizers 12; Raw sugar 7 (FAO estimate); Motor spirit 21; Kerosene 2; Gas-diesel oil 91; Cement 84; Ferro-chromium 30; Electric energy (million kWh) 5,068.

Sources (for 1997–98): FAO, *Production Yearbook*; IMF, *Albania: Recent Economic Developments and Statistical Appendix* (July 1999).

# Finance

## CURRENCY AND EXCHANGE RATES

**Monetary Units**

100 qindarka (qintars) = 1 new lek.

**Sterling, Dollar and Euro Equivalents** (30 September 1999)

£1 sterling = 220.8 lekë;
US $1 = 134.1 lekë;
€1 = 143.0 lekë;
1,000 lekë = £4.529 = $7.457 = €6.992.

**Average Exchange Rate** (lekë per US $)

1996 104.50
1997 148.93
1998 150.63

## STATE BUDGET (million lekë)

| Revenue | 1996 | 1997 | 1998 |
|---|---|---|---|
| Tax revenue | 42,884 | 46,298 | 72,572 |
| Turnover tax/value-added tax | 9,076 | 15,655 | 28,771 |
| Taxes on income and profits | 4,787 | 3,592 | 6,400 |
| Social security contributions | 12,688 | 13,143 | 15,828 |
| Import duties and export taxes | 7,708 | 8,960 | 12,615 |
| Excise taxes | 4,947 | 2,168 | 4,910 |
| Other revenue | 9,003 | 12,206 | 21,076 |
| Profit transfer from Bank of Albania | 3,859 | 8,067 | 16,400 |
| Income from budgetary institutions | 2,735 | 1,834 | 3,326 |
| Counterpart sales revenue | 266 | 256 | 137 |
| Privatization receipts | 546 | 910 | 133 |
| **Total** | 51,887 | 58,504 | 93,648 |

| Expenditure | 1996 | 1997 | 1998 |
|---|---|---|---|
| Current expenditure | 72,493 | 86,870 | 117,604 |
| Wages | 17,918 | 20,377 | 22,048 |
| Social security contributions | 5,062 | 5,167 | 6,288 |
| Interest | 8,571 | 18,779 | 36,086 |
| Operational and maintenance | 12,482 | 13,565 | 18,537 |
| Subsidies | 1,110 | 1,551 | 2,308 |
| Social security | 20,342 | 20,133 | 24,329 |
| Unemployment insurance | 2,163 | 2,204 | 1,621 |
| Social assistance | 3,795 | 4,274 | 6,168 |
| Capital expenditure (investment) | 12,752 | 13,751 | 23,789 |
| **Total** | 85,245 | 100,621 | 141,393 |

Source: IMF, *Albania: Recent Economic Developments and Statistical Appendix* (July 1999).

## INTERNATIONAL RESERVES (US $ million at 31 December)

| | 1996 | 1997 | 1998 |
|---|---|---|---|
| Gold* | 42.50 | 33.40 | 33.70 |
| IMF special drawing rights | 0.75 | 0.62 | 61.10 |
| Reserve position in IMF | 0.01 | 0.01 | 0.01 |
| Foreign exchange | 280.10 | 308.30 | 287.40 |
| **Total** | 323.36 | 342.33 | 382.20 |

* Valued at market-related prices.

Source: IMF, *International Financial Statistics*.

## MONEY SUPPLY ('000 million lekë at 31 December)

| | 1996 | 1997 | 1998 |
|---|---|---|---|
| Currency outside banks | 47.81 | 72.73 | 68.32 |
| Demand deposits at deposit money banks | 42.59 | 18.94 | 15.41 |
| **Total money** | 90.41 | 91.67 | 83.73 |

Source: IMF, *International Financial Statistics*.

## COST OF LIVING (Consumer price index; base: 1992 = 100)

| | 1996 | 1997 | 1998 |
|---|---|---|---|
| Food | 263.0 | 357.8 | 433.2 |
| **All items** (incl. others) | 275.5 | 366.9 | 442.6 |

Source: UN, *Monthly Bulletin of Statistics*.

## NATIONAL ACCOUNTS (million lekë at current prices)

**Gross Domestic Product by Economic Activity**

| | 1996 | 1997 | 1998 |
|---|---|---|---|
| Agriculture | 144,825 | 191,269 | 250,705 |
| Industry* | 34,309 | 42,351 | 55,047 |
| Construction | 31,360 | 38,423 | 58,037 |
| Transport | 9,006 | 9,362 | 14,024 |
| Other services | 61,498 | 60,311 | 82,817 |
| **GDP in purchasers' values** | 280,998 | 341,716 | 460,631 |
| **GDP at constant 1990 prices** | 16,478 | 15,325 | 16,548 |

* Comprising mining, manufacturing, electricity, gas and water.

Source: IMF, *Albania: Recent Economic Developments and Statistical Appendix* (July 1999).

**BALANCE OF PAYMENTS** (US $ million)

| | 1996 | 1997 | 1998 |
|---|---|---|---|
| Exports of goods f.o.b. | 243.7 | 158.6 | 208.0 |
| Imports of goods f.o.b. | −922.0 | −693.6 | −811.7 |
| **Trade balance** | −678.3 | −535.0 | −603.6 |
| Exports of services | 129.2 | 63.8 | 86.6 |
| Imports of services | −189.4 | −115.2 | −129.3 |
| **Balance on goods and services** | −738.5 | −586.4 | −646.3 |
| Other income received | 83.7 | 61.4 | 86.1 |
| Other income paid | −11.9 | −11.8 | −8.7 |
| **Balance on goods, services and income** | −666.7 | −536.8 | −569.0 |
| Current transfers received | 595.9 | 299.8 | 560.8 |
| Current transfers paid | −36.5 | −35.2 | −56.9 |
| **Current balance** | −107.3 | −272.2 | −65.1 |
| Capital account (net) | 4.8 | 2.0 | 31.0 |
| Direct investment from abroad | 90.1 | 47.5 | 45.0 |
| Other investment assets | −138.6 | 59.8 | −126.9 |
| Other investment liabilities | 110.0 | 44.1 | 97.3 |
| Net errors and omissions | 96.9 | 158.4 | 71.1 |
| **Overall balance** | 55.9 | 39.5 | 52.4 |

Source: IMF, *International Financial Statistics*.

# External Trade

**PRINCIPAL COMMODITIES** (million lekë)

| Imports c.i.f. | 1988 | 1989 | 1990 |
|---|---|---|---|
| Machinery and equipment | 1,160.9 | 1,070.0 | 1,174.8 |
| Fuels, minerals and metals | 742.3 | 984.1 | 931.0 |
| Chemical products | 409.7 | 458.0 | 354.0 |
| Raw materials of plant or animal origin | 347.2 | 573.8 | 385.7 |
| Unprocessed foodstuffs | 86.5 | 104.0 | 203.1 |
| Processed foodstuffs | 262.4 | 274.0 | 382.3 |
| Non-foodstuffs of mass consumption | 204.3 | 296.0 | 319.1 |
| **Total** (incl. others) | 3,217.4 | 3,792.0 | 3,795.3 |

| Exports f.o.b. | 1988 | 1989 | 1990 |
|---|---|---|---|
| Fuels, minerals and metals | 1,404.2 | 1,647.3 | 1,063.8 |
| Raw materials of plant or animal origin | 329.3 | 437.0 | 350.2 |
| Unprocessed foodstuffs | 62.1 | 50.3 | 44.6 |
| Processed foodstuffs | 431.4 | 521.5 | 456.0 |
| Non-foodstuffs of mass consumption | 246.3 | 295.4 | 269.2 |
| **Total** (incl. others) | 2,549.2 | 3,029.2 | 2,273.3 |

Source: *Statistical Yearbook of Albania*.

**Total imports f.o.b.** (US $ million): 281.0 in 1991; 540.5 in 1992; 601.5 in 1993; 601.0 in 1994; 679.7 in 1995; 922.0 in 1996; 693.6 in 1997; 811.7 in 1998.

**Total exports f.o.b.** (US $ million): 73.0 in 1991; 70.0 in 1992; 111.6 in 1993; 141.3 in 1994; 204.9 in 1995; 243.7 in 1996; 158.6 in 1997; 208.0 in 1998.

Source: IMF, *International Financial Statistics*.

**PRINCIPAL TRADING PARTNERS** (% of total trade)

| Imports f.o.b. | 1996 | 1997 | 1998 |
|---|---|---|---|
| Austria | 1.0 | 1.5 | 1.4 |
| Belgium-Luxembourg | 2.5 | 1.1 | 1.1 |
| Bulgaria | 4.0 | 2.7 | 2.8 |
| Czech Republic | 0.5 | 1.1 | 0.3 |
| Egypt | 1.0 | 0.2 | 0.8 |
| France | 3.1 | 0.1 | 0.2 |
| Germany | 4.1 | 1.1 | 0.9 |
| Greece | 21.2 | 26.6 | 29.2 |
| Hungary | 0.8 | 0.1 | 0.1 |
| Italy | 41.7 | 44.5 | 44.1 |
| Romania | 2.4 | 0.3 | 0.4 |
| Switzerland | 1.7 | 1.2 | 1.5 |
| Turkey | 4.4 | 4.4 | 3.4 |
| USA | 1.3 | 0.1 | 0.3 |
| **Total** (incl. others) | 100.0 | 100.0 | 100.0 |

| Exports f.o.b | 1996 | 1997 | 1998 |
|---|---|---|---|
| Austria | 1.1 | 1.5 | 1.6 |
| Belgium-Luxembourg | 1.3 | 0.5 | 1.5 |
| France | 2.0 | 1.9 | 1.2 |
| Germany | 6.9 | 6.9 | 5.7 |
| Greece | 13.0 | 20.5 | 19.8 |
| Italy | 57.9 | 49.4 | 60.1 |
| Netherlands | 2.9 | 5.6 | 0.9 |
| Turkey | 3.1 | 1.0 | 0.6 |
| USA | 1.2 | 1.5 | 1.7 |
| **Total** (incl. others) | 100.0 | 100.0 | 100.0 |

Source: IMF, *Albania: Recent Economic Developments and Statistical Appendix* (July 1999).

# Transport

**RAILWAYS** (traffic)

| | 1993 | 1994 | 1995 |
|---|---|---|---|
| Passengers-km (million) | 223 | 215 | 197 |
| Freight ton-km (million) | 54 | 53 | 53 |

Source: UN, *Statistical Yearbook*.

**ROAD TRAFFIC** (motor vehicles in use at 31 December)

| | 1994 | 1995 | 1996 |
|---|---|---|---|
| Passenger cars | 67,960 | 58,692 | 67,031 |
| Buses and coaches | 8,149 | 6,651 | 6,926 |
| Lorries and vans | 42,271 | 25,790 | 27,132 |
| Road tractors | 8,842 | 3,334 | 2,835 |
| Motorcycles and mopeds | 14,339 | 6,946 | 5,541 |

Source: International Road Federation, *World Road Statistics*.

**SHIPPING**

**Merchant Fleet** (registered at 31 December)

| | 1996 | 1997 | 1998 |
|---|---|---|---|
| Number of vessels | 33 | 32 | 25 |
| Displacement ('000 gross registered tons) | 43.4 | 30.4 | 28.7 |

Source: Lloyd's Register of Shipping, *World Fleet Statistics*.

**International Sea-borne Freight Traffic**
('000 metric tons)

| | 1988 | 1989 | 1990 |
|---|---|---|---|
| Goods loaded | 1,090 | 1,112 | 1,065 |
| Goods unloaded | 644 | 659 | 664 |

Source: UN, *Monthly Bulletin of Statistics*.

**CIVIL AVIATION** (traffic on scheduled services)

| | 1994 | 1995 |
|---|---|---|
| Passengers carried ('000) | 9 | 13 |
| Passenger-km (million) | 2 | 4 |

Source: UN, *Statistical Yearbook.*

# Tourism

**FOREIGN TOURIST ARRIVALS BY COUNTRY OF ORIGIN***

| | 1994 | 1995 | 1996 |
|---|---|---|---|
| Austria | 454 | 1,134 | 1,412 |
| Egypt | 61 | 1,364 | 3,205 |
| France | 1,742 | 1,497 | 1,477 |
| Germany | 1,862 | 2,184 | 2,552 |
| Greece | 3,098 | 2,244 | 4,424 |
| Italy | 6,609 | 7,476 | 8,088 |
| United Kingdom | 1,035 | 1,672 | 1,433 |
| USA | 2,374 | 4,176 | 3,927 |
| Yugoslavia | 4,682 | 2,076 | 2,645 |
| **Total** (incl. others) | 28,439 | 40,175 | 56,276 |

* Figures refer to arrivals in hotels.

**Tourism receipts** (US $ million): 5 in 1994; 7 in 1995; 11 in 1996.

Source: World Tourism Organization, *Yearbook of Tourism Statistics.*

# Communications Media

| | 1994 | 1995 | 1996 |
|---|---|---|---|
| Radio receivers ('000 in use) | 650 | 700 | 800 |
| Television receivers ('000 in use) | 310 | 350 | 400 |
| Telephones ('000 main lines in use) | 42 | 42 | n.a. |
| Daily newspapers: | | | |
| Number | 3 | 3 | 5 |
| Average circulation ('000 copies) | n.a. | 130 | 116 |

**Book production** (1991): 381 titles (including 18 pamphlets).

**Telefax stations** (number in use, 1992): 600.

Sources: UN, *Statistical Yearbook*, and UNESCO, *Statistical Yearbook.*

# Education

(1995/96, unless otherwise indicated)

| | Institutions | Teachers | Students | | |
|---|---|---|---|---|---|
| | | | Males | Females | Total |
| Pre-primary | 2,670 | 4,416 | 42,292 | 42,244 | 84,536 |
| Primary | 1,782* | 31,369 | 288,592 | 269,509 | 558,101 |
| Secondary | | | | | |
| General | 162† | 4,147 | 37,392 | 33,999 | 71,391 |
| Vocational | 259† | 2,174 | 12,758 | 5,746 | 18,504 |
| Higher‡§ | 10 | 1,774 | 14,116 | 16,069 | 30,185 |
| Universities, etc. | 8 | 1,596 | 8,656 | 10,430 | 19,086 |
| Other | 2 | 178 | 1,143 | 523 | 1,666 |

* 1994/95 figure.

† 1990 figure.

‡ Figures for students include those enrolled at distance-learning institutions, totalling 9,433 (males 4,317; females 5,116).

§ 1993/94 figures.

Sources: Ministry of Education, Tirana, and UNESCO, *Statistical Yearbook.*

# Directory

## The Constitution

In October 1998 the People's Assembly approved a new Constitution, which had been drafted by a parliamentary commission. The Constitution was endorsed at a national referendum on 22 November, and was officially adopted on 28 November.

### GENERAL PROVISIONS

Albania is a parliamentary republic. The Republic of Albania is a unitary state, with a system of government based on the separation and balancing of legislative, executive and judicial powers. Sovereignty is exercised by the people through their elected representatives. The Republic of Albania recognizes and protects the national rights of people who live outside the country's borders. Political parties are created freely, and are required to conform with democratic principles. The Republic off Albania does not have an official religion, and guarantees equality of religious communities. The economic system of the Republic of Albania is based on a market economy, and on freedom of economic activity, as well as on private and public property. The armed forces ensure the independence of the country, and protect its territorial integrity and constitutional order. Local government in the Republic of Albania is exercised according to the principle of decentralization of public power. The fundamental political, economic and social rights and freedoms of Albanian citizens are guaranteed under the Constitution.

### LEGISLATURE

The People's Assembly comprises at least 140 deputies, and is elected for a term of four years. One hundred deputies are elected directly in single-member constituencies, while parties receiving more than 3% of votes cast nationally are allocated further deputies in proportion to the number of votes won. The Council of Ministers, every deputy and 20,000 voters each have the right to propose legislation. The People's Assembly makes decisions by a majority of votes, when more than one-half of the deputies are present. The 25-member Council of the Assembly is elected by the members of the People's Assembly at the beginning of the first session. The Council of the Assembly reviews preliminary draft laws, and gives opinions on specific issues.

### PRESIDENT

The President of the Republic is the Head of State and represents the unity of the people. A candidate for President is proposed to the People's Assembly by a group of not less than 20 deputies. The President is elected by secret ballot by a majority of three-fifths of the members of the People's Assembly for a term of five years.

### COUNCIL OF MINISTERS

The Council of Ministers comprises the Prime Minister, Deputy Prime Minister and ministers. The President of the Republic nominates as Prime Minister the candidate presented by the party or coalition of parties that has the majority of seats in the People's Assembly. The Prime Minister, within 40 days of his appointment, forms a Council of Ministers, which is presented for approval to the People's Assembly.

### LOCAL GOVERNMENT

The units of local government are communes, municipalities and regions. The representative organs of the basic units of local government are councils, which are elected by general direct elections for a period of three years. The executive organ of a municipality or commune is the Chairman. The Council of Ministers appoints a Prefect in every region as its representative.

### JUDICIARY

Judicial power is exercised by the High Court, as well as by the Courts of Appeal and the Courts of First Instance. The Chairman and members of the High Court are appointed by the President of the Republic, with the approval of the People's Assembly, for a term of seven years. Other judges are appointed by the President upon the proposal of a High Council of Justice. The High Council of Justice comprises the Chairman of the High Court, the Minister of Justice, three members elected by the People's Assembly for a term of five years, and nine judges who are elected by a national judicial conference. The Constitutional Court arbitrates on constitutional issues, and determines the conformity of proposed legislation with the Constitution. The Constitutional Court comprises nine members, who are appointed by the President, with the approval of the People's Assembly, for a term of nine years.

# The Government

(January 2000)

### HEAD OF STATE

**President of the Republic:** Dr REXHEP MEJDANI (elected 24 July 1997).

### COUNCIL OF MINISTERS

A coalition of the Socialist Party of Albania (SPA), the Social Democratic Party of Albania (SDP), the Democratic Alliance Party (DAP), the Agrarian Party (AP), the Union for Human Rights Party (UHRP), and independents (Ind.).

**Prime Minister:** ILIR META (SPA).

**Deputy Prime Minister and Minister of Labour and Social Affairs:** MAKBULE CECO (SPA).

**Minister of Foreign Affairs:** PASKAL MILO (SDP).

**Minister of Public Order:** SPARTAK POCI (SPA).

**Minister of Defence:** LUAN HAJDARAGA (SPA).

**Minister of Finance:** ANASTAS ANGJELI (SPA).

**Minister of the Public Economy and Privatization:** ZEF PRECI (Ind.).

**Minister of Justice:** ILIR PANDA (Ind.).

**Minister of Education and Science:** ETHEM RUKA (SPA).

**Minister of Economic Co-operation and Trade:** ERMELINDA MEKSI (SPA).

**Minister of Transport:** INGRID SHULI (SDP).

**Minister of Construction:** ARBEN DEMETI (DAP).

**Minister of Agriculture and Food:** LUFTER XHUVELI (AP).

**Minister of Local Government:** BASHKIM FINO (SPA).

**Minister of Health:** LEONARD SOLIS (UHRP).

**Minister of Culture, Youth and Sports:** EDI RAMA (Ind.).

**Minister of State in the Office of the Prime Minister:** PREC ZOGAJ (DAP).

### MINISTRIES

**Council of Ministers:** Këshilli i Ministrave, Tirana; tel. (42) 28210; fax (42) 27888.

**Ministry of Agriculture and Food:** Ministria e Bujqësisë dhe Ushqimit, Tirana; tel. and fax (42) 23917.

**Ministry of Culture, Youth and Sports:** Ministria e Kulturës, Bulevardi Zhan D'Ark, Tirana; tel. (42) 29715; fax (42) 27878.

**Ministry of Defence:** Ministria e Mbrojtjes, Tirana; tel. (42) 25726; fax (42) 28325.

**Ministry of Economic Co-operation and Trade:** Tirana; tel. and fax (42) 62565.

**Ministry of Education and Science:** Ministria e Arsimit dhe Shkences, Rruga Durrësit 23, Tirana; tel. (42) 26307; fax (42) 32002; e-mail eruka@excite.com; f. 1912.

**Ministry of Finance:** Ministria e Financave, Tirana; tel. (42) 28405; fax (42) 28494.

**Ministry of Foreign Affairs:** Ministria e Punëve të Jashtme, Tirana; tel. (42) 34600; fax (42) 32971.

**Ministry of Health:** Ministria e Shendetesisë, Tirana; tel. and fax (42) 64632.

**Ministry of Information:** Tirana; tel. and fax (42) 56269.

**Ministry of the Interior:** Ministria e Brendshme, Sheshi Skënderbeu 3, Tirana; tel. (42) 28161; fax (42) 63607.

**Ministry of Justice:** Ministria e Drejtësisë, Tirana; tel. (42) 28378; fax (42) 28359.

**Ministry of Labour and Social Affairs:** Ministria e Punës dhe Ndihmës Sociale, Rruga e Kavajes, Tirana; tel. (42) 28340; fax (42) 27779.

**Ministry of Public Affairs and Transport:** Rruga Skënderbeu, Tirana; tel. and fax (42) 34954.

**Ministry of the Public Economy and Privatization:** Sheshi Skënderbeu 2, Tirana; tel. (42) 32833; fax (42) 34052; e-mail postmaster@mepptirana.al; internet www.mepp.gov.al.

**Ministry of Public Order:** Tirana.

**Ministry of Tourism:** Ministria e Turizmit, Bulevardi Deshmoret e Kombit, Tirana; tel. (42) 34668; fax (42) 34658.

**Ministry of Trade and Economic Co-operation:** Tirana; tel. (42) 34668; fax (42) 34658.

# Legislature

### KUVENDI POPULLOR

(People's Assembly)

**President (Speaker):** SKENDER GJINUSHI.

**Deputy President:** NAMIK DOKLE.

**General Election, 29 June and 6 July 1997**

| Party | Seats |
|---|---|
| Socialist Party of Albania | 101 |
| Democratic Party of Albania | 29 |
| Social Democratic Party of Albania | 8 |
| Union for Human Rights Party | 4 |
| National Front Party | 3 |
| Democratic Alliance Party | 2 |
| Legality Movement Party | 2 |
| Albanian Republican Party | 1 |
| Party of National Unity | 1 |
| Agrarian Party | 1 |
| Independents | 3 |
| **Total** | 155 |

# Political Organizations

**Agrarian Party (AP):** Rruga Budi 6, Tirana; tel. (42) 27481; fax (42) 27481; f. 1991; Chair. LUFTER XHUVELI.

**Albanian Civil Party:** Tirana; f. 1998; Chair. ROLAND VELKO; Sec. ETLEVA GJERMENI.

**Albanian Communist Party:** Tirana; f. 1991; granted legal recognition 1998; Chair. HYSNI MILLOSHI.

**Albanian Conservative Party** (Partia Konservatore Shqiptare): Tirana; Chair. ARMANDO RUCO.

**Albanian Ecological Party** (Partia Ekologjike Shqiptare): Rruga Aleksander Moissi 26, POB 135, Tirana; tel. (42) 22503; fax (42) 34413; environmental political party; Chair. Dr NAMIK VEHBI FADILE HOTI.

**Albanian Green Party** (Partia e Blertë Shqiptare): POB 749, Tirana; tel. and fax (42) 33309; f. 1991; campaigns on environmental issues; Chair. NEVRUZ MALUKA; Sec. SHYQRI KONDI.

**Albanian Helsinki Forum** (Forum Shqiptar i Helsinkit): Tirana; f. 1990; mem. International Federation of Helsinki; Chair. Prof. ARBEN PUTO.

**Albanian Liberal Party** (Partia Liberale Shqiptare): Tirana; f. 1991; Chair. VALTER FILE.

**Albanian National Democratic Party** (Partia Nacional Demokratike): Tirana; f. 1991; Chair. FATMIR ÇEKANI.

**Albanian Nationalist Party:** Tirana; f. 1993.

**Albanian New Socialist Party:** Tirana; f. 1996 by former mems of the SPA.

**Albanian Republican Party (ARP)** (Partia Republikane Shqiptare—PRS): Tirana; f. 1991; Gen. Council of 54 mems, Steering

Commission of 21 mems; Chair. SABRI GODO; Vice-Chair. FATMIR MEDIU; Sec. CERCIZ MINGOMATAS.

**Albanian Women's Federation** (Forum i Grus Shqiptare): Tirana; tel. (42) 28309; f. 1991; independent organization uniting women from various religious and cultural backgrounds; Chair. DIANA ÇULI.

**Alternative Republican Party:** Tirana; f. 1993.

**Çamëria Political and Patriotic Association** (Shoqata Politike-Patriotike Çamëria): Tirana; supports the rights of the Çam minority (an Albanian people) in northern Greece; f. 1991; Chair. Dr ABAZ DOJAKA.

**Christian Democratic Party of Albania (CDPA):** Rruga Dëshmorët e 4 Shkurtit, Tirana; tel. (42) 30042; fax (42) 34024; f. 1991; Pres. ZEF BUSHATI; Gen.-Sec. GASPER MOLNI.

**Democratic Alliance Party (DAP):** Tirana; f. 1992 by former members of the DPA; Chair. NERITAN ÇEKA; Sec.-Gen. EDMOND DRAGOTI.

**Democratic Alternative:** Tirana; f. 1999 by breakaway faction of reformist members of the Democratic Party of Albania; Leader GENC POLLO.

**Democratic Movement of the Unification of Albanians:** f. 1993.

**Democratic Party of Albania (DPA)** (Partia Demokratike e Shqipërisë—PDSH): Rruga Punetoret e Rilindjes; Tirana; tel. (42) 28091; fax (42) 23525; e-mail profsberisha@albaniaonline.net; f. 1990; committed to centre-right democratic ideals and market economics; Chair. Prof. Dr SALI BERISHA; Sec.-Gen. RIDVAN BODE.

**Democratic Prosperity Party** (Partia e Prosperitetit Demokratik): Tirana; f. 1991; Chair. YZEIR FETAHU.

**Democratic Party of the Right:** Tirana; Leader PETRIT KALAKULA.

**Democratic Union of the Greek Minority** (OMONIA—Bashkimia Demokratik i Minoritet Grek): Tirana; f. 1991; Chair. JORGO LABOVITJADHI.

**Democratic Unity Party** (Partia e Bashkimit Demokratik): Tirana; Chair. XHEVDET LIBOHOVA.

**Independent Party** (Partia Indipendente): Tirana; f. 1991; Chair. EDMOND GJOKRUSHI.

**Legality Movement Party** (Partia Lëvizja e Legalitetit): Tirana; f. 1992; monarchist; Chair. GURI DUROLLARI.

**Movement for Democracy** (Levizja per Democraci): Tirana; f. 1997 by former mems of the DPA; Leader DASHAMIR SHEHI.

**National Committee of the War Veterans of the Anti-Fascist National Liberation War of the Albanian People** (Komiteti Kombëtar i Veteranëve të Luftës Antifashiste Nacional Çlirimtare të Popullit Shqiptar): Rruga Dëshmorët e 4 Shkurtit, Tirana; f. 1957; Chair. PIRRO DODBIBA; Gen. Sec. QAMIL PODA.

**National Front** (Balli Kombëtar): c/o Kuvendi Popullor, Tirana; Chair. ABAZ ERMENJI.

**National Progress Party** (Partia e Perparimit Kombëtar): Tirana; f. 1991; Chair. MYRTO XHAFERRI.

**National Unity Party** (Partia e Unitetit Kombëtar): Rruga Alqi Kondi, Tirana; tel. (42) 27498; fax (42) 23929; f. 1991; Chair. of Steering Cttee IDAJET BEQIRI.

**New Party of Labour:** Tirana; f. 1998; left-wing; defines itself as successor to the former communist Party of Labour of Albania.

**People's Party** (Partia Popullore): Tirana; f. 1991; aims to eradicate communism; Chair. BASHKIM DRIZA.

**Republican Party:** Tirana; Chair. FATMIR MEDIU.

**Right National Party:** Tirana; f. 1998 by a breakaway faction of the National Front; Leader HYSEN SELFO.

**Social Democratic Party of Albania (SDP)** (Partia Social Demokratike e Shqipërise—PSDS): Rruga Asim Vokshi 26, Tirana; tel. (42) 26540; fax (42) 27485; f. 1991; advocates gradual economic reforms and social justice; 100-member National Managing Council; Chair. GRAMOZ PASHKO; Gen.-Sec. DHORI KULE.

**Social Justice Party** (Partia e Drejtesise Shogerore): Tirana.

**Social Labour Party of Albania** (Partia Socialpuntore Shqiptare): Burrel; f. 1992; Pres. RAMADAN NDREKA.

**Socialist Party of Albania (SPA)** (Partia Socialiste e Shqipërisë—PSS): Tirana; tel. (42) 27409; fax (42) 27417; f. 1941 as Albanian Communist Party, renamed Party of Labour of Albania (PLA) in 1948, adopted present name in 1991; now rejects Marxism-Leninism and claims commitment to democratic socialism and a market economy; Managing Cttee of 81 mems, headed by Presidency of 15 mems; Chair. FATOS NANO; Sec.-Gen. NAMIK DOKLE; 110,000 mems.

**Union for Human Rights Party (UHRP)** (Partia për Mbrojtjen e te Drejtave te Njeriut—PBDNj): Tirana; f. 1992; represents the Greek and Macedonian minorities; Chair. VASIL MELO; Sec.-Gen. THOMA MICO.

**Union of Social Democrats (USD):** Tirana; f. 1995; breakaway faction of the SDP; Leader TEODOR LACO.

# Diplomatic Representation

### EMBASSIES IN ALBANIA

**Austria:** Rruga Skënderbeu, Tirana; tel. (42) 33157; fax (42) 33140; e-mail austemb@adanet.com.al; Ambassador: ARNO RIEDEL.

**Bosnia and Herzegovina:** Rruga Themistokli Germenji 5, Tirana; tel. (42) 30454; fax (42) 34848; Chargé d'affaires a.i.: MUHAREM ZEJNULAHU.

**Bulgaria:** Rruga Skënderbeu 12, Tirana; tel. (42) 33155; Ambassador: STEFAN NAUMOV.

**China, People's Republic:** Rruga Skënderbeu 57, Tirana; tel. (42) 32077; Ambassador: MA WEIMAO.

**Croatia:** Rruga Abdyl Frashëri, Tirana; tel. (42) 28390; fax (42) 30577; Ambassador: MLLADEN JURIČIĆ.

**Czech Republic:** Rruga Skënderbeu 4, Tirana; tel. (42) 34004; fax (42) 32159; Chargé d'affaires a.i.: IMRICH SEDLÁK.

**Egypt:** Rruga Skënderbeu 43, Tirana; tel. (42) 33022; fax (42) 32295; Ambassador: ATTIA QARAM.

**France:** Rruga Skënderbeu 14, Tirana; tel. (42) 34250; Ambassador: PATRICK CHRISMANT.

**Germany:** Rruga Skënderbeu 8, Tirana; tel. (42) 32050; fax (42) 33497; Ambassador: HANNSPETER DISDORN.

**Greece:** Rruga Frederik Shiroka 3, Tirana; tel. (42) 34290; fax (42) 34443; Ambassador: CONSTANIN PREVEDOURAKIS.

**Holy See:** Rruga e Durrësit 13, POB 8355, Tirana; tel. (42) 33516; fax (42) 32001; Apostolic Nuncio: Most Rev. GIOVANNI BULAITIS, Titular Archbishop of Narona.

**Hungary:** Rruga Skënderbeu 16, Tirana; tel. (42) 32238; fax (42) 33211; Ambassador: ISTVÁN BOGNAR.

**Iran:** Rruga Skënderbeu 21, Tirana; tel. (42) 27869; fax (42) 30409; Chargé d'affaires a.i.: VAHID FARMAND.

**Italy:** Rruga Lek Dukagjini, Tirana; tel. (42) 34343; fax (42) 32507; Ambassador: MARCELLO SPATAFORA.

**Libya:** Rruga Sulejman Pasha 58, Tirana; tel. (42) 28101; fax (42) 34559; Bureau Chief: YOUSSEF OMAR SAGAR.

**Macedonia, former Yugoslav republic:** Skënderbeu 3/6, Tirana; tel. and fax (42) 33036; Ambassador: RISTO NIKOVSKI.

**Poland:** Rruga e Durrësit 123, Tirana; tel. (42) 34190; fax (42) 33464; Chargé d'affaires a.i.: ARTUR TOMASZEWSKI.

**Romania:** Rruga Themistokli Gërmenji 2, Tirana; tel. (42) 32287; Ambassador: FILIP TEODORESCU.

**Russia:** Rruga Asim Zeneli 5, Tirana; tel. (42) 56040; fax (42) 56046; Ambassador: IGOR A. SAPRYKIN.

**Switzerland:** Rruga e Elbasanit 81, Tirana; tel. (42) 34890; fax (42) 34889; e-mail swissemb@adanet.com.al; Ambassador THOMAS FELLER.

**Turkey:** Rruga Konferenca e Pezës 31, Tirana; tel. (42) 33399; fax (42) 32941; e-mail turemb@adanet.com.al; Ambassador: AHMET RIFAT OKCUN.

**United Kingdom:** Rruga Skënderbeu 12, Tirana; tel. and fax (42) 34973; Ambasssador: Dr PETER JANUARY.

**USA:** Rruga Labinoti 103, Tirana; tel. (42) 32875; fax (42) 32222; Ambassador: JOSEPH LIMPRECHT.

**Yugoslavia:** Rruga e Durrësit 192–196, Tirana; tel. and fax (42) 23042; Chargé d'affaires: STANIMIR VUKIČEVIĆ.

# Judicial System

The judicial structure comprises the High Court, the Courts of Appeal and the Courts of First Instance. The Chairman and members of the High Court are appointed by the President of the Republic, with the approval of the legislature, for a term of seven years. Other judges are appointed by the President upon the proposal of a High Council of Justice. The High Council of Justice comprises the Chairman of the High Court, the Minister of Justice, three members elected by the legislature for a term of five years, and nine judges of all levels who are elected by a national judicial conference.

**The Constitutional Court:** The Constitutional Court arbitrates on constitutional issues, and determines, *inter alia*, the conformity of proposed legislation with the Constitution. It is empowered to prohibit the activities of political organizations on constitutional grounds, and also formulates legislation regarding the election of the President of the Republic. The Constitutional Court comprises nine members, who are appointed by the President, with the approval of the legislature, for a term of nine years.

**Chairman of the Constitutional Court:** FEHMI ABDIU.

## Religion

All religious institutions were closed by the Government in 1967 and the practice of religion was prohibited. In May 1990, however, the prohibition on religious activities was revoked, religious services were permitted, and, from 1991, mosques and churches began to be reopened. Under the Constitution of November 1998, Albania is a secular state which observes freedom of religious belief. On the basis of declared affiliation in 1945, it is estimated that some 70% of the population are of Muslim background (mainly Sunni or adherents of the liberal Bektashi order), 20% Eastern Orthodox Christian (mainly in the south) and some 10% Roman Catholic Christian (mainly in the north).

### ISLAM

**Albanian Islamic Community** (Bashkesia Islamc c Shqipërisë): Rruga Puntoret e Rilindjes, Tirana; f. 1991; Chair. HAFIZ H. SABRI KOÇI; Grand Mufti of Albania HAFIZ SALIH TERMAT HOXHA.

#### Bektashi Sect

**World Council of Elders of the Bektashis:** Tirana; f. 1991; Chair. RESHAT Baba BARDHI.

### CHRISTIANITY

#### The Eastern Orthodox Church

**Orthodox Autocephalous Church of Albania** (Kisha Orthodhokse Autoqefale të Shqipërisë): Rruga Kavaja 151, Tirana; tel. (42) 34117; fax (42) 32109; e-mail arch-an@ocual.tirana.al; the Albanian Orthodox Church was proclaimed autocephalous at the Congress of Berat in 1922, its status was approved in 1929 and it was recognized by the Ecumenical Patriarchate in Istanbul (Constantinople), Turkey, in 1936; the Serbian, Macedonian and Greek churches do not recognize its separate existence; Archbishop ANASTAS JANULATOS.

#### The Roman Catholic Church

Many Roman Catholic churches have been reopened since 1990, and in September 1991 diplomatic relations were restored with the Holy See. Albania comprises two archdioceses, four dioceses and one apostolic administration. At 31 December 1997 the estimated number of adherents represented about 34.5% of the total population.

**Bishops' Conference:** Conferenza Episcopale dell'Albania, Rruga Labinoti, KP 1510, Tirana; tel. (42) 32082; fax (42) 30727; Pres. Most Rev. RROK K. MIRDITA, Archbishop of Durrës-Tirana.

**Archbishop of Durrës-Tirana:** Most Rev. RROK K. MIRDITA, Arqipeshkvia, Rruga Labinoti, Vilar e Gjermaneve 3, Tirana; tel. (42) 32082; fax (42) 30727.

**Archbishop of Shkodër:** Most Rev. ANGELO MASSAFRA, Kryeipeshkëvi, Sheshi Gijon Pali II, Shkodër; tel. (224) 2744.

## The Press

Until 1991 the Press was controlled by the Party of Labour of Albania, now the Socialist Party of Albania (SPA), and adhered to a strongly Marxist-Leninist line. From 1991 many new periodicals and newspapers were established by the newly emerging independent political organizations. In 1994 there were some 400 newspapers and periodicals in publication.

### PRINCIPAL DAILIES

**Koha Jonë** (Our Time): Tirana; f. 1991; independent; Editor-in-Chief BEN BLUSHI; circ. 400,000.

**Rilindja Demokratike** (Democratic Revival): Rruga Fortuzi, Tirana; tel. (42) 29609; fax (42) 42329; f. 1991; organ of the DPA; Editor-in-Chief LORENC LIGORI; circ. 50,000.

**Zëri i Popullit** (The Voice of the People): Bulevardi Zhan D'Ark, Tirana; tel. (42) 22192; fax (42) 27813; f. 1942; daily, except Mon.; organ of the SPA; Editor-in-Chief LUAN RAMA; circ. 105,000.

### PERIODICALS

#### Tirana

**Agrovizion:** Rruga d'Istria, Tirana: tel. (42) 26147; f. 1992; 2 a week; agricultural economic policies, new technology in farming, advice for farmers; circ. 3,000.

**Albania:** Tirana; f. 1991; weekly; organ of the Albanian Green Party; environmental issues.

**Albanian Daily News:** Rruga Hile Mosi, 5, Tirana; tel. and fax (42) 27639; e-mail adn@icc.al.eu.org; internet www.albaniannews.com.; f. 1995; weekly English-language newspaper; Editor ARBEN LESKAJ.

**Alternativa SD:** Tirana; f. 1991; 2 a week; organ of the Social Democratic Party.

**Arbër:** Tirana; f. 1992; fortnightly; social, literary and artistic review.

**The Balkans:** Tirana; f. 1993; humorous review; Editor-in-Chief NIKO NIKOLLA.

**Balli i Kombit** (The Head of the Nation): Tirana; f. 1991.

**Bashkimi Kombëtar:** Bulevardi Zhan D'Ark, Tirana; tel. (42) 28110; f. 1943; Editor-in-Chief QEMAL SAKAJEVA; circ. 30,000.

**Çamëria—Vatra Amtare** (Çamëria—Maternal Hearth): Tirana; f. 1991; weekly; organ of the Çamëria Political and Patriotic Association.

**Drita** (The Light): Rruga Konferenca e Pezës 4, Tirana; tel. (42) 27036; f. 1960; weekly; publ. by Union of Writers and Artists of Albania; Editor-in-Chief BRISEIDA MEMA; circ. 31,000.

**Ekonomia Botërore** (World Economics): Tirana; f. 1991; monthly; independent.

**Fatosi** (The Valiant): Tirana; tel. (42) 23024; f. 1959; fortnightly; literary and artistic magazine for children; Editor-in-Chief XHEVAT BEQARAJ; circ. 21,200.

**Filmi** (The Film): Rruga 'Aleksander Moisiu' 76; tel. and fax (42) 64971; f. 1998; annual; illustrated cinema review.

**Gazeta Shqiptare** (Albanian Gazette): Tirana; independent; Editor CARLO BOLLINO.

**Hosteni** (The Goad): Tirana; f. 1945; fortnightly; political review of humour and satire; publ. by the Union of Journalists; Editor-in-Chief NIKO NIKOLLA.

**The Hour of Albania:** Rruga Dëshmorët e 4 Shkurtit, Tirana; tel. (42) 42042; fax (42) 34024; weekly; organ of the Christian Democratic Party of Albania; Editor-in-Chief Dr FAIK LAMA; circ. 3,000.

**Kombi** (The Nation): Rruga Alqi Kondi, Tirana; tel. (42) 27498; fax (42) 23929; f. 1991; 2 a week; organ of the Party of National Unity; circ. 15,000.

**Kushtrim Brezash** (Clarion Call of Generations): Tirana; f. 1992; weekly; organ of the National Committee of the War Veterans of the Anti-Fascist National Liberation War of the Albanian People.

**Liria:** Tirana.

**Mbrojtja** (The Defence): Tirana; f. 1991; monthly; publ. by the Ministry of Defence; Editor-in-Chief XHELADIN ÇELMETA.

**Mësuesi** (The Teacher): Tirana; f. 1961; weekly; publ. by the Ministry of Education and Science; Editor-in-Chief THOMA QENDRO.

**Ndërtuesi** (The Builder): Tirana; quarterly.

**Official Gazette of the Republic of Albania:** Kuvendi Popullore, Tirana; tel. (42) 28668; fax (42) 27949; f. 1945; occasional government review.

**Panorama Agroushqimore** (Agro-food Panorama): Rruga d'Istria, Tirana; f. 1921, publ. under several names; monthly; specialist agricultural magazine; circ. 3,000.

**Pasqyra** (The Mirror): Bulevardi Zhan D'Ark, Tirana; f. 1991 to replace *Puna* (Labour—f. 1945); 2 a week; also 4 times a year in French; organ of the Confederation of Albanian Trade Unions; Editor-in-Chief KRISTAQ LAKA.

**Patrioti** (The Patriot): Tirana; f. 1992; organ of the Elez Isufi Patriotic Association; Editor-in-Chief VEDIP BRENSHI.

**Përmbledhje Studimesh** (Collection of Studies): Tirana; quarterly; summaries in French.

**Populli Po:** Tirana.

**Progresi** (Progress): Rruga Budi 6, Tirana; tel. (42) 27481; fax (42) 27481; f. 1991; 2 a week; organ of the Agrarian Party.

**Republika:** Bulevardi Zhan D'Ark 66, Tirana; tel. and fax (42) 25988; f. 1991; 2 a week; organ of the Albanian Republican Party; Editor-in-Chief YLLI RAKIPI.

**Revista Pedagogjike:** Naim Frashëri St 37, Tirana; fax (42) 56441; f. 1945; quarterly; organ of the Institute of Pedagogical Studies; educational development, psychology, didactic; Editor BUJAR BASKA; circ. 4,000.

**Rinia e Lire** (Free Youth): Tirana; f. 1992; organ of the Albanian Free Youth Federation.

**Shëndeti** (Health): M. Duri 2, Tirana; tel. (42) 27803; fax (42) 27803; f. 1949; monthly; publ. by the National Directorate of Health Education; issues of health and welfare, personal health care; Editors-in-Chief KORNELIA GJATA, AGIM XHUMARI.

**Shqiptarja e Re** (The New Albanian Woman): Tirana; f. 1943; monthly; political and socio-cultural review; Editor-in-Chief VALENTINA LESKAJ.

**Sindikalisti** (Trade Unionists): Tirana; f. 1991; newspaper; organ of the Union of Independent Trade Unions of Albania; Editor-in-Chief VANGJEL KOZMAI.

**Skena dhe Ekrani** (Stage and Screen): Tirana; quarterly; cultural review.

**Spektër** (The Spectre): Tirana; f. 1991; illustrated independent monthly; in Albanian and Italian.

**Sporti Shqiptar:** Rruga e Kavajës 23, Sheshi Ataturk, 2908 Tirana; tel. and fax (42) 20237; f. 1935; 3 a week; Editor BESNIK DIZDARI; circ. 10,000.

**Studenti** (The Student): Tirana; f. 1967; weekly.

**Tirana:** Tirana; f. 1987; independent; 2 a week; publ. by Tirana District SPA.

**Tregtia e Jashtme Popullore** (Albanian Foreign Trade): Rruga Konferenca e Pezës 6, Tirana; tel. (42) 22934; f. 1961; 6 a year; in English and French; organ of the Albanian Chamber of Commerce; Editor AGIM KORBI.

**Tribuna Demokratike** (Democratic Tribune): Tirana.

**Tribuna e Gazetarit** (The Journalist's Tribune): Tirana; 6 a year; publ. by the Union of Journalists of Albania; Editor NAZMI QAMILI.

**Ushtria dhe Koha** (Army and Time): Tirana; f. 1993; monthly; publ. by the Ministry of Defence; Editor-in-Chief AGRON MANÇE.

**Zeri i Atdheut** (The Voice of the Country): Tirana; f. 1992; weekly.

### Other Towns

**Adriatiku** (Adriatic): Durrës; f. 1967; independent; 2 a week.

**Dibra:** Dibër; f. 1991; independent; 2 a week.

**Egnatia:** Berat; f. 1991; independent; 2 a week.

**Korçë Demokratike** (Democratic Korça): Korça; f. 1992; organ of the Democratic Party of Albania; weekly.

**Ore** (The Clock): Shkodër; f. 1992; independent; 2 a week.

**Universi Rinor** (The Youth Universe): Korçë; f. 1991.

**Zëri i Vlorës** (The Voice of Vlorë): Vlorë; f. 1967; 2 a week; Editor-in-Chief DASHO METODASHAJ.

### NEWS AGENCIES

**Albanian Telegraphic Agency (ATA):** Bulevardi Zhan D'Ark 23, Tirana; tel. (42) 22929; fax (42) 34230; e-mail hola@ata.tirana.al; internet www.telpress.it/ata/ata.htm; f. 1929; domestic and foreign news; brs in provincial towns and in Kosovo, Yugoslavia; Dir-Gen. FRROK CUPI.

### Foreign Bureau

**Xinhua (New China) News Agency** (People's Republic of China): Rruga Zef Jubani 3, Apt 903, Tirana; tel. (42) 33139; fax (42) 48019; e-mail xinhua-tirana@china.com; Bureau Chief LI JIYU.

### PRESS ASSOCIATIONS

**League of Journalists of Albania** (Lidhja e Gazetarëve të Shqipërisë): Tirana.

**Union of Journalists of Albania** (Bashkimi i Gazetarëve të Shqipërisë): Tirana; tel. (42) 28020; f. 1949; Chair. MARASH HAJATI; Sec.-Gen. YMER MINXHOZI.

## Publishers

**Agjensia Qëndrore e Tregtimit të Librit Artistik dhe Shkencor** (Central Agency of the Artistic and Scientific Book Trade): Tirana; tel. and fax (42) 27246.

**Bota Sportive:** Tirana; f. 1991; sports.

**Botime të Akademisë së Shkencave të RSH:** Tirana; publishing house of the Albanian Academy of Sciences.

**Botime te Universitetit Bujqësor te Tiranës:** Kamzë, Tirana; publishing house of the Agricultural University of Tirana.

**Botime të Shtëpisë Botuese 8 Nëntori:** Tirana; tel. (42) 28064; f. 1972; books on Albania and other countries, political and social sciences, translations of Albanian works into foreign languages, technical and scientific books, illustrated albums, etc.; Dir XHEMAL DINI.

**Dituria Publishing House:** Rruga Dervish Hima 32, Tirana; tel. and fax (42) 25882; f. 1991; dictionaries, calendars, encyclopaedias, social sciences, biographies, fiction and non-fiction; Gen. Dir PETRIT YMERI.

**Dora d'Istria:** Tirana; f. 1991.

**Fan Noli:** Tirana; tel. (42) 42739; f. 1991; Albanian and foreign literature.

**Globus:** Tirana; f. 1991.

**Hasan Tahsini:** Tirana; f. 1991; humorous literature.

**Qendr e Informacionit për Bujsinë dhe Ushqimin** (Information Centre for Agriculture and Food): Rruga d'Istria, Tirana; tel. (42) 26147; f. 1970; publishes various agricultural periodicals; Gen. Dir SALI ÇELA.

**Shtëpia Botuese e Librit Shkollor:** Tirana; tel. (42) 22331; f. 1967; educational books; Dir SHPËTIM BOZDO.

**Shtëpia Botuese 'Libri Universitar':** Rruga Dora d'Istria, Tirana; tel. (42) 25659; fax (42) 29268; f. 1988; publishes university textbooks on science, medicine, engineering, geography, history, literature, foreign languages, economics, etc.; Dir MUSTAFA FEZGA.

**Shtëpia Botuese e Lidhjes së Shkrimtarëve:** Konferenca e Pezës 4, Tirana; tel. (42) 22691; fax (42) 25912; f. 1990; artistic and documentary literature; Dir ZIJA ÇELA.

**Shtëpia Botuese Naim Frashëri:** Tirana; tel. (42) 27906; f. 1947; fiction, poetry, drama, criticism, children's literature, translations; Dir GAQO BUSHAKA.

**Union of Writers and Artists Publishing House:** Tirana; f. 1991; fiction, poetry incl. foreign literature and works by the Albanian diaspora.

### WRITERS' UNIONS

**Independent Union of Writers** (Bashkimi i Shkrimtarëve te Pavarur): Tirana; f. 1991; Chair. AGIM SHEHU.

**Union of Writers and Artists of Albania** (Lidhja e Shkrimtarëve dhe e Artistëve të Shqipërisë): Rruga Konferenca e Pezës 4, Tirana; tel. (42) 29689; f. 1945; 26 brs; 1,750 mems; Chair. BARDHYL LONDO.

## Broadcasting and Communications

### TELECOMMUNICATIONS

**State Department of Posts and Telecommunications:** Rruga Myslym Shyri 42, Tirana; tel. (42) 27204; fax (42) 33772; e-mail kote@dshpt.tirana.al; Gen. Dir HYDAJET KOPANI; Man. Dir FREDERIK KOTE.

**Albanian Telekom:** Tirana; Dir-Gen. DHIMITRAQ RAFTI.

### BROADCASTING

In 1991 state broadcasting was removed from political control and made subordinate to the Parliamentary Commission for the Media.

**Radiotelevisioni Shqiptar:** Rruga Ismail Qemali 11, Tirana; tel. (42) 28310; fax (42) 27745; f. 1938; Chair. YLLI PANGO; Dir-Gen. ALBERT MINGA.

### Radio

**Radio Tirana:** Rruga Ismail Qemali 11, Tirana; tel. and fax (42) 28444; e-mail fabio@interalbnet; internet www.fabio.interalbnet; two channels broadcast 24 hours of internal programmes daily from Tirana; regional stations in Korçë, Gjirokastër, Kukës and Shkodër; in 1991 radio broadcasts in Macedonian began in the area of Korçë; in Gjirokastër, programmes in Greek are broadcast for 45 minutes daily; external service broadcasts for 20 hours daily in eight languages; Gen. Dir MARTIN LEKA; Dir of External Service SADI PETRELA.

**Kontakt Radio:** Tirana; independent radio station; commenced broadcasts Oct. 1997; Dir AGRON BALA.

### Television

**Alba Television:** International Centre of Culture, QNK, Tirana; private television station; broadcasts suspended Aug. 1997; Dir PAULIN SHKJEZI.

## Finance

(cap. = capital; dep. = deposits; res = reserves; m. = million; brs = branches; amounts in lekë, unless otherwise stated)

### BANKING

### Central Bank

**Bank of Albania:** Sheshi Skënderbeu 1, Tirana; tel. (42) 22752; fax (42) 23558; e-mail public@bankofalbania.org; f. 1992; cap. US $5.5m. (Nov. 1999), res $26.4m. (Oct. 1998); Gov. SHKËLQUIM CANI.

### State Banks

**National Commercial Bank of Albania:** Bulevardi Zhan D'Ark, Tirana; tel. (42) 50955; fax (42) 50948; e-mail julian@aedp.soros.al; internet www.come.to.ncba; f. 1993, following merger of National Bank of Albania and Commercial Bank of Albania; cap. 12,087.3m., dep. 34,886.8m. (Dec. 1997); Gen. Man. SPIRO BRUMBULLI; 37 brs.

**Rural Commercial Bank:** Bulevardi Zhan D'Ark, Tirana; tel. (42) 28331; fax (42) 28477; scheduled for liquidation during 1998.

**Savings Bank of Albania:** Rruga Deshmoret e 4 Shkurtit 6, Tirana; tel. (42) 23695; fax (42) 24972; f. 1991; 100% state-owned; cap. 3.2m., res 10.5m., dep. 1,127m. (August 1999); Gen. Man. ARTAN SANTO; 25 brs.

### Other Banks

**Arab-Albanian Islamic Bank:** Dëshmorët e Kombit 8, Tirana; tel. and fax (42) 28460; jt venture with National Commercial Bank of Albania.

**Dardania Bank:** Dëshmorët e Kombit 'VEVE' Center, Tirana; tel. and fax (42) 35053; f. 1994; privately-owned.

**Italian-Albanian Bank:** Rruga e Barrikadave, Tirana; tel. (42) 26262; fax (42) 33965; jt venture between the National Commercial Bank of Albania and Banca di Roma.

### INSURANCE

**Insurance Institute of Albania** (Instituti i Sigurimeve të Shqipërisë): Rruga Dibres 91, Tirana; tel. (42) 34170; fax (42) 34180; f. 1991; all types of insurance; Gen. Dir QEMAL DISHA; 28 brs.

### STOCK EXCHANGE

**Albanian Stock Exchange:** Sheshi Skënderbeu 1, Tirana; f. 1996.

## Trade and Industry

### PRIVATIZATION AGENCY

**National Agency for Privatization (NAP):** Tirana; tel. and fax (42) 27933; govt agency under the control of the Council of Ministers; prepares and proposes the legal framework concerning privatization procedures and implementation; Dir NIKO GLOZHENI.

### SUPERVISORY ORGANIZATIONS

**Albkontroll:** Rruga Skënderbeu 45, Durrës; tel. (52) 23377; fax (52) 22791; f. 1962; brs throughout Albania; independent control body for inspection of goods for import and export, means of transport, etc.; Gen. Man. DILAVER MEZINI; 15 brs.

**State Control Commission:** Bulevardi Deshmoret e Kombit, Tirana; tel. (42) 28306; fax (42) 32491; Chair. BLERIM ÇELA.

### DEVELOPMENT ORGANIZATIONS

**Albanian Centre for Foreign Investment Promotion (ACFIP):** Bulevardi Zhan D'Ark, Tirana; tel. (42) 30133; fax (42) 28439; e-mail xhepa@cpfi.tirana.al; f. 1993; govt agency to promote foreign investment in Albania and to provide practical support to foreign investors; Chair. SELAMI XHEPA; Vice-Chair. SELIM BELORTAJA.

**Enterprise Restructuring Agency** (Agjensia e Ristrukturimit te Ndermarrjeve): Rruga e Durresit 83, Tirana; tel. (42) 27878; fax (42) 25730; govt agency established to assist state-owned enterprises to become privately owned by offering enterprise sector surveys, strategic plans and consultations; provides technical assistance; Dir ADRIATIK BANKJA.

### CHAMBERS OF COMMERCE

**Union of Chambers of Commerce and Industry of Albania:** Rruga Kavajes 6, Tirana; tel. and fax (42) 22934; f. 1958; Pres. ANTON LEKA.

**Durrës Chamber of Commerce:** Durrës; f. 1988; promotes trade with southern Italy.

**Gjirokastër Chamber of Commerce:** Gjirokastër; f. 1988; promotes trade with Greek border area.

**Shkodër Chamber of Commerce:** Shkodër; promotes trade with Yugoslav border area.

There are also chambers of commerce in Korçë, Kukës, Peshkopi, Pogradec, Sarandë and Vlorë.

### UTILITIES

#### Electricity

**Korporata Elektroenergjetike Shqiptare (KESH):** Biloky 'Vasil Shanto', Tirana; tel. (42) 28434; fax (42) 32046; state corpn for the generation, transmission, distribution and export of electrical energy; govt-controlled; scheduled for transfer to private ownership; Chair. BASHKIM QATIPI; Gen. Dir Dr NAKO HOBDARI.

### TRADE UNIONS

Until 1991 independent trade-union activities were prohibited, the official trade unions being represented in every work and production centre. During 1991, however, independent unions were established. The most important of these was the Union of Independent Trade Unions of Albania. Other unions were established for workers in various sectors of the economy.

**Confederation of Albanian Trade Unions** (Konfederata e Sindikatave të Shqipërisë—KSSh): Bulevardi Zhan D'Ark, Tirana; f. 1991 to replace the official Central Council of Albanian Trade Unions (f. 1945); includes 17 trade union federations representing workers in different sectors of the economy; Chair. of Man. Council KASTRIOT MUÇO.

**Union of Independent Trade Unions of Albania** (Bashkimi i Sindikatave të Pavarura të Shqipërisë—BSPSh): Tirana; f. 1991; Chair. (vacant).

#### Other Trade Unions

**Agricultural Trade Union Federation** (Federata Sindikale e Bujqesise): Tirana; f. 1991; Leaders ALFRED GJOMO, NAZMI QOKU.

**Autonomous Union of Public-Service Workers:** Tirana; f. 1992; Chair. MINELLA KURETA.

**Free and Independent Miners' Union** (Sindikata e Lire dhe e Pavarur e Minatoreve): Tirana; f. 1991; Chair. GEZIM KALAJA.

**Independent Trade Union Federation of Workers in the Artistic Articles, Handicrafts, Glassware and Ceramics Industries:** Tirana; f. 1991.

**Independent Trade Union Federation of the Food Industry:** Tirana; f. 1991.

**Independent Trade Union of Dock Workers:** Durrës; f. 1992.

**Independent Trade Union of Radio and Television:** Tirana; f. 1991; represents interests of media workers.

**Trade Union of Army and Police Civilians:** Tirana; f. 1994.

**Trade Union Federation of Education and Science Workers:** Tirana; f. 1991; represents teachers and academics.

**Trade Union Federation of Health Workers:** Tirana; Chair. MINELLA MANO.

**Union of Oil Industry Workers:** seceded from the Confederation of Albanian Trade Unions in 1991; represents workers in the petroleum and natural gas industry; Chair. MENPOR XHEMALI.

## Transport

### RAILWAYS

In 1994 there were approximately 720 km of railway track, with lines linking Tirana–Vlorë–Durrës, Durrës–Kavajë–Rrogozhinë–Elbasan–Librazhd–Prenjas–Pogradec, Rrogozhinë–Lushnjë–Fier–Ballsh, Milot–Rrëshen, Vlorë–Laç–Lezhë–Shkodër and Selenicë–Vlorë. There are also standard-gauge lines between Fier and Selenicë and between Fier and Vlorë. A 50-km international freight link between Shkodër and Titograd (now Podgorica), Montenegro (Yugoslavia), opened in 1986.

**Albanian Railways:** Durrës; tel. (52) 22311; fax (52) 22037; Gen. Dir FERDINAND XHAFERRI; Deputy Gen. Dirs ALEKSANDËR SHELDIA, PETRAQ PANO.

### ROADS

In 1996 the road network comprised an estimated 18,000 km of classified roads, including 3,225 km of main roads and 4,300 km of secondary roads; about 30% of the total network was paved in 1995. All regions are linked by the road network, but many roads in mountainous districts are unsuitable for motor transport. Private cars were banned in Albania until 1991, but many have since been imported (estimated at over 120,000 by the end of 1993). A three-year public investment plan, which was initiated in 1995, included substantial funds for the rehabilitation of the road network; the principal projects were the creation of east–west (Durrës–Kapshtice) and north–south highways.

### SHIPPING

At December 1998 Albania's merchant fleet had 25 vessels, with a total displacement of 28,671 grt. The chief ports are those in Durrës, Vlorë, Sarandë and Shëngjin. In 1996 the port of Himare, which was closed in 1991, was reopened. Ferry services have been established between Durrës and three Italian ports (Trieste, Bari and Ancona) and between Sarandë and the Greek island of Corfu. There is also a service between Vlorë and Brindisi (Italy).

**Adetare Shipping Agency Ltd:** Durrës; tel. (52) 23883; fax (52) 23666.

**Albanian State Shipping Enterprise:** Porti Detar, Durrës; tel. (52) 22233; fax (52) 229111.

### CIVIL AVIATION

There is a small international airport at Rinas, 25 km from Tirana. Reconstruction of the airport was undertaken in the late 1990s. Total traffic averaged 300,000 passengers and 900,000 metric tons of goods carried per year.

**Albanian Airlines Mak:** Rruga Minepeza 2, Tirana; tel. (42) 27606; fax (42) 28461; e-mail tiadplvasita@msmail.com; f. 1992 as Albanian Airlines, a jt venture between the Albanian state-owned air agency, Albtransport, and the Austrian airline, Tyrolean Airways; acquired in 1995 by the Kuwaiti co, Aviation World Mak, and assumed present name; scheduled services to Germany, Italy and Turkey; Commercial Man. HANS MOOK.

**Arberia Airways:** Tirana; f. 1992.

# Tourism

In 1996 there were some 56,276 international tourist arrivals at hotels in Albania, compared with 40,175 in 1995 and 28,439 in 1994. In 1996 receipts from tourism totalled about US $11m. The main tourist centres include Tirana, Durrës, Sarandë, Shkodër and Pogradec. The Roman amphitheatre at Durrës is one of the largest in Europe. The ancient towns of Apollonia and Butrint are important archaeological sites and there are many other towns of historic interest. However, expansion of the tourist industry has as yet been limited by the inadequacy of Albania's infrastructure and a lack of foreign investment in the development of new facilities. Regional instability, particularly during the NATO air offensive against Yugoslavia in early 1999 (see Recent History), has also inhibited tourist activity.

**Albturist:** Bulevardi Zhan D'Ark 8, Tirana; tel. (42) 27958; fax (42) 34295; brs in main towns and all tourist centres; 28 hotels throughout the country; Dir-Gen. BESNIK PELLUMBI.

**Committee for Development and Tourism:** Tirana; govt body.

# ALGERIA

## Introductory Survey

**Location, Climate, Language, Religion, Flag, Capital**

The Democratic and People's Republic of Algeria lies in north Africa, with the Mediterranean Sea to the north, Mali and Niger to the south, Tunisia and Libya to the east, and Morocco and Mauritania to the west. The climate on the Mediterranean coast is temperate, becoming more extreme in the Atlas mountains immediately to the south. Further south is part of the Sahara, a hot and arid desert. Temperatures in Algiers, on the coast, are generally between 9°C (48°F) and 29°C (84°F), while in the interior they may exceed 50°C (122°F). Arabic is the official language, but French is still widely used. There is a substantial Berber minority, whose principal language is Tamazight. Islam is the state religion, and almost all Algerians are Muslims. The national flag (proportions 3 by 2) has two equal vertical stripes, of green and white, with a red crescent moon and a five-pointed red star superimposed in the centre. The capital is Algiers (el-Djezaïr).

**Recent History**

Algeria was conquered by French forces in the 1830s and annexed by France in 1842. For most of the colonial period, official policy was to colonize the territory with French settlers, and many French citizens became permanent residents. Unlike most of France's overseas possessions, Algeria was not formally a colony but was 'attached' to metropolitan France. However, political and economic power within Algeria was largely held by the white settler minority, as the indigenous Muslim majority did not have equal rights.

On 1 November 1954 the principal Algerian nationalist movement, the Front de libération nationale (FLN), began a war for national independence, in the course of which about 1m. Muslims were killed or wounded. Despite resistance from the Europeans in Algeria, the French Government agreed to a cease-fire in March 1962 and independence was declared on 3 July 1962. In August the Algerian provisional Government transferred its functions to the Political Bureau of the FLN, and in September a National Constituent Assembly was elected (from a single list of FLN candidates) and the Republic proclaimed. A new Government was formed, with Ahmed Ben Bella, founder of the FLN, as Prime Minister. As a result of the nationalist victory, about 1m. French settlers emigrated from Algeria.

A draft Constitution, providing for a presidential regime with the FLN as the sole party, was adopted by the Constituent Assembly in August 1963. In September the Constitution was approved by popular referendum and Ben Bella was elected President. Under his leadership, economic reconstruction was begun and the foundation was laid for a single-party socialist state. However, the failure of the FLN to function as an active political force left real power with the bureaucracy and the army. In June 1965 the Minister of Defence, Col Houari Boumedienne, deposed Ben Bella in a bloodless coup and took control of the country as President of a Council of the Revolution, which was composed of 26 members, chiefly army officers.

Boumedienne encountered considerable opposition from left-wing members of the FLN, but by 1971 the Government was confident enough to adopt a more active social policy. French petroleum interests were nationalized and an agrarian reform programme was initiated. In mid-1975 Boumedienne announced a series of measures to consolidate the regime and enhance his personal power, including the drafting of a National Charter and a new Constitution, and the holding of elections for a President and National People's Assembly. Following public discussion of the National Charter, which formulated the principles and plans for creating a socialist system and maintaining Islam as the state religion, a referendum was held in June 1976, at which the Charter was adopted by 98.5% of the electorate. In November a new Constitution (incorporating the principles of the Charter) was approved by another referendum, and in December Boumedienne was elected President unopposed, winning more than 99% of the votes cast. The new formal structure of power was completed in February 1977 by the election of FLN members to the National People's Assembly.

In December 1978 President Boumedienne died, and the Council of the Revolution (now comprising only eight members) took over the Government. In January 1979 the FLN adopted a new party structure, electing a Central Committee, which was envisaged as the highest policy-making body both of the party and of the nation as a whole: this Committee was to choose a party Secretary-General, who would automatically become the sole presidential candidate. The Committee was also to elect an FLN Political Bureau (nominated by the Secretary-General). The Committee's choice of Col Ben Djedid Chadli, commander of Oran military district, as presidential candidate was endorsed by a referendum in February, and was regarded as a compromise between liberal and radical aspirants. Unlike Boumedienne, Chadli appointed a Prime Minister, Col Muhammad Abd al-Ghani (who also retained his post as Minister of the Interior), anticipating constitutional changes that were approved by the National People's Assembly in June and which included the obligatory appointment of a Premier. In mid-1980 the FLN authorized Chadli to form a smaller Political Bureau, with more limited responsibilities, thereby increasing the power of the President. Membership of the National People's Assembly was increased to 281 for the legislative elections of March 1982, when the electorate was offered a choice of three candidates per seat.

At a presidential election, held in January 1984, Chadli's candidature was endorsed by 95.4% of the electorate. Immediately after his re-election, Chadli reorganized the Government, appointing Abd al-Hamid Brahimi as Prime Minister. In 1985 Chadli initiated a public debate on Boumedienne's National Charter, and this resulted in the adoption of a new National Charter at a special FLN Congress in December. The revised Charter, which envisaged a state ideology based on the twin principles of socialism and Islam, and encouraged the development of the private sector, was approved by a referendum in January 1986. The number of seats in the National People's Assembly was increased to 295, all candidates being nominated by the FLN, for a general election in February 1987. In July of that year the Assembly adopted legislation to permit the formation of local organizations without prior government approval: a ban remained, however, on associations that were deemed to oppose the policies of the Charter or to threaten national security.

During the 1980s the Government incurred criticism from a number of different groups. In 1985 22 Berber cultural and human rights activists were imprisoned after being convicted of belonging to illegal organizations, while 18 alleged supporters of the former President Ben Bella were also detained. In 1986 riots occurred at Constantine and Sétif, following student protests against inadequate facilities. In 1987 several leading activists of an Islamist group were killed by the security forces, and some 200 of the group's members were given prison sentences. From mid-1988 severe unemployment, high prices, and shortages of essential supplies (resulting from economic austerity measures imposed in 1987 in response to a decline in the price of petroleum) provoked a series of strikes, and in early October rioting erupted in Algiers, spreading to Oran and Annaba: a six-day state of emergency was imposed, and (according to official sources) 159 people were killed during confrontations with the security forces, while more than 3,500 were arrested. In response to the unrest, Chadli proposed constitutional amendments that would allow non-FLN candidates to participate in elections, and make the Prime Minister answerable to the National People's Assembly, rather than to the President. In November these reforms were approved by a referendum. In the same month Chadli appointed Col Kasdi Merbah, hitherto the Minister of Health, as Prime Minister, and a new Council of Ministers (of whom fewer than one-half had previously held government office) was formed. Also in November, Chadli relinquished the post of Secretary-General of the FLN. In December he was elected President for a third term of office, obtaining 81% of the votes cast.

In February 1989 a new Constitution, signifying the end of the one-party socialist state, was approved by referendum.

The formation of political associations outside the FLN was henceforth to be permitted, while the armed forces were no longer allocated a role in the development of socialism. The executive, legislative and judicial functions of the State were separated and subjected to the supervision of a Constitutional Council. In July legislation permitting the formation of political parties became effective (although they were still required to be licensed by the Government): by mid-1991 a total of 47 political parties had been registered, including a radical Islamist group, the Front islamique du salut (FIS), the Mouvement pour la démocratie en Algérie (MDA), which had been founded by Ben Bella in 1984, the Parti d'avant-garde socialiste (renamed Ettahaddi in 1993), the Parti social-démocrate (PSD) and the Berber Rassemblement pour la culture et la démocratie (RCD). Other legislation adopted in July 1989 further reduced state control of the economy, allowed the expansion of investment by foreign companies, and ended the state monopoly of the press (while leaving the principal newspapers under FLN control). Despite these changes, strikes and riots continued during 1989, in protest at alleged official corruption and the Government's failure to improve living conditions. In September Chadli again appointed a new Premier, Mouloud Hamrouche (hitherto a senior official in the presidential office), who made extensive changes to the Council of Ministers. A programme of economic liberalization was announced by the new Government. Municipal and provincial elections, scheduled to take place in December, were postponed until the following June, to allow the recently-registered parties time to organize. A new electoral law, adopted in March 1990, introduced a system of partial proportional representation for local elections.

At local elections, held in June 1990, the principal Islamist party, the FIS, received some 55% of total votes cast, while the FLN obtained about 32%. In July, following disagreement within the FLN concerning the pace of economic and political reform, the Prime Minister and four other ministers resigned from the party's Political Bureau. In the same month the Council of Ministers was reorganized, and the defence portfolio was separated from the presidency for the first time since 1965. Also in July, Chadli acceded to the demands of the FIS for an early general election, announcing that it was to take place in early 1991. In August 1990 a general amnesty permitted the release of thousands of 'political' prisoners, and in September the former President Ben Bella was allowed to return from exile.

In December 1990 the National People's Assembly adopted a law providing that, after 1997, Arabic would be Algeria's only official language and that the use of French and Berber in schools and in official transactions would be punished by substantial fines. In response, more than 100,000 people demonstrated in Algiers against political and religious intolerance.

In March 1991 the Union Générale des Travailleurs Algériens (UGTA), although affiliated to the FLN, organized a two-day general strike, the country's first since independence, in protest against recent price rises. The Government reacted by announcing increases in subsidies and other benefits. In April President Chadli declared that Algeria's first multi-party general election would take place in late June. The FIS argued that a presidential election should be held simultaneously with, or shortly after, the general election, and in May organized an indefinite general strike and held demonstrations, demanding the resignation of Chadli and changes in the electoral laws. In the wake of violent confrontations in June between Islamist activists and the security forces, Chadli declared a state of emergency and postponed the general election. He also announced that he had accepted the resignation of the Prime Minister and his Government. The former Minister of Foreign Affairs, Sid-Ahmad Ghozali, was appointed Premier. Following a further week of unrest, the FLN and the FIS reached a compromise, according to which the strike was abandoned and legislative and presidential elections were to be held before the end of 1991. In mid-June Ghozali appointed a new Council of Ministers, consisting mainly of political independents. In late June, following further violent incidents between Islamists and the security forces, Chadli resigned from his post as Chairman of the FLN. In early July army units arrested some 700 Islamists and occupied the headquarters of the FIS. Among those arrested were the President of the FIS, Abbasi Madani, who had earlier threatened to launch a jihad ('holy war') if the state of emergency were not ended, and the party's Vice-President, Ali Belhadj; the two men were charged with armed conspiracy against the State. In late September the state of emergency was revoked.

In October 1991, following the National People's Assembly's decision to enact a revised electoral law, President Chadli announced that the multi-party general election would take place in December. The revisions that were made to the electoral system included an increase in the number of seats in the Assembly, from 295 to 430, and a lowering of the minimum age for electoral candidates from 35 years to 28 years. On 26 December, in the first round of voting in the general election, at which 231 of the 430 seats in the National People's Assembly were won outright, the FIS took 188 seats (with 47.5% of the votes cast), the Front des forces socialistes (FFS) 25, the FLN just 15, and independents three. The FLN alleged that there had been widespread intimidation and electoral malpractice on the part of the FIS. A second round of voting, in the 199 remaining constituencies where no candidate had obtained an absolute majority, was scheduled for 16 January 1992. On 4 January the Assembly was dissolved by presidential decree, and on 11 January President Chadli resigned. On the following day the High Security Council, comprising the Prime Minister, three generals and two senior ministers, cancelled the second round of voting, and on 14 January a five-member High Council of State (HCS) was appointed to act as a collegiate presidency until the expiry of Chadli's term of office in December 1993, at the latest. The most influential figure in the HCS was believed to be Maj.-Gen. Khaled Nezzar, the Minister of Defence, but its Chairman was Muhammad Boudiaf, a veteran of the war of independence who had been in exile since 1964. The other members of the HCS were Ali Haroun (the Minister of Human Rights), Sheikh Tejini Haddam (the Rector of the Grand Mosque in Paris) and Ali Kafi (President of the war veterans' association, the Organisation nationale des moudjahidine—ONM); Ghozali was not included, although he remained Premier. The constitutional legality of the HCS was disputed by all the political parties, including the FLN. The 188 FIS deputies who had been elected in December 1991 formed a 'shadow' Assembly and demanded a return to legality.

Amid sporadic outbreaks of violence, the security forces took control of the FIS offices in February 1992. The HCS declared a 12-month state of emergency, detention centres were opened in the Sahara, and the FIS claimed that 150 people had been killed, and as many as 30,000 detained, since the military-sponsored take-over. In March the FIS was officially dissolved by the Government.

In April 1992 Boudiaf, as Chairman of the HCS, announced the creation of a National Human Rights' Monitoring Centre (to replace the Ministry of Human Rights) and a 60-member National Consultative Council (NCC), which was to meet each month in the building of the suspended Assembly, although it enjoyed no legislative powers. In the same month the trial of Maj.-Gen. Mustafa Beloucif, a former senior defence ministry official accused of embezzlement, was regarded as evidence of a genuine desire on Boudiaf's part to eradicate corruption. In June Boudiaf proposed the establishment of a National Patriotic Rally, with committees in every village and workplace, to prepare for genuine multi-party democracy, and promised a constitutional review, the dissolution of the FLN and a presidential election. Moreover, he ordered the release of 2,000 FIS detainees, despite the fact that the security forces continued to be the target of frequent attack.

In late June 1992 the FIS leaders, Madani and Belhadj, were brought before a military tribunal in Blida, accused of conspiracy against the State, but, following the withdrawal of the defence lawyers from the court, the trial was adjourned until July. On 29 June Boudiaf was assassinated while making a speech in Annaba. The HCS ordered an immediate inquiry into the assassination, for which the FIS denied all responsibility. Ali Kafi succeeded Boudiaf as Chairman of the HCS, and Redha Malek, the Chairman of the NCC, was appointed as a new member of the HCS. In June 1995 Lt Lembarek Boumâarafi was sentenced to death for Boudiaf's assassination. The trial revealed little new information, and some observers remained sceptical about the authorities' insistence that Boumâarafi had acted alone.

On 8 July 1992 Ghozali resigned in order to enable Kafi to appoint his own Prime Minister. He was replaced by Belaid Abd es-Salam, who, for almost 20 years after independence, had directed Algeria's petroleum and gas policy. In mid-July Abd es-Salam appointed a new Council of Ministers.

In late July 1992 Madani and Belhadj were sentenced to 12 years' imprisonment. Violent protest demonstrations erupted in Algiers and quickly spread to other cities. In August Kafi appealed for a multi-party dialogue to be held in September, in an attempt to end civil strife. However, the Government attracted widespread criticism for reinforcing its emergency powers to repress any person or organization whose activities were deemed to represent a threat to stability. In late August a bomb explosion at Algiers airport killed nine people and left many injured. The FIS denied any involvement in the incident. Political manoeuvring and attempts at reconciliation continued against a background of escalating violence throughout the country. In early December the Government imposed a curfew in Algiers and its six neighbouring departments.

In February 1993 the state of emergency was renewed for an indefinite period. Nevertheless, there was subsequently an assassination attempt against Maj.-Gen. Nezzar, followed by a series of attacks on other senior government officials. In May large demonstrations took place in Algiers, Constantine and Oran, to protest against terrorism and to demand that there be no negotiation with its perpetrators. In June the HCS appealed for a 'general mobilization' against terrorism, but in the same month Abd es-Salam expressed his willingness to open a dialogue with the militants. Meanwhile, violence continued unabated and several prominent officials were assassinated in July. Moreover, in what appeared to be a change of tactics, terrorist attacks were increasingly targeted against intellectual and civilian figures.

In March 1993 Kafi met representatives of the ONM and the FLN to discuss, *inter alia,* possible formulae for a transitional period and the amendment of the Constitution. In June the HCS announced that it would dissolve itself at the end of December, and that a modern democracy and free market economy would be created within three years of that date.

In July 1993 Liamine Zéroual (a retired general) replaced Maj.-Gen. Nezzar as Minister of Defence, although Nezzar retained his position within the HCS. In August Redha Malek, while also retaining his post within the HCS, was appointed to replace Abd es-Salam as Prime Minister. On the same day, Kasdi Merbah, the former Prime Minister and now leader of the Mouvement algérien pour la justice et le développement, was assassinated, together with several of his staff. In September Malek appointed a new Council of Ministers. He stated that the resolute stance against terrorism would be maintained, and rejected the possibility of dialogue with its perpetrators. In the following month Maj.-Gen. Nezzar announced that he would be withdrawing from political life following the expiry of the mandate of the HCS. Also in October, the HCS appointed an eight-member National Dialogue Commission (NDC), which included three generals and which was charged with the preparation of a political conference to organize the gradual transition to an elected and democratic form of government. In December it was announced that the HCS would not be disbanded until a new presidential body had been elected at the NDC conference in January 1994. However, all the main political parties (with the exception of the moderate Islamist party, Hamas) boycotted the conference. Liamine Zéroual was subsequently appointed as Head of State for a three-year term by the HCS, on the apparent recommendation of an eight-man High Security Council (composed mainly of senior army officers), and inaugurated on 31 January. Plans for a three-year transitional period, leading to a presidential election, and for the appointment of a National Transition Council were approved by the NDC. Zéroual retained the defence portfolio, and the Council of Ministers remained unchanged. In February Ali Djeddi and Abdelkader Boukhamkham, representing the second tier in the FIS leadership, were released from prison, and rumours circulated that divisions had occurred within the military as a result of high-ranking members of the regime, including President Zéroual, making contact with imprisoned Islamist leaders in an attempt to establish dialogue with them. Malek, who was known to be opposed to any compromise with the Islamist militants, resigned as Prime Minister on 11 April; Mokdad Sifi, the erstwhile Minister of Equipment, was appointed in his place. Only 12 ministers retained their portfolios in the new Council of Ministers, announced in mid-April, and the majority of new appointees were technocrats or senior civil servants. In May, in an apparent attempt to strengthen his authority, Zéroual appointed Maj.-Gen. Ahmed Gaïd, who was believed to be one of the President's close associates, Commander of the Land Force. In the same month the President inaugurated the National Transition Council (NTC), an interim legislature of 200 appointed members, the aim of which was to provide a forum for debate pending legislative elections. Most of the 21 parties that agreed to participate in the NTC were virtually unknown except for Hamas, and the 22 seats that were allocated to major parties remained vacant. Also in May, a group of six 'independent national figures', including former President Ben Bella, was commissioned by Zéroual to promote dialogue with Islamist militants and opposition groups.

In mid-1994 it was reported that about 490 death sentences had been imposed, and a total of 26 official executions carried out, since the institution in February 1993 of three special courts to try suspects accused of terrorist offences. (The courts were abolished in February 1995, following strong criticism of alleged cases of abuse of human rights.) It remained unclear whether the FIS actively supported the Groupe islamique armé (GIA—the most prominent and radical Islamist militant group) in its attacks on members of the security forces, local government and the judiciary, as well as prominent public figures, intellectuals, journalists and ordinary civilians. In March 1994 an attack by Islamist militants on the high-security Tazoult prison, near Batna, resulted in the release of more than 1,000 political prisoners. Certain towns and entire neighbourhoods in some cities were virtually controlled by Islamist activists, and the increasing number of murders of foreign nationals (60 killings, the majority perpetrated by the GIA, in the year to September 1994) led several countries to advise their citizens to leave. In response to the rise in violence, the security forces intensified their campaign against armed Islamist groups, resorting to air attacks, punitive raids, torture and psychological warfare. Thousands of militants were killed during 1994, including the GIA leader in February and his successor in September.

In August 1994 members of the FLN, the Parti du renouveau algérien (PRA), the MDA, Nahdah and Hamas engaged in national dialogue with the Government; the meetings were boycotted, however, by Ettahaddi, the FFS and the RCD. At further negotiations, held in early September, discussion focused on two letters sent to the President by Abbasi Madani, which allegedly offered a 'truce'. Madani and Belhadj were released from prison in mid-September and placed under house arrest; however, the FIS did not participate in the next round of national dialogue later that month, declaring that negotiations could take place only after the granting of a general amnesty, the rehabilitation of the FIS and the repeal of the state of emergency. The GIA threatened reprisals if the FIS entered into dialogue with the regime, and intensified its campaign of violence against secular society by targeting educational institutions. In addition to the upheaval caused by Islamist terrorism, the Berber RCD urged a boycott of the start of the school year, and in September a general strike was staged by Berber activists in the Kabyle, in protest at the exclusion of the Berber language, Tamazight, from the syllabus and at the prospect of the FIS entering the national dialogue. In May 1995 the RCD welcomed the establishment of a government body to oversee the teaching of Tamazight in schools and universities (commencing in October) and to promote its use in the official media. The Mouvement culturel berbère, however, appealed for the continuation of the school boycott and again demanded that Tamazight be recognized as an official language.

In October 1994 President Zéroual announced that a presidential election would be held before the end of 1995. The announcement was welcomed by many, but others questioned the purpose of any elections if the FIS were not included in the political process. In November representatives from most of the major Algerian parties, including the FIS, attended a two-day conference in Rome, Italy, organized by the Sant' Egidio Catholic community to foster discussion about the crisis in Algeria. The Sant' Egidio pact, endorsed by all the participants at a meeting in Rome in January 1995, rejected the use of violence to achieve or maintain power, and urged the Algerian regime to repeal the state of emergency and thereby facilitate negotiations between all parties. In April Zéroual resumed bilateral discussions with the legalized opposition parties in preparation for the presidential election. Talks with the FLN and the FFS quickly collapsed, however, as they rejected the prospect of participating in an election in which the FIS were excluded. In May the Government issued an electoral decree (promulgated by the NTC in July), stipulating that presidential candidates would be required to obtain the endorsement of 75,000 signatures from at least 25 provinces in order to qualify. There was speculation that the Government was still engaged in dialogue with the FIS leaders, who had once again reportedly been placed under house arrest (in March) and reimprisoned in June. In mid-July a co-founder of the FIS and prominent opposition spokesman in France,

Sheikh Sahraoui, was assassinated in a mosque in Paris. The FIS blamed the Algerian security forces for the murder, although some analysts considered it more likely to have been perpetrated by the GIA, angered by the dialogue between the Government and the FIS. The incident coincided with Zéroual's announcement that dialogue with the FIS had failed.

In August 1995 President Zéroual declared that the presidential election would take place on 16 November. As many as 40 people subsequently presented themselves as candidates, although in October it was announced that only four had succeeded in attaining the required number of signatures: President Zéroual; Saïd Saadi, Secretary-General of the RCD; Nourreddine Boukrouh, leader of the PRA; and Sheikh Mahfoud Nahnah, leader of Hamas. Redha Malek, who had established an anti-Islamist political party (the Alliance national républicaine) earlier in the year, failed to qualify as a presidential candidate. Despite an appeal by the FLN, the FFS and the FIS for voters to boycott the election, 75.7% of the electorate participated in the poll, which was monitored by observers from the Organization of African Unity (OAU), the Arab League and the UN. Zéroual won 61.0% of the valid votes cast, followed by Sheikh Mahfoud Nahnah (25.6%), Saïd Saadi (9.6%) and Nourreddine Boukrouh (3.8%). Notwithstanding initial suggestions that the election had not been conducted fairly, most opposition parties subsequently accepted the legitimacy of President Zéroual's victory. Zéroual was inaugurated on 27 November. Shortly afterwards, despite the assassination of a high-ranking military official, the Government announced the closure of the last of seven detention centres (all of which had opened since February 1992), thereby releasing as many as 650 prisoners, many of whom were Islamist sympathizers. In late December Ahmed Ouyahia, a career diplomat, replaced Mokdad Sifi as Prime Minister. In early January 1996 Ouyahia appointed a new Government, which included two members of Hamas and a dissident leader of the FIS.

During 1995–96 the violence in Algeria continued unabated, and both the Islamist militants and the security forces appeared determined to match the other in the intensity of their attacks. The GIA launched a series of car-bomb attacks, resulting in hundreds of deaths, while the security forces claimed to have killed 1,300 Islamists in March 1995 in a week-long campaign in the Ain-Defla, Jijel and Médéa regions. The spate of car-bomb attacks intensified during late 1995 and early 1996, and in February the Government imposed harsh censorship measures on the media in an attempt to suppress reports on the extent of the violence.

In January 1996 the FLN elected Boualem Benhamouda as its new Secretary-General, in place of Abd al-Hamid Mehiri, whose leadership had been questioned following his appeal for a boycott of the November 1995 presidential election. On his appointment, Benhamouda strove to distance the FLN from the Sant' Egidio pact, and in February he announced that the party was prepared to enter into dialogue with the Government. In April, in an attempt to foster national reconciliation, President Zéroual held bilateral discussions with more than 50 influential individuals, including leaders of trade unions, opposition parties and organizations. The FIS was not invited to participate. In the following month Zéroual announced his intention to hold legislative elections in early 1997. In addition, he proposed that a referendum be held on constitutional reform, prior to the elections. Recommended amendments to the Constitution included measures increasing the powers of the President, while limiting his tenure to a maximum of two consecutive mandates, creating a second parliamentary chamber, to be known as the Council of the Nation (one-third of whose members would be chosen by the President), establishing a State Council (to regulate the administrative judiciary) and a High State Court, and, significantly, banning political parties that were based on religion, language, gender or regional differences. It was also suggested that the electoral law be revised to allow for a system of full proportional representation. Several opposition parties reiterated their plea that the Government resume negotiations with the FIS, and argued that constitutional reform should be undertaken only after legislative elections.

A government-sponsored conference on national concord, held in September 1996, was attended by some 1,000 delegates, including representatives of the FLN, Nahdah and Hamas. The conference was boycotted by the FFS, the RCD, Ettahaddi and the MDA. Owing to their lack of support, Zéroual subsequently withdrew his offer to include members of opposition parties in an expanded Council of Ministers and NTC. The proposed constitutional amendments (see above) were duly approved by referendum on 28 November. According to official sources, some 79.8% of the electorate participated in the referendum, of whom 85.8% voted in favour of the changes; however, a number of opposition parties disputed the results, claiming that the Government had manipulated the figures concerning the rate of participation and the votes cast in favour. The constitutional amendments were promulgated in December.

In January 1997 the Secretary-General of the UGTA, Abd al-Hak Benhamouda (who had recently announced his intention to establish a centrist political party), was shot dead in Algiers. Although an Islamist group claimed responsibility for the assassination, there was speculation that it may have been perpetrated by opponents within the regime. In February President Zéroual announced that elections to the National People's Assembly would take place in late May or early June. Shortly afterwards the NTC adopted restrictive legislation concerning political parties in accordance with the amended Constitution. The new electoral law, replacing the majority system with proportional representation, was also adopted. Later in February Abdelkader Bensalah, the President of the NTC, formed a centrist grouping, the Rassemblement national démocratique (RND), which was originally to have been led by Adb al-Hak Benhamouda (see above). The RND received support from a wide range of organizations, including trade unions, anti-Islamist groups and the influential ONM, and was closely linked with Zéroual and the Government. In the following months several more political parties emerged, while certain existing parties changed their names to comply with the new legislation. Notably, Hamas became the Mouvement de la société pour la paix (MSP).

In April 1997 representatives of Algeria's principal opposition parties (including the FIS) attended a conference in Madrid, Spain, convened by Spanish non-governmental organizations, to discuss the situation in Algeria. During the conference the FIS strongly condemned the massacre of civilians by the GIA and it appealed to the Algerian Government to initiate dialogue with the banned opposition.

Some 39 political parties contested the elections to the National People's Assembly on 5 June 1997. The FIS and Ettahaddi appealed for a boycott of the elections, while the MDA was banned from participating after failing to comply with the new legislation concerning political parties. (Later in June the MDA and several small political groupings were formally dissolved by the Government.) As the preliminary results of the elections began to emerge, opposition leaders complained of irregularities during the electoral process, and accused officials of manipulating the results in favour of the RND. International observers were critical of the conduct of the elections and commented that the rate of voter participation (officially estimated at 65.5% of the electorate) seemed unrealistically high. According to the final official results, the RND won 156 of the Assembly's 380 seats, followed by the MSP (69), the FLN (62), Nahdah (34), the FFS (20), the RCD (19), and other small political groupings and independent candidates. In mid-June President Zéroual asked Ahmed Ouyahia (who had tendered his resignation following the election) to form a new Government. Later in the month Ouyahia announced a new Council of Ministers, comprising members of the RND, the FLN and the MSP.

In July 1997 Abdelkader Hachani, a high-ranking member of the FIS, was formally sentenced to five years' imprisonment and three years' deprivation of his civil rights; Hachani was released immediately as he had been in custody for five years. Shortly afterwards Abbasi Madani was conditionally released following a hearing at a military tribunal. The release of the two leaders was widely interpreted as a conciliatory gesture by the Government towards the Islamist opposition. In August Kofi Annan, the UN Secretary-General, angered the Algerian Government by suggesting that the UN might consider some form of intervention in Algeria in order to stem the violence, which had escalated dramatically. In September Madani responded by writing Annan an open letter offering to appeal for an immediate truce. Shortly afterwards Madani was once again confined to house arrest. (Annan subsequently announced that the UN would not be considering intervention in Algeria.)

The level of violence intensified in mid-1997, with civilians increasingly becoming the target of attacks by armed Islamists. There were numerous massacres in villages to the south and west of Algiers, resulting in the deaths of hundreds of civilians and the kidnapping of many young women for 'temporary marriage'. An estimated 300 civilians were killed in August during a massacre in the Blida region; in September another 200 died during an attack on a suburb of Algiers. In late September the Armée islamique du salut (AIS, the armed wing of the FIS) declared a cease-fire, effective from October, in an attempt to expose members of the GIA as the principal perpetrators of the recent civilian massacres. The GIA admitted responsibility for the massacres, which it insisted were 'God's work'.

Elections to regional and municipal authorities in Algeria took place on 23 October 1997. According to official results, the RND won more than one-half of the seats contested, followed by the FLN (20.8%) and the MSP (10.3%). All the main opposition parties, including the FLN and the MSP, accused the authorities of manipulating the results in favour of the RND, and disputed the reported high rate of voter participation (officially estimated at 66.2% of the electorate). In the following weeks several thousand people demonstrated in Algiers to protest against the alleged electoral fraud. In late December the Government announced the appointment of the Council of the Nation. Of the Council's 96 seats indirectly elected by regional and municipal authorities, 80 were won by the RND, followed by the FLN (10), the FFS (4) and the MSP (2); President Zéroual appointed the remaining 48 members. The RND thus became the dominant party in both parliamentary chambers.

In April 1998 the RND held its first congress, at which Abdelkader Bensalah resigned as the party's President. Muhammad Tahar Benbaibeche was appointed RND Secretary-General, but the election of a successor to Bensalah was postponed. In the following month the authorities disbanded some 30 political groupings, including Ettahaddi and the PSD, for failing to satisfy the legal requirements concerning political associations.

In late June 1998 there were violent protests in the Kabyle region following the assassination of Lounes Matoub, a popular Berber singer and an outspoken critic of both the Government and the Islamist movement. There were further protests in July when controversial legislation on the compulsory use of the Arabic language in public life (see above) came into effect. Berber activists in the Kabyle fiercely opposed the 'arabization' policy and demanded the recognition of Tamazight as an official language. The authorities narrowly averted an escalation of social unrest in September, when the UGTA agreed to cancel its planned general strike in return for direct negotiations with government officials.

In mid-September 1998 President Zéroual announced that a presidential election would be held before March 1999, nearly two years ahead of schedule. Although there were reports that Zéroual had been suffering from ill health, most analysts suggested that the announcement had been prompted primarily by a power struggle in the regime, between the faction loyal to the President (including his close adviser, Gen. Muhammad Betchine, and Prime Minister Ouyahia) and that of Lt-Gen. Muhammad Lamari, the Chief of Staff of the Army. In October both Betchine and Muhammad Adami, the Minister of Justice, resigned from their posts, following numerous media reports in which they were accused of corruption and abuse of office. In late October Zéroual declared that the presidential election would be postponed until April 1999 to allow political parties to prepare their campaigns. In December 1998 Ouyahia resigned as Premier; he was replaced by Smail Hamdani, a widely respected senior politician and former diplomat. A new, largely unaltered, Council of Ministers was subsequently appointed. Ouyahia was elected Secretary-General of the RND at the end of January 1999.

A total of 47 candidates registered to contest the presidential election; however, only seven were declared eligible to stand by the Constitutional Council. Abdelaziz Bouteflika, who commanded the support of the mainstream FLN and the RND, was also believed to have the support of the military establishment as he had declined a proposal by the armed forces to assume the presidency in 1994. The senior generals had decided not to nominate a member of the armed forces for the presidency in order to guarantee a civilian president to promote dialogue with the Islamist militants. However, public support for Bouteflika by retired members of the armed forces provoked widespread cynicism regarding the military's assurances of its neutrality. The other candidates comprised: the FFS leader, Hocine Aït Ahmed; former Prime Minister Mokdad Sifi; a veteran of the war of independence, Youcef Khateb; Mouloud Hamrouche, who enjoyed the support of the reformist wing of the FLN; Ahmad Taleb Ibrahimi, a former Minister of Foreign Affairs who received support from the proscribed FIS; and Abdallah Djaballah, the leader of Nahdah, who was subsequently removed from office following the decision of senior members of the party to support Bouteflika's candidacy, and who formed a new party, the Mouvement de la réforme nationale (MRN), to promote his candidature. Following the exclusion of its leader, Sheikh Mafoud Nahnah, from the presidential election, on the grounds that he had not taken part in the war of independence (despite his candidacy in the 1995 election), the Islamist MSP eventually announced its support for Bouteflika. Bouteflika thus enjoyed the support of the four main political parties, as well as that of the UGTA and several political associations.

On the eve of the election, which took place on 15 April 1999, Bouteflika's six rivals withdrew their candidacies following Zéroual's refusal to postpone the poll as a result of allegations of massive electoral fraud in favour of Bouteflika. Voting papers were, nevertheless, distributed for all seven candidates, and no official boycott of the election was organized. The credibility of the poll was, however, seriously diminished, and Bouteflika announced that he would accept the presidency only if there were both a high voter turn-out and a large majority in his favour. According to official results, Bouteflika won 73.8% of the votes cast (his closest rival, Ibrahimi, secured 12.5%). However, this figure, together with the estimated official turn-out of more than 60%, was immediately disputed by his opponents, who maintained that voter turn-out had reached only 23.3% and that Bouteflika had received only 28% of the votes cast, compared with 20% for Ibrahimi. Bouteflika, however, accepted the presidency on 16 April. Clashes took place on the following day between protesters and the security forces after the authorities banned a planned peaceful protest organized by the opposition parties. At his inaugural ceremony on 27 April, Bouteflika reiterated his commitment to national reconciliation to end the civil conflict in Algeria, but pledged to continue the military campaign against terrorists and reaffirmed that the FIS would not be legalized.

Following clandestine negotiations between the Government and representatives of the FIS, in June 1999 the armed wing of the FIS, the AIS, announced the permanent cessation of its armed struggle against the Government. In July President Bouteflika announced plans to launch an initiative for national reconciliation, which some believed to be linked to the AIS truce. Bouteflika's peace plans were incorporated in the Law on Civil Concord (promulgated in July), which contained provisions for a partial or total amnesty for Islamists belonging to armed forces (excluding the perpetrators of murder and rape and those who have planted incendiary devices) on condition that they accept the authority of the State. The 'civil concord' was to be subject to popular approval at a referendum held on 16 September. The opposition rejected the premise of the referendum, which they believed to have been organized solely to legitimize Bouteflika's appointment as President. At the referendum 98.6% of those who voted (85% of the electorate) indicated their support for Bouteflika's approach to restoring peace to Algeria.

In his first months in office Bouteflika exhibited unprecedented candour; in August 1999 he announced that at least 100,000 people had died in the previous seven years as a result of the civil conflict (rather than the 30,000 previously claimed by the Government), as well as acknowledging that state monopolies were being abused by 10 to 15 individuals. He replaced 22 of the 48 regional governors in August, in an attempt to eradicate corruption, and dismissed a further 20 provincial (wilayat) general secretaries and 318 heads of administrative districts (dairas) in October. Also in October Bouteflika invited Amnesty International and other human rights organizations to visit Algeria to confirm its progress and announced that he would resign in January 2000 if he had failed by then to restore peace in Algeria and 'revolutionize' its economy. At the end of October 1999 Bouteflika pardoned 5,000 prisoners (although including only 152 condemned for offences contained within the Law on Civil Concord), bringing the total released during his administration to 14,563.

Following Bouteflika's accession to the presidency in April 1999, there was constant media speculation concerning his failure to appoint a new government. Despite Bouteflika's repeated denials, many believed that the senior members of the armed forces were preventing the formation of a government by opposing its proposed composition. These reports intensified during October; however, in November Bouteflika announced that a new government would be formed by the end of the year.

In November 1999 the assassination of Hachani, the most senior member of the FIS at liberty (ranked third in the party), represented a serious reverse for hopes for national reconciliation. Hachani, who had favoured dialogue with all political forces and had urged the legalization of the FIS as a political party, was believed to have been involved in a secret political dialogue between the Government and the FIS. In mid-December a member of the GIA, Fouad Boulemia, was arrested and charged with the murder of Hachani, after having been found in possession of the alleged murder weapon and identity documents belonging to Hachani. Several of Hachani's relatives, however, claimed that the security forces, which had reportedly kept the FIS official under surveillance following his release from prison, had perpetrated the assassination. Later that month Bouteflika finally announced the formation of a new Council of Ministers, comprising members of the FLN, the MSP, Nahdah, the RCD, the ANR and the PRA, all of which had supported Bouteflika's presidential campaign. Ahmed Benbitour, a former Minister of Finance, was appointed to the post of Prime Minister.

In early January 2000, following discussions between representatives of the Government, the army and the AIS, an agreement was reached whereby the AIS pledged to dissolve itself in return for the restoration of full civil and political rights to its former members. It was estimated that some 1,500 rebels were to be granted a full pardon under the agreement and it was hoped that these former militants would assist the security forces in their attempts to apprehend members of the GIA and a breakaway group from the GIA, the Groupe salafiste pour la prédication et combat (GSPC). On 13 January the amnesty that had been granted to militant Islamists under the Law on Civil Concord expired, and thousands of government troops launched a concerted assault on rebel strongholds in the north-east and south-west of the country, in an attempt to eliminate remaining anti-Government factions. Despite the Law on Civil Concord, the Government estimated that around 600 people (many of them civilians) had been killed between July 1999 and January 2000, mostly in incidents connected to the GIA and the GSPC. In late January it was reported that the leader of the GSPC, Hassan Hattab, was negotiating the surrender of his group with the Government; however, the army onslaught against the rebels continued into February, with both parties to the conflict announcing heavy losses.

During the late 1970s and early 1980s the protracted struggle in Western Sahara embittered Algeria's relations with France, which supported the claims of Morocco. Algeria also criticized French military intervention elsewhere in Africa, while further grievances were the trade imbalance in favour of the former colonial power, and recurrent disputes over the price of Algerian exports of gas to France; the French Government's determination to reduce the number of Algerians residing in France was another source of contention. In 1986 the French Government co-operated with the Algerian authorities by expelling 13 members of the MDA, and in 1986–88 it suppressed three MDA newspapers that were being published in France. In 1987 the Algerian Government agreed to release the assets of former French settlers, which had been 'frozen' since independence, and to allow former settlers to sell their land to the Algerian State; in return, financial assistance was provided by France. The Algerian army's coup in January 1992 was welcomed by the French Government, which was rumoured to have been consulted beforehand. French economic and political support for the Algerian regime increased in early 1993, following the appointment of Edouard Balladur as Prime Minister of France. Alleged Islamist militants residing in France continued to be prosecuted, and in August 1994, following the killing of five French embassy employees in Algiers, 26 suspected Algerian extremists were interned in northern France; 20 of them were subsequently expelled to Burkina Faso. In September the French embassy in Algiers confirmed that entry visas would be issued to Algerians only in exceptional cases. By November, when the number of French nationals killed by Islamist militants in Algeria had reached 21, the French Government was urging its citizens to evacuate Algeria. An Air France aircraft was hijacked in Algiers in December by members of the GIA, resulting in the deaths of three passengers and, later, in the killing of the hijackers by French security forces when the aircraft landed in France. In retaliation, the GIA 'declared war' on France.

In early 1995 French police made a series of arrests across France in an attempt to dismantle support networks for Islamist militants in Algeria and Tunisia; however, this did not prevent the GIA from embarking on a ruthless campaign of violence in France in the following months. The GIA claimed responsibility for numerous bomb attacks across France between July and November, in which seven people were killed and more than 160 injured. The French authorities made a number of arrests and, in a widely-publicized attempted arrest, shot and killed an Algerian-born French resident, whom they alleged to be a leading figure in the bombing campaign. French authorities sought extradition orders for further suspects in Sweden and Britain. In November the French police arrested several alleged Islamist activists in France and seized explosive devices, reportedly foiling an imminent bomb attack in Lille. Meanwhile, British police arrested two Algerian nationals suspected of involvement in the French bomb attacks.

French nationals in Algeria continued to be the target of attacks by Islamist militants, and in May 1996 seven French clergymen (abducted by the GIA in March) were killed, despite apparent efforts by the French authorities to negotiate their release. In July Hervé de Charette, the French Minister of Foreign Affairs, made an official visit to Algeria, the first ministerial-level visit for three years. However, the success of the visit was marred by the assassination in August of Pierre Claverie, the French Roman Catholic Bishop of Oran, only hours after meeting de Charette. In December four people were killed and at least 45 were injured as a result of a bomb explosion on a passenger train in Paris, prompting speculation that the GIA had resumed its campaign of violence in France. The French authorities subsequently arrested numerous suspected Islamist activists. In early 1998 a French court sentenced 36 Islamist militants to terms of imprisonment of up to 10 years for providing logistical support for the bomb attacks in France in 1995. A further 138 people stood trial in France in September 1998, accused of criminal association with Algerian terrorists. Twenty-seven of the accused had been in custody for four years. In June 1999 the French National Assembly voted unanimously to abandon the official claim that the eight-year struggle between Algerian nationalists and French troops, which began in November 1954, had been no more than 'an operation for keeping order' and thus admitted that France had indeed fought in the Algerian war of independence. Later in June the French Minister of Foreign Affairs, Hubert Védrine, visited Algeria and discussed plans to reopen the French consulates in Annaba and Oran with President Bouteflika. Relations between the two countries appeared to be improving; in September Bouteflika and the French President, Jacques Chirac, met in New York (the first meeting between the leaders of the two countries since 1992), and Chirac announced his intention to visit Algeria in the near future. In November 1999 the President of the French Senate, Christian Poncelet, met Bouteflika in Algiers, and in January 2000 the Algerian Minister of Foreign Affairs, Youcef Yousfi, made the first official visit to France by an Algerian member of government for six years.

Relations with Spain were affected during the early 1980s by Spain's support for Morocco in the Western Sahara dispute, and by mutual suspicion that each country was harbouring opponents of the other's Government. In 1987 Algeria and Spain concluded an agreement allowing closer supervision of Algerian dissidents in Spain and of members of Euskadi ta Askatasuna (ETA, the Basque separatist movement) in Algeria; later in that year, an MDA activist was expelled from Spain, and in early 1989 Algeria ejected 16 ETA members. In late July 1999 the Spanish Minister of Foreign Affairs met President Bouteflika in Algiers for talks and delivered messages of support for Bouteflika's process of political and economic liberalization from King Juan Carlos and from José María Aznar López, the Spanish Prime Minister.

During the 1980s Algeria attempted to achieve a closer relationship with the other countries of the Maghreb (Libya, Mauritania, Morocco and Tunisia). In March 1983 Algeria and Tunisia signed the Maghreb Fraternity and Co-operation Treaty, establishing a basis for the creation of the long-discussed 'Great Arab Maghreb'; Mauritania signed the treaty in December. Relations with Morocco, however, continued to be affected by the dispute over Western Sahara (see chapter on Morocco). In May 1988 Algeria and Morocco re-established diplomatic relations at ambassadorial level (relations had been severed in 1976). In June the five Heads of State of the Maghreb countries met in Algiers, and announced the formation of a Maghreb commission, to examine areas of regional integration. In February 1989 the leaders signed a treaty establishing the Union du Maghreb arabe (UMA, see p. 293), with the aim of encouraging economic co-operation and eventually establishing a full customs union.

The Algerian army's intervention in January 1992, to prevent an FIS victory in the general election, was welcomed by nearly all Arab Governments (particularly Egypt), with the exception of Sudan. In February the Minister of Foreign Affairs, Lakhdar Brahimi, visited member states of the Gulf Co-operation Council (GCC, see p. 153) to explain the reasons behind the coup and to highlight Algeria's economic plight. Of Algeria's fellow Maghreb countries, Tunisia and Morocco were relieved that the establishment of a neighbouring fundamentalist state had been pre-empted, and diplomatic relations remained cordial.

Morocco imposed entry visas on Algerian nationals in August 1994, following the murder of two Spanish tourists in Morocco, allegedly by Algerian Islamist extremists. Algeria reciprocated by closing the border between the two countries and imposing entry visas on Moroccan nationals. Tensions eased slightly in September when Algeria announced the appointment of a new ambassador to Morocco, and in early 1995 Algerian–Moroccan negotiations commenced on the development of bilateral co-operation. However, in December King Hassan of Morocco expressed his disapproval at Algeria's alleged continuing support for the independence of Western Sahara, and he demanded that UMA activities be suspended. A UMA summit meeting, scheduled for later that month, was subsequently postponed. In December 1996 the Ministers of the Interior of Algeria and Morocco held a meeting in Rabat, prompting speculation of a *rapprochement* between the two countries. In August 1998 Prime Minister Ahmed Ouyahia held talks in Algeria with his Moroccan counterpart, Abd ar-Rahman el-Youssoufi, enhancing the prospects of the mutual border being reopened. Following his accession to the presidency, Bouteflika initially attempted further to improve bilateral relations in a visit to the Moroccan capital to attend the funeral of the Moroccan King, Hassan II. However, the *rapprochement* was halted following the GIA's massacre in August of 29 civilians in the region of Bechar, near the Moroccan border, on the day when the imminent reopening of the mutual border was announced. Bouteflika publicly accused Morocco of providing sanctuary for those responsible for the attack and also extended accusations to drugs-trafficking and arms-dealing on the Algerian border. Later in September Bouteflika accused both Morocco and Tunisia of acting against the interests of the UMA by negotiating separate agreements with the European Union (EU).

In December 1996 the EU and Algeria began negotiations on Algeria's participation in a Euro-Mediterranean free-trade zone. In early 1998 EU delegations visited Algeria to express concern about the escalation of violence in the country. In October the EU agreed to commence negotiations with the Algerian Government with the aim of concluding an association agreement. In November 1999 an EU delegation visited Algiers (following a meeting in Vienna in October) and it was agreed that negotiations on a trade partnership agreement would be resumed before March 2000.

In February 1995 the GIA claimed responsibility for an attack on a Tunisian border post, during which six Tunisian border guards were killed. The Tunisian Government initially denied that the incident had taken place; however, it later accepted that the guards had been killed, most probably by Islamist militants. Security measures were subsequently increased along the common border.

### Government

Under the 1976 Constitution (with modifications adopted by the National People's Assembly in June 1979 and with further amendments approved by popular referendum in November 1988, February 1989 and in November 1996), Algeria is a multi-party state, with parties subject to approval by the Ministry of the Interior. The Head of State is the President of the Republic, who is elected by universal adult suffrage for a five-year term, renewable once. The President presides over a Council of Ministers and a High Security Council. The President must appoint a Prime Minister as Head of Government, who appoints a Council of Ministers. The bicameral legislature consists of the 380-member National People's Assembly and the 144-member Council of the Nation. The members of the National People's Assembly are elected by universal, direct, secret suffrage for a five-year term. Two-thirds of the members of the Council of the Nation are elected by indirect, secret suffrage from regional and municipal authorities; the remainder are appointed by the President of the Republic. The Council's term in office is six years; one-half of its members are replaced every three years. Both the Head of Government and the parliamentary chambers may initiate legislation. Legislation must be deliberated upon respectively by the National People's Assembly and the Council of the Nation before promulgation. The country is divided into 48 departments (*wilayat*), which are, in turn, sub-divided into communes. Each *wilaya* and commune has an elected assembly.

### Defence

In August 1999 the estimated strength of the armed forces was 122,000 (including 75,000 conscripts), comprising an army of 105,000, a navy of about 7,000 and an air force of 10,000. The 1999 defence budget was estimated at 121,000m. dinars. Military service is compulsory for 18 months. There are para-military forces of 81,200, controlled by the Ministry of Defence and the Directorate of National Security, and an estimated 100,000 self-defence militia and communal guards.

### Economic Affairs

In 1997, according to estimates by the World Bank, Algeria's gross national product (GNP), measured at average 1995–97 prices, was US $43,927m., equivalent to $1,500 per head. During 1990–97, it was estimated, GNP per head declined, in real terms, at an average annual rate of 1.6%. Over the same period, the population increased at an average rate of 2.3% per year. In 1998 GNP was estimated at $46,500m. ($1,550 per head). Algeria's gross domestic product (GDP) increased, in real terms, at an average annual rate of 1.2% in 1990–98. Real GDP rose by 3.8% in 1996, by an estimated 1.3% in 1997 and, according to an IMF estimate, by 4% in 1998.

Agriculture (including forestry and fishing) is an important sector of the Algerian economy, employing 24.8% of the country's total labour force in 1998 and providing 12% of GDP in that year. The principal crops are wheat, barley and potatoes. Olives, citrus fruits and grapes are also grown. During 1990–98 agricultural GDP increased at an average annual rate of 2.6%. Agricultural GDP declined by 13.5% in 1997, but rose by 11.4% in 1998.

Industry (including mining, manufacturing, construction and power) contributed 47% of GDP in 1998, and engaged 31.2% of the employed population in 1987. During 1990–98 industrial GDP decreased at an average annual rate of 2.0%. However, industrial GDP rose by 4.3% in 1997 and by 4.1% in 1998.

The mining sector engaged only 1.6% of the employed population in 1987, but provides almost all of Algeria's export earnings. The major mineral exports are petroleum and natural gas. In November 1996 a 1,400-km gas pipeline became fully operational, transporting natural gas from Algeria to Spain. Reserves of iron ore, phosphates, lead and zinc are also exploited. In addition, Algeria has deposits of antimony, tungsten, manganese, mercury, copper and salt. The exploitation of gold reserves was expected to commence in the late 1990s. The extraction and processing of petroleum and natural gas provided 32.8% of GDP in 1997. In real terms, the GDP of the mining sector increased at an average annual rate of 2.3% in 1988–92. Mining GDP declined by 4.6% in 1996 and by 8.4% in 1997.

Manufacturing engaged 12.2% of the employed population in 1987 and provided 9% of GDP in 1998. In 1994 food products, beverages and tobacco accounted for 39.0% of the gross value of manufacturing output, while metals, metal products, machinery and transport equipment provided 27.5%. During 1990–97 the GDP of the manufacturing sector declined at an average annual rate of 10.2%. It fell by 3.8% in 1997, but increased by 8.4% in 1998.

Energy is derived principally from natural gas and petroleum. However, nuclear power is exploited as an additional source of energy; the first nuclear reactor was installed in 1989. Imports of fuel and energy comprised only 1.6% of the value of merchandise imports in 1995.

Services engaged 46.0% of the employed labour force in 1987 and provided 41% of GDP in 1998. During 1990–98 the combined GDP of the service sectors increased at an average annual rate of 4.8%. Services GDP rose by 2.6% in 1997 and by 4.4% in 1998.

In 1997 Algeria recorded a visible trade surplus of US $5,700m., and there was a surplus of $3,500m. on the current account of the balance of payments. In 1995 the principal source of imports continued to be France (providing 24.9% of the total), while Italy was the principal market for exports (22.4%). Other major trading partners were the USA, Spain and Germany. The principal exports in 1995 were mineral fuels, lubricants, etc., which accounted for 95.2% of total export revenue (petroleum and derivatives 64.7%, gas 30.4%). Other exports included vegetables, tobacco, hides and dates. The principal imports in that year were food and live animals, machinery and transport equipment, and basic manufactures.

In 1997 Algeria's overall budget surplus was 66,100m. dinars, equivalent to 2.4% of GDP. Algeria's total external debt at the end of 1997 amounted to US $30,921m., of which $28,741m. was long-term public debt. The cost of debt-servicing represented 27.2% of export earnings (goods and services) in that year. The annual rate of inflation averaged 20.4% in 1990–98. Consumer prices increased by an average of 5.7% in 1997 and by 5.0% in 1998. The inflation rate declined to 2.0% in the year ending August 1999. An estimated 28% of the labour force were unemployed in 1998.

Algeria is a member of the Union of the Arab Maghreb (see p. 293), which aims to promote economic integration of member states, and also of the Organization of the Petroleum Exporting Countries (OPEC, see p. 252).

The dramatic fall during 1998 in international prices for petroleum emphasized Algeria's continued over-dependence on the hydrocarbons sector: a decline of more than 25% in government revenue from oil and gas (which amounts to as much as 60% of total revenue) resulted in a fiscal deficit equivalent to some 3.9% of GDP (from a surplus of 2.4% in 1997), the current account of the balance of payments regressed from a surplus in 1997 to a deficit equivalent to 2% of GDP, and reserves of foreign exchange were eroded. None the less, a recovery in agricultural output, in conjunction with growth in the non-oil-related industrial sector (the first since 1991), contributed to the continued expansion of overall GDP. A credit equivalent to some US $300m., agreed in May 1999 by the IMF (which has been supporting Algeria's economic adjustment efforts since 1994) under its Compensatory and Contingency Financing Facility, was intended to relieve the shortfall in export revenue arising from the oil-price crisis. As a member of OPEC, Algeria assumed an active role during 1998–99 in efforts by the organization to reduce petroleum output in order to stimulate a recovery in world oil prices. By the time of Abdelaziz Bouteflika's inauguration as President in April 1999, there was a degree of optimism regarding Algeria's economic prospects, afforded by signs of a recovery in petroleum prices, together with hopes that a return of domestic political stability would attract foreign investment to both the hydrocarbons and non-oil sectors and thus enable economic reconstruction and form the basis for sustained growth. Bouteflika emphasized his commitment to the pursuit of policies of economic liberalization and diversification adopted by the administration of Liamine Zéroual, which had notably entailed strict controls on public expenditure and brought about a marked reduction in the rate of inflation. The privatization of state-owned enterprises and liberalization of the banking sector was to continue, while the commencement of trading on the Algiers Stock Exchange in mid-1999 was regarded as indicative of the commitment to the participation of private investors in the Algerian economy. None the less, serious inadequacies remain in terms of infrastructure and social and economic provisions, while a renewed decline in international petroleum prices could again jeopardize the process of economic recovery, notably Algeria's ability to service its sizeable public debt. Furthermore, the participation of private investors and of the international financial community, regarded as essential to long-term economic development, will largely depend on the new administration's ability to bring about a lasting civil peace.

### Social Welfare

Since 1974 all Algerian citizens have had the right to free medical care. In 1984 there were 9,056 physicians (4.3 per 10,000 population), 2,596 dentists, 1,174 pharmacists and 474 midwifery personnel working in the country. In 1996 the Government's current budgetary expenditure included about 28,500m. dinars (5.2% of total current expenditure) on hospitals, 36,400m. dinars (6.6%) on family allowances and 18,900m. dinars (3.4%) on war veterans' pensions.

### Education

Education, in the national language (Arabic), is officially compulsory for nine years between six and 15 years of age. Primary education begins at the age of six and lasts for six years. Secondary education begins at 12 years of age and lasts for up to six years (comprising two cycles of three years each). In 1996 the total enrolment at primary and secondary schools was equivalent to 86% of the school-age population (89% of boys; 82% of girls). Enrolment at primary schools in that year included 94% of children in the relevant age-group (97% of boys; 91% of girls). Enrolment at secondary schools in 1996 included 56% of children in the relevant age-group (58% of boys; 54% of girls). Some 12.5% of total planned expenditure in the 1997 administrative budget was allocated to education and training. Priority is being given to teacher-training, to the development of technical and scientific teaching programmes, and to adult literacy and training schemes. In addition to the 10 universities, there are seven other *centres universitaires* and a number of technical colleges. In 1995/96 a total of 347,410 students were enrolled in higher education. In 1995, according to UNESCO estimates, the average rate of adult illiteracy was 38.4% (males 26.1%; females 51.0%).

### Public Holidays

**2000:** 1 January (New Year), 8 January*† (Id al-Fitr, end of Ramadan), 16 March* (Id al-Adha, Feast of the Sacrifice), 6 April* (Islamic New Year), 15 April* (Ashoura), 1 May (Labour Day), 15 June* (Mouloud, Birth of Muhammad), 19 June (Ben Bella's Overthrow), 5 July (Independence), 26 October* (Leilat al-Meiraj, Ascension of Muhammad), 1 November (Anniversary of the Revolution), 28 November* (Ramadan begins), 28 December*† (Id al-Fitr, end of Ramadan).

**2001:** 1 January (New Year), 6 March* (Id al-Adha, Feast of the Sacrifice), 26 March* (Islamic New Year), 4 April* (Ashoura), 1 May (Labour Day), 4 June* (Mouloud, Birth of Muhammad), 19 June (Ben Bella's Overthrow), 5 July (Independence), 15 October* (Leilat al-Meiraj, Ascension of Muhammad), 1 November (Anniversary of the Revolution), 17 November* (Ramadan begins), 17 December* (Id al-Fitr, end of Ramadan).

* Religious holidays, which are dependent on the Islamic lunar calendar, may differ by one or two days from the dates given.

† This festival will occur twice (in the Islamic years AH 1420 and 1421) within the same Gregorian year.

### Weights and Measures

The metric system is in force.

# Statistical Survey

Source (unless otherwise stated): Office National des Statistiques, 8 rue des Moussebiline, BP 55, Algiers; tel. (2) 64-77-90; internet www.ons.dz.

## Area and Population

**AREA, POPULATION AND DENSITY**

| | |
|---|---|
| Area (sq km) | 2,381,741* |
| Population (census results)† | |
| 20 April 1987 | 23,038,942 |
| 25 June 1998 (provisional) | |
| Males | 14,766,371 |
| Females | 14,510,396 |
| Total | 29,276,767 |
| Density (per sq km) at 25 June 1998 | 12.3 |

* 919,595 sq miles.

† Excluding Algerian nationals residing abroad, numbering an estimated 828,000 at 1 January 1978.

**POPULATION BY WILAYA (ADMINISTRATIVE DISTRICT)**
(provisional census results, April 1987)*

| | Population |
|---|---|
| Adrar | 216,931 |
| el-Asnam (ech-Cheliff) | 679,717 |
| Laghouat | 215,183 |
| Oum el-Bouaghi (Oum el-Bouagul) | 402,683 |
| Batna | 757,059 |
| Béjaia | 697,669 |
| Biskra (Beskra) | 429,217 |
| Béchar | 183,896 |
| Blida (el-Boulaïda) | 704,462 |
| Bouira | 525,460 |
| Tamanrasset (Tamenghest) | 94,219 |
| Tébessa (Tbessa) | 409,317 |
| Tlemcen (Tilimsen) | 707,453 |

| *— continued* | Population |
|---|---|
| Tiaret (Tihert) | 574,786 |
| Tizi-Ouzou | 931,501 |
| Algiers (el-Djezaïr) | 1,687,579 |
| Djelfa (el-Djelfa) | 490,240 |
| Jijel | 471,319 |
| Sétif (Stif) | 997,482 |
| Saida | 235,240 |
| Skikda | 619,094 |
| Sidi-Bel-Abbès | 444,047 |
| Annaba | 453,951 |
| Guelma | 353,329 |
| Constantine (Qacentina) | 662,330 |
| Médéa (Lemdiyya) | 650,623 |
| Mostaganem (Mestghanem) | 504,124 |
| M'Sila | 605,578 |
| Mascara (Mouaskar) | 562,806 |
| Ouargla (Wargla) | 286,696 |
| Oran (Ouahran) | 916,678 |
| el-Bayadh | 155,494 |
| Illizi | 19,698 |
| Bordj Bou Arreridj | 429,009 |
| Boumerdes | 646,870 |
| el-Tarf | 276,836 |
| Tindouf | 16,339 |
| Tissemsilt | 227,542 |
| el-Oued | 379,512 |
| Khenchela | 243,733 |
| Souk-Ahras | 298,236 |
| Tipaza | 615,140 |
| Mila | 511,047 |
| Ain-Defla | 536,205 |
| Naama | 112,858 |
| Ain-Temouchent | 271,454 |
| Ghardaia | 215,955 |
| Relizane | 545,061 |
| **Total** | 22,971,558 |

* Excluding Algerian nationals abroad, estimated to total 828,000 at 1 January 1978.

**PRINCIPAL TOWNS** (population at 1987 census)

| | | | |
|---|---|---|---|
| Algiers (el-Djezaïr, capital) | 1,507,241 | Biskra (Beskra) | 128,281 |
| Oran (Ouahran) | 609,823 | Blida (el-Boulaïda) | 127,284 |
| Constantine (Qacentina) | 443,727 | Béjaia | 117,162 |
| Annaba | 222,518 | Mostaganem (Mestghanem) | 115,212 |
| Batna | 183,377 | Tébessa (Tbessa) | 112,007 |
| Sétif (Stif) | 179,055 | Tlemcen (Tilimsen) | 110,242 |
| Sidi-bel-Abbès | 153,106 | Béchar | 107,311 |
| Skikda | 128,747 | Tiaret (Tihert) | 100,118 |

**June 1998** (provisional census results, not including suburbs): Algiers 2,561,992.

**BIRTHS, MARRIAGES AND DEATHS***

| | Registered live births† | | Registered marriages | | Registered deaths† | |
|---|---|---|---|---|---|---|
| | Number | Rate (per 1,000) | Number | Rate (per 1,000) | Number | Rate (per 1,000) |
| 1990 | 775,000 | 31.0 | n.a. | n.a. | 151,000 | 6.0 |
| 1991 | 773,000 | 30.1 | 151,467 | 5.9 | 155,000 | 6.0 |
| 1992 | 799,000 | 30.4 | 159,380 | 6.1 | 160,000 | 6.1 |
| 1993 | 775,000 | 28.8 | 153,137 | 5.7 | 168,000 | 6.2 |
| 1994 | 776,000 | 28.2 | 147,851 | 5.4 | 180,000 | 6.5 |
| 1995 | 711,000 | 25.3 | n.a. | n.a. | 180,000 | 6.4 |
| 1996 | 733,375 | 25.7 | n.a. | n.a. | 172,000 | 6.0 |
| 1997 | 653,000 | 22.5 | n.a. | n.a. | 178,000 | 6.1 |

* Figures refer to the Algerian population only. Birth registration is estimated to be at least 90% complete, but the registration of marriages and deaths is incomplete. According to UN estimates, the average annual rates per 1,000 in 1990–95 were: births 30.8; deaths 6.4.

† Excluding live-born infants dying before registration of birth.

Source: UN, mainly *Demographic Yearbook* and *Population and Vital Statistics Report*.

**Expectation of life** (UN estimates, years at birth, 1990–95): 67.1 (males 66.0; females 68.3).

Source: UN, *World Population Prospects: The 1998 Revision*.

**ECONOMICALLY ACTIVE POPULATION** (1987 census)*

| | Males | Females | Total |
|---|---|---|---|
| Agriculture, hunting, forestry and fishing | 714,947 | 9,753 | 724,699 |
| Mining and quarrying | 64,685 | 3,142 | 67,825 |
| Manufacturing | 471,471 | 40,632 | 512,105 |
| Electricity, gas and water | 40,196 | 1,579 | 41,775 |
| Construction | 677,211 | 12,372 | 689,586 |
| Trade, restaurants and hotels | 376,590 | 14,399 | 390,990 |
| Transport, storage and communications | 207,314 | 9,029 | 216,343 |
| Financing, insurance, real estate and business services | 125,426 | 17,751 | 143,178 |
| Community, social and personal services | 945,560 | 234,803 | 1,180,364 |
| Activities not adequately defined | 149,241 | 83,718 | 232,959 |
| **Total employed** | 3,772,641 | 427,183 | 4,199,824 |
| Unemployed | 1,076,018 | 65,260 | 1,141,278 |
| **Total labour force** | 4,848,659 | 492,443 | 5,341,102 |

* Employment data relate to persons aged 6 years and over; those for unemployment relate to persons aged 16 to 64 years. Estimates have been made independently, so the totals may not be the sum of the component parts.

**1997** (sample survey, '000 persons, July–September): Total labour force 7,757 (employed 5,708; unemployed 2,049). Figures refer to males aged 15 to 60 years and females aged 15 to 55 years. Source: ILO, *Yearbook of Labour Statistics*.

**Mid-1998** (estimates in '000): Agriculture, etc. 2,420; Total labour force 9,754 (Source: FAO, *Production Yearbook*).

# Agriculture

**PRINCIPAL CROPS** ('000 metric tons)

| | 1996 | 1997 | 1998 |
|---|---|---|---|
| Wheat | 2,983 | 662 | 2,280† |
| Barley | 1,800 | 191 | 700 |
| Oats | 117 | 17 | 50* |
| Potatoes | 1,150 | 948 | 1,115 |
| Pulses | 68 | 28 | 27* |
| Rapeseed* | 100 | 100 | 100 |
| Olives | 313 | 319 | 124 |
| Tomatoes | 719 | 689 | 700* |
| Pumpkins, squash and gourds | 87 | 82 | 82* |
| Cucumbers and gherkins | 42 | 35 | 35* |
| Green chillies and peppers | 145 | 191 | 190* |
| Onions (dry) | 313 | 352 | 350* |
| Carrots | 129 | 125 | 125* |
| Other vegetables | 544 | 546 | 543* |
| Melons and watermelons | 455 | 401 | 400* |
| Grapes | 195 | 192 | 159 |
| Dates | 361 | 303 | 387 |
| Apples | 74 | 66 | 65* |
| Pears | 56 | 47 | 47* |
| Peaches and nectarines | 45 | 39 | 39* |
| Oranges | 237 | 243 | 280 |
| Tangerines, mandarins, clementines and satsumas | 80 | 90 | 111 |
| Apricots | 80 | 40 | 40* |
| Other fruits | 149 | 132 | 132 |
| Tobacco (leaves) | 6 | 7 | 7* |

* FAO estimate(s). † Unofficial figure.

Source: FAO, *Production Yearbook*.

**LIVESTOCK** ('000 head, year ending September)

| | 1996 | 1997 | 1998* |
|---|---|---|---|
| Sheep | 17,565 | 16,755 | 16,755 |
| Goats | 2,895 | 3,122 | 3,122 |
| Cattle | 1,228 | 1,255 | 1,250 |
| Horses | 60 | 60* | 60 |
| Mules | 76 | 75* | 75 |
| Asses | 210 | 210* | 210 |
| Camels | 136 | 141† | 140 |

Poultry (million): 111 in 1996; 132 in 1997; 132* in 1998.

* FAO estimate(s). † Unofficial figure.

Source: FAO, *Production Yearbook*.

**LIVESTOCK PRODUCTS** ('000 metric tons)

| | 1996 | 1997 | 1998 |
|---|---|---|---|
| Beef and veal | 104 | 119 | 120* |
| Mutton and lamb | 175 | 145 | 175* |
| Goat meat* | 9 | 9 | 9 |
| Poultry meat* | 210 | 220 | 220 |
| Other meat | 10 | 10 | 10* |
| Cows' milk* | 898 | 850 | 850 |
| Sheep's milk* | 175 | 175 | 180 |
| Goats' milk* | 142 | 145 | 145 |
| Poultry eggs* | 85 | 95 | 117 |
| Honey* | 2 | 2 | 2 |
| Wool: | | | |
| greasy* | 50 | 50 | 50 |
| clean* | 26 | 26 | 26 |
| Cattle hides* | 11 | 14 | 14 |
| Sheepskins* | 30 | 25 | 30 |
| Goatskins* | 2 | 2 | 2 |

* FAO estimate(s).

Source: FAO, *Production Yearbook*.

## Forestry

**ROUNDWOOD REMOVALS** ('000 cubic metres, excl. bark)

| | 1995 | 1996 | 1997 |
|---|---|---|---|
| Sawlogs, veneer logs and logs for sleepers | 40 | 40 | 68 |
| Pulpwood | 79 | 91 | 85 |
| Other industrial wood | 271 | 279 | 285 |
| Fuel wood | 2,141 | 2,192 | 2,245 |
| **Total** | 2,531 | 2,622 | 2,683 |

Sawnwood production ('000 cubic metres, incl. railway sleepers): 13 per year (FAO estimates) in 1980–97.

Source: FAO, *Yearbook of Forest Products*.

## Fishing

('000 metric tons, live weight)

| | 1995 | 1996* | 1997* |
|---|---|---|---|
| Bogue | 2.3 | 2.2 | 2.1 |
| Jack and horse mackerels | 6.6 | 6.2 | 6.1 |
| Sardinellas | 17.9 | 16.8 | 16.7 |
| European pilchard (sardine) | 59.0 | 55.5 | 55.2 |
| Other fishes | 17.2 | 16.2 | 16.1 |
| Crustaceans and molluscs | 3.0 | 2.8 | 2.8 |
| **Total catch** | 105.9 | 99.7 | 99.0 |

* FAO estimates.

Source: FAO, *Yearbook of Fishery Statistics*.

## Mining

('000 metric tons, unless otherwise indicated)

| | 1994 | 1995 | 1996 |
|---|---|---|---|
| Hard coal* | 20 | 22 | n.a. |
| Crude petroleum | 35,330 | 36,152 | 37,464 |
| Natural gas (petajoules) | 1,996 | 2,431 | n.a. |
| Iron ore: | | | |
| gross weight | 2,016 | 2,000* | 1,900* |
| metal content | 1,089 | 1,000*† | 1,000† |
| Lead ores or concentrates‡ | 1.1 | 0.8† | 0.9† |
| Zinc concentrates‡ | 5.6 | 3.7† | 3.7† |
| Mercury (metric tons) | 414† | 292† | 300† |
| Phosphate rock | 763 | 757 | 760† |
| Salt (unrefined) | 75 | n.a. | n.a. |

* Provisional or estimated data.

† Data from the US Bureau of Mines.

‡ Figures refer to the metal content of ores or concentrates.

Sources: UN, *Industrial Commodity Statistics Yearbook* and *Monthly Bulletin of Statistics*.

## Industry

**SELECTED PRODUCTS** ('000 metric tons, unless otherwise indicated)

| | 1993 | 1994 | 1995 |
|---|---|---|---|
| Olive oil (crude) | 27 | 23 | 15 |
| Refined sugar | 201 | 193 | 198* |
| Wine* | 65 | 50 | 57 |
| Beer ('000 hectolitres) | 421 | 398 | n.a. |
| Soft drinks ('000 hectolitres) | 1,007 | 901 | n.a. |
| Cigarettes (metric tons) | 16,260 | 16,345 | n.a. |
| Footwear—excl. rubber ('000 pairs) | 7,171 | 6,467 | n.a. |
| Nitrogenous fertilizers (a)† | 80 | 62 | n.a. |
| Phosphate fertilizers (b)† | 204 | 179 | n.a. |
| Naphthas‡ | 4,400 | 4,500 | 4,400 |
| Motor spirit (petrol) | 2,469 | 2,907 | 2,576 |
| Kerosene‡ | 129 | 200 | 250 |
| Jet fuel‡ | 350 | 900 | 784 |
| Distillate fuel oils | 7,543 | 6,896 | 7,189 |
| Residual fuel oils | 5,827 | 5,810 | 5,535 |
| Lubricating oils‡ | 140 | 140 | 150 |
| Petroleum bitumen (asphalt)‡ | 240 | 250 | 260 |
| Liquefied petroleum gas: | | | |
| from natural gas plants | 4,570 | 4,510 | 4,384 |
| from petroleum refineries | 430 | 520 | 510‡ |
| Cement | 6,951 | 6,093 | 6,200‡ |
| Pig-iron for steel-making | 925 | 919 | 940§ |
| Crude steel (ingots) | 798 | 772 | 827§ |
| Zinc—unwrought | 29.7 | 20.1 | 23.4§ |
| Refrigerators for household use ('000) | 183 | 119 | n.a. |
| Radio receivers ('000) | 109 | 107 | n.a. |
| Television receivers ('000) | 258 | 165 | n.a. |
| Buses and coaches—assembled (number) | 596 | 468 | n.a. |
| Lorries—assembled (number) | 2,304 | 1,230 | n.a. |
| Electric energy (million kWh) | 19,415 | 19,888 | 19,714 |

**1996** ('000 metric tons): Olive oil 48*; Refined sugar 362*; Wine 39*; Pig-iron for steel-making 850§; Crude steel (ingots) 675§; Zinc-unwrought 24.0§. **1997** ('000 metric tons)*: Olive oil 47; Wine 46.

* Data from FAO, *Production Yearbook*.

† Production in terms of (a) nitrogen or (b) phosphoric acid.

‡ Provisional or estimated data.

§ Data from the US Bureau of Mines.

Source: mainly UN, *Industrial Commodity Statistics Yearbook*.

# Finance

### CURRENCY AND EXCHANGE RATES

**Monetary Units**

100 centimes = 1 Algerian dinar (AD).

**Sterling, Dollar and Euro Equivalents** (30 September 1999)

£1 sterling = 110.49 dinars;
US $1 = 67.11 dinars;
€1 = 71.57 dinars;
1,000 Algerian dinars = £9.050 = $14.902 = €13.972.

**Average Exchange Rate** (dinars per US $)

1996 54.749
1997 57.707
1998 58.739

### BUDGET ('000 million AD)*

| Revenue | 1995 | 1996 | 1997 |
|---|---|---|---|
| Hydrocarbon revenue | 358.8 | 519.7 | 592.5 |
| Export taxes | 305.2 | 451.0 | 514.8 |
| Domestic receipts | 30.9 | 45.0 | 50.0 |
| Dividends and entry rights | 22.7 | 23.7 | 27.7 |
| Other revenue | 242.1 | 305.1 | 334.1 |
| Tax revenue | 233.2 | 290.5 | 313.9 |
| Taxes on income and profits | 53.6 | 67.5 | 81.8 |
| Taxes on goods and services | 99.9 | 129.5 | 148.0 |
| Customs duties | 73.3 | 84.4 | 73.5 |
| Non-tax revenue | 8.9 | 14.6 | 20.2 |
| **Total** | 600.9 | 824.8 | 926.6 |

| Expenditure† | 1995 | 1996 | 1997 |
|---|---|---|---|
| Current expenditure | 444.4 | 550.6 | 643.5 |
| Personnel expenditure | 187.5 | 222.8 | 245.2 |
| War veterans' pensions | 15.6 | 18.9 | 0.7 |
| Material and supplies | 29.4 | 34.7 | 25.0 |
| Public services | 55.4 | 69.9 | n.a. |
| Hospitals | 21.3 | 28.5 | n.a. |
| Current transfers | 94.2 | 115.4 | n.a. |
| Family allowances | 24.5 | 36.4 | n.a. |
| Public works and social assistance | 13.6 | 14.2 | 44.2 |
| Food subsidies | 18.3 | 11.9 | 12.0 |
| Housing | 7.9 | 18.1 | 28.7 |
| Interest payments | 62.2 | 89.0 | 109.4 |
| Capital expenditure | 144.7 | 174.0 | 201.6 |
| **Total** | 589.1 | 724.6 | 845.1 |

* Figures refer to operations of the central Government, excluding special accounts. The balance (revenue less expenditure) on such accounts (in '000 million AD) was: −0.7 in 1995; 1.5 in 1996; 1.1 in 1997.

† Excluding net lending by the Treasury ('000 million AD): 2.4 in 1995; 2.4 in 1996; 1.5 in 1997. Also excluded are allocations to the Rehabilitation Fund ('000 million AD): 36.9 in 1995; 24.4 in 1996; 18.0 in 1997.

Source: IMF, *Algeria: Selected Issues and Statistical Appendix* (September 1998).

### CENTRAL BANK RESERVES (US $ million at 31 December)

| | 1996 | 1997 | 1998 |
|---|---|---|---|
| Gold* | 281 | 264 | 275 |
| IMF special drawing rights | 5 | 1 | 2 |
| Foreign exchange | 4,230 | 8,046 | 6,844 |
| **Total** | 4,516 | 8,311 | 7,121 |

* Valued at SDR 35 per troy ounce.

Source: IMF, *International Financial Statistics*.

### MONEY SUPPLY (million AD at 31 December)*

| | 1996 | 1997 | 1998 |
|---|---|---|---|
| Currency outside banks | 290,880 | 337,620 | 390,780 |
| Demand deposits at deposit money banks | 234,030 | 254,830 | 334,520 |
| Checking deposits at post office | 57,960 | 71,680 | 81,050 |
| Private sector demand deposits at treasury | 6,220 | 7,430 | 7,330 |
| **Total money** (incl. others) | 589,990 | 675,960 | 817,260 |

* Figures are rounded to the nearest 10 million dinars.

Source: IMF, *International Financial Statistics*.

### COST OF LIVING (Consumer Price Index for Algiers; average of monthly figures; base: 1989 = 100)

| | 1996 | 1997 | 1998 |
|---|---|---|---|
| Foodstuffs, beverages and tobacco | 510.7 | 539.8 | 570.5 |
| Clothing and footwear | 347.7 | 369.6 | 385.5 |
| Housing costs | 454.0 | 541.7 | 580.6 |
| **All items** (incl. others) | 468.1 | 494.9 | 519.4 |

Source: partly IMF, *Algeria: Selected Issues and Statistical Appendix* (September 1998).

### NATIONAL ACCOUNTS

**National Income and Product** (million AD at current prices)

| | 1987 | 1988 | 1989 |
|---|---|---|---|
| Compensation of employees | 125,754.4 | 137,647.5 | 156,145.1 |
| Operating surplus | 92,417.5 | 99,899.8 | 142,711.2 |
| **Domestic factor incomes** | 218,171.9 | 237,547.3 | 298,856.3 |
| Consumption of fixed capital | 32,525.2 | 32,621.8 | 33,050.1 |
| **Gross domestic product (GDP) at factor cost** | 250,697.1 | 270,169.1 | 331,906.4 |
| Indirect taxes, *less* subsidies | 62,009.0 | 64,437.5 | 71,553.8 |
| **GDP in purchasers' values** | 312,706.1 | 334,606.6 | 403,460.2 |
| Net factor income from abroad | −7,267.7 | −11,744.7 | −13,178.4 |
| Reinsurance (net) | −76.0 | — | — |
| **Gross national product** | 305,362.4 | 322,861.9 | 390,281.8 |
| *Less* Consumption of fixed capital | 32,525.2 | 32,621.8 | 33,050.1 |
| **National income in market prices** | 272,837.2 | 290,240.1 | 357,231.7 |
| Other current transfers from abroad (net) | 2,358.2 | 2,067.7 | 3,850.4 |
| **National disposable income** | 275,195.4 | 292,307.8 | 361,082.1 |

**Expenditure on the Gross Domestic Product**
('000 million AD at current prices)

| | 1995 | 1996 | 1997 |
|---|---|---|---|
| Government final consumption expenditure | 309.7 | 356.4 | 391.4 |
| Private final consumption expenditure | 1,097.4 | 1,316.8 | 1,386.7 |
| Increase in stocks | 52.4 | −27.0 | −34.0 |
| Gross fixed capital formation | 580.0 | 688.1 | 733.0 |
| **Total domestic expenditure** | 2,039.4 | 2,334.3 | 2,477.1 |
| Exports of goods and services | 539.8 | 770.7 | 847.2 |
| *Less* Imports of goods and services | 612.7 | 610.1 | 607.9 |
| **GDP in purchasers' values** | 1,966.5 | 2,494.9 | 2,716.4 |

Source: IMF, *Algeria: Selected Issues and Statistical Appendix* (September 1998).

**Gross Domestic Product by Economic Activity**
('000 million AD at current prices)

| | 1995 | 1996 | 1997 |
|---|---|---|---|
| Agriculture, forestry and fishing | 190.0 | 271.9 | 254.9 |
| Hydrocarbons* | 503.4 | 727.7 | 818.5 |
| Mining (excl. hydrocarbons); Manufacturing (excl. hydrocarbons); Electricity and water | 208.1 | 230.5 | 244.6 |
| Construction and public works | 200.7 | 240.6 | 269.6 |
| Government services | 230.3 | 260.9 | 286.7 |
| Non-government services | 453.4 | 550.9 | 621.5 |
| **Sub-total** | 1,785.9 | 2,282.5 | 2,495.8 |
| Import taxes and duties | 180.6 | 212.3 | 220.6 |
| **GDP in purchasers' values** | 1,966.5 | 2,494.8 | 2,716.4 |

* Extraction and processing of petroleum and natural gas.

Source: IMF, *Algeria: Selected Issues and Statistical Appendix* (September 1998).

**BALANCE OF PAYMENTS** (US $ '000 million)

| | 1995 | 1996 | 1997 |
|---|---|---|---|
| Exports of goods f.o.b. | 10.3 | 13.2 | 13.8 |
| Imports of goods f.o.b. | -10.1 | -9.1 | -8.1 |
| **Trade balance** | 0.2 | 4.1 | 5.7 |
| Exports of services | 0.7 | 0.8 | 1.1 |
| Imports of services | -2.0 | -2.2 | -2.2 |
| **Balance on goods and services** | -1.1 | 2.7 | 4.6 |
| Other income received | 0.1 | 0.2 | 0.3 |
| Other income paid | -2.3 | -2.6 | -2.5 |
| **Balance on goods, services and income** | -3.3 | 0.3 | 2.4 |
| Transfers (net) | 1.1 | 0.9 | 1.1 |
| **Current balance** | -2.2 | 1.2 | 3.5 |
| Direct investment (net) | 0.0 | 0.3 | 0.3 |
| Official capital (net) | -3.9 | -3.4 | -2.5 |
| Short-term credit (net) | 0.1 | -0.2 | 0.0 |
| Net errors and omissions | -0.2 | 0.0 | 0.0 |
| **Overall balance** | -6.3 | -2.1 | 1.2 |

Source: IMF, *Algeria: Selected Issues and Statistical Appendix* (September 1998).

# External Trade

Note: Data exclude military goods. Exports include stores and bunkers for foreign ships and aircraft.

**PRINCIPAL COMMODITIES** (distribution by SITC, US $ million)

| Imports c.i.f. | 1993 | 1994 | 1995 |
|---|---|---|---|
| **Food and live animals** | 2,155.5 | 2,848.9 | 2,462.4 |
| Dairy products and birds' eggs | 654.0 | 540.8 | 434.8 |
| Milk and cream | 569.4 | 493.7 | 375.0 |
| Cereals and cereal preparations | 904.2 | 1,324.1 | 1,142.2 |
| Wheat and meslin (unmilled) | 353.8 | 602.4 | 662.7 |
| Meal and flour of wheat, etc. | 281.3 | 323.2 | 306.0 |
| Sugar, sugar preparations and honey | 253.3 | 298.1 | 295.8 |
| Sugar and honey | 253.3 | 297.3 | 290.5 |
| Coffee, tea, cocoa and spices | 113.9 | 336.7 | 185.3 |
| Coffee and coffee substitutes | 105.8 | 308.2 | 158.2 |
| **Crude materials (inedible) except fuels** | 386.0 | 378.6 | 378.6 |
| Cork and wood | 172.5 | 168.9 | 199.4 |
| **Animal and vegetable oils, fats and waxes** | 184.2 | 222.9 | 320.8 |
| Fixed vegetable oils and fats | 153.1 | 188.7 | 268.8 |
| **Chemicals and related products** | 895.4 | 1,027.0 | 1,094.6 |
| Medicinal and pharmaceutical products | 366.7 | 509.8 | 517.6 |
| Medicaments (incl. veterinary) | 334.7 | 473.9 | 460.0 |

| Imports c.i.f. — *continued* | 1993 | 1994 | 1995 |
|---|---|---|---|
| **Basic manufactures** | 1,905.6 | 2,087.4 | 2,038.1 |
| Rubber manufactures | 180.3 | 140.8 | 164.8 |
| Non-metallic mineral manufactures | 194.7 | 246.0 | 226.4 |
| Iron and steel | 740.3 | 913.6 | 820.2 |
| Bars, rods, angles, shapes and sections | 254.0 | 418.2 | 258.3 |
| Bars and rods (excl. wire rod) | 161.0 | 335.9 | 180.4 |
| Tubes, pipes and fittings | 224.8 | 325.3 | 408.1 |
| **Machinery and transport equipment** | 2,784.1 | 2,572.2 | 2,990.3 |
| Power-generating machinery and equipment | 355.6 | 398.5 | 273.1 |
| Machinery specialized for particular industries | 241.2 | 232.9 | 239.4 |
| General industrial machinery, equipment and parts | 974.1 | 739.5 | 981.1 |
| Heating and cooling equipment | 251.4 | 158.2 | 145.1 |
| Office machines and automatic data-processing equipment | 90.1 | 102.7 | 200.3 |
| Telecommunications and sound equipment | 135.9 | 134.1 | 295.1 |
| Other electrical machinery, apparatus, etc. | 508.4 | 507.9 | 481.4 |
| Switchgear, etc., and parts | 164.0 | 217.3 | 206.3 |
| Road vehicles and parts* | 351.7 | 348.2 | 408.8 |
| **Miscellaneous manufactured articles** | 299.9 | 321.8 | 353.6 |
| **Total** (incl. others) | 8,785.3 | 9,598.7 | 9,830.6 |

* Excluding tyres, engines and electrical parts.

| Exports f.o.b. | 1993 | 1994 | 1995 |
|---|---|---|---|
| **Mineral fuels, lubricants, etc.** | 9,679.2 | 8,342.0 | 8,146.2 |
| Petroleum, petroleum products, etc. | 6,339.7 | 5,585.5 | 5,537.4 |
| Crude petroleum oils, etc. | 4,448.7 | 3,924.5 | 3,940.7 |
| Refined petroleum products | 1,828.8 | 1,617.0 | 1,540.3 |
| Motor spirit (petrol) and other light oils | 539.8 | 564.2 | 498.4 |
| Gas oils (distillate fuels) | 677.0 | 494.1 | 477.9 |
| Residual fuel oils | 587.8 | 485.2 | 504.9 |
| Gas (natural and manufactured) | 3,329.9 | 2,677.6 | 2,597.4 |
| Liquefied petroleum gases | 2,198.8 | 1,773.9 | 1,404.7 |
| Petroleum gases, etc., in the gaseous state | 1,131.0 | 903.7 | 1,192.7 |
| **Total** (incl. others) | 10,097.7 | 8,593.8 | 8,555.5 |

Source: UN, *International Trade Statistics Yearbook*.

**PRINCIPAL TRADING PARTNERS** (US $ million)*

| Imports c.i.f. | 1993 | 1994 | 1995 |
|---|---|---|---|
| Austria | 172.5 | 286.6 | 200.2 |
| Belgium-Luxembourg | 164.6 | 214.7 | 225.9 |
| Brazil | 79.4 | 126.4 | 124.0 |
| Canada | 248.0 | 383.1 | 412.7 |
| China, People's Republic | 120.0 | 156.5 | 230.5 |
| France (incl. Monaco) | 2,240.6 | 2,376.3 | 2,449.7 |
| Germany | 469.1 | 517.1 | 672.2 |
| Indonesia | 216.5 | 240.2 | 106.4 |
| Italy | 952.1 | 931.4 | 947.3 |
| Japan | 375.9 | 254.0 | 333.5 |
| Morocco | 84.8 | 120.6 | 46.9 |
| Netherlands | 159.5 | 109.6 | 131.9 |
| New Zealand | 96.7 | 76.9 | 71.1 |
| Spain | 926.2 | 901.3 | 841.9 |
| Switzerland-Liechtenstein | 69.8 | 91.8 | 79.5 |
| Tunisia | 122.5 | 138.5 | 130.2 |
| Turkey | 108.5 | 250.4 | 278.1 |
| United Kingdom | 119.1 | 132.0 | 141.9 |
| USA | 1,311.5 | 1,371.9 | 1,292.8 |
| **Total** (incl. others) | 8,785.3 | 9,598.7 | 9,830.6 |

| Exports f.o.b. | 1993 | 1994 | 1995 |
|---|---|---|---|
| Austria | 67.2 | 161.2 | 106.3 |
| Belgium-Luxembourg | 627.8 | 528.4 | 335.7 |
| Brazil | 443.8 | 195.2 | 206.0 |
| Canada | 158.2 | 174.1 | 201.6 |
| France (incl. Monaco) | 1,688.6 | 1,326.2 | 1,203.0 |
| Germany | 504.2 | 524.8 | 156.8 |
| Italy | 2,219.7 | 1,535.1 | 1,919.0 |
| Korea, Republic | 34.2 | 20.7 | 111.5 |
| Morocco | 70.7 | 101.3 | 74.2 |
| Netherlands | 784.5 | 885.0 | 889.2 |
| Portugal | 284.7 | 285.0 | 130.2 |
| Russia | 126.3 | 40.0 | 121.1 |
| Singapore | 154.2 | 59.9 | 42.1 |
| Spain | 679.2 | 650.2 | 571.5 |
| Switzerland-Liechtenstein | 3.1 | 4.3 | 100.7 |
| Tunisia | 62.2 | 113.1 | 99.0 |
| Turkey | 7.2 | 49.5 | 287.5 |
| United Kingdom | 192.4 | 140.0 | 186.5 |
| USA | 1,608.7 | 1,414.0 | 1,429.4 |
| **Total** (incl. others) | 10,097.7 | 8,593.8 | 8,555.5 |

* Imports by country of production; exports by country of last consignment.

Source: UN, *International Trade Statistics Yearbook*.

**1996** (US $ million): Imports c.i.f. 8,690; Exports f.o.b. 12,621 (Source: UN, *Monthly Bulletin of Statistics*).

# Transport

**RAILWAYS** (traffic)

| | 1992 | 1993 | 1994 |
|---|---|---|---|
| Passengers carried ('000) | 58,422 | n.a. | n.a. |
| Freight carried ('000 metric tons) | 11,112 | n.a. | n.a. |
| Passenger-km (million) | 2,904 | 3,009 | 2,077 |
| Freight ton-km (million) | 2,523 | 2,296 | 2,082 |

Source: partly UN, *Statistical Yearbook*.

**ROAD TRAFFIC** ('000 motor vehicles in use)

| | 1993 | 1994 | 1995 |
|---|---|---|---|
| Passenger cars | 1,547.8 | 1,555.8 | 1,562.1 |
| Commercial vehicles | 926.0 | 930.8 | 933.1 |

Source: UN, *Statistical Yearbook*.

**SHIPPING**

**Merchant Fleet** (registered at 31 December)

| | 1996 | 1997 | 1998 |
|---|---|---|---|
| Number of vessels | 151 | 151 | 148 |
| Total displacement ('000 grt) | 982.5 | 982.5 | 1,004.7 |

Source: Lloyd's Register of Shipping, *World Fleet Statistics*.

**International Sea-borne Freight Traffic** (estimates, '000 metric tons)

| | 1991 | 1992 | 1993 |
|---|---|---|---|
| Goods loaded | 59,430 | 61,577 | 63,110 |
| Goods unloaded | 15,100 | 15,600 | 15,700 |

Source: UN Economic Commission for Africa, *African Statistical Yearbook*.

**CIVIL AVIATION** (traffic on scheduled services)

| | 1993 | 1994 | 1995 |
|---|---|---|---|
| Kilometres flown (million) | 36 | 36 | 31 |
| Passengers carried ('000) | 3,254 | 3,241 | 3,478 |
| Passenger-km (million) | 2,901 | 2,706 | 2,855 |
| Total ton-km (million) | 296 | 268 | 278 |

Source: UN, *Statistical Yearbook*.

# Tourism

**FOREIGN TOURIST ARRIVALS BY COUNTRY OF ORIGIN**

| | 1995 | 1996 | 1997 |
|---|---|---|---|
| France | 26,349 | 35,214 | 34,690 |
| Germany | 1,398 | 1,467 | 1,554 |
| Italy | 2,791 | 2,541 | 3,664 |
| Libya | 7,698 | 6,349 | 5,611 |
| Mali | 5,874 | 6,993 | n.a. |
| Morocco | 4,797 | 2,067 | 2,470 |
| Spain | 1,621 | 1,826 | n.a. |
| Tunisia | 24,207 | 19,966 | 17,734 |
| **Total** (incl. others) | 97,650 | 93,491 | n.a. |

**1998:** Total foreign tourist arrivals 107,214 (France 38,357; Mali 7,106; Tunisia 20,056).

Source: Ministère du Tourisme et de l'Artisanat.

**Tourism receipts** (US $ million): 36 in 1994; 27 in 1995; 24 in 1996 (Source: World Tourism Organization, *Yearbook of Tourism Statistics*).

# Communications Media

| | 1994 | 1995 | 1996 |
|---|---|---|---|
| Radio receivers ('000 in use) | 6,450 | 6,700 | 6,870 |
| Television receivers ('000 in use) | 2,150 | 2,500 | 3,000 |
| Telephones ('000 main lines in use) | 1,122 | 1,176 | n.a. |
| Telefax stations (number in use)* | 4,138 | 5,200 | n.a. |
| Mobile cellular telephones (subscribers) | 1,348 | 4,691 | n.a. |
| Book production: titles† | 323 | n.a. | 670 |
| Daily newspapers | | | |
| Number | 6 | 8 | 5 |
| Average circulation ('000 copies) | 1,250 | 1,440 | 1,080 |

**1990:** Non-daily newspapers 37 (average circulation 1,409,000 copies); Other periodicals 48 (average circulation 803,00 copies).

* Estimate(s).

† Excluding pamphlets.

Sources: UNESCO, *Statistical Yearbook*, and UN, *Statistical Yearbook*.

# Education

(1996/97)

| | Institutions | Teachers | Pupils |
|---|---|---|---|
| Pre-primary | n.a. | 1,333 | 33,503 |
| Primary | 15,426 | 170,956 | 4,674,947 |
| Secondary | | | |
| General | 4,138 | 145,160 | 2,480,168 |
| Vocational | | 6,788 | 138,074 |
| Higher | | | |
| Universities, etc.* | n.a. | 14,364 | 267,142 |
| Distance-learning institutions* | n.a. | 3,213 | 60,095 |
| Other* | n.a. | 2,333 | 20,173 |

* 1995/96.

Sources: UNESCO, *Statistical Yearbook*, and Ministère de l'Education nationale.

# Directory

## The Constitution

A new Constitution for the Democratic and People's Republic of Algeria, approved by popular referendum, was promulgated on 22 November 1976. The Constitution was amended by the National People's Assembly on 30 June 1979. Further amendments were approved by referendum on 3 November 1988, on 23 February 1989, and on 28 November 1996. The main provisions of the Constitution, as amended, are summarized below:

The preamble recalls that Algeria owes its independence to a war of liberation which led to the creation of a modern sovereign state, guaranteeing social justice, equality and liberty for all. It emphasizes Algeria's Islamic, Arab and Amazigh heritage, and stresses that, as an Arab Mediterranean and African country, it forms an integral part of the Great Arab Maghreb.

### FUNDAMENTAL PRINCIPLES OF THE ORGANIZATION OF ALGERIAN SOCIETY

#### The Republic

Algeria is a popular, democratic state. Islam is the state religion and Arabic is the official national language.

#### The People

National sovereignty resides in the people and is exercised through its elected representatives. The institutions of the State consolidate national unity and protect the fundamental rights of its citizens. The exploitation of one individual by another is forbidden.

#### The State

The State is exclusively at the service of the people. Those holding positions of responsibility must live solely on their salaries and may not, directly or by the agency of others, engage in any remunerative activity.

#### Fundamental Freedoms and the Rights of Man and the Citizen

Fundamental rights and freedoms are guaranteed. All discrimination on grounds of sex, race or belief is forbidden. Law cannot operate retrospectively and a person is presumed innocent until proved guilty. Victims of judicial error shall receive compensation from the State.

The State guarantees the inviolability of the home, of private life and of the person. The State also guarantees the secrecy of correspondence, the freedom of conscience and opinion, freedom of intellectual, artistic and scientific creation, and freedom of expression and assembly.

The State guarantees the right to form political associations (on condition that they are not based on differences in religion, language, race, gender or region), to join a trade union, the right to strike, the right to work, to protection, to security, to health, to leisure, to education, etc. It also guarantees the right to leave the national territory, within the limits set by law.

#### Duties of Citizens

Every citizen must respect the Constitution, and must protect public property and safeguard national independence. The law sanctions the duty of parents to educate and protect their children, as well as the duty of children to help and support their parents. Every citizen must contribute towards public expenditure through the payment of taxes.

#### The National Popular Army

The army safeguards national independence and sovereignty.

#### Principles of Foreign Policy

Algeria subscribes to the principles and objectives of the UN. It advocates international co-operation, the development of friendly relations between states, on the basis of equality and mutual interest, and non-interference in the internal affairs of states.

### POWER AND ITS ORGANIZATION

#### The Executive

The President of the Republic is Head of State, Head of the Armed Forces and responsible for national defence. He must be of Algerian origin, a Muslim and more than 40 years old. He is elected by universal, secret, direct suffrage. His mandate is for five years, and is renewable once. The President embodies the unity of the nation. The President presides over meetings of the Council of Ministers. He decides and conducts foreign policy and appoints the Head of Government, who is responsible to the National People's Assembly. The Head of Government must appoint a Council of Ministers. He drafts, co-ordinates and implements his government's programme, which he must present to the Assembly for ratification. Should the Assembly reject the programme, the Head of Government and the Council of Ministers resign, and the President appoints a new Head of Government. Should the newly-appointed Head of Government's programme be rejected by the Assembly, the President dissolves the Assembly, and a general election is held. Should the President be unable to perform his functions, owing to a long and serious illness, the President of the Council of the Nation assumes the office for a maximum period of 45 days (subject to the approval of a two-thirds majority in the National People's Assembly and the Council of the Nation). If the President is still unable to perform his functions after 45 days, the Presidency is declared vacant by the Constitutional Council. Should the Presidency fall vacant, the President of the Council of the Nation temporarily assumes the office and organizes presidential elections within 60 days. He may not himself be a candidate in the election. The President presides over a High Security Council which advises on all matters affecting national security.

#### The Legislature

The legislature consists of the Assemblée Nationale Populaire (National People's Assembly) and the Conseil de la Nation (Council of the Nation, which was established by constitutional amendments approved by national referendum in November 1996). The members of the lower chamber, the National People's Assembly, are elected by universal, direct, secret suffrage for a five-year term. Two-thirds of the members of the upper chamber, the Council of the Nation, are elected by indirect, secret suffrage from regional and municipal authorities; the remainder are appointed by the President of the Republic. The Council's term in office is six years; one-half of its members are replaced every three years. The deputies enjoy parliamentary immunity. The legislature sits for two ordinary sessions per year, each of not less than four months' duration. The commissions of the legislature are in permanent session. The two parliamentary chambers may be summoned to meet for an extraordinary session on the request of the President of the Republic, or of the Head of Government, or of two-thirds of the members of the National People's Assembly. Both the Head of Government and the parliamentary chambers may initiate legislation. Legislation must be deliberated upon respectively by the National People's Assembly and the Council of the Nation before promulgation. Any text passed by the Assembly must be approved by three-quarters of the members of the Council in order to become legislation.

#### The Judiciary

Judges obey only the law. They defend society and fundamental freedoms. The right of the accused to a defence is guaranteed. The Supreme Court regulates the activities of courts and tribunals, and the State Council regulates the administrative judiciary. The Higher Court of the Magistrature is presided over by the President of the Republic; the Minister of Justice is Vice-President of the Court. All magistrates are answerable to the Higher Court for the manner in which they fulfil their functions. The High State Court is empowered to judge the President of the Republic in cases of high treason, and the Head of Government for crimes and offences.

#### The Constitutional Council

The Constitutional Council is responsible for ensuring that the Constitution is respected, and that referendums, the election of the President of the Republic and legislative elections are conducted in accordance with the law. The Constitutional Council comprises nine members, of whom three are appointed by the President of the Republic, two elected by the National People's Assembly, two elected by the Council of the Nation, one elected by the Supreme Court and one elected by the State Council. The Council's term in office is six years; the President of the Council is appointed for a six-year term and one-half of the remaining members are replaced every three years.

#### The High Islamic Council

The High Islamic Council is an advisory body on matters relating to Islam. The Council comprises 15 members and its President is appointed by the President of the Republic.

#### Constitutional Revision

The Constitution can be revised on the initiative of the President of the Republic (subject to approval by the National People's Assembly and by three-quarters of the members of the Council of the Nation), and must be approved by national referendum. Should the Constitutional Council decide that a draft constitutional amendment does not in any way affect the general principles governing Algerian society, it may permit the President of the Republic to promulgate the amendment directly (without submitting it to referendum) if it has been approved by three-quarters of the members of both parliamentary chambers. Three-quarters of the members of both parliamentary chambers, in a joint sitting, may propose a constitutional amendment to the President of the Republic who may submit it to referendum. The basic principles of the Constitution may not be revised.

# The Government

### HEAD OF STATE

**President and Minister of Defence:** ABDELAZIZ BOUTEFLIKA (inaugurated 27 April 1999).

### COUNCIL OF MINISTERS
(January 2000)

A coalition of the Front de libération nationale (FLN), the Mouvement de la société pour la paix (MSP), Nahdah, the Rassemblement pour la culture et la démocratie (RCD), the Alliance nationale républicaine (ANR) and the Parti du renouveau algérien (PRA).

**Prime Minister:** AHMED BENBITOUR.

**Minister of State for Justice:** AHMED OUYAHIA.

**Minister of Interior and Local Authorities:** YAZID ZERHOUNI.

**Minister of Foreign Affairs:** YOUCEF YOUSFI.

**Minister of Finance:** ABDELLATIF BENACHENHOU.

**Minister of Participation and Co-ordination of Reforms:** HAMID TEMMAR.

**Minister of Water Resources:** SALIM SAADI.

**Minister of Small and Medium-sized Enterprises:** NOUREDDINE BOUKROUH.

**Minister of Energy and Mines:** CHAKIB KEHLIL.

**Minister of National Education:** BOUBEKEUR BENBOUZID.

**Minister of Culture and Communications:** ABEDLMADJID TEBBOUNE.

**Minister of Higher Education and Scientific Research:** AMMAR SAKHRI.

**Minister of Youth and Sports:** ABDELMALEK SELLAL.

**Minister of Commerce:** MOURAD MEDELCI.

**Minister of Posts and Telecommunications:** MUHAMMAD MAGHLAOUI.

**Minister of Vocational Training:** KARIM YOUNES.

**Minister of Religious Affairs and Endowments:** BOUABDELLAH GHLAMALLAH.

**Minister of Housing:** ABDELKADER BOUNEKRAF.

**Minister of Industry and Restructuring:** ABDELMADJID MENASRA.

**Minister of Labour and Social Protection:** BOUGUERRA SOLTANI.

**Minister in charge of National Solidarity:** DJAMEL OULD ABBES.

**Minister of War Veterans:** MUHAMMAD CHERIF ABBES.

**Minister of Agriculture:** SAÏD BERKAT.

**Minister in charge of Relations with Parliament:** ABDELWAHAB DERBAL.

**Minister of Health and Population:** AMARA BENYOUNES.

**Minister of Public Works, Territorial Management, Environment and Urban Planning:** MUHAMMAD ALI BOUGHAZI.

**Minister of Tourism and Handicrafts:** LAKHDAR DORBANI.

**Minister of Transport:** HAMID LOUNAOUCI.

**Minister of Fisheries and Marine Resources:** OMAR GHOUL.

**Minister at the Office of the Prime Minister in charge of Greater Algiers Governorate:** CHERIF RAHMANI.

**Minister-delegate to the Minister of Finance in charge of the Budget:** ALI BRAHITI.

**Minister-delegate to the Minister of Foreign Affairs in charge of the National Community Abroad and Regional Co-operation:** ABDELAZIZ ZIARI.

**Secretary-General of the Government:** AHMED NOUI.

### MINISTRIES

**Office of the President:** Présidence de la République, el-Mouradia, Algiers; tel. (2) 69-15-15; fax (2) 69-15-95.

**Office of the Prime Minister:** rue Docteur Saâdane, Algiers; tel. (2) 73-23-40; fax (2) 71-79-27.

**Ministry of Agriculture:** 4 route des Quatre Canons, Algiers; tel. (2) 71-17-12; fax (2) 61-57-39.

**Ministry of Commerce:** rue Docteur Saâdane, Algiers; tel. (2) 73-23-40; fax (2) 73-54-18.

**Ministry of Communications and Culture:** Palais de la Culture, Les Annassers, Kouba, Algiers; tel. (2) 69-22-01; fax (2) 68-40-41.

**Ministry of Defence:** Les Tagarins, el-Biar, Algiers; tel. (2) 71-15-15; fax (2) 64-67-26.

**Ministry of Energy and Mines:** 80 ave Ahmed Ghermoul, Algiers; tel. (2) 67-33-00; fax (2) 65-27-83.

**Ministry of Finance:** Immeuble Maurétania, place du Pérou, Algiers; tel. (2) 71-13-66; fax (2) 73-42-76.

**Ministry of Fisheries and Marine Resources:** Algiers.

**Ministry of Foreign Affairs:** place Mohamed Seddik Benyahia, el-Mouradia, Algiers; tel. (2) 69-23-33; fax (2) 69-21-61.

**Ministry of Health and Population:** 125 rue Abd ar-Rahmane Laâla, el-Madania, Algiers; tel. (2) 68-29-00; fax (2) 66-24-13.

**Ministry of Higher Education and Scientific Research:** 11 rue Doudou Mokhtar, Algiers; tel. (2) 91-12-56; fax (2) 91-11-97.

**Ministry of Housing:** 137 rue Didouche Mourad, Algiers; tel. (2) 74-07-22; fax (2) 74-53-83.

**Ministry of Industry and Restructuring:** Immeuble le Colisée, 4 rue Ahmed Bey, Algiers; tel. (2) 60-11-44; fax (2) 69-32-35.

**Ministry of the Interior and Local Authorities:** 18 rue Docteur Saâdane, Algiers; tel. (2) 73-23-40; fax (2) 73-43-67.

**Ministry of Justice:** 8 place Bir Hakem, el-Biar, Algiers; tel. (2) 92-41-83; fax (2) 92-25-60.

**Ministry of Labour and Social Protection:** 14 blvd Mohamed Belouizdad, Algiers; tel. (2) 68-33-66; fax (2) 66-28-11.

**Ministry of National Education:** 8 ave de Pékin, Algiers; tel. (2) 69-20-98; fax (2) 60-67-57.

**Ministry of National Solidarity:** Algiers.

**Ministry of Posts and Telecommunications:** 4 blvd Krim Belkacem, Algiers; tel. (2) 71-12-20; fax (2) 71-92-71.

**Ministry of Public Works, Territorial Management, Environment and Urban Planning:** Algiers.

**Ministry of Religious Affairs and Endowments:** 4 rue de Timgad, Hydra, Algiers; tel. (2) 60-85-55; fax (2) 60-09-36.

**Ministry of Small and Medium-sized Enterprises:** Immeuble le Colisée, 4 rue Ahmed Bey, Algiers; tel. (2) 60-11-44; fax (2) 59-40-50.

**Ministry of Tourism and Handicrafts:** 7 rue des Frères Ziata, el-Mouradia, 16000 Algiers; tel. (2) 60-33-55; fax (2) 59-13-15.

**Ministry of Transport:** 119 rue Didouche Mourad, Algiers; tel. (2) 74-06-99; fax (2) 74-33-95.

**Ministry of Vocational Training:** Algiers.

**Ministry of Water Resources:** BP 86, rue du Caire, Algiers; tel. (2) 68-95-00; fax (2) 58-63-64.

**Ministry of War Veterans:** 2 ave du Lt. Med Benarfa, el-Biar, Algiers; tel. (2) 92-23-55; fax (2) 92-35-16.

**Ministry of Youth and Sports:** 3 rue Mohamed Belouizdad, Algiers; tel. (2) 66-33-50; fax (2) 68-41-71.

# President and Legislature

### PRESIDENT

**Presidential Election, 15 April 1999**

| Candidate* | Votes | % of votes |
|---|---|---|
| ABDELAZIZ BOUTEFLIKA | 7,445,045 | 73.76 |
| AHMAD TALEB IBRAHIMI | 1,265,594 | 12.54 |
| Sheikh ABDALLAH DJABALLAH | 400,080 | 3.96 |
| HOCINE AÏT AHMED | 321,179 | 3.18 |
| MOULOUD HAMROUCHE | 314,160 | 3.11 |
| MOKDAD SIFI | 226,139 | 2.24 |
| YOUCEF KHATEB | 121,414 | 1.20 |
| **Total†** | 10,093,611 | 100.00 |

* Six of the seven presidential candidates withdrew prior to the election, leaving Abdelaziz Bouteflika as the only remaining official contestant.

† Excluding 559,012 invalid votes.

### LEGISLATURE

#### Assemblée Nationale Populaire

**President:** ABDELKADER BENSALAH.

**General Election, 5 June 1997**

| | Seats |
|---|---|
| Rassemblement national démocratique (RND) | 156 |
| Mouvement de la société pour la paix (MSP) | 69 |
| Front de libération nationale (FLN) | 62 |
| Nahdah | 34 |
| Front des forces socialistes (FFS) | 20 |
| Rassemblement pour la culture et la démocratie (RCD) | 19 |
| Independent | 11 |
| Parti des travailleurs (PT) | 4 |
| Parti républicain progressif (PRP) | 3 |
| Union pour la démocratie et les libertés (UDL) | 1 |
| Parti social-libéral (PSL) | 1 |
| **Total** | 380 |

#### Conseil de la Nation

**President:** BACHIR BOUMAAZA.

**Elections, 25 December 1997**

| | Seats* |
|---|---|
| Rassemblement national démocratique (RND) | 80 |
| Front de libération nationale (FLN) | 10 |
| Front des forces socialistes (FFS) | 4 |
| Mouvement de la société pour la paix (MSP) | 2 |
| Appointed by the President† | 48 |
| **Total** | 144 |

* Deputies of the Conseil de la Nation serve a six-year term; one-half of its members are replaced every three years. Elected representatives are selected by indirect, secret suffrage from regional and municipal authorities.

† Appointed on 27 December 1997.

# Political Organizations

Until 1989 the FLN was the only legal party in Algeria. The February 1989 amendments to the Constitution permitted the formation of other political associations, with some restrictions. The right to establish political parties was guaranteed by constitutional amendments in November 1996; however, political associations based on differences in religion, language, race, gender or region were proscribed. Some 39 political parties contested the legislative elections which took place in June 1997. The most important political organizations are listed below.

**Alliance nationale républicaine (ANR):** Algiers; f. 1995; anti-Islamist; Leader REDHA MALEK.

**Congrès national algérien:** Algiers; f. 1999; Leader ABDELKADER BELHAYE.

**Fidélité:** Algiers; f. 1999 by AHMAD TALEB IBRAHIMI.

**Front démocratique:** Algiers; f. 1999; Leader SID-AHMAD GHOZALI.

**Front des forces socialistes (FFS):** 56 ave Souidani Boudjemaâ, 16000 Algiers; tel. (2) 59-33-13; fax (2) 59-11-45; f. 1963; revived 1990; Leader HOCINE AÏT AHMED.

**Front islamique du salut (FIS):** Algiers; f. 1989; aims to emphasize the importance of Islam in political and social life; formally dissolved by the Algiers Court of Appeal in March 1992; Leader ABBASI MADANI.

**Armée islamique du salut (AIS):** Algiers; military wing of the FIS; agreed a cease-fire with the Govt in Sept. 1997, which was made permanent in June 1999 in order to promote a negotiated solution to the civil conflict; voluntarily dissolved in Jan. 2000; Cmmdr MADANI MEZRAG.

**Front de libération nationale (FLN):** 7 rue du Stade, Hydra, Algiers; tel. (2) 59-21-49. 1954; sole legal party until 1989; socialist in outlook, the party is organized into a Secretariat, a Political Bureau, a Central Committee, Federations, Kasmas and cells; under the aegis of the FLN are various mass political organizations, including the Union Nationale de la Jeunesse Algérienne (UNJA) and the Union Nationale des Femmes Algériennes (UNFA); Sec.-Gen. BOUALEM BENHAMOUDA.

**Front national algérien:** Algiers; f. 1999; advocates eradication of poverty and supports the Govt's peace initiative; Pres. MOUSSA TOUATI.

**Front national de renouvellement (FNR):** Algiers; Leader ZINEDDINE CHERIFI.

**Mouvement algérien pour la justice et le développement (MAJD):** Villa Laibi, Lot. Kapiot No. 5, Bouzaréah, Algiers; tel. (2) 60-58-00; fax (2) 78-78-72; f. 1990; reformist party supporting policies of fmr Pres. Boumedienne; Leader MOULAY HABIB.

**Mouvement pour la démocratie et la citoyenneté (MDC):** Tizi-Ouzou; f. 1997 by dissident members of the FFS; Leader SAÏD KHELIL.

**Mouvement démocratique et social (MDS):** Algiers; f. 1998 by fmr mems of Ettahadi; left-wing party; 4,000 mems; Sec.-Gen. HACHEMI CHERIF.

**Mouvement pour la liberté:** Algiers; f. 1999; in opposition to Pres. Bouteflika; Leader MOULOUD HAMROUCHE.

**Mouvement de la réforme nationale (MRN):** Algiers; f. 1998; Leader Sheikh ABDALLAH DJABALLAH.

**Mouvement de la société pour la paix (MSP):** 163 Hassiba Ben Bouali, Algiers; f. as Hamas; adopted current name in 1997; moderate Islamic party, favouring the gradual introduction of an Islamic state; Leader Sheikh MAHFOUD NAHNAH.

**Nahdah:** Algiers; fundamentalist Islamist group; Sec.-Gen. HABIB ADAMI.

**Parti démocratique progressif (PDR):** Algiers; f. 1990 as a legal party; Leader SACI MABROUK.

**Parti national pour la solidarité et le développement (PNSD):** Cité du 5 juillet 11, No. 22, Constantine; Leader MOHAMED CHERIF TALEB.

**Parti du renouveau algérien (PRA):** 29 rue des Frères Bouatik, el-Biar, Algiers; tel. (2) 56-62-78; Sec.-Gen. MUHAMMAD MENAI; Leader NOUREDDINE BOUKROUH.

**Parti républicain progressif (PRP):** 10 rue Ouahrani Abou-Mediêne, Cité Seddikia, Oran; tel. (5) 35-79-36; f. 1990 as a legal party; Sec.-Gen. SLIMANE CHERIF.

**Parti des travailleurs (PT):** Algiers; workers' party; Leader LOUISA HANOUNE.

**Rassemblement pour la culture et la démocratie (RCD):** 87A rue Didouche Mourad, Algiers; tel. (2) 73-62-01; fax (2) 73-62-20; f. 1989; secular party; advocates recognition of the Berber language, Tamazight, as a national language; Pres. SAÏD SAADI.

**Rassemblement national démocratique (RND):** Algiers; f. 1997; centrist party; Sec.-Gen. AHMED OUYAHIA.

**Union pour la démocratie et les libertés (UDL):** Algiers; f. 1997; Leader ABDELKRIM SEDDIKI.

The following groups are in armed conflict with the Government:

**Groupe islamique armé (GIA):** the most prominent and radical Islamist militant group; Leader ANTAR ZOUABRI.

**Groupe salafiste pour la prédication et combat (GSPC):** f. 1998; breakaway group from the GIA; particularly active in the east of Algiers and in the Kabyle; responds to preaching by Ali Belhadj, the second most prominent member of the proscribed FIS; Leader HASSAN HATTAB.

# Diplomatic Representation

### EMBASSIES IN ALGERIA

**Angola:** 14 rue Marie Curie, el-Biar, Algiers; tel. (2) 92-54-41; fax (2) 79-74-41; Ambassador: JOSÉ CÉSAR AUGUSTO.

**Argentina:** 26 rue Finaltieri, el-Biar, Algiers; tel. (2) 92-34-23; fax (2) 92-34-43; Ambassador: GERÓNIMO CORTES FUNES.

**Austria:** 17 chemin Abd al-Kader Gadouche, Hydra, Algiers; tel. (2) 69-10-86; fax (2) 56-73-52; Ambassador: BERNHARD ZIMBURG.

**Belgium:** 22 chemin Youcef Tayebi, el-Biar, Algiers; tel. (2) 92-24-46; fax (2) 92-50-36; Ambassador: DIRK LETTENS.

**Benin:** 36 Lot. du Stade, Birkhadem, Algiers; tel. (2) 56-52-71; Ambassador: LEONARD ADJIN.

**Brazil:** 10 chemin Laroussi Messaoud Les Glycines, BP 186, Algiers; tel. (2) 74-95-75; fax (2) 74-96-87; Ambassador: SÉRGIO THOMPSON-FLORES.

**Bulgaria:** 13 blvd Col Bougara, Algiers; tel. (2) 23-00-14; fax (2) 23-05-33; Ambassador: MARIN DIMITROV TODOROV.

**Burkina Faso:** 23 Lot. el Feth, Poirson el-Biar, BP 212 Didouche Mourade, Algiers; tel. (2) 92-33-39; fax (2) 79-38-53.

**Cameroon:** 26 chemin Cheick Bachir Ibrahimi, 16011 el-Biar, Algiers; tel. (2) 92-11-24; fax (2) 92-11-25; Chargé d'affaires: JEAN MISSOUP.

**Canada:** BP 225, 16000 Alger-Gare, 27 bis rue des Frères Benhafid, Algiers; tel. (2) 69-16-11; fax (2) 69-39-20; Ambassador: JACQUES NOISEUX.

**Chad:** Villa No. 18, Cité DNC, chemin Ahmed Kara, Hydra, Algiers; tel. (2) 69-26-62; fax (2) 69-26-63; Ambassador: El-Hadj MAHAMOUD ADJI.

**China, People's Republic:** 34 blvd des Martyrs, Algiers; tel. (2) 69-27-24; fax (2) 69-29-62; Ambassador: ZHENG AQUAN.

**Congo, Democratic Republic:** 5 rue Saint Georges, Kouba, Algiers; tel. (2) 59-12-27; Ambassador: IKAKI BOMELE MOLINGO.

**Congo, Republic:** 111 Parc Ben Omar, Kouba, Algiers; tel. (2) 58-68-00; Ambassador: PIERRE N'GAKA.

**Côte d'Ivoire:** Immeuble 'Le Bosquet', Le Paradou, BP 710 Hydra, Algiers; tel. (2) 69-23-78; fax (2) 69-36-83; Ambassador: GUSTAVE OUFFOUE-KOUASSI.

**Cuba:** 22 rue Larbi Alik, Hydra, Algiers; tel. (2) 69-21-48; fax (2) 69-32-81; Ambassador: RAFAEL POLANCO BRAHOJOS.

**Czech Republic:** BP 358, Villa Koudia, 3 chemin Ziryab, Algiers; tel. (2) 23-00-56; fax (2) 23-01-03; Chargé d'affaires a.i.: JOSEF BUZALKA.

**Denmark:** 12 ave Emile Marquis, Lot. Djenane el-Malik, 16035 Hydra, BP 384, 16000 Alger-Gare, Algiers; tel. (2) 69-27-55; fax (2) 69-28-46; Ambassador: HERLUF HANSEN.

**Egypt:** BP 297, 8 chemin Abdel-Kader Gadouche, 16300 Hydra, Algiers; tel. (2) 60-16-73; fax (2) 60-29-52; Ambassador: IBRAHIM YOUSSRI.

**Finland:** BP 256, 16035 Hydra, Algiers; tel. (2) 69-29-25; fax (2) 69-16-37; e-mail finamb@wissal.dz.

**France:** chemin Abd al-Kader Gadouche, Hydra, Algiers; tel. (2) 69-24-88; fax (2) 69-13-69; Ambassador: ALFRED SIEFER-GAILLARDIN.

**Gabon:** BP 125, Rostomia, 21 rue Hadj Ahmed Mohamed, Hydra, Algiers; tel. (2) 69-24-00; fax (2) 60-25-46; Ambassador: YVES ONGOLLO.

**Germany:** BP 664, Alger-Gare, 165 chemin Sfindja, Algiers; tel. (2) 74-19-56; fax (2) 74-05-21; Ambassador: STEFFEN RUDOLPH.

**Ghana:** 62 rue des Frères Benali Abdellah, Hydra, Algiers; tel. (2) 60-64-44; fax (2) 69-28-56; Ambassador: GEORGE A. O. KUGBLENU.

**Greece:** 60 blvd Col Bougara, Algiers; tel. (2) 92-34-91; fax (2) 69-16-55; Ambassador: IOANNIS DRAKOULARAKOS.

**Guinea:** 43 blvd Central Saïd Hamdine, Hydra, Algiers; tel. (2) 69-20-66; fax (2) 69-34-68; Ambassador: MAMADY CONDÉ.

**Guinea-Bissau:** 17 rue Ahmad Kara, BP 32, Colonne Volrol, Hydra, Algiers; tel. (2) 60-01-51; fax (2) 60-97-25; Ambassador: JOSÉ PEREIRA BATISTA.

**Holy See:** 1 rue Noureddine Mekiri, 16090 Bologhine, Algiers (Apostolic Nunciature); tel. (2) 95-45-20; fax (2) 95-40-95; Apostolic Nuncio: Most Rev. AUGUSTINE KASUJJA, Titular Archbishop of Caesarea in Numidia.

**Hungary:** BP 68, 18 ave des Frères Oughlis, el-Mouradia, Algiers; tel. (2) 69-79-75; fax (2) 69-81-86; Chargé d'affaires: Dr LÁSZLÓ MÁRTON.

**India:** BP 121, 119 rue Didouche Mourad, Algiers; tel. (2) 74-71-35; fax (2) 74-85-13; e-mail eoialg.ist.cerist.dz; Ambassador: JAYANT PRASAD.

**Indonesia:** BP 62, 16 chemin Abd al-Kader Gadouche, 16070 el-Mouradia, Algiers; tel. (2) 69-20-11; fax (2) 69-39-31; Ambassador: LILLAHI GRAHANA SIDHARTA.

**Iraq:** 4 rue Abri Arezki, Hydra, Algiers; tel. (2) 69-31-25; fax (2) 69-10-97; Ambassador: ABD AL-KARIM AL-MULLA.

**Italy:** 18 rue Muhammad Ouidir Amellal, el-Biar, Algiers; tel. (2) 92-23-30; fax (2) 92-59-86; e-mail ambitalgeri@ist.cerist.dz; Ambassador: ARMELLINI ANTONIO.

**Japan:** 1 chemin el-Bakri, el-Biar, Algiers; tel. (2) 91-20-04; fax (2) 91-20-46; Ambassador: YOSHIHISA ARA.

**Jordan:** 6 rue du Chenoua, Algiers; tel. (2) 60-20-31; Ambassador: KHALED ABIDAT.

**Korea, Democratic People's Republic:** 49 rue Hamlia, Bologhine, Algiers; tel. (2) 62-39-27; Ambassador: PAK HO IL.

**Korea, Republic:** BP 92, 17 chemin Abdelkader Gadouche, Hydra, Algiers; tel. (2) 69-36-20; fax (2) 69-16-03; Ambassador: JOON-KIL CHA.

**Kuwait:** chemin Abd al-Kader Gadouche, Hydra, Algiers; tel. (2) 59-31-57; Ambassador: YOUSSEFF ABDULLAH AL-AMIZI.

**Lebanon:** 9 rue Kaïd Ahmad, el-Biar, Algiers; tel. (2) 78-20-94; Ambassador: SALHAD NASRI.

**Libya:** 15 chemin Cheikh Bachir Ibrahimi, Algiers; tel. (2) 92-15-02; fax (2) 92-46-87; Ambassador: ABDEL-MOULA EL-GHADHBANE.

**Madagascar:** 22 rue Abd al-Kader Aouis, 16090 Bologhine, BP 65, Algiers; tel. (2) 95-03-74; fax (2) 95-17-76; Ambassador: LAURENT RADAODY-RAKOTONDRAVAO.

**Mali:** Villa 15, Cité DNC/ANP, chemin Ahmed Kara, Hydra, Algiers; tel. (2) 69-13-51; fax (2) 69-20-82; Ambassador: CHEICK S. DIARRA.

**Mauritania:** 107 Lot. Baranès, Air de France, Bouzaréah, Algiers; tel. (2) 79-21-39; fax (2) 78-42-74; Ambassador: SID AHMED OULD BABAMINE.

**Mexico:** BP 329, 21 rue du Commandant Amar Azzouz (ex rue Général Lapperine), el-Biar, Algiers; tel. (2) 92-40-23; fax (2) 92-34-51; e-mail mexiarl@ist.wissal.dz; Ambassador: FRANCISO CORREA VILLALOBOS.

**Morocco:** 8 rue des Cèdres, el-Mouradia, Algiers; tel. (2) 69-14-08; fax (2) 69-29-00; Ambassador: ABDERRAZAK DOGHMI.

**Netherlands:** BP 72, 23/27 chemin Cheikh Bachir Ibrahimi, el-Biar, Algiers; tel. (2) 92-28-28; fax (2) 92-37-70; e-mail nldalg@ist.cerist.dz; Ambassador: GERBEN MEIHUIZEN.

**Niger:** 54 rue Vercors Rostamia Bouzaréah, Algiers; tel. (2) 78-89-21; fax (2) 78-97-13; Ambassador: GOUROUZA OUMAROU.

**Nigeria:** BP 629, 27 bis rue Blaise Pascal, Algiers; tel. (2) 69-18-49; fax (2) 69-11-75; Ambassador: ALIYU MOHAMMED.

**Oman:** 53 rue Djamel Eddine, El Afghani, Bouzaréah, Algiers; tel. (2) 94-13-10; fax (2) 94-13-75; Ambassador: HELLAL AS-SIYABI.

**Pakistan:** BP 404, 62A Djenane el-Malik, Parc le Pardou, Hydra, Algiers; tel. (2) 69-37-81; fax (2) 69-22-12; e-mail parapalgiers@mail.wissal.dz; Ambassador: M. ASLAM RIZVI.

**Poland:** 37 ave Mustafa Ali Khodja, el-Biar, Algiers; tel. (2) 92-25-53; fax (2) 92-14-35; e-mail lupina@wissal.dz; Ambassador: ANDRZEJ MICHAL LUPINA.

**Portugal:** 7 rue Mohamed Khoudi, el-Biar, Algiers; tel. (2) 78-48-20; fax (2) 92-54-14; Ambassador: EDUARDO MANUEL FERNANDES.

**Qatar:** BP 118, 7 chemin Doudou Mokhtar, Algiers; tel. (2) 92-28-56; fax (2) 92-24-15; Ambassador: HOCINE ALI EDDOUSRI.

**Romania:** 24 rue Abri Arezki, Hydra, Algiers; tel. (2) 60-08-71; fax (2) 69-36-42; Ambassador: DUMITRU OLARU.

**Russia:** 7 chemin du Prince d'Annam, el-Biar, Algiers; tel. (2) 92-31-39; fax (2) 92-28-82; Ambassador: ALEKSANDR ADSENYONOK.

**Saudi Arabia:** 62 rue Med. Drafini, chemin de la Madeleine, Hydra, Algiers; tel. (2) 60-35-18; Ambassador: HASAN FAQQI.

**Senegal:** BP 379, Alger-Gare, 1 chemin Mahmoud Drarnine, Hydra, Algiers; tel. (2) 69-16-27; fax (2) 69-26-84; Ambassador: SAÏDOU NOUROU.

**Slovakia:** BP 84, 7 chemin du Ziryab, Didouche Mourad, 16006 Algiers; tel. (2) 22-01-31; fax (2) 23-00-51; Chargé d'affaires a.i.: TOMÁŠ FELIX.

**South Africa:** Sofitel Hotel, 172 rue Hassuba Ben Bouali, Algiers; tel. (2) 68-52-10; fax (2) 66-21-04.

**Spain:** 46 bis rue Mohamed Chabane, el-Biar, Algiers; tel. (2) 92-27-13; fax (2) 92-27-19; Ambassador: RICARDO ZALACAIN.

**Sudan:** 8 Shara Baski Brond, el-Yanabia, Bir Mourad Rais, Algiers; tel. (2) 60-95-35; fax (2) 69-30-19.

**Sweden:** rue Olof Palme, Nouveau Paradou, Hydra, Algiers; tel. (2) 69-23-00; fax (2) 69-19-17; Ambassador: KRISTEL GORANSSON.

**Switzerland:** BP 443, 2 rue Numéro 3, 16035 Hydra, Algiers; tel. (2) 60-04-22; fax (2) 60-98-54; Ambassador: ANDRÉ VON GRAFFENINED.

**Syria:** Domaine Tamzali, 11 chemin Abd al-Kader Gadouche, Hydra, Algiers; tel. (2) 91-20-26; fax (2) 91-20-30; Ambassador: ABELJABER ALDAHAK.

**Tunisia:** 11 rue du Bois de Boulogne, el-Mouradia, Algiers; tel. (2) 60-13-88; fax (2) 69-23-16; Ambassador: MOHAMED EL FADHAL KHALIL.

**Turkey:** Villa dar el Ouard, chemin de la Rochelle, blvd Col Bougara, Algiers; tel. (2) 69-12-57; fax (2) 69-31-61; Ambassador: UMIT PAMIR.

**United Arab Emirates:** BP 165, Alger-Gare, 14 rue Muhammad Drarini, Hydra, Algiers; tel. (2) 69-25-74; fax (2) 69-37-70; Ambassador: HAMAD SAÏD AZ-ZAABI.

**United Kingdom:** BP 08, Alger-Gare, 16000 Algiers, Résidence Cassiopée, Bâtiment B, 7 chemin des Glycines, Algiers; tel. (2) 23-00-92; fax (2) 23-00-69; Ambassador: WILLIAM B. SINTON.

**USA:** BP 549, 4 chemin Cheikh Bachir Ibrahimi, 16000 Alger-Gare, Algiers; tel. (2) 60-11-86; fax (2) 60-39-79; e-mail amembalg@ist.cerist.dz; Ambassador: CAMERON HUME.

**Venezuela:** BP 297, 3 impasse Ahmed Kara, Algiers; tel. (2) 69-38-46; fax (2) 69-35-55; Ambassador: EDUARDO SOTO ALVAREZ.

**Viet Nam:** 30 rue de Chenoua, Hydra, Algiers; tel. (2) 69-27-52; fax 69-37-78; Ambassador: TRAN XUAN MAN.

**Yemen:** Villa 19, Cité DNC, rue Ahmed Kara, Hydra, Algiers; tel. (2) 69-30-85; fax (2) 69-17-58; Ambassador: GASSEM ASKAR DJEBRANE.

**Yugoslavia:** BP 366, 7 rue des Frères Benhafid, Hydra, Algiers; tel. (2) 69-12-18; fax (2) 69-34-72; Chargé d'affaires a.i.: DIMITRIJE BABIĆ.

# Judicial System

The highest court of justice is the Supreme Court (Cour suprême) in Algiers. Justice is exercised through 183 courts (tribunaux) and 31 appeal courts (cours d'appel), grouped on a regional basis. New legislation, promulgated in March 1997, provided for the eventual establishment of 214 courts and 48 appeal courts. The Cour des comptes was established in 1979. Algeria adopted a penal code in 1966, retaining the death penalty. In February 1993 three special courts were established to try suspects accused of terrorist offences; however, the courts were abolished in February 1995. Constitutional amendments, introduced in November 1996, provided for the establishment of a High State Court (empowered to judge the President of the Republic in cases of high treason, and the Head of Government for crimes and offences), and a State Council to regulate the administrative judiciary. In addition, a Conflicts Tribunal is to be established to adjudicate in disputes between the Supreme Court and the State Council.

**Supreme Court:** ave du 11 décembre 1960, Ben Aknoun, Algiers; tel. and fax (2) 92-44-89.

**President of Supreme Court:** A. NASRI.

**Procurator-General:** M. DAHMANI.

# Religion

### ISLAM

Islam is the official religion, and the whole Algerian population, with a few rare exceptions, is Muslim.

**High Islamic Council:** place Cheikh Abd al-Hamid ibn Badis, Algiers.

**President of the High Islamic Council:** ABDELMAJID MEZIANE.

### CHRISTIANITY

The European inhabitants, and a few Arabs, are generally Christians, mostly Roman Catholics.

#### The Roman Catholic Church

Algeria comprises one archdiocese and three dioceses (including one directly responsible to the Holy See). In December 1997 there were an estimated 2,730 adherents in the country.

**Bishops' Conference:** Conférence des Evêques de la Région, Nord de l'Afrique (CERNA), 13 rue Khélifa-Boukhalfa, 16000 Alger-Gare, Algiers; tel. (2) 74-41-22; fax (2) 72-86-09; f. 1985; Pres. Most Rev. HENRI TEISSIER, Archbishop of Algiers; Sec.-Gen. Fr ROMAN STÄGER.

**Archbishop of Algiers:** Most Rev. HENRI TEISSIER, Archevêché, 13 rue Khélifa-Boukhalfa, 16000 Alger-Gare, Algiers; tel. (2) 72-87-29; fax (2) 72-86-09.

#### Protestant Church

**Protestant Church of Algeria:** 31 rue Reda Houhou, 16000 Alger-Gare, Algiers; tel. and fax (2) 71-62-38; three parishes; 1,500 mems; Pastor Dr HUGH G. JOHNSON.

# The Press

### DAILIES

**L'Authentique:** Algiers; French.

**Al-Badil:** Algiers; relaunched 1990; MDA journal in French and Arabic; circ. 130,000.

**Ach-Cha'ab** (The People): 1 place Maurice Audin, Algiers; f. 1962; FLN journal in Arabic; Dir KAMEL AVACHE; circ. 24,000.

**Al-Djeza'ir El-Ghad** (Algeria of Tomorrow): Algiers; f. 1999; Arabic; Editor MUSTAPHA HACINI.

**Al-Djeza'ir El-Youm:** Algiers; Arabic; circ. 54,000.

**Horizons:** 20 rue de la Liberté, Algiers; tel. (2) 73-47-25; fax (2) 73-61-34; f. 1985; evening; French; circ. 35,000.

**Le Jeune Indépendant:** Algiers; f. 1997; French; circ. 60,000.

**Al-Joumhouria** (The Republic): 6 rue Bensenouci Hamida, Oran; f. 1963; Arabic; Editor BOUKHALFA BENAMEUR; circ. 20,000.

**Le Journal:** Algiers; f. 1992; French.

**El Khabar:** Maison de la Presse 'Tahar Djaout', 1 rue Bachir Attar, place du 1er mai, Algiers; tel. (2) 67-07-05; fax (2) 67-07-10; e-mail admin@elkhabar.com; f. 1990; Arabic; Gen. Man. CHERIF REZKI; circ. 200,000.

**Liberté:** 37 rue Larbi Ben M'Hidi, BP 178, Alger-Gare, Algiers; tel. (2) 69-25-88; fax (2) 69-35-46; internet www.liberte-algerie.com; French; independent; Dir-Gen. ABROUS OUTOUDERT; circ. 20,000.

**Al-Massa:** Maison de la Presse, Abd al-Kader Safir, Kouba, Algiers; tel. (2) 59-54-19; fax (2) 59-64-57; f. 1977; evening; Arabic; circ. 45,000.

**Le Matin:** Maison de la Presse, 1 rue Bachir Attar, 16016 Algiers; tel. (2) 66-07-08; fax (2) 66-20-97; French; Dir MUHAMMAD BENCHICOU.

**Al-Moudjahid** (The Fighter): 20 rue de la Liberté, Algiers; tel. (2) 637030; f. 1965; govt journal in French and Arabic; Dir ZOUBIR ZEMZOUM; circ. 392,000.

**An-Nasr** (The Victory): BP 388, Zone Industrielle, La Palma, Constantine; tel. (4) 93-92-16; f. 1963; Arabic; Editor ABDALLAH GUETTAT; circ. 340,000.

**La Nouvelle République:** Algiers; French.

**Le Quotidien d'Oran:** Oran; French.

**Le Soir d'Algérie:** Algiers; f. 1990; evening; independent information journal in French; Editors ZOUBIR SOUISSI, MAAMAR FARRAH; circ. 80,000.

**La Tribune:** Algiers; internet www.latribune-online.com; f. 1994; current affairs journal in French; Editor BAYA GACEMI.

**El Watan:** Maison de la Presse, 1 rue Bachir Attar, 16016 Algiers; tel. (2) 68-21-83; fax (2) 68-21-87; internet www.elwatan.com; French; Dir OMAR BELHOUCHET.

### WEEKLIES

**Algérie Actualité:** 2 rue Jacques Cartier, 16000 Algiers; tel. (2) 63-54-20. 1965; French; Dir KAMEL BELKACEM; circ. 250,000.

**Al-Hadef** (The Goal): Algiers; tel. (4) 93-92-16; f. 1972; sports; French; Editor-in-Chief LARBI MOHAMED ABBOUD; circ. 110,000.

**Libre Algérie:** Algiers; French; organ of the FFS.

**La Nation:** Algiers; French; Editor SALIMA GHEZALI; circ. 35,000.

**Révolution Africaine:** Maison de la Presse, Kouba, Algiers; tel. (2) 59-77-91; fax (2) 59-77-92; current affairs journal in French; socialist; Dir FERRAH ABDELLALI; circ. 50,000.

**El Wadjh al-Akhar** (The Other Face): Algiers; Arabic.

### OTHER PERIODICALS

**Al-Acala:** 4 rue Timgad, Hydra, Algiers; tel. (2) 60-85-55; fax (2) 60-09-36; f. 1970; published by the Ministry of Religious Affairs; fortnightly; Editor MUHAMMAD AL-MAHDI.

**Algérie Médicale:** Algiers; f. 1964; publ. of Union médicale algérienne; 2 a year; circ. 3,000.

**Alouan** (Colours): 119 rue Didouche Mourad, Algiers; f. 1973; cultural review; monthly; Arabic.

**Bibliographie de l'Algérie:** Bibliothèque Nationale d'Algérie, BP 127, Hamma el-Annasser, 16000 Algiers; tel. (2) 67-18-67; fax (2) 67-29-99; f. 1963; lists books, theses, pamphlets and periodicals published in Algeria; 2 a year; Arabic and French; Dir-Gen. MOHAMED AÏSSA OUMOUSSA.

**Ach-Cha'ab ath-Thakafi** (Cultural People): Algiers; f. 1972; cultural monthly; Arabic.

**Ach-Chabab** (Youth): Algiers; journal of the UNJA; bi-monthly; French and Arabic.

**Al-Djeich** (The Army): Office de l'Armée Nationale Populaire, Algiers; f. 1963; monthly; Algerian army review; Arabic and French; circ. 10,000.

**Journal Officiel de la République Algérienne Démocratique et Populaire:** BP 376, Saint-Charles, Les Vergers, Bir Mourad Rais, Algiers; tel. (2) 54-35-06; fax (2) 54-35-12; f. 1962; French and Arabic.

**Nouvelles Economiques:** 6 blvd Amilcar Cabral, Algiers; f. 1969; publ. of Institut Algérien du Commerce Extérieur; monthly; French and Arabic.

**Révolution et Travail:** Maison du Peuple, 1 rue Abdelkader Benbarek, place du 1er mai, Algiers; tel. (2) 66-73-53; journal of UGTA (central trade union) with Arabic and French editions; monthly; Editor-in-Chief RACHIB AÏT ALI.

**Revue Algérienne du Travail:** Algiers; f. 1964; labour publication; quarterly; French.

**Ath-Thakafa** (Culture): 2 place Cheikh ben Badis, Algiers; tel. (2) 62-20-73; f. 1971; every 2 months; cultural review; Editor-in-Chief CHEBOUB OTHMANE; circ. 10,000.

### NEWS AGENCIES

**Algérie Presse Service (APS):** 4 rue Zouieche, Kouba, Algiers; tel. (2) 77-79-28; fax (2) 59-77-59; f. 1962.

#### Foreign Bureaux

**Agence France-Presse (AFP):** 6 rue Abd al-Karim el-Khettabi, Algiers; tel. (2) 63-62-01; Chief YVES LEERS.

**Agencia EFE** (Spain): 4 ave Pasteur, 15000 Algiers; tel. (2) 71-85-59; fax (2) 73-77-62; Chief MANUEL OSTOS LÓPEZ.

**Agenzia Nazionale Stampa Associata (ANSA)** (Italy): 4 ave Pasteur, Algiers; tel. (2) 63-73-14; fax (2) 61-25-84; Rep. CARLO DI RENZO.

**Associated Press (AP)** (USA): BP 769, 4 ave Pasteur, Algiers; tel. (2) 63-59-41; fax (2) 63-59-42; Rep. RACHID KHIARI.

**Bulgarska Telegrafna Agentsia (BTA)** (Bulgaria): Algiers; Chief GORAN GOTEV.

**Informatsionnoye Telegrafnoye Agentstvo Rossii—Telegrafnoye Agentstvo Suverennykh Stran (ITAR—TASS)** (Russia): 21 rue de Boulogne, Algiers; Chief KONSTANTIN DUDAREV.

**Reuters** (UK): Algiers; tel. (2) 74-70-53; fax (2) 74-53-75.

**Rossiiskoye Informatsionnoye Agentstvo—Novosti (RIA—Novosti)** (Russia): Algiers; Chief Officer YURII S. BAGDASAROV.

**Xinhua (New China) News Agency** (People's Republic of China): 32 rue de Carthage, Hydra, Algiers; tel. and fax (2) 69-27-12; Chief WANG LIANZHI.

Wikalat al-Maghreb al-Arabi (Morocco) and the Middle East News Agency (Egypt) are also represented.

# Publishers

**Entreprise Nationale du Livre (ENAL):** 3 blvd Zirout Youcef, BP 49, Algiers; tel. and fax (2) 73-58-41. 1966 as Société Nationale d'Edition et de Diffusion, name changed 1983; publishes books of all types, and imports, exports and distributes printed material, stationery, school and office supplies; Pres. and Dir-Gen. HASSEN BENDIF.

**Office des Publications Universitaires:** 1 place Centrale de Ben Aknoun, Algiers; tel. (2) 78-87-18; publishes university textbooks.

# Broadcasting and Communications

## TELECOMMUNICATIONS

**Entreprise Nationale des Télécommunications (ENTC):** 1 ave du 1er novembre, Tlemcen; tel. (7) 20-76-71; fax (2) 26-39-51; f. 1978; national telecommunications org; jt venture with Sweden: Dir-Gen. SIBAWAGHI SAKER.

## BROADCASTING

### Radio

**Arabic Network:** transmitters at Adrar, Aïn Beïda, Algiers, Béchar, Béni Abbès, Djanet, El Goléa, Ghardaia, Hassi Messaoud, In Aménas, In Salah, Laghouat, Les Trembles, Ouargla, Reggane, Tamanrasset, Timimoun, Tindouf.

**French Network:** transmitters at Algiers, Constantine, Oran and Tipaza.

**Kabyle Network:** transmitter at Algiers.

**Radio Algérienne:** 21 blvd des Martyrs, Algiers; tel. (2) 23-08-00; fax (2) 23-08-23; e-mail radioalg@ist.cerist.dz; govt-controlled; Dir-Gen. ABDELKADER LALMI.

### Television

The principal transmitters are at Algiers, Batna, Sidi-Bel-Abbès, Constantine, Souk-Ahras and Tlemcen. Television plays a major role in the national education programme.

**Télévision Algérienne:** 21 blvd des Martyrs, Algiers; tel. (2) 60-23-00; fax (2) 60-19-22; Dir-Gen. CHIKI ABDELMADJID (acting).

# Finance

(cap. = capital; res = reserves; dep. = deposits; brs = branches; m. = million; amounts in Algerian dinars)

## BANKING

### Central Bank

**Banque d'Algérie:** 38 ave Franklin Roosevelt, 16000 Algiers; tel. (2) 23-02-32; fax (2) 23-01-50; f. 1963 as Banque Centrale d'Algérie; present name adopted 1990; cap. 40m.; bank of issue; Gov. ABDELOUAHAB KERAMANE; 50 brs.

### Nationalized Banks

**Banque Al-Baraka d'Algérie:** Villa n°1, cité Bouteldja Houadef, Ben Aknoun, Algiers; tel. (2) 91-64-51; fax (2) 91-64-57; f. 1991; cap. 500m., total assets 9,932m. (Dec. 1998); Algeria's first Islamic financial institution; owned by the Jeddah-based Al-Baraka Investment and Development Co (50%) and the local Banque de l'Agriculture et du Développement Rural (BADR) (50%); Chair. MUHAMMAD TEWFIK AL-MAGHARIBI; Gen. Man. MUHAMMAD SEDDIK HAFID.

**Banque Extérieure d'Algérie (BEA):** BP 344, Alger-Gare, 11 blvd Col Amirouche, 16000 Algiers; tel. (2) 23-93-15; fax (2) 23-92-67; f. 1967; cap. 5,600m., res 31,269m., total assets 405,481m. (Dec. 1996); chiefly concerned with energy and maritime transport sectors; Chair. MUHAMMAD BENHALIMA; Dir-Gen. HOCINE HANNACHI; 80 brs.

**Banque du Maghreb Arabe pour l'Investissement et le Commerce:** 21 blvd des Trois Frères Bouadou, Bir Mourad Rais, Algiers; tel. (2) 56-04-46; fax (2) 56-60-12; owned by the Algerian Govt (50%) and the Libyan Govt (50%); Pres. M. HAKIKI; Dir-Gen. IBRAHIM ALBISHARY.

**Banque Nationale d'Algérie (BNA):** 8 blvd Ernesto Ché Guévara, 16000 Algiers; tel. (2) 71-55-64; fax (2) 71-47-59; f. 1966; cap. 8,000m., res 10,227m., dep. 68,920m. (Dec. 1995); specializes in industry, transport and trade sectors; scheduled for partial privatization in 1999; Chair. and Man. Dir MUHAMMAD TERBECHE; 163 brs.

**Crédit Populaire d'Algérie (CPA):** BP 1031, 2 blvd Col Amirouche, 16000 Algiers; tel. (2) 71-78-78; fax (2) 71-79-00; f. 1966; cap. 13,600m., total assets 353,863m. (Dec. 1996); specializes in light industry, construction and tourism; Chair. and Gen. Man. EL HACHEMI MEGHAOUI; 117 brs.

### Development Banks

**Banque de l'Agriculture et du Développement Rural (BADR):** BP 484, 17 blvd Col Amirouche, 16000 Algiers; tel. (2) 64-72-64; fax (2) 61-55-51; f. 1982; cap. 2,200m., res 1,942m., dep. 103,939m. (Dec. 1993); finance for the agricultural sector; Chair. and Man. Dir MOURAD DAMARDJI; 270 brs.

**Banque Algérienne de Développement (BAD):** 12 blvd Col Amirouche, 16000 Algiers; tel. (2) 73-89-50; fax (2) 74-51-36; f. 1963; cap. 100m., total assets 233,132.9m. (Dec. 1996); a public establishment with fiscal sovereignty; aims to contribute to Algerian economic devt through long-term investment programmes; Chair. SASSI AZIZA; Dir-Gen. MUHAMMAD KERKEBANE; 4 brs.

**Banque de Développement Local (BDL):** 5 rue Gaci Amar, Staouéli, Grand Governorat d'Alger; tel. (2) 39-28-01; fax (2) 39-37-66; f. 1985; regional devt bank; scheduled for partial privatization in 1999; cap. and res 6,555.4m. (1996); Dir-Gen. MUHAMMAD MALEK; 14 brs.

**Caisse Nationale d'Epargne et de Prévoyance (CNEP):** 42 blvd Khélifa Boukhalfa, Algiers; tel. (2) 71-33-53; fax (2) 71-70-22; f. 1964; 206,915.8m. (Dec. 1992); savings and housing bank; Dir-Gen. ABDELKRIM NAAS.

### Private Banks

**Mouna Bank:** Oran; f. 1998; cap. 260m.; Pres. AHMED BENSADOUN.

**Union Bank:** 5 bis, chemin Mackley, el-Biar, 16030 Algiers; tel. (2) 91-45-49; fax (2) 91-45-48; f. 1995; cap. 100m., total assets 992m. (Dec. 1996); principal shareholder Brahim Hadjas; Pres. SELIM BENATA.

### Foreign Banks

**Arab Banking Corpn** (Bahrain): 54 ave des Trois Frères Bouaddou, Bir Mourad Rais, Algiers; tel. (2) 54-15-15; fax (2) 54-16-04; e-mail abcbank@ist.cerist.dz; cap. US $20m.

**Natexis Al-Amana Banque** (France): Algiers; f. 1999; owned by Natexis Banques Populaires; Man. Dir HOCINE MOUFFOK.

## STOCK EXCHANGE

The Algiers Stock Exchange began trading in July 1999.

**Commission d'Organisation et de Surveillance des Opérations de Bourse (COSOB):** Algiers; tel. (2) 71-27-25; fax (2) 71-21-98; Chair. ALI BOUKRAMI; Gen. Sec. ABDELHAKIM BERRAH.

## INSURANCE

Insurance is a state monopoly; however, in 1997 regulations were drafted to permit private companies to enter the Algerian insurance market.

**Caisse Nationale de Mutualité Agricole:** 24 blvd Victor Hugo, Algiers; tel. (2) 73-46-31; fax (2) 73-31-07; f. 1972; Dir-Gen. YAHIA CHERIF BRAHIM; 47 brs.

**Cie Algérienne d'Assurance:** 48 rue Didouche Mourad, Algiers; tel. (2) 64-54-32; fax (2) 64-20-15; f. 1963 as a public corpn; Pres. ALI DJENDI.

**Cie Centrale de Réassurance (CCR):** 21 blvd Zirout Youcef, Algiers; tel. (2) 73-80-20; fax (2) 73-80-60; f. 1973; general; Chair. DJAMEL-EDDINE CHOUAÏB CHOUITER.

**Société Nationale d'Assurances (SNA):** 5 blvd Ernesto Ché Guévara, Algiers; tel. (2) 71-47-60; fax (2) 71-22-16; f. 1963; state-sponsored co; Pres. KACI AISSA SLIMANE; Chair. and Gen. Man. LATROUS AMARQ.

**Trust Algeria:** Algiers; f. 1997; 65% owned by Trust Insurance Co (Bahrain) and Qatar General Insurance and Reinsurance Co, 35% owned by Compagnie Algérienne d'Assurance.

# Trade and Industry

## GOVERNMENT AGENCY

**Centre Algérien pour la Promotion des Investissements (CALPI):** Algiers; f. 1994 to promote investment; offices in the 48 administrative districts.

## DEVELOPMENT ORGANIZATIONS

**Agence Nationale pour l'Aménagement du Territoire (ANAT):** 30 ave Muhammad Fellah, Algiers; tel. (2) 58-48-12; fax (2) 68-85-03; f. 1980; Pres. and Dir-Gen. KOUIDER DJEBLI.

**Engineering Environment Consult (EEC):** BP 395, Alger-Gare, 50 rue Khélifa Boukhalfa, Algiers; tel. (2) 73-33-90; fax (2) 73-24-81; e-mail eec@ist.wissal.dz; internet eldjazair.net.dz/economie/eec/eec.htm; f. 1982; Dir-Gen. MUHAMMAD BENTIR.

**Institut National de la Production et du Développement Industriel (INPED):** 126 rue Didouche Mourad, Boumerdès; tel. (2) 41-52-50.

## CHAMBERS OF COMMERCE

**Chambre Française de Commerce et d'Industrie en Algérie (CFCIA):** 1 rue Lt Mohamed Touileb, Algiers; tel. (2) 73-28-28; fax (2) 63-75-33; f. 1965; Pres. JEAN-PIERRE DEQUEKER; Dir JEAN-FRANÇOIS HEUGAS.

**Chambre Algérienne de Commerce et d'Industrie (CACI):** BP 100, Palais Consulaire, rue Amilcar Cabral, Algiers; tel. (2) 57-55-55; fax (2) 57-70-25; f. 1980; Dir-Gen. MUHAMMAD CHAMI.

## INDUSTRIAL AND TRADE ASSOCIATIONS

**Association Nationale des Fabrications et Utilisateurs d'Emballages Métalliques:** BP 245, rue de Constantine, Algiers; Pres. OTHMANI.

**Centre National des Textiles et Cuirs (CNTC):** BP 65, route du Marché, Boumerdes; tel. (2) 81-13-23; fax (2) 81-13-57.

**Entreprise Nationale de Développement des Industries Alimentaires (ENIAL):** 2 rue Ahmed Aït Muhammad, Algiers; tel. (2) 76-51-42; Dir-Gen. MOKRAOUI.

**Entreprise Nationale de Développement des Industries Manufacturières (ENEDIM):** 22 rue des Fusillés, El Anasser, Algiers; tel. (2) 68-13-43; fax (2) 67-55-26; f. 1983; Dir-Gen. FODIL.

**Entreprise Nationale de Développement et de Recherche Industriels des Matériaux de Construction (ENDMC):** BP 78, 35000 Algiers; tel. (2) 41-50-70. 1982; Dir-Gen. A. TOBBAL.

**Groupement pour l'Industrialisation du Bâtiment (GIBAT):** BP 51, 3 ave Colonel Driant, 55102 Verdun, France; tel. 29-86-09-76; fax 29-86-20-51; Dir JEAN MOULET.

**Institut Algérien de la Propriété Industrielle (INAPI):** 40–42 rue Larbi Ben M'hidi, 16000 Algiers; tel. (2) 73-60-84; fax (2) 73-55-81; f. 1973; Dir-Gen. M. BOUHNIK AMOR.

**Institut National Algérien du Commerce Extérieur (COMEX):** 6 blvd Anatole-France, Algiers; tel. (2) 62-70-44; Dir-Gen. SAAD ZERHOUNI.

**Institut National des Industries Manufacturières (INIM):** 35000 Boumerdès; tel. (2) 81-62-71; fax (2) 82-56-62; f. 1973; Dir-Gen. HOCINE HASSISSI.

### State Trading Organizations

Since 1970 all international trading has been carried out by state organizations, of which the following are the most important:

**Entreprise Nationale d'Approvisionnement en Bois et Dérivés (ENAB):** BP 166, Alger-Gare, 2 blvd Muhammad V, Algiers; tel. (2) 72-57-70; fax (2) 72-62-15; wood and derivatives and other building materials; Dir-Gen. El-Hadj REKHROUKH.

**Entreprise Nationale d'Approvisionnement en Outillage et Produits de Quincaillerie Générale (ENAOQ):** 5 rue Amar Semaous, Hussein-Dey, Algiers; tel. (2) 23-31-83; fax (2) 59-84-54; tools and general hardware; Dir-Gen. SMATI BAHIDJ FARID.

**Entreprise Nationale d'Approvisionnements en Produits Alimentaires (ENAPAL):** Algiers; tel. (2) 76-10-11. 1983; monopoly of import, export and bulk trade in basic foodstuffs; brs in more than 40 towns; Chair. LAID SABRI; Man. Dir BRAHIM DOUAOURI.

**Entreprise Nationale d'Approvisionnement et de Régulation en Fruits et Légumes (ENAFLA):** BP 42, 12 ave des Trois Frères Bouadou, Bir Mourad Rais, Algiers; tel. (2) 54-10-10; fax (2) 56-79-59; f. 1983; division of the Ministry of Commerce; fruit and vegetable marketing, production and export; Man. Dir RÉDHA KHELEF.

**Entreprise Nationale de Commerce:** 6–9 rue Belhaffat-Ghazali, Hussein Dey, Algiers; tel. (2) 77-43-20; monopoly of imports and distribution of materials and equipment; Dir-Gen. MUHAMMAD LAÏD BELARBIA.

**Office Algérien Interprofessionel des Céréales (OAIC):** 5 rue Ferhat-Boussaad, Algiers; tel. (2) 73-26-01; fax (2) 73-22-11; f. 1962; monopoly of trade in wheat, rice, maize, barley and products derived from these cereals; Gen. Man. LAÏD TALAMALI.

**Office National de la Commercialisation des Produits Viti-Vinicoles (ONCV):** 112 Quai-Sud, Algiers; tel. (2) 73-72-75; fax (2) 73-72-97; f. 1968; monopoly of importing and exporting products of the wine industry; Man. Dir SAÏD MEBARKI.

## UTILITIES

**Société Nationale de l'Electricité et du Gaz (SONELGAZ):** 2 blvd Colonel Krim Belkacem, Algiers; tel. (2) 74-82-60; fax (2) 61-54-77; monopoly of production, distribution and transportation of electricity and transportation and distribution of natural gas; Gen. Man. AÏSSA ABDELKRIM BENGHANEM.

### Electricity

**Entreprise de Travaux d'Electrification (KAHRIF):** Hai Ain d'Hab, Médéa; tel. (3) 58-51-67; fax (3) 58-31-14; f. 1982; study of electrical infrastructure.

### Gas

**Entreprise Nationale des Gaz Industriels (ENGI):** BP 247, Kouba, Algiers; tel. (2) 23-35-99; fax (2) 77-11-94; production and distribution of gas; Gen. Man. LAHOCINE BOUCHERIT.

### Water

**Agence Nationale de l'Eau Potable et Industrielle et de l'Assainissement (AGEP):** Algiers; state water co.

## HYDROCARBONS COMPANIES

**Société Nationale pour la Recherche, la Production, le Transport, la Transformation et la Commercialisation des Hydrocarbures (SONATRACH):** 10 rue du Sahara, Hydra, Algiers; tel. and fax (2) 60-20-21. 1963; exploration, exploitation, transport and marketing of petroleum, natural gas and their products; Chair. ABEDLHAK BOUHAFS.

Since 1980 the following associated companies have shared SONATRACH's functions:

**Entreprise Nationale de Canalisation (ENAC):** Algiers; tel. (2) 70-35-90; piping; Dir-Gen. HAMID MAZRI.

**Entreprise Nationale d'Engineering Pétrolier (ENEP):** 2 blvd Muhammad V, Algiers; tel. (2) 64-08-37; fax (2) 63-71-83; design and construction for petroleum-processing industry; Gen. Man. MUSTAPHA MEKIDECHE.

**Entreprise Nationale de Forage (ENAFOR):** BP 211, 30500 Hassi Messaoud, Algiers; tel. (2) 73-71-35; fax (2) 73-22-60; drilling; Dir-Gen. ABD AR-RACHID ROUABAH.

**Entreprise Nationale de Génie Civil et Bâtiments (GCB):** BP 23, route de Corso, Boudouaou, Algiers; tel. (2) 84-65-26; fax (2) 84-60-09; civil engineering; Dir-Gen. ABD EL-HAMID ZERGUINE.

**Entreprise Nationale de Géophysique (ENAGEO):** BP 140, Hassi Messaoud, Ouargla; tel. (9) 73-77-00; fax (9) 73-72-12; e-mail enageodg@ist.cerist.dz; geophysics; Dir-Gen. REDA RAHAL.

**Entreprise Nationale des Grands Travaux Pétroliers (ENGTP):** BP 09, Zone Industrielle, Reghaïa, Boumerdes; tel. (2) 85-24-50; fax (2) 85-14-70; f. 1980; major industrial projects; Dir-Gen. B. DRIAD.

**Entreprise Nationale des Plastiques & Caoutchoucs (ENPC):** BP 452–453, Zone industrielle, Sétif; tel. (5) 93-75-45; fax (5) 93-05-65; production and marketing of rubber and plastics products; Dir-Gen. MEDDOUR NOUREDDINE.

**Entreprise Nationale de Services Pétroliers (ENSP):** BP 83, Hassi Messaoud, Ouargla; tel. (9) 73-73-33; fax (9) 73-82-01; oil-well services; Dir-Gen. A. GASMI.

**Entreprise Nationale des Travaux aux Puits (ENTP):** BP 71, In-Amenas, Illizi; oil-well construction; Dir-Gen. ABD AL-AZIZ KRISSAT.

**Société Nationale de Commercialisation et de Distribution des Produits Pétroliers (NAFTAL, SpA):** BP 73, route des Dunes, Cheraga, Algiers; tel. (2) 36-09-69; fax (2) 37-57-11; f. 1987; international marketing and distribution of petroleum products; Gen. Man. NOREDINE CHEROUATI.

## TRADE UNIONS

**Union Générale des Travailleurs Algériens (UGTA):** Maison du Peuple, place du 1er mai, Algiers; tel. (2) 66-89-47. 1956; 800,000 mems; Sec.-Gen. ABDELMADJID SIDI SAID .

There are 10 national 'professional sectors' affiliated to UGTA. These are:

**Secteur Alimentation, Commerce et Tourisme** (Food, Commerce and Tourist Industry Workers): Gen. Sec. ABD AL-KADER GHRIBLI.

**Secteur Bois, Bâtiments et Travaux Publics** (Building Trades Workers): Gen. Sec. LAIFA LATRECHE.

**Secteur Education et Formation Professionnelle** (Teachers): Gen. Sec. SAÏDI BEN GANA.

**Secteur Energie et Pétrochimie** (Energy and Petrochemical Workers): Gen. Sec. ALI BELHOUCHET.

**Secteur Finances** (Financial Workers): Gen. Sec. MUHAMMAD ZAAF.

**Secteur Information, Formation et Culture** (Information, Training and Culture).

**Secteur Industries Légères** (Light Industry): Gen. Sec. ABD AL-KADER MALKI.

**Secteur Industries Lourdes** (Heavy Industry).

**Secteur Santé et Sécurité Sociale** (Health and Social Security Workers): Gen. Sec. ABD AL-AZIZ DJEFFAL.

**Secteur Transports et Télécommunications** (Transport and Telecommunications Workers): Gen. Sec. EL-HACHEMI BEN MOUHOUB.

**Al-Haraka al-Islamiyah lil-Ummal al-Jazarivia** (Islamic Movement for Algerian Workers): Tlemcen; f. 1990; based on teachings of Islamic faith and affiliated to the FIS.

**Union Nationale des Paysans Algériens (UNPA):** f. 1973; 700,000 mems; Sec.-Gen. AISSA NEDJEM.

# Transport

### RAILWAYS

A new authority, Infrafer (Entreprise Publique Economique de Réalisation des Infrastructures Ferroviaires), was established in 1987 to take responsibility for the construction of new track. In the following year a project to build an underground railway network in Algiers was revived in a modified form.

**Entreprise Métro d'Alger:** 4 chemin de Wilaya 13, Kouba, Algiers; tel. (2) 58-67-68; fax (2) 68-97-05; construction of a 26.5-km metro railway line began in 1989; initial 12.5-km section (16 stations) scheduled to open in two stages, starting in 2000; Dir-Gen. H. BELLIL.

**Infrafer (Entreprise Publique Economique de Réalisation des Infrastructures Ferroviaires):** BP 208, 35300 Rouiba; tel. (2) 85-27-47; fax (2) 85-17-55; f. 1987; Pres. and Dir-Gen. K. BENMAMI.

**Société Nationale des Transports Ferroviaires (SNTF):** 21–23 blvd Muhammad V, Algiers; tel. (2) 71-15-10; fax (2) 74-81-90; f. 1976 to replace Société Nationale des Chemins de Fer Algériens; 4,820 km of track, of which 304 km are electrified and 1,156 km are narrow gauge; daily passenger services from Algiers to the principal provincial cities and services to Tunisia and Morocco; Dir-Gen. A. LALAIMIA.

### ROADS

In 1996 there were an estimated 104,000 km of roads and tracks, of which 640 km were motorways, 25,200 km were main roads and 23,900 km were secondary roads. The French administration built a good road system (partly for military purposes), which, since independence, has been allowed to deteriorate in parts. New roads have been built linking the Sahara oil fields with the coast, and the Trans-Sahara highway is a major project. In 1996 it was estimated that the cost of renovating the national road system would total US $4,124m.

**Société Nationale des Transports Routiers (SNTR):** 27 rue des Trois Frères Bouadou, Bir Mourad Rais, Algiers; tel. (2) 54-06-00; fax (2) 56-53-73; f. 1967; holds a monopoly of goods transport by road; Chair. El-Hadj HAOUSSINE; Dir-Gen. ESSAID BENDAKIR.

**Société Nationale des Transports des Voyageurs (SNTV):** Algiers; tel. (2) 66-00-52. 1967; holds monopoly of long-distance passenger transport by road; Man. Dir M. DIB.

### SHIPPING

Algiers is the main port, with anchorage of between 23 m and 29 m in the Bay of Algiers, and anchorage for the largest vessels in Agha Bay. The port has a total quay length of 8,380 m. There are also important ports at Annaba, Arzew, Béjaia, Djidjelli, Ghazaouet, Mostaganem, Oran, Skikda and Ténés. Petroleum and liquefied gas are exported through Arzew, Béjaia and Skikda. Algerian crude petroleum is also exported through the Tunisian port of La Skhirra. In December 1998 Algeria's merchant fleet totalled 148 vessels, amounting to 1,004,690 grt.

**Cie Algéro-Libyenne de Transports Maritimes (CALTRAM):** 19 rue des Trois Frères Bouadou, Bir Mourad Rais, Algiers; tel. (2) 57-17-00; fax (2) 54-21-04; Man. Dir A. HASMIM.

**Entreprise Nationale de Réparations Navales (ERENAV):** quai no. 12, Algiers; tel. (2) 42-04-00; fax (2) 71-31-72; f. 1987; ship repairs; Dir-Gen. MOHAMED MOSLI.

**Entreprise Nationale de Transport Maritime de Voyageurs—Algérie Ferries (ENTMV):** BP 467, 5,6 Jawharlal Nehru, Algiers; tel. (2) 74-04-85; fax (2) 64-88-76; f. 1987 as part of restructuring of SNTM-CNAN; responsible for passenger transport; operates car ferry services between Algiers, Annaba, Skikda, Alicante, Marseilles and Oran; Dir-Gen. A. CHERIET.

**Entreprise Portuaire d'Alger (EPAL):** BP 16, 2 rue d'Angkor, Alger-Gare, Algiers; tel. (2) 71-54-39; fax (2) 71-54-52; e-mail portalg@ist.cerist.dz; f. 1982; responsible for management and growth of port facilities and sea pilotage; Dir-Gen. ALI FERRAH.

**Entreprise Portuaire d'Annaba (EPAN):** BP 1232, Môle Cigogne-Quai nord, Annaba; tel. (8) 86-31-31; fax (8) 86-54-15; e-mail epan@annaba-port.com; internet www.annaba.port.com; Man. Dir DJILANI SALHI.

**Entreprise Portuaire d'Arzew (EPA):** BP 46, 7 rue Larbi Tebessi, Arzew; tel. (6) 37-24-91; fax (6) 47-49-90; Man. Dir CHAIB OUMER.

**Entreprise Portuaire de Béjaia (EPB):** BP 94, Môle de la Casbah, Béjaia; tel. (5) 21-18-07; fax (5) 22-25-79; Man. Dir M. BOUMSILA.

**Entreprise Portuaire de Djen-Djen (EPDJ):** BP 87, El Achouat, Djen-Djen, Djidjelli; tel. (5) 45-00-36; fax (5) 44-02-72; f. 1984; Man. Dir MUHAMMAD ATMANE.

**Entreprise Portuaire de Ghazaouet (EPG):** BP 217, Enceinte Portuaire Môle de Batna, 13400 Ghazaouet; tel. (7) 32-11-75; fax (7) 32-11-75; Man. Dir B. ABDELMALEK.

**Entreprise Portuaire de Mostaganem (EPM):** BP 131, quai du Port, Mostaganem; tel. (6) 21-14-11; fax (6) 21-78-05; Dir-Gen. M. LAKEHAL.

**Entreprise Portuaire d'Oran (EPO):** BP 106, 6 blvd Mimouni Lahcène, Oran; tel. (6) 39-26-25; fax (6) 39-53-52; Man. Dir M. S. LOUHIBI.

**Entreprise Portuaire de Skikda (EPS):** BP 65, 46 ave Rezki Rahal, Skikda; tel. (8) 75-68-27; fax (8) 75-20-15; Man. Dir M. LEMRABET.

**Entreprise Portuaire de Ténès (EPT):** BP 18, 02200 Ténès; tel. (3) 76-72-76; fax (3) 76-61-77; Man. Dir K. EL-HAMRI.

**NAFTAL Division Aviation Marine:** BP 70, Aéroport Houari Boumedienne, Dar-el-Beïda, Algiers; tel. (2) 50-95-50; fax (2) 50-67-09; Dir HAMZA BELAIDI.

**Société Générale Maritime (GEMA):** 2 rue J. Nehru, Algiers; tel. (2) 74-73-00; fax (2) 74-76-73; f. 1987 as part of restructuring of SNTM-CNAN; responsible for merchant traffic; Dir-Gen. ABDULLAH SERIAI.

**Société Nationale de Transport Maritime et Cie Nationale Algérienne de Navigation (SNTM-CNAN):** BP 280, 2 quai no. 9, Nouvelle Gare Maritime, Algiers; tel. (2) 71-14-78; fax (2) 61-59-64; f. 1963; state-owned co which owns and operates fleet of freight ships; rep. office in Marseilles (France) and rep. agencies in Antwerp (Belgium), Valencia (Spain) and the principal ports in many other countries; Gen. Man. GHAZI REGAÏNIA.

**Société Nationale de Transports Maritimes des Hydrocarbures et des Produits Chimiques (SNTM-HYPROC):** BP 60, Arzew, 31200 Oran; tel. (6) 37-30-99; fax (6) 37-28-30; f. 1982; Dir-Gen. CHAÏB OUMEUR.

### CIVIL AVIATION

Algeria's principal international airport, Houari Boumedienne, is situated 20 km from Algiers. At Constantine, Annaba, Tlemcen and Oran there are also airports that meet international requirements. There are, in addition, 65 aerodromes, of which 20 are public, and a further 135 airstrips connected with the petroleum industry.

**Air Algérie (Entreprise Nationale d'Exploitation des Services Aériens):** BP 858, 1 place Maurice Audin, Immeuble el-Djazair, Algiers; tel. (2) 74-24-28; fax (2) 74-44-25; f. 1953 by merger; state-owned from 1972; internal services and extensive services to Europe, North and West Africa, and the Middle East; Sec.-Gen. ALI DJERABA; Dir-Gen. FAYSAL KHALIL.

**Air Maghreb:** planned consortium of the national airlines of Algeria, Libya, Mauritania, Morocco and Tunisia; the merger of the airlines has been delayed indefinitely.

**Antinea Airlines:** Algiers; domestic and international cargo and passenger services.

**Desert Aviation Co:** Touggourt; f. 1999; private co; internal flights; Exec. Dir CHOKRI MIAADI.

**Eco Air International:** Algiers; f. 1998; private co operating domestic and international passenger flights.

**Khalifa Airways:** Algiers; f. 1999; private co operating domestic and international passenger flights.

**Tassili Airlines:** Hassi Messaoud; f. 1997; jt venture between SONATRACH and Air Algérie; domestic passenger services.

# Tourism

Algeria's tourist attractions include the Mediterranean coast, the Atlas mountains and the desert. In 1998 a total of 107,214 tourists visited Algeria, compared with 722,682 in 1991. Receipts from tourism totalled US $24m. in 1996. In that year there were 737 hotels, with a total of 64,695 beds.

**Agence Nationale de Développement Touristique (ANDT):** BP 151, Sidi Fredj Staoueli, Algiers; tourism promotion; Dir-Gen. ABDELKRIM BOUCETTA.

**Office National du Tourisme (ONT):** 2 rue Ismail Kerrar, Algiers; tel. (2) 71-29-82; fax (2) 71-29-85; f. 1990; state institution; oversees tourism promotion policy; Dir-Gen. ABDELKADER GOUTI (acting).

**ONAT-TOUR (Opérateur National Algérien de Tourisme):** 126 bis A, rue Didouche Mourod, 16000 Algiers; tel. (2) 74-33-76; fax (2) 74-32-14; f. 1962; Dir-Gen. BELKACEMI HAMMOUCHE.

**Société de Développement de l'Industrie Touristique en Algérie (SODITAL):** 72 rue Asselah Hocine, Algiers; f. 1989; Dir-Gen. NOUREDDINE SALHI.

**TCA-TOUR (Touring Club d'Algérie):** BP 18, Birkhamden; rue Hacéne Benaamane, quartier les vergers, Algiers; tel. (2) 56-90-16; fax (2) 54-19-39; Dir-Gen. ABDERAHMANE ABD-EDDAIM.

# ANDORRA

## Introductory Survey

### Location, Climate, Language, Religion, Flag, Capital

The Principality of Andorra lies in the eastern Pyrenees, bounded by France and Spain, and is situated roughly midway between Barcelona and Toulouse. The climate is alpine, with much snow in winter and a warm summer. The official language is Catalan, but French and Spanish are also widely spoken. Most of the inhabitants profess Christianity, and about 94% are Roman Catholics. The civil flag (proportions 3 by 2) has three equal vertical stripes, of blue, yellow and red. The state flag has, in addition, the state coat of arms (a quartered shield above the motto *Virtus unita fortior*) in the centre of the yellow stripe. The capital is Andorra la Vella.

### Recent History

Owing to the lack of distinction between the authority of the General Council (Consell General) of Andorra and the Co-Princes (Coprínceps) who have ruled the country since 1278, the Andorrans encountered many difficulties in their attempts to gain international status for their country and control over its essential services.

Until 1970 the franchise was granted only to third-generation Andorran males who were more than 25 years of age. Thereafter, women, persons aged between 21 and 25, and second-generation Andorrans were allowed to vote in elections to the General Council. In 1977 the franchise was extended to include all first-generation Andorrans of foreign parentage who were aged 28 and over. The electorate remained small, however, when compared with the size of the population, and Andorra's foreign residents (who comprised 66.8% of the total population at December 1998) increased their demands for political and nationality rights. Immigration is on a quota system, being restricted primarily to French and Spanish nationals intending to work in Andorra.

Prior to 1993, political parties were not directly represented in the General Council, but there were loose groupings with liberal and conservative sympathies. The country's only political organization, the Partit Democràtic d'Andorra (PDA), was technically illegal, and in the 1981 elections to the General Council the party urged its supporters to cast blank votes.

In 1980, during discussions on institutional reform, representatives of the Co-Princes and the General Council agreed that an executive council should be formed, and that a referendum should be held on changes to the electoral system. In early 1981 the Co-Princes formally requested the General Council to prepare plans for reform, in accordance with these proposals. After the December elections to the General Council, in January 1982 the new legislature elected Oscar Ribas Reig as Head of Government (Cap de Govern). Ribas Reig appointed an executive of six ministers, who expressed their determination to provide Andorra with a written constitution. The formation of the executive body, known as the Govern, constituted the separation of powers between an executive and a legislature, and represented an important step towards institutional reform.

Severe storm damage in November 1982, and the general effects of the world-wide economic recession, led to a controversial vote by the General Council, in August 1983, in favour of the introduction of income tax, in an effort to alleviate Andorra's budgetary deficit and to provide the Government with extra revenue for development projects. Subsequent government proposals for an indirect tax on bank deposits, hotel rooms and property sales encountered strong opposition from financial and tourism concerns, and prompted the resignation of the Government in April 1984. Josep Pintat Solans, a local business executive, was elected unopposed by the General Council as Head of Government in May. In August, however, the Ministers of Finance and of Industry, Commerce and Agriculture resigned, following disagreements concerning the failure to implement economic reforms (including the introduction of income tax).

At the December 1985 elections to the General Council the electorate was increased by about 27%, as a result of the newly-introduced lower minimum voting age of 18 years. The Council re-elected Pintat Solans as Head of Government in January 1986, when he won the support of 27 of its 28 members.

In September 1986 President François Mitterrand of France and the Bishop of Urgel, Dr Joan Martí Alanis (respectively the French and Spanish Co-Princes), met in Andorra to discuss the principality's status in relation to the European Community (EC, now European Union—EU—see p. 172), as well as the question of free exchange of goods between the members of the EC and Andorra, following Spain's admission to the Community in January of that year.

In April 1987 the Consejo Sindical Interregional Pirineos-Mediterráneo, a collective of French and Spanish trade unions, in conjunction with the Andorran Asociación de Residentes Andorranos, began to claim rights, including those of freedom of expression and association and the right to strike, on behalf of 20,000 of its members who were employed as immigrant workers in Andorra.

Further proposals for institutional reforms were approved by the General Council in October 1987. The transfer to the Andorran Government of responsibility for such matters as public order was proposed, while the authority of the Co-Princes in the administration of justice was recognized. The drafting of a constitution for Andorra was also envisaged. The implementation of the reforms was, however, dependent on the agreement of the Co-Princes.

Municipal elections were held in December 1987, at which 80% of the electorate voted; however, the number of citizens eligible to vote represented only 13% of Andorra's total population. For the first time, the election campaign involved the convening of meetings and the use of the media, in addition to traditional canvassing. Although Andorra then had no political parties as such, four of the seven seats were won by candidates promoting a conservative stance.

In April 1988 Andorra enacted legislation recognizing the Universal Declaration of Human Rights, adopted by the UN General Assembly in 1948. In June 1988 the first Andorran trade union was established by two French union confederations and by the Spanish Unión General de Trabajadores. (There were about 26,000 salaried workers in Andorra at this time, 90% of whom were of French or Spanish origin.) In the following month, however, the General Council rejected the formation of the union, as it did not recognize workers' right of association and prohibited the existence of any union.

Elections to the General Council took place in December 1989, at which more than 80% of the electorate participated. In January 1990 the new Council elected the reformist Ribas Reig as Head of Government, with the support of 22 members. In June the Council voted unanimously to establish a special commission to draft a constitution. The proposed document was to promulgate popular sovereignty and to constitutionalize the Co-Princes. In April 1991 representatives of the Co-Princes agreed to recognize popular sovereignty in Andorra and to permit the drafting of a constitution, which would be subject to approval by referendum. In September, however, Ribas Reig was threatened with a vote of 'no confidence' by traditionalist members of the Council. There followed a period of political impasse, during which no official budget was authorized for the principality. In January 1992, following small, but unprecedented, public demonstrations in protest against the political deadlock, Ribas Reig and the General Council resigned. A general election took place in April, at which 82% of the electorate (of 8,592 voters) voted. However, the result was inconclusive, necessitating a second round of voting one week later, following which supporters of Ribas Reig controlled 17 of the 28 seats. Accordingly, Ribas Reig was re-elected as Head of Government.

At a referendum held in March 1993, in which 75.7% of the electorate participated, 74.2% of those who voted approved the draft Constitution. The document was signed by the Co-Princes in April, and was promulgated on 4 May. Under its provisions, the Co-Princes remained as Heads of State, but with greatly reduced powers, while Andorran nationals were afforded full sovereignty and (together with foreigners who had lived in Andorra for at least 20 years) were authorized to form and to join political parties and trade unions. The Constitution provided for the establishment of an independent judiciary, and permitted the principality to formulate its own foreign policy and to join international organizations. The Co-Princes were to retain a right of veto over treaties with France and Spain that affected Andorra's borders or security.

The first general election under the terms of the new Constitution took place on 12 December 1993. One-half of the General Council's 28 members were directly elected from the single national constituency, the remainder being elected by Andorra's seven parishes (two for each parish). No party won an overall majority of seats, the largest number (eight) being secured by Ribas Reig's Agrupament Nacional Democràtic (AND—the successor to the PDA); Nova Democràcia (ND) and the Unió Liberal (UL) each won five seats. Some 80.8% of the electorate participated in the election. In January 1994 Ribas Reig was re-elected Head of Government, supported by the AND and the ND, together with the two representatives of the Iniciatíva Democratica Nacional (IDN). He announced that it would be a priority of his administration to restore economic growth by means of financial reforms and infrastructural development. Opposition to Ribas Reig's proposed budget and tax legislation, however, led in November to the adoption by the General Council of a motion expressing 'no confidence' in the Government. Ribas Reig immediately submitted his resignation; Marc Forné Molne, the leader of the UL, was subsequently elected Head of Government, and was inaugurated in late December.

Forné Molne's Government lacked an overall majority in the General Council; however, the support of councillors from regional political organizations enabled the Government to adopt more than 30 acts (between December 1994 and July 1996), including controversial legislation regarding foreign nationals (see Economic Affairs). Municipal elections, at which some 77.7% of the electorate voted, took place in December 1995. Bibiana Rossa (a former Minister of Health) became the first woman in Andorra to be elected to the office of mayor (of Canillo). After being censured twice in one year by the General Council, Forné Molne was obliged to announce that a general election would be held in early 1997. Elections to the Council took place on 16 February 1997, at which 81.6% of the registered electorate (of 10,837 voters) participated. The UL won an overall majority of seats (16 of 28); six seats were secured by the AND, while the ND, the IDN and the Unió Parroquiai d'Ordino took two each. In April Forné Molne announced the formation of a new, expanded Government. The UL was subsequently renamed the Partit Liberal d'Andorra (PLA).

Following the referendum of March 1993, Andorra formally applied for membership of the Council of Europe (see p. 158), gaining entry in October 1994. In June 1993 the Andorran Government signed a treaty of co-operation with France and Spain which explicitly recognized the sovereignty of Andorra. In the following month Andorra became the 184th member of the UN. In late 1993 France and Spain established embassies in Andorra, and Andorra subsequently opened embassies in Paris and Madrid. In September 1997 Jacques Chirac made his first official visit to Andorra in his capacity as President of France.

## Government

Andorra is a co-principality, under the suzerainty of the President of France and the Spanish Bishop of Urgel. However, since May 1993, when the Constitution of the Principality of Andorra was promulgated, these positions have been almost purely honorary.

The General Council comprises 28 councillors, who are elected by universal suffrage for a four-year period. Two councillors are directly elected by each of the seven parishes of Andorra, and the remainder by a single national constituency. At its opening session the Council elects as its head the Speaker (Syndic General) and the Deputy Speaker (Subsyndic General), who cease to be members of the Council on their election. The General Council elects the Head of Government, who appoints ministers to the Govern.

Andorra is divided into seven parishes, each of which is administered by a Communal Council. Communal councillors are elected for a four-year term by direct universal suffrage. At its opening session each Communal Council elects two consuls, who preside over it.

## Defence

Andorra has no defence budget.

## Economic Affairs

In 1996 Andorra's national revenue totalled an estimated US $1,194m., equivalent to $18,514 per head. Traditionally an agricultural country, Andorra's principal crops are tobacco and potatoes; livestock-rearing is also of importance. However, the agricultural sector accounted for less than 1% of total employment in 1999, and Andorra is dependent on imports of foodstuffs to satisfy domestic requirements.

Industry in Andorra includes the manufacture of cigars and cigarettes, together with the production of textiles, leather goods, wood products and processed foodstuffs. Iron, lead, alum and stone are also produced. Including construction, industry provided 19.5% of total employment in 1999.

The country's hydroelectric power plant supplies only about one-quarter of domestic needs, and Andorra is dependent on imports of electricity and other fuels from France and Spain. Andorra's total electricity consumption in 1996 amounted to 357.0m. kWh.

After 1945 Andorra's economy expanded rapidly, as a result of the co-principality's development as a market for numerous European and overseas goods, owing to favourable excise conditions. The trade in low-duty consumer items and tourism are therefore the most important sources of revenue. An estimated 8m. tourists visited Andorra in 1995. The absence of income tax and other forms of direct taxation favoured the development of Andorra as a 'tax haven'. The banking sector makes a significant contribution to the economy.

Andorra's external trade is dominated by the import of consumer goods destined for sale to visitors. In 1998 imports were valued at 161,426m. pesetas and exports at 8,637m. pesetas. Spain and France are Andorra's principal trading partners, respectively providing 42.3% and 30.8% of imports and taking 50.4% and 29.6% of exports in 1998.

In 1996 Andorra recorded a budgetary surplus of 732m. pesetas. For 1999 expenditure was projected at 31,528m. pesetas and revenue at 28,770m. pesetas. In the absence of direct taxation, the Government derives its revenue from levies on imports and on financial institutions, indirect taxes on petrol and other items, stamp duty and the sale of postage stamps. There is reportedly no unemployment in Andorra: the restricted size of the indigenous labour force necessitates high levels of immigration.

In March 1990 Andorra approved a trade agreement with the EC (effective from July 1991), allowing for the establishment of a customs union with the EC and enabling Andorran companies to sell non-agricultural goods to the EU market without being subject to the external tariffs levied on third countries. Andorra benefits from duty-free transit for goods imported via EU countries. Notable impediments to growth in Andorra include the narrow economic base and the inability of the agricultural and manufacturing sectors to fulfil domestic needs. As part of initiatives to establish Andorra as a major financial centre, a law regulating financial services was approved in late 1993. In mid-1994 legislation was approved requiring banks to invest as much as 4% of their clients' deposits in a fund intended to alleviate the public debt. Controversial legislation was adopted in 1996 to allow certain foreign nationals to become 'nominal residents' (individuals who, for the purposes of avoiding taxation, establish their financial base in Andorra), on condition that they pay an annual levy of some 1m. pesetas, in addition to a deposit. The practice of granting this status (without the levy) had been suspended in 1992; however, in the mid-1990s those already accorded nominal residency were estimated to contribute 90% of Andorra's bank deposits. Plans were announced in 1997 to remove restrictions on foreign investment in the country, which currently limit investors to holding a maximum of one-third of the capital of any Andorran business. In October Andorra's request to commence negotiations for membership of the World Trade Organization (WTO, see p. 232) was approved by the WTO General Council. In late 1999 it was reported that the Government was considering the introduction of value-added tax and a duty on the sale of property.

## Social Welfare

In 1996 there was one hospital in Andorra, providing 2.2 beds per 1,000 inhabitants, and 148 registered medical practitioners. The 1999 budget allocated some 1,591m. pesetas (5.0% of total expenditure) to welfare and health services. A formal system of social security was established in 1966–68, and provides for sickness benefits, old-age pensions and workers' insurance. Contributions are made both by employers and workers.

### Education

Education is compulsory for children of between six and 16 years of age, and is provided free of charge by Catalan-, French- and Spanish-language schools. Six years of primary education are followed by four years of secondary schooling. University education is undertaken abroad, although there are two centres for vocational training in Andorra. In 1997/98 there were a total of 9,272 pupils attending Andorra's 33 schools, while 1,217 students were in higher education. The 1999 budget allocated some 4,902m. pesetas (15.5% of total expenditure) to education, youth and sports.

### Public Holidays

**2000:** 1 January (New Year's Day), 6 January (Epiphany), 14 March (Constitution Day), 21 April (Good Friday), 24 April (Easter Monday), 1 May (Labour Day), 12 June (Whit Monday), 15 August (Assumption), 8 September (National Holiday), 1 November (All Saints' Day), 8 December (Immaculate Conception), 25 December (Christmas), 26 December (St Stephen's Day).

**2001:** 1 January (New Year's Day), 6 January (Epiphany), 14 March (Constitution Day), 13 April (Good Friday), 16 April (Easter Monday), 1 May (Labour Day), 4 June (Whit Monday), 15 August (Assumption), 8 September (National Holiday), 1 November (All Saints' Day), 8 December (Immaculate Conception), 25 December (Christmas), 26 December (St Stephen's Day).

Each Parish also holds its own annual festival, which is taken as a public holiday, usually lasting for three days, in July, August or September.

### Weights and Measures

The metric system is in force.

# Statistical Survey

Source (unless otherwise stated): Servei d'Estudis, Ministeri de Finances, Carrer Dr Vilanova, 13 Edif. Thaïs, Esc. C5è, Andorra la Vella; tel. 865345; fax 867898; e-mail servest@andorra.ad.

## AREA AND POPULATION

**Area:** 467.76 sq km (180.6 sq miles).

**Population** (December 1998): 65,877 (males 34,493; females 31,384); comprising 21,866 Andorrans, 28,229 Spanish, 7,024 Portuguese, 4,420 French and 4,338 others. *Capital:* Andorra la Vella, population 21,513.

**Births, Marriages and Deaths** (1998): Registered live births 781; Registered marriages 208; Registered deaths 235.

**Employment** (July 1999): Agriculture, forestry and fishing 173; Industry (incl. construction) 6,744; Services 22,811; Other 1,834; Total 31,562.

## AGRICULTURE

**Principal Crop** (metric tons, 1997): Tobacco 1,047.0.

**Livestock** (1997/98): Cattle 1,199; Sheep 2,515; Horses 996; Goats 768.

## FINANCE

**Currency and Exchange Rates:** French and Spanish currencies are both in use. *French currency:* 100 centimes = 1 franc. *Sterling, Dollar and Euro Equivalents* (30 September 1999): £1 sterling = 10.1269 francs; US $1 = 6.1506 francs; €1 = 6.5596 francs; 1,000 French francs = £98.75 = $162.59 = €152.45. *Average Exchange Rate* (francs per US dollar): 5.1155 in 1996; 5.8367 in 1997; 5.8995 in 1998. *Spanish currency:* 100 céntimos = 1 peseta. *Sterling, Dollar and Euro Equivalents* (30 September 1999): £1 sterling = 256.87 pesetas; US $1 = 156.01 pesetas; €1 = 166.39 pesetas; 1,000 Spanish pesetas = £3.893 = $6.410 = €6.010. *Average Exchange Rate* (pesetas per US dollar): 126.66 in 1996; 146.41 in 1997; 149.40 in 1998.

**Budget** (million pesetas, 1999): *Expenditure:* Ministry of the Presidency and the Interior 4,400, Ministry of Agriculture and the Environment 869, Ministry of Foreign Affairs 527, Ministry of Finance 862, Ministry of Territorial Development 10,452, Ministry of Education, Youth and Sports 4,902, Ministry of the Economy 382, Ministry of Welfare and Public Health 1,591, Ministry of Tourism and Culture 1,673, Transfers to local authorities 5,780, Total (incl. others) 31,528; *Revenue:* Indirect taxes on commodities 21,340, Other taxes 1,318, Administrative fees and charges, sales and other receipts 1,057, Property income 5,055, Total 28,770.

## EXTERNAL TRADE

**Principal Commodities** (million pesetas, 1998): *Imports:* Live animals and animal products 9,680 (Milk and dairy products; eggs; natural honey 4,992); Prepared foodstuffs; beverages, spirits and vinegar; tobacco and manufactured substitutes 27,139 (Alcoholic and non-alcoholic beverages 9,366; Tobacco 6,205); Mineral products 6,976 (Mineral fuels and oils, etc. 5,689); Products of chemical or allied industries 15,666 (Perfumery products and toiletries 11,205); Wood pulp, etc.; paper and paperboard and articles thereof 4,879; Textiles and textile articles 17,043 (Non-knitted clothing and accessories 6,448); Base metals and articles thereof 5,475; Machinery and mechanical appliances; electrical equipment; sound and television apparatus 27,057 (Boilers, non-electric machinery and mechanical appliances 9,614; Electrical machinery and appliances; sound and television apparatus 17,443); Vehicles, aircraft, vessels and associated transport equipment 14,625 (Passenger motor cars, tractors and other road vehicles 14,190); Optical, photographic, cinematographic, precision and medical instruments, etc.; clocks and watches; musical instruments 8,714; Total (incl. others) 161,426. *Exports:* Prepared foodstuffs; beverages, spirits and vinegar; tobacco and manufactured substitutes 872 (Alcoholic and non-alcoholic beverages 418; Tobacco 432); Products of chemical or allied industries 405 (Perfumery products and toiletries 336); Raw hides and skins, leather, furskins and articles thereof; saddlery and harness; travel goods, handbags, etc. 1,117 (Leather objects 1,107); Wood pulp, etc.; paper and paperboard and articles thereof 1,094 (Printed matter 1,048); Textiles and textile articles 695 (Non-knitted clothing and accessories 391); Machinery and mechanical appliances; electrical equipment; sound and television apparatus 1,422 (Boilers, non-electric machinery and mechanical appliances 306; Electrical machinery and appliances; sound and television apparatus 1,116); Vehicles, aircraft, vessels and associated transport equipment 1,228 (Passenger motor cars, tractors and other road vehicles 1,143); Furniture, bed linen, etc.; lighting devices 326; Total (incl. others) 8,637.

**Principal Trading Partners** (million pesetas, 1998): *Imports:* China, People's Republic 1,849; France 49,733; Germany 7,105; Italy 6,024; Japan 5,204; Netherlands 2,131; Spain 68,253; Switzerland 3,070; United Kingdom 4,602; USA 3,642; Total (incl. others) 161,426. *Exports:* France 2,557; Italy 89; Japan 732; Netherlands 240; Spain 4,353; Total (incl. others) 8,637.

## TRANSPORT

**Road Traffic** (registered motor vehicles, 1998): Total 55,394. *1996:* Passenger cars 35,358; Commercial vehicles 4,238.

## TOURISM

**Tourist Arrivals** (1998): Passenger cars entering from Spain 2,544,726; Passenger cars entering from France 1,342,824.

## COMMUNICATIONS MEDIA

**Radio Receivers** (1996): 15,000 in use.

**Television Receivers** (1996): 26,000 in use.

Source: UNESCO, *Statistical Yearbook*.

**Daily Newspapers** (1997): 2 titles published.

**Telephones** (main lines in use, December 1998): 32,946.

**Telefax Stations** (number in use, 1996): 1,450.

**Mobile Cellular Telephones** (subscribers, December 1998): 14,117.

## EDUCATION*

**School enrolment** (1997/98): 3- to 6-year-olds 2,269; 7- to 15-year-olds 5,338; 16 and over 1,665; Total 9,272.

**Other students** (1997/98): 1,217.

* Part of the educational systems is undertaken by Spain and France.

# Directory

## The Constitution

The Constitution of the Principality of Andorra came into force on 4 May 1993, having been approved by the Andorran people in a referendum on 14 March. The official name of the independent state is Principat d'Andorra. The Constitution asserts that Andorra is 'a Democratic and Social independent state abiding by the Rule of Law', and defines the fundamental rights, freedoms and obligations of Andorran citizens and delineates the functions and competences of the organs of state.

In accordance with Andorran tradition, the Co-Princes (Coprínceps), respectively the Bishop of Urgel and the President of the French Republic, are titular Heads of State.

The legislature is the General Council (Consell General), one-half of whose members are elected from a single national constituency, the remainder being elected to represent Andorra's seven parishes (Parròquies); members are elected to the General Council for four years. Elections are on the basis of direct universal adult suffrage. The ruling organ of the General Council is the Sindicatura, headed by a Speaker (Syndic General).

The Govern (the executive organ of state) is directed by the Head of Government (Cap de Govern), who is elected by the General Council (and formally appointed by the Co-Princes) and who must command the support of the majority of the legislature's members. The Head of Government nominates government ministers, who may not at the same time be members of the General Council. The Head of Government is restricted to two consecutive full terms of office.

The Constitution defines the composition and powers of the judiciary, the highest organ of which is the Higher Court of Justice.

The Constitution defines the functions of the communal councils (Comuns), which are the organs of representation and administration of the parishes.

Revision of the Constitution shall require the approval of two-thirds of the members of the General Council and ratification by a referendum.

The Constitutional Court is the supreme interpreter of the Constitution. Its decisions are binding for public authorities and for individuals.

## The Government

(January 2000)

### HEADS OF STATE

**Episcopal Co-Prince:** Dr JOAN MARTÍ ALANIS, Bishop of Urgel.

**French Co-Prince:** JACQUES CHIRAC.

### GOVERNMENT

**Head of Government:** MARC FORNÉ MOLNE.

**Minister of the Presidency and the Interiror:** ESTANISLAU SANGRÀ CARDONA.

**Minister of Foreign Affairs:** ALBERT PINTAT SANTOLÀRIA.

**Minister of Finance:** SUSAGNA ARASANZ SERRA.

**Minister of the Economy:** ENRIC CASADEVALL MEDRANO.

**Minister of Territorial Development:** CÀNDID NAUDI MORA.

**Minister of Welfare and Public Health:** JOSEP GOICOECHEA UTRILLO.

**Minister of Education, Youth and Sports:** PERE CERVÓS CARDONA.

**Minister of Tourism and Culture:** ENRIC PUJAL ARENY.

**Minister of Agriculture and the Environment:** OLGA ADELLACH COMA.

### MINISTRIES

**Office of the Head of Government:** Govern d'Andorra, Carrer Prat de la Creu, 62–64, Andorra la Vella; tel. 875700; fax 822882.

**Ministry of Agriculture and the Environment:** Carrer Prat de la Creu 62–64, Andorra la Vella; tel. 875700; fax 828906.

**Ministry of the Economy:** Govern d'Andorra, Edif. Administratiu, Carrer Prat de la Creu 62–64, Andorra la Vella; tel. 875700; fax 861519.

**Ministry of Education, Youth and Sports:** Carrer Bonaventura Armengol 6, Edif. Crèdit Centre, Andorra la Vella; tel. 866585; fax 861229.

**Ministry of Finance:** Carrer Prat de la Creu 62–64, Andorra la Vella; tel. 875700; fax 860962.

**Ministry of Foreign Affairs:** Carrer Prat de la Creu 62–64, Andorra la Vella; tel. 875700; fax 869559.

**Ministry of the Presidency and the Interior:** Carrer Ciutat de Sabadell, Escaldes-Engordany; tel. 872080; fax 869250.

**Ministry of Territorial Development:** Carrer Prat de la Creu 62–64, Andorra la Vella; tel. 875700; fax 861313.

**Ministry of Tourism and Culture:** Carrer Prat de la Creu 62–64, Andorra la Vella; tel. 875700; fax 860184; e-mail turisme@andorra.ad; internet www.turisme.ad.

**Ministry of Welfare and Public Health:** Avinguda Príncep Benlloch 26, Andorra la Vella; tel. 860345; fax 861933.

## Legislature

### CONSELL GENERAL

(General Council)

**Syndic General (Speaker):** FRANCESC ARENY CASAL (PLA).

**General Election, 16 February 1997**

| Party | Seats |
|---|---|
| Unió Liberal (UL)* | 16 |
| Agrupament Nacional Democràtic (AND) | 6 |
| Nova Democràcia (ND) | 2 |
| Iniciatíva Democratica Nacional (IDN) | 2 |
| Unió Parroquiai d'Ordino (UPO) | 2 |
| **Total** | 28 |

* Subsequently renamed Partit Liberal d'Andorra (PLA).

## Political Organizations

The establishment of political parties was sanctioned under the Constitution that was promulgated in May 1993.

**Agrupament Nacional Democràtic (AND):** Andorra la Vella; tel. 821930; fax 864368; e-mail and@and.ad; internet www.and.ad; f. 1979; fmrly Partit Democràtic d'Andorra; Leader LADISLAU BARÓ SOLÀ.

**Iniciatíva Democratica Nacional (IDN):** Plaça Rebés 1, 2°, Andorra la Vella; tel. 866406; fax 866306; e-mail idn@andorra.ad; f. 1993; Leader VICENÇ MATEU ZAMORA.

**Nova Democràcia (ND):** Andorra la Vella; f. 1993; Leader JAUME BARTOMEU CASSANY.

**Partit Liberal d'Andorra (PLA):** Andorra la Vella; f. 1993 as Unió Liberal; Leader MARC FORNÉ MOLNE.

**Unió Parroquiai d'Ordino (UPO):** Leader SIMÓ DURÓ COMA.

## Diplomatic Representation

### EMBASSIES IN ANDORRA

**France:** Carrer-les-Canals 38–40, POB 155, Andorra la Vella; tel. 820809; Ambassador: HENRI LECLERCQ.

**Spain:** Carrer Prat de la Creu 34, Andorra la Vella; tel. 800030; fax 868500; Ambassador: JUAN MARÍA LÓPEZ-AGUILAR.

## Judicial System

The 1993 Constitution guarantees the independence of the judiciary.

Judicial power is vested, in the first instance, in the Magistrates' Courts (Batllia) and in the Judges' Tribunal (Tribunal de Batlles), the criminal-law courts (Tribunal de Corts) and the Higher Court of Justice (Tribunal Superior de la Justícia). The judiciary is represented, directed and administered by the Higher Council of Justice (Consell Superior de la Justícia), whose five members are appointed for single terms of six years. Final jurisdiction, in constitutional matters, is vested in the Constitutional Court (Tribunal Constitucional), whose four members hold office for no more than two consecutive eight-year terms.

## The Press

In 1996 the average weekly circulation of the local press totalled 10,000.

**7 DIES:** Avinguda Riberaygua 39, Andorra la Vella; tel. 863700; fax 863800; weekly; Catalan; Dir ROSA MARI SORRIBES.

**Butlletí Oficial de Principat d'Andorra:** Andorra la Vella; official govt gazette; tel. 861400; fax 864300.

**Diari d'Andorra:** Avinguda Riberaygua 39, Andorra la Vella; tel. 863700; fax 863800; f. 1991; daily; local issues; Catalan; Dir IGNASI PLANELL; circ. 3,000.

**El Periòdic d'Andorra:** Carrer Sant Salvador 10, Andorra la Vella; tel. 800555; fax 826777; daily; Catalan; Dir JOSEP ANTON ROSSELL.

# Broadcasting and Communications

## TELECOMMUNICATIONS

**Servei de Telecomunicacions d'Andorra (STA):** Avinguda Meritxell 112, Andorra la Vella; tel. 875000; fax 860600; e-mail sta@sta.ad; provides national and international telecommunications services; Dir RAMON PLA.

## BROADCASTING

### Radio

**Radio Andorra:** Baixada del Molí, Andorra la Vella; tel. 873777; fax 864999; e-mail ecastelletorta@andorra.ad; f. 1991 as an Andorran-owned commercial public broadcasting service, to replace two stations which closed in 1981, following the expiry of their contracts with French and Spanish companies; Dir ENRIC CASTELLET.

**Radio Valira:** Avinguda Meritxell 9, 1st Floor, Andorra la Vella; tel. 829600; fax 828273; e-mail r_valira@andornet.ad; internet www.andornet.ad/r_valira; f. 1985; public commercial broadcasting service; Dirs GUALBERTO OSSORIO, JOSÉ RABADA.

### Television

In 1996 Andorra was able to receive broadcasts from seven television stations (excluding channels received by satellite or cable).

**Andorra Televisió:** Baixada del Molí, Andorra la Vella; tel. 873777; fax 864999; e-mail ecastelletorta@andorra.ad; f. 1995 as an Andorran-owned commercial public broadcasting service; Dir ENRIC CASTELLET.

**Antena 7:** Avinguda les Escoles 16, Escaldes-Engordany; tel. 824433; fax 826088; private co; in 1987 began to transmit one hour of Andorran-interest programmes from the Spanish side of the border.

# Finance

(cap. = capital; res = reserves; dep. = deposits; m. = million; brs = branches; amounts in Spanish pesetas)

In 1997 there were seven banks, with a total of 48 branches, operating in Andorra.

## PRINCIPAL BANKS

**Banc Agricol i Comercial d'Andorra SA:** POB 49, Avinguda Fiter i Rossell, 4 bis, Escaldes-Engordany; tel. 873345; fax 873350; e-mail internacional@banc-agricol.ad; internet www.banc-agricol.ad; f. 1930; cap. 6,000m., res 22,049m., dep. 234,035m. (Dec. 1998); Pres. MANUEL CERQUEDA-DONADEU; Gen. Man. JAUME SABATER ROVIRA; 9 brs.

**Banc Internacional d'Andorra SA:** POB 8, Avinguda Meritxell 32, Andorra la Vella; tel. 884488; fax 884499; e-mail bibm@bibm.ad; internet www.bibm.ad; f. 1958; affiliated to Banco Bilbao Vizcaya, Spain; cap. 7,056m., res 17,971m., dep. 301,650m. (Dec. 1998); Hon. Chair. JOAN MORA FONT; Chair. of Bd of Dirs JORDI ARISTOT MORA; 4 brs.

**Banca Mora SA:** POB 8, Plaça Coprínceps 2, Escaldes-Engordany; tel. 884488; fax 884499; e-mail bibm@bibm.ad; internet www.bibm.ad; f. 1952; subsidiary of Banc Internacional d'Andorra SA; cap. 5,000m., res 5,346m., dep. 135,740m. (Dec. 1998); Chair. FRANCESC MORA FONT; CEO JORDI ARISTOT MORA; 7 brs.

**Banca Privada d'Andorra SA:** POB 25, Avinguda Carlemany 119, Escaldes-Engordany; tel. 873500; fax 873517; e-mail bpa@bpa.ad; internet www.bpa.ad; f. 1958; fmrly Banca Cassany SA; cap. 2,400m., res 842m., dep. 69,109m. (Dec. 1997); Pres. HIGINI CIERCO I GARCÍA; Gen. Man. JOAN PAU MIQUEL PRATS; 4 brs.

**Banca Reig SA:** Avinguda Meritxell 79, Andorra la Vella; tel. 872872; fax 872875; e-mail reigbank@andorra.ad; f. 1956; cap. 2,000m., res 10,269m., dep. 151,813m. (Dec. 1997); Pres. OSCAR RIBAS REIG; CEO ORIOL RIBAS DURÓ; 4 brs.

**Crèdit Andorrà:** Avinguda Meritxell 80, Andorra la Vella; tel. 888035; fax 888881; internet www.creditandorra.ad; f. 1955; cap. 10,000m., res 43,194m., dep. 521,529m. (Dec. 1998); Chair. J. CASAL; Gen. Man. J. PERALBA; 14 brs.

# Transport

## RAILWAYS

There are no railways in Andorra, but the nearest stations are Ax-les-Thermes, L'Hospitalet and La Tour de Carol, in France (with trains from Toulouse and Perpignan), and Puigcerdá, in Spain, on the line from Barcelona. There is a connecting bus service from all four stations to Andorra.

## ROADS

A good road connects the Spanish and French frontiers, passing through Andorra la Vella. In 1996 there were 279 national roads, 198 of which were tarmacked.

## CIVIL AVIATION

There is an airport at Seo de Urgel in Spain, 20 km from Andorra la Vella.

# Tourism

Andorra has attractive mountain scenery, and winter sports facilities are available at six skiing centres. Tourists are also attracted by Andorra's duty-free shopping facilities. In 1999 there were 267 hotels and hostels in Andorra. An estimated 8m. tourists visited Andorra in 1995.

**Sindicat d'Iniciativa Oficina de Turisme:** Carrer Dr Vilanova, Andorra la Vella; tel. 820214; fax 825823.

# ANGOLA

## Introductory Survey

### Location, Climate, Language, Religion, Flag, Capital

The Republic of Angola lies on the west coast of Africa. The Cabinda district is separated from the rest of the country by the estuary of the River Congo and territory of the Democratic Republic of the Congo (DRC—formerly Zaire), with the Republic of the Congo lying to its north. Angola is bordered by the DRC to the north, Zambia to the east and Namibia to the south. The climate is tropical, locally tempered by altitude. There are two distinct seasons (wet and dry) but little seasonal variation in temperature. It is very hot and rainy in the coastal lowlands but temperatures are lower inland. The official language is Portuguese, but African languages (mainly Umbundo, Kimbundo, Kikongo, Chokwe and Ganguela) are also in common use. Much of the population follows traditional African beliefs, although a majority profess to be Christians, mainly Roman Catholics. The flag (proportions 3 by 2) has two equal horizontal stripes, of red and black; superimposed in the centre, in gold, are a five-pointed star, half a cog-wheel and a machete. The capital is Luanda.

### Recent History

Formerly a Portuguese colony, Angola became an overseas province in 1951. African nationalist groups began to form in the 1950s and 1960s, including the Movimento Popular de Libertação de Angola (MPLA) in 1956, the Frente Nacional de Libertação de Angola (FNLA) in 1962 and the União Nacional para a Independência Total de Angola (UNITA) in 1966. There was an unsuccessful nationalist rebellion in 1961. Severe repression ensued but, after a new wave of fighting in 1966, nationalist guerrilla groups were able to establish military and political control in large parts of eastern Angola and to press westward. Following the April 1974 *coup d'état* in Portugal, Angola's right to independence was recognized, and negotiations between the Portuguese Government and the nationalist groups began in September. After the formation of a common front by these groups, it was agreed that Angola would become independent in November 1975.

In January 1975 a transitional Government was established, comprising representatives of the MPLA, the FNLA, UNITA and the Portuguese Government. However, violent clashes between the MPLA and the FNLA occurred in March, as a result of the groups' political differences, and continued throughout the country. By the second half of 1975 control of Angola was effectively divided between the three major nationalist groups, each aided by foreign powers. The MPLA (which held the capital) was supported by the USSR and Cuba, the FNLA by Zaire and Western powers (including the USA), while UNITA was backed by South African forces. The FNLA and UNITA formed a united front to fight the MPLA.

The Portuguese Government proclaimed Angola independent from 11 November 1975, transferring sovereignty to 'the Angolan people' rather than to any of the liberation movements. The MPLA proclaimed the People's Republic of Angola and the establishment of a government in Luanda under the presidency of the movement's leader, Dr Agostinho Neto. The FNLA and UNITA proclaimed the People's Democratic Republic of Angola and a coalition government, based in Nova Lisboa (renamed Huambo). The involvement of South African and Cuban troops caused an international furore. By the end of February 1976, however, the MPLA, aided by Cuban technical and military expertise, had effectively gained control of the whole country. South African troops were withdrawn from Angola in March, but Cuban troops remained to assist the MPLA regime in countering guerrilla activity by the remnants of the defeated UNITA forces.

In May 1977 an abortive coup, led by Nito Alves (a former minister), resulted in a purge of state and party officials. In December the MPLA was restructured as a political party, the Movimento Popular de Libertação de Angola—Partido do Trabalho (MPLA—PT), but further divisions became evident in December 1978, when President Neto abolished the post of Prime Minister and ousted several other ministers.

Neto died in September 1979, and José Eduardo dos Santos, hitherto the Minister of Planning, was unanimously elected party leader and President by the MPLA—PT Central Committee. Dos Santos continued to encourage strong links with the Soviet bloc, and led campaigns to eliminate corruption and inefficiency. Elections to the National People's Assembly, which replaced the Council of the Revolution, were first held in 1980. Fresh elections, due to be held in 1983, were postponed until 1986, owing to political and military problems.

The MPLA—PT Government's recovery programme was continually hindered by security problems. Although the FNLA rebel movement reportedly surrendered to the Government in 1984, UNITA conducted sustained and disruptive guerrilla activities, mainly in southern and central Angola, throughout the 1980s. In addition, forces from South Africa, which was providing UNITA with considerable military aid, made numerous armed incursions over the Angolan border with Namibia, ostensibly in pursuit of guerrilla forces belonging to the South West Africa People's Organisation (SWAPO), which was supported by the Angolan Government. In July 1983 regional military councils were established in the provinces affected by the fighting. Although the Government's military campaign against UNITA appeared to be increasingly successful during 1985, the rebels' position was strengthened in April 1986, when US military aid began to arrive. (The US Government continued to provide covert military aid to UNITA until 1990.) Nevertheless, UNITA was excluded from a series of major peace negotiations, between Angola, Cuba and South Africa (with the unofficial mediation of the USA), which commenced in May 1988. By mid-July the participants had agreed to a document containing the principles for a peace settlement which provided for independence for Namibia, the discontinuation of South African military support for UNITA and the withdrawal of Cuban troops from Angola. In July and August Dr Jonas Savimbi, the President of UNITA, travelled to the USA and to several European and African capitals to seek support for UNITA's demands to be included in the negotiations. Although movement for a negotiated settlement between the MPLA—PT Government and UNITA then gathered momentum, UNITA's position became vulnerable in August, when a cease-fire between Angola and South Africa was declared and when South African troops were withdrawn from Angola. UNITA refused to adhere to the cease-fire. Following the conclusion of the New York accords on Angola and Namibia in December the US Government renewed its commitment to the rebels.

During late 1988 peace initiatives emerged from within Africa with regard to the Angolan civil war. Several African states (including Zaire) were involved in efforts, supported by the USA, to pressurize the Angolan Government into negotiating an internal settlement with UNITA. In December the UN Security Council established the UN Angola Verification Mission (UNAVEM), to verify the phased withdrawal of Cuban troops from Angola, which was completed in May 1991.

In February 1989 the Angolan Government offered a 12-month amnesty to members of the rebel organization; UNITA, restating its aim of entering into a transitional coalition government with the MPLA—PT as a prelude to multi-party elections, responded to the amnesty by launching a major offensive against Angolan government targets. This was abandoned shortly afterwards, following the intercession of President Houphouët-Boigny of Côte d'Ivoire. In March dos Santos announced that he was willing to attend a regional summit conference on the Angolan civil war; Savimbi, in turn, announced that he would honour a unilateral moratorium on offensive military operations until mid-July. In May eight African Heads of State attended a conference in Luanda, at which dos Santos presented a peace plan that envisaged the cessation of US aid to UNITA and offered the rebels reintegration into society; this was rejected by UNITA. Nevertheless, in June both dos Santos and Savimbi attended a conference at Gbadolite, in Zaire, convened by the Zairean President, Mobutu Sese Seko, at which 18 African Heads of State were present. Mobutu succeeded in mediating a peace agreement between the Angolan Government and UNITA, in accordance with which a cease-fire came into effect on 24 June. The full terms of the accord were not, however, made public at that time, and it subsequently became apparent that these were interpreted differently by each party. Within one week, each side had accused the other of violating the cease-fire, and in late August Savimbi announced a resumption of hostilities.

In September 1989, after boycotting a conference of eight African Heads of State in Kinshasa, Zaire, at which the June peace accord had been redrafted, Savimbi announced a series of counter-proposals, envisaging the creation of an African peace-keeping force, to supervise a renewed cease-fire, and the commencement of negotiations between UNITA and the Angolan Government towards a settlement providing the foundation of a multi-party democracy in Angola. In October, following a meeting with President Bush of the USA, Savimbi agreed to resume peace talks with the Angolan Government, with Mobutu acting as mediator. In December dos Santos proposed a peace plan that envisaged some political reform, but did not include provisions for a multi-party political system; the plan was rejected by UNITA.

In July 1990 the Central Committee of the MPLA—PT announced that the Government would allow Angola to 'evolve towards a multi-party system'. In October the Central Committee proposed a general programme of reform, including the replacement of the party's official Marxist-Leninist ideology with a commitment to 'democratic socialism', the legalization of political parties, the transformation of the army from a party institution to a state institution, the introduction of a market economy, a revision of the Constitution and the holding of multi-party elections in 1994, following a population census. These proposals were formally approved by the third Congress of the MPLA—PT in December. However, the Government and UNITA continued to disagree over the timing of elections and the status of UNITA pending the elections. UNITA insisted on immediate political recognition as a precondition for a cease-fire, and the holding of elections by the end of 1991.

In March 1991 the People's Assembly approved legislation permitting the formation of political parties. On 1 May, as a result of the series of talks that commenced in April 1990, the Government and UNITA concluded a peace agreement in Estoril, Portugal. The agreement provided for a cease-fire from 15 May, which was to be monitored by a joint political and military commission, comprising representatives from the MPLA—PT, UNITA, the UN, Portugal, the USA and the USSR. A new national army of 50,000 men was to be established, comprising equal numbers of government and UNITA soldiers. Free and democratic elections were to be held by the end of 1992. In early May 1991 the Government approved legislation allowing all exiles one year in which to return to Angola. The cease-fire took effect, according to plan, on 15 May, despite an intensification of hostilities prior to that date. On 31 May the Government and UNITA signed a formal agreement in Lisbon, Portugal, ratifying the Estoril agreement. Meanwhile, all Cuban troops had been withdrawn from Angola, but the UN Security Council agreed to prolong the presence of the UN Angola Verification Mission (as UNAVEM II), with a mandate to ensure implementation of the peace accords. In July the Standing Commission of the People's Assembly approved a new amnesty law, under the terms of which amnesty would be granted for all crimes against state security as well as for military and common law offences committed before 31 May 1991.

A reshuffle of the Council of Ministers in July 1991 included the appointment of Fernando José França van-Dúnem to the post of Prime Minister, thus reintroducing the premiership to the Government. Supreme executive power remained, however, with the President.

In September 1991 Savimbi returned to Luanda for the first time since the civil war began in 1975; UNITA headquarters were transferred to the capital from Jamba in October. In the following month dos Santos announced that legislative and presidential elections were to take place in September 1992, subject to the extension of state administration to areas still under UNITA control and the confinement of all UNITA forces to assembly points by mid-December 1991. In January 1992, on the recommendation of the joint political and military commission, a monitoring task group was established to oversee the implementation of the peace agreement. The creation of the group, which included members of the Government, UNITA and UNAVEM II, followed growing concern over the reported decline in the number of government and UNITA troops in confinement areas and the reoccupation of territory by UNITA forces.

Representatives of the Government and 26 political parties met in Luanda in January 1992 to discuss the transition to multi-party democracy. UNITA boycotted the meeting, but in February it held talks with the Government, at which it was agreed that the elections would be conducted on the basis of proportional representation, with the President elected for a five-year term, renewable for a maximum of three terms. The legislature would be a national assembly, elected for a four-year term. In April the People's Assembly adopted electoral legislation incorporating these decisions and providing for the creation of a national assembly of 223 members (90 to be elected in 18 provincial constituencies and the remainder from national lists).

In April 1992 the Supreme Court approved UNITA's registration as a political party. In May the MPLA—PT held an extraordinary congress to prepare for the forthcoming elections. The delegates voted to enlarge the membership of the Central Committee to allow the inclusion of prominent dissidents who had returned to the party. The Central Committee recommended that the Political Bureau further expand its membership with a view to broadening the base of the party's support. During the congress the delegates also voted to remove the suffix Partido do Trabalho (Party of Labour or Workers' Party) from the organization's official name. In August the legislature approved a further revision of the Constitution, removing the remnants of the country's former Marxist ideology, and deleting the words 'People's' and 'Popular' from the Constitution and from the names of official institutions. The name of the country was changed from the People's Republic of Angola to the Republic of Angola.

Increased tension and outbreaks of violence in the period preceding the general election, which was due to be held on 29 and 30 September 1992, seriously threatened to disrupt the electoral process. In early September secessionist groups in Cabinda province, the enclave which provides most of Angola's petroleum revenue, intensified attacks on government troops. Following an offensive by guerrilla forces of the Frente de Libertação do Enclave de Cabinda (FLEC), government troops effectively lost control of Cabinda City for several days. In the same month, clashes between UNITA and government forces in Bié province resulted in the seizure of Kuito airport by UNITA.

On 27 September 1992 the government Forças Armadas Populares de Libertação de Angola (FAPLA) and the UNITA forces were formally disbanded, and the new national army, the Forças Armadas de Angola (FAA), was officially established. However, the process of training and incorporating FAPLA and UNITA troops into the new 50,000-strong national army had been hindered by delays in the demobilization programme. By 28 September fewer than 10,000 soldiers were ready to be sworn in as members of the FAA. Tens of thousands of government troops were reported to be awaiting demobilization or to have abandoned confinement areas, owing to poor conditions and non-payment of wages. Military observers reported that only a small percentage of UNITA soldiers had been demobilized, and that UNITA retained a heavily armed and disciplined force.

Presidential and legislative elections were held, as scheduled, on 29 and 30 September 1992. When preliminary results indicated victory in the elections to the new National Assembly for the MPLA, Savimbi accused the Government of electoral fraud, withdrew his troops from the FAA, and demanded the suspension of the official announcement of the election results until an inquiry into the alleged electoral irregularities had been conducted. According to the provisions of the electoral law, a second round of the presidential election was required to be held between dos Santos and Savimbi, as neither candidate had secured 50% of the votes cast in the first round. Savimbi, who had retreated to the UNITA-dominated province of Huambo, agreed to participate in this second round on the condition that it be conducted by the UN, while the Government insisted that the election should not take place until UNITA had satisfied the conditions of the Estoril peace agreement by transferring its troops to assembly points or to the FAA.

Following the announcement, on 17 October 1992, of the official results of the elections, which the UN had declared to have been free and fair, violence broke out between MPLA and UNITA supporters in the cities of Luanda and Huambo. By the end of October hostilities had spread throughout Angola, with the majority of UNITA's demobilized soldiers returning to arms. On 20 November, following negotiations with UN diplomats,

Savimbi issued a statement in which he agreed to abide by the results of the September elections, although he maintained that the ballot had been fraudulent. Subsequently dos Santos announced that the new National Assembly, which was to be formed in accordance with the results of the September elections, would be inaugurated on 26 November. On that day delegations from the Government and UNITA met in Namibe in an effort to resolve the crisis. A joint communiqué was issued, declaring full acceptance of the validity of the May 1991 Estoril peace agreement and the intention to implement immediately a nation-wide cease-fire. However, UNITA's 70 elected deputies failed to attend the inauguration of the National Assembly. On 27 November dos Santos announced the appointment of Marcolino José Carlos Moco, the Secretary-General of the MPLA, as Prime Minister. At the end of November, in violation of the recently-signed Namibe accord, hostilities broke out in the north of the country. On 2 December a new Council of Ministers was announced, including minor ministerial positions for members of the FNLA, the Fórum Democrático Angolano, the Partido Renovador Social and the Partido de Aliança de Juventude, Operários e Camponêses de Angola. In addition, one full and four deputy ministerial posts were reserved for UNITA, which was allowed a week to join the Government. UNITA subsequently issued a statement nominating a number of its officials to the reserved posts. According to a statement by the Prime Minister, however, the appointment of UNITA officials to the Government was entirely dependent upon the implementation of the Estoril peace agreement.

In December 1992 government forces launched a major nation-wide offensive against UNITA, in an effort to regain territory lost to the rebels in the wake of the September elections, when UNITA assumed control of some 65% of the country. By mid-January 1993 UNITA forces had been ousted from most major towns, but had captured the petroleum-producing centre of Soyo, on the Zaire border (the occupation of which was estimated to cost the Government some US $2m. per day in lost revenue). In late January peace talks between UNITA and the Government, convened by the UN, were conducted in Addis Ababa, Ethiopia, with Portugal, Russia and the USA attending as observers. Following two months of intense fighting for control of the country's second largest city, Huambo (a traditional UNITA stronghold), the Government confirmed in early March that it had withdrawn its forces. Some 10,000 people were thought to have died in the conflict. On 12 March the UN Security Council adopted a resolution condemning UNITA's violations of the peace accords. Peace talks, which resumed in Abidjan, Côte d'Ivoire, in mid-April, were frustrated by UNITA's insistence that a UN peace-keeping force be deployed prior to the negotiation of a formal cease-fire. The talks were finally suspended indefinitely on 21 May. On 19 May, prompted by UNITA's intransigence and apparent lack of commitment to peace, the US President, Bill Clinton, had announced that the USA was to recognize the Angolan Government. In mid-July the UN Security Council reiterated demands that UNITA cease military activity and abide by the results of the September 1992 elections, warning that an embargo would be enforced against UNITA unless an effective cease-fire had been established by 15 September. In early August the FAA launched a major bombing campaign against Huambo. In response, UNITA intensified its attacks on the besieged government garrison in the central city of Kuito. On 14 September UNITA announced that it would implement a unilateral cease-fire, to begin on 20 September, thus prompting the UN Security Council to delay its deadline for imposing an embargo against UNITA until 25 September. However, despite UNITA's claims that it was observing the cease-fire, diplomatic sources reported an intensification of UNITA activity beyond the UN deadline. Consequently, on 26 September the UN imposed an arms and petroleum embargo against UNITA. Observers calculated, however, that clandestine supplies of arms and petroleum from Zaire, in addition to UNITA's existing arms stockpiles, would ensure that the rebels' military capacity could be sustained for some years, despite the embargo. Further UN sanctions, including the expulsion of UNITA representatives from foreign capitals and the freezing of the rebels' assets abroad, were to be imposed on 1 November if UNITA should fail to cease hostilities. In late October exploratory peace talks began in Lusaka, Zambia, between the UN, the official observer nations, and representatives of the Government and UNITA. On 1 November the UN Secretary-General's special representative, Alioune Blondin Beye, informed the UN Security Council that UNITA had agreed to withdraw its forces to UN-monitored confinement areas. In response, the UN agreed to delay the imposition of further sanctions against UNITA until 15 December, on condition that the rebels comply with their undertakings.

Direct talks between UNITA and the Government, which had been adjourned in May, resumed in Lusaka in November 1993. By 10 December agreement had reportedly been reached on issues concerning the demobilization and confinement of UNITA troops, the surrender of UNITA weapons to the UN, and the integration of UNITA generals into the FAA. On 15 December the UN Security Council extended the mandate of UNAVEM II for a further three months and agreed to another postponement of additional sanctions against UNITA. The Lusaka talks resumed in January 1994, and that month an agreement was announced on the formation of a national police force of 26,700 members, of which UNITA was to provide 5,500, to be formed under UN supervision. Further talks culminated in the signing, on 17 February, of a document on national reconciliation incorporating five fundamental principles. Acceptance of the September 1992 election results by both sides was also reaffirmed. On 16 March 1994 the UN Security Council extended the mandate of UNAVEM II until 31 May. Progress at the Lusaka peace talks slowed as discussions moved on to the issue of the participation of UNITA in central and local government. Negotiations on the distribution of ministerial posts appeared to have reached an impasse in mid-March, and Beye announced at the end of March that negotiations would instead move on to discuss the conclusion of the electoral process: the second round of presidential elections between dos Santos and Savimbi. In early May agreement was officially confirmed regarding these elections, although some related issues remained to be discussed, including the role of the independent observers. Further talks, concerning the issues of UNITA's representation in the Council of Ministers and the status of Savimbi, reached an impasse in May. The talks took place against a background of intensified hostilities, particularly in Kuito and Malanje. On 31 May the UN Security Council extended the mandate of UNAVEM II until 30 June, when it was to reconsider the role of the UN if a peace accord had not been reached. In mid-June agreement was reached on the extension of state administration throughout the entire national territory. Talks continued in Lusaka in late June, culminating in the signing of an 18-point document on national reconciliation. At the same time, government forces were reported to have gained complete control of Kuito, ending an 18-month siege of the city by UNITA forces.

In early July 1994 President Mandela of South Africa hosted talks in Pretoria between the Presidents of Angola, Mozambique and Zaire. The discussions concentrated on allegations of Zairean support for UNITA and resulted in the re-establishment of a joint defence and security commission between Angola and Zaire, with the aim of curbing the supply of armaments to the rebels. In early August UNITA acceded to government insistence that its officials be permitted to participate in government institutions only after the total demilitarization of the movement. An 11-point procedural accord, enabling discussions on full reconciliation, was signed on 9 August. In mid-August UNITA officially acknowledged that it had lost control of the diamond-mining centre of Kafunfo (in the north-east of the country), an important source of funds for UNITA. Government troops were also reported to have taken control of the strategic diamond-producing town of Catoca, close to the border with Zaire, in a campaign to drive UNITA out of Lunda-Norte province.

Throughout July and August 1994 the question of the governorship of Huambo continued to constitute the main obstacle to the furtherance of the peace talks. On 8 September UNITA reportedly accepted a proposal by mediators for the allocation to UNITA of government positions that included some 170 posts in central and local administration but excluded the governorship of Huambo. On 9 September the UN Security Council announced that additional sanctions would not be imposed on UNITA. In mid-September the Government and UNITA agreed on the general principles governing the mandate of a new UN Angola Verification Mission—UNAVEM III. At the end of that month, following successive extensions since July, the UN Security Council further extended the mandate of UNAVEM II until 31 October and urged both sides to sign a peace accord by 15 October. However, talks continued throughout October, concentrating on the replacement of the joint political and

military commission with a new joint commission—to be chaired by Beye and comprise representatives of the Government and UNITA and observers from the USA, Russia and Portugal—and the issue of Savimbi's security. A peace accord was finally initialled on 31 October, and dos Santos and Savimbi were to sign it on 15 November in Lusaka. However, an intensified military campaign by the Government, which resulted in the seizure in early November of Soyo and the UNITA stronghold of Huambo, threatened to jeopardize the peace accord, and UNITA indicated that it was no longer disposed to sign the treaty. On 15 November, following mediation by President Mandela, government and UNITA generals signed a truce in Lusaka, which was to remain in force until 22 November, when a permanent cease-fire was to come into force. The formal signing of the peace accord was postponed until 20 November, to allow outstanding issues to be discussed. Despite the absence of Savimbi, the formal signing of the Lusaka peace accord took place on the designated date. However, hostilities continued beyond 22 November, notably in Huambo and in Bié province, and each side accused the other of violations of the permanent cease-fire.

In December 1994 the UN Security Council extended the mandate of UNAVEM II until 8 February 1995, when it was to be superseded by UNAVEM III, on condition that the cease-fire was observed. In January 1995, in the light of continuing fighting, a meeting took place at Chipipa, in Huambo province, between the Chief of General Staff of the FAA and his UNITA counterpart, at which agreement was reached on an immediate cessation of hostilities nation-wide. Despite this undertaking, however, the fighting continued.

In early February 1995 the UN Security Council adopted a resolution creating UNAVEM III. However, the deployment of the new peace-keeping mission remained conditional on the cessation of hostilities and the disengagement of government and UNITA forces. Also in February the UN conducted an appeal for humanitarian aid in excess of US $200m. to provide emergency assistance for more than 3m. people, to support the demobilization and reintegration of former combatants, and to finance a programme to clear the country of an estimated 10m. land-mines.

In March 1995 both the Government and UNITA came under criticism in a report made to the UN Security Council by the UN Secretary-General, Dr Boutros Boutros-Ghali, who accused the two sides of a lack of goodwill in implementing the peace process, and reiterated the conditions for the deployment of UNAVEM III, which required strict observance of the cease-fire. The report, which followed continued and widespread violations of the truce, set a deadline of 25 March for the two sides to demonstrate a genuine commitment to the peace process. It also appealed for preparations to be expedited to enable the prompt transfer of UNITA troops into the FAA. On 28 March, following a meeting of the joint commission, Beye announced that the initial stage of troop disengagement had been completed, allowing arrangements to proceed for the deployment of UNAVEM III. In the following month Beye confirmed that the majority of UNAVEM III personnel would begin arriving in early May. In late April the joint commission reported a significant reduction in violations of the cease-fire and a concomitant increase in the free movement of people and goods. However, at the same time Boutros-Ghali indicated that the fragility of the cease-fire and reports of military preparations, including the acquisition of arms from abroad, remained serious causes of concern.

In early May 1995, in what represented an important development in the peace process, dos Santos and Savimbi met in Lusaka for direct talks. The meeting, which had been achieved as the result of mediation by Beye, concluded with the ratification of the Lusaka peace accord. Notably, Savimbi recognized the status of dos Santos as President of Angola, addressing him as such, and pledged his full co-operation in the reconstruction of the nation. The two leaders agreed to accelerate the consolidation of the cease-fire, to create conditions for the deployment of UNAVEM III, to expedite the integration of UNITA troops into the FAA, and to establish a government of unity based on the provisions of the Lusaka accord (subsequent to the demobilization of the UNITA forces). Dos Santos requested that Savimbi nominate immediately the UNITA appointees to the new government.

In June 1995 the MPLA announced its decision to propose a revision of the Constitution to create two new posts of Vice-President, of which one was to be offered to Savimbi, conditional upon the prior disbanding of UNITA forces. The other vice-presidency was to be assumed by the then President of the National Assembly, Fernando José França van-Dúnem. Later that month Savimbi, who had publicly expressed his intention to accept the vice-presidency, declared the war in Angola to be at an end and appealed to neighbouring nations to prevent the traffic of arms to the country. In July the National Assembly approved the proposed constitutional amendment to create the two new vice-presidential positions, and Boutros-Ghali announced that the deployment of UNAVEM III personnel, which had fallen seriously behind schedule, would be completed by the end of August. In late July, at ongoing discussions between delegations of the Government and UNITA concerning the implementation of military aspects of the Lusaka accord, it was agreed that the FAA should be enlarged to 90,000 troops.

Direct talks between dos Santos and Savimbi resumed in August 1995 in Franceville, Gabon. At the meeting Savimbi agreed in principle to accept the vice-presidency but requested that the offer be formally extended to UNITA. The Government duly complied. Earlier in August the UN Security Council had extended the mandate of UNAVEM III until February 1996. In September 1995 the joint commission expressed concern at continuing violations of the cease-fire. However, in the following month, figures issued by UNAVEM III revealed that recorded cease-fire violations had decreased by approximately 50% between July and September. In late September the Government signed a four-month cease-fire agreement with FLEC—Renovada, a faction of FLEC, the secessionist group in Cabinda province. It was anticipated that the agreement, which followed an offensive by FLEC—Renovada on Cabinda City in the previous month, would facilitate the negotiation, between the Government and all factions of FLEC, of a pact aimed at national reconciliation.

In late September 1995 dos Santos and Savimbi met for direct talks in Brussels, Belgium, immediately prior to the convention there of an international donors' conference on Angola. At the conference donors pledged a total of US $997.5m. towards Angola's national rehabilitation and reconciliation programme, of which $200m. was to be allocated to emergency humanitarian assistance. The cantonment of UNITA forces began officially in late November. However, continued hostilities were reported that month, including confrontations in the diamond-producing areas of the north-east and in the Cabinda enclave. In early December, following concerted military operations by government forces aimed at occupying UNITA-controlled territory in Zaire province, UNITA suspended the confinement of its troops. In the light of this set-back, and in an effort to promote confidence in the peace process in advance of discussions to be conducted that month with US President Clinton, dos Santos promptly introduced a number of conciliatory measures, including the withdrawal of government troops from positions seized in Zaire province, and the confinement, which began the following month, of the paramilitary Rapid Intervention Force. In January 1996 UNITA resumed the process of confining its troops. By early February, however, UNITA had succeeded in confining only some 8,200 troops, prompting the UN Security Council to renew the mandate of UNAVEM III for a reduced term of only three months. In late January, following discussions conducted in Brazzaville, the Congo, the Government and FLEC–Renovada agreed to extend the cease-fire accord secured in September 1995. Discussions were to continue in pursuit of a definitive cease-fire agreement.

In March 1996 discussions between dos Santos and Savimbi, conducted in Libreville, Gabon, resulted in agreement on the establishment of a government of national unity, in accordance with the provisions of the Lusaka accord, by the end of July. Savimbi presented dos Santos with a proposal listing the UNITA nominees who would participate in such a government, while dos Santos in turn presented Savimbi with a formal invitation to assume the vice-presidency. (Later that month, however, Savimbi demanded the inclusion of other opposition parties in the government of national unity, presenting as a condition to his own participation the inclusion in the new administration of the President of the FNLA, Holden Roberto.) Agreement was also reached in Libreville on the formation of the unified national army, which, it was envisaged, would be concluded in June. In subsequent talks conducted in March between representatives of the Government and UNITA it was agreed that 18 UNITA generals would be appointed to command posts in the new unified FAA. It was also established that 26,300 of UNITA's total force of some 62,000 would be integrated into the FAA. In late March the Government began the phased withdrawal to barracks of its troops.

On 8 May 1996, in the light of further delays in the peace process, the UN Security Council extended the mandate of UNAVEM III by just two months. That month the National Assembly approved an amnesty law pardoning all crimes against internal state security committed since the signing of the Estoril peace agreement. In late May, following negotiations between the Government and UNITA, agreement was reached on a programme to integrate UNITA troops into the FAA. Selection of UNITA personnel was to begin on 1 June. During May Savimbi introduced further conditions for his acceptance of the vice-presidency and expressed his intention to retain control of diamond-producing areas in north-eastern Angola. In mid-May the Government and a Cabinda secessionist faction, FLEC—Forças Armadas Cabindesas (FLEC—FAC), signed an agreement outlining the principles of a cease-fire. However, following renewed fighting later that month between government troops and the secessionists, the leader of FLEC—FAC, Henrique N'zita Tiago, declared that a definitive cease-fire would only follow the withdrawal of the FAA from Cabinda.

In mid-1996 public protest at deteriorating economic conditions and the high level of corruption within the state apparatus placed increasing political pressure on dos Santos, who responded in early June with the dismissal of the Moco administration. Moco was succeeded as Prime Minister by the President of the National Assembly (and former Prime Minister), Fernando José França van-Dúnem. A new Government was sworn in on 8 June, with only limited changes to the previous administration.

On 11 July 1996 the UN Security Council extended the mandate of UNAVEM III by a further three months. In mid-August the Government approved the disbursement of US $65m. to finance the reintegration of as many as 100,000 government and UNITA soldiers into civilian society. A further $66m. was required from international donors to complete the programme. In late August, following its party congress, UNITA issued a communiqué declining the appointment of Savimbi to the position of national Vice-President. UNITA did not propose the appointment of another of its officials to the post, and in September Beye confirmed that the offer of the vice-presidency had become void.

In October 1996 delays in the implementation of the provisions of the Lusaka accord prompted the UN Security Council to threaten the imposition of sanctions against UNITA unless it met certain requirements by 20 November, including the surrender of weapons and the designation of those UNITA troops to be integrated into the FAA. In the following month the National Assembly adopted a constitutional revision extending its mandate, which was due to expire that month, for a period of between two and four years, pending the establishment of suitable conditions for the conduct of free and fair elections. On 11 December the UN Security Council extended the mandate of UNAVEM III until 28 February 1997, when the peace-keeping force was due to complete its mandate and begin withdrawing from Angola. Despite assertions by UNITA that it had fully disarmed in accordance with the terms of the Lusaka accord, UNAVEM III expressed concern in December 1996 that some 15,705 UNITA troops had deserted confinement areas. At the same time UN sources reported the existence of a residual UNITA force of some 15,000 well-armed troops in central and north-eastern Angola. Despite these apparent obstacles to the further implementation of the peace accord, the Government announced in the same month that the UNITA deputies who had been elected in 1992 would join the National Assembly in mid-January 1997, and that the new government of national unity and reconciliation would be inaugurated on 25 January. However, following the failure of the UNITA deputies to join the National Assembly, the Government postponed the inauguration of the new administration. In February UNITA asserted that it would only send its deputies and government nominees to the capital if the Government first agreed to negotiate a draft programme for the government of national unity and reconciliation. In mid-March the Government conceded to UNITA's demand and agreement was reached later that month on a basic programme. In the light of Savimbi's rejection of the vice-presidency, discussions concerning the special status to be conferred on him resulted, in early April, in an agreement according the UNITA leader the official title of 'leader of the opposition'. Subsequent to the arrival of the full contingent of UNITA deputies and government nominees in Luanda, on 11 April the new Government of National Unity and Reconciliation was inaugurated, although the ceremony was not attended by Savimbi who maintained that his personal security could not be guaranteed. As envisaged, UNITA assumed the ministerial portfolios of geology and mines, trade, health, and hotels and tourism, and a further seven deputy ministerial posts. Ten minor political parties were also represented in the 87-member Government.

In May 1997 the Angolan Government officially recognized the new Government of Laurent-Désiré Kabila in the Democratic Republic of the Congo (DRC, formerly Zaire). The Angolan Government had actively supported Kabila's rebels during the civil war in Zaire, while UNITA, which relied on Zaire as a conduit for exporting diamonds and importing arms, had reportedly sent some 2,000 troops to support President Mobutu. In the light of the defeat of UNITA's main ally, the Government subsequently launched a military offensive on UNITA strongholds in the north-eastern provinces of Lunda-Sul and Lunda-Norte in what appeared to be an attempt to eradicate UNITA as a military force.

On 30 June 1997 the UN Security Council unanimously approved the UN Secretary-General's recommendations that UNAVEM III be discontinued and replaced by a scaled-down observer mission, the United Nations Observer Mission in Angola (MONUA), with a seven-month mandate to oversee the implementation of the remaining provisions of the Lusaka accord, including the reinstatement of state administration throughout the country. MONUA began operating on 1 July. The remaining UNAVEM III personnel were to be withdrawn gradually. In late July the UN again condemned UNITA's failure to adhere to the Lusaka accord and threatened to impose further sanctions on the movement, including travel restrictions, if it did not take irreversible steps towards fulfilling its obligations. A deadline of 15 August was set by which date UNITA was to give a full account of its military strength and to allow for the disarmament of its troops and the extension of state administration into those areas under its control. According to government estimates, UNITA forces numbered some 25,000–35,000, whereas UNITA claimed to retain a force of only 2,963 'police'. By 15 August UNITA had failed to meet the requirements stipulated by the UN, which on 28 August unanimously adopted new sanctions. However, the implementation of the resolution was delayed until 30 September, allowing UNITA a further opportunity to resume the peace process. In addition, the withdrawal of some 2,650 UN military personnel was postponed until the end of October. At the end of August UNITA announced that it intended to comply with the demands of the UN in order to avoid the imposition of new sanctions.

In September 1997 the restoration of state administration proceeded in several districts, and, despite unsatisfactory progress in the demobilization of UNITA's residual force, was sufficient to prompt the UN Security Council, at the end of that month, to postpone the implementation of the sanctions for a further 30 days. In early October UNITA ceded control of one of the country's principal diamond mines, at Luzamba in Lunda-Norte, to the Government.

In July 1997 government delegations from Angola and the Republic of the Congo met in Cabinda to discuss the security situation along the border between the Angolan exclave and the Congo, in the light of armed clashes between Angolan soldiers and FLEC separatists apparently operating from Congolese territory. The talks resulted in proposals to strengthen border security, including the establishment of a joint police force, comprising representatives from both countries and UNHCR. However, in October it became evident that FAA troops were actively supporting the former Marxist ruler of the Congo, Gen. Denis Sassou-Nguesso, in his attempts to overthrow the Government of President Pascal Lissouba. Angola's involvement had been prompted by attacks on Cabinda by FLEC and UNITA forces operating from bases in the Congo provided by Lissouba. In mid-October Sassou-Nguesso's Cobra militia, with Angolan assistance, succeeded in securing his return to power in the Congo.

On 31 October 1997, as a result of UNITA's continued failure to meet its obligations under the peace process, the UN Security Council finally ordered the implementation of additional sanctions against the movement, including a ban on international travel for UNITA officials and the closure of UNITA offices abroad. In late November UNITA expressed its intention to continue to pursue a peaceful settlement, and during the ensuing months ceded further territory to state administration, including the important Cuango valley diamond mines in Lunda-Norte province.

In January 1998 a new schedule was agreed for the implementation of the Lusaka protocol, which stipulated a deadline of 28 February for its terms to be met. This schedule was subsequently revised, allowing UNITA until 16 March to complete its demobilization. In early March UNITA issued a declaration announcing the disbandment of its remaining forces, following which it received official recognition as a legally constituted party. Later that month the Government implemented the special status agreed for Savimbi, and legislation was adopted allowing him to retain a 400-strong personal guard. However, despite these developments, allegations persisted of preparations by UNITA for a resumption of hostilities. During May there were reports of escalating conflict in Lunda-Norte and Benguela provinces. By June fighting had spread to 14 of the country's 18 provinces resulting in the displacement of some 150,000 people. In a further reversal to the peace process, that month the UN Secretary-General's special representative, Alioune Blondin Beye, was killed in an air crash near Abidjan, Côte d'Ivoire. In July many members of UNITA were reported to have left Luanda and a meeting of the joint commission had to be postponed owing to the absence of UNITA's chief representative, Isaias Samakuva. Later that month the Southern African Development Community (SADC) issued a communiqué urging UNITA to resume negotiations with the Government. In early August Samakuva returned to Luanda and Issa Diallo was appointed by the UN Secretary-General to replace Beye. In mid-August the Government threatened to suspend UNITA's representatives in the Government and the legislature unless it had disarmed fully and ceded all remaining territory under its control by 28 August. In late August UNITA accused the observer countries in the joint commission (Portugal, Russia and the USA) of bias in the Government's favour and declared that it would no longer negotiate with them. On 31 August the Government suspended UNITA's government and parliamentary representatives from office.

On 2 September 1998 a group of five UNITA moderates, who were based in the capital and led by the suspended Minister of Hotels and Tourism, Jorge Alicerces Valentim, issued a manifesto declaring the suspension of Savimbi and the introduction of an interim UNITA leadership pending a general congress of the party. However, the group, which styled itself UNITA Renovada, commanded very limited support among UNITA's leaders in Luanda, while UNITA's Secretary-General dismissed the group as irrelevant. Conversely, the Government welcomed the development. In mid-September dos Santos announced that his Government had ceased dialogue with Savimbi and recognized UNITA Renovada as the sole and legitimate representative of UNITA in negotiations concerning the implementation of the Lusaka peace process. Dos Santos was supported in this decision by the SADC, which passed a resolution denouncing Savimbi and recognizing the new group. However, while UNITA Renovada pledged to implement the Lusaka peace accord, observers questioned its ability to influence UNITA members outside of the capital. The UN Security Council continued to seek a dialogue between dos Santos and Savimbi as the only solution to the conflict. In late September the Government revoked the suspension of UNITA's representatives in the Government and legislature, but dismissed UNITA's Minister of Geology and Mines, Marcos Samondo. In mid-October, following successive extensions, MONUA's mandate was further extended to 3 December.

In October 1998 the National Assembly revoked Savimbi's special status. In that month UNITA Renovada failed to impose its candidate to lead the UNITA parliamentary group when Abel Chivukuvuku was overwhelmingly re-elected as its Chairman. Chivukuvuku, who, while no longer claiming allegiance to Savimbi, was opposed to UNITA Renovada, subsequently announced the formation of his own wing of UNITA.

In November 1998, following increasingly frequent outbreaks of fighting in a number of regions, the UN Security Council demanded that UNITA withdraw immediately from territories that it had reoccupied through military action and complete the demilitarization of its troops. At the fourth congress of the MPLA, conducted in December, dos Santos asserted that military action was the only way to subdue UNITA and bring peace to Angola. João Manuel Gonçalves Lourenço was elected Secretary-General of the MPLA while dos Santos was re-elected unopposed as party President.

In December 1998 the military situation deteriorated considerably prompting the Government to approve the introduction of compulsory military service. According to observers, the scale and force of UNITA's operations indicated that the rebels had assembled massive supplies of military equipment. In a report made to the UN Security Council that month the UN Secretary-General, Kofi Annan, declared that Angola was once again at war and questioned whether the UN still had a role to play in the country. The UN also warned of a major humanitarian crisis in the country where more than 400,000 people were reported to have abandoned their homes to escape the fighting. However, in late December the UN World Food Programme was forced to suspend its flights in Angola following the shooting down by UNITA of a UN aircraft ealier in that month. In January 1999 a further UN aircraft was shot down by the rebels.

In late January 1999 dos Santos reorganized the Council of Ministers in an effort to address the prevailing military and economic crisis. Notably, the premiership was assumed by dos Santos himself. In that month UNITA Renovada conducted its first congress in Luanda, at which Euginio Manuvakola was elected leader of the breakaway faction. In a report to the UN Security Council issued in mid-January, Annan recommended the withdrawal of MONUA from Angola, declaring that, despite expenditure of US $1,500m. over the previous four years, conditions had deteriorated to such an extent that UN personnel were no longer able to function. Both the Government and UNITA had indicated that they favoured the withdrawal of the UN; dos Santos openly criticized the UN for having lost control of the peace process. In February the UN Security Council voted unanimously to end MONUA's mandate and withdraw its operatives by 20 March, although the UN expressed its intention to seek the Government's approval to maintain a presence in the country in the form of a 'follow-up' mission, intended to focus on issues concerning humanitarian assistance and human rights.

In the wake of the renewed hostilities, some 780,000 people were reported to have fled to government-occupied towns by late April 1999. The cities of Huambo, Kuito and Malanje were under siege by UNITA forces, and, with access to the cities impeded and food stocks declining, a major humanitarian crisis was developing. Some 10,000 people, including 4,000 civilians, were estimated to have died in the renewed fighting in the four months since the resumption of the war. In May the Government rejected an offer made by Savimbi for peace talks and announced that the FAA was preparing to mount a renewed offensive against the UNITA strongholds of Andulo and Bailundo. In June the Government agreed in principle to the presence of a small 'follow-up' mission of UN observers in Angola. (In October it was agreed that the mission would comprise some 30 UN officials.)

In October 1999, following a large-scale offensive by the FAA in northern, eastern and central Angola, the Government claimed to have made considerable gains, including, most notably, the capture of UNITA's headquarters in Andulo and Bailundo. While UNITA denied that the towns had fallen to the Government, there were reports that Savimbi had fled the area. In a letter to the Government received in late October, Savimbi warned that UNITA troops were approaching the capital and called for dialogue towards a 'national pact'. The Government, however, dismissed the possibility of further talks, demanding instead the full implementation of the Lusaka protocol. Also that month four UNITA members of the legislature, who had been detained by the security forces in January and charged with committing crimes against the security of the state, were released by order of the Supreme Court owing to insufficient evidence. The arrests had occurred following the refusal of the four deputies to join UNITA Renovada. In September a UNITA parliamentarian was found shot dead on the outskirts of Luanda.

During 1999 the UN increased its efforts to impose sanctions on UNITA, with the appointment of Canada's ambassador to the UN, Robert Fowler, as Chairman of the UN Sanctions Committee. Fowler toured southern Africa in May investigating the contravention of UN sanctions. In July the UN allocated US $1m. for a six-month investigation into UNITA's funding of its war effort, the source of its armaments and the inefficacy of the sanctions imposed against it. In October, following discussions with Fowler, the South African diamond company De Beers, which controls the majority of the international trade in diamonds, announced that it had placed a worldwide embargo on the purchase of all diamonds from Angola, except those whose acquisition was already under contract.

Following the internal uprising in August 1998 against the Kabila regime in the DRC, the Angolan Government moved swiftly to provide Kabila with military support against the rebels. In September the number of FAA troops in the DRC was estimated at 5,000. In October, as the conflict escalated in the east of the DRC, Angola, in alliance with Namibia and Zimbabwe, announced its intention to continue supporting Kabila until the rebels were defeated.

Relations with Zambia became tense during 1999 following persistent allegations that it was actively supporting UNITA and allowing its territory to be used as a transit point for the provision of arms and supplies to the rebels. It was further alleged that senior ministers in the Zambian Government had been personally involved in contravening sanctions. It was claimed that several explosions in the Zambian capital, Lusaka, in late February, including one at the Angolan embassy, were linked to this tension, and an Angolan national was arrested in connection with the incidents. In June, following co-operation talks between the respective governments, an agreement was signed putting aside past disputes.

In July 1996 Angola was among the five lusophone African countries which, together with Portugal and Brazil, formed the Comunidade dos Países de Língua Portuguesa (CPLP, see p. 300), a Portuguese-speaking commonwealth seeking to achieve collective benefits from co-operation in technical, cultural and social matters.

## Government

In March 1991 and in the first half of 1992 the Government of the Movimento Popular de Libertação de Angola—Partido do Trabalho (MPLA—PT) introduced a series of far-reaching amendments to the 1975 Constitution, providing for the establishment of a multi-party democracy (hitherto, no other political parties, apart from the ruling MPLA—PT, had been permitted). According to the amendments, legislative power was to be vested in the National Assembly, with 223 members elected for four years on the basis of proportional representation. Executive power was to be held by the President, who was to be directly elected for a term of five years (renewable for a maximum of three terms). As Head of State and Commander-in-Chief of the armed forces, the President was to govern with the assistance of an appointed Council of Ministers.

For the purposes of local government, the country is divided into 18 provinces, each administered by an appointed Governor.

Legislative elections, held in September 1992, resulted in victory for the MPLA. However, in the presidential election, which was held at the same time, the MPLA's candidate and incumbent President, José Eduardo dos Santos, narrowly failed to secure the 50% of the votes necessary to be elected President. Following a resumption of hostilities between UNITA and government forces, the conduct of a second round of presidential elections was held in abeyance, with dos Santos remaining in the presidency. The inauguration of the National Assembly took place, in the absence of UNITA's 70 elected delegates, in late November 1992. In accordance with the terms of the Lusaka peace accord of November 1994, in April 1997 a new Government of National Unity and Reconciliation was inaugurated in which UNITA held four portfolios. The second round of presidential elections having been abandoned, Savimbi was accorded the official title of 'leader of the opposition'. Meanwhile, in November 1996 the National Assembly had adopted a constitutional revision extending the parliamentary mandate, which was due to expire that month, for a period of between two and four years in order to allow for the establishment of suitable conditions for the conduct of elections. In November 1998 Savimbi's 'special status' as 'leader of the opposition' was revoked.

## Defence

In December 1990 the governing party, the Movimento Popular de Libertação de Angola—Partido do Trabalho (MPLA—PT), agreed to terminate the party's direct link with the armed forces. In accordance with the peace agreement concluded by the Government and the União Nacional para a Independência Total de Angola (UNITA) in May 1991 (see Recent History), a new 50,000-strong national army, the Forças Armadas de Angola (FAA), was to be established, comprising equal numbers of government forces, the Forças Armadas Populares de Libertação de Angola (FAPLA), and UNITA soldiers. The formation of the FAA was to coincide with the holding of a general election in late September 1992. Pending the general election, a cease-fire between FAPLA and UNITA forces, which commenced in mid-May 1991, was monitored by a joint political and military commission, comprising representatives of the MPLA—PT, UNITA, the UN, Portugal, the USA and the USSR. This commission was to oversee the withdrawal of FAPLA and UNITA forces to specific confinement areas, to await demobilization. Although not all troops had entered the confinement areas, demobilization began in late March 1992. Military advisers from Portugal, France and the United Kingdom were to assist with the formation of the new national army. However, the demobilization process and the formation of the FAA fell behind schedule and were only partially completed by the end of September and the holding of the general election. Following the election, UNITA withdrew its troops from the FAA, alleging electoral fraud on the part of the MPLA, and hostilities resumed. Following the signing of the Lusaka peace accord in November 1994, preparations for the confinement and demobilization of troops, and the integration of the UNITA contingent into the FAA, resumed. In mid-1995 agreement was reached between the Government and UNITA on the enlargement of the FAA to comprise a total of 90,000 troops, and discussions began concerning the potential formation of a fourth, non-combatant branch of the FAA, which would engage in public works projects. The internment of UNITA forces began in November 1995. In March 1996 agreement was reached that the unified FAA would include 26,300 UNITA troops. The process of selecting UNITA troops for integration into the FAA began in June. In December the UN Angola Verification Mission (UNAVEM III) expressed concern that, of a total of 70,336 UNITA troops registered at confinement areas, some 15,705 had deserted. At that time UN sources reported the existence of a residual UNITA force estimated at 15,000 well-armed troops operating in central and north-eastern Angola. In mid-1997 the Government estimated that UNITA's residual force numbered some 25,000–30,000 troops, while UNITA claimed to have retained a force of only 2,963 'police'. In March 1998 UNITA issued a declaration announcing the complete demobilization of its forces. However, military sources believed that, despite this declaration, UNITA retained a force of some 15,000 troops and substantial quantities of heavy weaponry. Evidence of the existence of a large UNITA force became apparent with the escalation of widespread hostilities in Angola from mid-1998.

In August 1999 the FAA had an estimated total strength of 112,500: army 100,000, navy 1,500 and air force 11,000. In addition, there was a paramilitary force numbering an estimated 15,000.

The defence budget for 1999 was US $574m.

## Economic Affairs

In 1997, according to estimates by the World Bank, Angola's gross national product (GNP), measured at average 1995–97 prices, was US $3,012m., equivalent to $260 per head. During 1990–97 GNP per head declined, in real terms, by an estimated average annual rate of 10.0%. Over the same period, Angola's population increased at an average annual rate of 3.3%. In 1998 GNP was estimated at $4,100m. ($340 per head). Angola's gross domestic product (GDP) declined, in real terms, by an average of 0.4% per year in 1990–98. However, according to the IMF, real GDP rose by 11.3% in 1995, by 11.7% in 1996 and by an estimated 6.6% in 1997.

Agriculture, forestry and fishing contributed an estimated 12.8% of GDP in 1998. An estimated 72.4% of the total working population were employed in the agricultural sector in that year. Coffee is the principal cash crop. The main subsistence crops are cassava, maize, sugar cane, bananas and sweet potatoes. During 1990–98 agricultural GDP declined at an average rate of 4.3% per year.

Industry (including mining, manufacturing, construction and power) provided an estimated 57.3% of GDP in 1998. Industrial GDP increased, in real terms, at an average rate of 3.6% per year in 1990–98. Industry employed an estimated 10.5% of the labour force in 1991.

Mining contributed an estimated 45.6% of GDP in 1998. Petroleum production (including liquefied petroleum gas) accounted for an estimated 48.5% of GDP in 1997. Angola's principal mineral exports are petroleum and diamonds. In addition, there are reserves of iron ore, copper, lead, zinc, gold, manganese, phosphates, salt and uranium.

The manufacturing sector provided an estimated 6% of GDP in 1998. According to the World Bank, during 1990–97 the GDP of the sector declined at an average annual rate of 4.2%; according to the IMF, it declined by 11.4% in 1995, before increasing by 2.6% in 1996 and by an estimated 9.3% in 1997. The principal branch of manufacturing is petroleum refining. Other manufacturing activities include food-processing, brewing, textiles and construction materials.

Energy is derived mainly from hydroelectric power. Angola's power potential exceeds its requirements.

Services accounted for an estimated 29.9% of GDP in 1998. In real terms, the combined GDP of the service sectors declined at an average rate of 5.7% per year in 1990–98. The service sectors employed an estimated 20.1% of the labour force in 1991.

In 1997 Angola recorded an estimated visible trade surplus of US $2,530m., while there was an estimated deficit of $866m. on the current account of the balance of payments. In 1997 the principal source of imports (20.6%) was Portugal; other major suppliers were South Africa and the USA. In that year the principal market for exports (63.6%) was the USA; other notable purchasers were the People's Republic of China and Belgium/Luxembourg. The principal exports in 1997 were petroleum and petroleum products, accounting for an estimated 92.5% of total export earnings. The principal imports in 1985 were foodstuffs, transport equipment, electrical equipment and base metals.

The 1997 state budget envisaged balanced expenditure and revenue of 694,600,000m. readjusted kwanza. The 1998 state budget envisaged expenditure of 1,348,205,000m. readjusted kwanza. Angola's total external debt at the end of 1997 was US $10,160m., of which $8,885m. was long-term public debt. In that year the cost of debt-servicing was equivalent to 15.9% of the value of exports of goods and services. The rate of inflation in the year to December was 3,783% in 1995, 1,650% in 1996 and 148% in 1997. Consumer prices increased by 92.9% in the year to October 1998.

Angola is a member of both the Common Market for Eastern and Southern Africa (COMESA, see p. 142) and the Southern African Development Community (SADC, see p. 263), which was formed with the aim of reducing the economic dependence of southern African states on South Africa.

Since independence, exploitation of Angola's extensive mineral reserves, hydroelectric potential and abundant fertile land has been severely impaired by internal conflict, as well as an acute shortage of skilled personnel. Angola's prospects depend greatly on a definitive resolution of the civil strife, the successful reintegration of the displaced population and the rehabilitation of the country's devastated infrastructure. In the late 1990s the development of the petroleum sector continued apace. In August 1997 the French company Elf Aquitaine announced the discovery of one of Africa's largest ever petroleum fields, with estimated reserves of 3,500m. barrels. Further significant discoveries were made in 1998–99. With increasing international investment in the sector, Angola's total daily output of crude petroleum was expected to reach 1.25m. barrels early in the 21st century. However, in 1999 the vast majority of petroleum revenue was being used to service loans, many of which had been put towards financing the Government's military expenditure following the resumption of full-scale hostilities in Angola in late 1998. In September 1999 the Government estimated that the number of people displaced by the war totalled 3.2m. The movement of people from the countryside to the towns was expected to have serious consequences for agricultural production. In August the budget projections for 1999 were revised in view of a recovery in formerly depressed world petroleum prices and of new monetary and fiscal policies adopted by the Government. Planned expenditure was increased by some 30%. Government revenues were also projected to receive a considerable boost in the second half of 1999 from down payments, expected to total about US $800m., from foreign petroleum companies in return for operating licences.

## Social Welfare

Medical care is provided free of charge, but its availability is limited by a shortage of trained personnel and medicines. In 1993 Angola had 31 hospitals, 246 health centres and 1,288 health posts, with a total of 12,297 beds. There were 630 doctors and 5,780 paramedics working in the country. The 1997 budget allocated an estimated 30,740,000m. readjusted kwanza (3.1% of total expenditure) to health. War veterans receive support from the Ministry of Defence.

## Education

Education is officially compulsory for eight years, between seven and 15 years of age, and is provided free of charge by the Government. Primary education begins at six years of age and lasts for four years. Secondary education, beginning at the age of 10, lasts for up to seven years, comprising a first cycle of four years and a second of three years. In 1973, under Portuguese rule, primary school pupils numbered only 300,000, but by 1991/92 there were 989,443 pupils. Enrolment at secondary schools (including students receiving vocational instruction and teacher-training) increased from 57,829 in 1970 to 218,987 in 1991/92. As a proportion of the school-age population, the total enrolment at primary and secondary schools was 45% in 1991. Higher education is being encouraged. The only university, Agostinho Neto University in Luanda, had 5,736 students in 1986/87. The number of students attending courses at the university and other equivalent institutions in 1991/92 was 6,331. Much education is now conducted in vernacular languages rather than Portuguese. At independence the estimated rate of adult illiteracy was more than 85%. A national literacy campaign was launched in 1976, and the average rate of adult illiteracy in 1990 was estimated by UNESCO to be 58.3% (males 44.4%, females 71.5%). The 1997 budget allocated an estimated 48,346,000m. readjusted kwanza (4.9% of total expenditure) to education.

In 1991 the People's Assembly approved legislation permitting the foundation of private educational establishments.

## Public Holidays

**2000:** 1 January (New Year's Day), 4 February (Anniversary of the outbreak of the armed struggle against Portuguese colonialism), 27 March (Victory Day), 14 April (Youth Day)*, 1 May (Workers' Day), 1 August (Armed Forces' Day)*, 17 September (National Hero's Day, birthday of Dr Agostinho Neto), 11 November (Independence Day), 1 December (Pioneers' Day)*, 10 December (Anniversary of the Foundation of the MPLA), 25 December (Family Day).

**2001:** 1 January (New Year's Day), 4 February (Anniversary of the outbreak of the armed struggle against Portuguese colonialism), 27 March (Victory Day), 14 April (Youth Day)*, 1 May (Workers' Day), 1 August (Armed Forces' Day)*, 17 September (National Hero's Day, birthday of Dr Agostinho Neto), 11 November (Independence Day), 1 December (Pioneers' Day)*, 10 December (Family Day).

* Although not officially recognized as public holidays, these days are popularly treated as such.

## Weights and Measures

The metric system is in force.

# Statistical Survey

Source (unless otherwise stated): Instituto Nacional de Estatística, Luanda.

## Area and Population

**AREA, POPULATION AND DENSITY**

| | |
|---|---|
| Area (sq km) | 1,246,700* |
| Population (census results) | |
| 30 December 1960 | 4,480,719 |
| 15 December 1970 | |
| Males | 2,943,974 |
| Females | 2,702,192 |
| Total | 5,646,166 |
| Population (official estimates at mid-year)† | |
| 1995 | 11,559,000 |
| 1996 | 11,895,000 |
| 1997 | 12,240,000 |
| Density (per sq km) at mid-1997 | 9.8 |

* 481,354 sq miles.

† Population figures are projected from the 1970 census. In mid-1996, according to a nation-wide survey, the population was an estimated 15,300,000.

**DISTRIBUTION OF POPULATION BY PROVINCE** (provisional estimates, mid-1995)

| | Area (sq km) | Population | Density (per sq km) |
|---|---|---|---|
| Luanda | 2,418 | 2,002,000 | 828.0 |
| Huambo | 34,274 | 1,687,000 | 49.2 |
| Bié | 70,314 | 1,246,000 | 17.7 |
| Malanje | 87,246 | 975,000 | 11.2 |
| Huíla | 75,002 | 948,000 | 12.6 |
| Uíge | 58,698 | 948,000 | 16.2 |
| Benguela | 31,788 | 702,000 | 22.1 |
| Cuanza-Sul | 55,660 | 688,000 | 12.4 |
| Cuanza-Norte | 24,110 | 412,000 | 17.1 |
| Moxico | 223,023 | 349,000 | 1.6 |
| Lunda-Norte | 102,783 | 311,000 | 3.0 |
| Zaire | 40,130 | 247,000 | 6.2 |
| Cunene | 88,342 | 245,000 | 2.8 |
| Cabinda | 7,270 | 185,000 | 25.4 |
| Bengo | 31,371 | 184,000 | 5.9 |
| Lunda-Sul | 56,985 | 160,000 | 2.8 |
| Cuando-Cubango | 199,049 | 137,000 | 0.7 |
| Namibe | 58,137 | 135,000 | 2.3 |
| **Total** | 1,246,600 | 11,561,000 | 9.3 |

**PRINCIPAL TOWNS** (population at 1970 census)

| | | | |
|---|---|---|---|
| Luanda (capital) | 480,613* | Benguela | 40,996 |
| Huambo (Nova Lisboa) | 61,885 | Lubango (Sá da Bandeira) | 31,674 |
| Lobito | 59,258 | Malanje | 31,559 |

* 1982 estimate: 1,200,000.

Source: Direcção dos Serviços de Estatística, Luanda.

**BIRTHS AND DEATHS** (UN estimates, annual averages)

| | 1980–85 | 1985–90 | 1990–95 |
|---|---|---|---|
| Birth rate (per 1,000) | 50.8 | 51.3 | 50.8 |
| Death rate (per 1,000) | 22.8 | 21.3 | 19.2 |

**Expectation of life** (UN estimates, years at birth, 1990–95): 46.5 (males 44.9; females 48.1).

Source: UN, *World Population Prospects: The 1998 Revision.*

**ECONOMICALLY ACTIVE POPULATION** (estimates, '000 persons, 1991)

| | Males | Females | Total |
|---|---|---|---|
| Agriculture, etc. | 1,518 | 1,374 | 2,892 |
| Industry | 405 | 33 | 438 |
| Services | 644 | 192 | 836 |
| **Total labour force** | 2,567 | 1,599 | 4,166 |

Source: UN Economic Commission for Africa, *African Statistical Yearbook.*

**Mid-1998** (estimates in '000): Agriculture, etc. 4,028; Total (incl. others) 5,564. Source: FAO, *Production Yearbook.*

## Agriculture

**PRINCIPAL CROPS** ('000 metric tons)

| | 1996 | 1997 | 1998 |
|---|---|---|---|
| Wheat* | 5* | 5* | 6 |
| Rice (paddy)* | 25 | 25 | 26 |
| Maize† | 398 | 370 | 505 |
| Millet and sorghum† | 102 | 62 | 89 |
| Potatoes* | 33 | 31 | 33 |
| Sweet potatoes* | 200 | 195 | 198 |
| Cassava (Manioc) | 2,500* | 2,326† | 3,211† |
| Dry beans† | 55 | 66 | 86 |
| Groundnuts (in shell)* | 23 | 22 | 23 |
| Sunflower seed* | 11 | 10 | 11 |
| Cottonseed† | 8 | 8 | 8 |
| Cotton (lint)† | 4 | 4 | 4 |
| Palm kernels* | 16 | 16 | 16 |
| Palm oil* | 54 | 53 | 54 |
| Vegetables* | 263 | 256 | 263 |
| Citrus fruit* | 82 | 80 | 82 |
| Pineapples* | 38 | 36 | 38 |
| Bananas* | 295 | 295 | 295 |
| Other fruits* | 31 | 30 | 31 |
| Sugar cane* | 290 | 310 | 330 |
| Coffee (green) | 4† | 5† | 6* |
| Tobacco (leaves) | 4† | 4† | 4* |
| Sisal* | 1 | 1 | 1 |

* FAO estimate(s). † Unofficial figure(s).

Source: FAO, *Production Yearbook.*

**LIVESTOCK** ('000 head, year ending September)

| | 1996 | 1997 | 1998 |
|---|---|---|---|
| Cattle | 3,309 | 3,556† | 3,500* |
| Pigs* | 810 | 820 | 810 |
| Sheep* | 245 | 250 | 245 |
| Goats* | 1,470 | 1,480 | 1,450 |

Poultry (million): 7* in 1996; 7* in 1997; 7* in 1998.

* FAO estimate(s). † Unofficial figure.

Source: FAO, *Production Yearbook.*

**LIVESTOCK PRODUCTS** (FAO estimates, '000 metric tons)

| | 1996 | 1997 | 1998 |
|---|---|---|---|
| Beef and veal | 58 | 61 | 60 |
| Goat meat | 4 | 4 | 4 |
| Pig meat | 22 | 23 | 22 |
| Poultry meat | 7 | 7 | 7 |
| Other meat | 8 | 8 | 9 |
| Cows' milk | 162 | 175 | 172 |
| Cheese | 1 | 1 | 1 |
| Poultry eggs | 4 | 4 | 4 |
| Honey | 23 | 23 | 22 |
| Cattle hides | 9 | 9 | 9 |

Source: FAO, *Production Yearbook*.

## Forestry

**ROUNDWOOD REMOVALS**
('000 cubic metres, excluding bark)

| | 1995 | 1996 | 1997 |
|---|---|---|---|
| Sawlogs, veneer logs and logs for sleepers* | 66 | 66 | 66 |
| Other industrial wood | 910 | 941 | 974 |
| Fuel wood | 5,893 | 6,057 | 6,229 |
| **Total** | 6,869 | 7,064 | 7,269 |

* Annual output assumed to be unchanged since 1990.

Source: FAO, *Yearbook of Forest Products*.

**SAWNWOOD PRODUCTION**
('000 cubic metres, including railway sleepers)

| | 1995 | 1996 | 1997 |
|---|---|---|---|
| **Total** | 5 | 5 | 5 |

Source: FAO, *Yearbook of Forest Products*.

## Fishing

('000 metric tons, live weight)

| | 1995 | 1996 | 1997 |
|---|---|---|---|
| Freshwater fishes | 6.0 | 6.0 | 6.0 |
| Cunene horse mackerel | 25.3 | 19.8 | 35.8 |
| Sardinellas | 34.2 | 17.5 | 21.0 |
| Other marine fishes (incl. unspecified) | 27.2 | 28.8 | 9.4 |
| **Total fish** | 92.7 | 72.1 | 72.2 |
| Crustaceans and molluscs | 1.1 | 0.8 | 0.0 |
| **Total catch** | 93.8 | 72.8 | 72.2 |

Source: FAO, *Yearbook of Fishery Statistics*.

## Mining

('000 metric tons, unless otherwise indicated)

| | 1994 | 1995 | 1996 |
|---|---|---|---|
| Crude petroleum | 27,193 | 32,132 | 34,777 |
| Natural gas (petajoules)* | 7 | 7 | 7 |
| Salt (unrefined)*† | 30 | 30 | 30 |
| Diamonds ('000 carats):† | | | |
| Industrial | 30 | 300 | 400* |
| Gem | 270 | 2,700 | 3,600* |
| Gypsum (crude)† | 50 | 50 | 50* |

* Estimate(s).

† Data from the US Bureau of Mines.

Source: UN, *Industrial Commodity Statistics Yearbook*.

**1997** ('000 metric tons): Crude petroleum 35,341 (Source: UN, *Monthly Bulletin of Statistics*).

## Industry

**SELECTED PRODUCTS**
('000 metric tons, unless otherwise indicated)

| | 1994 | 1995 | 1996 |
|---|---|---|---|
| Raw sugar* | 20 | 20 | 25 |
| Plywood ('000 cubic metres)*† | 10 | 10 | 10 |
| Chemical wood pulp*† | 15 | 15 | 15 |
| Jet fuels† | 160 | 158 | 160 |
| Motor spirit (petrol)† | 105 | 108 | 110 |
| Kerosene† | 50 | 50 | 55 |
| Distillate fuel oils† | 320 | 315 | 320 |
| Residual fuel oils† | 640 | 630 | 635 |
| Cement†‡ | 300 | 300 | n.a. |
| Crude steel† | 9 | 9 | 9‡ |
| Electric energy (million kWh)† | 1,865 | 1,870 | 1,885 |

* Data from the FAO.

† Estimates.

‡ Data from the US Bureau of Mines.

Source: UN, *Industrial Commodity Statistics Yearbook*.

## Finance

**CURRENCY AND EXCHANGE RATES**

**Monetary Units**

100 lwei = 1 readjusted kwanza.

**Sterling, Dollar and Euro Equivalents** (31 August 1999)

£1 sterling = 6,218,565 readjusted kwanza;
US $1 = 3,877,636 readjusted kwanza;
€1 = 4,099,825 readjusted kwanza;
10,000,000 readjusted kwanza = £1.608 = $2.579 = €2.439.

**Average Exchange Rate** (readjusted kwanza per US $)

1996 128,029
1997 229,040
1998 392,824

Note: An official exchange rate of US $1 = 29.62 kwanza was introduced in 1976 and remained in force until September 1990. In that month the kwanza was replaced, at par, by the new kwanza. At the same time, it was announced that the currency was to be devalued by more than 50%, with the exchange rate adjusted to US $1 = 60 new kwanza, with effect from 1 October 1990. This rate remained in force until 18 November 1991, when a basic rate of US $1 = 90 new kwanza was established. The currency underwent further devaluation, by 50% in December 1991, and by more than 67% on 15 April 1992, when a basic rate of US $1 = 550 new kwanza was established. In February 1993 the currency was again devalued, when a basic rate of US $1 = 7,000 new kwanza was established. In April 1993 this was adjusted to US $1 = 4,000 new kwanza, and in October to US $1 = 6,500 new kwanza, a devaluation of 38.5%. Following a series of four devaluations in February and March 1994, a rate of US $1 = 35,000 new kwanza was established in late March. In April 1994 the introduction of a new method of setting exchange rates resulted in an effective devaluation, to US $1 = 68,297 new kwanza, and provided for an end to the system of multiple exchange rates. Further substantial devaluations followed, and in July 1995 a 'readjusted' kwanza, equivalent to 1,000 new kwanza, was introduced. The currency, however, continued to depreciate. Between July 1997 and June 1998 a fixed official rate of US $1 = 262,376 'readjusted' kwanza was in operation. In May 1999 the Central Bank announced its decision to abolish the existing dual currency exchange rate system.

**BUDGET** ('000 million readjusted kwanza)

| Revenue | 1995 | 1996 | 1997* |
|---|---|---|---|
| Tax revenue | 4,074.0 | 374,404 | 496,528 |
| Income tax | 2,843.7 | 246,033 | 271,592 |
| Petroleum corporate tax | 1,508.1 | 106,459 | 195,286 |
| Petroleum transaction tax | 1,236.7 | 132,524 | 51,704 |
| Tax on goods and services | 935.0 | 105,499 | 171,169 |
| Petroleum sector | 835.3 | 96,580 | 143,955 |
| Diamond sector | 2.2 | 1,887 | — |
| Taxes on foreign trade | 201.0 | 16,086 | 33,830 |
| Other taxes | 94.3 | 6,786 | 19,937 |
| Stamp tax | 83.8 | 5,890 | 14,145 |
| Non-tax revenue | 41.5 | 1,856 | 141,387 |
| **Total** | 4,115.6 | 376,260 | 637,915 |

* Estimates.

| Expenditure* | 1995 | 1996 | 1997† |
|---|---|---|---|
| General public services | 1,513 | 64,628 | 173,598 |
| Defence and public order | 2,469 | 162,354 | 355,565 |
| Peace process | 39 | 3,666 | 6,097 |
| Education | 399 | 21,546 | 48,346 |
| Health | 450 | 13,909 | 30,740 |
| Social security, welfare and housing | 247 | 9,968 | 51,470 |
| Economic affairs and services | 523 | 39,385 | 85,192 |
| Interest payments | 1,483 | 97,391 | 97,247 |
| **Total** (incl. others) | 7,863 | 463,867 | 980,319 |

* Including adjustments for unrecorded transactions. The data include lending minus repayments.

† Estimates.

Source: IMF, *Angola: Statistical Annex* (April 1999).

**INTERNATIONAL RESERVES** (US $ million at 31 December)

| | 1996 | 1997 | 1998 |
|---|---|---|---|
| IMF special drawing rights | 0.16 | 0.16 | 0.17 |
| Foreign exchange | 551.46 | 396.27 | 203.29 |
| **Total** | 551.62 | 396.43 | 203.46 |

Source: IMF, *International Financial Statistics*.

**MONEY SUPPLY** ('000 million readjusted kwanza at 31 December)

| | 1996 | 1997 | 1998 |
|---|---|---|---|
| Currency outside banks | 42,166 | 101,619 | 165,686 |
| Demand deposits at banking institutions | 51,751 | 93,292 | 106,583 |
| **Total** (incl. others) | 93,918 | 195,165 | 272,432 |

Source: IMF, *International Financial Statistics*.

**COST OF LIVING**

(Consumer Price Index for Luanda at December; base: 1994 average = 100)

| | 1995 | 1996 | 1997 |
|---|---|---|---|
| Food | 10,425 | 170,984 | 318,793 |
| Clothing | 19,152 | 307,789 | 420,558 |
| Rent, fuel and light | 10,295 | 257,809 | 4,572,341 |
| **All items** (incl. others) | 11,642 | 203,768 | 504,818 |

Source: IMF, *Angola: Statistical Annex* (April 1999).

**NATIONAL ACCOUNTS**

**Composition of the Gross National Product** (US $ million)

| | 1987 | 1988 | 1989 |
|---|---|---|---|
| **Gross domestic product (GDP) at factor cost** | 6,482 | 6,877 | 7,682 |
| Indirect taxes | 94 | 95 | 117 |
| *Less* Subsidies | 189 | 122 | 93 |
| **GDP in purchasers' values** | 6,386 | 6,850 | 7,706 |
| Net factor income from abroad | −402 | −938 | −1,079 |
| **Gross national product** | 5,984 | 5,912 | 6,627 |

**Gross Domestic Product by Economic Activity**

('000 million readjusted kwanza at current prices)

| | 1996 | 1997 | 1998* |
|---|---|---|---|
| Agriculture, forestry and fishing | 62,113.5 | 166,032.7 | 300,921.4 |
| Mining | 518,629.4 | 908,348.6 | 1,073,894.4 |
| Processing industry | 28,789.1 | 76,700.3 | 141,397.2 |
| Electricity and water | 289.4 | 772.1 | 1,451.8 |
| Construction | 25,911.4 | 71,344.4 | 131,649.4 |
| Trade | 125,472.9 | 282,933.0 | 433,953.7 |
| Other services | 68,741.5 | 197,306.7 | 270,915.9 |
| **Sub-total** | 829,947.5 | 1,703,437.7 | 2,354,183.9 |
| Import duties | 15,931.6 | 33,829.7 | 35,250.7 |
| **GDP in purchasers' values** | 845,878.8 | 1,737,267.4 | 2,389,434.6 |

* Provisional figures.

**BALANCE OF PAYMENTS** (US $ million)

| | 1995 | 1996 | 1997* |
|---|---|---|---|
| Exports of goods f.o.b. | 3,723 | 5,095 | 5,008 |
| Imports of goods f.o.b. | −1,852 | −2,040 | −2,477 |
| **Trade balance** | 1,871 | 3,055 | 2,530 |
| Services (net)<br>Interest payments (net)<br>Unrequited transfers (net) | −2,864 | −3,378 | −3,397 |
| **Current balance** | −994 | −323 | −866 |
| Direct investment (net) | 303 | 588 | 492 |
| Other long-term capital (net) | −729 | −306 | 267 |
| Short-term capital (net) | 221 | −208 | −669 |
| Net errors and omissions | −20 | 31 | −30 |
| **Overall balance** | −1,218 | −218 | −806 |

* Estimates.

Source: IMF, *Angola: Statistical Annex* (April 1999).

# External Trade

**SELECTED COMMODITIES**

| Imports (million kwanza) | 1983 | 1984 | 1985 |
|---|---|---|---|
| Animal products | 1,315 | 1,226 | 1,084 |
| Vegetable products | 2,158 | 3,099 | 2,284 |
| Fats and oils | 946 | 1,006 | 1,196 |
| Food and beverages | 2,400 | 1,949 | 1,892 |
| Industrial chemical products | 1,859 | 1,419 | 1,702 |
| Plastic materials | 431 | 704 | 454 |
| Paper products | 376 | 380 | 411 |
| Textiles | 1,612 | 1,816 | 1,451 |
| Base metals | 1,985 | 3,730 | 2,385 |
| Electrical equipment | 3,296 | 2,879 | 2,571 |
| Transport equipment | 2,762 | 2,240 | 3,123 |
| **Total** (incl. others) | 20,197 | 21,370 | 19,694 |

**Total Imports** (million kwanza): 18,691 in 1986; 13,372 in 1987; 29,845 in 1988; 34,392 in 1989 (Source: UN, *Monthly Bulletin of Statistics*).

| Exports (US $ million) | 1995 | 1996 | 1997* |
|---|---|---|---|
| Crude petroleum | 3,425 | 4,651 | 4,507 |
| Refined petroleum products | 96 | 130 | 123 |
| Diamonds | 168 | 267 | 348 |
| **Total** (incl. others) | 3,723 | 5,095 | 5,008 |

* Estimates.

Source: IMF, *Angola: Statistical Annex* (April 1999).

**PRINCIPAL TRADING PARTNERS** (US $ million)

| Imports c.i.f. | 1987 | 1988 | 1989 |
|---|---|---|---|
| Belgium-Luxembourg | 17.9 | 22.9 | 99.9 |
| Brazil | 55.8 | 119.2 | 104.0 |
| France | 63.3 | 8.8 | 114.1 |
| German Dem. Repub. | 35.2 | 34.7 | 41.9 |
| Germany, Fed. Repub. | 51.0 | 149.0 | 178.4 |
| Italy | 19.0 | 19.3 | 35.2 |
| Japan | 8.1 | 39.7 | 34.5 |
| Netherlands | 20.6 | 148.3 | 160.5 |
| Portugal | 51.4 | 171.4 | 206.8 |
| Spain | 4.8 | 53.2 | 55.6 |
| United Arab Emirates | 70.5 | 25.1 | 23.1 |
| United Kingdom | 9.1 | 26.7 | 32.9 |
| **Total** (incl. others) | 442.6 | 987.9 | 1,139.6 |

**Total Imports** (US $ million): 1,139.5 in 1990; 457.9 in 1991; 728.7 in 1992.

| Exports f.o.b. | 1990 | 1991 | 1992 |
|---|---|---|---|
| Austria | 62.8 | — | — |
| Belgium-Luxembourg | 231.9 | 45.9 | 106.0 |
| Brazil | 80.0 | 210.2 | 46.0 |
| Canada | 28.1 | 37.1 | — |
| Chile | 76.7 | 22.2 | — |
| China, People's Repub. | — | — | 63.0 |
| France | 456.3 | 290.4 | 300.0 |
| Germany | 40.4 | 21.0 | — |
| Gibraltar | 72.8 | 12.5 | — |
| Italy | 143.9 | 82.6 | 37.0 |
| Netherlands | 414.0 | 206.2 | 167.1 |
| Portugal | 88.8 | 87.8 | 75.5 |
| Singapore | — | — | 49.0 |
| Spain | 2.5 | 40.5 | 50.1 |
| United Kingdom | 21.5 | 144.3 | 316.0 |
| USA | 2,067.6 | 2,094.6 | 2,460.0 |
| Yugoslavia | — | 62.2 | — |
| **Total** (incl. others) | 3,910.3 | 3,409.7 | 3,697.5 |

Source: UN, *International Trade Statistics Yearbook.*

# Transport

**GOODS TRANSPORT** ('000 metric tons)

| | 1988 | 1989 | 1990 |
|---|---|---|---|
| Road | 1,056.7 | 690.1 | 867.3 |
| Railway | 580.9 | 510.3 | 443.2 |
| Water | 780.8 | 608.6 | 812.1 |
| Air | 24.6 | 10.5 | 28.3 |
| **Total** | 2,443.0 | 1,819.5 | 2,150.9 |

Sources: Instituto Nacional de Estatística; Ministério de Transporte e Comunicações.

**PASSENGER TRANSPORT** ('000 journeys)

| | 1988 | 1989 | 1990 |
|---|---|---|---|
| Road | 12,699.2 | 32,658.7 | 48,796.1 |
| Railway | 6,659.7 | 6,951.2 | 6,455.8 |
| Water | 151.8 | 163.2 | 223.8 |
| Air | 608.9 | 618.4 | 615.9 |
| **Total** | 20,119.6 | 40,391.5 | 56,091.6 |

Sources: Instituto Nacional de Estatística; Ministério de Transporte e Comunicações, Luanda.

**ROAD TRAFFIC** (estimates, motor vehicles in use at 31 December)

| | 1994 | 1995 | 1996 |
|---|---|---|---|
| Passenger cars | 180,000 | 197,000 | 207,000 |
| Lorries and vans | 32,340 | 26,000 | 25,000 |
| **Total** | 212,340 | 223,000 | 232,000 |

Source: IRF, *World Road Statistics.*

**SHIPPING**

**Merchant Fleet** (registered at 31 December)

| | 1996 | 1997 | 1998 |
|---|---|---|---|
| Number of vessels | 113 | 109 | 123 |
| Total displacement (grt) | 81,856 | 68,031 | 73,907 |

Source: Lloyd's Register of Shipping, *World Fleet Statistics.*

**International Sea-borne Freight Traffic**
(estimates, '000 metric tons)

| | 1989 | 1990 | 1991 |
|---|---|---|---|
| Goods loaded | 19,980 | 21,102 | 23,288 |
| Goods unloaded | 1,235 | 1,242 | 1,261 |

Source: UN Economic Commission for Africa, *African Statistical Yearbook.*

**CIVIL AVIATION** (traffic on scheduled services)

| | 1993 | 1994 | 1995 |
|---|---|---|---|
| Kilometres flown (million) | 9 | 13 | 13 |
| Passengers carried ('000) | 334 | 519 | 545 |
| Passenger-km (million) | 948 | 1,594 | 1,708 |
| Total ton-km (million) | 113 | 197 | 212 |

Source: UN, *Statistical Yearbook.*

# Tourism

| | 1994 | 1995 | 1996 |
|---|---|---|---|
| Tourist arrivals ('000) | 11 | 8 | 8 |
| Tourism receipts (US $ million) | 13 | 10 | 9 |

Source: World Tourism Organization, *Yearbook of Tourism Statistics.*

## Communications Media

| | 1994 | 1995 | 1996 |
|---|---|---|---|
| Radio receivers ('000 in use) | 320 | 370 | 600 |
| Television receivers ('000 in use) | 70 | 80 | 300 |
| Telephones ('000 main lines in use) | n.a. | 60 | n.a. |
| Mobile cellular telephones (subscribers) | n.a. | 1,994 | n.a. |
| Daily newspapers | | | |
| Number | 4 | 5 | 5 |
| Average circulation ('000 copies) | 117 | 122 | 128 |

Book production: 47 titles (books 35, pamphlets 12) and 419,000 copies (books 338,000, pamphlets 81,000) in 1985; 14 titles (all books) and 130,000 copies in 1986; 22 titles (all books) in 1995.

Sources: UNESCO, *Statistical Yearbook*; UN, *Statistical Yearbook*.

## Education

(1991/92)

| | Teachers | Pupils |
|---|---|---|
| Pre-primary | n.a. | 214,867 |
| Primary | 31,062* | 989,443 |
| Secondary: | | |
| general | 5,138† | 196,099 |
| teacher training | 280‡ | 10,772 |
| vocational | 286† | 12,116 |
| Higher | 787 | 6,331 |

* Figure for school year 1990/91.

† Figure for school year 1989/90.

‡ Figure for school year 1987/88.

Source: mainly UNESCO, *Statistical Yearbook*.

# Directory

## The Constitution

The MPLA regime adopted an independence Constitution for Angola in November 1975. It was amended in October 1976, September 1980, March 1991, April and August 1992, and November 1996. The main provisions of the Constitution, as amended, are summarized below:

### BASIC PRINCIPLES

The Republic of Angola shall be a sovereign and independent state whose prime objective shall be to build a free and democratic society of peace, justice and social progress. It shall be a democratic state based on the rule of law, founded on national unity, the dignity of human beings, pluralism of expression and political organization, respecting and guaranteeing the basic rights and freedoms of persons, whether as individuals or as members of organized social groups. Sovereignty shall be vested in the people, which shall exercise political power through periodic universal suffrage.

The Republic of Angola shall be a unitary and indivisible state. Economic, social and cultural solidarity shall be promoted between all the Republic's regions for the common development of the entire nation and the elimination of regionalism and tribalism.

#### Religion

The Republic shall be a secular state and there shall be complete separation of the State and religious institutions. All religions shall be respected.

#### The Economy

The economic system shall be based on the coexistence of diverse forms of property—public, private, mixed, co-operative and family—and all shall enjoy equal protection. The State shall protect foreign investment and foreign property, in accordance with the law. The fiscal system shall aim to satisfy the economic, social and administrative needs of the State and to ensure a fair distribution of income and wealth. Taxes may be created and abolished only by law, which shall determine applicability, rates, tax benefits and guarantees for taxpayers.

#### Education

The Republic shall vigorously combat illiteracy and obscurantism and shall promote the development of education and of a true national culture.

### FUNDAMENTAL RIGHTS AND DUTIES

The State shall respect and protect the human person and human dignity. All citizens shall be equal before the law. They shall be subject to the same duties, without any distinction based on colour, race, ethnic group, sex, place of birth, religion, level of education, or economic or social status.

All citizens aged 18 years and over, other than those legally deprived of political and civil rights, shall have the right and duty to take an active part in public life, to vote and be elected to any state organ, and to discharge their mandates with full dedication to the cause of the Angolan nation. The law shall establish limitations in respect of non-political allegiance of soldiers on active service, judges and police forces, as well as the electoral incapacity of soldiers on active service and police forces.

Freedom of expression, of assembly, of demonstration, of association and of all other forms of expression shall be guaranteed. Groupings whose aims or activities are contrary to the constitutional order and penal laws, or that, even indirectly, pursue political objectives through organizations of a military, paramilitary or militarized nature shall be forbidden. Every citizen has the right to a defence if accused of a crime. Individual freedoms are guaranteed. Freedom of conscience and belief shall be inviolable. Work shall be the right and duty of all citizens. The State shall promote measures necessary to ensure the right of citizens to medical and health care, as well as assistance in childhood, motherhood, disability, old age, etc. It shall also promote access to education, culture and sports for all citizens.

### STATE ORGANS

#### President of the Republic

The President of the Republic shall be the Head of State, Head of Government and Commander-in-Chief of the Angolan armed forces. The President of the Republic shall be elected directly by a secret universal ballot and shall have the following powers:

- to appoint and dismiss the Prime Minister, Ministers and other government officials determined by law;
- to appoint the judges of the Supreme Court;
- to preside over the Council of Ministers;
- to declare war and make peace, following authorization by the National Assembly;
- to sign, promulgate and publish the laws of the National Assembly, government decrees and statutory decrees;
- to preside over the National Defence Council;
- to decree a state of siege or state of emergency;
- to announce the holding of general elections;
- to issue pardons and commute sentences;
- to perform all other duties provided for in the Constitution.

#### National Assembly

The National Assembly is the supreme state legislative body, to which the Government is responsible. The National Assembly shall be composed of 223 deputies, elected for a term of four years. The National Assembly shall convene in ordinary session twice yearly and in special session on the initiative of the President of the National Assembly, the Standing Commission of the National Assembly or of no less than one-third of its deputies. The Standing Commission shall be the organ of the National Assembly that represents and assumes its powers between sessions.

#### Government

The Government shall comprise the President of the Republic, the ministers and the secretaries of state, and other members whom the law shall indicate, and shall have the following functions:

- to organize and direct the implementation of state domestic and foreign policy, in accordance with decision of the National Assembly and its Standing Commission;

to ensure national defence, the maintenance of internal order and security, and the protection of the rights of citizens;

to prepare the draft National Plan and General State Budget for approval by the National Assembly, and to organize, direct and control their execution;

The Council of Ministers shall be answerable to the National Assembly. In the exercise of its powers, the Council of Ministers shall issue decrees and resolutions.

**Judiciary**

The organization, composition and competence of the courts shall be established by law. Judges shall be independent in the discharge of their functions.

**Local State Organs**

The organs of state power at provincial level shall be the Provincial Assemblies and their executive bodies. The Provincial Assemblies shall work in close co-operation with social organizations and rely on the initiative and broad participation of citizens. The Provincial Assemblies shall elect commissions of deputies to perform permanent or specific tasks. The executive organs of Provincial Assemblies shall be the Provincial Governments, which shall be led by the Provincial Governors. The Provincial Governors shall be answerable to the President of the Republic, the Council of Ministers and the Provincial Assemblies.

**National Defence**

The State shall ensure national defence. The National Defence Council shall be presided over by the President of the Republic, and its composition shall be determined by law. The Angolan armed forces, as a state institution, shall be permanent, regular and non-partisan. Defence of the country shall be the right and the highest indeclinable duty of every citizen. Military service shall be compulsory. The forms in which it is fulfilled shall be defined by the law.

Note: In accordance with the terms of the Lusaka peace accord of November 1994, in April 1997 a new Government of National Unity and Reconciliation was inaugurated in which UNITA held four portfolios. In November 1996 the National Assembly adopted a constitutional revision extending the parliamentary mandate, which was due to expire that month, for a period of between two and four years in order to allow for the establishment of suitable conditions for the conduct of elections.

# The Government

## HEAD OF STATE

**President:** José Eduardo dos Santos (assumed office 21 September 1979).

## COUNCIL OF MINISTERS

(January 2000)

**Prime Minister:** José Eduardo dos Santos.

**Minister of Defence:** Gen. Kundi Paihama.

**Minister of the Interior:** Fernando da Piedade Dias dos Santos.

**Minister of Foreign Affairs:** João Bernardo de Miranda.

**Minister of Territorial Administration:** Fernando Faustino Muteka.

**Minister of Finance:** Joaquim Duarte da Costa David.

**Minister of Economic Planning:** Ana Dias Lourenço.

**Minister of Petroleum:** José Botelho de Vasconcelos.

**Minister of Industry:** Albina Faria de Assis Pereira Africano.

**Minister of Agriculture and Rural Development:** Gilberto Buta Lutukuta.

**Minister of Fisheries and Environment:** Maria de Fátima Monteiro Jardim.

**Minister of Geology and Mines:** Manuel António Africano.

**Minister of Public Works and Housing:** António Henriques da Silva.

**Minister of Transport:** André Luís Brandão.

**Minister of Trade:** Victorino Domingos Hossi.

**Minister of Health:** Albertina Júlia Hamukuaya.

**Minister of Education and Culture:** António Burity da Silva Neto.

**Minister of Social Welfare:** Albino Malungo.

**Minister of Youth and Sports:** José Marcos Barrica.

**Minister of Justice:** Dr Paulo Tchipilica.

**Minister of Public Administration, Employment and Social Security:** Dr António Domingos Pitra Costa Neto.

**Minister of Social Communication:** Dr Pedro Hendrik Vaal Neto.

**Minister of Science and Technology:** João Baptista Nganda Gina.

**Minister of Post and Telecommunications:** Licínio Tavares Ribeiro.

**Minister of Family and the Promotion of Women:** Cândida Celeste da Silva.

**Minister of War Veterans:** Pedro José van-Dúnem.

**Minister of Hotels and Tourism:** Jorge Alicerces Valentim.

**Minister of Energy and Water:** Luis Filipe da Silva.

### Secretaries of State with Independent Charge

**Secretary of State for Coffee:** Gilberto Buta Lutukuta.

**Secretary of State for Environment:** Manuel David Mendes.

## MINISTRIES

All Ministries are located in Luanda.

**Ministry of Agriculture and Rural Development:** Avda Norton de Matos 2, Luanda.

**Ministry of Defence:** Rua Silva Carvalho ex Quartel General, Luanda.

**Ministry of Education and Culture:** Avda Comandante Jika, CP 1281, Luanda; tel. (2) 321592; fax (2) 321592.

**Ministry of Finance:** Avda 4 de Fevereiro, Luanda; tel. (2) 344628.

**Ministry of Fisheries and Environment:** Avda 4 de Fevereiro 25, Predio Atlântico, Luanda; tel. (2) 392782.

**Ministry of Foreign Affairs:** Avda Comandante Jika, Luanda.

**Ministry of Geology and Mines:** CP 1260, Luanda; tel. (2) 322766; fax (2) 321655.

**Ministry of Health:** Rua Diogo Cão, Luanda.

**Ministry of the Interior:** Avda 4 de Fevereiro, Luanda.

**Ministry of Justice:** Largo do Palácio, Luanda.

**Ministry of Petroleum:** Avda 4 de Fevereiro 105, CP 1279, Luanda; tel. (2) 337448.

**Ministry of Public Administration, Employment and Social Security:** Rua 17 de Setembro 32, CP 1986, Luanda; tel. (2) 339656; fax (2) 339054.

**Ministry of Social Communication:** Avda Comandante Valódia, CP 2608, Luanda; tel. (2) 343495.

**Ministry of Trade:** Largo Kinaxixi 14, Luanda; tel. (2) 344525.

**Ministry of Transport and Communications:** Avda 4 de Fevereiro 42, CP 1250-C, Luanda; tel. (2) 370061.

## PROVINCIAL GOVERNORS*

**Bengo:** Ezelino Mendes.

**Benguela:** Dumilde das Chagas Simões Rangel.

**Bié:** Luís Paulino dos Santos.

**Cabinda:** José Amaro Tati.

**Cuando-Cubango:** Manuel Gama

**Cuanza-Norte:** Manuel Pedro Pacavira.

**Cuanza-Sul:** Francisco Higino Lopes Carneiro.

**Cunene:** Pedro Mutinde.

**Huambo:** Paulo Kassoma.

**Huíla:** Francisco José Ramos da Cruz.

**Luanda:** José Aníbal Lopes Rocha.

**Lunda-Norte:** Manuel Francisco Gomes Maiato.

**Lunda-Sul:** Francisco Sozinho Chiubsa.

**Malanje:** Flavio Fernandes.

**Moxico:** João Ernesto dos Santos (Liberdade).

**Namibe:** Salomeo José Lueto Sirimbimbe.

**Uíge:** Cordero Ernesto Zacundomba.

**Zaire:** Ludi Kissassunda.

*All Governors are ex-officio members of the Government.

# President and Legislature

PRESIDENT*

**Presidential Election, 29 and 30 September 1992**

| | Votes | % of votes |
|---|---|---|
| José Eduardo dos Santos (MPLA) | 1,953,335 | 49.57 |
| Dr Jonas Malheiro Savimbi (UNITA) | 1,579,298 | 40.07 |
| António Alberto Neto (PDA) | 85,249 | 2.16 |
| Holden Roberto (FNLA) | 83,135 | 2.11 |
| Honorato Lando (PDLA) | 75,789 | 1.92 |
| Luís dos Passos (PRD) | 59,121 | 1.47 |
| Bengui Pedro João (PSD) | 38,243 | 0.97 |
| Simão Cacete (FPD) | 26,385 | 0.67 |
| Daniel Júlio Chipenda (Independent) | 20,646 | 0.52 |
| Anália de Victória Pereira (PLD) | 11,475 | 0.29 |
| Rui de Victória Pereira (PRA) | 9,208 | 0.23 |
| **Total** | 3,940,884 | 100.00 |

NATIONAL ASSEMBLY

**President:** Roberto de Almeida.

**Legislative Election, 29 and 30 September 1992**

| | Votes | % of votes | Seats† |
|---|---|---|---|
| MPLA | 2,124,126 | 53.74 | 129 |
| UNITA | 1,347,636 | 34.10 | 70 |
| FNLA | 94,742 | 2.40 | 5 |
| PLD | 94,269 | 2.39 | 3 |
| PRS | 89,875 | 2.27 | 6 |
| PRD | 35,293 | 0.89 | 1 |
| AD Coalition | 34,166 | 0.86 | 1 |
| PSD | 33,088 | 0.84 | 1 |
| PAJOCA | 13,924 | 0.35 | 1 |
| FDA | 12,038 | 0.30 | 1 |
| PDP–ANA | 10,620 | 0.27 | 1 |
| PNDA | 10,281 | 0.26 | 1 |
| CNDA | 10,237 | 0.26 | — |
| PSDA | 19,217 | 0.26 | — |
| PAI | 9,007 | 0.23 | — |
| PDLA | 8,025 | 0.20 | — |
| PDA | 8,014 | 0.20 | — |
| PRA | 6,719 | 0.17 | — |
| **Total** | 3,952,277 | 100.00 | 220 |

* Under the terms of the electoral law, a second round of presidential elections was required to take place in order to determine which of the two leading candidates from the first round would be elected. However, a resumption of hostilities between UNITA and government forces prevented a second round of presidential elections from taking place. The electoral process was to resume only when the provisions of the Estoril peace agreement, concluded in May 1991, had been fulfilled. However, provision in the Lusaka peace accord of November 1994 for the second round of presidential elections was not pursued.

† According to the Constitution, the total number of seats in the National Assembly is 223. On the decision of the National Electoral Council, however, elections to fill three seats reserved for Angolans resident abroad were abandoned.

# Political Organizations

**Aliança Democrática de Angola:** Leader Simba da Costa.

**Angolan Alliance and Hamista Party.**

**Angolan Democratic Coalition (AD Coalition):** Pres. Evidor Quiela (acting).

**Angolan Democratic Confederation:** f. 1994; Chair. Gaspar Neto.

**Angolan Democratic Unification:** Leader Eduardo Milton Sivi.

**Associação Cívica Angolana (ACA):** f. 1990; Leader Joaquim Pinto de Andrade.

**Centro Democrático Social (CDS):** Pres. Mateus José; Sec.-Gen. Delfina Francisco Capciel.

**Christian Democratic Convention:** Leader Gaspar Neto.

**Democratic Civilian Opposition:** f. 1994; opposition alliance including:

**Convenção Nacional Democrata de Angola (CNDA):** Leader Paulino Pinto João.

**Frente Nacional de Libertação de Angola (FNLA):** f. 1962; Pres. Lucas Ngonda.

**Frente para a Democracia (FPD):** Leader Nelso Pestana; Sec.-Gen. Filomeno Vieira Lopes.

**Movimento de Defesa dos Interesses de Angola—Partido de Consciência Nacional:** Leader Isidoro Klala.

**National Ecological Party of Angola:** Leader Sukawa Dizizeko Ricardo.

**National Union for Democracy:** Leader Sebastião Rogerio Suzama.

**Partido Renovador Social (PRS):** Pres. Eduardo Kwangana.

**Party of Solidarity and the Conscience of Angola:** Leader Fernando Dombassi Quiesse.

**Fórum Democrático Angolano (FDA):** Leader Jorge Rebelo Pinto Chicoti.

**Frente de Libertação do Enclave de Cabinda (FLEC):** f. 1963; comprises several factions, claiming total forces of c. 5,000 guerrillas, seeking the secession of Cabinda province; mem. groups include:

**Frente Democrática de Cabinda (FDC):** Leader Francisco Xavier Lubota.

**Frente de Libertação do Enclave de Cabinda–Forças Armadas Cabindesas (FLEC–FAC):** Chair. Henrique Tiago N'Zita; Chief-of-Staff (FAC) Commdr Estanislau Miguel Bomba.

**Frente de Libertação do Enclave de Cabinda–Renovada (FLEC–R):** Pres. António Bento Bembe; Sec.-Gen. Arturo Chibasa.

**Movimento Amplo para a Democracia:** Leader Francisco Viana.

**Movimento Popular de Libertação de Angola (MPLA)** (People's Movement for the Liberation of Angola): Luanda. 1956; in 1961–74 conducted guerrilla operations against Portuguese rule; governing party since 1975; known as Movimento Popular de Libertação de Angola–Partido do Trabalho (MPLA–PT) (People's Movement for the Liberation of Angola–Workers' Party) 1977–92; in Dec. 1990 replaced Marxist-Leninist ideology with commitment to 'democratic socialism'; Chair. José Eduardo dos Santos; Sec.-Gen. João Manuel Gonçalves Lourenço.

**Movimento de Unidade Democrática para a Reconstrução (Mudar):** Leader Manuel dos Santos Lima.

**National Union for the Light of Democracy and Development of Angola:** Pres. Miguel Muendo; Sec.-Gen. Domingos Chizela.

**Partido de Aliança de Juventude, Operários e Camponêses de Angola (PAJOCA)** (Angolan Youth, Workers' and Peasants' Alliance Party): Leader Miguel João Sebastião.

**Partido para a Aliança Popular:** Leader Campos Neto.

**Partido Angolano Independente (PAI):** Leader Adriano Parreira.

**Partido Democrático Angolano (PDA):** Leader António Alberto Neto.

**Partido Liberal Democrata (PLD):** Leader Anália de Victória Pereira.

**Partido Nacional Democrata de Angola (PNDA):** Sec.-Gen. Pedro João António.

**Partido Reformador de Angola (PRA):** Leader Rui de Victória Pereira.

**Partido Renovador Democrático (PRD):** Leader Luís dos Passos.

**Partido Republicano Conservador de Angola (PRCA):** Leader Martinho Mateus.

**Partido Social Democrata (PSD):** Leader Bengui Pedro João.

**Partido do Trabalho de Angola (PTA):** Leader Agostinho Paldo.

**Patriotic Front:** f. 1995; opposition alliance including:

**Partido Angolano Liberal (PAL):** Leader Manuel Francisco Lulo (acting).

**Partido Democrático Liberal de Angola (PDLA):** Leader Honorato Lando.

**Partido Democrático para o Progresso–Aliança Nacional de Angola (PDP–ANA):** Leader Mfufumpinga Nlandu Victor.

**Partido Social Democrata de Angola (PSDA):** Leader André Milton Kilandonoco.

**Peaceful Democratic Party of Angola:** Leader António Kunzolako.

**Unangola:** Leader André Franco de Sousa.

**União Nacional para a Independência Total de Angola (UNITA):** f. 1966 to secure independence from Portugal; later received Portuguese support to oppose the MPLA; UNITA and the Frente Nacional de Libertação de Angola conducted guerrilla campaign against the MPLA Govt with aid from some Western countries, 1975–76; supported by South Africa until 1984 and in 1987–88, and by USA after 1986; obtained legal status in March

1998; support drawn mainly from Ovimbundu ethnic group; Pres. Dr JONAS MALHEIRO SAVIMBI; Sec.-Gen. PAULO LUKAMBA 'GATO'.

**UNITA Renovada:** f. 1998; splinter group claiming to be legitimate leadership of UNITA and recognized as such by MPLA, although commanding minority support among UNITA members; Leader EUGINIO MANUVAKOLA.

**United Front for the Salvation of Angola:** Leader JOSÉ AUGUSTO DA SILVA COELHO.

**Vofangola:** Leader LOMBY ZUENDOKI.

# Diplomatic Representation

### EMBASSIES IN ANGOLA

**Algeria:** Luanda; Ambassador: HANAFI OUSSEDIK.

**Belgium:** Avda 4 de Fevereiro 93, CP 1203, Luanda; tel. (2) 336437; fax (2) 336438; e-mail luanda@diplobel.org; Ambassador: MICHEL VANTROYEN.

**Brazil:** Rua Houari Boumedienne 132, CP 5428, Luanda; tel. (2) 344848; Ambassador: PAULO DYRCEU PINHEIRO.

**Bulgaria:** Rua Fernão Mendes Pinto 35, CP 2260, Luanda; tel. (2) 321010; Chargé d'affaires a.i.: LILO TOCHEV.

**Cape Verde:** Rua Alexandre Peres 29, Luanda; tel. (2) 333211; Ambassador: JOSÉ LUÍS JESUS.

**China, People's Republic:** Rua Houari Boumedienne 196, Luanda; tel. (2) 344185; Ambassador: XIAO SIJIN.

**Congo, Democratic Republic:** Rua Cesario Verde 24, Luanda; tel. (2) 361953; Ambassador: MUNDINDI DIDI KILENGO.

**Congo, Republic:** Rua 4 de Fevereiro 3, Luanda; Ambassador: ANATOLE KHONDO.

**Côte d'Ivoire:** Rua Karl Marx 43, Luanda; tel. (2) 333992; fax (2) 333997; Ambassador: ETIENNE MIEZAN EZO.

**Cuba:** Rua Che Guevara 42, Bairro Ingombotas, Luanda; tel. (2) 339165; Ambassador: JUAN B. PUJOL-SÁNCHEZ.

**Egypt:** Rua Comandante Stona 247, Luanda; tel. (2) 321590; Ambassador: ANWAR DAKROURY.

**France:** Rua Reverendo Pedro Agostinho Neto 31–33, Luanda; tel. (2) 334335; fax (2) 391949; Ambassador: ANDRÉ CIRA.

**Gabon:** Avda 4 de Fevereiro 95, Luanda; tel. (2) 372614; Ambassador: RAPHAËL NKASSA-NZOGHO.

**Germany:** Avda 4 de Fevereiro 120, CP 1295, Luanda; tel. (2) 334516; fax (2) 334516; Ambassador: Dr HENDRIK DANE.

**Ghana:** Rua Cirilo da Conceição e Silva 5, CP 1012, Luanda; tel. (2) 339222; fax (2) 338235; Ambassador: SIMON S. PULI.

**Guinea:** Luanda.

**Holy See:** Rua Luther King 123, CP 1030, Luanda (Apostolic Delegation); tel. (2) 336289; fax (2) 332378; Apostolic Delegate: Most Rev. ALDO CAVALLI, Titular Archbishop of Vibo Valentia.

**Hungary:** Rua Comandante Stona 226-228, Luanda; tel. (2) 32313; fax (2) 322448; Ambassador: Dr GÁBOR TÓTH.

**India:** Prédio dos Armazens Carrapas 81, 1°, D, CP 6040, Luanda; tel. (2) 345398; fax (2) 342061; Ambassador: BALDEV RAJ GHULIANI.

**Italy:** Edif. Importang 7°, Rua Kinaxixi, Luanda; tel. (2) 393533; Ambassador: PAOLA SANNELLA.

**Korea, Democratic People's Republic:** Rua Cabral Moncada 116–120, CP 599, Luanda; tel. (2) 395575; fax (2) 332813; Ambassador: HYON SOK.

**Morocco:** Largo 4 de Fevereiro 3, Luanda; tel. (2) 338847.

**Mozambique:** Luanda; tel. (2) 330811; Ambassador: M. SALESSIO.

**Namibia:** Rua dos Coqueiros, Luanda; tel. (2) 339234; fax (2) 394730.

**Netherlands:** Edif. Secil, Avda 4 de Fevereiro 42, CP 3624, Luanda; tel. (2) 333540; fax (2) 333699; e-mail lua@gg.lua.minbuza.nl; Ambassador: H. KROON.

**Nigeria:** Rua Houari Boumedienne 120, CP 479, Luanda; tel. (2) 340084; Ambassador: AGWOM GOKIR GOTIP.

**Poland:** Rua Comandante N'zaji 21–23, CP 1340, Luanda; tel. (2) 323086; Ambassador: JAN BOJKO.

**Portugal:** Rua Karl Marx 50, CP 1346, Luanda; tel. (2) 333027; Ambassador: RAMALHO ORTIGÃO.

**Romania:** Ramalho Ortigão 30, Alvalade, Luanda; tel. and fax (2) 321076; Ambassador: MARIN ILIESCU.

**Russia:** Rua Houari Boumedienne 170, CP 3141, Luanda; tel. (2) 345028; Ambassador: YURII KAPRALOV.

**São Tomé and Príncipe:** Rua Armindo de Andrade 173–175, Luanda; tel. (2) 345677; Ambassador: ARIOSTO CASTELO DAVID.

**Slovakia:** Rua Amílcar Cabral 5, CP 2691, Luanda; tel. (2) 334456.

**South Africa:** Rua Manuel Fernandes Caldeira 6B, CP 6212 Luanda; tel. (2) 397391; fax (2) 339126; Ambassador: R. J. M. MAMPANE.

**Spain:** Avda 4 de Fevereiro 95, 1°, CP 3061, Luanda; tel. (2) 391187; fax (2) 391188; Ambassador: ALVARO IRANZO.

**Sweden:** Rua Garcia Neto 9, Luanda; tel. (2) 340424; Ambassador: LENA SUND.

**Switzerland:** Avda 4 de Fevereiro 129, 2°, CP 3163, Luanda; tel. (2) 338314; fax (2) 336878; Chargé d'affaires a.i.: ARNOLDO LARDI.

**Tanzania:** Rua Joaquim Kapango 57–63, Luanda; tel. (2) 330536.

**United Kingdom:** Rua Diogo Cão 4, CP 1244, Luanda; tel. (2) 392991; fax (2) 333331; Ambassador: CAROLINE ELMES.

**USA:** Rua Houari Boumedienne 32, Miramar, CP 6468, Luanda; tel. (2) 346418; Ambassador: JOSEPH SULLIVAN.

**Viet Nam:** Rua Comandante N'zaji 66–68, CP 75, Luanda; tel. (2) 323388; Ambassador: NGUYEN HUY LOI.

**Yugoslavia:** Rua Comandante N'zaji 25–27, Luanda; tel. (2) 321421; fax (2) 321724; Chargé d'affaires a.i.: BRANKO MARKOVIĆ.

**Zambia:** Rua Rei Katyavala 106–108, CP 1496, Luanda; tel. (2) 331145; Ambassador: BONIFACE ZULU.

**Zimbabwe:** Edif. do Ministério de Transportes e Comunicações, Avda 4 de Fevereiro 42, CP 428, Luanda; tel. (2) 310125; fax (2) 311528; Ambassador: B. G. CHIDYAUSIKU.

# Judicial System

There is a Supreme Court and Court of Appeal in Luanda. There are also civil, criminal and military courts.

**Chief Justice of the Supreme Court:** JOÃO FELIZARDO.

# Religion

Much of the population follows traditional African beliefs, although a majority profess to be Christians, mainly Roman Catholics.

### CHRISTIANITY

**Conselho de Igrejas Cristãs em Angola** (Council of Christian Churches in Angola): Rua Amílcar Cabral 182, 1° andar, CP 1659, Luanda; tel. (2) 330415; fax (2) 393746; f. 1977; 14 mem. churches; five assoc. mems; one observer; Pres. Rev. ALVARO RODRIGUES; Gen. Sec. Rev. AUGUSTO CHIPESSE.

#### Protestant Churches

**Evangelical Congregational Church in Angola (Igreja Evangélica Congregacional em Angola:** CP 551, Huambo; tel. 3087; 100,000 mems; Gen. Sec. Rev. JÚLIO FRANCISCO.

**Evangelical Pentecostal Church of Angola (Missão Evangélica Pentecostal de Angola):** CP 219, Porto Amboim; 13,600 mems; Sec. Rev. JOSÉ DOMINGOS CAETANO.

**United Evangelical Church of Angola (Igreja Evangélica Unida de Angola):** CP 122, Uíge; 11,000 mems; Gen. Sec. Rev. A. L. DOMINGOS.

Other active denominations include the African Apostolic Church, the Church of Apostolic Faith in Angola, the Church of Our Lord Jesus Christ in the World, the Evangelical Baptist Church, the Evangelical Church in Angola, the Evangelical Church of the Apostles of Jerusalem, the Evangelical Reformed Church of Angola, the Kimbanguist Church in Angola and the United Methodist Church.

#### The Roman Catholic Church

Angola comprises three archdioceses and 12 dioceses. At 31 December 1997 an estimated 49.5% of the total population were adherents.

**Bishops' Conference:** Conferência Episcopal de Angola e São Tomé, CP 87, Luanda; tel. (2) 343686; fax (2) 345504; f. 1967; Pres. Most Rev. ZACARIAS KAMWENHO, Archbishop of Lubango.

**Archbishop of Huambo:** Most Rev. FRANCISCO VITI, Arcebispado, CP 10, Huambo; tel. 20130.

**Archbishop of Luanda:** Cardinal ALEXANDRE DO NASCIMENTO, Arcebispado, CP 87, 1230-C, Luanda; tel. (2) 334640; fax (2) 334433.

**Archbishop of Lubango:** Most Rev. ZACARIAS KAMWENHO, Arcebispado, CP 231, Lubango; tel. 20405; fax 23547.

# The Press

The press was nationalized in 1976.

### DAILIES

**Diário da República:** CP 1306, Luanda; official govt bulletin.

**O Jornal de Angola:** Rua Rainha Ginga 18–24, CP 1312, Luanda; tel. (2) 338947; fax (2) 333342; f. 1923; Dir-Gen. LUÍS FERNANDO; mornings and Sun.; circ. 41,000.

Newspapers are also published in several regional towns.

### PERIODICALS

**Angola Norte:** CP 97, Malanje; weekly.

**Angolense:** Luanda; weekly.

**A Célula:** Luanda; political journal of MPLA; monthly.

**Comércio Externo:** Rua da Missão 85, CP 6375, Luanda; tel. (2) 334060; fax (2) 392216.

**Correio da Semana:** Rua Rainha Ginga 18–24, CP 1213, Luanda; tel. (2) 331623; fax (2) 333342; f. 1992; owned by *O Jornal de Angola*; weekly. Editor-in-Chief MANUEL DIONISIO.

**Eme:** Rua Ho Chi Minh, Luanda; tel. (2) 321130; f. 1996; MPLA publ.

**Folha 8:** Rua Conselheiro Julio de Vilhena 24, 5° andar, Luanda; tel. (2) 391943; fax (2) 392289; two a week.

**Horizonte:** Rua da Samba 144, 1° andar, Luanda.

**Jornal de Benguela:** CP 17, Benguela; 2 a week.

**Lavra & Oficina:** CP 2767-C, Luanda; tel. (2) 322155; f. 1975; journal of the Union of Angolan Writers; monthly; circ. 5,000.

**Militar:** Luanda; f. 1993; Editor-in-Chief CARMO NETO.

**Noticias de Angola:** Calçada G. Ferreira, Luanda; weekly.

**Novembro:** CP 3947, Luanda; tel. (2) 331660; monthly; Dir ROBERTO DE ALMEIDA.

**O Planalto:** CP 96, Huambo; 2 a week.

**Tempos Novos:** Avda Combatentes 244, 2° andar, CP 16088, Luanda; tel. (2) 349534; fax (2) 349534.

**A Voz do Povo:** Rua João de Deus 99-103, Vila Alice, Luanda.

**A Voz do Trabalhador:** Avda 4 de Fevereiro 210, CP 28, Luanda; journal of União Nacional de Trabalhadores Angolanos (National Union of Angolan Workers); monthly.

### NEWS AGENCIES

**ANGOP:** Rua Rei Katiavala 120, CP 2181, Luanda; tel. (2) 391525; fax (2) 391537; Dir-Gen. and Editor-in-Chief AVELINO MIGUEL.

#### Foreign Bureaux

**Agence France-Presse (AFP):** Prédio Mutamba, CP 2357, Luanda; tel. (2) 334939; Bureau Chief MANUELA TEIXEIRA.

**Allgemeiner Deutscher Nachrichtendienst (ADN)** (Germany): CP 3193, Luanda; Correspondent GUDRUN GROSS.

**Informatsionnoye Telegrafnoye Agentstvo Rossii—Telegrafnoye Agentstvo Suverennykh Stran (ITAR—TASS)** (Russia): Rua Marechal Tito 75, CP 3209, Luanda; tel. (2) 342524; Correspondent VLADIMIR BORISOVICH BUYANOV.

**Inter Press Service (IPS)** (Italy): c/o Centro de Imprensa Anibal de Melo, Rua Cequeira Lukoki 124, Luanda; tel. (2) 334895; fax: (2) 393445; Correspondent CHRIS SIMPSON.

**Prensa Latina** (Cuba): Rua D. Miguel de Melo 92-2, Luanda; tel. (2) 336804; Chief Correspondent LUÍS MANUEL SÁEZ.

**Reuters** (UK): c/o Centro de Imprensa Anibal de Melo, Rua Cequeira Lukoki 124, Luanda; tel. (2) 334895; fax (2) 393445; Correspondent CRISTINA MULLER.

**Rossiyskoye Informatsionnoye Agentstvo—Novosti (RIA—Novosti)** (Russia): Luanda; Chief Officer VLADISLAV Z. KOMAROV.

**Xinhua (New China) News Agency** (People's Republic of China): Rua Karl Marx 57-3, andar E, Bairro das Ingombotas, Zona 4, Luanda; tel. (2) 332415; Correspondent ZHAO XIAOZHONG.

## Publishers

**Empresa Distribuidora Livreira (EDIL), UEE:** Rua da Missão 107, CP 1245, Luanda; tel. (2) 334034.

**Neográfica, SARL:** CP 6518, Luanda; publrs of *Novembro*.

**Nova Editorial Angolana, SARL:** CP 1225, Luanda; f. 1935; general and educational; Man. Dir POMBO FERNANDES.

**Offsetográfica Gráfica Industrial Lda:** CP 911, Benguela; tel. 32568; f. 1966; Man. FERNANDO MARTINS.

#### Government Publishing House

**Imprensa Nacional, UEE:** CP 1306, Luanda; f. 1845; Gen. Man. Dr ANTÓNIO DUARTE DE ALMEIDA E CARMO.

## Broadcasting and Communications

### TELECOMMUNICATIONS

**Empresa Pública de Telecomunicações (EPTEL), UEE:** Rua I Congresso 26, CP 625, Luanda; tel. (2) 392285; fax (2) 391688; international telecommunications.

### BROADCASTING

#### Radio

**Rádio Nacional de Angola:** Rua Comandante Jika, CP 1329, Luanda; tel. (2) 320192; fax (2) 324647; broadcasts in Portuguese, English, French, Spanish and vernacular languages (Chokwe, Kikongo, Kimbundu, Kwanyama, Fiote, Ngangela, Luvale, Songu, Umbundu); Dir-Gen. AGOSTINHO VIEIRA LOPES.

**Luanda Antena Comercial (LAC):** Praceta Luther King 5, Luanda; tel. (2) 396229; e-mail lac@ebonet.net.

#### Television

**Televisão Popular de Angola (TPA):** Rua Ho Chi Minh, CP 2604, Luanda; tel. (2) 320025; fax (2) 391091; f. 1975; state-controlled; Man. Dir CARLOS CUNHA.

## Finance

(cap. = capital; res = reserves; dep. = deposits; m. = million; brs = branches; amounts in old kwanza)

### BANKING

All banks were nationalized in 1975. In 1995 the Government authorized the formation of private banks.

#### Central Bank

**Banco Nacional de Angola:** Avda 4 de Fevereiro 151, CP 1298, Luanda; tel. (2) 332633; fax (2) 390579; e-mail bnagab@ebonet; internet www.ebonet.net/bna; f. 1976; bank of issue; cap. and res 7,657m.; dep. 111,975m. (1983); Gov. AGUINALDO JAIME.

#### Commercial Banks

**Banco de Crédito Comercial e Industrial:** CP 1395, Luanda.

**Banco de Poupança e Crédito (BPC):** Largo Saydi Mingas, CP 1343, Luanda; tel. (2) 339158; fax (2) 393790; cap. 10,000m. (Dec. 1992); Chair. AMILCAR S. AZEVEDO SILVA; brs throughout Angola.

**Caixa de Crédito Agro-Pecuario e Pescas (CCAPP):** Rua Rainha Ginga 83; tel. (2) 392749; fax (2) 392225; f. 1991; assumed commercial operations of Banco Nacional de Angola in 1996.

#### Development Bank

**Banco de Comércio e Indústria SARL:** Avda 4 de Fevereiro 86, CP 1395, Luanda; tel. (2) 333684; fax (2) 333839; f. 1991; provides loans to businesses in all sectors; cap. 1,000m., dep. 424,591.3m. (1992); Chair. PEDRO MAIANGALA PUNA; 2 brs.

#### Investment Bank

**Banco Africano de Investimentos SARL (BAI):** Rua Major Kanhangulo 34, CP 6022, Luanda; tel. (2) 335749; fax (2) 335486; f. 1996; 37.5% interest owned by Angolan shareholders; Pres. MÁRIO ABILIO PALHARES.

#### Foreign Banks

**Banco Espírito Santo e Comercial de Lisboa SA:** 5-3°, Rua Cirilo da Conceição Silva, CP 1471, Luanda; tel. (2) 392287; fax (2) 391484; Rep. JOSÉ RIBEIRO DA SILVA.

**Banco de Fomento e Exterior SA:** Edifício BPA, 7° andar, Rua Dr Alfredo Troni, Luanda; tel. (2) 394275; fax (2) 397090; Man. TERESA MATEUS.

**Banco Português do Atlântico:** Largo Rainha Ginga 6–8, CP 5726, Luanda; tel. (2) 397946; fax (2) 397397.

**Banco Totta e Açores SA:** Avda 4 de Fevereiro 99, CP 1231, Luanda; tel. (2) 336440; fax (2) 333233; e-mail totta-ang@edonet.net; Gen. Man. Dr MÁRIO NELSON MAXIMINO.

### INSURANCE

**Empresa Nacional de Seguros e Resseguros de Angola (ENSA), UEE:** Avda 4 de Fevereiro 93, CP 5778, Luanda; tel. (2) 332991.

## Trade and Industry

### SUPERVISORY BODY

**National Supplies Commission:** Luanda; f. 1977 to combat sabotage and negligence.

### CHAMBERS OF COMMERCE

**Angolan Chamber of Commerce and Industry:** Largo do Kinaxixi 14, 1° andar, CP 92, Luanda; tel. (2) 344506; fax (2) 344629; Pres. ANTÓNIO JOÃO DOS SANTOS.

**Associação Comercial de Luanda:** Edifício Palácio de Comércio, 1° andar, CP 1275, Luanda; tel. (2) 322453.

### STATE TRADING ORGANIZATIONS

**Angomédica, UEE:** Rua do Sanatório, Bairro Palanca, CP 2698, Luanda; tel. (2) 363765; fax (2) 362336; f. 1981 to import pharmaceutical goods; Gen. Dir Dr FÁTIMA SAIUNDO.

**Direcção dos Serviços de Comércio** (Dept of Trade): Largo Diogo Cão, CP 1337, Luanda; f. 1970; brs throughout Angola.

**Epmel, UEE:** Rua Karl Marx 35–37, Luanda; tel. (2) 330943; industrial agricultural machinery.

**Exportang, UEE:** Rua dos Enganos 1A, CP 1000, Luanda; tel. (2) 332363; co-ordinates exports.

**Importang, UEE:** Calçada do Município 10, CP 1003, Luanda; tel. (2) 337994. 1977; co-ordinates majority of imports; Dir-Gen. SIMÃO DIOGO DA CRUZ.

**Maquimport, UEE:** Rua Rainha Ginga 152, CP 2975, Luanda; tel. (2) 339044. 1981 to import office equipment.

**Mecanang, UEE:** Rua dos Enganos, 1°–7° andar, CP 1347, Luanda; tel. (2) 390644. 1981 to import agricultural and construction machinery, tools and spare parts.

### STATE INDUSTRIAL ENTERPRISES

**Companhia do Açúcar de Angola:** Rua Direita 77, Luanda; production of sugar.

**Companhia Geral dos Algodões de Angola (COTONANG):** Avda da Boavista, Luanda; production of cotton textiles.

**Empresa Abastecimento Técnico Material (EMATEC), UEE:** Largo Rainha Ginga 3, CP 2952, Luanda; tel. (2) 338891; technical and material suppliers to the Ministry of Defence.

**Empresa Açucareira Centro (OSUKA), UEE:** Estrada Principal do Lobito, CP 37, Catumbela; tel. 24681; sugar industry.

**Empresa Açucareira Norte (ACUNOR), UEE:** Rua Robert Shilds, Caxito, Bengo; tel. 71720; sugar production.

**Empresa Angolana de Embalagens (METANGOL), UEE:** Rua Estrada do Cacuaco, CP 151, Luanda; tel. (2) 370680; production of non-specified metal goods.

**Empresa de Cimento de Angola (CIMANGOLA), UEE:** Avda 4 de Fevereiro 42, Luanda; tel. (2) 371190. 1954; 69% state-owned; cement production; exports to several African countries.

**Empresa de Construção de Edificações (CONSTROI), UEE:** Rua Alexandre Peres, CP 2566, Luanda; tel. (2) 333930; construction.

**Empresa de Pesca de Angola (PESCANGOLA), UEE:** Luanda; f. 1981; state fishing enterprise, responsible to Ministry of Fisheries and Environment.

**Empresa de Rebenefício e Exportação do Café de Angola (CAFANGOL), UEE:** Rua Robert Shields 4/6, CP 342, Luanda; tel. (2) 337916; fax (2) 334742; f. 1983; nat. coffee-processing and trade org; proposed transfer to private sector announced in 1991.

**Empresa de Tecidos de Angola (TEXTANG), UEE:** Rua N'gola Kiluanji-Kazenga, CP 5404, Luanda; tel. (2) 381134; production of textiles.

**Empresa Nacional de Cimento (ENCIME), UEE:** CP 157, Lobito; tel. (711) 2325; cement production.

**Empresa Nacional de Comercialização e Distribuição de Produtos Agrícolas (ENCODIPA):** Luanda; central marketing agency for agricultural produce; numerous brs throughout Angola.

**Empresa Nacional de Diamantes de Angola (ENDIAMA), UEE:** Rua Major Kanhangulo 100, Luanda; tel. (2) 392336; fax (2) 337276; f. 1981 as the sole diamond-mining concession; commenced operations 1986; Dir-Gen. AUGUSTO PAULINO ALMEIDA NETO.

**Empresa Nacional de Ferro de Angola (FERRANGOL):** Rua João de Barros 26, CP 2692, Luanda; tel. (2) 373800; iron production; Dir ARMANDO DE SOUSA (MACHADINHO).

**Empresa Nacional de Manutenção (MANUTECNICA), UEE:** Rua 7, Avda do Cazenga 10, CP 3508, Luanda; tel. (2) 383646; assembly of machines and specialized equipment for industry.

**Empresa Texteis de Angola (ENTEX), UEE:** Avda Comandante Kima Kienda, CP 5720, Luanda; tel. (2) 336182; weaving and tissue finishing.

**Fina Petróleos de Angola SARL:** CP 1320, Luanda; tel. (2) 336869; fax (2) 391031; e-mail carlos.alves@fpa.ebonet.net; f. 1957; petroleum production, refining and exploration; operates Luanda petroleum refinery, Petrangol, with capacity of 40,000 b/d; also operates Quinfuquena terminal; Man. CARLOS ALVES.

**Siderurgia Nacional, UEE:** CP Zona Industrial do Forel das Lagostas, Luanda; tel. (2) 373028. 1963, nationalized 1980; steelworks and rolling mill plant.

**Sociedade Nacional de Combustíveis de Angola (SONANGOL):** Rua I Congresso do MPLA, CP 1318, Luanda; tel. (2) 331690. 1976 for exploration, production and refining of crude petroleum, and marketing and distribution of petroleum products; sole concessionary in Angola, supervises on- and offshore operations of foreign petroleum cos; holds majority interest in jt ventures with Cabinda Gulf Oil Co (Cabgoc), Fina Petróleos de Angola and Texaco Petróleos de Angola; Dir-Gen. JOAQUIM DAVID.

**Sociedade Unificada de Tabacos de Angola, Lda (SUT):** Rua Deolinda Rodrigues 530/537, CP 1263, Luanda; tel. (2) 360180; fax (2) 362138; f. 1919; tobacco products; Gen. Man. Dr MANUEL LAMAS.

### UTILITIES

#### Electricity

**Empresa Nacional de Construções Eléctricas (ENCEL), UEE:** Rua Comandante Che Guevara 185/7, Luanda; tel. (2) 346712; fax (2) 346759; e-mail encel.dg@netangola.com; f. 1982.

**Empresa Nacional de Electricidade (ENE), UEE:** Edifício Geominas, 6°–7° andar, CP 772, Luanda; tel. (2) 321529; fax (2) 323382; e-mail enedg@netangola.com; f. 1980; production and distribution of electricity; Dir-Gen. Eng. MARIO FERNANDO PONTES MOREIRA FONTES.

### TRADE UNIONS

**Angolan General Independent and Free Trade Union Confederation:** Chair. MANUEL DIFUILA.

**União Nacional de Trabalhadores Angolanos (UNTA)** (National Union of Angolan Workers): Avda 4 de Fevereiro 210, CP 28, Luanda; tel. (2) 334670; fax (2) 393590; f. 1960; Pres. MANUEL DIOGO DA SILVA NETO; Gen. Sec. MANUEL AUGUSTO VIAGE; 600,000 mems.

## Transport

The transport infrastructure has been severely dislocated by the civil war.

### RAILWAYS

The total length of track operated was 2,952 km in 1987. There are plans to extend the Namibe line beyond Menongue and to construct north–south rail links.

**Caminhos de Ferro de Angola:** Avda 4 de Fevereiro 42, CP 1250-C, Luanda; tel. (2) 339794; fax (2) 339976; f. 1975; nat. network operating four fmrly independent systems covering 2,952 track-km; Nat. Dir R. M. DA CONCEIÇÃO JUNIOR.

**Amboim Railway:** Porto Amboim; f. 1922; 123 track-km; Dir A. GUIA.

**Benguela Railway (Companhia do Caminho de Ferro de Benguela):** Rua Praça 11 Novembro 3, CP 32, Lobito; tel. (711) 22645; fax (711) 22865; f. 1903, line completed 1928; owned 90% by Tank Consolidated Investments (a subsidiary of Société Générale de Belgique), 10% by Govt of Angola; line carrying passenger and freight traffic from the port of Lobito across Angola, via Huambo and Luena, to the border of the Democratic Republic of the Congo (fmrly Zaire) where it connects with that country's railway system, which, in turn, links with Zambia Railways, thus providing the shortest west coast route for central African trade; 1,394 track-km; guerrilla operations by UNITA suspended all international traffic from 1975, with only irregular services from Lobito to Huambo being operated; a declaration of intent to reopen the cross-border lines was signed in 1987 by Angola, Zambia and Zaire, and the rehabilitation of the railway was a priority of a 10-year programme, planned by the SADCC (now SADC), to develop the 'Lobito corridor'; In 1997 an Italian company, Tor di Vale, began a US $450m.-programme of repairs to the railway. Minimum repairs allowing the resumption of freight traffic were expected to take three years to complete, to be followed by further modernization, including the reconstruction of 22 passenger stations; Dir-Gen. DANIEL QUIPAXE.

**Luanda Railway (Empresa de Caminho de Ferro de Luanda, UEE):** CP 1250-C, Luanda; tel. (2) 370061. 1886; serves an iron, cotton and sisal-producing region between Luanda and Malanje; reconstruction of Luanda-Dondo rail link completed 1997, rehabilitation of Dondo-Malanje section proceeding in 1999; 536 track-km; Man. A. ALVARO AGANTE.

**Namibe Railway:** CP 130, Lubango; f. 1905; main line from Namibe to Menongue, via Lubango; br. lines to Chibia and iron ore mines at Cassinga; 899 track-km; Gen. Man. J. SALVADOR.

### ROADS

In 1996 Angola had 72,626 km of roads, of which 7,955 km were main roads and 15,571 km were secondary roads. About 25% of roads were paved. In 1997 the state-owned road construction and maintenance company, the Instituto de Estradas de Angola, reported that 80% of the country's road network was in disrepair and that the cost of rebuilding the roads and bridges damaged during the civil conflict would total some US $4,000m.

### SHIPPING

The main harbours are at Lobito, Luanda and Namibe; the commercial port of Porto Amboim, in Cuanza-Sul province, has been closed for repairs since 1984. The expansion of port facilities in Cabinda was due to begin in late 1995 and was expected to be completed within two years. In 1983 a regular shipping service began to operate between Luanda and Maputo (Mozambique). Under the emergency transport programme launched in 1988, refurbishment work was to be undertaken on the ports of Luanda and Namibe. The first phase of a 10-year SADCC (now SADC) programme to develop the 'Lobito corridor', for which funds were pledged in January 1989, was to include the rehabilitation of the ports of Lobito and Benguela.

**Angonave—Linhas Marítimas de Angola, UEE:** Rua Serqueira 31, CP 5953, Luanda; tel. (2) 330144. shipping line; Dir-Gen. FRANCISCO VENÂNCIO.

**Cabotang—Cabotagem Nacional Angolana, UEE:** Avda 4 de Fevereiro 83A, Luanda; tel. (2) 373133; operates off the coasts of Angola and Mozambique; Dir-Gen. JOÃO OCTAVIO VAN-DÚNEM.

**Empresa Portuária do Lobito, UEE:** Avda da Independência, CP 16, Lobito; tel. (711) 2710; long-distance sea transport; Gen. Man. JOSÉ CARLOS GOMES.

**Empresa Portuária de Moçâmedes—Namibe, UEE:** Rua Pedro Benje 10A and 10C, CP 49, Namibe; tel. (64) 60643; long-distance sea transport; Dir HUMBERTO DE ATAIDE DIAS.

**Linhas Marítimas de Angola, UEE:** Rua Serqueira 31, CP 5953, Luanda; tel. (2) 30144.

**Secil Marítima SARL, UEE:** Avda 4 de Fevereiro 42, 1° andar, CP 5910, Luanda; tel. (2) 335230.

### CIVIL AVIATION

**Air Nacoia:** Rua Comandante Che Guevara 67, 1° andar, Luanda; tel. and fax (2) 395477; f. 1993; Pres. SALVADOR SILVA.

**TAAG—Linhas Aéreas de Angola:** Rua da Missão 123, CP 79, Luanda; tel. (2) 334889; fax (2) 332714; f. 1939; internal scheduled passenger and cargo services, and services from Luanda to destinations within Africa and to Europe, South America and the Caribbean; Chair. MIGUEL COSTA; Commercial Dir. ERNESTO MONIMAMBO.

**Angola Air Charter:** Aeroporto Internacional 4 de Fevereiro, CP 5433, Luanda; tel. (2) 350559; fax (2) 392229; f. 1992; subsidiary of TAAG.

**Transafrik International:** Rua Joaquim Kapango, CP 2839, Luanda; tel. (2) 352141; fax (2) 351723; f. 1986; operates contract cargo services mainly within Africa; Man. Dir ERICH F. KOCH; Gen. Man. PIMENTAL ARAUJO.

## Tourism

**National Tourist Agency:** Palácio de Vidro, CP 1240, Luanda; tel. (2) 372750.

# ANTARCTICA

Source: Scientific Committee on Antarctic Research, Scott Polar Research Institute, Lensfield Rd, Cambridge, CB2 1ER, England; tel. (1223) 362061; fax (1223) 336549; e-mail execsec@scar.demon.co.uk; internet www.scar.org.

The Continent of Antarctica is estimated to cover 13,661,000 sq km. There are no indigenous inhabitants, but a number of permanent research stations have been established. W. S. Bruce, of the Scottish National Antarctic Expedition (1902–04), established a meteorological station on Laurie Island, South Orkney Islands, on 1 April 1903. After the expedition, this was transferred to the Argentine authorities (the British Government having declined to operate the station), who have maintained the observatory since 22 February 1904 (see Orcadas, below). The next permanent stations were established in 1944 by the United Kingdom, and then subsequently by other countries.

## Wintering Stations

(The following list includes wintering stations south of latitude 60° occupied during austral winter 1999)

| | Latitude | Longitude |
|---|---|---|
| **ARGENTINA** | | |
| General Belgrano II, Bertrab Nunatak, Luitpold Coast | 77° 52′ S | 34° 38′ W |
| Esperanza, Hope Bay | 63° 24′ S | 57° 00′ W |
| Teniente Jubany, King George Island | 62° 14′ S | 58° 40′ W |
| Vicecomodoro Marambio, Seymour Island | 64° 15′ S | 56° 39′ W |
| Orcadas, Laurie Island | 60° 44′ S | 44° 44′ W |
| General San Martín, Barry Island | 68° 08′ S | 67° 06′ W |

**AUSTRALIA**

| | | |
|---|---|---|
| Casey, Vincennes Bay, Budd Coast | 66° 17′ S | 110° 31′ E |
| Davis, Ingrid Christensen Coast | 68° 35′ S | 77° 58′ E |
| Mawson, Mac. Robertson Land | 67° 36′ S | 62° 52′ E |

In a report published in 1997 the Australian Government's advisory body on the Antarctic proposed that future research work might be concentrated at the Davis station, thus enabling Casey and Mawson to be leased to other countries or to strictly regulated tour operators. (In 1998/99 the total number of tourists visiting Antarctica—mainly on special 'eco-cruises'—amounted to about 10,000.)

**BRAZIL**

| | | |
|---|---|---|
| Comandante Ferraz, King George Island | 62° 05′ S | 58° 23′ W |

**CHILE**

| | | |
|---|---|---|
| Capitán Arturo Prat, Greenwich Island | 62° 30′ S | 59° 41′ W |
| General Bernardo O'Higgins, Cape Legoupil | 63° 19′ S | 57° 54′ W |
| Presidente Eduardo Frei, King George Island | 62° 12′ S | 58° 58′ W |
| Professor Julio Escudero, King George Island | 62° 12′ S | 58° 59′ W |

**PEOPLE'S REPUBLIC OF CHINA**

| | | |
|---|---|---|
| Chang Cheng (Great Wall), King George Island | 62° 13′ S | 58° 58′ W |
| Zhongshan, Princess Elizabeth Land | 69° 22′ S | 76° 23′ E |

**FRANCE**

| | | |
|---|---|---|
| Dumont d'Urville, Terre Adélie | 66° 40′ S | 140° 00′ E |

A new research station, Concorde (at Dome C—75° 06′ S 123° 23′ E), was officially open for summer routine operations in December 1997 as a joint venture with Italy; the station was expected to be opened year round from 2003.

**GERMANY**

| | | |
|---|---|---|
| Neumayer, Ekstrømisen | 70° 38′ S | 8° 16′ W |

**INDIA**

| | | |
|---|---|---|
| Maitri, Schirmacheroasen | 70° 46′ S | 11° 44′ E |

**JAPAN**

| | | |
|---|---|---|
| Syowa, Ongul | 69° 00′ S | 39° 35′ E |

**REPUBLIC OF KOREA**

| | | |
|---|---|---|
| King Sejong, King George Island | 62° 13′ S | 58° 47′ W |

**NEW ZEALAND**

| | | |
|---|---|---|
| Scott Base, Ross Island | 77° 51′ S | 166° 46′ E |

**POLAND**

| | | |
|---|---|---|
| Henryk Arctowski, King George Island | 62° 10′ S | 58° 28′ W |

**RUSSIA**

| | | |
|---|---|---|
| Bellingshausen, King George Island | 62° 12′ S | 58° 58′ W |
| Mirnyy, Queen Mary Land | 66° 33′ S | 93° 01′ E |
| Molodezhnaya, Enderby Land | 67° 40′ S | 45° 51′ E |
| Novolazarevskaya, Prinsesse Astrid Kyst | 70° 46′ S | 11° 50′ E |
| Progress, Princess Elizabeth Land | 69° 23′ S | 76° 23′ E |
| Vostok, East Antarctica | 78° 28′ S | 106° 48′ E |

**SOUTH AFRICA**

| | | |
|---|---|---|
| SANAE, Vesleskarvet | 71° 41′ S | 2° 50′ W |

**UKRAINE**

| | | |
|---|---|---|
| Vernadsky, Argentine Islands | 65° 15′ S | 64° 15′ W |

**UNITED KINGDOM**

| | | |
|---|---|---|
| Halley, Brunt Ice Shelf, Caird Coast | 75° 35′ S | 26° 30′ W |
| Rothera, Adelaide Island | 67° 34′ S | 68° 07′ W |

In May 1990 the UK built an airstrip at the Rothera scientific station.

**USA**

| | | |
|---|---|---|
| McMurdo, Ross Island | 77° 51′ S | 166° 40′ E |
| Palmer, Anvers Island | 64° 47′ S | 64° 03′ W |
| Amundsen-Scott | South Pole* | |

* The precise co-ordinates of the location of this station are: 89° 59′ 51″ S, 139° 16′ 22″ E.

**URUGUAY**

| | | |
|---|---|---|
| Artigas, King George Island | 62° 11′ S | 58° 54′ W |

## Territorial Claims

| Territory | Claimant State |
|---|---|
| Antártida Argentina | Argentina |
| Australian Antarctic Territory | Australia |
| British Antarctic Territory | United Kingdom |
| Dronning Maud Land | Norway |
| Ross Dependency | New Zealand |
| Terre Adélie | France |
| Territorio Chileno Antártico | Chile |

These claims are not recognized by the USA or Russia. No formal claims have been made in the sector of Antarctica between 90° W and 150° W.

See also Article 4 of the Antarctic Treaty below.

## Research

**Scientific Committee on Antarctic Research (SCAR)** of the **International Council of Scientific Unions (ICSU):** Secretariat: Scott Polar Research Institute, Lensfield Rd, Cambridge, CB2 1ER, England; tel. (1223) 362061; fax (1223) 336549; e-mail execsec@scar.demon.co.uk; internet www.scar.org; f. 1958 to initiate, promote and co-ordinate scientific research in the Antarctic, and to provide scientific advice to the Antarctic Treaty System; 26 full mems; six assoc. mems.

**President:** Dr R. H. Rutford (USA).

**Vice-Presidents:** Dr R. Schlich (France), Dr J. Valencia (Chile), Prof. A. D. M. Walker (South Africa), Dr F. J. Davey (New Zealand).

**Executive Secretary:** Dr P. D. Clarkson.

# The Antarctic Treaty

The Treaty (summarized below) was signed in Washington, DC, on 1 December 1959 by the 12 nations co-operating in the Antarctic during the International Geophysical Year, and entered into force on 23 June 1961. The Treaty made provision for a review of its terms, 30 years after ratification; however, no signatory to the Treaty has requested such a review.

Article 1. Antarctica shall be used for peaceful purposes only.

Article 2. On freedom of scientific investigation and co-operation.

Article 3. On exchange of information and personnel.

Article 4. i. Nothing contained in the present Treaty shall be interpreted as:

(a) a renunciation by any Contracting Party of previously asserted rights of or claims to territorial sovereignty in Antarctica;

(b) a renunciation or diminution by any Contracting Party of any basis of claim to territorial sovereignty in Antarctica which it may have whether as a result of its activities or those of its nationals in Antarctica, or otherwise;

(c) prejudicing the position of any Contracting Party as regards its recognition or non-recognition of any other State's right of or claim or basis of claim to territorial sovereignty in Antarctica.

ii. No acts or activities taking place while the present Treaty is in force shall constitute a basis for asserting, supporting or denying a claim to territorial sovereignty in Antarctica or create any rights of sovereignty in Antarctica. No new claim, or enlargement of an existing claim, to territorial sovereignty in Antarctica shall be asserted while the present Treaty is in force.

Article 5. Any nuclear explosions in Antarctica and the disposal there of radioactive waste material shall be prohibited.

Article 6. On geographical limits and rights on high seas.

Article 7. On designation of observers and notification of stations and expeditions.

Article 8. On jurisdiction over observers and scientists.

Article 9. On consultative meetings.

Articles 10–14. On upholding, interpreting, amending, notifying and depositing the Treaty.

### ORIGINAL SIGNATORIES

| | | |
|---|---|---|
| Argentina | France | South Africa |
| Australia | Japan | USSR (former) |
| Belgium | New Zealand | United Kingdom |
| Chile | Norway | USA |

### ACCEDING STATES

Austria, Brazil, Bulgaria, Canada, the People's Republic of China, Colombia, Cuba, the Czech Republic, Denmark, Ecuador, Finland, Germany, Greece, Guatemala, Hungary, India, Italy, the Democratic People's Republic of Korea, the Republic of Korea, the Netherlands, Papua New Guinea, Peru, Poland, Romania, Slovakia, Spain, Sweden, Switzerland, Turkey, Ukraine, Uruguay, Venezuela.

Brazil, Bulgaria, the People's Republic of China, Ecuador, Finland, Germany, India, Italy, the Republic of Korea, the Netherlands, Peru, Poland, Spain, Sweden and Uruguay have achieved consultative status under the Treaty, by virtue of their scientific activity in Antarctica.

### ANTARCTIC TREATY CONSULTATIVE MEETINGS

Meetings of representatives from all the original signatory nations of the Antarctic Treaty and acceding nations accorded consultative status (27 in 1999), are held every one to two years to discuss scientific, environmental and political matters. The 23nd meeting was held in Lima, Peru, in May–June 1999. The representatives elect a Chairman and Secretary. Committees and Working Groups are established as required.

Among the numerous measures that have been agreed and implemented by the Consultative Parties are several designed to protect the Antarctic environment and wildlife. These include Agreed Measures for the Conservation of Antarctic Flora and Fauna, the designation of Specially Protected Areas and Sites of Special Scientific Interest, a Convention for the Conservation of Antarctic Seals, and a Convention on the Conservation of Antarctic Marine Living Resources.

A Convention on the Regulation of Antarctic Mineral Resource Activities (the Wellington Convention) was adopted in June 1988 and was opened for signature in November. To enter into force, the Wellington Convention required the ratification of 16 of the Consultative Parties (then numbering 22). However, France and Australia opposed the Convention, which would permit mineral exploitation (under stringent international controls) in Antarctica, and proposed the creation of an Antarctic wilderness reserve. An agreement was reached at the October 1989 Consultative Meeting, whereby two extraordinary meetings were to be convened in Chile in November 1990, one to discuss the protection of the environment and the other to discuss the issue of liability for environmental damage within the framework of the Wellington Convention. In September 1990 the Government of New Zealand, which played a major role in drafting the Wellington Convention, reversed its policy, stating that it was no longer willing to ratify the Convention. At the same time, it introduced legislation in the New Zealand House of Representatives to ban all mining and prospecting activities from its territories in Antarctica. At the extraordinary meetings, which were held in Chile in November–December, the Consultative Parties failed to reach an agreement regarding the protection of Antarctica's environment. However, a draft protocol was approved. This formed the basis for a further meeting in Madrid, Spain, in April 1991. France, Australia and 16 other countries supported a permanent ban on mining, whereas the USA, the United Kingdom, Japan, Germany and four others were in favour of a moratorium. Subsequently, however, Japan and Germany transferred their allegiance to the Australian-French initiative, exerting considerable pressure on the USA and the United Kingdom, whose position became increasingly isolated. Agreement was eventually reached on a ban on mining activity for 50 years, and mechanisms for a review of the ban after 50 years, or before if all Parties agree. This agreement is embodied in Article 7 of the Protocol on Environmental Protection to the Antarctic Treaty, which was adopted by the original signatory nations in October 1991, immediately prior to the 16th Consultative Meeting. By late 1997 the Protocol had been ratified by all of the Consultative Parties (then numbering 26), and entered into force on 14 January 1998. Thus there can be mining in the Antarctic only with the consent of all the present Consultative Parties and, even then, only when a regulatory regime is in place. The first four annexes to the Protocol, providing for environmental impact assessment, conservation of fauna and flora, waste disposal, and monitoring of marine pollution, entered into force with the Protocol, but the fifth annex, on area protection, agreed after the adoption of the Protocol, has yet to take effect. A sixth annex on environmental liability is currently being negotiated. At the 22nd Consultative Meeting in mid-1998 the Committee for Environmental Protection was established, under the provisions of the Protocol on Environmental Protection, and held its first meeting. In January 1999 the first ever political meeting held in Antarctica took place at the US McMurdo Station on Ross Island and was attended by representatives of 24 of the then 43 countries acceding to the Antarctic Treaty; all of the participants reaffirmed their commitment to the protection of the Antarctic environment under the terms of the Treaty. Of especial concern in the late 1990s was the threat posed to stocks of fish—and, in particular, to the Patagonian toothfish—by illegal fishing.

At a meeting of the International Whaling Commission (see p. 284), held in Mexico in May 1994, it was agreed to establish a whale sanctuary around Antarctica below 40° S. The sanctuary, which was expected to protect about 80% of the world's remaining whales from commercial hunting, came into effect in December.

In May 1997 the World Meteorological Organization (see p. 110) suggested that long-term prospects for the rate of depletion of the ozone layer over Antarctica might be improving, but that strong statistical evidence of such a trend might not become apparent for at least five years. In late 1998 the New Zealand Government reported that the largest ozone hole on record, covering more than 27m. sq km, had formed over Antarctica. In late 1999, however, the US National Aeronautics and Space Administration (NASA) reported that the ozone hole had decreased in size to 25.4m. sq km.

There has been speculation that the calving of a 1,300-sq km iceberg from the Larsen A ice-shelf at the northern Antarctic Peninsula in early 1995 may have been attributable to the normal cycle of loss by calving; however, there is stronger evidence that the disintegration of a further considerable area of the ice shelf during the past 50 years was the result of climate warming. Research published by British scientists in October 1998, based on measurements of the Antarctic ice taken by satellite between 1992 and 1996, indicated, however, that the Antarctic ice sheet was not melting to any significant extent, as had been feared. Despite this, it was anticipated that average sea levels throughout the world would rise in the 21st century by more than had previously been predicted, as a result of other factors, including the thermal expansion of the oceans. According to the results of joint research by British and American scientists announced in early 1999, the Larsen B and Wilkins ice-shelves were reported to have lost nearly 3,000 sq km of their total area during the preceding year. This calving constituted a rate of loss much greater than predicted and was proffered by some experts as evidence of climate warming on a global scale.

# ANTIGUA AND BARBUDA

## Introductory Survey

### Location, Climate, Language, Religion, Flag, Capital

The country comprises three islands: Antigua (280 sq km—108 sq miles), Barbuda (161 sq km—62 sq miles) and the uninhabited rocky islet of Redonda (1.6 sq km—0.6 sq mile). They lie along the outer edge of the Leeward Islands chain in the West Indies. Barbuda is the most northerly (40 km—25 miles north of Antigua), and Redonda is 40 km south-west of Antigua. The French island of Guadeloupe lies to the south of the country, the United Kingdom Overseas Territory of Montserrat to the south-west and Saint Christopher and Nevis to the west. The climate is tropical, although tempered by constant sea breezes and the trade winds, and the mean annual rainfall of 1,000 mm (40 ins) is slight for the region. The temperature averages 27°C (81°F), but can rise to 33°C (93°F) during the hot season between May and October. English is the official language, but an English patois is commonly used. The majority of the inhabitants profess Christianity, and are mainly adherents of the Anglican Communion. The national flag consists of an inverted triangle centred on a red field; the triangle is divided horizontally into three unequal bands, of black, blue and white, with the black stripe bearing a symbol of the rising sun in gold. The capital is St John's, on Antigua.

### Recent History

Antigua was colonized by the British in the 17th century. The island of Barbuda, formerly a slave stud farm for the Codrington family, was annexed to the territory in 1860. Until December 1959 Antigua and other nearby British territories were administered, under a federal system, as the Leeward Islands. The first elections under universal adult suffrage were held in 1951. The colony participated in the West Indies Federation, which was formed in January 1958 but dissolved in May 1962.

Attempts to form a smaller East Caribbean Federation failed, and most of the eligible colonies subsequently became Associated States in an arrangement that gave them full internal self-government while the United Kingdom retained responsibility for defence and foreign affairs. Antigua attained associated status in February 1967. The Legislative Council was replaced by a House of Representatives, the Administrator became Governor and the Chief Minister was restyled Premier.

In the first general election under associated status, held in February 1971, the Progressive Labour Movement (PLM) ousted the Antigua Labour Party (ALP), which had held power since 1946, by winning 13 of the 17 seats in the House of Representatives. George Walter, leader of the PLM, replaced Vere C. Bird, Sr, as Premier. However, a general election in February 1976 was won by the ALP, with 11 seats, while the seat representing Barbuda was won by an independent. Vere Bird, the ALP's leader, again became Premier, while Lester Bird, one of his sons, became Deputy Premier.

In 1975 the Associated States agreed to seek independence separately. In the 1976 elections the PLM campaigned for early independence while the ALP opposed it. In September 1978, however, the ALP Government declared that the economic foundation for independence had been laid, and a premature general election was held in April 1980, when the ALP won 13 of the 17 seats. There was strong opposition in Barbuda to gaining independence as part of Antigua, and at local elections in March 1981 the Barbuda People's Movement (BPM), which continued to campaign for secession from Antigua, won all the seats on the Barbuda Council. However, the territory finally became independent, as Antigua and Barbuda, on 1 November 1981, remaining within the Commonwealth. The grievances of the Barbudans concerning control of land and devolution of power were unresolved, although the ALP Government had conceded a certain degree of internal autonomy to the Barbuda Council. The Governor, Sir Wilfred Jacobs, became Governor-General, while the Premier, Vere Bird, Sr, became the country's first Prime Minister.

Following disagreements within the opposition PLM, George Walter formed his own political party, the United People's Movement (UPM), in 1982. In April 1984, at the first general election since independence, divisions within the opposition allowed the ALP to win all of the 16 seats that it contested. The remaining seat, representing Barbuda, was retained by an unopposed independent (who subsequently formed the Barbuda National Party—BNP). A new opposition party, the National Democratic Party (NDP), was formed in Antigua in 1985. In April 1986 it merged with the UPM to form the United National Democratic Party (UNDP). Dr Ivor Heath, who had led the NDP, was elected leader of the new party.

In November 1986 controversy surrounding a rehabilitation scheme at the international airport on Antigua led to an official inquiry, which concluded that Vere Bird, Jr (a senior minister and the eldest son of the Prime Minister), had acted inappropriately by awarding part of the contract to a company with which he was personally involved. The affair divided the ALP, with eight ministers (including Lester Bird, the Deputy Prime Minister) demanding the resignation of Vere Bird, Jr, and Prime Minister Bird refusing to dismiss him. The rifts within the ALP and the Bird family continued into 1988, when new allegations of corruption implicated Lester Bird. At a general election in March 1989 the ALP remained the ruling party by retaining 15 of the 16 seats that it had held previously. The UNDP won more than 30% of the total votes, but only one seat. The Barbuda seat was won by the BPM.

In April 1990 the Government of Antigua and Barbuda received a diplomatic note of protest from the Government of Colombia regarding the sale of weapons to the Medellín cartel of drugs-traffickers in Colombia. The weapons had originally been sold by Israel to Antigua and Barbuda but, contrary to regulation, were then immediately shipped on to Colombia in April 1989. The communication from the Colombian Government implicated Vere Bird, Jr, and the Prime Minister eventually agreed to establish a judicial inquiry. In October 1990 the Chamber of Commerce recommended the resignation of the Government. In the following month a news agency obtained a copy of the unpublished report of the inquiry, which accused Antigua and Barbuda of having become 'engulfed in corruption'. In addition, the report revealed the activities of a number of British mercenaries on Antigua, involved in the training of paramilitary forces employed by Colombian drugs-trafficking organizations. Also in November, acting upon the recommendations of the report, the Government of Antigua and Barbuda dismissed Vere Bird, Jr, and banned him for life from holding office in the Government. The head of the defence force, Col Clyde Walker, was also dismissed.

Discontent within the ALP (including dissatisfaction with the leadership of Vere Bird, Sr), provoked a serious political crisis in early 1991. The Minister of Finance, John St Luce, resigned in February, after claiming that his proposals for a restructuring of government were ignored by the Prime Minister. A subsequent cabinet reshuffle (in which Lester Bird lost his deputy premiership) provoked the immediate resignation of three ministers. In September, however, Lester Bird and John St Luce accepted invitations from the Prime Minister to rejoin the Cabinet.

In early 1992 further reports of corruption involving Vere Bird, Sr, provoked public unrest and demands for his resignation. In April the Antigua Caribbean Liberation Movement (ACLM), the PLM and the UNDP consolidated their opposition to the Government by merging to form the United Progressive Party (UPP). In response to mounting public pressure, the ALP convened in May to elect a new leader. However, Vere Bird, Sr, retained the post, following an inconclusive result after the two candidates, Lester Bird and John St Luce, received an equal number of votes. In August further controversy arose when proposed anti-corruption legislation (which had been recommended following the Colombian arms scandal in 1991) was withdrawn as a result of legal intervention by the Prime Minister.

On 10 June 1993 James (later Sir James) Carlisle took office as Governor-General, replacing Sir Wilfred Jacobs. In September the ALP convened in order to hold further leadership elections. As a result of the vote, Lester Bird became leader of the party, while Vere Bird, Jr, was elected as Chairman.

At a general election in March 1994 the ALP remained the ruling party, although with a reduced majority, having secured 11 seats; the UPP won five and the BPM retained the Barbuda seat. Following the election, Lester Bird assumed the premiership. Despite some criticism regarding inaccuracies in the electoral register and the fact that the opposition was denied access to the state-owned media during its campaign, the election was generally thought to have been free and fair.

Controversy continued to surround the Government in 1995. In February of that year an ALP activist, Leonard Aaron, was charged with threatening to murder Tim Hector, editor of an opposition newspaper, *The Outlet*. It was reported that Hector's house had been burgled on several occasions, when material containing allegedly incriminating information relating to members of the Government had been stolen. Aaron was subsequently released, following the intervention of the Prime Minister. Furthermore, in May the Prime Minister's brother, Ivor Bird, was arrested following an incident in which he collected luggage at V. C. Bird International Airport from a Barbadian citizen from Venezuela, which contained 12 kg of cocaine. *The Outlet* claimed that such an exchange had occurred on at least three previous occasions. Ivor Bird's subsequent release from police custody, upon payment of a fine of EC $200,000, attracted considerable criticism. In an attempt to improve the country's worsening reputation as a centre for drugs-trafficking, the Government proposed legislation in early 1996 which aimed to curb the illegal drugs trade. Moreover, later that year Wrenford Ferrance, a former financial controller at the Organisation of Eastern Caribbean States (OECS—see p. 292), was appointed to the newly-created position of Special Adviser to the Government on 'money-laundering' and on the control of illicit drugs. However, a report published by the US Government in early 1998 found Antigua and Barbuda to be 'of primary concern' with regard to both of these illegal activities.

Meanwhile, in September 1995 Antigua and Barbuda suffered extensive damage when the islands were struck by 'Hurricane Luis'. The storm, which caused damage estimated at US $300m., seriously affected some 75% of buildings and left almost one-half of the population homeless. Discussions between the Government and the World Bank, the IMF and other financial institutions took place in late 1995, in an attempt to resolve some of the economic problems caused by the hurricane.

A major cabinet reorganization, effected in May 1996, was controversial because of the appointment to the post of Special Adviser to the Prime Minister of Vere Bird, Jr, who had been declared unfit for public office following a judicial inquiry in 1990 (see above). In September 1996 Molwyn Joseph resigned as Minister of Finance over allegations that he had used his position in order to evade the payment of customs duties on the import of a vintage motor car. His resignation followed an opposition protest, at which the UPP leader, Baldwin Spencer, and seven other party members, including Tim Hector, were arrested (charges brought against them were later dismissed). A further demonstration took place at the end of the month, when some 10,000 people demanded a full inquiry into the affair and an early general election. In early December 1997, however, Joseph was reinstated in the Cabinet, assuming the new post of Minister of Planning, Implementation and the Environment; the appointment was vehemently condemned by the opposition.

In March 1997 the opposition BPM defeated the ALP's ally, the New Barbuda Development Movement, in elections to the Barbuda Council, winning all five of the contested seats and thus gaining control of all the seats in the nine-member Council. In the same month the High Court upheld a constitutional motion presented by Baldwin Spencer seeking the right of expression for the opposition on state-owned radio and television (denied during the electoral campaign in March 1994). In late May and early June the UPP boycotted sittings of the House of Representatives (the first legislative boycotts in the country's history) during a parliamentary debate on a proposed US $300m.-tourism development on Guiana Island, which was to be constructed by a Malaysian company. The opposition claimed that the Prime Minister had failed to publish the proposals for public discussion prior to the parliamentary debate and that the 2,000-room hotel project would have adverse effects on the island's ecology. The project was, none the less, endorsed by the legislature. In September Spencer applied to the High Court to have the hotel project agreement declared illegal and unconstitutional. However, his objections were overruled by the High Court in November, and a subsequent appeal, made to the Eastern Caribbean Court of Appeal, was also dismissed in April 1998. (The Prime Minister had rejected demands for a referendum on the controversial scheme in October 1997.) Meanwhile, in August 1997 *The Outlet* published further allegations regarding government-supported drugs-trafficking, including a claim that a Colombian drug cartel had contributed US $1m. to the ALP's election campaign in 1994. In response, Prime Minister Lester Bird obtained a High Court injunction in early September prohibiting the newspaper from publishing further material relating to the allegations.

In February 1997 the Government announced that four Russian and one Ukrainian 'offshore' banks were to be closed down, amid suspicions of 'money-laundering' for the Russian mafia. Wrenford Ferrance, the government Special Adviser, stated that, since the country's 'offshore' banking system (which had expanded rapidly in the mid-1990s) lacked adequate regulation, no new 'offshore' banking applications would be accepted until new legislation was passed. In April Ferrance was appointed to the post of superintendent of 'offshore' banks and insurance companies and director of international business corporations. Following the collapse, under suspicious circumstances, of the Antigua-based European Union Bank in August, the 51 remaining 'offshore' banks in Antigua and Barbuda were requested to submit full details of their operations in an attempt to combat further fraud. However, in May 1998 two more 'offshore' banks were implicated in a 'money-laundering' case. In October the Government introduced legislation aimed at preventing such irregularities, while simultaneously promoting the development of the 'offshore' financial sector. However, in March 1999 the US Government published a report which claimed that the recent Antiguan legislation had weakened regulations concerning 'money-laundering' and increased the secrecy surrounding 'offshore' banks. It also advised US banks to scrutinize all financial dealings with Antigua and Barbuda, which was described as a potential 'haven for money-laundering activities'. In April the United Kingdom issued a similar financial advisory to its banks. In response, in September the Antiguan Government announced the establishment of an independent body to regulate 'offshore' banking, and promised to make existing controls more stringent.

During 1998 the Guiana Island project continued to provoke controversy. In December 1997 Vere Bird, Jr, was slightly wounded in a shooting incident on the same day as the Government agreed terms for the compulsory resettlement of the island's sole occupants, Cyril 'Taffy' Bufton and his wife. Bufton was subsequently charged with attempted murder, but was acquitted in October 1998. The UPP denied government allegations of its involvement in the attack.

In August 1998 the House of Representatives approved an amendment to voting regulations, granting the right to vote to all citizens who had been born abroad (including non-Commonwealth citizens) but who had been resident in Antigua and Barbuda for more than three years. Opposition members accused the Government of enlarging the electoral register for political advantage; these allegations were strenuously denied.

In November 1998 the printing presses of *The Outlet* were destroyed by fire, two days after the newspaper's editor, Tim Hector, had publicly alleged that a large consignment of 'sophisticated' weaponry had entered Antigua. The Government denied allegations that it was responsible for the fire, and stated that a shipment of 'basic' arms had been imported for police use.

At a general election held on 9 March 1999, the ALP increased its representation in the 17-seat House of Representatives from 11 to 12, at the expense of the UPP, which secured four seats; the BPM retained its single seat. Following the election, Lester Bird was reappointed Prime Minister, and a new Cabinet was duly appointed, which controversially included Vere Bird, Jr, as Minister of Agriculture, Lands and Fisheries (despite the 1990 ruling declaring him unfit to hold public office, see above). The UPP subsequently filed electoral petitions alleging breaches of electoral law in six constituencies (all of which were either dismissed or withdrawn in July 1999). Independent observers, meanwhile, declared the election to have been free, although they expressed reservations concerning its fairness, owing to the ALP's large-scale expenditure and use of the media during its electoral campaign. In June Vere Bird, Sr, Antigua's first premier and the founder of the ALP, died in St John's. At the fourth convention of the UPP, held in November, Vincent Derrick was re-elected as Chairman of the party, while its deputy leader, Tim Hector, announced his resignation.

In foreign relations the ALP Government follows a policy of non-alignment, although the country has strong links with the

USA, and actively assisted in the US military intervention in Grenada in October 1983 as a member of the OECS. Antigua and Barbuda is also a member of the Caribbean Community and Common Market (CARICOM—see p. 136), but in 1988 proved to be a leading opponent of closer political federation within either organization. The Government did, however, agree to the reduction of travel restrictions between OECS members (which took effect in January 1990). Following a period of political unrest in Haiti in mid-1994 the Government of Antigua and Barbuda agreed to accept 2,000 refugees from that country. In mid-1997 Antigua and Barbuda appointed its first ambassador to Cuba, serving on a non-resident basis.

### Government

Antigua and Barbuda is a constitutional monarchy. Executive power is vested in the British sovereign, as Head of State, and exercised by the Governor-General, who represents the sovereign locally and is appointed on the advice of the Antiguan Prime Minister. Legislative power is vested in Parliament, comprising the sovereign, a 17-member Senate and a 17-member House of Representatives. Members of the House are elected from single-member constituencies for up to five years by universal adult suffrage. The Senate is composed of 11 members (of whom one must be an inhabitant of Barbuda) appointed on the advice of the Prime Minister, four appointed on the advice of the Leader of the Opposition, one appointed at the discretion of the Governor-General and one appointed on the advice of the Barbuda Council. Government is effectively by the Cabinet. The Governor-General appoints the Prime Minister and, on the latter's recommendation, selects the other ministers. The Prime Minister must be able to command the support of a majority of the House, to which the Cabinet is responsible. The Barbuda Council has nine seats, with partial elections held every two years.

### Defence

There is a small defence force of 150 men (army 125, navy 25). The US Government leases two military bases on Antigua. Antigua and Barbuda participates in the US-sponsored Regional Security System. Military expenditure in 1999 was projected to total an estimated EC $11.0m.

### Economic Affairs

In 1997, according to estimates by the World Bank, Antigua and Barbuda's gross national product (GNP), measured at average 1995–97 prices, was US $489m., equivalent to US $7,380 per head. During 1990–97, it was estimated, GNP per head increased, in real terms, at an average annual rate of 1.8%. Over the same period, the population increased at an average rate of 0.5% per year. Estimated GNP in 1998 was US $555m. (US $8,300 per head). Measured at factor cost, the country's gross domestic product (GDP) increased, in real terms, at an average annual rate of 2.9% in 1990–97. According to the Eastern Caribbean Central Bank, real GDP increased by 6.1% in 1996, by an estimated 5.6% in 1997, and by 3.9% in 1998.

Agriculture (including forestry and fishing) engaged 3.9% of the labour force in 1991. The sector contributed 3.8% of GDP in 1997. Agricultural GDP increased, in real terms, between 1990 and 1997 at an average rate of 0.6% per year. It declined by 2.0% in 1996, but rose by an estimated 4.8% in 1997 and by 4.2% in 1998. The principal crops are cucumbers, pumpkins, sweet potatoes, mangoes, coconuts, limes, melons and the speciality 'Antigua Black' pineapple. Lobster, shrimp and crab farms are in operation, and further projects to develop the fishing industry were undertaken in the mid-1990s.

Industry (comprising mining, manufacturing, construction and utilities) employed 18.9% of the labour force in 1991 and provided 18.2% of GDP in 1997. The principal industrial activity is construction, accounting for 11.6% of total employment in 1991. Industrial GDP increased, in real terms, at an average rate of 3.0% per year during 1990–97. It rose by 2.1% in 1995, by 10.6% in 1996, and by 8.3% in 1997.

Mining and quarrying employed only 0.2% of the labour force in 1991 and contributed 1.6% of GDP in 1997. The real GDP of the mining sector increased at an average rate of 2.0% per year during 1990–97. It rose by 6.1% in 1996, by an estimated 5.0% in 1997 and by 8.0% in 1998.

The manufacturing sector consists of some light industries producing garments, paper, paint, furniture, food and beverage products, and the assembly of household appliances and electrical components for export. Manufacturing contributed 2.1% of GDP in 1997, when construction provided 10.3%. In real terms, the GDP of the manufacturing sector declined at an average rate of 1.4% per year during 1990–97. Real GDP in manufacturing increased by 4.0% in 1996, while construction activity increased by 12.0% (mainly due to ongoing rehabilitation projects necessitated by 'Hurricane Luis'). In 1997 real GDP growth in the manufacturing and construction sectors was estimated to be, respectively, 6.0% and 8.0%. Manufacturing GDP increased by 5.5% in 1998, when construction growth was 10.0%.

Most of the country's energy production is derived from imported fuel. Imports of mineral fuels accounted for 9.9% of total imports in 1991. However, this included petroleum products for re-export to neighbouring islands.

Services provided 70.2% of employment in 1991 and 78.0% of GDP in 1997. The combined GDP of the service sectors increased, in real terms, at an average rate of 3.4% per year during 1990–97. It declined by 4.8% in 1995 (when the hotels and restaurants sector fell by 21.1%), but rose by 4.9% in 1996 and by 5.2% in 1997. Tourism is the main economic activity, providing approximately 35% of employment in 1991, and accounted (directly and indirectly) for some 60% of GDP in the mid-1990s. By 1998 the industry showed significant signs of recovery, following the severe effects of 'Hurricane Luis' (despite suffering a minor set-back in September 1998, when 'Hurricane Georges' resulted in the closure of several hotels). Tourist arrivals increased from 470,975 in 1995 to 577,024 in 1998, while expenditure by tourists rose from EC $666.1 in 1995 to EC $749.3m. in 1997. The real GDP of the hotels and restaurants sector increased by 5.6% in 1996 and by an estimated 5.7% in 1997; however, it fell by 2.2% in 1998. Most tourists are from the USA (31% in 1997), the United Kingdom (27%), Canada (9%) and other Caribbean countries (18%).

In 1997 Antigua and Barbuda recorded a visible trade deficit of EC $777.4m. and a deficit of EC $189.4m. on the current account of the balance of payments. The country's principal trading partners are the other members of CARICOM (see p. 136), the USA, the United Kingdom and Canada. In 1987 the USA provided 29.5% of total imports and was also one of the main markets for exports (mainly re-exports).

In 1998 there was an estimated budgetary deficit of EC $67.9m. Budget proposals for the financial year ending 31 March 1999 envisaged total expenditure of EC $414.9m., compared with revenue of EC $391.7m., resulting in a deficit of EC $23.2m. In that year debt-servicing costs were expected to account for EC $83.9m. By the end of 1998 total external debt amounted to US $357.0m. The estimated annual average rate of inflation was 2.7% in 1995 and 3.5% in 1996. The consumer price index declined during 1997. The rate of unemployment at the end of 1998 was reported to be 5% of the labour force.

Antigua and Barbuda is a member of CARICOM, the OECS, the Organization of American States (see p. 245), and is a signatory of the Lomé Conventions with the EU (see p. 196).

In the 1980s and 1990s the Government sought to diversify the economy, which is dominated by tourism. In May 1993 the Senate approved legislation to allow the establishment of a free-trade zone, to encourage the manufacture of goods for export, in the north-east of Antigua. Consumption taxes were introduced in January 1995 (to coincide with the implementation of the CARICOM common external tariff) and provoked widespread public unrest. In April 1996 the Government introduced a programme of economic austerity, which included a public-sector pay 'freeze'. By 1997 the country was experiencing a degree of economic recovery, and in July 1998 it joined fellow members of the OECS in applying for group membership of the Inter-American Development Bank (IBD, see p. 202). Despite a deceleration in economic growth in 1998 (largely as a result of infrastructural damage caused by 'Hurricane Georges'), the economy was expected to recover in 1999, with continued buoyancy in the construction sector and increased tourist arrivals. In September 1999 the Government announced plans to transfer the state broadcasting service to private ownership. In the following month it was reported that all but two of the country's external debts had been rescheduled. In the late 1990s the Government's attempts to develop the 'offshore' financial sector were restricted, following several cases of 'money-laundering' (see History).

### Social Welfare

There are two state welfare schemes, both funded by contributions from employers and employees. The Social Security Scheme provides pensions and benefits for maternity, disability and sickness, while the Medical Benefits Scheme awards grants for the treatment of specific chronic diseases. Antigua has a 220-bed general hospital and 25 health centres and clinics. In 1997 work began on the construction of a new hospital, the Mount St John's Medical Complex, near the capital; the project, estimated to cost EC $80m., was to be financed by a US company and was nearing completion in late 1999. In 1993 there was one physician for every 1,316 inhabitants.

### Education

Education is compulsory for 11 years between five and 16 years of age. Primary education begins at the age of five and normally lasts for seven years. Secondary education, beginning at 12 years of age, lasts for five years, comprising a first cycle of three years and a second cycle of two years. In 1987/88 there were 43 primary and 15 secondary schools; the majority of schools are administered by the Government. In 1991/92 some 9,298 primary school pupils and 5,845 secondary school pupils were enrolled. Teacher-training and technical training are available at the Antigua State College in St John's. An extra-mural department of the University of the West Indies offers several foundation courses leading to higher study at branches elsewhere. The adult literacy rate in Antigua and Barbuda is more than 90%, one of the highest rates in the Eastern Caribbean. Current government expenditure on education in 1993/94 was projected at EC $37.1m., equivalent to 12.8% of total budgetary expenditure.

### Public Holidays

**2000:** 3 January (for New Year's Day), 21 April (Good Friday), 24 April (Easter Monday), 1 May (Labour Day), 10 June (Queen's Official Birthday), 12 June (Whit Monday), 3 July (CARICOM Day), 31 July–1 August (Carnival), 1 November (Independence Day), 25–26 December (Christmas).

**2001:** 1 January (New Year's Day), 13 April (Good Friday), 16 April (Easter Monday), 7 May (Labour Day), 4 June (Whit Monday), 9 June (Queen's Official Birthday), 2 July (CARICOM Day), 6–7 August (Carnival), 1 November (Independence Day), 25–26 December (Christmas).

### Weights and Measures

The imperial system is in use, but a metrication programme is being introduced.

# Statistical Survey

Source (unless otherwise stated): Ministry of Finance, High St, St John's; tel. 462-4860; fax 462-1622.

## AREA AND POPULATION

**Area:** 441.6 sq km (170.5 sq miles).

**Population:** 65,525 (males 31,054, females 34,471) at census of 7 April 1970; 62,922 (provisional result) at census of 28 May 1991; 68,612 (official estimate) at mid-1996.

**Density** (estimate, mid-1996): 155.4 per sq km.

**Principal Town:** St John's (capital), population 22,342 at 1991 census.

**Births, Marriages and Deaths** (registrations): Live births (provisional, 1997) 1,448 (birth rate 21.6 per 1,000); Marriages (1987) 343 (marriage rate 5.4 per 1,000); Deaths (1995) 434 (death rate 6.4 per 1,000). Source: UN, *Demographic Yearbook*.

**Expectation of Life** (World Bank estimate, years at birth, 1997): 75.

**Employment** (persons aged 15 years and over, census of 28 May 1991): Agriculture, forestry and fishing 1,040; Mining and quarrying 64; Manufacturing 1,444; Electricity, gas and water 435; Construction 3,109; Trade, restaurants and hotels 8,524; Transport, storage and communications 2,395; Finance, insurance, real estate and business services 1,454; Community, social and personal services 6,406; Activities not adequately defined 1,882; Total employed 26,753 (males 14,564, females 12,189). Source: ILO, *Yearbook of Labour Statistics*.

## AGRICULTURE, ETC.

**Principal Crops** (FAO estimates, '000 metric tons, 1998): Vegetables 1; Melons 1; Mangoes 1; Other fruits 6. Source: FAO, *Production Yearbook*.

**Livestock** (FAO estimates, '000 head, year ending September 1998): Asses 1; Cattle 16; Pigs 2; Sheep 12; Goats 12. Source: FAO, *Production Yearbook*.

**Livestock Products** (FAO estimates, '000 metric tons, 1998): Beef and veal 1; Cows' milk 6. Source: FAO, *Production Yearbook*.

**Fishing** (metric tons, live weight): Total catch 470 in 1995; 530 in 1996 (FAO estimate); 500 (Marine fishes 380, Caribbean spiny lobster 65, Stromboid conchs 55) in 1997 (FAO estimates). Source: FAO, *Yearbook of Fishery Statistics*.

## INDUSTRY

**Production** (estimates, 1988): Rum 4,000 hectolitres; Wines and vodka 2,000 hectolitres; Electric energy (1995) 98m. kWh. Source: UN, *Industrial Commodity Statistics Yearbook*.

## FINANCE

**Currency and Exchange Rates:** 100 cents = 1 Eastern Caribbean dollar (EC $). *Sterling, US Dollar and Euro Equivalents* (30 September 1999): £1 sterling = EC $4.446; US $1 = EC $2.700; €1 = EC $2.880; EC $100 = £22.49 = US $37.04 = €34.73. *Exchange rate:* Fixed at US $1 = EC $2.700 since July 1976.

**Budget** (provisional, EC $ million, 1998): *Revenue:* Tax revenue 292.6 (Taxes on income and profits 27.2, Taxes on domestic goods and services 64.2, Taxes on international transactions 197.1); Other current revenue 49.6; Capital revenue 9.3; Total 351.6, excluding grants received (15.7). *Expenditure:* Current expenditure 364.0 (Personal emoluments 206.3, Other goods and services 78.9, Interest payments 40.3, Transfers and subsidies 38.5); Capital expenditure 71.2; Total 435.2. Source: Eastern Caribbean Central Bank, *Report and Statement of Accounts*.

**International Reserves** (US $ million at 31 December 1998): IMF special drawing rights 0.01; Foreign exchange 59.36; Total 59.37. Source: IMF, *International Financial Statistics*.

**Money Supply** (EC $ million at 31 December 1998): Currency outside banks 79.78; Demand deposits at deposit money banks 250.64; Total money (incl. others) 330.47. Source: IMF, *International Financial Statistics*.

**Cost of Living** (Consumer Price Index; base: 1990 = 100): 93.5 in 1989; 100.0 in 1990; 105.7 in 1991. Source: ILO, *Yearbook of Labour Statistics*.

**Expenditure on the Gross Domestic Product** (provisional, EC $ million at current prices, 1997): Government final consumption expenditure 324.7; Private final consumption expenditure 756.2; Gross capital formation 648.3; *Total domestic expenditure* 1,729.2; Exports of goods and services 1,174.9; *Less* Imports of goods and services 1,328.0; *GDP in purchasers' values* 1,576.0. Source: IMF, *International Financial Statistics*.

**Gross Domestic Product by Economic Activity** (provisional, EC $ million at current prices, 1997): Agriculture, hunting, forestry and fishing 54.0; Mining and quarrying 22.0; Manufacturing 29.2; Electricity and water 60.0; Construction 146.0; Trade 140.1; Restaurants and hotels 175.4; Transport and communications 254.3; Finance, insurance, real estate and business services 205.3; Government services 229.5; Other community, social and personal services 98.1; *Sub-total* 1,414.1; *Less* Imputed bank service charges 91.0; *GDP at factor cost* 1,323.1; Indirect taxes, *less* subsidies 252.9; GDP in purchasers' values 1,576.0. Source: Eastern Caribbean Central Bank, *Statistical Digest*.

**Balance of Payments** (EC $ million, 1997): Exports of goods f.o.b. 102.26; Imports of goods f.o.b. −879.70; *Trade balance* −777.44; Exports of services 1,072.60; Imports of services −448.30; *Balance on goods and services* −153.14; Other income received 10.0; Other income paid −79.49; *Balance on goods, services and income* −222.62; Current transfers received 60.40; Current transfers paid −27.19; *Current balance* −189.42; Capital account (net) 24.76; Direct investment from abroad (net) 63.48; Other investments (net) 121.96; Net errors and omissions −12.80; *Overall balance* 7.99. Source: Eastern Caribbean Central Bank, *Balance of Payments*.

### EXTERNAL TRADE

**Total Trade** (EC $ million, incl. stores and bunkers): *Imports c.i.f.:* 933.42 in 1995; 970.16 in 1996; 988.71 (provisional) in 1997. *Exports f.o.b.:* 143.49 in 1995; 145.91 in 1996; 102.26 in 1997. Source: Eastern Caribbean Central Bank, *Balance of Payments*.

**Principal Commodities** (US $ million, 1991): *Imports:* Food and live animals 30.4; Beverages and tobacco 8.2; Mineral fuels, lubricants, etc. 24.3; Chemicals 15.3; Basic manufactures 66.5; Machinery and transport equipment 65.8; Miscellaneous manufactured articles 30.2. Total (incl. others) 245.9. *Exports:* Food and live animals 1.1; Mineral fuels, lubricants, etc. 10.0; Chemicals 2.8; Basic manufactures 3.3; Machinery and transport equipment 12.0; Miscellaneous manufactured articles 9.9; Total (incl. others) 39.8. Source: UN, *International Trade Statistics Yearbook*.

**Principal Trading Partners** (EC $ million, 1987): *Imports:* Italy 166.5; Trinidad and Tobago 42.5; United Kingdom 70.6; USA 197.0; Total (incl. others) 666.9. *Exports:* CARICOM 24.7; United Kingdom 4.7; USA 8.1; Total (incl. others) 52.5. Source: OECS, *Digest of Trade Statistics*.

### TRANSPORT

**Road Traffic** (registered vehicles, 1995): Passenger motor cars 15,100; Commercial vehicles 4,700. Source: UN, *Statistical Yearbook*.

**Shipping** (international freight traffic, '000 metric tons, 1990): Goods loaded 28; Goods unloaded 113 (Source: UN, *Monthly Bulletin of Statistics*). *Arrivals* (vessels, 1987): 3,940. *Merchant Fleet* (registere at 31 December): 575 vessels (total displacement 2,787,829 grt) in 1998. (Source: Lloyd's Register of Shipping, *World Fleet Statistics*).

**Civil Aviation** (traffic on scheduled services, 1995): Kilometres flown (million) 12; Passengers carried ('000) 1,050; Passenger-km (million) 252; Total ton-km (million) 23. Source: UN, *Statistical Yearbook*.

### TOURISM

**Visitor Arrivals:** 470,975 in 1995; 522,438 in 1996; 540,773 (232,141 stop-overs, 285,489 cruise-ship passengers, 18,558 yacht passengers, 4,585 excursionists) in 1997.

*1998:* 577,024 visitor arrivals (incl. 222,958 stop-overs, 336,066 cruise-ship passengers).

**Tourism Receipts** (EC $ million): 666.1 in 1995; 696.5 in 1996; 749.3 in 1997.

Source: Eastern Caribbean Central Bank, *Statistical Digest*, *Balance of Payments* and *Report and Statement of Accounts*.

### COMMUNICATIONS MEDIA

**Daily Newspaper** (1996): 1 (estimated circulation 6,000)*.

**Non-Daily Newspapers** (1990): 4*.

**Radio Receivers** (1996): 35,000 in use*.

**Television Receivers** (1996): 31,000 in use*.

**Telephones** (1996): 27,556 in use.

**Telefax stations** (year ending 31 March 1991): 350 in use (Source: UN, *Statistical Yearbook*).

* Source: UNESCO, *Statistical Yearbook*.

### EDUCATION

**Pre-primary** (1983): 21 schools; 23 teachers; 677 pupils.

**Primary** (1987/88): 43 schools; 446 teachers; 9,298 students (1991/92).

**Secondary** (1991/92): 15 schools (1987/88); 400 teachers (estimate); 5,845 students.

**Tertiary** (1986): 2 colleges; 631 students.

# Directory

## The Constitution

The Constitution, which came into force at the independence of Antigua and Barbuda on 1 November 1981, states that Antigua and Barbuda is a 'unitary sovereign democratic state'. The main provisions of the Constitution are summarized below:

### FUNDAMENTAL RIGHTS AND FREEDOMS

Regardless of race, place of origin, political opinion, colour, creed or sex, but subject to respect for the rights and freedoms of others and for the public interest, every person in Antigua and Barbuda is entitled to the rights of life, liberty, security of the person, the enjoyment of property and the protection of the law. Freedom of movement, of conscience, of expression (including freedom of the press), of peaceful assembly and association is guaranteed and the inviolability of family life, personal privacy, home and other property is maintained. Protection is afforded from discrimination on the grounds of race, sex, etc., and from slavery, forced labour, torture and inhuman treatment.

### THE GOVERNOR-GENERAL

The British sovereign, as Monarch of Antigua and Barbuda, is the Head of State and is represented by a Governor-General of local citizenship.

### PARLIAMENT

Parliament consists of the Monarch, a 17-member Senate and the House of Representatives composed of 17 elected members. Senators are appointed by the Governor-General: 11 on the advice of the Prime Minister (one of whom must be an inhabitant of Barbuda), four on the advice of the Leader of the Opposition, one at his own discretion and one on the advice of the Barbuda Council. The Barbuda Council is the principal organ of local government in that island, whose membership and functions are determined by Parliament. The life of Parliament is five years.

Each constituency returns one Representative to the House who is directly elected in accordance with the Constitution.

The Attorney-General, if not otherwise a member of the House, is an ex-officio member but does not have the right to vote.

Every citizen over the age of 18 is eligible to vote.

Parliament may alter any of the provisions of the Constitution.

### THE EXECUTIVE

Executive authority is vested in the Monarch and exercisable by the Governor-General. The Governor-General appoints as Prime Minister that member of the House who, in the Governor-General's view, is best able to command the support of the majority of the members of the House, and other ministers on the advice of the Prime Minister. The Governor-General may remove the Prime Minister from office if a resolution of no confidence is passed by the House and the Prime Minister does not either resign or advise the Governor-General to dissolve Parliament within seven days.

The Cabinet consists of the Prime Minister and other ministers and the Attorney-General.

The Leader of the Opposition is appointed by the Governor-General as that member of the House who, in the Governor-General's view, is best able to command the support of a majority of members of the House who do not support the Government.

### CITIZENSHIP

All persons born in Antigua and Barbuda before independence who, immediately prior to independence, were citizens of the United Kingdom and Colonies automatically become citizens of Antigua and Barbuda. All persons born outside the country with a parent or grandparent possessing citizenship of Antigua and Barbuda automatically acquire citizenship as do those born in the country after independence. Provision is made for the acquisition of citizenship by those to whom it would not automatically be granted.

## The Government

**Head of State:** HM Queen ELIZABETH II (succeeded to the throne 6 February 1952).

**Governor-General:** Sir JAMES CARLISLE (took office 10 June 1993).

### CABINET
(January 2000)

**Prime Minister and Minister of Foreign Affairs, Caribbean Community Affairs, Defence and Security, and Merchant Shipping:** LESTER BIRD.

**Minister of Justice and Legal Affairs, and Attorney-General:** Dr ERROL CORT.

**Minister of Public Utilities, Aviation, Transport and Housing:** ROBIN YEARWOOD.

**Minister of Finance:** JOHN ST LUCE.

**Minister of Tourism and the Environment:** MOLWYN JOSEPH.

**Minister of Health and Social Improvement:** BERNARD PERCIVAL.

**Minister of Education, Culture and Technology:** Dr Rodney Williams.

**Minister of Agriculture, Lands and Fisheries:** Vere Bird, Jr.

**Minister of Trade, Industry and Business Development:** Hilroy Humphreys.

**Minister of Labour, Home Affairs and Co-operatives:** Steadroy Benjamin.

**Minister of Planning, Implementation and Public Service Affairs:** Gatson Brown.

**Minister of Youth Affairs and Sports:** Sen. Guy Yearwood.

**Minister of Public Works, Communications and Insurance:** Sen. Asot Michael.

**Minister of State in the Ministry of Trade with responsibility for Industrial Development and Manufacturing:** Jeremy Longford.

**Minister of State in the Ministry of Finance:** Sherfield Bowen.

**Minister of State in the Office of the Prime Minister with responsibility for Urban Development, Information and Broadcasting:** Sen. George Bernard Walker.

### MINISTRIES

**Office of the Prime Minister:** Factory Rd, St John's; tel. 462-4956; fax 462-3225.

**Ministry of Agriculture, Lands and Fisheries:** Queen Elizabeth Highway, St John's; tel. 462-1543; fax 462-6104.

**Ministry of Education, Culture and Technology:** Church St, St John's; tel. 462-4959; fax 462-4970.

**Ministry of Finance:** High St, St John's; tel. 462-4860; fax 462-1622.

**Ministry of Health and Social Improvement:** St John's St, St John's; tel. 462-1600; fax 462-5003.

**Ministry of Justice and Legal Affairs, and Office of the Attorney-General:** Hadeed Bldg, Redcliffe St, St John's; tel. 462-0017; fax 462-2465.

**Ministry of Labour, Home Affairs and Co-operatives:** Redcliffe St, St John's; tel. 462-0011; fax 462-1595.

**Ministry of Planning, Implementation and Public Service Affairs:** St John's.

**Ministry of Public Utilities, Aviation, Transport and Housing:** St John's St, St John's; tel. 462-0894; fax 462-1529.

**Ministry of Tourism and the Environment:** Queen Elizabeth Highway, St John's; tel. 462-0787; fax 462-2836.

**Ministry of Trade, Industry and Business Development:** Redcliffe St, St John's; tel. 462-1543; fax 462-5003.

**Ministry of Youth Affairs and Sports:** St John's.

## Legislature

### PARLIAMENT

#### Senate

**President:** Millicent Percival.

There are 17 nominated members.

#### House of Representatives

**Speaker:** Bridgette Harris.

**Ex-Officio Member:** The Attorney-General.

**Clerk:** L. Dowe.

**General Election, 9 March 1999**

| Party | Votes cast | % | Seats |
|---|---|---|---|
| Antigua Labour Party | 17,417 | 52.6 | 12 |
| United Progressive Party | 14,817 | 44.8 | 4 |
| Barbuda People's Movement | 418 | 1.3 | 1 |
| Independents and others | 439 | 1.3 | — |
| **Total** | 33,091 | 100.0 | 17 |

## Political Organizations

**Antigua Freedom Party (AFP):** St. John's.

**Antigua Labour Party (ALP):** St Mary's St, POB 948, St John's; tel. 462-2235; f. 1968; Leader Lester Bird; Chair. Vere Bird, Jr.

**Barbuda Independence Movement:** Codrington; f. 1983 as Organisation for National Reconstruction, re-formed 1988; advocates self-government for Barbuda; Pres. Arthur Shabazz-Nibbs.

**Barbuda National Party:** Codrington; Leader Eric Burton.

**Barbuda People's Movement (BPM):** Codrington; campaigns for separate status for Barbuda; Parliamentary Leader Thomas Hilbourne Frank; Chair. Fabian Jones.

**National Reform Movement (NRM).**

**New Barbuda Development Movement:** Codrington; linked with the Antigua Labour Party.

**People's Democratic Movement (PDM):** St John's; f. 1995; Leader Hugh Marshall.

**United Progressive Party (UPP):** St John's; f. 1992 by merger of the Antigua Caribbean Liberation Movement (f. 1979), the Progressive Labour Movement (f. 1970) and the United National Democratic Party (f. 1986); Leader Baldwin Spencer; Dep. Leader (vacant); Chair. Vincent Derrick.

## Diplomatic Representation

### EMBASSIES AND HIGH COMMISSION IN ANTIGUA AND BARBUDA

**China, People's Republic:** The Heritage Hotel, POB 1446, St John's; tel. 462-1125; (Ambassador resident in Barbados).

**United Kingdom:** British High Commission, Price Waterhouse Centre, 11 Old Parham Rd, POB 483, St John's; tel. 462-0008; fax 462-2806; (High Commissioner resident in Barbados).

**Venezuela:** Cross and Redcliffe Sts, POB 1201, St John's; tel. 462-1574; fax 462-1570; e-mail venezuela@mail.candw.ag; Ambassador: Alberto Garantón.

## Judicial System

Justice is administered by the Eastern Caribbean Supreme Court, based in Saint Lucia, which consists of a High Court of Justice and a Court of Appeal. One of the Court's Puisne Judges is resident in and responsible for Antigua and Barbuda, and presides over the Court of Summary Jurisdiction on the islands. There are also Magistrates' Courts for lesser cases.

**Chief Justice:** Dennis Byron.

**Solicitor-General:** Lebrecht Hesse.

**Attorney-General:** Dr Errol Cort.

## Religion

The majority of the inhabitants profess Christianity, and the largest denomination is the Church in the Province of the West Indies (Anglican Communion).

### CHRISTIANITY

**Antigua Christian Council:** POB 863, St John's; tel. 462-0261; f. 1964; five mem. churches; Pres. Most Rev. Dr Orland U. Lindsay (Anglican Church); Exec. Sec. Edris Roberts.

#### The Anglican Communion

Anglicans in Antigua and Barbuda are adherents of the Church in the Province of the West Indies. The diocese of the North Eastern Caribbean and Aruba comprises 12 islands: Antigua, Saint Christopher (St Kitts), Nevis, Anguilla, Barbuda, Montserrat, Dominica, Saba, St Maarten/St Martin, Aruba, St Bartholomew and St Eustatius; the total number of Anglicans is about 60,000. The See City is St John's, Antigua.

**Bishop of the North Eastern Caribbean and Aruba:** Rt Rev. Leroy Errol Brooks, Bishop's Lodge, POB 23, St John's; tel. 462-0151; fax 462-2090; e-mail dioceseneca@candw.ag.

#### The Roman Catholic Church

The diocese of St John's-Basseterre, suffragan to the archdiocese of Castries (Saint Lucia), includes Anguilla, Antigua and Barbuda, the British Virgin Islands, Montserrat and Saint Christopher and Nevis. At 31 December 1997 there were an estimated 14,222 adherents in the diocese. The Bishop participates in the Antilles Episcopal Conference (whose Secretariat is based in Port of Spain, Trinidad).

**Bishop of St John's-Basseterre:** Rt Rev. Donald James Reece, Chancery Offices, POB 836, St John's; tel. 461-1135; fax 462-2383; e-mail djr@candw.ag.

#### Other Christian Churches

**Antigua Baptist Association:** POB 277, St John's; tel. 462-1254; Pres. Ivor Charles.

**Evangelical Lutheran Church:** Woods Centre, POB W77, St John's; tel. 462-2896; e-mail lutheran@candw.ag; Pastors M. HENRICH, D. KEHL.

**Methodist Church:** c/o POB 863, St John's; Superintendent Rev. ELOY CHRISTOPHER.

There are also Pentecostal, Seventh-day Adventist, Moravian, Nazarene, Salvation Army and Wesleyan Holiness places of worship.

# The Press

**Antigua Sun:** Woods Mall, POB W263, Friar's Hill Rd, St John's; tel. 480-5960; fax 480-5968; internet www.antol.ag; twice weekly; Publr ALLEN STANFORD.

**Business Expressions:** POB 774, St John's; tel. 462-0743; fax 462-4575; monthly; organ of the Antigua and Barbuda Chamber of Commerce and Industry.

**Daily Observer:** Fort Rd, POB 1318, St John's; fax 462-5561; Publr SAMUEL DERRICK; Editor WINSTON DERRICK.

**The Herald:** Redcliffe House, 2nd Floor, Cross 8, Redcliffe St, St John's; tel. 462-3752; weekly.

**The Nation's Voice:** Public Information Division, Church St and Independence Ave, POB 590, St John's; tel. 462-0090; weekly.

**National Informer:** St John's; weekly.

**The Outlet:** Marble Hill Rd, McKinnons, POB 493, St John's; tel. 462-4453; fax 462-0438; e-mail outletpub@candw.ag; f. 1975; weekly; publ. by the Antigua Caribbean Liberation Movement (founder member of the United Progressive Party in 1992); Editor TIM HECTOR; circ. 5,000.

**The Worker's Voice:** Emancipation House, 46 North St, POB 1281, St John's; tel. 462-0090; f. 1943; twice weekly; official organ of the Antigua Labour Party and the Antigua Trades and Labour Union; Editor NOEL THOMAS; circ. 6,000.

### FOREIGN NEWS AGENCY

**Inter Press Service (IPS)** (Italy): Old Parham Rd, St John's; tel. 462-3602; Correspondent LOUIS DANIEL.

# Publishers

**Antigua Printing and Publishing Ltd:** POB 670, St John's; tel. 462-1265; fax 462-6200.

**Wadadli Productions Ltd:** POB 571, St John's; tel. 462-4489.

# Broadcasting and Communications

### TELECOMMUNICATIONS

Most telephone services are provided by the Antigua Public Utilities Authority (see Trade and Industry).

**Cable & Wireless (Antigua and Barbuda) Ltd:** 42–44 St Mary's St, St John's; internet www.cwantigua.com; owned by Cable & Wireless PLC (United Kingdom).

### RADIO

**ABS Radio:** POB 590, St John's; tel. 462-3602; f. 1956; subsidiary of Antigua and Barbuda Broadcasting Service (see Television, below); Programme Man. D. L. PAYNE.

**Caribbean Radio Lighthouse:** POB 1057, St John's; tel. 462-1454; e-mail cradiolight@candw.ag; f. 1975; religious broadcasts; operated by Baptist Int. Mission Inc. (USA); Dir CURTIS L. WAITE.

**Caribbean Relay Co Ltd:** POB 1203, St John's; tel. 462-0994; fax 462-0487; e-mail cm-crc@candw.ag; jtly-operated by British Broadcasting Corpn and Deutsche Welle.

**Radio ZDK:** Grenville Radio Ltd, POB 1100, St John's; tel. 462-1100; f. 1970; commercial; Programme Dir IVOR BIRD; CEO E. PHILIP.

**Sun FM Radio:** St John's; commercial.

### TELEVISION

**Antigua and Barbuda Broadcasting Service (ABS):** Directorate of Broadcasting and Public Information, POB 590, St John's; tel. 462-0010; fax 462-4442; scheduled for privatization; Dir-Gen. HOLLIS HENRY; CEO DENIS LEANDRO; subsidiary:

**ABS Television:** POB 1280, St John's; tel. 462-0010; fax 462-1622; f. 1964; Programme Man. JAMES TANNY ROSE.

**CTV Entertainment Systems:** 25 Long St, St John's; tel. 462-0346; fax 462-4211; cable television co; transmits 13 channels of US television 24 hours per day to subscribers; Programme Dir J. COX.

# Finance

(cap. = capital; res = reserves; dep. = deposits; brs = branches)

### BANKING

The Eastern Caribbean Central Bank (see p. 294), based in Saint Christopher, is the central issuing and monetary authority for Antigua and Barbuda.

**Antigua Barbuda Investment Bank Ltd:** High St and Corn Alley, POB 1679, St John's; tel. 480-2700; fax 480-2750; e-mail aob@candw.ag; f. 1990; cap. EC $6.3m., res EC $2.3m., dep. EC $107.5m. (Sept. 1997); three subsidiaries: Antigua Overseas Bank Ltd, ABI Trust Ltd and AOB Holdings Ltd; Chair. EUSTACE FRANCIS; Man. Dir MCALISTER ABBOTT; 2 brs.

**Antigua Commercial Bank:** St Mary's and Thames Sts, POB 95, St John's; tel. 462-1217; fax 462-1220; f. 1955; auth. cap. EC $5m.; Man. JOHN BENJAMIN; 2 brs.

**Antigua and Barbuda Development Bank:** 27 St Mary's St, POB 1279, St John's; tel. 462-0838; fax 462-0839; f. 1974; Man. S. ALEX OSBORNE.

**Bank of Antigua:** 1000 Airport Blvd, Coolidge, POB 315, St John's; tel. 462-4282; fax 462-4718; internet www.bankofantigua.com; Chair. ALLEN STANFORD; 1 br.

#### Foreign Banks

**Bank of Nova Scotia** (Canada): High St, POB 342, St John's; tel. 480-1500; fax 480-1554; Man. LEN WRIGHT.

**Barclays Bank PLC** (UK): High St, POB 225, St John's; tel. 480-5000; fax 462-4910; Man. WINSTON ST AGATHE.

**Canadian Imperial Bank of Commerce:** High St and Corn Alley, POB 28, St John's; tel. 462-0836; fax 462-4439; Man. G. R. HILTS.

**Caribbean Banking Corporation Ltd** (Trinidad and Tobago): 45 High St, POB 1324, St John's; tel. 462-4217; fax 462-5040; Man. B. P. DE CASTRO.

**Royal Bank of Canada:** High and Market Sts, POB 252, St John's; tel. 480-1151; offers a trustee service.

**Swiss American National Bank of Antigua Ltd:** High St, POB 1302, St John's; tel. 462-4460; fax 462-0274; f. 1983; cap. US $1.0m., res US $2.1m., dep. US $31.9m. (Dec. 1993); Gen. Man. JOHN GREAVES; 3 brs.

In mid-1997 there were 51 registered 'offshore' banks in Antigua and Barbuda.

### INSURANCE

Several foreign companies have offices in Antigua. Local insurance companies include the following:

**Diamond Insurance Co Ltd:** St Mary's St, St John's; tel. 462-3474.

**General Insurance Co Ltd:** Upper Redcliffe St, POB 340, St John's; tel. 462-2346; fax 462-4482.

**Sentinel Insurance Co Ltd:** Coolidge, POB 207, St John's; tel. 462-4603.

**State Insurance Corpn:** Redcliffe St, POB 290, St John's; tel. 462-0110; fax 462-2649; f. 1977; Chair. Dr VINCENT RICHARDS; Gen. Man. ROLSTON BARTHLEY.

# Trade and Industry

### DEVELOPMENT ORGANIZATIONS

**Barbuda Development Agency:** St John's; economic development projects for Barbuda.

**Development Control Authority:** St John's.

**Industrial Development Board:** Newgate St, St John's; tel. 462-1038; fax 462-1033; f. 1984 to stimulate investment in local industries.

**St John's Development Corporation:** Heritage Quay, POB 1473, St John's; tel. 462-3925; fax 462-3931; e-mail stjohnsdevcorp@candw.ag; f. 1986; manages the Heritage Quay duty-free complex.

### CHAMBER OF COMMERCE

**Antigua and Barbuda Chamber of Commerce and Industry Ltd:** Redcliffe St, POB 774, St John's; tel. 462-0743; fax 462-4575; f. 1944 as Antigua Chamber of Commerce Ltd; name changed as above in 1991, following the collapse of the Antigua and Barbuda Manufacturers' Assn; Pres. CLARVIS JOSEPH.

### INDUSTRIAL AND TRADE ASSOCIATIONS

**Antigua Cotton Growers' Association:** Dunbars, St John's; tel. 462-4962; Chair. FRANCIS HENRY; Sec. PETER BLANCHETTE.

**Antigua Fisheries Corpn:** St John's; e-mail fisheries@candw.ag; partly funded by the Antigua and Barbuda Development Bank; aims to help local fishermen.

**Antigua Sugar Industry Corpn:** Gunthorpes, POB 899, St George's; tel. 462-0653.

**Private Sector Organization of Antigua and Barbuda:** St John's.

### EMPLOYERS' ORGANIZATION

**Antigua Employers' Federation:** Factory Rd, POB 298, St John's; tel. 462-0449; fax 462-0449; e-mail aempfed@candw.ag; f. 1950; 120 mems; Chair. RENÉE PHILLIPS; Exec. Sec. HENDERSON BASS.

### UTILITIES

**Antigua Public Utilities Authority (APUA):** St Mary's St, POB 416, St John's ; tel. 480-7000; fax 462-2782; generation, transmission and distribution of electricity; internal telecommunications; collection, treatment, storage and distribution of water; Gen. Man. PETER BENJAMIN.

### TRADE UNIONS

**Antigua and Barbuda Public Service Association (ABPSA):** POB 1285, St John's; Pres. JAMES SPENCER; Gen. Sec. ELLOY DE FREITAS; 550 mems.

**Antigua Trades and Labour Union (ATLU):** 46 North St, St John's; tel. 462-0090; f. 1939; affiliated to the Antigua Labour Party; Pres. WIGLEY GEORGE; Gen. Sec. NATALIE PAYNE; about 10,000 mems.

**Antigua Workers' Union (AWU):** Freedom Hall, Newgate St, St John's; tel. 462-2005; f. 1967 after a split with ATLU; not affiliated to any party; Pres. MAURICE CHRISTIAN; Gen. Sec. KEITHLYN SMITH; 10,000 mems.

## Transport

### ROADS

There are 384 km (239 miles) of main roads and 781 km (485 miles) of secondary dry-weather roads.

### SHIPPING

The main harbour is the St John's Deep Water Harbour. It is used by cruise ships and a number of foreign shipping lines. There are regular cargo and passenger services internationally and regionally. At Falmouth, on the south side of Antigua, is a former Royal Navy dockyard in English Harbour. The harbour is now used by yachts and private pleasure craft.

**Antigua and Barbuda Port Authority:** Deep Water Harbour, POB 1052, St John's; tel. 462-4243; fax 462-2510; f. 1968; responsible to Ministry of Finance; Chair. LLEWELLYN SMITH; Port Man. LEROY ADAMS.

**Joseph, Vernon, Toy Contractors Ltd:** Nut Grove St, St John's.

**Parenzio Shipping Co Ltd:** Nevis St, St John's.

**Vernon Edwards Shipping Co:** Thames St, POB 82, St John's; tel. 462-2034; fax 462-2035; weekly cargo service to Dominica.

**The West Indies Oil Co Ltd:** Friars Hill Rd, POB 230, St John's; tel. 462-0140; fax 462-0543.

### CIVIL AVIATION

Antigua's V.C. Bird (formerly Coolidge) International Airport, 9 km (5.6 miles) north-east of St John's, is modern and accommodates jet-engined aircraft. There is a small airstrip at Codrington on Barbuda. Antigua and Barbuda Airlines, a nominal company, controls international routes, but services to Europe and North America are operated by American Airlines (USA), Continental Airlines (USA), Lufthansa (Germany) and Air Canada. Antigua and Barbuda is a shareholder in, and the headquarters of, the regional airline, LIAT. Other regional services are operated by BWIA (Trinidad and Tobago) and Air BVI (British Virgin Islands).

**LIAT (1974) Ltd:** POB 819, V.C. Bird Int. Airport; tel. 480-5600; fax 480-5635; e-mail li.sales.mrkting@candw.ag; f. 1956 as Leeward Islands Air Transport Services, jointly-owned by 11 regional Govts; privatized in 1995; shares are held by the Govts of Antigua and Barbuda, Montserrat, Grenada, Barbados, Trinidad and Tobago, Jamaica, Guyana, Dominica, Saint Lucia, Saint Vincent and the Grenadines and Saint Christopher and Nevis (30.8%), BWIA (29.2%), LIAT employees (13.3%) and private investors (26.7%); scheduled passenger and cargo services to 19 destinations in the Caribbean; charter flights are also undertaken; Chair. AZIZ HADEED; Exec. Dir DAVID JARDINE.

**Carib Aviation Ltd:** V.C. Bird Int. Airport; tel. 462-3147; fax 462-3125; e-mail caribav@candw.ag; charter co; operates regional services.

## Tourism

Tourism is the country's main industry. Antigua offers a reputed 365 beaches, an annual international sailing regatta and Carnival week, and the historic Nelson's Dockyard in English Harbour (a national park since 1985). Barbuda is less developed but is noted for its beauty, wildlife and beaches of pink sand. In 1986 the Government established the St John's Development Corporation to oversee the redevelopment of the capital as a commercial duty-free centre, with extra cruise-ship facilities. In 1998 there were 577,024 tourist arrivals, including 336,066 cruise-ship passengers. In 1997 some 31% of stop-over visitors came from the USA, 27% from the United Kingdom, 18% from other Caribbean countries and 9% from Canada. There were an estimated 3,225 hotel rooms in 1996.

**Antigua and Barbuda Department of Tourism:** Nevis St and Friendly Alley, POB 363, St John's; tel. 462-0029; fax 462-2483; e-mail info@antigua-barbuda.org; internet www.antigua-barbuda.org; Dir-Gen. MADELINE BLACKMAN; Asst Man. IRMA TOMLINSON.

**Antigua Hotels and Tourist Association (AHTA):** Lower St Mary's St, POB 454, St John's; tel. 462-3703; fax 462-3702; Chair. PETER RAMRATTAN.

# ARGENTINA

## Introductory Survey

### Location, Climate, Language, Religion, Flag, Capital

The Argentine Republic occupies almost the whole of South America south of the Tropic of Capricorn and east of the Andes. It has a long Atlantic coastline stretching from Uruguay and the River Plate to Tierra del Fuego. To the west lie Chile and the Andes mountains, while to the north are Bolivia, Paraguay and Brazil. Argentina also claims the Falkland Islands (known in Argentina as the Islas Malvinas), South Georgia, the South Sandwich Islands and part of Antarctica. The climate varies from sub-tropical in the Chaco region of the north to sub-arctic in Patagonia, generally with moderate summer rainfall. Temperatures in Buenos Aires are usually between 5°C (41°F) and 29°C (84°F). The language is Spanish. The great majority of the population profess Christianity: more than 90% are Roman Catholics and about 2% Protestants. The national flag (proportions 14 by 9) has three equal horizontal stripes, of light blue (celeste), above white, above light blue. The state flag (proportions 2 by 1) has the same design with, in addition, a gold 'Sun of May' in the centre of the white stripe. The capital is Buenos Aires.

### Recent History

During the greater part of the 20th century, government in Argentina has tended to alternate between military and civilian rule. In 1930 Hipólito Yrigoyen, a member of the reformist Unión Cívica Radical (UCR), who in 1916 had become Argentina's first President to be freely elected by popular vote, was overthrown by an army coup, and the country's first military regime was established. Civilian rule was restored in 1932, only to be supplanted by further military intervention in 1943. A leading figure in the new military regime, Col (later Lt-Gen.) Juan Domingo Perón Sosa, won a presidential election in 1946. As President, he established the Peronista party in 1948 and pursued a policy of extreme nationalism and social improvement, aided by his second wife, Eva ('Evita') Duarte de Perón, whose popularity (particularly among industrial workers and their families) greatly enhanced his position and contributed to his re-election as President in 1951. In 1954, however, his promotion of secularization and the legalization of divorce brought him into conflict with the Roman Catholic Church. In September 1955 President Perón was deposed by a revolt of the armed forces. He went into exile, eventually settling in Spain, from where he continued to direct the Peronist movement.

Following the overthrow of Perón, Argentina entered another lengthy period of political instability. Political control continued to pass between civilian (mainly Radical) and military regimes during the late 1950s and the 1960s. This period was also characterized by increasing guerrilla activity, particularly by the Montoneros, a group of left-wing Peronist sympathizers, and urban guerrilla groups intensified their activities in 1971 and 1972.

Congressional and presidential elections were conducted in March 1973. The Frente Justicialista de Liberación, a Peronist coalition, won control of the National Congress (Congreso Nacional), while the presidential election was won by the party's candidate, Dr Héctor Cámpora, who assumed the office in May. However, Cámpora resigned in July, to enable Gen. Perón, who had returned to Argentina in June, to contest a fresh presidential election. In September Perón was returned to power, with more than 60% of the votes. He took office in October, with his third wife, María Estela ('Isabelita') Martínez de Perón, as Vice-President.

Gen. Perón died in July 1974 and was succeeded as President by his widow. The Government's economic austerity programme and the soaring rate of inflation caused widespread strike action, prompted dissension among industrial workers, and led to demands for the resignation of 'Isabelita' Perón. In March 1976 the armed forces, led by Gen. Jorge Videla (Commander of the Army), overthrew the President and installed a three-man junta: Gen. Videla was sworn in as President. The junta made substantial alterations to the Constitution, dissolved Congress, suspended all political and trade union activity and removed most government officials from their posts. Several hundred people were arrested, while 'Isabelita' Perón was detained and later went into exile.

The military regime launched a successful, although ferocious, offensive against left-wing guerrillas and opposition forces. The imprisonment, torture and murder of suspected left-wing activists by the armed forces provoked domestic and international protests against violations of human rights. Repression eased in 1978, after all armed opposition had been eliminated.

In March 1981 Gen. Roberto Viola, a former member of the junta, succeeded President Videla and made known his intention to extend dialogue with political parties as a prelude to an eventual return to democracy. Owing to ill health, he was replaced in December by Lt-Gen. Leopoldo Galtieri, the Commander-in-Chief of the Army, who attempted to cultivate popular support by continuing the process of political liberalization initiated by his predecessor.

In April 1982, in order to distract attention from an increasingly unstable domestic situation, and following unsuccessful negotiations with the United Kingdom in February over Argentina's long-standing sovereignty claim, President Galtieri ordered the invasion of the Falkland Islands (Islas Malvinas) (see chapter on the Falkland Islands, Vol. II). The United Kingdom recovered the islands after a short conflict, in the course of which about 750 Argentine lives were lost. Argentine forces surrendered in June 1982, but no formal cessation of hostilities was declared until October 1989. Humiliated by the defeat, Galtieri was forced to resign, and the members of the junta were replaced. The army, under the control of Lt-Gen. Cristino Nicolaides, installed a retired general, Reynaldo Bignone, as President in July 1982. The armed forces were held responsible for the disastrous economic situation, and the transfer of power to a civilian government was accelerated. Moreover, in 1983 a Military Commission of Inquiry into the Falklands conflict concluded in its report that the main responsibility for Argentina's defeat lay with members of the former junta, who were recommended for trial. Galtieri was sentenced to imprisonment, while several other officers were put on trial for corruption, murder and insulting the honour of the armed forces. Meanwhile, in August 1983 the regime approved the Ley de Pacificación Nacional, an amnesty law which granted retrospective immunity to the police, the armed forces and others for political crimes that had been committed over the previous 10 years.

In February 1983 the Government announced that general and presidential elections would be held on 30 October. At the elections, the UCR defeated the Peronist Partido Justicialista (PJ), attracting the votes of many former Peronist supporters. The UCR won 317 of the 600 seats in the presidential electoral college, and 129 of the 254 seats in the Chamber of Deputies (Cámara de Diputados), although the PJ won a narrow majority of provincial governorships. Dr Raúl Alfonsín, the UCR candidate, took office as President on 10 December. President Alfonsín promptly announced a radical reform of the armed forces, which led to the immediate retirement of more than one-half of the military high command. In addition, he repealed the Ley de Pacificación Nacional and ordered the court martial of the first three military juntas to rule Argentina after the 1976 coup, for offences including abduction, torture and murder. Public opposition to the former military regime was reinforced by the discovery and exhumation of hundreds of bodies from unmarked graves throughout the country. (It was believed that 15,000–30,000 people 'disappeared' during the so-called 'dirty war' between the former military regime and its opponents in 1976–83.) In December the Government announced the formation of the National Commission on the Disappearance of Persons to investigate the events of the 'dirty war'. The trial of the former leaders began in April 1985. Several hundred prosecution witnesses gave testimonies which revealed the systematic atrocities and the campaign of terror perpetrated by the former military leaders. In December four of the accused were acquitted, but sentences were imposed on the remaining five, including sentences of life imprisonment for Gen. Videla and Adm. Eduardo Massera. The court martial of the members of the junta that had held power during the Falklands conflict was conducted concurrently with the trial of the former military leaders. In May 1986 all three members of the junta were found guilty of negligence and received prison sentences, including a term of 12 years for Galtieri.

In late 1986 the Government sought approval for the Punto Final ('Full Stop') Law, whereby civil and military courts were to begin new judicial proceedings against members of the armed forces accused of violations of human rights, within a 60-day period ending on 22 February 1987. The pre-emptive nature of the legislation provoked widespread popular opposition but was, nevertheless, approved by Congress in December 1986. However, in May 1987, following a series of minor rebellions at army garrisons throughout the country, the Government announced new legislation, known as the Obediencia Debida ('Due Obedience') law, whereby an amnesty was to be declared for all but senior ranks of the police and armed forces. Therefore, under the new law, of the 350–370 officers hitherto due to be prosecuted for alleged violations of human rights, only 30–50 senior officers were now to be tried. The legislation provoked great controversy, and was considered to be a decisive factor in the significant gains made by the PJ at gubernatorial and legislative elections conducted in September. The UCR's defeat was also attributed to its imposition, in July, of an unpopular economic programme of strict austerity measures.

Two swiftly-suppressed army rebellions in January and December 1988 (led by Lt-Col Aldo Rico and Col Mohamed Ali Seineldín respectively) demonstrated continuing military disaffection. In both incidents, the rebel military factions demanded higher salaries for soldiers, an increase in the military budget and some form of amnesty for officers awaiting trial for violations of human rights during the 'dirty war'.

In January 1989 the army quickly repelled an attack by 40 left-wing activists on a military base at La Tablada, in which 39 lives were lost. Many of the guerrilla band were identified as members of the Movimiento Todos por la Patria.

In the campaign for the May 1989 elections, Carlos Saúl Menem headed the Frente Justicialista de Unidad Popular (FREJUPO) electoral alliance, comprising his own PJ grouping, the Partido Demócrata Cristiano (PDC) and the Partido Intransisigente (PI). On 14 May the Peronists were guaranteed a return to power, having secured, together with the two other members of the FREJUPO alliance, 48.5% of the votes cast in the presidential election and 310 of the 600 seats in the electoral college. The Peronists were also victorious in the election for 127 seats (one-half of the total) in the Chamber of Deputies, winning 45% of the votes and 66 seats, in contrast to the 29% (41 seats) obtained by the UCR. The failure of attempts by the retiring and incoming administrations to collaborate, and the reluctance of the Alfonsín administration to continue in office with the prospect of further economic embarrassment, left the nation in a political vacuum. Menem was due to take office as President on 10 December 1989, but the worsening economic situation compelled Alfonsín to resign five months earlier than scheduled. Menem took office on 8 July.

Rumours of a possible amnesty, agreed between the newly-elected Government and military leaders, prompted the organization of a massive demonstration in support of human rights in Buenos Aires in September 1989. In October, however, the Government issued decrees whereby 210 officers, NCOs and soldiers who had been involved in the 'dirty war', the governing junta during the Falklands conflict (including Gen. Galtieri) and leaders of three recent military uprisings (including Lt-Col Rico and Col Seineldín) were pardoned.

Economic affairs dominated the latter half of 1989 and much of 1990. The Minister of the Economy, Nestór Rapanelli, introduced several measures, including the devaluation of the austral, but these failed to reverse the trend towards hyperinflation, and Rapanelli resigned in December 1989. His successor, Antonio Erman González, introduced a comprehensive plan for economic readjustment, incorporating the expansion of existing plans for the transfer to private ownership of many state-owned companies, the rationalization of government-controlled bodies, and the restructuring of the nation's financial systems. In August 1990 Erman González appointed himself head of the Central Bank and assumed almost total control of the country's financial structure. Public disaffection with the Government's economic policy was widespread. Failure to contain the threat of hyperinflation led to a loss in purchasing power, and small-scale food riots and looting became more frequent. The Government's rationalization programme proved unpopular with public-sector employees, and resulted in industrial action and demonstrations, organized from within the sector with the support of trade unions, political opposition parties and human rights groups.

In August 1990, following a formal declaration by the PI and the PDC of their intention to leave the 1989 (FREJUPO) alliance, Menem announced his readiness to enter into electoral alliances with centre-right parties for congressional elections due to be held in 1991.

Widespread public concern at the apparent impunity of military personnel increased following President Menem's suggestion that a further military amnesty would be granted before the end of 1990, and was exacerbated by rumours of escalating military unrest (which were realized in December 1990 when 200–300 rebel soldiers staged a swiftly-suppressed uprising at the Patricios infantry garrison in Buenos Aires). A second round of presidential pardons was announced in late December. More than 40,000 demonstrators gathered in Buenos Aires to protest against the release of former military leaders, including Gen. Videla, Gen. Viola and Adm. Massera. Critics and political opponents dismissed Menem's claims that such action was essential for the effective 'reconciliation' of the Argentine people. In mid-1991 it was announced that the number of armed forces personnel was to be reduced by some 20,000 men; military spending was also to be restricted.

During 1991 the popularity and the political reputation of President Menem were dramatically undermined by the highly-publicized deterioration in marital relations between the President and his wife, Zulema Yoma, and by a succession of corruption scandals in which members of the Yoma family were implicated. In January 1991 Menem was obliged to reorganize the Cabinet, following allegations that government ministers and officials had requested bribes from US businessmen during the course of commercial negotiations. Later in the month, the President was forced to implement a second cabinet reshuffle when his economic team, led by Erman González, resigned following a sudden spectacular decline in the value of the austral in relation to the US dollar.

In mid-1991, following congressional approval of an amendment to the electoral law, it was announced that gubernatorial and congressional elections would take place later in the year. In the first two rounds of voting, the Peronists were unexpectedly successful, wresting the governorship of San Juan from the provincial Bloquista party in August, and securing control of nine of the 12 contested provinces (including the crucial province of Buenos Aires) in September. The third and fourth rounds of voting, in October and December respectively, proved less successful for the PJ. Overall, however, the Peronists secured control of 14 of the 24 contested territories and increased their congressional representation by seven seats, compared with a five-seat reduction in the congressional representation of the UCR.

The success of the Peronist campaign was widely attributed to the popularity of the Minister of the Economy, Domingo Cavallo, and the success of the economic policies that he had implemented since succeeding Erman González. New economic measures included the abolition of index-linked wage increases and, most dramatically, the announcement that the austral would become freely convertible from April. This new initiative soon achieved considerable success in reducing inflation, and impressed international finance organizations sufficiently to secure the negotiation of substantial loan agreements. In October 1991 the President issued a comprehensive decree ordering the removal of almost all of the remaining bureaucratic apparatus of state regulation of the economy, and in November the Government announced plans to accelerate the transfer to private ownership of the remaining public-sector concerns. Continuing economic success in 1992 helped to secure agreements for the renegotiation of repayment of outstanding debts with the Government's leading creditor banks and with the 'Paris Club' of Western creditor governments.

However, in November 1992 the Confederación General del Trabajo (CGT—General Confederation of Labour) organized a one-day general strike, in protest at the Government's continuing programme of economic austerity. The strike, which was well-supported in the provinces but only partially observed in the capital, was precipitated by revelations that senior government officials were to receive pay increases of as much as 200%.

Meanwhile, President Menem sought to consolidate his own position and to increase the popularity of his party in the months preceding legislative elections scheduled for late 1993, at which the Peronists hoped to make significant gains in order to facilitate Menem's wish to effect a constitutional amendment that would allow him to pursue a second, consecutive presidential term. In December 1992 the President reorganized the Cabinet, replacing three unpopular ministers with close associates.

Legislative elections to renew 127 seats in the Chamber of Deputies, conducted on 3 October 1993, were won convincingly by the ruling PJ party, with 42.3% of the votes, while the UCR obtained 30% of the votes.

An unexpected development in November 1993 was the return to political prominence of former President Alfonsín. While UCR opposition to Menem's presidential ambitions had remained vociferous, several opposition leaders, notably Alfonsín, feared that the UCR would be excluded from negotiations on constitutional reform, should the unorthodox political manoeuvring of the Peronists, largely orchestrated by the President of the Senate, Menem's brother Eduardo, succeed in propelling the reform proposal through the legislature. Alfonsín, also anxious to avoid another humiliating defeat for the UCR at a national referendum which Menem had elected to organize in late 1993 on the question of constitutional reform, entered into a dialogue with the President, which resulted in a declaration, in early November, that a framework for consensual reform had been negotiated, apparently in return for Menem's postponement of the referendum and acceptance of modified reform proposals. Hopes for the successful conclusion of a bilateral agreement on constitutional reform were further encouraged, later in November, by the election of Alfonsín to the presidency of the UCR. The terms of the agreement, detailing the central reform issues of the possibility of re-election of the President for one consecutive term, a reduction in the presidential term, to four years, the abolition of the presidential electoral college, the delegation of some presidential powers to a Chief of Cabinet, an increase in the number of seats in the Senate and a reduction in the length of the mandate of all senators, a reform of the procedure for judicial appointments, the removal of religious stipulations from the terms of eligibility for presidential candidates, and the abolition of the President's power to appoint the mayor of the federal capital, were endorsed by the UCR national convention in early December, and the need for constitutional reform was approved by Congress later in the month. Elections to a 305-member constituent assembly were to be conducted in early 1994. Menem immediately declared his intention to seek re-election in 1995.

Elections to the Constituent Assembly took place in April 1994. While the Peronists won the largest share of the vote (37.8%—136 seats), they failed to secure an absolute majority in the Assembly. The UCR won only 19.9% of the votes, equivalent to 75 seats in the Assembly, while a centre-left coalition, Frente Grande, established in mid-1993 to contest the October 1993 legislative elections, emerged unexpectedly as the third political force (with 12.5% of the votes and 31 seats), having campaigned against institutionalized corruption. The Assembly was inaugurated in May 1994, and by mid-August it had successfully incorporated the crucial recommendations of the December 1993 constitutional reform pact between the PJ and the UCR (see above) into the 1853 Constitution. On 24 August 1994 a new Constitution, containing 19 new articles, 40 amendments to existing articles and a new chapter on civil rights and guarantees, was duly promulgated. An electoral timetable was also established by the Assembly, with presidential, legislative and provincial elections all scheduled for May 1995. In December 1994 the Senate approved the new electoral code providing for the direct election of a president and a vice-president and for a second round of voting for the first- and second-placed candidates in the event of a closely contested election.

In January 1995 Carlos Ruckauf, the Minister of the Interior, was named as President Menem's running mate for the new post of vice-president. Menem's campaign for re-election concentrated on the economic success of his previous administration and, despite the increasingly precarious condition of the economy during 1995 (see below), was sufficiently successful to secure 49.9% of the votes at the presidential election conducted on 14 May, thereby avoiding a second ballot. José Octavio Bordón, the candidate of the Frente del País Solidario (Frepaso—a centre-left alliance of socialist, communist, Christian Democrat and dissident Peronist groups formed in late 1994) was second with 29.3% of the votes, ahead of the UCR candidate, Horacio Massaccesi, who received 17.0% of the votes. The Peronists were also successful in nine of the 14 gubernatorial contests; however, Frepaso, with almost 35% of the votes, won the largest share of the 130 contested seats in the Chamber of Deputies at legislative elections conducted concurrently, and significantly increased its representation in the Senate (as did the Peronists) largely at the expense of the UCR. (In September 1995 Alfonsín resigned as UCR party leader in response to dwindling popular support for the party's policies; Rodolfo Terragno was elected as his successor in November.) Menem was inaugurated as President for a four-year term on 8 July 1995. The composition of a largely unaltered Cabinet was announced simultaneously, led by Eduardo Bauzá, in the new post of Cabinet Chief. The Peronists performed well at gubernatorial elections conducted in late 1995, but suffered an unexpected defeat at senatorial elections in the capital in October at which the Peronist candidate was beaten into third place by the Frepaso and UCR candidates respectively. Menem's executive power was increased in February 1996 when Congress endorsed the Administrative Reform Act, enabling the Government to merge certain state agencies and reduce public expenditure considerably.

Meanwhile, the Government's ongoing programme of economic austerity continued to provoke violent opposition, particularly from the public sector, where redundancies and a 'freeze' on salaries had been imposed in many provinces. A protest march in the capital in July 1994 and a general strike in August were organized by two of Argentina's dissident trade union confederations, the Congreso de los Trabajadores Argentinos (CTA) and the Movimiento de Trabajadores Argentinos (MTA), and were well supported despite opposition from the country's largest trade union confederation, the CGT. However, in August a 12-month moratorium on appointments in the public sector was announced, as were plans to privatize several more state enterprises. In March 1995 the Government presented an economic consolidation programme aimed at protecting the Argentine currency against devaluation and supporting the ailing banking sector, which had been adversely affected by the financial crisis in Mexico in late 1994. Subsequent austerity measures adopted by provincial governments, together with a dramatic increase in the rate of unemployment, provoked widespread social unrest in the city of Córdoba in mid-1995 (prompting the resignation of the incumbent Governor six months before the scheduled inauguration of the Governor-elect) and in the province of Río Negro in September. The publication of official unemployment figures for July of 18.6% led Menem to announce, in August, a series of employment initiatives. General strikes organized in April and September were only partially observed, principally in those provinces already experiencing social unrest.

In February 1996 it was revealed that Domingo Cavallo, the Minister of the Economy, had paid a minimal amount of income tax in 1994. Cavallo, whose economic reform programme had concentrated on combating tax evasion and corruption, denounced the claims and insisted that he was the victim of a campaign to discredit him. Cavallo's position was undermined further in March 1996, when President Menem dismissed one of Cavallo's close associates, Haroldo Grisanti, the Postmaster-General (indicted on charges of fraudulent actions against the public administration), and when responsibility for telecommunications was transferred from the Ministry of the Economy to the Secretary-General of the Presidency. Later in the month Jorge Rodríguez, hitherto Minister of Education and Culture, was appointed Cabinet Chief in place of Bauzá, who had resigned citing ill health. Meanwhile, internal divisions in Frepaso led to the resignation from the alliance in February of José Octavio Bordón (the Frepaso presidential candidate in the 1995 elections); shortly afterwards Bordón resigned from the leadership of his own party (Política Abierta para la Integridad Social), and from the Senate.

In June 1996 the Government suffered a serious political defeat when a UCR candidate, Fernando de la Rúa, won almost 40% of the votes cast in the first direct elections for the Mayor of the Federal District of Buenos Aires; a Frepaso candidate secured 26.5% of the votes, while the incumbent Peronist Mayor, Jorge Domínguez, received only 18% of the ballot. In concurrent elections to the 60-member Constituent Assembly (which was charged with drafting a constitution for the newly-autonomous Federal District of Buenos Aires), Frepaso candidates secured 25 seats, the UCR 19, the PJ 11 and the recently-formed Nueva Dirigencia (ND, led by a former Peronist, Gustavo Béliz) five. The results were widely believed to reflect growing discontent with the Government's inability to redress the problems of recession and high levels of unemployment. In July the Government was again undermined by the resignations of Rodolfo

Barra, the Minister of Justice (who had been criticized for the slow progress made in resolving anti-semitic attacks and who had subsequently conceded that he had belonged to a fascist group in his youth), and that of Oscar Camilión, the Minister of Defence, whose parliamentary immunity was to be removed to allow investigations in connection with the illegal sale of armaments to Ecuador and Croatia. More significant, however, was the dismissal of Cavallo from the post of Minister of the Economy, following months of bitter dispute with the President and other cabinet members. Roque Fernández, hitherto President of the Central Bank, assumed the economy portfolio. Cavallo became increasingly vociferous in his attacks against the integrity of certain cabinet members, and, in October, as Menem launched a well-publicized campaign against corruption after the discovery of wide-scale malpractice within the customs service, he accused the Government of having links with organized crime.

Industrial unrest continued during 1996, and in August a 24-hour general strike, organized by the CGT, the MTA and the CTA, received widespread support. A 36-hour strike in September was also widely observed, and was supported by Frepaso, the UCR and several Peronist deputies and senators. None the less, in that month taxation and austerity measures secured congressional approval, albeit with significant amendments. In October relations between the Government and the trade unions deteriorated, following the submission to Congress of controversial labour reform legislation. In December, owing to the slow pace at which debate on the bill was progressing in Congress, President Menem introduced part of the reforms by decree. Although three decrees were signed, radically altering labour contracts, in January 1997 a court declared that they were unconstitutional.

In January 1997 there was public outcry at the mafia-style murder of an investigative news photographer who had been examining alleged links between drugs-traffickers and policemen in the province of Buenos Aires, as well as between certain provincial officials and Alfredo Yabrán, a controversial businessman whom Cavallo had accused of corruption. Policemen from the province of Buenos Aires and Yabrán's chief of security were subsequently implicated in the murder. (In May 1998, shortly after a warrant had been issued for his arrest in connection with the murder, Yabrán committed suicide.) In March 1997 Eduardo Duhalde, the Peronist Governor of the province of Buenos Aires, initiated a radical reorganization of the provincial police in an attempt to avert attention from the politically sensitive issue of corruption, with which the PJ was increasingly associated. Nevertheless, in June Elías Jassan, the Minister of Justice, tendered his resignation after admitting maintaining links with Yabrán, having previously denied that he had ever met him.

The popularity of the PJ was undermined further by an upsurge in social and industrial unrest during 1997, which was primarily the result of widespread discontent with proposed labour reforms, reductions in public expenditure and the high level of unemployment. In May violent protests erupted across Argentina as police clashed with thousands of demonstrators who had occupied government buildings and blockaded roads and bridges. In July some 30,000 people demonstrated in the capital to protest at the high level of unemployment, which was estimated at more than 17%. However, a general strike in August, organized by the MTA and the CTA, was only partially observed and was not supported by the CGT, which in May was reported to have reached a compromise agreement with the Government concerning labour reforms.

In March 1997 Cavallo founded his own political party, Acción por la República (AR), and in July he and Béliz of the ND formed an alliance to contest the forthcoming congressional elections. In the following month the leaders of Frepaso and the UCR confirmed that they had agreed to an electoral pact, known as the Alianza por el Trabajo, la Justicia y la Educación (ATJE), in order to present joint lists in certain constituencies, notably in the province of Buenos Aires, and to remain in alliance subsequently.

At the mid-term congressional elections, held on 26 October 1997, the UCR and Frepaso (in both separate and joint lists) won 45.6% of the votes and 61 of the 127 seats contested, in contrast to the 36.3% (51 seats) obtained by the PJ; of the remaining 15 seats, three were secured by AR–ND. The PJ thus lost its overall majority in the Chamber of Deputies (its total number of seats in the Chamber being reduced to 118), while the UCR and Frepaso together increased their representation to 110 seats. More significant was the PJ's poor performance in the critical constituency of the province of Buenos Aires, where it received only 41.3% of the votes, compared with the ATJE's 48.3%.

In December 1997 President Menem appointed Erman González as Minister of Labour and Social Security, following the resignation of Armando Caro Figueroa, who had been criticized for failing to introduce labour reforms. Legislation concerning labour reforms, including the elimination of short-term contracts and a reduction in redundancy payments, was finally approved by Congress in September 1998.

Preparations for the 1999 presidential election gained momentum in April 1998 with the UCR's selection of Fernando de la Rúa as the party's candidate. In a nation-wide primary in November, de la Rúa was elected as the ATJE presidential candidate, defeating Graciela Fernández Meijide, the highly-regarded Frepaso nominee. In December Carlos 'Chacho' Alvarez of Frepaso was formally nominated as de la Rúa's running mate, while Fernández Meijide was to contest the governorship of Buenos Aires. In July President Menem abandoned a controversial campaign to amend the Constitution in order to allow him to contest the presidency for a third consecutive term of office. The campaign was vociferously opposed by the leading PJ contender, Eduardo Duhalde, who had threatened to hold a provincial plebiscite on the issue. Duhalde's main rival for the PJ presidential nomination was Ramón 'Palito' Ortega, a former Governor of Tucumán, who had been appointed Secretary of Social Development in April. The popularity of the PJ remained low, not least because of the corruption scandals that had beset the Menem administration, and in November the President was accused of seeking to undermine the independence of the judiciary when he demanded the investigation of a prosecutor probing allegations of government involvement in the sale of armaments to Ecuador and Croatia. In September a judge had ordered that Erman González, who had held the defence portfolio at the time of the alleged incidents, be summoned to testify in the investigation. Guido di Tella, the Minister of Foreign Affairs, and Menem's brother-in-law, Emir Yoma, a former presidential adviser, were also implicated in the case. (The investigations continued in 1999.) An agreement reached by Duhalde and Ortega to run jointly in the PJ presidential primary seemed to restore some unity to the party, although it was apparent that Menem had not entirely abandoned the idea of a re-election bid. In March 1999, however, the Supreme Court rejected appeals for Menem to be allowed to stand in the October elections.

In May 1999 a decision to reduce substantially the education budget by presidential decree prompted Susana Decibe, the Minister of Culture and Education, to resign in protest. The Government was subsequently forced to reverse the cuts, in response to widespread political and public discontent. Later that month the ruling administration was further undermined by the scandal surrounding the resignation of Erman González, the Minister of Labour and Social Security, following revelations that he was being paid a generous special pension (granted by Menem in recognition of his years of service), in addition to his ministerial salary.

In June 1999 Duhalde officially received the PJ presidential nomination after the only other contender, Adolfo Rodríguez Saa, the Governor of San Luis, withdrew from the contest. Moreover, in August Duhalde's candidacy was publicly endorsed by Menem, who pledged to campaign for his former rival. Meanwhile, however, social unrest escalated in several provinces, as economic recession led to rising levels of unemployment and non-payment of public-sector salaries.

At the presidential election, conducted on 24 October 1999, de la Rúa (with 48.50% of the votes) defeated Duhalde (who secured 38.09%), thereby ending 10 years of Menem's Peronist rule. The ATJE also performed well in concurrent elections to renew 130 of the 257 seats in the Chamber of Deputies, winning 63 seats, while the PJ secured 50 seats and Cavallo's AR won nine. The ATJE's total number of seats in the Chamber increased to 127—only two short of an absolute majority—in contrast to the PJ, whose representation was reduced to 101 seats. However, in gubernatorial elections held on the same day, the ATJE candidate, Graciela Fernández Meijide, failed to secure the critical province of Buenos Aires, where Carlos Ruckauf, the outgoing Vice-President, was elected. As a result of the elections the PJ controlled 14 of the 24 provincial administrations, while the ATJE held only six. On 24 November de la Rúa formally annouced the composition of his new Cabinet,

which significantly comprised a large number of economists. De la Rúa took office as President on 10 December, with Alvarez as his Vice-President.

Despite the public expressions of regret (in 1995) by the heads of the navy, the army and the air force for crimes committed by the armed forces during 1976–83, issues concerning the 'dirty war' remained politically sensitive in the late 1990s. Plans announced in January 1998 by President Menem to demolish the Naval Mechanics School (formerly the principal torture centre used by the military) and replace it with a monument to national reconciliation had to be suspended after protesters demanded that the premises be converted into a museum, as a reminder to future generations of the atrocities committed. Later in January Alfredo Astiz, a notorious former naval captain, was deprived of his rank and pension after he defended the elimination of political opponents during the dictatorship. In the following month the Swiss authorities revealed that they had discovered a number of Swiss bank accounts belonging to former Argentine military officials, including Astiz and Antonio Domingo Bussi, then Governor of Tucumán. It was rumoured that the accounts contained funds stolen by the military regime from Argentines who had been detained or 'disappeared'. In March Congress approved legislation repealing the Punto Final and Obediencia Debida laws (adopted in 1986 and 1987, respectively); however, the new legislation was not retrospective and would not affect those who had already received an amnesty. In June Gen. Videla was arrested in connection with the abduction and illegal adoption of children whose parents had 'disappeared' during the dictatorship, and in November Adm. Massera was summoned to give evidence. As many as 300 infants born in special holding centres during the 'dirty war' were believed to have been abducted by the military. In the following months further arrests were made in connection with the alleged kidnappings, including that of former President Reynaldo Bignone, former army chief Lt-Gen. Cristino Nicolaides and former navy chief Vice-Adm. Rubén Oscar Franco. By November 1999 seven officers had been placed under house arrest and were awaiting trial on charges of abduction and illegal adoption, while three others had avoided detention and remained in hiding.

In May 1985 a treaty was formally ratified by representatives of the Argentine and Chilean Governments, concluding the territorial dispute over three small islands in the Beagle Channel, south of Tierra del Fuego. The islands were awarded to Chile, while Argentine rights to petroleum and other minerals in the disputed waters were guaranteed. In August 1991 Argentina and Chile reached a settlement regarding disputed claims to territory in the Antarctic region; however, the sovereignty of the territory remained under dispute, necessitating the signing of an additional protocol in late 1996. In December 1998 the Presidents of the two countries signed a new agreement on the border demarcation of the contested 'continental glaciers' territory in the Antarctic region (despite the 1991 treaty); the accord became effective in June 1999 following ratification by the Argentine and Chilean legislatures. Meanwhile, the two countries' navies held joint exercises for the first time in August 1998. In February 1999, during a meeting held in Ushuaia, southern Argentina, President Menem and the Chilean President, Eduardo Frei Ruiz-Tagle, signed a significant defence agreement and issued a joint declaration on both countries' commitment to the consolidation of their friendship.

Full diplomatic relations were restored with the United Kingdom in February 1990, following senior-level negotiations in Madrid, Spain. The improvement in relations between Argentina and the United Kingdom prompted the European Community (now European Union) to sign a new five-year trade and co-operation agreement with Argentina in April. In November Argentina and the United Kingdom concluded an agreement for the joint administration of a comprehensive protection programme for the lucrative South Atlantic fishing region. Subsequent agreements to regulate fishing in the area were concluded in December 1992 and November 1993. A diplomatic accord, signed in September 1991, significantly reduced military restrictions in the region, which the United Kingdom had imposed on Argentina following the Falklands conflict. The question of sovereignty over the disputed islands was not resolved. The results of preliminary seismic investigations (published in late 1993), which indicated rich petroleum deposits in the region, were expected to further complicate future negotiations. Although a comprehensive agreement on exploration was signed by both countries in New York in September 1995, negotiations on fishing rights in the region remained tense. In late 1996 the Argentine Government suggested, for the first time, that it might consider shared sovereignty of the Falkland Islands with the United Kingdom. The proposal was firmly rejected by the British Government and by the Falkland Islanders, who reiterated their commitment to persuading the UN Special Political and Decolonization Committee to adopt a clause allowing the Islanders the right to self-determination. Anglo-Argentine relations improved in November 1996 when Lt-Gen. Martín Balza, the Chief of Staff of the Argentine Army, became the first high-ranking Argentine military official to visit the United Kingdom since 1982. Relations between Argentina and the United Kingdom were consolidated further in January 1997 when the two countries agreed to resume negotiations on a long-term fisheries accord. Moreover, in October 1998 President Menem made an official visit to the United Kingdom, during which he held talks with the British Prime Minister, Tony Blair, on issues including the arms embargo, defence, trade and investment. Notably, Menem paid tribute to the British servicemen who died during the 1982 conflict, while he also appealed for an 'imaginative' solution to the Falkland Islands sovereignty issue. Earlier in 1998 relations with the United Kingdom had been strained by the presentation of draft legislation to the Argentine Congress on the imposition of sanctions on petroleum companies and fishing vessels operating in Falkland Island waters without Argentine authorization. In late 1998 the United Kingdom announced the partial lifting of its arms embargo against Argentina. There were also reports that Argentina and the United Kingdom were considering the establishment of an advisory council, based in the Falkland Islands, as part of negotiations on a new status for the territory. In March 1999, during an official visit to Argentina, Prince Charles, heir to the British throne, paid tribute to the Argentine soldiers who died in the Falklands conflict, although his apparent support for the Islanders' right to self-detemination provoked some controversy. In May formal negotiations were held in London between the British and Argentine Governments and members of the Falkland Islands legislature. Following further talks in July, an agreement was reached providing for an end to the ban on Argentine citizens visiting the Falkland Islands and for the restoration of air links between the islands and South America, with stopovers in Argentina to be introduced from mid-October. (Chile had suspended flights to the islands in March in protest at the British Government's continued detention of Gen. (retd) Augusto Pinochet Ugarte, the former Chilean President.) In September 1999 Argentine and British government officials reached an understanding on co-operation against illegal fishing in the South Atlantic, and naval forces from both countries held joint exercises in the region in November.

In March 1991 the Presidents of Argentina, Brazil, Paraguay and Uruguay signed the Asunción treaty in Paraguay, thereby confirming their commitment to the creation of a Southern Common Market, Mercosur (Mercado Común del Sur). Mercosur duly came into effect on 1 January 1995. While a complete common external tariff was not expected until 2006, customs barriers on 80%–85% of mutually exchanged goods were removed immediately. The effects of economic recession and the devaluation of the Brazilian currency in January 1999 provoked a series of trade disputes within Mercosur during that year, particularly between Argentina and Brazil, the two largest members. Meanwhile, relations with Paraguay were strained by Argentina's refusal, in September 1999, to extradite Gen. Lino César Oviedo Silvo, who had been granted asylum in March following the assassination of the Paraguayan Vice-President Luis María Argaña. Relations improved to some extent at the end of September as a result of Oviedo's relocation to the remote territory of Tierra del Fuego. Oviedo disappeared on 9 December, the day before de la Rúa took office.

In late 1997, following a visit to Argentina by President Bill Clinton of the USA, the US Congress declared Argentina a 'special non-NATO ally', affording the country privileged access to US surplus defence supplies and certain military funding. Chile and Brazil criticized the granting of the special status, claiming it would lead to a regional imbalance. In January 1999, during a visit by President Menem to Washington, DC, a number of US-Argentine defence agreements were signed, which aimed to enhance military co-operation between the two countries.

In late 1996 a criminal investigation was begun in Spain regarding the torture, disappearance and killing of several hundred Spanish citizens in Argentina during 1976–83. A parallel investigation was instigated into the abduction of 54 children of Spanish victims during this period. In October 1997

Adolfo Scilingo, a former Argentine military official, was arrested in Madrid, Spain, after admitting to his involvement in the 'dirty war'. During that year a Spanish High Court judge issued international arrest warrants for several other Argentine officers, including Adm. Massera and Gen. Galtieri. The investigations continued in 1998–99, and by October 1999 a reported 192 Argentines had been indicted on charges of genocide, terrorism and torture. In November international arrest warrants were issued for 98 of those accused, although any request for extradition was likely to be refused by the Argentine Government. Shortly afterwards Adolfo Scilingo, now on bail in Spain awaiting trial, was reported to have retracted his earlier confession, claiming that he had been pressured to lie under oath.

In May 1998 diplomatic relations with Iran were reduced to a 'minimum level' after evidence emerged of Iranian involvement in a bomb attack on a Jewish social centre in Buenos Aires in 1994, which resulted in 86 fatalities. In September 1999 the Argentine Supreme Court issued an arrest warrant for Imad Mughniyah, a leader of the fundamentalist Shi'ite Hezbollah, who was suspected of involvement in a bomb attack on the Israeli embassy in Buenos Aires in 1992.

## Government

For administrative purposes Argentina comprises 1,617 municipalities located in 22 provinces, the Federal District of Buenos Aires, and the National Territory of Tierra del Fuego.

Legislative power is vested in the bicameral Congress (Congreso): the Chamber of Deputies (Cámara de Diputados) has 257 members, elected by universal adult suffrage for a term of four years (with approximately one-half of the seats renewable every two years). In accordance with the amended Constitution, promulgated in August 1994, from 1995 legislative elections provided for an expanded Senate (Senado), which was eventually to have 72 members, with three members drawn from each of the 22 provinces, the Federal District of Buenos Aires and the National Territory of Tierra del Fuego. A reduced, six-year term of office would be in place by 2001, with one-third of the Senate elected every three years. The President is directly elected for a four-year term, renewable once. Each province has its own elected Governor and legislature, concerned with all matters not delegated to the Federal Government.

## Defence

Conscription was ended on 1 April 1995. The total strength of the regular armed forces in August 1999 was 70,500, comprising a 40,000-strong army with a further 375,000 trained reservists, a 20,000-strong navy and an air force of 10,500 men. There were also paramilitary forces numbering 31,240 men. Budget forecasts for 2000 envisaged defence expenditure of 4,000m. new pesos.

## Economic Affairs

In 1997, according to estimates by the World Bank, Argentina's gross national product (GNP), measured at average 1995–97 prices, was US $319,293m., equivalent to $8,950 per head. During 1990–97, it was estimated, GNP per head increased, in real terms, at an average annual rate of 4.2%. Over the same period, Argentina's population increased at an average rate of 1.3% per year. In 1998 GNP was $324,100m., equivalent to $8,970 per head. The country's gross domestic product (GDP) increased, in real terms, at an average annual rate of 5.3% during 1990–98. Real GDP increased by 8.1% in 1997 and by 3.9% in 1998.

Agriculture (including forestry and fishing) contributed 5.7% of GDP in 1998 and employed an estimated 10.2% of the labour force. The principal cash crops are wheat, maize, sorghum and soybeans. Beef production is also important. During 1990–98 agricultural GDP increased at an average annual rate of 2.1%. The GDP of the sector increased by 10.3% in 1998.

Industry (including mining, manufacturing, construction and power) engaged 25.3% of the employed labour force in 1991 and provided 28.7% of GDP in 1998. During 1990–98 industrial GDP increased, in real terms, at an estimated average annual rate of 4.6%.

Mining contributed 1.5% of GDP in 1998, and employed 0.4% of the working population in 1991. Argentina has substantial deposits of petroleum and natural gas, as well as steam coal and lignite. In late 1997 the Bajo de la Alumbrera open-pit gold and copper mine became operational, leading to forecasts of a substantial rise in mineral output in the late 1990s. The GDP of the mining sector increased, in real terms, at an average rate of 7.3% per year during 1993–98; growth of 2.3% was recorded in 1998.

Manufacturing contributed 19.1% of GDP in 1998, and employed 17.3% of the working population in 1991. In 1993 the most important branches of manufacturing, measured by gross value of output, were food products and beverages (accounting for 26.4% of the total), chemical products (10.5%), transport equipment (9.9%) and petroleum refineries. During 1993–98 manufacturing GDP increased, in real terms, at an estimated average annual rate of 2.8%. Manufacturing GDP increased by 9.2% in 1997, and by 1.6% in 1998.

Energy is derived principally from hydroelectric power (responsible for the production of 38.5% of total electricity in 1998) and coal. In 1998 9.8% of Argentina's total energy requirements were produced by its two nuclear power stations. In that year imports of mineral fuels comprised 10.5% of the country's total energy requirements.

Services engaged 62.7% of the employed labour force in 1991 and accounted for 65.6% of GDP in 1998. The combined GDP of the service sectors increased, in real terms, at an estimated average rate of 3.9% per year during 1990–98; growth of 4.7% was recorded in 1998.

In 1998 Argentina recorded a visible trade deficit of US $3,014m., and there was a deficit of $14,697m. on the current account of the balance of payments. In 1998 (according to provisional figures) the principal source of imports (22.5%) was Brazil, just ahead of the USA (19.8%). Brazil also accounted for 30.1% of exports. Other major trading partners in 1998 were Italy, Chile and Germany. The principal exports in that year were food and live animals, machinery and transport equipment, basic manufactures and animal and vegetable oils and fats. The principal imports were machinery and transport equipment, chemical and mineral products, and basic manufactures.

In 1996 there was a budget deficit of 5,233.6m. new Argentine pesos, equivalent to 1.9% of GDP. Argentina's total external debt was US $123,221m. at the end of 1997, of which $73,955m. was long-term public debt. In that year the total cost of debt-servicing was equivalent to 58.7% of revenue from exports of goods and services. The annual rate of inflation averaged 19.3% in 1990–98, although consumer prices increased by an annual average of only 0.5% and 0.9% in 1997 and 1998, respectively. Record national unemployment of 18.6% (equivalent to 2.2m. workers) was reported in May 1995; by May 1999, however, the level had declined to 14.5%.

During 1986–90 Argentina signed a series of integration treaties with neighbouring Latin American countries, aimed at increasing bilateral trade and establishing the basis for a Latin American economic community. Argentina is a member of ALADI (see p. 292) and of Mercosur (see p. 267).

Economic growth in Argentina in the 1980s was hampered primarily by massive external debt obligations, limited access to financial aid and a scarcity of raw materials. In 1989, however, the IMF approved a stand-by loan of US$ 1,400m. in recognition of the austerity measures adopted under the Menem administration. Further deregulation of the economy, and the success of new economic measures introduced by the Government in the early 1990s (including a programme of privatization), drastically reduced inflation and helped to secure agreements to reschedule debt repayments and the disbursement of loans from international financial organizations. Attempts to support the Argentine peso in the aftermath of the collapse of the Mexican currency in early 1995 imposed severe restrictions on public expenditure, which, together with a dramatic rise in the rate of unemployment, led to widespread social unrest. Real GDP declined by 2.8% in 1995, but it subsequently recovered, and economic growth of 8.1% was recorded in 1997. From mid-1998, however, the economy began to contract, with both trade and budget deficits widening, as international prices for certain commodities fell, adversely affecting exports. Exports declined further in 1999 following the devaluation of the Brazilian currency in January, and the economy entered recession; GDP fell by 4.6% in the second quarter of the year and was forecast to decline by at least 3% for 1999 as a whole. In August Congress approved fiscal convertibility legislation, which imposed limitations on public expenditure, with the aim of achieving a balanced budget by 2003. President Fernando de la Rúa's administration, which came to power in late 1999, inherited a problematic economic situation, not least a mounting fiscal deficit, which was expected to exceed the ceiling of US $5,100m. agreed with the IMF. Labour and tax reforms were identified as priorities for the new Government.

## Social Welfare

Social welfare benefits comprise three categories: retirement, disability and survivors' pensions; family allowances; and health insurance. The first is administered by the Administración Nacional de Seguridad Social (part of the Ministry of Labour and Social Security) and funded by compulsory contributions from all workers, employed and self-employed, over 18 years of age. The second is supervised by the Administración Nacional de Seguridad Social and funded by employers. The third is administered by the Administración Nacional del Seguro de Salud, by means of public funds, and may be provided only by authorized public institutions. Work insurance is the responsibility of the employer. In 1993 the Government approved reforms to the pension system, which offered contributors a choice between privately-managed and state-operated schemes. In the case of privately-managed pension funds (Administradoras de Fondos de Jubilación y Pensión—AFJPs), employees set aside 11% of their monthly salaries, 7.5% of which goes toward retirement. On retirement (at 65 years of age for men and 60 years of age for women), employees can use these funds to purchase an annuity from an insurance company or begin to withdraw funds at a specified monthly rate. Pension managers are required to maintain sufficient reserves to honour a minimum pension guaranteed by the Government. AFJPs are monitored by a government supervisory body. There is considerable foreign participation in the management of the AFJPs and the country's three most successful funds, Consolidar, Máxima, SA and Siembra, have strong links with Dresdner Bank AG, Deutsche Bank AG and Citibank NA, respectively. Of total government expenditure in 1996, 1,058.0m. new pesos (2.5%) was for health, and a further 22,339.0m. new pesos (53.3%) was for social security and welfare.

In the early 1990s there were 268 physicians for every 100,000 inhabitants in Argentina (one of the best doctor-patient ratios of any country in Latin America) and 54 nurses per 100,000 inhabitants. In 1995 there were 155,822 hospital beds in Argentina.

## Education

Education from pre-school to university level is available free of charge. Education is officially compulsory for all children at primary level, between the ages of six and 14 years. Secondary education lasts for between five and seven years, depending on the type of course: the normal certificate of education (bachillerato) course lasts for five years, whereas a course leading to a technical or agricultural bachillerato lasts for six years. Technical education is supervised by the Consejo Nacional de Educación Técnica. The total enrolment at primary and secondary schools in 1996 was estimated at 99.4% and 67.2% of the school-age population, respectively. Non-university higher education, usually leading to a teaching qualification, is for three or four years, while university courses last for four years or more. There are 36 state universities and 48 private universities. Central government expenditure on education in 1996 was 2,402.7m. new pesos (5.7% of total public expenditure).

According to estimates by UNESCO, the average rate of adult illiteracy in 1995 was only 3.8%.

## Public Holidays

**2000:** 1 January (New Year's Day), 21 April (Good Friday), 1 May (Labour Day), 25 May (Anniversary of the 1810 Revolution), 13 June (for Occupation of the Islas Malvinas), 20 June (Flag Day), 9 July (Independence Day), 15 August (for Death of Gen. José de San Martín), 10 October (for Columbus Day), 25 December (Christmas).

**2001:** 1 January (New Year's Day), 13 April (Good Friday), 1 May (Labour Day), 25 May (Anniversary of the 1810 Revolution), 14 June (for Occupation of the Islas Malvinas), 20 June (for Flag Day), 9 July (Independence Day), 17 August (for Death of Gen. José de San Martín), 12 October (for Columbus Day), 25 December (Christmas).

## Weights and Measures

The metric system is in force.

# Statistical Survey

Sources (unless otherwise stated): Instituto Nacional de Estadística y Censos, Avda Julio A. Roca 609, 1067 Buenos Aires; tel. (11) 4349-9652; fax (11) 4349-9621; e-mail ces@indec.mecon.ar; internet www.indec.mecon.ar; and Banco Central de la República Argentina, Reconquista 266, 1003 Buenos Aires; tel. (11) 4394-8111; fax (11) 4334-5712.

## Area and Population

**AREA, POPULATION AND DENSITY**

| | |
|---|---|
| Area (sq km) | 2,780,400* |
| Population (census results)† | |
| 22 October 1980 | 27,949,480 |
| 15 May 1991 | |
| Males | 15,937,980 |
| Females | 16,677,548 |
| Total | 32,615,528 |
| Population (official estimates at mid-year) | |
| 1996 | 35,219,612 |
| 1997 | 35,671,894 |
| 1998 | 36,124,933 |
| Density (per sq km) at mid-1997 | 13.0 |

* 1,073,518 sq miles. The figure excludes the Falkland Islands (Islas Malvinas) and Antarctic territory claimed by Argentina.

† Figures exclude adjustment for underenumeration, estimated to have been 1% at the 1980 census and 0.9% at the 1991 census.

**PROVINCES** (census of 15 May 1991)

| | Area (sg km) | Population* | Density (per sq km) | Capital |
|---|---|---|---|---|
| Buenos Aires—Federal District | 200 | 2,965,403 | 14,827.0 | |
| Buenos Aires—Province | 307,571 | 12,594,974 | 40.9 | La Plata |
| Catamarca | 102,602 | 264,234 | 2.6 | San Fernando del Valle de Catamarca |
| Chaco | 99,633 | 839,677 | 8.4 | Resistencia |
| Chubut | 224,686 | 357,189 | 1.6 | Rawson |
| Córdoba | 165,321 | 2,766,683 | 16.7 | Córdoba |
| Corrientes | 88,199 | 795,594 | 9.0 | Corrientes |
| Entre Ríos | 78,781 | 1,020,257 | 13.0 | Paraná |
| Formosa | 72,066 | 398,413 | 5.5 | Formosa |
| Jujuy | 53,219 | 512,329 | 9.6 | San Salvador de Jujuy |
| La Pampa | 143,440 | 259,996 | 1.8 | Santa Rosa |
| La Rioja | 89,680 | 220,729 | 2.5 | La Rioja |
| Mendoza | 148,827 | 1,412,481 | 9.5 | Mendoza |
| Misiones | 29,801 | 788,915 | 26.5 | Posadas |
| Neuquén | 94,078 | 388,833 | 4.1 | Neuquén |
| Río Negro | 203,013 | 506,772 | 2.5 | Viedma |
| Salta | 155,488 | 866,153 | 5.6 | Salta |
| San Juan | 89,651 | 528,715 | 5.9 | San Juan |
| San Luis | 76,748 | 286,458 | 3.7 | San Luis |
| Santa Cruz | 243,943 | 159,839 | 0.7 | Río Gallegos |
| Santa Fe | 133,007 | 2,798,422 | 21.0 | Santa Fe |
| Santiago del Estero | 136,351 | 671,988 | 4.9 | Santiago del Estero |
| Tucumán | 22,524 | 1,142,105 | 50.7 | San Miguel de Tucumán |
| *Territory* | | | | |
| Tierra del Fuego | 21,571 | 69,369 | 3.2 | Ushuaia |
| **Total** | 2,780,400 | 32,615,528 | 11.7 | Buenos Aires |

* Excluding adjustment for underenumeration.

**PRINCIPAL TOWNS** (provisional population, census of 15 May 1991)

| | | | |
|---|---|---|---|
| Buenos Aires (capital) | 2,960,976* | Corrientes | 257,766 |
| Córdoba | 1,148,305 | Bahía Blanca | 255,145 |
| La Matanza | 1,111,811 | Resistencia | 228,199 |
| Rosario | 894,645 | Paraná | 206,848 |
| Morón | 641,541 | Posadas | 201,943 |
| Lomas de Zamora | 572,769 | Santiago del Estero | 189,490 |
| La Plata | 520,647 | San Salvador de Jujuy | 181,318 |
| Mar del Plata | 519,707 | Neuquén | 167,078 |
| Quilmes | 509,445 | Formosa | 153,855 |
| San Miguel de Tucumán | 470,604 | San Fernando | 141,496 |
| Lanús | 466,755 | Río Cuarto | 133,741 |
| General San Martín | 407,506 | Comodoro Rivadavia | 123,672 |
| Salta | 367,099 | Mendoza | 121,739 |
| Avellaneda | 346,620 | San Juan | 119,492 |
| Santa Fe | 342,796 | Concordia | 116,491 |
| San Isidro | 299,022 | San Nicolás | 114,752 |
| Vicente López | 289,142 | San Fernando del Valle de Catamarca | 110,269 |

* Figure for urban agglomeration: 10,686,163.

**BIRTHS AND DEATHS**

| | Registered live births | | Registered deaths | |
|---|---|---|---|---|
| | Number | Rate (per 1,000) | Number | Rate (per 1,000) |
| 1989 | 667,058 | 20.9 | 252,302 | 7.9 |
| 1990 | 678,644 | 21.0 | 259,683 | 8.0 |
| 1991 | 694,776 | 21.1 | 255,609 | 7.8 |
| 1992 | 678,761 | 20.3 | 262,287 | 7.9 |
| 1993 | 667,518 | 19.8 | 267,286 | 7.9 |
| 1994 | 707,869 | 20.7 | 260,245 | 7.6 |
| 1995 | 658,735 | 18.9 | 268,997 | 7.7 |
| 1996 | 675,437 | 19.2 | 268,715 | 7.6 |

Marriages: 186,337 (marriage rate 5.7 per 1,000) in 1990; 158,805 (marriage rate 4.6 per 1,000) in 1995; 148,721 in 1996 (4.2 per 1,000).

Source: mainly UN, *Demographic Yearbook* and *Population and Vital Statistics Report*.

**Expectation of life** (UN estimates, years at birth, 1990–95): 71.9 (males 68.6; females 75.7). Source: UN, *World Population Prospects: The 1998 Revision*.

**ECONOMICALLY ACTIVE POPULATION**
(persons aged 14 years and over, census of 15 May 1991)

| | Males | Females | Total |
|---|---|---|---|
| Agriculture, hunting, forestry and fishing | 1,142,674 | 222,196 | 1,364,870 |
| Mining and quarrying | 43,905 | 3,525 | 47,430 |
| Manufacturing | 1,590,713 | 546,090 | 2,136,803 |
| Electricity, gas and water | 92,469 | 11,318 | 103,787 |
| Construction | 818,831 | 17,617 | 836,448 |
| Wholesale and retail trade, restaurants and hotels | 1,730,600 | 808,702 | 2,539,302 |
| Transport, storage and communication | 583,938 | 54,024 | 637,962 |
| Finance, insurance, real estate and business services | 432,264 | 222,757 | 655,021 |
| Community, social and personal services | 1,459,492 | 2,464,552 | 3,924,044 |
| Activities not adequately described | 81,013 | 41,648 | 122,661 |
| **Total employed** | 7,975,899 | 4,392,429 | 12,368,328 |
| Unemployed | 447,488 | 386,384 | 833,872 |
| **Total labour force** | 8,423,387 | 4,778,813 | 13,202,200 |

**1995** (provisional figures, sample survey, persons aged 15 years and over): Total active population 14,345,171 (males 9,087,075; females 5,258,096) (Source: ILO, *Yearbook of Labour Statistics*).

**Mid-1998** (estimates in '000): Agriculture, etc. 1,469; Total labour force 14,393 (Source: FAO, *Production Yearbook*).

# Agriculture

**PRINCIPAL CROPS** ('000 metric tons)

| | 1996 | 1997 | 1998 |
|---|---|---|---|
| Wheat | 15,914 | 14,800 | 10,000* |
| Rice (paddy) | 974 | 1,205 | 1,036 |
| Barley | 537 | 926 | 500* |
| Maize | 10,518 | 15,536 | 19,100 |
| Rye | 36 | 62 | 62* |
| Oats | 310 | 512 | 300* |
| Millet | 47 | 44 | 46 |
| Sorghum | 2,132 | 2,499 | 3,720 |
| Potatoes | 2,275 | 2,376 | 3,100 |
| Sweet potatoes | 340 | 340† | 340† |
| Cassava (Manioc)† | 160 | 160 | 160 |
| Dry beans† | 227 | 269 | 290 |
| Other pulses | 57 | 59 | 61 |
| Soybeans | 12,448 | 11,000 | 18,718 |
| Groundnuts (in shell) | 660 | 403 | 929 |
| Sunflower seed | 5,558 | 5,450 | 5,400 |
| Linseed | 153 | 72 | 75 |
| Cottonseed | 748 | 564 | 452* |
| Cotton (lint) | 432 | 300* | 300* |
| Olives | 92 | 92† | 92† |
| Tomatoes | 662 | 675 | 675† |
| Pumpkins, squash and gourds† | 400 | 428 | 428 |
| Onions (dry) | 605 | 629 | 699 |
| Carrots | 200* | 200† | 200† |
| Watermelons† | 130 | 130 | 130 |
| Grapes | 2,040† | 2,500† | 2,021† |
| Sugar cane† | 17,600 | 19,450 | 19,400 |
| Apples | 1,219 | 1,306 | 1,347* |
| Pears | 484 | 523 | 540* |
| Peaches and nectarines* | 281 | 290 | 280 |
| Oranges | 504 | 841 | 841† |
| Tangerines, mandarins, clementines and satsumas | 253 | 410 | 410† |
| Lemons and limes | 801 | 871 | 871† |
| Grapefruit and pomelos | 167 | 229 | 230† |
| Bananas† | 170 | 170 | 170 |
| Tea (made) | 47 | 46 | 44 |
| Tobacco (leaves) | 98 | 123 | 117* |

* Unofficial figure. † FAO estimate(s).

Source: FAO, *Production Yearbook*.

**LIVESTOCK** ('000 head, year ending September)

| | 1996 | 1997 | 1998 |
|---|---|---|---|
| Horses* | 3,300 | 3,300 | 3,300 |
| Cattle | 54,000 | 54,500 | 54,600 |
| Pigs | 3,100 | 3,200 | 3,200* |
| Sheep† | 17,956 | 17,295 | 16,432 |
| Goats | 3,374 | 3,428 | 3,428* |

Chickens (million)*: 54 in 1996; 55 in 1997; 55 in 1998.
Ducks (million)*: 2 in 1996; 2 in 1997; 2 in 1998.
Turkeys (million)*: 3 in 1996; 3 in 1997; 3 in 1998.

* FAO estimate(s). † Unofficial figure.

Source: FAO, *Production Yearbook*.

**LIVESTOCK PRODUCTS** ('000 metric tons)

| | 1996 | 1997 | 1998 |
|---|---|---|---|
| Beef and veal | 2,374 | 2,336 | 2,250* |
| Mutton and lamb | 64 | 52* | 46* |
| Goat meat† | 7 | 7 | 7 |
| Pig meat | 148 | 137 | 137† |
| Horse meat† | 50 | 50 | 50 |
| Poultry meat | 587 | 615 | 615† |
| Cows' milk* | 9,140 | 9,405 | 9,750* |
| Butter* | 52 | 49 | 52 |
| Cheese | 376 | 445 | 420 |
| Hen eggs | 256* | 256* | 256† |
| Wool: | | | |
| greasy | 70 | 64 | 64 |
| scoured† | 39 | 35 | 35 |
| Cattle hides (fresh)† | 388 | 384 | 330 |

* Unofficial figure. †FAO estimate(s).

Source: FAO, *Production Yearbook*.

# Forestry

**ROUNDWOOD REMOVALS** ('000 cubic metres, excl. bark)

| | 1995 | 1996 | 1997 |
|---|---|---|---|
| Sawlogs, veneer logs and logs for sleepers | 2,844 | 3,575 | 3,575 |
| Pulpwood | 3,463 | 3,685 | 3,685 |
| Other industrial wood | 609 | 427 | 427 |
| Fuel wood | 4,615 | 5,505 | 5,505 |
| **Total** | 11,531 | 13,192 | 13,192 |

Source: FAO, *Yearbook of Forest Products*.

**SAWNWOOD PRODUCTION**
('000 cubic metres, incl. railway sleepers)

| | 1995 | 1996 | 1997* |
|---|---|---|---|
| Coniferous (softwood) | 625 | 594 | 594 |
| Broadleaved (hardwood) | 704 | 1,117 | 1,117 |
| **Total** | 1,329 | 1,711 | 1,711 |

* FAO estimates.

Source: FAO, *Yearbook of Forest Products*.

# Fishing

('000 metric tons, live weight)

| | 1995 | 1996 | 1997 |
|---|---|---|---|
| Freshwater fishes | 11.8 | 11.8 | 11.9 |
| Southern blue whiting | 104.2 | 85.0 | 79.9 |
| Argentine hake | 574.3 | 597.6 | 584.0 |
| Patagonian grenadier | 22.8 | 44.1 | 41.8 |
| Whitemouth croaker | 30.0 | 23.5 | 26.1 |
| Pink cusk-eel | 23.3 | 21.9 | 21.9 |
| Argentine anchovy | 24.4 | 21.0 | 25.2 |
| Other marine fishes | 145.8 | 136.4 | 133.1 |
| Crustaceans | 7.8 | 10.7 | 7.8 |
| Argentine shortfin squid | 199.0 | 292.6 | 412.0 |
| Other molluscs | 3.9 | 4.0 | 7.2 |
| **Total catch** | 1,147.4 | 1,248.7 | 1,351.1 |
| Inland waters | 11.9 | 11.9 | 12.0 |
| Atlantic Ocean | 1,135.5 | 1,236.9 | 1,339.1 |

Source: FAO, *Yearbook of Fishery Statistics.*

**1998** (estimate): Total catch 1,117,375 metric tons.

# Mining

('000 metric tons, unless otherwise indicated)

| | 1994 | 1995 | 1996 |
|---|---|---|---|
| Hard coal | 348 | 305 | 311 |
| Crude petroleum | 34,278 | 35,888 | 40,311 |
| Natural gas ('000 terajoules) | 996 | 1,062* | 1,032 |
| Iron ore†‡ | 28 | 0 | 0 |
| Lead ore† | 10.0 | 10.5 | 11.3* |
| Zinc ore† | 26.9 | 32.1 | 31.1* |
| Silver ore (metric tons) | 38 | 48 | 50 |
| Uranium ore (metric tons)† | 79 | 70 | n.a. |
| Gold ore (kilograms)† | 937 | 837 | 723 |

* Estimate.

† Figures refer to the metal content of ores and concentrates.

‡ Data from US Bureau of Mines.

Source: UN, *Industrial Commodity Statistics Yearbook*.

**1997** (estimates, '000 metric tons, unless otherwise stated): Crude petroleum ('000 cu metres) 48,403; Natural gas (million cu metres) 37,073; Zinc ore 33.4; Gold ore (kilograms) 2,289; Silver ore (metric tons) 52.6; Lead ore 13.8; Uranium ore (metric tons) 41.

**1998** (estimates, '000 metric tons, unless otherwise stated): Crude petroleum ('000 cu metres) 49,149; Natural gas (million cu metres) 38,631; Zinc ore 35.6; Gold ore (kilograms) 19,500; Silver ore (metric tons) 36.2; Lead ore 15.0; Uranium ore 41.

# Industry

**SELECTED PRODUCTS** ('000 metric tons, unless otherwise indicated)

| | 1994 | 1995 | 1996 |
|---|---|---|---|
| Wheat flour | 3,292 | 3,240 | 3,481 |
| Beer ('000 hectolitres) | 11,272 | 10,422 | 10,286 |
| Cigarettes (million units) | 1,975 | 1,963 | 1,971 |
| Paper and paper products | 970 | 1,021 | 1,121 |
| Wood pulp, sulphate and soda | 477 | 437 | 437 |
| Non-cellulosic continuous fibres | 37.0 | 43.6* | 42.3* |
| Sulphuric acid | 204 | 226 | 220 |
| Rubber tyres for motor vehicles ('000) | 7,083 | 6,940 | 7,297 |
| Portland cement | 6,306 | 5,477 | 5,117 |
| Distillate fuel oils | 8,793 | 8,627 | 9,487 |
| Residual fuel oils | 2,748 | 2,282 | 1,924 |
| Motor spirit (petrol) | 6,057 | 6,444 | 5,160 |
| Kerosene | 346 | 263 | 200 |
| Liquefied petroleum gas: | | | |
| from natural gas plants | 681 | 1,009 | 1,054 |
| from petroleum refineries | 869 | 758 | 830 |
| Passenger motor vehicles ('000 units) | 338 | 227 | 269 |
| Refrigerators ('000 units) | 494 | 389 | 379 |
| Washing machines ('000 units) | 702 | 458 | 524 |
| Television receivers ('000) | 1,523 | 949 | 1,089 |
| Electric energy (million kWh)† | 66,196 | 67,169 | 69,746 |

* Data from Fiber Economics Bureau, Inc. (USA).

† Provisional figures.

Source: mainly UN, *Industrial Commodity Statistics Yearbook.*

**1997** ('000 metric tons, unless otherwise indicated): Wheat flour 3,640; Beer ('000 hectolitres) 12,687*; Cigarettes (million units) 1,940; Paper and paper products 1,143; Rubber tyres for motor vehicles ('000) 8,138; Portland cement 6,769; Television receivers ('000) 1,601; Washing machines ('000 units) 603*; Passenger motor vehicles ('000 units) 366.

**1998** ('000 metric tons, unless otherwise indicated): Wheat flour 3,675*; Beer ('000 hectolitres) 12,395*; Cigarettes (million units) 1,967; Paper and paper products 1,159*; Rubber tyres for motor vehicles ('000) 9,190; Portland cement 7,092; Television receivers ('000) 1,592; Washing machines ('000 units) 624; Passenger motor vehicles ('000 units) 353.

* Provisional figure.

# Finance

**CURRENCY AND EXCHANGE RATES**

**Monetary Units:**

100 centavos = 1 nuevo peso argentino (new Argentine peso).

**Sterling, Dollar and Euro Equivalents** (30 September 1999)

£1 sterling = 1.6457 nuevos pesos;
US $1 = 99.95 centavos;
€1 = 1.0660 nuevos pesos;
100 nuevos pesos = £60.77 = $100.05 = €93.81.

**Average Exchange Rate** (pesos argentinos per US $)

| | |
|---|---|
| 1996 | 0.99966 |
| 1997 | 0.99950 |
| 1998 | 0.99950 |

Note: The nuevo peso argentino was introduced on 1 January 1992, replacing the austral at a rate of 1 nuevo peso = 10,000 australes. The austral had been introduced on 15 June 1985, replacing the peso argentino at the rate of 1 austral = 1,000 pesos argentinos. The peso argentino, equal to 10,000 former pesos, had itself been introduced on 1 June 1983. The official exchange rate has been fixed at US $1 = 99.95 centavos since April 1996.

**BUDGET** (million new pesos)*

| Revenue | 1994 | 1995 | 1996 |
|---|---|---|---|
| Taxation | 35,005.6 | 33,380.3 | 32,869.1 |
| Taxes on income, profits, etc. | 4,065.6 | 3,730.6 | 4,689.8 |
| Social security contributions | 14,084.9 | 12,597.5 | 10,629.6 |
| Taxes on property | 706.6 | 934.6 | 1,203.0 |
| Domestic taxes on goods and services | 12,778.2 | 13,203.7 | 13,931.4 |
| Value-added tax | 8,846.4 | 9,145.8 | 10,589.4 |
| Excises | 3,822.8 | 3,923.5 | 3,141.8 |
| Taxes on international trade and transactions | 2,791.8 | 1,890.7 | 2,326.2 |
| Import duties | 1,687.6 | 1,596.1 | 1,928.2 |
| Export duties | 34.1 | 35.3 | 104.8 |
| Property income | 1,191.4 | 1,050.7 | 1,394.4 |
| Administrative fees and charges, etc. | 1,548.9 | 1,335.3 | 952.3 |
| Other current revenue | 518.4 | 421.3 | 266.2 |
| Capital revenue | 53.8 | 24.1 | 65.9 |
| **Total revenue** | 38,318.1 | 36,211.7 | 35,547.9 |

| Expenditure† | 1994 | 1995 | 1996 |
|---|---|---|---|
| General public services | 3,677.2 | 3,765.5 | 4,191.3 |
| Defence | 2,007.5 | 2,084.5 | 2,012.1 |
| Public order and safety | 1,430.3 | 1,464.0 | 1,416.5 |
| Education | 2,146.8 | 2,231.3 | 2,402.7 |
| Health | 960.3 | 1,097.1 | 1,058.0 |
| Social security and welfare | 21,072.4 | 21,859.4 | 22,339.0 |
| Housing and community amenities | 1,169.4 | 1,205.0 | 1,023.3 |
| Recreational, cultural and religious affairs and services | 155.3 | 178.4 | 147.8 |
| Economic affairs and services | 3,583.2 | 2,835.1 | 2,629.8 |
| Agriculture, forestry and fishing | 386.0 | 373.3 | 373.1 |
| Fuel and energy | 1,309.0 | 479.2 | 478.8 |
| Transportation and communication | 1,409.3 | 1,483.3 | 1,405.8 |
| Mining, manufacturing and construction | 175.0 | 187.2 | 121.2 |
| Other purposes | 3,219.1 | 4,083.1 | 4,676.2 |
| Interest payments | 3,192.0 | 4,083.1 | 4,628.1 |
| **Sub-total** | 39,421.5 | 40,803.4 | 41,896.7 |
| Adjustment to cash basis | −264.0 | −158.8 | −29.8 |
| **Total expenditure** | 39,157.5 | 40,644.6 | 41,866.9 |
| Current | 36,689.7 | 37,663.5 | 38,394.7 |
| Capital | 2,467.8 | 2,981.1 | 3,472.2 |

* Budget figures refer to the consolidated accounts of the central Government, including special accounts, government agencies and the national social security system. The budgets of provincial and municipal governments are excluded.

† Excluding net lending (million new pesos): 423.1 in 1994; 1,457.2 in 1995; 299.2 in 1996.

Source: IMF, *Government Finance Statistics Yearbook.*

**INTERNATIONAL RESERVES** (US $ million at 31 December)

| | 1996 | 1997 | 1998 |
|---|---|---|---|
| Gold* | 1,611 | 120 | 124 |
| IMF special drawing rights | 399 | 167 | 264 |
| Foreign exchange | 17,705 | 22,153 | 24,488 |
| **Total** | 19,715 | 22,440 | 24,876 |

* Valued at US $388 per troy ounce in 1996, at $331 per ounce in 1997 and at $294 per ounce in 1998.

Source: IMF, *International Financial Statistics.*

**MONEY SUPPLY** (million new pesos at 31 December)

| | 1996 | 1997 | 1998 |
|---|---|---|---|
| Currency outside banks | 11,736 | 13,331 | 13,503 |
| Demand deposits at commercial banks | 7,305 | 8,151 | 7,986 |
| **Total money** | 19,042 | 21,482 | 21,489 |

Source: IMF, *International Financial Statistics.*

**COST OF LIVING** (Consumer Price Index for Buenos Aires metropolitan area; annual averages; base: 1988 = 100)

| | 1996 | 1997 | 1998 |
|---|---|---|---|
| Food | 276,443 | 274,621 | 279,216 |
| Clothing | 181,480 | 176,184 | 171,767 |
| Housing | 325,439 | 323,543 | 320,884 |
| **All items** (incl. others) | 321,966 | 323,668 | 326,661 |

**NATIONAL ACCOUNTS** (million new pesos at current prices)

**Expenditure on the Gross Domestic Product**

| | 1996 | 1997 | 1998 |
|---|---|---|---|
| Government final consumption expenditure | 34,023 | 35,325 | 35,474 |
| Private final consumption expenditure | 190,522 | 207,108 | 210,857 |
| Gross fixed capital formation | 49,211 | 56,727 | 59,276 |
| **Total domestic expenditure** | 273,756 | 299,160 | 305,607 |
| Exports of goods and services | 28,470 | 30,939 | 31,019 |
| *Less* Imports of goods and services | 30,077 | 37,240 | 38,494 |
| **GDP in purchasers' values** | 272,150 | 292,859 | 298,131 |
| **GDP at constant 1993 prices** | 256,626 | 277,441 | 288,195 |

Source: IMF, *International Financial Statistics.*

**Gross Domestic Product by Economic Activity**

| | 1996 | 1997 | 1998 |
|---|---|---|---|
| Agriculture, hunting and forestry | 14,664 | 14,625 | 15,275 |
| Fishing | 606 | 668 | 647 |
| Mining and quarrying | 5,889 | 5,633 | 4,291 |
| Manufacturing | 47,723 | 53,382 | 53,266 |
| Electricity, gas and water supply | 5,232 | 5,502 | 5,749 |
| Construction | 13,527 | 15,080 | 16,635 |
| Wholesale and retail trade | 37,754 | 41,477 | 42,385 |
| Hotels and restaurants | 6,787 | 7,644 | 8,110 |
| Transport, storage and communications | 20,501 | 22,952 | 23,631 |
| Financial intermediation | 9,832 | 10,116 | 10,393 |
| Real estate, renting and business activities | 42,543 | 44,567 | 45,522 |
| Public administration and defence* | 15,497 | 15,860 | 16,463 |
| Education, health and social work | 20,452 | 21,366 | 22,155 |
| Other community, social and personal service activities† | 13,600 | 14,221 | 14,111 |
| **Sub-total** | 254,609 | 273,093 | 278,632 |
| Value-added tax | 12,564 | 12,776 | 13,162 |
| Import duties | 8,486 | 10,525 | 10,437 |
| *Less* Imputed bank service charge | 3,509 | 3,534 | 4,099 |
| **GDP in purchasers' values** | 272,150 | 292,859 | 298,131 |

* Including extra-territorial organizations and bodies.

† Including private households with employed persons.

**BALANCE OF PAYMENTS** (US $ million)

| | 1996 | 1997 | 1998 |
|---|---|---|---|
| Exports of goods f.o.b. | 24,043 | 26,431 | 26,434 |
| Imports of goods f.o.b. | -22,283 | -28,554 | -29,448 |
| **Trade balance** | 1,760 | -2,123 | -3,014 |
| Exports of services | 4,428 | 4,510 | 4,660 |
| Imports of services | -7,794 | -8,687 | -9,045 |
| **Balance on goods and services** | -1,606 | -6,300 | -7,399 |
| Other income received | 4,504 | 5,448 | 5,914 |
| Other income paid | -9,782 | -11,619 | -13,600 |
| **Balance on goods, services and income** | -6,884 | -12,471 | -15,085 |
| Current transfers received | 510 | 542 | 490 |
| Current transfers paid | -94 | -106 | -102 |
| **Current balance** | -6,468 | -12,035 | -14,697 |
| Direct investment abroad | -1,576 | -3,170 | -1,973 |
| Direct investment from abroad | 6,513 | 8,094 | 6,150 |
| Portfolio investment assets | -2,421 | -1,231 | -1,068 |
| Portfolio investment liabilities | 12,200 | 12,346 | 10,831 |
| Other investment assets | -5,232 | -7,112 | 402 |
| Other investment liabilities | 1,977 | 7,739 | 4,542 |
| Net errors and omissions | -1,655 | -1,257 | -69 |
| **Overall balance** | 3,338 | 3,374 | 4,118 |

Source: IMF, *International Financial Statistics*.

# External Trade

**PRINCIPAL COMMODITIES** (distribution by SITC, US $ '000)

| Imports c.i.f. | 1994 | 1995 | 1996 |
|---|---|---|---|
| **Food and live animals** | 992,607 | 969,714 | 1,025,634 |
| **Crude materials (inedible) except fuels** | 591,619 | 714,088 | 787,308 |
| **Mineral fuels, lubricants, etc.** | 645,657 | 859,002 | 885,800 |
| Petroleum, petroleum products, etc. | 487,133 | 623,960 | 616,694 |
| Refined petroleum products | 382,372 | 475,807 | 448,530 |
| **Chemicals and related products** | 2,933,092 | 3,482,324 | 4,264,041 |
| Organic chemicals | 866,994 | 1,053,378 | 1,226,892 |
| Medicinal and pharmaceutical products | 495,061 | 488,826 | 582,580 |
| Artificial resins, plastic materials, etc. | 535,438 | 679,265 | 770,889 |
| Products of polymerization, etc. | 337,577 | 426,948 | 479,527 |
| **Basic manufactures** | 2,854,621 | 3,023,690 | 3,544,722 |
| Paper, paperboard and manufactures | 524,493 | 665,674 | 721,732 |
| Textile yarn, fabrics, etc. | 485,520 | 428,685 | 609,698 |
| Iron and steel | 487,569 | 514,292 | 524,908 |
| **Machinery and transport equipment** | 11,188,152 | 8,930,585 | 10,901,953 |
| Power-generating machinery and equipment | 660,762 | 767,264 | 887,448 |
| Machinery specialized for particular industries | 1,132,190 | 814,516 | 1,090,943 |
| General industrial machinery, equipment and parts | 1,559,845 | 1,691,779 | 1,866,929 |
| Office machines and automatic data-processing equipment | 927,403 | 707,632 | 815,211 |
| Automatic data-processing machines, etc. | 670,504 | 469,076 | 543,049 |
| Telecommunications and sound equipment | 1,495,055 | 1,028,652 | 1,083,050 |
| Other electrical machinery, apparatus, etc. | 1,504,753 | 1,338,292 | 1,604,211 |

| Imports c.i.f. — *continued* | 1994 | 1995 | 1996 |
|---|---|---|---|
| Road vehicles and parts* | 3,330,590 | 2,118,971 | 2,983,694 |
| Passenger motor cars (excl. buses) | 1,394,468 | 773,204 | 1,198,389 |
| Motor vehicles for goods transport, etc. | 558,680 | 310,998 | 532,857 |
| Goods vehicles (lorries and trucks) | 519,705 | 284,389 | 509,322 |
| Parts and accessories for cars, buses, lorries, etc.* | 968,052 | 867,733 | 1,061,325 |
| **Miscellaneous manufactured articles** | 2,236,232 | 1,996,846 | 2,209,614 |
| **Total** (incl. others) | 21,581,084 | 20,121,670 | 23,761,588 |

| Exports f.o.b. | 1994 | 1995 | 1996 |
|---|---|---|---|
| **Food and live animals** | 5,584,425 | 7,214,582 | 9,241,573 |
| Meat and meat preparations | 918,088 | 1,229,138 | 1,073,840 |
| Fresh, chilled or frozen meat | 627,906 | 848,098 | 780,996 |
| Boneless meat (bovine) | 470,400 | 653,341 | 583,536 |
| Meat and edible meat offals, prepared or preserved | 289,991 | 381,013 | 292,733 |
| Fish and fish preparations | 725,169 | 914,291 | 1,003,813 |
| Fish, fresh (live or dead), chilled or frozen | 365,653 | 501,564 | 494,855 |
| Cereals and cereal preparations | 1,456,331 | 2,017,775 | 2,802,887 |
| Wheat (including spelt) and meslin, unmilled | 669,979 | 1,005,372 | 1,065,647 |
| Maize (corn), unmilled | 491,845 | 682,289 | 1,239,350 |
| Vegetables and fruit | 699,238 | 1,034,940 | 1,180,466 |
| Fruit and nuts, fresh or dried | 275,728 | 444,813 | 508,676 |
| Feeding-stuff for animals | 1,348,966 | 1,254,639 | 2,366,909 |
| Oilcake and other residues | 1,301,788 | 1,196,120 | 2,293,308 |
| **Crude materials (inedible) except fuels** | 1,446,894 | 1,767,938 | 1,869,110 |
| Oil seeds and oleaginous fruit | 943,600 | 875,059 | 955,076 |
| Soya beans | 690,463 | 535,966 | 588,186 |
| Textile fibres and waste | 318,971 | 582,196 | 625,426 |
| Cotton | 179,153 | 437,489 | 500,701 |
| **Mineral fuels, lubricants, etc.** | 1,657,123 | 2,175,369 | 3,096,115 |
| Petroleum, petroleum products, etc. | 1,580,964 | 2,088,659 | 2,973,320 |
| Crude petroleum | 1,125,573 | 1,591,855 | 2,319,964 |
| Refined petroleum products | 413,556 | 435,540 | 584,876 |
| **Animal and vegetable oils, fats and waxes** | 1,518,934 | 2,077,340 | 1,882,531 |
| Fixed vegetable oils and fats | 1,498,542 | 2,043,852 | 1,857,181 |
| Soya bean oil | 859,437 | 942,993 | 900,771 |
| Sunflower seed oil | 546,835 | 973,681 | 832,082 |
| **Chemicals and related products** | 918,947 | 1,314,779 | 1,320,071 |
| **Basic manufactures** | 2,095,484 | 2,972,490 | 2,851,956 |
| Leather, leather manufactures and dressed furskins | 876,354 | 989,161 | 926,412 |
| Leather | 733,416 | 893,786 | 823,788 |
| Iron and steel | 467,998 | 731,961 | 797,759 |
| Tubes, pipes and fittings | 273,386 | 334,442 | 457,840 |
| 'Seamless' tubes and pipes | 261,574 | 315,006 | 417,163 |
| **Machinery and transport equipment** | 1,770,733 | 2,275,227 | 2,592,458 |
| Road vehicles and parts* | 863,390 | 1,233,141 | 1,514,509 |
| Parts and accessories for cars, buses, lorries, etc.* | 456,722 | 546,161 | 440,791 |
| **Miscellaneous manufactured articles** | 642,324 | 889,997 | 666,930 |
| **Total** (incl. others) | 15,838,665 | 20,962,590 | 23,809,643 |

* Excluding tyres, engines and electrical parts.

Source: UN, *International Trade Statistics Yearbook*.

**1997** (US $ million): Imports c.i.f. 30,450; Exports f.o.b. 26,431.
**1998** (US $ million): Imports c.i.f. 31,404; Exports f.o.b. 26,441.

**PRINCIPAL TRADING PARTNERS** (US $ million)

| Imports c.i.f. | 1996 | 1997 | 1998* |
|---|---|---|---|
| Brazil | 5,326 | 6,914 | 7,055 |
| Canada | 275 | 450 | 385 |
| Chile | 559 | 688 | 708 |
| China, People's Republic | 698 | 1,006 | 1,167 |
| France (incl. Monaco) | 1,181 | 1,375 | 1,584 |
| Germany | 1,427 | 1,655 | 1,876 |
| Italy | 1,503 | 1,747 | 1,605 |
| Japan | 725 | 1,150 | 1,453 |
| Mexico | 541 | 610 | 603 |
| Paraguay | 182 | 320 | 348 |
| Spain | 1,064 | 1,256 | 1,311 |
| United Kingdom | 563 | 802 | 797 |
| USA | 4,749 | 6,095 | 6,227 |
| Uruguay | 293 | 371 | 528 |
| **Total** (incl. others) | 23,762 | 30,450 | 31,404 |

| Exports f.o.b. | 1996 | 1997 | 1998* |
|---|---|---|---|
| Belgium | 269 | 304 | 278 |
| Bolivia | 292 | 464 | 431 |
| Brazil | 6,615 | 8,133 | 7,949 |
| Chile | 1,766 | 1,932 | 1,864 |
| China, People's Republic | 607 | 871 | 682 |
| France (incl. Monaco) | 297 | 310 | 315 |
| Germany | 565 | 503 | 564 |
| Iran | 637 | 659 | 476 |
| Italy | 721 | 730 | 753 |
| Japan | 512 | 554 | 657 |
| Mexico | 248 | 216 | 261 |
| Netherlands | 1,225 | 880 | 1,100 |
| Paraguay | 584 | 624 | 622 |
| Peru | 254 | 306 | 326 |
| South Africa | 247 | 304 | 253 |
| Spain | 724 | 623 | 839 |
| United Kingdom | 355 | 320 | 256 |
| USA | 1,973 | 2,204 | 2,211 |
| Uruguay | 719 | 840 | 843 |
| Venezuela | 351 | 315 | 364 |
| **Total** (incl. others) | 23,811 | 26,431 | 26,441 |

* Provisional.

# Transport

**RAILWAYS** (traffic)

| | 1994 | 1995 | 1996 |
|---|---|---|---|
| Passengers carried (million) | 248 | 349 | 416 |
| Freight carried ('000 tons) | 13,174 | 15,196 | 17,017 |
| Passenger-km (million) | 6,460 | n.a. | n.a. |
| Freight ton-km (million) | 6,663 | 7,613 | 8,506 |

**1997:** Passengers carried (million) 459; Freight carried ('000 tons) 18,912; Freight ton-km (million) 9,835.

**1998:** Passengers carried (million) 480; Freight carried ('000 tons) 18,838; Freight ton-km (million) 9,824.

**ROAD TRAFFIC** (motor vehicles in use)

| | 1993 | 1994 | 1995 |
|---|---|---|---|
| Passenger cars | 4,556,000 | 4,426,706 | 4,665,329 |
| Commercial vehicles | n.a. | 1,203,908 | 1,181,569 |

Source: Secretaría de Obras Públicas y Transporte.

**1996:** (motor vehicles in use at 31 December, estimates): Passenger cars 4,459,000; Buses and coaches 12,000; Lorries and vans 943,000; Motorcycles and mopeds 35,640 (Source: International Road Federation, World Road Statistics).

**SHIPPING**

**Merchant Fleet** (registered at 31 December)

| | 1996 | 1997 | 1998 |
|---|---|---|---|
| Number of vessels | 480 | 513 | 501 |
| Total displacement ('000 grt) | 586.3 | 579.4 | 498.7 |

Source: Lloyd's Register of Shipping, *World Fleet Statistics*.

**International Sea-borne Freight Traffic** ('000 metric tons)

| | 1993 | 1994 | 1995 |
|---|---|---|---|
| Goods loaded | 38,032 | 40,025 | 48,538 |
| Goods unloaded | 10,831 | 14,202 | 15,146 |

Source: Secretaría de Obras Públicas y Transporte.

**CIVIL AVIATION** (scheduled airline traffic)

| | 1993 | 1994 | 1995 |
|---|---|---|---|
| Passengers carried ('000) | 6,191 | 6,359 | 6,798 |
| Passenger-km (million) | 9,272 | 11,305 | 12,190 |
| Kilometres flown (million) | 78 | 90 | 113 |
| Freight ('000 metric tons) | 120 | 123 | 109 |
| Total ton-km (million)* | 1,117 | 1,289 | 1,338 |

* Source: UN, *Statistical Yearbook*.

Source: Secretaría de Obras Públicas y Transporte.

# Tourism

| | 1996 | 1997 | 1998 |
|---|---|---|---|
| Tourist arrivals ('000) | 4,286 | 4,540 | 4,860 |
| Tourist receipts (US $ million) | 4,572 | 4,069 | 5,363 |

## Communications Media

| | 1994 | 1995 | 1996 |
|---|---|---|---|
| Radio receivers ('000 in use) | 23,000 | 23,500 | 23,850 |
| Television receivers ('000 in use) | 7,500 | 7,600 | 7,800 |
| Telephones* ('000 main lines in use) | 4,834 | 5,532 | 6,120 |
| Telefax stations*† ('000 in use) | 40 | 50 | n.a. |
| Mobile cellular telephones* ('000 subscribers) | 202.2 | 340.7 | 667.0 |
| Daily newspapers | 187 | 190† | 181 |
| Books (number of titles) | 9,065 | 9,113 | 9,850 |

* Year ending September.

† Provisional.

Sources: mainly UNESCO, *Statistical Yearbook*, and UN, *Statistical Yearbook*.

**1997:** Telephones ('000 main lines in use) 6,824; Mobile cellular telephones ('000 subscribers) 2,009; Books (number of titles) 11,919.

**1998:** Books (number of titles) 13,156

## Education

(1997)

| | Institutions*† | Students | Teachers‡ |
|---|---|---|---|
| Pre-primary | 14,064 | 1,145,919 | 65,708 |
| Primary | 27,146 | 5,153,256 | 295,488 |
| Secondary | 7,623 | 2,463,608 | 238,791 |
| Universities§ | 36 | 812,302* | n.a. |
| Colleges of higher education | 1,795 | 356,585 | 43,921 |

* 1996 figure(s).

† Provisional.

‡ 1994 figures.

§ State universities only.

Source: Ministerio de Cultura y Educación.

# Directory

## The Constitution

The return to civilian rule in 1983 represented a return to the principles of the 1853 Constitution, with some changes in electoral details. In August 1994 a new Constitution was approved, which contained 19 new articles, 40 amendments to existing articles and the addition of a chapter on New Rights and Guarantees. The Constitution is summarized below:

### DECLARATIONS, RIGHTS AND GUARANTEES

Each province has the right to exercise its own administration of justice, municipal system and primary education. The Roman Catholic religion, being the faith of the majority of the nation, shall enjoy state protection; freedom of religious belief is guaranteed to all other denominations. The prior ethnical existence of indigenous peoples and their rights, as well as the common ownership of lands they traditionally occupy, are recognized. All inhabitants of the country have the right to work and exercise any legal trade; to petition the authorities; to leave or enter the Argentine territory; to use or dispose of their properties; to associate for a peaceable or useful purpose; to teach and acquire education, and to express freely their opinion in the press without censorship. The State does not admit any prerogative of blood, birth, privilege or titles of nobility. Equality is the basis of all duties and public offices. No citizens may be detained, except for reasons and in the manner prescribed by the law; or sentenced other than by virtue of a law existing prior to the offence and by decision of the competent tribunal after the hearing and defence of the person concerned. Private residence, property and correspondence are inviolable. No one may enter the home of a citizen or carry out any search in it without his consent, unless by a warrant from the competent authority; no one may suffer expropriation, except in case of public necessity and provided that the appropriate compensation has been paid in accordance with the provisions of the laws. In no case may the penalty of confiscation of property be imposed.

### LEGISLATIVE POWER

Legislative power is vested in the bicameral Congreso (Congress), comprising the Cámara de Diputados (Chamber of Deputies) and the Senado (Senate). The Chamber of Deputies has 257 directly-elected members, chosen for four years and eligible for re-election; approximately one-half of the membership of the Chamber shall be renewed every two years. Until October 1995 the Senate had 48 members, chosen by provincial legislatures for a nine-year term, with one-third of the seats renewable every three years. Since October 1995 elections have provided for a third senator, elected by provincial legislatures. By 2001 the members of the expanded Senate will henceforth serve a six-year term.

The powers of Congress include regulating foreign trade; fixing import and export duties; levying taxes for a specified time whenever the defence, common safety or general welfare of the State so requires; contracting loans on the nation's credit; regulating the internal and external debt and the currency system of the country; fixing the budget and facilitating the prosperity and welfare of the nation. Congress must approve required and urgent decrees and delegated legislation. Congress also approves or rejects treaties, authorizes the Executive to declare war or make peace, and establishes the strength of the Armed Forces in peace and war.

### EXECUTIVE POWER

Executive power is vested in the President, who is the supreme head of the nation and controls the general administration of the country. The President issues the instructions and rulings necessary for the execution of the laws of the country, and himself takes part in drawing up and promulgating those laws. The President appoints, with the approval of the Senate, the judges of the Supreme Court and all other competent tribunals, ambassadors, civil servants, members of the judiciary and senior officers of the Armed Forces and bishops. The President may also appoint and remove, without reference to another body, his cabinet ministers. The President is Commander-in-Chief of all the Armed Forces. The President and Vice-President are elected directly for a four-year term, renewable only once.

### JUDICIAL POWER

Judicial power is exercised by the Supreme Court and all other competent tribunals. The Supreme Court is responsible for the internal administration of all tribunals. In April 1990 the number of Supreme Court judges was increased from five to nine.

### PROVINCIAL GOVERNMENT

The 22 provinces, the Federal District of Buenos Aires and the National Territory of Tierra del Fuego retain all the power not delegated to the Federal Government. They are governed by their own institutions and elect their own governors, legislators and officials.

## The Government

### HEAD OF STATE

**President of the Republic:** FERNANDO DE LA RÚA (took office 10 December 1999).

**Vice-President of the Republic:** CARLOS 'CHACHO' ALVAREZ.

### CABINET

(January 2000)

**Cabinet Chief:** RODOLFO TERRAGNO.

**Minister of the Interior:** FEDERICO STORANI.

**Minister of Foreign Affairs:** ADALBERTO RODRÍGUEZ GIAVARINI.

**Minister of Education:** JUAN JOSÉ LLACH.

**Minister of Defence:** RICARDO LÓPEZ MURPHY.

**Minister of the Economy:** JOSÉ LUIS MACHINEA.
**Minister of Labour:** ALBERTO FLAMARIQUE.
**Minister of Social Action:** GRACIELA FERNÁNDEZ MEIJIDE.
**Minister of Health:** HÉCTOR LOMBARDO.
**Minister of Infrastructure:** NICOLÁS GALLO.
**Minister of Justice:** RICARDO GIL LAVEDRA.

### MINISTRIES

**General Secretariat to the Presidency:** Balcarce 50, 1064 Buenos Aires; tel. (11) 446-9841.

**Ministry of Defence:** Avda Paseo Colón 255, 9°, 1063 Buenos Aires; tel. (11) 4343-1560; fax (11) 4331-7745.

**Ministry of the Economy:** Hipólito Yrigoyen 250, 1310 Buenos Aires; tel. (11) 4342-6411; fax (11) 4331-7426.

**Ministry of Education:** Pizzurno 935, 1020 Buenos Aires; tel. (11) 442-4551; fax (11) 4812-8905.

**Ministry of Foreign Affairs:** Reconquista 1088, 1003 Buenos Aires; tel. (11) 4311-0071; fax (11) 4311-5730.

**Ministry of Health:** 9 de Julio 1925, 1332 Buenos Aires; tel. (11) 4381-8911; fax (11) 4381-2182.

**Ministry of Infrastructure:** Buenos Aires.

**Ministry of the Interior:** Balcarce 50, 1064 Buenos Aires; tel. (11) 446-9841; fax (11) 4331-6376.

**Ministry of Justice:** Talcahuano 550, 1013 Buenos Aires; tel. (11) 4803-4051; fax (11) 4803-3955.

**Ministry of Labour:** Leandro N. Alem 650, 1001 Buenos Aires; tel. (11) 4311-2913; fax (11) 4312-7860.

**Ministry of Social Action:** Buenos Aires.

# President and Legislature

### PRESIDENT

**Election, 24 October 1999**

| Candidates | Votes | % votes cast |
|---|---|---|
| FERNANDO DE LA RÚA (ATJE) | 9,039,892 | 48.50 |
| EDUARDO DUHALDE (PJ) | 7,100,678 | 38.09 |
| DOMINGO CAVALLO (AR) | 1,881,417 | 10.09 |
| Others | 618,846 | 3.32 |
| **Total** | 18,640,833 | 100.00 |

### CONGRESO

**Cámara de Diputados**
(Chamber of Deputies)

**President:** ALBERTO PIERRI.

The Chamber has 257 members, who hold office for a four-year term, with approximately one-half of the seats renewable every two years.

**Legislative Elections, 24 October 1999***

| | Seats |
|---|---|
| Alianza para el Trabajo, la Justícia y la Educación (ATJE)† | 127 |
| Partido Justicialista (PJ) | 101 |
| Acción por la República (AR) | 12 |
| Others | 17 |
| **Total** | 257 |

* The table indicates the distribution of the total number of seats, following the elections for 130 seats.
† Alliance comprising Frente del País Solidario and the Unión Cívica Radical.

**Senado**
(Senate)

**President:** EDUARDO MENEM.

**Distribution of Seats, November 1997***

| | Seats |
|---|---|
| Partido Justicialista (PJ) | 36 |
| Unión Cívica Radical (UCR) | 15 |
| Frente del País Solidario (Frepaso) | 2 |
| Provincial parties | 10 |
| **Total** | 63 |

* Until October 1995 the Senate comprised 48 members, who were nominated by the legislative bodies of the Federal District, the National Territory, and each province (two Senators for each), with the exception of Buenos Aires, which elected its Senators by means of a special Electoral College. The Senate's term of office was nine years, with one-third of the seats renewable every three years. Since October 1995 elections have provided for an expanded Senate (three members from each region) with a six-year term of office (one-third of the seats being renewable every three years).

### PROVINCIAL ADMINISTRATORS
(January 2000)

**Mayor of the Federal District of Buenos Aires:** ENRIQUE OLIVERA.
**Governor of the Province of Buenos Aires:** CARLOS RUCKAUF.
**Governor of the Province of Catamarca:** OSCAR CASTILLO.
**Governor of the Province of Chaco:** ANGEL ROZAS.
**Governor of the Province of Chubut:** JOSÉ LUIS LIZURUME.
**Governor of the Province of Córdoba:** JOSÉ MANUEL DE LA SOTA.
**Governor of the Province of Corrientes:** (vacant)*.
**Governor of the Province of Entre Ríos:** SERGIO MONTIEL.
**Governor of the Province of Formosa:** GILDO INSFRÁN.
**Governor of the Province of Jujuy:** EDUARDO FELLNER.
**Governor of the Province of La Pampa:** RUBÉN HUGO MARIN.
**Governor of the Province of La Rioja:** ANGEL MAZA.
**Governor of the Province of Mendoza:** ROBERTO IGLESIAS.
**Governor of the Province of Misiones:** CARLOS ROVIRA.
**Governor of the Province of Neuquén:** JORGE SOSBICH.
**Governor of the Province of Río Negro:** PABLO VERANI.
**Governor of the Province of Salta:** JUAN CARLOS ROMERO.
**Governor of the Province of San Juan:** ALFREDO AVELÍN.
**Governor of the Province of San Luis:** ADOLFO RODRÍGUEZ SAA.
**Governor of the Province of Santa Cruz:** NÉSTOR KIRSCHNER.
**Governor of the Province of Santa Fe:** CARLOS REUTEMANN.
**Governor of the Province of Santiago del Estero:** CARLOS JUÁREZ.
**Governor of the Province of Tucumán:** JULIO MIRANDA.
**Governor of the Territory of Tierra del Fuego:** CARLOS MANFREDOTTI.

* RAMÓN MESTRE was appointed as mediator of Corrientes in December 1999.

# Political Organizations

**Acción por la República–Nueva Dirigencia (AR–ND):** Buenos Aires; f. 1997; electoral alliance; Leaders DOMINGO CAVALLO, GUSTAVO BÉLIZ.

**Acción por la República (AR):** Buenos Aires; e-mail accion republic@geocities.com; f. 1997; right-wing; Leader DOMINGO CAVALLO.

**Nueva Dirigencia (ND):** Buenos Aires; f. 1996; centre-right; Leader GUSTAVO BÉLIZ.

**Alianza para el Trabajo, la Justícia y la Educación (ATJE):** Buenos Aires; f. 1997; electoral alliance comprising the UCR and Frepaso.

**Frente del País Solidario (Frepaso):** Buenos Aires; internet www.visit-ar.com/nuevoespacio/frepaso.htm; f. 1994; centre-left coalition of socialist, communist and Christian Democrat groups; Leader CARLOS ÁLVAREZ.

**Unión Cívica Radical (UCR):** Buenos Aires; tel. (11) 449-0036; e-mail info@ucr.org.ar; internet www.ucr.org.ar; moderate; f. 1890; Pres. RODOLFO TERRAGNO; 1,410,000 mems.

**Movimiento por la Dignidad y la Independencia (Modin):** Buenos Aires; f. 1991; right-wing; Leader Col ALDO RICO.

**Movimiento de Integración y Desarrollo (MID):** Buenos Aires; f. 1963; Leader ARTURO FRONDIZI; 145,000 mems.

**Movimiento al Socialismo (MAS):** Chile 1362, 1098 Buenos Aires; tel. (11) 4381-2718; fax (11) 4381-2976; e-mail mas@giga.com.ar; internet www.wp.com/mas; Leaders RUBÉN VISCONTI, LUIS ZAMORA; 55,000 mems.

**Partido Comunista de Argentina:** Buenos Aires; f. 1918; Leader PATRICIO ECHEGARAY; Sec.-Gen. ATHOS FAVA; 76,000 mems.

**Partido Demócrata Cristiano (PDC):** Combate de los Pozos 1055, 1222 Buenos Aires; fax (11) 426-3413; f. 1954; Leader ESIO ARIEL SILVEIRA; 85,000 mems.

**Partido Demócrata Progresista (PDP):** Chile 1934, 1227 Buenos Aires; Leader RAFAEL MARTÍNEZ RAYMONDA; 97,000 mems.

**Partido Intransigente:** Buenos Aires; f. 1957; left-wing; Leaders Dr Oscar Alende, Lisandro Viale; Sec. Mariano Lorences; 90,000 mems.

**Partido Justicialista (PJ):** Buenos Aires; Peronist party; f. 1945; Pres. Carlos Saúl Menem; 3m. mems; three factions within party:

**Frente Renovador, Justicia, Democracia y Participación—Frejudepa:** f. 1985; reformist wing; Leaders Carlos Saúl Menem, Antonio Cafiero, Carlos Grosso.

**Movimiento Nacional 17 de Octubre:** Leader Herminio Iglesias.

**Oficialistas:** Leaders José María Vernet, Lorenzo Miguel.

**Partido Nacional de Centro:** Buenos Aires; f. 1980; conservative; Leader Raúl Rivanera Carles.

**Partido Nacionalista de los Trabajadores (PNT):** Buenos Aires; f. 1990; extreme right-wing; Leader Alejandro Biondini.

**Partido Obrero:** Ayacucho 444, Buenos Aires; tel. (11) 4953-3824; fax (11) 4953-7164; internet www.po.org.ar; f. 1982; Trotskyist; Leaders Jorge Altamira, Christian Rath; 61,000 mems.

**Partido Popular Cristiano:** Leader José Antonio Allende.

**Partido Socialista Democrático:** Rivadavia 2307, 1034 Buenos Aires; Leader Américo Ghioldi; 39,000 mems.

**Partido Socialista Popular:** f. 1982; Leaders Guillermo Estévez Boero, Edgardo Rossi; 60,500 mems.

**Política Abierta para la Integridad Social (PAIS):** Buenos Aires; f. 1994 following split with the PJ.

**Unión del Centro Democrático (UCeDé):** Buenos Aires; f. 1980 as coalition of eight minor political organizations to challenge the 'domestic monopoly' of the populist movements; Leader Alvaro Alsogaray.

**Unión para la Nueva Mayoría:** Buenos Aires; f. 1986; centre-right; Leader José Antonio Romero Feris.

The following political parties and groupings contested the 1999 presidential elections: Alianza Cristiana Social, Frente para la Resistencia Social, Izquierda Unida, Partido Humanista, Partido Obrero, Partido Socialista Auténtico and the Partido de Trabajadores Socialistas.

Other parties and groupings include: Afirmación Peronista, Alianza Socialista, Confederación Socialista Argentina, Cruzada Renovadora (San Juan), Frente Cívica y Socialista (Catamarca), Fuerza Republicana (Tucumán), Movimiento Línea Popular, Movimiento Patriótico de Liberación, Movimiento Peronista, Movimiento Popular Neuquino, Movimiento Popular (Tierra del Fuego), Partido Autonomista (Corrientes), Partido Bloquista de San Juan, Partido Conservador Popular, Partido Izquierda Nacional, Partido Liberal (Corrientes), Partido Obrero Comunista Marxista-Leninista, Partido Socialista Unificado and Renovador de Salta.

The following political parties and guerrilla groups are illegal:

**Intransigencia y Movilización Peronista:** Peronist faction; Leader Nilda Garres.

**Movimiento Todos por la Patria (MTP):** left-wing movement.

**Partido Peronista Auténtico (PPA):** f. 1975; Peronist faction; Leaders Mario Firmenich, Óscar Bidegain, Ricardo Obregón Cano.

**Partido Revolucionario de Trabajadores:** political wing of the **Ejército Revolucionario del Pueblo (ERP)**; Leader Luis Mattini.

**Triple A—Alianza Anticomunista Argentina:** extreme right-wing; Leader Aníbal Gordon (in prison).

# Diplomatic Representation

### EMBASSIES IN ARGENTINA

**Algeria:** Montevideo 1889, 1021 Buenos Aires; tel. (11) 4815-1271; fax (11) 4815-8837; Ambassador: Abdelkader Rashi.

**Armenia:** Avda Roque S. Peña 570, 3°, 1035 Buenos Aires; tel. (11) 4345-2051; fax (11) 4343-2467; Ambassador: Vahan Ter-Ghevondian.

**Australia:** Villanueva 1400, 1426 Buenos Aires; tel. (11) 4777-6580; fax (11) 4776-0960; e-mail martine.letts@dfat.gov.ar; Ambassador: Martine Letts.

**Austria:** French 3671, 1425 Buenos Aires; tel. (11) 4802-7195; fax (11) 4805-4016; Ambassador: Dr Wolfgang Kriechbaum.

**Belgium:** Defensa 113, 8°, 1065 Buenos Aires; tel. (11) 4331-0066; fax (11) 4311-0814; Ambassador: Paul Duqué.

**Bolivia:** Avda Corrientes 545, 2°, 1043 Buenos Aires; tel. (11) 4394-6042; Ambassador: Agustín Saavedra Weise.

**Brazil:** Arroyo 1142, 1007 Buenos Aires; tel. (11) 444-0035; fax (11) 4814-4085; Ambassador: Sebastião do Rego Barros Netto.

**Bulgaria:** Mariscal A. J. de Sucre 1568, 1428 Buenos Aires; tel. (11) 4781-8644; fax (11) 4786-6273; Ambassador: Vassiliy Takev.

**Canada:** Tagle 2828, 1425 Buenos Aires; tel. (11) 4805-3032; fax (11) 4806-1209; Ambassador: Robert Rochon.

**Central African Republic:** Marcelo T. de Alvear 776, Edif. Charcas, Buenos Aires; tel. (11) 4312-2051.

**Chile:** Tagle 2762, 1425 Buenos Aires; tel. (11) 4802-7020; Ambassador: Edmundo Pérez Yoma.

**China, People's Republic:** Avda Crisólogo Larralde 5349, 1431 Buenos Aires; tel. (11) 4543-8862; Ambassador: Xu Yicong.

**Colombia:** Carlos Pellegrini 1363, 3°, 1011 Buenos Aires; tel. (11) 4325-0494; fax (11) 4322-9370; Ambassador: Víctor G. Ricardo.

**Congo, Democratic Republic:** Buenos Aires; tel. (11) 4792-9989; Ambassador: Badassa-Bahaduka.

**Costa Rica:** Uruguay 292, 14°G, 1015 Buenos Aires; tel. (11) 449-4731; Ambassador: Fernando Salazar Navarrete.

**Cuba:** Virrey del Pino 1810, 1426 Buenos Aires; tel. (11) 4782-9049; fax (11) 4786-7713; e-mail embcuba@teletel.com.ar; Ambassador: Nicolás Rodríguez Astiazaraín.

**Czech Republic:** Avda Figueroa Alcorta 3240, 1425 Buenos Aires; tel. (11) 4801-3804; Ambassador: Ian Kopecky.

**Denmark:** Avda Leandro N. Alem 1074, 9°, 1001 Buenos Aires; tel. (11) 4312-6901; fax (11) 4312-7857; Ambassador: Jens Peter Larsen.

**Dominican Republic:** Avda Santa Fe 1206, 2°c, 1059 Buenos Aires; tel. (11) 441-4669; Ambassador: Jesús M. Hernández Sánchez.

**Ecuador:** Quintana 585, 9° y 10°, 1129 Buenos Aires; tel. (11) 4804-0073; Ambassador: Luis Valencia Rodríguez.

**Egypt:** Juez Tedín 2795, 1425 Buenos Aires; tel. (11) 4801-6145; Ambassador: Hassan I. Abdel Hadi.

**El Salvador:** Avda Santa Fe 882, 12°A, 1059 Buenos Aires; tel. (11) 4394-7628; Ambassador: Horacio Trujillo.

**Finland:** Avda Santa Fe 846, 5°, 1059 Buenos Aires; tel. (11) 4312-0600; fax (11) 4312-0670; Ambassador: Erkki Kivimäki.

**France:** Cerrito 1399, 1010 Buenos Aires; tel. (11) 4819-2930; fax (11) 4393-1235; e-mail ambafr@impsat1.com.ar; internet www.embafrancia-argentina.org; Ambassador: Paul Dijoud.

**Gabon:** Avda Figueroa Alcorta 3221, 1425 Buenos Aires; tel. (11) 4801-9840; Ambassador: J.-B. Eyi-Nkoumou.

**Germany:** Villanueva 1055, 1426 Buenos Aires; tel. (11) 4778-2500; fax (11) 4778-2550; Ambassador: Adolf von Wagner.

**Greece:** Avda Roque S. Peña 547, 4°, 1035 Buenos Aires; tel. (11) 434-4598; fax (11) 434-2838; Ambassador: Apostolos Anninos.

**Guatemala:** Avda Santa Fe 830, 5°, 1059 Buenos Aires; tel. (11) 4313-9160; fax (11) 4313-9181; Ambassador: Leslie Mishaan de Kirkvoorde.

**Haiti:** Avda Figueroa Alcorta 3297, 1425 Buenos Aires; tel. (11) 4802-0211; Ambassador: Frank Paul.

**Holy See:** Avda Alvear 1605, 1014 Buenos Aires; tel. (11) 4813-9697; fax (11) 4815-4097; Apostolic Nuncio: Most Rev. Ubaldo Calabresi, Titular Archbishop of Fundi (Fondi).

**Honduras:** Paraná 275, 4°, Of. 7, 1017 Buenos Aires; tel. (11) 4813-2800; fax (11) 4371-4885; Ambassador: Rafael Leiva Vivas.

**Hungary:** Coronel Díaz 1874, 1425 Buenos Aires; tel. (11) 4822-0767; fax (11) 4805-3918; Ambassador: Károly Misley.

**India:** Córdoba 950, 4°, 1054 Buenos Aires; tel. (11) 4393-4001; fax (11) 4393-4063; Ambassador: M. K. Khisha.

**Indonesia:** Mariscal Ramón Castilla 2901, 1425 Buenos Aires; tel. (11) 4807-2211; fax (11) 4802-4448; Chargé d'affaires: Eddy S. Suryodiningrat.

**Iran:** Avda Figueroa Alcorta 3229, 1425 Buenos Aires; tel. (11) 4802-1470; fax (11) 4805-4409; Chargé d'affaires a.i.: Mr Sadatifar.

**Ireland:** Suipacha 1380, 2°, 1011 Buenos Aires; tel. (11) 4325-8588; fax (11) 4325-7572; Ambassador: Art Agnew.

**Israel:** Arroyo 910, 1007 Buenos Aires; tel. (11) 4325-2502; Ambassador: Itzhak Aviran.

**Italy:** Billinghurst 2577, 1425 Buenos Aires; tel. (11) 4802-0071; e-mail stampa@sminter.com.ar; Ambassador: Giuseppe Maria Borga.

**Japan:** Bouchard 547, 17°, Buenos Aires; tel. (11) 4318-8200; fax (11) 4318-8210; Ambassador: Teruo Kijima.

**Korea, Republic:** Avda del Libertador 2257, 1425 Buenos Aires; tel. (11) 4802-9665; Ambassador: Sang Chin Lee.

**Lebanon:** Avda del Libertador 2354, 1425 Buenos Aires; tel. (11) 4802-4492; fax (11) 4802-2909; Ambassador: Riad Kantar.

**Libya:** Lapampa 3121, Buenos Aires; tel. (11) 4788-3760; fax (11) 4788-9394; Chargé d'affaires a.i.: Assed Mohamed Almutaa.

**Malaysia:** Villanueva 1040-1048, 1062 Buenos Aires; tel. (11) 4776-0504; Ambassador: Dennis Joachim Ignatius.

**Mexico:** Larrea 1230, 1117 Buenos Aires; tel. (11) 4821-7172; fax (11) 4821-7251; Ambassador: Jesús Puente Leyva.

**Morocco:** Mariscal Ramón Castilla 2952, 1425 Buenos Aires; tel. (11) 4801-8154; fax (11) 4802-0136; e-mail sifamabueno@tournet.com.ar; Ambassador: ABDESLAM BARAKA.

**Netherlands:** Avda de Mayo 701, 19°, 1084 Buenos Aires; tel. (11) 4334-4000; fax (11) 4334-2717; e-mail nlgovbue@informatic.com.ar; Ambassador: J. E. CRAANEN.

**New Zealand:** Buenos Aires; tel. (11) 4328-0747; fax (11) 4328-0757; Ambassador: CAROLINE FORSYTH.

**Nicaragua:** Avda Corrientes 2548, 4°I, 1426 Buenos Aires; tel. (11) 4951-3463; Ambassador: ARIEL RAMÓN GRANERA SACASA.

**Nigeria:** Rosales 2674, 1636 Olivos, Buenos Aires; tel. (11) 4771-6541; Ambassador: OKON EDET UYA.

**Norway:** Esmeralda 909, 3°B, 1007 Buenos Aires; tel. (11) 4312-2204; fax (11) 4315-2831; Ambassador: ERIK TELLMANN.

**Pakistan:** Gorostiaga 2176, 1426 Buenos Aires; tel. (11) 4782 7663; Ambassador: ZAFAR HABIB.

**Panama:** Avda Santa Fe 1461, 5°, 1060 Buenos Aires; tel. (11) 4811-1254; fax (11) 4814-0450; e-mail epar@ba.net; Ambassador: MERCEDES ALFARO DE LÓPEZ.

**Paraguay:** Avda Las Heras 2545, 1425 Buenos Aires; tel. (11) 4802-3826; fax (11) 4801-0657; Ambassador: OSCAR FACUNDO YNSFRÁN.

**Peru:** Avda del Libertador 1720, 1425 Buenos Aires; tel. (11) 4802-2000; Ambassador: ALFONSO GRADOS BERTORINI.

**Philippines:** Juramento 1945, 1428 Buenos Aires; tel. (11) 4781-4173; Ambassador: SIME D. HIDALGO.

**Poland:** Alejandro M. de Aguado 2870, 1425 Buenos Aires; tel. (11) 4802-9681; fax (11) 4802-9683; Ambassador: ANDRZEJ WRÓBEL.

**Portugal:** Córdoba 315, 3°, 1054 Buenos Aires; tel. (11) 4311-2586; Ambassador: ANTÓNIO BAPTISTA MARTINS.

**Romania:** Arroyo 962-970, 1007 Buenos Aires; tel. and fax (11) 4322-2630; Ambassador: STELIAN OANCEA.

**Russia:** Rodríguez Peña 1741, 1021 Buenos Aires; tel. (11) 4813-1552; fax (11) 4812-1794; Ambassador: IAN A. BURLIAY.

**Saudi Arabia:** Alejandro M. de Aguado 2881, 1425 Buenos Aires; tel. (11) 4802-4735; Ambassador: FUAD A. NAZIR.

**Slovakia:** Avda Figueroa Alcorta 3240, 1425 Buenos Aires; tel. (11) 4786-0692; fax (11) 4786-0938; Ambassador: MARIÁN MASARIK.

**South Africa:** Marcelo T. de Alvear 590, 8°, 1058 Buenos Aires; tel. (11) 4317-2900; fax (11) 4317-2951; e-mail saemba@slcoar.com; Ambassador: AUBREY X. NKOMO.

**Spain:** Mariscal Ramón Castilla 2720, 1425 Buenos Aires; tel. (11) 4802-6031; fax (11) 4802-0719; Ambassador: CARLOS CARDERERA SOLER.

**Sweden:** Casilla 3599, Correo Central 1000, Buenos Aires; tel. (11) 4311-3088; fax (11) 4311-8052; Ambassador: PETER LANDELIUS.

**Switzerland:** Avda Santa Fe 846, 10°, 1059 Buenos Aires; tel. (11) 4311-6491; fax (11) 4313-2998; Ambassador: JEAN-MARC BOILLAT.

**Syria:** Calloa 956, 1023 Buenos Aires; tel. (11) 442-2113; Ambassador: ABDUL HASSIB ITSWANI.

**Thailand:** Virrey del Pino 2458, 6°, 1426 Buenos Aires; tel. (11) 4785-6504; fax (11) 4785-6548; e-mail thbsemb@tournet.com.ar; Ambassador: KRIENGSAK DEESRISUK.

**Turkey:** 11 de Setiembre 1382, 1426 Buenos Aires; tel. (11) 4788-3239; fax (11) 4784-9179; e-mail iyihava@ba.net; Ambassador: ERHAN YIGITBASIOGLU.

**United Kingdom:** Dr Luis Agote 2412/52, 1425 Buenos Aires; tel. (11) 4803-7070; fax (11) 4806-5713; e-mail ukembarg@starnet.net.ar; Ambassador: WILLIAM MARSDEN.

**USA:** Avda Colombia 4300, 1425 Buenos Aires; tel. (11) 4774-7611; fax (11) 4775-4205; Ambassador: (vacant).

**Uruguay:** Avda Las Heras 1907, 1127 Buenos Aires; tel. (11) 4803-6030; Ambassador: ADOLFO CASTELLS MENDIVIL.

**Venezuela:** Virrey Loreto 2035, 1428 Buenos Aires; tel. (11) 4788-4944; fax (11) 4784-4311; e-mail embvenez@ba.net; Ambassador: REINALDO LEANDRO RODRÍGUEZ.

**Yugoslavia:** Marcelo T. de Alvear 1705, 1060 Buenos Aires; tel. (11) 441-2860; Ambassador: RUDOLF HAZURAN.

# Judicial System

### SUPREME COURT

**Corte Suprema:** Talcahuano 550, 4°, 1013 Buenos Aires; tel. (11) 440-0837; fax (11) 440-2270.

The nine members of the Supreme Court are appointed by the President, with the agreement of at least two-thirds of the Senate. Members are dismissed by impeachment.

**President:** JULIO SALVADOR NAZARENO.

**Justices:** CARLOS SANTIAGO FAYT, AUGUSTO CÉSAR BELLUSCIO, ENRIQUE SANTIAGO PETRACCHI, EDUARDO MOLINÉ O'CONNOR, ADOLFO VÁZQUEZ, ANTONIO BOGGIANO, GUILLERMO A. F. LÓPEZ, GUSTAVO A. BOSSERT.

### OTHER COURTS

Judges of the lower, national or further lower courts are appointed by the President, with the agreement of the Senate, and are dismissed by impeachment. From 1999, however, judges were to retire on reaching 75 years of age.

The Federal Court of Appeal in Buenos Aires has three courts: civil and commercial, criminal, and administrative. There are six other courts of appeal in Buenos Aires: civil, commercial, criminal, peace, labour, and penal-economic. There are also federal appeal courts in: La Plata, Bahía Blanca, Paraná, Rosario, Córdoba, Mendoza, Tucumán and Resistencia. In August 1994, following constitutional amendments, the Office of the Attorney-General was established as an independent entity and a Council of Magistrates was envisaged. In December 1997 the Senate adopted legislation to create the Council.

The provincial courts each have their own Supreme Court and a system of subsidiary courts. They deal with cases originating within and confined to the provinces.

**Attorney-General:** OSCAR LUJÁN FAPPIANO.

# Religion

### CHRISTIANITY

More than 90% of the population are Roman Catholics and about 2% are Protestants.

**Federación Argentina de Iglesias Evangélicas** (Argentine Federation of Evangelical Churches): José María Moreno 873, 1424 Buenos Aires; tel. and fax (11) 4922-5356; e-mail faie@faie.com.ar; f. 1938; 29 mem. churches; Pres. Rev. EMILIO N. MONTI (Argentine Evangelical Methodist Church); Exec. Sec. Rev. ENRIQUE LAVIGNE.

#### The Roman Catholic Church

Argentina comprises 14 archdioceses, 49 dioceses (including one each for Uniate Catholics of the Ukrainian rite, of the Maronite rite and of the Armenian rite) and three territorial prelatures. The Archbishop of Buenos Aires is also the Ordinary for Catholics of Oriental rites, and the Bishop of San Gregorio de Narek en Buenos Aires is also the Apostolic Exarch of Latin America and Mexico for Catholics of the Armenian rite.

**Bishops' Conference:** Conferencia Episcopal Argentina, Suipacha 1034, 1008 Buenos Aires; tel. (11) 4328-2015; fax (11) 4328-9570; f. 1959; Pres. Mgr ESTANISLAO ESTEBAN KARLIC, Archbishop of Paraná.

*Armenian Rite*

**Bishop of San Gregorio de Narek en Buenos Aires:** VARTAN WALDIR BOGHOSSIAN, Charcas 3529, 1425 Buenos Aires; tel. (11) 4824-1613; fax (11) 4827-1975; e-mail exarmal@usa.net; internet www.fast.to/exarcado.

*Latin Rite*

**Archbishop of Bahía Blanca:** RÓMULO GARCÍA, Avda Colón 164, 8000 Bahía Blanca; tel. (291) 455-0707; fax (291) 452-2070; e-mail arzobispado@bblanca.com.ar.

**Archbishop of Buenos Aires:** JORGE BERGOGLIO, Arzobispado, Rivadavia 415, 1002 Buenos Aires; tel. (11) 4343-3925; fax (11) 4334-8373.

**Archbishop of Córdoba:** CARLOS JOSÉ ÑÁÑEZ, Hipólito Yrigoyen 98, 5000 Córdoba; tel. (351) 422-1015; fax (351) 425-5082.

**Archbishop of Corrientes:** DOMINGO SALVADOR CASTAGNA, 9 de Julio 1543, 3400 Corrientes; tel. and fax (3783) 422436.

**Archbishop of La Plata:** CARLOS GALÁN, Arzobispado, Calle 14, 1009, 1900 La Plata; tel. (221) 425-1656; fax (221) 425-8269.

**Archbishop of Mendoza:** JOSÉ MARÍA ARANCIBIA, Catamarca 98, 5500 Mendoza; tel. (261) 423-3862; fax (261) 429-5415; e-mail archimza@satlink.com.

**Archbishop of Mercedes-Luján:** EMILIO OGÑÉNOVICH, Calle 22, No 745, 6600 Mercedes, Buenos Aires; tel. (2324) 432-412; fax (2324) 432-104.

**Archbishop of Paraná:** Mgr ESTANISLAO ESTEBAN KARLIC, Monte Caseros 77, 3100 Paraná; tel. (343) 431-1440; fax (343) 423-0372; e-mail arzparan@satlink.com.ar.

**Archbishop of Resistencia:** CARMELO JUAN GIAQUINTA, Bartolomé Mitre 363, Casilla 35, 3500 Resistencia; tel. and fax (3722) 434573.

**Archbishop of Rosario:** EDUARDO VICENTE MIRÁS, Córdoba 1677, 2000 Rosario; tel. (341) 425-1298; fax (341) 425-1207.

**Archbishop of Salta:** MOISÉS JULIO BLANCHOUD, España 596, 4400 Salta; tel. (387) 421-4306; fax (387) 421-3101.

**Archbishop of San Juan de Cuyo:** ITALO SEVERINO DI STÉFANO, Bartolomé Mitre 250 Oeste, 5400 San Juan de Cuyo; tel. (264) 422-2578; fax (264) 427-3530.

**Archbishop of Santa Fe de la Vera Cruz:** EDGARDO GABRIEL STORNI, Avda General López 2720, 3000 Santa Fe; tel. (342) 459-5791; fax (342) 459-4491; e-mail arzobsfe@infovia.com.ar.

**Archbishop of Tucumán:** ARSENIO RAÚL CASADO, Avda Sarmiento 895, 4000 San Miguel de Tucumán; tel. (381) 422-6345; fax (381) 431-0617.

*Maronite Rite*

**Bishop of San Charbel en Buenos Aires:** CHARBEL MERHI, Eparquía Maronita, Paraguay 834, 1057 Buenos Aires; tel. (11) 4311-7299; fax (11) 4312-8348; e-mail meharbel@hotmail.com; internet www.intra-next.com/sanmaron.

*Ukrainian Rite*

**Bishop of Santa María del Patrocinio en Buenos Aires:** (vacant); Apostolic Administrator: Rt Rev. MIGUEL MYKYCEJ (Titular Bishop of Nazianzus), Ramón L. Falcón 3950, Casilla 28, 1407 Buenos Aires; tel. (11) 4671-4192.

### The Anglican Communion

The Iglesia Anglicana del Cono Sur de América (Anglican Church of the Southern Cone of America) was formally inaugurated in Buenos Aires in April 1983. The Church comprises seven dioceses: Argentina, Northern Argentina, Chile, Paraguay, Peru, Bolivia and Uruguay. The Primate is the Bishop of Northern Argentina.

**Bishop of Argentina:** Rt Rev. DAVID LEAKE, 25 de Mayo 282, 1002 Buenos Aires; Casilla 4293, Correo Central 1000, Buenos Aires; tel. (11) 4342-4618; fax (11) 4331-0234; e-mail diocesisanglibue@arnet.com.ar.

**Bishop of Northern Argentina:** Rt Rev. MAURICE SINCLAIR, Casilla 187, 4400 Salta; jurisdiction extends to Jujuy, Salta, Tucumán, Catamarca, Santiago del Estero, Formosa and Chaco; tel. (387) 431-1718; fax (387) 431-2622; e-mail sinclair@salnet.com.ar.

### Protestant Churches

**Convención Evangélica Bautista Argentina** (Baptist Evangelical Convention): Virrey Liniers 42, 1174 Buenos Aires; tel. and fax (11) 4864-2711; e-mail ceba@sion.com; f. 1909; Pres. CARLOS A. CARAMUTTI.

**Iglesia Evangélica Congregacionalista** (Evangelical Congregational Church): Perón 525, 3100 Paraná; tel. (43) 21-6172; f. 1924; 100 congregations, 8,000 mems, 24,000 adherents; Supt Rev. REYNOLDO HORSTT.

**Iglesia Evangélica Luterana Argentina** (Evangelical Lutheran Church of Argentina): Ing. Silveyra 1639-41, 1607 Villa Adelina, Buenos Aires; tel. (11) 4766-7948; fax (11) 4766-7948; f. 1905; 30,000 mems; Pres. WALDOMIRO MAILI.

**Iglesia Evangélica del Río de la Plata** (Evangelical Church of the River Plate): Mariscal Sucre 2855, 1428 Buenos Aires; tel. (11) 4787-0436; fax (11) 4787-0335; e-mail ierp@ierp.org.ar; f. 1899; 40,000 mems; Pres. JUAN PEDRO SCHAAD.

**Iglesia Evangélica Metodista Argentina** (Methodist Church of Argentina): Rivadavia 4044, 3°, 1205 Buenos Aires; tel. (11) 4982-3712; fax (11) 4981-0885; e-mail iema@iema.com.ar; internet www.iema.com.ar; f. 1836; 6,040 mems, 9,000 adherents, seven regional superintendents; Bishop ALDO M. ETCHEGOYEN; Exec. Sec.-Gen. Bd DANIEL A. FAVARO.

## JUDAISM

**Delegación de Asociaciones Israelitas Argentinas—DAIA** (Delegation of Argentine Jewish Associations): Pasteur 633, 7°, 1028 Buenos Aires; tel. and fax (11) 4953-1785; e-mail daia@infovia.com.ar; f. 1935; there are about 250,000 Jews in Argentina, mostly in Buenos Aires; Pres. Dr RUBÉN E. BERAJA; Sec.-Gen. Dr JOSÉ KESTELMAN.

# The Press

## PRINCIPAL DAILIES

### Buenos Aires

**Ambito Financiero:** Avda Paseo Colón 1196, 1063 Buenos Aires; tel. (11) 4349-1500; fax (11) 4349-1505; e-mail correo@afinanciero.com; internet www.afinanciero.com; f. 1976; morning (Mon.–Fri.); business; Dir JULIO A. RAMOS; circ. 115,000.

**Buenos Aires Herald:** Azopardo 455, 1107 Buenos Aires; tel. (11) 4342-1535; fax (11) 4334-7917; e-mail info@buenosairesherald.com; internet www.buenosairesherald.com; f. 1876; English; morning; independent; Editor-in-Chief ANDREW GRAHAM YOOLL; circ. 20,000.

**Boletín Oficial de la República Argentina:** Suipacha 767, 1008 Buenos Aires; tel. (11) 4322-3982; fax (11) 4322-3982; f. 1893; morning (Mon.–Fri.); official records publication; Dir RUBÉN ANTONIO SOSA; circ. 15,000.

**Clarín:** Piedras 1743, 1140 Buenos Aires; tel. (11) 4309-7500; fax (11) 4309-7559; e-mail lectores@www.clarin.com; internet www.clarin.com; f. 1945; morning; independent; Dir ERNESTINA L. HERRERA DE NOBLE; circ. 616,000 (daily), 1.0m. (Sunday).

**Crónica:** Avda Juan de Garay 40, 1063 Buenos Aires; tel. (11) 4361-1001; fax (11) 4361-4237; f. 1963; morning and evening; Dir MARIO ALBERTO FERNÁNDEZ (morning), RICARDO GANGEME (evening); circ. 330,000 (morning), 190,000 (evening), 450,000 (Sunday).

**El Cronista:** Honduras 5663, 1414 Buenos Aires; tel. (11) 4778-6789; fax (11) 4778-6727; e-mail cronista@sadei.org.ar; f. 1908; morning; Dir NÉSTOR SCIBONA; circ. 65,000.

**Diario Popular:** Beguiristain 142, 1872 Sarandí, Avellaneda, Buenos Aires; tel. (11) 4204-2778; fax (11) 4205-2376; e-mail redacpop@inea.net.ar; f. 1974; morning; Dir ALBERTO ALBERTENGO; circ. 145,000.

**La Gaceta:** Beguiristain 182, 1870 Avellaneda, Buenos Aires; Dir RICARDO WEST OCAMPO; circ. 35,000.

**La Nación:** Bouchard 551, 1106 Buenos Aires; tel. (11) 4319-1600; fax (11) 4319-1969; e-mail cescribano@lanacion.com.ar; internet www.lanacion.com.ar; f. 1870; morning; independent; Dir BARTOLOMÉ MITRE; circ. 184,000.

**Página 12:** Avda Belgrano 671, 1092 Buenos Aires; tel. (11) 4334-2334; fax (11) 4334-2335; e-mail lectores@pagina12.com.ar; internet www.pagina12.com.ar; f. 1987; morning; independent; Dir ERNESTO TIFFEMBERG; Editor FERNANDO SOKOLOWICZ; circ. 280,000.

**La Prensa:** Azopardo 715, 1107 Buenos Aires; tel. (11) 4349-1000; fax (11) 4349-1025; e-mail laprensa@interlink.com; internet www.interlink.com.ar/laprensa; f. 1869; morning; independent; Dir FLORENCIO ALDREY IGLESIAS; circ. 100,000.

**La Razón:** Río Cuarto 1242, 1168 Buenos Aires; tel. and fax (11) 4309-6000; e-mail larazon@arnet.com.ar; internet www.larazon.com.ar; f. 1992; evening; Dir OSCAR MAGDALENA; circ. 62,000.

**El Sol:** Hipólito Yrigoyen 122, Quilmes, 1878 Buenos Aires; tel. and fax (11) 4257-6325; e-mail elsol@elsolquilmes.com.ar; internet www.elsolquilmes.com.ar; f. 1927; Dir RODRIGO GHISANI; circ. 25,000.

**Tiempo Argentino:** Buenos Aires; tel. (11) 428-1929; Editor Dr TOMÁS LEONA; circ. 75,000.

## PRINCIPAL PROVINCIAL DAILIES

### Catamarca

**El Ancasti:** Sarmiento 526, 1°, 4700 Catamarca; tel. and fax (3833) 431385; e-mail ancasti@satlink.com; f. 1988; morning; Dir ROQUE EDUARDO MOLAS; circ. 8,000.

### Chaco

**Norte:** Carlos Pellegrini 744, 3500 Resistencia; tel. (3722) 428204; fax (3722) 426047; e-mail prensanorte@diarionorte.com.ar; f. 1968; Dir MIGUEL A. FERNÁNDEZ; circ. 14,000.

### Chubut

**Crónica:** Impresora Patagónica, Namuncurá 122, 9000 Comodoro Rivadavia; tel. (297) 447-1200; fax (297) 447-1780; e-mail cronica@arnet.com.ar; f. 1962; morning; Dir Dr DIEGO JOAQUÍN ZAMIT; circ. 15,000.

### Córdoba

**Comercio y Justicia:** Mariano Moreno 378, 5000 Córdoba; tel. and fax (351) 422-0202; e-mail sistemas@powernet.com.ar; internet www.powernet.com.ar/cyj; f. 1939; morning; economic and legal news; Editor PABLO EGUÍA; circ. 5,800.

**La Voz del Interior:** Avellaneda 1661, 5000 Córdoba; tel. (351) 4757200; fax (351) 4757201; e-mail lavoz@satlink.com; internet www.intervoz.com.ar; f. 1904; morning; independent; Dir Dr CARLOS HUGO JORNET; circ. 68,000.

### Corrientes

**El Litoral:** Hipólito Yrigoyen 990, 3400 Corrientes; tel. and fax (3783) 422227; e-mail el-litoral@compunort.com.ar; internet www.corrientes.com.ar/el-litoral; f. 1960; morning; Dir CARLOS A. ROMERO FERIS; circ. 25,000.

**El Territorio:** Avda Quaranta 4307, 3300 Posadas; tel. and fax (3752) 452100; e-mail elterritorio@elterritorio.com.ar; internet www.elterritorio.com.ar; f. 1925; Dir GONZALO PELTZER; circ. 22,000 (Mon.–Fri.), 28,000 (Sunday).

### Entre Ríos

**El Diario:** Buenos Aires y Urquiza, 3100 Paraná; tel. (343) 423-1000; fax (343) 431-9104; e-mail saer@satlink.com; internet www.eldiario.com.ar; f. 1914; morning; democratic; Dir Dr LUIS F. ETCHEVEHERE; circ. 25,000.

**El Heraldo:** Quintana 42, 3200 Concordia; tel. (345) 421-5304; fax (345) 421-1397; e-mail elheraldo@concordia.com.ar; internet www.paginasamarillas.com.ar/elheraldo; f. 1915; evening; Editor Dr Carlos Liebermann; circ. 10,000.

### Mendoza

**Los Andes:** Avda San Martín 1049, 5500 Mendoza; tel. (261) 4491200; fax (261) 4202011; e-mail amartinez@losandes.com.ar; internet www.losandes.net; f. 1982; morning; Dir Jorge Enrique Oviedo; circ. 107,000.

### Provincia de Buenos Aires

**El Atlántico:** Bolívar 2975, 7600 Mar del Plata; tel. (223) 435462; f. 1938; morning; Dir Oscar Alberto Gastiarena; circ. 20,000.

**La Capital:** Avda Champagnat 2551, 7600 Mar del Plata; tel. (223) 478-8490; fax (223) 478-1038; e-mail diario@lacapitalnet.com.ar; internet www.lacapitalnet.com.ar; f. 1905; Dir Florencio Aldrey Iglesias; circ. 32,000.

**El Día:** Avda A. Diagonal 80, 817-21, 1900 La Plata; tel. (221) 425-0101; fax (221) 423-2996; e-mail redaccion@eldia.com; f. 1884; morning; independent; Dir Raúl E. Kraiselburd; circ. 54,868.

**Ecos Diarios:** Calle 62, No 2486, 7630 Necochea; tel. (2262) 430754; fax (2262) 420485; e-mail ecosdiar@satlink.com; internet www.ecosdiarios.com.ar; f. 1921; morning; independent; Dir Guillermo Ignacio; circ. 6,000.

**La Nueva Provincia:** Sarmiento 54–64, 8000 Bahía Blanca; tel. (291) 459-0000; fax (291) 459-0001; e-mail nprovin@relay.startel; internet www.lanueva.com.ar; f. 1898; morning; independent; Dir Diana Julio de Massot; circ. 36,000 (Mon.–Fri.), 55,000 (Sunday).

**La Voz del Pueblo:** Avda San Martín 991, 7500 Tres Arroyos; tel. (2983) 430680; fax (2938) 430682; e-mail redaccion@lavozdelpueblo.com.ar; f. 1902; morning; independent; Dir Alberto Jorge Maciel; circ. 8,500.

### Río Negro

**Río Negro:** 9 de Julio 733, 8332, Gen. Roca, Río Negro; tel. (2941) 439300; fax (2941) 430517; e-mail rnredaccion@rionet.rionegro.com.ar; internet www.rionegro.com.ar; f. 1912; morning; Editor Nélida Rajneri de Gamba.

### Salta

**El Tribuno:** Avda Ex Combatientes de Malvinas 3890, 4400 Salta; tel. (387) 424-0000; fax (387) 424-1382; e-mail tribuno@salnet.com.ar; internet www.eltribuno.com.ar; f. 1949; morning; Dir Roberto Eduardo Romero; circ. 25,000.

### San Juan

**Diario de Cuyo:** Mendoza 380 Sur, 5400 San Juan; tel. (264) 429-0016; fax (264) 429-0004; e-mail diarcuyo@esternet.net.ar; f. 1947; morning; independent; Dir Francisco Montes; circ. 25,000.

### San Luis

**El Diario de La República:** Junín 741, 5700 San Luis; tel. (2623) 422037; fax (2623) 428770; e-mail paynesa@infovia.com.ar; f. 1966; Dir Zulema A. Rodríguez Saa de Divizia; circ. 12,000.

### Santa Fe

**La Capital:** Sarmiento 763, 2000 Rosario; tel. (341) 420-1100; fax (341) 420-1114; e-mail elagos@lacapital.com.ar; f. 1867; morning; independent; Dir Carlos María Lagos; circ. 65,000.

**El Litoral:** Avda 25 de Mayo 3536, 3000 Santa Fe; tel. (342) 450-2500; fax (342) 450-2530; e-mail litoral@litoral.com.ar; internet www.litoral.com.ar; f. 1918; morning; independent; Dir Gustavo Víttori; circ. 37,000.

### Santiago del Estero

**El Liberal:** Libertad 263, 4200 Santiago del Estero; tel. (385) 422-4400; fax (385) 422-4538; e-mail liberal@teletel.com.ar; internet www.sdnet.com.ar; f. 1898; morning; Exec. Dir José Luis Castiglione; Editorial Dir Dr Julio César Castiglione; circ. 20,000.

### Tucumán

**La Gaceta:** Mendoza 654, 4000 San Miguel de Tucumán; tel. (381) 431-1111; fax (381) 431-1597; e-mail redaccion@lagaceta.com.ar; internet www.lagaceta.com.ar; f. 1912; morning; independent; Dir Alberto García Hamilton; circ. 70,000.

## WEEKLY NEWSPAPER

**El Informador Público:** Uruguay 252, 3°F, 1015 Buenos Aires; tel. (11) 4476-3551; fax (11) 4342-2628; f. 1986.

## PERIODICALS

**Aeroespacio:** Casilla 37, Sucursal 12B, 1412 Buenos Aires; tel. and fax (11) 4514-1562; e-mail info@aeroespacio.com.ar; internet www.aeroespacio.com.ar; f. 1940; bimonthly, aeronautics; Dir Jorge A. Cuadros; circ. 24,000.

**Billiken:** Azopardo 579, 1307 Buenos Aires; tel. (11) 4342-7071; fax (11) 4343-7040; e-mail artebilliken@atlántida.com.ar; f. 1919; weekly; children's magazine; Dir Juan Carlos Porras. circ. 240,000.

**Casas y Jardines:** Sarmiento 643, 1382 Buenos Aires; tel. (11) 445-1793; f. 1932; every 2 months; houses and gardens; publ. by Editorial Contémpora SRL; Dir Norberto M. Muzio.

**Chacra y Campo Moderno:** Editorial Atlántida, SA, Azopardo 579, 1307 Buenos Aires; tel. (11) 4331-4591; fax (11) 4331-3272; f. 1930; monthly; farm and country magazine; Dir Constancio C. Vigil; circ. 35,000.

**Claudia:** Avda Córdoba 1345, 12°, Buenos Aires; tel. (11) 442-3275; fax (11) 4814-3948; f. 1957; monthly; women's magazine; Dir Ana Torrejón; circ. 150,000.

**El Economista:** Avda Córdoba 632, 2°, 1054 Buenos Aires; tel. (11) 4322-7360; fax (11) 4322-8157; f. 1951; weekly; financial; Dir Dr D. Radonjic; circ. 37,800.

**Fotografía Universal:** Buenos Aires; monthly; circ. 39,500.

**Gente:** Azopardo 579, 3°, 1307 Buenos Aires; tel. (11) 433-4591; f. 1965; weekly; general; Dir Jorge de Luján Gutiérrez; circ. 133,000.

**El Gráfico:** Paseo Colón 505, 2°, 1063 Buenos Aires; tel. (11) 4341-5100; fax (11) 4341-5137; f. 1919; weekly; sport; Dir Aldo Proietto; circ. 127,000.

**Guía Latinoamericana de Transportes:** Florida 8287 esq. Portinari, 1669 Del Viso (Ptdo de Pilar), Provincia de Buenos Aires; tel. (11) 4320-7004; fax (11) 4307-1956; f. 1968; every 2 months; travel information and timetables; Editor Dr Armando Schlecker Hirsch; circ. 7,500.

**Humor:** Venezuela 842, 1095 Buenos Aires; tel. (11) 4334-5400; fax (11) 411-2700; f. 1978; every 2 weeks; satirical revue; Editor Andrés Cascioli; circ. 180,000.

**Legislación Argentina:** Talcahuano 650, 1013 Buenos Aires; tel. (11) 4371-0528; e-mail jurispru@lvd.com.ar; f. 1958; weekly; law; Dir Ricardo Estévez Boero; circ. 15,000.

**Mercado:** Rivadavia 877, 2°, 1002 Buenos Aires; tel. (11) 4346-9400; fax (11) 4343-7880; e-mail mdiez@mercado.com.ar; internet www.mercado.com.ar; f. 1969; monthly; business; Dir Miguel Angel Diez; circ. 28,000.

**Mundo Israelita:** Pueyrredón 538, 1°B, 1032 Buenos Aires; tel. (11) 4961-7999; fax (11) 4961-0763; f. 1923; weekly; Editor Dr José Kestelman; circ. 15,000.

**Nuestra Arquitectura:** Sarmiento 643, 5°, 1382 Buenos Aires; tel. (11) 445-1793; f. 1929; every 2 months; architecture; publ. by Editorial Contémpora SRL; Dir Norberto M. Muzio.

**Para Ti:** Azopardo 579, 1307 Buenos Aires; tel. (11) 4331-4591; fax (11) 4331-3272; f. 1922; weekly; women's interest; Dir Aníbal C. Vigil; circ. 104,000.

**Pensamiento Económico:** Avda Leandro N. Alem 36, 1003 Buenos Aires; tel. (11) 4331-8051; fax (11) 4331-8055; e-mail cac@cac.com.ar; internet www.cac.com.ar; f. 1925; quarterly; review of Cámara Argentina de Comercio; Dir Dr Carlos L. P. Antonucci.

**La Prensa Médica Argentina:** Junín 845, 1113 Buenos Aires; tel. (11) 4961-9793; fax (11) 4961-9494; f. 1914; monthly; medical; Editor Dr P. A. López; circ. 8,000.

**Prensa Obrera:** Ayacucho 444, Buenos Aires; tel. (11) 4953-3824; fax (11) 4953-7164; f. 1982; weekly; publication of Partido Obrero; circ. 16,000.

**La Semana:** Sarmiento 1113, 1041 Buenos Aires; tel. (11) 435-2552; general; Editor Daniel Pliner.

**La Semana Médica:** Arenales 3574, 1425 Buenos Aires; tel. (11) 4824-5673; f. 1894; monthly; Dir Dr Eduardo F. Mele; circ. 7,000.

**Siete Días Ilustrados:** Avda Leandro N. Alem 896, 1001 Buenos Aires; tel. (11) 432-6010; f. 1967; weekly; general; Dir Ricardo Cámara; circ. 110,000.

**Técnica e Industria:** Buenos Aires; tel. (11) 446-3193; f. 1922; monthly; technology and industry; Dir E. R. Fedele; circ. 5,000.

**Visión:** French 2820, 2°A, 1425 Buenos Aires; tel. (11) 4825-1258; fax (11) 4827-1004; e-mail edlatin@visionmag.com.ar; f. 1950; fortnightly; Latin American affairs, politics; Editor Luis Vidal Rucabado.

**Vosotras:** Avda Leandro N. Alem 896, 3°, 1001 Buenos Aires; tel. (11) 432-6010; f. 1935; women's weekly; Dir Abel Zanotto; circ. 33,000. Monthly supplements: **Labores:** circ. 130,000; **Modas:** circ. 70,000.

## NEWS AGENCIES

**Agencia TELAM, SA:** Bolívar 531, 1066 Buenos Aires; tel. (11) 4342-2161; fax (11) 4339-0353; Dir Omar Cerigliano.

**Diarios y Noticias (DYN):** Avda Julio A. Roca 636, 8°, 1067 Buenos Aires; tel. (11) 4342-3040; fax (11) 4342-3043; e-mail info@dyn.com.ar; internet www.dyn.com.ar; Editor Santiago González.

**Noticias Argentinas, SA (NA):** Suipacha 570, 3°B, 1008 Buenos Aires; tel. (11) 4394-7522; fax (11) 4394-7648; f. 1973; Dir LUIS FERNANDO TORRES.

### Foreign Bureaux

**Agence France-Presse (AFP):** Avda Corrientes 456, 3°, Of. 34/37, 1366 Buenos Aires; tel. (11) 4394-8169; fax (11) 4393-9912; e-mail afp-baires@tournet.com.ar; internet www.afp.com; Bureau Chief JEAN VIREBAYRE.

**Agencia EFE** (Spain): Guido 1770, 1016 Buenos Aires; tel. (11) 4812-9596; fax (11) 4815-8691; Bureau Chief AGUSTÍN DE GRACIA.

**Agenzia Nazionale Stampa Associata (ANSA)** (Italy): San Martín 320, 6°, 1004 Buenos Aires; tel. (11) 4394-7568; fax (11) 4394-5214; e-mail ansabaires@infovia.com.ar; Bureau Chief ALBERTO PIAZZA.

**Associated Press (AP)** (USA): Bouchard 551, 5°, Casilla 1296, 1106 Buenos Aires; tel. (11) 4311-0081; fax (11) 4311-0082; Bureau Chief WILLIAM H. HEATH.

**Deutsche Presse-Agentur (dpa)** (Germany): Buenos Aires; tel. (11) 4311-5311; e-mail msvgroth@ba.net; Bureau Chief Dr HENDRIK GROTH.

**Informatsionnoye Telegrafnoye Agentstvo Rossii-Telegrafnoye Agentstvo Suverennykh Stran (ITAR-TASS)** (Russia): Avda Córdoba 652, 11°E, 1054 Buenos Aires; tel. (11) 4392-2044; Dir ISIDORO GILBERT.

**Inter Press Service (IPS)** (Italy): Buenos Aires; tel. (11) 4394-0829; Bureau Chief RAMÓN M. GORRIARÁN; Correspondent GUSTAVO CAPDEVILLA.

**Magyar Távirati Iroda (MTI)** (Hungary): Marcelo T. de Alvear 624, 3° 16, 1058 Buenos Aires; tel. (11) 4312-9596; Correspondent ENDRE SIMÓ.

**Prensa Latina** (Cuba): Buenos Aires; tel. (11) 4394-0565; Correspondent MARIO HERNÁNDEZ DEL LLANO.

**Reuters** (United Kingdom): Avda Eduardo Madero 940, 25°, 1106 Buenos Aires; tel. (11) 4318-0600; fax (11) 4318-0698; Dir CARLOS PÍA MANGIONE.

**United Press International (UPI)** (USA): Avda Belgrano 271, Casilla 796, Correo Central 1000, 1092 Buenos Aires; tel. (11) 434-5501; fax (11) 4334-1818; Dir ALBERTO J. SCHAZÍN.

**Xinhua (New China) News Agency** (People's Republic of China): Tucumán 540, 14°, Apto D, 1049 Buenos Aires; tel. (11) 4313-9755; Bureau Chief JU QINGDONG.

The following are also represented: Central News Agency (Taiwan), Interpress (Poland), Jiji Press (Japan).

### PRESS ASSOCIATION

**Asociación de Entidades Periodísticas Argentinas (ADEPA):** Chacabuco 314, 3°, 1069 Buenos Aires; tel. and fax (11) 4331-1500; e-mail adepa@ciudad.com.ar; internet www.adepa.com.ar; f. 1962; Pres. GUILLERMO IGNACIO.

## Publishers

**Editorial Abril, SA:** Suipacha 664, 1093 Buenos Aires; tel. (11) 4331-0112; f. 1961; fiction, non-fiction, children's books, textbooks; Dir ROBERTO M. ARES.

**Editorial Acme, SA:** Santa Magdalena 635, 1277 Buenos Aires; tel. (11) 428-2014; f. 1949; general fiction, children's books, agriculture, textbooks; Man. Dir EMILIO I. GONZÁLEZ.

**Aguilar, Altea, Taurus, Alfaguara, SA de Ediciones:** Beazley 3860, 1437 Buenos Aires; tel. (11) 491-4111; fax (11) 4953-3716; f. 1946; general, literature, children's books; Gen. Man. ENRIQUE DE POLANCO.

**Editorial Albatros, SACI:** Hipólito Yrigoyen 3920, 1208 Buenos Aires; tel. (11) 4982-5439; fax (11) 4981-1161; f. 1967; technical, non-fiction, social sciences, sport, children's books, medicine and agriculture; Pres. ANDREA INÉS CANEVARO.

**Amorrortu Editores, SA:** Paraguay 1225, 7°, 1057 Buenos Aires; tel. (11) 4393-8812; fax (11) 4325-6307; f. 1967; anthropology, religion, economics, sociology, philosophy, psychology, pschoanalysis, current affairs; Man. Dir HORACIO DE AMORRORTU.

**Angel Estrada y Cía, SA:** Bolívar 462-66, 1066 Buenos Aires; tel. (11) 4331-6521; fax (11) 4331-6527; f. 1869; textbooks, children's books; Gen. Man. OSCAR DOMECQ.

**Editorial El Ateneo, Librerías Yenny, SA:** Patagones 2463, 1282 Buenos Aires; tel. (11) 4942-9002; fax (11) 4942-9162; e-mail librerías@yenny.com.ar; f. 1912; medicine, engineering, economics and general; Pres. EDUARDO CARLOS GRUNEISEN; Commercial Dir JORGE GONZÁLEZ.

**Editorial Atlántida, SA:** Azopardo 579, 1307 Buenos Aires; tel. (11) 4346-0100; fax (11) 4331-3272; internet www.atlantida.com; f. 1918; fiction and non-fiction, children's books; Chair. JORGE CONSTANCIO TERRA.

**Ediciones La Aurora:** Buenos Aires; tel. and fax (11) 4941-8940; f. 1925; general, religion, spirituality, theology, philosophy, psychology, history, semiology, linguistics; Dir Dr HUGO O. ORTEGA.

**Az Editora, SA:** Paraguay 2351, 1121 Buenos Aires; tel. (11) 961-4036; fax (11) 961-0089; f. 1976; social sciences and medicine; Pres. DANTE OMAR VILLALBA.

**Biblioteca Nacional de Maestros:** c/o Ministry of Education and Culture, Pizzurno 935, Planta baja, 1020 Buenos Aires; tel. (11) 4811-0275; e-mail gperrone@mcye.gov.ar; internet www.bnm.mcye.gov.ar; Dir GRACIELA PERRONE.

**Centro Editor de América Latina, SA:** Salta 38, 3°, 1074 Buenos Aires; tel. (11) 435-9449; f. 1967; literature, history; Man. Dir JOSÉ B. SPIVACOW.

**Editorial Claretiana:** Lima 1360, 1138 Buenos Aires; tel. (11) 427-9250; fax (11) 427-4015; f. 1956; Catholicism; Dir EDUARDO RIGHETTI.

**Editorial Claridad, SA:** Viamonte 1730, 1°, 1055 Buenos Aires; tel. (11) 4371-6402; fax (11) 4375-1659; e-mail editorial@heliasta.com.ar; internet www.heliasta.com.ar; f. 1922; literature, biographies, social science, politics, reference, dictionaries; Pres. Dra ANA MARÍA CABANELLAS.

**Club de Lectores:** Avda de Mayo 624, 1084 Buenos Aires; tel. (11) 434-6251; f. 1938; non-fiction; Dir JUAN MANUEL FONTENLA.

**Club de Poetas:** Casilla 189, 1401 Buenos Aires; f. 1975; poetry and literature; Exec. Dir JUAN MANUEL FONTENLA.

**Editorial Columba, SA:** Sarmiento 1889, 5°, 1044 Buenos Aires; tel. (11) 445-4297; f. 1953; classics in translation, 20th century; Man. Dir CLAUDIO A. COLUMBA.

**Editorial Contémpora, SRL:** Sarmiento 643, 5°, 1382 Buenos Aires; tel. (11) 445-1793; architecture, town-planning, interior decoration and gardening; Dir NORBERTO C. MUZIO.

**Cosmopolita, SRL:** Piedras 744, 1070 Buenos Aires; tel. and fax (11) 4361-8049; f. 1940; science and technology; Man. Dir RUTH F. DE RAPP.

**Depalma, SA:** Talcahuano 494, 1013 Buenos Aires; tel. (11) 4371-7306; fax (11) 4371-6913; e-mail info@ed-depalma.com; internet www.ed-depalma.com; f. 1944; periodicals and books covering law, politics, sociology, philosophy, history and economics; CEO ALBERTO O. ERMILIO; Dir NICOLAS VON DER PAHLEN.

**Editorial Difusión, SA:** Sarandi 1065–67, Buenos Aires; tel. (11) 4941-0088; f. 1937; literature, philosophy, religion, education, textbooks, children's books; Dir DOMINGO PALOMBELLA.

**Edicial, SA:** Rivadavia 739, 1002 Buenos Aires; tel. (11) 4342-8481; fax (11) 4343-1151; e-mail edicial@ssdnet.com.ar; internet www.ssdnet.com.ar/edicial; f. 1931; education; Man. Dir J. A. MUSSET.

**Emecé Editores, SA:** Alsina 2062, 1090 Buenos Aires; tel. (11) 4954-0105; fax (11) 4953-4200; e-mail editorial@emece.com.ar; internet www.emece.com.ar; f. 1939; fiction, non-fiction, biographies, history, art, essays; Pres. ALFREDO DEL CARRIL.

**Espasa Calpe Argentina, SA:** Buenos Aires; tel. (11) 4342-0073; fax (11) 4345-1776; f. 1937; literature, science, dictionaries; publ. *Colección Austral*; Dir GUILLERMO SCHAUELZON.

**Angel Estrada y Cía, SA:** Bolivar 462-466, 1066 Buenos Aires; tel. (11) 331-6521; f. 1869; education; Gen. Man. ZSOLT ARÁRDY.

**EUDEBA—Editorial Universitaria de Buenos Aires:** Rivadavia 1573, 1033 Buenos Aires; tel. (11) 4383-8025; fax (11) 4383-2202; e-mail eudeba@eudeba.com.ar; internet www.eudeba.com.ar; f. 1958; university text books and general interest publications; Pres. Dr LUIS YANES.

**Fabril Editora, SA:** Buenos Aires; tel. (11) 421-3601; f. 1958; non-fiction, science, arts, education and reference; Editorial Man. ANDRÉS ALFONSO BRAVO; Business Man. RÓMULO AYERZA.

**Editorial Glem, SACIF:** Avda Caseros 2056, 1264 Buenos Aires; tel. (11) 426-6641; f. 1933; psychology, technology; Pres. JOSÉ ALFREDO TUCCI.

**Editorial Guadalupe:** Mansilla 3865, 1425 Buenos Aires; tel. (11) 4826-8587; fax (11) 4805-4112; e-mail ventas@editorialguadalupe.com.ar; f. 1895; social sciences, religion, anthropology, children's books, and pedagogy; Dir P. LORENZO GOYENECHE.

**Editorial Heliasta, SRL:** Viamonte 1730, 1°, 1055 Buenos Aires; tel. (11) 4371-6402; fax (11) 4375-1659; e-mail editorial@heliasta.com.ar; internet www.heliasta.com.ar; f. 1944; literature, biography, dictionaries, legal; Pres. Dra ANA MARÍA CABANELLAS.

**Editorial Hemisferio Sur, SA:** Pasteur 743, 1028 Buenos Aires; tel. (11) 4952-9825; fax (11) 4952-8454; e-mail informe@hemisferiosur.com.ar; internet www.hemisferiosur.com.ar; f.1966; agriculture, veterinary and food science; Man. Dir ADOLFO JULIÁN PEÑA.

**Editorial Hispano-Americana, SA (HASA):** Alsina 731, 1087 Buenos Aires; tel. (11) 4331-5051; f. 1934; science and technology; Pres. Prof. HÉCTOR OSCAR ALGARRA.

**Editorial Inter-Médica, SAICI:** Junín 917, 1°, Casilla 4625, 1113 Buenos Aires; tel. (11) 4961-9234; fax (11) 4961-5572; e-mail info@inter-medica.com.ar; internet www.inter-medica.com.ar; f. 1959; medicine, dentistry, psychology, psychiatry, veterinary; Pres. JORGE MODYEIEVSKY.

**Editorial Inter-Vet, SA:** Avda de los Constituyentes 3141, Buenos Aires; tel. (11) 451-2382; f. 1987; veterinary; Pres. JORGE MODYEIEVSKY.

**Kapelusz Editora, SA:** Buenos Aires; tel. (11) 4342-6450; fax (11) 4331-9352; f. 1905; textbooks, psychology, pedagogy, children's books; Gen. Man. TOMÁS CASTILLO.

**Editorial Kier, SACIFI:** Avda Santa Fe 1260, 1059 Buenos Aires; tel. (11) 4811-0507; fax (11) 4811-3395; e-mail info@kier.com.ar; internet www.kier.com.ar; f. 1907; Eastern doctrines and religions, astrology, parapsychology, tarot, I Ching, occultism, cabbala, freemasonry and natural medicine; Pres. HECTOR S. PIBERNUS; Mans SERGIO PIBERNUS, OSVALDO PIBERNUS, CRISTINA GRIGNA.

**Ediciones Librerías Fausto:** Avda Corrientes 1316, 1043 Buenos Aires; tel. (11) 4476-4919; fax (11) 4476-3914; f. 1943; fiction and non-fiction; Man. RAFAEL ZORRILLA.

**Carlos Lohlé, SA:** Tacuarí 1516, 1139 Buenos Aires; tel. (11) 427-9969; f. 1953; philosophy, religion, belles-lettres; Dir FRANCISCO M. LOHLÉ.

**Editorial Losada, SA:** Moreno 3362/64, 1209 Buenos Aires; tel. (11) 4863-8608; fax (11) 4864-0434; f. 1938; general; Pres. JOSÉ JUAN FERNÁNDEZ REGUERA.

**Ediciones Macchi, SA:** Alsina 1535/37, 1088 Buenos Aires; tel. (11) 446-2506; fax (11) 446-0594; f. 1947; economic sciences; Pres. RAÚL LUIS MACCHI; Dir JULIO ALBERTO MENDONÇA.

**Editorial Médica Panamericana, SA:** Marcelo T. de Alvear 2145, 1122 Buenos Aires; tel. (11) 4821-5520; fax (11) 4825-5006; e-mail info@medicapanamericana.com.ar; internet www.medicapanamericana.com.ar; f. 1962; medicine and health sciences; Pres. HUGO BRIK.

**Ediciones Nueva Visión, SAIC:** Tucumán 3748, 1189 Buenos Aires; tel. (11) 4864-5050; fax (11) 4863-5980; f. 1954; psychology, education, social sciences, linguistics; Man. Dir HAYDÉE P. DE GIACONE.

**Editorial Paidós:** Defensa 599, 1°, 1065 Buenos Aires; tel. (11) 4331-2275; fax (11) 4345-6769; f. 1945; social sciences, medicine, philosophy, religion, history, literature, textbooks; Man. Dir MARITA GOTTHEIL.

**Plaza y Janés, SA:** Buenos Aires; tel. (11) 486-6769; popular fiction and non-fiction; Man. Dir JORGE PÉREZ.

**Editorial Plus Ultra, SA:** Callao 575, 1022 Buenos Aires; tel. (11) 4374-2953; f. 1964; literature, history, textbooks, law, economics, politics, sociology, pedagogy, children's books; Man. Editors RAFAEL ROMÁN, LORENZO MARENGO.

**Editorial Santillana:** Buenos Aires; f. 1960; education; Pres. JESÚS DE POLANCO GUTÉRREZ.

**Schapire Editor, SRL:** Uruguay 1249, 1016 Buenos Aires; tel. (11) 4812-0765; fax (11) 4815-0369; f. 1941; music, art, theatre, sociology, history, fiction; Dir MIGUEL SCHAPIRE DALMAT.

**Editorial Sigmar, SACI:** Belgrano 1580, 7°, 1093 Buenos Aires; tel. (11) 4383-3045; fax (11) 411-2662; e-mail editorial@sigmar.com.ar; f. 1941; children's books; Man. Dir ROBERTO CHWAT.

**Editorial Sopena Argentina, SACI e I:** Buenos Aires; tel. (11) 438-7182; f. 1918; dictionaries, classics, chess, health, politics, history, children's books; Exec. Pres. DANIEL CARLOS OLSEN.

**Editorial Stella:** Viamonte 1984, 1056 Buenos Aires; tel. (11) 446-0346; general non-fiction and textbooks; owned by Asociación Educacionista Argentina.

**Editorial Sudamericana, SA:** Humberto 545, 1°, 1103 Buenos Aires; tel. (11) 4300-5400; fax (11) 4362-7364; e-mail edsudame@satlink.com; f. 1939; general fiction and non-fiction; Gen. Man. OLAF HANTEL.

**Editorial Troquel, SA:** Dr E. Finochietto 473, 1143 Buenos Aires; tel. (11) 427-1116; fax (11) 423-9350; f. 1954; general literature, and textbooks; Pres. GUSTAVO A. RESSIA.

### PUBLISHERS' ASSOCIATION

**Cámara Argentina de Publicaciones:** Reconquista 1011, 6°, 1003 Buenos Aires; tel. (11) 4311-6855; f. 1970; Pres. AGUSTÍN DOS SANTOS; Man. LUIS FRANCISCO HOULIN.

# Broadcasting and Communications

**Secretaría de Comunicaciones:** Sarmiento 151, 4°, 1000 Buenos Aires; tel. (11) 4318-9410; fax (11) 4318-9432; co-ordinates 30 stations and the international service; Sec. Dr GERMÁN KAMMERATH.

**Subsecretaría de Planificación y Gestión Tecnológica:** Sarmiento 151, 4°, 1000 Buenos Aires; tel. (11) 4311-5909; Under-Sec. Ing. LEONARDO JOSÉ LEIBSON.

**Subsecretaría de Radiocomunicaciones:** Sarmiento 151, 4°, 1000 Buenos Aires; tel. (11) 4311-5909; Under-Sec. Ing. ALFREDO R. PARODI.

**Subsecretaría de Telecomunicaciones:** Sarmiento 151, 4°, 1000 Buenos Aires; tel. (11) 4311-5909; Under-Sec. JULIO I. GUILLÁN.

**Comité Federal de Radiodifusión (COMFER):** Suipacha 765, 9°, 1008 Buenos Aires; tel. (11) 4320-4900; fax (11) 4394-6866; f. 1972; controls various technical aspects of broadcasting and transmission of programmes; Head JOSÉ AIELLO.

### TELECOMMUNICATIONS

**Cámara de Informática y Comunicaciones de la República Argentina (CICOMRA):** Avda Córdoba 744, 2°, 1054 Buenos Aires; tel. (11) 4325-8839; fax (11) 4325-9604; e-mail cicomra@starnet.net.ar.

**Comisión Nacional de Comunicaciones (CNC):** Perú 103, 9°, 1067 Buenos Aires; tel. (11) 4347-9242; fax (11) 4347-9244; Pres. Dr ROBERTO CATALÁN.

**Cía Ericsson SACI:** Avda Madero, 1020 Buenos Aires; tel. (11) 4319-5500; fax (11) 4315-0629; Dir-Gen. Ing. ROLANDO ZUBIRÁN.

**Cía de Radiocomunicaciones Móviles SA:** Tucumán 744, 9°, 1049 Buenos Aires; tel. (11) 4325-5006; fax (11) 4325-5334; mobile telecommunications co; Pres. Lic. MAURICIO E. WIOR.

**Empresa Nacional de Telecomunicaciones (ENTEL):** Defensa 143, 7°, 1065 Buenos Aires; tel. (11) 4499-571; f. 1956; telecommunications services; Gen. Man. GUILLERMO GUSTAVO KLEIN.

**Movicom:** Tucumán 744, 2°, 1049 Buenos Aires; tel. (11) 4978-4773; fax (11) 4978-7373; e-mail rree@movi.com.ar; internet www.movi.com.ar; telecommunications services, including cellular phones, trunking, paging and wireless access to the internet; Pres. Lic. MAURICIO WIOR.

**Telecom Argentina:** Maipú 1210, 9°, 1006 Buenos Aires; tel. (11) 4968-4000; fax (11) 4968-1420; e-mail rkustra@starnet.net.ar; internet www.telecom.com.ar; provision of telecommunication services in the north of Argentina; Pres. JUAN CARLOS MASJOAN.

**Telecomunicaciones Internacionales de Argentina TELINTAR SA:** 25 de Mayo 457, 7°, 1002 Buenos Aires; tel. (11) 4318-0500; fax (11) 4313-4924; e-mail mlamas@telintar.com.ar; internet www.telintar.com.ar; Sec.-Gen. Dr MARCELO MIGUEL LAMAS.

**Telefónica de Argentina SA (TASA):** Tucumán 1, 17°, 1049 Buenos Aires; tel. (11) 4345-5772; fax (11) 4345-5771; e-mail gabello@telefonica.com.ar; internet www.telefonica.com.ar; provision of telecommunication services in the south of Argentina; Pres. CARLOS FERNÁNDEZ PRIDA.

### RADIO

There are three privately-owned stations in Buenos Aires and 72 in the interior. There are also 37 state-controlled stations, four provincial, three municipal and three university stations. The principal ones are Radio Antártida, Radio Argentina, Radio Belgrano, Radio Ciudad de Buenos Aires, Radio Excelsior, Radio Mitre, Radio El Mundo, Radio Nacional, Radio del Plata, Radio Rivadavia and Radio Splendid, all in Buenos Aires.

**Servicio Oficial de Radiodifusión (SOR):** Maipú 555, 1006 Buenos Aires; tel. (11) 4325-1969; fax (11) 4325-9433; e-mail rna@mecon.ar; Dir PATRICIA IVONE BARRAL; controls:

**Cadena Argentina de Radiodifusión (CAR):** Avda Entre Ríos 149, 3°, 1079 Buenos Aires; tel. (11) 4325-9100; fax (11) 4325-9433; groups all national state-owned commercial stations which are operated directly by the Subsecretaría Operativa.

**LRA Radio Nacional de Buenos Aires:** Maipú 555, 1006 Buenos Aires; tel. and fax (11) 4325-9433; e-mail rna@mecon.ar; f. 1937; Dir PATRICIA IVONE BARRAL.

**Radiodifusión Argentina al Exterior (RAE):** Maipú 555, 1006 Buenos Aires; tel. (11) 4325-6368; fax (11) 4325-9433; e-mail rna@mecon.ar; f. 1958; broadcasts in 8 languages to all areas of the world; Dir-Gen. PERLA DAMURI.

**Asociación de Radiodifusoras Privadas Argentinas (ARPA):** Juan D. Perón 1561, 8°, 1037 Buenos Aires; tel. (11) 4382-4412; f. 1958; an association of all but 3 of the privately-owned commercial stations; Pres. DOMINGO F. L. ELÍAS.

### TELEVISION

There are 44 television channels, of which 29 are privately-owned and 15 are owned by provincial and national authorities. The national television network is regulated by the Comité Federal de Radiodifusión (see above).

The following are some of the more important television stations in Argentina: Argentina Televisora Color LS82 Canal 7, LS83 (Canal 9 Libertad), LS84 (Canal 11 Telefé), LS85 Canal 13 ArTeAr SA, LV80 Telenueva, LU81 Teledifusora Bahiense SA, LV81 Canal 12 Telecor SACI, Dicor Difusión Córdoba, LV80 TV Canal 10 Universidad Nacional Córdoba, and LU82 TV Mar del Plata SA.

**Asociación de Teleradiodifusoras Argentinas (ATA):** Avda Córdoba 323, 6°, 1054 Buenos Aires; tel. (11) 4312-4208; fax (11) 4315-4681; e-mail ata@giga.com.ar; f. 1959; asscn of 22 private television channels; Pres. EDUARDO FARLEY.

**ATC—Argentina Televisora Color LS82 TV Canal 7:** Avda Figueroa Alcorta 2977, 1425 Buenos Aires; tel. (11) 4802-6001; fax (11) 4802-9878; state-controlled channel; Dir RENÉ JOLIVET.

**LS83 (Canal 9 Libertad):** Bernardo de Irigoyén 610, Buenos Aires; tel. (11) 4334-4568; fax (11) 4334-3248; private channel; Dir ALEJANDRO RAMAY.

**LS84 (Canal 11 Telefé):** Pavón 2444, 1248 Buenos Aires; tel. (11) 4941-9549; fax (11) 4942-6773; leased to a private concession in 1992; Pres. PEDRO SIMONCINI.

**LS85: Canal 13 (ArTeAr SA):** Avda San Juan 1170, 1147 Buenos Aires; tel. (11) 4305-0013; fax (11) 4307-0315; e-mail webmaster@webtv.artear.com; internet www.webtv.artear.com.ar; f. 1989; leased to a private concession in 1992; Dir-Gen. LUCIO PAGLIARO.

# Finance

(cap. = capital; res = reserves; dep. = deposits; m. = million; amounts in nuevos pesos argentinos—$, unless otherwise stated)

## BANKING

At the end of 1998 there were three public banks, 14 municipal banks, 44 domestic private banks, 39 foreign private banks and four co-operative banks.

### Central Bank

**Banco Central de la República Argentina:** Reconquista 266, 1003 Buenos Aires; tel. (11) 4348-3500; fax (11) 4348-3955; e-mail sistema@bcra.gov.ar; internet www.bcra.gov.ar; f. 1935 as a central reserve bank; it has the right of note issue; all capital is held by the State; Gov. ROQUE BENJAMIN FERNÁNDEZ; Pres. PEDRO POU.

### Government-owned Commercial Banks

**Banco de la Ciudad de Buenos Aires:** Florida 302, 1313 Buenos Aires; tel. (11) 4329-8600; fax (11) 4112-098; municipal bank; f. 1878; cap. and res $200.0m., dep. $2,836.3m. (Oct. 1998); Chair. HORACIO CHIGHIZOLA; 31 brs.

**Banco de la Nación Argentina:** Bartolomé Mitre 326, 1036 Buenos Aires; tel. (11) 4347-6000; fax (11) 4347-8078; internet www.bna.com.ar; f. 1891; national bank; cap. $319.0m., res $1,604.2m., dep. $10,484.5m. (Dec. 1997); Pres. Dr ROQUE MACCARONE; 541 brs.

**Banco de la Pampa:** Carlos Pellegrini 255, 6300 Santa Rosa; tel. (2954) 433008; fax (2954) 433196; f. 1958; cap. $5.7m., res $110.2m., dep. $882.4m. (June 1998); Pres. NÉSTOR MARIO BOSIO; 70 brs.

**Banco de la Provincia de Buenos Aires:** Avda San Martín 137, 1004 Buenos Aires; tel. (11) 4331-2561; fax (11) 4331-5154; e-mail baprocri@internet.siscotel.com; internet www.bpba.com; f. 1822; provincial bank; cap. $750.0m., res $371.0m., dep. $11,055.3m. (Dec. 1997); Pres. Dr CARLOS EDUARDO SÁNCHEZ; 313 brs.

**Banco de la Provincia del Chubut:** Rivadavia 615, 9103 Rawson; tel. (2965) 482506; dep. $170.0m., total assets $456.8m. (May 1995); Principal Officer FREDERICO G. POLAK.

**Banco de la Provincia de Córdoba:** San Jerónimo 166, 5000 Córdoba; tel. (351) 420-7200; fax (351) 422-9718; f. 1873; provincial bank; cap. $47.6m., res $142.8m., dep. $1,036.1 (Dec. 1994); Pres. Dr OSCAR MACARIO CARRIZO; 151 brs.

**Banco de la Provincia de Jujuy:** Alvear 999, 4600 San Salvador de Jujuy; tel. (3882) 423003; f. 1933; dep. $87.9m., total assets $134.8m. (May 1995); Pres. Dr ARMANDO EDUARDO FERNÁNDEZ.

**Banco de la Provincia del Neuquén:** Avda Argentina 41/45, 8300 Neuquén; tel. (299) 434221; fax (299) 4480439; f. 1960; dep. $232.8m., total assets $388.6m. (March 1995); Pres. ÓMAR SANTIAGO NEGRETTI; 21 brs.

**Banco de la Provincia de San Luis:** Rivadavia 602, 5700 San Luis; tel. (2623) 425013; fax (2623) 424943; dep. $88.8m., total assets $107.8m. (May 1995); Principal Officer SALVADOR OMAR CAMPO.

**Banco de la Provincia de Santa Cruz:** Avda General Roca 802, 9400 Río Gallegos; tel. (2966) 420845; dep. $211.7m., total assets $382.1m. (June 1995); Govt Admin. EDUARDO LABOLIDA.

**Banco de la Provincia de Santiago del Estero:** Avda Belgrano 529 Sur, 4200 Santiago del Estero; tel. (385) 422-2300; dep. $69.9m., total assets $101.6m. (Jan. 1995); Pres. AMÉRICO DAHER.

**Banco de la Provincia de Tucumán:** San Martín 362, 4000 San Miguel de Tucumán; tel. (381) 431-1709; dep. $164.7m., total assets $359.5m. (March 1995); Govt Admin. EMILIO APAZA.

**Banco Provincial de Salta:** España 550, 4400 Salta; tel. (387) 422-1300; fax (387) 431-0020; f. 1887; dep. $40.7m., total assets $125.0m. (June 1995); Pres. Dr REYNALDO ALFREDO NOGUEIRA; 19 brs.

**Banco de Santa Fe:** San Martín 715, 2000 Rosario; tel. (342) 4402400; fax (342) 4401750; f. 1874; provincial bank; dep. $40.7m., total assets $773.3m. (June 1995); Chair. FERNANDO JUAN VINALS; 103 brs.

**Banco Social de Córdoba:** 27 de Abril 185, 1°, 5000 Córdoba; tel. (351) 422-3367; dep. $187.3m., total assets $677.3m. (June 1995); Pres. Dr JAIME POMPAS.

**Banco del Territorio Nacional de Tierra del Fuego, Antártida e Islas del Atlántico Sur:** San Martín, esq. Roca, 9410 Ushuaia; tel. (2901) 424087; national bank; cap. and res $21.8m., dep. $54.2m. (June 1992); Pres. OSVALDO MANUEL RODRÍGUEZ.

### Private Commercial Banks

**Banco BI Creditanstalt, SA:** Bouchard 547, 24°, 1106 Buenos Aires; tel. (11) 4319-8400; fax (11) 4319-8230; e-mail bi_credit@impsat1.com.ar; f. 1971; fmrly Banco Interfinanzas; cap. and res $51.8m., dep. $103.0m. (Aug. 1998); Pres. Dr MIGUEL ANGEL ANGELINO.

**Banco Baires, SA:** Buenos Aires; tel. (11) 4394-5851; fax (11) 4325-8548; f. 1956 as Baires Exchange House, adopted current name in 1992 following merger with Banco Mediterráneo, SA; cap. $11.6m., res $1.3m., dep. $56.5m. (Dec. 1994); Pres. G. ANÍBAL MENÉNDEZ.

**Banco Bansud, SA:** Sarmiento 447, 1041 Buenos Aires; tel. (11) 4348-6500; fax (11) 4325-5641; internet www.bansud.com; f. 1995 after merger of Banesto Banco Shaw, SA and Banco del Sud, SA; cap. $44.4m., res $302.2m., dep. $1,432.7m. (June 1997); Pres. LEONARDO ANIDJAR; 39 brs.

**Banco Comercial Israelita, SA:** Bartolomé Mitre 702, 2000 Rosario; tel. (341) 420-0557; fax (341) 420-0517; f. 1921; cap. $4.3m., res $20.5m., dep. $232.0m. (June 1998); Pres. Ing. DAVID ZCARNY; 4 brs.

**Banco de Corrientes:** 9 de Julio 1099, esq. San Juan, 3400 Corrientes; tel. (3783) 479200; fax (3783) 479283; f. 1951 as Banco de la República de Corrientes; adopted current name in 1993, after transfer to private ownership; cap. and res $38.5m., dep. $126.7m. (June 1995); Pres. JUAN RAMÓN BRANCHI; 33 brs.

**Banco Crédito Provincial SA:** Calle 7, esq. 50, Casilla 54, 1900 La Plata; tel. and fax (221) 429-2000; f. 1911; cap. $2.5m., res $40.5m., dep. $160.5m. (June 1995); Pres. ANTONIO R. FALABELLA; 47 brs.

**Banco de Entre Ríos SA:** Monte Caseros 128, 3100 Paraná; tel. (343) 423-1200; fax (343) 421-1221; e-mail bersaext@satlink.com; f. 1935; provincial bank; transferred to private ownership in 1995; cap. $53.7m., res $2.9m., dep. $685.6m. (June 1998); Pres. EDMUNDO JUSTO MUGURUZA; 29 brs.

**Banco Florencia, SA:** Reconquista 353, 1003 Buenos Aires; tel. (11) 4325-5949; fax (11) 4325-5849; f. 1984; cap. and res $8.8m., dep. $11.8m. (Dec. 1993); Chair. ALBERTO BRUNET; Vice-Chair. JORGE GONZÁLEZ.

**Banco Francés, SA:** Reconquista 199, 1003 Buenos Aires; tel. (11) 4346-4000; fax (11) 4346-4320; internet www.bancofrances.com; f. 1886 as Banco Francés del Río de la Plata, SA; adopted current name in 1998 following merger with Banco de Crédito Argentino; dep. US $5,883.6m., total assets US $9,447.4m. (March 1999); Chair. GERVÂSIO COLLAR ZAVALETA; 75 brs.

**Banco de Galicia y Buenos Aires SA:** Juan D. Perón 407, Casilla 86, 1038 Buenos Aires; tel. (11) 4394-7080; fax (11) 4393-1603; internet www.bancogalicia.com.ar; f. 1905; cap. $371.9m., res $473.8m., dep. $6,396.0m. (June 1998); Chair. EDUARDO J. ESCASANY; 165 brs.

**Banco General de Negocios, SA:** Esmeralda 120/38, 1035 Buenos Aires; tel. (11) 4320-6100; fax (11) 4334-6422; f. 1978; cap. $73.0m., res $38.5m., dep. $329.2m. (Dec. 1997); Chair. JOSÉ E. ROHM.

**Banco Israelita de Cordoba, SA:** Ituzaingó 60, 5000 Córdoba; tel. (351) 420-3200; fax (351) 424-3616; f. 1942; cap. $9.0m., res $18.3m., dep. $160.5m. (June 1995); Pres. JUAN MACHTEY; 20 brs.

**Banco Macro Misiones, SA:** Sarmiento 735, 1041 Buenos Aires; tel. (11) 4323-6300; fax (11) 4325-6935; f. 1997 by merger of Banco Macro, SA (f. 1988) and Banco de Misiones, SA; cap. $6.1m., res $29.5m., dep. $400.5m. (Dec. 1997); Pres. JORGE HORACIO BRITO.

**Banco Mariva, SA:** Sarmiento 500, 1041 Buenos Aires; tel. (11) 4331-7571; fax (11) 4321-2222; f. 1980; cap. $30.0m., res $10.0m., dep. $206.3m. (Dec.1994); Pres. RICARDO MAY.

**Banco Mercantil Argentino, SA:** Avda Corrientes 629, 1324 Buenos Aires; tel. (11) 4323-5000; fax (11) 4323-5073; f. 1923; cap. $0.1m., res $61.4m., dep. $587.3m. (Dec. 1997); Pres. NOEL WERTHEIN; 60 brs.

**Banco Popular Financiero:** Sobremonte 801, Casilla 5800, Río Cuarto, Córdoba; tel. (3586) 430001; f. 1964; cap. and res $8.8m., dep. $41.2m. (June 1992); Pres. José Osvaldo Travaglia; Vice-Pres. Hugo Ricardo Lardone.

**Banco Quilmes, SA:** Juan D. Perón 564, 2°, 1038 Buenos Aires; tel. (11) 4331-8111; fax (11) 4334-5235; f. 1907; cap. $81.7m., res $51.3m., dep. $2,383.5m. (June 1998); Chair. William P. Sutton; 88 brs.

**Banco Río de la Plata, SA:** Bartolomé Mitre 480, 1036 Buenos Aires; tel. (11) 4341-1000; fax (11) 4341-1554; internet www.bancorio.com.ar; f. 1908; cap. $150.0m., res $269.1m., dep. $5,372.6m. (Dec. 1996); Pres. Jorge Gregorio Pérez Compaño; 169 brs.

**Banco Suquía, SA:** 25 de Mayo 160, 5000 Córdoba; tel. (351) 420-0200; fax (351) 420-0443; internet www.bancosuquia.com.ar; f. 1961 as Banco del Suquía, SA; adopted current name in 1998; cap. $80.6m., res $66.1m., dep. $1,481.5m. (June 1998); Pres. Vito Remo Roggio; Gen. Man. Raúl Fernández; 98 brs.

**Banco de Valores, SA:** Sarmiento 310, 1041 Buenos Aires; tel. (11) 4323-6900; fax (11) 4334-1731; e-mail bcoval@internet.siscotel.com; internet www.bancodevalores.com; f. 1978; cap. $10.0m., res $5.8m., dep. $219.1m. (Dec. 1996); Pres. Miguel A. Amoretti; 1 br.

**Banco Velox, SA:** San Martín 298, 1004 Buenos Aires; tel. (11) 4320-0200; fax (11) 4393-7672; f. 1983; cap. and res $97.4m., dep. $261.0m. (June 1999); Pres. Juan Peirano; 8 brs.

**HSBC Banco Roberts, SA:** 25 de Mayo 701, 26°, 1084 Buenos Aires; tel. (11) 4344-3333; fax (11) 4334-6404; f. 1978 as Banco Roberts, SA; adopted current name in 1998; cap. $175.0m., res $102.2m., dep. $3,003.1m. (June 1998); Chair. and CEO Jorge A. Heinze; 62 brs.

**Nuevo Banco del Chaco, SA:** Güemes 40, 3500 Resistencia; tel. (3722) 424888; f. 1958 as Banco del Chaco; transferred to private ownership and adopted current name in 1994; cap. $10.5m., dep. $45.4m. (June 1995); 28 brs.

**Nuevo Banco de Formosa:** 25 de Mayo 102, 3600 Formosa; tel. (3717) 426030; transferred to private ownership in 1995; dep. $145.3m., total assets $235.7m. (May 1995); Pres. José Manuel Pablo Viudes.

### Co-operative Banks

**Banco Almafuerte Cooperativo Ltdo:** Corrales Viejos 64, 1437 Buenos Aires; tel. (11) 4911-5153; fax (11) 4911-6887; f. 1978; cap. $18.3m., res $38.1m., dep. $378.4m. (Dec. 1997); Pres. Dr Elias Farah; 27 brs.

**Banco Mayo Cooperativo Ltdo:** Sarmiento 706, 1041 Buenos Aires; tel. (11) 4329-2400; fax (11) 4326-8080; f. 1978; cap. $83.4m., res $32.4m., dep. $904.2m. (June 1997); Chair. Rubén E. Beraja; 106 brs.

**Banco Patricios:** Florida 101, 1005 Buenos Aires; tel. (11) 4331-1786; fax (11) 4331-6887; f. 1927; cap. and res $19.1m., dep. $144.0m. (Dec. 1993); Pres. Dr Alberto Spolski.

**Banco Roco Cooperativo Ltdo:** 25 de Mayo 122, 1002 Buenos Aires; tel. (11) 4342-0051; fax (11) 4331-6596; f. 1961; cap. and res $10.8m., dep. $58.1m. (Dec. 1992); Pres. Alfredo B. Arregui.

### Other National Banks

**Banco Hipotecario Nacional:** Alsina 353, 1087 Buenos Aires; tel. (11) 4347-5470; fax (11) 4347-5416; f. 1886; partially privatized in Jan. 1999; mortgage bank; cap. and res $322.4m., dep. $83.6m. (April 1992); Govt Admin. Horacio José Agustín Alvarez Rivero; 23 brs.

**Caja Nacional de Ahorro y Seguro:** Hipólito Yrigoyen 1770, 1308 Buenos Aires; tel. (11) 4457-260; fax (11) 4111-568; f. 1915; state-owned; savings bank and insurance institution; cap. and res $143.5m., dep. $307.6m. (May 1994); Pres. Dr Carlos Augusto Font; 44 brs.

### Foreign Banks

**ABN Amro Bank N.V.** (Netherlands): Florida 361, Casilla 171, 1005 Buenos Aires; tel. (11) 4320-0600; fax (11) 4322-0839; f. 1914; cap. and res $37.7m., dep. $94.5m. (June 1992); Gen. Man. César A. Deymonnaz.

**Banca Nazionale del Lavoro, SA—BNL** (Italy): Florida 40, 1005 Buenos Aires; tel. (11) 4323-4400; fax (11) 4323-4689; internet www.bnl.com.ar; cap. $272m., dep. $2,306m. (June 1999); took over Banco de Italia y Río de la Plata in 1987; Pres. Ademaro Lanzara; Gen. Man. Niccolo Pandolfiu; 136 brs.

**Banco do Brasil, SA** (Brazil): Sarmiento 487, Casilla 2684, 1041 Buenos Aires; tel. (11) 4394-0939; fax (11) 4394-9577; f. 1960; cap. and res $33.9m., dep. $2.0m. (June 1992); Gen. Man. Hélio Testoni.

**Banco do Estado de São Paulo** (Brazil): Tucumán 821, Casilla 2177, 1049 Buenos Aires; tel. (11) 4325-9533; fax (11) 4325-9527; cap. and res $11.7m., dep. $6.7m. (June 1992); Gen. Man. Carlos Alberto Bergamasco.

**Banco Europeo para América Latina (BEAL), SA:** Juan D. Perón 338, 1038 Buenos Aires; tel. (11) 4331-6544; fax (11) 4331-2010; e-mail bealbsa@inter.prov.com; f. 1914; cap. and res $60m., dep. $121m. (Nov. 1996); Gen. Mans Jean Pierre Smerd, Klaus Krüger.

**Banco Itaú Buen Ayre, SA** (Brazil): 25 de Mayo 476, 2°, 1002 Buenos Aires; tel. (11) 4325-6698; fax (11) 4394-1057; internet www.itau.com.ar; fmrly Banco Itaú Argentina, SA, renamed as above following purchase of Banco del Buen Ayre, SA, in May 1998; cap. and res $20.2m., dep. $1.2m. (June 1992); Dir-Gen. Antonio Carlos B. de Oliveira; 94 brs.

**Banco Sudameris Argentina, SA:** Juan D. Perón 500, 1038 Buenos Aires; tel. (11) 4329-5200; fax (11) 4331-2793; f. 1912; cap. $59.0m., res $8.9m., dep. $562.4m. (Dec. 1997); Exec.-Dir Carlos González Taboada.

**Banco Supervielle-Société Générale, SA:** Reconquista 330, 1003 Buenos Aires; tel. (11) 4329-8000; fax (11) 4329-8080; internet www.supervielle.com.ar; f. 1887 as Banco Supervielle de Buenos Aires, SA, adopted current name in 1979; cap. $50.5m., res $25.7m., dep. $649.7m. (Dec. 1997); Chair. and Gen. Man. Marc-Emmanuel Vives; 40 brs.

**Bank of Tokyo-Mitsubishi, Ltd** (Japan): Avda Corrientes 420, 1043 Buenos Aires; tel. (11) 4348-2001; fax (11) 4322-6607; f. 1956; cap. and res $20m., dep. $81m. (Sept. 1994); Gen. Man. Kazuo Omi.

**BankBoston NA** (USA): Florida 99, 1005 Buenos Aires; tel. (11) 4346-2000; fax (11) 4346-3200; f. 1784; cap. $456.8m., dep. $4,012m.; total assets $8,677m. (Sept. 1998); Pres. Ing. Manuel Sacerdote; 139 brs.

**Banque Nationale de Paris, SA** (France): 25 de Mayo 471, 1002 Buenos Aires; tel. (11) 4318-0318; fax (11) 4311-1368; f. 1981; cap. and res $29.4m., dep. $86.7m. (June 1992); Gen. Man. Chislain de Beaucé.

**Chase Manhattan Bank** (USA): Arenales 707, 5°, 1061 Buenos Aires; tel. (11) 4319-2400; fax (11) 4319-2416; f. 1904; cap. and res $46.3m., dep. $12,387m. (Sept. 1992); Gen. Man. Marcelo Podestá.

**Citibank, NA** (USA): Colón 58, Bahía Blanca, 8000 Buenos Aires; tel. (11) 4331-8281; f. 1914; cap. and res $172.8m., dep. $660.8m. (June 1992); Pres. Ricardo Angles; Vice-Pres. Guillermo Stanley; 16 brs.

**Deutsche Bank Argentina, SA** (Germany): Bartolomé Mitre 401, Casilla 995, 1036 Buenos Aires; tel. (11) 4343-2510; fax (11) 4343-3536; f. 1960; cap. and res $123.6m., dep. $801.0m. (June 1994); Gen. Man. Gerardo Greiser; 47 brs.

**Lloyds Bank (Bank of London and South America) Ltd** (United Kingdom): Tronador 4890, 13°, Casilla 128, 1003 Buenos Aires; tel. (11) 4335-3551; fax (11) 4342-7487; f. 1862; subsidiary of Lloyds Bank TSB Group; cap. and res $108.1m., dep. $583.4m. (Sept. 1997); Gen. Man. for Argentina Colin J. Mitchell; 31 brs.

**Morgan Guaranty Trust Co of New York** (USA): Avda Corrientes 411, 1043 Buenos Aires; tel. and fax (11) 4325-8046; cap. and res $29.1m., dep. $11.6m. (June 1992); Gen. Man. José McLoughlin.

**Republic National Bank of New York** (USA): Bartolomé Mitre 343, 1036 Buenos Aires; tel. (11) 4343-0161; fax (11) 4331-6064; cap. and res $17.2m., dep. $13.6m. (March 1994); Gen. Man. Alberto Muchnick.

### Bankers' Associations

**Asociación de Bancos de la Argentina (ABA):** San Martín 229, 10°, 1004 Buenos Aires; tel. (11) 4394-1430; fax (11) 4394-6340; e-mail webmaster@aba-argentina.com; internet www.aba-argentina.com; f. 1999 by merger of Asociación de Bancos de la República Argentina (f. 1919) and Asociación de Bancos Argentinos (f. 1972); Pres. Lic. Eduardo J. Escasany; Exec. Dir Dr Norberto Carlos Peruzzotti.

**Asociación de Bancos del Interior de la República Argentina (ABIRA):** Avda Corrientes 538, 4°, 1043 Buenos Aires; tel. (11) 4394-3439; fax (11) 4394-5682; f. 1956; Pres. Dr Jorge Federico Christensen; Dir Raúl Passano; 30 mems.

**Asociación de Bancos de Provincia de la República Argentina (ABAPRA):** Florida 470, 1°, 1005 Buenos Aires; tel. (11) 4322-6321; fax (11) 4322-6721; f. 1959; Pres. José Manuel Pablo Viudes; Man. Luis B. Bucafusco; 31 mems.

**Federación de Bancos Cooperativos de la República Argentina (FEBANCOOP):** Maipú 374, 9°/10°, 1006 Buenos Aires; tel. (11) 4394-9949; f. 1973; Pres. Omar C. Trillo; Exec. Sec. Juan Carlos Romano; 32 mems.

## STOCK EXCHANGES

**Mercado de Valores de Buenos Aires, SA:** 25 de Mayo 367, 8°–10°, 1002 Buenos Aires; tel. (11) 4313-6021; fax (11) 4313-4472; internet www.merval.sba.com.ar; Pres. Eugenio de Bary.

There are also stock exchanges at Córdoba, Rosario, Mendoza and La Plata.

### Supervisory Authority

**Comisión Nacional de Valores (CNV):** 25 de Mayo 175, 1002 Buenos Aires; tel. (11) 4342-4607; fax (11) 4331-0639; e-mail gharte@mecon.ar; internet www.cnv.gob.ar; monitors capital markets; Pres. GUILLERMO HARTENECK.

## INSURANCE

**Superintendencia de Seguros de la Nación:** Avda Julio A. Roca 721, 1°, 1067 Buenos Aires; tel. (11) 4331-9821; fax (11) 4331-8733; f. 1938; Superintendent Dr ALBERTO ANGEL FERNÁNDEZ.

In December 1993 there were 249 insurance companies operating in Argentina, of which 11 were foreign. The following is a list of those offering all classes or a specialized service.

**La Agrícola, SA:** Buenos Aires; tel. (11) 4394-5031; f. 1905; associated co La Regional; all classes; Pres. LUIS R. MARCO; First Vice-Pres. JUSTO J. DE CORRAL.

**Aseguradora de Créditos y Garantías, SA:** Avda Corrientes 415, 4°, 1043 Buenos Aires; tel. (11) 4394-4037; fax (11) 4394-0320; e-mail acgtias@infovia.com.ar; internet www.acg.com.ar; f. 1965; Pres. Lic. HORACIO SCAPPARONE; Exec. Vice-Pres. Dr ANÍBAL E. LÓPEZ.

**Aseguradora de Río Negro y Neuquén:** Avda Alem 503, Cipolletti, Río Negro; tel. (299) 477-2725; fax (299) 477-0321; f. 1960; all classes; Gen. Man. ERNESTO LÓPEZ.

**Aseguradores de Cauciones, SA:** Paraguay 580, 1057 Buenos Aires; tel. (11) 4318-3700; fax (11) 4318-3799; e-mail directorio@caucion.com.ar; internet www.caucion.com.ar; f. 1968; all classes; Pres. JOSÉ DE VEDIA.

**Aseguradores Industriales, SA:** Juan D. Perón 650, 6°, 1038 Buenos Aires; tel. (11) 4326-8881; fax (11) 4326-3742; f. 1961; all classes; Exec. Pres. Dir LUIS ESTEBAN LOFORTE.

**La Austral:** Buenos Aires; tel. (11) 442-9881; fax (11) 4953-4459; f. 1942; all classes; Pres. RODOLFO H. TAYLOR.

**Colón, Cía de Seguros Generales, SA:** San Martín 548–550, 1004 Buenos Aires; tel. (11) 4320-3800; fax (11) 4320-3802; f. 1962; all classes; Gen. Man. L. D. STÜCK.

**Columbia, SA de Seguros:** Juan D. Perón 690, 1038 Buenos Aires; tel. (11) 4325-0208; fax (11) 4326-1392; f. 1918; all classes; Pres. MARTA BLANCO; Gen. Man. HORACIO H. PETRILLO.

**El Comercio, Cía de Seguros a Prima Fija, SA:** Avda Corrientes 415, 3° y 5°, 1043 Buenos Aires; tel. (11) 4394-9111; fax (11) 4393-1207; f. 1889; all classes; Pres. DONALD JOSÉ SMITH BALMACEDA; Man. PABLO DOMINGO F. LONGO.

**Cía Argentina de Seguros de Créditos a la Exportación, SA:** Corrientes 345, 7°, 1043 Buenos Aires; tel. (11) 4313-3048; fax (11) 4313-2919; f. 1967; covers credit and extraordinary and political risks for Argentine exports; Pres. LUIS ORCOYEN; Gen. Man. Dr MARIANO A. GARCÍA GALISTEO.

**Cía Aseguradora Argentina, SA:** Avda Roque S. Peña 555, 1035 Buenos Aires; tel. (11) 430-1571; fax (11) 430-5973; f. 1918; all classes; Man. GUIDO LUTTINI; Vice-Pres. ALBERTO FRAGUIO.

**La Continental, Cía de Seguros Generales SA:** Avda Corrientes 655, 1043 Buenos Aires; tel. (11) 4393-8051; fax (11) 4325-7101; f. 1912; all classes; Pres. RAÚL MASCARENHAS.

**La Franco-Argentina, SA:** Buenos Aires; tel. (11) 430-3091; f. 1896; all classes; Pres. Dr GUILLERMO MORENO HUEYO; Gen. Man. Dra HAYDÉE GUZIAN DE RAMÍREZ.

**Hermes, SA:** Edif. Hermes, Bartolomé Mitre 754/60, 1036 Buenos Aires; tel. (11) 4331-4506; fax (11) 4343-5552; e-mail hermes@mbox.servicenet.com.ar; f. 1926; all classes; Pres. DIONISIO KATOPODIS; Gen. Man. FRANCISCO MARTÍN ZABALO.

**India, Cía de Seguros Generales SA:** Avda Roque S. Peña 728/36, 1035 Buenos Aires; tel. (11) 4328-6001; fax (11) 4328-5602; f. 1950; all classes; Pres. ALFREDO JUAN PRIESSE; Vice-Pres. Dr RAÚL ALBERTO GUARDIA.

**Instituto Italo-Argentino de Seguros Generales, SA:** Avda Roque S. Peña 890, 1035 Buenos Aires; tel. (11) 4320-9200; fax (11) 4320-9229; f. 1920; all classes; Pres. ALEJANDRO A. SOLDATI.

**La Meridional, Cía Argentina de Seguros SA:** Juan D. Perón 646, 1038 Buenos Aires; tel. (11) 4909-7000; fax (11) 4909-7274; e-mail meridi@starnet.net.ar; f. 1949; life and general; Pres. GUILLERMO V. LASCANO QUINTANA; Gen. Man. PETER HAMMER.

**Plus Ultra, Cía Argentina de Seguros, SA:** San Martín 548–50, 1004 Buenos Aires; tel. (11) 4393-5069; f. 1956; all classes; Gen. Man. L. D. STÜCK.

**La Primera, SA:** Blvd Villegas y Oro, Trenque Lauquén, Prov. Buenos Aires; tel. (11) 4393-8125; all classes; Pres. ENRIQUE RAÚL U. BOTTINI; Man. Dr RODOLFO RAÚL D'ONOFRIO.

**La Rectora, SA:** Avda Corrientes 848, 1043 Buenos Aires; tel. (11) 4394-6081; fax (11) 4394-3251; f. 1951; all classes; Pres. PEDRO PASCUAL MEGNA; Gen. Man. ANTONIO LÓPEZ BUENO.

**La República Cía Argentina de Seguros Generales, SA:** San Martín 627/29, 1374 Buenos Aires; tel. (11) 4314-1000; fax (11) 4318-8778; f. 1928; group life and general; Pres. JUAN E. CAMBIASO; Gen. Man. EDUARDO ESCAFFI.

**Sud América Terrestre y Marítima Cía de Seguros Generales, SA:** Florida 15, 2°, Galería Florida 1, 1005 Buenos Aires; tel. (11) 4340-5100; fax (11) 4340-5380; f. 1919; all classes; Pres. EMA SÁNCHEZ DE LARRAGOITI; Vice-Pres. ALAIN HOMBREUX.

**La Unión Gremial, SA:** Mitre 665/99, 2000 Rosario, Santa Fe; tel. (341) 426-2900; fax (341) 425-9802; f. 1908; general; Gen. Man. EDUARDO IGNACIO LLOBET.

**La Universal:** Buenos Aires; tel. (11) 442-9881; fax (11) 4953-4459; f. 1905; all classes; Pres. RODOLFO H. TAYLOR.

**Zurich-Iguazú Cía de Seguros, SA:** San Martín 442, 1004 Buenos Aires; tel. (11) 4329-0400; fax (11) 4322-4688; f. 1947; all classes; Pres. RAMÓN SANTAMARINA.

### Reinsurance

**Instituto Nacional de Reaseguros:** Avda Julio A. Roca 694, 1067 Buenos Aires; tel. (11) 4334-0084; fax (11) 4334-5588; f. 1947; reinsurance in all branches; Pres. and Man. REINALDO A. CASTRO.

### Insurance Associations

**Asociación Argentina de Cías de Seguros (AACS):** 25 de Mayo 565, 2°, 1002 Buenos Aires; tel. (11) 4312-7790; fax (11) 4312-6300; e-mail secret@aacsra.org.ar; f. 1894; 60 mems; Pres. ROBERTO F. E. SOLLITTO.

**Asociación de Entidades Aseguradoras Privadas de la República Argentina (EAPRA):** Esmeralda 684, 4°, 1007 Buenos Aires; tel. (11) 4393-2268; fax (11) 4393-2283; f. 1875; asscn of 12 foreign insurance cos operating in Argentina; Pres. Dr PIERO ZUPPELLI; Sec. BERNARDO VON DER GOLTZ.

# Trade and Industry

## GOVERNMENT AGENCIES

**Cámara de Exportadores de la República Argentina:** Avda Roque S. Peña 740, 1°, 1035 Buenos Aires; tel. (11) 4328-8556; fax (11) 4328-1003; e-mail contacto@cera.org.ar; internet www.cera.org.ar; f. 1943 to promote exports; 700 mems.

**Consejo Federal de Inversiones:** San Martín 871, 1004 Buenos Aires; tel. (11) 4313-5557; fax (11) 4313-4486; federal board to co-ordinate domestic and foreign investment and provide technological aid for the provinces; Sec.-Gen. Ing. JUAN JOSÉ CIÁCERA.

**Dirección de Forestación (DF):** Avda Paseo Colón 982, anexo jardin, 1063 Buenos Aires; tel. (11) 4349-2124; fax (11) 4349-2102; e-mail fsanti@sagyp.mecon.ar; assumed the responsibilities of the national forestry commission (Instituto Forestal Nacional—IFONA) in 1991, following its dissolution; supervised by the Secretaría de Agricultura, Ganaderia y Pesca; maintains the Centro de Documentación e Información Forestal; Library Man. NILDA E. FERNÁNDEZ.

**Instituto de Desarrollo Económico y Social (IDES):** Araoz 2838, 1425 Buenos Aires; tel. (11) 4804-4949; fax (11) 4804-5856; e-mail ides@clasco.edu.ar; internet www.clacso.edu.ar/~ides; f. 1960; investigation into social sciences and promotion of social and economic devt; 700 mems; Pres. BERNARDO KOSACOFF; Sec. ADRIANA MARSHALL.

**Junta Nacional de Granos:** Avda Paseo Colón 359, 1063 Buenos Aires; tel. (11) 430-0641; national grain board; supervises commercial practices and organizes the construction of farm silos and port elevators; Pres. JORGE CORT.

**Secretaría de Agricultura, Ganadería, Pesca y Alimentación:** Avda Paseo Colón 922, primera planta, Of. 146, 1063 Buenos Aires; tel. (11) 4349-2291; fax (11) 4349-2292; e-mail mpelle@sagyp.mecon.ar; internet www.siiap.sagyp.mecon.ar; f. 1871; undertakes regulatory, promotional, advisory and administrative responsibilities on behalf of the meat, livestock and fisheries industries; Sec. FELIPE C. SOLA.

**Sindicatura General de Empresas Públicas:** Lavalle 1429, 1048 Buenos Aires; tel. (11) 449-5415; fax (11) 4476-4054; f. 1978; to exercise external control over wholly-or partly-owned public enterprises; Pres. ALBERTO R. ABAD.

## DEVELOPMENT ORGANIZATIONS

**Instituto Argentino del Petróleo y Gas:** Maipú 645, 3°, 1006 Buenos Aires; tel. (11) 4325-8008; fax (11) 4393-5494; f. 1957; established to promote the devt of petroleum exploration and exploitation; Pres. Ing. E. J. ROCCHI.

**Secretario de Programación Económica:** Hipólito Yrigoyen 250, 8°, Of. 819, Buenos Aires; tel. (11) 4349-5710; fax (11) 4349-5714; f. 1961 to formulate national long-term devt plans; Sec. Dr JUAN JOSÉ LACH.

**Sociedad Rural Argentina:** Florida 460, 1005 Buenos Aires; tel. (11) 4324-4700; fax (11) 4324-4774; f. 1866; private org. to promote the devt of agriculture; Pres. ENRIQUE C. CROTTO; 9,400 mems.

## CHAMBERS OF COMMERCE

**Cámara Argentina de Comercio:** Avda Leandro N. Alem 36, 1003 Buenos Aires; tel. (11) 4331-8051; fax (11) 4331-8055; e-mail cac@cac.com.ar; f. 1924; Pres. JORGE LUIS DI FIORI.

**Cámara de Comercio, Industria y Producción de la República Argentina:** Florida 1, 4°, 1005 Buenos Aires; tel. (11) 4331-0813; fax (11) 4331-9116; f. 1913; Pres. JOSÉ CHEDIEK; Vice-Pres. Dr FAUSTINO S. DIÉGUEZ, Dr JORGE M. MAZALAN; 1,500 mems.

**Cámara de Comercio Exterior de Rosario:** Avda Córdoba 1868, 2000 Rosario, Santa Fe; tel. and fax (341) 425-7147; e-mail ccer@commerce.com.ar; internet www.commerce.com.ar; f. 1958; deals with imports and exports; Pres. JUAN CARLOS RETAMERO; Vice-Pres. EDUARDO C. SALVATIERRA; 150 mems.

Similar chambers are located in most of the larger centres and there are many foreign chambers of commerce.

## INDUSTRIAL AND TRADE ASSOCIATIONS

**Asociación de Importadores y Exportadores de la República Argentina:** Avda Belgrano 124, 1°, 1092 Buenos Aires; tel. (11) 4342-0010; fax (11) 4342-1312; f. 1966; Pres. HÉCTOR MARCELLO VIDAL; Man. ESTELIA D. DE AMATI.

**Asociación de Industriales Textiles Argentinos:** Buenos Aires; tel. (11) 4373-2256; fax (11) 4373-2351; f. 1945; textile industry; Pres. BERNARDO ABRAMOVICH; 250 mems.

**Asociación de Industrias Argentinas de Carnes:** Buenos Aires; tel. (11) 4322-5244; meat industry; refrigerated and canned beef and mutton; Pres. JORGE BORSELLA.

**Asociación Vitivinícola Argentina:** Güemes 4464, 1425 Buenos Aires; tel. (11) 4774-3370; f. 1904; wine industry; Pres. LUCIANO COTUMACCIO; Man. Lic. MARIO J. GIORDANO.

**Cámara de Sociedades Anónimas:** Florida 1, 3°, 1005 Buenos Aires; tel. (11) 4342-9013; fax (11) 4342-9225; Pres. Dr ALFONSO DE LA FERRERE; Man. CARLOS ALBERTO PERRONE.

**Centro de Exportadores de Cereales:** Bouchard 454, 7°, 1106 Buenos Aires; tel. (11) 4311-1697; fax (11) 4312-6924; f. 1943; grain exporters; Pres. RAUL S. LOEH.

**Confederaciones Rurales Argentinas:** México 628, 2°, 1097 Buenos Aires; tel. (11) 4261-1501; Pres. ARTURO J. NAVARRO.

**Coordinadora de Actividades Mercantiles Empresarias:** Buenos Aires; Pres. OSVALDO CORNIDE.

**Federación Lanera Argentina:** Avda Paseo Colón 823, 5°, 1063 Buenos Aires; tel. (11) 4300-7661; fax (11) 4361-6517; f. 1929; wool industry; Pres. JULIO AISENSTEIN; Sec. RICHARD VON GERSTENBERG; 80 mems.

## EMPLOYERS' ORGANIZATION

**Unión Industrial Argentina (UIA):** Avda Leandro N. Alem 1067, 11°, 1001 Buenos Aires; tel. (11) 4313-4474; fax (11) 4313-2413; e-mail uia01@act.net.ar; f. 1887; re-established in 1974 with the fusion of the Confederación Industrial Argentina (CINA) and the Confederación General de la Industria; following the dissolution of the CINA in 1977, the UIA was formed in 1979; assen of manufacturers, representing industrial corpns; Pres. OSVALDO RIAL; Sec.-Gen. Dr JOSÉ I. DE MENDIGUREN.

## UTILITIES

**Agua y Energía Eléctrica Sociedad del Estado (AyEE):** Avda Leandro N. Alem 1134, 1001 Buenos Aires; tel. (11) 4311-6364; fax (11) 4312-2236; f. 1947; scheduled for transfer to private ownership; state water and electricity board; Principal Officer HAROLDO H. GRISANTI.

### Electricity

**Central Costanera, SA (CECCO):** Avda España 3301, 1107 Buenos Aires; tel. (11) 4307-3040; fax (11) 4307-1706; generation, transmission, distribution and sale of thermal electric energy; Chair. JAIME BAUZÁ BAUZÁ.

**Central Puerto, SA (CEPU):** Avda Tomás Edison 2701, 1104 Buenos Aires; tel. (11) 4317-5000; fax (11) 4317-5099; electricity generating co; CEO ANTONIO BÜCHI BUĆ.

**Comisión Nacional de Energía Atómica (CNEA):** Avda del Libertador 8250, 1429 Buenos Aires; tel. (11) 4704-1384; fax (11) 4704-1176; e-mail freijo@cnea.edu.ar; internet www.cnea.gov.ar; f. 1950; scheduled for transfer to private ownership; nuclear energy science and technology; Pres. JACOBO DAN BENINSON.

**Comisión Técnica Mixta de Salto Grande (CTMSG):** Avda Leandro N. Alem 449, 1003 Buenos Aires; operates Salto Grande hydroelectric station, which has an installed capacity of 650 MW; joint Argentine-Uruguayan project.

**Dirección de Energía de la Provincia de Buenos Aires:** Calle 55, No. 570, La Reja, 1900 Buenos Aires; tel. (11) 4415-000; fax (11) 4216-124; f. 1957; electricity co for province of Buenos Aires; Dir AGUSTÍN NÚÑEZ.

**Empresa Distribuidora Norte, SA (EDENOR):** Avda de Mayo 70, 22°, 1084 Buenos Aires; tel. (11) 4348-2121; fax (11) 4334-0805; distribution of electricity.

**Empresa Distribuidora Sur, SA (EDESUR):** San José 140, 1076 Buenos Aires; tel. (11) 4381-8981; fax (11) 4383-3699; distribution of electricity; Chair. MARCOS ZIBERBERG.

**Entidad Binacional Yacyretá:** Avda Eduardo Madero 942, 21°–22°, 1106 Buenos Aires; tel. (11) 4510-7500; e-mail rrpp@eby.org.ar; internet www.yacyreta.org.ar; operates the hydroelectic dam at Yacyretá on the Paraná river, owned jointly by Argentina and Paraguay. Completed in 1998, it is one of the world's largest hydroelectric complexes, consisting of 20 generators with a total generating capacity of 18,100 GWh.

**Hidroeléctrica Norpatagónica, SA (HIDRONOR):** Avda Leandro N. Alem 1074, 1001 Buenos Aires; tel. (11) 4312-6031; fax (11) 4313-0734; formerly the largest producer of electricity in Argentina; responsible for developing the hydroelectric potential of the Limay and neighbouring rivers; transferred to private ownership in 1992 and divided into the following companies:

**Central Hidroeléctrica Alicurá, SA:** Avda Leandro N. Alem 712, 7°, 1001 Buenos Aires.

**Central Hidroeléctrica Cerros Colorados, SA:** Avda Leandro N. Alem 690, 12°, 1001 Buenos Aires.

**Central Hidroeléctrica El Chocón, SA:** Suipacha 268, 9°, Of. A, Buenos Aires.

**Hidroeléctrica Piedra del Aguila, SA:** Avda Tomás Edison 1251, 1104 Buenos Aires; tel. (11) 4315-2586; fax (11) 4317-5174; Pres. Dr URIEL FEDERICO O'FARRELL; Gen. Man. IGNACIO J. ROSNER.

**Transener, SA:** Avda Paseo Colón 728, 6°, 1063 Buenos Aires; tel. (11) 4342-6925; fax (11) 4342-7147; energy transmission co.

**Hidroeléctrica Pichi Picún Leufu, SA:** Avda Leandro N. Alem 1074, 6°, Buenos Aires; fax (11) 4313-0734; state-owned co, responsible for the construction of the Pichi Picún dam; Pres. Ing. ALBERTO A. HEVIA; Vice-Pres. Dr CARLOS E. BASANTA.

**Servicios Eléctricos del Gran Buenos Aires, SA (SEGBA):** Balcarce 184, 1002 Buenos Aires; tel. (11) 4331-1901; Principal Officer CARLOS A. MATTAUSCH.

### Gas

**Distribuidora de Gas del Centro, SA:** Avda Hipólito Yrigoyen 475, 5000 Córdoba; tel. (351) 4688-100; fax (351) 4681-568; state-owned co, distributes natural gas.

**Gas del Estado, SA:** Alsina 1169, 1069 Buenos Aires; tel. (11) 4383-2091; fax (11) 4982-3848; f. 1946; operates integrated natural-gas network and produces liquefied gas and by-products.

**Metrogás, SA:** Avda Montes de Oca 1120, 1271 Buenos Aires; tel. (11) 4309-1000; fax (11) 4309-1366; internet www.metrogas.com; gas distribution; Dir-Gen. WILLIAM ADAMSON.

**Transportadora de Gas del Norte, SA:** Don Bosco 3672, 3°, 1206 Buenos Aires; tel. (11) 4959-2000; fax (11) 4959-2253; state-owned co, distributes natural gas; Gen. Man. FREDDY CAMEO.

**Transportadora de Gas del Sur, SA (TGS):** Don Bosco 3672, 5°, 1206 Buenos Aires; tel. (11) 4865-9050; fax (11) 4865-9059; e-mail totgs@tgs.com.ar; internet www.tgs.com.ar; processing and transport of natural gas; Gen. Dir EDUARDO OJEA QUINTANA.

**Aguas Argentinas:** Buenos Aires; distribution of water in Buenos Aires; privatized in 1993; Dir-Gen. JEAN-LOUIS CHAUSSADE.

### Water

**Obras Sanitarias de la Nación:** Marcelo T. de Alvear 1840, 1122 Buenos Aires; tel. (11) 441-1081; fax (11) 441-4050; sanitation; transferred to private ownership in 1992.

## TRADE UNIONS

**Congreso de los Trabajadores Argentinos (CTA):** Buenos Aires; dissident trade union confederation; Leader VÍCTOR DE GENARO.

**Confederación General del Trabajo—CGT** (General Confederation of Labour): Buenos Aires; f. 1984; Peronist; represents approx. 90% of Argentina's 1,100 trade unions; Sec.-Gen. HUGO MOYANO.

**Movimiento de Trabajadores Argentinos (MTA):** Buenos Aires; dissident trade union confederation.

# Transport

**Secretaría de Energía:** Paseo Colón 171, 8°, Of. 803, Buenos Aires; tel. (11) 4349-8005; e-mail energia@mecon.ar; internet www.ar/energia; Sec. Ing. ALFREDO HÉCTOR MIRKIN.

**Secretaría de Obras Públicas y Transporte:** Hipólito Yrigoyen 250, 12°, 1310 Buenos Aires; tel. (11) 4349-7254; fax (11) 4349-7201; Sec. Ing. Armando Guibert.

**Secretaría de Transporte Metropolitano y de Larga Distancia:** Hipólito Yrigoyen 250, 12°, 1310 Buenos Aires; tel. (11) 4349-7162; fax (11) 4349-7146; Under-Sec. Dr Armando Canosa.

**Secretaría de Transporte Aero-Comercial:** Hipólito Yrigoyen 250, 12°, 1310 Buenos Aires; tel. (11) 4349-7203; fax (11) 4349-7206; Under-Sec. Arq. Fermín Alarcia.

**Dirección de Estudios y Proyectos:** Hipólito Yrigoyen 250, 12°, 1310 Buenos Aires; tel. (11) 4349-7127; fax (11) 4349-7128; Dir Ing. José Luis Jagodnik.

## RAILWAYS

Lines: General Belgrano (narrow-gauge), General Roca, General Bartolomé Mitre, General San Martín, Domingo Faustino Sarmiento (all wide-gauge), General Urquiza (medium-gauge) and Línea Metropolitana, which controls the railways of Buenos Aires and its suburbs. There are direct rail links with the Bolivian Railways network to Santa Cruz de la Sierra and La Paz; with Chile, through the Las Cuevas–Caracoles tunnel (across the Andes) and between Salta and Antofagasta; with Brazil, across the Paso de los Libres and Uruguayana bridge; with Paraguay (between Posadas and Encarnación by ferry-boat); and with Uruguay (between Concordia and Salto). In 1995 there were 33,000 km of tracks. In the Buenos Aires commuter area 270.4 km of wide-gauge track and 52 km of medium gauge track are electrified.

Plans for the eventual total privatization of Ferrocarriles Argentinos (FA) were initiated in 1991, with the transfer to private ownership of the Rosario-Bahía Blanca grain line and with the reallocation of responsibility for services in Buenos Aires to the newly-created Ferrocarriles Metropolitanos, prior to its privatization.

In early 1993 central government funding for the FA was suspended and responsibility for existing inter-city passenger routes was devolved to respective provincial governments. However, owing to lack of resources, few provinces have successfully assumed the operation of services, and many trains have been suspended. At the same time, long-distance freight services were sold as six separate 30-year concessions (including lines and rolling stock) to private operators. By late 1996 all freight services had been transferred to private management, with the exception of Ferrocarril Belgrano, SA, which was in the process of undergoing privatization. The Buenos Aires commuter system was divided into eight concerns (one of which incorporates the underground railway system) and was offered for sale to private operators as 10- or 20-year (subsidized) concessions. The railway network is currently regulated by the National Commission for Transport Regulation.

**Ferrocarriles Argentinos (FA):** Salta 1929, 1137 Buenos Aires; tel. (11) 4304-1557; fax (11) 4313-3129; f. 1948 with the nationalization of all foreign property; autonomous body but policies established by the Secretaría de Obras Públicas y Transporte; dismantled and responsibilities transferred in 1993 (see above); Trustee Daniel Oscar Halperin; Gen. Man. P. Suárez.

**Ferrocarriles Metropolitanos, SA (FEMESA):** Bartolomé Mitre 2815, Buenos Aires; tel. (11) 4865-4135; fax (11) 4861-8757; f. 1991 to assume responsibility for services in the capital; 820 km of track; Pres. Matías Ordóñez; concessions to operate services have been awarded to:

**Metrovías.**

**Trainmet.**

**Ferrovías.**

**Cámara de Industriales Ferroviarios:** Alsina 1609, 1°, Buenos Aires; tel. (11) 4371-5571; private org. to promote the devt of Argentine railway industries; Pres. Ing. Ana María Guibaudi.

The following consortia were awarded 30-year concessions to operate rail services, during 1991–94:

**Consorcio Nuevo Central Argentino (CNCA):** Buenos Aires; operates freight services on the Bartolomé Mitre lines; 5,011 km of track; Pres. H. Urquia.

**Ferrocarril Buenos Aires al Pacífico/San Martín (BAP):** Avda Santa Fe 4636, 3°, Buenos Aires; tel. (11) 4778-2486; fax (11) 4778-2493; operates services on much of the San Martín line, and on 706 km of the Sarmiento line; 6,106 km of track; Pres. and Gen. Man. E. Glezer.

**Ferrocarril General Belgrano, SA (FGB):** Maipú 88, 1084 Buenos Aires; tel. and fax (11) 4343-7220; fax (11) 4343-7229; f. 1993; operates freight services; Pres. Dr Ignacio A. Ludveña.

**Ferrocarril Mesopotámico General Urquiza (FMGU):** Avda Santa Fe 4636, 3°, 1425 Buenos Aires; tel. (11) 4778-2425; fax (11) 4778-2493; operates freight services on the Urquiza lines; 2,272 km of track; Pres. and Gen. Man. E. Glezer.

**Ferroexpreso Pampeano (FEPSA):** Bouchard 680, 9°, 1106 Buenos Aires; tel. (11) 4318-4900; fax (11) 4510-4945; operates services on the Rosario–Bahía Blanca grain lines; 5,193 km of track; Pres. H. Masoero.

**Ferrosur Roca (FR):** Bouchard 680, 8°, 1106 Buenos Aires; tel. (11) 4319-3900; fax (11) 4319-3901; e-mail ferrosur@impsat1.com.ar; operator of freight services on the Roca lines since 1993; 3,000 km of track; Pres. Amelia Lacroze de Fortabat; Gen. Man. Sergio do Rego.

Buenos Aires also has an underground railway system:

**Subterráneos de Buenos Aires:** Bartolomé Mitre 3342, 1201 Buenos Aires; tel. (11) 4862-6844; fax (11) 4864-0633; f. 1913; became completely state-owned in 1951; fmrly controlled by the Municipalidad de la Ciudad de Buenos Aires; responsibility for operations was transferred, in 1993, to a private consortium (Metrovías) with a 20-year concession; five underground lines totalling 36.5 km, 63 stations, and a 7.4 km light rail line with 13 stations, which was inaugurated in 1987; Pres. A. Verra.

## ROADS

In 1996 there were 218,276 km of roads, of which 29.1% were paved. Four branches of the Pan-American highway run from Buenos Aires to the borders of Chile, Bolivia, Paraguay and Brazil. In 1996 9,932 km of main roads were under private management. Construction work on a 41-km bridge across the River Plate (linking Punta Lara in Argentina with Colonia del Sacramento in Uruguay) was scheduled to begin in the late 1990s.

**Dirección Nacional de Vialidad:** Avda Julio A. Roca 378, Buenos Aires; tel. (11) 4343-2838; fax (11) 4343-7292; controlled by the Secretaría de Transportes; Gen. Man. Ing. Elio Vergara.

**Asociación Argentina de Empresarios Transporte Automotor (AAETA):** Bernardo de Irigoyen 330, 6°, 1072 Buenos Aires; e-mail aaeta@sei.com.ar; internet www.aaeta.org.ar; Gen. Man. Ing. Marcelo González.

**Federación Argentina de Entidades Empresarias de Autotransporte de Cargas (FADEAC):** Avda de Mayo 1370, 3°, 1372 Buenos Aires; tel. (11) 4383-3635; Pres. Rogelio Cavalieri Iribarne.

There are several international passenger and freight services including:

**Autobuses Sudamericanos, SA:** Buenos Aires; tel. (11) 4307-1956; fax (11) 4307-1956; f. 1928; international bus services; car and bus rentals; charter bus services; Pres. Armando Schlecker Hirsch; Gen. Man. Miguel Angel Ruggiero.

## INLAND WATERWAYS

There is considerable traffic in coastal and river shipping, mainly carrying petroleum and its derivatives.

**Dirección Nacional de Construcciones Portuarias y Vías Navegables:** Avda España 221, 4°, Buenos Aires; tel. (11) 4361-5964; responsible for the maintenance and improvement of waterways and dredging operations; Dir Ing. Enrique Casals de Alba.

## SHIPPING

There are more than 100 ports, of which the most important are Buenos Aires, Quequén and Bahía Blanca. There are specialized terminals at Ensenada, Comodoro Rivadavia, San Lorenzo and Campana (petroleum); Bahía Blanca, Rosario, Santa Fe, Villa Concepción, Mar del Plata and Quequén (cereals); and San Nicolás and San Fernando (raw and construction materials). In 1998 Argentina's merchant fleet totalled 501 vessels amounting to 498,715 grt.

**Administración General de Puertos:** Avda Julio A. Roca 734/42, 1344 Buenos Aires; tel. (11) 4342-5621; fax (11) 4331-0298; f. 1956; state enterprise for direction, administration and exploitation of all national sea- and river-ports; scheduled for transfer to private ownership; Pres. Luis A. Roura.

**Capitanía General del Puerto:** Avda Julio A. Roca 734, 2°, 1067 Buenos Aires; tel. (11) 434-9784; f. 1967; co-ordination of port operations; Port Captain Capt. Pedro Taramasco.

**Administración General de Puertos (Santa Fe):** Duque 1 Cabacera, Santa Fe; tel. (42) 41732.

**Consorcio de Gestión del Puerto de Bahía Blanca:** Avda Dr Mario M. Guido s/n, 8103 Provincia de Buenos Aires; tel. (91) 57-3213; Pres. José E. Conte; Sec.-Gen. Claudio Marcelo Conte.

**Terminales Portuarias Argentinas:** Buenos Aires; operates one of five recently privatized cargo and container terminals in the port of Buenos Aires.

**Terminales Río de la Plata:** Buenos Aires; operates one of five recently privatized cargo and container terminals in the port of Buenos Aires.

**Empresa Líneas Marítimas Argentinas, SA (ELMA):** Avda Corrientes 389, 1327 Buenos Aires; tel. (11) 4312-9245; fax (11) 4311-7954; f. 1941 as state-owned org.; transferred to private ownership in 1994; operates vessels to northern Europe, the Mediterranean, west and east coasts of Canada and the USA, Gulf of Mexico,

Caribbean ports, Brazil, Pacific ports of Central and South America, Far East, northern and southern Africa and the Near East; Pres. PABLO DOMINGO DE ZORZI.

Other private shipping companies operating on coastal and overseas routes include:

**Antártida Pesquera Industrial:** Moreno 1270, 5°, 1091 Buenos Aires; tel. (11) 4381-0167; fax (11) 4381-0519; Pres. J. M. S. MIRANDA; Man. Dir J. R. S. MIRANDA.

**Astramar Cía Argentina de Navegación, SAC:** Buenos Aires; tel. (11) 4311-3678; fax (11) 4311-7534; Pres. ENRIQUE W. REDDIG.

**Bottacchi SA de Navegación:** Maipú 509, 2°, 1006 Buenos Aires; tel. (11) 4392-7411; fax (11) 411-1280; Pres. ANGEL L. M. BOTTACCHI.

**Maruba S. en C. por Argentina:** Maipú 535, 7°, 1006 Buenos Aires; tel. (11) 4322-7173; fax (11) 4322-3353; Chartering Man. R. J. DICKIN.

**Yacimientos Petrolíferos Fiscales (YPF):** Avda Roque S. Peña 777, 1364 Buenos Aires; tel. (11) 446-7271; privatization finalized in 1993; Pres. NELLS LEÓN.

### CIVIL AVIATION

Argentina has 10 international airports (Aeroparque Jorge Newbery, Córdoba, Corrientes, El Plumerillo, Ezeiza, Jujuy, Resistencia, Río Gallegos, Salta and San Carlos de Bariloche). Ezeiza, 35 km from Buenos Aires, is one of the most important air terminals in Latin America. More than 30 airports were scheduled for transfer to private ownership in the late 1990s.

**Aerolíneas Argentinas:** Bouchard 547, 9°, 1063 Buenos Aires; tel. (11) 4317-3201; fax (11) 4317-3581; internet www.aeorlineas.com.ar; f. 1950; transfer to private ownership initiated in 1990; services to North and Central America, Europe, the Far East, New Zealand, South Africa and destinations throughout South America; the internal network covers the whole country; passengers, mail and freight are carried; Pres. MANUEL MORÁN.

**Austral Líneas Aéreas (ALA):** Avda Corrientes 485, 9°, 1398 Buenos Aires; tel. (11) 4317-3922; fax (11) 4317-3991; internet www.austral.com.ar; f. 1971; domestic flights linking 27 cities in Argentina; Pres. MANUEL A. M. CASERO.

**CATA Líneas Aéreas S.A.C.I.F.I.:** Cerrito 1320, 3°, 1010 Buenos Aires; tel. (11) 4812-3390; fax (11) 4627-3721; e-mail cataaer@satlink.com; internet www.webs.satlink.com/usuarios/c/cataaer; f. 1978; domestic passenger flights; Pres. ROQUE PUGLIESE.

**Líneas Aéreas Entre Ríos:** Salvador Caputo, Paraná, Entre Ríos; tel. (343) 436-2013; fax (343) 436-2177; f. 1988; scheduled domestic passenger services; Pres. PEDRO PEDRINIL.

**Líneas Aéreas del Estado (LADE):** Perú 710, 1068 Buenos Aires; tel. (11) 4362-1853; fax (11) 4300-0031; e-mail director@lade.com.ar; Dir GUILLERMO JOSÉ TESTONI.

**Líneas Aéreas Privadas Argentinas (LAPA):** Avda Santa Fe 1970, 2°, 1123 Buenos Aires; tel. (11) 4812-0953; fax (11) 4814-2100; e-mail gcaputi@lapa.com.ar; f. 1976; domestic scheduled passenger services, and international routes to Uruguay; Pres. GUSTAVO ANDRÉS DEUTSCH.

**Transporte Aéreo Costa Atlántica (TACA):** Bernardo de Yrigoyen 1370, 1°, Ofs 25-26, 1138 Buenos Aires; tel. (11) 4307-1956; fax (11) 4307-8899; f. 1956; domestic and international passenger and freight services between Argentina and Bolivia, Brazil and the USA; Pres. DR ARMANDO SCHLECKER HIRSCH.

**Transportes Aéreos Neuquén:** Diagonal 25 de Mayo 180, 8300 Neuquén; tel. (299) 4423076; fax (299) 4488926; e-mail tancentr@satlink.com.ar; domestic routes; Pres. JOSÉ CHALÉN; Gen. Man. PATROCINIO VALVERDE MORAIS.

**Valls Líneas Aéreas:** Río Grande, Tierra del Fuego; f. 1995; operates three routes between destinations in southern Argentina, Chile and the South Atlantic islands.

## Tourism

Argentina's superb tourist attractions include the Andes mountains, the lake district centred on Bariloche (where there is a National Park), Patagonia, the Atlantic beaches and Mar del Plata, the Iguazú falls, the Pampas and Tierra del Fuego. Tourist arrivals in Argentina in 1998 totalled 4,859,867. In the same year tourist receipts were US $5,363m.

**Secretaría de Turismo de la Nación:** Suipacha 1111, 20°, 1368 Buenos Aires; tel. (11) 4312-5611; fax (11) 4313-6834; internet www.turismo.gov.ar; Sec. FRANCISCO MAYORGA.

**Asociación Argentina de Agencias de Viajes y Turismo (AAAVYT):** Viamonte 640, 10°, 1053 Buenos Aires; tel. (11) 4325-4691; fax (11) 4322-9641; e-mail aaavyt@tournet.com.ar; f. 1951; Pres. HUGO E. COPERTARI; Gen. Man. GERARDO BELO.

# ARMENIA

## Introductory Survey

**Location, Climate, Language, Religion, Flag, Capital**

The Republic of Armenia is situated in south-west Transcaucasia, on the north-eastern border of Turkey. Its other borders are with Iran to the south, Azerbaijan to the east, and Georgia to the north. The Nakhichevan Autonomous Republic, an Azerbaijani territory, is situated to the south, separated from the remainder of Azerbaijan by Armenian territory. The climate is typically continental: dry, with wide temperature variations. Winters are cold, the average January temperature in Yerevan being −3°C (26°F), but summers can be very warm, with August temperatures averaging 25°C (77°F), although high altitude moderates the heat in much of the country. Precipitation is low in the Yerevan area (annual average 322 mm), but much higher in the mountains. The official language is Armenian, the sole member of a distinct Indo-European language group. It is written in the Armenian script. Kurdish is used in broadcasting and publishing for some 56,000 Kurds inhabiting Armenia. Most of the population are adherents of Christianity, the largest denomination being the Armenian Apostolic Church. There are also Russian Orthodox, Protestant, Islamic and Yazidi communities. The national flag (approximate proportions 3 by 2) consists of three equal horizontal stripes, of red, blue and orange. The capital is Yerevan.

**Recent History**

Although Armenia was an important power in ancient times, for much of its history it has been ruled by foreign states. In 1639 Armenia was partitioned, with the larger, western part being annexed by Turkey and the eastern region becoming part of the Persian Empire. In 1828, after a period of Russo–Persian conflict, eastern Armenia was ceded to the Russian Empire by the Treaty of Turkmanchai, and subsequently became a province of the empire. At the beginning of the 20th century Armenians living in western, or Anatolian, Armenia, under Ottoman rule, were subject to increasing persecution by the Turks. As a result of brutal massacres and deportations (particularly in 1915), the Anatolian lands were largely emptied of their Armenian population, and it was estimated that during the period 1915–22 some 1.5m. Armenians perished. After the collapse of Russian imperial power in 1917, Russian Armenia joined the anti-Bolshevik Transcaucasian Federation, which included Georgia and Azerbaijan. This collapsed when threatened by Turkish forces, and on 28 May 1918 Armenia was proclaimed an independent state. Without Russian protection, however, the newly-formed republic was almost defenceless against Turkish expansionism and was forced to cede the province of Kars and other Armenian lands to Turkey. Armenia was recognized as an independent state by the Allied Powers and by Turkey in the Treaty of Sèvres, signed on 10 August 1920. However, the rejection of the Treaty by the new Turkish ruler, Mustafa Kemal, left Armenia vulnerable to renewed Turkish threats. In September Turkish troops attacked Armenia, but they were prevented from establishing full control over the country by the invasion of Armenia, from the east, by Russian Bolshevik troops, and the founding, on 29 November 1920, of a Soviet Republic of Armenia. In December 1922 the republic became a member, together with Georgia and Azerbaijan, of the Transcaucasian Soviet Federative Socialist Republic (TSFSR), which, in turn, became a constituent republic of the USSR. In 1936 the TSFSR was dissolved and Armenia became a full union republic of the USSR.

Although many Armenians suffered under communist rule, advances were made in economic and social development. During the period of tsarist rule Russian Armenia had been an underdeveloped region of the empire, with very little infrastructure; however, in the Armenian Soviet Socialist Republic (SSR), the authorities implemented a policy of forced modernization, which expanded communications and introduced industrial plants. Literacy and education were also improved. A programme to collectivize agriculture, initiated on a voluntary basis in 1928, engèndered little enthusiasm; collectivization was enforced in 1930, and many thousands of peasants who still opposed it were deported. Armenians experienced further suffering during the Stalinist purges of the late 1930s, in which thousands of people were executed or imprisoned. Unlike many western parts of the USSR during the Second World War (1939–45), Armenia was not occupied by German forces following their invasion of the USSR in June 1941. Consequently, the republic provided an essential source of labour for the Soviet economy, and as many as 600,000 Armenians served in the Soviet armies (of whom an estimated 350,000 were killed). In the immediate post-war period the Soviet Government gave priority to developing the industrial sector in Armenia, while also expanding the agricultural collectivization programme. In the late 1940s an estimated 150,000 Armenians of the 'diaspora' returned to the republic.

The Soviet leader Mikhail Gorbachev's policies of *perestroika* (restructuring) and *glasnost* (openness) (introduced following his accession to power in 1985) had little initial impact in Armenia. The first manifestations of the new policies were campaigns against corruption in the higher echelons of the Communist Party of Armenia (CPA). On a more public level, environmental problems became a focus for popular protest. The first demonstrations against ecological degradation took place in September 1987, but the demands of protesters soon began to include the redress of historical and political grievances.

Of the historical and ethnic issues discussed in late 1987 and early 1988, the most significant was the status of Nagornyi Karabakh, an autonomous oblast (region) within neighbouring Azerbaijan, largely populated by (non-Muslim) Armenians, control of which had been ceded to Azerbaijan in 1921 (see chapter on Azerbaijan). Demands for the incorporation of Nagornyi Karabakh into the Armenian SSR began within the enclave itself in early 1988. In February as many as 1m. people took part in demonstrations in Yerevan, the Armenian capital, in support of these demands. The demonstrations were organized by Yerevan intellectuals, who formed a group known as the Karabakh Committee. In response to increased unrest within Armenia, many Azerbaijanis began to leave the republic. Rumours of ill-treatment of the refugees led to anti-Armenian riots in Sumgait (Azerbaijan) in late February, in which 26 Armenians died. This event provoked further Armenian anger, which was compounded by the decision of the Presidium of the USSR's Supreme Soviet (legislature) not to transfer Nagornyi Karabakh to Armenia. Strikes and rallies continued under the leadership of the officially-outlawed Karabakh Committee, and the inability of the local authorities to control the unrest led to the dismissal, in May, of the First Secretary (leader) of the CPA. In December, however, the issue of Nagornyi Karabakh was temporarily subordinated to the problems of overcoming the effects of a severe earthquake which had struck northern Armenia. Some 25,000 people were reported to have been killed and many thousands more were made homeless. In the chaos following the earthquake the members of the Karabakh Committee were arrested, ostensibly for interfering in relief work. They were released only in May 1989, after huge demonstrations took place, protesting against their continued internment. Meanwhile, in January 1989, the Soviet Government had formed a Special Administration Committee of the Council of Ministers to preside over Nagornyi Karabakh, although the enclave remained under formal Azerbaijani jurisdiction.

Throughout 1989 unrest continued both in Armenia and within Nagornyi Karabakh, but there were other significant political developments within the republic. *Glasnost* allowed a much fuller examination of Armenian history and culture, and several unofficial groups, concerned with both cultural and political issues, were formed. In May the *yerakuyn*, the national flag of independent Armenia, was flown again, and 28 May, the anniversary of the establishment of independent Armenia, was declared a national day. However, internal politics continued to be dominated by events in Nagornyi Karabakh. In September Azerbaijan implemented an economic blockade against Armenia, seriously affecting the reconstruction programme required after the 1988 earthquake. In November 1989 the Special Administration Committee was disbanded, and Azerbaijan resumed control over Nagornyi Karabakh. This prompted the Armenian Supreme Soviet to declare the enclave part of a 'unified Armenian Republic'. In January 1990 this declaration was declared unconstitutional by the USSR's Supreme Soviet. The Armenian Supreme Soviet responded by granting itself the power to veto any legislation approved by the central authorities.

The increasing disillusionment among Armenians with the Soviet Government was apparently responsible for the low level of participation in the elections to the Armenian Supreme Soviet, which took place in May–July 1990. No party achieved an overall majority, but the Armenian Pan-National Movement (APNM), the successor to the Karabakh Committee, was the largest single party, with some 35% of the seats in the legislature. Supported by other non-communist groups, Levon Ter-Petrossian, a leader of the APNM, defeated Vladimir Movsisian, the First Secretary of the CPA, in elections to the chairmanship of the Supreme Soviet. Vazgen Manukian, also a leader of the APNM, was appointed Prime Minister. On 23 August the legislature adopted a declaration of sovereignty, including a claim to the right to maintain armed forces and a demand for international recognition that the Turkish massacres of Armenians in 1915 constituted genocide. The Armenian SSR was renamed the Republic of Armenia. The new Government began to establish political and commercial links with the Armenian diaspora, and several prominent exiles returned to the republic. In late November 1990 the CPA, after heated debate, voted to become an independent organization within the Communist Party of the Soviet Union (CPSU).

The Armenian Government refused to enter into the negotiations between Soviet republics on a new treaty of union, which took place in late 1990 and early 1991, and officially boycotted the referendum on the renewal of the USSR, which was held in March 1991 in nine of the other republics. Instead, the legislature decided to conduct a referendum on Armenian secession from the USSR, to be held in September. Initially, it was planned that the referendum would be conducted within the provisions of the Soviet law on secession, adopted in April by the all-Union Supreme Soviet. This entailed a transitional period of at least five years before full independence could be achieved.

In late April 1991 there was an escalation of tension in the Nagornyi Karabakh region. The Armenian Government continued to deny any direct involvement in the violence, claiming that the attacks were outside its control, being organized by units of the ethnic Armenian 'Nagornyi Karabakh self-defence forces'. However, Azerbaijan countered that Armenia was, in fact, playing an aggressive role in the conflict, making reference to 'Armenian expeditionary forces'. In a further complication, Armenia suggested that the Soviet leadership was supporting Azerbaijan, following the latter's agreement to sign the new union treaty, and punishing Armenia for its moves towards independence, for its refusal to take part in discussions on the union treaty and for its nationalization of CPA property.

The moderate policies of the new APNM-led Government, especially in developing relations with Turkey, attracted criticism from more extreme nationalist groups, notably the Union for National Self-Determination (UNS), which continued to seek the recovery of lands lost to Turkey after the First World War. The CPA attacked the Government for its willingness to promote relations with Turkey, as did the Armenian Revolutionary Federation (ARF, or Dashnaktsutyun, which had formed the Government of independent Armenia during 1918–20). The CPA also strongly opposed the idea of secession, while the ARF advocated a more gradual process towards independence. The UNS campaigned for immediate secession, which was in breach of the constitutional procedure.

The attempted coup in Moscow, and subsequent events of August 1991, forced the Government to accelerate the moves towards secession, and provided further support for those advocating complete independence for Armenia. The referendum on independence took place, as scheduled, on 21 September. According to official returns, 94.4% of the electorate took part, and 99.3% of voters supported Armenia's becoming 'an independent, democratic state outside the Union'. On 23 September, instead of conforming to the Soviet law on secession, the Supreme Soviet declared Armenia to be thenceforth a fully independent state. Meanwhile, in early September, a congress of the CPA voted to dissolve the party.

The independence declaration was followed, on 16 October 1991, by elections to the post of President of the Republic. Six candidates participated in the poll, but it was won overwhelmingly by the incumbent, Ter-Petrossian (with some 87% of the total votes). The President continued to demand international recognition of Armenia, but on 18 October, with the leaders of seven other Soviet republics, he signed a treaty to establish an economic community, stressing, however, that it did not encroach on Armenia's political independence, and refusing to sign a new treaty on political union. The Armenian leadership did, nevertheless, join the Commonwealth of Independent States (CIS, see p. 150), and signed the founding Alma-Ata Declaration, on 21 December. In early 1992 Armenia was admitted to the Conference on Security and Co-operation in Europe (CSCE, which was renamed the Organization for Security and Co-operation in Europe—OSCE—in December 1994, see p. 237) and the UN.

Economic conditions in Armenia deteriorated alarmingly during 1992, and there were widespread shortages of foodstuffs and fuel. The situation was exacerbated not only by the continuing conflict in Nagornyi Karabakh (see below), but also by the fighting in neighbouring Georgia (impeding supplies to Armenia), and the ongoing economic blockade by Azerbaijan (and its ally, Turkey). Compounding the economic crisis was the enormous influx of refugees from Nagornyi Karabakh and Azerbaijan. There were also growing signs of public dissatisfaction with the Ter-Petrossian administration, and in mid-August mass rallies were staged in Yerevan to demand the President's resignation. In the same month, however, a proposal to hold a referendum to decide the President's future was rejected during an emergency session of the legislature.

In February 1993 there were further large-scale rallies in Yerevan, at which demonstrators protested at the continuing energy crisis and reiterated demands for Ter-Petrossian to resign. Earlier in the month Ter-Petrossian had dismissed the Prime Minister, Khosrov Arutyunian, following disagreements over economic and social policy. A new Council of Ministers was subsequently announced; it was headed by Hrant Bagratian, who was widely known as an economic reformist.

Armenia's economic crisis deteriorated further during 1993. In 1993/94 Armenians endured their third successive winter without heating or lighting for long periods. Popular resentment against Ter-Petrossian's leadership increased, and hundreds of thousands of Armenians were reported to have emigrated, owing to the level of economic hardship. In the latter half of 1994 thousands of people participated in anti-Government protests and rallies, which were organized at regular intervals by the Union of Civic Accord (UCA), an association of opposition groups. Within the legislature—now known as the Supreme Council—opposition deputies were vocal in criticizing APNM-supported proposals for the new Constitution (under discussion since late 1992), which envisaged extensive presidential powers and a restricted role for the legislature.

The assassination in December 1994 of a former mayor of Yerevan prompted the Government to effect a number of measures aimed at eliminating terrorism. By far the most radical of these was the suspension in late December of the leading opposition party, the ARF. The party was officially charged with having engaged in 'terrorist activities, political murders and drugs-trafficking'. Anti-Government forces condemned these measures and monthly rallies were organized by the UCA in early 1995 in protest at official harassment of opposition activists.

Armenia's first post-Soviet legislative elections were held in July 1995. Thirteen parties and organizations contested the 190 seats of the new National Assembly under a mixed system of voting (150 seats to be filled by majority vote and the remaining 40 by proportional representation on the basis of party lists). Nine parties, including the ARF, were barred from participation. The Republican bloc (an alliance of six groups, led by the APNM) won an overwhelming majority of the seats in the Assembly (119). Eight seats were won by the Shamiram Women's Party, while the revived CPA achieved seven. The UNS took three seats and the ARF, despite the official ban, succeeded in winning one seat. Forty-five independent candidates won representation in the Assembly. Some irregularities were reported by OSCE observers, and opposition parties contested the authenticity of the election results. In late July President Ter-Petrossian appointed the new Government, in which Hrant Bagratian remained as Prime Minister. A referendum on the new Armenian Constitution was held simultaneously with the general election. Of the 56% of the electorate who participated in the plebiscite, some 68% voted in favour of the Constitution, which granted wide-ranging executive authority to the President. Under the existing electoral law, the National Assembly comprised 190 deputies; however, the new Constitution provided for an Assembly of 131 deputies (effective from the next general election, which was due to be held in 1999).

The presidential election was held on 22 September 1996. Ter-Petrossian was the candidate of the Republican bloc, while five opposition parties united to support Vazgen Manukian, the Chairman of the National Democratic Union (NDU). Preliminary results indicated that Ter-Petrossian had been re-elected; however, the opposition alleged that widespread electoral malpractice had been perpetrated, and several thousand opposition supporters staged protest rallies in Yerevan, demanding the President's resignation. International observers reported that there had been serious irregularities in the electoral proceedings, which cast doubt on the validity of the result. On 25 September supporters of Manukian stormed the National Assembly building, injuring, among others, the Chairman and his deputy. A temporary ban on rallies was imposed, and large numbers of opposition supporters, including parliamentary deputies, were arrested. According to the final election results, Ter-Petrossian received 51.8% of votes cast, while Manukian secured 41.3% (although he achieved a significantly higher percentage than Ter-Petrossian in Yerevan). Despite the decision in November by the Constitutional Court to reject an appeal by Manukian and another unsuccessful presidential candidate that the election results be annulled and that new elections be held, opposition parties maintained their demand for fresh elections. A number of them had also boycotted the elections to the new bodies of local government, established by the Constitution in 1995, which were held earlier in that month. The resignation of Bagratian as Prime Minister, allegedly in response to opposition to his programme of economic reforms, was announced in November 1996; he was replaced by Armen Sarkissian. The latter resigned in March 1997 on grounds of ill health, and was replaced by Robert Kocharian, hitherto the President of Nagornyi Karabakh, in what was regarded as an attempt by Ter-Petrossian to reduce the pressure from opposition parties to hold fresh presidential elections. Disagreements within the ruling APNM, which had developed since the re-election of Ter-Petrossian in September 1996, became apparent in mid-1997 during legislative discussions on compulsory military conscription and during elections to the chairmanship of the party.

Following the unexpected resignation of Ter-Petrossian on 3 February 1998, as a result of government disputes over his support of the OSCE plan for a peaceful, step-by-step settlement in Nagornyi Karabakh (see below), a presidential election was held on 16 March. The acting President and incumbent Prime Minister, Robert Kocharian, achieved the greatest number of votes, but did not gain an overall majority. In the requisite second ballot, which was consequently conducted on 30 March, Kocharian was victorious over the former Soviet-era CPA leader, Karen Demirchian, winning 59.5% of the votes. The results were declared valid despite some OSCE-reported electoral irregularities, and Kocharian was inaugurated as President on 9 April. On the following day Kocharian appointed Armen Darbinian, the erstwhile Minister of Finance and the Economy, as Prime Minister to head a new Government.

In early May 1998 Kocharian relegalized the ARF, and appointed two more members of the party, including its leader, Vahan Hovhanissian, to positions in the Government (one member of the ARF had been included in the Government on its appointment the previous month). Later in May the President announced the formation of a commission whose task it was to formulate constitutional amendments. In March 1999 six amendments were submitted to President Kocharian by the commission for consideration (including proposals to reduce the size of the National Assembly by a further 30 deputies), and were approved by him. If passed by the National Assembly, the proposed amendments were to be subject to a national referendum. Meanwhile, in early July 1998 it was announced that, as part of a major reform to the judicial and legal system (which was due to be implemented in January 1999), the Supreme Court was to be disbanded and replaced by a Court of Cassation.

The controversial new law, regarding electoral procedure, which had been approved by the National Assembly in November 1998 (despite fierce opposition from a number of deputies), providing for a 131-member legislature composed of 75 deputies elected by majority vote through single-mandate constitutencies and the remaining 56 chosen under a system of proportional representation on the basis of party lists, was fully adopted in February 1999; shortly afterwards it was announced that legislative elections were to be held on 30 May. In April the Republican Party of Armenia (RPA) and the People's Party of Armenia (PPA) formed an electoral alliance, the Unity bloc (Miasnutiun), which was to campaign as a single party. The Unity bloc proved highly successful in the elections, winning a total of 55 seats in the 131-seat National Assembly. The CPA secured 11 seats and the ARF obtained nine, while the Law and Unity bloc, the Law-governed Country Party and the NDU won six seats each; the APNM, the Armenian Democratic Party, the Mission Party and the National Concord Party each secured one seat, and independents accounted for the remaining 32. By-elections were called in two constituencies where the results had been annulled; otherwise, the results were declared valid by the Central Electoral Commission, despite the disenfranchisement of many citizens owing to inaccuracies in the electoral register. Independents won the two remaining seats in the by-elections, which were held in July. Meanwhile in early June Darbinian was replaced as Prime Minister by Vazgen Sarkissian, the unofficial leader of the RPA and hitherto Minister of Defence; Darbinian was demoted to the post of Minister of the Economy. At the first session of the new National Assembly, which was held several days later, Karen Demirchian, a former communist leader but now head of the PPA, was elected Chairman of the legislature. Later in June a government reorganization was conducted, including the division of a number of ministries.

In January 1999 the Prosecutor-General petitioned the National Assembly for permission to arrest the Chairman of the PNM and former Minister of the Interior, Vano Siradeghian, thereby removing his parliamentary immunity, for his alleged participation in a number of political murders in the mid-1990s. The petition was rejected, and Siradeghian left the country, reportedly for medical treatment, shortly afterwards. In February, however, the legislature, under threat of dissolution, endorsed the petition, and on his return to Armenia in May, Siradeghian (who had been re-elected Chairman of the PNM *in absentia*) was placed under arrest; his trial commenced in Yerevan in January 2000.

Politically-motivated attacks and murders were rife in Armenia during late 1998 and 1999. One of the most serious incidents occurred in February 1999, when the Deputy Minister of the Interior and National Security and commander of Armenia's internal troops, Maj.-Gen. Artsrun Makarian, was found shot dead. The victim's bodyguards were subsequently charged with the murder, and there was some speculation that Makarian had been killed to prevent him from giving evidence against Siradeghian.

On 27 October 1999 Armenia was thrown into political turmoil when five gunmen, led by ardent nationalist Nairi Unanian, besieged the National Assembly debating chamber. Eight people were killed during the attack, including Prime Minister Sarkissian, the Chairman of the legislature, Karen Demirchian, and his two deputies, and the Minister for Urgent Issues, Leonard Petrossian. The gunmen (who claimed no political affiliation) held some 50 hostages for several hours; their stated aim was to seek revenge against the 'corrupt political elite'. Having voluntarily surrendered, following overnight negotiations with President Kocharian, the assailants were subsequently charged with terrorist offences and with deliberate murder (with aggravating circumstances). In the aftermath of the attack, the Minister of the Interior and the Minister of National Security both tendered their resignations (which were later accepted, following the appointment of a new Prime Minister). At the beginning of November the National Assembly held an extraordinary sitting, at which Armen Khachatrian, who was a member of the PPA, was elected as Chairman of the legislature. On the following day President Kocharian appointed Aram Sarkissian, the younger brother of Vazgen and a political novice, as the new Prime Minister, on the recommendation of members of the Unity bloc. A number of new ministers were appointed in mid-November; at the same time the post of Minister for Urgent Issues was abolished.

The proclamation of Armenia's independence in September 1991 led to an escalation of hostilities in the disputed enclave of Nagornyi Karabakh. In that month the territory declared itself an independent republic, and the violence intensified following the dissolution of the USSR in December. In January 1992 the President of Azerbaijan, Ayaz Mutalibov, placed the region under direct presidential rule; in the same month Azerbaijani forces surrounded and attacked Stepanakert, the capital of Nagornyi Karabakh, while the Armenians laid siege to Shusha, a town with a mainly Azerbaijani population. In May the Nagornyi Karabakh self-defence forces (which the Armenian Government continued to claim to be operating without its military support) captured Shusha, thereby gaining complete control of the enclave and ending the bombardment of Stepanakert. With the capture of the strategically-important Lachin valley, the Armenian militia then succeeded in opening a 'corridor' inside Azerbaijan, linking Nagornyi Karabakh with Armenia proper.

In June 1992 Azerbaijani forces launched a sustained counter-offensive in Nagornyi Karabakh, recapturing villages both inside and around the enclave, and expelling several thousand inhabitants, thus exacerbating the already urgent refugee crisis. In early August Azerbaijani forces resumed the bombardment of Stepanakert. In response to the escalation of attacks and ensuing military gains by Azeri forces, the Nagornyi Karabakh legislature declared a state of martial law, and a state defence committee, in close alignment with the Ter-Petrossian administration, replaced the enclave's government.

In early 1993 the military situation in Nagornyi Karabakh was reversed, as Armenian forces undertook a series of successful offensives, regaining territory that they had lost in 1992 and also taking control of large areas of Azerbaijan surrounding the enclave. With the capture of the Kelbajar district of Azerbaijan in April 1993, the Armenians succeeded in creating a second 'corridor' linking the enclave with Armenia and effectively securing the whole swath of Azerbaijani territory extending south to the Lachin 'corridor'. Many thousands of Azeris fled or were expelled from their homes. The Armenian position was only strengthened by the growing political turmoil in Azerbaijan in mid-1993 (q.v.), and by late June Armenian forces had secured full control of Nagornyi Karabakh.

The Armenian seizure of Azerbaijani territory prompted widespread international condemnation, particularly by neighbouring Turkey and Iran, the latter fearing a massive influx of refugees from south-western Azerbaijan. Resolutions adopted by the UN Security Council, demanding the withdrawal of Armenian forces from Azerbaijan, went unheeded; by late August 1993 as much as 20% of Azerbaijan's total territory was reported to have been captured by the Nagornyi Karabakh Armenian forces. In late October the Turkish leadership stated that no normalization of relations between Turkey and Armenia could occur until Armenian aggression in Azerbaijan had ceased. Nevertheless, hostilities reintensified: yet more Azerbaijani territory came under the control of the Armenians, who had extended their operations as far south as the Azerbaijan-Iran border. Azeri forces launched a major new counter-offensive in December, recapturing some of the territory that they had lost to the Armenians during the year. A series of cease-fire agreements was reached in the first half of 1994, but none was lasting. In February it was reported that as many as 18,000 people had been killed since 1988, with a further 25,000 wounded. The number of displaced Azeris was now believed to have exceeded 1m.

However, in early May 1994, following protracted mediation by the CSCE and Russia, a new cease-fire agreement was signed by the Ministers of Defence of Armenia and Azerbaijan and representatives of Nagornyi Karabakh. Although some violations of the cease-fire were subsequently reported, the agreement was formalized in late July. Ter-Petrossian held talks with the President of Azerbaijan, Heydar Aliyev, in Moscow in early September. Although agreement was reached on some key provisions of a future peace treaty, Aliyev stated that his willingness to negotiate such an accord depended on the unconditional withdrawal of Armenian forces from occupied Azerbaijani territory. Negotiations were held at regular intervals throughout 1995 under the aegis of the 'Minsk Group' of the OSCE. However, progress towards reaching a political settlement was hampered by Azerbaijan's demand for the return of Lachin and Shusha regions, as well as by its apparent unwillingness to recognize the Nagornyi Karabakh leadership as an equal party in the negotiations. Nevertheless, the cease-fire continued to be observed, with only sporadic violations reported, and in May the three sides carried out a large-scale exchange of prisoners of war. Direct discussions between Armenia and Azerbaijan, which were held in conjunction with the OSCE negotiations, were initiated in December.

Ter-Petrossian and Aliyev met, together with President Shevardnadze of Georgia, in April 1996 in Luxembourg, where they signed an agreement on partnership and co-operation with the European Union (EU, see p. 172), and affirmed their commitment to the 1994 cease-fire. A further exchange of prisoners of war occurred in May 1996. Little progress was made in the negotiations in the following months, and elections to the post of President of Nagornyi Karabakh, held in November, were condemned by Azerbaijan and criticized by the 'Minsk Group' as a hindrance to the peace process. Robert Kocharian, the incumbent President, was re-elected with some 86% of the vote. He subsequently appointed Leonard Petrossian as Prime Minister.

In December 1996 Ter-Petrossian and Aliyev attended an OSCE summit meeting in Lisbon, Portugal. Following demands by Azerbaijan, the OSCE Chairman issued a statement recommending three principles that would form the basis of a future political settlement in the enclave: the territorial integrity of Armenia and Azerbaijan; the legal status of Nagornyi Karabakh, which would be granted broad autonomy within Azerbaijan; and security guarantees for the population of Nagornyi Karabakh. Armenia, however, refused to accept the terms of the statement.

Relations between the two countries deteriorated in early 1997, with mutual accusations of the stockpiling of weapons in preparation for the renewal of military conflict in Nagornyi Karabakh. In April Armenia temporarily withdrew from the direct negotiations that were being held in conjunction with the OSCE talks, and this was followed by a series of clashes on the Armenian-Azerbaijani border, which left many people killed and wounded. Negotiations under the auspices of the OSCE continued, however, and it was reported in late May that new proposals for a settlement to the conflict had been offered to the participants. Fresh elections to the post of President of Nagornyi Karabakh in early September, which were called following the appointment of Kocharian as Prime Minister of Armenia, were won by Arkadyi Gukasian, with some 90% of the vote, but were criticized by the international community. Gukasian reportedly rejected the OSCE peace settlement on the grounds that the proposals presupposed Azerbaijan's sovereignty over the enclave. However, in late September it was reported that Armenia had accepted, in principle, the OSCE's plan for a stage-by-stage settlement of the conflict, which entailed the withdrawal of Armenian forces from six districts around Nagornyi Karabakh, to be followed by a decision on the status of the Shusha and Lachin 'corridors', and on the status of Nagornyi Karabakh itself. A statement by President Ter-Petrossian that Nagornyi Karabakh could neither hope to gain full independence, nor be united with Armenia, was severely condemned by opposition parties, and appeared to indicate a significant change in policy on the part of the President. Ter-Petrossian's cautious and moderate approach to the Nagornyi Karabakh crisis provoked much government disapproval and led to the President's resignation in early February 1998. His replacement, Kocharian, who was born in Nagornyi Karabakh, was expected to adopt a more belligerent and nationalistic stance towards resolving the situation in the disputed enclave. In June Leonard Petrossian resigned as Prime Minister of Nagornyi Karabakh, following a rift with his Minister of Defence; the erstwhile Deputy Prime Minister, Zhirayr Pogossian, replaced him in the premiership and a government reorganization was carried out. In late November the Armenian Government announced that, despite some reservations, it officially accepted the latest proposals put forward by the 'Minsk Group' regarding a settlement of the conflict in Nagornyi Karabakh, which were based on the principle of a 'common state'; Azerbaijan, however, rejected the proposals. Minor cease-fire violations were committed by both sides during late 1998. Following an escalation in hostilities in mid-1999, both sides made mutual accusations that the other was attempting to destroy the 1994 cease-fire agreement. Despite a series of meetings between Presidents Kocharian and Aliyev in the second half of 1999, no substantive progress was made regarding the conflict. Meanwhile, in June President Gukasian dismissed Prime Minister Pogossian and the Government of Nagornyi Karabakh on the grounds of their failure to resolve the enclave's economic problems. At the end of that month Anashavan Danielian was appointed to head a new administration. In July Pogossian was arrested and charged with illegally possessing arms and ammunition, and with losing a state document. He was released from detention a few days later, but was not allowed to leave Nagornyi Karabakh; the former Prime Minister was expected to be put on trial in the near future.

Armenia's relations with Russia in 1997 focused on the ratification by the Armenian legislature in April of a treaty allowing Russia to maintain military bases in Armenia for a period of 25 years, and on the signing of a treaty of 'friendship, co-operation and mutual understanding' in August, during a state visit by Ter-Petrossian to Moscow. Armenia's close diplomatic and military links with Russia during the late 1990s (including reports of large supplies of Russian armaments to Armenia) were met with disapproval and suspicion on the part of the Azerbaijani Government. Armenia's relations with Georgia were furthered by the visit of the Georgian President, Eduard Shevardnadze, in May 1997, during which several co-operation agreements were signed. Relations were somewhat strained during late 1998 and 1999, owing to the sporadic nature of Armenia's supply of electricity to Georgia (initiated only in September 1998), due to the latter's non-payment of bills. In September 1999, however, the two countries signed a declaration on the basic principles of co-operation.

### Government

Under the Constitution of 1995, the President of the Republic is Head of State and Supreme Commander-in-Chief of the armed forces, but also holds broad executive powers. The President is directly elected for a term of five years (and for no more than two consecutive terms of office). The President appoints the Prime Minister and, on the latter's recommendation, the members of the Government. Legislative power is vested in the 131-member National Assembly, which is elected for a four-year term by universal adult suffrage. For administrative purposes, Armenia is divided into 11 regions (*marz*), including the capital, Yerevan. The regions are subdivided into communities (*hamaynk*).

### Defence

Following the dissolution of the USSR in December 1991, Armenia became a member of the Commonwealth of Independent States and its collective security system. The country also began to establish its own armed forces (estimated to number some 53,400 in August 1999). Military service is compulsory and lasts for 18 months. Some mobilization of reserves by conscription was reported. There is also a paramilitary force of an estimated 1,000, attached to the Ministry of National Security. In August 1999 there were approximately 3,100 Russian troops stationed on Armenian territory. The budget for 1999 allocated an estimated US $75m. to defence. In October 1994 Armenia joined NATO's 'Partnership for Peace' programme of military co-operation (see p. 228).

### Economic Affairs

In 1997, according to estimates by the World Bank, Armenia's gross national product (GNP), measured at average 1995–97 prices, was US $2,112m., equivalent to $560 per head. During 1990–97, it was estimated, GNP per head declined at an average annual rate of 10.7% in real terms, while the population increased at an average rate of 0.9% per year. According to preliminary estimates, GNP in 1998 was about $1,800m. ($480 per head). During 1990–97, it was estimated, Armenia's gross domestic product (GDP) decreased, in real terms, by an average of 10.3% annually. However, GDP increased by 5.8% in 1996, by 3.1% in 1997 and by 7.2% in 1998. GDP growth of 4.0% was forecast for 1999.

According to government figures, agriculture and forestry contributed 33.2% of GDP in 1998 and employed 40.8% of the working population in 1996. The FAO estimated the proportion of the working population employed in agriculture at 13.6% in 1998. The principal crops are potatoes and other vegetables, cereals and fruit. By late 1996 privatization of arable land was near to completion. Private farms accounted for some 98% of agricultural production in 1998. During 1990–97, according to estimates by the World Bank, agricultural GDP increased, in real terms, at an average annual rate of 0.2%. The GDP of the sector increased by 4.0% in 1995 and by 1.7% in 1996.

According to government figures, in 1998 industry (including mining, manufacturing, construction and power) contributed 32.5% of GDP. In 1996 the sector employed 22.5% of the working population. According to the World Bank, industrial GDP increased at an average annual rate of 5.1% during 1980–90. However, during 1990–97 industrial GDP declined by an average of 18.1% annually. The GDP of the sector increased by 1.0% in 1995 and by 5.4% in 1996. According to government figures, industrial GDP grew by 2.5% in 1998, compared with 1997.

Armenia's mining sector has not yet been extensively developed. Copper, molybdenum, gold, silver and iron are extracted on a small scale, and there are reserves of lead and zinc. There are also substantial, although largely unexploited, reserves of mineral salt, calcium oxide and carbon. Production of gold decreased significantly in the 1990s, but the Government hoped to encourage a recovery in the industry, following the conclusion in 1996 of an agreement with a US company to develop new extraction facilities, which went into production in 1998.

In 1997, according to the World Bank, the manufacturing sector provided 25% of Armenia's GDP. In 1995 the principal branches of manufacturing, measured by gross value of output, were food-processing and beverages (accounting for 40.5% of the total), machinery and metal products (13.0%), textiles and clothing (8.0%), chemicals (5.2%), and non-metallic mineral products (5.5%). Shortages of energy and raw materials in the mid-1990s resulted in a change of emphasis in industrial production, with the production of textiles and jewellery, for example, increasing, while traditional industries declined. During 1990–97 the GDP of the manufacturing sector declined at an average annual rate of 13.1%.

Armenia is heavily dependent on imported energy. The two principal suppliers of energy products are Russia (petroleum and derivatives) and Turkmenistan (natural gas). It is, however, thought probable that Armenia has significant reserves of petroleum and natural gas. Hydroelectricity was the only significant domestic source of energy in 1994, providing 63.1% of Armenia's electricity supply. The country's sole nuclear power station, at Medzamor, was closed following the earthquake of 1988. However, in late 1995, in view of Armenia's worsening energy crisis, the station's second generating unit resumed operations, following restoration work. By 1995, with the recommissioning of the Medzamor power station, hydroelectricity provided only 35% of the country's electricity supply, and nuclear power contributed 5.5%. The nuclear share increased to 40.5% in the first six months of 1999. In 1996 proposals were made for the construction of a new nuclear power plant, scheduled for completion in 2010. By July 1999 Armenia had a surplus of electricity, some of which was exported to Georgia. In September 1999 Armenia signed an agreement with the EU Department for Relations with the CIS on shutting down the Medzamor power station by 2004. The agreement was, however, dependent on the construction of adequate alternative energy facilities. Imports of energy products comprised 31.3% of the value of merchandise imports in 1995.

The services sector contributed an estimated 34.3% of GDP in 1998, and engaged 36.7% of the employed labour force in 1996. During 1980–90 the GDP of the sector increased by an annual average of 4.6%. However, services GDP declined by an average of 10.8% annually during 1990–97. The GDP of the sector increased by 23.2% in 1995 and by 13.6% in 1996. According to official sources, growth of sectoral GDP was 8.5% in 1998, compared with 1997.

In 1998 Armenia recorded a visible trade deficit of US $577.5m., while the deficit on the current account of the balance of payments was $390.3m. In 1998 the principal source of imports, according to official statistics, was Russia, which provided 20.4% of the total; other main sources were the USA, Belgium and the United Kingdom. In that year the major market for exports was Russia. Other important purchasers were Turkmenistan, the USA, Belgium and Iran. The principal exports in 1995 were pearls, precious and semi-precious stones, precious metals, imitation jewellery and coin; machinery and electrical equipment; and base metals. The principal imports in that year were mineral products, vegetable products, and live animals and animal products.

In 1998, according to official sources, there was a budgetary deficit of 36,000m. drams (equivalent to 3.8% of GDP). At the end of 1997 Armenia's total external debt was US $665.5m., of which $511.5m. was long-term public debt. In that year the cost of debt-servicing was equivalent to 5.8% of the value of exports of goods and services. At the end of 1998 external debt amounted to $828m. (equivalent to 43.9% of GDP). The average annual rate of inflation was 176.0% in 1995, 18.7% in 1996, 13.9% in 1997 and 8.7% in 1998. In the first six months of 1999, however, consumer prices decreased by 2.4%. At 1 April 1999 some 159,721 people were officially registered as unemployed, giving an unemployment rate of 10.5%.

Armenia is a member of the IMF, the World Bank and the European Bank for Reconstruction and Development (EBRD, see p. 168). It is also a member of the Black Sea Economic Co-operation organization (BSEC, see p. 135), and is pursuing membership of the World Trade Organization (WTO, see p. 274).

The collapse of the Soviet central planning system and internal trading structures exacerbated an already critical economic situation in Armenia. The decline was compounded by the severe effects of the earthquake in 1988 and of the conflict in Nagornyi Karabakh, which resulted in a massive influx of refugees from the enclave and from Azerbaijan. The economic blockade of Armenia by Azerbaijan and, subsequently, Turkey, as well as the civil war in Georgia, resulted in widespread shortages of food and fuel, and a concomitant decline in industrial production, owing to a lack of essential raw materials. A wide-ranging programme of economic reforms was initiated in the early 1990s, which included price liberalization, the promotion of privatization and a rationalization of the taxation system. By 1994 the first signs of economic recovery were observed, with growth in GDP and a decrease in the rate of inflation. The Government expanded its reform programme in the mid-1990s, to include a review of public-sector administration and expenditure, and reform of the energy sector. New agreements, which provided for the supply to Armenia of nuclear fuel and electricity, were concluded with Russia and Iran, respectively, in 1997, and a further agreement was reached with a Russian company, Gazprom, and an international energy corporation concerning deliveries of natural gas and the upgrading of Armenia's gas infrastructure. The privatization programme was well advanced by late 1998. In July 1999, however, the Minister of Finance announced that the Armenian economy was in recession, having been affected by the ongoing Russian economic crisis to a much greater extent than had been anticipated. In addition, problems had been compounded by a prevailing climate of political uncertainty associated with the legislative elections in May. The IMF and the World Bank continued to support Armenia, regularly disbursing loans and credits during the latter half of 1999. In September an agreement was reached with the World Bank that preferential credits worth US $238m. would be allocated to Armenia in 2000–2003, which were to be used for medium-term economic programmes. The Government's key objectives were to ensure price stability, enhance Armenia's external competitiveness, reform the education and health systems, extend the restructuring of the energy and financial sectors, and accelerate the privatization process.

### Social Welfare

Much of Armenia's expenditure on health and welfare services during the last decade has been directed towards the victims of the 1988 earthquake, which caused an estimated 25,000 deaths and 8,500m. roubles' worth of damage. However, the collapse of the USSR and the escalation of the conflict in Nagornyi Karabakh encouraged a large number of refugees to flee to Armenia, creating new demands of social expenditure at a time of restricted government revenue. Furthermore, the adaptation to a market economy and the economic blockade on the country also exacerbated the situation. In 1992 it was estimated that about one-seventh of the population was 'in need' (excluding refugees—estimated at some 350,000). The Government sought to control social expenditure by targeting resources, as well as encouraging private and voluntary involvement.

A Pension Fund was created in 1991, and was subsequently merged with the Employment Fund, to create the Pension and Employment Fund, which, in 1992, was the only extrabudgetary fund remaining in Armenia. In September 1997 607,111 people were in receipt of state pensions, of which 71.7% were provided on account of old age. In 1993 there was one physician for every 261 people. In 1995 there were 90 hospital beds per 10,000 inhabitants. Current expenditure on health by all levels of government in 1993 was 32,744m. roubles.

### Education

Education is compulsory for nine years, to be undertaken between the ages of six and 17 years. Until the early 1990s the general education system conformed to that of the centralized Soviet system, but extensive changes were then introduced, with greater emphasis placed on Armenian history and culture. Primary education usually begins at seven years of age and lasts for four years. Secondary education, beginning at 11 years of age, comprises a first cycle of four years and a second of two years. In 1996 total enrolment at primary and secondary schools was equivalent to 87% of the school-age population. Primary enrolment in that year was equivalent to 86% of children in the relevant age-group, while the comparable ratio for secondary enrolment was 88%. Most instruction in higher institutions is in Armenian, although Russian is widely taught as a second language. In addition to Yerevan State University and the State Engineering University, higher education is provided at 13 institutes of higher education, with a total enrolment, in the 1996/97 academic year, of 35,517 students. Current expenditure on education by all levels of government in 1996 was 3,418.6m. drams. In 1989, according to census results, the rate of adult illiteracy in Armenia was 1.2% (males 0.6%; females 1.9%).

### Public Holidays

**2000:** 1–2 January (New Year), 6 January (Christmas), 22–23 April (Easter), 24 April (Armenian Genocide Commemoration Day), 9 May (Victory Day), 28 May (Declaration of the First Armenian Republic Day), 21 September (Independence Day), 7 December (Day of Remembrance of the 1988 Earthquake), 31 December (New Year's Eve).

**2001:** 1–2 January (New Year), 6 January (Christmas), 14–15 April (Easter), 24 April (Armenian Genocide Commemoration Day), 9 May (Victory Day), 28 May (Declaration of the First Armenian Republic Day), 21 September (Independence Day), 7 December (Day of Remembrance of the 1988 Earthquake), 31 December (New Year's Eve).

### Weights and Measures

The metric system is in force.

# Statistical Survey

Principal sources: IMF, *Armenia, Economic Review, Recent Economic Developments* and *International Financial Statistics: Supplement on Countries of the Former Soviet Union*; World Bank, *Statistical Handbook: States of the Former USSR* and *World Tables.*

## Area and Population

**AREA, POPULATION AND DENSITY**

| | |
|---|---|
| Area (sq km) | 29,800* |
| Population (census results)† | |
| 17 January 1979 | 3,037,259 |
| 12 January 1989 | |
| Males | 1,619,308 |
| Females | 1,685,468 |
| Total | 3,304,776 |
| Population (official estimates at 1 January) | |
| 1995 | 3,754,300 |
| 1996 | 3,766,400 |
| 1997 | 3,782,400 |
| Density (per sq km) at 1 January 1997 | 126.9 |

* 11,500 sq miles.

† Figures refer to *de jure* population. The *de facto* total at the 1989 census was 3,287,677.

**POPULATION BY NATIONALITY**
(permanent inhabitants, 1989 census)

| | % |
|---|---|
| Armenian | 93.3 |
| Azerbaijani | 2.6 |
| Kurdish | 1.7 |
| Russian | 1.5 |
| Others | 0.9 |
| **Total** | **100.0** |

**PRINCIPAL TOWNS**
(estimated population at 1 July 1990)

Yerevan (capital) 1,254,400; Gyumri (formerly Leninakan) 206,600; Vanadzor (formerly Kirovakan) 170,200.

Source: UN, *Demographic Yearbook.*

**BIRTHS, MARRIAGES AND DEATHS**

| | Registered live births | | Registered marriages | | Registered deaths | |
|---|---|---|---|---|---|---|
| | Number | Rate (per 1,000) | Number | Rate (per 1,000) | Number | Rate (per 1,000) |
| 1988 | 74,707 | 22.1 | 26,581 | 7.9 | 35,567 | 10.5 |
| 1989 | 75,250 | 21.6 | 27,257 | 7.8 | 20,853 | 6.0 |
| 1990 | 79,882 | 22.5 | 28,233 | 8.0 | 21,993 | 6.2 |
| 1991 | 77,825 | 21.5 | 28,023 | 7.8 | 23,425 | 6.5 |
| 1992 | 70,581 | 19.1 | 22,955 | 6.2 | 25,824 | 7.0 |
| 1993 | 59,041 | 15.8 | 21,514 | 5.8 | 27,500 | 7.4 |
| 1994 | 51,143 | 13.6 | 17,074 | 4.6 | 24,648 | 6.6 |

**1996:** Live births 48,134; Marriages 14,200 (provisional); Deaths 24,396.

**Expectation of life** (years at birth, 1997): Males 70; Females 77 (Source: World Bank, *World Development Indicators*).

**ECONOMICALLY ACTIVE POPULATION**
(annual averages, '000 persons)

| | 1994 | 1995 | 1996 |
|---|---|---|---|
| Material sphere | 1,077 | 1,071.3 | 1,055.8 |
| Agriculture | 502 | 549.6 | 583.5 |
| Forestry | 2 | 2.3 | 2.5 |
| Industry* | 355 | 302.9 | 255.0 |
| Construction | 97 | 76.0 | 68.0 |
| Transport and communications† | 30 | 26.6 | 24.0 |
| Trade and catering‡ | 64 | 100.0 | 110.2 |
| Other activities | 27 | 13.7 | 12.6 |
| Non-material sphere | 411 | 405.1 | 379.8 |
| Transport and communications† | 25 | 26.6 | 24.0 |
| Public education | 147 | 147.5 | 142.1 |
| Culture and art | 34 | 32.7 | 31.7 |
| Science | 25 | 22.8 | 14.7 |
| Health, physical culture and social welfare | 84 | 85.5 | 81.7 |
| Housing and personal services | 58 | 52.2 | 50.6 |
| General administration | 30 | 29.3 | 28.6 |
| Financing and insurance | 8 | 8.5 | 6.4 |
| **Total employed** | 1,488 | 1,476.4 | 1,435.6 |
| Registered unemployed | 106 | 106.0 | 147.9 |
| **Total labour force** | 1,594 | 1,582.4 | 1,583.5 |

* Comprising manufacturing (except printing and publishing), mining and quarrying, electricity, gas, water, logging and fishing.

† Transport and communications servicing material production are included in activities of the material sphere. Other branches of the sector are considered to be non-material services.

‡ Including material supply and procurement.

# Agriculture

**PRINCIPAL CROPS** ('000 metric tons)

| | 1996 | 1997 | 1998 |
|---|---|---|---|
| Wheat | 212 | 184 | 244 |
| Barley | 105 | 59 | 71 |
| Maize | 4 | 10 | 6 |
| Other cereals | 47 | 25 | 39 |
| Potatoes | 423 | 360 | 425 |
| Pulses | 5 | 5* | 5* |
| Sunflower seed | n.a. | n.a. | 11* |
| Cabbages | 82 | 88† | 87* |
| Tomatoes | 180 | 141 | 145† |
| Cauliflowers | 6† | 4† | 5* |
| Cucumbers and gherkins | 48† | 35† | 28* |
| Onions (dry) | 39 | 32† | 36* |
| Garlic | 15† | 12† | 12* |
| Peas (green) | 8† | 6† | 5* |
| Carrots | 12 | 10† | 11* |
| Other vegetables | 54 | 42 | 65 |
| Watermelons‡ | 61 | 62 | 60 |
| Grapes | 158 | 134 | 106 |
| Apples | 80 | 49 | 56† |
| Pears† | 14 | 10 | 16 |
| Peaches and nectarines† | 22 | 20 | 21 |
| Plums† | 20 | 14 | 14 |
| Apricots† | 21 | 16 | 19 |
| Almonds* | 2 | 2 | 2 |

* FAO estimate(s). † Unofficial figure(s).

‡ Including melons, pumpkins and squash.

Source: FAO, *Production Yearbook*.

**LIVESTOCK** ('000 head, year ending September)

| | 1996 | 1997 | 1998 |
|---|---|---|---|
| Horses* | 11 | 11 | 12 |
| Asses* | 3 | 3 | 3 |
| Cattle | 497 | 510 | 505* |
| Pigs | 79 | 55 | 52* |
| Sheep | 590 | 566† | 550* |
| Goats | 14 | 13† | 12* |

Poultry (million): 3† in 1996; 3* in 1997; 3* in 1998.

* FAO estimate(s). † Unofficial figure.

Source: FAO, *Production Yearbook*.

**LIVESTOCK PRODUCTS** ('000 metric tons)

| | 1996 | 1997 | 1998 |
|---|---|---|---|
| Beef and veal | 33 | 30* | 30† |
| Mutton and lamb | 6 | 6* | 5† |
| Pig meat | 6 | 4* | 3† |
| Poultry meat | 4 | 3† | 3† |
| Cows' milk | 421 | 425 | 455 |
| Sheep's milk | 10 | 10* | 12* |
| Cheese† | 9 | 9 | 9 |
| Hen eggs* | 11 | 11 | 12 |
| Wool: | | | |
| greasy | 1 | 1† | 1† |
| clean | 1 | 1† | 1† |

* Unofficial figure. † FAO estimate(s).

Source: FAO, *Production Yearbook*.

# Fishing

(FAO estimates, metric tons, live weight)

| | 1995 | 1996 | 1997 |
|---|---|---|---|
| Crucian carp | 60 | 50 | 45 |
| Goldfish | 230 | 200 | 180 |
| Other cyprinids | 60 | 50 | 45 |
| Whitefishes | 170 | 140 | 130 |
| **Total catch** | 520 | 440 | 400 |

Source: FAO, *Yearbook of Fishery Statistics*.

# Mining

('000 metric tons)

| | 1994 | 1995 | 1996 |
|---|---|---|---|
| Salt (unrefined) | 47 | 33 | 26 |
| Gypsum (crude) | 35 | 34 | 17 |

Source: UN, *Industrial Commodity Statistics Yearbook*.

# Industry

**SELECTED PRODUCTS** ('000 metric tons, otherwise indicated)

| | 1994 | 1995 | 1996 |
|---|---|---|---|
| Margarine | n.a. | 0.1 | n.a. |
| Wheat flour | 290 | 265 | 156 |
| Ethyl alcohol ('000 hectolitres) | 7 | 2 | 0 |
| Wine ('000 hectolitres) | 227 | 102 | 48 |
| Beer ('000 hectolitres) | 70 | 53 | 29 |
| Mineral water ('000 hectolitres) | 48 | 78 | 119 |
| Soft drinks ('000 hectolitres) | 13 | 12 | 59 |
| Cigarettes (million) | 2,014 | 1,043 | 152 |
| Wool yarn—pure and mixed (metric tons) | 200 | 200 | 200 |
| Cotton yarn—pure and mixed (metric tons) | 400 | 200 | 300 |
| Woven cotton fabrics ('000 metres) | 200 | 100 | 600 |
| Silk fabrics ('000 sq metres) | 653 | 370 | 143 |
| Woven woollen fabrics ('000 sq metres) | 300 | 100 | 200 |
| Carpets ('000 sq metres) | 35 | 29 | 23 |
| Leather footwear ('000 pairs) | 1,612 | 656 | 305 |
| Caustic soda (Sodium hydroxide) | 4 | 4 | 4 |
| Synthetic rubber | 2.1 | 1.5 | 2.8 |
| Non-cellulosic continuous fibres (metric tons) | 200 | 300 | 400 |
| Rubber tyres ('000)* | 104 | 90 | 54 |
| Rubber footwear ('000 pairs) | 205 | 79 | 56 |
| Quicklime | 3 | 3 | 2 |
| Cement | 122 | 228 | 281 |
| Aluminium plates, sheets, strip and foil | 1.1 | 1.4 | 0.4 |
| Domestic washing machines ('000) | n.a. | 1 | n.a. |
| Lorries (number) | 446 | 232 | 114 |
| Bicycles ('000) | 12 | 8 | 7 |
| Watches ('000) | 3 | 1 | 2 |
| Clocks ('000)† | 362 | 392 | 216 |
| Electric energy (million kWh) | 5,658 | 5,561 | n.a. |

* For road motor vehicles.
† Including electric clocks.

Source: UN, *Industrial Commodity Statistics Yearbook*.

**1996:** Electric energy (million kWh) 6,215 (Source: IMF, *Republic of Armenia: Recent Economic Developments*, April 1998).

# Finance

**CURRENCY AND EXCHANGE RATES**

**Monetary Units**

100 louma = 1 dram.

**Sterling, Dollar and Euro Equivalents** (30 September 1999)

£1 sterling = 848.1 drams;
US $1 = 515.1 drams;
€1 = 549.4 drams;
1,000 drams = £1.179 = $1.941 = €1.820.

**Average Exchange Rate** (drams per US $)

1996 414.04
1997 490.85
1998 504.92

Note: The dram was introduced on 22 November 1993, replacing the Russian (formerly Soviet) rouble at a conversion rate of 1 dram = 200 roubles. The initial exchange rate was set at US $1 = 14.3 drams, but by the end of the year the rate was $1 = 75 drams. After the introduction of the dram, Russian currency continued to circulate in Armenia. The rouble had been withdrawn from circulation by March 1994.

**STATE BUDGET** (million drams)*

| Revenue | 1994 | 1995 | 1996 |
|---|---|---|---|
| Tax revenue | 24,431 | 66,457 | 85,051 |
| Value-added tax | 5,076 | 17,019 | 21,520 |
| Excises | 836 | 2,388 | 11,323 |
| Enterprise profits tax | 10,712 | 23,868 | 16,761 |
| Personal income tax | 2,275 | 6,826 | 8,795 |
| Land tax | 405 | 1,721 | 1,940 |
| Customs duties | 789 | 2,707 | 5,875 |
| Payroll taxes | 2,836 | 10,680 | 14,717 |
| Other taxes | 1,502 | 1,249 | 4,120 |
| Other revenue | 5,179 | 18,346 | 21,884 |
| Grants | 22,147 | 19,031 | 9,671 |
| **Total** | 51,756 | 103,834 | 116,606 |

| Expenditure† | 1994 | 1995 | 1996 |
|---|---|---|---|
| Current expenditure | 64,134 | 117,725 | 129,740 |
| Wages | 3,443 | 13,528 | 18,983 |
| Subsidies | 24,032 | 4,916 | 815 |
| Interest | 3,642 | 16,112 | 17,273 |
| Transfers | 7,484 | 31,084 | 32,009 |
| Pensions and social protection | 5,690 | 27,289 | 28,840 |
| Goods and services | 25,533 | 47,085 | 60,660 |
| Health and education | 3,931 | 12,866 | 9,725 |
| Other | 21,602 | 34,219 | 50,935 |
| Capital expenditure | 17,913 | 35,383 | 26,794 |
| Net lending | 531 | 2,575 | 16,062 |
| Restructuring expenses | — | — | 855 |
| **Total** | 82,578 | 150,684 | 173,450 |

* Figures refer to the consolidated accounts of republican and local authorities, including the operations of the Pension and Employment Fund.
† Excluding adjustment for changes in arrears. The net change (in million drams) was: 11,900 in 1994; –11,274 in 1995; –4,832 in 1996 (minus sign indicates additional expenditure).

**INTERNATIONAL RESERVES** (US $ million at 31 December)

| | 1996 | 1997 | 1998 |
|---|---|---|---|
| Gold* | 12.82 | 10.72 | 12.37 |
| IMF special drawing rights | 41.50 | 37.28 | 28.00 |
| Reserve position in IMF | 0.01 | 0.01 | 0.01 |
| Foreign exchange | 114.14 | 191.46 | 287.28 |
| **Total** | 168.47 | 239.47 | 327.66 |

* National valuation.
Source: IMF, *International Financial Statistics*.

**MONEY SUPPLY** (million drams at 31 December)

| | 1996 | 1997 | 1998 |
|---|---|---|---|
| Currency outside banks | 34,784 | 37,596 | 41,370 |
| Demand deposits at commercial banks | 4,968 | 6,372 | 11,216 |
| **Total money** | 39,752 | 43,969 | 52,586 |

Source: IMF, *International Financial Statistics*.

**COST OF LIVING**

(Consumer Price Index; base: 1995 = 100)

| | 1996 | 1997 | 1998 |
|---|---|---|---|
| **All items** | 119 | 135 | 147 |

Source: IMF, *International Financial Statistics*.

**NATIONAL ACCOUNTS** (million drams at current prices)

**Expenditure on the Gross Domestic Product**

| | 1995 | 1996 | 1997 |
|---|---|---|---|
| Government final consumption expenditure | 58,336 | 81,668 | 94,596 |
| Private final consumption expenditure | 555,056 | 665,488 | 814,891 |
| Increase in stocks | 11,858 | 13,021 | 12,084 |
| Gross fixed capital formation | 84,365 | 107,470 | 156,840 |
| **Total domestic expenditure** | 709,615 | 867,647 | 1,078,411 |
| Exports of goods and services | 124,965 | 153,665 | 163,099 |
| *Less* Imports of goods and services | 324,775 | 370,208 | 471,628 |
| **Sub-total** | 509,805 | 651,104 | 769,882 |
| Statistical discrepancy* | 12,451 | 9,206 | 28,673 |
| **GDP in purchasers' values** | 522,256 | 660,310 | 798,555 |

* Referring to the difference between the sum of the expenditure components and official estimates of GDP, compiled from the production approach.

Source: IMF, *International Financial Statistics.*

**Gross Domestic Product by Economic Activity**

| | 1994 | 1995 | 1996 |
|---|---|---|---|
| Agriculture and forestry | 81,304 | 202,135 | 217,594 |
| Industry* | 54,495 | 126,731 | 156,980 |
| Construction | 12,508 | 44,512 | 63,124 |
| Transport and communications | 7,838† | 22,646† | 31,023 |
| Trade and catering | 8,423 | 49,781 | 63,262 |
| Other services | 22,496 | 76,451 | 128,327 |
| **Total** | 187,064 | 522,256 | 660,310 |

* Principally mining, manufacturing, electricity, gas and water.

† Includes passenger transport only.

**BALANCE OF PAYMENTS** (US $ million)

| | 1996 | 1997 | 1998 |
|---|---|---|---|
| Exports of goods f.o.b. | 290.4 | 233.6 | 228.9 |
| Imports of goods f.o.b. | –759.6 | –793.1 | –806.4 |
| **Trade balance** | –469.2 | –559.5 | –577.5 |
| Exports of services | 77.7 | 96.6 | 130.7 |
| Imports of services | –128.5 | –159.4 | –181.3 |
| **Balance on goods and services** | –520.0 | –622.2 | –628.1 |
| Other income received | 78.0 | 139.0 | 103.9 |
| Other income paid | –33.3 | –40.4 | –43.5 |
| **Balance on goods, services and income** | –475.3 | –523.7 | –567.7 |
| Current transfers received | 199.0 | 252.4 | 203.0 |
| Current transfers paid | –14.4 | –35.2 | –25.6 |
| **Current balance** | –290.7 | –306.5 | –390.3 |
| Capital account (net) | 13.4 | 10.9 | 9.7 |
| Direct investment abroad | n.a. | n.a. | –11.6 |
| Direct investment from abroad | 17.6 | 51.9 | 232.4 |
| Portfolio investment assets | –0.1 | –0.1 | –0.6 |
| Portfolio investment liabilities | 7.2 | 15.9 | –16.6 |
| Other investment assets | 35.3 | 40.8 | 20.0 |
| Other investment liabilities | 156.6 | 226.4 | 165.6 |
| Net errors and omissions | 15.1 | 10.8 | –9.3 |
| **Overall balance** | –45.5 | 50.0 | 0.6 |

Source: IMF, *International Financial Statistics.*

# External Trade

**PRINCIPAL COMMODITIES** (US $ million)

| Imports c.i.f. | 1994 | 1995 |
|---|---|---|
| Live animals and animal products | 46.1 | 63.3 |
| Vegetable products | 64.3 | 85.6 |
| Animal or vegetable fats and oils; prepared edible fats; animal or vegetable waxes | 11.9 | 25.1 |
| Prepared foodstuffs; beverages, spirits and vinegar; tobacco and manufactured substitutes | 32.4 | 51.5 |
| Mineral products | 161.0 | 224.7 |
| Products of chemical or allied industries | 9.1 | 55.4 |
| Textiles and textile articles | 8.6 | 7.8 |
| Natural or cultured pearls, precious and semi-precious stones, precious metals and articles thereof; imitation jewellery; coin | 31.8 | 62.4 |
| Base metals and articles thereof | 3.6 | 15.9 |
| Machinery and mechanical appliances; electrical equipment; sound and television apparatus | 8.0 | 49.6 |
| **Total** (incl. others) | 393.8 | 673.9 |

| Exports f.o.b. | 1994 | 1995 |
|---|---|---|
| Prepared foodstuffs; beverages, spirits and vinegar; tobacco and manufactured substitutes | 12.9 | 12.6 |
| Mineral products | 17.8 | 28.8 |
| Products of chemical or allied industries | 3.9 | 14.5 |
| Plastics, rubber and articles thereof | 7.9 | 10.8 |
| Textiles and textile articles | 15.8 | 15.2 |
| Footwear, headgear, umbrellas, walking-sticks, whips, etc.; prepared feathers; artificial flowers; articles of human hair | 15.9 | 5.4 |
| Articles of stone, plaster, cement, asbestos, mica, etc.; ceramic products; glass and glassware | 12.7 | 2.1 |
| Natural or cultured pearls, precious and semi-precious stones, precious metals and articles thereof; imitation jewellery; coin | 75.2 | 89.6 |
| Base metals and articles thereof | 9.4 | 30.5 |
| Machinery and mechanical appliances; electrical equipment; sound and television apparatus | 30.9 | 39.1 |
| Vehicles, aircraft, vessels and associated transport equipment | 1.7 | 11.4 |
| Miscellaneous manufactured articles | 5.5 | 3.4 |
| **Total** (incl. others) | 215.5 | 270.9 |

**PRINCIPAL TRADING PARTNERS** (US $ million)

| Imports | 1994 | 1995 | 1996 |
|---|---|---|---|
| France | 10.7 | 16.0 | 12.1 |
| Germany | 6.9 | 11.0 | 17.3 |
| Iran | 42.5 | 90.0 | 149.7 |
| Russia | 110.4 | 133.7 | 125.4 |
| Turkmenistan | 69.4 | 129.2 | 86.3 |
| Other CIS | 39.7 | 71.1 | 66.0 |
| USA | 96.1 | 114.0 | 103.6 |
| **Total** (incl. others) | 401.2 | 672.9 | 855.8 |

| Exports | 1994 | 1995 | 1996 |
|---|---|---|---|
| Belgium | 20.8 | 30.6 | 44.8 |
| Germany | 7.1 | 10.0 | 3.7 |
| Iran | 16.1 | 35.1 | 39.9 |
| Russia | 92.8 | 88.3 | 96.1 |
| Turkmenistan | 43.7 | 67.2 | 17.5 |
| Other CIS | 8.9 | 10.2 | 14.5 |
| **Total** (incl. others) | 209.3 | 270.9 | 290.3 |

**1997** (US $ million): Total imports c.i.f. 892.3; Total exports f.o.b. 232.5.

**1998** (US $ million): Total imports c.i.f. 895.7; Total exports f.o.b. 223.5 (Source: IMF, *International Financial Statistics*).

## Transport

**RAILWAYS** (traffic)

| | 1993 | 1994 | 1995 |
|---|---|---|---|
| Passenger-km (million) | 435 | 353 | 166 |
| Freight ton-km (million) | 451 | 378 | 403 |

Source: UN, *Statistical Yearbook*.

## Tourism

| | 1995 | 1996 |
|---|---|---|
| Tourism receipts (US $ million) | 1 | 12 |

Source: World Tourism Organization, *Yearbook of Tourism Statistics*.

## Communications Media

| | 1994 | 1995 | 1996 |
|---|---|---|---|
| Television receivers ('000 in use) | 800 | 815 | 820 |
| Book production†: | | | |
| Titles | 224 | n.a. | 396 |
| Copies ('000) | 1,739 | n.a. | 20,212 |
| Daily newspapers: | | | |
| Titles | 7 | 7 | 11 |
| Average circulation ('000 copies) | 80* | 85 | n.a. |
| Non-daily newspapers: | | | |
| Titles | n.a. | n.a. | 112 |
| Average circulation ('000 copies) | n.a. | n.a. | 304* |
| Other periodicals: | | | |
| Titles | n.a. | n.a. | 44 |
| Average circulation ('000 copies) | n.a. | n.a. | 541 |

* Provisional.

† Including pamphlets (27 titles and 83,000 copies in 1994).

Source: UNESCO, *Statistical Yearbook*.

**Telephones** ('000 main lines in use): 583 in 1993; 587 in 1994; 583 in 1995 (Source: UN, *Statistical Yearbook*).

**Telefax stations** (number in use): 180 in 1992; 220 in 1993; 300 in 1994 (Source: UN, *Statistical Yearbook*).

## Education

(1996/97, unless otherwise indicated)

| | Institutions | Teachers | Students |
|---|---|---|---|
| Pre-primary | 978 | 9,981 | 68,426 |
| Primary | 1,402 | 13,620 | 256,475 |
| Secondary: | | | |
| General | 1,456 | 57,325 | 365,025 |
| Vocational | | n.a. | 7,162 |
| Higher schools (incl. universities) | 15 | 4,065 | 35,517 |

Sources: Ministry of Education and Science; UNESCO, *Statistical Yearbook*.

# Directory

## The Constitution

The Constitution was approved by some 68% of the electorate in a national referendum, held on 5 July 1995. It replaced the amended Soviet Constitution of 1978. The following is a summary of the new Constitution's main provisions:

### GENERAL PROVISIONS OF CONSTITUTIONAL ORDER

The Republic of Armenia is an independent democratic state; its sovereignty is vested in the people, who execute their authority through free elections, referendums and local self-government institutions and officials, as defined by the Constitution. Referendums, as well as elections of the President of the Republic, the National Assembly and local self-government bodies, are carried out on the basis of universal, equal, direct suffrage by secret ballot. Through the Constitution and legislation, the State ensures the protection of human rights and freedoms, in accordance with the principles and norms of international law. A multi-party political system is guaranteed. The establishment of political parties is a free process, but the activities of political parties must not contravene the Constitution and the law. The right to property is recognized and protected. Armenia conducts its foreign policy based on the norms of international law, seeking to establish neighbourly and mutually beneficial relations with all countries. The State ensures the protection of the environment, historical and cultural monuments, as well as cultural values. The official language is Armenian.

### FUNDAMENTAL HUMAN AND CIVIL RIGHTS AND FREEDOMS

The acquisition and loss of citizenship are prescribed by law. A citizen of the Republic of Armenia may not be simultaneously a citizen of another country. The rights, liberties and duties of citizens of Armenia, regardless of nationality, race, sex, language, creed, political or other convictions, social origin, property and other status, are guaranteed. No one shall be subject to torture or cruel treatment. Every citizen has the right to freedom of movement and residence within the republic, as well as the right to leave the republic. Every citizen has the right to freedom of thought, speech, conscience and religion. The right to establish or join associations, trade unions, political organizations, etc., is guaranteed, as is the right to strike for protection of economic, social and labour interests. Citizens of the republic who have attained 18 years of age are entitled to participate in state government through their directly-elected representatives or by expression of free will.

Every citizen has the right to social insurance in the event of old age, disability, sickness, widowhood, unemployment, etc. Every citizen has the right to education. Education is provided free at elementary and secondary state educational institutions. Citizens belonging to national minorities have the right to preserve their traditions and to develop their language and culture. Everyone charged with a penal offence has the right to be presumed innocent until proved guilty. The advocacy of national, racial and religious hatred, and the propagation of violence and war, are prohibited.

### THE PRESIDENT OF THE REPUBLIC

The President of the Republic of Armenia ensures the observance of the Constitution and the effective operation of the legislative, executive and juridical authorities. The President is the guarantor of the independence, territorial integrity and security of the republic. He/she is elected by citizens of the republic for a period of five years. Any person who has the right to participate in elections, has attained the age of 35 years, and has been a resident citizen of Armenia for the preceding 10 years is eligible for election to the office of President. No person may be elected to the office for more than two successive terms.

The President signs and promulgates laws adopted by the National Assembly, or returns draft legislation to the National Assembly for reconsideration; may dismiss the National Assembly and declare special elections to it, after consultation with the Prime Minister and the Chairman of the National Assembly; appoints and dismisses the Prime Minister; appoints and dismisses the members of the Government, upon the recommendation of the Prime Minister; appoints civil service officials; establishes deliberation bodies; represents Armenia in international relations, co-ordinates foreign policy, concludes international treaties, signs international treaties ratified by the National Assembly, and ratifies agreements between governments; appoints and recalls diplomatic representatives of Armenia to foreign countries and international organizations, and receives the credentials of diplomatic representatives of foreign countries; appoints the Procurator-General, as nominated by the Prime Minister; appoints members and the Chairman of the Constitutional Court; is the Supreme Commander-in-Chief of the armed forces; takes decisions on the use of the armed forces; grants titles of honour; and grants amnesties to convicts.

### THE NATIONAL ASSEMBLY

Legislative power in the Republic of Armenia is executed by the National Assembly. The Assembly comprises 131 deputies, elected for a four-year term. Any person who has attained the age of 25 years and has been a permanent resident and citizen of Armenia for the preceding five years is eligible to be elected a deputy.

The National Assembly deliberates and enacts laws; has the power to express a vote of 'no confidence' in the Government; confirms the state budget, as proposed by the Government; supervises the implementation of the state budget; elects its Chairman (Speaker) and two Deputy Chairmen; appoints the Chairman and Deputy Chairman of the Central Bank, upon the nomination of the President; and appoints members of the Constitutional Court.

At the suggestion of the President of the Republic, the National Assembly declares amnesties; ratifies or declares invalid international treaties; and declares war. Upon the recommendation of the Government, the National Assembly confirms the territorial and administrative divisions of the republic.

### THE GOVERNMENT

Executive power is realized by the Government of the Republic of Armenia, which is composed of the Prime Minister and the Ministers. The Prime Minister is appointed by the President; upon the recommendation of the Prime Minister, the President appoints the remaining Ministers. The Prime Minister directs the current activities of the Government and co-ordinates the activities of the Ministers.

The Government presents the programme of its activities to the National Assembly for approval; presents the draft state budget to the National Assembly for confirmation, ensures implementation of the budget and presents a report on its implementation to the National Assembly; manages state property; ensures the implementation of state fiscal, loan and tax policies; ensures the implementation of state policy in the spheres of science, education, culture, health care, social security and environmental protection; ensures the implementation of defence, national security and foreign policies; and takes measures to strengthen adherence to the laws, to ensure the rights and freedoms of citizens, and to protect public order and the property of citizens.

### JUDICIAL POWER*

In the Republic of Armenia the courts of general competence are the tribunal courts of first instance, the review courts and the courts of appeal. There are also economic, military and other courts. The guarantor of the independence of judicial bodies is the President of the Republic. He/she is the Head of the Council of Justice. The Minister of Justice and the Procurator-General are the Deputy Heads of the Council of Justice. Fourteen members appointed by the President of the Republic for a period of five years are included in the Council. The Constitutional Court is composed of nine members, of whom the National Assembly appoints five and the President of the Republic appoints four. The Constitutional Court, *inter alia*, determines whether decisions of the National Assembly, decrees and orders of the President, and resolutions of the Government correspond to the Constitution; decides, prior to ratification of an international treaty, whether the obligations created in it correspond to the Constitution; resolves disputes relating to referendums and results of presidential and legislative elections; and decides on the suspension or prohibition of the activity of a political party.

### TERRITORIAL ADMINISTRATION AND LOCAL SELF-GOVERNMENT

The administrative territorial units of the Republic of Armenia are regions and communities. Regions are comprised of rural and urban communities. Local self-government takes place in the communities. Bodies of local self-government, community elders and the community head (city mayor or head of village) are elected for a three-year period to administer community property and solve issues of community significance. State government is exercised in the regions. The Government appoints and dismisses regional governors, who carry out the Government's regional policy and co-ordinate the performance of regional services by state executive bodies. The city of Yerevan has the status of a region.

* The new judicial system came into force in January 1999. The Supreme Court was replaced by the Court of Cassation, and Appellate Courts were to operate in the place of People's Courts. Members of the Court of Cassation were to be appointed by the President, for life.

## The Government

### HEAD OF STATE

**President:** ROBERT KOCHARIAN (acting from 3 February 1998, elected 30 March, inaugurated 9 April).

### GOVERNMENT

(January 2000)

**Prime Minister:** ARAM SARKISSIAN.

**Minister of Foreign Affairs:** VARTAN OSKANIAN.

**Minister of Internal Affairs:** HAYK HAROUTUNIAN.

**Minister of National Security:** KARLOS PETROSSIAN.

**Minister of Defence:** VAGARSHAK HAROUTUNIAN.

**Minister of Finance:** LEVON BARKHOUDARIAN.

**Minister of the Economy:** ARMEN DARBINIAN.

**Minister of Justice:** DAVID HAROUTUNIAN.

**Minister of Economic and Infrastructural Reforms:** VAHAN SHIRKHANIAN.

**Minister of Energy:** DAVID ZADOIAN.

**Minister of Urban Development:** HRAYR HOVHANISSIAN.

**Minister of Social Security:** RAZMIK MARTIROSSIAN.

**Minister of Health:** HAYK NIKOGHOSIAN.

**Minister of Territorial Administration:** KHOSROV HAROUTUNIAN.

**Minister of Agriculture:** GAGIK SHAHBAZIAN.

**Minister of Environmental Protection:** GEVORK VARDANIAN.

**Minister of Industry and Trade:** KAREN CHSHMARITIAN.

**Minister of Education and Science:** EDUARD GHAZARIAN.

**Minister of Post and Telecommunications:** RUBEN TONOIAN.

**Minister of Culture, Youth Affairs and Sports:** ROLAND SHAROIAN.

**Minister of Transport:** YERVAND ZAKARIAN.

**Minister of Privatization:** PAVEL GHALTAKHCHIAN.

**Minister of Statistics, the State Register and Analysis:** STEPAN MNATSAKANIAN.

**Minister of State Revenues:** SMBAT AYVAZIAN.

**Minister without Portfolio:** GAGIK MARTIROSSIAN.

**Chief of Staff at the Office of the Prime Minister:** SHAHEN KARAMANOUKIAN.

**Mayor of Yerevan:** SOUREN ABRAHAMIAN.

### MINISTRIES

**Office of the Prime Minister:** 375010 Yerevan, Republic Sq. 1, Government House; tel. (2) 52-03-60; fax (2) 15-10-35.

**Ministry of Agriculture:** 375010 Yerevan, Republic Sq. 1, Government House; tel. (2) 52-46-41; fax (2) 15-10-86.

**Ministry of Culture, Youth Affairs and Sports:** 375010 Yerevan, Tumanian St 5; tel. (2) 52-88-69; fax (2) 52-39-22.

**Ministry of Defence:** Yerevan, Proshian Settlement, G. Shaush St 60G; tel. (2) 35-78-22; fax (2) 52-65-60.

**Ministry of Economic and Infrastructural Reforms:** Yerevan; fax (2) 15-10-69.

**Ministry of the Economy:** Yerevan.

**Ministry of Education and Science:** 375010 Yerevan, Movses Khorenatsi St 13; tel. (2) 52-66-02; fax (2) 15-11-50.

**Ministry of Energy:** 375010 Yerevan, Republic Sq. 2, Government House 2; tel. (2) 52-19-64; fax (2) 15-10-36.

**Ministry of Environmental Protection:** 375012 Yerevan, Moskovian St 35; tel. (2) 53-07-41; fax (2) 53-49-02; e-mail femini@nature.arminco.com.

**Ministry of Finance:** 375010 Yerevan, Melik-Adamian St 1; tel. (2) 52-70-82; fax (2) 15-11-54; e-mail mfeinf@hotmail.com.

**Ministry of Foreign Affairs:** 375010 Yerevan, Republic Sq. 1, Government House 2; tel. (2) 52-35-31; fax (2) 15-10-42.

**Ministry of Health:** 375001 Yerevan, Tumanian St 8; tel. (2) 58-24-13; fax (2) 15-10-97.

**Ministry of Industry and Trade:** 375008 Yerevan, Terian St 69; tel. (2) 50-61-34; fax (2) 15-16-75.

**Ministry of Internal Affairs:** 375025 Yerevan, Nalbandian St 2; tel. (2) 52-97-33; fax (2) 57-84-40.

**Ministry of Justice:** 375010 Yerevan, Parliament St 8; tel. (2) 58-21-57; fax (2) 56-56-40.

**Ministry of National Security:** Yerevan.

**Ministry of Operational Affairs and Office of the Chief of Staff of Government:** Yerevan 375010, Republic Sq., Government House 1; tel. (2) 52-03-21; fax (2) 15-10-36.

**Ministry of Post and Telecommunications:** 375010 Yerevan, Nalbandian St 28; tel. (2) 52-66-32; fax (2) 15-14-46; e-mail armoc@mbox.amilink.net.

**Ministry of Privatization:** 375010 Yerevan, Republic Sq., Government House 2; tel. (2) 52-18-77; fax (2) 50-61-72; e-mail root@minprv.arminco.com.

**Ministry of Social Security:** 375025 Yerevan, Issahakian St 18; tel. (2) 52-68-31; fax (2) 15-19-20.

**Ministry of State Revenues:** 375015 Yerevan, Movses Khorenatsi St 3; tel. (2) 53-91-95; fax (2) 53-82-26.

**Ministry of Statistics, the State Register and Analysis:** 375010 Yerevan, Republic. Sq.; tel. (2) 52-42-13.

**Ministry of Territorial Administration:** 375010 Yerevan, Republic Sq. 1, Government House 2; tel (2) 52-52-74; fax (2) 50-67-54.

**Ministry of Transport:** 375015 Yerevan, Zakian St 10; tel. (2) 56-33-91; fax (2) 52-52-68.

**Ministry of Urban Development:** 375010 Yerevan, Republic Sq., Government House 3; tel. (2) 58-90-80; fax (2) 52-32-00.

**Office of the Mayor of Yerevan:** Yerevan, Grigor Lousavoritch St; tel. (2) 52-58-47.

**Office of the State Department for Emergency Situations:** Yerevan 375010, Republic Sq., Government House; tel. (2) 53-16-12; fax (2) 15-10-36.

# President and Legislature

### PRESIDENT

**Presidential Election, First Ballot, 16 March 1998**

| Candidates | % of votes |
|---|---|
| ROBERT KOCHARIAN | 38.76 |
| KAREN DEMIRCHIAN | 30.67 |
| VAZGEN MANUKIAN (National Democratic Union) | 12.24 |
| SERGEI BADALIAN (Communist Party of Armenia) | 11.01 |
| PARUIR HAIRIKIAN (Union for National Self-Determination) | 5.41 |
| Others | 1.91 |
| **Total** | 100.0 |

**Second Ballot, 30 March 1998**

| Candidates | % of votes |
|---|---|
| ROBERT KOCHARIAN | 59.49 |
| KAREN DEMIRCHIAN | 40.51 |
| **Total** | 100.0 |

### NATIONAL ASSEMBLY

**Chairman:** ARMEN KHACHATRIAN.

**Deputy Chairmen:** TIGRAN TOROSSIAN, GAGIK ASLANIAN.

**General Election, 30 May 1999**

| Parties and blocs | % of vote for seats by proportional representation | Total seats |
|---|---|---|
| Unity bloc* | 41.2 | 55 |
| Communist Party of Armenia | 12.1 | 11 |
| Armenian Revolutionary Federation | 7.7 | 9 |
| Law and Unity bloc | 8.0 | 6 |
| Law-governed Country Party of Armenia | 5.3 | 6 |
| National Democratic Union | 5.2 | 6 |
| Armenian Pan-National Movement | 1.2 | 1 |
| Armenian Democratic Party | 1.0 | 1 |
| Mission Party | 0.8 | 1 |
| National Concord Party | — | 1 |
| Independents | — | 32 |
| **Total** (incl. others) | 100.0 | 131† |

* A coalition of the Republican Party of Armenia and the People's Party of Armenia.

† Results were annulled in two constituencies; the subsequent by-elections, which were held in July, were won by independents.

# Political Organizations

**Armenian Christian Democratic Union:** Yerevan, Nubarashen St 16; tel. (2) 47-68-68; Chair. AZAD ARSHAKIAN.

**Armenian Democratic Agricultural Party:** Yerevan, Kutuzov St 1/7; tel. (2) 26-40-03; Chair. TELMAN DILANIAN.

**Armenian Democratic Party:** Yerevan, Koriun St 14; tel. (2) 52-52-73; f. 1992 by elements of Communist Party of Armenia; Chair. ARAM SARKISSIAN.

**Armenian Monarchists Party:** Aparan, Garegin Nejdeh St 13/11; tel. (520) 85-20; Chair. TIGRAN PETROSSIAN.

**Armenian National Democratic Party–21st Century:** Yerevan; f. 1998; Chair. DAVID SHAKHNAZARYAN.

**Armenian National Party:** Yerevan; f. 1996.

**Armenian Pan-National Movement (APNM)** (Haiots Hamazgaien Sharjoum): 375019 Yerevan, Khanjian St 27; tel. (2) 57-04-70; f. 1989; Pres. LEVON TER-PETROSSIAN; Chair. VANO SHIRADEGHIAN.

**Armenian Revolutionary Federation (ARF)** (Hai Heghapokhakan Dashnaktsutyun): 375025 Yerevan, Myasnyak Ave 2; f. 1890; formed the ruling party in independent Armenia, 1918–20; prohibited under Soviet rule, but continued its activities in other countries; permitted to operate legally in Armenia from 1991; suspended in December 1994; legally reinstated 1998; 40,000 mems; Chair. RUBEN HAGOBIAN, VAHAN HOVHANISSIAN.

**Azatutyun** (Freedom): Yerevan; f. 1997; liberal, right-wing; Leader HRANT BAGRATIAN.

**Communist Party of Armenia (CPA):** Yerevan, Marshal Baghramian St 10; tel. (2) 56-79-33; fax (2) 53-38-55; f. 1920; dissolved 1991, relegalized 1992; c. 50,000 mems; Chair. (vacant).

**Haykandoukht Women's Party:** Yerevan; Leader ARMENOUHI KAZARIAN.

**Hnchak Armenian Social Democratic Party:** Yerevan, Aghbiur Serob St 7; tel. (2) 27-33-15; Chair. ERNEST SOGOMONYAN.

**Law-Governed Country Party of Armenia** (Orinats Yerkir): Yerevan; f. 1998; centrist; 1,100 mems; Head ARTUR BAGDASARIAN.

**Liberal Democratic Party** (Ramgavar Azadagan): 375009 Yerevan, Koryun St 19A; tel. (2) 52-64-03; fax (2) 52-53-23; f. 1991; Leader HARUTYUN KARAPETIAN.

**Mission Party** (Arakelutun): c/o National Assembly, Yerevan.

**National Concord Party:** c/o National Assembly, Yerevan; f. 1998; Leaders GARNIK ISAGULYAN, IGOR MURADYAN, GRANT KHACHATRYAN.

**National Democratic Union:** Yerevan, Abovian St 12; tel. and fax (2) 56-31-88; e-mail adjm@arminco.com; f. 1991 as a splinter party of the PNM (see below); Leader DAVIT VARDANIAN; Chair. VAZGEN MANUKIAN.

**New Way Party** (Nor Ugi): Yerevan; f. 1998; Leader ASHOT BLEYAN.

**People's Party of Armenia (PPA):** Yerevan; f. 1998; Chair. STEPAN DEMIRCHIAN (acting); Sec. AMAYAK OVANESYAN.

**Republican Party of Armenia:** Yerevan, Tumanian St 23; tel. (2) 58-00-31; fax (2) 56-60-34; f. 1990 following a split in the UNS (see below); merged with Yerkrapah Union of Volunteers in 1999; 13 territorial orgs; 5,500 mems; Chair. ANDRANIK MARKARIAN.

**Shamiram Women's Party:** Yerevan; f. 1995.

**Union for National Self-Determination (UNS):** 375013 Yerevan, Gregory the Illuminator St 15; tel. (2) 52-55-38; Chair. PARUIR HAIRIKIAN.

**Union of Socialist Forces:** Yerevan; f. 1997 as an alliance of several left-wing parties; Leader ASHOT MANUCHARIAN.

# Diplomatic Representation

### EMBASSIES IN ARMENIA

**China, People's Republic:** Yerevan, Bagramian Ave 12; tel. (2) 56-00-67; fax (2) 15-11-43; Ambassador: ZHU ZHAOSHUN.

**Egypt:** Yerevan, Pionerakan St 72, Hotel Hrazdan, 10th Floor; tel. (2) 53-73-04; fax (2) 15-11-60; Ambassador: SAID IMAM MAHMOUD SAID.

**France:** 375015 Yerevan, Grigor Lusavorichy St 8; tel. (2) 56-11-03; fax (2) 15-11-05; Ambassador: MICHEL LEGRAS.

**Georgia:** Yerevan, Aramy St 42; tel. 56-43-57; Ambassador: NIKOLOZ NIKOLOZISHVILI.

**Germany:** Yerevan, Charents St 29; tel. (2) 52-32-79; fax (2) 15-11-12; e-mail germemb@arminco.com; Ambassador: VOLKER SEITZ.

**Greece:** Yerevan, Pionerakan St 72, Hotel Hrazdan, 5th Floor; tel. (2) 53-00-51; fax (2) 15-11-70; Ambassador: PANAYOTIS ZOGRAFOS.

**Iran:** Yerevan, Budaghian St 1; tel. (2) 52-98-30; fax (2) 15-13-85; Ambassador: HAMIDREZA ESFAHANI.

**Lebanon:** Yerevan, Vardanants St 7; tel (2) 52-65-40; fax (2) 15-11-28; Chargé d'affaires a.i.: SAAD ZAKHIA.

**Russia:** Yerevan, Grigor Lusavorichy St 13A; tel. (2) 56-74-27; fax (2) 50-52-37; Ambassador: ANATOLII DRYUKOV.

**Ukraine:** Yerevan, Erznkian St 58; tel. and fax (2) 56-24-36; Ambassador: OLEKSANDR BOZHKO.

**United Arab Emirates:** Yerevan.

**United Kingdom:** Yerevan, Charents St 28; tel. (2) 15-18-41; fax (2) 15-18-07; Ambassador: TIMOTHY JONES.

**USA:** Yerevan, Bagramian St 18; tel. (2) 15-15-51; fax (2) 15-15-50; e-mail lemmonmc@wo_state.gov; Ambassador: MICHAEL LEMMON.

# Judicial System

A new judicial and legal system came into force in January 1999. The Supreme Court was replaced by the Court of Cassation, and Appellate Courts were to operate in the place of People's Courts. Members of the Court of Cassation were to be appointed by the President, for life.

**Chairman of the Constitutional Court:** GAGIK ARUTYUNIAN.

**Chairman of the Court of Cassation:** TARIEL K. BARSEGIAN.

**Prosecutor-General:** AGHVAN HOVSEPIAN.

# Religion

The major religion is Christianity. The Armenian Apostolic Church is the leading denomination and was widely identified with the movement for national independence. There are also Russian Orthodox and Islamic communities, although the latter lost adherents as a result of the departure of large numbers of Muslim Azeris from the republic. Most Kurds are also adherents of Islam, although some are Yazidis.

### GOVERNMENT AGENCY

**Council for the Affairs of the Armenian Church:** 375001 Yerevan, Abovian St 3; tel. (2) 56-46-34; fax (2) 56-41-81.

### CHRISTIANITY

**Armenian Apostolic Church:** Etchmiadzin, Vagharshapat City; tel. (2) 15-11-98; fax (2) 15-10-77; e-mail mairator@arminco.com; nine dioceses in Armenia, four in other ex-Soviet republics and 25 dioceses and bishoprics in the rest of the world; 7m. members worldwide (some 4m. in Armenia); 15 monasteries and three theological seminaries in Armenia; Supreme Patriarch GAREGIN II, Catholicos of All Armenians.

#### The Roman Catholic Church

*Armenian Rite*

Armenian Catholics in Eastern Europe are under the jurisdiction of an Ordinary (equivalent to a bishop with direct authority). At 31 December 1997 there were an estimated 220,000 adherents within this jurisdiction, including about 30,000 in Armenia itself.

**Ordinary:** Most Rev. NERSES TER-NERSESSIAN (Titular Archbishop of Sebaste), Gyumri, Atarbekian St 82; tel. (69) 22-115; fax (69) 21-839; e-mail armorda@shirak.am.

*Latin Rite*

The Apostolic Administrator of the Caucasus is the Apostolic Nuncio (Ambassador of the Holy See) to Georgia, Armenia and Azerbaijan, who is resident in Tbilisi, Georgia.

# The Press

### PRINCIPAL NEWSPAPERS

In Armenian except where otherwise stated.

**Ankakhutiun** (Independence): 375013 Yerevan, Gregory the Illuminator St 15; tel. (2) 58-18-64; daily; organ of the Union for National Self-Determination; Editor PARUIR HAIRIKIAN.

**Aravot:** 375023 Yerevan, Arshakunyats Ave 2, 10th Floor; tel. (2) 52-87-52; Editor A. ABRAMIAN.

**Avangard:** 375023 Yerevan, Arshakunyats Ave 2; f. 1923; 3 a week; organ of the Youth League of Armenia; Editor M. K. ZOHRABIAN.

**Azg** (The Nation): 375010 Yerevan, Hanrapetoutian St 47; tel. (2) 52-16-35; f. 1990; Editor S. SARKISSIAN.

**Bravo:** Yerevan, Abovian St 12, Hotel Yerevan; tel. (2) 55-44-05; weekly; Editor K. KAZARIAN.

**Delovoi Express:** Yerevan, Zarian St 22, 2nd Floor; tel. (2) 25-26-83; fax (2) 25-90-23; e-mail eis@arminco.com; f. 1992; weekly; Editor E. NAGDALIAN.

**Epokha** (Epoch): 375023 Yerevan, Arshakunyats Ave 2; f. 1938; fmrly *Komsomolets*; weekly; Russian; organ of the Youth League of Armenia; Editor V. S. GRIGORIAN.

**Golos Armenii** (The Voice of Armenia): 375023 Yerevan, Arshakunyats Ave 2, 7th Floor; tel. (2) 52-77-23; f. 1934 as *Kommunist;* 3 a week; Russian; Editor F. NASHKARIAN.

**Grakan Tert** (Literary Paper): 375019 Yerevan, Marshal Baghramian St 3; tel. (2) 52-05-94; f. 1932; weekly; organ of the Union of Writers; Editor F. H. MELOIAN.

**Hanrapetakan:** Yerevan, Tumanian St 23; tel. (2) 58-00-31; fax (2) 56-60-34; organ of the Republican Party of Armenia.

**Hayastan** (Armenia): 375023 Yerevan, Arshakunyats Ave 2; tel. (2) 52-84-50; f. 1920; 6 a week; Russian; Editor G. ABRAMIAN.

**Hayastani Hanrapetoutian** (Republic of Armenia): 375023 Yerevan, Arshakunyats Ave 2, 13th–14th Floors; f. 1990; tel. and fax (2) 52-69-74; 6 a week; also in Russian (as *Respublika Armeniya*); Editor M. HAROUTUNIAN.

**Hayk** (Armenia): 375023 Yerevan, Arshakunyats Ave 2, 11th Floor; tel. (2) 52-77-01; weekly; organ of the Armenian Pan-National Movement; Editor V. DAVTIAN; circ. 30,000.

**Hayots Ashkhar:** Yerevan, Tumanian St 38; tel. (2) 53-88-65; Editor G. MKRTCHIAN.

**Hazatamart** (The Battle for Freedom): 375070 Yerevan, Atarbekian 181; organ of the Armenian Revolutionary Federation; Editor M. MIKAYELIAN.

**Hnchak Hayastani** (The Bell of Armenia): 375019 Yerevan, Lord Byron St 12; weekly.

**Marzakan Hayastan:** 375023 Yerevan, Arshakunyats Ave 5; tel. (2) 52-62-41; weekly; Editor S. MOURADIAN.

**Molorak:** 375023 Yerevan, Arshakunyats Ave 5; tel. (2) 52-62-12; daily; Editor H. GHAGHRINIAN.

**Respublika Armenia:** 375023 Yerevan, Arshakunyats Ave 2, 9th Floor; tel. (2) 52-69-69; Editor A. KHANBABIAN.

**Ria Taze** (New Way): Yerevan; 2 a week; Kurdish.

**Vozny** (Hedgehog): 375023 Yerevan, Arshakunyats Ave 2, 12th Floor; tel. (2) 52-63-83; f. 1954; Editor A. SAHAKIAN.

**Yerevanyan Orer** (Yerevan Days): Yerevan; Editor M. AIRAPETIAN.

**Yerkir** (Country): 375009 Yerevan, Yeznik Koghbatsi St 50A; tel. (2) 53-05-70; daily; organ of the Armenian Revolutionary Federation.

**Yerokoyan Yerevan** (Evening Yerevan): 375023 Yerevan, Arshakunyats Ave 2, 10th Floor; tel. (2) 52-97-52; weekly; organ of Yerevan City Council; Editor N. YENGIBARIAN.

**Yeter:** Yerevan, Manukian St 5; tel. (2) 55-34-13; weekly; Editor G. KAZARIAN.

**Zroutsakits:** 375023 Yerevan, Arshakunyats Ave 2, 2nd Floor; tel. (2) 52-84-30; weekly; Editor M. MIRIDJANIAN.

### PRINCIPAL PERIODICALS

**Aghbiur** (Source): Yerevan; f. 1923, fmrly *Pioner*; monthly; for teenagers; Editor T. V. TONOIAN.

**Armenian Kommersant:** Yerevan, Koriuny St 19A; tel. (2) 52-79-77; monthly; Editor M. VARTANIAN.

**Aroghchapakutyun** (Health): 375001 Yerevan, Tumanian St 8; f. 1956; monthly; journal of the Ministry of Health; Editor M. A. MURADIAN.

**Arvest** (Art): 375001 Yerevan, Tumanian St 5; f. 1932, fmrly *Sovetakan Arvest* (Soviet Art); monthly; publ. by the Ministry of Culture, Youth Affairs and Sports; Editor G. A. AZAKELIAN.

**Chetvertaya Vlast:** Yerevan, Abovian St 12, Hotel Yerevan, Room 105; tel. (2) 59-73-81; monthly; Editor A. GEVORKIAN.

**Ekonomika** (Economics): Yerevan, Vardanants St 2; tel. (2) 52-27-95; f. 1957; monthly; organ of the Ministry of the Economy; Editor R. H. SHAKHKULIAN; circ. 1,500–2,000.

**Garun** (Spring): 375015 Yerevan, Karmir Banaki St 15; tel. (2) 56-29-56; f. 1967; monthly; independent; fiction and socio-political issues; Editor L. Z. ANANIAN.

**Gitutyun ev Tekhnika** (Science and Technology): 375048 Yerevan, pr. Komitasa 49/3; tel. (2) 23-37-27; f. 1963; quarterly; journal of the Research Institute of Scientific-Technical Information and of Technological and Economic Research; Dir M. B. YEDILIAN; Editor M. A. CHUGURIAN; circ. 1,000.

**Hayastani Ashkhatavoruhi** (Working Women of Armenia): Yerevan; f. 1924; monthly; Editor A. G. CHILINGARIAN.

**Hayreniky Dzayn** (Voice of the Motherland): Yerevan; f. 1965; weekly; organ of the Armenian Committee for Cultural Relations with Compatriots Abroad; Editor L. H. ZAKARIAN.

**Iravounk:** 375002 Yerevan, Yeznik Koghbatsu St 50A; tel. (2) 53-27-30; fax (2) 53-26-76; e-mail iravunk@sim.arminco.com; f. 1989; monthly; Editor H. BABUKHANIAN; circ. 18,000.

**Literaturnaya Armeniya** (Literature of Armenia): 375019 Yerevan, Marshal Baghramian St 3; tel. (2) 56-36-57; f. 1958; monthly; journal of the Union of Writers; fiction; Russian; Editor A. M. NALBANDIAN.

**Nork:** Yerevan; f. 1934; fmrly *Sovetakan Grakanutyun* (Soviet Literature); monthly; journal of the Union of Writers; fiction; Russian; Editor R. G. OVSEPIAN.

**Novoye Vremya:** 375023 Yerevan, Arshakunyats Ave 2, 3rd Floor; tel. (2) 52-29-61; 2 a week; Editor R. SATIAN.

**Veratsnvats Hayastan** (Reborn Armenia): Yerevan; f. 1945 as *Sovetakan Hayastan* (Soviet Armenia); monthly; journal of the Armenian Committee for Cultural Relations with Compatriots Abroad; fiction; Editor V. A. DAVITIAN.

**The Yerevan Times:** 375009 Yerevan, Isaahakian St 28, 3rd Floor; tel. (2) 52-82-70; fax (2) 15-17-38; e-mail yertime@armpress.arminco.com; weekly; English; Editor T. HAKOBIAN.

### NEWS AGENCIES

**Armenpress** (Armenian Press Agency): 375009 Yerevan, Isaahakian St 28, 4th Floor; tel. (2) 52-67-02; fax (2) 15-17-38; e-mail root@armpress.arminco.com; state information agency, transformed into state joint-stock company in 1997; Dir T. HAKOBIAN.

**Noyan Tapan** (Noah's Ark): 375009 Yerevan, Isaahakian St 28, 3rd Floor; tel. and fax (2) 52-42-18; Dir TIGRAN HARUTYUNIAN.

**Past:** 375023 Yerevan, Arshakunyats Ave 2, 15th Floor; tel. (2) 53-86-18; Dir T. NAGDALIAN.

**Snark:** 375009 Yerevan, Isaahakian St 28, 1st Floor; tel. (2) 52-99-42; fax (2) 56-22-51; Dir V. OGHANIAN.

## Publishers

**Academy of Sciences Publishing House:** 375019 Yerevan, Marshal Baghramian St 24G; Dir KH. H. BARSEGHIAN.

**Ajstan:** 375009 Yerevan, Isaahakian St 28; tel. (2) 52-85-20; f. 1921; government, politics, law, science, literature; Dir. D. M. SARKISSIAN.

**Anait:** Yerevan; art publishing.

**Arevik** (Sun Publishing House): 375009 Yerevan, Terian St 91; tel. (2) 52-45-61; f. 1986; political, scientific, fiction for children; Dir V. S. KALANTARIAN.

**Hayastan** (Armenia Publishing House): 375009 Yerevan, Isaahakian St 91; tel. (2) 52-85-20; f. 1921; political and fiction; Dir DAVID SARKISSIAN.

**Haykakan Hanragitaran** (Armenian Encyclopedia): 375001 Yerevan 1, Tumanian St 17; tel. (2) 52-43-41; f. 1967; encyclopaedias and other reference books; Editor K. S. KHUDAVERDIAN.

**Luys** (Enlightenment Publishing House): Yerevan, Kirov St 19A; textbooks; Dir S. M. MOVSISSIAN.

**Nairi:** Yerevan, Terian St 91; fiction; Dir H. H. FELEKHIAN.

## Broadcasting and Communications

### TELECOMMUNICATIONS

**ArmenTel:** Yerevan; transferred to private ownership in 1998; 10% state-owned, 90% owned by Hellenic Telecommunications Organization (Greece); Exec. Dir GAREGIN MOVSESSIAN; Dep. Exec. Dir ANDRANIK POGOSSIAN.

### BROADCASTING

#### Radio

**Armenian Radio:** 375025 Yerevan, A. Manukian St 5; tel. (2) 55-80-10; fax (2) 55-15-13; 3 programmes; broadcasts inside the republic in Armenian, Russian and Kurdish; external broadcasts in Armenian, Russian, Kurdish, Azeri, Arabic, English, French, Spanish and Farsi; transformed into state joint-stock company in 1997; Dir-Gen. ARMEN AMIRIAN.

#### Television

**Armenian Television:** 375025 Yerevan, A. Manukian St 5; tel. (2) 55-25-02; fax (2) 55-15-13; broadcasts in Armenian and occasionally in Russian; transformed into state joint-stock company in 1997; Dir TIGRAN NAGDALYAN.

## Finance

(cap. = capital; res = reserves; dep. = deposits; m. = million; brs = branches; amounts in drams, unless otherwise stated)

### BANKING

#### Central Bank

**Central Bank of the Republic of Armenia:** 375010 Yerevan, Nalbandian St 6; tel. (2) 58-38-41; fax (2) 15-11-07; e-mail cba@mbox.amilink.net; f. 1991; cap. 100m., res 162.2m. (Nov. 1998); Chair. TIGRAN SARKISSIAN.

#### Commercial Banks

In late 1997 there were reported to be 30 commercial banks in operation in Armenia. Some of the most influential of these are listed below:

**Agrobank Open Joint-Stock Company (Armagrobank):** 375015 Yerevan, M. Khorenatsi St 7A; tel. (2) 53-63-61; fax (2) 90-71-24; e-mail agrobank@mbox.amilink.net; f. 1988, incorporated as joint-stock co in 1992; cap. 279m.; Chair. A. ARZOUMANIAN; 49 brs.

**Ardshinbank (ASHB):** 375010 Yerevan, Deghatan St 3; tel. and fax (2) 15-11-55; e-mail office@ashb.infocom.amilink.net; f. 1922, reorganized as joint-stock commercial bank for industry and construction in 1992; restructured 1997; largest bank in Armenia; cap. 500.0m., res 216.2m., dep. 2,492.8m. (Sept. 1998); Chair. LEVON FARMANYAN; 36 brs.

**Armaviabank:** 375014 Yerevan, Sevaki St 1; tel. (2) 28-88-57; fax (2) 28-19-40.

**Armenian Development Bank:** 375015 Yerevan, Paronian St 21/7; tel. (2) 53-00-94; fax (2) 53-03-12; cap 573.2m., res 51m., dep. 1.2m. (Nov. 1998).

**Armenian Economy Development Bank (Armeconombank):** 375002 Yerevan, Amirian St 23/1; tel. (2) 53-88-00; fax (2) 15-11-49; e-mail bank@aeb.am; internet www.aeb.am; incorporated as joint-stock co in 1992; corporate banking; cap. 1,000m., res 52.8m., dep. 1,462.9m. (Nov. 1998); Chair. of Bd SARIBEK SUKIASSIAN; 22 brs.

**Armenian Import-Export Bank CjSC (Armimpexbank):** 375010 Yerevan, Nalbandian St 2; tel. (2) 58-99-27; fax (2) 15-18-13; e-mail jav@impex.infocom.amilink.net; f. 1992 by reorganization of Armenian br. of the Vneshekonombank of the former USSR; joint-stock co with foreign shareholding; cap. US $2.1m., dep. US $16.6m. (Nov. 1998); Chair. of Bd E. ARABKHANIAN; 10 brs.

**Arminvestbank:** 375010 Yerevan, Vardanants St 13; tel. (2) 52-37-18; fax (39) 07-210; e-mail ibank@aics.am; f. 1992; Chair. of Bd VAROUZHAN AMIRAGIAN.

**Credit-Yerevan Joint-Stock Commercial Bank:** 375010 Yerevan, Amirian 2/8; tel. (2) 58-90-65; fax (2) 15-18-20; e-mail garik@mail.creyer.am; f. 1993; cap. US $2.1m. (Nov. 1998); Pres. MARTIN HOVHANNISIAN.

**HSBC Bank of Armenia:** 375010 Yerevan, Amirian St 1; tel. (2) 56-32-29; fax (2) 15-18-58; f. 1996; cap. 2,438m., res 858.7m., dep. 11,423m. (Nov. 1998); CEO J. A. J. HUNT; 1 br.

**Shirakinvestbank:** 377500 Gyumri, G. Njdeh St 7; tel. (69) 23-86-5; fax (69) 34-88-3; e-mail shib@shirak.am; internet www.shirak.am/bus/shib/shib.html; f. 1996; cap. and res 338.3m., dep. 943.6m. (Dec. 1997); Chair. GRIGOR KONJEIAN; Pres. MESROP KARAPETIAN.

#### Savings Bank

**Armsavingbank:** 375010 Yerevan, Nalbandian St 46; tel. (2) 58-04-51; fax (2) 56-55-78; e-mail root@sberbank.armenia.su; reorganized 1996; cap. 444.4m., res 138.6m., dep. 3,320.1m. (November 1998); Chair. HOVHANNES MANDAKUNI; 35 regional brs.

#### Banking Association

**Association of Banks of Armenia:** Yerevan; Pres. TIGRAN SARKISSIAN.

### COMMODITY AND STOCK EXCHANGES

**Adamand Stock Exchange:** Adamand.

**Gyumri Stock Exchange:** Gyumri, Abovian St 244; tel. (69) 2-31-09; fax (69) 2-10-23; f. 1995; Dir SISAK MCHITARIAN.

**Yerevan Commodity and Raw Materials Exchange:** 375051 Yerevan, Aram Khachaturian St 31/1; tel. (2) 25-26-00; fax (2) 25-09-93; f. 1991; authorized cap. 5m.; Gen. Man. ARA ARZUMANAIAN.

**Yerevan Stock Exchange:** 375010 Yerevan, Hanrapetoutian St 5; tel. (2) 52-32-01; fax (2) 15-15-48; f. 1993; Pres. DR SEDRAK SEDRAKIAN.

### INSURANCE

**Iran-Armenian Insurance Co:** Yerevan; f. 1997.

**Armenian Financial Insurance Co (AFIC):** 375010 Yerevan, Hanrapetoutian St 5; tel. (2) 52-77-93; f. 1996; Exec. Man. LEVON MAMIKONIAN.

## Trade and Industry

### CHAMBER OF COMMERCE

**Chamber of Commerce and Industry of the Republic of Armenia:** 375033 Yerevan, Hanrapetoutian St 39; tel. (2) 56-54-38; fax (2) 56-50-71; Chair. ASHOT SARKISSIAN.

### INDUSTRIAL AND TRADE ASSOCIATION

**Armenintorg—Armenian State Foreign Economic and Trade Association:** 375012 Yerevan, Hr. Kochar St 25; tel. (2) 22-43-10; fax (2) 22-00-34; f. 1987; import and export of all types of goods, marketing, consultancy, auditing and other services, conducts training programmes, arranges international exhibitions and trade fairs; Gen. Dir DR ARMEN R. DARBINIAN; 20 employees.

### EMPLOYERS' ORGANIZATIONS

**Armenian Business Forum:** Yerevan; tel. (2) 52-75-43; fax (2) 52-43-32; f. 1991; promotes joint ventures, foreign capital investments; Pres. VAHE JAZMADARIAN.

**Armenian Union of Industrialists and Entrepreneurs:** Yerevan; Chair. ARAM VARDANIAN.

### UTILITIES

**Armenian Energy Commission:** Yerevan; Chair. VARDAN MOVSISIAN.

#### Electricity

**Medzamor Nuclear Plant:** Medzamor; VVER-440 pressurized water-reactor, with a 410 MW operating capacity.

#### Gas

**Armgazprom:** Yerevan; state gas company; Dir ROLAND ADONTS.

**Armrosgazprom:** Yerevan; f. 1997; Armenian-Russian joint-stock co; Exec. Chair. ROLAND ADONTS; Dep. Exec. Chair. VIKTOR BRLYANSKIKH.

### TRADE UNIONS

**General Confederation of Armenian Trade Unions:** 375010 Yerevan, Hanrapetoutian Sq.; tel. (2) 58-42-78; fax (2) 15-18-78; Chair. MARTIN ARUTYUNIAN.

## Transport

### RAILWAYS

In 1995 there were 806 km of railway track. There are international lines to Iran and Georgia; lines to Azerbaijan and Turkey remained closed in late 1999, as a result of those countries' continuing economic blockade of Armenia.

**Armenia Railways:** 375005 Yerevan, Tigran the Great St 50; tel. (2) 54-42-28; f. 1992 following the dissolution of the former Soviet Railways; Pres. G. G. BERIAN.

#### Metropolitan Railway

An initial 10-km route, with nine stations, opened in 1981, and a 10-km extension, with two stations, is currently under construction. A second line is planned, and ultimate proposals envisage the installation of a 47-km network.

**Yerevan Metro:** 375033 Yerevan, Marshal Bagramian Ave 76; tel. (2) 27-45-43; fax (2) 15-13-95; f. 1981; Gen. Man. H. BEGLARIAN.

### ROADS

In 1997 there were 8,431 km of roads in Armenia (including 3,361 km of highways and 4,206 km of secondary roads). In the mid-1990s some 40% of the network was estimated to be in poor condition and in need of repair. In 1996 plans were made to upgrade existing roads, and to construct some 1,400 km of new roads over the next four years, with financial assistance from various international organizations. As a result of the economic blockade imposed in 1989 by Azerbaijan (and subsequently reinforced by Turkey), the Kajaran highway linking Armenia with Iran emerged as Armenia's most important international road connection; in December 1995 a permanent road bridge over the Araks (Aras) river was opened, strengthening this link. In mid-1997 a bus route to Syria was opened—the first overland route between the two countries.

### CIVIL AVIATION

**Armenian Airlines:** 375042 Yerevan, Zvarnots Airport; tel. (2) 28-28-60; fax (2) 15-13-93; f. 1993; operates scheduled and charter passenger services to countries of the CIS, Europe and the Middle East; Man. Dir VYACHESLAV YARALOV.

## Tourism

Prior to secession from the USSR in 1991, Armenia attracted a number of tourists from the other Soviet republics. Following its independence, however, tourism severely declined, although in the late 1990s some European firms were beginning to introduce tours to the country. According to the World Tourism Organization, tourism receipts increased from about US $1m. in 1995 to $12m. in 1996. The major tourist attractions were the capital, Yerevan; Artashat, an early trading centre on the 'Silk Road'; and medieval monasteries. There was, however, little accommodation available outside the capital.

# AUSTRALIA

## Introductory Survey

### Location, Climate, Language, Religion, Flag, Capital

The Commonwealth of Australia occupies the whole of the island continent of Australia, lying between the Indian and Pacific Oceans, and its offshore islands, principally Tasmania to the south-east. Australia's nearest neighbour is Papua New Guinea, to the north. In the summer (November–February) there are tropical monsoons in the northern part of the continent (except for the Queensland coast), but the winters (July–August) are dry. Both the north-west and north-east coasts are liable to experience tropical cyclones between December and April. In the southern half of the country, winter is the wet season; rainfall decreases rapidly inland. Very high temperatures, sometimes exceeding 50°C (122°F), are experienced during the summer months over the arid interior and for some distance to the south, as well as during the pre-monsoon months in the north. The official language is English; 170 indigenous languages are spoken by Aboriginal and Torres Strait Islander peoples. At the census of 1996 70.9% of the population professed Christianity (of whom 27.0% were Roman Catholic and 22.0% Anglican). The national flag (proportions 2 by 1) is blue, with a representation of the United Kingdom flag in the upper hoist, a large seven-pointed white star in the lower hoist and five smaller white stars, in the form of the Southern Cross constellation, in the fly. The capital, Canberra, lies in one of two enclaves of federal territory known as the Australian Capital Territory (ACT).

### Recent History

Since the Second World War, Australia has played an important role in Asian affairs, and has strengthened its political and economic ties with Indonesia, and the other countries of South-East Asia, and with Japan. The country co-operates more closely than formerly with the USA (see ANZUS, p. 300), and has given much aid to Asian and Pacific countries.

At the election of December 1949 the ruling Australian Labor Party (ALP) was defeated by the Liberal Party, in coalition with the Country Party. In January 1966 Sir Robert Menzies resigned after 16 years as Prime Minister, and was succeeded by Harold Holt, who was returned to office at elections in December of that year. However, Holt died in December 1967. His successor, Senator John Gorton, took office in January 1968 but resigned, after losing a vote of confidence, in March 1971. William McMahon was Prime Minister from March 1971 until December 1972, when, after 23 years in office, the Liberal-Country Party coalition was defeated at a general election for the House of Representatives. The ALP, led by Gough Whitlam, won 67 of the 125 seats in the House. Following a conflict between the Whitlam Government and the Senate, both Houses of Parliament were dissolved in April 1974, and a general election was held in May. The ALP was returned to power, although with a reduced majority in the House of Representatives. However, the Government failed to gain a majority in the Senate, and in October 1975 the Opposition in the Senate obstructed legislative approval of budget proposals. The Government was not willing to consent to a general election over the issue, but in November the Governor-General, Sir John Kerr, intervened and took the unprecedented step of dismissing the Government. A caretaker Ministry was installed under Malcolm Fraser, the Liberal leader, who formed a coalition Government with the Country Party. This coalition gained large majorities in both Houses of Parliament at a general election in December 1975, but the majorities were progressively reduced at general elections in December 1977 and October 1980.

Fraser's coalition Government was defeated by the ALP at a general election in March 1983. Robert (Bob) Hawke, who had replaced William (Bill) Hayden as Labor leader in the previous month, became the new Prime Minister and immediately organized a meeting of representatives of government, employers and trade unions to reach agreement on a prices and incomes policy (the 'Accord') that would allow economic recovery. Hawke called a general election for December 1984, 15 months earlier than necessary, and the ALP was returned to power with a reduced majority in the House of Representatives. The opposition coalition between the Liberal Party and the National Party (formerly known as the Country Party) collapsed in April 1987, when 12 National Party MPs withdrew from the agreement and formed the New National Party (led by the right-wing Sir Johannes Bjelke-Petersen, the Premier of Queensland), while the remaining 14 National Party MPs continued to support their leader, Ian Sinclair, who wished to remain within the alliance. Parliament was dissolved in June, in preparation for an early general election in July. The election campaign was dominated by economic issues. The ALP was returned to office with an increased majority, securing 86 of the 148 seats in the House of Representatives. The Liberal and National Parties announced the renewal of the opposition alliance in August. Four months later, Bjelke-Petersen was forced to resign as Premier of Queensland, under pressure from National Party officials.

During 1988 the Hawke Government suffered several defeats at by-elections, seemingly as a result of a decline in living standards and an unpopular policy of wage restraint. The ALP narrowly retained power at state elections in Victoria, but was defeated in New South Wales, where it had held power for 12 years. In May 1989 the leader of the Liberal Party, John Howard, was replaced by Andrew Peacock, and Charles Blunt succeeded Ian Sinclair as leader of the National Party. In July a commission of inquiry into alleged corruption in Queensland published its report. The Fitzgerald report documented several instances of official corruption and electoral malpractice by the Queensland Government, particularly during the administration of Bjelke-Petersen. Following the publication of the report, support for the National Party within Queensland declined once more, and in December the ALP defeated the National Party in the state election (the first time that it had defeated the National Party in Queensland since 1957). By the end of 1991 four former members of the Queensland Cabinet and the former chief of the state's police force had received custodial sentences. The trial of Bjelke-Petersen, initially on charges of perjury and corruption but subsequently of perjury alone, resulted in dismissal of the case, when the jury failed to reach a verdict.

In August 1989 the popularity of the Hawke Government was further damaged by a dispute between the major domestic airlines and the airline pilots' federation. The pilots had resigned *en masse* when both Ansett and Australian Airlines, with government approval, had rejected their claim for a 29.5% increase in wages. In September Hawke announced that the Government was to award substantial compensation to the airlines. In November the airlines intensified overseas recruitment initiatives, while maintaining a very limited service. By February 1990 the airlines claimed to have restored their operations, and in March the remaining rebel pilots ended their strike.

In February 1990 Hawke announced that a general election for the House of Representatives and for 40 of the 76 seats in the Senate was to be held on 24 March. The Government's position in the period preceding the election had been strengthened by the ALP's victory in Queensland in December 1989, the removal of an unpopular Labor leadership in Western Australia and its replacement by the first female Premier, Dr Carmen Lawrence, and by the support that it secured from environmental groups as a result of its espousal of 'green' issues. Although the opposition parties won the majority of the first-preference votes in the election for the House of Representatives, the endorsement of the environmental groups delivered a block of second-preference votes to the ALP, which was consequently returned to power, albeit with a reduced majority, securing 78 of the 148 seats. Following its defeat, Peacock immediately resigned as leader of the Liberal Party and was replaced by Dr John Hewson, a former professor of economics. Blunt lost his seat in the election and was succeeded as leader of the National Party by Timothy Fischer.

In September 1990, at a meeting of senior ALP members, government proposals to initiate a controversial programme of privatization were endorsed, effectively ending almost 100 years of the ALP's stance against private ownership. In October plans for constitutional and structural reform were approved in principle by the leaders of the six state and two territory governments. The proposed reforms envisaged the creation of national standards in regulations and services. They also aimed to alleviate the financial dependence of the states and territories on the Federal Government. These suggested reforms, however, encountered strong opposition from sections of the public services, the trade unions and the business community. In July 1991 the leaders of the federal and state Governments finally agreed to reforms in the country's systems of marketing, transport, trade and taxation, with the aim of creating a single national economy from 1992.

In April 1991, as a result of preliminary investigations by a Royal Commission into the financial dealings of the Labor Government of Western Australia in the 1980s, Brian Burke, the former state Premier, resigned as Australia's ambassador to Ireland and the Holy See. Owing to the alleged irregularities, more than $A1,000m. of public funds were believed to have been lost. In May the Premier of New South Wales called a state election, 10 months earlier than was necessary, in an attempt to capitalize on the problems of Labor administrations at federal and state level. However, the Liberal-National Party Government lost its overall majority and was able to retain power only with the support of independent members of the state legislature.

In June 1991, following months of divisions within the ALP, Hawke narrowly defeated a challenge to his leadership from Paul Keating, the Deputy Prime Minister and Treasurer, who accused the Prime Minister of reneging on a promise to resign in his favour before the next general election. This cast doubt on Hawke's credibility, as he had assured Parliament and the public in 1990 that he would continue as leader for the whole of the parliamentary term. Following his defeat, Keating resigned. In December Hawke dismissed John Kerin, Keating's replacement as Treasurer, following a series of political and economic crises. Hawke called another leadership election, but, on this occasion, he was defeated by Keating, who accordingly became Prime Minister. A major reorganization of the Cabinet followed. John Dawkins, a staunch supporter of Keating, was appointed Treasurer.

Following the ALP's recent defeat in state elections in Tasmania, the party encountered further embarrassment in April 1992, when a by-election in Melbourne to fill the parliamentary seat vacated by Bob Hawke was won by a local football club coach, standing as an independent candidate. In May the Prime Minister suffered another set-back, when Graham Richardson, the Minister for Transport and Communications, resigned, owing to his implication in a scandal involving a relative who was alleged to have participated in an illegal scheme whereby Taiwanese investors were able to secure US residency rights via the Marshall Islands. In the following month Nick Greiner, the Liberal-National Premier of New South Wales, was obliged to resign, as a result of accusations of corruption. In August, however, he was exonerated by the state's Supreme Court.

Meanwhile, Brian Burke, the former Premier of Western Australia, had been arrested. It was alleged that, during his term of office, he had misappropriated more than $A17,000 from a parliamentary expense account. In October 1992 the conclusions of the inquiry into the ALP's alleged involvement in corrupt practices in Western Australia were released. The Royal Commission was highly critical of the improper transactions between successive governments of Western Australia and business entrepreneurs. The conduct of Brian Burke drew particular criticism. (In July 1994 Burke received a prison sentence of two years upon conviction on four charges of fraud; he was released in February 1995, but was sentenced to three years' imprisonment in February 1997 for the theft of $A122,000 from ALP funds.) Furthermore, in February 1995 Ray O'Connor, Premier of Western Australia between 1982 and 1983, received a prison sentence of 18 months, having been found guilty of the theft in 1984 of $A25,000, intended as a donation to the Liberal Party. He was released in August 1995.

In September 1992 John Bannon became the seventh state Premier since 1982 to leave office in disgrace. The resignation of the ALP Premier of South Australia was due to a scandal relating to attempts to offset the heavy financial losses incurred by the State Bank of South Australia. At state elections in Queensland in mid-September, the ALP administration of Wayne Goss was returned to power. In the following month, however, the ruling ALP was defeated in state elections in Victoria. Furthermore, in November a new financial scandal emerged: the federal Treasurer was alleged to have suppressed information pertaining to the former ALP Government of Victoria which, in a clandestine manner prior to the state elections, was believed to have exceeded its borrowing limits.

By late 1992, therefore, the ALP's prospects of being returned to office at the forthcoming general election appeared to have been seriously damaged. Proposals for radical tax and economic reforms that were advocated by the federal opposition leader, Dr John Hewson, attracted much attention. At state elections in Western Australia in February 1993, the incumbent Labor Government was defeated. Dr Carmen Lawrence was replaced as Premier by Richard Court of the Liberal-National coalition.

Nevertheless, at the general election, held on 13 March 1993, the ALP was unexpectedly returned to office, for a fifth consecutive term, having secured 80 of the 147 seats in the House of Representatives. The new Government, appointed later that month, included many younger members, although several senior ministers were retained. John Dawkins resigned as Treasurer in December 1993. A government reorganization followed, in which Dawkins was replaced by Ralph Willis.

In January 1994 the Government was embarrassed by the resignation of the Minister of Industry, Technology and Regional Development, Alan Griffiths, as a result of allegations that public funds and ALP resources had been misappropriated in order to meet the private business debts incurred by his Melbourne sandwich shop. In the following month Ros Kelly, the Minister for Environment, Sport and Territories and close associate of the Prime Minister, yielded to pressure to resign, owing to a scandal relating to the alleged use of community sports grants to attempt to influence voters in vulnerable ALP-held constituencies prior to the 1993 general election. In March 1994 Graham Richardson, the Minister for Health, resigned. In the ensuing government reorganization, Dr Carmen Lawrence, former Premier of Western Australia, joined the Cabinet as Minister for Health.

In May 1994 Dr John Hewson was replaced as leader of the Liberal Party by Alexander Downer, a supporter of the monarchy. Downer was therefore expected to lead the campaign against Paul Keating's proposal that Australia become a republic by the year 2001 (see below). In January 1995, however, Downer resigned. The party leadership was resumed by John Howard, also a monarchist.

At state elections in New South Wales in March 1995 the ALP defeated the ruling Liberal-National coalition. Robert (Bob) Carr was appointed Premier. At a federal by-election in Canberra, however, the ALP suffered a serious reverse when, for the first time in 15 years, the seat fell to the Liberal Party. In July, at state elections in Queensland, the ALP Government of Wayne Goss was narrowly returned to office, only to be ousted following a by-election defeat in February 1996. In June 1995, meanwhile, the Deputy Prime Minister, Brian Howe, who intended to retire at the next general election, announced his resignation from the Cabinet. He was replaced by the Minister for Finance, Kim Beazley.

At the general election held on 2 March 1996 the Liberal-National coalition achieved a decisive victory, securing a total of 94 of the 148 seats in the House of Representatives. The ALP won only 49 seats. In the Senate the minor parties and independent members retained the balance of power. John Howard of the Liberal Party became Prime Minister, and immediately promised to give priority to the issues of industrial relations, the transfer to partial private ownership of the state telecommunications company, Telstra, and to expanding relations with Asia. The leader of the National Party, Tim Fischer, was appointed Deputy Prime Minister and Minister for Trade. Paul Keating was replaced as leader of the ALP by Kim Beazley.

In August 1996, in an unprecedented display of violence, demonstrators protesting against proposed budget cuts stormed the Parliament building in Canberra. Clashes between the police and the protesters resulted in many injuries. Meanwhile, fears for Australia's tradition of racial tolerance continued to grow. In October Pauline Hanson, a newly-elected independent member of the House of Representatives, aroused much controversy when, in a speech envisaging 'civil war', she reiterated her demands for the ending of immigration from Asia and for the elimination of special funding for Aboriginal people. The Prime Minister attracted criticism for his failure to issue a direct denunciation of the views of Pauline Hanson, a former member of the Liberal Party. The increasingly bitter debate also damaged Australia's image in the countries of Asia, a vital source of investment and of tourist revenue. In March 1997, moreover, the One Nation Party was established by Pauline Hanson and rapidly attracted support. In May, while attending a fund-raising rally in Perth, Pauline Hanson was besieged by more than 1,000 opponents. Larger protests against her policies followed in Melbourne and Canberra. Meanwhile, after his initial weak response, the Prime Minister condemned the views of the founder of the One Nation Party. In August, as fears for Australian revenue from Asian investment, trade and tourism grew, the Government issued a document on foreign policy, in which Pauline Hanson's views were strongly repudiated and in which Australia's commitment to racial equality was reiterated. In order to counter the negative impact of the activities of the One Nation Party, a special diplomatic unit was established. In November 1997, furthermore, former Prime Ministers Keating, Hawke and Whitlam published a statement denouncing Pauline Hanson.

In July 1997 the Minister for Small Business and Consumer Affairs was obliged to resign amid controversy over a conflict of interest. In September a scandal arising from apparently illicit claims for parliamentary travel allowances led to further resignations, and in October the Prime Minister announced major changes in the composition of his Government. These included the removal of the employment portfolio from Senator Amanda Vanstone, the post being regarded as of vital importance as the next general election approached and as the issue of unemployment remained a principal concern. In October Senator Cheryl Kernot, leader of the Australian Democrats Party, announced her defection to the ALP, from where she hoped better to oppose the Liberal-National Government.

In early 1998 the long-standing tension between the National Farmers' Federation and the powerful Maritime Union of Australia (MUA) developed into a bitter dispute over trade unionists' rights when farmers established their own non-unionized stevedoring operation in Melbourne to handle their exports, in protest at high dockside costs and alleged inefficiency. The confrontation escalated in April, when Patrick Stevedores, a major cargo-handling company based in Sydney, dismissed its entire unionized work-force of 1,400 dockers, with the intention of replacing them with secretly-trained contract workers. As part of its campaign to break the MUA monopoly (the offensive being supported by the Government), Patrick Stevedores drafted in hundreds of security guards to its 14 terminals around Australia, in an operation to lock out the dockers. The Federal Court, however, subsequently ruled that Patrick Stevedores had acted illegally and ordered the company to reinstate the 1,400 trade unionists. Following the rejection of an appeal to the High Court by Patrick Stevedores and the return to work of the dockers in May, the Prime Minister nevertheless pledged to press ahead with waterfront reform. Although the majority of Australians appeared to support the reform of labour practices in the country's ports, the Government's handling of the dispute had attracted much criticism.

In December 1997 the New One Nation Party was established by former supporters of Pauline Hanson, who had apparently become disillusioned with her autocratic style of leadership. In June 1998, at state elections in Queensland, the One Nation Party won 23% of first-preference votes, thus unexpectedly securing 11 of the 89 seats in the legislature and leading to renewed concern among tourism and business leaders. In August it was announced that an early general election was to be held in October. As the campaign commenced, former Prime Ministers Whitlam, Fraser, Hawke and Keating signed an open letter urging citizens not to support racist candidates at the forthcoming election.

At the election, conducted on 3 October 1998, the Liberal-National coalition was narrowly returned to office, winning a total of 80 of the 148 seats in the House of Representatives. The ALP, led by Kim Beazley, increased its representation to 67 seats. Contrary to expectations, the One Nation Party failed to win any representation in the lower house, the controversial Pauline Hanson losing her Queensland seat. (The one seat secured by the One Nation Party in the Senate was subsequently subjected to a legal challenge, owing to the candidate's apparent failure to meet citizenship requirements—see below.) In a referendum held on the same day, the electorate of the Northern Territory unexpectedly rejected a proposal for the territory's elevation to full statehood. In mid-October the Prime Minister announced the composition of his new Cabinet; most senior ministers retained their portfolios. Changes included the establishment of a special portfolio (transport and regional services) to focus on rural issues, in response to the ruling coalition's poor electoral performance in rural areas. John Howard also created a new Ministry of Financial Services and Regulation. The incoming Government's programme incorporated the implementation of a controversial 10% goods-and-services tax (GST) and the transfer to the private sector of the remaining two-thirds of the assets of Telstra.

In February 1999 Pauline Hanson was re-elected leader of the One Nation Party, despite a series of defections, including the departure from the party of several of the 11 One Nation members of the Queensland legislature. At state elections in New South Wales in March, at which the ALP was returned to power, the One Nation Party won two seats in the 42-member upper chamber. In June a court ruled that the One Nation Senator was ineligible to occupy her seat in the federal upper house, owing to her failure to renounce her British citizenship prior to the general election. She was subsequently replaced by another member of the One Nation Party.

Following a protracted debate, in June 1999 the Senate narrowly approved the Government's proposal to dispose of a further 16.6% of the assets of Telstra (to bring the total transferred to the private sector to 49.9%). Two independent Senators, including the veteran Brian Harradine of Tasmania, had initially opposed the plan, but reversed their stance in exchange for commitments of additional funding for their respective regions. Kim Beazley, leader of the opposition ALP, denounced the arrangement as 'shameful'. The Treasurer, however, maintained that the sale of a further tranche of the telecommunications corporation would permit the Government drastically to reduce public debt. The Senate subsequently approved proposals to introduce the GST.

In June 1999 Tim Fischer, Deputy Prime Minister and Minister for Trade and leader of the National Party, unexpectedly announced his resignation. He was replaced as leader of the National Party by John Anderson, hitherto Minister for Transport and Regional Services, those portfolios being retained upon his subsequent appointment as Deputy Prime Minister. Mark Vaile, hitherto Minister for Agriculture, Forestry and Fisheries, became Minister for Trade.

Following state elections in Victoria in September 1999, the Liberal-National Premier, Jeffrey Kennett, was replaced by Stephen Bracks of the ALP. The defeat of the Liberal-National coalition was regarded as a set-back to the Federal Government's programme of economic reform, the transfer of public utilities to the private sector having been particularly unpopular among the voters of Victoria.

In March 1986, meanwhile, Australia's constitutional links with the United Kingdom (UK) were reduced by the Australia Act, which abolished the British Parliament's residual legislative, executive and judicial controls over Australian state law. In February 1992, shortly after a visit by Queen Elizabeth, Paul Keating caused a furore by accusing the UK of abandoning Australia to the Japanese threat during the Second World War. Following a visit to the UK in September 1993, Keating announced that Australia was to become a republic by the year 2001, subject to approval by referendum. Sir William Deane succeeded William Hayden as Governor-General in February 1996, the former's term of office being scheduled to expire at the end of the year 2000. Although John Howard personally favoured the retention of the monarchy, in 1996 the new Prime Minister announced plans for a constitutional convention, prior to the holding of a referendum on the issue if necessary. In an unexpected development in January 1997, the Deputy Prime Minister put forward proposals for the removal from the Constitution of all references to the monarch and for the transfer of the Queen's functions to Australia's Chief Justice.

Voluntary postal voting to select, from among 609 candidates, 76 delegates who were to attend the constitutional convention (scheduled for February 1998) commenced in November 1997. The complex system of preferential voting, however, appeared to give rise to much confusion, particularly in New South Wales where a total of 174 candidates were contesting 20 places at the forthcoming convention. In addition to the official groupings, the Australian Republican Movement (ARM) and Australians for a Constitutional Monarchy (ACM), numerous other republican and monarchist, as well as individual, candidates were standing for election. Only 42.6% of registered voters were reported to have returned their ballot papers, the participation rate in New South Wales being only 39.9%. In February 1998, following nine days of debate, a majority of the 152 delegates (a further 76 having been appointed by the Government) endorsed proposals to adopt a republican system and to replace the British monarch as Head of State. Although the Constitutional

Convention was dominated by Republicans, delegates were divided over the method of election of a future head of state.

In December 1998 it was confirmed that a referendum on the republican issue would be held in late 1999. In August 1999 the Federal Parliament gave approval to the wording of the question to be posed to the electorate, which was to be asked if support was forthcoming for an 'act to alter the Constitution to establish the Commonwealth of Australia as a republic with the Queen and Governor-General being replaced by a President appointed by a two-thirds majority of the members of the Commonwealth Parliament'. At the referendum, conducted on 6 November 1999, 55% of voters favoured the retention of the monarchy. Many observers, however, interpreted the result as a rejection of the particular republican system offered, opinion polls having indicated that more than two-thirds of Australians would support the introduction of a republican system of government if the President were to be directly elected.

In May 1987 Australia and the UK began a joint operation to ascertain the extent of plutonium contamination resulting from British nuclear weapons testing at Maralinga in South Australia between 1956 and 1963. Many Australians were highly critical of the UK's apparent disregard for the environmental consequences of the tests and of the British authorities' failure to make adequate arrangements to protect the local Aboriginal people, who were now campaigning for a thorough decontamination of their traditional lands. In June 1993 Australia announced its acceptance of $A45m. in compensation from the British Government for the cost of the decontamination. In December 1994 the displaced Aboriginal people and the federal Government reached agreement on a compensation settlement of $A13.5m., to be spent on health, employment and infrastructural projects. In January 1999, furthermore, it was announced that the Australian and British Governments were to conduct separate inquiries into research linking the nuclear tests to the numerous cases of a rare form of cancer in servicemen who had witnessed the explosions.

The sensitive issue of Aboriginal land rights was addressed by the Government in August 1985, when it formulated proposals for legislation that would give Aboriginal people inalienable freehold title to national parks, vacant Crown land and former Aboriginal reserves, in spite of widespread opposition from state governments (which had previously been responsible for their own land policies), from mining companies and from the Aboriginal people themselves, who were angered by the Government's withdrawal of its earlier support for the Aboriginal right to veto mineral exploitation. In October 1985 Ayers Rock, in the Northern Territory, was officially transferred to the Mutijulu Aboriginal community, on condition that continuing access to the rock (the main inland tourist attraction) be guaranteed. In 1986, however, the Government abandoned its pledge to impose such federal legislation on unwilling state governments, and this led to further protests from Aboriginal leaders. In June 1991 the Government imposed a permanent ban on mining at an historical Aboriginal site in the Northern Territory.

An important precedent was established in June 1992, when the High Court overruled the concept of *terra nullius* (unoccupied land) by recognizing the existence of land titles that predated European settlement in 1788 in cases where a close association with the land in question had been continued; however, land titles legally acquired since 1788 were to remain intact. As a result of the 'Mabo' decision of 1992 (named after the Aboriginal claimant, Eddie Mabo), in December 1993 Parliament approved the Native Title Act, historic legislation granting Aboriginal people the right to claim title to their traditional lands. Despite the Prime Minister's personal involvement in the issue, the legislation aroused much controversy, particularly in Western Australia (vast areas of the state being vacant Crown land) where rival legislation to replace native title rights with lesser rights to traditional land usage, such as access for ceremonial purposes only, had been enacted. In March 1995 the High Court declared the Native Title Act to be valid, rejecting as unconstitutional Western Australia's own legislation. The ruling was expected to have widespread implications for the mining industry.

In October 1996, following protracted delays in the development of a valuable zinc mine in Queensland owing to Aboriginal land claims, the Howard Government announced proposals to amend the Native Title Act to permit federal ministers to overrule Aboriginal concerns if a project of 'major economic benefit' to Australia were threatened. Other proposed amendments included the simplification of the process of negotiation between potential developers and Aboriginal claimants. In December the Larrakia people of the Northern Territory presented a claim under the Native Title Act. The area in question incorporated the city of Darwin and was thus the first such claim to encompass a provincial capital. In the same month the federal High Court upheld an appeal by two Aboriginal communities in Queensland (including the Wik people of Cape York) against an earlier ruling that prevented them from submitting a claim to land leased by the state Government to cattle and sheep farmers. The Court's decision, known as the Wik judgment, was expected to encourage similar challenges to 'pastoral' leases, which covered 40% of Australia. Vociferous protests from farmers, who were strongly opposed to the co-existence of native title and pastoral leases, followed.

In April 1997 the first native title deed to be granted on mainland Australia was awarded to the Dunghutti people of New South Wales. In the same month the Prime Minister announced the introduction of legislation to clarify the issue of land tenure; a 10-point plan was to be drawn up in consultation with state governments and with representatives of the Aboriginal community. In September the Government introduced the Wik Native Title Bill, which was subsequently passed by the House of Representatives. In November, however, the Senate questioned the constitutional validity of the proposed legislation, whereby pastoralists' rights and activities would prevail over, but not extinguish (as had been assumed), the Aboriginal people's rights to Native Title. In December the Government refused to accept the Senate's proposed amendments to the legislation, thus raising the possibility of an early general election dominated by Aboriginal issues. In April 1998 the Senate rejected the legislation for a second time. Finally, in July, following a protracted and acrimonious debate, the Senate narrowly approved the Native Title Amendment Bill, thereby restricting the Aboriginal people's rights to claim access to Crown land leased to farmers. The passage of the controversial legislation was immediately denounced by Aboriginal leaders, who threatened to enlist international support for their cause. In the same month, however, the federal court of Darwin granted communal (but not exclusive) native title to the waters and seabed around Croker Island in the Northern Territory to five Aboriginal groups. With about 140 similar claims over Australian waters pending, the historic ruling represented the first recognition of native title rights over the sea. In March 1999, in a conciliatory gesture that settled a land claim case outstanding since 1845, the Tasmanian Government relinquished the site of a mission station at Wybellena, where 200 Aboriginal people had been forcibly resettled; most had subsequently died of disease and maltreatment.

In November 1987 an official commission of inquiry into the cause of the high death rate among Aboriginal prisoners recommended immediate government action, and in July 1988 it was announced that 108 cases remained to be investigated. In August 1988 a UN report accused Australia of violating international human rights in its treatment of the Aboriginal people. In November the Government announced an inquiry into its Aboriginal Affairs Department, following accusations, made by the opposition coalition, of nepotism and misuse of funds. The commission of inquiry published its first official report in February 1989. Following the report's recommendations, the Government announced the creation of a $A10m. programme to combat the high death rate among Aboriginal prisoners. In October an unofficial study indicated that Aboriginal people, although accounting for only 1% of the total population of Australia, comprised more than 20% of persons in prison. In May 1991 the report of the Royal Commission into Aboriginal Deaths in Custody was published, after three years of investigation. The report outlined evidence of racial prejudice in the police force and included more than 300 recommendations for changes in policies relating to Aboriginal people, aimed at improving relations between the racial groups of Australia and granting Aboriginal people greater self-determination and access to land ownership. In June Parliament established a Council for Aboriginal Reconciliation. In March 1992, Aboriginal deaths in custody having continued, radical plans for judicial, economic and social reforms, aimed at improving the lives of Aboriginal people, were announced. The Government made an immediate allocation of $A150m.; a total of $A500m. was to be made available over the next 10 years. In February 1993 the human rights organization, Amnesty International, issued a highly critical report on the prison conditions of Aboriginal people. In March 1996 Amnesty International claimed that

Australia had made little progress with regard to its treatment of Aboriginal prisoners.

In July 1996 the Roman Catholic Church issued an apology for its role in the forcible removal from their parents of tens of thousands of Aboriginal children, in a controversial practice of placement in white foster homes, where many were abused. This policy of assimilation had continued until the late 1960s. In August 1996 the new Governor-General, Sir William Deane, urged all state parliaments to affirm their support for reconciliation with the Aboriginal people. The legislature of South Australia was the first to do so, in November. In May 1997 the publication of the findings of a two-year inquiry into the removal of as many as 100,000 Aboriginal children from their families had profound political repercussions. The author of the report, a distinguished former judge and President of the Human Rights and Equal Opportunities Commission, urged the Government to issue a formal apology to the 'stolen generation'. At a conference on reconciliation at the end of the month, the Prime Minister made an unexpected personal apology. The Government, however, repudiated the commission's assertion that the policy of assimilation had been tantamount to genocide and rejected recommendations that compensation be paid to victims. In July 1997, furthermore, with more than 1,000 claims pending, the federal High Court ruled that a group of Aboriginal applicants could not sue for compensation for their removal from their parents. In December the Government reaffirmed that it would not issue a formal apology to the 'stolen generation'. A $A63m. programme to help reunite divided Aboriginal families was nevertheless announced. In February 1998 the Anglican Church apologized unreservedly for its part in the removal of Aboriginal children from their families. In May, on the occasion of 'National Sorry Day' during which thousands of Australians accepted an invitation to sign books of apology, the Prime Minister continued to refuse to grant a formal apology, maintaining that the issue was best addressed by means of health, housing and education programmes. In August 1999, in a Darwin court, a test case against the Federal Government opened: two members of the 'stolen generation' were suing the authorities for compensation and punitive damages for the trauma occasioned by their forcible removal from their families. About 30,000 similar cases were believed to be pending. In the same month the Prime Minister expressed his regret that indigenous Australians had suffered injustices under the practices of previous generations. His motion was approved by both chambers of Parliament.

In foreign affairs, the Hawke and Keating Governments placed greater emphasis on links with South-East Asia. This policy was continued by John Howard, who pledged to expand relations with Asia. In January 1989 Hawke proposed the creation of an Asia-Pacific Economic Co-operation forum (APEC, see p. 122) to facilitate the exchange of services, tourism and direct foreign investment in the region. The inaugural APEC conference took place in Canberra in November 1989.

Australian relations with Indonesia, which had been strained since the Indonesian annexation of the former Portuguese colony of East Timor in 1976, improved in August 1985, when Hawke made a statement recognizing Indonesian sovereignty over the territory, but subsequently deteriorated, following the publication in a Sydney newspaper, in April 1986, of an article containing allegations of corruption against the Indonesian President, Gen. Suharto. Relations between Australia and Indonesia improved in December 1989, when they signed an accord regarding joint exploration for petroleum and gas reserves in the Timor Gap, an area of sea forming a disputed boundary between the two countries. Portugal, however, withdrew its ambassador from Canberra in protest, and in February 1991 instituted proceedings against Australia at the International Court of Justice. In June 1995 the Court refused to invalidate the exploration treaty. In April 1992 Paul Keating's visit to Indonesia, the new Prime Minister's first official overseas trip, aroused controversy, owing to the repercussions of the massacre of unarmed civilians in East Timor by Indonesian troops in November 1991. On another visit to Jakarta in June 1994, the Australian Prime Minister attempted to concentrate on economic issues. In July 1995, owing to strong opposition in Australia, Indonesia was obliged to withdraw the appointment as ambassador to Canberra of Lt-Gen. (retd) Herman Mantiri, a former Chief of the General Staff of the Armed Forces and an apparent supporter of the November 1991 Dili massacre. Nevertheless, in December 1995 Australia and Indonesia unexpectedly signed a joint security treaty. In March 1996 a new Indonesian ambassador took up his appointment in Canberra, and in September, following a visit to Jakarta by John Howard, Indonesia accepted Australia's ambassador-designate.

Meanwhile, the investigation into the deaths of six Australia-based journalists (including two Britons) in East Timor in 1975 had been reopened, and in June 1996 a government report concluded that they had been murdered by Indonesian soldiers. In October 1996, as Canberra continued to fail to denounce the Suharto Government's violations of human rights, Australian senators from all parties urged the Government to withdraw its recognition of Indonesian sovereignty over East Timor. In March 1997 Australia and Indonesia signed a treaty defining their seabed and 'economic zone' boundaries. The political unrest in Indonesia in early 1998, culminating in President Suharto's replacement in May, caused deep concern in Australia. In August the International Commission of Jurists, the Geneva-based human-rights organization, reported that five of the six journalists had been murdered in an East Timorese village in October 1975 in an attempt to conceal the invasion of the territory, while the sixth man was killed in Dili in December of that year. Furthermore, it was claimed that the Australian embassy in Jakarta had been aware of the forthcoming invasion of East Timor but had failed to give adequate warning to the journalists. In October 1998, as newly-emerging evidence continued to suggest that the truth had been suppressed and as interest in the matter was renewed in the United Kingdom, the Indonesian Government declared that it would not open an inquiry into the deaths of the two British journalists, maintaining that they and their colleagues had been killed in cross-fire. Australia, however, announced that its judicial inquiry was to be reopened.

In January 1999, in a significant shift in its policy, Australia announced that henceforth it would support eventual self-determination for East Timor. (Australia had been the only developed nation to recognize Indonesia's annexation of the territory.) In late January, furthermore, Australia welcomed the Indonesian Government's declaration of its willingness to consider the possibility of full independence, if proposals for autonomy were rejected by the East Timorese people. During 1999, however, Australia became increasingly concerned at the deteriorating security situation in East Timor. The announcement of the result of the referendum on the future of East Timor, held in late August, at which the territory's people voted overwhelmingly in favour of independence (see chapter on Indonesia) led to a rapid escalation of the violence. As pro-Jakarta militias embarked upon a campaign of murder and arson against innocent civilians, most of whom were forced to flee their homes, thousands of refugees were airlifted to safety in northern Australia. With a commitment of 4,500 troops in its largest operation since the Viet Nam War, Australia took a leading role in the deployment of a multinational peace-keeping force, the first contingent of which landed in East Timor on 20 September 1999. Several Asian countries, however, in particular Malaysia and Thailand, along with Indonesia itself (which earlier in the month had suspended its security pact with Australia), were critical of Australia's bias towards pro-independence groups and of the country's apparent aggressive approach to its role in the operation, which some observers considered would have been more appropriately led by the Association of South East Asian Nations (ASEAN).

A crisis in Australia's relations with Malaysia arose in late 1993, when Keating described the Malaysian Prime Minister as a 'recalcitrant' for his failure to attend the APEC summit meeting in Seattle, USA, in November. Relations subsequently improved, however, and in January 1996 Keating paid the first official visit to Malaysia by an Australian Prime Minister since 1984. In March 1996, furthermore, the Malaysian Prime Minister travelled to Brisbane for a meeting with his newly-elected Australian counterpart. During 1999 Australia was critical of the continued detention and the trials of Anwar Ibrahim, the former Deputy Prime Minister and Minister of Finance (see chapter on Malaysia).

During an official visit to Hanoi in April 1994 Keating had discussions with his Vietnamese counterpart. Australia's relations with the People's Republic of China continued to be strained by the issue of China's nuclear-testing programme, and deteriorated further in September 1996 when the Dalai Lama, the exiled spiritual leader of Tibet, was received in Sydney by the Prime Minister. In March 1997, however, the Australian Prime Minister began a six-day official visit to China, where he had discussions with Premier Li Peng. In July 1999, during a visit to Beijing by the Australian Minister of Foreign Affairs, Australia endorsed China's bid for membership of the World Trade Organization (WTO). The two countries also signed a bilateral trade pact. In September, however, President Jiang Zemin's visit to Australia was disrupted by pro-Tibet and Taiwan activists. Australia's relations with Japan were strained in the late 1990s by a fishing dispute relating to the latter's failure to curb its catches of the endangered southern bluefin tuna, as agreed in a treaty of 1993, of which New Zealand was also a signatory. In August 1999, however, an international tribunal ruled in favour of Australia and New Zealand.

The viability of the ANZUS military pact, which was signed in 1951, linking Australia, New Zealand and the USA, was disputed by the US Government following the New Zealand Government's declaration, in July 1984, that vessels which were believed to be powered by nuclear energy, or to be carrying nuclear weapons, would be barred from the country's ports. Hawke did not support the New Zealand initiative, and Australia continued to participate with the USA in joint military exercises from which New Zealand had been excluded. However, the Hawke Government declined directly to endorse US retaliation against New Zealand, and in 1986 stated that Australia regarded its 'obligations to New Zealand as constant and undiminishing'. In late 1988 Australia signed a 10-year agreement with the USA, extending its involvement in the management of US-staffed military bases in Australia. In March 1987 proposals for an ambitious new defence strategy were published, following the recommendations of a government commissioned report advocating a comprehensive restructuring of the country's military forces, on the basis of greater self-reliance. The cost of the plan, however, was estimated at $A25,000m. over 15 years. In September 1990 Australia and New Zealand signed an agreement to establish a joint venture to construct as many as 12 naval frigates to patrol the South Pacific. In February 1994 the USA announced its decision to resume senior-level contacts with New Zealand. In July 1996 Australia and the USA upgraded their defence alliance. Training facilities were to be expanded, and major joint military exercises were to be held in Queensland in early 1997. In 1999 Australia's trading relations with the USA were strained by the latter's imposition of tariffs on imports of Australian lamb. In October Australia urged that the dispute be settled by means of a WTO panel.

Owing to Australian opposition to French test explosions of nuclear weapons at Mururoa Atoll (French Polynesia) in the South Pacific Ocean, a ban on uranium sales to France was introduced in 1983. However, in August 1986 the Government announced its decision to resume uranium exports, claiming that the sanction had been ineffective and that the repeal of the ban would increase government revenue. In December Australia ratified a treaty declaring the South Pacific area a nuclear-free zone. France's decision, in April 1992, to suspend its nuclear-testing programme was welcomed by Australia. In June 1995, however, the French President's announcement that the programme was to be resumed provoked outrage throughout the Pacific region. The Australian ambassador to France was recalled, and the French consulate in Perth was destroyed in an arson attack. Further widespread protests followed the first of the new series of tests in September. Australia's relations with the UK were strained by the British Government's refusal to join the condemnation of France's policy. The final test was conducted in January 1996. On an official visit to Paris in September, the Australian Minister for Foreign Affairs adopted a conciliatory stance (which drew much criticism from anti-nuclear groups). A ban on new contracts for the supply of uranium to France, imposed in September 1995, was removed in October 1996. Meanwhile, Australia remained committed to achieving the elimination of all nuclear testing. In August, following a veto of the draft text by India and Iran at the UN Conference on Disarmament in Geneva, Australia took the initiative in leading an international effort to secure the passage of the Comprehensive Test Ban Treaty. In an unusual procedure, the Treaty was referred to the UN General Assembly, which voted overwhelmingly in its favour in September.

Relations with neighbouring Pacific island states were strained in mid-1997. In July Australia was embarrassed by the unauthorized publication of a secret official document in which certain regional politicians were described as corrupt and incompetent. At a meeting of the South Pacific Forum in September, the member countries failed to reach agreement on a common policy regarding mandatory targets for the reduction of emissions of the so-called 'greenhouse gases'. The low-lying nation of Tuvalu was particularly critical of Australia's refusal to compromise, the Australian Prime Minister declaring that the Pacific islands' concerns over rising sea levels were exaggerated.

Australia's relations with Papua New Guinea were strained in early 1997 as a result of the latter's decision to engage the services of a group of mercenaries in the Government's operations against secessionists on the island of Bougainville. Fearing for the stability of the South Pacific region, the Australian Prime Minister denounced the use of foreign forces as unacceptable. As the crisis escalated (see chapter on Papua New Guinea), Australia continued its attempts to mediate, while reportedly placing its troops on alert. Following the suspension of the mercenaries' contract by the Prime Minister of Papua New Guinea in March, Australia remained committed to a peaceful settlement of the Bougainville dispute, and in November 1997 offered a venue for the next round of peace talks. In the same month Australian forces played a leading role in drought-relief operations in Papua New Guinea. In January 1998 a permanent ceasefire agreement between the Papua New Guinea Government and the Bougainville secessionists, which was to take effect in April, was signed in New Zealand. Australia reaffirmed its commitment to the provision of a peace-monitoring force. In July Australian forces responded promptly to an appeal for assistance following a series of tsunami, which killed thousands of villagers on the north-west coast of Papua New Guinea. Australia subsequently provided substantial relief aid.

## Government

Australia comprises six states and three territories. Executive power is vested in the British monarch and exercised by the monarch's appointed representative, the Governor-General, who normally acts on the advice of the Federal Executive Council (the Ministry), led by the Prime Minister. The Governor-General appoints the Prime Minister and, on the latter's recommendation, other Ministers.

Legislative power is vested in the Federal Parliament. This consists of the monarch, represented by the Governor-General, and two chambers elected by universal adult suffrage (voting is compulsory). The Senate has 76 members (12 from each state and two each from the Northern Territory and the Australian Capital Territory), who are elected by a system of proportional representation for six years when representing a state, with half the seats renewable every three years, and for a term of three years when representing a territory. The House of Representatives has 148 members, elected for three years (subject to dissolution) from single-member constituencies. The Federal Executive Council is responsible to Parliament.

Each state has a Governor, representing the monarch, and its own legislative, executive and judicial system. The state governments are essentially autonomous, but certain powers are placed under the jurisdiction of the Federal Government. All states except Queensland have an Upper House (the Legislative Council) and a Lower House (the Legislative Assembly or House of Assembly). The chief ministers of the states are known as Premiers, as distinct from the Federal Prime Minister. The Northern Territory (self-governing since 1978) and the Australian Capital Territory (self-governing since 1988) have unicameral legislatures, and each has a government led by a Chief Minister. The Jervis Bay Territory is not self-governing.

## Defence

Australia's defence policy is based on collective security, and it is a member of the British Commonwealth Strategic Reserve and of ANZUS, with New Zealand and the USA. Australia also participates in the Five-Power Defence Arrangements, with New Zealand, Malaysia, Singapore and the United Kingdom. In August 1999 Australia's armed forces numbered 55,200 (army 25,200, navy 14,200, air force 15,800). Defence expenditure for 2000 was budgeted at $A11,200m. Service in the armed forces is voluntary. In September 1999 Australia committed 4,500 troops to the peace-keeping operation in East Timor.

## Economic Affairs

In 1997, according to estimates by the World Bank, Australia's gross national product (GNP), measured at average 1995–97 prices, was US $382,705m., equivalent to US $20,650 per head. It was estimated that Australia's GNP per head increased, in real terms, at an average rate of 2.4% per year between 1990 and 1997. Over the same period, the population increased at an average annual rate of 1.2%. In 1998 GNP totalled an estimated US $380,600m. (US $20,300 per head). The country's gross domestic product (GDP) increased, in real terms, by an annual average of 3.6% in 1990–98.

Agriculture (including forestry, hunting and fishing) contributed 4.0% of GDP in 1996/97, and engaged 5.0% of the employed labour force in August 1998. The principal crops are wheat, fruit, sugar and cotton, and Australia is the world's leading producer of wool (export earnings from greasy wool, however, declining from $A2,446m. in 1997 to $A1,712m. in 1998). The export of wine is of increasing importance, rising from 10m. litres in 1986 to 155m. litres in 1996/97. The value of wine exports was projected to reach $A700m. in 1997/98. Beef production is also important, contributing an estimated 12.1% of the value of gross farm output in 1996/97. Between 1989/90 and 1996/97 agricultural GDP increased at an average annual rate of 3.0%, rising by 13.7%, compared with the previous year, in 1996/97.

Industry (comprising mining, manufacturing, construction and utilities) employed 21.9% of the working population in 1998, and provided 27.2% of GDP in 1996/97. Industrial GDP increased at an average rate of 1.4% per year between 1989/90 and 1996/97.

The mining sector employed 1.0% of the working population in 1998, and contributed 4.3% of GDP in 1996/97. Australia is one of the world's leading exporters of coal. Earnings from coal and related products in 1997/98 reached $A9,588m., more than 10.9% of total export receipts in that year. The other principal minerals extracted are iron ore, gold, silver, petroleum and natural gas. Bauxite, zinc, copper, titanium, nickel, tin, lead, zirconium and diamonds are also mined. Between 1989/90 and 1996/97 the GDP of the mining sector increased at an average annual rate of 2.9%, rising by 3.2% in 1996/97.

Manufacturing contributed 13.5% of GDP in 1996/97. The sector employed 12.8% of the working population in 1998. Measured by the value of sales, the principal branches of manufacturing in 1996/97 were food, beverages and tobacco (21.6%), equipment and machinery (19.8%), metal products (18.2%), petroleum, coal and chemical products (15.8%), printing, publishing and recording (7.1%) and wood and paper products (5.5%). The manufacturing sector's GDP grew at an average annual rate of 1.2% between 1989/90 and 1996/97, increasing by 1.1% in 1996/97.

Energy is derived principally from petroleum, natural gas and coal. Production of petroleum declined from 31,301m. litres in 1994/95 to 30,763m. litres in 1995/96, while that of black coal increased from 191.9m. metric tons in 1994/95 to 194.5m. tons in 1995/96.

The services sector provided 68.8% of GDP in 1996/97, and engaged 72.8% of the employed labour force in 1998. The tourism industry is of growing significance. The number of visitor arrivals, however, declined from 4.3m. in 1997 to fewer than 4.2m. in 1998, when tourist receipts reached $A16,300m. It was estimated that in 1995/96 the tourism sector contributed 7.4% of GDP and accounted for 8.4% of total employment. The GDP of the services sector increased at an average annual rate of 4.2% between 1989/90 and 1996/97.

In 1998 Australia recorded a visible trade deficit of US $5,397m., and there was a deficit of US $17,484m. on the current account of the balance of payments. In the year ending 30 June 1998 the principal source of imports was the USA (21.9%), followed by Japan (13.7%). Japan was the principal market for exports in that year (20.0%), followed by the Republic of Korea (7.3%) and New Zealand (6.4%). Other major trading partners are the United Kingdom, Singapore, Taiwan, the People's Republic of China and Germany. The principal exports were metalliferous ores (sales of gold being of increasing significance), coal, machinery, non-ferrous metals, textile fibres (mainly wool), and meat (mainly beef). The principal imports were machinery and transport equipment, basic manufactures, and chemicals and related products.

In the 1998/99 financial year an estimated budgetary surplus of $A2,880m. (excluding sales of government assets) was recorded. A surplus of $A5,210m. was projected for 1999/2000. In mid-1997 Australia's net external debt stood at $A203,732m. (equivalent to 39.5% of annual GDP). An estimated 8.0% of the labour force were unemployed in 1998, the rate declining to 6.6% in July 1999. The annual rate of inflation averaged 3.3% in 1988–97. Consumer prices rose by 0.9% in 1998 and by 1.7% in the 12 months to September 1999.

Australia is a member of the Asian Development Bank (see p. 125), the South Pacific Forum (to become the Pacific Islands' Forum, see p. 260) and the Pacific Community (formerly the South Pacific Commission—see p. 257). In 1989 Australia played a major role in the creation of the Asia-Pacific Economic Co-operation group (APEC, see p. 122), which aimed to stimulate economic development in the region. Australia is also a member of the OECD (see p. 232), of the Cairns Group (see p. 338) and of the International Grains Council (see p. 288).

Upon taking office in March 1996, the Howard Government confirmed its determination to achieve fiscal balance. One of the principal aims of the administration's programme was the transfer to the private sector of Telstra, the state-owned telecommunications company. The sale of one-third of the company's assets took place in November 1997, raising revenue of $A14,300m. and representing the most successful Australian flotation to date. Following its re-election in October 1998, the Government reaffirmed its commitment to the disposal of the remaining two-thirds of Telstra's assets, and in late 1999 a further 16.6% was sold. The Government also remained committed to the deregulation of the labour market. The 1997/98 budget resulted in the first surplus for many years. The 1998/99 budget aimed to prepare the way for radical tax reforms, including the introduction of a controversial 10% goods-and-services tax (GST). Legislation to implement the GST from mid-2000 received the Senate's approval in June 1999. The 1999/2000 budget, presented in May 1999, allocated additional funding (of $A800m.) to the biotechnology industry, the sector being regarded as a significant source of future economic growth. In late 1999, as the cost of Australia's involvement in East Timor (see History) continued to rise, with the agreement of the opposition the Government announced the imposition in 2001 of a special levy on middle- and high-income taxpayers, in order to maintain the budgetary surplus. Meanwhile, revenues from exports of commodities were constrained by global surpluses, low international prices for gold, coal and iron ore, in particular, and by the increasing strength of the Australian dollar. The deteriorating current-account deficit, which by 1999 had exceeded the equivalent of 6% of GDP, also remained a cause for concern. Furthermore, the repercussions of the Asian financial crisis of 1997/98 continued to depress Australia's major markets. These losses, however, were partly offset by increased exports to the more buoyant markets of Europe and the USA. GDP expanded by an estimated 4.25% in 1998/99. A growth rate of 3.5% was projected for 1999/2000.

## Social Welfare

Australia provides old-age, invalid and widows' pensions, unemployment, sickness and supporting parents' benefits, family allowances and other welfare benefits and allowances. Reciprocal welfare agreements operate between Australia and New Zealand and the United Kingdom. In 1993/94 Australia had 1,142 hospitals, with a total of 78,298 beds. In 1997/98 there were 34,600 general practitioners and 12,800 specialist practitioners. There were 148,300 nurses registered in the country. The desert interior is served by the Royal Flying Doctor Service. Expenditure on health by both the public and private sectors in 1996/97 was estimated at $A43,204m. Public expenditure on social security and welfare totalled an estimated $A50,400m. in 1997/98.

In February 1984 the Government introduced a system of universal health insurance, known as Medicare, whereby every Australian is protected against the costs of medical and hospital care. Where medical expenses are incurred, Medicare covers patients for 85% of the government-approved Schedule Fee for services. For private in-patients in hospitals, 75% of the Schedule Fee for services is payable. The Medicare scheme is financed in part by a levy, normally of 1.5%, on taxable incomes above a certain level.

## Education

Education is the responsibility of each of the states and the Federal Government. It is compulsory, and available free of charge, for all children from the ages of six to 15 years (16 in Tasmania). Primary education generally begins at six years of age and lasts for six years. Secondary education, beginning at the age of 12, usually lasts for five years. As a proportion of children in the relevant age-groups, the enrolment ratios in 1996 were 97% in primary schools and 92% in secondary schools. In 1997 there were 1,367,007 children enrolled in government primary schools and 863,045 in secondary schools, while 941,572 children were attending private schools (488,782 primary and 452,790 secondary). Special services have been developed to fulfil the requirements of children living in the remote 'outback' areas, notably Schools of the Air, using two-way receiver sets.

A system of one-teacher schools and correspondence schools also helps to satisfy these needs. Under a major reform programme initiated in 1988, the binary system of universities and colleges of advanced education was replaced by a unified national system of fewer and larger institutions. In 1997 there were 36 publicly-funded institutions of higher education. In the same year students totalled 658,827. Most courses last from three to six years. Expenditure on education by all levels of government in the financial year 1996/97 was $A24,480m.

### Public Holidays*

**2000:** 3 January (for New Year's Day), 26 January (Australia Day), 21–24 April (Easter), 25 April (Anzac Day), 12 June (Queen's Official Birthday, except Western Australia), 25–26 December (Christmas Day, Boxing Day).

**2001** (provisional): 1 January (New Year's Day), 26 January (Australia Day), 13–16 April (Easter), 25 April (Anzac Day), 11 June (Queen's Official Birthday, except Western Australia), 25–26 December (Christmas Day, Boxing Day).

* National holidays only. Some states observe these holidays on different days.

There are also numerous individual state holidays.

### Weights and Measures

The metric system is in force.

# Statistical Survey

Source (unless otherwise stated): Australian Bureau of Statistics, POB 10, Belconnen, ACT 2616; tel. (2) 6252-7911; fax (2) 6251-6009; internet www.abs.gov.au.

## Area and Population

**AREA, POPULATION AND DENSITY**

| | |
|---|---|
| Area (sq km) | 7,692,030* |
| Population (census results)† | |
| 6 August 1991 | |
| Males | 8,361,798 |
| Females | 8,485,512 |
| Total | 16,847,310 |
| 6 August 1996 (provisional) | |
| Total | 17,752,800 |
| Population (official estimates at mid-year)† | |
| 1995 | 18,071,800 |
| 1996 | 18,310,700 |
| 1997 (provisional) | 18,532,200 |
| Density (per sq km) at mid-1997 | 2.4 |

* 2,969,909 sq miles.

† Census results exclude, and estimates include, an adjustment for under-enumeration, estimated to have been 1.9% in 1991. Estimates also exclude overseas visitors in Australia and include Australian residents temporarily overseas. On this basis, the adjusted census total was 17,317,800 (provisional) in 1991.

**STATES AND TERRITORIES** (30 June 1997)

| | Area (sq km) | Estimated Population | Density (per sq km) |
|---|---|---|---|
| New South Wales (NSW) | 800,640 | 6,274,400 | 7.8 |
| Victoria | 227,420 | 4,605,100 | 20.2 |
| Queensland | 1,730,650 | 3,401,200 | 2.0 |
| South Australia | 983,480 | 1,479,800 | 1.5 |
| Western Australia | 2,529,880 | 1,798,100 | 0.7 |
| Tasmania | 68,400 | 473,500 | 6.9 |
| Northern Territory | 1,349,130 | 187,100 | 0.1 |
| Australian Capital Territory (ACT) | 2,360 | 309,800 | 131.3 |
| Jervis Bay Territory | 70 | n.a. | n.a. |
| **Total** | 7,692,030 | 18,532,200* | 2.4 |

* Includes populations of Jervis Bay Territory, Christmas Island and the Cocos (Keeling) Islands.

**PRINCIPAL TOWNS** (estimated population at 30 June 1997)*

| | |
|---|---|
| Canberra (national capital) | 309,500 |
| Sydney (capital of NSW) | 3,934,700 |
| Melbourne (capital of Victoria) | 3,321,700 |
| Brisbane (capital of Queensland) | 1,548,300 |
| Perth (capital of W Australia) | 1,319,000 |
| Adelaide (capital of S Australia) | 1,083,100 |
| Newcastle | 468,900 |
| Gold Coast-Tweed | 367,700 |
| Wollongong | 258,100 |
| Hobart (capital of Tasmania) | 195,500 |
| Sunshine Coast | 162,100 |
| Geelong | 153,100 |
| Townsville | 123,600 |
| Cairns | 109,500 |

* Figures refer to metropolitan areas, each of which normally comprises a municipality and contiguous urban areas.

**BIRTHS, MARRIAGES AND DEATHS***

| | Registered live births | | Registered marriages | | Registered deaths | |
|---|---|---|---|---|---|---|
| | Number | Rate (per 1,000) | Number | Rate (per 1,000) | Number | Rate (per 1,000) |
| 1990 | 262,648 | 15.4 | 116,959 | 6.9 | 120,062 | 7.0 |
| 1991 | 257,247 | 14.9 | 113,869 | 6.6 | 119,146 | 6.9 |
| 1992 | 264,151 | 15.1 | 114,752 | 6.6 | 123,660 | 7.1 |
| 1993 | 260,229 | 14.7 | 113,255 | 6.4 | 121,599 | 6.9 |
| 1994 | 258,051 | 14.5 | 111,174 | 6.2 | 126,692 | 7.1 |
| 1995 | 256,190 | 14.2 | 109,386 | 6.1 | 125,133 | 6.9 |
| 1996 | 253,834 | 13.9 | 106,103 | 5.8 | 128,719 | 7.0 |
| 1997 | 253,673 | 13.7 | 106,735 | 5.8 | 128,944 | 7.0 |

* Data are tabulated by year of registration rather than by year of occurrence.

**Expectation of life** (years at birth, 1996): males 75.22, females 81.05.

**PERMANENT AND LONG-TERM MIGRATION*** (year ending 31 December)

| | 1992 | 1993 | 1994 |
|---|---|---|---|
| **Permanent** | | | |
| Arrivals | 107,390 | 76,330 | 69,770 |
| Departures | 29,120 | 27,910 | 27,280 |
| **Other long-term** | | | |
| Arrivals | 126,780 | 127,440 | 137,600 |
| Departures | 115,160 | 113,190 | 112,710 |

* Persons intending to remain in Australia, or Australian residents intending to remain abroad, for 12 months or more. Figures are rounded to the nearest 10.

**ECONOMICALLY ACTIVE POPULATION**
('000 persons aged 15 years and over, excluding armed forces, at August)

| | 1996 | 1997 | 1998 |
|---|---|---|---|
| Agriculture, forestry and fishing | 427.8 | 423.1 | 426.6 |
| Mining | 90.2 | 80.7 | 86.7 |
| Manufacturing | 1,122.6 | 1,145.9 | 1,101.7 |
| Electricity, gas and water supply | 67.8 | 65.5 | 68.8 |
| Construction | 605.3 | 566.4 | 628.5 |
| Wholesale trade | 495.5 | 472.1 | 510.9 |
| Retail trade | 1,256.4 | 1,212.0 | 1,268.2 |
| Accommodation, cafés and restaurants | 382.6 | 397.5 | 407.9 |
| Transport and storage | 396.9 | 395.3 | 383.3 |
| Communication services | 170.9 | 157.7 | 155.8 |
| Finance and insurance | 311.3 | 313.3 | 322.4 |
| Property and business services | 807.3 | 878.4 | 927.8 |
| Government administration and defence | 377.4 | 342.2 | 334.4 |
| Education | 578.7 | 574.3 | 594.3 |
| Health and community services | 759.7 | 780.6 | 809.4 |
| Cultural and recreational services | 191.5 | 198.6 | 203.0 |
| Personal and other services | 314.8 | 344.5 | 351.3 |
| **Total employed** (incl. others) | 8,381.1 | 8,375.9 | 8,611.2 |
| Unemployed | 807.1 | 798.7 | 761.0 |
| **Total labour force** | 9,188.2 | 9,174.6 | 9,372.2 |
| Males | 5,238.7 | 5,218.7 | 5,299.6 |
| Females | 3,949.5 | 3,955.8 | 4,072.6 |

Source: *ABS Labour Force Australia.*

# Agriculture

**PRINCIPAL CROPS** ('000 metric tons)

| | 1996 | 1997 | 1998 |
|---|---|---|---|
| Wheat | 22,924 | 19,417 | 21,855 |
| Rice (paddy) | 966 | 1,255 | 1,335 |
| Barley | 6,696 | 6,429 | 5,395 |
| Maize | 311 | 398 | 340 |
| Oats | 1,653 | 1,583 | 1,252 |
| Sorghum | 1,592 | 1,425 | 1,065 |
| Potatoes | 1,308 | 1,286 | 1,300* |
| Dry peas | 454 | 303 | 343 |
| Other pulses | 2,056 | 1,820 | 1,885 |
| Soybeans (Soya beans) | 45 | 74 | 93 |
| Sunflower seed | 68 | 143 | 98 |
| Rapeseed | 623 | 860 | 1,614 |
| Cottonseed | 542 | 860 | 941 |
| Cotton (lint) | 381 | 608 | 666 |
| Cabbages | 76 | 66 | 66* |
| Tomatoes | 393 | 400* | 400* |
| Cauliflower | 109 | 105 | 110* |
| Pumpkins, squash and gourds | 110 | 101 | 105* |
| Onions (dry) | 196 | 200* | 210* |
| Green peas | 81 | 95 | 97* |
| Carrots | 250 | 257 | 270* |
| Watermelons | 79 | 87 | 88* |
| Grapes | 1,087 | 943 | 1,097 |
| Sugar cane | 35,889 | 38,633 | 41,044 |
| Apples | 280 | 353 | 360* |
| Pears | 156 | 168 | 172* |
| Peaches and nectarines | 94 | 95* | 96* |
| Oranges | 523 | 559* | 369* |
| Pineapples | 123 | 120* | 123* |
| Bananas | 200 | 210* | 215* |

* FAO estimate.

Source: FAO, *Production Yearbook.*

**LIVESTOCK** ('000 head at 31 March)

| | 1996 | 1997 | 1998 |
|---|---|---|---|
| Horses* | 230 | 230 | 230 |
| Cattle | 26,377 | 26,780 | 26,710 |
| Pigs | 2,526 | 2,555 | 2,680 |
| Sheep | 121,116 | 120,228 | 119,600 |
| Goats* | 230 | 230 | 230 |
| Chickens | 76,000 | 81,000 | 83,000* |

* FAO estimate(s).

Source: mainly FAO, *Production Yearbook.*

**LIVESTOCK PRODUCTS** ('000 metric tons)

| | 1996 | 1997 | 1998 |
|---|---|---|---|
| Beef and veal | 1,745 | 1,816 | 1,955 |
| Mutton and lamb | 574 | 574 | 615 |
| Goat meat* | 9 | 9 | 9 |
| Pig meat | 334 | 326 | 343 |
| Horse meat* | 22 | 22 | 22 |
| Poultry meat | 503 | 520 | 573 |
| Cows' milk | 8,986 | 9,304 | 9,731 |
| Butter | 145 | 147 | 161 |
| Cheese | 264 | 285 | 295 |
| Hen eggs* | 185 | 190 | 190 |
| Honey | 26 | 27 | 27* |
| Wool: | | | |
| greasy* | 703 | 728 | 687 |
| clean* | 457 | 473 | 473 |
| Cattle hides* | 198 | 211 | 211 |
| Sheepskins* | 130 | 132 | 141 |

* FAO estimate(s).

Note: Figures for meat and milk refer to the 12 months ending 30 June of the year stated.

Source: FAO, *Production Yearbook.*

# Forestry

**ROUNDWOOD REMOVALS** ('000 cubic metres, excl. bark)

| | 1995 | 1996 | 1997 |
|---|---|---|---|
| Sawlogs, veneer logs and logs for sleepers | 9,589 | 9,675 | 10,201 |
| Pulpwood | 9,383 | 9,065 | 9,414 |
| Other industrial wood | 588 | 600 | 540 |
| Fuel wood | 2,898 | 2,904 | 2,904 |
| **Total** | 22,458 | 22,244 | 23,059 |

Source: FAO, *Yearbook of Forest Products.*

**SAWNWOOD PRODUCTION** ('000 cubic metres, incl. sleepers)

| | 1995 | 1996 | 1997 |
|---|---|---|---|
| Coniferous (softwood) | 2,121 | 2,053 | 2,062 |
| Broadleaved (hardwood) | 1,570 | 1,477 | 1,393 |
| **Total** | 3,691 | 3,530 | 3,455 |

Source: FAO, *Yearbook of Forest Products.*

# Fishing

('000 metric tons, live weight, year ending 30 June)

| | 1994/95 | 1995/96 | 1996/97 |
|---|---|---|---|
| Inland waters | 1.7 | 1.8 | 1.5 |
| Indian Ocean* | 108.0 | 106.8 | 92.5 |
| Pacific Ocean* | 93.7 | 94.6 | 93.7 |
| **Total catch** | 203.4 | 203.2 | 187.7 |

* FAO estimates.

Source: FAO, *Yearbook of Fishery Statistics.*

# Mining*

(year ending 30 June, '000 metric tons, unless otherwise indicated)

| | 1993/94 | 1994/95 | 1995/96 |
|---|---|---|---|
| Coal (black) | 177,874 | 191,903 | 194,492 |
| Coal, brown (lignite) | 49,684 | 50,679 | 54,281 |
| Bauxite | 43,306 | 45,384 | 50,724 |
| Mineral sands† | 2,252 | 2,375 | 2,491 |
| Iron ore (incl. pellets) | 123,631 | 137,525 | 137,267 |
| Lead concentrate | 873 | 766 | 774 |
| Zinc concentrate‡ | 1,890 | 1,699 | 1,295 |
| Copper concentrate and precipitate§ | 1,338 | 9,424 | 1,317 |
| Antimony (metric tons)‖ | 1,700¶ | 1,700** | 900†† |
| Cadmium (refined, metric tons)‡‡ | 951¶ | 910** | 838 |
| Cobalt (metric tons)‡‡§§ | 1,800¶ | 2,200** | 2,200†† |
| Manganese ore | 1,043.0¶ | 944.0**⦀ | 1,066.0††⦀ |
| Ilmenite | 1,870.0¶ | 1,764.0** | 1,808.0††⦀ |
| Tin (metric tons)¶¶ | 7,972 | 9,057 | 11,568 |
| Crude petroleum (incl. condensate, million litres) | 29,583 | 31,301 | 30,763 |
| Natural gas (million cu m) | 24,855 | 28,176 | 29,985 |
| Gold (kg) | 255,757 | 243,213 | 263,916 |
| Silver (metric tons)‖ | 1,152¶ | 1,045** | 920†† |
| Nickel¶¶ | 66 | 98 | 113‖ |
| Tungsten (metric tons)‡‡ | 11¶ | —** | —†† |
| Uranium concentrate (metric tons) | 1,457[1] | n.a. | 3,200[1] |
| Diamonds—industrial ('000 carats)¶¶ | 23,000¶ | 23,800** | 22,381††⦀ |
| Diamonds—gem ('000 carats)‡‡ | 18,800¶ | 19,500** | 18,300†† |

* Figures for metallic minerals represent metal contents based on chemical assay, except figures for bauxite, iron and manganese, which are in terms of gross quantities produced.

† Includes ilmenite, beneficiated ilmenite, leucoxene, monazite, rutile and zircon.

‡ Includes zinc-lead concentrate.

§ Excluding copper concentrate of South Australia.

‖ Data from *World Metal Statistics* (London). (Source: UN, *Industrial Commodity Statistics Yearbook.*)

¶ January–December 1993.

** January–December 1994.

†† January–December 1995.

‡‡ Estimated by US Bureau of Mines (Source: UN, *Industrial Commodity Statistics Yearbook*).

§§ Provisional figures. Content of nickel concentrates.

⦀ Provisional figure(s).

¶¶ Source: UN, *Industrial Commodity Statistics Yearbook.*

[1] Excluding South Australia.

# Industry

**SELECTED PRODUCTS**

(year ending 30 June, '000 metric tons, unless otherwise indicated)

| | 1994/95 | 1995/96 | 1996/97 |
|---|---|---|---|
| Pig-iron | 7,449 | 7,553 | 7,346 |
| Blooms and slabs from continuous casting | 7,807 | 7,951 | 7,775 |
| Aluminium—unwrought* | 1,285† | 1,331 | n.a. |
| Copper—unwrought | 281† | 282 | 305 |
| Lead—unwrought* | 205† | 223 | 202 |
| Zinc—unwrought* | 312† | 330 | 319 |
| Tin—unwrought (metric tons)* | 455† | 550 | 570 |
| Motor spirit (petrol—million litres) | 17,911† | 18,358 | 18,084 |
| Fuel oil (million litres) | 2,431† | 1,998 | 1,795 |
| Diesel-automotive oil (million litres) | 11,365† | 12,202 | 12,968 |
| Aviation turbine fuel (million litres) | n.a. | 4,882 | 5,284 |
| Electric motors ('000) | 3,099 | 2,850 | 2,669 |
| Clay bricks (million) | 1,860 | 1,455 | 1,468 |
| Superphosphate† | 1,590 | 1,697 | n.a. |
| Refrigerators ('000) | 408 | 414 | 398 |
| Woven man-made fibres ('000 sq metres) | 185,171 | 149,066 | 142,194 |
| Woven cotton fabrics (incl. towelling, '000 sq metres) | 51,938 | 63,886 | 60,616 |
| Woven woollen fabrics (incl. blanketing, '000 sq metres) | 8,189 | 6,523 | 6,300 |
| Cotton yarn (metric tons) | 37,643 | 36,955 | 39,853 |
| Wool yarn (metric tons) | 23,093 | 20,063 | 18,284 |
| Textile floor coverings ('000 sq metres) | 47,258 | 42,683 | 44,681 |
| Electricity (million kWh) | 165,063 | 167,544 | 168,415 |
| Cement | 7,124 | 6,397 | 6,701 |
| Concrete—ready-mixed ('000 cu m) | 15,892 | 14,556 | 15,393 |
| Newsprint | 423 | 446 | 422 |
| Motor vehicles ('000) | 328 | 328 | 331 |
| Wheat flour‡ | 1,403§ | 1,351‖ | 1,488¶ |
| Plastics in primary forms | 1,240 | 1,222 | 1,235 |
| Non-laminated particle board ('000 sq metres) | 846 | 804 | 774 |
| Domestic washing machines ('000) | 305 | 297 | 268 |
| Confectionery | 182.4 | 187.0 | 181.1 |
| Beer (million litres) | 1,788 | 1,743 | 1,735 |
| Tobacco and cigarettes (metric tons) | 23,083 | 20,390 | 22,193 |

* Primary refined metal only.

† Source: Australian Bureau of Agricultural and Resource Economics (ABARE), ACT.

‡ Source: UN, *Industrial Commodity Statistics Yearbook.*

§ January–December 1994.

‖ January–December 1995.

¶ January–December 1996.

**1997/98** ('000 metric tons, unless otherwise indicated): Pig-iron 7,928; Blooms and slabs from continuous casting 8,356; Motor spirit (million litres) 18,589; Fuel oil (million litres) 1,662; Diesel-automotive fuel (million litres) 13,183; Aviation turbine fuel (million litres) 5,423; Clay bricks (million) 1,532; Electricity (million kWh) 179,239; Cement 7,236; Newsprint 402; Beer (million litres) 1,757; Tobacco and cigarettes (metric tons) 21,275.

# Finance

**CURRENCY AND EXCHANGE RATES**

**Monetary Units**

100 cents = 1 Australian dollar ($A).

**Sterling, US Dollar and Euro Equivalents** (30 September 1999)

£1 sterling = $A2.5191;
US $1 = $A1.5300;
€1 = $A1.6317;
$A100 = £39.70 = US $65.36 = €61.28.

**Average Exchange Rate** (US $ per Australian dollar)

| | |
|---|---|
| 1996 | 0.7829 |
| 1997 | 0.7441 |
| 1998 | 0.6294 |

**COMMONWEALTH GOVERNMENT BUDGET**
($A '000 million, year ending 30 June)

| Revenue | 1995/96 | 1996/97 | 1997/98* |
|---|---|---|---|
| Tax revenue | 116.4 | 125.8 | 130.8 |
| Direct taxes | 85.5 | 93.8 | 97.2 |
| Individuals | 60.4 | 66.5 | 70.2 |
| Companies | 18.3 | 19.2 | 18.8 |
| Indirect taxes, etc. | 30.9 | 32.0 | 33.6 |
| Sales Tax | 13.0 | 13.3 | 14.1 |
| Excise | 12.8 | 13.3 | 13.6 |
| Non-tax revenue | 5.3 | 5.2 | 4.6 |
| Interest | 1.4 | 1.1 | 1.0 |
| **Total** | 121.7 | 131.0 | 135.4 |

| Expenditure† | 1995/96 | 1996/97 | 1997/98* |
|---|---|---|---|
| Defence | 10.1 | 10.1 | 10.4 |
| Education | 10.1 | 10.3 | 10.8 |
| Health | 18.6 | 19.2 | 20.7 |
| Social security and welfare | 46.8 | 49.6 | 50.4 |
| Economic services | 9.3 | 8.6 | 8.4 |
| Public-debt interest | 9.1 | 9.4 | 8.3 |
| General purpose transfers to other governments | 17.8 | 18.2 | 17.9 |
| Other | 4.9 | 3.1 | -4.2 |
| **Total** | 126.7 | 128.5 | 122.7 |

* Forecasts.

† Including net lending ($A '000 million): -5.3 in 1995/96; -7.5 in 1996/97; -13.9 in 1997/98.

Source: Commonwealth of Australia, *Budget Strategy and Outlook, 1998/99*.

**OFFICIAL RESERVES** (US $ million at 31 December)

| | 1996 | 1997 | 1998 |
|---|---|---|---|
| Gold* | 2,918 | 740 | 737 |
| IMF special drawing rights | 37 | 19 | 18 |
| Reserve position in IMF | 482 | 727 | 1,256 |
| Foreign exchange | 13,967 | 16,099 | 14,133 |
| **Total** | 17,404 | 17,585 | 16,144 |

* Valued at market-related prices.

Source: IMF, *International Financial Statistics*.

**MONEY SUPPLY** ($A million at 31 December)

| | 1996 | 1997 | 1998 |
|---|---|---|---|
| Currency outside banks | 19,628 | 21,098 | 22,766 |
| Demand deposits at trading and savings banks | 75,801 | 86,965 | 91,864 |
| **Total money** (incl. others) | 95,641 | 108,352 | 114,776 |

Source: IMF, *International Financial Statistics*.

**COST OF LIVING** (Consumer Price Index*; base: 1990 = 100)

| | 1995 | 1996 | 1997 |
|---|---|---|---|
| Food | 112.9 | 116.1 | 119.0 |
| Fuel and light | 117.6 | 118.8 | 120.4 |
| Clothing | 104.4 | 104.8 | 104.9 |
| Rent† | 101.6 | 102.1 | 93.9 |
| **All items** (incl. others) | 113.2 | 116.1 | 116.4 |

* Weighted average of six state capitals.

† Including expenditure on maintenance and repairs of dwellings.

Source: ILO, *Yearbook of Labour Statistics*.

**1998:** Food 122.3; All items 117.3 (Source: UN, *Monthly Bulletin of Statistics*).

**NATIONAL ACCOUNTS** ($A million, year ending 30 June)

**National Income and Product** (at current prices)

| | 1994/95 | 1995/96 | 1996/97 |
|---|---|---|---|
| Compensation of employees | 225,705 | 241,374 | 257,597 |
| Operating surplus | 111,617 | 120,570 | 122,994 |
| **Domestic factor incomes** | 337,322 | 361,944 | 380,591 |
| Consumption of fixed capital | 66,799 | 69,530 | 72,407 |
| **Gross domestic product (GDP) at factor cost** | 404,121 | 431,474 | 452,998 |
| Indirect taxes | 62,403 | 66,806 | 70,369 |
| *Less* Subsidies | 6,233 | 6,167 | 7,061 |
| **GDP in purchasers' values** | 460,291 | 492,113 | 516,306 |
| Net factor income from abroad | -15,826 | -16,702 | -18,126 |
| **Gross national product** | 444,465 | 475,411 | 498,180 |
| *Less* Consumption of fixed capital | 66,799 | 69,530 | 72,407 |
| **National income in market prices** | 377,666 | 405,881 | 425,773 |

**Expenditure on the Gross Domestic Product** (at current prices)

| | 1994/95 | 1995/96 | 1996/97 |
|---|---|---|---|
| Government final consumption expenditure | 79,341 | 83,437 | 86,419 |
| Private final consumption expenditure | 286,830 | 306,369 | 318,480 |
| Increase in stocks | 2,581 | 2,239 | -1,410 |
| Gross fixed capital formation | 97,926 | 100,286 | 105,534 |
| Statistical discrepancy | 2,203 | 361 | 4,373 |
| **Total domestic expenditure** | 468,881 | 492,692 | 513,396 |
| Exports of goods and services | 87,090 | 98,528 | 104,601 |
| *Less* Imports of goods and services | 95,680 | 99,107 | 101,691 |
| **GDP in purchasers' values** | 460,291 | 492,113 | 516,306 |
| **GDP at constant 1989/90 prices** | 420,838 | 437,264 | 450,575 |

**Gross Domestic Product by Economic Activity**
(provisional, at constant 1989/90 prices)

| | 1994/95 | 1995/96 | 1996/97 |
|---|---|---|---|
| Agriculture, hunting, forestry and fishing | 13,068 | 15,873 | 18,218 |
| Mining and quarrying | 17,813 | 18,668 | 19,307 |
| Manufacturing | 58,605 | 59,184 | 61,138 |
| Electricity, gas and water | 13,680 | 13,707 | 14,271 |
| Construction | 26,826 | 27,147 | 28,177 |
| Wholesale and retail trade | 70,585 | 74,547 | 77,612 |
| Transport, storage and communications | 37,621 | 40,642 | 42,959 |
| Finance, insurance, real estate and business services | 50,057 | 51,878 | 63,054 |
| Ownership of dwellings | 40,470 | 41,905 | 44,124 |
| Public administration and defence | 14,803 | 15,393 | 15,471 |
| Other community, recreational and personal services (incl. restaurants and hotels) | 64,756 | 67,268 | 68,305 |
| **Sub-total** | 408,284 | 426,212 | 452,636 |
| Import duties | 5,316 | 5,439 | 5,935 |
| *Less* Imputed bank service charge | 7,583 | 8,259 | 9,844 |
| Statistical discrepancy | 12,813 | 10,500 | 1,848 |
| **GDP in purchasers' values** | 418,830* | 433,892† | 450,575 |

* Revised total is $A420,838 million.

† Revised total is $A437,264 million.

**BALANCE OF PAYMENTS** (US $ million)

| | 1996 | 1997 | 1998 |
|---|---|---|---|
| Exports of goods f.o.b. | 60,397 | 64,893 | 55,839 |
| Imports of goods f.o.b. | -61,032 | -63,044 | -61,236 |
| **Trade balance** | -635 | 1,849 | -5,397 |
| Exports of services | 18,542 | 18,810 | 16,325 |
| Imports of services | -18,606 | -18,847 | -17,157 |
| **Balance on goods and services** | -699 | 1,812 | -6,229 |
| Other income received | 6,019 | 6,894 | 6,820 |
| Other income paid | -21,417 | -21,167 | -18,041 |
| **Balance on goods, services and income** | -16,097 | -12,461 | -17,450 |
| Current transfers received | 2,683 | 2,665 | 2,436 |
| Current transfers paid | -2,601 | -2,935 | -2,470 |
| **Current balance** | -16,015 | -12,731 | -17,484 |
| Capital account (net) | 967 | 903 | 672 |
| Direct investment abroad | -5,843 | -5,905 | -2,569 |
| Direct investment from abroad | 5,159 | 8,612 | 6,425 |
| Portfolio investment assets | -1,227 | -40 | -991 |
| Portfolio investment liabilities | 21,861 | 11,374 | 3,367 |
| Other investment assets | -5,727 | -5,003 | -330 |
| Other investment liabilities | 2,813 | 5,792 | 9,198 |
| Net errors and omissions | 483 | 487 | -168 |
| **Overall balance** | 2,471 | 3,488 | -1,879 |

Source: IMF, *International Financial Statistics.*

# External Trade

**PRINCIPAL COMMODITIES** ($A million, year ending 30 June)

| Imports f.o.b. | 1995/96 | 1996/97 | 1997/98 |
|---|---|---|---|
| **Food and live animals** | 2,894 | 2,985 | 3,460 |
| **Beverages and tobacco** | 503 | 502 | 574 |
| **Crude materials (inedible) except fuels** | 1,576 | 1,487 | 1,605 |
| **Mineral fuels, lubricants, etc.** | 4,312 | 5,164 | 4,412 |
| Petroleum, petroleum products, etc. | 4,234 | 5,055 | 4,312 |
| **Animal and vegetable oils, fats and waxes** | 268 | 266 | 258 |
| **Chemicals and related products** | 8,901 | 9,028 | 10,277 |
| Organic chemicals | 1,919 | 2,040 | 2,135 |
| Medicinal and pharmaceutical products | 1,830 | 1,998 | 2,544 |
| **Basic manufactures** | 11,039 | 10,724 | 12,533 |
| Paper, paperboard and manufactures | 1,942 | 1,769 | 1,991 |
| Textile yarn, fabrics, etc. | 2,359 | 2,284 | 2,522 |
| **Machinery and transport equipment** | 36,458 | 36,782 | 41,926 |
| Power-generating machinery and equipment | 1,998 | 1,895 | 2,054 |
| Machinery specialized for particular industries | 3,924 | 4,043 | 4,245 |
| General industrial machinery and equipment and parts | 4,470 | 4,649 | 5,440 |
| Office machines and automatic data-processing machines | 6,033 | 5,984 | 6,956 |

| Imports f.o.b. — *continued* | 1995/96 | 1996/97 | 1997/98 |
|---|---|---|---|
| Telecommunications and sound-recording and reproducing apparatus and equipment | 3,759 | 3,669 | 3,986 |
| Other electrical machinery, apparatus, appliances and parts | 5,316 | 4,912 | 5,428 |
| Road vehicles | 7,980 | 8,579 | 11,301 |
| Other transport equipment | 2,487 | 2,443 | 1,936 |
| **Miscellaneous manufactured articles** | 11,035 | 11,349 | 13,458 |
| Clothing and accessories | 1,766 | 1,841 | 2,277 |
| Professional, scientific and controlling instruments and apparatus | 1,911 | 1,944 | 2,294 |
| **Other commodities and transactions** | 804 | 712 | 2,178 |
| Non-monetary gold (excl. gold ores and concentrates) | 708 | 590 | 2,006 |
| **Total** | 77,792 | 78,998 | 90,680 |

| Exports f.o.b. | 1995/96 | 1996/97 | 1997/98 |
|---|---|---|---|
| **Food and live animals** | 15,272 | 16,311 | 16,034 |
| Meat and meat preparations | 3,296 | 2,958 | 3,730 |
| Dairy products and birds' eggs | 1,673 | 1,759 | 1,907 |
| Cereals and cereal preparations | 4,929 | 5,954 | 5,094 |
| Sugars, sugar preparations and honey | 1,710 | 1,695 | 1,340 |
| **Beverages and tobacco** | 605 | 714 | 994 |
| **Crude materials (inedible) except fuels** | 14,752 | 15,615 | 17,884 |
| Textile fibres and waste* | 4,065 | 4,619 | 5,102 |
| Metalliferous ores and metal scrap | 8,666 | 9,051 | 10,433 |
| **Mineral fuels, lubricants, etc.** | 12,591 | 13,705 | 15,402 |
| Coal, coke and briquettes | 7,840 | 8,005 | 9,588 |
| Petroleum, petroleum products, etc. | 3,188 | 3,805 | 3,846 |
| Gas (natural and manufactured) | 1,562 | 1,895 | 1,968 |
| **Animal and vegetable oils, fats and waxes** | 238 | 232 | 333 |
| **Chemicals and related products** | 3,015 | 3,045 | 3,298 |
| **Basic manufactures** | 9,844 | 9,257 | 10,595 |
| Iron and steel | 1,757 | 1,623 | 1,859 |
| Non-ferrous metals | 5,043 | 4,434 | 5,375 |
| **Machinery and transport equipment** | 9,720 | 10,666 | 11,071 |
| Office machines and automatic data-processing machines | 1,903 | 1,627 | 1,724 |
| Other machinery | 5,323 | 5,402 | 5,788 |
| Transport equipment | 2,494 | 3,637 | 3,559 |
| **Miscellaneous manufactured articles** | 2,718 | 2,844 | 3,217 |
| **Other commodities and transactions** | 7,208 | 6,476 | 8,872 |
| Non-monetary gold (excl. gold ores and concentrates) | 5,545 | 4,717 | 6,263 |
| **Total** | 76,004 | 78,885 | 87,766 |

* Excluding wool tops.

**PRINCIPAL TRADING PARTNERS** ($A million, year ending 30 June)

| Imports f.o.b. | 1995/96 | 1996/97 | 1997/98 |
|---|---|---|---|
| Canada | 1,557 | 1,265 | 1,450 |
| China, People's Republic | 4,010 | 4,203 | 5,304 |
| France | 1,867 | 1,980 | 2,030 |
| Germany | 4,862 | 4,558 | 5,209 |
| Hong Kong | 970 | 900 | 1,031 |
| Indonesia | 1,522 | 1,864 | 2,869 |
| Italy | 2,231 | 2,304 | 2,615 |
| Japan | 10,816 | 10,241 | 12,663 |
| Korea, Republic | 2,293 | 2,550 | 3,759 |
| Malaysia | 1,636 | 1,891 | 2,405 |
| Netherlands | 702 | 817 | 847 |
| New Zealand | 3,591 | 3,685 | 3,723 |
| Papua New Guinea | 1,220 | 1,091 | 768 |
| Saudi Arabia | 874 | 858 | 634 |
| Singapore | 2,613 | 2,620 | 2,641 |
| Sweden | 1,617 | 1,497 | 1,557 |
| Switzerland | 966 | 895 | 950 |
| Taiwan | 2,585 | 2,522 | 2,809 |
| Thailand | 1,005 | 1,201 | 1,475 |
| United Arab Emirates | 475 | 800 | 495 |
| United Kingdom | 4,882 | 5,182 | 5,595 |
| USA | 17,545 | 17,642 | 19,833 |
| **Total** (incl. others) | 77,792 | 78,998 | 90,680 |

| Exports f.o.b. | 1995/96 | 1996/97 | 1997/98 |
|---|---|---|---|
| Belgium-Luxembourg | 668 | 923 | 1,154 |
| Canada | 1,267 | 1,178 | 1,282 |
| China, People's Republic | 3,781 | 3,584 | 3,874 |
| France | 727 | 799 | 864 |
| Germany | 1,152 | 1,058 | 1,236 |
| Hong Kong | 3,052 | 3,105 | 4,138 |
| India | 1,185 | 1,493 | 1,852 |
| Indonesia | 2,716 | 3,305 | 2,751 |
| Italy | 1,282 | 1,354 | 1,751 |
| Japan | 16,429 | 15,377 | 17,583 |
| Korea, Republic | 6,615 | 7,134 | 6,396 |
| Malaysia | 2,289 | 2,332 | 2,097 |
| Netherlands | 695 | 584 | 828 |
| New Zealand | 5,609 | 6,214 | 5,662 |
| Papua New Guinea | 1,048 | 1,272 | 1,151 |
| Philippines | 1,075 | 1,226 | 1,165 |
| Singapore | 3,556 | 3,410 | 3,697 |
| South Africa | 776 | 1,014 | 1,096 |
| Switzerland | 519 | 237 | 1,097 |
| Taiwan | 3,452 | 3,620 | 4,179 |
| Thailand | 1,779 | 1,693 | 1,390 |
| United Arab Emirates | 542 | 665 | 1,066 |
| United Kingdom | 2,829 | 2,357 | 3,039 |
| USA | 4,619 | 5,526 | 7,794 |
| **Total** (incl. others) | 76,005 | 78,932 | 87,766 |

# Transport

**RAILWAYS***

| | 1994/95 | 1995/96 | 1996/97 |
|---|---|---|---|
| Passengers carried ('000) | 434,209 | 446,927 | 467,038 |
| Freight carried ('000 metric tons) | 214,986 | 215,724 | 235,372 |
| Freight ton-km (million) | 61,617 | 63,488 | 68,176 |

* Traffic on government railways only.

**ROAD TRAFFIC** ('000 vehicles registered at 31 October)

| | 1995* | 1996 | 1997 |
|---|---|---|---|
| Passenger vehicles | 8,660.6 | 9,021.5 | 9,239.5 |
| Light commercial vehicles | 1,527.2 | 1,601.4 | 1,632.2 |
| Trucks | 410.9 | 415.4 | 418.4 |
| Buses | 52.2 | 58.8 | 61.1 |
| Motor cycles | 296.6 | 303.9 | 313.1 |

* At 31 May.

**SHIPPING**

**Merchant Fleet** (registered at 31 December)

| | 1996 | 1997 | 1998 |
|---|---|---|---|
| Number of vessels | 625 | 617 | 617 |
| Total displacement ('000 grt) | 2,717.9 | 2,606.6 | 2,188.1 |

Source: Lloyd's Register of Shipping, *World Fleet Statistics.*

**INTERNATIONAL SEA-BORNE TRAFFIC** ('000 metric tons, year ending 30 June)

| | 1990/91 | 1991/92 | 1992/93 |
|---|---|---|---|
| Goods loaded | 304,439 | 316,729 | 327,097 |
| Goods unloaded | 32,202 | 34,396 | 38,757 |

**1995/96:** Total goods loaded and unloaded ('000 metric tons): 419,965.

**CIVIL AVIATION** (traffic)*

| | 1995 | 1996 | 1997 |
|---|---|---|---|
| International services: | | | |
| Passenger arrivals | 12,086,675 (arrivals and departures combined) | 6,714,037 | 7,090,979 |
| Passenger departures | | 6,588,465 | 7,010,931 |
| Freight carried (metric tons) | n.a. | 585,487 | 649,371 |
| Mail carried (metric tons) | n.a. | 20,238 | 21,975 |
| Domestic services†: | | | |
| Passengers carried | 22,789,674 | 23,678,307 | 23,322,436 |
| Passenger-km ('000) | 24,625,411 | 26,191,426 | 26,299,206 |
| Freight and mail carried (metric tons) | 169,446 | 172,761 | 190,667 |

* Includes Christmas Island and Norfolk Island.
† Year ending 30 June.

# Tourism

**VISITOR ARRIVALS BY COUNTRY OF ORIGIN***

| | 1996 | 1997 | 1998 |
|---|---|---|---|
| Canada | 61,119 | 64,752 | 71,690 |
| China, People's Republic | 53,968 | 65,843 | 76,543 |
| Germany | 125,402 | 128,874 | 127,381 |
| Hong Kong | 153,204 | 151,737 | 143,428 |
| Indonesia | 154,451 | 160,366 | 93,032 |
| Japan | 813,113 | 813,892 | 751,107 |
| Korea, Republic | 227,850 | 233,815 | 66,635 |
| Malaysia | 134,408 | 143,683 | 112,074 |
| New Zealand | 671,889 | 685,655 | 709,390 |
| Papua New Guinea | 43,482 | 43,957 | 44,924 |
| Singapore | 222,819 | 239,306 | 247,079 |
| Taiwan | 159,415 | 153,247 | 149,958 |
| Thailand | 88,918 | 68,569 | 49,124 |
| United Kingdom | 367,550 | 410,620 | 467,535 |
| USA | 316,881 | 329,586 | 373,911 |
| **Total** (incl. others) | 4,164,825 | 4,317,870 | 4,167,206 |

* Visitors intending to stay for less than one year.

**Receipts from tourism** ($A million): 16,101 in 1996; 16,452 in 1997; 16,300 in 1998.

Source: Australian Tourist Commission, Sydney.

## Communications Media

('000 at 30 June)

| | 1993 | 1994 | 1995 |
|---|---|---|---|
| Telephone services in operation | 8,540 | 8,850 | 9,200 |
| Telefax stations in use | 425 | 450 | 475 |
| Mobile telephones (subscribers) | 760 | 1,220 | 2,305 |

Source: UN, *Statistical Yearbook.*

**Radio receivers** (1996): 25,000,000 in use.

**Television receivers** (1996): 10,000,000 in use.

**Book production** (1994): 10,835 titles.

**Newspapers** (1996): 65 dailies (estimated combined circulation 5,370,000); (1988, estimates): 460 non-dailies (circulation 17,204,000).

Source: mainly UNESCO, *Statistical Yearbook.*

## Education

(1997)

| | Institutions | Teaching staff | Students |
|---|---|---|---|
| Government schools | 7,029 | 145,536* | 2,230,052† |
| Non-government schools | 2,580 | 61,523* | 941,572‡ |
| Higher educational institutions | 36§ | 81,404‖ | 658,827 |

* Full-time teaching staff and full-time equivalent of part-time teaching staff.

† Comprising 1,367,007 primary and 863,045 secondary students.

‡ Comprising 488,782 primary and 452,790 secondary students.

§ Public institutions only.

‖ Full-time staff and full-time equivalent of part-time and casual staff.

# Directory

## The Constitution

The Federal Constitution was adopted on 9 July 1900 and came into force on 1 January 1901. Its main provisions are summarized below:

### PARLIAMENT

The legislative power of the Commonwealth of Australia is vested in a Federal Parliament, consisting of HM the Queen (represented by the Governor-General), a Senate, and a House of Representatives. The Governor-General may appoint such times for holding the sessions of the Parliament as he or she thinks fit, and may also from time to time, by proclamation or otherwise, prorogue the Parliament, and may in like manner dissolve the House of Representatives. By convention, these powers are exercised on the advice of the Prime Minister. After any general election Parliament must be summoned to meet not later than 30 days after the day appointed for the return of the writs.

### THE SENATE

The Senate is composed of 12 senators from each state, two senators representing the Australian Capital Territory and two representing the Northern Territory. The senators are directly chosen by the people of the state or territory, voting in each case as one electorate, and are elected by proportional representation. Senators representing a state have a six-year term and retire by rotation, one-half from each state on 30 June of each third year. The term of a senator representing a territory is limited to three years. In the case of a state, if a senator vacates his or her seat before the expiration of the term of service, the houses of parliament of the state for which the senator was chosen shall, in joint session, choose a person to hold the place until the expiration of the term or until the election of a successor. If the state parliament is not in session, the Governor of the state, acting on the advice of the state's executive council, may appoint a senator to hold office until parliament reassembles, or until a new senator is elected.

The Senate may proceed to the dispatch of business notwithstanding the failure of any state to provide for its representation in the Senate.

### THE HOUSE OF REPRESENTATIVES

In accordance with the Australian Constitution, the total number of members of the House of Representatives must be as nearly as practicable double that of the Senate. The number in each state is in proportion to population, but under the Constitution must be at least five. The House of Representatives is composed of 148 members, including two members for the Australian Capital Territory and one member for the Northern Territory.

Members are elected by universal adult suffrage and voting is compulsory. Only Australian citizens are eligible to vote in Australian elections. British subjects, if they are not Australian citizens or already on the rolls, have to take out Australian citizenship before thay can enrol and before they can vote.

Members are chosen by the electors of their respective electorates by the preferential voting system.

The duration of the Parliament is limited to three years.

To be nominated for election to the House of Representatives, a candidate must be 18 years of age or over, an Australian citizen, and entitled to vote at the election or qualified to become an elector.

### THE EXECUTIVE GOVERNMENT

The executive power of the Federal Government is vested in the Queen, and is exercisable by the Governor-General, advised by an Executive Council of Ministers of State, known as the Federal Executive Council. These ministers are, or must become within three months, members of the Federal Parliament.

The Australian Constitution is construed as subject to the principles of responsible government and the Governor-General acts on the advice of the ministers in relation to most matters.

### THE JUDICIAL POWER

See Judicial System, p. 501.

### THE STATES

The Australian Constitution safeguards the Constitution of each state by providing that it shall continue as at the establishment of the Commonwealth, except as altered in accordance with its own provisions. The legislative power of the Federal Parliament is limited in the main to those matters that are listed in section 51 of the Constitution, while the states possess, as well as concurrent powers in those matters, residual legislative powers enabling them to legislate in any way for 'the peace, order and good Government' of their respective territories. When a state law is inconsistent with a law of the Commonwealth, the latter prevails, and the former is invalid to the extent of the inconsistency.

The states may not, without the consent of the Commonwealth, raise or maintain naval or military forces, or impose taxes on any property belonging to the Commonwealth of Australia, nor may the Commonwealth tax state property. The states may not coin money.

The Federal Parliament may not enact any law for establishing any religion or for prohibiting the exercise of any religion, and no religious test may be imposed as a qualification for any office under the Commonwealth.

The Commonwealth of Australia is charged with protecting every state against invasion, and, on the application of a state executive government, against domestic violence.

Provision is made under the Constitution for the admission of new states and for the establishment of new states within the Commonwealth of Australia.

### ALTERATION OF THE CONSTITUTION

Proposed laws for the amendment of the Constitution must be passed by an absolute majority in both Houses of the Federal Parliament, and not less than two or more than six months after its passage through both Houses the proposed law must be submitted in each state to the qualified electors.

In the event of one House twice refusing to pass a proposed amendment that has already received an absolute majority in the other House, the Governor-General may, notwithstanding such refusal, submit the proposed amendment to the electors. By convention, the Governor-General acts on the advice of the Prime Minister. If in a majority of the states a majority of the electors voting approve the proposed law and if a majority of all the electors voting also approve, it shall be presented to the Governor-General for Royal Assent.

No alteration diminishing the proportionate representation of any state in either House of the Federal Parliament, or the minimum number of representatives of a state in the House of Representatives, or increasing, diminishing or altering the limits of the state, or in any way affecting the provisions of the Constitution in relation thereto, shall become law unless the majority of the electors voting in that state approve the proposed law.

### STATES AND TERRITORIES

**New South Wales**

The state's executive power is vested in the Governor, appointed by the Crown, who is assisted by an Executive Council composed of cabinet ministers.

The state's legislative power is vested in a bicameral Parliament, composed of the Legislative Council and the Legislative Assembly. The Legislative Council consists of 42 members directly elected for the duration of two parliaments (i.e. eight years), 21 members retiring every four years. The Legislative Assembly consists of 99 members and sits for four years.

**Victoria**

The state's legislative power is vested in a bicameral Parliament: the Upper House, or Legislative Council, of 44 members, elected for two terms of the Legislative Assembly; and the Lower House, or Legislative Assembly, of 88 members, elected for a minimum of three and maximum of four years. One-half of the members of the Council retires every three–four years.

In the exercise of the executive power the Governor is assisted by a cabinet of responsible ministers. Not more than six members of the Council and not more than 17 members of the Assembly may occupy salaried office at any one time.

The state has 88 electoral districts, each returning one member, and 22 electoral provinces, each returning two Council members.

**Queensland**

The state's executive power is vested in the Governor, appointed by the Crown, who is assisted by an Executive Council composed of Ministers. The state's legislative power is vested in the Parliament comprising the Legislative Assembly (composed of 89 members who are elected at least every three years to represent 89 electoral districts) and the Governor, who assents to bills passed by the Assembly. The state's Constitution anticipates that Ministers are also members of the Legislative Assembly and provides that up to 18 members of the Assembly can be appointed Ministers.

**South Australia**

The state's Constitution vests the legislative power in a Parliament elected by the people and consisting of a Legislative Council and a House of Assembly. The Council is composed of 22 members, one-half of whom retires every three years. Their places are filled by new members elected under a system of proportional representation, with the whole state as a single electorate. The executive has no authority to dissolve this body, except in circumstances warranting a double dissolution.

The 45 members of the House of Assembly are elected for three years from 45 electoral districts.

The executive power is vested in a Governor, appointed by the Crown, and an Executive Council consisting of 10 responsible ministers.

**Western Australia**

The state's administration is vested in the Governor, a Legislative Council and a Legislative Assembly.

The Legislative Council consists of 34 members, two of the six electoral regions returning seven members on a proportional representation basis, and four regions returning five members. Election is for a term of four years.

The Legislative Assembly consists of 57 members, elected for four years, each representing one electorate.

**Tasmania**

The state's executive authority is vested in a Governor, appointed by the Crown, who acts upon the advice of his premier and ministers, who are elected members of either the Legislative Council or the House of Assembly. The Council consists of 15 members who sit for six years, retiring in rotation. The House of Assembly has 25 members elected for four years.

**Northern Territory**

On 1 July 1978, the Northern Territory was established as a body politic with executive authority for specified functions of government. Most functions of the Federal Government were transferred to the Territory Government in 1978 and 1979, major exceptions being Aboriginal affairs and uranium mining.

The Territory Parliament consists of a single house, the Legislative Assembly, with 25 members. The first Parliament stayed in office for three years. As from the election held in August 1980, members are elected for a term of four years.

The office of Administrator continues. The Northern Territory (Self-Government) Act provides for the appointment of an Administrator by the Governor-General charged with the duty of administering the Territory. In respect of matters transferred to the Territory Government, the Administrator acts with the advice of the Territory Executive Council; in respect of matters retained by the Commonwealth, the Administrator acts on Commonwealth advice.

**Australian Capital Territory**

On 29 November 1988 the Australian Capital Territory (ACT) was established as a body politic. The ACT Government has executive authority for specified functions, although a number of these were to be retained by the Federal Government for a brief period during which transfer arrangements were to be finalized.

The ACT Parliament consists of a single house, the Legislative Assembly, with 17 members. The first election was held in March 1989. Members are elected for a term of four years.

The Federal Government retains control of some of the land in the ACT for the purpose of maintaining thc Seat of Government and the national capital plan.

**Jervis Bay Territory**

Following the attainment of self-government by the ACT (see above), the Jervis Bay Territory, which had formed part of the ACT since 1915, remained a separate Commonwealth Territory, administered by the then Department of the Arts, Sport, the Environment and Territories. The area is governed in accordance with the Jervis Bay Territory Administration Ordinance, issued by the Governor-General on 17 December 1990.

## The Government

**Head of State:** HM Queen Elizabeth II (succeeded to the throne 6 February 1952).

**Governor-General:** Sir William Deane (took office 16 February 1996).

### THE MINISTRY
(January 2000)

**Cabinet Ministers**

**Prime Minister:** John Howard.

**Deputy Prime Minister and Minister for Transport and Regional Services:** John Anderson.

**Minister for Foreign Affairs:** Alexander Downer.

**Treasurer:** Peter Costello.

**Minister for Trade:** Mark Vaile.

**Minister for the Environment and Heritage, Leader of the Government in the Senate:** Senator Robert Hill.

**Minister for Communications, Information Technology and the Arts, Deputy Leader of the Government in the Senate:** Senator Richard Alston.

**Minister for Employment, Workplace Relations and Small Business, Leader of the House:** Peter Reith.

**Minister for Family and Community Services:** Senator Jocelyn Newman.

**Minister for Defence:** John Moore.

**Minister for Health and Aged Care:** Dr Michael Wooldridge.

**Minister for Finance and Administration:** John Fahey.

**Minister for Education, Training and Youth Affairs:** David Kemp.

**Minister for Industry, Science and Resources:** Senator Nick Minchin.

**Attorney-General:** Daryl Williams.

**Minister for Agriculture, Forestry and Fisheries:** Warren Truss.

**Minister for Immigration and Multicultural Affairs:** Phillip Ruddock.

**Other Ministers**

**Minister of Aboriginal Affairs and Torres Strait Islander Affairs:** John Herron.

**Minister Assisting the Prime Minister and Minister for Forestry and Conservation:** Wilson Tuckey.

**Assistant Treasurer:** Senator Rod Kemp.

**Minister for Financial Services and Regulation:** Joe Hockey.

**Minister for Regional Services, Territories and Local Government:** Senator Ian MacDonald.

**Minister for the Arts and the Centenary of Federation, Deputy Leader of the House:** Peter McGauran.

**Minister for Employment Services:** Tony Abbott.

**Minister for Community Services:** Larry Anthony.

**Minister Assisting the Prime Minister for Defence and Minister for Veterans' Affairs:** BRUCE SCOTT.

**Minister for Aged Care:** BRONWYN BISHOP.

**Special Minister of State:** Senator CHRIS ELLISON.

**Minister Assisting the Prime Minister for the Public Service:** TRISH WORTH.

**Minister for Sport and Tourism:** JACKIE KELLY.

**Minister Assisting the Prime Minister for the Sydney 2000 Games:** WARREN ENTSCH.

**Minister for Justice and Customs:** Senator AMANDA VANSTONE.

**Minister Assisting the Prime Minister for Reconciliation:** Senator KAY PATTERSON.

### DEPARTMENTS

**Department of the Prime Minister and Cabinet:** 3–5 National Circuit, Barton, ACT 2600; tel. (2) 6271-5111; fax (2) 6271-5414; internet www.dpmc.gov.au.

**Aboriginal and Torres Strait Islander Commission:** MLC Tower, Woden Town Centre, Phillip, ACT 2606; tel. (2) 6289-1222; fax (2) 6282-4541; internet www.atsic.gov.au.

**Department of Agriculture, Fisheries and Forestry:** GPOB 858, Canberra, ACT 2601; tel. (2) 6272-3933; fax (2) 6272-5161; internet www.affa.gov.au/home.html.

**Attorney-General's Department:** Robert Garran Offices, Barton, ACT 2600; tel. (2) 6250-6666; fax (2) 6250-5900; internet www.law.gov.au.

**Department of Communications, Information Technology and the Arts:** GPOB 2154, Canberra, ACT 2601; tel. (2) 6271-1000; fax (2) 6271-1901; internet www.dca.gov.au.

**Department of Defence:** Russell Offices, Canberra, ACT 2600; tel. (2) 6265-9111; e-mail mpi@spirit.com.au; internet www.defence.gov.au.

**Department of Education, Training and Youth Affairs:** GPOB 9880, Canberra, ACT 2601; tel. (2) 6240-8848; fax (2) 6240-8861; e-mail library@detya.gov.au; internet www.detya.gov.au.

**Department of Employment, Workplace Relations and Small Business:** GPO Box 9879, Canberra, ACT 2601; tel. (2) 6121-7547; fax (2) 6121-7542; e-mail webmaster@dewrsb.gov.au.

**Department of the Environment and Heritage:** GPOB 787, Canberra, ACT 2601; tel. (2) 6274-1111; fax (2) 6274-1123; internet www.environment.gov.au.

**Department of Family and Community Services:** Box 7788, Canberra Mail Centre, ACT 2610; tel. (2) 6244-7788; fax (2) 6244-5540; internet www.facs.gov.au.

**Department of Finance and Administration:** King Edward Tce, Parkes, ACT 2600; tel. (2) 6263-2222; fax (2) 6273-3021; internet www.dofa.gov.au.

**Department of Foreign Affairs and Trade:** GPO Box 12, Canberra City, ACT 2601; tel. (2) 6261-1111; fax (2) 6261-3959; internet www.dfat.gov.au.

**Department of Health and Aged Care:** GPOB 9848, Canberra, ACT 2601; tel. (2) 6289-1555; fax (2) 6281-6946; internet www.health.gov.au.

**Department of Immigration and Multicultural Affairs:** Benjamin Offices, Chan St, Belconnen, ACT 2617; tel. (2) 6264-1111; fax (2) 6264-2670; internet www.immi.gov.au.

**Department of Industry, Science and Resources:** 20 Allara St, Canberra, ACT 2601; tel. (2) 6213-6000; fax (2) 6213-7000; e-mail distpubs@isr.gov.au; internet www.isr.gov.au.

**Department of Transport and Regional Services:** GPOB 594, Canberra, ACT 2601; tel. (2) 6274-7111; fax (2) 6257-2505; e-mail public affairs@dotrs.gov.au; internet www.dotrs.gov.au.

**Department of the Treasury:** Parkes Place, Parkes, ACT 2600; tel. (2) 6263-2111; fax (2) 6273-2614; internet www.treasury.gov.au.

**Department of Veterans' Affairs:** POB 21, Woden, ACT 2606; tel. (2) 6289-1111; fax (2) 6289-6025; internet www.dva.gov.au.

## Legislature

### FEDERAL PARLIAMENT

#### Senate

**President:** Senator MARGARET REID.

**Election, 3 October 1998**

| Party | Seats* |
|---|---|
| Liberal Party of Australia | 31 |
| Australian Labor Party | 29 |
| Australian Democrats Party | 9 |
| National Party of Australia | 4 |
| Greens | 1 |
| Independent | 1 |
| One Nation | 1 |
| **Total** | 76 |

* Party representation from 1 July 1999. The election was for 36 of the 72 seats held by state senators and for all four senators representing the Northern Territory and the Australian Capital Territory (the terms of the latter being limited to three years). The figures for seats refer to the totals held after the election.

#### House of Representatives

**Speaker:** IAN SINCLAIR.

**Election, 3 October 1998**

| Party | Seats |
|---|---|
| Australian Labor Party | 67* |
| Liberal Party of Australia | 64 |
| National Party of Australia | 16 |
| Independent | 1 |
| **Total** | 148 |

* Owing to the death of a candidate shortly before the election, polling for one seat was postponed until 21 November.

## State and Territory Governments

(January 2000)

### NEW SOUTH WALES

**Governor:** GORDON SAMUELS, Level 3, Chief Secretary's Bldg, 121 Macquarie St, Sydney, NSW 2000; tel. (2) 9242-4200; fax (2) 9242-4266; e-mail ersm1@waratah.www.nsw.gov.au; internet www.nsw.gov.au.

**Premier:** ROBERT (BOB) J. CARR (Labor).

### VICTORIA

**Governor:** Sir JAMES AUGUSTINE GOBBO, Government House, Melbourne, Vic 3004; tel. (3) 9651-4211; fax (3) 9651-9050; internet www.vic.gov.au.

**Premier:** STEPHEN P. BRACKS (Labor).

### QUEENSLAND

**Governor:** Maj.-Gen. PETER M. ARNISON, Government House, Brisbane, Qld 4001; tel. (7) 3858-5700; fax (7) 3858-5701; e-mail govhouse@govhouse.qld.gov.au; internet www.govhouse.qld.gov.au.

**Premier:** PETER D. BEATTIE (Labor).

### SOUTH AUSTRALIA

**Governor:** Sir ERIC JAMES NEAL, Government House, North Terrace, Adelaide, SA 5000; tel. (8) 8203-9800; fax (8) 8203-9899; internet www.sa.gov.au.

**Premier:** JOHN W. OLSEN (Liberal-National).

### WESTERN AUSTRALIA

**Governor:** Maj.-Gen. PHILIP MICHAEL JEFFERY, Government House, Perth, WA 6000; tel. (8) 9429-9199; fax (8) 9325-4476; e-mail govhouse@govhouse.wa.gov.au; internet www.wa.gov.au.

**Premier:** RICHARD COURT (Liberal-National).

### TASMANIA

**Governor:** Sir GUY STEPHEN MONTAGUE GREEN, Government House, Hobart, Tas 7000; tel. (3) 6234-2611; fax (3) 6234-2556; internet www.tas.gov.au.

**Premier:** JAMES A. BACON (Labor).

### NORTHERN TERRITORY

**Administrator:** Dr NEIL RAYMOND CONN, Government House, The Esplanade, Darwin, NT 0800; tel. (8) 8999-7103; fax (8) 8981-9379; internet www.nt.gov.au/administrator.

**Chief Minister:** DENIS G. BURKE (Liberal-National).

### AUSTRALIAN CAPITAL TERRITORY

**Chief Minister:** A. KATHERINE (KATE) CARNELL (Liberal-National); Legislative Assembly Bldg, Civic Square, London Circuit, Canberra, ACT 2601; tel. (2) 6205-0101; fax (2) 6205-0399; e-mail carnell@dpa.act.gov.au; internet www.act.gov.au.

## Political Organizations

**Australian Democrats Party:** Victorian Division, G1/Eastbourne House, 62 Wellington Pde, East Melbourne, Vic 3002; tel. (3) 9419-5808; fax (3) 9419-5697; e-mail senator.lees@democrats.org.au; internet www.democrats.org.au/; f. 1971; comprises the fmr Liberal Movement and the Australia Party; Leader Senator MEG LEES.

**Australian Labor Party (ALP):** Centenary House, 19 National Circuit, Barton, ACT 2600; tel. (2) 6273-3133; fax (2) 6273-2031; e-mail natsect@alp.org.au; internet www.alp.org.au/; f. 1891; advocates social democracy; trade unions form part of its structure; Fed. Parl. Leader KIM BEAZLEY; Nat. Pres. BARRY O. JONES; Nat. Sec. GARY GRAY.

**Communist Party of Australia:** 65 Campbell St, Surry Hills, NSW 2010; tel. (2) 9212-6855; fax (2) 9281-5795; e-mail cpa@cpa.org.au; internet www.cpa.org.au; f. 1971; fmrly Socialist Party; advocates public ownership of the means of production, working-class political power; Pres. Dr H. MIDDLETON; Gen. Sec. P. SYMON.

**Liberal Party of Australia:** Federal Secretariat, Cnr Blackall and Macquarie Sts, Barton, ACT 2600; tel. (2) 6273-2564; fax (2) 6273-1534; e-mail libadm@liberal.org.au; internet www.liberal.org.au; f. 1944; advocates private enterprise, social justice, individual liberty and initiative; committed to national development, prosperity and security; Fed. Dir LYNTON CROSBY; Fed. Parl. Leader JOHN HOWARD.

**National Party of Australia:** John McEwen House, National Circuit, Barton, ACT 2600; tel. (2) 6273-3822; fax (2) 6273-1745; e-mail npafed@ozemail.com.au; internet www.ozemail.com.au/~npafed; f. 1916 as the Country Party of Australia; adopted present name in 1982; advocates balanced national development based on free enterprise, with special emphasis on the needs of people outside the major metropolitan areas; Fed. Pres. HELEN DICKIE; Fed. Parl. Leader JOHN ANDERSON; Fed. Dir PAUL DAVEY.

**One Nation Party:** c/o The Senate, Canberra; e-mail senator.harris@aph.gov.au; f. 1997; opposes immigration and special funding for Aboriginal people; Leader PAULINE HANSON.

Other political organizations include the Green Party, the Australian Republican Movement (Chair. MALCOLM TURNBULL) and No Republic (formerly Australians for a Constitutional Monarchy—Exec. Dir KERRY JONES).

## Diplomatic Representation

### EMBASSIES AND HIGH COMMISSIONS IN AUSTRALIA

**Argentina:** POB 4835, Kingston, ACT 2604; tel. (2) 6282-4855; fax (2) 6285-3062; e-mail eaust@canberra.teknet.net.au; Ambassador: NÉSTOR E. STANCANELLI.

**Austria:** POB 3375, Manuka, ACT 2603; tel. (2) 6295-1533; fax (2) 6239-6751; e-mail austria@dynamite.com.au; internet www.austriaemb.org.au/; Ambassador: Dr OTMAR KOLER.

**Bangladesh:** POB 5, Red Hill, ACT 2603; tel. (2) 6295-3328; fax (2) 6295-3351; e-mail bdoot.canberra@cyberone.com.au; High Commissioner: Q. A. M. A. RAHIM.

**Belgium:** 19 Arkana St, Yarralumla, ACT 2600; tel. (2) 6273-2501; fax (2) 6273-3392; e-mail belgemb@spirit.com.au; Ambassador: BERNARD LAUWAERT.

**Bosnia and Herzegovina:** 15 State Circle, Forrest, ACT 2603; tel. (2) 6239-5955; fax (2) 6239-5793; e-mail bihembcbr@webone.com.au; Chargé d'affaires a.i.: FUAD DJIDIĆ.

**Brazil:** GPOB 1540, Canberra, ACT 2601; tel. (2) 6273-2372; fax (2) 6273-2375; e-mail aasbrem@interconnect.com.au; internet brazil.org.au; Ambassador: ANTÔNIO AUGUSTO DAYRELL DE LIMA.

**Brunei:** 16 Bulwarra Close, O'Malley, ACT 2606; tel. (2) 6290-1801; fax (2) 6286-1554; High Commissioner: Pehin Dato' Haji HUSIN AHMAD.

**Cambodia:** 5 Canterbury Crescent, Deakin, ACT 2600; tel. (2) 6273-1259; fax (2) 6273-1053; e-mail cambodia@embassy.net.au; Ambassador: HOR NAMBORA.

**Canada:** Commonwealth Ave, Canberra, ACT 2600; tel. (2) 6270-4000; fax (2) 6273-3285; internet www.canada.org.au; High Commissioner: JAMES BARTLEMAN.

**Chile:** POB 69, Red Hill, ACT 2603; tel. (2) 6286-2430; fax (2) 6286-1289; e-mail echileau@dynamite.com.au; internet www.users.netinfo.com.au/chile; Ambassador: JORGE TARUD.

**China, People's Republic:** 15 Coronation Drive, Yarralumla, ACT 2600; tel. (2) 6273-4780; fax (2) 6273-4235; Ambassador: ZHOU WENZHONG.

**Colombia:** GPOB 2892, Canberra City, ACT 2601; tel. (2) 6257-2027; fax (2) 6257-1448; Ambassador: JUAN SANTIAGO URIBE.

**Croatia:** 14 Jindalee Crescent, O'Malley, ACT 2606; tel. (2) 6286-6988; fax (2) 6286-3544; e-mail croemb@dynamite.com.au; Chargé d'affaires: BRANIMIR MULLER.

**Cyprus:** 30 Beale Crescent, Deakin, ACT 2600; tel. (2) 6281-0832; fax (2) 6281-0860; e-mail cyphicom@dynamite.com.au; High Commissioner: ANDREAS GEORGIADES.

**Czech Republic:** 38 Culgoa Circuit, O'Malley, ACT 2606; tel. (2) 6290-1386; fax (2) 6290-0006; e-mail canberra@embassy.mzv.cz; Ambassador: JOSEF SLÁDEK.

**Denmark:** 15 Hunter St, Yarralumla, ACT 2600; tel. (2) 6273-2195; fax (2) 6273-3864; e-mail dkembact@dynamite.com.au; Ambassador: JENS OSTENFELD.

**Ecuador:** 1st Floor, Law Society Bldg of Canberra, 11 London Circuit, ACT 2601; tel. (2) 6262-5282; fax (2) 6262-5285; e-mail embecu@canberra.hotkey.net.au; Ambassador: ABELARDO POSSO-SERRANO.

**Egypt:** 1 Darwin Ave, Yarralumla, ACT 2600; tel. (2) 6273-4437; fax (2) 6273-4279; Ambassador: GILLANE ALLAM.

**Fiji:** POB 159, Deakin West, ACT 2600; tel. (2) 6260-5115; fax (2) 6260-5105; e-mail fhc@cyberone.com.au; High Commissioner: Ratu ISOA GAVIDI.

**Finland:** 10 Darwin Ave, Yarralumla, ACT 2600; tel. (2) 6273-3800; fax (2) 6273-3603; e-mail finland@dynamite.com.au; internet www.finland.org.au; Ambassador: ESKO HAMILO.

**France:** 6 Perth Ave, Yarralumla, ACT 2600; tel. (2) 6216-0100; fax (2) 6216-0127; e-mail embassy@france.net.au; internet www.france.net.au; Ambassador: PIERRE VIAUX.

**Germany:** 119 Empire Circuit, Yarralumla, ACT 2600; tel. (2) 6270-1911; fax (2) 6270-1951; e-mail embgerma@dynamite.com.au; Ambassador: Dr HORST BÄCHMANN.

**Greece:** 9 Turrana St, Yarralumla, ACT 2600; tel. (2) 6273-3011; fax (2) 6273-2620; e-mail greekemb@dynamite.com.au; Ambassador: IOANNIS BEVERATOS.

**Holy See:** POB 3633, Manuka, ACT 2603 (Apostolic Nunciature); tel. (2) 6295-3876; Apostolic Nuncio: Most Rev. FRANCESCO CANALINI, Titular Archbishop of Valeria.

**Hungary:** 17 Beale Crescent, Deakin, ACT 2600; tel. (2) 6282-3226; fax (2) 6285-3012; e-mail huembcbr@attmail.com.au; Ambassador: Dr ISTVÁN GYÜRK.

**India:** 3–5 Moonah Place, Yarralumla, ACT 2600; tel. (2) 6273-3999; fax (2) 6273-3328; e-mail hciisi@cyberone.com.au; High Commissioner: C. P. RAVINDRANATHAN.

**Indonesia:** 8 Darwin Ave, Yarralumla, ACT 2600; tel. (2) 6273-3222; fax (2) 6250-8600; e-mail kbricbr@dynamite.com.au; Ambassador: SASTROHANDOJO WIRYONO.

**Iran:** POB 3219, Manuka, ACT 2603; tel. (2) 6290-2421; fax (2) 6290-2431; internet www.mfa.gov.ir; Ambassador: Dr GHOLAMALI KHOSHROO.

**Iraq:** 48 Culgoa Circuit, O'Malley, ACT 2606; tel. (2) 6286-1333; fax (2) 6290-1788; Chargé d'affaires: NATIK A. RADHI.

**Ireland:** 20 Arkana St, Yarralumla, ACT 2600; tel. (2) 6273-3022; fax (2) 6273-3741; e-mail irishemb@computech.com.au; Ambassador: RICHARD A. O'BRIEN.

**Israel:** 6 Turrana St, Yarralumla, ACT 2600; tel. (2) 6273-1309; telex 62224; fax (2) 6273-4273; e-mail israel.aust@embassy.net.au; internet www.mfa.gov.il; Ambassador: GABBY LEVY.

**Italy:** 12 Grey St, Deakin, ACT 2600; tel. (2) 6273-3333; fax (2) 6273-4223; e-mail embassy@ambitalia.org.au; internet www.ambitalia.org.au; Ambassador: GIOVANNI CASTELLANETA.

**Japan:** 112 Empire Circuit, Yarralumla, ACT 2600; tel. (2) 6273-3244; fax (2) 6273-1848; Ambassador: MASAJI TAKAHASHI.

**Jordan:** 20 Roebuck St, Red Hill, ACT 2603; tel. (2) 6295-9951; fax (2) 6239-7236; Ambassador: Dr KHALDOUN THARWAT TALHOUNI.

**Kenya:** GPOB 1990, Canberra, ACT 2601; tel. (2) 6247-4788; fax (2) 6257-6613; High Commissioner: FRANKLIN K. ARAP BETT.

**Korea, Republic:** 113 Empire Circuit, Yarralumla, ACT 2600; tel. (2) 6270-4100; fax (2) 6273-4839; e-mail adm2@embrok-canberra.org.au; internet www.mofat.go.kr/en–australia.htm; Ambassador: SHIN HYO-HUN.

**Laos:** 1 Dalman Crescent, O'Malley, ACT 2606; tel. (2) 6286-4595; fax (2) 6290-1910; Ambassador: SOUTSAKHONE PATHAMMAVONG.

**Lebanon:** 27 Endeavour St, Red Hill, ACT 2603; tel. (2) 6295-7378; fax (2) 6239-7024; Ambassador: MICHEL BITAR.

**Malaysia:** 7 Perth Ave, Yarralumla, ACT 2600; tel. (2) 6273-1543; fax (2) 6273-2496; e-mail malaysia@aucom.com.au; High Commissioner: Dato' ADNAN OTHMAN.

**Malta:** 261 La Perouse St, Red Hill, ACT 2603; tel. (2) 6295-1586; fax (2) 6239-6084; e-mail maltahc@cs.net.au; internet www.embassies-online.com.au/malta; High Commissioner: IVES DE BARRO.

**Mauritius:** 2 Beale Crescent, Deakin, ACT 2600; tel. (2) 6281-1203; fax (2) 6282-3235; e-mail Mauritius@caber.net; High Commissioner: PATRICE CURÉ.

**Mexico:** 14 Perth Ave, Yarralumla, ACT 2600; tel. (2) 6273-3905; fax (2) 6273-1190; e-mail embmex@enternet.com.au; internet people.enternet.com.au/~embmex; Ambassador: RAPHAEL STEGER-CATAÑO.

**Myanmar:** 22 Arkana St, Yarralumla, ACT 2600; tel. (2) 6273-3811; fax (2) 6273-4357; Ambassador: U MAUNG MAUNG LAY.

**Netherlands:** 120 Empire Circuit, Yarralumla, ACT 2600; tel. (2) 6273-3111; fax (2) 6273-3206; e-mail nlgovcan@ozemail.com.au; Ambassador: ALBERTUS J. A. M. NOOIJ.

**New Zealand:** Commonwealth Ave, Canberra, ACT 2600; tel. (2) 6270-4211; fax (2) 6273-3194; e-mail nzhccba@dynamite.com.au; High Commissioner: SIMON MURDOCH.

**Nigeria:** POB 241, Civic Square, ACT 2608; tel. (2) 6286-1322; fax (2) 6286-5332; e-mail nigeriaACT@netinfo.com.au; High Commissioner: MUSTAFA SAM.

**Norway:** 17 Hunter St, Yarralumla, ACT 2600; tel. (2) 6273-3444; fax (2) 6273-3669; e-mail noramb@ibm.net; internet www.members.tripod.com/~norembassy/; Ambassador: KJELL-MARTIN FREDERIKSEN.

**Pakistan:** POB 684, Mawson, ACT 2607; tel. (2) 6290-1676; fax (2) 6290-1073; e-mail parepcanberra@actonline.com.au; High Commissioner: KHAWAR ZAMAN.

**Papua New Guinea:** POB E432, Queen Victoria Terrace, Kingston, ACT 2600; tel. (2) 6273-3322; fax (2) 6273-3732; High Commissioner: RENAGI R. LOHIA.

**Peru:** POB 106, Red Hill, ACT 2603; tel. (2) 6290-0922; fax (2) 6290-0924; e-mail emperuau@dynamite.com.au; internet www.users.netinfo.com.au/~embaperuaussie; Ambassador: JOSÉ LUIS GARAYCOCHEA.

**Philippines:** POB 3297, Manuka, ACT 2603; tel. (2) 6273-2536; fax (2) 6273-3984; e-mail embaphil@iaccess.com.au; Ambassador: DELIA DOMINGO-ALBERT.

**Poland:** 7 Turrana St, Yarralumla, ACT 2600; tel. (2) 6273-1208; fax (2) 6273-3184; e-mail beata@clover.com.au; Ambassador: Dr TADEUSZ SZUMOWSKI.

**Portugal:** 23 Culgoa Circuit, O'Malley, ACT 2606; tel. (2) 6290-1733; fax (2) 6290-1957; e-mail embport@dynamite.com.au; Ambassador: Dr ZÓZIMO JUSTO DA SILVA.

**Romania:** 4 Dalman Crescent, O'Malley, ACT 2606; tel. (2) 6286-2343; fax (2) 6286-2433; e-mail roembcbr@cyberone.com.au; Chargé d'affaires a.i.: DAN SITARU.

**Russia:** 78 Canberra Ave, Griffith, ACT 2603; tel. (2) 6295-9033; fax (2) 6295-1847; e-mail rusemb@dynamite.com.au; Ambassador: RASHIT KHAMIDULIN.

**Samoa:** POB 3274, Manuka, ACT 2603; tel. (2) 6286-5505; fax (2) 6286-5678; e-mail samoahcaussi@netspeed.com.au; High Commissioner: Leiataua Dr KILIFOTI S. ETEUATI.

**Saudi Arabia:** POB 63, Garran, ACT 2605; tel. (2) 6282-6999; fax (2) 6282-8911; e-mail saudiemb@hotmail.com; Ambassador: MOHAMAD I. AL-HEJAILAN.

**Singapore:** 17 Forster Crescent, Yarralumla, ACT 2600; tel. (2) 6273-3944; fax (2) 6273-3260; e-mail shc.cbr@u030.aone.net.au; High Commissioner: LOW CHOON MING.

**Slovakia:** 47 Culgoa Circuit, O'Malley, ACT 2606; tel. (2) 6290-1516; fax (2) 6290-1755; e-mail slovak.embassy@cs.net.au; Chargé d'affaires: Dr ANNA TURENIČOVÁ.

**Slovenia:** POB 284, Civic Square, Canberra, ACT 2608; tel. (2) 6243-4830; fax (2) 6243-4827; e-mail Embassyofslovenia@webone.com.au; internet www.slovenia.webone.com.au; Chargé d'affaires: HELENA DRNOVŠEK ZORKO.

**Solomon Islands:** Unit 4, JAA House, 19 Napier Close, Deakin, ACT 2600; tel. (2) 6282-7030; fax (2) 6282-7040; e-mail info@solomon.emb.gov.au; High Commissioner: (vacant).

**South Africa:** cnr State Circle and Rhodes Place, Yarralumla, ACT 2600; tel. (2) 6273-2424; fax (2) 6273-3543; e-mail info@rsa.emb.gov.au; internet www.rsa.emb.gov.au; High Commissioner: Dr BHADRA G. RANCHOD.

**Spain:** POB 9076, Deakin, ACT 2600; tel. (2) 6273-3555; fax (2) 6273-3918; e-mail embespau@mail.mae.es; Ambassador: EMILIO FERNÁNDEZ CASTAÑO.

**Sri Lanka:** 35 Empire Circuit, Forrest, ACT 2603; tel. (2) 6239-7041; fax (2) 6239-6166; e-mail slhc@atrax.net.au; internet www.slhccanberra.wejump.com; High Commissioner: H. K. J. R. BANDARA.

**Sweden:** 5 Turrana St, Yarralumla, ACT 2600; tel. (2) 6270-2700; fax (2) 6270-2755; e-mail sweden@netinfo.com.au; Ambassador: GÖRAN HASSELMARK.

**Switzerland:** 7 Melbourne Ave, Forrest, ACT 2603; tel. (2) 6273-3977; fax (2) 6273-3428; e-mail swiemcan@dynamite.com.au; Ambassador: Dr BERNHARD MARFURT.

**Thailand:** 111 Empire Circuit, Yarralumla, ACT 2600; tel. (2) 6273-1149; fax (2) 6273-1518; e-mail thai@csccs.com.au; Ambassador: LAXANACHANTORN LAOHAPHAN.

**Turkey:** 60 Mugga Way, Red Hill, ACT 2603; tel. (2) 6295-0227; fax (2) 6239-6592; e-mail turkembs@ozemail.com.au; internet www.ozemail.com.au/~turkembs; Ambassador: UMUT ARIK.

**United Arab Emirates:** 36 Culgoa Circuit, O'Malley, ACT 2606; tel. (2) 6286-8802; fax (2) 6286-8804; e-mail UAEAUS@interact.net.au; internet www.users.bigpond.com/UAEAUS; Ambassador: KHALIFA MOHAMMED BAKHIT AL-FALASI.

**United Kingdom:** Commonwealth Ave, Canberra, ACT 2600; tel. (2) 6270-6666; fax (2) 6273-3236; e-mail BHC.Canberra@uk.emb.gov.au; internet www.uk.emb.gov.au; High Commissioner: Sir ALASTAIR GOODLAD.

**USA:** Moonah Place, Yarralumla, ACT 2600; tel. (2) 6270-5000; fax (2) 6270-5970; Ambassador: GENTA HAWKINS HOLMES.

**Uruguay:** POB 5058, Kingston, ACT 2604; tel. (2) 6273-9100; fax (2) 6273-9099; e-mail urucan@interconnect.com.au; Ambassador: PABLO SADER.

**Venezuela:** 5 Culgoa Circuit, O'Malley, ACT 2606; tel. (2) 6290-2968; fax (2) 6290-2911; e-mail embaustralia@venezuelaemb-org.au; internet www.venezuela-emb.org.au; Chargé d'affaires: RAMÓN E. TOVAR ROBLES.

**Viet Nam:** 6 Timbarra Crescent, O'Malley, ACT 2606; tel. (2) 6286-6059; fax (2) 6286-4534; e-mail vemembassy@webone.com.au; Ambassador: TRAN VAN TUNG.

**Yugoslavia:** POB 728, Mawson, ACT 2607; tel. (2) 6290-2630; fax (2) 6290-2631; Ambassador: DRAGAN DRAGOJLOVIĆ.

**Zimbabwe:** 11 Culgoa Circuit, O'Malley, ACT 2606; tel. (2) 6286-2700; fax (2) 6290-1680; e-mail zimbabwe@dynamite.com.au; High Commissioner: Prof. HASU H. PATEL.

## Judicial System

The judicial power of the Commonwealth of Australia is vested in the High Court of Australia, in such other Federal Courts as the Federal Parliament creates, and in such other courts as it invests with Federal jurisdiction.

The High Court consists of a Chief Justice and six other Justices, each of whom is appointed by the Governor-General in Council, and has both original and appellate jurisdiction.

The High Court's original jurisdiction extends to all matters arising under any treaty, affecting representatives of other countries, in which the Commonwealth of Australia or its representative is a party, between states or between residents of different states or between a state and a resident of another state, and in which a writ of mandamus, or prohibition, or an injunction is sought against an officer of the Commonwealth of Australia. It also extends to matters arising under the Australian Constitution or involving its interpretation, and to many matters arising under Commonwealth laws.

The High Court's appellate jurisdiction has, since June 1984, been discretionary. Appeals from the Federal Court, the Family Court and the Supreme Courts of the states and of the territories may now be brought only if special leave is granted, in the event of a legal question that is of general public importance being involved, or of there being differences of opinion between intermediate appellate courts as to the state of the law.

Legislation enacted by the Federal Parliament in 1976 substantially changed the exercise of Federal and Territory judicial power, and, by creating the Federal Court of Australia in February 1977, enabled the High Court of Australia to give greater attention to its primary function as interpreter of the Australian Constitution. The Federal Court of Australia has assumed, in two divisions, the jurisdiction previously exercised by the Australian Industrial Court and the Federal Court of Bankruptcy and was additionally given jurisdiction in trade practices and in the developing field of administrative law. In 1987 the Federal Court of Australia acquired jurisdiction in federal taxation matters and certain intellectual property matters. In 1991 the Court's jurisdiction was expanded to include civil proceedings arising under Corporations Law. Jurisdiction has also been conferred on the Federal Court of Australia, subject to a number of exceptions, in matters in which a writ of mandamus, or prohibition, or an injunction is sought against an officer of the Commonwealth of Australia. The Court also hears appeals from the Court constituted by a single Judge, from the Supreme Courts of the territories, and in certain specific matters from State Courts, other than a Full Court of the Supreme Court of a state, exercising Federal jurisdiction.

In March 1986 all remaining categories of appeal from Australian courts to the Queen's Privy Council in the UK were abolished by the Australia Act.

### FEDERAL COURTS

#### High Court of Australia

POB E435, Kingston, Canberra, ACT 2604; tel. (2) 6270-6811; fax (2) 6270-6868; internet www.hcourt.gov.au.

**Chief Justice:** ANTHONY MURRAY GLEESON.

**Justices:** MARY GAUDRON, MICHAEL MCHUGH, WILLIAM GUMMOW, MICHAEL DONALD KIRBY, KENNETH MADISON HAYNE, IAN DAVID FRANCIS CALLINAN.

#### Federal Court of Australia

**Chief Justice:** MICHAEL ERIC JOHN BLACK.

In 1999 there were 49 other judges.

#### Family Court of Australia

**Chief Justice:** ALISTAIR BOTHWICK NICHOLSON.

In 1999 there were more than 50 other judges.

### NEW SOUTH WALES

#### Supreme Court

**Chief Justice:** JAMES JACOB SPIGELMAN.

**President:** KEITH MASON.

**Chief Judge in Equity:** DAVID HARGRAVES HODGSON.

**Chief Judge at Common Law:** JAMES ROLAND TOMSON WOOD.

**Chief Judge of the Commercial Division:** (vacant).

### VICTORIA

#### Supreme Court

**Chief Justice:** JOHN HARBER PHILLIPS.

**President of the Court of Appeal:** JOHN SPENCE WINNEKE.

### QUEENSLAND

#### Supreme Court

**Chief Justice:** PAUL DE JERSEY.

**President of the Court of Appeal:** MARGARET MCMURDO.

**Senior Judge Administrator, Trial Division:** MARTIN PATRICK MOYNIHAN.

Central District (Rockhampton)

**Resident Judge:** ALAN GEORGE DEMACK.

Northern District (Townsville)

**Resident Judge:** KEIRAN ANTHONY CULLINANE.

### SOUTH AUSTRALIA

#### Supreme Court

**Chief Justice:** JOHN JEREMY DOYLE.

### WESTERN AUSTRALIA

#### Supreme Court

**Chief Justice:** DAVID KINGSLEY MALCOLM.

### TASMANIA

#### Supreme Court

**Chief Justice:** WILLIAM JOHN ELLIS COX.

### AUSTRALIAN CAPITAL TERRITORY

#### Supreme Court

**Chief Justice:** JEFFREY ALLAN MILES.

### NORTHERN TERRITORY

#### Supreme Court

**Chief Justice:** BRIAN FRANK MARTIN.

## Religion

### CHRISTIANITY

According to the population census of August 1996, Christians numbered an estimated 12,582,764.

**National Council of Churches in Australia:** Private Bag 199, QVB PO, Sydney, NSW 1230; tel. (2) 9299-2215; fax (2) 9262-4514; f. 1946; 14 mem. churches; Pres. Archbishop JOHN BATHERSBY; Gen. Sec. Rev. DAVID GILL.

#### The Anglican Communion

The constitution of the Church of England in Australia, which rendered the church an autonomous member of the Anglican Communion, came into force in January 1962. The body was renamed the Anglican Church of Australia in August 1981. The Church comprises five provinces (together containing 22 dioceses) and the extra-provincial diocese of Tasmania. At the 1996 population census there were 3,903,324 adherents.

**National Office of the Anglican Church:** General Synod Office, Box Q190, QVB PO, Sydney, NSW 1230; tel. (2) 9265-1525; fax (2) 9264-6552; e-mail gensec@anglican.org.au; internet www.anglican.org.au; Gen. Sec. Rev. Dr B. N. KAYE.

**Archbishop of Adelaide and Metropolitan of South Australia:** Most Rev. IAN G. C. GEORGE, Bishop's Court, 45 Palmer Place, North Adelaide, SA 5006; fax (8) 8305-9399; e-mail anglade@camtech.net.au.

**Archbishop of Brisbane and Metropolitan of Queensland:** Most Rev. PETER J. HOLLINGWORTH, Bishopsbourne, Box 421, GPO, Brisbane, Qld 4001; fax (7) 3832-5030; e-mail relliott@anglicanbrisbane.org.au.

**Archbishop of Melbourne and Metropolitan of Victoria and Primate:** (vacant), Bishopscourt, 120 Clarendon St, East Melbourne, Vic 3002.

**Archbishop of Perth and Metropolitan of Western Australia:** Most Rev. PETER F. CARNLEY, GPOB W2067, Perth, WA 6846; e-mail abcsuite@iinet.net.au; internet www.perth.anglican.org; also has jurisdiction over Christmas Island and the Cocos (Keeling) Islands.

**Archbishop of Sydney and Metropolitan of New South Wales:** Most Rev. R. H. GOODHEW, POB Q190, QVB Post Office, Sydney, NSW 1230; tel. (2) 9265-1521; fax (2) 9265-1504; e-mail archbishop@sydney.anglican.asn.au; internet www.anglicanmediasydney.asn.au.

#### The Roman Catholic Church

Australia comprises five metropolitan archdioceses, two archdioceses directly responsible to the Holy See and 25 dioceses, including one diocese each for Catholics of the Maronite, Melkite and Ukrainian rites, and one military ordinariate. At the census of 1996 there were 4.8m. adherents in the country.

**Australian Catholic Bishops' Conference:** GPO Box 368, Canberra, ACT 2601; tel. (2) 6201-9845; fax (2) 6247-6083; e-mail gensec@catholic.org.au; internet www.catholic.org.au; f. 1979; Pres. Cardinal EDWARD BEDE CLANCY, Archbishop of Sydney; Sec. Most Rev. BRIAN V. FINNIGAN.

**Archbishop of Adelaide:** Most Rev. LEONARD A. FAULKNER, GPO Box 1364, Adelaide, South Australia 5001; tel. (8) 8210-8108; fax (8) 8223-2307.

**Archbishop of Brisbane:** Most Rev. JOHN A. BATHERSBY, Archbishop's House, 790 Brunswick St, New Farm, Brisbane, Qld 4005; tel. (7) 3224-3364; fax (7) 3358-1357; e-mail archbish@bne.catholic.net.au.

**Archbishop of Canberra and Goulburn:** Most Rev. FRANCIS P. CARROLL, GPOB 89, Canberra, ACT 2601; tel. (2) 6248-6411; fax (2) 6247-9636.

**Archbishop of Hobart:** Most Rev. ADRIAN DOYLE, GPOB 62A, Hobart, Tas 7001; tel. (3) 6225-1920; fax (3) 6225-3865; e-mail archbishop.hobart@cathtas.com; internet www.busker.trumpet.com.au/cathtas/.

**Archbishop of Melbourne:** Most Rev. GEORGE PELL, GPOB 146, East Melbourne, Vic 3002; tel. (3) 9926-5677; fax (3) 9926-5617.

**Archbishop of Perth:** Most Rev. BARRY J. HICKEY, St Mary's Cathedral, Victoria Sq., Perth, WA 6000; tel. (8) 9223-1350; fax (8) 9221-1716; e-mail archsec@perth.catholic.org.au; internet www.perth.catholic.org.au.

**Archbishop of Sydney:** Cardinal EDWARD BEDE CLANCY, Archdiocesan Chancery, Polding House, 13th Floor, 276 Pitt St, Sydney, NSW 2000; tel. (2) 9390-5100; fax (2) 9261-8312.

#### Orthodox Churches

**Greek Orthodox Archdiocese of Australia:** 242 Cleveland St, Redfern, Sydney, NSW 2016; tel. (2) 9698-5066; fax (2) 9698-5368; f. 1924; 700,000 mems; Primate His Eminence Archbishop STYLIANOS.

The Antiochian, Coptic, Romanian, Serbian and Syrian Orthodox Churches are also represented.

#### Other Christian Churches

**Baptist Union of Australia:** POB 377, Hawthorn, Vic 3122; tel. (3) 9818-0341; fax (3) 9818-1041; f. 1926; 64,159 mems; 883 churches; Nat. Pres. Rev. TIM COSTELLO; Nat. Sec. C. K. MOSS.

**Churches of Christ in Australia:** POB 55, Helensburgh, NSW 2508; tel. (2) 4294-1913; fax (2) 4294-1914; e-mail bobsmit@ozemail.com.au; 36,000 mems; Pres. Rev. BARRY RYALL; Co-ordinator Rev. ROBERT SMITH.

**Lutheran Church of Australia:** National Office, 197 Archer St, North Adelaide, SA 5006; tel. (8) 8267-7300; fax (8) 8267-7310; e-mail president@lca.org.au; internet www.lca.org.au; f. 1966; 98,191 mems; Pres. Rev. Dr L. G. STEICKE.

**Uniting Church in Australia:** POB A2266, Sydney South, NSW 1235; tel. (2) 8267-4200; fax (2) 8267-4222; e-mail assysec@nat.uca.org.au; internet www.nat.uca.org.au; f. 1977 with the union of Methodist, Presbyterian and Congregational Churches; 1.4m. mems; Pres. Rev. JOHN MAVOR; Sec. Rev. GREGOR HENDERSON.

Other active denominations include the Pentecostal Church (174,720 adherents in 1996), the Armenian Apostolic Church, the Assyrian Church of the East and the Society of Friends (Quakers).

### JUDAISM

**Great Synagogue:** 166 Castlereagh St, Sydney, NSW; tel. (2) 9267-2477; fax (2) 9264-8871; e-mail admin@greatsynagogue.com.au; internet www.greatsynagogue.com.au; f. 1828; Sr Minister Rabbi RAYMOND APPLE.

### OTHER FAITHS

According to the provisional results of the August 1996 census, Muslims numbered 200,185, Buddhists 199,812 and Hindus 67,279.

## The Press

The total circulation of Australia's daily newspapers is very high, but in the remoter parts of the country weekly papers are even more popular. Most of Australia's newspapers are published in sparsely populated rural areas where the demand for local news is strong. The only newspapers that may fairly claim a national circulation are the dailies *The Australian* and *Australian Financial Review*, and the weekly magazines *The Bulletin, Time Australia* and *Business Review Weekly*, the circulation of most newspapers being almost entirely confined to the state in which each is produced.

**ACP Publishing Pty Ltd:** 54–58 Park St, Sydney, NSW 2000; tel. (2) 9282-8000; fax (2) 9267-4371; fmrly Australian Consolidated Press Ltd; publishes *Australian Women's Weekly, The Bulletin with Newsweek, Cleo, Cosmopolitan, Woman's Day, Dolly, Belle, Street Machine* and more than 70 other magazines.

**APN News and Media Ltd:** 10th Floor, 300 Ann St, Brisbane, Qld 4000; tel. (7) 3307-0300; fax (7) 3307-0307; Chair. L. P. HEALY; Chief Exec. VINCENT CROWLEY.

**John Fairfax Holdings Ltd:** POB 506, Sydney, NSW 2001; tel. (2) 9282-2833; fax (2) 9282-3133; f. 1987; Chair. BRIAN POWERS; Chief Exec. FREDERICK G. HILMER; controls *The Sydney Morning Herald, The Australian Financial Review* and *Sun-Herald* (Sydney), *The Age, The Sunday Age* and BRW Publications (Melbourne), *Illawarra Mercury* (Wollongong), *The Newcastle Herald* (Newcastle).

**The Herald and Weekly Times Ltd:** POB 14999, Melbourne MC, Vic 8001; tel. (3) 9292-2000; fax (3) 9292-2002; e-mail newspapers@hwt.newsltd.com.au; acquired by News Ltd in 1987; Chair. JANET CALVERT-JONES; Man. Dir JULIAN CLARKE; publs include *Herald Sun, Sunday Herald Sun, The Weekly Times*.

**The News Corporation:** 2 Holt St, Surry Hills, Sydney, NSW 2010; tel. (2) 9288-3000; fax (2) 9288-2300; Chair. and CEO K. RUPERT MURDOCH; controls *The Australian* and *The Weekend Australian* (national), *Daily Telegraph, Sunday Telegraph* (Sydney), *The Herald Sun* and *Sunday Herald Sun* (Victoria), *Northern Territory News* (Darwin), *Sunday Times* (Perth), *Townsville Bulletin, Courier Mail, Sunday Mail* (Queensland), *The Mercury* (Tasmania), *The Advertiser, Sunday Mail* (South Australia).

**Rural Press Ltd:** 159 Bells Line of Road, North Richmond, NSW 2754; tel. (2) 4570-4444; fax (2) 4570-4663; Chair. JOHN B. FAIRFAX; Man. Dir B. K. MCCARTHY.

**West Australian Newspapers Holdings Ltd:** Newspaper House, 50 Hasler Rd, Osborne Park, WA 6017; tel. (8) 9482-3111; fax (8) 9482-9080; Chair. T. R. EASTWOOD; Man. Dir D. W. THOMPSON.

Other newspaper publishers include Federal Capital Press (K. Stokes).

### NEWSPAPERS

#### Australian Capital Territory

**The Canberra Times:** 9 Pirie St, Fyshwick, ACT 2609; POB 7155, Canberra Mail Centre, ACT 2610; tel. (2) 6280-2122; fax (2) 6280-2282; f. 1926; daily and Sun.; morning; Editor JACK WATERFORD; circ. 42,444 (Mon.–Fri.), 72,008 (Sat.), 40,488 (Sun.).

#### New South Wales

Dailies

**The Australian:** News Ltd, 2 Holt St, Surry Hills, NSW 2010, POB 4245; tel. (2) 9288-3000; fax (2) 9288-3077; f. 1964; edited in Sydney, simultaneous edns in Sydney, Melbourne, Perth, Townsville, Adelaide and Brisbane; Editor-in-Chief DAVID ARMSTRONG; Editor CAMPBELL REID; circ. 122,500 (Mon.–Fri.); *The Weekend Australian* (Sat.) 311,000.

**Australian Financial Review:** 201 Sussex St, GPOB 506, Sydney, NSW 2000; tel. (2) 9282-2512; fax (2) 9282-3137; f. 1951; Mon.–Fri.; distributed nationally; Editor-in-Chief GREG HYWOOD; Editor DEBORAH LIGHT; circ. 85,000.

**The Daily Telegraph:** 2 Holt St, Surry Hills, NSW 2010; tel. (2) 9288-3000; fax (2) 9288-2300; f. 1879, merged in 1990 with Daily Mirror (f. 1941); 24-hour tabloid; CEO LACHLAN MURDOCH; circ. 442,000.

**The Manly Daily:** Level 1, 39 East Esplanade, Manly, NSW 2095; tel. (2) 9977-3333; fax (2) 9977-2831; f. 1906; Tue.–Sat.; Editor STEVE STICKNEY; circ. 89,326.

**The Newcastle Herald:** 28–30 Bolton St, Newcastle, NSW 2300; tel. (2) 4979-5000; fax (2) 4979-5888; f. 1858; morning; 6 a week; Editor-in-Chief JOHN MCCLUSKEY; circ. 45,253.

**The Sydney Morning Herald:** 201 Sussex St, GPOB 506, Sydney, NSW 2001; tel. (2) 9282-2822; fax (2) 9282-3253; internet www.smh.com.au; f. 1831; morning; Editor-in-Chief (vacant); circ. 231,508 (Mon.–Fri.), 400,000 (Sat.).

Weeklies

**Bankstown Canterbury Torch:** Nabberly House, Cnr Marion St and Airport Ave, Bankstown, NSW 2200; tel. (2) 9795-0000; fax (2) 9795-0096; f. 1920; Wed.; Editor CHARLES ELIAS; circ. 86,577.

**Northern District Times:** 79 Rowe St, Eastwood, NSW 2122; tel. (2) 9858-1766; fax (2) 9804-6901; f. 1921; Wed.; Editor D. BARTOK; circ. 55,302.

**The Parramatta Advertiser:** 142 Macquarie St, Parramatta, NSW 2150; tel. (2) 9689-5370; fax (2) 9689-5353; Wed.; Editor LES POBJIE; circ. 96,809.

**St George and Sutherland Shire Leader:** 182 Forest Rd, Hurstville, NSW 2220; tel. (2) 9598-3999; fax (2) 9598-3987; f. 1960; Tue. and Thur.; Editor PETER ALLEN; circ. 143,595.

**Sun-Herald:** 201 Sussex St, GPOB 506, Sydney, NSW 2001; tel. (2) 9282-2822; fax (2) 9282-2151; f. 1953; Sun.; Editor and Publr ALAN REVELL; circ. 612,000.

**Sunday Telegraph:** 2 Holt St, Surry Hills, NSW 2010; tel. (2) 9288-3000; fax (2) 9288-3311; f. 1938; Editor ROY MILLER; circ. 710,000.

#### Northern Territory

Daily

**Northern Territory News:** Printers Place, POB 1300, Darwin, NT 0801; tel. (8) 8944-9900; fax (8) 8981-6045; f. 1952; Mon.–Sat.; Gen. Man. D. KENNEDY; circ. 24,470.

Weekly

**Sunday Territorian:** Printers Place, GPOB 1300, Darwin, NT 0801; tel. (8) 8944-9900; fax (8) 8981-6045; Sun.; Editor DAVID COREN; circ. 26,437.

#### Queensland

Daily

**Courier-Mail:** 41 Campbell St, Bowen Hills, Brisbane, Qld 4006; tel. (7) 3252-6011; fax (7) 3252-6696; f. 1933; morning; Editor-in-Chief C. MITCHELL; circ. 250,875.

Weekly

**Sunday Mail:** Campbell St, Bowen Hills, Brisbane, Qld 4006; tel. (7) 3666-6011; fax (7) 3252-6692; f. 1923; Editor MICHAEL PRAIN; circ. 598,065.

#### South Australia

Daily

**Advertiser:** 121 King William St, Adelaide, SA 5001; tel. (8) 8206-2220; fax (8) 8206-3669; f. 1858; morning; Editor STEVE HOWARD; circ. 199,689 (Mon.–Fri.), 264,876 (Sat.).

Weekly

**Sunday Mail:** 9th Floor, 121 King William St, Adelaide, SA 5000; tel. (8) 8206-2000; fax (8) 8206-3646; e-mail sullivank@adv.newsltd.com.au; f. 1912; Editor KERRY SULLIVAN; circ. 346,220.

#### Tasmania

Dailies

**The Advocate:** POB 63, Burnie 7320; tel. (3) 6440-7409; fax (3) 6440-7461; f. 1890; morning; Editor M. D. CHERRY; circ. 25,623.

**Examiner:** 71–75 Paterson St, POB 99A, Launceston, Tas 7250; tel. (3) 6331-5111; fax (3) 6334-7328; e-mail mail@examiner.com.au; internet www.examiner.com.au/examiner/; f. 1842; morning; independent; Editor R. J. SCOTT; circ. 38,721.

**Mercury:** 91–93 Macquarie St, Hobart, Tas 7000; tel. (3) 6230-0622; fax (3) 6230-0711; e-mail mercuryedletter@dbl.newsltd.com.au; internet www.news.com.au; f. 1854; morning; Man. Dir REX GARDNER; Editor I. MCCAUSLAND; circ. 52,199.

Weeklies

**Sunday Examiner:** 71–75 Paterson St, Launceston, Tas 7250; tel. (3) 6315-111; fax (3) 6347-328; e-mail@examiner.com.au; f. 1924; Editor R. J. SCOTT; circ. 42,000.

**Sunday Tasmanian:** 91–93 Macquarie St, Hobart, Tas 7000; tel. (3) 6230-0622; fax (3) 6230-0711; e-mail mercuryedletter@trump.net.au; f. 1984; morning; Man. Dir REX GARDNER; Editor IAN MCCAUSLAND; circ. 53,449.

### Victoria

Dailies

**The Age:** 250 Spencer St (cnr Lonsdale St), Melbourne, Vic 3000; tel. (3) 9600-4211; fax (3) 9601-2327; e-mail DPearson@theage.com.au; internet www.theage.com.au; f. 1854; independent; morning, incl. Sun.; Publr and Editor-in-Chief STEVE HARRIS; Editor MICHAEL GAWENDA; circ. 237,474.

**Herald Sun:** HWT Tower, 40 City Rd, Southbank, Vic 3006; tel. (3) 9292-2000; fax (3) 9292-2112; f. 1840 as The Herald, merged with the Sun-News Pictorial (f. 1922) in 1990; 24-hour tabloid; Editor PETER BLUNDEN; circ. 575,317.

Weeklies

**Progress Press:** 360 Burwood Rd, Hawthorn, Vic 3122; tel. (3) 9818-0555; fax (3) 9818-0029; e-mail editor@ldr.newsltd.com.au; f. 1960; Tue.; Editor LYNNE KINSEY; circ. 74,829.

**Sunday Herald Sun:** HWT Tower, 40 City Rd, Southbank, Vic 3006; tel. (3) 9292-2000; fax (3) 9292-2080; e-mail sundayhs@hwt.newsltd.com.au; f. 1991; Editor ALAN HOWE; circ. 500,000.

### Western Australia

Daily

**The West Australian:** POB D162, Perth, WA 6001; tel. (8) 9482-3111; fax (8) 9482-3399; e-mail editor@wanews.com.au; f. 1833; morning; Editor P. R. MURRAY; circ. 221,282 (Mon.–Fri.), 389,810 (Sat.).

Weekly

**Sunday Times:** 34–42 Stirling St, Perth, WA 6000; tel. (8) 9326-8326; fax (8) 9221-1121; f. 1897; Gen. Man. BILL REPARD; Man. Editor DON SMITH; circ. 346,014.

## PRINCIPAL PERIODICALS

### Weeklies and Fortnightlies

**Australasian Post:** 32 Walsh St, West Melbourne, Vic 3003; tel. (3) 9320-7000; fax (3) 9320-7020; f. 1864; factual, general interest, Australiana; Mon.; Editor GRAEME JOHNSTONE; circ. 81,640.

**The Bulletin:** 54 Park St, Sydney, NSW 2000; tel. (2) 9282-8227; fax (2) 9267-4359; f. 1880; Wed.; Editor-in-Chief GERALD STONE; circ. 91,771.

**Business Review Weekly:** Level 2, 469 La Trobe St, Melbourne, Vic 3000; tel. (3) 9603-3888; fax (3) 9670-4328; f. 1981; Chair. and Editorial Dir ROBERT GOTTLIEBSEN; Editor ROSS GREENWOOD; circ. 75,166.

**The Countryman:** 219 St George's Terrace, Perth, WA 6000; GPO Box D162, Perth 6001; tel. (8) 9482-3322; fax (8) 9482-3324; e-mail countryman@wanews.com.au; f. 1885; Thur.; farming; Editor GARY MCGAY; circ. 13,444.

**The Medical Journal of Australia:** Private Bag 901, North Sydney, NSW 2059; tel. (2) 9954-8666; fax (2) 9954-7644; e-mail mja@ampco.com.au; internet www.mja.com.au; f. 1914; fortnightly; Editor Dr MARTIN VAN DER WEYDEN; circ. 25,937.

**New Idea:** 35–51 Mitchell St, McMahons Point, NSW 2060; tel. (3) 9464-3450; fax (3) 9464-3203; e-mail newidea@pacpubs.com.au; weekly; women's; Editorial Dir BUNTY AVIESON; circ. 512,000.

**News Weekly:** POB 186, North Melbourne, Vic 3051; tel. (3) 9326-5757; fax (3) 9328-2877; e-mail freedom@connexus.net.au; f. 1943; publ. by National Civic Council; fortnightly; Sat.; political, social, educational and trade union affairs; Editor PETER WESTMORE; circ. 12,000.

**People:** 54 Park St, Sydney, NSW 2000; tel. (2) 9282-8743; fax (2) 9267-4365; e-mail sbutler-white@acp.com.au; weekly; Editor SIMON BUTLER-WHITE; circ. 70,000.

**Picture:** GPOB 5201, Sydney, NSW 1028; tel. (2) 9282-8367; fax (2) 9267-4372; e-mail picture@acp.com.au; weekly; men's; Editor TIM SCOTT; circ. 162,864.

**Queensland Country Life:** POB 586, Cleveland, Qld 4163; tel. (7) 3826-8200; fax (7) 3821-1236; f. 1935; Thur.; Editor CHRIS GRIFFITH; circ. 33,900.

**Stock and Land:** 200 Rouse St, Port Melbourne, Vic 3207; tel. (3) 9287-0900; fax (3) 9287-0999; e-mail stockland@rpl.com.au; f. 1914; weekly; agricultural and rural news; Editor JOHN CARSON; circ. 12,608.

**That's Life!:** 35–51 Mitchell St, McMahons Point, NSW 2060; tel. (2) 9464-3300; fax (2) 9464-3480; f. 1994; weekly; features; Editor BEV HADGRAFT; circ. 465,500 (incl. New Zealand).

**Time Australia Magazine:** GPOB 3873, Sydney, NSW 2001; tel. (2) 9925-2646; fax (2) 9954-0828; e-mail time.letters@time.com.au; internet www.time.com.au; Editor STEVE WATERSON; circ. 111,000.

**TV Week:** 32 Walsh St, Melbourne, Vic 3000; tel. (3) 9320-7000; fax (3) 9320-7409; f. 1957; Wed.; colour national; Editor KATIE EKBERG; circ. 364,044.

**The Weekly Times:** POB 14999, Melbourne City MC, Vic 8001; tel. (3) 9292-2000; fax (3) 9292-2697; e-mail wtimes@hwt.newsltd.com.au; internet www.news.com.au; f. 1869; farming, regional issues, gardening, country life; Wed.; Editor PETER FLAHERTY; circ. 81,134.

**Woman's Day:** 54–58 Park St, POB 5245, Sydney, NSW 1028; tel. (2) 9282-8000; fax (2) 9267-4360; e-mail Womansday@publishing.acp.com.au; weekly; circulates throughout Australia and NZ; Editor MICHELE CRAWSHAW; circ. 765,170.

### Monthlies and Others

**Architecture Australia:** Architecture Media Pty Ltd, Level 3, 4 Princes St, Port Melbourne, Vic 3207; tel. (3) 9596-8904; fax (3) 9596-8913; e-mail aa@archmedia.com.au; internet www.archmedia.com.au; f. 1904; 6 a year; Editor DAVINA JACKSON; Man. CAROLYN WINTON; circ. 14,363.

**Australian Hi-Fi:** POB 5555, St Leonards, NSW 1590; tel. (2) 9901-6100; fax (2) 9901-6198; e-mail hifi@horwitz.com.au; f. 1970; every 2 months; consumer tests on hi-fi and home theatre equipment; Editor GREG BORROWMAN; circ. 11,800.

**Australian Home Beautiful:** 35–51 Mitchell St, McMahons Point, NSW 2059; tel. (2) 9464-3300; fax (2) 9464-3263; e-mail homebeaut@pacpubs.com.au; f. 1925; monthly; Editor ANDREA JONES; circ. 81,496.

**Australian House and Garden:** 54 Park St, Sydney, NSW 2000; tel. (2) 9282-8456; fax (2) 9267-4912; e-mail h&g@acp.com.au; f. 1948; monthly; design, decorating, renovating, gardens, food and travel; Editor ANNY FRIIS; circ. 113,046.

**Australian Journal of Mining:** IBC Australia Pty Ltd, Level 2, 120 Sussex St, Sydney, NSW 2000; e-mail charles.macdonald@informa.com.au; f. 1986; monthly; mining and exploration throughout Australia and South Pacific; Editor CHARLES MCDONALD; circ. 6,771.

**Australian Journal of Pharmacy:** 100 Harris St, Pyrmont, NSW 2009; tel. (2) 8587-7000; fax (2) 8587-7100; f. 1886; monthly; journal of the associated pharmaceutical orgs; Man. Editor DAVID WESTON; circ. 6,443.

**Australian Law Journal:** 100 Harris St, Pyrmont, NSW 2009; tel. (2) 8587-7000; fax (2) 8587-7104; f. 1927; monthly; Editor Justice P. W. YOUNG; circ 4,500.

**Australian Photography:** POB 606, Sydney, NSW 1041; tel. (2) 9281-2333; fax (2) 9281-2750; monthly; Editor ROBERT KEELEY; circ. 9,010.

**The Australian Women's Weekly:** 54–58 Park St, Sydney, NSW 2000; tel. (2) 9282-8000; fax (2) 9267-4459; e-mail FDaniele@acp.com.au; f. 1933; monthly; Editor DEBORAH THOMAS; circ. 890,000.

**Belle:** 54 Park St, Sydney, NSW 2000; tel. (2) 9282-8000; fax (2) 9267-8037; f. 1975; every 2 months; Editor MICHAELA DUNWORTH; circ. 44,663.

**Better Homes and Gardens:** 45 Jones St, Ultimo, NSW 2007; tel. (2) 9692-2000; fax (2) 9692-2264; e-mail philippah@mm.com.au; f. 1978; 13 a year; Editor TONI EATTS; circ. 340,133.

**Cleo:** 54 Park St, Sydney, NSW 2000; POB 4088, Sydney, NSW 2001; tel. (2) 9282-8617; fax (2) 9267-4368; f. 1972; women's monthly; Editor DEBORAH THOMAS; circ. 263,353.

**Commercial Photography:** GPOB 606, Sydney, NSW 1041; tel. (2) 9281-2333; fax (2) 9281-2750; e-mail yaffa@flex.com.au; every 2 months; journal of the Professional Photographers Asscn of Australia and Photographic Industry Marketing Asscn of Australia; Editor SAIMA MOREL; circ. 3,835.

**Cosmopolitan:** 54 Park St, Sydney, NSW 2000; tel. (2) 9282-8000; fax (2) 9267-4457; e-mail cosmo@publishing.acp.com.au; f. 1973; monthly; Editor MIA FREEDMAN; circ. 237,579.

**Dolly:** 54–58 Park St, Sydney, NSW 1028; tel. (2) 9282-8437; fax (2) 9267-4911; e-mail dolly@ninemsn.com.au; internet www.dolly.ninemsn.com.au; f. 1970; monthly; for young women; Editor SUSIE PITTS; circ. 195,000.

**Ecos:** CSIRO, POB 1139, Collingwood, Vic 3066; tel. (3) 9662-7500; fax (3) 9662-7555; internet www.publish.csiro.au/ecos; f. 1974; quarterly; reports of CSIRO environmental research findings for the non-specialist reader; Editor BRYONY BENNETT; circ. 8,000.

**Electronics Australia:** POB 199, Alexandria, NSW 1435; tel. (2) 9353-0620; fax (2) 9353-0613; e-mail info@electronicsaustralia.com.au; internet www.electronicsaustralia.com.au; f. 1922; monthly; technical, radio, television, microcomputers, hi-fi and electronics; Editor GRAHAM CATTLEY; circ. 20,900.

**Elle:** 54 Park St, Sydney, NSW 2000; tel. (2) 9282-8790; fax (2) 9267-4375; f. 1990; monthly; Editor MARINA GO; circ. 68,154.

**Family Circle:** 45 Jones St, Ultimo, NSW 2007; tel. (2) 9692-2000; fax (2) 9692-2020; e-mail family-circle@mm.com.au; 13 a year; circ. 235,860.

**Gardening Australia:** POB 199, Alexandria, NSW 1435; tel. (2) 9353-6666; fax (2) 9317-4615; f. 1991; monthly; Editor ANNE LAWTON; circ. 93,000.

**Houses:** Architecture Media Pty Ltd, Level 3, 4 Princes St, Port Melbourne, Vic 3207; tel. (3) 9646-4760; fax (3) 9646-4918; e-mail houses@archmedia.com.au; internet www.archmedia.com.au; f. 1989; 4 a year; Editor SUE HARRIS; circ. 22,569.

**HQ:** 54 Park St, Sydney, NSW 1028; tel. (2) 9282-8260; fax (2) 9267-3616; e-mail hq@publishing.acp.com.au; internet www.hq.ninemsn.com.au; f. 1989; every 2 months; Publr JOHN ALEXANDER; Editor KATHY BAIL; circ. 32,837.

**Manufacturers' Monthly:** 46 Porter St, Prahran, Vic 3181; tel. (3) 9245-7777; fax (3) 9245-7750; f. 1961; Editor GREG VIDEON; circ. 14,091.

**Modern Boating:** The Federal Publishing Co Pty Ltd, 180 Bourke Rd, Alexandria, NSW 2015; tel. (2) 9353-6666; fax (2) 9353-0613; f. 1965; every 2 months; Editor MARK ROTHFIELD; circ. 9,007.

**Motor:** Locked Bag 12, Oakleigh, Vic 3166; tel (3) 9567-4200; fax (3) 9563-4554; e-mail motor@acpaction.com.au; f. 1954; monthly; Editor GED BULMER; circ. 40,500.

**New Woman:** Murdoch Magazines, 45 Jones St, Ultimo, NSW 2007; tel. (2) 9692-2000; fax (2) 9692-2488; monthly; Editor-in-Chief GAY BRYANT; circ. 108,444.

**The Open Road:** L27, 388 George St, Sydney, NSW 2000; tel. (2) 9292-9275; fax (2) 9292-9069; f. 1927; every 2 months; journal of National Roads and Motorists' Asscn (NRMA); Editor LEE ATKINSON; circ. 1,555,917.

**Personal Investor:** Level 2, 469 La Trobe St, Melbourne, Vic 3000; tel. (3) 9603-3888; fax (3) 9670-4328; e-mail pieditor@brw.fairfax.com.au; internet www.personalinvestor.com.au; monthly; Editor ROBIN BOWERMAN; circ. 66,097.

**Reader's Digest:** 26–32 Waterloo St, Surry Hills, NSW 2010; tel. (2) 9690-6111; fax (2) 9690-6211; monthly; Editor-in-Chief BRUCE HEILBUTH; circ. 508,142.

**Street Machine:** Locked Bag 756, Epping, NSW 2121; tel. (2) 9868-4832; fax (2) 9869-7390; e-mail streetmachine@acpaction.com.au; Editor MARK OASTLER; circ. 55,000.

**TV Hits:** Private Bag 9900, North Sydney, NSW 2059; tel. (2) 9464-3300; fax (2) 9464-3508; f. 1988; monthly; circ. 114,509.

**TV Soap:** 55 Chandos St, St Leonards, NSW 2065; tel. (2) 9901-6100; fax (2) 9901-6166; f. 1983; monthly; Editor BEN MITCHELL; circ. 85,751.

**Vogue Australia:** Level 2, 170 Pacific Highway, Greenwich, NSW 2065; tel. (2) 9964-3888; fax (2) 9964-3879; f. 1959; monthly; fashion; Editor JULIET ASHWORTH; circ. 54,705.

**Wheels:** Locked Bag 756, Epping, NSW 2121; tel. (2) 9870-0017; fax (2) 9869-4137; f. 1953; monthly; international motoring magazine; circ. 60,286.

**Wildlife Research:** CSIRO Publishing, 150 Oxford St, POB 1139, Collingwood, Vic 3066; tel. (3) 9662-7622; fax (3) 9662-7611; e-mail ajsr@publish.csiro.au; internet www.publish.csiro.au/journals/wr; f. 1974; 6 a year; Man. Editor D. W. MORTON; circ. 1,000.

**Your Garden:** 35–51 Mitchell St, McMahons Point, NSW 2060; tel. (2) 9464-3586; fax (2) 9464-3487; e-mail yg@pacpubs.com.au; monthly; Editor KANDY SHEPHERD; circ. 60,246.

### NEWS AGENCIES

**AAP Information Services:** Locked Bag 21, Grosvenor Place, Sydney, NSW 2000; tel. (2) 9322-8000; fax (2) 9322-8888; f. 1983; owned by major daily newspapers of Australia; Chair. and CEO C. L. CASEY.

#### Foreign Bureaux

**Agence France-Presse (AFP):** 7th Floor, 259 George St, Sydney, NSW 2000; tel. (2) 9251-1544; fax (2) 9251-5230; e-mail afpsydney@compuserve.com; internet www.afp.com; Bureau Chief RON WALL.

**Agenzia Nazionale Stampa Associata (ANSA)** (Italy): Suite 4, 2 Grosvenor St, Bondi Junction, NSW 2022; tel. (2) 9369-1427; fax (2) 9369-4351; e-mail ansasyd@ozemail.com.au; Bureau Chief CLAUDIO MARCELLO.

**Deutsche Presse-Agentur (dpa)** (Germany): 36 Heath St, Mona Vale, NSW 2103; tel. (2) 9979-8253; fax (2) 9997-3154; e-mail hofman@zip.com.au; Correspondent ALEXANDER HOFMAN.

**Jiji Press (Australia) Pty Ltd** (Japan): GPOB 2584, Sydney, NSW 2001; tel. (2) 9299-5404; fax (2) 9299-5405; e-mail jijiaust@bigpond.com; Bureau Chief SATOSHI MIYAUCHI.

**Kyodo News Service** (Japan): Level 7, 9 Lang St, Sydney, NSW 2000; tel. (2) 9251-5240; fax (2) 9251-4980; Bureau Chief MICHITAKA YAMADA.

**Reuters Australia Pty Ltd:** Level 30, 60 Margaret St, Sydney, NSW 2000; Bureau Chief RUTH PITCHFORD.

**Xinhua (New China) News Agency** (People's Republic of China): 50 Russell St, Hackett, Canberra, ACT 2602; tel. (2) 6248-6369; fax (2) 6257-4706; Chief Correspondent LIN ZHENXI.

The Central News Agency (Taiwan) and the New Zealand Press Association are represented in Sydney, and Antara (Indonesia) is represented in Canberra.

### PRESS ASSOCIATIONS

**Australian Press Council:** Suite 303, 149 Castlereagh St, Sydney, NSW 2000; tel. (2) 9261-1930; fax (2) 9267-6826; e-mail info@presscouncil.org.au; internet www.presscouncil.org.au; Chair. Prof. DENNIS PEARCE.

**Australian Suburban Newspapers Association:** POB 58, St Leonards, NSW 1590; tel. (2) 9372-1222; fax (2) 9372-1288; Sec. DANIELLE FRANKS.

**Country Press Association of New South Wales Inc:** POB Q182, Queen Victoria Bldg, Sydney, NSW 2000; tel. (2) 9299-4658; fax (2) 9299-1892; f. 1900; Exec. Dir D. J. SOMMERLAD; 120 mems.

**Country Press Association of SA Incorporated:** 198 Greenhill Rd, Eastwood, SA 5063; tel. (8) 8373-6533; fax (8) 8373-6544; f. 1912; represents South Australian country newspapers; Pres. B. PRICE; Exec. Dir M. R. TOWNSEND.

**Country Press Australia:** POB Q182, Queen Victoria Bldg, Sydney, NSW 2000; tel. (2) 9299-4658; fax (2) 9299-1892; f. 1906; Exec. Dir D. J. SOMMERLAD; 420 mems.

**Queensland Country Press Association:** POB 103, Paddington, Qld 4064; tel. (7) 3356-0033; Pres. W. CREIGHTON; Sec. N. D. MCLARY.

**Tasmanian Press Association Pty Ltd:** 71–75 Paterson St, Launceston, Tas 7250; tel. (3) 6320-255; Sec. L. WHISH-WILSON.

**Victorian Country Press Association Ltd:** 33 Rathdowne St, Carlton, Vic 3053; tel. (3) 9662-3244; fax (3) 9663-7433; e-mail vcpa@vcpa.com.au; f. 1910; Pres. B. C. ELLEN; Exec. Dir J. E. RAY; 114 mems.

## Publishers

**Addison Wesley Longman Australia Pty Ltd:** 95 Coventry St, South Melbourne, Vic 3205; tel. (3) 9697-0666; fax (3) 9699-2041; e-mail awlaus@awl.com.au; internet www.awl.com.au; f. 1957; mainly educational, academic, computer, some general; Man. Dir ROBERT W. FISHER.

**Allen and Unwin Pty Ltd:** 9 Atchison St, St Leonards, NSW 2065; tel. (2) 8425-0100; fax (2) 9906-2218; e-mail frontdesk@allen-unwin.com.au; internet www.allen-unwin.com.au; fiction, trade, academic, children's; Man. Dir PATRICK A. GALLAGHER.

**Australasian Medical Publishing Co Ltd:** Level 1, 76 Berry St, North Sydney, NSW 2060; tel. (2) 9954-8666; fax (2) 9956-7644; e-mail ampco@ampco.com.au; internet www.ampco.com.au; f. 1913; scientific, medical and educational; CEO Dr MARTIN VAN DER WEYDEN.

**Britannica.com.au:** Locked Bag 927, North Sydney, NSW 2060; tel. (2) 9923-5600; fax (2) 9929-3753; e-mail ebsales@eba.com.au; internet www.britannica.com; reference, education, art, science and commerce; Man. Dir COOMA CHELLIAH.

**Butterworths:** Tower 2, 475 Victoria Ave, Chatswood, NSW 2067; tel. (2) 9422-2222; fax (2) 9422-2444; internet www.butterworths.com.au; f. 1910; div. of Reed International Books Australia Pty Ltd; legal and commercial; Man. Dir MURRAY HAMILTON.

**Cambridge University Press (Australia):** 10 Stamford Road, Oakleigh, Melbourne, Vic 3166; tel. (3) 9568-0322; fax (3) 9569-9292; e-mail info@cup.edu.au; internet www.cup.edu.au; scholarly and educational; Dir SANDRA MCCOMB.

**Commonwealth Scientific and Industrial Research Organisation (CSIRO Publishing):** 150 Oxford St, POB 1139, Collingwood, Vic 3066; tel. (3) 9662-7500; fax (3) 9662-7555; e-mail info@publish.csiro.au; internet www.publish.csiro.au; f. 1926; scientific and technical journals, books, magazines, videos, CD-ROMs; Gen. Man. P. W. REEKIE.

**Doubleday Australia Pty Ltd:** 91 Mars Rd, Lane Cove, NSW 2066; tel. (2) 9427-0377; fax (2) 9427-6973; educational, trade, non-fiction, Australiana; Man. Dir DAVID HARLEY.

**Gordon and Gotch Ltd:** 25–37 Huntingdale Rd, Private Bag 290, Burwood, Vic 3125; tel. (3) 9805-1700; fax (3) 9808-0714; general; Chair. and Man. Dir I. D. GOLDING.

**Harcourt Australia Pty Ltd:** 30–52 Smidmore St, Marrickville, NSW 2204; tel. (2) 9517-8999; fax (2) 9517-2249; e-mail service@harcourt.com.au; business, science, humanities, social science, engineering, medicine, etc.; Man. Dir BRIAN M. BRENNAN.

**Harlequin Enterprises (Australia) Pty Ltd:** Unit 3, 3 Gibbes St, Chatswood, NSW 2067; tel. (2) 9417-7333; fax (2) 9417-5232; e-mail harlequin@romance.net.au; internet www.romance.net.au; romantic fiction; Man. Dir NANCY PETERS.

**Hodder Headline Australia Pty Ltd:** Level 22, 201 Kent, Sydney, NSW 2000; tel. (2) 8248-0800; fax (2) 8248-0810; e-mail auspub@hha.com.au; internet www.hha.com.au; fiction, general, technical, children's; Man. Dir MALCOLM EDWARDS.

**Hyland House Publishing Pty Ltd:** Hyland House, 387–389 Clarendon St, South Melbourne, Vic 3205; tel. (3) 9696-9064; fax (3) 9696-9065; e-mail hyland@al.com.au; f. 1976; trade, general, gardening, pet care, Aboriginal, Asian-Pacific and children's; Rep. NAJIYE NIHAT.

**Jacaranda Wiley Ltd:** POB 1226, Milton, Qld 4064; tel. (7) 3859-9755; fax (7) 3859-9715; e-mail headoffice@jacwiley.com.au; f. 1954; educational, reference and trade; Man. Dir PETER DONOUGHUE.

**Lansdowne Publishing:** Level 1, 18 Argyle St, The Rocks, NSW 2000; tel. (2) 9240-9222; fax (2) 9241-4818; e-mail reception@lanspub.com.au; Australiana, cookery, gardening, health, history, pet care; Chief Exec. MARGARET SEALE.

**LBC Information Services:** 100 Harris St, Pyrmont, NSW 2009; tel. (2) 8587-7000; fax (2) 8587-7100; e-mail lbccustomer@thomson.com.au; legal and professional; Man. Dir E. J. COSTIGAN.

**Lothian Books:** 11 Munro St, Port Melbourne, Vic 3207; tel. (3) 9645-1544; fax (3) 9646-4882; e-mail books@lothian.com.au; f. 1888; gardening, health, craft, business, New Age, self-help, general non-fiction and children's picture books; Man. Dir PETER LOTHIAN.

**McGraw-Hill Book Publishing Co Australia Pty Ltd:** 4 Barcoo St, Roseville, Sydney, NSW 2069; tel. (2) 9415-9899; fax (2) 9417-8872; e-mail sydney.reception@mcgraw-hill.com; internet www.mcgraw-hill.com.au; educational, professional and technical; Man. Dir FIRGAL ADAMS.

**Melbourne University Press:** 268 Drummond St, Carlton South, Vic 3053; tel. (3) 9347-3455; fax (3) 9349-2527; e-mail info@mup.unimelb.edu.au; internet www.mup.com.au; f. 1922; academic, educational, Australiana; Chair. Prof. BARRY SHEEHAN; Dir JOHN MECKAN.

**Murdoch Books:** Level 5, 45 Jones St, Ultimo, NSW 2007; tel. (2) 9692-2000; fax (2) 9692-2558; e-mail markn@mm.com.au; general non-fiction; Publr ANNE WILSON.

**National Library of Australia:** Parkes Place, Canberra, ACT 2600; tel. (2) 6262-1111; fax (2) 6257-1703; e-mail www@nla.gov.au; internet www.nla.gov.au; f. 1960; national bibliographic service, etc.

**Nelson Thomson Learning:** 102 Dodds St, South Melbourne, Vic 3205; tel. (3) 9685-4111; fax (3) 9685-4199; e-mail customerservice@nelson.com.au; internet www.nelsonitp.com; educational; Man. Dir G. J. BROWNE.

**Oxford University Press:** 253 Normanby Rd, South Melbourne, Vic 3205; tel. (3) 9934-9123; fax (3) 9934-9100; f. 1908; general non-fiction and educational; Man. Dir MAREK PALKA.

**Pan Macmillan Australia Pty Ltd:** Level 18, St Martin's Tower, 31 Market St, Sydney, NSW 2000; tel. (2) 9261-5611; fax (2) 9261-5047; e-mail publicity@macmillan.wm.au; general, reference, children's, fiction, non-fiction; Chair. R. GIBB.

**Penguin Books Australia Ltd:** 487/493 Maroondah Highway, POB 257, Ringwood, Vic 3134; tel. (3) 9871-2400; fax (3) 9870-9618; internet www.penguin.com.au; f. 1946; general; Man. Dir PETER FIELD; Publishing Dir ROBERT SESSIONS.

**Random House Australia Pty Ltd:** 20 Alfred St, Milsons Point, NSW 2061; tel. (2) 9954-9966; fax (2) 9954-4562; e-mail random@randomhouse.com.au; internet www.randomhouse.com.au; fiction, non-fiction, general and children's; Man. Dir JULIET ROGERS.

**Reader's Digest (Australia) Pty Ltd:** POB 4353, Sydney, NSW 2000; tel. (2) 9690-6111; fax (2) 9699-8165; general; Man. Dir WILLIAM B. TOOHEY.

**Reed Educational & Professional Publishing:** POB 460, Port Melbourne, Vic 3207; tel. (3) 9245-7111; fax (3) 9245-7333; e-mail admin@reededucation.com.au; primary, secondary and tertiary educational, incl. electronic; division of Reed International; Man. Dir DAVID O'BRIEN.

**Scholastic Australia Pty Ltd:** Railway Crescent, Lisarow, POB 579, Gosford, NSW 2250; tel. (2) 4328-3555; fax (2) 4323-3827; internet www.scholastic.com.au; f. 1968; educational and children's; Man. Dir KEN JOLLY.

**Schwartz Publishing (Victoria) Pty Ltd:** 45 Flinders Lane, Melbourne, Vic 3000; tel. (3) 9654-2000; fax (3) 9650-5418; fiction, non-fiction; Dir MORRY SCHWARTZ.

**Simon and Schuster Australia:** 20 Barcoo St, POB 507, East Roseville, NSW 2069; tel. (2) 9417-3255; fax (2) 9417-3188; educational, trade, reference and general; Man. Dir JON ATTENBOROUGH.

**Thames and Hudson (Australia) Pty Ltd:** 11 Central Boulevard, Portside Business Park, Fishermans Bend, Vic 3207; tel. (3) 9646-7788; fax (3) 9646-8790; e-mail thaust@thaust.com.au; art, history, archaeology, architecture, photography, design, fashion, textiles, lifestyle; Man. Dir PETER SHAW.

**D. W. Thorpe:** 18 Salmon St, Locked Bag 20, Port Melbourne, Vic 3207; tel. (3) 9245-7370; fax (3) 9245-7395; e-mail customer.service@thorpe.com.au; bibliographic, library and book trade reference; Publishing Man. PAULENE MOREY.

**Time Life Australia Pty Ltd:** 3 Talavera Rd, North Ryde, NSW 2113; tel. (2) 9856-2212; fax (2) 9856-2255; general and educational; Man. Dir ROBERT HARDY.

**Transworld Publishers (Australia) Pty Ltd:** 40 Yeo St, Neutral Bay, NSW 2089; tel. (2) 9908-9900; fax (2) 9953-8563; fiction and non-fiction, romance, politics, humour, health, juvenile, etc.; Man. Dir GEOFFREY S. RUMPF.

**University of New South Wales Press Ltd:** University of New South Wales, Sydney, NSW 2052; tel. (2) 9664-0999; fax (2) 9664-5420; e-mail info.press@unsw.edu.au; f. 1961; scholarly, general and tertiary texts; Man. Dir Dr ROBIN DERRICOURT.

**University of Queensland Press:** POB 42, St Lucia, Qld 4067; tel. (7) 3365-2127; fax (7) 3365-7579; e-mail rosichay@uqp.uq.edu.au; f. 1948; scholarly and general cultural interest, incl. Black Australian writers, adult and children's fiction; Gen. Man. LAURIE MULLER.

**University of Western Australia Press:** c/o University of Western Australia, Nedlands, WA 6907; tel. (8) 9380-3670; fax (8) 9380-1027; e-mail uwap@cyllene.uwa.edu.au; internet www.uwapress.uwa.edu.au; f. 1954; natural history, history, literary studies, Australiana, children's, general non-fiction; Dir Dr JENNY GREGORY.

### Government Publishing House

**AusInfo:** GPOB 1920, Canberra, ACT 2601; tel. (2) 6275-3442; fax (2) 6275-3682; internet www.ausinfo.gov.au; f. 1970; fmrly Australian Govt Publishing Service; Assistant Sec. MICHELLE KINNANE.

### PUBLISHERS' ASSOCIATION

**Australian Publishers Association Ltd:** Suite 59, Level 3, 89 Jones St, Ultimo, NSW 2007; tel. (2) 9281-9788; fax (2) 9281-1073; e-mail apa@magna.com.au; internet www.publishers.asn.au; f. 1949; c. 150 mems; Pres. SANDY GRANT; Dir SUSAN BLACKWELL.

# Broadcasting and Communications

### TELECOMMUNICATIONS

By July 1999 a total of 31 licensed telecommunication carriers were in operation.

**Cable & Wireless Optus Ltd:** POB 1, North Sydney, NSW 2059; tel. (2) 9342-7800; fax (2) 9342-7100; internet www.cwo.net.au; general and mobile telecommunications, data and internet services, pay-TV; Chair. Sir RALPH ROBINS; Chief Exec. CHRIS ANDERSON.

**Telstra Corpn Ltd:** Level 14, 231 Elizabeth St, Sydney, NSW 2000; tel. (2) 9287-4677; fax (2) 9287-5869; internet www.telstra.com.au; general and mobile telecommunication services; Man. Dir and Chief Exec. ZIGGY SWITKOWSKI.

**Vodafone Australia:** Tower A, 799 Pacific Highway, Chatswood, NSW 2067; tel. (2) 9878-7000; fax (2) 9878-7788; mobile telecommunication services.

### Regulatory Authority

**Australian Communications Authority (ACA):** POB 13112, Law Courts, Melbourne, Vic 8010; tel. (3) 9963-6800; fax (3) 9963-6899; e-mail candinfo@aca.gov.au; internet www.aca.gov.au; f. 1997 through merger of Australian Telecommunications Authority and Spectrum Management Agency; regulator for telecommunications and radiocommunications; Chair. TONY SHAW.

## BROADCASTING

Many programmes are provided by the non-commercial statutory corporation, the Australian Broadcasting Corporation (ABC). Commercial radio and television services are provided by stations operated by companies under licences granted and renewed by the Australian Broadcasting Authority (ABA). They rely for their income on the broadcasting of advertisements. In mid-1993 there were 166 commercial radio stations in operation, and 44 commercial television stations.

In 1996 there were an estimated 25.0m. radio receivers and 10.0m. television receivers in use.

**Australian Broadcasting Corporation (ABC):** 700 Harris St, Ultimo, POB 9994, Sydney, NSW 2001; tel. (2) 9333-1500 (radio), telex 176464 (radio), 120432 (television); fax (2) 9333-2603 (radio), (2) 9950-3050 (television); e-mail comments@your.abc.net.au; internet www.abc.net.au; f. 1932 as Australian Broadcasting Commission; one national television network operating on about 600 transmitters and six radio networks operating on more than 6,000 transmitters; Chair. DONALD MCDONALD; Man. Dir BRIAN JOHNS.

**Radio Australia:** international service broadcast by short wave and satellite in English, Indonesian, Standard Chinese, Khmer, Tok Pisin and Vietnamese.

### Radio

**Federation of Australian Radio Broadcasters Ltd:** POB 299, St Leonards, NSW 1590; tel. (2) 9906-5866; fax (2) 9906-5152; e-mail rmb@radiomarketing.com.au; internet www.radiomarketing.com.au; asscn of privately-owned commercial stations; CEO D. BACON.

Major Commercial Broadcasting Station Licensees

**5AD Broadcasting Co Pty Ltd:** 201 Tynte St, Nth Adelaide, SA 5006; tel. (8) 8300-1000; fax (8) 8300-1020; internet www.5adfm.com.au; also operates 5DN; Gen. Man. GRAEME TUCKER.

**Associated Communications Enterprises (ACE) Radio Broadcasters Pty Ltd:** POB 7515, Melbourne, Vic 3004; tel. (3) 9645-9877; fax (3) 9645-9886; operates six stations; Man. Dir S. EVERETT.

**Austereo Pty Ltd:** Ground Level, 180 St Kilda Rd, St Kilda, Vic 3182; tel. (3) 9230-1051; fax (3) 9593-9007; operates 11 stations; Man. Dir PETER HARVIE.

**Australian Radio Network Pty Ltd:** Level 8, 99 Mount St, North Sydney, NSW 2060; tel. (2) 9464-1000; fax (2) 9464-1010; operates nine stations; CEO NEIL MOUNT.

**Australian Regional Broadcasters:** 1 June Rd, Gooseberry Hill, WA 6076; tel. (8) 9472-8900; fax (8) 9472-8911; operates three stations; Man. Dir NICK RINGROSE.

**Bass Strait Media:** 109 York St, Launceston, Tas 7250; tel. (3) 6431-1651; fax (3) 6431-3188; operates four radio stations; Man. Dir JOHN JOST.

**Capital Radio:** 28 Sharp St, Cooma, NSW 2630; tel. (2) 6452-1521; fax (2) 6452-1006; operates four stations; Man. Dir KEVIN BLYTON.

**DMG Regional Radio Pty Ltd:** Level 9, 2 Bridge St, Sydney, NSW 2000; tel. (2) 9258-4999; fax (2) 9241-2224; operates 30 stations; Chief Exec. ROB GAMBLE.

**Grant Broadcasting:** 63 Minimbah Rd, Northbridge, NSW 2063; tel. (2) 9958-7301; fax (2) 9958-6906; operates seven stations; Gen. Man. JANET CAMERON.

**Greater Cairns Radio Ltd:** Virginia House, Abbott St, Cairns, Qld 4870; tel. (7) 4050-0846; fax (7) 4051-8060; Gen. Man. J. ELLER.

**Macquarie Radio Network Pty Ltd:** POB 4290, Sydney, NSW 2001; tel. (2) 9269-0646; fax (2) 9287-2772; operates 2GB and 2CH; CEO GEORGE BUSCHMAN.

**Moree Broadcasting and Development Company Ltd:** 87–89 Balo St, Moree, NSW 2400; tel. (2) 6752-1155; fax (2) 6752-2601; operates two stations; Man. KEN BIRCH.

**Radio 2SM Gold 1269:** 186 Blues Point Rd, North Sydney, NSW 2060; tel. (2) 9922-1269; fax (2) 9954-3117; f. 1931; CEO and Chair. C. M. MURPHY.

**RadioWest Hot FM:** POB 10067, Kalgoorlie, WA 6430; tel. (8) 9021-2666; fax (8) 9091-2209; e-mail radio6KG@gold.net.au; f. 1931.

**Regional Broadcasters (Australia) Pty:** McDowal St, Roma, Qld 4455; tel. (7) 4622-1800; fax (7) 4622-3697; Chair. G. MCVEAN.

**RG Capital Radio Pty Ltd:** Level 2, Seabank Bldg, 12–14 Marine Parade, Southport, Qld 4215; tel. (7) 5591-5000; fax (7) 5591-2869; operates 14 stations; Man. Dir RHYS HOLLERAN.

**Rural Press Ltd:** Cnr Pine Mt Rd and Hill St, Raymonds Hill, Qld 4305; tel. (7) 3201-6000; fax (7) 3812-3060; internet www.rpl.com.au; f. 1911; operates five stations; Gen. Man. RICHARD BURNS.

**SEA FM Pty Ltd:** POB 5910, Gold Coast Mail Centre, Bundall, Qld 4217; tel. (7) 5591-5000; fax (7) 5591-6080; operates six stations; Chair. S. J. WILLMOTT.

**Southern Cross Broadcasting (Australia) Ltd:** see under Television.

**Supernetwork Radio Pty Ltd:** POB 97, Coolangatta, Qld 4225; tel. (7) 5524-4497; fax (7) 5554-3970; operates 15 stations; Chair. W. CARALIS.

**Tamworth Radio Development Company Pty Ltd:** POB 497, Tamworth, NSW 2340; tel. (2) 6765-7055; fax (2) 6765-2762; operates five stations; Man. W. A. MORRISON.

**Tasmanian Broadcasting Network (TBN):** POB 665G, Launceston, Tas 7250; tel. (3) 6431-2555; fax (3) 6431-3188; operates three stations; Chair. K. FINDLAY.

**Wesgo Ltd:** POB 234, Seven Hills, NSW 2147; tel. (2) 9831-7611; fax (2) 9831-2001; operates eight stations; CEO G. W. RICE.

### Television

**Federation of Australian Commercial Television Stations (FACTS):** 44 Avenue Rd, Mosman, NSW 2088; tel. (2) 9960-2622; fax (2) 9969-3520; f. 1960; represents all commercial television stations; Chair. JOHN MCALPINE; Gen. Man. TONY BRANIGAN.

Commercial Television Station Licensees

**Amalgamated Television Services Pty Ltd:** Mobbs Lane, Epping, NSW 2121; tel. (2) 9877-7777; fax (2) 9877-7888; f. 1956; originating station for Seven Network TV programming; Exec. Chair. KERRY STOKES; CEO JULIAN MOUNTER.

**Australian Capital Television Pty Ltd (Ten Capital):** Private Bag 10, Dickson, ACT 2602; tel. (2) 6242-2400; fax (2) 6241-7230; f. 1962; Gen. Man. ERIC PASCOE.

**Brisbane TV Ltd:** GPOB 604, Brisbane, Qld 4001; tel. (7) 3369-7777; fax (7) 3368-2970; f. 1959; operates one station; mem. of Seven Network; Man. Dir L. M. RILEY.

**Broken Hill Television Ltd:** POB 472, Rocky Hill, Broken Hill, NSW 2880; tel. (8) 8087-6013; fax (8) 8087-8492; f. 1968; operates one station; Chair. PETER STORROCK; Chief Exec. D. WESTON.

**Channel 9 South Australia Pty Ltd:** 202 Tynte St, North Adelaide 5006; tel. (8) 8267-0111; fax (8) 8267-3996; f. 1959; Gen. Man. M. COLSON.

**General Television Corporation Pty Ltd:** 22–46 Bendigo St, POB 100, Richmond, Vic 3121; tel. (3) 9429-0201; fax (3) 9429-3670; internet www.nine.msn.com.au; f. 1957; operates one station; Man. Dir I. J. JOHNSON.

**Golden West Network:** POB 5090, Geraldton, WA 6531; tel. (8) 9921-4422; fax (8) 9921-8096.

**Golden West Network Pty Ltd:** POB 1062, West Perth, WA 6872; tel. (8) 9481-0050; fax (8) 9321-2470; f. 1967; operates three stations (SSW10, VEW and WAW); Gen. Man. W. FENWICK.

**HSV Channel 7 Pty Ltd:** 119 Wells St, Southbank, Vic 3205; tel. (3) 9697-7777; fax (3) 9697-7888; e-mail rob.smithwick@hsvpo.ccmail.compuserve.com; f. 1956; operates one station; Chair. KERRY STOKES; Gen. Man. ROBERT SMITHWICK.

**Imparja Television Pty Ltd:** POB 52, Alice Springs, NT 0871; tel. (8) 8950-1411; fax (8) 8953-0322; e-mail imparja@ozemail.com.au; internet www.imparja.com.au; CEO CORALLIE FERGUSON.

**Independent Broadcasters of Australia Pty Ltd:** POB 285, Sydney, NSW 2001; tel. (2) 9264-9144; fax (2) 9264-6334; fmrly Regional Television Australia Pty Ltd; Chair. GRAEME J. GILBERTSON; Sec. JEFF EATHER.

**Mt Isa Television Pty Ltd:** 110 Canooweal St, Mt Isa, Qld 4825; tel. (7) 4743-8888; fax (7) 4743-9803; f. 1971; operates one station; Station Man. LYALL GREY.

**NBN Ltd:** Mosbri Crescent, POB 750L, Newcastle, NSW 2300; tel. (2) 4929-2933; fax (2) 4926-2936; f. 1962; operates one station; Man. Dir DENIS LEDBURY.

**Network Ten Ltd:** GPOB 10, Sydney, NSW 2001; tel. (2) 9650-1010; fax (2) 9650-1170; operates Australian TV network and commercial stations in Sydney, Melbourne, Brisbane, Perth and Adelaide; CEO JOHN MCALPINE.

**Nine Network Australia Pty Ltd:** POB 27, Willoughby, NSW 2068; tel. (2) 9906-9999; fax (2) 9958-2279; internet www.ninemsn.com.au; f. 1956; division of Publishing and Broadcasting Ltd; operates three stations: TCN Channel Nine Pty Ltd (Sydney), Queensland Television Ltd (Brisbane) and General Television Corporation Ltd (Melbourne); CEO DAVID LECKIE.

**Northern Rivers Television Pty Ltd:** Peterson Rd, Locked Bag 1000, Coffs Harbour, NSW 2450; tel. (2) 6652-2777; fax (2) 6652-3034; f. 1965; CEO GARRY DRAFFIN.

**Prime Television Group:** Level 6, 1 Pacific Highway, North Sydney, NSW 2060; tel. (2) 9965-7700; fax (2) 9965-7729; e-mail primetv@primetv.com.au; internet www.primetv.com.au; Chair. PAUL RAMSAY; CEO GEORGE BROWN.

**Prime Television (Northern) Pty Ltd:** POB 2077, Elermore Vale, NSW 2287; tel. (2) 4952-0500; fax (2) 4952-0502; internet www.primetv.com.au; Gen. Man. BRAD JONES.

**Prime Television (Southern) Pty Ltd:** POB 465, Orange, NSW 2800; tel. (2) 6361-6888; fax (2) 6363-1889; Gen. Man. D. THISTLETHWAITE.

**Prime Television (Victoria) Pty Ltd:** Sunraysia Highway, Ballarat, Vic 3350; tel. (3) 5337-1777; fax (3) 5337-1700; Gen. Man. WARWICK FENWICK.

**Queensland Television Ltd:** POB 72, GPO Brisbane, Qld 4001; tel. (7) 3214-9999; fax (7) 3369-3512; f. 1959; operates one station; Gen. Man. IAN R. MÜLLER.

**Riverland Television Pty Ltd:** Murray Bridge Rd, POB 471, Loxton, SA 5333; tel. (8) 8584-6891; fax (8) 8584-5062; f. 1976; operates one station; Exec. Chair. E. H. URLWIN; Gen. Man. W. L. MUDGE.

**Seven Network Ltd:** Television Centre, Mobbs Lane, Epping, NSW 2121; owns Amalgamated Television Services Pty Ltd (Sydney), Brisbane TV Ltd (Brisbane), HSV Channel 7 Pty Ltd (Melbourne), South Australian Telecasters Ltd (Adelaide) and TVW Enterprises Ltd (Perth); Exec. Chair. KERRY STOKES.

**Australia Television:** international satellite service; broadcasts to more than 30 countries and territories in Asia and the Pacific.

**Seven Queensland:** 140–142 Horton Parade, Maroochydore, Qld 4558; tel. (7) 5430-1777; fax (7) 5479-1767; f. 1965; fmrly Sunshine Television Network Ltd; Gen. Man. LAURIE PATTON.

**South Australian Telecasters Ltd:** 45–49 Park Terrace, Gilberton, SA 5081; tel. (8) 8342-7777; fax (8) 8342-7717; f. 1965; operates SAS Channel 7; mem. of Seven Network; Man. Dir (vacant).

**Southern Cross Broadcasting (Australia) Ltd:** 41–49 Bank St, South Melbourne, Vic 3205; tel. (3) 9243-2100; fax (3) 9690-0937; internet www.southcrossbroad.com.au; f. 1932; operates four TV and four radio stations; Man. Dir A. E. BELL.

**Southern Cross Television (TNT9) Pty Ltd:** Watchorn St, Launceston, Tas 7250; tel. (3) 6344-0202; fax (3) 6343-0340; f. 1962; operates one station; Gen. Man. BRUCE ABRAHAM.

**Special Broadcasting Service (SBS):** Locked Bag 028, Crows Nest, NSW 1585; tel. (2) 9430-2828; fax (2) 9430-3700; e-mail sbs.com.au; internet www.sbs.com.au; f. 1980; national multi-cultural broadcaster of TV and radio; Man. Dir NIGEL MILAN.

**Spencer Gulf Telecasters Ltd:** POB 305, Port Pirie, SA 5540; tel. (8) 8632-2555; fax (8) 8633-0984; e-mail dweston@centralonline.com.au; internet www.centralonline.com.au; f. 1968; operates two stations; Chair. P. M. STURROCK; Chief Exec. D. WESTON.

**Swan Television & Radio Broadcasters Pty Ltd:** POB 99, Tuart Hill, WA 6939; tel. (8) 9449-9999; fax (8) 9449-9900; Gen. Man. P. BOWEN.

**Telecasters Australia Ltd:** Level 8, 1 Elizabeth Plaza, North Sydney, NSW 2060; tel. (2) 9922-1011; fax (2) 9922-1033; internet www.telecasters.com.au; operates commercial TV services of TEN Queensland, TEN Northern NSW, Seven Central and Seven Darwin.

**Territory Television Pty Ltd:** POB 1764, Darwin, NT 0801; tel. (8) 8981-8888; fax (8) 8981-6802; f. 1971; operates one station; Gen. Man. A. G. BRUYN.

**TVW Enterprises Ltd:** POB 77, Tuart Hill, WA 6060; tel. (8) 9344-0777; fax (8) 9344-0670; f. 1959; Chair. DAVID ASPINALL.

**WIN Television Griffith Pty Ltd:** 161 Remembrance Driveway, Griffith, NSW 2680; tel. (2) 6962-4500; fax (2) 6962-0979; e-mail mtntv@ozemail.com.au; fmrly MTN Television; Man. Dir G. RAYMENT.

**WIN Television Mildura Pty Ltd:** 18 Deakin Ave, Mildura, Vic 3500; tel. (3) 5023-0204; fax (3) 5022-1179; f. 1965; Chair. JOHN RUSHTON; Man. NOEL W. HISCOCK.

**WIN Television NSW Network:** Television Ave, Mt St Thomas, Locked Bag 8800, South Coast Mail Centre, NSW 2521; tel. (2) 4223-4199; fax (2) 4227-3682; f. 1962; Man. Dir K. KINGSTON; CEO JOHN RUSHTON.

**WIN Television Qld Pty Ltd:** POB 568 Rockhampton, Qld 4700; tel. (7) 4930-4499; fax (7) 4930-4490; Station Man. R. HOCKEY.

**WIN Television Tas Pty Ltd:** 52 New Town Rd, Hobart, Tas 7008; tel. (3) 6228-8999; fax (3) 6228-8991; e-mail wintas.com.au; internet www.wintv.com.au; f. 1959; Gen. Man. GREG RAYMENT.

**WIN Television Vic Pty Ltd:** POB 464, Ballarat, Vic 3353; tel. (3) 5320-1366; fax (3) 5333-1598; f. 1961; operates five stations; Gen. Man. DAVID LANGSFORD.

#### Satellite, Cable and Digital Television

Digital television was to become available in metropolitan areas from January 2001.

**Austar United Communications:** Level 29, AAP Centre, 259 George St, Sydney NSW 2000, tel. (2) 9251-6999; fax (2) 9251-6136; internet www.austar.com.au; began operations in 1995; sole provider of pay-TV (satellite and cable) services to rural Australia; 325,000 subscribers (March 1999); CEO JOHN C. PORTER.

**Foxtel:** Foxtel Television Centre, Pyrmont, Sydney; internet www.foxtel.com.au; owned by the News Corpn, Telstra Corpn and PBL; 534,000 subscribers (Sept. 1999).

**Optus Vision:** Tower B, Level 15, 16 Zenith Centre, 821–841 Pacific Highway, Chatswood, NSW 2067; commenced cable services on 11 channels in 1995; 210,000 subscribers (March 1999).

#### Regulatory Authority

**Australian Broadcasting Authority:** POB Q500, QVB Post Office, NSW 1230; tel. (2) 9334-7700; fax (2) 9334-7799; e-mail info@aba.gov.au; internet www.aba.gov.au; regulates radio and TV broadcasting; Chair. Prof. DAVID FLINT.

## Finance

Radical reforms of the financial sector, to be introduced from 1998, were announced in September 1997. The banking system was to be opened up to greater competition. The licensing and regulation of deposit-taking institutions was to be supervised by the new Australian Prudential Regulation Authority, while consumer protection was to be the responsibility of the Australian Corporations and Financial Services Commission.

(cap. = capital; p.u. = paid up; res = reserves; dep. = deposits; m. = million; brs = branches; amounts in Australian dollars)

### BANKING

#### Central Bank

**Reserve Bank of Australia:** GPOB 3947, Sydney, NSW 2001; tel. (2) 9551-8111; fax (2) 9551-8000; e-mail rbainfo.@rba.gov.au; internet www.rba.gov.au; f. 1911; responsible for monetary policy, financial system stability, payment system development; cap. and res 7,237m., dep. 10,383m., total assets 49,073m., notes on issue 23,552m. (June 1999); Gov. IAN MACFARLANE.

#### Development Banks

**Commonwealth Development Bank of Australia:** GPOB 2719, Sydney, NSW 2001; tel. (2) 9378-2000; fax (2) 9312-9905; f. 1960; cap. and res 295.2m., dep. 550.0m. (June 1996); Gen. Man. R. H. WEAVER.

**Primary Industry Bank of Australia Ltd:** GPOB 4577, Sydney, NSW 1042; tel. (2) 9234-4200; fax (2) 9221-6218; f. 1978; cap. 123.2m., res 2.5m., dep. 1,683.5m. (Dec. 1997); Chair. H. G. GENTIS; Man. Dir B. H. WALTERS; 24 brs.

#### Trading Banks

**ABN AMRO Australia Ltd:** NAB House, 255 George St, Sydney, NSW 2000; tel. (2) 9259-5711; fax (2) 9259-5444; f. 1983; cap. 70m., res 65m. (Dec. 1997); CEO STEVE CRANE.

**ABN AMRO Finance (Aust.) Ltd:** Level 40, Governor Phillip Tower, 1 Farrer Place, Sydney, NSW 2000; tel. (2) 9375-5555; fax (2) 9251-1473; f. 1985 as Lloyds Bank NZA Ltd, name changed 1997; cap. 48.1m., res 46.7m., dep. 681.8m. (Dec. 1995); Chair. P. M. MCCAW; CEO DAVID S. WILLIS.

**Arab Bank Australia Ltd:** GPOB N645, Level 9, Grosvenor Place, 200 George St, Sydney, NSW 1220; tel. (2) 9377-8900; fax (2) 9221-5428; cap. 55.0m., dep. 217.2m. (Dec. 1997); Chair. KHALID SHOMAN; Man. Dir JACK BEIGHTON.

**Australia and New Zealand Banking Group Ltd:** 100 Queen St, Melbourne, Vic 3000; POB 537 E, Melbourne, Vic 3001; tel. (3) 9273-5555; fax (3) 9273-4909; internet www.anz.com; f. 1835; present name adopted in 1970; cap. 5,226.0m., res 697.0m., dep. 105,357.0m. (Sept. 1998); 806 brs; Chair. C. B. GOODE; CEO JOHN MCFARLANE.

**BA Australia Ltd:** Level 63, MLC Centre, 19–29 Martin Place, Sydney, NSW 2000; tel. (2) 9931-4200; fax (2) 9221-1023; f. 1964; cap. 150.3m. (Dec. 1998); Man. Dir TERRY FRANCIS.

**Bank of Melbourne:** 360 Collins St, Melbourne, Vic 3000; tel. (3) 9608-3222; fax (3) 9608-3700; f. 1989; cap. 752m., dep. 8,706m. (1997); Chair. CHRIS STEWART; CEO MATTHEW SLATTER; 129 brs.

**Bank of Queensland Ltd:** 229 Elizabeth St, POB 898, Brisbane, Qld 4001; tel. (7) 3212-3333; fax (7) 3212-3399; f. 1874; cap. 120.9m., res 1.2m., dep. 2,404.9m. (Aug. 1998); Chair. NEIL ROBERTS; Chief Exec. JOHN K. DAWSON; 95 brs.

**Bank of Tokyo-Mitsubishi (Australia) Ltd:** Level 26, Gateway, 1 Macquarie Place, Sydney, NSW 2000; tel. (2) 9255-1111; fax (2) 9247-4266; cap. 150.0m., res 2.9m., dep. 2,228.3m. (Dec. 1997); f. 1985; Chair. R. NICOLSON; Man. Dir H. YOKOYAMA.

**Bank of Western Australia Ltd:** 108 St George's Terrace, POB E237, Perth, WA 6001; tel. (8) 9449-7000; fax (8) 9449-7050; internet www.bankwest.com.au; f. 1895 as Agricultural Bank of Western

Australia, 1945 as Rural and Industries Bank of Western Australia; present name adopted in 1994; cap. and res 629.8m., dep. 9,130.1m. (Feb. 1998); Chair. IAN C. R. MACKENZIE; Man. Dir TERRY C. BUDGE; 109 brs.

**Bankers' Trust Australia Ltd:** GPOB H4, Australia Sq., Sydney, NSW 2000; tel. (2) 9259-3555; fax (2) 9259-9800; f. 1986; cap. 273.3m., dep. 6,266.8m. (Dec. 1997); Man. Dir R. A. FERGUSON; 5 brs.

**The Chase Manhattan Bank:** GPOB 9816, NSW 2001; tel. (2) 9250-4111; fax (2) 9250-4554; internet www.chase.com; Man. Dir W. SCOTT REID.

**Citibank Ltd:** GPOB 40, Sydney, NSW 1027; tel. (2) 9239-9100; fax (2) 9239-9110; internet www.citibank.com.au; f. 1954; cap. 457m., res 1m., dep. 5,619m. (Dec. 1998); Country Corporate Officer WILLIAM W. FERGUSON.

**Colonial State Bank:** GPOB 41, Sydney, NSW 2001; tel. (2) 9226-8000; fax (2) 9798-1184; internet www.colonial.com.au; f. 1933; fmrly State Bank of New South Wales; cap. and res 1,541.6m., dep. 7,211m. (1997); Chair. PETER SMEDLEY; Man. Dir STUART JAMES; 340 brs in Australia.

**Commonwealth Bank of Australia:** GPOB 2719, Sydney, NSW 2001; tel. (2) 9378-2000; fax (2) 9378-3317; f. 1912; cap. 1,845.0m., res 4,112.0m., dep. 87,283m. (June 1998); Chair. TIM BESLEY; CEO Dir D. V. MURRAY; more than 1,500 brs world-wide.

**HSBC Bank Australia Ltd:** Level 10, 1 O'Connell Street, Sydney, NSW 2000; tel. (2) 9255-2888; fax (2) 9255-2332; internet www.hsbc.com.au; f. 1985; fmrly HongkongBank of Australia; cap. 500.0m., res 60.1m., dep. 4,237.6m. (Dec. 1997); CEO CHRIS CROOK; Man. Dir PHILIP HOLBERTON; 16 brs.

**IBJ Australia Bank Ltd:** 21st Level, State Bank Centre, 52 Martin Place, Sydney, NSW 2000; tel. (2) 9377-8888; fax (2) 9377-8884; f. 1985; subsidiary of Industrial Bank of Japan; cap. 104.1m., res 67.2m., dep. 1,822.1m. (Dec. 1997); Chair. M. J. PHILLIPS; Man. Dir K. TSUJI.

**ING Mercantile Mutual Bank Ltd:** Level 1, 347 Kent St, Sydney, NSW 2000; tel. (2) 9234-8444; fax (2) 9290-3683; cap. 60m., res 1.5m., dep. 374.9m. (Sept. 1996); Gen. Man. JULIE BROWN.

**Macquarie Bank Ltd:** Level 22, 20 Bond St, Sydney, NSW 2000; tel. (2) 9237-3333; fax (2) 9237-3350; internet www.macquarie .com.au; f. 1969 as Hill Samuel Australia Ltd; present name adopted in 1985; cap. 160.5m., res 420.4m., dep. 4,310.6m. (March 1998); Chair. DAVID S. CLARKE; Man. Dir ALLAN E. MOSS; 4 brs.

**National Australia Bank Ltd:** 500 Bourke St, Melbourne, Vic 3000; tel. (3) 8641-3500; fax (3) 8641-4916; internet www .national.com.au/; f. 1858; cap. 6,675m., res 1,782m., dep. 158,084m. (Sept. 1998); Chair. M. R. RAYNER; Exec. Dir FRANK CICUTTO; 2,349 brs.

**N. M. Rothschild & Sons (Australia) Ltd:** 1 O'Connell St, Sydney, NSW 2000; tel. (2) 9323-2000; fax (2) 9323-2323; f. 1967 as International Pacific Corpn; cap. 130m., dep. 606m. (March 1998); Chair. PHILIP BRASS; Man. Dir RICHARD LEE.

**SG Australia Ltd:** Level 21, 400 George St, Sydney, NSW 2000; tel. (2) 9210-8000; fax (2) 9231-2196; internet www.sgal@zip.com.au; f. 1981; fmrly Société Générale; cap. 21.5m., res 170.5m., dep. 5,509.0m. (Dec. 1998); CEO MICHEL L. MACAGNO.

**St George Bank Ltd:** Locked Bag 1, PO, Kogarah, NSW 1485; tel. (2) 9236-1111; fax (2) 9952-1066; e-mail stgeorge@stgeorge.com.au; internet www.stgeorge.com.au; f. 1937 as building society; cap. 3,249m., res 69m., dep. 32,537m. (Sept. 1999); Chair. F. J. CONROY; CEO and Man. Dir EDWARD O'NEAL; 421 brs.

**Standard Chartered Bank Australia Ltd:** 345 George St, Sydney, NSW; tel. (2) 9232-6599; fax (2) 9232-9345; f. 1986; cap. 226.2m., dep. 939.0m. (Dec. 1998); Chair. Sir BRUCE MACKLIN; CEO DAVID MANSON.

**Toronto Dominion Australia Ltd:** 36th Floor, 385 Bourke St, Melbourne, Vic 3000; tel. (3) 9602-1344; fax (3) 9670-3779; f. 1970; cap. 191.5m., res 6.0m., dep. 3,435.4m. (Oct. 1997); Man. Dir W. C. JACOBSON.

**Westpac Banking Corporation:** 60 Martin Place, Sydney, NSW 2000; tel. (2) 9226-3311; fax (2) 9226-4128; internet www.westpac .com.au; f. 1817; cap. 1,899m., res 4,466m., dep. 77,479m. (Sept. 1998); Chair. JOHN UHRIG; Man. Dir D. R. MORGAN.

### Savings Bank

**Trust Bank:** 39 Murray St, Hobart, Tas 7000; tel. (3) 131828; fax (3) 6223-2279; e-mail trustbank@trustbank.com.au; internet www.trustbank.com.au; f. 1845; cap. and res 137.4m., dep. 1,818.3m. (Aug. 1998); Chair. G. N. LOUGHRAN; Man. Dir P. W. KEMP; 47 brs.

### Foreign Banks

**Bank of China** (People's Republic of China): 39–41 York St, Sydney, NSW 2000; tel. (2) 9267-5188; fax (2) 9262-1794; e-mail bocsyd@bigpond.com.au; Gen. Man. GAO JI LU.

**Bank of New Zealand:** 9th Floor, BNZ House, 333–339 George St, Sydney, NSW 2000; tel. (2) 9290-6666; fax (2) 9290-3414; Chief Operating Officer G. ARMBRUSTER.

**Banque Nationale de Paris** (France): 60 Castlereagh St, Sydney, NSW 2000; POB 269, Sydney, NSW 2001; tel. (2) 9232-8733; fax (2) 9221-3026; e-mail bnp@bnp.com.au; Gen. Man. ROLAND GIRAULT; 4 brs.

**BOSA Ltd:** 75 Castlereagh St, Sydney, NSW 2000; tel. (2) 9235-2022; fax (2) 9221-4360; e-mail ocbcau@ozmail.com.au; f. 1986; fmrly Bank of Singapore (Australia); Gen. Man. ONG SING YIK; 4 brs.

**Deutsche Bank AG** (Germany): GPOB 7033, Sydney, NSW 2001; tel. (2) 9258-3666; fax (2) 9241-2565; Man. Dir Dr KLAUS ALBRECHT.

## STOCK EXCHANGE

**Australian Stock Exchange Ltd (ASX):** Level 9, 20 Bridge St, Sydney, NSW 2000; tel. (2) 9227-0000; fax (2) 9235-0056; e-mail info@asx.com.au; internet www.asx. com.au; f. 1987 by merger of the stock exchanges in Sydney, Adelaide, Brisbane, Hobart, Melbourne and Perth, to replace the fmr Australian Associated Stock Exchanges; demutualized Oct. 1998; 104 participating orgs; Chair. MAURICE NEWMAN; Man. Dir and CEO RICHARD HUMPHRY.

### Supervisory Body

**Australian Securities and Investments Commission:** POB 4866, Sydney, NSW 2001; tel. (2) 9911-2000; fax (2) 9911-2030; internet www.asic.gov.au; f. 1990; corporations and financial products regulator; Chair. ALAN CAMERON.

## PRINCIPAL INSURANCE COMPANIES

**Allianz Australia Ltd:** 2 Market St, Sydney, NSW 2000; tel. (2) 9390-6222; fax (2) 9390-6425; internet www.allianz.com.au; f. 1914; workers' compensation; fire, general accident, motor and marine; Chair. J. S. CURTIS; Man. Dir T. TOWELL.

**AMP Ltd:** AMP Bldg, 33 Alfred St, Sydney, NSW 2000; tel. (2) 9257-5000; fax (2) 9257-7886; internet www.amplimited.com.au; f. 1849; fmrly Australian Mutual Provident Society; life insurance; Chair. IAN BURGESS; Man. Dir PAUL BATCHELOR.

**AMP General Insurance Ltd:** 10 Loftus St, Sydney Cove, NSW 2000; tel. (2) 9257-2500; fax (2) 9257-2199; internet www.amp.com.au; f. 1958; Chair. GREG COX; Man. Dir GAVIN PEACE.

**Australian Guarantee Corpn Ltd:** 130 Phillip St, Sydney, NSW 2000; tel. (2) 9234-1122; fax (2) 9234-1225; f. 1925; Chair. J. A. UHRIG; Man. Dir R. THOMAS.

**Australian Unity General Insurance Ltd:** 114–124 Albert Rd, South Melbourne, Vic 3205; tel. (3) 9285-0285; fax (3) 9690-5556; f. 1948; Chair. C. S. VINCENT; Chief Exec. M. W. SIBREE.

**Catholic Church Insurances Ltd:** 324 St Kilda Rd, Melbourne, Vic 3004; tel. (3) 9934-3000; fax (3) 9934-3460; f. 1911; Chair. Most Rev. KEVIN MANNING, Bishop of Parramatta; Gen. Man. PETER RUSH.

**Colonial Ltd:** 330 Collins St, Melbourne, Vic 3000; tel. (3) 9200-6111; fax (3) 9200-6294; internet www.colonial.com.au; f. 1873; Chair. D. S. ADAM; Group Man. Dir and CEO PETER SMEDLEY.

**Commercial Union Assurance Co of Australia Ltd:** Commercial Union Centre, 485 La Trobe St, Melbourne, Vic 3000; tel. (3) 9601-8222; fax (3) 9601-8366; f. 1960; fire, accident, marine; Chair. A. F. GUY; Man. Dir I. M. BALFE.

**The Copenhagen Reinsurance Co Ltd:** 60 Margaret St, Sydney, NSW 2000; tel. (2) 9247-7266; fax (2) 9235-3320; internet www .copre.com; reinsurance; Gen. Man. ANDREW ALLISON.

**FAI Insurances Ltd:** FAI Insurance Group, 333 Kent St, Sydney, NSW 1026; tel. (2) 9274-9000; fax (2) 9274-9900; internet www.fai .com.au; f. 1953; Chair. JOHN LANDERER; CEO RODNEY ADLER.

**Fortis Australia Ltd:** 464 St Kilda Rd, Melbourne, Vic 3004; tel. (3) 9869-0300; fax (3) 9820-8537; CEO R. B. WILLING..

**General and Cologne Reinsurance Australasia Ltd:** Level 13, 225 George St, Sydney, NSW 2000; tel. (2) 9336-8100; fax (2) 9251-1665; f. 1961; reinsurance, fire, accident, marine; Chair. F. A. MCDONALD; Man. Dir G. C. BARNUM.

**GIO Australia Holdings Ltd:** Level 39, Governor Phillip Tower, 1 Farrer Place, Sydney, NSW 2000; tel. (2) 9255-8090; fax (2) 9251-2079; internet www.gio.com.au; f. 1926; CEO PETER CORRIGAN.

**Guild Insurance Ltd:** Guild House, 40 Burwood Rd, Hawthorn, Vic 3122; tel. (3) 9810-9820; fax (3) 9819-5670; f. 1963; Man. Dir W. K. BASTIAN.

**HIH Insurance Ltd:** AMP Centre, 50 Bridge St, Sydney, NSW 2000; tel. (2) 9650-2000; fax (2) 9650-2030; internet www.hih.com.au; f. 1968; Chair. G. A. COHEN; CEO R. R. WILLIAMS.

**Lumley General Insurance Ltd:** Lumley House, 309 Kent St, Sydney, NSW 1230; tel. (2) 9248-1111; fax (2) 9248-1122; e-mail general@lumley.com.au; Man. Dir D. M. MATCHAM.

**Mercantile Mutual Holdings Ltd:** 347 Kent St, Sydney, NSW; tel. (2) 9234-8111; fax (2) 9299-3979; f. 1878; Chair. J. B. STUDDY; Man. Dir R. J. ATFIELD.

**The National Mutual Life Association of Australasia Ltd:** 447 Collins St, Melbourne, Vic 3000; tel. (3) 9616-3911; fax (3) 9614-2240; internet www.nm.com.au; f. 1869; life insurance, superannuation, income protection; Chair. D. R. Wills; Man. Dir J. A. Killen.

**NRMA Insurance Ltd:** 151 Clarence St, Sydney, NSW 2000; tel. (2) 9292-9222; fax (2) 9292-8472; f. 1926; CEO Malcolm Jones.

**NZI Insurance Australia Ltd:** 9th Floor, 10 Spring St, Sydney, NSW 2000; tel. (2) 9551-5000; fax (2) 9551-5865; Man. Dir H. D. Smith.

**QBE Insurance Group Ltd:** 82 Pitt St, Sydney, NSW 2000; tel. (2) 9375-4444; fax (2) 9235-3166; internet www.qbe.com.au; f. 1886; general insurance; Chair. E. J. Cloney; Man. Dir F. M. O'Halloran.

**RAC Insurance Pty Ltd:** 228 Adelaide Terrace, Perth, WA 6000; tel. (8) 9421-4444; fax (8) 9421-4593; f. 1947; Gen. Man. Tony Carter.

**RACQ-GIO Insurance Ltd:** POB 4, Springwood, Qld 4127; tel. (7) 3361-2444; fax (7) 3361-2199; f. 1995; CEO I. W. Norris.

**RACV Insurance:** 550 Princes Highway, Noble Park, Vic 3174; tel. (3) 9790-2211; fax (3) 9790-3091; Gen. Man. D. C. Hurford.

**Sun Alliance and Royal Insurance Australia Ltd:** 465 Victoria Ave, Chatswood, NSW 2067; tel. (2) 9978-9000; fax (2) 9978-9807; fire, accident and marine insurance; Gen. Man. E. Kulk.

**Suncorp Metway:** 36 Wickham Tce, Brisbane, Queensland 4001; tel. (7) 3835-5355; fax (7) 3362-2890; f. *c.* 1916; Chair. John Lamble; CEO Steve Jones.

**Swiss Re Australia Ltd:** 31 Queen St, Melbourne, Vic 3000; tel. (3) 9616-9200; fax (3) 9621-2446; f. 1962; fmrly Australian Reinsurance Co Ltd; reinsurance; Chair. R. H. Syme; Man. Dir R. G. Watts.

**Transport Industries Insurance Co Ltd:** 310 Queen St, Melbourne, Vic 3000; tel. (3) 9623-3355; fax (3) 9623-2624; f. 1960; Chair. R. H. Y. Syme; Man. Dir R. G. Watts.

**Wesfarmers Federation Insurance Ltd:** 184 Railway Parade, Bassendean, WA 6054; tel. (8) 9273-5333; fax (8) 9273-5290; Gen. Man. R. J. Buckley.

**Westpac Life Ltd:** 35 Pitt St, Sydney, NSW 2000; tel. (2) 9220-4768; f. 1986; CEO David White.

**World Marine & General Insurances Ltd:** 600 Bourke St, Melbourne, Vic 3000; tel. (3) 9609-3333; fax (3) 9609-3634; f. 1961; Chair. G. W. McGregor; Man. Dir A. E. Reynolds.

**Zurich Financial Services Australia Ltd:** 5 Blue St, North Sydney, NSW 2060; tel. (2) 9391-1111; fax (2) 9922-4630; CEO Malcolm M. Jones.

### Insurance Associations

**Australian Insurance Association:** GPOB 369, Canberra, ACT 2601; tel. (2) 6274-0609; fax (2) 6274-0666; f. 1968; Pres. Raymond Jones; Exec. Sec. P. M. Murphy.

**Australian Insurance Institute:** Level 17, 31 Queen St, Melbourne, Vic 3000; tel. (3) 9629-4021; fax (3) 9629-4204; e-mail ceo@aii.com.au; internet www.aii.com.au; f. 1919; Pres. Rhys Withers; CEO Joan Fitzpatrick; 11,984 mems.

**Insurance Council of Australia Ltd:** Level 3, 56 Pitt St, Sydney, NSW 2000; tel. (2) 9252-5100; fax (2) 9253-5111; internet www.ica.com.au; f. 1975; CEO Alan Mason.

**Investment and Financial Services Ltd (IFSA):** Level 24, 44 Market St, Sydney, NSW 2000; tel. (2) 9299-3022; fax (2) 9299-3198; e-mail ifsa@ifsa.com.au; f. 1996; fmrly Life, Investment and Superannuation Asscn of Australia Inc; Chair. Ian Martin; CEO Lynn Ralph.

# Trade and Industry

## CHAMBERS OF COMMERCE

**International Chamber of Commerce:** POB E118, Kingston, Canberra, ACT 2604; tel. (2) 6295-1961; fax (2) 6295-0170; f. 1927; 65 mems; Chair. C. S. Cullen; Sec.-Gen. H. C. Grant.

**Australian Chamber of Commerce and Industry (ACCI):** POB E14, Kingston, ACT 2604; tel. (2) 6273-2311; fax (2) 6273-3286; e-mail acci@acci.asn.au; internet www.acci.asn.au; Pres. Rob Gerard; CEO Philip Holt.

**Chamber of Commerce and Industry of Western Australia (CCIWA):** POB 6209, East Perth, WA 6892; tel. (8) 9365-7555; fax (8) 9481-0980; e-mail whitaker@cciwa.asn.au; internet www.cciwa.asn.au; f. 1890; 6,000 mems; Chief Exec. Lyndon Rowe; Pres. Graham Greig.

**Queensland Chamber of Commerce and Industry:** Industry House, 375 Wickham Terrace, Brisbane, Qld 4000; tel. (7) 3842-2244; fax (7) 3832-3195; e-mail qcci@qcci.com.au; internet www.qcci.com.au; f. 1868; operates World Trade Centre, Brisbane; 3,800 mems; CEO Clive Bubb.

**South Australian Employers' Chamber of Commerce and Industry Inc:** Enterprise House, 136 Greenhill Road, Unley, SA 5061; tel. (8) 8300-0000; fax (8) 8300-0001; e-mail saecci@dove.net.au; internet www.saecci.asn.au; 4,700 mems; CEO P. Vaughan.

**State Chamber of Commerce (New South Wales):** Level 12, 83 Clarence St, GPO 4280, Sydney, NSW 2001; tel. (2) 9350-8100; fax (2) 9350-8199; operates World Trade Centre, Sydney; Deputy Gen. Man. Diane Hacking.

**Tasmanian Chamber of Commerce and Industry:** GPOB 793H, Hobart, Tas 7001; tel. (3) 6234-5933; fax (3) 6231-1278; CEO Tim Abey.

**Victorian Employers' Chamber of Commerce and Industry:** Employers' House, 50 Burwood Rd, Hawthorn, Vic 3122; tel. (3) 9251-4333; fax (3) 9819-3826; e-mail itd@vecci.org.au; f. 1885; CEO N. Feely.

## AGRICULTURAL, INDUSTRIAL AND TRADE ASSOCIATIONS

**The Agriculture and Resource Management Council of Australia and New Zealand:** Dept of Agriculture, Fisheries and Forestry—Australia, Barton, Canberra, ACT 2600; tel. (2) 6272-5216; fax (2) 6272-4772; e-mail armcanz.contact@affa.gov.au; internet www.affa.gov.au/armcanz; f. 1992 to develop integrated and sustainable agricultural and land and water management policies, strategies and practices; mems comprising the Commonwealth/state/territory and New Zealand ministers responsible for agriculture, soil conservation, water resources and rural adjustment matters; Sec. J. W. Graham.

**Standing Committee on Agriculture and Resource Management:** f. 1992; an advisory body to the Agriculture and Resource Management Council of Australia and New Zealand; comprises the heads of Commonwealth/state/territory and New Zealand agencies responsible for agriculture, soil conservation and water resources and representatives from CSIRO, Bureau of Meteorology and rural adjustment authorities; Sec. J. W. Graham.

**Australian Business Ltd:** Private Bag 938, North Sydney, NSW 2059; tel. (2) 9927-7500; fax (2) 9923-1166; f. 1885; fmrly Chamber of Manufactures of NSW; CEO P. M. Holt.

**Australian Dairy Corporation:** Locked Bag 104, Flinders Lane, Vic 8009; tel. (3) 9694-3777; fax (3) 9694-3888; internet www.dairy.com.au/adc; provides export agency and market devt services, and promotes domestic consumption; Chair. Des Nicholl; Man. Dir Grahame Tonkin.

**Australian Manufacturers' Export Council:** POB E14, Queen Victoria Terrace, ACT 2600; tel. (2) 6273-2311; fax (2) 6273-3196; f. 1955; Exec. Dir G. Chalker.

**Australian Trade Policy Advisory Council:** c/o Dept of Foreign Affairs and Trade, Canberra, ACT 2600; tel. (2) 6261-2125; fax (2) 6261-2465; f. 1958; advises the Minister for Trade on policy issues; Chair. R. B. Vaughan.

**Australian Wool Research & Promotion Organisation:** Wool House, 369 Royal Parade, Parkville, Vic 3052; tel. (3) 9341-9111; fax (3) 9341-9273; internet www.wool.co.au; f. 1993; operates as The Woolmark Co; responsible for building sustainable demand via research and development, marketing and promotion, Chair. Tony Sherlock.

**AWB Ltd:** Ceres House, 528 Lonsdale St, Melbourne, Vic 3000; tel. (3) 9209-2000; fax (3) 9670-2782; e-mail awb@awb.com.au; internet www.awb.com.au; f. 1939; fmrly Australian Wheat Board; national and international marketing of grain, financing and marketing of wheat and other grains for growers; 12 mems; Chair. Trevor Flugge; CEO Murray Rogers.

**Business Council of Australia:** 15th Floor, 10 Queens Rd, Melbourne, Vic 3004; tel. (3) 9274-7777; fax (3) 9274-7744; public policy research and advocacy; governing council comprises chief execs of Australia's major cos; Pres. Stan Wallis; Exec. Dir David Buckingham.

**Meat and Livestock Australia:** 165 Walker St, North Sydney, NSW 2060; tel. 1800-023-100; internet www.mla.com.au; producer-owned co; represents, promotes, protects and furthers interests of industry in both the marketing of meat and livestock and devt of industry-based research and devt activities; Chair. David Crombie.

**National Farmers' Federation:** POB E10, Kingston, ACT 2604; tel. (2) 6273-3855; fax (2) 6273-2331; e-mail nff@nff.org.au; internet www.nff.org.au; Pres. Ian Donges; Exec. Dir Dr Wendy Craik.

**Wool Council Australia:** POB E10, Kingston, Canberra, ACT 2604; tel. (2) 6273-2531; fax (2) 6273-1120; e-mail woolcouncil@nff.org.au; internet www.farmwide.com.au/nff/wool/wool/htm; comprises 20 mems; represents wool-growers in dealings with the Federal Govt and industry; consults with Australian Wool Research and Promotion Organisation/Woolmark Co and Wool International; Pres. David Wolfenden.

### EMPLOYERS' ORGANIZATIONS

**Australian Co-operative Foods Ltd:** Level 12, 168 Walker St, North Sydney, NSW 2060; tel. (2) 9903-5222; fax (2) 9957-3530; f. 1900; Man. Dir A. R. TOOTH.

**Australian Industry Group:** 51 Walker St, North Sydney, NSW 2060; tel. (2) 9466-5566; fax (2) 9466-5599; e-mail louisep@aignsw.aigroup.asn.au; internet www.aigroup.asn.au; f. 1998 through merger of MTIA and ACM; 11,500 mems; Nat. Pres. G. J. ASHTON; CEO ROBERT N. HERBERT; 11,500 mems.

**National Meat Association:** 25–27 Albany St, Crows Nest, NSW 2065; POB 1208, Crows Nest, NSW 1585; tel. (2) 9906-7767; fax (2) 9906-8022; e-mail meat@magna.com.au; f. 1928; Pres. GARY HARDWICK; CEO G. JUREIDINI.

**NSW Farmers' Association:** 1 Bligh St, Sydney, NSW 2001; GPOB 1068, Sydney, NSW 1041; tel. (2) 9251-1700; fax (2) 9221-6913; e-mail emailus@nswfarmers.org.au; internet www.nswfarmers.org.au; f. 1978; CEO (vacant).

### UTILITIES

**Australian Gas Association (AGA):** GPOB 323, Canberra, ACT 2600; tel. (2) 6247-3955; fax (2) 6249-7402; e-mail canberra@gas.asn.au; internet www.gas.asn.au; 1,000 mems, incl. 290 corporate mems; Chair. GRANT KING; Chief Exec. BRIAN ROCHFORD (acting).

**Australian Institute of Energy:** POB 268, Toukley, NSW 2263; tel. 1800-629-945; fax (2) 4393-1114; e-mail aie@tpgi.com.au.

**Electricity Supply Association of Australia:** POB A2492, Sydney South, NSW 1235; tel. (2) 9233-7222; fax (2) 9233-7244; internet www.esaa.com.au; CEO KEITH ORCHISON.

#### Electricity Companies

**ACTEW Corpn Ltd:** GPOB 366, Canberra City, ACT 2601; tel. (2) 6248-3111; e-mail actew.energy@actew.com.au; internet www.actew.com.au; f. 1988 by amalgamation of the ACT's water and electricity authorities.

**Delta Electricity:** POB Q863, QVB, NSW 1230; tel. (2) 9285-2700; fax (2) 9285-2777; internet www.de.com.au; f. 1996; Chief Exec. JIM HENNESS.

**ENERGEX:** GPOB 1461, Brisbane, Qld 4001; tel. (7) 3407-4000; fax (7) 3407-4609; e-mail energex@energex.com.au; internet www.energex.com.au; largest electricity distribution corpn in Queensland; CEO BRIAN BLINCO.

**EnergyAustralia:** 145 Newcastle Rd, Wallsend, NSW 2287; tel. (2) 4951-9346; fax (2) 4951-9351; e-mail energy@energy.com.au; internet www.energy.com.au; supplies customers in NSW; CEO PETER HEADLEY; Man. Dir PAUL BROAD.

**Ergon Energy:** POB 107, Albert St, Brisbane, Qld 4002; tel. (7) 3228-8222; fax (7) 3228-8118; internet www.ergon.com.au; national retailer of electricity.

**Great Southern Energy:** Level 1, Citilink Plaza, Morriset St, Queanbeyan, NSW 2620; tel. (2) 6214-9600; fax (2) 6214-9860; e-mail mail@gsenergy.com.au; internet www.gsenergy.com.au; state-owned electricity and gas distributor; Chair. BRUCE RODELY.

**Snowy Mountains Hydro-electric Authority:** POB 332, Cooma, NSW 2630; tel. (2) 6452-1777; fax (2) 6452-3794; e-mail info@snowyhydro.com.au; internet www.snowyhydro.com.au.

**United Energy Ltd:** Level 13, 101 Collins St, Melbourne, Vic 3000; fax (3) 9222-8588; e-mail info@mail.ue.com.au; internet www.ue.com.au; f. 1994, following division of State Electricity Commission of Victoria; transferred to private sector; distributor of electricity and gas.

**Western Power Corpn:** GPOB L921, Perth, WA 6842; tel. (8) 9326-4911; fax (8) 9326-4595; e-mail info@wpcorp.com.au; internet www.wpcorp.com.au; f. 1995; principal supplier of electricity in WA; Chair. HECTOR STEBBINS (acting); Man. Dir DAVID EISZELE.

#### Gas Companies

**Alinta Gas:** GPOB W2030, Perth, WA 6846; internet www.alintagas.com.au; f. 1995; CEO PHIL HARVEY.

**Australian Gas Light Co:** AGL Centre, Corner Pacific Highway and Walker St, North Sydney, NSW 2060; tel. (2) 9922-0101; fax (2) 9957-3671; Chair. M. J. PHILLIPS; Man. Dir. L. F. BLEASEL.

**Envestra:** 10th Floor, 81 Flinders St, Adelaide, SA 5000; tel. (8) 8227-1500; fax (8) 8277-1511; e-mail petherick@envestra.com.au; internet www.envestra.com.au; f. 1997 by merger of South Australian Gas Co, Gas Corpn of Queensland and Centre Gas Pty Ltd; Chair. R. W. PIPER; Man. Dir O. G. CLARK.

**Epic Energy:** GPOB 657, Brisbane, Qld 4001; tel. (7) 3218-1600; fax (7) 3218-1650; internet www.epicenergy.com.au; Australia's largest gas transmission co; privately owned.

### TRADE UNIONS

**Australian Council of Trade Unions (ACTU):** North Wing, Trades Hall, 54 Victoria St, Carlton South, Vic 3053; tel. (3) 9663-5266; fax (3) 9663-4051; e-mail mailbox@actu.asn.au; internet www.worksite.actu.asn.au; f. 1927; br. in each state, generally known as a Trades and Labour Council; 51 affiliated trade unions; Pres. JENNIE GEORGE; Sec. GREGORY COMBET.

#### Principal Affiliated Unions

**Association of Professional Engineers, Scientists & Managers, Australia (APESMA):** POB 1272L, Melbourne, Vic 3001; tel. (3) 9695-8800; fax (3) 9696-9312; e-mail info@apesma.asn.au; internet www.apesma.asn.au; Pres. ROB J. ALLEN; Sec. GREG SUTHERLAND; 24,000 mems.

**Australasian Meat Industry Employees' Union (AMIEU):** 377 Sussex St, Sydney, NSW 2000; tel. (2) 9264-2279; fax (2) 9261-1970; e-mail amieu-fed@bigpond.com; Fed. Pres. JOHN PYSING; Fed. Sec. T. R. HANNAN; 27,500 mems.

**Australian Education Union:** POB 1158, South Melbourne, Vic 3205; tel. (3) 9254-1800; fax (3) 9254-1805; e-mail aeu@edunions.labor.net.au; internet www.edunions.labor.net.auaeu; f. 1984; Fed. Pres. SHARAN BURROW; Fed. Sec. ROBERT DURBRIDGE; 157,388 mems.

**Australian Manufacturing Workers' Union/AMWU:** POB 160, Granville, NSW 2142; tel. (2) 9897-9133; fax (2) 9897-9274; e-mail amwu2@amwu.asn.au; internet www.amwu2@amwu.asn.au; Nat. Pres. DAVE GOODGER; Nat. Sec. DOUG CAMERON; 189,000 mems.

**Australian Services Union (ASU):** Ground Floor, 116 Queensberry St, Carlton South, Vic 3053; tel. (3) 9342-1400; fax (3) 9342-1499; e-mail asunatm@asu.asn.au; Nat. Sec. PAUL SLAPE; 165,000 mems.

**Australian Workers' Union (AWU):** Suite 15, 245 Chalmers St, Redfern, NSW 2016; tel. (2) 9690-1022; fax (2) 9690-1020; e-mail nat.office@awu.net.au; internet www.awu.net.au; f. 1886; Nat. Pres. GRAHAM ROBERTS; Nat. Sec. TERRY MUSCAT; 160,000 mems.

**Communications, Electrical, Electronic, Energy, Information, Postal, Plumbing and Allied Services Union of Australia (CEPU):** POB 812, Rockdale, NSW 2216; tel. (2) 9597-4499; fax (2) 9597-6354; e-mail edno@cepu.mpx.com.au; internet www.cepu.asn.au; Nat. Sec. PETER TIGHE; 180,000 mems.

**Community and Public Sector Union (CPSU):** Level 5, 191–199 Thomas St, Haymarket, NSW 2000; tel. (2) 9334-9200; fax (2) 9334-9250; e-mail cpsu@cpsu.org; internet www.cpsu.org; Nat. Pres. MARGARET SEXTON; Nat. Sec. WENDY CRAIG; 250,000 mems.

**Construction, Forestry, Mining and Energy Union (CFMEU):** Box Q235, Queen Victoria Bldg PO, Sydney, NSW 2000; tel. (2) 9290-3699; fax (2) 9299-1685; internet www.cfmeu.asn.au; f. 1992 by amalgamation; Pres. T. SMITH; Sec. J. MAITLAND; 120,000 mems.

**Finance Sector Union of Australia (FSU):** 341 Queen St, Melbourne, Vic 3000; tel. (3) 9261-5300; fax (3) 9670-2940; e-mail fsuinfo@fsunion.org.au; internet www.fsunion.org.au; f. 1991; Nat. Pres. JOY MCSHANE; Nat. Sec. TONY BECK; 85,000 mems.

**Health Services Union of Australia (HSUA):** POB 560, Flemington, Vic 3031; tel. (3) 9376-8242; fax (3) 9376-8243; e-mail hsuno@c031.aone.net.au; Nat. Pres. MICHAEL WILLIAMSON; Nat. Sec. ROBERT ELLIOTT; 90,000 mems.

**Independent Education Union of Australia (IEU):** POB 1301, South Melbourne, Vic 3205; tel. (3) 9254-1830; fax (3) 9254-1835; e-mail ieu@edunions.labor.net.au; internet www.edunions.labor.net.au/ieu; Fed. Sec. LYNNE ROLLEY; Fed. Pres. RICHARD SHEARMAN; 44,000 mems.

**Liquor, Hospitality and Miscellaneous Workers Union (LHMU):** Locked Bag 9, Haymarket, NSW 1240; tel. (2) 9281-9511; fax (2) 9281-4480; e-mail lhmu@lhmu.com.au; internet www.lhmu.org.au; f. 1992; Nat. Pres CHRIS RAPER; Nat. Sec. JEFF LAWRENCE; 150,000 mems.

**Maritime Union of Australia (MUA):** 365 Sussex St, Sydney, NSW 2000; tel. (2) 9267-9134; fax (2) 9261-3481; e-mail muano@mua.asn.au; internet www.mua.tcp.net.au; f. 1993; Nat. Sec. JOHN COOMBS; 10,619 mems.

**Media, Entertainment & Arts Alliance (MEAA):** POB 723, Strawberry Hills, NSW 2012; tel. (2) 9333-0999; fax (2) 9333-0933; e-mail meaa@alliance.aust.com; internet www.alliance.aust.com; Jt Fed. Secs ANNE BRITTON, CHRISTOPHER WARREN; 30,000 mems.

**National Union of Workers (NUW):** POB 343, North Melbourne, Vic 3051; tel. (3) 9287-1850; fax (3) 9287-1818; e-mail nuw@c031.aone.net.au; Gen. Sec. GREG SWORD; Gen. Pres. DENIS LENNEN; 100,000 mems.

**Rail, Tram and Bus Union (RTBU):** 83–89 Renwick St, Redfern, NSW 2016; tel. (2) 9310-3966; fax (2) 9319-2096; e-mail publictu@magna.com.au; internet www.ptuwa.asn.au; Nat. Pres. R. PLAIN; Nat. Sec. R. G. JOWETT; 38,000 mems.

**Shop, Distributive & Allied Employees Association (SDA):** 5th Floor, 53 Queen St, Melbourne, Vic 3000; tel. (3) 9629-2299; fax (3) 9629-2646; e-mail sdanat@c031.aone.net.au; internet www.sda.org.au; f. 1908; Nat. Pres. DON FARRELL; Nat. Sec. JOE DE BRUYN; 230,000 mems.

**Textile, Clothing and Footwear Union of Australia (TCFUA):** Ground Floor, 28 Anglo Rd, Campsie, NSW 2194; tel. (2) 9789-4188; fax (2) 9789-6510; e-mail tcfua@tcfua.org.au; f. 1919; Pres. BARRY TUBNER; 25,403 mems.

**Transport Workers' Union of Australia (TWU):** Level 2, 18–20 Lincoln Sq., North Carlton, Vic 3053; tel. (3) 9347-0099; fax (3) 9347-2502; e-mail info@twu-federal.asn.au; internet www.twu-federal.asn.au; Fed. Pres. BILL NOONAN; Fed. Sec. JOHN ALLAN; 71,000 mems.

**United Firefighters' Union of Australia (UFU of A):** POB 289, Torrensville, SA 5031; tel. (8) 8352-7211; fax (8) 8234-1031; e-mail ufua@senet.com.au; Nat. Pres. SIMON FLYNN; Nat. Sec. PAUL CAICA; 11,000 mems.

# Transport

**Australian Transport Council:** POB 594, Canberra, ACT 2601; tel. (2) 6274-7851; fax (2) 6274-7703; internet www.dot.gov.au/atc/atchome.htm; f. 1993; mems include: Federal Minister for Transport and Regional Services, State, Territory and New Zealand Ministers responsible for transport, roads and marine and ports; initiates discussion, and reports as necessary, on any matter relating to better co-ordination of transport development, while encouraging modernization and innovation; promotes research; Sec. D. JONES.

**State Transit Authority of New South Wales:** 100 Miller St, North Sydney, NSW 2060; tel. (2) 9245-5777; fax (2) 9245-5710; internet www.sta.nsw.gov.au; operates government buses and ferries in Sydney and Newcastle metropolitan areas; Chair. DAVID HERLIHY; CEO JOHN STOTT.

**TransAdelaide (South Australia):** GPOB 2351, Adelaide, SA 5001; tel. (8) 8218-2200; fax (8) 8218-4399; e-mail info@transadelaide.sa.gov.au; internet www.transadelaide.com.au; f. 1994; fmrly State Transport Authority; operates metropolitan train, bus, tram and Busway services; Gen. Man. SUE FILBY.

### RAILWAYS

In 1997 there were 33,099 km of government-operated railways in Australia.

**National Rail Corporation Ltd:** 85 George St, Parramatta, NSW 2150; tel. (2) 9685-2555; fax (2) 9687-1808; e-mail information@nrc.com.au; internet www.nationalrail.com.au; freight; Chair. P. YOUNG; Man. Dir V. J. GRAHAM.

**Public Transport Corporation (Victoria):** 15th Floor, 589 Collins St, Melbourne, Vic 3000; tel. (3) 9619-1111; f. 1989; Chief Exec. ANDREW NEAL.

**Queensland Rail:** POB 1429, Brisbane, Qld 4001; tel. (7) 3235-2222; fax (7) 3235-1799; Chief Exec. VINCE O'ROURKE.

**State Rail Authority of New South Wales:** POB K349, Haymarket, NSW 1238; tel. (2) 9379-3000; fax (2) 9379-2090; internet www.staterail.nsw.gov.au; f. 1980; responsible for passenger rail and associated coach services in NSW; Chief Exec. SIMON LANE.

**Western Australian Government Railways (Westrail):** Westrail Centre, POB S1422, Perth 6845, WA; tel. (8) 9326-2222; fax (8) 9326-2589; internet www.westrail.wa.gov.au; statutory authority competing in the freight, passenger and related transport markets in southern WA; operates 5,369 main line route-km of track; Commr WAYNE JAMES (acting).

### ROADS

In 1996 there were 810,000 km of roads, including 1,000 km of freeways, a further 103 km of toll roads, 45,889 km of highways, 77,045km of arterial and major roads and 30,596 of secondary tourist and other roads. Local roads in urban areas account for 93,677 km of the network and those in rural localities for 537,278 km.

**Austroads Inc:** POB K659, Haymarket, NSW 2000; tel. (2) 9264-7088; fax (2) 9264-1657; e-mail austroads@austroads.com.au; internet www.austroads.com.au; f. 1989; asscn of road transport and traffic authorities.

### SHIPPING

In December 1998 the Australian merchant fleet comprised 617 vessels, with a total displacement of 2,188,146 grt.

**Adsteam Marine Ltd:** Level 22, 6 O'Connell St, Sydney, NSW 2000; tel. (2) 9232-3955; fax (2) 9232-3988; e-mail info@adsteam.com.au; f. 1875; fmrly Adelaide Steamship Co; Man. Dir DAVID RYAN; Chief Exec. CLAY FREDERICK.

**ANL Ltd (Australian National Line):** POB 2238T, Melbourne, Vic 3001; tel. (3) 9257-0555; fax (3) 9257-0619; f. 1956; shipping agents; coastal and overseas container shipping and coastal bulk shipping; container management services; overseas container services to Hong Kong, Taiwan, the Philippines, Korea, Singapore, Malaysia, Thailand, Indonesia and Japan; extensive transhipment services; Chair. E. G. ANSON; CEO R. B. PERKINS.

**BHP Transport Pty Ltd:** 27th Level, 600 Bourke St, POB 86A, Melbourne, Vic 3000; tel. (3) 9609-3333; fax (3) 9609-2400; Chair. JEREMY ELLIS; Man. Dir JOHN B. PRESCOTT.

**William Holyman and Sons Pty Ltd:** No. 3 Berth, Bell Bay, Tas 7253; tel. (3) 6382-2383; fax (3) 6382-3391; coastal services; Chair. R. J. HOY.

**Howard Smith Ltd:** POB N364, Grosvenor Place, Sydney, NSW 2000; tel. (2) 9230-1777; fax (2) 9251-1190; e-mail info@hst.com.au; harbour towage and other services; Chair. FRANCIS JOHN CONROY; CEO KENNETH JOHN MOSS.

### CIVIL AVIATION

In the sparsely-populated areas of central and western Australia, air transport is extremely important, and Australia has pioneered services such as the Flying Doctor Service to overcome the problems of distance. The country is also well served by international airlines.

**Ansett Australia (Ansett Australia Holdings Ltd):** 501 Swanston St, Melbourne, Vic 3000; tel. (3) 9623-3333; e-mail tracy-Barrie@ansett.com.au; f. 1936; domestic and international passenger and cargo services; Exec. Chair. ROD EDDINGTON.

**Eastern Australia Airlines:** POB 538, Mascot, Sydney, NSW 2020; tel. (2) 9691-2333; fax (2) 9693-2715; internet www.qantas.com.au; subsidiary of Qantas; domestic flights; Gen. Man. NEIL SHEA.

**National Jet Systems:** Level 9, Southgate House, 435 King William St, Adelaide, SA 5000; tel. (8) 8304-5600; fax (8) 8304-5650; internet www.natjet.com.au; f. 1989; domestic services; Chair. and Chief Exec. WARREN SEYMOUR.

**Qantas Airways Ltd:** Qantas Centre, 203 Coward St, Mascot, NSW 2020; tel. (2) 9691-3636; fax (2) 9691-3339; internet www.qantas.com.au; f. 1920 as Queensland and Northern Territory Aerial Services; Australian Govt became sole owner in 1947; merged with Australian Airlines in Sept. 1992; British Airways purchased 25% in March 1993; remaining 75% transferred to private sector in 1995; services throughout Australia and to 36 countries, including destinations in Europe, Africa, the USA, Canada, South America, Asia, the Pacific and New Zealand; Chair. GARY PEMBERTON; CEO JAMES STRONG.

**Sunstate Airlines:** Lobby 3, Level 2, 153 Campbell St, Bowen Hills, Qld 4006; tel. (7) 3308-9022; fax (7) 3308-9088; f. 1982; wholly owned by Qantas; operates passenger services within Queensland and to Newcastle (NSW) and Lord Howe Island; Gen. Man. ASHLEY KILROY.

# Tourism

The main attractions are the cosmopolitan cities, the Great Barrier Reef, the Blue Mountains, water sports and also winter sports in the Australian Alps, notably the Snowy Mountains. The town of Alice Springs, the Aboriginal culture and the sandstone monolith of Ayers Rock (Uluru) are among the attractions of the desert interior. Much of Australia's wildlife is unique to the country. Australia received 4,167,206 foreign visitors in 1998. The majority of visitors come from Japan (751,107 in 1998) and other Asian countries, New Zealand (709,390 in 1998), Europe and the USA. Receipts totalled $A16,300m. in 1998. The 2000 Olympic Games were to be held in Sydney in September.

**Australian Tourist Commission:** GPO 2721, Sydney, NSW 1006; Level 4, 80 William St, Woolloomooloo, Sydney, NSW 2011; tel. (2) 9360-1111; fax (2) 9331-6469; internet www.atc.net.au; f. 1967 for promotion of international inbound tourism; 11 offices, of which 10 are overseas; Chair. DON MORRIS; Man. Dir JOHN MORSE.

# AUSTRALIAN EXTERNAL TERRITORIES

# CHRISTMAS ISLAND

## Introduction

Christmas Island lies 360 km south of Java Head (Indonesia) in the Indian Ocean. The nearest point on the Australian coast is North West Cape, 1,408 km to the south-east. Christmas Island has no indigenous population. The population was 1,906 at the 1996 census (compared with 1,275 in 1991), comprising mainly ethnic Chinese (some 70%), but there were large minorities of Malays (about 10%) and Europeans (about 20%). A variety of languages are spoken, but English is the official language. The predominant religious affiliation is Buddhist (55% in 1991). The principal settlement and only anchorage is Flying Fish Cove.

Following annexation by the United Kingdom in 1888, Christmas Island was incorporated for administrative purposes with the Straits Settlements (now Singapore and part of Malaysia) in 1900. Japanese forces occupied the island from March 1942 until the end of the Second World War, and in 1946 Christmas Island became a dependency of Singapore. Administration was transferred to the United Kingdom on 1 January 1958, pending final transfer to Australia, effected on 1 October 1958. The Australian Government appointed Official Representatives to the Territory until 1968, when new legislation provided for an Administrator, appointed by the Governor-General. Responsibility for administration lies with the Minister for Regional Services, Territories and Local Government. In 1980 an Advisory Council was established for the Administrator to consult. In 1984 the Christmas Island Services Corporation was created to perform those functions which are normally the responsibility of municipal government. This body was placed under the direction of the Christmas Island Assembly, the first elections to which took place in September 1985. Nine members were elected for one-year terms. In November 1987 the Assembly was dissolved, and the Administrator empowered to perform its functions. The Corporation was superseded by the Christmas Island Shire Council in 1992.

In May 1994 an unofficial referendum on the island's status was held concurrently with local government elections. At the poll, sponsored by the Union of Christmas Island Workers, the islanders rejected an option to secede from Australia, but more than 85% of voters favoured increased local government control. The referendum was prompted, in part, by the Australian Government's plans to abolish the island's duty-free status (which had become a considerable source of revenue).

Since 1981 all residents of the island have been eligible to acquire Australian citizenship. In 1984 the Australian Government extended social security, health and education benefits to the island, and enfranchised Australian citizens resident there. Full income-tax liability was introduced in the late 1980s.

The economy has been based on the recovery of phosphates. During the year ending 30 June 1984 about 463,000 metric tons were exported to Australia, 332,000 tons to New Zealand and 341,000 tons to other countries. Reserves were estimated to be sufficient to enable production to be maintained until the mid-1990s. In November 1987 the Australian Government announced the closure of the phosphate mine, owing to industrial unrest, and mining activity ceased in December. In 1990, however, the Government allowed private operators to recommence phosphate extraction, subject to certain conditions such as the preservation of the rainforest. A total of 220,000 metric tons of phosphates were produced in 1995. In that year an estimated 100 people were employed in the phosphate industry (whose activities consisted largely of the removal of stockpiles). A new 21-year lease, drawn up by the Government and Phosphate Resources Ltd, took effect in February 1998. The agreeement incorporated environmental safeguards and provided for a conservation levy, which was to finance a programme of rainforest rehabilitation.

Efforts have been made to develop the island's considerable potential for tourism. In 1989, in an attempt to protect the natural environment and many rare species of flora and fauna (including the Abbott's Booby and the Christmas frigate bird), the National Park was extended to cover some 70% of the island. A hotel and casino complex, covering 47 ha of land, was opened in November 1993. In 1994 revenue from the development totalled $A500m. A 50-room extension to the complex was constructed in 1995. In early 1997, however, fears for the nascent industry were expressed, following the decision by Ansett Australia to discontinue its twice-weekly air service to the island from September of that year. Despite the subsequent commencement of a weekly flight from Perth, Australia, operated by National Jet Systems, the complex was closed down in April 1998 and some 350 employees were made redundant. The resort's casino licence was cancelled and a liquidator was appointed to realize the complex's assets. The closure of the resort had serious economic and social repercussions for the island.

Proposals for the development of a communications satellite launching facility on the island were under consideration in 1998. An assessment of the environmental impact of the proposed scheme was scheduled for completion by mid-1999.

Between 1992 and 1999 the Australian Government invested an estimated $A110m. in the development of Christmas Island's infrastructure as part of the Christmas Island Rebuilding Programme. The main areas of expenditure under this programme have been a new hospital, the upgrading of ports facilities, school extensions, the construction of housing, power, water supply and sewerage, and the repair and construction of roads. The cost of the island's imports from Australia declined from $A17m. in 1996/97 to $A15m. in 1997/98 when the Territory's exports to that country earned $A7m.

## Statistical Survey

### AREA AND POPULATION

**Area:** 135 sq km (52 sq miles).

**Population:** 2,871 (males 1,918, females 953) at census of 30 June 1981; 1,275 at August 1991 census; 1,906 at 1996 census. *Ethnic Groups* (1981): Chinese 1,587; Malay 693; European 336; Total (incl. others) 2,871. Source: mainly UN, *Demographic Yearbook*.

**Density** (1996): 14.1 per sq km.

**Births and Deaths** (1985): Registered live births 36 (birth rate 15.8 per 1,000); Registered deaths 2.

### MINING

**Natural Phosphates** (official estimates, '000 metric tons): 285 in 1994; 220 in 1995.

### FINANCE

**Currency and Exchange Rates:** Australian currency is used (see p. 493).

### EXTERNAL TRADE

**Principal Trading Partners** (phosphate exports, '000 metric tons, year ending 30 June 1984): Australia 463; New Zealand 332; Total (incl. others) 1,136.

**1997/98** ($A'000): *Imports:* Australia 15,000. *Exports:* Australia 7,000. Source: *Year Book Australia*.

### TRANSPORT

**International Sea-borne Shipping** (estimated freight traffic, '000 metric tons, 1990): Goods loaded 1,290; Goods unloaded 68. Source: UN, *Monthly Bulletin of Statistics*.

### TOURISM

**Visitor Arrivals and Departures by Air:** 27,479 in 1995; 14,513 in 1996; 3,895 in 1997. Source: *Year Book Australia*.

### COMMUNICATIONS MEDIA

**Radio Receivers** (1997): 1,000 in use.

**Television Receivers** (1997): 600 in use.

### EDUCATION

**Pre-primary** (1992): 53 pupils.
**Primary** (1992): 253 pupils.
**Secondary** (1992): 53 pupils.
Source: *The Commonwealth Yearbook*.

## Directory

### The Government

The Administrator, appointed by the Governor-General of Australia and responsible to the Minister for Regional Services, Territories and Local Government, is the senior government representative on the island.

**Administrator:** WILLIAM TAYLOR.

**Administration Headquarters:** POB AAA, Christmas Island 6798, Indian Ocean; tel. (8) 9164-7901; fax (8) 9164-8524.

**Shire of Christmas Island:** George Farm Centre, POB 863, Christmas Island 6798, Indian Ocean; tel.(8) 9164-8300; fax (8) 9164-8304; e-mail soci@iocomm.com.au.

## Judicial System

The judicial system comprises the Supreme Court, District Court, Magistrate's Court and Children's Court.

**Supreme Court:** c/o Govt Offices, Christmas Island 6798, Indian Ocean; tel. (8) 9164-7911; fax (8) 9164-8530; Judges (non-resident): ROBERT SHERATON FRENCH, MALCOLM CAMERON LEE.

**Managing Registrar:** JEFFERY LOW; Govt Offices, Christmas Island 6798, Indian Ocean; tel. (8) 9164-7911; fax (8) 9164-8530.

## Religion

According to the census of 1991, of the 1,275 residents of Christmas Island, some 55% were Buddhists, 10% were Muslims, and 15% were Christians. Within the Christian churches, Christmas Island lies in the jurisdiction of both the Anglican and Roman Catholic Archbishops of Perth, in Western Australia.

## Broadcasting and Communications

### BROADCASTING

#### Radio

**Christmas Island Community Radio Service:** POB AAA, Christmas Island 6798, Indian Ocean; tel. (8) 9164-8316; fax (8) 9164-8315; f. 1967; operated by the Administration since 1991; daily broadcasting service by Radio VLU-2 on 1422 KHz and 102 MHz FM, in English, Malay, Cantonese and Mandarin; Station Man. The Administrator.

**Christmas Island Tropical Radio VLU2:** POB AAA, Christmas Island 6798, Indian Ocean; tel. (8) 9164-8316; fax (8) 9164-8315; Chair. DAVID MASTERS; Station Man. The Administrator.

#### Television

**Christmas Island Television:** POB AAA, Christmas Island 6798, Indian Ocean.

## Finance

### BANKING

#### Commercial Bank

**Westpac Banking Corpn (Australia):** Flying Fish Cove, Christmas Island, Indian Ocean.

## Trade and Industry

**Shire of Christmas Island:** George Farm Centre, POB 863, Christmas Island 6798, Indian Ocean; tel. (8) 9164-8300; fax (8) 9164-8304; e-mail soci@iocomm.com.au; f. 1992 by Territories Law Reform Act to replace Christmas Island Services Corpn; provides local govt services; manages tourism and economic development; Pres. DAVID MCLANE; CEO ANDREW SMOLDERS (acting).

**Christmas Island Chamber of Commerce:** Christmas Island 6798, Indian Ocean; tel. (8) 9164-8249.

**Christmas Island Utilities:** Christmas Island 6798, Indian Ocean; tel. (8) 9164-8504; operates power, port and airport facilities; Gen. Man. BRYN MARTIN.

**Union of Christmas Island Workers—UCIW:** Poon Saan Rd, POB 84, Christmas Island 6798, Indian Ocean; tel. (8) 9164-8471; fax (8) 9164-8470; fmrly represented phosphate workers; Pres. CHAN BOO HWA; Gen. Sec. GORDON THOMSON; 800 mems.

## Transport

There are good roads in the developed areas. National Jet Systems operate a weekly flight from Perth, via the Cocos (Keeling) Islands, and a private Christmas Island-based charter company operates services to Jakarta, Indonesia. In 1997 arrivals and departures by air in Christmas Island totalled 3,895 (compared with 14,513 in the previous year). The Australian National Line (ANL) operates ships to the Australian mainland. Cargo vessels from Perth deliver supplies to the island every four to six weeks. The Joint Island Supply System, established in 1989, provides a shipping service for Christmas Island and the Cocos Islands. The only anchorage is at Flying Fish Cove.

## Tourism

Tourism is a growing sector of the island's economy. Visitors are attracted by the unique flora and fauna, as well as the excellent conditions for scuba-diving and game-fishing.

**Christmas Island Tourism Association/Christmas Island Visitor Information Centre:** POB 63, Christmas Island 6798, Indian Ocean; tel. (8) 9164-8382; fax (8) 9164-8080.

**Christmas Island Tours and Travel:** Christmas Island 6798, Indian Ocean; Dir TAN SIM KIAT.

# COCOS (KEELING) ISLANDS

## Introduction

The Cocos (Keeling) Islands are 27 in number and lie 2,768 km north-west of Perth, in the Indian Ocean. The islands form two low-lying coral atolls, densely covered with coconut palms. The climate is equable, with temperatures varying from 21°C (69°F) to 32°C (88°F), and rainfall of 2,000 mm per year. In 1981 some 58% of the population were of the Cocos Malay community, and 26% were Europeans. The Cocos Malays are descendants of the people brought to the islands by Alexander Hare and of labourers who were subsequently introduced by the Clunies-Ross family (see below). English is the official language, but Cocos Malay and Malay are also widely spoken. Most of the inhabitants are Muslims (56.8% in 1981). Home Island, which had a population of 446 in mid-1992, is where the Cocos Malay community is based. The only other inhabited island is West Island, with a population of 147 in mid-1992, and where most of the European community lives, the administration is based and the airport is located. The total population of the islands was 655 at the 1996 cansus.

The islands were uninhabited when discovered by Capt. William Keeling, of the British East India Company, in 1609, and the first settlement was not established until 1826, by Alexander Hare. The islands were declared a British possession in 1857 and came successively under the authority of the Governors of Ceylon (now Sri Lanka), from 1878, and the Straits Settlements (now Singapore and part of Malaysia), from 1886. Also in 1886 the British Crown granted all land on the islands above the high-water mark to John Clunies-Ross and his heirs and successors in perpetuity. In 1946, when the islands became a dependency of the Colony of Singapore, a resident administrator, responsible to the Governor of Singapore, was appointed. Administration of the islands was transferred to the Commonwealth of Australia on 23 November 1955. The agent of the Australian Government was known as the Official Representative until 1975, when an Administrator was appointed. The Minister for Regional Services, Territories and Local Government is responsible for the governance of the islands. The Territory is part of the Northern Territory Electoral District.

In June 1977 the Australian Government announced new policies concerning the islands, which resulted in its purchase from John Clunies-Ross of the whole of his interests in the islands, with the exception of his residence and associated buildings. The purchase for $A6.5m. took effect on 1 September 1978. An attempt by the Australian Government to acquire Clunies-Ross' remaining property was deemed by the Australian High Court in October 1984 to be unconstitutional.

In July 1979 the Cocos (Keeling) Islands Council was established, with a wide range of functions in the Home Island village area (which the Government transferred to the Council on trust for the benefit of the Cocos Malay community) and, from September 1984, in the greater part of the rest of the Territory.

On 6 April 1984 a referendum to decide the future political status of the islands was held by the Australian Government, with UN observers present. A large majority voted in favour of integration with Australia. As a result, the islanders were to acquire the rights, privileges and obligations of all Australian citizens. In July 1992 the Cocos (Keeling) Islands Council was replaced by the Cocos (Keeling) Islands Shire Council, modelled on the local government and state law of Western Australia.

Following unsuccessful investment in a shipping venture, the Clunies-Ross family was declared bankrupt in mid-1993, and the Australian Government took possession of its property.

Although local fishing is good, some livestock is kept and domestic gardens provide vegetables, bananas and papayas (pawpaws), the islands are not self-sufficient, and other foodstuffs, fuels and consumer items are imported from mainland Australia. A Cocos postal service (including a philatelic bureau) came into operation in September 1979, and revenue from the service is used for the benefit of the community.

Coconuts, grown throughout the islands, are the sole cash crop: total output was an estimated 6,000 metric tons in 1996. Total exports of coconuts in 1984/85 were 202 metric tons. The cost of the islands' imports from Australia increased from $A2m. in 1996/97 to $A5m. in 1997/98. Exports to Australia totalled $A2m. in 1996/97. It was hoped that a tourist industry could be developed to provide an additional source of revenue for the islands by the late 1990s.

Primary education is provided at the schools on Home and West Islands. Secondary education is provided to the age of 16 years on West Island. A bursary scheme enables Cocos Malay children to continue their education on the Australian mainland.

# Statistical Survey

### AREA AND POPULATION

**Area:** 14.2 sq km (5.5 sq miles).

**Population:** 555 (males 298, females 257) at census of 30 June 1981; 647 at census of 1991; 593 (Home Island residents 446, West Island residents 147) at mid-1992; 655 at census of 1996. *Ethnic Groups* (1981): Cocos Malay 320; European 143; Total (incl. others) 555. Source: mainly UN, *Demographic Yearbook*.

**Density** (1996): 46.1 per sq km.

**Births and Deaths** (1986): Registered live births 12 (birth rate 19.8 per 1,000); Registered deaths 2.

### AGRICULTURE

**Production** (FAO estimates, metric tons, 1998): Coconuts 6,000; Copra 1,000. Source: FAO, *Production Yearbook*.

### FINANCE

**Currency and Exchange Rates:** Australian currency is used (see p. 493).

### COMMUNICATIONS MEDIA

**Radio Receivers** (1992): 300 in use.

### EXTERNAL TRADE

**Principal Commodities** (metric tons, year ending 30 June 1985): *Exports*: Coconuts 202. *Imports*: Most requirements come from Australia. The trade deficit is offset by philatelic sales and Australian federal grants and subsidies.

**1996/97** ($A '000): *Imports:* Australia 2,000. *Exports:* Australia 2,000. Source: *Year Book Australia*.

**1997/98** ($A '000): *Imports:* Australia 5,000. *Exports:* Australia n.a. Source: *Year Book Australia*.

# Directory

## The Government

The Administrator, appointed by the Governor-General of Australia and responsible to the Minister for Regional Services, Territories and Local Government, is the senior government representative in the islands.

**Administrator:** WILLIAM TAYLOR (non-resident).

**Administrative Headquarters:** West Island, Cocos (Keeling) Islands 6799, Indian Ocean; tel. (8) 9162-6660; fax (8) 9162-6697.

**Cocos (Keeling) Islands Shire Council:** POB 94, Home Island, Cocos (Keeling) Islands 6799, Indian Ocean; tel. (8) 9162-6649; fax (8) 9162-6668; e-mail info@shire.cc; f. 1992 by Territories Law Reform Act; Pres. MOHAMMED SAID CHONGKIN; CEO BOB JARVIS.

## Judicial System

**Supreme Court, Cocos (Keeling) Islands:** West Island Police Station, Cocos (Keeling) Islands 6799, Indian Ocean; tel. (8) 9162-6660; fax (8) 9162-6691; Judge: ROBERT SHERATON FRENCH; Additional Judge: MALCOLM CAMERON LEE.

**Magistrates' Court, Cocos (Keeling) Islands:** Special Magistrate: (vacant).

**Managing Registrar:** DEB BLASKETT; Cocos (Keeling) Islands 6799, Indian Ocean; tel. (8) 9162-6661; fax (8) 9162-6697.

## Religion

According to the census of 1981, of the 555 residents, 314 (some 57%) were Muslims and 124 (22%) Christians. The majority of Muslims live on Home Island, while most Christians are West Island residents. The Cocos Islands lie within both the Anglican and the Roman Catholic archdioceses of Perth (Western Australia).

## Broadcasting and Communications

### BROADCASTING

#### Radio

**Radio VKW Cocos:** POB 33, Cocos (Keeling) Islands 6799, Indian Ocean; tel. (8) 9162-6666; non-commercial; daily broadcasting service in Cocos Malay and English; Station Man. SEAN LAVERY.

#### Television

A television service, broadcasting Indonesian, Malaysian and Australian satellite television programmes and videotapes of Australian television programmes, began operating on an intermittent basis in September 1992.

## Industry

**Cocos (Keeling) Islands Co-operative Society Ltd:** Home Island, Cocos (Keeling) Islands 6799, Indian Ocean; tel. (8) 9162-6702; fax (8) 9162-6764; f. 1979; conducts the business enterprises of the Cocos Islanders; activities include boat construction and repairs, copra and coconut production, sail-making, stevedoring and airport operation; owns and operates a supermarket and tourist accommodation; Chair. MOHAMMED SAID BIN CHONGKIN; Gen. Man. RONALD TAYLOR.

## Transport

National Jet Systems operate a weekly service from Perth, via Christmas Island, for passengers, supplies and mail to and from the airport on West Island. Cargo vessels from Perth deliver supplies, at intervals of four to six weeks.

**Cocos Trader:** Cocos (Keeling) Islands 6799, Indian Ocean; tel. (8) 9162-6612; shipping agent.

## Tourism

**Cocos Island Tourism Association:** POB 31, Cocos (Keeling) Islands 6799, Indian Ocean; tel. and fax (8) 9162-6790; e-mail jenny.freshwater@cocos-tourism.cc.

# NORFOLK ISLAND

## Introductory Survey

### Location, Climate, Language, Religion, Capital

Norfolk Island lies off the eastern coast of Australia, about 1,400 km east of Brisbane, to the south of New Caledonia and 640 km north of New Zealand. The Territory also comprises uninhabited Phillip Island and Nepean Island, 7 km and 1 km south of the main island respectively. Norfolk Island is hilly and fertile, with a coastline of cliffs and an area of 34.6 sq km (13.3 sq miles). It is about 8 km long and 4.8 km wide. The climate is mild and subtropical, and the average annual rainfall is 1,350 mm, most of which occurs between May and August. The resident population, which numbered 1,772 in August 1996, consists of 'islanders' (descendants of the mutineers from HMS *Bounty*, evacuated from Pitcairn Island, who numbered 683 in 1996) and 'mainlanders' (originally from Australia, New Zealand or the United Kingdom). English is the official language, but a local Polynesian dialect (related to Pitcairnese) is also spoken. Most of the population (70.4% at the 1996 census) adhere to the Christian religion. The capital of the Territory is Kingston.

### Recent History and Economic Affairs

The island was uninhabited when discovered in 1774 by a British expedition, led by Capt. James Cook. Norfolk Island was used as a penal settlement from 1788 to 1814 and again from 1825 to 1855, when it was abandoned. In 1856 it was resettled by 194 emigrants from Pitcairn Island, which had become overpopulated. Norfolk Island was administered as a separate colony until 1897, when it became a dependency of New South Wales. In 1913 control was transferred to the Australian Government. Norfolk Island has a continuing dispute with the Australian Government concerning the island's status as a territory of the Commonwealth of Australia. There have been successive assertions of Norfolk Island's right to self-determination, as a distinct colony.

Under the Norfolk Island Act 1979, Norfolk Island is progressing to responsible legislative and executive government, enabling the Territory to administer its own affairs to the greatest practicable extent. Wide powers are exercised by the nine-member Legislative Assembly and by the Executive Council, comprising the executive members of the Legislative Assembly who have ministerial-type responsibilities. The Act preserves the Australian Government's responsibility for Norfolk Island as a territory under its authority, with the Minister for Regional Services, Territories and Local Government as the responsible minister. The Act indicated that consideration would be given within five years to an extension of the powers of the Legislative Assembly and the political and administrative institutions of Norfolk Island. In 1985 legislative and executive responsibility was assumed by the Norfolk Island government for public works and services, civil defence, betting and gaming, territorial archives and matters relating to the exercise of executive authority. In 1988 further amendments empowered the Legislative Assembly to select a Norfolk Island government auditor (territorial accounts were previously audited by the Commonwealth Auditor-General). The office of Chief Minister was replaced by that of the President of the Legislative Assembly. David Ernest Buffett was reappointed to this post following the May 1992 general election. A lack of consensus among members of the Executive Council on several major issues prompted early legislative elections in April 1994. The newly-elected seventh Legislative Assembly was significant in having three female members. Following elections in April 1997, in which 22 candidates contested the nine seats, George Smith was appointed President (subsequently reverting to the title of Speaker and Chief Minister) of the eighth Legislative Assembly.

In December 1991 the population of Norfolk Island overwhelmingly rejected a proposal, made by the Australian Government, to include the island in the Australian federal electorate. The outcome of the poll led the Australian Government, in June 1992, to announce that it had abandoned the plan. Similarly, in late 1996 a proposal by the Australian Government to combine Norfolk Island's population with that of Canberra for record-keeping purposes was strongly opposed by the islanders.

In late 1997 the Legislative Assembly debated the issue of increased self-determination for the island. Pro-independence supporters argued that the Territory could generate sufficient income by exploiting gas- and oilfields in the island's exclusive economic zone.

Despite the island's natural fertility, agriculture is no longer the principal economic activity. About 400 ha of land are arable. The main crops are Kentia palm seed, cereals, vegetables and fruit. Cattle and pigs are farmed for domestic consumption. Development of a fisheries industry is restricted by the lack of a harbour. Some flowers and plants are grown commercially. The administration is increasing the area devoted to Norfolk Island pine and hardwoods. Seed of the Norfolk Island pine is exported. Potential oil- and gas-bearing sites in the island's waters may provide a possible future source of revenue. A re-export industry has been developed to serve the island's tourist industry. In early 1999 the Norfolk Island Legislative Assembly announced plans to seek assistance from the Australian Government to establish an offshore financial centre on the island.

In 1997/98 imports from Australia cost $A17.6m. (compared with $A23.4m. in the previous year). In 1997/98 imports from New Zealand totalled $NZ7.6m. (compared with $A7.9m. in the previous year). In 1998/99 the cost of imports totalled $A28.7m., while revenue from exports amounted to $A3.0m. The authorities receive revenue from customs duties (some $A3.0m., equivalent to 30.8% of total revenue in 1997/98) and the sale of postage stamps, but tourism is the island's main industry. In 1998/99 there were 36,514 tourist arrivals on the island. In 1985 and 1986 the Governments of Australia and Norfolk Island jointly established the 465-ha Norfolk Island National Park. This was to protect the remaining native forest, which is the habitat of several unique species of flora (including the largest fern in the world) and fauna (such as the Norfolk Island green parrot, the guavabird and the boobook owl). Conservation efforts include the development of Phillip Island as a nature reserve.

### Education

Education is free and compulsory for all children between the ages of six and 15. Pupils attend the government school from infant to secondary level. A total of 328 pupils were enrolled at infant, primary and secondary levels in 1997. Students wishing to follow higher education in Australia are eligible for bursaries and scholarships. The budgetary allocation for education was $A1,524,837 in 1997/98 (equivalent to 15.7% of total expenditure).

### Weights and Measures

The metric system is in force.

## Statistical Survey

Source: The Administration of Norfolk Island, Administration Offices, Kingston, Norfolk Island 2899; tel. 22001; fax 23177.

### AREA AND POPULATION

**Area:** 34.6 sq km (13.3 sq miles).

**Population:** 2,285 (males 1,111, females 1,174), including 373 visitors, at census of 6 August 1991; 1,896 (resident population) at 30 June 1993; 2,181 (males 1,039, females 1,142), including 409 visitors, at census of 6 August 1996.

**Density** (resident population, 1996): 51.2 per sq km.

**Births, Marriages and Deaths** (1996): Live births 15; Marriages 34; Deaths 21.

**Economically Active Population** (persons aged 10 years and over, 1996 census): 1,273 (males 629, females 644).

### FINANCE

**Currency and Exchange Rates:** Australian currency is used (see p. 493).

**Budget** (year ending 30 June 1998): Revenue $A9,780,400 (Customs duties $A3,016,500); Expenditure $A9,685,916 (Education $A1,524,837).

### EXTERNAL TRADE

**1998/99** (year ending 30 June): *Imports*: $A28,669,888, mainly from Australia and New Zealand. *Exports*: $A3,031,725.

### TOURISM

**Visitors** (year ending 30 June): 32,089 in 1996/97; 35,626 in 1997/98; 36,514 in 1998/99.

### COMMUNICATIONS MEDIA

**Radio Receivers** (1996): 2,500 in use.

**Television Receivers** (1996): 1,200 in use.

**Non-daily Newspaper** (1996): 1 (estimated circulation 1,000).

### EDUCATION

**Institution** (1997): 1 state school incorporating infant, primary and secondary levels.

**Teachers** (1997): Full-time 21; Part-time 2.

**Students** (1997): Infants 87; Primary 106; Secondary 135.

# Directory

## The Constitution

The Norfolk Island Act 1979 constitutes the administration of the Territory as a body politic and provides for a responsible legislative and executive system, enabling it to administer its own affairs to the greatest practicable extent. The preamble of the Act states that it is the intention of the Australian Parliament to consider the further extension of powers.

The Act provides for an Administrator, appointed by the Australian Government, who shall administer the government of Norfolk Island as a territory under the authority of the Commonwealth of Australia. The Administrator is required to act on the advice of the Executive Council or the responsible Commonwealth Minister in those matters specified as within their competence. Every proposed law passed by the Legislative Assembly must be effected by the assent of the Administrator, who may grant or withhold that assent, reserve the proposed law for the Governor-General's pleasure or recommend amendments.

The Act provides for the Legislative Assembly and the Executive Council, comprising the executive members of the Assembly who have ministerial-type responsibilities. Both bodies are led by the Speaker of the Legislative Assembly. The nine members of the Legislative Assembly are elected for a term of not more than three years under a cumulative method of voting: each elector is entitled to as many votes (all of equal value) as there are vacancies, but may not give more than four votes to any one candidate. The nine candidates who receive the most votes are declared elected.

## The Government

The Administrator, who is the senior representative of the Commonwealth Government, is appointed by the Governor-General of Australia and is responsible to the Minister for Regional Services, Territories and Local Government. A form of responsible legislative and executive government was extended to the island in 1979, as outlined above.

**Administrator:** Tony Messner (assumed office on 4 August 1997).

### EXECUTIVE COUNCIL
(January 2000)

**Speaker of the Legislative Assembly, Chief Minister and Minister for Finance and Strategic Planning:** George Charles Smith.

**Deputy Speaker:** David Ernest Buffett.

**Minister for Immigration and Resource Management:** Cedric Newton Ion-Robinson.

**Minister for Tourism and Commerce:** James Gary Robertson.

**Minister for Health:** Geoffrey Robert Gardner.

### MINISTRIES

All Ministries are located at: Old Military Barracks, Kingston, Norfolk Island 2899.

### GOVERNMENT OFFICES

**Office of the Administrator:** New Military Barracks, Norfolk Island 2899; tel. 22152; fax 22681.

**Administration of Norfolk Island:** Administration Offices, Kingston, Norfolk Island 2899; tel. 22001; fax 23177; all govt depts; Chief Administrative Officer: Ivens F. Buffett.

## Legislature

### LEGISLATIVE ASSEMBLY

Nine candidates are elected for not more than three years. The most recent general election was held on 30 April 1997.

**Speaker:** George Charles Smith.

**Members:** David Ernest Buffett, John T. Brown, James Gary Robertson, Cedric Newton Ion-Robinson, Geoffrey Robert Gardner, Ronald C. Nobbs, Brian G. Bates, John McCoy.

## Judicial System

**Supreme Court of Norfolk Island:** Kingston; appeals lie to the Federal Court of Australia.

**Judges:** Bryan Alan Beaumont (Chief Justice), Murray Rutledge Wilcox.

## Religion

The majority of the population professes Christianity (70.4%, according to the census of 1996), with the principal denominations being the Church of England (38%), the Uniting Church (14%) and the Catholic Church (11%).

## The Press

**Norfolk Island Government Gazette:** Kingston, Norfolk Island 2899; tel. 22001; fax 23177; weekly.

**Norfolk Islander:** Greenways Press, POB 150, Norfolk Island 2899; tel. 22159; fax 22948; f. 1965; weekly; Co-Editors Tom Lloyd, Tim Lloyd; circ. 1,000.

## Broadcasting and Communications

### BROADCASTING

#### Radio

**Norfolk Island Broadcasting Service:** New Cascade Rd, POB 456, Norfolk Island 2899; tel. 22137; fax 23298; e-mail 2niradio@ni.net.nf; govt-owned; non-commercial; broadcasts 112 hours per week; relays television programmes from Australia; Broadcasting Man. Margaret Meadows.

**Radio VL2NI:** New Cascade Rd, POB 456, Norfolk Island 2899; tel. 22137; fax 23298; e-mail 2niradio@ni.net.nf.

#### Television

**Norfolk Island Broadcasting Service:** (see Radio).

**Norfolk Island Television Service:** f. 1987; govt-owned; relays programmes of Australian Broadcasting Corpn and Special Broadcasting Service Corpn by satellite.

**TV Norfolk (TVN):** locally-operated service featuring programmes of local events and information for tourists.

## Finance

### BANKING

**Commonwealth Banking Corpn** (Australia): Burnt Pine, Norfolk Island 2899; tel. 22144; fax 22805.

**Westpac Banking Corpn Savings Bank Ltd** (Australia): Burnt Pine, Norfolk Island 2899; tel. 22120; fax 22808.

## Trade

**Norfolk Island Chamber of Commerce:** POB 370, Norfolk Island 2899; tel. 22018; fax 23106; e-mail monica@worldtraders.nf; f. 1966; affiliated to the Australian Chamber of Commerce; 60 mems; Pres. Bruce Walker; Sec. Monica Anderson.

## Transport

### ROADS

There are about 100 km of roads, including 85 km of sealed road.

### SHIPPING

Norfolk Island is served by the three shipping lines, Neptune Shipping, Pacific Direct Line and Roslyndale Shipping Company Pty Ltd. A small tanker from Nouméa (New Caledonia) delivers petroleum products to the island and another from Australia delivers liquid propane gas.

### CIVIL AVIATION

Norfolk Island has one airport, with two runways (of 1,900 m and 1,550 m), capable of taking medium-sized jet-engined aircraft. Air New Zealand operates a twice-weekly direct service between Christchurch and Norfolk Island (via Auckland). Charter flights from New Caledonia also serve the island. The cessation of scheduled services from Australia by Ansett Australia in 1997 had an adverse effect on the island's important tourist industry. As a consequence, Norfolk Jet Express was established to provide a weekly service to Australia, and Flight West Airlines began to operate a flight from Brisbane and Sydney (Australia) to the island. In early 1999 Air Nauru announced its decision to operate a twice-weekly charter flight service from Sydney, under contract with Norfolk Jet Express.

## Tourism

Visitor arrivals totalled 36,514 in 1998/99.

**Norfolk Island Visitors Information Centre:** Taylors Rd, Burnt Pine, POB 211, Norfolk Island 2899; tel. 22147; fax 23109; e-mail info@nigtb.gov.nf; internet www.norfolkisland.nf; Gen. Man. JOANNE LIBLINE.

# OTHER TERRITORIES

## Territory of Ashmore and Cartier Islands

The Ashmore Islands (known as West, Middle and East Islands) and Cartier Island are situated in the Timor Sea, about 850 km and 790 km west of Darwin respectively. The Ashmore Islands cover some 93 ha of land and Cartier Island covers 0.4 ha. The islands are small and uninhabited, consisting of sand and coral, surrounded by shoals and reefs. Grass is the main vegetation. Maximum elevation is about 2.5 m above sea-level. The islands abound in birdlife, sea-cucumbers (*bêches-de-mer*) and, seasonally, turtles.

The United Kingdom took formal possession of the Ashmore Islands in 1878, and Cartier Island was annexed in 1909. The islands were placed under the authority of the Commonwealth of Australia in 1931. They were annexed to, and deemed to form part of, the Northern Territory of Australia in 1938. On 1 July 1978 the Australian Government assumed direct responsibility for the administration of the islands, which rests with a parliamentary secretary appointed by the Minister for Regional Services, Territories and Local Government. Periodic visits are made to the islands by the Royal Australian Navy and aircraft of the Royal Australian Air Force, and the Civil Coastal Surveillance Service makes aerial surveys of the islands and neighbouring waters. The oilfields of Jabiru and Challis are located in waters adjacent to the Territory.

In August 1983 Ashmore Reef was declared a national nature reserve. An agreement between Australia and Indonesia permits Indonesian traditional fishermen to continue fishing in the territorial waters and to land on West Island to obtain supplies of fresh water. In 1985 the Australian Government extended the laws of the Northern Territory to apply in Ashmore and Cartier, and decided to contract a vessel to be stationed at Ashmore Reef during the Indonesian fishing season (March–November) to monitor the fishermen.

## Australian Antarctic Territory

The Australian Antarctic Territory was established by Order in Council in February 1933 and proclaimed in August 1936, subsequent to the Australian Antarctic Territory Acceptance Act (1933). It consists of the portion of Antarctica (divided by the French territory of Terre Adélie) lying between 45°E and 136°E, and between 142°E and 160°E. The Antarctic Division of the Department of the Environment, Sport and Territories (subsequently renamed the Department of the Environment and Heritage) was established in 1948 as a permanent agency, and to administer and provide support for the Australian National Antarctic Research Expeditions (ANARE), which maintains three permanent scientific stations (Mawson, Davis and Casey) in the Territory. The area of the Territory is estimated to be 5,896,500 sq km (2,276,650 sq miles), and there are no permanent inhabitants, although there is a permanent presence of scientific personnel. In late 1997 the Antarctic Science Advisory Committee suggested closing two of Australia's three research stations (Mawson and Casey), partly as a result of the increasing automation of data-gathering, and the establishment of an airline service and a base for adventure tourism. Environmentalists expressed alarm at proposals in the late 1990s to encourage tourism in the Territory, which, they claimed, could damage the area's sensitive ecology. The Territory is administered by the Antarctic Division of the Department of the Environment and Heritage. Australia is a signatory to the Antarctic Treaty (see p. 433).

## Coral Sea Islands Territory

The Coral Sea Islands became a Territory of the Commonwealth of Australia under the Coral Sea Islands Act of 1969. The Territory lies east of Queensland, between the Great Barrier Reef and longitude 156° 06'E, and between latitude 12°S and 24°S, and comprises several islands and reefs. The islands are composed largely of sand and coral, and have no permanent fresh water supply, but some have a cover of grass and scrub. The area has been known as a notorious hazard to shipping since the 19th century, the danger of the reefs being compounded by shifting sand cays and occasional tropical cyclones. The Coral Sea Islands have been acquired by Australia by numerous acts of sovereignty since the early years of the 20th century.

Spread over a sea area of approximately 780,000 sq km (300,000 sq miles), all the islands and reefs in the Territory are very small, totalling only a few sq km of land area. They include Cato Island, Chilcott Islet in the Coringa Group, and the Willis Group. In 1997 the Coral Sea Islands Act was amended to include Elizabeth and Middleton Reefs. A meteorological station, operated by the Commonwealth Bureau of Meteorology and with a staff of four, has provided a service on one of the Willis Group since 1921. The other islands are uninhabited. There are eight automatic weather stations (on Cato Island, Flinders Reef, Frederick Reef, Holmes Reef, Lihou Reef, Creal Reef, Marion Reef and Gannet Cay) and several navigation aids distributed throughout the Territory.

The Act constituting the Territory did not establish an administration on the islands, but provides means of controlling the activities of those who visit them. The Lihou Reef and Coringa-Herald National Nature Reserves were established in 1982 to provide protection for the wide variety of terrestrial and marine wildlife, which include rare species of birds and sea turtles (one of which is the largest, and among the most endangered, of the world's species of sea turtle). The Australian Government has concluded agreements for the protection of endangered and migratory birds with Japan and the People's Republic of China. The Governor-General of Australia is empowered to make ordinances for the peace, order and good government of the Territory and, by ordinance, the laws of the Australian Capital Territory apply. The Supreme Court and Court of Petty Sessions of Norfolk Island have jurisdiction in the Territory. The Territory is administered by a parliamentary secretary appointed by the Minister for Regional Services, Territories and Local Government, and the area is visited regularly by the Royal Australian Navy.

## Territory of Heard Island and the McDonald Islands

These islands are situated about 4,000 km (2,500 miles) south-west of Perth, Western Australia. The Territory, consisting of Heard Island, Shag Island (8 km north of Heard) and the McDonald Islands, is almost entirely covered in ice and has a total area of 369 sq km (142 sq miles). The Territory has been administered by the Australian Government since December 1947, when it established a scientific research station on Heard Island (which functioned until 1955) and the United Kingdom ceded its claim to sovereignty. There are no permanent inhabitants, but Australian expeditions visit occasionally. The island is of considerable scientific interest, as it is believed to be one of the few Antarctic habitats uncontaminated by introduced organisms. Heard Island is about 44 km long and 20 km wide and possesses an active volcano, named Big Ben. In January 1991 an international team of scientists travelled to Heard Island to conduct research involving the transmission of sound waves, beneath the surface of the ocean, in order to monitor any evidence of the 'greenhouse effect' (melting of polar ice and the rise in sea-level as a consequence of pollution). The pulses of sound, which travel at a speed largely influenced by temperature, were to be received at various places around the world, with international co-operation. Heard Island was chosen for the experiment because of its unique location, from which direct paths to the five principal oceans extend. The McDonald Islands, with an area of about 1 sq km (0.4 sq miles), lie some 42 km west of Heard Island. In late 1997 Heard Island and the McDonald Islands were accorded World Heritage status by UNESCO in recognition of their outstanding universal significance as a natural landmark. In mid-1999 concern was expressed that stocks of the Patagonian toothfish in the waters around the islands were becoming depleted as a result of over-exploitation, mainly by illegal operators. The islands are administered by the Antarctic Division of the Department of the Environment and Heritage.

# AUSTRIA

## Introductory Survey

**Location, Climate, Language, Religion, Flag, Capital**

The Republic of Austria lies in central Europe, bordered by Switzerland and Liechtenstein to the west, by Germany and the Czech Republic to the north, by Hungary and Slovakia to the east, and by Italy and Slovenia to the south. The climate varies sharply, owing to great differences in elevation. The mean annual temperature lies between 7°C and 9°C (45°F and 48°F). The population is 99% German-speaking, with small Croat and Slovene-speaking minorities. The majority of the inhabitants profess Christianity: about 74% are Roman Catholics and about 5% are Protestants. The national flag (proportions 3 by 2) consists of three equal horizontal stripes, of red, white and red. The state flag has, in addition, the coat of arms (a small shield, with horizontal stripes of red separated by a white stripe, superimposed on a black eagle, wearing a golden crown and holding a sickle and a hammer in its feet, with a broken chain between the legs) in the centre. The capital is Vienna (Wien).

**Recent History**

Austria was formerly the centre of the Austrian (later Austro-Hungarian) Empire, which comprised a large part of central Europe. The Empire, under the Habsburg dynasty, was dissolved in 1918, at the end of the First World War, and Austria proper became a republic. The first post-war Council of Ministers was a coalition led by Dr Karl Renner, who remained Chancellor until 1920, when a new Constitution introduced a federal form of government. Many of Austria's inhabitants favoured union with Germany but this was forbidden by the post-war peace treaties. In March 1938, however, Austria was occupied by Nazi Germany's armed forces and incorporated into the German Reich, led by the Austrian-born Adolf Hitler.

After Hitler's defeat in Austria, a provisional Government, under Dr Renner, was established in April 1945. In July, following Germany's surrender to the Allied forces, Austria was divided into four zones, occupied by forces of the USA, the USSR, the United Kingdom and France. At the first post-war elections to the 165-seat Nationalrat (National Council), held in November 1945, the conservative Österreichische Volkspartei (ÖVP, Austrian People's Party) won 85 seats and the Sozialistische Partei Österreichs (SPÖ, Socialist Party of Austria) secured 76. The two parties formed a coalition Government. In December Dr Renner became the first Federal President of the second Austrian Republic, holding office until his death in December 1950. However, it was not until May 1955 that the four powers signed a State Treaty with Austria, ending the occupation and recognizing Austrian independence, effective from 27 July; occupation forces left in October.

More than 20 years of coalition government came to an end in April 1966 with the formation of a Council of Ministers by the ÖVP alone. Dr Josef Klaus, the Federal Chancellor since April 1964, remained in office. The SPÖ achieved a relative majority in the March 1970 general election and formed a minority Government, with Dr Bruno Kreisky (a former Minister of Foreign Affairs, who had been party leader since 1967) as Chancellor. In April 1971 the incumbent President, Franz Jonas of the SPÖ, was re-elected, defeating the ÖVP candidate, Dr Kurt Waldheim, a former Minister of Foreign Affairs (who subsequently served two five-year terms as UN Secretary-General, beginning in January 1972). The SPÖ won an absolute majority of seats in the Nationalrat at general elections in October 1971 (when the number of seats was increased from 165 to 183) and October 1975. President Jonas died in April 1974, and the subsequent presidential election, held in June, was won by Dr Rudolf Kirchschläger, the Minister of Foreign Affairs since 1970. He was re-elected for a second six-year term in 1980.

In November 1978 a government proposal to commission Austria's first nuclear power plant was defeated in a national referendum. Despite expectations that Chancellor Kreisky would resign, he received full support from the SPÖ and emerged in an apparently even stronger position. At the general election in May 1979 the SPÖ increased its majority in the Nationalrat. The general election of April 1983, however, marked the end of the 13-year era of one-party government: the SPÖ lost its absolute majority in the Nationalrat and Kreisky, unwilling to participate in a coalition, resigned as Chancellor. The reduction in the SPÖ's representation was partly attributed to the emergence of two environmentalist 'Green' parties, both founded in 1982. The two parties together received more than 3% of the total votes, but failed to win any seats. Kreisky's successor, Dr Fred Sinowatz (the former Vice-Chancellor and Minister of Education), took office in May, leading a coalition of the SPÖ and the right-of-centre Freiheitliche Partei Österreichs (FPÖ, Freedom Party of Austria). The new Government continued the social welfare policy that had been pursued by its predecessor, in addition to maintaining Austria's foreign policy of 'active neutrality'.

A presidential election was held in May 1986 to choose a successor to Kirchschläger. The SPÖ candidate was Dr Kurt Steyrer (the Minister of Health and Environment), while Dr Waldheim, the former UN Secretary-General, stood as an independent candidate, although with the support of the ÖVP. The campaign was dominated by allegations that Waldheim, a former officer in the army of Nazi Germany, had been implicated in atrocities committed by the Nazis in the Balkans during 1942–45; the ensuing controversy divided the country and brought unexpected international attention to the election. Waldheim won a run-off ballot in June 1986, with 54% of the votes. The defeat of the SPÖ presidential candidate led Chancellor Sinowatz and four of his ministers to resign. Dr Franz Vranitzky, hitherto the Minister of Finance, became the new Chancellor. In September the FPÖ elected a controversial new leader, Dr Jörg Haider, who represented the far right wing of his party. This precipitated the end of the partnership between the SPÖ and the FPÖ, and the general election for the Nationalrat, scheduled for April 1987, was brought forward to November 1986. No party won an absolute majority: the SPÖ took 80 seats, the ÖVP 77, the FPÖ 18 and an alliance of three 'Green' parties eight. Following several weeks of negotiations, a 'grand coalition' of the SPÖ and the ÖVP, with Vranitzky as Chancellor, was formed in January 1987.

Waldheim's election to the presidency was controversial both domestically and internationally, and Austria's relations with Israel and the USA, in particular, were severely strained. In February 1988 a specially-appointed international commission of historians concluded that Waldheim must have been aware of the atrocities that had been committed. Waldheim refused to resign, but in June 1991 he announced that he would not seek a second presidential term.

At the general election held in October 1990 the SPÖ retained its position as the largest single party, securing 43% of the votes and increasing its number of seats in the Nationalrat by one, to 81. The ÖVP, however, suffered a considerable reverse: with 32% of the votes, it obtained 60 seats in the Nationalrat, a loss of 17. The FPÖ received 17% of the votes, increasing its representation in the Nationalrat by 15 seats, to 33. The FPÖ's success was attributed, in large part, to its support of restricted immigration, especially from eastern Europe. The Grüne Alternative Liste (GAL, Green Alternative List), an informal electoral alliance comprising Die Grüne Alternative (The Green Alternative) and the Vereinte Grüne Österreichs (United Green Party of Austria), increased 'Green' representation by one seat, to nine. In December, following several weeks of negotiations, the SPÖ and the ÖVP formed a new coalition Government, again led by Vranitzky.

A congress of the SPÖ held in June 1991 voted to revert to the party's original name, the Sozialdemokratische Partei Österreichs (SPÖ, Social-Democratic Party of Austria). In the same month the FPÖ leader, Dr Haider, was dismissed as Governor of Carinthia (Kärnten) after publicly praising Hitler's employment policies. In December the Nationalrat approved government legislation whereby Austria became the only country in Europe able to reject asylum requests from individuals without identity papers. Following the imprisonment, in January 1992, of a prominent right-wing activist for demanding the restoration of the Nazi party, and the subsequent fire-bombing of a refugee hostel by neo-Nazis in northern Austria, the Nationalrat voted unanimously in February to amend anti-Nazi legislation. The minimum prison sentence for Nazi agitation was reduced from five years to one year (in order to increase the number of successful prosecutions) and denial of the Nazi Holocaust was made a criminal offence.

At the presidential election held in April 1992 the two main candidates were Dr Rudolf Streicher (hitherto the Minister of Public Economy and Transport), for the SPÖ, and Dr Thomas Klestil (a former ambassador to the USA), representing the ÖVP. No candidate achieved the required 50% of the vote at the first ballot, but in the second 'run-off' ballot, held in May, Klestil received almost 57% of the votes; he assumed the presidency in July.

In June 1992 a 32-year-old dispute between Austria and Italy was resolved when Austria formally accepted autonomy proposals for Italy's German-speaking Trentino-Alto Adige (South Tyrol) region. In January 1993 the FPÖ organized a national petition seeking to require the Nationalrat to debate the introduction of legislation that would halt immigration into Austria and impose stricter controls on foreign residents in the country (the estimated number of whom had increased from 350,000 to 600,000 since 1989). Although the petition was signed by 7.4% of the electorate (417,000 signatures, compared with the constitutional requirement of 100,000 to force parliamentary debate), the result was considered disappointing by the FPÖ. The initiative was strongly opposed by a broad coalition of politicians, church leaders and intellectuals. In February 1993 five FPÖ deputies in the Nationalrat left the party, partly in protest at the petition on immigration, and formed a new political organization, the Liberales Forum (LiF, Liberal Forum), under the leadership of Dr Heide Schmidt, hitherto the Vice-President of the FPÖ. In December four campaigners for tolerance towards immigrant and refugee communities, including the Mayor of Vienna, were injured by letter-bombs. (In March 1999 a lone right-wing extremist was sentenced to life imprisonment, having been found guilty of perpetrating these and other bomb attacks during the 1990s against members and supporters of ethnic minorities, including an assault in February 1995 which killed four gypsies.)

In late 1993 an ongoing debate over Austria's future in Europe intensified when the European Union (EU, see p. 172) set a deadline of 1 March 1994 by which time the conditions of Austria's entry into the Union (pending a national referendum) were to be agreed. Austria strongly defended its right to preserve its neutrality, to uphold higher environmental standards and to impose restrictions on the transit of road-freight traffic through the Austrian Alps. Eventually a number of compromises were reached, including an extension of the existing limit on lorry transit traffic until 2001. At the ensuing national referendum on the terms of Austria's membership of the EU, held in June 1994, some two-thirds of voters (66.4%) supported Austria's entry into the Union. Following the referendum Austria announced plans to sign NATO's Partnership for Peace programme (see p. 228). Austria was formally admitted to the EU on 1 January 1995. Observer status at Western European Union (see p. 268) was subsequently granted.

At the general election held in October 1994 the ruling coalition lost its two-thirds' majority in the Nationalrat. The SPÖ obtained 66 seats (winning 35% of the votes), the ÖVP took 52 seats (with 28% of the votes), and the FPÖ (which had campaigned against Austria's accession to the EU) increased its share of the votes by 6%, to 23%, securing 42 seats. The GAL and the LiF also made gains, winning 13 and 10 seats respectively. The success of the FPÖ's populist campaign, which had concentrated on countering corruption and immigration and had advocated referendum- rather than parliamentary-based governance, unsettled the Austrian political establishment after years of relative consensus. At the end of November, following protracted negotiations, the SPÖ and ÖVP finally agreed to form a new coalition Government, with Vranitzky remaining as Chancellor.

The new SPÖ-ÖVP coalition was beleaguered by disagreements, mainly concerning differences in approach to the urgent need to reduce the annual budgetary deficit in compliance with Austria's commitment, as a member of the EU, to future economic and monetary union (EMU). In March 1995 four ministers resigned from the Government, including the Minister of Finance, Ferdinand Lacina, whose draft 1995 budget, containing several economic austerity measures, had generated widespread adverse criticism. In April Dr Erhard Busek, the Vice-Chancellor and Minister of Education and Culture, resigned from both posts and was replaced as Chairman of the ÖVP by Dr Wolfgang Schüssel; Busek had been widely blamed for the ruling coalition's poor performance at the October 1994 election. A reorganization of ministerial posts was undertaken at the end of April 1995. In October a deepening rift between the SPÖ and ÖVP regarding the means of curtailing the 1996 budgetary deficit (with the former advocating increased taxation measures and the latter proposing to restrain public expenditure) proved irreconcilable, culminating in the collapse of the coalition. Consequently a new general election was held in December 1995. The SPÖ improved upon its disappointing performance at the previous election, receiving 38.1% of the votes cast and winning 71 of the 183 seats in the Nationalrat. The ÖVP secured 28.3% of the votes (obtaining 53 seats), the Freiheitlichen (as the FPÖ had been popularly restyled in January 1995) 21.9% (40 seats), the LiF 5.5% (10 seats) and the GAL 4.8% (nine seats). In early March 1996, following lengthy negotiations, the SPÖ and ÖVP agreed an economic programme and formed a new coalition Government, with Vranitzky remaining as Chancellor. In June the Minister of Economic Affairs, Johannes Ditz of the ÖVP, resigned, reportedly following disagreements within his party over the pace of economic reform. In December tensions arose in the governing coalition regarding the impending sale of Creditanstalt-Bankverein (traditionally aligned with the ÖVP) to Bank Austria AG (controlled by the SPÖ-dominated Vienna city council); in the following month (when the sale was concluded) an agreement was reached, whereby the ownership of both banks was to be substantially depoliticized. In mid-January 1997 Vranitzky unexpectedly resigned as Chancellor. Viktor Klima, the Minister of Finance, was appointed as his successor, both as Chancellor and as Chairman of the SPÖ, and the Council of Ministers was reorganized.

Meanwhile, mounting popular disillusionment with Austria's membership of the EU was reflected in the results of the first national elections to the European Parliament, which took place in October 1996. The Freiheitlichen, which continued to oppose EU membership, won an unprecedented 27.6% of the votes cast, at the expense of the SPÖ, which registered its worst ever election performance, with 29.1% of the votes. The ÖVP secured 29.6% of the votes. At concurrent elections to the Vienna city administration the SPÖ lost the absolute majority of seats that it had held since the end of the Second World War, while the Freiheitlichen increased their representation. The election results were regarded as a protest against the ruling coalition's alleged misrepresentation, prior to the June 1994 referendum, of the immediate effects of admission to the EU; the Government's programme of economic austerity measures was particularly unpopular, while demands by the Union that Austria abolish anonymously-held bank accounts were also resented. In early 1998 the Freiheitlichen abandoned an attempt to petition the Nationalrat to force a referendum on EMU, as the initiative did not receive significant support. During the first half of that year several of the party's functionaries were implicated in a financial scandal. Austria assumed the EU presidency for the first time in July 1998.

In March 1998, following months of debate, the Government announced that Austria would not apply to join NATO, and would thereby preserve its traditional neutrality (as favoured by the SPÖ, but opposed by the ÖVP). Nevertheless, in early April 1999 Austria, in conjunction with the three other officially neutral EU member states, signed an EU declaration stating that the ongoing bombing of Serbia by NATO forces was 'both necessary and warranted'.

At the presidential election held in April 1998, which was contested by five candidates, Klestil was re-elected emphatically, winning 63.5% of the votes. The Freiheitlichen made significant gains at regional elections in early March 1999, becoming the dominant party, with 42.1% of the votes, in Dr Haider's home province of Carinthia; Haider was subsequently elected Governor of Carinthia (having previously been dismissed from that post in 1991—see above). At elections to the European Parliament, which took place in June 1999, the SPÖ and ÖVP showed improved performances, securing 31.7% and 30.6% of the votes respectively. The Freiheitlichen took 23.5% of the votes cast. The turn-out was, however, relatively low (49.0%). The general election held in early October resulted in unprecedented success for the Freiheitlichen, which, by a narrow margin of 415 votes, took second place ahead of the ÖVP. The SPÖ won 65 of the 183 seats in the Nationalrat (with 33.2% of the votes cast), while the FPÖ and ÖVP both secured 52 seats (with

26.9% of the votes each). The GAL took 14 seats (7.4%). The Freiheitlichen had campaigned for a programme which included a halt to immigration, the obstruction of the projected eastwards expansion of the EU, the radical deregulation of the business sector and the introduction of a uniform low rate of income tax and of hugely increased child allowances for Austrian citizens. Dr Haider appeared to have inflamed popular fears that the planned admission to the EU of Austria's eastern neighbours would flood the domestic market with cheap labour, thereby causing the level of unemployment to rise. During the Freiheitlichen campaign Haider allegedly revived nationalist terminology previously employed by the Nazi regime; nevertheless, he consistently denied embracing neo-Nazi ideology. The election result was most widely regarded as a protest against the 12-year old 'grand' SPÖ-ÖVP coalition, which had acquired a reputation for unwieldy bureaucracy and for sanctioning politically-motivated appointments to public companies. Following the election, protracted negotiations took place with a view to forming a new administration. In late January 2000, following a failed attempt to reconstruct the SPÖ-ÖVP coalition, the SPÖ announced that it would not attempt to form a minority government. At the beginning of February President Klestil reluctantly presided over the inauguration of a Freiheitlichen-ÖVP coalition Government, under the Chancellorship of Dr Schüssel, the ÖVP leader. Dr Haider elected not to participate directly in the new administration, which comprised a Freiheitlichen Vice-Chancellor, Dr Susanne Riess-Passer, and five Freiheitlichen Ministers (including those of Finance, Justice and Defence). Although the new coalition had committed itself to respecting human rights and had adopted a relatively moderate political programme, the participation in government of the Freiheitlichen provoked strong opposition both within Austria (where numerous demonstrations were organized) and abroad. Israel and the USA immediately recalled their ambassadors from Vienna, pending a reassessment of bilateral relations, while Austria's 14 fellow EU member states each suspended bilateral political co-operation, maintaining diplomatic relations at a 'technical' level. It was feared that international disapproval could have a detrimental impact on Austria's tourism sector.

During the late 1990s a number of lawsuits were filed by US interests against several Austrian banks, which were accused of having profited during the Second World War from handling stolen Jewish assets. In November 1999 Bank Austria AG agreed to pay US $33m. in compensation to Holocaust survivors and, furthermore, to establish a humanitarian fund to assist survivors resident in Austria.

The Heads of Government of Austria, Hungary and Slovakia met on several occasions during the late 1990s in order to pursue co-operation on security and economic issues. In September 1999, however, Austria threatened to hinder Slovakia's entry into the EU, in protest at the alleged inadequacy of that country's nuclear safety standards.

## Government

Austria is a federal republic, divided into nine provinces, each with its own provincial assembly and government. Legislative power is held by the bicameral Federal Assembly. The first chamber, the Nationalrat (National Council), has 183 members, elected by universal adult suffrage for four years (subject to dissolution) on the basis of proportional representation. The second chamber, the Bundesrat (Federal Council), has 64 members, elected for varying terms by the provincial assemblies. The Federal President, elected by popular vote for six years, is the Head of State, and normally acts on the advice of the Council of Ministers, which is led by the Federal Chancellor, and which is responsible to the Nationalrat.

## Defence

After the ratification of the State Treaty in 1955, Austria declared its permanent neutrality. To protect its independence, the armed forces were instituted. Austria reaffirmed its neutrality in March 1998, having evaluated the possibility of joining NATO. Military service is compulsory and normally consists of seven months' initial training, followed by a maximum of 30 days' reservist training over 10 years (officers, non-commissioned officers and specialists undergo 60–90 days' reservist training). In August 1999 the total armed forces numbered 40,500 (including 16,600 conscripts).The air force (numbering 4,250, of whom 3,400 were conscripts) is an integral part of the army. Total reserves numbered 100,700, compared with 200,000 in June 1992. The estimated defence budget for 1999 amounted to 21,800m. Schilling.

## Economic Affairs

In 1997, according to estimates by the World Bank, Austria's gross national product (GNP), measured at average 1995–97 prices, was US $225,373m., equivalent to $27,920 per head. During 1990–97, it was estimated, GNP per head increased, in real terms, by an average annual rate of 1.1%. Over the same period, the population increased at an average rate of only 0.6% per year. In 1998, according to preliminary World Bank data, GNP totalled $217,200m. ($26,850 per head). Austria's gross domestic product (GDP) grew, in real terms, at an average annual rate of 2.0% in 1990–97. Real GDP grew by 2.0% in 1996, by 1.2% in 1997 and by 2.9% in 1998.

The contribution of agriculture (including hunting, forestry and fishing) to GDP was 2.3% in 1998. In that year some 6.3% of the economically active population were engaged in the agricultural sector. Austrian farms produce more than 90% of the country's food requirements, and surplus dairy products are exported. The principal crops are wheat, barley, maize and sugar beet. Agricultural production increased at an average annual rate of 0.1% in 1990–97. Compared with the previous year, output remained static in 1996, but rose by 1.6% in 1997. The GDP of the agricultural sector increased, in real terms, by 4.9% in 1998.

Industry (including mining and quarrying, manufacturing, construction and power) contributed 31.4% of GDP in 1998, in which year it engaged 30.5% of the economically active population. Industrial production (not including construction) increased at an average annual rate of 2.7% in 1990–97. Industrial output rose by 0.7% in 1996, by 6.5% in 1997 and by 9.8% in 1998.

In 1998 mining and quarrying contributed 0.4% of GDP and employed 0.3% of the economically active population. The most important indigenous mineral resource is iron ore (2.1m. metric tons, with an iron content of 31%, were mined in 1995). Austria also has deposits of petroleum, lignite, magnesite, lead and some copper. The output of the mining sector declined at an average rate of 2.2% per year during 1990–97, but increased by 10.0% in 1998.

Manufacturing contributed 20.0% of GDP and engaged 20.5% of the economically active population in 1998. Measured by the value of output, the principal branches of manufacturing in 1995 were metals and metal products (accounting for 15.1% of the total), food products (11.7%), wood and paper products (10.1%), non-electric machinery (9.9%) and electrical machinery and telecommunications equipment (9.8%). The production of chemicals and road vehicles are also important activities. The output of the manufacturing sector increased at an average annual rate of 2.8% during 1990–97. It increased by 0.7% in 1996, by 6.8% in 1997 and by 9.1% in 1998.

Power supplies in Austria are provided by petroleum, natural gas, coal and hydroelectric plants. Hydroelectric power resources provide the major domestic source of energy, accounting for 71% of total electricity production in 1986. Austria is heavily dependent on imports of energy, mainly from eastern Europe. Imports of mineral fuels accounted for 4.2% of the total cost of imports in 1998.

The services sector contributed 66.3% of GDP and employed 63.2% of the economically active population in 1998. Tourism has traditionally been a leading source of revenue, providing receipts of about 139,200m. Schilling in 1998.

In 1998 Austria recorded a visible trade deficit of US $4,072m., and the current account of the balance of payments showed a deficit of $4,425m. Much of Austria's trade is conducted with other member countries of the European Union (EU, see p. 172), which accounted for 70.8% of Austria's imports and 64.2% of exports in 1996. In 1998 the principal source of imports (41.8%) was Germany, which was also the principal market for exports (36.0%); Italy is another major trading partner. In mid-1998 about 15,000 joint ventures were reportedly under way between Austrian and eastern European companies.

The federal budget for 1998 produced a deficit of 82,100m. Schilling, equivalent to 3.1% of GDP. The central Government's debt was 1,475,900m. Schilling at 31 December 1997, equivalent to 58.5% of annual GDP. The average annual rate of inflation was 2.8% in 1990–97. Consumer prices increased by 1.8% in 1996, by 1.3% in 1997, and by 0.9% in 1998. In November 1999 some 4.4% of the labour force were unemployed.

Austria joined the EU on 1 January 1995, having resigned its membership of the European Free Trade Association at the end of 1994. The country is also a member of the Organisation for Economic Co-operation and Development (OECD—see p. 232).

In November 1993, following a major restructuring of the state sector during the 1980s, the Government announced further wide-ranging privatization measures, with the dual aim of attracting foreign investors and stimulating the domestic capital market. The measures included the gradual dissolution of the state holding company, Österreichische Industrieholding AG (ÖIAG), and full privatization of the petroleum and chemicals group ÖMV and of two major banks, one of which, Creditanstalt-Bankverein, was acquired by the other, Bank Austria AG, in January 1997, in anticipation of the sale of publicly-held Bank Austria stocks, which took place in February. Upon joining the EU in January 1995 the Government committed itself to compensating certain economic sectors, particularly agriculture, which were likely to be initially adversely affected by alignment with prices in the other EU countries and the removal of protective trade barriers. During the mid-1990s the Government implemented a far-reaching austerity programme, including large reductions in public expenditure, with the aim of curtailing the expanding budget deficit prior to the introduction of a single currency (the euro), which constituted the third stage of economic and monetary union (EMU) among the 15 EU states. The reduction in the general government budgetary deficit from 5.1% of GDP in 1995 to only 2.1% of GDP in 1998 represented a considerable success in this objective. Stage III of EMU, the launch of the euro, commenced (with 11 initial participants, including Austria) at the beginning of January 1999. By the late 1990s foreign investment in Austria had reached an unprecedented level, GDP growth was buoyant, and the country's economic performance was described as 'impressive' by the IMF. Nevertheless, there was some concern that the favourable economic situation was over-reliant on the state of Austria's eastern European export markets.

### Social Welfare

The social insurance system covers all wage-earners and salaried employees, agricultural and non-agricultural self-employed and dependants, regardless of nationality. The coverage is compulsory and provides earnings-related benefits in the event of old age, invalidity, death, sickness, maternity and injuries at work. About 99% of the population are protected. There are separate programmes which provide unemployment insurance, family allowance, long-term care allowances, benefits for war victims, etc. In 1998 Austria had 74,810 hospital beds (one for every 105 inhabitants), and in December 1998 there were 33,700 physicians working in the country. Of total expenditure by the central Government in 1996, 130,800m. Schilling (13.0%) was for health services, while a further 416,070m. Schilling (41.2%) was for social security and welfare. In 1997 total expenditure by the central Government on social welfare amounted to some 725,000m. Schilling.

### Education

The central controlling body is the Federal Ministry of Education and Cultural Affairs. Higher education and research are the responsibility of the Federal Ministry of Science and Transport. Provincial boards (Landesschulräte) supervise school education in each of the nine federal provinces. Expenditure on education by all levels of government in 1997 was 161,308m. Schilling (equivalent to 6.4% of GDP).

Education is free and compulsory between the ages of six and 15 years. All children undergo four years' primary education at a Volksschule, after which they choose between two principal forms of secondary education. This may be a Hauptschule which, after four years, may be followed by one of a variety of schools offering technical, vocational and other specialized training, some of which provide a qualification for university. Alternatively, secondary education may be obtained in an Allgemeinbildende höhere Schule, which provides an eight-year general education covering a wide range of subjects, culminating in the Reifeprüfung or Matura. This gives access to all Austrian universities. In addition, all Austrian citizens over the age of 24, and with professional experience, may attend certain university courses in connection with their professional career or trade.

Opportunities for further education exist at 18 universities as well as 13 colleges of technology, all of which have university status, and schools of art and music. Institutes of adult education (Volkshochschulen) are found in all provinces, as are other centres operated by public authorities, church organizations and the Austrian Trade Union Federation.

### Public Holidays

**2000:** 1 January (New Year's Day), 6 January (Epiphany), 24 April (Easter Monday), 1 May (Labour Day), 1 June (Ascension Day), 12 June (Whit Monday), 22 June (Corpus Christi), 15 August (Assumption), 26 October (National Holiday), 1 November (All Saints' Day), 8 December (Immaculate Conception), 25 December (Christmas Day), 26 December (St Stephen's Day).

**2001:** 1 January (New Year's Day), 6 January (Epiphany), 16 April (Easter Monday), 1 May (Labour Day), 24 May (Ascension Day), 4 June (Whit Monday), 14 June (Corpus Christi), 15 August (Assumption), 26 October (National Holiday), 1 November (All Saints' Day), 8 December (Immaculate Conception), 25 December (Christmas Day), 26 December (St Stephen's Day).

### Weights and Measures

The metric system is in force.

# Statistical Survey

Source (unless otherwise stated): Austrian Central Statistical Office, 1033 Vienna, Hintere Zollamtsstr. 2b; tel. (222) 711-28-76-55; fax (222) 715-68-28; e-mail info@oestat.gv.at; internet www.oestat.gv.at.

## Area and Population

**AREA, POPULATION AND DENSITY**

| | |
|---|---|
| Area (sq km) | 83,858* |
| Population (census results)† | |
| 12 May 1981 | 7,555,338 |
| 15 May 1991 | |
| Males | 3,753,989 |
| Females | 4,041,797 |
| Total | 7,795,786 |
| Population (official estimates at mid-year) | |
| 1996 | 8,067,800 |
| 1997 | 8,072,182 |
| 1998 | 8,078,449 |
| Density (per sq km) at mid-1998 | 96.3 |

* 32,378 sq miles.

† Figures include all foreign workers.

**PROVINCES** (31 December 1998)

| | Area (sq km) | Population ('000) | Density (per sq km) | Capital (with population) |
|---|---|---|---|---|
| Burgenland | 3,965.4 | 279.5 | 70.5 | Eisenstadt (11,706) |
| Kärnten (Carinthia) | 9,533.0 | 564.1 | 59.2 | Klagenfurt (90,765) |
| Niederösterreich (Lower Austria) | 19,173.3 | 1,538.3 | 80.2 | Sankt Pölten (49,099) |
| Oberösterreich (Upper Austria) | 11,979.6 | 1,375.3 | 114.8 | Linz (189,073) |
| Salzburg | 7,154.2 | 514.0 | 71.8 | Salzburg (143,991) |
| Steiermark (Styria) | 16,388.1 | 1,203.6 | 73.4 | Graz (240,513) |
| Tirol (Tyrol) | 12,647.8 | 665.4 | 52.6 | Innsbruck (110,997) |
| Vorarlberg | 2,601.4 | 346.9 | 133.3 | Bregenz (26,452) |
| Wien (Vienna) | 415.0 | 1,606.8 | 3,871.9 | |
| **Total** | 83,858.1 | 8,094.1 | 96.5 | |

**PRINCIPAL TOWNS**
(population at 31 December 1998)

| | | | |
|---|---|---|---|
| Vienna (capital) | 1,606,843 | Klagenfurt | 90,765 |
| Graz | 240,513 | Villach | 57,301 |
| Linz | 189,073 | Wels | 56,558 |
| Salzburg | 143,991 | Sankt Pölten | 49,099 |
| Innsbruck | 110,997 | Dornbirn | 41,541 |

**BIRTHS, MARRIAGES AND DEATHS**

| | Registered live births | | Registered marriages | | Registered deaths | |
|---|---|---|---|---|---|---|
| | Number | Rate (per 1,000) | Number | Rate (per 1,000) | Number | Rate (per 1,000) |
| 1991 | 94,629 | 12.1 | 44,106 | 5.6 | 83,428 | 10.7 |
| 1992 | 95,302 | 12.1 | 45,701 | 5.8 | 83,162 | 10.5 |
| 1993 | 95,227 | 11.9 | 45,014 | 5.6 | 82,517 | 10.3 |
| 1994 | 92,415 | 11.5 | 43,284 | 5.4 | 80,684 | 10.0 |
| 1995 | 88,669 | 11.0 | 42,946 | 5.3 | 81,171 | 10.1 |
| 1996 | 88,809 | 10.9 | 42,298 | 5.2 | 80,790 | 9.9 |
| 1997 | 84,045 | 10.4 | 41,394 | 5.1 | 79,432 | 9.8 |
| 1998 | 81,233 | 10.1 | 39,143 | 4.8 | 78,339 | 9.7 |

**Expectation of life** (years at birth, 1997): Males 74.3; females 80.6.

**ECONOMICALLY ACTIVE POPULATION***
(ISIC Major Divisions, '000 persons aged 15 years and over)

| | 1996 | 1997 | 1998 |
|---|---|---|---|
| Agriculture, hunting, forestry and fishing | 275.3 | 256.0 | 246.4 |
| Mining and quarrying | 10.7 | 9.5 | 11.9 |
| Manufacturing | 824.6 | 795.5 | 795.4 |
| Electricity, gas and water | 35.3 | 38.5 | 36.5 |
| Construction | 341.4 | 334.9 | 341.4 |
| Trade, restaurants and hotels | 825.3 | 845.7 | 848.0 |
| Transport, storage and communications | 237.5 | 239.5 | 250.0 |
| Financing, insurance, real estate and business services | 386.3 | 397.0 | 387.8 |
| Community, social and personal services | 933.8 | 967.8 | 970.7 |
| **Total labour force** | 3,870.2 | 3,884.0 | 3,888.2 |
| Males | 2,216.9 | 2,216.3 | 2,214.1 |
| Females | 1,653.3 | 1,667.8 | 1,674.1 |

* Yearly averages, based on the results of quarterly sample surveys. The figures include unemployed persons ('000): 160.4 in 1996.

# Agriculture

**PRINCIPAL CROPS** ('000 metric tons)

| | 1996 | 1997 | 1998 |
|---|---|---|---|
| Wheat | 1,239.7 | 1,352.3 | 1,341.8 |
| Barley | 1,082.8 | 1,257.8 | 1,211.6 |
| Maize | 1,735.6 | 1,841.7 | 1,646.3 |
| Rye | 156.2 | 207.2 | 236.4 |
| Oats | 152.7 | 196.7 | 164.2 |
| Mixed grain | 50.0 | 47.2 | 43.0 |
| Potatoes | 769.0 | 676.9 | 646.9 |
| Sugar beet | 3,131.3 | 3,011.9 | 3,314.1 |
| Apples | 367.6 | 477.3 | 416.5 |
| Pears | 78.2 | 69.9 | 132.4 |
| Plums | 54.4 | 76.7 | 49.5 |
| Cherries | 21.6 | 21.3 | 30.7 |
| Currants | 15.6 | 19.5 | 19.5 |

Grapes ('000 metric tons): 274 in 1996; 234 in 1997. Source: FAO, *Production Yearbook*.

**LIVESTOCK** ('000 head at December)

| | 1996 | 1997 | 1998 |
|---|---|---|---|
| Horses | 73.2 | 74.2 | 75.3 |
| Cattle | 2,271.9 | 2,197.9 | 2,171.7 |
| Pigs | 3,663.7 | 3,679.9 | 3,810.3 |
| Sheep | 380.9 | 383.7 | 360.8 |
| Goats | 54.5 | 58.3 | 54.2 |
| Chickens | 12,215.2 | 13,949.6 | 13,539.7 |
| Ducks | 101.6 | 95.3 | 95.5 |
| Geese | 20.7 | 22.0 | 26.4 |
| Turkeys | 642.5 | 693.0 | 645.3 |

**LIVESTOCK PRODUCTS** ('000 metric tons)

| | 1996 | 1997 | 1998 |
|---|---|---|---|
| Milk | 3,054.9 | 3,089.8 | 3,279.2 |
| Butter | 41.6 | 41.8 | 42.4 |
| Cheese | 103.6 | 110.7 | 117.4 |
| Hen eggs* | 1,640.1 | 1,668.8 | 1,656.8 |
| Beef and veal | 238.8 | 220.8 | 210.4 |
| Pig meat | 461.9 | 465.4 | 488.1 |
| Poultry meat | 98.1 | 103.8 | 107.2 |

* Millions.

# Forestry

**ROUNDWOOD REMOVALS** ('000 cubic metres, excl. bark)

| | 1996 | 1997 | 1998 |
|---|---|---|---|
| Sawlogs, veneer logs and logs for sleepers | 8,195 | 8,530 | 8,165 |
| Pitprops (mine timber), pulpwood, and other industrial wood | 3,018 | 2,772 | 2,693 |
| Fuel wood | 3,797 | 3,423 | 3,176 |
| **Total** | 15,010 | 14,726 | 14,033 |

**SAWNWOOD PRODUCTION** ('000 cubic metres, incl. railway sleepers)

| | 1995 | 1996 | 1997 |
|---|---|---|---|
| Coniferous (softwood) | 7,552 | 7,950 | 8,122 |
| Broadleaved (hardwood) | 252 | 250 | 185 |
| **Total** | 7,804 | 8,200 | 8,307 |

Source: FAO, *Yearbook of Forest Products*.

# Fishing

('000 metric tons)

| | 1995 | 1996 | 1997 |
|---|---|---|---|
| Total catch | 4.5 | 4.5 | 4.7 |

# Mining

('000 metric tons, unless otherwise indicated)

| | 1993 | 1994 | 1995 |
|---|---|---|---|
| Brown coal (incl. lignite) | 1,691 | 1,369 | 1,283 |
| Crude petroleum | 1,155 | 1,100 | 1,035 |
| Iron ore: | | | |
| gross weight | 1,427 | 1,644 | 2,107 |
| metal content | 448 | 515 | 656 |
| Magnesite (crude) | 627 | 654 | 785 |
| Salt (unrefined) | 712 | 786 | 834 |
| Lead ore (metric tons)* | 2,047 | n.a. | n.a. |
| Zinc ore (metric tons)* | 20,014 | n.a. | n.a. |
| Graphite (natural) | 4 | 12 | 12 |
| Gypsum (crude) | 874 | 1,012 | 975 |
| Kaolin | 346 | 467 | 479 |
| Natural gas (million cu metres) | 1,488 | 1,350 | 1,480 |

* Figures refer to the metal content of ores.

**1996** ('000 metric tons): Brown coal 843 (estimate); Crude petroleum 989; Iron ore (metal content) 600; Graphite 12 (Source: UN, *Industrial Commodity Statistics Yearbook*, partly quoting US Bureau of Mines).

Tungsten ore (metric tons): 0 in 1994; 188 in 1995; 360 in 1996 (Figures refer to metal content; source: UN, *Industrial Commodity Statistics Yearbook*, quoting US Bureau of Mines).

# Industry

## SELECTED PRODUCTS

('000 metric tons, unless otherwise indicated)

| | 1996 | 1997 | 1998* |
|---|---|---|---|
| Wheat flour | 297 | 272 | 274 |
| Raw sugar | 535 | 526 | n.a. |
| Wine ('000 hectolitres) | 2,110 | 1,801 | 2,703 |
| Beer ('000 hectolitres) | 9,427 | 9,304 | 8,948 |
| Cotton yarn—pure and mixed (metric tons) | 19,639 | 21,849 | 24,829 |
| Woven cotton fabrics—pure and mixed ('000 sq metres) | 97,726 | 100,076 | 101,133 |
| Wool yarn—pure and mixed (metric tons) | 2,537 | 2,692 | n.a. |
| Woven woollen fabrics—pure and mixed ('000 sq metres) | 17,515 | 22,279 | 26,594 |
| Mechanical wood pulp | 344 | 378 | n.a. |
| Chemical and semi-chemical wood pulp | 1,051 | 1,097 | n.a. |
| Newsprint | 361 | 397 | n.a. |
| Other printing and writing paper | 1,787 | 1,826 | n.a. |
| Other paper and paperboard | 1,505 | 1,593 | n.a. |
| Plastics and resins | 993 | 1,035 | 1,074 |
| Motor spirit (petrol) | 2,299 | n.a. | n.a. |
| Jet fuel | 478 | n.a. | n.a. |
| Distillate fuel oils | 3,604 | n.a. | n.a. |
| Residual fuel oils | 1,421 | n.a. | n.a. |
| Cement | 3,900 | 3,944 | 3,958 |
| Crude steel | 4,442 | n.a. | n.a. |
| Refined copper—unwrought (metric tons): secondary | 76,000 | n.a. | n.a. |
| Refined lead—unwrought (metric tons): secondary | 22,900 | n.a. | n.a. |
| Passenger motor cars (number) | 97,386 | 97,774 | n.a. |
| Motorcycles, etc. (number) | 18,618 | 18,652 | n.a. |
| Construction: new dwellings completed (number) | 57,984 | 58,029 | 57,450 |
| Electric energy (million kWh) | 54,835 | 56,851 | 57,394 |
| Manufactured gas (terajoules)† | 27,730 | 30,132 | 30,076 |

* Provisional figures.

† Production of blast-furnace gas and coke-oven gas.

Sources: mainly Austrian Central Statistical Office, Vienna; FAO, *Yearbook of Forest Products*; UN, *Industrial Commodity Statistics Yearbook* and *Monthly Bulletin of Statistics*; International Road Federation, *World Road Statistics*.

# Finance

## CURRENCY AND EXCHANGE RATES

**Monetary Units**

100 Groschen = 1 Schilling.

**Sterling, Dollar and Euro Equivalents** (30 September 1999)

£1 sterling = 21.244 Schilling;
US $1 = 12.902 Schilling;
€1 = 13.760 Schilling;
1,000 Schilling = £47.07 = $77.51 = €72.67.

**Average Exchange Rate** (Schilling per US $)

1996 10.587
1997 12.204
1998 12.379

## FEDERAL BUDGET (million Schilling)*

| Revenue | 1996 | 1997 | 1998 |
|---|---|---|---|
| Direct taxes on income and wealth | 235,141 | 258,700 | 272,442 |
| Social security contributions—unemployment insurance | 45,300 | 45,926 | 47,709 |
| Indirect taxes | 204,257 | 211,454 | 245,613 |
| Current transfers | 61,935 | 72,685 | 72,646 |
| Sales and charges | 18,777 | 14,770 | 16,293 |
| Interest, shares of profit and other income | 37,092 | 118,594 | 35,243 |
| Sales of assets | 10,523 | 18,681 | 7,483 |
| Repayments of loans granted | 634 | 395 | 701 |
| Capital transfers | 386 | 285 | 391 |
| Borrowing | 219,596 | 234,553 | 401,967 |
| Other revenue | 7,869 | 3,936 | 4,076 |
| **Total** | 841,510 | 979,979 | 1,104,564 |

| Expenditure | 1996 | 1997 | 1998 |
|---|---|---|---|
| Current expenditure on goods and services | 168,954 | 253,447 | 176,989 |
| Interest on public debt | 96,974 | 97,274 | 102,316 |
| Current transfers to: | | | |
| Regional and local authorities | 55,381 | 68,341 | 76,145 |
| Other public bodies | 136,847 | 136,241 | 148,940 |
| Households | 126,085 | 121,250 | 116,473 |
| Other | 51,942 | 53,367 | 53,530 |
| Deficits of government enterprises | 2,429 | 2,279 | 2,339 |
| Gross capital formation | 12,742 | 10,176 | 10,409 |
| Capital transfers | 47,590 | 48,456 | 49,282 |
| Acquisition of assets | 6,073 | 14,992 | 33,045 |
| Loans granted | 358 | 483 | 273 |
| Debt redemption | 130,231 | 167,334 | 319,867 |
| Other expenditure | 5,904 | 6,339 | 14,956 |
| **Total** | 841,510 | 979,979 | 1,104,564 |

* Figures refer to federal government units covered by the general budget. The data exclude the operations of social insurance institutions and other units with their own budgets.

## NATIONAL BANK RESERVES (US $ million at 31 December)

| | 1996 | 1997 | 1998 |
|---|---|---|---|
| Gold* | 1,805 | 1,168 | 2,795 |
| IMF special drawing rights | 195 | 168 | 149 |
| Reserve position in IMF | 809 | 963 | 1,365 |
| Foreign exchange | 21,861 | 18,605 | 20,918 |
| **Total** | 24,670 | 20,904 | 25,227 |

* Valued at 60,000 Schilling per kilogram.

Source: IMF, *International Financial Statistics*.

## MONEY SUPPLY ('000 million Schilling at 31 December)

| | 1995 | 1996 | 1997 |
|---|---|---|---|
| Currency outside banks | 168.6 | 176.7 | 178.8 |
| Demand deposits at deposit money banks | 244.0 | 255.2 | 273.5 |
| **Total money** | 412.6 | 431.9 | 452.3 |

Source: IMF, *International Financial Statistics*.

**COST OF LIVING** (Consumer Price Index; base: 1986 = 100)

| | 1996 | 1997 | 1998 |
|---|---|---|---|
| Food and beverages | 120.3 | 122.3 | 124.5 |
| Rent (incl. maintenance and repairs) | 152.6 | 156.0 | 160.4 |
| Fuel and light | 103.8 | 107.2 | 105.1 |
| Clothing | 129.3 | 129.7 | 129.6 |
| **Total** (incl. others) | 130.8 | 132.5 | 133.7 |

**NATIONAL ACCOUNTS** ('000 million Schilling at current prices)

**National Income and Product**

| | 1996 | 1997 | 1998 |
|---|---|---|---|
| Compensation of employees | 1,290.93 | 1,310.51 | 1,365.72 |
| Operating surplus* | 538.61 | 547.72 | 563.60 |
| **Domestic factor incomes** | 1,829.54 | 1,858.23 | 1,929.32 |
| Consumption of fixed capital | 324.67 | 335.03 | 347.58 |
| **Gross domestic product at factor cost** | 2,154.21 | 2,193.26 | 2,276.90 |
| Indirect taxes<br>*Less* Subsidies | 299.03 | 328.97 | 334.02 |
| **GDP in purchasers' values** | 2,453.24 | 2,522.22 | 2,610.91 |
| Factor income received from abroad | 122.90 | 145.55 | 152.28 |
| *Less* Factor income paid abroad | 134.43 | 159.71 | 175.73 |
| **Gross national product** | 2,441.71 | 2,508.06 | 2,587.46 |
| *Less* Consumption of fixed capital | 324.67 | 335.03 | 347.58 |
| **National income in market prices** | 2,117.04 | 2,173.03 | 2,239.89 |
| Other current transfers from abroad | 19.83 | 23.26 | 24.43 |
| *Less* Other current transfers paid abroad | 31.30 | 33.49 | 40.26 |
| **National disposable income** | 2,105.58 | 2,162.80 | 2,224.06 |

* Including a statistical discrepancy.

**Expenditure on the Gross Domestic Product**

| | 1996 | 1997 | 1998 |
|---|---|---|---|
| Government final consumption expenditure | 496.68 | 499.10 | 516.48 |
| Private final consumption expenditure | 1,406.86 | 1,433.70 | 1,465.76 |
| Increase in stocks<br>Gross fixed capital formation | 581.24 | 600.32 | 645.77 |
| **Total domestic expenditure** | 2,484.78 | 2,533.12 | 2,628.02 |
| Exports of goods and services | 969.94 | 1,074.26 | 1,172.44 |
| *Less* Imports of goods and services | 996.22 | 1,110.69 | 1,186.42 |
| Statistical discrepancy | –5.25 | 25.54 | –3.12 |
| **GDP in purchasers' values** | 2,453.24 | 2,522.22 | 2,610.91 |
| **GDP at constant 1995 prices** | 2,422.23 | 2,451.02 | 2,521.51 |

**Gross Domestic Product by Economic Activity**

| | 1996 | 1997 | 1998 |
|---|---|---|---|
| Agriculture, hunting, forestry and fishing | 57.66 | 56.88 | 56.75 |
| Mining and quarrying | 8.50 | 8.74 | 8.76 |
| Manufacturing | 450.98 | 472.42 | 492.47 |
| Electricity, gas and water | 65.99 | 62.57 | 63.90 |
| Construction | 187.07 | 190.92 | 205.58 |
| Wholesale and retail trade | 294.77 | 301.23 | 308.15 |
| Restaurants and hotels | 89.17 | 91.66 | 96.79 |
| Transport, storage and communications | 168.98 | 177.34 | 184.05 |
| Finance and insurance | 164.48 | 173.81 | 173.20 |
| Real estate and business services* | 327.75 | 352.83 | 367.02 |
| Public administration and defence | 158.82 | 160.90 | 164.01 |
| Other services | 348.84 | 326.22 | 335.52 |
| **Sub-total** | 2,323.02 | 2,375.53 | 2,456.21 |
| *Less* Imputed bank service charges | 117.59 | 127.35 | 127.56 |
| **GDP at basic prices** | 2,205.43 | 2,248.18 | 2,328.65 |
| Taxes on products<br>*Less* Subsidies on products | 247.80 | 274.04 | 282.26 |
| **GDP in purchasers' values** | 2,453.24 | 2,522.22 | 2,610.91 |

* Including imputed rents of owner-occupied dwellings.

**BALANCE OF PAYMENTS** (US $ million)

| | 1996 | 1997 | 1998 |
|---|---|---|---|
| Exports of goods f.o.b. | 57,937 | 58,662 | 62,458 |
| Imports of goods f.o.b. | –65,252 | –62,936 | –66,530 |
| **Trade balance** | –7,315 | –4,274 | –4,072 |
| Exports of services | 33,977 | 29,603 | 32,905 |
| Imports of services | –29,331 | –28,510 | –30,260 |
| **Balance on goods and services** | –2,669 | –3,180 | –1,426 |
| Other income received | 9,852 | 10,296 | 10,678 |
| Other income paid | –10,291 | –10,417 | –11,755 |
| **Balance on goods, services and income** | –3,107 | –3,302 | –2,503 |
| Current transfers received | 3,145 | 2,912 | 2,911 |
| Current transfers paid | –4,928 | –4,606 | –4,834 |
| **Current balance** | –4,890 | –4,996 | –4,425 |
| Capital account (net) | 78 | 29 | –162 |
| Direct investment abroad | –1,848 | –1,944 | –3,030 |
| Direct investment from abroad | 4,485 | 2,354 | 6,031 |
| Portfolio investment assets | –8,081 | –10,254 | –12,176 |
| Portfolio investment liabilities | 5,607 | 11,224 | 16,391 |
| Other investment assets | 719 | –5,292 | –1,521 |
| Other investment liabilities | 4,442 | 5,415 | 2,049 |
| Net errors and omissions | 562 | 412 | 347 |
| **Overall balance** | 1,075 | –3,053 | 3,503 |

Source: IMF, *International Financial Statistics*.

# External Trade

Note: Austria's customs territory excludes Mittelberg im Kleinen Walsertal (in Vorarlberg) and Jungholz (in Tyrol). The figures also exclude trade in silver specie and monetary gold.

**PRINCIPAL COMMODITIES**
(distribution by SITC, million Schilling)

| Imports c.i.f. | 1996 | 1997 | 1998 |
|---|---|---|---|
| **Food and live animals** | 38,611.3 | 44,285.8 | 45,556.4 |
| **Crude materials (inedible) except fuels** | 26,791.2 | 32,417.3 | 32,716.9 |
| **Mineral fuels, lubricants, etc.** (incl. electric current) | 38,079.5 | 41,691.1 | 35,292.8 |
| Petroleum, petroleum products, etc. | 23,137.6 | 26,429.8 | 21,052.0 |
| **Chemicals and related products** | 73,741.9 | 83,792.2 | 90,081.5 |
| Medicinal and pharmaceutical products | 19,515.0 | 23,334.6 | 27,460.3 |
| Artificial resins, plastic materials, etc. | 19,931.2 | 22,270.1 | 23,603.0 |
| **Basic manufactures** | 129,508.3 | 144,583.1 | 152,127.4 |
| Paper, paperboard and manufactures | 14,979.0 | 16,580.4 | 17,656.0 |
| Textile yarn, fabrics, etc. | 20,067.5 | 21,725.8 | 21,615.6 |
| Non-metallic mineral manufactures | 14,317.3 | 15,914.7 | 15,520.0 |
| Iron and steel | 17,367.3 | 19,270.6 | 22,032.7 |
| Non-ferrous metals | 15,748.3 | 19,733.7 | 20,276.5 |
| Other metal manufactures | 30,184.4 | 32,042.0 | 34,560.0 |
| **Machinery and transport equipment** | 269,884.3 | 301,564.2 | 334,650.8 |
| Power-generating machinery and equipment | 17,130.9 | 20,532.7 | 23,270.3 |
| Machinery specialized for particular industries | 23,525.7 | 26,299.2 | 26,697.6 |
| General industrial machinery, equipment and parts | 40,659.1 | 43,720.4 | 45,361.1 |
| Office machines and automatic data-processing equipment | 21,496.7 | 24,681.9 | 27,149.5 |
| Telecommunications and sound equipment | 17,474.8 | 22,096.0 | 29,912.0 |
| Other electrical machinery, apparatus, etc. | 48,447.2 | 57,297.4 | 63,774.7 |
| Road vehicles and parts (excl. tyres, engines and electrical parts) | 86,168.9 | 86,793.4 | 97,016.5 |
| **Miscellaneous manufactured articles** | 126,791.7 | 133,825.0 | 140,751.5 |
| Furniture and parts | 16,228.3 | 16,503.1 | 17,064.2 |
| Clothing and accessories (excl. footwear) | 33,730.4 | 35,497.9 | 36,636.5 |
| **Total** (incl. others) | 712,759.6 | 790,250.8 | 842,128.0 |

| Exports f.o.b. | 1996 | 1997 | 1998 |
|---|---|---|---|
| **Food and live animals** | 22,928.1 | 27,082.1 | 29,010.0 |
| **Crude materials (inedible) except fuels** | 22,239.7 | 25,712.7 | 26,190.0 |
| **Chemicals and related products** | 57,187.0 | 69,319.5 | 72,128.0 |
| Medicinal and pharmaceutical products | 14,550.8 | 18,752.0 | 19,117.1 |
| Artificial resins, plastic materials, etc. | 19,044.9 | 21,974.2 | 22,595.3 |
| **Basic manufactures** | 166,295.3 | 185,320.9 | 204,586.3 |
| Paper, paperboard and manufactures | 34,263.5 | 36,290.8 | 38,416.3 |
| Textile yarn, fabrics, etc. | 21,220.9 | 23,647.5 | 24,751.9 |
| Non-metallic mineral manufactures | 16,273.9 | 18,717.6 | 17,828.8 |
| Iron and steel | 29,443.1 | 33,039.1 | 45,276.3 |
| Non-ferrous metals | 13,694.7 | 16,008.0 | 16,863.1 |
| Other metal manufactures | 30,380.6 | 34,848.2 | 37,091.9 |
| **Machinery and transport equipment** | 248,833.5 | 293,110.2 | 321,215.4 |
| Power-generating machinery and equipment | 38,368.7 | 39,107.6 | 41,033.4 |

| Exports f.o.b. — *continued* | 1996 | 1997 | 1998 |
|---|---|---|---|
| Machinery specialized for particular industries | 34,083.7 | 39,511.6 | 42,723.1 |
| General industrial machinery, equipment and parts | 39,495.5 | 44,074.6 | 47,441.2 |
| Telecommunications and sound equipment | 18,681.0 | 25,993.7 | 28,624.8 |
| Other electrical machinery, apparatus, etc. | 45,941.2 | 54,854.6 | 61,503.2 |
| Road vehicles and parts (excl. tyres, engines and electrical parts) | 54,156.2 | 61,530.3 | 68,490.7 |
| **Miscellaneous manufactured articles** | 81,148.3 | 99,379.3 | 106,256.9 |
| Clothing and accessories (excl. footwear) | 14,716.6 | 16,557.3 | 17,003.0 |
| **Total** (incl. others) | 612,189.8 | 715,016.2 | 774,738.0 |

**PRINCIPAL TRADING PARTNERS** (million Schilling)*

| Imports c.i.f. | 1996 | 1997 | 1998 |
|---|---|---|---|
| Belgium-Luxembourg | 16,327.4 | 18,970.8 | 20,171.2 |
| China, People's Republic | 8,990.3 | 10,784.6 | 11,099.6 |
| Czech Republic | 14,363.6 | 17,581.4 | 19,934.2 |
| France | 34,214.7 | 36,980.1 | 41,317.3 |
| Germany | 305,559.6 | 329,322.7 | 351,881.7 |
| Hungary | 19,151.6 | 24,412.3 | 27,629.2 |
| Italy | 62,742.4 | 66,803.5 | 67,511.9 |
| Japan | 17,211.5 | 17,345.5 | 19,708.9 |
| Netherlands | 22,889.2 | 26,229.3 | 28,978.3 |
| Russia | 11,271.9 | 11,888.0 | 10,556.9 |
| Spain | 10,197.4 | 11,842.0 | 12,898.5 |
| Sweden | 10,979.4 | 10,543.1 | 12,139.4 |
| Switzerland-Liechtenstein | 24,890.2 | 26,269.3 | 29,997.0 |
| United Kingdom | 21,477.5 | 24,050.6 | 25,657.7 |
| USA | 31,780.3 | 42,308.4 | 40,643.7 |
| **Total** (incl. others) | 712,759.6 | 790,250.8 | 842,128.0 |

| Exports f.o.b. | 1996 | 1997 | 1998 |
|---|---|---|---|
| Belgium-Luxembourg | 11,806.3 | 12,318.3 | 13,876.7 |
| Czech Republic | 17,751.7 | 21,005.6 | 21,816.6 |
| France | 26,186.6 | 29,479.8 | 34,756.3 |
| Germany | 229,041.8 | 250,854.6 | 278,550.8 |
| Hungary | 24,338.1 | 34,978.4 | 38,251.3 |
| Italy | 51,313.2 | 59,316.9 | 66,574.1 |
| Japan | 9,457.7 | 8,976.0 | 7,172.8 |
| Netherlands | 15,833.9 | 19,292.0 | 18,723.2 |
| Poland | 9,057.8 | 11,823.1 | 12,395.6 |
| Russia | 7,946.3 | 9,974.6 | 7,380.0 |
| Slovenia | 9,864.3 | 12,904.8 | 12,962.0 |
| Spain | 13,638.1 | 16,139.4 | 20,859.3 |
| Sweden | 8,082.3 | 9,027.4 | 9,310.5 |
| Switzerland-Liechtenstein | 30,303.7 | 34,822.9 | 41,972.9 |
| United Kingdom | 21,649.3 | 29,640.3 | 32,464.8 |
| USA | 14,487.9 | 26,210.2 | 31,365.0 |
| **Total** (incl. others) | 612,189.8 | 715,016.2 | 774,738.0 |

* Imports by country of production; exports by country of consumption.

# Transport

**RAILWAYS** (Federal Railways only)

| | 1996 | 1997 | 1998 |
|---|---|---|---|
| Passenger-km (millions) | 9,689 | 8,647.3 | n.a. |
| Freight net ton-km (millions) | 13,909.0 | 14,791.1 | 15,347.8 |
| Freight tons carried ('000) | 69,948.0 | 74,346.6 | 76,508.4 |

**ROAD TRAFFIC** (motor vehicles in use at 31 December)

| | 1996 | 1997 | 1998 |
|---|---|---|---|
| Private cars | 3,690,692 | 3,782,544 | 3,887,174 |
| Buses and coaches | 9,740 | 9,718 | 9,675 |
| Goods vehicles | 293,614 | 300,726 | 309,630 |
| Motorcycles and scooters | 193,685 | 212,791 | 237,767 |
| Mopeds | 366,506 | 362,953 | 362,864 |

**SHIPPING**

**Merchant Fleet** (registered at 31 December)

| | 1996 | 1997 | 1998 |
|---|---|---|---|
| Number of vessels | 29 | 13 | 22 |
| Total displacement ('000 grt) | 94.7 | 83.4 | 68.0 |

Source: Lloyd's Register of Shipping, *World Fleet Statistics*.

**Freight Traffic** ('000 metric tons)

| | 1995 | 1996 | 1997 |
|---|---|---|---|
| Goods loaded | 1,311 | 1,352 | 1,479 |
| Goods unloaded | 5,122 | 5,830 | 5,766 |

**CIVIL AVIATION** (Austrian Airlines, '000)

| | 1996 | 1997 | 1998 |
|---|---|---|---|
| Kilometres flown | 57,400 | 59,735 | 64,595 |
| Passenger ton-km | 523,765 | 597,875 | 695,046 |
| Cargo ton-km | 124,510 | 158,726 | 160,319 |
| Mail ton-km | 7,322 | 7,308 | 9,535 |

# Tourism

**FOREIGN TOURIST ARRIVALS** (by country of origin)*

| | 1996 | 1997 | 1998 |
|---|---|---|---|
| Belgium-Luxembourg | 415,844 | 391,336 | 339,734 |
| France-Monaco | 536,819 | 486,862 | 505,454 |
| Germany | 9,877,394 | 9,391,361 | 9,667,328 |
| Italy | 856,354 | 896,158 | 950,632 |
| Netherlands | 1,073,008 | 1,031,979 | 1,045,377 |
| Switzerland-Liechtenstein | 746,106 | 699,543 | 700,643 |
| United Kingdom | 512,578 | 531,926 | 562,407 |
| USA | 575,178 | 578,581 | 662,837 |
| **Total** (incl. others) | 17,089,973 | 16,642,400 | 17,269,097 |

* Arrivals at accommodation establishments.

**Receipts from tourism** (US $ million): 13,152 in 1994; 14,593 in 1995; 13,990 in 1996 (Source: World Tourism Organization, *Yearbook of Tourism Statistics*).

# Communications Media

| | 1996 | 1997 | 1998 |
|---|---|---|---|
| Telephones (individual lines in use) | 3,779,000 | 3,726,000 | 3,570,000 |
| Radio licences issued | 2,792,584 | 2,769,705 | 2,778,912 |
| Television licences issued | 2,641,367 | 2,636,677 | 2,673,765 |
| Book titles produced | 20,653 | 20,942 | 21,428 |
| Daily newspapers | 17 | 17 | 17 |
| Weekly newspapers | 153 | 151 | 155 |
| Other periodicals | 2,617 | 2,637 | 2,685 |

**Telefax stations** ('000 in use): 210.0 in 1993; 240.0 in 1994; 284.7 in 1995 (Source: UN, *Statistical Yearbook*).

**Mobile cellular telephones** ('000 subscribers): 220.9 in 1993; 278.2 in 1994; 383.5 in 1995 (Source: UN, *Statistical Yearbook*).

# Education

(1998/99)

| | Institutions | Staff | Students |
|---|---|---|---|
| Primary | 3,720 | 35,923 | 396,245 |
| General secondary and upper primary | 1,711 | 59,147 | 480,137 |
| Compulsory vocational | 189 | 4,558 | 131,196 |
| Technical and vocational | 718 | 19,864 | 189,117 |
| Teacher training: | | | |
| second level | 39 | 1,401 | 13,137 |
| third level | 33 | 2,460 | 11,578 |
| Universities | 18 | 17,378 | 222,163 |
| Tertiary vocational | 46 | 1,216* | 7,867 |

* 1997/98 figure.

# Directory

## The Constitution

The Austrian Constitution of 1920, as amended in 1929, was restored on 1 May 1945. Its main provisions, with subsequent amendments, are summarized below:

Austria is a democratic republic, having a Federal President (Bundespräsident), elected directly by the people, and a two-chamber legislature, the Federal Assembly (Bundesversammlung), consisting of the National Council (Nationalrat) and the Federal Council (Bundesrat). The republic is organized on the federal system, comprising the nine federal provinces (Bundesländer) of Burgenland, Carinthia (Kärtnen), Lower Austria (Niederösterreich), Upper Austria (Oberösterreich), Salzburg, Styria (Steiermark), Tyrol (Tirol), Vorarlberg and Vienna (Wien). There is universal suffrage for men and women who are more than 18 years of age.

The Nationalrat consists of 183 members, elected by universal direct suffrage, according to a system of proportional representation. It functions for a maximum period of four years.

The Bundesrat represents the Bundesländer. Lower Austria sends 12 members, Vienna and Upper Austria 11 each, Styria 10, Carinthia and Tyrol five each, Salzburg four, and Burgenland and Vorarlberg three each, making 64 in all. The seats are divided between the parties according to the number of seats that they control in each Provincial Assembly (Landtag) and are held during the life of the provincial government (Landesreigerung) that they represent. Each Länder, in turn, provides the Chairman for six months.

The Bundesversammlung meets for certain matters of special importance, for example to witness the swearing-in of the President. It can also be convened to declare war or to demand a referendum on the deposition of the President, if demanded by the Nationalrat.

The Federal President, elected by popular vote, is the head of state and holds office for a term of six years. The President is eligible for re-election only once in succession. Although invested with special emergency powers, the President normally acts on the authority of the Council of Ministers, which is responsible to the Nationalrat for governmental policy.

The Government consists of the Federal Chancellor, the Vice-Chancellor and the other ministers and state secretaries, who may vary in number. The Chancellor is chosen by the President, usually from the party with the strongest representation in the newly elected Nationalrat, and the other ministers are then chosen by the President on the advice of the Chancellor.

If the Nationalrat adopts an explicit motion expressing 'no confidence' in the Federal Government or individual members thereof, the Federal Government or the federal minister concerned is removed from office.

All new legislative proposals must be read and submitted to a vote in both chambers of the Bundesversammlung. A new draft law is presented first to the Nationalrat, where it usually has three readings, and secondly to the Bundesrat, where it can be delayed, but not vetoed.

The Constitution also provides for appeals by the Government to the electorate on specific points by means of referendum. If a petition supported by 100,000 electors or more is presented to the Government, the Government must submit it to the Nationalrat.

The Landtag exercises the same functions in each province as the Nationalrat does in the State. The members of the Landestag elect the Landesregierung consisting of a provincial governor (Landeshauptmann) and his or her councillors (Landesräte). They are responsible to the Landtag.

The spheres of legal and administrative competence of both national and provincial governments are clearly defined. The Constitution distinguishes four groups:

1. Law-making and administration are the responsibility of the State: e.g. foreign affairs, justice and finance.
2. Law-making is the responsibility of the State, administration is the responsibility of the provinces: e.g. elections, population matters and road traffic.
3. The State formulates the rudiments of the law, the provinces enact the law and administer it: e.g. charity, rights of agricultural workers, land reform.
4. Law-making and administration are the responsibility of the provinces in all matters not expressly assigned to the State: e.g. municipal affairs.

# The Government

### HEAD OF STATE

**Federal President:** Dr THOMAS KLESTIL (sworn in 8 July 1992; re-elected 19 April 1998).

### COUNCIL OF MINISTERS
(February 2000)

A coalition of the Freiheitliche Partei Österreichs (FPÖ) and the Österreichische Volkspartei (ÖVP).

**Federal Chancellor:** Dr WOLFGANG SCHÜSSEL (ÖVP).

**Vice-Chancellor:** Dr SUSANNE RIESS-PASSER (FPÖ).

**Minister of Foreign Affairs:** Dr BENITA FERRERO-WALDNER (ÖVP).

**Minister of Economic Affairs:** Dr MARTIN BARTENSTEIN (ÖVP).

**Minister of Labour, Health and Social Affairs:** Dr ELISABETH SICKL (FPÖ).

**Minister of Finance:** Mag. KARL-HEINZ GRASSER (FPÖ).

**Minister of the Interior:** Dr ERNST STRASSER (ÖVP).

**Minister of Justice:** Dr MICHAEL KRÜGER (FPÖ).

**Minister of Defence:** HERBERT SCHEIBNER (FPÖ).

**Minister of Agriculture and Forestry:** Mag. WILHELM MOLTERER (ÖVP).

**Minister of Education and Cultural Affairs:** ELISABETH GEHRER (ÖVP).

**Minister of Science and Transport:** MICHAEL SCHMID (FPÖ).

**Secretary of State in the Federal Chancellery:** FRANZ MORAK (ÖVP).

**Secretary of State in the Ministry of Economic Affairs:** MARES ROSSMANN (FPÖ).

**Secretary of State in the Ministry of Labour, Health and Social Affairs:** Prof. Dr REINHART WANECK (FPÖ).

**Secretary of State in the Ministry of Finance:** Dr ALFRED FINZ (ÖVP).

### MINISTRIES

**Office of the Federal President:** 1010 Vienna, Hofburg; tel. (1) 534-22-0; fax (1) 535-65-12; internet hofburg.at.

**Office of the Federal Chancellor:** 1014 Vienna, Ballhausplatz 2; tel. (1) 531-15-0; fax (1) 535-03-380; internet www.austria .gv.at.

**Ministry of Agriculture and Forestry:** 1010 Vienna, Stubenring 1; tel. (1) 711-00-0; fax (1) 710-32-54; internet www.bmlf.gv.at.

**Ministry of Defence:** 1030 Vienna, Dampfschiffstr. 2; tel. (1) 515-95; fax (1) 515-95-17033.

**Ministry of Economic Affairs:** 1010 Vienna, Stubenring 1; tel. (1) 711-00-0; fax (1) 713-79-95; e-mail post@bmwa.gv.at; internet www.bmwa.gv.at.

**Ministry of Education and Cultural Affairs:** 1014 Vienna, Minoritenplatz 5; tel. (1) 531-20-00; fax (1) 531-20-00; internet www.bmuk.gv.at.

**Ministry of the Environment, Youth and Family Affairs:** 1010 Vienna, Cobdengasse 2; tel. (1) 515-22-0; fax (1) 515-22-72-32; internet www.bmu.gv.at.

**Ministry of Finance:** 1010 Vienna, Himmelpfortgasse 4–8B; tel. (1) 514-33-0; fax (1) 512-78-69; internet www.bmf.gov.at.

**Ministry of Foreign Affairs:** 1014 Vienna, Ballhausplatz 2; tel. (1) 531-15-0; fax (1) 535-45-30; internet www.bmaa.gv.at.

**Ministry of the Interior:** 1014 Vienna, Herrengasse 7; tel. (1) 531-26-0; fax (1) 531-26-39-10; internet www.bmi.gv.at.

**Ministry of Justice:** 1016 Vienna, Museumstr. 7; tel. (1) 521-52-0; fax (1) 521-52-72-7.

**Ministry of Labour, Health and Social Affairs:** 1010 Vienna, Stubenring 1; tel. (1) 711-00; fax (1) 711-00-64-69; internet www.bmags.gv.at.

**Ministry of Science and Transport:** 1030 Vienna, Radetzkystr. 2; tel. (1) 71162-0; fax (1) 531-20-4499; internet www.bmwv.gv.at.

**Ministry of Women's Issues and Consumer Protection:** 1014 Vienna, Ballhausplatz 1; tel. (1) 536-33-23; fax (1) 536-33-36; e-mail hmffpost@bmff.bka.hka.gr.at.

# President and Legislature

### PRESIDENT

**Presidential Election, 19 April 1998**

| Candidates | Votes | % |
|---|---|---|
| Dr THOMAS KLESTIL (ÖVP) | 2,626,860 | 63.5 |
| GERTRAUD KNOLL (Independent) | 559,943 | 13.5 |
| Dr HEIDE SCHMIDT (FPÖ) | 458,491 | 11.1 |
| RICHARD LUGNER (Independent) | 411,378 | 9.9 |
| KARL WALTER NOVAK (Independent) | 80,741 | 2.0 |
| **Total** | 4,137,413 | 100.0 |

### FEDERAL ASSEMBLY

**Nationalrat**
(National Council)

**President of the Nationalrat:** Dr HEINZ FISCHER.

**General Election, 3 October 1999**

| | Votes | % of Total | Seats |
|---|---|---|---|
| Social-Democratic Party (SPÖ) | 1,532,448 | 33.15 | 65 |
| Freedom Party (FPÖ) | 1,244,087 | 26.91 | 52 |
| People's Party (ÖVP) | 1,243,672 | 26.91 | 52 |
| Green Alternative List (GAL)* | 342,260 | 7.40 | 14 |
| Liberal Forum (LiF) | 168,612 | 3.65 | — |
| The Independents (DU) | 46,943 | 1.02 | — |
| Others | 44,332 | 0.96 | — |
| **Total** | 4,622,354 | 100.00 | 183 |

* An informal electoral alliance comprising Die Grüne Alternative (Green Alternative) and Vereinte Grüne Österreichs (United Green Party of Austria).

**Bundesrat**
(Federal Council)
(February 2000)

**Chairman of the Bundesrat:** ANNA ELISABETH HASELBACH (Jan. 2000–June 2000).

| Provinces | Total seats | SPÖ | ÖVP | FPÖ |
|---|---|---|---|---|
| Burgenland | 3 | 2 | 1 | – |
| Carinthia | 5 | 1 | 1 | 3 |
| Lower Austria | 12 | 5 | 6 | 1 |
| Upper Austria | 11 | 4 | 5 | 2 |
| Salzburg | 4 | – | 3 | 1 |
| Styria | 10 | 4 | 4 | 2 |
| Tyrol | 5 | 1 | 3 | 1 |
| Vorarlberg | 3 | – | 2 | 1 |
| Vienna | 11 | 5 | 2 | 4 |
| **Total** | 64 | 22 | 27 | 15 |

# Political Organizations

**Freiheitliche Partei Österreichs (FPÖ/Die Freiheitlichen)** (Freedom Party): 1010 Vienna, Kärntnerstr. 28; tel. (1) 512-35-35; fax (1) 513-88-58; internet www.fpoe.at; f. 1955, partially succeeding the Verband der Unabhängigen (League of Independents, f. 1949); popularly known as Die Freiheitlichen; populist right-wing party advocating the participation of workers in management, stricter immigration controls and deregulation in the business sector; opposes Austria's membership of the EU; Chair. Dr JÖRG HAIDER; Gen. Sec. PETER WESTENTHELER.

**Die Grünen–Die Grüne Alternative** (Greens–Green Alternative): 1070 Vienna, Lindengasse 40; tel. (1) 521-25-0; fax (1) 526-91-10; e-mail bundesbuero@gruene.at; internet www.gruene.at; f. 1986; campaigns for environmental protection, peace and social justice; Chair. and Leader of Parliamentary Group Prof. Dr ALEXANDER VAN DER BELLEN.

**Kommunistische Partei Österreichs (KPÖ)** (Communist Party of Austria): 1040 Vienna, Weyringergasse 33/5; tel. (1) 503-65-80; fax (1) 503-65-80-411; e-mail kpoe@magnet.at; internet www.kpoenet.at; f. 1918; strongest in the industrial centres and trade unions; advocates a policy of strict neutrality and opposes Austria's membership of the EU; Chair. WALTER BAIER.

**Liberales Forum (LiF)** (Liberal Forum): 1010 Vienna, Reichsratstr. 7/10; tel. (1) 402-78-81; fax (1) 402-78-89; e-mail bund@lif.or.at; internet www.lif.or.at; f. 1993 by fmr mems of Freiheitliche Partei Österreichs; Leader Dr HEIDE SCHMIDT.

**Österreichische Volkspartei (ÖVP)** (Austrian People's Party): 1010 Vienna, Lichtenfelsgasse 7; tel. (1) 401-26; fax (1) 401-26-32-9; internet www.oevp.or.at; f. 1945; Christian-Democratic party; advocates an ecologically-orientated social market economy; 760,000 mems; Chair. Dr WOLFGANG SCHÜSSEL; Secs-Gen. OTHMAR KARAS, MARIA RAUCH-KALLAT.

**Sozialdemokratische Partei Österreichs (SPÖ)** (Social-Democratic Party of Austria): 1014 Vienna, Löwelstr. 18; tel. (1) 534-27-0; fax (1) 535-96-83; internet www.spoe.at; f. as the Social-Democratic Party in 1889, subsequently renamed the Socialist Party, reverted to its original name in 1991; advocates democratic socialism and Austria's permanent neutrality; 500,000 mems; Chair. Mag. VIKTOR KLIMA; Sec. ANDREAS RUDAS.

**Die Unabhängigen (DU)** (Independents): 1015 Vienna, Gablenzgasse 11; tel. (1) 981-40-202; fax (1) 981-40-99; e-mail service@ldu.at; f. 1999; Chair. RICHARD LUGNER.

**Vereinte Grüne Österreichs (VGÖ)** (United Green Party of Austria): Linz; tel. (732) 66-83-91; fax (732) 65-06-68; f. 1982; ecologist party; Chair. ADI PINTER; Gen. Secs WOLFGANG PELIKAN, GÜNTER OFNER.

# Diplomatic Representation

## EMBASSIES IN AUSTRIA

**Afghanistan:** 1070 Vienna, Kaiserstr. 84/1/3; tel. (1) 524-78-06; fax (1) 524-78-07; Chargé d'affaires: FARID A. AMIN.

**Albania:** 1190 Vienna, An den langen Lüssen 1; tel. (1) 328-86-56; fax (1) 328-86-58; Ambassador: ALBERT SEJDIAJ.

**Algeria:** 1190 Vienna, Rudolfinergasse 16–18; tel. (1) 369-88-53; fax (1) 369-88-56; Ambassador: MOKHTAR REGUIEG.

**Angola:** 1030 Vienna, Strohgasse 45; tel. (1) 718-74-88; fax (1) 718-74-86; e-mail embangola.vienna@magnet.at; Ambassador: Dr FIDELINO LOY DE JESUS FIGUEIREDO.

**Argentina:** 1010 Vienna, Goldschmiedgasse 2/1; tel. (1) 533-85-77; fax (1) 533-87-97; e-mail argvienna@ping.at; Ambassador: (vacant).

**Armenia:** 1070 Vienna, Neubaugasse 12–14/1/16; tel. (1) 522-74-79; fax (1) 522-74-81; Chargé d'affaires: SAMUEL MKRTCHIAN.

**Australia:** 1040 Vienna, Mattiellistr. 2–4/III; tel. (1) 512-85-80; fax (1) 504-11-78; Ambassador: LANCE LOUIS JOSEPH.

**Azerbaijan:** 1080 Vienna, Strozzigasse 10; tel. (1) 403-13-22; fax (1) 403-13-23; e-mail azerbembvienna@compuserve.com; Ambassador: VAGIF SADYKHOV.

**Belarus:** 1140 Vienna, Hüttelbergstr. 6; tel. (1) 419-96-30; fax (1) 416-53-45; Ambassador: VALYANTSIN M. FISENKA.

**Belgium*:** 1040 Vienna, Wohllebengasse 6; tel. (1) 502-07; fax (1) 502-07-11; Ambassador: MICHEL ADAM.

**Bolivia:** 1040 Vienna, Waaggasse 10/4; tel. (1) 587-46-75; fax (1) 586-68-80; e-mail embol.austria@chello.at; Ambassador: JAIME NIÑO DE GUZMÁN QUIROZ.

**Bosnia and Herzegovina:** 1120 Vienna, Tivoligasse 54; tel. (1) 811-85-55; fax (1) 811-85-69; Ambassador: Prof. Dr EMINA KEČO-ISAKOVIĆ.

**Brazil:** 1010 Vienna, Lugeck 1/V/15; tel. (1) 512-06-31; fax (1) 513-83-74; e-mail ausbrem@xpoint.at; Ambassador: AFFONSO CELSO DE OURO-PRETO.

**Bulgaria:** 1040 Vienna, Schwindgasse 8; tel. (1) 505-64-44; fax (1) 505-14-23; e-mail bulgamb@eunet.at; Ambassador: Dr KIRIL KALEV.

**Burkina Faso:** 1040 Vienna, Prinz-Eugen-Str. 18; tel. and fax (1) 503-82-64; Ambassador: THOMAS SANON.

**Canada:** 1010 Vienna, Laurenzerberg 2; tel. (1) 531-38-30-00; fax (1) 531-38-33-21; internet www.kanada.at; Ambassador: PAUL DUBOIS.

**Cape Verde:** 1040 Vienna, Schwindgasse 20; tel. (1) 503-87-27; fax (1) 503-87-29; Ambassador: LUIŚ DE MATOS MONTEIRO DA FONSECA.

**Chile:** 1010 Vienna, Lugeck 1/III/10; tel. (1) 512-92-08-0; fax (1) 512-92-08-33; e-mail echileat@netway.at; Ambassador: OSVALDO PUCCIO HUIDOBRO.

**China, People's Republic:** 1030 Vienna, Metternichgasse 4; tel. (1) 714-31-49; fax (1) 713-68-16; Ambassador: LIU CHANGYE.

**Colombia:** 1010 Vienna, Stadiongasse 6–8; tel. (1) 406-44-46; fax (1) 408-83-03; e-mail embcol@atnet.at; Ambassador: HÉCTOR CHARRY SAMPER.

**Costa Rica:** 1120 Vienna, Schlöglgasse 10; tel. (1) 804-05-37; fax (1) 804-90-71; e-mail aviram@aktiv.co.at; Chargé d'affaires: STELLA AVIRAM NEUMAN.

**Croatia:** 1170 Vienna, Heuberggasse 10; tel. (1) 480-20-83; fax (1) 480-29-42; Ambassador: Prof. Dr IVAN ILIĆ.

**Cuba:** 1130 Vienna, Himmelhofgasse 40 a-c, PF 36; tel. (1) 877-81-98; fax (1) 877-77-03; Ambassador: LUIS GARCÍA PERAZA.

**Cyprus:** 1010 Vienna, Parkring 20; tel. (1) 513-06-30; fax (1) 513-06-32; e-mail embassy@cyprus.vienna.at; Ambassador: NICOLAS D. MAGRIS.

**Czech Republic:** 1140 Vienna, Penzinger Str. 11–13; tel. (1) 894-21-25; fax (1) 894-12-00; Ambassador: JIŘÍ GRUSA.

**Denmark*:** 1015 Vienna, Führichgasse 6, PF 298; tel. (1) 512-79-04-0; fax (1) 513-81-20; Ambassador: HENRIK WÖHLK.

**Ecuador:** 1010 Vienna, Goldschmiedgasse 10/2/24; tel. (1) 535-32-08; fax (1) 535-08-97; e-mail embaustria@council.net; Ambassador: PATRICIO PALACIOS.

**Egypt:** 1190 Vienna, Hohe Warte 52; tel. and fax (1) 370-81-04; Ambassador: Dr MOSTAFA M. EL-FEKI.

**Estonia:** 1040 Vienna, Wohllebengasse 9/13; tel. (1) 503-77-61; fax (1) 503-77-62; Ambassador: TOIVO TASA.

**Ethiopia:** 1030 Vienna, Zaunergasse 1–3; tel. (1) 710-21-68; fax (1) 710-21-71; Ambassador: MENBERE ALEMAYEHU.

**Finland*:** 1010 Vienna, Gonzagagasse 16; tel. (1) 531-59-0; fax (1) 535-57-03; Ambassador: TOM CARL ERNST GRÖNBERG.

**France*:** 1040 Vienna, Technikerstr. 2; tel. (1) 502-75-0; fax (1) 502-75-168; Ambassador: JEAN CADET.

**Georgia:** 1030 Vienna, Marokkanergasse 16; tel. (1) 710-36-11; fax (1) 710-36-10; Ambassador: LEVAN MIKELADZE.

**Germany*:** 1030 Vienna, Metternichgasse 3; tel. (1) 711-54; fax (1) 713-83-66; internet www.deubowien.magnet.at; Ambassador: URSULA SEILER-ALBRING.

**Greece*:** 1040 Vienna, Argentinierstr. 14; tel. (1) 505-57-91; fax (1) 505-62-17; Ambassador: JEAN YENNIMATAS.

**Guatemala:** 1030 Vienna, Salesianergasse 25/1/5; tel. (1) 714-35-70; fax (1) 714-35-70-15; Ambassador: FEDERICO ADOLFO URRUELA PRADO.

**Guinea-Bissau:** 1190 Vienna, Kaasgrabengasse 61; tel. (1) 328-80-62; fax (1) 328-80-63; Chargé d'affaires: EDUARD W. BURGE.

**Holy See:** 1040 Vienna, Theresianumgasse 31; tel. (1) 505-13-27; fax (1) 505-61-40; Apostolic Nuncio: Most Rev. DONATO SQUICCIARINI, Titular Archbishop of Tiburnia.

**Hungary:** 1010 Vienna, Bankgasse 4–6; tel. (1) 537-80-300; fax (1) 535-99-40; e-mail ungboa@eunet.at; Ambassador: Dr SÁNDOR PEISCH.

**India:** 1015 Vienna, Kärntner Ring 2a; tel. (1) 505-86-66; fax (1) 505-92-19; Ambassador: YOGESH MOHAN TIWARI.

**Indonesia:** 1180 Vienna, Gustav-Tschermak-Gasse 5–7; tel. (1) 479-05-37; fax (1) 310-99-78; Ambassador: RHOUSDY SOERIATMADJA.

**Iran:** 1030 Vienna, Jaurèsgasse 9; tel. (1) 712-26-57; fax (1) 713-46-94; e-mail botschaft.d.islam.rep.iran@acv.at; Ambassador: EBRAHIM RAHIM POUR.

**Iraq:** 1010 Vienna, Johannesgasse 26; tel. (1) 713-81-95; fax (1) 713-67-20; Chargé d'affaires: KHALID A. NASIR.

**Ireland*:** 1030 Vienna, Hilton Centre, 16th Floor; tel. (1) 715-42-46; fax (1) 713-60-04; Ambassador: THELMA MARIA DORAN.

**Israel†:** 1180 Vienna, Anton-Frank-Gasse 20; tel. (1) 470-47-41; fax (1) 470-47-46; Ambassador: NATHAN MERON.

**Italy*:** 1030 Vienna, Rennweg 27; tel. (1) 712-51-21; fax (1) 713-97-19; e-mail ambitalviepress@via.at; Ambassador: Dr PIER LUIGI RACHELE.

**Japan:** 1010 Vienna, Heßgasse 6; tel. (1) 531-92-0; fax (1) 532-05-90; internet www.embjapan.at; Ambassador: YUSHU TAKASHIMA.

**Jordan:** 1010 Vienna, Doblhoffgasse 3/2; tel. (1) 405-10-25; fax (1) 405-10-31; Ambassador: Dr MAZEN ARMOUTI.

**Kazakhstan:** 1190 Vienna, Billrothstr. 2/23; tel. (1) 367-68-93; fax (1) 367-68-95; Ambassador Dr SAGYNBEK T. TURSYNOV.

**Korea, Democratic People's Republic:** 1140 Vienna, Beckmanngasse 10–12; tel. (1) 894-23-11; fax (1) 894-31-74; Ambassador: KIM KWANG SOP.

**Korea, Republic:** 1180 Vienna, Gregor-Mendel-Str. 25; tel. (1) 478-19-91; fax (1) 478-10-13; Ambassador: BAN KI-MOON.

**Kuwait:** 1010 Vienna, Universitätsstr. 5; tel. (1) 405-56-46; fax (1) 408-56-00; Ambassador: FAISAL R. AL-GHAIS.

**Kyrgyzstan:** 1010 Vienna, Naglergasse 25/5; tel. (1) 535-03-78; fax (1) 535-03-79-13; e-mail kyrbot@kyrbotwien.or.at; Ambassador: KAMIL BAIALINOV.

**Latvia:** 1090 Vienna, Währinger Str. 3/8; tel. (1) 403-31-12; fax (1) 403-31-12/27; e-mail lettbox@netway.at; Ambassador: Dr MĀRTIŅŠ VIRSIS.

**Lebanon:** 1010 Vienna, Oppolzergasse 6/3; tel. (1) 533-88-22; fax (1) 533-49-84; e-mail ambassade.liban@vienna.telecom.at; Ambassador: Dr WILLIAM HABIB.

**Libya:** 1190 Vienna, Blaasstr. 33; tel. (1) 367-76-39; fax (1) 367-76-01; Secretary of People's Bureau: Dr SAID ABDULAATI MOHAMED.

**Liechtenstein:** 1010 Vienna, Löwelstr. 8/7; tel. (1) 535-92-11; fax (1) 535-92-114; Ambassador: Princess MARIA-PIA KOTHBAUER OF LIECHTENSTEIN.

**Lithuania:** 1030 Vienna, Löwengasse 47; tel. (1) 718-54-67; fax (1) 718-54-69; e-mail chancery@mail.austria.eu.net; Ambassador: GINTĖ DAMUSIS.

**Luxembourg*:** 1180 Vienna, Sternwartestr. 81; tel. (1) 478-21-42; fax (1) 478-21-44; Ambassador: GEORGES SANTER.

**Macedonia, former Yugoslav republic:** 1070 Vienna, Kaiserstr. 84/1/5; tel. (1) 524-87-56; fax (1) 524-87-53; e-mail macembassy@aon.at; Ambassador: OGNEN MALESKI.

**Malaysia:** 1040 Vienna, Prinz-Eugen-Str. 18; tel. (1) 505-10-42; fax (1) 505-79-42; e-mail malaysia@netway.at; Ambassador: MELANIE LEONG SOOK LEI.

**Malta:** 1010 Vienna, Opernring 5/1; tel. (1) 586-50-10; fax (1) 586-50-109; Ambassador: MAURICE ABELA.

**Mexico:** 1090 Vienna, Türkenstr. 15; tel. (1) 310-73-83; fax (1) 310-73-87; e-mail embamex@embamex.or.at; Ambassador: ROBERTA LAJOUS.

**Moldova:** 1020 Vienna, Taborstr. 24a; tel. (1) 216-60-03; fax (1) 214-19-97; e-mail amda@netway.at; Ambassador: Dr VALENTIN CIUMAC.

**Morocco:** 1010 Vienna, Opernring 3–5/I/4; tel. (1) 586-66-50; fax (1) 586-76-67; Ambassador: ABDERRAHIM BENMOUSSA.

**Namibia:** 1080 Vienna, Strozigasse 10/14; tel. (1) 402-93-71; fax (1) 402-93-70; Ambassador: HINYANGERWA P. ASHEEKE.

**Netherlands*:** 1010 Vienna, Opernring 3–5; tel. (1) 589-39; fax (1) 589-39-265; e-mail nlgovwen@eunet.at; internet www.netherlands-embassy.at; Ambassador: JAAP RAMAKER.

**Nicaragua:** 1010 Vienna, Ebendorferstr. 10/3/12; tel. (1) 403-18-38; fax (1) 403-27-52; e-mail 113350.2341@compuserve.com; Ambassador: SUYAPA INDIANA PADILLA TERCERO.

**Nigeria:** 1030 Vienna, PF 183, Rennweg 25; tel. (1) 712-66-85; fax (1) 714-14-02; Ambassador: ALBERT AZUBOGU ANOPUECHI.

**Norway:** 1030 Vienna, Bayerngasse 3; tel. (1) 715-66-92; fax (1) 712-65-52; e-mail ambvie@chello.at; Ambassador: HELGA HERNES.

**Oman:** 1090 Vienna, Währingerstr. 2–4/24–25; tel. (1) 310-86-43; fax (1) 310-72-68; Ambassador: SALIM M. AL-RIYAMI.

**Pakistan:** 1190 Vienna, Hofzeile 13; tel. (1) 368-73-81; fax (1) 368-73-76; e-mail parep.vienna@telecom.at; Ambassador: (vacant).

**Panama:** 1010 Vienna, Elisabethstr. 4–5/4/10; tel. (1) 587-23-47; fax (1) 586-30-80; e-mail mail@empanvienna.co.at; Ambassador: Dr JORGE ENRIQUE HALPHEN PÉREZ.

**Paraguay:** Vienna; tel. (1) 715-56-08; fax (1) 715-56-09; e-mail embapar@abacus.at; Chargé d'affaires: MARIA CHRISTINA ACOSTA-ALVAREZ.

**Peru:** 1030 Vienna, Gottfried-Keller-Gasse 2/8; tel. (1) 713-43-77; fax (1) 712-77-04; e-mail peru.emb@xpoint.at; Ambassador: GILBERT CHAUNY DE PORTURAS-HOYLE.

**Philippines:** 1010 Vienna, Laurenzerberg 2; tel. (1) 533-24-01; fax (1) 533-24-01-24; e-mail phat@ping.at; Ambassador: JOSÉ A. ZAIDE.

**Poland:** 1130 Vienna, Hietzinger Hauptstr. 42c; tel. (1) 870-15; fax (1) 870-15-22-2; Ambassador: Prof. Dr JAN BARCZ.

**Portugal*:** 1010 Vienna, Opernring 3/1; tel. (1) 586-75-36; fax (1) 586-75-36-99; e-mail embport@via.at; Ambassador: ÁLVARO DE MENDONÇA E MOURA.

**Qatar:** Vienna; tel. (1) 479-98-03; fax (1) 478-49-66; Chargé d'affaires: SALEH ABDULLAH AL-BOUANIN.

**Romania:** 1040 Vienna, Prinz-Eugen-Str. 60; tel. (1) 505-32-27; fax (1) 504-14-62; Ambassador: ION NEAMTU.

**Russia:** 1030 Vienna, Reisnerstr. 45–47; tel. (1) 712-12-29; fax (1) 712-33-88; e-mail russia@embassy.vienna.at; Ambassador: VLADIMIR M. GRININ.

**San Marino:** 1010 Vienna, Getreidemarkt 12; tel. (1) 586-21-80; fax (1) 586-22-35; Ambassador: GIOVANNI VITO MARCUCCI.

**Saudi Arabia:** 1190 Vienna, Formanekgasse 38; tel. (1) 368-23-16; fax (1) 368-25-60; Ambassador: OMER MUHAMMED KURDI.

**Slovakia:** 1190 Vienna, Armbrustergasse 24; tel. (1) 318-90-55; fax (1) 318-90-60; Ambassador: ĽUBOR BYSTRICKÝ.

**Slovenia:** 1010 Vienna, Nibelungengasse 13/3; tel. (1) 586-13-07; fax (1) 586-12-65; Ambassador: IVO VAJGL.

**South Africa:** 1190 Vienna, Sandgasse 33; tel. (1) 326-49-3; fax (1) 326-49-35-1; e-mail saembvie@ins.at; internet www.saembvie.ins.at; Ambassador: N. J. MXAKATO-DISEKO.

**Spain*:** 1040 Vienna, Argentinierstr. 34; tel. (1) 505-57-80; fax (1) 505-57-88-25; Ambassador: RICARDO DÍEZ-HOCHLEITNER RODRÍGUEZ.

**Sri Lanka:** 1040 Vienna, Rainergasse 1/2/5; tel. (1) 503-79-88; fax (1) 503-79-93; e-mail embassy@srilanka.at; Ambassador: C. S. POOLOKASINGHAM.

**Sudan:** 1030 Vienna, Reisnerstr. 29/5; tel. (1) 710-23-43; fax (1) 710-23-46; e-mail sudan-embassy-vienna@aon.at; internet www.members.aon.at/sudanivienna; Ambassador: ABD EL-GHAFFAR ABD EL-RAHMAN HASSAN.

**Sweden*:** 1025 Vienna, Obere Donaustr. 49–51; tel. (1) 217-53-0; fax (1) 217-53-370; e-mail office@swedemb.or.at; Ambassador: BJÖRN SKALA.

**Switzerland:** 1030 Vienna, Prinz-Eugen-Str. 7; tel. (1) 795-05; fax (1) 795-05-21; Chargé d'affaires: MARKUS PETER.

**Syria:** 1010 Vienna, Wallnerstr. 8; tel. (1) 533-46-33; fax (1) 533-46-32; Ambassador: Dr RIAD SIAGE.

**Tajikistan:** 1090 Vienna, Wallnergasse 8; tel. and fax (1) 409-82-66; Ambassador: KHAMROKHON ZARIPOV.

**Thailand:** 1180 Vienna, Cottagegasse 48; tel. (1) 478-27-97; fax (1) 478-29-07; e-mail thai.vn@embthai.telecom.at; Ambassador: SORAYOUTH PROMPOJ.

**Tunisia:** 1010 Vienna, Opernring 5/3; tel. (1) 581-52-81; fax (1) 581-55-92; Ambassador: ABDELAZIZ CHAABANE.

**Turkey:** 1040 Vienna, Prinz-Eugen-Str. 40; tel. (1) 505-73-38-0; fax (1) 505-36-60; Ambassador: ÖMER ERSAN.

**Turkmenistan:** 1040 Vienna, Argentinierstr. 22/11/EG; tel. (1) 503-64-70; fax (1) 503-64-73; Ambassador: BATYR BERDYEV.

**Ukraine:** 1180 Vienna, Naaffgasse 23; tel. (1) 479-71-72; fax (1) 479-71-72-47; Ambassador: MYKOLA P. MAKAREVYCH.

**United Arab Emirates:** 1190 Vienna, Peter-Jordan-Str. 66; tel. (1) 368-14-55; fax (1) 368-44-85; Chargé d'affaires: AHMED RASHED AL-DOSARI.

**United Kingdom*:** 1030 Vienna, Jaurèsgasse 12; tel. (1) 716-13-0; fax (1) 716-13-69-00; e-mail britem@netway.at; internet www.britishembassy.at; Ambassador: Sir ANTHONY FIGGIS.

**USA†:** 1090 Vienna, Boltzmanngasse 16; tel. (1) 313-39; fax (1) 310-06-82; Ambassador: KATHRYN WALT HALL.

**Uruguay:** 1010 Vienna, Palais Esterhazy, Wallnerstr. 4/3/17; tel. (1) 535-66-36; fax (1) 535-66-18; e-mail uruvien@embuy.or.at; Ambassador: FRUCTUOSO PITTALUGA.

**Uzbekistan:** 1090 Vienna, Porzellangasse 32/5; tel. (1) 315-39-94; fax (1) 315-39-93; e-mail botschaft.usbekistan@aon.at; Chargé d'affaires: SHUKRAT KHAKIMOV.

**Venezuela:** 1030 Vienna, Marokkanergasse 22; tel. (1) 712-26-38; fax (1) 715-32-19; Ambassador: Prof. Dr DEMETRIO BOERSNER.

**Viet Nam:** 1190 Vienna, Félix-Mottl-Str. 20; tel. (1) 368-07-55; fax (1) 368-07-54; e-mail embassyofvietnam@netway.at; Ambassador: NGUYEN XUAN HONG.

**Yemen:** 1040 Vienna, Karolinengasse 5/7; tel. (1) 503-29-30; fax (1) 505-31-59; e-mail vienna@yemen-embassy.at; Ambassador: Dr HASSAN MOHAMED MAKKI.

**Yugoslavia:** 1030 Vienna, Rennweg 3; tel. (1) 713-25-95; fax (1) 713-25-97; e-mail yuambaus@ins.at; Ambassador: Dr RADOS SMILJKOVIĆ.

**Zimbabwe:** 1080 Vienna, Strozzigasse 10/15; tel. (1) 407-92-36; fax (1) 407-92-38; Ambassador: EVELYN LILLIAN KAWONZA.

* In February 2000 Austria's 14 fellow EU member states suspended bilateral political co-operation, maintaining diplomatic contact at a 'technical' level.

† In February 2000 the Governments of Israel and the USA withdrew their ambassadors from Austria for consultations, pending the reassessment of bilateral relations.

# Judicial System

The Austrian legal system is based on the principle of a division between legislative, administrative and judicial power. There are three supreme courts (Verfassungsgerichtshof, Verwaltungsgerichtshof and Oberster Gerichtshof). The judicial courts are organized into about 200 local courts (Bezirksgerichte), 17 provincial and district courts (Landes- und Kreisgerichte), and four higher provincial courts (Oberlandesgerichte) in Vienna, Graz, Innsbruck and Linz.

### SUPREME ADMINISTRATIVE COURTS

**Verfassungsgerichtshof** (Constitutional Court): 1010 Vienna, Judenplatz 11; fax (1) 531-22-499; e-mail vfgh@vfgh.gv.at; internet www.vfgh.gv.at; f. 1919; deals with matters affecting the Constitution, examines the legality of legislation and administration; Pres. Prof. Dr LUDWIG ADAMOVICH; Vice-Pres. Prof. Dr KARL KORINEK.

**Verwaltungsgerichtshof** (Administrative Court): 1010 Vienna, Judenplatz 11; tel. (1) 531-11; fax (1) 531-11-135; deals with matters affecting the legality of administration; Pres. Prof. Dr CLEMENS JABLONER; Vice-Pres. Prof. Dr WOLFGANG PESENDORFER.

### SUPREME JUDICIAL COURT

**Oberster Gerichtshof:** 1016 Vienna, Schmerlingplatz 10–11; tel. (1) 521-52-0; fax (1) 521-52-37-10; Pres. Dr ERWIN FELZMANN; Vice-Pres Dr HORST SCHLOSSER, Hon. Prof. Dr KONRAD BRUSTBAUER.

# Religion

### CHRISTIANITY

**Ökumenischer Rat der Kirchen in Österreich** (Ecumenical Council of Churches in Austria): 1010 Vienna, Fleischmarkt 13; tel. (1) 533-29-65; fax (1) 533-38-89; f. 1958; 14 mem. Churches, 11 observers; Hon. Pres. Bishop MICHAEL STAIKOS (Greek Orthodox Church); Vice-Pres Dr JOHANNES DANTINE (Protestant Church of the Augsburgian Confession), Mother Superior CHRISTINE GLEIXNER (Roman Catholic Church); Sec. Superintendent HELMUT NAUSNER (United Methodist Church).

#### The Roman Catholic Church

Austria comprises two archdioceses, seven dioceses and the territorial abbacy of Wettingen-Mehrerau (directly responsible to the Holy See). The Archbishop of Vienna is also the Ordinary for Catholics of the Byzantine rite in Austria (totalling an estimated 5,000 at 31 December 1997). At 31 December 1997 there were an estimated 5,967,497 adherents (about 74% of the population).

**Bishops' Conference:** Österreichische Bischofskonferenz, 1010 Vienna, Wollzeile 2; tel. (1) 515-52-280; fax (1) 515-52-436; e-mail sekretariat@bischofskonferenz.at; internet www.bischofskonferenz.at; f. 1849; Pres. Cardinal Dr CHRISTOPH SCHÖNBORN, Archbishop of Vienna; Sec. ÄGIDIUS ZSIFKOVICS.

**Archbishop of Salzburg:** Most Rev. Dr GEORG EDER, 5020 Salzburg, Kapitelplatz 2; 5010 Salzburg, PF 62; tel. (662) 80-47-200; fax (662) 80-47-213; e-mail erzbischof-eder@kirchen.net; internet www.kirchen.net.

**Archbishop of Vienna:** Cardinal Dr CHRISTOPH SCHÖNBORN, 1010 Vienna, Wollzeile 2; tel. (1) 515-52-0; fax (1) 515-52-37-28.

#### Orthodox Churches

The Armenian Apostolic Church and the Bulgarian, Coptic, Greek, Romanian, Russian, Serbian and Syrian Orthodox Churches are active in Austria.

#### The Anglican Communion

Within the Church of England, Austria forms part of the diocese of Gibraltar in Europe. The Bishop is resident in London.

**Archdeacon of the Eastern Archdeaconry:** Ven. JEREMY PEAKE, 1020 Vienna, Thugutstr. 2/12; tel. and fax (1) 663-92-09-264.

#### Protestant Churches

**Bund der Baptistengemeinden in Österreich** (Fed. of Baptist Communities): 1030 Vienna, Krummgasse 7/4; tel. (1) 713-68-28; fax (1) 713-68-28-4; Pres. Rev. HORST FISCHER.

**Evangelische Kirche Augsburgischen Bekenntnisses in Österreich** (Protestant Church of the Augsburgian Confession): 1180 Vienna, Severin-Schreiber-Gasse 3; tel. (1) 479-15-23; fax (1) 479-15-23-330; e-mail bischof@okr-evang.at; internet www.evang.at; 340,422 mems; Bishop Mag. HERWIG STURM.

**Evangelische Kirche HB (Helvetischen Bekenntnisses)** (Protestant Church of the Helvetic Confession): 1010 Vienna, Dorotheergasse 16; tel. (1) 513-65-64; fax (1) 512-44-90; e-mail kirche-hb@evang.at; 15,863 mems; Landessuperintendent Pfr. PETER KARNER.

**Evangelisch-methodistische Kirche** (United Methodist Church): 1100 Vienna, Landgutgasse 39/7; tel. (1) 604-53-47; fax (1) 606-67-17; Superintendent HELMUT NAUSNER.

#### Other Christian Churches

**Altkatholische Kirche Österreichs** (Old Catholic Church in Austria): 1010 Vienna, Schottenring 17; tel. (1) 317-83-94; fax (1) 317-83-95-9; c. 18,000 mems; Bishop BERNHARD HEITZ.

### JUDAISM

There are about 10,000 Jews in Austria.

**Israelitische Kultusgemeinde** (Jewish Community): 1010 Vienna, Seitenstettengasse 4; tel. (1) 531-04-0; fax (1) 533-15-77; Pres. Dr ARIEL MUZICANT.

# The Press

Austria's first newspaper was published in 1605. The *Wiener Zeitung*, founded in 1703, is the world's oldest daily paper. Restrictions on press freedom are permissible only within the framework of Article 10 (2) of the European Convention of Human Rights.

The Austrian Press Council (Presserat), founded in 1961, supervises the activities of the press. Vienna is the focus of newspaper and periodical publishing, although there is also a strong press in some provinces. The three highest circulation dailies are the *Neue Kronen-Zeitung,* the *Kurier,* and the *Kleine Zeitung* (Graz).

### PRINCIPAL DAILIES

#### Bregenz

**Neue Vorarlberger Tageszeitung:** 6901 Bregenz, Arlbergstr. 117; tel. (5574) 40-90; fax (5574) 40-93-00; f. 1972; morning; independent; Editor (vacant); circ. 20,136.

**Vorarlberger Nachrichten:** 6901 Bregenz, Kirchstr. 35; tel. (5574) 51-22-27; fax (5574) 51-22-30; internet www.vol.at; morning; Editor EUGEN A. RUSS; circ. 74,948.

#### Graz

**Kleine Zeitung:** 8011 Graz, Schönaugasse 64; tel. (316) 87-50; fax (316) 87-54-03-4; internet www.kleine.co.at; f. 1904; independent; Chief Editor Dr ERWIN ZANKEL; circ. 177,050.

**Neue Zeit:** 8054 Graz, Ankerstr. 4; tel. (316) 28-08-0; fax (316) 28-08-32-5; f. 1945; morning; Editor JOSEF RIEDLER.

#### Innsbruck

**Tiroler Tageszeitung:** 6020 Innsbruck, Ing.-Etzel-Str. 30; tel. (512) 53-54-0; fax (512) 57-59-24; e-mail tt.redaktion@tirol.com; internet www.tirol.com.tt; morning; independent; Chief Editor CLAUS REITEN; circ. 103,630.

#### Klagenfurt

**Kärntner Tageszeitung:** 9020 Klagenfurt, Viktringer Ring 28; tel. (463) 58-66-0; fax (463) 58-66-32-1; f. 1946; morning except Monday; Socialist; Chief Editor Dr HELLWIG VALENTIN.

**Kleine Zeitung:** 9020 Klagenfurt, Funderstr. 1A; tel. (463) 200-58-00; fax (463) 56-50-0; independent; Editor Dr HORST PIRKER; circ. 99,380.

#### Linz

**Neues Volksblatt:** 4010 Linz, Hafenstr. 1–3; tel. (732) 76-06-0; fax (732) 77-92-42; e-mail volksblatt@volksblatt.at; internet www.volksblatt.at; f. 1869; Austrian People's Party; Chief Editor Dr FRANZ ROHRHOFER.

**Oberösterreichische Nachrichten:** 4010 Linz, Promenade 23; tel. (732) 78-05-41-0; fax (732) 78-05-21-7; internet www.oon.at; f. 1865; morning; independent; Chief Editor Dr HANS KÖPPL; circ. 123,470.

### Salzburg

***Salzburger Nachrichten:** 5021 Salzburg, Karolingerstr. 40; tel. (662) 83-73-0; fax (662) 83-73-39-9; e-mail service@salzburg.com; internet www.salzburg.com; f. 1945; morning; independent; Editor-in-Chief RONALD ARAZON; circ. 99,123.

**Salzburger Volkszeitung:** 5020 Salzburg, Bergstr. 12; tel. (662) 87-94-91; fax (662) 87-94-91-13; Austrian People's Party; Editor HELMUT MÖDLHAMMER; circ. weekdays 12,030.

### Vienna

***Kurier:** 1072 Vienna, Lindengasse 52; tel. (1) 521-00; fax (1) 521-00-22-63; e-mail leser@kurier.at; internet www2.kurier.at; f. 1954; independent; Chief Editor PETER RABL; circ. weekdays 334,204, Sunday 545,700.

***Neue Kronen-Zeitung:** 1190 Vienna, Muthgasse 2; tel. (1) 360-10; fax (1) 369-83-85; internet www.krone.at; f. 1900; independent; Editor HANS DICHAND; circ. weekdays 510,226, Sunday 751,296.

***Die Presse:** 1015 Vienna, Parkring 12a; tel. (1) 514-14; fax (1) 514-14-400; e-mail chefredaktion@presse-wien.at; internet www.diepresse.at; f. 1848; morning; independent; Editors JULIUS KAINZ, Dr THOMAS CHORHERR; circ. Mon.–Wed. 96,000, Thur.–Fri. 105,000; Sat. 156,000.

***Der Standard:** 1014 Vienna, Herrengasse 19–21; tel. (1) 531-70; fax (1) 531-70-13-1; e-mail documentation@derstandard.at; internet www.derstandard.at; f. 1988; independent; Editors-in-Chief OSCAR BRONNER, Dr GERFRIED SPERL; circ. 104,050.

***Wiener Zeitung:** 1037 Vienna, Rennweg 16; tel. (1) 797-89; fax (1) 797-89-43-3; internet www.wienerzeitung.at; f. 1703; morning; official govt paper; Editor HORST TRAXLER; circ. 20,020.

* National newspapers.

## PRINCIPAL WEEKLIES

**Blickpunkt:** 6020 Innsbruck, E.-Bodem-Gasse 6; tel. (512) 32-00; fax (512) 32-01-20; Editor OTTO STEIXNER.

**Die Furche:** 1010 Vienna, Lobkowitzplatz 1, Singerstr. 7; tel. (1) 512-52-61; fax (1) 512-82-15; f. 1945; Catholic; Editor Dr GOTTFRIED MOIK.

**Die ganze Woche:** 1210 Vienna, Ignaz-Köck Str. 17; tel. (1) 391-60-0; fax (1) 391-60-06-4; circ. 582,060.

**industrie:** 1030 Vienna, Reisnerstr. 40/2; tel. (1) 711-95-0; fax (1) 711-95-52-99; Editor MILAN FRÜHBAUER; circ. 14,330.

**IW-Internationale Wirtschaft:** 1051 Vienna, Nikolsdorfer Gasse 7–11; tel. (1) 546-64-346; fax (1) 546-64-342; economics; Editor NIKOLAUS GERSTMAYER; circ. 13,430.

**Kärntner Nachrichten:** 9010 Klagenfurt, Waagplatz 7; tel. (463) 51-14-17-22; fax (463) 50-41-85; f. 1954; Editor HANS RIEPAN.

**Die neue Wirtschaft:** 1051 Vienna, Nikolsdorfer Gasse 7–11; tel. (1) 546-64-24-7; fax (1) 546-64-34-7; economics; circ. 25,650.

**Neue Wochenschau:** 7210 Mattersburg, J. N. Bergerstr. 2; tel. and fax (2622) 67-47-3; f. 1908; Editor HELMUT WALTER; circ. 128,500.

**NFZ—Neue Freie Zeitung:** 1010 Vienna, Grillparzerstr. 7/7A; tel. (1) 402-35-85-0; fax (1) 408-68-38-31; organ of Freedom Party; Chief Editor MICHAEL A. RICHTER; circ. 60,000.

**Niederösterreichische Nachrichten:** 3100 St Pölten, Gutenbergstr. 12; tel. (2742) 80-20; fax (2742) 80-21-48-0; e-mail chefredaktion@noen.at; internet www.noen.at; Editor HARALD KNABL; circ. 158,972.

**Oberösterreichische Rundschau:** 4010 Linz, Hafenstr. 1–3; tel. (732) 76-16-0; fax (732) 76-16-30-7; Editor-in-Chief RUDOLF CHMELIR; circ. 284,650.

**Der Österreichische Bauernbündler:** 1014 Vienna, Schenkenstr. 2; tel. (1) 533-16-76-16; fax (1) 533-16-76-45; Editor Prof. PAUL GRUBER; circ. 70,000.

**Präsent:** 6020 Innsbruck, Exlgasse 20; tel. (512) 22-33; fax (512) 22-33-50-1; f. 1892; independent Catholic; Chief Editor PAUL MVIGG.

**Samstag:** 1081 Vienna, Faradaygasse 6; tel. (1) 795-94-13-5; e-mail samstag@heroldwien.at; f. 1951; weekly; independent; Chief Editor GERLINDE KOLANDA; circ. 41,000.

**Tiroler Bauernzeitung:** 6021 Innsbruck, Brixner Str. 1; tel. (512) 59-90-00; fax (1) 59-90-03-1; publ. by Tiroler Bauernbund; Chief Dir GEORG KEUSCHNIGG; circ. 23,000.

**Volksstimme:** 1040 Vienna, Weyringergasse 35/DG; tel. (1) 503-68-28; fax (1) 503-66-38; e-mail redaktion@volksstimme.at; f. 1994; Chief Editor WALTER BAIER.

## POPULAR PERIODICALS

**Agrar Post:** Vienna, 2103 Langenzersdorf, Schulstr. 80; tel. (2244) 46-47; f. 1924; monthly; agriculture.

**Austria-Ski:** 6020 Innsbruck, Olympiastr. 10; tel. (512) 335-01-0; 6 a year; official journal of Austrian Skiing Asscn; Editor Mag. JOSEF SCHMID.

**auto touring:** 3400 Klosterneuburg, Tauchnergasse 5; tel. (2243) 40-40; fax (2243) 40-43-72-1; e-mail ottoburghart@oeamtc.at; monthly; official journal of the Austrian Automobile Organizations; Editor-in-Chief OTTO BURGHART; circ. 1,180,000.

**Bunte Österreich:** 1010 Vienna, Karl Luegel Platz 2; tel. (1) 513-88-33; fax (1) 513-88-38; illustrated weekly.

**Frauenblatt:** 1032 Vienna, Faradaygasse 6; tel. (1) 795-94-13-5; e-mail samstag@heroldwien.at; women's weekly; Editor GERLINDE KOLANDA; circ. 22,300.

**Die Neue Sportzeitung:** 1080 Vienna, Piaristengasse 16; tel. (1) 405-55-88; fax (1) 402-49-60; e-mail redaktion@sportzeitung.at; internet www.sportzeitung.at; f. 1949; weekly sports illustrated; Editor HORST HÖTSCH; circ. 28,330.

**News:** 1020 Vienna, Praterstr. 31; tel. (1) 213-12-0; fax (1) 213-12-30-0; weekly; illustrated; Editor WOLFGANG FELLNER; circ. 342,244.

**Profil:** 1010 Vienna, Marc-Aurel-Str. 10–12; tel. (1) 534-70-0; fax (1) 535-32-50; e-mail redaktion@profil.at; f. 1970; weekly; political, general; independent; circ. 98,490.

**RZ—Wochenschau:** Vienna; tel. (1) 523-56-46; fax (1) 523-56-46-22; f. 1936; weekly illustrated; Chief Editor PAUL WEISS.

**Trend:** 1010 Vienna, Marc-Aurel-Str. 10–12; tel. (1) 534-70; monthly; economics.

**TV Media:** 1020 Vienna, Praterstr. 31; tel. (1) 213-120; weekly; illustrated; Editor WOLFGANG FELLNER; circ. 210,150.

**Vídeňské svobodné listy:** 1050 Vienna, Margaretenplatz 7/2; tel. (1) 587-83-08; fortnightly for Czech and Slovak communities in Austria; Editor HEINRICH DRAZDIL.

**Welt der Frau:** 4020 Linz, Lustenauerstr. 21; tel. (732) 77-00-01-11; fax (732) 77-00-01-24; women's monthly magazine; circ. 73,530.

**Wiener:** 3400 Klosterneuburg, Büropark Donau, Donaustr. 102; tel. (1) 88-60-0; fax (1) 88-60-01-99; monthly; Chief Editor HANS SCHMID; circ. 130,530.

## SPECIALIST PERIODICALS

**Eurocity:** 1110 Vienna, Leberstr. 122; tel. (1) 740-95-0; fax (1) 740-95-49-1; e-mail eurocity.zv@bohmann.co.at; f. 1928; every 2 months; Editor-in-Chief GEORG KARP.

**Forum:** 1070 Vienna, Museumstr. 5; tel. (1) 932-73-3; fax (1) 938-36-8; f. 1954; every 2 months; international magazine for cultural freedom, political equality and labour solidarity; Editor-in-Chief GERHARD OBERSCHLICK.

**itm praktiker:** ZB-Verlag, 1125 Vienna, Marochallplatz 23/1/21; tel. (1) 804-04-74; fax (1) 804-44-39; technical hobbies; Chief Editor GERHARD K. BUCHBERGER; circ. 18,800.

**Juristische Blätter (mit Beilage 'Wirtschaftsrechtliche Blätter'):** Springer Verlag, 1201 Vienna, Sachsenplatz 4; tel. (1) 330-24-15-0; f. 1872; monthly; Editors F. BYDLINSKI, M. BURGSTALLER.

**Die Landwirtschaft:** 1010 Vienna, Löwelstr. 16; tel. (1) 534-41; fax (1) 534-41-45-0; f. 1923; monthly; agriculture and forestry; owned and publ. by Österreichischer Agrarverlag; Editor GERD RITTENAUER.

**Liberal Konkret:** 1010 Vienna, Reichsratstr. 7/10; tel. (1) 402-78-81; fax (1) 402-78-89; e-mail bund@lif.or.at; internet www.lif.or.at; 10 a year; organ of Liberal Forum.

**Literatur und Kritik:** Otto-Müller-Verlag, 5020 Salzburg, Ernest-Thun-Str. 11; tel. (662) 88-19-74; fax (662) 87-23-87; f. 1966; 5 a year; Austrian and European literature and criticism; Editor KARL-MARKUS GAUSS.

**Monatshefte für Chemie:** 1201 Vienna, Sachsenplatz 4–6; tel. (1) 330-24-15-0; f. 1880; monthly; chemistry; Man. Editor K. SCHLÖGL.

**Österreichische Ärztezeitung:** 1010 Vienna, Weihburggasse 9; tel. (1) 512-44-86; fax (1) 512-44-86-24; e-mail presse.verlags@oak.at; f. 1945; 21 a year; organ of the Austrian Medical Board; Editor MARTIN STICKLER.

**Österreichische Ingenieur- und Architekten-Zeitschrift (ÖIAZ):** 1010 Vienna, Eschenbachgasse 9; tel. (1) 587-35-36-28; fax (1) 587-35-36; e-mail office@oiav.at; internet www.members.eunct.at/oiavi; f. 1849; 6 a year; Editor Dr GEORG WIDTMANN; circ. 4,000.

**Österreichische Monatshefte:** 1010 Vienna, Lichtenfelsgasse 7; tel. (1) 401-26-53-2. 1945; monthly; organ of Austrian People's Party; Editor GERHARD WILFLINGER.

**Österreichische Musikzeitschrift:** 1010 Vienna, Hegelgasse 13; tel. (1) 512-68-69; fax (1) 512-46-29; f. 1946; monthly; Editor Dr M. DIEDERICHS-LAFITE; circ. 5,000.

**Reichsbund-Aktuell mit SPORT:** 1080 Vienna, Laudongasse 16/3/2a; tel. and fax (1) 405-54-06; f. 1917; monthly; Catholic; organ of Reichsbund, Bewegung für christliche Gesellschaftspolitik und Sport; Editor WALTER RAMING; circ. 12,000.

**Welt der Arbeit:** 1230 Vienna, Altmannsdorferstr. 154-156; tel. (1) 662-32-96; socialist industrial journal; Editor WALTER KRATZER; circ 64,350.

**Wiener klinische Wochenschrift:** 1201 Vienna, Sachsenplatz 4–6; tel. (1) 330-24-15; fax (1) 330-24-26; f. 1888; medical bi-weekly; Editors O. KRAUPP, H. SINZINGER.

**Die Zukunft:** 1014 Vienna, Loewelstr. 18; tel. (1) 534-27-20-6; fax (1) 535-96-83; monthly; organ of Social-Democratic Party of Austria; Editor ALBRECHT K. KONECNY; circ. 15,000.

## NEWS AGENCIES

**APA (Austria Presse-Agentur):** Internationales Pressezentrum (IPZ), 1199 Vienna, Gunoldstr. 14; tel. (1) 360-60-0; fax (1) 360-60-30-99; e-mail marketing@apa.at; internet www.apa.at; f. 1946; co-operative agency of the Austrian Newspapers and Broadcasting Co (private co); 37 mems; Man. Dir Dr WOLFGANG VYSLOZIL; Chief Editor WOLFGANG MAYR.

### Foreign Bureaux

**Agence France-Presse (AFP)** (France): IPZ, 1199 Vienna, Gunoldstr. 14; tel. (1) 368-31-87; fax (1) 368-31-88-20; e-mail afpvie@afp.com; Bureau Chief PATRICK RAHIR.

**Agenzia Nazionale Stampa Associata (ANSA)** (Italy): IPZ, 1199 Vienna, Gunoldstr. 14; tel. (1) 368-13-00; fax (1) 368-79-35; Bureau Chief ROBERTO PAPI.

**Associated Press (AP)** (USA): IPZ, 1199 Vienna, Gunoldstr. 14; tel. (1) 368-41-56; fax (1) 369-15-58; Bureau Chief ROBERT REID.

**Central News Agency (CNA)** (Taiwan): 1030 Vienna, Trubelgasse 17-4-40; tel. (1) 799-17-02; fax (1) 798-45-98; Bureau Chief OU CHUN-LIN.

**Česká tisková kancelář (ČTK)** (Czech Republic): Vienna; tel. and fax (1) 439-21-8.

**Deutsche Presse-Agentur (dpa)** (Germany): IPZ, 1199 Vienna, Gunoldstr. 14; tel. (1) 368-21-58; fax (1) 369-85-49.

**Informatsionnoye Telegrafnoye Agentstvo Rossii–Telegrafnoye Agentstvo Suverennykh Stran (ITAR–TASS)** (Russia): 1040 Vienna, Grosse Neugasse 28; tel. (1) 810-43-1; fax (1) 566-53-6; Correspondent ALEKSANDR S. KUZMIN.

**Jiji Tsushin-Sha** (Japan): IPZ, 1199 Vienna, Gunoldstr. 14; tel. (1) 369-17-97; fax (1) 369-10-52; Bureau Chief SATO NOBUYUKI.

**Kyodo Tsushin** (Japan): IPZ, 1199 Vienna, Gunoldstr. 14/130; tel. (1) 368-15-20; fax (1) 369-92-52-2; e-mail nagatarr@kyodonews.or.jp; Bureau Chief MASATOSHI NAGATA.

**Magyar Távirati Iroda (MTI)** (Hungary): Vienna, Premreinergasse, tel. and fax (1) 876-69-94; Correspondent ZSÓFIA FÜLEP.

**Novinska Agencija Tanjug (Tanjug)** (Yugoslavia): Vienna; tel. (1) 37-60-82; fax (1) 368-11-80.

**Reuters** (UK): 1010 Vienna, Börsegasse 11; tel. (1) 531-12-0; fax (1) 531-12-5; Bureau Chief DAVID T. CROUCH.

**Xinhua (New China) News Agency** (People's Republic of China): 1030 Vienna, Reisnerstr. 15/8; tel. (1) 713-41-40; fax (1) 714-14-57; Chief Correspondent YANG HUANQIN.

## PRESS ASSOCIATIONS

**Österreichischer Zeitschriften-Verband** (Asscn of Periodical Publrs): 1090 Vienna, Hörlgasse 18/5; tel. and fax (1) 319-70-01; e-mail oezv@teleweb.at; internet www.oezv.or.at; f. 1946; 190 mems; Pres. Dr RUDOLF BOHMANN; Vice-Pres. and Man. Dir Dr WOLFGANG BRANDSTETTER.

**Verband Österreichischer Zeitungen** (Newspaper Asscn of Austria): 1010 Vienna, Renngasse 12; tel. (1) 533-79-79-0; fax (1) 533-79-79-22; e-mail gs@voez.co.at; internet www.voez.at; f. 1946; 14 daily and most weekly papers are mems; Pres. Dr MAX DASCH; Sec.-Gen. Dr WALTER SCHAFFELHOFER.

# Publishers

**Akademische Druck- und Verlagsanstalt:** 8010 Graz, Auersperggasse 12, PF 598; tel. (316) 36-44; fax (316) 36-44-24; e-mail info@adeva.com; internet www.adeva.com; f. 1949; scholarly reprints and new works, facsimile editions of Codices; Dir Dr URSULA STRUZL.

**Alekto Verlag GmbH:** 9020 Klagenfurt, Radetzkystr. 10; tel. (463) 515230; fax (463) 503351; e-mail bali@bali.co.at; literature; Man. Dir STEFAN ZEFFERER.

**Betz, Annette, Verlag GmbH:** 1091 Vienna, Alser Str. 24; tel. (1) 404-44-0; fax (1) 404-44-5; f. 1962; Man. Dir Dr JOHANNA RACHINGER.

**Blackwell Wissenschafts-Verlag GmbH:** 1130 Vienna, Firmiangasse 7; tel. (1) 877-93-51-0; fax (1) 877-93-51-24; e-mail verlag@blackwis.at; internet www.blackwis.de; f. 1989; medicine, medical journals; Dir MARTIN WILKINSON.

**Böhlau Verlag GmbH & Co KG:** 1201 Vienna, Sachsenplatz 4–6; tel. (1) 330-24-27; fax (1) 330-24-32; e-mail dr.rauch@boehlau.at; f. 1947; history, law, philology, the arts, sociology; Dirs Dr PETER RAUCH, RUDOLF SIEGLE.

**Bohmann Druck und Verlag GmbH & Co KG:** 1010 Vienna, Universitätsstr. 11; tel. (1) 407-27-08; fax (1) 407-27-08-88; e-mail buchverlag@bohmann.at; internet www.bohmann-buch.at; f. 1936; trade, technical and educational books and periodicals.

**Christian Brandstätter, Verlag und Edition:** 1070 Vienna, Schwarzenbergstr. 5; tel. (1) 514-05-233; fax (1) 514-05-231; e-mail books@cbv.co.at; f. 1982; art books; Chair. Dr CHRISTIAN BRANDSTÄTTER.

**Wilhelm Braumüller Universitätsverlagsbuchhandlung, GmbH:** 1092 Vienna, Servitengasse 5; tel. (1) 319-14-82; fax (1) 310-28-05; e-mail braumueller@mis.magnet.at; f. 1783; sociology, politics, history, law, ethnology, linguistics, journalism, communications, psychology, philosophy, literature and theatre; university publrs; Dir BRIGITTE PFEIFER.

**Czernin Verlag GmbH:** 1010 Vienna, Stallburggasse 2; tel. (1) 512-07-32; fax (1) 512-01-32.

**Franz Deuticke Verlagsgesellschaft mbH:** 1010 Vienna, Hegelgasse 21; tel. (1) 514-05-281; fax (1) 514-05-289; e-mail schmidt@oebv.co.at; f. 1878; culture, literature, travel guides; Dirs WALTER AMON, Dr MARTINA SCHMIDT.

**Ludwig Doblinger Musikhaus-Musikverlag:** 1010 Vienna, Dorotheergasse 10; tel. (1) 515-03-0; fax (1) 515-03-51; e-mail music@doblinger.co.at; f. 1876; music; Dir HELMUTH PANY.

**Freytag-Berndt und Artaria KG Kartographische Anstalt:** 1231 Vienna, Brunnerstr. 69; tel. (1) 869-90-90; fax (1) 869-88-55; f. 1879 (1770–Artaria); geography, maps and atlases; Chair. FRANZ LEBER.

**Gerold & Co:** 1011 Vienna, Graben 31; tel. (1) 533-50-14; fax (1) 533-50-14; f. 1867; philology, literature, eastern Europe, sociology and philosophy; Dir PETER NEUSSER.

**Verlag Kerle im Verlag Herder & Co:** 1010 Vienna, Wollzeile 33; tel. (1) 512-14-65; fax (1) 512-14-13-60; f. 1886; children's books, juvenile.

**Verlagsbuchhandlung Brüder Hollinek und Co GmbH:** 3002 Purkersdorf, Luisenstr. 20; tel. and fax (2231) 673-65; f. 1872; science, law and administration, printing, reference works, dictionaries; Dir RICHARD HOLLINEK.

**Jugend and Volk GmbH:** 1016 Vienna,Universitätsstr. 11; tel. (1) 407-27-07; fax (1) 407-27-07-22; e-mail verlag@jugendvolk.co.at; internet www.jugendvolk.co.at; f. 1921; pedagogics, art, literature, children's books.

**Verlag Kremayr & Scheriau:** 1121 Vienna, Niederhofstr. 37; tel. (1) 811-02; fax (1) 811-02-616; f. 1951; non-fiction, history.

**Kunstverlag Wolfrum:** 1010 Vienna, Augustinerstr. 10; tel. (1) 512-53-98-0; fax (1) 512-53-98-57; f. 1919; art; Dir HUBERT WOLFRUM.

**Leykam Verlag:** 8011 Graz, Stempfergasse 3; tel. (316) 80-76; fax (316) 80-76-39; f. 1585; art, literature, academic, law; Dir Dr KLAUS BRUNNER.

**Linde Verlag Wien:** 1211 Vienna, Scheydgasse 24; tel. (1) 278-05-26; fax (1) 278-05-26-23; e-mail info.service@linde-verlag.telecom.at; f. 1925; business; Man. Dir HEIDELINDE LANGMAYR.

**Manz'sche Verlags- und Universitätsbuchhandlung GmbH:** 1014 Vienna, Kohlmarkt 16; tel. (1) 531-61-0; fax (1) 531-61-181; e-mail verlag@manz.at; f. 1849; law, political and economic sciences; textbooks and schoolbooks; Man. Dir Dr WOLFGANG PICHLER.

**Wilhelm Maudrich:** 1096 Vienna, Spitalgasse 21a; tel. (1) 408-58-92; fax (1) 408-50-80; e-mail medbook@maudrich.com; internet www.maudrich.com; f. 1909; medical; Man. Dir GERHARD GROIS.

**Molden Verlag GmbH:** 1010 Vienna, Stadiongasse 6–8; tel. (1) 403-94-09; fax (1) 402-97-55.

**Otto Müller Verlag:** 5021 Salzburg, Ernest-Thun-Str. 11; tel. (662) 88-19-74; fax (662) 87-23-87; f. 1937; general; Man. ARNO KLEIBEL.

**öbv & hpt Verlags-gesellschaft mbH:** 1096 Vienna, Frankgasse 4; tel. (1) 407-36; fax (1) 401-36-185; e-mail office@oebvhpt.at.

**Verlag Oldenbourg:** 1030 Vienna, Neulinggasse 26/12; tel. (1) 712-62-58; fax (1) 712-62-58-19; e-mail gala@oldenbourg.co.at; f. 1959; Dir Dr THOMAS CORNIDES.

**Verlag Orac:** 1010 Vienna, Graben 17; tel. (1) 534-52; fax (1) 534-52-14-1; e-mail bestellung@orac.at; internet www.orac.at; f. 1946; Dir Dr DIETRICH SCHERF.

**Anna Pichler Verlag GmbH:** 1060 Vienna, Marchettigasse 6; tel. (1) 597-16-52.

**Pinguin Verlag Pawlowski GmbH:** 6021 Innsbruck, Lindenbühelweg 2; tel. (512) 28-11-83; fax (512) 29-32-43; f. 1945; illustrated books; Dirs OLAF PAWLOWSKI, HELLA PFLANZER.

**Residenz Verlag GmbH:** 5020 Salzburg, Gaisbergstr. 6; tel. (662) 64-19-86; fax (662) 64-35-48; e-mail residenz@oebv.co.at; f. 1956; Dir Dr JOCHEN JUNG.

**Anton Schroll & Co:** 1051 Vienna, Spengergasse 37; tel. (1) 544-56-41; fax (1) 544-56-41-66; f. 1884; also in Munich; art books; Man. F. GEYER.

**Springer-Verlag KG:** 1201 Vienna, Sachsenplatz 4–6; tel. (1) 330-24-15; fax (1) 330-24-26; f. 1924; medicine, science, technology, law, sociology, economics, periodicals; Man. Dir RUDOLF SIEGLE.

**Leopold Stocker Verlag:** 8011 Graz, Hofgasse 5; tel. (316) 82-16-36; fax (316) 83-56-12; f. 1917; history, nature, hunting, fiction, agriculture, textbooks; Dir WOLFGANG DVORAK-STOCKER.

**Verlag Styria:** 8011 Graz, Schönaugasse 64; tel. (316) 80-63-0; fax (316) 80-63-70-04; e-mail skaiser@styria.co.at; f. 1869; literature, history, theology, philosophy; Chair. Dr REINHARD HABER-FELLNER.

**Verlagsanstalt Tyrolia GmbH:** 6020 Innsbruck, Exlgasse 20, PF 220; tel. (512) 22-33; fax (512) 22-33-50-1; e-mail tyrolia@tyrolia-verlagsanstalt.co.at; f. 1888; geography, history, science, children's, religion, fiction; Chair. Dr RAIMUND TISCHLER.

**Carl Ueberreuter Verlag:** 1091 Vienna, Alser Str. 24; tel. (1) 404-44-0; fax (1) 404-44-5; e-mail office@vcu.ueberreuter.com; non-fiction, children's, economics; CEO JOHANNA RACHINGER.

**Universal Edition:** 1040 Vienna, Brucknerstr. 6; tel. (1) 505-86-95; fax (1) 505-27-20; e-mail uemusic@uemusic.at; internet www.uemusic.at; f. 1901; music; Dir Dr J. JURANEK; Dir. MARION VON HARTLIEB.

**Urban & Schwarzenberg GmbH:** 1096 Vienna, Frankgasse 4; tel. (1) 405-27-31; fax (1) 405-27-24-41; f. 1866; science, medicine; Dir GUNTER ROYER.

**Paul Zsolnay Verlag GmbH:** 1041 Vienna, Prinz Eugen-Str. 30; tel. (1) 505-76-61; fax (1) 505-76-61-10; e-mail pzsolnay@aol.com; f. 1923; fiction, non-fiction; Dirs MICHAEL KRÜGER, STEPHAN D. JOSS.

### Government Publishing House

**Verlag Österreich** (Austrian Publishing House): 1037 Vienna, Rennweg 12A; tel. (1) 797-89-41-9; fax (1) 797-89-104; e-mail verlag-oesterreich@verlag.oesd.co.at; f. 1804; law, CD-ROMs.

### PUBLISHERS' ASSOCIATION

**Hauptverband des Österreichischen Buchhandels** (Asscn of Austrian Publrs and Booksellers): 1010 Vienna, Grünangergasse 4; tel. (1) 512-15-35; fax (1) 512-84-82; e-mail sekretariat@hvb.at; internet www.buecher.at; f. 1859; Pres. Dr ANTON C. HILSCHER; 605 mems.

# Broadcasting and Communications

### TELECOMMUNICATIONS

**Telekom-Control Österreichische Gesellschaft für Telekommunikationsregulierung mbH:** 1060 Vienna, Mariahilfer Str. 77–79; tel. (1) 580-58-0; fax (1) 580-58-9-191; e-mail tkc@tkc.at; internet www.tkc.at; f. 1997; regulatory body for the telecommunications sector.

**Telekom Austria AG:** 1090 Vienna, Nordbergstr. 15; tel. (0800) 100-800; e-mail kundenservice@telekom.at; internet www.telekom.at; f. 1998; 75%-owned by PTA AG (Austria), 25%-owned by Telecom Italia/STET International; Dir-Gen. WERNER KETZLER.

**Connect Austria Gesellschaft für Telekommunikation GmbH:** 1210 Vienna, Brunnerstr. 52; tel. (1) 277-28-0; internet www.connectaustria.at; Chair. FRANZ GEIGER.

**max.mobil Telekommunikation Service GmbH:** 1030 Vienna, Kelsenstr. 5–7; tel. (1) 795-85-0; fax (1) 795-85-53-2; internet www.maxmobil.at; Chair. Dr STEPHAN HUXOLD.

**mobilkom Austria AG:** 1200 Vienna, Treustr. 43; tel. (1) 331-61-0; internet www.mobilkom.at.

**tele.ring Telekom Service GmbH & Co KG:** 1140 Vienna, Linzer Str. 221; tel. (1) 931-01-20; internet www.1012privat.at; 54%-owned by Mannesmann AG (Germany).

### RADIO AND TELEVISION

In December 1996 there were 1,757 radio and television transmitters in Austria. The state-owned Österreichischer Rundfunk (ORF) provides three national and nine regional radio channels, as well as an overseas service. The ORF also has two terrestrial television channels, and operates a satellite station in conjunction with German and Swiss companies. While the ORF retains a monopoly over television broadcasting in Austria, the provision of radio services was liberalized in 1998, when a number of commercial radio stations were launched.

**Österreichischer Rundfunk (ORF)** (Austrian Broadcasting Company): 1136 Vienna, Würzburggasse 30; tel. (1) 878-78-0; fax (1) 878-78-22-50; internet www.orf.at; f. 1955; state-owned; Dir-Gen. GERHARD ZEILER; Dirs Dr RUDOLF NAGILLER, KATHRIN ZECHNER (Television), GERHARD WEIS (Radio).

# Finance

(cap. = capital; res = reserves; dep. = deposits; m. = million; brs = branches; amounts in Schilling)

### BANKS

Banks in Austria, apart from the National Bank, belong to one of five categories. The first category comprises banks that are organized as corporations (i.e. joint-stock and private banks), and special-purpose credit institutions. In December 1993 these numbered, respectively, 56 and 95. The second category comprises savings banks, which numbered 80. The third category comprises co-operative banks. These include rural credit co-operatives (Raiffeisenbanken), which numbered 728 in December 1994, and industrial credit co-operatives (Volksbanken), which numbered 80. The remaining two categories comprise the mortgage banks of the various Austrian Länder, which numbered 9 in December 1994, and the building societies, which numbered five. The majority of Austrian banks (with the exception of the building societies) operate on the basis of universal banking, although certain categories have specialized. Banking operations are governed by the Banking Act of 1993 (Bankwesengesetz–BWG).

### Central Bank

**Oesterreichische Nationalbank** (Austrian National Bank): 1090 Vienna, Otto Wagner-Platz 3, PF 61; tel. (1) 404-20-0; fax (1) 404-66-96; internet www.oenb.at; f. 1922; cap. 150m. (Dec. 1997), res 126,216m., dep. 224,009m. (Dec. 1998); Pres. ADOLF WALA; Gov. Dr KLAUS LIEBSCHER; 8 brs.

### Commercial Banks

**Adria Bank AG:** 1010 Vienna, Tegetthoffstr. 1; tel. (1) 514-09; fax (1) 514-09-43; f. 1980; cap. 170m., res 238m., dep. 2,545m. (Dec. 1998); Mans CIRIL KRPAC, Dr ALFRED SCHERHAMMER.

**Anglo Irish Corporate Bank (Austria) AG:** 1010 Vienna, Rathaustr. 20, PF 306; tel. (1) 406-61-61; fax (1) 405-81-42; e-mail pb@angloirishbank.at; f. 1998; cap. 190m., res 104m., dep. 3,035m. (Dec. 1998); Gen. Mans T. CARROLL, E. TRAUN.

**Bank Austria AG:** 1010 Vienna, Am Hof 2; tel. (1) 711-91-0; fax (1) 711-91-61-55; internet www.bankaustria.com; f. 1991 by merger of Österreichische Länderbank and Zentralsparkasse und Kommerzialbank; cap. 18,023m., res 36,848m., dep. 704,286m. (Dec. 1997); Chair. Bd of Man. Dir GERHARD RANDA; 529 brs.

**Bank Austria Creditanstalt International AG:** 1010 Vienna, Am Hof 2; tel. (1) 711-91-0; e-mail margit.györög@at.bacai.com; f. 1998 through merger of international business of Bank Austria AG (see above) with Creditanstalt AG (f. 1855); wholly owned by Bank Austria AG.

**Bank Austria Handelsbank AG:** 1015 Vienna, Operngasse 6, PF 83; tel. (1) 514-40-0; fax (1) 512-66-01; f. 1935, present name adopted 1994; cap. 331m., res 273m., dep. 8,207m. (Dec. 1998); Chair. KARL SAMSTAG.

**Bank für Arbeit und Wirtschaft AG (BAWAG):** 1010 Vienna, Seitzergasse 2–4; tel. (1) 534-53-0; fax (1) 534-53-2840; e-mail bawag@bawag.com; internet www.bawag.com; f. 1947; present name adopted 1963; cap. 7,487m., res 9,101m., dep. 230,062m. (Dec. 1997); Chair. and Gen. Man. HELMUT ELSNER; 154 brs.

**Bank Winter und Co AG:** 1011 Vienna, Singerstr. 10; tel. (1) 515-04-0; fax (1) 515-04-21-3; f. 1959; cap. 650m., res 1,226m., dep. 22,714m. (June 1998); Chair. THOMAS MOSKOVICS; 1 br.

**Bankhaus Schelhammer und Schattera AG:** 1010 Vienna, Goldschmiedgasse 3; 1011 Vienna, PF 618; tel. (1) 534-34; fax (1) 534-34-64; e-mail foreign-dept@schelhammer.at; internet www.schelhammer.at; f. 1832; cap. 410m., res 268m., dep. 3,984m. (Dec. 1997); Chair. Dr HEINZ BURGMANN; 1 br.

**Central Wechsel- und Creditbank AG:** 1015 Vienna, Kärntner Str. 43, PF 140; tel. (1) 515-66-0; fax (1) 515-66-9; f. 1918; cap. 400m., res 276m., dep. 9,860m. (Dec. 1997); Chair. Dr LÁSZLO LÁNG.

**Centro Internationale Handelsbank AG:** 1015 Vienna, Tegetthoffstr. 1; tel. (1) 515-20-0; fax (1) 513-43-96; e-mail voelket.centrobank@telecom.at; internet www.centrobank.com; f. 1973; cap. 650m., res 227m., dep. 4,616m. (Dec. 1998); Exec. Bd Dr GERHARD VOGT (Chair.), JERZY PLUSA, CHRISTIAN SPERK.

**Citibank International Plc (Austria):** 1015 Vienna, Lothringer str. 7; tel. (1) 717-17-0; fax (1) 713-92-06; f. 1959 as Internationale

Investitions- und Finanzierungs Bank AG; present name adopted 1978; wholly-owned subsidiary of Citibank Overseas Investment Corpn; Gen. Man. ALBRECHT STAERKER.

**Deutsche Bank (Austria) AG:** 1010 Vienna, Hohenstaufengasse 4; tel. (1) 531-81-0; fax (1) 531-81-114; f. 1989; cap. 250m., res 386m., dep. 10,200m. (Dec. 1994); Mans Dr WOLFGANG HABERMAYER, CHRISTOPH BREWKA.

**Donau-Bank AG:** 1011 Vienna, Parkring 6, PF 1451; tel. (1) 515-35; fax (1) 515-35-29-7; e-mail donau-bank.allgem@telecom.at; f. 1974; cap. 1,105m., res 855m., dep. 6,832m. (Dec. 1997); Chair. ANDREI E. TCHETYRKIN.

**Kathrein und Co Privatgeschäftsbank AG:** 1013 Vienna, Wipplingerstr. 25, PF 174; tel. (1) 534-51-0; fax (1) 534-51/384; e-mail maximilian.hahn@kathrein.at; f. 1924; cap. 440m., res 70m., dep. 1,817m. (Dec. 1997); Chair. Dr CHRISTOPH KUNATH.

**Meinl Bank AG:** 1015 Vienna, Bauernmarkt 2, PF 99; tel. (1) 531-88; fax (1) 531-88-44; f. 1922; cap. 328m., res 445m., dep. 4,093m. (Dec. 1998); Chair. Dr ANTON OSOND; 2 brs.

**SKWB Schoellerbank AG:** 1010 Vienna, Renngasse 1–3; tel. (1) 534-71-43-2; fax (1) 534-71-435; internet www.skwbschoellerbank.at; f. 1998 by merger of Schoellerbank AG (f. 1833) and Salzburger Kredit-und Wechsel-Bank AG (f. 1922); Chair. MARTIN KÖLSCH.

### Regional Banks

**Allgemeine Sparkasse Oberösterreich Bank AG:** 4041 Linz, Promenade 11–13, PF 92, tel. (732) 73-91-26-81; fax (732) 78-44-04; internet www.ask.co.at; f. 1849; cap. 1,722m., res 2,136m., dep. 57,147m. (Dec. 1997); Gen. Man. MANFRED REITINGER; 121 brs.

**Bank für Kärnten und Steiermark AG:** 9020 Klagenfurt, St. Veiter Ring 43; tel. (463) 58-58; fax (463) 58-58-80-3; e-mail bks@bks.at; internet www.bks.at; f. 1922; cap. 1,086m., res 1,667m., dep. 32,021m. (Dec. 1997); Dirs Dr HEIMO PENKER, MARKUS ORSINI-ROSENBERG; 6 brs.

**Bank für Tirol und Vorarlberg AG:** 6020 Innsbruck, Erlerstr. 5–9; tel. (512) 53-33-0; fax (512) 533-31-33; internet www.btv.at; f. 1904; cap. 1,799m., res 1,936m., dep. 50,121m. (Dec. 1998); Man. Dirs PETER GAUGG, MATTHIAS MONCHER; 35 brs.

**Bankhaus Krentschker und Co AG:** 8010 Graz, Am Eisernen Tor 3; tel. (316) 80-30-0; fax (316) 80-30-94-9; f. 1924; cap. 315m., res 334m., dep. 9,264m. (Dec. 1997); Chair. Dr JÖRG BRUCKBAUER; 3 brs.

**Bankhaus Carl Spängler und Co AG:** 5020 Salzburg, Schwarzstr. 1; 5024 Salzburg, PF 41; tel. (662) 86-86-0; fax (662) 86-86-15-8; e-mail bankhaus@spaengler.co.at internet www.spaengler.co.at; f. 1828; cap. 738m., res 205m., dep. 4,748m. (Dec. 1998); Gen. Man. HEINRICH SPANGLER; 12 brs.

**Kärntner Landes- und Hypothekenbank AG:** 9020 Klagenfurt, Alpe-Adria-Platz 1, PF 517; tel. (463) 58-60; fax (463) 58-60-50; internet www.hypo-alpe-adria.com; f. 1896; cap. 458m., res 827m., dep. 38,047m. (Dec. 1997); Man. Dirs Dr WOLFGANG KULTERER, Dr JÖRG SCHUSTER; 10 brs.

**Landes-Hypothekenbank Tirol AG:** 6020 Innsbruck, Meraner Str. 8, PF 524; tel. (512) 59-11-0; fax (512) 59-11-21-21; e-mail office@hypotirol.at; internet www.hypotirol.at; f. 1901; cap. 538m., res 2,141m., dep. 56,238m. (Dec. 1998); Pres. Dr JOSEF PRADER; 23 brs.

**Niederösterreichische Landesbank-Hypothekenbank AG:** 3101 St Pölten, Kremser Gasse 20; tel. (2742) 49-20; e-mail hypobank@hypobank.co.at; internet www.hypobank.co.at; f. 1889; cap. 553m., res 1,176m., dep. 42,981m. (Dec. 1998); Chair. Dr OTTO BERNAU; Gen. Man. WERNER SCHMITZER; 27 brs.

**Oberbank AG:** 4020 Linz, Hauptplatz 10–11; tel. (732) 78-02-0; fax (732) 78-58-17; e-mail tre@oberbank.at; internet www.oberbank.at; f. 1869 as Bank für Oberösterreich und Salzburg AG; present name adopted 1998; cap. 3,395m., res 3,926m., dep. 92,278m. (Dec. 1998); Chair. Dr HERMANN BELL; 96 brs and sub-brs.

**Oberösterreichische Landesbank AG:** 4010 Linz, Landstr. 38; tel. (70) 76-39-0; fax (70) 76-39-20-5; e-mail 3v@hypo-ooe.at; internet www.hypo.at; f. 1891; cap. 442m., res 1,192m., dep. 34,671m. (Dec. 1997); Chair. Dr WOLFGANG STAMPFL; Gen. Man. Dr WOLFGANG LANGBAUER; 14 brs.

**Privatinvest Bank AG:** 5020 Salzburg, Griesgasse 11, PF 16; tel. (662) 80-48-0; fax (662) 80-48-33-3; e-mail piag@piag.at; internet www.privatinvestbank.com; f. 1885 as Bankhaus Daghofer & Co; present name adopted 1990; cap. 80m., res 72m., dep. 2,327m. (Dec. 1998); Chair. HANS-WERNER ZESCHKY.

**Quelle Bank C. A. Steinhäusser:** 4060 Leonding, Kornstr. 4; tel. (732) 68-67-0; fax (732) 68-67-15-0; f. 1856; cap. 130m. (1994); Mans BERND SCHADRACK, KARL-HEINZ STOIBER.

**Salzburger Landes-Hypothekenbank AG:** 5010 Salzburg, Residenzplatz 7; tel. (662) 804-60; fax (662) 804-65-69-2; cap. 864m., res 817m., dep. 32,437m. (Dec. 1997); Gen. Man. Dr KURT ADELSBURG.

**Steiermärkische Bank und Sparkassen AG:** 8011 Graz, Landhausgasse 16, Sparkassenplatz 4, PF 844; tel. (316) 80-33-0; fax (316) 80-33-30; e-mail bankstyria@bank-styria.co.at; internet www.bank-styria.co.at; f. 1825; cap. 558m., res 2,999m., dep. 57,991m. (Dec. 1998); Man. Dir JOSEPH KASSLER; 95 brs.

**Tiroler Sparkasse-Bankaktiengesellschaft Innsbruck:** 6020 Innsbruck, Sparkassenplatz 1; tel. (512) 59-05; fax (512) 59-10-50-0; f. 1822 as Sparkasse der Stadt Innsbruck; present name adopted 1990, following merger in 1975; cap. 1,950m., res 1,765m., dep. 35,489m. (Dec. 1997); Chair. and Gen. Man. Dr E. WUNDERBALDINGER; 49 brs.

**Volkskreditbank AG:** 4010 Linz, Rudigierstr. 5–7, PF 116; tel. (732) 76-37-0; fax (732) 76-37-20-0; e-mail international@vkb-bank.at; internet www.vkb-bank.at; f. 1872; cap. 260m., res 1,294m., dep. 17,767m. (Dec. 1997); Gen. Man. Dr GERNOT KRENNER; 45 brs.

**Vorarlberger Landes- und Hypothekenbank AG:** 6900 Bregenz, Hypo-Passage 1; tel. (5574) 414-0; fax (5574) 414-21-4; e-mail info@hypovbg.at; internet www.hypovbg.at; f. 1899; cap. 1,702m., res 1,980m., dep. 41,963m. (Dec. 1997); Chair. Dr KURT RUPP; 22 brs.

### Specialized Banks

**CAIB Investment Bank AG:** 1011 Vienna, Nibelungengasse 15; tel. (1) 588-84-0; fax (1) 585-42-42; e-mail ca-ib@ca-ib.com; f. 1997; wholly owned by Bank Austria Creditanstalt International AG; cap. 400m., res 227m., dep. 3,117m. (Dec. 1997); Chair. WILHELM HEMETSBERGER.

**Internationale Bank für Aussenhandel AG:** 1011 Vienna, Neuer Markt 1; tel. (1) 515-56-0; fax (1) 515-56-50; f. 1970; cap. 75m., res 123m., dep. 5,229m. (Dec. 1994); Mans Dr WALTER BEYER, ILSE SMEYKAL.

**Oesterreichische Kontrollbank AG:** 1010 Vienna, Am Hof 4, PF 70; tel. (1) 531-27-0; fax (1) 531-27-0; e-mail oeffentlichkeitsarbeit@oekb.co.at; internet www.oekb.co.at; f. 1946; export financing, stock exchange clearing, money market operations; cap. 440m., res 2,101m., dep. 6,078m. (Dec. 1997); Mans Dr JOHANNES ATTEMS, Dr RUDOLF SCHOLTEN.

**Österreichische Investitionskredit AG:** 1013 Vienna, Renngasse 10; tel. (1) 531-35-0; fax (1) 531-35-99-3; cap. 3,007m. (1994); Gen. Man. Dkfm. ALFRED REITER.

**Österreichische Kommunalkredit AG:** 1092 Vienna, Türkenstr. 9; tel. (1) 316-31-0; fax (1) 316-31-10-5; e-mail kommunal@kommunalkredit.at; internet www.kommunalkredit.at; f. 1958; cap. 374m., dep. 5,727m. (1994); Mans Dr REINHARD PLATZER, GERHARD GANGL.

**Österreichischer Exportfonds GmbH:** 1031 Vienna, Neulinggasse 29; tel. (1) 712-61-51-0; fax (1) 712-61-51-30; cap. 122m. (1994); Mans HERBERT NIEMETZ, BRIGITTE BRUCK.

### Savings Banks

**Dornbirner Sparkasse:** 6850 Dornbirn, Bahnhofstr. 2; tel. (5572) 381-10; fax (5572) 381-15-0; e-mail spk.dornbirn@telecom.at; internet www.dornbirn.sparkasse.at; cap. 150m., res 1,295m., dep. 14,196m. (Dec. 1997); Chair. RUDOLF SOHM; 15 brs.

**Erste Bank der oesterreichischen Sparkassen AG (Erste Bank)** (First Austrian Savings Bank): 1010 Vienna, Graben 21, PF 162; tel. (1) 531-00-0; fax (1) 531-00-22-72; internet www.erstebank.at; f. 1819, present name adopted 1997; cap. 11,855m., res 19,850m., dep. 532,037m. (Dec. 1998); Chair. and CEO ANDREAS TREICHL; 357 brs.

**Kärntner Sparkasse:** 9020 Klagenfurt, Neuer Platz 14; tel. (463) 588-80; fax (463) 588-82-91; e-mail info@kaerntnersparkasse.co.at; internet www.kaerntnersparkasse.at; f. 1835; cap. 1,221m., res 1,124m., dep. 24,453m. (Dec. 1997); Pres. HANS LETTNER; Gen. Man. MICHAEL KRAINZ; 57 brs.

**Österreichische Postsparkasse AG (PSK):** 1018 Vienna, Georg-Coch Platz 2; tel. (1) 51-40-00; fax (1) 514-00-17-00; internet www.psk.co.at/psk; f. 1883; cap. 2,563m., res 6,508m., dep. 247,595m. (Dec. 1997); CEO MAX KOTHBAUER.

**Salzburger Sparkasse Bank AG:** 5021 Salzburg, Alter Markt 3, PF 5000; tel. (662) 80-40-0; fax (662) 80-40-21-89; internet www.salzburger-sparkasse.co.at; f. 1855; cap. 1,369m., res 1,619m., dep. 37,017m. (Dec. 1997); Gen. Man. WALTER SCHWIMBERSKY; 79 brs.

### Co-operative Banks

**Österreichische Volksbanken-AG:** 1090 Vienna, Peregringasse 3; tel. (1) 313-40-34-12; fax (1) 313-40-36-43; e-mail info@oevag.volksbank.at; internet www.oevag.volksbank.at; f. 1922; cap. 2,701m., res 3,124m., dep. 82,387m. (Dec. 1998); Chair. and CEO Dr KLAUS THALHAMMER.

**Raiffeisenlandesbank Kärnten rGmbH:** 9020 Klagenfurt, St. Veiter Ring 53; tel. (463) 581-52-28-5; fax (463) 581-57-0; internet www.raiffeisen.at; cap. 145m., res 588m., dep. 12,963m. (Dec. 1997); Chair. Dr KLAUS PEKAREK.

**Raiffeisenlandesbank Niederösterreich-Wien rGmbH:** 1020 Vienna, Friedrich-Wilhelm-Raiffeisen-Platz 1, Raiffeisenhaus; tel.

(1) 21-13-60; fax (1) 21-13-62-22-3; internet www.rlbnoew.at; f. 1898; cap. 1,597m., res 3,296m., dep. 78,200m. (Dec. 1996); Chair. HANS WINDBICHLER.

**Raiffeisenlandesbank Oberösterreich rGmbH:** 4021 Linz, Raiffeisenplatz 1, PF 455; tel. (732) 65-96-0; fax (732) 65-96-35-29; e-mail rlbl@rlb.linz.raffeisen.at; internet www.rlbooe.at; f. 1900; cap. 2,811m., res 3,447m., dep. 86,070m. (Dec. 1997); Chair. Dr LUDWIG SCHARINGER.

**Raiffeisenlandesbank Steiermark rGmbH:** 8010 Graz, Kaiserfeldgasse 5–7; tel. (316) 80-36-0; fax (316) 80-36-17-11-3; internet www.raffeisen.at; f. 1927; cap. 853m., res 1,944m., dep. 33,461m. (Dec. 1997); Chair. JOSEF RIEGLER.

**Raiffeisenlandesbank Vorarlberg Gen mbH:** 6901 Bregenz, Rheinstr. 11; tel. (5574) 4050; fax (5574) 405-333; internet www.vol.at; cap. 199m., res 567m., dep. 17,220m. (Dec. 1997); Chair. VIKTOR RINDERER.

**Raffeisenverband Salzburg Gen mbH:** 5024 Salzburg, Schwarzstr. 13–15; tel. (662) 88860; fax (662) 888-65-24; f. 1905; present name adopted 1949; cap. 409m., res 1,739m., dep. 38,848m. (Dec. 1997); Chair. MANFRED HOLZTRATTNER.

**Raiffeisen Zentralbank Österreich AG (RZB-Austria):** 1030 Vienna, Am Stadtpark 9; tel. (1) 717-07-0; fax (1) 717-07-17-15; internet www.rzb.at; f. 1927; cap. 4,995m., res 8,499m., dep. 266,689m. (Dec. 1998); central institute of the Austrian Raiffeisen banking group; Chair. Supervisory Bd Dr CHRISTIAN KONRAD; Chair. Bd of Management Dr WALTER ROTHENSTEINER.

### Bankers' Organization

**Verband österreichischer Banken und Bankiers** (Asscn of Austrian Banks and Bankers): 1013 Vienna, Börsegasse 11; tel. (1) 535-17-71; fax (1) 535-17-71/38; e-mail voebb@voebb.at; internet www.voebb.at; f. 1945; Pres. HELMUT ELSNER; Gen. Sec. FRANZ OVESNY; 54 mems.

## STOCK EXCHANGES

**Wiener Börse** (Vienna Stock Exchange): 1013 Vienna, Wipplingerstr. 34; tel. (1) 534-99; fax (1) 535-68-57; e-mail communications @vienna-stock-exchange.at; internet www.wbag.at; f. 1771; 50% state-owned; two sections: Stock Exchange, Commodity Exchange; Pres. GERHARD REIDLINGER; Gen. Sec. Dr ULRICH KAMP.

**Österreichische Termin- und Optionenbörse** (Austrian Futures and Options Exchange): 1014 Vienna, PF 192, Strauchgasse 1-3; tel. (1) 531-65-0; fax (1) 532-97-40; f. 1991; by appointment to the Vienna Stock Exchange, provides a fully automated screen-based trading system, the Austrian Traded Index (ATX), and acts as clearing house for options and futures; trades futures on the Austrian Govt Bond (Bond-Futures) and options on six Austrian stocks listed on the Vienna Stock Exchange; CEO Dr CHRISTIAN IMO.

## INSURANCE COMPANIES

A selection of companies is given below.

**Allianz Elementar Versicherungs-AG:** 1130 Vienna, Hietzinger Kai 101–105; tel. (1) 878-07-0; fax (1) 878-07-53-90; e-mail 106534.1555@compuserv.com; internet www.allianz.co.at; f. 1860; all classes except life insurance; Gen. Man. Dr ALEXANDER HOYOS.

**Allianz Elementar Lebensversicherung-AG:** 1130 Vienna, Hietzinger Kai 101–105; tel. (1) 878-07-0; fax (1) 878-07-27-03; e-mail 106534.1555@compuserv.com; internet www.allianz.co.at; life insurance; Gen. Man. Dr ALEXANDER HOYOS.

**Austria-Collegialität Österreichische Versicherungs-AG:** 1021 Vienna, Untere Donaustr. 25; tel. (1) 211-75-0; fax (1) 211-75-19-99; e-mail ac.kommunikation@austriacoll.at; internet www .austriacoll.at; f. 1936; Gen. Man. HERBERT SCHIMETSCHEK.

**Donau Allgemeine Versicherungs-AG:** 1010 Vienna, Schottenring 15; tel. (1) 313-11; fax (1) 310-77-51; e-mail donau@ donauversicherung.co.at; internet www.donauversicherung.at; f. 1867; all classes; Gen. Man. Dr GÜNTER GEYER.

**Generali Versicherung AG:** 1011 Vienna, Landskrongasse 1–3; tel. (1) 534-01; fax (1) 534-01/12-26; e-mail headoffice@generali.at; internet www.generali.co.at; f. 1882 as Erste Österreichische Allgemeine Unfall-Versicherungs-Gesellschaft; Gen. Man. Dr HANS PEER.

**Grazer Wechselseitige Versicherung:** 8011 Graz, Herrengasse 18–20; tel. (316) 80-37-0; fax (316) 80-37-41-4; f. 1828; all classes; Gen. Man. Dr FRIEDRICH FALL.

**Interunfall Versicherungs-AG:** 1011 Vienna, Tegetthoffstr. 7; tel. (1) 514-03-0; fax (1) 514-03-500; e-mail w-k@interunfall .telecom.at; internet www.telecom.at/wkims/interunfall; all classes of insurance (including reinsurance); Man. Dr HANS PEER.

**Raffeisen-Versicherung AG:** 1020 Wien, Taborstr. 2–6; tel. (1) 211-19-0; fax (1) 211-19-11-34; e-mail rv-kommunikation@rvag .co.at; Dir Dr CHRISTIAN SEDLNITZKY.

**Sparkassen Versicherung AG:** 1011 Wien, Wipplinger-Str. 36-38; tel. (1) 313-81-0; fax (1) 313-81-300; Gen. Man. Dr MICHAEL HARRER.

**Uniqa Versicherungen AG:** 1021 Vienna, Praterstr. 1–7; tel. (1) 211-11-0; fax (1) 214-33-36; present name adopted 1999, fmrly Versicherungsanstalt der österreichischen Bundesländer Versicherungs-AG; Chair. HERBERT SCHIMETSCHEK.

**Wiener Städtische Allgemeine Versicherung AG:** 1010 Vienna, Schottenring 30, Ringturm; tel. (1) 531-39-0; fax (1) 535-34-37; e-mail mail-us@wr.staedtische.co.at; internet www.staedtische .co.at; f. 1824; all classes; CEO Dr SIEGFRIED SELLITSCH.

**Wüstenrot Versicherungs-AG:** 5033 Salzburg, Alpenstr. 61; tel. (662) 638-60; fax (662) 638-66-52; e-mail versicherung@wuestenrot .co.at; internet www.wuestenrot.co.at; Gen. Man. HELMUT GEIER.

**Zürich Kosmos Versicherungen AG:** 1015 Vienna I, Schwarzenbergplatz 15; tel. (1) 501-25-0; fax (1) 505-04-85; f. 1910; all classes; Gen. Man. FRANZ WIPFLI.

### Insurance Organization

**Verband der Versicherungsunternehmen Österreichs** (Asscn of Austrian Insurance Cos): 1030 Vienna, Schwarzenbergplatz 7; tel. (1) 711-56-0; fax (1) 711-56-27-0; e-mail versver@ibm.net; internet www.vvo.at; f. 1945; Pres. Dr ALEXANDER HOYOS; Gen. Sec. HERBERT RETTER; 87 mems.

# Trade and Industry

## GOVERNMENT AGENCIES

**Austrian Business Agency (ABA):** 1010 Vienna, Opernring 3; fax (1) 586-86-59; e-mail austrian.business@telecom.at; internet www .aba.gv.at; Man. Dir RENÉ SIEGL.

**Österreichische Industrieholding AG (ÖIAG):** 1015 Vienna, Kantgasse 1, PF 99; tel. (1) 711-14-0; fax (1) 711-14-37-8; f. 1970; Mans. KARL HOLLWEGER, Dr ERICH BECKER.

## CHAMBERS OF COMMERCE

All Austrian enterprises must by law be members of the Economic Chambers. The Federal Economic Chamber promotes international contacts and represents the economic interests of trade and industry on a federal level. Its Foreign Trade Organization includes about 90 offices abroad.

**Wirtschaftskammer Österreich** (Austrian Federal Economic Chamber): 1045 Vienna, Wiedner Hauptstr. 63; tel. (1) 501-05; fax (1) 502-06-25-0; e-mail mservice@wkoe.wk.or.at; f. 1946; six depts: Commerce, Industry, Small-scale Production, Banking and Insurance, Transport and Tourism; these divisions are subdivided into branch asscns; Local Economic Chambers with divisions and branch asscns in each of the nine Austrian provinces; Pres. LEOPOLD MADERTHANER; Sec.-Gen. GÜNTER STUMMVOLL; c. 300,000 mems.

## INDUSTRIAL AND TRADE ASSOCIATIONS

**Wirtschaftskammer Österreich—Bundessektion Industrie:** 1045 Vienna, Wiedner Hauptstr. 63; tel. (1) 501-05-34-57; fax (1) 501-05-27-3; e-mail bsi@wkoesk.wk.or.at; internet www.wk.or.at/ bsi; f. 1896 as Zentralverband der Industrie Österreichs (Central Fed. of Austrian Industry), merged into present org. 1947; Chair. HEINZ KESSLER; Dir JOACHIM LAMEL; comprises the following industrial feds:

**Fachverband der Audiovisions-und Filmindustrie Österreichs** (Film): 1045 Vienna, Wiedner Hauptstr. 63, PF 327; tel. (1) 501-05/30-10; fax (1) 501-05/27-6; e-mail film@fafo.at; Chair. MICHAEL WOLKENSTEIN, Prof. Dr ELMAR A. PETERLUNGER; 1,700 mems.

**Fachverband der Bauindustrie** (Building): 1040 Vienna, Karlsgasse 5; tel. (1) 504-15-51; fax (1) 504-15-55; e-mail sekretariat @bauindustrie.at; internet www.bauindustrie.at; Chair. Ing. ERNST NUSSBAUMER; Dir Dr JOHANNES SCHENK; 150 mems.

**Fachverband der Bekleidungsindustrie** (Clothing): 1037 Vienna, Schwarzenbergplatz 4; tel. (1) 712-12-96; fax (1) 713-92-04; e-mail office@fashion-industry.at; internet www .fashion-industry.at; Chair. WILHELM EHRLICH; Dir CHRISTOPH HAIDINGER; 280 mems.

**Fachverband der Bergwerke und Eisenerzeugenden Industrie** (Mining and Steel Production): 1015 Vienna, Goethegasse 3, PF 300; tel. (1) 512-46-01; fax (1) 512-46-01-20; e-mail fvil@ wkoesk.wk.or.at; internet www.wk-or.at/ergbau-stahl; Chair. Pres. Dr HELLMUT LONGIN; Sec. Ing. Mag. HERMANN PRINZ; 51 mems.

**Fachverband der Chemischen Industrie** (Chemicals): 1045 Vienna, Wiedner Hauptstr. 63; tel. (1) 501-05-0; fax (1) 502-06-28-0; e-mail fcio@wkoesk.wk.or.at; Pres. JOSEF FRICK; Gen. Dir Dr WOLFGANG EICKHOFF; 530 mems.

**Fachverband der Eisen- und Metallwarenindustrie Österreichs** (Iron and Metal Goods): 1045 Vienna, Wiedner Hauptstr.

63, PF 335; tel. (1) 501-05; fax (1) 505-09-28; internet www.fmwi.at; f. 1908; Chair. REINHARD JORDAN; Gen. Man. Dr WOLFGANG LOCKER; 800 mems.

**Fachverband der Elektro- und Elektronikindustrie** (Electrical): 1060 Vienna, Mariahilferstr. 37–39; tel. (1) 588-39-0; fax (1) 586-69-71; Chair. Dr WALTER WOLFSBERGER; Dir Dr HEINZ RASCHKA; 558 mems.

**Fachverband der Erdölindustrie** (Oil): 1031 Vienna, Erdbergstr. 72; tel. (1) 713-23-48; fax (1) 713-05-10; e-mail fv_erdoel@telenetz.com; f. 1947; Gen. Dirs Dr RICHARD SCHENZ, Dr RUDOLF MERTEN; 21 mems.

**Fachverband der Fahrzeugindustrie** (Vehicles): 1045 Vienna, Wiedner Hauptstr. 63; tel. (1) 501-05; fax (1) 502-06-28-9; Pres. Dr RICHARD DAIMER; Gen. Sec. ERIK BAIER; 160 mems.

**Fachverband der Gas- und Wärmeversorgungsunternehmungen** (Gas and Heating): 1010 Vienna, Schubertring 14; tel. (1) 513-15-88; fax (1) 513-15-88-25; e-mail info@fv.ovgw.or.at; Gen. Dir Dr KARL SKYBA; 190 mems.

**Fachverband der Giessereiindustrie** (Foundries): 1045 Vienna, Wiedner Hauptstr. 63, PF 339; tel. (1) 501-05-34-63; fax (1) 502-06-27-9; Chair. MICHAEL ZIMMERMANN; Dir Dipl. Ing. Dr HANSJÖRG DICHTL; 60 mems.

**Fachverband der Glasindustrie** (Glass): 1045 Vienna, Wiedner Hauptstr. 63; tel. (1) 501-05/3428; fax (1) 502-05/281; e-mail office@fvglas.at; Chair. RUDOLF SCHRAML; Dir ALEXANDER KRISSMANEK; 65 mems.

**Fachverband der Holzverarbeitenden Industrie** (Wood Processing): 1037 Vienna, Schwarzenbergplatz 4, PF 123; tel. (1) 712-26-01; fax (1) 713-03-09; e-mail office@holzindustrie.at; f. 1946; Chair. Dr ERICH WIESNER; Dir Dr CLAUDIUS KOLLMANN; 360 mems.

**Fachverband der Ledererzeugenden Industrie** (Leather Production): 1045 Vienna 4, Wiedner Hauptstr. 63, PF 312; tel. (1) 501-05-34-53; fax (1) 501-05-278; e-mail fvleder@wkoesk.wk.or.at; f. 1945; Chair. HELMUT SCHMIDT; Dir PETER KOVACS; 8 mems.

**Fachverband der Lederverarbeitenden Industrie** (Leather Processing): 1045 Vienna, PF 313, Wiedner Hauptstr. 63; tel. (1) 501-05; fax (1) 501-05-278; e-mail fvleder@wkoesk.wk.or.at; f. 1945; Chair. Gen. Dir GERHARD WALLNER; Dir PETER KOVACS; 47 mems.

**Fachverband der Maschinen- und Stahlbauindustrie** (Machinery and Steel Construction): 1045 Vienna, Wiedner Hauptstr. 63; tel. (1) 502-25; fax (1) 505-10-20; Pres. Dr JOSEF BERTSCH; Dir Dr RUDOLF TUPPA; 850 mems.

**Fachverband der Metallindustrie** (Metals): 1045 Vienna, Wiedner Hauptstr. 63, PF 338; tel. (1) 501-05/33-09; fax (1) 501-05-33-78; e-mail nemetall@wkoesk.wk.or.at; f. 1946; Chair. Dr OTHMAR RANKL; Dir Dr GÜNTER GREIL; 69 mems.

**Fachverband der Nahrungs- und Genussmittelindustrie** (Provisions): Vienna, Zaunergasse 1-3; tel. (1) 712-21-21; fax (1) 713-18-02; Chair. Dr ERWIN BUNDSCHUH; Dir Dr MICHAEL BLASS; 674 mems.

**Fachverband der Papier und Pappe verarbeitenden Industrie** (Paper and Board Processing): 1041 Vienna, Brucknerstr. 8; tel. (1) 505-53-82-0; fax (1) 505-90-18; e-mail ppv@ppv.at; Chair. GUSTAV GLÖCKLER; 134 mems.

**Fachverband der Papierindustrie** (Paper): 1061 Vienna, Gumpendorferstr. 6; tel. (1) 588-86-0; fax (1) 588-86-22-2; e-mail fvpapier@cafvpapier.wk.or.at; Chair. Dr ROBERT LAUNSKY-TIEFFENTHAL; Dir Dr GEROLF OTTAWA; 30 mems.

**Fachverband der Sägeindustrie Österreichs** (Sawmills): 1011 Vienna, Uraniastr. 4/1, PF 156; tel. (1) 712-04-74-0; fax (1) 713-10-18; e-mail info@proholz.at; internet www.proholz.at; f. 1947; Chair. Dipl. Ing. HANS MICHAEL OFFNER; Dir Dr GERHARD ALTRICHTER; 1,700 mems.

**Fachverband der Stein- und keramischen Industrie** (Stone and Ceramics): 1045 Vienna, PF 329, Wiedner Hauptstr. 63; tel (1) 501-05-35-31; fax (1) 505-62-40; e-mail steine@wkoesk.wk.or.at; internet www.wk.or.at/stein-keramik; f. 1946; Chair. Dr CARL HENNRICH; Pres. Sen. LEOPOLD HELBICH; 400 mems.

**Fachverband der Textilindustrie** (Textiles): 1013 Vienna, Rudolfsplatz 12; tel. (1) 533-37-26-0; fax (1) 533-37-26-40; e-mail fvtextil@fvtextil.wk.or.at; internet www.wk.or.at; Pres. Dr PETER PFNEISL; Dir Dr F. PETER SCHINZEL; 265 mems.

## UTILITIES

### Electricity

**Energie-Versorgung-Niederösterreich AG (EVN):** 2344 Maria Enzersdorf, Johann-Steinboeck-Str. 1; tel. (2742) 80-00; fax (2742) 80-03-60; Chair. Dr RUDOLF GRUBER.

**Burgenländische Elektrizitätswirtschafts-AG:** 7001 Eisenstadt, Kasemenstr. 9; tel. (2682) 900-01-02-1; fax (2682) 900-01-91-0; e-mail guenther.ofner@bewag.co.at; Chair. Dr GÜNTHER OFNER.

**Kärntner Elektrizitäts-AG:** 9020 Klagenfurt, Arnulfplatz 2; tel. (463) 52-50; fax (463) 52-51-59-6; Chair. Dr GÜNTHER BRESITZ.

**Oberösterreichische Kraftwerke AG:** 4020 Linz, Böhmerwaldstr. 3; tel. (732) 65-93-0; fax (732) 65-93-36-00; Chair. Dr LEOPOLD WINDTNER.

**Österreichische Elektrizitätswirtschafts-AG:** 1010 Vienna, Am Hof 6A; tel. (1) 531-13-0; fax (1) 531-13-41-91; e-mail info@pol.verbund.co.at; internet www.verbund.co.at/verbund; federal electricity authority; operates national grid, wholesales electricity to the nine regional operators; Dir HANS HAIDER.

**Salzburger AG für Energiewirtschaft:** 5021 Salzburg, Bayerhamerstr. 16; tel. (662) 88-84-0; fax (662) 88-84-17-0; e-mail safe.post@safe.at; internet www.safe.at; Chair. Dr JOHANN OBERHAMBERGER.

**Steirische Wasserkraft- und Elektrizitäts-AG:** 8011 Graz, Leonhardgurtel 10; tel. (316) 3870; fax (316) 387290; Chair. Dr OSWIN KOIS.

**Tiroler Wasserkraftwerke AG:** 6010 Innsbruck, Landhausplatz; tel. (512) 50-60; fax (512) 50-62-12-6; Chair. Dr HELMUT MAYR.

**Vorarlberger Kraftwerke AG:** 6900 Bregenz, Weidachstr. 6; tel. (5574) 601-0; fax (5574) 60-15-00; e-mail energie@vkw.at; internet www.vkw.at; Chair. Dr LEO WAGNER, Dr OTTO WAIBEL.

**WienStrom:** 1010 Vienna, Schottenring 30; tel. (1) 531-23-0; fax (1) 531-23-73-99-9; Chair. Dr KARL SKYBA.

### Gas

**BEGAS-Burgenländische Erdgasversorgungs-AG:** 7000 Eisenstadt, Kasernenstr. 10; tel. (2682) 70-9; fax (2682) 70-91-74; Chair. HERIBERT ARTINGER.

**Oberösterreichische Ferngas-AG:** 4030 Linz, Neubauzeile 99; tel. (732) 38-83; fax (732) 37-72-19; Chair. MAX DOBRUCKT.

**Steirische Ferngas-AG:** 8041 Graz, Gaslaternenweg 4; tel. (316) 476-0; fax (316) 476-30; e-mail office@steirische-ferngas.at; internet www.steirische.ferngas; Chair. BERNARD ALRAN, PETER KOBERL, MAX POLZL.

## TRADE UNIONS

**Österreichischer Gewerkschaftsbund (ÖGB)** (Austrian Trade Union Fed.): 1010 Vienna, Hohenstaufengasse 10–12; tel. (1) 534-44; fax (1) 534-44-20-4; e-mail oegb@oegb.or.at; internet www.oegb.or.at; non-party union org. with voluntary membership; f. 1945; org. affiliated with ICFTU and the European Trade Union Confederation (ETUC); Pres. FRIEDRICH VERZETNITSCH; Exec. Secs KARL DROCHTER, Dr RICHARD LEUTNER; 1,497,584 mems (Dec. 1997); comprises the following 14 trade unions:

**Gewerkschaft Agrar-Nahrung-Genuss** (Agricultural, Food, Beverage and Tobacco Workers): 1081 Vienna, Albertgasse 35; tel. (1) 401-49; fax (1) 401-49-20; e-mail ang@ang.oegb.or.at; Chair. Dr LEOPOLD SIMPERL; 40,113 mems (1989).

**Gewerkschaft Bau-Holz** (Building Workers and Woodworkers): 1010 Vienna, Ebendorferstr. 7; tel. (1) 401-47; fax (1) 401-47-25-8; e-mail johann-driemer@gbh.oegb.or.at; Chair. JOHANN DRIEMER; 171,000 mems (1997).

**Gewerkschaft der Chemiearbeiter** (Chemical Workers): 1060 Vienna, Stumpergasse 60; tel. (1) 597-15-01; fax (1) 597-21-01-23; Chair. GERHARD LINNER; 51,172 mems (1993).

**Gewerkschaft Druck und Papier** (Printing and Paper Trade Workers): 1070 Vienna, PF 91, Seidengasse 15–17; tel. (1) 523-82-31; fax (1) 523-81-32-28; e-mail gewdu@netway.at; f. 1842; Chair. FRANZ BITTNER; 18,023 mems (1999).

**Gewerkschaft der Eisenbahner** (Railwaymen): 1051 Vienna, Margaretenstr. 166; tel. (1) 546-41-50-0; fax (1) 546-41-50-4; e-mail gde@gde.oegb.or.at; Chair. GERHARD NOWAK; 105,000 mems (1997).

**Gewerkschaft der Gemeindebediensteten** (Municipal Employees): 1090 Vienna, Maria-Theresien-Str. 11; tel. (1) 313-16-83-00; fax (1) 313-16-7701; e-mail gdg@gdg.oegb.or.at; internet www.oegb.or.at/gdg; Chair. GÜNTER WENINGER; 176,623 mems (1998).

**Gewerkschaft Handel, Transport, Verkehr** (Workers in Commerce and Transport): 1010 Vienna, Teinfaltstr. 7; tel. (1) 534-54; fax (1) 534-54-32-5; f. 1904; Chair. PETER SCHNEIDER; 37,846 mems (1989).

**Gewerkschaft Hotel, Gastgewerbe, Persönlicher Dienst** (Hotel and Restaurant Workers): 1013 Vienna, Hohenstaufengasse 10; tel. (1) 534-44; fax (1) 534-44-50-5; e-mail hgpd@cahgpd.oegb.or.at; f. 1906; Chair. RUDOLF KASKE; 50,977 mems (1997).

**Gewerkschaft Kunst, Medien, freie Berufe** (Musicians, Actors, Artists, Journalists, etc.): 1090 Vienna, Maria-Theresien-Str. 11; tel. (1) 313-16; fax (1) 313-16-77-00; e-mail kmfb@kmfb.oegb.or.at; f. 1945; Chair. ERNST KÖRMER; Sec.-Gen. THOMAS LINZBAUER; 16,202 mems (1998).

**Gewerkschaft Metall-Bergbau-Energie** (Metal Workers, Miners and Power Supply Workers): 1041 Vienna, Plösslgasse 15; tel. (1) 501-46-0; fax (1) 501-46-13-30-0; e-mail gmbe@gmbe.oegb.or.at; f. 1890; Chair. RUDOLF NÜRNBERGER; 206,241 mems (1997).

**Gewerkschaft Öffentlicher Dienst** (Public Employees): 1010 Vienna, Teinfaltstr. 7; tel. (1) 534-54-0; fax (1) 534-54-20-7; e-mail goed@goed.or.at; internet www.goed.or.at; f. 1945; Chair. FRITZ NEUGEBAUER; Gen. Secs Dr MANFRED MÖGELE, GERHARD NEUGEBAUER, Dr ANDRÉ ALVARADO-DUPUY; 228,000 mems (1993).

**Gewerkschaft der Post- und Fernmeldebediensteten** (Postal and Telegraph Workers): 1010 Vienna, Biberstr. 5, PF 343; tel. (1) 512-55-11; fax (1) 512-55-11/52; e-mail gpf@gpf.oegb.or.at; Chair. HANS-GEORG DÖRFLER; 78,436 mems (1998).

**Gewerkschaft der Privatangestellten** (Commercial, Clerical and Technical Employees): 1013 Vienna, Deutschmeisterplatz 2; tel. and fax (1) 313-93; Chair. HANS SALLMUTTER; 301,046 mems (1997).

**Gewerkschaft Textil, Bekleidung, Leder** (Textile, Garment and Leather Workers): 1010 Vienna, Hohenstaufengasse 10; tel. (1) 534-44; fax (1) 534-44-49-8; e-mail tbl@tbl.oegb.or.at; f. 1945; Chair. HARALD ETTL; 38,580 mems (1989).

**Bundesfraktion Christlicher Gewerkschafter im Österreichischen Gewerkschaftsbund** (Christian Trade Unionists' Section of the Austrian Trade Union Fed.): 1010 Vienna, Hohenstaufengasse 12; tel. (1) 534-44; organized in Christian Trade Unionists' Sections of the above 14 trade unions; affiliated with WCL; Sec.-Gen. KARL KLEIN.

# Transport

## RAILWAYS

Austrian Federal Railways operates more than 90% of all the railway routes in Austria. There are 5,600 km of track and all main lines are electrified.

**Österreichische Bundesbahnen (ÖBB)** (Austrian Federal Railways): Head Office: 1010 Vienna, Elisabethstr. 9; tel. (1) 58-00-0; fax (1) 58-00/25-00-1; Gen. Dir Dr HELMUT DRAXLER.

**Innsbruck Divisional Management:** 6020 Innsbruck, Claudiastr. 2; tel. (512) 50-33-00-0; fax (512) 50-35-00-5; Dir JOHANN LINDENBERGER.

**Linz Divisional Management:** 4021 Linz, Bahnhofstr. 3; tel. (732) 69-09-0; fax (732) 69-09-18-33; Dir HELMUTH AFLENZER; Vice-Dir KLAUS SEEBACHER.

**Vienna Divisional Management:** 1020 Vienna, Nordbahnstr. 50; fax (1) 580-05-00-00; fax (1) 580-02-56-01; Dir FRANZ POLZER.

**Villach Divisional Management:** 9501 Villach, 10-Oktober-Str. 20; tel. (4242) 20-20-32-00; fax (4242) 20-20-32-29; e-mail willibald.schicho@gv.oebb.at; internet www.railcargo.at; Dir WILLIBALD SCHICHO.

Other railway companies include: Achenseebahn AG, AG der Wiener Lokalbahnen, Graz-Köflacher Eisenbahn- und Bergbau GmbH, Lokalbahn, Montafonerbahn AG, Raab-Oedenburg-Ebenfurter Eisenbahn, Salzburger Stadtwerke AG-Verkehrsbetriebe, Steiermärkische Lokalbahnen, Stern & Hafferl Verkehrs GmbH, Zillertaler Verkehrsbetriebe AG.

## ROADS

At 31 December 1997 Austria had about 200,000 km of classified roads, of which 1,613 km were modern motorways, 9,970 km main roads, 19,822 km secondary roads and 98,000 km other roads.

## INLAND WATERWAYS

The Danube (Donau) is Austria's only navigable river. It enters Austria from Germany at Passau and flows into Slovakia near Hainburg. The length of the Austrian section of the river is 351 km. Danube barges carry up to 1,800 metric tons, but loading depends on the water level, which varies considerably throughout the year. Cargoes are chiefly petroleum and derivatives, coal, coke, iron ore, iron, steel, timber and grain. Transport on the Danube was severely disrupted by the NATO bombing of Serbian bridges in early 1999. The Rhine-Main-Danube Canal opened in 1992. A passenger service is maintained on the Upper Danube and between Vienna and the Black Sea. Passenger services are also provided on Bodensee (Lake Constance) and Wolfgangsee by Austrian Federal Railways, and on all the larger Austrian lakes.

**Ministry of Science and Transport:** 1030 Vienna, Radetzkystr. 2; tel. (1) 71162-0; fax (1) 531-20-44-99; internet www.bmwv.gv.at; responsible for the administration of inland waterways.

**DDSG-Cargo GmbH:** 1021 Vienna; tel. (1) 217-10-0; fax (1) 217-10-25-0; Man. Dir HERBERT PETSUIG.

## CIVIL AVIATION

The main international airport, at Schwechat, near Vienna, handled more than 8m. passengers in 1995. There are also international flights from Graz, Innsbruck, Klagenfurt, Linz and Salzburg, and internal flights between these cities.

### Principal Airlines

**Austrian Airlines** (Österreichische Luftverkehrs AG): 1107 Vienna, Fontanastr. 1; tel. (1) 176-6; fax (1) 688-55-05; e-mail public.relations@aua.com; internet www.aua.com; f. 1957; 39.7% state-owned; serves 123 cities in 67 countries world-wide; Chair. Dr RUDOLF STREICHER; Pres Dr HERBERT BAMMER, MARIO REHULKA.

**Austrian Airtransport (AAT):** 1107 Vienna, Fontanastr. 1, PF 50; tel. (1) 688-16-91; fax (1) 688-11-91; f. 1964; 80% owned by Austrian Airlines, from which it leases most of its aircraft; operates scheduled and charter flights for passengers and cargo, and tour services; Man Dir Dr HERBERT KOSCHIER.

**Lauda Air Luftfahrt AG:** 1300 Vienna-Schwechat, Lauda Air Bldg, PF 56; tel. (1) 7000-0; fax (1) 7000-790-15; e-mail office@laudaair.com; internet www.laudaair.com; f. 1979; became a scheduled carrier 1987; operates scheduled passenger services and charter flights to Europe, Australia, the Far East and the USA; Chair. NIKI LAUDA.

**Tiroler Luftfahrt AG** (Tyrolean Airways): 6026 Innsbruck, Fürstenweg 176, PF 98; tel. (512) 22-2-0; fax (512) 22-22-90-05; internet www.telecom.at/tyrolean; f. 1958 as Aircraft Innsbruck; adopted present name 1980; operates scheduled services and charter flights within Austria and to other European countries; Pres. and CEO FRITZ FEITL.

# Tourism

Tourism plays an important part in the Austrian economy. However, receipts from the sector, estimated at 161,000m. Schilling in 1991, declined during the 1990s, and stood at 134,100m. Schilling in 1997 and an estimated 139,200m. Schilling in 1998. In 1998 Austria received 17.3m. foreign visitors at accommodation establishments (compared with 19.1m. visitors in 1992). The country's mountain scenery attracts visitors in both summer and winter, while Vienna and Salzburg, hosts to a number of internationally-renowned art festivals, are important cultural centres.

**Österreich Werbung** (Austrian National Tourist Office): 1040 Vienna, Margaretenstr. 1; tel. (1) 588-66-0; fax (1) 588-66-20; internet www.austria-tourism.at; f. 1955.

# AZERBAIJAN

## Introductory Survey

### Location, Climate, Language, Religion, Flag, Capital

The Azerbaijan Republic is situated in eastern Transcaucasia, on the western coast of the Caspian Sea. To the south it borders Iran, to the west Armenia, to the north-west Georgia, and to the north the Republic of Dagestan, in Russia. The Nakhichevan Autonomous Republic is part of Azerbaijan, although it is separated from the rest of Azerbaijan by Armenian territory. Azerbaijan also includes the Nagorno-Karabakh Autonomous Oblast (Nagornyi Karabakh), which is largely populated by Armenians but does not legally constitute part of Armenia. The Kura plain has a dry, temperate climate with an average July temperature of 27°C (80°F) and an average January temperature of 1°C (34°F). Average annual rainfall on the lowlands is 200 mm–300 mm, but the Lenkoran plain normally receives between 1,000 mm and 1,750 mm. The official language is Azerbaijani (Azeri), one of the South Turkic group of languages; in 1992 the Turkish version of the Latin script replaced the Cyrillic alphabet (which had been in use since 1939). Religious adherence corresponds largely to ethnic origins: almost all ethnic Azerbaijanis are Muslims, some 70% being Shi'ite and 30% Sunni. There are also Christian communities, mainly representatives of the Russian Orthodox and Armenian Apostolic denominations. The national flag (proportions 2 by 1) consists of three equal horizontal stripes, of pale blue, red and green, with a white crescent moon framing a white eight-pointed star on the central red stripe. The capital is Baku.

### Recent History

An independent state in ancient times, Azerbaijan was dominated for much of its subsequent history by foreign powers. Under the Treaty of Turkmanchai of 1828, Azerbaijan was divided between Persia (which was granted southern Azerbaijan) and Russia (northern Azerbaijan). During the latter half of the 19th century petroleum was discovered in Azerbaijan, and by 1900 the region had become one of the world's leading petroleum producers. Immigrant Slavs began to dominate Baku and other urban areas.

After the October Revolution of 1917 in Russia, there was a short period of pro-Bolshevik rule in Baku before a nationalist Government took power and established an independent state on 28 May 1918, with Gyanja (formerly Elisavetpol, but renamed Kirovabad in 1935) as the capital. Azerbaijan was occupied by troops of both the Allied and Central Powers during its two years of independence; after their withdrawal, Azerbaijan was invaded by the Red Army in April 1920, and on 28 April a Soviet Republic of Azerbaijan was established. In December 1922 the republic became a member of the Transcaucasian Soviet Federative Socialist Republic (TSFSR), which entered the USSR as a constituent republic on 31 December. The TSFSR was disbanded in 1936, and Azerbaijan became a full union republic, the Azerbaijan Soviet Socialist Republic (SSR).

Following the Soviet seizure of power in 1920, many nationalist and religious leaders and their followers were persecuted or killed. Religious intolerance was particularly severe in the 1930s, and many mosques and religious sites were destroyed. In 1930–31 forced collectivization of agriculture led to peasant uprisings, which were suppressed by Soviet troops. The Stalinist purges of 1937–38 involved the execution or imprisonment of many members of the Communist Party of Azerbaijan (CPA), including Sultan Mejit Efendiyev, the republic's leader, and two republican premiers. In 1945 the Soviet Government attempted to unite the Azerbaijani population of northern Iran with the Azerbaijan SSR, by supporting a local 'puppet' government in Iran with military forces, but Soviet troops were forced to withdraw from northern Iran in the following year by US-British opposition.

The most influential of Azerbaijan's communist leaders in the period following the Second World War was Heydar Aliyev, who was installed as First Secretary of the CPA in 1969. He greatly increased the all-Union sector of the economy at the expense of republican industry, while retaining popularity with his liberal attitude to local corruption. Attempts to address corruption in the CPA followed the accession to power of Mikhail Gorbachev, who became leader of the USSR in 1985. Aliyev was dismissed in October 1987, but popular dissatisfaction with the poor state of the economy and the party élite became more vocal. Unlike most Soviet republics, Azerbaijan had an annual trade surplus with the rest of the USSR, and yet its income per head was the lowest outside Central Asia. Public grievances over economic mismanagement and the privileges enjoyed by the party leadership were expressed at demonstrations in November 1988. Protesters occupied the main square in Baku, the capital, for 10 days before being dispersed by troops, who arrested the leaders of the demonstrations.

The initial impetus, however, for the demonstrations was the debate on the status of Nagornyi Karabakh (an autonomous region within Azerbaijan) and Nakhichevan (an autonomous republic of Azerbaijan, separated from it by Armenian land). Both territories were claimed by Armenia, on historical grounds, and Nagornyi Karabakh still had an overwhelming majority of (non-Muslim) Armenians in its population. Nakhichevan, despite an apparent surrender of Azerbaijan's claims to the territory in 1920, never became part of Soviet Armenia. The Soviet-Turkish Treaty of March 1921 included a clause guaranteeing Azerbaijani jurisdiction over Nakhichevan. The 45%–50% of the republic's population that had been ethnically Armenian in 1919 was reduced to less than 5% by 1989. Nagornyi Karabakh had been a disputed territory during the period of Armenian and Azerbaijani independence (1918–20), but in June 1921 the Bureau for Caucasian Affairs (the Kavburo) voted to unite Nagornyi Karabakh with Armenia. However, some days after the Kavburo vote, following an intervention by Stalin, the decision was reversed. In 1923 the territory was declared an autonomous oblast (region) within the Azerbaijan SSR. There were attempts to challenge Azerbaijan's jurisdiction over the region, including two petitions by the inhabitants of Nagornyi Karabakh in the 1960s, but they were strongly opposed by the Soviet and Azerbaijani authorities.

Conflict over the territory began again in February 1988, when the Nagornyi Karabakh regional soviet (council) requested the Armenian and Azerbaijani Supreme Soviets to agree to the transfer of the territory to Armenia. The Soviet and Azerbaijani authorities rejected the request, thus provoking huge demonstrations by Armenians, not only in Nagornyi Karabakh, but also in the Armenian capital, Yerevan. Azerbaijanis began leaving Armenia, and rumours that refugees had been attacked led to three days of anti-Armenian violence in the Azerbaijani town of Sumgait. According to official figures, 32 people died, 26 of whom were Armenians. Disturbances over the issue of Nagornyi Karabakh continued throughout 1988, leading to a large-scale exodus of refugees from both Armenia and Azerbaijan.

In January 1989, in an attempt to end the tension, the Soviet Government suspended the activities of the local authorities in Nagornyi Karabakh and established a Special Administration Committee (SAC), responsible to the USSR Council of Ministers. Although it was stressed that the region would formally retain its status as an autonomous oblast within Azerbaijan, the decision was widely viewed by Azerbaijanis as an infringement of Azerbaijan's territorial integrity. This imposition of 'direct rule' from Moscow and the dispatch of some 5,000 Soviet troops did little to reduce tensions within Nagornyi Karabakh, where Armenians went on strike from May until September.

In mid-1989 the nationalist Popular Front of Azerbaijan (PFA) was established. Following sporadic strikes and demonstrations throughout August, the PFA organized a national strike in early September and demanded discussion on the issue of sovereignty, the situation in Nagornyi Karabakh, the release of political prisoners and official recognition of the PFA. After a week of the general strike, the Azerbaijan Supreme Soviet agreed to concessions to the PFA, including official recognition. In addition, draft laws on economic and political sovereignty were published, and on 23 September the Supreme Soviet adopted the 'Constitutional Law on the Sovereignty of the Azerbaijan SSR', effectively a declaration of sovereignty. The conflict with

Armenia continued, with the imposition by Azerbaijan of an economic blockade of Armenia.

In November 1989 the Soviet Government transferred control of Nagornyi Karabakh from the SAC to an Organizing Committee, which was dominated by ethnic Azerbaijanis. This decision was denounced by the Armenian Supreme Soviet, which declared Nagornyi Karabakh to be part of a 'unified Armenian republic', prompting further outbreaks of violence in Nagornyi Karabakh and along the Armenian–Azerbaijani border. Growing unrest within Azerbaijan, exacerbated by the return of refugees from Armenia to Baku, was directed both at the local communist regime and at ethnic Armenians.

In January 1990 radical members of the PFA led assaults on CPA and government buildings in Baku and other towns. Border posts were attacked on the Soviet–Iranian border, and nationalist activists seized CPA buildings in Nakhichevan and declared its secession from the USSR. In addition, renewed violence against Armenians, with some 60 people killed in rioting in Baku, led to a hasty evacuation of the remaining non-Azerbaijanis, including ethnic Russians, from the city. On 19 January a state of emergency was declared in Azerbaijan, and Soviet troops were ordered into Baku, where the PFA was in control. According to official reports, 131 people were killed, and some 700 wounded, during the Soviet intervention. The inability of the CPA to ensure stability in the republic led to the dismissal of Abdul Vezirov as First Secretary of the party; he was replaced by Ayaz Mutalibov. Order was restored in Azerbaijan by the end of January, following the arrest of leading members of the PFA, the outlawing of other radical nationalist organizations, and the issuing of decrees banning all strikes, rallies and demonstrations.

The continuing unrest caused the elections to the republic's Supreme Soviet (held in most of the other Soviet republics in February 1990) to be postponed. When the elections did take place, in September–October 1990, the CPA won an overall majority. The opposition Democratic Alliance (which included the PFA), however, questioned the validity of the elections. In addition, the continuing state of emergency, which prohibited large public meetings, severely disrupted campaigning by the opposition. When the new Supreme Soviet convened in February 1991, some 80% of the deputies were members of the CPA. The small group of opposition deputies united as the Democratic Bloc of Azerbaijan.

Unlike the other Caucasian republics (Armenia and Georgia), Azerbaijan declared a willingness to sign a new Union Treaty and participated in the all-Union referendum concerning the preservation of the USSR, which took place in March 1991. Official results of the referendum demonstrated a qualified support for the preservation of the USSR, with 75.1% of the electorate participating, of whom 93.3% voted for a 'renewed federation'. In Nakhichevan, however, only some 20% of eligible voters approved President Gorbachev's proposal. Opposition politicians also contested the results of the referendum, claiming that only 15%–20% of the electorate had actually participated.

In August 1991, when the State Committee for the State of Emergency seized power in Moscow, Mutalibov issued a statement that appeared to demonstrate support for the coup. Despite denials that he had supported the coup leaders, large demonstrations took place, demanding his resignation, the declaration of Azerbaijan's independence, the repeal of the state of emergency, and the postponement of the presidential elections, scheduled for 8 September. The opposition was supported by Heydar Aliyev, the former First Secretary of the CPA, and now the Chairman of the Supreme Majlis (legislature) of Nakhichevan, who had become increasingly critical of Mutalibov's leadership. Mutalibov responded by ending the state of emergency and resigning as First Secretary of the CPA; on 30 August the Azerbaijani Supreme Soviet voted to 'restore the independent status of Azerbaijan'.

Despite continued protests from the PFA, the elections to the presidency proceeded, although they were boycotted by the opposition, with the result that Mutalibov was the only candidate. According to official results, he won 84% of the total votes cast. At a congress of the CPA, held later in September, it was agreed to dissolve the party.

Independence was formally restored on 18 October 1991. The Supreme Soviet voted not to sign the treaty to establish an economic community, which was signed by the leaders of eight other Soviet republics on the same day. In a further move towards full independence, the Supreme Soviet adopted legislation allowing for the creation of national armed forces, and Azerbaijani units began to take control of the Soviet Army's military facilities in the republic. However, Azerbaijan did join the Commonwealth of Independent States (CIS, see p. 150), signing the Alma-Ata Declaration on 21 December.

Following the dissolution of the USSR, hostilities intensified in Nagornyi Karabakh in early 1992. In March President Mutalibov resigned, owing to military reverses suffered by Azeri forces. He was replaced, on an interim basis, by Yagub Mamedov, the Chairman of the Milli Majlis, or National Assembly (which had replaced the Supreme Soviet following its suspension in late 1991), pending a presidential election in June. However, further military set-backs prompted the Majlis to reinstate Mutalibov as President in mid-May. His immediate declaration of a state of emergency and the cancellation of the forthcoming presidential election outraged the opposition PFA, which organized a large-scale protest rally in Baku. The demonstrators occupied both the Majlis building and the presidential palace, and succeeded in deposing Mutalibov, who had held office for only one day. (He subsequently took refuge in Russia.) The PFA's effective takeover was consolidated in the following month, when the party's leader, Abulfaz Elchibey, was elected President of Azerbaijan by direct popular vote, defeating four other candidates by a substantial margin.

During 1992 the Government had to contend with a steadily deteriorating economic situation, largely the result of the continuing conflict in Nagornyi Karabakh and the collapse of the former Soviet economic system. Severe shortages of food and fuel were reported throughout the country, and the Government's failure to provide adequate support for an estimated 500,000 refugees from Nagornyi Karabakh and from Armenia prompted a number of protest actions in Baku from mid-1992.

The background of military defeats and continuing economic decline severely undermined the Government and led to divisions within the PFA in early 1993. In June a rebel army, led by Col Surat Husseinov (the former Azerbaijani military commander in Nagornyi Karabakh), seized the city of Gyanja and advanced towards the capital, with the apparent intention of deposing Elchibey. In an attempt to bolster his leadership, Elchibey summoned Heydar Aliyev to Baku. In mid-June Aliyev was elected Chairman of the legislature. Following Elchibey's subsequent flight from the capital, Aliyev announced that he had assumed the powers of the presidency. There ensued what appeared to be a power struggle between Aliyev and Husseinov, following the bloodless capture of Baku by the rebel forces. However, in late June virtually all presidential powers were transferred, on an acting basis, to Aliyev by the Milli Majlis (which had voted to impeach Elchibey), while Husseinov was appointed Prime Minister, with control over all security services.

A referendum of confidence in Elchibey (who had taken refuge in Nakhichevan and still laid claim to the presidency) was held in late August 1993; of the 92% of the electorate that participated, 97.5% voted against him. The Milli Majlis endorsed the result and announced the holding of a direct presidential election. This took place on 3 October: Aliyev was elected President of Azerbaijan, against two other candidates, with 98.8% of the votes cast. In the months preceding the election there had been an escalation of harassment of opposition members, particularly the PFA. Several leading supporters of Elchibey were arrested, while PFA rallies were violently dispersed. The PFA boycotted the election in protest.

The domestic political situation remained tense during 1994. There was a noticeable increase in organized crime (drugs-trafficking, in particular) as well as political violence. Opponents of President Aliyev and his New Azerbaijan Party (NAP) were subject to increasing harassment, and their media activities were severely restricted. In February more than 40 members of the PFA were arrested at a regional conference of the party. In the following month police raided the PFA headquarters in Baku, arresting more than 100 people; the PFA, it was claimed, had been planning to overthrow the Government. The signature, in May, of a cease-fire in Nagornyi Karabakh (see below) led to further unrest in Azerbaijan. Nationalist opposition leaders claimed that the cease-fire would result in humiliating concessions by Azerbaijan and would be followed by the deployment of Russian troops as peace-keepers in Azerbaijan. Large-scale, anti-Government demonstrations were organized by the PFA in Baku in May and September. On both occasions many people were reported to have been injured or arrested.

A new political crisis arose in late September 1994 when the Deputy Chairman of the Milli Majlis and Aliyev's security chief were assassinated. Three members of the special militia (known as OPON) attached to the Ministry of Internal Affairs were arrested on suspicion of involvement in the murders. In early October some 100 OPON troops, led by Rovshan Javadov (a Deputy Minister of Internal Affairs), stormed the office of the Procurator-General, taking him and his officials hostage and demanding the release of the three OPON members in custody. These were released, and the OPON militia withdrew to their base. President Aliyev described the incident as an attempted coup and declared a state of emergency in Baku and Gyanja.

In the immediate aftermath of these events, other forces mutinied in Baku and elsewhere in Azerbaijan. In Gyanja, rebel forces, reportedly led by a relative of Surat Husseinov, occupied government and strategic buildings, although troops loyal to Aliyev quickly re-established control. Despite Husseinov's assurances of allegiance to Aliyev, the President dismissed him as Prime Minister, replacing him, on an acting basis, with Fuad Kuliyev. However, Aliyev stated that he himself would head the Government for the immediate future. The President then initiated a series of purges of senior members of the Government and the armed forces. In mid-October 1994 the Milli Majlis voted unanimously to remove Husseinov's parliamentary immunity from prosecution, in order that he could be arrested on charges of treason. However, Husseinov was rumoured to have fled to Russia.

Azerbaijan experienced only a short period of calm before political turmoil occurred again. In March 1995, following a decree by the Government to disband the OPON militia (which had remained under the control of Javadov), OPON forces seized government and police buildings in Baku and in north-western Azerbaijan. Many casualties were reported as government forces clashed with the OPON units, but the rebellion was crushed when government troops stormed the OPON headquarters near Baku; Javadov and many of his men were killed, while some 160 rebels were arrested. Aliyev accused former President Elchibey and Surat Husseinov of collusion in the attempted coup. In the aftermath of the unrest the PFA was also accused of involvement, and the party was banned. In early April Aliyev extended the state of emergency in Baku (introduced in October 1994) until June. However, the state of emergency in Gyanja was lifted. In May Fuad Kuliyev was confirmed as Prime Minister.

Political life in the latter half of 1995 was dominated by preparations for Azerbaijan's first post-Soviet legislative election in November. However, unrest continued: in late July a new plot to overthrow Aliyev was allegedly uncovered. This was again linked to Elchibey, Husseinov and other anti-Aliyev forces based in exile in Moscow. The harassment of opposition parties in Azerbaijan intensified, and in August–October a number of parties, as well as independent candidates, were refused permission to participate in the forthcoming election. In response, opposition parties staged protest actions in Baku.

The election of the new 125-member Milli Majlis took place, as scheduled, on 12 November 1995. Of Azerbaijan's 31 officially-registered parties, as few as eight were, in the event, permitted to participate; of these, only two were opposition parties—the PFA (recently relegalized) and the National Independence Party (NIP). Almost 600 independent candidates were barred from participation. The election was held under a mixed system of voting: 25 seats were to be filled by proportional representation of parties and the remaining 100 by majority vote in single-member constituencies. These included the constituencies of Nagornyi Karabakh and of the other Armenian-occupied territories (refugees from those regions voted in areas under Azerbaijani control, in anticipation of the eventual restoration of the country's territorial integrity). The result demonstrated widespread support for President Aliyev and his NAP, which won 19 of the 25 party seats (with the PFA and the NIP receiving three seats each). The NAP and independent candidates supporting Aliyev won an overwhelming majority of single-constituency seats. Of the remaining 28 seats in the Majlis, 27 were filled at 'run-off' elections held in late November 1995 and in February 1996, while one seat remained vacant. Some international observers monitoring the election declared that it had not been conducted in a free and fair manner and that 'serious electoral violations' had occurred. The Round Table bloc (a loose association of 21 opposition parties) claimed that the new legislature was 'illegal' and demanded the holding of fresh elections.

On the same occasion as the election of the Milli Majlis, Azerbaijan's new Constitution was approved by an overwhelming majority of the electorate (91.9%, according to official data) in a national referendum. The Constitution, which replaced the 1978 Soviet version, provided for a secular state, headed by the President, who was accorded wide-ranging executive powers.

In early 1996 supporters of Surat Husseinov and former President Elchibey received lengthy custodial sentences for their involvement in the alleged coup attempts of October 1994 and March 1995. In February 1996 two former members of the Government were sentenced to death on charges of treason, and were executed shortly afterwards. Several other former government members were sentenced to death on charges of conspiracy in the following months. Former President Mutalibov, whom Aliyev had accused of conspiring with Javadov, was arrested in Russia in April. He remained in Moscow, however, for medical treatment. The Russian authorities later refused to extradite Mutalibov on the grounds that there was insufficient evidence against him.

Repressive measures against the opposition continued, with the seizure by the police of the PFA headquarters in April 1996. Several members of the party were later arrested, one for an alleged attempt to assassinate Aliyev in 1993, and the others on charges of establishing illegal armed groups. In July 1996 Aliyev criticized the Cabinet of Ministers for failing to implement economic reform proposals, and dismissed several senior government officials for corruption. Fuad Kuliyev resigned from the office of Prime Minister, officially on grounds of ill health, after he was accused by Aliyev of hindering the process of reform; Artur Rasizade, hitherto first Deputy Prime Minister, was appointed acting Prime Minister. (His appointment as Prime Minister was confirmed in November.) This was followed, in September, by the resignation, also allegedly on grounds of ill health, of the Chairman of the Milli Majlis, Rasul Kuliyev, who had been criticized by the NAP. Murtuz Aleskerov, a staunch supporter of Aliyev, was elected in his place.

In January 1997 the Azerbaijani authorities released details of an abortive coup in October 1996, which had reportedly been organized by, amongst others, Mutalibov and Surat Husseinov. Charges were subsequently brought against some 40 alleged conspirators; in early 1997 many people, including 31 former members of the Baku police force, received prison sentences for their part in the attempted coups of October 1994 and March 1995. Husseinov was extradited from Russia to Azerbaijan in March 1997, and his trial, on charges of treason, began in July 1998. (In February 1999 he was sentenced to life imprisonment.) Meanwhile, in February 1997 four leading members of the opposition Islamic Party of Azerbaijan, including its Chairman, Ali Akram Aliyev, went on trial on charges of espionage on behalf of Iran (which denied any involvement). The trial concluded in April, and the four men received lengthy terms of imprisonment.

In April 1997 President Aliyev established a Security Council, the creation of which was stipulated in the 1995 Constitution. The formation in that month of an informal alliance of 10 parties (including the ruling NAP) to support Aliyev's policies, and to unite behind him in the 1998 presidential election, was criticized as unrepresentative by the opposition PFA; nevertheless, in May 1997, following a renewed outbreak of hostilities on the Armenian–Azerbaijani border (see below), many opposition parties issued a statement expressing their intention to support the Government, should war be declared on Armenia. Meanwhile, former President Elchibey was elected Chairman of the Democratic Congress, an opposition alliance.

In January 1998 the Azerbaijani authorities accused the former Chairman of the Milli Majlis, Rasul Kuliyev (who was now resident in the USA), of organizing a conspiracy to depose President Aliyev. In April Kuliyev, who denied the accusations, was charged *in absentia* with alleged abuses of power while in office. Meanwhile, in February the Minister of Foreign Affairs, Hassan Hassanov, was dismissed from his post for allegedly misappropriating government funds; criminal proceedings were subsequently instigated against him. In May legislation was passed creating a 24-member Central Electoral Commission, 12 of whose members would be directly appointed by the President, and 12 by the legislature. Opposition parties that had demanded that 17 of the 24 members should be representatives of political parties protested against the passage of the controversial piece of legislation. A law regarding presidential elections was approved in June, requiring candidates to collect 50,000 signatures to stand, and setting a minimum level of voter participation of 50%. This was reduced to 25% when the bill was amended in July, and each voter was allowed to endorse more than one candidate. The opposition protested that the law favoured Aliyev's re-election, and launched a series of rallies and demonstrations demanding the cancellation of the presidential elections, which were scheduled to be held in October. On 12 September police and demonstrators clashed violently in Baku, resulting in some 70–100 injuries and a number of arrests. Subsequent demonstrations in September and October were conducted peacefully following the imposition of new restrictions on public protests. Meanwhile, in August, Aliyev issued a decree dismantling the General Directorate of State Secrets, thereby effectively abolishing media censorship. Harassment of the independent media continued, however. In November a number of employees of independent newspapers staged a hunger strike in the capital to protest at alleged police brutality towards journalists and the instigation of libel proceedings against the opposition media.

The presidential election was held, as planned, on 11 October 1998, despite continuing opposition; according to official results, Heydar Aliyev was re-elected, with 77.6% of the total votes cast. Five other candidates contested the election. The polls were criticized by the Organization for Security and Co-operation in Europe (OSCE) and the Council of Europe for failing to meet international standards. Unrest continued, owing to the opposition's dissatisfaction with the validity of the results, and in November the Prosecutor-General announced that criminal proceedings would be instigated against a number of opposition leaders for their seditious pronouncements at protest rallies. The Cabinet of Ministers resigned shortly after the presidential election, as required by the Constitution. In late October the majority of ministers, including Prime Minister Rasizade, were reconfirmed in their positions by President Aliyev. In late December the Milli Majlis approved a revised Constitution for Nakhichevan, which defined the enclave as 'an autonomous state' within Azerbaijan. The amended Constitution had earlier been endorsed by the Nakhichevan legislature. The revisions were opposed by a number of deputies on the grounds that the enclave's redefined status as a state within a state could set an undesirable precedent. In the same month the opposition alliance the Round Table bloc announced its dissolution; the erstwhile component parties of the alliance stated that they intended to work with a new opposition coalition, known as the Movement for Democratic Elections and Electoral Reform, which was established in November and was composed of 23 opposition groups. It was reported that the new movement's primary aim was to campaign for the annulment of the recent presidential election.

President Aliyev's poor health caused widespread concern in the first half of 1999. Amid fears of instability arising from the possibility of the impending demise of the President, rumours abounded that Aliyev was grooming his son Ilham (the Vice-Chairman of the State Oil Company of the Azerbaijan Republic) to assume the presidency. Following medical treatment in the USA in April, however, the President's health improved and he retained his hold on power, making a number of cabinet changes in the following months and announcing, in September, that he was prepared to stand for a third term. Meanwhile, a newly-founded opposition grouping in the legisature, entitled the Democratic bloc, which comprised the PFA and the Civic Solidarity Party (some 17 deputies in total), began a boycott of the Milli Majlis in April on the grounds that the Government had violated the rights of opposition deputies by refusing to discuss draft laws on municipal elections. The boycott was ended in late June following negotiations with the Government. In July it was announced that local elections were to be held in December. The OSCE would not send observers, but was to assist with preparations for the polls. In October Tofik Zulfugarov resigned as Minister of Foreign Affairs (reportedly following disagreements with the President regarding Nagornyi Karabakh) and was replaced by Vilayat Mukhtar oglu Guliyev.

At the time of the disintegration of the USSR in late 1991, the leadership of Nagornyi Karabakh declared the enclave to be an independent republic. Azerbaijan refused to accept the territory's attempts to secede, and in January 1992 Nagornyi Karabakh was placed under direct presidential rule. International efforts to negotiate a peace settlement foundered, owing to Azerbaijan's insistence that the conflict was a domestic problem. Military successes by the ethnic Armenian forces of Nagornyi Karabakh in early 1992 culminated in the creation, in May, of a 'corridor' through Azerbaijani territory to link Nagornyi Karabakh with Armenia proper. Despite a successful Azerbaijani counter-offensive in late 1992, ethnic Armenian forces were able to open a second 'corridor' in early 1993, following which they extended their operations into Azerbaijan itself, apparently in an attempt to create a secure zone around Nagornyi Karabakh. By August some 20% of Azerbaijan's territory had been seized by Armenian units, while all of Nagornyi Karabakh had already come under their control. The Armenian military gains prompted mounting alarm among the Azeri population, and there was a massive new movement of refugees fleeing from Armenian-occupied territory. The Armenian offensive in Azerbaijan continued, despite widespread international condemnation. Although it did not directly accuse Armenia itself of aggression, the UN Security Council adopted a series of resolutions demanding an immediate cease-fire and the withdrawal of all Armenian units from Azerbaijan. There were also strong protests by Turkey and Iran, both of which mobilized troops in regions bordering Armenia and Azerbaijan in September. In December Azeri forces launched a new counter-offensive in Nagornyi Karabakh, recapturing some areas that they had lost to Armenian control, although suffering heavy casualties. Meanwhile, international efforts to halt the conflict continued. These were led by the 'Minsk Group', which had been established by the Conference on Security and Co-operation in Europe (CSCE) in 1992 to provide a framework for peace negotiations between the parties. However, all cease-fire agreements that were reached were quickly violated. In early 1994 it was estimated that, since the conflict began in 1988, some 18,000 people had been killed and a further 25,000 had been wounded. The number of Azeri refugees was believed to have exceeded 1m.

However, in early May 1994 a major breakthrough was achieved with Azerbaijan's signature of the so-called Bishkek Protocol, which had been adopted several days previously at a meeting of the CIS Inter-Parliamentary Assembly, with the approval of representatives of both Armenia and Nagornyi Karabakh. The protocol, although not legally binding, was regarded as an expression of willingness by the warring factions to negotiate a lasting peace accord. On 8 May the Nagornyi Karabakh leadership ordered its forces to cease hostilities, in accordance with the protocol. Although isolated violations were subsequently reported, the cease-fire remained in force. In the latter half of the year efforts were made to co-ordinate the separate peace proposals of the CSCE 'Minsk Group' and Russia. However, Azerbaijan refused either to negotiate a peace settlement or to discuss the future status of Nagornyi Karabakh until Armenian forces were withdrawn entirely from occupied Azerbaijani territory and Azerbaijani refugees had returned to their homes. Azerbaijan also insisted that international peacekeeping forces be deployed in Nagornyi Karabakh (as opposed to the Russian- and CIS-led force favoured by Armenia). In December, at a summit meeting of the CSCE (subsequently known as the OSCE), delegates agreed in principle to deploy a 3,000-strong multinational peace-keeping force in Nagornyi Karabakh; the agreement had apparently received the approval of the Russian Government, which was to contribute not more than 30% of the peacekeepers.

The cease-fire was maintained in Nagornyi Karabakh throughout 1995, with only minor violations reported. However, no real progress towards a full political settlement was achieved, although negotiations continued to be held under the aegis of the OSCE. Nevertheless, in May the exchange of prisoners of war and other hostages was commenced. In April–June a new 33-seat republican legislature was elected in Nagornyi Karabakh (replacing the former 81-member Supreme Soviet). Robert Kocharian, hitherto Chairman of the State Defence Committee, was appointed to the new office of an executive presidency. In August the new legislature extended martial law in Nagornyi Karabakh until January 1996 (this was subsequently extended until December 1997).

Efforts to reach a political settlement continued throughout 1996, with negotiations being held both under the auspices of the 'Minsk Group', and through direct discussions. Aliyev, who met President Ter-Petrossian of Armenia on several occasions, continued to affirm his commitment to Azerbaijan's territorial integrity, reiterating that Nagornyi Karabakh could be granted autonomy within Azerbaijan, but not full independence. The cease-fire remained in force and a further exchange of prisoners of war was carried out in May. The election to the office of President of Nagornyi Karabakh was held in November, despite earlier criticism from the OSCE and condemnation by Azerbaijan, and Kocharian, the incumbent President, was re-elected with more than 85% of votes cast. Azerbaijani refugees from the enclave staged protests in Baku, while Azerbaijan declared that it would not recognize the election results. Kocharian subsequently appointed Leonard Petrossian as Prime Minister of Nagornyi Karabakh.

In December 1996 Aliyev and Ter-Petrossian attended a summit meeting of the OSCE, in Lisbon, Portugal. Following demands by Azerbaijan, a statement was released by the OSCE Chairman, recommending three principles that would form the basis of a political settlement to the conflict: the territorial integrity of Armenia and Azerbaijan; legal status for Nagornyi Karabakh, which would be granted self-determination within Azerbaijan; and security guarantees for the population of Nagornyi Karabakh. However, Armenia refused to accept the terms of the statement.

Relations between Azerbaijan and Armenia deteriorated in February 1997, when Azerbaijan expressed concern at the provision of weapons to Armenia by several countries, including Russia, and condemned it as a violation of the Conventional Forces in Europe (CFE) Treaty. Armenia retaliated by accusing Azerbaijan of preparing for a military offensive against Nagornyi Karabakh to regain the territory. The admission by the Russian Minister of Defence that weapons had been delivered to Armenia in 1994–96 without the authorization, or knowledge, of the Russian Government, resulted in a deterioration in relations between Russia and Azerbaijan, particularly since Russia, as a participant in the 'Minsk Group', was expected to act as an impartial mediator. Azerbaijan demanded that the issue be investigated by the signatories to the CFE Treaty. It also criticized the appointment in March 1997 of Robert Kocharian, hitherto President of Nagornyi Karabakh, as Prime Minister of Armenia. Negotiations under the auspices of the OSCE resumed in Moscow in April, but little progress was made, and later in that month a series of clashes, which left many people killed or wounded, occurred on the Armenian–Azerbaijani border, with each side accusing the other of initiating the hostilities.

In late May 1997 a draft peace settlement for the disputed enclave was presented by the 'Minsk Group' to Armenia and Azerbaijan. The proposals were initially rejected by the two parties, but a revised plan, issued in July, received the qualified support of President Aliyev. The proposals provided for a stage-by-stage settlement of the conflict: Nagornyi Karabakh would receive autonomous status within Azerbaijan, and the withdrawal of Armenian forces from the enclave was to be followed by the deployment of OSCE peace-keeping troops, which would guarantee freedom of movement through the Lachin 'corridor' linking Armenia with Nagornyi Karabakh. The proposed presidential elections in Nagornyi Karabakh, scheduled for September, following the appointment of Kocharian as Prime Minister of Armenia, were severely criticized by Aliyev; the Azerbaijani authorities also expressed concern at the conclusion of a partnership treaty between Armenia and Russia, fearing that a strengthening of relations between the two countries was a hindrance to the peace process.

The election of Arkadyi Gukasian to the post of President of Nagornyi Karabakh, in September 1997, was not recognized by the international community and threatened to hamper further progress on reaching a settlement, owing to his outright dismissal of the OSCE proposals; it was reported later in that month, however, that both Azerbaijan and Armenia had accepted the revised plan drawn up by the 'Minsk Group'. In addition, in an apparently significant change in policy, President Ter-Petrossian of Armenia publicly admitted that Nagornyi Karabakh could expect neither to gain full independence, nor to be united with Armenia. Moreover, the Azerbaijani authorities indicated that they would be willing to discuss with the leadership of Nagornyi Karabakh the level of autonomy to be granted to the enclave, providing that the principles of the Lisbon statement were accepted, having previously refused to recognize the Nagornyi Karabakh administration as an equal party in the negotiations.

Ter-Petrossian's cautious and moderate approach to the Nagornyi Karabakh crisis provoked much governmental disapproval and led to the President's resignation in early February 1998. His replacement, Kocharian, who was born in Nagornyi Karabakh, was expected to adopt a more belligerent and nationalistic stance towards resolving the situation in the disputed enclave. In June Leonard Petrossian resigned as Prime Minister of Nagornyi Karabakh, following a rift with his Minister of Defence; the erstwhile Deputy Prime Minister, Zhirayr Pogossian, replaced him in the premiership and a government reorganization was carried out. In late November the Armenian Government announced that, despite some reservations, it officially accepted the latest proposals put forward by the 'Minsk Group' regarding a settlement of the conflict in Nagornyi Karabakh, which were based on the principle of a 'common state' (comprising Azerbaijan and Nagornyi Karabakh). The Azerbaijani Government, however, rejected the proposals, claiming that they threatened the territorial integrity of Azerbaijan. Minor cease-fire violations were committed by both sides in late 1998.

An escalation in hostilities in mid-1999 prompted mutual accusations by Azerbaijan and Armenia that the other was attempting to destroy the 1994 cease-fire agreement. Presidents Kocharian and Aliyev met on several occasions in the latter half of 1999, but no substantive progress was made towards resolving the crisis. Meanwhile, in June of that year President Gukasian dismissed the Government of Nagornyi Karabakh for failing to remedy the enclave's economic problems; at the end of that month Anushavan Danielian was appointed to head a new administration. In July former Prime Minister Zhirayr Pogossian was arrested and charged with the illegal possession of arms and ammunition, and also with having been responsible for losing a state document. He was released from detention a few days later, but was not permitted to leave the enclave, pending a likely trial in the coming months.

Although it signed the Alma-Ata Declaration in December 1991, Azerbaijan's subsequent attitude towards its membership of the CIS was equivocal. Indeed, the Milli Majlis failed to ratify the Commonwealth's founding treaty, and in October 1992 it voted overwhelmingly against further participation in the CIS. However, with the overthrow of the nationalist PFA Government and the accession to power of Heydar Aliyev, the country's position regarding the CIS was again reversed, and in September 1993 Azerbaijan was formally admitted to full membership of the body. In February 1999, however, it was reported that Azerbaijan would not renew its membership of the CIS collective security treaty because of the continued occupation of Nagornyi Karabakh by Armenian troops, and in protest against Russia's continuing supply of armaments to Armenia. Negotiations concerning the repair and reopening of an existing oil pipeline from Azerbaijan, via Chechnya, to Novorossiisk on Russia's Black Sea coast, were the focus of Azerbaijani-Russian relations in 1997. Security guarantees for personnel working on the pipeline were an essential part of the discussions (due to the ongoing conflict in Chechnya), and Azerbaijan actively pursued the development of alternative, new pipelines, primarily through Georgia and Turkey (see Economic Affairs). Agreements were concluded with a number of Russian companies concerning both the extraction and the transportation of crude petroleum from the offshore oilfields in the Caspian Sea, and in October the first delivery of crude petroleum was consigned to Novorossiisk through the refurbished pipeline. By April 1999, however, a pipeline carrying crude petroleum from Baku to the Georgian port of Supsa was fully operational, and supplies to Novorossiisk were discontinued. In October 1999 relations between Russia and Azerbaijan were further strained when it was reported that a Russian military aircraft had accidentally bombed a village in northern Azerbaijan. Meanwhile, a dispute with Turkmenistan concerning ownership of the Kyapaz offshore oilfield (the legal status of the Caspian Sea has yet to be established by the littoral states, following the dissolution of the USSR) appeared to threaten the conclusion of a contract with Russia to develop the area. In February 1998 Azerbaijan and Turkmenistan held talks regarding the delineation of their disputed border in the Caspian Sea, and in 1999 a mutually acceptable resolution to the problem was achieved.

In early 1999 the speakers of the Azerbaijani, Armenian and Georgian legislatures met under the auspices of the Parliamentary Assembly of the Council of Europe (see p. 158). A succession of tripartite meetings were to be held in the capitals of the three countries in turn.

The strengthening of relations with Turkey, which had been cultivated by successive leaderships following independence in 1991, continued under Aliyev. Throughout the conflict over Nagornyi Karabakh, Azerbaijan was supported by Turkey, which provided humanitarian and other aid, and reinforced Azerbaijan's economic blockade of Armenia. Proposals were made in 1997 for the construction of an oil pipeline from the Azerbaijani oilfields to the Turkish port of Ceyhan via Tbilisi, Georgia; an agreement was signed by the Azerbaijani and Turkish Presidents regarding the building of the pipeline at a summit meeting in Istanbul in November 1999. Concerning relations with neighbouring Iran, it was believed that the large Azeri minority there (numbering an estimated 20m.) might prove to be a potential source of tension. In early 1995 it was reported that ethnic Azeri organizations in northern areas of Iran had established a 'national independence front' in order to achieve unification with Azerbaijan. Nevertheless, official relations between Iran and Azerbaijan remained amicable, and bilateral trade increased significantly in the 1990s, with Iran becoming one of Azerbaijan's largest trading partners by 1997. Relations deteriorated in 1999, however, following Azerbaijani allegations, which were denied by Iran, that Iranian spies had been operating in Azerbaijan to supply Armenia with military intelligence and that Islamist guerrillas had been trained in Iran as part of a plot against the Azerbaijani Government.

Relations with the USA expanded significantly in the mid-1990s, and in July 1997 President Aliyev visited the USA, the first visit by an Azerbaijani Head of State since the country regained its independence. An agreement was signed on military co-operation between the two countries, and four contracts between the Azerbaijani State Oil Company, SOCAR, and US petroleum companies to develop offshore oilfields in the Caspian Sea were also concluded. The USA assumed co-chairmanship of the 'Minsk Group' in early 1997, together with Russia and France. US-Azerbaijani relations were strengthened in 1999. New contracts for the development of the petroleum industry worth US $10m. were signed during a visit to Washington, DC, by Aliyev in April, and the USA expressed its support for the proposed Baku-Ceyhan pipeline (see above).

In March 1992 Azerbaijan was admitted to the UN; it subsequently became a member of the CSCE (now OSCE). In April 1996, together with Georgia and Armenia, Azerbaijan signed a co-operation agreement with the European Union (see p. 172), and in June the Council of Europe granted Azerbaijan special 'guest status'. Azerbaijan sent 30 troops to be part of the NATO peace-keeping force in Kosovo, Yugoslavia, in July 1999, and the attainment of full membership of the organization was a government priority in that year (Azerbaijan had been given observer status by NATO in June).

### Government

Under the Constitution of November 1995, the President of the Azerbaijan Republic is Head of State and Commander-in-Chief of the armed forces. The President, who is directly elected for a five-year term of office, holds supreme executive authority in conjunction with the Cabinet of Ministers, which is appointed by the President and is headed by the Prime Minister. Supreme legislative power is vested in the 125-member Milli Majlis (National Assembly), which is directly elected (under a mixed system of voting) for a five-year term.

### Defence

After gaining independence in 1991, Azerbaijan began the formation of national armed forces. In August 1999 these numbered 69,900 (including 4,000 Ministry of Defence and centrally-controlled units): an army of 55,600, a navy of 2,200 and an air force of 8,100. Military service is for 17 months (but may be extended for ground forces). The Ministry of Internal Affairs controls a militia of an estimated 10,000 and a border guard of some 5,000. As a member of the CIS, Azerbaijan's naval forces operate under CIS (Russian) control. In May 1994 Azerbaijan became the 15th country to join NATO's 'Partnership for Peace' (see p. 228) programme of military co-operation. The 1999 budget allocated an estimated US $120m. to defence.

### Economic Affairs

In 1997, according to World Bank estimates, Azerbaijan's gross national product (GNP), measured at average 1995–97 prices, was US $3,886m., equivalent to $510 per head. During 1990–97, it was estimated, GNP per head declined at an average annual rate of 16.0% in real terms. Over the same period the population increased at an average rate of 0.9% per year. In 1998, according to preliminary World Bank data, GNP was about $3,900m. ($490 per head). During 1990–98 Azerbaijan's gross domestic product (GDP) decreased, in real terms, at an average rate of 10.5% annually. Real GDP declined by 11.8% in 1995, but increased by 1.3% in 1996, by 5.8% in 1997 and by 10.0% in 1998.

Agriculture (including forestry) contributed 20.3% of GDP in 1998. In that year some 22.6% of the working population were employed in the sector. The principal crops are grain, grapes and other fruit, vegetables and cotton. By mid-1999 some 80% of state-owned agriculture had passed into private ownership, and land reform was expected to be complete by the end of that year. More than 80% of the production of vegetables, fruit, livestock and animal products was generated by private farms by the end of 1997. During 1993–98 Azerbaijan's gross agricultural output decreased at an average annual rate of 4.2%. In 1996, according to the IMF, agricultural GDP grew by 3.0%, but in 1997 it decreased by 6.9%. In 1998 agricultural production was estimated to have increased by 4%.

Industry (including mining, manufacturing, construction and power) contributed 38.7% of GDP in 1998. In that year, according to official sources, 10.7% of the working population were employed in industry. The real GDP of the industrial sector increased by 16.8% in 1997 and by 19.9% in 1998.

Azerbaijan is richly endowed with mineral resources, the most important of which is petroleum. The country's known reserves of petroleum were estimated to total 1,300m.–1,500m. metric tons in December 1996, of which more than 95% was located in offshore fields in the Caspian Sea. Production of crude petroleum declined by 1% in 1996 (compared with the previous year), and also decreased in 1997, owing mainly to inefficient technology and poor maintenance of the oilfields. In September 1994 the Azerbaijani Government and a consortium of international oil companies, the Azerbaijan International Operating Company (AIOC), concluded an agreement to develop these offshore oilfields. By late 1998 a number of agreements had been signed between the State Oil Company (SOCAR) and international consortia, and negotiations were under way with Russia, Georgia, Turkey and Iran concerning the pipeline routes for the export of the crude petroleum. Production of 'early' oil began in October 1997 and was transported to the Russian Black Sea port of Novorossiisk, via Chechnya, and the first shipment of petroleum from AIOC-operated fields was made in November. During 1999, however, technical problems with the pipeline and the conflict in Chechnya caused regular closures, and, following the opening of a pipeline transporting petroleum from Baku to the Georgian port of Supsa in April 1999, it was decided to redirect supplies from the Chechnya route to the less hazardous new route. It was envisaged that production of crude petroleum would exceed 1m. barrels per day when all the fields were developed. Azerbaijan also has substantial reserves of natural gas, most of which are located off shore. In July 1999 a massive gasfield was discovered at Shah Deniz in the Caspian Sea, with sufficient reserves (estimated to be in excess of 400,000m. cu m) for major exports to Turkey. Other minerals extracted include gold, silver, iron ore, alunite (alum-stone), iron pyrites, barytes, cobalt and molybdenum.

Production in the manufacturing sector has declined significantly since 1991, owing to the collapse of the Soviet internal trading systems and the increasing cost of energy products. In 1996 the principal branches of manufacturing, measured by gross value of output, were petroleum refineries (accounting for 47.6% of the total), textiles (13.0%), chemicals (3.2%) and food products and beverages (1.3%).

In 1992 Azerbaijan's supply of primary energy was provided by natural gas (58%), nuclear power (31%), petroleum and petroleum products (6%) and hydroelectric and other sources (5%). In 1997 some 85% of electricity generation was provided by thermal power stations, while the remaining 15% was provided by hydroelectric stations. In 1994 some 30% of gas used for domestic purposes was imported from Turkmenistan. However, in 1995 imports of gas from Turkmenistan ceased, owing to the increase in gas prices to world market levels.

The services sector has expanded since 1991, with retail trade, restaurants and hotels gaining in importance in the mid-1990s. In 1998, according to official sources, services accounted for 66.7% of employment and provided 41.1% of GDP. According to the World Bank, the real GDP of the services sector increased by 8.9% in 1997 and by 0.9% in 1998.

In 1998 Azerbaijan recorded a visible trade deficit of US $1,046m., and there was a deficit of $1,365m. on the current account of the balance of payments. In 1998 the principal source of imports was Turkey (20.4%). Other major sources of imports were Russia, Ukraine, the United Kingdom and Germany. The main market for exports in that year was Turkey (22.4%). Other important purchasers were Russia, Georgia, Italy, Iran and the United Kingdom. The major exports in 1998 were petroleum products (accounting for 69.0% of the total) and cotton. The principal imports in that year were machinery and transport equipment (42.5%) and food.

Azerbaijan's overall budget deficit for 1998 was some 545,000m. manats. At the end of 1997 the country's total external debt was estimated to be US $503.7m., of which $232.9m. was long-term public debt. The cost of debt-servicing in that year was equivalent to only 6.7% of the value of exports of goods and services. The annual rate of inflation averaged 333.7% during 1990–97. Consumer prices increased by an average of 1,664% in 1994 and by 412% in 1995. However, the average inflation rate declined to 19.8% in 1996 and to 3.7% in 1997, and in 1998 deflation of 0.8% was recorded. In November 1999, according to government figures, some 1.8m. people (42.4% of the labour force) were unemployed or underemployed; however, only 42,329 were actually registered as unemployed at the end of 1998.

Azerbaijan became a member of the IMF and the World Bank in 1992. It also joined the Islamic Development Bank (see p. 216), the European Bank for Reconstruction and Development (EBRD, see p. 168), the Economic Co-operation Organization (ECO, see p. 167) and the Black Sea Economic Co-operation organization (BSEC, see p. 135).

The dissolution of the USSR in 1991, the conflict in Nagornyi Karabakh and the disruption of trade routes through Georgia and Chechnya have all caused significant economic problems for Azerbaijan. However, owing to its enormous mineral wealth, Azerbaijan's prospects for eventual economic prosperity are considered to be favourable, although major investment and foreign technological expertise are required for the full potential of the country's unexploited mineral reserves to be realized. The agreements that have been concluded with international consortia to develop these reserves were expected greatly to improve Azerbaijan's economic situation, as was the endorsement of the TRACECA (Transport Corridor Europe–Caucasus–Asia) project by the 12 countries along the route of the ancient 'Silk Road', which was signed in Baku in September 1998. The Government's stabilization and reform programme, adopted in early 1995, had achieved considerable success by late 1997. In 1998 Azerbaijan enjoyed negative growth in the rate of inflation and strong GDP expansion. However, in 1999 the rate of growth decelerated, in response to low petroleum prices, and doubts were raised as to the profitability of proposed oil pipelines via Azerbaijan. On the other hand, the discovery of massive reserves of natural gas in the Caspian Sea in July of that year looked certain to boost revenue (see above). By 1999 Azerbaijan's privatization programme, now in its second phase, was well advanced, but greater reform in the banking sector was required. The current-account deficit widened further in 1999, and revenue collection was persistently weak. Unemployment remained extremely prevalent, and living standards for much of the population were low. Nevertheless, the IMF, the World Bank and other international organizations continued to endorse Azerbaijan's programme of economic restructuring.

## Social Welfare

Azerbaijan has a comprehensive social security system, which aims to ensure that no citizen receives less than a subsistence income and that health care and education are freely available to all. However, in the late 1990s Azerbaijan's social welfare system was under enormous strain, owing to the conflict in Nagornyi Karabakh (see Recent History) and the massive influx of refugees into the republic, as well as the effects of comprehensive economic reforms. Among the most important provisions of the system are: old-age, disability, and survivor pensions; birth, child, and family allowances, as well as benefits for sick leave, maternity leave, temporary disability, and burial; unemployment compensation; price subsidies; and tax exemptions for specific social groups. The above social benefits are financed by three extrabudgetary funds, the Social Protection Fund, the Employment Fund and the Disabled Persons' Fund. The Social Protection Fund receives transfers from the republican budget, and the Employment Fund is financed by social insurance contributions from employers. In 1998 government expenditure on health care amounted to 1.0% of GDP. Transfers to households by the Social Protection Fund in 1998 totalled 1,096,000m. manats (16% of total government expenditure), including 528,000m. manats in pensions. At the end of 1998, according to official figures, some 1.2m. people were receiving pensions, 727,000 of whom were old-age pensioners.

Azerbaijan's first private hospital was opened, in the Nakhichevan Autonomous Republic, in May 1998. In mid-1998 it was reported that, under the state health-care system, there were 79,000 hospital beds and at the end of that year there were 28,850 physicians working in the country.

## Education

Before 1918 Azerbaijan was an important centre of learning among Muslims of the Russian Empire. Under Soviet rule, a much more extensive education system was introduced. In the early 1990s this was reorganized, as part of overall economic and political reforms. Education is officially compulsory between the ages of six and 17 years. Primary education begins at six years of age and lasts for four years. Secondary education, beginning at 10, comprises a first cycle of five years and a second cycle of two years. In 1996 total enrolment at primary and secondary schools was equivalent to 89% of the school-age population (males 87%; females 91%). Approximately 85% of secondary schools use Azerbaijani as the medium of instruction, while some 13% use Russian. Since 1992 a Turkic version of the Latin alphabet has been used in Azerbaijani-language schools (replacing the Cyrillic script). There were 17 institutions of higher education in 1992; courses of study for full-time students last between four and five years. Higher education institutes include Baku State University, which specializes in the sciences, and the State Petroleum Academy, which trains engineers for the petroleum industry. In 1995 it was estimated that the rate of adult illiteracy in Azerbaijan was only 0.4% (males 0.3%; females 0.5%). Government expenditure on education in 1995 was 375,820m. manats (17.5% of total government expenditure). Such spending was estimated to total 3.6% of GDP in 1998.

## Public Holidays

**2000:** 1 January (New Year), 8 January*† (Ramazan Bayramy, end of Ramadan), 20 January (Day of Sorrow), 8 March (International Women's Day), 16 March* (Kurban Bayramy, Sacrifice Day), 28 May (Republic Day), 15 June (Day of Liberation of the Azerbaijani People), 9 October (Day of the Armed Services), 18 October (Day of Statehood), 12 November (Constitution Day), 17 November (Day of National Survival), 28 December*† (Ramazan Bayramy, end of Ramadan), 31 December (Day of Azerbaijani Solidarity World-wide).

**2001:** 1 January (New Year), 20 January (Day of Sorrow), 8 March (International Women's Day), 16 March* (Kurban Bayramy, Sacrifice Day), 28 May (Republic Day), 15 June (Day of Liberation of the Azerbaijani People), 9 October (Day of the Armed Services), 18 October (Day of Statehood), 12 November (Constitution Day), 17 November (Day of National Survival), 17 December* (Ramazan Bayramy, end of Ramadan), 31 December (Day of Azerbaijani Solidarity World-wide).

* These holidays are dependent on the Islamic lunar calendar and may vary by one or two days from the dates given.

† This festival will occur twice (in the Islamic years AH 1420 and AH 1421) within the same Gregorian year.

## Weights and Measures

The metric system is in force.

# Statistical Survey

Source (unless otherwise stated): State Statistical Committee of Azerbaijan Republic, 370136 Baku, Inshatchilar St; tel. (12) 38-64-98; fax (12) 38-24-42; internet www.statcom.baku-az.com.

## Area and Population

### AREA, POPULATION AND DENSITY

| | |
|---|---|
| Area (sq km) | 86,600* |
| Population (census results)† | |
| 17 January 1979 | 6,026,515 |
| 12 January 1989 | |
| Males | 3,423,793 |
| Females | 3,597,385 |
| Total | 7,021,178 |
| Population (official estimates at 31 December) | |
| 1996 | 7,799,800 |
| 1997 | 7,876,700 |
| 1998 | 7,953,000 |
| Density (per sq km) at 31 December 1998 | 91.8 |

* 33,400 sq miles.

† Figures refer to *de jure* population. The *de facto* total at the 1989 census was 7,037,867.

### ETHNIC GROUPS

(permanent inhabitants, 1989 census)

| | % |
|---|---|
| Azeri | 82.7 |
| Russian | 5.6 |
| Armenian | 5.6 |
| Lezghi | 2.4 |
| Others | 3.7 |
| **Total** | **100.0** |

### PRINCIPAL TOWNS

(estimated population at 1 January 1990)

Baku (capital) 1,149,000; Gyanja (formerly Kirovabad) 281,000; Sumgait 235,000.

**1999** (estimated population at 22 February): Baku 1,708,000.

### BIRTHS, MARRIAGES AND DEATHS

| | Registered live births | | Registered marriages | | Registered deaths | |
|---|---|---|---|---|---|---|
| | Number | Rate (per 1,000) | Number | Rate (per 1,000) | Number | Rate (per 1,000) |
| 1987 | 184,585 | 26.9 | 68,031 | 9.9 | 45,744 | 6.7 |
| 1988 | 184,350 | 26.4 | 68,887 | 9.9 | 47,485 | 6.8 |
| 1989 | 181,631 | 25.6 | 71,874 | 10.1 | 44,016 | 6.2 |

**1996:** Registered deaths 48,242 (death rate 6.4 per 1,000).

Source: UN, *Population and Vital Statistics Report*.

**1997** (provisional): Registered births 132,100 (birth rate 17.3 per 1,000); Registered marriages 47,000 (marriage rate 6.2 per 1,000).

Source: UN, *Demographic Yearbook*.

**Expectation of life** (official estimates, years at birth, 1989): 70.6 (males 66.6; females 74.2) (Source: Goskomstat USSR).

### ECONOMICALLY ACTIVE POPULATION*

(ISIC Major Divisions, annual average, '000 persons)

| | 1995 | 1996 | 1997 |
|---|---|---|---|
| Agriculture, hunting, forestry and fishing | 874.0 | 921.3 | 967.4 |
| Mining and quarrying }<br>Manufacturing } | 352.1 | 282.9 | 257.4 |
| Electricity, gas and water | 81.8 | 86.1 | 90.4 |
| Construction | 185.1 | 164.1 | 151.0 |
| Trade, restaurants and hotels | 396.2 | 456.6 | 511.4 |
| Transport, storage and communications | 159.1 | 168.3 | 175.0 |
| Financing, insurance, real estate and business services | 14.2 | 14.0 | 13.9 |
| Community, social and personal services | 613.7 | 625.4 | 635.2 |
| Activities not adequately defined | 161.1 | 176.7 | 98.3 |
| **Total employed** | 2,837.3 | 2,895.4 | 2,900.0 |
| Unemployed | 28.3 | 31.9 | 38.3 |
| **Total labour force** | 2,865.6 | 2,927.3 | 2,938.3 |
| Males | n.a. | n.a. | 1,573.5 |
| Females | n.a. | n.a. | 1,364.8 |

* Figures refer to males aged 16 to 59 years and females aged 16 to 54 years.

Source: ILO, *Yearbook of Labour Statistics*.

## Agriculture

### PRINCIPAL CROPS ('000 metric tons)

| | 1996 | 1997 | 1998 |
|---|---|---|---|
| Wheat | 729 | 896 | 798 |
| Barley | 213 | 145 | 167* |
| Maize | 14 | 19 | 30 |
| Potatoes | 215 | 223 | 310 |
| Cottonseed | 170* | 77† | 69† |
| Cabbages | 66 | 44 | 65† |
| Tomatoes | 246 | 206 | 235† |
| Cucumbers and gherkins | 57 | 65* | 65† |
| Onions (dry) | 59 | 40 | 66† |
| Other vegetables | 152 | 171 | 193† |
| Watermelons† ‡ | 150 | 165 | 145 |
| Grapes | 275 | 145 | 144 |
| Apples | 209* | 189* | 125† |
| Pears | 18* | 7 | 8† |
| Peaches and nectarines | 18* | 13 | 15† |
| Plums | 30* | 22 | 25† |
| Citrus fruits | 14* | 8† | 9† |
| Apricots | 16* | 15 | 15† |
| Tea (made) | 3 | 2 | 1 |
| Tobacco (leaves) | 11 | 15 | 15† |
| Cotton (lint) | 74 | 69 | 45 |

* Unofficial figure. † FAO estimate(s).

‡ Including melons, pumpkins and squash.

Source: FAO, *Production Yearbook*.

**LIVESTOCK** ('000 head, year ending September)

| | 1996 | 1997 | 1998 |
|---|---|---|---|
| Horses | 49 | 47 | 46* |
| Asses* | 7 | 6 | 6 |
| Cattle | 1,682 | 1,780 | 1,843 |
| Buffaloes | 298 | 303 | 293 |
| Camels* | 25 | 24 | 24 |
| Pigs | 30 | 23 | 21 |
| Sheep | 4,644 | 4,922 | 5,867 |
| Goats | 210 | 274 | 371 |
| Chickens (million)† | 13 | 12 | 13 |

* FAO estimate(s). † Unofficial figures.

Source: FAO, *Production Yearbook*.

**LIVESTOCK PRODUCTS** ('000 metric tons)

| | 1996 | 1997 | 1998 |
|---|---|---|---|
| Beef and veal | 44 | 48 | 51 |
| Mutton and lamb | 26 | 26 | 27 |
| Pig meat | 2 | 2 | 2 |
| Poultry meat | 15 | 15 | 15 |
| Cows' milk | 843 | 854 | 854* |
| Cheese | 2 | 1 | 1* |
| Butter* | n.a. | 1 | 1 |
| Hen eggs† | 27 | 27 | 28 |
| Honey | 1 | n.a. | 1* |
| Wool: | | | |
| greasy | 9 | 10 | 10 |
| clean | 5 | 6 | 6 |
| Cattle and buffalo hides* | 8 | 8 | 9 |

* FAO estimates. † Unofficial figure.

Source: FAO, *Production Yearbook*.

# Fishing

(metric tons, live weight)

| | 1995 | 1996 | 1997 |
|---|---|---|---|
| Freshwater bream* | 110 | 100 | 94 |
| Azov sea sprat* | 9,010 | 8,275 | 7,777 |
| Other fishes* | 151 | 137 | 129 |
| **Total catch** | 9,271 | 8,512* | 8,000* |

* FAO estimate(s).

Source: FAO, *Yearbook of Fishery Statistics*.

# Mining

| | 1996 | 1997 | 1998 |
|---|---|---|---|
| Crude petroleum ('000 metric tons) | 9,100 | 9,100 | 11,400 |
| Natural gas (million cu metres) | 6,300 | 6,000 | 5,600 |

# Industry

**SELECTED PRODUCTS** ('000 metric tons, unless otherwise indicated)

| | 1994 | 1995 | 1996 |
|---|---|---|---|
| Steel | 37 | 19 | — |
| Cement | 467 | 196 | 223 |
| Fertilizers | 33 | 12 | 10 |
| Pesticides | 1 | — | n.a. |
| Sulphuric acid | 56 | 24 | 31 |
| Caustic soda | 40 | 36 | 33 |
| Sulphanol | 7 | — | n.a. |
| Concrete (reinforced, million cu m) | 250 | 91 | n.a. |
| Bricks (million) | 62 | 26 | 11 |
| Radio receivers ('000) | 3 | — | — |
| Bicycles ('000) | 213 | 4 | 2 |
| Electric motors ('000) | 834 | 512 | n.a. |
| Electric energy (million kWh) | 17,600 | 17,040 | 17,090 |
| Jet fuels | 419 | 500 | n.a. |
| Motor spirit (petrol) | 1,073 | 900 | n.a. |
| Kerosene | 562 | 550 | 700 |
| Diesel oil | 2,300 | 2,200 | 2,100 |
| Lubricants | 230 | 100 | 100 |
| Residual fuel oil (Mazout) | 4,149 | 4,290 | 4,000 |

Source: partly UN, *Industrial Commodity Statistics Yearbook*.

# Finance

**CURRENCY AND EXCHANGE RATES**

**Monetary Units**

100 gopik = 1 Azerbaijani manat.

**Sterling, Dollar and Euro Equivalents** (30 September 1999)

£1 sterling = 7,112.9 manats;
US $1 = 4,320.0 manats;
€1 = 4,607.3 manats;
10,000 manats = £1.406 = $2.315 = €2.170.

**Average Exchange Rate** (Azerbaijani manats per US $)

1996 4,301.3
1997 3,985.4
1998 3,869.0

Note: The Azerbaijani manat was introduced in August 1992, initially to circulate alongside the Russian (formerly Soviet) rouble, with an exchange rate of 1 manat = 10 roubles. In December 1993 Azerbaijan left the rouble zone, and the manat became the country's sole currency.

**STATE BUDGET** ('000 million manats)

| Revenue | 1996 | 1997 | 1998 |
|---|---|---|---|
| Individual income tax | 213.0 | 331.1 | 408 |
| Enterprise profits tax | 586.0 | 443.6 | 327 |
| Social security contributions | 310.3 | 387.6 | 405 |
| Value-added tax | 467.6 | 654.2 | 719 |
| Excises | 206.3 | 221.7 | 95 |
| Royalties | 41.6 | 341.9 | 171 |
| Customs revenue | 111.8 | 233.8 | 293 |
| Other receipts | 464.5 | 409.2 | 337 |
| **Total** | 2,401.0 | 3,023.2 | 2,755 |

| Expenditure* | 1996 | 1997 | 1998 |
|---|---|---|---|
| Wages and salaries | 482.8 | 701.3 | 811 |
| Purchases of goods and services | 943.8 | 1,161.3 | 942 |
| Interest payments | 43.7 | 18.5 | 17 |
| Transfers to households | 872.3 | 958.8 | 1,096 |
| Social protection fund | 793.5 | 841.5 | 947 |
| Pensions | 366.2 | 421.4 | 528 |
| Cash compensations | 307.4 | 320.1 | 290 |
| Other compensations and allowances | 119.9 | 100.0 | 129 |
| Current transfers abroad | 0.0 | 14.8 | n.a. |
| Subsidies | 285.4 | 105.9 | 20 |
| Capital investment | 68.0 | 200.6 | 185 |
| Other purposes | 1.7 | 27.2 | 12 |
| **Total** | 2,699.7 | 3,188.4 | 3,300 |

* Excluding lending minus repayments ('000 million manats): 83.0 in 1996; 91.5 in 1997; 130 in 1998.

Source: partly IMF, *Azerbaijan Republic: Selected Issues* (August 1999).

**1999** (forecasts, '000 million manats): Total revenue 3,228; Total expenditure 3,969 (legislative and executive agencies 34.7, central executive authority 179.2, science 43.4, courts and law-enforcement and security agencies 362.9, education 860.2, health 220.4, social security 462.0, social welfare 137.4, state debt payments 324.9).

**INTERNATIONAL RESERVES** (US $ million at 31 December)

| | 1996 | 1997 | 1998 |
|---|---|---|---|
| Gold* | 2.38 | 1.38 | 1.37 |
| IMF special drawing rights | 20.82 | 5.59 | 0.11 |
| Reserve position in IMF | 0.01 | 0.01 | 0.01 |
| Foreign exchange | 190.45 | 460.49 | 447.20 |
| **Total** | 213.66 | 467.47 | 448.69 |

* National valuation.

Source: IMF, *International Financial Statistics*.

**MONEY SUPPLY** ('000 million manats at 31 December)

| | 1996 | 1997 | 1998 |
|---|---|---|---|
| Currency outside banks | 865.4 | 1,170.5 | 926.0 |
| Demand deposits at commercial banks | 250.1 | 323.8 | 203.0 |
| **Total money** (incl. others) | 1,119.7 | 1,524.1 | 1,134.5 |

Source: IMF, *International Financial Statistics*.

**COST OF LIVING** (Consumer Price Index; base: 1993 = 100)

| | 1996 | 1997 | 1998 |
|---|---|---|---|
| Food | 11,016.2 | 10,964.0 | 10,816.9 |
| **All items** (incl. others) | 10,816.5 | 11,217.7 | 11,131.0 |

Source: UN, *Monthly Bulletin of Statistics*.

## NATIONAL ACCOUNTS

**Expenditure on the Gross Domestic Product**
('000 million manats at current prices)

| | 1996 | 1997 | 1998 |
|---|---|---|---|
| Government final consumption expenditure | 1,642.0 | 1,828.7 | 2,039.9 |
| Private final consumption expenditure | 11,980.0 | 12,043.6 | 12,893.7 |
| Increase in stocks | −14.7 | 70.7 | −5.3 |
| Gross fixed capital formation | 3,976.8 | 5,800.2 | 6,471.0 |
| **Total domestic expenditure** | 17,584.1 | 19,743.2 | 21,399.3 |
| Exports of goods and services | 3,406.0 | 4,396.0 | 4,037.8 |
| *Less* Imports of goods and services | 7,640.4 | 8,599.6 | 9,288.6 |
| **Sub-total** | 13,349.7 | 15,539.6 | 16,148.5 |
| Statistical discrepancy* | 313.5 | −187.4 | −218.8 |
| **GDP in purchasers' values** | 13,663.2 | 15,352.2 | 15,929.7 |

* Referring to the difference between the sum of the expenditure components and official estimates of GDP, compiled from the production approach.

Source: partly IMF, *Azerbaijan Republic: Selected Issues* (August 1999).

**Gross Domestic Product by Economic Activity**
('000 million manats at current prices)

| | 1993 | 1994 | 1995 |
|---|---|---|---|
| Agriculture and forestry | 42,562 | 605,996 | 2,837,056 |
| Industry* | 39,127 | 309,639 | 2,306,855 |
| Construction | 11,759 | 138,755 | 274,172 |
| Trade and catering† | 8,451 | 117,419 | 735,534 |
| Transport and communications‡ | 12,532 | 230,046 | 2,659,713 |
| Other activities of the material sphere | 732 | 4,371 | 32,276 |
| Finance and insurance | 11,277 | 104,951 | 432,693 |
| Housing | 1,109 | 19,416 | 71,508 |
| General administration and defence | 9,415 | 96,018 | 392,271 |
| Other community, social and personal services | 22,260 | 228,460 | 894,859 |
| Private non-profit institutions serving households | 220 | 515 | 2,400 |
| **Sub-total** | 159,445 | 1,855,586 | 10,639,337 |
| *Less* Imputed bank service charge | 10,045 | 91,383 | 375,211 |
| **GDP at factor cost** | 149,400 | 1,764,203 | 10,264,126 |
| Indirect taxes | 20,468 | 105,223 | 604,074 |
| *Less* Subsidies | 12,786 | 68,622 | 299,967 |
| **GDP in purchasers' values** | 157,082 | 1,800,804 | 10,568,233 |

* Comprising manufacturing (except printing and publishing), mining and quarrying, electricity, gas, water, logging and fishing.
† Including material supply and procurement.
‡ Including road maintenance.

**BALANCE OF PAYMENTS** (US $ million)

| | 1996 | 1997 | 1998 |
|---|---|---|---|
| Exports of goods f.o.b. | 643.7 | 808.3 | 677.8 |
| Imports of goods f.o.b. | −1,337.6 | −1,375.2 | −1,723.9 |
| **Trade balance** | −693.9 | −566.9 | −1,046.2 |
| Exports of services | 149.3 | 341.8 | 331.7 |
| Imports of services | −440.9 | −726.0 | −700.8 |
| **Balance on goods and services** | −985.6 | −951.1 | −1,415.2 |
| Other income received | 15.1 | 22.8 | 38.3 |
| Other income paid | −27.2 | −32.3 | −51.6 |
| **Balance on goods, services and income** | −997.7 | −960.6 | −1,428.5 |
| Current transfers received | 107.2 | 95.7 | 145.0 |
| Current transfers paid | −40.7 | −50.9 | −80.9 |
| **Current balance** | −931.2 | −915.8 | −1,364.5 |
| Capital account (net) | — | −10.2 | −0.7 |
| Direct investment from abroad | 627.3 | 1,114.8 | 1,023.0 |
| Portfolio investment assets | — | 1.1 | — |
| Portfolio investment liabilities | — | — | 0.4 |
| Other investment assets | −216.8 | −102.6 | 22.3 |
| Other investment liabilities | 412.0 | 78.8 | 280.4 |
| Net errors and omissions | 23.6 | −27.0 | −20.1 |
| **Overall balance** | −85.0 | 139.2 | −59.2 |

Source: IMF, *International Financial Statistics*.

# External Trade

**PRINCIPAL COMMODITIES** (US $ million)

| Imports c.i.f.* | 1996 | 1997 | 1998 |
|---|---|---|---|
| Food | 383 | 181 | 175 |
| Metals and metal products | 87 | 109 | 127 |
| Chemicals and petrochemicals† | 60 | 50 | 79 |
| Machinery and transport equipment | 226 | 219 | 458 |
| **Total** (incl. others) | 961 | 794 | 1,077 |

| Exports f.o.b. | 1996 | 1997 | 1998 |
|---|---|---|---|
| Food | 29 | 55 | 47 |
| Cotton | 59 | 123 | 49 |
| Petroleum products | 395 | 452 | 418 |
| Metals and metal products | 6 | 15 | 13 |
| Chemicals and petrochemicals† | 20 | 13 | 11 |
| Machinery and transport equipment | 48 | 41 | 41 |
| **Total** (incl. others) | 631 | 781 | 606 |

* Excluding shuttle trade.

† Including pharmaceutical products.

Source: partly IMF, *Azerbaijan Republic: Selected Issues* (August 1999).

**PRINCIPAL TRADING PARTNERS** (US $ million)

| Imports c.i.f. | 1996 | 1997 | 1998 |
|---|---|---|---|
| Georgia | 28* | 37* | 25.2 |
| Germany | n.a. | n.a. | 46.7 |
| Iran | 66 | 49 | 42.6 |
| Kazakhstan | 19 | 30 | 44.4 |
| Russia | 158 | 152 | 193.8 |
| Switzerland | n.a. | n.a. | 12.8 |
| Turkey | 216 | 180 | 220.1 |
| Turkmenistan | 13 | 25 | 26.4 |
| Ukraine | 94 | 86 | 93.0 |
| United Arab Emirates | 109* | 42* | 45.6 |
| United Kingdom | 15* | 14* | 69.9 |
| USA | n.a. | n.a. | 39.8 |
| **Total** (incl. others) | 961 | 794 | 1,077.2 |

| Exports f.o.b. | 1996 | 1997 | 1998 |
|---|---|---|---|
| Georgia | 92 | 133 | 76.9 |
| Iran | 226 | 190 | 44.5 |
| Italy | n.a. | n.a. | 45.1 |
| Kazakhstan | 15 | 9 | 10.6 |
| Russia | 111 | 181 | 105.8 |
| Switzerland | n.a. | n.a. | 17.1 |
| Turkey | 39 | 41 | 135.8 |
| Turkmenistan | n.a. | n.a. | 13.9 |
| Ukraine | 22 | 32 | 12.0 |
| United Kingdom | 13 | 1 | 40.4 |
| USA | n.a. | n.a. | 13.9 |
| **Total** (incl. others) | 631 | 781 | 606.2 |

* Source: IMF, *Azerbaijan Republic: Selected Issues* (August 1999).

Source: partly Azerbaijan State Committee for Statistics.

# Transport

**RAILWAYS**

| | 1996 | 1997 | 1998 |
|---|---|---|---|
| Passenger-kilometres (million) | 558 | 489 | 550 |
| Freight carried (million metric tons) | 9.6 | 9.2 | 10.6 |
| Freight ton-kilometres (million) | 2,777 | 3,514 | 4,613 |

**ROAD TRAFFIC** (vehicles in use at 31 December)

| | 1995 | 1996 | 1997 |
|---|---|---|---|
| Passenger cars | 278,285 | 273,656 | 271,265 |
| Buses | 12,768 | 12,925 | 12,053 |
| Lorries and vans | 79,673 | 77,710 | 71,938 |

Source: International Road Federation, *World Road Statistics*.

**1998:** Passenger cars 281,100; Lorries 77,800 (Source: Azerbaijan State Committee for Statistics).

**SHIPPING**

**Merchant Fleet** (registered at 31 December)

| | 1996 | 1997 | 1998 |
|---|---|---|---|
| Number of vessels | 289 | 288 | 287 |
| Total displacement ('000 grt) | 636.1 | 632.7 | 650.9 |

Source: Lloyd's Register of Shipping, *World Fleet Statistics*.

**CIVIL AVIATION** (traffic on scheduled services)

| | 1993 | 1994 | 1995 |
|---|---|---|---|
| Kilometres flown (million) | 23 | 23 | 21 |
| Passengers carried ('000) | 1,383 | 1,380 | 1,156 |
| Passenger-km (million) | 1,738 | 1,731 | 1,650 |
| Total ton-km (million) | 184 | 183 | 183 |

Source: UN, *Statistical Yearbook*.

# Tourism

| | 1994 | 1995 | 1996 |
|---|---|---|---|
| Tourist arrivals ('000) | 321 | 149 | 145 |
| Tourism receipts (US $ million) | 64 | 146 | 158 |

Source: World Tourism Organization, *Yearbook of Tourism Statistics*.

**Tourist arrivals:** 305,830 in 1997; 483,162 in 1998 (Source: Azerbaijan State Committee for Statistics).

## Communications Media

| | 1994 | 1995 | 1996 |
|---|---|---|---|
| Daily newspapers: | | | |
| Titles | 3 | 3 | 6 |
| Average circulation ('000 copies) | 210 | 210* | n.a. |
| Book production†: | | | |
| Titles | 375 | 498 | 542 |
| Copies ('000) | 5,557 | 3,592 | 2,643 |

* Provisional.

† Figures include pamphlets: 46 titles and 424,000 copies in 1994.

**1992:** Non-daily newspapers 273 (average circulation 3,476,000 copies); Other periodicals 49 (average circulation 801,000 copies).

Source: UNESCO, *Statistical Yearbook.*

**Telephones** ('000 main lines in use): 647 in 1993; 635 in 1994; 640 in 1995 (Source: UN, *Statistical Yearbook*).

**Telefax stations** (number in use): 2,500 in 1994 (Source: UN, *Statistical Yearbook*).

**Mobile cellular telephones** (subscribers): 500 in 1994; 6,000 in 1995 (Source: UN, *Statistical Yearbook*).

## Education

(1996/97, unless otherwise indicated)

| | Institutions | Teachers | Students |
|---|---|---|---|
| Pre-primary | 1,867 | 13,033 | 96,318 |
| Primary | 4,454 | 35,514 | 719,013 |
| Secondary | n.a. | 105,656* | 819,625 |
| General | n.a. | 85,001 | 802,338 |
| Teacher-training | n.a. | n.a. | 721† |
| Vocational | 167‡ | n.a. | 17,287 |
| Higher | 17§ | 15,929** | 115,116 |

* 1995/96. † 1993/94. ‡ 1991. § 1992. ** provisional.

Source: mainly UNESCO, *Statistical Yearbook*.

# Directory

## The Constitution

The new Constitution was endorsed by 91.9% of the registered electorate in a national referendum, held on 12 November 1995. It replaced the amended Soviet Constitution of 1978. The following is a summary of the 1995 Constitution's main provisions:

The Azerbaijan Republic is a democratic, secular and unitary state. The President, who is directly elected for a term of five years, is Head of State and Commander-in-Chief of the armed forces. Executive power is held by the President, who acts as guarantor of the independence and territorial integrity of the republic. The President appoints the Cabinet of Ministers, headed by the Prime Minister, which is the highest executive body. The President proposes candidates for the Constitutional Court and the Supreme Court, and may call legislative elections. The supreme legislative body is the 125-member Milli Majlis (National Assembly), which is directly elected for a five-year term. Three types of ownership—state, private and municipal—are recognized. The state is committed to a market economic system and to freedom of entrepreneurial activity.

## The Government

### HEAD OF STATE

**President:** HEYDAR A. ALIYEV (elected by direct popular vote, 3 October 1993; inaugurated on 10 October 1993; re-elected 11 October 1998; inaugurated on 18 October 1998).

### CABINET OF MINISTERS

(January 2000)

**Prime Minister:** ARTUR RASIZADE.

**First Deputy Prime Minister:** ABBAS A. ABBASSOV.

**Deputy Prime Ministers:** ELCHIN I. EFENDIYEV, IZZET A. RUSTAMOV, ABID G. SHARIFOV, ALI HASANOV, YAGUB ABDULLA OGLU EYYUBOV.

**Minister of the Economy:** NAMIK N. NASRULLAYEV.

**Minister of Public Health:** ALI BINNET OGLY INSANOV.

**Minister of Foreign Affairs:** VILAYAT MUKHTAR OGLU KULIYEV.

**Minister of Agriculture and Produce:** IRSHAD N. ALIYEV.

**Minister of Internal Affairs:** RAMIL I. USUBOV.

**Minister of Culture:** POLAD BYUL-BYUL OGLY.

**Minister of Education:** MISIR MARDANOV.

**Minister of Communications:** NADIR AKHMEDOV.

**Minister of Trade:** (vacant).

**Minister of Finance:** AVAZ ALEKPEROV.

**Minister of Justice:** SUDABA D. HASANOVA.

**Minister of Labour and Social Protection:** ALI NAGIYEV.

**Minister of National Security:** NAMIG R. ABBASOV.

**Minister of Defence:** Lt-Gen. SAFAR A. ABIYEV.

**Minister of Information and the Press:** SIRUS TEBRIZLI.

**Minister of Youth and Sport:** ABULFAZ M. KARAYEV.

### Chairmen of State Committees

**Chairman of the State Tax Inspection Committee:** FAZIL MAMMADOV.

**Chairman of the State Committee for Securities:** HEYDAR BABAYEV.

**Chairman of the State Committee for Inter-ethnic Relations:** ABBAS ABBASSOV.

**Chairman of the State Committee for Property:** FARKHAD ALIYEV.

**Chairman of the State Committee for Construction and Architectural Affairs:** ABID G. SHARIFOV.

**Chairman of the State Committee for Anti-monopoly Policy and Enterprise Support:** RAHIB GULIYEV.

**Chairman of the State Committee for Statistics:** ARIF A. VELIYEV.

**Chairman of the State Committee for Geology and Mineral Resources:** ISLAM TAGIYEV.

**Chairman of the State Committee for Ecology and Use of Natural Resources:** (vacant).

**Chairman of the State Committee for Supervision of Safety at Work in Industry and Mining:** YAGUB EYYUBOV.

**Chairman of the State Committee for Geodesy and Cartography:** ADIL SULTANOV.

**Chairman of the State Committee for Material Resources:** HULMAMMAD JAVADOV.

**Chairman of the State Committee for Specialized Machinery:** SABIR ALEKPEROV.

**Chairman of the State Committee for Science and Technology:** AZAD MIRZAJANZADE.

**Chairman of the State Land Committee:** HARIB MAMMADOV.

**Chairman of the State Customs Committee:** KAMALEDDIN HEYDAROV.

**Chairman of the State Committee for Veterinary Affairs:** MIRSALEH HUSEYNOV.

**Chairman of the State Committee for Hydrometeorology:** ZULFUGAR MUSAYEV.

**Chairman of the State Committee for the Protection and Refurbishment of Historical and Cultural Monuments:** FAKHREDDIN MIRALIYEV.

**Chairman of the State Committee for Refugees and Involuntary Migrants:** ALI HASANOV.

**Chairman of the State Committee for Improvements in the Water Industry:** AHMED AHMEDZADE.

### MINISTRIES

**Office of the Prime Minister:** 370066 Baku, Lermontov St 63; tel. (912) 92-66-23; fax (12) 92-91-79.

**Ministry of Agriculture and Food:** 370016 Baku, Azadlyg Sq. 1, Government House; tel. (12) 93-53-55.

**Ministry of Communications:** 370139 Baku, Azerbaijan Ave 33; tel. (12) 93-00-04; fax (12) 98-42-85; e-mail behm@azerin.com.

**Ministry of Culture:** 370016 Baku, Azadlyg Sq. 1, Government House; tel. (12) 93-43-98; fax (12) 93-56-05.

**Ministry of Defence:** 370139 Baku, Azerbaijan Ave.

**Ministry of the Economy:** 370016 Baku, Azadlyg Sq. 1, Government House; tel. (12) 93-61-62; fax (12) 93-20-25.

**Ministry of Education:** 370016 Baku, Azadlyg Sq. 1, Government House; tel. (12) 93-72-66.

**Ministry of Finance:** 370022 Baku, Samed Vurghun St 83; tel. (12) 93-30-12; fax (12) 98-71-84; e-mail adalet-ferd@artel.net.az.

**Ministry of Foreign Affairs:** 370004 Baku, Ghanjlar meydani 3; tel. (12) 92-68-56.

**Ministry of Information and the Press:** 370001 Baku, A. Karayev St 12; tel. (12) 92-63-57; fax (12) 92-93-33.

**Ministry of Internal Affairs:** 370005 Baku, Gusi Hajiyev St 7; tel. (12) 92-57-54.

**Ministry of Justice:** 370601 Baku, Bul-Bul Ave 13; tel. (12) 93-97-85.

**Ministry of Labour and Social Protection:** 370016 Baku, Azadlyg Sq. 1, Government House; tel. (12) 93-05-42; fax (12) 93-94-72.

**Ministry of National Security:** 370602 Baku, Parliament Ave 2; tel. (12) 95-01-63.

**Ministry of Public Health:** 370014 Baku, Malaya Morskaya St 4; tel. (12) 93-29-77.

**Ministry of Trade:** 370016 Baku, Uzevir Hajibeyov St 40; tel. (12) 98-50-74; fax (12) 98-74-31.

**Ministry of Transport:** Baku.

**Ministry of Youth and Sport:** 370072 Baku, Fhataly Khan Khoyski Ave 98A; tel. (12) 90-64-42; fax (12) 90-64-38; e-mail mys@azeri.com; internet www.mys.azeri.com.

## President and Legislature

### PRESIDENT

**Presidential Election, 11 October 1998**

| Candidates | Votes | % of votes |
|---|---|---|
| HEYDAR ALIYEV (New Azerbaijan Party) | 2,556,059 | 77.61 |
| ETIBAR MAMEDOV (National Independence Party) | 389,662 | 11.83 |
| NIZAMI SULEYMANOV (Independent Azerbaijan Party) | 270,709 | 8.22 |
| FIRUDIN HASANOV (Communist Party of Azerbaijan-2) | 29,244 | 0.89 |
| ASHRAF MEHDIYEV (Association of Victims of Illegal Political Repressions) | 28,809 | 0.87 |
| KHANHUSEIN KAZYMLY (Social Welfare Party) | 8,254 | 0.25 |
| Blank or spoiled | 10,910 | 0.33 |
| **Total** | 3,293,647 | 100.0 |

### MILLI MAJLIS
(National Assembly)

Elections to Azerbaijan's new 125-member Milli Majlis were held on 12 November 1995. The electoral law of August 1995 provided for a mixed system of voting: 25 seats to be filled by proportional representation according to party lists, the remaining 100 deputies to be elected in single-member constituencies. The latter included the constituencies of Armenian-held Nagornyi Karabakh and other occupied territories: refugees from those regions cast their votes in other parts of Azerbaijan (in anticipation of the eventual return of occupied areas to Azerbaijani jurisdiction). All 25 party seats were filled: New Azerbaijan Party (NAP) 19, Popular Front of Azerbaijan (PFA) three, National Independence Party (Istiklal) three. However, only 72 of the 100 constituency seats were filled. Of these, the overwhelming majority were taken by the NAP and by independent candidates supporting the NAP's leader, the President of the Republic, HEYDAR ALIYEV. A further round of voting was held on 26 November in order to elect members for 20 of the 28 vacant seats (the respective seats being contested by the two leading candidates in the first round). However, only 12 of these were filled. On 4 February 1996 a further 14 deputies were elected—12 from the NAP, one from the PFA and one from the Muslim Democratic Party (Musavat)—and on 18 February one more seat was filled. Thus, following all the rounds of voting, only one seat in the Majlis remained vacant (representing the Khankendi-Khojali-Khojavend constituency in Nagornyi Karabakh).

**Chairman (Speaker):** MURTUZ ALESKEROV.

**First Deputy Chairman:** A. RAHIMZADE.

## Political Organizations

**Alliance for Azerbaijan Party:** Baku; f. 1994; Leader ABUTALYB SAMADOV.

**Azerbaijan Democratic Independence Party:** Baku; Chair. LEYLA YUNUSOVA; Leader VAGIF KERIMOV.

**Azerbaijan National Equality Party:** Leader FAHRADDIN AYDAYEV.

**Azerbaijani Democratic Left Party:** Baku; f. 1999; Chair. MEHMAN AMIRALIYEV.

**Azerbaijani Salvation Party:** Baku; f. 1999; nationalist; supports united Azerbaijan; Chair. ELDAR GARADAGLY.

**Civic Solidarity Party:** Baku; Chair. SABIR RUSTAMKHANLY.

**Communist Party of Azerbaijan (CPA):** Baku; disbanded Sept. 1991, re-established Nov. 1993; Chair. RAMIZ AHMADOV.

**Communist Party of Azerbaijan-2 (CPA-2):** Baku; Chair. FIRUDIN HASANOV.

**Democratic Development Party:** Baku; f. 1999; Leader SABUHI ABDINOV.

**Democratic Party of Azerbaijan:** Baku; f. 1994; unregistered; Co-Chair. ILIAS ISMAILOV, RASUL GULIYEV; Gen. Sec. SARDAR JALALOGLU.

**Equality:** Baku; f. 1998 to represent interests of those displaced as a result of conflict in Nagornyi Karabakh.

**Grey Wolves Party** (Boz Gurd): Baku; Leader BAKHTIYAR A. AHMADOV.

**Heyrat Party:** Baku; Sec.-Gen. ASHRAF MEHDIYEV.

**Independent Azerbaijan Party:** Baku; Chair. NIZAMI SULEYMANOV.

**Islamic Party of Azerbaijan:** Baku; f. 1992; Leader ALI AKRAM ALIYEV (ALIYEV imprisoned 1997 on charges of treason. A temporary supreme council was established to lead the party); 50,000 mems (1997).

**Labour Party of Azerbaijan:** Baku; Leader SABUTAY MARNEDOV.

**Liberal Democratic Party:** Baku; Chair. ZAKIR MAMEDOV.

**Liberal Party of Azerbaijan:** Chair. LALA SHOVKAT HAJIYEVA.

**Motherland Party** (Ana Vatan): Baku; Leader FAZAIL AGAMALIYEV.

**Muslim Democratic Party (Musavat):** Baku, Azerbaijan Ave 37; tel. (12) 98-18-70; fax (12) 98-31-66; f. 1911; in exile from 1920; re-established 1992; Chair. ISA GAMBAR; Gen. Sec. VURGUN EYYUB.

**National Congress Party:** Baku; f. 1997 by disaffected members of Muslim Democratic Party; Chair. IHTIYAR SHIRINOV.

**National Independence Party (Istiklal):** c/o Milli Majlis, 370152 Baku, Mehti Hussein St 2; f. 1992; Chair. ETIBAR MAMEDOV.

**National Statehood Party:** Baku; f. 1994; Chair. HAFIZ AGAYARZADE.

**New Azerbaijan Party (NAP)** (Yeni Azerbaijan): c/o Milli Majlis, 370152 Baku, Mehti Hussein St 2; f. 1992; Chair. HEYDAR ALIYEV; Dep. Chair. ALI NAGIYEV.

**People's Freedom Party** (Halg Azadlyg): Baku; Leader PANAH SHAHSEVENLI.

**People's Party of Azerbaijan:** Baku; f. 1998; Chair. PANAH HUSEYNOV.

**Popular Front of Azerbaijan (PFA):** c/o Milli Majlis, 370152 Baku, Mehti Hussein St 2; f. 1989; Chair. ABULFAZ ELCHIBEY; Dep. Chair. ALIMAMMAD NURIYEV.

**Republican Party:** f. 1999.

**Social Democratic Party:** 370014 Baku, 28 May St 3–11; tel. (12) 93-33-78; fax (12) 98-75-55; e-mail asdp@ngonet.baku.az; f. 1989; Chair. ARAZ ALIZADEH, ZARDUSHT ALIZADE; 2,000 mems (1990).

**Social Justice Party:** Baku; Leader MATLAB MUTALLIMOV.

**Social Welfare Party:** Baku; Chair. KHANHUSEIN KAZYMLY.

**Socialist Party of Azerbaijan:** Baku; f. 1997; Co-Chair. SHAPUR GASIMI, MUBARIZ IBADOV; 2,000 mems.

**Turkic Nationalist Party:** Baku; Leader VUGAR BEYTURAN.

**Umid Party** (Hope Party): Baku; f. 1993; socialist; Leader ABULFAR AHMADOV; 5,000 mems (1998).

**United Communist Party of Azerbaijan:** Baku; Leader SAYYAD SAYYADOV.

**Vahdat Party** (Unity Party): Baku; unregistered; Chair. BEYDULLA ABDULLAYEV.

**Workers' Party of Azerbaijan:** Sumgait; f. 1999; socialist; Chair. AKIF HASANOGLU.

Other political groups include the Ana Toprag (Native Soil) party, the Azeri Party of Popular Revival, the Democratic Party of Azerbaijan Business People, the Green Party of Azerbaijan, the Modern Turan Party, the National Resistance Movement and the Yurdash (Compatriot) party.

# Diplomatic Representation

### EMBASSIES IN AZERBAIJAN

**China, People's Republic:** Baku, Azadlyg Ave 1, Hotel Azerbaijan, Rm 831; tel. (12) 98-90-10; Ambassador: ZHANG GUOQIANG.

**Egypt:** Baku, Azadlyg Ave 1, Hotel Azerbaijan, Rms 1434, 1439 and 1441; tel. (12) 98-92-14; Ambassador: FARUK AMIN AL-HAVARI.

**France:** Baku, Hotel Respublika, Rms 8 and 17; tel. (12) 92-89-77; fax (12) 98-92-53; Ambassador: JEAN-PIERRE GUINHUT.

**Georgia:** Baku, Azadlyg Ave 1, Hotel Azerbaijan, Rms 1322–1325; tel. (12) 98-17-79; fax (12) 98-94-40; Ambassador: GYORGI CHANTURIA.

**Germany:** 370000 Baku, Mamedaliyev St 15; tel. (12) 98-78-19; fax (12) 98-54-19; Ambassador: Dr CHRISTIAN SIEBECK.

**Greece:** Baku, Hotel Respublika, Rms 19–20; tel. (12) 92-17-56; Ambassador: PANAYOTIS KARAKASSIS.

**Iran:** Baku, B. Sadarov St 4; tel. (12) 92-64-53; Ambassador: ALIREZA BIGDELI.

**Iraq:** 370000 Baku, Khagani St 9; tel. (12) 93-72-07; Chargé d'affaires a.i.: FARUQ SALMAN DAVUD.

**Israel:** Baku, Inshaatchylar Ave 1; tel. (12) 38-52-82; fax (12) 98-92-83; Chargé d'affaires: ARKADII MIL-MAN.

**Kazakhstan:** Baku, Azadlyg Ave 1, Hotel Azerbaijan, Rms 1524 and 1529; tel. (12) 98-87-08; fax (12) 98-87-08.

**Pakistan:** Baku, Azadlyg Ave 1, Hotel Azerbaijan, Rms 541 and 534; tel. (12) 98-90-04; fax (12) 98-94-85; Ambassador: PERVEZ KHANZADA.

**Russia:** Baku, Azadlyg Ave 1, Hotel Azerbaijan, Rms 1102, 1104 and 1123; tel. (12) 98-90-04; fax (12) 98-60-83; Ambassador: ALEKSANDR BLOKHIN.

**Spain:** Baku; Ambassador: JESÚS ATIENZA SERNA.

**Sudan:** Baku, Neftchilar Ave 60; tel. (12) 98-48-97; fax (12) 93-40-47; Ambassador: HASSAN BESHIR ABDELWAHAB.

**Turkey:** 370000 Baku, Khagani St 57; tel. (12) 98-81-33; Ambassador: KADRI ECVET TEZCAN.

**United Kingdom:** 370065 Baku, Izmir St 5; tel. (12) 92-48-13; fax (12) 91-65-92; e-mail office@britemb.baku.az; Ambassador: ROGER THOMAS.

**USA:** 370007 Baku, Azadlyg Ave 83; tel. (12) 98-03-36; fax (12) 98-37-55; Ambassador: STANLEY ESCUDERO.

# Judicial System

**Constitutional Court:** comprises a Chairman and eight judges, who are nominated by the President and confirmed in office by the Milli Majlis for a term of office of 10 years. Only the President, the Milli Majlis, the Cabinet of Ministers, the Procurator-General, the Supreme Court and the legislature of the Autonomous Republic of Nakhichevan are permitted to submit cases to the Constitutional Court.

**Chairman of the Constitutional Court and of the Supreme Court:** KHANLAR HAJIYEV.

**Prosecutor-General:** ELDAR HASSANOV.

# Religion

### ISLAM

The majority (some 70%) of Azerbaijanis are Shi'ite Muslims; most of the remainder are Sunni (Hanafi school). The Spiritual Board of Muslims of the Caucasus is based in Baku. It has spiritual jurisdiction over the Muslims of Armenia, Georgia and Azerbaijan. The Chairman of the Directorate is normally a Shi'ite, while the Deputy Chairman is usually a Sunni.

**Spiritual Board of Muslims of the Caucasus:** Baku; Chair. Sheikh ALLASHUKUR PASHEZADE.

### CHRISTIANITY

#### The Roman Catholic Church

The Apostolic Administrator of the Caucasus is the Holy See's Apostolic Nuncio to Georgia, Armenia and Azerbaijan, who is resident in Tbilisi, Georgia.

# The Press

In 1995 there were 276 newspaper titles and 49 periodicals officially registered in Azerbaijan. Owing to financial, political and technical difficulties, many publications have reportedly suffered a sharp decrease in circulation. In August 1998 President Aliyev signed a decree abolishing censorship and ordering government bodies to provide support to the independent media.

### PRINCIPAL NEWSPAPERS

In Azerbaijani, except where otherwise stated.

**Adabiyat:** 370146 Baku, Metbuat Ave, Block 529; tel. (12) 39-50-37; organ of the Union of Writers of Azerbaijan.

**Azadliq** (Liberty): 370000 Baku, Khaqani St 33; tel. (12) 98-90-81; fax (12) 93-40-01; e-mail azadliq@azeri.com; f. 1989; weekly; organ of the Popular Front of Azerbaijan; in Azerbaijani and Russian; Editor-in-Chief GUHDUZ TAHIRLY; circ. 9,034.

**Azerbaijan:** Baku, Metbuat Ave, Block 529; f. 1991; 5 a week; publ. by the National Assembly; in Azerbaijani and Russian; Editor-in-Chief A. MUSTAFAYEV; circ. 10,242 (Azerbaijani), 3,040 (Russian).

**Azerbaijan Ganjlyari** (Youth of Azerbaijan): Baku; f. 1919; 3 a week; Editor YU. A. KERIMOV.

**Bakinskii Rabochii** (Baku Worker): 370146 Baku, Metbuat Ave, Block 529; tel. (12) 38-00-29; f. 1906; 5 a week; govt newspaper; in Russian; Editor I. VEKILOVA; circ. 4,776.

**Hayat** (Life): 370146 Baku, Metbuat Ave, Block 529; f. 1991; 5 a week; publ. by the National Assembly of Azerbaijan; Editor-in-Chief A. H. ASKEROV.

**Intibah** (Revival): Baku; independent; 3 a week; Editor-in-Chief FAKHRI UGURLU; circ. 10,000.

**Istiklal** (Independence): 370014 Baku, 28 May St 3–11; tel. (12) 93-33-78; fax (12) 98-75-55; e-mail istiklal@ngonet.baku.az; 4 a month; organ of the Social Democratic Party; Editor ZARDUSHT ALIZADEH; circ. 5,000.

**Khalg Gazeti:** Baku; f. 1919; fmrly *Kommunist*; 6 a week; Editor M. ISMAYILOGLU.

**Millat:** Baku.

**Molodezh Azerbaijana** (Youth of Azerbaijan): 370146 Baku, Metbuat Ave, Block 529, 8th Floor; tel. (12) 39-00-51; f. 1919; weekly; in Russian; Editor V. EFENDIYEV; circ. 7,000.

**Panorama:** 370146 Baku, Metbuat Ave, Block 529; f. 1995; 5 a week; organ of the Centre of Strategic and International Investigations; in Azerbaijani and Russian; Editor-in-Chief A. ZEYNALOV; circ. 8,000.

**Respublika** (Republic): 370146 Baku, Metbuat Ave, Block 529; tel. (12) 38-01-14; fax (12) 38-01-31; f. 1996; daily; govt newspaper; Editor-in-Chief T. AHMADOV; circ. 5,500.

**Veten Sesi** (Voice of the Motherland): 370146 Baku, Metbuat Ave, Block 529; f. 1990; weekly; publ. by the Society of Refugees of Azerbaijan; in Azerbaijani and Russian; Editor-in-Chief T. A. AHMEDOV.

**Vyshka** (Tower): 370146 Baku, Metbuat Ave, Block 529; tel. and fax (12) 39-96-97; e-mail vyska@azevt.cam; f. 1928; weekly; independent social-political newspaper; in Russian; Editor M. E. GASANOVA.

**Yeni Azerbaijan:** Baku, Metbuat Ave, Block 529; f. 1993; weekly; organ of the New Azerbaijan Party; Editor A. HASANOGLU; circ. 2,493.

**Yeni Musavat:** Baku; Editor-in-Chief RAUF ARIFOGLU.

### PRINCIPAL PERIODICALS

**Azerbaijan:** Baku; tel. (12) 92-59-63; f. 1923; monthly; publ. by the Union of Writers of Azerbaijan; recent works by Azerbaijani authors; Editor-in-Chief YUSIF SAMEDOGLU.

**Azerbaijan Gadyny** (Woman of Azerbaijan): Baku; f. 1923; monthly; illustrated; Editor H. M. HASILOVA.

**Dialog** (Dialogue): Baku; f. 1989; fortnightly; in Azerbaijani and Russian; Editor R. A. ALEKPEROV.

**Iki Sahil:** Baku, Nobel Ave 64; f. 1965; weekly; organ of the New Baku Oil-Refining Plant; Editor-in-Chief V. RAHIMZADEH; circ. 2,815.

**Kend Khayaty** (Country Life): Baku; f. 1952; monthly; journal of the Ministry of Agriculture and Food; advanced methods of work in agriculture; in Azerbaijani and Russian; Editor D. A. DAMIRLI.

**Kirpi** (Hedgehog): Baku; f. 1952; fortnightly; satirical; Editor A. M. AIVAZOV.

**Literaturnyi Azerbaijan** (Literature of Azerbaijan): 370001 Baku, Istiglaliyat St 31; tel. (12) 92-39-31; f. 1931; monthly; journal of the Union of Writers of Azerbaijan; fiction; in Russian; Editor-in-Chief I. P. TRETYAKOV.

**Monitor:** Baku; f. 1996; social and political monthly; Editor-in-Chief ELMAR HUSEYNOV; circ. 3,000.

**Ulus:** Baku; tel. (12) 92-27-43; monthly; Editor Tofik Dadashev.

### NEWS AGENCIES

**AzerTAJ** (Azerbaijan State News Agency): 370000 Baku, Bul-Bul Ave 18; tel. (12) 93-59-29; fax (12) 93-62-65; e-mail office@azertac.baku.az; f. 1919; Gen. Dir Shamil Mammad oglu Shahmammadov.

**Bilik Dunyasi:** Baku.**Sharg News Agency:** Baku; Correspondent K. Mustafayeva.

**Trend News Agency:** Baku; Correspondent E. Huseynov.

**Turan News Agency:** Baku, Khagani St 33; tel. (12) 98-42-26; fax (12) 98-38-17; e-mail root@turan.azerbaijan.su; internet www.intrans.baku.az; f. 1990; independent news agency; Dir Mehman Aliyev.

## Publishers

**Azerbaijan Ensiklopediyasy** (Azerbaijan Encyclopedia): 370004 Baku, Boyuk Gala St 41; tel. (12) 92-87-11; f. 1965; Editor-in-Chief I. O. Veliyev (acting).

**Azerneshr** (State Publishing House): 370005 Baku, Gusi Hajiyev St 4; tel. (12) 92-50-15; f. 1924; various; Dir A. Mustafazade; Editor-in-Chief A. Kuseinzade.

**Elm** (Azerbaijani Academy of Sciences Publishing House): 370073 Baku, Narimanov Ave 37; scientific books and journals.

**Gyanjlik** (Youth): 370005 Baku, Gusi Hajiyev St 4; books for children and young people; Dir E. T. Aliyev.

**Ishyg** (Light): 370601 Baku, Gogol St 6; posters, illustrated publs; Dir G. N. Ismailov.

**Maarif** (Education): 370122 Baku, Tagizade St 4; educational books.

**Madani-maarif Ishi** (Education and Culture): 370146 Baku, Metbuat Ave, Block 529; tel. (12) 32-79-17; Editor-in-Chief Alovsat Atamaly ogly Bashirov.

**Medeniyyat** (Publishing House of the 'Culture' Newspaper): 370146 Baku, Metbuat Ave 146; tel. (12) 32-98-38; Dir Shakmar Akper ogly Akperzade.

**Sada, Literaturno-Izdatelskyi Centr:** 370004 Baku, Bolshaya Krepostnaya St 28; tel. (12) 92-75-64; fax (12) 92-98-43; reference.

**Shur:** 370001 Baku, M. Muchtarov St 6; tel. (12) 92-93-72; f. 1992; Dir Gasham Isa ogly Isabeyli.

**Yazychy** (Writer): 370005 Baku, Natavan St 1; fiction; Dir F. M. Melikov.

## Broadcasting and Communications

### TELECOMMUNICATIONS

**Baku Telegraph:** 370000 Baku, Azerbaijana Ave 41; tel. (12) 93-61-42; fax (12) 98-55-25; operates international telegraph and telex services.

### RADIO AND TELEVISION

**Radio and Television Company of Azerbaijan:** 370011 Baku, Mekhti Hussein St 1; tel. (12) 92-72-53; fax (12) 39-54-52; state-owned; Dir Nizami Manaf ogly Khudiyev.

**Radio Baku:** f. 1926; broadcasts in Azerbaijani, Arabic, English and Turkish.

**Azerbaijan National Television:** f. 1956; programmes in Azerbaijani and Russian (14 hours a day).

**BM–TI TV:** Baku; f. 1993; first privately-owned TV station in Azerbaijan; broadcasts in Azerbaijani and Russian, five hours a day; Dir Mahmud Mammadov.

## Finance

(cap. = capital; res = reserves; dep. = deposits; m. = million; brs = branches; amounts in manats, unless otherwise stated)

### BANKING

#### Central Bank

**National Bank of Azerbaijan:** 370070 Baku, Bjul-Bjul Ave 19; tel. (12) 93-50-58; fax (12) 93-55-41; f. 1992 as central bank and supervisory authority; Chair. Elman Roustamov.

#### State-owned Banks

**Agroprombank (Agricultural Bank):** 370006 Baku, Kadyrly St 125; tel. (12) 38-93-48; fax (12) 38-91-15; f. 1992 from br of USSR Agroprombank; 51% state-owned; cap. 10,000m. (June 1995); Chair. Mamed Gurban Musayev; 69 brs.

**Amanatbank:** 370014 Baku, Fizuli St 71; tel. (12) 93-18-26; fax (12) 98-31-80; f. 1992 to replace br of USSR Sberbank; 361 brs.

**International Bank of Azerbaijan:** 370005 Baku, Nizami St 67; tel. (12) 93-03-07; fax (12) 93-40-91; e-mail ibar@ibar.az; internet www.ibar.az; f. 1992 to succeed br of USSR Vneshekonombank; 51% state-owned; carries out all banking services; cap. 11,393m., res 20,628m., dep. 1,263,681m. (Dec. 1997); Chair. Fuad Akhoundov; First Dep. Chair. Zahir Aliyev; 26 brs.

**Prominvestbank (Industrial Investment Bank):** 370014 Baku, Fizuli St 71; tel. (12) 98-79-46; fax (12) 98-12-66; f. 1992 to succeed br of USSR Prominvestbank.

#### Other Banks

In January 2000 there were 70, mainly small, registered commercial banks operating in Azerbaijan, some of the most prominent of which are listed below:

**Azakbank:** 370070 Baku, Bebutov St 8; tel. (12) 98-31-09; fax (12) 93-20-85; f. 1991; joint-stock bank with 100% private ownership; first Azerbaijani bank with foreign shareholders; deals with crediting and settlements carried out in local currency and trade and retail banking involving all major operations in foreign currencies; cap. 1,273.5m., plus US $2.6m. (Nov. 1995); Chair. Fuad S. Ysif-Zadeh.

**Azerbaijan Central Republican Bank:** 370088 Baku, Fizuli St 71; tel. (12) 93-05-61; fax (12) 93-94-89.

**Azerbaijan Industrial Bank:** 370010 Baku, Fizuli St 71; tel. (12) 93-17-01; fax (12) 93-12-66; f. 1992; joint-stock commercial bank; Chair. Oruj H. Heydarov; 40 brs.

**Azerdemiryolbank:** Baku; f. 1989; largest private commercial bank; operates mainly in transport sector.

**Azerigazbank:** 370073 Baku, Inshaatchylar Ave 3; tel. (12) 97-50-17; fax (12) 39-26-03; e-mail agbbank@azeri.com; f. 1992; joint-stock investment bank; Chair. Azer Movsumov.

**Bakcoopbank (Baku Co-operative Bank):** 370025 Baku, Barinov St 12; tel. (12) 67-45-46; Gen. Dir Alim I. Azimov.

**Baybank:** 370000 Baku, S. Vurgun St 14; tel. (12) 93-50-07; fax (12) 98-57-76; e-mail baybank@artel.net.az; f. 1995; joint-stock bank, carries out all baking services; cap. 4,865m., res 584m., dep. 6,450m. (Dec. 1997); Pres. and CEO A. Kemal Tosyali; Chair. Huseyin Bayraktar.

**Günay Bank:** 370095 Baku, Rasul Rza St 4/6; tel. (12) 98-14-29; fax (12) 98-14-39; f. 1992; first privately owned bank in Azerbaijan; cap. 3,433m., res 477m., dep. 991.7m.; Chair. Aloisat Godjaev; 2 brs.

**Inpatbank Investment Commercial Bank:** 370125 Baku, Istiglaliyat St 9; tel. (12) 98-48-37.

**Rabitabank:** Baku; f. 1993; operates mainly in telecommunications sector.

**Ruzubank:** 370055 Baku, Istiglaliyat St 27; tel. (12) 92-42-58; fax (12) 92-78-12; f. 1992; joint-stock bank; cap. 216m., res 30.4m., dep. 1,834m.; Pres. S. A. Aliyev; Chair. of Bd V. N. Musayev.

**Universal Commercial Bank:** Baku; fax (12) 92-92-15; f. 1988; Pres. Felix V. Mamedov.

**Vostochniy Bank:** 370070 Baku, Kirova Ave 19; tel. (12) 93-22-47; fax 912) 93-11-81; Gen. Dir Ragimov A. Abbal.

**Yuzhniy Bank:** 373230 Shemakha, Bakiyskaya St 32.

#### Foreign Banks

In August 1997 there were seven foreign banks licensed to operate in Azerbaijan.

**Bank Melli Iran:** 370009 Baku, Salatin Askerova 85; tel. (12) 95-70-18; fax (12) 98-04-37; Man. Hassan Bahadory.

**HSBC Bank Middle East:** 37000 Baku, The Landmark, Nizami St 96, POB 132; tel. (12) 97-08-08; fax (12) 97-17-30; e-mail hsbc@hsbc.baku.az; internet www.hsbc.com; CEO Zaki Anderson.

#### Association

**Azerbaijani Association of Banks:** Baku; 49 mems.

### INSURANCE

In February 1999 64 insurance companies were licensed to operate in Azerbaijan.

**Azersigorta:** Baku.

**Günay Anadolu Sigorta JV:** Baku, Terlan Aliyarbekov St 3; tel. (12) 98-13-56; fax (12) 98-13-60; f. 1992; serves major international cos operating in Azerbaijan.

**Shafag:** Baku; f. 1998; medical insurance.

## Trade and Industry

### CHAMBER OF COMMERCE

**Chamber of Commerce and Industry:** 370601 Baku, Istiglaliyat St 31/33; tel. (12) 92-89-12; fax (12) 98-93-24; e-mail expo@chamber.baku.az; Pres. Suleyman Bayram ogly Tatliyev.

### INDUSTRIAL AND TRADE ASSOCIATIONS

**Azerbintorg:** 370004 Baku, Nekrasov St 7; tel. (12) 93-71-69; fax (12) 98-32-92; imports and exports a wide range of goods (90.4% of exports in 1995); Dir E. M. HUREYNOV.

**Azerkontract:** 370141 Baku, A. Alekperov St 83/23; tel. (12) 39-42-96; fax (12) 39-91-76; Chair. Minister of Trade.

**Azertijaret:** 370004 Baku, Genjler Sq. 3; tel (12) 92-66-67; fax (12) 98-07-56; e-mail aztij@azeri.com; Dir R. SH. ALIYEV.

**Improtex:** 370000 Baku, Azi Aslanov St 115; tel. (12) 98-02-27; fax (12) 90-92-25; e-mail haliyev@improtex.baku.az; internet www.improtex.baku-az.com; imports and exports a wide range of goods, incl. chemical and construction products; retail trade in consumer electronics and automobile dealership; Pres. FIZULI HASAN OGLY ALEKPEROV.

**MIT International Trade Co:** 370148 Baku, Mehti Guseyn St, Hotel Anba; tel. (12) 98-45-20; fax (12) 98-45-19; f. 1993; food products and consumer goods; Dir TAIR RAMAZAN OGLY ASADOV.

### UTILITIES

#### Electricity

**BakGES:** Baku; electricity supply co; Head of Planning TAMILLA GULIYEVA.

#### Gas

**Azerigaz:** 370025 Baku, Yusif Safarov St 23; tel. (12) 67-74-47; fax (12) 65-12-01; f. 1992; Pres. TARIEL ABULFAZ OGLY HUSSEINOV.

### MAJOR STATE-OWNED INDUSTRIAL COMPANIES

**Bakinsky Rabochy Engineering:** 370034 Baku, Proletar St 10; tel. (12) 25-93-75; fax (12) 25-93-82; equipment for the petroleum industry, including pumping units and pipe transporters; Dir MAMED AKPER OGLY VELIYEV; 1,200 employees.

**State Oil Company of the Azerbaijan Republic (SOCAR):** 370004 Baku, Neftchilar Ave 73; tel. (12) 92-07-45; fax (12) 93-64-92; f. 1992 following merger; conducts production and exploration activities, oversees refining and capital construction activities; Pres. NATIK ALIYEV; First Vice-Pres. ILHAM ALIYEV.

### TRADE UNIONS

**Association of Independent Workers of Azerbaijan:** Baku; Chair. NEYMAT PANAKHLI.

**Confederation of Azerbaijan Trade Unions:** Baku; tel. and fax (12) 92-72-68; Chair. SATTAR MEHBALIYEV.

**Free Trade Union of Teachers:** Baku; Chair. SEYRAN SEYRANOV.

**Free Trade Unions of Oil and Gas Industry Workers:** mems are employees of c. 118 enterprises in petroleum and gas sectors; Chair. JAHANGIR ALIYEV.

**Trade Union of Journalists:** 370105 Baku, A. Haqverdiyev St 3A/5; tel. and fax (12) 38-32-56; e-mail azeri@ajip.baku.az; f. 1998; 212 mems; Chair. AZER HASRET; not permitted to register by Govt.

## Transport

### RAILWAYS

In 1995 there were 2,123 km of railway track, of which 1,277 km were electrified. The overwhelming majority of total freight traffic is carried by the railways (some 78% in 1991). Railways connect Baku with Tbilisi (Georgia), Makhachkala (Dagestan, Russia) and Yerevan (Armenia). In 1997 passenger rail services between Moscow and Baku were resumed, and a service to Kiev (Ukraine) was inaugurated. The rail link with Armenia runs through the Autonomous Republic of Nakhichevan, but is currently disrupted, owing to Azerbaijan's economic blockade of Armenia. From Nakhichevan an international line links Azerbaijan with Tabriz (Iran). In 1991 plans were agreed with the Iranian Government for the construction of a rail line between Azerbaijan and Nakhichevan, which would pass through Iranian territory, thus bypassing Armenia. There is an underground railway in Baku (the Baku Metro); it comprises two lines (total length 28 km) with 19 stations. A further 4.1 km, with three stations, is currently under construction.

**Azerbaijani Railways:** 370010 Baku, 1 May St 230; tel. (12) 98-44-67; fax (12) 98-85-47; f. 1992, following the dissolution of the former Soviet Railways; Pres. ZIYA MAMEDOV; First Dep. Pres. and Chief Eng. M. M. MEHTIEV.

**Bakinskii Metropolitan** (Baku Metro): 370602 Baku, G. Javid Ave 33A; Gen. Man. Y. I. USIFOV.

### ROADS

At 31 December 1997 the total length of roads in Azerbaijan was 45,870 km (22,935 km main roads, 6,057 km secondary roads and 16,878 km other roads).

### SHIPPING

Shipping services on the Caspian Sea link Baku with Astrakhan (Russia), Turkmenbashy (Turkmenistan) and the Iranian ports of Bandar Anzali and Bandar Nowshar. At 31 December 1998 the Azerbaijani merchant fleet comprised 287 vessels, with a combined displacement of 650,933 grt. The total included 39 petroleum tankers (176,101 grt).

#### Shipowning Company

**Caspian Shipping Company (Caspar):** 370005 Baku, Mammademin Resulzade St 5; tel. (12) 93-20-58; fax (12) 93-53-39; f. 1858; nationalized by the Azerbaijani Govt in 1991; transports crude petroleum and petroleum products; operates cargo and passenger ferries; Pres. A. A. BASHIROV.

### CIVIL AVIATION

**Azerbaijan Airlines** (Azerbaijan Hava Yollari): 370000 Baku, Azadlyg Ave 11; tel. (12) 93-44-34; fax (12) 96-52-37; f. 1992; state airline operating scheduled and charter passenger and cargo services to the CIS, Europe and the Middle East.

## Tourism

Tourism is not widely developed. However, there are resorts on the Caspian Sea, including the Ganjlik international tourist centre, on the Apsheron Peninsula, near Baku, which has four hotels as well as camping facilities.

# THE BAHAMAS

## Introductory Survey

### Location, Climate, Language, Religion, Flag, Capital

The Commonwealth of the Bahamas consists of about 700 islands and more than 2,000 cays and rocks, extending from east of the Florida coast of the USA to just north of Cuba and Haiti, in the West Indies. The main islands are New Providence, Grand Bahama, Andros, Eleuthera and Great Abaco. Almost 70% of the population reside on the island of New Providence. The remaining members of the group are known as the 'Family Islands'. A total of 29 of the islands are inhabited. The climate is mild and sub-tropical, with average temperatures of about 30°C (86°F) in summer and 20°C (68°F) in winter. The average annual rainfall is about 1,000 mm (39 ins). The official language is English. Most of the inhabitants profess Christianity, the largest denominations being the Anglican, Baptist, Roman Catholic and Methodist Churches. The national flag comprises three equal horizontal stripes, of blue, gold and blue, with a black triangle at the hoist, extending across one-half of the width. The capital is Nassau, on the island of New Providence.

### Recent History

A former British colonial territory, the Bahamas attained internal self-government in January 1964, although the parliamentary system dates back to 1729. The first elections under universal adult suffrage were held in January 1967 for an enlarged House of Assembly. The Progressive Liberal Party (PLP), supported mainly by Bahamians of African origin and led by Lynden (later Sir Lynden) Pindling, won 18 of the 38 seats, as did the ruling United Bahamian Party (UBP), dominated by those of European origin. With the support of another member, the PLP formed a Government and Pindling became Primier (he was restyled Prime Minister in September 1968). At the next elections, in April 1968, the PLP won 29 seats and the UBP only seven.

Following a constitutional conference in September 1968, the Bahamas Government was given increased responsibility for internal security, external affairs and defence in May 1969. In the elections of September 1972, which were dominated by the issue of independence, the PLP maintained its majority. Following a constitutional conference in December 1972, the Bahamas became an independent nation, within the Commonwealth, on 10 July 1973. Pindling remained Prime Minister. The PLP increased its majority in the elections of July 1977 and was again returned to power in the June 1982 elections, with 32 of the 43 seats in the enlarged House of Assembly. The remaining 11 seats were won by the Free National Movement (FNM), which had reunited for the elections after splitting into several factions over the previous five years.

Trading in illicit drugs, mainly for the US market, has become a major problem for the country, since many of the small islands and cays are used by drugs-traffickers in their smuggling activities. According to estimates by the US Government, some 70% of cocaine and 50% of marijuana entering the USA between the early 1970s and the early 1990s passed through the Bahamas. In 1983 allegations of widespread corruption, and the abuse of Bahamian bank secrecy laws by drugs-traffickers and US tax evaders, led Pindling to appoint a Royal Commission to investigate thoroughly the drugs trade in the Bahamas. The Commission's hearings revealed the extent to which money deriving from this trade had permeated Bahamian social and economic affairs. In October 1984 two cabinet ministers, implicated by the evidence presented to the Commission, resigned, and by November 1985 a total of 51 suspects had been indicted, including the assistant police commissioner. The Commission also revealed that Pindling had received several million dollars in gifts and loans from business executives, although it found no evidence of a link to the drugs trade. After unsuccessfully demanding Pindling's resignation, the Deputy Prime Minister, Arthur Hanna, resigned, and two other ministers, Perry Christie and Hubert Ingraham, were dismissed.

Although the issue of the illegal drugs trade and of drugs-related corruption within the Government dominated the general election campaign, the PLP was returned to power for a fifth consecutive term in June 1987, winning 31 of the 49 seats in the enlarged House of Assembly. The FNM won 16 seats, while the remaining two seats were secured by Christie and Ingraham as independents.

Statistics relating to crime in 1987 indicated unprecedented levels of violent and drugs-related offences, and in February 1988 new claims of official corruption were made at the trial in Florida, USA, of a leading Colombian drugs-trafficker. Pindling and the Deputy Prime Minister were alleged to have accepted bribes, but this was vehemently denied. In March 1990 the Minister of Agriculture, Trade and Industry, Ervin Knowles, resigned, following allegations of nepotism and the misuse of public funds. He was replaced by Christie, who rejoined the PLP. The other independent member, Ingraham, subsequently joined the FNM and became its leader in May, upon the death of Sir Cecil Wallace-Whitfield.

The general election campaign in mid-1992 was disrupted by industrial unrest in the country's telephone and electricity companies, and by the continuing problems of the state airline, Bahamasair. Despite predictions of a PLP victory, the FNM won the general election on 19 August, securing 33 seats, while Pindling's party won the remaining 16. Ingraham replaced Pindling as Prime Minister, and announced a programme of measures aimed at increasing the accountability of government ministers, combating corruption and revitalizing the economy. Acknowledging responsibility for his party's defeat in the election, Pindling resigned as leader of the PLP, but, at the party's annual convention in January 1993, agreed to continue in office.

The resignation of Orville Turnquest, the Deputy Prime Minister, Minister of Foreign Affairs and Attorney-General, in January 1995, in order to assume the post of Governor-General, prompted an extensive cabinet reorganization.

In March 1995 a marked increase in violent crime in parts of New Providence led the Government to announce the creation of a special police unit to tackle the problem. Meanwhile, the trade in illegal drugs remained widespread in the country, and in late 1995 several local business leaders, as well as close relatives of a member of Parliament, were arrested in connection with a large seizure of cocaine. In October of that year the Prime Minister introduced further legislation that aimed to prevent the abuse of Bahamian banks by drugs-traffickers, and thus improve the reputation of the country's financial sector, particularly in the USA.

The decision in March 1996 to hang a man convicted of murder in early 1991 was controversial, owing to the fact that the period spent awaiting execution had exceeded five years. In recognition of a prisoner's suffering in anticipation of execution, previous cases had held five years to constitute the maximum term after which the case should be subject to review with a possible commutation to life imprisonment. However, in October 1996 the Judicial Committee of the Privy Council ruled that to await execution for more than three and a half years would amount to inhuman punishment, and that all such cases should be commuted. The ruling was believed to affect 22 of the 39 prisoners under sentence of death in the Bahamas at that time.

At a general election held on 14 March 1997, in which 91.7% of the electorate participated, the FNM won 34 of the 40 seats in a reduced House of Assembly, and the PLP six. The FNM's overwhelming victory in the election was attributed both to the Prime Minister's success in reversing the economic decline and the involvement of the PLP in various financial scandals. Most notably, Pindling was implicated in February in the findings of a public inquiry (instituted in 1993) to investigate alleged corruption and misappropriation of funds in the three principal state corporations. Following the election, Pindling, who had retained his seat in the House of Assembly, resigned as leader of the PLP and was replaced by Christie. In July Pindling announced his retirement from parliamentary politics, and his seat was won by the FNM at a by-election in September.

In the late 1990s violent crime continued to be of major concern to Bahamians. In April 1998 the Government signed a convention drawn up by the Organization of American States to ban illegal guns, amid a disturbing increase in gun-related crime. The murders of several tourists in 1998 shocked the local community and provoked fears regarding the future of the tourism industry. In September the Prime Minister increased security in tourist areas, and announced plans to limit the right of appeal against death sentences (17 prisoners had had their sentences commuted in January). The hanging in October of two convicted murderers caused controversy, despite growing public demand for execution as a deterrent against crime. In carrying out the executions, the Government rejected a last-minute plea for clemency from the European Union (EU), on the grounds that both men had appeals pending at the Inter-American Commission on Human Rights (IACHR) in Washington, DC, USA. In August 1999 the Bahamian authorities were strongly criticized by human rights groups, after they announced their intention to execute another two convicted murderers who had also submitted petitions to the IACHR. The Government justified its decision, however, by referring to a 1998 court ruling that executions could be carried out if appeals had been pending at the IACHR for more than 18 months. Despite attempts to reduce levels of crime, police in New Providence reported 25 murders (many of which were drugs-related) in the first six months of 1999, compared with 29 during the whole of 1998.

In mid-1999 there was vigorous public opposition in the Bahamas to the impending privatization of the state-owned telecommunications company, BaTelCo. Meanwhile, in August the Prime Minister announced plans to establish an agency that would investigate and prosecute suspected 'money-launderers'.

The Bahamas suffered considerable damage in September 1999 when 'Hurricane Floyd' struck the islands; one person died and at least 2,000 were made homeless as a result of the storm. In the following month 'Hurricane Irene' caused another four deaths and inflicted further structural damage on the Bahamas.

In mid-December 1999 the Prime Minister dismissed the Minister of Consumer Welfare and Aviation, Pierre Dupuch. Later in the month the Attorney-General and Minister of Justice, Tennyson Wells, announced his resignation from both positions, in order to challenge Ingraham for the leadership of the FNM. This announcement prompted the Prime Minister, in early January 2000, to effect an extensive cabinet reorganization. In a slightly reduced Cabinet, eight ministers retained their portfolios unchanged, while the Minister of Foreign Affairs, Janet Bostwick, also assumed that of Attorney-General. Several ministries were restructured, leading to the creation of new ministries, including a Ministry of Commerce, Agriculture and Industry, aimed at the promotion of small business.

The Bahamas' traditionally close relationship with the USA has been strained by the increasingly aggressive attitude of the US Government towards the bank secrecy laws and the drugs-smuggling in the islands. Bilateral relations were damaged in August 1997, when an incendiary device exploded at a travel agency in Nassau commonly used by US tourists. Nevertheless, the USA and the Bahamas have collaborated in a series of operations to intercept drugs-traffickers, and in late 1998 the USA commended the Bahamian authorities for their efforts to curb this illegal trade.

Relations with the Bahamas' other neighbours, Haiti and Cuba, have been strained by the influx of large numbers of illegal immigrants from both countries. In 1994 the Government announced that it would increase its efforts to deport approximately 40,000 Haitian immigrants residing illegally in the islands. During 1996 and the first half of 1997 more than 800 Haitian and some 100 Cuban immigrants were deported. However, despite the Government's rigorous deportation policy, the number of Haitian immigrants reportedly increased during August and September 1997, when more than 500 immigrants were detained over a five-week period. In June 1998 the Bahamian Government agreed to inform Cuba of the arrival of illegal Cuban immigrants within 72 hours of their discovery, while Cuba agreed to their repatriation within 15 days. In mid-1998 many Cubans were deported from the Bahamas, despite an offer by Nicaragua of temporary asylum for 200 detainees.

### Government

Legislative power is vested in the bicameral Parliament. The Senate has 16 members, of whom nine are appointed by the Governor-General on the advice of the Prime Minister, four by the Leader of the Opposition and three after consultation with the Prime Minister. The House of Assembly has 40 members, elected for five years (subject to dissolution) by universal adult suffrage. Executive power is vested in the British monarch, represented by a Governor-General, who is appointed on the Prime Minister's recommendation and who acts, in almost all matters, on the advice of the Cabinet. The Governor-General appoints the Prime Minister and, on the latter's recommendation, selects the other ministers. The Cabinet is responsible to the House of Assembly.

### Defence

The Royal Bahamian Defence Force, a paramilitary coastguard, is the only security force in the Bahamas, and numbered 860 (including 70 women) in August 1999. Defence expenditure in 1999 was budgeted at B $23m.

### Economic Affairs

In 1995, according to estimates by the World Bank, the Bahamas' gross national product (GNP), measured at average 1993–95 prices, was US $3,297m., equivalent to US $11,940 per head (the highest level among Caribbean countries). During 1985–95, it was estimated, GNP per head decreased, in real terms, at an average rate of 1.0% per year. The population increased at an average annual rate of 1.7% over the same period, and by the same rate during 1990–97. In 1997, according to preliminary World Bank data, GNP totalled US $3,288m. (US $11,830 per head). During 1990–95 the Bahamas' gross domestic product (GDP) declined, in real terms, at an average rate of 2.6% per year. According to IMF estimates, real GDP rose by 4.2% in 1996, by 3.3% in 1997 and by 3.0% in 1998.

Agriculture, hunting, forestry and fishing, which together accounted for only 3.4% of GDP in 1992 and engaged an estimated 5.4% of the employed labour force in 1994, have been developed by the Government in an attempt to reduce dependence on imports (80% of food supplies were imported in the 1980s). In 1997, however, agricultural production accounted for only 1.0% of total land area. By the late 1990s, according to official estimates, agriculture contributed less than 3% of GDP and provided only 4% of employment. The increase in agricultural output has resulted in the export of certain crops, particularly of cucumbers, tomatoes, pineapples, papayas, avocados, mangoes, limes and other citrus fruits. The development of commercial fishing has concentrated on conchs and crustaceans. In 1995 exports of Caribbean spiny lobster (crawfish) provided 60.6% of total domestic export earnings. There is also some exploitation of pine forests in the northern Bahamas.

Industry (comprising mining, manufacturing, construction and utilities) employed 12.9% of the working population in 1994 (construction accounted for 7.1%) and provided 10.9% of GDP in 1992.

Mining and manufacturing together contributed only 4.0% of GDP in 1992. Mining provided 0.2% of employment, and manufacturing 4.1%, in 1994. The islands' principal mineral resources are salt (which provided 14.5% of domestic export earnings in 1995) and aragonite.

The manufacturing sector contributed some 10% of GDP in 1982, since when it has declined, owing to the closure, in 1985, of the country's petroleum refinery. In 1992 the principal branches of manufacturing, based on the value of output, were beverages (accounting for 44.7% of the total), chemicals (16.2%) and printing and publishing. Exports of rum provided 27.5% of domestic export earnings in 1991, but the proportion declined to only 3.1% in 1995. Petroleum transhipment on Grand Bahama remains an important activity (crude petroleum accounted for some 53% of total trade in 1990, and petroleum products for about 11% in 1988). The construction sector has, since 1986, experienced much activity, owing to hotel-building and harbour developments. In the late 1990s several major projects guaranteed strong growth in the sector.

Most of the energy requirements of the Bahamas are fulfilled by the petroleum that Venezuela and, particularly, Mexico provide under the San José Agreement (originally negotiated in 1980), which commits both the petroleum-producers to selling subsidized supplies, on favourable terms, to the developing countries of the region. Excluding transhipments of petroleum, imports of mineral fuels accounted for 12.6% of total imports in 1995.

Service industries constitute the principal sectors of the economy, providing 85.7% of GDP in 1992 and 81.1% of total employment in 1994. The Bahamas established its own shipping registry in 1976, and by 1983 had one of the largest 'open-registry' fleets in the world. At the end of 1998 a total of 1,286 vessels were registered under the Bahamian flag. With a combined displacement of 27.7m. grt, the fleet was the third largest in the world. In 1996 the country was ranked as the 12th largest 'offshore' financial centre in the world. Banking is the second most important economic activity in the Bahamas.

Tourism is the predominant sector of the economy, directly accounting for about 27% of GDP in 1992, and employing some 30% of the working population in 1994. In 1997 81% of stop-over arrivals were from the USA, although attempts are being made to attract visitors from other countries and improve air access to resorts. Tourist arrivals increased steadily during the 1980s, and by 1991 amounted to some 3.7m. However, figures declined somewhat during the 1990s, as a result of recession in the important US market, an increase in the incidence of crime in the islands and competition from alternative destinations. In 1996–98 the average annual number of tourist arrivals totalled about 3.4m. Total arrivals were expected to increase to 4m.–5m. per year by 2000 (with projected growth of some 15% for 1999). Receipts from tourism fell slightly in 1998, to an estimated B $1,408m., compared with B $1,416m. in 1997.

In 1998 the Bahamas recorded a visible trade deficit (excluding figures for petroleum and petroleum products not for domestic consumption) of US $1,060.5m., and there was a deficit of US $593.5m. on the current account of the balance of payments. The USA is the principal trading partner of the Bahamas, providing 92.8% of non-petroleum imports and taking 81.1% of total exports in 1995. Excluding the trade in petroleum and its products, the principal exports (including re-exports) in 1995 were food and live animals (36.8% of the total), machinery and transport equipment (26.1%) and inedible crude materials. In that year the principal imports were machinery and transport equipment (24.8% of the total), food and live animals, miscellaneous manufactured articles and basic manufactures.

In the year ending 30 June 1998 there was an estimated budgetary deficit of B $71.3m. The deficit declined to an estimated B $23.5m. in 1998/99. At 31 December 1998 the external debt of the central Government was B $85.0m. The annual rate of inflation averaged 2.8% during 1990–98; consumer prices increased by 1.3% in 1998, and were forecast to rise by an annual average of 1.3% in 1999. The rate of unemployment declined from 13.3% of the labour force in April 1994 to an estimated 7.8% in 1998.

The Bahamas is a member of the Caribbean Community and Common Market (CARICOM, see p. 136) and the Organization of American States (OAS, see p. 245), the Association of Caribbean States (see p. 290) and is a signatory of the Lomé Conventions with the EU (see p. 196).

Despite increasing competition, the Bahamas continues to be the principal tourist destination of the Caribbean. However, the tourism sector was severely affected by world recession in the early 1990s and, as a result, many hotels and casinos were closed. By 1999 investment in tourism appeared to have effected a recovery in the sector. Although in 1998 visitor arrivals decreased by 3.1% and tourist receipts by 0.6% (owing mainly to the closure of several hotels for refurbishment), tourist arrivals rose sharply in 1999. Meanwhile, economic expansion through foreign investment continued to be restricted by fears of widespread corruption and instability, caused by the activities of illegal drugs-trafficking networks in the islands (although investor confidence was reported to be increasing by 1999). In 1995 measures were introduced in an attempt to combat corruption in the financial sector and thus improve the reputation of the country's economic institutions. In May 1999 a Securities Industry Bill was adopted. By mid-1999 all but one of the state-owned hotels had been transferred to private ownership, under a privatization programme launched in 1993, with a number of foreign companies investing in large-scale projects. The divestment of the state telecommunications and electricity companies was scheduled for 1999 and 2000 respectively. In the late 1990s the Government maintained a policy of fiscal prudence, with the aim of eliminating the recurrent budget deficit by 2001. The budget proposals for 1999/2000 included measures to raise further revenue, such as an increase in the hotel occupancy tax rate from 4% to 6%. The establishment of a stock exchange, for both offshore and domestic dealings, was planned for 1999.

## Social Welfare

The health service is centralized in Nassau at the government general hospital, which has 484 beds. There is also a mental hospital and rehabilitation unit (with 477 beds), a geriatric hospital (with 170 beds) and two private clinics on New Providence. There is a 92-bed hospital on Grand Bahama, and in the Family Islands several cottage hospitals and medical centres operate. A Flying Doctor Service supplies medical attention to islands that lack resident personnel. Flying Dental Services and nursing personnel from the Community Nursing Service are also provided. In 1993 there was one physician for every 692 inhabitants, and one hospital bed for every 258. A National Insurance Scheme, established in 1972, provides a wide range of benefits, including sickness, maternity, retirement and widows' pensions as well as social assistance payments. The scheme is administered by the National Insurance Board (NIB), which is funded mainly by contributions and investment income. Total expenditure by the NIB in 1994 was B $74.9m., including B $56.4m. in benefit payments. An Industrial Injuries Scheme has also been established. In addition to payments by the NIB, there is some government expenditure on social welfare from the General Budget: in 1998/99 this included B $134.3m. on health (15.6% of total expenditure) and B $47.5m. on social services (5.5%).

## Education

Education is compulsory between the ages of five and 16 years, and is provided free of charge in government schools. There are several private and denominational schools. Primary education begins at five years of age and lasts for six years. In 1995 enrolment at primary level was equivalent to 100% of children in the relevant age-group. Secondary education, beginning at the age of 11, also lasts for six years and is divided into two equal cycles. In 1995 enrolment at secondary level was equivalent to 86% of children in the relevant age-group. The University of the West Indies has an extra-mural department in Nassau, offering degree courses in hotel management, tourism and law. The Bahamas Law School opened, as part of the University of the West Indies, in 1998. The Bahamas Hotel Training College was established in 1992. Technical, teacher-training and professional qualifications can be obtained at the two campuses of the College of the Bahamas. In 1999 plans were under way to upgrade the college to full university status in the near future.

In 1995, according to UNESCO estimates, the average rate of adult illiteracy was 1.8% (males 1.5%; females 2.0%). Government expenditure on education in 1998/99 was B $164.7m. (or 19.1% of total spending from the General Budget).

## Public Holidays

**2000:** 3 January (for New Year's Day), 21 April (Good Friday), 24 April (Easter Monday), 2 June (Labour Day), 12 June (Whit Monday), 10 July (Independence Day), 7 August (Emancipation Day), 13 October (Discovery Day/Columbus Day), 25–26 December (Christmas).

**2001:** 1 January (New Year's Day), 13 April (Good Friday), 16 April (Easter Monday), 1 June (Labour Day), 4 June (Whit Monday), 10 July (Independence Day), 6 August (Emancipation Day), 12 October (Discovery Day/Columbus Day), 25–26 December (Christmas).

## Weights and Measures

The imperial system is used.

# Statistical Survey

Source (unless otherwise stated): Central Bank of the Bahamas, Frederick St, POB N-4868, Nassau; tel. 322-2193; fax 322-4321.

## AREA AND POPULATION

**Area:** 13,939 sq km (5,382 sq miles).

**Population:** 209,505 at census of 12 May 1980; 255,095 (males 124,992, females 130,103) at census of 2 May 1990; 288,862 (official estimate) at mid-1997. *By island* (1990): New Providence 172,196 (including the capital, Nassau); Grand Bahama 40,898; Andros 8,187; Eleuthera 10,586.

**Density** (mid-1997): 20.7 per sq km.

**Principal Town:** Nassau (capital), population 172,000 (1997).

**Births, Marriages and Deaths** (1996): Registered live births 5,873 (birth rate 20.7 per 1,000); Registered marriages 2,628 (marriage rate 9.3 per 1,000); Registered deaths 1,537 (death rate 5.4 per 1,000). Source: UN, *Demographic Yearbook* and *Population and Vital Statistics Report*.

**Expectation of Life** (UN estimates, years at birth, 1990–95): 72.2 (males 69.3; females 76.1). Source: UN, *World Population Prospects: The 1998 Revision*.

**Economically Active Population** (sample survey, persons aged 15 years and over, excl. armed forces, April 1994): Agriculture, hunting and forestry 4,375; Fishing 2,130; Mining and quarrying 285; Manufacturing 4,980; Electricity, gas and water supply 1,690; Construction 8,515; Wholesale and retail trade; repair of motor vehicles, motorcycles and personal and household goods 20,415; Hotels and restaurants 18,215; Transport, storage and communications 10,650; Financial intermediation 6,090; Real estate, renting and business activities 5,660; Public administration and defence; compulsory social security 10,685; Education 6,265; Health and social work 5,260; Other community, social and personal service activities 6,625; Private households with employed persons 7,735; Activities not adequately defined 725; *Total employed* 120,300 (males 63,710, females 56,590); Unemployed 18,400 (males 9,150, females 9,250). *Total labour force* 138,700 (males 72,860, females 65,840). Source: ILO, *Yearbook of Labour Statistics*.

## AGRICULTURE, ETC.

**Principal Crops** ('000 metric tons, 1998): Roots and tubers 1*; Sugar cane 40*; Tomatoes 3*; Other vegetables 18; Lemons and limes 8; Grapefruit and pomelos 12; Bananas 1; Other fruits 4. *FAO estimate. Source: FAO, *Production Yearbook*.

**Livestock** (FAO estimates, '000 head, year ending September 1998): Cattle 1; Pigs 5; Sheep 6; Goats 16; Poultry (million) 4 (FAO estimate). Source: FAO, *Production Yearbook*.

**Livestock Products** ('000 metric tons, 1998): Poultry meat 11; Cows' milk 1*; Goats' milk 1*; Hen eggs 1. *FAO estimate. Source: FAO, *Production Yearbook*.

**Forestry** ('000 cu m, 1997): Roundwood removals: Sawlogs and veneer logs 17; Pulpwood 100; Total 117; Sawnwood production: Coniferous (softwood) 1. Source: FAO, *Yearbook of Forest Products*.

**Fishing** (metric tons, live weight): Total catch 9,557 in 1995; 9,866 in 1996; 10,439 (Caribbean spiny lobster 7,799) in 1997. Source: FAO, *Yearbook of Fishery Statistics*.

## MINING AND INDUSTRY

**Production** (estimates, '000 metric tons, unless otherwise indicated): Unrefined salt 900* in 1996; Sulphur 48* in 1990; Electric energy 1,028m. kWh in 1995 (UN estimate). *Data from the US Bureau of Mines. Source: UN, *Industrial Commodity Statistics Yearbook*.

## FINANCE

**Currency and Exchange Rates:** 100 cents = 1 Bahamian dollar (B $). *Sterling, US Dollar and Euro Equivalents* (30 September 1999): £1 sterling = B $1.6465; US $1 = B $1.0000; €1 = B $1.0665; B $100 = £60.73 = US $100.00 = €93.76. *Exchange Rate:* Since February 1970 the official exchange rate, applicable to most transactions, has been US $1 = B $1, i.e., the Bahamian dollar has been at par with the US dollar. There is also an investment currency rate, applicable to certain capital transactions between residents and non-residents and to direct investments outside the Bahamas. Since 1987 this exchange rate has been fixed at US $1 = B $1.225.

**General Budget** (estimates, B $ million, year ending 30 June 1999): *Revenue:* Total 839.1. *Expenditure:* Education 164.7; Uniformed services 90.6; Health 134.3; Tourism 57.3; Public works 55.7; Social services 47.5; Public debt interest 106.6; Total (incl. other) 862.6 (current 767.1; capital 95.5).

*1999/2000* (forecasts, B $ million): Recurrent revenue 895.6; Recurrent expenditure 838.7; Capital expenditure 95.8.

**International Reserves** (US $ million at 31 December 1998): Reserve position in IMF 8.8; Foreign exchange 337.7; Total 346.5. Source: IMF, *International Financial Statistics*.

**Money Supply** (B $ million at 31 December 1998): Currency outside banks 126.0; Demand deposits at deposit money banks 459.9; Total money (incl. others) 593.1. Source: IMF, *International Financial Statistics*.

**Cost of Living** (consumer price index; base: 1995 = 100): 101.4 in 1996; 101.9 in 1997; 103.3 in 1998. Source: IMF, *International Financial Statistics*.

**Gross Domestic Product** (B $ million at current prices): 2,853.6 in 1993; 3,053.1 in 1994; 3,069.4 in 1995. Source: IMF, *International Financial Statistics*.

**Expenditure on the Gross Domestic Product** (B $ million at current prices, 1995): Government final consumption expenditure 483.9; Private final consumption expenditure 2,077.4; Increase in stocks 13.8; Gross fixed capital formation 698.5; *Total domestic expenditure* 3,273.6; Exports of goods and services 1,680.1; *Less* Imports of goods and services 1,819.6; Statistical discrepancy −64.7; *GDP in purchasers' values* 3,069.4. Source: IMF, *International Financial Statistics*.

**Gross Domestic Product by Economic Activity** (B $ million at current prices, 1992): Agriculture, hunting, forestry and fishing 89; Manufacturing (incl. mining and quarrying) 105; Electricity, gas and water 88; Construction 91; Trade, restaurants and hotels 705; Transport, storage and communications 227; Finance, insurance, real estate and business services 610; Government services 336; Other community, social and personal services 310; Other services 55; Statistical discrepancy 13; *Sub-total* 2,629; Import duties 268; Other indirect taxes 162; *GDP in purchasers' values* 3,059. Source: UN, *National Accounts Statistics*.

**Balance of Payments*** (US $ million, 1998): Exports of goods f.o.b. 311.4; Imports of goods f.o.b. −1,371.9; *Trade balance* −1,060.5; Exports of services 1,580.8; Imports of services −958.2; *Balance on goods and services* −437.9; Other income received 147.9; Other income paid −337.7; *Balance on goods, services and income* −627.7; Current transfers received 45.0; Current transfers paid −10.8; *Current balance* −593.5; Capital account (net) −11.7; Direct investment abroad −1.0; Direct investment from abroad 235.4; Other investment assets −4,872.0; Other investment liabilities 5,139.7; Net errors and omissions 222.3; *Overall balance* 119.2. Source: IMF, *International Financial Statistics*.

* The figures for merchandise imports and exports exclude petroleum and petroleum products, except imports for local consumption.

## EXTERNAL TRADE*

**Principal Commodities** (US $ million, 1995): *Imports c.i.f.:* Food and live animals 209.0; Crude materials (inedible) except fuels 26.2; Mineral fuels, lubricants etc. 156.4; Chemicals 100.7; Basic manufactures 194.0; Machinery and transport equipment 308.6; Miscellaneous manufactured articles 202.9; Total (incl. others) 1,243.1. *Exports f.o.b.:* Food and live animals 64.8; Beverages and tobacco 3.5; Crude materials (inedible) except fuels 31.2; Chemicals 16.8; Basic manufactures 7.4; Machinery and transport equipment 46.0; Miscellaneous manufactured articles 6.0; Total (incl. others) 175.9.

*Total Imports c.i.f.* (US $ million): 1,343 in 1996; 1,622 in 1997; 1,872 in 1998.

*Total Exports f.o.b.* (US $ million): 180 in 1996; 181 in 1997; 300 in 1998.

Source (for 1996–98): IMF, *International Financial Statistics*.

**Principal Trading Partners** (US $ million, 1991): *Imports c.i.f.:* Aruba 52.2; Canada 21.2; Denmark 23.7; France 20.8; Nigeria 23.9; USA 866.0; Total (incl. others) 1,091.2. *Exports f.o.b.:* Canada 6.7; France 14.5; Germany 6.2; Mexico 4.0; United Kingdom 27.2; USA 142.5; Total (incl. others) 225.1. Source: UN, *International Trade Statistics Yearbook*.

*1995* (US $ million): *Imports c.i.f.* (excl. mineral fuels): Canada 11.3; USA 1,008.7; Total (incl. others) 1,086.7. *Exports f.o.b.:* Canada 3.4; United Kingdom 4.0; USA 142.6; Total (incl. others) 175.9.

* The data exclude imports and exports of crude petroleum and residual fuel oils that are brought into the Bahamas for storage on behalf of foreign companies abroad. Also excluded is trade in certain chemical products. In 1991 total imports were valued at US $1,801.2m. and total exports at US $1,517.1m.

### TRANSPORT

**Road Traffic** (vehicles in use, 1995): 67,100 passenger cars; 13,700 commercial vehicles. Source: UN, *Statistical Yearbook*.

**Shipping:** *Merchant fleet* (displacement, '000 grt at 31 December): 24,409 in 1996; 25,523 in 1997; 27,716 in 1998. (Source: Lloyd's Register of Shipping, *World Fleet Statistics*). *International sea-borne freight traffic* (estimates, '000 metric tons, 1990): Goods loaded 5,920; Goods unloaded 5,705. Source: UN, *Monthly Bulletin of Statistics*.

**Civil Aviation** (1995): Kilometres flown (million) 4; Passengers carried ('000) 937; Passenger-km (million) 220; Total ton-km (million) 20. Source: UN, *Statistical Yearbook*.

### TOURISM

**Tourist Arrivals:** 3,415,858 in 1996; 3,453,769 in 1997; 3,346,329 (1,304,531 by air, 2,041,798 by sea) in 1998.

**Tourism Receipts** (estimates, B $ million): 1,398 in 1996; 1,416 in 1997; 1,408 in 1998.

### COMMUNICATIONS MEDIA

**Radio Receivers** (1996): 210,000 in use.

**Television Receivers** (1996): 66,000 in use.

**Telephones** (estimate, 1994): 77,000 main lines in use.

**Telefax Stations** (1993): 550 in use.

**Mobile Cellular Telephones** (1993): 2,400 subscribers.

**Daily Newspapers** (1996): 3 titles (total circulation 28,000 copies).

Sources: UN, *Statistical Yearbook*; UNESCO, *Statistical Yearbook*.

### EDUCATION

**Pre-primary** (1996/97): 20 schools; 76 teachers; 1,094 pupils.

**Primary** (1996/97): 113 schools; 1,540 teachers (estimate); 34,199 students.

**Secondary** (1996/97): 37 junior/senior high schools (1990); 1,352 teachers (public education only); 27,970 students (public education only).

**Tertiary** (1987): 249 teachers; 5,305 students.

In 1993 there were 3,201 students registered at the College of the Bahamas.

Source: mainly UNESCO, *Statistical Yearbook*.

# Directory

## The Constitution

A representative House of Assembly was first established in 1729, although universal adult suffrage was not introduced until 1962. A new Constitution for the Commonwealth of the Bahamas came into force at independence, on 10 July 1973. The main provisions of the Constitution are summarized below:

Parliament consists of a Governor-General (representing the British monarch, who is Head of State), a nominated Senate and an elected House of Assembly. The Governor-General appoints the Prime Minister and, on the latter's recommendation, the remainder of the Cabinet. Apart from the Prime Minister, the Cabinet has no fewer than eight other ministers, of whom one is the Attorney-General. The Governor-General also appoints a Leader of the Opposition.

The Senate (upper house) consists of 16 members, of whom nine are appointed by the Governor-General on the advice of the Prime Minister, four on the advice of the Leader of the Opposition and three on the Prime Minister's advice after consultation with the Leader of the Opposition. The House of Assembly (lower house) has 40 members. A Constituencies Commission reviews numbers and boundaries at intervals of not more than five years and can recommend alterations for approval of the House. The life of Parliament is limited to a maximum of five years.

The Constitution provides for a Supreme Court and a Court of Appeal.

## The Government

**Head of State:** HM Queen ELIZABETH II (succeeded to the throne 6 February 1952).

**Governor-General:** Sir ORVILLE TURNQUEST (appointed 22 February 1995).

### THE CABINET
(January 2000)

**Prime Minister:** HUBERT ALEXANDER INGRAHAM.

**Deputy Prime Minister and Minister of National Security:** FRANK HOWARD WATSON.

**Attorney-General and Minister of Foreign Affairs:** JANET G. BOSTWICK.

**Minister of Tourism:** CORNELIUS ALVIN SMITH.

**Minister of Finance:** WILLIAM C. ALLEN.

**Minister of Education and Youth:** Sen. Dame IVY LEONA DUMONT.

**Minister of Housing and Social Development:** ALGERNON SIDNEY PATRICK BENEDICT ALLEN.

**Minister of Commerce, Agriculture and Industry:** THERESA MOXEY-INGRAHAM.

**Minister of Public Service, Immigration and National Insurance:** TOMMY TURNQUEST.

**Minister of Works and Transport:** JAMES F. KNOWLES.

**Minister of Health:** Sen. Dr RONALD KNOWLES.

**Minister of Local Government, Sports and Culture:** DAVID C. THOMPSON.

**Minister of Labour and Maritime Affairs:** DION A. FOULKES.

**Minister of Economic Affairs:** CARL W. BETHEL.

**Minister of State for Education and Youth:** ZHIVARGO LAING.

### MINISTRIES

**Attorney-General's Office and Ministry of Justice:** East Hill, POB N-3007, Nassau; tel. 322-1141; fax 356-4179.

**Office of the Prime Minister:** Cecil V. Wallace-Whitfield Centre, POB CB-10980, Nassau; tel. 327-5826; fax 327-5806.

**Office of the Deputy Prime Minister:** POB N-3217, Nassau; tel. 356-6792; fax 356-6087.

**Ministry of Commerce, Agriculture and Industry:** East Bay St, POB N-3028, Nassau; tel. 325-7502; fax 322-1767.

**Ministry of Consumer Welfare and Aviation:** Thompson Blvd, POB N-3002, Nassau; tel. 326-4550; fax 328-1160.

**Ministry of Education and Youth:** Shirley St, POB N-3913, Nassau; tel. 322-8140; fax 322-8491.

**Ministry of Finance:** Rawson Sq., POB N-3017, Nassau; tel. 327-1530; fax 327-1618.

**Ministry of Foreign Affairs:** East Hill St, POB N-3746, Nassau; tel. 322-7624; fax 328-8212.

**Ministry of Health:** Royal Victoria Gardens, East Hill St, POB N-3730, Nassau; tel. 322-7425; fax 322-7788.

**Ministry of Housing and Social Development:** Frederick House, Frederick St, POB N 3206, Nassau; tel. 356-0765; fax 323-3883.

**Ministry of Labour and Maritime Affairs:** POB N-4891, Nassau; tel. 322-6250; fax 322-6546.

**Ministry of Local Government, Sports and Culture:** Pilot House, East Bay St, POB N-10114, Nassau; tel. 394-0451; fax 394-0428; e-mail minyouth.mail@batelnet.bs.

**Ministry of National Security:** POB N-3217, Nassau; tel. 356-6792; fax 326-7344.

**Ministry of Public Works:** John F. Kennedy Drive, POB N-8156, Nassau; tel. 323-7240; fax 326-7344.

**Ministry of Tourism:** Bay St, POB N-3701, Nassau; tel. 322-7500; fax 328-0945; internet www.bahamas.com.

**Ministry of Transport:** Post Office Bldg, East Hill St, POB N-3008, Nassau; tel. 322-1112; fax 325-2016.

# Legislature

### PARLIAMENT

**Houses of Parliament:** Parliament Sq., Nassau.

### Senate

**President:** J. HENRY BOSTWICK.

There are 16 nominated members.

### House of Assembly

**Speaker:** ROME ITALIA JOHNSON.

The House has 40 members.

**General Election, 14 March 1997**

| Party | Seats* |
|---|---|
| Free National Movement (FNM) | 34 |
| Progressive Liberal Party (PLP) | 6 |
| **Total** | 40 |

* In a by-election in September 1997 an FNM member replaced the former PLP leader, Sir Lynden Pindling, who announced his retirement from parliamentary politics in July.

# Political Organizations

**Bahamian Freedom Alliance:** Nassau; f. 1994; Leader HALSON MOULTRIE.

**Free National Movement (FNM):** POB N-10713, Nassau; tel. 393-7863; fax 393-7914; f. 1970; Leader HUBERT A. INGRAHAM.

**Progressive Liberal Party (PLP):** Nassau; tel. 325-2900; f. 1953; centrist party; Leader PERRY CHRISTIE; Chair. OBIE WILCHCOMBE.

# Diplomatic Representation

### EMBASSY AND HIGH COMMISSION IN THE BAHAMAS

**United Kingdom:** Ansbacher Bldg, 3rd Floor, East St, POB N-7516, Nassau; tel. 325-7471; fax 323-3871; High Commissioner: PETER HEIGL.

**USA:** Mosmar Bldg, Queen St, POB N-8197, Nassau; tel. 322-1183; fax 328-7838; Ambassador: ARTHUR SCHECHTER.

# Judicial System

The Judicial Committee of the Privy Council (based in the United Kingdom), the Bahamas Court of Appeal, the Supreme Court and the Magistrates' Courts are the main courts of the Bahamian judicial system.

All courts have both a criminal and civil jurisdiction. The Magistrates' Courts are presided over by professionally qualified Stipendiary and Circuit Magistrates in New Providence and Grand Bahama, and by Island Administrators sitting as Magistrates in most of the other Family Islands.

Whereas all magistrates are empowered to try offences which may be tried summarily, a Stipendiary and Circuit Magistrate may, with the consent of the accused, also try certain less serious indictable offences. The jurisdiction of magistrates is, however, limited by law.

The Supreme Court consists of the Chief Justice, two Senior Justices and six Justices. The Supreme Court also sits in Freeport, with one Justice.

Appeals in almost all matters lie from the Supreme Court to the Court of Appeal, with further appeal in certain instances to the Judicial Committee of the Privy Council.

**Supreme Court of the Bahamas:** Parliament Sq., POB N-8167, Nassau; tel. 322-3315; fax 323-6895; Chief Justice JOAN SAWYER.

**Court of Appeal:** POB N-8167, Nassau; tel. 322-3315; fax 325-6895; Pres. JOHAQUIM C. GONZALES-SABOLA.

**Magistrates' Courts:** POB N-421, Nassau; tel. 325-4573; fax 323-1446; 15 magistrates and a circuit magistrate.

**Registrar of the Supreme Court:** STEVEN ISAACS; POB N-167, Nassau.

**Attorney-General:** JANET G. BOSTWICK.

**Office of the Attorney-General:** East Hill, POB N-3007, Nassau; tel. 322-1141; fax 322-2255; Dir of Legal Affairs RHONDA BAIN; Dir of Public Prosecutions BERNARD TURNER (acting).

**Registrar-General:** STERLING QUANT, POB N-532, Nassau.

# Religion

Most of the population profess Christianity, but there are also small communities of Jews and Muslims.

### CHRISTIANITY

According to the census of 1990, there were 79,465 Baptists (31.2% of the population), 40,894 Roman Catholics (16.0%) and 40,881 Anglicans (16.0%). Other important denominations include the Pentecostal Church (5.5%), the Church of Christ (5.0%) and the Methodists (4.8%).

**Bahamas Christian Council:** POB SS-5863, Nassau; tel. 393-3946; f. 1948; 10 mem. churches; Pres. Rev. SIMEON HALL.

### The Roman Catholic Church

The Bahamas comprises the single diocese of Nassau, suffragan to the archdiocese of Kingston in Jamaica. At 31 December 1997 there were an estimated 31,290 adherents in the Bahamas. The Bishop participates in the Antilles Episcopal Conference (whose Secretariat is based in Port of Spain, Trinidad). The Turks and Caicos Islands are also under the jurisdiction of the Bishop of Nassau.

**Bishop of Nassau:** Rt Rev. LAWRENCE A. BURKE, The Hermitage, West St, POB N-8187, Nassau; tel. 322-8919; fax 322-2599; e-mail rcchancery@batelnet.bs.

### The Anglican Communion

Anglicans in the Bahamas are adherents of the Church in the Province of the West Indies. The diocese also includes the Turks and Caicos Islands.

**Archbishop of the West Indies, and Bishop of the Bahamas and the Turks and Caicos Islands:** Most Rev. DREXEL GOMEZ, Bishop's Lodge, POB N-7107, Nassau; tel. 322-3015; fax 322-7943.

### Other Christian Churches

**Bahamas Conference of Methodist Churches:** POB SS-5103, Nassau; Pres. Rev. CHARLES SWEETING.

**Bahamas Conference of Seventh-day Adventists:** Shirley St, POB N-356, Nassau; tel. 322-3032; fax 325-7248.

**Bahamas Evangelical Church Association:** Carmichael Rd, POB N-1224, Nassau; tel. 362-1024.

**Greek Orthodox Church:** Church of the Annunciation, West St, POB N-823, Nassau; tel. 322-4382; f. 1928; part of the Archdiocese of North and South America, based in New York (USA); Priest Rev. THEOPHANIS KULYVAS.

**Methodist Church Conference in the Bahamas:** POB F-40021, Nassau; Superintendent Rev. RAYMOND NEILY.

Other denominations include the Assemblies of Brethren, the Jehovah's Witnesses, the Salvation Army, Pentecostal, Presbyterian, Baptist, Lutheran and Assembly of God churches.

### BAHÁ'Í FAITH

**Bahá'í National Spiritual Assembly:** Shirley St, POB N-7105, Nassau; tel. 326-0607; e-mail nsabaha@hotmail.com.

### OTHER RELIGIONS

**Islam:** there is a small community of Muslims in the Bahamas.

**Judaism:** most of the Bahamian Jewish community are based on Grand Bahama. There were 126 Jews, according to the 1990 census.

# The Press

### NEWSPAPERS

**Bahama Journal:** Media House, POB N-8610, Nassau; tel. 325-3082; fax 356-7256; daily.

**Freeport News:** Cedar St, POB F-40007, Freeport; tel. 352-8321; fax 352-3449; f. 1961; daily; Gen. Man. DORLAN COLLIE; Editor ROBYN ADDERLEY; circ. 6,000.

**The Nassau Guardian:** 4 Carter St, Oakes Field, POB N-3011, Nassau; tel. 323-5654; fax 363-3783; internet www.thenassauguardian.com; f. 1844; daily; Gen. Man. PATRICK WALKES; Editor OSWALD BROWN; circ. 12,277.

**The Punch:** POB N-4081, Nassau; tel. 322-7112; fax 323-5268; twice weekly; Editor IVAN JOHNSON.

**The Tribune:** Shirley St, POB N-3207, Nassau; tel. 322-1986; fax 328-2398; e-mail tribune@100jamz.com; f. 1903; daily; Publr and Editor EILEEN DUPUCH CARRON; circ. 13,500.

### PERIODICALS

**The Bahamas Financial Digest:** Miramar House, Bay and Christie Sts, POB N-4271, Nassau; tel. 356-2981; fax 356-7118; e-mail michael.symonette@batelnet.bs; f. 1973; 4 a year; business and investment; Publr and Editor MICHAEL A. SYMONETTE; circ. 15,890.

**Bahamas Tourist News:** Bayparl Bldg, Parliament St, POB N-4855, Nassau; tel. 322-4528; fax 322-4527; f. 1962; monthly; Editor BOBBY BOWER; circ. 360,000 (annually).

**Nassau City Magazine:** Miramar House, Bay and Christie Sts, POB N-4824, Nassau; tel. 356-2981; fax 326-2849.

**Official Gazette:** c/o Cabinet Office, POB N-7147, Nassau; tel. 322-2805; weekly; publ. by the Cabinet Office.

**What's On Magazine:** Woodes Rogers Wharf, POB CB-11713, Nassau; tel. 323-2323; fax 322-3428; e-mail whatson@batelnet.bs; internet www.whatsonbahamas.com; monthly; Publr NEIL ABERLE.

# Publishers

**Bahamas Free Press Ltd:** POB CB-13309, Nassau; tel. 323-8961.

**Etienne Dupuch Jr Publications Ltd:** Oakes Field, POB N-7513, Nassau; tel. 323-5665; fax 323-5728; e-mail dupuch@bahamasnet.com; internet www.bahamasnet.com; publishes *Bahamas Handbook*, *Trailblazer* maps, *What To Do* magazines, *Welcome Bahamas*, *Tadpole* (educational colouring book) series and *Dining and Entertainment Guide*; Dirs ETIENNE DUPUCH, Jr, S. P. DUPUCH.

**Printing Tours and Publishing:** Miramar House, Bay and Christie Sts, POB N-4846, Nassau; tel. 356-2981; fax 356-7118; e-mail michael.symonette@batelnet.bs.

**Sacha de Frisching Publishing:** POB N-7776, Nassau; tel. 362-6230; fax 362-6274; children's books.

**Star Publishers Ltd:** POB N-4855, Nassau; tel. 322-3724; fax 322-4537.

# Broadcasting and Communications

### TELECOMMUNICATIONS

**Bahamas Telecommunications Co (BaTelCo):** POB N-3048, JFK Dr, Nassau; tel. 302-7000; fax 326-7474; e-mail info@batelnet.bs; internet www.batelnet.bs; state-owned; scheduled for partial privatization in late 1999.

### BROADCASTING

#### Radio

**Broadcasting Corporation of the Bahamas:** POB N-1347, Centreville, New Providence; tel. 322-4623; fax 322-3924; f. 1936; govt-owned; commercial; Chair. MICHAEL D. SMITH; Gen. Man. EDWIN LIGHTBOURNE.

**Radio Bahamas:** f. 1936; broadcasts 24 hours per day on four stations: the main Radio Bahamas (ZNS1), Radio New Providence (ZNS2), which are both based in Nassau, Radio Power 104.5 FM, and the Northern Service (ZNS3—Freeport; f. 1973; Station Man. ANTHONY FORSTER); Programme Man. TANYA PINDER.

#### Television

**Broadcasting Corporation of the Bahamas:** (see Radio).

**Bahamas Television:** f. 1977; broadcasts for Nassau, New Providence and the Central Bahamas; transmitting power of 50,000 watts; full colour; Programme Man. CARL BETHEL.

US television programmes and some satellite programmes can be received. Most islands have a cable-television service.

# Finance

In recent years the Bahamas has developed into one of the world's foremost financial centres (there are no corporation, income, capital gains or withholding taxes or estate duty), and finance has become a significant feature of the economy. At June 1999 there were 416 banks and trust companies operating in the Bahamas, of which 199 had a physical presence in the islands.

### BANKING

(cap. = capital; dep. = deposits; res = reserves; m. = million; brs = branches)

#### Central Bank

**The Central Bank of the Bahamas:** Frederick St, POB N-4868, Nassau; tel. 322-2193; fax 322-4321; f. 1973; bank of issue; cap. B $3.0m., res B $76.8m., dep. B $124.4m. (Dec. 1997); Gov. JULIAN W. FRANCIS; Dep. Gov. WENDY CRAIG.

#### Development Bank

**The Bahamas Development Bank:** Cable Beach, West Bay St, POB N-3034, Nassau; tel. 327-5780; fax 327-5047; f. 1978 to fund approved projects and channel funds into appropriate investments; Chair. FREDERICK GOTTLIEB.

#### Principal Bahamian-based Banks

**Bank of the Bahamas Ltd:** Shirley and Charlotte Sts, POB N-7118, Nassau; tel. 326-2560; fax 325-2762; f. 1970, name changed as above in 1988, when Bank of Montreal Bahamas Ltd became jointly owned by Govt and Euro Canadian Bank; 50% owned by Govt, 50% owned by c. 4,000 Bahamian shareholders; cap. B $10.0m., res B $1.0m., dep. B $171.8m. (June 1999); Chair. HUGH G. SANDS; Man. Dir P. M. ALLEN-DEAN; 8 brs.

**Commonwealth Bank Ltd:** 610 Bay St, POB SS-5541, Nassau; tel. 394-7373; f. 1960; Pres. WILLIAM SANDS; 8 brs.

**Eurobanco Bank Ltd:** 3rd Floor, Bolan House, King and George Sts, POB N-3026, Nassau; tel. 356-5454; fax 356-9432; f. 1992; cap. US $3.0m., dep. US $136.3m. (Dec. 1994); Pres. CHRISTOPHER GEOFFREY DOUGLAS HOOPER.

**Finance Corporation of the Bahamas Ltd (FinCo):** Charlotte and Shirley Sts, POB N-3038, Nassau; tel. 322-4822; fax 326-3031; f. 1953; Man. Dir PETER THOMPSON; 4 brs.

**Private Investment Bank and Trust (Bahamas) Ltd:** Cumberland House, 27 Cumberland St, POB N-3918, Nassau; tel. 326-0282; fax 326-5213; f. 1984 as Bank Worms and Co International Ltd;renamed in 1990, 1996 and 1998; cap. US $3.0m., res US $1.8m., dep. US $247.7m. (Dec. 1997); Chair. and Dir FRANÇOIS ROUGE.

#### Principal Foreign Banks

**Bank Leu Ltd** (Switzerland): Norfolk House, Frederick St, POB N-3926, Nassau; tel. 326-5054; fax 323-8828; subsidiary of Bank Leu AG, Zurich.

**Bank of Nova Scotia International Ltd** (Canada): Scotiabank Bldg, Rawson Sq., POB N-7545, Nassau; tel. 322-4631; fax 328-8473; Man. Dir C. A. BARNES; 13 brs.

**Barclays Bank PLC** (United Kingdom): Charlotte House, Shirley St, POB N-3221, Nassau; tel. 325-7384; fax 322-8267; internet www.bahamas.barclays.com; Dir SHARON BROWN.

**BSI Overseas (Bahamas) Ltd** (Italy): Norfolk House, Frederick St, POB N-7130, Nassau; tel. 394-9200; fax 394-9220; f. 1990; wholly-owned subsid. of Banca della Svizzera Italiana; cap. US $10.0m., res US $33.9m., dep. US $1,111.8m. (Dec. 1997); Chair. Dr A. GYSI; Man. IVOR J. HERRINGTON.

**Canadian Imperial Bank of Commerce** (Canada): 4th Floor, 308 East Bay St, POB N-8329, Nassau; tel. 393-4710; fax 393-4280; internet www.cibc.com; Area Man. TERRY HILTS; 9 brs.

**Citibank NA** (USA): Citibank Bldg, Thompson Blvd, Oakes Field, POB N-8158, Nassau; tel. 322-8510; fax 302-8555; internet www.citibank.com; Gen. Man. ALISON JOHNSTON; 2 brs.

**Credit Suisse (Bahamas) Ltd** (Switzerland): Frederick St., POB N-4928, Nassau; tel. 356-8100; fax 326-6589; f. 1968; subsidiary of Credit Suisse Zurich; portfolio and asset management, offshore company management, trustee services; cap. US $12.0m., res US $20.0m., dep. US $500.7m. (Dec. 1997); Man. Dir GREGOR MAISSEN.

**Handelsfinanz-CCF Bank International Ltd** (Switzerland): Third Floor, Maritime House, Frederick St, POB N-10441, Nassau; tel. 328-8644; fax 328-8600; f. 1971; cap. US $5.0m., res US $8.1m., dep. US $659.4m. (Dec. 1997); Pres. and Gen. Man. FERDINANDO M. MENCONI.

**Lloyds TSB Bank International (Bahamas) Ltd** (United Kingdom): Bolam House, King and George Sts, POB N-4843, Nassau; tel. 322-8711; fax 322-8719; f. 1977; cap. US $25.0m., dep. US $342.6 (Dec. 1996); Gen. Man. A. B. HOWELLS.

**Overseas Union Bank and Trust (Bahamas) Ltd** (Switzerland): 250 Bay St, POB N-8184, Nassau; tel. 322-2476; fax 323-8771; f. 1980; cap. US $5.0m., res US $6.2m., dep. US $97.9m. (Dec. 1997); Chair. Dr CARLO SGANZINI; Gen. Man. URS FREI.

**Pictet Bank and Trust Ltd** (Switzerland): Charlotte House, Charlotte St, POB N-4837, Nassau; tel. 322-3938; fax 323-7986; e-mail pbtbah@bahamas.net.bs; internet www.pictet.com/nassau.htm; f. 1978; cap. US $1.0m., res US $10.0m., dep. US $126.2m. (Dec. 1995); Chair. and Dir CLAUDE DEMOLE.

**Royal Bank of Canada Ltd** (Canada): 323 Bay St, POB N-7537, Nassau; tel. 322-8700; fax 323-6381; internet www.royalbank.com; Vice-Pres. MICHAEL F. PHELAN; 16 brs.

**Royal Bank of Scotland (Nassau) Ltd** (United Kingdom): 3rd Floor, Bahamas Financial Centre, Shirley and Charlotte Sts, POB N-3045, Nassau; tel. 322-4643; fax 326-7559; e-mail info@rbsint.bs; f. 1951 as E. D. Sassoon Bank and Trust Ltd, name changed 1978, 1986 and 1989; cap. US $2.0m., res US $7.3m., dep. US 289.5m. (Sept. 1998); Chair. JAMES D. PATON; CEO DAVID BARRON.

**UBS (Bahamas) Ltd** (Switzerland): Swiss Bank House, East Bay St, POB N-7757, Nassau; tel. 394-9300; fax 394-9333; f. 1968 as

Swiss Bank Corpn (Overseas) Ltd, name changed as above 1998; cap. US $4.0m., dep. US $420.2m. (Dec. 1997); Chair. ERNST BALSIGER; Exec. Dir and Pres. PHILIP WHITE.

### Principal Bahamian Trust Companies

**Ansbacher (Bahamas) Ltd:** Ansbacher House, Bank Lane, POB N-7768, Nassau; tel. 322-1161; fax 326-5020; e-mail ansbbah@batelnet.bs; incorporated 1957 as Bahamas International Trust Co Ltd, name changed 1994; cap. B $1.0m., res B $9.7m., dep. B $190.3m. (Sept. 1998); Chair. PETER N. SCAIFE; Man. Dir DAVID L. E. FAWKES.

**Chase Manhattan Trust Corpn:** Shirley and Charlotte Sts, POB N-3708, Nassau; tel. 356-1305; fax 325-1706; Gen. Man. KEN BROWN; 4 brs.

**Leadenhall Bank and Trust Co Ltd:** IBM Bldg, Bay St at Church St, POB N-1965, Nassau; tel. 325-5508; fax 328-7030; e-mail drounce@leadentrust.com; f. 1976; Man. Dir DAVID J. ROUNCE.

**MeesPierson (Bahamas) Ltd:** POB SS-5539, Nassau; tel. 393-8777; fax 393-0582; internet www.mpbahamas.com; f. 1987; subsidiary of MeesPierson International AG of Zug, Switzerland; Chair. IAN D. FAIR; Gen. Man. RONALD J. A. DE GRAAF.

**Oceanic Bank and Trust:** Euro Canadian Centre, POB N-8327, Nassau; tel. 322-7461; fax 326-6177; f. 1969.

**SG Hambros Bank and Trust (Bahamas) Ltd:** West Bay St, POB N-7788, Nassau; tel. 326-0404; fax 326-6709; e-mail sghbahamas@socgen.com.bs; f. 1936; previously Coutts (Bahamas) Ltd; sold 1998 to Hambros Bank Ltd, a subsidiary of Société Générale (Paris); cap. US $17.7m., dep. US $410.6m. (Oct. 1999); Chair. WARRICK NEWBURY; Man. Dir PASCAL HAMMERER.

**Winterbotham Trust Co Ltd:** Bolam House, King and George Sts, POB N-3026, Nassau; tel. 356-5454; fax 356-9432; e-mail nassau@winterbotham.com; cap. US $2.8m.; CEO GEOFFREY HOOPER; 2 brs.

### Bankers' Organizations

**Association of International Banks and Trust Companies in the Bahamas:** POB N-7880, Nassau; tel. 394-6755; Chair. BRUCE BELL.

**Bahamas Institute of Bankers:** Royal Palm Mall, Mackey St, POB N-3202, Nassau; tel. 393-0456; fax 394-3503; Pres. KIM BODIE.

## INSURANCE

The leading British and a number of US and Canadian companies have agents in Nassau and Freeport. Local insurance companies include the following:

**Allied Bahamas Insurance Co Ltd:** 93 Collins Ave, POB N-121, Nassau; tel. 326-3537; fax 356-2192; general, aviation and marine.

**Bahamas First General Insurance Co Ltd:** 93 Collins Ave, POB N-1216, Nassau; tel. 326-5439; fax 326-5472.

**Colina Insurance Co Ltd:** 12 Village Rd, POB N-4728, Nassau; tel. 393-2224; fax 393-1710.

**The Family Guardian Insurance Co Ltd:** East Bay St, POB SS-6232, Nassau; tel. 393-1023; f. 1965.

### Association

**Bahamas General Insurance Association:** POB N-860, Nassau; tel. 323-2596; fax 328-4354; Co-ordinator Dr ROGER G. BROWN.

# Trade and Industry

## DEVELOPMENT ORGANIZATIONS

**Bahamas Agricultural and Industrial Corpn (BAIC):** BAIC Bldg, East Bay St, POB N-4940, Nassau; tel. 322-3740; fax 322-2123; f. 1981 as an amalgamation of Bahamas Development Corpn and Bahamas Agricultural Corpn for the promotion of greater co-operation between tourism and other sectors of the economy through the development of small- and medium-sized enterprises; Exec. Chair. ALVIN SMITH.

**Bahamas Investment Authority:** Cecil V. Wallace-Whitfield Centre, POB CB-10980, Nassau; tel. 327-5970; fax 327-5907; Exec. Dir BASIL H. ALBURY.

**Bahamas Light Industries Development Council:** POB SS-5599, Nassau; tel. 394-1907; Pres. LESLIE MILLER.

**Nassau Paradise Island Promotion Board:** Dean's Lane, Fort Charlotte, POB N-7799, Nassau; tel. 322-8381; fax 325-8998; f. 1970; Chair. HOWARD KARAWAN; Sec. MICHAEL C. RECKLEY; 30 mems.

## CHAMBER OF COMMERCE

**Bahamas Chamber of Commerce:** Shirley St, POB N-665, Nassau; tel. 322-2145; fax 322-4649; f. 1935 to promote, foster and protect trade, industry and commerce; Pres. A. BISMARK COAKLEY; Exec. Dir RUBY L. SWEETING; 450 mems.

## EMPLOYERS' ASSOCIATIONS

**Bahamas Association of Land Surveyors:** POB N-10147, Nassau; tel. 322-4569; Pres. DONALD THOMPSON; Vice-Pres. GODFREY HUMES; 30 mems.

**Bahamas Boatmen's Association:** POB ES-5212, Nassau; f. 1974; Pres. and Sec. FREDERICK GOMEZ.

**Bahamas Contractors' Association:** POB N-8049, Nassau; Pres. BRENDON C. WATSON; Sec. EMMANUEL ALEXIOU.

**Bahamas Employers' Confederation:** POB N-166, Nassau; tel. 393-5613; fax 322-4649; f. 1963; Pres. REGINALD LOBOSKY.

**Bahamas Hotel Employers' Association:** Dean's Lane, Fort Charlotte, POB N-7799, Nassau; tel. 322-2262; fax 326-5346; f. 1958; Pres. J. BARRIE FARRINGTON; Exec. Dir MICHAEL C. RECKLEY; 26 mems.

**Bahamas Institute of Chartered Accountants:** Star Plaza, Mackey St, POB N-7037, Nassau; tel. 394-3439; fax 394-3629; f. 1971; Pres. L. EDGAR MOXEY.

**Bahamas Institute of Professional Engineers:** Nassau; tel. 322-3356; fax 323-8503; Pres. ANTHONY DEAN.

**Bahamas Motor Dealers' Association:** POB N-3919, Nassau; tel. 328-7671; fax 328-1922; Pres. HARRY ROBERTS.

**Bahamas Petroleum Retailers' Association:** Nassau; tel. 325-1141; fax 325-3936.

**Bahamas Real Estate Association:** Bahamas Chamber Bldg, POB N-8860, Nassau; tel. 325-4942; fax 322-4649; Pres. PATRICK STRACHAN.

## UTILITIES

### Electricity

**The Bahamas Electricity Corpn (BEC):** POB N-7509, Pond and Tucker Rd, Nassau; tel. 325-4101; fax 323-6852; state-owned; scheduled for privatization in 2000; provides 70% of the islands' power-generating capacity.

**Freeport Power and Light Co Ltd:** POB F-888, Mercantile Bldg, Cedar St, Freeport; tel. 352-6611; privately-owned.

### Gas

**Bahamas Gas Ltd:** Nassau; tel. 325-6401.

**Tropigas:** Nassau; tel. 322-2404.

### Water

**Bahamas Water and Sewerage Corpn:** John F. Kennedy Dr., POB N-3905, Nassau; tel. 323-3944; Chair. FREDERICK GOTTLIEB.

## TRADE UNIONS

All Bahamian unions are members of one of the following:

**National Congress of Trade Unions:** Horseshoe Drive, POB GT-2887, Nassau; tel. 356-7457; Pres. LEROY HANNA; 20,000 mems.

**Trade Union Congress:** Warwick St, Nassau; tel. 394-6301; fax 394-7401; Pres. OBIE FERGUSON; 12,500 mems.

The main unions are as follows:

**Bahamas Airport and Allied Workers' Union:** Workers House, Harrold Rd, POB N-3364, Nassau; tel. 323-5030; f. 1958; Pres. FRANKLYN CARTER; Gen. Sec. PATRICE TYNES-RODGERS; 550 mems.

**Bahamas Brewery, Distillers and Allied Workers' Union:** Nassau; f. 1968; Pres. BRADICK CLEARE; Gen. Sec. DAVID KEMP; 140 mems.

**Bahamas Communications and Public Officers' Union:** Farrington Rd, POB N-3190, Nassau; tel. 322-1537; fax 323-8719; e-mail prebcpou@batelnet.bs; f. 1973; Pres. D. SHANE GIBSON; Sec.-Gen. ROBERT A. FARQUHARSON; 2,100 mems.

**Bahamas Doctors' Union:** Nassau; Pres. Dr EUGENE NEWERY; Gen. Sec. GEORGE SHERMAN.

**Bahamas Electrical Workers' Union:** East West Highway, POB GT-2535, Nassau; tel. 393-1431; Pres. SAMUEL MITCHELL; Gen. Sec. JONATHAN CAMBRIDGE.

**Bahamas Hotel Catering and Allied Workers' Union:** POB GT-2514, Nassau; tel. 323-5933; fax 325-6546; f. 1958; Pres. THOMAS BASTIAN; Gen. Sec. LEO DOUGLAS; 6,500 mems.

**Bahamas Maritime Port and Allied Workers' Union:** POB SS-6501, Nassau; tel. 328-7502; Pres. ANTHONY WILLIAMS; Sec.-Gen. FREDERICK N. RODGERS.

**Bahamas Musicians' and Entertainers' Union:** Horseshoe Drive, POB N-880, Nassau; tel. 322-3734; fax 323-3537; f. 1958; Pres. LEROY (DUKE) HANNA; Gen. Sec. PORTIA NOTTAGE; 410 mems.

**Bahamas Public Services Union:** Wulff Rd, POB N-4692, Nassau; tel. 325-0038; fax 323-5287; f. 1959; Pres. WILLIAM MCDONALD; Sec.-Gen. SYNIDA DORSETT; 4,247 mems.

**Bahamas Taxi-Cab Union:** POB N-1077, Nassau; tel. 323-5952; Pres. FELIX ROLLE (acting); Gen. Sec. ROSCOE WEECH.

**Bahamas Union of Teachers:** 104 Bethel Ave, Stapledon Gardens, POB N-3482, Nassau; tel. 323-7085; fax 323-7086; f. 1945; Pres. KINGSLEY BLACK; Gen. Sec. HELENA CARTWRIGHT; 2,600 mems.

**Eastside Stevedores' Union:** POB N-1176, Nassau; f. 1972; Pres. SALATHIEL MACKEY; Gen. Sec. CURTIS TURNQUEST.

**Grand Bahama Construction, Refinery and Maintenance Workers' Union:** 33A Kipling Bldg, POB F-839, Freeport; tel. 352-7438; f. 1971; Pres. JAMES TAYLOR; Gen. Sec. EPHRAIM BLACK.

**United Brotherhood of Longshoremen's Union:** Wulff Rd, POB N-7317, Nassau; f. 1959; Pres. J. MCKINNEY; Gen. Sec. W. SWANN; 157 mems.

# Transport

## ROADS

There are about 966 km (600 miles) of roads in New Providence and 1,368 km (850 miles) in the Family Islands, mainly on Grand Bahama, Cat Island, Eleuthera, Exuma and Long Island.

## SHIPPING

The principal seaport is at Nassau (New Providence), which can accommodate the very largest cruise ships. Passenger arrivals exceed two million annually. The other main ports are at Freeport (Grand Bahama), where a container terminal opened in 1997, and Matthew Town (Inagua). There are also modern berthing facilities for cruise ships at Potters Cay (New Providence), Governor's Harbour (Eleuthera), Morgan's Bluff (North Andros) and George Town (Exuma).

The Bahamas converted to free-flag status in 1976, and by 1983 possessed the world's third-largest open-registry fleet. The fleet's displacement was 27,715,783 grt in December 1998 (the third-largest national fleet in the world).

There is a weekly cargo and passenger service to all the Family Islands.

**Bahamas Maritime Authority:** POB N-4679, Nassau; tel. 394-5022; fax 394-5023; f. 1995; promotes ship registration and co-ordinates maritime administration.

**Freeport Harbour Co Ltd:** POB F-42465, Freeport; tel. 352-9651; fax 352-6888; e-mail fhcol@batelnet.bs; Gen. Man. MICHAEL J. POWER.

**Nassau Port Authority:** Prince George Wharf, POB N-8175, Nassau; tel. 356-7354; fax 322-5545; regulates principal port of the Bahamas; Port Dir ANTHONY ALLENS.

### Principal Shipping Companies

**Bahamas Ranger Ltd:** POB N-3709, Nassau.

**Cavalier Shipping:** Arawak Cay, POB N-8170, New Providence; tel. 328-3035.

**Dockendale Shipping Co Ltd:** Bitco Bldg, Bank Lane, POB N-10455, Nassau; tel. 325-0448; fax 328-1542; e-mail dockship@bahamas.net.bs; f. 1973; ship management; Man. Dir L. J. FERNANDES; Tech. Dir K. VALLURI.

**Eleuthera Express Shipping Co:** POB N-4201, Nassau.

**R. R. Farrington & Sons:** Union Dock, POB N-93, Nassau; tel. 322-2203.

**Grand Master Shipping Co:** POB N-4208, Nassau.

**Grenville Ventures Ltd:** 43 Elizabeth Ave, POB CB-13022, Nassau.

**HJH Trading Co Ltd:** POB N-4402, Nassau; tel. 392-3939; fax 392-1828.

**Gladstone Patton:** POB SS-5178, Nassau.

**Pioneer Shipping Ltd:** Union Wharf, POB N-3044, Nassau; tel. 325-7889; fax 325-2214.

**Seaboard Marine:** POB N-9087, Nassau; tel. 356-7624; fax 356-7804.

**Taylor Corporation:** POB N-1195, Nassau.

**Teekay Shipping Corporation:** 4th Floor, Euro Canadian Centre, Marlborough St & Lion Rd, POB SS-6293, Nassau; tel. 322-8020; fax 328-7330; internet www.teekay.com; Pres. and CEO BJORN MOLLER.

**Tropical Shipping Co Ltd:** POB N-8183, Nassau; tel. 322-1012; fax 323-7566.

**United Shipping Co Ltd:** POB F-42552, Freeport; tel. 352-9315; fax 352-4034.

## CIVIL AVIATION

Nassau International Airport (15 km (9 miles) outside the capital) and Freeport International Airport (5 km (3 miles) outside the city, on Grand Bahama) are the main terminals for international and internal services. There are also important airports at West End (Grand Bahama) and Rock Sound (Eleuthera) and some 50 smaller airports and landing strips throughout the islands.

**Bahamasair Holdings Ltd:** Coral Harbour Rd, POB N-4881, Nassau; tel. 377-8451; fax 377-8550; e-mail astuart@bahamasair.com; internet www.bahamasair.com; f. 1973; scheduled services between Nassau, Freeport, destinations within the USA and 20 locations within the Family Islands; Chair. ANTHONY MILLER; Man. Dir PAT ROLLE (acting).

# Tourism

The mild climate and beautiful beaches attract many tourists. In 1998 tourist arrivals decreased by 3.1%, compared with the previous year, to 3,346,329 (including 2,041,798 visitors by sea). The majority of stop-over arrivals (81% in 1997) were from the USA. Receipts from the tourist industry decreased by 0.6% in 1998, compared with the previous year, to B $1,408m. In September 1999 there were 223 hotels in the country, with a total of 14,080 rooms.

**Ministry of Tourism:** Bay St, POB N-3701, Nassau; tel. 322-7500; fax 328-0945; internet www.bahamas.com; Dir-Gen. VINCENT VANDERPOOL-WALLACE.

**Bahamas Hotel Association:** Dean's Lane, Fort Charlotte, POB N-7799, Nassau; tel. 322-8381; fax 326-5346; e-mail bhainfo@batelnet.bs; Exec. Vice-Pres. E. JOHN DELEVEAUX.

**Bahamas Tourism and Development Authority:** POB SS-5256, Nassau; tel. 394-3575; Exec. Dir DIANE PHILLIPS.

**Hotel Corporation of the Bahamas:** West Bay St, POB N-9520, Nassau; tel. 327-8395; fax 327-6978; Chair. GEOFFREY JOHNSTONE; Chief Exec. WARREN ROLLE.

# BAHRAIN

## Introductory Survey

### Location, Climate, Language, Religion, Flag, Capital

The State of Bahrain consists of a group of about 35 islands, situated midway along the Persian (Arabian) Gulf, approximately 24 km (15 miles) from the east coast of Saudi Arabia (to which it is linked by a causeway), and 28 km (17 miles) from the west coast of Qatar. There are six principal islands in the archipelago, and the largest of these is Bahrain itself, which is about 50 km (30 miles) long and between 13 km and 25 km (8 miles and 15 miles) wide. To the north-east of Bahrain island, and linked to it by a causeway and road, lies Muharraq island, which is approximately 6 km (4 miles) long. Another causeway links Bahrain with Sitra island. The climate is temperate from December to the end of March, with temperatures ranging between 19°C (66°F) and 25°C (77°F), but becomes very hot and humid during the summer months. In August and September temperatures can rise to 40°C (104°F). The official language is Arabic, but English is also widely spoken. Almost all Bahraini citizens are Muslims, divided into two sects: Shi'ites (almost 60%) and Sunnis (more than 40%). Non-Bahrainis comprised 36.4% of the total population at the 1991 census. The national flag (proportions 5 by 3) is red, with a vertical white stripe at the hoist, the two colours being separated by a straight or (more frequently) serrated line. The capital is Manama.

### Recent History

Bahrain, a traditional Arab monarchy, became a British Protected State in the 19th century. Under this arrangement, government was shared between the ruling sheikh and his British adviser. Following a series of territorial disputes in the 19th century, Persia (now Iran) made renewed claims to Bahrain in 1928. This disagreement remained unresolved until May 1970, when Iran accepted the findings of a report, commissioned by the UN, which showed that the inhabitants of Bahrain overwhelmingly favoured complete independence, rather than union with Iran.

During the reign of Sheikh Sulman bin Hamad al-Khalifa, who became ruler of Bahrain in 1942, social services and public works were considerably expanded. Sheikh Sulman died in November 1961 and was succeeded by his eldest son, Sheikh Isa bin Sulman al-Khalifa. Extensive administrative and political reforms were implemented in January 1970, when a supreme executive authority, the 12-member Council of State, was established, representing the first formal derogation of the ruler's powers. Sheikh Khalifa bin Sulman al-Khalifa, the ruler's eldest brother, was appointed President of the Council.

Meanwhile, in January 1968 the United Kingdom had announced its intention to withdraw British military forces from the area by 1971. In March 1968 Bahrain joined the nearby territories of Qatar and the Trucial States (now the United Arab Emirates), which were also under British protection, in the Federation of Arab Emirates. It was intended that the Federation should become fully independent, but the interests of Bahrain and Qatar proved to be incompatible with those of the smaller sheikhdoms, and both seceded from the Federation. Bahrain thus became a separate independent state on 15 August 1971, when a new treaty of friendship was signed with the United Kingdom. Sheikh Isa took the title of Amir, while the Council of State became the Cabinet, with Sheikh Khalifa as Prime Minister. A Constituent Assembly, convened in December 1972, formulated a new Constitution providing for a National Assembly to be comprised of 14 cabinet ministers and 30 elected members. On 6 December 1973 the Constitution came into force, and on the following day elections to the new Assembly were conducted. In the absence of political parties, candidates sought election in an individual capacity. In August 1975 the Prime Minister submitted his resignation, complaining that the National Assembly was obstructing the Government's initiatives for new legislation, particularly regarding national security. However, Sheikh Khalifa was reappointed and, at his request, the Assembly was dissolved by Amiri decree. New elections were to be conducted following minor changes to the Constitution and to the electoral law, but there were few subsequent signs that the National Assembly would be reconvened.

With no elected legislative body, the ruling family exercises near-absolute power. On 16 January 1993 a 30-member Consultative Council—appointed by the ruling authorities and comprising a large number of business executives and some members of the old National Assembly—held its inaugural meeting. As in other Gulf states, the Council acts in a purely advisory capacity, with no legislative powers.

Although major international territorial claims were brought to an end by the 1970 agreement with Iran, the Iranian revolution of 1979 led to uncertainty about possible future claims to Bahrain. There has also been evidence of tension between Shi'ite Muslims, who form a slender majority in Bahrain (and many of whom are of Iranian descent), and the dominant Sunni Muslims, the sect to which the ruling family belongs. During the 1980s two plots to overthrow the Government, one of which was alleged to have Iranian support, were uncovered, as was a plan to sabotage Bahrain's petroleum installations, which was also widely reported to have received Iranian support. In December 1993 the human rights organization Amnesty International published a report criticizing the Bahraini Government's treatment of Shi'ite Muslims, some of whom had been forcibly exiled. In March 1994, apparently in response to this criticism, the Amir issued a decree pardoning 64 Bahrainis who had been in exile since the 1980s and permitting them to return to Bahrain. In December Sheikh Ali Salman Ahmad Salman, a Muslim cleric, was arrested following his criticism of the Government and his public appeal for reform, particularly the restoration of the National Assembly. Widespread rioting ensued throughout Bahrain, especially in Shi'ite districts, and large-scale demonstrations were held in Manama in support of Sheikh Salman's demands and to petition for his release. Civil unrest ensued despite the Amir's pledge, in mid-December, to extend the powers of the Consultative Council; some 2,500 demonstrators were arrested and as many as 12 people were killed during clashes with the security forces in December and early January 1995. Sheikh Salman sought asylum in the United Kingdom, following his deportation in January. The unprecedented scale of the disturbances was widely attributed to a marked deterioration in socio-economic conditions in Bahrain, and in particular to a high level of unemployment.

Anti-Government demonstrations erupted in Shi'ite districts in late March 1995, and again in April, following a police search of the property of an influential Shi'ite clergyman, Sheikh Abd al-Amir al-Jamri, who was subsequently placed under house arrest and later imprisoned. In mid-April, after Bahrain convened a meeting of Ministers of the Interior of member states of the Gulf Co-operation Council (GCC—see below), the Governments of the GCC countries issued a statement supporting the measures adopted by Bahrain to quell civil disturbances. In May and July several people were sentenced to terms of imprisonment, ranging from one year to life imprisonment, for damaging public installations, and one Bahraini was sentenced to death for the murder of a police officer in March. In late June, in an apparent attempt to appease Shi'ite opposition leaders, the Prime Minister announced the first major cabinet reshuffle for 20 years. However, the important portfolios, of the interior, defence, finance and national economy, and foreign affairs, remained unchanged.

In mid-August 1995 the Government initiated talks with Shi'ite opposition leaders in an effort to foster reconciliation. In the same month the Amir issued a decree pardoning 150 people detained since the disturbances. A report issued by Amnesty International in September indicated that as many as 1,500 demonstrators remained in detention in Bahrain, and that two prisoners (including a 16-year-old student) had died in police custody following torture. In mid-September talks between the Government and opposition leaders collapsed. None the less, more than 40 political prisoners were released from detention later in the month, including Sheikh al-Jamri. In late October al-Jamri and six other opposition figures began a hunger strike in protest at the Government's refusal to concede to their demands, which included the release of all political prisoners and the restoration of the National Assembly. In early November, following a large demonstration to mark the end of the hunger strike, the Government announced that it would take 'necessary action' to prevent future 'illegal' gatherings. In December the Amir declared an amnesty for nearly 150 prisoners, mostly people arrested during the disturbances earlier in the year. Large-scale demonstrations were staged in late December and in early January 1996, in protest at the heavy deployment of security forces in Shi'ite districts and at the closure of two mosques. Opposition figures strongly criticized the use of tear-gas and plastic bullets to disperse protesters. It was also suggested that both Saudi Arabian and Indian security officers had been dispatched to reinforce the Bahrain police. In mid-January eight opposition leaders, including Sheikh al-Jamri, were arrested and accused of inciting unrest. In early February Ahmad ash-Shamlan, a noted lawyer and writer, became the first prominent Sunni to be arrested in connection with the disturbances, following his distribution of a statement criticizing the authoritarian actions of the Government. A number of car-bomb and fire-bomb explosions in February and early March culminated in an arson attack on a restaurant in Sitra, which resulted in the deaths of seven Bangladeshi workers. Also in March, jurisdiction with regard to a number of criminal offences was transferred from ordinary courts to the High Court of Appeal, acting in the capacity of State Security Court. This move effectively accelerated court proceedings, while removing the right of appeal and limiting the role of the defence. In late March Isa Ahmad Hassan Qambar was executed by firing squad, having been condemned to death for killing a policeman during clashes with security forces in March 1995 (see above). The execution was the first to be performed in Bahrain since 1977, and provoked massive popular protest and condemnation by international human rights organizations, which challenged the validity of Qambar's confession and trial. Civil disturbances continued during 1996, and tensions were exacerbated by the Government's announcement, in April, of the creation of a Higher Council of Islamic Affairs (to be appointed by the Prime Minister and headed by the Minister of Justice and Islamic Affairs), to supervise all religious activity (including that of the Shi'ite community) in the country. In early June, however, the Amir sought to appease the demands of opposition reformers by announcing the future expansion of the Consultative Council from 30 to 40 members. A new 40-member Council was appointed by the Amir in late September. In July the State Security Court imposed the death sentence on three of the eight Bahrainis convicted of the arson attack in Sitra. Another four men were sentenced to life imprisonment. The death sentences provoked widespread domestic protests and international criticism. In response the Government agreed to allow an appeal against the ruling. In October the Court of Cassation ruled that it had no jurisdiction to overturn the verdict, and the fate of the three men seemed likely to be decided by the Amir. Towards the end of the year government plans to close a number of Shi'ite mosques resulted in further unrest. Demonstrators who had gathered at the Ras Roman mosque in central Manama became involved in a violent confrontation with the security forces during which police fired tear-gas at worshippers. The continuing unrest in December and in early 1997 prompted rumours of division within the ruling family concerning the use of force in response to the crisis. In January 1997 a National Guard was created, to provide support for the Bahraini Defence Force and the security forces of the Ministry of the Interior. The Amir's son, Hamad, was appointed to command the new force, prompting speculation that its primary duty would be to protect the ruling family. In March a week of anti-Government protests marked the first anniversary of the execution of Isa Ahmad Hassan Qambar. It was reported that since the outbreak of civil unrest at the end of 1994, some 28 people had been killed and 220 imprisoned in connection with the disturbances. In July and August 1997 two human rights groups produced reports criticizing the Bahraini police for allegedly making arbitrary arrests, using torture, and arresting children as young as seven years of age. The Government rejected these reports, claiming that they were based on dishonest sources. The Government, however, appeared to respond to these criticisms when, in November, the trial *in absentia* of eight prominent exiled activists (including Sheikh Ali Salman Ahmad Salman) resulted in the imposition of prison sentences of between five and 15 years. Although the activists claimed not to have been summoned to stand trial, their sentences were considered lenient, in view of the severity of the offences with which they were charged, which included attempting to overthrow the regime. In addition, during 1997 publishing restrictions were relaxed, and in December the Amir announced plans to enlarge further the Consultative Council and to allow greater media coverage of its affairs. In February 1998 opposition groups welcomed the appointment of Khalid bin Muhammad al-Khalifa as the new head of the State Security Investigation Directorate (the previous, long-serving, incumbent was not a Bahraini national) and urged the continuing 'Bahrainization' of the security apparatus as a precondition for the initiation of dialogue between the regime and the opposition.

On 6 March 1999 Sheikh Isa died and was succeeded as Amir by his son, the Crown Prince, Sheikh Hamad bin Isa al-Khalifa, hitherto Commander-in-Chief of the Bahrain Defence Force and the National Guard; Sheikh Hamad was replaced in both his previous offices by his eldest son, Sheikh Salman bin Hamad al-Khalifa. Opposition groups welcomed Sheikh Hamad's accession which raised expectations of political change. In his first months in office Sheikh Hamad permitted Shi'ites to join the armed forces, allowed an investigation by Amnesty International into alleged brutality by the Sunni security forces and released more than 300 Shi'ite prisoners being held on security-related charges. However, the opposition claimed that 1,200–1,500 political prisoners remained in detention and, despite the initial optimism among opposition groups, Sheikh Hamad failed promptly to initiate negotiations to end political unrest. On 31 May Sheikh Hamad announced a cabinet reorganization in which three new ministers were appointed, including the former Governor of the Bahrain Monetary Agency, Abdullah Hassan Saif, as Minister of Finance. However, few significant changes were effected and, despite tension in relations between the new Amir and the hardline Sheikh Khalifa, Sheikh Khalifa retained his position as Prime Minister. In July Sheikh al-Jamri, who was brought to trial in February, having been detained since 1996 under the terms of the State Security Act (which provides for the imprisonment of suspects without trial for a period of up to three years) was sentenced to 10 years' imprisonment for spying and inciting anti-Government unrest; a substantial fine was also imposed. Following intense international pressure Sheikh Hamad granted him an official pardon the following day, although Sheikh al-Jamri was first required to read a public apology to the Amir on national television. In December 1999 the Amir announced his intention to introduce elected municipal councils on the basis of universal suffrage. He indicated that the councils could lead to fuller popular representation in Bahrain, although no timescale was given for their establishment.

Although relations between Bahrain and Iran were upgraded to ambassadorial level in late 1990, the situation between the two countries began to deteriorate in the mid-1990s. While there was sufficient evidence to suggest largely domestic motivation for the recent increase in popular disaffection, the Bahraini authorities continued to imply that the disturbances were the result of the efforts of Iranian-backed Shi'ite fundamentalist terrorists to destabilize the country. These allegations were frequently dismissed by the Iranian press. In early June 1996 the Bahraini Government announced that it had uncovered details of a carefully-planned terrorist campaign, initiated in 1993 with support from fundamentalist Shi'ite groups in Iran, which sought to oust the Government and ruling family in Bahrain and replace them with a pro-Iranian administration. It was claimed that a previously unknown Shi'ite terrorist group, Hezbollah Bahrain, had been established and financed by Iran's Revolutionary Guard. Young Bahraini Shi'ites were alleged to have received military training in Iran and at guerrilla bases in Lebanon, in preparation for a terrorist offensive in Bahrain, which had culminated in the disturbances of the previous 18 months. Within days of the Government's announcement more than 50 Bahrainis had been arrested in connection with the plot. Many of the detained persons admitted membership of Hezbollah Bahrain, including six prisoners who made confessions on national television. The Iranian authorities denied any involvement in the planned insurrection, but bilateral relations were severely undermined by the unprecedented directness of the Bahraini Government's accusations, and diplomatic relations between the two countries were downgraded in early June. While the national press congratulated the Government and the security services for discovering the conspiracy, independent observers were again sceptical of the validity of confessions obtained during detention with no legal representation, and further doubts were expressed that the inexpert execution of recent terrorist acts in Bahrain was inconsistent with the involvement of an established movement such as Hezbollah. During June more than 30 Bahrainis received prison sentences of between one and 13 years—for offences connected to the disturbances—from the State Security Court (and were therefore denied the right of appeal). In March 1997 59 Bahraini Shi'ites accused of belonging to Hezbollah Bahrain were brought to trial. The State Security Court sentenced 37 of the defendants to terms of imprisonment ranging from three to 15 years, and acquitted the others. Following talks in December, relations at ambassadorial level were re-established between Bahrain and Iran.

In March 1981 Bahrain was one of the six founder-members of the Co-operation Council for the Arab States of the Gulf (more generally known as the Gulf Co-operation Council—GCC, see p. 153), which was established in order to co-ordinate defence strategy and to promote freer trading and co-operative economic protection among Gulf states.

In common with other Gulf states, Bahrain consistently expressed support for Iraq at the time of the Iran–Iraq war (1980–88). However, following the Iraqi invasion of Kuwait in August 1990, Bahrain firmly supported the implementation of UN economic sanctions against Iraq and permitted the stationing of US troops and combat aircraft in Bahrain. (Military co-operation with the USA had been close for many years.) In June 1991, following the liberation of Kuwait in February, it was confirmed that Bahrain would remain a regional support base for the USA, and later in the year the two countries signed a defence co-operation agreement. In January 1994 Bahrain signed further accords of military co-operation with the USA and the United Kingdom. Relations with Iraq, however, remained strained, and in October hopes of improved relations receded when Iraqi forces were again deployed in the Iraq–Kuwait border area, in an apparent threat to Kuwait's sovereignty. In response, Bahrain deployed combat aircraft and naval units to join GCC and US forces in the defence of Kuwait. In late 1995 Bahrain agreed to the temporary deployment on its territory of US fighter aircraft in order to deter any possible military threat from Iraq. In February 1998 Bahrain strongly advocated a diplomatic solution to the ongoing dispute between Iraq and the UN weapons inspectors (see chapter on Iraq) and refused to allow US military aircraft to launch attacks on Iraq from Bahraini bases. In June, as part of a wider US effort to reduce its military presence in the region, US military aircraft were withdrawn from Bahrain. In December a further US-led military campaign against Iraq was supported by the Bahraini authorities (the operation was centred in Manama where the US Fifth Fleet is based) although Bahrain refrained from any public endorsement of the air strikes; in August 1999 it was reported that Bahrain desired a further reduction of the US military presence in Bahrain, particularly that of the Fifth Fleet.

In April 1986 Qatari military forces raided the island of Fasht ad-Dibal, which had been artificially constructed on a coral reef (submerged at high tide), situated midway between Bahrain and Qatar; both countries claimed sovereignty over the island. Following GCC mediation, in May the two Governments agreed to destroy the island. Other areas of dispute between the two countries are Zubara (which was part of Bahraini territory until the early 20th century), in mainland Qatar, and the region of the Hawar islands, which is believed to contain potentially valuable reserves of petroleum and natural gas. In July 1991 Qatar instituted proceedings at the International Court of Justice (ICJ) regarding the issue of the Hawar islands (in 1939 a British judgment had awarded sovereignty of the islands to Bahrain), the shoals of Dibal and Qit'at Jaradah (over which the British had recognized Bahrain's 'sovereign rights' in 1947), together with the delimitation of the maritime border between Qatar and Bahrain. The question of sovereignty was further confused in April 1992, when the Government of Qatar issued a decree redefining its maritime borders to include territorial waters claimed by Bahrain, and tensions were exacerbated by Qatar's persistent rejection of Bahrain's insistence that the two countries should seek joint recourse to the ICJ. Moreover, it was reported that Bahrain had attempted to widen the issue to include its claim to the Zubara region. Qatar applied unilaterally to the Court and in February 1995 the ICJ ruled that it would have authority to adjudicate in the dispute. Relations between Bahrain and Qatar deteriorated in September, following the Bahraini Government's decision to construct a tourist resort on the Hawar islands, and remained tense subsequently, with the Bahraini Government advocating a regional solution to the dispute in preference to ICJ jurisdiction. In December 1996 Bahrain boycotted the GCC annual summit convened in Doha, Qatar, at which it was decided to establish a quadripartite committee (comprising those GCC members not involved in the dispute) to facilitate a solution. The committee reportedly made some progress towards resolving the territorial dispute, and following meetings between prominent government ministers from Bahrain and Qatar in London, United Kingdom, and Manama in early 1997, it was announced that diplomatic relations at ambassadorial level were to be established between the two countries. Qatar nominated its diplomatic representative shortly after the exchange of ambassadors was agreed, but by late 1998 Bahrain had yet to nominate its candidate. By November regional attempts to find a solution to the territorial dispute had not proved successful, and the announcement of Bahraini construction plans on the Hawar islands (which, in addition to the opening of a hotel in mid-1997, included a housing complex and a causeway linking the islands to Bahrain) did little to further relations between the two countries. Bahrain has stated that it will disregard any ruling by the ICJ, and has also dismissed as a forgery a series of documents supporting the Qatari claim, which was submitted to the ICJ by the Qatari Government. In September 1998 Qatar presented a report to the ICJ in support of the legitimacy of the documents, although it subsequently agreed to withdraw them from evidence. At the end of 1999 the Amir of Qatar made his first official visit to Manama, during which it was agreed that a joint committee, headed by the Crown Princes of Bahrain and Qatar, would be established to encourage co-operation between the two countries. Qatar also agreed to withdraw its petition from the ICJ in the event of the joint committee reaching a solution to the territorial disputes. A second senior-level meeting was held in early January 2000, when the new Amir of Bahrain, Sheikh Hamad, made his first visit to Qatar. The two countries agreed to hasten the opening of embassies in Manama and Doha; Bahrain reportedly nominated an ambassador to Qatar. It was also reported that a date had been set for the inaugural meeting of the afore-mentioned joint committee.

**Government**

Bahrain is ruled by an Amir through an appointed Cabinet.

**Defence**

Military service is voluntary. In August 1999 the Bahraini Defence Force consisted of some 11,000 men (8,500 army, 1,000 navy, 1,500 air force). There were also paramilitary forces of an estimated 10,150 men (9,000 police, 900 national guard, 250 coastguard). The defence budget for 1999 was estimated at BD 115m.

**Economic Affairs**

In 1995, according to estimates by the World Bank, Bahrain's gross national product (GNP), measured at average 1993–95 prices, was US $4,525m., equivalent to $7,840 per head. During 1985–95, it was estimated, GNP per head increased, in real terms, at an average rate of 0.6% per year, while the population increased at an average annual rate of 3.4%. In 1998 GNP was estimated at $4,912m. ($7,660 per head). During 1991–96 the country's gross domestic product (GDP) increased, in real terms, an average rate of 4.7% per year.

Agriculture and fishing engaged an estimated 1.1% of the employed labour force in 1998, and contributed 1.0% of GDP in 1995. The principal crops are dates and tomatoes. Poultry production is also important. Agricultural GDP increased, in real terms, at an average annual rate of 2.4% during 1985–94.

Industry (comprising mining, manufacturing, construction and utilities) engaged 28.2% of the employed labour force in 1991, and provided 44.0% of GDP in 1995. Industrial GDP increased, in real terms, at an average annual rate of 4.0% during 1985–94.

Mining and quarrying engaged 1.7% of the employed labour force in 1991, and contributed 15.8% of GDP in 1995. The major mining activities are the exploitation of petroleum and natural gas. At 1994 levels of production (105,000 barrels per day), Bahrain's known reserves of crude petroleum will have been exhausted by 2000. By the end of 1998 petroleum production had declined to 37,674 barrels per day. There are sufficient reserves of natural gas to maintain the 1998 output level (7,900m. cu m) for 15.0 years. In real terms, the GDP of the mining sector increased at an average rate of 2.0% per year during 1985–94.

In 1991 manufacturing engaged 12.6% of the employed labour force; the sector provided 20.5% of GDP in 1995. Important industries include the petroleum refinery at Sitra, aluminium (Bahrain is the region's largest producer) and aluminium-related enterprises, shipbuilding, iron and steel and chemicals. Since the mid-1980s the Government has encouraged the development of light industry. Manufacturing GDP increased at an average annual rate of 7.1% during 1985–94.

Industrial expansion has resulted in energy demands which threaten to exceed the country's 1,126-MW total installed generating capacity, particularly as not all of the installed capacity is operational, owing to the advanced age of a number of stations. A programme of refurbishment and expansion, which included private-sector funding, had begun by 1999. Despite these improvements, and an agreement with Aluminium Bahrain to provide an additional 275 MW annually until 2004, it was estimated that a further 560 MW would be required by 2006.

Banking is a major source of Bahrain's prosperity. Since the mid-1970s the Government has licensed 'offshore' banking units (OBUs). Largely owing to regional instability, by 1997 the number of OBUs had declined to 47, compared with 56 prior to the Iraqi invasion and occupation of Kuwait in 1990–91, and 74 in mid-1985. Despite the decline in banking activity, the GDP of the services sector increased, in real terms, at an average annual rate of 2.6% during 1985–94. The sector contributed 54.9% of GDP in 1995. A stock exchange was inaugurated in Bahrain in 1989. It has since been linked to the Oman and Jordan Stock Exchanges (with each other's shares listed under reciprocal agreements), and in 1997 plans were announced to link it to the Kuwait Stock Exchange.

In 1998 Bahrain recorded a visible trade surplus of US $71.3m. and there was a deficit of $1,042.0m. on the current account of the balance of payments. In 1998 the principal sources of non-petroleum imports were Japan (accounting for 11.5% of the total), the USA (10.4%), Australia, the United Kingdom, Saudi Arabia, Italy and Germany. Saudi Arabia also provided most of Bahrain's petroleum imports (and accounted for 50.8% of all imports in 1990). Saudi Arabia was the principal customer for Bahrain's non-petroleum exports (18.0% of the total) in 1998; other important markets were the USA (13.3%), Japan, India and Taiwan. The principal exports are petroleum, petroleum products and aluminium. Sales of petroleum and petroleum products provided 67.2% of total export earnings in 1996. The principal import is crude petroleum (for domestic refining), accounting for 41.8% of total imports in 1996. The main category of non-petroleum imports (21.4% in 1997) is machinery and transport equipment.

In the financial year ending 31 December 1997 there was a budgetary deficit of BD 125.2m. (equivalent to 5.5% of GDP). The average annual rate of inflation was 1.1% in 1990–96; consumer prices increased by an annual average of 2.7% in 1995, but decreased by an annual average of 0.2% in 1996. About 60% of the labour force were expatriates in 1994. The official rate of unemployment among the national labour force was 1.8% in late 1995; however, Western diplomats estimated the level of unemployment to have reached 25%–30%.

Bahrain is a member of the Gulf Co-operation Council (GCC, see p. 153), which seeks to co-ordinate defence strategy and to promote freer trading and co-operative economic protection among Gulf states. The country is also a member of the Organization of Arab Petroleum Exporting Countries (OAPEC, see p. 248), the Arab Monetary Fund (see p. 290) and the Islamic Development Bank (see p. 216).

In recognition of the fact that Bahrain's reserves of petroleum and natural gas are nearing exhaustion, the Government has introduced measures both to diversify the country's industrial base and to attract wider foreign investment. During the 1990s the Government continued to encourage the greater participation of the private sector in economic development and indicated that it would adopt a gradual approach to the privatization of state enterprises (excluding the petroleum sector), and would prioritize employment opportunities for Bahraini nationals. By early 1997 the Government had announced a three-year development programme, which included the proposed creation of a port and free-trade zone at Hidd on Muharraq island, a new power-station and desalination plant, and the renovation of Bahrain's international airport. In 1998 plans were announced for the expansion of tourism facilities on Ad-Dar island, and for a seven-year investment programme in the power and water sector, projected to cost an estimated BD 700m. By 1999 work had begun on the port and industrial area at Hidd as well as on the power and water complex, which was scheduled for completion by 2005. The two-year budget for 1999–2000 forecast a deficit of some BD 320m., double that forecast for 1997–98, as a result of a sharp decline in world petroleum prices in 1998. However, following an agreement by both OPEC and non-OPEC producers to cut production from April 1999, petroleum prices improved considerably and seemed likely to result in a greatly reduced deficit for 1999.

## Social Welfare

The state-administered medical service provides comprehensive treatment for all residents, including expatriates. There are also physicians, dentists and opticians in private practice. In 1988 Bahrain had 1,445 hospital beds. In that year there were seven hospitals, 19 government health centres and seven government maternity centres. A social security law covers pensions, industrial accidents, sickness, unemployment, maternity and family allowances. In the early 1990s there were 11 physicians per 100,000 inhabitants and 289 nursing personnel per 100,000 inhabitants working in the country. Of total expenditure by the central Government in 1997, BD 61.2m. (10.1%) was for health, and a further BD 24.4m. (3.9%) for social security and welfare.

## Education

Education is compulsory for nine years between the ages of six and 14 and is available free of charge. Private and religious education are also available. The education system is composed of three different stages: primary and intermediate schooling, which together form 'basic education', and secondary schooling. Primary education lasts for six years from the age of six; it is divided into two cycles, each comprising three years. Intermediate education lasts for three years, between the ages of 12 and 14. Entry to secondary education, which comprises three years between the ages of 15 and 17, is conditional on obtaining the Intermediate School Certificate or its equivalent. The student chooses between five curriculums: science, literature, commerce, applied curriculums (five branches) and a technical curriculum. The University of Bahrain, established by Amiri decree in 1986, comprises five colleges: the College of Engineering, the College of Arts, the College of Science, the College of Education and the College of Business and Management. About 8,160 students were enrolled at the university in 1998. The Arabian Gulf University (AGU), funded by seven Arab governments, also provides higher education. In 1998 it comprised two colleges: the Medicine and Medical Sciences College and the Post-Graduate College. The University campus is due to be completed at the end of 2006, and will accommodate 5,000 students. In 1998 557 students were enrolled at the AGU. The College of Health Sciences provides post-secondary education and was attended by 696 students in 1998. In 1996 enrolment at primary, intermediate and secondary levels was 97.8% (males 97.6%; females 97.9%), 96.0% (males 96.4%; females 95.5%) and 95.0% (males 90.2%; females 99.9%), respectively, of the relevant age-groups. Expenditure on education by the central Government in 1997 was BD 84.8m. (13.7% of total expenditure). According to UNESCO estimates, the average rate of adult illiteracy in 1995 was 14.8% (males 10.9%; females 20.6%).

## Public Holidays

**2000:** 1 January (New Year's Day), 8 January*† (Id al-Fitr, end of Ramadan), 16 March* (Id al-Adha, Feast of the Sacrifice), 6 April* (Muharram, Islamic New Year), 15 April* (Ashoura), 15 June* (Mouloud, Birth of the Prophet), 16 December (National Day), 28 December*† (Id al-Fitr, end of Ramadan).

**2001:** 1 January (New Year's Day), 6 March* (Id al-Adha, Feast of the Sacrifice), 26 March* (Muharram, Islamic New Year), 4 April* (Ashoura), 4 June* (Mouloud, Birth of the Prophet), 16 December (National Day), 17 December* (Id al-Fitr, end of Ramadan).

* These holidays are dependent on the Islamic lunar calendar and may vary by one or two days from the dates given.

† This festival will occur twice (in the Islamic years AH 1420 and AH 1421) within the same Gregorian year.

## Weights and Measures

The metric system is being introduced.

# Statistical Survey

Source (unless otherwise stated): Central Statistics Organization, POB 5835, Manama; tel. 725725; fax 728989.

## AREA AND POPULATION

**Area** (1995): 707.3 sq km (273.1 sq miles).

**Population:** 350,798 (males 204,793, females 146,005) at census of 5 April 1981; 508,037 (males 294,346, females 213,691), comprising 323,305 Bahrainis (males 163,453, females 159,852) and 184,732 non-Bahraini nationals (males 130,893, females 53,839), at census of 16 November 1991; 640,000 (official estimate) at mid-1998.

**Density** (mid-1998): 904.8 per sq km.

**Principal Towns** (population in 1991): Manama (capital) 136,999; Muharraq Town 74,245. *Mid-1992:* Manama 140,401.

**Births, Marriages and Deaths** (1995): Registered live births 13,481 (birth rate 23.3 per 1,000); Registered marriages 3,321 (marriage rate 5.7 per 1,000); Registered deaths 1,910 (death rate 3.3 per 1,000).

**Expectation of Life** (UN estimates, years at birth, 1990–95): 71.6 (males 69.8; females 74.1). Source: UN, *World Population Prospects: The 1998 Revision*.

**Economically Active Population** (persons aged 15 years and over, 1991 census): Agriculture, hunting, forestry and fishing 5,108; Mining and quarrying 3,638; Manufacturing 26,618; Electricity, gas and water 2,898; Construction 26,738; Trade, restaurants and hotels 29,961; Transport, storage and communications 13,789; Financing, insurance, real estate and business services 17,256; Community, social and personal services 83,944; Activities not adequately defined 2,120; *Total employed* 212,070 (males 177,154; females 34,916); Unemployed 14,378 (males 9,703; females 4,675); *Total labour force* 226,448 (males 186,857; females 39,591), comprising 90,662 Bahrainis (males 73,118, females 17,544) and 135,786 non-Bahraini nationals (males 113,739, females 22,047). *Mid-1998* (estimates): Agriculture, etc. 3,000; Total 268,000 (Source: FAO, *Production Yearbook*).

## AGRICULTURE, ETC.

**Principal Crops** ('000 metric tons, 1998): Tomatoes 5; Other vegetables 7; Dates 16*; Other fruits 5*. *FAO estimate. Source: FAO, *Production Yearbook*.

**Livestock** ('000 head, year ending September 1998): Cattle 13; Camels 1*; Sheep 17; Goats 16. * FAO estimate. Source: FAO, *Production Yearbook*.

**Livestock Products** ('000 metric tons, 1998): Mutton and lamb 5*; Goat meat 2*; Poultry meat 5; Milk 14; Poultry eggs 3. * FAO estimate. Source: FAO, *Production Yearbook*.

**Fishing** ('000 metric tons, live weight): Total catch 9.4 in 1995; 12.9 in 1996; 10.1 in 1997. Source: FAO, *Yearbook of Fishery Statistics*.

## MINING

**Production** (1995): Crude petroleum 14,459,000 barrels; Natural gas 7,701.7 million cubic metres.

## INDUSTRY

**Production** ('000 barrels, unless otherwise indicated, 1995): Liquefied petroleum gas 365; Naphtha 12,772; Motor spirit (Gasoline) 7,766; Kerosene 11,327; Jet fuel 6,219; Fuel oil 20,807; Diesel oil and gas oil 31,024; Petroleum bitumen (asphalt) 1,399; Electric energy 4,611.9 million kWh; Aluminium (unwrought) 461,245 metric tons (1996).

## FINANCE

**Currency and Exchange Rates:** 1,000 fils = 1 Bahraini dinar (BD). *Sterling, Dollar and Euro Equivalents* (30 September 1999): £1 sterling = 619.1 fils; US $1 = 376.0 fils; €1 = 401.0 fils; 100 Bahraini dinars = £161.53 = $265.96 = €249.37. *Exchange Rate:* Fixed at US $1 = 376.0 fils (BD 1 = $2.6596) since November 1980.

**Budget** (BD million, 1997): *Revenue:* Taxation 154.7 (Taxes on income and profits 31.9, Social security contributions 33.0, Domestic taxes on goods and services 19.6, Import duties 55.5); Entrepreneurial and property income 446.3; Other current revenue 32.1; Capital revenue 0.1; Total 633.2, excl. grants from abroad (46.9). *Expenditure:* General public services 73.8; Defence 109.0; Public order and safety 91.4; Education 84.8; Health 61.2 Social security and welfare 24.4; Housing and community amenities 22.3; Recreational, cultural and religious affairs and services 10.5; Economic affairs and services 121.1 (Fuel and energy 89.1, Transport and communications 23.4); Interest payments 21.5; Total 620.0 (Current 516.3, Capital 103.7), excl. lending minus repayments (185.3). Source: IMF, *Government Finance Statistics Yearbook*.
*1998* (forecasts, BD million): Revenue 630; Expenditure 705.

**International Reserves** (US $ million at 31 December 1998): Gold (valued at $44 per troy oz) 6.6; IMF special drawing rights 17.1; Reserve position in IMF 68.3; Foreign exchange 993.8; Total 1,085.8. Source: IMF, *International Financial Statistics*.

**Money Supply** (BD million at 31 December 1998): Currency outside banks 93.30; Demand deposits at commercial banks 272.30; Total money 365.60. Source: IMF, *International Financial Statistics*.

**Cost of Living** (Consumer Price Index for Bahraini nationals; base: 1995 = 100): 97.3 in 1994; 100.0 in 1995; 99.8 in 1996. Source: IMF, *International Financial Statistics*.

**Expenditure on the Gross Domestic Product** (BD million, 1998): Government final consumption expenditure 482.8; Private final consumption expenditure 1,193.8; Increase in stocks 83.6; Gross fixed capital formation 326.2; *Total domestic expenditure* 2,086.4; Exports of goods and services 1,818.9; *Less* Imports of goods and services 1,580.1; *GDP in purchasers' values* 2,325.2. Source: IMF, *International Financial Statistics*.

**Gross Domestic Product by Economic Activity** (BD million at current prices, 1995): Agriculture, hunting, forestry and fishing 20.5; Mining and quarrying 316.6; Manufacturing 412.1; Electricity, gas and water 58.4; Construction 97.9; Trade, restaurants and hotels 151.0; Transport, storage and communications 158.2; Finance, insurance, real estate and business services 328.0; Government services 369.5; Other community, social and personal services 97.2; *Sub-total* 2,009.4; *Less* Imputed bank service charge 170.7; *GDP at factor cost* 1,838.7; Indirect taxes (net) 61.6; *GDP in purchasers' values* 1,900.2.

**Balance of Payments** (US $ million, 1998): Exports of goods f.o.b. 3,270.2; Imports of goods f.o.b. –3,198.9; *Trade balance* 71.3; Exports of services 769.1; Imports of services –739.9; *Balance on goods and services* 100.5; Other income received 4,768.1; Other income paid –5,250.8; *Balance on goods, services and income* –382.2; Current transfers received 65.2; Current transfers paid –725.0; *Current balance* –1,042.0; Capital account (net) 100.0; Direct investment abroad –180.9; Direct investment from abroad –2,135.6; Portfolio investment assets –1,221.3; Portfolio investment liabilities 608.5; Other investment assets –14,636.4; Other investment liabilities 17,692.3; Net errors and omissions 798.8; *Overall balance* –16.6. Source: IMF, *International Financial Statistics*.

## EXTERNAL TRADE

**Total Trade** (BD million): *Imports c.i.f.:* 1,606.6 in 1996; 1,513.6 in 1997; 1,301.9 in 1998. *Exports:* 1,767.1 in 1996; 1,648.2 in 1997; 1,229.2 in 1998. Source: IMF, *International Financial Statistics*.

**Principal Commodities** (BD million, 1997): *Imports c.i.f.:* Live animals and animal products 45.6; Vegetable products 53.0; Prepared foodstuffs, beverages, spirits, vinegar and tobacco 65.0; Mineral products 50.6; Products of chemical or allied industries 142.3; Plastics, rubber and articles thereof 32.2; Paper-making material, paper and paperboard and articles thereof 28.4; Textiles and textile articles 70.3; Articles of stone, plaster, cement, asbestos, mica, etc., ceramic products, glass and glassware 23.2; Base metals and articles thereof 95.7; Machinery and mechanical appliances, electrical equipment, sound and television apparatus 210.5; Vehicles, aircraft, vessels and associated transport equipment 76.0; Optical, photographic, cinematographic, measuring, precision and medical apparatus, clocks and watches, musical instruments 21.5; Miscellaneous manufactured articles 30.4; Total (incl. others) 984.5. *Exports f.o.b.:* Products of chemicals and allied industries 56.4; Paper-making material, paper and paperboard, and articles thereof 14.7; Textiles and textile articles 54.0; Base metals and articles of base metal 416.4; Machinery and mechanical appliances, electrical equipment, sound and television apparatus 13.4; Vehicles, aircraft, vessels and associated transport equipment 12.7; Total (incl. others) 627.5. Note: Figures exclude trade in petroleum.

**Principal Trading Partners** (provisional figures, BD million, 1998): *Imports c.i.f.:* Australia 104.0; France 38.0; Germany 60.6; India 33.5; Italy 61.4; Japan 122.4; Saudi Arabia 76.4; United Arab Emirates 35.7; United Kingdom 79.3; USA 110.5; Total (incl. others) 1,066.9. *Exports f.o.b.:* India 34.5; Italy 14.4; Japan 54.2; Republic of Korea 25.9; Kuwait 17.9; Netherlands 17.7; Saudi Arabia 100.5; Taiwan 32.1; United Arab Emirates 25.7; USA 74.0; Total (incl. others) 556.9, excl. re-exports (35.7). Note: Figures exclude trade in petroleum.

### TRANSPORT

**Road Traffic** (registered motor vehicles, 31 December 1997): Passenger cars 149,636; Buses and coaches 4,490; Lorries and vans 27,723; Motorcycles 1,846. Source: IRF, *World Road Statistics*.

**Shipping** (international sea-borne freight traffic, '000 metric tons, 1990): *Goods loaded:* Dry cargo 1,145; Petroleum products 12,140. *Goods unloaded:* Dry cargo 3,380; Petroleum products 132. Source: UN, *Monthly Bulletin of Statistics*. *Merchant Fleet* (31 December 1998): Registered vessels 110; Total displacement 283,704 grt. Source: Lloyd's Register of Shipping, *World Fleet Statistics*.

**Civil Aviation** (1995): Kilometres flown (million) 21; Passengers carried ('000) 1,073; Passenger-km (million) 2,766; Total ton-km (million) 395. Figures include an apportionment (equivalent to one-quarter) of the traffic of Gulf Air, a multinational airline with its headquarters in Bahrain. Source: UN, *Statistical Yearbook*.

### TOURISM

**Tourist Arrivals** (1996): 1,757,000.

**Tourist Receipts** (1996): US $258 million.

Source: World Tourism Organization, *Yearbook of Tourism Statistics*.

### COMMUNICATIONS MEDIA

**Radio Receivers** (1996): 330,000 in use.

**Television Receivers** (1996): 268,000 in use.

**Telephones** (1995): 141,000 main lines in use.

**Telefax Stations** (number in use, 1995): 5,730.

**Mobile Cellular Telephones** (subscribers, 1995): 27,600.

**Book Production** (1996, first editions only): 40 titles.

**Daily Newspapers** (1996): 4 (circulation 67,000 copies).

**Non-daily Newspapers** (1993): 5 (circulation 17,000 copies).

**Other Periodicals** (1993): 26 (circulation 73,000 copies).

Sources: UNESCO, *Statistical Yearbook*; UN, *Statistical Yearbook*.

### EDUCATION

**Pre-Primary:** 90 schools (1996/97); 449 teachers (1995/96); 12,308 pupils (1996/97).

**Primary** (1996/97): 72,876 pupils.

**General Secondary** (1996/97): 49,897 pupils.

**Vocational Secondary** (1996/97): 7,287 pupils.

Source: UNESCO, *Statistical Yearbook*.

# Directory

## The Constitution

A 108-article Constitution was ratified in June 1973. It states that 'all citizens shall be equal before the law' and guarantees freedom of speech, of the press, of conscience and religious beliefs. Other provisions include the outlawing of the compulsory repatriation of political refugees. The Constitution also states that the country's financial comptroller should be responsible to the legislature and not to the Government, and allows for national trade unions 'for legally justified causes and on peaceful lines'. Compulsory free primary education and free medical care are also laid down in the Constitution. The Constitution, which came into force on 6 December 1973, also provided for a National Assembly, composed of 14 members of the Cabinet and 30 members elected by popular vote, although this was dissolved in August 1975.

## The Government

### HEAD OF STATE

**Amir:** Sheikh HAMAD BIN ISA AL-KHALIFA (succeeded to the throne on 6 March 1999).

**Crown Prince and Commander-in-Chief of Bahraini Defence Force and National Guard:** Sheikh SALMAN BIN HAMAD AL-KHALIFA.

### CABINET
(January 2000)

**Prime Minister:** Sheikh KHALIFA BIN SULMAN AL-KHALIFA.

**Minister of Justice and Islamic Affairs:** Sheikh ABDULLAH BIN KHALIFA KHALID AL-KHALIFA.

**Minister of Foreign Affairs:** Sheikh MUHAMMAD BIN MUBARAK BIN HAMAD AL-KHALIFA.

**Minister of the Interior:** Sheikh MUHAMMAD BIN KHALIFA BIN HAMAD AL-KHALIFA.

**Minister of Transport:** Sheikh ALI BIN KHALIFA BIN SALMAN AL-KHALIFA.

**Minister of State:** JAWAD SALIM AL-ARRAYEDH.

**Minister of Housing, Municipalities and Environment:** Sheikh KHALID BIN ABDULLAH BIN KHALID AL-KHALIFA.

**Minister of State:** MAJID JAWAD AL-JISHI.

**Minister of Public Works and Agriculture:** ALI IBRAHIM AL-MAHROUS.

**Minister of Finance and National Economy:** ABDULLAH HASSAN SAIF.

**Minister of Defence:** Maj.-Gen. Sheikh KHALIFA BIN AHMAD AL-KHALIFA.

**Minister of Cabinet Affairs and Information:** MUHAMMAD IBRAHIM AL-MUTAWA.

**Minister of Oil and Industry:** Sheikh ISA BIN ALI AL-KHALIFA.

**Minister of Commerce:** ALI SALEH ABDULLAH AS-SALEH.

**Minister of Education:** Brig.-Gen. ABD AL-AZIZ BIN MUHAMMAD AL-FADHIL.

**Minister of Health:** Dr FAISAL RADHI AL-MOUSAWI.

**Minister of Power and Water:** Sheikh DAIJ BIN KHALIFA BIN MUHAMMAD AL-KHALIFA.

**Minister of Labour and Social Affairs:** ABD AN-NABI ASH-SHULA.

**Minister of Amiri Court Affairs:** Sheikh ALI BIN ISA BIN SULMAN AL-KHALIFA.

### MINISTRIES

**Amiri Court:** POB 555, Riffa Palace, Manama; tel. 661252.

**Office of the Prime Minister:** POB 1000, Government House, Government Rd, Manama; tel. 225522; fax 229022.

**Ministry of Cabinet Affairs and Information:** POB 26613, Government House, Government Rd, Manama; tel. 223366; fax 225202.

**Ministry of Commerce:** POB 5479, Diplomatic Area, Manama; tel. 531531; fax 530455.

**Ministry of Defence:** POB 245, West Rifa'a; tel. 665599; fax 662854.

**Ministry of Education:** POB 43, Isa Town; tel. 685558; fax 680161.

**Ministry of Finance and National Economy:** POB 333, Diplomatic Area, Manama; tel. 530800; fax 532853.

**Ministry of Foreign Affairs:** POB 547, Government House, Government Rd, Manama; tel. 227555; fax 212603.

**Ministry of Health:** POB 12, Sheikh Sulman Rd, Manama; tel. 255555; fax 254459.

**Ministry of Housing, Municipalities and Environment:** POB 11802, Diplomatic Area, Manama; tel. 533000; fax 534115.

**Ministry of the Interior:** POB 13, Police Fort Compound, Manama; tel. 272111; fax 262169.

**Ministry of Justice and Islamic Affairs:** POB 450, Diplomatic Area, Manama; tel. 531333; fax 532984.

**Ministry of Labour and Social Affairs:** POB 32333, Isa Town; tel. 687800; fax 686954.

**Ministry of Oil and Industry:** POB 1435, Manama; tel. 291511; fax 290302.

**Ministry of Power and Water:** POB 2, Manama; tel. 533133; fax 537151.

**Ministry of Public Works and Agriculture:** POB 5, Muharraq Causeway Rd, Manama; tel. 535222; fax 533095.

**Ministry of Transport:** POB 10325, Diplomatic Area, Manama; tel. 534534; fax 537537.

### CONSULTATIVE COUNCIL

The Consultative Council is an advisory body of 40 members appointed by the ruling authorities for a four-year term, which is empowered to advise the Government but has no legislative powers. The Council held its inaugural session on 16 January 1993.

**President:** IBRAHIM MUHAMMAD HUMAIDAN.

# Legislature

### NATIONAL ASSEMBLY

In accordance with the 1973 Constitution, elections to a National Assembly took place in December 1973. About 30,000 electors elected 30 members for a four-year term. Since political parties are not allowed, all 114 candidates stood as independents but, in practice, the National Assembly was divided almost equally between conservative, moderate and more radical members. In addition to the 30 elected members, the National Assembly contained 14 members of the Cabinet. In August 1975 the Prime Minister resigned because, he complained, the National Assembly was preventing the Government from carrying out its functions. The Amir invited the Prime Minister to form a new Cabinet, and two days later the National Assembly was dissolved by Amiri decree. It has not been revived.

# Diplomatic Representation

### EMBASSIES IN BAHRAIN

**Algeria:** POB 2604, Villa 579, Rd 3622, Adliya, Manama; tel. 713669; fax 713662; Ambassador: LAHSSAN BOUFARES.

**Bangladesh:** POB 26718, House 2280, Rd 2757, Area 327, Adliya, Manama; tel. 714717; fax 710031; e-mail bangla@batelco.com.bh; Ambassador: ANWAR UL-ALAM.

**China, People's Republic:** POB 3150, Bldg 158, Road 382, Juffair Ave, Block 341, Manama; tel. 723800; fax 727304; Ambassador: PAN XIANGKANG.

**Egypt:** POB 818, Adliya; tel. 720005; fax 721518; Ambassador: MUHAMMAD ELSAYED ABBAS.

**France:** POB 11134, Road 1901, Building 51, Block 319, Diplomatic Area, Manama; tel. 291734; fax 293655; Ambassador: GEORGES DUQUIN.

**Germany:** POB 10306, Al-Hasan Bldg, Sheikh Hamad Causeway, Manama; tel. 530210; fax 536282; Ambassador: NORBERT HEINZE.

**India:** POB 26106, Bldg 182, Rd 2608, Area 326, Adliya, Manama; tel. 712785; fax 715527; e-mail indemb@batelco.com.bh; internet www.indianembassy-bh.com; Ambassador: S. S. GILL.

**Iran:** POB 26365, Entrance 1034, Rd 3221, Area 332, Mahooz, Manama; tel. 722400; fax 722101; Ambassador: MUHAMMAD JALAL FIROUZNIA.

**Iraq:** POB 26477, Ar-Raqib Bldg, No 17, Rd 2001, Comp 320, King Faysal Ave, Manama; tel. 786929; fax 786220; Chargé d'affaires: AWAD FAKHRI.

**Japan:** POB 23720, 55 Salmaniya Ave, Manama Tower 327, Manama; tel. 716565; fax 712950; Ambassador: TOSHIAKI TANABE.

**Jordan:** POB 5242, Villa 43, Rd 915, Area 309, Hoora; tel. 291109; fax 291280; Ambassador: Dr SHAKER ARABIAT.

**Kuwait:** POB 786, Rd 1703, Diplomatic Area, Manama; tel. 534040; fax 533579; Ambassador: ABD AL-MUHSIN SALIM AL-HARUN.

**Lebanon:** POB 32474, Manama; tel. 786994; fax 784998; Ambassador: ZUHAIR A. QAZAZ.

**Morocco:** POB 26229, Manama; tel. 740566; fax 740178; Ambassador: OMER AN-NAJEY.

**Oman:** POB 26414, Bldg 37, Rd 1901, Diplomatic Area, Manama; tel. 293663; fax 293540; Ambassador: RASHID BIN OBAID AL-GHARAIBI.

**Pakistan:** POB 563, Bldg 261, Rd 2807, Block 328, Segeiya, Manama; tel. 244113; fax 255960; Ambassador: (vacant).

**Philippines:** POB 26681, Bldg 81, Rd 3902, Block 339, Umm Al-Hassan; tel. 710200; fax 710300; Ambassador: AKMAD ATLAH SAKKAM.

**Russia:** POB 26612, House 877, Rd 3119, Block 331, Zinj, Manama; tel. 725222; fax 725921; Ambassador: ALEKSANDR NOVOZHILOV.

**Saudi Arabia:** POB 1085, Bldg 1450, Rd 4043, Area 340, Juffair, Manama; tel. 537722; fax 533261; Ambassador: ABDULLAH BIN ABD AR-RAHMAN ASH-SHEIKH.

**Tunisia:** POB 26911, House 54, Rd 3601, Area 336, Manama; tel. 714149; fax 715702; Ambassador: MAINSI ABD AL-AZIZ.

**Turkey:** POB 10821, Flat 10, Bldg 81, Rd 1702, Area 317, Manama; tel. 533448; fax 536557; e-mail tcbahrbe@batelco.com.bh; Ambassador: ENGIN TÜRKER.

**United Arab Emirates:** POB 26505, Manama; tel. 723737; fax 727343; Ambassador: AL-ASRI SAEED AHMAD ADH-DHAHIRI.

**United Kingdom:** POB 114, 21 Government Ave, Area 306, Manama; tel. 534404; fax 531273; e-mail britemb@batelco.com.bh; internet www.ukembassy.gov.bh; Ambassador: PETER FORD.

**USA:** POB 26431, Bldg 979, Rd 3119, Block 331, Zinj, Manama; tel. 273300; fax 272594; Ambassador: JOHNY YOUNG.

**Yemen:** POB 26193, House 1048, Rd 1730, Area 517, Saar; tel. 277072; fax 262358; Ambassador: NASSER M. Y. ALGAADANI.

# Judicial System

Since the termination of British legal jurisdiction in 1971, intensive work has been undertaken on the legislative requirements of Bahrain. The Criminal Law is at present contained in various Codes, Ordinances and Regulations. All nationalities are subject to the jurisdiction of the Bahraini courts which guarantee equality before the law irrespective of nationality or creed.

**Directorate of Courts:** POB 450, Government House, Government Rd, Manama; tel. 531333.

# Religion

At the November 1991 census the population was 508,037, distributed as follows: Muslims 415,427; Christians 43,237; Others 49,373.

### ISLAM

Muslims are divided between the Sunni and Shi'i sects. The ruling family is Sunni, although the majority of the Muslim population (estimated at almost 60%) are Shi'ite.

### CHRISTIANITY

#### The Anglican Communion

Within the Episcopal Church in Jerusalem and the Middle East, Bahrain forms part of the diocese of Cyprus and the Gulf. There are two Anglican churches in Bahrain: St Christopher's Cathedral in Manama and the Community Church in Awali. The congregations are entirely expatriate. The Bishop and Archdeacon in Cyprus and the Gulf are both resident in Cyprus.

**Provost:** Very Rev. KEITH W. T. W. JOHNSON, St Christopher's Cathedral, POB 36, Al-Mutanabi Ave, Manama; tel. 253866; fax 246436; e-mail provost@batelco.com.bh; internet www.stchcathedral.org.bh.

#### Roman Catholic Church

A small number of adherents, mainly expatriates, form part of the Apostolic Vicariate of Arabia. The Vicar Apostolic is resident in the United Arab Emirates.

# The Press

### DAILIES

**Akhbar al-Khalij** (Gulf News): POB 5300, Manama; tel. 620111; fax 624312; f. 1976; Arabic; Chair. IBRAHIM AL-MOAYED; Man. Dir and Editor-in-Chief Dr HILAL ASH-SHAIJI; circ. 17,000.

**Al-Ayam** (The Days): POB 3232, Manama; tel. 727111; fax 727552; e-mail alayam@batelco.com.bh; internet www.alayam.com; f. 1989; publ. by Al-Ayam Establishment for Press and Publications; Chair. and Editor-in-Chief NABIL YAQUB AL-HAMER; circ. 37,000.

**Bahrain Tribune:** POB 3232, Manama; tel. 827111; fax 827222; e-mail tribune@batelco.com.bh; internet www.bahraintribune.com; f. 1997; English; Editor DAVID THOMPSON; circ. 12,500.

**Gulf Daily News:** POB 5300, Manama; tel. 620222; fax 622141; e-mail gdn1@batelco.com.bh; internet www.gulf-daily-news.com; f. 1978; English; Editor-in-Chief GEORGE WILLIAMS; Deputy Editor LES HORTON; circ. 50,000.

**Khaleej Times:** POB 26707, City Centre Bldg, Suite 403, 4th Floor, Government Ave, Manama; tel. 213911; fax 211819; f. 1978; English; circ. 72,565.

### WEEKLIES

**Al-Adhwaa'** (Lights): POB 250, Old Exhibition Rd, Manama; tel. 290942; fax 293166; f. 1965; Arabic; publ. by Arab Printing and Publishing House; Chair. RAID MAHMOUD AL-MARDI; Editor-in-Chief MUHAMMAD QASSIM SHIRAWI; circ. 7,000.

**Akhbar BAPCO** (BAPCO News): Bahrain Petroleum Co BSC, POB 25149, Awali; tel. 755055; fax 755047; e-mail khalidfm@batelco.com.bh; f. 1981; formerly known as *an-Najma al-Usbou'* (The Weekly Star); Arabic; house journal; Editor KHALID F. MEHMAS; circ. 3,000.

**Al-Bahrain ath-Thaqafya:** POB 26613, Manama; tel. 290210; fax 292678; Arabic; publ. by the Ministry of Cabinet Affairs and Information; Editor ABDULLAH YATIM.

**BAPCO Weekly News:** POB 25149, Awali; tel. 755049; fax 755047; English; publ. by the Bahrain Petroleum Co BSC; Editor KATHLEEN CROES; circ. 800.

**Huna al-Bahrain:** POB 26005, Isa Town; tel. 731888; fax 681292; Arabic; publ. by the Ministry of Cabinet Affairs and Information; Editor HAMAD AL-MANNAI.

**Al-Mawakif** (Attitudes): POB 1083, Manama; tel. 231231; fax 271720; f. 1973; Arabic; general interest; Editor-in-Chief MANSOOR M. RADHI; circ. 6,000.

**Oil and Gas News:** POB 224, Bldg 149, Exhibition Ave, Manama; tel. 293131; fax 293400; e-mail hilalmag@batelco.com.bh; English; publ. by Al-Hilal Publishing and Marketing Co; Editor-in-Chief CLIVE JACQUES.

**Sada al-Usbou'** (Weekly Echo): POB 549, Bahrain; tel. 291234; fax 290507; f. 1969; Arabic; Owner and Editor-in-Chief ALI SAYYAR; circ. 40,000 (in various Gulf states).

### OTHER PERIODICALS

**Arab Agriculture:** POB 10131, Manama; tel. 213900; fax 211765; e-mail fanar@batelco.com.bh; annually; English and Arabic; publ. by Fanar Publishing WLL; Editor-in-Chief ABD AL-WAHED AL-ALWANI; Gen. Man. FAYEK AL-ARRAYED.

**Arab World Agribusiness:** POB 10131, Manama; tel. 213900; fax 211765; e-mail fanar@batelco.com.bh; nine per year; English and Arabic; publ. by Fanar Publishing WLL; Editor-in-Chief ABD AL-WAHED AL-ALWANI; Gen. Man. FAYEK AL-ARRAYED.

**Discover Bahrain:** POB 10704, Manama; tel. 534587; fax 531296; f. 1988; publ. by G. and B. Media Ltd; Publr and Editor ROBERT GRAHAM.

**Gulf Construction:** POB 224, Exhibition Ave, Manama; tel. 293131; fax 293400; e-mail hilalmag@batelco.com.bh; monthly; English; publ. by Al-Hilal Publishing and Marketing Group; Editor BINA PRABHU GOVEAS; circ. 12,485.

**Gulf Economic Monitor:** POB 224, Exhibition Ave, Manama; tel. 293131; fax 293400; e-mail hilalmag@batelco.com.bh; weekly; English; published by Al-Hilal Publishing and Marketing Group; Man. Dir RONNIE MIDDLETON.

**Al-Hayat at-Tijariya** (Commerce Review): POB 248, Manama; tel. 229555; fax 224985; e-mail bahcci@batelco.com.bh; monthly; English and Arabic; publ. by Bahrain Chamber of Commerce and Industry; Editor KHALIL YOUSUF; circ. 7,500.

**Al-Hidayah** (Guidance): POB 450, Manama; tel. 727100; fax 729819; f. 1978; monthly; Arabic; publ. by Ministry of Justice and Islamic Affairs; Editor-in-Chief ABD AR-RAHMAN BIN MUHAMMAD RASHID AL-KHALIFA; circ. 5,000.

**Al-Mohandis** (The Engineer): POB 835, Manama; e-mail mohandis@batelco.com.bh; internet www.mohandis.org; f. 1972; quarterly; Arabic and English; publ. by Bahrain Society of Engineers; Editor MUHAMMAD K. AS-SAYED.

**Al-Musafir al-Arabi** (Arab Traveller): POB 10131, Manama; tel. 213900; fax 211765; e-mail fanar@batelco.com.bh; f. 1984; six per year; Arabic; publ. by Fanar Publishing WLL; Editor-in-Chief ABD AL-WAHED AL-ALWANI; Gen. Man. FAYEK AL-ARRAYED.

**Panorama:** POB 3232, Manama; tel. 727111; fax 729009; monthly; Editor IBRAHIM BASHMI; circ. 15,000.

**Profile:** POB 10243, Manama; tel. 291110; fax 294655; f. 1992; monthly; English; publ. by Bahrain Market Promotions; Editor ISA KHALIFA AL-KHALIFA.

**Al-Quwwa** (The Force): POB 245, Manama; tel. 291331; fax 659596; f. 1977; monthly; Arabic; publ. by Bahrain Defence Force; Editor-in-Chief Maj. AHMAD MAHMOUD AS-SUWAIDI.

**Shipping and Transport News International:** POB 224, Exhibition Ave, Manama; tel. 293131; fax 293400; six per year; English; publ. by Al-Hilal Publishing and Marketing Group; Editor FREDERICK ROCQUE; circ. 5,500.

**Travel and Tourism News Middle East:** POB 224, Exhibition Ave, Manama; tel. 293131; fax 293400; e-mail hilalmag@batelco.com.bh; f. 1983; monthly; English; travel trade; publ. by Al-Hilal Publishing and Marketing Group; Editorial Man. SHILPI PILLAI; circ. 6,050.

### NEWS AGENCIES

**Agence France-Presse (AFP):** POB 5890, Kanoo Tower, Phase 3, Tijaar Ave, Manama; tel. and fax 403446; Dir JEAN-PIERRE PERRIN.

**Associated Press (AP)** (USA): POB 26940, Mannai Bldg, Manama; tel. 530101; fax 530249.

**Gulf News Agency:** POB 5421 Manama; tel. 689044; fax 683825; e-mail brctnews@batelco.com.bh; internet www.gna.gov.bh.

**Reuters** (United Kingdom): POB 1030, UGB Bldg, 6th Floor, Diplomatic Area, Manama; tel. 536111; fax 536192; Bureau Man. KENNETH WEST.

## Publishers

**Arab Communicators:** POB 551, Manama; tel. 534664; fax 531837; publrs of annual Bahrain Business Directory; Dirs AHMAD A. FAKHRI, HAMAD A. ABUL.

**Falcon Publishing WLL:** POB 5028, Manama; tel. 253162; fax 259695; business magazines and directories; Chair. ABD AN-NABI ASH-SHOALA.

**Gulf Advertising:** POB 5518, Manama; tel. 226262; fax 228660; e-mail gulfad@batelco.com.bh; f. 1974; advertising and marketing communications; Chair. and Man. Dir KHAMIS AL-MUQLA.

**Al-Hilal Publishing and Marketing Group:** POB 224, Exhibition Ave, Manama; tel. 293131; fax 293400; e-mail hilalmag@batelco.com.bh; f. 1977; specialist magazines and newspapers of commercial interest; Chair. A. M. ABD AR-RAHMAN; Man. Dir R. MIDDLETON.

**Manama Publishing Co WLL:** POB 1013, Manama; tel. 213223; fax 211548.

**Al-Masirah Journalism, Printing and Publishing House:** POB 5981, Manama; tel. 258882; fax 276178.

**Tele-Gulf Directory Publications, WLL:** POB 2738, 3rd Floor, Bahrain Tower, Manama; tel. 213301; fax 210503; e-mail telegulf@batelco.com.bh; f. 1977; publrs of annual *Gulf Directory* and *Arab Banking and Finance*; Chair. ABD AN-NABI ASH-SHOALA.

### Government Publishing House

**Directorate of Publications:** POB 26005, Manama; tel. 689077; Dir MUHAMMAD AL-KHOZAI.

## Broadcasting and Communications

### TELECOMMUNICATIONS

**Bahrain Telecommunications Co BSC (BATELCO):** POB 14, Manama; tel. 884557; fax 611898; e-mail batelco@btc.com.bh; internet www.batelco.com.bh; f. 1981; operates all telecommunications services; cap. BD 100m.; 80% owned by Government of Bahrain, financial institutions and public of Bahrain, 20% by Cable and Wireless PLC (United Kingdom); Chair. Sheikh ALI BIN KHALIFA BIN SALMAN AL-KHALIFA; CEO ANDREW HEARN.

**Telecommunications Directorate:** POB 11170, Manama; tel. 534534; fax 533544; regulatory body; Dir Dr RASHID JASSIM ASHOOR.

### BROADCASTING

#### Radio

English language radio programmes, broadcast from Saudi Arabia by the US Air Force in Dhahran and by Saudi Aramco, can be received in Bahrain.

**Bahrain Radio and Television Corpn:** POB 702, Manama; tel. 781888; f. 1955; state-owned and -operated enterprise; two 10-kW transmitters; programmes are in Arabic and English, and include news, plays and discussions; Dir of Broadcasting ABD AR-RAHMAN ABDULLAH.

**Radio Bahrain:** POB 702, Manama; tel. 781888; fax 780911; e-mail brtcnews@batelco.com.bh; f. 1977; commercial radio station in English language; Head of Station SALAH KHALID.

#### Television

English language television programmes, broadcast from Saudi Arabia by Saudi Aramco, can be received in Bahrain.

**Bahrain Radio and Television Corpn:** POB 1075, Manama; tel. 781888; fax 681544; commenced colour broadcasting in 1973; broadcasts on five channels, of which the main Arabic and the main English channel accept advertising; covers Bahrain, eastern Saudi Arabia, Qatar and the UAE; an Amiri decree in early 1993 established the independence of the Corpn, which was to be controlled by a committee; Dir H. AL-UMRAN.

## Finance

(cap. = capital; p.u. = paid up; res = reserves; dep. = deposits; m. = millions; brs = branches; amounts in Bahraini dinars unless otherwise stated)

### BANKING

#### Central Bank

**Bahrain Monetary Agency (BMA):** POB 27, Manama; tel. 535535; fax 534170; e-mail bmalbr@batelco.com.bh; internet www.bma.gov.bh; f. 1973, in operation from January 1975; controls issue of currency, regulates exchange control and credit policy, organization and control of banking system and bank credit; cap. and res 294.9m., dep. 104.9m. (March 1999); Governor Sheikh ABDULLAH AL-KHALIFA; Chair. Sheikh KHALIFA BIN SULMAN AL-KHALIFA.

### Locally-incorporated Commercial Banks

**Al-Ahli Commercial Bank BSC:** POB 5941, Bahrain Car Park Bldg, Government Rd, Manama; tel. 224333; fax 224322; e-mail alahli@al-ahlibank.com; internet www.al-ahlibank.com; f. 1977; full commercial bank; cap. 13.2m., res 31.4m., dep. 254.6m. (Dec. 1998); Chair. MUHAMMAD Y. JALAL; CEO MICHAEL J. FULLER; 9 brs.

**Bahrain Islamic Bank BSC:** POB 5240, Government Rd, Manama; tel. 223402; fax 223956; e-mail bahisl@batelco.com.bh; f. 1979; cap. 11.5m., res 2.7m., dep. 137.7m. (April 1998); Chair. Sheikh ABD AR-RAHMAN AL-KHALIFA; Gen. Man. ABD AL-LATIF ABD AR-RAHIM JANAHI; 5 brs.

**Bahraini Saudi Bank BSC (BSB):** POB 1159, Government Rd, Manama; tel. 211010; fax 210989; e-mail bsbbahr@batelco .com.bh; f. 1983; commenced operations in early 1985; licensed as a full commercial bank; cap. 20.0m., res 7.5m., dep. 111.3m. (Dec. 1998); Chair. Sheikh IBRAHIM BIN HAMAD AL-KHALIFA; Gen. Man. MANSOOR AS-SAYED ALI; 4 brs.

**Bank of Bahrain and Kuwait BSC (BBK):** POB 597, Manama; tel. 223388; fax 229822; e-mail bbk@batelco.com.bh; internet www.bbkonline.com; f. 1971; cap. 56.9m., res 34.5m., dep. 821.2m. (Dec. 1998); Chair. HASSAN KHALIFA AL-JALAHMA; Gen. Man. and CEO MURAD ALI MURAD; 22 local brs, 2 brs overseas.

**Faysal Islamic Bank of Bahrain EC:** Chamber of Commerce Bldg, POB 3005, King Faysal Rd, Manama; tel. 211373; fax 210717; e-mail fibbrn@batelco.com.bh; f. 1982 as Massraf Faysal Al-Islami of Bahrain EC; renamed as above in 1987; cap. US $100.00m., res US $20.2m., dep. US $114.3m. (Dec. 1997); Pres. and CEO NABIL ABD AL-ILLAH NASEER; 2 brs.

**Grindlays Bahrain Bank BSC:** POB 793, Manama; tel. 225999; fax 224482; e-mail grindlay@batelco.com.bh; internet www .grndbah.com; f. 1984; owned by Bahraini shareholders (60%) and ANZ Grindlays Bank PLC, London (40%); cap. 6.0m., res 4.8m., dep. 82.4m. (Dec. 1998); Chair. MUHAMMAD ABDULLAH AZ-ZAMIL; Gen. Man. PETER TOMKINS; 6 brs.

**National Bank of Bahrain BSC (NBB):** POB 106, Government Ave, Manama; tel. 228800; fax 263876; e-mail nbb@nbbonline.com; internet www.nbbonline.com; f. 1957; 49% govt-owned; cap. 40.0m., res 51.0m., dep. 742.4m. (Dec. 1998); Gen. Man. ABD AR-RAZAK A. HASSAN; Man. Dir HASSAN ALI JUMA; 25 brs.

### Foreign Commercial Banks

**ABN AMRO Bank NV** (Netherlands): POB 350, Manama; tel. 255420; fax 262241; e-mail abnamro@batelco.com.bh; internet www.abnamro.com; Country Man. G. LOET KNIPHORST; 1 br.

**Arab Bank PLC** (Jordan): POB 395, Government Rd, Manama; tel. 229988; fax 210443; internet www.arabbank.com; Chair. ABD AL-MAJEED SHOMAN; 4 brs.

**Bank Melli Iran:** POB 785, Government Rd, Manama; tel. 259910; fax 270768; Gen. Man. ALI ASGHAR KAMALI ROUSTA; 2 br.

**Bank Saderat Iran:** POB 825, Government Rd, Manama; tel. 210003; fax 210398; Man. MUHAMMAD JAVAD NASSIRI; 2 brs.

**Banque du Caire** (Egypt): POB 815, Manama; tel. 227454; fax 213704; Man. ES-SAYED MOUSTAFA EL-DOKMAWEY.

**Citibank NA** (USA): POB 548, Government Rd, Manama; tel. 223344; fax 211323; Gen. Man. MUHAMMAD ASH-SHROOGI; 1 br.

**Habib Bank Ltd** (Pakistan): POB 566, Manama Centre, Manama; tel. 227118; fax 213421; f. 1941; Exec. Vice-Pres. and Gen. Man. ASHRAF BIDIWALA; 5 brs.

**HSBC Bank Middle East** (United Kingdom): POB 57, Al-Khalifa Rd, Manama; tel. 242555; fax 256822; e-mail bbmemnm@batelco .com.bh; internet www.britishbank.com; CEO ROGER J. JORDAN; 4 brs.

**Paribas** (France): POB 5241, Manama; tel. 225275; fax 224697; Gen. Man. N. NAHAWI.

**Rafidain Bank** (Iraq): POB 607, Manama; tel. 275796; fax 255656; f. 1969; Man. IBTISAM NAJEM ABOUD; 1 br.

**Standard Chartered Bank** (United Kingdom): POB 29, Government Rd, Manama; tel. 255946; fax 230503; f. in Bahrain 1920; Man. PETER RAWLINGS; 5 brs.

**United Bank Ltd** (Pakistan): POB 546, Government Rd, Manama; tel. 224032; fax 224099; e-mail askubl@batelco.com.bh; Gen. Man. ZAFAR AL-HAQ MEMON; 3 brs.

### Specialized Financial Institutions

**Bahrain Development Bank (BDB):** POB 20501, Manama; tel. 537007; fax 534005; internet www.bd-bank.com; f. 1992; invests in manufacturing, agribusiness and services; cap. 10.0m., res 0.1m., dep. 0.1m. (Dec. 1998); Chair. Sheikh IBRAHIM BIN KHALIFA AL-KHALIFA.

**The Housing Bank:** POB 5370, Diplomatic Area, Manama; tel. 534443; fax 533437; f. 1979; provides housing loans for Bahraini citizens and finances construction of commercial properties. Chair. Sheikh KHALID BIN ABDULLAH BIN KHALID AL-KHALIFA; Gen. Man. ISA SULTAN ADH-DHAWADI.

### 'Offshore' Banking Units

Bahrain has been encouraging the establishment of 'offshore' banking units (OBUs) since 1975. An OBU is not permitted to provide local banking services, but is allowed to accept deposits from governments and large financial organizations in the area and make medium-term loans for local and regional capital projects. Prior to the Iraqi invasion of Kuwait in August 1990, there were 56 OBUs in operation in Bahrain. By 1997, however, the number of OBUs had declined to 47.

### Investment Banks

**Al-Baraka Islamic Bank BSC (EC):** POB 1882, 1 Al-Hedaya Bldg, Government Rd, Manama; tel. 274488; fax 274499; e-mail baraka@batelco.com.bh; internet www.barakaonline.com; f. 1984; cap. US $50.0m., res US $5.0m., dep. US $33.9m. (Dec. 1998); Chair. Sheikh SALEH ABDULLAH KAMEL; 17 brs.

**INVESTCORP Bank EC:** POB 5340, Diplomatic Area, Manama; tel. 532000; fax 530816; f. 1982 as Arabian Investment Banking Corpn (INVESTCORP) EC, current name adopted in 1990; cap. US $100.0m., res US $79.1m., dep. US $525.7m. (Dec. 1998); Pres. and CEO NEMIR A. KIRDAR.

**Nomura Investment Banking (Middle East) EC:** POB 26893, 10th and 11th floor, BMB Centre, Diplomatic Area, Manama; tel. 530531; fax 530365; f. 1982; cap. US $25m., res US $107.1m., dep. US $37.1m. (Dec. 1997); Chair. TAKASHI TSUTSUI.

**TAIB Bank EC:** POB 20485, Sehl Centre, Diplomatic Area, Manama; tel. 533334; fax 533174; e-mail taib@batelco.com.bh; internet www.taib.com; f. 1979 as Trans-Arabian Investment Bank EC; current name adopted in 1994; cap. US $84.4m., res US $16.8m., dep. US $246.8m. (Dec. 1997); Chair. ABD AR-RAHMAN AL-JERAISY; Vice-Chair. and CEO IQBAL G. MAMDANI.

**United Gulf Bank (BSC) EC:** POB 5964, UGB Tower, Diplomatic Area, Manama; tel. 533233; fax 533137; e-mail ugbbah@ batelco.com.bh; f. 1980; cap. US $200.0m., res US $14.9m., dep. US $147.3m. (Dec. 1997); Chair. FAISAL H. ALAYYAR; Gen. Man. MUHAMMAD HAROUN.

Other investment banks operating in Bahrain include the following: ABC Islamic Bank EC, Amex (Middle East) EC, Arab Financial Services Co EC, Bahrain Investment Bank BSC, Bahrain Islamic Investment Co BSC, Capital Union EC, Daiwa Middle East EC, Faysal Investment Bank of Bahrain EC, First Islamic Investment Bank EC, Islamic Investment Company of the Gulf—Bahrain EC, Man-Ahli Investment Bank EC, Merrill Lynch Int. Bank Ltd, Nikko Europe Plc, Okasan Int. (Middle East) EC, Sumitomo Finance (Middle East) EC, Turk-Gulf Merchant Bank EC, Yamaichi Int. (Middle East) EC.

## STOCK EXCHANGE

**Bahrain Stock Exchange:** POB 3203, Manama; tel. 259690; fax 276181; internet www.bahrainstock.com; f. 1989; nine mems; linked to Muscat Securities Market (Oman) in 1995, and to Amman Financial Market (Jordan) in 1996; Dir-Gen. Sheikh AHMAD BIN MUHAMMAD AL-KHALIFA.

## INSURANCE

**Abdullah Yousuf Fakhro Corpn:** POB 39, Government Ave, Manama; tel. 275000; fax 273947; general.

**Al-Ahlia Insurance Co BSC:** POB 5282, Manama; tel. 225860; fax 224870; internet www.alahlia.com; f. 1976; Chair. TAQI MUHAMMAD AL-BAHARNA.

**Arab Insurance Group BSC (ARIG):** POB 26992, Arig House, Diplomatic Area, Manama; tel. 544444; fax 531155; e-mail info@arig.com.bh; internet www.arig.com.bh; f. 1980; owned by Governments of Kuwait, Libya and the UAE (49.5%), and other shareholders; reinsurance and insurance; Chair. NASSER M. AN-NOWAIS.

**Arab International Insurance Co EC (AIIC):** POB 10135, Manama; tel. 530087; fax 530122; f. 1981; non-life reinsurance; Chair. and Man. Dir Sheikh KHALID J. AS-SABAH.

**Bahrain Kuwait Insurance Co BSC:** POB 10166, Diplomatic Area, Manama; tel. 542222; fax 530799; e-mail bkicbah@ batelco.com.bh; internet www.bkic.com; f. 1975; Gen. Man. HAMEED AL-NASSER.

**Bahrain National Insurance (BNI):** POB 843, Manama; tel. 227800; fax 224385; internet www.bahins.com; f. 1998 by merger of Bahrain Insurance Co and National Insurance Co; all classes including life insurance; Chair. MUHAMMAD FAKHRO; Gen. Man. SAMIR AL-WAZZAN.

**Gulf Union Insurance and Reinsurance Co:** POB 10949, Ground Floor, Manama Centre, Manama; tel. 215622; fax 215421; e-mail guirco@batelco.com.bh; internet www.gulfunion-bah.com; Chair. IBRAHIM BIN HAMAD AL-KHALIFA.

# Trade and Industry

### GOVERNMENT AGENCIES

**Bahrain Promotions and Marketing Board:** POB 11299, Manama; tel. 533886; fax 531117; internet www.bpmb.com; f. 1993; provides national focus for Bahraini marketing initiatives; attracts inward investment; encourages development and expansion of Bahraini exports; Chair. Minister of Commerce.

**Supreme Council for Oil:** Manama; formulates Bahrain's petroleum policy; Chair. Prime Minister.

### CHAMBER OF COMMERCE

**Bahrain Chamber of Commerce and Industry:** POB 248, New Chamber of Commerce Bldgs, King Faysal Rd, Manama; tel. 229555; fax 224985; e-mail bahcci@batelco.com.bh; internet www.bahchamber.com; f. 1939; 7,300 mems (1996); Pres. ALI BIN YOUSUF FAKHROO; Sec.-Gen. JASSIM MUHAMMAD ASH-SHATTI.

### STATE HYDROCARBONS COMPANIES

**Bahrain National Gas Co BSC (BANAGAS):** POB 29099, Rifa'a; tel. 756222; fax 756991; f. 1979; responsible for extraction, processing and sale of hydrocarbon liquids from associated gas derived from onshore Bahraini fields; ownership is 75% Government of Bahrain, 12.5% Caltex and 12.5% Arab Petroleum Investments Corpn (APICORP); produced 202,955 metric tons of LPG and 189,803 tons of naphtha in 1996; Chair. Sheikh HAMAD BIN IBRAHIM AL-KHALIFA; Gen. Man. Dr. Sheikh MUHAMMAD BIN KHALIFA AL-KHALIFA.

**Bahrain National Oil Co (BANOCO):** POB 25504, Awali; tel. 754666; fax 753203; f. 1976; to merge with BAPCO in 2000; responsible for exploration, production, processing, transportation and storage of petroleum and petroleum products; distribution and sales of petroleum products (including natural gas), international marketing of crude petroleum and petroleum products, supply and sales of aviation fuels; average production 40,000 barrels per day; Man. Dir MUHAMMAD SALEH SHEIKH ALI; Gen. Man. Dr FAYEZ HASHIM AS-SADAH.

**Bahrain Petroleum Co BSC (BAPCO):** POB 25504, Manama; tel. 754444; fax 752924; e-mail kathleen_croes@bapco.net; f. 1980; to merge with BANOCO in 2000; a refining company wholly owned by the Government of Bahrain; refined 92m. barrels of crude petroleum in 1997; Chair. Minister of Oil and Industry; Chief Exec. JOHANN F. LUBBE.

**Gulf Petrochemical Industries Co BSC (GPIC):** POB 26730, Sitra; tel. 731777; fax 731047; f. 1979 as a joint venture between the Governments of Bahrain, Kuwait and Saudi Arabia, each with one-third equity participation; a petrochemical complex at Sitra, inaugurated in 1981; produces 1,200 tons of both methanol and ammonia per day (1990); Chair. Sheikh ISA BIN ALI AL-KHALIFA; Gen. Man. MUSTAFA AS-SAYED.

### UTILITIES

**Ministry of Power and Water:** (see Ministries, above); provides electricity and water throughout Bahrain.

#### Electricity

**Directorate of Electricity:** King Faysal Rd, POB 2, Manama; tel. 533133; supplies domestic and industrial power and street lighting.

#### Water

**Directorate of Water Supply:** POB 326, Manama; tel. 727009; responsible for water supply to all areas except Awali.

### TRADE UNIONS

There are no trade unions in Bahrain.

# Transport

### RAILWAYS

There are no railways in Bahrain.

### ROADS

At 31 December 1997 Bahrain had 3,103 km of roads, of which 77% were hard-surfaced. Most inhabited areas of Bahrain are linked by bitumen-surfaced roads. A modern network of dual highways is being developed, and a 25-km causeway link with Saudi Arabia was opened in 1986. A three-lane dual carriageway links the causeway to Manama. Other causeways link Bahrain with Muharraq island and with Sitra island. In March 1997 the Government approved the construction of a US $80m.-causeway linking Hidd on Muharraq island with the port of Mina Salman; the new causeway was scheduled to be completed in 2001. A second 2.5-km Manama-to-Muharraq causeway was opened in early 1997.

**Directorate of Roads:** POB 5, Sheikh Hamad Causeway, Manama; tel. 535222; fax 532565; responsible for traffic engineering, safety, planning, road design, maintenance and construction; Dir ESSAM A. KHALAF.

### SHIPPING

Numerous shipping services link Bahrain and the Gulf with Europe, the USA, Pakistan, India, the Far East and Australia.

The deep-water harbour of Mina Salman was opened in 1962; it has 13 conventional berths, two container terminals (one of which has a 400-m quay—permitting two 180-m container ships to be handled simultaneously) and a roll-on/roll-off berth. Two nearby slipways can accommodate vessels of up to 1,016 tons and 73m in length, and services are available for ship repairs afloat. During 1992 Mina Salman handled about 90,000 TEUs (20-ft equivalent units).

By 1999 work had begun on the construction of a new port and industrial zone at Hidd, on Muharraq island, which had been approved by the Cabinet in March 1997. At an estimated total cost of US $330m., the port was to have an annual handling capacity of 234,000 TEUs and was to include a general cargo berth and two container berths with roll-on/roll-off facilities.

**Directorate of Customs and Ports:** POB 15, Manama; tel. 725555; fax 725534; responsible for customs activities and acts as port authority; Pres. of Customs and Ports EID ABDULLAH YOUSUF; Dir-Gen. of Ports Capt. MAHMOOD Y. AL-MAHMOOD; Dir-Gen. of Customs JASSIM JAMSHEER.

**Arab Shipbuilding and Repair Yard Co (ASRY):** POB 50110, Hidd; tel. 671111; fax 670236; e-mail asry@batelco.com.bh; internet www.asry.net; f. 1974 by OAPEC members; 500,000-ton dry dock opened 1977; two floating dry docks in operation since 1992; repaired 119 ships in 1998; Chair. Sheikh DAIJ BIN KHALIFA AL-KHALIFA; CEO MUHAMMAD M. AL-KHATEEB.

#### Principal Shipping Agents

**Dilmun Shipping Agency:** POB 11664, Manama; tel. 534530; fax 531287; e-mail dilmun@batelco.com.bh; Chair. Capt. P. CARR.

**The Gulf Agency Co (Bahrain) Ltd:** POB 412, Manama; tel. 530022; fax 530063; Man. Dir SKJALM BANG.

**Al-Jazeera Shipping Co WLL:** POB 302, Manama; tel. 728837; fax 728217.

**Al-Sharif Group:** POB 1322, Manama; tel. 530535; fax 537637; e-mail general@bahragents.com; Dirs ALI ABDURASOOL ASH-SHARIF, KHALID ABDURASOOL ASH-SHARIF.

**UCO Marine Contracting WLL:** POB 1074, Manama; tel. 730816; fax 83213; e-mail ucomarin@batelco.com.bh; Man. Dirs BADER A. KAIKSOW, HASSAN AS-SABAH, ALI AL-MUSALAM.

**Yusuf bin Ahmad Kanoo:** POB 45, Al-Khalifa Rd, Manama; tel. 727881; fax 727024; air and shipping cargo services; Dir AHMAD KANOO.

### CIVIL AVIATION

Bahrain International Airport has a first-class runway, capable of taking the largest aircraft in use. In 1997 there were 54,314 flights to and from the airport, and in 1996 a total of 3.4m. passengers were carried. Extension work to the airport's main terminal building has been carried out during the 1990s, in order to increase the airport's cargo-handling facilities.

**Department of Civil Aviation Affairs:** POB 586, Bahrain International Airport, Muharraq; tel. 321095; fax 321139; e-mail bahintapt@bahrainairport.co; internet www.bahrainairport.com; Under-Sec. IBRAHIM ABDULLAH AL-HAMER.

**Gulf Air Co GSC (Gulf Air):** POB 138, Manama; tel. 322200; fax 338033; e-mail gfpr@batelco.com.bh; internet www.gulfairco.com.; f. 1950; jointly owned by Govts of Bahrain, Oman, Qatar and Abu Dhabi (part of the United Arab Emirates) since 1974; services to the Middle East, South-East Asia, the Far East, Australia, Africa and Europe; Chair. Sheikh ALI BIN KHALIFA AL-KHALIFA (Bahrain); Pres. and Chief Exec. Sheikh AHMAD BIN SAIF AN-NAHYAN (Abu Dhabi).

# Tourism

There are several archaeological sites of importance in Bahrain, which is the site of the ancient trading civilization of Dilmun. There is a wide selection of hotels and restaurants, and a new national museum opened in 1989. In 1996 some 1.8m. tourists visited Bahrain, and income from tourism totalled some US $258m.

**Bahrain Tourism Co (BTC):** POB 5831, Manama; tel. 530530; fax 530867; e-mail bahtours@batelco.com.bh; Chair. MUHAMMAD YOUSUF JALAL.

**Tourism Affairs:** Ministry of Cabinet Affairs and Information, POB 26613, Manama; tel. 201203; fax 211717; e-mail btour@bahraintourism.com; internet www.bahraintourism.com; Asst Under-Sec. for Tourism Dr KADHIM RAJAB.

# BANGLADESH

## Introductory Survey

### Location, Climate, Language, Religion, Flag, Capital

The People's Republic of Bangladesh lies in southern Asia, surrounded by Indian territory except for a short south-eastern frontier with Myanmar (formerly Burma) and a southern coast fronting the Bay of Bengal. The country has a tropical monsoon climate and suffers from periodic cyclones. The average temperature is 19°C (67°F) from October to March, rising to 29°C (84°F) between May and September. The average annual rainfall in Dhaka is 188 cm (74 ins), of which about three-quarters occurs between June and September. About 95% of the population speak Bengali, the state language, while the remainder mostly use tribal dialects. More than 85% of the people are Muslims, Islam being the state religion, and there are small minorities of Hindus, Buddhists and Christians. The national flag (proportions 5 by 3) is dark green, with a red disc slightly off-centre towards the hoist. The capital is Dhaka (Dacca).

### Recent History

Present-day Bangladesh was formerly East Pakistan, one of the five provinces into which Pakistan was divided at its initial creation, when Britain's former Indian Empire was partitioned in August 1947. East Pakistan and the four western provinces were separated by about 1,000 miles (1,600 km) of Indian territory. East Pakistan was created from the former Indian province of East Bengal and the Sylhet district of Assam. Although the East was more populous, government was based in West Pakistan. Dissatisfaction in East Pakistan at its dependence on a remote central Government flared up in 1952, when Urdu was declared Pakistan's official language. Bengali, the main language of East Pakistan, was finally admitted as the joint official language in 1954, and in 1955 Pakistan was reorganized into two wings, east and west, with equal representation in the central legislative assembly. However, discontent continued in the eastern wing, particularly as the region was under-represented in the administration and armed forces, and received a disproportionately small share of Pakistan's development expenditure. The leading political party in East Pakistan was the Awami League (AL), led by Sheikh Mujibur (Mujib) Rahman, who demanded autonomy for the East. A general election in December 1970 gave the AL an overwhelming victory in the East, and thus a majority in Pakistan's National Assembly; Sheikh Mujib should then, by right, have been appointed Prime Minister, but Pakistan's President, Gen. Yahya Khan, would not accept this, and negotiations on a possible constitutional compromise broke down. The convening of the new National Assembly was postponed indefinitely in March 1971, leading to violent protests in East Pakistan. The AL decided that the province should unilaterally secede from Pakistan, and on 26 March Sheikh Mujib proclaimed the independence of the People's Republic of Bangladesh ('Bengal Nation').

Civil war immediately broke out. President Yahya Khan outlawed the AL and arrested its leaders. By April 1971 the Pakistan army dominated the eastern province. In August Sheikh Mujib was secretly put on trial in West Pakistan. Resistance continued, however, from the Liberation Army of East Bengal (the Mukhti Bahini), a group of irregular fighters, who launched a major offensive in November. As a result of the conflict, an estimated 9.5m. refugees crossed into India. On 4 December India declared war on Pakistan, with Indian forces intervening in support of the Mukhti Bahini. Pakistan surrendered on 16 December and Bangladesh's independence became a reality. Pakistan was thus confined to its former western wing. In January 1972 Sheikh Mujib was freed by Pakistan's new President, Zulfiqar Ali Bhutto, and became Prime Minister of Bangladesh. Under a provisional Constitution, Bangladesh was declared to be a secular state and a parliamentary democracy. The new nation quickly achieved international recognition, causing Pakistan to withdraw from the Commonwealth in January 1972. Bangladesh joined the Commonwealth in April. The members who had been elected from the former East Pakistan for the Pakistan National Assembly and the Provincial Assembly in December 1970 formed the Bangladesh Constituent Assembly. A new Constitution was approved by this Assembly in November 1972 and came into effect in December. A general election for the country's first Jatiya Sangsad (Parliament) was held in March 1973. The AL received 73% of the total votes and won 292 of the 300 directly-elective seats in the legislature. Bangladesh was finally recognized by Pakistan in February 1974. Internal stability, however, was threatened by opposition groups which resorted to terrorism and included both political extremes (i.e. Islamic fundamentalists and Maoists). In December a state of emergency was declared and constitutional rights were suspended. In January 1975 parliamentary government was replaced by a presidential form of government. Sheikh Mujib became President, assuming absolute power, and created the Bangladesh Peasants' and Workers' Awami League. In February Bangladesh became a one-party state.

In August 1975 Sheikh Mujib and his family were assassinated in a right-wing coup, led by a group of Islamic army officers. Khandakar Mushtaq Ahmed, the former Minister of Commerce, was installed as President, declared martial law and banned political parties. A counter-coup on 3 November brought to power Brig. Khalid Musharaf, the pro-Indian commander of the Dhaka garrison, who was appointed Chief of Army Staff; on 7 November a third coup overthrew Brig. Musharaf's four-day-old regime and power was assumed by the three service chiefs jointly, under a non-political President, Abusadet Mohammed Sayem, the Chief Justice of the Supreme Court. A neutral non-party Government was formed, in which the reinstated Chief of Army Staff, Major-Gen. Ziaur Rahman (Gen. Zia), took precedence over his colleagues. Political parties were legalized again in July 1976.

An early return to representative government was promised, but in November 1976 elections were postponed indefinitely and, in a major shift of power, Gen. Zia took over the role of Chief Martial Law Administrator from President Sayem, assuming the presidency also in April 1977. He amended the Constitution, making Islam, instead of secularism, its first basic principle. In a national referendum in May 99% of voters affirmed their confidence in President Zia's policies, and in June 1978 the country's first direct presidential election resulted in a clear victory for Zia, who formed a Council of Ministers to replace his Council of Advisers. Parliamentary elections followed in February 1979 and, in an attempt to persuade opposition parties to participate in the elections, President Zia met some of their demands by repealing 'all undemocratic provisions' of the 1974 constitutional amendment, releasing political prisoners and withdrawing press censorship. Consequently, 29 parties contested the elections, in which President Zia's Bangladesh Nationalist Party (BNP) received 49% of the total votes and won 207 of the 300 contested seats in the Jatiya Sangsad. In April 1979 a new Prime Minister was appointed, and martial law was repealed. The state of emergency was revoked in November.

Political instability recurred, however, when Gen. Zia was assassinated on 30 May 1981 during an attempted military coup, allegedly led by Maj.-Gen. Mohammad Abdul Manzur, an army divisional commander who was himself later killed in confused circumstances. The elderly Vice-President, Justice Abdus Sattar, assumed the role of acting President but was confronted by strikes and demonstrations in protest against the execution of several officers who had been involved in the coup, and pressure from opposition parties to have the date of the presidential election moved. As the only person acceptable to the different groups within the BNP, Sattar was nominated as the party's presidential candidate, gaining an overwhelming victory at the November election. President Sattar announced his intention of continuing the policies of the late Gen. Zia. He found it increasingly difficult, however, to retain civilian control over the country, and in January 1982 he formed a National Security Council, which included military personnel, led by the Chief of Army Staff, Lt-Gen. Hossain Mohammad Ershad. On 24 March Gen. Ershad seized power in a bloodless coup, claiming that political corruption and economic mismanagement had become intolerable. The country was placed under martial law, with Ershad as Chief Martial Law Administrator (in October his title was changed to Prime Minister), aided by a mainly military Council of Advisers; a retired judge, Justice Abul Chowdhury, was nominated as President by Ershad. Political activities were banned. Later in the year, several former ministers were tried and imprisoned on charges of corruption.

Although the Government's economic policies achieved some success and gained a measure of popular support for Ershad, there were increasing demands in 1983 for a return to democratic government. The two principal opposition groups that emerged were an eight-party alliance, headed by the AL under Sheikh Hasina Wajed (daughter of the late Sheikh Mujib), and a seven-party group, which was led by the BNP under the former President Sattar (who died in 1985) and Begum Khaleda Zia (widow of Gen. Zia). In September 1983 the two groups formed an alliance, the Movement for the Restoration of Democracy (MRD), and jointly issued demands for an end to martial law, for the release of political prisoners and for the holding of parliamentary elections before any others. In November the resumption of political activity was permitted, and it was announced that a series of local elections between December 1983 and March 1984 were to precede a presidential election and parliamentary elections later in the year. A new political party, the Jana Dal (People's Party), was formed in November 1983 to support Ershad as a presidential candidate. Following demonstrations demanding civilian government, the ban on political activity was reimposed at the beginning of December, only two weeks after it had been rescinded, and leading political figures were detained. On 11 December Ershad declared himself President.

Bangladesh remained disturbed in 1984, with frequent strikes and political demonstrations. Local elections, due to take place in March, were postponed, as the opposition objected to their being held before the presidential and parliamentary elections, on the grounds that Ershad was trying to strengthen his power-base. The presidential and parliamentary elections, scheduled for May, were also postponed, until December, because of persistent opposition demands for the repeal of martial law and for the formation of an interim neutral government to oversee a fair election. In October Ershad offered to repeal martial law if the opposition would participate in the elections. They responded with an appeal for a campaign of civil disobedience, which led to the elections being indefinitely postponed.

In January 1985 it was announced that parliamentary elections would be held in April, to be preceded by a partial relaxation of martial law: the Constitution was to be fully restored after the elections. The announcement was followed by the formation of a new Council of Ministers, composed entirely of military officers and excluding all members of the Jana Dal, in response to demands by the opposition parties for a neutral government during the pre-election period. Once more, the opposition threatened to boycott the elections, as President Ershad would not relinquish power to an interim government, and in March the elections were abandoned and political activity was again banned. This was immediately followed by a referendum, held in support of the presidency, in which Ershad reportedly received 94% of the total votes. Local elections were held in May, without the participation of the opposition, and Ershad claimed that 85% of the elected council chairmen were his supporters, although not necessarily of his party. In September a new five-party political alliance, the National Front (comprising the Jana Dal, the United People's Party, the Gonotantrik Party, the Bangladesh Muslim League and a breakaway section of the BNP), was established to promote government policies.

In January 1986 the 10-month ban on political activity was ended. The five components of the National Front formally became a single pro-Government entity, named the Jatiya Dal (National Party). In March President Ershad announced that parliamentary elections were to be held (under martial law) at the end of April. He relaxed martial law, however, by removing all army commanders from important civil posts and by abolishing more than 150 military courts and the martial law offices. These concessions fulfilled some of the opposition's demands and, as a result, candidates from the AL alliance (including Sheikh Hasina Wajed herself), the Jamaat-e-Islami Bangladesh and other smaller opposition parties participated in the parliamentary elections in May (postponed from April). However, the BNP alliance, led by Begum Khaleda Zia, boycotted the polls. The elections were characterized by allegations of extensive fraud, violence and intimidation. The Jatiya Dal won 153 of the 300 directly-elective seats in the Jatiya Sangsad. In addition, the 30 seats reserved for women in the legislature were filled by nominees of the Jatiya Dal. In July a mainly civilian Council of Ministers was sworn in. Mizanur Rahman Chowdhury, former General Secretary of the Jatiya Dal, was appointed Prime Minister.

In order to be eligible to stand as a candidate in the presidential election in October 1986, Ershad retired as Chief of Army Staff in August, while remaining Chief Martial Law Administrator and Commander-in-Chief of the Armed Forces. In early September Ershad officially joined the Jatiya Dal, being elected as Chairman of the party and nominated as its presidential candidate. At the presidential election in mid-October, which was boycotted by both the BNP and the AL, Ershad won an overwhelming victory over his 11 opponents.

In November 1986 the Jatiya Sangsad approved indemnity legislation, legalizing the military regime's actions since March 1982. Ershad repealed martial law and restored the 1972 Constitution. The opposition alliances criticized the indemnity law, stating that they would continue to campaign for the dissolution of the Jatiya Sangsad and the overthrow of the Ershad Government. In December 1986, in an attempt to curb increasing dissension, President Ershad formed a new Council of Ministers, including four MPs from the AL. The Minister of Justice, Justice A. K. M. Nurul Islam, was appointed Vice-President.

In 1987 the opposition groups continued to hold anti-Government strikes and demonstrations, often with the support of the trade unions and student groups. In July the Jatiya Sangsad approved a bill, enabling army representatives to participate in the district councils, along with the elected representatives. The adoption of this controversial legislation led to widespread and often violent strikes and demonstrations, organized by the opposition groups, which claimed that the bill represented an attempt by the President to secure an entrenched military involvement in the governing of the country, despite the ending of martial law in November 1986. Owing to the intensity of public opposition, President Ershad was forced to withdraw the bill in August 1987 and return it to the Jatiya Sangsad for reconsideration. Political events were overshadowed in August and September, however, when the most severe floods in the region for 40 years resulted in widespread devastation. In a renewed effort to oust President Ershad, the opposition groups combined forces and organized further protests in November. Thousands of activists were detained, but demonstrations, strikes and opposition rallies continued, leading to numerous clashes between police units and protesters. The unrest caused considerable economic dislocation, and the Government claimed that the country was losing US $50m. per day. As a result of this, and in an attempt to forestall another general strike being planned by opposition groups, President Ershad declared a nation-wide state of emergency on 27 November, suspending political activity and civil rights, and banning all anti-Government protests. In spite of the imposition of curfews on the main towns, reports of disturbances continued, as the opposition maintained its campaign to force Ershad's resignation. In early December, when about 6,000 people were being detained in prison as a result of the unrest, opposition parties in the Jatiya Sangsad announced that their representatives intended to resign their seats. On 6 December, after 12 opposition members had resigned and the 73 AL members had agreed to do likewise, President Ershad dissolved the Jatiya Sangsad. In January 1988 the President announced that parliamentary elections would be held on 28 February, but leaders of the main opposition parties declared their intention to boycott the proposed poll while Ershad remained in office. Local elections, which were held throughout Bangladesh in February and which were not boycotted by the opposition, were marred by serious outbreaks of violence. The parliamentary elections (postponed until 3 March) were also characterized by widespread violence, as well as by alleged fraud and malpractice. The opposition's boycott campaign proved to be highly successful and the actual level of participation by the electorate appeared to have been considerably lower than the Government's estimate of 50%. As expected, the Jatiya Dal won a large majority of the seats.

In late March 1988 a radical reshuffle of the Council of Ministers included the appointment of a new Prime Minister, Moudud Ahmed, a long-time political ally of Ershad and hitherto the Minister of Industry and a Deputy Prime Minister, in place of Mizanur Rahman Chowdhury. Owing to an abatement in the opposition's anti-Government campaign, Ershad repealed the state of emergency in April. Despite strong condemnation by the opposition and sections of the public, legislation to amend the

Constitution, establishing Islam as Bangladesh's state religion, was approved by an overall majority in the Jatiya Sangsad in June. By early September, however, political events had been completely overshadowed by a new wave of disastrous monsoon floods, which began in August and proved to be the most severe in the area's recorded history. Bangladesh suffered further flooding in December 1988 and January 1989, following a devastating cyclone in late November. The resultant economic problems undoubtedly compounded the political unrest in Bangladesh. In late 1988 the Government established a national Disaster Prevention Council and urged the use of regional co-operation to evolve a comprehensive solution to the problem of flooding.

The Government claimed that it was reinforcing constitutionality and democracy when, in July 1989, the Jatiya Sangsad approved legislation limiting the tenure of the presidency to two electoral terms of five years each and creating the post of a directly-elected Vice-President (previously appointed by the President). In August Ershad appointed Moudud Ahmed, hitherto the Prime Minister, as Vice-President, to replace Justice A.K.M. Nurul Islam, who was dismissed following charges of inefficiency. Kazi Zafar Ahmed, formerly the Minister of Information and a Deputy Prime Minister, was promoted to the post of Prime Minister. Local elections were held in March 1990. These elections were officially boycotted by the opposition parties, but, in fact, many of their members participated on an individual basis. In April Ershad announced that he would present himself as a candidate in the presidential election, which was scheduled to be held in mid-1991.

In late 1990 the opposition groups, with the support of thousands of students, worked more closely together and increased the intensity of their anti-Government campaign of strikes and demonstrations. In October at least eight demonstrators were shot dead by riot police, more than 500 people were arrested and Ershad announced the closure of Dhaka University and other educational institutions. Violent incidents also occurred in Chittagong and in several other towns in southern and central Bangladesh. On 27 November President Ershad proclaimed a nationwide state of emergency for the second time in three years, suspending civil rights, imposing strict press censorship and enforcing an indefinite curfew throughout the country. On the following day, however, army units were summoned to impose order in the capital when crowds of thousands defied the curfew and attacked police in protest at the imposition of the state of emergency. The death toll in resultant clashes between the troops and demonstrators was variously estimated at between 20 and 70. Under intensifying pressure from the opposition groups, President Ershad resigned on 4 December and declared that parliamentary elections would be held before the presidential election. At the same time, the state of emergency was revoked, and the Jatiya Sangsad was dissolved. Following his nomination by the opposition, Justice Shahabuddin Ahmed, the Chief Justice of the Supreme Court, was appointed Vice-President. He assumed the responsibilities of acting President and was placed at the head of a neutral caretaker Government, pending fresh parliamentary elections. Shahabuddin Ahmed dismissed heads of financial institutions, purged local government and ordered a massive reshuffle in the civil service to remove persons appointed by Ershad from important posts. The opposition parties welcomed all these dramatic political developments and abandoned their protest campaigns, while appealing for calm. They also demanded that Ershad should be tried for alleged corruption and abuse of power. In the week following his resignation, Ershad was put under house arrest (he was later sentenced to 20 years' imprisonment for illegal possession of firearms and other offences).

Fresh parliamentary elections were held in February 1991. The BNP alliance won an overall majority and, following discussions with the Jamaat-e-Islami, as a result of which the BNP was ensured a small working majority in the Jatiya Sangsad, Begum Khaleda Zia assumed office as Prime Minister. In May the new Government was faced with the immense problems caused by a devastating cyclone which killed up to 250,000 people and wrought massive economic damage. In August the Jatiya Sangsad approved a constitutional amendment ending 16 years of presidential rule and restoring the Prime Minister as executive leader (under the previous system, both the Prime Minister and the Council of Ministers had been answerable to the President). The amendment, which was formally enforced when it was approved by national referendum in the following month, reduced the role of the President, who was now to be elected by the Jatiya Sangsad for a five-year term, to that of a titular Head of State. Accordingly, a new President was elected by the Jatiya Sangsad in October. The successful candidate was the BNP nominee, the erstwhile Speaker of the Jatiya Sangsad, Abdur Rahman Biswas. In September the BNP had gained an absolute majority in the Jatiya Sangsad, following the party's victory in a number of by-elections. In late November, despite strong protest from the opposition parties, the Government abolished the *upazilla* (sub-district) system of rural administration, introduced by Ershad in 1982. Henceforth, all public functions at *upazilla* level were to be performed through executive orders of the central Government, pending the introduction of a new system of rural administration. To this end, the Government established a special committee to review all aspects of local government.

In early 1992 measures to transfer public-sector industries to private ownership and to curb endemic labour unrest led to strong political resistance from the opposition. In April, in an apparent attempt to destabilize the Government, accusations were made against the leader of the Jamaat-e-Islami, Golam Azam, of complicity in Pakistani war crimes in 1971 and of having remained a Pakistani citizen while participating in Bangladesh politics. The AL MPs boycotted the Jatiya Sangsad over the issue and demanded that Azam be put on trial immediately before a special tribunal. Eventually a compromise was reached in late June 1992, whereby charges were to be brought against him, but only through the highly dilatory regular courts. In mid-August the Government survived a parliamentary motion of 'no confidence', introduced by the AL, by 168 votes to 122. The opposition accused the Government of failing to curb the increasing lawlessness in the country, notably amongst university students. The stringent anti-terrorism measures introduced by the Government in November, however, were widely criticized as being excessively harsh and undemocratic. Subsequently, the opposition parties sank their differences in pursuit of a common demand that the general election due in 1996 be held under the auspices of a neutral, caretaker government. From late 1993 and into the first half of 1994 large-scale anti-Government demonstrations were organized by the opposition, which initiated a boycott of parliamentary proceedings in February 1994. In January the AL won the mayoralties of Dhaka and Chittagong, the country's two largest cities, but a by-election success in March revealed the continuing strength of the BNP elsewhere.

In 1993–94 the apparently increasing influence and popularity of Islamic fundamentalism in Bangladesh was reflected in the high-profile campaign against the feminist author Taslima Nasreen, who angered certain traditionalist sectors of the population with her allegedly anti-Islamic public stance and statements. Despite her claim that she had been misquoted in the national press, there were demands from Islamic bodies, often expressed at large demonstrations, that Nasreen should be executed. The Government issued a warrant for the author's arrest on blasphemy-related charges, although she had gone into hiding before it could be implemented. In August 1994, with the apparent complicity of government officials, Nasreen secretly fled Bangladesh and was granted refuge in Sweden.

The number of strikes and violent protests staged by the opposition increased in the latter half of 1994, and culminated in the resignation of all the opposition members from the Jatiya Sangsad *en masse* in December. In spite of the political chaos, compounded by the holding of further general strikes by the opposition, the Prime Minister, with her party's parliamentary majority, pledged to maintain constitutional government.

In June 1995 former President Ershad was acquitted of illegally possessing arms; his sentence was thus reduced to 10 years. In the following month, however, Ershad was sentenced to a further three years' imprisonment for criminal misconduct.

The opposition caused more general disruption in September–October 1995 by organizing nation-wide strikes, which were, at times, marked by outbreaks of violence between police and demonstrators. In response to the intensification of the anti-Government campaign and in an attempt to break the political impasse (the opposition parties were refusing to take part in the coming by-elections), the Jatiya Sangsad was dissolved in November at the request of the Prime Minister, pending the holding of a general election in early 1996. Despite opposition demands for a neutral interim government to oversee the election, the President requested that Begum Khaleda Zia's administration continue in office in an acting capacity. Strikes and demonstrations aimed at obstructing the electoral process were organized by the opposition throughout December 1995 and into January 1996. All of the main opposition parties boycotted the general election, which was held in mid-February, and independent monitors estimated the turn-out at only about 10%–15% of the electorate. Of the 207 legislative seats declared by the end of February, the BNP had won 205 (a partial repoll had been ordered in most of the 93 remaining constituencies where violence had disrupted the electoral process). The opposition refused to recognize the legitimacy of the polls and announced the launch of a 'non-co-operation' movement against the Government. Renewed street protest made the country virtually ungovernable and, finally, pressure from the army and other sources forced Begum Khaleda Zia to agree to the holding of fresh elections under neutral auspices, as the opposition had demanded all along. The Prime Minister and her Government duly resigned from their posts on 30 March and the Jatiya Sangsad was dissolved. President Biswas appointed the former Chief Justice Muhammad Habibur Rahman as acting Prime Minister and requested that a fresh general election be held, under the auspices of an interim neutral government, within three months. In the general election, which was held on 12 June, the AL won 146 of the 300 elective seats in the Jatiya Sangsad, the BNP 116, the Jatiya Dal 32 and the Jamaat-e-Islami three. An understanding was rapidly reached between the AL and the Jatiya Dal, whose major interest was the release of Ershad, who had gained a legislative seat from within prison. (The former President was released on bail in January 1997.) Sheikh Hasina Wajed was sworn in as the new Prime Minister on 23 June 1996. Her Council of Ministers incorporated one member from the Jatiya Dal; it also included a number of retired officials and army officers.

During the electoral campaign an unsuccessful military coup attempt was carried out (on 20 May 1996), which indicated the continuing fragility of the country's institutions. The Chief of Army Staff, Lt-Gen. Abu Saleh Mohammed Nasim, who had objected to the action of the President (who retained direct control of the armed forces during the caretaker period prior to the general election) in dismissing some senior officers for political activity, endeavoured to seize power, but was unable to mobilize sufficient support to achieve his aim. Lt-Gen. Nasim was immediately dismissed, and a new Chief of Army Staff was appointed.

On 23 July 1996 the AL's presidential nominee, retired Chief Justice and former acting President, Shahabuddin Ahmed, was elected unopposed (the opposition did not present any candidates) as Bangladesh's new Head of State. In early September the AL won eight of the 15 seats contested in by-elections; this result gave the AL, which was also allocated 27 of the 30 nominated women's parliamentary seats in July, an absolute majority in the Jatiya Sangsad.

On assuming power, Sheikh Hasina Wajed had vowed to bring to justice those responsible for the assassination of her father, Sheikh Mujibur Rahman, in 1975. In November 1996 the Jatiya Sangsad voted unanimously to repeal the indemnity law that had been enacted in 1975 to protect the perpetrators of the military coup in that year; the BNP and the Jamaat-e-Islami, however, boycotted the vote. The trial of 19 people accused of direct involvement in Sheikh Mujib's assassination began in March 1997, with 14 of the defendants being tried *in absentia*.

Agitational politics continued throughout 1997; in March the opposition launched a campaign to protest against the Government's agreement with India with regard to the sharing of the Ganga (Ganges) waters (see below), and during an anti-Government strike held at the end of the month one person was killed and many were injured. The opposition organized further disruptive general strikes in July and August in protest at the Government's imposition of higher taxes and the increase in fuel prices. Despite a subsequent government ban on street rallies and processions, a series of strikes and demonstrations, organized by the BNP in conjunction with Islamic and right-wing groups, ensued. In addition to the disruption caused by such actions (which frequently involved violent clashes between demonstrators and police), the efficacy of the Jatiya Sangsad was limited by several boycotts of parliamentary proceedings organized by BNP deputies throughout the year and in early 1998. In mid-1998 the opposition organized public demonstrations in protest at problems of law and order and power failures. The BNP's foremost demand was for the holding of fresh elections, echoing the AL's earlier campaign. The AL, however, strengthened its position through a series of by-election victories. The departure, therefore, of the Jatiya Dal from the coalition in March had little effect on the ruling party's hold on power. In June and August Begum Khaleda Zia was indicted on charges of corruption and abuse of power, allegedly perpetrated during her tenure of the premiership.

In August 1998 the Government appealed for international aid following devastating floods (the worst since 1988), which had caused more than 500 deaths (this figure later rose to more than 1,500) and infrastructural damage estimated at about US $220m. By late August more than 60% of the country was submerged, including large parts of the capital, and the flooding lasted an unprecedented 11 weeks.

In September 1998 the controversial author Taslima Nasreen was reported to have secretly returned to Bangladesh after four years in self-imposed exile. On her return, a fresh warrant for Nasreen's arrest on charges of blasphemy was issued by a Dhaka court and the police launched a hunt for her. Islamic extremists reiterated their demand for Nasreen's immediate arrest and execution and organized street protests. In late November Nasreen voluntarily surrendered herself before the High Court in Dhaka, where she was granted bail. In January 1999 the author left Bangladesh for Sweden, following renewed death threats from Muslim fanatics.

In September 1998 three former ministers, including the former Prime Minister Shah Moazzem Hossain and a prominent member of the BNP, K. M. Obaidur Rahman, were arrested in connection with the murder in 1975 of four former government ministers, who were shot dead in Dhaka two months after the murder of Bangladesh's founder, Sheikh Mujib. In November 1998 a Dhaka court sentenced to death 15 of the 19 people accused of Mujib's assassination; four of the defendants were acquitted. Only four of those convicted, however, were actually in custody in Bangladesh; the 11 others remained fugitives abroad.

In November 1998 the BNP organized a three-day, nationwide general strike in protest at alleged government repression. At least two people were killed and many injured when the police clashed with protestors in Dhaka (the tension was exacerbated by the BNP's disapproval of the death sentences imposed on Mujib's assassins). The Government, in response, accused the opposition of disrupting vital post-flood rehabilitation work. In mid-December at least 100 people were injured in Dhaka in further violent clashes between police and opposition activists, following protests against alleged electoral fraud on the part of the Government during a recent by-election. Later in the month the opposition was strengthened by a decision by the BNP and the Jamaat-e-Islami to accept Ershad and the Jatiya Dal in the anti-Government movement without any condition. In March 1999 the Minister of Home Affairs was forced to resign following an escalation in violence and political instability, culminating in two bomb explosions in Jessore as a result of which 11 people died. In July the opposition condemned the Government's proposals to spend US $115m. on eight Russian fighter aircraft as expensive and unnecessary. The announcement the following month of government plans to permit the transshipment of Indian goods through Bangladesh to the remote states in north-eastern India provoked further protests and strikes by the opposition, which claimed that the transit proposals would pose a threat to Bangladesh's sovereignty and would allow India to transport troops across Bangladesh's borders to suppress separatists in the adjacent Indian states. In retaliation, the Government claimed that the transshipment plans could earn Bangladesh US $400m. per year and boost the importance of the port of Chittagong. The Government was also criticized in August for its plans to evict thousands of people from Dhaka's slums in response to the increasing environmental risks and rising levels of crime; a major rehabilitation programme was to be instigated for those who were displaced. Political unrest and strikes continued throughout the latter half of 1999 and into 2000. The opposition parties boycotted parliamentary proceedings in January 2000 and persisted in their demands for the holding of early elections.

In foreign affairs Bangladesh has traditionally maintained a policy of non-alignment. Relations with Pakistan improved in 1976: ambassadors were exchanged, and trade, postal and telecommunication links were resumed. In September 1991 Pakistan finally agreed to initiate a process of phased repatriation and rehabilitation of some 250,000 Bihari Muslims (who supported Pakistan in Bangladesh's war of liberation in 1971) still remaining in refugee camps in Bangladesh. The first group of Bihari refugees returned to Pakistan from Bangladesh in January 1993, but the implementation of the repatriation process has since been very slow.

Relations with India have been strained over the questions of cross-border terrorism (especially around the area of the Chittagong Hill Tracts, where Buddhist tribal rebels, the Shanti Bahini, have been waging guerrilla warfare against the Bangladeshi police and the Bengali settlers for several years) and of the Farrakka barrage, which was constructed by India on the Ganga river in 1975, so depriving Bangladesh of water for irrigation and river transport during the dry season. In December 1996, however, Indo-Bangladesh relations were given a major boost following the signing of an historic 30-year water-sharing agreement. In January 1997 the Indian Prime Minister, H. D. Deve Gowda, paid an official visit to Bangladesh, the first Indian Premier to do so for 20 years. In June 1999, during a visit to Dhaka by the Indian Prime Minister, Atal Bihari Vajpayee, to celebrate the inauguration of the first direct passenger bus service between Bangladesh and India, Vajpayee promised Bangladesh greater access to Indian markets and announced that India would give its neighbour US $50m. in credits over three years to help develop its transport and industrial infrastructure. In August the Bangladesh Government was criticized by the opposition for its approval of proposals to permit the transshipment of Indian goods through Bangladesh to the north-eastern states of India by Bangladeshi transport companies.

In 1985 Bangladesh and Burma (now Myanmar) completed work on the demarcation of their common border, in accordance with a 1979 agreement. During 1991 more than 50,000 Rohingya Muslims, a Myanma ethnic minority, crossed into Bangladesh to escape political persecution in Myanmar. Despite the signing of an agreement by the Governments of Bangladesh and Myanmar in April 1992 regarding the repatriation of the Rohingyas, the influx of refugees continued unabated (by the end of June the number of Rohingya refugees in Bangladesh had increased to about 270,000). By early September 1994 about 65,000 refugees had reportedly been voluntarily repatriated. Meanwhile, in December 1993 Bangladesh and Myanmar had signed an agreement to instigate bilateral border trade. By the end of May 1995, according to government figures, more than 216,000 Rohingyas had been repatriated. In July 1999, however, about 20,000 Rohingya refugees remained in camps in Bangladesh, despite the expiry of the official deadline for their repatriation in August 1997.

In 1989 the Government attempted to suppress the continuing insurgency being waged by the Shanti Bahini in the Chittagong Hill Tracts, by introducing concessions providing limited autonomy to the region in the form of three new semi-autonomous hill districts. In June voting to elect councils for the districts took place reasonably peacefully, despite attempts at disruption by the Shanti Bahini, who continued to demand total autonomy for the Chakma tribals. The powers vested in the councils were designed to give the tribals sufficient authority to regulate any further influx of Bengali settlers to the districts (the chief complaint of the tribals since Bengalis were settled in the Chittagong Hill Tracts, as plantation workers and clerks, by the British administration in the 19th century). Despite these concessions, the violence continued unabated, and refugees continued to flee across the border into India (the number of refugees living in camps in Tripura reached about 56,000). In May 1992 the Governments of Bangladesh and India negotiated an agreement which was intended to facilitate the refugees' return. However, the refugees, fearing persecution by the Bangladesh security forces, proved reluctant to move. Following the conclusion of a successful round of negotiations in early 1994, the process of repatriation, which was to be carried out in phases, commenced in mid-February. By August, however, only about 2,000 refugees had returned. In December 1997 the Bangladesh Government signed a peace agreement with the political wing of the Shanti Bahini ending the insurgency in the Chittagong Hill Tracts. The treaty offered the rebels a general amnesty in return for the surrender of their arms and gave the tribal people greater powers of self-governance through the establishment of three new elected district councils (to control the area's land management and policing) and a regional council (the chairman of which was to enjoy the rank of a state minister). The peace agreement, which was strongly criticized by the opposition for representing a 'sell-out' of the area to India and a threat to Bangladesh's sovereignty, was expected to accelerate the process of repatriating the remaining refugees from Tripura (who totalled about 31,000 at the end of December 1997). According to official Indian sources, only about 5,500 refugees remained in Tripura by early February 1998. All of the Chakma refugees were expected to be repatriated by February 1999.

In June 1992 the Indian Government, under the provisions of an accord signed with Bangladesh in 1974, formally leased the Tin Bigha Corridor (a small strip of land covering an area of only 1.5 ha) to Bangladesh for 999 years. India maintained sovereignty over the corridor, but the lease gave Bangladesh access to its enclaves of Dahagram and Angarpota. In September 1997 India granted Nepal a transit route through a 60-km corridor in the Indian territory joining Nepal and Bangladesh, thus facilitating trade between the latter two countries.

Bangladesh is a member of the South Asian Association for Regional Co-operation (SAARC, see p. 259), formally constituted in 1985, with Bhutan, India, Maldives, Nepal, Pakistan and Sri Lanka. Included in SAARC's charter are pledges of non-interference by members in each other's internal affairs and a joint effort to avoid 'contentious' issues whenever the association meets. The SAARC Preferential Trading Arrangement (SAPTA) was signed in April 1993 and came into effect in December 1995. It was also agreed that members should work towards the objective of establishing a South Asian Free Trade Area (SAFTA) by 2005.

## Government

The role of the President, who is elected by the Jatiya Sangsad (Parliament) for a five-year term, is essentially that of a titular Head of State. Executive power is held by the Prime Minister, who heads the Council of Ministers. The President appoints the Prime Minister and, on the latter's recommendation, other ministers. Three hundred of the 330-member Jatiya Sangsad are elected by universal suffrage. An additional 30 women members are appointed by the other members. The Jatiya Sangsad serves a five-year term, subject to dissolution.

For purposes of local government, the country is divided into 64 administrative districts.

## Defence

Military service is voluntary. In August 1999 the armed forces numbered 137,000: an army of 120,000, a navy of 10,500 and an air force of 6,500. The paramilitary forces totalled 55,200, and included the Bangladesh Rifles (border guard) of 30,000. Budget expenditure on defence was estimated at 30,000m. taka for 1999.

## Economic Affairs

In 1997, according to estimates by the World Bank, Bangladesh's gross national product (GNP), measured at average 1995–97 prices, was US $44,090m., equivalent to $360 per head. During 1990–97, it was estimated, GNP per head increased, in real terms, at an average annual rate of 3.3%. Over the same period, the population increased at an average annual rate of 1.6%. In 1998 GNP was estimated at $44,000m. ($350 per head). Bangladesh's gross domestic product (GDP) increased at an average annual rate of 4.8% in 1990–98; GDP grew by 5.7% in 1996/97, by 5.6% in 1997/98 and by 4.2% in 1998/99.

Agriculture (including hunting, forestry and fishing) contributed an estimated 28.9% of total GDP in 1997/98. About 58% of the economically active population were employed in agriculture in 1998. The principal sources of revenue in the agricultural sector are jute (which accounted for an estimated 7.6% of total export earnings in 1997/98), fish and tea. In 1990–98 agricultural GDP rose at an average annual rate of 1.5%. Despite severe flooding, agricultural output rose by about 3% in 1998/99 (the flood waters destroyed the summer crops, but led to bumper winter crops).

Industry (including mining, manufacturing, power and construction) employed 9.6% of the working population in 1995/96, and contributed an estimated 17.5% of total GDP in 1997/98. During 1990–98 industrial GDP increased at an average annual rate of 7.0%; industrial output grew by only about 3% in 1998/99 (compared with around 7% in 1997/98), largely owing to a deceleration in export growth in the ready-made garments sector as competition increased from South-East Asia.

Manufacturing contributed an estimated 9.4% of total GDP in 1997/98, and employed 7.5% of the working population in 1995/96. Based on a census of establishments engaged in manufacturing (excluding hand-loom weaving), the principal branches of the sector, measured by value of output, in 1991/92 were textiles (accounting for 23.8% of the total), food products (20.4%), wearing apparel (excluding footwear) (13.6%) and chemicals (11.4%). During 1990–97 manufacturing GDP increased at an average annual rate of 7.5%. Manufacturing output grew by 3.3% in 1996/97 and by 11.5% in 1997/98.

Mineral resources in Bangladesh are few. There are, however, large but underdeveloped reserves of natural gas (see below) and smaller deposits of coal (estimated at more than 1,000m. metric tons) and petroleum.

Energy is derived principally from natural gas and petroleum. In 1999 natural gas provided about 70% of the country's commercial energy requirement, compared with less than 40% in the early 1980s. Total proven reserves of natural gas in Bangladesh currently amount to around 25,000,000m. cu ft, but, in the light of recent discoveries of vast gas fields, actual reserves may be twice as large or more. Imports of petroleum products and crude petroleum comprised an estimated 6.7% of the cost of total imports in 1997/98.

In 1998, according to the IMF, Bangladesh recorded a visible trade deficit of US $1,720.6m., and there was a deficit of $189.8m. on the current account of the balance of payments. In 1997/98 the principal source of imports was India (which contributed an estimated 15% of the total), while Western Europe was the principal market for exports (accounting for an estimated 49% of the total). Other major trading partners were the USA, Japan, the People's Republic of China and Hong Kong. The principal exports in 1997/98 were ready-made garments (accounting for an estimated 54.8% of export revenue), knitwear and hosiery products, raw jute and jute goods, and frozen shrimp and fish. The principal imports were capital goods (an estimated 25.5% of the total), textiles, yarn and petroleum products.

In 1999/2000 the overall budgetary deficit was projected to amount to 91,490m. taka. Bangladesh's total external debt, according to the World Bank, was US $15,125m. at the end of 1997, of which $14,578m. was long-term public debt. In that year the cost of debt-servicing was equivalent to 10.6% of the total revenue from exports of goods and services. The annual rate of inflation averaged 4.2% in 1990–97; consumer prices increased by 3.4% in the twelve months ending November 1999. About 2.5% of the total labour force were unemployed in 1996. Remittances from Bangladeshis working abroad, which are Bangladesh's second-largest source of foreign revenue after ready-made garments, rose by about 4.9% in 1998, compared with the previous year, to an estimated $1,600m.

Bangladesh is a member of the South Asian Association for Regional Co-operation (SAARC, see p. 259), which seeks to improve regional co-operation, particularly in economic development.

The problems of developing Bangladesh are manifold, in view of the widespread poverty, malnutrition and underemployment superimposed on an increasing population and a poor resource base. There are grounds, however, for cautious optimism. Despite the frequency of natural disasters, food production has improved somewhat in recent years, the birth rate has decreased considerably, owing to a successful nation-wide birth control campaign, and quite remarkable achievements have been made in the field of export-promotion, especially in non-traditional items (notably cotton garments). Bangladesh remains, however, heavily dependent on large amounts of foreign aid. The World Bank-led Paris aid group, which co-ordinates annual aid flows to Bangladesh, commits about US $2,000m. in aid every year, of which around $1,700m.–$1,800m. is actually disbursed. In 1994 Bangladesh's economy showed clear signs of stabilization as a result of the Government's reform and liberalization programme, which was introduced in 1991. In 1995–99, however, the social and political unrest (including frequent general strikes) had a negative impact on the level of foreign investment. The Awami League Government, which came to power in 1996, has emphasized its commitment to rehabilitating the weak banking sector and, despite resistance from trade unionists, to accelerating the process of privatizing the country's chronically infirm state-owned enterprises. In September 1999, however, Bangladesh's international aid donors warned that funds would be reduced if the Government failed to accelerate the implementation of economic reforms, particularly in the financial sector and in the extremely tardy privatization process. It was estimated that the state-owned commercial banks had outstanding bad loans of about US $3,000m. The donors also criticized the Government for increasing expenditure on defence, while the education and health sectors remained under-funded. On a more positive note, the recently-discovered huge reserves of natural gas appeared to offer Bangladesh the opportunity to transform itself into a middle-income country. However, international gas and oil companies that were interested in acquiring exploration licences met with a worrying lack of transparency and accountability on the part of the Bangladesh Government. An additional problem was the Government's reluctance to commit itself to allowing gas exports to India, the most obvious large market for the product.

## Social Welfare

Basic health services remain relatively undeveloped. Health programmes give particular priority to the popularization of birth control (an estimated 4.2% of public-sector development expenditure was allocated to family planning in 1997/98. In 1981 Bangladesh had 504 hospital establishments, with a total of only 19,727 beds, equivalent to one for every 4,545 inhabitants: one of the lowest levels of health-care provision in the world. In the early 1990s there were 18 physicians per 100,000 inhabitants and five nurses per 100,000 inhabitants. Government development expenditure on health totalled 13,700m. taka in 1998/99 (equivalent to 10.1% of total public-sector development expenditure); an additional 1,900m. taka was allocated to social welfare. In late 1996 about 20m. children were inoculated against poliomyelitis as part of a mass campaign by the Bangladeshi authorities to eradicate the disease.

## Education

The Government provides free schooling for children of both sexes for eight years. Primary education, which is compulsory, begins at six years of age and lasts for five years. Secondary education, beginning at the age of 11, lasts for up to seven years, comprising a first cycle of five years and a second cycle of two further years. In 1990 an estimated 62% of children (66% of boys; 58% of girls) in the relevant age-group attended primary schools, while the enrolment ratio at secondary schools was 20% of children (26% of boys; 14% of girls) in the relevant age-group. Secondary schools and colleges in the private sector vastly outnumber government institutions. There are seven state universities, including one for agriculture, one for Islamic studies and one for engineering. The Government launched an Open University Project in 1992 at an estimated cost of US $34.3m. In 1990 the Government initiated the Primary Education Sector Project, which aimed to help to achieve universal primary education and the eradication of illiteracy by the year 2000. In 1995, according to UNESCO estimates, the rate of adult illiteracy was 61.9% (males 50.6%; females 73.9%). Government development expenditure on education was set at 19,291m. taka for 1999/2000 (equivalent to 12.4% of total public-sector development expenditure).

## Public Holidays

**2000:** 1 January (New Year's Day), 8 January*† (Id al-Fitr, end of Ramadan), 21 February (National Mourning Day), 16 March* (Id al-Adha, Feast of the Sacrifice), 26 March (Independence Day), 6 April* (Muharram, Islamic New Year), 21 April (Good Friday), 24 April (Easter Monday), May* (Buddha Purinama), 1 May (May Day), 15 June* (Birth of the Prophet), July* (Jamat Wida), August/September (Janmashtami), September* (Shab-i-Bharat), September/October* (Durga Puja), 7 November (National Revolution Day), 16 December (National Day), 25 December (Christmas), 26 December (Boxing Day), 28 December*† (Id al-Fitr, end of Ramadan).

**2001:** 1 January (New Year's Day), 21 February (National Mourning Day), 26 March (Independence Day), 6 March* (Id al-Adha, Feast of the Sacrifice), 26 March* (Muharram, Islamic New Year), 13 April (Good Friday), 16 April (Easter Monday), May* (Buddha Purinama), 1 May (May Day), 4 June* (Birth of the Prophet), July* (Jamat Wida), August/September (Janmashtami), September* (Shab-i-Bharat), September/October* (Durga Puja), 7 November (National Revolution Day), 16 December (National Day), 17 December* (Id al-Fitr, end of Ramadan), 25 December (Christmas), 26 December (Boxing Day).

* Dates of certain religious holidays are subject to the sighting of the moon, and there are also optional holidays for different religious groups.

† This festival will occur twice (in the Islamic years AH 1420 and AH 1421) within the same Gregorian year.

## Weights and Measures

The imperial system of measures is in force, pending the introduction of the metric system. The following local units of weight are also used:

1 maund = 82.28 lb (37.29 kg).
1 seer = 2.057 lb (932 grams).

# Statistical Survey

Source (unless otherwise stated): Bangladesh Bureau of Statistics, Industry, Trade, Labour Statistics and National Income Wing, 14/2 Topkhana Rd, Dhaka 1000; tel. (2) 409871.

## Area and Population

**AREA, POPULATION AND DENSITY**

| | |
|---|---|
| Area (sq km) | 147,570* |
| Population (census results) | |
| 6 March 1981 | 89,912,000† |
| 11 March 1991‡ | |
| Males | 57,313,929 |
| Females | 54,141,256 |
| Total | 111,455,185 |
| Population (UN estimates at mid-year)§ | |
| 1996 | 120,594,000 |
| 1997 | 122,650,000 |
| 1998 | 124,774,000 |
| Density (per sq km) at mid-1998 | 845.5 |

* 56,977 sq miles.
† Including adjustment for net underenumeration, estimated to have been 3.2%. The enumerated total was 87,119,965.
‡ Including adjustment for net underenumeration.
§ Source: UN, *World Population Prospects: The 1998 Revision.*

**POPULATION BY DIVISIONS***

| | 1981 Census | 1991 Census† |
|---|---|---|
| Chittagong | 23,322,000 | 28,811,446 |
| Dhaka | 27,091,000 | 33,593,103 |
| Khulna | 17,695,000 | 20,804,515 |
| Rajshahi | 21,804,000 | 26,667,913 |
| **Total** | 89,912,000 | 109,876,977 |

* Including adjustments for net underenumeration.
† Figures are provisional. The revised total is 111,455,185.

**PRINCIPAL TOWNS** (population at 1991 census)

| | | | |
|---|---|---|---|
| Dhaka (capital) | 3,637,892* | Barisal | 180,014 |
| Chittagong | 1,566,070 | Jessore | 176,398 |
| Khulna | 601,051 | Comilla | 164,509 |
| Rajshahi | 324,532 | Sylhet | 114,284 |
| Rangpur | 220,849 | Saidpur | 110,494 |

* Including Narayanganj (population 270,680 in 1974).

**BIRTHS AND DEATHS***

| | Registered live births Rate (per 1,000) | Registered deaths Rate (per 1,000) |
|---|---|---|
| 1990 | 32.8 | 11.4 |
| 1991 | 31.6 | 11.2 |
| 1992 | 30.8 | 11.0 |
| 1993 | 28.8 | 10.0 |
| 1994 | 27.8 | 9.0 |
| 1995 | 26.5 | 8.4 |
| 1996 | 25.6 | 8.1 |

* Registration is incomplete. According to UN estimates, the average annual rates per 1,000 were: Births 38.1 in 1985–90, 27.8 in 1990–95; Deaths 13.9 in 1985–90, 10.8 in 1990–95 (Source: UN, *World Population Prospects: The 1998 Revision*).

**1997** (provisional): Registered live births 3,057,000 (birth rate 25.1 per 1,000); Registered deaths 958,000 (death rate 7.9 per 1,000) (Source: UN, *Population and Vital Statistics Report*).

**Expectation of life** (UN estimates, years at birth, 1990–95): 55.6 (males 55.6; females 55.6). Source: UN, *World Population Prospects: The 1998 Revision.*

**ECONOMICALLY ACTIVE POPULATION***
(sample survey, '000 persons aged 10 years and over, year ending June 1996)

| | Males | Females | Total |
|---|---|---|---|
| Agriculture, hunting, forestry and fishing | 18,382 | 16,148 | 34,530 |
| Mining and quarrying | 22 | 1 | 23 |
| Manufacturing | 2,586 | 1,499 | 4,085 |
| Electricity, gas and water | 90 | 13 | 103 |
| Construction | 936 | 80 | 1,015 |
| Trade, restaurants and hotels | 5,573 | 488 | 6,060 |
| Transport, storage and communications | 2,263 | 45 | 2,308 |
| Financing, insurance, real estate and business services | 197 | 16 | 213 |
| Community, social and personal services | 3,343 | 1,748 | 5,092 |
| Activities not adequately defined | 373 | 795 | 1,168 |
| **Total employed** | 33,765 | 20,832 | 54,597 |
| Unemployed | 933 | 484 | 1,417 |
| **Total labour force** | 34,698 | 21,317 | 56,014 |

* Figures exclude members of the armed forces.
Source: ILO, *Yearbook of Labour Statistics.*

## Agriculture

**PRINCIPAL CROPS**
(million metric tons, unless otherwise indicated, year ending 30 June)

| | 1995/96 | 1996/97 | 1997/98‡ |
|---|---|---|---|
| Rice (milled) | 17.7 | 18.9 | 18.8 |
| Wheat | 1.4 | 1.5 | 1.8 |
| Jute (million bales*) | 4.1 | 4.9 | 5.8 |
| Tea ('000 metric tons) | 47.7 | 53.0 | 54.0 |
| Cotton ('000 bales†) | 75.9 | 95.8 | 100.0 |
| Oilseed | 0.5 | 0.4 | 0.5 |
| Pulses | 0.5 | 0.5 | 0.7 |
| Potatoes | 1.9 | 1.9 | 2.4 |
| Other vegetables | 1.2 | 1.2 | 1.5 |
| Tobacco ('000 metric tons) | 39.4 | 38.0 | 38.0 |
| Sugar cane | 7.2 | 7.5 | 10.9 |
| Fruit | 1.6 | 1.5 | 2.4 |

* Each of 400 lb (181.4 kg).
† Each of 500 lb (226.8 kg) gross or 480 lb (217.7 kg) net.
‡ Estimates.

**LIVESTOCK** ('000 head, year ending September)

| | 1996 | 1997 | 1998 |
|---|---|---|---|
| Cattle | 23,573 | 23,962 | 23,400 |
| Buffaloes | 828 | 854* | 854† |
| Sheep | 1,124 | 1,158 | 1,158† |
| Goats | 33,312 | 34,478 | 33,500 |
| Chickens | 143,000 | 153,000 | 153,000† |
| Ducks | 14,000 | 13,000 | 13,000† |

* Unofficial figure. † FAO estimate.

Source: FAO, *Production Yearbook.*

**LIVESTOCK PRODUCTS** ('000 metric tons)

| | 1996 | 1997 | 1998 |
|---|---|---|---|
| Beef and veal | 171 | 183* | 161 |
| Buffalo meat | 4 | 4* | 4* |
| Mutton and lamb | 3 | 3* | 3* |
| Goat meat | 115 | 116* | 126 |
| Poultry meat* | 118 | 124 | 124 |
| Cows' milk* | 770 | 770 | 770 |
| Buffalo milk* | 22 | 22 | 22 |
| Sheeps' milk* | 22 | 22 | 22 |
| Goats' milk* | 1,280 | 1,328 | 1,328 |
| Butter and ghee* | 16 | 16 | 16 |
| Cheese* | 1 | 1 | 1 |
| Hen eggs* | 95 | 104 | 104 |
| Other poultry eggs* | 28 | 28 | 28 |
| Wool: | | | |
| greasy* | 1 | 1 | 1 |
| clean* | 1 | 1 | 1 |
| Cattle and buffalo hides* | 35 | 32 | 32 |
| Goatskins* | 37 | 39 | 39 |

* FAO estimate(s).

Source: FAO, *Production Yearbook*.

# Forestry

**ROUNDWOOD REMOVALS**
('000 cubic metres, excl. bark)

| | 1995 | 1996 | 1997 |
|---|---|---|---|
| Sawlogs, veneer logs and logs for sleepers | 155 | 174 | 174 |
| Pulpwood* | 69 | 69 | 69 |
| Other industrial wood | 354 | 360 | 366 |
| Fuel wood | 30,739 | 31,218 | 31,723 |
| **Total** | 31,317 | 31,821 | 32,332 |

* Annual output assumed to be unchanged since 1986.

Source: FAO, *Yearbook of Forest Products*.

**SAWNWOOD PRODUCTION** ('000 cubic metres, incl. railway sleepers)

| | 1995 | 1996 | 1997 |
|---|---|---|---|
| **Total** | 70 | 70 | 70 |

Source: FAO, *Yearbook of Forest Products*.

# Fishing

('000 metric tons, live weight)

| | 1995 | 1996 | 1997 |
|---|---|---|---|
| Freshwater fishes | 443.3 | 445.4 | 451.1 |
| Hilsa shad | 213.5 | 225.6 | 215.0 |
| Other marine fishes | 115.2 | 119.5 | 135.9 |
| Crustaceans | 20.4 | 24.3 | 28.0 |
| **Total** | 792.4 | 814.8 | 830.0 |

Source: FAO, *Yearbook of Fishery Statistics*.

# Mining

(petajoules, year ending 30 June)

| | 1993/94 | 1994/95 | 1995/96 |
|---|---|---|---|
| Natural gas | 233 | 270 | 264 |

Source: UN, *Statistical Yearbook for Asia and the Pacific*.

# Industry

**SELECTED PRODUCTS** ('000 metric tons, unless otherwise indicated; public sector only, year ending 30 June)

| | 1994/95 | 1995/96 | 1996/97 |
|---|---|---|---|
| Jute textiles | 276 | 275 | 269 |
| Hessian | 89 | 81 | 73 |
| Sacking | 145 | 152 | 157 |
| Carpet backing | 35 | 35 | 33 |
| Others | 7 | 7 | 6 |
| Woven cotton fabrics (million metres) | 17 | 10 | 11 |
| Pure cotton yarn | 49 | 50 | 50 |
| Newsprint | 43 | 40 | 28 |
| Other paper | 40 | 42 | 40 |
| Cement | 316 | 426 | 611 |
| Steel ingots | 25 | 21 | 16 |
| Re-rolled steel products | 10 | 33 | 27 |
| Petroleum products | 1,371 | 1,160 | 1,310 |
| Urea fertilizer | 1,981 | 2,134 | 1,631 |
| Ammonium sulphate | 5 | 7 | 9 |
| Chemicals | 20 | 25 | 19 |
| Refined sugar | 270 | 184 | 135 |
| Wine and spirits ('000 litres) | 3,650 | 2,196 | 2,747 |
| Tea | 47 | 51 | 53 |
| Edible oil and vegetable ghee | 30 | 31 | 26 |
| Cigarettes ('000 million) | 17 | 16 | 19 |
| Electric energy (million kWh) | 10,806 | 11,474 | 11,492 |

**1997/98** ('000 metric tons, unless otherwise indicated): Pure cotton yarn 53.5, Woven cotton fabrics 10.7 million metres, Petroleum products 1,400, Cement 574.3, Refined sugar 195.4.

# Finance

**CURRENCY AND EXCHANGE RATES**

**Monetary Units**
100 poisha = 1 taka.

**Sterling, Dollar and Euro Equivalents** (30 September 1999)
£1 sterling = 81.50 taka;
US $1 = 49.50 taka;
€1 = 52.79 taka;
1,000 taka = £12.27 = $20.20 = €18.94.

**Average Exchange Rate** (taka per US $)
1996 41.794
1997 43.892
1998 46.906

**BUDGET** (million taka, year ending 30 June)

| Revenue | 1996/97 | 1997/98* | 1998/99† |
|---|---|---|---|
| Taxation | 133,100 | 147,000 | 167,300 |
| Customs duties | 40,100 | 43,500 | 50,300 |
| Income and profit taxes | 16,400 | 20,000 | 24,500 |
| Excise duties | 2,000 | 2,200 | 2,300 |
| Value-added tax | 63,800 | 69,800 | 78,500 |
| Non-tax | 32,800 | 38,500 | 42,700 |
| Profits from non-financial enterprises | 2,200 | 3,400 | 4,200 |
| Profits from financial institutions | 4,500 | 4,800 | 5,700 |
| Interest receipts | 5,300 | 5,700 | 5,900 |
| Registration fees | 1,700 | 1,800 | 1,900 |
| Services | 8,900 | 9,700 | 10,400 |
| Bangladesh Telephone and Telegraph Board | 6,300 | 7,700 | 9,100 |
| **Total** | 165,900 | 185,500 | 210,000 |

* Revised figures. † Estimates.

**1999/2000** (million taka, year ending 30 June): Total projected revenue 241,510.

| Expenditure | 1996/97 | 1997/98* | 1998/99† |
|---|---|---|---|
| Goods and services | 76,000 | 78,600 | 82,500 |
| Pay and allowances | 43,900 | 46,500 | 48,600 |
| Operations and maintenance | 8,400 | 6,200 | 6,200 |
| Works | 2,100 | 2,300 | 2,300 |
| Interest payments | 17,600 | 23,300 | 25,700 |
| Domestic | 10,800 | 16,000 | 18,500 |
| Foreign | 6,800 | 7,300 | 7,300 |
| Subsidies and current transfers | 31,900 | 41,300 | 44,700 |
| Local government transfers | 700 | 700 | 700 |
| Grants in aid | 16,300 | 24,700 | 26,500 |
| Pensions and gratuities | 7,100 | 7,800 | 8,700 |
| Targeted food distribution | 4,700 | 5,200 | 5,000 |
| Subsidies for fertilizer | 1,600 | 1,200 | 1,300 |
| Other subsidies | 300 | 400 | 1,400 |
| Operational deficits | 1,200 | 1,200 | 1,200 |
| Unallocated | 300 | 700 | 5,300 |
| **Gross current expenditure** | 125,800 | 143,900 | 158,200 |
| *Less* Recoveries | 2,100 | 700 | 700 |
| **Net current expenditure** | 123,600 | 143,200 | 157,500 |

* Revised figures. †Estimates.

Source: IMF, *Bangladesh—Statistical Appendix* (December 1998).

**1999/2000** (million taka, year ending 30 June): Total projected expenditure 178,000.

**PUBLIC-SECTOR DEVELOPMENT EXPENDITURE**
(estimates, million taka, year ending 30 June)

| | 1996/97 | 1997/98‡ | 1998/99 |
|---|---|---|---|
| Agriculture | 6,400 | 6,000 | 7,400 |
| Rural development | 10,300 | 9,000 | 11,100 |
| Water and flood control | 10,600 | 10,400 | 8,800 |
| Industry | 1,900 | 1,200 | 1,400 |
| Power, scientific research and natural resources | 19,300 | 18,800 | 21,200 |
| Transport* | 23,300 | 22,600 | 23,900 |
| Communications | 2,700 | 3,900 | 5,100 |
| Physical planning and housing | 6,800 | 6,000 | 8,000 |
| Education | 15,800 | 14,900 | 16,800 |
| Health | 5,800 | 5,300 | 13,700 |
| Family planning | 4,900 | 6,300 | — |
| Social welfare† | 1,900 | 1,600 | 1,900 |
| Other sectoral | 100 | 200 | 400 |
| **Total sectoral allocations** | 109,800 | 106,400 | 119,700 |
| Block allocations | 2,400 | 10,900 | 11,300 |
| Food for Work | — | 5,700 | 5,400 |
| Technical assistance | 3,200 | 3,000 | 3,200 |
| Domestic self-financing | 1,600 | 1,700 | 1,800 |
| **Total development expenditure** | 117,000 | 122,000 | 136,000 |

* Includes Jamuna Bridge.
† Includes employment.
‡ Revised figures.

Source: Ministry of Planning (Implementation, Monitoring and Evaluation Division).

**1999/2000** (estimates, million taka, year ending 30 June): Education 19,291, Agriculture 8,350; **Total** (incl. others) 155,000.

**INTERNATIONAL RESERVES** (US $ million at 31 December)

| | 1996 | 1997 | 1998 |
|---|---|---|---|
| Gold* | 28.0 | 25.3 | 22.3 |
| IMF special drawing rights | 109.6 | 29.2 | 12.9 |
| Reserve position in IMF | 0.2 | 0.1 | 0.2 |
| Foreign exchange | 1,724.9 | 1,552.1 | 1,892.3 |
| **Total** | 1,862.7 | 1,606.7 | 1,927.7 |

* Valued at market-related prices.

Source: IMF, *International Financial Statistics*.

**MONEY SUPPLY** (million taka at 31 December)

| | 1996 | 1997 | 1998 |
|---|---|---|---|
| Currency outside banks | 68,195 | 76,074 | 80,756 |
| Demand deposits at deposit money banks* | 73,481 | 76,559 | 83,214 |
| **Total money** | 141,676 | 152,633 | 163,970 |

* Comprises the scheduled banks plus the agricultural and industrial development banks.

Source: IMF, *International Financial Statistics*.

**COST OF LIVING** (Consumer Price Index for middle-class families in Dhaka, year ending 30 June; base: 1973/74 = 100)

| | 1994/95 | 1995/96 | 1996/97 |
|---|---|---|---|
| Food | 732 | 774 | 812 |
| Fuel and lighting | 1,014 | 1,030 | 1,056 |
| Housing and household requisites | 1,040 | 1,047 | 1,067 |
| Clothing and footwear | 439 | 439 | 439 |
| Miscellaneous | 860 | 883 | 883 |
| **All items** | 786 | 818 | 850 |

**NATIONAL ACCOUNTS** (million taka at current prices, year ending 30 June)

**Expenditure on the Gross Domestic Product**

| | 1995/96 | 1996/97 | 1997/98* |
|---|---|---|---|
| Government final consumption expenditure | 177,655 | 198,225 | 227,584 |
| Private final consumption expenditure | 1,026,129 | 1,099,416 | 1,191,606 |
| Gross capital formation | 224,370 | 214,272 | 223,380 |
| **Total domestic expenditure** | 1,428,154 | 1,511,913 | 1,642,570 |
| Exports of goods and services | 184,359 | 216,723 | 258,948 |
| *Less* Imports of goods and services | 310,913 | 325,591 | 360,595 |
| **GDP in purchasers' values** | 1,301,600 | 1,403,045 | 1,540,923 |

* Estimates.

**Gross Domestic Product by Economic Activity**

| | 1995/96 | 1996/97 | 1997/98* |
|---|---|---|---|
| Agriculture and hunting | 282,057 | 294,605 | 312,519 |
| Forestry and logging | 43,059 | 45,531 | 50,096 |
| Fishing | 64,870 | 71,496 | 82,182 |
| Mining and quarrying | 282 | 365 | 457 |
| Manufacturing | 124,411 | 130,496 | 145,115 |
| Electricity, gas and water | 28,630 | 30,318 | 32,918 |
| Construction | 76,599 | 82,863 | 91,544 |
| Wholesale and retail trade | 117,461 | 124,996 | 137,433 |
| Transport, storage and communications | 148,238 | 161,161 | 172,946 |
| Owner-occupied dwellings | 124,567 | 135,106 | 146,597 |
| Finance, insurance and business services | 26,373 | 28,512 | 30,285 |
| Public administration and defence | 70,742 | 79,950 | 91,577 |
| Other services | 194,311 | 217,646 | 247,254 |
| **Total** | 1,301,600 | 1,403,045 | 1,540,923 |

* Provisional figures.

**BALANCE OF PAYMENTS** (US $ million)

| | 1996 | 1997 | 1998 |
|---|---|---|---|
| Exports of goods f.o.b. | 4,009.3 | 4,839.9 | 5,141.4 |
| Imports of goods f.o.b. | −6,284.6 | −6,587.6 | −6,862.1 |
| **Trade balance** | −2,275.3 | −1,747.7 | −1,720.6 |
| Exports of services | 604.8 | 687.3 | 723.9 |
| Imports of services | −1,166.0 | −1,287.9 | −1,253.3 |
| **Balance on goods and services** | −2,836.5 | −2,348.3 | −2,250.0 |
| Other income received | 129.4 | 86.5 | 90.0 |
| Other income paid | −193.1 | −196.1 | −197.5 |
| **Balance on goods, services and income** | −2,900.2 | −2,457.9 | −2,357.5 |
| Current transfers received | 1,912.8 | 2,134.9 | 2,173.6 |
| Current transfers paid | −4.0 | −4.3 | −5.9 |
| **Current balance** | −991.4 | −327.3 | −189.8 |
| Capital account (net) | 371.2 | 368.1 | 238.7 |
| Direct investment abroad | — | −3.1 | −3.0 |
| Direct investment from abroad | 13.5 | 141.3 | 307.9 |
| Portfolio investment assets | — | — | −0.3 |
| Portfolio investment liabilities | −117.0 | −14.5 | 0.9 |
| Other investment assets | −426.7 | −674.6 | −876.0 |
| Other investment liabilities | 622.6 | 451.1 | 596.6 |
| Net errors and omissions | 113.5 | −77.3 | 215.2 |
| **Overall balance** | −414.3 | −136.3 | 290.2 |

Source: IMF, *International Financial Statistics*.

**FOREIGN AID DISBURSEMENTS** (US $ million, year ending 30 June)

| | 1995/96 | 1996/97 | 1997/98* |
|---|---|---|---|
| Bilateral donors | 756.9 | 717.2 | 608.8 |
| Australia | 11.1 | 15.7 | 9.1 |
| Canada | 24.8 | 30.4 | 21.1 |
| Denmark | 13.6 | 22.7 | 25.0 |
| France | 9.7 | 27.0 | 20.6 |
| Germany | 64.1 | 33.8 | 40.0 |
| Japan | 331.1 | 368.2 | 301.7 |
| Netherlands | 32.9 | 71.9 | 25.0 |
| Norway | 29.8 | 16.7 | 29.3 |
| Saudi Arabia | 30.8 | 10.1 | 7.0 |
| Sweden | 5.2 | 22.1 | 23.4 |
| United Kingdom | 33.3 | 20.6 | 28.0 |
| USA | 51.3 | 35.3 | 38.6 |
| Multilateral donors | 686.9 | 764.0 | 809.8 |
| Asian Development Bank | 279.0 | 254.9 | 310.0 |
| International Development Association | 225.6 | 313.8 | 327.0 |
| European Union | 90.9 | 62.0 | 60.0 |
| World Food Programme | 34.3 | 18.3 | 43.2 |
| UNICEF | 20.9 | 60.2 | 22.0 |
| Islamic Development Bank | 11.0 | 19.3 | 16.3 |
| OPEC Fund | 15.9 | 17.4 | 3.0 |
| **Total aid disbursements** | 1,443.8 | 1,481.2 | 1,418.6 |

* Estimates.

Source: Ministry of Finance (Economic Relations Division).

# External Trade

**PRINCIPAL COMMODITIES** (US $ million, year ending 30 June)

| Imports | 1995/96 | 1996/97 | 1997/98* |
|---|---|---|---|
| Rice | 358 | 28 | 195 |
| Wheat | 228 | 156 | 155 |
| Edible oil | 179 | 216 | 220 |
| Petroleum products | 290 | 341 | 350 |
| Crude petroleum | 166 | 174 | 157 |
| Cotton | 185 | 195 | 205 |
| Yarn | 296 | 395 | 380 |
| Fertilizer | 97 | 150 | 125 |
| Cement | 171 | 156 | 140 |
| Textiles | 1,043 | 1,098 | 1,425 |
| Capital goods | 1,918 | 1,937 | 1,917 |
| **Total** (incl. others) | 6,881 | 7,162 | 7,525 |

| Exports | 1995/96 | 1996/97 | 1997/98* |
|---|---|---|---|
| Raw jute | 90.7 | 116.0 | 112.8 |
| Jute goods (excl. carpets) | 324.8 | 313.3 | 276.0 |
| Leather and leather products | 211.7 | 195.0 | 188.4 |
| Frozen shrimp and fish | 313.7 | 320.0 | 320.0 |
| Ready-made garments | 1,948.0 | 2,238.0 | 2,800.0 |
| Knitwear and hosiery products | 598.3 | 763.3 | 905.1 |
| Chemical fertilizers | 94.7 | 104.1 | 80.0 |
| **Total** (incl. others) | 3,882.4 | 4,418.3 | 5,110.7 |

* Estimates.

Source: Bangladesh Bank.

**PRINCIPAL TRADING PARTNERS** (%, year ending 30 June)

| Imports c.i.f. | 1995/96 | 1996/97 | 1997/98* |
|---|---|---|---|
| Australia | 1.0 | 2.5 | 2.0 |
| Canada | 1.0 | 1.1 | 1.0 |
| China, People's Republic | 10.0 | 8.6 | 10.0 |
| Eastern Europe | 1.0 | 1.8 | 2.0 |
| Hong Kong | 6.0 | 6.1 | 6.0 |
| India | 16.0 | 13.8 | 15.0 |
| Indonesia | 1.0 | 1.9 | 1.0 |
| Japan | 9.0 | 8.8 | 9.0 |
| Korea, Republic | 5.0 | 5.4 | 7.0 |
| Malaysia | 1.0 | 2.9 | 3.0 |
| Pakistan | 2.0 | 1.0 | 1.0 |
| Saudi Arabia | 1.0 | 1.3 | 1.0 |
| Singapore | 5.0 | 4.4 | 5.0 |
| Thailand | 1.0 | 1.2 | 1.0 |
| USA | 5.0 | 4.5 | 5.0 |
| Western Europe | 11.0 | 12.7 | 13.0 |
| **Total** (incl. others) | 100.0 | 100.0 | 100.0 |

* Estimates.

| Exports f.o.b. | 1995/96 | 1996/97 | 1997/98* |
|---|---|---|---|
| Canada | 2.0 | 1.7 | 2.0 |
| China, People's Republic | 1.0 | 1.2 | 1.0 |
| Eastern Europe | 1.0 | 1.3 | 1.0 |
| Hong Kong | 4.0 | 2.8 | 3.0 |
| India | 1.0 | 0.8 | 1.0 |
| Iran | 1.0 | 1.2 | 1.0 |
| Japan | 4.0 | 2.5 | 2.7 |
| Pakistan | 1.0 | 1.2 | 1.2 |
| Singapore | 1.0 | 0.5 | 1.0 |
| USA | 30.0 | 31.3 | 32.0 |
| Western Europe | 49.0 | 47.9 | 49.0 |
| **Total** (incl. others) | 100.0 | 100.0 | 100.0 |

* Estimates.

Source: Bangladesh Bank.

# Transport

**RAILWAYS** (traffic, year ending 30 June)

| | 1994/95 | 1995/96 | 1996/97 |
|---|---|---|---|
| Passenger-kilometres (million) | 4,037 | 3,333 | 3,754 |
| Freight ton-kilometres (million) | 760 | 689 | 782 |

Source: Bangladesh Railway.

**ROAD TRAFFIC** (motor vehicles in use at 31 December)

| | 1995 | 1996 | 1997 |
|---|---|---|---|
| Passenger cars | 51,114 | 55,034 | 54,784 |
| Buses and coaches | 27,453 | 28,347 | 29,310 |
| Lorries and vans | 35,145 | 37,322 | 40,084 |
| Road tractors | 2,638 | 2,667 | 2,769 |
| Motor cycles and mopeds | 134,303 | 140,864 | 145,259 |
| **Total** | 250,653 | 264,234 | 272,206 |

Source: International Road Federation, *World Road Statistics*.

**SHIPPING**

**Merchant Fleet** (registered at 31 December)

| | 1996 | 1997 | 1998 |
|---|---|---|---|
| Number of vessels | 317 | 314 | 309 |
| Total displacement ('000 grt) | 435.7 | 419.2 | 413.8 |

Source: Lloyd's Register of Shipping, *World Fleet Statistics*.

**International Sea-borne Freight Traffic**

('000 long tons, year ending 30 June)

| | 1994/95 | 1995/96 | 1996/97 |
|---|---|---|---|
| Mongla | | | |
| Goods loaded | 725 | 396 | 520 |
| Goods unloaded | 2,322 | 2,443 | 2,174 |
| Chittagong | | | |
| Goods loaded | 1,417 | 1,451 | 1,435 |
| Goods unloaded | 8,638 | 8,738 | 9,063 |
| **Total goods loaded** | 2,142 | 1,847 | 1,955 |
| **Total goods unloaded** | 10,960 | 11,181 | 11,237 |

**CIVIL AVIATION**

(million, traffic on scheduled Bangladesh Biman services)

| | 1992 | 1993 | 1994 |
|---|---|---|---|
| Kilometres flown | 15 | 17 | 19 |
| Passenger-km | 2,303 | 2,556 | 2,936 |
| Freight ton-km | 82.6 | 47.7 | n.a. |

Source: UN, *Statistical Yearbook for Asia and the Pacific*.

## Tourism

**TOURIST ARRIVALS BY COUNTRY OF NATIONALITY**

| | 1994 | 1995 | 1996 |
|---|---|---|---|
| China, People's Republic | 2,936 | 3,408 | 4,016 |
| India | 47,349 | 46,015 | 53,007 |
| Japan | 5,749 | 5,600 | 5,716 |
| Korea, Republic | 4,635 | 5,251 | 6,017 |
| Malaysia | 2,425 | 2,209 | 3,927 |
| Nepal | 2,288 | 2,995 | 3,628 |
| Netherlands | 2,780 | 3,279 | 3,511 |
| Pakistan | 14,194 | 12,903 | 7,070 |
| United Kingdom | 17,332 | 31,984 | 33,463 |
| USA | 9,735 | 10,541 | 11,033 |
| **Total** (incl. others) | 140,122 | 156,231 | 165,887 |

**Tourism receipts** (US $ million): 19 in 1994; 23 in 1995; 34 in 1996.

Source: World Tourism Organization, *Yearbook of Tourism Statistics*.

**Hotel rooms***: 3,190 in 1994; 4,085 in 1995.

**Hotel beds:** 6,434 in 1994; 8,224 in 1995.

* Including rooms of similar establishments.

Source: UN, *Statistical Yearbook for Asia and the Pacific*.

**1997:** Tourist arrivals 182,420.

## Communications Media

| | 1994 | 1995 | 1996 |
|---|---|---|---|
| Radio receivers ('000 in use) | 5,500 | 5,600 | 6,000 |
| Television receivers ('000 in use) | 685 | 700 | 750 |
| Telephones ('000 in use) | 296 | 315 | 388 |
| Telefax stations (number in use)*† | 2,000 | 4,000 | n.a. |
| Mobile cellular telephones (subscribers)* | 1,104 | 2,500 | n.a. |
| Daily newspapers: | | | |
| Number of titles | 51 | 51 | 37 |
| Average circulation ('000) | 710‡ | 950 | 1,117 |

* Twelve months ending 30 June of year stated.

† Provisional figures.

‡ Estimate.

**1997:** 389,000 telephones in use.

Sources: mainly UNESCO, *Statistical Yearbook*; UN, *Statistical Yearbook*.

## Education

(1995/96)

| | Institutions | Students |
|---|---|---|
| Primary schools | 75,595 | 17,580,000 |
| Secondary schools | 12,858 | 5,788,000 |
| Universities (government) | 11 | 118,945 |

Technical colleges and institutes (government, 1990/91)*: 141 institutions, 23,722 students.

* In addition to government-owned and managed institutes, there are many privately-administered vocational training centres.

# Directory

## The Constitution

The members who were returned from East Pakistan (now Bangladesh) for the Pakistan National Assembly and the Provincial Assembly in the December 1970 elections formed the Bangladesh Constituent Assembly. A new Constitution for the People's Republic of Bangladesh was approved by this Assembly on 4 November 1972 and came into effect on 16 December 1972. Following the military coup of 24 March 1982, the Constitution was suspended, and the country was placed under martial law. On 10 November 1986 martial law was repealed and the suspended Constitution was revived. The main provisions of the Constitution, including amendments, are listed below.

### SUMMARY

**Fundamental Principles of State Policy**

The Constitution was initially based on the fundamental principles of nationalism, socialism, democracy and secularism, but in 1977 an amendment replaced secularism with Islam. The amendment states that the country shall be guided by 'the principles of absolute trust and faith in the Almighty Allah, nationalism, democracy and socialism'. A further amendment in 1988 established Islam as the state religion. The Constitution aims to establish a society free from exploitation in which the rule of law, fundamental human rights and freedoms, justice and equality are to be secured for all citizens. A socialist economic system is to be established to ensure the attainment of a just and egalitarian society through state and co-operative ownership as well as private ownership within limits prescribed by law. A universal, free and compulsory system of education shall be established. In foreign policy the State shall endeavour to consolidate, preserve, and strengthen fraternal relations among Muslim countries based on Islamic solidarity.

**Fundamental Rights**

All citizens are equal before the law and have a right to its protection. Arbitrary arrest or detention, discrimination based on race, age, sex, birth, caste or religion, and forced labour are prohibited. Subject to law, public order and morality, every citizen has freedom of movement, of assembly and of association. Freedom of conscience, of speech, of the press and of religious worship are guaranteed.

### GOVERNMENT

**The President**

The President is the constitutional Head of State and is elected by Parliament (Jatiya Sangsad) for a term of five years. He is eligible for re-election. The supreme control of the armed forces is vested in the President. He appoints the Prime Minister and other Ministers as well as the Chief Justice and other judges.

**The Executive**

Executive authority shall rest in the Prime Minister and shall be exercised by him either directly or through officers subordinate to him in accordance with the Constitution.

There shall be a Council of Ministers to aid and advise the Prime Minister.

**The Legislature**

Parliament (Jatiya Sangsad) is a unicameral legislature. It comprises 300 members and an additional 30 women members elected by the other members. Members of Parliament, other than the 30 women members, are directly elected on the basis of universal adult franchise from single territorial constituencies. Persons aged 18 and over are entitled to vote. The parliamentary term lasts for five years. War can be declared only with the assent of Parliament. In the case of actual or imminent invasion, the President may take whatever action he may consider appropriate.

### THE JUDICIARY

The Judiciary comprises a Supreme Court with High Court and an Appellate Division. The Supreme Court consists of a Chief Justice and such other judges as may be appointed by the President. The High Court division has such original appellate and other jurisdiction and powers as are conferred on it by the Constitution and by other law. The Appellate Division has jurisdiction to determine appeals from decisions of the High Court division. Subordinate courts, in addition to the Supreme Court, have been established by law.

### ELECTIONS

An Election Commission supervises elections, delimits constituencies and prepares electoral rolls. It consists of a Chief Election Commissioner and other Commissioners as may be appointed by the President. The Election Commission is independent in the exercise of its functions. Subject to the Constitution, Parliament may make provision as to elections where necessary.

## The Government

### HEAD OF STATE

**President:** SHAHABUDDIN AHMED (elected 23 July 1996; took office 9 October 1996).

### COUNCIL OF MINISTERS

(January 2000)

All ministers are members of the Awami League, with the exception of the two specified.

**Prime Minister and Minister of the Armed Forces Division, of the Cabinet Division, of Special Affairs, of Defence, of Planning, of Power, Energy and Mineral Resources, and of the Establishment:** Sheikh HASINA WAJED.

**Minister of Foreign Affairs:** ABDUS SAMAD AZAD.

**Minister of Local Government, Rural Development and Co-operatives:** MOHAMMAD ZILLUR RAHMAN.

**Minister of Finance:** S. A. M. S. KIBRIA.

**Minister of Education, and of the Primary and Mass Education Division:** A. S. H. K. SADEQUE.

**Minister of Labour and Manpower:** M. A. MANNAN.

**Minister of Science and Technology:** Lt-Gen. (retd) MOHAMMAD NOORUDDIN KHAN.

**Minister of Water Resources and Flood Control:** ABDUR RAZZAK.

**Minister of Commerce and Industry:** TOFAEL AHMED.

**Minister of Home Affairs and of Post and Telecommunications:** MOHAMMAD NASIM.

**Minister of Agriculture, Food, Disaster Management and Relief:** MATIA CHOUDHRY.

**Minister of Civil Aviation and Tourism and of Public Works:** Eng. MOSHARRAF HOSSAIN.

**Minister of Law, Justice and Parliamentary Affairs:** ABDUL MATIN KHASRU.

**Minister of Communications:** ANWAR HUSSAIN MANJU (Jatiya Dal).

**Minister of Health and Family Welfare:** SALAHUDDIN YOUSUF.

**Minister of the Environment and Forests:** Syeda SAJEDA CHOWDHURY.

**Minister of Shipping:** A. S. M. ABDUR RAB (Jatiya Samajtantrik Dal—Rab).

**Minister of Chittagong Hill Tracts Affairs:** KALPARANJAN CHAKMA.

**Minister without Portfolio:** Maj.-Gen. (retd) RAVIQUL ISLAM BIR UTTAM.

**Minister of State for Women's and Children's Affairs:** MOZAMMEL HOSSAIN.

**Minister of State for Youth and Sports and Cultural Affairs:** OBAIDUL KADER.

**Minister of State for Fisheries and Livestock:** SATISH CHANDRA RAY.

**Minister of State for Religious Affairs:** MOHAMMAD NURUL ISLAM.

**Minister of State for Women's Affairs:** Begum SARWARI RAHMAN.

**Minister of State for Industry:** LUTFUR RAHMAN KHAN.

### MINISTRIES

All ministries are situated in Dhaka.

**Prime Minister's Office:** Old Sangsad Bhaban, Tejgaon, Dhaka; tel. (2) 814100; fax (2) 813244.

**Ministry of Agriculture, Food, Disaster Management and Relief:** Bangladesh Secretariat, Bhaban 4, 2nd 9-Storey Bldg, Dhaka; tel. (2) 832137.

**Ministry of Civil Aviation and Tourism:** Bangladesh Secretariat, Bhaban 6, 19th Floor, Dhaka 1000; tel. (2) 866485.

**Ministry of Commerce:** Bangladesh Secretariat, Bhaban 3, Dhaka 1000; tel. (2) 862826; fax (2) 865741.

**Ministry of Communications:** Bangladesh Secretariat, Bhaban 7, 1st 9-Storey Bldg, 8th Floor, Dhaka 1000; tel. (2) 868752; fax (2) 866636.

**Ministry of Cultural Affairs:** Dhaka; tel. (2) 402133.

**Ministry of Defence:** Old High Court Bldg, Dhaka; tel. (2) 259082.

**Ministry of Education:** Bangladesh Secretariat, Bhaban 7, 2nd 9-Storey Bldg, 6th Floor, Dhaka; tel. (2) 404162.

**Ministry of Energy and Mineral Resources:** Bangladesh Secretariat, Bhaban 6, First Floor, Dhaka 1000; tel. (2) 865918; fax (2) 861110.

**Ministry of Finance:** Bangladesh Secretariat, Bhaban 7, 1st 9-Storey Bldg, 3rd Floor, Dhaka 1000; tel. (2) 8690202; fax (2) 865581.

**Ministry of Foreign Affairs:** Segunbagicha, Dhaka 1000; tel. (2) 9562950; fax (2) 833597.

**Ministry of Health and Family Welfare:** Bangladesh Secretariat, Main Bldg, 3rd Floor, Dhaka; tel. (2) 832079.

**Ministry of Home Affairs:** Bangladesh Secretariat, School Bldg, 2nd and 3rd Floors, Dhaka; tel. (2) 404142.

**Ministry of Housing and Public Works:** Bangladesh Secretariat, Bhaban 5, Dhaka; tel. (2) 834494; fax (2) 861290.

**Ministry of Industry:** Shilpa Bhaban, 91 Motijheel C/A, Dhaka 1000; tel. (2) 9564250; fax (2) 860588.

**Ministry of Information:** Bangladesh Secretariat, 2nd 9-Storey Bldg, 8th Floor, Dhaka; tel. (2) 235111; fax (2) 834535.

**Ministry of Labour and Manpower:** Bangladesh Secretariat, 1st 9-Storey Bldg, 4th Floor, Dhaka; tel. (2) 404106; fax (2) 813420.

**Ministry of Land:** Bangladesh Secretariat, Bhaban 4, 2nd 9-Storey Bldg, 3rd Floor, Dhaka.

**Ministry of Local Government, Rural Development and Co-operatives:** Bangladesh Secretariat, Bhaban 7, 1st 9-Storey Bldg, 6th Floor, Dhaka.

**Ministry of Planning:** Block No. 7, Sher-e-Bangla Nagar, Dhaka; tel. (2) 815142; fax (2) 822210.

**Ministry of Post and Telecommunications:** Bangladesh Secretariat, Bhaban 7, 6th Floor, Dhaka 1000; tel. (2) 864800; fax (2) 865775.

**Ministry of Religious Affairs:** Dhaka; tel. (2) 404346.

**Ministry of Shipping:** Bangladesh Secretariat, Bhaban 6, 8th Floor, Dhaka 1000; tel. (2) 861275.

**Ministry of Social Welfare and Women's Affairs:** Bangladesh Secretariat, Bhaban 6, New Bldg, Dhaka; tel. (2) 402076.

**Ministry of Textiles:** Bangladesh Secretariat, Bhaban 6, 11th Floor, Dhaka 1000; tel. (2) 862051; fax (2) 860600.

**Ministry of Youth and Sports:** Dhaka; tel. (2) 407670.

# President and Legislature

### PRESIDENT

On 23 July 1996 the Awami League's presidential candidate, SHAHABUDDIN AHMED, was elected unopposed as Bangladesh's new Head of State by the Jatiya Sangsad.

### JATIYA SANGSAD
(Parliament)

**Speaker:** HUMAYUN RASHID CHOWDHURY.

**General Election, 12 June 1996**

| | Seats |
|---|---|
| Awami League (AL) | 146 |
| Bangladesh Jatiyatabadi Dal (Bangladesh Nationalist Party—BNP) | 116 |
| Jatiya Dal | 32 |
| Jamaat-e-Islami Bangladesh | 3 |
| Jatiya Samajtantrik Dal (Rab) | 1 |
| Islami Oikya Jote | 1 |
| Independent | 1 |
| **Total** | 300 |

In addition to the 300 directly-elected members, a further 30 seats are reserved for women members.

# Political Organizations

**Awami League (AL):** 23 Bangabandhu Ave, Dhaka; f. 1949; supports parliamentary democracy; advocates socialist economy, but with a private sector, and a secular state; pro-Indian; 28-member central executive committee, 15-member central advisory committee and a 13-member presidium; Pres. Sheikh HASINA WAJED; Gen.-Sec. ZILLUR RAHMAN; c. 1,025,000 mems.

**Bangladesh Jatiya League:** 500A Dhanmandi R/A, Rd 7, Dhaka; f. 1970 as Pakistan National League, renamed in 1972; supports parliamentary democracy; Leader ATAUR RAHMAN KHAN; c. 50,000 mems.

**Bangladesh Jatiyatabadi Dal** (Bangladesh Nationalist Party—BNP): 29 Minto Rd, Dhaka; f. 1978 by merger of groups supporting Ziaur Rahman, including Jatiyatabadi Gonotantrik Dal (Jagodal—Nationalist Democratic Party); right of centre; favours multiparty democracy and parliamentary system of govt; Chair. Begum KHALEDA ZIA; Sec.-Gen. ABDUL MANNAN BHUIYAN.

**Bangladesh Khelafat Andolon:** 314/2 Lalbagh Kellar Morr, Dhaka 1211; tel. (2) 862465; fax (2) 9881436; Supreme Leader SHAH AHMADULLAH ASHRAF IBN HAFEZZEE; Sec.-Gen. Maulana MUHAMMAD ZAFRULLAH KHAN.

**Bangladesh Krishak Sramik Party** (Peasants' and Workers' Party): Sonargaon Bhavan, 99 South Kamalapur, Dhaka 1217; tel. (2) 834512; f. 1914, renamed 1953; supports parliamentary democracy, non-aligned foreign policy, welfare state, guarantee of fundamental rights for all religions and races, free market economy and non-proliferation of nuclear weapons; 15-mem. exec. council; Pres. A. S. M. SULAIMAN; Sec.-Gen. RASHEED KHAN MEMON; c. 125,000 mems.

**Bangladesh Muslim League:** Dhaka; Sec.-Gen. Alhaj MOHAMMAD ZAMIR ALI.

**Bangladesh People's League:** Dhaka; f. 1976; supports parliamentary democracy; Leader KHANDAKER SABBIR AHMED; c. 75,000 mems.

**Communist Party of Bangladesh:** 21/1 Purana Paltan, Dhaka 1000; tel. (2) 9558612; fax (2) 837464; e-mail manzur@bangla.net; f. 1948; Pres. SHAHIDULLAH CHOWDHURY; Gen. Sec. MUJAHIDUL ISLAM SELIM; c. 22,000 mems.

**Democratic League:** 68 Jigatola, Dhaka 9; tel. (2) 507994; f. 1976; conservative; Leader ABDUR RAZZAK.

**Freedom Party:** f. 1987; Islamic; Co-Chair. Lt-Col (retd) SAID FARUQ RAHMAN, Lt-Col (retd) KHANDAKAR ABDUR RASHID.

**Gonoazadi League:** 30 Banagran Lane, Dhaka.

**Islamic Solidarity Movement:** 84 East Tejturi Bazar, Tejgaon, Dhaka 1215; tel. (2) 325886; fmrly known as Islamic Democratic League; renamed as above in 1984; Chair. HAFIZ MUHAMMAD HABIBUR RAHMAN.

**Jamaat-e-Islami Bangladesh:** 505 Elephant Rd, Bara Maghbazar, Dhaka 1217; tel. (2) 401581; f. 1941; Islamic fundamentalist; Chair. Prof. GHULAM AZAM; Sec.-Gen. Maulana MATIUR RAHMAN NIZAMI; Asst Sec.-Gen. MUHAMMAD QUAMARUZZAMAN.

**Jatiya Dal** (National Party): c/o Jatiya Sangsad, Dhaka; f. 1983 as Jana Dal; reorg. 1986, when the National Front (f. 1985), a five-party alliance of the Jana Dal, the United People's Party, the Gonotantrik Dal, the Bangladesh Muslim League and a breakaway section of the Bangladesh Nationalist Party, formally converted itself into a single pro-Ershad grouping; advocates nationalism, democracy, Islamic ideals and progress; Chair. Lt-Gen. HOSSAIN MOHAMMAD ERSHAD; Sec.-Gen. NAZIUR RAHMAN MONZUR; in April 1999 a group of dissidents, led by MIZANUR RAHMAN CHOWDHURY and ANWAR HUSSAIN MANJU, formed a rival faction.

**Jatiya Samajtantrik Dal (Rab):** breakaway faction of JSD; Pres. A. S. M. ABDUR RAB; Gen. Sec. HASANUL HAQUE INU.

**Jatiya Samajtantrik Dal (JSD—(S))** (National Socialist Party): 23 DIT Ave, Malibagh Choudhury Para, Dhaka; f. 1972; left-wing; Leader SHAJAHAN SIRAJ; c. 5,000 mems.

**Jatiyo Gonotantrik Party (JAGPA):** Purana Paltan, Dhaka; Jt Gen. Secs AZIZUR RAHMAN, SARDAR SHAHJAHAN.

**Jatiyo Janata Party:** Janata Bhaban, 47A Toyenbee Circular Rd, Dhaka 1203; tel. (2) 9567315; f. 1976; social democratic; Leader ABDULLAH NASER; Gen. Sec. MUJIBUR RAHMAN HIRO; c. 30,000 mems.

**National Awami Party—Bhashani (NAP):** Dhaka; f. 1957; Maoist; Leader NAZRUL ISLAM; Gen. Sec. ABDUS SUBHANI.

**National Awami Party—Muzaffar (NAP—M):** 21 Dhanmandi Hawkers' Market, 1st Floor, Dhaka 5; f. 1957, reorg. 1967; c. 500,000 mems; Pres. MUZAFFAR AHMED; Sec.-Gen. PANKAJ BHATTACHARYA.

**Parbattya Chattagram Jana Sanghati Samity:** f. 1972; political wing of the Shanti Bahini; represents interests of Buddhist tribals in Chittagong Hill Tracts; Leader JATINDRA BODDHIPRIYA ('SHANTU') LARMA.

**Samyabadi Dal:** Dhaka; Maoist; Leader MOHAMMAD TOAHA.

**Zaker Party:** f. 1989; supports sovereignty and the introduction of an Islamic state system; Leader SYED HASMATULLAH; Mem. of the Presidium MUSTAFA AMIR FAISAL.

# Diplomatic Representation

### EMBASSIES AND HIGH COMMISSIONS IN BANGLADESH

**Afghanistan:** House CWN(C)-2A Gulshan Ave, Gulshan Model Town, Dhaka 1212; tel. (2) 603232; Chargé d'affaires a.i.: ABDUL AHAD WOLASI.

**Australia:** 184 Gulshan Ave, Gulshan Model Town, Dhaka 1212; tel. (2) 873101; fax (2) 871125; e-mail peter.doyle@dfat.gov.au; High Commissioner: CHARLES STUART.

**Belgium:** Gulshan Model Town, Dhaka 1212; tel. (2) 600138; Ambassador: Baron OLIVIER GILLES.

**Bhutan:** House No. F5 (SE), Gulshan Ave, Dhaka 1212; tel. (2) 8827160; fax (2) 8823939; e-mail bhtemb@bdmail.net; Ambassador: LHATU WANGCHUK.

**Canada:** House 16A, Rd 48, Gulshan Model Town, POB 569, Dhaka 1212; tel. (2) 607071; fax (2) 883043; High Commissioner: JON SCOTT.

**China, People's Republic:** Plot NE(L)6, Rd 83, Gulshan Model Town, Dhaka 1212; tel. (2) 884862; Ambassador: WANG CHUNGUI.

**Czech Republic:** Dhaka; tel. (2) 601673.

**Denmark:** House NW(H)1, Rd 51, Gulshan Model Town, POB 2056, Dhaka 1212; tel. (2) 881799; fax (2) 883638; e-mail dandhaka@mail.citechco.net; Ambassador: FINN THILSTED.

**Egypt:** House NE(N)-9, Rd 90, Gulshan Model Town, Dhaka 1212; tel. (2) 882766; fax (2) 884883; Ambassador: OSSAMA MOHAMED TAWFIK.

**France:** POB 22, House 18, Rd 108, Gulshan Model Town, Dhaka 1212; tel. (2) 607083; Ambassador: ALAIN BRIOTTET.

**Germany:** 178 Gulshan Ave, Gulshan Model Town, POB 108, Dhaka 1212; tel. (2) 884735; fax (2) 883141; Ambassador: BRUNO WEBER.

**Holy See:** Lake Rd 2, Diplomatic Enclave, Baridhara Model Town, POB 6003, Dhaka 1212; tel. (2) 8822018; fax (2) 8823574; e-mail ve@bdonline.com; Apostolic Nuncio: Most Rev. EDWARD JOSEPH ADAMS, Titular Archbishop of Scala.

**Hungary:** House 14, Rd 68, Gulshan Model Town, POB 6012, Dhaka 1212; tel. (2) 608101; fax (2) 883117; Chargé d'affaires a.i.: I. B. BUDAY.

**India:** House 120, Rd 2, Dhanmandi R/A, Dhaka 1205; tel. (2) 503606; fax (2) 863662; High Commissioner: DEV MUKHERJEE.

**Indonesia:** CWS (A)-10, 75 Gulshan Ave, Gulshan Model Town, Dhaka 1212; tel. (2) 600131; fax (2) 885391; Ambassador: HADI A. WAYARABI ALHADAR.

**Iran:** CWN(A)-12 Kamal Ataturk Ave, Gulshan Model Town, Dhaka 1212; tel. (2) 601432; Ambassador: MOHAMMAD SADEQ FAYAZ.

**Iraq:** 112 Gulshan Ave, Gulshan Model Town, Dhaka 1212; tel. (2) 600298; Ambassador: ZUHAIR MUHAMMAD ALOMAR.

**Italy:** Plot No. 2 & 3, Rd 74/79, Gulshan Model Town, Dhaka 1212; tel. (2) 600152; fax (2) 882578; Ambassador: Dr RAFFAELE MINIERO.

**Japan:** 5 & 7, Dutabash Rd, Baridhara, Dhaka; tel. (2) 870087; fax (2) 886737; Ambassador: YOSHIKAZU KANEKO.

**Korea, Democratic People's Republic:** House 6, Rd 7, Baridhara Model Town, Dhaka; tel. (2) 601250; Ambassador: KIM KI DUK.

**Korea, Republic:** 4 Madani Ave, Diplomatic Enclave, Baridhara, Dhaka; tel. (2) 872088; fax (2) 883871; e-mail rokdhaka@bangla.net; Ambassador: HAN TAE-KYU.

**Kuwait:** Plot 39, Rd 23, Block J, Banani, Dhaka 13; tel. (2) 600233; Ambassador: AHMAD MURSHED AL-SULIMAN.

**Libya:** NE(D), 3A, Gulshan Ave (N), Gulshan Model Town, Dhaka 1212; tel. (2) 600141; Secretary of People's Committee: MUSBAH ALI A. MAIMOON (acting).

**Malaysia:** House 4, Rd 118, Gulshan Model Town, Dhaka 1212; tel. (2) 887759; fax (2) 883115; High Commissioner: Dato' ZULKIFLY IBRAHIM BIN ABDUR RAHMAN.

**Myanmar:** 89(B), Rd 4, Banani, Dhaka; tel. (2) 601915; Ambassador: U TINT LWIN.

**Nepal:** United Nations Rd, Rd 2, Diplomatic Enclave, Baridhara, Dhaka; tel. (2) 601790; fax (2) 8826401; e-mail rnedhaka@bdmail.net; Ambassador: MADHU RAMAN ACHARYA.

**Netherlands:** House 49, Rd 90, Gulshan Model Town, POB 166, Dhaka 1212; tel. (2) 882715; fax (2) 883326; e-mail nlgovdha@bangla.net; Ambassador: D.C.B. DEN HAAS.

**Pakistan:** House NEC-2, Rd 71, Gulshan Model Town, Dhaka 1212; tel. (2) 885388; High Commissioner: KARAM ELAHI.

**Philippines:** House NE(L) 5, Rd 83, Gulshan Model Town, Dhaka 1212; tel. (2) 605945; Ambassador: CESAR C. PASTORES.

**Poland:** House 111, Rd 4, Banani, POB 6089, Dhaka 1213; tel. (2) 608503; fax (2) 8827568; e-mail plembres@bdmail.net; Chargé d'affaires a.i.: JERZY SADOWSKI.

**Qatar:** House 23, Rd 108, Gulshan Model Town, Dhaka 1212; tel. (2) 604477; Chargé d'affaires a.i.: ABDULLAH AL-MUTAWA.

**Romania:** House 33, Rd 74, Gulshan Model Town, Dhaka 1212; tel. (2) 601467; Chargé d'affaires a.i.: ALEXANDRU VOINEA.

**Russia:** NE(J) 9, Rd 79, Gulshan Model Town, Dhaka 1212; tel. (2) 8828147; fax (2) 8823735; e-mail rusemb@citechco.net; Chargé d'affaires: GENNADII P. TROTSENKO.

**Saudi Arabia:** House 12, Rd 92, Gulshan (North), Dhaka 1212; tel. (2) 889124; fax (2) 883616; Ambassador: ABDULLAH OMAR BARRY.

**Sri Lanka:** House 15(NW), Rd 50, Gulshan 2, Dhaka; tel. (2) 882790; fax (2) 883971; e-mail slhc@citechco.net; High Commissioner: S. B. ATUGODA.

**Sweden:** House 1, Rd 51, Gulshan, Dhaka 1212; tel. (2) 884761; fax (2) 883948; Ambassador: ANDERS JOHNSON.

**Thailand:** House NW (E) 12, Rd 59, Gulshan Model Town, Dhaka 1212; tel. (2) 601475; Ambassador: CHAIYA CHINDAWONGSE.

**Turkey:** House 7, Rd 62, Gulshan Model Town, Dhaka 1212; tel. (2) 882198; fax (2) 883873; Ambassador: K. OZCAN DAVAZ.

**United Arab Emirates:** House CEN(H) 41, Rd 113, Gulshan Model Town, Dhaka 1212; tel. (2) 604775; Chargé d'affaires a.i.: ABDUL RAZAK HADI.

**United Kingdom:** United Nations Rd, Baridhara, Dhaka 1212; tel. (2) 8822705; fax (2) 8823437; e-mail ppabhcbd@citechco.net; High Commissioner: Dr DAVID CARTER.

**USA:** Diplomatic Enclave, Madani Ave, Baridhara Model Town, POB 323, Dhaka 1212; tel. (2) 884700; fax (2) 883744; Ambassador: JOHN C. HOLZMAN.

# Judicial System

A judiciary, comprising a Supreme Court with High Court and Appellate Divisions, is in operation (see under Constitution).

**Supreme Court:** Dhaka 2; tel. (2) 433585.

**Chief Justice:** MUSTAFA KAMAL.

**Attorney-General:** MAHMUDUL ISLAM.

**Deputy Attorney-General:** A. M. FAROOQ.

# Religion

Preliminary results of the 1981 census classified 86.6% of the population as Muslims, 12.1% as caste Hindus and scheduled castes, and the remainder as Buddhists, Christians and tribals.

Freedom of religious worship is guaranteed under the Constitution but, under the 1977 amendment to the Constitution, Islam was declared to be one of the nation's guiding principles and, under the 1988 amendment, Islam was established as the state religion.

## BUDDHISM

**World Federation of Buddhists Regional Centre:** Buddhist Monastery, Kamalapur, Dhaka 14; Leader Ven. VISUDDHANANDA MAHATHERO.

## CHRISTIANITY

**Jatiyo Church Parishad** (National Council of Churches): 395 New Eskaton Rd, Moghbazar, Dhaka 2; tel. (2) 402869; f. 1949 as East Pakistan Christian Council; four mem. churches; Pres. Dr SAJAL DEWAN; Gen. Sec. M. R. BISWAS.

### Church of Bangladesh—United Church

After Bangladesh achieved independence, the Diocese of Dacca (Dhaka) of the Church of Pakistan (f. 1970 by the union of Anglicans, Methodists, Presbyterians and Lutherans) became the autonomous Church of Bangladesh. In 1986 the Church had an estimated 12,000 members. In 1990 a second diocese, the Diocese of Kushtia, was established.

**Bishop of Dhaka:** Rt Rev. BARNABAS DWIJEN MONDAL, St Thomas's Church, 54 Johnson Rd, Dhaka 1100; tel. (2) 236546; fax (2) 238218; e-mail cbdacdio@bangla.net.

**Bishop of Kushtia:** Rt Rev. MICHAEL BAROI, Church of Bangladesh, 94 N.S. Rd, Thanapara, Kushtia; tel. (71) 3603.

### The Roman Catholic Church

For ecclesiastical purposes, Bangladesh comprises one archdiocese and five dioceses. At 31 December 1997 there were an estimated 247,650 adherents in the country.

**Catholic Bishops' Conference:** Archbishop's House, 1 Kakrail Rd, Ramna, POB 3, Dhaka 1000; tel. (2) 408879; fax (2) 834993; f. 1978; Pres. Most Rev. MICHAEL ROZARIO, Archbishop of Dhaka.

**Archbishop of Dhaka:** Most Rev. MICHAEL ROZARIO, Archbishop's House, 1 Kakrail Rd, Ramna, POB 3, Dhaka 1000; tel. (2) 408879.

### Other Christian Churches

**Bangladesh Baptist Sangha:** 33 Senpara, Parbatta, Mirpur 10, POB 8018, Dhaka 1216; tel. (2) 802967; fax (2) 803556; f. 1922; 26,500 mems (1985); Pres. M. S. ADHIKARI; Gen. Sec. Rev. MARTIN ADHIKARY.

Among other denominations active in Bangladesh are the Bogra Christian Church, the Evangelical Christian Church, the Garo Baptist Union, the Reformed Church of Bangladesh and the Sylhet Presbyterian Synod.

# The Press

## PRINCIPAL DAILIES

### Bengali

**Azadi:** 9 C.D.A. C/A, Momin Rd, Chittagong; tel. (31) 224341; f. 1960; Editor Prof. MOHAMMAD KHALED; circ. 13,000.

**Banglar Bani:** 81 Motijheel C/A, Dhaka 1000; tel. (2) 237548; f. 1972; Editor Sheikh FAZLUL KARIM SALIM; circ. 20,000.

**Dainik Bangla:** Dhaka; tel. (2) 864748; f. 1964; Editor AHMED HUMAYUN; circ. 65,000.

**Dainik Bhorer Kagoj:** 8 Link Rd, Banglamotor, Dhaka; tel (2) 868802; fax (2) 868801; Editor MATIUR RAHMAN; circ. 50,000.

**Dainik Birol:** 26 R. K. Mission Rd, Dhaka 1203; tel. (2) 9567152; fax (2) 9567153; Chair. of Editorial Bd ABDULLAH AL-NASER.

**Dainik Inquilab:** 2/1 Ramkrishna Mission Rd, Dhaka 1203; tel. (2) 9563162; fax (2) 9552881; e-mail inquilab1@bangla.net; Editor A. M. M. BAHAUDDIN; circ. 180,025.

**Dainik Ittefaq:** 1 Ramkrishna Rd, Dhaka 1203; tel. (2) 256075; f. 1953; Propr/Editor ANWAR HUSSAIN MANJU; circ. 200,000.

**Dainik Jahan:** 3/B Shehra Rd, Mymensingh; tel. (91) 5677; f. 1980; Editor MUHAMMAD HABIBUR RAHMAN SHEIKH; circ. 4,000.

**Dainik Janakantha** (Daily People's Voice): Dhaka; f. 1993; Man. Editor TOAB KHAN; Exec. Editor BORHAN AHMED; circ. 100,000.

**Dainik Janata:** 24 Aminbagh, Shanti Nagar, Dhaka 1217; tel. (2) 400498; Editor Dr M. ASADUR RAHMAN.

**Dainik Janmobhumi:** 110/1 Islampur Rd, Khulna; tel. (41) 721280; fax (41) 724324; f. 1982; Editor HUMAYUN KABIR; circ. 30,000.

**Dainik Karatoa:** Chalkjadu Rd, Bogra; tel. (51) 3660; fax (51) 5898; f. 1976; Editor MOZAMMEL HAQUE LALU; circ. 40,000.

**Dainik Khabar:** 137 Shanti Nagar, Dhaka 1217; tel. (2) 406601; f. 1985; Editor MIZANUR RAHMAN MIZAN; circ. 18,000.

**Dainik Millat:** Dhaka; tel. (2) 242351; Editor CHOWDHURY MOHAMMAD FAROOQ.

**Dainik Nava Avijan:** Lalkuthi, North Brook Hall Rd, Dhaka; tel. (2) 257516; Editor A. S. M. REZAUL HAQUE; circ. 15,000.

**Dainik Patrika:** 85 Elephant Rd, Maghbazar, Dhaka 1217; tel. (2) 415057; fax (2) 841575; e-mail patrika@citechco.net; Publr and Chief Editor MIA MUSA HOSSAIN; Editor M. FAISAL HASSAN (acting).

**Dainik Probaha:** 3 KDA Ave, Khulna; tel. (41) 722552; f. 1977; Editor ASHRAF-UL-HAQUE; circ. 11,400.

**Dainik Purbanchal:** 38 Iqbal Nagar Mosque Lane, Khulna 9100; tel. (41) 22251; fax (41) 21432; f. 1974; Editor LIAQUAT ALI; circ. 42,000.

**Dainik Rupashi Bangla:** Abdur Rashid Rd, Natun Chowdhury Para, Bagicha Gaon, Comilla 3500; tel. (81) 6689; f. 1972 (a weekly until 1979); Editor Prof. ABDUL WAHAB; circ. 10,000.

**Dainik Sangram:** 423 Elephant Rd, Baramaghbazar, Dhaka 1217; tel. (2) 9330579; fax (2) 831250; f. 1970; Chair. MOHAMMAD YOUNUS; Editor ABUL ASAD; circ. 45,000.

**Dainik Sphulinga:** Amin Villa, P-5 Housing Estate, Jessore 7401; tel. (421) 6433; f. 1971; Editor Mian ABDUS SATTAR; circ. 14,000.

**Dainik Uttara:** Bahadur Bazar, Dinajpur Town, Dinajpur; tel. (531) 4326; f. 1974; Editor Prof. MUHAMMAD MOHSIN; circ. 8,500.

**Ganakantha:** Dhaka; tel. (2) 606784; f. 1979; morning; Editor JAHANGIR KABIR CHOWDHURY; Exec. Editor SAIYED RABIUL KARIM; circ. 15,000.

**Jaijaidin Protidin:** 3/4-B Purana Paltan, Dhaka 1000; Editor SHAFIK REHMAN.

**Janabarta:** 5 Babu Khan Rd, Khulna; tel. (41) 21075; f. 1974; Editor SYED SOHRAB ALI; circ. 4,000.

**Jugabheri:** Sylhet; tel. (821) 5461; f. 1931; Editor FAHMEEDA RASHEED CHOUDHURY; circ. 6,000.

**Manav Jomeen** (Human Land): Dhaka; f. 1998; tabloid.

**Naya Bangla:** 101 Momin Rd, Chittagong; tel. (31) 206247; f. 1978; Editor ABDULLAH AL-SAGIR; circ. 12,000.

**Protidin:** Ganeshtola, Dinajpur; tel. (531) 4555; f. 1980; Editor KHAIRUL ANAM; circ. 3,000.

**Runner:** Pyari Mohan Das Rd, Bejpara, Jessore; tel. (421) 6943; f. 1980; circ. 2,000.

**Sangbad:** 36 Purana Paltan, Dhaka 1000; tel. (2) 9558147; fax (2) 9562882; e-mail sangbad@bangla.net; f. 1952; Editor AHMADUL KABIR; circ. 71,050.

**Swadhinata:** Chittagong; tel. (31) 209644; f. 1972; Editor ABDULLAH-AL-HARUN; circ. 4,000.

### English

**Bangladesh Observer:** Observer House, 33 Toyenbee Circular Rd, Motijheel C/A, Dhaka 1000; tel. (2) 235105; f. 1949; morning; Editor S. M. ALI; circ. 43,000.

**The Bangladesh Times:** Dhaka; tel. (2) 233195; f. 1975; morning; Editor MAHBUB ANAM; circ. 35,000.

**Daily Evening News:** 26 R. K. Mission Rd, Dhaka 1203; tel. (2) 9567152; fax (2) 9567153; Chair. of Editorial Bd ABDULLAH AL-NASER.

**Daily Star:** House 11, Rd 3, Dhanmandi R/A, Dhaka 1205; tel.(2) 866772; fax (2) 863035; e-mail dstar@bangla.net; internet www .dailystarnews.com; f. 1991; Publr and Editor MAHFUZ ANAM; circ. 30,000.

**Daily Tribune:** 38 Iqbal Nagar Mosque Lane, Khulna 9100; tel. (41) 21944; fax (41) 22251; f. 1978; morning; Editor FERDOUSI ALI; circ. 22,000.

**Financial Express:** Dhaka; f. 1994.

**The Independent:** Beximco Media Complex, 32 Kazi Nazrul Islam Ave, Karwan Bazar, Dhaka 1215; tel. (2) 9129938; fax (2) 9127722; e-mail ind@citechco.net; internet independent-bangladesh.com; f. 1995; Editor MAHBUBUL ALAM.

**New Nation:** 1 Ramkrishna Mission Rd, Dhaka 1203; tel. (2) 245011; fax (2) 245536; f. 1981; Editor ALAMGIR MOHIUDDIN; circ. 15,000.

**People's View:** 102 Siraj-ud-Daulla Rd, Chittagong; tel. (31) 227403; f. 1969; Editor SABBIR ISLAM; circ. 3,000.

## PERIODICALS

### Bengali

**Aachal:** 100B Malibagh Chowdhury Para, Dhaka 1219; tel. (2) 414043; weekly; Editor FERDOUSI BEGUM.

**Adhuna:** 1/3 Block F, Lalmatia, Dhaka 1207; tel. (2) 812353; fax (2) 813095; e-mail adab@bdonline.com; f. 1974; quarterly; publ. by the Asscn of Devt Agencies in Bangladesh (ADAB); Exec. Editor MINAR MONSUR; circ. 10,000.

**Ahmadi:** 4 Bakshi Bazar Rd, Dhaka 1211; f. 1925; fortnightly; Editor MOQBUL AHMAD KHAN.

**Alokpat:** 166 Arambagh, Dhaka 1000; tel. (2) 413361; fax (2) 863060; fortnightly; Editor RABBANI JABBAR.

**Amod:** Chowdhury Para, Comilla 3500; tel. (81) 5193; f. 1955; weekly; Editor SHAMSUN NAHAR RABBI; circ. 6,000.

**Ananda Bichitra:** Dhaka; tel. (2) 241639; f. 1986; fortnightly; Editor SHAHADAT CHOWDHURY; circ. 32,000.

**Begum:** 66 Loyal St, Dhaka 1; tel. (2) 233789; f. 1947; women's illustrated weekly; Editor NURJAHAN BEGUM; circ. 25,000.

**Bichitra:** Dhaka; tel. (2) 232086; f. 1972; weekly; Editor SHAHADAT CHOWDHURY; circ. 42,000.

**Chakra:** 242A Nakhalpara, POB 2682, Dhaka 1215; tel. (2) 604568; social welfare weekly; Editor HUSNEARA AZIZ.

**Chitra Desh:** 24 Ramkrishna Mission Rd, Dhaka 1203; weekly; Editor HENA AKHTAR CHOWDHURY.

**Chitrali:** Observer House, 33 Toyenbee Circular Rd, Motijheel C/A, Dhaka 1000; tel. (2) 9550938; fax (2) 9562243; f. 1953; film weekly; Editor PRODIP KUMAR DEY; circ. 25,000.

**Ekota:** 15 Larmini St, Wari, Dhaka; tel. (2) 257854; f. 1970; weekly; Editor MATIUR RAHMAN; circ. 25,000.

**Fashal:** 28J Toyenbee Circular Rd, Motijheel C/A, Dhaka 1000; tel. (2) 233099; f. 1965; agricultural weekly; Chief Editor ERSHAD MAZUMDAR; circ. 8,000.

**Ispat:** Majampur, Kushtia; tel. (71) 3676; f. 1976; weekly; Editor WALIUR BARI CHOUDHURY; circ. 3,000.

**Jaijaidin:** 15 New Bailey Rd, Dhaka 1000; weekly; Editor SHAFIK REHMAN.

**Jhorna:** 4/13 Block A, Lalmatia, Dhaka; tel. (2) 415239; Editor MUHAMMAD JAMIR ALI.

**Kalantar:** 87 Khanjahan Ali Rd, Khulna; tel. (41) 61424; f. 1971; weekly; Editor NOOR MOHAMMAD; circ. 12,000.

**Kankan:** Nawab Bari Rd, Bogra; tel. (51) 6424; f. 1974; weekly; Editor Mrs SUFIA KHATUN; circ. 6,000.

**Kirajagat:** National Sports Control Board, 62/63 Purana Paltan, Dhaka; f. 1977; weekly; Editor ALI MUZZAMAN CHOWDHURY; circ. 7,000.

**Kishore Bangla:** Observer House, Motijheel C/A, Dhaka 1000; juvenile weekly; f. 1976; Editor RAFIQUL HAQUE; circ. 5,000.

**Moha Nagar:** 4 Dilkusha C/A, Dhaka 1000; tel. (2) 255282; Editor SYED MOTIUR RAHMAN.

**Moshal:** 4 Dilkusha C/A, Dhaka 1000; tel. (2) 231092; Editor MUHAMMAD ABUL HASNAT; circ. 3,000

**Muktibani:** Toyenbee Circular Rd, Motijheel C/A, Dhaka 1000; tel. (2) 253712; f. 1972; weekly; Editor NIZAM UDDIN AHMED; circ. 35,000.

**Natun Bangla:** 44/2 Free School St Bylane, Hatirpool, Dhaka 1205; tel. (2) 866121; fax (2) 863794; e-mail mujib@bangla.net; f. 1971; weekly; Editor MUJIBUR RAHMAN.

**Natun Katha:** 31E Topkhana Rd, Dhaka; weekly; Editor HAJERA SULTANA; circ. 4,000.

**Nipun:** 520 Peyarabag, Magbazar, Dhaka 11007; tel. (2) 312156; monthly; Editor SHAJAHAN CHOWDHURY.

**Parikrama:** 65 Shanti Nagar, Dhaka; tel. (2) 415640; Editor MOMTAZ SULTANA.

**Prohar:** 35 Siddeswari Rd, Dhaka 1217; tel. (2) 404206; Editor MUJIBUL HUQ.

**Protirodh:** Dept of Answar and V.D.P. Khilgoan, Ministry of Home Affairs, School Bldg, 2nd and 3rd Floors, Bangladesh Secretariat, Dhaka; tel. (2) 405971; f. 1977; fortnightly; Editor ZAHANGIR HABIBULLAH; circ. 20,000.

**Purbani:** 1 Ramkrishna Mission Rd, Dhaka 1203; tel. (2) 256503; f. 1951; film weekly; Editor KHONDKER SHAHADAT HOSSAIN; circ. 22,000.

**Robbar:** 1 Ramkrishna Mission Rd, Dhaka; tel. (2) 256071; f. 1978; weekly; Editor ABDUL HAFIZ; circ. 20,000.

**Rokshena:** 13B Avoy Das Lane, Tiktuli, Dhaka; tel. (2) 255117; Editor SYEDA AFSANA.

**Sachitra Bangladesh:** 112 Circuit House Rd, Dhaka 1000; tel. (2) 402129; f. 1979; fortnightly; Editor A. B. M. ABDUL MATIN; circ. 8,000.

**Sachitra Sandhani:** 68/2 Purana Paltan, Dhaka; tel. (2) 409680; f. 1978; weekly; Editor GAZI SHAHABUDDIN MAHMUD; circ. 13,000.

**Sandip:** 28/A/3 Toyenbee Circular Rd, Dhaka; tel. (2) 235542; weekly; Editor MOHSEN ARA RAHMAN.

**Shishu:** Bangladesh Shishu Academy, Old High Court Compound, Dhaka 1000; tel. (2) 230317; f. 1977; children's monthly; Editor GOLAM KIBRIA; circ. 5,000.

**Sonar Bangla:** 423 Elephant Rd, Mogh Bazar, Dhaka 1217; tel. (2) 400637; f. 1961; Editor MUHAMMED QAMARUZZAMAN; circ. 25,000.

**Swadesh:** 19 B.B. Ave, Dhaka; tel. (2) 256946; weekly; Editor ZAKIUDDIN AHMED; circ. 8,000.

**Tarokalok:** Tarokalok Complex, 25/3 Green Rd, Dhaka 1205; tel. (2) 506583; fax (2) 864330; weekly; Editor AREFIN BADAL.

**Tide:** 56/57 Motijheel C/A, Dhaka 1000; tel. (2) 259421; Editor ENAYET KARIM.

**Tilotwoma:** 14 Bangla Bazar, Dhaka; Editor ABDUL MANNAN.

#### English

**ADAB News:** 1/3, Block F, Lalmatia, Dhaka 1207; tel. (2) 327424; f. 1974; 6 a year; publ. by the Asscn of Devt Agencies in Bangladesh (ADAB); Editor-in-Chief AZFAR HUSSAIN; circ. 10,000.

**Bangladesh:** 112 Circuit House Rd, Dhaka 1000; tel. (2) 402013; fortnightly; Editor A. B. M. ABDUL MATIN.

**Bangladesh Gazette:** Bangladesh Government Press, Tejgaon, Dhaka; f. 1947, name changed 1972; weekly; official notices; Editor M. HUDA.

**Bangladesh Illustrated Weekly:** Dhaka; tel. (2) 23358; Editor ATIQUZZAMAN KHAN; circ. 3,000.

**Cinema:** 81 Motijheel C/A, Dhaka 1000; Editor SHEIKH FAZLUR RAHMAN MARUF; circ. 11,000.

**Detective:** Polwell Bhaban, Naya Paltan, Dhaka 2; tel. (2) 402757; f. 1960; weekly; also publ. in Bengali; Editor SYED AMJAD HOSSAIN; circ. 3,000.

**Dhaka Courier:** Cosmos Centre, 69/1 New Circular Rd, Malibagh, Dhaka 1217; tel. (2) 408420; fax (2) 831942; weekly; Editor ENAYETULLAH KHAN; circ. 18,000.

**Holiday:** Holiday Bldg, 30 Tejgaon Industrial Area, Dhaka 1208; tel. (2) 9122950; fax (2) 833113; e-mail holiday@bangla.net; f. 1959; weekly; independent; Editor-in-Chief ENAYETULLAH KHAN; circ. 18,000.

**Motherland:** Khanjahan Ali Rd, Khulna; tel. (41) 61685; f. 1974; weekly; Editor M. N. KHAN.

**Tide:** 56/57 Motijheel C/A, Dhaka; tel. (2) 259421; Editor ENAYET KARIM.

**Voice From the North:** Dinajpur Town, Dinajpur; tel. (531) 3256; f. 1981; weekly; Editor Prof. MUHAMMAD MOHSIN; circ. 5,000.

### NEWS AGENCIES

**Bangladesh Sangbad Sangstha (BSS)** (Bangladesh News Agency): 68/2 Purana Paltan, Dhaka 1000; tel. (2) 235036; Man. Dir and Chief Editor MAHBUBUL ALAM; Gen. Man. D. P. BARUA.

**Eastern News Agency (ENA):** Dhaka; tel. (2) 234206; f. 1970; Man. Dir and Chief Editor GOLAM RASUL MALLICK.

**Islamic News Society (INS):** 24 RK Mission Rd, Dhaka 1203; tel. (2) 9567152; fax (2) 9567153; Editor ABDULLAH AL-NASER.

**United News of Bangladesh:** Dhaka.

#### Foreign Bureaux

**Agence France-Presse (AFP):** Shilpa Bank Bldg, 5th Floor, 8 DIT Ave, nr Dhaka Stadium, Dhaka 1000; tel. (2) 242234; Bureau Chief GOLAM TAHABOOR.

**Associated Press (AP)** (USA): 69/1 New Circular Rd, Dhaka 1217; tel. (2) 833717; Representative HASAN SAEED FARID HOSSAIN.

**Inter Press Service (IPS)** (Italy): c/o Bangladesh Sangbad Sangstha, 68/2 Purana Paltan, Dhaka 1000; tel. (2) 235036; Correspondent A. K. M. TABIBUL ISLAM.

**Reuters Ltd** (UK): POB 3993, Dhaka; tel. (2) 864088; fax (2) 832976; Bureau Chief ATIQUL ALAM.

**South Asian News Agency (SANA):** Dhaka.

**United Press International (UPI)** (USA): Dhaka; tel. (2) 233132.

### PRESS ASSOCIATIONS

**Bangladesh Council of Newspapers and News Agencies:** Dhaka; tel. (2) 413256; Pres. Kazi SHAHED AHMED; Sec.-Gen. HABIBUL BASHAR.

**Bangladesh Federal Union of Journalists:** National Press Club Bldg, 18 Topkhana Rd, Dhaka 1000; tel. (2) 254777; f. 1973; Pres. REAZUDDIN AHMED; Sec.-Gen. SYED ZAFAR AHMED.

**Bangladesh Sangbadpatra Karmachari Federation** (Newspaper Employees' Fed.): Dhaka; tel. (2) 235065; f. 1972; Pres. RAFIQUL ISLAM; Sec.-Gen. MIR MOZAMMEL HOSSAIN.

**Bangladesh Sangbadpatra Press Sramik Federation** (Newspaper Press Workers' Federation): 1 Ramkrishna Mission Rd, Dhaka 1203; f. 1960; Pres. M. ABDUL KARIM; Sec.-Gen. BOZLUR RAHMAN MILON.

**Dhaka Union of Journalists:** National Press Club, Dhaka; f. 1947; Pres. ABEL KHAIR; Gen.-Sec. ABDUL KALAM AZAD.

**Overseas Correspondents' Association of Bangladesh (OCAB):** 18 Topkhana Rd, Dhaka 1000; e-mail naweed@bdonline.com; f. 1979; Pres. ZAGLUL A. CHOWDHURY; Gen. Sec. NADEEM QADIR; 60 mems.

## Publishers

**Academic Publishers:** 2/7 Nawab-Habibullah Rd, Dhaka 1000; tel. (2) 507355; fax (2) 863060; f. 1982; social sciences and sociology; Jt Man. Dir HABIBUR RAHMAN.

**Agamee Prakashani:** 36 Bangla Bazar, Dhaka 1100; tel. (2) 231332; fax (2) 9562018; fiction and academic; Owner OSMAN GANI.

**Ahmed Publishing House:** 7 Zindabahar 1st Lane, Dhaka 1; tel. (2) 36492; f. 1942; literature, history, science, religion, children's, maps and charts; Man. Dir KAMALUDDIN AHMED; Man. MESBAHUDDIN AHMED.

**Ankur Prakashani:** 38/4 Bangla Bazar, Dhaka 1100; tel. (2) 250132; f. 1986; academic and general.

**Ashrafia Library:** 4 Hakim Habibur Rahman Rd, Chawk Bazar, Dhaka 1000; Islamic religious books, texts, and reference works of Islamic institutions.

**Asiatic Society of Bangladesh:** 5 Old Secretariat Rd, Ramna, Dhaka; tel. (2) 9560500; f. 1952; periodicals on science, Bangla and humanities; Pres. Prof. WAKIL AHMED; Admin. Officer MD ABDUL AWAL MIAH.

**Bangla Academy (National Academy of Arts and Letters):** Burdwan House, 3 Kazi Nazrul Islam Ave, Dhaka 1000; tel. (2) 869577; f. 1955; higher education textbooks in Bengali, research works in language, literature and culture, language planning, popular science, drama, encyclopaedias, translations of world classics, dictionaries; Dir-Gen. Prof. MONSUR MUSA.

**Bangladesh Publishers:** 45 Patuatully Rd, Dhaka 1100; tel. (2) 233135; f. 1952; textbooks for schools, colleges and universities, cultural books, journals, etc.; Dir MAYA RANI GHOSAL.

**Bangladesh Books International Ltd:** Ittefaq Bhaban, 1 Ramkrishna Mission Rd, POB 377, Dhaka 3; tel. (2) 256071; f. 1975; reference, academic, research, literary, children's in Bengali and English; Chair. MOINUL HOSSEIN; Man. Dir ABDUL HAFIZ.

**Gatidhara:** 38/2-Ka Bangla Bazar, Dhaka 1100; tel. (2) 247515; fax (2) 956600; f. 1988; academic, general and fiction.

**Gono Prakashani:** 14/E Dhanmondhi R/A, Dhaka 1205; tel. (2) 9332245; fax (2) 863567; e-mail gk.mail@drik.bgd.toolnet.org; f. 1978; science and medicine; Man. Dir SHAFIO KHAN; Editor BAZLUR RAHIM.

**International Publications:** 8 Baitul Mukarram, 1st Floor, GPO Box 45, Dhaka 1000.

**Muktadhara:** 74 Farashganj, Dhaka 1100; tel. (2) 231374; f. 1971; educational, literary and general; Bengali and English; Dir J. L. SAHA; Man. Dir C. R. SAHA.

**Mullick Brothers:** 3/1 Bangla Bazar, Dhaka 1100; tel. (2) 232088; fax (2) 833983; educational.

**Osmania Book Depot:** 30/32 North Brook Hall Rd, Dhaka 1100.

**Puthighar Ltd:** 74 Farashganj, Dhaka 1100; tel. (2) 231374; f. 1951; educational; Bengali and English; Dir J. L. SAHA; Man. Dir C. R. SAHA.

**Rahman Brothers:** 5/1 Gopinath Datta, Kabiraj St, Babu Bazar, Dhaka; tel. (2) 282633; educational.

**Royal Library:** Ispahani Bldg, 31/32 P. K. Roy Rd, Banglabazar, Dhaka 1; tel. (2) 250863.

**Shahitya Prakash:** 51 Purana Paltan, Dhaka 1000; tel. (2) 9560485; fax (2) 9565506; f. 1970; Prin. Officer MOFIDUL HOQUE.

**University Press Ltd:** Red Crescent Bldg, 114 Motijheel C/A, POB 2611, Dhaka 1000; tel. (2) 9565441; fax (2) 9565443; e-mail upl@bangla.net; internet www.uplbooks.com; f. 1975; educational, academic and general; Man. Dir MOHIUDDIN AHMED; Editor ABDAR RAHMAN.

#### Government Publishing Houses

**Bangladesh Bureau of Statistics:** Bldg 8, Room 14, Bangladesh Secretariat, Dhaka 1000; tel. (2) 8612833; f. 1971; statistical year book and pocket book, censuses, surveys, agricultural year book and special reports; Jt Dir S. M. TAJUL ISLAM; Sec. MAMUN-UR-RASHID.

**Bangladesh Government Press:** Tejgaon, Dhaka 1209; tel. (2) 606316; f. 1972.

**Department of Films and Publications:** 112 Circuit House Rd, Dhaka 1000; tel. (2) 402263.

**Press Information Department:** Bhaban 6, Bangladesh Secretariat, Dhaka 1000; tel. (2) 400958.

### PUBLISHERS' ASSOCIATIONS

**Bangladesh Publishers' and Booksellers' Association:** 3rd Floor, 3 Liaquat Ave, Dhaka 1; f. 1972; Pres. JANAB JAHANGIR MOHAMMED ADEL; 2,500 mems.

**National Book Centre of Bangladesh:** 67A Purana Paltan, Dhaka 1000; f. 1963 to promote the cause of 'more, better and cheaper books'; organizes book fairs, publs a monthly journal; Dir FAZLE RABBI.

## Broadcasting and Communications

### TELECOMMUNICATIONS

**Bangladesh Telegraph and Telephone Board:** Central Office, Telejogajog Bhaban, 37/E Eskaton Garden, Dhaka 1000; tel. (2) 831500; fax (2) 832577; Chair. M.A. MANNAN CHOWDHURY; Dir (International) MD HASSANUZZAMAN.

**Grameen Telecom:** Dhaka; f. 1996 by Grameen Bank to expand cellular telephone service in rural areas; Head NAJMUL HUDA.

### BROADCASTING

#### Radio

**Bangladesh Betar:** NBA House, 121 Kazi Nazrul Islam Ave, Shahabag, Dhaka 1000; tel. (2) 865294; fax (2) 862021; e-mail dgradio@drik.bgd.toolnet.org; f. 1971; govt-controlled; regional stations at Dhaka, Chittagong, Khulna, Rajshahi, Rangpur, Sylhet, Rangamati and Thakurgaon broadcast a total of approximately 160 hours daily; transmitting centres at Lalmai and Rangamati; external service broadcasts 8 transmissions daily in Arabic, Bengali, English, Hindi, Nepalese and Urdu; Dir-Gen. M.I. CHOWDHURY; Dep. Dir-Gen. (Programmes) ASHFAQUR RAHMAN KHAN.

#### Television

**Bangladesh Television (BTV):** Television House, Rampura, Dhaka 1219; tel. (2) 866606; fax (2) 832927; f. 1964; govt-controlled; daily broadcasts on one channel from Dhaka station for 10 hours; transmissions also from nationwide network of 14 relay stations; Dir-Gen. SAYED SALAHUDDIN ZAKI; Gen. Man. NAWAZISH ALI KHAN.

## Finance

(cap. = capital; p.u. = paid up; res = reserves; dep. = deposits; m. = million; brs = branches; amounts in taka)

### BANKING

#### Central Bank

**Bangladesh Bank:** Motijheel C/A, POB 325, Dhaka 1000; tel. (2) 9555000; fax (2) 9566212; e-mail banglabank@bangla.net; f. 1971; cap. 30m., res 7,757.9m., dep. 78,401.8m. (June 1998); Gov. Dr MOHAMED FARASUDDIN; 9 brs.

#### Nationalized Commercial Banks

**Agrani Bank:** Agrani Bank Bhaban, Motijheel C/A, POB 531, Dhaka 1000; tel. (2) 9566160; fax (2) 9563662; f. 1972; 100% state-owned; cap. 2,484m., res 314m., dep. 86,914m. (Dec. 1998); Chair. MD MATIUR RAHMAN; Man. Dir M. ENAMUL HAQ CHOUDHURY; 903 brs.

**Janata Bank:** 110 Motijheel C/A, Motijheel, POB 468, Dhaka 1000; tel. (2) 9565041; fax (2) 9564644; e-mail jbcomp@citecho.net; f. 1972; 100% state-owned; cap. 2,594m., res 124m., dep. 69,115m. (June 1996); Chair. MUHAMMED ALI; Man. Dir and CEO MD AMINUL ISLAM; 893 brs in Bangladesh, 4 brs in the UAE.

**Rupali Bank Ltd:** 34 Dilkusha C/A, POB 719, Dhaka 1000; tel. (2) 9551624; fax (2) 9564148; f. 1972; 51% state-owned, 49% by public; cap. 1,250m., res 76.1m., dep. 29,585m. (June 1996); Chair. M. ABU SYEED; Man. Dir A. K. M. NOZMUL HAQUE; 516 brs in Bangladesh, 1 br. in Pakistan.

**Sonali Bank:** 35–44 Motijheel C/A, POB 3130, Dhaka 1000; tel. (2) 9550426; fax (2) 9561410; f. 1972; 100% state-owned; cap. 3,272.2m., res 1,866.3m., dep. 142,128.5m. (Dec. 1997); Chair. MOHAMMAD ASAFUDDOWLAH; Man. Dir KHONDKER IBRAHIM KHALED; 1,313 brs in Bangladesh, 6 brs in United Kingdom and 1 br. in India.

#### Private Commercial Banks

**Al-Arafah Islami Bank Ltd:** Rahman Mansion, 161 Motijheel C/A, Dhaka; tel. (2) 9560198; f. 1995; 100% owned by 23 sponsors; cap. 101.2m., res 10m., dep. 534.4m. (Aug. 1996); Chair. A. Z. M. SHAMSUL ALAM; Man. Dir M. M. NURUL HAQUE.

**Al-Baraka Bank Bangladesh Ltd:** Kashfia Plaza, 35C Naya Paltan (VIP Rd), POB 3467, Dhaka 1000; tel. (2) 410050; fax (2) 834943; f. 1987 on Islamic banking principles; 34.68% owned by Al-Baraka Group, Saudi Arabia, 5.78% by Islamic Development Bank, Jeddah, 45.91% by local sponsors, 5.75% by Bangladesh Govt., 7.8% by general public; cap. 259.6m., res 14.9m., dep. 4,898.1m. (June 1996); Chair. Dr SALEH J. MALAIKAH; Man. Dir ANOWAR AHMED; 33 brs.

**Arab Bangladesh Bank Ltd:** BCIC Bhaban, 30–31 Dilkusha C/A, POB 3522, Dhaka 1000; tel. (2) 9560312; fax (2) 9564122; e-mail abbank@citecho.net; f. 1981; 95% owned by Bangladesh nationals and 5% by Bangladesh Govt; cap. 372.7m., res 286.3m., dep. 11,370.6m. (Dec. 1997); Chair. M. MORSHED KHAN; Man. Dir A. RAHIM CHOWDHURY; 58 brs.

**City Bank Ltd:** Jiban Bima Tower, 10 Dilkusha C/A, POB 3381, Dhaka 1000; tel. (2) 9565925; fax (2) 9562347; f. 1983; 50% owned by sponsors, 45% by general public and 5% by Govt; cap. p.u. 160.0m., res 125m., dep. 7,050m. (June 1996); Chair. IBRAHIM MIA; Pres. and Gen. Man. QUAZI BAHARUL ISLAM; 60 brs.

**Dhaka Bank Ltd:** 1st Floor, Biman Bhaban, 100 Motijheel C/A, Dhaka 1000; tel. (2) 9556592; fax (2) 9556584; e-mail dhakabnk@bdonline.com; f. 1995; cap. 270m., res 69m., dep. 6,170m. (June 1999); Chair. ABDUL HAI SARKER; Man. Dir A. I. M. IFTIKAR RAHMAN; 11 brs.

**Eastern Bank Ltd:** Jiban Bima Bhaban, 2nd Floor, 10 Dilkusha C/A, POB 896, Dhaka 1000; tel. (2) 9556360; fax (2) 9562364; f. 1992; appropriated assets and liabilities of fmr Bank of Credit and Commerce International (Overseas) Ltd; 20% govt.-owned; cap. 600m., res 432.1m., dep. 10,013.8m. (Dec. 1998); Chair. NURUL HUSAIN KHAN; Man. Dir M. KHAIRUL ALAM; 21 brs.

**International Finance Investment and Commerce Bank Ltd (IFICB):** BSB Bldg, 17th–19th Floors, 8 Rajuk Ave, POB 2229, Dhaka 1000; tel. (2) 9563020; fax (2) 9562015; f. 1983; 40% state-owned; cap. 279.4m., res 311.1m., dep. 17,229.5m. (Dec. 1998); Chair. A.S.F. RAHMAN; Man. Dir MD SHAWKAT ALI; 52 brs in Bangladesh, 2 brs in Pakistan.

**Islami Bank Bangladesh Ltd (IBBL):** Head Office, 71 Dilkusha C/A, POB 233, Dhaka 1000; tel. (2) 9563046; fax (2) 9564532; e-mail ibbl@ncll.com; f. 1983 on Islamic banking principles; cap. 318m., res 1,011.8m., dep. 20,021.7m. (Dec. 1998); Chair. Cdre (retd) MOHAMMAD ATAUR RAHMAN; Exec. Pres. and CEO M. KAMALUDDIN CHOWDHURY; 110 brs.

**National Bank Ltd:** 18 Dilkusha C/A, POB 3424, Dhaka 1000; tel. (2) 9557045; fax (2) 9563953; e-mail nblho@citechco.net; f. 1983; 50% owned by sponsors, 45% by general public and 5% by Govt; cap. 391.2m., res 943.9m., dep. 17,364.7m. (Dec. 1998); Chair. M. NURUL ISLAM; Man. Dir RAFIQUL ISLAM KHAN; 66 brs.

**National Credit and Commerce Bank Ltd:** 7–8 Motijheel C/A, POB 2920, Dhaka 1000; tel. (2) 9561902; fax (2) 9566290; e-mail nccbl@bdmail.net; f. 1993; 50% owned by sponsors, 45% by general public and 5% by Govt; cap. 195m., res 54m., dep. 6,898.1m. (Dec. 1998); Chair. MIR ZAHIR HOSSAIN; Man. Dir MD SAJIDUL HAQ; 27 brs.

**Prime Bank Ltd:** Adamjee Court Annex Bldg No. 2, 119–20 Motijheel C/A, Dhaka 1000; tel. (2) 9567265; fax (2) 9567230; e-mail primebnk@bangla.net; f. 1995; cap. p.u. 400m., res 175.9m., dep. 7,058.4m. (Sept. 1999); Chair. MD NADER KHAN; Man. Dir Kazi ABDUL MAZID; 20 brs.

**Pubali Bank Ltd:** Pubali Bank Bhaban, 26 Dilkusha C/A, POB 853, Dhaka 1000; tel. (2) 9551614; fax (2) 9564009; e-mail pubali@

bdmail.net; f. 1959 as Eastern Mercantile Bank Ltd; name changed to Pubali Bank in 1972; 95% privately-owned, 5% state-owned; cap. p.u. 160m., res 357m., dep. 21,091m. (Sept. 1998); Chair. EMADUDDIN AHMED CHAUDHURY; Man. Dir MOHAMMAD QAMRUL HUDA; 350 brs.

**Social Investment Bank:** 15 Dilkusha C/A, Dhaka 1000; tel. (2) 881654; fax (2) 881654; f. 1995; cap. p.u. 118.4m., dep. 322.4m. (July 1996); Chair. Dr M. A. MANNAN; Man. Dir M. AZIZUL HUQ; 5 brs.

**Southeast Bank Ltd:** 1 Dilkusha C/A, Dhaka 1000; tel. (2) 9550081; fax (2) 9550093; e-mail seastbk@citechco.net; f. 1995; cap. 100m., dep. 3,341m. (Dec. 1997); Chair. M. A. KASHEM; CEO SYED ANISUL HUQ; 10 brs.

**United Commercial Bank Ltd:** Federation Bhaban, 60 Motijheel C/A, POB 2653, Dhaka 1000; tel. (2) 232217; fax (2) 9560587; f. 1983; 50% owned by sponsors, 45% by general public and 5% by Govt; cap. 230.2m., res 265.7m., dep. 9,451.2m. (Dec. 1997); Chair. AKHTARUZZAMAN CHOWDHURY BABU; 78 brs.

**Uttara Bank Ltd:** 90 Motijheel C/A, POB 818, Dhaka 1000; tel. (2) 9551162; fax (2) 863529; e-mail uttara@citecho.net; f. 1965 as Eastern Banking Corpn Ltd; name changed to Uttara Bank in 1972 and to Uttara Bank Ltd in 1983; 5% state-owned; cap. 99.8m., res 204.4m., dep. 16,882.6m. (Dec. 1997); Chair. A. M. ANISUZZAMAN; Man. Dir and CEO M. AMINUZAMMAN; 198 brs.

#### Foreign Commercial Banks

**American Express Bank Ltd** (USA): ALICO Bldg, 18–20 Motijheel C/A, POB 420, Dhaka 1000; tel. (2) 9561496; fax (2) 863808; res 537.5m., dep. 6,236.5m. (Dec. 1995); Chair. JOHN A. WARD III; Gen. Man. STEVEN R. BRITTAINS; 2 brs.

**ANZ Grindlays Bank Ltd** (UK): 2 Dilkusha C/A, POB 502, Dhaka 1000; tel. (2) 9550181; fax (2) 9562332; e-mail choudhun@anz.com; res 60.5m., dep. 20,060m. (1999); Gen. Man. MUHAMMAD A. ALI; 9 brs.

**Citibank, NA (USA):** 122–124 Motijheel C/A, POB 1000, Dhaka 1000; tel. (2) 9550060; fax (2) 642611; f. 1995; cap. p.u. 209.5m., res 5.5m., dep. 648.8m. (July 1996); Chair. JOHN S. REED; Man. Dir S. SRIDHAR; 1 br.

**Crédit Agricole Indosuez** (France): 47 Motijheel C/A, POB 3490, Dhaka 1000; tel. (2) 9566566; fax (2) 9565707; res 591m., dep. 5,302m. (Dec. 1997); Country Man. FRANCIS DUBUS; Chief Operating Officer S. R. VATOVEY; 2 brs.

**Habib Bank Ltd** (Pakistan): 53 Motijheel C/A, POB 201, Dhaka 1000; tel. (2) 9555091; fax (2) 9561784; cap. 80.5m., res 14.3m., dep. 578.6m. (Dec. 1996); Man. Dir J. A. SHAHID; 2 brs.

**The Hongkong and Shanghai Banking Corpn Ltd** (Hong Kong): Dhaka; CEO for Bangladesh DAVID HUMPHREYS.

**Muslim Commercial Bank Ltd** (Pakistan): 4 Dilkusha C/A, POB 7213, Dhaka 1000; tel. (2) 9568871; fax (2) 860671; cap. p.u. 100m., res 4m., dep. 650.3m. (July 1996); Man. Dir HADI ALI KHAN; 2 brs.

**Standard Chartered Bank** (UK): ALICO Bldg, 18–20 Motijheel C/A, POB 420, Dhaka 1000; tel. (2) 9561465; fax (2) 9561758; cap. p.u. 215m., dep. 5,850m. (Dec. 1995); Chief Exec. (Bangladesh) GEOFF WILLIAMS; 3 brs.

**State Bank of India:** 24–25 Dilkusha C/A, POB 981, Dhaka 1000; tel. (2) 9559935; fax (2) 9563992; e-mail sbibd@bangla.net; cap. 190.4m., dep. 557.1m. (March 1997); CEO K. K. CHATTOPADHYAY; 1 br.

#### Development Finance Organizations

**Bangladesh House Building Finance Corpn (BHBFC):** HBFC Bldg, 22 Purana Paltan, POB 2167, Dhaka 1000; tel. (2) 9562767; f. 1952; provides low-interest credit for residential house-building; 100% state-owned; cap. p.u. 972.9m., res 2,937.8m. (June 1996); Chair. AMINUL ISLAM; Man. Dir MD HELAL UDDIN; 9 zonal offices, 12 regional offices and 6 camp offices.

**Bangladesh Krishi Bank (BKB):** 84 Motijheel C/A, POB 357, Dhaka 1000; tel. (2) 9560031; fax (2) 95661211; e-mail bkb@ citecho.net; f. 1961 as the Agricultural Development Bank, name changed as above in 1973; provides credit for agricultural and rural devt; 100% state-owned; cap. 1,000m., res 820.5m., dep. 43,365.2m. (June 1997); Chair. Dr MIRZA A. JALIL; Man. Dir SHOAIB AHMED; 836 brs.

**Bangladesh Samabaya Bank Ltd (BSBL):** 'Samabaya Sadan', 9D Motijheel C/A, POB 505, Dhaka 1000; tel. (2) 9564628; f. 1948; provides credit for agricultural co-operatives; cap. p.u. 31.6m., res 558m., dep. 22m. (June 1996); Chair. Dr ABDUL MOYEEN KHAN; Gen. Man. MD ABDUL WAHED.

**Bangladesh Shilpa Bank (BSB)** (Industrial Development Bank): 8 Rajuk Ave, POB 975, Dhaka; tel. (2) 9555151; fax (2) 9562061; f. 1972; fmrly Industrial Devt Bank; provides long- and short-term financing for industrial devt in the private and public sectors; also provides underwriting facilities and equity support; 51% state-owned; cap. 1,320.0m., res 643.6m., dep. 8,882.5m. (June 1997); Chair. Prof. M. SHAMSUL HAQ; 15 brs.

**Bangladesh Shilpa Rin Sangstha (BSRS)** (Industrial Loan Agency): BIWTA Bhaban, 5th Floor, 141-143 Motijheel C/A, POB 473, Dhaka 1000; tel. (2) 9565046; fax (2) 956705; f. 1972; 100% state-owned; cap. p.u. 700m., res 462.8m. (June 1996); Chair. Dr M. FARASHUDDIN; Man. Dir AL-AMEEN CHAUDHURY; 4 brs.

**Bank of Small Industries and Commerce Bangladesh Ltd (BASIC):** Suite 601/602, Sena Kalyan Bhaban, 6th Floor, 195 Motijheel C/A, Dhaka 1000; tel. (2) 956430; fax (2) 9564829; f. 1988; 100% state-owned; cap. p.u. 80m., res 106m., dep. 2,738m. (Dec. 1995); Chair. A. M. AKHTER; Man. Dir ALAUDDIN A. MAJID; 19 brs.

**Grameen Bank:** Head Office, Mirpur-2, POB 1216, Dhaka 1216; tel. (2) 801138; fax (2) 803559; e-mail grameen.bank@grameen.net; f. 1976; provides credit for the landless rural poor; 6.97% owned by Govt; cap. p.u. 258.1m., res 188.2m., dep. 6,063.2m. (Dec. 1998); Chair. REHMAN SOBHAN; Man. Dir Dr MUHAMMAD YUNUS; 1,140 brs.

**Infrastructure Development Co Ltd (IDCOL):** Dhaka; f. 1999; state-owned.

**Investment Corpn of Bangladesh (ICB):** BSB Bldg, 12th–14th Floor, 8 Rajuk Ave, POB 2058, Dhaka 1000; tel. (2) 9563455; fax (2) 865684; f. 1976; provides devt financing; 27% owned by Govt; cap. p.u. 200.0m., res 315.2m. (June 1996); Chair. HEDAYAT AHMED; Man. Dir KHAIRUL HUDA; 5 brs.

**Rajshahi Krishi Unnayan Bank:** Sadharan Bima Bhaban, Kazihata, Greater Rd, Rajshahi 6000; tel. (721) 775759; fax (721) 775947; f. 1987; 100% state-owned; cap. p.u. 980m., res 208.4m., dep. 2,622.7m. (June 1996); Chair. MD EMRAN ALI SARKAR; Man. Dir SHAHIDUL HAQ KHAN.

### STOCK EXCHANGES

**Chittagong Stock Exchange:** Kashfia Plaza, 923/A, Sk Mujib Rd, Agrabad, Chittagong; tel. (31) 714632; fax (31) 714101.

**Dhaka Stock Exchange Ltd:** 9F Motijheel C/A, Dhaka 1000; tel. (2) 9559118; fax (2) 9564727; f. 1960; 196 listed cos; Chair. ABDUL HUQ HOWLADAR.

#### Regulatory Authority

**Bangladesh Securities and Exchange Commission:** Jiban Bima Tower, 15th–16th Floor, 10 Dilkush C/A, Dhaka 1000; tel. (2) 9568101; fax (2) 867940; CEO M. ABU SAYEED.

### INSURANCE

**Bangladesh Insurance Association:** Dhaka; Chair. MAYEEDUL ISLAM.

**Department of Insurance:** 74 Motijheel C/A, Dhaka 1000; attached to Ministry of Commerce; supervises activities of domestic and foreign insurers; Controller of Insurance SHAMSUDDIN AHMAD.

In 1973 the two corporations below were formed, one for life insurance and the other for general insurance:

**Jiban Bima Corpn:** 24 Motijheel C/A, POB 346, Dhaka 1000; tel. (2) 256876; fax (2) 868112; state-owned; comprises 37 national life insurance cos; life insurance; Man. Dir A. K. M. MOSTAFIZUR RAHMAN.

**Sadharan Bima Corpn:** 33 Dilkusha C/A, POB 607, Dhaka 1000; tel. (2) 9552070; state-owned; general insurance; Man. Dir M. LUTFAR RAHMAN.

## Trade and Industry

### GOVERNMENT AGENCIES

**Board of Investment:** Jiban Bima Tower, 19th Floor, 10 Dilkusha C/A, Dhaka 1000; tel. (2) 9563570; fax (2) 9562312; e-mail ec@boi.bdmail.net; Exec. Chair. FAROOQ SOBHAN; Dep. Dir LUTFUR RAHMAN BHUIYA.

**Export Promotion Bureau:** 122–124 Motijheel C/A, Dhaka 1000; tel. (2) 9552245; fax (2) 9568000; e-mail epb.tic@pradeshta.net; f. 1972; attached to Ministry of Commerce; regional offices in Chittagong, Khulna and Rajshahi; brs in Comilla, Sylhet, Barisal and Bogra; Dir-Gen. TAJUL ISLAM; Vice-Chair. A. B. CHOWDHURY.

**Petrobangla:** Dhaka; fax (2) 811613; organizes exploration for natural gas, petroleum and minerals; Gen. Man. (Petroleum Concession Division) M. FARIDUDDIN.

**Planning Commission:** Planning Commission Secretariat, G.O. Hostel, Sher-e-Bangla Nagar, Dhaka; f. 1972; govt agency responsible for all aspects of economic planning and development including the preparation of the five-year plans and annual development programmes (in conjunction with appropriate govt ministries), promotion of savings and investment, compilation of statistics and evaluation of development schemes and projects.

**Privatization Board:** Jiban Bima Tower, 14th Floor, 10 Dilkusha C/A, Dhaka 1000; tel. (2) 9563723; fax (2) 9563766; f. 1993; Chair. KAZI ZAFRULLAH; Sec. A. M. M. NASIR UDDIN.

**Trading Corpn of Bangladesh:** Kawranbazar, Dhaka; tel. (2) 811516; fax (2) 813582; f. 1972; imports, exports and markets goods through appointed dealers and agents; Chair. SHOAIB AHMED; Sec. NIRMAL CHANDRA SARKER.

## DEVELOPMENT ORGANIZATIONS

**Bangladesh Chemical Industries Corpn:** BCIC Bhaban, 30–31 Dilkusha C/A, Dhaka; tel. (2) 259852; Chair. A. K. M. MOSHARRAF HOSSAIN.

**Bangladesh Export Processing Zones Authority:** 222 New Eskaton Rd, Dhaka 1000; tel. (2) 832553; fax (2) 834967; e-mail bepza@bdmail.net; internet www.bangladesh-epz.com; f. 1983 to plan, develop, operate and manage export processing zones (EPZs) in Bangladesh; in mid-1999 two state-owned EPZs (one in Chittagong and the other in Dhaka) were in operation, and another three EPZs were at the implementation stage; Exec. Chair. MAB SIDDIQUE TALUKDAR.

**Bangladesh Fisheries Development Corpn:** 24–25 Dilkusha C/A, Motijheel, Dhaka 1000; tel. (2) 9552689; fax (2) 9563990; e-mail bfdc@citecho.net; f. 1964; under Ministry of Fisheries and Livestock; development and commercial activities; Chair. MOHAMMED SHAH ALAM; Sec. SHEIKH MONJURUL HOQUE.

**Bangladesh Forest Industries Development Corpn:** Dhaka; Chair. M. ATIKULLAH.

**Bangladesh Jute Mills Corpn:** Adamjee Court (Annexe), 115–120 Motijheel C/A, Dhaka 1000; tel. (2) 861980; fax (2) 863329; f. 1972; operates 35 jute mills, incl. 2 carpet mills; world's largest manufacturer and exporter of jute goods; bags, carpet backing cloth, yarn, twine, tape, felt, floor covering, etc.; Chair. MANIRUDDIN AHMAD; Man. (Marketing) MD JAHIRUL ISLAM.

**Bangladesh Small and Cottage Industries Corpn (BSCIC):** 137/138 Motijheel C/A, Dhaka 1000; tel. (2) 233202; f. 1957; Chair. MUHAMMAD SIRAJUDDIN.

**Bangladesh Steel and Engineering Corpn (BSEC):** BSEC Bhaban, 102 Kazi Nazrul Islam Ave, Dhaka 1215; tel. (2) 814616; fax (2) 812846; 16 industrial units; sales US $83m. (1994); cap. US $52m.; Chair. A. I. M. NAZMUL ALAM; Gen. Man. (Marketing) ASHRAFUL HAQ; 8,015 employees.

**Bangladesh Sugar and Food Industries Corpn:** Shilpa Bhaban, Motijheel C/A, Dhaka 1000; tel. (2) 258084; f. 1972; Chair. M. NEFAUR RAHMAN.

**Bangladesh Textile Mills Corpn:** Shadharan Bima Bhaban, 33 Dilkusha C/A, Dhaka 1000; tel. (2) 252504; f. 1972; Chair. M. NURUNNABI CHOWDHURY.

## CHAMBERS OF COMMERCE

**Federation of Bangladesh Chambers of Commerce and Industry (FBCCI):** Federation Bhaban, 60 Motijheel C/A, 4th Floor, POB 2079, Dhaka 1000; tel. (2) 250566; fax (2) 863213; f. 1973; comprises 135 trade asscns and 58 chambers of commerce and industry; Pres. ABDUL AWAL MINTOO.

**Barisal Chamber of Commerce and Industry:** Asad Mansion, 1st Floor, Sadar Rd, Barisal; tel. (431) 3984; Pres. Qazi ISRAIL HOSSAIN.

**Bogra Chamber of Commerce and Industry:** Chamber Bhaban, 2nd Floor, Kabi Nazrul Islam Rd, Jhawtola, Bogra 5800; tel. (51) 4138; fax (51) 6257; f. 1963; Pres. AMJAD HOSSAIN TAJMA; Sr Vice-Pres. Alhaj ABUL KALAM AZAD.

**Chittagong Chamber of Commerce and Industry:** Chamber House, Agrabad C/A, POB 481, Chittagong; tel. (31) 713366; fax (31) 710183; f. 1959; 4,000 mems; Pres. SARWAR JAMAL NIZAM: Sec. M. H. CHOWDHURY.

**Comilla Chamber of Commerce and Industry:** Rammala Rd, Ranir Bazar, Comilla; tel. (81) 5444; Pres. AFZAL KHAN.

**Dhaka Chamber of Commerce and Industry:** Dhaka Chamber Bldg, 1st Floor, 56–66 Motijheel C/A, POB 2641, Dhaka 1000; tel. (2) 9552808; fax (2) 9560830; f. 1958; 5,000 mems; Pres. M. H. RAHMAN; Sr Vice-Pres. ASHRAF IBN NOOR.

**Dinajpur Chamber of Commerce and Industry:** Jail Rd, Dinajpur; tel. (531) 3189; Pres. KHAIRUL ANAM.

**Faridpur Chamber of Commerce and Industry:** Chamber House, Niltuly, Faridpur; tel. 3530; Pres. KHANDOKER MOHSIN ALI.

**Foreign Investors' Chamber of Commerce and Industry:** 'Mahbub Castle', 4th Floor, 35-1 Purana Paltan Line, Inner Circular Rd, GPO Box 4086, Dhaka 1000; tel. (2) 412877; fax (2) 839449; e-mail ficci@fsbd.net; f. 1963 as Agrabad Chamber of Commerce and Industry, name changed as above in 1987; Pres. A.K.M. SHAMSUDDIN; Sec. JAHANGIR BIN ALAM.

**Khulna Chamber of Commerce and Industry:** 6 Lower Jessore Rd, Khulna; tel. (41) 24135; f. 1934; Pres. S. K. ZAHOIUL ISLAM.

**Khustia Chamber of Commerce and Industry:** 15, NS Rd, Kushtia; tel. (71) 3448; Pres. DIN MOHAMMAD.

**Metropolitan Chamber of Commerce and Industry:** Chamber Bldg, 4th Floor, 122–124 Motijheel C/A, Dhaka 1000; tel. (2) 9565208; fax (2) 9565212; e-mail sg@citechco.net; internet www.mcci-bd.org; f. 1904; 279 mems; Sec.-Gen. C. K. HYDER.

**Noakhali Chamber of Commerce and Industry:** Noakhali Pourshara Bhaban, 2nd Floor, Maiydee Court, Noakhali; tel. 5229; Pres. MOHAMMAD NAZIBUR RAHMAN.

**Rajshahi Chamber of Commerce and Industry:** Chamber Bhaban, Station Rd, P.O. Ghoramara, Rajshahi 6100; tel. (721) 772115; fax (721) 2412; f. 1960; 800 mems; Pres. MOHAMMAD ALI SARKER.

**Sylhet Chamber of Commerce and Industry:** Chamber Bldg, Jail Rd, POB 97, Sylhet 3100; tel. (821) 714403; fax (821) 715210; e-mail scci@btsnet.net; Pres. MOHD SAFWAN CHOUDHURY.

## INDUSTRIAL AND TRADE ASSOCIATIONS

**Bangladesh Garment Manufacturers and Exporters Association:** Dhaka; Pres. MOSTAFA GOLAM QUDDUS; Vice-Pres. NURUL HAQ SIKDAR.

**Bangladesh Jute Association:** BJA Bldg, 77 Motijheel C/A, Dhaka; tel. (2) 256558; Chair. M.A. MANNAN; Sec. S. H. PRODHAN.

**Bangladesh Jute Goods Association:** 3rd Floor, 150 Motijheel C/A, Dhaka 1000; tel. (2) 253640; f. 1979; 17 mems; Chair. M. A. KASHEM, Haji MOHAMMAD ALI.

**Bangladesh Jute Mills Association:** Adamjee Court, 4th Floor, 115–120 Motijheel C/A, Dhaka 1000; tel. (2) 9560071; fax (2) 9566472; Chair. A. M. ZAHIRUDDIN KHAN.

**Bangladesh Jute Spinners Association:** 55 Purana Paltan, 3rd Floor, Dhaka 1000; tel. (2) 9551317; fax (2) 9562772; f. 1979; 34 mems; Chair. SHABBIR YUSUF; Sec. SHAHIDUL KARIM.

**Bangladesh Tea Board:** 171–172 Baizid Bostami Rd, Nasirabad, Chittagong; tel. (31) 682903; fax (31) 682863; f. 1951; regulates, controls and promotes the cultivation and marketing of tea, both in Bangladesh and abroad; Chair. MUSIB UDDIN CHOWDHURY; Sec. M. ALI AHMED.

**Bangladeshiyo Cha Sangsad** (Tea Association of Bangladesh): 'Dar-e-Shahidi', 3rd Floor, 69 Agrabad C/A, POB 287, Chittagong 4100; tel. (31) 501009; f. 1952; Chair. QUAMRUL CHOWDHURY; Sec. G. S. DHAR.

## UTILITIES

### Electricity

**Bangladesh Atomic Energy Commission (BAEC):** 4 Kazi Nazrul Islam Ave, POB 158, Dhaka 1000; tel. (2) 502600; fax (2) 863051; f. 1964 as Atomic Energy Centre of the fmr Pakistan Atomic Energy Comm. in East Pakistan; reorg. 1973; operates an atomic energy research establishment and a 3-MW research nuclear reactor (inaugurated in January 1987) at Savar, an atomic energy centre at Dhaka, one nuclear medicine institute at IPGMR, Dhaka, nine nuclear medicine centres, and a beach-sand exploitation centre at Cox's Bazar; nuclear mineral project involving the exploitation of uranium and thorium; gamma radiation sources for food preservation and industrial radiography; Chair. M. A. QUAIYUM; Sec. RAFIQUL ALAM.

**Bangladesh Power Development Board:** Dhaka; e-mail webmaster@bd-pdb.org; f. 1972; under Ministry of Energy and Mineral Resources; installed capacity 3,603 MW (1999); Chair. QUAMRUL ISLAM SIDDIQUE.

**Dhaka Electric Supply Authority:** Dhaka; under Ministry of Energy and Mineral Resources.

**Powergrid Company of Bangladesh:** Dhaka; f. 1996; responsible for power transmission throughout Bangladesh.

**Rural Electrification Board:** Dhaka; under Ministry of Energy and Mineral Resources.

### Water

**Chittagong Water Supply and Sewerage Authority:** Dampara, Chittagong; tel. (31) 621606; fax (31) 610465; f. 1963; govt corpn; Chair. SULTAN MAHMUD CHOWDHURY.

**Dhaka Water Supply and Sewerage Authority:** 98 Kazi Nazrul Islam Ave, Kawran Bazar, Dhaka 1215; tel. (2) 816792; fax (2) 812109; f. 1963; govt corpn; Man. Dir K. AZHARUL HAQ.

## TRADE UNIONS

In 1986 only about 3% of the total labour force was unionized. There were 2,614 registered unions, organized mainly on a sectoral or occupational basis. There were about 17 national trade unions to represent workers at the national level.

# Transport

## RAILWAYS

In late 1999 an Indian company announced plans to construct a 245-km railway line between Dhaka and Kolkata/Culcutta at a projected cost of US $58m.

**Bangladesh Railway:** Rail Bhaban, Abdul Ghani Rd, Dhaka 1000; tel. (2) 9561200; fax (2) 9563413; e-mail systcan@citechco.net; f. 1862; supervised by the Railway and Road Transport Division of the Ministry of Communications; divided into East and West zones, with HQ at Chittagong (tel. (31) 711294) and Rajshahi (tel. (721) 761576; fax (721) 761982); total length of 2,706 route km (June 1997); 489 stations; Dir-Gen. M. A. MANAF; Gen. Man. (East Zone) M. FARHAD REZA; Gen. Man. (West Zone) A.T.M. NURUL ISLAM.

## ROADS

In 1995 the total length of roads in use was 223,391 km (16,070 km of highways, 22,780 km of secondary roads and 184,541 km of other roads), of which 7.2% were paved. In 1992 the World Bank approved Bangladesh's US $700m. Jamuna Bridge Project. The construction of the 4.8-km bridge, which was, for the first time, to link the east and the west of the country with a railway and road network, was begun in early 1994. The bridge, which was renamed the Bangabandhu Jamuna Multipurpose Bridge, was officially opened in June 1998.

In June 1999 the first direct passenger bus service between Bangladesh (Dhaka) and India (Kolkata/Calcutta) was inaugurated.

**Bangladesh Road Transport Corpn:** Paribhaban, DIT Ave, Dhaka; f. 1961; state-owned; operates transport services, incl. truck division; transports govt foodgrain; Chair. AZMAN HOSSAIN CHOWDHURY.

## INLAND WATERWAYS

In Bangladesh there are some 8,433 km of navigable waterways, which transport 70% of total domestic and foreign cargo traffic and on which are located the main river ports of Dhaka, Narayanganj, Chandpur, Barisal and Khulna. A river steamer service connects these ports several times a week. Vessels of up to 175-m overall length can be navigated on the Karnaphuli river.

**Bangladesh Inland Water Transport Corpn:** 5 Dilkusha C/A, Dhaka 1000; tel. (2) 257092; f. 1972; 273 vessels (1986).

## SHIPPING

The chief ports are Chittagong, where the construction of a second dry-dock is planned, and Chalna. A modern seaport is being developed at Mongla.

**Atlas Shipping Lines Ltd:** Atlas House, 7 Sk. Mujib Rd, Agrabad C/A, Chittagong 2; tel. (31) 504287; fax (31) 225520; Man. Dir S. U. CHOWDHURY; Gen. Man. M. KAMAL HAYAT.

**Bangladesh Shipping Corpn:** BSC Bhaban, Saltgola Rd, POB 641, Chittagong 4100; tel. (31) 713277; fax (31) 710506; e-mail bsc-ctg@spnetctg.com; f. 1972; maritime shipping; 15 vessels, 210,672 dwt capacity (1999); Chair. MOFAZZAL HOSSAIN CHOWDHURY MAYA; Man. Dir ZULFIQAR HAIDAR CHAUDHURY.

**Bengal Shipping Line Ltd:** Palm View, 100A Agrabad C/A, Chittagong 4100; tel. (31) 714800; fax (31) 710362; e-mail mgt@mkrbd.com; Chair. MOHAMMED ABDUL AWWAL; Man. Dir MOHAMMED ABDUL MALEK.

**Blue Ocean Lines Ltd:** 1st Floor, H.B.F.C. Bldg, 1D Agrabad C/A, Agrabad, Chittagong; tel. (31) 501567; fax (31) 225415.

**Broadway Shipping Line:** Hafiz Estate, 65 Shiddeswari Rd, Dhaka; tel. (2) 404598; fax (2) 412254.

**Chittagong Port Authority:** POB 2013, Chittagong 4100; tel. (31) 505041; f. 1887; provides bunkering, ship repair, towage and lighterage facilities as well as provisions and drinking water supplies; Chair. MD SHAHADAT HUSSAIN.

**Continental Liner Agencies:** 3rd Floor, Facy Bldg, 87 Agrabad C/A, Chittagong; tel. (31) 721572; fax (31) 710965; Man. SAIFUL AHMED; Dir (Technical and Operations) Capt. MAHFUZUL ISLAM.

**Nishan Shipping Lines Ltd:** 1st Floor, Monzoor Bldg, 67 Agrabad C/A, Chittagong; tel. (31) 710855; fax (31) 710044; Dir Capt. A. K. M. ALAMGIR.

## CIVIL AVIATION

There is an international airport at Dhaka (Zia International Airport) situated at Kurmitola, with the capacity to handle 5m. passengers annually. There are also airports at all major towns. In 1997 the civil aviation industry was deregulated to permit domestic competition to Biman Bangladesh Airlines.

**Biman Bangladesh Airlines:** Head Office, Balaka, Kurmitola, Dhaka 1229; tel. (2) 8917400; fax (2) 8913005; f. 1972; 100% state-owned; domestic services to seven major towns; international services to the Middle East, the Far East, Europe, and North America; Chair. Minister of Civil Aviation and Tourism; Man. Dir Air Cmmdre M. RAFIQUL ISLAM.

**GMG Airlines:** Dhaka; tel. (2) 889019; fax (2) 895214; f. 1997; Dir (Flight Operations) Capt. M. ELIASH; Man. Dir SHAHAB SATTAR.

# Tourism

Tourist attractions include the cities of Dhaka and Chittagong, Cox's Bazar—which has the world's longest beach (120 km)—on the Bay of Bengal, and Teknaf, at the southernmost point of Bangladesh. Tourist arrivals totalled 165,887 in 1996 and earnings from tourism reached about US $34m. The majority of visitors are from India, Pakistan, Japan, the United Kingdom and the USA.

**Bangladesh Parjatan Corpn** (National Tourism Organization): 233 Airport Rd, Tejgaon, Dhaka 1215; tel. (2) 8117855; fax (2) 8117235; there are four tourist information centres in Dhaka, and one each in Bogra, Chittagong, Cox's Bazar, Dinajpur, Khulna, Kuakata, Rangamati, Rangpur, Rajshahi and Sylhet; Chair. MD ABU SALEH; Man. (Public Relations Division) MOHAMMAD AHSAN ULLAH.

# BARBADOS

## Introductory Survey

**Location, Climate, Language, Religion, Flag, Capital**

Barbados is the most easterly of the Caribbean islands, lying about 320 km (200 miles) north-east of Trinidad. The island has a total area of 430 sq km (166 sq miles). There is a rainy season from July to November and the climate is tropical, tempered by constant sea winds, during the rest of the year. The mean annual temperature is about 26°C (78°F). Average annual rainfall varies from 1,250 mm (49 ins) on the coast, to 1,875 mm (74 ins) in the interior. The official language is English. Almost all of the inhabitants profess Christianity, but there are small groups of Hindus, Muslims and Jews. The largest denomination is the Anglican church, but about 90 other Christian sects are represented. The national flag (proportions 3 by 2) has three equal vertical stripes, of blue, gold and blue; superimposed on the centre of the gold band is the head of a black trident. The capital is Bridgetown.

**Recent History**

Barbados was formerly a British colony. The Barbados Labour Party (BLP) won a general election in 1951, when universal adult suffrage was introduced, and held office until 1961. Although the parliamentary system dates from 1639, ministerial government was not established until 1954, when the BLP's leader, Sir Grantley Adams, became the island's first Premier. He was subsequently Prime Minister of the West Indies Federation from January 1958 until its dissolution in May 1962.

Barbados achieved full internal self-government in October 1961. An election in December was won by the Democratic Labour Party (DLP), formed in 1955 by dissident members of the BLP. The DLP's leader, Errol Barrow, became Premier, succeeding Dr Hugh Cummins of the BLP. When Barbados achieved independence on 30 November 1966, Barrow became the island's first Prime Minister, following another electoral victory by his party earlier in the month.

The DLP retained power in 1971, but in the general election of September 1976 the BLP, led by J. M. G. M. ('Tom') Adams (Sir Grantley's son), ended Barrow's 15-year rule. The BLP successfully campaigned against alleged government corruption, winning a large majority over the DLP. At a general election in June 1981 the BLP was returned to office with 17 of the 27 seats in the newly-enlarged House of Assembly. The DLP won the remainder of the seats. Adams died suddenly in March 1985 and was succeeded as Prime Minister by his deputy, Bernard St John, a former leader of the BLP.

At a general election in May 1986 the DLP won a decisive victory, receiving 59.4% of the total votes and winning 24 seats in the House of Assembly. Bernard St John and all except one of his cabinet ministers lost their seats, and Errol Barrow returned as Prime Minister after 10 years in opposition. In June it was announced that Barrow was to review Barbados' participation in the US-supported Regional Security System (RSS), the defence force that had been established soon after the US invasion of Grenada in October 1983. Barbados, under Adams, was one of the countries whose troops had supported the invasion. In November 1986 Barrow announced a halt in recruitment to the Barbados Defence Force. In June 1987 Barrow died suddenly; he was succeeded by L. Erskine Sandiford (hitherto the Deputy Prime Minister), who pledged to continue Barrow's economic and social policies. In September 1987, however, the Minister of Finance, Dr Richard (Richie) Haynes, resigned, accusing Sandiford of failing to consult him over financial appointments. Sandiford assumed the finance portfolio, but acrimony over government policy continued to trouble the DLP. In February 1989 Haynes and three other members of Parliament resigned from the DLP and announced the formation of the National Democratic Party (NDP). Haynes was subsequently appointed as leader of the parliamentary opposition.

At a general election in January 1991 the DLP won 18 of the 28 seats in the enlarged House of Assembly, while the BLP secured the remaining 10. The creation of a Ministry of Justice and Public Safety by the new Government, and the reintroduction of flogging for convicted criminals, reflected widespread concern over increased levels of violent crime on the island. Moreover, as a result of serious economic problems, a series of austerity measures were proposed in September. However, the proposals resulted in public unrest, which continued in 1992, as large numbers of civil servants and agricultural workers were made redundant. The increasing unpopularity of Sandiford's premiership provoked continued demands for his resignation during 1993, and at the DLP's annual convention in August a leadership challenge was mounted. However, Sandiford remained in office, and he subsequently announced a major reallocation of cabinet portfolios. Moreover, a controversial reorganization of the Barbados Tourist Authority prompted the resignation of three cabinet ministers in early 1994. Increasing dissatisfaction with the Prime Minister culminated in his defeat, by 14 votes to 12, in a parliamentary motion of confidence in June. Despite intense speculation that he would resign, Sandiford remained in office, but announced the dissolution of Parliament in preparation for a general election, which was to take place in September. At the DLP annual conference in August, David Thompson defeated Brandford Taitt in a leadership contest.

A general election took place on 6 September 1994, at which the BLP won a decisive victory, securing 19 seats in the House of Assembly, compared with the DLP's eight and the NDP's one. Owen Arthur was subsequently appointed as Prime Minister.

In May 1995 Arthur announced the formation of a 10-member commission to advise the Government on possible reforms of the country's Constitution and political institutions. In July 1996 the commission was asked to consider, in particular, the continuing role of the British monarch as Head of State in Barbados. The commission's report, which was published in December 1998, recommended, as expected, the replacement of the British monarch with a ceremonial President. It also proposed changes in the composition of the Senate and the substitution of a jointly-administered Caribbean Court for the existing highest judicial body, the Privy Council. In July 1999 Caribbean leaders agreed to establish such a court.

In December 1996 the DLP retained a seat in a by-election. This development resulted in renewed pressure for the reunification of the DLP and the NDP, which together secured more votes (though fewer seats) than the BLP in the general election. In mid-1997 two prominent members of the NDP (including the influential General Secretary of the National Union of Public Workers, Joseph Goddard) rejoined the DLP. The NDP lost a further electoral candidate to the ruling BLP in November. In September two candidates (one of whom subsequently joined the DLP) resigned from the BLP, attributing their decision to the Prime Minister's lack of control over the party. In September 1998 Hamilton Lashley, a prominent DLP member of the House of Assembly, accepted the post of consultant to the Prime Minister on matters of poverty alleviation. In October Lashley transferred political allegiance to the governing BLP.

In late December 1998 the Prime Minister called a general election, to be held on 20 January 1999, although elections were not constitutionally due until September of that year. Although the BLP was widely expected to win a second term in government, the scale of its election victory was unprecedented. The BLP received 64.8% of the total votes cast, winning 26 of the 28 seats in the House of Assembly, while the DLP received 35.1% of the votes and won only two seats (the NDP did not contest the election). The result represented an even greater defeat for the DLP than the BLP had itself experienced in the elections of 1986 (see above), and was largely attributed to the Government's recent successes in reviving the Barbadian economy, particularly in reducing unemployment. (However, although there were severe doubts over his political future, David Thompson was re-elected as the leader of the DLP in August 1999.) On 24 January the Prime Minister announced an expanded 14-member Cabinet, including the new post of Minister of Social Transformation (to which Lashley was appointed), whose major concern was to be poverty alleviation. Arthur promised to create a 'new and unprecedented prosperity' in Barbados, and declared his Government's commitment to transforming Barbados into a republic (although he simultaneously pledged to keep the country within the Commonwealth).

In April 1999 Trafalgar Square, in the centre of Bridgetown, was renamed National Heroes Square, and the decision was made to replace the statue of the British Admiral Lord Horatio Nelson which stood there, with one of Errol Barrow, the country's first Prime Minister. These developments, which reinforced existing differences between Barbados' two main ethnic communities, were seen as evidence that the country was beginning its transformation into a republic. With the aim of resolving any growing divisions, the Government organized a day of national reconciliation in July, while a 13-member Committee for National Reconciliation was also established.

In August 1999 the long-serving Minister of Health, Elizabeth Thompson, was unexpectedly dismissed by the Prime Minister. Reasons for her dismissal were unspecified, although it apparently followed derogatory remarks made by the minister about the opposition leader, David Thompson. Phillip Goddard was appointed the new Minister of Health, while the Public Works and Transport portfolio was assumed by Rommell Marshall. In November two former electoral candidates for the DLP, who had been unsuccessful in January's general election, announced their resignation from the party. One of the candidates stated that he intended to join the ruling BLP, claiming that the DLP lacked direction.

In late 1997 the Government established a committee to examine alternative methods of punishing offenders, following a report which found Barbados' only prison to be grossly overcrowded. In October 1998, owing to a recent significant increase in the number of violent crimes involving firearms, the Government announced a temporary amnesty for individuals surrendering illegally-owned weapons; tougher penalties for unlawful possession were introduced as part of new firearms-control legislation enacted in November. Amid a further escalation in violent crime and fears that the country's tourism industry might be affected, it was announced in October 1999 that an anti-firearms unit was to be established in the police force.

Relations with Trinidad and Tobago were strained between 1982 and 1985 by publicly-stated differences over the 1983 intervention in Grenada (q.v.), and by Trinidad and Tobago's imposition of import restrictions (a compromise on this was reached in August 1986). In November 1990 the two Governments signed a bilateral fishing agreement; they also agreed, in late 1999, to draft a boundary delimitation treaty and to establish a negotiating mechanism to resolve trade disputes. In late 1996 Barbados signed an agreement with the USA to co-operate with a regional initiative to combat the illegal drugs trade. In mid-1998 the Government announced its intention to develop relations with countries in Asia, the Pacific region and Latin America, in order to pursue a foreign policy based on economic considerations. In March of that year Barbados began negotiations with the Organisation of Eastern Caribbean States (OECS, see p. 292) concerning the country's eventual membership in a confederation, and possible political union, of Eastern Caribbean states. Areas under discussion included health, education, diplomatic representation and the judiciary. A 14-member joint 'task force' had been appointed in February to discuss the possible incorporation of Barbados into the OECS. An inaugural meeting of the discussion group took place in April, when it was suggested that a working confederation could be instituted within 2–3 years. Although monetary union was not to be a prior condition to membership, OECS spokesmen described the adoption of a single currency as highly desirable.

## Government

Executive power is vested in the British monarch, represented by a Governor-General, who acts on the advice of the Cabinet. The Governor-General appoints the Prime Minister and, on the latter's recommendation, other members of the Cabinet. Legislative power is vested in the bicameral Parliament, comprising a Senate of 21 members, appointed by the Governor-General, and a House of Assembly with 28 members, elected by universal adult suffrage for five years (subject to dissolution) from single-member constituencies. The Cabinet is responsible to Parliament. In 1969 elected local government bodies were abolished in favour of a division into 11 parishes, all of which are administered by the central Government.

## Defence

The Barbados Defence Force was established in 1978. The total strength of the Barbados armed forces in August 1999 was estimated at 610; the army consisted of 500 members and the navy (coastguard) 110. There was also a reserve force of 430. Government spending on defence in the year ending 31 March 1999 was budgeted at Bds $27.8m.

## Economic Affairs

In 1995, according to estimates by the World Bank, the island's gross national product (GNP), measured at average 1993–95 prices, was US $1,745m., equivalent to US $6,560 per head. Between 1985 and 1995, it was estimated, GNP per head decreased, in real terms, at an average annual rate of 0.2%. Between 1990 and 1997 the population increased at an average rate of 0.4% per year. According to preliminary estimates, GNP totalled US $2,096m. (US $7,890 per head) in 1998. Barbados' gross domestic product (GDP), at factor cost, increased, in real terms, at an average rate of 0.7% per year during 1990–97. Real GDP increased by 4.1% in 1996, by 3.0% in 1997 and by an estimated 4.9% in 1998.

Agriculture (including forestry and fishing) contributed 4.0% of GDP and engaged 4.3% of the employed labour force in 1998. Sugar remains the main commodity export, earning Bds $56.6m. in 1998; in that year, however, raw sugar production decreased by 25.7% to an estimated 48,000 metric tons. Sea-island cotton, once the island's main export crop, was revived in the mid-1980s. The other principal crops, primarily for local consumption, are sweet potatoes, carrots, yams and other vegetables and fruit. Fishing was also developed in the 1980s, and in 1988 there was a fleet of about 750 fishing vessels. The GDP of the agricultural sector declined, in real terms, at an average rate of 0.5% per year during 1990–97. Agricultural GDP rose by 17% in 1996, but fell by 0.8% in 1997.

In 1998 industry accounted for an estimated 16.1% of GDP, and 20.9% of the working population were employed in all industrial activities (manufacturing, construction, quarrying and utilities). In real terms, industrial GDP increased at an average rate of 0.9% annually in 1990–97. Industrial GDP rose by 7.3% in 1995, by 2.1% in 1996 and by 4.8% in 1997.

Owing to fluctuations in international prices, the production of crude petroleum declined substantially from its peak in 1985, to 454,424 barrels in 1990, or 31% of Barbados' requirements. In late 1996 the Barbados National Oil Company signed a five-year agreement with a US company to intensify exploration activity, with the aim of increasing petroleum production from 1,000 barrels per day (b/d) to 10,000 b/d by 2001. Total annual extraction was expected to reach more than 850,000 barrels in 1999, equivalent to more than 50% of local consumption. Production of natural gas was 24.2m. cu m in 1998. Mining and construction contributed 6.6% of GDP and employed 10.5% of the working population in 1998.

Manufacturing contributed an estimated 6.2% of GDP and employed 8.9% of the working population in 1998. Excluding sugar factories and refineries, the principal branches of manufacturing, measured by the value of output, in 1994 were chemical, petroleum, rubber and plastic products (accounting for 27.3% of the total), food products (26.9%), and beverages and tobacco (15.0%). Manufacturing GDP increased, in real terms, at an average rate of 0.2% per year during 1990–97; it rose by 4.3% in 1997.

Service industries are the main sector of the economy, accounting for an estimated 79.9% of GDP and 74.4% of employment in 1998. The combined GDP of the service sectors increased, in real terms, at an average rate of 0.7% per year during 1990–97. Finance, insurance, real estate and business services contributed an estimated 18.2% of GDP in 1998. The Government has encouraged the growth of 'offshore' financial facilities, particularly through the negotiation of double taxation agreements with other countries. At the end of 1998 there were 3,073 international business companies and 2,608 foreign sales corporations operating in the country. It was estimated that the 'offshore' sector contributed almost US $150m. in foreign earnings in 1995. In the following year the Government announced a series of proposals which aimed to expand the industry.

Tourism made a direct contribution of 12.3% to GDP and employed 11.5% of the working population in 1998. Receipts from the tourist industry almost doubled between 1980 and 1988, and in 1998 totalled some Bds $1,500m. Stop-over tourist arrivals increased by 8.5% in 1998 compared with the previous year, to 512,397, while cruise-ship passenger arrivals decreased by 2.2%, to 506,610. In 1998 some 36.4% of stop-over arrivals were from the United Kingdom.

In 1998 Barbados recorded a visible trade deficit of US $644.1m. and there was a deficit of US $55.9m. on the current account of the balance of payments. In 1998 the principal source of imports (40.9%) was the USA, which also received 14.5% of exports. The principal single market for exports (16.3%) in 1998 was the United Kingdom, which accounted for 9.3% of imports. Other major trading partners included the CARICOM countries (see below), especially Trinidad and Tobago. The principal commodity exports were provided by the sugar industry (sugar, molasses, syrup and rum), which together accounted for some 22% of total receipts from exports in 1998. The principal imports were machinery, transport equipment and basic manufactures.

For the financial year ending 31 March 2000 there was a projected total budgetary deficit of Bds $346.1m. At December 1997 the total external debt of Barbados was US $644.3m., of which US $350.0m. was long-term public debt. In 1996 the cost of foreign debt-servicing was equivalent to 7.5% of the value of exports of goods and services. The average annual rate of inflation was 3.0% in 1990–98; however, average consumer prices declined by 1.3% in 1998. In early 1999 an estimated 11.1% of the labour force were unemployed.

Barbados is a member of the Caribbean Community and Common Market (CARICOM, see p. 136), of the Inter-American Development Bank (IDB, see p. 202), of the Latin American Economic System (SELA, see p. 292) and of the Association of Caribbean States (see p. 290).

Political stability and consensus have contributed to the economic strengths of Barbados. Tourism dominates the economy but 'offshore' banking and sugar production are also important. During 1998 the tourism sector continued to expand, with stop-over arrivals reaching record levels. An increase in US visitors was forecast for 1999, although the closure of major hotels for refurbishment was expected to bring about a temporary decline in tourism earnings. Despite the thriving tourism sector, in early 1998 the Government voiced concerns over the incidence of poverty in Barbados and established a US $5m.-Social Investment Fund and a Poverty Eradication Fund. In 1998, for the first time since 1991, a balance-of-payments deficit was recorded, owing largely to the high level of import demand in the construction sector. Moreover, the expansion of private credit, which had resulted in a significant decrease in international reserves in 1998, led the Central Bank to raise the discount rate to commercial banks in May 1999, in order to curb the excess demand. The 1999/2000 budget proposals, which were announced in August 1999, were less expansionary than previous budgets; however, they included a decrease in fuel taxation, as well as incentives for the tourism, agricultural and manufacturing sectors to allow them to raise their levels of competitiveness within the planned CARICOM single market and economy (see p. 138). The rate of inflation grew during 1997, in response to the introduction in January of value-added tax (VAT) of 15%, to replace other indirect taxes on sales and consumption. However, following the removal of VAT from several basic food items, in 1998 prices decreased by an average of 1.3%. The year 1998 was the sixth successive year of economic expansion, with real GDP growth of some 4.9%. By early 1999 unemployment was reportedly at its lowest level since the early 1980s. In early 1998 negotiations were initiated regarding the proposed confederation of Barbados and the OECS (see p. 292), following the 1995 economic co-operation agreement between the two parties.

### Social Welfare

A social security scheme was established in 1967, and a National Drug Plan was introduced in 1980. Old-age pensions and unemployment insurance are available. The Government has also created a building scheme of group housing for lower-income families. In 1993 Barbados had one hospital bed for every 119 citizens, and one physician for every 1,100 inhabitants on the island. Of total current budgetary expenditure by the central Government in the 1998/99 financial year, Bds $248.0m. (16.1%) was for health services and Bds $148.3m. (9.6%) was for social security and welfare. In addition, the national insurance scheme, funded by contributions, provides pensions and other benefits (totalling Bds $221.2m. in 1996/97).

### Education

Education is compulsory for 12 years, between five and 16 years of age. Primary education begins at the age of five and lasts for seven years. Secondary education, beginning at 12 years of age, lasts for six years. In 1998 enrolment of children in the primary age-group was 97% (males 99%; females 95%), while enrolment at secondary level included 69% of children in the relevant age-group (males 67%; females 71%). In that year enrolment at tertiary level was equivalent to 33.7% of the relevant age-group (males 22.2%; females 34.2%). According to UNESCO estimates, in 1996/97 3,275 students were enrolled at universities or similar institutions. Degree courses in arts, law, education, natural sciences and social sciences are offered at the Barbados branch of the University of the West Indies. The faculty of medicine administers the East Caribbean Medical Scheme, while an in-service training programme for secondary-school teachers is provided by the School of Education.

In 1995, according to UNESCO estimates, adult illiteracy in Barbados was 2.6% (males 2.0%; females 3.2%).

Current expenditure on education by the central Government in 1998/99 was Bds $289.7m. (equivalent to 18.8% of total current spending).

### Public Holidays

**2000:** 1 January (New Year's Day), 21 January (Errol Barrow Day), 21 April (Good Friday), 24 April (Easter Monday), 28 April (National Heroes' Day), 1 May (Labour Day), 12 June (Whit Monday), 1 August (Emancipation Day), 7 August (Kadooment Day), 30 November (Independence Day), 25–26 December (Christmas).

**2001:** 1 January (New Year's Day), 21 January (Errol Barrow Day), 13 April (Good Friday), 16 April (Easter Monday), 28 April (National Heroes' Day), 3 May (for Labour Day), 4 June (Whit Monday), 1 August (Emancipation Day), 6 August (Kadooment Day), 30 November (Independence Day), 25–26 December (Christmas).

### Weights and Measures

The metric system is used.

# Statistical Survey

Sources (unless otherwise stated): Barbados Statistical Service, National Insurance Bldg, 3rd Floor, Fairchild St, Bridgetown; tel. 427-7841; fax 435-2198; e-mail barstats@caribsurf.com; internet www.barbadosgov.bb/stats.
Central Bank of Barbados, Spry St, POB 1016, Bridgetown; tel. 436-6870; fax 427-1431; e-mail cbb.libr@caribsurf.com; internet www.centralbank.org.bb.

## AREA AND POPULATION

**Area:** 430 sq km (166 sq miles).

**Population:** 252,029 (males 119,665, females 132,364) at census of 12 May 1980; 257,082 (provisional) at census of 2 May 1990; 266,900 (official estimate; males 128,300, females 138,600) at 31 December 1998.

**Density** (31 December 1998): 620.7 per sq km.

**Ethnic Groups** (*de jure* population, excl. persons resident in institutions, 1990 census): Black 228,683; White 8,022; Mixed race 5,886; Total (incl. others) 247,288.

**Principal Town:** Bridgetown (capital), population 5,928 at 1990 census.

**Births, Marriages and Deaths** (provisional registrations, 1998): Live births 3,612 (birth rate 13.6 per 1,000); Marriages (1997) 3,377 (marriage rate 12.7 per 1,000); Deaths 2,471 (death rate 9.3 per 1,000).

**Expectation of Life** (UN estimates, years at birth, 1990–95): 75.3 (males 72.9; females 77.9). Source: UN, *World Population Prospects: The 1998 Revision*.

**Economically Active Population** (labour force sample survey, '000 persons aged 15 years and over, excl. armed forces, 1998): Agriculture, forestry and fishing 5.2; Manufacturing 10.7; Electricity, gas and water 1.8; Construction and quarrying 12.5; Wholesale and retail trade 18.2; Tourism 13.8; Transport, storage and communications 5.1; Financing, insurance, real estate and business services 7.5; Community, social and personal services 44.4; Total employed 119.6 (males 64.4, females 55.2); Unemployed 16.7 (males 5.9, females 10.8); Total labour force 136.3 (males 70.3, females 66.0).

## AGRICULTURE, ETC.

**Principal Crops** (FAO estimates '000 metric tons, 1998): Maize 2; Sweet potatoes 5; Cassava 1; Yams 1; Pulses 1; Coconuts 2; Cabbages 1; Tomatoes 1; Pumpkins 1; Cucumbers 1; Peppers 1; Carrots 1; Other vegetables 6; Sugar cane 571; Bananas 1; Other fruits 2. Source: FAO, *Production Yearbook*.

**Livestock** (FAO estimates, '000 head, year ending September 1998): Horses 1; Mules 2; Asses 2; Cattle 22; Pigs 30; Sheep 41; Goats 5; Poultry (million) 3. Source: FAO, *Production Yearbook*.

**Livestock Products** (FAO estimates, '000 metric tons, 1998): Beef and veal 1; Pig meat 4; Poultry meat 11; Cows' milk 9; Hen eggs 1. Source: FAO, *Production Yearbook*.

**Forestry** ('000 cubic metres): Roundwood removals 5 in 1995; 5 in 1996; 5 in 1997. Source: FAO, *Yearbook of Forest Products*.

**Fishing** (metric tons, live weight): Total catch 3,284 in 1995; 3,439 in 1996; 2,764 (Flying fishes 1,566, Common dolphinfish 721) in 1997. Source: FAO, *Yearbook of Fishery Statistics*.

## MINING

**Production** (1998): Natural gas 24.2 million cu m; Crude petroleum 576,636 barrels.

## INDUSTRY

**Selected Products** (official estimates, 1998): Raw sugar 48,000 metric tons; Rum 8,830,000 litres; Beer (1995) 7,429,000 litres; Cigarettes (1995) 65 metric tons; Batteries 17,165; Electric energy 715m. kWh.

## FINANCE

**Currency and Exchange Rates:** 100 cents = 1 Barbados dollar (Bds $). *Sterling, US Dollar and Euro Equivalents* (30 September 1999): £1 sterling = Bds $3.293; US $1 = Bds $2.000; €1 = Bds $2.133; Bds $100 = £30.37 = US $50.00 = €46.88. *Exchange Rate*: Fixed at US $1 = Bds $2.000 since 1986.

**Budget** (estimates, Bds $ million, year ending 31 March 1999): *Revenue*: Tax revenue 1,420.2 (Taxes on income and profits 449.3, Taxes on property 85.7, Domestic taxes on goods and services 735.4, Taxes on international trade 136.7); Other current revenue 81.8; Special receipts 54.1; Total 1,556.1. *Expenditure:* General public services 247.6, Defence and security 27.8, Education 289.7, Health 248.0, Social security and welfare 148.3, Housing and community amenities 54.4, Other community and social services 51.2, Economic services 303.6; Other purposes (incl. lending and debt charges) 414.0; Total 1,784.7.

**1999/2000** (projections, Bds $ million): Total revenue 1,630.0; Total expenditure 1,976.1 (Capital expenditure 318.6).

Note: Budgetary data refer to current and capital budgets only and exclude operations of the National Insurance Fund and other central government units with their own budgets.

**International Reserves** (US $ million at 31 December 1998): IMF special drawing rights 0.03; Reserve position in IMF 0.04; Foreign exchange 253.16; Total 253.23. Source: IMF, *International Financial Statistics*.

**Money Supply** (Bds $ million at 31 December 1998): Currency outside banks 268.2; Demand deposits at commercial banks 493.3; Total money (incl. others) 767.1. Source: IMF, *International Financial Statistics*.

**Cost of Living** (Index of Retail Prices; base: 1995 = 100): 102.4 in 1996; 110.3 in 1997; 108.9 in 1998. Source: IMF, *International Financial Statistics*.

**Expenditure on the Gross Domestic Product** (provisional, Bds $ million at current prices, 1998): Government final consumption expenditure 974.6; Private final consumption expenditure 2,977.2; Increase in stocks 9.9; Gross fixed capital formation 909.0; *Total domestic expenditure* 4,870.7; Exports of goods and services 2,470.7; *Less* Imports of goods and services 2,564.5; *GDP in purchasers' values* 4,776.9.

**Gross Domestic Product by Economic Activity** (Bds $ million at current prices, 1998): Agriculture, hunting, forestry and fishing 158.1; Mining and quarrying 20.1; Manufacturing 243.5; Electricity, gas and water 126.4; Construction 240.6; Wholesale and retail trade 702.2; Tourism 482.2; Transport, storage and communications 381.7; Finance, insurance, real estate and business services 715.7; Government services 674.5; Other community, social and personal services 179.8; *GDP at factor cost* 3,924.8; Indirect taxes, *less* subsidies 852.1; *GDP in purchasers' values* 4,776.9.

**Balance of Payments** (US $ million, 1998): Exports of goods f.o.b. 257.1; Imports of goods f.o.b. –901.1; *Trade balance* –644.1; Exports of services 1,023.6; Imports of services –432.2; *Balance on goods and services* –52.6; Other income received 63.4; Other income paid –119.5; *Balance on goods, services and income* –108.7; Current transfers received 78.9; Current transfers paid –26.2; *Current balance* –55.9; Capital account (net) 0.7; Direct investment abroad –1.0; Direct investment from abroad 15.8; Portfolio investment assets –23.1; Portfolio investment liabilities –1.5; Other investment assets –19.5; Other investment liabilities 45.3; Net errors and omissions –5.4; *Overall balance* –44.7.

## EXTERNAL TRADE*

**Principal Commodities** (US $ '000, 1996): *Imports:* Food and live animals 120,881; Beverages and tobacco 14,096; Crude materials (inedible) except fuels 31,941; Mineral fuels, lubricants, etc. 82,038; Animal and vegetable oils and fats 5,541; Chemicals 97,383; Basic manufactures 132,153; Machinery and transport equipment 229,361; Miscellaneous manufactured articles 112,997; Goods not classified by kind 2,585; Total 828,975. *Exports:* Food and live animals 87,292 (Sugar 35,805); Beverages and tobacco 15,600; Petroleum and products 36,965; Chemicals 33,966; Basic manufactures 39,623; Machinery and transport equipment 38,938; Miscellaneous manufactured articles 22,436; Total (incl. others) 279,049.

**Principal Trading Partners** (US $ '000, 1996): *Imports:* Canada 42,465; Japan 41,877; Trinidad and Tobago 89,336; United Kingdom 69,363; USA 360,846; Total (incl. others) 828,975. *Exports:* Canada 12,177; Jamaica 24,990; Saint Lucia 12,409; Trinidad and Tobago 20,462; United Kingdom 46,401; USA 39,245; Total (incl. others) 279,049.

* Source: UN, *International Trade Statistics Yearbook*. Note: Figures for imports exclude crude petroleum.

## TRANSPORT

**Road Traffic** (motor vehicles in use, 1995): Private cars 43,711; Taxis 1,405; Buses and minibuses 390; Lorries 2,215; Vans and pick-ups 3,967; Total 55,665.

**Shipping** (estimated freight traffic, '000 metric tons, 1990): Goods loaded 206; Goods unloaded 538. Source: UN, *Monthly Bulletin of Statistics*. *Merchant Fleet* (vessels registered at 31 December 1998): Number of vessels 69; Total displacement 687,586 grt. Source: Lloyd's Register of Shipping, *World Fleet Statistics*.

**Civil Aviation** (1994): Aircraft movements 36,100; Freight loaded 5,052.3 metric tons; Freight unloaded 8,548.3 metric tons.

## TOURISM

**Tourist Arrivals:** *Stop-overs:* 447,083 in 1996; 472,290 in 1997; 512,397 in 1998. *Cruise-ship passengers*: 509,975 in 1996; 517,888 in 1997; 506,610 in 1998.

## COMMUNICATIONS MEDIA

**Radio Receivers** (1996): 236,000 in use.

**Television Receivers** (1996): 75,000 in use.

**Telephones** (1996): 127,495 in use.

**Telefax Stations** (year ending 31 March 1996): 1,781 in use.

**Mobile Cellular Telephones** (year ending 31 March 1996): 4,614 subscribers.

**Book Production** (1983): 87 titles (18 books, 69 pamphlets).

**Newspapers:** *Daily* (1996): 2 (circulation 53,000). *Non-daily* (1990): 4 (estimated circulation 95,000).

Sources: partly UNESCO, *Statistical Yearbook*, and UN, *Statistical Yearbook*.

## EDUCATION

**Pre-primary** (1995/96): 84 schools; 529 teachers; 4,689 pupils.

**Primary** (1995/96): 79 schools; 944 teachers; 18,513 pupils.

**Secondary** (1995/96): 21 schools; 1,263 teachers; 21,455 pupils.

**Tertiary** (1995/96): 4 schools; 544 teachers (1984); 6,622 students.

# Directory

## The Constitution

The parliamentary system has been established since the 17th century, when the first Assembly sat, in 1639, and the Charter of Barbados was granted, in 1652. A new Constitution came into force on 30 November 1966, when Barbados became independent. Under its terms, protection is afforded to individuals from slavery and forced labour, from inhuman treatment, deprivation of property, arbitrary search and entry, and racial discrimination; freedom of conscience, of expression, assembly, and movement are guaranteed.

Executive power is nominally vested in the British monarch, as Head of State, represented in Barbados by a Governor-General, who appoints the Prime Minister and, on the advice of the Prime Minister, appoints other ministers and some senators.

The Cabinet consists of the Prime Minister, appointed by the Governor-General as being the person best able to command a majority in the House of Assembly, and not fewer than five other ministers. Provision is also made for a Privy Council, presided over by the Governor-General.

Parliament consists of the Governor-General and a bicameral legislature, comprising the Senate and the House of Assembly. The Senate has 21 members: 12 appointed by the Governor-General on the advice of the Prime Minister, two on the advice of the Leader of the Opposition and seven as representatives of such interests as the Governor-General considers appropriate. The House of Assembly has (since January 1991) 28 members, elected by universal adult suffrage for a term of five years (subject to dissolution). The minimum voting age is 18 years.

The Constitution also provides for the establishment of Service Commissions for the Judicial and Legal Service, the Public Service, the Police Service and the Statutory Boards Service. These Commissions are exempt from legal investigation; they have executive powers relating to appointments, dismissals and disciplinary control of the services for which they are responsible.

## The Government

**Head of State:** HM Queen ELIZABETH II (succeeded to the throne 6 February 1952).

**Governor-General:** Sir CLIFFORD HUSBANDS (appointed 1 June 1996).

### THE CABINET
(January 2000)

**Prime Minister and Minister of Finance and Economic Affairs, of Defence and Security and for the Civil Service:** OWEN S. ARTHUR.

**Deputy Prime Minister and Minister of Foreign Affairs and Foreign Trade:** BILLIE A. MILLER.

**Attorney-General and Minister of Home Affairs:** DAVID A. C. SIMMONS.

**Minister of Education, Youth Affairs and Culture:** MIA A. MOTTLEY.

**Minister of Health:** Sen. PHILLIP GODDARD.

**Minister of the Environment, Energy and Natural Resources:** RAWLE C. EASTMOND.

**Minister of Agriculture and Rural Development:** ANTHONY P. WOOD.

**Minister of Social Transformation:** HAMILTON F. LASHLEY.

**Minister of Tourism and of International Transport:** GEORGE W. PAYNE.

**Minister of Housing and Lands:** GLINE A. CLARKE.

**Minister of Commerce, Consumer Affairs and Business Development:** RONALD TOPPIN.

**Minister of Industry and International Business:** REGINALD R. FARLEY.

**Minister of Labour, Sports and Public-Sector Reform:** RUDOLPH N. GREENIDGE.

**Minister of Public Works and Transport:** ROMMELL MARSHALL.

**Minister of State in the Office of the Prime Minister and the Ministry for the Civil Service (with responsibility for Information):** GLYNE S. H. MURRAY.

### MINISTRIES

**Office of the Prime Minister:** Government Headquarters, Bay St, St Michael; tel. 436-6435; fax 436-9280; e-mail info@primeminister.gov.bb; internet www.primeminister.gov.bb.

**Ministry of Agriculture and Rural Development:** Graeme Hall, POB 505, Christ Church; tel. 428-4150; fax 420-8444; internet www.barbados.gov.bb/minagri.

**Ministry for the Civil Service:** Government Headquarters, Bay St, St Michael; tel. 426-2390; fax 228-0093.

**Ministry of Commerce, Consumer Affairs and Business Development:** Government Headquarters, Bay St, St Michael; tel. 436-6435.

**Ministry of Defence and Security:** Government Headquarters, Bay St, St Michael; tel. 436-1970.

**Ministry of Education, Youth Affairs and Culture:** Elsie Payne Complex, Constitution Rd, Bridgetown; tel. 430-2700; fax 436-2411.

**Ministry of Finance and Economic Affairs:** Government Headquarters, Bay St, St Michael; tel. 436-6435; fax 429-4032.

**Ministry of Foreign Affairs and Foreign Trade:** 1 Culloden Rd, St Michael; tel. 436-2990; fax 429-6652; e-mail foreign@foreign.barbadosgov.org; internet www.foreign.barbadosgov.org.

**Ministry of Health and the Environment:** Jemmott's Lane, St Michael; tel. 426-5080; fax 426-5570.

**Ministry of Home Affairs:** General Post Office Bldg, Level 5, Cheapside, Bridgetown; tel. 228-8961; fax 437-3794; e-mail mha@caribsurf.com.

**Ministry of Housing and Lands:** Culloden Rd, St Michael; tel. 431-7600; fax 435-0174; e-mail psmhl@caribsurf.com.

**Ministry of Industry and International Business:** The Business Centre, Upton, St Michael; tel. 430-2200; fax 223-6167; e-mail mtb-bax@caribsurf.com.

**Ministry of International Transport:** Port Authority Bldg, University Row, Bridgetown; tel. 426-9144; fax 429-3809.

**Ministry of Labour, Sports and Public-Sector Reform:** National Insurance Bldg, 5th Floor, Fairchild St, Bridgetown; tel. 436-6320; fax 426-8959; internet www.labour.gov.bb.

**Ministry of Public Works and Transport:** The Pine, St Michael; tel. 429-2191; fax 437-8133; internet www.publicworks.gov.bb.

**Ministry of Social Transformation:** Government Headquarters, Bay St, St Michael; tel. 436-6435.

**Ministry of Tourism:** Sherbourne Conference Centre, Two Mile Hill, St Michael; tel. 430-7500; fax 436-4828.

**Office of the Attorney-General:** Sir Frank Walcott Bldg, Culloden Rd, St Michael; tel. 431-7707; fax 435-9533; e-mail attygen@caribsurf.com.bb.

## Legislature

### PARLIAMENT

#### Senate

**President:** FRED GOLLOP.

There are 21 members.

#### House of Assembly

**Speaker:** ISHMAEL ROETT.

**Clerk of Parliament:** GEORGE BRANCKER.

**General Election, 20 January 1999**

| Party | Votes | % | Seats |
|---|---|---|---|
| Barbados Labour Party (BLP) . . | 83,085 | 64.85 | 26 |
| Democratic Labour Party (DLP) . | 44,974 | 35.10 | 2 |
| Others . . . . . . . . | 64 | 0.05 | – |
| **Total** . . . . . . | 128,123 | 100.00 | 28 |

## Political Organizations

**Barbados Labour Party:** Grantley Adams House, 111 Roebuck St, Bridgetown; tel. 429-1990; e-mail hq@blp.org.bb; internet www.blp.org.bb; f. 1938; moderate social democrat; Leader OWEN ARTHUR; Chair. DAVID SIMMONS; Gen. Sec. GEORGE PAYNE.

**Democratic Labour Party:** George St, Belleville, St Michael; tel. 429-3104; fax 429-3007; e-mail dlp@dlpbarbados.bb; internet www.dlpbarbados.org; f. 1955; Leader DAVID THOMPSON.

**National Democratic Party:** 'Sueños', 3 Sixth Ave, Belleville; tel. 429-6882; f. 1989 by split from Democratic Labour Party; Leader Dr RICHARD (RICHIE) HAYNES.

**Workers' Party of Barbados:** Bridgetown; tel. 425-1620; f. 1985; small left-wing organization; Gen. Sec. Dr GEORGE BELLE.

# Diplomatic Representation

### EMBASSIES AND HIGH COMMISSIONS IN BARBADOS

**Australia:** Bishops Court Hill, Pine Rd, St Michael; tel. 435-2834; High Commissioner: P. M. SMITH.

**Brazil:** Sunjet House, 3rd Floor, Fairchild St, Bridgetown; tel. 427-1735; fax 427-1744; Ambassador: CARLOS ALFREDO PINTO DA SILVA.

**Canada:** Bishops Court Hill, Pine Rd, POB 404, St Michael; tel. 429-3550; fax 429-3780; High Commissioner: DUANE VAN BESELAERE.

**China, People's Republic:** 17 Golf View Terrace, Rockley, Christ Church; tel. 435-6890; fax 435-8300; Ambassador: ZHAN DAODE.

**Colombia:** 'Rosemary', Dayrells Rd, Rockley, POB 37W, Christ Church; tel. 429-6821; fax 429-6830; e-mail colombiaembassy@sunbeach.net; Ambassador: JOSÉ JOAQUÍN GORI.

**Costa Rica:** Cuba Erin Court, Collymore Rock, St Michael; tel. 435-2769; Ambassador: JOSÉ DE J. CONEJO.

**Cuba:** Collymore Rock, St Michael; tel. 435-2769.

**Guatemala:** Trident House, 2nd Floor, Broad St, Bridgetown; tel. 435-3542; fax 435-2638; Ambassador: JULIO ROBERTO PALOMO.

**United Kingdom:** Lower Collymore Rock, POB 676, St Michael; tel. 430-7800; fax 430-7826; e-mail britishhc@sunbeach.net; High Commissioner: GORDON M. BAKER.

**USA:** Canadian Imperial Bank of Commerce Bldg, Broad St, POB 302, Bridgetown; tel. 436-4950; fax 429-5246; Ambassador: (vacant).

**Venezuela:** Hastings, Main Rd, Christ Church; tel. 435-7619; fax 435-7830; e-mail embaven@sunbeach.net; Ambassador: ANGEL BRITO VILLARROEL.

# Judicial System

Justice is administered by the Supreme Court of Judicature, which consists of a High Court and a Court of Appeal. Final appeal lies with the Judicial Committee of the Privy Council, in the United Kingdom. There are Magistrates' Courts for lesser offences, with appeal to the Court of Appeal.

**Supreme Court:** Judiciary Office, Coleridge St, Bridgetown; tel. 426-3461; fax 246-2405.

**Chief Justice:** Sir DENYS WILLIAMS.

**Justices of Appeal:** G. C. R. MOE, ERROL DA COSTA CHASE, COLIN A. WILLIAMS.

**Judges of the High Court:** FREDERICK A. WATERMAN, MARIE A. MACCORMACK, E. GARVEY HUSBANDS, CARLISLE PAYNE, SHERMAN MOORE, LIONEL DACOSTA GREENIDGE.

**Registrar of the Supreme Court:** SANDRA MASON.

**Office of the Attorney-General:** Sir Frank Walcott Bldg, Culloden Rd, St Michael; tel. 431-7707; fax 435-9533; e-mail attygen@caribsurf.com.bb; Dir of Public Prosecutions CHARLES LEACOCK; e-mail cbleacock@inaccs.com.bb.

# Religion

More than 100 religious denominations and sects are represented in Barbados, but the vast majority of the population profess Christianity. According to the 1980 census, there were 96,894 Anglicans (or some 40% of the total population), while the Pentecostal (8%) and Methodist (7%) churches were next in importance. The regional Caribbean Conference of Churches is based in Barbados. There are also small groups of Hindus, Muslims and Jews.

### CHRISTIANITY

#### The Anglican Communion

Anglicans in Barbados are adherents of the Church in the Province of the West Indies, comprising eight dioceses. The Archbishop of the Province is the Bishop of the Bahamas and the Turks and Caicos Islands, resident in Nassau, the Bahamas. In Barbados there is a Provincial Office (St George's Church, St George) and an Anglican Theological College (Codrington College, St John).

**Bishop of Barbados:** (vacant), Diocesan Office, Mandeville House, Bridgetown; tel. 426-2761; fax 427-5867.

#### The Roman Catholic Church

Barbados comprises a single diocese (formed in January 1990, when the diocese of Bridgetown-Kingstown was divided), which is suffragan to the archdiocese of Port of Spain (Trinidad and Tobago). At 31 December 1997 there were an estimated 10,000 adherents in the diocese. The Bishop participates in the Antilles Episcopal Conference (currently based in Port of Spain, Trinidad and Tobago).

**Bishop of Bridgetown:** Rt Rev. MALCOLM GALT, St Patrick's Presbytery, Jemmott's Lane, POB 1223, Bridgetown; tel. 426-3510; fax 429-6198.

#### Protestant Churches

**Baptist Churches of Barbados:** National Baptist Convention, President Kennedy Dr., Bridgetown; tel. 429-2697.

**Church of God (Caribbean Atlantic Assembly):** St Michael's Plaza, St Michael's Row, POB 1, Bridgetown; tel. 427-5770; Pres. Rev. VICTOR BABB.

**Church of Jesus Christ of Latter-day Saints (Mormons)—West Indies Mission:** Bridgetown; tel. 435-8595; fax 435-8278.

**Church of the Nazarene:** District Office, Eagle Hall, Bridgetown; tel. 425-1067.

**Methodist Church:** Bethel Church Office, Bay St, Bridgetown; tel. 426-2223.

**Moravian Church:** Roebuck St, Bridgetown; tel. 426-2337; Superintendent Rev. ERROL CONNOR.

**Seventh-day Adventists (East Caribbean Conference):** Brydens Ave, Brittons Hill, POB 223, St Michael; tel. 429-7234; fax 429-8055.

**Wesleyan Holiness Church:** General Headquarters, Bank Hall; tel. 429-4864.

Other denominations include the Apostolic Church, the Assemblies of Brethren, the Salvation Army, Presbyterian congregations, the African Methodist Episcopal Church, the Mt Olive United Holy Church of America and Jehovah's Witnesses.

### ISLAM

In 1996 there were an estimated 2,000 Muslims in Barbados.

**Islamic Teaching Centre:** Harts Gap, Hastings; tel. 427-0120.

### JUDAISM

**Jewish Community:** Nidhe Israel and Shaara Tzedek Synagogue, Rockley New Rd, POB 651, Bridgetown; tel. 437-1290; fax 437-1303; there were 60 Jews in Barbados in 1997; Pres. RACHELLE ALTMAN; Sec. SHARON ORAN.

**Caribbean Jewish Congress:** POB 1331, Bridgetown; tel. 436-8163; f. 1994; aims to foster closer relations between Jewish communities in the region and to promote greater understanding of the Jewish faith; Chair. BENNY GILBERT; Sec.-Gen. MICHAEL DAVIS.

### HINDUISM

**Hindu Community:** Bridgetown; there were 411 Hindus at the census of 1980.

# The Press

**Barbados Advocate:** POB 230, St Michael; tel. 434-2000; fax 434-2020; e-mail advocate@sunbeach.net; internet www.advocatenews.com; f. 1895; daily; Pres. and CEO HUMPHREY METZGEN; Editor REUDON EVERSLEY; circ. 11,413.

**The Beacon:** 111 Roebuck St, Bridgetown; organ of the Barbados Labour Party; weekly; circ. 15,000.

**The Broad Street Journal:** Letchworth Complex, Garrison, St Michael; tel. 437-8770; fax 437-8772; internet www.bsj.gocarib.com; f. 1993; weekly; business; Editor PATRICK HOYOS.

**Caribbean Week:** Lefferts Place, River Rd, St Michael; tel. 436-1902; fax 436-1904; e-mail cweek@sunbeach.net; internet www.sunbeach.net/st.html; f. 1989; fortnightly; Editor-in-Chief JOHN E. LOVELL; Publr TIMOTHY C. FORSYTHE; circ. 56,200.

**The Nation:** Nation House, Fontabelle, St Michael; tel. 430-5400; fax 427-6968; e-mail nationnews@sunbeach.net; internet www.sunbeach.net/comp/nation; f. 1973; daily; Pres. and Editor-in-Chief HAROLD HOYTE; circ. 23,144 (weekday), 33,084 (weekend).

**Official Gazette:** Government Printing Office, Bay St, St Michael; tel. 436-6776; Mon. and Thur.

**Sunday Advocate:** POB 230, St Michael; tel. 434-2000; fax 434-2020; e-mail advocate@sunbeach.net; internet www.advocatenews.com; f. 1895; CEO HUMPHREY METZGEN; Editor REUDON EVERSLEY; circ. 17,490.

**The Sunday Sun:** Fontabelle, St Michael; tel. 436-6240; fax 427-6968; e-mail subs@sunbeach.net; f. 1977; Dir HAROLD HOYTE; circ. 42,286.

**Weekend Investigator:** POB 230, St Michael; tel. 434-2000; circ. 14,305.

### NEWS AGENCIES

**Caribbean News Agency (CANA):** Culloden View, Beckles Rd, St Michael; tel. 429-2903; fax 429-4355; f. 1976; internet www.cananews.com; public and private shareholders from English-speaking Caribbean; Chair. COLIN D. MURRAY; Gen. Man. TREVOR SIMPSON.

#### Foreign Bureaux

**Inter Press Service (IPS)** (Italy): POB 697, Bridgetown; tel. 426-4474; Correspondent MARVA COSSY.

**United Press International (UPI)** (USA): Bridgetown; tel. 436-0465; Correspondent RICKEY SINGH.

**Xinhua (New China) News Agency** (People's Republic of China): Christ Church; Chief Correspondent DING BAOZHONG.

Agence France-Presse (AFP) is also represented.

## Publishers

**The Advocate Publishing Co Ltd:** POB 230, St Michael; tel. 434-2000; fax 434-2020.

**Business Tutors:** POB 800E St Michael; tel. 428-5664; fax 429-4854; e-mail pchad@caribsurf.com; business, management, computers.

**Carib Research and Publications Inc:** POB 556, Bridgetown; tel. 438-0580; f. 1986; regional interests; CEO Dr FARLEY BRAITHWAITE.

**Nation Publishing Co Ltd:** Nation House, Fontabelle, St Michael; tel. 436-6240; fax 427-6968.

## Broadcasting and Communications

### TELECOMMUNICATIONS

**Cable & Wireless BET Ltd:** POB 32, Wildey, St Michael; tel. 292-6000; fax 427-5808; e-mail bdsinfo@caribsurf.com; internet www.candwbet.com.bb; fmrly Barbados External Telecommunications Ltd; provides international telecommunications services; owned by Cable & Wireless PLC (United Kingdom).

**Barbados Telephone Co Ltd (Bartel):** The Windsor Lodge, Government Hill, St Michael; tel. 429-5050; fax 436-5036; provides domestic telecommunications services; subsidiary of Cable & Wireless BET Ltd.

### BROADCASTING

#### Regulatory Authority

**Caribbean Broadcasting Corporation (CBC):** The Pine, POB 900, Bridgetown; tel. 429-2041; fax 429-4795; f. 1963; Chair. F. BREWSTER.

#### Radio

**Barbados Broadcasting Service Ltd:** Astoria St George, Bridgetown; tel. 437-9550; fax 437-9554; f. 1981; FM station.

Faith 102 FM; religious broadcasting.

**Barbados Rediffusion Service Ltd:** River Rd, Bridgetown; tel. 430-7300; fax 429-8093; f. 1935; public company; Gen. Man. VIC FERNANDES.

HOTT FM, at River Rd, Bridgetown (f. 1998), is a commercial station.

Voice of Barbados, at River Rd, Bridgetown (f. 1981), is a commercial station covering Barbados and the eastern Caribbean.

YESS Ten-Four FM, at River Rd, Bridgetown (f. 1988), is a commercial station.

**CBC Radio:** POB 900, Bridgetown; tel. 429-2041; fax 429-4795; e-mail CBC.@.CaribNet.Net; f. 1963; commercial; Programme Man. W. CALLENDER.

CBC Radio 900, f. 1963, broadcasts 21 hours daily.

Radio Liberty FM, f. 1984, broadcasts 24 hours daily.

#### Television

**CBC TV:** POB 900, Bridgetown; tel. 429-2041; fax 429-4795; f. 1964; Channel Eight is the main national service, broadcasting 24 hours daily; a maximum of 30 subscription channels are available through Multi Choice; Gen. Man. MELBA SMITH; Programme Man. HILDA COX.

## Finance

In December 1998 there were 3,073 international business companies, 2,608 foreign sales corporations and 44 offshore banks registered in Barbados.

### BANKING

(cap. = capital; auth. = authorized; dep. = deposits; res = reserves; brs = branches; m. = million; amounts in Barbados dollars)

#### Central Bank

**Central Bank of Barbados:** Tom Adams Financial Centre, POB 1016, Spry St, Bridgetown; tel. 436-6870; fax 427-1431; e-mail cbb.libr@caribsurf.com; f. 1972; bank of issue; cap. 2.0m., res 10.0m., dep. 400.5m. (Dec. 1996); Gov. MARION WILLIAMS.

#### Commercial Bank

**Caribbean Commercial Bank Ltd:** Broad St, POB 1007C, Bridgetown; tel. 431-2500; fax 431-2530; f. 1984; cap. 25.0m., res 4.4m., dep. 145.6m. (Dec. 1998); Pres. and CEO MARIANO R. BROWNE; 4 brs.

#### Regional Development Bank

**Caribbean Development Bank:** Wildey, POB 408, St Michael; tel. 431-1600; fax 426-7269; f. 1970; cap. 143.4m., res 6.3m. (Dec. 1997); Pres. Sir NEVILLE V. NICHOLLS.

#### National Bank

**Barbados National Bank (BNB):** 1 Broad St, POB 1002, Bridgetown; tel. 431-5739; fax 426-5037; f. 1978 by merger; cap 47.5m., res 22.5m., dep. 586.8m., total assets 702.3m. (Dec. 1997); identified for privatization; Chair. GRENVILLE PHILLIPS; CEO and Man. Dir LOUIS GREENIDGE; 6 brs.

#### Foreign Banks

**Bank of Nova Scotia** (Canada): Broad St, POB 202, Bridgetown; tel. 431-3000; fax 228-8574; Man. PETER F. VAN SCHIE; 8 brs.

**Barclays Bank PLC** (United Kingdom): Broad Street, POB 301, Bridgetown; tel. 431-5262; fax 429-4785; f. 1837; Man. P. A. WEATHERHEAD; 12 brs.

**CIBC West Indies Holdings** (Canada): Broad St, POB 405, Bridgetown; tel. 426-0571; affiliated to the Canadian Imperial Bank of Commerce; Man. T. MULLOY; 9 brs.

**Royal Bank of Canada:** Trident House, Broad St, POB 68, Bridgetown; tel. 431-6700; fax 426-4139; e-mail roycorp@caribsurf.com; f. 1911; Man. C. D. MALONEY; 7 brs.

#### Trust Companies

**Bank of Nova Scotia Trust Co (Caribbean) Ltd:** Bank of Nova Scotia Bldg, Broad St, POB 1003B, Bridgetown; tel. 431-3120; fax 426-0969.

**Barbados International Bank and Trust Co:** Price Waterhouse Centre, POB 634C, Collymore Rock, St Michael; tel. 436-7000; fax 436-7057.

**Barclays Finance Corporation of Barbados Ltd (BARFINCOR):** Roebuck St, POB 180, Bridgetown; tel. 426-1608.

**Clico Mortgage & Finance Corporation:** C L Duprey Financial Centre, Walrond St, Bridgetown; tel. 431-4719; fax 426-6168; e-mail cmfc@sunbeach.net.

**Ernst & Young Trust Corporation:** Bush Hill, Garrison, St Michael; tel. 430-3900.

**Royal Bank of Canada Financial Corporation:** Bldg 2, Chelston Park, Collymore Rock, St Michael; tel. 431-6580; fax 429-3800; e-mail roycorp@caribsurf.com; Man. N. L. SMITH.

### STOCK EXCHANGE

**Securities Exchange of Barbados (SEB):** Tom Adams Financial Centre, 5th Floor, Church Village, Bridgetown; tel. 436-9871; fax 429-8942; e-mail sebd@caribsurf.com; f. 1987; in 1989 the Govts of Barbados, Trinidad and Tobago and Jamaica agreed to link exchanges; cross-trading began in April 1991; Chair. NEVILLE LEROY SMITH; Gen. Man. VIRGINIA MAPP.

### INSURANCE

The leading British and a number of US and Canadian companies have agents in Barbados. At the end of 1995 230 captive insurance companies were registered in the country. Local insurance companies include the following:

**Barbados Fire & Commercial Insurance Co:** Beckwith Place, Broad St, POB 150, Bridgetown; tel. 431-2800; fax 426-0752; e-mail bf&c@caribsurf.com; f. 1996, following merger of Barbados Commercial Insurance Co. Ltd and Barbados Fire and General Insurance Co (f. 1880).

**Barbados Mutual Life Assurance Society:** Collymore Rock, St Michael; tel. 431-7000; fax 436-8829; f. 1840; Chair. COLIN G. GODDARD; Pres. J. ARTHUR L. BETHELL.

**Insurance Corporation of Barbados:** Roebuck St, Bridgetown; tel. 427-5590; fax 426-3393; f. 1978; cap. Bds $3m.; Man. Dir WISMAR GREAVES; Gen. Man. MONICA SKINNER.

**Life of Barbados Ltd:** Wildey, POB 69, St Michael; tel. 426-1060; fax 436-8835; f. 1971; Pres. and CEO STEPHEN ALLEYNE.

**United Insurance Co Ltd:** United Insurance Centre, Lower Broad St, POB 1215, Bridgetown; tel. 430-1900; fax 436-7573; e-mail united@caribsurf.com; f. 1976; Man. Dir DAVE A. BLACKMAN.

#### Insurance Association

**Insurance Association of the Caribbean:** IAC Bldg, St Michael; Collymore Rock, St Michael; tel. 427-5608; fax 427-7277; regional asscn.

# Trade and Industry

### GOVERNMENT AGENCIES

**Barbados Agricultural Management Co Ltd:** Warrens, POB 719c, St Michael; tel. 425-0010; fax 425-0007; Exec. Chair. Dr ATTLEE BRATHWAITE; Gen. Man. K. C. WARD.

**Barbados Sugar Industry Ltd:** POB 719c, Warrens, St Thomas; tel. 422-8725; fax 422-5357; Lt-Col STEPHEN F. CAVE.

### DEVELOPMENT ORGANIZATIONS

**Barbados Agriculture Development and Marketing Corpn:** Fairy Valley, Christ Church; tel. 428-0250; fax 428-0152; f. 1993 by merger; programme of diversification and land reforms; Chair. TYRONE POWER; CEO E. LEROY ROACH.

**Barbados Investment and Development Corpn:** Pelican House, Princess Alice Highway, Bridgetown; tel. 427-5350; fax 426-7802; e-mail bidc@bidc.org; internet www.bidc.com; f. 1992 by merger; facilitates the devt of the industrial sector, especially in the areas of manufacturing, information technology and financial services; offers free consultancy to investors; provides factory space for lease or rent; administers the Fiscal Incentives Legislation; Chair. TREVOR CLARKE; CEO ERROL HUMPHREY.

**Commonwealth Development Corporation:** Culloden Complex, Culloden Rd, St Michael; tel. 436-9890; fax 436-1504.

**Department for International Development in the Caribbean:** Collymore Rock, POB 167, St Michael; tel. 436-9873; fax 426-2194; Head BRIAN THOMSON.

### CHAMBER OF COMMERCE

**Barbados Chamber of Commerce and Industry:** Nemwil House, 1st Floor, Lower Collymore Rock, POB 189, St Michael; tel. 426-2056; fax 429-2907; e-mail bdscham@caribsurf.com; f. 1825; 176 mem. firms, 276 reps; Pres. HALLAM EDWARDS; Exec. Dir ROLPH JORDAN.

### INDUSTRIAL AND TRADE ASSOCIATIONS

**Barbados Agricultural Society:** The Grotto, Beckles Rd, St Michael; tel. 436-6683; fax 435-0651; e-mail heshimu@sunbeach.net; Pres. TYRONE POWER.

**Barbados Association of Medical Practitioners:** BAMP Complex, Spring Garden, St Michael; tel. 429-7569; fax 435-2328; e-mail bamp@infinetworx.com; Pres. JEROME WALCOTT.

**Barbados Association of Professional Engineers:** POB 666, Bridgetown; tel. 425-6105; fax 425-6673; f. 1964; Pres. GLYNE BARKER; Sec. PATRICK CLARKE.

**Barbados Builders' Association:** POB RW 93; Bridgetown; tel. 437-8383; Pres. KEITH CODRINGTON.

**Barbados Hotel and Tourism Association:** Fourth Ave, Belleville, St Michael; tel. 426-5041; fax 429-2845; e-mail bhta@maccs.com.bb; Pres. SUSAN SPRINGER; Exec. Vice-Pres. NOEL LYNCH.

**Barbados Manufacturers' Association:** Bldg 1, Pelican Industrial Park, St Michael; tel. 426-4474; fax 436-5182; e-mail bmex-products@sunbeach.net; internet www.bma.org.bb; f. 1964; Pres. IAN PICKUP; Exec. Dir CLIFTON E. MAYNARD; 100 mem. firms.

**West Indian Sea Island Cotton Association (Inc):** c/o Barbados Agricultural Development and Marketing Corpn, Fairy Valley, Christ Church; tel. 428-0250; Pres. E. LEROY WARD; Sec. MICHAEL I. EDGHILL; 11 mem. asscns.

### EMPLOYERS' ORGANIZATION

**Barbados Employers' Confederation:** Nemwil House, 1st Floor, Collymore Rock, St Michael; tel. 426-1574; fax 429-2907; f. 1956; Pres. HARCOURT SANDIFORD; 235 mems (incl. associate mems).

### UTILITIES

#### Electricity

**Barbados Light and Power Co (BL & P):** POB 142, Garrison Hill, St Michael; tel. 436-1800; fax 436-9933; electricity generator and distributor; operates two stations with a combined capacity of 152,500 kW.

**Public Utilities Board:** cnr Pine Plantation Rd, Collymore Rock, St Michael; tel. 427-5693; f. 1955; electricity regulator.

#### Gas

**Barbados National Oil Co Ltd (BNOCL):** POB 175, Woodbourne, St Philip; tel. 423-0918; fax 423-0166; f. 1979; extraction of petroleum and natural gas; state-owned, scheduled for privatization; Chair. HARCOURT LEWIS; 166 employees.

**National Petroleum Corporation:** Wildey; tel. 430-4000; gas production and distribution.

#### Water

**Barbados Water Authority:** The Pine, St Michael; tel. 427-3990.

### TRADE UNIONS

Principal unions include:

**Barbados Secondary Teachers' Union:** Ryeburn, Eighth Ave, Belleville, St Michael; tel. 429-7676; e-mail bstumail@caribsurf.com; f. 1949; Pres. WAYNE WILLOCK; Gen. Sec. PATRICK FROST; 382 mems.

**Barbados Union of Teachers:** Welches, POB 58, St Michael; tel. 436-6139; f. 1974; Pres. RONALD DAC. JONES; Gen. Sec. HARRY HUSBANDS; 2,000 mems.

**Barbados Workers' Union:** Solidarity House, Harmony Hall, POB 172, St Michael; tel. 426-3492; fax 436-6496; f. 1941; operates a Labour College; Sec.-Gen. LEROY TROTMAN; 20,000 mems.

**Caribbean Association of Media Workers (Camwork):** Bridgetown; f. 1986; regional; Pres. RICKEY SINGH.

**National Union of Public Workers:** Dalkeith Rd, POB 174, Bridgetown; tel. 426-1764; fax 436-1795; e-mail nupwbarbados@sunbeach.net; f. 1944; Pres. MILLICENT M. B. SMALL; Gen. Sec. JOSEPH E. GODDARD; 6,000 mems.

**National Union of Seamen:** Bridgetown; tel. 436-6137; Pres. LORENZO COWARD.

# Transport

### ROADS

**Ministry of Public Works and Transport:** The Pine, St Michael; tel. 429-2191; fax 437-8133; internet www.publicworks.gov.bb; maintains a network of 1,573 km (977 miles) of roads, of which 1,496 km (930 miles) are paved; Chief Tech. Officer C. H. ARCHER.

### SHIPPING

Inter-island traffic is catered for by a fortnightly service of one vessel of the West Indies Shipping Corpn (WISCO, the regional shipping company, based in Trinidad and Tobago, in which the Barbados Government is a shareholder) operating from Trinidad as far north as Jamaica. The CAROL container service consortium connects Bridgetown with western European ports and several foreign shipping lines call at the port. Bridgetown harbour has berths for eight ships and simultaneous bunkering facilities for five. A four-year project to extend the harbour, providing increased capacity for cruise ships, was due to begin in 1997 at a cost of Bds $120m.

**Barbados Port Authority:** University Row, Bridgetown Harbour; tel. 430-4700; fax 429-5348; internet www.barbadosport.com; Gen. Man. EVERTON WALTERS; Port Dir Capt. H. L. VAN SLUYTMAN.

**Shipping Association of Barbados:** Trident House, 2nd Floor, Broad St, Bridgetown; tel. 427-9860; fax 426-8392; e-mail shasba@caribsurf.com.

#### Principal Shipping Companies

**Barbados Shipping and Trading Co Ltd:** Musson Bldg, Hincks St, POB 1227c, Bridgetown; tel. 426-3844; fax 427-4719; e-mail richard_marshall@bsandtco.com; f. 1920; Chair. C. D. BYNOE; Man. Dir A. C. FIELDS.

**DaCosta Mannings Ltd:** Carlisle House, Hincks St, POB 103, Bridgetown; tel. 431-8700; fax 431-0051; shipping company.

**T. Geddes Grant Bros:** White Park Rd, Bridgetown; tel. 631-3343.

**Hassell, Eric and Son Ltd:** Carlisle House, Hincks St, Bridgetown; tel. 436-6102; fax 429-3416; e-mail hassric@sunbeach.net; internet www.erichassell.com; shipping agent, stevedoring contractor and cargo fowarder.

**Maersk:** James Fort Bldg, Hincks St, Bridgetown; tel. 430-4816.

**Tec Marine:** Carlisle House, Hincks St, Bridgetown; tel. 430-4816.

**Tropical Shipping Kensington:** Fontabelle Rd, St Michael; tel. 426-9990.

**Windward Lines Ltd:** 10 James Fort Bldg, Hincks St, Bridgetown; tel. 431-0449.

### CIVIL AVIATION

The principal airport is Grantley Adams International Airport, at Seawell, 18 km (11 miles) from Bridgetown.

## Tourism

The natural attractions of the island consist chiefly of the warm climate and varied scenery. In addition, there are many facilities for outdoor sports of all kinds. Revenue from tourism increased from Bds $13m. in 1960 to some Bds $1,500m. in 1998. The number of stop-over tourist arrivals increased by 8.5%, compared with the previous year, to 512,397 in 1998, while the number of visiting cruise-ship passengers decreased by 2.2%, to 506,610. There were some 6,000 hotel rooms on the island in 1999.

**Barbados Tourism Authority:** Harbour Rd, POB 242, Bridgetown; tel. 427-2623; fax 426-4080; internet www.barbados.org; f. 1993 to replace Barbados Board of Tourism; offices in London, New York, Montreal, Miami, Toronto, California and Frankfurt; Chair. Sen. DALE MARSHALL; Pres. and CEO EARLYN SHUFFLER.

# BELARUS

## Introductory Survey

**Location, Climate, Language, Religion, Flag, Capital**

The Republic of Belarus is a land-locked state in north-eastern Europe. It is bounded by Lithuania and Latvia to the north-west, by Ukraine to the south, by the Russian Federation to the east, and by Poland to the west. The climate is of a continental type, with an average January temperature, in Minsk, of -5°C (23°F) and an average for July of 19°C (67°F). Average annual precipitation is between 560 mm and 660 mm. The official languages of the republic are Belarusian and Russian. The major religion is Christianity—the Roman Catholic Church and the Eastern Orthodox Church being the largest denominations. There are also small Muslim and Jewish communities. The national flag (proportions 2 by 1) consists of two unequal horizontal stripes, of red over light green, with a red-outlined white vertical stripe at the hoist, bearing in red a traditional embroidery pattern. The capital is Minsk (Miensk).

**Recent History**

Following periods of Lithuanian and Polish rule, Belarus became a part of the Russian Empire in the late 18th century. During the 19th century there was a growth of national consciousness in Belarus and, as a result of industrialization, significant migration of people from rural to urban areas. After the February Revolution of 1917 in Russia, Belarusian nationalists and socialists formed a rada (council), which sought a degree of autonomy from the Provisional Government in Petrograd (St Petersburg). In November, after the Bolsheviks had seized power in Petrograd, Red Army troops were dispatched to Minsk, and the rada was dissolved. However, the Bolsheviks were forced to withdraw by the invasion of the German army. The Treaty of Brest-Litovsk, signed in March 1918, assigned most of Belarus to the Germans. On 25 March Belarusian nationalists convened to proclaim a Belarusian National Republic, but it achieved only limited autonomy. After the Germans had withdrawn, the Bolsheviks easily reoccupied Minsk, and the Belarusian Soviet Socialist Republic (BSSR) was declared on 1 January 1919.

In February 1919 the BSSR was merged with neighbouring Lithuania in a Lithuanian-Belarusian Soviet Republic (known as 'Litbel'). In April, however, Polish armed forces entered Lithuania and Belarus, and both were declared part of Poland. In July 1920 the Bolsheviks recaptured Minsk, and in August the BSSR was re-established; Lithuania became an independent state. However, the BSSR comprised only the eastern half of the lands populated by Belarusians. Western Belarus was granted to Poland by the Treaty of Riga, signed on 18 March 1921. The Treaty also assigned Belarus's easternmost regions to the Russian Federation, but they were returned to the BSSR in 1924 and 1926. Meanwhile, the BSSR, with Ukraine and Transcaucasia, had joined with the Russian Federation to form the Union of Soviet Socialist Republics (USSR), established in December 1922.

The Soviet leadership's New Economic Policy of 1921–28, which permitted some liberalization of the economy, brought a measure of prosperity, and there was significant cultural and linguistic development, with the use of the Belarusian language officially encouraged. This period ended in 1929 with the emergence of Iosif Stalin as the dominant figure in the USSR. In that year Stalin began a campaign to collectivize agriculture, which was strongly resisted by the peasantry. In Belarus, as in other parts of the USSR, there were frequent riots and rebellions in rural areas, and many peasants were deported or imprisoned. The purges of the early 1930s were initially targeted against Belarusian nationalists and intellectuals, but by 1936–38 they had widened to include all sectors of the population.

After the invasion of Poland by German and Soviet forces in September 1939, the BSSR was enlarged by the inclusion of the lands that it had lost to Poland and Lithuania in 1921. Between 1941 and 1944 the BSSR was occupied by Nazi German forces; an estimated 2.2m. people died during this period, including most of the republic's large Jewish population. At the Yalta conference, in February 1945, the Allies agreed to recognize the 'Curzon line' as the western border of the BSSR, thus endorsing the unification of western and eastern Belarus. As a result of the Soviet demand for more voting strength in the UN, the Western powers permitted the BSSR to become a member of the UN in its own right.

The immediate post-war period was dominated by the need to rehabilitate the republic's infrastructure. The reconstruction programme's requirements and the local labour shortage led to an increase in Russian immigration into the republic, thus discouraging use of the Belarusian language. During the 1960s and 1970s the process of 'russification' continued; there was a decrease in the use of Belarusian in schools, and in the media. The republic was, however, one of the most prosperous in the USSR, with a wider variety of consumer goods available than in other republics.

This relative prosperity was one reason why the ruling Communist Party of Belarus (CPB) was initially able to resist implementing the economic and political reforms that were proposed by the Soviet leader, Mikhail Gorbachev, from 1985 onwards. By 1987, however, the CPB was being criticized in the press for its stance on cultural and ecological issues. Intellectuals and writers campaigned for the greater use of Belarusian in education. Campaigners also demanded more information about the consequences of the explosion at the Chornobyl nuclear power station, in Ukraine in April 1986, which had affected large areas of southern Belarus. Not surprisingly, the two most important unofficial groups that emerged in the late 1980s were the Belarusian Language Association and the Belarusian Ecological Union.

There was, however, little opportunity for overt political opposition. A Belarusian Popular Front (BPF) was established in October 1988, but the CPB severely restricted its activities and refused to permit reports about the new group in the republican media. At the end of the month riot police were used to disperse a pro-BPF demonstration in Minsk. The BPF did have some success in the elections to the all-Union Congress of People's Deputies, which took place in March 1989, persuading voters to reject several leading officials of the CPB. However, the inaugural congress of the BPF took place in Vilnius (Lithuania) in June, the Front having been refused permission to meet in Minsk.

In early 1990, in anticipation of the elections to the republican Supreme Soviet, or Supreme Council (legislature), the CPB adopted some of the BPF's policies regarding the Belarusian language. In January the authorities approved a law declaring Belarusian to be the state language, effective from 1 September. (However, Russian was reinstated as a second state language, following the adoption of a new Constitution in November 1996.) The BPF was not officially permitted to participate in the elections to the Belarusian Supreme Council, which took place in March 1990. Instead, its members joined other pro-reform groups in a coalition known as the Belarusian Democratic Bloc (BDB). The BDB won about one-quarter of the 310 seats that were decided by popular election; most of the remainder were won by CPB members loyal to the republican leadership. The opposition won most seats in the large cities, notably Gomel (Homiel) and Minsk, where Zyanon Paznyak, the leader of the BPF, was elected. When the new Supreme Council first convened in May the BDB deputies immediately demanded the adoption of a declaration of sovereignty. The CPB initially opposed such a move, but on 27 July, apparently after consultations with the leadership of the Communist Party of the Soviet Union in Moscow, a Declaration of State Sovereignty of the BSSR was adopted unanimously by the Supreme Council. The declaration asserted the republic's right to maintain armed forces, to establish a national currency and to exercise full control over its domestic and foreign policies. On the insistence of the opposition, the declaration included a clause stating the right of the republic to compensation for the damage caused by the accident at the Chornobyl nuclear power station. The issue of the Chornobyl accident united both communist and opposition deputies. The Belarusian Government appealed to the all-Union Government for a minimum of 17,000m. roubles to address the consequences of the disaster, but was offered only 3,000m. roubles in compensation.

The 31st congress of the CPB, which took place in November 1990, was notable for delegates' criticisms of Gorbachev's reforms, in particular his foreign policy towards Eastern Europe. Yefrem Sakalau, who had led the CPB since 1987, did not seek re-election as First Secretary. He was replaced by Anatol Malafeyeu, who only narrowly defeated an outspoken critic of Gorbachev, Uladzimir Brovikou.

The Belarusian Government took part in the negotiation of a new Treaty of Union and signed the protocol to the draft treaty on 3 March 1991. The all-Union referendum on the preservation of the USSR took place in the BSSR on 17 March; of the 83% of the electorate who participated, 83% voted in favour of Gorbachev's proposals for a 'renewed federation of equal sovereign republics'. Members of the BPF conducted a campaign advocating rejection of Gorbachev's proposals, but complained that they were denied the opportunity to present their views to the general public.

In April 1991 a series of strikes threatened the continued power of the CPB. On 10 April a general strike took place, and an estimated 100,000 people attended a demonstration in Minsk. The Government finally agreed to certain economic concessions, including high wage increases, but the strikers' political demands, including the resignation of the Belarusian Government and the depoliticization of republican institutions, were rejected. Some 200,000 workers were estimated to have taken part in a second general strike on 23 April, in protest at the legislature's refusal to reconvene. The Supreme Council, which was still dominated by members of the CPB, was eventually convened in May. The authority of the conservative CPB, however, was threatened by increased internal dissent. In June 33 deputies joined the opposition as a 'Communists for Democracy' faction, led by Alyaksandr Lukashenka.

The Belarusian leadership did not strongly oppose the attempted coup in Moscow in August 1991. The Presidium of the Supreme Council released a neutral statement on the last day of the coup, but the Central Committee of the CPB issued a declaration unequivocally supporting the coup. Following the failure of the coup attempt, an extraordinary session of the Supreme Council was convened. Mikalay Dzemyantsei, the Chairman of the Supreme Council (republican head of state), was forced to resign. He was replaced by Stanislau Shushkevich, a respected centrist politician, pending an election to the office. In addition, the Supreme Council agreed to nationalize all CPB property, to prohibit the party's activities in law-enforcement agencies, and to suspend the CPB, pending an investigation into its role in the coup. On 25 August the legislature voted to grant constitutional status to the July 1990 Declaration of State Sovereignty, and declared the political and economic independence of Belarus.

On 19 September 1991 the Supreme Council voted to rename the BSSR the Republic of Belarus. The Council also elected Shushkevich as its Chairman. Shushkevich demonstrated his strong support for the continuation of some form of union by signing, in October, a treaty to establish an economic community and by agreeing, in November, to the first draft of the Treaty on the Union of Sovereign States. On 8 December Shushkevich, with the Russian and Ukrainian Presidents, signed the Minsk Agreement establishing a new Commonwealth of Independent States (CIS—see p. 150). On 21 December the leaders of 11 former Soviet republics confirmed this decision by the Alma-Ata Declaration. The proposal that the headquarters of the CIS should be in Minsk was widely welcomed in Belarus as a means of attracting foreign political and economic interest.

By comparison with other former Soviet republics, Belarus experienced relative stability in domestic affairs during 1992, which was attributed to the country's more favourable social and economic policies, as well as to the comparatively homogenous nature of the population. In governmental affairs, the opposition BPF censured the continued dominance of the communists in both the Supreme Council and the Cabinet of Ministers, notwithstanding the temporary suspension of the CPB itself. (In February 1993, however, the suspension was lifted and the CPB was permitted to re-establish itself.) In addition, the BPF campaigned insistently for the holding of a referendum to assess the electorate's confidence in the Supreme Council and the Government. In June 1992, having collected the required number of signatures, the BPF accused the Supreme Council of seeking to obstruct such a referendum. In October the Council voted against the holding of a referendum, owing to alleged irregularities in the collection of signatures.

Divisions between the various branches of government in Belarus became more pronounced during 1993. A major source of controversy was the drafting of Belarus's new Constitution, three separate versions of which were submitted to the Supreme Council in 1991–93. Shushkevich and the BPF strongly opposed the establishment of Belarus as a presidential republic; nevertheless, the new Constitution, which provided for a presidential system, was adopted in March 1994. A further point of dispute was the question of whether Belarus should adopt closer economic, military and other relations with the Russian Federation and the CIS (as advocated by the Supreme Council). Shushkevich and the BPF were opposed to Belarus's signing the Treaty on Collective Security (which had been concluded by six other CIS states in May 1992), on the grounds that this would contravene the Declaration of State Sovereignty which defined Belarus as a neutral state, and would also lead to renewed Russian domination. None the less, in April the Supreme Council voted to sign the Treaty. Three months later the legislature passed a vote of 'no confidence' in Shushkevich, in response to his continued opposition to the Treaty; he remained in office, however, as the Council had been inquorate at the time of the vote. A second vote of confidence in Shushkevich was held in January 1994; this time the Council voted overwhelmingly to dismiss him, on charges of corruption. He was replaced by Mechislau Gryb, formerly a senior police official. The premier, Vyacheslau Kebich, survived a similar vote of confidence.

Support for the CPB increased substantially during 1993: the party's popularity was attributed in large part to nostalgia for the relative prosperity enjoyed under communist rule, as well as regret for the demise of the USSR. In March the CPB formed, with 17 other parties and groups opposed to Belarusian independence, an informal coalition, the Popular Movement of Belarus.

Renewed allegations of corruption against Kebich and leading members of the Cabinet of Ministers, coupled with the worsening economic situation, culminated in a BPF-led general strike in Minsk in February 1994. Protesters returned to work only when Gryb announced that the presidential election would be brought forward to mid-1994. Six candidates collected the requisite number of signatures, including Kebich, Shushkevich, Paznyak and Lukashenka, who, as head of the Supreme Council's anti-corruption committee, had been responsible for bringing the corruption charges against Shushkevich. In the first ballot, held in late June, no candidate gained an overall majority, although Lukashenka, with 47% of the valid votes, led by a considerable margin. In the second ballot, between Lukashenka and Kebich (held in early July), Lukashenka received 85% of the votes, and he was inaugurated as the first President of Belarus on 20 July. Mikhail Chigir, an economic reformist, replaced Kebich as Chairman of a new Cabinet of Ministers. In December one of the Deputy Chairmen of the Cabinet of Ministers, Viktar Ganchar, tendered his resignation in protest at what he perceived as the President's disregard for the Cabinet. Later in the month a report to the Supreme Council by a BPF deputy alleged widespread corruption in the presidential administration.

In early 1995 there were repeated confrontations between President Lukashenka and the Supreme Council over constitutional issues. In late January the Council voted for a second time to adopt legislation whereby the President could be removed by a two-thirds vote of the Council. In March Lukashenka announced that, simultaneously with the legislative elections scheduled to take place in May, a referendum would be held on four policy questions. In early April, following the Council's rejection of all but one of the proposed questions (on closer integration with Russia), Lukashenka threatened to dissolve the legislature. A number of opposition deputies (including Paznyak) were forcibly evicted from the Supreme Council building, where they had declared a hunger strike in protest at the referendum. Shortly after this action, deputies voted in favour of the inclusion in the referendum of the remaining three questions: to give the Russian language equal status with Belarusian as an official language; to abandon the state insignia and flag of independent Belarus in favour of a modified version of those used in the republic during the Soviet era; and to amend the Constitution in order to empower the President to suspend the Supreme Council in the event of unconstitutional acts. Some 65% of the electorate participated in the referendum, which was held, as scheduled, on 14 May. All four questions received overwhelming popular support.

On the same occasion as the referendum, Belarus's first post-Soviet legislative elections were held. However, owing to the stringent electoral regulations, only 18 of the total 260 seats in the Supreme Council were filled. At 'run-off' elections, held on 28 May 1995, a further 101 deputies were elected, but the two rounds of voting failed to produce the necessary two-thirds quorum, and a further round was scheduled for November. In the mean time, the confrontation between Lukashenka and the incumbent Supreme Council intensified. The Chairman of the Supreme Council, Mechislau Gryb, requested the Constitutional Court to examine the legality of a number of decrees issued by Lukashenka, five of which were subsequently found to be unconstitutional. A quorum was finally achieved in the Supreme Council at two further rounds of voting, held on 29 November and 10 December 1995. Seventy-nine new deputies were elected to the Council, bringing the total to 198. The CPB emerged with the largest number of seats in the new legislature (42), followed by the Agrarian Party (AP) (33), the United Civic Party of Belarus (nine) and the Party of People's Accord (eight). Independent candidates accounted for 95 seats. The BPF failed to win representation in the Council as the 62 seats remaining vacant, largely owing to low electoral participation, were mostly in areas where the BPF commanded its strongest support. No announcements were made concerning elections to fill those seats. The Supreme Council held its inaugural session in early January 1996. Syamyon Sharetski, the leader of the AP, was appointed Chairman of the Council, replacing Gryb. With the realignment of independent candidates and parties into parliamentary factions, five major groupings emerged: Accord (59 deputies), Agrarians (47), Communists (44), People's Unity (17) and Social Democrats 'Belarus' (15).

Relations between the Constitutional Court and President Lukashenka deteriorated in early 1996, with the Court declaring the observance of constitutional law in 1995 to have been unsatisfactory. Lukashenka extended his authority over the security services and over the state-owned media, giving control of editorial appointments to the Cabinet of Ministers. Despite strong opposition and protests against government proposals to sign a new union treaty with Russia, President Lukashenka and the President of the Russian Federation, Boris Yeltsin, signed the Treaty on the Formation of a Community of Sovereign Republics in Moscow on 2 April 1996. Although not actually establishing a single state, the treaty included extensive provisions covering military, economic and political co-operation between the two component parts of the new Community of Sovereign Republics (CSR). Following the endorsement of this important document, confrontation between Lukashenka and the opposition parties increased. A warrant was issued in April for the arrest of Paznyak, who was accused of organizing the anti-union treaty demonstrations. The offices of the BPF were searched, but Paznyak fled the country and later applied for political asylum in the USA. Several activists were arrested, and riot police clashed with demonstrators demanding their release. (They were later released on health grounds after staging a hunger strike.) Unauthorized rallies, organized by the opposition movement, were held in Minsk at the end of the month to commemorate the 10th anniversary of the disaster at the Chornobyl nuclear power station. The demonstrators used the opportunity to express publicly their dissatisfaction with the Government and, in particular, with the formation of the CSR. It was reported that the rallies were brutally dispersed by the police, and about 200 people were arrested.

In early August 1996 the President, seeking to enhance his powers further, scheduled another national referendum, for early November, which was to contain, amongst other questions, proposed amendments to the 1994 Constitution. In September demands for the impeachment of the President became more insistent, and protesters carrying the red and white flag of independent Belarus appealed for the Supreme Council to begin proceedings to remove Lukashenka. The Presidium of the Supreme Council proposed three further questions for the referendum, seeking to curtail the President's powers. Despite disagreement between Lukashenka and the Supreme Council over the date of the referendum, it was eventually scheduled for 24 November (with polling stations to be open from 9 November for those unable to vote on the later date). Elections for the remaining vacant seats in the Supreme Council were also due to be held on 24 November. Relations between Lukashenka and the Constitutional Court deteriorated in November, following a ruling by the Court that the results of the referendum questions concerning amendments to the Constitution could be used only for consultative purposes and would not be legally binding. Lukashenka's revocation of this decision by presidential decree provoked fierce criticism.

The referendum ballot papers contained seven questions, four of which were proposed by Lukashenka: whether amendments should be made to the 1994 Constitution to extend the President's term of office from 1999 to 2001, to enable the President to issue decrees that would carry legal force, and to grant him extensive powers of appointment both to the judiciary and to the envisaged bicameral National Assembly, which would replace the Supreme Council; whether the Belarusian Independence Day should be moved from 27 July (the anniversary of the Declaration of State Sovereignty) to 3 July (the anniversary of the liberation from the Nazis); whether there should be an unrestricted right to purchase and sell land; and whether the death penalty should be abolished. The remaining three questions were submitted by the Supreme Council and proposed that there be a significant reduction in the powers of the President (in effect, virtually abolishing the presidency); that the Supreme Council should be allowed to elect heads of local administration (currently appointed by the President); and that state institutions should be funded from the budget instead of from a non-budgetary fund controlled by the President.

Despite the inclusion of questions concerning proposed constitutional changes, copies of the draft Constitution were not available to the public by the time that voting began on 9 November 1996. The Chairman of the Central Electoral Commission, Viktar Ganchar, stated that he would not approve the results of the voting, owing to this and other electoral violations; he was shortly afterwards dismissed by President Lukashenka. The crisis worsened in mid-November, when the Chairman of the Cabinet of Ministers, Mikhail Chigir, resigned, urging that the referendum be cancelled; he was replaced, in an acting capacity, by Syargey Ling. Some 10,000 people attended an anti-Government rally in Minsk, protesting at the restrictions on their freedom of expression. Independent radio stations were closed down, and as many as 200,000 issues of *Nasha Niva*, an independent newspaper containing criticisms of Lukashenka, were confiscated at the Lithuanian border. Widespread violations of the law were reported by parliamentary electoral observers—in particular, no record was kept of those who had voted early. The Organization for Security and Co-operation in Europe (OSCE, see p. 237) refused to send observers to monitor the referendum, and the Council of Europe declared that the presidential draft of the amended Constitution did not comply with European standards. Meanwhile, 75 deputies in the Supreme Council submitted a motion to the Constitutional Court to begin impeachment proceedings against the President. The Court had already found 17 decrees issued by Lukashenka to be unconstitutional.

The outcome of the voting revealed considerable support for the President, although, owing to the reported widespread electoral violations, accuracy of this result was disputed by opposition movements and electoral observers. According to official figures, some 84% of the electorate took part, 70.5% of whom voted for the President's constitutional amendments, while only 7.9% voted for those of the Supreme Council. More than 88% of those who participated voted to transfer the Belarusian Independence Day to 3 July, while the remaining motions were all rejected. The Constitutional Court was forced to abandon the impeachment proceedings against the President, as deputies withdrew their signatures from the motion. The amended Constitution was published on 27 November 1996 and came into immediate effect.

Following the referendum, the Supreme Council divided into two factions. More than 100 deputies declared their support for Lukashenka, and adopted legislation abolishing the Supreme Council and establishing a 110-member House of Representatives, the lower chamber of the new National Assembly. Some 50 other deputies denounced the referendum as invalid and declared themselves to be the legitimate legislature. The House of Representatives convened shortly afterwards and elected Anatol Malafeyeu as its Chairman. Deputies were granted a four-year mandate, while the term of office of those opposed to the new legislature was curtailed to two months. Deputies elected in the by-elections held simultaneously with the referendum were denied registration. Legislation governing the formation of the upper house of the National Assembly, the 64-member Council of the Republic, was approved by Lukashenka in early December 1996: eight members were appointed by the President, while the remaining 56 were elected by regional councils. In the event, no deputies from the former Supreme Council participated in the Council of the Republic, which convened for the first time in mid-January 1997, and elected Pavel Shypuk as its Chairman. Meanwhile, in protest at the constitutional amendments introduced through the referendum, the Chairman of the Constitutional Court, Valery Tsikhinya, and several other judges announced their resignations.

Continued opposition to the provisions of the referendum from deputies of the former legislature resulted in the formation in early January 1997 of the Public Coalition Government–National Economic Council, a form of 'shadow' cabinet, chaired by Genadz Karpenka. Structural changes to the Belarusian Government were implemented by Lukashenka, with the Chairmen of State Committees henceforth to be included in the Cabinet of Ministers; the President also made several ministerial and judicial appointments. Doubts about the legitimacy of the referendum were expressed by international organizations, including the Council of Europe, which suspended Belarus's 'guest status', citing the lack of democracy in the new political structures, and the Permanent Council of the Parliamentary Assembly of the OSCE, which recognized the right of a delegation from the former Supreme Council, rather than members of the new House of Representatives, officially to represent Belarus at that organization. In February Syargey Ling was confirmed as Chairman of the Cabinet of Ministers by the legislature.

Repression against opponents of the new Constitution was maintained throughout early 1997, despite the conclusion by international observers from the OSCE and the Council of Europe that the referendum and subsequent legislative elections could not be deemed legal, and that the provisions of the 1994 Constitution should be restored. Several opposition members were brought to trial for organizing unauthorized rallies, and in early March 1997 a presidential decree restricted further the right to demonstrate. Moves towards greater integration with Russia (see below) continued to provoke protest from opposition parties, led, in particular, by the BPF, and in late March an anti-Lukashenka demonstration, which attracted some 10,000 participants, was violently dispersed by security forces.

The signing with Russia of the Treaty of Union, and initialling of the Charter of the Union, on 2 April 1997, by Presidents Lukashenka and Yeltsin (see below) prompted a further anti-Union demonstration in Minsk, which was violently suppressed by the police, and which resulted in many arrests. Charges of violating the presidential decree on demonstrations were subsequently brought against opposition members, including Mikalay Statkevich, leader of the Belarusian Social Democratic Party. Nevertheless, support for the union treaty appeared widespread, with some 15,000 people participating in a pro-Union rally in Minsk in mid-May. The Charter of the Union was signed in Moscow on 23 May. The Treaty and Charter were ratified shortly afterwards by the respective legislatures, and came into effect in mid-June.

Negotiations mediated by the Council of Europe and the European Union (EU, see p. 172) to end the confrontation between the deputies of the former Supreme Council and the new legislature were held in June 1997. A second round of talks collapsed in July, following disagreement over which constitution was to form the basis of the discussions. Despite a statement by the EU that it was willing to assist Belarus in redrafting the new Constitution, while still recognizing the 1994 version as legitimate, negotiations between the deputies of the former and current legislatures, scheduled to recommence in September, were postponed indefinitely following a severe breakdown in relations between the EU and the Belarusian authorities.

Harassment and suppression of the independent media became more persistent in mid-1997. International concern at Belarus's failure to observe human rights was expressed in August in the report of one organization, Human Rights Watch, which declared that Lukashenka had reversed most of the progress achieved during the *perestroika* (restructuring) period. In November the UN Commission on Human Rights echoed this concern. Opposition to the Belarusian authorities descended into violence in September, when responsibility for an explosion at the Minsk District Court was claimed by the Belarusian Liberation Army, which subsequently issued a statement demanding the restoration of the 1994 Constitution and the cessation of harassment of the opposition. In October 1997 Lukashenka issued a presidential decree providing for more severe measures to combat terrorism and violent crime, following the death in a bomb attack of a senior law enforcement official in the Mogilev region.In November, amid allegations of a connection with this murder, the Minister of Agriculture and Food was arrested on charges of embezzlement. (He was sentenced to four-and-a-half years' imprisonment in January 2000.)

In November 1997 pro-Lukashenka rallies were held to commemorate the first anniversary of the referendum that dissolved the legislature. In the same month the opposition launched a petition movement called Charter-97 (Khartyya-97–a title reminiscent of the Czechoslavak Charter 77 pro-democracy movement), which called for greater democracy in Belarus and for presidential elections to be held in 1999 as required by the 1994 Constitution. However, later that month *Svaboda*, the largest independent newspaper, was closed, following its publication of an article by the exiled Chairman of the BPF, Paznyak, advocating Lukashenka's resignation. Repression of opposition figures continued unabated in 1998. A number of senior BFP members were among 40 protesters arrested in April during an unauthorized rally to protest against the Treaty of Union between Russia and Belarus, which was held on the anniversary of the signing of the treaty. A further 30 demonstrators were arrested later in the month at a rally led by former members of the disbanded legislature, the Supreme Council, urging Lukashenka's resignation for mismanaging the economy and destroying national culture. Lukashenka's campaign to institutionalize the use of the Russian language had successfully marginalized Belarusian, which had become widely associated with the opposition.

The discovery of alleged coup plots by the opposition in January and October 1998 was widely regarded as a further attempt to discredit and persecute the opposition, who remained without access to the media or representation in public institutions. Freedom of expression was further eroded in 1998. In May instructions were issued banning government agencies from making official documents available to the independent media and forbidding government officials to comment for them. In June legislation was approved which rendered defamation of the President an offence punishable by up to five years' imprisonment.

In late 1998 Lukashenka effected a limited reorganization of the state administration. The formation of a special committee to address the country's economic problems was decreed by the President in November, relegating the Cabinet of Ministers to a subordinate role in economic policy; the new body was to be known as the National Headquarters. The following month the Ministry of Foreign Affairs was expanded to incorporate the Ministers for CIS Affairs and for Foreign Economic Relations. The former Minister of Foreign Affairs, Ivan Antanovich, was dismissed and was replaced by Prof. Ural Latypaw, a former assistant to the President on foreign policy. Latypaw was promoted to Deputy Prime Minister in January 1999.

In September 1998 about 30 left-wing and centrist parties, including the CPB and the Liberal Democratic Party of Belarus formed a new alliance to promote further integration with Russia and to support Lukashenka's candidacy in the presidential election scheduled for 2001. The alliance, which was styled the Belarusian People's Patriotic Union, elected the CPB leader, Viktar Chykin, as its Executive Secretary and declared its intention to contest future legislative elections as a single bloc.

A new law on local elections was approved by the House of Representatives in December 1998, effectively banning candidates with a police record or fine from standing in the local elections which were to be held in April 1999. Numerous opposition candidates who had incurred fines for participating in anti-Lukashenka demonstrations were thus excluded from the polls. In the event, the majority of the seats in the elections were each contested by a single candidate, since the opposition organized an electoral boycott owing to the non-compliance of the polls with international standards. International observers noted irregularities in the voting procedure, in particular with regard to turn-out, which was believed to be much lower than the officially-reported 66.9% of the electorate.

Meanwhile, in January 1999 the Central Electoral Commission of the former Supreme Council called a presidential election, in accordance with the 1994 Constitution, to be held on 16 May. Throughout March the Government harrassed members of the Commission and its Chairman, Viktar Ganchar, was arrested. He was charged with the offence of 'appointing oneself as an official', but was released on health grounds after a 10-

day hunger strike. Nevertheless, during March the Commission registered two presidential candidates, the exiled Paznyak and former Chairman of the Cabinet of Ministers Mikhail Chigir. The latter was arrested in April and charged with large-scale embezzlement and abuse of office (the embezzlement charges were later dropped). Speculation naturally arose that Chigir had been arrested in order to prevent his participation in the election. The Chairman of the Public Coalition Government–National Economic Council, Genadz Karpenka, died in April and was replaced, in an acting capacity, by Mechislau Gryb (who was officially elected to the post in November). In May the Central Electoral Commission of the Supreme Council was unable to organize fixed polling stations for the presidential election, which was not recognized by Lukashenka's Government or by the international community. Activists with ballot boxes therefore visited voters in their homes during 6–16 May. Paznyak withdrew his candidacy in mid-May, stating that the voting procedure had violated the law. The election results were declared invalid later in the month owing to alleged irregularities in the polling, despite a reported turn-out of 53%. The Commission announced that the election was to be repeated within three months. In July the Chairman of the Supreme Council, Syamyon Sharetski, fled to Lithuania amid rumours of a warrant for his arrest in Belarus, following his appointment by the Supreme Council as acting President of Belarus (according to the 1994 Constitution Lukashenka's legitimate term of office expired in mid-July 1999).

The opposition suffered increased repression in 1999. In January Lukashenka decreed that political parties, trade unions and other organizations were required to re-register by 1 July; those failing to do so were to be disbanded. Stringent minimum levels of membership penalized several political parties, and by September only 17 of the 28 existing official parties had been re-registered. In early September OSCE-mediated negotiations between the Government and the opposition concerning legislative elections in 2000 began, and it was rumoured that they prompted an increased determination on Lukashenka's part to restrict opposition activity. (Further rounds of talks were subject to government-proposed postponements.) Stricter security measures were implemented following a stampede in a Minsk metro station in May, which resulted in 52 deaths (caused, according to Lukashenka, by 'an excess of democracy'), and following a series of bombing incidents in Russia in September. The independent press sector also came under greater scrutiny and a number of publications were closed down or had their registration revoked. Amid this atmosphere of increased control, the Government unexpectedly made a statement in August 1999 committing itself to a number of measures to defend and improve human rights in Belarus. Meanwhile, a number of outspoken critics of the President had seemingly disappeared, in strange circumstances. In May a former Minister of the Interior and campaigner for Chigir, Yuriy Zakharenka, went missing. His disappearance was followed in the next few months by those of Tamara Vinnikava, the former head of the central bank who had been under house arrest since January 1997, an independent publisher and Viktar Ganchar. It was officially claimed that the four had voluntarily gone into hiding to attract attention to their political cause. In October 1999 15,000 people were estimated to have taken part in an anti-Government demonstration in Minsk (this constituted the largest opposition demonstration to have taken place in Belarus since April 1996). One of the protesters' demands was the release of political prisoners. Chigir, who had been held in detention for more than six months, was released in late November pending trial, which began in January 2000.

The opposition was weakened by internal divisions in 1999. In late July the BPF held a leadership vote, called by members disaffected by Paznyak, which proved inconclusive and was to be repeated in October. In September supporters of Paznyak formed a breakaway faction known as the Conservative Christian Party of the BPF, with Paznyak as Chairman. At the end of October Vintsuk Vyachorka was elected Chairman of the 'rump' BPF (he had previously held the deputy chairmanship).

In February 2000 Syargey Ling resigned as Chairman of the Cabinet of Ministers, owing to his failure to resolve Belarus's economic problems. He was replaced, in an acting capacity, by Uladzimir Yermashin, hitherto the Mayor of Minsk.

Following the dissolution of the USSR in 1991, Belarus's closest relations continued to be with member states of the CIS, in particular the neighbouring Russian Federation. In April 1993 Belarus signed the CIS Treaty on Collective Security (see above), and accords on closer economic co-operation with CIS member states followed. In April 1994 Belarus and Russia concluded an agreement on an eventual monetary union. In March 1996 Belarus, Kazakhstan, Kyrgyzstan and Russia signed the Quadripartite Treaty, which envisaged a common market and a customs union between the four countries, as well as joint transport, energy and communications systems. (Tajikistan signed the Treaty in 1998.)

In April 1996 Belarus and Russia concluded the far-reaching and controversial Treaty on the Formation of a Community of Sovereign Republics, providing for closer economic, political and military integration between the two countries. On 2 April 1997 a further Treaty of Union was signed by Yeltsin and Lukashenka in Moscow, and a Charter of the Union, detailing the process of integration, was also initialled. The stated aim of the Union was for the 'voluntary unification of the member states', and was to include the development of a common infrastructure, a single currency and a joint defence policy. The Union's ruling body was to be a Supreme Council, chaired alternately by the Presidents of the member states, and comprising the Heads of State and Government, the leaders of the legislatures and the Chairman of the Executive Committee. The Executive Committee was to be appointed by the Supreme Council. The Parliamentary Assembly (provision for which had been made in the 1996 Treaty and which had convened in March) comprised 36 members from the legislature of each country. The Charter was submitted for nation-wide discussion in both countries, before being signed in Moscow on 23 May. Ratification of the documents by the respective legislatures took place in June, and the first official session of the Parliamentary Assembly followed shortly afterwards, with the Assembly adopting the anthem of the former Soviet Union as its national anthem.

Progress towards further integration appeared threatened by the deterioration in relations caused by the arrest of two Russian television crews in Belarus in mid-1997. The incidents led to strong exchanges of opinion between the two Presidents, and the subsequent cancellation of two visits by Lukashenka to Russia. Despite this affair, the new Russian Prime Minister, Yevgenii Primakov, selected Minsk as the destination of his first foreign trip in September 1998, and Lukashenka declared his support for Yeltsin, amid demands for Yeltsin's resignation, but expressed dissatisfaction with the progress of unification with Russia. In November the Parliamentary Assembly of the Russia-Belarus Union voted for the creation of a unified parliament, to consist of two chambers. The upper chamber was to include deputies delegated by the legislatures of the two countries, and the lower chamber, comprising 25 Belarusian and 75 Russian deputies, was to be elected by direct universal suffrage. The first elections to the union Parliament were expected to coincide with elections to the Russian and Belarusian legislatures. On 25 December, at a meeting in Moscow, Presidents Lukashenka and Yeltsin signed a document providing for equal rights for their citizens in Russia and Belarus and the creation of a union state within a year. A treaty on unification was to be drafted and submitted for national discussion by mid-1999. Provisions were to include the formation of the necessary governing bodies and a mechanism for pursuing a common policy in international affairs and defence and security matters, as well as further moves towards economic integration. The opposition in Belarus criticized the agreement as representing a loss of sovereignty. Agreements on enhanced military co-operation between Belarus and Russia were signed in April 1999. Lukashenka's hopes for the formation of a single state, which were much contested by the Belarusian opposition, were also not shared by Russia itself, and the draft treaty on unification, which was submitted for public inspection in October, did not fully satisfy the wishes of the Belarusian President. In addition, the then Russian Prime Minister, Vladimir Putin, warned that the implementation process might take several years. The signing of the treaty took place in Moscow on 8 December, having been postponed from November (owing to President Yeltsin's ill health). The unification treaty was ratified by the two countries' respective legislatures and by Lukashenka later in December and by Putin, who had replaced Yeltsin as the President of Russia (following the latter's unexpected resignation on 31 December), on 3 January 2000. Lukashenka stressed that the appointment of Putin as Russia's new President was confirmation of Russia's continuity of policy and expressed confidence that the new Head of State would further promote integration between Russia and Belarus.

Relations with Poland deteriorated sharply in February 1998, when Poland introduced visas for travellers from Belarus, Russia and Ukraine in preparation for EU membership and the standardization of controls. The introduction of a new visa system in Latvia with regard to seven CIS states, including Belarus, in April 1999 caused tension between Belarus and Latvia, as the former was not informed of the changes prior to their implementation.

In June 1998 a diplomatic scandal resulted from the enforced eviction of 22 diplomatic families from their residences in the Drazdy Government Complex outside Minsk for 'essential repairs'. This violation of the Vienna Convention, guaranteeing the inviolability of diplomatic residences, led to the recall from Belarus of the ambassadors from members of the EU, a number of other European states and the USA and Japan. In a retaliatory act, Belarus envoys were expelled from the EU in June, and in the following month Belarusian officials (including the President) were barred from entering its member states. The ban was subsequently adopted by several other European countries and the USA. The situation had been largely resolved by December, however, as Belarus undertook compensation procedures for those families who had been forced to relocate and Lukashenka gave assurances that henceforth he would comply with international agreements. All heads of diplomatic missions accredited to Belarus, with the exception of the US ambassador, returned to Minsk in January 1999. The EU ban on Belarusian officials entering its territory was repealed in February, and the US ambassador returned to Minsk in September.

In late 1999 international organizations, including the OSCE, continued to recognize the former Supreme Council as the legitimate legislature of Belarus. The OSCE, however, opened a bureau in Minsk in February 1998, whose mission was to encourage democratization, to promote a dialogue between the Government and the oppositon and to monitor human rights. In September 1998 Belarus became a permanent member of the Non-aligned Movement (see p. 302).

With the dissolution of the USSR in December 1991, Belarus effectively became a nuclear power, with approximately 80 SS-25 intercontinental ballistic missiles stationed on its territory. However, the Government of independent Belarus has consistently stressed that, under the Declaration of State Sovereignty of July 1990, Belarus is a neutral and non-nuclear state. Accordingly, in May 1992 Belarus signed the Lisbon Protocol to the Treaty on the Non-Proliferation of Nuclear Weapons (see under International Atomic Energy Agency, p. 74), under which it pledged to transfer all nuclear missiles to the Russian Federation by 1999. In February 1993 the Supreme Council ratified the first Strategic Arms Reduction Treaty (START 1—for further details, see chapter on the USA). Substantial amounts of financial and technical aid were pledged by the USA to help Belarus dismantle its nuclear arsenal. The last remaining nuclear warhead was removed from Belarus and transported to Russia in late November 1996. In 1998 Belarus signed the International Convention on Nuclear Safety, adopted in June 1994 in Vienna.

## Government

Under the Constitution of March 1994, which was amended in November 1996, legislative power is vested in the bicameral National Assembly. The lower chamber, the 110-member House of Representatives, is elected by universal adult suffrage for a term of four years. The upper chamber, the Council of the Republic, comprises 64 members: 56 members elected by organs of local administration, and eight members appointed by the President. The President is the Head of State, and is elected by popular vote for five years. Executive authority is exercised by the Cabinet of Ministers, which is led by the Chairman (Prime Minister) and which is responsible to the National Assembly. For administrative purposes, Belarus is divided into six regions (*oblasts*) and the capital city of Minsk; the regions are divided into districts (*rayons*).

## Defence

In August 1999 the total strength of Belarus's armed forces was 80,900, comprising an army of 43,350, an air force of 22,450 (including air defence of 10,200), as well as 15,100 in centrally controlled units and Ministry of Defence staff. There is also a border guard numbering 8,000, which is controlled by the Ministry of Internal Affairs. Military service is compulsory and lasts for 18 months. In May 1996 it was reported that the term of military service would be reduced to 12 months from the year 2000. In October 1994 it was announced that two Russian non-nuclear military installations were to remain in Belarus. The defence budget for 1999 was projected at 22,565,000m. new roubles. In January 1995 Belarus joined NATO's 'Partnership for Peace' programme of military co-operation (see p. 228).

## Economic Affairs

In 1997, according to estimates by the World Bank, Belarus's gross national product (GNP), measured at average 1995–97 prices, was US $22,082m., equivalent to $2,150 per head. During 1990–97, it was estimated, GNP per head declined at an average annual rate of 5.6%. Over the same period, the population increased at an average annual rate of less than 0.05%. In 1998 total GNP was estimated at $22,500m., equivalent to $2,200 per head. During 1990–97 Belarus's gross domestic product (GDP) declined, in real terms, by an average of 6.1% annually. However, GDP increased by 2.8% in 1996, by 11.4% in 1997 and by 8.3% in 1998.

Agriculture and forestry contributed an estimated 12.4% of GDP in 1998, and 16.4% of the employed labour force were engaged in the sector in that year. The principal crops are potatoes, grain and sugar beet. The livestock sector accounted for some 37% of agricultural output in 1995. Large areas of arable land (some 1.6m. ha) are still unused after being contaminated in 1986, following the accident at the Chornobyl nuclear power station in Ukraine. The Belarusian authorities have largely opposed private farming, and in 1997 collective and state farms still accounted for some 82.3% of agricultural land. However, 40.4% of total crop output was produced by private farms in that year. During 1990–97, according to the World Bank, agricultural GDP decreased at an average annual rate of 5.9%; agricultural output declined by 0.2% in 1997.

Industry (comprising mining, manufacturing, construction and power) provided an estimated 42.7% of GDP in 1998, and engaged 35.1% of the employed labour force in that year. According to the World Bank, industrial GDP decreased at an average annual rate of 7.8% during 1990–97. However, it was estimated that industrial output increased by 3.0% in 1996 and by 17.6% in 1997.

According to the World Bank, the manufacturing sector contributed an estimated 21.1% of GDP in 1995, and employed 26.5% of the labour force in 1994. Machine-building, power generation and chemicals are the principal branches of the sector. During 1990–97, according to the World Bank, manufacturing GDP decreased at an average annual rate of 6.5%. After several years of decline, production increased in 1996. The greatest advance was recorded in the iron and steel industry, where output rose by 23.4% in that year. According to the Government, all branches of the manufacturing sector were expected to record growth in 1998.

Belarus has relatively few mineral resources, although there are small deposits of petroleum and natural gas, and important peat reserves. Peat extraction, however, was severely affected by the disaster at Chornobyl, since contaminated peat could not be burned. Belarus produced 50% of the former Soviet Union's output of potash. However, production of potash has declined in recent years. In 1994 only 0.6% of the labour force were engaged in mining and quarrying.

In 1996 Belarus's supply of energy was provided by petroleum and petroleum products (58%), natural gas (34%) and electricity (8%). In 1997 the country imported 89% of its crude oil consumption, 99% of its natural gas consumption and 31% of its electricity consumption. In the latter half of the 1990s Belarus's principal gas supplier, the Russian company Gazprom, threatened to reduce supplies to Belarus, owing to continuing substantial arrears in the payment of a debt estimated at US $250m. Having failed to comply with previous settlements, Belarus agreed in December 1998 to supply Russia with foodstuffs to repay the remainder of the debt. In January 1999, however, Gazprom reduced its gas supplies to Belarus by 12%. Imports of energy products comprised 40.2% of the total value of imports in 1995. There are two large petroleum refineries, at Novopolotsk and Mozyr.

Services accounted for 48.5% of total employment in 1998, and provided an estimated 44.9% of GDP in that year. The services sector is led by transport and communications and trade and catering, which accounted for 11.5% and 10.0% of GDP, respectively, in 1998. Trade and catering GDP increased by 23.0% in 1996, compared with a decline of 24.0% in 1995. During 1990–97 the GDP of the services sector declined at an average annual rate of 3.8%.

In 1998 Belarus recorded a visible trade deficit of US $1,358.5m., and there was a deficit of $862.1.m. on the current account of the balance of payments. Since the dissolution of the USSR in December 1991, Belarus has endeavoured to promote economic links with non-traditional trading partners. In 1998 these partners accounted for an estimated 32.6% of Belarus's total trade (35.7% of imports, 29.5% of exports), the remaining 67.4% being conducted with former Soviet republics. Belarus's principal trading partners amongst countries constituting the former USSR in 1998 were Russia (which accounted for 54.1% of total imports and 62.3% of exports) and Ukraine; outside the former USSR the most important trading partners are Germany, Poland and the USA. In 1997 the principal exports were trucks, potassium fertilizers, tractors, tyres and refrigerators. The principal imports were petroleum and natural gas, machinery, chemicals, iron and steel, and grain.

The 1998 state budget registered a deficit of 9,995,517m. new roubles. Belarus's total external debt was US $1,162m. at the end of 1997, of which $675m. was long-term public debt. In that year the cost of debt-servicing was equivalent to 1.8% of the value of exports of goods and services. During 1990–98 consumer prices increased at an average rate of 365% per year. The average annual rate of inflation was 52.7% in 1996, but it increased to 63.8% in 1997 and to 73.0% in 1998. In the year to September 1999 average prices rose by 335.8%. In April 1998 the unemployment rate was 2.2% of the labour force. In May 1999 103,100 people were officially registered as unemployed.

Belarus joined the IMF and the World Bank in 1992. It also became a member of the European Bank for Reconstruction and Development (EBRD, see p. 168).

Prior to 1991, Belarus was widely considered to have the most stable republican economy of the Soviet Union, supported largely by a comparatively advanced engineering sector. Following the dissolution of the USSR, however, Belarus experienced serious economic problems comparable to those prevalent in other former Soviet republics, and suffered a severe contraction in output in all sectors. The introduction of market economic principles was effectively halted in 1995, causing the IMF to suspend credit to Belarus. Belarus's economic policy was influenced by its aim of integration with Russia, as envisaged in a number of treaties and agreements signed in the mid-1990s to early 2000. A treaty signed in December 1998 (although not ratified) provided for the completion (by July 1999 at the earliest) of a single customs area, unified civil and tax legislation, the standardization of monetary and credit systems, the imposition of a single legal environment for companies and the adoption of a common currency. Despite the Russian economic crisis in 1998, GDP continued to expand, although the standard of living in Belarus declined significantly, with consumer prices rising rapidly in comparison with real incomes. Price rises and severe food shortages continued in 1999. A decree compelling farmers to sell their produce to the State failed to resolve the crisis, which deepened following a poor grain harvest in August. In that month 75% of households in Belarus were classified as 'poor'. While economic growth had been achieved in 1998 (largely owing to short-term factors such as the boost to exports resulting from the depreciation of the currency), prospects for the Belarusian economy in 1999 were not favourable. There was an absence of significant structural reform in most sectors of the economy, which in July 1999 led to a refusal by the IMF to give any further aid or to send any more missions to Belarus. In addition, the World Bank, which had re-established permanent representation in the country in June, was rapidly losing patience with the slow pace of reform by the end of the year. At the end of 1999 it was announced that the currency was to be redenominated over a three-year period. One new rouble was to be equivalent to 1,000 current roubles.

## Social Welfare

Since 1993 the social security system has been financed by two principal funds: the Social Protection Fund (covering family allowances, pensions and sickness and disability benefits), and the Employment Fund (directing employment schemes, retraining projects and unemployment benefits). More than 2.5m. people were receiving pensions in 1998. A variety of benefits, financed through the Chornobyl tax, are paid to victims of the accident at the Chornobyl power station in April 1986. In 1996 government expenditure on social protection was 22,954,000m. new roubles (12.8% of GDP), and expenditure on health from the state budget was 9,402,000m. new roubles (5.2% of GDP). In 1995 there were 41.2 physicians and 117.1 hospital beds per 10,000 inhabitants.

## Education

Education is officially compulsory for nine years. Generally, education lasts for 11 years from six to 17 years of age. In 1999 the total enrolment at pre-primary level was equivalent to 71% of children in the relevant age group (males 72.7%; females 62.7%). Primary education generally begins at six years of age and lasts for four years (Grades 1–4). In 1999 the total enrolment at primary level was equivalent to 99.3% of the school-age population (males 99.9%; females 98.8%). Secondary education, beginning at the age of 10, lasts for a further seven years (Grades 5–11), comprising a first cycle of five years and a second of two years. In 1999 enrolment at secondary level was equivalent to 99.9% of those in the relevant age group (males 99.7%; females 99.9%). In 1998 a transition towards compulsory education for 10 years and general education lasting 12 years began. In the early 1990s, in response to public demand, the Government began to introduce greater provision for education in the Belarusian language and more emphasis on Belarusian, rather than Soviet or Russian, history and literature. In 1998/99 30.5% of all pupils were taught in Belarusian, and 69.4% were taught in Russian. Higher education institutions include seven general and 12 specialized universities, as well as nine academies. In 1999 262,000 students were enrolled in higher education. In 1996 enrolment at tertiary level was equivalent to 44.0% of people in the relevant age group (males 38.8%; females 49.3%). Research is co-ordinated by the Belarusian Academy of Sciences. Proposed expenditure on education by all levels of government was 16,630,000m. new roubles (6.6% of projected GDP) in 1999. In 1989, according to census results, the average rate of adult illiteracy was 2.1% (males 0.6%; females 3.4%).

## Public Holidays

**2000:** 1 January (New Year's Day), 7 January (Orthodox Christmas), 8 March (International Women's Day), 15 March (Constitution Day), 24 April (Catholic Easter), 28 April (Memorial Day), 1 May (Labour Day and Orthodox Easter), 9 May (Victory Day), 3 July (Anniversary of Liberation from the Nazis), 2 November (Day of Commemoration), 7 November (October Revolution Day), 25 December (Catholic Christmas).

**2001:** 1 January (New Year's Day), 7 January (Orthodox Christmas), 8 March (International Women's Day), 15 March (Constitution Day), 16 April (Catholic and Orthodox Easter), 28 April (Memorial Day), 1 May (Labour Day), 9 May (Victory Day), 3 July (Anniversary of Liberation from the Nazis), 2 November (Day of Commemoration), 7 November (October Revolution Day), 25 December (Catholic Christmas).

## Weights and Measures

The metric system is in force.

# Statistical Survey

Source: mainly Ministry of Statistics and Analysis, 220070 Minsk, pr. Partizanski 12; tel. (17) 249-52-00; fax (17) 249-22-04.

## Area and Population

**AREA, POPULATION AND DENSITY**

| | |
|---|---|
| Area (sq km) | 207,595* |
| Population (census results)† | |
| 12 January 1989 | 10,151,806 |
| 16 February 1999‡ | |
| Males | 4,718,000 |
| Females | 5,327,000 |
| Total | 10,045,000 |
| Population (official estimates at 1 January)§ | |
| 1997 | 10,236,127 |
| 1998 | 10,203,837 |
| 1999 | 10,179,121 |
| Density (per sq km) at 16 February 1999 | 48.3 |

* 80,153 sq miles.

† Figures refer to the *de jure* population. The *de facto* total was 10,199,709 in 1989.

‡ Preliminary results.

§ Not revised to take account of the February 1999 census.

**POPULATION BY NATIONALITY** (1989 census)

| | % |
|---|---|
| Belarusian | 77.9 |
| Russian | 13.2 |
| Polish | 4.1 |
| Ukrainian | 2.9 |
| Others | 1.9 |
| **Total** | 100.0 |

**PRINCIPAL TOWNS***
(estimated population at 1 January 1999)

| | | | |
|---|---|---|---|
| Minsk (Miensk, capital) | 1,725,100 | Baranovichi (Baranavichy) | 173,800 |
| Gomel (Homiel) | 503,700 | Borisov (Barysau) | 153,500 |
| Mogilev (Mahilou) | 371,300 | Pinsk | 133,500 |
| Vitebsk (Viciebsk) | 358,700 | Orsha (Vorsha) | 124,300 |
| Grodno (Horadnia) | 308,900 | Mozyr (Mazyr) | 110,000 |
| Brest (Bierascie)† | 300,400 | Soligorsk | 101,700 |
| Bobruysk (Babrujsk) | 228,000 | Lida | 99,600 |

* The Belarusian names of towns, in Latin transliteration, are given in parentheses after the more widely used Russian names.

† Formerly Brest-Litovsk.

**1999 census** (provisional): Minsk 1,680,000.

**BIRTHS, MARRIAGES AND DEATHS**

| | Registered live births | | Registered marriages | | Registered deaths | |
|---|---|---|---|---|---|---|
| | Number | Rate (per 1,000) | Number | Rate (per 1,000) | Number | Rate (per 1,000) |
| 1991 | 132,045 | 12.9 | 94,760 | 9.2 | 114,650 | 11.2 |
| 1992 | 127,971 | 12.4 | 79,813 | 7.7 | 116,674 | 11.3 |
| 1993 | 117,384 | 11.3 | 82,326 | 7.9 | 128,544 | 12.4 |
| 1994 | 110,599 | 10.7 | 75,540 | 7.3 | 130,003 | 12.6 |
| 1995 | 101,144 | 9.8 | 77,027 | 7.5 | 133,775 | 13.0 |
| 1996 | 95,798 | 9.3 | 63,677 | 6.2 | 133,422 | 13.0 |
| 1997 | 89,586 | 8.8 | 69,735 | 6.8 | 136,653 | 13.4 |
| 1998 | 92,645 | 9.1 | 71,354 | 7.0 | 137,296 | 13.5 |

**Expectation of life** (official estimates, years at birth, 1998): 68.4 (males 62.7, females 74.4).

**EMPLOYMENT** (annual averages, '000 persons)

| | 1996 | 1997 | 1998 |
|---|---|---|---|
| Agriculture | 760.4 | 735.1 | 695.3 |
| Forestry | 26.4 | 27.4 | 28.7 |
| Industry* | 1,202.0 | 1,204.3 | 1,221.0 |
| Construction | 314.1 | 311.8 | 329.5 |
| Trade and communications | 311.2 | 309.1 | 321.4 |
| Trade and public catering† | 460.1 | 461.6 | 483.2 |
| Housing, public utilities and personal services | 195.5 | 197.6 | 193.4 |
| Health care | 253.8 | 259.9 | 262.0 |
| Physical culture and social security | 45.8 | 48.0 | 51.6 |
| Education | 433.0 | 441.1 | 454.5 |
| Culture and arts | 69.8 | 71.1 | 73.9 |
| Science | 47.8 | 44.6 | 43.7 |
| Credit and insurance | 50.4 | 50.7 | 53.2 |
| Other activities | 194.5 | 207.6 | 205.2 |
| **Total** | 4,364.8 | 4,369.9 | 4,416.6 |
| Males | 2,128.0 | 2,128.6 | 2,146.5 |
| Females | 2,236.8 | 2,241.3 | 2,270.1 |

* Comprising manufacturing (except printing and publishing), mining and quarrying, electricity, gas, logging and fishing.

† Including material and technical supply and procurement.

**Unemployment** ('000 persons registered at December): 182.5 (males 66.1, females 116.4) in 1996; 126.2 (males 42.1, females 84.1) in 1997; 105.9 (males 35.3, females 70.6) in 1998.

## Agriculture

**PRINCIPAL CROPS** ('000 metric tons)

| | 1996 | 1997 | 1998 |
|---|---|---|---|
| Wheat | 600 | 744 | 570† |
| Barley | 2,194 | 2,359 | 1,850† |
| Maize | 5 | 5† | 4† |
| Rye | 1,794 | 1,788 | 1,370† |
| Oats | 707 | 822 | 628† |
| Other cereals | 178 | 201 | 162 |
| Potatoes | 10,881 | 6,942 | 10,000* |
| Dry beans | 129 | 205 | 155† |
| Dry peas | 181 | 287 | 217† |
| Rapeseed | 19 | 21 | 19* |
| Linseed* | 20 | 18 | 15 |
| Cabbages | 500† | 490† | 505* |
| Tomatoes | 120† | 114† | 120* |
| Cucumbers and gherkins | 140† | 135† | 120* |
| Onions (dry) | 50† | 55† | 50* |
| Carrots | 54 | 54† | 55* |
| Other vegetables | 340 | 328† | 325* |
| Sugar beet | 1,011 | 1,262 | 1,200* |
| Apples | 294† | 243† | 215* |
| Pears | 20† | 16† | 14* |
| Plums | 60† | 49† | 45* |
| Other fruits and berries | 65† | 55† | 49* |
| Walnuts* | 9 | 10 | 10 |
| Tobacco (leaves)* | 2 | 2 | 2 |
| Flax fibre | 49 | 50* | 50* |

* FAO estimate(s). † Unofficial figure.

Source: FAO, *Production Yearbook*.

**LIVESTOCK** ('000 head at 1 January)

| | 1997 | 1998 | 1999 |
|---|---|---|---|
| Horses | 232 | 233 | 229 |
| Cattle | 4,855 | 4,802 | 4,686 |
| Pigs | 3,715 | 3,686 | 3,698 |
| Sheep | 155 | 127 | 106 |
| Goats | 59 | 59 | 56 |
| Chickens | 31,540 | 29,871 | 30,425 |

**LIVESTOCK PRODUCTS** ('000 metric tons)

| | 1996 | 1997 | 1998† |
|---|---|---|---|
| Beef and veal | 277 | 282* | 285 |
| Mutton and lamb | 4 | 3* | 3 |
| Pig meat | 273 | 278* | 280 |
| Poultry meat | 64 | 63* | 65 |
| Cows' milk | 4,908 | 5,088 | 5,088 |
| Cheese | 39 | 51 | 51 |
| Butter | 61 | 72 | 72 |
| Hen eggs | 192 | 194* | 194 |
| Honey | 4 | 4† | 4 |
| Cattle and buffalo hides† | 30 | 31 | 31 |

* Unofficial figure. † FAO estimate(s).

Source: partly FAO, *Production Yearbook*, and Ministry of Statistics and Analysis, Minsk.

## Forestry

**ROUNDWOOD REMOVALS** ('000 cubic metres, excl. bark)

| | 1995 | 1996 | 1997 |
|---|---|---|---|
| Sawlogs, veneer logs and logs for sleepers | 3,920 | 9,142 | 11,020 |
| Other industrial wood | 5,286 | 5,286 | 5,286 |
| Fuel wood | 809 | 809 | 809 |
| **Total** | 10,015 | 15,707 | 17,585 |

Source: FAO, *Yearbook of Forest Products*.

**SAWNWOOD PRODUCTION** ('000 cubic metres, incl. railway sleepers)

| | 1995 | 1996 | 1997 |
|---|---|---|---|
| Coniferous (softwood)* | 938 | 938 | 938 |
| Broadleaved (hardwood)* | 607 | 607 | 607 |
| **Total** | 1,545 | 1,545 | 1,545 |

* FAO estimates.

Source: FAO, *Yearbook of Forest Products*.

## Fishing

(metric tons, live weight)

| | 1995 | 1996 | 1997 |
|---|---|---|---|
| Freshwater bream* | 50 | 50 | 60 |
| Roaches* | 124 | 120 | 140 |
| Other fishes* | 82 | 81 | 100 |
| **Total catch** | 256 | 251* | 300* |

* FAO estimate(s).

Source: FAO, *Yearbook of Fishery Statistics*.

## Mining

('000 metric tons, unless otherwise indicated)

| | 1996 | 1997 | 1998 |
|---|---|---|---|
| Crude petroleum | 1,860 | 1,822 | 1,830 |
| Natural gas (million cu metres) | 249 | 246 | 252 |
| Chalk | 64 | 75 | 79 |
| Gypsum (crude) | 21 | 23 | 17 |
| Peat: for fuel | 2,847 | 2,768 | 2,035 |
| for agriculture | 533 | 253 | 99 |

## Industry

**SELECTED PRODUCTS** ('000 metric tons, unless otherwise indicated)

| | 1996 | 1997 | 1998 |
|---|---|---|---|
| Refined sugar | 226 | 352 | 476 |
| Margarine | 25.3 | 22.7 | 15.0 |
| Wheat flour | 1,397 | 1,274 | 1,159 |
| Ethyl alcohol ('000 hectolitres) | 1,025 | 1,312 | 1,051 |
| Wine ('000 hectolitres) | 868.7 | 1,256.5 | 1,733.4 |
| Beer ('000 hectolitres) | 2,012.5 | 2,412.6 | 2,603.7 |
| Mineral water ('000 hectolitres) | 295.8 | 548.3 | 886.4 |
| Soft drinks ('000 hectolitres) | 1,627.0 | 2,031.1 | 1,942.0 |
| Cigarettes (million) | 6,267 | 6,787 | 7,296 |
| Cotton yarn (pure and mixed) | 11.4 | 10.2 | 18.6 |
| Flax yarn | 16.1 | 16.8 | 17.4 |
| Wool yarn (pure and mixed) | 12.8 | 15.5 | 16.3 |
| Woven cotton fabrics (million sq metres) | 42.8 | 47.4 | 66.9 |
| Woven woollen fabrics (million sq metres) | 7.0 | 8.9 | 9.5 |
| Linen fabrics (million sq metres) | 43.0 | 45.1 | 50.1 |
| Woven fabrics of cellulosic fibres (million sq metres) | 39.5 | 66.7 | 77.2 |
| Carpets ('000 sq metres) | 5,612 | 6,861 | 8,145 |
| Footwear (excluding rubber, '000 pairs) | 11,381 | 15,587 | 16,159 |
| Plywood ('000 cu metres) | 103 | 121 | 139 |
| Paper | 30 | 36 | 45 |
| Paperboard | 112 | 135 | 150 |
| Benzene (Benzol) | 34.7 | 35.9 | 16.7 |
| Ethylene (Ethene) | 78.9 | 104.0 | 108.1 |
| Propylene (Propene) | 55.1 | 69.8 | 70.5 |
| Xylenes (Xylol) | 7.6 | 9.3 | — |
| Sulphuric acid (100%) | 549 | 698 | 640 |
| Nitrogenous fertilizers (a)[1] | 565 | 490 | 559 |
| Phosphate fertilizers (b)[1] | 100 | 136 | 130 |
| Potash fertilizers (c)[1] | 2,716 | 3,247 | 3,451 |
| Non-cellulosic continuous fibres | 46.6 | 64.2 | 66.2 |
| Cellulosic continuous filaments | 10.7 | 13.2 | 14.3 |
| Soap | 29.7 | 33.7 | 26.1 |
| Rubber tyres ('000)[2] | 1,916 | 2,355 | 2,324 |
| Rubber footwear ('000 pairs) | 3,054 | 4,376 | 5,036 |
| Quicklime | 450 | 551 | 684 |
| Cement | 1,467 | 1,876 | 2,035 |
| Concrete blocks ('000 cu metres) | 1,370 | 1,996 | 2,134 |
| Crude steel | 886 | 1,220 | 1,412 |
| Tractors ('000) | 26.8 | 27.4 | 26.9 |
| Refrigerators ('000) | 754 | 795 | 802 |
| Domestic washing machines ('000) | 60.5 | 88.2 | 90.8 |
| Television receivers ('000) | 314 | 454 | 468 |
| Radio receivers ('000) | 138 | 170 | 114 |
| Lorries (number) | 10,671 | 13,002 | 12,792 |
| Motor cycles ('000) | 30.1 | 22.6 | 20.4 |
| Bicycles ('000) | 280 | 317 | 452 |
| Cameras ('000) | 35 | 15 | 5 |
| Watches ('000) | 4,809 | 4,956 | 4,847 |
| Electric energy (million kWh) | 23,728 | 26,057 | 23,492 |

[1] Production in terms of (a) nitrogen; (b) phosphoric acid; or (c) potassium oxide.

[2] For lorries and farm vehicles.

# Finance

## CURRENCY AND EXCHANGE RATES

**Monetary Units:**
100 kopeks = 1 new Belarusian rouble (rubel).

**Sterling, Dollar and Euro Equivalents** (30 September 1999)
£1 sterling = 477,485 new roubles;
US $1 = 290,000 new roubles;
€1 = 309,285 new roubles;
1,000,000 new Belarusian roubles = £2.094 = $3.448 = €3.233.

**Average Exchange Rate** (new Belarusian roubles per US $)
1997 25,964

Note: The Belarusian rouble was introduced in May 1992, initially as a coupon currency, to circulate alongside (and at par with) the Russian (formerly Soviet) rouble. Following the dissolution of the USSR in December 1991, Russia and several other former Soviet republics retained the rouble as their monetary unit. The parity between Belarusian and Russian currencies was subsequently ended, and the Belarusian rouble was devalued. At 30 September 1993 the exchange rate was 1 Russian rouble = 2 Belarusian roubles. The rate per Russian rouble was adjusted to 3 Belarusian roubles in October 1993, and to 4 Belarusian roubles in November. In April 1994 Belarus and Russia signed a treaty providing for the eventual union of their monetary systems. However, it was subsequently recognized that, under the prevailing economic conditions, such a union was not practicable. In August a new Belarusian rouble, equivalent to 10 old roubles, was introduced. On 1 January 1995 the Belarusian rouble became the sole national currency, while the circulation of Russian roubles ceased. In October 1999 it was announced that a readjusted Belarusian rouble, equivalent to 1,000 current roubles, would be introduced over a three-year period, beginning on 1 January 2000.

## STATE BUDGET (million roubles)*

| Revenue | 1996 | 1997 | 1998 |
|---|---|---|---|
| Tax revenue | 43,486,194 | 96,932,523 | 183,818,268 |
| Income taxes | 5,297,023 | 11,372,646 | 24,984,554 |
| Value-added tax | 14,273,982 | 33,538,879 | 61,813,955 |
| Excises | 6,335,907 | 14,615,432 | 26,605,166 |
| Fuel tax | 252,465 | — | — |
| Chornobyl tax† | 3,821,430 | 5,634,228 | 6,237,805 |
| Other taxes | 13,505,387 | 31,771,338 | 64,176,788 |
| Non-tax revenue | 7,182,437 | 15,953,828 | 14,979,250 |
| **Total** | 50,668,631 | 112,886,351 | 239,581,995 |

| Expenditure | 1996 | 1997 | 1998 |
|---|---|---|---|
| National economy | 10,815,565 | 19,463,192 | 39,056,727 |
| Socio-cultural activities | 26,430,607 | 51,545,908 | 94,936,760 |
| Administration, law and order | 5,755,691 | 11,342,588 | 20,676,847 |
| Chornobyl fund† | 4,164,652 | 7,561,416 | 13,100,982 |
| **Total** (incl. others) | 54,314,594 | 120,832,143 | 249,577,512 |

* Excluding the operations of social funds and extrabudgetary accounts. In 1996 the consolidated totals of government transactions (in '000 million new roubles) were: Revenue and grants 75,410; Expenditure and net lending 78,370 (Source: IMF Staff Country Report, November 1997).

† Relating to measures to relieve the effects of the accident at the Chornobyl nuclear power station, in northern Ukraine, in April 1986.

Source: Ministry of Finance, Minsk.

## INTERNATIONAL RESERVES (US $ million at 31 December)

| | 1996 | 1997 | 1998 |
|---|---|---|---|
| IMF special drawing rights | 0.14 | — | 0.42 |
| Reserve position in IMF | 0.03 | 0.03 | 0.03 |
| Foreign exchange | 468.98 | 393.67 | 338.39 |
| **Total** | 469.15 | 393.70 | 338.83 |

Source: IMF, *International Financial Statistics*.

## MONEY SUPPLY (million new roubles at 31 December)

| | 1996 | 1997 | 1998 |
|---|---|---|---|
| Currency outside banks | 6,199,400 | 12,300,000 | 27,074,000 |
| Demand deposits at deposit money banks | 9,240,100 | 21,052,000 | 52,487,000 |
| **Total money** (incl. others) | 15,708,400 | 33,852,000 | 80,932,000 |

Source: IMF, *International Financial Statistics*.

## COST OF LIVING (Consumer price index; base: 1992 = 100)

| | 1996 | 1997 | 1998 |
|---|---|---|---|
| Food (incl. beverages) | 427,096 | 725,423 | 1,275,657 |
| Fuel and light | 1,122,403 | 1,883,617 | 2,675,490 |
| Clothing (incl. footwear) | 193,950 | 275,293 | 442,424 |
| Rent | 4,661,974 | 5,415,815 | 7,002,649 |
| **All items** (incl. others) | 370,067 | 606,280 | 1,049,047 |

## NATIONAL ACCOUNTS ('000 million new roubles at current prices)

### Expenditure on the Gross Domestic Product

| | 1996 | 1997 | 1998* |
|---|---|---|---|
| Government final consumption expenditure | 36,627 | 72,441 | 128,921 |
| Private final consumption expenditure | 109,603 | 202,875 | 389,564 |
| Increase in stocks | 4,681 | 5,891 | 685 |
| Gross fixed capital formation | 40,438 | 92,555 | 172,338 |
| **Total domestic expenditure** | 191,349 | 373,762 | 691,508 |
| Exports of goods and services | 88,876 | 217,574 | 410,684 |
| *Less* Imports of goods and services | 96,051 | 239,975 | 450,252 |
| Statistical discrepancy | — | 4,718 | 10,430 |
| **GDP in purchasers' values** | 184,174 | 356,079 | 662,370 |

* Figures are preliminary.

### Gross Domestic Product by Economic Activity

| | 1996 | 1997 | 1998* |
|---|---|---|---|
| Agriculture | 24,769.9 | 43,134.6 | 67,336.1 |
| Forestry | 1,303.6 | 2,401.9 | 4,252.8 |
| Industry† | 56,518.8 | 110,727.0 | 205,735.6 |
| Construction | 8,943.0 | 20,274.7 | 39,848.4 |
| Transport | 17,382.6 | 31,741.0 | 55,272.8 |
| Communications | 3,663.6 | 5,804.5 | 10,761.3 |
| Trade and catering | 14,335.8 | 26,401.3 | 57,497.0 |
| Material supply | 2,274.4 | 4,518.9 | 8,430.9 |
| Procurement | 491.9 | 903.5 | 1,417.4 |
| Housing | 4,077.8 | 7,608.9 | 12,654.5 |
| Public utilities | 3,130.4 | 6,114.2 | 11,554.1 |
| Health care | 5,694.7 | 11,523.3 | 19,203.2 |
| Education | 7,630.8 | 15,454.4 | 27,588.2 |
| Culture and science | 2,278.4 | 3,385.4 | 5,726.7 |
| Banks and insurance | 4,354.2 | 7,208.8 | 16,306.3 |
| Public administration and defence | 6,959.0 | 11,620.2 | 20,231.6 |
| Other services | 2,598.2 | 5,692.8 | 11,769.8 |
| **Sub-total** | 166,406.9 | 314,515.4 | 575,586.7 |
| *Less* Imputed bank service charge | 3,056.4 | 5,190.0 | 11,205.4 |
| **GDP at factor cost** | 163,350.5 | 309,325.4 | 564,381.3 |
| Indirect taxes, *less* subsidies | 20,823.4 | 46,753.9 | 97,988.6 |
| **GDP in purchasers' values** | 184,173.9 | 356,079.3 | 662,369.9 |

* Figures are preliminary.

† Principally mining, manufacturing, electricity, gas and water.

**BALANCE OF PAYMENTS** (US $ million)

| | 1996 | 1997 | 1998 |
|---|---|---|---|
| Exports of goods f.o.b. | 5,790.1 | 7,382.6 | 7,123.2 |
| Imports of goods f.o.b. | −6,938.6 | −8,718.0 | −8,481.7 |
| **Trade balance** | −1,148.5 | −1,335.4 | −1,358.5 |
| Exports of services | 908.0 | 918.8 | 940.7 |
| Imports of services | −335.9 | −364.8 | −449.7 |
| **Balance on goods and services** | −576.4 | −781.4 | −867.5 |
| Other income received | 74.1 | 31.2 | 26.1 |
| Other income paid | −104.9 | −115.8 | −116.3 |
| **Balance on goods, services and income** | −607.2 | −866.0 | −957.7 |
| Current transfers received | 135.5 | 106.1 | 120.9 |
| Current transfers paid | −44.2 | −27.7 | −25.3 |
| **Current balance** | −515.9 | −787.6 | −862.1 |
| Capital account (net) | 101.1 | 133.2 | 170.1 |
| Direct investment abroad | n.a. | −2.1 | −2.3 |
| Direct investment from abroad | 72.6 | 200.0 | 149.2 |
| Portfolio investment assets | −17.7 | −61.6 | 28.0 |
| Portfolio investment liabilities | 3.2 | 41.8 | −13.4 |
| Other investment assets | −131.5 | 25.2 | 239.6 |
| Other investment liabilities | 420.2 | 357.6 | −55.5 |
| Net errors and omissions | −146.2 | 157.0 | 26.8 |
| **Overall balance** | −214.2 | 63.5 | −319.6 |

Source: IMF, *International Financial Statistics*.

# External Trade

**PRINCIPAL COMMODITIES** (million new roubles at domestic prices)*

| Imports | 1996 | 1997 | 1998 |
|---|---|---|---|
| Industrial products | 88,229,269 | 221,827,000 | 414,174,700 |
| Electric energy | 2,414,738 | 4,515,000 | 11,364,500 |
| Petroleum and gas | 24,656,946 | 55,299,000 | 86,540,400 |
| Iron and steel | 8,897,745 | 23,239,000 | 44,936,500 |
| Chemical and petroleum products | 15,293,645 | 38,802,000 | 65,748,500 |
| Machinery and metalworking | 17,554,312 | 49,934,000 | 112,649,900 |
| Wood and paper products | 2,378,800 | 6,436,000 | 12,756,000 |
| Light industry | 3,934,900 | 10,584,000 | 21,888,900 |
| Food and beverages | 8,179,958 | 22,093,000 | 39,080,600 |
| Agricultural products (unprocessed) | 4,565,600 | 8,465,000 | 11,565,300 |
| **Total** (incl. others) | 92,850,698 | 230,294,000 | 431,446,600 |
| USSR (former)† | 61,430,171 | 153,831,000 | 277,517,600 |
| Other countries | 31,420,527 | 76,463,000 | 153,929,000 |

| Exports | 1996 | 1997 | 1998 |
|---|---|---|---|
| Industrial products | 73,632,505 | 189,810,000 | 303,443,200 |
| Petroleum and gas | 8,802,010 | 14,198,800 | 27,760,800 |
| Iron and steel | 4,778,700 | 15,599,000 | 24,924,400 |
| Chemical and petroleum products | 16,962,400 | 40,440,000 | 78,227,800 |
| Machinery and metalworking | 23,650,400 | 64,957,100 | 63,097,800 |
| Wood and paper products | 4,255,200 | 13,732,000 | 24,517,000 |
| Construction materials | 1,754,800 | 4,808,900 | 9,967,100 |
| Light industry | 6,106,900 | 18,289,000 | 36,364,400 |
| Food and beverages | 5,647,900 | 14,599,000 | 34,900,000 |
| Agricultural products (unprocessed) | 1,467,200 | 3,273,000 | 6,292,400 |
| **Total** (incl. others) | 75,142,300 | 193,084,000 | 367,896,800 |
| USSR (former)† | 49,774,300 | 142,583,000 | 259,282,200 |
| Other countries | 25,368,000 | 50,501,000 | 108,614,600 |

* Figures relating to trade with Russia are compiled from enterprise surveys, while data on trade with other countries are calculated on the basis of customs declarations.

† Excluding trade with Estonia, Latvia and Lithuania.

**PRINCIPAL TRADING PARTNERS**

**Trade with the former USSR** (excluding trade with Estonia, Latvia and Lithuania; million roubles at domestic prices)*

| Imports c.i.f. | 1996 | 1997 | 1998 |
|---|---|---|---|
| Kazakhstan | 762,711 | 1,525,869 | 1,513,100 |
| Moldova | 649,962 | 1,581,235 | 2,479,400 |
| Russia | 47,142,914 | 124,082,200 | 233,201,000 |
| Ukraine | 12,174,038 | 25,113,457 | 37,154,500 |
| Uzbekistan | 493,672 | 841,644 | 1,961,400 |
| **Total** (incl. others) | 61,430,171 | 153,830,400 | 277,517,600 |

| Exports f.o.b. | 1996 | 1997 | 1998 |
|---|---|---|---|
| Kazakhstan | 1,103,172 | 1,416,576 | 2,705,600 |
| Moldova | 920,260 | 1,646,513 | 3,185,400 |
| Russia | 39,953,600 | 126,763,100 | 229,083,200 |
| Ukraine | 6,378,435 | 11,181,745 | 21,082,400 |
| Uzbekistan | 1,020,625 | 796,466 | 995,000 |
| **Total** (incl. others) | 49,774,300 | 142,583,100 | 259,282,200 |

* Figures relating to trade with Russia are compiled from enterprise surveys, while data on trade with other countries are calculated on the basis of customs declarations.

**Trade with Other Countries** (US $ million)*

| Imports | 1996 | 1997 | 1998 |
|---|---|---|---|
| Europe | 1,947 | 2,266 | 2,423 |
| Austria | 54 | 63 | 61 |
| Germany | 601 | 691 | 758 |
| Poland | 195 | 250 | 283 |
| Switzerland | 38 | 42 | 49 |
| USA | 152 | 138 | 125 |
| **Total** (incl. others) | 2,369 | 2,872 | 2,995 |

| Exports | 1996 | 1997 | 1998 |
|---|---|---|---|
| Europe | 1,316 | 1,176 | 1,238 |
| Austria | 15 | 16 | 20 |
| Germany | 198 | 217 | 200 |
| Italy | 57 | 64 | 73 |
| Poland | 338 | 246 | 185 |
| Switzerland | 20 | 21 | 8 |
| Turkey | 30 | 33 | 27 |
| USA | 84 | 93 | 103 |
| **Total** (incl. others) | 1,889 | 1,922 | 1,910 |

* Figures are calculated on the basis of customs declarations.

# Transport

**RAILWAYS** (traffic)

| | 1996 | 1997 | 1998 |
|---|---|---|---|
| Passenger-km (million) | 11,657 | 12,909 | 13,268 |
| Freight ton-km (million) | 26,018 | 30,636 | 30,370 |

**ROAD TRAFFIC** (motor vehicles in use at 31 December)

| | 1996 | 1997 | 1998 |
|---|---|---|---|
| Passenger cars | 1,035,750 | 1,132,843 | 1,279,208 |
| Buses and coaches | 8,922 | 8,867 | 8,768 |

**CIVIL AVIATION** (traffic on scheduled services)

| | 1996 | 1997 | 1998 |
|---|---|---|---|
| Passengers carried ('000) | 362 | 327 | 274 |
| Passenger-km (million) | 1,085 | 910 | 729 |
| Total ton-km (million) | 123 | 84 | 12 |

# Tourism

**ARRIVALS BY NATIONALITY**

| | 1994 | 1995 | 1996 |
|---|---|---|---|
| Germany | 8,702 | 9,673 | 12,740 |
| Italy | 3,181 | 5,460 | 5,004 |
| Lithuania | 3,109 | 4,528 | 6,747 |
| Moldova | 2,987 | 3,606 | 2,359 |
| Poland | 39,130 | 32,334 | 30,216 |
| Russia | 66,892 | 57,859 | 112,678 |
| Ukraine | 28,344 | 15,006 | 15,115 |
| United Kingdom | 5,500 | 6,040 | 9,024 |
| USA | 4,251 | 4,960 | 6,870 |
| **Total** (incl. others) | 184,200 | 161,397 | 234,226 |

**Tourism receipts** (US $ million): 39 in 1994; 23 in 1995; 48 in 1996.

Source: World Tourism Organization, *Yearbook of Tourism Statistics*.

# Communications Media

| | 1996 | 1997 | 1998 |
|---|---|---|---|
| Telephones ('000 main lines in use) | 2,128 | 2,313 | 2,490 |
| Telefax stations (number in use) | 12,259 | 15,610 | 19,466 |
| Book production*: | | | |
| titles | 3,809 | 5,331 | 6,073 |
| copies ('000) | 59,073 | 67,632 | 60,022 |
| Daily newspapers: | | | |
| number | 12 | 19 | 20 |
| average circulation ('000) | 1,261 | 1,437 | 1,559 |
| Non-daily newspapers: | | | |
| number | 500 | 539 | 560 |
| average circulation ('000) | 7,825 | 7,824 | 8,973 |
| Other periodicals: | | | |
| number | 269 | 302 | 318 |
| average circulation ('000) | 1,424 | 1,647 | 1,687 |

* Including pamphlets (1,015 titles and 16,789,000 copies in 1996).

**Mobile cellular telephones** (subscribers): 324 in 1993; 1,724 in 1994; 5,897 in 1995 (Source: UN, *Statistical Yearbook*).

**Radio receivers** ('000 in use): 3,138 in 1994; 3,031 in 1995; 3,021 in 1996.

**Television receivers** ('000 in use): 3,337 in 1994; 3,139 in 1995; 3,040 in 1996.

# Education

(1998/99)

| | Institutions | Teachers | Students |
|---|---|---|---|
| Pre-primary | 4,483 | 53,700 | 416,700 |
| Primary (Grades 1–4)<br>Secondary (Grades 5–11) | 4,796 | 149,600 | 1,601,600 |
| Vocational and technical | 249 | 14,000 | 130,700 |
| Specialized secondary | 157 | 12,400 | 138,400 |
| Higher | 58 | 18,500 | 244,000 |
| Institutions offering post-graduate studies | 103 | 2,600 | 4,400 |

# Directory

## The Constitution

A new Constitution came into effect on 30 March 1994. An amended version of the 1994 Constitution became effective on 27 November 1996, following a referendum held on 24 November. The following is a summary of its main provisions:

### PRINCIPLES OF THE CONSTITUTIONAL SYSTEM

The Republic of Belarus is a unitary, democratic, social state based on the rule of law. The people are the sole source of state power and the repository of sovereignty in the Republic of Belarus. The people shall exercise their power directly through representative and other bodies in the forms and within the bounds specified by the Constitution. Democracy in the Republic of Belarus is exercised on the basis of diversity of political institutions, ideologies and opinions. State power in the Republic of Belarus is exercised on the principle of division of powers between the legislature, executive and judiciary, which are independent of one another. The Republic of Belarus is bound by the principle of supremacy of law; it recognizes the supremacy of the universally acknowledged principles of international law and ensures that its laws comply with such principles. Property may be the ownership of the State or private. The mineral wealth, waters and forests are the sole and exclusive property of the State. Land for agricultural use is the property of the State. All religions and creeds are equal before the law. The official languages of the Republic of Belarus are Belarusian and Russian. The Republic of Belarus aims to make its territory a neutral, nuclear-free state. The capital is Minsk.

### THE INDIVIDUAL, SOCIETY AND THE STATE

All persons are equal before the law and entitled without discrimination to equal protection of their rights and legitimate interests. Every person has the right to life. Until its abolition, the death penalty may be applied in accordance with the verdict of a court of law as an exceptional penalty for especially grave crimes. The State ensures the freedom, inviolability and dignity of the individual. No person may be subjected to torture or cruel, inhuman or humiliating treatment or punishment. Freedom of movement is guaranteed. Every person is guaranteed freedom of opinion and beliefs and their free expression. The right to assemble publicly is guaranteed, as is the right to form public associations, including trade unions. Citizens of the Republic of Belarus have the right to participate in the solution of state matters, both directly and through freely elected representatives; the right to vote freely and to be elected to state bodies on the basis of universal, equal, direct or indirect suffrage by secret ballot. The State shall create the conditions necessary for full employment. The right to health care is guaranteed, as is the right to social security in old age, in the event of illness, disability and in other instances. Each person has the right to housing and to education. Everyone has the right to preserve his or her ethnic affiliation, to use his or her native language and to choose the language of communication. Payment of statutory taxes and other levies is obligatory. Every person is guaranteed the protection of his or her rights and freedom by a competent, independent and impartial court of law, and every person has the right to legal assistance.

### THE ELECTORAL SYSTEM AND REFERENDUMS

Elections and referendums are conducted by means of universal, free, equal and secret ballot. Citizens of the Republic of Belarus who have reached the age of 18 years are eligible to vote. Deputies are elected by direct ballot. Referendums may be held to resolve the most important issues of the State and society. National referendums may be called by the President of the Republic of Belarus, by the National Assembly or by no fewer than 450,000 citizens eligible to vote. Local referendums may be called by local representative bodies or on the recommendation of no less than 10% of the citizens who are eligible to vote and resident in the area concerned. Decisions adopted by referendum may be reversed or amended only by means of another referendum.

### THE PRESIDENT

The President of the Republic of Belarus is Head of State, the guarantor of the Constitution of the Republic of Belarus, and of the rights and freedoms of its citizens. The President is elected for a term of five years by universal, free, equal, direct and secret ballot for no more than two terms.

The President calls national referendums; calls elections to the National Assembly and local representative bodies; dissolves the chambers of the National Assembly, as determined by the Constitution; appoints six members to the Central Electoral Commission; forms, dissolves and reorganizes the Administration of the President, as well as other bodies of state administration; appoints the Chairman of the Cabinet of Ministers (Prime Minister) of the Republic of Belarus with the consent of the House of Representatives; determines the structure of the Government, appoints and dismisses Ministers and other members of the Government, and considers the resignation of the Government; appoints, with the consent of the Council of the Republic, the Chairman of the Constitutional, Supreme and Economic Courts, the judges of the Supreme and Economic Courts, the Chairman of the Central Electoral Commission, the Procurator General, the Chairman and members of the board of the National Bank, and dismisses the aforementioned, having notified the Council of the Republic; appoints six members of the Constitutional Court, and other judges of the Republic of Belarus; appoints and dismisses the Chairman of the State Supervisory Committee; reports to the people of the Republic of Belarus on the state of the nation and on domestic and foreign policy; may chair meetings of the Government of the Republic of Belarus; conducts negotiations and signs international treaties, appoints and recalls diplomatic representatives of the Republic of Belarus; in the event of a natural disaster, a catastrophe, or unrest involving violence or the threat of violence that may endanger people's lives or jeopardize the territorial integrity of the State, declares a state of emergency; has the right to abolish acts of the Government and to suspend decisions of local councils of deputies; forms and heads the Security Council of the Republic of Belarus, and appoints and dismisses the Supreme State Secretary of the Security Council; is the Commander-in-Chief of the Armed Forces and appoints and dismisses the Supreme Command of the Armed Forces; imposes, in the event of military threat or attack, martial law in the Republic of Belarus; issues decrees and orders which are mandatory in the Republic of Belarus. In instances determined by the Constitution, the President may issue decrees which have the force of law. The President may be removed from office for acts of state treason and other grave crimes, by a decision of the National Assembly.

### THE NATIONAL ASSEMBLY

The National Assembly is a representative and legislative body of the Republic of Belarus, consisting of two chambers: the House of Representatives and the Council of the Republic. The term of the National Assembly is four years. The House of Representatives comprises 110 deputies. Deputies are elected by universal, equal, free, direct suffrage and by secret ballot. The Council of the Republic is a chamber of territorial representation with 64 members, consisting of eight deputies from every region and from Minsk, elected by deputies of local councils. Eight members of the Council of the Republic are appointed by the President. Any citizen who has reached the age of 21 years may become a deputy of the House of Representatives. Any citizen who has reached the age of 30 years, and who has been resident in the corresponding region for no less than five years, may become a member of the Council of the Republic. The chambers of the National Assembly elect their Chairmen.

The House of Representatives considers draft laws concerning amendments and alterations to the Constitution; domestic and foreign policy; the military doctrine; ratification and denunciation of international treaties; the approval of the republican budget; the introduction of national taxes and levies; local self-government; the administration of justice; the declaration of war and the conclusion of peace; martial law and a state of emergency; and the interpretation of laws. The House of Representatives calls elections for the presidency; grants consent to the President concerning the appointment of the Chairman of the Cabinet of Ministers; accepts the resignation of the President; together with the Council of the Republic, takes the decision to remove the President from office.

The Council of the Republic approves or rejects draft laws adopted by the House of Representatives; consents to appointments made by the President; elects six judges of the Constitutional Court and six members of the Central Electoral Commission; considers charges of treason against the President; takes the decision to remove the President from office; considers presidential decrees on the introduction of a state of emergency, martial law, and general or partial mobilization.

Any proposed legislation is considered initially in the House of Representatives and then in the Council of the Republic. On the proposal of the President, the House of Representatives and the Council of the Republic may adopt a law, delegating to him legislative powers to issue decrees which have the power of a law. However, he may not issue decrees making alterations or addenda to the Constitution or to policy laws.

### THE GOVERNMENT

Executive power in the Republic of Belarus is exercised by the Cabinet of Ministers. The Government is accountable to the President and responsible to the National Assembly. The Chairman of the Cabinet of Ministers is appointed by the President with the consent of the House of Representatives. The Government of the Republic of Belarus formulates and implements domestic and foreign policy; submits the draft national budget to the President; and issues acts that have binding force.

### THE JUDICIARY

Judicial authority in the Republic of Belarus is exercised by the courts. Justice is administered on the basis of adversarial proceedings and equality of the parties involved in the trial. Supervision of the constitutionality of enforceable enactments of the State is exercised by the Constitutional Court, which comprises 12 judges (six of whom are appointed by the President and six are elected by the Council of the Republic).

### LOCAL GOVERNMENT AND SELF-GOVERNMENT

Citizens exercise local and self-government through local councils of deputies, executive and administrative bodies and other forms of direct participation in state and public affairs. Local councils of deputies are elected by citizens for a four-year term, and the heads of local executive and administrative bodies are appointed and dismissed by the President of the Republic of Belarus.

### THE PROCURATOR'S OFFICE AND THE STATE SUPERVISORY COMMITTEE

The Procurator's office exercises supervision over the implementation of the law. The Procurator General is appointed by the President with the consent of the Council of the Republic, and is accountable to the President. The Supervisory Authority monitors the implementation of the national budget and the use of public property. The State Supervisory Committee is formed by the President, who appoints the Chairman.

### APPLICATION OF THE CONSTITUTION AND THE PROCEDURE FOR AMENDING THE CONSTITUTION

The Constitution has supreme legal force. Amendments and supplements to the Constitution are considered by the chambers of the National Assembly on the initiative of the President, or of no fewer than 150,000 citizens of the Republic of Belarus who are eligible to vote. The Constitution may be amended or supplemented via a referendum.

## The Government

### HEAD OF STATE

**President:** ALYAKSANDR R. LUKASHENKA (took office 20 July 1994).

### CABINET OF MINISTERS
(February 2000)

**Chairman:** ULADZIMIR YERMOSHIN (acting).

**First Deputy Chairman:** VASIL DALGALYOU.

**Deputy Chairmen:** ULADZIMIR ZAMYATALIN, VALERY KOKARAU, LEANID KOZIK, ALYAKSANDR PAPKOW.

**Minister of Agriculture and Food:** YURIY D. MOROZ.

**Minister of Architecture and Construction:** GENADZ F. KURACHKIN.

**Minister of Culture:** ALYAKSANDR U. SASNOUSKI.

**Minister of Defence:** Lt-Gen. ALYAKSANDR CHUMAKOU.

**Minister of the Economy:** ULADZIMIR SHYMAU.

**Minister of Education:** VASIL I. STRAZHAU.

**Minister for Emergency Situations:** VALERY P. ASTAPOU.

**Minister of Entrepreneurship and Investments:** ALYAKSANDR YU. SASONAU.

**Minister of Finance:** MIKALAI P. KORBUT.

**Minister of Foreign Affairs:** Prof. URAL LATYPAW.

**Minister of Forestry:** VALYANTSIN P. ZORYN.

**Minister of Fuel and Energy:** VALYANTSIN V. GERASIMAU.

**Minister of Health Care:** IGAR ZELYANKEVICH.

**Minister of Housing and Municipal Services:** BARYS V. BATURA.

**Minister of Industry:** ANATOL KHARLAP.

**Minister of Internal Affairs:** YURIY SIVAKOW.

**Minister of Justice:** GENADZ VARANTSOU.

**Minister of Labour:** IVAN LYAKH.

**Minister for Natural Resources and Environmental Protection:** MIKHAIL I. RUSY.

**Minister of Telecommunications and Information:** MIKALAI KRUKOUSKI.

**Minister for Social Protection:** OLGA B. DARGEL.

**Minister of Sports and Tourism:** YAWHEN N. VORSIN.

**Minister of State Property Management and Privatization:** VASIL A. NOVAK.

**Minister of Statistics and Analysis:** VLADIMIR I. ZINOVSKY.

**Minister of Trade:** PYOTR A. KAZLOU.

**Minister of Transport and Communications:** ALYAKSANDR LUKASHOU.

**Presidential Administrator of Affairs:** ULADZIMIR I. GANCHARENKA.

### Chairmen of State Committees

**Chairman of the State Security Committee:** ULADZIMIR MATSKEVICH.

**Chairman of the State Committee for the Press:** ZINOVI PRYGODZICH (acting).

**Chairman of the State Committee for Aviation:** RYGOR FYODARAW.

**Chairman of the State Committee for Youth Affairs:** ALYAKSANDR PAZNYAK.

**Chairman of the State Customs Committee:** VIKENTSI MAKAREVICH (acting).

**Chairman of the State Taxation Committee:** MIKALAY DZYAMCHUK.

**Chairman of the State Committee for Border Troops:** ALYAKSANDR PAWLOUWKI.

**Chairman of the State Committee for Land Resources, Geodesy and Cartography:** GEORGIY KUZNYATSOW.

**Chairman of the State Committee for Energy and Energy Supervision:** LEW DUBOVIK.

**Chairman of the State Committee for Archives and Records:** ALYAKSANDR MIKHALCHANKA.

**Chairman of the State Patents Committee:** VALERY KUDASHOW.

**Chairman of the State Committee for Standardization, Metrology and Certification:** VALERY KARASHKOW.

**Chairman of the State Committee for Hydrometeorology:** YURY PAKUMEYKA.

**Chairman of the State Higher Appraisal Committee:** ANATOL DASTANKA.

**Chairman of the State Committee for Science and Technology:** VIKTAR GAYSYONAK.

**Chairman of the State Committee for Religious and Ethnic Affairs:** ALYAKSANDR BELYK.

**Chairman of the State Control Committee:** MIKALAY DAMASHKEVICH.

**Chairman of the State Committee for Material Resources:** ULADZIMIR I. YARMOLIK.

## MINISTRIES AND STATE COMMITTEES

### Ministries

**Cabinet of Ministers of the Republic of Belarus:** 220010 Minsk, pl. Nezalezhnasti, Dom Urada; tel. (17) 222-69-05; fax (17) 222-66-65; e-mail contact@udsm.belpak.minsk.by; internet www.president.gov.by.

**Ministry of Agriculture and Food:** 220050 Minsk, vul. Kirava 15; tel. (17) 227-37-51; fax (17) 227-43-88.

**Ministry of Architecture and Construction:** 220048 Minsk, vul. Myasnikova 39; tel. (17) 227-26-42; fax (17) 220-74-24.

**Ministry of Culture:** 220600 Minsk, pr. Masherava 11; tel. (17) 223-75-74; fax (17) 223-85-15.

**Ministry of Defence:** 220003 Minsk, vul. Kamunistychnaya 1; tel. (17) 239-23-79; fax (17) 227-35-64.

**Ministry of the Economy:** 220050 Minsk, vul. Stankevicha 14; tel. (17) 222-60-48; fax (17) 222-63-35.

**Ministry of Education:** 220010 Minsk, vul. Savetskaya 9; tel. (17) 227-47-36; fax (17) 227-17-36; e-mail root@minedu.unibel.by.

**Ministry for Emergency Situations:** 220030 Minsk, vul. Lenina 14; tel. (17) 227-58-63; fax (17) 229-34-39.

**Ministry of Entrepreneurship and Investments:** 220050 Minsk, vul. Myasnikova 39; tel. (17) 220-16-23; fax (17) 227-22-40.

**Ministry of Finance:** 220010 Minsk, vul. Savetskaya 7; tel. (17) 2222-61-37; fax (17) 220-21-72; e-mail mofb@office.un.minsk.by.

**Ministry of Foreign Affairs:** 220030 Minsk, vul. Lenina 19; tel. (17) 227-29-22; fax (17) 227-45-21.

**Ministry of Forestry:** 220039 Minsk, vul. Chkalova 6; tel. (17) 224-47-05; fax (17) 224-41-83.

**Ministry of Fuel and Energy:** 220050 Minsk, vul. K. Marksa 14; tel. (17) 229-83-59; fax (17) 229-84-68.

**Ministry of Health Care:** 220010 Minsk, vul. Myasnikova 39; tel. (17) 222-60-95; fax (17) 222-62-97.

**Ministry of Housing and Municipal Services:** 220640 Minsk, vul. Bersana 16; tel. (17) 220-15-45; fax (17) 220-38-94.

**Ministry of Industry:** 220033 Minsk, pr. Partizanski 2-4; tel. (17) 224-95-95; fax (17) 224-87-84.

**Ministry of Internal Affairs:** 220615 Minsk, Gorodskoy Val 4; tel. (17) 229-78-08; fax (17) 223-99-18.

**Ministry of Justice:** 220048 Minsk, vul. Kalektarnaya 10; tel. and fax (17) 220-97-55.

**Ministry of Labour:** 220004 Minsk, pr. Masherava 23/2; tel. (17) 223-11-71; fax (17) 223-45-21.

**Ministry for Natural Resources and Environmental Protection:** 220048 Minsk, vul. Kalektarnaya 10; tel. (17) 220-66-91; fax (17) 220-55-83; e-mail minproos@minproos.belpak.minsk.by.

**Ministry for Social Protection:** 220010 Minsk, vul. Savetskaya 9; tel. (17) 222-69-90; fax (17) 222-62-55.

**Ministry of Sports and Tourism:** 220600 Minsk, vul. Kirava 8-2; tel. (17) 227-72-37; fax (17) 227-76-22.

**Ministry of State Property Management and Privatization:** 220050 Minsk, vul. Myasnikova 39; tel. (17) 276-81-78; fax (17) 220-65-47.

**Ministry of Statistics and Analysis:** 220070 Minsk, pr. Partizanski 12; tel. (17) 249-52-00; fax (17) 249-22-04; e-mail esis@stat.belpak.minsk.by; internet www.president.gov.by/Minstat/en/main.html.

**Ministry of Telecommunications and Information:** 220050 Minsk, pr. F. Skaryny 10; tel. (17) 227-38-61; fax (17) 226-08-48.

**Ministry of Trade:** 220050 Minsk, vul. Kirava 8, kor. 1; tel. (17) 227-08-97; fax (17) 227-24-80.

**Ministry of Transport and Communications:** 220030 Minsk, vul. Lenina 17; tel. (17) 234-11-52; fax (17) 232-83-91.

### State Committees

All State Committees are in Minsk.

**State Customs Committee:** 220029 Minsk, vul. Kamunistychnaya 11; tel. (17) 233-23-16; fax (17) 234-68-93.

**State Security Committee:** 220050 Minsk, pr. F. Skaryny 17; tel. (17) 229-94-01; fax (17) 226-00-38.

**State Committee for Religious and Ethnic Affairs:** 220029 Minsk, vul. Kamunistychnaya 11A; tel. and fax (17) 284-89-65; internet www.lingoo.minsk.by/kamitet/.

# President and Legislature

## PRESIDENT

**Presidential Election, First Ballot, 23 June 1994**

| Candidates | Votes | % |
|---|---|---|
| ALYAKSANDR LUKASHENKA | 2,646,140 | 47.10 |
| VYACHESLAU KEBICH | 1,023,174 | 18.21 |
| ZYANON PAZNYAK | 757,195 | 13.48 |
| STANISLAU SHUSHKEVICH | 585,143 | 10.42 |
| ALYAKSANDR DUBKO | 353,119 | 6.29 |
| VASIL NOVIKAU | 253,009 | 4.50 |
| **Total** | 5,617,780 | 100.00 |

**Second Ballot, 10 July 1994** (preliminary result)

| Candidates | Votes | % |
|---|---|---|
| ALYAKSANDR LUKASHENKA | 4,219,991 | 84.95 |
| VYACHESLAU KEBICH | 747,793 | 15.05 |
| **Total** | 4,967,784 | 100.00 |

## NATIONAL ASSEMBLY*

### Council of the Republic

**Chairman:** PAVEL SHYPUK.

**Deputy Chairman:** (vacant).

The Council of the Republic is the upper chamber of the legislature and comprises 64 deputies. Of the total, 56 deputies are elected by regional councils and eight deputies are appointed by the President.

### House of Representatives

**Chairman:** ANATOL MALAFEYEU.

**Deputy Chairman:** ULADZIMIR KANAPLYOW.

The House of Representatives is the lower chamber of the legislature and comprises 110 deputies elected by universal, equal, free, direct electoral suffrage and by secret ballot.

* The National Assembly was formed following a referendum held on 24 November 1996. Deputies who had been elected to the Supreme Council at the general election held in late 1995 were invited to participate in the new legislative body. However, many deputies regarded the new National Assembly as unconstitutional and declared themselves to be the legitimate legislature. A form of 'shadow' cabinet, the Public Coalition Government—National Economic Council, chaired by Genadz Karpenka, was established in January 1997 by opposition deputies. Following Karpenka's death in April 1999, the chairmanship of the Council was assumed, in an acting capacity, by Mechislau Gryb (he was officially elected to the post in November). International organizations continued to urge President Lukashenka to recognize the legitimacy of the Supreme Council.

# Political Organizations

Following the Government's imposition of stringent measures for re-registration in January 1999, in September of that year there were only 17 political parties officially registered with the Ministry of Justice (28 had previously been registered).

**Agrarian Party (AP)** (Agrarnaya Partya): 220050 Minsk, vul. Kazintsa 86-2; tel. (17) 220-38-29; fax (17) 249-50-18; f. 1992; Leader SYAMYON SHARETSKI.

**Belarusian Christian-Democratic Party** (Belaruskaya Khrystsiyanska-Demakratychnaya Partya): Minsk, vul. Bagdanovicha 7A; f. 1994; Leader MIKALAI KRUKOUSKI.

**Belarusian Christian-Democratic Union** (Belaruskaya Khrystsiyanska-Demakratychnaya Zluchnasts): 220065 Minsk, vul. Avakyana 38-59; tel. and fax (17) 229-67-56; f. 1991; nationalist, reformist; Leader PETR SILKO.

**Belarusian Ecological Green Party:** Minsk; f. 1998 by the merger of the Belarusian Ecological Party and the Green Party of Belarus.

**Belarusian Greenpeace Party** (Belaruskaya Partya Zyaleny Mir): 246023 Gomel, vul. Brestskaya 6; tel. (232) 47-08-08; fax (232) 47-96-96; f. 1994; Leaders OLEG GROMYKA, NICK LEKUNOVICH.

**Belarusian National Party** (Belaruskaya Natsiyanalnaya Partya): 220094 Minsk, vul. Plekhanava 32-198; tel. (17) 227-43-76; f. 1994; Leader ANATOL ASTAPENKA.

**Belarusian Party of Labour** (Belaruskaya Partya Pratsy): Minsk, vul. Kazintsa 21-3; tel. (17) 223-82-04; fax (17) 223-97-92; e-mail acmbel@glas.apc.org; f. 1993; Leader ALYAKSANDR BUKHVOSTAU.

**Belarusian Party of Women 'Hope'** (Belaruskaya Partya Zhanchyn 'Nadzeya'): 220099 Minsk, vul. Kazintsa 21-3; f. 1994; Leader VALENTINA PALEVIKOVA.

**Belarusian Patriotic Party** (Belaruskaya Patryatychnaya Partya): 220050 Minsk, vul. Myasnikova 38; tel. (17) 220-27-57; f. 1994; Leader ANATOL BARANKEVICH.

**Belarusian Peasant Party** (Belaruskaya Syalyanskaya Partya): 220068 Minsk, vul. Gaya 38-1; tel. (17) 277-19-05; fax (17) 277-96-51; f. 1991; advocates agricultural reforms; 7,000 mems; Leader YAUGEN M. LUGIN.

**Belarusian People's Patriotic Union:** Minsk; f. 1998; a pro-Lukashenka alliance supportive of further integration with Russia, comprising 30 left-wing and centrist organizations, incl. the CPB, the Belarusian Patriotic Party, the Liberal Democratic Party of Belarus, the White Rus Slavonic Council and the Union of Reserve Officers; Exec. Sec. VIKTAR CHYKIN.

**Belarusian Popular Party** (Belaruskaya Narodnaya Partya): 220050 Minsk, vul. K. Marksa 18; tel. (17) 227-89-52; fax (17) 227-13-30; e-mail imi@imibel.belpak.minsk.by; f. 1994; Leader VIKTAR TERESCHENKO.

**Belarusian Republican Party** (Belaruskaya Respublikanskaya Partya): 220100 Minsk, vul. Kulman 13-71; tel. (17) 234-07-49; f. 1994; Leaders VALERY ARTYSHEUSKI, ULADZIMIR RAMANAU.

**Belarusian Social Democratic Assembly** (Belaruskaya Satsyal-demakratychnaya Hramada): 220017 Minsk, pr. Partizanski 28-2-322; tel. (17) 226-74-37; f. 1998; Leader STANISLAU SHUSHKEVICH.

**Belarusian Social Democratic Party (National Assembly)** (Belaruskaya Satsyal-demakratychnaya Partya (Narodnaya Hramada): 220114 Minsk, pr. F. Skaryny 153-2-107; tel. and fax (17) 263-37-48; e-mail bsdp@infonet.by; f. 1903, re-established 1991; merged with Party of People's Accord (f. 1992) in 1996; centrist; Leader MIKALAI STATKEVICH; c. 2,500 mems.

**Belarusian Socialist Party** (Belaruskaya Satsyalistychnaya Partya): Minsk, pr. F. Skaryny 25; tel. (17) 229-37-38; f. 1994; aims for a civilized society, where rights and freedoms are guaranteed for all; Leader MICHAIL PADGAINY.

**Belarusian Social-Sports Party** (Belaruskaya Satsyalna-Spartyunaya Partya): 220000 Minsk, pr. Partizanski 89A; tel. (17) 226-93-15; f. 1994; Leader ULADZIMIR ALYAKSANDROVICH.

**Christian-Democratic Choice** (Khrystsiyanska-Demakratychny Vybar): 220050 Minsk, vul. Leningradskaya 3-1; tel. (17) 220-17-67; f. 1995; Leader VALERY SAROKA.

**Communist Party of Belarus (CPB)** (Kamunistychnaya Partya Belarusi): 220007 Minsk, vul. Varanyanskaga 52; tel. (17) 226-64-22; fax (17) 232-31-23; Leader VIKTAR CHYKIN.

**Liberal Democratic Party of Belarus** (Liberalna-Demakratychnaya Partya Belarusi): 220056 Minsk, vul. Platonava 22, 12th Floor; tel. and fax (17) 231-63-31; e-mail tsar@-mail.ru; f. 1994; advocates continued independence of Belarus, increased co-operation with other European countries and expansion of the private sector; Leader SYARGEY GAYDUKEVICH; 28,943 mems (1999).

**National Democratic Party of Belarus** (Natsyanalna-Demakratychnaya Partya Belarusi): Minsk, vul. Labanka 97-140 ; tel. (17) 271-95-16; fax (17) 236-99-72; f. 1990; Leader VIKTAR NAVUMENKA.

**Party of Belarusian Popular Front (BPF)** (Partya Belaruskaga Narodnaga Frontu): 220005 Minsk, vul. Varvasheni 8; tel. (17) 231-48-93; fax (17) 239-58-69; f. 1988; anti-communist movement campaigning for democracy, genuine independence for Belarus and national and cultural revival; Chair. VINTSUK VYACHORKA; Exec. Sec. ANATOL KRYVAROT.

**Conservative Christian Party of the BPF:** Minsk; f. 1999 as a breakaway faction of the BPF; Chair. ZYANON PAZNYAK; Dep. Chair. MIKALAI ANTSIPOVICH, YURIY BELENKI, SYARGEY PAPKOW, ULADZIMIR STARCHANKA.

**Party of Common Sense** (Partya Zdarovaga Sensu): 220094 Minsk, pr. Rakasouskaga 37-40; tel. (17) 247-08-68; f. 1994; Leader IVAN KARAVAYCHYK.

**Party of Communists of Belarus** (Partya Kamunistau Belaruskaya): 220013 Minsk, vul. Y. Kolas 10-8; tel. (17) 232-25-73; fax (17) 231-80-36; f. 1991; Leader SERGEY KALYAKIN.

**Republican Party** (Respublikanskaya Partya): 220000 Minsk, vul. Pershamayskaya 18; tel. (17) 236-50-71; fax (17) 236-32-14; f. 1994; aims to build a neutral, independent Belarus; Leader ULADZIMIR BELAZOR.

**Republican Party of Labour and Justice** (Respublikanskaya Partya Pratsy i Spravyadlivasti): 220004 Minsk, vul. Amuratarskaya 7; tel. (17) 223-93-21; fax (17) 223-86-41; f. 1993; Leader ANATOL NYATYLKIN.

**Social-Democratic Party of Popular Accord** (Satsiyal-Demakratychnaya Partya Narodnay Zgody): 220050 Minsk, vul. K. Marksa 10; tel. (17) 248-02-21; f. 1997; Leader LEANID SECHKA.

**United Civic Party of Belarus** (Abyadnanaya Hramadzyanskaya Partya Belarusi): 220033 Minsk, vul. Sudmalisa 10-4; tel. (17) 229-08-34; fax (17) 227-29-12; e-mail ucp@ucp.minsk.by; f. 1990; liberal-conservative; Chair. STANISLAU A. BAHDANKEVICH; Dep. Chair. ALYAKSANDR A. DABRAVOLSKI, VASILY SHLYNDZIKAV, ANATOL U. LIABEDZKA.

**White Rus Slavonic Council** (Slavyanski Sabor 'Belaya Rus'): 220088 Minsk, vul. Pershamayskaya 24-1-80; tel. (17) 239-52-32; fax (17) 270-09-28; f. 1992; Leader MIKALAY SYARGEEU.

# Diplomatic Representation

### EMBASSIES IN BELARUS

**Armenia:** 220050 Minsk, vul. Kirava 17; tel. and fax (17) 227-51-53; Ambassador: SUREN HARUTYUNIAN.

**Bulgaria:** 220034 Minsk, Branyavy per. 5; tel. (17) 227-55-02; fax (17) 236-56-61; Chargé d'affaires a.i.: VASIL PETKOV.

**China, People's Republic:** 220071 Minsk, vul. Berestyanskaya 22; tel. (17) 285-36-82; fax (17) 285-36-81; Ambassador: WU XIAOQUI.

**Cuba:** 220050 Minsk, pr. Skaryny 11, Hotel Minsk, Room 389; tel. (17) 220-03-83; fax (17) 220-23-45; Chargé d'affaires a.i.: JOSÉ FERNÁNDEZ.

**Czech Republic:** 220034 Minsk, Branyavy per. 5A; tel. (17) 226-52-43; fax (17) 211-01-37; Chargé d'affaires a.i.: ALES FOJTIK.

**France:** 220030 Minsk, pl. Svabody 11; tel. (17) 210-28-68; fax (17) 210-25-48; Ambassador: BERNARD FASSIER.

**Germany:** 220034 Minsk, vul. Zakharava 26B; tel. (17) 213-37-52; fax (17) 236-85-52; Ambassador: HORST WINKELMANN.

**Greece:** 220030 Minsk, vul. Engelsa 13, Hotel Oktyabrskaya, Room 515; tel. (17) 227-27-60; fax (17) 226-08-05; Ambassador: PANAYOTIS GOUMAS.

**Holy See:** Minsk, vul. Volodarsky 6, 3rd Floor; tel. (17) 289-15-84; fax (17) 289-15-17; Apostolic Nuncio: Most Rev. HRUŠOVSKÝ DOMINIK, Titular Archbishop of Tubia.

**India:** 220090 Minsk, vul. Kaltsova 4, kor. 5; tel. (17) 262-93-99; fax (17) 262-97-99; e-mail ambsdr@indemb.minsk.by; Ambassador: MADHU BHADURI.

**Israel:** 220033 Minsk, pr. Partizanski 6A; tel. (17) 230-44-44; fax (17) 210-52-70; Ambassador: MARTIN PELED-FLAX.

**Italy:** 220030 Minsk, vul. K. Marska 37, Hotel Belarus; tel. (17) 229-29-69; fax (17) 234-30-46; Ambassador: GIOVANNI CERUTI.

**Japan:** 220030 Minsk, vul. Engelsa 13, Hotel Oktyabrskaya, Room 303; tel. (17) 223-60-37; fax (17) 210-41-80; Chargé d'affaires a.i.: NAOTAKE YAMASHITA.

**Kazakhstan:** 220029 Minsk, vul. Kuibysheva 12; tel. (17) 213-30-26; fax (17) 234-96-50; Ambassador: VLADIMIR ALESIN.

**Kyrgyzstan:** 220002 Minsk, vul. Staravilenskaya 57; tel. (17) 234-91-17; fax (17) 234-16-02; e-mail manas@nsys.minsk.by; Chargé d'affaires a.i.: BUBUIRA ABDYJAPAROVA.

**Latvia:** 220013 Minsk, vul. Doroshevicha 6A; tel. (17) 284-93-93; fax (17) 284-73-34; Chargé d'affaires a.i.: INGRĪDA LEVRENCE.

**Lithuania:** 220029 Minsk, vul. Varvasheni 17; tel. (17) 234-77-84; fax (17) 289-34-71; Ambassador: JONAS PASLAUKAS.

**Moldova:** 220030 Minsk, vul. Belaruskaya 2; tel. (17) 289-14-41; fax (17) 289-11-47; Ambassador: NIKOLAE DUDAU.

**Peru:** 220082 Minsk, vul. Pritytskogo 34; tel.(17) 216-91-14; fax (17) 283-28-62.

**Poland:** 220034 Minsk, vul. Rumyantsava 6; tel. (17) 213-43-13; fax (17) 236-49-92; Ambassador: MARIUSZ MASZKIEWICZ.

**Romania:** 220035 Minsk, per. Moskvina 4; tel. (17) 223-77-26; fax (17) 210-40-85; Chargé d'affaires a.i.: LEONTIN PASTOR.

**Russia:** 220002 Minsk, vul. Staravilenskaya 48; tel. (17) 234-54-97; fax (17) 250-36-64; Ambassador: VYACHESLAV DOLGOV.

**Tajikistan:** 220050 Minsk, vul. Kirava 17; tel. (17) 222-37-98; fax (17) 227-76-13; Chargé d'affaires: OLIM RAKHIMOV.

**Turkey:** 220050 Minsk, vul. Volodarsky 6, 4th Floor; tel. (17) 227-13-83; fax (17) 227-27-46; e-mail dtmin@comco.belpak.minsk.by; Ambassador: SULE SOYSAL.

**Turkmenistan:** 220050 Minsk, vul. Kirava 17; tel. (17) 222-34-27; fax (17) 222-33-67; Ambassador: ILYA VELDJANOV.

**Ukraine:** 220050 Minsk, vul. Kirava 17; tel. (17) 227-23-54; fax (17) 227-28-61; e-mail postmaster@am.minsk.mfa.ua; Ambassador: ANATOLIY DRON.

**United Kingdom:** 220030 Minsk, vul. K. Marksa 37; tel. (17) 210-59-20; fax (17) 229-23-06; e-mail pia@bepost.belpak.minsk.by; Ambassador: IAIN KELLY.

**USA:** 220002 Minsk, vul. Staravilenskaya 46; tel. (17) 210-12-83; fax (17) 234-78-53; Ambassador: DANIEL V. SPECKHARD.

**Yugoslavia:** 220012 Minsk, vul. Surganova 28A; tel. (17) 239-90-90; fax (17) 232-51-54; Ambassador: NIKOLA PEJAKOVICH.

# Judicial System

In May 1999 there were 154 courts in Belarus, employing some 200 judges.

**Supreme Court:** 220030 Minsk, vul. Lenina 28; tel. (17) 226-12-06; fax (17) 227-12-25; Chair. VALENTIN SUKALO.

**Supreme Economic Court:** 22050 Minsk, vul. Valadarskaga 8; tel. and fax (17) 227-16-41; Chair ULADZIMIR BOYKA.

**Procuracy:** 220050 Minsk, vul. Internatsionalnaya 22; tel. (17) 226-41-66; Procurator General ALEG BAZHELKA.

**Constitutional Court:** Minsk, vul. K. Marksa 32; tel. and fax (17) 227-80-12; e-mail ksrb@user.unibel.by; 12 mem. judges; Chair. RYHOR VASILEVICH: Dep. Chair. ALYAKSANDR MARYSKIN.

# Religion

**State Committee for Religious and Ethnic Affairs:** see section on The Government.

### CHRISTIANITY

The major denomination is the Eastern Orthodox Church, but there are also an estimated 1.1m. adherents of the Roman Catholic Church. Of these, some 25% are ethnic Poles and there is a significant number of Uniates or 'Greek Catholics'. There is also a growing number of Baptist churches.

#### The Eastern Orthodox Church

In 1990 Belarus was designated an exarchate of the Russian Orthodox Church, thus creating the Belarusian Orthodox Church.

**Belarusian Orthodox Church:** 220004 Minsk, vul. Osvobozhdeniya 10; tel. (17) 223-44-95; Patriarch and Exarch of All Belarus FILARET.

#### The Roman Catholic Church

Although five Roman Catholic dioceses, embracing 455 parishes, had officially existed since the Second World War, none of them had a bishop. In 1989 a major reorganization of the structure of the Roman Catholic Church in Belarus took place. The dioceses of Minsk and Mogilev (Mahilou) were merged, to create an archdiocese, and two new dioceses were formed, in Grodno (Horadnia) and Pinsk. The Eastern-rite, or Uniate, Church was abolished in Belarus in 1839, but was re-established in the early 1990s. At 31 December 1997 the Roman Catholic Church had an estimated 1.1m. adherents in Belarus.

*Latin Rite*

**Archdiocese of Minsk and Mogilev:** 220030 Minsk, pl. Svabody 9; tel. (17) 226-61-27; fax (17) 226-90-92; Archbishop: Cardinal KAZIMIERZ SWIATEK.

*Byzantine Rite*

**Belarusian Greek Catholic (Uniate) Church:** 220030 Minsk, vul. Hertsena 1.

#### Protestant Churches

**Union of Evangelical Christian Baptists of Belarus:** 220093 Minsk, POB 108; tel. (17) 253-92-67; fax (17) 253-82-49.

### ISLAM

There are small communities of Azeris and Tatars, who are adherents of Islam. In 1994 the supreme administration of Muslims in Belarus, which had been abolished in 1939, was reconstituted. In mid-1998 there were some 4,000 Muslims and four mosques.

**Muslim Society:** 220004 Minsk, vul. Zaslavskaya 11, kor. 1, kv. 113; tel. (17) 226-86-43; f. 1991; Chair. ALI HALIMBERK.

### JUDAISM

Before Belarus was occupied by Nazi German forces, in 1941–44, there was a large Jewish community, notably in Minsk. There were some 142,000 Jews at the census of 1989, but many have since emigrated.

**Jewish Religious Society:** 220030 Minsk, pr. F. Skaryny 44A.

# The Press

In October 1998 there were a total of 1,001 registered periodicals in Belarus, of which 116 were in Belarusian and 295 in Russian, and 447 were in both Belarusian and Russian. Most daily newspapers are government-owned.

### PRINCIPAL DAILIES

In Russian, except where otherwise stated.

**Belorusskaya Niva** (Belarusian Cornfield): 220013 Minsk, vul. B. Hmyalnitskaga 10A; tel. (17) 268-26-20; fax (17) 268-26-43; f. 1921; 5 a week; organ of the Cabinet of Ministers; in Belarusian and Russian; Editor E. SEMASHKO; circ. 80,000 (1998).

**Narodnaya Hazeta** (The People's Newspaper): 220013 Minsk, vul. B. Hmyalnitskaga 10A; tel. (17) 268-28-75; fax (17) 268-26-24; f. 1990; 5–6 a week; in Belarusian and Russian; Editor-in-Chief M. SHIMANSKIY; circ. 180,000 (1998).

**Respublika** (Republic): 220013 Minsk, vul. B. Hmyalnitskaga 10A; tel. (17) 268-26-12; fax (17) 268-26-15; organ of the Cabinet of Ministers; 5 a week; in Belarusian and Russian; Editor SERGEY DUBOVIK; circ. 130,000 (1998).

**Sovetskaya Belorussiya** (Soviet Belorussia): 220013, Minsk, vul. B. Hmyalnitskaga 10A; tel. (17) 232-14-32; fax (17) 232-14-51; 5 a week; organ of the Cabinet of Ministers; Editor-in-Chief PAVEL YAKUBOVICH; circ. 330,000 (1998).

**Vechernii Minsk** (Evening Minsk): 220805 Minsk, pr. F. Skaryny 44; tel. (17) 213-30-54; fax (17) 276-80-05; e-mail omp@nsys.minsk.by; internet www.belarus.net/minsk-evl; Editor S. SVERKUNOU; circ. 111,000 (1998).

**Znamya Yunosti** (Banner of Youth): 220013 Minsk, vul. B. Hmyalnitskaga 10A; tel. (17) 268-26-84; fax (17) 232-24-96; f. 1938; 5 a week; organ of the Cabinet of Ministers; Editor-in-Chief ELENA PHILIPTCHIK; circ. 30,000 (1998).

**Zvyazda** (Star): 220013 Minsk, vul. B. Hmyalnitskaga 10A; tel. (17) 268-29-19; fax (17) 268-27-79; f. 1917 as *Zvezda*; 5 a week; organ of the Cabinet of Ministers; in Belarusian; Editor ULADZIMIR B. NARKEVICH; circ. 90,000 (1998).

### PRINCIPAL PERIODICALS

In Belarusian, except where otherwise stated.

**Advertisements Weekly;** 220805 Minsk, pr. F. Skaryny 44; tel. and fax (17) 213-45-25; e-mail omp@bm.belpak.minsk.by; Editor T. ANANENKO; circ. 21,500 (1997).

**Alesya:** 220013 Minsk, pr. F. Skaryny 77; tel. (17) 232-20-51; f. 1924; monthly; Editor MARYA KARPENKA; circ. 17,000 (1998).

**Belarus:** 220005 Minsk, vul. Zakharava 19, tel. (17) 284-80-01; f. 1930; monthly; publ. by the State Publishing House; journal of the Union of Writers of Belarus and the Belarusian Society of Friendship and Cultural Links with Foreign Countries; fiction and political essays; in Belarusian and Russian; Editor-in-Chief A. A. SHABALIN.

**Belaruskaya Krinitsa:** 220065 Minsk, vul. Avakyana 38-59; tel. and fax (17) 229-67-56; f. 1991; monthly; journal of the Belarusian Institute of Social Development and Co-operation; Editor-in-Chief MIKHAIL MALKO; circ. 5,000.

**Byarozka** (Birch Tree): 220013 Minsk, pr. F. Skaryny 77; tel. (17) 232-94-66; f. 1924; monthly; fiction; illustrated; for 10–15-year-olds; Editor-in-Chief VL. I. JAGOVDZIK.

**Chyrvonaya Zmena** (Red Rising Generation): 220013 Minsk, vul. B. Hmyalnitskaga 10A; tel. and fax (17) 232-21-03; f. 1921; weekly; Editor A. KARLUKIEVICH.

**Gramadzyanin:** 220033 Minsk, vul. Sudmalisa 10; tel. (17) 229-08-34; fax (17) 272-95-05; publ. by the United Civic Party of Belarus.

**Holas Radzimy** (Voice of the Motherland): 220005 Minsk, pr. F. Skaryny 44; tel. (17) 213-37-82; f. 1955; weekly; articles of interest to Belarusians in other countries; Editor-in-Chief (vacant).

**Krynitsa** (Spring): 220807 Minsk, vul. Kiseleva 11; tel. (17) 236-60-71; f. 1988; monthly; political and literary; in Belarusian and Russian; Editor GALINA BULYKO.

**Litaratura i Mastatstva** (Literature and Art): 220600 Minsk, vul. Zakharava 19; tel. (17) 284-84-61; f. 1932; weekly; publ. by the Ministry of Culture and the Union of Writers of Belarus; Editor ALYAKSANDR PISMENKOV; circ. 5,000 (1998).

**Maladosts** (Youth): 220016 Minsk, vul. B. Hmyalnitskaga 10A; tel. (17) 268-27-54; f. 1953; monthly; journal of the Union of Writers of Belarus; novels, short stories, essays, translations, etc., for young people; Editor-in-Chief G. DALIDOVICH.

**Mastatstva** (Art): 220029 Minsk, vul. Chicherina 1; tel. (17) 276-94-67; fax (17) 276-94-67; monthly; illustrated; Editor-in-Chief ALYAKSEY DUDARAU.

**Narodnaya Asveta** (People's Education): 220023 Minsk, vul. Makaenka 12; tel. (17) 264-62-68; f. 1924; publ. by the Ministry of Education; Editor-in-Chief N. I. KALESNIK.

**Neman** (The River Nieman): 220005 Minsk, pr. F. Skaryny 39; tel. (17) 233-40-72; f. 1945; monthly; publ. by the Polymya (Flame) Publishing House; journal of the Union of Writers of Belarus; fiction; in Russian; Editor-in-Chief A. ZHOUK.

**Polymya** (Flame): 220005 Minsk, vul. Zakharava 19; tel. (17) 284-80-12; f. 1922; monthly; publ. by the Polymya (Flame) Publishing House; journal of the Union of Writers of Belarus; fiction; Editor-in-Chief S. I. ZAKONNIKOU.

**Vozhyk** (Hedgehog): 220013 Minsk, pr. F. Skaryny 77; tel. (17) 232-41-92; f. 1941; fortnightly; satirical; Editor-in-Chief VALYANTSIN V. BOLTACH; circ. 12,000 (1998).

**Vyaselka** (Rainbow): 220004 Minsk, vul. Kalektarnaya 10; tel. (17) 220-92-61; f. 1957; monthly; popular, for 5–10-year-olds; Editor-in-Chief V. S. LIPSKI; circ. 30,000 (1999).

### PRESS ASSOCIATIONS

**Belarusian Journalists' Association:** Minsk; tel. (17) 227-05-58; f. 1995; Pres. ZHANNA LITVINA.

**Belarusian Union of Journalists:** 220005 Minsk, vul. Rumyantsava 3; tel. and fax (17) 236-51-95; 3,000 mems; Pres. L. EKEL.

### NEWS AGENCY

**BelTa** (Belarusian News Agency): 220600 Minsk, vul. Kirava 26; tel. (17) 222-30-40; fax (17) 227-13-46; Dir YAKAU ALAKSEYCHYK.

## Publishers

In 1998 there were 6,073 titles (books and pamphlets) published in Belarus (60m. copies).

**Belarus:** 220600 Minsk, pr. F. Skaryny 79; tel. (17) 223-87-42; fax (17) 223-87-31; f. 1921; social, political, technical, medical and musical literature, fiction, children's, reference books, art reproductions, etc.; Dir MIKALAY KAVALEVSKI; Editor-in-Chief ELENA ZAKONNIKOVA.

**Belaruskaya Entsiklopediya** (Belarusian Encyclopaedia): 220072 Minsk, pr. F. Skaryny 15A; tel. (17) 284-06-00; fax (17) 239-31-44; f. 1967; encyclopaedias, dictionaries, directories and scientific books; Editor-in-Chief G. P. PASHKOV.

**Belaruskaya Navuka** (Science and Technology Publishing House): 220067 Minsk, vul. Zhodinskaya 18; tel. (17) 263-76-18; f. 1924; scientific, technical, reference books, educational literature and fiction in Belarusian and Russian; Dir LUDMILA PIETROVA.

**Belaruski Dom Druku** (Belarusian House of Printing): 220013 Minsk, pr. F. Skaryny 79; tel. (17) 268-27-03; fax (17) 231-67-74; f. 1917; social, political, children's and fiction in Belarusian, Russian and other European languages; Dir BARYS KUTAVY.

**Belblankavyd:** 220035 Minsk, vul. Timirazeva 2; tel. (17) 226-71-22; reference books in Belarusian and Russian; Dir VALENTINA MILOVANOVA.

**Mastatskaya Litaratura** (Art Publishing House): 220600 Minsk, pr. Masherava 11; tel. (17) 223-48-09; f. 1972; fiction in Belarusian and Russian; Dir GEORGE MARCHUK.

**Narodnaya Asveta** (People's Education Publishing House): 220600 Minsk, pr. Masherava 11; tel. and fax (17) 223-61-84; e-mail igpna@asveta.belpak.minsk.by; f. 1951; scientific, educational, reference literature and fiction in Belarusian, Russian and other European languages; Dir IGAR N. LAPTSYONAK.

**Polymya** (Flame Publishing House): 220600 Minsk, pr. Masherava 11; tel. and fax (17) 223-52-85; f. 1950; social, political, scientific, technical, religious, children's and fiction; Dir MIKHAIL A. IVANOVICH.

**Universitetskae** (University Publishing House): 220048 Minsk, pr. Masherava 11; tel. and fax (17) 223-58-51; f. 1967; scientific, educational, art and fiction; Dir ULADZIMIR K. KASKO.

**Uradzhay** (Harvest Publishing House): 220048 Minsk, pr. Masherava 11; tel. (17) 223-64-94; fax (17) 223-80-23; f. 1961; scientific, technical, educational, books and booklets on agriculture; in Belarusian and Russian; Dir YAUGEN MALASHEVICH.

**Vysheyshaya Shkola** (Higher School Publishing House): 220048 Minsk, pr. Masherava 11; tel. and fax (17) 223-54-15; f. 1954; textbooks and science books for higher educational institutions; in Belarusian, Russian and other European languages; Dir ANATOL A. ZHADAN; Editor-in-Chief T. K. MAIBORODA.

**Yunatstva** (Youth Publishing House): 220600 Minsk, pr. Masherava 11; tel. (17) 223-24-30; fax (17) 223-31-16; f. 1981; fiction and children's books; Dir ALYAKSANDR KOMAROVSKY; Vice Dir MIKHAIL POZDNIAKOV.

## Broadcasting and Communications

### BROADCASTING

**National State Television and Radio Company of Belarus:** 220807 Minsk, vul. A. Makayenka 9; tel. (17) 264-75-05; fax (17) 264-81-82; Chair. RYGOR KISEL.

**Belarusian Television:** 220807 Minsk, vul. A. Makayenka 9; tel. (17) 233-45-01; fax (17) 264-81-82; f. 1956; Pres. A. R. SITYLAROU.

**Belarusian Radio:** 220807 Minsk, vul. Chyrvonaya 4; tel. (17) 233-39-22; fax (17) 236-66-43; Gen. Dir A. S. ULASENKA.

### Television

**Television Broadcasting Network (TBN):** 220072 Minsk, pr. F. Skaryny 15a; tel. and fax (17) 239-41-71; e-mail mmc@glas.apc.org; comprises 12 private television cos in Belarus's largest cities.

**Minsk Television Company:** Minsk; private; broadcasts to CIS, western Europe and North America.

A second national television channel, BT-2, was to be established in 1997. It was to use networks currently used by Russian Public Television (ORT) and was expected to commence broadcasting by 2000.

## Finance

(cap. = capital; dep. = deposits; res = reserves; m. = million; brs = branches; amounts in new Belarusian roubles)

### BANKING

After Belarus gained its independence, the Soviet-style banking system was restructured and a two-tier system was introduced. In November 1998 there were 26 universal commercial banks operating in Belarus.

### Central Bank

**National Bank of Belarus:** 220008 Minsk, pr. F. Skaryny 20; tel. (17) 227-64-31; fax (17) 227-48-79; e-mail nbrb@nbrb.belpak .minsk.by; f. 1990; cap. 1,000,000m., res 5,517,686m., dep. 18,185,469m. (Dec. 1997); Chair. PYOTR PRAKAPOVICH; 6 brs.

### Commercial Banks

**Absolutbank:** 220023 Minsk, pr. F. Skaryny 115; tel. (17) 263-24-43; fax (17) 264-60-43; f. 1993; cap. 39,234m. (Dec. 1997); Chair. DANIIL P. SVIRID; 1 br.

**Bank for Foreign Economic Affairs (Belvneshekonombank—BVEB):** 220050 Minsk, vul. Myasnikova 32; tel. (17) 226-59-09; fax (17) 226-48-09; e-mail chernik@bveb.belpak.minsk.by; f. 1991; cap. 401,351m., res 197,353m., dep. 7,764,240m. (Dec. 1997); Chair. GEORGIY YEGOROV; 23 brs.

**Bank Poisk:** 220090 Minsk, vul. Gamarnik 9/4; tel. (17) 228-32-49; fax (17) 228-32-48; f. 1974 (as a regional branch of Gosbank of the USSR); renamed Housing and Communal Bank (Zhilsotsbank) in 1989; present name adopted in 1992; cap. 171,820m., res 323,590m., dep. 3,896,172m. (Dec. 1998); Chair. TIMOFEL DVOSKIN; 17 brs.

**Belarusbank:** 220050 Minsk, vul. Myasnikova 32; tel. (17) 220-18-31; fax (17) 223-91-00; e-mail info@belarusbank.minsk.by; internet www.belarusbank.minsk.by; f. 1995 following merger with Sberbank (Savings Bank; f. 1926); cap. 786,018m. res 1,299,329m., dep. 105,195,823m. (Dec. 1998); Chair. NADEZHDA A. YERMAKOVA; 178 brs.

**Belaruski Bank Razvitiya:** 220004 Minsk, vul. Melnikaite 2; tel. (17) 226-09-59; fax (17) 220-98-20; e-mail bbr@belinv.minsk.by; f. 1993; cap. 1,071,334m., dep. US $2.3m. (Jan. 1999); Chair. ALYAKSANDR Y. RUTKOVSKY; 6 brs.

**Belaruski Birzhevoy Bank:** 220013 Minsk, vul. Surganova 48A; tel. (17) 232-47-86; fax (17) 232-67-00; e-mail kuzar@exchbank.org.by; f. 1992; cap. 50,568m. (Dec. 1997); Chair. ANDREY L. MARKOVSKY; 7 brs.

**Belaruski Narodnyi Bank:** 220004 Minsk, vul. Tankovaya 1; tel. and fax (17) 223-84-57; f. 1992; cap. 69,937m. (Dec. 1997); Chair. ANDREY S. TARATUKHIN; 1 br.

**Belbaltia:** 220050 Minsk, Privokzalnaya pl., Express Hotel, 8th Floor; tel. (17) 226-58-88; fax (17) 226-49-18; f. 1994; cap. 32,821.2m. (Dec. 1997); Chair. DMITRIY V. OMELYANOVICH; 1 br.

**Belcombank:** 220007 Minsk, vul. Mogilevskaya 43; tel. (17) 229-25-28; fax (17) 229-21-94; e-mail bkb780@iname.com; f. 1991; cap. 78,265.5m. (Dec. 1997); Chair. ALYAKSANDR E. KIRNOZHITSKY; 14 brs.

**Belgazprombank:** 220121 Minsk, vul. Pritytskiy 60/2; tel. (17) 259-40-24; fax (17) 259-45-25; e-mail olmpbank@olimp2.belpak.minsk.by; f. 1990; cap. 160,393m., res 37,031m., dep. 7,724,396m. (Nov. 1999); Chair. ALEKSEY M. ZADOIKO; 5 brs.

**Belkoopbank:** 220121 Minsk, pr. Masherava 17; tel. (17) 226-96-96; fax (17) 226-97-93; f. 1992; cap. 50,741.8m. (Dec. 1997); Chair. LIDIYA A. NIKITENKO; 12 brs.

**Djembank:** 220012 Minsk, vul. Surganava 28; tel. (17) 268-81-15; fax (17) 268-81-90; e-mail main@djem.com.by; internet www.djem .com.by; f. 1991; cap. 132,723m., res. 3,448m., dep. 909,680m. (Dec. 1998); Pres. ALYAKSANDR V. TATARINTSEV.

**Infobank:** 220035 Minsk, vul. Ignatenka 11; tel. and fax (17) 253-43-88; e-mail infobk.belpak.minsk.by; f. 1994; cap. 82,875m. (Dec. 1997); Chair. ALYAKSANDR D. OSMOLOVSKIY; 3 brs.

**Joint-Stock Commercial Agricultural and Industrial Bank (Belagroprombank):** 220073 Minsk, vul. Olshevskaga 24; tel. (17) 228-50-01; fax (17) 228-53-19; e-mail frk@agrbank2.belpak .minsk.by; f. 1991; cap. 122,777.3m., res 1,978,070.8m., dep. 19,424,020.2m. (Dec. 1998); Chair. ALYAKSANDR GAVRUSHEV; 132 brs.

**Joint-Stock Commercial Bank for Industry and Construction (Belpromstroibank):** 220678 Minsk, pr. Lunacharskaga 6; tel. (17) 213-39-93; fax (17) 231-44-76; e-mail teletype@belpsb.minsk.by; internet www.belpsb.minsk.by; f. 1991; provides credit to enterprises undergoing privatization and conversion to civil production; cap. 95,911m., res. 1,142,275.6m., dep. 9,812,427.1m. (Dec. 1997); Chair. NIKOLAY YA. RAKOV; 60 brs.

**Joint-Stock Commercial Bank for Reconstruction and Development (Belbiznesbank):** 220002 Minsk, vul. Varvasheni 81; tel. (17) 289-35-42; fax (17) 289-35-46; e-mail root@bbb.belpak.minsk.by; f. 1992; cap. 218,855m., res 766,564m., dep. 13,319,330m. (Dec. 1998); Chair. KAZIMIR V. TURUTO; 51 brs.

**MinskComplexbank** (Joint Byelorusian-Russian Bank): 220050 Minsk, vul. Myasnikova 40; tel. (17) 228-20-50; fax (17) 228-20-60; e-mail administrator@complex.nsys.minsk.by; f. 1992; cap. 153,000m. (Dec. 1997); Chair. YEVGENII I. KRAVTSOV.

**Minski Tranzitnyi Bank:** 220033 Minsk, pr. Partizanski 6A; tel. (17) 213-29-14; fax (17) 213-29-09; e-mail cor@mtb.minsk.by; f. 1994; cap. 36,001.9m. (Dec. 1997), res 6,570.2m., dep. 656,300m. (Dec. 1997); Chair. ANNA G. GRINKEVICH; 5 brs.

**Priorbank:** 220002 Minsk, vul. V. Khoruzhey 31A; tel. (17) 234-01-35; fax (17) 234-15-54; e-mail root@prior.minsk.by; internet www.prior.minsk.by; f. 1989, present name since 1992; cap. 117,743m., res 269,653m., dep. 4,928,580m. (Dec. 1997); Pres. MIKHAIL F. LAVRINOVICH; Chair. SYARGEY A. KOSTYUCHENKA; 29 brs.

**Profbank:** 220126 Minsk, vul. Melnikaite 8; tel. (17) 223-95-78; fax (17) 222-26-15; f. 1991; cap. 42,336.4m. (Dec. 1997); Chair. MIKHAIL P. SLESAREV; 5 brs.

**RRB-Bank:** 220037 Minsk, pr. Masherava 23; tel. (17) 226-57-27; fax (17) 226-63-93; f. 1994; cap. 51,003.3m. (Dec. 1997); Chair. IRINA A. VERETELNIKOVA.

**Slavneftebank:** 220007 Minsk, vul. Fabritsius 8; tel. (17) 222-07-09; fax (17) 222-07-52; e-mail snb@snbank.belpak.minsk .by; f. 1996; total assets 6,033,143.6m., cap. 82,200m. (Dec. 1998); Chair. VLADIMIR V. IVANOV.

**Tekhnobank:** 220002 Minsk, vul. Krapotkina 44; tel. and fax (17) 283-15-10; e-mail tex182new@belabm.x400.rosprint.ru; f. 1994; cap. 85,410.8m. (Dec. 1997); Chair. ZOYA I. LISHAY; 6 brs.

**Trade and Industrial Bank SA:** 220141 Minsk, vul. Russiyanov 8; tel. (17) 268-03-45; fax (17) 260-34-02; f. 1994 as Novokom; cap. 1,141,435m. (Nov. 1999); Chair. FELIKS I. CHERNYAVSKY.

**Zolotoy Taler:** 220035 Minsk, vul. Tatarskaya 3; tel. (17) 226-62-98; fax (17) 223-06-40; e-mail gt_bank2@gtp.by; f. 1994; cap. and res –224,338.2m., dep. 832,387.2m. (Oct. 1999); Chair. ALYAKSANDR A. ZHILINSKIY.

### BANKING ASSOCIATION

**Association of Belarusian Banks:** 220071 Minsk, vul. Smolyachkova 9; tel. (17) 210-10-37; fax (17) 227-58-41; Char. ANNA G. GRINKEVICH.

### COMMODITY AND STOCK EXCHANGES

**Belagroprambirzha** (Belarusian Agro-Industrial Trade and Stock Exchange): 220108 Minsk, vul. Kazintsa 86, kor. 2; tel. (17) 277-07-26; fax (17) 277-01-37; f. 1991; trade in agricultural products, industrial goods, shares; 900 mems; Pres. ANATOL TIBOGANOU; Chair. of Bd ALYAKSANDR P. DECHTYAR.

**Belarusian Currency and Stock Exchange:** 220004 Minsk, vul. Melnikaite 2; tel. (17) 276-91-21; fax (17) 229-25-66; f. 1991; Gen. Dir VYACHESLAV A. KASAK.

**Belarusian Universal Exchange (BUE):** 220099 Minsk, vul. Kazintsa 4; tel. (17) 278-11-21; fax (17) 278-85-16; f. 1991; Pres. ULADZIMIR SHEPEL.

**Gomel Regional Commodity and Raw Materials Exchange (GCME):** 246000 Gomel, vul. Savetskaya 16; tel. (232) 55-73-28; fax (232) 55-70-07; f. 1991; Gen. Man. ANATOL KUZILEVICH.

### INSURANCE

**Belarusian Insurance Co:** 220141 Minsk, vul. Zhodinskaya 1-4; tel. (17) 263-38-57; fax (17) 268-80-17; e-mail reklama@belinscosc.belpak.minsk.by; f. 1992; Dir-Gen. LEONID M. STATKEVICH.

**Belgosstrakh** (State Insurance Co): 220036 Minsk, vul. K. Libknekht 70; tel. (17) 259-10-32; fax (17) 259-10-22; Dir-Gen. VICTOR I. SHOUST.

**Belingosstrakh:** 220078 Minsk, pr. Masherava 19; tel. and fax (17) 226-98-04; f. 1977; non-life, property, vehicle and cargo insurance; Dir-Gen. YURI A. GAVRILOV.

**GARIS:** 220600 Minsk, vul. Myasnikova 32; tel. (17) 220-37-01.

**Polis:** 220087 Minsk, pr. Partizansky 81; tel. (17) 245-02-91; Dir DANUTA I. VORONOVICH.

**SNAMI:** 220040 Minsk, vul. Nekrasova 40A; tel. and fax (17) 231-63-86; f. 1991; Dir S. N. SHABALA.

## Trade and Industry

### CHAMBERS OF COMMERCE

**Belarusian Chamber of Commerce and Industry:** 220035 Minsk, pr. Masherava 14; tel. (17) 226-91-27; fax (17) 226-98-60; e-mail gpp@cci.belpak.minsk.by; f. 1953; brs in Brest, Gomel, Grodno, Mogilev and Vitebsk; Pres. ULADZIMIR K. LESUN.

**Minsk Branch:** 220113 Minsk, vul. Kolasa 65; tel. (17) 266-04-73; fax (17) 266-26-04; Man. Dir P. A. YUSHKEVICH.

### EMPLOYERS' ORGANIZATION

**Confederation of Industrialists and Entrepreneurs:** 220004 Minsk, vul. Kalvaryskaya 1-410; tel. (17) 222-47-91; fax (17) 222-47-91; e-mail belka@belpak.minsk.by; f. 1990; Pres. MAX KUNYAVSKI.

### UTILITIES

#### Electricity

In November 1999 an agreement was signed on the unification of Russia and Belarus's energy systems (including a power-grid merger).

**Institute of Nuclear Energy:** 223061 Minsk, Sosny Settlement; tel. (17) 246-77-12.

#### Gas

**Belnaftagaz:** Minsk; tel. (17) 233-06-75.

**Beltopgaz:** distributes natural gas to end-users.

**Beltransgaz:** imports natural gas; acts as holding co for regional transmission and storage enterprises.

### TRADE UNIONS

**Belarusian Congress of Democratic Trade Unions:** 220005 Minsk, vul. Zaharova 24; tel. (17) 233-31-82; fax (17) 210-15-00; f. 1993; Chair. ALYAKSANDR LYSENKA; 18,000 mems.

**Free Trade Union of Belarus:** 220030 Minsk, pl. Svabody 23; tel. (17) 284-31-82; fax (17) 210-15-00; e-mail spb@user.unibel.by; f. 1992; Chair. GENADZ BYKAU; Vice-Chair. NOVIKOV JURI; 8,000 mems.

**Independent Trade Union of Belarus:** 223710 Soligorsk, vul. Lenina 42; tel. and fax (1710) 20-059; f. 1991; Chair. VIKTAR BABAYED; Sec. NIKOLAY ZIMIN; 10,000 mems.

**Belarusian Organization of Working Women:** 220030 Minsk, pl. Svabody 23; (17) 227-57-78; fax (17) 227-13-16; f. 1992; 7,000 mems.

**Belarusian Peasants' Union** (Syalanski Sayuz): 220199 Minsk, vul. Brestskaya 64-327; tel. (17) 277-99-93; Chair. KASTUS YARMOLENKA.

**Federation of Trade Unions of Belarus:** Minsk; Chair. ULADZIMIR GANCHARYK.

**Independent Association of Industrial Trade Unions of Belarus:** 220013 Minsk, vul. Kulman 4; tel. (17) 223-80-74; fax (17) 223-82-04; f. 1992; Chairs ALYAKSANDR I. BUKHVOSTOU, G. F. FEDYNICH; 380,000 mems; derecognized by Govt in 1999.

**Union of Electronic Industry Workers:** Minsk; Leader G. F. FEDYNICH.

**Union of Motor Car and Agricultural Machinery Construction Workers:** Minsk; largest industrial trade union in Belarus; Leader ALYAKSANDR I. BUKHVOSTOU; 200,000 mems.

**Union of Small Ventures:** 220010 Minsk, vul. Sukhaya 7; tel. (17) 220-23-41; fax (17) 220-93-41; f. 1990; legal, business; Gen. Dir VIKTAR F. DROZD.

## Transport

### RAILWAYS

In 1995 the total length of railway lines in use was 5,543 km. Minsk is a major railway junction, situated on the east-west line between Moscow and Warsaw, and north-south lines linking the Baltic countries and Ukraine. There is an underground railway in Minsk, the Minsk Metro, which has two lines (total length 20 km), with 18 stations.

**Belarusian State Railways:** 220745 Minsk, vul. Lenina 17; tel. (17) 296-44-00; fax (17) 227-56-48; f. 1992, following the dissolution of the former Soviet Railways; Pres. E. I. VOLODKO; First Vice-Pres. V. BORISUK.

### ROADS

At 31 December 1997 the total length of roads in Belarus was 53,407 km (including 15,460 km main roads and 37,497 km secondary roads). Some 98.2% of the total network was hard-surfaced. In September 1999 it was estimated that more than 28,000 km of Belarus' road network was in need of repair.

### CIVIL AVIATION

Minsk has two airports, one largely for international flights and one for domestic connections.

**Belair Belarussian Airlines:** 222039 Minsk, vul. Korotkevicha 5; tel. (17) 225-07-02; fax (17) 225-30-45; f. 1991; operates regional and domestic charter services.

**Belavia:** 220004 Minsk, vul. Nemiga 14; tel. (17) 229-24-24; fax (17) 229-23-83; e-mail belaviamarket@infonet.by; internet www.belavia.infonet.by; f. 1993 from former Aeroflot division of the USSR; became state national carrier in 1996; operates services in Europe and selected destinations in Asia; Gen. Dir A. GUSAROV.

**Gomel Air Detachment:** 246011 Gomel, Gomel Airport; tel. (23) 251-14-07; fax (23) 253-14-15. 1944; CEO VALERY N. KULAKOUSKI.

## Tourism

**Belintourist:** 220078 Minsk, pr. Masherava 19; tel. (17) 226-98-40; fax (17) 223-11-43; e-mail belintrst@nttcmk.belpak.minsk.by; f. 1992; leading tourist org. in Belarus; Dir-Gen. VYACHESLAV V. IVANOV.

# BELGIUM

## Introductory Survey

### Location, Climate, Language, Religion, Flag, Capital

The Kingdom of Belgium lies in north-western Europe, bounded to the north by the Netherlands, to the east by Luxembourg and Germany, to the south by France, and to the west by the North Sea. The climate is temperate. Temperatures in the capital, Brussels, are generally between 0°C (32°F) and 23°C (73°F). Flemish (closely related to Dutch), spoken in the north (Flanders), and French, spoken in the south (Wallonia), are the two main official languages. Brussels (which is situated in Flanders) has bilingual status. Nearly 60% of the population are Flemish-speaking, about 40% are French-speaking and less than 1% have German as their mother tongue. The majority of the inhabitants profess Christianity, and about four-fifths are Roman Catholics. The national flag (proportions 15 by 13) consists of three equal vertical stripes, of black, yellow and red.

### Recent History

Since the Second World War, Belgium has become recognized as a leader of international co-operation in Europe. It is a founder member of many important international organizations, including the North Atlantic Treaty Organization (NATO, see p. 226), the Council of Europe (see p. 158), the European Union (EU, see p. 172) and the Benelux Economic Union (see p. 290).

In the latter half of the 20th century linguistic divisions were exacerbated by the political and economic polarization of Flemish-speaking Flanders in the north and francophone Wallonia in the south. The faster-growing and relatively prosperous population of Flanders has traditionally supported the conservative Flemish Christelijke Volkspartij (CVP—Christian People's Party) and the nationalist Volksunie—Vlaamse Vrije Democraten (VU) (People's Union—Flemish Free Democrats), while Wallonia has traditionally been a stronghold of socialist political sympathies. Most major parties have both French and Flemish sections, as a result of a trend away from centralized administration towards greater regional control. Moderate constitutional reforms, introduced in 1971, were the first steps towards regional autonomy; in the following year further concessions were made, with the German-speaking community being represented in the Cabinet for the first time, and in 1973 linguistic parity was assured in central government. Provisional legislation, adopted in 1974, established separate Regional Councils and Ministerial Committees. The administrative status of Brussels remained contentious: the majority of the city's inhabitants are francophone, but the Flemish parties were, until the late 1980s, unwilling to grant the capital equal status with the other two regional bodies (see below).

In June 1977 the Prime Minister, Leo Tindemans, formed a coalition composed of the CVP and the francophone Parti Social Chrétien (PSC—Christian Social Party), which were collectively known as the Christian Democrats, the Socialists, the Front Démocratique des Francophones (FDF—French-speaking Democratic Front) and the VU. The Cabinet, in what became known as the Egmont Pact, proposed the abolition of the virtually defunct nine-province administration, and devolution of power from the central Government to create a federal Belgium, comprising three political and economic regions (Flanders, Wallonia and Brussels), and two linguistic communities. However, these proposals were not implemented. Tindemans resigned in October 1978 and the Minister of Defence, Paul Vanden Boeynants, was appointed Prime Minister in a transitional Government. Legislative elections in December caused little change to the distribution of seats in the Chamber of Representatives. Four successive Prime Ministers-designate failed to form a new government, the main obstacle being the future status of Brussels. The six-month crisis was finally resolved when a new coalition Government was formed in April 1979 under Dr Wilfried Martens, the President of the CVP.

During 1980 the linguistic conflict worsened, sometimes involving violent incidents. Legislation was formulated, under the terms of which Flanders and Wallonia were to be administered by regional assemblies, with control of cultural matters, public health, roads, urban projects and 10% of the national budget, while Brussels was to retain its three-member executive.

Belgium suffered severe economic difficulties during the late 1970s and early 1980s, and internal disagreement over Martens' proposals for their resolution resulted in the formation of four successive coalition Governments between April 1979 and October 1980. Proposed austerity measures, including a 'freeze' on wages and reductions in public expenditure at a time of high unemployment, provoked demonstrations and lost Martens the support of the Socialist parties. Martens also encountered widespread criticism over plans to install NATO nuclear missiles in Belgium. In April 1981 a new Government was formed, comprising a coalition of the Christian Democrats and the Socialist parties and led by Mark Eyskens (of the CVP), hitherto Minister of Finance. However, lack of parliamentary support for his policies led to Eyskens' resignation in September. In December Martens formed a new centre-right Government, comprising the Christian Democrats and the two Liberal parties. In 1982 Parliament granted special powers for the implementation of economic austerity measures; these were effective until 1984, and similar powers were approved in March 1986. Opposition to reductions in public spending was vigorous, with public-sector unions undertaking damaging strike action throughout the 1980s.

In November 1983 the Chamber of Representatives debated the controversial proposed installation of 48 US 'cruise' nuclear missiles on Belgian territory, deferring a final decision on the issue until 1985. A series of bombings, directed against NATO-connected targets, occurred during 1984. Responsibility for the attacks was claimed by an extreme left-wing organization. In March 1985 the Chamber finally adopted a majority vote in favour of the cruise sitings, and 16 missiles were installed at Florennes. Further terrorist attacks against NATO targets were perpetrated in 1985, before a number of arrests were made. The missiles were removed in December 1988, under the terms of the Intermediate-range Nuclear Forces treaty concluded by the USA and the USSR in December 1987.

In May 1985 a riot at a football match between English and Italian clubs at the Heysel Stadium in Brussels, which resulted in 39 deaths, precipitated demands for the resignation of the Minister of the Interior, Charles-Ferdinand Nothomb, over accusations of inefficient policing. In July the resignation, in connection with the issue, of six Liberal cabinet members (including the Deputy Prime Minister, Jean Gol) led to the collapse of the coalition. Martens offered the resignation of his Government, but this was 'suspended' by King Baudouin pending a general election, which was called for October. Meanwhile, however, controversy regarding educational reform provoked a dispute between the two main linguistic groups and caused the final dissolution of Parliament in September. The general election returned the Christian Democrats-Liberal alliance to power, and in November Martens formed his sixth Cabinet.

The Government collapsed in October 1987, as a result of continuing division between the French- and Flemish-speaking parties of the coalition. At the ensuing general election in December, the CVP sustained significant losses in Flanders, while the French-speaking Parti Socialiste (PS—Socialist Party) gained seats in Wallonia, and the Socialists became the largest overall grouping in the Chamber of Representatives. No party, however, had a clear mandate for power, and negotiations for a new coalition lasted 146 days. During this time, Martens assumed a caretaker role, while a series of mediators, appointed by the King, attempted to reach a compromise. In May 1988 Martens was sworn in at the head of his eighth administration, after agreement was finally reached by the French- and Flemish-speaking wings of both the Christian Democrats and Socialist parties and by the VU.

The five-party coalition agreement committed the new Government to a programme of further austerity measures, together with tax reforms and increased federalization. In August 1988 Parliament approved the first phase of the federalization plan, intended ultimately to lead to a constitutional amendment, whereby increased autonomy would be granted to the country's Communities and Regions in several areas of jurisdiction, including education and socio-economic policy. It was also agreed that Brussels would have its own Regional Council, with an executive responsible to it, giving the city equal status with Flanders and Wallonia. In January 1989 Parliament approved the second phase of the federalization programme, allocating the public funds necessary to give effect to the regional autonomy that had been approved in principle in August 1988. The federal Constitution formally came into effect in July 1989.

A brief constitutional crisis in 1990 provoked widespread demands for a review of the powers of the Monarch, as defined by the Constitution. In March proposals for the legalization of abortion (in strictly-controlled circumstances) completed their passage through Parliament. However, King Baudouin had previously stated that his religious convictions would render him unable to give royal assent to any such legislation. A compromise solution was reached in early April, whereby Article 82 of the Constitution, which makes provision for the Monarch's 'incapacity to rule', was invoked. Baudouin thus abdicated for 36 hours, during which time the new legislation was promulgated. A joint session of Parliament was then convened to declare the resumption of Baudouin's reign. However, the incident prompted considerable alarm within Belgium: it was widely perceived as setting a dangerous precedent for the reinterpretation of the Constitution.

The Government was weakened by the resignation of both VU ministers in September 1991 and by the resultant loss of its two-thirds parliamentary majority, necessary for the implementation of the third stage of the federalization programme. Further linguistic conflict between the remaining coalition partners led to Martens' resignation as Prime Minister in October and the subsequent collapse of the Government. However, King Baudouin rejected the resignations of Martens and the Cabinet. The Government remained in office until the next general election, which took place in November. The results of the election reflected a significant decline in popular support for all five parties represented in the outgoing Government. The Socialist parties remained the largest overall grouping in the Chamber of Representatives, although they sustained the highest combined loss of seats (nine). The Christian Democrats and the Liberal parties remained, respectively, the second and third largest groupings, while the two ecologist parties (Anders Gaan Leven—Agalev, and the Ecologistes Confédéres pour l'Organisation des Luttes Originales—Ecolo) increased their representation in the Chamber to become the fourth strongest grouping. The Vlaams Blok (Flemish Bloc), an extreme right-wing party advocating Flemish separatism and the repatriation of immigrants, obtained 12 seats, recording the highest increase (10 seats) of any party. Following the election, the political parties conducted protracted negotiations, during which Martens' interim Cabinet continued in office. In early March 1992 four of the five parties that had composed the previous Government, the CVP, the PSC, the Socialistische Partij (SP) and the PS (which together controlled 120 seats in the 212-member Chamber of Representatives), agreed to form a new administration; a leading member of the CVP, Jean-Luc Dehaene, was appointed Prime Minister. The new Government committed itself to the completion of the constitutional reforms that had been initiated under Martens' premiership. For several months, however, the coalition partners repeatedly failed to reach agreement, both on proposals for the implementation of the third stage of the federalization programme and on amendments to the 1993 budget. A compromise on both issues was eventually reached at the end of September 1992.

In July 1992 the Chamber of Representatives voted, by 146 to 33, in favour of ratifying the Treaty on European Union, agreed by the heads of government of member states of the European Community (now EU) at Maastricht, in the Netherlands, in December 1991. The Senate approved ratification in November 1992.

In February 1993 (in accordance with the constitutional reforms agreed in September 1992) Parliament voted to amend the Constitution to create a federal state of Belgium, comprising the largely autonomous regions of Flanders, Wallonia and (bilingual) Brussels. The three regions, and the country's three linguistic groups, were to be represented by the following directly-elected administrations: a combined administration for Flanders and the Flemish-speaking community, regional administrations for Wallonia and Brussels, and separate administrations for French- and German-speakers. The regional administrations were to assume sole responsibility for the environment, housing, transport and public works, while the language community administrations were to supervise education policy and culture. Legislation to implement the reforms was enacted in July 1993.

In March 1993 Dehaene offered to resign as Prime Minister, owing to continuing failure by the ruling coalition to agree measures to reduce the level of the budget deficit. At the end of that month, however, a solution was achieved; Dehaene remained in his post and, in early April, Parliament adopted a vote of confidence in his Government.

In July 1993 King Baudouin died; Baudouin was succeeded by his brother, hitherto Prince Albert of Liège, in August.

In November 1993 trade union movements united to organize several one-day strikes, including a general strike, in protest at the Dehaene administration's intention to implement a series of severe economic austerity measures and at the relatively high rate of unemployment; the strike action was suspended in mid-December, when the Government agreed to negotiate with the unions.

In January 1994 three government ministers who were members of the PS (including a Deputy Prime Minister, Guy Coëme) resigned from their posts, following allegations that they had been involved in a bribery scandal concerning the apparently illegal receipt by the SP (the Flemish section of the party) of a substantial sum of money in connection with the award, in 1988, of a defence contract to an Italian helicopter company. The PS (the Walloon section of the party) was subsequently implicated in a similar scandal involving a French aviation company. In April 1996 Coëme and seven others were found guilty of fraud and abuse of public office; Coëme, who received a two-year suspended prison sentence, subsequently resigned from the Chamber of Representatives.

At elections to the European Parliament in June 1994 all four parties of the governing coalition registered a decline in support, while the Liberal parties increased their number of seats. Extreme right-wing parties also performed well: the Vlaams Blok and the Wallonia-based Front National (FN—National Front) together gained more than 10% of the total votes.

The investigation into the PS/SP bribery scandal (see above) intensified during 1995 as increasing numbers of people became implicated. In March a retired Chief of Staff of the Air Force, who had been in office at the time of the illegal financial transaction, committed suicide, having been arrested and questioned in connection with the inquiry. In the same month Frank Vandenbroucke, a Deputy Prime Minister and the Minister of Foreign Affairs, and a member of the SP, resigned from the Cabinet, claiming that he had participated unwittingly in the affair. Meanwhile, Willy Claes, a prominent SP official and former Deputy Prime Minister and Minister of Foreign Affairs, who had been elected Secretary-General of NATO in 1994, came under increasing pressure to resign from his post, owing to allegations of his involvement in the scandal. In May 1995 Claes was questioned about the affair by the Supreme Court, and in October, following the withdrawal by Parliament of his immunity from prosecution (held by all serving and retired government ministers under Belgian law), Claes was committed to trial on charges of corruption, fraud and forgery. Immediately afterwards he resigned as Secretary-General of NATO. Proceedings against Claes commenced in September 1998, and in February 1999 he received a three-year suspended prison sentence for his part in the affair.

At a general election held in May 1995 the ruling centre-left coalition retained significant support, securing a total of 82 seats in the Chamber of Representatives (membership of which had been reduced from 208 to 150), despite the ongoing investigation into allegedly illegal activities by officials of the two Socialist parties. The performance of the extreme right-wing Vlaams Blok was not as strong as had been anticipated: although the party won nearly 28% of the votes cast in Antwerp, Belgium's second largest city, it received only 12% of the votes overall in Flanders. Elections to the regional assemblies took place concurrently with the national legislative elections. Following an unusually short period of negotiations the CVP-PSC-PS-SP coalition was reformed and in mid-June a new Cabinet was appointed, with Dehaene remaining as Prime Minister. The Government, which continued to be strongly committed to meeting the economic targets for future European economic and monetary union, introduced several strict economic austerity measures in late 1995; public-sector unions responded by organizing protest strike action. In April 1996 the Government, employers and trade unions agreed a package of measures which aimed to reduce the high level of unemployment. The agreement was, however, short-lived, owing to the subsequent withdrawal of one of the main trade unions, on the grounds that the proposals for job creation were not sufficiently detailed. In the following month Parliament granted the Dehaene administration special emergency powers to implement economic austerity measures by decree.

The latter half of 1996 was dominated by extreme public concern over allegations of endemic official corruption, following the discovery, in August, of an international paedophile network based in Belgium, and subsequent widespread speculation (fuelled by the arrests in early September of several police officers) that this had received protection from the police force and from senior figures in the judicial and political establishment, who were allegedly implicated in the activities of organized crime syndicates. During September King Albert promised a thorough investigation of the network and, in an unprecedented gesture, demanded a review of the judicial system. In October, however, allegations of a judicial and political conspiracy to impede the progress of the investigation were prompted by the removal from the case of Jean-Marc Connerotte, a widely-respected senior investigating judge. The prevailing mood of national crisis was heightened by the arrests, during September, of Alain van der Biest of the PS (a former federal Minister of Pensions) and four others, on charges connected with the assassination in 1991 of a former Deputy Prime Minister, André Cools. It was alleged that Cools' murder had been ordered by PS colleagues, in order to prevent him from disclosing corruption within the party. In June 1998 a Tunisian court found two Tunisian citizens guilty of the murder; however, the background to the assassination remained unclear.

During 1997 the sense of national malaise was exacerbated by industrial unrest. In February demonstrations in protest at the closure of a Wallonian steelworks, Forges de Clabecq (which had employed some 1,800 people), received much popular support. At the end of the same month the French automobile manufacturer Renault announced the impending closure of its Belgian factory, with the loss of more than 3,000 jobs in a town in which it was the principal employer. Strikes and widely-attended demonstrations ensued, while the Belgian Government mounted an ultimately unsuccessful legal challenge to Renault's action. Concerns were raised that the cost to employers of Belgian social welfare contributions was prompting businesses to relocate elsewhere within the EU.

Meanwhile, in March 1997 Guy Spitaels (a former Deputy Prime Minister and an erstwhile President of the PS), having resigned in the previous month as President of the Walloon regional assembly, was indicted on bribery charges relating to the political scandals of 1994–95 (see above). In April 1997 a parliamentary committee, which had been established in October 1996 to investigate allegations of official corruption and mismanagement, issued a report which claimed that rivalry between the country's various police and judicial divisions often prevented their effective co-operation; it recommended the establishment of a single integrated national police force. However, the committee found little evidence that paedophile networks had received official protection. In February 1998 the Government announced that, in place of the recommended integrated national police force, efforts would be made to facilitate 'voluntary co-operation contracts' between the various law enforcement services.

In April 1998 Marc Dutroux, a convicted paedophile whose arrest in August 1996 on charges of child kidnapping and murder had prompted the ongoing scrutiny of Belgium's national institutions, briefly escaped from police custody. The incident incited renewed public anger and precipitated the resignations of several high-ranking figures, including the commander of the national gendarmerie and the Ministers of the Interior and of Justice. A proposed vote of 'no confidence' in the Dehaene Government, also ensuing from Dutroux's escape, was defeated in the Chamber of Representatives. Dehaene immediately reaffirmed his commitment to restructuring the police and judiciary.

In mid-June 1998 a reorganization of the Cabinet included the appointment of a new (socialist) Minister of Finance. In late September Louis Tobback, who had been appointed Deputy Prime Minister and Minister of the Interior in April, resigned, following protests at the death of a Nigerian woman during an attempt forcibly to deport her from Belgium. Two police officers were subsequently charged with involuntary manslaughter, and the Government suspended the forced repatriation of asylum-seekers, pending further investigations.

Preparations for the general election scheduled to be held in mid-June 1999 were overshadowed by the public announcement in late May that animal feed contaminated with industrial oil containing dioxin (a carcinogenic chemical) had been supplied to farms throughout Belgium from a factory near Ghent. Following the announcement, many Belgium food products, particularly poultry and egg-based products, were withdrawn from sale in Belgium and elsewhere in Europe, while production was suspended at farms across Belgium. There was widespread public anger that, although veterinary inspectors had identified a problem as early as mid-March, it was not until May that the Ministry of Agriculture had suspended sales from the affected animal-feed suppliers, and had informed government officials in neighbouring countries. On 1 June Karel Pinxten, the Minister of Agriculture and Small and Medium-sized Enterprises, and Marcel Colla, the Minister of Consumer Affairs, Public Health and the Environment, who had been jointly blamed for the delay in informing the public of the contamination, resigned from their posts. In early June the EU announced that it was to demand the removal from sale, and subsequent destruction, of poultry, pork and cattle products from farms whose feed had been contaminated with dioxin. The Belgian Government subsequently introduced a total ban on the slaughter and transportation of all poultry, cattle and pigs until it could confirm which farms had received the infected feed. On 7 June Dehaene took the unprecedented step of halting his electoral campaign, and announced an official parliamentary enquiry into the contamination. On 10 June, in an apparent attempt to assuage farmers who were losing large amounts of income on a daily basis and demanding compensation, the Government announced that slaughtering and exports could resume at farms that had not received the contaminated feed, despite the lack of a definitive list of dioxin-free farms. This relaxation of the temporary ban on production contravened the advice of the European Commission, which had recommended that the ban should remain in place while there continued to be uncertainty about which farms had received the contaminated feed. It was alleged that the Government had believed that, for political reasons, it could not wait for the convening of the Commission's scientific and veterinary committee, whose meeting was scheduled to take place after the Belgian general election. Confusion, however, remained within Belgium as to the identification of the affected farms, and Belgian farmers blocked the roads into the country from France and the Netherlands, in an attempt to prevent agricultural imports. The Commission later announced that it was to initiate legal proceedings against the Belgian Government over its handling of the crisis, which had led to imports of European food products being banned by many non-European countries (including the USA).

At the general election, which was held on 13 June 1999, the Christian Democrats suffered heavy losses, mainly at the hands of the Liberals and the ecologist parties. The Vlaams Blok also showed significant gains, winning more than 10% of the vote in many areas. The Vlaamse Liberalen en Demokraten—Partij van de Burger (VLD—Flemish Liberals and Democrats—Citizens' Party) emerged as the largest single party, with 23 seats in the 150-member Chamber of Representatives (having received 14.3% of the total votes cast), while the ecologist parties almost doubled their representation, to 20 seats (with 14.4%), and the Vlaams Blok became the fifth largest party in the lower house, with 15 seats (9.9%). The CVP secured 22 seats (14.1% of the total votes) and the PSC won 10 seats (5.9%), while the Socialist parties obtained a combined total of 33 seats (19.8%). The VLD also performed well in the elections to the Senate, which (together with elections to the assemblies for the regions and linguistic communities) were held on the same day as the elections to the Chamber of Representatives; the VLD won the largest number of votes in the polling for the 40 directly-elective seats in the upper house (with 15.4% of the total votes). The defeat of the outgoing coalition in the general election was largely attributed to public anger at the authorities' perceived incompetence in their response to the dioxin scandal (which compounded general disquiet over the earlier corruption and paedophile scandals). Dehaene, who had held the premiership for eight years, tendered his resignation on 14 June and announced that he was considering leaving national politics. On 23 June the King asked the President of the VLD, Guy Verhofstadt, to form a new government. Following intensive negotiations, a new six-party coalition Government, comprising the VLD, the francophone Parti Réformateur Libéral (PRL), the two Socialist parties and the two ecologist parties, was sworn in on 12 July. The new administration was of historic note in that it was the first Belgian Government in 40 years not to include the Christian Democrats, the first to include the ecologist parties, and the first to be headed by a Liberal Prime Minister since 1884. Reflecting the right-wing programme of the Liberal parties, the new Government promised to reduce the social charges payable by employers and to reduce levels of public debt through the privatization of state assets. The Government also committed itself to the gradual abandonment of nuclear power (prompted by the greatly strengthened ecologist lobby), the further liberalization of the electricity sector and greater investment in the railway network.

Despite demonstrations staged by farmers (many of whom were reportedly on the brink of bankruptcy) in late June and in early July 1999, in protest at the authorities' handling of the dioxin crisis, the new Government announced that it was to add a further 400 farms to the list of 800 already forbidden to sell their produce. The Government also announced that it was to buy back and destroy some 80,000 metric tons of pork. In early August, in response to recommendations made by scientific advisers from the European Commission, the Belgian Government agreed to add beef to the list of livestock exports that were banned until definitively cleared of contamination. A few days later the Government promulgated a decree banning the export of food products, containing more than 2% animal fat (except dairy products) that did not have a certificate guaranteeing their safety. Although the Minister of Consumer Affairs, Public Health and the Environment described the decree as unnecessarily harsh, representatives of the agricultural industry subsequently persuaded her that stringent procedures were required in order to regain consumer confidence and to avoid the imposition of a total ban on all Belgian agricultural exports by the EU. The Government, none the less, announced that, while it would comply with EU directives, it would mount a legal challenge in the hope of reducing their severity.

In late September 1999 the Belgian Government announced that some 500 Slovak gypsies who had applied for political asylum were to be repatriated. In the following month the Minister of the Interior ordered an official investigation into criticisms made by human rights groups regarding the tactics used by the authorities in Ghent to assemble the gypsies prior to deportation. In mid-October the Government announced that legislation was to be introduced, aimed at reforming the procedure of applying for asylum. The new procedure was to take no longer than one month, including the appeals process, and those applicants not granted asylum were to be repatriated without delay. The Government also announced that all outstanding asylum applications would be processed within one year, while asylum-seekers resident in Belgium for five years and illegal immigrants resident in Belgium for six years were to be granted permanent residence.

From late 1988 Belgium's hitherto cordial relations with its former colonies underwent considerable strain. Proposals that Prime Minister Martens made in November 1988 regarding the relief of public and commercial debts owed to Belgium by Zaire (formerly the Belgian Congo) were opposed by the Socialist parties and provoked allegations in the Belgian press of corruption within the Zairean Government and of the misappropriation of development aid. President Mobutu Sese Seko of Zaire responded by ordering the withdrawal of all Zairean state-owned businesses from Belgium and by demanding that all Zairean nationals resident in Belgium remove their assets from, and leave, their host country. In July 1989 the situation was apparently resolved following meetings between Martens and Mobutu, at which a new debt-servicing agreement was signed. However, relations again deteriorated when, in May 1990, the Mobutu regime refused to accede to demands for an international inquiry into the alleged massacre of as many as 150 students by the Zairean security forces. Mobutu accused Belgium of interfering in his country's internal affairs, and ordered the expulsion from Zaire of some 700 Belgian technical workers, together with the closure of three of Belgium's four consular offices. Following the collapse of public order in Zaire in September 1991, the Belgian Government dispatched 1,000 troops to Zaire for the protection of the estimated 11,000 Belgian nationals resident there. By the end of 1991 all the troops had been withdrawn and about 8,000 Belgian nationals had been evacuated. Prospects for the normalization of relations improved following the establishment of a transitional Government in Zaire in July 1992 and the removal of Zairean sanctions against Belgium. Relations deteriorated again, however, in January 1993, when, in response to rioting by troops loyal to President Mobutu, Belgium dispatched 520 troops to evacuate the remaining 3,000 Belgian nationals in Zaire. In October 1994 the Belgian Government pledged to resume humanitarian aid to Zaire. In August 1997, following the deposition of Mobutu's regime in May by the forces of Laurent-Désiré Kabila, it was announced that normal relations between Belgium and the Democratic Republic of the Congo (DRC—as Zaire was now renamed) would be gradually restored. In October 1999 a high-level Belgian delegation visited the capital of the DRC, Kinshasa, to express the willingness of the Belgian Government to mediate in the ongoing crisis in the troubled African state; relations between the two countries were reported to have greatly improved since the election of the new Government in Belgium in June.

In October 1990 the Martens Government dispatched 600 troops to protect some 1,600 Belgian nationals resident in Rwanda (part of the former Belgian territory of Ruanda-Urundi), when that country was invaded by exiled opponents of the incumbent regime. The Belgian Government insisted that the deployment was a purely humanitarian action, and stated that it would not agree to a request from the Rwandan Government for military assistance, citing unacceptable violations of human rights by the authorities. In late October a cease-fire agreement came into effect, and in early November Belgian forces were withdrawn from Rwanda. Nevertheless, the conflict in Rwanda continued during 1991–94. Following the signing of a peace accord in August 1993, some 420 Belgian troops were redeployed as part of a UN peace-keeping force; this was, however, unable to prevent an outbreak of extreme violence, beginning in April 1994, which resulted in the deaths of many hundreds of thousands of people. Following the execution of 10 Belgian troops in April, the Belgian Government withdrew its peace-keeping contingent. It also dispatched some 800 paratroopers to Rwanda to co-ordinate the evacuation of the estimated 1,500 Belgian expatriates remaining in the country, as well as other foreign nationals. In October 1998 three Belgian army officers were demoted, having been found negligent in not preventing the 10 troop fatalities in April 1994.

## Government

Belgium is a constitutional and hereditary monarchy, consisting of a federation of the largely autonomous regions of Brussels, Flanders and Wallonia and of the Flemish-, French- and German-speaking language communities. The central legislature consists of a bicameral Parliament (the Chamber of Representatives and the Senate). The Chamber has 150 members, all directly elected for a term of four years by universal adult suffrage, on the basis of proportional representation. The Senate has 71 normal members, of whom 40 are directly elected at intervals of four years, also by universal suffrage on the basis of proportional representation, 21 are appointed by the legislative bodies of the three language communities (see below), and 10 are co-opted by the elected members. In addition, children of the King are entitled to honorary membership of the Senate from 18 years of age and acquire voting rights at the age of 21. Members of both Houses serve for up to four years. Executive power, nominally vested in the King, is exercised by the Cabinet. The King appoints the Prime Minister and, on the latter's advice, other Ministers. The Cabinet is responsible to the Chamber of Representatives. The three regions and three linguistic communities are represented by the following directly-elected legislative administrations: a combined administration for Flanders and the Flemish-speaking community, regional administrations for Wallonia and Brussels, and separate administrations for French- and German-speakers. The regional administrations have sole responsibility for the environment, housing, transport and public works, while the language community administrations supervise education policy and culture.

## Defence

Belgium is a member of NATO. In 1999 the total strength of the armed forces was 41,191, including an army of 26,193, a navy of 2,475 and an air force of 10,631. The defence budget for 2000 was estimated at BF 102,300m. Compulsory military service was abolished in 1995. A reduction in the size of the country's armed forces to 40,000 was under way during the late 1990s. In 1996 the Belgian and Netherlands navies came under a joint operational command, based at Den Helder, the Netherlands.

## Economic Affairs

In 1997, according to estimates by the World Bank, Belgium's gross national product (GNP), measured at average 1995–97 prices, was US $272,382m., equivalent to $26,730 per head. During 1990–97, it was estimated, GNP per head increased at an average rate of 1.3% per year, in real terms. Over the same period, the population increased at an average rate of 0.3% per year. Belgium's GNP totalled an estimated $259,000m. in 1998, equivalent to $25,380 per head. The country's gross domestic product (GDP) increased, in real terms, at an average annual rate of 1.8% in 1990–98. GDP rose by 0.9% in 1996, by 3.2% in 1997 and by 2.9% in 1998.

Agriculture (including forestry and fishing) contributed a provisional 1.5% of GDP in 1998. An estimated 2.4% of the employed labour force were engaged in the sector in 1996. The principal agricultural products are sugar beet, cereals and potatoes. Pig meat, beef and dairy products are also important. Exports of live animals and animal and vegetable products accounted for 5.7% of Belgium's total export revenue in 1998. It was expected that agricultural exports in 1999 would be severely affected by the dioxin contamination scandal (see Recent History). Agricultural GDP increased, in real terms, at an average annual rate of 4.0% in 1990–94. It increased slightly, by 0.5% in 1995, declined by 4.3% in 1996, and increased by 3.1% in 1997; in 1998, however, an estimated decrease of 6.8% was recorded.

Industry (including mining and quarrying, manufacturing, power and construction) contributed a provisional 28.2% of GDP in 1998. An estimated 26.1% of the employed labour force were engaged in industry in 1996. Industrial production (excluding construction) increased at an average rate of 1.2% per year in 1990–98. It rose by 0.8% in 1996, by 4.5% in 1997 and by 3.4% in 1998.

Belgium has few mineral resources, and the country's last coal-mine closed in 1992. In 1997 extractive activities accounted for only 0.3% of GDP. Belgium is, however, an important producer of copper, zinc and aluminium, smelted from imported ores. An estimated 0.2% of the employed labour force worked in the mining sector in 1995. The sector's output increased at an average rate of 6.8% per year during 1990–98. It rose by 6.7% in 1996, by 6.3% in 1997 and by 2.7% in 1998.

Manufacturing contributed 22.3% of GDP in 1997. The sector accounted for an estimated 18.8% of the employed labour force in 1995. In 1996 the main branches of manufacturing, in terms of value added, were fabricated metal products, machinery and equipment (accounting for 29.7% of the total), food products (16.7%) and chemical products (15.4%). During 1990–98 manufacturing production increased at an average annual rate of 1.8%. It rose by 0.5% in 1996, by 4.9% in 1997 and by 2.9% in 1998.

Belgium's seven nuclear reactors accounted for 60% of total electricity generation in 1997 (one of the highest levels in the world). The country's dependence on imported petroleum and natural gas has, however, increased, following the announcement by the Government in 1988 of the indefinite suspension of its nuclear programme and of the construction of a gas-powered generator. In 1999 the Government announced that it would phase out nuclear power from 2015. Imports of mineral fuels comprised 6.2% of the value of the Belgium's total imports in 1998.

The services sector contributed a provisional 70.4% of GDP in 1998, and engaged an estimated 71.5% of the employed labour force in 1996. The presence in Belgium of the offices of many international organizations and businesses is a significant source of revenue. The output of the services sector increased by 3.5% in 1997, and by a provisional 4.0% in 1998.

In 1998 the Belgo-Luxembourg Economic Union (BLEU) recorded a visible trade surplus of US $7,561m., while there was a surplus of US $12,111m. on the current account of the balance of payments. In 1998 Belgium's three major trading partners (Germany, the Netherlands and France) together accounted for 48.1% of imports as well as 49.4% of exports. The principal exports in 1998 were basic manufactures (including gem diamonds and iron and steel), machinery and transport equipment, chemicals and related products, food and live animals and miscellaneous manufactured articles. The principal imports in that year were machinery and transport equipment, basic manufactures, chemicals and related products, miscellaneous manufactured articles and food and live animals.

In 1995 there was a budget deficit of BF 259,100m., equivalent to 3.2% of GDP. By means of strict austerity measures, however, the budget deficit had decreased to 1.3% of GDP by 1998. The annual rate of inflation averaged 2.1% in 1990–98. Consumer prices increased by an annual average of 2.1% in 1996, 1.6% in 1997 and 0.9% in 1998. According to IMF figures, the rate of unemployment declined from 13.3% in 1997 to 12.6% in 1998.

Belgium is a member of the European Union (EU—see p. 172), including the European Monetary System (EMS, see p. 189), and of the Benelux Economic Union (see p. 290). Belgium is also a member of the European System of Central Banks (ESCB), which was inaugurated in 1998 (see European Central Bank, p. 178).

Following strong and sustained economic growth during the late 1980s, the Belgian economy entered recession in 1991. By the end of 1994 economic growth appeared to have regained momentum, although the improved economic performance was accompanied by continuing high unemployment, and severe structural weaknesses remained, notably the chronic public-sector debt. Belgium's economic priorities were dominated in the mid-1990s by the need to reduce the budget deficit and public-sector debt in order to qualify for the final stage of economic and monetary union (EMU) within the EU. The two Dehaene administrations succeeded in reducing the budget deficit from 7% of GDP in 1993 to 1.3% in 1998, and the level of public debt from 135% of GDP in 1993 to 116.5% in 1998. These achievements, in part facilitated by the privatization of state assets, enabled Belgium to participate in the introduction of the European single currency, the euro, which came into effect on 1 January 1999 (in 11 of the countries participating in EMU). Despite the damage to the economy caused by the food contamination scandal in mid-1999 (see Recent History), greater fiscal consolidation, allied to a general economic recovery in Europe, permitted the new Government, which came to power in June (under the leadership of the head of the Flemish-speaking Liberal party, Guy Verhofstadt), to reduce the social charges payable by employers, currently among the highest in the EU, and to inaugurate a youth employment programme. A reduction in the rate of unemployment was considered essential if the long-term prospects for the Belgian economy were to be favourable, as increased social security and, in particular, pension payments remained a serious and growing burden on public finances. It was also hoped that the new Government would address imbalances in the performances of the regional economies, since the relative weakness of the Walloon economy had encouraged Flemish demands for greater devolution of fiscal control to the regions.

## Social Welfare

Belgium maintains a very comprehensive system of social welfare, which is administered mainly by the National Office for Social Security. Contributions are paid by employers and employees towards family allowances, health insurance, unemployment benefit and pensions. Self-employed people's contributions cover only family allowances, pensions and a more limited level of health insurance. Most allowances and pensions are periodically adjusted in accordance with changes to the consumer price index. Workers and employees are entitled to four weeks' holiday for every 12-month period of work. They are insured against accidents occurring on the work premises or on the way to and from work. Unemployment benefit is paid by trade unions to their affiliates on behalf of the National Employment Office; unemployed people without trade union affiliation are paid from a public fund. A higher rate of medical reimbursement applies to widows, pensioners, orphans and the disabled, if they fall within a designated income bracket. Ordinary and supplementary family allowances are the entitlement of all families. Social welfare is also administered at a local level by Public Assistance Commissions, which have been established in every municipality. In 1982 Belgium had 531 hospital establishments, with a total of 92,686 beds (one for every 106 inhabitants), and in 1998 there were 364 physicians and 70 dentists per 100,000 inhabitants. Current legislation restricts the number of hospital beds and establishments to the 1982 level. Government expenditure on social security, health benefits, family allowances and pensions was curtailed during the 1990s. In 1996 total expenditure by the central Government on health was equivalent to some 6.1% of GDP.

## Education

Legislation granting responsibility for the formulation of education policy to the administrations of the Flemish-, French- and German-speaking communities came into effect in 1993. Education may be provided by the Communities, by public authorities or by private interests. All educational establishments, whether official or 'free' (privately-organized), receive most of their funding from the Communities. Roman Catholic schools constitute the greatest number of 'free' establishments.

Full-time education in Belgium is compulsory between the ages of six and 16 years. Thereafter, pupils must remain in part-time education for a further two-year period. About 90% of infants attend state-financed nursery schools. Elementary education begins at six years of age and consists of three courses of two years each. Secondary education, beginning at the age of 12, lasts for six years and is divided into three two-year cycles or, in a few cases, two three-year cycles. Enrolment at elementary schools in 1994 included 98% of children in the relevant age-group, while the comparable ratio at secondary schools was 99%.

The requirement for university entrance is a pass in the 'examination of maturity', taken after the completion of secondary studies. Courses are divided into 2–3 years of general preparation followed by 2–3 years of specialization. The French Community controls four universities, while the Flemish Community controls three such institutions; in addition, there are 11 university centres or faculties (six French, five Flemish). In 1997/98 an estimated total of 130,000 students were enrolled in university-level establishments. Non-university institutions of higher education provide arts education, technical training and teacher training; in 1997/98 an estimated 175,000 students were enrolled in such institutions. A national study fund provides grants where necessary and almost 20% of students receive scholarships.

Expenditure on education by all levels of government was 439,608m. francs in 1994 (equivalent to 10.2% of total government spending).

### Public Holidays

**2000:** 1 January (New Year's Day), 24 April (Easter Monday), 1 May (Labour Day), 1 June (Ascension Day), 12 June (Whit Monday), 11 July (Flemish-speaking Community), 21 July (Independence Day), 15 August (Assumption), 27 September (French-speaking Community), 1 November (All Saints' Day), 11 November (Armistice Day), 15 November (German-speaking Community), 25 December (Christmas Day).

**2001:** 1 January (New Year's Day), 16 April (Easter Monday), 1 May (Labour Day), 24 May (Ascension Day), 4 June (Whit Monday), 11 July (Flemish-speaking Community), 21 July (Independence Day), 15 August (Assumption), 27 September (French-speaking Community), 1 November (All Saints' Day), 11 November (Armistice Day), 15 November (German-speaking Community), 25 December (Christmas Day).

### Weights and Measures

The metric system is in force.

# Statistical Survey

Source: mainly Institut National de Statistique, 44 rue de Louvain, 1000 Brussels; tel. (2) 548-62-11; fax (2) 548-63-67; e-mail info@statbel.mineco.fgov.be; internet statbel.fgov.be.

## Area and Population

**AREA, POPULATION AND DENSITY**

| | |
|---|---|
| Area (sq km) | 30,528* |
| Population (census results)† | |
| 1 March 1981 | 9,848,647 |
| 1 March 1991 | |
| Males | 4,875,982 |
| Females | 5,102,699 |
| Total | 9,978,681 |
| Population (official estimates at 31 December)† | |
| 1996 | 10,170,226 |
| 1997 | 10,192,264 |
| 1998 | 10,213,752 |
| Density (per sq km) at 31 December 1998 | 334.6 |

* 11,787 sq miles. † Population is *de jure*.

**PROVINCES** (population at 31 December 1998)

| | Population | Capital (with population) |
|---|---|---|
| Flemish region | 5,926,838 | |
| Antwerp | 1,640,966 | Antwerp (447,632*) |
| Brabant (Flemish) | 1,011,588 | Leuven (88,245) |
| Flanders (East) | 1,359,702 | Ghent (224,074) |
| Flanders (West) | 1,127,091 | Brugge (115,991) |
| Limburg | 787,491 | Hasselt (67,777) |
| Walloon region | 3,332,454 | |
| Brabant (Walloon) | 347,423 | Wavre (30,656) |
| Hainaut | 1,280,427 | Mons (91,187) |
| Liège | 1,018,259 | Liège (187,538) |
| Luxembourg | 245,140 | Arlon (24,685) |
| Namur | 441,205 | Namur (104,994) |
| Brussels (capital) | 954,460 | |
| **Total** | 10,213,752 | |

* Including suburbs.

**PRINCIPAL TOWNS** (population at 31 December 1998)

| | |
|---|---|
| Bruxelles (Brussel, Brussels) | 954,460* |
| Antwerpen (Anvers, Antwerp) | 447,632† |
| Gent (Gand, Ghent) | 224,074 |
| Charleroi | 202,020 |
| Liège (Luik) | 187,538 |
| Brugge (Bruges) | 115,991 |
| Namur (Namen) | 104,994 |
| Mons (Bergen) | 91,187 |
| Leuven (Louvain) | 88,245 |
| Aalst (Alost) | 76,223 |
| Mechelen (Malines) | 75,418 |
| Kortrijk (Courtrai) | 75,099 |
| Sint-Niklaas (Saint-Nicolas) | 68,119 |
| Hasselt | 67,777 |
| Tournai | 67,611 |
| Oostende (Ostende, Ostend) | 67,304 |

* Including Schaerbeek, Anderlecht and other suburbs.
† Including Deurne and other suburbs.

**BIRTHS, MARRIAGES AND DEATHS**

| | Registered live births | | Registered marriages* | | Registered deaths† | |
|---|---|---|---|---|---|---|
| | Number | Rate (per 1,000) | Number | Rate (per 1,000) | Number | Rate (per 1,000) |
| 1991 | 125,924 | 12.6 | 60,740 | 6.1 | 104,149 | 10.4 |
| 1992 | 124,774 | 12.4 | 58,156 | 5.8 | 104,200 | 10.4 |
| 1993 | 120,848 | 12.0 | 54,112 | 5.4 | 106,834 | 10.6 |
| 1994 | 116,449 | 11.5 | 51,962 | 5.1 | 104,894 | 10.4 |
| 1995 | 115,638 | 11.4 | 51,402 | 5.1 | 105,933 | 10.5 |
| 1996 | 116,208 | 11.4 | 50,552 | 5.0 | 105,322 | 10.4 |
| 1997 | 116,244 | 11.4 | 47,759 | 4.7 | 104,190 | 10.2 |
| 1998 | 114,276 | 11.2 | 44,460 | 4.4 | 104,583 | 10.3 |

* Including marriages among Belgian armed forces stationed outside the country and alien armed forces in Belgium, unless performed by local foreign authority.
† Including Belgian armed forces stationed outside the country but excluding alien armed forces stationed in Belgium.

**Expectation of life** (official estimates, years at birth, 1996–98): Males 74.81; Females 81.08.

**ECONOMICALLY ACTIVE POPULATION**
(estimates, '000 persons aged 15 years and over, at 30 June each year)

| | 1994 | 1995 |
|---|---|---|
| Agriculture, hunting and forestry | 89.4 | 88.9 |
| Fishing | 2.2 | 2.1 |
| Mining and quarrying | 5.9 | 5.6 |
| Manufacturing | 699.0 | 694.2 |
| Electricity, gas and water supply | 28.9 | 28.3 |
| Construction | 256.7 | 252.9 |
| Wholesale and retail trade; repair of motor vehicles, motorcycles and personal and household goods | 562.3 | 559.1 |
| Hotels and restaurants | 116.9 | 117.6 |
| Transport, storage and communications | 241.2 | 244.6 |
| Financial intermediation | 133.4 | 132.7 |
| Real estate, renting and business activities | 260.8 | 276.5 |
| Public administration and defence; compulsory social security | 282.4 | 279.2 |
| Education | 307.5 | 308.6 |
| Health and social work | 357.9 | 365.2 |
| Other community, social and personal service activities | 150.9 | 154.5 |
| Private households with employed persons | 85.7 | 87.5 |
| Activities not adequately defined | 95.5 | 97.8 |
| **Total in home employment** | 3,676.5 | 3,695.4 |
| Persons working abroad (net) | 49.9 | 50.3 |
| **Total in employment** | 3,726.4 | 3,745.7 |
| Unemployed | 554.0 | 555.3 |
| **Total labour force** | 4,280.4 | 4,300.9 |

**1996** ('000 persons at 30 June): Home employment 3,710.2; Working abroad (net) 51.1; Total in employment 3,761.3; Unemployed 544.9; Total labour force 4,306.2 (males 2,426.1, females 1,880.2).

**1997** ('000 persons at 1 January): Total in employment 3,839.0; Unemployed (ILO definition) 375.1; Total labour force 4,214.2 (males 2,450.2, females 1,764.0) (Source: partly ILO, *Yearbook of Labour Statistics*).

# Agriculture

(Figures include totals for Luxembourg)

**PRINCIPAL CROPS** ('000 metric tons)

| | 1996 | 1997 | 1998 |
|---|---|---|---|
| Wheat and spelt | 1,909 | 1,661 | 1,803 |
| Barley | 445 | 432 | 411 |
| Maize | 48 | 50* | 251 |
| Oats | 49 | 55 | 50† |
| Other cereals | 111 | 103 | 118 |
| Potatoes | 2,806 | 2,822 | 2,700† |
| Rapeseed | 27 | 24† | 22† |
| Cabbages | 89 | 85 | 85* |
| Tomatoes | 286 | 303 | 300* |
| Cauliflowers | 86 | 90 | 90* |
| Cucumbers and gherkins | 33 | 29 | 30* |
| Beans (green) | 59 | 72 | 60* |
| Peas (green) | 165 | 166 | 165* |
| Carrots | 133 | 136 | 135* |
| Other vegetables | 753 | 796 | 775* |
| Sugar beet | 6,125 | 6,545 | 5,216 |
| Apples | 302 | 373 | 413 |
| Pears | 138 | 131 | 151 |
| Strawberries | 43 | 36 | 36* |
| Other fruits and berries | 39 | 17 | 23 |

* FAO estimate. † Unofficial figure.

Source: FAO, *Production Yearbook*.

**LIVESTOCK** ('000 head, year ending September)

| | 1996 | 1997 | 1998 |
|---|---|---|---|
| Horses | 24 | 24 | 25 |
| Cattle | 3,363 | 3,280 | 3,184 |
| Pigs | 7,225 | 7,194 | 7,436 |
| Sheep | 161 | 162 | 155† |
| Goats | 9 | 10 | 10* |
| Chickens (million) | 49 | 48 | 48* |

* FAO estimate. † Unofficial figure.

Source: FAO, *Production Yearbook*.

**LIVESTOCK PRODUCTS** ('000 metric tons)

| | 1996 | 1997 | 1998 |
|---|---|---|---|
| Beef and veal | 362 | 340 | 298† |
| Mutton and lamb | 5 | 4† | 5* |
| Pig meat | 1,070 | 1,033 | 1,070* |
| Horse meat | 4 | 5† | 4* |
| Poultry meat | 338 | 337 | 337* |
| Other meat | 25 | 26 | 27 |
| Cows' milk | 3,681 | 3,477 | 3,700* |
| Butter | 97 | 107 | 105* |
| Cheese | 75† | 78† | 78* |
| Hen eggs | 220 | 228 | 228* |
| Cattle hides* | 33 | 31 | 29 |

* FAO estimate(s). † Unofficial figure.

Source: FAO, *Production Yearbook*.

# Forestry

(Figures include totals for Luxembourg)

**ROUNDWOOD REMOVALS**
('000 cubic metres, excluding bark)

| | 1995 | 1996 | 1997 |
|---|---|---|---|
| Sawlogs, veneer logs and logs for sleepers | 2,550 | 2,400 | 2,400 |
| Pulpwood | 850 | 875 | 875 |
| Other industrial wood | 210 | 210 | 210 |
| Fuel wood | 500 | 500 | 500 |
| **Total** | 4,110 | 3,985 | 3,985 |

Source: FAO, *Yearbook of Forest Products*.

**SAWNWOOD PRODUCTION**
('000 cubic metres, including railway sleepers)

| | 1995 | 1996 | 1997 |
|---|---|---|---|
| Coniferous (softwood) | 880 | 830 | 830 |
| Broadleaved (hardwood) | 270 | 270 | 270 |
| **Total** | 1,150 | 1,100 | 1,100 |

Source: FAO, *Yearbook of Forest Products*.

# Fishing

('000 metric tons, live weight)

| | 1995 | 1996 | 1997 |
|---|---|---|---|
| European plaice | 9.3 | 7.7 | 7.5 |
| Lemon sole | 1.0 | 1.1 | 1.0 |
| Common sole | 5.5 | 5.2 | 4.5 |
| Atlantic cod | 5.9 | 4.5 | 5.7 |
| Whiting | 1.3 | 1.3 | 1.0 |
| Angler (Monk) | 1.8 | 1.4 | 1.1 |
| Rays | 1.3 | 1.4 | 1.3 |
| Other fishes | 6.5 | 6.3 | 6.6 |
| **Total fish** | 32.5 | 28.7 | 28.6 |
| Common shrimp | 1.6 | 0.9 | 0.7 |
| Other crustaceans | 0.7 | 0.4 | 0.5 |
| Molluscs | 0.9 | 0.9 | 0.6 |
| **Total catch** | 35.6 | 30.8 | 30.5 |

Source: FAO, *Yearbook of Fishery Statistics*.

# Mining

('000 metric tons, unless otherwise indicated)

| | 1993 | 1994 | 1995 |
|---|---|---|---|
| Lignite | 862 | 753 | 637 |
| Uranium (metric tons) | 34 | 40 | 24 |
| Kaolin | 139 | n.a. | n.a. |
| Chalk | 5,409 | 2,100 | 2,186 |

**1996:** Chalk ('000 metric tons) 2,139.
**1997:** Chalk ('000 metric tons) 2,071.
**1998:** Chalk ('000 metric tons) 2,099.

Source: partly UN, *Industrial Commodity Statistics Yearbook*.

# Industry

**SELECTED PRODUCTS**

('000 metric tons, unless otherwise indicated)

| | 1996 | 1997 | 1998 |
|---|---|---|---|
| Wheat flour[1] | 1,319 | 1,343 | 1,332 |
| Raw sugar | 979 | 1,034 | 995 |
| Margarine | 351.5 | 341.5 | 304.3 |
| Beer ('000 hectolitres) | n.a. | 14,758.3 | 14,815.7 |
| Cigarettes (million) | 20,554.7 | n.a. | n.a. |
| Cotton yarn—pure and mixed (metric tons) | 20,208 | 22,206 | 20,371 |
| Woven cotton fabrics—pure and mixed (metric tons)[2] | 37,126 | 37,590 | 39,281 |
| Flax yarn (metric tons)[3] | 2,453 | 2,920 | 3,027 |
| Wool yarn—pure and mixed (metric tons) | 12,587 | 13,146 | 14,868 |
| Woven woollen fabrics—pure and mixed (metric tons)[2] | 2,106 | 2,632 | 2,971 |
| Woven rayon and acetate fabrics—pure and mixed (metric tons)[4] | 68,189 | 70,757 | 73,440 |
| Mechanical wood pulp[5] | 173 | 173 | n.a. |
| Chemical and semi-chemical wood pulp[5] | 209 | 209 | n.a. |
| Newsprint[5] | 104 | 104 | n.a. |
| Other paper and paperboard | 1,455.6 | 1,621.3 | 1,742.3 |
| Ethyl alcohol—Ethanol ('000 hectolitres) | 150.1 | 64.1 | 102.4 |
| Sulphuric acid (100%) | 677.7 | 648.8 | 587.4 |
| Nitric acid (100%) | 48.0 | 50.4 | 55.7 |
| Liquefied petroleum gas | 605 | 578 | 598 |
| Naphtha | 1,148 | 1,407 | 1,524 |
| Motor spirit (petrol) | 5,947 | 6,103 | 6,431 |
| Kerosene | 100 | 113 | 128 |
| White spirit | 112 | 164 | 157 |
| Jet fuel | 1,739 | 1,644 | 2,067 |
| Distillate fuel oils | 12,619 | 12,520 | 12,447 |
| Residual fuel oil | 6,949.8 | 7,694.3 | 8,349.2 |
| *— continued* | **1996** | **1997** | **1998** |
| Petroleum bitumen (asphalt) | 771.8 | 951.5 | 956.8 |
| Coke-oven coke | 3,551 | 3,402 | 300.3 |
| Cement | 9,822 | 9,926 | 9,875 |
| Pig-iron | 8,626.7 | 8,076.5 | 8,618.1 |
| Crude steel | 10,751.7 | 10,717.6 | 11,403.8 |
| Refined copper—unwrought (metric tons)[6] | 593,070 | 619,187 | 637,992 |
| Refined lead—unwrought (metric tons)[7] | 142,178 | 142,901 | 111,858 |
| Tin: secondary (metric tons)[8] | 3,000 | 3,000 | 2,500 |
| Passenger motor cars ('000)[9] | 1,153.4 | 1,020.4 | 974.9 |
| Commercial motor vehicles ('000)[9] | 78.0 | 81.7 | n.a. |
| Electric energy (million kWh) | 76,147.4 | 78,891.7 | 79,492.4 |
| Manufactured gas (million cu metres) | 1,510 | 1,366 | 1,334 |

[1] Industrial production only.
[2] Including blankets and carpets.
[3] Including yarn made from tow.
[4] Including fabrics of natural silk and blankets and carpets of cellulosic fibres.
[5] Including production in Luxembourg. Source: FAO, *Yearbook of Forest Products*.
[6] Including alloys and the processing of refined copper imported from the Democratic Republic of the Congo.
[7] Primary and secondary production, including alloys and remelted lead.
[8] Estimated production. Source: US Geological Survey.
[9] Assembled wholly or mainly from imported parts.

# Finance

**CURRENCY AND EXCHANGE RATES**

**Monetary Units**

100 centimes (centiemen) = 1 franc belge (frank) or Belgian franc (BF).

**Sterling, Dollar and Euro Equivalents** (30 September 1999)

£1 sterling = 62.278 francs;
US $1 = 37.825 francs;
€1 = 40.340 francs;
1,000 Belgian francs = £16.06 = $26.44 = €24.79.

**Average Exchange Rate** (francs per US $)

1996 30.962
1997 35.774
1998 36.299

**BUDGET** ('000 million Belgian francs)*

| Revenue† | 1993 | 1994 | 1995 |
|---|---|---|---|
| Tax revenue | 3,112.9 | 3,342.4 | 3,462.5 |
| Taxes on income, profits and capital gains | 1,070.9 | 1,202.8 | 1,262.0 |
| Social security contributions | 1,155.3 | 1,181.1 | 1,221.1 |
| Taxes on property | 85.1 | 92.9 | 89.0 |
| Domestic taxes on goods and services | 801.6 | 865.6 | 890.4 |
| General sales, turnover or value-added taxes | 511.5 | 550.9 | 553.9 |
| Excises | 173.9 | 190.3 | 193.2 |
| Other current revenue | 137.3 | 123.4 | 86.1 |
| Entrepreneurial and property income | 68.9 | 50.2 | 53.4 |
| Capital revenue | 13.2 | 10.6 | 18.9 |
| **Total** | 3,263.4 | 3,476.4 | 3,567.5 |

| Expenditure‡ | 1993 | 1994 | 1995 |
|---|---|---|---|
| Current expenditure | 3,532.1 | 3,650.7 | 3,694.0 |
| Expenditure on goods and services | 665.5 | 692.8 | 714.3 |
| Wages and salaries | 527.9 | 555.0 | 577.0 |
| Interest payments | 737.2 | 750.9 | 695.8 |
| Subsidies and other current transfers | 2,129.4 | 2,207.0 | 2,283.9 |
| Subsidies | 142.2 | 145.5 | 149.4 |
| Transfers to other levels of national government | 212.5 | 223.5 | 228.4 |
| Transfers to non-profit institutions and households | 1,740.4 | 1,797.9 | 1,871.9 |
| Capital expenditure | 167.4 | 170.6 | 191.6 |
| Capital transfers | 103.3 | 104.9 | 118.7 |
| **Total** | 3,699.5 | 3,821.3 | 3,885.6 |

* Figures refer to the consolidated transactions of the central Government. In addition to the general budget, the data include the operations of social security funds, government agencies and other extrabudgetary funds.
† Excluding grants received ('000 million Belgian francs): 4.6 in 1993; 5.7 in 1994; 11.1 in 1995.
‡ Excluding lending minus repayments ('000 million Belgian francs): 18.7 in 1993; -14.3 in 1994; -47.9 in 1995.

Source: IMF, *Government Finance Statistics Yearbook*.

**NATIONAL BANK RESERVES** (US $ million at 31 December)

| | 1996 | 1997 | 1998 |
|---|---|---|---|
| Gold*† | 6,171 | 5,140 | 2,565 |
| IMF special drawing rights | 498 | 489 | 610 |
| Reserve position in IMF | 1,075 | 1,182 | 1,899 |
| Foreign exchange† | 15,380 | 14,159 | 15,763 |
| **Total** | 23,124 | 20,970 | 20,837 |

* Valued at market-related prices.
† Figures for gold and foreign exchange refer to the monetary association between Belgium and Luxembourg and exclude deposits made with the European Monetary Institute (now the European Central Bank).

Source: IMF, *International Financial Statistics*.

**MONEY SUPPLY** ('000 million Belgian francs at 31 December)

| | 1995 | 1996 | 1997 |
|---|---|---|---|
| Currency outside banks | 465.9 | 486.2 | 501.1 |
| Demand deposits at commercial banks | 1,152.7 | 1,200.0 | 1,237.0 |
| **Total money** | 1,618.6 | 1,686.2 | 1,738.1 |

**1998** ('000 million Belgian francs at 31 December): Currency outside banks 505.8.

Source: IMF, *International Financial Statistics*.

**COST OF LIVING** (Consumer Price Index; base: 1990 = 100)

| | 1996 | 1997 | 1998 |
|---|---|---|---|
| Food | 104.8 | 107.1 | 109.0 |
| Fuel and light | 107.0 | 109.5 | 105.5 |
| Clothing | 113.4 | 114.1 | 115.6 |
| Rent | 126.5 | 128.7 | 130.2 |
| **All items** (incl. others) | 115.2 | 117.1 | 118.2 |

Source: mainly ILO, *Yearbook of Labour Statistics*.

**NATIONAL ACCOUNTS**
('000 million Belgian francs at current prices)

**National Income and Product**

| | 1996 | 1997 | 1998 |
|---|---|---|---|
| Compensation of employees | 4,274 | 4,417 | 4,575 |
| Operating surplus | 2,234 | 2,365 | 2,491 |
| **Domestic factor incomes** | 6,508 | 6,782 | 7,066 |
| Consumption of fixed capital | 953 | 1,012 | 1,027 |
| **Gross domestic product (GDP) at factor cost** | 7,461 | 7,794 | 8,093 |
| Indirect taxes / *Less* Subsidies | 871 | 932 | 971 |
| **GDP in purchasers' values** | 8,332 | 8,726 | 9,064 |
| Factor income from abroad (net) | 127 | 114 | 125 |
| **Gross national product (GNP)** | 8,459 | 8,840 | 9,189 |
| *Less* Consumption of fixed capital | 953 | 1,012 | 1,027 |
| **National income in market prices** | 7,506 | 7,828 | 8,162 |
| Current transfers from abroad (net) | -135 | -133 | -142 |
| **National disposable income** | 7,371 | 7,695 | 8,020 |

Source: Service Statistiques financières et économiques, Banque Nationale de Belgique.

**Expenditure on the Gross Domestic Product**

| | 1996 | 1997 | 1998 |
|---|---|---|---|
| Government final consumption expenditure | 1,804 | 1,843 | 1,910 |
| Private final consumption expenditure | 4,526 | 4,704 | 4,897 |
| Increase in stocks | -20 | -26 | 25 |
| Gross fixed capital formation | 1,687 | 1,811 | 1,879 |
| **Total domestic expenditure** | 7,997 | 8,332 | 8,711 |
| Exports of goods and services | 5,917 | 6,623 | 6,832 |
| *Less* Imports of goods and services | 5,583 | 6,228 | 6,479 |
| **GDP in purchasers' values** | 8,331 | 8,727 | 9,064 |
| **GDP at constant 1995 prices** | 8,203 | 8,466 | 8,712 |

Source: Service Statistiques financières et économiques, Banque Nationale de Belgique.

**Gross Domestic Product by Economic Activity** (provisional)

| | 1995 | 1996 | 1997 |
|---|---|---|---|
| Agriculture and livestock | 92.3 | 92.2 | 94.2 |
| Forestry and logging | 7.2 | 7.2 | 7.2 |
| Fishing | 2.4 | 2.4 | 2.7 |
| Mining and quarrying | 20.3 | 20.6 | 22.1 |
| Manufacturing[1] | 1,753.8 | 1,752.0 | 1,846.6 |
| Electricity, gas and water | 196.9 | 205.4 | 213.0 |
| Construction | 401.0 | 396.1 | 424.2 |
| Wholesale and retail trade | 758.1 | 794.0 | 806.4 |
| Distribution of petroleum products | 215.2 | 234.6 | 242.5 |
| Transport, storage and communications | 628.4 | 632.5 | 675.5 |
| Finance and insurance | 464.7 | 511.4 | 515.2 |
| Real estate | 650.0 | 676.6 | 698.2 |
| Business services | 500.8 | 524.9 | 568.8 |
| Public administration and defence | 573.6 | 590.4 | 610.2 |
| Education | 443.7 | 445.6 | 458.1 |
| Health services | 232.5 | 243.5 | 244.3 |
| Other community, social and personal services[2] | 704.4 | 757.3 | 788.5 |
| Domestic service of households | 60.7 | 62.5 | 64.3 |
| **Sub-total** | 7,705.9 | 7,949.1 | 8,282.1 |
| Imputed bank service charge | -217.4 | -261.0 | -240.6 |
| Value-added tax and import duties | 610.0 | 635.7 | 669.3 |
| Statistical discrepancy[3] | -30.3 | -18.7 | -35.4 |
| **GDP in purchasers' values** | 8,068.1 | 8,305.1 | 8,675.5 |

[1] Including garages.
[2] Including restaurants and hotels.
[3] Including a correction to compensate for the exclusion of certain own-account capital investments ('000 million francs): 11.4 in 1995; 13.3 in 1996; 13.8 in 1997.

**BALANCE OF PAYMENTS** (US $ million)*

| | 1996 | 1997 | 1998 |
|---|---|---|---|
| Exports of goods f.o.b. | 154,695 | 149,968 | 153,160 |
| Imports of goods f.o.b. | −146,004 | −142,168 | −145,599 |
| **Trade balance** | 8,690 | 7,800 | 7,561 |
| Exports of services | 35,766 | 35,447 | 36,814 |
| Imports of services | −32,837 | −31,697 | −34,258 |
| **Balance on goods and services** | 11,620 | 11,550 | 10,117 |
| Other income received | 61,195 | 55,751 | 59,596 |
| Other income paid | −54,157 | −49,464 | −53,182 |
| **Balance on goods, services and income** | 18,658 | 17,837 | 16,530 |
| Current transfers received | 7,474 | 7,193 | 6,993 |
| Current transfers paid | −12,081 | −11,091 | −11,412 |
| **Current balance** | 14,051 | 13,939 | 12,111 |
| Capital account (net) | 179 | 405 | −42 |
| Direct investment abroad | −8,026 | −7,713 | −23,272 |
| Direct investment from abroad | 14,064 | 12,352 | 20,824 |
| Portfolio investment assets | −49,379 | −62,861 | −97,339 |
| Portfolio investment liabilities | 37,149 | 54,486 | 61,967 |
| Other investment assets | −14,979 | −48,928 | 6,121 |
| Other investment liabilities | 8,911 | 40,320 | 16,713 |
| Net errors and omissions | −1,377 | −944 | 823 |
| **Overall balance** | 593 | 1,056 | −2,095 |

* Data refer to the Belgium-Luxembourg Economic Union and exclude transactions between the two countries.

Source: IMF, *International Financial Statistics.*

# External Trade

**PRINCIPAL COMMODITIES**
('000 million Belgian francs)

| Imports c.i.f. | 1996 | 1997 | 1998 |
|---|---|---|---|
| Live animals and animal products | 139.1 | 148.1 | 151.2 |
| Vegetable products | 201.7 | 208.2 | 207.3 |
| Prepared foodstuffs; beverages, spirits and vinegar; tobacco and manufactured substitutes | 221.8 | 246.5 | 260.1 |
| Mineral products | 408.2 | 464.1 | 367.8 |
| Products of the chemical or allied industries | 588.0 | 674.1 | 790.7 |
| Plastics, rubber and articles thereof | 317.9 | 349.8 | 377.4 |
| Paper-making material; paper and paperboard and articles thereof | 156.3 | 165.0 | 183.5 |
| Textiles and textile articles | 295.3 | 329.7 | 345.6 |
| Natural or cultured pearls, precious or semi-precious stones, precious metals and articles thereof; imitation jewellery; coin | 384.8 | 423.6 | 389.3 |
| Base metals and articles thereof | 385.1 | 430.5 | 476.2 |
| Machinery and mechanical appliances; electrical equipment; sound and television apparatus | 871.1 | 976.5 | 1,073.5 |
| Vehicles, aircraft, vessels and associated transport equipment | 659.8 | 701.3 | 757.8 |
| Optical, photographic, measuring, precision and medical apparatus; clocks and watches; musical instruments | 108.2 | 122.2 | 132.8 |
| Miscellaneous manufactured articles | 113.9 | 128.4 | 138.2 |
| **Total** (incl. others) | 5,065.5 | 5,619.2 | 5,902.5 |

| Exports f.o.b. | 1996 | 1997 | 1998 |
|---|---|---|---|
| Live animals and animal products | 177.9 | 188.2 | 183.7 |
| Vegetable products | 163.2 | 172.4 | 182.2 |
| Prepared foodstuffs; beverages, spirits and vinegar; tobacco and manufactured substitutes | 260.6 | 300.1 | 305.3 |
| Mineral products | 226.3 | 254.3 | 212.9 |
| Products of the chemical or allied industries | 746.3 | 872.3 | 943.1 |
| Plastics, rubber and articles thereof | 437.2 | 499.1 | 526.4 |
| Paper-making material; paper and paperboard and articles thereof | 147.0 | 158.1 | 171.1 |
| Textiles and textile articles | 348.6 | 383.4 | 409.5 |
| Natural or cultured pearls, precious or semi-precious stones, precious metals and articles thereof; imitation jewellery; coin | 386.4 | 443.9 | 412.1 |
| Base metals and articles thereof | 499.1 | 546.9 | 583.8 |
| Machinery and mechanical appliances; electrical equipment; sound and television apparatus | 747.5 | 878.1 | 953.1 |
| Vehicles, aircraft, vessels and associated transport equipment | 845.4 | 924.4 | 975.1 |
| **Total** (incl. others) | 5,430.1 | 6,142.8 | 6,396.7 |

**PRINCIPAL TRADING PARTNERS** ('000 million Belgian francs)*

| Imports c.i.f. | 1997 | 1998 |
|---|---|---|
| China, People's Repub. | 91.2 | 93.5 |
| France | 779.1 | 797.4 |
| Germany | 971.2 | 1,057.1 |
| Ireland | 96.1 | 153.1 |
| Italy | 216.5 | 233.5 |
| Japan | 137.2 | 150.3 |
| Netherlands | 1,011.7 | 983.6 |
| Spain | 98.5 | 110.3 |
| Sweden | 143.1 | 160.7 |
| Switzerland | 61.0 | 59.0 |
| United Kingdom | 510.8 | 507.0 |
| USA | 431.1 | 467.3 |
| **Total** (incl. others) | 5,619.2 | 5,902.5 |

| Exports f.o.b. | 1996 | 1997 | 1998 |
|---|---|---|---|
| Austria | n.a. | 65.1 | 72.4 |
| France | 981.1 | 1,063.5 | 1,132.2 |
| Germany | 1,089.1 | 1,146.7 | 1,213.2 |
| India | 77.5 | 102.5 | 96.9 |
| Israel | n.a. | 113.9 | 97.8 |
| Italy | 293.4 | 329.9 | 366.5 |
| Luxembourg | 115.3 | 118.0 | 116.2 |
| Netherlands | 730.0 | 789.3 | 802.4 |
| Spain | 162.9 | 189.6 | 226.2 |
| Sweden | n.a. | 88.0 | 95.4 |
| Switzerland | 91.1 | 101.2 | 102.3 |
| United Kingdom | 483.7 | 607.3 | 628.7 |
| USA | 223.2 | 299.6 | 330.0 |
| **All countries** (incl. others) | 5,407.3 | 6,119.4 | 6,366.7 |
| Not distributed | 22.8 | 23.4 | 30.0 |
| **Total** | 5,430.1 | 6,142.8 | 6,396.7 |

* Imports by country of production; exports by country of last consignment.

# Transport

**RAILWAYS** (traffic)

| | 1996 | 1997 | 1998 |
|---|---|---|---|
| Passenger-km (million) | 6,788 | 6,980 | 7,097 |
| Freight ton-km (million) | 7,244 | 7,465 | 7,600 |

Source: Ministère des Communications et de l'Infrastructure.

**ROAD TRAFFIC** (motor vehicles in use at 1 August)

| | 1996 | 1997 | 1998 |
|---|---|---|---|
| Private cars | 4,339,231 | 4,415,343 | 4,491,734 |
| Buses and coaches | 14,660 | 14,667 | 14,566 |
| Goods vehicles | 416,716 | 435,237 | 453,122 |
| Tractors (non-agricultural) | 40,449 | 41,346 | 42,342 |
| Motorcycles and mopeds | 209,015 | 221,623 | 238,053 |

Source: Ministère des Communications et de l'Infrastructure.

**SHIPPING**

**Fleet** (at 30 June)

| | 1997 | 1998 | 1999 |
|---|---|---|---|
| Merchant shipping: | | | |
| Steamships: | | | |
| number | 1 | 1 | 1 |
| displacement* | 81.8 | 81.8 | 81.8 |
| Motor vessels: | | | |
| number | 27 | 24 | 14 |
| displacement* | 524 | 344 | 259 |
| Inland waterways: | | | |
| Powered craft: | | | |
| number | 1,264 | n.a. | n.a. |
| displacement* | 1,041 | n.a. | n.a. |
| Non-powered craft: | | | |
| number | 157 | n.a. | n.a. |
| displacement* | 384 | n.a. | n.a. |

* '000 gross registered tons.

Source: Ministère des Communications et de l'Infrastructure.

**Freight Traffic** ('000 metric tons)

| | 1996 | 1997 | 1998 |
|---|---|---|---|
| Sea-borne shipping: | | | |
| Goods loaded | 57,703 | 61,856 | 60,430 |
| Goods unloaded | 95,598 | 100,208 | 111,129 |
| Inland waterways: | | | |
| Goods loaded | 53,106 | 54,418 | n.a. |
| Goods unloaded | 68,826 | 68,418 | n.a. |

Source: Ministère des Communications et de l'Infrastructure.

**CIVIL AVIATION** (traffic)

| | 1996 | 1997 | 1998 |
|---|---|---|---|
| Kilometres flown ('000) | 118,218 | 121,556 | 167,464 |
| Passenger-km ('000) | 9,099,901 | 11,273,577 | 16,971,798 |
| Ton-km ('000) | 818,990 | 1,014,622 | 1,527,490 |
| Mail ton-km ('000) | 16,231 | 13,090 | n.a. |

Figures refer to SABENA Belgian Airlines.

Source: Ministère des Communications et de l'Infrastructure.

# Tourism

**NUMBER OF TOURIST NIGHTS BY COUNTRY OF ORIGIN***

| | 1995 | 1996† | 1998 |
|---|---|---|---|
| France | 1,382,982 | 1,450,277 | 1,604,108 |
| Germany | 2,889,675 | 2,737,254 | 2,523,475 |
| Italy | 377,853 | 419,325 | 412,927 |
| Japan | 248,505 | 273,413 | 274,197 |
| Netherlands | 4,428,559 | 4,610,188 | 4,502,548 |
| Spain | 265,195 | 305,120 | 314,311 |
| United Kingdom | 1,513,222 | 1,640,723 | 2,126,911 |
| USA | 580,579 | 638,099 | 704,789 |
| **Total** (incl. others) | 13,877,622 | 14,440,943 | 14,838,367 |

* Nights spent by foreign visitors in hotels and similar establishments.

† 1997 figures not available.

**Total number of tourist arrivals:** 5,559,875 in 1995; 5,829,257 in 1996; 6,037,031 in 1997; 6,179,254 in 1998.

Sources: World Tourism Organization, *Yearbook of Tourism Statistics*; Office de Promotion du Tourisme Wallonie-Bruxelles.

# Communications Media

| | 1994 | 1995 | 1996 |
|---|---|---|---|
| Telephones ('000 main lines in use) | 4,526 | 4,632 | 4,818 |
| Mobile cellular telephones ('000 subscribers) | 128.1 | 235.3 | 478.1 |
| Radio receivers ('000 in use) | 7,800 | 8,000 | 8,050 |
| Television receivers ('000 in use) | 4,565 | 4,600 | 4,700 |
| Daily newspapers: | | | |
| Titles | 32 | 31 | 30 |
| Average circulation ('000 copies) | n.a. | 1,628 | 1,625 |

Telefax stations ('000 in use): 165 in 1993.

Telephones ('000 main lines in use): 4,939 in 1997.

Mobile cellular telephones ('000 subscribers): 974.5 in 1997; 1,756.3 in 1998.

Sources: mainly UN, *Statistical Yearbook*; UNESCO, *Statistical Yearbook*.

# Education

(1996/97)

| | Institutions | | Students | |
|---|---|---|---|---|
| | French* | Flemish | French* | Flemish |
| Pre-primary | 1,932 | 2,175 | 171,478 | 253,043 |
| Primary | 2,023 | 2,378 | 320,454 | 417,369 |
| Secondary | 648 | 1,079 | 349,170 | 447,775 |
| Non-university higher education | 105 | 29 | 73,359 | 94,140 |
| University level | 9 | 8 | 62,300 | n.a. |

* Figures for 1995/96.

**Teachers:** French (1995/96): Pre-primary and primary 38,150; Secondary 57,555; Higher education 20,927. Flemish (1996/97): Pre-primary and primary 44,018; Secondary 57,707; Higher education 17,087.

# Directory

## The Constitution

The Belgian Constitution has been considerably modified by amendments since its creation in 1831. Belgium is a constitutional monarchy. The central legislature consists of a bicameral Parliament (the Chamber of Representatives and Senate). In July 1993 the Constitution was amended to provide for a federation of the largely autonomous regions of Brussels, Flanders and Wallonia and of the Flemish-, French- and German-speaking language communities. Article 1 of the Constitution states 'Belgium is a federal state which consists of communities and regions'. The three regions and three linguistic groups are represented by the following directly-elected legislative assemblies: a combined assembly for Flanders and the Flemish-speaking community, regional assemblies for Wallonia and Brussels, and separate assemblies for French- and German-speakers. Each assembly is elected for a term of four years. The regional administrations have sole responsibility for the local economy, the environment, housing, transport and public works, while the language community administrations supervise education policy and culture.

### ELECTORAL SYSTEM

Members of Parliament must be 25 years of age, and they are elected by secret ballot according to a system of proportional representation. Suffrage is universal for citizens of 18 years or over, and voting is compulsory.

The Chamber of Representatives consists of 150 members, who are elected for four years unless the Chamber is dissolved before that time has elapsed. The Senate comprises 71 normal members, of whom 40 are directly elected, usually at intervals of four years, 21 are appointed by the legislative assemblies of the three language communities (10 each from the Flemish- and French-speaking communities and one from the German-speaking community), and 10 are co-opted by the elected members. Children of the King are entitled to honorary membership of the Senate from 18 years of age and acquire voting rights at the age of 21.

### THE CROWN

The King has the right to veto legislation, but, in practice, he does not exercise it. The King is nominally the supreme head of the executive, but, in fact, he exercises his control through the Cabinet, which is responsible for all acts of government to the Chamber of Representatives. According to the Constitution, the King appoints his own ministers, but in practice, since they are responsible to the Chamber of Representatives and need its confidence, they are generally the choice of the Representatives. Similarly, the royal initiative is in the control of the ministry.

### LEGISLATION

Legislation is introduced either by the federal Government or the members in the two Houses, and as the party complexion of both Houses is generally almost the same, measures passed by the Chamber of Representatives are usually passed by the Senate. Each House elects its own President at the beginning of the session, who acts as an impartial Speaker, although he is a party nominee. The Houses elect their own committees, through which all legislation passes. They are so well organized that through them the Legislature has considerable power of control over the Cabinet. Nevertheless, according to the Constitution (Article 68), certain treaties must be communicated to the Chamber only as soon as the 'interest and safety of the State permit'. Further, the Government possesses an important power of dissolution which it uses; a most unusual feature is that it may be applied to either House separately or to both together (Article 71).

Revision of the Constitution is to be first settled by an ordinary majority vote of both Houses, specifying the article to be amended. The Houses are then automatically dissolved. The new Chambers thereupon determine the amendments to be made, with the provision that in each House the presence of two-thirds of the members is necessary for a quorum, and a two-thirds majority of those voting is required.

## The Government

### HEAD OF STATE

**King of the Belgians:** HM King ALBERT II (took the oath 9 August 1993).

### THE CABINET

(January 2000)

A coalition of Vlaamse Liberalen en Demokraten—Partij van de Burger (VLD), the Parti Réformateur Libéral (PRL), the Parti Socialiste (PS), the Socialistische Partij (SP), Anders Gaan Leven (Agalev) and the Ecologistes Confédérés pour l'Organisation des Luttes Originales (Ecolo).

**Prime Minister:** GUY VERHOFSTADT (VLD).

**Deputy Prime Minister, Minister of Employment and Equal Opportunities:** LAURETTE ONKELINX (PS).

**Deputy Prime Minister, Minister of Foreign Affairs:** LOUIS MICHEL (PRL).

**Deputy Prime Minister, Minister of the Budget, Social Integration and Social Economy:** JOHAN VANDE LANOTTE (SP).

**Deputy Prime Minister, Minister of Mobility and Transport:** ISABELLE DURANT (Ecolo).

**Minister of Consumer Affairs, Public Health and the Environment:** MAGDA AELVOET (Agalev).

**Minister of the Interior:** ANTOINE DUQUESNE (PRL).

**Minister of Social Affairs and Pensions:** FRANK VANDENBROUCKE (SP).

**Minister of the Civil Service and Modernization of the Public Administration:** LUC VAN DEN BOSSCHE (SP).

**Minister of Defence:** ANDRÉ FLAHAUT (PS).

**Minister of Agriculture and Small and Medium-sized Enterprises:** JAAK GABRIELS (VLD).

**Minister of Justice:** MARK VERWILGHEN (VLD).

**Minister of Finance:** DIDIER REYNDERS (PRL).

**Minister of Telecommunications, Public Enterprises and Participation:** RIK DAEMS (CVD).

**Minister of Economic Affairs and Scientific Research:** RUDY DEMOTTE (PS).

**Secretary of State for Foreign Trade:** PIERRE CHEVALIER (VLD).

**Secretary of State for Development Co-operation:** EDDY BOUTMANS (Agalev).

**Secretary of State for Energy and Sustainable Development:** OLIVIER DELEUZE (Agalev).

### MINISTRIES

**Office of the Prime Minister:** 16 rue de la Loi, 1000 Brussels; tel. (2) 501-02-11; fax (2) 512-69-53; internet www.premier.fgov.be.

**Department of Development Co-operation:** 45–46 blvd du Régent, 1000 Brussels; tel. (2) 519-02-11; fax (2) 519-05-85.

**Department of Energy and Sustainable Development:** 56 rue des Colonies, 1000 Brussels; tel. (2) 227-07-00; fax (2) 219-79-30.

**Department of Foreign Trade:** 15 rue des Petits Carmes, 6th floor, 1000 Brussels; tel. (2) 501-83-11; fax (2) 512-72-21.

**Ministry of Agriculture and Small and Medium-sized Enterprises:** 1 rue Marie-Thérèse, 1000 Brussels; tel. (2) 211-06-11; fax (2) 219-61-30.

**Ministry of the Budget, Social Integration and Social Economy:** 180 rue Royale, 1000 Brussels; tel. (2) 210-19-11; fax (2) 217-33-28.

**Ministry of the Civil Service and Modernization of Public Administration:** Résidence Palais, 9th floor, 155 rue de la Loi, 1040 Brussels; tel. (2) 233-05-11; fax (2) 233-05-90.

**Ministry of Consumer Affairs, Public Health and the Environment:** Bâtiment Amazone, 33 ave Bischoffsheim, 1000 Brussels; tel. (2) 220-20-11; fax (2) 220-20-67.

**Ministry of Defence:** 8 rue Lambermont, 1000 Brussels; tel. (2) 550-28-11; fax (2) 550-29-19.

**Ministry of Economic Affairs and Scientific Research:** 23 square de Meeûs, 1000 Brussels; tel. (2) 506-51-11; fax (2) 511-86-56.

**Ministry of Employment and Equal Opportunities:** 51–53 rue Belliard, 1040 Brussels; tel. (2) 233-51-11; fax (2) 230-10-67; e-mail info@meta.fgov.be.

**Ministry of Finance:** 12 rue de la Loi, 1000 Brussels; tel. (2) 233-81-11; fax (2) 233-80-03.

**Ministry of Foreign Affairs:** 15 rue des Petits Carmes, 1000 Brussels; tel. (2) 501-82-11; fax (2) 511-63-85.

**Ministry of the Interior:** 60–62 rue Royale, 1000 Brussels; tel. (2) 504-85-11; fax (2) 504-85-00; e-mail henri.maes@mibz.fgov.be; internet mibz.fgov.be.

**Ministry of Justice:** 115 blvd de Waterloo, 1000 Brussels; tel. (2) 542-79-11; fax (2) 538-07-67; internet www.just.fgov.be.

**Ministry of Mobility and Transport:** 65 rue de la Loi, 1040 Brussels; tel. (2) 237-67-11; fax (2) 231-18-24.

**Ministry of Social Affairs and Pensions:** 66 rue de la Loi, 1040 Brussels; tel. (2) 238-28-11; fax (2) 230-38-62.

**Ministry of Telecommunications, Public Enterprises and Participation:** 7 place Quetelet, 1210 Brussels; tel. (2) 250-03-03; fax (2) 219-09-14.

# Legislature

### CHAMBRE DES REPRÉSENTANTS/KAMER VAN VOLKSVERTEGENWOORDIGERS
(Chamber of Representatives)

**General Election, 13 June 1999**

| | % of votes | Seats |
|---|---|---|
| VLD | 14.3 | 23 |
| CVP | 14.1 | 22 |
| PS | 10.2 | 19 |
| PRL-FDF | 10.1 | 18 |
| Vlaams Blok | 9.9 | 15 |
| SP | 9.6 | 14 |
| Ecolo | 7.4 | 11 |
| PSC | 5.9 | 10 |
| Agalev | 7.0 | 9 |
| VU-ID21 | 5.6 | 8 |
| FN | 1.5 | 1 |
| **Total** (incl. others) | 100.0 | 150 |

### SÉNAT/SENAAT

**General Election, 13 June 1999**

| | % of votes | Seats |
|---|---|---|
| VLD | 15.4 | 6 |
| CVP | 14.7 | 6 |
| PRL-FDF | 10.6 | 5 |
| PS | 9.7 | 4 |
| Vlaams Blok | 9.4 | 4 |
| SP | 8.9 | 4 |
| Ecolo | 7.4 | 3 |
| Agalev | 7.1 | 3 |
| PSC | 6.0 | 3 |
| VU-ID21 | 5.1 | 2 |
| **Total** (incl. others) | 100.0 | 40 |

In addition, the Senate has 21 members appointed by the legislative assemblies of the three language communities and 10 members co-opted by the elected members. Children of the King are entitled to honorary membership of the Senate from 18 years of age and acquire voting rights at the age of 21.

# Advisory Councils

**Conseil Central de l'Economie/Centrale Raad voor het Bedrijfsleven:** 17–21 ave de la Joyeuse entrée, 1040 Brussels; e-mail mail@ccecrb.fgov.be; internet www.ccecrb.fgov.be; f. 1948; representative and consultative body; advises the authorities on economic issues; 50 mems; Pres. Baron ROBERT TOLLET.

**Conseil d'Etat/Raad van Staat:** 33 rue de la Science, 1040 Brussels; tel. (2) 234-96-11; e-mail webmaster@raadvst-consetat.be; internet www.raadvst.consetat.be; f. 1946; advisory body on legislative and regulatory matters; supreme administrative court; hears complaints against the actions of the legislature; 38 mems; Pres. JEAN-JACQUES STRYCKMANS.

# Regional and Community Administrations

Belgium is a federal state, and considerable power has been devolved to the regional administrations of Brussels, Wallonia and Flanders, and to the French-, German- and Flemish-speaking communities. The regional authorities have sole responsibility for the environment, housing, transport and public works, and for certain aspects of social welfare, while the community administrations are primarily responsible for cultural affairs and for education. The administrations of Flanders and of the Flemish-speaking community are, however, homologous.

### REGION OF FLANDERS AND THE FLEMISH-SPEAKING COMMUNITY

**Minister-President:** PATRICK DEWAEL (VLD).

**Vlaams Parlement** (Flemish Parliament): 27 Leuvensweg, 1011 Brussels; tel. (2) 552-16-51; fax (2) 513-74-80; internet www.vlaamsparlement.be; f. 1980; 124 mems.

**Vlaamse Overheid** (Flemish Authority): 19 Martelaarsplein, 1000 Brussels; tel. (2) 553-29-11; fax (2) 553-29-05; e-mail kabinet.dewael@vlaanderen.be; internet www.vlaanderen.be.

### REGION OF WALLONIA

**Minister-President:** ELIO DI RUPO (PS).

**Le Parlement Wallon** (Walloon Parliament): 24 rue Saint-Nicolas, 5000 Namur; tel. (81) 23-10-36; fax (2) 23-12-20; internet parlement.wallonie.be; elects Government of Wallonia; 75 mems.

**Gouvernement Wallon** (Walloon Government): internet www.wallonie.org; 9 mems.

### REGION OF BRUSSELS-CAPITAL

**Minister-President:** JACQUES SIMONET (PRL-FDF).

**Conseil de la Région de Bruxelles-Capitale/Brussels Hoofdstedelijke Raad** (Council of the Region of Brussels-Capital): 1005 Brussels; tel. (2) 549-62-11; fax (2) 549-62-12; e-mail Parlement@parlbru.irisnet.be; internet www.parlbru.irisnet.be.

**Gouvernement de la Région de Bruxelles-Capitale/Brusselse Hoofdstedelijke Regering** (Government of Brussels-Capital): 7–9 rue Ducale, 1000 Brussels; tel. (2) 506-32-11; fax (2) 514-40-22; internet www.bruxelles.irisnet.be.

### FRENCH-SPEAKING COMMUNITY

**Minister-President:** ELIO DI RUPO (PS).

**Parlement de la Communauté française de Belgique** (Parliament of the French-speaking Community): 6 rue de la Loi, 1000 Brussels; fax (2) 506-38-08; internet www.pcf.be; comprises mems of the Walloon Parliament and the 19 francophone mems of the Council of the Region of Brussels-Capital; 94 mems.

**Gouvernement de la Communauté française de Belgique** (Government of the French-speaking Community): 15–17 place Surlet de Chokier, 1040 Brussels; tel. (2) 227-32-11; fax (2) 227-33-53; internet www.cfwb.be.

### GERMAN-SPEAKING COMMUNITY

**Minister-President:** KARL-HEINZ LAMBERTZ (PS).

**Rat der Deutschsprachigen Gemeinschaft Belgiens** (Council of the German-speaking Community): 8 Kaperberg, 4700 Eupen; tel. and fax (87) 55-59-70; e-mail rdg@euregio.net; internet www.euregio.net/rdg.

**Regierung der Deutschsprachigen Gemeinschaft Belgiens** (Government of the German-speaking Community): 32 Klötzerbahn, 4700 Eupen; tel. (87) 59-64-00; fax (87) 74-02-58; e-mail juergen.heck@grenzecho.be; internet www.dglive.be.

# Political Organizations

**Anders Gaan Leven (Agalev)** (Ecologist Party—Flemish-speaking): 23 Brialmontstraat, 1210 Brussels; tel. (2) 219-19-19; fax (2) 223-10-90; e-mail agalev@agalev.be; internet www.agalev.be; f. 1982; Pres. WILFRED BERVOETS.

**Christelijke Volkspartij (CVP)/Parti Social Chrétien (PSC)** (Christian Democrats): 89 Wetstraat, 1040 Brussels; tel. (2) 238-38-11; fax (2) 230-43-60 (CVP); 45 rue des Deux-Eglises, 1040 Brussels; tel. (2) 238-01-11; fax (2) 238-01-29 (PSC); e-mail inform@cvp.be; internet www.cvp.be; f. 1945; Pres. (CVP) MARC VAN PEEL; Pres. (PSC) PHILIPPE MAYSTADT; 186,000 mems.

**Ecologistes Confédérés pour l'Organisation des Luttes Originales (Ecolo)** (Ecologist Party—French-speaking): 12 rue Charles VI, 1210 Brussels; tel. (2) 218-30-35; fax (2) 217-52-90; internet www.ecolo.be; Fed. Secs ISABELLE DURANT, JACKY MORAEL, JEAN-LUC ROLAND.

**Front Démocratique des Francophones (FDF)** (French-speaking Democratic Front): 127 chaussée de Charleroi, 1060 Brussels; tel. (2) 538-83-20; fax (2) 539-36-50; e-mail fdf@fdf.be; internet www.fdf.be; f. 1964; aims to preserve the French character of Brussels; Pres. OLIVIER MAINGAIN; Sec.-Gen. SERGE DE PATOUL.

**Front National (FN):** Clos du Parnasse 12, 1040 Brussels; tel. (2) 512-05-75; e-mail daniel.feret@frontnational.be; internet www.frontnational.be; f. 1985; extreme right-wing nationalist party; Pres. DANIEL FERET.

**ID21:** 80 Noordstraat, 1000 Brussels; e-mail info@id21.be; internet www.id21.be.

**Partei der Deutschsprachigen Belgier (PDB)** (German-speaking Party): 6 Kaperberg, 4700 Eupen; tel. (87) 55-59-87; fax (87) 55-59-84; internet users.skynet.be/pdb; f. 1971; promotes equality for the German-speaking minority; Pres. GUIDO BREVER.

**Parti Communiste (PC)** (Communist Party): 4 rue Rouppe, 1000 Brussels; tel. (2) 548-02-90; fax (2) 548-02-95; f. 1921 as Parti Communiste de Belgique–Kommunistische Partij van België, name changed 1990; Pres. PIERRE BEAUVOIS; 5,000 mems.

**Parti de la Liberté du Citoyen/Parti Libéral Chretien/Partij der Liberale Christenen (PLC):** 46 ave de Scheut, 1070 Brussels; tel. (2) 524-39-66; fax (2) 521-60-71; Pres. LUC EYKERMAN, PAUL MOORS.

**Parti Féministe Humaniste:** 35 ave des Phalènes, bte 14, 1050 Brussels; tel. (2) 648-87-38; f. 1972 as Parti Féministe Unifié, name changed 1990; aims to create a humanistic and egalitarian republic where the fundamental rights of the individual and of society are respected.

**Parti Humaniste de Belgique:** 131 rue du Noyer, 1000 Brussels; tel. (2) 734-37-84; fax (2) 426-03-78; e-mail parti.humaniste@euronet.be; internet www.multimania.com/phum; f. 1994; promotes social equality and human rights.

**Parti Réformateur Libéral (PRL)** (Liberal Party—French-speaking wing): 41 rue de Naples, 1050 Brussels; tel. (2) 500-35-11; fax (2) 500-35-09; e-mail prl@prl.be; internet www.prl.be; f. 1846 as Parti Libéral; Pres. DANIEL DUCARNE; 50,000 mems.

**Parti Socialiste (PS)** (Socialist Party—French-speaking wing): Maison du PS, 13 blvd de l'Empereur, 1000 Brussels; tel. (2) 548-32-11; fax (2) 548-33-80; e-mail secretariat@ps.be; internet www.ps.be; f. 1885 as the Parti Ouvrier Belge; split from the Flemish wing 1979; Pres. ELIO DI RUPO; Sec. JEAN-POL BARAS.

**Parti Wallon (PW)** (Walloon Party): 14 rue du Faubourg, 1430 Quenast; tel. (6) 767-00-19; f. 1985 by amalgamation of the Rassemblement Wallon (f. 1968), the Rassemblement Populaire Wallon and the Front Indépendantiste Wallon; left-wing socialist party advocating an independent Walloon state; Pres. JEAN-CLAUDE PICCIN.

**Partij van de Arbeid van België (PvdA)/Parti du Travail de Belgique (PTB)** (Belgian Labour Party): blvd M. Lemonnier 171, 1000 Brussels; tel. (2) 513-77-60; fax (2) 513-98-31; e-mail wpb@wpb.be; internet www.wpb.be; f. 1979; Marxist-Leninist; Gen. Sec. NADINE ROSA-ROSSO.

**Socialistische Partij (SP)** (Socialist Party—Flemish wing): 13 blvd de l'Empereur, 1000 Brussels; tel. (2) 548-32-11; fax (2) 548-35-90; e-mail info@sp.be; internet www.sp.be; f. 1885; Pres. LOUIS TOBBACK; Sec. LINDA BLOMME.

**Vlaams Blok** (Flemish Bloc): 8 Madouplein, bus 9, 1210 Brussels; tel. (2) 219-60-09; fax (2) 217-52-75; e-mail vlblok@vlaams-blok.be; internet www.vlaams-blok.be; f. 1979; advocates Flemish separatism; Chair. FRANK VANHECKE; Chief Officer ROELAND RAES.

**Vlaamse Liberalen en Demokraten—Partij van de Burger (VLD)** (Flemish Liberals and Democrats—Citizens' Party: Liberal Party—Flemish-speaking wing): 34 Melsensstraat, 1000 Brussels; tel. (2) 549-00-20; fax (2) 512-60-25; f. 1961 as Partij voor Vrijheid en Vooruitgang; name changed 1992; Chair. RIK DAEMS; Pres. GUY VERHOFSTADT; 85,000 mems.

**Volksunie—Vlaamse Vrije Democraten (VU)** (People's Union—Flemish Free Democrats): 12 Barrikadenplein, 1000 Brussels; tel. (2) 219-49-30; fax (2) 217-35-10; e-mail secretariaat@vu.be; internet www.volksunie.be; f. 1954; Flemish nationalist party supporting national and European federalism; Pres. PATRIK VANKRUNKELSVEN; Sec. LAURENS APPELTANS; 16,000 mems.

# Diplomatic Representation

## EMBASSIES IN BELGIUM

**Albania:** 42 rue Alphonse Hottat, 1050 Brussels; tel. (2) 640-14-22; fax (2) 640-28-58; e-mail amba.brux@skynet.be; Ambassador: IPRIZ BASHA.

**Algeria:** 209 ave Molière, 1050 Brussels; tel. (2) 343-50-78; fax (2) 343-51-68; Ambassador: MISSOUM SBIH.

**Andorra:** 10 rue de la Montagne, 1000 Brussels; tel. (2) 513-28-06; fax (2) 513-07-41; e-mail meri.matev@skynet.be; Ambassador: MERITXELL MATEV.

**Angola:** 182 rue Franz Merjay, 1180 Brussels; tel. (2) 346-18-72; fax (2) 344-08-94; Ambassador: JOSÉ GUERREIRO ALVES PRIMO.

**Argentina:** 225 ave Louise, bte 3, 1050 Brussels; tel. (2) 647-78-12; fax (2) 647-93-19; e-mail ebelg@mrecic.gov.ar; Ambassador: EDUARDO M. DE L. AIRALDI.

**Armenia:** 157 rue Franz Merjay, 1050 Brussels; tel. and fax (2) 346-56-67; Ambassador: V. TCHITETCHIAN.

**Australia:** 6–8 rue Guimard, 1040 Brussels; tel. (2) 231-05-00; fax (2) 230-68-02; Ambassador: DONALD KENYON.

**Austria:** 5 place du Champs de Mars, 1050 Brussels; tel. (2) 289-07-00; fax (2) 513-66-41; Ambassador: WINFRIED LANG.

**Azerbaijan:** 464 ave Molière, 1060 Brussels; tel. (2) 345-26-60; fax (2) 345-91-58; Ambassador: MIR-HAMZA EFENDIEV.

**Bangladesh:** 29–31 rue Jacques Jordaens, 1000 Brussels; tel. (2) 640-55-00; fax (2) 646-59-98; Ambassador: A. S. M. KHAIRHUL ANAM.

**Barbados:** 78 ave Général Lartigue, 1200 Brussels; tel. (2) 732-17-37; fax (2) 732-32-66; e-mail embar@pophost.eunet.be; internet www.foreign.barbadosgov.org; Ambassador: MICHAEL IAN KING.

**Belarus:** 192 ave Molière, 1050 Brussels; tel. (2) 340-02-71; fax (2) 340-02-87; Ambassador: ULADZIMIR A. LABUNOU.

**Benin:** 5 ave de l'Observatoire, 1180 Brussels; tel. (2) 374-91-92; fax (2) 375-83-26; Ambassador: SALIOU ABOUDOU.

**Bolivia:** 176 ave Louise, bte 6, 1050 Brussels; tel. (2) 627-00-10; fax (2) 647-47-82; Chargé d'affaires a.i.: ARTURO LIEBERS BALDIVIESO.

**Bosnia and Herzegovina:** 9 rue Paul Lauters, 1000 Brussels; tel. (2) 644-20-08; fax (2) 644-16-98; Ambassador: MILES V. RAGUZ.

**Botswana:** 169 ave de Tervueren, 1150 Brussels; tel. (2) 735-20-70; fax (2) 735-63-18; Ambassador: SASARA CHASALA GEORGE.

**Brazil:** 350 ave Louise, bte 5, 1050 Brussels; tel. (2) 640-20-15; fax (2) 640-81-34; e-mail 100653.665@compuserve.com; Ambassador: MARCIO DE OLIVEIRA DIAS.

**Brunei:** 238 ave F. D. Roosevelt, 1050 Brussels; tel. (2) 675-08-78; fax (2) 672-93-58; e-mail kedutaan-brunei.brussels@skynet.be; Ambassador: Dato KASSIM DAUD.

**Bulgaria:** 58 ave Hamoir, 1180 Brussels; tel. (2) 374-59-63; fax (2) 374-84-94; e-mail bgemb@club.innet.be; Ambassador: BOYKO NOEV.

**Burkina Faso:** 16 place Guy d'Arezzo, 1180 Brussels; tel. (2) 345-99-12; fax (2) 345-06-12; Ambassador: YOUSSOUF OUÉDRAOGO.

**Burundi:** 46 square Marie-Louise, 1000 Brussels; tel. (2) 230-45-35; fax (2) 230-78-83; Ambassador: JONATHAN NIYUNGEKO.

**Cameroon:** 131 ave Brugmann, 1190 Brussels; tel. (2) 345-18-70; fax (2) 344-57-35; Ambassador: ISABELLE BASSONG.

**Canada:** 2 ave de Tervueren, 1040 Brussels; tel. (2) 741-06-11; fax (2) 741-06-09; Ambassador: CLAUDE LAVERDURE.

**Cape Verde:** 29 ave Jeanne, 1050 Brussels; tel. (2) 643-62-70; fax (2) 646-33-85; Ambassador: JOSÉ LUIS ROCHA.

**Central African Republic:** 416 blvd Lambermont, 1030 Brussels; tel. (2) 242-28-80; fax (2) 242-30-81; Chargé d'affaires a.i.: JEAN-PIERRE MBAZOA.

**Chad:** 52 blvd Lambermont, 1030 Brussels; tel. (2) 215-19-75; fax (2) 216-35-26; Chargé d'affaires: IDRISS ADJIDEYE.

**Chile:** 40 rue Montoyer, 1000 Brussels; tel. (2) 280-16-20; fax (2) 280-14-81; Ambassador: HUGO CUBILLOS BRAVO.

**China, People's Republic:** 443 ave de Tervueren, 1150 Brussels; tel. (2) 771-33-09; fax (2) 772-37-45; Ambassador: DING YUANHONG.

**Colombia:** 96A ave F. D. Roosevelt, 1050 Brussels; tel. (2) 649-56-79; fax (2) 646-54-91; e-mail colombia@emcolbru.org; Ambassador: ROBERTO ARENAS BONILLA.

**Congo, Democratic Republic:** 30 rue Marie de Bourgogne, 1000 Brussels; tel. (2) 513-66-10; fax (2) 514-04-03; Ambassador: JUSTINE MPOYO KASAVUBU.

**Congo, Republic:** 16–18 ave F. D. Roosevelt, 1050 Brussels; tel. (2) 648-38-56; fax (2) 648-42-13; Ambassador: PAUL ALEXANDRE MAPINGOU.

**Costa Rica:** 489 ave Louise, bte 13, 1050 Brussels; tel. (2) 640-55-41; fax (2) 648-31-92; e-mail embcrbel@infonie.be; Ambassador: MARIO FERNÁNDEZ SILVA.

**Côte d'Ivoire:** 234 ave F. D. Roosevelt, 1050 Brussels; tel. (2) 672-23-57; fax (2) 672-04-91; Ambassador: ANET N'ZI NANAN KOLIABO.

**Croatia:** 50 ave des Arts, 1000 Brussels; tel. (2) 500-09-20; fax (2) 512-03-38; Ambassador: ŽJKO MATIÉ.

**Cuba:** 77 rue Roberts-Jones, 1180 Brussels; tel. (2) 343-00-20; fax (2) 344-96-91; Ambassador: RENÉ JUAN MUJICA CANTELAR.

**Cyprus:** 2 square Ambiorix, 1000 Brussels; tel. (2) 735-35-10; fax (2) 735-45-52; e-mail chypre.pio.bxl@skynet.be; Ambassador: NICOS AGATHOCLEOUS.

**Czech Republic:** 555 rue Engeland, 1080 Brussels; tel. (2) 374-12-03; fax (2) 375-92-72; Ambassador: KATEŘINA LUKEŠOVÁ.

**Denmark:** 73 rue d'Arlon, 1040 Brussels; tel. (2) 626-07-70; fax (2) 230-93-84; Ambassador: ALF JÖNSSON.

**Dominican Republic:** 12 ave Bel Air, 1180 Brussels; tel. (2) 346-49-35; fax (2) 346-51-52; Ambassador: CLARA JOSELYN QUIÑONES DE LONGO.

**Ecuador:** 363 ave Louise, 1050 Brussels; tel. (2) 644-30-50; fax (2) 644-28-13; Ambassador: MENTO P. VILLAGOMEZ MERINO.

**Egypt:** 44 ave Léo Errera, 1180 Brussels; tel. (2) 340-78-24; fax (2) 343-65-33; Ambassador: RAOUF SAAD.

**El Salvador:** 171 ave de Tervueren, 1150 Brussels; tel. (2) 733-04-85; fax (2) 735-02-11; Ambassador: Joaquín Rodezno Munguia.

**Equatorial Guinea:** 295 ave Brugman, 1180 Brussels; tel. (2) 346-25-09; fax (2) 346-33-09; Ambassador: Aurelio Mba Olo.

**Eritrea:** Brussels; tel. (2) 374-44-34; fax (2) 372-07-30; Ambassador: Hanna Simon Ghebremedhin.

**Estonia:** 1 ave Isidore Gérard, 1160 Brussels; tel. (2) 779-07-55; fax 779-28-17; e-mail saatkond@estemb.be; Ambassador: Sulev Kannike.

**Ethiopia:** 231 ave de Tervueren, 1150 Brussels; tel. (2) 771-32-94; fax (2) 771-49-14; Ambassador: Dr Peter Gabriel Robleh.

**Fiji:** 66 ave de Cortenberg, 1000 Brussels; tel. (2) 736-90-50; fax (2) 736-14-58; e-mail fijimission.brussels@skynet.be; Ambassador: Isikeli U. Mataitoga.

**Finland:** 58 ave des Arts, 1000 Brussels; tel. (2) 287-12-12; fax (2) 287-12-00; Ambassador: Leif Blomqvist.

**France:** 65 rue Ducale, 1000 Brussels; tel. (2) 548-87-11; fax (2) 548-87-32; internet www.ambafrance.be; Ambassador: Jacques Runnelhardt.

**Gabon:** 112 ave Winston Churchill, 1180 Brussels; tel. (2) 343-00-55; fax (2) 346-46-69; Ambassador: Jean Robert Goulongana.

**Gambia:** 126 ave F. D. Roosevelt, 1050 Brussels; tel. (2) 640-10-49; fax (2) 646-32-77; e-mail bs175335@skynet.be; Ambassador: Maudo H. N. Touray.

**Georgia:** 15 rue Vergote, 1030 Brussels; tel. (2) 732-85-50; fax (2) 732-85-47; Ambassador: Zurab Abachidze.

**Germany:** 190 ave de Tervueren, 1150 Brussels; tel. (2) 774-19-11; fax (2) 772-36-92; Ambassador: Rolf Hofstetter.

**Ghana:** blvd Général Wahis, 1030 Brussels; tel. (2) 705-82-20; fax (2) 705-66-53; Ambassador: Alex Ntim Abankwa.

**Greece:** 2 ave F. D. Roosevelt, 1050 Brussels; tel. (2) 648-17-30; fax (2) 647-45-25; e-mail ambagre@skynet.be; Ambassador: John Cambolis.

**Grenada:** Brussels; tel. (2) 514-12-42; fax (2) 513-87-24; Chargé d'affaires a.i.: Joan-Marie Coutain.

**Guatemala:** 53 blvd Général Wahis, 1030 Brussels; tel. (2) 705-39-40; fax (2) 705-78-89; Ambassador: Claudio Riedel Telge.

**Guinea:** 75 ave Roger Vandendriessche, 1150 Brussels; tel. (2) 771-01-26; fax (2) 762-60-36; Ambassador: Naby Moussa Soumah.

**Guinea-Bissau:** 70 ave F. D. Roosevelt, 1050 Brussels; tel. (2) 647-13-51; fax (2) 640-43-12; Chargé d'affaires: José Fonseca.

**Guyana:** 12 ave du Brésil, 1050 Brussels; tel. (2) 675-62-16; fax (2) 675-55-98; Ambassador: Havelock Brewster.

**Haiti:** 160A ave Louise, bte 25, 1050 Brussels; tel. (2) 649-73-81; fax (2) 640-60-80; Ambassador: Yolette Azor-Charles .

**Holy See:** 9 ave des Franciscains, 1150 Brussels (Apostolic Nunciature); tel. (2) 762-20-05; fax (2) 762-20-32; Apostolic Nuncio: Most Rev. Pier Luigi Celata, Titular Archbishop of Doclea.

**Honduras:** 3 ave des Gaulois (5e étage), 1040 Brussels; tel. (2) 734-00-00; fax (2) 735-26-26; Ambassador: Ivan Romero Martínez.

**Hungary:** 41 rue Edmond Picard, 1050 Brussels; tel. (2) 343-67-90; fax (2) 347-60-28; Ambassador: S. E. M. Tibor Kiss.

**Iceland:** 74 rue de Trèves, 1040 Brussels; tel. (2) 286-17-00; fax (2) 286-17-70; Ambassador: Gunnar Snorri Gunnarsson.

**India:** 217 chaussée de Vleurgat, 1050 Brussels; tel. (2) 640-91-40; fax (2) 648-96-38; e-mail eoibru@mail.interpac.be; Ambassador: Chandrashekhara Dasgupta.

**Indonesia:** 294 ave de Tervueren, 1150 Brussels; tel. (2) 771-20-14; fax (2) 771-22-91; Ambassador: H. Sabana Kartasasmita.

**Iran:** 415 ave de Tervueren, 1150 Brussels; tel. (2) 762-37-45; fax (2) 762-39-15; Ambassador: Hamid Aboutalébi.

**Iraq:** 23 ave des Aubépines, 1180 Brussels; tel. (2) 374-59-92; fax (2) 374-76-15; Chargé d'affaires a.i.: Tarik M. Yahya.

**Ireland:** 89 rue Froissard, 1040 Brussels; tel. (2) 230-53-37; fax (2) 286-17-70; Ambassador: Padraic Cradock.

**Israel:** 40 ave de l'Observatoire, 1180 Brussels; tel. (2) 373-55-00; fax (2) 373-56-17; Ambassador: Senny Omer.

**Italy:** 28 rue Emile Claus, 1050 Brussels; tel. (2) 649-97-00; fax (2) 648-54-85; e-mail ambit.bxl@ibm.net; internet www.pi.cnr.it/ambitbe; Ambassador: Francesco Corrias.

**Jamaica:** 2 ave Palmerston, 1000 Brussels; tel. (2) 230-11-70; fax (2) 230-37-09; e-mail emb.jam.brussels@skynet.be; Ambassador: Douglas Saunders.

**Japan:** 58 ave des Arts, bte 17/18, 1000 Brussels; tel. (2) 513-23-40; fax (2) 513-15-56; Ambassador: Junichi Nakamura.

**Jordan:** 104 ave F. D. Roosevelt, 1050 Brussels; tel. (2) 640-77-55; fax (2) 640-27-96; Ambassador: Dr Umayya Toukan.

**Kazakhstan:** 30 ave Van Bever, 1180 Brussels; tel. (2) 374-95-62; fax (2) 374-50-91; Ambassador: Akhmetzhan S. Yesimov.

**Kenya:** 208 ave Winston Churchill, 1180 Brussels; tel. (2) 340-10-40; fax (2) 340-10-50; Ambassador: Dr Philip M. Mwanzia.

**Korea, Republic:** 173–5 Chaussée de la Hulpe, 1170 Brussels; tel. (2) 662-23-03; fax (2) 675-52-21; Ambassador: Lee Jai Chun.

**Kuwait:** 43 ave F. D. Roosevelt, 1050 Brussels; tel. (2) 647-79-50; fax (2) 646-12-98; Ambassador: Ahmad A. K. al-Ebrahim.

**Kyrgyzstan:** 133 rue Tenbosch, 1050 Brussels; tel. (2) 534-63-99; fax (2) 534-23-25; Ambassador: Chingiz Torekulovitch Aitmatov.

**Latvia:** 158 ave Molière, 1050 Brussels; tel. (2) 344-16-82; fax (2) 344-74-78; e-mail lvembassybenelux@arcadis.be; Ambassador: Imants Liegis.

**Lebanon:** 2 rue Guillaume Stocq, 1050 Brussels; tel. (2) 649-94-60; fax (2) 649-90-02; Ambassador: Jihad Mortada.

**Lesotho:** 45 blvd Général Wahis, 1030 Brussels; tel. (2) 705-39-76; fax (2) 705-67-79; Ambassador: R. V. Lechesa.

**Liberia:** 50 ave du Château, 1081 Brussels; tel. (2) 411-09-12; fax (2) 411-01-12; Ambassador: Youngor Telewoda.

**Libya:** 28 ave Victoria, 1000 Brussels; tel. (2) 647-37-37; fax (2) 640-90-76; Sec. of People's Bureau: Hamed Ahmed Elhouderi.

**Liechtenstein:** 1 place du Congrès, 1000 Brussels; tel. (2) 229-39-00; fax (2) 219-35-45; Ambassador: Prince Nikolaus von Liechtenstein.

**Lithuania:** 48 rue Maurice Liétart, 1150 Brussels; tel. (2) 772-27-50; fax (2) 772-17-01; Chargé d'affaires: Arvydas Daunoravičius.

**Luxembourg:** 75 ave de Cortenbergh, 1000 Brussels; tel. (2) 737-57-00; fax (2) 737-57-10; Ambassador: Jean-Jacques Kasel.

**Macedonia, former Yugoslav republic:** 276 ave de Tervueren, 1150 Brussels; tel. (2) 732-91-08; fax (2) 732-91-11; Ambassador: Jovan Tegovski.

**Madagascar:** 276 ave de Tervueren, 1150 Brussels; tel. (2) 770-17-26; fax (2) 772-37-31; Ambassador: Jean Omer Beriziky.

**Malawi:** 15 rue de la Loi, 1040 Brussels; tel. (2) 231-09-80; fax (2) 231-10-66; Ambassador: Julie Nanyoni Mphande.

**Malaysia:** 414A ave de Tervueren, 1150 Brussels; tel. (2) 762-67-67; fax (2) 762-50-49; Ambassador: Dato Martyn M. Sathiah.

**Mali:** 487 ave Molière, 1060 Brussels; tel. (2) 345-74-32; fax (2) 344-57-00; Ambassador: Ahmed Mohamed ag Hamani.

**Malta:** 44 rue Jules Lejeune, 1050 Brussels; tel. (2) 343-01-95; fax (2) 343-01-06; e-mail victor.camilleri@magnet.mt; Ambassador: Victor Camilleri.

**Mauritania:** 6 ave de la Colombie, 1000 Brussels; tel. (2) 672-47-47; fax (2) 672-20-51; Ambassador: Mohamed Salem Ould Lekhal.

**Mauritius:** 68 rue des Bollandistes, 1040 Brussels; tel. (2) 733-99-88; fax (2) 734-40-21; Ambassador: T. W. Wan Chat Kwong.

**Mexico:** 94 ave F. D. Roosevelt, 1050 Brussels; tel. (2) 629-07-77; fax (2) 646-87-68; e-mail embamexbel@pophost.eunet.be; Ambassador: Manuel Rodríguez Arriaga.

**Moldova:** 175 ave Emile Max, 1030 Brussels; tel. (2) 732-93-00; fax (2) 732-96-60; e-mail molda@skynet.be; Ambassador: Ion Capatina.

**Monaco:** 17 place Guy d'Arezzo, bte 7, 1180 Brussels; tel. (2) 347-49-87; fax (2) 343-49-20; Ambassador: Jean André Gréther.

**Mongolia:** 18 ave Besme, 1190 Brussels; tel. (2) 344-69-74; fax (2) 344-32-15; e-mail embassy.mongolia@skynet.be; Ambassador: Jagvaralyn Hanibal.

**Morocco:** 29 blvd St-Michel, 1040 Brussels; tel. (2) 736-11-00; fax (2) 734-64-68; Ambassador: Rachad Bouhlal.

**Mozambique:** 97 blvd St-Michel, 1040 Brussels; tel. (2) 736-25-64; fax (2) 735-62-07; Ambassador: Alvaro O. da Silva.

**Namibia:** 454 ave de Tervueren, 1150 Brussels; tel. (2) 771-14-10; fax (2) 771-96-89; Ambassador: Dr Zedekia J. Ngavirue.

**Nepal:** 68 ave Winston Churchill, 1180 Brussels; tel. (2) 346-26-58; fax (2) 344-13-61; e-mail rne.bru@skynet.be; Ambassador: Kedar Bhakta Shrestha.

**Netherlands:** 48 ave Hermann Debroux, 1160 Brussels; tel. (2) 679-17-11; fax (2) 679-17-71; Ambassador: E. Röell.

**New Zealand:** 47–48 blvd du Régent, 1000 Brussels; tel. (2) 512-10-40; fax (2) 513-48-56; e-mail nzembbru@compuserve.com; Ambassador: Dell Higge.

**Nicaragua:** 55 ave de Wolvendael, 1180 Brussels; tel. (2) 375-65-00; fax (2) 375-71-88; Ambassador: Roger Quant Pallavicini.

**Niger:** 78 ave F. D. Roosevelt, 1050 Brussels; tel. (2) 648-61-40; fax (2) 648-27-84; Ambassador: Housseini Abdou-Saleye.

**Nigeria:** 288 ave de Tervueren, 1150 Brussels; tel. (2) 762-52-00; fax (2) 762-37-63; Ambassador: Prof. Alaba Ogunsanwo.

**Norway:** 130A ave Louise (6e étage), 1050 Brussels; tel. (2) 646-07-80; fax (2) 646-28-82; e-mail ambassade-brussel@ud.dep.telemax.no; Ambassador: Tor B. Naess.

**Pakistan:** 57 ave Delleur, 1170 Brussels; tel. (2) 673-80-07; fax (2) 675-83-94; Ambassador: SAIDULLA KHAN DEHLAVI.

**Panama:** 390–392 ave Louise, 1150 Brussels; tel. (2) 647-07-29; fax (2) 648-92-16; e-mail panama@antrasite.be; Chargé d'affaires: ELENA BARLETTA DE NOTTEBOHM.

**Papua New Guinea:** 430 ave de Tervueren, 1150 Brussels; tel. (2) 779-08-26; fax (2) 772-70-88; Ambassador: GABRIEL KOIBA PEPSON.

**Paraguay:** 475 ave Louise, 1050 Brussels; tel. (2) 649-90-55; fax (2) 647-42-48; e-mail embapar.belgica@skynet.be; Ambassador: MANUEL M. CÁCERES.

**Peru:** 179 ave de Tervueren, 1150 Brussels; tel. (2) 733-33-19; fax (2) 733-48-19; e-mail embassy.of.peru@unicall.be; Ambassador: JOSÉ ANTONIO ARROSPIDE DEL BUSTO.

**Philippines:** 297 ave Molière, 1050 Brussels; tel. (2) 340-33-77; fax (2) 345-64-24; e-mail bleu.pe@skynet.be; Ambassador: JOSÉ U. FERNANDEZ.

**Poland:** 29 ave des Gaulois, 1040 Brussels; tel. (2) 735-72-12; fax (2) 736-18-81; e-mail 106032.2752@compuserve.com; Ambassador: JAN W. PIEKARSKI.

**Portugal:** 55 ave de la Toison d'Or, 1060 Brussels; tel. (2) 533-07-00; fax (2) 539-07-73; Ambassador: FRANCISCO PESSANHA DE QUEVEDO CRESPO.

**Qatar:** 71 ave F. D. Roosevelt, 1050 Brussels; tel. (2) 640-29-00; fax (2) 648-40-78; e-mail qatar.amb.bru@skynet.be; Chargé d'affaires: MOHAMED AL-HAIYKI.

**Romania:** 105 rue Gabrielle, 1180 Brussels; tel. (2) 345-26-80; fax (2) 346-23-45; e-mail sagesse@infonie.be; Ambassador: VIRGIL N. CONSTANTINESCU.

**Russia:** 66 ave de Fré, 1180 Brussels; tel. (2) 374-34-00; fax (2) 374-26-13; Ambassador: SERGEI KISLYAK.

**Rwanda:** 1 ave des Fleurs, 1150 Brussels; tel. (2) 763-07-05; fax (2) 763-07-53; Ambassador: MANZI BAKURAMUTZA.

**Saint Lucia:** 42 rue de Livourne, 1000 Brussels; tel. (2) 534-26-11; fax (2) 539-40-09; e-mail ecs.embassies@skynet.be; Ambassador: EDWIN PONTIEN JOSEPH LAURENT.

**Saint Vincent and the Grenadines:** 42 rue de Livourne, 1000 Brussels; tel. (2) 534-26-11; fax (2) 539-40-09; e-mail ecs.embassies@skynet.be; Ambassador: EDWIN PONTIEN JOSEPH LAURENT.

**Samoa:** 123 ave F. D. Roosevelt, bte 14, 1050 Brussels; tel. (2) 660-84-54; fax (2) 675-03-36; e-mail samoa.emb.bxl@skynet.be; Ambassador: TAU'ILI'ILI UILI MEREDITH.

**San Marino:** 62 ave F. D. Roosevelt, 1050 Brussels; tel. (2) 644-22-24; fax (2) 644-20-57; Ambassador: SAVINA ZAFFERANI.

**São Tomé and Príncipe:** 175 ave de Tervueren, 1150 Brussels; tel. (2) 734-88-15; fax (2) 734-88-15; Chargé d'affaires a.i.: ANTÓNIO DE LIMA VIEGAS.

**Saudi Arabia:** 45 ave F. D. Roosevelt, 1050 Brussels; tel. (2) 649-20-44; fax (2) 647-24-92; Ambassador: NASSER ASSAF HUSSEIN AL-ASSAF.

**Senegal:** 196 ave F. D. Roosevelt, 1050 Brussels; tel. (2) 673-00-97; fax (2) 675-04-60; Ambassador: SALOUM KANDE.

**Sierra Leone:** 410 ave de Tervueren, 1150 Brussels; tel. (2) 771-00-53; fax (2) 771-11-80; Chargé d'affaires a.i.: JAMES GOODWILL.

**Singapore:** 198 ave F. D. Roosevelt, 1050 Brussels; tel. (2) 660-29-79; fax (2) 660-86-85; e-mail amb.eu@singembbru.be; Ambassador: PANG ENG FONG.

**Slovakia:** 195 ave Molière, 1050 Brussels; tel. (2) 346-40-45; fax (2) 346-63-85; e-mail ambassade.slovaque@euronet.be; Ambassador: FRANTIŠEK LIPKA.

**Slovenia:** 179 ave Louise, 1050 Brussels; tel. (2) 646-90-99; fax (2) 646-36-67; Ambassador: JAŠA ZLOBEC-LUKIČ.

**Solomon Islands:** ave de l'Yser, 13, bte 3, 1040 Brussels; tel. (2) 732-70-85; fax (2) 732-68-85; Ambassador: ROBERT SISILO.

**South Africa:** 26 rue de la Loi, btes 7–8, 1040 Brussels; tel. (2) 285-44-00; fax (2) 285-44-02; e-mail samission@village.uunet.be; Ambassador: Dr ELIAS LINKS.

**Spain:** 19 rue de la Science, 1040 Brussels; tel. (2) 230-03-40; fax (2) 230-93-80; Ambassador: MANUEL BENAVIDES.

**Sri Lanka:** 27 rue Jules Lejeune, 1050 Brussels; tel. (2) 344-53-94; fax (2) 344-67-37; e-mail sri.lanka@euronet.be; Ambassador: (vacant).

**Sudan:** 124 ave F. D. Roosevelt, 1050 Brussels; tel. (2) 647-94-94; fax (2) 648-34-99; Ambassador: ABDELRAHIM AHMED KHALIL.

**Suriname:** 379 ave Louise, 1050 Brussels; tel. (2) 640-11-72; fax (2) 646-39-62; Chargé d'affaires a.i.: CARLO R. SPIER.

**Swaziland:** 188 ave Winston Churchill, 1180 Brussels; tel. (2) 347-47-71; fax (2) 347-46-23; Ambassador: Dr THEMBAYENA ANNASTASIA DLAMINI.

**Sweden:** 3 rue de Luxembourg, 1050 Brussels; tel. (2) 289-57-60; fax (2) 289-57-90; e-mail embassy.sweden@euronet.be; Ambassador: ANDERS OIJELUND.

**Switzerland:** 26 rue de la Loi, bte 9, 1040 Brussels; tel. (2) 285-43-50; fax (2) 230-37-81; e-mail vertretung@bru.rep.admin.ch; Ambassador: ANTON THALMANN.

**Syria:** 3 ave F. D. Roosevelt, 1050 Brussels; tel. (2) 648-01-35; fax (2) 646-40-18; Chargé d'affaires a.i.: SAMI SALAMEH.

**Tanzania:** 363 ave Louise (7e étage), 1050 Brussels; tel. (2) 640-65-00; fax (2) 640-80-26; Ambassador: ALI ABEID KARUME.

**Thailand:** 2 square du Val de la Cambre, 1050 Brussels; tel. (2) 640-68-10; fax (2) 648-30-66; e-mail thaibxl@pophost.eunet.be; internet www.waw.be/rte-be; Ambassador: SURAPONG POSAYANOND.

**Togo:** 264 ave de Tervueren, 1150 Brussels; tel. (2) 770-17-91; fax (2) 771-50-75; Ambassador: FOLLY-GLIDJITO AKAKPO.

**Trinidad and Tobago:** 14 ave de la Faisanderie, 1150 Brussels; tel. (2) 762-94-00; fax (2) 772-27-83; Ambassador: LINGSTON LLOYD CUMBERBATCH.

**Tunisia:** 278 ave de Tervueren, 1150 Brussels; tel. (2) 771-73-95; fax (2) 771-94-33; Ambassador: TAHAR SIOUD.

**Turkey:** 4 rue Montoyer, 1000 Brussels; tel. (2) 513-40-95; fax (2) 514-07-48; e-mail turkdelegeu@euronet.be; Ambassador: TEMEL ISKIT.

**Uganda:** 317 ave de Tervueren, 1150 Brussels; tel. (2) 762-58-25; fax (2) 763-04-38; Ambassador: KAKIMA NTAMBI.

**Ukraine:** 28–32 ave Lancaster, 1180 Uccle; tel. (2) 344-40-20; fax (2) 344-44-66; e-mail embukr@planetintemet.be; Ambassador: KOSTYANTYN GRYSHCHENKO.

**United Arab Emirates:** 73 ave F. D. Roosevelt, 1050 Brussels; tel. (2) 640-60-00; fax (2) 646-24-73; e-mail emirates.bxl@infonie.be; Ambassador: ABDULHADI AL-KHAJAH.

**United Kingdom:** 85 rue d'Arlon, 1040 Brussels; tel. (2) 287-62-11; fax (2) 287-63-55; internet www.british.embassy.be; Ambassador: DAVID HUGH COLVIN.

**USA:** 27 blvd du Régent, 1000 Brussels; tel. (2) 508-21-11; fax (2) 511-27-25; e-mail ic@usinfo.be; internet www.usinfo.be; Ambassador: PAUL L. CEJAS.

**Uruguay:** 22 ave F. D. Roosevelt, 1050 Brussels; tel. (2) 640-11-69; fax (2) 648-29-09; e-mail uruemb@euronet.be; Ambassador: GUILLERMO E. VALLES GALMES.

**Uzbekistan:** 99 ave F. D. Roosevelt, 1050 Brussels; tel. (2) 672-88-44; fax (2) 672-39-46; Ambassador: SHAVKAT KHAMRAKULOV.

**Venezuela:** 10 ave F. D. Roosevelt, 1050 Brussels; tel. (2) 639-03-40; fax (2) 647-88-20; e-mail 100775.1735@compuserve.com; Ambassador: LUIS XAVIER GRISANTI.

**Viet Nam:** 130 ave de la Floride, 1180 Brussels; tel. (2) 374-91-33; fax (2) 374-93-76; Ambassador: HUYNH ANH DZUNG.

**Yemen:** 114 ave F. D. Roosevelt, 1050 Brussels; tel. (2) 646-52-90; fax (2) 646-29-11; Ambassador: A. K. AL-AGHBARI.

**Yugoslavia:** 11 ave Emile de Mot, 1000 Brussels; tel. (2) 647-57-81; fax (2) 647-29-41; Chargé d'affaires a.i.: DRAGAN MOMCILOVIĆ.

**Zambia:** 469 ave Molière, 1050 Brussels; tel. (2) 343-56-49; fax (2) 347-43-33; Ambassador: ISAIAH ZIMBA CHABALA.

**Zimbabwe:** 11 square Joséphine Charlotte, 1200 Brussels; tel. (2) 762-58-08; fax (2) 762-96-05; Ambassador: SIMBARASHE S. MUMBENGEGWI.

## Judicial System

The independence of the judiciary is based on the constitutional division of power between the legislative, executive and judicial bodies, each of which acts independently. Judges are appointed by the crown for life, and cannot be removed except by judicial sentence. The judiciary is organized on four levels, from the judicial canton to the district, regional and national courts. The lowest courts are those of the Justices of the Peace and the Police Tribunals. Each district has one of each type of district court, including the Tribunals of the First Instance, Tribunals of Commerce, and Labour Tribunals, and there is a Court of Assizes in each province. There are Courts of Appeal and Labour Courts in each region. The highest courts are the national civil and criminal Courts of Appeal, Labour Courts and the Supreme Court of Justice. The Military Court of Appeal is in Brussels.

### COUR DE CASSATION/HOF VAN CASSATIE (SUPREME COURT OF JUSTICE)

**First President:** PIERRE MARCHAL.

**President:** D. HOLSTERS.

**Counsellors:** P. GHISLAIN, M. CHARLIER, M. LAHOUSSE, Y. BELLEJEANMART, T. VERHEYDEN, I. VEROUGSTRAETE, E. FORRIER, F. FISCHER, C. PARMENTIER, R. BOES, E. WAÛTERS, G. DHAEYER, G. SUETENS-BOURGEOIS, L. HUYBRECHTS, E. GOETHALS, J.-P. FRÈRE, P. ECHEMENT, CHR.

STORCK, J. DE CODT, F. CLOSE, G. LONDERS, P. MATHIEU, E. DIRIX, D. BATSELE, P. MAFFEI, E. CHEVALIER, D. DEBRUYNE.

**Attorney-General:** JEAN-MARIE PIRET.

**First Advocate-General:** J. DU JARDIN.

**Advocates-General:** J.-F. LECLERQ, P. GOEMINNE, M. DE SWAEF, G. BRESSELEERS, A. DE RAEVE, G. DUBRULLE, X. DE RIEMAECKER, J. SPREUTELS.

### COURS D'APPEL/HOVEN VAN BEROEP (CIVIL AND CRIMINAL HIGH COURTS)

**Antwerp:** First Pres. LUCIEN JANSSENS; Attorney-Gen. CHRISTINE DEKKERS.

**Brussels:** First Pres. JACQUELINE COPPIN; Attorney-Gen. ANDRÉ VAN OUDENHOVE.

**Ghent:** First Pres. JACQUES DEGRAEVE; Attorney-Gen. FRANK SCHINS.

**Liège:** First Pres. ANNE MOUREAU; Attorney-Gen. ANDRÉ THILY.

**Mons:** First Pres. CHRISTIAN JASSOGNE; Attorney-Gen. GASTON LADRIERE.

### COURS DU TRAVAIL/ARBEIDSHOVEN (LABOUR COURTS)

**Antwerp:** First Pres. JULES BEULS.

**Brussels:** First Pres. PIETER TAELMAN.

**Ghent:** First Pres. WALTER DECRAEYE.

**Liège:** First Pres. JOEL HUBIN.

**Mons:** First Pres. JOSEPH GILLAIN.

# Religion

## CHRISTIANITY

### The Roman Catholic Church

Belgium comprises one archdiocese and seven dioceses. At 31 December 1997 there were an estimated 8,273,876 adherents (about four-fifths of the total population).

**Bishops' Conference:** Bisschoppenconferentie van België/Conférence Episcopale de Belgique, 1 rue Guimard, 1040 Brussels; tel. (2) 509-96-94; fax (2) 509-96-95; e-mail ce.belgica@catho.kerknet.be; internet www.kerknet.be; f. 1981; Pres. Cardinal GODFRIED DANNEELS, Archbishop of Mechelen-Brussels.

**Archbishop of Mechelen-Brussels:** Cardinal GODFRIED DANNEELS, Aartsbisdom, 15 Wollemarkt, 2800 Mechelen; tel. (15) 21-65-01; fax (15) 20-94-85; e-mail aartsbisdom@kerknet.be.

### Protestant Churches

**Belgian Evangelical Lutheran Church:** Brussels; tel. (2) 511-92-47; f. 1950; 425 mems; Pres C. J. HOBUS.

**Church of England:** 29 rue Capitaine Crespel, 1050 Brussels; tel. (2) 511-71-83; fax (2) 511-10-28; e-mail holy.trinity@arcadis.be; internet www.arcadis.be/htb; Rev. Canon NIGEL WALKER, Chaplain and Chancellor of the Pro-Cathedral of the Holy Trinity, Brussels.

**Eglise Protestante Unie de Belgique:** 5 rue du Champ de Mars, 1050 Brussels; tel. (2) 510-61-66; fax (2) 510-61-64; e-mail belpro.epub@skynet.be; internet www.protestanet.be; Pres. Rev. DANIEL VANESCOTE; Sec. Mrs B. SMETRYNS-BAETENS; 35,000 mems.

**Mission Evangélique Belge:** 158 blvd Lambermont, 1030 Brussels; tel. (2) 241-30-15; fax (2) 245-79-65; e-mail 100307.2377@compuserve.com; internet www.m-e-b.org; f. 1919; Pres. JOHANN LUKASSE; about 12,000 mems.

**Union of Baptists in Belgium (UBB):** 85 A. Liebaertstraat, 8400 Ostend; tel. (59) 32-46-10; fax (59) 32-46-10; e-mail 106466.3510@compuserve.com; f. 1922 as Union of Protestant Baptists in Belgium; Pres. SAMUEL VERHAEGHE; Sec. PATRICK DENEUT.

## ISLAM

There are some 350,000 Muslims in Belgium. In December 1998 the Belgian Islamic community elected an Islamic representative body.

**Leader of the Islamic Community:** Imam Prof. SALMAN AL-RAHDI.

## JUDAISM

There are about 35,000 Jews in Belgium.

**Consistoire Central Israélite de Belgique** (Central Council of the Jewish Communities of Belgium): 2 rue Joseph Dupont, 1000 Brussels; tel. (2) 512-21-90; fax (2) 512-35-78; f. 1808; Chair. M. GEORGES SCHNEK; Sec. MICHEL LAUB.

# The Press

Article 25 of the Belgian Constitution states: 'The Press is free; no form of censorship may ever be instituted; no cautionary deposit may be demanded from writers, publishers or printers. When the author is known and is resident in Belgium, the publisher, printer or distributor may not be prosecuted.'

There were an estimated 30 general information dailies in 1996, with an estimated combined circulation of 1,625,000 copies per issue.

There is a trend towards concentration. The Rossel ('Le Soir') group and the Médiabel group control the majority of francophone newspapers, while the principal publisher of Flemish newspapers is the VUM ('De Standaard') group. The Roularta media group is an important publisher of regional newspapers and periodicals, and the Mediaxis group is an important magazine publisher.

The most widely-circulating dailies in French in 1995 were: *Le Soir* (182,520), *L'Avenir de Luxembourg / Vers l'Avenir* (139,960) and *La Lanterne, La Meuse, La Wallonie* (129,840). (*La Wallonie* was subsequently superseded by *Le Matin.*) The corresponding figures for Flemish-language dailies were: *De Standaard / Nieuwsblad / De Gentenaar* (372,410) and, *Het Laatste Nieuws / De Nieuwe Gazet* (306,240), The major weeklies include *De Bond, Flair, Humo* and *Télémoustique*. Some periodicals are printed in both French and Flemish.

## PRINCIPAL DAILIES

### Antwerp

**De Financieel Economische Tijd:** Franklin Bldg, 3 Posthoflei, 2600 Berchem; tel. (3) 286-02-11; fax (3) 286-02-10; e-mail tijd@tijd.be; internet www.tijd.be; f. 1968; economic and financial; Gen. Man. HANS MAERTENS; circ. 45,858.

**Gazet van Antwerpen:** 2 Katwilgweg, 2050 Antwerp; tel. (3) 210-02-10; fax (3) 219-40-41; e-mail webmaster@gva.be; internet www.gva.be; f. 1891; Christian Democrat; Gen. Man. P. BAERT; Editor LUC VAN LOON; circ. 123,000.

**De Lloyd/Le Lloyd:** 18 Vleminckstraat, 2000 Antwerp; tel. (3) 234-05-50; fax (3) 234-25-93; f. 1858; Flemish and French edns, with supplements in English; shipping, commerce, industry, finance; Dir GUY DUBOIS; Editor BERNARD VAN DEN BOSSCHE; circ. 10,600.

**De Nieuwe Gazet:** 5 Posthhoflei, 2600 Berchem; tel. (3) 286-89-30; fax (3) 286-89-40; f. 1897; liberal; Chief Editor MARCEL WILMET.

### Arlon

**L'Avenir du Luxembourg:** 38 rue des Déportés, 6700 Arlon; tel. (63) 22-03-49; fax (63) 22-05-16; f. 1897; Catholic; Chief Editor JEAN-LUC HENQUINET; circ. 139,960 (with *Vers l'Avenir*).

### Brussels

**La Dernière Heure/Les Sports:** 127 blvd Emile Jacqmain, 1000 Brussels; tel. (2) 211-28-88; fax (2) 211-28-70; f. 1906; independent Liberal; Dir FRANÇOIS LE HODEY; Chief Editor DANIEL VAN WYLICK; circ. 73,130.

**L'Echo:** 131 rue de Birmingham, 1070 Brussels; tel. (2) 526-55-11; fax (2) 526-55-26; f. 1881; economic and financial; Dir R. WATSON; Editor F. MELAET; circ. 22,230.

**Het Laatste Nieuws:** 347 Brusselsesteenweg, 1730 Asse-Kobbegem; tel. (2) 454-22-11; fax (2) 454-28-22; e-mail redactie.hln@persgroep.be; f. 1888; Flemish; independent; Dir-Gen. R. BERTELS; Editors JAAK SMEETS, PAUL DAENEN; circ. 306,279.

**La Lanterne:** 134 rue Royale, 1000 Brussels; tel. (2) 225-56-00; fax (2) 225-59-13; f. 1944; independent; Dir-Gen. M. FROMONT; Chief Editor GUY DEBISSCHOP.

**La Libre Belgique:** 127 blvd Emile Jacqmain, 1000 Brussels; tel. (2) 211-27-77; fax (2) 211-28-32; f. 1884; Catholic; independent; Chief Editor JEAN-PAUL DUCHATEAU; circ. 80,000 (with *La Libre Belgique*—Liège).

**De Morgen:** 54 Brogniezstraat, 1070 Brussels; tel. (2) 556-68-11; fax (2) 520-35-15; Dir-Gen. KOEN CLEMENT; Editor YVES DESMET; circ. 35,000.

**Het Nieuwsblad:** 30 Gossetlaan, 1702 Groot Bijgaarden; tel. (2) 467-22-11; fax (2) 466-30-93; e-mail nieuwsblad@vum.be; internet www.vum.be; f. 1923; Dir-Gen. GUIDO VERDEYEN; Chief Editor RIK VANWALLEGHEM; circ. 372,410 (with *De Standaard* and *De Gentenaar*).

**Le Soir:** 120 rue Royale, 1000 Brussels; tel. (2) 225-54-32; fax (2) 225-59-14; e-mail journal@lesoir.be; internet www.lesoir.com; f. 1887; independent; Chief Editor GUY DUPLAT; circ. 178,569.

**De Standaard:** 28 Gossetlaan, 1702 Groot Bijgaarden; tel. (2) 467-22-11; fax (2) 467-26-96; internet www.standaard.be; f. 1914; Dir-Gen. GUIDO VERDEYEN; Publisher DIRK ACHTEN; Chief Editor PIETER VANDERMEERSCH; circ. 77,000.

### Charleroi

**La Nouvelle Gazette (Charleroi, La Louvière, Philippeville, Namur, Nivelles); La Province (Mons):** 2 quai de Flandre, 6000 Charleroi; tel. (71) 27-64-11; fax (71) 27-65-67; internet www.charline.be/gazette; f. 1878; Man. Dir PATRICK HURBAIN; Editor M. FROHONT.

**Le Rappel:** 24 rue de Montigny, 6000 Charleroi; tel. (71) 31-22-80; fax (71) 31-43-61; f. 1900; Dir-Gen. JACQUES DE THYSEBAERT; Chief Editor CARL VAN DOORNE.

### Eupen

**Grenz-Echo:** 8 Marktplatz, 4700 Eupen; tel. (87) 59-13-00; fax (87) 74-38-20; e-mail info@grenzecho.be; f. 1927; German; independent Catholic; Dir A. KÜCHENBERG; Chief Editor HEINZ WARNY; circ. 12,040.

### Ghent

**De Gentenaar:** 102 Lousbergskaai, 9000 Ghent; tel. (9) 265-68-51; fax (9) 265-68-50; e-mail gentenaar@vum.be; f. 1879; Catholic; Dir-Gen. GUIDO VERDEYEN; Chief Editor RIK VANWALLEGHEN; circ. 366,665 (with *Het Nieuwsblad* and *De Standaard*).

**Het Volk:** 22 Forelstraat, 9000 Ghent; tel. (9) 265-61-11; fax (9) 225-35-27; e-mail redactie.gent@hetvolk.be; internet www.hetvolk.be; f. 1891; Catholic; Publisher JAKI LOUAGE; Dir-Gen. GUIDO VERDEYEN; circ. 114,473.

### Hasselt

**Het Belang van Limburg:** 10 Herckenrodesingel, 3500 Hasselt; tel. (11) 87-81-11; fax (11) 87-82-04; internet www.hbvl.be; f. 1879; Dir FELIX PORTERS; Editors LUC VAN LOON, MARCEL GRAULS, RICHARD SWARTENBROEKX; circ. 100,980.

### Liège

**La Libre Belgique—Gazette de Liège:** 26 blvd d'Avroy, 4000 Liège; tel. (4) 223-19-33; fax (4) 222-41-26; f. 1840; Dir-Gen. F. LE HODEY; Editor LOUIS MARAITE; circ. 80,000 (with *La Libre Belgique*—Brussels).

**Le Matin:** 55 rue de la Régence, 4000 Liège; tel. (4) 230-56-56; fax (4) 223-31-17; e-mail redaction@lematin.be; f. 1998; progressive; Dir JOSÉ VERDIN; Editor FABRICE JACQUEMART; circ. 8,000.

**La Meuse:** 8–12 blvd de la Sauvenière, 4000 Liège; tel. (4) 220-08-01; fax (4) 220-08-40; f. 1855; independent; Editor-in-Chief MARC DURAND; circ. 129,840 (with *La Lanterne*).

### Mons

**La Province:** 29 rue des Capucins, 7000 Mons; tel. (65) 39-49-70; fax (65) 33-84-77; internet charline.be/gazette; Dir PHILIPPE DAUTEZ; Chief Editor JEAN GODIN.

### Namur

**Vers l'Avenir:** 12 blvd Ernest Mélot, 5000 Namur; tel. (81) 24-88-11; fax (81) 22-60-24; f. 1918; Editor JO MOTTET; circ. 139,960 (with *L'Avenir du Luxembourg*).

### Tournai

**Le Courrier de l'Escaut:** 24 rue du Curé Notre-Dame, 7500 Tournai; tel. (69) 88-96-20; fax (69) 88-96-61; f. 1829; Chief Editor WILLY THOMAS.

### Verviers

**Le Jour/Le Courrier:** 14 rue du Brou, 4800 Verviers; tel. (87) 32-20-90; fax (87) 31-67-40; f. 1894; independent; Dir JACQUES DE THYSEBAERT; Chief Editor THIERRY DEGIVES.

## WEEKLIES

**Atlas Weekblad:** Condédreef 89, 8500 Kortrijk; tel. (56) 26-10-10; fax (56) 21-35-93; e-mail atlas@atlasweekblad.be; internet www.atlasweekblad.be; classified advertising, regional news and sports.

**De Boer en de Tuinder:** 8 Minderbroedersstraat, 3000 Leuven; tel. (16) 24-21-60; fax (16) 24-21-68; f. 1891; agriculture and horticulture; circ. 38,000.

**De Bond:** 170 Langestraat, 1150 Brussels; tel. (2) 779-00-00; fax (2) 779-16-16; e-mail com@publicants.be; f. 1921; general interest; circ. 318,537.

**Brugsch Handelsblad:** 20 Sint-Jorisstraat, 8000 Brugge; tel. (50) 44-21-55; fax (50) 44-21-66; e-mail redactie.bhblad@roularta.be; f. 1906; local news; includes the Krant van West-Vlaanderen as a supplement; Dir EDDY BROUCKAERT; Editor-in-Chief HEDWIG DACQUIN; circ. 40,000.

**Ciné Télé Revue:** 101 ave Reine Marie-Henriette, 1190 Brussels; tel. (2) 345-99-68; fax (2) 343-12-72; e-mail redaction@cinetelerevue.be; internet www.cinetelerevue.be; f. 1944 as Theatra Ciné Revue, current name adopted 1984; TV listings, celebrity news, family issues; circ. 2,000,000.

**La Cité:** 26 rue St Laurent, 1000 Brussels; tel. (2) 217-23-90; fax (2) 217-69-95; f. 1950 as daily, weekly 1988; Christian Democrat; Editor JOS SCHOONBROODT; circ. 20,000.

**European Voice:** 17–19 rue Montoyer, 1000 Brussels; tel. (2) 540-90-90; fax (2) 540-90-71; e-mail europeanvoice@compuserve.com; internet www.european-voice.com; f. 1995; EU news; Editor JACKI DAVIS; circ 18,000.

**Femmes d'Aujourd'hui:** 109 rue Neewald, 1200 Brussels; tel. (2) 776-28-50; fax (2) 776-28-58; f. 1933; women's magazine; Chief Editor ROBERT MALIES; circ. 160,000.

**Flair:** 7 Jan Blockxstraat, 2018 Antwerp; tel. (3) 247-45-11; fax (3) 237-95-19; Flemish and French; women's magazine; Chief Editor A. BROUCKMANS; circ. 239,858.

**Foot/Voetbal Magazine:** 50 Raketstraat, 1130 Brussels; tel. (2) 702-45-71; fax (2) 702-45-72; e-mail voetbal@roularta.be.

**Humo:** 109 Neerveldstraat, 1200 Brussels; tel. (2) 776-24-20; fax (2) 776-23-24; e-mail humo@mediaxis.be; internet www.humo.be; general weekly and TV and radio guide in Flemish; Chief Editor GUY MORTIER; circ. 278,350.

**Joepie TV Plus:** 2 Brandekensweg, 2627 Schelle; tel. (3) 880-84-65; fax (3) 844-61-52; f. 1973; teenagers' interest; Chief Editor GUIDO VAN LIEFFERINGE; circ. 144,841.

**Kerk en Leven:** 92 Halewijnlaan, 2050 Antwerp; tel. (3) 210-08-40; fax (3) 210-08-36; e-mail redaktie.kerklev@kerknet.be; internet www.kerknet.be; f. 1942; Catholic; five regional edns; circ. 620,000.

**Knack:** 50–52 Raketstraat, 1130 Brussels; tel. (2) 702-46-51; fax (2) 702-46-52; e-mail knack@knack.be; internet www.knack.be; f. 1971; news magazine; Dir HUBERT VAN HUMBEECK; Chief Editors RIK VAN CAUWELAERT, FRANK DE MOOR; circ. 145,000.

**Kontakt Lier:** 14 Centrale Weg, 2560 Nijlen; tel. (3) 481-89-58; fax (3) 481-71-22; f. 1967; Antwerp local news.

**De Kortrijks Handelsblad:** 83B Doorniksewijk, 8500 Kortrijk; tel. (56) 27-00-30; fax (56) 27-00-39; regional news; owned by Roularta media group; includes De Krant van West-Vlaanderen as a supplement.

**De Krant van West-Vlaanderen:** 33 Meiboomlaan, 8800 Roeselares; tel. (51) 26-61-11; fax (51) 26-65-87; e-mail kvwvl@roularta.be; internet www.krantvanwestvlaanderen.be; national news and sport; owned by Roularta media group; included as a supplement with regional newspapers; Dir EDDY BROUCKAERT; circ. 331,600.

**Kwik:** Brusselsesteenweg 347, 1730 Kobbegem; tel. (2) 454-25-01; fax (2) 454-28-28; f. 1962; men's interest; Dir CHRISTIAN VAN THILLO; Editor FRANK SCHRAETS; circ. 55,000.

**Landbouwleven/Le Sillon Belge:** 92 ave Léon Grosjean, 1140 Brussels; tel. (2) 730-33-00; fax (2) 726-91-34; e-mail erulu@euronet.be; f. 1952; agriculture; Gen. Dir P. CALLEBAUT; Editorial Man. ANDRÉ DE MOL; circ. 37,300.

**Libelle (Het Rijk der Vrouw):** 7 Jan Blockxstraat, 2018 Antwerp; tel. (3) 247-48-51; fax (3) 247-46-88; f. 1945; Flemish; women's interest; Dir JAN VANDENWYNGAERDEN; Chief Editor KARIN BODEGOM; circ. 250,668.

**Le Soir Illustré:** 21 place de Louvain, 1000 Brussels; tel. (2) 225-55-55; fax (2) 225-59-11; f. 1928; independent illustrated; Chief Editor STEVE POLUS; circ. 87,000.

**Spirou/Robbedoes:** rue Jules Deserée 52, 6001 Marcinelle; tel. (71) 60-05-00; children's interest; circ. 80,000.

**TeVe-Blad:** 7 Jan Blockxstraat, 2018 Antwerp; tel. (3) 231-47-90; fax (3) 234-34-66; f. 1981; illustrated; Chief Editor ROB JANS.

**Télémoustique:** Brussels; tel. (2) 537-08-00; fax (2) 537-45-63; f. 1924; radio and TV; Dir LOUIS CROONEN; Editor ALAIN DE KUYSSCHE; circ. 120,000.

**Télépro/Telepro:** 31 rue Saint Remacle, 4800 Verviers; tel. (87) 30-70-24; fax (87) 31-35-37; f. 1954; TV listings; owned by Roularta media group; Chief Editor GUY DARRENOUGUÉ; circ. 185,000.

**Trends/Tendances:** Research Park Zellik, De Haak, 1731 Zellik; tel. (2) 467-59-00; fax (2) 467-57-59; e-mail tendances@roularta.be; internet www.trends.be; economic analysis and business news; owned by Roularta media group; Dir TONY COENJAERTS; Chief Editor HENRI DUPUIS; circ. 43,514.

**TV Ekspres:** 7 Jan Blockxstraat, 2018 Antwerp; tel. (3) 247-46-77; fax (3) 247-45-89; e-mail tvexpress@mediaxis.be; Chief Editor ROB JANS; circ. 95,000.

**TV Story:** 7 Jan Blockxstraat, 2018 Antwerp; tel. (3) 247-45-11; fax (3) 216-17-67; f. 1975; Flemish; women's interest; Dir J. VANDENWYNGAERDEN; Chief Editor L. VAN RAAK; circ. 175,111.

**Le Vif/L'Express:** 33 place de Jamblinne de Meux, 1030 Brussels; tel. (2) 739-65-11; fax (2) 734-30-40; f. 1971; current affairs; owned by Roularta media group; Dir Gen. PATRICK DE BORCHGRAVE; Chief Editors JACQUES GEVERS, STÉPHANE RENARD; circ. 83,816.

**De Weekbode:** 33 Meiboomlaan, 8800 Roeselare; tel. (51) 26-61-11; fax (51) 26-65-87; regional news; owned by Roularta media group; includes De Krant van West-Vlaanderen as a supplement; Chief Editor NOËL MAES.

**De Weekkrant:** 10 Herckenrodesingel, 3500 Hasselt; tel. (11) 87-81-11; fax (11) 87-82-04; f. 1949; Brabant and Limburg local news.

**Het Wekelijks Nieuws:** 5 Nijverheidslaan, 8970 Poperinge; tel. (57) 33-67-21; fax (57) 33-40-18; Christian news magazine; Dir WIM WAUTERS; Editor HERMAN SANSEN; circ. 56,000.

**De Zeewacht:** 72 Nieuwpoortsesteenweg, 8400 Ostend; tel. (59) 56-07-21; fax (59) 27-00-39; Ostend local news; owned by Roularta media group; includes De Krant van West-Vlaanderen as a supplement.

**ZIE-Magazine:** Antwerp; tel. (3) 231-47-90; fax (3) 234-34-66; f. 1930; illustrated; Dir JAN MERCKX; Chief Editor ROB JANS.

**Zondag Nieuws:** 2 Brandekensweg, 2627 Schelle; tel. (2) 220-22-11; fax (2) 217-98-46; f. 1958; general interest; Dir RIK DUYCK; Chief Editor LUC VANDRIESSCHE; circ. 113,567.

**Zondagsblad:** 22 Forelstraat, 9000 Ghent; tel. (9) 265-68-02; fax (9) 223-16-77; f. 1949; Gen. Man. WIM SCHAAP; Editor JEF NIJS; circ. 75,000.

### SELECTED OTHER PERIODICALS

**Alternative Libertaire:** BP 103, 1050 Ixelles 1; internet www.users.skynet.be/AL; 11 a year; radical social criticism and debate.

**Axelle:** 170 Langestraat, 1150 Brussels; tel. (2) 799-00-00; fax (2) 799-16-16; e-mail com@publicants.be; f. 1917; monthly; women's interest; circ. 54,876.

**Het Beste uit Reader's Digest:** 20 blvd Paepsem, 1070 Brussels; tel. (2) 526-81-85; fax (2) 526-81-89; f. 1968; monthly; general; Man. Dir CAREL ROG; circ. 80,000.

**Le Cri du Citoyen:** BP 1607, 1000 Brussels 1; tel. and fax (2) 217-48-31; e-mail redaction@lecriducitoyen.com; internet www.chez.com/lecriducitoyen; social comment; 10 a year; Editor FRANCESCO PAOLO CATANIA.

**Eigen Aard:** 170 Langestraat, 1150 Brussels; tel. (2) 799-00-00; fax (2) 799-16-16; e-mail com@publicants.be; f. 1911; monthly; women's interest; circ. 141,414.

**International Engineering News:** 216 rue Verte, 1030 Brussels; tel. (2) 240-26-11; fax (2) 242-71-11; e-mail pepco@pepco.be; internet www.pepco.be; f. 1975; 9 a year; Man. Dir A. ROZENBROEK; circ. 53,000.

**Jet Limburg:** 10 Herckenrodesingel, 3500 Hasselt; tel. (11) 87-84-85; fax (11) 87-84-84; fortnightly; general interest; circ. 292,000.

**Marie Claire:** Brussels; tel. (2) 776-25-91; monthly; women's interest; circ. 80,000.

**Le Moniteur Belge/Belgisch Staatsblad:** 40–42 rue de Louvain, 1000 Brussels; tel. (2) 552-24-59; fax (2) 511-01-84; internet moniteur.be; legislation and official documents; up to 5 a week.

**Le Moniteur de l'Automobile:** Brussels; tel. (2) 660-19-20; fortnightly; motoring; Editor ÉTIENNE VISART; circ. 85,000.

**Notre Temps/Onze Tijd:** 33 rue de la Concorde, 1050 Brussels; tel. (2) 514-24-24; fax (2) 514-22-44; e-mail Redaction.NT@bayard-presse.be; senior citizen's interests; monthly; circ. 96,672.

**Passie/Passion:** T & M, place du Congrès, 4020 Luik; tel. (4) 343-50-50; fax (4) 342-70-00; 6 a year; luxury goods; owned by Roularta media group; Dir and Chief Editor JEAN PERINI; circ. 20,000.

**PC World Belgium:** 70 rue Rederbachstraat, 1190 Brussels; tel. (2) 346-48-50; fax (2) 346-43-65; internet www.best.be; f. 1998; monthly; Pres. JEAN DE GHELDERE; circ. 35,000.

**Santé:** Drogenbos; tel. (2) 331-06-13; fax (2) 331-23-33; monthly; popular health, diet, fitness; circ. 200,000.

**Sélection du Reader's Digest:** 20 blvd Paepsem, 1070 Brussels; tel. (2) 526-81-85; fax (2) 526-81-89; f. 1947; monthly; general; Man. Dir CAREL ROG; circ. 80,000.

**Vrouw & Wereld:** 170 Langestraat, 1150 Brussels; tel. (2) 799-00-00; fax (2) 799-16-16; e-mail com@publicants.be; f. 1920; monthly; women's interest; circ. 197,794.

### NEWS AGENCIES

**Agence Belga (Agence Télégraphique Belge de Presse SA)—Agentschap Belga (Belgisch Pers-telegraafagentschap NV):** 8B rue F. Pelletier, 1030 Brussels; tel. (2) 743-13-11; fax (2) 735-18-74; f. 1920; largely owned by daily newspapers; Chair. L. NEELS; Gen. Man. E. HANS.

**Agence Europe SA:** 36 rue de la Gare, 1040 Brussels; tel. (2) 737-94-94; fax (2) 736-37-00; internet www.agenceurope.com; f. 1952; daily bulletin on EU activities.

**Centre d'Information de Presse (CIP):** 199 blvd du Souverain, 1160 Brussels; tel. (2) 675-25-79; f. 1946; Dir T. SCHOLTES.

#### Foreign Bureaux

**Agence France-Presse (AFP):** 17 rue Archimède, 1000 Brussels; tel. (2) 230-83-94; fax (2) 230-23-04; e-mail afp.bru@euronet.be; internet www.afp.com; Dir JEAN BURNER.

**Agencia EFE** (Spain): 1 blvd Charlemagne, bte 20, 1041 Brussels; tel. (2) 285-48-30; Dir JOSÉ MANUEL SANZ MINGOTE.

**Agenzia Nazionale Stampa Associata (ANSA)** (Italy): 1 blvd Charlemagne, bte 7, 1040 Brussels; tel. (2) 230-81-92; fax (2) 230-60-82; Dir FABIO CANNILLO.

**Algemeen Nederlands Persbureau (ANP)** (Netherlands): 1 blvd Charlemagne, bte 6, 1041 Brussels; tel. (2) 230-11-88; fax (2) 231-18-04; Correspondents TON VAN LIEROP, KEES PIJNAPPELS, WILMA VAN MELEREN.

**Allgemeiner Deutscher Nachrichtendienst (ADN)** (Germany): Brussels; tel. (2) 734-59-57; fax (2) 736-27-11; Correspondents BARBARA SCHUR, ULLRICH SCHUR.

**Associated Press (AP)** (USA): 1 blvd Charlemagne, bte 49, 1041 Brussels; tel. (2) 230-52-49; Dir ROBERT WIELAARD.

**Česká tisková kancelář (ČTK)** (Czech Republic): 2 rue des Egyptiens, bte 6, 1050 Brussels; tel. (2) 648-01-33; fax (2) 640-31-91; Correspondent M. BARTAK.

**Deutsche Presse-Agentur (dpa)** (Germany): 1 blvd Charlemagne, bte 17, 1041 Brussels; tel. (2) 230-36-91; fax (2) 230-98-96; e-mail dpa@dpa.be; Dir HEINZ-PETER DIETRICH.

**Informatsionnoye Telegrafnoye Agentstvo Rossii-Telegrafnoye Agentstvo Suverennykh Stran (ITAR-TASS)** (Russia): 103 rue Général Lotz, bte 10, 1180 Brussels; tel. (2) 343-86-70; fax (2) 344-83-76; e-mail mineev@arcadis.be; Correspondent ALEKSANDR I. MINEYEV.

**Inter Press Service-Vlaanderen (IPS)** (Italy): 21 Inquisitiestraat, 1000 Brussels; tel. (2) 736-18-31; fax (2) 735-20-89; e-mail ips@ips.ngonet.be; internet www.ips.ngonet.be; Dir LUC VERHEYEN.

**Jiji Tsushin** (Japan): 1 blvd Charlemagne, bte 26, 1041 Brussels; tel. (2) 285-09-48; fax (02) 230-14-50; Dir HIROSHI MASUDA.

**Kyodo News Service** (Japan): 1 blvd Charlemagne, bte 37, 1041 Brussels; tel. (2) 285-09-10; fax (02) 230-53-34; Dir MASARU IWATA.

**Magyar Távirati Iroda (MTI)** (Hungary): 41 rue Jean Chapelie, 1050 Brussels; tel. and fax (2) 343-75-35; Correspondents BÉLA VERES, BALÁZS LÁSZLÓ.

**Reuters** (United Kingdom): 61 rue de Trèves, 1040 Brussels; tel. (2) 287-66-11; fax (2) 230-55-40; Man. Dir PETER KAYER.

**Rossiyskoye Informatsionnoye Agentstvo—Novosti (RIA—Novosti)** (Russia): 74 rue du Merlot, 1180 Brussels; tel. (2) 332-24-35; fax 332-17-29; e-mail novosti@village.uunet.be; Dir VIKTOR ONOUTCHKO.

**Xinhua (New China) News Agency** (People's Republic of China): 32 square Ambiorix, Résidence le Pavois, bte 4, 1040 Brussels; tel. (2) 230-32-54; Chief Correspondent LE ZUDE.

### PRESS ASSOCIATIONS

**Association belge des Editeurs de Journaux/Belgische Vereniging van de Dagbladuitgevers:** 22 blvd Paepsem, bte 7, 1070 Brussels; tel. (2) 522-96-60; fax (2) 522-60-04; e-mail abej.bvdu@village.uunet.be; f. 1964; 17 mems; Pres KOEN CLEMENT; Gen. Secs ALEX FORDYN (Flemish), MARGARET BORIBON (French).

**Association générale des Journalistes professionnels de Belgique/Algemene Vereniging van de Beroepsjournalisten in België:** 9B Quai à la Houille, 1000 Brussels; tel. (2) 229-14-60; fax (2) 223-02-72; f. 1978 by merger; 4,000 mems; affiliated to IFJ (International Federation of Journalists); Pres. PHILIPPE LERUTH; Vice-Pres. GERRIT LUTS.

**Fédération Belge des Magazines/Federatie van de Belgische Magazines:** 22/8 blvd Paepsemlaan, 1070 Brussels; tel. (2) 522-57-91; fax (2) 522-85-27; e-mail magazines@febelma.be; Pres. PATRICK DE BORCHGRAVE; Sec. Gen. ALAIN LAMBRECHTS.

**Fédération de la Presse Périodique de Belgique/Federatie van de periodieke pers van België (FPPB):** 54 rue Charles Martel, 1000 Brussels; tel. (2) 230-09-99; fax (2) 231-14-59; f. 1891; Pres. P. VAN SINT JAN; Sec.-Gen. JOHAN VAN CLEEMPUT.

## Principal Publishers

**Acco CV:** 134–136 Tiensestraat, 3000 Louvain; tel. (16) 29-11-00; fax (16) 20-73-89; e-mail rob.berrevoets@acco.be; f. 1960; general reference, scientific books, periodicals; Dir ROB BERREVOETS.

**Uitgeverij Altiora Averbode NV** (Publishing Dept): 1 Abdijstraat, bte 54, 3271 Averbode; tel. (13) 78-01-02; fax (13) 78-01-79; e-mail averbode.publ@verbode.be; internet www.averbode-online.be; f. 1993; children's fiction and non-fiction, religious; Man. P. HERMANS.

**De Boeck & Larcier SA:** 39 rue des Minimes, 1000 Brussels; tel. (10) 48-25-11; fax (10) 48-26-50; f. 1795; school, technical and university textbooks, youth, nature, legal publs and documentaries; Dirs CHR. DE BOECK, G. HOYOS.

**Brepols NV:** 68 Steenweg op Tielen, 2300 Turnhout; tel. (14) 40-25-00; fax (14) 42-20-22; e-mail postmaster@brepols.com; internet www.brepols.com; f. 1796; humanities, diaries; Dir PAUL VANGERVEN.

**Casterman SA:** 28 rue des Soeurs Noires, 7500 Tournai; tel. (69) 25-42-11; fax (69) 25-42-29; f. 1780; fiction, encyclopaedias, education, history, comic books and children's books; Man. Dir J. SIMON.

**D2H Didier Hatier Hachette Education SA:** 412c Chaussée de Waterloo, 1050 Brussels; tel. (2) 539-26-79; fax (2) 539-26-79; e-mail d2h@infoboard.be; internet www.d2h.be; f. 1979; school books, general literature; Dir B. DELGORD.

**Davidsfonds vzw:** 79 Blijde Inkomststraat, 3000 Louvain; tel. (16) 31-06-00; fax (16) 31-06-08; f. 1875; general, reference, textbooks; Dir J. RENS.

**Editions Dupuis SA:** 52 rue Jules Destrée, 6001 Marcinelle; tel. (71) 60-50-00; fax (71) 60-05-99; f. 1898; children's fiction, periodicals and comic books for children and adults, multimedia and audio-visual; Dir JEAN DENEUMOSTIER.

**Etablissements Emile Bruylant:** 67 rue de la Régence, 1000 Brussels; tel. (2) 512-98-45; fax (2) 511-72-02; e-mail bruylant@pophost.eunet.be; internet www.bruylant.be; f. 1838; law; Chief Man. Dir J. VANDEVELD.

**Halewijn NV:** 92 Halewijnlaan, 2050 Antwerp; tel. (3) 210-08-11; fax (3) 210-08-36; e-mail Jo.Cornille@kerknet.be; f. 1953; general, periodicals; Dir-Gen. J. CORNILLE.

**Editions Hemma SA:** 106 rue de Chevron, 4987 Chevron; tel. (86) 43-01-01; fax (86) 43-36-40; f. 1956; juveniles, educational books and materials; Dir A. HEMMERLIN.

**Houtekiet NV:** 33 Vrijheidstraat, 2000 Antwerp; tel. (3) 238-12-96; fax (3) 238-80-41; e-mail info@houtekiet.com; f. 1983; Dir L. DE HAES.

**Die Keure NV:** 108 Oude Gentweg, 8000 Brugge; tel. (50) 33-12-35; fax (50) 34-37-68; e-mail die.keure@pophost.eunet.be; f. 1948; textbooks, law, political and social sciences; Dirs J. P. STEEVENS (textbooks), R. CARTON (law, political and social sciences).

**Uitgeverij De Klaproos:** 4 Hostenstraat, 8670 Koksijde; tel. (58) 51-85-30; fax (58) 51-29-42; internet www.klaproos.be; f. 1992; historical works.

**Kritak NV:** 249 Diestsestraat, 3000 Louvain; tel. (16) 23-12-64; fax (16) 22-33-10; f. 1976; art, law, social sciences, education, humanities, literature, periodicals; Dir ANDRÉ VAN HALEWIJCK.

**Editions Labor:** 156–158 chaussée de Haecht, 1030 Brussels; tel. (2) 240-05-70; fax (2) 216-34-47; f. 1925; general; *L'Ecole 2000* (periodical); Gen. Man. MARIE-PAULE ESKÉNAZI.

**Lannoo Uitgeverij NV:** 97 Kasteelstraat, 8700 Tielt; tel. (51) 42-42-11; fax (51) 40-11-52; e-mail lannoo@lannoo.be; internet www.lannoo.be; f. 1909; general, reference.

**Editions du Lombard SA:** 1–11 ave Paul-Henri Spaak, 1070 Brussels; tel. (2) 526-68-11; f. 1946; juveniles, games, education, geography, history, religion; Man. Dir ROB HARREU.

**Imprimerie Robert Louis Editions:** 35–43 rue Borrens, 1050 Brussels; tel. (2) 640-10-40; fax (2) 640-07-39; f. 1952; science and technical; Man. PIERRE LOUIS.

**Manteau NV:** 147A Belgiëlei, 2018 Antwerp; tel. (3) 285-72-26; fax (3) 285-72-99; e-mail algem@standaard.com; internet www.standaard.com; f. 1932; literature, periodicals; Dir R. VANSCHOONBEEK.

**Mercatorfonds:** 85 Meir, 2000 Antwerp; tel. (3) 202-72-60; fax (3) 231-13-19; f. 1965; art, ethnography, literature, music, geography and history; Dir JAN MARTENS.

**Nouvelles Editions Marabout SA:** 30 ave de l'Energie, 4432 Alleur; tel. (41) 246-38-63; fax (41) 263-88-63; f. 1977; paperbacks; Man. Dir J. FIRMIN; Dir JEAN ARCACHE.

**Peeters pvba:** 153 Bondgenotenlaan, 3000 Louvain; tel. (16) 23-51-70; fax (16) 22-85-00; f. 1970; general, reference; Dir M. PEETERS-LISMOND.

**Uitgeverij Pelckmans NV:** 222 Kapelsestraat, 2950 Kapellen; tel. (3) 664-53-20; fax (3) 655-02-63; f. 1893 as De Nederlandsche Boekhandel, name changed 1988; school books, scientific, general; Dirs J. and R. PELCKMANS.

**Roularta Books:** 33 Meiboomlaan, 8800 Roeselare; tel. (51) 26-63-32; fax (51) 26-64-87; e-mail roulartabooks@roularta.be; f. 1988; owned by Roularta media group; Publr JAN INGELBEEN.

**De Sikkel:** 8 Nijverheidsstraat, 2390 Malle; tel. (3) 309-13-30; fax (3) 311-77-39; e-mail info@desikkel.be; internet www.desikkel.be; f. 1919; educational books and magazines; Dir K. DE BOCK.

**Snoeck-Ducaju en Zoon NV:** 464 Begijnhoflaan, 9000 Ghent; tel. (9) 23-48-97; fax (9) 23-68-30; f. 1948; art books, travel guides; Pres. SERGE SNOECK.

**Société Belgo-Française de Presse et de Promotion (SBPP) SA:** Brussels; tel. (2) 349-00-90; fax (2) 344-28-27; periodicals; Dir CLAUDE CUVELIER.

**Standaard Uitgeverij NV:** 147A Belgiëlei, 2018 Antwerp; tel. (3) 285-72-00; fax (3) 285-72-99; e-mail info@standaard.com; internet www.standaard.com; f. 1924; general, fiction, non-fiction, comics, dictionaries; Dirs WILFRIED CAROT, RUDY VANSCHOONBECK, DIRK WILLEMSE.

**Vlaamse Uitgeversmaatschappij (VUM):** 30 Gossetlaan, 1702 Groot-Bijgaarden; tel. (2) 467-22-11; internet www.vum.be; f. 1976; newspaper and magazine publishing group; Dir-Gen. GUIDO VERDEYEN.

**Wolters Kluwer Belgie NV:** Kovterveldstraat 14, 1831 Diegem; tel. (2) 723-11-11; fax (2) 725-13-06; e-mail ben.houdmont@wkb.be; internet www.wkb.be; law, business, school books, scientific; Dir B. HAUDMONT.

**Wolters Plantyn:** 21–25 Santvoortbeeklaan, 2100 Deurne; tel. (3) 360-03-37; fax (3) 360-03-30; e-mail wolters.plantyn@wpeu.wkb.be; internet www.wpeu.be; f. 1959; education; Dir JACQUES GERMONPREZ.

**Zuidnederlandse Uitgeverij NV:** 7 Vluchtenburgstraat, 2630 Aartselaar; tel. (3) 887-14-64; fax (3) 877-21-15; f. 1956; general fiction and non-fiction, children's books; Dir J. VANDE VELDEN.

### PUBLISHERS' ASSOCIATIONS

**Association des Editeurs Belges (ADEB):** 140 blvd Lambermont, 1030 Brussels; tel. (2) 241-65-80; fax (2) 216-71-31; f. 1922; asscn of French-language book publrs; Dir BERNARD GÉRARD.

**Cercle Belge de la Librairie:** 35 rue de la Chasse Royale, 1160 Brussels; tel. (2) 640-52-41; f. 1883; asscn of Belgian booksellers and publrs; 205 mems; Pres. M. DESTREBECQ.

**Vlaamse Uitgevers Vereniging:** Antwerp; tel. (3) 230-89-23; fax (3) 281-22-40; asscn of Flemish-language book publrs; Sec. WIM DE MONT.

## Broadcasting and Communications

### TELECOMMUNICATIONS

In January 1998 the Belgian telecommunications sector was fully opened to private-sector competition. More than 300 private companies have subsequently registered as service providers.

#### Regulatory Authority

**Institut Belge des Services Postaux et de Télécommunications (IBPT)/Belgisch Instituut voor Postdiensten en Telecommunicatie (BIPT):** 14 ave de l'Astronomie, 1210 Brussels; tel. (2) 226-88-88; fax (2) 223-24-78; e-mail eric.van.heesvelde@bipt.be; internet www.bipt.be; Administrator-Gen. ERIC VAN HEESVELDE.

#### Major Service Providers

**Belgacom:** 177 blvd Emile Jacqmain, 1030 Brussels; tel. (2) 202-41-11; fax (2) 203-54-93; e-mail contact@is.belgacom.be; internet www.belgacom.be; 50.1% state owned; total service operator; Chair. MICHEL DUSSENNE; Pres. and CEO JOHN J. GOOSSENS.

**Belgacom Mobile SA:** 177 blvd Emile Jacqmain, 1130 Brussels; tel. (2) 205-40-00; fax (2) 205-40-40; 75% owned by Belgacom, 25% by AirTouch; mobile cellular telephone operator.

**BT (Worldwide) Ltd:** 48–50 Excelsiorlaan, 1930 Zaventem; tel. (2) 718-22-11; e-mail olivier.servais@bt.be; internet www.bt.be.

**Cable & Wireless Belgium SA:** Blue Tower, 326 ave Louise, BP 17, 1050 Brussels; tel. (2) 629-03-11; fax (2) 646-82-24; internet www.cweurope.com.

**Esprit Telecom Belgium BV:** Bâtiment Radius, 44–46 Excelsiorlaan, 1930 Zaventem; tel. (2) 720-35-45; fax (2) 720-01-02; e-mail belgiuminfo@esprittele.com; internet www.esprittele.com; f. 1995.

**KPN-Orange Belgium:** 115 rue Colonel Bourg, 1140 Brussels; tel. (2) 702-42-00; fax (2) 702-42-01; mobile cellular telephone operator.

**Mobistar:** 149 rue Colonel Bourg, 1140 Brussels; tel. (2) 745-71-11; fax (2) 745-70-00; f. 1995; 51% owned by FTMI group; mobile cellular telephone and fixed-line operator; Pres. J. CORDIER; Dir-Gen. B. GHILLEBAERT.

**Telenet Operaties NV:** 4 Liersesteenweg, 2800 Mechelen; tel. (1) 533-30-00; e-mail communicatie@telenet.be; internet www.telenet.be; f. 1996; telecommunications and cable service provider; CEO PAUL VAN DER SPIEGEL.

**Unisource Belgium NV:** 50 Medialaan, 1800 Vilvoorde; internet www.unisource.be; subsidiary of KPN Belgium; Man. Dir PIERRE VERBRUGEN.

**VersaTel Telecom Belgium NV:** 133 Noorderlaan, 2030 Antwerp; internet www.versatel.be; f. 1995.

**WorldCom NV:** 37 Wetenschapstraat, 1040 Brussels; tel. (2) 400-83-00; e-mail worldcom.info@wcom.be; internet www.worldcom.be; subsidiary of MCI WorldCom.

### STATE BROADCASTING ORGANIZATIONS

#### Flemish

**Vlaamse Radio- en Televisieomroep NV (VRT):** 52 Auguste Reyerslaan, 1043 Brussels; tel. (2) 741-31-11; fax (2) 734-93-51;

e-mail info@vrt.be; internet www.vrt.be; f. 1998; shares held by Flemish Community; operates five radio stations and three television stations; Pres. of Board of Dirs BART DE SCHUTTER; Man. Dir BERT DE GRAEVE; Dir of Radio Programmes FRANS IEVEN; Dir of Television Programmes CHRISTINA VON WACKERBARTH.

#### French

**Radio-Télévision Belge de la Communauté Française (RTBF):** 52 blvd Auguste Reyers, 1044 Brussels; tel. (2) 737-21-11; fax (2) 737-43-57; internet www.rtbf.be; operates five radio stations and two television stations; Chair. EDOUARD DESCAMPE; Admin-Gen. CHRISTIAN DRUITTE; Dir of Radio Programmes CLAUDE DELACROIX; Dir of Television Programmes GERRARD LOVERIOUS.

#### German

**Belgisches Rundfunk- und Fernsehzentrum der Deutschsprachigen Gemeinschaft (BRF):** 11 Kehrweg, 4700 Eupen; tel. (87) 59-11-11; fax (87) 59-11-99; e-mail info@brf.be; internet www.brf.be; Dir H. ENGELS.

### COMMERCIAL, CABLE AND PRIVATE BROADCASTING

Numerous private radio stations operate in Belgium. Television broadcasts, including foreign transmissions, are received either directly or via cable.

**Canal Plus Belgique:** 656 chaussée de Louvain, 1030 Brussels; tel. (2) 730-02-11; fax (2) 730-03-79; f. 1989; 42% owned by Canal Plus Europe; broadcasts to Brussels region and Wallonia.

**Event TV:** 135 rue Bertelot, 1190 Brussels; tel. (2) 345-15-13; e-mail event@skypro.be; internet www.event-tv.be; f. 1999; commercial station; broadcasts in French and Flemish.

**Regionale TV Media:** Brussels; tel. (2) 467-58-77; fax (2) 467-56-54; e-mail contact@rtvm.be; internet www.rtvm.be; group of 11 regional news broadcasters within Flanders; commercial.

**Télévision Indépendante (TVI):** 1 ave Ariane, 1201 Brussels; tel. (2) 778-68-11; fax (2) 778-68-12; commercial station; broadcasts in French.

**Vlaamse Media Maatschappij:** 1 Medialaan, 1800 Vilvoorde; tel. (2) 255-32-11; fax (2) 252-37-87; f. 1987; commercial; broadcasts in Flemish; Gen. Man. ERIC CLAEYS.

## Finance

(cap. = capital; m. = million; res = reserves; dep. = deposits; brs = branches; amounts in Belgian francs, unless otherwise indicated)

### BANKING

**Commission bancaire et financière/Commissie voor het Bank- en Financiewezen:** 99 ave Louise, 1050 Brussels; tel. (2) 535-22-11; fax (2) 535-23-23; f. 1935 to supervise the application of legislation relating to the legal status of credit institutions and to the public issue of securities; Chair. JEAN-LOUIS DUPLAT; CEOs M. CARDON, R. BONTE, C. LEMPEREUR, A. NIESTEN.

#### Central Bank

**Banque Nationale de Belgique:** 14 blvd de Berlaimont, 1000 Brussels; tel. (2) 221-21-11; fax (2) 221-31-01; e-mail secretariat@bnbb.be; internet www.bnb.be; f. 1850; bank of issue; cap. 400m., res 53,184m., total assets 1,006,809m. (Dec. 1998); Gov. GUY QUADEN; Vice-Gov. WILLIAM FRAEYS; Exec. Dirs J.-P. PAUWELS, J.-J. REY, R. REYNDERS; 2 brs.

#### Development Bank

**Investeringsmaatschappij voor Vlaanderen (GIMV):** 37 Karel Oomsstraat, 2018 Antwerp; tel. (3) 290-21-00; fax (3) 290-21-05; e-mail gimv@gimv.be; internet www.gimv.com; f. 1980; promotes creation, restructuring and expansion of private cos; cap. 8,800,000m. (1999); Chair. HERMAN DAEMS; Dir-Gen. GERARD VAN ACKER.

#### Major Commercial Banks

**ABN AMRO Bank NV:** 53 Regentlaan, 1000 Brussels; tel. (2) 546-04-60; fax (2) 546-04-00; internet www.abnamro.be; cap. 1,050m., res 1,887m., dep. 106,649m. (Dec. 1996); Chair. J. KOOPMAN; Dir J. J. W. ZWEEGERS; 7 brs.

**Anhyp Spaarbank NV/Anhyp Banque d'Epargne SA:** 214 Grotesteenweg, 2600 Berchem; tel. (3) 286-22-11; fax (3) 286-24-07; e-mail info@anhyp.be; internet www.anhyp.be; f. 1881; owned by Royale Belge, Brussels; cap. 1,000m., res 14,583m., dep. 279,886m. (Dec. 1997); Chair. of Bd of Dirs PATRICK DE COURCEL; Chair. of Exec. Cttee CARL HOLSTERS.

**Antwerpse Diamantbank NV/Banque Diamantaire Anversoise SA:** 54 Pelikaanstraat, 2018 Antwerp; tel. (3) 204-72-04; fax (3) 233-90-95; e-mail info@adia.be; f. 1934; cap. 1,386m., res 2,064m., dep. 27,249m. (Dec. 1998); Chair. JAN VANHEVEL; Man. Dir and Chair. of Exec. Cttee PAUL C. GORIS.

**Antwerpse Hypotheekkas/Caisse Hypothécaire Anversoise (ANHYP):** 214 Grotesteenweg, 2600 Antwerp; tel. (3) 286-22-11; fax (3) 286-24-07; e-mail contact@anyhp.be; internet www.anhyp.be; f. 1881; savings bank; cap. 1,000m., res 14,263m., dep. 254,133m. (Dec. 1997); Chair. ALFRED BOUCKAERT; Gen. Man. CARL HOLSTERS.

**Artesia Banking Corporation:** W.T.C. Tower 1, 30 B2 Koning Albert II-laan, 1000 Brussels; tel. (2) 204-41-11; fax (2) 203-20-14; e-mail info@artesiabc.be; internet www.artesiabc.be; f. 1999; owns Artesia Bank, BACOB Bank and DVV/AP insurance co; cap. and res 54,413m., total assets 2,605,352m. (Dec. 1998); Chair. DIRK BRUNEEL.

**Artesia Bank SA/NV:** 162 blvd Emile Jacqmain, 1000 Brussels; tel. (2) 204-41-11; fax (2) 203-20-14; e-mail bel_mail@artesia.be; f. 1968; specialized merchant bank and portfolio manager; Chair. WILLEM MOESEN; 49 brs.

**BACOB Bank SC:** 25 Trierstraat, 1040 Brussels; tel. (2) 285-20-20; fax (2) 230-71-78; e-mail bacob@bacob.be; internet www.bacob.be; f. 1924 as BACOB Savings Bank SC; Chair. DIRK BRUNEEL; 559 brs.

**Banca Monte Paschi Belgio SA/NV:** 24 rue Joseph II, 1000 Brussels; tel. (2) 220-72-11; fax (2) 218-83-91; f. 1947 as Banco di Roma (Belgique), name changed 1992; cap. 1,050m., res 950m., dep. 83,596m. (Dec. 1997); Chair. of Exec. Cttee and Gen. Man. CARLO FIABANE; 6 brs.

**Bank J. van Breda & Co GCV:** 295 Plantin en Moretuslei, 2140 Borgerhout; tel. (3) 217-51-11; fax (3) 235-37-84; e-mail mail@bank.vanbreda.be; internet www.bank.vanbreda.be; f. 1930; cap. 650m., res 1,567m., dep. 54,193m. (Dec. 1997); Gen. Man. CARLO HENRIKSEN; 32 brs.

**Bank Brussels Lambert:** 24 ave Marnix, 1000 Brussels; tel. (2) 547-21-11; fax (2) 547-38-44; e-mail info@bbl.be; internet www.bbl.be; f. 1975; taken over by ING Bank NV (the Netherlands) Jan. 1998; cap. 34,074m., res 79,620m., dep. 3,373,000m. (Dec. 1998); Chair. of Bd JACQUES MOULAERT; Pres. and CEO MICHEL TILMANT; 953 brs.

**Bank Degroof SA/Banque Degroof SCS:** 44 rue de l'Industrie, 1040 Brussels; tel. (2) 287-91-11; fax (2) 230-67-00; internet www.degroof.be; f. 1871, present name adopted 1998; cap. 1,250m., res 1,923m., dep. 35,091m. (Sept. 1998); Man. Dir ALAIN PHILIPPSON.

**Bank of Yokohama (Europe) SA:** 287 ave Louise, BP 1, 1050 Brussels; tel. (2) 648-82-85; fax (2) 647-72-77; f. 1983; cap. 875m., res 99m., dep. 7,962m. (Dec. 1997); Chair. JIRO GOTO; Man. Dir and Gen. Man. AKIO KAWACHI.

**Bankunie NV:** 46 Parklaan, 2300 Turnhout; tel. (14) 44-32-00; fax (14) 42-78-51; internet www.bankunie.be; f. 1966; cap. 320m., res 383m., dep. 28,810m. (Dec. 1997); Chair. ALBERT BARROO; CEO ROBERT CUYPERS.

**Banque Belgolaise SA:** 1 Cantersteen, bte 807, 1000 Brussels; tel. (2) 551-72-11; fax (2) 551-75-15; e-mail belgolaise.brussels@belgolaise.com; f. 1960 as Banque Belgo-Congolaise SA, present name adopted 1991; cap. 1,000m., res 2,146m., dep. 75,725m. (Dec. 1998); Chair. MARC YVES BLANPAIN; Vice-Chair. ANDRÉ BERGEN; 1 br.

**Banque Européenne pour l'Amérique Latine (BEAL) SA:** 166 chaussée de la Hulpe, 1170 Brussels; tel. (2) 663-69-00; fax (2) 663-69-59; internet www.westlb.com/beal; f. 1974; cap. 3,200m., res 1,598m., dep. 139,516m. (Dec. 1997); Chair. HANS-JÜRGEN SENGERA; Man. Dirs PHILIP WYKES, HORST R. MAGIERA.

**Banque Nagelmackers 1747 SA:** 23 ave de l'Astronomie, 1210 Brussels; tel. (2) 229-76-00; fax (2) 229-76-99; e-mail hilde.vernaillen@nagelmackers.be; internet www.nagelmackers.be; f. 1747; cap. 1,849m., res 1,966m., dep. 88,255m. (Dec. 1997); Pres. Exec. Cttee JEAN-LOUIS LUYCKX; 67 brs.

**BCH Benelux SA/NV:** 227 rue de la Loi, 1040 Brussels; tel. (2) 286-54-11; fax (2) 230-09-40; f. 1914, present name adopted 1998; cap. 1,000m., res 580m., dep. 77,266m. (Dec. 1997); Pres. LEOPOLDO CALVO SOTELO Y BUSTELO; Man. Dir MIGUEL SÁNCHEZ TÓVAR

**CBC Banque SA:** 5 Grand-Place, 1000 Brussels; tel. (2) 547-12-11; fax (2) 547-11-62; internet www.cbc.be; f. 1958, name changed as above 1998; cap. 3,000m., res 3,461m., dep. 261,818m. (Dec. 1997); Chair. JAN HUYGHEBAERT; 71 brs.

**Citibank Belgium NV/SA:** 263 blvd Général Jacques, 1050 Brussels; tel. (2) 626-51-11; fax (2) 626-55-84; internet www.citibank.be; f. 1919, present name adopted 1992; Gen. Man. JACK WRIGHT.

**Crédit Communal de Belgique SA/Gemeentekrediet van België NV:** 44 blvd Pachéco, 1000 Brussels; tel. (2) 222-11-11; fax (2) 222-40-32; internet www.creditcommunal.be; f. 1860; merged with Crédit Locale de France in 1996; cap. 59,421m., res 5,896m., dep. 2,758,928m. (Dec. 1998); Chair. M. DECONINCK; Man. Dir FRANÇOIS NARMON; 959 brs.

**Crédit à l'Industrie/Krediet aan de Nijverheid:** 14 ave de l'Astronomie, 1210 Brussels; tel. (2) 214-12-11; fax (2) 218-04-78; f. 1919; share capital 98% owned by private interests; cap. 4,500m., res 7,554m., dep. 511,133m. (Dec. 1995); Chair. WIM COUMANS; 4 brs.

**Crédit Professionnel SA/Beroepskrediet NV:** 16 blvd de Waterloo, 1000 Brussels; tel. (2) 289-89-89; fax (2) 289-89-90; e-mail info@bkcp.be; internet www.bkcp.be; f. 1946 as Caisse Nationale de Crédit Professionel SA; name changed as above 1997; cap. 2,445m., res 52m., dep. 141,280m. (Dec. 1997); Chair. of Supervisory Bd GUIDO VERHAEGEN; Chair. of Exec. Cttee THIERRY FAUT.

**Deutsche Bank SA/NV:** 9 Lange Gasthuisstraat, 2000 Antwerp 1; tel. (2) 551-65-11; fax (2) 551-66-66; f. 1893 as Banque de Commerce SA (Handelsbank NV), renamed Crédit Lyonnais Belgium 1989, bought by Deutsche Bank 1999; cap. 6,587m., res 3,847m., dep. 406,231m. (Dec. 1997); Chair. CARL L. VON BOEHM-BEZING; Chief Exec. PHILIPPE CLOËS; 40 brs.

**Europabank NV:** 170 Burgstraat, 9000 Ghent; tel. (9) 224-73-11; tel. (9) 224-73-11; fax (9) 223-34-72; e-mail europabank@village .eunet.be; f. 1964; owned by Staal Bank NV, The Hague; cap. 64m., res. 1,151m., total assets 17,229m. (Dec. 1998); Chair. of Supervisory Board RAOUL WIJNAKKER; 26 brs.

**Fortis Bank NV/Fortis Banque SA:** 3 Montagne du Parc, 1000 Brussels; tel. (2) 565-11-11; fax (2) 565-42-22; e-mail fortisbank@ gbank.com; internet www.fortisbank.com; f. 1999 by merger of Generale Bank/Générale de Banque and ASLK-CGER Bank/Banque with the Fortis Group; total assets €303,966m. (Oct. 1999); banking, insurance and investments; Chair. of Bd of Dirs Count MAURICE LIPPENS; Chair. of Exec. Cttee HERMAN VERWILST; 3,000 brs.

**ING Bank (Belgium) SA/NV:** 1 rue de Ligne, 1000 Brussels; tel. (2) 229-87-11; fax (2) 229-88-10; f. 1934, present name adopted 1995; wholly-owned subsidiary of Bank Brussels Lambert; cap. 540m., res 1,560m., dep. 50,914m. (Dec. 1997); Chair. E. DRALANS; Man. Dirs G. COLONNA, J. DE VAUCLEROY; 1 br.

**Ippa Bank NV/SA:** 23 blvd du Souverain, 1170 Brussels; tel. (2) 678-69-11; fax (2) 678-66-05; e-mail webmaster@ippa.be; internet www.ippa.be; f. 1969; cap. 4,000m., res 905m., dep. 267,190m. (Dec. 1998); Chair. A. BOUCKAERT; Man. Dir C. HOLSTERS; 30 brs.

**KBC Bank NV:** 2 Havenlaan, 1080 Brussels 8; tel. (2) 429-71-11; fax (2) 429-81-31; e-mail kbc.telecenter@kbc.be; internet www.kbc.be; f. 1935 as Kredietbank NV; merged with Bank von Roeselare NV and CERA Investment Bank NV in 1998; cap. 23,425m., res 186,970m., dep. 4,882,300m. (Dec. 1998); Pres. REMI VERMEIREN.

**Mitsubishi Trust and Banking Corporation (Europe) SA:** 40 blvd du Régent, 1000 Brussels; tel. (2) 511-22-00; fax (2) 511-26-13; f. 1976; cap. 600m., res 1,573m., dep. 27,470m. (Dec. 1996); Chair. T. SUZUKI; Man. Dir SHIGEO SEKIJIMA.

**Parfibank SA:** 40 blvd du Régent, 1000 Brussels; tel. (2) 513-90-20; fax (2) 512-73-20; e-mail roland_deras@artesia.be; f. 1976 as Nippon European Bank SA, present name adopted 1996; cap. 3,000m., res 705m., dep. 21,693m. (Dec. 1997); Chair. RENAUD GREINDL; Man. Dir ROLAND DERAS.

### Banking Association

**Association Belge des Banques/Belgische Vereniging van Banken (ABB):** 36 rue Ravenstein, 1000 Brussels; tel. (2) 507-68-11; fax (2) 512-58-61; e-mail abb-bvb@abb-bvb.be; f. 1936; 137 mems; affiliated to Fédération des Entreprises de Belgique and Fédération Bancaire de l'UE; Pres. KAREL DE BOECK; Dir-Gen. GUIDO RAVOET.

## STOCK EXCHANGE

**Brussels Exchanges (BXS):** Palais de la Bourse, 1000 Brussels; tel. (2) 509-12-11; fax (2) 509-12-12; e-mail info@bxs.be; internet www.bxs.be; Pres. O. LEFEBVRE; Dir E. COOREMANS.

## HOLDING COMPANY

**Société Générale de Belgique:** 30 rue Royale, 1000 Brussels; tel. (2) 507-02-11; fax 512-18-95; f. 1822; investment and holding co with substantial interests in banking and finance, industry, mining and energy; CEO PHILIPPE LIOTIER.

## INSURANCE

In 1998 there were 234 registered insurance companies active in Belgium, of which 150 were Belgian-owned.

### Regulatory Authority

**Office de Contrôle des Assurances/Controledienst voor de Verzekeringen:** 61 ave de Cortenbergh,1000 Brussels; tel. (2) 737-07-11; fax (2) 736-88-17; internet www.cdv-oca.be; f. 1975; supervises insurance funds and mortgage and pension cos; Chair. WILLY P. LENAERTS; Dir-Gen. GUIDO VERNAILLEN.

### Principal Insurance Companies

**Assurances Groupe Josi SA:** 135 rue Colonel Bourg, 1140 Brussels; tel. (2) 730-12-11; fax (2) 730-16-00; f. 1955; accident, fire, marine, general, life; Pres. and Dir-Gen. J. P. LAURENT JOSI.

**Aviabel, Compagnie Belge d'Assurances Aviation, SA:** 10 ave Brugmann, 1060 Brussels; tel. (2) 349-12-11; fax (2) 349-12-99; f. 1935; aviation, insurance, reinsurance; Chair. P. GERVY; Gen. Man. J. VERWILGHEN.

**AXA Royale Belge:** 25 blvd du Souverain, 1170 Brussels; tel. (2) 678-61-11; fax (2) 678-93-40; f. 1853; member of the AXA group; all branches; Pres. Comte JEAN-PIERRE DE LAUNOIT; Man. Dir ALFRED BOUCKAERT.

**Belgamar, Compagnie Belge d'Assurances Maritimes SA:** 66 Mechelsesteenweg, 2018 Antwerp; tel. (3) 247-36-11; fax (3) 247-35-90; f. 1945; marine insurance; Chair. P. H. SAVERYS; Man. Dir A. THIÈRY.

**Compagnie d'Assurance de l'Escaut:** 10 rue de la Bourse, Antwerp; f. 1821; fire, accident, life, burglary, reinsurance; Man E. DIERCXSENS.

**Compagnie de Bruxelles 1821 SA d'Assurances:** Brussels; tel. (2) 237-12-11; fax (2) 237-12-16; f. 1821; fire, life, general; Pres. C. BASECQ.

**DVV Verzekeringen NV/Les AP Assurances SA:** 6 ave Livingston, 1000 Brussels; tel. (2) 286-61-11; fax (2) 286-15-15; f. 1929; all branches; 82% owned by Artesia Banking Corporation.

**EULER-COBAC Belgium NV/SA:** 15 rue Montoyer, 1000 Brussels; tel. (2) 289-31-11; fax (2) 289-32-99; f. 1929 as Compagne Belge d'Assurance-Crédit; name changed 1998; CEO PHILIPPE MUÊLE.

**Fortis AG:** 53 blvd Emile Jacqmain, 1000 Brussels; tel. (2) 220-81-11; fax (2) 220-81-50; e-mail info@fortis.com; internet www.fortis .com; f. 1990; owned by the Fortis Group; Chair. MAURICE LIPPENS, HANS BARTELDS.

**Generali Belgium SA:** 149 ave Louise, 1050 Brussels; tel. (2) 533-81-11; fax (2) 533-88-99; fire, accident, marine, life, reinsurance; Pres. G. BECKERS; Dir-Gen. R. GRANDI.

**KBC SA/NV:** Havenlaan 2, 1080 Brussels; tel. (2) 429-71-11; fax (2) 429-81-31; e-mail kbc.telecenter@kbc.be; internet www.kbc.be; f. 1998.

**Mercator & Noordstar NV:** 302 Kortrijksesteenweg, 900 Ghent; tel. (9) 242-37-11; fax (9) 242-36-36; internet www.mercator.be; all branches.

**Société Mutuelle des Administrations Publiques (SMAP):** 24 rue des Croisiers, 4000 Liège; tel. (41) 220-31-11; institutions, civil service employees, public administration and enterprises.

**Victoire, Société Anonyme Belge d'Assurances:** Brussels; tel. (2) 286-24-11; fax (2) 230-94-73; life and non-life; Chair. M. P. DE COURCEL; Gen. Man. G. DUPIN.

### Insurance Associations

**Fédération des Producteurs d'Assurances de Belgique (FEPRABEL):** 40 ave Albert-Elisabeth, 1200 Brussels; tel (2) 743-25-60; fax (2) 735-44-58; e-mail info@feprabel.be; internet www .feprabel.be; f. 1934; Pres. RÉGINALD VAN INGELGEM; 500 mems.

**Union Professionnelle des Entreprises d'Assurances Belges et Etrangères Opérant en Belgique/Beroepsvereniging der Belgische en in België werkzame Buitenlandse Verzekeringsondernemingen:** 29 square de Meeûs, 1040 Brussels; tel. (2) 547-56-11; fax (2) 547-56-01; f. 1921; affiliated to Fédération des Entreprises de Belgique; Pres. JEAN-PIERRE GÉRARD; Man. Dir MICHEL BAECKER; 137 mems.

# Trade and Industry

## GOVERNMENT AGENCIES

**Investeren in Vlaanderen–Flanders Foreign Investment Office:** 4 Leuvenseplein 1000 Brussels; tel. (2) 227-53-11; fax (2) 227-53-10; e-mail flanders@ffio.be; internet www.ffio.com; f. 1988; promotes investment in Flanders; Man. Dir JEAN-PIERRE VANDELOO.

**Société Développement Régionale de Bruxelles (SDRB):** 6 rue Gabrielle Petit, 1080 Brussels; tel. (2) 422-51-11; fax (2) 422-51-12; e-mail info.sdrb@sdrb.irisnet.be; internet www.brda.irisnet.be; f. 1974; promotes economic development in the capital; Chair. P. MOUREAUX.

**Société Régionale d'Investissement de Wallonie:** 13 ave Destenay, 4000 Liège; tel. (4) 221-98-11; fax (4) 221-99-99; e-mail cdelevoy@sriw.be; f. 1979; promotes private enterprise in Wallonia; Pres. JEAN-CLAUDE DEHOVRE.

## PRINCIPAL CHAMBERS OF COMMERCE

There are chambers of commerce and industry in all major towns and industrial areas.

**Kamer van Koophandel en Nijverheid van Antwerpen:** 12 Markgravestraat, 2000 Antwerp; tel. (3) 232-22-19; fax (3) 233-64-42; f. 1969; Pres. LUC MEURRENS; Gen. Man. L. LUWEL.

**Chambre de Commerce et d'Industrie de Bruxelles:** 500 ave Louise, 1050 Brussels; tel. (2) 648-50-02; fax (2) 640-93-28; f. 1875; Pres. JACQUES-ISAAC CASTIAU.

**Chambre de Commerce et d'Industrie de Liège:** Palais de Congrès, 2 Esplanade de l'Europe, 4020 Liège; tel. (43) 43-92-92; fax (43) 43-92-67; e-mail info@ccilg.be; internet www.ccilg.be; f. 1866; Pres. Jacques Arnolis.

## INDUSTRIAL AND TRADE ASSOCIATIONS

**Fédération des Entreprises de Belgique** (Federation of Belgian Companies): 4 rue Ravenstein, 1000 Brussels; tel. (2) 515-08-11; fax (2) 515-09-99; e-mail red@vbo-feb.be; internet www.vbo-feb.be; f. 1895; federates all the main industrial and non-industrial asscns; Pres. Karel Boone; Man. Dir Tony Vandeputte; 35 full mems.

**Association Belge des Banques/Belgische Vereniging van Banken (ABB):** (see Finance above).

**Association des Exploitants de Carrières de Porphyre** (Porphyry): 64 rue de Belle-Vue, 1000 Brussels; tel. (2) 648-68-60; f. 1967; Pres. Georges Hansen.

**Association des Fabricants de Pâtes, Papiers et Cartons de Belgique (COBELPA)** (Paper): Brussels; tel. (2) 646-64-50; fax (2) 646-82-97; f. 1940; Pres. Frans Walters.

**Confédération des Brasseries de Belgique (CBB)** (Breweries): Maison des Brasseurs, 10 Grand' Place, 1000 Brussels; tel. (2) 511-49-87; fax (2) 511-32-59; e-mail cbb@beerparadise.be; internet www.beerparadise.be; f. 1971; Pres. Yannick Boes.

**Confédération Nationale de la Construction (CNC)** (Civil Engineering, Road and Building Contractors and Auxiliary Trades): 34–42 rue du Lombard, 1000 Brussels; tel. (2) 545-56-00; fax (2) 545-59-00; f. 1946; Pres. Rob Lenaers.

**Confédération Professionnelle du Sucre et de ses Dérivés** (Sugar): 182 ave de Tervueren, 1150 Brussels; tel. (2) 775-80-69; fax (2) 775-80-75; e-mail info@subel.be; f. 1938; mems 10 groups, 66 firms; Pres. E. Kessels; Dir-Gen. M. Rosiers.

**Fédération Belge de la Brique** (Bricks): 13 rue des Poissonniers, bte 22, 1000 Brussels; tel. (2) 511-25-81; fax (2) 513-26-40; e-mail pub02424@innet.be; internet www.brique.be; f. 1947; Pres. Gilbert de Baere.

**Fédération Belge des Dragueurs de Gravier et de Sable (BELBAG-DRAGBEL)** (Quarries): Hasselt; tel. (89) 56-73-45; fax (89) 56-45-42; f. 1967; Pres. Charles Lecluyse.

**Fédération Belge des Entreprises de la Transformation du Bois (FEBELBOIS)** (Wood): 109–111 rue Royale, 1000 Brussels; tel. (2) 217-63-65; fax (2) 217-59-04; Pres. Gustaaf Neyt.

**Fédération Belge des Industries Graphiques (FEBELGRA)** (Graphic Industries): 20 rue Belliard, bte 16, 1040 Brussels; tel. (2) 512-36-38; fax (2) 513-56-76; f. 1978; Pres. Francis Maes.

**Fédération Belge des Industries de l'Habillement** (Clothing): 24 rue Montoyer, 1040 Brussels; tel. (2) 238-10-11; fax (2) 230-47-00; e-mail info@febelgra.be; internet www.febelgra.be; f. 1946; Pres. Alain Chauveheid.

**Fédération Belgo-Luxembourgeoise des Industries du Tabac (FEDETAB)** (Tobacco): 7 ave Lloyd George, 1050 Brussels; tel. (2) 646-04-20; fax (2) 646-22-13; f. 1947; Pres. Claude de Mapnée.

**Fédération Charbonnière de Belgique** (Coal): Brussels; tel. (2) 230-37-40; fax (2) 230-88-50; f. 1909; Pres. Yves Sleuwaegen; Dir Jos van den Broeck.

**Fédération des Carrières de Petit Granit** (Limestone): 245 rue de Cognebeau, 7060 Soignies; tel. (67) 34-78-00; fax (67) 33-00-59; f. 1948; Pres. J.-F. Abraham.

**Fédération d'Employeurs pour le Commerce International, le Transport et les Branches d'Activité Connexes** (Employers' Federation of International Trade, Transport and Related Activities): 33 Brouwersvliet, bus 7, 2000 Antwerp; tel. (3) 221-99-90; fax (3) 226-83-71; f. 1937; Pres. François van Geel; Dir Frans Gielen.

**Fédération des Entreprises de l'Industrie des Fabrications Métalliques, Mécaniques, Electriques, Electroniques et de la Transformation des Matières Plastiques (FABRIMETAL)** (Metalwork, Engineering, Electrics, Electronics and Plastic Processing): 21 rue des Drapiers, 1050 Brussels; tel. (2) 510-23-11; fax (2) 510-23-01; e-mail info@fabrimetal.be; internet www.fabrimetal.be; f. 1946; Pres. Julien de Wilde.

**Fédération de l'Industrie Alimentaire/Federatie Voedingsindustrie (FEVIA)** (Food and Agriculture): 172 Kortenberglaan, bte 7, 1000 Brussels; tel. (2) 743-08-00; fax (2) 733-94-26; e-mail info@fevia.be; internet www.fevia.be; f. 1937; Pres. Eric Swenden; Dir-Gen. Chris Moris.

**Fédération de l'Industrie du Béton (FeBe)** (Precast Concrete): 207–209 blvd August Reyers, 1030 Brussels; tel. (2) 735-80-15; fax (2) 734-77-95; e-mail mail@febe.be; internet www.febe.be; f. 1936; Pres. P. Declerck; Dir Willy Simons.

**Fédération des Industries Chimiques de Belgique (Fedichem)** (Chemical Industries): 49 square Marie-Louise, 1000 Brussels; tel. (2) 238-97-11; fax (2) 231-13-01; e-mail postmaster@fedichem.be; internet www.fedichem.be; f. 1919; Pres. Jacques van Bost; Man. Dir Jean-Marie Biot.

**Fédération de l'Industrie Cimentière Belge** (Cement): 8 rue Volta, 1050 Brussels; tel. (2) 645-52-11; fax (2) 640-06-70; e-mail febelcem@febelcem.be; internet www.febelcem.be; f. 1949; Pres. Paul Vanfrachem; Dir-Gen. Jean-Pierre Jacobs.

**Fédération des Industries Extractives et Transformatrices de Roches non Combustibles (FEDIEX)** (Extraction and processing of non-fuel rocks): 61 rue du Trône, 1050 Brussels; tel. (2) 511-61-73; fax (2) 511-12-84; f. 1942 as Union des Producteurs Belges de Chaux, Calcaires, Dolomies et Produits Connexes, name changed 1990; co-operative society; Pres. Gilles Plaquet.

**Fédération de l'Industrie du Gaz (FIGAZ)** (Gas): 4 ave Palmerston, 1000 Brussels; tel. (2) 237-11-11; fax (2) 230-44-80; f. 1946; Pres. Jean-Pierre Depaemelaere.

**Fédération de l'Industrie Textile Belge (FEBELTEX)** (Textiles): 24 rue Montoyer, 1000 Brussels; tel. (2) 287-08-11; fax (2) 230-65-85; e-mail info@febeltex.be; f. 1945; Pres. Filiep Libeert; Dir-Gen. Jean-François Quix; 500 mems.

**Fédération des Industries Transformatrices de Papier et Carton (FETRA)** (Paper and Cardboard): 715 chaussée de Waterloo, BP 25, 1180 Brussels; tel. (2) 344-19-62; fax (2) 344-86-61; f. 1976; Pres. Paul Pissens.

**Fédération de l'Industrie du Verre** (Glass): 89 ave Louise, 1050 Brussels; tel. (2) 542-61-20; fax (2) 542-61-21; e-mail info@vgi-fiv.be; internet www.vgi-fiv.be; f. 1947; Pres. R. Buekenhout; Man. Dir Roland Deridder.

**Fédération Patronale des Ports Belges** (Port Employers): 33 Brouwersvliet, bus 7, 2000 Antwerp; tel. (3) 221-99-85; fax (3) 226-83-71; f. 1937; Pres. François van Geel; Secs Frans Gielen, Guy Vankrunkelsven.

**Fédération Pétrolière Belge** (Petroleum): 4 rue de la Science, 1000 Brussels; tel. (2) 512-30-03; fax (2) 511-05-91; f. 1926; Pres. E. de Menten de Horne; Sec.-Gen. G. van de Werve.

**Groupement des Sablières** (Sand and Gravel): 49 Quellinstraat, 2018 Antwerp; tel. (3) 223-66-83; fax (3) 223-66-47; e-mail pdn@sibelco.be; f. 1937; Pres. B. de Caritat de Peruzzis; Sec. Paul de Nie.

**Groupement de la Sidérurgie** (Iron and Steel): 47 rue Montoyer, 1000 Brussels; tel. (2) 509-14-11; fax (2) 509-14-00; f. 1953; Pres. Paul Matthys.

**Union des Armateurs Belges** (Shipowners): 9 Lijnwaadmarkt, 2000 Antwerp; tel. (3) 232-72-31; fax (3) 225-28-36; e-mail bru@afsnet.be; Chair. Nicolas Saverys; Man. C. Betrains.

**Union des Carrières et Scieries de Marbres de Belgique (UCSMB)** (Marble): 8 Heideveld, 1654 Huizingen; tel. (2) 361-36-81; fax (2) 361-31-55; Pres. P. Stone.

**Union des Exploitations Electriques et Gazières en Belgique (UEGB)** (Electricity and Gas): 8 blvd du Régent, 1000 Brussels; tel. (2) 518-67-07; fax (2) 518-64-58; f. 1911; Pres. André Marchal.

**Industrie des Huiles Minérales de Belgique (IHMB—IMOB)** (Mineral Oils): 49 square Marie-Louise, 1000 Brussels; tel. (2) 238-97-11; fax (2) 230-03-89; f. 1921; Pres. J. Vercheval; Sec. D. de Hemptinne; 65 mems.

**Union Professionnelle des Producteurs de Fibres-Ciment** (Fibre-Cement): 361 ave de Tervueren, 1150 Brussels; tel. (2) 778-12-11; fax (2) 778-12-12; f. 1941; Pres. Jean Beeckman; Sec. Annie Naus.

**Union de la Tannerie et de la Mégisserie Belges (UNITAN)** (Tanning and Tawing): c/o 140 rue des Tanneurs, 7730 Estaimbourg; tel. (69) 36-23-23; fax (69) 36-23-10; f. 1962; Pres. Bruno Colle; Sec. Anne Vandeputte; 5 mems.

## UTILITIES

### Electricity

**Electrabel:** 8 Regentlaan, 1000 Brussels; tel. (2) 518-61-11; fax (2) 518-64-00; www.electrabel.com; f. 1905; 40% owned by Tractebel.

### Gas

**Distrigas:** 31 Kunstlaan, 1040 Brussels; tel. (2) 282-72-11; fax (2) 230-02-39.

### Water

**Société Wallonne des Distributions d'Eau:** 41 rue de la Concorde, 4800 Verviers; tel. (87) 34-28-11; fax (87) 34-28-00; f. 1986; Dir-Gen. Marc Deconinck.

**Vlaamse Maatschappij voor Watervoorziening:** 73 Belliardstraat, 1040 Brussels; tel. (2) 238-94-11; fax (2) 230-97-98.

### TRADE UNIONS

**Fédération Générale du Travail de Belgique (FGTB)/Algemeen Belgisch Vakverbond (ABVV):** 42 rue Haute, 1000 Brussels; tel. (2) 506-82-11; fax (2) 513-47-21; f. 1899; affiliated to ICFTU; Pres. MICHEL NOLLET; Gen. Sec. MIA DE VITS; has nine affiliated unions with an estimated total membership of 1,176,701 (1995). Affiliated unions:

**Belgische Transportarbeidersbond/Union Belge des Ouvriers du Transport** (Belgian Transport Workers' Union): 66 Paardenmarkt, 2000 Antwerp: tel. (3) 224-34-11; fax (3) 234-01-49; f. 1913; Pres. ALFONS GEERAERTS; 24,000 mems (1990).

**La Centrale Générale/De Algemene Centrale** (Central Union, building, timber, glass, paper, chemicals and petroleum industries): 26–28 rue Haute, 1000 Brussels; tel. (2) 549-05-49; fax (2) 514-16-91; e-mail info@accg.be; internet www.accg.be; Pres. MAURICE CORBISIER; Sec. Gen. DAN PLAUM; Fed. Secs HANS RAES, PAUL LOOTENS, FERDY DE WOLF, JACQUES MICHIELS, RENÉ GEYBELS, JEAN CLAUDE HUMBERT; 300,000 mems (1998).

**Centrale Générale des Services Publics/Algemene Centrale der Openbare Diensten** (Public Service Workers): Maison des Huit Heures, 9–11 place Fontainas, 1000 Brussels; tel. (2) 508-58-11; fax (2) 508-59-02; f. 1945; Pres. HENRI DUJARDIN; Vice-Pres. F. FERMON; Gen. Secs J. DUCHESNE, A. MORDANT, K. STESSENS, T. BERGS.

**Centrale de l'Industrie du Métal de Belgique/Centrale der Metaalindustrie van België** (Metal Workers): 17 rue Jacques Jordaens, 1000 Brussels; tel. (2) 627-74-11; fax (2) 627-74-90; f. 1887; Pres. HERWIG JORISSEN; 185,570 mems (1993).

**Centrale Syndicale des Travailleurs des Mines de Belgique/Belgische Mijnwerkerscentrale** (Miners): 26-28 rue Haute, 1000 Brussels; tel. (2) 549-05-49; f. 1889; Pres. M. CORBISIER.

**Centrale Voeding-Horeca-Diensten** (Catering and Hotel Workers): 18 rue des Alexiens, 1000 Brussels; tel. (2) 512-97-00; fax (2) 512-53-68; f. 1912; Pres. F. DE MEY; Nat. Sec. J. PASCHENKO.

**FGTB–Textile, Vêtement, et Diamant/ABVV–Textiel, Kleding–Diamant** (Textile, Clothing and Diamond Workers): 143 Opvoedingstraat, 9000 Ghent; tel. (9) 242-86-86; fax (9) 242-86-96; e-mail abvvtkd.fgtbtvd@glo.be; f. 1994; Pres. DONALD WITTEVRONGEL; 60,000 mems (1999).

**SETCA/Livre-BBTK/Boek** (Graphical and Paper Workers): Brussels; tel. (2) 512-13-90; fax (2) 512-57-85; e-mail jmcappoen@setca-fgtb.be; f. 1945; Sec.-Gen. ROGER SAGON; Nat. Sec. JEAN-MICHEL CAPPOEN; 13,000 mems (1998).

**Syndicat des Employés, Techniciens et Cadres de Belgique/Bond der Bedienden, Technici en Kaders van België** (Employees, Technicians and Administrative Workers): 42 rue Haute, 1000 Brussels; tel. (2) 512-52-50; fax (2) 511-05-08; e-mail nationaal@setca-fgtb.be; internet www.setca-fgtb.be; f. 1891; Pres. CHRISTIAN ROLAND; Gen. Sec. ROBERT WITTEBROUCK.

**Les Cadets**, an organization for students and school pupils, is also affiliated to the FGTB/ABVV.

**Confédération des Syndicats Chrétiens (ACV-CSC):** 579 Haachtsesteenweg, POB 10, 1031 Brussels; tel. (2) 246-36-00; fax (2) 246-30-10; e-mail international@acv-csc.be; internet www.acv-csc.be; Pres. LUC CORTEBEECK; has 18 affiliated unions with an estimated total membership of 1,546,360 (1993). Affiliated unions:

**CSC Bâtiment et Industrie** (Building and Industrial Workers): 31 rue de Trèves, 1040 Brussels; tel. (2) 285-02-11; fax (2) 230-74-43; e-mail cchb@acv-csc.be; Pres. J. Jackers; Sec.-Gen. RAYMOND JONGEN; 225,000 mems (1999).

**Centrale Chrétienne de l'Alimentation et des Services** (Food and Service Industries): Brussels; tel. (2) 218-21-71; f. 1919; Pres. W. VIJVERMAN; Sec.-Gen. F. BOCKLANDT.

**Centrale Chrétienne des Métallurgistes de Belgique** (Metal Workers): 127 rue de Heembeek, 1120 Brussels; tel. (2) 244-99-11; fax (2) 241-48-27; Pres. T. JANSSEN.

**Centrale Chrétienne des Mines, de l'Energie, de la Chimie et du Cuir (CCMECC)** (Mines, Power, Chemical and Leather Workers): 26 ave d'Auderghem, 1040 Brussels; tel. (2) 238-73-32; f. 1912; Pres. A. VAN GENECHTEN; Gen. Sec. M. ANDRÉ; Nat. Sec. A. CUYVERS; 63,155 mems (1993).

**Centrale Chrétienne des Ouvriers du Textile et du Vêtement de Belgique** (Textile and Clothing Workers): 27 Koning Albertlaan, 9000 Ghent; tel. (91) 22-57-01; fax (91) 20-45-59; f. 1886; Pres. A. DUQUET; Gen. Sec. L. MEULEMAN.

**Centrale Chrétienne des Ouvriers du Transport et des Ouvriers du Diamant** (Transport and Diamond Workers): 12 Entrepotplaats, 2000 Antwerp; tel. (3) 206-95-41; fax (3) 206-95-50; e-mail cvd@acv-csc.be; Pres. JOHN JANSSENS.

**Centrale Chrétienne du Personnel de l'Enseignement Moyen et Normal Libre** (Lay Teachers in Secondary and Teacher-Training Institutions): 26 ave d'Auderghem, 1040 Brussels; tel. and fax (2) 238-72-31; f. 1924; f. 1950; Pres. WILLEM MILLER.

**Centrale Chrétienne du Personnel de l'Enseignement Technique** (Teachers in Technical Education): 16 rue de la Victoire, 1060 Brussels; tel. (2) 542-09-00; fax (2) 542-09-08; Pres. J.-L. MASUY; Sec.-Gen. PROSPER BOULANGE; 8,000 mems (1993).

**Centrale Chrétienne des Services Publics–Christelijke Centrale van de Openbare Diensten** (Public Service Workers): 26-32 ave d'Auderghem, 1040 Brussels; tel. (2) 231-00-90; f. 1921; Pres. FILIP WIEERS; Sec.-Gen. GUY RASNEUR.

**Christelijke Centrale van Diverse Industrieen** (Miscellaneous): 26–32 Oudergemselaan, 1040 Brussels; tel. (2) 238-72-11; fax (2) 238-73-12; Pres. LEO DUSOLEIL; Nat. Secs FRANÇOIS LICATA, LEON VAN HAUDT.

**Christelijk Onderwijzersverbond van België** (School teachers): 203 Koningsstraat, 1210 Brussels; tel. (2) 227-41-11; fax (2) 219-47-61; e-mail rmaes.cov@acv-csc.be; internet www.cov.be; f. 1893; Pres. G. BOURDEAUD'HUI; Sec.-Gen. R. MAES; 41,000 mems (1999).

**Fédération des Instituteurs Chrétiens** (School teachers): 16 rue de la Victoire, 1060 Brussels; tel. (2) 539-00-01; fax (2) 534-13-36; f. 1893; publishes twice monthly periodical 'L'éducateur'; Sec.-Gen. R. DOHOGNE; 17,000 mems (1999).

**Service Syndical Sports** (Sport): 59 Beukenlaan, 9051 Ghent; tel. (9) 222-45-54; fax (9) 222-45-54; e-mail sporta@aw.csc.be; Nat. Sec. M. VAN MOL; Sec. M. LIPPENS.

**Syndicat Chrétien des Communications et de la Culture** (Christian Trade Unions of Railway, Post and Telecommunications, Shipping, Civil Aviation, Radio, TV and Cultural Workers): Galerie Agora, 105 rue du Marché aux Herbes, bte 40, 1000 Brussels; tel. (2) 549-07-62; fax (2) 512-85-91; f. 1919; Pres. M. BOVY; Vice-Pres. P. BERTIN.

**Union Chrétienne des Membres du Personnel de l'Enseignement Officiel:** 16 rue de la Victoire, 1060 Brussels; tel. (2) 542-09-00; fax (2) 542-09-08; Pres. G. BULTOT; Sec. Gen. P. BOULANGE.

**Centrale Générale des Syndicats Libéraux de Belgique (CGSLB)** (General Federation of Liberal Trade Unions of Belgium): 95 Koning Albertlaan, 9000 Ghent; tel. (9) 222-57-51; fax (9) 221-04-74; e-mail cgslb@cgslb.be; internet www.cgslb.be; f. 1891; Nat. Pres. GUY HAAZE; 220,000 mems.

**Fédération Nationale des Unions Professionnelles Agricoles de Belgique:** 47 chaussée de Namur, 5030 Gembloux; tel. (81) 60-00-60; e-mail upa@euronet.be; Pres. L. FRANC; Sec.-Gen. J. P. CHAMPAGNE.

**Landelijke Bediendencentrale-Nationaal Verbond voor Kaderpersoneel (LBC-NVK)** (Employees): 5 Sudermanstraat, 2000 Antwerp; tel. (3) 220-87-11; fax (2) 231-66-64; e-mail vakbond@ibc-nvk.be; f. 1912; Sec-Gen. M. MAMPUYS; 270,000 (1998).

**Nationale Unie der Openbare Diensten (NUOD)/Union Nationale des Services Publics (UNSP):** 25 rue de la Sablonnière, 1000 Brussels; tel. (2) 219-88-02; fax (2) 223-38-36; f. 1983; Pres. GÉRALD VAN ACKER; Sec.-Gen. FRANCIS SACRE.

## Transport

### RAILWAYS

The Belgian railway network is one of the densest in the world. The main lines are operated by the Société Nationale des Chemins de Fer Belges (SNCB) under lease from the State Transport Administration. Construction of the Belgian section of a high-speed railway network for northern Europe, which will eventually link Belgium, France, Germany, the Netherlands and the United Kingdom, is expected to be completed by 2005. A high-speed link between Brussels and Paris was completed in 1997.

**Société Nationale des Chemins de Fer Belges (SNCB)/Nationale Maatschappij der Belgische Spoorwegen (NMBS):** 85 rue de France, 1060 Brussels; tel. (2) 525-21-11; fax (2) 525-40-45; internet www.sncb.be; f. 1926; 146m. passengers were carried in 1995; 3,479 km of lines, of which 2,293 km are electrified; Chair. MICHEL DAMAR; Man. Dir ETIENNE SCHOUPPE.

### ROADS

At 1 January 1998 there were 1,682 km of motorways and some 12,542 km of other main or national roads. There were also 1,326 km of secondary or regional roads and an additional 130,300 km of minor roads.

**Société Régionale Wallonne du Transport:** 96 ave Gouverneur Bovesse, 5100 Namur; tel. (81) 32-27-11; fax (81) 32-27-10; f. 1991; operates light railways, buses and trams; Dir-Gen. JEAN-CLAUDE PHLYPO.

**Société des Transports Intercommunaux de Bruxelles:** 15 ave de la Toison d'or, 1050 Brussels; tel. (2) 515-20-51; fax (2) 515-32-85; operates a metro service, buses and trams; Dir-Gen. J. DEVROYE.

**VVM-De Lijn:** 1 Hendrik Consciencestraat, 2800 Mechelen; tel. (15) 44-07-11; fax (15) 44-07-09; f. 1991; public transport; Dir-Gen. HUGO VAN WESEMAEL.

### INLAND WATERWAYS

There are over 1,520 km of inland waterways in Belgium, of which 660 km are navigable rivers and 860 km are canals. In 1996 an estimated 107.8m. metric tons of cargo were carried on the inland waterways.

In 1989 waterways administration was divided between the Flemish region (1,055 km), the Walloon region (450 km) and the Brussels region (15 km):

Flemish region:

**Departement Leefmilieu en Infrastructuur Administratie Waterwegen en Zeewezen:** Graaf de Ferraris-Gebouw, 156 ave Emile Jacqmain, bte 5, 1000 Brussels; tel. (2) 553-77-11; fax (2) 553-77-05; e-mail janej.strubbe@lin.vlaanderen.be; Dir-Gen. JAN STRUBBE.

Walloon region:

**Direction Générale des Voies Hydrauliques:** W. T. C. Tour 3, 30 blvd S. Bolivar, 1000 Brussels; tel. (2) 208-41-36; fax (2) 208-41-41; Dir-Gen. B. FAES.

Brussels region:

**Haven van Brussel:** 6 place des Armateurs, 1000 Brussels; tel. (2) 420-67-00; fax (2) 420-69-74; f. 1993; Gen. Man. STEVEN VANACKERE; Dep. Man. Dir CHARLES HUYGENS.

### SHIPPING

The modernized port of Antwerp is the second biggest in Europe and handles about 80% of Belgian foreign trade by sea and inland waterways. It is also the largest railway port and has one of the largest petroleum refining complexes in Europe. Antwerp has 98 km of quayside and 17 dry docks, and is currently accessible to vessels of up to 75,000 metric tons: extensions are being carried out which will increase this limit to 125,000 tons. Other ports include Zeebrugge, Ostend, Ghent, Liège and Brussels.

**Ahlers Shipping NV:** 139 Noorderlaan, 2030 Antwerp; tel. (3) 543-72-11; fax (3) 541-23-09; services to Finland, Poland, Latvia, Morocco; Chair. ALBERT WEYNEN; Man. Dirs LUC NATON, YVES VAN BAVEL.

**ESSO Belgium:** POB 100, 2060 Antwerp; tel. (3) 543-31-11; fax (3) 543-34-95; refining and marketing of petroleum products; Pres. K. O. GILJE.

**De Keyser Thornton:** 38 Huidevettersstraat, 2000 Antwerp; tel. (3) 205-31-00; fax (3) 234-27-86; e-mail info@multimodal.be; f. 1853; shipping agency, forwarding and warehousing services; Chair. and CEO M. P. INGHAM.

**Northern Shipping Service NV:** 54 St Katelijnevest, 2000 Antwerp; tel. (3) 204-78-78; fax (3) 231-30-51; forwarding, customs clearance, liner and tramp agencies, chartering, Rhine and inland barging, multi-purpose bulk/bags fertilizer terminal; Pres. and Man. Dir BERNARD MONTALDIER.

**P&O North Sea Ferries Ltd:** Leopold II Dam, 13, 8380 Zeebrugge; tel. (50) 54-34-11; fax (50) 54-68-35; roll-on/roll-off ferry services between Zeebrugge, Felixstowe, Hull and Middlesbrough; Dirs P. V. D. BROMDHOF, R. B. LOUGH.

**TotalFina SA:** 52 rue de l'Industrie, 1040 Brussels; tel. (2) 288-94-49; fax (2) 288-34-45; integrated petroleum co active in exploration and production, transportation and petroleum refining, petrochemicals, etc., marketing of petroleum products and research; Vice-Chair. and Man. Dir FRANÇOIS CORNELIS.

### CIVIL AVIATION

The main international airport is at Brussels, with a direct train service from the air terminal. A major programme of expansion, more than doubling the airport's passenger-handling capacity, was completed in 1994. Further expansion work was to include the construction of a new concourse by 2002. There are also international airports at Antwerp, Liège, Charleroi and Ostend.

**SABENA Belgian Airlines (Société anonyme belge d'exploitation de la navigation aérienne):** 2 ave E. Mounierlaan, 1200 Brussels; tel. (2) 723-31-11; fax (2) 723-80-99; internet www.sabena.com; f. 1923; 49.5% owned by Swissair; services to most parts of the world; Chair. and CEO PAUL REUTLINGER.

**Delta Air Transport (DAT) NV:** Airport Bldg 117, 1820 Melsbroek; tel. (2) 754-19-00; fax (2) 754-19-99; f. 1966; 100% owned by SABENA; scheduled and charter services from Brussels to many European destinations; Gen. Dir WILLY BUYSSE.

**Sobelair (Société Belge de Transports par Air) NV:** Bldg 45, Brussels National Airport, 1930 Zaventem; tel. (2) 754-12-11; fax (2) 754-12-88; f. 1946; 72.5% owned by SABENA; operates charter flights; Pres. and CEO SYLVIANE LUST.

**Virgin Express:** Airport Bldg 116, 1820 Melsbroek; tel. (2) 752-05-11; fax (2) 752-05-06; f. 1991 as EuroBelgium Airlines, name changed as above 1996; 51% owned by Virgin Group (UK), scheduled and charter services to European destinations; CEO JIM SWIGART; Man. Dir JONATHAN ORNSTEIN.

## Tourism

Belgium has several towns of rich historic and cultural interest, such as Antwerp, Bruges, Brussels, Durbuy, Ghent, Liège, Namur and Tournai. The country's seaside towns attract many visitors. The forest-covered Ardennes region is renowned for hill-walking and gastronomy. In 1998 tourist arrivals totalled an estimated 6,179,254.

**Office de Promotion du Tourisme Wallonie–Bruxelles:** 61 rue Marché-aux-Herbes, 1000 Brussels; tel. (2) 504-02-00; fax (2) 513-69-50; internet www.belgique-tourisme.net; f. 1981; promotion of tourism in French-speaking Belgium; Dir-Gen. VIVIANE JACOBS.

**Tourist Information Office for Brussels (TIB):** Hôtel de Ville, Grand-Place, 1000 Brussels; tel. (2) 513-89-40; fax (2) 514-45-38; Dirs A. VRYDAGH, G. RENDERS.

**Tourist Office for Flanders:** 61 Grasmarkt, 1000 Brussels; tel. (2) 504-03-00; fax (2) 504-03-77; internet www.visitflanders.be; f. 1985; official promotion and policy body for tourism in Flemish region of Belgium; Gen. Commissioner URBAIN CLAEYS.

# BELIZE

## Introductory Survey

### Location, Climate, Language, Religion, Flag, Capital

Belize lies on the Caribbean coast of Central America, with Mexico to the north-west and Guatemala to the south-west. The climate is sub-tropical, tempered by trade winds. The temperature averages 24°C (75°F) from November to January, and 27°C (81°F) from May to September. Annual rainfall ranges from 1,290 mm (51 ins) in the north to 4,450 mm (175 ins) in the south. The average annual rainfall in Belize City is 1,650 mm (65 ins). Belize is ethnically diverse, the population (according to the 1991 census) consisting of 44% Mestizos (Maya-Spanish), 30% Creoles (those of predominantly African descent), 11% Amerindian (mainly Maya), 7% Garifuna ('Black Caribs', descendants of those deported from the island of Saint Vincent in 1797) and communities of Asians, Portuguese, German Mennonites and others of European descent. English is the official language and an English Creole is widely understood. Spanish is the mother-tongue of some 15% of the population but is spoken by many others. There are also speakers of Garifuna (Carib), Maya and Ketchi, while the Mennonites speak a German dialect. Most of the population profess Christianity, with about 58% being Roman Catholics in 1997. The national flag (proportions usually 5 by 3) is dark blue, with narrow horizontal red stripes at the upper and lower edges; at the centre is a white disc containing the state coat of arms, bordered by an olive wreath. The capital is Belmopan.

### Recent History

Belize, known as British Honduras until June 1973, was first colonized by British settlers (the 'Baymen') in the 17th century, but was not recognized as a British colony until 1862. In 1954 a new Constitution granted universal adult suffrage and provided for the creation of a legislative assembly. The territory's first general election, in April 1954, was won by the only party then organized, the People's United Party (PUP), led by George Price. The PUP won all subsequent elections until 1984. In 1961 Price was appointed First Minister under a new ministerial system of government. The colony was granted internal self-government in 1964, with the United Kingdom retaining responsibility for defence, external affairs and internal security. Following an election in 1965, Price became Premier and a bicameral legislature was introduced. In 1970 the capital of the territory was moved from Belize City to the newly-built town of Belmopan.

Much of the recent history of Belize has been dominated by the territorial dispute with Guatemala, particularly in the years prior to Belize's independence (see below). This was achieved on 21 September 1981, within the Commonwealth, and with Price becoming Prime Minister. However, the failure of the 1981 draft treaty with Guatemala, and the clash of opposing wings within the ruling party, undermined the dominance of the PUP. Internal disputes within the PUP intensified during 1983, although Price succeeded in keeping the factions together. However, at the general election held in December 1984 the PUP's 30 years of rule ended when the United Democratic Party (UDP) received 53% of the total votes and won 21 of the 28 seats in the enlarged House of Representatives. The remaining seven seats were won by the PUP, with 44% of the votes, but Price and several of his ministers lost their seats. The UDP's leader, Manuel Esquivel, was appointed Prime Minister. The new Government pledged itself to reviving Belize's economy through increased foreign investment.

A general election was held in September 1989. The UDP underwent a damaging selection process for candidates to contest the election, and encountered criticism that its economic successes had benefited only foreign investors and a limited number of Belizeans. The PUP campaigned for a more liberal broadcasting policy, including the establishment of a broadcasting corporation independent of direct government control, and against the sale of citizenship, of which many Hong Kong Chinese had taken advantage. At the election the PUP obtained almost 51% of the total valid votes cast, and won 15 seats in the 28-member House of Representatives. The UDP received 49% of the votes and retained 13 seats, although one of their members subsequently joined the PUP. Price was again appointed Prime Minister, and his new Government immediately began moves to end the issue of citizenship bonds.

A general election was held in June 1993. The UDP formed an alliance with the National Alliance for Belizean Rights (NABR) to contest the election, and their campaign concentrated on concern about the security situation in the light of the imminent withdrawal of British troops and the prevailing political crisis in neighbouring Guatemala (see below). The PUP had called the election 15 months before it was constitutionally due, following recent successes at local and by-elections. However, at the election the PUP secured only 13 seats in the House of Representatives, despite obtaining more than 51% of the votes. The UDP/NABR alliance received 48.7% of the votes but secured 16 seats (the total number of seats having been increased from 28 to 29). Esquivel was sworn in as Prime Minister on 2 July. In November, at Esquivel's request, Dame Minita Gordon, who had been the Governor-General since independence, resigned from her position. She was replaced by Dr (later Sir) Colville Young, formerly President of the University College of Belize. In the same month the leader of the PUP and former Minister of Foreign Affairs, Said Musa, was among five members of the PUP who were arrested for allegedly attempting to bribe two government ministers to transfer parliamentary allegiance to the PUP. Musa was acquitted in July 1994.

In June 1994 the sale of citizenship was officially ended, following criticism that the system was open to corruption. However, a revised economic citizenship programme, including mechanisms to prevent corruption, received government approval in early 1995. In January of that year Esquivel conducted a redistribution of cabinet portfolios. The changes included the replacement of the Ministry of Defence with a new portfolio, of National Security, with responsibility for defence and the police. In June the Minister of Human Resources, Community and Youth Development, Culture and Women's Affairs, Philip S. W. Goldson, was relieved of responsibility for immigration and nationality affairs, following allegations implicating him in the sale of false residence and visitor permits to nationals of the People's Republic of China and the Republic of China (Taiwan). Reportedly some 5,000 such permits had been issued over the previous 12-month period, and the recipients then smuggled into the USA. In August the Judicial Committee of the Privy Council in the United Kingdom (the final court of appeal for Belize) issued stays of execution for two convicted murderers. The ruling, which came amid growing concern at rising crime in Belize, prompted widespread criticism of the British court, which was considered to be undermining the authority of the Belizean judiciary, and demands for a revision of the appeals system.

Popular discontent at economic austerity measures implemented by the Government was reflected at local elections conducted in March 1997, when the opposition PUP recorded a resounding victory over the ruling alliance. In April Esquivel conducted a reorganization of the Cabinet and created a new ministry, of National Co-ordination and Mobilisation.

In November 1997 the PUP presented proposals for the reform of the political system, including the establishment of a republican form of government, with the Governor-General to be replaced by a president elected by the National Assembly. The proposals were rejected by the Government. However, the leader of the PUP, Said Musa, pledged that, if his party should gain power at the forthcoming general election (which was due to be held in August 1998), preliminary proposals for political reform would be introduced within 100 days of taking office.

At the general election of August 1998 the PUP won an overwhelming victory, securing 26 of the 29 seats in the House of Representatives. The UDP obtained the remaining three seats. The result reflected popular discontent with the outgoing Government's structural adjustment policies, including the introduction of value-added tax (VAT), which the PUP had pledged to repeal. The PUP had also promised to create 15,000 new jobs, to build 10,000 new houses and to reduce public utility tariffs. Following the defeat of his party, Esquivel, who had lost his seat in the House of Representatives, resigned as leader of the UDP. He was succeeded by Dean Barrow. On 1 September Said Musa was sworn in as Prime Minister, and the new Cabinet was inaugurated.

In January 1999 a 14-member Political Reform Commission was established in order to review the system of governance in Belize. The commission, which included representatives of the two principal political parties and of non-governmental organizations, was expected to complete its work within a year. In July Musa issued a statement rejecting allegations published in the British press that Michael Ashcroft, who had extensive business and banking interests in Belize and was its ambassador to the UN, as well as being treasurer of the British Conservative Party, had used improper influence in Belizean affairs and that he may have been involved in money 'laundering'. In October Musa conducted a reorganization of the Cabinet.

The frontier with Guatemala was agreed by a convention in 1859 but this was declared invalid by Guatemala in 1940. Guatemalan claims to sovereignty of Belize date back to the middle of the 19th century and were written into Guatemala's Constitution in 1945. In November 1975 and July 1977 British troops and aircraft were sent to protect Belize from the threat of Guatemalan invasion, and a battalion of troops and a detachment of fighter aircraft remained in the territory. Negotiations between the United Kingdom and Guatemala began in 1977. In 1980 the United Kingdom warned that it might unilaterally grant independence to Belize if no settlement with Guatemala were forthcoming, and later that year the British Government finally excluded the possibility of any cession of land to Guatemala, although offering economic and financial concessions. In November the UN General Assembly overwhelmingly approved a resolution urging that Belize be granted independence (similar resolutions having been adopted in 1978 and 1979), and the United Kingdom decided to proceed with a schedule for independence. A tripartite conference in March 1981 appeared to produce a sound basis for a final settlement, with Guatemala accepting Belizean independence in exchange for access to the Caribbean Sea through Belize and the use of certain offshore cayes and their surrounding waters. A constitutional conference began in April. Further tripartite talks in May and July collapsed, however, as a result of renewed claims by Guatemala to Belizean land. With Belizean independence imminent, Guatemala made an unsuccessful appeal to the UN Security Council to intervene, severing diplomatic relations with the United Kingdom and sealing its border with Belize on 7 September. However, on 21 September, as scheduled, Belize achieved independence. Guatemala alone refused to recognize Belize's new status, and during 1982 requested the reopening of negotiations with the United Kingdom, alleging that Belize was not legally independent. Tripartite talks in January 1983 collapsed when Belize rejected Guatemala's proposal that Belize should cede the southern part of the country. This claim was subsequently suspended. Belize is a member of the Caribbean Community and Common Market (CARICOM—see p. 136), whose summit conferences have consistently expressed support for Belize's territorial integrity against claims by Guatemala.

At independence the United Kingdom had agreed to leave troops as protection and for training of the Belize Defence Force 'for an appropriate time'. In 1984 Prime Minister Esquivel was given renewed assurances from the British Government as regards its commitment to keep British troops in Belize until the resolution of the territorial dispute with Guatemala. Discussions with Guatemala resumed in February 1985, with greater optimism shown by all three parties. In July the new draft Guatemalan Constitution omitted the previous unconditional claim to Belize, while Esquivel had previously acknowledged Guatemala's right of access to the Caribbean Sea, but no settlement was forthcoming. In January 1986 Dr Marco Vinicio Cerezo was inaugurated as the elected President of Guatemala, representing a change from military to civilian government. In August the United Kingdom and Guatemala renewed diplomatic relations at consular level, and in December the restoration of full diplomatic relations was announced. In March 1987 the first Guatemalan trade delegation since independence visited Belize, and in April renewed discussions were held between Guatemala, the United Kingdom and Belize (although Belize was still regarded by Guatemala as being only an observer at the meetings). Tripartite negotiations continued, and in May 1988 the formation of a permanent joint commission (which, in effect, entailed a recognition of the Belizean state by Guatemala) was announced.

In the latter half of 1991 relations between Belize and Guatemala showed considerable signs of improvement, and in September the two countries signed an accord under the terms of which Belize pledged to legislate to reduce its maritime boundaries and to allow Guatemala access to the Caribbean Sea and use of its port facilities. In return, President Jorge Serrano Elías of Guatemala officially announced his country's recognition of Belize as an independent state and established diplomatic relations. The Maritime Areas Bill was approved in January 1992 by 16 votes to 12 in the Belizean House of Representatives. The legislation, however, had caused serious divisions within the UDP, leading to the formation, in December 1991, of the Patriotic Alliance for Territorial Integrity (PATI) by certain members of the party to co-ordinate opposition to the bill. Further disagreement between PATI activists and the leaders of the UDP resulted in the expulsion or resignation of five UDP members (including two members of Parliament) in January 1992. In February these members formed a new organization, the NABR (see above), led by the former UDP Deputy Leader and Minister of Transport, Derek Aikman. In November 1992 the Guatemalan legislature voted to ratify Serrano's decision to recognize Belize. Serrano, however, indicated that the accord was not definitive and that Guatemala maintained its territorial claim over Belize.

In April 1993 Belize and Guatemala signed a non-aggression pact, affirming their intent to refrain from the threat or use of force against each other, and preventing either country from being used as a base for aggression against the other. Relations between the two countries were jeopardized when, in June, President Serrano was ousted following an attempt to suspend certain articles of the Constitution and dissolve Congress. However, in late June the new Guatemalan President, Ramiro de León Carpio, announced that Guatemala would continue to respect Belize's independence. In July the Belizean Prime Minister, Manuel Esquivel, reportedly suspended the September 1991 accord, which had been signed by the previous administration and had still not been formally ratified, stating that it involved too many concessions on the part of Belize and that the issue should be put to a referendum.

On 1 January 1994 responsibility for the defence of Belize was transferred to the Belize Defence Force, and all of the British troops were withdrawn by October, with the exception of some 100 troops, who remained to organize training for jungle warfare.

In March 1994, in a letter to the UN Secretary-General, Guatemala formally reaffirmed its territorial claim to Belize, prompting the Belizean Minister of Foreign Affairs to seek talks with the British Government regarding assistance with national defence. Concern was also expressed by the Standing Committee of CARICOM Ministers of Foreign Affairs, which reaffirmed its support for Belizean sovereignty. In mid-1994 Esquivel accused Guatemala of employing destabilizing tactics against Belize by encouraging Guatemalans to occupy and settle in areas of Belizean forest. In September 1996 the Ministers of Foreign Affairs of Belize and Guatemala conducted preliminary talks in New York, USA, concerning a resumption of negotiations on the territorial dispute. Further such discussions, involving representatives of the Governments and armed forces of both countries, were conducted in Miami, USA, in February 1997. In November 1998, at a meeting of ambassadors and officials of both countries, conducted in Miami, agreement was reached on the establishment of a joint commission to deal with immigration, cross-border traffic and respect for the rights of both countries' citizens.

## Government

Belize is a constitutional monarchy, with the British sovereign as Head of State. Executive authority is vested in the sovereign and is exercised by the Governor-General, who is appointed on the advice of the Prime Minister, must be of Belizean nationality, and acts, in almost all matters, on the advice of the Cabinet. The Governor-General is also advised by an appointed Belize Advisory Council. Legislative power is vested in the bicameral National Assembly, comprising a Senate (eight members appointed by the Governor-General) and a House of Representatives (29 members elected by universal adult suffrage for five years, subject to dissolution). The Governor-General appoints the Prime Minister and, on the latter's recommendation, other ministers. The Cabinet is responsible to the House of Representatives.

## Defence

The Belize Defence Force was formed in 1978 and was based on a combination of the existing Police Special Force and the Belize Volunteer Guard. Military service is voluntary. Provision has been made for the establishment of National Service if necessary to supplement normal recruitment. In August 1999 the regular armed forces totalled 1,050 (including 50 in the maritime wing), with some 700 militia reserves. In 1994 all British forces were withdrawn from Belize, with the exception of some 100 troops who remained to organize training for jungle warfare. The defence budget for 1999 was an estimated BZ $17m.

## Economic Affairs

In 1997, according to estimates by the World Bank, the country's gross national product (GNP), measured at average 1995–97 prices, was US $614m., equivalent to US $2,670 per head. During 1990–97, it was estimated, GNP per head increased, in real terms, at an average rate of 0.3% per year. Over this period, Belize's population grew at an average rate of 2.8% per year. In 1998 GNP was estimated at $615m. ($2,610 per head). Belize's gross domestic product (GDP) increased, in real terms, at an average rate of 3.8% per year in 1990–96, by 4.0% in 1997 and by 1.4% in 1998.

Although 38% of the country is considered suitable for agriculture, only an estimated 3.9% of total land area was used for agricultural purposes in 1997. Nevertheless, agriculture, forestry and fishing employed 31.1% of the working population in 1998, and contributed an estimated 21.7% of GDP, measured at constant 1984 prices, in 1997. The principal cash crops are sugar cane (sugar and molasses accounted for an estimated 30.4% of total domestic exports in 1997), citrus fruits (citrus concentrates accounted for an estimated 14.9%) and bananas (an estimated 16.1%). Maize, red kidney beans and rice are the principal domestic food crops, and the development of other crops, such as cocoa, coconuts and soybeans (soya beans), is being encouraged. The country is largely self-sufficient in fresh meat and eggs. Belize has considerable timber reserves, particularly of tropical hardwoods, and the forestry sector is being developed. In 1997 fishing provided export earnings of an estimated US $17.7m. (10.9% of total domestic export revenue). According to the IMF, the real GDP of the agricultural sector increased at an average rate of 6.1% per year during 1990–96 and by an estimated 9.4% in 1997.

Industry (including mining, manufacturing, construction, water and electricity) employed 18.2% of the working population and contributed an estimated 24.7% of GDP at constant prices in 1997. Manufacturing alone, particularly of clothing, accounted for an estimated 16.2% of GDP and employed 11.3% of the working population in 1997. The processing of agricultural products is important, particularly sugar cane (for sugar and rum). According to the IMF, industrial GDP increased at an average annual rate of 3.6% during 1990–96 and by an estimated 1.5% in 1997. Manufacturing GDP increased at an average rate of 3.9% per year during 1990–96, and by an estimated 1.9% in 1997. Mining accounted for an estimated 0.6% of GDP and only 0.1% of employment in 1997.

Belize has no indigenous energy resources other than wood. Exploration for petroleum in the interior of Belize continued in the 1990s, despite increasing concern for the impact of such activity on the environment. Imports of mineral fuels and lubricants accounted for 8.3% of the total cost of retained imports in 1997. Hydroelectric power was to be developed in the 1990s.

The services sector employed 51.8% of the working population and contributed 53.6% of GDP at constant prices in 1997. Tourist development is concentrated on promoting 'eco-tourism', based on the attraction of Belize's natural environment, particularly its rain forests and the barrier reef, the second largest in the world. Tourist arrivals totalled an estimated 112,191 in 1997, which represented an increase of 3.7% compared with the previous year. According to the IMF, the GDP of the services sector increased, in real terms, at an average rate of 3.4% per year during 1990–96 and by an estimated 1.2% in 1997.

In 1998 Belize recorded a trade deficit of US $104.7m., and a deficit of US $59.8m. on the current account of the balance of payments. According to preliminary figures, in 1997 the principal source of imports was the USA (accounting for 51.5% of the total), while the principal markets for exports were the USA (45.5%) and the United Kingdom (30.0%). Other important trading partners are Mexico and Canada. The principal exports in 1997 were agricultural products (84.5%, including forestry and fish products). The principal imports in that year were machinery and transport equipment, basic manufactures, food and live animals and miscellaneous manufactured articles.

For the financial year ending 31 March 1998 there was a projected budgetary deficit of BZ $37.7m. (equivalent to 3.0% of GDP). Budget proposals for the financial year ending 31 March 2000 envisaged an operating surplus of BZ $11.8m., with the overall deficit expected to be equivalent to less than 4.0% of GDP. Belize's total external debt was US $383.4m. at the end of 1997, of which US $199.1m. was long-term public debt. In that year the cost of debt-servicing was equivalent to 9.2% of the value of exports of goods and services. The annual rate of inflation averaged 2.7% in 1990–97. Consumer prices declined by an average of 0.8% in 1998. In mid-1998 an estimated 12.7% of the economically active population were unemployed. Many Belizeans, however, work abroad, and remittances to the country from such workers are an important source of income. Emigration, mainly to the USA, is offset by the number of immigrants and refugees from other Central American countries, particularly El Salvador.

Belize is a member of the Caribbean Community and Common Market (CARICOM, see p. 136), and in 1991 acceded to the Organization of American States (OAS, see p. 245). In September 1992 Belize was granted membership of the Inter-American Development Bank (IDB, see p. 202).

Agriculture is the dominant sector of the Belizean economy. As a member of the Commonwealth, Belize enjoys low tariffs on its exports to the European Union (EU) under the Lomé Convention, and tariff-free access to the USA under the Caribbean Basin Initiative. The development of tourism and the availability of foreign investment have been hindered by the uncertainties arising from the territorial dispute with Guatemala. In an effort to develop service industries, an international shipping register was established in 1989 and legislation on 'offshore' financial services was introduced in 1990. The withdrawal of British troops from Belize in 1994 had serious economic repercussions, with the loss of an estimated BZ $60m. annually to the economy. In late 1995 some 870 civil service employees (equivalent to 9% of the total central government work-force) were made redundant as the initial phase of a structural adjustment programme, introduced to address the country's serious budget deficit. As part of a reform of the tax system, value-added tax (VAT), at a basic rate of 15%, was introduced with effect from April 1996. Real GDP growth declined from 4.0% in 1997 to 1.4% in 1998, reflecting high interest rates and low commodity prices. On taking office in September 1998 the Musa administration inherited an extremely weak fiscal position, including a public-sector deficit of some BZ $51m. (equivalent to 4.0% of GDP). Despite this the new Government proceeded to implement its manifesto pledges, including a restructuring of the tax system: in April 1999 VAT was replaced with a broad-based 8% sales tax. Plans for a large-scale public investment programme were also initiated. By mid-1999 prospects for economic growth had improved, based on the moderation of interest rates, expanded market opportunities for bananas and increased investment in the tourism sector.

## Social Welfare

There were six district hospitals, a referral hospital in Belize City, and more than 30 urban and rural health centres in Belize in 1999; pre-natal and child welfare clinics are sponsored by the Ministry of Health, Public Services, Labour and Civil Society. In 1996 there were 554 hospital beds and 142 registered physicians. The infant mortality rate declined from 51 per 1,000 live births in 1970 to 18.2 per 1,000 in 1995. Of total projected budgetary expenditure by the central Government for the financial year 1997/98, BZ $29.6m. (8.2%) was for health and a further BZ $21.4m. (5.9%) for social security and welfare. The Social Security Board, established in 1981, is funded by contributions from employers and employees, as well as investment income, and provides maternity, invalidity and retirement benefits.

## Education

Education is compulsory for all children for a period of 10 years between the ages of five and 14 years. Primary education, beginning at five years of age and lasting for eight years, is provided free of charge, principally through subsidized denominational schools under government control. There were 53,110 pupils enrolled at 280 primary schools in 1996/97. Secondary education, beginning at the age of 13, lasts for four years. There were 10,912 students enrolled in 30 general secondary schools in 1996/97. In 1994 primary enrolment included an estimated 99% of children in the relevant age-group (males 100%; females

98%), while secondary enrolment in that year was equivalent to 49% (males 47%; females 52%).

In 1996/97 there were 2,500 students enrolled in 11 other educational institutions, which included technical, vocational and teacher-training colleges. The University College of Belize was established in 1986 and there is also an extra-mural branch of the University of the West Indies in Belize. Budgetary expenditure on education in the financial year 1997/98 was projected at BZ $74.2m., representing 20.5% of total spending by the central Government. In 1991 the average rate of adult illiteracy was 29.7% (males 29.7%; females 29.7%).

### Public Holidays

**2000:** 1 January (New Year's Day), 9 March (Baron Bliss Day), 21–24 April (Easter), 1 May (Labour Day), 24 May (Commonwealth Day), 10 September (St George's Caye Day), 21 September (Independence Day), 12 October (Columbus Day, anniversary of the discovery of America), 19 November (Garifuna Settlement Day), 25–26 December (Christmas).

**2001:** 1 January (New Year's Day), 9 March (Baron Bliss Day), 13–16 April (Easter), 1 May (Labour Day), 24 May (Commonwealth Day), 10 September (St George's Caye Day), 21 September (Independence Day), 12 October (Columbus Day, anniversary of the discovery of America), 19 November (Garifuna Settlement Day), 25–26 December (Christmas).

### Weights and Measures

Imperial weights and measures are used, but petrol and paraffin are measured in terms of the US gallon (3.785 litres).

# Statistical Survey

Source (unless otherwise stated): Central Statistical Office, Ministry of Finance, Belmopan; tel. (8) 22207; fax (8) 23206; e-mail csogob@blt.net.

## AREA AND POPULATION

**Area:** 22,965 sq km (8,867 sq miles).

**Population:** 144,857 at census of 12 May 1980; 189,774 (males 96,289, females 93,485) at census of 12 May 1991; 228,695 at April 1997 (official estimate).

**Density** (April 1997): 10.0 per sq km.

**Principal Towns** (estimated population, April 1997): Belmopan (capital) 6,785; Belize City (former capital) 53,915; Orange Walk 15,035; San Ignacio/Santa Elena 11,375; Corozal 7,715; Dangriga (formerly Stann Creek) 7,110; Benque Viejo 5,995; Punta Gorda 4,770.

**Births, Marriages and Deaths** (1996, provisional figures): Registered live births 5,163 (birth rate 23.3 per 1,000); Registered marriages (1995) 1,347 (marriage rate 6.2 per 1,000); Registered deaths 964 (death rate 4.3 per 1,000). Source: partly UN, *Population and Vital Statistics Report*.

**Expectation of Life** (years at birth, 1991): Males 69.95; Females 74.07. Source: UN, *Demographic Yearbook*.

**Economically Active Population** (sample survey, April 1997): Agriculture, hunting, forestry and fishing 21,140; Mining and quarrying 95; Manufacturing 7,980; Electricity, gas and water 985; Construction 3,835; Trade, restaurants and hotels 15,155; Transport, storage and communications 3,655; Financing, insurance, real estate and business services 2,360; Community, social and personal services 12,225; Private households 2,915; Other 335; Total employed 70,680.

## AGRICULTURE, ETC.

**Principal Crops** ('000 metric tons unless otherwise stated, 1998): Sugar cane 1,208 (FAO estimate); Red kidney beans (million lb) 9.3 (1997, provisional figure); Maize 37 (FAO estimate); Rice (paddy) 17 (FAO estimate); Roots and tubers 4 (FAO estimate); Pulses (dry beans) 5; Coconuts 3 (FAO estimate); Vegetables and melons 5 (FAO estimate); Oranges 170; Grapefruit and pomelo 41; Bananas 81 (FAO estimate); Other fruit 4 (FAO estimate). Source: mainly FAO, *Production Yearbook*.

**Livestock** (FAO estimates, '000 head, year ending September 1998): Horses 5; Mules 4; Cattle 60; Pigs 23; Sheep 3; Goats 1; Chickens 2. Source: FAO, *Production Yearbook*.

**Livestock Products** (FAO estimates, '000 metric tons, 1998): Meat 10; Cows' milk 7; Hen eggs 2. Source: FAO, *Production Yearbook*.

**Forestry** ('000 cu m): *Roundwood removals* (1987): Industrial wood (Sawlogs) 62, Fuel wood 126 (FAO estimate), Total 188 (FAO estimated annual production in 1988–97 as in 1987). *Sawnwood* (1997): 20. Source: FAO, *Yearbook of Forest Products*.

**Fishing** (metric tons, live weight): Total catch: 1,229 in 1995; 977 in 1996; 1,223 in 1997. Source: FAO, *Yearbook of Fishery Statistics*.

## INDUSTRY

**Production** (preliminary figures, 1997): Raw sugar 123,782 long tons; Molasses 51,773 long tons; Cigarettes 88 million; Beer 817,000 gallons; Batteries 7,967; Flour 25,623,000 lb; Fertilizers 21,525 metric tons; Garments 1,968,000 items; Citrus concentrate 3,756,000 gallons; Soft drinks 1,330,000 cases.

## FINANCE

**Currency and Exchange Rates:** 100 cents = 1 Belizean dollar (BZ $). *Sterling, US Dollar and Euro Equivalents* (30 September 1999): £1 sterling = BZ $3.293; US $1 = BZ $2.000; €1 = BZ $2.133; BZ $100 = £30.37 = US $50.00 = €46.88. *Exchange rate:* Fixed at US $1 = BZ $2.000 since May 1976.

**Budget** (BZ $ million, year ending 31 March): *1997/98* (projections): *Revenue:* Taxation 251.3 (Taxes on income, profits, etc. 52.3, Domestic taxes on goods and services 101.3, Import duties 83.6); Other current revenue 29.8 (Entrepreneurial and property income 10.2, Administrative fees, etc. 14.9); Capital revenue 2.2; Total 283.4, excl. grants (41.2). *Expenditure:* General public services 41.3; Defence 19.7; Public order and safety 25.7; Education 74.2; Health 29.6; Social security and welfare 21.4; Housing and community amenities 9.3; Recreational, cultural and religious affairs 4.8; Economic services 101.9 (Agriculture, forestry, fishing and hunting 22.5, Transport and communications 60.8); Other purposes 34.3 (Interest payments 29.0); Total 362.3 (Current 244.8, Capital 117.4), excl. lending minus repayments (–5.1). Source: IMF, *Government Finance Statistics Yearbook*.

**International Reserves** (US $ million at 31 December 1998): IMF special drawing rights 1.16; Reserve position in the IMF 4.10; Foreign exchange 38.82; Total 44.09. Source: IMF, *International Financial Statistics*.

**Money Supply** (BZ $ million at 31 December 1998): Currency outside banks 70.38; Demand deposits at commercial banks 115.85; Total money (incl. others) 186.65. Source: IMF, *International Financial Statistics*.

**Cost of Living** (Consumer Price Index; base: 1995 = 100): 106.4 in 1996; 107.5 in 1997; 106.6 in 1998. Source: IMF, *International Financial Statistics*.

**Expenditure on the Gross Domestic Product** (BZ $ million at current prices, 1998): Government final consumption expenditure 219.1; Private final consumption expenditure 852.2; Increase in stocks 38.5; Gross fixed capital formation 265.5; *Total domestic expenditure* 1,375.3; Exports of goods and service 666.2; *Less* Imports of goods and services 781.6; *GDP in purchasers' values* 1,259.9. Source: IMF, *International Financial Statistics*.

**Gross Domestic Product by Economic Activity** (BZ $ million at constant 1984 prices, 1997, preliminary figures): Agriculture 125.1; Forestry and logging 15.6; Fishing 26.0; Mining 4.9; Manufacturing 124.8; Electricity and water 17.0; Construction 43.3; Trade, restaurants and hotels 125.8; Transport and communications 107.1; Finance, insurance, real estate and business services 72.8; Public administration 55.4; Other services 51.0; *Sub-total* 768.9; *Less* Imputed bank service charges 22.7; *GDP at factor cost* 746.2; Indirect taxes, *less* subsidies 133.4; *GDP in purchasers' values* 879.6. Source: IMF, *Recent Economic Developments* (October 1998).

**Balance of Payments** (US $ million, 1998): Exports of goods f.o.b. 186.2; Imports of goods c.i.f. –290.9; *Trade balance* –104.7; Exports of services 140.5; Imports of services –99.0; *Balance on goods and services* –63.3; Other income received 7.2; Other income paid –39.3; *Balance on goods, services and income* –95.4; Current transfers received 38.4; Current transfers paid –2.8; *Current balance* –59.8; Capital account (net) –1.9; Direct investment abroad –4.5; Direct investment from abroad 17.7; Portfolio investment liabilities 12.5; Other investment liabilities –2.2; Net errors and omissions 24.5;

*Overall balance* –13.7. Source: IMF, *International Financial Statistics*.

## EXTERNAL TRADE

**Principal Commodities** (preliminary figures, US $ million, 1997): *Imports c.i.f.:* Food and live animals 47.6; Beverages and tobacco 2.4; Mineral fuels, lubricants, etc. 22.6; Chemicals 32.9; Basic manufactures 55.4; Machinery and transport equipment 73.2; Miscellaneous manufactured articles 33.0; Total (incl. others) 271.5. *Exports f.o.b.:* Food and live animals 136.9 (Sugar 46.0, Seafood products 17.7, Banana 26.1, Citrus concentrates 24.1, Single strength juices 11.4); Miscellaneous manufactured articles 19.6 (Garments 18.5); Total (incl. others) 162.0. Note: Figures refer to retained imports and domestic exports. The data exclude re-exports (US $17.2m.). Source: IMF, *Belize: Recent Economic Development* (October 1998) *1998* (BZ $ million): Total imports c.i.f. 649.9; Total exports f.o.b. 335.0 (Source: IMF, *International Financial Statistics*).

**Principal Trading Partners** (preliminary figures, US $ million, 1997): *Imports c.i.f.:* Canada 7.9; Mexico 36.5; United Kingdom 15.4; USA 148.6; Total (incl. others) 288.7. *Exports f.o.b.* (excl. re-exports): Canada 5.4; Mexico 5.4; United Kingdom 48.7; USA 73.7; Total (incl. others) 162.0. Source: IMF, *Belize: Recent Economic Developments* (October 1998).

## TRANSPORT

**Road Traffic** (motor vehicles licensed, 1997): 22,450.

**Shipping** (sea-borne freight traffic, '000 short tons, 1996): Goods loaded 281.5; Goods unloaded 305.4. *Merchant Fleet* (vessels registered at 31 December 1998): Number of vessels 1,308; Total displacement 2,382,478 grt. Source: Lloyd's Register of Shipping, *World Fleet Statistics*.

**Civil Aviation** (preliminary, 1997): Passenger arrivals 95,337.

## TOURISM

**Tourist Arrivals:** 104,553 in 1995; 108,189 in 1996; 112,191 in 1997 (preliminary figure).

**Tourist Receipts** (preliminary 1997): BZ $181.4m.

**Hotels** (1996): 360.

## COMMUNICATIONS MEDIA

**Radio Receivers** (1996): 129,000 in use*.

**Television Receivers** (1996): 40,000 in use*.

**Telephones** (1996): 29,439 main lines in use.

**Telefax Stations** (1993): 538 in use†.

**Mobile Cellular Telephones** (1995): 1,237 subscribers†.

**Book Production** (1996): 107 titles*.

**Newspapers:** *Non-daily* (1996): 6 (circulation 80,000)*.

* Source: UNESCO, *Statistical Yearbook*.

† Source: UN, *Statistical Yearbook*.

## EDUCATION

**Pre-primary*** (1994/95): 90 schools, 190 teachers, 3,311 students.

**Primary** (1996/97): 280 schools, 1,966 teachers (1995/96), 53,110 students.

**Secondary** (1996/97): 30 schools, 697 teachers (1995/96), 912 students.

**Higher** (1996/97): 11 institutions, 254 teachers (1995/96), 2,500 students.

* Source: UNESCO, *Statistical Yearbook*.

# Directory

## The Constitution

The Constitution came into effect at the independence of Belize on 21 September 1981. Its main provisions are summarized below:

### FUNDAMENTAL RIGHTS AND FREEDOMS

Regardless of race, place of origin, political opinions, colour, creed or sex, but subject to respect for the rights and freedoms of others and for the public interest, every person in Belize is entitled to the rights of life, liberty, security of the person, and the protection of the law. Freedom of movement, of conscience, of expression, of assembly and association and the right to work are guaranteed and the inviolability of family life, personal privacy, home and other property and of human dignity is upheld. Protection is afforded from discrimination on the grounds of race, sex, etc., and from slavery, forced labour and inhuman treatment.

### CITIZENSHIP

All persons born in Belize before independence who, immediately prior to independence, were citizens of the United Kingdom and Colonies automatically become citizens of Belize. All persons born outside the country having a husband, parent or grandparent in possession of Belizean citizenship automatically acquire citizenship, as do those born in the country after independence. Provision is made which permits persons who do not automatically become citizens of Belize to be registered as such. (Belizean citizenship was also offered, under the Belize Loans Act 1986, in exchange for interest-free loans of US $25,000 with a 10-year maturity. The scheme was officially ended in June 1994, following sustained criticism of alleged corruption on the part of officials. However, a revised economic citizenship programme, offering citizenship in return for a minimum investment of US $75,000, received government approval in early 1995.)

### THE GOVERNOR-GENERAL

The British monarch, as Head of State, is represented in Belize by a Governor-General, a Belizean national.

**Belize Advisory Council**

The Council consists of not less than six people 'of integrity and high national standing', appointed by the Governor-General for up to 10 years upon the advice of the Prime Minister. The Leader of the Opposition must concur with the appointment of two members and be consulted about the remainder. The Council exists to advise the Governor-General, particularly in the exercise of the prerogative of mercy, and to convene as a tribunal to consider the removal from office of certain senior public servants and judges.

### THE EXECUTIVE

Executive authority is vested in the British monarch and exercised by the Governor-General. The Governor-General appoints as Prime Minister that member of the House of Representatives who, in the Governor-General's view, is best able to command the support of the majority of the members of the House, and appoints a Deputy Prime Minister and other Ministers on the advice of the Prime Minister. The Governor-General may remove the Prime Minister from office if a resolution of 'no confidence' is passed by the House and the Prime Minister does not, within seven days, either resign or advise the Governor-General to dissolve the National Assembly. The Cabinet consists of the Prime Minister and other Ministers.

The Leader of the Opposition is appointed by the Governor-General as that member of the House who, in the Governor-General's view, is best able to command the support of a majority of the members of the House who do not support the Government.

### THE LEGISLATURE

The Legislature consists of a National Assembly comprising two chambers: the Senate, with eight nominated members; and the House of Representatives, with 29 elected members. The Assembly's normal term is five years. Senators are appointed by the Governor-General: five on the advice of the Prime Minister; two on the advice of the Leader of the Opposition or on the advice of persons selected by the Governor-General; and one after consultation with the Belize Advisory Council. If any person who is not a Senator is elected to be President of the Senate, he or she shall be an ex-officio Senator in addition to the eight nominees.

Each constituency returns one Representative to the House, who is directly elected in accordance with the Constitution.

If a person who is not a member of the House is elected to be Speaker of the House, he or she shall be an ex-officio member in addition to the 29 members directly elected. Every citizen older than 18 years is eligible to vote. The National Assembly may alter any of the provisions of the Constitution.

## The Government

**Head of State:** HM Queen ELIZABETH II (succeeded to the throne 6 February 1952).

**Governor-General:** Sir COLVILLE YOUNG (appointed 17 November 1993).

### THE CABINET
(January 2000)

**Prime Minister and Minister of Finance and of Foreign and Latin American Affairs:** SAID MUSA.

**Deputy Prime Minister and Minister of Natural Resources, the Environment and Industry:** JOHN BRICEÑO.

**Senior Minister:** GEORGE CADLE PRICE.

**Minister of National Security and Immigration:** JORGE ESPAT.

**Minister of Public Utilities, Energy and Communications:** MAXWELL SAMUELS.

**Minister of Budget Planning, Economic Development, Investment and Trade:** RALPH FONSECA.

**Minister of Health and Public Services:** JOSE COYE.

**Minister of the Sugar Industry, Labour and Local Government:** VALDEMAR CASTILLO.

**Minister of Human Development, Civil Society and Women:** DOLORES BALDERAMOS GARCIA.

**Minister of Agriculture, Fisheries and Co-operatives:** DANIEL SILVA, Jr.

**Minister of Public Works, Transport and Citrus and Banana Industries:** HENRY CANTON.

**Minister of Education and Sports:** CORDEL HYDE.

**Minister of Youth and Tourism:** MARK ESPAT.

**Minister of Rural Development and Culture:** MARCIAL MES.

**Attorney-General and Minister of Information:** GODFREY SMITH.

**Minister of Housing, Urban Renewal and Home Affairs:** RICHARD BRADLEY.

### MINISTRIES

**Office of the Prime Minister:** New Administrative Bldg, Belmopan; tel. (8) 22346; fax (8) 20071; e-mail prime-minister@belize.gov.bz.

**Ministry of Agriculture, Fisheries and Co-operatives:** Belmopan; tel. (8) 22241; fax (8) 22432.

**Ministry of the Attorney-General:** Belmopan; tel. (8) 22504; fax (8) 23390.

**Ministry of Budget Planning, Economic Development, Investment and Trade:** New Administrative Bldg, Belmopan; tel. (8) 22526; fax (8) 20158.

**Ministry of Education and Sports:** Belmopan; tel. (8) 22380; fax (8) 23389; e-mail educate@btl.net.

**Ministry of Finance:** New Administrative Bldg, Belmopan; tel. (8) 22152; fax (8) 22886; e-mail finsecmof@btl.net.

**Ministry of Foreign and Latin American Affairs:** Belmopan; tel. (8) 22322; fax (8) 22854; e-mail belizemfa@btl.net.

**Ministry of Health and Public Services:** Belmopan; tel. (8) 23325; fax (8) 22942.

**Ministry of Housing, Urban Renewal and Home Affairs:** Belmopan; tel. (1) 23338; fax (8) 23298.

**Ministry of Human Development, Civil Society and Women:** Belmopan; tel. (8) 22684; fax (8) 23175.

**Ministry of National Security and Immigration:** New Administrative Bldg, POB 174, Belmopan; tel. (8) 22423; fax (8) 22615.

**Ministry of Natural Resources, the Environment and Industry:** Market Sq., Belmopan; tel. (8) 22249; fax (8) 22333; e-mail lincenbze@btl.net.

**Ministry of Public Utilities, Energy and Communications:** Belmopan; tel. (8) 22435; fax (8) 23317.

**Ministry of Public Works, Transport and Citrus and Banana Industries:** Belmopan; tel. (8) 22136; fax (8) 23282; e-mail peumow@btl.net.

**Ministry of Rural Development and Culture:** Belmopan; tel. (8) 22444; fax (8) 20317; e-mail ruraldev@btl.net.

**Ministry of the Sugar Industry, Labour and Local Government:** Belmopan.

**Ministry of Youth and Tourism:** Constitution Drive, Belmopan; tel. (8) 23393; fax (8) 23815; e-mail tourismmdpt@btl.net.

## Legislature

### NATIONAL ASSEMBLY

#### The Senate

**President:** ELIZABETH ZABANEH.

There are eight nominated members.

#### House of Representatives

**Speaker:** SYLVIA FLORES.

**Clerk:** JESUS KEN.

**General Election, 27 August 1998**

| | Votes cast | % of total | Seats |
|---|---|---|---|
| People's United Party (PUP) | 50,330 | 59.30 | 26 |
| United Democratic Party (UDP) | 33,237 | 39.16 | 3 |
| Others | 1,309 | 1.54 | – |
| **Total** | 84,876 | 100.00 | 29 |

## Political Organizations

**National Alliance for Belizean Rights (NABR):** Belize City; f. 1992 by UDP members opposed to compromise over territorial dispute with Guatemala; Chair. (vacant); Co-ordinator PHILIP S. W. GOLDSON.

**People's United Party (PUP):** Belize City; tel. (2) 45886; fax (2) 31940; f. 1950; based on organized labour; merged with Christian Democratic Party in 1988; Leader SAID MUSA; Chair. JORGE ESPAT; Deputy Leaders MAX SAMUELS, JOHN BRICEÑO.

**United Democratic Party (UDP):** 19 King St, POB 1143, Belize City; tel. (2) 72576; fax (2) 31004; f. 1974 by merger of People's Development Movement, Liberal Party and National Independence Party; conservative; Leader DEAN BARROW; Chair. ELODIO ARAGON.

## Diplomatic Representation

### EMBASSIES AND HIGH COMMISSION IN BELIZE

**Belgium:** 126 Freetown Rd, Belize City; tel. (2) 30748; fax (2) 30750; Ambassador: WILLY VERRIEST.

**China (Taiwan):** 3rd Floor, Blake's Bldg, cnr Hutson and Eyre Sts, POB 1020, Belize City; tel. (2) 78744; fax (2) 33082; e-mail embroc@btl.net; Ambassador: KUO-HSIUNG SHEN.

**Colombia:** 168 Newtown Barracks, POB 1805, Belmopan; tel. (8) 35623; fax (8) 31972; e-mail colombia@btl.net; Chargé d'affaires: PABLO ANTONIO REBOLLEDO.

**Costa Rica:** 2 Sapodilla St, Belmopan; tel. (8) 23801; fax (8) 23805; Ambassador: ROBERTO FRANCISCO ANGLEDA SOLER.

**El Salvador:** 2 Lubantum St, Piccini Site, POB 215, Belmopan; tel. (8) 35162; fax (8) 23404.

**Germany:** 57 South Foreshore, POB 1021, Belize City; tel. (2) 77282; fax (2) 24375; Ambassador: Dr NILS GRÜBER.

**Guatemala:** 8 'A' St, POB 1771, Belize City; tel. (2) 33150; fax (2) 35140; e-mail guatemb.bz@btl.net; Ambassador: RAFAEL A. SALAZAR.

**Honduras:** 22 Gabourel Lane, POB 285, Belize City; tel. (2) 45889; fax (2) 30562; Chargé d'affaires: CARLOS AUGUSTO MATUTÉ RIVERA.

**Mexico:** 20 North Park St, POB 754, Belize City; tel. (2) 30193; fax (2) 78742; Ambassador: FEDERICO URUCHUA.

**Panama:** 79 Unity Blvd, POB 1692, Belize City; tel. (2) 44991; fax (2) 30654; Chargé d'affaires: JOSÉ DE LA CRUZ PAREDES.

**United Kingdom:** Embassy Sq., POB 91, Belmopan; tel. (8) 22146; fax (8) 22761; e-mail britmail@btl.net; High Commissioner: TIMOTHY J. DAVID.

**USA:** 29 Gabourel Lane, POB 286, Belize City; tel. (2) 77161; fax (2) 30802; e-mail amboffice@btl.net; internet www.usemb-belize.gov; Ambassador: CAROLYN CURIEL.

**Venezuela:** 18–20 Unity Blvd, POB 49, Belmopan; tel. (8) 22384; fax (8) 22022; e-mail embaven@btl.net; Ambassador: CHRISTIAAN VAN DER REE.

## Judicial System

Summary Jurisdiction Courts (criminal jurisdiction) and District Courts (civil jurisdiction), presided over by magistrates, are established in each of the six judicial districts. Summary Jurisdiction Courts have a wide jurisdiction in summary offences and a limited jurisdiction in indictable matters. Appeals lie to the Supreme Court, which has jurisdiction corresponding to the English High Court of Justice and where a jury system is in operation. From the Supreme Court further appeals lie to a Court of Appeal, established in 1967, which holds an average of four sessions per year. Final appeals are made to the Judicial Committee of the Privy Council in the United Kingdom.

**Court of Appeal:** KENNETH GEORGE, Dr NICHOLAS LIVERPOOL, MANUEL SOSA.

**Chief Justice:** TROADIO GONZALEZ (acting).

**Supreme Court:** Supreme Court Bldg, Belize City; tel. (2) 77256; fax (2) 70181; internet www.supremecourt.com; Registrar RAYMOND A. USHER.

**Chief Magistrate:** HERBERT LORD, Paslow Bldg, Belize City; tel. (2) 77164.

# Religion

## CHRISTIANITY

Most of the population are Christian, the largest denomination being the Roman Catholic Church (62% of the population, according to the census of 1980). The other main groups were the Anglican (12% in 1980), Methodist (6%), Mennonite (4%), Seventh-day Adventist (3%) and Pentecostal (2%) churches.

**Belize Council of Churches:** 149 Allenby St, POB 508, Belize City; tel. (2) 77077; f. 1957 as Church World Service Committee, present name adopted 1984; eight mem. Churches, four assoc. bodies; Pres. Maj. ERROL ROBATEAU (Salvation Army); Gen. Sec. SADIE VERNON.

### The Roman Catholic Church

Belize comprises the single diocese of Belize City-Belmopan, suffragan to the archdiocese of Kingston in Jamaica. In December 1997 it was estimated that there were 132,940 adherents in the diocese. The Bishop participates in the Antilles Episcopal Conference (whose secretariat is based in Port of Spain, Trinidad and Tobago).

**Bishop of Belize City-Belmopan:** OSMOND PETER MARTIN, Bishop's House, 144 North Front St, POB 616, Belize City; tel. (2) 72122; fax (2) 31922.

### The Anglican Communion

Anglicans in Belize belong to the Church in the Province of the West Indies, comprising eight dioceses. The Archbishop of the Province is the Bishop of North Eastern Caribbean and Aruba, resident in St John's, Antigua.

**Bishop of Belize:** Rt Rev. SYLVESTRE DONATO ROMERO-PALMA, Bishopthorpe, 25 Southern Foreshore, POB 535, Belize City; tel. (2) 73029; fax (2) 76898; e-mail bzediocese@btl.net.

### Protestant Churches

**Methodist Church (Belize/Honduras District Conference):** 88 Regent St, POB 212, Belize City; tel. (2) 77173; fax (2) 75870; f. 1824; c. 2,620 mems; District Pres. Rev. Dr LESLEY G. ANDERSON.

**Mennonite Congregations in Belize:** POB 427, Belize City; tel. (8) 30137; fax (8) 30101; f. 1958; four main Mennonite settlements: at Spanish Lookout, Shipyard, Little Belize and Blue Creek; Bishops J. B. LOEWEN, J. K. BARKMAN, P. THIESSEN, H. R. PENNER, CORNELIUS ENNS.

Other denominations active in the country include the Seventh-day Adventists, Pentecostals, Presbyterians, Baptists, Moravians, Jehovah's Witnesses, the Church of God, the Assemblies of Brethren and the Salvation Army.

## OTHER RELIGIONS

There are also small communities of Hindus (106, according to the census of 1980), Muslims (110 in 1980), Jews (92 in 1980) and Bahá'ís.

# The Press

**Amandala:** Amandala Press, 3304 Partridge St, POB 15, Belize City; tel. (2) 24476; fax (2) 24702; f. 1969; weekly; independent; Editor EVAN X. HYDE; circ. 45,000.

**The Belize Times:** 3 Queen St, POB 506, Belize City; tel. (2) 45757; fax (2) 31940; f. 1956; weekly; party political paper of PUP; Editor MICHAEL RUDON; circ. 6,000.

**Belize Today:** Belize Information Service, East Block, POB 60, Belmopan; tel. (8) 22159; fax (8) 23242; monthly; official; Editor MIGUEL H. HERNÁNDEZ, Jr; circ. 17,000.

**Government Gazette:** Government Printery, Power Lane, Belmopan; tel. (8) 22127; official; weekly.

**The Reporter:** 147 cnr Allenby and West Sts, POB 707, Belize City; tel. (2) 72503; f. 1968; weekly; Editor HARRY LAWRENCE; circ. 6,500.

**The San Pedro Sun:** POB 35, San Pedro Town, Ambergris Caye; fax (26) 2905; e-mail sanpedrosun@btl.net; weekly; Editors DAN JAMISON, EILEEN JAMISON.

## NEWS AGENCY

**Agencia EFE** (Spain): c/o POB 506, Belize City; tel. (2) 45757; Correspondent AMALIA MAI.

# Publisher

**Government Printery:** Power Lane, Belmopan; tel. (8) 22293; f. 1871; responsible for printing, binding and engraving requirements of all govt depts and ministries; publications include annual govt estimates, govt magazines and the official *Government Gazette*.

# Broadcasting and Communications

## TELECOMMUNICATIONS

**Belize Telecommunications Ltd:** Esquivel Telecom Centre, St Thomas St, POB 603, Belize City; tel. (2) 32868; fax (2) 31800; e-mail educ@btl.net; Chair. ERNESTO VASQUEZ; CEO EDBERTO TESECUM.

## RADIO

**Broadcasting Corporation of Belize (BCB):** Albert Cattouse Bldg, Regent St, POB 89, Belize City; tel. (2) 72468; fax (2) 75040; e-mail rbgold@btl.net; f. 1937; privatized in 1998; broadcasts in English (75%) and Spanish; also transmits programmes in Garifuna and Maya; Gen. Man. (vacant).

**Love FM:** Belize City; purchased Friends FM in 1998.

**Radio Krem Ltd:** 3304 Partridge St, POB 15, Belize City; tel. (2) 75929; fax (2) 74079; commercial; purchased Radio Belize in 1998; Man. EVA S. HYDE.

There are a further three private radio stations broadcasting in Belize.

## TELEVISION

In August 1986 the Belize Broadcasting Authority issued licences to eight television operators for 14 channels, which mainly retransmit US satellite programmes, thus placing television in Belize on a fully legal basis for the first time.

**BCB Teleproductions:** POB 89, Belize City; govt-owned; video production unit; local programmes for broadcasting.

**CTV (Channel 9):** 27 Dayman Ave, Belize City; tel. (2) 44400; commercial; Man. MARIE HOARE.

**Tropical Vision (Channels 7 and 11):** 73 Albert St, Belize City; tel. (2) 73988; fax (2) 78583; commercial; Man. NESTOR VASQUEZ.

# Finance

(cap. = capital; res = reserves; dep. = deposits; brs = branches)

## BANKING

### Central Bank

**Central Bank of Belize:** Gabourel Lane, POB 852, Belize City; tel. (2) 36194; fax (2) 36226; e-mail governor@cenbank.gov.bz; f. 1982; cap. BZ $10m., res 10.8m., dep. 82.2m. (1997); Gov. Sir KEITH A. ARNOLD.

### Development Bank

**Development Finance Corporation:** Bliss Parade, Belmopan; tel. (8) 22350; fax (8) 23096; f. 1972; issued cap. BZ $10m.; Chair. JOY GRANT; Gen. Man. DOUGLAS SINGH; 5 brs.

### Other Banks

**Barclays Bank PLC** (United Kingdom): 21 Albert St, POB 363, Belize City; tel. (2) 77211; fax (2) 78572; Man. TILVAN KING; 3 brs.

**Belize Bank Ltd:** 60 Market Sq., POB 364, Belize City; tel. (2) 77132; fax (2) 72712; e-mail bzbank@btl.net; cap. BZ $4.3m., res BZ $4.3m., dep. BZ $280.1m. (April 1997); Chair. Sir EDNEY CAIN; Senior Vice-Pres. and Gen. Man. LOUIS ANTHONY SWASEY; 11 brs.

**Scotiabank** (Canada): Albert St, POB 708, Belize City; tel. (2) 77027; fax 77416; e-mail cmobel@btl.net; Gen. Man. C. E. MARCEL; 6 brs.

There is also a government savings bank.

## INSURANCE

General insurance is provided by local companies, and British, US and Jamaican companies are also represented.

## Trade and Industry

### STATUTORY BODIES

**Banana Control Board:** c/o Dept of Agriculture, West Block, Belmopan; management of banana industry; in 1989 it was decided to make it responsible to growers, not an independent executive; Head LALO GARCIA.

**Belize Beef Corporation:** c/o Dept of Agriculture, West Block, Belmopan; f. 1978; semi-governmental organization to aid development of cattle-rearing industry; Dir DEEDIE RUNKEL.

**Belize Marketing Board:** 117 North Front St, POB 633, Belize City; tel. (2) 77402; fax (2) 77656; f. 1948 to encourage the growing of staple food crops; purchases crops at guaranteed prices, supervises processing, storing and marketing intelligence; Chair. SILAS C. CAYETANO.

**Belize Sugar Board:** 7, 2nd St South, Corozal Town; tel. (4) 22005; fax (4) 22672; f. 1960 to control the sugar industry and cane production; includes representatives of the Government, sugar manufacturers, cane farmers and the public sector; Chair. ORLANDO PUGA; Exec. Sec. MARIA PUERTO.

**Citrus Control Board:** c/o Dept of Agriculture, West Block, Belmopan; tel. (8) 22199; f. 1966; determines basic quota for each producer, fixes annual price of citrus; Chair. C. SOSA.

### DEVELOPMENT ORGANIZATIONS

**Belize Reconstruction and Development Corporation:** 36 Trinity Blvd, POB 1, Belmopan; tel. (8) 22271; fax (8) 23992; e-mail recondev@btl.net; Gen. Man. ALOYSIUS PALACIO.

**Belize Trade and Investment Promotion Service:** 14 Orchid Gorden St, Belmopan; tel. (8) 23737; fax (8) 20595; e-mail tipsbze@btl.net; f. 1986 as a joint government and private-sector institution to encourage export and investment; Gen. Man. HUGH FULLER.

**Department of Economic Development:** Ministry of Budget Planning, Economic Development, Investment and Trade, New Administrative Bldg, Belmopan; tel. (8) 22526; fax (8) 23111; administration of public and private-sector investment and planning; statistics agency; Head HUMBERTO PAREDES.

### CHAMBER OF COMMERCE

**Belize Chamber of Commerce and Industry:** 63 Regent St, POB 291, Belize City; tel. (2) 73148; fax (2) 74984; e-mail bcci@btl.net; f. 1920; Pres. GODWIN HULSE; Gen. Man. MERILYN YOUNG (acting); 626 mems.

### EMPLOYERS' ASSOCIATIONS

**Banana Growers' Association:** Big Creek, Independence Village, Stann Creek District; tel. (6) 22001; fax (6) 22112; e-mail banana@btl.net.

**Belize Cane Farmers' Association:** 34 San Antonio Rd, Orange Walk; tel. (3) 22005; fax (3) 23171; f. 1959 to assist cane farmers and negotiate with the Sugar Board and manufacturers on their behalf; Chair. PABLO TUN; 16 district brs.

**Belize Livestock Producers' Association:** 47.5 miles Western Highway, POB 183, Belmopan; tel. (8) 23202; fax (8) 23886; e-mail blpa@btl.net; Chair. PETE LIZARRAGA.

**Citrus Growers' Association:** 9 miles Stann Creek Valley Rd, POB 7, Stann Creek District; tel. (5) 23585; fax (5) 22686; e-mail cga@btl.net; f. 1966; Chair. LEROY DIAZ; Gen. Man. CLINTON HERNANDEZ.

### UTILITIES

#### Electricity

**Office of Electricity Supply:** Mahogany St, POB 1846, Belize City; tel. (2) 24995; fax (2) 24994; f. 1992; Dir-Gen. GREGORY GILL.

**Belize Electricity Co Ltd (BECOL):** 115 Barrack Rd, POB 327, Belize City; tel. (2) 70954; fax (2) 30891; e-mail bel@btl.net; Chair. NESTOR VASQUEZ; CEO LUIS LUE.

#### Water

**Water and Sewer Authority (WASA):** 44 Regent St, Belize City; tel. (2) 77097; fax (2) 77092; f. 1971; Man. WINSTON W. MICHAEL.

### TRADE UNIONS

**National Trades Union Congress of Belize (NTUCB):** POB 2359, Belize City; tel. (2) 71596; fax (2) 72864; Pres. RAY DAVIS; Gen. Sec. DORENE QUIROS.

#### Principal Unions

**United General Workers' Union:** 1259 Lakeland City, Dangriga; tel. (5) 22105; f. 1979 by amalgamation of the Belize General Development Workers' Union and the Southern Christian Union; three branch unions affiliated to the central body; affiliated to ICFTU; Pres. FRANCIS SABAL; Gen. Sec. CONRAD SAMBULA.

**Belize National Teachers' Union:** POB 382, Belize City; tel. (2) 72857; Pres. HELEN STUART; Sec. MIGUEL WONG; 1,000 mems.

**Christian Workers' Union:** 107B Cemetery Rd, Belize City; tel. (2) 72150; f. 1962; general; Pres. JAMES MCFOY; Gen. Sec. ANTONIO GONZALEZ; 1,000 mems.

**Democratic Independent Union:** Belize City; Pres. CYRIL DAVIS; 1,250 mems.

**Public Service Union of Belize:** 81 Almara Ave, POB 45, Belize City; tel. (2) 72318; fax (2) 70029; f. 1922; public workers; Pres. HUBERT ENRIQUEZ; Sec.-Gen. PATRICIA BENNETT; 1,236 mems.

**United Banners Banana Workers' Union:** Dangriga; f. 1995; Pres. MARCIANA FUNEZ.

## Transport

### RAILWAYS

There are no railways in Belize.

### ROADS

There are 1,419 km (882 miles) of all-weather main and feeder roads and 651 km (405 miles) of cart roads and bush trails. About 805 km (500 miles) of logging and forest tracks are usable by heavy-duty vehicles in the dry season.

### SHIPPING

There is a deep-water port at Belize City and a second port at Commerce Bight, near Dangriga (formerly Stann Creek), to the south of Belize City. There is a port for the export of bananas at Big Creek. Nine major shipping lines operate vessels calling at Belize City, including the Carol Line (consisting of Harrison, Hapag-Lloyd, Nedlloyd and CGM).

**Belize Port Authority:** Caesar Ridge Rd, POB 633, Belize City; tel. (2) 72439; fax (2) 73571; e-mail portbz@btl.net; f. 1980; Chair. KAY MENZIES; Ports Commr ALFRED B. COYE.

**Belize Lines Ltd:** 37 Regent St, Belize City.

### CIVIL AVIATION

Philip S. W. Goldson International Airport, 14 km (9 miles) from Belize City, can accommodate medium-sized jet-engined aircraft. A new terminal was completed in 1990. There are airstrips for light aircraft on internal flights near the major towns and offshore islands.

**Maya Island Air:** Municipal Airport, POB 458, Belize City; tel. (2) 35795; fax (2) 30585; e-mail mayair@btl.net; internet www.ambergriscaye.com/islandair; f. 1997 as merger between Maya Airways Ltd and Island Air; operated by Belize Air Group; internal services, centred on Belize City, and charter flights to neighbouring countries; Exec. Dir TREVOR ROE; Gen. Man. PABLO ESPAT.

**Tropical Air Services (Tropic Air):** San Pedro, POB 20, Ambergris Caye; tel. (2) 62012; fax (2) 62338; f. 1979; operates internal services and services to Mexico and Guatemala; Chair. CELI MCCORKLE; Man. Dir JOHN GREIF.

## Tourism

The main tourist attractions are the beaches and the barrier reef, diving, fishing and the Mayan archaeological sites. There are nine major wildlife reserves (including the world's only reserves for the jaguar and for the red-footed booby), and government policy is to develop 'eco-tourism', based on the attractions of an unspoilt environment and Belize's natural history. The country's wildlife also includes howler monkeys and 500 species of birds, and its barrier reef is the second largest in the world. There were 360 hotels in Belize in 1996. In 1997 there were an estimated 112,191 tourist arrivals and tourist receipts totalled an estimated BZ $181.4m. In February 1996 the Mundo Maya Agreement was ratified, according to which Belize, El Salvador, Guatemala, Honduras and Mexico would co-operate in the management of Mayan archaeological remains.

**Belize Tourist Board:** Level 2, Central Bank Bldg, POB 325, Belize City; tel. (2) 31913; fax (2) 31943; e-mail btbb@btl.net; internet www.travelbelize.org; f. 1964; fmrly Belize Tourist Bureau; eight mems; Chair. PATTY ARCEO; Dir TRACY TAEGAR.

**Belize Tourism Industry Association (BTIA):** 10 North Park St, POB 62, Belize City; tel. (2) 75717; fax (2) 78710; e-mail btia@btl.net; Pres. WADE BEVIER (acting).

# BENIN

## Introductory Survey

### Location, Climate, Language, Religion, Flag, Capital

The Republic of Benin (known as the People's Republic of Benin between 1975 and 1990) is a narrow stretch of territory in West Africa. The country has an Atlantic coastline of about 100 km (60 miles), flanked by Nigeria to the east and Togo to the west; its northern borders are with Burkina Faso and Niger. Benin's climate is tropical, and is divided into three zones: the north has a rainy season between July and September, with a hot, dry season in October–April; the central region has periods of abundant rain in May–June and in October, while there is year-round precipitation in the south, the heaviest rains being in May–October. Average annual rainfall in Cotonou is 1,300 mm. French is the official language, but each of the indigenous ethnic groups has its own language. Bariba and Fulani are the major languages in the north, while Fon and Yoruba are widely spoken in the south. It is estimated that 35% of the people follow traditional beliefs and customs; about 35% are Christians, mainly Roman Catholics, and the majority of the remainder are Muslims. The national flag (proportions 3 by 2) has a vertical green stripe at the hoist, with equal horizontal stripes of yellow over red in the fly. The administrative capital is Porto-Novo, but most government offices and other state bodies are presently in the economic capital, Cotonou.

### Recent History

Benin, called Dahomey until 1975, was formerly part of French West Africa. It became a self-governing republic within the French Community in December 1958, and an independent state on 1 August 1960. The early years of independence were characterized by chronic political instability and by periodic regional unrest, fuelled by long-standing rivalries between north and south.

Elections in December 1960 were won by the Parti dahoméen de l'unité, whose leader, Hubert Maga (a northerner), became the country's first President. In October 1963, following riots by workers and students, Maga was deposed in a coup led by Col (later Gen.) Christophe Soglo, Chief of Staff of the Army. Soglo served as interim Head of State until January 1964, when Sourou-Migan Apithy, a southerner who had been Vice-President under Maga, was elected President. Another southerner, Justin Ahomadegbé, became Prime Minister. In November 1965, following a series of political crises, Gen. Soglo forced Apithy and Ahomadegbé to resign. A provisional Government was formed, but the army intervened again in December, and Soglo assumed power at the head of a military regime. In December 1967 industrial unrest, following a ban on trade union activity, precipitated another coup, led by Maj. (later Lt-Col) Maurice Kouandété. Lt-Col Alphonse Alley, hitherto Chief of Staff, became interim Head of State, and Kouandété Prime Minister.

A return to civilian rule was attempted in 1968. A referendum in March approved a new Constitution, and a presidential election followed in May. All former Heads of State and other leading politicians, banned from contesting the presidency, urged their supporters to boycott the election. Only about 26% of the electorate voted, with the abstention rate reaching 99% in the north. The election was declared void, and in June the military regime nominated Dr Emile-Derlin Zinsou, a former Minister of Foreign Affairs, as President; he was confirmed in office by referendum in the following month. In December 1969 Zinsou was deposed by Lt-Col Kouandété, then Commander-in-Chief of the Army, and a three-member military Directoire assumed power.

In March 1970 a presidential election was held amid violent incidents and widespread claims of irregularities. The poll was abandoned when counting revealed roughly equal support for the three main candidates—Ahomadegbé, Apithy and Maga—to whom the Directoire ceded power in May: it was intended that each member of this Presidential Council would act as Head of State, in rotation, for a two-year period. Maga was the first to hold this office (a concession to the north) and was succeeded in May 1972 by Ahomadegbé. In October, however, the civilian leadership was deposed by Maj. (later Brig.-Gen.) Mathieu Kérékou, Deputy Chief of Staff of the armed forces. Kérékou, a northerner, asserted that his military regime would be based on equal representation between northern, central and southern regions. In September 1973 a Conseil national révolutionnaire (CNR), comprising representatives from each of these regions, was established.

Kérékou pursued a Marxist-based policy of 'scientific socialism'. Strategic sectors and financial institutions were acquired by the State. Between 1974 and 1978 a decentralized local administration was established, the education system was placed under government control, and the legal system was revised. A restructuring of the armed forces followed an unsuccessful coup attempt in January 1975. A further plot to depose Kérékou, allegedly initiated by the exiled Zinsou, was disclosed in October. In late 1975 the Parti de la révolution populaire du Bénin (PRPB) was established as the sole party, and Dahomey was renamed the People's Republic of Benin.

In January 1977 an airborne attack on Cotonou, led by a French mercenary, Col Robert Denard, was repelled by the armed forces. In August the CNR adopted a *Loi fondamentale* decreeing new structures in government. Elections to a new 'supreme authority', the Assemblée nationale révolutionnaire (ANR), took place in November 1979, when a single list of 336 'People's Commissioners' was approved by 97.5% of voters. At the same time a Comité exécutif national (CEN) was established to replace the CNR. The PRPB designated Kérékou as the sole candidate for President of the Republic, and in February 1980 he was unanimously elected to this office by the ANR. In April 1981 it was announced that Ahomadegbé, Apithy and Maga, imprisoned following the coup of 1972, had been released from house arrest. A gradual moderation in Benin's domestic policies followed, and subsequent ministerial changes reflected a government campaign against corruption and inefficiency. Members of the extreme left lost influence, as did the army, whose officers were by now outnumbered by civilians in the Government.

In February 1984 the ANR amended the *Loi fondamentale*, increasing the mandates of People's Commissioners and of the President from three years to five, while reducing the number of Commissioners to 196. At legislative elections in June 98% of voters approved the single list of People's Commissioners, and in July the ANR re-elected Kérékou, again the sole candidate, as President. Kérékou subsequently consolidated his position, reducing the membership of the CEN and effectively depriving southern communities of influence in government.

In January 1987 Kérékou resigned from the army to become a civilian Head of State. Concern among army officers at perceived corruption within Kérékou's civilian Government, together with opposition to the proposed establishment of a Court of State Security, were the apparent catalysts for a coup attempt in March 1988: almost 150 officers, including members of the Presidential Guard, were reportedly arrested. There were reports of a further coup attempt in June, while Kérékou was attending a regional conference in Togo.

Chronic economic difficulties, compounded by Nigeria's closure of the two countries' joint border in 1984–86, caused Benin to seek stronger ties with the West in the second half of the 1980s. In early 1989 delays in the payment of salaries and of education grants and scholarships provoked strike action by public-sector employees and students. In June, after three years of negotiations, economic adjustment measures were agreed with the IMF and the World Bank, prompting fears of further austerity measures. At elections to the ANR in that month a relative decline in support for the single list of PRBP-approved candidates (which was endorsed by 89.6% of voters) was attributed to dissatisfaction with the country's economic difficulties. Unrest escalated in July: civil servants at several government ministries withdrew their labour, teaching staff were suspended, and the 1988/89 academic year was declared invalid in all institutions where strikes had taken place.

In August 1989 the ANR re-elected Kérékou (the sole candidate) to the presidency. An ensuing reorganization of the CEN included the appointment of several known proponents of political reform. In September the Government promised partial payment to teachers of outstanding salaries, following pledges of financial assistance from overseas creditors. In the following month the Union nationale des syndicats de travailleurs du Bénin (UNSTB), the sole officially-recognized trade union, announced that it was to sever its ties with the PRPB. The Government's renewed failure to meet its salary commitments resulted in further disruption in December. Kérékou then yielded to domestic pressure and to demands made by France and other external creditors, instituting radical political changes and abandoning Marxism-Leninism as the official ideology of the State. Foreign donors subsequently agreed to contribute towards the payment of outstanding salaries.

A national conference of what were termed the 'active forces of the nation' was convened in Cotonou in February 1990. Delegates voted to abolish the 1977 *Loi fondamentale* and its institutions: all resolutions adopted by the conference were incorporated in a 'national charter' that was to form the basis of a new constitution. An Haut conseil de la République (HCR) was appointed to assume the functions of the ANR pending the appointment of a new legislature. Among the members of the HCR were former Presidents Ahomadegbé, Maga and Zinsou, all of whom had recently returned to Benin to lead opposition parties. Presidential and legislative elections, to be held on the basis of universal suffrage, in the context of a multi-party political system, were scheduled for early 1991. A former official of the World Bank (who had briefly been Minister of Finance and Economic Affairs in the mid-1960s), Nicéphore Soglo, was designated interim Prime Minister, and Kérékou, who reluctantly acceded to the conference's decisions, subsequently relinquished the defence portfolio to the new premier. The conference also voted to change the country's name to the Republic of Benin.

In March 1990 an amnesty was announced for all political dissidents. The HCR was inaugurated, and Soglo appointed a transitional, civilian Government. Thus, of the previous administration, only Kérékou remained in office. In May civilian administrators were appointed to replace the military prefects in Benin's six provinces. In June the Government undertook an extensive restructuring of the armed forces. Legislation permitting the registration of political parties was promulgated in August. (The PRPB had itself been succeeded by a new party, the Union des forces du progrès, in May.)

After considerable delay, a national referendum on the draft Constitution was conducted on 2 December 1990. Voters were asked to choose between two proposed documents, one of which incorporated a clause stipulating upper and lower age-limits for presidential candidates (and would therefore exclude Ahomadegbé, Maga and Zinsou from contesting the presidency). It was reported that 95.8% of those who voted approved one or other of the versions, with 79.7% of voters favouring the age-restriction clause.

As many as 24 political parties (many of which had formed electoral alliances) contested the legislative election, which took place on 17 February 1991. No party or group of parties won an overall majority in the 64-member Assemblée nationale, the greatest number of seats (12) being secured by an alliance of three pro-Soglo parties.

Kérékou and Soglo were among 13 candidates at the first round of the presidential election, on 10 March 1991. The distribution of votes largely reflected ethnic divisions: of the leading candidates, Soglo, who took 36.2% of the total votes cast, received his greatest support in the south of the country, while Kérékou, who received 27.3% of the overall vote, was reported to have secured the support of more than 80% of voters in the north. Soglo and Kérékou proceeded to a second round of voting, which was conducted two weeks later amid violence and allegations of electoral malpractice. Despite strong support for Kérékou in the north, Soglo was elected President, obtaining 67.7% of the total votes cast. In late March, prior to its own dissolution, the HCR granted Kérékou immunity from any legal proceedings connected with actions committed since the *coup d'état* of October 1972.

Soglo was inaugurated as President on 4 April 1991. Shortly afterwards he relinquished the defence portfolio to Désiré Vieyra (his brother-in-law), who was designated Minister of State. In July the defence portfolio was transferred to Florentin Feliho, while Vieyra took the post of Senior Minister, Secretary-General at the Office of the President of the Republic.

As President, Soglo furthered attempts that had been initiated by his transitional administration to address Benin's economic problems and to recover state funds allegedly embezzled by former members of the Kérékou regime. None the less, the new administration's inability immediately to pay public-sector salary arrears which had accumulated during the late 1980s provoked intermittent labour unrest. There was, moreover, considerable opposition in the Assemblée nationale to elements of the Government's programme of economic reform, notably the sale of former state-owned enterprises to foreign interests, and during the first six months of 1992 the legislature refused to ratify that year's budget proposals. Tensions between the executive and legislature were temporarily resolved following the formation, in June, of a 34-member pro-Soglo grouping, styled Le Renouveau, in the Assemblée nationale. However, the Soglo administration's pursuit of economic reforms, while favourably received by the international financial community, continued to be a source of domestic disquiet.

In May 1992, meanwhile, several army officers were arrested following an incident outside the presidential palace in Cotonou. In August it was reported that some of the detainees, including their leader, Capt. Pascal Tawes (formerly deputy commander of the now-disbanded Presidential Guard), had escaped from custody and that Tawes was leading a mutiny at an army camp in the northern town of Natitingou. The rebellion was quickly suppressed, but Tawes was among those who evaded arrest. In March 1993 more than 100 prisoners, including several soldiers who were implicated in the previous year's disturbances, escaped from detention in Ouidah, in the south-west. The dismissal, shortly afterwards, of the armed forces Chief of Staff and of other senior members of the security forces prompted Feliho to resign the defence portfolio, protesting that Soglo had acted unconstitutionally by making new appointments to the military command without consulting him. Following a reorganization of the Council of Ministers in September, Vieyra, now Minister of State in charge of National Defence, remained the most senior member of the Government. The Assemblée nationale delayed the official publication of the new government list for several days, reportedly because deputies felt that Soglo had been discourteous in leaving Benin for a visit to Europe without first having presented the list to parliament. In the following month 15 assembly members withdrew from Le Renouveau, alleging that Soglo was consistently excluding the legislature from the decision-making process. In July Soglo, who had previously asserted his political neutrality, had made public his membership of the (Parti de la) Renaissance du Bénin (RB), an organization formed by his wife, Rosine Vieyra Soglo, in the previous year. President Soglo was appointed leader of the RB in July 1994.

Social tensions re-emerged following the 50% devaluation of the CFA franc in January 1994. In late January the deployment of security forces in Cotonou to disperse an unauthorized demonstration by union activists (who were demanding 30% salary increases) prompted workers' representatives to withdraw contacts with the authorities. Strike action during March caused widespread disruption. Meanwhile, student protests were ended by force. In May the Government announced salary increases of 10% for all state employees, as well as the reintroduction of housing allowances (abolished in 1986) and an end to the eight-year freeze on promotions within the civil service. In July, however, the Assemblée nationale approved increases in salaries and student grants that exceeded those provided for in the Government's draft budget. Soglo announced his intention to impose the draft budget by decree, on the grounds that the imbalanced budget arising from the legislature's amendments was unconstitutional, and would, moreover, result in the loss of funding and debt relief already agreed with external creditors. The Assemblée nationale referred the matter to the Constitutional Court, which effectively ruled that presidential recourse to the relevant article of the Constitution could not be subject to legal control. The payment of salary arrears from 1983–91 began in November 1994.

In September 1994 Tawes and 15 others were sentenced *in absentia* to life imprisonment with hard labour, after having been convicted of plotting to overthrow the Government in 1992; eight of those who were present at the trial received lesser custodial sentences, while three defendants were acquitted.

In November 1994 the Assemblée nationale voted to establish an independent electoral supervisory body, the Commission électorale nationale autonome (CENA). Soglo, who was known to have opposed such a body, had also objected to the planned increase in the number of parliamentary deputies from 64 to 83. Legislative voting, twice postponed because of organizational difficulties, took place on 28 March 1995. Some 31 political organizations had been authorized to participate, and a total of 5,580 candidates contested seats in the enlarged assembly.

Provisional results indicated that the RB had won the largest number of seats in the Assemblée nationale, but that opposition parties were likely, in alliance, to outnumber the President's supporters. The final composition of the new parliament remained uncertain, as the results of voting for 13 seats were annulled by the Constitutional Court on the grounds of irregularities. Voting for three seats was repeated in May, although one of the newly elected deputies (a member of the RB) was immediately disqualified by the Constitutional Court, which judged that he had failed to fulfil the necessary residency criteria. In the following month Soglo accused the President of the Constitutional Court, Elisabeth Kayssan Pognon, of incitement to riot and rebellion, after she criticized the RB for organizing a demonstration to protest against the annulment of the by-election result.

The RB thus held 20 seats in the Assemblée nationale, and other supporters of Soglo a total of 13. Opposition parties held, in all, 49 seats, the most prominent organizations being the Parti du renouveau démocratique (PRD), with 19 seats, and the Front d'action pour le renouveau et le développement—Alafia (FARD—Alafia), which had attracted considerable support among supporters of Kérékou in the north (although the former President had not actively campaigned in the election), with 10. In June 1995 Bruno Amoussou, the leader of the opposition Parti social-démocrate, was elected President of the Assemblée nationale, after Soglo's supporters voted for Amoussou in preference to the PRD leader, Adrien Houngbédji, who had held this post in the outgoing assembly. A new Government was formed later in June 1995 by the RB.

In late 1995 rumours circulated of a coup plot and of attempts to sabotage a conference of Heads of State and Government of the Conseil permanent de la francophonie, which was due to take place in Cotonou, under the chairmanship of ex-President Zinsou, in December. The Government denied allegations that a plot had been discovered, although it was confirmed that members of the military had been among several people arrested in security operations. Tensions escalated following a rocket attack in November on the newly-built conference centre at which the francophone summit was to take place. Although the authorities dismissed the attack as a minor act of sabotage, it was subsequently announced that one person had been killed and several arrested, and that munitions stolen during a raid on the Ouidah barracks in early 1994 had been recovered, as part of operations to apprehend the perpetrators of the attack. Among those detained was Soulé Dankoro, a former minister under Kérékou.

Despite Kérékou's effective withdrawal from active politics following his defeat in 1991, the success of his supporters at the 1995 parliamentary elections prompted speculation that Kérékou might again contest the presidency in 1996, and in January 1996 he announced his candidature. While Soglo's economic policies had earned his regime the respect of the international financial community, there was disquiet within Benin that strong growth had been achieved at the expense of social concerns; moreover, criticism was increasingly levelled at what was termed the regime's 'authoritarian drift' and nepotism. Soglo, meanwhile, asserted that the economic successes now attained would henceforth permit his administration to address unemployment and other social problems exacerbated by the adjustment policies of the first half of the decade.

In December 1995 the Assemblée nationale decided to delay ratification of the third phase of the country's structural adjustment programme, the most contentious element of which was the planned restructuring of the state company responsible for the distribution of petroleum products. Deputies rejected ratification of a modified programme twice during January 1996, and also rejected the Government's draft budget for that year, prompting Soglo, citing the national interest, to implement the budget and adjustment programme by decree.

The first round of the presidential election, on 3 March 1996, was contested by seven candidates. As had been expected, Soglo and Kérékou emerged as the leading candidates, although Soglo's supporters alleged widespread vote-rigging. Some 22.8% of the votes cast were subsequently invalidated by the Constitutional Court prior to the announcement of the official results, whereby Soglo secured 35.7% of the valid votes and Kérékou 33.9%, followed by Houngbédji (19.7%) and Amoussou (7.8%). The rate of participation by voters was high, at 86.9%. Most of the defeated candidates quickly expressed their support for Kérékou, among them Houngbédji (who had in 1975 been sentenced *in absentia* to death for his part in a plot to overthrow Kérékou's military regime), who stated that the electorate clearly desired a change of regime.

Indications of a clear victory for Kérékou at the second round of voting, which took place on 18 March 1996, were denounced by Soglo's supporters as being attributable to 'massive fraud', and Soglo himself spoke of an international plot to end democracy in Benin. Prior to the official announcement of the results, a gun attack was reported on the home of a member of the Constitutional Court, while members of the court were said to have received intimidatory letters, signed by 'southerners in rebellion', accusing them of plotting against democracy. (International monitors stated, however, that any irregularities in the conduct of voting did not affect the overall credibility of the result.) On 24 March the Constitutional Court issued the official results, announcing Kérékou's election with the support of 52.5% of the valid votes. Some 78.1% of those eligible had voted, and less than 3% of the votes had been disallowed. Kérékou won the support of a majority of voters in four of the country's six provinces, and secured more than 90% of the votes in his home province of Atakora; Soglo won some 80% of the votes in his native Zou province, in central Benin, and (despite a high rate of unemployment) also performed strongly in Cotonou and other areas of Atlantique province. On 1 April the Court stated that it had rejected all appeals against the outcome of the election, and accordingly endorsed Kérékou's victory. Soglo conceded defeat the following day; he left the country shortly afterwards, and remained abroad for several months. Speaking in Washington, DC, in mid-June, he expressed his desire to lead Benin's opposition. He subsequently indicated his recognition of the legitimacy of Kérékou's election. Meanwhile, Zinsou was named as an adviser to the President in late August; Ahomadegbé was among other former opponents of the military regime who had come to support Kérékou.

Having sought authorization by the Constitutional Court for the appointment of a Prime Minister (provision for such a post is not stipulated in the Constitution), in April 1996 Kérékou named Houngbédji as premier in a Government mostly composed of representatives of those parties that had supported his presidential campaign; a former associate of Soglo, Moïse Mensah, was named Minister of Finance. Kérékou assumed personal responsibility for defence. The Government's stated priorities were to strengthen the rule of law, and to promote economic revival and social development. Addressing a national economic conference in December, Kérékou stated that the maintenance of democracy was vital to Benin's future prosperity. He also recognized the need further to develop the private sector, and pledged measures to combat corruption in all areas of public life.

Seven of those detained in late 1995, including Soulé Dankoro, were released on bail in April 1996. The authorities stated, none the less, that no political pressure had been exerted to secure their release, and it was emphasized that applications for bail made by five other defendants had been rejected. In September three defendants were sentenced to five years' enforced labour, and one to a year's imprisonment, having been convicted of involvement in the rocket attack; a fifth defendant was sentenced *in absentia* to 15 years' imprisonment. In September 1997 the Assemblée nationale approved an amnesty for all acts seeking to undermine state security, for electoral and media crimes committed between January 1990 and June 1996. The amnesty, which most notably benefited members of the military as well as civilians implicated in the events of late 1995, provoked protests by the RB, which warned that the measure would exacerbate ethnic and regional divisions, as well as tensions and indiscipline within the army. The law was promulgated by Kérékou shortly afterwards, but in October 1997 the Constitutional Court invalidated the amnesty legislation, on the grounds that the Government had not consulted the Supreme Court, whose participation in the formulation of such legislation the Constitutional Court judged obligatory.

The Government was obliged to revise its budgetary provisions for 1998 at the end of 1997, after the Assemblée nationale rejected proposals to end automatic promotions within the civil service. The proposed emphasis (in accordance with IMF recommendations) on promotions according to merit had prompted strike action by state employees during previous weeks. In March 1998, following several weeks of disruption by some 37,000 civil servants, agreement was reached on the payment of salary arrears, valued by the Government at 5,000m. francs CFA, which had accumulated since 1992, as well as on efforts to preserve jobs in recently privatized enterprises. In early May, however, civil servants announced their intention to resume strike action, in protest at the State's failure to honour its commitment to pay arrears. Kérékou met with trade union leaders, undertaking personally to address the issue of salary arrears, and, moreover, invited the unions to nominate a new minister with responsibility for the civil service. A general strike none the less proceeded in mid-May. Meanwhile, Houngbédji, who was apparently dissatisfied at his exclusion from the drafting of the 1998 budget, and who was reportedly concerned that an impending government reshuffle would result in a loss of influence for himself and the PRD, resigned the premiership. Kérékou named a new Government in which there was no Prime Minister, the most senior minister being Pierre Otcho (hitherto Minister of Foreign Affairs and Co-operation) as Minister-delegate to the Presidency, in charge of Defence and Relations with the Institutions.

In early March 1999 six people were sentenced to prison terms of between two and 12 years, having been convicted on charges involving forgery and fraudulent distribution of voting cards and falsification of voters' lists, in advance of legislative elections scheduled for later in the month; charges in connection with similar offences remained against about 40 defendants. Voting, originally planned for 28 March, was postponed by two days, as the earlier date coincided with Islamic and Christian religious festivals. A three-day strike by workers at the state radio and television broadcasting company caused some disruption to campaigning immediately prior to the elections. Polling none the less proceeded on 30 March, with more than 2,900 candidates, representing 35 parties and alliances, contesting the 83 seats in the Assemblée nationale. International monitors reported that the elections had been conducted peacefully and democratically. Official results, issued by the CENA on 3 April and confirmed by the Constitutional Council one week later, indicated that the combined opposition parties had won a slender majority in the legislature, with 42 seats. Voting was generally divided along clear regional lines. The largest number of seats was won by the RB, principally in the south and centre (including eight of Cotonou's nine seats); Rosine Soglo was expected to remain as the party's parliamentary leader. FARD—Alafia (10 seats), the PSD (nine seats) and other parties loyal to the President performed very strongly in the north and west. The PRD, which won 11 seats, was, however, strongly challenged in the east, particularly by the pro-Kérékou Mouvement africain pour la démocratie et le progrès (which won six seats overall). The rate of participation by voters was in excess of 70%. Both the presidential group and the new parliamentary majority expressed optimism regarding the forthcoming period of institutional 'cohabitation'. In late April Houngbédji was elected Speaker of the new assembly, defeating Amoussou.

In late June 1999 Kérékou implemented a government reshuffle, increasing the number of parties represented in the Council of Ministers from seven to 10, in an apparent effort to consolidate his support in the Assemblée nationale. Five new ministers were appointed, most notably Bruno Amoussou, who became Minister of State, in charge of Co-ordinating Government Action, Planning, Development and Promotion of Employment; Pierre Otcho remained in place as Minister-delegate at the Presidency, in charge of National Defence, while Abdoulaye Bio Tchang retained the finance and economy portfolio.

The findings of a commission of inquiry into official corruption in Benin, established by Kérékou following his election in 1996, were published in early July 1999. The commission, which had investigated 167 suspected cases of corruption, revealed that public funds valued at more than 70,000m. francs CFA had been embezzled in the three years to April 1999. At the end of July the Government instituted a code of ethics which was intended to curb corruption by excluding those convicted of corruption from public office, and by obliging the disclosure of all payments made during tendering for state projects.

In early October 1999 some 20,000 people attended a rally in Lokosso (in south-west Benin) to denounce Benin's judicial system. The rally was organized by local vigilante groups, who were reported to have been responsible for the burning alive of about 100 alleged thieves and bandits in the previous two months. The Government, while critical of the vigilantes' actions, expressed its understanding of their frustrations and refrained from suggesting that action would be taken against them. Human rights activists, meanwhile, criticized the Government for its failure to curb the vigilantes, accusing the authorities of tacit complicity in their activities. In mid-October the Government dispatched troops to restore peace to the region. The leader of the vigilantes subsequently urged his supporters to cease extrajudicial executions, stating that suspects should in future be surrendered to the authorities; in subsequent weeks 150 suspects were handed over to the armed forces by militia groups.

In late October 1999 an estimated 32,000 civil servants undertook a three-day general strike after talks between public-sector unions and the Government failed to reach agreement on the payment of salary arrears (valued by the unions at some 18,000m. francs CFA) and the abolition of the new system of promotions according to merit. The Government, while deploring the strike action, expressed willingness to pursue negotiations with workers' representatives. In early November, however, some unions began further industrial action, claiming that offers made by the Government were not satisfactory. Agreement was subsequently reached on the creation of a bipartite commission to investigate a new system of remuneration and promotion for the civil service, and on the payment of salary arrears. None the less, one trade union federation, the Centrale des organisations syndicales indépendantes, resumed strike action the following week, demanding the immediate implementation of the provisions of the agreement.

Under the Soglo administration extensive efforts were made to foster harmonious trading and diplomatic relations with external creditors. Relations with France (Benin's principal trading partner and supplier of aid, and a prominent advocate of Benin's transition to multi-party democracy) were generally cordial, as were links with the USA and other creditors. Following Kérékou's election to the presidency in March 1996, there was some initial uncertainty regarding his Government's likely conduct of external political and economic relations, particularly with the IMF (which stipulated continued spending restraint as a precondition for assistance). However, Kérékou swiftly demonstrated a pragmatic approach to international economic relations. Kérékou made an official visit to France in October 1996, during which he requested French assistance in transferring the economic capital from Cotonou to the administrative capital, Porto-Novo.

As part of its stated policy of countering violent crime in Benin, the Kérékou administration expelled some 700 foreign nationals in October 1996. In October 1998 it was announced that more than 500 illegal immigrants had been returned to Nigeria, and that a further 1,000 West Africans were awaiting repatriation. The deportation of more than 500 Nigerians was reported in mid-1999. In August 1996 the Governments of Benin and Nigeria had agreed to review the demarcation of disputed areas of their joint border, and in 1997 a joint border commission was established.

Benin has in recent years played an active role in efforts to co-ordinate regional peace-keeping and humanitarian assistance operations. In late 1998 Benin contributed some 140 troops to the peace-keeping operations in Guinea-Bissau undertaken by the ECOWAS Cease-Fire Monitoring Group (ECOMOG, see p. 165), although the force was withdrawn in mid-1999 following the *coup d'état* in Guinea-Bissau.

**Government**

The Constitution of the Republic of Benin, which was approved in a national referendum on 2 December 1990, provides for a civilian, multi-party political system. Executive power is vested in the President of the Republic, who is elected by direct universal adult suffrage with a five-year mandate, renewable only once. The legislature is the 64-member Assemblée nationale, which is similarly elected, for a period of four years, by universal suffrage. The President of the Republic appoints the Council of Ministers, subject to formal parliamentary approval.

For the purposes of local administration, Benin is divided into 12 departments, each administered by a civilian prefect.

**Defence**

In August 1999 the Beninois Armed Forces numbered an estimated 4,800 in active service (land army 4,500, navy about 150, air force 150). Paramilitary forces comprised a 2,500-strong gendarmerie. Military service is by selective conscription, and lasts for 18 months. The estimated defence budget for 1999 was 21,000m. francs CFA.

**Economic Affairs**

In 1997, according to estimates by the World Bank, Benin's gross national product (GNP), measured at average 1995–97 prices, was US $2,227m., equivalent to $380 per head. During 1990–97, it was estimated, GNP per head increased at an average annual rate of 1.7% in real terms. Over the same period the population was estimated to have increased at an average rate of 2.9% per year. GNP in 1998 was estimated at $2,300m., equivalent to $380 per head. Benin's gross domestic product (GDP) increased, in real terms, by an average of 4.6% per year in 1990–98. GDP growth in 1997 was estimated at 5.6%, allthough growth slowed to an estimated 4.4% in 1998.

Agriculture (including forestry and fishing) contributed 41.1% of GDP in 1997. In 1998 an estimated 55.9% of the labour force were employed in the sector. The principal cash crops are cotton (exports of which accounted for an estimated 83.9% of domestic exports and 51.6% of total exports in 1997) and oil palm. Benin is normally self-sufficient in basic foods; the main subsistence crops are yams, cassava and maize. The World Bank estimated that agricultural GDP increased at an average annual rate of 5.2% in 1990–98.

Industry (including mining, manufacturing, construction and power) contributed 14.9% of GDP in 1997, and engaged 10.4% of the employed labour force at the time of the 1992 census. According to the World Bank, industrial GDP increased at an average annual rate of 4.0% in 1990–98.

According to estimates published by the IMF, mining contributed only 0.4% of GDP in 1997, and engaged less than 0.1% of the employed labour force in 1992. Petroleum reserves at Semé had been exhausted by 1998, leaving marble and limestone as the only minerals currently exploited commercially. There are also deposits of gold, phosphates, natural gas, iron ore, silica sand, peat and chromium. The GDP of the mining sector was estimated to have declined by an average of 8.8% per year in 1990–97.

The manufacturing sector, which contributed 8.8% of GDP in 1996, engaged 7.8% of the employed labour force in 1992. The sector is based largely on the processing of primary products (principally cotton-ginning and oil-palm processing). Construction materials and some simple consumer goods are also produced for the domestic market. According to IMF data, manufacturing GDP increased at an average annual rate of 4.0% in 1990–96, with growth estimated at 4.2% in 1996.

Benin is at present highly dependent on imports of electricity from Ghana (which supplied some 85% of total available production in 1996). It is envisaged that a hydroelectric installation on the Mono river, constructed and operated jointly with Togo, will reduce Benin's dependence on imported electricity, and a second such installation is under construction downstream. It is also planned to construct a pipeline to supply natural gas from Nigeria to Benin, Togo and Ghana. Imports of petroleum products accounted for some 9.5% of the value of domestic imports in 1997.

The services sector contributed 43.9% of GDP in 1997, and engaged 31.8% of the employed labour force in 1992. The port of Cotonou is of considerable importance as an entrepôt for regional trade: re-exports comprised an estimated 38.5% of the value of total exports in 1997. According to the World Bank, the GDP of the services sector increased by an average of 4.3% per year in 1990–98.

In 1998 Benin recorded a visible trade deficit of an estimated 98,900m. francs CFA, while there was a deficit of an estimated 54,200m. francs CFA on the current account of the balance of payments. In 1995 the principal source of imports (34.8%) was France; other major sources were Thailand, the USA and the Netherlands. The principal market for exports in that year was Brazil (20.0%); other important purchasers were Portugal, Morocco, India and Thailand. The principal exports in 1990 were ginned cotton, fuels and palm products. The main imports in that year were miscellaneous manufactured articles (most notably cotton yarn and fabrics), foodstuffs (particularly cereals), fuels, machinery and transport equipment, chemical products and beverages and tobacco.

In 1997 Benin recorded an overall budget deficit of 66,900m. francs CFA (equivalent to 5.4% of GDP). The country's total external debt at the end of 1997 was US $1,624m., of which $1,393m. was long-term public debt. In that year the cost of debt-servicing was equivalent to 9.1% of the value of exports of goods and services. The annual rate of inflation, which had been negligible prior to the 50% devaluation of the CFA franc in January 1994, increased to 38.5% in 1994, but slowed to an average of 4.7% per year in 1995–98; average inflation was 5.8% in 1998. About one-quarter of the urban labour force was estimated to be unemployed in 1997.

Benin is a member of the Economic Community of West African States (ECOWAS, see p. 163), of the West African organs of the Franc Zone (see p. 200), of the African Petroleum Producers' Association (APPA, see p. 287), of the Conseil de l'Entente (see p. 291) and of the Niger Basin Authority (see p. 292).

Benin has experienced considerable economic growth since the beginning of the 1990s. Economic liberalization measures undertaken by the Kérékou regime in the second half of the 1980s were extended by the Soglo administration, and considerable success was achieved in strengthening public finances, improving the external balance-of-payments position and in reforming the financial sector. The enhanced competitiveness of cotton and other agricultural exports was, moreover, among the principal benefits to the economy of the devaluation of the CFA franc in 1994. At his election to the presidency in March 1996 Kérékou undertook to address unemployment and other socio-economic problems arising from the rigorous adjustment measures implemented by his predecessor, and to eliminate corruption in public and economic life, identified as a major obstacle to sustained growth. A new three-year (1996–99) Enhanced Structural Adjustment Facility (ESAF) was agreed with the IMF in August 1996, envisaging average annual growth of almost 6%. The renewal of co-operation with the IMF ensured debt relief measures, notably along concessionary terms by the 'Paris Club' of official creditors. GDP growth neared this level in 1997, but slowed in 1998, mainly reflecting severe electricity shortages in March–June caused by generating difficulties in Ghana. In the latter year Benin was also affected by a decline in cotton production and in revenue from cotton exports, while the higher price of petroleum supplies from Nigeria contributed to an increase in the rate of inflation. Furthermore, the Government's slow progress in the privatization of a number of major state enterprises and in the reform of the civil service led the IMF to suspend disbursements during 1998. The facility was, however, resumed in January 1999, after the Government agreed to implement the agreed structural reforms. Strike action by public-sector workers in October and November of that year indicated, however, the difficulties faced by the Kérékou administration in the introduction of the reforms demanded by their external creditors.

## Social Welfare

In 1995 Benin had one doctor per 20,000 people and one midwife per 12,000 people. In that year only 42% of the population had access to health care. In mid-1995 the International Development Association approved funding of US $27.8m., in support of a health and population project (costing $33.4m.) a principal aim of which was to be the establishment of a nation-wide family planning programme. Moreover, a particular emphasis of economic policy for the second half of the 1990s was to be the improvement of health care and social services provisions for the poorest sectors of the population. There is a minimum wage for workers (which stood at 21,924 francs CFA per month in 1997). In 1996 the Social Security Fund's total expenditure was 5,382m. frans CFA. Spending on health in 1997 amounted to 15,100m. francs CFA.

## Education

The Constitution of Benin obliges the state to make a quality compulsory primary education available to all children. All public primary and secondary schools in Benin finance themselves through school fees. Primary education begins at six years of age and lasts for six years. Secondary education, beginning at 12 years of age, lasts for up to seven years, comprising a first cycle of four years and a second of three years. Primary enrolment in 1996 included only 62% of children in the appropriate age-group (males 78%; females 46%). Enrolment at secondary schools in that year was equivalent to only 17% (males 23%; females 10%). In the 1990s the Government has sought to extend the provision of education. In 1993 girls in rural areas were exempted from school fees, and in 1999 the Government created a 500m. francs CFA fund to increase female enrolment. The University of Benin, at Cotonou, was founded in 1970. In 1996 14,055 students were enrolled at tertiary institutions. Adult illiteracy at the time of the 1992 census was 72.7% (males 60.0%; females 83.3%). In 1995, according to UNESCO estimates, the average rate of adult illiteracy was 63.0% (males 51.3%; females 74.2%). In 1995 the Government spent 31,074m. francs CFA on education (equivalent to 15.2% of total expenditure by the central Government).

## Public Holidays

**2000:** 1 January (New Year's Day), 10 January (*Vodoun* national holiday), 8 January*† (Id al-Fitr, end of Ramadan), 16 January

(Martyrs' Day, anniversary of mercenary attack on Cotonou), 16 March* (Id al-Adha, Feast of the Sacrifice), 1 April (Youth Day), 21 April (Good Friday), 24 April (Easter Monday), 1 May (Workers' Day), 1 June (Ascension Day), 12 June (Whit Monday), 1 August (Independence Day), 15 August (Assumption), 26 October (Armed Forces Day), 1 November (All Saints' Day), 30 November (National Day), 25 December (Christmas Day), 28 December*† (Id al-Fitr, end of Ramadan), 31 December (Harvest Day).

**2001:** 1 January (New Year's Day), 10 January (*Vodoun* national holiday), 16 January (Martyrs' Day, anniversary of mercenary attack on Cotonou), 6 March* (Id al-Adha, Feast of the Sacrifice), 1 April (Youth Day), 13 April (Good Friday), 16 April (Easter Monday), 1 May (Workers' Day), 24 May (Ascension Day), 4 June (Whit Monday), 1 August (Independence Day), 15 August (Assumption), 26 October (Armed Forces Day), 1 November (All Saints' Day), 30 November (National Day), 17 December* (Id al-Fitr, end of Ramadan), 25 December (Christmas Day), 31 December (Harvest Day).

* These holidays are dependent on the Islamic lunar calendar and may vary by one or two days from the dates given.

† This festival will occur twice (in the Islamic years AH 1420 and 1421) within the same Gregorian year.

### Weights and Measures

The metric system is in force.

# Statistical Survey

Source (unless otherwise stated): Institut National de la Statistique et de l'Analyse Economique, Ministère du Plan, de la Restructuration Economique et de la Promotion de l'Emploi, BP 342, Cotonou; tel. 31-05-41; internet planben.intnet.bj.

## Area and Population

**AREA, POPULATION AND DENSITY**

| | |
|---|---|
| Area (sq km) | 112,622* |
| Population (census results) | |
| 20–30 March 1979 | |
| Total | 3,331,210 |
| 15–29 February 1992 | |
| Males | 2,390,336 |
| Females | 2,525,219 |
| Total | 4,915,555 |
| Population (official estimates at mid-year) | |
| 1996 | 5,594,000 |
| 1997 | 5,828,000 |
| 1998 | 6,100,799 |
| Density (per sq km) at mid-1998 | 54.2 |

* 43,484 sq miles.

**ETHNIC GROUPS**

1992 census (percentages): Fon 42.2; Adja 15.6; Yoruba 12.1; Bariba 8.6; Otamari 6.1; Peulh 6.1; Yoa-Lokpa 3.8; Dendi 2.8; Others 2.7.

**POPULATION BY PROVINCE** (1992 census)

| | |
|---|---|
| Atakora | 649,308 |
| Atlantique | 1,066,373 |
| Borgou | 827,925 |
| Mono | 676,377 |
| Ouémé | 876,574 |
| Zou | 818,998 |
| **Total** | 4,915,555 |

Note: Legislation was approved in August 1997 whereby Benin was reorganized into 12 administrative departments: Alibori, Atacora, Atlantique, Borgou, Collines, Donga, Kouffo, Lama, Mono, Ouémé, Plateau, Zou.

**PRINCIPAL TOWNS** (official estimates, 1994)

| | | | |
|---|---|---|---|
| Cotonou | 750,000 | Djougou | 132,000 |
| Porto-Novo (capital) | 200,000 | Parakou | 120,000 |

**BIRTHS AND DEATHS** (UN estimates, annual averages)

| | 1980–85 | 1985–90 | 1990–95 |
|---|---|---|---|
| Birth rate (per 1,000) | 51.4 | 49.0 | 44.2 |
| Death rate (per 1,000) | 17.7 | 16.2 | 14.4 |

**Expectation of life** (UN estimates, years at birth, 1990–95): 52.5 (males 50.7; females 54.5).

Source: UN, *World Population Prospects: The 1998 Revision*.

**1998** (official estimates at mid-year): Birth rate (per 1,000) 45.82; Death rate (per 1,000) 12.77; Expectation of life (years at birth) 53.61.

**ECONOMICALLY ACTIVE POPULATION**
(persons aged 10 years and over, 1992 census)

| | Males | Females | Total |
|---|---|---|---|
| Agriculture, hunting, forestry and fishing | 780,469 | 367,277 | 1,147,746 |
| Mining and quarrying | 609 | 52 | 661 |
| Manufacturing | 93,157 | 67,249 | 160,406 |
| Electricity, gas and water | 1,152 | 24 | 1,176 |
| Construction | 50,959 | 696 | 51,655 |
| Trade, restaurants and hotels | 36,672 | 395,829 | 432,501 |
| Transport, storage and communications | 52,228 | 609 | 52,837 |
| Finance, insurance, real estate and business services | 2,705 | 401 | 3,106 |
| Community, social and personal services | 126,122 | 38,422 | 164,544 |
| Activities not adequately defined | 25,579 | 12,917 | 38,496 |
| **Total employed** | 1,169,652 | 883,476 | 2,053,128 |
| Unemployed | 26,475 | 5,843 | 32,318 |
| **Total labour force** | 1,196,127 | 889,319 | 2,085,446 |

Source: ILO, *Yearbook of Labour Statistics*.

**Mid-1998** (estimates in '000): Agriculture, etc. 1,472; Total 2,631 (Source: FAO, *Production Yearbook*).

# Agriculture

**PRINCIPAL CROPS** ('000 metric tons)

| | 1996 | 1997 | 1998* |
|---|---|---|---|
| Rice (paddy) | 22 | 27 | 27 |
| Maize | 504 | 514 | 514 |
| Millet | 29 | 28† | 28 |
| Sorghum | 112 | 120 | 120 |
| Sweet potatoes | 68 | 57 | 57 |
| Cassava (Manioc) | 1,452 | 1,625* | 1,625 |
| Yams | 1,346 | 1,408 | 1,408 |
| Taro (Coco yam) | 3* | 4 | 4 |
| Dry beans | 59 | 74 | 74 |
| Groundnuts (in shell) | 84 | 102 | 102 |
| Cottonseed | 252 | 220* | 220 |
| Cotton (lint) | 166 | 175* | 175 |
| Coconuts | 20† | 20* | 20 |
| Palm kernels* | 16 | 14 | 14 |
| Tomatoes | 72 | 121 | 121 |
| Chillies and peppers (green)* | 12 | 12 | 12 |
| Other vegetables* | 155 | 146 | 146 |
| Oranges* | 12 | 12 | 12 |
| Mangoes* | 12 | 12 | 12 |
| Bananas | 13† | 13* | 13 |
| Pineapples* | 3 | 3 | 3 |
| Other fruit* | 109 | 108 | 108 |

* FAO estimate(s). † Unofficial figure.

Source: FAO, *Production Yearbook*.

**LIVESTOCK** ('000 head, year ending September)

| | 1996 | 1997 | 1998* |
|---|---|---|---|
| Horses* | 6 | 6 | 6 |
| Asses* | 1 | 1 | 1 |
| Cattle | 1,350 | 1,400* | 1,400 |
| Pigs | 584 | 580* | 580 |
| Sheep | 601 | 605* | 605 |
| Goats | 1,013 | 1,020* | 1,020 |

Poultry (million): 25† in 1996; 27* in 1997; 27* in 1998.

* FAO estimate(s). † Unofficial figure.

Source: FAO, *Production Yearbook*.

**LIVESTOCK PRODUCTS** (FAO estimates, '000 metric tons)

| | 1996 | 1997 | 1998 |
|---|---|---|---|
| Beef and veal | 18 | 18 | 18 |
| Mutton and lamb | 3 | 3 | 3 |
| Goat meat | 4 | 4 | 4 |
| Pig meat | 8 | 8 | 7 |
| Poultry meat | 28 | 30 | 33 |
| Other meat | 5 | 5 | 5 |
| Cows' milk | 20 | 20 | 20 |
| Goats' milk | 7 | 7 | 7 |
| Poultry eggs | 18 | 20 | 20 |
| Cattle hides | 3 | 3 | 3 |
| Goatskins | 1 | 1 | 1 |

Source: FAO, *Production Yearbook*.

# Forestry

**ROUNDWOOD REMOVALS**
('000 cubic metres, excl. bark)

| | 1995 | 1996 | 1997 |
|---|---|---|---|
| Sawlogs, veneer logs and logs for sleepers | 50 | 50 | 50 |
| Other industrial wood | 271 | 278 | 286 |
| Fuel wood | 5,580 | 5,742 | 5,901 |
| **Total** | 5,901 | 6,070 | 6,237 |

Source: FAO, *Yearbook of Forest Products*.

**SAWNWOOD PRODUCTION**
('000 cubic metres, incl. railway sleepers)

| | 1995 | 1996 | 1997 |
|---|---|---|---|
| **Total** (all broadleaved) | 24 | 24 | 24 |

Source: FAO, *Yearbook of Forest Products*.

# Fishing

('000 metric tons, live weight)

| | 1995 | 1996* | 1997* |
|---|---|---|---|
| Tilapias | 11.7 | 10.7 | 10.3 |
| Black catfishes | 1.3 | 1.2 | 1.1 |
| Torpedo-shaped catfishes | 2.3 | 2.1 | 2.0 |
| Freshwater gobies | 0.9 | 0.8 | 0.8 |
| Other freshwater fishes | 10.4 | 9.4 | 9.1 |
| Groupers and seabasses* | 1.3 | 1.6 | 2.2 |
| Threadfins and tasselfishes* | 1.0 | 1.1 | 1.5 |
| Sardinellas* | 1.4 | 1.6 | 2.2 |
| Bonga shad | 2.0 | 1.8 | 1.7 |
| Other marine fishes* | 4.2 | 4.6 | 5.8 |
| **Total fish*** | 36.6 | 34.9 | 36.7 |
| Freshwater crustaceans | 4.7 | 4.3 | 4.1 |
| Marine crustaceans* | 3.2 | 3.0 | 2.9 |
| **Total catch** | 44.4 | 42.2 | 43.8 |

* FAO estimate(s).

Note: Figures exclude catches by Beninois canoes operating from outside the country.

Source: FAO, *Yearbook of Fishery Statistics*.

# Mining

('000 barrels)

| | 1996 | 1997 | 1998 |
|---|---|---|---|
| Crude petroleum | 552.1 | 455.1 | 355.9 |

Source: Banque centrale des états de l'Afrique de l'ouest.

# Industry

**SELECTED PRODUCTS** ('000 metric tons, unless otherwise indicated)

| | 1993 | 1994 | 1995 |
|---|---|---|---|
| Salted, dried or smoked fish* | 2.0 | 2.0 | 2.0 |
| Cement† | 380 | 380 | 380 |
| Electric energy (million kWh)‡ | 5 | 6 | 6 |

* Data from FAO.

† Data from the US Bureau of Mines.

‡ Provisional or estimated figures.

Source: UN, *Industrial Commodity Statistics Yearbook*.

**Palm oil and palm kernel oil** ('000 metric tons): 10.8 in 1993; 10.3 in 1994; 5.4 in 1995; 7.4 in 1996; 6.6 in 1997 (Source: IMF, *Benin: Selected Issues and Statistical Appendix*, September 1998).

# Finance

### CURRENCY AND EXCHANGE RATES

**Monetary Units**

100 centimes = 1 franc de la Communauté financière africaine (CFA).

**Sterling, Dollar and Euro Equivalents** (30 September 1999)

£1 sterling = 1,012.69 francs CFA;
US $1 = 615.06 francs CFA;
€1 = 655.96 francs CFA;
10,000 francs CFA = £9.875 = $16.259 = €15.245.

**Average Exchange Rate** (francs CFA per US $)

| | |
|---|---|
| 1996 | 511.55 |
| 1997 | 583.67 |
| 1998 | 589.95 |

Note: An exchange rate of 1 French franc = 50 francs CFA, established in 1948, remained in force until January 1994, when the CFA franc was devalued by 50%, with the exchange rate adjusted to 1 French franc = 100 francs CFA.

### BUDGET ('000 million francs CFA)

| Revenue | 1995 | 1996 | 1997 |
|---|---|---|---|
| Tax revenue | 123.0 | 142.6 | 158.8 |
| Direct taxation | 42.4 | 46.3 | 42.7 |
| Indirect taxation | 80.6 | 96.3 | 116.1 |
| Taxes on goods and services | 20.3 | 26.0 | 33.4 |
| Import duties | 60.0 | 70.3 | 82.7 |
| Export duties | 0.3 | 0.0 | 0.0 |
| Non-tax revenue | 26.1 | 29.3 | 23.1 |
| **Total** | 149.1 | 171.9 | 181.9 |

| Expenditure* | 1995 | 1996 | 1997 |
|---|---|---|---|
| Current expenditure | 140.8 | 147.9 | 151.4 |
| Salaries | 53.9 | 58.2 | 62.0 |
| Social security payments | 11.5 | 16.9 | 16.2 |
| Interest due | 27.9 | 27.3 | 21.1 |
| Domestic debt | 2.7 | 3.2 | 2.7 |
| External debt | 25.2 | 24.1 | 18.4 |
| Other current expenditure | 47.3 | 45.5 | 52.1 |
| Capital expenditure | 78.2 | 71.8 | 83.6 |
| Internal financing | 13.2 | 7.3 | 11.9 |
| External financing | 65.0 | 64.5 | 71.7 |
| **Total** | 219.0 | 219.7 | 235.0 |

* Excluding net lending ('000 million francs CFA): 3.0 in 1995; 0.7 in 1996; –0.7 in 1997.

Source: Banque centrale des états de l'Afrique de l'ouest.

**1998** (draft budget, '000 million francs CFA): Revenue 203.2; Expenditure 317.3.

**1999** (draft budget, '000 million francs CFA): Revenue 235.0; Expenditure 335.2.

### INTERNATIONAL RESERVES (US $ million at 31 December)

| | 1995 | 1996 | 1997 |
|---|---|---|---|
| Gold* | 4.3 | 4.2 | 3.4 |
| IMF special drawing rights | 0.1 | 0.3 | 0.1 |
| Reserve position in IMF | 3.2 | 3.1 | 2.9 |
| Foreign exchange | 194.7 | 258.4 | 250.1 |
| **Total** | 202.2 | 266.0 | 256.5 |

* Valued at market-related prices.

Source: IMF, *International Financial Statistics.*

### MONEY SUPPLY ('000 million francs CFA at 31 December)

| | 1996 | 1997 | 1998 |
|---|---|---|---|
| Currency outside banks | 68.9 | 80.7 | 70.7 |
| Demand deposit at deposit money banks | 114.8 | 107.5 | 108.4 |
| Checking deposits at post office | 5.3 | 4.5 | n.a. |
| **Total money** (incl. others) | 189.5 | 193.4 | 185.5 |

Source: IMF, *International Financial Statistics.*

### COST OF LIVING

(Consumer price index; base: 1995 = 100)

| | 1996 | 1997 | 1998 |
|---|---|---|---|
| **All items** | 104.9 | 108.6 | 114.8 |

Source: IMF, *International Financial Statistics.*

### NATIONAL ACCOUNTS

('000 million francs CFA at current prices)

**Expenditure on the Gross Domestic Product**

| | 1996 | 1997 | 1998 |
|---|---|---|---|
| Government final consumption expenditure | 108.3 | 113.8 | 119.6 |
| Private final consumption expenditure | 913.9 | 1,017.2 | 1,099.4 |
| Increase in stocks | 5.6 | 6.2 | 6.8 |
| Gross fixed capital formation | 196.7 | 223.1 | 242.0 |
| **Total domestic expenditure** | 1,224.4 | 1,360.3 | 1,467.8 |
| Exports of goods and services | 300.2 | 337.2 | 367.8 |
| *Less* Imports of goods and services | 395.1 | 447.7 | 474.8 |
| **GDP in purchasers' values** | 1,129.5 | 1,249.8 | 1,360.6 |

Source: IMF, *International Financial Statistics.*

**Gross Domestic Product by Economic Activity**

| | 1995 | 1996 | 1997 |
|---|---|---|---|
| Agriculture, livestock, forestry and fishing | 341.3 | 425.4 | 479.8 |
| Mining | 5.0 | 4.9 } | 109.4 |
| Manufacturing and handicrafts | 86.7 | 93.4 } | |
| Water, gas and electricity | 7.5 | 8.2 | 10.1 |
| Construction and public works | 46.9 | 48.6 | 54.6 |
| Trade and hotels | 191.4 | 205.6 | 222.5 |
| Transport and communications | 81.2 | 82.7 | 87.8 |
| Financial services | 106.1 | 111.2 | 115.7 |
| Other services | 76.1 | 82.3 | 86.7 |
| **GDP at factor cost** | 942.2 | 1,062.2 | 1,166.6 |
| Indirect taxes, *less* subsidies | 60.7 | 67.3 | 83.2 |
| **GDP in purchasers' values** | 1,002.9 | 1,129.5 | 1,249.8 |

Source: mainly Banque centrale des états de l'Afrique de l'ouest.

### BALANCE OF PAYMENTS ('000 million francs CFA)

| | 1996 | 1997 | 1998* |
|---|---|---|---|
| Exports of goods f.o.b. | 269.9 | 247.5 | 227.5 |
| Imports of goods f.o.b. | –286.3 | –336.7 | –326.4 |
| **Trade balance** | –16.4 | –89.2 | –98.9 |
| Services and other income (net) | –42.7 | –44.5 | –43.9 |
| **Balance on goods, services and income** | –59.1 | –133.7 | –142.8 |
| Private unrequited transfers (net) | 32.1 | 38.2 | 44.5 |
| Public unrequited transfers (net) | 62.9 | 55.0 | 44.1 |
| **Current balance** | 35.9 | –40.5 | –54.2 |
| Long-term capital (net) | –17.7 | 13.5 | 36.8 |
| Short-term capital (net) | 0.8 | 68.7 | 5.9 |
| Net errors and omissions | 3.2 | 3.9 | — |
| **Overall balance** | 22.2 | 45.7 | –11.5 |

Source: Banque centrale des états de l'Afrique de l'ouest.

# External Trade

**PRINCIPAL COMMODITIES** (million francs CFA)

| Imports c.i.f.* | 1988 | 1989 | 1990 |
|---|---|---|---|
| **Food products** | 25,743 | 12,814 | 17,863 |
| Food products of animal origin | 2,856 | 2,040 | 1,300 |
| Food products of plant origin | 19,655 | 8,579 | 15,020 |
| Rice | 13,523 | 4,753 | 9,110 |
| Wheat | 2,170 | 1,769 | 3,562 |
| Processed foodstuffs | 3,222 | 2,195 | 1,543 |
| **Beverages and tobacco** | 4,643 | 4,688 | 5,268 |
| Alcoholic beverages | 1,863 | 1,199 | 2,241 |
| Manufactured tobacco products | 2,760 | 3,482 | 2,983 |
| **Energy products** | 13,343 | 10,113 | 10,393 |
| Refined petroleum products | 9,355 | 5,795 | 6,158 |
| **Other raw materials (inedible)** | 4,500 | 2,449 | 2,410 |
| **Machinery and transport equipment** | 13,302 | 9,593 | 7,860 |
| Non-electrical machinery | 5,478 | 3,486 | n.a. |
| Electrical machinery | 4,239 | 2,251 | n.a. |
| Road transport equipment | 3,454 | 3,812 | n.a. |
| **Other industrial products** | 34,774 | 25,036 | 28,026 |
| Chemical products | 7,726 | 4,710 | 7,235 |
| Fertilizers | 866 | 3 | 1,533 |
| Miscellaneous manufactured articles | 27,048 | 20,326 | 20,791 |
| Cotton yarn and fabrics | 14,988 | 11,160 | 7,715 |
| **Total** (incl. others) | 97,257 | 66,132 | 72,192 |

| Exports f.o.b.† | 1988 | 1989 | 1990 |
|---|---|---|---|
| **Food products** | 517 | 228 | 266 |
| **Energy products** | 6,388 | 6,636 | 7,765 |
| Crude petroleum | 6,314 | 6,636 | 7,765 |
| **Other raw materials (inedible)** | 8,772 | 20,007 | 18,734 |
| Cottonseed | 717 | 1,119 | 68 |
| Cotton (ginned) | 7,725 | 18,681 | 16,792 |
| **Oils and fats** | 2,243 | 1,951 | 1,191 |
| Palm and palm-kernel oil | 1,586 | 1,437 | 1,181 |
| **Machinery and transport equipment** | 1,278 | 613 | 460 |
| **Other industrial products** | 1,756 | 1,505 | 4,833 |
| Miscellaneous manufactured articles | 1,337 | 1,378 | 4,704 |
| Cotton yarn and fabrics | 189 | 1,008 | 4,021 |
| **Total** (incl. others) | 20,995 | 31,090 | 33,254 |

* Excluding imports for re-export.
† Excluding re-exports.
Source: Banque centrale des états de l'Afrique de l'ouest.

**PRINCIPAL TRADING PARTNERS** (US $ '000)

| Imports c.i.f. | 1993 | 1994 | 1995 |
|---|---|---|---|
| China, People's Repub. | 33,151 | 17,730 | 20,420 |
| Côte d'Ivoire | 10,138 | 12,506 | 23,353 |
| France (incl. Monaco) | 148,499 | 111,522 | 225,347 |
| Germany | 16,798 | 21,588 | 22,758 |
| Japan | 33,844 | 24,772 | 28,637 |
| Netherlands | 52,046 | 22,749 | 31,125 |
| Senegal | 8,988 | 5,675 | 21,596 |
| Thailand | 99,249 | 69,562 | 64,459 |
| United Kingdom | 15,502 | 14,265 | 21,833 |
| USA | 24,175 | 18,519 | 31,755 |
| **Total** (incl. others) | 571,719 | 431,558 | 647,065 |

| Exports f.o.b. | 1993 | 1994 | 1995 |
|---|---|---|---|
| Brazil | 10,662 | 31,162 | 32,914 |
| China, People's Repub. | 13,298 | 966 | 4,147 |
| France (incl. Monaco) | 5,953 | 11,586 | 4,578 |
| India | 7,199 | 3,635 | 10,597 |
| Indonesia | 2,579 | 7,138 | 7,258 |
| Italy | 13,476 | 7,141 | 7,064 |
| Morocco | 63,923 | 15,091 | 16,801 |
| Nigeria | 5,873 | 11,654 | 4,336 |
| Portugal | 9,230 | 17,868 | 24,242 |
| Southern African Customs Union* | 5,199 | 2,500 | 4,291 |
| Thailand | 3,390 | 4,806 | 8,419 |
| **Total** (incl. others) | 181,589 | 163,260 | 164,955 |

* Comprising Botswana, Lesotho, Namibia, South Africa and Swaziland.
Source: UN, *International Trade Statistics Yearbook*.

# Transport

**RAILWAYS** (traffic)

| | 1995 | 1996 | 1997 |
|---|---|---|---|
| Passenger-km (million) | 116.0 | 117.0 | 121.8 |
| Freight ton-km (million) | 388.4 | 269.7 | 311.4 |

Source: IMF, *Benin—Selected Issues and Statistical Appendix* (September 1998).

**ROAD TRAFFIC** (motor vehicles in use)

| | 1994 | 1995 | 1996 |
|---|---|---|---|
| Passenger cars | 26,507 | 30,346 | 37,772 |
| Buses and coaches | 353 | 405 | 504 |
| Lorries and vans | 5,301 | 6,069 | 7,554 |
| Road tractors | 2,192 | 2,404 | 2,620 |
| Motor cycles and mopeds | 220,800 | 235,400 | 250,000 |

Source: IRF, *World Road Statistics*.

**SHIPPING**

**Merchant Fleet** (registered at 31 December)

| | 1996 | 1997 | 1998 |
|---|---|---|---|
| Number of vessels | 7 | 8 | 6 |
| Total displacement ('000 grt) | 1.0 | 1.2 | 0.9 |

Source: Lloyd's Register of Shipping, *World Fleet Statistics*.

**International Sea-borne Freight Traffic**
(at Cotonou, including goods in transit, '000 metric tons)

| | 1995 | 1996 | 1997 |
|---|---|---|---|
| Goods loaded | 338.5 | 423.9 | 370.3 |
| Goods unloaded | 1,738.4 | 1,795.8 | 1,877.9 |

Source: IMF, *Benin—Selected Issues and Statistical Appendix* (September 1998).

**CIVIL AVIATION** (traffic on scheduled services)*

| | 1993 | 1994 | 1995 |
|---|---|---|---|
| Kilometres flown (million) | 2 | 2 | 3 |
| Passengers carried ('000) | 68 | 69 | 74 |
| Passenger-km (million) | 207 | 215 | 223 |
| Total ton-km (million) | 33 | 34 | 36 |

* Including an apportionment of the traffic of Air Afrique.
Source: UN, *Statistical Yearbook*.

## Tourism

| | 1994 | 1995 | 1996 |
|---|---|---|---|
| Tourist arrivals ('000) | 111 | 138 | 147 |
| Tourism receipts (US $ million) | 22 | 27 | 29 |

Source: World Tourism Organization, *Yearbook of Tourism Statistics*.

## Communications Media

| | 1994 | 1995 | 1996 |
|---|---|---|---|
| Radio receivers ('000 in use) | 480 | 500 | 600 |
| Television receivers ('000 in use) | 29 | 32 | 100 |
| Telephones ('000 main lines in use) | 24 | 28 | n.a. |
| Telefax stations (number in use) | 600 | 800 | n.a. |
| Mobile cellular telephones (subscribers) | n.a. | 1,050 | n.a. |
| Daily newspapers | | | |
| Number | 1 | 1 | 1 |
| Average circulation ('000 copies) | 12 | 3 | 12 |
| Non-daily newspapers | | | |
| Number | n.a. | n.a. | 4 |
| Average circulation ('000 copies) | n.a. | n.a. | 66 |
| Book production* | | | |
| Titles | 84 | n.a. | n.a. |
| Copies ('000) | 42 | n.a. | n.a. |

* First editions.

Sources: UNESCO, *Statistical Yearbook*; UN, *Statistical Yearbook*.

## Education

(1996/97)

| | Institutions | Teachers | Students Males | Students Females | Students Total |
|---|---|---|---|---|---|
| Pre-primary | 283* | 622 | 9,106 | 8,335 | 17,441 |
| Primary | 3,088* | 13,957 | 492,826 | 286,503 | 779,329 |
| Secondary | | | | | |
| General | 145§ | 5,352 | 102,011 | 44,124 | 146,135 |
| Vocational§ | 14 | 283 | 3,553 | 1,320 | 4,873 |
| Higher | 9 | 962‡ | 11,398† | 2,657† | 14,055† |

*1995/96. †1996. ‡1995. §1993/94.

Source: mainly UNESCO, *Statistical Yearbook*.

# Directory

## The Constitution

A new Constitution was approved in a national referendum on 2 December 1990.

The Constitution of the Republic of Benin guarantees the basic rights and freedoms of citizens. The functions of the principal organs of state are delineated therein.

The President of the Republic, who is Head of State and Head of Government, is directly elected, by universal adult suffrage, for a period of five years, renewable only once. The President appoints government members, who are responsible to the Head of State. The legislature is the 83-member Assemblée nationale, which is elected, also by direct universal suffrage, for a period of four years.

The Constitution upholds the principle of an independent judiciary. The Constitutional Court, the Economic and Social Council and Higher Audiovisual and Communications Authority are intended to counterbalance executive authority.

## The Government

### HEAD OF STATE

**President:** Gen. (retd) MATHIEU KÉRÉKOU (took office 4 April 1996).

### COUNCIL OF MINISTERS

(January 2000)

**President:** Gen. (retd) MATHIEU KÉRÉKOU.

**Minister of State in charge of Co-ordinating Government Action, Planning, Development and Promotion of Employment:** BRUNO AMOUSSOU.

**Minister-delegate at the Presidency, in charge of National Defence:** PIERRE OTCHO.

**Minister of the Interior, Security and Local Government:** DANIEL TAWÉMA.

**Minister of Foreign Affairs and Co-operation:** ANTOINE IDJI.

**Minister of Justice, Legislation and Human Rights:** JOSEPH GNONLONFOUN.

**Minister of Finance and the Economy:** ABDOULAYE BIO TCHANE.

**Minister of Relations with the Institutions, Civil Society and Benin Nationals Abroad:** SYLVAIN ADEKPEDJOU AKINDES.

**Minister of the Civil Service, Labour and Administrative Reform:** OUSMANE BATOKO.

**Minister of Rural Development:** THÉOPHILE NATA.

**Minister of Trade, Handicrafts and Tourism:** SÉVÉRIN ADJOVI.

**Minister of Mining, Energy and Water:** FÉLIX ESSOU.

**Minister of Public Works and Transport:** JOSEPH SOUROU ATTIN.

**Minister of the Environment, Housing and Urban Development:** LUC-MARIE CONSTANT GNACADJA.

**Minister of Youth, Sports and Recreation:** VALENTIN ADITI HOUDE.

**Minister of Culture and Communication, Spokesman for the Government:** GASTON ZOSSOU.

**Minister of Education and Scientific Research:** DAMIEN ZINSOU ALAHASSA.

**Minister of Industry and Small and Medium-Sized Enterprises:** PIERRE JOHN IGUE.

**Minister of Public Health:** MARINA D'ALMEIDA MASSOUGBODJI.

**Minister of Social and Family Affairs:** RAMATOU BABA MOUSSA.

### MINISTRIES

**Office of the President:** BP 1288, Cotonou; tel. 30-02-28.

**Ministry of the Civil Service, Labour and Administrative Reform:** BP 907, Cotonou; tel. 31-26-18.

**Ministry of Culture and Communication:** BP 120, Cotonou; fax. 31-59-31.

**Ministry of Education and Scientific Research:** BP 348, Cotonou; tel. 30-06-81; fax 30-18-48.

**Ministry of the Environment, Housing and Urban Development:** 01 BP 3621, Cotonou; tel. 31-55-96; fax 31-50-81.

**Ministry of Finance and the Economy:** BP 302, Cotonou; tel. 30-10-20; fax 31-58-98.

**Ministry of Foreign Affairs and Co-operation:** BP 318, Cotonou; tel. 30-04-00.

**Ministry of Industry and Small and Medium-sized Enterprises:** BP 363, Cotonou; tel. 30-16-46.

**Ministry of the Interior, Security and Local Government:** BP 925, Cotonou; tel. 30-10-06.

**Ministry of Justice, Legislation and Human Rights:** BP 967, Cotonou; tel. 31-31-46; fax 31-34-48.

**Ministry of Mining, Energy and Water:** 04 BP 1412, Cotonou; tel. 31-41-19; fax 31-35-46.

**Ministry of National Defence:** BP 2493, Cotonou; tel. 30-08-90.

**Ministry of Planning, Economic Restructuring and Employment Promotion:** BP 342, Cotonou; tel. 30-05-41; internet planben .intnet.bj.

**Ministry of Public Health:** BP 882, Cotonou; tel. 33-08-70.

**Ministry of Public Works and Transport:** BP 351, Cotonou; tel. 31-56-96.

**Ministry of Rural Development:** 03 BP 2900, Cotonou; tel. 30-19-55; fax 30-03-26.

**Ministry of Social and Family Affairs:** Cotonou.

**Ministry of Trade, Handicrafts and Tourism:** Cotonou.

**Ministry of Youth, Sports and Recreation:** 03 BP 2103, Cotonou; tel. 31-46-00.

# President and Legislature

## PRESIDENT

**Presidential Election, First Ballot, 3 March 1996**

| Candidate | % of votes |
|---|---|
| Nicéphore Soglo | 35.69 |
| Mathieu Kérékou | 33.94 |
| Adrien Houngbédji | 19.71 |
| Bruno Amoussou | 7.76 |
| Pascal Fantondji | 1.08 |
| Léandre Djagoue | 0.92 |
| Jacques Lionel Agbo | 0.90 |
| **Total** | 100.00 |

**Second Ballot, 18 March 1996**

| Candidate | Votes | % of votes |
|---|---|---|
| Mathieu Kérékou | 999,453 | 52.49 |
| Nicéphore Soglo | 904,626 | 47.51 |
| **Total** | 1,904,079 | 100.00 |

## ASSEMBLÉE NATIONALE

**President:** Adrien Houngbédji (PSD).

**Elections, 30 March 1999**

| Party | Seats |
|---|---|
| RB | 27 |
| PRD | 11 |
| FARD—Alafia | 10 |
| PSD | 9 |
| MADEP | 6 |
| Alliance Etoile | 4 |
| Alliance IPD | 4 |
| CAR—DUNYA | 3 |
| MERCI | 2 |
| Alliance RPR—UNSD | 1 |
| Alliance SURU | 1 |
| PDB | 1 |
| PN Ensemble | 1 |
| PS | 1 |
| RDP | 1 |
| RUND | 1 |
| **Total** | 83 |

# Advisory Councils

**Cour Constitutionnelle:** (see Judicial System, below).

**Conseil Economique et Social (ECOSOC):** Cotonou; f. 1994; 30 mems, representing the executive, legislature and 'all sections of the nation'; reviews all legislation relating to economic and social affairs; competent to advise on proposed economic and social legislation, as well as to recommend economic and social reforms; Pres. Raphiou Toukourou.

# Political Organizations

The registration of political parties commenced in August 1990. By October 1999 there were 116 registered parties. The following 35 parties and coalitions contested the 1999 legislative election:

The **Alliance étoile**; the **Alliance fraternité**; the **Alliance pour la démocratie et le progrès (ADP):** Leader Adekpedjou S. Akindes; the **Alliance des patriotes**; the **Alliance impulsion pour le progrès et la démocratie (Alliance IPD)**; the **Alliance pour le progrès (Alliance APP)**; eight mem. parties: Leader Emile Derlin Zinsou: the **Alliance rassemblement pour la république—Union nationale pour la solidarité et le développement (Alliance RPR—UNSD)**; the **Alliance républicaine**; the **Alliance SURU**; four mem. parties: Leader Gado Guirigissiou; the **Alliance union pour le développement économique et social (Alliance UDES)**; the **Congrès africain pour le renouveau—DUNYA (CAR—DUNYA)**; the **Congrès du peuple pour le progrès (CPP)**; the **Front d'action pour le renouveau, la démocratie et le développement—Alafia (FARD—Alafia):** Leader Saka Kina; the **Front pour la république (FPR)**; the **Mouvement africain pour la démocratie et le progrès (MADEP):** Leader Sefou Fagbohoun; the **Mouvement africain pour le progrès (MAP)**; the **Mouvement pour l'engagement et le réveil des citoyens (MERCI)**; five mem. parties; **Notre cause commune (NCC):** Leader François Odjo Tankpinon; the **Parti africain pour la rédemption et l'indépendance (PARI)**; the **Parti communiste du Bénin (PCB):** Leader Pascal Fantondji; the **Parti démocratique du Bénin (PDB)**; the **Parti national campagne pour la moralité et la démocratie (PN CMD)**; the **Parti national 'ensemble' (PN Ensemble)**; the **Parti du renouveau démocratique (PRD):** Leader Adrien Houngbédji; the **Parti du salut (PS)**; the **Parti social démocrate (PSD):** Leader Bruno Amoussou; the **Parti social démocrate—Bélier (PSD—Bélier)**; the **Parti socialiste du Bénin (PSB)**; the **Rassemblement pour la démocratie et le panafricanisme (RDP)**; the **Rassemblement pour l'unité nationale et la démocratie (RUND)**; the **Rassemblement national pour la démocratie (RND)**; the **Renaissance du Bénin (RB):** Leader Nicéphore Soglo; the **Union pour la patrie et le travail (UPT)**; the **Union républicaine du peuple (URP)**; the **Union pour le triomphe de la république (UTR)**.

The **Coalition des forces démocratiques** (Pres. Gatien Houngbédji) is an alliance of parties and organizations supporting President Kérékou.

# Diplomatic Representation

## EMBASSIES IN BENIN

**China, People's Republic:** 2 blvd de France, 01 BP 196, Cotonou; tel. 30-12-92; fax 30-08-41; Ambassador: Chunlai Duan.

**Congo, Democratic Republic:** Carré 221, Ayélawadjè, Derrière la maison du Peuple d'Akpakpa à côté de l'école Ronsard, Cotonou; tel. 30-00-01; Chargé d'affaires: Ndompetelo Deka.

**Cuba:** ave de la Marina, face Hôtel du Port, 01 BP 948, Cotonou; tel. and fax 31-52-97; Ambassador: Fernando Prats Mari.

**Denmark:** Lot P7, Les Cocotiers, 04 BP 1223, Cotonou; tel. 30-38-62; fax 30-38-60; e-mail ambdan@bow.intnet.bj; Chargé d'affaires: Johnny Flentø.

**Egypt:** route de l'Aéroport, Lot G26, BP 1215, Cotonou; tel. 30-08-42; fax 30-14-25; Ambassador: Mohamed Mahmoud Naguib.

**France:** ave Jean-Paul II, BP 966, Cotonou; tel. 30-08-24; fax 30-15-47; Ambassador: Jacques Courbin.

**Germany:** 7 ave Jean-Paul II, 01 BP 504, Recette Principale, Cotonou; tel. 31-29-68; fax 31-29-62; Ambassador: Volker Seitz.

**Ghana:** route de l'Aéroport, Lot F, Les Cocotiers, BP 488, Cotonou; tel. 30-07-46; fax 30-03-45; Ambassador: Agyogbe Achaab.

**Libya:** Les Cocotiers, BP 405, Cotonou; tel. 30-04-52; Ambassador: Toufik Ashour Adam.

**Netherlands:** ave Jean-Paul II, 08 BP 0783, Cotonou; tel. 30-41-52; fax 30-41-50; e-mail nlgovcot@intnet.bj; Chargé d'affaires: Saskia Bakker.

**Niger:** derrière l'Hôtel de la Plage, BP 352, Cotonou; tel. 31-56-65; Ambassador: Mahaman Bachir Zadaa.

**Nigeria:** blvd de France–Marina, BP 2019, Cotonou; tel. 30-11-42; Chargé d'affaires a.i.: M. S. Adoli.

**Russia:** BP 2013, Cotonou; tel. 31-28-34; fax 31-28-35; Ambassador: Yurii Tchepik.

**USA:** rue Caporal Anani Bernard, BP 2012, Cotonou; tel. 30-06-50; fax 30-19-74; e-mail usis.cotonou@bow.intnet.bj; Ambassador: John M. Yates.

# Judicial System

The Constitution of December 1990 establishes the judiciary as an organ of state whose authority acts as a counterbalance to that of the executive and of the legislature.

**Cour Constitutionnelle:** BP 2050, Cotonou; tel. 31-16-10; fax 31-37-12; f. 1990, inaug. 1993; seven mems (four appointed by the Assemblée nationale, three by the President of the Republic); exercises highest jurisdiction in constitutional affairs; determines the constitutionality of legislation, oversees and proclaims results of national elections and referendums, responsible for protection of individual and public rights and obligations, charged with regulating functions of organs of state and authorities; Pres. CONCEPTIA OUINSOU; Sec.-Gen. JEAN-BAPTISTE MONSI.

**Haute Cour de Justice:** comprises the members of the Cour constitutionnelle (other than its President), six deputies of the Assemblée nationale and the President of the Cour suprême; competent to try the President of the Republic and members of the Government in cases of high treason, crimes committed in, or at the time of, the exercise of their functions, and of plotting against state security.

**Cour Suprême:** highest juridical authority in administrative and judicial affairs and in matters of public accounts; competent in disputes relating to local elections; advises the executive on jurisdiction and administrative affairs; comprises a President (appointed by the President of the Republic, after consultation with the President of the Assemblée nationale, senior magistrates and jurists), presidents of the component chambers and counsellors; Pres. ABRAHAM ZINZINDOHOUE.

**Attorney-General:** LUCIEN DEGENO.

# Religion

At the time of the 1992 census it was estimated that some 35% of the population held animist beliefs; another 35% were Christians (mainly Roman Catholics) and the remainder were mostly Muslims. Religious and spiritual cults, which were discouraged under Kérékou's military regime, re-emerged as a prominent force in Beninois society during the early 1990s.

## CHRISTIANITY

### The Roman Catholic Church

Benin comprises two archdioceses and seven dioceses. At 31 December 1997 there were an estimated 1.3m. Roman Catholics (about 21.0% of the population), mainly in the south of the country.

**Bishops' Conference:** Conférence Episcopale du Bénin, Archevêché, BP 491, Cotonou; tel. 31-31-45; fax 30-07-07; Pres. Rt Rev. LUCIEN MONSI-AGBOKA, Bishop of Abomey.

**Archbishop of Cotonou:** (vacant), Archevêché, BP 491, Cotonou; tel. 30-01-45; fax 30-07-07.

**Archbishop of Parakou:** Most Rev. NESTOR ASSOGBA, Archevêché, BP 75, Parakou; tel. 61-02-54; fax 61-01-99.

### Protestant Church

There are 257 Protestant mission centres, with a personnel of about 120.

**Eglise protestante méthodiste en République du Bénin:** 54 ave Mgr Steinmetz, BP 34, Cotonou; tel. 31-11-42; fax 31-25-20; f. 1843; Pres. Rev. Dr MOÏSE SAGBOHAN; Sec. Rev. MATHIEU D. OLODO; 95,827 mems (1996).

## VODOUN

The origins of the traditional *vodoun* religion can be traced to the 14th century. Its influence is particularly strong in Latin America and the Caribbean, owing to the shipment of slaves from the West African region to the Americas in the 18th and 19th centuries.

**Grand conseil de la religion vodoun du Bénin:** Ouidah; Supreme Chief DAAGBO HOUNON HOUNA.

# The Press

## DAILIES

**L'Aurore:** Face Clinique Boni, Akpakpa, 05 BP 464, Cotonou; tel. 33-70-43; Dir PATRICK ADJAMONSI.

**Bénin-Presse Info:** 01 BP 72, Cotonou; tel. 31-26-55; Dir YAOVI HOUNKPONOU; Chief Editor AMÈGNIHOUÉ HOUNDJI.

**Le Citoyen:** Akpakpa, 06 BP 723, Cotonou; tel. and fax 33-59-33, e-mail lecitoyen@intnet.bj; Dir MARTIN FABOMY; Editor-in-Chief HERVÉ JOSSE.

**La Cloche:** Carré 2248, Zogbo, 07 BP65, Cotonou; tel. 30-56-04; e-mail lacloche@h2com.com; Dir VINCENT METONNOU; Chief Editor GASPARD C. KODJO.

**La Dépêche du Soir:** Carré 555, Akpakpa, 03 BP 1100, Cotonou; tel. 33-51-53; Dir MOULÉRO SOTON.

**Les Echos du Jour:** Akpakpa, 08 BP 718, Cotonou; tel. 33-18-33; fax 33-17-06; e-mail echos@intnet.bj; Dir MAURICE CHABI; Editor-in-Chief MICHEL TCHANOU.

**Le Journal:** Cotonou; f. 1999; independent; Chief Editor LUC AIMÉ DANSOU.

**Liberté:** Carré 1094, Wologuèdè, 03 BP 3555; tel. 32-55-19; Dir SYLVESTE FOHOUNGO.

**Le Matin:** Carré 8116, Guinkomey, Cotonou; tel. 31-10-80; fax 33-42-62; f. 1994; Dir MOÏSE DATO; Editor-in-Chief PIERRE MATCHOUDO.

**Le Matinal:** 06 BP 1969, Cotonou; tel. 31-49-20; fax 31-49-19; Dir CHARLES TOKO; Editor-in-Chief AGAPIT N. MAFORIKAN.

**Le Matinal Sport:** 06 BP 1989, Cotonou; tel. 31-49-20; fax 31-49-19.

**L'Oeil du Peuple:** rue PTT, Gbégamey, Carré 743, 08 BP 0131; tel. 30-22-07; Dir CÉLESTIN ABISSI.

**La Nation:** Cadjèhoun, 01 BP 1210, Cotonou; tel. 30-02-99; fax 30-34-63; e-mail lanation@elodia.intnet.bj; internet www.elodia.intnet.bj/nation.htm; f. 1990; official newspaper; Dir INNOCENT M. ADJAHO; Editor-in-Chief ALFRED AHOUNOU.

**Le Point au Quotidien:** 322 rue du Renouveau, 05 BP 934, Cotonou; tel. 32-50-55; fax 32-25-31; Dir VINCENT FOLY; Editor-in-Chief CÉLESTIN AKPOVO.

**Le Progrès:** 05 BP 708, Cotonou; Dir EDOUARD LOKO; Chief Editors SEPTIME TOLLI, MAURILLE GNANSOUNOU.

## PERIODICALS

**Africa Visages:** BP 2297, Porto-Novo; tel. 22-40-25; fax 21-25-25; fortnightly; Dir ERICK HOUNTONDJI.

**L'Autre Gazette:** 02 BP 1537, Cotonou; tel. 32-59-97; e-mail collegi@beninweb.org; fmrly Le Collégien; 2 a month; Dir WILFRIDO AYIBATIN; circ. 2,500.

**L'Avenir:** 02 BP 8143, Cotonou; tel. 30-29-70; fortnightly; Dir FIRMIN GANGBE.

**Bénin Info:** 06 BP 590, Cotonou; tel. 32-52-64; fortnightly; Dir ROMAIN TOI.

**Bénin Santé:** 06 BP 1905, Cotonou, tel. 33-26-38; fax 33-18-23; bi-monthly.

**Le Continental:** BP 4419, Cotonou; Dir ARNAULD HOUNDETE.

**La Croix du Bénin:** 01 BP 105, Cotonou; tel. and fax 32-11-19; f. 1946; fortnightly; Roman Catholic; Dir BARTHÉLEMY ASSOGBA CAKPO.

**Le Démocrate:** Carré 637, Gbégamey, BP 1538, Cotonou; tel. 30-52-27.

**L'Essor:** Carré 497, Jéricho, 06 BP 1182, Cotonou; tel. 32-43-13; monthly; Dir JEAN-BAPTISTE HOUNKONNOU.

**Exécutif Info:** 04 BP 1379, Cotonou; tel. 30-08-13; fax 30-33-15; monthly; Editor-in-Chief FRÉJUS BOCCO.

**Le Forum de la Semaine:** 04 BP 0301, Cotonou; tel. 30-26-23; weekly; Dir FRANCK AGBANGLAN.

**La Gazette du Golfe:** Carré 902 E Sikècodji, 03 BP 1624, Cotonou; tel. 32-42-08; fax 32-52-26; f. 1987; weekly; Dir ISMAËL Y. SOUMANOU; Editor MARCUS BONI TEIGA; circ. 18,000 (nat. edn), 5,000 (international edn).

**Initiatives:** 01 BP 2093, Cotonou; tel. 31-44-47; quarterly; Dir THÉOPHILE CAPO-CHICHI.

**Journal Officiel de la République du Bénin:** BP 59, Porto-Novo; tel. 21-39-77; f. 1890; official govt bulletin; fortnightly; Dir AFIZE D. ADAMON.

**Labari:** BP 816, Parakou; tel. and fax 61-09-10; f. 1997; weekly; Dir DRAMANE AMITOURE; circ. 3,000.

**Le Label:** 03 BP 3190, Cotonou; tel. 30-04-72; weekly; Dir GASPARD KODJO; Chief Editor YVES AGONDANOU.

**Le Messager du Jeudi:** 01 BP 4419, Cotonou; tel. 30-04-37; fax 30-03-21; weekly.

**Les Lumières de l'Islam:** 08 BP 0430, Cotonou; tel. 31-34-59.

**Le Pélican:** 03 BP 0432, Cotonou; tel. 30-33-97; monthly; Dir OSCAR S. GBAGUIDI.

**Le Perroquet:** Carré 478, 03 BP 0880, Cotonou; tel. 32-18-54; f. 1996; 2 a month; Dir DAMIEN HOUESSOU; Chief Editor ADRIEN HOUNKOUÉ.

**Préférence Magazine:** Carré 2202, 08 BP 0185, Cotonou; sporting and cultural; monthly.

**La Pyramide:** BP 2560, Cotonou; tel. 33-38-33; monthly; Dir CHRISTOPHE HODONOU.

**La Région:** Carré 1439, Akpakpa centre, 05 BP 708, Cotonou; tel. 30-20-09; monthly; Dir AGAPIT N. MAFORIKAN.

**Le Soleil:** 02 BP 8187, Cotonou; tel. 31-11-99; fax 30-61-56-49; weekly; Dir EDGARD KAHO.

**Le Tam-Tam-Express:** BP 2302, Cotonou; tel. 30-12-05; fax 30-39-75; f. 1988; fortnightly; Dir DENIS HODONOU; circ. 8,000.

**Le Télégramme:** 06 BP 1519, Cotonou; tel. 33-04-18; fortnightly; Dir ETIENNE HOUESSOU; Chief Editor RAYMOND MONOKE.

**La Tribune de l'Economie:** BP 31, Cotonou; tel. 31-20-81; fax 31-22-99; monthly; Dir MOUFTAOU WASSI.

### NEWS AGENCIES

**Agence Bénin-Presse (ABP):** BP 72, Cotonou; tel. 31-26-55; fax 31-12-26; e-mail abpben@bow.intnet.bj; f. 1961; national news agency; section of the Ministry of Culture and Communication; Dir YAOVI R. HOUNKPONOU.

#### Foreign Bureaux

**Agence France-Presse (AFP):** 06 BP 1382, Cotonou; tel. 33-51-32; fax 33-39-23; Correspondent VIRGILE C. AHISSOU.

Associated Press (USA) and Reuters (UK) are also represented in Benin.

## Publishers

**Les Editions du Flamboyant:** 08 BP 271, Cotonou; tel. 31-02-20; fax 31-20-79; f. 1989.

**Graphitec:** 04 BP 825, Cotonou; tel. and fax 30-46-04; e-mail padonou@bow.intnet.bj.

#### Government Publishing House

**Office National de Presse et d'Imprimerie (ONPI):** BP 1210, Cotonou; tel. 30-11-52; f. 1975; Dir-Gen. INNOCENT ADJAHO.

## Broadcasting and Communications

### TELECOMMUNICATIONS

**Office des Postes et des Télécommunications (OPT):** Cotonou; tel. 31-20-45; fax 31-38-43; internet www.opt.bj; Dir-Gen. BARTHÉLEMY AGNAN.

### BROADCASTING

#### Regulatory Authority

Since 1997 the HAAC has issued licences to private radio and television stations.

**Haute Autorité de l'Audiovisuel et de la Communication (HAAC):** Cotonou; f. in accordance with the 1990 Constitution to act as the highest authority for the media; Pres. RENÉ M. DOSSA.

#### Radio

**Office de Radiodiffusion et de Télévision du Bénin (ORTB):** 01 BP 366, Cotonou; tel. 30-10-96; state-owned; radio programmes broadcast from Cotonou and Parakou in French, English and 18 local languages; Dir-Gen. JEAN N'TCHA; Dir of Radio PELU C. DIOGO.

**Radio Régionale de Parakou:** BP 128, Parakou; tel. 61-07-73; Dir DIEUDONNÉ METOZOUNVÉ.

**Ahémé FM:** Centre Africa OBOTA, Possotomè; Promoter RUFIN GODJO.

**CAPP FM:** 06 BP 2076, Cotonou; tel. 31-08-10; Promoter JERÔME CARLOS.

**Radio Cotonou:** 01 BP 306, Cotonou; tel. 30-04-81; Dir PELU CHRISTOPHE DIOGO.

**Golfe FM:** 03 BP 1624, Cotonou; tel. 32-42-08; fax 32-52-26; internet www.eit.bj/golfefm.htm; Promoter ISMAËL SOUMANOU.

**Radio Iléma:** 01 BP 3609, Cotonou; tel. 32-46-67; fax 53-01-37; Promoter FRANÇOIS SOUROU OKIOH.

**Radio Immaculée Conception:** BP 49, Cotonou; tel. 37-10-23; operated by the Roman Catholic Church of Benin; Promoter Mgr ISADORE DE SOUZA.

**Radio Maranatha:** 03 BP 4113, Cotonou; tel. 32-53-23; operated by the Conseil des Eglises Protestantes évangéliques du Bénin; promoter Rev. ROMAIN ZANNOU.

**Radio Solidarité FM:** BP 135, Djougou; tel. 80-01-95; fax 80-15-63; Promoter DAOUDA TAKPARA.

**Radio Star:** 04 BP 0553, Cotonou; tel. 32-53-22; Promoter MARCELLIN Y. ATINDEGLA.

**La Voix de l'Islam:** 08 BP 134, Cotonou; tel. 31-11-34; operated by the Communauté musulmane de Zongo; Man. El Hadj MAMAN YARO.

**Radio Wêkê:** 03 BP 2753, Cotonou; tel. 33-13-82; Promoter SOULÉ ISSA BADAROU.

#### Television

**ORTB:** (see radio); Dir of Television MAMA SOUMAÏLA.

**ATVS:** Cotonou; owned by African Television System-Sobiex; Promoter JACOB AKINOCHO.

**La Chaîne 2 (LC2):** 05 BP 427, Cotonou; tel. 33-47-49; fax 33-46-76; e-mail lc2@intnet.bj; commenced broadcasts 1997; Promoter CHRISTIAN LAGNIDÉ.

**Telco:** Cotonou: Promoter JOSEPH JÉBARA.

**TV+ International:** Cotonou; Promoter CLUADE KARAM.

## Finance

(cap. = capital; res = reserves; m. = million; br. = branch; amounts in francs CFA)

### BANKING

#### Central Bank

**Banque Centrale des Etats de l'Afrique de l'Ouest (BCEAO):** ave Jean-Paul II, BP 325, Cotonou; tel. 31-24-66; fax 31-24-65; HQ in Dakar, Senegal; f. 1962; bank of issue for the mem. states of the Union économique et monétaire ouest-africaine (UEMOA, comprising Benin, Burkina Faso, Côte d'Ivoire, Guinea-Bissau, Mali, Niger, Senegal and Togo); cap. and res 806,918m., total assets 4,084,464m. (Dec. 1998); Gov. CHARLES KONAN BANNY; Dir in Benin IDRISS LYASSOU DAOUDA; br. at Parakou.

#### Commercial Banks

**Bank of Africa—Bénin:** ave Jean-Paul II, 08 BP 0879, Cotonou; tel. 31-32-28; fax 31-31-17; e-mail boa.benin@elodia.intnet.bj; f. 1990; 28% owned by African Financial Holding; cap. and res 12,153m., total assets 129,334m. (Dec. 1998); Pres. FRANÇOIS TANKPINOU; Man. Dir RENÉ FORMEY DE SAINT-LOUVENT.

**Banque Internationale du Bénin (BIBE):** Carrefour des Trois Banques, ave Giran, 03 BP 2098, Jéricho, Cotonou; tel. 31-55-49; fax 31-23-65; e-mail bibe@intnet.bj; f. 1989; owned by Nigerian commercial interests; cap. 3,000m., res 1,047m., dep. 33,179m. (Dec. 1997); Pres. Chief JOSEPH OLADÉLÉ SANUSI; Man. Dir RANSOME OLADÉLÉ ADEBOLU; 4 brs.

**Continental Bank—Bénin:** ave Jean-Paul II, carrefour des Trois Banques, 01 BP 2020, Cotonou; tel. 31-24-24; fax 31-51-77; e-mail contbk@intnet.bj; f. 1995 to assume activities of Crédit Lyonnais Bénin; 46% state-owned; cap. and res 3,398m., total assets 22,932m. (Dec. 1996); Pres. WASSI MOUFTAOU; Man. Dir MICHEL SABATH D'ALMEIDA.

**Ecobank—Bénin SA:** rue du Gouverneur Bayol, 01 BP 1280, Cotonou; tel. 31-40-33; fax 31-33-85; e-mail ecobnet@bow.intnet.bj; f. 1989; 72% owned by Ecobank Transnational Inc (operating under the auspices of the Economic Community of West African States); cap. and res 3,212m., total assets 83,758m. (Dec. 1997); Pres. GILBERT MEDJE; Gen. Man. RIZWAN HAIDER; 1 br.

**Financial Bank:** Immeuble Adjibi, rue du Commandant Decoeur, 01 BP 2700 RP, Cotonou; tel. 31-31-00; fax 31-31-02; e-mail financial@ment.fr; f. 1988; 99.99% owned by Financial BC (Switzerland); cap. and res 1,072m., total assets 26,648m. (Dec. 1996); Pres. and Man. Dir RÉMY BAYSSET; 8 brs.

#### Savings Bank

**Caisse Nationale d'Epargne:** Cadjéhoun, route Inter-Etat Cotonou-Lomé, Cotonou; tel. 30-18-35; fax 31-38-43; state-owned; cap. and res 736m., total assets 15,738m. (Dec. 1997); Pres. MARCELLIN DOSSOU KPANOU; Dir ANDRÉ H. AFFEDJOU.

#### Credit Institutions

**Crédit du Bénin:** 06- BP 172, Cotonou; tel. 31-31-44; fax 31-31-66.

**Crédit Promotion du Bénin:** 03 BP 1672, Cotonou; tel. 31-31-44; fax 31-31-66; wholly owned by private investors; cap. 150m., total assets 335m. (Dec. 1997); Pres. BERNARD ADIKPETO; Man. Dir DÉNIS OBA CHABI.

#### Financial Institution

**Caisse Autonome d'Amortissement du Bénin:** BP 59, Cotonou; tel. 31-47-81; fax 31-53-56; manages state funds; Man. Dir IBRAHIM PEDRO-BONI.

### STOCK EXCHANGE

**Bourse Régionale des Valeurs Mobilières (BRVM):** Cotonou; tel. 31-21-39; fax 33-34-44; f. 1998; national branch of BRVM (regional stock exchange based in Abidjan, Côte d'Ivoire, serving the member states of UEMOA); Man. in Benin YVETTE AISSI.

### INSURANCE

**A&C Benin SA:** Cotonou; internet elodia.intnet.bj/acb/index.htm; all branches; Dir Gen. Justin Herbert Agboton.

**Gras Savoye Benin:** Immeuble Goussanou, rue du Rev. Père Colineau, BP 294, Cotonou; tel. 31-24-34; fax 31-25-32; Man. Yves Mehou-Loko.

**Société Nationale d'Assurances et de Reassurances (SONAR):** BP 2030, Cotonou; tel. 30-16-49; fax 30-09-84; parastatal co.

**Union Béninoise d'Assurance-Vie:** Cotonou; f. 1994; cap. 400m.; 51% owned by Union Africaine Vie (Côte d'Ivoire).

## Trade and Industry

### GOVERNMENT AGENCIES

**Centre Béninois du Commerce Extérieur:** Place du Souvenir, BP 1254, Cotonou; tel. 30-13-20; fax 30-04-36; provides information to export cos.

**Centre de Promotion pour l'Emploi, la Petite et Moyenne Entreprise (CEPEPE):** Face à la Mairie de Xlacondji, BP 2093, Cotonou; tel. 31-44-47; fax 31-59-50; promotes business and employment.

**Office Béninois de Recherches Géologiques et Minières (OBRGM):** Ministère des mines, de l'energie et de l'hydraulique, 04 BP 249, Cotonou; tel. 31-03-09; fax 31-41-20; f. 1996 as govt agency responsible for mining policy, exploitation and research.

**Office National du Bois (ONAB):** BP 1238, Recette Principale, Cotonou; tel. 33-16-32; fax 33-19-56; f. 1983; forest development and management, manufacture and marketing of wood products; transfer of industrial activities to private ownership pending; Man. Dir Pascal Patinvoh.

**Société Nationale pour l'Industrie des Corps Gras (SONICOG):** BP 312, Cotonou; tel. 33-07-01; fax 33-15-20; f. 1962; state-owned; processes shea-nuts (karité nuts), palm kernels and cottonseed; Man. Dir Joseph Gabin Dossou.

**Société Nationale pour la Promotion Agricole (SONAPRA):** BP 933, Cotonou; tel. 33-08-20; fax 33-19-48; f. 1983; state-owned; manages five cotton-ginning plants and one fertilizer plant; distributes fertilizers and markets agricultural products; Pres. Imorou Salley; Man. Dir Michel Dassi.

### DEVELOPMENT ORGANIZATIONS

**Agence Française de Développement (AFD):** blvd Jean-Paul II, BP 38, Cotonou; tel. 31-35-80; fax 31-20-18; fmrly Caisse Française de Développement; Dir Henri Philippe de Clercq.

**Mission de Coopération et d'Action Culturelle** (Mission Française d'Aide et de Coopération): BP 476, Cotonou; tel. 30-08-24; administers bilateral aid from France according to the co-operation agreement of 1975; Dir Bernard Hadjadj.

### CHAMBER OF COMMERCE

**Chambre de Commerce, d'Agriculture et d'Industrie de la République du Bénin (CCIB):** ave du Général de Gaulle, BP 31, Cotonou; tel. 31-32-99; fax 31-32-99; Pres. Wassi Mouftatou; Sec.-Gen. N. A. Viadenou.

### EMPLOYERS' ORGANIZATIONS

**Association des Syndicats du Bénin (ASYNBA):** Cotonou; Pres. Pierre Fourn.

**Groupement Interprofessionnel des Entreprises du Bénin (GIBA):** BP 6, Cotonou; Pres. A. Jeukens.

**Organisation Nationale des Employeurs du Bénin (ONEB):** BP 41, Cotonou; tel. 33-13-00; fax 31-39-50.

**Syndicat des Commerçants Importateurs et Exportateurs du Bénin:** BP 6, Cotonou; Pres. M. Benchimol.

**Syndicat Interprofessionnel des Entreprises Industrielles du Bénin:** Cotonou; Pres. M. Doucet.

**Syndicat National des Commerçants et Industriels Africains du Bénin (SYNACIB):** BP 367, Cotonou; Pres. Urbain da Silva.

### UTILITIES

#### Electricity and Water

**Communauté Electrique du Bénin (CEB):** BP 385, Cotonou; see the chapter on Togo.

**Société Béninoise d'Electricité et d'Eau (SBEE):** BP 123, Cotonou; tel. 31-21-45; fax 31-50-28; f. 1973; cap. 10,000m. francs CFA; state-owned; production and distribution of electricity and water; Man. Dir Godefroy Chekete.

### TRADE UNIONS

**Confédération Générale des Travailleurs du Bénin (CGTB):** Sec.-Gen. Pascal Todjinou.

**Confédération des Syndicats Autonomes du Bénin (CSAB):** Cotonou; First Sec. Albert Gougan.

**Confédération des Syndicats des Travailleurs du Bénin (CSTB):** Cotonou; Sec.-Gen. Gaston Azoua.

**Union Nationale des Syndicats de Travailleurs du Bénin (UNSTB):** 1 blvd Saint-Michel, BP 69, Cotonou; tel. and fax 30-36-13; sole officially-recognized trade union 1974–90; Sec.-Gen. Amidou Lawani.

Other autonomous labour organizations include the **Collectif des Syndicats Indépendants** and the **Centrale des Organisations Syndicales Indépendants (COSI)**.

## Transport

In October 1996 the World Bank approved a credit of US $40m., to be issued through the International Development Association, in support of a major programme of investment in Benin's transport network. The integrated programme aimed to enhance Benin's status as an entrepôt for regional trade, and also to boost domestic employment and, by improving the infrastructure and reducing transport costs, agricultural and manufacturing output.

### RAILWAYS

In 1997 the network handled 311,400 metric tons of goods. Plans for a 650-km extension, linking Parakou to Niamey (Niger), via Gaya, were postponed in the late 1980s, owing to lack of finance. In January 1999 the line between Cotonou and Porto-Novo was re-opened after nine years of closure.

**Organisation Commune Bénin-Niger des Chemins de Fer et des Transports (OCBN):** BP 16, Cotonou; tel. 31-33-80; fax 31-41-50; f. 1959; 50% owned by Govt of Benin, 50% by Govt of Niger; total of 579 track-km; main line runs for 438 km from Cotonou to Parakou in the interior; br. line runs westward via Ouidah to Segboroué (34 km); also line of 107 km from Cotonou via Porto-Novo to Pobé (near the Nigerian border); Man. Dir Isaac Enidé Kilanyossi.

### ROADS

In 1996 there were 6,787 km of roads, including 10 km of motorway, 3,425 km of main roads and 3,352 km of secondary roads. About one-fifth of the network was paved.

**AGETRAC:** BP 1933, Cotonou; tel. 31-32-22; e-mail agetrac@leland.bj; f. 1967; goods transportation and warehousing.

**Compagnie de Transit et de Consignation du Bénin (CTCB Express):** route de l'Aéroport, BP 7079, Cotonou; f. 1986; Pres. Souléman Koura Zoumarou.

### SHIPPING

The main port is at Cotonou. In 1997 the port handled some 2,248,200 metric tons of goods.

**Port Autonome de Cotonou:** BP 927, Cotonou; tel. 31-28-90; fax 31-28-91; f. 1965; state-owned port authority; Man. Dir Issa Badarou-Soulé.

**Association pour la Défense des Intérêts du Port de Cotonou (AIPC) (Communauté Portuaire du Bénin):** BP 927, Cotonou; tel. 31-17-26; fax 31-28-91; f. 1993; promotes, develops and co-ordinates of port activities at Cotonou; Pres. Issa Badarou-Soulé; Sec.-Gen. Camille Médégan.

**Compagnie Béninoise de Navigation Maritime (COBENAM):** Place Ganhi, 01 BP 2032, Cotonou; tel. 31-32-87; fax 31-09-78; f. 1974; 51% state-owned, 49% by Govt of Algeria; Pres. Abdel Kader Allal; Man. Dir Cocou Théophile Hounkponou.

**SDV Bénin:** route du Collège de l'Union, Akpakpa, 01 BP 433, Cotonou; tel. 33-11-78; fax 33-06-11; e-mail sdvbenin@bow.intnet.bj; f. 1986; Pres. J. F. Mignonneau; Dir-Gen. R. Ph. Ranjard.

**Société Béninoise d'Entreprises Maritimes:** blvd de France, Zone Portuaire, BP 1733, Cotonou; tel. 31-21-19; fax 31-59-26; warehousing, storage and transportation.

**Société Béninoise des Manutentions Portuaires (SOBEMAP):** place des Martyrs, BP 35, Cotonou; tel. 31-39-83; state-owned; Pres. Georges Sekloka; Man. Dir Théodore Ahouménou Ahouassou.

### CIVIL AVIATION

The international airport at Cotonou (Cotonou-Cadjehoun) has a 2.4-km runway, and there are secondary airports at Parakou, Natitingou, Kandi and Abomey.

**Air Afrique:** ave du Gouverneur Ballot, BP 200, Cotonou; tel. 31-21-07; fax 31-53-41; see the chapter on Côte d'Ivoire; Dir in Benin JOSEPH KANZA.

**Bénin Inter-Régional:** Cotonou; f. 1991 as a jt venture by private Beninois interests and Aeroflot (then the state airline of the USSR); operates domestic and regional flights.

## Tourism

Benin's rich cultural diversity and its national parks and game reserves are the principal tourist attractions. About 147,000 tourists visited Benin in 1996, when receipts from tourism were estimated at US $29m.

**Conseil National du Tourisme:** Cotonou; f. 1993.

# BHUTAN

## Introductory Survey

### Location, Climate, Language, Religion, Flag, Capital

The Kingdom of Bhutan lies in the Himalaya range of mountains, with Tibet (the Xizang Autonomous Region), in China, to the north and India to the south. Average monthly temperature ranges from 4.4°C (40°F) in January to 17°C (62°F) in July. Rainfall is heavy, ranging from 150 cm (60 ins) to 300 cm (120 ins) per year. The official language is Dzongkha, spoken mainly in western Bhutan. Written Dzongkha is based on the Tibetan script. The state religion is Mahayana Buddhism, primarily the Drukpa school of the Kagyupa sect, although Nepalese settlers, who comprise about one-quarter of the country's total population, practise Hinduism. The Nepali-speaking Hindus dominate southern Bhutan and are referred to as southern Bhutanese. The national flag (proportions 3 by 2) is divided diagonally from the lower hoist to the upper fly, so forming two triangles, one orange and the other maroon, with a white dragon superimposed in the centre. The capital is Thimphu.

### Recent History

The first hereditary King of Bhutan was installed in December 1907. An Anglo-Bhutanese Treaty, signed in 1910, placed Bhutan's foreign relations under the supervision of the Government of British India. After India became independent, that treaty was replaced in August 1949 by the Indo-Bhutan Treaty of Friendship, whereby Bhutan agrees to seek the advice of the Government of India with regard to its foreign relations, but remains free to decide whether or not to accept such advice. King Jigme Dorji Wangchuk, installed in 1952, established the National Assembly (Tshogdu Chenmo) in 1953 and a Royal Advisory Council (Lodoi Tsokde) in 1965. He formed the country's first Council of Ministers (Lhengye Zhungtshog) in 1968. He died in 1972 and was succeeded by the Western-educated 16-year-old Crown Prince, Jigme Singye Wangchuk. The new King stated his wish to preserve the Indo-Bhutan Treaty and further to strengthen friendship with India. In 1979, however, during the Non-Aligned Conference and later at the UN General Assembly, Bhutan voted in opposition to India, in favour of Chinese policy. In 1983 India and Bhutan signed a new trade agreement concerning overland trade with Bangladesh and Nepal. India raised no objection to Bhutan's decision to negotiate directly with the People's Republic of China over the Bhutan–China border, and discussions between Bhutan and China were begun in 1984 (see below).

When Chinese authority was established in Tibet (Xizang) in 1959, Bhutan granted asylum to more than 6,000 Tibetan refugees. As a result of the discovery that many refugees were allegedly engaged in spying and subversive activities, the Bhutan Government decided in 1976 to disperse them in small groups, introducing a number of Bhutanese families into each settlement. In June 1979 the National Assembly approved a directive establishing the end of the year as a time-limit for the refugees to decide whether to acquire Bhutanese citizenship or accept repatriation to Tibet. By September 1985 most of the Tibetans had chosen Bhutanese citizenship, and the remainder were to be accepted by India. A revised Citizenship Act, adopted by the National Assembly in 1985, confirmed residence in Bhutan in 1958 as a fundamental basis for automatic citizenship (as provided for by the 1958 Nationality Act), but this was to be flexibly interpreted. Provision was also made for citizenship by registration for Nepalese immigrants who had resided in the country for at least 20 years (15 years if employed by the Government) and who could meet linguistic and other tests of commitment to the Bhutanese community.

The violent ethnic Nepalese agitation in India for a 'Gurkha homeland' in the Darjeeling-Kalimpong region during the late 1980s and the populist movement in Nepal in 1988–90 (see chapters on India and Nepal respectively) spread into Bhutan in 1990. Ethnic unrest became apparent in that year when a campaign of intimidation and violence, directed by militant Nepalese against the authority of the Government in Thimphu, was initiated. In September thousands of southern Bhutanese villagers, and Nepalese who entered Bhutan from across the Indian border, organized demonstrations in border towns in southern Bhutan to protest against domination by the indigenous Buddhist Drukpa. The 'anti-nationals' ('ngolops'), as they were called by the Bhutanese authorities, demanded a greater role in the country's political and economic life and were bitterly opposed to official attempts to strengthen the Bhutanese sense of national identity through an increased emphasis on Tibetan-derived, rather than Nepalese, culture and religion (including a formal dress code, Dzongkha as the sole official language, etc.). Bhutanese officials, on the other hand, viewed the southerners as recent arrivals who abused the hospitality of their hosts through acts of violence and the destruction of development infrastructure.

Most southern villagers are relatively recent arrivals from Nepal and many of them have made substantial contributions to the development of the southern hills. The provision of free education and health care by the Bhutan Government acted for many years as a magnet for Nepalese who were struggling to survive in their own country and who came to settle illegally in Bhutan. This population movement was largely ignored by local administrative officials, many of whom accepted incentives to disregard the illegal nature of the influx. The Government's policy of encouraging a sense of national identity, together with rigorous new procedures (introduced in 1988) to check citizenship registration, revealed thousands of illegal residents in southern Bhutan, many of whom had lived there for a decade or more, married local people and raised families. During the ethnic unrest in September 1990, the majority of southern villagers were coerced into participating in the demonstrations by groups of armed and uniformed young men (including many of Nepalese origin who were born in Bhutan). Many of these dissidents, including a large number of students and former members of the Royal Bhutan Army and of the police force, had fled Bhutan in 1989 and early 1990. In 1988–90 a large number of the dissidents resided in the tea gardens and villages adjoining southern Bhutan. Following the demonstrations that took place in Bhutan in September–October 1990, other ethnic Nepalese left Bhutan. In January 1991 some 234 persons, who claimed to be Bhutanese refugees, reportedly arrived in the Jhapa district of eastern Nepal. In September, at the request of the Nepalese Government, the United Nations High Commissioner for Refugees (UNHCR) inaugurated a relief programme providing food and shelter for more than 300 people in the *ad hoc* camps. By December the number of people staying in the camps had risen to about 6,000. The sizes of these camps have been substantially augmented by landless and unemployed Nepalese, who have been expelled from Assam and other eastern states of India. The small and faction-ridden ethnic Nepalese Bhutan People's Party (BPP), which was founded in Kathmandu in 1990 (as a successor to the People's Forum on Democratic Rights, an organization established in 1989), purported to lead the agitation for 'democracy', but presented no clear set of objectives and attracted little support from within Bhutan itself. Schools and bridges became principal targets for arson and looting during 1990–92, and families known to be loyal to the Bhutan Government were robbed of their valuables. Most of the schools in southern Bhutan were closed indefinitely from the end of September 1990, in response to threats to the lives of teachers and students' families, but the majority of pupils affected by these closures were provided with temporary places in schools in northern Bhutan. By mid-1995, despite the continuing security problems, some 74 schools and 89 health facilities had been reopened in the five southern districts.

Since 1988 King Jigme has personally authorized the release of 1,685 militants captured by the authorities. He has stated that, while he has an open mind regarding the question of the pace and extent of political reform (including a willingness to hold discussions with any minority group that has grievances), his Government cannot tolerate pressures for change that are based on intimidation and violence. Although several important leaders of the dissident movement remain in custody, the King has said that they will be released when conditions of law and order return to normal. Some leaders of the BPP have stated that they have no quarrel with the King, but with 'corrupt officials'; on the other hand, certain militants strongly condemn the King as their 'main enemy'.

A number of southern Bhutanese officials (including the Director-General of Power, Bhim Subba, and the Managing Director of the State Trading Corporation, R. B. Basnet) absconded in June 1991 (on the eve of the publication of departmental audits) and went directly to Nepal, where they reportedly sought political asylum on the grounds of repression and atrocities against southern Bhutanese. These accusations were refuted by the Government in Thimphu. The former Secretary-General of the BPP, D. K. Rai, was tried by the High Court in Thimphu in May 1992 and was sentenced to life imprisonment for terrorist acts; a further 35 defendants received lesser sentences. The alleged master-mind behind the ethnic unrest, Teknath Rizal, who had been held in prison since November 1989, came to trial, and was sentenced to life imprisonment in November 1993 after having been found guilty of offences against the Tsawa Sum ('the country, the King, and the people). (Rizal, together with 40 other 'political prisoners', was pardoned by the King and released from prison in December 1999.)

Violence continued in the disturbed areas of Samtse, Chhukha, Tsirang, Sarpang and Gelephu throughout the early 1990s, and companies of trained militia volunteers were posted to these areas to relieve the forces of the regular army. The state government of West Bengal in India, whose territory abuts much of southern Bhutan, reaffirmed in 1991 and 1992 that its land would not be used as a base for any agitation against Bhutan.

In late 1991 and throughout 1992 several thousand legally-settled villagers left southern Bhutan for the newly-established refugee camps in eastern Nepal. The Bhutan Government alleged that the villagers were being enticed or threatened to leave their homes by militants based outside Bhutan, in order to augment the population of the camps and gain international attention; the dissidents, on the other hand, claimed that the Bhutan Government was forcing the villagers to leave. The formation of the Bhutan National Democratic Party (BNDP), including members drawn from supporters of the BPP and with the leading dissident R. B. Basnet as its President, was announced in Kathmandu in February 1992. Incidents of ethnic violence, almost all of which involved infiltration from across the border by ethnic Nepalese who had been trained and dispatched from the camps in Nepal, reportedly diminished substantially in the first half of 1993 as talks continued between Bhutanese and Nepalese government officials regarding proposals to resolve the issues at stake. The Nepalese Government steadfastly refused to consider any solution that did not include the resettlement in Bhutan of all ethnic Nepalese 'refugees' living in the camps (by November 1993 the number of alleged ethnic Nepalese refugees from Bhutan totalled about 85,000). This proposal was rejected by the Bhutan Government, which maintained that the majority of the camp population merely claimed to be from Bhutan, had absconded from Bhutan (and thus forfeited their citizenship, according to Bhutan's citizenship laws), or had voluntarily departed after selling their properties and surrendering their citizenship papers and rights. The apparent deadlock was broken, however, when a joint statement was signed by the Ministers of Home Affairs of Bhutan and Nepal in July, which committed each side to establishing a 'high-level committee' to work towards a settlement and, in particular, to fulfilling the following mandate prior to undertaking any other related activity: to determine the different categories of people claiming to have come from Bhutan in the refugee camps in eastern Nepal (which now numbered eight); and to specify the positions of the two Governments on each of these categories, which would provide the basis for the resolution of the problem. The two countries held their first ministerial-level meeting regarding the issue in Kathmandu in October, at which it was agreed that four categories would be established among the people in the refugee camps — '(i) bona fide Bhutanese who have been evicted forcefully; (ii) Bhutanese who emigrated; (iii) non-Bhutanese; and (iv) Bhutanese who have committed criminal acts.' (These categories are henceforth referred to as Category I, II, III and IV.) Further meetings were held in 1994. Following the election of a new Government in Nepal in November of that year, however, little progress was made at joint ministerial meetings held in the first half of 1995. Nepal's communist Government demanded that all persons in the camps be accepted by Bhutan; the Bhutanese authorities, on the other hand, were prepared to accept only the unconditional return of any bona fide Bhutanese citizens who had left the country involuntarily. Nevertheless, diplomatic exchanges continued in the latter half of the year, despite serious political instability in Nepal.

In January 1996 the new Nepalese Prime Minister, Sher Bahadur Deuba, proposed a resumption of intergovernmental talks, this time at foreign minister level. King Jigme welcomed the proposal, but the seventh round of talks, which was held in April, resulted in demands by Nepal that went beyond the mandate drawn up by the joint ministerial committee in mid-1993. It was widely understood that the Nepalese Government had again reverted to a requisition that all persons in the camps be accepted by Bhutan, regardless of status. This demand remained unacceptable to Bhutanese Government, which stated that the problem of the people in the camps would not have arisen in the first place, if conditions (such as prospects of free food, shelter, health and education, and 'moral support' by the Nepalese authorities for all persons claiming to be Bhutanese refugees) had not been created when there were reportedly only 234 persons in Jhapa making such claims. In addition, the Bhutanese Government stated that even with such conditions attracting people to the refugee camps, a well-organized screening process would have prevented the sheer scale of ethnic Nepalese claiming to be Bhutanese refugees. (Until June 1993 no screening of claimants to refugees status had been enforced on the Indo-Nepalese border). In August 1996 a UNHCR delegation visited Bhutan at the invitation of the authorities and received detailed information from the Bhutan Government regarding the issue of the camps. Talks at ministerial level were held in 1997, without any public communiqué. Following informal meetings during the SAARC summit in Colombo in July 1998, the new Chairman of the Council of Ministers and Head of Government in Bhutan, Lyonpo Jigmi Y. Thinley, held talks with the Nepalese Prime Minister, G. P. Koirala; both leaders stated that their meeting had been 'very positive.' Thinley and Koirala agreed that bilateral negotiations would continue through their respective Foreign Ministers on the issue of persons claiming refugee status in Nepal (who now numbered about 100,000). The 77th National Assembly session, which took place in June–August 1999, unanimously reiterated that the Bhutanese Government accepted full responsibility for any Bhutanese found to have been forcefully evicted (Category I—see above): such persons would be recognized and accepted as genuine refugees, while those responsible for their eviction would be punished. Category II people who had voluntarily emigrated from the country would be dealt with according to the respective immigration and citizenship laws of Bhutan and Nepal; Category III people 'must return to their own country'; and the repatriation of those in Category IV was to be conducted in accordance with the laws of the two countries. At the eighth round of joint ministerial negotiations between Bhutan and Nepal, which were held in Kathmandu in September, the Bhutanese Minister of Foreign Affairs agreed that some of those previously classified as voluntary emigrants (under Category II) might be reclassified as belonging to Category I (according to the Bhutanese Government, the number of people in this category totalled only about 3,000, while the Nepalese Government claimed that all of the camp dwellers had been compelled to leave Bhutan). In 1999 the Bhutan Government was reported to have resettled people from the central and eastern hill regions of Bhutan in the southern areas of the country. No real progress was reported to have been made with regard to the refugee crisis at the ninth round of joint ministerial talks held in Thimphu in February 2000.

From December 1995 terrorist incidents in Bhutan were fewer, coinciding with the adoption of the 'peace march' tactic by persons claiming to be Bhutanese and seeking to travel from Nepal into Bhutan. These marches contined throughout 1996; a small group of marchers actually reached Phuentsholing in mid-August and again in December before being forced to return to India (which has adopted a neutral stance with regard to the refugee issue). The Bhutanese Minister of Home Affairs asserted that those participating in the marches were not Bhutanese, but were non-nationals and emigrants who were attempting to enter the country illegally. A number of isolated bombing incidents occurred in Bhutan during 1998–99, most notably in Thimphu's main stadium in November 1998; the Government claimed that Nepalese militants were responsible for the attacks. In June 1999 it was reported that the Bhutanese police had arrested 80 alleged Bhutanese refugees who were conducting a peaceful demonstration (organized by the Bhutan Gurkha National Liberation Front) in Phuentsholing; the demonstrators claimed to be genuine Bhutanese citizens who were seeking to travel from the camps in Nepal back into Bhutan.

In 1991 'Rongthong' Kinley Dorji (also styled Kuenley or Kunley), a former Bhutanese businessman accused of unpaid loans and of acts against the State, had absconded to Nepal and joined the anti-Government movement. In 1992 he established and became President of the Druk National Congress, claiming human-rights violations in Bhutan. The Bhutan Goverment's 74th Assembly held in July 1996 discussed Kinley Dorji's case at length, and unanimously demanded his extradition from Nepal in conjunction with the Bhutan-Nepal talks. Following the signing of an extradition treaty between India and Bhutan in December, Kinley was arrested by the Indian authorities during a visit to Delhi in April 1997, and remained in detention until June 1998, when he was released on bail while his case was being examined by the Indian courts. Meanwhile, the extradition treaty was read to the 75th Assembly in July 1997, when Kinley Dorji's case was again discussed at length and demands for his return to Bhutan for trial were unanimously supported (as they were also at the 76th Assembly in mid-1998 and the 77th Assembly in mid-1999). At the same time the Assembly resolved that all relatives of alleged 'anti-national militants' in government service should be compulsorily retired as soon as possible. The 75th Assembly also discussed the intrusions into Bhutan's south-eastern border forests by Bodo and Maoist extremists from the neighbouring Indian state of Assam. In September a group of Bodo militants attacked a Bhutanese police station in the south-eastern district of Samdrup Jongkhar, killing four policemen and looting large quantities of arms and ammunition.

During 1997 anti-Government activities (culminating in rallies in south-eastern Bhutan in October) were alleged to have been organized by several lay-preacher (Gomchen) students of Lam Dodrup in Sikkim, India; a number of arrests were subsequently made. Part of the famous historic retreat of Taktsang Monastery was badly damaged by fire under suspicious circumstances in April 1998. Despite the instability of the cliff face on which the monastry is positioned, reconstruction work was expected to commence in late 1999.

Important institutional changes were introduced in mid-1998, whereby King Jigme relinquished his role as Head of Government (while remaining Head of State) in favour of a smaller elected Council of Ministers, which was to enjoy full executive power under the leadership of a Chairman (elected by ministers, on a rotational basis, for a one-year term in office) who would be Head of Government. On 16 June the King informed the members of the existing Council of Ministers that it was to be dissolved on 26 June, and stated that he had issued a royal decree to the Speaker of the National Assembly, which was to be discussed at the pending 76th session. In the decree the King stressed the necessity to promote greater popular participation in the decision-making process, to strengthen the Government's mandate, and to enhance the administration's transparency and efficiency with integral checks and balances. He said that the Council of Ministers should now be restructured as an elected body 'vested with full executive powers', and he presented three key points—(i) All government ministers should henceforth be elected by the National Assembly, with the first election to take place during the 76th session; (ii) a decision should be taken on the exact role and responsibilities of the Council of Ministers; and (iii) the National Assembly should have a mechanism to move a vote of confidence in the King. In elaboration, King Jigme advised that the Council of Ministers should henceforth consist of six elected ministers and all nine members of the Royal Advisory Council, ministers should be elected by secret ballot, candidates should be selected from those who had held senior government posts at the rank of Secretary or above, and a candidate must secure a majority of the votes cast to be considered elected. The portfolios for the elected ministers were to be awarded by the King. A minister's term in office was to be five years, after which he would undergo a vote of confidence in the National Assembly (previously there was no time limit on the tenure of ministerial posts). All decisions adopted by the Council of Ministers were to be based on consensus, and, while the Council was to govern Bhutan with full executive powers, it was also to be obliged to keep the King fully informed on all matters concerning the security and sovereignty of the country. The procedures of the Council of Ministers were to be supervised by a Cabinet Secretary appointed by the Council. The 76th session of the National Assembly voted by secret ballot on six new ministerial nominees; all were successful, but all received some negative votes.

An act to regulate the Council of Ministers, which was framed by a committee comprising members of the Government, clergy and people's representatives of the 20 districts, was presented to the 77th session of the National Assembly in mid-1999 and was subjected to extensive discussion and amendment. The rules as finally endorsed explicitly specified that the King had full power to dissolve the Council of Ministers. Procedures for a confidence vote (with regard to the King) were also drafted by the aforementioned committee and presented to the 77th session of the National Assembly, where members unanimously expressed regret over (and opposition to) the draft and repeatedly requested that King Jigme withdraw the proposal. Following a further earnest plea by the King, however, a key draft provision that a confidence vote regarding the monarch should only be placed on the agenda of an assembly session if a minimum of 50% of the districts requested it, was amended to allow the initiative if supported by at least one-third of the assembly members. The 77th session also agreed that ministers should serve a maximum of two consecutive five-year terms.

King Jigme told the Council of Ministers at a special sitting in mid-August 1999 (held for the formal change of Chairman) that it should streamline the Government and create mobility in the higher levels of the civil service when staffing ministries and other organizations, and that it must be responsive to the needs of the people. He also stressed that while governance was the responsibility of the Council of Ministers, the Royal Advisory Council was empowered to ensure that all the policies, laws and resolutions passed by the National Assembly were implemented by the Government. The outgoing Chairman of the Council, Lyonpo Jigmi Yozer Thinley, stated that all the elements were now in place for a democratic system of decision-making, while government was being institutionalized and made more accountable and transparent.

The activities of the militant 'anti-nationals' were unanimously condemned at the 76th session of the National Assembly in mid-1998, but the most pressing security issue was judged to be the perceived threat from the presence of Assamese tribal (Bodo) and Maoist (United Liberation Front of Assam—ULFA) militants, who had established military training bases in the jungle border regions of south-eastern Bhutan. Particular concern was expressed regarding the Indian military incursions into Bhutanese territory in an attempt to expel the militants. A serious incident, which took place in May in Sarpang and was reported to have involved 165 armed Indian soldiers, was discussed during the session, and was to be investigated by the Bhutanese and Indian authorities. In late November Bhutan and India launched an unprecedented joint military offensive against tribal insurgents, following an attack on a Bhutanese army convoy in Assam by Bodo guerrillas which left four soldiers dead. In mid-1999 the Minister of Home Affairs reported that talks with ULFA leaders (in November 1998 and May 1999) had elicited the response that members of the ULFA had been forced to enter Bhutanese territory in 1992, but that they were not ready to leave Bhutanese territory for at least another 18 months. They asserted that they were determined to fight until independence for Assam was achieved, but offered to reduce their military presence in Bhutan. The Bhutan Government reiterated to the ULFA leaders that its concern was at the very presence of any number of armed militants on Bhutanese soil. After detailed discussion, assembly members decided that all supplies of food and other essentials to the ULFA and Bodo militants must be stopped, that any Bhutanese who assisted the militants should be punished according to the National Security Act, and that discussions should continue with the ULFA to seek a peaceful withdrawal of these foreign forces from Bhutan.

Reflecting the increasing complexities of contemporary administration, the 77th Assembly also passed an unprecedented number of acts in mid-1999 to enhance the prevailing legal framework relating to telecommunications (providing for the creation of a state-owned public corporation, Bhutan Telecom, from the existing Telecommunications Division), the postal sector (enabling Bhutan Post to become an autonomous public-sector corporation), bankruptcy (giving a contemporary context for the rights and duties of borrowers and lenders), property (setting a legal framework for the management of loans, mortgages and related securities and financial services), legal deposit, municipalities (establishing legal authority for municipalities to enforce rules relating to urban development), and road safety. Further indications of the modernization of Bhutan were the inauguration of (limited) television and internet services in mid-1999, and the election of nine women to attend the 1999 session of the National Assembly. At the end of 1999 a government-endorsed report proposed the rationalization of government under 10 ministries; the proposals were to be implemented during 2000. In addition, in late 1999 two new government agencies—the Office of Legal Affairs and the National Employment Board—were established, and a new Department of Aid and Debt Management was created. Among the proposed legislative acts to be discussed by the National Assembly in mid-2000 was one regarding the environment and another regarding judicial procedure.

Following the relaxation of many policies in the People's Republic of China since 1978, and looking forward to improved relations between India and China, Bhutan has moved cautiously to assert positions on regional and world affairs that take into account those of India but are not necessarily identical to them. Discussions with China regarding the formal delineation and demarcation of Bhutan's northern border were begun in 1984, and substantive negotiations began in 1986. At the 12th round of talks, held in Beijing in December 1998, the Foreign Ministers of Bhutan and China signed an official interim agreement (the first agreement ever to be signed between the two countries) to maintain peace and tranquillity in the Bhutan–China border area and to observe the status quo of the border as it was prior to May 1959, pending a formal agreement on the border alignment. The disputed area, which was 1,128 sq km during the early rounds of bilateral talks, has since been reduced to 269 sq km in three areas in the north-west of Bhutan. Demarcation of Bhutan's southern border has been agreed with India, except for small sectors in the middle zone (between Sarpang and Gelephu) and in the eastern zone of Arunachal Pradesh and the *de facto* Sino-Indian border.

Bhutan has asserted itself as a fully sovereign, independent state, becoming a member of the UN in 1971 and of the Non-aligned Movement in 1973. By 1993 Bhutan had established diplomatic relations with 17 countries and with the European Union, and maintained diplomatic missions at the UN in New York and Geneva, in New Delhi, Dhaka and Kuwait; it is also represented by several honorary consulates.

In 1983 Bhutan was an enthusiastic founder-member of the South Asian Regional Co-operation (SARC) organization, with Bangladesh, India, Maldives, Nepal, Pakistan and Sri Lanka. In 1985 Bhutan was host to the first meeting of ministers of foreign affairs from SARC member countries, which agreed to give their grouping the formal title of South Asian Association for Regional Co-operation (SAARC, see p. 259). Bhutan's international profile is expected to be raised when it hosts the SAARC summit meeting in 2002.

## Government

Bhutan's state system is a modified form of constitutional monarchy, without a formal, written constitution. The system of government is unusual in that power is shared by the monarchy (assisted by the Royal Advisory Council—Lodoi Tsokde), the Council of Ministers (Lhengye Zhungtshog), the National Assembly (Tshogdu Chenmo) and the Head Abbot (Je Khempo) of Bhutan's 3,000–4,000 Buddhist monks.

Important institutional changes were introduced at the 76th session of the National Assembly in July 1998. In accordance with a royal decree, King Jigme relinquished his role as Head of Government (while remaining Head of State) in favour of an elected Council of Ministers, which was to enjoy full executive powers (although the King was to retain authority with regard to strategic security issues) and was to be headed by a Chairman (elected by ministers, on a rotational basis, for a one-year period), who would be Head of Government. The new Council of Ministers was subsequently elected by the National Assembly by secret ballot and the portfolios of the elected ministers were awarded by the King. The term in office of a minister was to be five years, after which he would be obliged to undergo a vote of confidence in the National Assembly. In 1999 the National Assembly agreed that ministers should serve a maximum of two consecutive five-year terms.

The National Assembly, which serves a three-year term, has 150 members, including 105 directly elected by adult suffrage. Ten seats in the Assembly are reserved for religious bodies, while the remainder are occupied by officials, ministers and members of the Royal Advisory Council.

## Defence

The strength of the Royal Bhutanese Army, which is under the direct command of the King, is officially said to number just over 6,000, and is based on voluntary recruitment augmented by a form of conscription. Army training facilities are provided by an Indian military training team. Although India is not directly responsible for the country's defence, the Indian Government has indicated that any act of aggression against Bhutan would be regarded as an act of aggression against India. Militia courses, lasting up to two years, have been provided since 1990 with the aim of establishing a 'home guard' corps to protect public and government installations and facilities.

## Economic Affairs

In 1997, according to estimates by the World Bank, Bhutan's gross national product (GNP), measured at average 1995–97 prices, was US $315m., equivalent to $430 per head. In 1990–97 GNP per head increased, in real terms, at an average annual rate of 2.0%. During the same period the population increased by an average rate of 2.9% per year. Bhutan's gross domestic product (GDP) increased, in real terms, at an average annual rate of an estimated 5.9% in 1990–98. GDP grew by 6.0% in 1996, by 7.3% in 1997 and by an estimated 5.8% in 1998.

Agriculture (including livestock and forestry) contributed an estimated 36.7% of GDP in 1998. About 94% of the economically active population were employed in agriculture in that year. The principal sources of revenue in the agricultural sector are apples, oranges and cardamom. Timber production is also important; about 60% of the total land area is covered by forest. Agricultural GDP increased at an average annual rate of an estimated 3.2% in 1990–98.

Industry (including mining, manufacturing, utilities and construction) employed only about 1% of the labour force in 1981/82, but contributed an estimated 35.1% of GDP in 1998. The production of low-cost electricity by the Chhukha hydroelectric project (see below) helped to stimulate growth in the industrial sector in the 1990s. Industrial GDP increased at an average annual rate of an estimated 9.3% in 1990–98.

Mining and quarrying contributed an estimated 2.4% of GDP in 1998. Calcium carbide was the major mineral export in 1997 (contributing about 12.8% of total export revenue). Gypsum, coal, limestone, slate and dolomite are also mined. Mining GDP increased by an average rate of an estimated 12.3% per year in 1990–98.

Manufacturing contributed an estimated 11.1% of GDP in 1998. The most important sector is cement production. Commercial production began at a calcium carbide plant and a ferro-alloy plant at Pasakha, near Phuentsholing, in 1988 and 1995, respectively. Bhutan also has some small-scale manufacturers, producing, for example, textiles, soap, matches, candles and carpets. Manufacturing GDP increased at an average annual rate of an estimated 11.1% in 1990–98.

The services sector, which employed only about 3.4% of the labour force in 1981/82, contributed an estimated 28.2% of GDP in 1998. The GDP of the services sector increased at an average annual rate of an estimated 7.4% in 1990–98.

Energy is derived principally from hydroelectric power. The Chhukha hydroelectric project, with a generating capacity of about 338 MW, began production in 1986 and was formally inaugurated in 1988. The project provides about 40% of Bhutan's national revenue. The Indian-financed Tala hydroelectric project, when completed in 2004 at an estimated cost of Nu 20,000m., was to have an installed capacity of 1,020 MW. In 1997 the cost of imports of diesel oil and petroleum totalled Nu 236.2m. (equivalent to 4.7% of total import costs).

In the financial year ending 30 June 1999, according to official projections, Bhutan recorded a visible trade deficit of US $56.4m., and there was a deficit of $86.9m. on the current account of the balance of payments. In 1997/98 the principal source of imports (70.5%) was India, which was also the principal market for exports (94.5%). The principal exports in 1997 were electricity, calcium carbide and cement. Exports of electric energy to India commenced in 1988, with the inauguration of the Chhukha hydroelectric project. The principal imports in 1997 were telecommunications equipment, rice and diesel oil.

The 1998/99 budget envisaged a deficit of Nu 200m. (revenue Nu 6,844m., expenditure Nu 7,044m.). Bhutan's total external debt amounted to US $89.3m. at the end of 1997, of which $87.0m. was long-term public debt. In that year the cost of debt-servicing was equivalent to 5.1% of the value of exports of goods and services. For 1998/99, grants from the Government of India provided an estimated 33.2% of total budgetary revenue, and grants from the UN and other international agencies amounted to 21.6%. The average annual rate of inflation was 11.6% in 1990–94; consumer prices rose by by 8.3% in 1996, by an estimated 7.0% in 1997 and by an estimated 12.1% in 1998.

Bhutan is a member of the South Asian Association for Regional Co-operation (SAARC, see p. 259), which seeks to improve regional co-operation, particularly in economic development.

The Seventh Plan (1992–97) asserted seven main objectives: self-reliance, with emphasis on internal resource mobilization; sustainability, with emphasis on environmental protection; private-sector development; decentralization and popular participation; human resources' development; balanced development in all districts; and national security. The Eighth Plan (1997–2002) further refined the seven objectives of the Seventh Plan and explicitly added another: 'the preservation and promotion of cultural and traditional values'. During these five years, GDP was expected to grow at an average annual rate of 6.7%, while the population growth rate was projected to decline to 2.56%. Revenue, which was forecast to reach Nu 15,912m. during the plan, was to cover 53% of the total plan outlay of Nu 30,000m. The agriculture sector was projected to grow by 2.5% per year over the plan period through productivity gains and horticultural development. Exports to India and third countries were expected to increase by 15% and 10%, respectively, by 2002. The guiding goal was declared as the establishment of sustainability in development, while balancing achievements with the popular sense of contentment. Core areas were to be the further development of hydro-power (long-term potential was assessed at 20,000 MW) and further industrialization. The Plan also provided for further development of the infrastructure (18.6% of outlay) and social services (22%), human resource development (10.7%), and renewable natural resources. Development partners meeting in Geneva, Switzerland, in January 1997 pledged US $450m. (about 50% of the projected plan outlay). The mid-term review of the Eighth Plan, which was carried out in February 2000, was to serve as the basis for the Ninth Plan (2002–07), which was expected to give greater autonomy to local bodies with regard to project development.

Multilateral investment in Bhutan's financial sector was agreed by the Government for the first time in September 1998, when the Asian Development Bank and Citibank purchased shares in the Bhutan National Bank. Two major economic developments were implemented in Bhutan in 1999: a proper personal income tax (to be levied only on the wealthier inhabitants) was introduced, and the country was opened up to foreign investment (foreign investors were to be permitted up to 51% ownership in a joint venture).

## Social Welfare

In December 1997 there were 28 hospitals (including one indigenous and five leprosy hospitals, providing general health services also), with a total of 865 beds (one for every 737 inhabitants, on the basis of the estimated 1998 population figure), and there were 101 doctors (one for every 6,380 inhabitants) and 1,093 village health workers in the country. Because of a shortage of medical personnel and a lack of funds, local dispensaries are being converted into basic health units (of which there were 145 by the end of 1997), providing basic medical services. In 1990 the World Health Organization declared that universal child immunization had been achieved in Bhutan. Malaria and tuberculosis are, however, still widespread. The budget for the financial year 1998/99 allocated an estimated Nu 883m. (12.5% of total projected expenditure) to health. A national pension plan was due to be implemented in mid-2000.

## Education

Education is not compulsory. Pre-primary education usually lasts for one year. Primary education begins at six years of age and lasts for seven years. Secondary education, beginning at the age of 13, lasts for a further four years, comprising two cycles of two years each. Virtually free education is available (nominal fees are demanded), but there are insufficient facilities to accommodate all school-age children. In order to accommodate additional children, community schools (established in 1989 as 'extended classrooms'—ECRs, but renamed, as above, in 1991) were set up as essentially one-teacher schools for basic primary classes, whence children were to be 'streamed' to other schools. In 1988 the total enrolment at primary schools was equivalent to an estimated 26% of children in the relevant age-group (31% of boys; 20% of girls), while the comparable ratio for secondary schools was only 5% (boys 7%; girls 2%). All schools are co-educational. English is the language of instruction and Dzongkha is a compulsory subject. Bhutan has no mission schools. Since 1988 seven privately-operated schools have been established (the majority in Thimphu); these schools are under the supervision of the Department of Education. Owing to a shortage of qualified staff (despite the existence of two teacher-training institutes with a combined enrolment of 660 students in 1999), many Indian teachers are employed. In April 1999 the total number of enrolled pupils was 107,632, and the total number of teachers was 3,554. In 1999 there were more than 320 educational institutions under the supervision of the Department of Education, including 254 community and primary schools, 51 junior high schools, 21 high schools, one degree college and nine other post-secondary institutions. Some Bhutanese students were receiving higher education abroad. The 1998/99 budget allocated an estimated Nu 912m. (12.9% of total projected expenditure) to education. In 1995, according to UNESCO estimates, the rate of adult illiteracy in Bhutan averaged 57.8% (males 43.8%; females 71.9%).

## Public Holidays

**2000 and 2001:** The usual Buddhist holidays are observed, as well as the Birthday of HM Jigme Singye Wangchuck (11 November), the movable Hindu feast of Dussehra and the National Day of Bhutan (17 December).

## Weights and Measures

The metric system is in operation.

# Statistical Survey

Source (unless otherwise stated): Royal Government of Bhutan, Thimphu.

## Area and Population

**AREA, POPULATION AND DENSITY**

| | |
|---|---|
| Area (sq km) | 46,500* |
| Population (official estimates)† | |
| 1997 | 618,643 |
| 1998 | 637,821 |
| 1999 | 657,594 |
| Density (per sq km) in 1999 | 14.1 |

* 17,954 sq miles.

† These figures (which are based on the 1995 estimate of 582,000 and assume an annual population growth rate of 3.1%) are much lower than former estimates. It was previously reported that a census in 1969 enumerated a population of 931,514, and a 1980 census recorded a total of 1,165,000. On the basis of the latter figure, a mid-1988 population of 1,375,400 was projected. Other figures in this Survey are derived from the earlier, higher estimates of Bhutan's population.

**Capital:** Thimphu (estimated population 27,000 at 1 July 1990).

**POPULATION OF DISTRICTS*** (mid-1985 estimates, based on 1980 census)

| | |
|---|---|
| Bumthang | 23,842 |
| Dagana | 28,352 |
| Gasa† | 16,907 |
| Gelephu | 111,283 |
| Ha | 16,715 |
| Lhuentse | 39,635 |
| Mongar | 73,239 |
| Paro | 46,615 |
| Pemagatshel | 37,141 |
| Punakha† | 16,700 |
| Samdrup Jongkhar | 73,044 |
| Samtse | 172,109 |
| Zhemgang | 44,516 |
| Thimphu | 58,660 |
| Trashigang | 177,718 |
| Trongsa | 26,017 |
| Tsirang | 108,807 |
| Wangdue Phodrang | 47,152 |
| **Total rural population** | 1,119,452 |
| **Total urban population** | 167,823 |
| **Total** | 1,286,275 |

* The above figures are approximate, and predate the creation of a new district, Chhukha, in 1987. Chhukha has an estimated total population of about 13,372 (based on the figure of 3,343 households, with an estimated average of four persons per household), who were formerly included in Samtse, Paro or Thimphu districts. The above figures also predate the creation of a further two new districts, Gasa (previously within Punakha) and Trashi Yangtse (previously within Trashigang), in 1992.

† Gasa and Punakha were merged into a single district, which was to be known as Punakha, in 1987.

**BIRTHS AND DEATHS** (UN estimates, annual averages)

| | 1980–85 | 1985–90 | 1990–95 |
|---|---|---|---|
| Birth rate (per 1,000) | 41.5 | 40.9 | 39.8 |
| Death rate (per 1,000) | 17.6 | 14.4 | 11.5 |

Source: UN, *World Population Prospects: The 1998 Revision*.

**Infant mortality rate** (1997): 87 per 1,000 live births (Source: UNDP, *Human Development Report 1999*).

**LIFE EXPECTANCY** (UN estimates, years at birth)

57.6 (males 56.5; females 59.0) in 1990–95. Source: UN, *World Population Prospects: The 1998 Revision*.

**ECONOMICALLY ACTIVE POPULATION** (estimates, '000 persons, 1981/82)

| | |
|---|---|
| Agriculture, etc. | 613 |
| Industry | 6 |
| Trade | 9 |
| Public services | 22 |
| **Total** | 650 |

**1984** (estimates, '000 persons): Agriculture, hunting, forestry and fishing 629; Total 721 (Source: UN, *Statistical Yearbook for Asia and the Pacific*).

## Agriculture

**PRINCIPAL CROPS** (FAO estimates, '000 metric tons)

| | 1996 | 1997 | 1998 |
|---|---|---|---|
| Rice (paddy) | 50 | 50 | 50 |
| Wheat | 5 | 5 | 5 |
| Barley | 4 | 4 | 4 |
| Maize | 39 | 39 | 39 |
| Millet | 7 | 7 | 7 |
| Other cereals | 7 | 7 | 7 |
| Potatoes | 34 | 34 | 34 |
| Other roots and tubers | 22 | 22 | 22 |
| Pulses | 2 | 2 | 2 |
| Vegetables and melons | 10 | 10 | 10 |
| Oranges | 58 | 58 | 58 |
| Other fruits (excl. melons) | 6 | 6 | 6 |

Source: FAO, *Production Yearbook*.

**LIVESTOCK** (FAO estimates, '000 head, year ending September)

| | 1996 | 1997 | 1998 |
|---|---|---|---|
| Horses | 30 | 30 | 30 |
| Mules | 10 | 10 | 10 |
| Asses | 18 | 18 | 18 |
| Cattle | 435 | 435 | 435 |
| Buffaloes | 4 | 4 | 4 |
| Pigs | 75 | 75 | 75 |
| Sheep | 59 | 59 | 59 |
| Goats | 42 | 42 | 42 |

Source: FAO, *Production Yearbook*.

**Yaks** ('000 head): 35 in 1993; 39* in 1994; 40† in 1995.
**Poultry** ('000 head): 170 in 1993; 166* in 1994; 171† in 1995.

* Provisional. † Estimate.
Source: IMF, *Bhutan – Selected Issues* (February 1997).

**LIVESTOCK PRODUCTS** (FAO estimates, '000 metric tons)

| | 1996 | 1997 | 1998 |
|---|---|---|---|
| Beef and veal | 6 | 6 | 6 |
| Pigmeat | 1 | 1 | 1 |
| Other meat | 1 | 1 | 1 |
| Cows' milk | 29 | 29 | 29 |
| Buffaloes' milk | 3 | 3 | 3 |
| Cheese | 2 | n.a. | n.a. |
| Cattle and buffalo hides | 1 | 1 | 1 |

Source: FAO, *Production Yearbook*.

# Forestry

**ROUNDWOOD REMOVALS** ('000 cubic metres, excl. bark)

| | 1995 | 1996 | 1997 |
|---|---|---|---|
| Sawlogs, veneer logs and logs for sleepers | 18 | 18 | 18 |
| Other industrial wood | 27 | 27 | 27 |
| Fuel wood | 1,463 | 1,498 | 1,539 |
| **Total** | 1,508 | 1,543 | 1,584 |

**Sawnwood production** ('000 cubic metres, incl. railway sleepers): 18 in 1995; 18 in 1996; 18 in 1997.

Source: FAO, *Yearbook of Forest Products*.

# Fishing

(FAO estimates, metric tons, live weight)

| | 1995 | 1996 | 1997 |
|---|---|---|---|
| Total catch (freshwater fishes) | 310 | 300 | 300 |

Source: FAO, *Yearbook of Fishery Statistics*.

# Mining

(metric tons, unless otherwise indicated, year ending 30 June)

| | 1995/96 | 1996/97 | 1997/98 |
|---|---|---|---|
| Dolomite | 249,253 | 276,700 | 240,300 |
| Limestone | 266,591 | 297,900 | 376,700 |
| Gypsum | 52,102 | 66,600 | 62,300 |
| Coal | 67,994 | 63,900 | 53,200 |
| Marble chips (sq ft) | 12,841 | 35,400 | n.a. |
| Slate (sq ft) | 92,148 | 44,100 | 48,400 |
| Quartzite | 50,226 | 98,100 | 39,500 |
| Talc | 9,158 | 9,200 | 11,400 |
| Iron ore | 5,516 | 4,000 | 5,000 |
| Pink shale/quartzite | 5,112 | 1,400 | 2,700 |

Source: Geology and Mines Division, Ministry of Trade and Industry, Royal Government of Bhutan.

# Industry

**GROSS SALES AND OUTPUT OF SELECTED INDUSTRIES**
(million ngultrum)

| | 1996 | 1997 | 1998* |
|---|---|---|---|
| Penden Cement Authority | 209.5 | 265.5 | 564.7 |
| Bhutan Ferro Alloys | 497.1 | 522.9 | 488.4 |
| Bhutan Fruit Products | 133.2 | 107.2 | 112.3 |
| Army Welfare Project† | 198.6 | 232.0 | 237.9 |
| Bhutan Carbide and Chemicals | 561.2 | 560.3 | 583.6 |
| Bhutan Board Products | 348.0 | 428.7 | 383.8 |

* Provisional figures.

† Manufacturer of alcoholic beverages.

Source: Ministry of Trade and Industry, Royal Government of Bhutan.

**Electric energy** (million kWh, year ending 30 June): 1,972.2 in 1995/96; 1,838.4 in 1996/97; 1,800.0 in 1997/98.

**Revenue from the Chhukha Hydroelectric Project** (million ngultrum): 857.6 (Internal consumption 110.0, Exports 747.6) in 1996; 1,404.8 (Internal consumption 116.7, Exports 1,288.1) in 1997; 1,489.6 (Internal consumption 150.8, Exports 1,338.8) in 1998.

Source: Department of Power, Royal Government of Bhutan.

# Finance

**CURRENCY AND EXCHANGE RATES**

**Monetary Units**

100 chetrum (Ch) = 1 ngultrum (Nu).

**Sterling, Dollar and Euro Equivalents** (30 September 1999)

£1 sterling = 71.80 ngultrum;
US $1 = 43.61 ngultrum;
€1 = 46.51 ngultrum;
1,000 ngultrum = £13.93 = $22.93 = €21.50.

**Average Exchange Rate** (ngultrum per US $)

| | |
|---|---|
| 1996 | 35.433 |
| 1997 | 36.313 |
| 1998 | 41.259 |

Note: The ngultrum is at par with the Indian rupee, which also circulates freely within Bhutan. The foregoing figures relate to the official rate of exchange, which is applicable to government-related transactions alone. Since April 1992 there has also been a market rate of exchange, which values foreign currencies approximately 20% higher than the official rate of exchange.

**BUDGET** (estimates, million ngultrum, year ending 30 June)

| Revenue | 1996/97 | 1997/98* | 1998/99† |
|---|---|---|---|
| Domestic revenue | 2,425 | 3,079 | 3,094 |
| Tax | 869 | 1,246 | 1,285 |
| Non-tax | 1,556 | 1,832 | 1,809 |
| Grants from Government of India | 948 | 1,335 | 2,271 |
| Grants from UN and other international agencies | 1,284 | 820 | 1,479 |
| **Total** | 4,657 | 5,234 | 6,844 |

| Expenditure | 1996/97 | 1997/98* | 1998/99† |
|---|---|---|---|
| General public services | 1,427 | 1,562 | 1,985 |
| Economic services | 2,205 | 1,834 | 3,187 |
| Agriculture and irrigation | 430 | 199 | 320 |
| Animal husbandry | 135 | 78 | 149 |
| Forestry | 122 | 132 | 190 |
| Industries, mining, trade and commerce | 36 | 34 | 74 |
| Public works, roads and housing | 668 | 502 | 626 |
| Transport and communication | 252 | 250 | 161 |
| Power | 562 | 639 | 1,667 |
| Social services | 999 | 1,119 | 1,827 |
| Education | 517 | 543 | 912 |
| Health | 469 | 558 | 883 |
| Urban development and municipal corporations | 13 | 17 | 32 |
| Net lending | 327 | 231 | 45 |
| **Total expenditure and net lending** | 4,958 | 4,745 | 7,044 |

* Provisional figures. † Projected figures.

Source: IMF, *Bhutan—Statistical Annex* (July 1999).

**FOREIGN EXCHANGE RESERVES** (at 30 June)

| | 1997 | 1998 | 1999† |
|---|---|---|---|
| Indian rupee reserves (million Indian rupees) | 958.6 | 1,629.1 | 3,520.4 |
| Royal Monetary Authority | 39.2 | 152.8 | 222.7 |
| Bank of Bhutan | 913.8 | 1,404.4 | 2,795.6 |
| Bhutan National Bank | 5.7 | 72.0 | 502.1 |
| Convertible currency reserves (US $ million) | 145.4 | 177.2 | 197.5 |
| Royal Monetary Authority* | 137.8 | 171.0 | 187.8 |
| Bank of Bhutan | 6.7 | 4.0 | 6.3 |
| Bhutan National Bank | 0.8 | 2.2 | 3.4 |
| Royal Insurance Corporation of Bhutan | — | — | 0.1 |

* Includes tranche position in the International Monetary Fund.

† Figures at 31 March.

Source: Royal Monetary Authority of Bhutan.

**MONEY SUPPLY** (million ngultrum at 31 December)

| | 1996 | 1997 | 1998 |
|---|---|---|---|
| Currency outside banks* | 422.5 | 720.9 | 768.8 |
| Demand deposits at the Bank of Bhutan | 1,651.6 | 1,447.2 | 1,860.4 |
| **Total money†** | 2,098.3 | 2,196.5 | 2,792.0 |

* Including an estimate for Indian rupees.
† Including non-monetary deposits with the Royal Monetary Authority by financial institutions.

Source: Royal Monetary Authority of Bhutan.

**COST OF LIVING**
(Consumer Price Index at 31 December; base: 1979 = 100)

| | 1996 | 1997 | 1998 |
|---|---|---|---|
| **All items** (excl. rent) | 474.1 | 501.2 | 561.7 |

Source: Central Statistical Office of the Planning Commission, Royal Government of Bhutan.

**NATIONAL ACCOUNTS** (million ngultrum at current prices)

**Expenditure on the Gross Domestic Product**

| | 1994 | 1995 | 1996 |
|---|---|---|---|
| Government final consumption expenditure | 2,106.0 | 2,727.0 | 3,445.0 |
| Private final consumption expenditure | 3,136.0 | 3,147.0 | 4,224.0 |
| Increase in stocks | 229.3 | 155.7 | 157.3 |
| Gross fixed capital formation | 3,871.1 | 4,416.5 | 5,046.4 |
| **Total domestic expenditure** | 9,342.4 | 10,446.2 | 12,872.7 |
| Exports of goods and services | 2,508.0 | 3,712.0 | 3,973.0 |
| *Less* Imports of goods and services | 3,349.0 | 4,190.0 | 5,133.0 |
| **GDP in purchasers' values** | 8,501.4 | 9,968.2 | 11,712.7 |
| **GDP at constant 1990 prices** | 5,917.8 | 6,362.3 | 6,767.6 |

**GDP in purchasers' values** (million ngultrum): 14,477 in 1997; 16,420 in 1998.

Source: IMF, *International Financial Statistics*.

**Gross Domestic Product by Economic Activity**

| | 1996 | 1997* | 1998† |
|---|---|---|---|
| Agriculture, forestry and livestock | 4,538.0 | 5,276.0 | 5,975.9 |
| Mining and quarrying | 269.8 | 308.7 | 385.9 |
| Manufacturing | 1,393.4 | 1,588.5 | 1,810.9 |
| Electricity | 1,101.6 | 1,729.5 | 1,784.9 |
| Construction | 1,040.0 | 1,466.4 | 1,730.4 |
| Trade, restaurants and hotels | 903.5 | 1,014.4 | 1,146.2 |
| Transport, storage and communications | 855.8 | 1,022.6 | 1,216.9 |
| Finance, insurance and real estate | 441.9 | 729.2 | 838.6 |
| Community, social and personal services | 1,013.7 | 1,362.7 | 1,398.2 |
| **Sub-total** | 11,557.7 | 14,498.0 | 16,287.9 |
| *Less* Imputed bank service charges | 203.0 | 526.9 | 627.0 |
| **GDP at factor cost** | 11,354.7 | 13,971.1 | 15,660.9 |
| **GDP at constant 1980 factor cost** | 3,094.6 | 3,320.1 | 3,514.1 |

* Adjusted figures.
† Projected figures.

Source: Royal Monetary Authority of Bhutan.

**BALANCE OF PAYMENTS** (US $ million, year ending 30 June)

| | 1996/97 | 1997/98* | 1998/99† |
|---|---|---|---|
| Merchandise exports f.o.b.‡ | 99.3 | 111.3 | 108.8 |
| Merchandise imports c.i.f.‡ | –131.2 | –136.1 | –165.2 |
| **Trade balance** | –31.9 | –24.8 | –56.4 |
| Services and transfers: | | | |
| Receipts | 27.8 | 45.2 | 47.7 |
| Payments | –52.2 | –66.9 | –78.2 |
| **Current balance** | –56.4 | –46.5 | –86.9 |
| Grants | 74.4 | 85.4 | 124.8 |
| Loans (net) | 5.4 | 4.4 | 2.3 |
| Foreign direct investment | — | — | 1.1 |
| Net errors and omissions | –1.2 | 2.1 | — |
| **Total** (net monetary movements) | 22.2 | 45.4 | 41.4 |

* Provisional figures.
† Projected figures.
‡ On a calendar year basis.

Source: IMF, *Bhutan—Statistical Annex* (July 1999).

**OFFICIAL DEVELOPMENT ASSISTANCE** (US $ million)

| | 1993 | 1994 | 1995 |
|---|---|---|---|
| Bilateral donors | 43.5 | 57.3 | 55.3 |
| Multilateral donors | 22.3 | 19.2 | 18.5 |
| **Total** | 65.8 | 76.5 | 73.8 |
| Grants | 62.0 | 72.0 | 68.5 |
| Loans | 3.8 | 4.5 | 5.3 |
| Per caput assistance (US $) | 41.2 | 47.4 | 45.1 |

Source: UN, *Statistical Yearbook for Asia and the Pacific*.

**SELECTED COMMODITIES** (million ngultrum)

| Imports c.i.f. | 1995 | 1996 | 1997 |
|---|---|---|---|
| Wood charcoal | n.a. | 122.3 | 139.6 |
| Telecommunications equipment | n.a. | 302.0 | 491.0 |
| Beer | n.a. | 66.0 | 86.3 |
| Coal | n.a. | 44.6 | 103.3 |
| Diesel oil | 136.1 | 138.8 | 163.2 |
| Petroleum | 64.0 | 67.4 | 73.0 |
| Rice | 217.3 | 209.1 | 215.3 |
| Wheat | 39.3 | 89.0 | 100.0 |
| Vegetable fats and oils | 134.7 | 134.4 | 121.1 |
| Cotton fabric | 41.9 | 38.2 | n.a. |
| Industrial machinery | 142.0 | 77.5 | 54.3 |
| Tyres for buses and trucks | 37.5 | 34.5 | n.a. |
| Iron and steel | 115.4 | 109.6 | 117.0 |
| Electricity | 10.7 | 7.6 | n.a. |
| **Total** (incl. others) | 3,802.3 | 4,250.0 | 4,980.0 |

| Exports f.o.b. | 1995 | 1996 | 1997 |
|---|---|---|---|
| Electricity | 721.9 | 747.6 | 1,290.0 |
| Calcium carbide | 497.9 | 533.0 | 546.3 |
| Cement | 278.4 | 253.0 | 371.4 |
| Particle board | 329.1 | 286.0 | 329.0 |
| Non-coniferous plywood | 32.8 | 2.2 | n.a. |
| Sawn logs (hard) | 71.8 | 79.1 | 78.1 |
| Sawn timber (soft) | 60.7 | 27.1 | 76.5 |
| Cardamom | 73.8 | 68.2 | 36.9 |
| Wheat and flour | 23.8 | 58.0 | n.a. |
| Mixed fruit/vegetable juice | 119.5 | 86.7 | 7.8 |
| Coal (bituminous) | n.a. | 19.9 | 25.6 |
| Rum | n.a. | 65.0 | 58.8 |
| **Total** (incl. others) | 3,349.1 | 3,553.8 | 4,270.0 |

**PRINCIPAL TRADING PARTNERS**
(estimates, US $ million, year ending 30 June)

| Imports c.i.f. | 1995/96 | 1996/97 | 1997/98 |
|---|---|---|---|
| India | 81.4 | 85.8 | 96.0 |
| Other countries | 29.5 | 45.5 | 40.1 |
| **Total** | 110.9 | 131.3 | 136.1 |

| Exports f.o.b. | 1995/96 | 1996/97 | 1997/98 |
|---|---|---|---|
| India | 89.8 | 90.2 | 105.3 |
| Other countries | 7.9 | 9.1 | 6.1 |
| **Total** | 97.7 | 99.4 | 111.4 |

Source: Royal Monetary Authority of Bhutan.

# Transport

**ROAD TRAFFIC**

In 1997 there were 2,559 registered, roadworthy vehicles—764 light four-wheeled vehicles, 1,170 two-wheeled vehicles (motor cycles and scooters), 442 heavy vehicles (trucks, buses, bulldozers, etc.) and 183 taxis. Source: Central Statistical Office, Ministry of Planning.

**CIVIL AVIATION** (traffic, year ending 30 June)

| | 1985 | 1986 | 1987 |
|---|---|---|---|
| Kilometres flown ('000) | 152 | 201 | n.a. |
| Passengers | 5,928 | 7,776 | 8,700 |
| Passenger-km ('000) | 3,349 | 4,381 | n.a. |

Paying passengers: 19,608 in 1993, 21,115 in 1994, 22,286 in 1995.
Revenue (million ngultrum, year ending 30 June): 241.5 in 1992/93, 188.3 in 1993/94, 210.0 in 1994/95.

Source: Central Statistical Office, Ministry of Planning, Royal Government of Bhutan.

# Tourism

**FOREIGN VISITORS BY COUNTRY OF ORIGIN***

| | 1995 | 1996 | 1997 |
|---|---|---|---|
| Australia | 142 | 71 | 121 |
| Austria | 200 | 161 | n.a. |
| France | 338 | 331 | 229 |
| Germany | 500 | 722 | 533 |
| Italy | 202 | 242 | 186 |
| Japan | 1,192 | 1,211 | 1,173 |
| Netherlands | 100 | 131 | n.a. |
| Switzerland | 218 | 160 | n.a. |
| Thailand | 57 | 181 | n.a. |
| United Kingdom | 418 | 384 | n.a. |
| USA | 865 | 963 | 910 |
| **Total** (incl. others) | 4,765 | 5,138 | 5,363 |

* Figures relate to tourists paying in convertible currency.

**Receipts** (US $ million): 6.45 in 1996; 6.55 in 1997; 7.84 in 1998.

**Arrivals:** 6,208 in 1998.

Sources: Tourism Authority of Bhutan; World Tourism Organization, *Yearbook of Tourism Statistics*.

**Government hotel rooms:** 560 in 1996; 560 in 1997; 560 (provisional) in 1998 (Source: IMF, *Bhutan—Statistical Annex* (July 1999)).

# Communications Media

In 1985 there were 200 television receivers. In 1994 there were 9,126 telephones and 300 telefax stations in use. There were 35,000 radio receivers in 1996. A television service commenced operations in Thimphu in June 1999.

# Education

(at 1 April 1999)

| | |
|---|---|
| Primary schools (incl. community schools) | 254 |
| Junior high schools | 51 |
| High schools | 21 |
| Degree college* | 1 |
| Other post-secondary institutions (incl. Sanskrit Pathsalas) | 9 |
| Private schools | 7 |
| Non-formal education (NFE) centres | 81 |
| Total pupils | 107,632† |
| Total teachers | 3,554 |

* Affiliated with University of Delhi.
† Including 2,922 pupils in NFE centres.

Source: Department of Education, Royal Government of Bhutan.

# Directory

## The Constitution

The Kingdom of Bhutan has no formal constitution. However, the state system is a modified form of constitutional monarchy. Written rules, which are changed periodically, govern procedures for the election of members of the Council of Ministers, the Royal Advisory Council and the Legislature, and define the duties and powers of those bodies.

## The Government

**Head of State:** HM Druk Gyalpo ('Dragon King') Jigme Singye Wangchuk (succeeded to the throne in July 1972).

### LODOI TSOKDE
(Royal Advisory Council)
(November 1999)

The Royal Advisory Council (Lodoi Tsokde), established in 1965, comprises nine members: two monks representing the Central and District Monastic Bodies (Rabdeys), six people's representatives and a Chairman (Kalyon), nominated by the King. Each geog (group of villages, known also as a block) within a dzongkhag (district) selects one representative, from whom the respective Dzongkhag Yargye Tshogchungs (DYTs—District Development Committees) each agree on one nomination to be forwarded to the National Assembly (Tshogdu Chenmo). From these 20 nominees, the National Assembly, in turn, elects six persons to serve on the Royal Advisory Council as people's representatives for the whole country. The Council's principal task is to advise the Chairman of the Council of Ministers (Lhengye Zhungtshog), as head of government, and to supervise all aspects of administration. The Council is in permanent session, virtually as a government department, and acts, on a daily basis, as the *de facto* Standing Committee of the National Assembly. Representatives of the monastic bodies serve for one year, representatives of the people for three years, and the duration of the Chairman's term of office is at the discretion of the King. Representatives may be re-elected, but not for consecutive terms; they are all full members of the Council of Ministers.

**Chairman:** Dasho Rinzin Gyeltshen.

**Councillors:** Dasho PHANCHUNG*, Dasho TASHI DORJI*, Dasho JAMBAY NGEDUB*, Dasho PENPA*, Dasho NOB TSHERING*, Dasho UGYEN DORJI*, Lopon UGYEN†, Lam KARMA GYELTSHEN†.

* From November 1998 to November 2001.
† From November 1998 to November 1999.

### LHENGYE ZHUNGTSHOG
(Council of Ministers)
(February 2000)

**Chairman** (July 1999–June 2000) **and Minister of Health and Education:** Lyonpo SANGYE NGEDUP DORJI.

**Minister of Finance:** Lyonpo YESHEY ZIMBA.

**Minister of Agriculture:** Lyonpo KUNZANG DORJI.

**Minister of Trade and Industry:** Lyonpo KHANDU WANGCHUK.

**Minister of Home Affairs:** Lyonpo THINLEY GYAMTSHO.

**Minister of Foreign Affairs:** Lyonpo JIGMI YOZER THINLEY.

**Cabinet Secretary:** NETEN ZANGMO.

All members of the Royal Advisory Council are also members of the Council of Ministers.

### MINISTRIES AND OTHER MAJOR GOVERNMENT BODIES

**Ministry of Agriculture:** POB 252, Thimphu; tel. 322129; fax 323153.

**Ministry of Communications:** Tashichhodzong, POB 278, Thimphu; tel. 322218; fax 322184; Dep. Minister Dasho LEKI DORJI.

**Ministry of Finance:** Tashichhodzong, POB 117, Thimphu; tel. 322223; fax 323154.

**Ministry of Foreign Affairs:** Convention Centre, POB 103, Thimphu; tel. 324119; fax 323240.

**Ministry of Health and Education:** Tashichhodzong, POB 726, Thimphu; tel. 322351; fax 324649.

**Ministry of Home Affairs:** Tashichhodzong, POB 133, Thimphu; tel. 322301; fax 322214.

**Ministry of Trade and Industry:** Tashichhodzong, POB 141, Thimphu; tel. 322211; fax 323617.

**National Environment Commission:** Thimphu; tel. 323384; fax 323385; Hon. Dep. Minister Dasho NADO RINCHEN.

**Office of the Royal Advisory Council:** Tashichhodzong, POB 200, Thimphu; tel. 312339; fax 325343.

**Special Commission for Cultural Affairs:** Thimphu; tel. 322001; fax 323040; Chair. Lyonpo THINLEY GYAMTSHO; Sec. Dasho SANGAY WANGCHUK.

## Legislature

### TSHOGDU CHENMO

A National Assembly (Tshogdu Chenmo) was established in 1953. The Assembly has a three-year term and meets at least once a year, in spring (May–July) and/or autumn (October–November), although in recent years the Assembly has met for a longer session once a year only. The size of the membership is based, in part, on the population of the districts; although the size is, in principle, subject to periodic revision, in practice the popular representation has remained unchanged since 1953. In 1999 the Assembly had 150 members, of whom 105 were elected by direct popular consensus (formal voting is used, however, in the event of a deadlock). Ten seats were reserved for religious bodies, one was reserved for a representative of industry (elected by the Bhutan Chamber of Commerce and Industry), and the remainder were occupied by officials nominated by the Government (including the Dzongdas—see below). Not all of the 105 public members (chimis) are elected simultaneously; there are, therefore, overlaps in tenure. The Assembly elects its own Speaker from among its members. It enacts laws, advises on constitutional and political matters and debates all important issues. There is provision for a secret ballot on controversial issues, but, in practice, decisions are reached by consensus. Both the Royal Advisory Council and the Council of Ministers are responsible to the Assembly.

**Speaker:** Lyonpo KUNZANG DORJI.

**Deputy Speaker:** Dasho (Gup) UGYEN DORJI.

### LOCAL ADMINISTRATION

There are 20 districts (dzongkhags), each headed by a Dzongda (district officer) (in charge of administration and law and order) and a Thrimpon (magistrate) (in charge of judicial matters). Dzongdas were previously appointed by the King, but are now appointed by the Royal Civil Service Commission, established in 1982. The Dzongdas are responsible to the Royal Civil Service Commission and the Ministry of Home Affairs, while the Thrimpons are responsible to the High Court. The principal officers under the Dzongda are the Dzongda Wongma and the Dzongrab, responsible for locally administered development projects and fiscal matters respectively. Seven of the districts are further sub-divided into sub-districts (dungkhags), and the lowest administrative unit in all districts is the block (geog) of several villages.

In July 1991 Geog Yargye Tshogchungs (GYTs—Geog Development Committees) were established in each of the geogs in Bhutan (of which there were 202 in July 1998). Membership of these committees consists of between five and 13 members (geog yargye tshogpas), depending on the size of the block. Members are directly elected, on the basis of merit, by the villagers. Each GYT also elects a representative to the Dzongkhag Yargye Tshogchungs (DYTs—District Development Committees).

In 1987 Gasa and Punakha were amalgamated into a single district, known as Punakha, and a new district, named Chhukha, was created from portions of three existing districts in western Bhutan. Two new districts, Gasa and Trashi Yangtse, were created in 1992. There are two municipal corporations (in Thimphu and Phuentsholing), each of which is headed by a Thrompon (mayor) and is composed of government officials from the Urban Development and Housing Division in the Ministry of Communications.

## Political Organizations

Political parties are banned in Bhutan, in accordance with long-standing legislation. There are, however, a small number of anti-Government organizations, composed principally of Nepali-speaking former residents of Bhutan, which are based in Kathmandu, Nepal.

**Bhutan Gurkha National Liberation Front (BGNLF):** Nepal; f. 1994; Sec.-Gen. R. P. SUBBA.

**Bhutan National Democratic Party (BNDP):** POB 3334, Kathmandu, Nepal; tel. 525682; f. 1992; also has offices in Delhi and Varanasi, India, and in Thapa, Nepal; Pres. R. B. BASNET; Gen. Secs HARI P. ADHIKARI (Organization), Dr D. N. S. DHAKAL (Planning and External Affairs).

**Bhutan People's Party (BPP):** f. 1990 as a successor to the People's Forum on Democratic Rights (f. 1989); advocates unconditional release of all political prisoners, judicial reform, freedom of religious practices, linguistic freedom, freedom of press, speech and expression, and equal rights for all ethnic groups; Pres. R. K. BUDATHOKI; Gen. Sec. R. K. CHETTRI.

**Druk National Congress (DNC):** Maharagunj, Chakrapath, Kathmandu, Nepal; f. 1992; claims to represent 'all the oppressed people of Bhutan'; Pres. 'RONGTHONG' KINLEY DORJI.

**Human Rights Organization of Bhutan (HUROB):** POB 172, Patan Dhoka, Lalitpur, Kathmandu, Nepal; tel. 525046; fax 526038; f. 1991; documents alleged human rights violations in Bhutan and co-ordinates welfare activities in eight refugee camps in Nepal for ethnic Nepalese claiming to be from Bhutan; Chair. S. B. SUBBA; Gen. Sec. OM DHUNGEL.

**United Liberation People's Front:** f. 1990; Leader BALARAM POUDYAL.

## Diplomatic Representation

### EMBASSIES IN BHUTAN

**Bangladesh:** POB 178, Upper Choubachu, Thimphu; tel. 322362; fax 322629; Ambassador: SARADINDU SEKHAR CHAKMA.

**India:** India House, Lungtenzampa, Thimphu; tel. 322100; fax 323195; Ambassador: PRADEEP KUMAR SINGH.

## Judicial System

Bhutan has Civil and Criminal Codes, which are based on those laid down by the Shabdrung Ngawang Namgyal in the 17th century. An independent judicial authority was established in 1961, but law was mostly administered at the district level until 1968, when the High Court was set up. Existing laws were consolidated in 1982, although annual or biennial conferences of Thrimpons are held to keep abreast of changing circumstances and to recommend (in the first instance, to the King) amendments to existing laws. Most legislation is sent by the Council of Ministers to the National Assembly for approval and enactment. During 1995–99 substantial revisions to the civil and criminal codes were being drafted.

**Appeal Court:** The Supreme Court of Appeal is the King.

**High Court** (Thrimkhang Gongma): Thimphu; tel. 322344; fax 322921; established 1968 to review appeals from Lower Courts, although some cases are heard at the first instance. The Full Bench is presided over by the Chief Justice. There are normally seven other judges, who are appointed by the King on the recommendation of the Chief Justice and who serve until their superannuation. Three judges form a quorum. The judges are assisted by senior rabjams/

ramjans (judges in training). Assistance to defendants is available through jabmis (certificated pleaders). The operation of the legal system and proposed amendments are considered by regular meetings of all the judges and Thrimpons (usually annually, or at least once every two years). Under the mid-1998 grant of governance to an elected Council of Ministers and pending the adoption of detailed regulations, proposed amendments are expected to be submitted to the Council of Ministers for consideration.

**Chief Justice:** Lyonpo SONAM TOBGYE.

**Judges of the High Court:** Dasho THINLEY YOEZER, Dasho PASANG TOBGYE, Dasho KARMA D. SHERPA, Dasho D. N. KATWAL*, Dasho K. B. GHALEY*, Dasho GAGEY LHAM, Dasho DORJI WANGDI.

* Originally nominated as public representative.

**Magistrates' Courts** (Dzongkhag Thrimkhang): Each district has a court, headed by the thrimpon (magistrate) and aided by a junior rabjam/ramjam, which tries most cases. Appeals are made to the High Court, and less serious civil disputes may be settled by a gup or mandal (village headman) through written undertakings by the parties concerned.

All citizens have the right to make informal appeal for redress of grievances directly to the King, through the office of the gyalpoi zimpon (court chamberlain).

# Religion

The state religion is Mahayana Buddhism, but the southern Bhutanese are predominantly followers of Hinduism. Buddhism was introduced into Bhutan in the eighth century AD by the Indian saint Padmasambhava, known in Bhutan as Guru Rimpoche. In the 13th century Phajo Drugom Shigpo made the Drukpa school of Kagyupa Buddhism pre-eminent in Bhutan, and this sect is still supported by the dominant ethnic group, the Drukpas. The main monastic group, the Central Monastic Body (comprising 1,160 monks), is led by an elected Head Abbot (Je Khenpo), is directly supported by the State and spends six months of the year at Tashichhodzong and at Punakha respectively. A further 2,120 monks, who are members of the District Monastic Bodies, are sustained by the lay population. The Council for Ecclesiastical Affairs oversees all religious bodies. Monasteries (Gompas) and shrines (Lhakhangs) are numerous. Religious proselytizing, in any form, is illegal.

**Council for Ecclesiastical Affairs** (Dratshang Lhentshog): POB 254, Thimphu; tel. 322754; fax 323867; f. 1984, replacing the Central Board for Monastic Studies, to oversee all Buddhist meditational centres and schools of Buddhist studies, as well as the Central and District Monastic Bodies; daily affairs of the Council are run by the Central Monastic Secretariat; Chair. His Holiness the Je Khenpo JIGME CHOEDRA; Sec. SANGAY WANGCHUK; Dep. Sec. SANGAY TENZIN.

# The Press

**The Bhutan Review:** POB 172, Patan Dhoka, Lalitpur, Kathmandu, Nepal; tel. 525046; fax 523819; f. 1993; monthly organ of the Human Rights Organization of Bhutan (HUROB); opposed to existing government policies.

**Kuensel:** POB 204, Thimphu; tel. 323043; fax 322975; internet www.kuensel.com.bt; f. 1965 as a weekly govt bulletin; reorg. as a national weekly newspaper in 1986; became autonomous corporation in 1992 (previously under Dept of Information), incorporating former Royal Government Press; in English, Dzongkha and Nepali; Editor-in-Chief KINLEY DORJI; Editors R. N. MISHRA (Nepali), TENZIN RIGDEN (English), MINDU DORJI (Dzongkha); circ. 331 (Nepali), 8,102 (English), 2,729 (Dzongkha).

# Broadcasting and Communications

## TELECOMMUNICATIONS

**Bhutan Telecom Corporation:** POB 134, Thimphu; tel. 322678; fax 323041; e-mail director@telecom.net.bt; f. 2000; state-owned public corpn; regulation authority; Dir THINLEY DORJI.

**DrukNet:** Thimphu; f. 1999; internet service provider; Head GANGA SHARMA.

## BROADCASTING

### Radio

In 1994 there were 52 radio stations for administrative communications. Of these, 34 were for internal communications (to which the public had access), and three were external stations serving Bhutan House at Kalimpong and the Bhutanese diplomatic missions in India and Bangladesh. A further 11 stations are for hydrological and meteorological purposes.

**BBS Corporation (Bhutan Broadcasting Service):** POB 101, Thimphu; tel. 323071; fax 323073; f. 1973 as Radio National Youth Association of Bhutan (NYAB); became autonomous corporation in 1992 (previously under Dept of Information); short-wave radio station broadcasting 30 hours per week in Dzongkha, Sharchopkha, Nepali (Lhotsamkha) and English; a daily FM programme (for Thimphu only) began in 1987; Chair. Lyonpo YESHEY ZIMBA; Exec. Dir KINGA SINGYE.

### Television

In June 1999 the BBS Corporation started operating a television service (in Dzongkha and English) in Thimphu; the service was gradually to be expanded throughout the country. Broadcasts were to be limited to a few hours a day and were to consist entirely of national news and documentaries about the Bhutanese themselves.

# Finance

(cap. = capital; auth. = authorized; p.u. = paid up; res = reserves; dep. = deposits; m. = million; brs = branches; amounts in ngultrum)

## BANKING

### Central Bank

**Royal Monetary Authority (RMA):** POB 154, Thimphu; tel. 322540; fax 322847; f. 1982; bank of issue; frames and implements official monetary policy, co-ordinates the activities of financial institutions and holds foreign-exchange deposits on behalf of the Govt; cap. 1.5m.; Chair. Lyonpo YESHEY ZIMBA; Man. Dir SONAM WANGCHUK.

### Commercial Banks

**Bank of Bhutan:** POB 75, Phuentsholing; tel. 252300; fax 252641; f. 1968; 20%-owned by the State Bank of India and 80% by the Govt of Bhutan; wholly managed by Govt of Bhutan from 1997; auth. cap. 100m., cap. p.u. 50m., res 354.3m., dep. 4,921.5m. (Dec. 1998); Dirs nominated by the Bhutan Govt: Chair. Lyonpo YESHEY ZIMBA; Dirs KINLEY D. DORJI, SONAM WANGCHUK, Dasho UGYEN DORJI; Dirs nominated by the State Bank of India: D. K. JAIN, V. RAMAMOORTY; Man. Dir TSHERING DORJI; 25 brs and 3 extension counters.

**Bhutan National Bank (BNB):** POB 439, Thimphu; tel. 322767; fax 323601; f. as Unit Trust of Bhutan (a savings institution); reorganized, as Bhutan's second commercial bank, in 1996; partially privatized in 1998; 27% owned by Govt, 20.1% by Asian Development Bank and 19.9% by Citibank; auth. cap. 200m., cap. p.u. 59.5m. (1999); Chair. Lyonpo YESHEY ZIMBA; Man. Dir KIPCHU TSHERING; 4 brs.

### Development Bank

**Bhutan Development Finance Corporation (BDFC):** POB 256, Thimphu; tel. 322579; fax 323428; e-mail karmarangdol@bdfc.org.bt; f. 1988; provides industrial loans and short- and medium-term agricultural loans; cap. p.u. 100m., loans 422m. (1998); Chair. Lyonpo YESHEY ZIMBA; Man. Dir KARMA RANGDOL.

## STOCK EXCHANGE

**Royal Securities Exchange of Bhutan Ltd:** POB 742, Thimphu; tel. 323995; fax 323849; f. 1993; under temporary management of the Royal Monetary Authority; 13 listed cos (1998); Chair. SONAM WANGCHUK; Man. TASHI YEZER.

## INSURANCE

**Royal Insurance Corporation of Bhutan:** POB 77, Phuentsholing; tel. 252869; fax 252640; f. 1975; Chair. Lyonpo YESHEY ZIMBA; Man. Dir SANGAY KHANDU; 10 brs and development centres.

# Trade and Industry

## GOVERNMENT AGENCIES

**Food Corporation of Bhutan (FCB):** POB 80, Phuentsholing; tel. 252375; fax 252289; f. 1974; activities include procurement and distribution of food grains and other essential commodities through appointed Fair Price Shop Agents; marketing of surplus agricultural and horticultural produce through FCB-regulated market outlets; logistics concerning World Food Programme food aid; accumulation of buffer stocks to offset any emergency food shortages; maintenance of SAARC Food Security Reserve Stock; Man. Dir TSHERING WANGDI.

**Forestry Development Corporation:** Man. Dir NAMGAY WANGCHUK.

**Planning Commission:** Convention Centre, POB 127, Thimphu; tel. 322832; fax 322928; e-mail plansect@druknet.net.bt; headed by the King until 1991, formally reconstituted 1999; consists of 17 officials; proposes socio-economic policy guidelines, issues directives for the formulation of development plans, ensures efficient and judicious allocation of resources, directs socio-economic research, studies and surveys, and appraises the Government on the progress of development plans and programmes; Chair. Lyonpo YESHEY ZIMBA; Sec. DAW TENZIN.

**State Trading Corpn of Bhutan Ltd (STCB):** POB 76, Phuentsholing; tel. 252713; fax 252618; e-mail stcbl@druknet.net.bt; manages imports and exports on behalf of the Govt; Man. Dir Dasho DORJI NAMGAY; Jt Man. Dir (Automobile Div.) SONAM GYAMTSHO; brs in Thimphu (POB 272; tel. 322953; fax 323781; e-mail stcbthim@druknet.net.bt) and Kolkata, India.

### CHAMBER OF COMMERCE

**Bhutan Chamber of Commerce and Industry (BCCI):** POB 147, Thimphu; tel. 322742; fax 323936; e-mail bcci@druknet.net.bt; f. 1980; reorg. 1988; promotion of trade and industry, information dissemination, private-sector human resource development; 434 registered mems; 12-mem. technical advisory committee; 25-mem. executive committee; 20 liaison offices; Pres. Dasho UGYEN DORJI; Sec.-Gen. Dasho TSHERING DORJI.

### UTILITIES

#### Electricity

**Department of Power:** c/o Ministry of Trade and Industry, Tashichhodzong, POB 141, Thimpu; tel. 22159; fax 223507.

**Chhukha Hydropower Corporation:** Phuentsholing; tel. 252575; fax 252582; f. 1991; state-owned; Chair. Lyonpo YESHEY ZIMBA; Man. Dir YESHEY WANGDI.

**Kurichu Project Authority:** Mongar; tel. 641145; co-ordinates construction of dam and hydroelectric power-generating facilities at Kurichu; Gen. Man. TSHEWANG RINZIN.

**Tala Hydroelectric Project:** Tala; tel. 325498; fax 325499; co-ordinates construction of dam and hydroelectric power-generating facilities; Gen. Man. R. N. KHAZANCHI.

#### Water

**Thimphu City Corporation (Water Supply Unit):** POB 215, Thimphu; tel. 22265; fax 24315; f. 1982; responsible for water supply of Thimphu municipality (population 32,000); Head BHIMLAL DHUNGEL.

### TRADE UNIONS

Under long-standing legislation, trade union activity is illegal in Bhutan.

## Transport

### ROADS AND TRACKS

In December 1997 there were 3,375 km of roads in Bhutan, of which 65.9% were paved. Surfaced roads link the important border towns of Phuentsholing, Gelephu, Sarpang and Samdrup Jongkhar in southern Bhutan to towns in West Bengal and Assam in India. There is a shortage of road transport. Yaks, ponies and mules are still the chief means of transport on the rough mountain tracks. By 1990 most of the previously government-operated transport facilities (mainly buses and minibuses) on major and subsidiary routes had been transferred to private operators on the basis of seven-year contracts.

**Road Safety and Transport Authority:** Thimphu; tel. 321282; fax 322538; under Ministry of Communications; regulates condition of goods and passenger transport services; Dir YESHI TSHERING.

**Transport Corpn of Bhutan:** Phuentsholing; tel. 252476; f. 1982; subsidiary of Royal Insurance Corpn of Bhutan; operates direct coach service between Phuentsholing and Kolkata (Calcutta) via Siliguri.

Other operators are Barma Travels (f. 1990), Dawa Transport (Propr SHERUB WANGCHUCK), Dhendup Travel Service (Phuentsholing; tel. 252437), Gyamtsho Transport, Gurung Transport Service, Namgay Transport, Nima Travels (Phuentsholing; tel. 252384), and Rimpung Travels (Phuentsholing; tel. 252354).

Lorries for transporting goods are operated by the private sector.

### CIVIL AVIATION

There is an international airport at Paro. There are also numerous helicopter landing pads, which are used, by arrangement with the Indian military and aviation authorities, solely by government officials.

**Department of Civil Aviation:** c/o Ministry of Communications, Tashichhodzong, POB 278, Thimphu; tel. 22499; fax 22987; Dir RIN GYELTSHEN.

**Druk-Air Corpn Ltd** (Royal Bhutan Airlines): POB 209, Old Bhutan Hotel, Thimphu; tel. 322825; fax 322775; internet www.drukair.com; national airline; f. 1981; became fully operational in 1983; services from Paro to Bangladesh, India, Nepal and Thailand; charter services also undertaken; Chair. Dasho LEKI DORJI; Man. Dir (vacant).

## Tourism

Bhutan was opened to tourism in 1975. In 1998 the total number of foreign visitors was 6,208 and receipts from tourism totalled US $7.84m. Tourists travel in organized 'package' or trekking tours, or individually, accompanied by government-appointed guides. Hotels have been constructed at Phuentsholing, Paro, Bumthang and Thimphu, with lodges at Trongsa, Trashigang and Mongar. In addition, there are many small privately-operated hotels and guest-houses. The Government exercises close control over the development of tourism. In 1987 the National Assembly resolved that all monasteries, mountains and other holy places should be inaccessible to tourists from 1988 (this resolution is flexibly interpreted, however—e.g. Japanese Buddhist tour groups are permitted to visit 'closed' monasteries). In 1991 the Government began transferring the tourism industry to the private sector and licences were issued to new private tourism operators. New rules were introduced in 1995, asserting more stringent controls over private operators, through the Tourism Authority of Bhutan.

**Tourism Authority of Bhutan:** POB 126, Thimphu; tel. 323252; fax 323695; f. 1991; under regulatory authority of Ministry of Trade and Industry; exercises overall authority over tourism policy, pricing, hotel, restaurant and travel agency licensing, visa approvals, etc.; Man. Dir TSHERING YONTEN; Dep. Man. Dir THUJI D. NADIK.

# BOLIVIA

## Introductory Survey

**Location, Climate, Language, Religion, Flag, Capital**

The Republic of Bolivia is a land-locked state in South America, bordered by Chile and Peru to the west, by Brazil to the north and east, and by Paraguay and Argentina to the south. The climate varies, according to altitude, from humid tropical conditions in the northern and eastern lowlands, which are less than 500 m (1,640 ft) above sea-level, to the cool and cold zones at altitudes of more than 3,500 m (about 11,500 ft) in the Andes mountains. The official languages are Spanish, Quechua and Aymará. Almost all of the inhabitants profess Christianity, and the great majority are adherents of the Roman Catholic Church. The national civil flag (proportions 3 by 2) has three equal horizontal stripes, of red, yellow and green. The state flag has, in addition, the national coat of arms in the centre of the yellow stripe. The legal capital is Sucre. The administrative capital and seat of government is La Paz.

**Recent History**

The Incas of Bolivia were conquered by Spain in 1538 and, although there were many revolts against Spanish rule, independence was not achieved until 1825. Bolivian history has been characterized by recurrent internal strife, resulting in a lengthy succession of presidents, and frequent territorial disputes with its neighbours, including the 1879–83 War of the Pacific between Bolivia, Peru and Chile, and the Chaco Wars of 1928–30 and 1932–35 against Paraguay.

At a presidential election in May 1951 the largest share of the vote was won by Dr Víctor Paz Estenssoro, the candidate of the Movimiento Nacionalista Revolucionario (MNR), who had been living in Argentina since 1946. He was denied permission to return to Bolivia and contested the election *in absentia*. However, he failed to gain an absolute majority, and the incumbent President transferred power to a junta of army officers. This regime was itself overthrown in April 1952, when a popular uprising, supported by the MNR and a section of the armed forces, enabled Dr Paz Estenssoro to return from exile and assume the presidency. His Government, a coalition of the MNR and the Labour Party, committed itself to profound social revolution. The coalition nationalized the tin mines and introduced universal suffrage (the franchise had previously been limited to literate adults) and land reform. Dr Hernán Siles Zuazo, a leading figure in the 1952 revolution, was elected President for the 1956–60 term, and Dr Paz Estenssoro was again elected President in 1960. However, the powerful trade unions came into conflict with the Government, and in November 1964, following widespread strikes and disorder, President Paz Estenssoro was overthrown by the Vice-President, Gen. René Barrientos Ortuño, who was supported by the army. After serving with Gen. Alfredo Ovando Candía as Co-President under a military junta, Gen. Barrientos resigned in January 1966 to campaign for the presidency; he was elected in July 1966.

President Barrientos encountered strong opposition from left-wing groups, including mineworkers' unions. There was also a guerrilla uprising in south-eastern Bolivia, led by Dr Ernesto ('Che') Guevara, the Argentine-born revolutionary who had played a leading role in the Castro regime in Cuba. However, the insurgency was suppressed by government troops, with the help of US advisers, and guerrilla warfare ended in October 1967, when Guevara was captured and killed. In April 1969 President Barrientos was killed in an air crash and Dr Luis Adolfo Siles Salinas, the Vice-President, succeeded to the presidency. In September, however, President Siles Salinas was deposed by the armed forces, who reinstated Gen. Ovando. He was forced to resign in October 1970, when, after a power struggle between right-wing and left-wing army officers, Gen. Juan José Torres González, who had support from leftists, emerged as President, pledging support for agrarian reform and worker participation in management. A 'People's Assembly', formed by Marxist politicians, radical students and leaders of trade unions, was allowed to meet and demanded the introduction of extreme socialist measures, causing disquiet in right-wing circles. President Torres was deposed in August 1971 by Col (later Gen.) Hugo Bánzer Suárez, who drew support from the right-wing Falange Socialista Boliviana and a section of the MNR, as well as from the army. In June 1973 President Bánzer announced an imminent return to constitutional government, but elections were later postponed to June 1974. The MNR withdrew its support and entered into active opposition.

Following an attempted military coup in June 1974, all portfolios within the Cabinet were assigned to military personnel. After another failed coup attempt in November, President Bánzer declared that elections had been postponed indefinitely and that his military regime would retain power until at least 1980. All political and union activity was banned. Political and industrial unrest in 1976, however, led President Bánzer to announce that elections would be held in July 1978. Allegations of fraud rendered the elections void, but Gen. Juan Pereda Asbún, the armed forces candidate in the elections, staged a successful military coup. In November 1978 his right-wing Government was overthrown in another coup, led by Gen. David Padilla Aranciba, Commander-in-Chief of the Army, with the support of national left-wing elements.

Presidential and congressional elections were held in July 1979. The presidential poll resulted in almost equal support for two ex-Presidents, Dr Siles Zuazo (with 36.0% of the vote) and Dr Paz Estenssoro (with 35.9%), who were now leading rival factions of the MNR. Congress, which was convened in August to resolve the issue, failed to award a majority to either candidate. An interim Government was formed under Walter Guevara Arce, President of the Senate (the upper house of Congress), but this administration was overthrown on 1 November by a right-wing army officer, Col Alberto Natusch Busch. He withdrew 15 days later after failing to gain the support of Congress, which elected Dra Lidia Gueiler Tejada, President of the Chamber of Deputies (the lower house of Congress), as interim Head of State pending presidential and congressional elections scheduled for June 1980.

The result of the 1980 presidential election was inconclusive, and in July, before Congress could meet to decide between the two main contenders (again Siles Zuazo and Paz Estenssoro), a military junta led by an army commander, Gen. Luis García Meza, staged a coup—the 189th in Bolivia's 154 years of independence. In August 1981 a military uprising forced Gen. García to resign. In September the junta transferred power to another army commander, Gen. Celso Torrelio Villa, who declared his intention to fight official corruption and to return the country to democracy within three years. Labour unrest, provoked by Bolivia's severe economic crisis, was appeased by restitution of trade union and political rights, and a mainly civilian Cabinet was appointed in April 1982. Elections were scheduled for April 1983. The political liberalization disturbed the armed forces, who attempted to create a climate of violence, and President Torrelio resigned in July 1982, amid rumours of an impending coup. The junta installed the less moderate Gen. Guido Vildoso Calderón, the Army Chief of Staff, as President. Unable to resolve the worsening economic crisis or to control a general strike, in September the military regime announced that power would be handed over in October to the Congress that had originally been elected in 1980. Dr Siles Zuazo, who had obtained most votes in both 1979 and 1980, was duly elected President by Congress, and was sworn in for a four-year term in October 1982.

President Siles Zuazo appointed a coalition Cabinet consisting of members of his own party, the Movimiento Nacionalista Revolucionario de Izquierda (MNRI), the Movimiento de la Izquierda Revolucionaria (MIR) and the Partido Comunista de Bolivia (PCB). Economic aid from the USA and Europe was resumed, but the Government found itself unable to fulfil the expectations that had been created by the return to democratic rule. The entire Cabinet resigned in August 1983, and the President appointed a Cabinet in which the number of portfolios that were held by the right-wing of the MNRI, the Partido Demócrata Cristiano (PDC) and independents was increased. The MIR joined forces with the MNR and with business interests in rejecting the Government's policy of complying with IMF conditions for assistance, which involved harsh economic measures. The Government lost its majority in Congress and was confronted by strikes and mass labour demonstrations. In November the opposition-dominated Senate approved an increase of 100% in the minimum wage, in defiance of the Government's austerity measures. Following a 48-hour general strike, the whole Cabinet resigned once again in December, in anticipation of an opposition motion of censure; the ministers accused the Senate of planning a 'constitutional coup' and urged the formation of a government of 'national unity'. In January 1984 President Siles Zuazo appointed a new coalition Cabinet, including 13 members of the previous Government.

The new Cabinet's main priority was to reverse Bolivia's grave economic decline. However, constant industrial agitation by the trade union confederation, the Central Obrera Boliviana (COB), coupled with rumours of an imminent coup, seriously undermined public confidence in the President. In June 1984 the country was again thrown into turmoil by the temporary abduction of President Siles Zuazo. Two former cabinet ministers and some 100 right-wing army officers were arrested in connection with the kidnapping, which was believed to have been supported by leading figures in the illicit drugs trade.

In September 1984 another crisis beset the Government following the discovery of a plot by extreme right-wing groups to overthrow the President. The disclosure that Congress had ordered an inquiry into suspected links between the Government and cocaine-dealers prompted President Siles Zuazo to undertake a five-day hunger strike in a bid to secure national unity and stability. In January 1985 a new Cabinet was formed, comprising only members of the MNRI and independents. In the same month it was announced that an attempted coup by former military officers had been thwarted.

At elections in July 1985, amid reports of electoral malpractice and poor organization, the right-wing Acción Democrática Nacionalista (ADN), whose presidential candidate was Gen. Hugo Bánzer Suárez (the former dictator), received 28.6% of the votes cast, and the MNR obtained 26.4%, while the MIR was the leading left-wing party. At a further round of voting in Congress in August, an alliance between the MNR and the leading left-wing groups, including the MIR, enabled Dr Víctor Paz Estenssoro of the MNR to secure the presidency (which he had previously held in 1952–56 and 1960–64). The armed forces pledged their support for the new Government.

On taking office in August 1985, the new Government immediately introduced a very strict economic programme, designed to reduce inflation, which was estimated to have reached 14,173% in the year to August. The COB rejected the programme and called an indefinite general strike in September. The Government responded by declaring the strike illegal and by ordering a 90-day state of siege throughout Bolivia. Leading trade unionists were detained or banished, and thousands of strikers were arrested. The strike was called off in October, when union leaders agreed to hold talks with the Government. The conclusion of the strike was regarded as a considerable success for the new administration which, in spite of having achieved office with the assistance of left-wing parties, had subsequently found a greater ally in the right-wing ADN.

In July 1986 the Government was strongly criticized by opposition groups and trade unions when 160 US soldiers arrived in Bolivia to participate in a joint campaign with the Bolivian armed forces to eradicate illegal coca plantations. The Government was accused of having contravened the Constitution and of compromising national sovereignty. The allocation of US aid, however, was to be conditional upon the elimination of Bolivia's illegal cocaine trade. In October the US administration agreed to provide more than US $100m. in aid to continue the coca-eradication campaign, and US troops were withdrawn, so that the Bolivian authorities could assume responsibility for the campaign. However, within a few months of the troops' withdrawal, cocaine production was once again flourishing.

Throughout 1986 demonstrations and strikes were held by the COB in protest at the Government's austerity measures. Following a general strike in August, the Government imposed another 90-day state of siege. Social discontent persisted in 1987 and extensive unrest continued in 1988 (following a further increase in the price of petrol in February of that year), which culminated in April with a national hunger strike, called by the COB, to protest against the continuing austerity measures. These problems led to the resignation of the Cabinet in August, although all except four ministers were reappointed.

Presidential and congressional elections took place in May 1989. Of the votes cast in the presidential election, Gonzalo Sánchez de Lozada of the MNR obtained 23.1%, Gen. Hugo Bánzer Suárez of the ADN 22.7%, and Jaime Paz Zamora of the MIR 19.6%. As no candidate had gained the requisite absolute majority, responsibility for the choice of President passed to the newly-elected Congress, which was to convene in August. Political uncertainty prevailed in the interim, and this led, in turn, to economic stagnation. Shortly before the second stage of the election, Bánzer withdrew his candidacy in order to support his former adversary, Paz Zamora. The 46 ADN and 41 MIR seats in Congress were sufficient to assure a majority vote for Paz Zamora, who assumed the presidency. A coalition Government of 'national unity', the Acuerdo Patriótico, was then formed. At the same time, a joint political council (with undefined powers), headed by Bánzer, was established. In his inaugural speech, President Paz Zamora gave assurances that fiscal discipline would be maintained, and a state of siege, banning strikes, was imposed in November.

Meanwhile, further measures to reduce the production of coca were taken during 1988. An anti-narcotics department was established in April. The drugs-control troops, Unidad Móvil de Patrullaje Rural (UMOPAR), were provided with greater resources and were further supported by a coca limitation law, restricting the area of land allowed for coca production (the leaves to be used for 'traditional' purposes only). In the same month, Roberto Suárez, Bolivia's leading cocaine-trafficker, was arrested and imprisoned for trading in illicit drugs. Suárez's arrest led to the exposure of drugs-trading involving leading members of the ADN, and was linked to a bomb attack on US Secretary of State George Shultz's motorcade in La Paz in August, during a visit undertaken to demonstrate support for the campaign against coca production.

By mid-1989, however, the Government had failed to attain the targets of its coca-eradication programme, having encountered staunch opposition from the powerful coca-growers' organizations. Clashes between UMOPAR and drugs-traffickers had become increasingly violent, especially in the coca-processing region of northern Beni. Paz Zamora was critical of the militaristic approach of the USA to coca eradication and emphasized the need for economic and social support. In May 1990, however, he accepted US $35m. in military aid from the USA. In late 1990 reaction to US involvement in Bolivia became increasingly violent. The left-wing Nestor Paz Zamora guerrilla group claimed responsibility for several bomb attacks, declaring that its actions were in response to the violation of Bolivia's political and territorial sovereignty by the USA.

In December 1989 a serious institutional conflict arose when the Government allowed a former Minister of the Interior, Migration and Justice, Col Luis Arce Gómez, to be taken to Miami, Florida (USA), to be tried on drugs-trafficking charges, despite the absence of a formal extradition treaty between Bolivia and the USA. Arce Gómez had been on trial in Bolivia since 1986, accused of violating human rights. His extradition, therefore, constituted a contravention of Bolivian law, which states that a Bolivian cannot be extradited while undergoing trial in Bolivia. Following an acrimonious conflict between the Government and the judiciary, Congress temporarily suspended eight of the 12 supreme court judges in late 1990. In retaliation, the court threatened to annul the 1989 elections. The conflict was resolved in early 1991 with the signing by the country's five main political parties of a pact affirming the independence of the Supreme Court. In January 1991 a federal jury in Miami found Arce Gómez guilty on two charges of drugs-trafficking, and in March he was sentenced to 30 years' imprisonment. (In July 1997 the Bolivian Government officially requested his extradition to Bolivia.)

In March 1991 the reputation of the Government was seriously undermined when three of its senior officials were forced to resign amid allegations of corruption. Moreover, the appointment in February of Col. Faustino Rico Toro as the new head of Bolivia's Special Force for the Fight Against Drugs-Trafficking (FELCN) had provoked widespread outrage. In addition to his alleged connections with illegal drugs-traffickers, Rico was accused of having committed human rights abuses during his tenure as chief of army intelligence under the regime of Gen. Luis García Meza (1980–81). On 4 March, after considerable pressure from the USA (including the suspension of all military and economic aid), Rico resigned from his new position. On 13 March, following accusations by the USA linking them with illegal drugs-traffickers, the Minister of the Interior, Migration and Justice and the Chief of Police resigned from their posts, although both maintained their innocence. In July the Government announced a decree granting a period of amnesty, lasting

120 days, for drugs-traffickers to surrender voluntarily. A condition of the amnesty was that those giving themselves up confess their crimes and contribute effectively to the apprehension of other such criminals. In return, they were offered minimum prison sentences and the guarantee that they would not risk extradition to the USA. In the months that followed, as many as seven of the country's most powerful drugs-traffickers were reported to have taken advantage of the amnesty.

Government plans to privatize state-owned enterprises, including the state mining corporation, COMIBOL, resulted in a series of strikes, organized by the COB, in late 1991 and early 1992. In July the COB called a further general strike, and in October, in what was regarded as a major reversal for the Government and a considerable victory for the mining union, Federación Sindical de Trabajadores Mineros de Bolivia (FSTMB), the Government suspended its programme of joint ventures between COMIBOL and private companies. Continued social unrest led to violent confrontation between protesters and troops throughout the country in early 1993, and the military occupation of La Paz in March of that year.

In April 1993 the Supreme Court found the former military dictator Gen. Luis García Meza guilty on 49 charges of murder, human rights abuses, corruption and fraud, and sentenced him, *in absentia*, to 30 years' imprisonment. Similar sentences were imposed on 14 of his collaborators. García Meza was arrested in Brazil in March 1994 and, following his extradition to Bolivia in October of that year, began his prison sentence in March 1995.

Presidential and congressional elections were held in June 1993. Sánchez de Lozada was presented as the MNR's presidential candidate, while Bánzer Suárez was supported by both the ADN and the MIR, owing to the fact that Paz Zamora was ineligible for re-election. Of the votes cast in the presidential election, Sánchez received 33.8%, Bánzer secured 20.0% and Carlos Palenque Aviles, a popular television presenter and leader of Conciencia de Patria (Condepa), received 13.6%. Since no candidate had secured the requisite absolute majority, a congressional vote was scheduled to take place in August to decide between the two main contenders. However, Bánzer withdrew from the contest, thereby leaving Sánchez de Lozada's candidacy unopposed. At legislative elections, conducted simultaneously, the MNR secured 69 of the 157 seats in the bicameral Congress, while the ruling Acuerdo Patriótico coalition won only 43. The MNR subsequently concluded a pact with the Unión Cívica Solidaridad (UCS) and the Movimiento Bolivia Libre, thus securing a congressional majority. Sánchez de Lozada was sworn in as President on 6 August.

In March 1994 the leader of the opposition MIR, former President Jaime Paz Zamora, announced his retirement from political life. His statement followed the presentation of a report by the FELCN to Congress alleging his co-operation with drugs-traffickers. The report, which also implicated several of Paz Zamora's political allies and family members, was largely based on information provided by one of the country's most notorious drugs-traffickers, Carmelo 'Meco' Domínguez, and his former associate, Isaac 'Oso' Chavarría, who had been a paramilitary leader during Gen. García Meza's military regime in 1980–81 and was arrested in January 1994. Despite his earlier statement, Paz Zamora announced his return to political life in January 1995, while denying the allegations against him in the FELCN report.

Despite the new Government's stated intention to combat corruption in Bolivia's political and public life, evidence of fraudulent practice continued to feature widely in the country's affairs. In June 1994 the President of the Supreme Court and its third judge were found guilty of bribery by the Senate and were dismissed and banned from holding public office for 10 years. In the same month it was revealed that a large proportion of the US $20m. seized from drugs-traffickers between 1988 and 1993 had disappeared. Members of the FELCN, trustees from the Attorney-General's office and local government officials were implicated in the affair.

Meanwhile, the US-funded coca-eradication programme (see above) continued to cause serious unrest during 1994, particularly in the Chapare valley of Cochabamba, where UMOPAR forces were occupying the area. Large-scale demonstrations throughout the year culminated in August and September in protests across the country by teachers, students and COB members, as well as coca producers. The unrest subsided in late September, when the Government pledged to cease forcible eradication of coca and to withdraw its forces gradually from Chapare.

In early 1995 some 80,000 teachers across the country undertook a campaign of industrial action in opposition to a proposed programme of education reforms, which advocated the privatization of much of the education system and the restriction of teachers' rights to union membership. In March the COB called an indefinite strike after a demonstration by 3,000 teachers in La Paz was violently disrupted by police and army personnel. In response to the strike, and in an attempt to quell several weeks of civil unrest, the Government declared a state of siege for 90 days. Military units were deployed throughout the country, and 370 union leaders (including the Secretary-General of the COB, Oscar Salas) were arrested and banished to remote areas. However, protests continued nation-wide, and some 70,000 teachers remained on strike. In April COB leaders agreed to sign a memorandum of understanding with the Government to end the strike in return for the release of trade union officials and the initiation of negotiations. The state of siege, however, was extended by a further 90 days in July, owing to continued civil unrest, which had become particularly intense in the Chapare valley, where, despite of the introduction of a voluntary coca-eradication programme, UMOPAR forces had begun to occupy villages and to destroy coca plantations. Violent clashes between peasant farmers and UMOPAR personnel between July and September resulted in the arrest of almost 1,000 coca-growers. Human rights organizations expressed alarm at the force with which UMOPAR was conducting its operations and at the number of peasants killed and injured in the campaign. In October the state of siege was revoked, and negotiations between the Government and the coca-growers were undertaken, although the talks soon broke down, and further violent clashes were reported. Despite sustained resistance by coca-growers throughout 1995, a total of 5,520 ha of the crop were destroyed during the year (some 120 ha more than the target set by the US Government in its eradication programme).

Meanwhile, allegations implicating senior public officials in the illegal drugs trade continued to emerge in 1995. Four members of the FELCN, including the organization's second-in-command, Col Fernando Tarifa, were dismissed in September, following an investigation into their links with drugs-traffickers. A further 100 FELCN members were detained in November on drugs-related charges. Also in September, 13 police officers and 10 civilians were arrested in connection with a large haul of cocaine seized from a Bolivian aircraft in Peru. Moreover, a serious political scandal erupted in October, following allegations that Guillermo Bedregal, the President of the Senate and a deputy leader of the MNR, had co-operated with leading drugs-traffickers. The MNR suffered serious losses in municipal elections held in December, winning control in only one of the 10 principal cities.

In December 1995 a team of experts from Argentina began a search for the body of the guerrilla leader and revolutionary, Ernesto ('Che') Guevara, at the request of Sánchez de Lozada, following revelations by a retired general concerning the whereabouts of his remains. The Government of Cuba had long sought to recover Guevara's remains. In July 1997 Guevara's remains, together with those of three of his comrades, were finally located and returned to Cuba.

The issue of fraudulent practice in political and public life re-emerged in early 1996, when allegations concerning the abuse of the personal expenses system resulted in the resignation of 10 MNR members of Congress and the suspension of 12 others on criminal charges. Moreover, a supreme court judge who had presided over numerous cases involving drugs-related offences was arrested by the FELCN in March after having been filmed accepting money from a defendant's relative.

Continued opposition to the Government's capitalization programme led to further industrial unrest in early 1996. Strikes by teachers and doctors in March culminated in a general strike at the end of the month. In April more than 100,000 transport workers undertook a series of strikes and demonstrations in protest at the sale of the Eastern Railway to a Chilean company. Riots in La Paz resulted in damage to Chilean-owned railway property, which prompted threats from the Chilean Government to withdraw its investment from Bolivia. During violent clashes with the police several protesters were injured and one was killed. The dispute ended later in the month, when the COB signed an agreement with the Government which provided for modest public-sector wage increases, but did not include concessions in the Government's plans to continue implementation of its capitalization policies.

The proposed introduction of an agrarian reform law proved highly controversial and led to a series of protests in September and October 1996 by indigenous and peasant groups who feared that their land rights would be undermined by measures contained in the proposed legislation. In early October the leaders of several peasant farmers' groups began a hunger strike, while the COB called an indefinite general strike. Shortly afterwards Sánchez de Lozada agreed to hold discussions with representatives of some of the indigenous and peasant groups (although not with the COB) and subsequently secured their support for the law by making a number of significant concessions. The most important of these was the modification of the proposed role of the Agrarian Superintendency, such that it would not be authorized to rule on issues of land ownership. The law was approved by Congress later that month.

Dissatisfaction with the continued privatization of major industrial companies in Bolivia, particularly in the mining sector, resulted in further unrest in late 1996. In mid-December a group of miners occupied a pit at Amayapampa in northern Potosí to protest at the actions of the mine's Canadian operators, who, they alleged, had failed to pay local taxes and had caused damage to the environment. When troops arrived at the site to remove the miners 10 protesters were killed and 50 others injured in ensuing violent clashes. The incident provoked outrage throughout the country and was the subject of an investigation by the Organization of American States' Inter-American Human Rights Commission in early 1997. A similar occupation by miners opposed to private development of the Cerro Rico site in Potosí took place in January 1997.

Ten presidential candidates announced their intention to contest the elections scheduled for 1 June 1997. The MNR confirmed Juan Carlos Durán as its candidate (owing to the fact that Sánchez de Lozada was ineligible for re-election), the MIR presented Paz Zamora, while Bánzer Suárez was to make a fourth attempt to gain the presidency by democratic means, on behalf of the ADN. An often acrimonious election campaign was characterized by expressions of increasing discontent with the Government's radical economic reform programme and repeated criticism of Bánzer, who was held responsible for numerous human rights abuses during his dictatorship in the 1970s. In the event, Bánzer secured 22.3% of the total votes, Durán won 17.7% and Paz Zamora received 16.7%. At legislative elections held concurrently the ADN won a total of 46 congressional seats, the MIR won 31, the MNR secured 29 and the UCS and Condepa secured 23 and 20 seats respectively. The ADN subsequently concluded a pact with the MIR, the UCS and Condepa to form a congressional majority. The inclusion of the MIR in the coalition prompted concern among some observers, as it was feared that previous allegations of corruption and of involvement in the illegal drugs trade against the party and, in particular, against Paz Zamora (see above) would jeopardize the country's ability to attract international aid and investment. However, the grouping remained, and on 5 August Bánzer was elected President for a newly-extended term of five years with 118 congressional votes. The new administration pledged to consolidate the free-market reforms introduced by the previous Government and sought to assure the USA that the alliance with the MIR would not compromise its commitment to combating the illegal drugs trade.

In late August 1997 the newly-elected Government signed a financial co-operation agreement with the USA for continued action to combat the illegal drugs trade. The agreement, which provided finance for the implementation of eradication programmes, was criticized for its emphasis on the suppression of coca cultivation rather than on the development of alternative crops. The previous Government's commitment to destroy 7,000 ha of coca plantations during 1997 in order to keep Bolivia's 'certification' status led to concern that violence might erupt if the new Government felt under pressure to implement an aggressive eradication programme in order to meet this target (particularly as only 3,600 ha had been destroyed by September of that year). Moreover, many observers believed the policy to be ineffective, as, despite the provision of US finance worth US $500m. since 1990 to eradicate the crop, there had been no net reduction in coca production in Bolivia. There was also evidence that compensation payments given to coca growers for the destruction of their crops had been used to replant coca in more remote areas. Meanwhile, discontent with some of the new Government's economic policies, particularly an increase in petrol prices and taxes announced in November, prompted several strikes, organized by the COB in late 1997 and early 1998.

In February 1998 coca-producers in the Cochabamba region announced their rejection of the Government's new anti-coca policy (the so-called 'Dignity Plan', which aimed to eradicate all illegal coca plantations by 2002), claiming that an agreement, signed in October 1997, to provide alternative development programmes had not been honoured. Coca-growers also stated that groups of peasant farmers, styled 'self-defence committees', created to defend the coca crop but disbanded in mid-1997, would be reactivated. Violent clashes ensued, in which some 13 peasant farmers were killed and many more injured, when army and police personnel converged on the region in April to implement the eradication programme. In the following month the Government agreed temporarily to suspend the measures. Further clashes, however, were reported in May.

In late May 1998 central Bolivia was struck by a series of earthquakes which left more than 120 people dead and some 15,000 homeless.

In July 1998 Freddy Conde, the Minister of Agriculture, resigned his post after publicly criticizing the leaders of his party, Condepa. Internal divisions within Condepa subsequently led Bánzer to announce the removal of the party from the governing coalition, and to make several new appointments to the Cabinet.

More than 1,000 coca-growers undertook a 800-km march of protest from Chapare to La Paz in August 1998. The protesters demanded that the Government review its coca-eradication programme and denounced new measures including the confiscation of land used for coca cultivation, the incarceration of new coca-growers and the reduction, by more than 50%, of compensation rates paid to farmers who voluntarily ceased to grow coca. The Government rejected the demands of the coca-producers, reiterating its intention to eradicate more than 9,000 ha of the crop by the end of the year. Demonstrations and roadblocks by protesters in La Paz and Cochabamba during September were disrupted by security forces, leading to violent confrontation in many cases. The announcement in late 1998 that the headquarters of the armed forces were to be moved from La Paz to Cochabamba during 1999 was interpreted by some observers as a further measure to suppress the activities of the coca-growing community. The Government, however, denied that a process of militarization of the Cochabamba region was being implemented. In late 1998 it was announced that the 'Dignity Plan' was progressing successfully, with more than 11,500 ha of coca having been destroyed during that year. The Bolivian Government stated that funding for the programme had been received from the USA and the European Union (EU), but that a further US $300m. was required to develop alternative resources to replace revenue lost from the illegal sale of coca.

During the first half of 1999 there were a number of high-profile resignations: in March the Minister of Labour, Leopoldo López, resigned following revelations, in a report published by the Ministry of Finance, that he had been involved in smuggling activities; in the subsequent month the commander of the national police force, Ivar Narváez, was forced to stand down from his post as a result of accusations of corruption and misuse of funds; and in June the resignation of the Minister of the Interior, Guido Nayor, prompted a major cabinet reorganization, including the appointment of eight new ministers. In mid-1999 a number of reforms of the judicial system were announced, including the appointment of a people's ombudsman, a constitutional tribunal and an independent judicial council. It was hoped that these measures would help to reduce levels of corruption, particularly with regard to the accountability of the police force. The new system was not expected to be fully implemented, however, until 2001. Bolivia's new penal code, which came into effect at the end of May 1999, was groundbreaking in that it formally incorporated into the country's legal system the customary law of indigenous Indian peoples.

In September 1990, following the completion of a 650-km march of protest by 700 indigenous Indians from the town of Trinidad, in Beni, to the capital, La Paz, the Government issued four decrees in an unprecedented act of recognition of Indian land rights. Besides acknowledging as Indian territory more than 1.6m. ha of tropical rainforest in northern Bolivia, a multi-party commission was to be established in order to draft a new Law for Indigenous Indians of the East and Amazonia.

Bolivia's relations with Peru and Chile have been dominated by the long-standing issue of possible Bolivian access to the

Pacific Ocean. An agreement with Peru, completed in 1993, granted Bolivia free access from the border town of Desaguadero, Bolivia, to the Pacific port of Ilo, Peru, until 2091. Bolivia's desire to regain sovereign access to the sea, however, continued to impair relations with Chile in 1997, when the Bolivian Government repeatedly requested that discussions on the subject take place and sought Peru's assistance as a mediator in the dispute. In February Bolivia's Minister of Foreign Affairs directly accused Gen. Augusto Pinochet Ugarte, the Commander-in-Chief of the Chilean Army, of being the main obstacle in Bolivia's quest for access to the sea. Moreover, talks which aimed to improve trade arrangements between the two countries were suspended in March and again in May following failure to reach agreement. Relations deteriorated further in late 1997 when the Bolivian Government filed an official protest note to Chile regarding its failure to remove land-mines along the common border (planted during the 1970s). However, following a meeting between government representatives in August 1998 Bolivia announced that it was to abandon its policy of actively pursuing access to the sea in Chile and, after discussions with the Chilean Minister of Foreign Affairs in June 1999, President Bánzer announced that Bolivia was considering the resumption of diplomatic relations with Chile. However, subsequent talks between representatives of the two countries appeared to collapse later in the year, when the Chilean Government indicated that it would not be willing to resume negotiations over Bolivia's access to the Chilean coastline.

In 1992 Bolivia signed an agreement with Brazil for the construction of a 3,150-km pipeline to carry natural gas from Bolivia to southern Brazil. The outlines of the project, which was expected to cost US $1,800m. and was the largest of its kind in South America, were finalized, following considerable delay, in mid-1996. The pipeline (the first 1,970 km of which were completed in early 1999) was expected to transport an initial 3.7m. cu m of natural gas per day to Brazil, increasing to 9.1m. cu m by 2000, when the pipeline was due to be fully operational. Concern was expressed by numerous environmental groups throughout the world in mid-1999 that the project would threaten the tropical Chiquitano forest, through which the pipeline was to pass. Protests groups claimed that the scheme was in breach of a US law prohibiting support for projects harmful to the environment. However, these claims were rejected by the US Overseas Private Investment Corporation, which was expected to approve a US $200m.-loan for the construction of the pipeline.

In November 1994 an agreement to provide a waterway linking Bolivia with the Atlantic coast in Uruguay was concluded. The controversial project, which involved dredging a deep-water channel in the Paraguay and Paraná Rivers was postponed repeatedly, owing to Brazilian fears that the scheme would devastate a large, undeveloped area of ecological importance in south-western Brazil, known as the Pantanal.

### Government

Legislative power is held by the bicameral Congress, comprising a Senate (27 members) and a Chamber of Deputies (130 members). Both houses are elected for a four-year term by universal adult suffrage. Executive power is vested in the President and the Cabinet, which is appointed by the President. The President is directly elected for five years (extended from four years in 1997). If no candidate gains an absolute majority of votes, the President is chosen by Congress. The country is divided, for administrative purposes, into nine departments, each of which is governed by a prefect, appointed by the President.

### Defence

Military service, for one year, is selective. In August 1999 the armed forces numbered 32,500 men (there were plans to increase this to 35,000), of whom the army had 25,000 (including 18,000 conscripts), the air force 3,000, and the navy 4,500. Expenditure on defence by the central Government in 1997 was 783.7m. bolivianos, equivalent to 8.3% of total spending.

### Economic Affairs

In 1997, according to World Bank estimates, Bolivia's gross national product (GNP), measured at average 1995–97 prices, totalled US $7,564m., equivalent to about $970 per head. In the period 1990–97 real GNP per head grew by an average of 2.0% per year. During the same period the population increased at an average annual rate of 2.4%. In 1998 total GNP was estimated at $7,900m., equivalent to about $1,000 per head. Bolivia's gross domestic product (GDP) increased, in real terms, at an average annual rate of 4.2% in 1990–98; GDP increased by some 4.7% in 1998.

Agriculture (including forestry and fishing) contributed an estimated 15.8% of GDP (at constant 1990 prices) in 1997. In 1998 an estimated 44.7% of the economically active population were employed in agriculture. Wood accounted for 6.3% of export earnings in 1997. The principal cash crops are soybeans (which, together with soybean oil, accounted for 20.9% of export earnings in 1997), sugar, chestnuts and coffee. Beef and hides are also important exports. In the period 1990–96 agricultural GDP increased at an average annual rate of 3.7%; it rose by 3.6% in 1996 and by 4.9% in 1997.

Industry (including mining, manufacturing, construction and power) provided some 34.2% of GDP (at constant 1990 prices) in 1997. In 1997 18.4% of the working population were employed in industry. During the period 1990–97 industrial GDP increased at an average annual rate of 4.3%; it rose by 3.3% in 1996 and by 3.5% in 1997.

Mining (including petroleum exploration) contributed an estimated 9.9% of GDP (at constant 1990 prices) in 1997 and employed about 1% of the working population in that year. Investment in mineral exploitation increased 10-fold between 1991 and 1996. Funding for gold exploration projects, however, decreased from US $45m. in 1996 to US $20m. in 1997, while investment in polymetallic projects increased from US $8m. in 1996 to US $15m. in the following year. Investment in petroleum exploration totalled US $129m. in 1997. Zinc, tin, silver, gold, lead and antimony are the major mineral exports. Tungsten and copper continue to be mined. Exports of zinc and tin earned US $153.8m. and US $81m., respectively, in 1997. In 1990–97 the GDP of the mining sector increased at an average annual rate of 2.7%; mining GDP decreased by 1.0% in 1996 and by 0.3% in 1997.

In 1997 manufacturing accounted for some 18.1% of GDP (at constant 1990 prices), and in that year some 11.0% of the working population were employed in manufacturing. The GDP of this sector increased during 1990–97 at an average annual rate of 4.2%; it rose by 3.9% in 1996 and by 4.2% in 1997. Measured by the value of output, the principal branches of manufacturing in 1995 were food products (30.9%—including meat preparations 10.5% and beverages 9.1%), petroleum refineries (20.7%), jewellery and related articles (5.7%) and cement (3.8%).

Energy is derived principally from petroleum and natural gas, although hydroelectricity is also important. In 1997 production of crude petroleum increased by an estimated 2.8% to 11m. barrels. In 1997 imports of fuels comprised an estimated 6.8% of total merchandise imports. Earnings from exports of petroleum and petroleum products accounted for 2.4% of the total in 1997, compared with 3.4% in the previous year. Exports of natural gas accounted for 26.1% of total export earnings in 1991, but only 5.9% in 1997. Reserves of natural gas were estimated at 4,600,000m. cu ft at the end of 1997. During the late 1990s several major new natural gas deposits were discovered, which significantly increased the country's total known reserves.

The services sector accounted for some 49.9% of GDP (at constant 1990 prices) in 1997 and engaged 38.5% of the employed population in that year. During the period 1990–97 the GDP of this sector increased at an average annual rate of 4.4%; services GDP increased by 4.9% in 1996 and by 5.1% in 1997.

In 1998 Bolivia recorded a visible trade deficit of US $655.4m., and there was a deficit of $673.1m. on the current account of the balance of payments. In 1997 the main sources of imports were the USA (21.9%), Brazil (12.6%), Japan (12.4%) and Argentina (8.5%). The USA, Argentina, Peru and the United Kingdom were the major recipients of Bolivian exports in 1996 (21.8%, 13.2%, 12.8% and 14.3% respectively). The principal imports in that year included industrial materials and machinery, transport equipment and consumer goods. The principal legal exports were metallic minerals, natural gas, soybeans and wood. In 1990 government sources estimated that around US $600m. (almost equivalent to annual earnings from official exports) were absorbed annually into the economy as a result of the illegal trade in coca and its derivatives (mainly cocaine).

In 1998 Bolivia's overall budget deficit (including regional and local governments) amounted to 1,275m. bolivianos (equivalent to 2.7% of GDP). Bolivia's total external debt at the end of 1997 was US $5,248m., of which $4,144m. was long-term public debt. The cost of debt-servicing in that year was equivalent to

32.5% of the total value of exports of goods and services. In 1990–98 the average annual rate of inflation was 8.0%. Consumer prices increased by an average of 12.4% in 1996, 4.7% in 1997 and 7.7% in 1998. In 1996 an estimated 4.2% of the labour force were unemployed.

In May 1991 Bolivia was one of five Andean Pact countries to sign the Caracas Declaration providing the foundation for a common market. In October 1992 Bolivia officially joined the Andean free-trade area, removing tariff barriers to imports from Colombia, Ecuador and Venezuela. Bolivia also agreed to sign a free-trade accord with Mexico in September 1994. In late 1996 Bolivia concluded a free-trade agreement with Mercosur (see p. 267), equivalent to associate membership of the organization, with effect from January 1997. In mid-1999 an agreement on the rationalization of their respective customs systems (thus moving closer to the formation of a regional free-trade area) was reached between Mercosur and the Andean Community (see p. 119); the two-year accord came into effect in August. Bolivia is a member of the Andean Community), and in 1989 the Andean Social Development Fund was established. The country is also a member of the Organization of American States (OAS, see p. 245), and of the Latin American Integration Association (ALADI, see p. 292). Bolivia became the 97th contracting party to GATT (which was superseded by the World Trade Organization, WTO, in 1995—see p. 274) in 1989.

A public-sector capitalization programme, which aimed to attract more private-sector involvement in Bolivia's principal industries by selling a 50% controlling share in several state-owned companies to private investors, began in early 1995; the process was expected to be completed by the end of 2002.

The continued success of exploratory missions in locating new sources of petroleum and natural gas, in particular, resulted in a series of projects in the late 1990s, which aimed to develop Bolivia's potential as one of the region's most important energy-producing countries. A major new gas deposit near Santa Cruz, with total reserves estimated at 1,700,000m. cu ft, was discovered in 1998. Official development assistance was equivalent to some 10% of GNP annually in the mid-1990s. The country's severe debt burden is widely acknowledged to be a major factor in inhibiting economic growth, and in recognition of this the World Bank and the IMF approved a debt-relief package worth US $760m. (under its Heavily Indebted Poor Countries' Initiative), which was released in October 1998. Also in late 1998 a three-year loan worth US $138m. was secured from the IMF. In early 1999 the Government announced that, despite severe drought conditions, the economy had again shown strong growth in 1998 and that the rate of inflation had fallen to its lowest level for nine years. It also confirmed that the programme for the transfer of state-owned companies to private ownership (launched in 1990) was expected to be finally completed by mid-2000, and that the process would provide an estimated US $150m. in revenue. However, on the negative side, the trade deficit in 1998 rose to its highest level for several years, partly owing to a 10.5% decrease in export revenue (one of the reasons for which was the effects of the Asian financial crisis).

### Social Welfare

There are benefits for unemployment, accident, sickness, old age and death. In 1993 there were 51 physicians and 25 nurses for every 100,000 inhabitants. A privately-managed national pension scheme was established in 1995, as a result of the Government's capitalization programme, in which a 50% share in several state-owned industries was sold to private-sector investors while the remaining 50% was invested in a pension fund for all Bolivian citizens. In May 1997 some 300,000 Bolivians over the age of 65 years began to receive a bonus payment (*bono solidaridad*) of US $248 from the pension fund. Of total expenditure by the central Government in 1997, 329.9m. bolivianos (3.5%) was for health, and a further 2,543.7m. bolivianos (26.8%) for social security and welfare.

### Education

Primary education, beginning at six years of age and lasting for eight years, is officially compulsory and is available free of charge. Secondary education, which is not compulsory, begins at 14 years of age and lasts for up to four years. In 1990 the total enrolment at primary and secondary schools was equivalent to 77% of the school-age population (81% of boys; 73% of girls). In that year enrolment at primary schools included an estimated 91% of children in the relevant age-group (95% of boys; 87% of girls), while the comparable ratio for secondary enrolment was only 29% (32% of boys; 27% of girls). There are eight state universities and two private universities. In 1995, according to UNESCO estimates, the average rate of adult illiteracy was 16.9% (males 9.5%; females 24.0%). Expenditure on education by the central Government in 1997 was 1,830.3m. bolivianos, representing 19.3% of total spending.

### Public Holidays

**2000:** 1 January (New Year), 4–7 February (Carnival), 22 February (Oruro only), 15 April (Tarija only), 21 April (Good Friday), 1 May (Labour Day), 25 May (Sucre only), 22 June (Corpus Christi), 16 July (La Paz only), 6 August (Independence), 14 September (Cochabamba only), 24 September (Santa Cruz and Pando only), 1–2 November (All Saints' Day), 10 November (Potosí only), 18 November (Beni only), 25 December (Christmas).

**2001:** 1 January (New Year), 4–7 February (Carnival), 22 February (Oruro only), 13 April (Good Friday), 15 April (Tarija only), 1 May (Labour Day), 25 May (Sucre only), 14 June (Corpus Christi), 16 July (La Paz only), 6 August (Independence), 14 September (Cochabamba only), 24 September (Santa Cruz and Pando only), 1–2 November (All Saints' Day), 10 November (Potosí only), 18 November (Beni only), 25 December (Christmas).

### Weights and Measures

The metric system is officially in force, but various old Spanish measures are also used.

# Statistical Survey

Sources (unless otherwise indicated): Instituto Nacional de Estadística, Plaza Mario Guzmán Aspiazu No. 1, Casilla 6129, La Paz; tel. (2) 36-7443; internet www.ine.gov.bo; Banco Central de Bolivia, Ayacucho esq. Mercado, Casilla 3118, La Paz; tel. (2) 37-4151; fax (2) 39-2398.

## Area and Population

**AREA, POPULATION AND DENSITY**

| | |
|---|---|
| Area (sq km) | |
| Land | 1,084,391 |
| Inland water | 14,190 |
| Total | 1,098,581* |
| Population (census results)† | |
| 29 September 1976 | 4,613,486 |
| 3 June 1992 | |
| Males | 3,171,265 |
| Females | 3,249,527 |
| Total | 6,420,792 |
| Population (official estimates at mid-year) | |
| 1995 | 7,413,834 |
| 1996 | 7,588,392 |
| 1997 | 7,767,059 |
| Density (per sq km) at mid-1997 | 7.1 |

* 424,164 sq miles.

† Figures exclude adjustment for underenumeration. This was estimated at 6.99% in 1976 and at 6.92% in 1992.

**DEPARTMENTS** (1992 census)*

| | Area (sq km) | Population | Density (per sq km) | Capital |
|---|---|---|---|---|
| Beni | 213,564 | 276,174 | 1.3 | Trinidad |
| Chuquisaca | 51,524 | 453,756 | 8.8 | Sucre |
| Cochabamba | 55,631 | 1,110,205 | 20.0 | Cochabamba |
| La Paz | 133,985 | 1,900,786 | 14.2 | La Paz |
| Oruro | 53,588 | 340,114 | 6.3 | Oruro |
| Pando | 63,827 | 38,072 | 0.6 | Cobija |
| Potosí | 118,218 | 645,889 | 5.5 | Potosí |
| Santa Cruz | 370,621 | 1,364,389 | 3.7 | Santa Cruz de la Sierra |
| Tarija | 37,623 | 291,407 | 7.7 | Tarija |
| **Total** | 1,098,581 | 6,420,792 | 5.8 | |

* Excluding adjustment for underenumeration.

**PRINCIPAL TOWNS** (estimated population at November 1997)

| | |
|---|---|
| Santa Cruz de la Sierra | 914,795 |
| La Paz (administrative capital) | 758,141 |
| Cochabamba | 560,284 |
| El Alto | 523,280 |
| Oruro | 202,548 |
| Sucre (legal capital) | 163,563 |
| Potosí | 122,962 |

**BIRTHS AND DEATHS** (UN estimates, annual averages)

| | 1980–85 | 1985–90 | 1990–95 |
|---|---|---|---|
| Birth rate (per 1,000) | 38.2 | 36.6 | 35.7 |
| Death rate (per 1,000) | 13.5 | 11.5 | 10.2 |

**Expectation of life** (UN estimates, years at birth, 1990–95): 59.3 (males 57.7, females 61.0).

Source: UN, *World Population Prospects: The 1998 Revision.*

**ECONOMICALLY ACTIVE POPULATION**
(labour force surveys, '000 persons aged 10 years and over, at November)

| | 1996 | 1997 |
|---|---|---|
| Agriculture | 1,620.7 | 1,518.7 |
| Forestery and fishing | 14.6 | 23.1 |
| Mining and quarrying | 53.7 | 63.9 |
| Manufacturing | 403.6 | 393.5 |
| Electricity, gas and water supply | 9.9 | 11.0 |
| Construction | 172.4 | 187.0 |
| Wholesale and retail trade; repair of motor vehicles, motorcycles and personal and household goods | 562.3 | 505.9 |
| Hotels and restaurants | 135.2 | 126.5 |
| Transport, storage and communications | 147.6 | 170.5 |
| Financial intermediation | 18.1 | 20.1 |
| Real estate, renting and business activities | 51.9 | 58.8 |
| Public administration and defence; compulsory social security | 91.8 | 78.8 |
| Education | 137.9 | 158.8 |
| Health and social work | 59.9 | 62.9 |
| Other community, social and personal service activities | 67.5 | 70.4 |
| Private households with employed persons | 127.0 | 117.8 |
| Extra-territorial organizations and bodies | 1.6 | 2.1 |
| **Total employed** | 3,675.7 | 3,569.7 |
| Unemployed | 65.0 | 75.4 |
| **Total labour force** | 3,740.7 | 3,645.2 |
| Males | 2,008.7 | 2,048.8 |
| Females | 1,731.9 | 1,596.4 |

# Agriculture

**PRINCIPAL CROPS** ('000 metric tons)

| | 1996 | 1997 | 1998 |
|---|---|---|---|
| Wheat | 99 | 143 | 164 |
| Rice (paddy) | 344 | 253 | 301 |
| Barley | 64 | 69 | 40 |
| Maize | 613 | 678 | 424 |
| Sorghum | 105 | 100 | 59† |
| Potatoes | 715 | 843 | 495 |
| Cassava (Manioc) | 311 | 348 | 357 |
| Other roots and tubers | 105 | 104 | 92 |
| Pulses | 27 | 27 | 27 |
| Soya beans | 862 | 1,038 | 1,071 |
| Groundnuts (in shell) | 12 | 13 | 13 |
| Sunflower seeds | 33 | 81 | 115 |
| Cottonseed | 15 | 12 | 11 |
| Cotton (lint) | 10 | 8 | 7 |
| Tomatoes | 59 | 80 | 80 |
| Pumpkins, squash and gourds | 103 | 105 | 108 |
| Onions (dry) | 47 | 48 | 48 |
| Peas (green) | 20 | 25 | 20 |
| Carrots | 33 | 33 | 33 |
| Other vegetables | 170 | 185 | 172 |
| Watermelons | 21 | 21 | 21 |
| Sugar cane | 4,120 | 4,126 | 4,241 |
| Oranges | 94 | 94 | 94 |
| Tangerines, mandarins, clementines and satsumas | 50 | 50 | 48 |
| Lemons and limes | 61 | 62 | 61 |
| Grapefruit and pomelos | 28 | 29 | 29 |
| Pineapples | 22 | 23 | 23* |
| Papayas | 22 | 22 | 22 |
| Peaches and nectarines | 36 | 36 | 36 |
| Grapes | 21 | 23 | 23 |
| Bananas | 279 | 336† | 368† |
| Plantains† | 215 | 230 | 154 |
| Other fruits and berries | 47 | 44 | 44 |
| Chestnuts | 40 | 40 | 44 |
| Coffee (green) | 22 | 23 | 24 |
| Natural rubber | 10 | 10 | 11 |

* FAO estimate. † Unofficial figure(s).

Source: FAO, *Production Yearbook*.

**LIVESTOCK** ('000 head, year ending September)

| | 1996 | 1997 | 1998 |
|---|---|---|---|
| Horses* | 322 | 322 | 322 |
| Mules* | 81 | 81 | 81 |
| Asses* | 631 | 631 | 631 |
| Cattle | 6,118 | 6,238 | 6,387 |
| Pigs | 2,482 | 2,569 | 2,637 |
| Sheep | 8,039 | 8,232 | 8,409 |
| Goats* | 1,496 | 1,496 | 1,496 |
| Poultry (million) | 59 | 58 | 59 |

* FAO estimates.

Source: FAO, *Production Yearbook*.

**LIVESTOCK PRODUCTS** ('000 metric tons)

| | 1996 | 1997 | 1998 |
|---|---|---|---|
| Beef and veal | 143 | 147 | 151 |
| Mutton and lamb | 14 | 15 | 15 |
| Goat meat* | 6 | 6 | 6 |
| Pig meat* | 66 | 69 | 72 |
| Poultry meat | 108 | 118 | 127 |
| Cows' milk | 195 | 200 | 205 |
| Sheep's milk* | 29 | 29 | 29 |
| Goats' milk* | 11 | 11 | 11 |
| Cheese* | 7 | 7 | 7 |
| Hen eggs* | 68 | 68 | 68 |
| Wool: greasy* | 8 | 8 | 8 |
| scoured* | 4 | 4 | 4 |
| Cattle hides (fresh)* | 18 | 17 | 18 |
| Sheepskins (fresh)* | 5 | 5 | 5 |

* FAO estimates.

Source: FAO, *Production Yearbook*.

# Forestry

**ROUNDWOOD REMOVALS** ('000 cubic metres, excl. bark)

| | 1995 | 1996 | 1997 |
|---|---|---|---|
| Sawlogs, veneer logs and logs for sleepers | 449 | 491 | 489 |
| Pulpwood | 383 | 383 | 383 |
| Other industrial wood | 18 | 18 | 18 |
| Fuel wood | 1,358 | 1,389 | 1,425 |
| **Total** | 2,208 | 2,281 | 2,315 |

Source: FAO, *Yearbook of Forest Products*.

**SAWNWOOD PRODUCTION** ('000 cubic metres, incl. railway sleepers)

| | 1995 | 1996 | 1997 |
|---|---|---|---|
| Coniferous (softwood)* | 10 | 15 | 15 |
| Broadleaved (hardwood) | 152 | 166 | 165 |
| **Total** | 162 | 181 | 180 |

* FAO estimates.

Source: FAO, *Yearbook of Forest Products*.

# Fishing

('000 metric tons, live weight)

| | 1995 | 1996 | 1997 |
|---|---|---|---|
| **Total catch** | 5.7 | 6.0 | 6.0 |

Source: FAO, *Yearbook of Fishery Statistics*.

# Mining*

(metric tons, unless otherwise indicated)

| | 1995 | 1996 | 1997 |
|---|---|---|---|
| Crude petroleum ('000 metric tons) | 1,417 | 1,463 | 1,503 |
| Natural gas (million cu metres) | 3,295 | 3,329 | 3,010 |
| Copper | 127 | 60 | 190 |
| Tin | 14,419 | 14,802 | 12,922 |
| Lead | 20,387 | 16,538 | 18,671 |
| Zinc | 146,131 | 145,092 | 154,030 |
| Tungsten (Wolfram) | 826 | 733 | 647 |
| Antimony | 6,426 | 6,487 | 6,478 |
| Silver | 425 | 386 | 401 |
| Gold | 14.4 | 12.6 | 13.5 |

**1998** (metric tons): Tin 11,305 (Source: US Geological Survey).

* Figures for metallic minerals refer to the metal content of ores.

# Industry

**SELECTED PRODUCTS** ('000 metric tons, unless otherwise indicated)

| | 1995 | 1996 | 1997* |
|---|---|---|---|
| Flour | 412 | 446 | 465 |
| Cement | 719 | 774 | 869 |
| Refined sugar | 332 | 350 | 332 |
| Carbonated drinks ('000 hectolitres) | 1,493 | 1,747 | 1,867 |
| Beer ('000 hectolitres) | 1,596 | 1,722 | 1,702 |
| Cigarettes (packets) | 82,084 | 68,835 | 73,166 |
| Alcohol ('000 litres) | 23,694 | 27,351 | 27,678 |
| Diesel oil | 470 | 504 | 540 |
| Motor spirit (petrol) | 368 | 409 | 393 |
| Electric energy (million kWh) | 3,020 | 3,222 | 3,528 |

**Tin** (primary metal, metric tons): 17,709 in 1995; 16,733 in 1996; 16,853 in 1997; 11,102 in 1998 (Source: US Geological Survey).

# Finance

## CURRENCY AND EXCHANGE RATES

**Monetary Units**

100 centavos = 1 boliviano (B).

**Sterling, Dollar and Euro Equivalents** (30 September 1999)

£1 sterling = 9.747 bolivianos;
US $1 = 5.920 bolivianos;
€1 = 6.314 bolivianos;
1,000 bolivianos = £102.59 = $168.92 = €158.39.

**Average Exchange Rate** (bolivianos per US $)

| | |
|---|---|
| 1996 | 5.0746 |
| 1997 | 5.2543 |
| 1998 | 5.5101 |

## BUDGET (million bolivianos)*

| Revenue† | 1995 | 1996 | 1997 |
|---|---|---|---|
| Taxation | 3,476.9 | 5,483.9 | 6,562.2 |
| Taxes on income, profits and capital gains | 132.1 | 416.6 | 524.2 |
| Social security contributions | 342.9 | 869.2 | 1,306.6 |
| Taxes on property | 536.5 | 604.6 | 562.5 |
| Sales taxes | 1,552.7 | 2,553.6 | 2,880.4 |
| Excises | 514.2 | 618.9 | 787.6 |
| Import duties | 349.8 | 377.9 | 472.0 |
| Entrepreneurial and property income | 1,293.6 | 575.3 | 181.0 |
| Administrative fees, charges, etc. | 303.9 | 243.8 | 421.4 |
| Other current revenue | 78.8 | 141.2 | 280.0 |
| Capital revenue | 102.9 | 120.5 | 22.3 |
| **Total** | 5,256.1 | 6,564.7 | 7,466.9 |

| Expenditure‡ | 1995 | 1996 | 1997 |
|---|---|---|---|
| General public services | 950.6 | 1,037.1 | 1,219.9 |
| Defence | 572.9 | 630.2 | 783.7 |
| Public order and safety | 549.1 | 650.8 | 782.9 |
| Education | 1,313.3 | 1,511.9 | 1,830.3 |
| Health | 420.6 | 347.0 | 329.9 |
| Social security and welfare | 1,085.3 | 1,672.8 | 2,543.7 |
| Housing and community amenities | 54.1 | 35.0 | 74.7 |
| Recreational, cultural and religious affairs and services | 33.4 | 27.5 | 35.3 |
| Economic services | 1,094.6 | 1,827.6 | 1,131.9 |
| Fuel and energy | 5.7 | 25.2 | 13.8 |
| Agriculture, forestry and fishing | 70.1 | 69.6 | 90.3 |
| Mining and mineral resources, manufacturing and construction | 27.9 | 68.4 | 47.2 |
| Transport and communications | 835.0 | 1,028.1 | 573.1 |
| Other purposes | 727.7 | 979.8 | 757.3 |
| **Total** | 6,801.6 | 8,719.7 | 9,489.6 |
| Current§ | 5,498.6 | 6,841.5 | 7,812.7 |
| Capital | 1,303.1 | 1,878.2 | 1,676.9 |

* Figures refer to the transactions of central government units covered by the General Budget, plus the operations of other units (government agencies and social security institutions) with their own budgets.

† Excluding grants received (million bolivianos): 646.8 in 1995; 1,185.4 in 1996; 738.0 in 1997.

‡ Excluding lending minus repayments (million bolivianos): –149.7 in 1995; –74.9 in 1996; –312.0 in 1997.

§ Including interest payments (million bolivianos): 727.7 in 1995; 749.5 in 1996; 709.2 in 1997.

Source: IMF, *Government Finance Statistics Yearbook*.

## INTERNATIONAL RESERVES (US $ million at 31 December)

| | 1996 | 1997 | 1998 |
|---|---|---|---|
| Gold* | 39.6 | 39.6 | 234.9 |
| IMF special drawing rights | 38.5 | 36.2 | 37.7 |
| Reserve position in IMF | 12.8 | 12.0 | 12.5 |
| Foreign exchange | 903.7 | 1,038.5 | 834.4 |
| **Total** | 994.6 | 1,126.2 | 1,119.5 |

* National valuation (939,000 troy oz each year).

Source: IMF, *International Financial Statistics*.

## MONEY SUPPLY (million bolivianos at 31 December)

| | 1996 | 1997 | 1998 |
|---|---|---|---|
| Currency outside banks | 1,802 | 2,061 | 2,193 |
| Demand deposits at commercial banks | 867 | 1,036 | 1,124 |
| **Total money** | 3,055 | 3,636 | 3,895 |

Source: IMF, *International Financial Statistics*.

## COST OF LIVING

(Consumer Price Index for urban areas; base: 1990 = 100)

| | 1994 | 1995 | 1996 |
|---|---|---|---|
| Food | 160.5 | 179.8 | 205.4 |
| Clothing | 112.8 | 113.9 | 114.2 |
| Rent | 105.7 | 107.3 | 108.7 |
| **All items** (incl. others) | 159.3 | 175.5 | 197.3 |

Source: ILO, *Yearbook of Labour Statistics*.

**1997** (1991 = 100): Food 176.3; All items 171.6 (Source: UN, *Monthly Bulletin of Statistics*).

**1998** (1991 = 100): Food 185.7; All items 184.9 (Source: UN, *Monthly Bulletin of Statistics*).

## NATIONAL ACCOUNTS

**Expenditure on the Gross Domestic Product**

(million bolivianos at current prices)

| | 1996 | 1997 | 1998 |
|---|---|---|---|
| Government final consumption expenditure | 5,003 | 5,755 | 6,604 |
| Private final consumption expenditure | 28,201 | 30,662 | 34,203 |
| Increase in stocks | 23 | 192 | –193 |
| Gross fixed capital formation | 6,072 | 8,105 | 10,943 |
| **Total domestic expenditure** | 39,299 | 44,714 | 51,557 |
| Exports of goods and services | 8,476 | 9,284 | 9,309 |
| *Less* Imports of goods and services | 10,238 | 12,139 | 13,642 |
| **GDP in purchasers' values** | 37,537 | 41,860 | 47,225 |
| **GDP at constant 1990 prices** | 19,701 | 20,577 | 21,554 |

Source: IMF, *International Financial Statistics*.

**Gross Domestic Product by Economic Activity**

(million bolivianos at constant 1990 prices)

| | 1995 | 1996 | 1997* |
|---|---|---|---|
| Agriculture, hunting, forestry and fishing | 2,810 | 2,911 | 3,053 |
| Mining and quarrying | 1,925 | 1,906 | 1,901 |
| Manufacturing | 3,220 | 3,346 | 3,488 |
| Electricity, gas and water | 389 | 423 | 455 |
| Construction | 634 | 699 | 752 |
| Trade | 1,622 | 1,692 | 1,779 |
| Restaurants and hotels | 609 | 632 | 649 |
| Transport, storage and communications | 1,880 | 2,044 | 2,183 |
| Finance, insurance, real estate and business services | 2,029 | 2,153 | 2,274 |
| Government services | 1,766 | 1,785 | 1,857 |
| Other community, social and personal services | 718 | 743 | 770 |
| Other producers | 104 | 106 | 109 |
| **Sub-total** | 17,706 | 18,440 | 19,270 |
| Import duties | 1,625 | 1,723 | 1,793 |
| *Less* Imputed bank service charge | 454 | 513 | 588 |
| **Total** | 18,877 | 19,651 | 20,474 |

* Estimates.

**BALANCE OF PAYMENTS** (US $ million)

| | 1996 | 1997 | 1998 |
|---|---|---|---|
| Exports of goods f.o.b. | 1,132.0 | 1,166.5 | 1,104.0 |
| Imports of goods f.o.b. | −1,368.0 | −1,643.6 | −1,759.4 |
| **Trade balance** | −236.0 | −477.1 | −655.4 |
| Exports of services | 180.9 | 246.7 | 253.3 |
| Imports of services | −363.4 | −449.5 | −441.3 |
| **Balance on goods and services** | −418.5 | −679.9 | −843.4 |
| Other income received | 28.6 | 101.0 | 129.6 |
| Other income paid | −236.8 | −294.8 | −289.2 |
| **Balance on goods, services and income** | −626.7 | −873.6 | −1,003.0 |
| Current transfers received | 226.2 | 332.6 | 341.6 |
| Current transfers paid | −3.8 | −9.7 | −11.7 |
| **Current balance** | −404.3 | −550.8 | −673.1 |
| Capital account (net) | 2.8 | 25.3 | 9.9 |
| Direct investment abroad | −2.1 | −2.5 | −2.6 |
| Direct investment from abroad | 474.1 | 730.7 | 872.4 |
| Portfolio investment assets | 0.3 | — | — |
| Portfolio investment liabilities | — | −53.0 | −74.5 |
| Other investment assets | 12.2 | −19.9 | −106.2 |
| Other investment liabilities | 216.5 | 234.1 | 309.9 |
| Net errors and omissions | −31.6 | −262.9 | −234.2 |
| **Overall balance** | 268.0 | 101.0 | 101.5 |

Source: IMF, *International Financial Statistics.*

# External Trade

**PRINCIPAL COMMODITIES** (distribution by SITC, US $ '000)

| Imports c.i.f. | 1994 | 1995 | 1996 |
|---|---|---|---|
| **Food and live animals** | 112,395 | 124,577 | 156,606 |
| Cereals and cereal preparations | 63,858 | 70,205 | 86,341 |
| Wheat (including spelt) and meslin, unmilled | 42,385 | 42,928 | 60,233 |
| Durum wheat, unmilled | 32,769 | 26,132 | 29,214 |
| **Crude materials (inedible) except fuels** | 43,499 | 51,175 | 51,988 |
| **Mineral fuels, lubricants, etc.** | 60,441 | 63,768 | 47,979 |
| Petroleum, petroleum products, etc. | 59,915 | 63,728 | 47,935 |
| Refined petroleum products | 56,989 | 58,306 | 39,771 |
| Gas oils (distillate fuels) | 30,053 | 36,081 | 30,860 |
| **Chemicals and related products** | 152,714 | 185,488 | 202,659 |
| Medical and pharmaceutical products | 23,466 | 28,518 | 28,228 |
| Essential oils, perfume materials and cleansing preparations | 28,503 | 23,678 | 31,252 |
| Artificial resins, plastic materials, etc. | 29,590 | 41,513 | 42,631 |
| Products of polymerization, etc. | 24,598 | 33,665 | 34,184 |
| **Basic manufactures** | 203,221 | 216,809 | 229,998 |
| Paper, paperboard and manufactures | 26,387 | 38,696 | 35,826 |
| Paper and paperboard (not cut to size or shape) | 20,954 | 30,408 | 25,842 |
| Textile yarn, fabrics, etc. | 28,392 | 28,753 | 29,658 |
| Iron and steel | 59,703 | 60,990 | 68,861 |
| Tubes, pipes and fittings | 24,155 | 15,110 | 18,298 |
| **Machinery and transport equipment** | 515,972 | 645,499 | 788,775 |
| Power-generating machinery and equipment | 18,787 | 50,284 | 47,212 |
| Machinery specialized for particular industries | 90,731 | 107,377 | 101,431 |
| Civil engineering and contractors' plant and equipment | 28,557 | 43,876 | 35,202 |
| Construction and mining machinery | 23,320 | 34,554 | 24,428 |
| General industrial machinery, equipment and parts | 62,556 | 64,803 | 67,905 |
| Telecommunications and sound equipment | 26,852 | 48,342 | 117,202 |
| Other electrical machinery, apparatus, etc. | 36,091 | 50,841 | 49,725 |
| Road vehicles and parts* | 249,390 | 234,190 | 233,284 |
| Passenger motor cars (excl. buses) | 109,709 | 100,072 | 107,319 |
| Motor vehicles for the transport of goods, etc. | 82,734 | 82,263 | 75,663 |
| Goods vehicles | 78,854 | 75,875 | 69,255 |
| Other road motor vehicles | 31,275 | 26,210 | 32,125 |
| Other transport equipment and parts* | 11,054 | 69,821 | 150,424 |
| Aircraft, associated equipment and parts* | 8,628 | 68,421 | 149,945 |
| **Miscellaneous manufactured articles** | 83,425 | 92,451 | 113,053 |
| **Non-monetary gold (excl. ores and concentrates** | 13,938 | 9,039 | 41,984 |
| **Total** (incl. others) | 1,196,345 | 1,396,260 | 1,643,051 |

* Excluding tyres, engines and electrical parts.

| Exports f.o.b. | 1994 | 1995 | 1996 |
|---|---|---|---|
| **Food and live animals** | 157,690 | 113,616 | 179,126 |
| Cereals and cereal preparations | 28,769 | 4,757 | 4,675 |
| Vegetables and fruit | 28,847 | 29,879 | 42,252 |
| Fresh or dried fruit and nuts (excl. oil nuts) | 17,277 | 19,042 | 29,384 |
| Edible nuts | 15,775 | 18,702 | 28,616 |
| Brazil nuts | 3,153 | 2,250 | 27,787 |
| Sugar, sugar preparations and honey | 45,506 | 16,968 | 28,121 |
| Sugar and honey | 45,486 | 16,766 | 27,855 |
| Refined sugars (solid) | 45,430 | 16,545 | 19,465 |
| Feeding-stuff for animals (excl. unmilled cereals) | 31,046 | 39,346 | 81,708 |
| Oil-cake and other residues from the extraction of vegetable oils | 30,998 | 39,241 | 81,108 |
| Oil-cake and residues from soya beans | 30,882 | 38,507 | 78,161 |
| **Crude materials (inedible) except fuels** | 329,889 | 415,289 | 428,712 |
| Oil seeds and oleaginous fruit | 44,244 | 69,509 | 84,638 |
| Soya beans | 43,174 | 46,716 | 64,794 |
| Cork and wood | 78,548 | 66,115 | 68,964 |
| Simply worked wood and railway sleepers | 78,548 | 66,057 | 68,935 |
| Sawn non-coniferous wood | 70,534 | 63,202 | 64,598 |
| Textile fibres (excl. wool tops) and waste | 15,373 | 31,003 | 32,385 |
| Cotton | 13,954 | 29,960 | 31,282 |
| Raw cotton (excl. linters) | 13,876 | 29,960 | 31,282 |
| Metalliferous ores and metal scrap | 180,852 | 240,199 | 235,042 |
| Base metal ores and concentrates | 132,709 | 182,758 | 182,485 |
| Zinc ores and concentrates | 105,334 | 151,346 | 151,741 |
| Precious metal ores and concentrates | 48,011 | 57,374 | 52,162 |
| **Mineral fuels, lubricants etc.** | 107,047 | 152,875 | 142,106 |
| Petroleum, petroleum products, etc. | 15,144 | 60,176 | 47,346 |
| Crude petroleum oils, etc. | 6,577 | 48,109 | 38,494 |
| Gas (natural and manufactured) | 91,621 | 92,407 | 94,539 |
| Petroleum gases and other gaseous hydrocarbons | 91,621 | 92,407 | 94,539 |
| **Animal and vegetable oils, fats and waxes** | 21,613 | 35,559 | 40,537 |
| Fixed vegetable oils and fats | 21,561 | 35,476 | 40,500 |
| Soya bean oil | 20,451 | 34,679 | 39,484 |
| **Basic manufactures** | 157,891 | 154,103 | 144,959 |
| Non-ferrous metals | 133,171 | 128,022 | 113,854 |
| Tin and tin alloys | 110,032 | 112,926 | 101,223 |
| Unwrought tin and alloys | 109,631 | 112,386 | 100,226 |

| Exports f.o.b. — *continued* | 1994 | 1995 | 1996 |
|---|---|---|---|
| **Machinery and transport equipment** | 28,714 | 38,134 | 76,728 |
| Transport equipment and parts* | 11,869 | 22,614 | 62,050 |
| Aircraft, associated equipment and parts* | 8,789 | 18,531 | 59,310 |
| **Miscellaneous manufactured articles** | 190,360 | 117,879 | 49,602 |
| Clothing and accessories (excl. footwear) | 18,333 | 17,938 | 28,543 |
| Jewellery, goldsmiths' and silversmiths' wares, etc. | 164,314 | 90,927 | 11,400 |
| **Non-monetary gold (excl. ores and concentrates)** | 119,088 | 130,802 | n.a. |
| **Total** (incl. others) | 1,124,232 | 1,181,213 | 1,086,945 |

* Excluding tyres, engines and electrical parts.

Source: UN, *International Trade Statistics Yearbook.*

**PRINCIPAL TRADING PARTNERS** (US $ '000)*

| Imports c.i.f. | 1994 | 1995 | 1996 |
|---|---|---|---|
| Argentina | 117,483 | 117,416 | 136,637 |
| Belgium-Luxembourg | 6,677 | 54,727 | 9,565 |
| Brazil | 178,613 | 174,202 | 181,635 |
| Canada | 10,591 | 22,418 | 42,722 |
| Chile | 93,962 | 104,786 | 110,641 |
| China, People's Republic | 10,044 | 14,504 | 12,446 |
| Colombia | 22,729 | 22,947 | 33,779 |
| Germany | 17,192 | 36,918 | 60,870 |
| Italy | 17,192 | 36,918 | 55,622 |
| Japan | 181,826 | 171,699 | 199,118 |
| Korea, Republic | 14,453 | 18,069 | 20,350 |
| Mexico | 16,657 | 19,457 | 25,509 |
| Peru | 65,060 | 73,042 | 89,141 |
| Spain | 16,869 | 19,314 | 35,004 |
| Sweden | 32,380 | 38,752 | 48,197 |
| United Kingdom | 13,053 | 26,253 | 12,400 |
| USA | 235,075 | 312,647 | 455,726 |
| Venezuela | 12,621 | 10,930 | 13,172 |
| **Total** (incl. others) | 1,196,345 | 1,396,260 | 1,643,051 |

| Exports f.o.b. | 1994 | 1995 | 1996 |
|---|---|---|---|
| Argentina | 160,110 | 142,657 | 143,425 |
| Belgium-Luxembourg | 26,592 | 40,392 | 49,349 |
| Brazil | 35,369 | 23,441 | 36,316 |
| Chile | 19,202 | 25,834 | 43,453 |
| Colombia | 63,940 | 64,368 | 115,995 |
| Ecuador | 14,562 | 7,346 | 7,755 |
| France (incl. Monaco) | 47,402 | 41,233 | 2,108 |
| Germany | 54,037 | 57,076 | 24,404 |
| Mexico | 13,080 | 1,398 | 11,847 |
| Peru | 122,916 | 144,377 | 138,745 |
| Switzerland-Liechtenstein | 14,497 | 81,003 | 51,951 |
| United Kingdom | 150,641 | 153,297 | 155,605 |
| USA | 360,919 | 331,680 | 237,423 |
| **Total** (incl. others) | 1,124,232 | 1,181,213 | 1,086,945 |

* Imports by country of provenance; exports by country of last consignment.

Source: UN, *International Trade Statistics Yearbook.*

# Transport

**RAILWAYS** (traffic)

| | 1993 | 1994 | 1995 |
|---|---|---|---|
| Passenger-kilometres (million) | 288 | 276 | 240 |
| Freight ton-kilometres (million) | 692 | 782 | 758 |

Source: UN, *Statistical Yearbook.*

**ROAD TRAFFIC** (motor vehicles in use at 31 December)

| | 1994 | 1995 | 1996 |
|---|---|---|---|
| Passenger cars | 198,734 | 213,666 | 223,829 |
| Buses | 18,884 | 19,627 | 20,322 |
| Lorries and vans | 108,214 | 114,357 | 118,214 |
| Tractors | 9 | 9 | 10 |
| Motorcycles | 62,725 | 64,936 | 66,113 |

Source: IRF, *World Road Statistics.*

**CIVIL AVIATION** (traffic on scheduled services)

| | 1993 | 1994 | 1995 |
|---|---|---|---|
| Kilometres flown (million) | 11 | 14 | 16 |
| Passengers carried ('000) | 1,117 | 1,175 | 1,224 |
| Passenger-km (million) | 1,092 | 1,139 | 1,234 |
| Freight ton-km (million) | 120 | 151 | 187 |

Source: UN, *Statistical Yearbook.*

# Tourism

**ARRIVALS AT HOTELS** (regional capitals only, '000)

| Country of origin | 1994 | 1995 | 1996 |
|---|---|---|---|
| Argentina | 33.1 | 35.4 | 41.0 |
| Brazil | 25.2 | 32.5 | 34.8 |
| Chile | 21.0 | 23.6 | 23.4 |
| France | 14.7 | 16.1 | 20.2 |
| Germany | 23.3 | 25.0 | 23.8 |
| Israel | 7.3 | 11.5 | 12.7 |
| Italy | 7.3 | 7.4 | 8.4 |
| Japan | 6.9 | 7.1 | 7.7 |
| Netherlands | 5.7 | 10.3 | 10.9 |
| Peru | 55.0 | 56.7 | 56.2 |
| Spain | 9.3 | 9.9 | 11.4 |
| Switzerland | 8.6 | 9.7 | 10.8 |
| United Kingdom | 12.3 | 12.7 | 12.2 |
| USA | 35.3 | 35.5 | 39.6 |
| **Total** (incl. others) | 319.6 | 350.7 | 376.9 |

**Total tourism receipts** (US $ million): 131 in 1994; 146 in 1995; 161 in 1996.

Source: World Tourism Organization, *Yearbook of Tourism Statistics.*

## Communications Media

| | 1994 | 1995 | 1996 |
|---|---|---|---|
| Radio receivers ('000 in use) | 4,850 | 4,980 | 5,100 |
| Television receivers ('000 in use) | 820 | 850 | 875 |
| Telephones ('000 main lines in use) | 250* | 348† | n.a. |
| Mobile cellular telephones (subscribers) | 4,056 | 7,229 | n.a. |
| Daily newspapers: | | | |
| Number | n.a. | 17 | 18 |
| Average circulation ('000 copies) | n.a. | 410 | 420 |

* Estimate.

† Installed lines.

Sources: UNESCO, *Statistical Yearbook*; UN, *Statistical Yearbook*.

## Education

(1990)

| | Institutions | Teachers | Students |
|---|---|---|---|
| Pre-primary | 2,294* | 2,895 | 121,132 |
| Primary | 12,639† | 51,763 | 1,278,775 |
| Secondary | n.a. | 12,434 | 219,232 |
| Higher | | | |
| Universities and equivalent | n.a. | 4,234 | 102,001 |
| Other | n.a. | 1,302‡ | 34,889‡ |

* 1988. † 1987. ‡ 1989.

**1991:** Universities and equivalent institutions: 4,261 teachers; 109,503 students.

Source: UNESCO, *Statistical Yearbook*.

# Directory

## The Constitution

Bolivia became an independent republic in 1825 and received its first Constitution in November 1826. Since that date a number of new Constitutions have been promulgated. Following the *coup d'état* of November 1964, the Constitution of 1947 was revived. Under its provisions, executive power is vested in the President, who chairs the Cabinet. According to the revised Constitution, the President is elected by direct suffrage for a five-year term (extended from four years in 1997) and is not eligible for immediate re-election. In the event of the President's death or failure to assume office, the Vice-President or, failing the Vice-President, the President of the Senate becomes interim Head of State.

The President has power to appoint members of the Cabinet, diplomatic representatives and archbishops and bishops from a panel proposed by the Senate. The President is responsible for the conduct of foreign affairs and is also empowered to issue decrees, and initiate legislation by special messages to Congress.

Congress consists of a Senate (27 members) and a Chamber of Deputies (130 members). Congress meets annually and its ordinary sessions last only 90 working days, which may be extended to 120. Each of the nine departments (La Paz, Chuquisaca, Oruro, Beni, Santa Cruz, Potosí, Tarija, Cochabamba and Pando), into which the country is divided for administrative purposes, elects three senators. Members of both houses are elected for four years.

The supreme administrative, political and military authority in each department is vested in a prefect appointed by the President. The sub-divisions of each department, known as provinces, are administered by sub-prefects. The provinces are further divided into cantons. There are 94 provinces and some 1,000 cantons. The capital of each department has its autonomous municipal council and controls its own revenue and expenditure.

Public order, education and roads are under national control.

A decree issued in July 1952 conferred the franchise on all persons who had reached the age of 21 years, whether literate or illiterate. Previously the franchise had been restricted to literate persons. (The voting age for married persons was lowered to 18 years at the 1989 elections.)

The death penalty was restored in October 1971 for terrorism, kidnapping and crimes against government and security personnel. In 1981 its scope was extended to drugs trafficking.

## The Government

### HEAD OF STATE

**President:** HUGO BÁNZER SUÁREZ (ADN) (took office 6 August 1997).

**Vice-President:** JORGE FERNANDO QUIROGA RAMÍREZ (ADN).

### THE CABINET
(January 2000)

A coalition comprising members of the Acción Democrática Nacionalista (ADN), the Nueva Fuerza Republicana (NFR), the Movimiento de la Izquierda Revolucionaria (MIR), the Unión Cívica Solidaridad (UCS) and Independents (Ind.).

**Minister of Foreign Affairs and Worship:** JAVIER MURILLO DE LA ROCHA (ADN).

**Minister of the Interior:** WALTER GUITERAS DENNIS (ADN).

**Minister of National Defence:** JORGE CRESPO VELASCO (MIR).

**Minister of the Presidency:** FRANZ ONDARZA LINARES (ADN).

**Minister of Sustainable Development and Planning:** ERICK REYES VILLA (NFR).

**Minister of Justice and Human Rights:** JUAN CHAIN (UCS).

**Minister of Finance:** HERBERT MÜLLER COSTAS (Ind.).

**Minister of Health and Social Welfare:** GUILLERMO CUENTAS YAÑEZ (MIR).

**Minister of Labour and Small Enterprises:** LUIS VÁSQUEZ VILLAMOR (MIR).

**Minister of Education, Culture and Sport:** TITO HOZ DE VILA (ADN).

**Minister of Agriculture, Livestock and Rural Development:** OSWALDO ANTEZANA VACA DÍEZ (ADN).

**Minister of Foreign Trade and Investment:** CARLOS SAAVEDRA BRUNO (MIR).

**Minister for Economic Development:** JOSÉ LUIS LUPO FLORES (Ind.).

**Minister of Housing and Basic Services:** RUBÉN POMA ROJAS (UCS).

**Minister without Portfolio, responsible for Government Information:** JOSÉ LANDÍVAR ROCA (ADN).

### MINISTRIES

**Office of the President:** Palacio de Gobierno, Plaza Murillo, La Paz; tel. (2) 37-1317.

**Ministry of Agriculture, Livestock and Rural Development:** Avda Camacho 1471, La Paz.

**Ministry of Economic Development:** Edif. Palacio de Comunicaciones, Avda Mariscal Santa Cruz, La Paz; tel. (2) 37-7234; fax (2) 35-9955.

**Ministry of Education, Culture and Sport:** Casilla 6500, La Paz.

**Ministry of Finance:** Edif. Palacio de Comunicaciones, Avda Mariscal Santa Cruz, La Paz; tel. (2) 37-7234; fax (2) 35-9955.

**Ministry of Foreign Affairs and Worship:** Calle Ingavi, esq. Junin, La Paz; tel. (2) 37-1150; fax (2) 37-1155.

**Ministry of Foreign Trade and Investment:** Edif. Palacio de las Comunicaciones, Avda Mariscal Santa Cruz, La Paz; tel. (2) 37-7222; fax (2) 37-7451; e-mail despacho@mcei-bolivia.com; internet www.mcei-bolivia.com.

**Ministry of Health and Social Welfare:** Plaza del Estudiante, La Paz; tel. (2) 37-1373; fax (2) 39-1590.

**Ministry of Housing and Basic Services:** Avda Saavedra 2273, La Paz.

**Ministry of the Interior:** Avda Arce 2409, esq. Belisario Salinas, La Paz; tel. (2) 37-0460; fax (2) 37-1334.

**Ministry of Justice and Human Rights:** Casilla 6966, La Paz; tel. (2) 36-1083; fax (2) 36-530.

**Ministry of Labour and Small Enterprises:** Calle Yanacocha, esq. Mercado, La Paz; tel. (2) 36-4164; fax (2) 37-1387.

**Ministry of National Defence:** Plaza Avaroa, esq. 20 de Octubre, La Paz; tel. (2) 37-7130; fax (2) 35-3156.

**Ministry of the Presidency:** Plaza Murillo, La Paz; tel. (2) 35-9956; fax (2) 37-1388.

**Ministry of Sustainable Development and Planning:** Avda Arce 2147, Casilla 3116, La Paz; tel. (2) 35-9820; fax (2) 39-2892.

# President and Legislature

### PRESIDENT

At the presidential election that took place on 1 June 1997 the majority of votes were spread between five of the 10 candidates. Gen. (retd) Hugo Bánzer Suárez of the Acción Democrática Nacionalista (ADN) obtained 22.3% of the votes cast, Juan Carlos Durán of the Movimiento Nacionalista Revolucionario (MNR) won 17.7%, Jaime Paz Zamora of the Movimiento de la Izquierda Revolucionaria (MIR) won 16.7%, Ivo Kuljis of the Unión Cívica Solidaridad (UCS) secured 15.9% and Remedios Loza of Conciencia de Patria (Condepa) won 15.8%. As no candidate obtained the requisite absolute majority, responsibility for the selection of the President passed to the new National Congress. As a result of the formation of a coalition between the ADN, the MIR, the UCS, the NFR, Condepa and an Independent, Bánzer was elected President with 118 votes on 5 August and took office the following day. Condepa was removed from the governing coalition in mid-1998.

### CONGRESO NACIONAL

**President of the Senate:** LEOPOLDO FERNÁNDEZ.

**President of the Chamber of Deputies:** HUGO CARVAJAL.

**General Election, 1 June 1997**

| Party | Seats | |
|---|---|---|
| | Chamber of Deputies | Senate |
| Acción Democrática Nacionalista (ADN) | 33 | 13 |
| Movimiento Nacionalista Revolucionario (Histórico) (MNR) | 26 | 3 |
| Movimiento de la Izquierda Revolucionaria (MIR) | 25 | 6 |
| Unión Cívica Solidaridad (UCS) | 21 | 2 |
| Conciencia de Patria (Condepa) | 17 | 3 |
| Movimiento Bolivia Libre (MBL) | 4 | — |
| Izquierda Unida | 4 | — |
| **Total** | 130 | 27 |

# Political Organizations

**Acción Democrática Nacionalista (ADN):** La Paz; f. 1979; right-wing; Leader HUGO BÁNZER SUÁREZ; Nat. Exec. Sec. JORGE LANDÍVAR.

**Bolivia Insurgente:** La Paz; f. 1996; populist party; Leader MÓNICA MEDINA.

**Conciencia de Patria (Condepa):** La Paz; f. 1988; populist party; Leader REMEDIOS LOZA.

**Frente Revolucionario de Izquierda (FRI):** La Paz; left-wing; Leader OSCAR ZAMORA.

**Movimiento Bolivariano:** La Paz; f. 1999; Leader CRISTINA CORRALES.

**Movimiento Bolivia Libre (MBL):** Edif. Camiri, Of. 601, Calle Comercio 972 esq. Yanacocha, Casilla 10382, La Paz; tel. (2) 34-0257; fax (2) 39-2242; f. 1985; left-wing; breakaway faction of MIR; Pres. MIGUEL URIOSTE.

**Movimiento Hacia el Socialismo (MAS):** La Paz; left-wing.

**Movimiento de la Izquierda Revolucionaria (MIR):** Avda América 119, 2°, La Paz. 1971; split into several factions in 1985; left-wing; Leader JAIME PAZ ZAMORA; Sec.-Gen. OSCAR EID FRANCO.

**Movimiento sin Miedo:** La Paz; f. 1999; left-wing; Leader JUAN DEL GRANADO.

**Movimiento Nacionalista Revolucionario (Histórico)—MNR:** Genaro Sanjines 541, Pasaje Kuljis, La Paz; formerly part of the Movimiento Nacionalista Revolucionario (MNR, f. 1942); centre-right; Leader GONZALO SÁNCHEZ DE LOZADA; Sec.-Gen. JUAN CARLOS DURÁN; 700,000 mems.

**Movimiento Revolucionario Túpac Katarí de Liberación (MRTKL):** Avda Baptista 939, Casilla 9133, La Paz; tel. 35-4784; f. 1978; peasant party; Leader VÍCTOR HUGO CÁRDENAS CONDE; Sec.-Gen. NORBERTO PÉREZ HIDALGO; 80,000 mems.

**Nueva Fuerza Republicana (NFR):** Cochabamba; Leader MANFRED REYES VILLA.

**Partido Comunista de Bolivia (PCB):** La Paz; f. 1950; Leader MARCOS DOMIC; First Sec. SIMÓN REYES RIVERA.

**Partido Demócrata Cristiano (PDC):** Casilla 4345, La Paz; f. 1954; Pres. BENJAMÍN MIGUEL HARB; Sec. ANTONIO CANELAS-GALATOIRE; 50,000 mems.

**Partido Obrero Revolucionario (POR):** Correo Central, La Paz; f. 1935; Trotskyist; Leader GUILLERMO LORA.

**Partido Revolucionario de la Izquierda Nacionalista (PRIN):** Calle Colón 693, La Paz; f. 1964; left-wing; Leader JUAN LECHIN OQUENDO.

**Partido Socialista-Uno (PS-1):** La Paz; Leader JERJES JUSTINIANO.

**Partido de Vanguardia Obrera:** Plaza Venezuela 1452, La Paz; Leader FILEMÓN ESCOBAR.

**Unión Cívica Solidaridad (UCS):** Calle Mercado 1064, 6°, La Paz; tel. (2) 36-0297; fax (2) 37-2200; f. 1989; populist; Leader JOHNNY FERNÁNDEZ.

**Vanguardia Revolucionaria 9 de Abril:** Avda 6 de Agosto 2170, Casilla 5810, La Paz; tel. (2) 32-0311; fax 39-1439; Leader Dr CARLOS SERRATE REICH.

Other parties include the Alianza de Renovación Boliviana, the Alianza Democrática Socialista and the Eje Patriótica.

# Diplomatic Representation

### EMBASSIES IN BOLIVIA

**Argentina:** Calle Aspiazu 497, La Paz; tel. (2) 32-2102; fax (2) 39-1083; Ambassador: MARÍA DEL CARMEN ECHEVERRÍA.

**Belgium:** Avda Hernando Siles 5290, Casilla 2433, La Paz; tel. (2) 78-4925; fax (2) 78-6764; Ambassador: CHRISTINE STEVENS.

**Brazil:** Edif. Foncomin, 9°, Avda 20 de Octubre 2038, Casilla 429, La Paz; tel. (2) 35-0718; fax (2) 39-1258; Ambassador: LUIZ ORLANDO C. GELIO.

**China, People's Republic:** La Paz; Ambassador: WU CHANGSHENG.

**Colombia:** Calle 20 de Octubre 2427, Casilla 1418, La Paz; tel. (2) 35-9658; Ambassador: CARLOS EDUARDO LOZANO TOVAR.

**Costa Rica:** Avda 14 de Septiembre 4850, Casilla 2780, La Paz; tel. and fax (2) 78-6751; Ambassador: JUAN RAMÓN GUTIÉRREZ ARAYA.

**Cuba:** Avda Arequipa 8037, Calacoto, La Paz; tel. (2) 79-2616; Ambassador: GUSTAVO BRUGUÉS-PÉREZ.

**Denmark:** Avda 6 de Agosto 2577, Casilla 9860, La Paz; tel. (2) 43-0046; fax (2) 43-0064; e-mail ambdklp@ceibo.entelnet.bo; Chargé d'affaires: MICHAEL HJORTSØ.

**Ecuador:** Edif. Herrman, 14°, Plaza Venezuela, Casilla 406, La Paz; tel. (2) 32-1208; Ambassador: OLMEDO MONTEVERDE PAZ.

**Egypt:** Avda Ballivián 599, Casilla 2956, La Paz; tel. (2) 78-6511; Ambassador: Dr GABER SABRA.

**France:** Avda Hernando Silés 5390, esq. Calle 8, Obrajes, Casilla 717, La Paz; tel. (2) 78-6114; fax (2) 78-6746; e-mail amfrabo@ceibo.entelnet.bo; internet www.consulfrance.int.bo; Ambassador: GÉRARD DUMONT.

**Germany:** Avda Arce 2395, Casilla 5265, La Paz; tel. (2) 43-0850; fax (2) 43-1297; Ambassador: JOACHIM KAUSCH.

**Holy See:** Avda Arce 2990, Casilla 136, La Paz; tel. (2) 43-1007; fax (2) 43-2120; e-mail nunzibol@caoba.entelnet.bo; Apostolic Nuncio: Most Rev. JÓZEF WESOŁOWSKI, Titular Archbishop of Slebte (Slebty).

**Israel:** Edif. Esperanza, 10°, Avda Mariscal Santa Cruz, Casilla 1309, La Paz; tel. (2) 37-4239; fax 39-1712; Ambassador: VAIR RECANATI.

**Italy:** Avda 6 de Agosto 2575, Casilla 626, La Paz; tel. (2) 36-1129; Ambassador: Dr ENRIC ANGIOLO FERRONI CARLI.

**Japan:** Calle Rosendo Gutiérrez 497, Casilla 2725, La Paz; tel. (2) 37-3152; Ambassador: HIROSHI IKEDA.

**Korea, Democratic People's Republic:** La Paz; Ambassador: KIM CHAN SIK.

**Korea, Republic:** Avda 6 de Agosto 2592, Casilla 1559, La Paz; tel. (2) 36-4485; Ambassador: CHO KAB-DONG.

**Mexico:** Avda 6 de Agosto 2652, Casilla 430, La Paz; tel. (2) 32-9505; Ambassador: Lic. MARCELO VARGAS CAMPOS.

**Panama:** Calle Potosí 1270, Casilla 678, La Paz; tel. (2) 37-1277; Chargé d'affaires a.i.: Lic. JOSÉ RODRIGO DE LA ROSA.

**Paraguay:** Edif. Illimani II, Avda 6 de Agosto y Pedro Salazar, Casilla 882, La Paz; tel. (2) 43-3176; fax (2) 43-2201; e-mail emparabo@ceibo.entelnet.bo; Ambassador: HORACIO NOGUES ZUBIZARRETA.

**Peru:** Calle F. Guachalla 300, Casilla 668, La Paz; tel. (2) 35-3550; fax (2) 36-7640; e-mail embbol@caoba.entelnet.bo; Ambassador: Dr HARRY BELEVAN-MCBRIDE.

**Romania:** Avda Ecuador 2286, Sopocachi, Casilla 12280, La Paz; tel. (2) 37-7265; Ambassador: VASILE LUCA.

**Russia:** Avda Walter Guevara Arce 8129, Casilla 5494, La Paz; tel. (2) 78-6419; fax (2) 78-6531; e-mail embrusia@ceibo.entelnet .bo; Ambassador: GUENNADI VASILIEVICH SIZOV.

**South Africa:** Calle 22, Calacoto 7810, La Paz; tel. (2) 79-2101; Chargé d'affaires a.i.: J. S. ALDRICH.

**Spain:** Avda 6 de Agosto 2860, Casilla 282, La Paz; tel. (2) 43-3518; fax (2) 43-2752; Ambassador: MANUEL VITURRO DE LA TORRE.

**Switzerland:** Edif. Petrolero, Avda 16 de Julio 1616, Casilla 657, La Paz; tel. (2) 35-3091; Chargé d'affaires a.i.: FERMO GEROSA.

**United Kingdom:** Avda Arce 2732–2754, Casilla 694, La Paz; tel. (2) 43-3424; fax (2) 43-1073; e-mail ppa@mail.rds.org.bo; Ambassador: GRAHAM MINTER.

**USA:** Avda Arce 2780, Casilla 425, La Paz; tel. (2) 43-0251; fax (2) 43-3900; Ambassador: DONNA J. HRINAK.

**Uruguay:** Avda 6 de Agosto 2577, Casilla 441, La Paz; tel. (2) 43-0080; fax 43-0087; Ambassador: HOMAR MURDOCH SCARONI.

**Venezuela:** Edif. Illimani, 4°, Avda Arce esq. Campos, Casilla 960, La Paz; tel. (2) 43-1365; Ambassador: OTTO R. VEITIA MATOS.

# Judicial System

## SUPREME COURT

**Corte Suprema:** Calle Pilinco 352, Sucre; tel. (64) 21883; fax (64) 32696.

Judicial power is vested in the Supreme Court. There are 12 members, appointed by Congress for a term of 10 years. The court is divided into four chambers of three justices each. Two chambers deal with civil cases, the third deals with criminal cases and the fourth deals with administrative, social and mining cases. The President of the Supreme Court presides over joint sessions of the courts and attends the joint sessions for cassation cases.

**President of the Supreme Court:** Dr HUGO ROSALES LIGERÓN.

## DISTRICT COURTS

There is a District Court sitting in each Department, and additional provincial and local courts to try minor cases.

## ATTORNEY-GENERAL

In addition to the Attorney-General at Sucre (appointed by the President on the proposal of the Senate), there is a District Attorney in each Department as well as circuit judges.

**Attorney-General:** OSCAR CRESPO.

# Religion

The majority of the population are Roman Catholics; there were an estimated 6.9m. adherents at 31 December 1997, equivalent to 89.5% of the population. Religious freedom is guaranteed. There is a small Jewish community, as well as various Protestant denominations, in Bolivia.

## CHRISTIANITY

### The Roman Catholic Church

Bolivia comprises four archdioceses, six dioceses, two Territorial Prelatures and five Apostolic Vicariates.

**Bishops' Conference:** Conferencia Episcopal Boliviana, Calle Potosí 814, Casilla 2309, La Paz; tel. (2) 32-4535; fax (2) 34-0604; e-mail comceb@ceibo.entelnet.bo; f. 1972; Pres. Most Rev. JULIO TERRAZAS SANDOVAL, Archbishop of Santa Cruz de la Sierra.

**Archbishop of Cochabamba:** Most Rev. RENÉ FERNÁNDEZ APAZA, Avda Heroínas esq. Zenteno Anaya, Casilla 129, Cochabamba; tel. (42) 56562; fax (42) 50522.

**Archbishop of La Paz:** Most Rev. EDMUNDO LUIS FLAVIO ABASTOFLOR MONTERO, Calle Ballivián 1277, Casilla 259, La Paz; tel. (2) 34-1920; fax (2) 39-1244.

**Archbishop of Santa Cruz de la Sierra:** Most Rev. JULIO TERRAZAS SANDOVAL, Calle Ingavi 49, Casilla 25, Santa Cruz; tel. (3) 32-4286; fax (3) 33-0181.

**Archbishop of Sucre:** Most Rev. JESÚS GERVASIO PÉREZ RODRÍGUEZ, Calle Bolívar 702, Casilla 205, Sucre; tel. (64) 51587; fax (64) 60336.

### The Anglican Communion

Within the Iglesia Anglicana del Cono Sur de América (Anglican Church of the Southern Cone of America), Bolivia forms part of the diocese of Peru. The Bishop is resident in Lima, Peru.

### Protestant Churches

**Baptist Union of Bolivia:** Casilla 1408, La Paz; Pres. Rev. AUGUSTO CHUIJO.

**Convención Bautista Boliviana** (Baptist Convention of Bolivia): Casilla 3147, Santa Cruz; tel. (3) 340717; fax (3) 340717; f. 1947; Pres. EIRA SORUCO DE FLORES.

**Iglesia Evangélica Metodista en Bolivia** (Evangelical Methodist Church in Bolivia): Casillas 356 y 8347, La Paz; tel. (2) 34-2702; fax (2) 35-7046; autonomous since 1969; 10,000 mems; Bishop Rev. EFRAÍN YANAPA.

## BAHÁ'Í FAITH

**National Spiritual Assembly of the Bahá'ís of Bolivia:** Casilla 1613, La Paz; tel. (2) 78-5058; fax (2) 78-2387; e-mail aebahais@ caoba.entelnet.bo; mems resident in 6,229 localities.

# The Press

## DAILY NEWSPAPERS

### Cochabamba

**Opinión:** General Acha 0252, Casilla 287, Cochabamba; tel. (42) 54402; fax (42) 15121; f. 1985; Dir EDWIN TAPIA FRONTANILLA; Man. Editor JAIME BUITRAGO.

**Los Tiempos:** Plaza Quintanilla-Norte, Casilla 525, Cochabamba; tel. (42) 54561; fax (42) 54577; e-mail lostiempos@lostiempos.bo.net; internet www.lostiempos.com; f. 1943; morning; independent; Dir CARLOS CANELAS; Man. Editor JOSÉ NOGALES; circ. 19,000.

### La Paz

**El Diario:** Calle Loayza 118, Casilla 5, La Paz; tel. (2) 39-0900; fax (2) 36-3846; e-mail contacto@eldiario.net; internet www.eldiario.net; f. 1904; morning; conservative; Dir JORGE CARRASCO JAHNSEN; Man. Editor JOSÉ MANUEL LOZA OBLITAS; circ. 55,000.

**Hoy:** Pasaje Carrasco 1718, Casilla 477, La Paz; tel. (2) 24-4154; fax (2) 24-4147; e-mail hoy@wara.bolnet.bo; f. 1968; morning and midday editions; independent; Pres. SAMUEL DORIA MEDINA; Dir HERNÁN PAREDES MUÑOZ; circ. 12,000.

**Jornada:** Edif. Almirante Grau 672, Casilla 1628, La Paz; tel. (2) 35-3844; fax (2) 35-6213; f. 1964; evening; independent; Dir JAIME RÍOS CHACÓN; circ. 11,500.

**Presencia:** Avda Mariscal Santa Cruz 2150, Casilla 3276, La Paz; tel. (2) 37-2340; fax (2) 39-1040; e-mail prsencia@caoba.entelnet.bo; f. 1952; morning and evening; Catholic; Pres. JESÚS LÓPEZ DE LAMA; Dir Lic. JUAN CRISTÓBAL SORUCO; Man. Lic. MARÍA LUISA URDAY; circ. 20,000.

**La Razón:** Jorge Sáenz 1330, Casilla 13100, La Paz; tel. (2) 22-2727; fax (2) 22-2049; f. 1990; Pres. RAÚL GARAFULIC GUTIÉRREZ; Dir JORGE CANELAS SÁENZ; circ. 27,000.

**Ultima Hora:** Avda Camacho 1372, Casilla 5920, La Paz; tel. (2) 39-2115; fax (2) 39-2139; e-mail uhora@wara.bolnet.bo; f. 1939; evening; independent; Propr LUIS MERCADO ROCABADO; Pres. MAURO BERTERO; Dir MARIANO BAPTISTA GUMUCIO; circ. 15,000.

### Oruro

**El Expreso:** Potosí 4921 esq. Villarroel, Oruro; f. 1973; morning; independent; right-wing; Dir ALBERTO FRONTANILLA MORALES; circ. 1,000.

**La Patria:** Avda Camacho 1892, Casilla 48, Oruro; tel. (52) 50761; fax (52) 50781; f. 1919; morning; independent; Pres. MARCELO MIRRALLES BOVÁ; Dir ENRIQUE MIRALLES BONNECARRERE; circ. 6,000.

### Potosí

**El Siglo:** Calle Linares 99, Casilla 389, Potosí; f. 1975; morning; Dir WILSON MENDIETA PACHECO; circ. 1,500.

### Santa Cruz

**El Deber:** Avda El Trompillo 1144, Casilla 2144, Santa Cruz; tel. (3) 53-8000; fax (3) 53-9053; e-mail info.eldeber@eldeber.com; internet www.eldeber.com; f. 1955; morning; independent; Dir PEDRO RIVERO MERCADO; Man. Editor GUILLERMO RIVERO JORDÁN; circ. 35,000.

**La Estrella del Oriente:** Calle Sucre 558, Casilla 736, Santa Cruz; tel. (3) 37-0707; fax (3) 37-0557; e-mail estrella@mitai.nrs.bolnet.bo; internet www.laestrella.com; f. 1864; Pres. JORGE LANDÍVAR ROCA; Man. Editor TUFFI ARÉ.

**El Mundo:** Parque Industrial PI-7, Casilla 1984, Santa Cruz; tel. (3) 46-4646; fax (3) 46-5057; e-mail elmundo@mitai.nrs.bolnet.bo; f. 1979; morning; owned by Santa Cruz Industrialists' Association; Pres. WALTER PAREJAS MORENO; Dir JUAN JAVIER ZEBALLOS GUTIÉRREZ; circ. 15,000.

**El Nuevo Día:** Calle Independencia 470, Casilla 5344, Santa Cruz; tel. (3) 33-7474; fax (3) 36-0303; f. 1987; Dir NANCY EKLUND VDA DE GUTIÉRREZ; Man. Editor JORGE ORÍAS HERRERA.

### Trinidad

**La Razón:** Avda Bolívar 295, Casilla 166, Trinidad; tel. (46) 21377; f. 1972; Dir CARLOS VÉLEZ.

### PERIODICALS

**Actualidad Boliviana Confidencial (ABC):** Fernando Guachalla 969, Casilla 648, La Paz; f. 1966; weekly; Dir HUGO GONZÁLEZ RIOJA; circ. 6,000.

**Aquí:** Casilla 10937, La Paz; tel. (2) 34-3524; fax (2) 35-2455; f. 1979; weekly; circ. 10,000.

**Bolivia Libre:** Edif. Esperanza, 5°, Avda Mariscal Santa Cruz 2150, Casilla 6500, La Paz; fortnightly; govt organ.

**Carta Cruceña de Integración:** Casilla 3531, Santa Cruz de la Sierra; weekly; Dirs HERNÁN LLANOVARCED A., JOHNNY LAZARTE J.

**Comentarios Económicos de Actualidad (CEA):** Casilla 312097, La Paz; tel. (2) 43-0122; fax (2) 43-2554; e-mail veceba@caoba.entelnet.bo; f. 1983; fortnightly; articles and economic analyses; Editor GUIDO CESPEDES.

**Información Política y Económica (IPE):** Calle Comercio, Casilla 2484, La Paz; weekly; Dir GONZALO LÓPEZ MUÑOZ.

**Informe R:** La Paz; weekly; Editor SARA MONROY.

**Notas:** Casilla 5782, La Paz; tel. (2) 37-3773; fax (2) 36-5153; weekly; political and economic analysis; Editor JOSÉ GRAMUNT DE MORAGAS.

**El Noticiero:** Sucre; weekly; Dir DAVID CABEZAS; circ. 1,500.

**Prensa Libre:** Sucre; tel. (64) 41293; fax (64) 32768; f. 1989; weekly; Dir JORGE ENCERAS DIAZ.

**Servicio de Información Confidencial (SIC):** Elías Sagárnaga 274, Casilla 5035, La Paz; weekly; publ. by Asociación Nacional de Prensa; Dir JOSÉ CARRANZA.

**Siglo XXI:** La Paz; weekly.

**Unión:** Sucre; weekly; Dir JAIME MERILES.

**Visión Boliviana:** Calle Loayza 420, Casilla 2870, La Paz; 6 a year.

### PRESS ASSOCIATIONS

**Asociación Nacional de la Prensa:** Avda 6 de Agosto 2170, Casilla 477, La Paz; tel. (2) 36-9916; Pres. Dr CARLOS SERRATE REICH.

**Asociación de Periodistas de La Paz:** Avda 6 de Agosto 2170, Casilla 477, La Paz; tel. (2) 36-9916; fax (2) 32-3701; f. 1929; Pres. MARIO MALDONADO VISCARRA; Vice-Pres. MARÍA EUGENIA VERASTEGUI A.

### NEWS AGENCIES

**Agencia de Noticias Fides (ANF):** Edif. Mariscal de Ayacucho, 5°, Of. 501, Calle Loayza, Casilla 5782, La Paz; tel. (2) 36-5152; fax (2) 36-5153; owned by Roman Catholic Church; Dir JOSÉ GRAMUNT DE MORAGAS.

#### Foreign Bureaux

**Agencia EFE** (Spain): Edif. Esperanza, Avda Mariscal Santa Cruz 2150, Casilla 7403, La Paz; tel. (2) 36-7205; fax (2) 39-1441; e-mail fvv@caoba.entelnet.bo; Bureau Chief FERNANDO DE VALENZUELA.

**Agenzia Nazionale Stampa Associata (ANSA)** (Italy): La Paz; tel. (2) 35-5521; fax (2) 36-8221; Correspondent RAÚL PENARANDA UNDURRAGA.

**Associated Press (AP)** (USA): Edif. Mariscal de Ayacucho, Of. 1209, Calle Loayza, Casilla 9569, La Paz; tel. (2) 37-0128; Correspondent PETER J. MCFARREN.

**Deutsche Presse-Agentur (dpa)** (Germany): Edif. Esperanza, 9°, Of. 3, Av. Mariscal Santa Cruz 2150, Casilla 13885, La Paz; tel. (2) 35-2684; fax (2) 39-2488; Correspondent ROBERT BROCKMANN.

**Informatsionnoye Telegrafnoye Agentstvo Rossii-Telegrafnoye Agentstvo Suverennykh Stran (ITARTASS)** (Russia): Casilla 6839, San Miguel, Bloque 0–33, Casa 958, La Paz; tel. (2) 79-2108; Correspondent ELDAR ABDULLAEV.

**Inter Press Service (IPS)** (Italy): Edif. Esperanza, 6°, Of. 6, Casilla 4313, La Paz; tel. (2) 36-1227; Correspondent RONALD GREBE LÓPEZ.

**Prensa Latina** (Cuba): La Paz; tel. (2) 32-3479; Correspondent MANUEL ROBLES SOSA.

**Reuters** (United Kingdom): Edif. Loayza, 3°, Of. 301, Calle Loayza 349, Casilla 4057, La Paz; tel. (2) 35-1106; fax (2) 39-1366; Correspondent RENÉ VILLEGAS MONJE.

**Rossiyskoye Informatsionnoye Agentstvo—Novosti (RIA—Novosti)** (Russia): La Paz; tel. (2) 37-3857; Correspondent VLADIMIR RAMÍREZ.

**United Press International (UPI)** (USA): Plaza Venezuela 1479, 7°, Of. 702, Casilla 1219, La Paz; tel. (2) 78-4172; fax (2) 78-4066; Correspondent ALBERTO ZUAZO NATHES.

Agence France-Presse and Telam (Argentina) are also represented.

## Publishers

**Editora Khana Cruz SRL:** Avda Camacho 1372, Casilla 5920, La Paz; tel. (2) 37-0263; Dir GLADIS ANDRADE.

**Editora Lux:** Edif. Esperanza, Avda Mariscal Santa Cruz, Casilla 1566, La Paz; tel. (2) 32-9102; fax (2) 34-3968; f. 1952; Dir FELICISIMO TARILONTE PÉREZ.

**Editorial los Amigos del Libro:** Avda Heroínas E-0311, Casilla 450, Cochabamba; tel. (42) 51140; fax (41) 15128; e-mail amigol@amigol.bo.net; f. 1945; general; Man. Dir WERNER GUTTENTAG.

**Editorial Bruño:** Calle Mercado esq. Loayza, Casilla 4809, La Paz; tel. (2) 32-0198; f. 1964; Dir IRINEO LOMAS.

**Editorial Don Bosco:** Calle Tiahuanacu 116, Casilla 4458, La Paz; tel. (2) 37-1757; fax (2) 36-2822; f. 1896; social sciences and literature; Dir GIAMPAOLO MARIO MAZZON.

**Editorial Icthus:** La Paz; tel. (2) 35-4007; f. 1967; general and textbooks; Man. Dir DANIEL AQUIZE.

**Editorial y Librería Juventud:** Plaza Murillo 519, Casilla 1489, La Paz; tel. (2) 34-1694; f. 1946; textbooks and general; Dirs RAFAEL URQUIZO, GUSTAVO URQUIZO.

**Editorial Popular:** Plaza Pérez Velasco 787, Casilla 4171, La Paz; tel. (2) 35-0701; f. 1935; textbooks, postcards, tourist guides, etc; Man. Dir GERMÁN VILLAMOR.

**Editorial Puerta del Sol:** Edif. Litoral Sub Suelo, Avda Mariscal Santa Cruz, La Paz; tel. (2) 36-0746; f. 1965; Man. Dir OSCAR CRESPO.

**Empresa Editora Proinsa:** Avda Saavedra 2055, Casilla 7181, La Paz; tel. (2) 22-7781; fax (2) 22-6671; f. 1974; school books; Dirs FLOREN SANABRIA G., CARLOS SANABRIA C.

**Gisbert y Cía, SA:** Calle Comercio 1270, Casilla 195, La Paz; tel. (2) 39-0056; fax (2) 39-1522; f. 1907; textbooks, history, law and general; Pres. JAVIER GISBERT; Dirs CARMEN G. DE SCHULCZEWSKI, ANTONIO SCHULCZEWSKI.

**Ivar American:** Calle Potosí 1375, Casilla 6016, La Paz; tel. (2) 36-1519; Man. Dir HÉCTOR IBÁÑEZ.

**Librería El Ateneo SRL:** Calle Ballivián 1275, Casilla 7917, La Paz; tel. (2) 36-9925; fax (2) 39-1513; Dirs JUAN CHIRVECHES D., MIRIAN C. DE CHIRVECHES.

**Librería Dismo Ltda:** Calle Comercio 806, Casilla 988, La Paz; tel. (2) 35-3119; fax (2) 31-6545; Dir TERESA GONZÁLEZ DE ALVAREZ.

**Librería La Paz:** Calle Campos y Villegas, Edif. Artemis, Casilla 539, La Paz; tel. (2) 43-4927; fax (2) 43-5004; e-mail liblapaz@ceibo.entelnet.bo; f. 1900; Dirs EDUARDO BURGOS R., CARLOS BURGOS M.

**Librería La Universal SRL:** Calle Genaro Sanjines 538, Casilla 2888, La Paz; tel. (2) 34-2961; f. 1958; Man. Dir ROLANDO CONDORI.

**Librería San Pablo:** Calle Colón 627, Casilla 3152, La Paz; tel. (2) 32-6084; f. 1967; Man. Dir MARÍA DE JESÚS VALERIANO.

### PUBLISHERS' ASSOCIATION

**Cámara Boliviana del Libro:** Calle Capitán Ravelo 2116, Casilla 682, La Paz; tel. (2) 32-7039; fax (2) 32-7039; f. 1947; Pres. FREDDY CARRASCO JARA; Vice-Pres. ANDRÉS CARDÓ SORIA.

## Broadcasting and Communications

### TELECOMMUNICATIONS

**Cámara Nacional de Medios de Comunicación:** Casilla 2431, La Paz.

**Empresa Nacional de Telecomunicaciones (ENTEL):** Edif. Palacio de Comunicaciones, Avda Mariscal Santa Cruz esq. Oruro, Casilla 4450, La Paz; tel. (2) 35-5908; fax (2) 39-1789; internet www.entelnet.bo; f. 1965; privatized under the Govt's capitalization programme in 1995; Exec. Pres. GERMÁN MEDRANO KREIDLER.

**Superintendencia de Telecomunicaciones:** Edif. M. Cristina, Plaza España, Casilla 6692, La Paz; tel. (2) 41-6641; fax (2) 41-8183; e-mail supertel@ceibo.entelnet.bo; f. 1995; govt-controlled broadcasting authority; Superintendent Ing. GUIDO LOAYZA.

### BROADCASTING

#### Radio

There were 145 radio stations in 1990, the majority of which were commercial. Broadcasts are in Spanish, Aymará and Quechua.

**Asociación Boliviana de Radiodifusoras (ASBORA):** Edif. Jazmin, 10°, Avda 20 de Octubre 2019, Casilla 5324, La Paz; tel. (2) 36-5154; fax (2) 36-3069; broadcasting authority; Pres. TERESA SANJINÉS L.; Vice-Pres. LUIS ANTONIO SERRANO.

**Educación Radiofónica de Bolivia (ERBOL):** Calle Ballivian 1323, 4°, Casilla 5946, La Paz; tel. (2) 35-4142; fax (2) 39-1985; asscn of 28 educational radio stations in Bolivia; Gen. Sec. RONALD GREBE LÓPEZ.

### Television

**Corporación Boliviana de Televisión Canal 30:** Calle Obispo Cárdenas 1475, Casilla 8980, La Paz; tel. (2) 31-5031; fax (2) 31-9563; f. 1996; Pres. RICARDO CLAURE; Dir ALEX MEJÍA.

**Empresa Nacional de Televisión Boliviana Canal 7:** Edif. La Urbana, 6° y 7°, Avda Camacho 1486, Casilla 900, La Paz; tel. (2) 37-6356; fax (2) 35-9753; f. 1969; govt network operating stations in La Paz, Oruro, Cochabamba, Potosí, Chuquisaca, Pando, Beni, Tarija and Santa Cruz; Gen. Man. MIGUEL N. MONTERO VACA.

**Televisión Boliviano Canal 2:** Casilla 4837, La Paz.

**Televisión Universitaria Canal 13:** Edif. 'Hoy', 12°–13°, Avda 6 de Agosto 2170, Casilla 13383, La Paz; tel. (2) 35-9297; fax (2) 35-9298; f. 1980; educational programmes; stations in Oruro, Cochabamba, Potosí, Sucre, Tarija, Beni and Santa Cruz; Dir Lic. ROBERTO CUEVAS RAMÍREZ.

# Finance

(cap. = capital; p.u. = paid up; res = reserves; dep. = deposits; m. = million; brs = branches; amounts are in bolivianos unless otherwise stated)

## BANKING

### Supervisory Authority

**Superintendencia de Bancos y Entidades Financieras:** Plaza Isabel la Católica 2507, Casilla 447, La Paz; tel. (2) 43-1919; fax (2) 43-0028; e-mail supban@lp.superbancos.gov.bo; f. 1928; Supt Lic. JACQUES TRIGO LOUBIÈRE.

### State Banks

**Banco Central de Bolivia:** Avda Ayacucho esq. Mercado, Casilla 3118, La Paz; tel. (2) 37-4151; fax (2) 39-2398; e-mail vmarquez@mail.bcb.gov.bo; internet www.bcb.gov.bo; f. 1911 as Banco de la Nación Boliviana, name changed as above 1928; bank of issue; cap. 96.6m., res 215.6m. (Dec. 1996); Pres. Dr JUAN ANTONIO MORALES ANAYA; Gen. Man. Lic. JAIME VALENCIA VALENCIA.

**Banco del Estado:** Calle Colón esq. Mercado, Casilla 1401, La Paz; tel. (2) 35-2868; fax (2) 39-1682; f. 1970; state bank incorporating banking department of Banco Central de Bolivia; cap. and res 51.1m., dep. 92.5m. (June 1990); Pres. Lic. RAMÓN RADA VELASCO; Gen. Man. JUAN LUIS PACHECO RAMÍREZ; 55 brs.

**Banco Agrícola de Bolivia:** Avda Mariscal Santa Cruz esq. Almirante Grau, Casilla 1179, La Paz; tel. (2) 36-5876; fax (2) 35-5940; f. 1942; cap. and res 100.4m. (June 1990); Pres. Lic. WALTER NÚÑEZ R.; Gen. Man. Lic. JUAN CARLOS PEREDO P.

**Banco Minero de Bolivia:** Calle Comercio 1290, Casilla 1410, La Paz; tel. (2) 35-2168; fax (2) 36-8870; f. 1936; finances private mining industry; cap. and res 44.6m. (June 1990); Pres. Ing. JAIME ASCARRUNZ E.; Gen. Man. Ing. RENÉ SANZ M.

**Banco de la Vivienda:** La Paz; tel. (2) 34-3510. 1964; to encourage and finance housing developments; 51% state participation; initial cap. 100m. Bolivian pesos; Pres. (vacant); Gen. Man. Lic. JOSÉ RAMÍREZ MONTALVA.

### Commercial Banks

**Banco Bisa SA:** Avda 16 de Julio 1628, Casilla 1290, La Paz; tel. (2) 35-9471; fax (2) 39-1735; e-mail bancbisa@caoba.entelnet.bo; f. 1963; cap. 285m., res 34m., dep. 2,800m. (Dec. 1998); Pres. Ing. JULIÓ LEÓN PRADO; Gen. Man. JOSÉ LUIS ARANGUREN AGUIRRE.

**Banco Boliviano Americano:** Avda Camacho esq. Loayza, Casilla 478, La Paz; tel. (2) 35-0860; fax (2) 35-3984; f. 1957; cap. and res US $13.4m., dep. US $186m. (June 1997); Pres. DAVID BLANCO; Gen. Man. FERNANDO CALVO UNZUETA (acting); 5 brs.

**Banco de Cochabamba, SA:** Warnes 40, Casilla 4107, Santa Cruz; tel. (3) 351036; fax (3) 340871; f. 1962; cap. 7.8m., dep. 112.0m. (July 1994); Exec. Pres. GUILLERMO GUTIÉRREZ SOSA; Gen. Man. MARÍA ELENA BLANCO DE ESTENSSORO; 5 brs.

**Banco de Crédito de Bolivia, SA:** Calle Colón esq. Mercado 1308, Casilla 907, La Paz; tel. (2) 36-0025; fax (2) 39-1044; f. 1993 as Banco Popular, SA, name changed as above 1994; 61% owned by Banco de Crédito del Perú; cap. 75.4m., res 21.0m., dep. 1,361.5m. (Dec. 1996); Chair. DIONISIO ROMERO SEMINARIO; Gen. Man. JAVIER SÁNCHEZ-GRIÑÁN CABALLERO; 6 brs.

**Banco Económico SA-SCZ:** Calle Ayacucho 166, Santa Cruz; tel. (3) 36-1177; fax (3) 36-1184; e-mail baneco@roble-scz.entelnet.bo; Pres. ALEX JOSÉ CUÉLLAR CHÁVEZ; Gen. Man. Ing. JUSTO YEPEZ KAKUDA.

**Banco de Financiamiento Industrial, SA:** Plaza 10 de Febrero acera Adolfo Mier esq. La Plata, Casilla 51, Oruro; tel. (52) 53759; f. 1974 to encourage and finance industrial development; cap. p.u. 2.6m. Bolivian pesos, dep. 1.1m. Bolivian pesos; Pres. Lic. HUGO CAMPOS; Man. FRANCISCO BERMÚDEZ.

**Banco Ganadero SA-Santa Cruz:** Calle 24 de Septiembre 110, Casilla 4492, Santa Cruz; tel. (3) 36-1616; fax (3) 36-1617; e-mail bangan@roble-scz.entelnet.bo; Pres. FERNANDO MONASTERIO NIEME; Gen. Man. JUAN OTERO STEINHART.

**Banco Industrial, SA:** Avda 16 de Julio 1628, 12°, Casilla 1290, La Paz; tel. (2) 31-7272; fax (2) 39-2013; f. 1963; industrial credit bank; cap. 153.2m., res 16.7m., dep. 2,194.2m. (Dec. 1996); Pres. JULIO LEÓN PRADO; CEO JUAN OTERO; 14 brs.

**Banco Industrial y Ganadero del Beni, SA:** Edif. Bigbeni, Avda 6 de Agosto, Casilla 54, Trinidad; tel. (46) 21476; cap. and res 22.4m., dep. 121.8m. (June 1990); Pres. Dr ISAAC SHIRIQUI V.; 11 brs.

**Banco Internacional de Desarrollo, SA:** Calle Nuflo de Chávez 150, Santa Cruz; tel. (3) 361555; fax (3) 338485; f. 1991; cap. 13.5m., res 11.8m., dep. 545.2m. (Dec. 1993); Pres. CARLOS LANDIVAR GIL; Gen. Man. Lic. ROBERTO LANDIVAR ROCA; 2 brs.

**Banco de Inversión Boliviano, SA:** Avda 16 de Julio 1571, Casilla 8639, La Paz; tel. (2) 35-4233; fax (2) 32-6536; f. 1977; cap. and res 11.2m., dep. 126.8m. (June 1991); Pres. JAIME GUTIÉRREZ MOSCOSO; Exec. Vice-Pres. MAURICIO URQUIDI URQUIDI.

**Banco de La Paz, SA:** Avda 16 de Julio 1473, Casilla 6826, La Paz; tel. (2) 36-4142; fax (2) 32-6536; f. 1975; cap. 53.1m., res 8.4m., dep. 767.5m. (Dec. 1995); Exec. Pres. Lic. GUIDO E. HINOJOSA CARDOSO; First Vice-Pres. Dr JORGE RENGEL SILLERICO; 11 brs.

**Banco Mercantil, SA:** Calle Ayacucho esq. Mercado 295, Casilla 423, La Paz; tel. (2) 31-5131; fax (2) 37-1279; e-mail bercant@caoba.entelnet.bo; f. 1905; cap. and res 38.5m., dep. 379m. (Sept. 1997); Pres. EDUARDO QUINTANILLA; Gen. Man. MARCELO DÍEZ DE MEDINA; 6 brs.

**Banco Nacional de Bolivia:** Avda Camacho esq. Colón, Casilla 360, La Paz; tel. (2) 35-4616; fax (2) 35-9146; e-mail info@bnb.com.bo; internet www.bnb.bolivia.com; f. 1872; cap. 59.9m., res 7.2m., dep. 344.7m. (Dec. 1998); Pres. FERNANDO BEDOYA B.; Gen. Man. EDUARDO ALVAREZ LEMAITRE; 33 brs.

**Banco de Santa Cruz de la Sierra, SA:** Calle Junín 154,Casilla 865, Santa Cruz; tel. (3) 33-9911; fax (3) 35-0114; e-mail bancruz@mail.bsc.com.bo; f. 1966; 90% owned by Banco Hispano (Spain); cap. and res 44.2m., dep. 315.4m. (June 1990); Pres. ANTONIO ESCÁMEZ TORRES; Gen. Man. ALFONSO ALVAREZ NÚÑEZ; 18 brs.

**Banco Solidario, SA:** Calle Nicolás Acosta esq. Cañada strongest 289, Casilla 13176, La Paz; tel. (2) 39-2810; fax (2) 39-1941; e-mail info@bancosol.com.bo; Pres. ROBERTO CAPRILES; Gen. Man. HERMANN KRUTZFELDT.

**Banco Unión, SA:** Avenida Libertad 156, Casilla 4057, Santa Cruz; tel. (3) 36-6869; fax (3) 34-0684; e-mail info@bancounion.com.bo; f. 1982; cap. 48.8m., res 7.6m., dep. 1,056.5m. (Dec. 1994); Pres. Ing. ANDRÉS PETRICEVIC; Gen. Man. Ing. LUIS SAAVEDRA BRUNO; 6 brs.

**Caja Central de Ahorros y Préstamos para la Vivienda:** Avda Mariscal Santa Cruz 1364, 20°, Casilla 4808, La Paz; tel. (2) 37-1280; fax (2) 36-1346; f. 1967; assets US $51m. (1993); Gen. Man. EDUARDO FRIAS T.

### Foreign Banks

**Banco do Brasil, SA:** Avda Camacho 1468, Casilla 1650, La Paz; tel. (2) 37-7272; fax (2) 39-1036; f. 1960; Man. LEO SCHNEIDERS; 3 brs.

**Banco de la Nación Argentina:** Avda 16 de Julio 1486, Casilla 2745-4312, La Paz; tel. (2) 35-9211; fax (2) 39-1392; e-mail bancnalp@caoba.entelnet.bo; internet www.bna.com.ar; f. 1891; Man. EDUARDO CASADO; 2 brs.

**Banco Real, SA:** Avda 16 de Julio 1642, Casilla 20270, La Paz; tel. (2) 36-6606; fax (2) 36-6607; Gen. Man. JOSÉ ROBERTO DO NASCIMENTO.

**Citibank NA** (USA): Edif. Multicentro Torre B, Rosendo Gutiérrez esq. Arce 146, La Paz; tel. (2) 43-0099; fax (2) 35-4645; Gen. Man. MARCELO CELLERINO.

**Dresdner Bank Lateinamerika AG:** Calle Rosendo Gutiérrez esq. Arce 136, Edif. Multicentro Torre B, La Paz; tel. (2) 43-4114; fax (2) 43-4115; fmrly Deutsch-Südamerikanische Bank AG and Dresdner Bank AG; Gen. Man. NILS HUPKA.

### Banking Association

**Asociación de Bancos Privados de Bolivia (ASOBAN):** Edif. Cámara Nacional de Comercio, 15°, Avda Mariscal Santa Cruz esq. Colombia 1392, Casilla 5822, La Paz; tel. (2) 36-1308; fax (2) 39-1093; e-mail asoban@wara.bdnet.bo; f. 1957; Pres. JAVIER ZUAZO CH.; Exec. Sec. CARLOS ITURRALDE B.; 18 mems.

## STOCK EXCHANGE

### Supervisory Authority

**Superintendencia de Pensiones, Valores y Seguros:** Calle Reyes Ortiz esq. Federico Zuazo, Torres Gundlach, piso 3, Casilla 6118, La Paz; tel. (2) 33-1212; fax (2) 33-0001; e-mail spvs@mail.spvs.gov.bo; Superintendent Dr PABLO GOTTRET VALDÉS; Intendent JOSÉ LUIS CONTRERAS.

**Bolsa Boliviana de Valores SA:** Edif. Zambrana P.B., Calle Montevideo 142, Casilla 12521, La Paz; tel (2) 39-2911; fax (2) 35-2308; e-mail info@bolsa-valores-bolivia.com; internet www.bolsa-valores-bolivia.com; f. 1989; Pres. Lic. LUIS FELIPE RIVERO MENDOZA; Gen. Man. Lic. ARMANDO ALVAREZ ARNAL.

### INSURANCE

#### Supervisory Authority

**Superintendencia de Pensiones, Valores y Seguros:** (see above).

#### National Companies

**Adriatica Seguros y Reaseguros, SA:** Avda Cristóbal de Mendoza 250, Santa Cruz; tel. (3) 36-6667; fax (3) 36-0600; Pres. ANTONIO OLEA BAUDOIN; Gen. Man. EDUARDO LANDÍVAR ROCA.

**Alianza, Cía de Seguros y Reaseguros, SA:** Avda 20 de Octubre 2680, esq. Campos Zona San Jorge, Casilla 11873, La Paz; tel. (2) 43-2121; fax (2) 43-2713; Pres. JUAN MANUEL PEÑA ROCA; Gen. Man. CÉSAR EYZAGUIRRE ANGELES.

**Aseguranza Internacional, SA:** Avda San Martín 1000-B esq. Calle Pablo Sanz, Casilla 1188, Santa Cruz; tel. (3) 43-7443; fax (3) 43-7439; Pres. MARCELO GOLDMANN P.

**Bisa Seguros y Reaseguros, SA:** Edif. San Pablo, 13°, Avda 16 de Julio 1479, Casilla 3669, La Paz; tel. (2) 35-2123; fax (2) 39-2500; Pres. JULIO LEÓN PRADO; Exec. Vice-Pres. ALEJANDRO MACLEAN C.

**La Boliviana Ciacruz de Seguros y Reaseguros, SA:** Calle Colón esq. Mercado 288, Casilla 628, La Paz; tel. (2) 37-9438; fax (2) 39-1309; e-mail bolseg@wara.bolnet.bo; f. 1946; all classes; Pres. GONZALO BEDOYA HERRERA.

**Compañía de Seguros y Reaseguros Cruceño, SA:** Calle René Moreno esq. Lemoyne 607, Santa Cruz; tel. (3) 33-8985; fax (3) 33-8984; Pres. Lic. GUIDO HINOJOSA; Gen. Man. NELSON HINOJOSA.

**Credinform International SA de Seguros:** Edif. Credinform, Calle Potosí esq. Ayacucho 1220, Casilla 1724, La Paz; tel. (2) 31-5566; fax (2) 39-1225; e-mail credinfo@cdobd.entelnet.bo; f. 1954; all classes; Pres. Dr ROBÍN BARRAGÁN PELÁEZ; Gen. Man. MIGUEL ANGEL BARRAGÁN IBARGUEN.

**Delta Insurance Co, SA:** Calle España, Casilla 920, Cochabamba; tel. (42) 25-7765; fax (42) 22-0451; f. 1965; all classes except life; Pres. CARLOS CHRISTIE JUSTINIANO.

**La Fenix Boliviana, SA de Seguros y Reaseguros:** Calle Potosí, Edif. Naira Mezzanine Of 5, Casilla 4409, La Paz; tel. (2) 35-3708; fax (2) 37-0167; Pres. ORLANDO NOGALES.

**Nacional de Seguros y Reaseguros, SA:** Edif. Aspiazu, Avda 20 de Octubre 2095, Casilla 14, La Paz; tel. (2) 31-2312; fax (2) 31-0011; f. 1977; fmrly known as Condor, SA de Seguros y Reaseguros; Pres. TONCHI ETEROVIC NIEGOVIC; Gen. Man. LUIS ALBERTO FLOR CORTEZ.

**Seguros Illimani, SA:** Edif. Mariscal de Ayacucho, 10°, Calle Loayza, Casilla 133, La Paz; tel. (2) 37-1090; fax (2) 39-1149; f. 1979; all classes; Pres. FERNANDO ARCE GRANDCHANT; Gen. Man. RAÚL UGARTE.

**Unicruz Cía de Seguros de Vida, SA:** Zona El Trompillo 76 Perimetral y Río Grande, Santa Cruz; tel. (3) 54-0707; fax (3) 53-9549; Pres. Lic. JOSÉ CAMACHO PARADA.

**Unión de Seguros, SA:** Edif. El Cóndor, 16°, Calle Batallón Colorados, Casilla 2922, La Paz; tel. (2) 35-8155; fax (2) 39-2049; all classes; Pres. Dr JORGE RENGEL SILLERICO; Man. VÍCTOR ROSAS.

**La Vitalicia Seguros y Reaseguros de Vida, SA:** Avda 6 de Agosto 2170, Edif. Hoy Mezzanine, La Paz; tel. (2) 33-4303; fax (2) 33-3792; Pres. RUDDY EDUARDO RIVERA D.

There are also four foreign-owned insurance companies operating in Bolivia: American Life Insurance Co, American Home Assurance Co, United States Fire Insurance Co and International Health Insurance Danmarck.

#### Insurance Association

**Asociación Boliviana de Aseguradores:** Edif. Castilla, 5°, Of. 506, Calle Loayza esq. Mercado 250, Casilla 4804, La Paz; tel. (2) 32-8804; fax (2) 37-9154; f. 1962; Pres. ALFONSO IBÁÑEZ; Exec. Sec. BLANCA M. DE OTERMIN.

## Trade and Industry

### GOVERNMENT AGENCIES

**Cámara Nacional de Exportadores (CAMEX):** Avda Arce 2017, esq. Goitia, Casilla 12145, La Paz; tel. (2) 34-1220; fax (2) 36-1491; e-mail camex@caoba.entelnet.bo; internet www.camex-lpb.com; f. 1970; Pres. LUIS NEMTALA YAMIN; Gen. Man. JORGE ADRIAZOLA REIMERS.

**Instituto Nacional de Inversiones (INI):** Edif. Cristal, 10°, Calle Yanacocha, Casilla 4393, La Paz; tel. (2) 37-5730; fax (2) 36-7297; e-mail abeseg@kolla.net.bo; f. 1971; state institution for the promotion of new investments and the application of the Investment Law; Exec. Dir Ing. JOSÉ MARIO FERNÁNDEZ IRAHOLA.

**Instituto Nacional de Promoción de Exportaciones (INPEX):** Calle Federico Zuazo esq. Reyes Ortiz, Casilla 10871, La Paz; tel. (2) 37-8000; fax (2) 39-1226.

**Sistema de Regulación Sectorial (SIRESE):** Superintendencia General, Edif. Cámara Nacional de Comercio, 16°, Casilla 9647, La Paz; tel. (2) 33-2525; fax (2) 33-3108; e-mail sirese@ceibo.entelnet.bo; f. 1994; regulatory body for the formerly state-owned companies and utilities; oversees the general co-ordination and growth of the regulatory system and the work of its Superintendencies of Electricity, Hydrocarbons, Telecommunications, Transport and Water; Superintendent Gen. CLAUDE BESSE ARZE.

### DEVELOPMENT ORGANIZATIONS

**Consejo Nacional de Acreditación y Medición de la Calidad Educativa (CONAMED):** La Paz; f. 1994; education quality board.

**Consejo Nacional de Planificación (CONEPLAN):** Edif. Banco Central de Bolivia, 26°, Calle Mercado esq. Ayacucho, Casilla 3118, La Paz; tel. (2) 37-4151; fax (2) 35-3840; e-mail claves@mail.bcb.gov.bo; internet www.bcb.gov.bo; f. 1985.

**Corporación de las Fuerzas Armadas para el Desarrollo Nacional (COFADENA):** Avda 6 de Agosto 2649, Casilla 1015, La Paz; tel. (2) 37-7305; fax (2) 36-0900; f. 1972; industrial, agricultural and mining holding company and development organization owned by the Bolivian armed forces; Gen. Man. EDGAR AMPUERO ANGULO.

**Corporación Regional de Desarrollo de La Paz (CORDEPAZ):** Calle Comercio 1200 esq. Ayacucho, Casilla 6102, La Paz; tel. (2) 37-1524; fax (2) 39-2283; f. 1972; decentralized government institution to foster the development of the La Paz area; Pres. Lic. RICARDO PAZ BALLIVIÁN; Gen. Man. Ing. JUAN G. CARRASCO R.

**Instituto para el Desarrollo de la Pequeña Unidad Productiva:** La Paz.

### CHAMBERS OF COMMERCE

**Cámara Nacional de Comercio:** Edif. Cámara Nacional de Comercio, Avda Mariscal Santa Cruz 1392, 1°, Casilla 7, La Paz; tel. (2) 35-0042; fax (2) 39-1004; f. 1890; 30 brs and special brs; Pres. GUILLERMO MORALES F.; Exec. Sec. FERNANDO CÁCERES PACHECO.

**Cámara de Comercio de Oruro:** Pasaje Guachalla s/n, Casilla 148, Oruro; tel. and fax (52) 50606; f. 1895; Pres. ALVARO CORNEJO GAZCÓN; Gen. Man. LUIS CAMACHO VARGAS.

**Cámara Departamental de Industria y Comercio de Santa Cruz:** Calle Suárez de Figueroa 127, 3°, Casilla 180, Santa Cruz; tel. (3) 33-4555; fax (3) 34-2353; e-mail cainco@cainco.org.bo; internet www.cainco.org.bo; f. 1915; Pres. Ing. CLAUDIO MANSILLA PEÑA; Gen. Man. Lic. OSCAR ORTIZ ANTELO.

**Cámara Departamental de Comercio de Cochabamba:** Calle Sucre E-0336, Casilla 493, Cochabamba; tel. (42) 57715; fax (42) 57717; f. 1922; Pres. RAQUEL ALEN DE SABA; Gen. Man. Lic. JUAN CARLOS AVILA S.

**Cámara Departamental de Comercio e Industria de Potosí:** Casilla 149, Potosí; tel. (62) 22641; fax (62) 22641; Pres. OSCAR VARGAS IPORRE; Gen. Man. WALTER ZABALA AYLLON.

**Cámara Departamental de Industria y Comercio de Chuquisaca:** Calle España 64, Casilla 33, Sucre; tel. (64) 51194; fax (64) 51850; e-mail cicch@camara.scr.entelnet.bo; f. 1923; Pres. JUAN CARLOS SABAT CASAP; Gen. Man. Lic. ALFREDO YÁÑEZ MERCADO.

**Cámara Departamental de Comercio e Industria de Cobija—Pando:** Cobija; tel. (842) 2153; fax (842) 2291; Pres. DULFREDO CÁRDENAS BERRIOS.

**Cámara Departamental de Industria y Comercio de Tarija:** Avda Bolívar 0413, 1°, Casilla 74, Tarija; tel. (66) 22737; fax (66) 24053; Pres. MILTON CASTELLANOS; Gen. Man. VÍCTOR ARAMAYO.

**Cámara Departamental de Comercio de Trinidad—Beni:** Casilla 96, Trinidad; tel. (46) 22365; fax (46) 21400; Pres. ALCIDES ALPIRE DURÁN.

### INDUSTRIAL AND TRADE ASSOCIATIONS

**Cámara Agropecuaria del Oriente:** 3 anillo interno zona Oeste, Casilla 116, Santa Cruz; tel. (3) 52-2200; fax (3) 52-2621; e-mail caosrz@bibosi.scz.entelnet.bo; f. 1964; agriculture and livestock association for eastern Bolivia; Pres. LUIS NUÑEZ RIBERO; Gen. Man. Lic. GUILLERMO RIBERA CUÉLLAR.

**Cámara Agropecuaria de La Paz:** Calle Loayza 250, Casilla 6297, La Paz; tel. (2) 32-3178; fax (2) 35-3942; Pres. FERNANDO PALACIOS; Gen. Man. HARLEY RODRÍGUEZ.

**Cámara Forestal de Bolivia:** Prolongación Manuel Ignacio Salvatierra 1055, Casilla 346, Santa Cruz; tel. (3) 33-2699; fax (3) 33-1456; e-mail foresbol@cotas.com.bo; f. 1969; represents the interests of the Bolivian timber industry; Pres. MARIO BARBERY SCIARONI; Gen. Man. Lic. ARTURO BOWLES OLHAGARAY.

**Cámara Nacional de Industrias:** Edif. Cámara Nacional de Comercio, 14°, Avda Mariscal Santa Cruz 1392, Casilla 611, La Paz; tel. (2) 37-4476; fax (2) 35-0620; internet www.bolivia-industry.com; f. 1931; Pres. GARY LACUNZA V.; Man. DR ALFREDO ARANA RUCK.

**Cámara Nacional de Minería:** Pasaje Bernardo Trigo 429, Casilla 2022, La Paz; tel. (2) 35-0623; f. 1953; mining institute; Pres. Ing. LUIS PRADO BARRIENTOS; Sec.-Gen. GERMÁN GORDILLO S.

**Comité Boliviano de Productores de Antimonio:** Pasajes Bernardo Trigo 429, Casilla 14451, La Paz; tel. (2) 44-2140; fax (2) 44-1653; f. 1978; controls the marketing, pricing and promotion policies of the antimony industry; Pres. ALBERTO BARRIOS MORALES; Sec.-Gen. DR ALCIDES RODRÍGUEZ J.

**Comité Boliviano del Café (COBOLCA):** Calle Nicaragua 1638, Casilla 9770, La Paz; tel. (2) 22-3883; fax (2) 24-4591; e-mail cobolca@ceibo.entelnet.bo; controls the export, quality, marketing and growing policies of the coffee industry; Gen. Man. MAURICIO VILLARROEL.

### EMPLOYERS' ASSOCIATIONS

**Asociación Nacional de Mineros Medianos:** Calle Pedro Salazar 600 esq. Presbítero Medina, Casilla 6190, La Paz; tel. (2) 41-2232; fax (2) 41-4123; f. 1939; association of the 14 private medium-sized mining companies; Pres. RAÚL ESPAÑA-SMITH; Sec.-Gen. ROLANDO JORDÁN.

**Confederación de Empresarios Privados de Bolivia (CEPB):** Edif. Cámara Nacional de Comercio, 7°, Avda Mariscal Santa Cruz 1392, Casilla 20439, La Paz; tel. (2) 35-6831; e-mail cepbol@ceibo .entelnet.bo; largest national employers' organization; Pres. Lic. CARLOS CALVO GALINDO; Exec. Sec. Lic. JOHNNY NOGALES VIRUEZ.

There are also employers' federations in Santa Cruz, Cochabamba, Oruro, Potosí, Beni and Tarija.

### UTILITIES

#### Electricity

**Superintendencia de Electricidad:** Avda 16 de Julio 1571, La Paz; tel. (2) 31-2401; fax (2) 31-2393; e-mail rlopez@antares .superele.gov.bo; internet www.superele.gov.bo; f. 1996; regulates the electricity sector; Superintendent ALEJANDRO NOWOTNY VERA; Gen. Sec. ROLANDO LÓPEZ.

**Compañía Boliviana de Energía Eléctrica, SA (COBEE):** Avda Hernando Siles 5635, Casilla 353, La Paz; tel. (2) 78-2474; fax (2) 78-5920; e-mail cobee@cobee.com; f. 1925; second largest private producer and distributor of electricity serving the areas of La Paz and Oruro; in 1998 the company generated 25.9% of all electricity produced in Bolivia; Chair. D. H. BUSWELL.

**Electropaz:** La Paz; tel. (2) 35-6911; Gen. Man. Ing. JOSÉ MARÍA CIRUJANO.

**Empresa Nacional de Electricidad, SA (ENDE):** Colombia 655, esq. Falsuri, Casilla 565, Cochabamba; tel. (42) 46322; fax (42) 42700; f. 1962; former state electricity company; privatized under the Govt's capitalization programme in 1995 and divided into three arms concerned with generation, transmission and distribution, respectively; Pres. Ing. CLAUDE BESSE ARZE; Gen. Man. Ing. JOHNNY COSCIO MALDONADO.

#### Gas

Numerous distributors of natural gas exist throughout the country, many of which are owned by the petroleum distributor, Yacimientos Petrolíferos Fiscales Bolivianos (YPFB).

### CO-OPERATIVES

**Instituto Nacional de Co-operativas (INALCO):** Edif. Lotería Nacional, 4°, Avda Mariscal Santa Cruz y Cochabamba, La Paz; tel. (2) 37-4366; fax (2) 35-9741; f. 1974; Exec. Dir DAVID E. MÁRQUEZ.

### TRADE UNIONS

**Central Obrera Boliviana (COB):** Edif. COB, Calle Pisagua 618, Casilla 6552, La Paz; tel. (2) 35-2426; fax (2) 32-4740; f. 1952; main union confederation; 800,000 mems; Exec. Sec. EDGAR RAMÍREZ SANTIESTÉBAN; Sec.-Gen. OSCAR SALAS MOYA.

Affiliated unions:

**Central Obrera Departamental de La Paz:** Estación Central 284, La Paz; tel. (2) 35-2898; Exec. Sec. FLAVIO CLAVIJO.

**Confederación Sindical Unica de los Trabajadores Campesinos de Bolivia (CSUTCB):** Calle Sucre, esq. Yanacocha, La Paz; tel. (2) 36-9433; f. 1979; peasant farmers' union; Exec. Sec. JUAN DE LA CRUZ VILLCA.

**Federación de Empleados de Industria Fabril:** Edif. Fabril, 5°, Plaza de San Francisco, La Paz; tel. (2) 37-2759; Exec. Sec. CARLOS SOLARI.

**Federación Sindical de Trabajadores Mineros de Bolivia (FSTMB):** Plaza Venezuela 1470, Casilla 14565, La Paz; tel. (2) 35-9656; f. 1944; mineworkers' union; Exec. Sec. VÍCTOR LÓPEZ ARIAS; Gen. Sec. EDGAR RAMÍREZ SANTIESTÉBAN; 27,000 mems.

**Federación Sindical de Trabajadores Petroleros de Bolivia:** Calle México 1504, La Paz; tel. (2) 35-1748; Exec. Sec. NEFTALYMENDOZA DURÁN.

**Confederación General de Trabajadores Fabriles de Bolivia (CGTFB):** Avda Armentia 452, Casilla 21590, La Paz; tel. (2) 37-1603; fax (2) 32-4302; e-mail dirabc@bo.net; f. 1951; manufacturing workers' union; Exec. Sec. ANGEL ASTURIZAGA; Gen. Sec. ROBERTO ENCINAS.

## Transport

### RAILWAYS

**Empresa Nacional de Ferrocarriles (ENFE):** Estación Central de Ferrocarriles, Plaza Zalles, Casilla 428, La Paz; tel. (2) 32-7401; fax (2) 39-2677; f. 1964; administers most of the railways in Bolivia; privatized under the Government's capitalization programme in 1995. Total networks: 3,698 km (1995); Andina network: 2,274 km; Eastern network: 1,424 km; Pres. ABRAHAM MONASTERIOS.

A former private railway, Machacamarca–Uncia, owned by Corporación Minera de Bolivia (105 km), merged with the Andina network of ENFE in 1987. There are plans to construct a railway line with Brazilian assistance, to link Cochabamba and Santa Cruz. The Government was expected to invite bids in early 1999 for the construction of a rail link between Santa Cruz and Mutún on the border with Brazil.

### ROADS

In 1996 Bolivia had some 49,400 km of roads, of which an estimated 2,500 km were paved. Almost the entire road network is concentrated in the altiplano region and the Andes valleys. A 560-km highway runs from Santa Cruz to Cochabamba, serving a colonization scheme on virgin lands around Santa Cruz. The Pan-American Highway, linking Argentina and Peru, crosses Bolivia from south to north-west. In late 1997 the Government announced the construction of 1,844 km of new roads in the hope of improving Bolivia's connections with neighbouring countries.

### INLAND WATERWAYS

By agreement with Paraguay in 1938 (confirmed in 1939), Bolivia has an outlet on the River Paraguay. This arrangement, together with navigation rights on the Paraná, gives Bolivia access to the River Plate and the sea. The River Paraguay is navigable for vessels of 12-ft draught for 288 km beyond Asunción, in Paraguay, and for smaller boats another 960 km to Corumbá in Brazil. In late 1994 plans were finalized to widen and deepen the River Paraguay, providing a waterway from Bolivia to the Atlantic coast in Uruguay. However, in 1999 work on the project had still not begun, owing largely to environmental concerns.

In 1974 Bolivia was granted free duty access to the Brazilian coastal ports of Belém and Santos and the inland ports of Corumbá and Port Velho. In 1976 Argentina granted Bolivia free port facilities at Rosario on the River Paraná. In 1992 an agreement was signed with Peru, granting Bolivia access to (and the use, without customs formalities, of) the Pacific port of Ilo. Most of Bolivia's foreign trade is handled through the ports of Matarani (Peru), Antofagasta and Arica (Chile), Rosario and Buenos Aires (Argentina) and Santos (Brazil). An agreement signed between Bolivia and Chile in mid-1995 to reform Bolivia's access arrangements to the port of Arica came into effect in January 1996.

Bolivia has over 14,000 km of navigable rivers, which connect most of Bolivia with the Amazon basin.

**Bolivian River Navigation Company:** f. 1958; services from Puerto Suárez to Buenos Aires (Argentina).

### OCEAN SHIPPING

**Líneas Navieras Bolivianas (LINABOL):** Edif. Hansa, 16°, Avda Mariscal Santa Cruz, Apdo 11160, La Paz; tel. (2) 37-9459; fax (2) 39-1079; Pres. Vice-Adm. LUIS AZURDUY ZAMBRANA; Vice-Pres. WOLFGANG APT.

### CIVIL AVIATION

Bolivia has 30 airports including the two international airports at La Paz (El Alto) and Santa Cruz (Viru-Viru).

**Dirección General de Aeronaútica Civil:** La Paz.

**AeroSur:** Calle Colón y Avda Irala, Casilla 3104, Santa Cruz; tel. (3) 36-4446; fax (3) 33-0666; e-mail javiedr.gonzalez@aerosur.com; f. 1992 by the merger of existing charter cos following deregulation; privately-owned; Pres. OSCAR ALCOCER; Gen. Man. FERNANDO PRUDENCIO.

**Lloyd Aéreo Boliviano, SAM (LAB):** Casilla 132, Aeropuerto 'Jorge Wilstermann', Cochabamba; tel. (42) 50750; fax (42) 50744; e-mail lider@labairlines.bo.net; internet www.labairlines.bo.net; f. 1925; privatized under the Government's capitalization programme in 1995; owned by Bolivian Govt (48.3%), VASP-Brazil (49%), private interests (2.7%); operates a network of scheduled services to 12 cities within Bolivia and to 17 international destinations in South America, Central America and the USA; Pres. ULISSES CANHEDO AZEVEDO; CEO ANTONIO SPAGNUOLO SÁNCHEZ.

**Transportes Aéreos Bolivianos (TAB):** Casilla 12237, La Paz; tel. (42) 37-8325; fax (42) 35-9660; f. 1977; regional scheduled and charter cargo services; Gen. Man. LUIS GUERECA PADILLA; Chair. CARLO APARICIO.

**Transportes Aéreos Militares:** Avda Panamericana Alto, La Paz; tel. (2) 84-2205; internal passenger and cargo services; Dir-Gen. Lt Col. LUIS A. TRIGO ANTELO.

## Tourism

Bolivia's tourist attractions include Lake Titicaca, at 3,810 m (12,500 ft) above sea-level, pre-Incan ruins at Tiwanaku, Chacaltaya in the Andes mountains, which has the highest ski-run in the world, and the UNESCO World Cultural Heritage Sites of Potosí and Sucre. In 1996 376,855 foreign visitors arrived at hotels in Bolivian regional capitals. In that year receipts from tourism totalled US $161m. Tourists come mainly from South American countries, the USA and Europe.

**Asociación Boliviana de Agencias de Viajes y Turismo:** Edif. Litoral, Avda Mariscal Santa Cruz 1351, Casilla 3967, La Paz; f. 1984; Pres. EUGENIO MONROY VÉLEZ.

**Secretaría Nacional de Turismo:** Calle Mercado 1328, Casilla 1868, La Paz; tel. (2) 36-7463; fax (2) 37-4630; e-mail turismo@mcei-bolivia.com; internet www.mcei-boliviacom/turismo /turismo.htm; f. 1977; Dir Lic. OSCAR ANGEL JORDÁN BACIGALUPO.

# BOSNIA AND HERZEGOVINA

## Introductory Survey

**Location, Climate, Language, Religion, Flag, Capital**

Bosnia and Herzegovina is situated in south-eastern Europe. It is bounded by Croatia to the north and west, by Serbia to the east and by Montenegro to the south-east, and has a short (20 km—12 miles) western coastline on the Adriatic Sea. It is a largely mountainous territory with a continental climate and steady rainfall throughout the year; in areas nearer the coast, however, the climate is more Mediterranean. The principal language is Serbo-Croat. Although it is a single spoken language, Serbo-Croat has two written forms: the Muslims (Bosniaks) and Croats use the Roman alphabet, while the Serbs use Cyrillic script. The Muslims (the majority of whom belong to the Sunni sect) are the largest religious grouping in Bosnia and Herzegovina, comprising 43.7% of the population in 1991. Religious affiliation is roughly equated with ethnicity, the Serbs (31.4% of the population) belonging to the Serbian Orthodox Church and the Croats (17.3%) being members of the Roman Catholic Church. The national flag (proportions 2 by 1) consists of two unequal vertical sections of blue, separated by a yellow triangle, which is bordered on the left by a diagonal line of nine white five-pointed stars. The capital is Sarajevo.

**Recent History**

The provinces of Bosnia and Herzegovina formed part of the Turkish (Ottoman) Empire for almost 400 years before annexation to the Austro-Hungarian Empire in 1878. The population of the provinces was composed of an ethnic mixture of Orthodox Serbs, Roman Catholic Croats and Muslims (mainly Bosnian Slavs who had converted to Islam). Serbian expansionist aims troubled the area from the beginning of the 20th century, and Austria-Hungary attempted to end the perceived Serbian threat in 1914 by declaring war on Serbia; this conflict was to escalate into the First World War. On 4 December 1918 the Kingdom of Serbs, Croats and Slovenes was proclaimed when the Serbs and Croats agreed with other ethnic groups to establish a common state under the Serbian monarchy. The provinces of Bosnia and Herzegovina formed part of the new kingdom. Bitter disputes ensued between Serbs and Croats, however, and in January 1929 King Alexander imposed a dictatorship, changing the name of the country to Yugoslavia later the same year.

Though officially banned in 1921, the Communist Party of Yugoslavia (CPY) operated clandestinely, and in 1937 Josip Broz (alias Tito) became the General Secretary of the CPY. During the Second World War (1939–45) Tito's communist-led Partisan movement, whose members were from a variety of ethnic groups, dominated most of Bosnia and Herzegovina, simultaneously waging war against invading German and Italian troops, the 'Ustaša' regime in Croatia and the Serb-dominated 'Chetniks'. On Tito's victory, after the War, Bosnia and Herzegovina became one of the six constituent republics of the Yugoslav federation (despite Serbian pressure to limit the region to provincial status, as with Kosovo and the Vojvodina). In the 1960s Tito established Muslim power in Bosnia and Herzegovina in an effort to counter the growing ethnic tension between the Serbs and Croats of the republic. Slav Muslims were granted a distinct ethnic status, as a nation of Yugoslavia, for the 1971 census, and a collective state presidency was established in that year, with a regular rotation of posts.

Increasing ethnic tension in Bosnia and Herzegovina, potentially the most dangerous in the various ethnic groups of Yugoslavia, became evident in September 1990. Followers of the Party of Democratic Action (PDA), the principal Muslim party of the republic, demonstrated in the neighbouring Sandjak area of Serbia in support of Muslim rights in the Novi Pazar district, clashing with Serb nationalists. Later that year ethnic affiliation proved to be a decisive factor in the republican elections in November and December. The ruling League of Communists of Bosnia and Herzegovina was ousted, and the three main parties to emerge were all nationalist: the Muslim (Bosniak) PDA, with 86 seats; the Serbian Democratic Party (SDP), with 72 seats; and the Croatian Democratic Union of Bosnia and Herzegovina (CDU—BH), an affiliate of the ruling CDU party of Croatia, with 44 seats. The three nationalist parties also took all seven seats on the directly-elected collective Presidency and formed a coalition administration for the republic. On 20 December they announced that Dr Alija Izetbegović of the PDA was to be President of the Presidency, Jure Pelivan of the CDU—BH was to be President of the Executive Council (Prime Minister) and Momčilo Krajišnik of the SDP was to be President of the Assembly.

In 1991 the politics of Bosnia and Herzegovina were increasingly dominated by the Serb–Croat conflict. Following the declarations of independence by Slovenia and Croatia in June, Serb-dominated territories in Bosnia and Herzegovina declared their intent to remain within the Yugoslav federation (or in a 'Greater Serbia'). On 27 June the self-proclaimed Serb 'Municipal Community of Bosanska Krajina' in Bosnia announced its unification with the 'Serbian Autonomous Region (SAR) of Krajina' in Croatia. An SAR of Bosanska Krajina was proclaimed on 16 September. The republican Government rejected these moves and declared the inviolability of the internal boundaries of Yugoslavia. Armed incidents contributed to the rising tension throughout mid-1991 and many Serb areas announced the formation of other 'Autonomous Regions'. Other ethnic groups accused the Serbs of planning a 'Greater Serbia', with the support of the Jugoslavenska Narodna Armija (JNA, Yugoslav People's Army). In October the JNA assumed effective control of Mostar, to the north-west of the Serb 'Old' Herzegovina, and began a siege of the Croatian city of Dubrovnik.

In October 1991 both the republican Presidency (with the dissenting votes of the Serb members) and the PDA proposed to the Assembly that the republic declare its independence (Macedonia had already done so in September). The proposals favoured a renewed federation, but one in which the republic had equal relations with both Serbia and Croatia. On 14 October, during the debate in the Assembly, the Serbs (mainly the SDP) rejected any such declaration as a move towards secession, claiming that all Serbs should live in one state. No compromise was reached, and the Serb representatives subsequently withdrew from the chamber. However, the other deputies, dominated by the members of the PDA and the CDU—BH, continued the session; on 15 October the remaining members of the Assembly approved a resolution declaring that the Republic of Bosnia and Herzegovina was a sovereign state within its existing borders.

The deputies of the three main parties continued to negotiate, but the PDA condemned what it described as the threats of the SDP leader, Dr Radovan Karadžić. The 'Autonomous Regions' of the Serbs rejected the republican Assembly's resolution and declared that only the federal laws and Constitution would apply on their territory. On 24 October 1991 the Serb deputies of the Bosnia and Herzegovina Assembly constituted an 'Assembly of the Serb Nation' (Serb Assembly). In early November another SAR was proclaimed, consisting of the Serbs of Northern Bosnia, with an Assembly based in Doboj (an area without a Serb majority). On 9–10 November a referendum, organized by the Serb Assembly, indicated overwhelming support for remaining in a common Serb State. However, in another referendum on 29 February and 1 March 1992, which was open to all ethnic groups but was boycotted by the Serbs, 99.4% of the 63% of the electorate who participated were in favour of full independence. President Izetbegović immediately declared the republic's independence and omitted the word 'socialist' from the new state's official title.

Following the declaration of independence, there was renewed Serb–Muslim tension, leading to clashes in Sarajevo, the republican capital, and elsewhere. On 18 March 1992, following mediation by the European Community (EC, now European Union—EU—see p. 172), the leaders of the Serb, Croat and Muslim communities of Bosnia and Herzegovina signed an agreement providing for the division of the republic into three autonomous units. The EC and the USA recognized Bosnia and Herzegovina's independence on 7 April. On 27 March the Serbs announced the formation of a 'Serbian Republic of Bosnia and Herzegovina', which comprised Serbian-held areas of the republic (about 65% of the total area), including the SARs, and which was to be headed by Karadžić. The Bosnian Government immediately declared this breakaway republic, the headquarters of which were based in Banja Luka, to be illegal. In April fighting between the Serbian-dominated JNA in Bosnia and Herzegovina and Muslim and Croatian forces intensified; several cities, including Sarajevo, were besieged by Serbian troops. In early May, however, the newly-established Federal Republic of Yugoslavia (FRY—composed solely of the republics of Serbia and Montenegro), in an apparent attempt to disclaim any responsibility for Bosnia and Herzegovina's internal strife, ordered all of its citizens in the JNA to withdraw from the republic within 15 days. Early EC and UN efforts at mediation proved unsuccessful, and their respective peace monitors were withdrawn from Sarajevo in mid-May after a state of emergency had been declared and successive cease-fires had failed to take effect. Izetbegović requested foreign military intervention, but the UN, while deploying 14,000 troops (the United Nations Protection Force—UNPROFOR, see p. 60) in Croatia and demanding a halt to the fighting and the withdrawal of Yugoslav and Croat troops from Bosnia and Herzegovina, decided against the deployment of a peace-keeping force in the republic under prevailing conditions. On 20 May the Government of Bosnia and Herzegovina declared the JNA to be an 'occupying force' and announced the formation of a republican army. Two days later Bosnia and Herzegovina was accepted as a member of the UN. On 30 May the UN imposed economic sanctions against the FRY for its continuing involvement in the Bosnian conflict. In early June, in an apparent effort to placate the UN, Serb leaders in Belgrade (the FRY capital) ordered the Bosnian Serbs to end the siege of Sarajevo and to surrender Sarajevo airport to UN control. In the same month the UN Security Council decided to redeploy 1,000 of the UNPROFOR troops in Croatia to protect Sarajevo airport. An additional 500 troops were dispatched to Sarajevo in mid-July.

On 7 July 1992 there was a major development in the Bosnian conflict, when a breakaway Croat state, 'The Croatian Union of Herzeg-Bosna', was declared. The new state covered about 30% of the territory of Bosnia and Herzegovina and was headed by Mate Boban. Izetbegović's Government promptly declared it illegal, while Karadžić proposed that Serbs and Croats partition Bosnia and Herzegovina among themselves. Despite their political differences, Izetbegović and President Franjo Tudjman of Croatia (who supported the establishment of 'The Croatian Union of Herzeg-Bosna'), signed a treaty of friendship and co-operation in late July.

Revelations concerning the predominantly Serb policy of 'ethnic cleansing' (involving the expulsion by one ethnic group of other ethnic groups in an attempt to create a homogenous population) and the discovery of a number of detention camps in Bosnia and Herzegovina led to the unanimous adoption by the UN Security Council, in early August 1992, of a resolution condemning the camps and those responsible for abuses of human rights. A further resolution, adopted in mid-August, demanded unimpeded access to the detention camps for the International Committee of the Red Cross (ICRC), and reiterated that those abusing human rights in the former Yugoslavia would be held personally responsible.

In an annex to the agreement signed in July 1992, the Governments of Croatia and of Bosnia and Herzegovina formed a Joint Defence Committee in late September, and repeated demands that the UN remove its arms embargo on Croatia and Bosnia and Herzegovina (the embargo was imposed on the whole of the former Yugoslavia in September 1991). Within Bosnia and Herzegovina itself, however, hostilities erupted between Bosnian Croats and Muslims in mid-October, and the towns of Mostar, Novi Travnik and Vitez were captured by the Croats. Mostar was subsequently proclaimed the capital of 'The Croatian Union of Herzeg-Bosna'. In early November the Croat Jure Pelivan resigned as Prime Minister of Bosnia and Herzegovina, and was replaced by Mile Akmadžić. In mid-November the Croatian Government admitted for the first time that Croatian regular army units had been deployed in Bosnia and Herzegovina, and agreed to withdraw them. In accordance with this official admission, Croatia became a signatory to the latest cease-fire agreement in Bosnia and Herzegovina. In early December the UN Human Rights Commission, echoing a statement made by the ICRC in October, declared that the Serbs were largely responsible for violations of human rights in Bosnia and Herzegovina. Following allegations of the organized rape of more than 20,000 Muslim women by Serb forces, the UN Security Council unanimously adopted, in mid-December, a resolution condemning the atrocities and demanding access to all Serb detention camps.

Meanwhile, in mid-December 1992 the Serbian enclave in Bosnia and Herzegovina, now calling itself the 'Serbian Republic', unilaterally declared that the conflict was at an end and that the Serbs had won their own 'independent and sovereign state'. However, by late December Muslim forces appeared to be regaining territory. In early January 1993 the co-Chairmen of the Geneva Peace Conference (a permanent forum for talks on the conflict, established in 1992), Lord (formerly David) Owen (a former British Secretary of State for Foreign and Commonwealth Affairs) and Cyrus Vance (the UN mediator and a former US Secretary of State), visited Belgrade for talks with the newly re-elected President of Serbia, Slobodan Milošević. Their aim was to persuade him to convince the Bosnian Serbs to agree to a division of Bosnia and Herzegovina into 10 provinces (with three provinces allocated to each faction and Sarajevo as a province with special status). The peace plan was approved by the leader of the Bosnian Croats, Mate Boban, and, in part, by Izetbegović, but was rejected by the Bosnian Serb leader, Karadžić, who insisted on the establishment of an autonomous Serbian state within the territory of Bosnia and Herzegovina.

In mid-January 1993 Milošević attended the peace talks in Geneva for the first time. Karadžić, under pressure from Milošević and President Dobrica Cosić of the FRY, agreed to the constitutional proposals included in the plan and subsequently to the military arrangements. On 19–20 January the Bosnian Serb Assembly voted to accept the general outline of the Vance-Owen plan. Hostilities between Croats and Muslims intensified, however, in central Bosnia.

In February 1993 the UN Security Council adopted a resolution providing for the establishment of an international court to try alleged war criminals for acts committed since 1991 in the former Yugoslav republics. In the following month the UN Security Council adopted a resolution to allow aircraft under the command of NATO to fire on any aircraft violating the 'no-fly zone' imposed on Bosnian airspace in October 1992.

During March 1993, at further peace talks, Izetbegović agreed to both the military arrangements and the proposed territorial divisions included in the Vance-Owen plan, leaving the Bosnian Serbs as the only party not to have signed the section on the division of Bosnia and Herzegovina. In April the Bosnian Serb Assembly rejected the territorial arrangements, incurring international disapproval (including that of Serbia, which had endorsed the plan under pressure from UN and EC sanctions). In early May Karadžić signed the Vance-Owen plan in Geneva, but two days later it was decisively rejected by the Serb Assembly at Pale, since under the terms of the plan the Bosnian Serbs would be forced to surrender some territory that they had seized during the fighting. In late May the USA, France, Russia, Spain and the United Kingdom signed a communiqué declaring that the arms embargo on the former Yugoslavia would continue and that international armed forces would not intervene in the conflict on behalf of the Muslims; they proposed instead the creation of six UN 'safe areas' (Sarajevo, Bihać, Tuzla, Goražde, Srebreniča and Zepa) to protect the Muslim population from Serb attack, to take effect from 22 July. UN-negotiated cease-fires collapsed in May, as both the Bosnian Serbs and Croats initiated offensives to expand and consolidate their territorial holdings. In mid-June new peace proposals were announced in Geneva by Lord Owen and Thorvald Stoltenberg (formerly Norwegian Minister of Foreign Affairs, who had replaced Vance as the UN mediator in May), under which Bosnia and Herzegovina would become a confederation of three states divided on ethnic grounds. Izetbegović refused to discuss the tripartite division of Bosnia and boycotted the remainder of the Geneva talks, although other members of the Presidency continued discussions.

In early June 1993 the UN adopted a resolution to allow UNPROFOR to use force, including air power, in response to attacks against 'safe areas', but later that month failed to approve a resolution, supported by the USA, on the exemption of the Bosnian Muslims from the UN arms embargo. In late June a joint Serb-Croat offensive began against the northern Muslim town of Maglaj, and in the following month Muslims and Croats began a fierce battle for control of the city of Mostar. On 30 July the three warring factions reached a constitutional agreement in Geneva on the reconstruction of Bosnia and Herzegovina into a confederation of three ethnically-based states, styled the 'Union of Republics of Bosnia and Herzegovina', under a central government with powers limited to foreign policy and foreign trade. Under this agreement, Sarajevo, except for the municipality of Pale, would be placed under UN administration during a two-year transitional period. Despite this agreement and numerous negotiated cease-fires, fighting continued, and in early August the three Croat members of the Bosnian State Presidency (including Mile Akmadžić, the Prime Minister of Bosnia and Herzegovina) left the Bosnian Geneva delegation in protest at Muslim attacks on Croat populations and joined the Croatian negotiating team. On 27 August Akmadžić was dismissed from the premiership. On the following day the 'Croatian Republic of Herzeg-Bosna' was proclaimed by a Croat 'House of Representatives of the Assembly of the Croatian Republic of Herzeg-Bosna' (Croat Assembly) in Grude, which proceeded to accept the Owen-Stoltenberg plan on condition that the Serbs and Muslims also accepted it. On the same day the Serb Assembly in Pale also voted in favour of the plan. On 31 August, however, a session of the Assembly of Bosnia and Herzegovina rejected the Geneva plan in its existing form, while agreeing to use it as a basis for further peace negotiations.

On 10 September 1993 Fikret Abdić, a Muslim member of the Bosnian State Presidency and a rival of President Izetbegović, announced the creation of an 'Autonomous Province of Western Bosnia' in the Muslim region around Bihać, which was to form part of the 'Union of Republics of Bosnia and Herzegovina'. On 27 September, in Velika Kladusa, the province was declared to have been established and Abdić was elected President by a 'Constituent Assembly'. Abdić was subsequently dismissed from the Bosnian State Presidency, Izetbegović imposed martial law on the area, and fighting erupted between Abdić's followers and government forces. The Muslim Democratic Party was founded in Bihać, with Abdić as Chairman.

In late September 1993 the Croat and Serb Assemblies announced their intention to withdraw concessions offered during negotiations earlier that month: the Croats had allowed Bosnian access to the sea; the Serbs had agreed to accept a territorial division awarding them 52% of Bosnia's territory compared with the 70% they currently controlled. During September Izetbegović had agreed, in a significant concession, that after two years the Serb and Croat republics in a future confederation would be permitted to hold a referendum on whether to remain in the 'Union' or to join Serbia and Croatia respectively.

On 23 October 1993 Fikret Abdić and the Bosnian Croat leader, Mate Boban, officially declared their intent to establish peace in Western Bosnia; two days later Abdić and the Bosnian Serb leader, Karadžić, announced their commitment to peace between their two 'republics'. Later in the month two Croats and one Muslim were elected to the three vacant positions in the Bosnian State Presidency, while Dr Haris Silajdžić, formerly the Minister of Foreign Affairs, was appointed Prime Minister of the Bosnian Government, replacing Akmadžić. Silajdžić's Government took office on 30 October.

At further talks in late December 1993 the Bosnian Serbs refused to accept the establishment of a UN administration in Sarajevo and the reopening of Tuzla airport (which was surrounded by Serb positions) to accelerate the passage of aid. The Bosnians demanded access through Croatian territory to the Adriatic (thus interrupting continuous Croatian control of the coast) and, although they accepted the proposed division of the country (whereby Bosnian Muslims were to receive 33.3% of the territory, Croats 17.5% and Serbs 49.2%), they remained opposed to the specific areas allocated to Bosnian Muslims.

The massacre, in early February 1994, of 68 civilians in Sarajevo prompted the EU and the USA to draft a joint French-US proposal that NATO set a deadline for Serb forces to cease their bombardment or risk being subjected to air attacks. Following a Russian initiative, the Bosnian Serbs withdrew most of their heavy weaponry, and Russian peace-keeping troops were deployed in the 'exclusion zone' around Sarajevo. However, the city remained effectively blockaded. In late February NATO aircraft shot down four Serb light attack aircraft near Banja Luka, which had violated the UN 'no-fly zone' over Bosnia and Herzegovina. The incident represented the first aggressive military action taken by NATO since its establishment. There was continuous Serb shelling of the Maglaj area in northern Bosnia throughout March, while Goražde, Bihać and other UN-designated 'safe areas' were also shelled. In the same month UNHCR officials accused the Serbs of the 'ethnic cleansing' of Banja Luka's Muslim population.

Following a cease-fire, which was agreed by the Bosnian Government and the Bosnian Croats in late February 1994, Silajdžić and Kresimir Zubak (who had replaced Mate Boban as the leader of the Bosnian Croats) signed an agreement on 18 March, in Washington, USA, providing for the creation of a Federation of Bosnia and Herzegovina, with power shared equally between Muslims and Croats. Under the federal Constitution (which had been finalized earlier in the month), a federal government was to be responsible for defence, foreign affairs and the economy. Greater executive power was to be vested in the prime ministerial post than in the presidency; the offices were to rotate annually between the two ethnic groups. Until the full implementation of the Federation and the holding of elections, Izetbegović was to remain President of the collective Presidency of Bosnia and Herzegovina; the emerging federal institutions were to operate in parallel during the interim period. At the same ceremony a second 'preliminary' agreement was signed by Presidents Izetbegović and Tudjman, which provided for the eventual creation of a loose confederation of the Federation and Croatia. As well as the establishment of a 'Confederative Council', closer economic ties between the two states were to be introduced, with the eventual aim of establishing a common market and monetary union. In late March the accords were approved by the Bosnian Croat Assembly, while the new Constitution was ratified by the Bosnian Assembly. However, the Bosnian Serb Assembly in Pale vetoed Serb participation in the agreements.

In April 1994, in response to the continued shelling of the 'safe area' of Goražde by Bosnian Serb forces, UN-sanctioned air strikes were launched by NATO aircraft on Serb ground positions. However, Serb forces captured Goražde later that month, prompting strong criticism from the Russian Government, which hitherto had been perceived as sympathetic towards the Serbs, but which now indicated that it would not oppose the use of force against them. Bosnian Serb forces withdrew from Goražde in late April. On 26 April a new negotiating forum was established in London, United Kingdom, following an appeal by President Yeltsin of Russia for an international summit to bring peace to Bosnia and Herzegovina. The 'Contact Group' comprised representatives from Russia, the USA, France, Germany and the United Kingdom.

In late May 1994 the Constituent Assembly of the Federation of Bosnia and Herzegovina held its inaugural meeting, at which it elected Kresimir Zubak to the largely ceremonial post of President of the Federation. Ejup Ganić, a Muslim, was elected Vice-President of the Federation (he was concurrently Vice-President of the collective Presidency of Bosnia and Herzegovina), while Silajdžić was appointed Prime Minister of the Federation. A joint Government of the Republic of Bosnia and Herzegovina and the Federation, led by Silajdžić, was appointed in late June. Earlier in the month it was announced that the existing Bosnian Assembly would act additionally as the interim legislature of the Federation.

Following peace negotiations in Geneva in early June 1994, a one-month cease-fire was declared throughout Bosnia and Herzegovina. Repeated violations were reported by the end of the month, however, by which time Bosnian government forces had captured Serb-held areas of central Bosnia in an attempt to link the region with the Adriatic coast. Fighting also escalated in the Bihać enclave between the Bosnian army and rebel forces led by Fikret Abdić.

The Contact Group presented new peace proposals in early July 1994, after its members had reached agreement on a territorial division of Bosnia and Herzegovina in late June. According to the new plan, the Federation of Bosnia and Herzegovina would be granted 51% of the territory of Bosnia and Herzegovina, while the Bosnian Serbs would yield approximately one-third of the territory they currently controlled. Key sensitive areas, including Sarajevo, Srebreniča, Goražde and Brčko, would be placed under UN and EU administration. In an indication of the international community's increasing impatience with the warring factions, the Contact Group warned of various measures that would be taken in the event of the parties' refusal of the plan. These included the relaxation of economic sanctions against Serbia and Montenegro if the Bosnian Government rejected the proposal, and the lifting of the arms embargo against Bosnia and Herzegovina in the event of Bosnian Serb refusal.

On 17 July 1994 Izetbegović and Tudjman endorsed the Contact Group plan, which was also approved by the Bosnian Assembly. However, the proposed territorial division was rejected by the Bosnian Serb Assembly at Pale. The Serbs' refusal to accept the plan centred on the question of Serb access to the Adriatic Sea, the status of Sarajevo and the right of the Bosnian Serbs to enter a confederation with the FRY. President Milošević of Serbia subsequently criticized the Bosnian Serbs for rejecting the plan, and in early August the FRY announced the closure of its border with Serb-occupied Bosnia and Herzegovina, blocking transits into the area with the exception of humanitarian aid convoys. On 5 August further NATO air strikes (the first since April) were launched against Bosnian Serb targets, following Serb attacks against UN forces and the renewed shelling of Sarajevo. In late August the Bosnian Serbs held a referendum in which 96% of participants voted to reject the Contact Group plan; the result was unanimously approved by the Bosnian Serb Assembly on 1 September. Meanwhile, on 21 August, the Bihać enclave, held by Abdić's forces, fell to the Bosnian government army.

In August and September 1994 tensions emerged between Muslims and Croats over the establishment of the Federation of Bosnia and Herzegovina. Contentious issues were addressed at a meeting between Izetbegović and Tudjman in Zagreb (Croatia) in mid-September, when it was agreed that interim municipal governments should be established by 30 September and cantonal authorities by 31 October. It was also agreed that a joint command of the Bosnian government army and the Bosnian Croat army should be instituted as soon as possible.

In early October 1994 Bosnian government troops infiltrated the demilitarized zone of Mount Igman, near Sarajevo, and attacked Serb forces there, to be repelled shortly afterwards by UNPROFOR troops. Later in the month government forces took control of tracts of Serb-held land around the Bihać enclave. In early November government forces, supported by Bosnian Croat troops, launched offensives on three fronts: in central Bosnia, in the Bihać area and around Sarajevo. The fall of the strategic Serb-held town of Kupres on 3 November represented the first significant military gain for the Muslim-Croat alliance (and the first decisive victory for government forces since the beginning of the conflict). By late November, however, the Serbs had regained most of the Bihać territory. Meanwhile, in early November the USA announced that its warships in the Adriatic Sea would no longer police the international arms embargo.

On 30 November 1994 an attempt by the UN Secretary-General, Dr Boutros Boutros-Ghali, to protect the Bihać 'safe area' from further Bosnian Serb attack and to salvage the UN peace-keeping operation in Bosnia and Herzegovina met with failure when Karadžić refused to meet him at Sarajevo airport. (Karadžić boycotted the proposed discussions owing to the UN's refusal to recognize the 'Serbian Republic'.) In early December the Contact Group issued a text based on the July peace plan (dividing Bosnia between the Federation and the Bosnian Serbs), which indicated the possibility of confederal links between the Bosnian Serbs and the FRY. President Milošević supported the proposals. In mid-December the former US President, Jimmy Carter (acting in a non-official capacity), visited Bosnia and Herzegovina with the aim of persuading the Bosnian Serb leadership to accept the Contact Group plan. The Bosnian Serbs and the Bosnian Government subsequently agreed to a four-month cease-fire, to take effect from 1 January 1995. Both sides expressed their readiness to resume peace negotiations based on the revised Contact Group plan; there were also agreements on the exchange of prisoners. The cease-fire agreement was formally signed by both parties on 31 December.

The cease-fire was generally observed throughout Bosnia and Herzegovina during January 1995. However, intense fighting continued in the Bihać enclave between government forces and troops loyal to Abdić, supported by troops from the self-proclaimed 'Republic of Serbian Krajina' (RSK) in Croatia (adjoining the Bihać enclave). There were renewed disagreements between Muslims and Croats over the implementation of the new Federation, the most controversial issues being the co-ordination of a joint military command, the division of power, and territorial reorganization. In early February, however, Zubak and Silajdžić were signatories to an accord allowing grievances concerning the implementation of the Federation of Bosnia and Herzegovina to be submitted to some form of (as yet unspecified) international arbitration. In the same month the USA refused to continue negotiations with Karadžić until the Bosnian Serbs accepted the Contact Group plan.

In early 1995 hostilities continued in the Bihać enclave, where Bosnian Serb and Bosnian government troops had resumed fighting around Bosanska Krupa, with the 'safe area' of Bihać town being directly targeted by the Serbs. In mid-February the UN announced that Serb and rebel Muslim attacks on humanitarian aid convoys into the Bihać enclave were resulting in the starvation of Muslim civilians within the 'safe area'. On 20 February representatives of the Bosnian Serbs and the Croatian Serbs signed a military pact, guaranteeing mutual assistance in the event of attack and providing for the establishment of a joint Supreme Defence Council, which was to be led by Karadžić and the Croatian Serb leader, Milan Martić. In late February the Bosnian Government introduced new restrictions on the movements of peace-keepers within its borders, preventing UN observers from monitoring front lines. In early March, following talks in Zagreb, Croatia, a formal military alliance was announced between the armies of Croatia, the Bosnian Croats and the Bosnian Government.

In late March 1995 the UN threatened to order further NATO air strikes against Serb targets unless the Bosnian Serbs halted their shelling of the UN 'safe areas' of Sarajevo, Tuzla, Bihać and Goražde. The Contact Group appealed to the warring factions to respect and work towards the extension of the four-month cease-fire, while Russia presented a fresh peace plan to the US Secretary of State, Warren Christopher, in Geneva. The plan, involving Serbian recognition of Bosnia and Herzegovina in exchange for the simultaneous lifting of UN sanctions against the FRY, had reportedly been drafted by President Milošević and the Russian Minister of Foreign Affairs, Andrey Kozyrev.

Attacks by government forces against the Serbs in the Majevica mountains, near Tuzla, continued in April 1995. Intense fighting also persisted in the Bihać enclave, where government forces came under attack from rebel Muslims and their Serb allies. The Serbs intensified their besiegement of Sarajevo in mid-April, attacking the only land route out of the capital and forcing the closure of the airport through their refusal to guarantee the safe passage of aircraft.

On 8 April 1995 an agreement was signed between President Zubak of the Federation and Ejup Ganić, Vice-President of both the Federation and of Bosnia and Herzegovina, aimed at accelerating the establishment of federal institutions. The inaugural session of the Federation's Constituent Assembly duly took place in Novi Travnik on 4 May, during which the Bonn Agreement on the implementation of federal principles was unanimously adopted. In mid-May heavy fighting was reported around the Serb-held corridor near Brčko, while hostilities intensified around Sarajevo, with Bosnian government forces regaining territory to the south-east of the capital. In a move reflecting increasing UN impatience at the situation, Lt-Gen. Smith issued a formal ultimatum to both the Bosnian Serbs and the Bosnian Government on 24 May, which threatened NATO air strikes unless all heavy weapons were removed from the 20-km 'exclusion zone' around Sarajevo (or surrendered to peace-keepers) by midday on 26 May. On 25 May, however, NATO aircraft carried out strikes on Serb ammunition depots near Pale, a move which was openly criticized by Russia. Within hours of the NATO air strikes, Serb forces responded by shelling five of the six UN 'safe areas' and, following further NATO air strikes against Serb positions on 26 May, retaliated with a massive bombardment of Tuzla, which resulted in at least 70 deaths. Over the next few days Serb troops disarmed and took hostage 222 UNPROFOR personnel in the Goražde 'safe area', thereby preventing the UN and NATO from taking retaliatory action against fighting in the region. However, the UN rejected the Serbs' offer of conditional negotiations on the release of the hostages. In the mean time, on 3 June defence ministers from NATO and some other European states agreed on the creation of a 10,000-strong 'rapid reaction force', which was to operate in Bosnia and Herzegovina under UN command from mid-July and the mandate of which was to provide 'enhanced protection' to UNPROFOR. The ongoing hostage crisis, led, however, to a withdrawal of UNPROFOR troops from Bosnian Serb territory around Sarajevo in mid-June and the consequent collapse of the 20-km 'exclusion zone'. Although the UN denied that any deal had been struck with the Bosnian Serbs, the release of the remaining hostages roughly coincided with the withdrawal of UNPROFOR from around the capital.

On 11 July 1995 the 'safe area' of Srebreniča in south-eastern Bosnia was captured by the Bosnian Serbs after Dutch peace-keeping troops based in the town were taken hostage, prompting NATO air strikes on Serb tanks approaching the town. The fall of Srebreniča was followed by the capture of the nearby 'safe area' of Zepa on 25 July. Another 'safe area', Bihać, was attacked on 20 July; the assault involved a concerted effort by Bosnian Serbs, Croatian Serbs and rebel Bosnian Muslims led by Fikret Abdić. The situation in Bihać prompted the signature of a military co-operation agreement between Bosnian President Alija Izetbegović and Croatian President Franjo Tudjman in Split, Croatia, on 22 July. Croatian and Bosnian Croat troops subsequently launched attacks on Serb positions around Bihać, as a result of which Serb supply routes into the Krajina enclave were blocked.

Croatian government forces invaded Serb-held Krajina on 4 August 1995; by 9 August the whole of the enclave had been recaptured by Croatia, resulting in a massive exodus of Serb civilians from the region into Serb-held areas of Bosnia and Herzegovina and into Serbia itself. On 6–7 August the siege of Bihać was effectively broken by Bosnian government and Croatian troops. On 9 August a fresh peace initiative, known as the 'Holbrooke initiative' (devised by Richard Holbrooke, the US Assistant Secretary of State for European and Canadian Affairs) was announced by the US Government; the proposals, which were based on the Contact Group plan of 1994, allowed the Bosnian Serbs to retain control of Srebrenića and Zepa.

On 28 August 1995 a suspected Serb mortar attack near a market place in central Sarajevo resulted in 37 deaths, prompting Bosnian Prime Minister Silajdžić to demand a clarification of the UN peace-keeping role in the 'safe area' of Sarajevo. NATO responded to the mortar attack by launching a series of air strikes (codenamed 'Operation Deliberate Force') on Serb positions across Bosnia and Herzegovina on 30 August and 5 September.

On 8 September 1995 major progress in the peace process was achieved when, at a meeting in Geneva, Switzerland, chaired by the Contact Group, the Ministers of Foreign Affairs of Bosnia and Herzegovina, Croatia and the FRY (the latter acting on behalf of the Bosnian Serbs), signed an agreement determining basic principles for a peace accord. These principles incorporated the territorial division of Bosnia and Herzegovina as earlier proposed by the Contact Group, with 51% apportioned to the Federation and 49% to the Bosnian Serbs. They also included the continuing existence of Bosnia and Herzegovina within its present borders, but the country was to be composed of two entities, namely the Federation of Bosnia and Herzegovina (as stated in the Washington Agreements of 1994) and a Serb Republic, with each entity existing under its present Constitution. In mid-September 'Operation Deliberate Force' was suspended, following the withdrawal of Bosnian Serb weaponry from the 'exclusion zone' around Sarajevo. Agreement on further basic principles for a peace accord was reached by the foreign ministers of Bosnia and Herzegovina, Croatia and the FRY, meeting in New York on 26 September. These included a one-third share in the republican parliamentary seats for the Serb Republic, while the Federation would control two-thirds of the seats (legislative decisions would only be implemented, however, with the approval of at least one-third of the deputies of each entity). A collective presidency would also be organized according to the one-third Serb to two-thirds Muslim-Croat proportional division, with all decisions being taken by majority vote. It was decided, furthermore, that free elections, under international auspices, would be held in Bosnia and Herzegovina at the earliest opportunity.

On 5 October 1995 a 60-day cease-fire was announced by President Clinton in Washington, DC, USA, which came into effect in Bosnia and Herzegovina on 12 October. The UN simultaneously announced its intention to reduce the number of peace-keeping troops in the area. In late October, at a summit meeting between Presidents Yeltsin and Clinton, it was agreed that Russian peace implementation troops would co-operate with, but work independently of, the NATO Peace Implementation Force, which was to be deployed in the country following the signature of a formal peace accord.

On 1 November 1995 peace negotiations between the three warring parties in the Bosnian conflict began in Dayton, Ohio, USA, and were attended by Presidents Izetbegović, Tudjman and Milošević (the latter representing both the FRY and the Bosnian Serbs) and representatives of the Contact Group and the EU. On 10 November Izetbegović and Tudjman signed an accord aimed at reinforcing the 1994 federation agreement, which included a provision for the unification of the divided city of Mostar as the federal capital and seat of the federal presidency. The Croatian Government and the Croatian Serbs of Eastern Slavonia subsequently concluded an accord providing for the eventual reintegration of Serb-held Eastern Slavonia into Croatia. The most comprehensive peace agreement was achieved on 21 November, when Izetbegović, Tudjman and Milošević initialled a definitive accord, dividing Bosnia and Herzegovina between the Federation, with 51% of the territory, and the Serb Republic (Republika Srpska), which would control 49% of the area; it was stressed, however, that any relations with neighbouring countries should honour the sovereignty and territorial integrity of Bosnia and Herzegovina. The Dayton agreement, which was based on the agreements on the principles that had been signed in Geneva and New York in September, included provisions for a central government with a democratically-elected collective presidency and a parliament, based in Sarajevo, and provisions for a single monetary system and central bank, and other institutions for the economic reconstruction of Bosnia and Herzegovina. It also stipulated the right of all refugees and displaced persons to return to their homes and to have seized property returned to them, or else receive fair compensation. Sarajevo was granted special status as a united city within the Federation, while it was also envisaged that each of the warring factions would relinquish some of the territory under its control at the time of the October cease-fire. Serb-held suburbs of Sarajevo were to be transferred to the administration of the Federation, while Bosnian Serbs were to retain control of Srebrenića and Zepa; Goražde was to remain under the control of the Federation and was to be linked to Sarajevo via a Federation-administered land corridor. No agreement was reached, however, regarding the width of the strategically vital Posavina corridor, connecting the northern sector of the Serb Republic with the southern sector, and control of the town of Brčko which is located at this point; the three sides agreed to place the issue under international arbitration. Under the Dayton agreement, UNPROFOR troops were to be replaced by an international NATO-commanded 60,000-strong 'Implementation Force' (IFOR, see p. 229). The agreement provided IFOR with a mandate to oversee the withdrawal of the warring parties from zones of separation and to monitor the agreed exchanges of territory.

Following the initialling of the Dayton peace agreement, the UN voted to suspend the remaining economic sanctions against the FRY and to phase out gradually the arms embargo imposed on all of the former Yugoslav republics in September 1991. At the end of November 1995 the deadline of 31 January 1996 was set by the UN Security Council for the withdrawal of UNPROFOR troops from Bosnia and Herzegovina. At a conference, on the implementation of the Dayton peace agreement, which took place in London in early December 1995, it was agreed that an OSCE mission would organize and oversee parliamentary elections in Bosnia and Herzegovina and that the Contact Group would be replaced by a Peace Implementation Council (notably including no UN representatives) based in Brussels, Belgium. The former Swedish Prime Minister and EU envoy to the Bosnian peace talks, Carl Bildt, was appointed High Representative of the International Community in Bosnia and Herzegovina, with responsibility for the implementation of the civilian aspects of the Dayton agreement. On 14 December the Dayton peace agreement was formally signed by Izetbegović, Tudjman and Milošević and by President Clinton and a number of European political leaders in Paris, France. The formal transfer of power from UNPROFOR to IFOR took place on 20 December.

In mid-December 1995 the People's Assembly of the Serb Republic elected a new Government, headed by Rajko Kasagić. On 30 January 1996 Hasan Muratović was elected by the republican Assembly as Prime Minister of the Republic of Bosnia and Herzegovina, following the resignation from the premiership of Haris Silajdžić; a new central Government was appointed on the same day. Silajdžić was reportedly rejecting the increasing Bosniak nationalism of the ruling PDA. On 31 January the Constituent Assembly of the Federation appointed a new federal Government, with Izudin Kapetanović as Prime Minister. In mid-February, in response to unrest in the city of Mostar and isolated attacks elsewhere, an emergency summit meeting took place in Rome, Italy, during which Izetbegović, Tudjman and Milošević reaffirmed their adherence to the Dayton agreement. A joint Croat-Muslim police patrol, accompanied by officers from the UN International Police Task Force (IPTF) and Western European Union (WEU) subsequently began operating in Mostar.

By the end of April 1996 substantial progress had been made in the implementation of the military aspects of the Dayton agreement. The former warring parties completed staged withdrawals from the IFOR-controlled zone of separation; agreement was reached, under the auspices of the OSCE in Vienna, on the exchange of information on weaponry and the submission of arsenals to OSCE inspection; and the majority of prisoners of war were released, albeit with some delays. However, the exchange of territory between the two Bosnian 'entities' did not proceed as envisaged in the peace agreement. From mid-January there was a mass exodus from the Serb-held suburbs of Sarajevo that were passing to the control of the Bosnian Federation. The Serb authorities in Pale were criticized for using intimidation to coerce the Serb inhabitants of these districts into leaving and to resettle in towns in the Serb Republic from which Muslims had been driven during the war. By late March only about 10% of the previous Serb population in the Sarajevo area remained.

In early April 1996 Muslim and Croat leaders agreed on a customs union linking the two parts of the Bosnian Federation. They also agreed on a single state budget and a unitary banking system. In mid-May further agreement was reached betwen the two sides, meeting in Washington, on the merger of their armed forces and the return of refugees. The agreement on a unified federation army was the principal precondition for the implementation of the controversial US programme to train and equip the Federation's army in order to place it on an equal military footing with that of the Serb Republic. Also in mid-May Karadžić dismissed Kasagić as Serb Prime Minister and appointed Gojko Klicković, a former Serb Minister for Health, in his place; Klicković's appointment was endorsed by the Bosnian Serb People's Assembly. Kasagić, who was considered a moderate among Serbs, had been co-operating to a large extent with the international community, and high-level diplomatic efforts were undertaken both to effect Kasagić's reinstatement and to oust Karadžić from the presidency. Karadžić had been indicted by the International Criminal Tribunal for the former Yugoslavia (ICTY, see p. 16), based in The Hague, the Netherlands, for his part in the siege of Sarajevo and the alleged massacre at Srebreniča in July 1995. His continued position as President—as well as that of Gen. Ratko Mladić, also indicted for war crimes, as head of the armed forces—was in breach of the Dayton agreement, which prohibited indicted war criminals from holding public office. In response to international pressure, Karadžić announced the delegation of some of his powers to his deputy, Dr Biljana Plavšić. In early June 1996 the USA threatened Milošević with renewed sanctions against the FRY unless he effect the removal from office of Karadžić and Mladić and their extradiction to the Netherlands to stand trial. At the Peace Implementation Conference on Bosnia and Herzegovina held in Florence, Italy, in mid-June, the holding of all-Bosnia elections in September was approved. Later in the same month the Chairman-in-Office of the OSCE, which was given responsibility under the Dayton accord for the organization and supervision of the Bosnian elections, formally announced that these would proceed on 14 September.

In mid-June 1996 Bosnian Croats in Mostar announced a new government of Herzeg-Bosna, in defiance of agreements that the separate Croat state would be dissolved; Pero Marković was named as Prime Minister of the new Government. Municipal elections in Mostar were held on 30 June: the PDA-dominated List for a United Mostar gained 21 of the council seats, while the CDU—BH secured 16 seats. At a summit meeting of the Presidents of Bosnia and Herzegovina, Croatia and Serbia, which was convened by the USA in Geneva in mid-August, Tudjman and Izetbegović agreed on the full establishment of the Bosnian Federation by the end of the month. Tudjman vouched for the dismantling of Herzeg-Bosna, while Izetbegović agreed that the functions of the current Bosnian Government that would not pass to the tripartite Presidency would revert to the Federation. The three Presidents signed a fresh declaration committing themselves to the Dayton agreement.

In late June 1996 Western European countries issued an ultimatum to Karadžić to resign, on penalty of the reimposition of sanctions against the Serb Republic (suspended in April, following the Serb withdrawal behind IFOR's line of separation). In defiance of this, the SDP re-elected Karadžić as their party leader. At the end of June Karadžić sent a letter to Bildt announcing his temporary resignation and the appointment of Plavšić as the acting Serb President. It was then confirmed that Karadžić would not stand in the election to the Serb presidency in September, and Plavšić was nominated as the SDP candidate. None the less, it was deemed unacceptable that Karadžić should retain the powerful position of party leader, and the OSCE Bosnian mission declared that the SDP would be excluded from the elections if Karadžić retained any office in the party. In mid-July the ICTY issued arrest warrants for Karadžić and Mladić; however, IFOR's mandate was not changed, and NATO remained cautious regarding pursuit of the indicted men. A few days later the USA dispatched former Assistant Secretary of State, Richard Holbrooke, to the former Yugoslavia in an attempt to engineer Karadžić's removal. Following intensive negotiations with Milošević and Bosnian Serb leaders, Holbrooke secured Karadžić's resignation on 19 July both from the presidency and as head of the SDP. Plavšić remained acting President, while Aleksa Buha succeeded Karadžić as leader of the SDP.

During the electoral campaign there were increasing reports of harassment and violence perpetrated by the PDA and its supporters against members of the opposition. Opposition candidates in the Serb Republic were also subjected to intimidation, and many international observers, as well as opposition activists, protested that the conditions would prevent free and fair elections from being conducted. In late August the OSCE announced that the Bosnian municipal elections, which were to have been held concurrently with the other elections, were to be postponed, in response to evidence that the Serb authorities were forcibly registering displaced Serbs in formerly Muslim-dominated localities. This arose from the provision included in the Dayton agreement permitting refugees and displaced persons to vote either in their former homes or in the place where they chose to settle. National elections were held on 14 September for the republican Presidency and legislature, the presidency and legislature of the Serb Republic, and the legislature and cantonal authorities of the Bosnian Federation. The elections were monitored by about 1,200 OSCE observers, while IFOR and the IPTF forces maintained security. In the elections for the republican Presidency Izetbegović won 80% of the Bosniak vote; Kresimir Zubak (CDU—BH) 88% of the Croat vote; and Momčilo Krajišnik (SDP), the former Speaker of the Serb Assembly, 67% of the Serb vote. Having received the largest number of votes of the three winning presidential candidates, Izetbegović became Chairman of the Presidency. The Federation section of the republican House of Representatives and the Federation's own House of Representatives were dominated by the PDA and the CDU—BH. None the less, the Joint List of Bosnia and Herzegovina, comprising an alliance of social-democrat Bosniak and Croat parties, and the Party for Bosnia and Herzegovina (established earlier that year by the former Prime Minister, Haris Silajdžić) won a significant number of votes in the elections to both the republican and federation Houses. Although the SDP secured a majority of votes in both the Serb section of the House of Representatives and in the Serb National Assembly, the PDA polled about one-sixth of the votes cast on the territory of the Serb Republic. The People's Alliance for Peace and Progress also gained a significant share of the Serb vote in the elections to the House of Representatives and the Serb National Assembly. Plavšić was elected President of the Serb Republic and Dragolub Mirjanić her Vice-President, securing some 59% of the votes cast. The validity of the election results was questioned by the International Crisis Group, comprising senior Western European politicians, who claimed that a large number of voting papers had been fraudulently added to the ballot boxes. The OSCE subsequently revised its estimate of the Bosnian electorate upwards and refused to order a recount of the ballot papers. Following the OSCE's endorsement of the election results, the UN Security Council decided on 1 October to remove the sanctions imposed against the FRY and the Serb Republic. A few days later Izetbegović and Milošević, meeting in Paris, agreed to establish full diplomatic relations; Milošević pledged to respect the territorial integrity of Bosnia and Herzegovina, while Izetbegović consented to recognize the FRY as the successor state to Yugoslavia. The inaugural session of the Presidency was held on 5 October; however, Krajišnik failed to attend, claiming that his personal safety might be threatened in Sarajevo (where the ceremony was held). The inaugural session of the republican Assembly was to have been held on the same day, but was boycotted by the Serb deputies. The new National Assembly of the Serb Republic held its inaugural session on 19 October; the inaugural session of the federation House of Representatives took place on 6 November.

In mid-October 1996 the OSCE changed the regulations regarding voting in the delayed municipal elections, ruling that people could only vote in their places of residence prior to 1992. The municipal elections, which were due to have taken place in November 1996, were rescheduled for early 1997 (when, however, they were again postponed). In early November 1996

Plavšić announced that she had dismissed Gen. Mladić as commander of the Serb armed forces, replacing him with a little-known officer, Maj.-Gen. Pero Colić. A large number of the members of Mladić's general staff were also replaced, but Mladić and the other officers refused to accept their dismissal. After a power struggle, during which the Minister of Defence of the Serb Republic was taken captive for a short time by Mladić's supporters, Mladić agreed to surrender his position at the end of November.

In mid-November 1996 clashes were reported between Muslims and Serbs along the inter-entity boundary near the Serb-held village of Gajevi, to which the Muslims were attempting to return. There were repeated incidents in which Muslims attempting to return home on Serb-held territory were forcibly repulsed. In many parts of the country hostility between the ethnic groups continued, with minority elements being intimidated and often driven out from their homes. At a conference on Bosnia and Herzegovina, hosted by the French Government in mid-November, it was agreed that the post of High Representative of the International Community would be maintained for a further two years, and that Bildt's powers would be increased to make him the final arbiter in the interpretation of the civilian provisions of the Dayton agreement. A Bosnian Peace Implementation Conference was held in London in early December; the NATO Secretary-General announced that a successor to IFOR, to be known as the Stabilization Force (SFOR), was to be established. SFOR was to be about one-half the size of IFOR and was to have a mandate of 18 months, with six-monthly reviews. SFOR officially replaced IFOR on 20 December. In mid-December, after some delay, the Presidency appointed the two Co-Prime Ministers of the republican Council of Ministers: Haris Silajdžić of the Party for Bosnia and Herzegovina and Boro Bosić of the SDP. One week later the federal House of Representatives elected Edhem Bičakčić as the federal Prime Minister, replacing Izudin Kapetanović. (On the previous day the Bosnian Croats had announced that 'Herzeg-Bosna' had ceased to exist.) The republican Council of Ministers was appointed by the Co-Prime Ministers and approved by the inaugural session of the Bosnian Assembly, which was finally held on 3 January 1997. The Council of Ministers comprised Ministers for Foreign Affairs, for Foreign Trade and Economic Relations, and for Communications and Civilian Affairs. Each post had two Deputy Ministers, with each of the Bosnian ethnic groups holding an equal number of offices. In February a ruling on the future status of the disputed town of Brčko was postponed until March 1998 by an international arbitration commission, and in the following month Robert Farrand, a US diplomat, was appointed to act as supervisor of the town in the interim period. In March 1997 Vladimir Soljić was elected to replace Kresimir Zubak as President of the Federation. (Soljić, in turn, was succeeded by the Vice-President, Dr Ejup Ganić, in December.)

On 28 February 1997 Krajišnik signed, on behalf of the Serb Republic, an agreement with the FRY to foster mutual economic co-operation and to collaborate on regional security. The accord was ratified by the National Assembly of the Serb Republic in March, despite opposition voiced by Plavšić and by a number of Bosnian Muslim and Bosnian Croat leaders. In June Plavšić suspended Dragan Kilac as Minister of Internal Affairs, following the alleged failure of Kilac to consult Plavšić on important issues. The suspension was opposed by the National Assembly, which contested the constitutional legality of the decision. Plavšić responded by accusing Karadžić of corruption and of orchestrating the opposition to her in the Bosnian Serb legislature. In the following month Plavšić announced the dissolution of the National Assembly and scheduled parliamentary elections for the beginning of September. Although this action was supported by both the UN and the OSCE, it was sharply criticized by Gojko Klicković, the Prime Minister of the Serb Republic, and a number of resolutions designed to undermine Plavšić were approved by the National Assembly. In mid-August the Constitutional Court ruled that Plavšić's decision to dissolve the legislature had been illegal: the Assembly proceeded to vote to disregard future decrees by Plavšić. (It subsequently emerged that one of the Constitutional Court judges had been subject to physical intimidation, allegedly by supporters of Karadžić, prior to the judgment.) Plavšić's position was strengthened in August, following a decision by the Serb Republic's Vice-President, Dragolub Mirjanić, to abandon the Assembly in Pale and join the presidential team in Banja Luka. Later in the month Plavšić appointed Mark Pavić to replace Kilac as Minister of Internal Affairs; however, the appointment was rejected by the Assembly, which subsequently promoted Kilac to the post of Deputy Prime Minister and appointed an alternative to Pavić to head the interior ministry. In late September a constitutional crisis was averted, following a meeting in Belgrade hosted by President Milošević and attended by Plavšić and Krajišnik. A joint statement was issued detailing an agreement, whereby elections to the National Assembly would be held in November under the aegis of the OSCE, and presidential elections for both the Serb Republic and the Bosnian collective Presidency would be held on 7 December. In October Carlos Westendorp, who had replaced Bildt as High Representative in June, announced his intention to reorganize the Bosnian Serb television service and to demand the resignation of the management board, including Krajišnik.

At a further Bosnian Peace Implementation Conference, held in Sintra, Portugal, in May 1997, NATO stipulated deadlines for the approval by the entities of a number of laws on property, passports and citizenship. In addition a new list of ambassadors was demanded better to reflect the ethnic diversity of the country. Following the expiry on 1 August of the deadline for the submission of the new diplomatic list, the USA and the EU suspended recognition of Bosnia and Herzegovina's ambassadors. In July, at a conference of international donors, the Serb Republic was warned that the supply of economic aid might be disrupted if suspected war criminals were not extradited to the ICTY. Earlier in the month the EU had announced the suspension of aid to the republic for its failure to comply with this requirement. In late November the collective Presidency accepted a Croatian proposal for the creation of a joint committee to improve co-operation between the two countries. On 17 December the Bosnian Assembly approved the law on passports within the deadline established by the international community, but failed to ratify the law on citizenship; the following day Westendorp announced that the citizenship law would be imposed on Bosnian territory from 1 January 1998. (An agreement had been signed earlier in the month by Krajišnik and the FRY Government, which accorded Bosnian Serbs citizenship of both Bosnia and Herzegovina and the FRY.) In late December it was announced that NATO had agreed to extend indefinitely the mandate of the peace-keeping forces; in November Westendorp had warned that renewed hostilities might ensue, following the scheduled withdrawal of SFOR troops at the expiry of their mandate in June 1998. In February 1998 NATO formally approved the establishment of a new peace-keeping force for Bosnia and Herzegovina, which was to be deployed in the country following the expiry of SFOR's mandate; the force was to comprise 33,000 troops, but was to be reduced after presidential and legislative elections in September of that year.

Municipal elections for both entities finally took place in September 1997 under the aegis of the OSCE. Although some 91 parties contested the elections (in which voter participation was estimated at about 60%) the three main nationalist parties, the PDA, the CDU—BH and the SDP, received the vast majority of the votes cast. Parliamentary elections to the National Assembly of the Serb Republic were held during 22–23 November, under the supervision of the OSCE. Participating parties included the Serb National Alliance (SNA), which had been established by Plavšić in September, following her expulsion from the SDP in July. In the elections the SDP secured 24 seats (compared with 45 in 1996), but still remained the largest party in the Assembly. A newly-formed electoral alliance, the Coalition for a Single and Democratic Bosnia and Herzegovina, which included the PDA and the Party for Bosnia and Herzegovina, secured 16 seats, while the SNA and the Serb Radical Party (SRP) each achieved 15 seats. At the inaugural session of the new Assembly on 27 December, Plavšić nominated as prime minister-designate Mladen Ivanić, an economist with no political affiliation. The nomination was immediately challenged by the leadership of the SDP, which considered that as the largest party in the new Assembly it should have the first opportunity to propose a new prime minister and government; accordingly, the SDP proposed Klicković, the outgoing Prime Minister, and Aleksa Buha, the acting Chairman of the party. Ivanić declared, however, that he would continue negotiating with all the parties represented in the new Assembly to try to form an interim government of 'national unity'. On 18 January 1998, however, following the failure of Ivanić's inter-party talks, Milorad Dodik, who was considered to be a proponent of moderate rather than extremist policies, secured sufficient parliamentary support to form a new government. Following the announcement of the new administration, which contained a large number of Bosnian Muslims, Dodik assured the international community of his determination to govern according to the terms of the Dayton peace agreement. His appointment was condemned, however, by Krajišnik who warned that it would lead to the destabilization of the Serb Republic. At the end of January Dodik announced that government bodies were to be transferred from Pale to Banja Luka.

A number of accused war criminals were put on trial in the Hague in 1997. In May Dušan Tadić, who had been indicted in 1996 for organizing 'ethnic cleansing' in Omarska concentration camp (see above), was convicted of torturing Bosnian Muslims and sentenced to 20 years' imprisonment. In July 1997 an indicted Serbian war criminal, Simo Drljaca, was killed following an exchange of fire with SFOR members, who had sought to arrest him. For many observers the operation demonstrated an increased determination on the part of the international community, and in particular Westendorp, to enforce indictments issued by the ICTY; to this end it had been decided not to publish the identity of accused war criminals (the policy was entitled 'sealed indictments') to facilitate their apprehension. The shooting of Drljaca was condemned as murder, however, by President Plavšić and other Bosnian Serb leaders, and the actions of SFOR were strongly criticized by Russia, which claimed that SFOR had exceeded its mandate. In February 1998 the arrest by SFOR troops of two Bosnian Serb suspected war criminals at the boundary between the Serb and Muslim regions of Sarajevo prompted protests from Bosnian Serbs in the town. In the same month three Bosnian Serbs who had been indicted for war crimes were the first to surrender to SFOR troops for trial at the Hague. In early April SFOR forces surrounded Karadžić's headquarters in Pale, in an apparent attempt to increase pressure on him to submit to trial at the ICTY.

In mid-March 1998 the international arbitration commission which was considering the future status of the town of Brčko announced a further deferral of judgment until after the presidential and legislative elections in September. In early April the OSCE dissolved the Serb-dominated municipal assembly of Srebrenića, owing to its failure to assist in the resettlement of displaced Muslims in the town; a provisional executive council, headed by a senior OSCE official, was established to replace the assembly. In May the Government issued a warrant for the arrest of Gojko Klicković (who had served as Prime Minister of the Serb Republic in 1996–97) on charges of embezzlement and abuse of office. In mid-June the UN Security Council officially voted in favour of extending the mandate of SFOR to remain in the country indefinitely, with six-monthly reviews.

In June 1998 Krajišnik criticized a motion by the National Assembly of the Serb Republic expressing 'no confidence' in its Speaker, Dragan Kalinić, and Deputy Speaker. Buha subsequently resigned from the chairmanship of the SDP, citing what he claimed to be interference in his leadership by Krajišnik; Kalinić was subsequently elected as the new Chairman of the SDP. In early September, following lengthy negotiations, the Governments of Bosnia and Croatia signed an agreement (subject to approval by the legislatures of both countries) which would allow Bosnia and Herzegovina to use the Croatian port of Ploce, while permitting Croatia transit through the village of Neum (Bosnia's only access to the Adriatic Sea).

In September 1998 elections took place, as scheduled, for a new Bosnian collective Presidency and national legislature, for the presidency and National Assembly of the Serb Republic, and for the Federation House of Representatives. Izetbegović was re-elected as the Bosniak member of the collective Presidency, while the Chairman of the Socialist Party of the Bosnian Serb Republic (Socijalistička partija za Republiku Srpsku—SPRS), which was a member of the SNA-led Accord Coalition, Zivko Radišić, replaced Krajišnik, and the Chairman of the CDU—BH, Ante Jelavić, was elected as the Croat member of the Presidency. In the election to the Serb presidency the Chairman of the SRP, Dr Nikola Poplasen (who represented a coalition of the SRP and the SDP), defeated Plavšić. The SDP retained 19 of the 83 seats in the National Assembly of the Serb Republic, while the Coalition for a Single and Democratic Bosnia and Herzegovina won 15 seats. The Coalition for a Single and Democratic Bosnia and Herzegovina secured 14 of the 42 seats in the Bosnian House of Representatives, and 68 of the 140 seats in the Federation House of Representatives.

On 13 October 1998 the newly-elected Presidency of Bosnia and Herzegovina was inaugurated. Radišić became the first Serb to chair the Presidency (replacing Izetbegović) for an eight-month term, in accordance with the rotational schedule. At the end of October Dodik replaced the Serbian Minister of the Interior and Minister of Justice. Poplasen was inaugurated as President of the Serb Republic; he pledged to maintain good relations with Western Governments and to comply with the Dayton agreement. The major parties represented in the Serb National Assembly subsequently conducted negotiations regarding the appointment of a new Council of Ministers in the Serb Republic. The Accord Coalition, which held 32 seats in the National Assembly, rejected Poplasen's nomination of Kalinić as Prime Minister, while supporting the reappointment of Dodik to the post.

In December 1998 the Federation Parliament re-elected Ganić as President, while Ivo Andrić-Luzanski (a member of the CDU—BH) became Federation Vice-President; a new Federation Council of Ministers, nominated by Bičakčić, was established. Following the continued failure of the National Assembly of the Serb Republic to agree on a new government, in early January 1999 Poplasen nominated Brane Miljus, a member of the Party of Independent Social Democrats (Stranko Nezavisnih Socijaldemokrata—SNSD) as Prime Minister Designate. The Accord Coalition objected to Miljus' candidacy, and Dodik (the leader of the SNSD) announced his expulsion from the party. (Miljus subsequently formed a breakaway organization, which was entitled the Party of Independent Social Democrats of the Serb Republic.) Later in January the National Assembly rejected Miljus' nomination to the office of Prime Minister (while continuing to support Dodik). Also in January SFOR troops killed a Bosnian Serb suspected of war crimes, after he resisted arrest near the town of Foca, in the east of the country; Bosnian Serbs subsequently staged violent protests at UN headquarters in Foca.

In February 1999 the Council of Ministers of the Presidency was reorganized. Later that month Westendorp declared that supreme command of the armed forces of the Federation and the Serb Republic was to be transferred to the members of the collective Presidency. However, the Government of the Serb Republic contested the decision, and announced that Poplasen would remain Commander of the Serb armed forces, pending a ruling by the Constitutional Court of Bosnia and Herzegovina. In early March Poplasen proposed a motion in the Serb Republic National Assembly in an attempt to instigate Dodik's dismissal. Westendorp announced Poplasen's removal from office, on the grounds that he had exceeded his authority. In the same month international arbitrators, who had met in Vienna, Austria, in February, ruled that Serb control of Brčko would end, and that the town would henceforth be governed jointly by the Serb Republic and the Federation, under international supervision. Dodik tendered his resignation (which he later withdrew) in protest at the announcement, and the National Assembly rejected both the ruling on Brčko and Westendorp's decision to remove Poplasen from office. (The National Assembly subsequently withdrew its opposition to Poplasen's dismissal, and Mirko Sarović, the incumbent Vice-President, provisionally assumed the presidential office.) In mid-April a new municipal government, comprising Serbs, Muslims and Croats, was elected in Brčko, with an SPRS candidate as mayor.

In May 1999 the ICTY sentenced a former Bosnian Croat detention camp commander to 30 months' imprisonment for war crimes, but acquitted him of charges brought under the 1949 Geneva Convention governing international warfare, on the grounds that the Muslim–Croat conflict had been internal. In June, in accordance with the Constitution, Jelavić became Chairman of the Bosnia and Herzegovina Presidency, replacing Radišić. In the same month the UN Security Council voted to extend the mandate of SFOR and the principally civilian security force, the UN Mission in Bosnia and Herzegovina (UNMIBH), for a further year; NATO announced that the strength of the SFOR contingent was to be reduced to about 16,500. In July SFOR members arrested Radislav Brdjanin, a former Bosnian Serb official (who had served as Deputy Prime Minister under Karadžić), following his indictment by the ICTY in connection with massacres of Muslims and Croats near Banja Luka by Serb forces in 1992. In August 1999 a prominent Bosnian Serb army commander, Col-Gen. Momir Talić, was arrested in Vienna, Austria (where he was attending a military conference), prompting protests from the Serb Republic Government; Talić had been secretly indicted by the ICTY for war crimes committed against Muslims and Croats during the Bosnian conflict.

In August 1999 Wolfgang Petritsch, hitherto the Austrian ambassador to the FRY, succeeded Westendorp as High Representative in Bosnia (following Westendorp's appointment to the

European Parliament). In September Plavšić was re-elected leader of the SNA at a party congress. In October Petritsch prohibited Poplasen and a further two SRP officials from contesting forthcoming local elections, on the grounds that they had obstructed the implementation of the Dayton peace agreement. Later that month a former Bosnian Serb detention camp commander, who had been seized by SFOR troops in early 1998, was indicted by the ICTY for crimes against humanity, although charges of genocide against him were abandoned. In December 1999 Andrić-Luzanski assumed the Federation presidency, in accordance with the one-year rotational mandate stipulated in the Constitution. In February 2000 Izetbegović replaced Jelavić as Chairman of the collective Presidency. The Presidency proposed the establishment of a reconstituted Bosnian Council of Ministers, which would have one Prime Minister (with a rotational mandate) and two Deputy Prime Ministers.

## Government

In accordance with the General Framework Agreement for Peace in Bosnia and Herzegovina, signed in December 1995, Bosnia and Herzegovina is a single state, which consists of two independent political entities: the Federation of Bosnia and Herzegovina, comprising the Bosniak (Muslim)- and Croat-majority areas, and the Serb Republic (Republika Srpska), comprising the Serb-majority area. The central Government of Bosnia and Herzegovina has a three-member collective presidency of one Bosniak, one Croat and one Serb. Members of the Presidency are directly elected for a term of four years, and are eligible to serve for only two consecutive terms. Chairmanship of the Presidency is rotated between the members every eight months. The bicameral Parliamentary Assembly of Bosnia and Herzegovina comprises the House of Peoples and the House of Representatives. The House of Representatives has 42 deputies, of whom 28 are directly elected from the Federation and 14 directly elected from the Serb Republic for a two-year term. The House of Peoples has 15 deputies, of whom 10 are selected by the Federation legislature and five by the Serb Republic legislature for a two-year term. The Presidency appoints two co-Prime Ministers, who subsequently appoint the national Council of Ministers, subject to the approval of the House of Representatives.

The Federation of Bosnia and Herzegovina and the Serb Republic each retain an executive presidency, government and legislature. The bicameral parliament of the Federation comprises a 140-member House of Representatives, which is elected for a two-year term by proportional representation, and a 74-member House of Peoples, which has one-half Bosniak and one-half Croat representation. The unicameral legislature of the Serb Republic, known as the National Assembly, has 83 deputies, who are elected for a two-year term by porportional representation. The Federation is divided into 10 cantons, each headed by a zupan or governor.

## Defence

In late 1995 it was estimated that government forces in Bosnia and Herzegovina numbered about 40,000 (with some 100,000 reserves), the army of the 'Serbian Republic of Bosnia and Herzegovina' totalled more than 30,000 and Croatian forces (comprising the Croatian Defence Council—HVO) around 16,000. In May 1996 agreement was reached on the merger of the Bosniak and Croat armed forces, to form a Federation army. In October 1997 it was reported that the merger had been completed, and that the armed forces numbered some 45,000.

On 20 December 1995, following the signing of the Dayton peace agreement (see Recent History), the United Nations Protection Force (UNPROFOR), deployed in Bosnia and Herzegovina, formally transferred power to an international NATO-commanded 60,000-strong 'Implementation Force' (IFOR), which was granted wide-ranging authority to oversee the implementation of the peace accord. In December 1996 IFOR was superseded by a Stabilization Force (SFOR), which comprised about 33,000 troops. In early 1998 NATO agreed to extend SFOR's mandate to remain in the region indefinitely, with six-monthly reviews. About 2,300 members of the International Police Task Force were deployed in Bosnia and Herzegovina in 1998. In that year the UN Mission in Bosnia and Herzegovina (UNMIBH) comprised 1,976 civilian police officers and three army personnel. In mid-1999 NATO announced that SFOR would be reduced to number about 16,500. Government expenditure on defence was estimated at 394m. Deutsche Marks in 1997.

## Economic Affairs

In 1997, according to official estimates, Bosnia and Herzegovina's gross domestic product (GDP) was US $4,455m., equivalent to $1,086 per head. GDP increased, in real terms, by an average of 31.4% annually during 1994–97. According to the World Bank, the population of Bosnia and Herzegovina declined at an average annual rate of 9.1% in 1990–97. According to official estimates, real GDP growth in Bosnia and Herzegovina was 34% in 1997; growth in the Bosnian Federation in that year was estimated at 21%, while growth in the Serb Republic was estimated at 54%.

Agriculture (including forestry and fishing) contributed an estimated 13.6% of GDP in the Federation of Bosnia and Herzegovina and an estimated 32.7% of GDP in the Serb Republic in 1997. In 1998 about 6.1% of the labour force were employed in the agricultural sector in Bosnia and Herzegovina. The major agricultural products were tobacco and fruit, while the livestock sector was also significant. Imports of foodstuffs comprised 4.1% of total imports in 1997. According to official estimates, agricultural GDP in the Federation declined slightly, by 1.1%, in 1995, but increased by 5.9% in 1996 and by 0.5% in 1997. It was estimated that agricultural GDP in the Serb Republic declined by 39.5% in 1995, but increased by 27.3% in 1996 and by 25.2% in 1997.

Industry (including mining and manufacturing) contributed an estimated 21.4% of GDP in the Federation of Bosnia and Herzegovina and 22.3% of GDP in the Serb Republic. Construction accounted for an estimated 4.9% of GDP in the Federation and 4.5% of GDP in the Serb Republic. According to official estimates, industrial GDP in the Federation increased by 59.5% in 1995, by 34.7% in 1996, and by 33.4% in 1997. It was estimated that industrial GDP in the Serb Republic declined by 12.2% in 1995, but increased slightly, by 1.3% in 1996 and by 2.7% in 1997.

The mining and manufacturing sectors accounted for an estimated 70.7% of total exports in 1997. Bosnia and Herzegovina possesses extensive mineral resources, including iron ore, lignite, copper, lead, zinc and gold, The manufacturing sector is based largely on the processing of iron ore, non-ferrous metals, coal, and wood and paper products.

The civil conflict in 1992–95 resulted in the destruction of much of the electric power system in Bosnia and Herzegovina. Prior to the the conflict, the system comprised 13 hydroelectric installations and 12 coal- and lignite-fuelled thermal power installations. Imports of electric power accounted for 3.2% of total imports in 1997.

The services sector contributed an estimated 60.0% of GDP in the Federation of Bosnia and Herzegovina and 40.4% of GDP the Serb Republic in 1997. In that year entrepôt trade accounted for an estimated 19.6% of GDP in the Federation and 9.8% of GDP in the Serb Republic. The GDP of the services sector increased by 21.8% in the Federation in 1997, according to official estimates.

In 1997 Bosnia and Herzegovina recorded a visible trade deficit of US $1,628m., while there was a deficit of $1,046m. on the current account of the balance of payments. The principal exports in 1997 were wood and paper products, iron and steel, electric power and fabricated metal products. The main imports in that year were foodstuffs and electric power.

Bosnia and Herzegovina's overall budget deficit for 1997 was estimated at 91m. Deutsche Marks. The country's total external debt was estimated at US $4,076m. at the end of 1997 (equivalent to some 91% of annual GDP). In that year the cost of debt-servicing was equivalent to about 31% of the value of exports of goods and services. Total foreign debt amounted to 3,700m. KM in May 1999. Consumer prices in the Federation of Bosnia and Herzegovina declined by 4.4% in 1995 and by 24.5% in 1996, but increased by an estimated 14.3% in 1997. The annual rate of inflation in the Serb Republic averaged 117.6% in 1995, but fell to 65.9% in 1996 and to an estimated 2.7% in 1997. The rate of unemployment in Bosnia and Herzegovina was estimated at 40% in late 1999.

Bosnia and Herzegovina became a member of the IMF in December 1995 and was admitted to the International Bank for Reconstruction and Development (the World Bank) in April 1996.

The civil conflict in 1992–95 resulted in extensive damage to the economy of Bosnia and Herzegovina. Following the signing of the Dayton peace agreement in December 1995, the official reconstruction of the economy commenced; Bosnia and Herzegovina was admitted to the IMF, and an emergency credit was subsequently approved. An early priority of the reconstruction programme was the resolution of the considerable foreign debt that Bosnia and Herzegovina had inherited from the former Yugoslavia. In May 1998 the IMF approved a stand-by credit to support the Bosnian Government's economic programme for 1998–99. The World Bank subsequently granted further assistance in economic reconstruction and development. A new national currency, the convertible mark (which was fixed at par with the German Deutsche Mark) was officially introduced in June 1998. In October agreement was reached with the Paris Club of creditor governments on the reorganization and reduction of external debt. In May 1999 a donor conference for Bosnia and Herzegovina pledged US $1,050m. to finance the 1999 programme of economic reconstruction and reform, which was to support rehabilitation projects, and the state budget and balance of payments; 40% of this aid was allocated to the Serb Republic. In June the IMF approved an augmentation and an extension (until April 2000) of stand-by credit to the Bosnian Government. However, corruption remained a major impediment to economic development; it was reported that an estimated $1,800m. of public funds and aid had been lost as a result of fraudulent practices since 1995. At the end of 1999 the economy remained largely dependent on international aid, while the absence of a commercial banking system, and lack of progress in implementing economic reforms (including privatization measures) continued to deter foreign investors.

### Social Welfare

There is a state-administered health service, which is open to all. Before the civil war the number of doctors in Bosnia and Herzegovina was equivalent to approximately one for every 636 inhabitants. The health service was greatly disrupted by the war. During the conflict basic humanitarian welfare became increasingly dependent on international relief organizations. Following the end of hostilities in December 1995, budgetary funds allocated to the health service were used principally for emergency relief and humanitarian aid. At the end of 1999 economic and social reconstruction continued to be supported by international aid.

### Education

Elementary education is free and compulsory for all children between the ages of seven and 15 years, when children attend the 'eight-year school'. Various types of secondary education are available to all who qualify, but the vocational and technical schools are the most popular. Alternatively, children may attend a general secondary school (gymnasium), where they follow a four-year course to prepare them for university entrance. At the secondary level there are also a number of art schools, apprentice schools and teacher-training schools. There are four universities, situated in Sarajevo, Banja Luka, Mostar and Tuzla, with a combined total of about 40,000 students. The educational system in Bosnia and Herzegovina was severely disrupted by the civil war (1992–95).

### Public Holidays

**2000:** 1–2 January (New Year), 1 March (Independence Day), 1 May (Labour Day), 9 May (V. E. Day), 21 November (National Statehood Day).

**2001:** 1–2 January (New Year), 1 March (Independence Day), 1 May (Labour Day), 9 May (V. E. Day), 21 November (National Statehood Day).

### Weights and Measures

The metric system is in force.

# Statistical Survey

Source (unless otherwise stated): *Yugoslav Survey*, Belgrade, POB 677, Moše Pijade 8/I; tel. (11) 333610; fax (11) 332295.

## Area and Population

**AREA, POPULATION AND DENSITY**

| | |
|---|---|
| Area (sq km) | 51,129* |
| Population (census results) | |
| 31 March 1981 | 4,124,008 |
| 31 March 1991 | |
| Males | 2,183,795 |
| Females | 2,193,238 |
| Total | 4,377,033 |
| Population (official estimates at mid-year)† | |
| 1997 | 4,204,000 |
| Density (per sq km) at mid-1997 | 82.2 |

* 19,741 sq miles.

† Figures include refugees outside the country. The number of people living in the country was estimated to be 3,250,000 in early 1996.

Source: mainly UN, *Demographic Yearbook* and *Population and Vital Statistics Report*.

**PRINCIPAL ETHNIC GROUPS** (1991 census, provisional)

| | Number | % of total population |
|---|---|---|
| Muslims | 1,905,829 | 43.7 |
| Serbs | 1,369,258 | 31.4 |
| Croats | 755,892 | 17.3 |
| 'Yugoslavs' | 239,845 | 5.5 |
| **Total** (incl. others) | 4,364,574 | 100.0 |

**PRINCIPAL TOWNS** (population at 1991 census): Sarajevo (capital) 415,631; Banja Luka 142,644 (Source: *Statistički godišnjak Jugoslavije*—Statistical Yearbook of Yugoslavia).

**1991** (estimates): Doboj 102,624; Mostar 127,034; Prijedor 112,635 (Source: UN, *Demographic Yearbook*).

Sarajevo (estimated population in 1993): 383,000.

**BIRTHS, MARRIAGES AND DEATHS**

**1989:** Registered live births 66,809 (birth rate 14.9 per 1,000); Registered deaths 30,383 (death rate 6.8 per 1,000).

**1990:** Registered live births 66,952; Registered marriages 29,990; Registered deaths 29,093.

**1995:** Registered deaths 114,670 (death rate 13.6 per 1,000) (Source: UN, *Demographic Yearbook*).

**1990–95** (UN estimates, annual averages): Birth rate 12.6 per 1,000; Death rate 7.1 per 1,000 (Source: UN, *World Population Prospects: The 1998 Revision*).

**Expectation of life** (UN estimates, years at birth, 1990–95): 72.2 (males 69.5; females 75.1) (Source: UN, *World Population Prospects: The 1998 Revision*).

**EMPLOYMENT** (Bosniak-majority area, average for December)

| | 1995 | 1996 | 1997 |
|---|---|---|---|
| Activities of the material sphere | 172,085 | 170,102 | 173,790 |
| Non-material services | 48,311 | 74,386 | 78,790 |
| **Total** | 220,396 | 244,488 | 252,580 |

Source: IMF, *Bosnia and Herzegovina: Selected Issues* (August 1998).

**1996:** Total formal employment 506,000: Bosniak-majority area 255,000 (excluding Ministry of Defence and Interior) in September; Croat-majority area 52,000 (including 19,000 soldiers and police) in April; Republika Srpska 199,000 (Source: World Bank, *Bosnia and Herzegovina: From Recovery to Sustainable Growth*, May 1997).

# Agriculture

**PRINCIPAL CROPS** ('000 metric tons)

| | 1996 | 1997 | 1998 |
|---|---|---|---|
| Wheat | 166 | 63 | 63* |
| Barley | 47 | 20* | 20* |
| Maize | 589 | 173 | 173* |
| Rye | 5 | 5* | 5* |
| Oats | 36 | 36* | 36* |
| Potatoes | 347 | 188 | 188* |
| Dry beans | 13 | 12* | 12* |
| Soybeans (Soya beans) | 4 | 4* | 4* |
| Rapeseed | 2 | 2* | 2* |
| Cabbages | 66 | 66* | 66* |
| Tomatoes | 29 | 29* | 29* |
| Green chillies and peppers | 4 | n.a. | n.a. |
| Onions (dry) | 27 | 27* | 27* |
| Garlic* | 2 | 2 | 2 |
| Beans (green)* | 2 | 2 | 2 |
| Carrots | 8 | 8* | 8* |
| Watermelons* | 3 | 3 | 3 |
| Grapes | 17 | 17* | 17* |
| Sugar beets | 1 | n.a. | n.a. |
| Apples | 18 | 18* | 18* |
| Pears* | 10 | 10 | 10 |
| Peaches and nectarines* | 2 | 2 | 2 |
| Plums | 25* | 23 | 23* |
| Strawberries* | 5 | 5 | 5 |
| Tobacco (leaves) | 4 | 4* | 4* |

* FAO estimate(s).

Source: FAO, *Production Yearbook*.

**LIVESTOCK** ('000 head, unless otherwise indicated, year ending September)

| | 1996 | 1997 | 1998* |
|---|---|---|---|
| Horses* | 50 | 50 | 50 |
| Cattle | 314 | 260* | 260 |
| Pigs | 165 | 70* | 70 |
| Sheep | 276 | 276* | 276 |
| Chickens (million) | 4 | 4* | 4 |

* FAO estimate(s).

Source: FAO, *Production Yearbook*.

**LIVESTOCK PRODUCTS** ('000 metric tons)

| | 1996 | 1997 | 1998* |
|---|---|---|---|
| Beef and veal | 18 | 13 | 9 |
| Mutton and lamb | 3 | 3* | 3 |
| Pig meat | 16 | 5 | 5 |
| Poultry meat | 11 | 8 | 8 |
| Cows' milk | 292 | 202 | 202 |
| Sheep's milk | 3 | 3* | 3 |
| Cheese | 14* | 14* | 14 |
| Eggs | 7 | 7* | 7 |
| Cattle and buffalo hides | 4* | 3* | 3 |

* FAO estimate(s).

Source: FAO, *Production Yearbook*.

# Fishing

(FAO estimates, '000 metric tons, live weight)

| | 1995 | 1996 | 1997 |
|---|---|---|---|
| **Total catch** (freshwater fish) | 2.5 | 2.6 | 2.6 |

Source: FAO, *Yearbook of Fishery Statistics*.

# Mining

('000 metric tons)

| | 1992 | 1993 | 1994 |
|---|---|---|---|
| Lignite | 2,000* | 1,500* | 1,400 |
| Barytes | 10 | n.a. | n.a. |
| Gypsum (crude) | 150 | n.a. | n.a. |

* Estimated production.

**Lignite** ('000 metric tons): 1,640 in 1995.

Source: UN, *Industrial Commodity Statistics Yearbook*.

# Industry

**SELECTED PRODUCTS** ('000 metric tons, unless otherwise indicated)

| | 1990 |
|---|---|
| Electric energy (million kWh) | 14,632 |
| Crude steel | 1,421 |
| Aluminium | 89 |
| Machines | 16 |
| Tractors (number) | 34,000 |
| Lorries (number) | 16,000 |
| Motor cars (number) | 38,000 |
| Cement | 797 |
| Paper and paperboard | 281 |
| Television receivers (number) | 21,000 |

**Electric energy** (million kWh): 3,500 (estimate) in 1993; 1,921 in 1994; 2,203 in 1995 (Source: UN, *Industrial Commodity Statistics Yearbook*).

# Finance

**CURRENCY AND EXCHANGE RATES**

**Monetary Units**

100 pfeninga = 1 konvertibilna marka (KM or convertible marka).

**Sterling, Dollar and Euro Equivalents** (30 September 1999)

£1 sterling = KM 3.0195;
US \$1 = KM 1.8339;
€1 = KM 1.9558;
KM 100 = £33.12 = \$54.53 = €51.13.

**Average Exchange Rate** (KM per US \$)

| | |
|---|---|
| 1996 | 1.5048 |
| 1997 | 1.7341 |
| 1998 | 1.7597 |

Note: The new Bosnia and Herzegovina dinar (BHD) was introduced in August 1994, with an official value fixed at 100 BHD = 1 Deutsche Mark (DM). The DM, the Croatian kuna and the Yugoslav dinar also circulated within Bosnia and Herzegovina. On 22 June 1998 the BHD was replaced by the KM, equivalent to 100 of the former units. The KM was thus at par with the DM.

**BUDGET** (million Deutsche Marks)*

| Revenue | 1995 | 1996 | 1997 |
|---|---|---|---|
| Tax revenue | 573.7 | 1,381 | 1,615 |
| Sales tax and excise taxes | 318.4 | 767 | 976 |
| Enterprise tax | 20.2 | 296 | 284 |
| Wage tax and tax for reconstruction | 82.1 | | |
| Customs duties | 111.4 | 296 | 349 |
| Social security contributions | 244.3 | 609 | 813 |
| Other revenue | 56.3 | | |
| Grants | 168.5 | | |
| **Total** | 1,042.8 | 1,991 | 2.428 |

| Expenditure† | 1995 | 1996 | 1997 |
|---|---|---|---|
| Wages and contributions | 87.0 | 235 | 325 |
| Goods and services | 580.3 | 280 | 478 |
| Military‡ | 461.9 | 188 | 394 |
| Education | 69.6 | n.a. | n.a. |
| Interest payments§ | 0.8 | | |
| Social Fund expenditure | 217.3 | | |
| Transfers to households (incl. subsidies) | | 1,658 | 1,716 |
| Other expenditure (incl. unallocated)‖ | 166.0 | | |
| **Total** | 1,051.4 | 2,173 | 2,519 |

* Figures represent a consolidation of the budgetary accounts of the central Government and the authorities in the Federation of Bosnia and Herzegovina and (except for local and district administration) the Serb Republic. The data for 1995 exclude the operations of all local and district administrations. Owing to lack of data, some military expenditure and associated external grant financing are excluded. Source: IMF, *Bosnia and Herzegovina—Recent Economic Developments* (October 1996) and *Bosnia and Herzegovina: Selected Issues* (August 1998).

† Figures are on a cash basis.

‡ Military expenditure includes only reported cash payments.

§ Unpaid arrears of external interest totalled 258 million DM in 1995.

‖ Figures for 1996 and 1997 include expenditure by district, canton and municipal authorities, for which sufficient data are not available to allocate to other categories.

**MONEY SUPPLY** (million Deutsche Marks at 31 December)

| | 1995 | 1996 | 1997 |
|---|---|---|---|
| Currency outside banks | 27.6 | 96.0 | 112.5 |
| Demand deposits at banks | 28.8 | 258.0 | 141.4 |
| **Total money** | 56.4 | 354.0 | 253.9 |

Source: IMF, *Bosnia and Herzegovina: Selected Issues* (August 1998).

**NATIONAL ACCOUNTS**
(estimates, US $ million at current prices)

| | 1995 | 1996 | 1997 |
|---|---|---|---|
| Gross domestic product | 2,157 | 3,327 | 4,455 |

Source: IMF, *Bosnia and Herzegovina: Selected Issues* (August 1998).

**BALANCE OF PAYMENTS** (estimates, US $ million).

| | 1995 | 1996 | 1997 |
|---|---|---|---|
| Exports of goods f.o.b. | 152 | 336 | 570 |
| Imports of goods f.o.b. | −1,082 | −1,882 | −2,199 |
| **Trade balance** | −930 | −1,546 | −1,628 |
| Exports of services | 229 | 322 | 427 |
| Imports of services | −252 | −396 | −388 |
| **Balance on goods and services** | −953 | −1,620 | −1,590 |
| Other income (net) | −242 | −222 | −228 |
| **Balance on goods, services and income** | −1,195 | −1,842 | −1,818 |
| Unrequited transfers received | 1,073 | 1,251 | 852 |
| Unrequited transfers paid | −71 | −157 | −80 |
| **Current balance** | −193 | −748 | −1,046 |
| Capital account (net) | −271 | 1,310 | 743 |
| Net errors and omissions | 100 | −90 | 223 |
| **Overall balance** | −364 | 471 | −80 |

Source: IMF, *Bosnia and Herzegovina: Selected Issues* (August 1998).

# External Trade

**SELECTED COMMODITIES** (US $ million)*

| Imports | 1996 | 1997 |
|---|---|---|
| Electric power | 19.7 | 39.6 |
| Fabricated metal products | 33.9 | 22.9 |
| Electrical machinery and equipment | 5.1 | 28.7 |
| Wood and paper products | 11.5 | 29.9 |
| Foodstuffs | 39.9 | 50.2 |
| **Total** (inc. others) | 1,172.6 | 1,225.0 |

| Exports | 1996 | 1997 |
|---|---|---|
| Electric power | 0.3 | 5.7 |
| Iron and steel | 7.0 | 12.4 |
| Non-metallic minerals | 1.3 | 0.9 |
| Fabricated metal products | 4.5 | 5.3 |
| Transport equipment | 6.5 | 3.4 |
| Electrical machinery and equipment | 0.3 | 4.6 |
| Chemical products | 1.4 | 1.6 |
| Wood and paper products | 18.2 | 18.1 |
| Textile products | 2.1 | 0.8 |
| Footwear and fancy goods | 1.6 | 2.2 |
| **Total** (incl. others) | 57.8 | 87.3 |

* Figures are provisional and refer only to the Federation of Bosnia and Herzegovina (the Bosniak- and Croat-majority areas, excluding the Serb Republic).

# Communications Media

| | 1993 | 1994 | 1995 |
|---|---|---|---|
| Telephones ('000 main lines in use) | 600 | 250 | 238 |
| Radio receivers ('000 in use) | n.a. | 800 | 840 |
| Daily newspapers*: | | | |
| Number | n.a. | n.a. | 2 |
| Average circulation ('000 copies) | n.a. | n.a. | 520 |

* Figures refer to government-controlled areas only.

**Non-daily newspapers** (1992): 22 (average circulation 2,508,000 copies).

Sources: UN, *Statistical Yearbook*; UNESCO, *Statistical Yearbook*.

# Directory

## The Constitution

The Constitution of Bosnia and Herzegovina was Annexe 4 to the General Framework Agreement for Peace in Bosnia and Herzegovina, signed in Paris (France) on 14 December 1995. These peace accords were negotiated at Dayton, Ohio (USA), in November and became the Elysées or Paris Treaty in December. Annexe 4 took effect as a constitutional act upon signature, superseding and amending the Constitution of the Republic of Bosnia and Herzegovina.

The previous organic law, an amended version of the 1974 Constitution of the then Socialist Republic of Bosnia and Herzegovina (part of the Socialist Federal Republic of Yugoslavia—the name was changed to the Republic of Bosnia and Herzegovina upon the declaration of independence following a referendum on 29 February–1 March 1992), provided for a collective State Presidency, a Government headed by a Prime Minister and a bicameral Assembly.

The institutions of the Republic continued to function until the firm establishment of the bodies provided for by the Federation of Bosnia and Herzegovina, which was formed on 31 March 1994. This was an association of the Muslim- or Bosniak-led Republic and the Croat Republic of Herzeg-Bosna. The federal Constitution provided for a balance of powers between Bosniak and Croat elements in a Federation divided into cantons. The federal Government was to be responsible for defence, foreign and economic affairs, and its head, the Prime Minister, was to have a greater executive role than the President. These two posts were to rotate between the two ethnic groups.

According to the General Framework Agreement, the Federation was one of the two constituent 'entities' of the new union of Bosnia and Herzegovina, together with the Serb Republic (Republika Srpska) of Bosnia and Herzegovina. The Serb Republic was proclaimed by the Serb deputies of the old Bosnian Assembly on 27 March 1992. Its Constitution provided for an executive President (with two Vice-Presidents), a Government headed by a Prime Minister and a unicameral National Assembly. Under the terms of the General Framework Agreement, known as the Dayton accords (after Dayton, Ohio, the US town where the treaty was negotiated in November 1995), the two Entities were to exist under their current Constitutions, which were to be amended to conform with the peace agreement.

The Dayton accords included 12 annexes on: the military aspects of the peace settlement (including the establishment of an international Implementation Force—IFOR); regional stabilization; inter-entity boundaries; elections; arbitration; human rights; refugees and displaced persons; a Commission to Preserve National Monuments; Bosnia and Herzegovina public corporations (specifically a Transportation Corporation); civilian implementation (including the office of a High Representative of the International Community); and an international police task force. One of the annexes was the Constitution of Bosnia and Herzegovina, summarized below, and it was signed by representatives of the Republic, the Federation and the Serb Republic.

### CONSTITUTION OF BOSNIA AND HERZEGOVINA

The Preamble declares the basic, democratic principles of the country and its conformity with the principles of international law. The Bosniaks, Croats and Serbs are declared to be the constituent peoples (along with Others) of Bosnia and Herzegovina.

Article I affirms the continuation of Bosnia and Herzegovina with the Republic of Bosnia and Herzegovina, within its existing international boundaries, but with its internal structure modified. Bosnia and Herzegovina is a democratic state, consisting of two Entities, the Federation of Bosnia and Herzegovina and the Serb Republic. The capital of the country is Sarajevo and the symbols are to be determined by the legislature. Citizenship is to exist both for Bosnia and Herzegovina and for the Entities.

Article II guarantees human rights and fundamental freedoms, and makes specific mention of the Human Rights Commission to be established under Annexe 6 of the General Framework Agreement. The provisions of a number of international agreements are assured and co-operation and access for the international war-crimes tribunal specified. The provisions of this Article, according to Article X, are incapable of diminution or elimination by any amendment to the Constitution.

The responsibilities of and relations between the Entities and the institutions of Bosnia and Herzegovina are dealt with in Article III. The institutions of Bosnia and Herzegovina are responsible for foreign policy (including trade and customs), overall financial policy, immigration and refugee issues, international and inter-entity law enforcement, common and international communications facilities, inter-entity transportation and air-traffic control. Any governmental functions or powers not reserved to the institutions of Bosnia and Herzegovina by this Constitution are reserved to the Entities, unless additional responsibilities are agreed between the Entities or as provided for in the General Framework Agreement (Annexes 5–8). The Entities may establish special, parallel relations with neighbouring states, provided this is consistent with the sovereignty and territorial integrity of Bosnia and Herzegovina. The Constitution of Bosnia and Herzegovina has primacy over any inconsistent constitutional or legal provisions of the Entities.

#### The Parliamentary Assembly

Bosnia and Herzegovina has a bicameral legislature, known as the Parliamentary Assembly. It consists of a House of Peoples and a House of Representatives. The House of Peoples comprises 15 members, five each from the Bosniaks, the Croats and the Serbs. The Bosniak and Croat Delegates are selected by, respectively, the Bosniak and Croat Delegates to the House of Representatives of the Federation, and the Serb Delegates by the National Assembly of the Serb Republic. The first House of the Peoples selected under the Constitution is protected from an early dissolution.

The House of Representatives consists of 42 Members, two-thirds to be directly elected from the territory of the Federation and one-third from the territory of the Serb Republic. The first general election was conducted in September 1998 in accordance with Annexe 3 of the General Framework Agreement, which provided for a Permanent Election Commission then to be appointed.

The Parliamentary Assembly convenes in Sarajevo and each chamber rotates its chair between three members, one from each of the constituent peoples. The Parliamentary Assembly is responsible for: necessary legislation under the Constitution or to implement Presidency decisions; determining a budget for the institutions of Bosnia and Herzegovina; and deciding whether to ratify treaties.

#### The Presidency

Article V concerns the state Presidency of Bosnia and Herzegovina. The head of state consists of three Members: one Bosniak and one Croat, each directly elected from the Federation; and one Serb, directly elected from the Serb Republic. Elections will be in accordance with legislation of the Parliamentary Assembly, but the first elections, in September 1998, were held as agreed in Annexe 3 of the General Framework Agreement. The first elected Members will have a term of two years, but, thereafter, a Member's term shall be for four years. The Chair for the first term of the Presidency will be the Member to receive the largest number of votes, thereafter the method of selection must be determined by parliamentary legislation. A Presidency decision, if declared to be destructive of a vital interest of an Entity, can be vetoed by a two-thirds majority in the relevant body: the National Assembly of the Serb Republic if the declaration was made by the Serb Member; or by the Bosniak or Croat Delegates in the Federation House of Peoples if the declaration was made by, respectively, the Bosniak or Croat Members of the Presidency. The Presidency is responsible for the foreign policy and international relations of Bosnia and Herzegovina. It is required to execute the decisions of the Parliamentary Assembly and to propose an annual central budget to that body, upon the recommendation of the Council of Ministers.

The Chair of the Council of Ministers is nominated by the Presidency and confirmed in office by the House of Representatives. Other Ministers, including, specifically, a foreign minister and a foreign-trade minister, are nominated by the Chair of the Council of Ministers, and also approved by the House of Representatives. The Council of Ministers is responsible for carrying out the policies and decisions of Bosnia and Herzegovina and reporting to the Parliamentary Assembly. There are also guarantees that no more than two-thirds of Ministers be from the territory of the Federation, and Deputy Ministers are to be from a different constituent people to their Minister.

Each Member of the Presidency has, *ex officio*, civilian command authority over armed forces. Each Member is a member of a Standing Committee on Military Matters, appointed by the Presidency and responsible for co-ordinating the activities of armed forces in the country. The inviolability of each Entity to any armed force of the other is assured.

#### Other Institutions and Provisions

Article VI is on the Constitutional Court, which is to have nine members, four selected by the House of Representatives of the Federation and two by the National Assembly of the Serb Republic. The three remaining judges, at least initially, are to be selected by the President of the European Court of Human Rights. The first judges will have a term of office of five years; thereafter judges will usually serve until they are 70 years of age (unless they retire or are removed by the consensus of the other judges). The Constitutional Court of Bosnia and Herzegovina is to uphold the Constitution, to resolve the jurisdictions of the institutions of Bosnia and Herzegovina and the Entities, to ensure consistency with the Constitution and to guarantee the legal sovereignty and territorial integrity of the country. Its decisions are final and binding.

The Central Bank of Bosnia and Herzegovina is the sole authority for issuing currency and for monetary policy in Bosnia and Herzegovina. For the first six years of the Constitution, however, it is not authorized to extend credit by creating money; moreover, during this period the first Governing Body will consist of a Governor, appointed by the International Monetary Fund, and three members appointed by the Presidency (a Bosniak and a Croat, sharing one vote, from the Federation, and one from the Serb Republic). The Governor, who may not be a citizen of Bosnia and Herzegovina or any neighbouring state, will have a deciding vote. Thereafter, the Governing Body shall consist of five members, appointed by the Presidency for a term of six years, with a Governor selected by them from among their number.

Article VIII concerns the finances of Bosnia and Herzegovina and its institutions. Article IX concerns general provisions, notably forbidding anyone convicted or indicted by the International Tribunal on war crimes in the former Yugoslavia from standing for or holding public office in Bosnia and Herzegovina. These provisions also guarantee the need for all public appointments to be generally representative of the peoples of Bosnia and Herzegovina. Amendments to the Constitution need a two-thirds majority of those present and voting in the House of Representatives.

The penultimate Article XI is on transitional arrangements provided for in an annexe to the Constitution. This is mainly concerned to legitimize the parallel competence of existing authorities and legislation until such time as the institutions of Bosnia and Herzegovina are properly established. A Joint Interim Commission is to co-ordinate the implementation of the Constitution of Bosnia and Herzegovina and of the General Framework Agreement and its Annexes. It is to be composed of four members from the Federation, three from the Serb Republic and one representative of Bosnia and Herzegovina. Meetings of the Commission are to be chaired by the High Representative of the International Community.

# The Government

(February 2000)

### HIGH REPRESENTATIVE OF THE INTERNATIONAL COMMUNITY IN BOSNIA AND HERZEGOVINA

Under the terms of the treaty and annexes of the General Framework Agreement for Peace in Bosnia and Herzegovina, signed in December 1995, the international community, as authorized by the UN Security Council, was to designate a civilian representative to oversee the implementation of the peace accords and the establishment of the institutions of the new order in Bosnia and Herzegovina.

**High Representative:** WOLFGANG PETRITSCH; 71000 Sarajevo, trg Djece Sarajeva bb; tel. (71) 447275; fax (71) 447420.

### BOSNIA AND HERZEGOVINA

#### Presidency

The Dayton accords, which were signed into treaty in December 1995, provide for a three-member Presidency for the state, comprising one Bosniak (Muslim), one Croat and one Serb. The Presidency has responsibility for governing Bosnia and Herzegovina at the state level. The members of the second Presidency were elected by their respective constituencies in the Bosnian elections that were held on 12–13 September 1998. The Presidency appoints two Co-Prime Ministers who, in turn, appoint the national Council of Ministers.

**President and Chairman of the Presidency:** Dr ALIJA IZETBEGOVIĆ (PDA).

**Co-Presidents:** ANTE JELAVIĆ (CDU—BH), ZIVKO RADIŠIĆ (Socialist Party of the Bosnian Serb Republic).

#### Council of Ministers

(January 2000)

**Co-Prime Ministers:** Dr HARIS SILAJDŽIĆ, SVETOZAR MIHAJLOVIĆ.

**Deputy Prime Minister:** NEVEN TOMIĆ.

**Minister for Foreign Affairs:** Dr JADRANKO PRLIĆ.

**Deputy Ministers for Foreign Affairs:** HUSEIN ŽIVALJ, DRAGAN BOŽANIĆ.

**Minister for Foreign Trade and Economic Relations:** MIRSAD KURTOVIĆ.

**Deputy Ministers for Foreign Trade and Economic Relations:** ŽELJKO ŠUMAN, GOJKO MILINKOVIĆ.

**Minister for Civil Affairs and Communications:** MARKO AŠANIN.

**Deputy Ministers for Civil Affairs and Communications:** NUDŽEIM REČICA, VALENTIN ĆORIĆ.

#### Ministries

**Office of the Presidency:** 71000 Sarajevo, Musala 5; tel. (71) 664941; fax (71) 472491.

**Office of the Prime Ministers:** 71000 Sarajevo, Vojvode Putnika 3; tel. (71) 664941; fax (71) 443446.

**Ministry of Civil Affairs and Communications:** 71000 Sarajevo, Vojvode Putnika 3; tel. (71) 786822; fax (71) 786944.

**Ministry of Foreign Affairs:** 71000 Sarajevo, Musala 2; tel. (71) 663813; fax (71) 472188.

**Ministry of Foreign Trade and Economic Relations:** 71000 Sarajevo, trg Oktobra bb; tel. (71) 445750; fax (71) 655060.

### THE FEDERATION OF BOSNIA AND HERZEGOVINA

Following an agreement reached in Washington, DC (USA), by representatives of the Republic of Bosnia and Herzegovina and the 'Croat Republic of Herzeg-Bosna' (declared on 28 August 1993), the Federation of Bosnia and Herzegovina was formed on 31 March 1994. The President and Vice-President of the Federation were elected in May 1994. The Federation was reorganized as one of the two constituent entities of Bosnia and Herzegovina in the peace agreements of 1995.

**President:** IVO ANDRIĆ-LUZANSKI (CDU—BH).

**Vice-President:** Dr EJUP GANIĆ (PDA).

#### Government

(January 2000)

**Prime Minister:** EDHEM BIČAKČIĆ.

**Deputy Prime Minister and Minister of Finance:** DRAGAN ČOVIĆ.

**Minister of Internal Affairs:** MEHMED ŽILIĆ.

**Minister of Defence:** MIROSLAV PRCE.

**Minister of Justice:** IGNJAC DODIK.

**Minister of Energy, Mining and Industry:** MIRSAD SALKIĆ.

**Minister of Transport and Communications:** BESIM MEHMEDIĆ.

**Minister for Social Welfare, Displaced Persons and Refugees:** SULEJMAN GARIB.

**Minister of Health:** Dr BOŽO LJUBIĆ.

**Minister of Education, Science, Culture and Sport:** Dr FAHRUDIN RIZVANBEGOVIĆ.

**Minister of Trade:** BRANKO IVKOVIĆ.

**Minister of Physical Planning and the Environment:** RAMIZ MEHMEDAGIĆ.

**Minister of Agriculture, Water Management and Forestry:** Dr AHMED SMAJIĆ.

**Ministers without Portfolio:** NIKOLA ANTUNOVIĆ, NEDELJKO DESPOTOVIĆ.

#### Ministries

**Office of the President:** 71000 Sarajevo; tel. and fax (71) 472618.

**Office of the Prime Minister:** 71000 Sarajevo, Zmaja od Bosne 3; tel. (71) 650457; fax (71) 664816.

**Ministry of Agriculture, Water Management and Forestry:** 71000 Sarajevo; tel. (71) 443338; fax (71) 663659.

**Ministry of Defence:** 71000 Sarajevo, Zmaja od Bosne 3A; tel. (71) 664926; fax (71) 663785.

**Ministry of Education, Science, Culture and Sport:** 71000 Sarajevo, Zmaja od Bosne 3; tel. (71) 202750; fax (71) 664381.

**Ministry of Energy, Mining and Industry:** 71000 Sarajevo, Alipašina 41; tel. (71) 663779; fax (71) 672067.

**Ministry of Finance:** 71000 Sarajevo, Zmaja od Bosne 3; tel. (71) 203149; fax (71) 664863.

**Ministry of Health:** 71000 Sarajevo, Alipašina 41; tel. (71) (71) 663701; fax (71) 664245; e-mail moh@bih.net.ba.

**Ministry of Internal Affairs:** 71000 Sarajevo, Boriše Kovačevića 7; tel. (71) 667246; fax (71) 472976.

**Ministry of Justice:** 71000 Sarajevo, Zmaja od Bosne 3; tel. and fax (71) 656743.

**Ministry of Physical Planning and the Environment:** 71000 Sarajevo; tel. (71) 473124; fax (71) 663548.

**Ministry for Social Welfare, Displaced Persons and Refugees:** 71000 Sarajevo, Alipašina 41 II; tel. (71) 204552; fax (71) 663977.

**Ministry of Trade:** 71000 Sarajevo; tel. and fax (71) 312191.

**Ministry of Transport and Communications:** 71000 Sarajevo; tel. (71) 668907; fax (71) 667866.

### SERB REPUBLIC (REPUBLIKA SRPSKA) OF BOSNIA AND HERZEGOVINA

On 27 March 1992 a 'Serb Republic of Bosnia and Herzegovina' was proclaimed. It was immediately declared illegal by the President of the State Presidency. The Republic comprised Serb-held areas of Bosnia and Herzegovina, including the 'Serb Autonomous Regions' of Eastern and Old Herzegovina, Bosanska Krajina, Romanija and Northern Bosnia. According to the peace treaty of December 1995, the Serb Republic was to constitute one of the two territorial entities comprising Bosnia and Herzegovina, with 49% of the country's area. It was to retain its own executive presidency, government and parliament (henceforth known as the National Assembly—see below).

**President:** MIRKO SAROVIĆ (acting).

#### Government
(January 2000)

**Prime Minister:** MILORAD DODIK.

**Deputy Prime Minister and Minister of Industry and Technology:** DJURADJ BANJAC.

**Deputy Prime Minister and Minister of Administration and Local Government:** OSTOJA KREMENOVIĆ.

**Deputy Prime Minister and Minister of Foreign Economic Relations:** SAVO LONČAR.

**Deputy Prime Minister and Minister for War Veterans and Casualties, and Labour Affairs:** TIHOMIR GLIGORIĆ.

**Minister of Defence:** Col-Gen. (retd) MANOJLO MILOVANOVIĆ.

**Minister of Internal Affairs:** SREDOJE NOVIĆ.

**Minister of Justice:** MILAN TRBOJEVIĆ.

**Minister of Finance:** NOVAK KONDIĆ.

**Minister of Trade and Tourism:** NIKOLA KRAGULJ.

**Minister of Energy and Mining:** VLADIMIR DOKIĆ.

**Minister of Transport and Communications:** MARKO PAVIĆ.

**Minister of Agriculture, Water Resources and Forestry:** MILENKO SAVIĆ.

**Minister of Urban Planning, Utilities and the Environment:** JOVO BASIĆ.

**Minister of Education:** NENAD SUZIĆ.

**Minister of Refugees and Displaced Persons:** MILADIN DRAGIČEVIĆ.

**Minister of Health and Social Welfare:** ŽELJKO RODIĆ.

**Minister of Science and Culture:** ŽIVOJIN ERIĆ.

**Minister of Information:** RAJKO VASIĆ.

**Minister of Sports and Youth:** MILORAD KARALIĆ.

**Minister of Religion:** JOVO TURANJANIN.

#### Ministries

**Office of the Prime Minister:** 78000 Banja Luka; tel. (78) 46474; fax (78) 30103.

**Ministry of Administration and Local Government:** 78000 Banja Luka; tel. (78) 218641; fax (78) 218674.

**Ministry of Agriculture, Water Resources and Forestry:** 76000 Bijelina; tel. (76) 471412; fax (76) 472353.

**Ministry of Defence:** 78000 Banja Luka; tel. and fax (78) 12025.

**Ministry of Education:** 78000 Banja Luka, Vuka Karadžica 1; tel. and fax (78) 218287.

**Ministry of Energy and Mining:** 78000 Banja Luka, trg Srpskih Junaka 4/3; tel. (78) 15118; fax (78) 218657.

**Ministry of Finance:** 78000 Banja Luka, Vuka Karadžica 4; tel. (78) 17626; fax (78) 218634.

**Ministry of Foreign Economic Relations:** 78000 Banja Luka, Srpska 2; tel. (78) 30963; fax (78) 218657.

**Ministry of Health and Social Welfare:** 78000 Banja Luka, Zdravke Korde 8; tel. (78) 36740; fax (78) 36472.

**Ministry of Industry and Technology:** 78000 Banja Luka; tel. (78) 218649; fax (78) 218657.

**Ministry of Information:** 78000 Banja Luka, Vuka Karadžica 4; tel. (78) 218816; fax (78) 218831.

**Ministry of the Interior:** Neznanih junaka, 76000 Bijeljina; tel. (76) 471633; fax (76) 472685.

**Ministry of Justice:** 78000 Banja Luka; tel. (78) 218835; fax (78) 218847.

**Ministry of Refugees and Displaced Persons:** 78000 Banja Luka, Kralja Petra I; tel. (78) 43224; fax (78) 17924.

**Ministry of Religion:** 78000 Banja Luka; tel. and fax (78) 17262.

**Ministry of Science and Culture:** 78000 Banja Luka; tel. (78) 17071; fax (78) 17003.

**Ministry of Sports and Youth:** 78000 Banja Luka; tel. (78) 18689; fax (78) 30103.

**Ministry of Trade and Tourism:** 78000 Banja Luka; tel. and fax (78) 12720.

**Ministry of Transport and Communications:** 78000 Banja Luka; tel. and fax (78) 18912.

**Ministry of Urban Planning, Utilities and the Environment:** 78000 Banja Luka; tel. (78) 39287; fax (78) 47218.

**Ministry of War Veterans and Casualties, and Labour Affairs:** 78000 Banja Luka; tel. (78) 17074; fax (78) 17003.

# Presidency and Legislature

### PRESIDENCY OF BOSNIA AND HERZEGOVINA

**Election, 12–13 September 1998**

| | Votes |
|---|---|
| Bosniak Candidates | |
| DR ALIJA IZETBEGOVIĆ (Party for Democratic Action) | 511,309 |
| FIKRET ABDIĆ (Democratic People's Union) | 36,446 |
| SEFER HALILOVIĆ | 33,680 |
| HARIJA HALILOVIĆ | 7,690 |
| Croat Candidates | |
| ANTE JELAVIĆ (Croatian Democratic Union of Bosnia and Herzegovina) | 189,408 |
| GRADIMIR GOJER | n.a. |
| KRESIMIR ZUBAK (New Croat Initiative) | 40,811 |
| Serb Candidates | |
| ZIVKO RADIŠIĆ (Socialist Party of the Bosnian Serb Republic) | 360,286 |
| MOMČILO KRAJIŠNIK (Serb Democratic Party) | 315,480 |
| ZORAN TADIĆ | 27,427 |

### PARLIAMENTARY ASSEMBLY

The General Framework Agreement, signed in December 1995, provided for a Parliamentary Assembly of Bosnia and Herzegovina, comprising two chambers, the House of Peoples and the House of Representatives. In both houses two-thirds of the deputies were to be drawn from the territory of the Federation of Bosnia and Herzegovina, while one-third were to come from the Serb Republic.

#### Dom Naroda
(House of Peoples)

There are 15 deputies in the House of Peoples, of whom 10 are elected by the Federation legislature and five by the Serb Republic legislature.

**Speaker:** VLADIMIR SOLJIĆ.

**Zastupnièki dom**
(House of Representatives)

There are 42 deputies in the House of Representatives.

**Speaker:** Dr HALID GENJAC.

**Election, 12–13 September 1998**

| Party | Votes | Seats |
|---|---|---|
| Federation of Bosnia and Herzegovina | | |
| Coalition for a Single and Democratic Bosnia and Herzegovina* | 455,403 | 14 |
| Croatian Democratic Union of Bosnia and Herzegovina | 187,152 | 6 |
| Social Democratic Party | 137,990 | 4 |
| Social Democrats of Bosnia and Herzegovina | 28,740 | 2 |
| New Croat Initiative | 28,572 | 1 |
| Democratic People's Union | n.a. | 1 |
| Serb Republic | | |
| Accord Coalition† | 214,948 | 4 |
| Serb Democratic Party of Bosnia and Herzegovina | 163,436 | 4 |
| Coalition for a Single and Democratic Bosnia and Herzegovina* | 128,277 | 3 |
| Serb Radical Party of the Serb Republic | 119,026 | 2 |
| Radical Party of the Serb Republic | 27,753 | 1 |

* Comprised the Civic Democratic Party, the Liberal Party, the Party for Bosnia and Herzegovina and the Party of Democratic Action.

† An electoral coalition comprising the Socialist Party of the Bosnian Serb Republic, the Serb National Alliance and the Party of Independent Social Democrats of the Serb Republic.

**ZASTUPNIÈKI DOM FEDERACIJE**
(House of the Representatives of the Federation)

There are 140 deputies in the House of Representatives.

**Speaker:** ENVER KRESO.

**Election, 12–13 September 1998**

| Party | Votes | Seats |
|---|---|---|
| Coalition for a Single and Democratic Bosnia and Herzegovina* | 456,387 | 68 |
| Croatian Democratic Union of Bosnia and Herzegovina | 184,569 | 28 |
| Social Democratic Party | 126,630 | 19 |
| Social Democrats of Bosnia and Herzegovina | 29,427 | 6 |
| New Croat Initiative | 27,357 | 4 |
| Democratic People's Union | 19,491 | 3 |
| Patriotic Party of Bosnia and Herzegovina | 12,581 | 2 |
| Socialist Party of the Bosnian Serb Republic | 10,742 | 2 |
| Pensioners' Party | 10,125 | 2 |
| Croatian Rights Party | n.a. | 2 |
| Bosnian Rights Party of Bosnia and Herzegovina | n.a. | 1 |
| Croatian Peasants' Party | n.a. | 1 |
| Bosnian Party | n.a. | 1 |
| Centre Coalition† | n.a. | 1 |

* Comprised the Civic Democratic Party, the Liberal Party, the Party for Bosnia and Herzegovina and the Party of Democratic Action.

† Allied with the Social Democrats of Bosnia and Herzegovina.

**PRESIDENCY OF THE SERB REPUBLIC (REPUBLIKA SRPSKA)**

**Election, 12–13 September 1998**

| Candidate | Votes |
|---|---|
| Dr NIKOLA POPLASEN (Serb Coalition of the Serb Republic*) | 324,033 |
| DR BILJANA PLAVŠIĆ (Accord Coalition†) | 286,914 |

* Comprised the Serb Radical Party of the Serb Republic and the Serb Democratic Party of Bosnia and Herzegovina.

† An electoral coalition comprising the Socialist Party of the Bosnian Serb Republic, the Serb National Alliance and the Party of Independent Social Democrats of the Serb Republic.

**NARODNA SKUPŠTINA REPUBLIKA SRPSKA**
(National Assembly of the Serb Republic)

There are 83 deputies in the National Assembly.

**Speaker:** PETAR DJOKIĆ.

**Election, 12–13 September 1998**

| Party | Votes | Seats |
|---|---|---|
| Serb Democratic Party of Bosnia and Herzegovina | 161,499 | 19 |
| Coalition for a Single and Democratic Bosnia and Herzegovina* | 125,546 | 15 |
| Serb National Alliance | 97,644 | 12 |
| Serb Radical Party of the Serb Republic | 95,840 | 11 |
| Socialist Party of the Bosnian Serb Republic | 79,253 | 10 |
| Party of Independent Social Democrats of the Serb Republic | 54,074 | 6 |
| Radical Party of the Serb Republic | 27,206 | 3 |
| Social Democratic Party | 19,894 | 2 |
| Serb Coalition of the Serb Republic† | 19,208 | 2 |
| Croatian Democratic Union of Bosnia and Herzegovina | n.a. | 1 |
| New Croat Initiative | n.a. | 1 |
| Coalition for King and Homeland | n.a. | 1 |

* Comprised the Civic Democratic Party, the Liberal Party, the Party for Bosnia and Herzegovina and the Party of Democratic Action.

† Comprised the Serb Radical Party of the Serb Republic and the Serb Democratic Party of Bosnia and Herzegovina.

# Political Organizations

**Association of the Democratic Initiative of Sarajevo Serbs** (Udruženje demokratske inicijative Srba iz Sarajeva): Sarajevo; f. 1996 to affirm and protect the rights of Serbs in Muslim-held Sarajevo; Chair. MAKSIM STANISIĆ.

**Bosnia and Herzegovina Democratic Alternative:** Sarajevo; f. 1990; Chair. MUHAMED CENGIĆ.

**Bosnian Party** (Bosanska Stranka): Chair. MIRNES AJANOVIĆ.

**Bosnian Rights Party of Bosnia and Herzegovina** (Bosanska Stranka Prava Bosne i Hercegovine—BSP BiH): Sarajevo.

**Civic Democratic Party** (Gradjanska Demokratska Stranka): member of the Coalition for a Single and Democratic Bosnia electoral alliance; Chair. IBRAHIM SPAHIĆ.

**Croat National Council of Bosnia and Herzegovina:** Sarajevo; f. 1993; established by Bosnian Croats opposed to Croatia's official policy towards Bosnia and Herzegovina as well as to radical Bosnian Muslims; Chair. IVO KOMSIĆ, IVAN LOVRENOVIĆ.

**Croatian Democratic Union of Bosnia and Herzegovina (CDU—BH)** (Hrvatska Demokratska Zajednica Bosne i Hercegovine—HDZ BiH): 71000 Sarajevo; f. 1990; affiliate of the CDU in Croatia; Croat nationalist party; Chair. ANTE JELAVIĆ; Gen.-Sec. MARKO TOKIĆ.

**Croatian Peasants' Party** (Hrvatska Seljacka Stranka): affiliated to Croatian Peasants' Party in Croatia; Chair. ILIJA SIMIĆ.

**Croatian Rights Party** (Hrvatska Stranka Prava): contested 1996 elections; nationalist; Pres. STANKO SLISKOVIĆ.

**Democratic Party for Banja Luka and Krajina:** Banja Luka; f. 1997, by fmr mems of Serb Radical Party (q.v.); Chair. NIKOLA SPIRIĆ.

**Democratic Patriotic Bloc of the Serb Republic** (Demokratski Patriotski Blok Republike Srpske): contested 1996 elections; Chair. PREDRAG RADIĆ.

**Democratic People's Union** (Narodna Demokratska Zajednica—NDZ): f. 1996; Chair. FIKRET ABDIĆ; Vice-Chair. ZLATKO JUSIĆ.

**Eastern Bosnian Muslim Party** (Istocnobosanska Muslimanska Stranka): Sarajevo; f. 1997; Chair. IBRAN MUSTAFIĆ.

**Homeland Party:** Banja Luka; f. 1996 by fmr members of Serb Democratic Union—Homeland Front; nationalist; Chair. PREDRAG RASIĆ.

**Liberal Bosniak Organization (LBO)** (Liberalna Bosnjacka Organizacija): 71000 Sarajevo; f. 1992; secular Muslim party; Pres. MUHAMED FILIPOVIĆ; Vice-Pres. SALIH FOCO.

**Liberal Party** (Liberalna Stranka): member of the Coalition for a Single and Democratic Bosnia electoral alliance; Pres. RASIM KADIĆ.

**Liberal Social Party of Bosnia and Herzegovina** (Liberalno Socijalna Partija—LSP): Sarajevo; f. 1998; centre party; Chair. HIDAJET REPOVAĆ; Deputy Chairs JADRANKA MIKIĆ, NAMIK TERZIMEHEC, VINKO CURO.

**Muslim Democratic Alliance** (Muslimanski Demokratski Savez—MDS): Bihać; f. 1994; seeks to promote equality between the ethnic groups of Bosnia and Herzegovina.

**New Croat Initiative:** (Nova Hrvatska Inicijativa): f. 1998 by fmr mems of the Croatian Democratic Union of Bosnia and Herzegovina (q.v.); Pres. KRESIMIR ZUBAK; Chair. IVO LOZANCIĆ.

**New Radical Party:** member of the People's Alliance for Peace and Progress electoral coalition.

**Party for Bosnia and Herzegovina:** Sarajevo; f. 1996; integrationist; member of the Coalition for a Single and Democratic Bosnia electoral alliance; Pres. Dr HARIS SILAJDŽIĆ; Sec. SAFET REDZEPAGIĆ.

**Party of Democratic Action (PDA)** (Stranka Demokratske Akcije—SDA): c/o 71000 Sarajevo, Mehmeda Spahe 14; internet www.bih.net.ba/~sda; f. 1990; leading Muslim nationalist party; has brs in Yugoslavia; member of the Coalition for a Unified and Democratic Bosnia electoral alliance; Chair. Dr ALIJA IZETBEGOVIĆ; Deputy Chair. EDHEM BIČAKČIĆ, Dr HALID GENJAC, Dr EJUP GANIĆ; Sec.-Gen. MIRSAD CEMAN.

**Party of Democratic Progress of the Serb Republic:** Banja Luka; Chair. MLADEN IVANIĆ.

**Party of Economic Prosperity** (Stranka Privednog Prosperita—SPP): Zenica; f. 1996; Chair. PANE SKRBIĆ; Sec.-Gen. SAFET REDZEPAGIĆ.

**Party of Independent Social Democrats** (Stranka Nezavisnih Socijaldemokrata—SNSD): Banja Luka; member of the Accord Coalition; Chair. MILORAD DODIK; Deputy Chair. BRANKO DOKIĆ; Sec.-Gen. NENAD BASTINAĆ.

**Party of Independent Social Democrats of the Serb Republic:** f. 1999; breakaway faction of the Party of Independent Social Democrats; Leader BRANE MILJUS.

**Party of Serb Unity** (Stranka Srpskog Jedinstva): Bijeljina; extreme nationalist; Chair. ZELKO RAZNJATOVIĆ ('Arkan').

**Patriotic Party of Bosnia and Herzegovina** (Patriotska Stranka BiH): Sarajevo.

**People's Party of the Serb Republic** (Narodna Stranka Republicka Srpska): Leader MILAN TRBOJEVIĆ.

**Radical Party of the Serb Republic** (Radikalna Stranka Republika Srpska).

**Republican Party:** Sarajevo; integrationist; Chair. STJEPAN KLJUIĆ.

**Serb Civic Council:** Sarajevo; anti-nationalist; org. of Serbs in the Federation of Bosnia and Herzegovina; Chair. Dr MIRKO PEJANOVIĆ.

**Serb Democratic Party of Bosnia and Herzegovina (SDP)** (Srpska Demokratska Stranka Bosne i Hercegovine—SDS BiH): c/o Pale, National Assembly of the Serb Republic; f. 1990; allied to SDP of Croatia; Serb nationalist party; member of the Serb Coalition of the Serb Republic electoral alliance; Chair. ALEXANDER BUHA (acting); Deputy Chair. DRAGAN CAVIĆ.

**Serb Democratic Union—Homeland Front:** nationalist; Pres. BOŽIDAR BOJANIĆ.

**Serb National Alliance (SNA)** (Srpski Narodni Savez—SNS): Banja Luka; f. 1997; member of the Accord Coalition; Chair. Dr BILJANA PLAVŠIĆ.

**Serb Patriotic Party** (Srpska Patriotska Stranka): contested 1996 elections; Chair. STOJAN ZUPLJANIN; Vice-Chair. PETAR DJAKOVIĆ.

**Serb Party of Krajina** (Srpska Stranka Krajina—SSK): Banja Luka; f. 1996; regional party in favour of the creation of clear borders between nations; Pres. PREDRAG LAZAREVIĆ; Chair. of Exec. Cttee DJORDJE UMICEVIĆ.

**Serb Radical Party of the Serb Republic** (Srpska Radikalna Stranka Srpske Republike—SRS SR): br. of SRS in Serbia; member of the Serb Coalition of the Serb Republic; Chair. MIRKO BLAGOJEVIĆ (acting); Vice-Chair. PANTELIJA DAMJANOVIĆ; Gen. Sec. OGNJEN TADIĆ.

**Social Alliance:** c/o 71000 Sarajevo, trg Dure Pucara bb; fmr communist mass organization; allies of Social Democratic Party; left-wing.

**Socialdemocratic Party** (Socijaldemokratska Partija BiH): 71000 Sarajevo, Alipašina 41; tel. (71) 664044; fax (71) 664042; f. 1908; merged with Social Democrats of Bosnia and Herzegovina; Chair. Dr ZLATKO LAGUMDŽIJA; Sec.-Gen. KARLO FILIPOVIĆ.

**Social Liberal Party:** Banja Luka; reintegrationist; member of the People's Alliance for Peace and Progress electoral coalition; Chair. MIODRAG ZIVANOVIĆ; Gen. Sec. MILAN TUKIĆ.

**Socialist Party of the Bosnian Serb Republic** (Socijalistička partija za Republiku Srpsku—SPRS): Kralja Petra 1 Karađorđevića 103/1; tel. and fax (51) 231643; e-mail sprs@inecco.net; f. 1993; br. of the Socialist Party of Serbia; member of the Accord Coalition; Chair. ZIVKO RADIŠIĆ; Sec.-Gen. ŽELJKO MIRJANIĆ; 40,000 mems.

**Yugoslav Left of the Serb Republic:** Bijeljina; f. 1996; branch of pro-communist party based in Belgrade (Yugoslavia); Pres. MILORAD IVOSEVIĆ.

# Diplomatic Representation

### EMBASSIES IN BOSNIA AND HERZEGOVINA

**Austria:** 71000 Sarajevo, Džidžikovac 7; tel. (71) 668337; fax (71) 668339; Ambassador: Dr VALENTIN INZKO.

**Bulgaria:** Sarajevo, Trampina 14/11; tel. (71) 668191; fax (71) 668182; Ambassador: MARKO MARKOV.

**Canada:** Sarajevo, Logavina 7; tel. (71) 447900; fax (71) 447901; Ambassador: SERGE MARCOUX.

**China, People's Republic:** Sarajevo, Pavla Lukača 16b; tel. (71) 654666; fax (71) 652972; Ambassador: WEN XIGUI.

**Croatia:** 71000 Sarajevo, Mehmeda Spahe 20; tel. (71) 444330; fax (71) 472434; Ambassador: DAMIR ZORIĆ.

**Czech Republic:** 71000 Sarajevo, Potoklinica 6; tel. (71) 447525; fax (71) 447526; Ambassador: JIŘÍ KUDĚLA.

**Denmark:** 71000 Sarajevo, Skenderija 4; tel. (71) 665901; fax (71) 665902; e-mail danamb@bih.net.ba; Ambassador: HENRIK WØHLK.

**Egypt:** Sarajevo, Ejuba Ademovića 19; tel. and fax (71) 666499; Ambassador AHMED ABDUL RAHMAN.

**France:** 71000 Sarajevo, Kapetanović Ljubušaka 18; tel. (71) 668149; fax (71) 668103; e-mail france-1@bih.net.ba; internet www.ambafrance.com.ba; Ambassador: BERNARD BAJOLET.

**Germany:** 71000 Sarajevo, Ulica Buka bb; tel. (71) 275000; Ambassador: Graf VON HENNECKE BASSEWITZ.

**Greece:** Sarajevo, Obala Maka Dizdara I; tel. (71) 203516; fax (71) 203512; Ambassador: PROCOPIOS MANTZOURANIS.

**Holy See:** Pehlivanuša 9, 71000 Sarajevo, Nadbiskupa Josipa Stadlera 5; tel. (71) 207867; fax (71) 207863; e-mail apnunbh@utic.net.ba; Apostolic Nuncio: Mgr GIUSEPPE LEANZA.

**Hungary:** 71000 Sarajevo; Armaganuša 32; tel. (71) 205302; fax (71) 205303; Ambassador: KÁLMÁN KOCSIS.

**Iran:** 71000 Sarajevo, Obala Maka Dizdara 6; tel. (71) 650210; fax (71) 663910; e-mail iries1@bih.net.ba; Ambassador: SEYED HOMAYOUN AMIRKHALILI.

**Italy:** 71000 Sarajevo, Čekaluša 39; tel. (71) 533765; fax (71) 659368; e-mail ambsara@bih.net.ba; Ambassador: ENRICO PIETROMARCHI.

**Japan:** Sarajevo, Mula Mustafe Bašeskije 2; tel. (71) 209580; fax (71) 209583; Ambassador: TAKASHIMA YUSHU.

**Libya:** 71000 Sarajevo, Tahtali sokak 17; tel. (71) 657534; fax (71) 663620; Head of People's Bureau: IBRAHIM ALI TAGIURI.

**Macedonia, former Yugoslav republic:** Sarajevo, Splitska 6; tel. (71) 206004; Chargé d'affaires a.i.: STOJAN RUMENOVSKI.

**Malaysia:** Sarajevo, UNIS Business Centre, Fra Anđela Zvizdovića 1; tel. (71) 667712; fax 667713; Ambassador: HUSSIN BIN NAYAN.

**Malta:** 71000 Sarajevo, Mula Mustafe Baseskije 12; tel. (71) 668632; Ambassador: Dr LORENZO TACCHELLA.

**Netherlands:** Sarajevo, Obala Kulina Bana 4/2; tel. (71) 668422; fax (71) 668423; Ambassador: VALERIE STEFANIE MARIE SLUITER.

**Norway:** 71000 Sarajevo, Ferhadija 20; tel. (71) 666373; fax (71) 666505; Ambassador: KNUT MØRKVED.

**Pakistan:** 71000 Sarajevo, Emerika Bluma 17; tel. (71) 211836; fax (71) 211837; Ambassador: Maj.-Gen. (retd) SYED ZAFAR MEHDI.

**Romania:** Sarajevo, Isaka Samokovlije 89; tel. and fax (71) 679344; Chargé d'affaires a.i.: Dr VASILE LECA.

**Russia:** Sarajevo, Kemal Begova 4; tel. (71) 668147; fax (71 668148; Ambassador: FILIP FILIPOVICH SIDORSKII.

**Saudi Arabia:** Sarajevo, Koševo 44; tel. (71) 211861; fax (71) 211744; Chargé d'affaires a.i.: HAZEM KARAKOTLY.

**Slovenia:** 71000 Sarajevo, Bentbaša 7; tel. (71) 271260; fax (71) 271270; Ambassador: DRAGO MIROŠIĆ.

**Spain:** Sarajevo, Maka Dizdara 5/1; tel. (71) 208754; fax (71) 208758; Ambassador: JOSÉ ANGEL LÓPEZ JORRÍN.

**Sweden:** 71000 Sarajevo, Ferhadija 20; tel. (71) 276030; fax (71) 276060; Ambassador: NILS ELIASSON.

**Switzerland:** 71000 Sarajevo, Josipa Štadlera 15; tel. (71) 665250; fax (71) 665246; Ambassador: WILHELM SCHMID.

**Turkey:** 71000 Sarajevo, Hamdije Kreševljakovića 5; tel. (71) 445260; fax (71) 472437; Ambassador: AHMET EROZAN.

**United Kingdom:** 71000 Sarajevo, Tina Vjevica 8; tel. (71) 444429; fax (71) 666131; Ambassador: GRAHAM HAND.

**USA:** 71000 Sarajevo, Alipašina 43; tel. (71) 659969; fax (71) 659722; Ambassador: THOMAS MILLER.

# Judicial System

The courts in Bosnia and Herzegovina are supervised by the Ministries of Justice of each entity. The Constitutional Court has competence regarding constitutional matters in both entities, but there are separate judicial systems in the Bosnian Federation and the Serb Republic.

**Constitutional Court of the Republic of Bosnia and Herzegovina:** 71000 Sarajevo, Save Kovačevića 6; tel. (71) 214555; nine mems; mems elected for five-year term; Pres. Dr KASIM TRNKA: Vice-Pres. VITOMIR POPOVIĆ.

**Constitutional Court of the Serb Republic:** Banja Luka; eight mems; Pres. RAJKO KUZMANOVIĆ; Sec. MIODRAG SIMOVIĆ.

**Supreme Court of the Federation of Bosnia and Herzegovina:** 71000 Sarajevo, Valtera Perića 15; tel. (71) 664754; Pres. VENCESLAV ILIĆ.

**Supreme Court of the Serb Republic:** Banja Luka; Pres. JOVO ROSIĆ.

**Office of the Federal Prosecutor:** 71000 Sarajevo, Valtera Perića 11; tel. (71) 214990; Federal Prosecutor SULJO BABIĆ.

# Religion

Bosnia and Herzegovina has a diversity of religious allegiances. Just over one-half of the inhabitants are nominally Christian, but these are divided between the Serbian Orthodox Church and the Roman Catholic Church. The dominant single religion is Islam. The Reis-ul-ulema, the head of the Muslims in the territory comprising the former Yugoslavia, is resident in Sarajevo. Most of the Muslims are ethnic Muslims or Bosniaks (Slavs who converted to Islam under the Ottomans). There are, however, some ethnic Albanian and Turkish Muslims. Virtually all are adherents of the Sunni persuasion. There is a small Jewish community; since 1966, however, there has been no rabbi in the community. In June 1997 an agreement to establish an interreligious council was signed by the leaders of the Roman Catholic, Serbian Orthodox, Jewish and Islamic communities.

## ISLAM

**Islamic Community of the Sarajevo Region:** 71000 Sarajevo, Save Kovačevića 2; Pres. of Massahat SALIH EFENDIJA COLAKOVIĆ; Mufti of Bosnia and Herzegovina Hadži MUSTAFA TIRIĆ; Reis-ul-ulema MUSTAFA EFENDI CERIĆ.

## CHRISTIANITY

### The Serbian Orthodox Church

**Metropolitan of Dabrobosna:** NICOLAJ; (c/o Serbian Patriarchate, 11001 Belgrade, Kralja Petra 5, POB 182; Yugoslavia).

### The Roman Catholic Church

For ecclesiastical purposes, Bosnia and Herzegovina comprises one archdiocese and three dioceses. At 31 December 1997 adherents of the Roman Catholic Church represented about 9.0% of the total population.

**Bishops' Conference:** Biskupska Konferencija Bosne i Hercegovine, Nadbiskupski Ordinarijat, 71000 Sarajevo, Kaptol 7; tel. and fax (71) 472178; f. 1995; Pres. Cardinal VINKO PULJIĆ, Archbishop of Vrhbosna-Sarajevo; Vice-Pres. Rt Rev. FRANJO KOMARICA, Bishop of Banja Luka.

**Archbishop of Vrhbosna-Sarajevo:** Cardinal VINKO PULJIĆ, Nadbiskupski Ordinarijat Vrhbosanski, 71000 Sarajevo, Kaptol 7; tel. (71) 663512; fax (71) 472429.

## JUDAISM

**Jewish Community of the Sarajevo Region:** 71000 Sarajevo, Hamdije Kreševljekoviće 59; tel. (71) 663472; fax (71) 663473; Pres. JAKOB FINCI.

# The Press

During the civil conflict in 1992–95 the majority of publications were obliged to cease production, although the broadcast media sector expanded. Whereas 377 publications, 54 radio stations, four television stations and one news agency were officially registered prior to the civil conflict, in early 1997 145 publications, 92 radio stations, 29 television stations and six news agencies were in existence in Bosnia and Herzegovina.

## PRINCIPAL DAILIES

**Dnevni Avaz:** 71000 Sarajevo.

**Glas Srpski:** Banja Luka; Serb Republic government newspaper; Editor-in-Chief TOMO MARIĆ; Deputy Editor-in-Chief NIKOLA GUZIJAN.

**Horizont:** Mostar; f. 1996; Croat independent.

**Oslobodjenje** (Liberation): 71000 Sarajevo, Džemala Bijedića 185; tel. (71) 454144; fax (71) 460982; e-mail info@obodjenje.net; f. 1943; morning; Editor MEHMED HALILOVIĆ; circ. 56,000.

**Slobodna Dalmacija BH:** 71000 Sarajevo; f. 1998; aimed at Croat population in Bosnia and Herzegovina; Exec. Editor ANTE SULJAK; Deputy Editor JOSKO DADIĆ.

**Večernje novine:** 71000 Sarajevo, Pruščakova St 13; tel. (71) 664874; fax (71) 664875; f. 1964; special edition published daily in Serb Republic; Editor-in-Chief FETO RAMOVIĆ; Exec. Editor BERIN EKMEČIĆ; circ. 15,000.

## WEEKLY NEWSPAPERS

**Hratska Rijec:** 71000 Sarajevo; Croat weekly.

**Ljiljan:** 71000 Sarajevo; official newspaper of the PDA; Chair. MENSUR BRDAR; Editor-in-Chief DŽEMALUDIN LATIĆ.

**Nezavisne novine** (The Independent): Banja Luka; f. 1995; Editor-in-Chief ŽELJKO KOPANJA.

## PERIODICALS

**Alternativa:** Doboj; f. 1996; fortnightly; Editor-in-Chief PAVLE STANISIĆ; Deputy Editor-in-Chief ZIVKO SAVKOVIĆ; Dir SLOBODAN BABIĆ; circ. 5,000.

**Dani:** 71000 Sarajevo; e-mail bhdani@bih.net.ba; independent; political and cultural; 4 a week; Editor-in-Chief SENAD PECANIN.

**Front Slobode:** Tuzla; formerly communist; became independent in 1993; 2 a week.

**Novi prelom:** Banja Luka; monthly.

**Reporter:** Banja Luka; independent; Editor PERICA VUCINIĆ.

**Slobodna Bosna:** 71000 Sarajevo, Muhameda Kantardžića 3; tel. (71) 444041; fax (71) 444895; e-mail slobo-bosna@zamir-sa.ztn.atc.-org; fortnightly; Editor SENAD AVDIĆ.

**Svijet:** Sarajevo; illustrated; weekly; Editor-in-Chief JELA JEVREMOVIĆ; circ. 115,000.

**Tuzla List:** Tuzla; f. 1993; independent; regional political information.

**Zadrugar:** Sarajevo, Omladinska 1; f. 1945; weekly; journal for farmers; Editor-in-Chief FADIL ADEMOVIĆ; circ. 34,000.

## NEWS AGENCIES

**Alternativna Informativna Mreza (AIM—Alternative Information Network):** Sarajevo; exchange of information between independent media in the former Yugoslavia; non-commercial and dependent on financial support from abroad.

**BH Press:** Sarajevo; state news agency.

**HABENA:** 88000 Mostar, Kralja Tvrtka 9; tel. (88) 319222; fax (88) 319422; e-mail habena@habena.ba; f. 1993; Bosnian Croat news agency, Man. MARKO DRAGIĆ; Editor-in-Chief ZDRAVKO NIKIĆ.

**ONASA** (Oslobodjenje News Agency): Sarajevo, Hasana Kikića 3; tel. (71) 276580; fax (71) 276590; e-mail onasa@onasa.com.ba; internet www.onasa.com.ba; f. 1994; Gen. Man. MEHMED HUSIĆ.

**SNRA:** Banja Luka; Bosnian Serb news agency; Man. Dir DRAGAN DAVIDOVIĆ.

# Publishers

**Novi Glas:** 78000 Banja Luka, Borisa Kidriča 1; tel. (78) 12766; fax (78) 12758; general literature; Dir MIODRAG ŽIVANOVIĆ.

**Public Company for Newspaper Publication Organization, Official Gazette of Bosnia and Herzegovina:** Sarajevo, Magribija 3; tel. (71) 663470; e-mail slist@bih.net.ba; publishes legislation for official newspapers, and books and other material from the field of newspaper-publication activities.

**Student's Printing House of the University of Sarajevo:** Sarajevo, Obala Kulina Bana 7; tel. and fax (71) 526138; university textbooks; Dir EMIR KADRIĆ; Chief Editor DRAGAN S. MARKOVIĆ.

**Svjetlost:** 71000 Sarajevo, Petra Preradovića 3; tel. (71) 212144; fax (71) 272352; f. 1945; textbooks and literature; Dir SAVO ZIROJEVIĆ.

**Veselin Masleša (Sarajevo Publishing):** 71000 Sarajevo, Obala Kulina Bana 4; tel. (71) 521476; fax (71) 272369; f. 1950; school and university textbooks, general literature; Dir RADOSLAV MIJATOVIĆ.

## PUBLISHERS' ASSOCIATION

**Association of Publishers and Booksellers of Bosnia and Herzegovina:** 71000 Sarajevo, M. Tita brigade 9a; tel. and fax (71) 207945; Pres. IBRAHIM SPAHIĆ; Gen. Sec. DRAGAN S. MARKOVIĆ.

# Broadcasting and Communications

## TELECOMMUNICATIONS

**Director of Telecommunications:** 71000 Sarajevo, Musala 2; tel. (71) 472657; fax (71) 441248; Dir EMIN SKOPLJAK.

### BROADCASTING

In 1997 broadcasting in Bosnia and Herzegovina was largely controlled by the three nationalist parties: the Party of Democratic Action (PDA); the Croatian Democratic Union of Bosnia and Herzegovina (CDU—BH); and the Serb Democratic Party (SDP). There were, however, a number of locally based independent radio and television stations. In May 1996 two such organizations, NTV Zetel and ITV Hayat (both television companies), had created, with the Mostar and Tuzla branches of Radio-Televizija Bosne i Hercegovine, the TVIN-TV International Network. This was to be open to media and correspondents from the Bosniak–Croat Federation and the Serb Republic, in accordance with the aims of the Dayton accords.

#### Regulatory Authority

**Open Media Commission:** Sarajevo; Dir-Gen. KRISTER THELIN.

#### Radio

**Croat Radio Herzeg-Bosna:** Mostar; Dir TOMISLAV MAZALO; Editor-in-Chief IVAN KRISTIĆ.

**Open Serb Network (OSM):** Pale; Editor-in-Chief MIRKO DESPIĆ.

**Radio Kameleon:** Milana Jovanovića 6, 75000 Tuzla; tel. and fax (75) 250055; e-mail kameleon@kameleon.ba; internet www.kameleon.ba; f. 1992; independent radio station; Gen. Dir ZLATKO BERBIĆ.

**Radio-Televizija (RTV) Bosne i Hercegovine:** 71000 Sarajevo, VI Proleterske brigade 4; tel. (71) 652333; fax (71) 461569; f. 1969; 2 TV programmes; Dir-Gen. MIRSAD PURIVATRA; Dir of TV AMILA OMERSOFTIĆ; Editor-in-Chief ESAD CEROVIĆ.

**Radio ZID:** Sarajevo; f. Dec. 1992; commenced broadcasts March 1993; independent radio station; cultural and educative programmes; Chair. ZDRAVKO GREBO; Editor-in-Chief VLADO AZINOVIĆ.

**Serb Radio Banja Luka:** Banja Luka; f. 1997 as independent radio station following breakaway from Serb Radio and Television (q.v.); eight-mem. editorial council; Chair. RADOMIR NESKOVIĆ.

**Studio 99:** Sarajevo; f. 1991; independent radio station; broadcast political information during the civil conflict; Editor-in-Chief ADIL KULENOVIĆ; Editor of Programmes ZORAN ILIĆ.

#### Television

**Independent TV Tuzla:** Tuzla; f. 1991 by a group of journalists; promotes the values of democratic society.

**ITV Hayat:** Sarajevo; e-mail itvhayat@bih.net.ba; internet www.ntvhayat.com; Muslim influences; broadcasts 18 hours daily; Dir and Editor-in-Chief ELVIR SVRAKIĆ.

**NTV Zetel:** Zenica; f. 1991; cultural, political, educative and sports programmes.

**Radio-Televizija (RTV) Bosne i Hercegovine:** 71000 Sarajevo, Bulevar Meše Šelimouića 12; tel. (71) 455124; fax (71) 455104; f. 1945; 4 radio programmes; broadcasts in Serbo-Croat; Dir-Gen. MIRSAD PURIVATRA; Dir of Radio NADJA PAŠIĆ; Editor-in-Chief ESAD CEROVIĆ.

**Serb Radio and Television (SRT):** Pale; Dir-Gen. SLAVIŠA SABLJIĆ; Chair. of Man. Bd MOMČILO KRAJIŠNIK; Editor-in-Chief DUSKO OLJACA.

## Finance

(d.d. = dioničko društvo (joint-stock company); cap. = capital; res = reserves; dep. = deposits; m. = million; amounts in Yugoslav dinars unless otherwise stated; brs = branches)

### BANKING

At the end of 1997 there were 63 banks in Bosnia and Herzegovina, of which 50 operated in the Federation and 13 in the Serb Republic. Public enterprises were majority owners of 18 banks in the Federation and seven banks in the Serb Republic, and were minority owners of an additional eight banks in the Federation. Total assets in Bosnia and Herzegovina amounted to 4,800m. Deutsche Marks.

#### Central Bank

**Central Bank of Bosnia and Herzegovina:** 71000 Sarajevo, 25 Maršala Tita; tel. (71) 663630; fax (71) 201517; e-mail contact@cbb; internet www.cbbh; replaced the National Bank of the Federation of Bosnia and Herzegovina, and the National Bank of the Republika Srpska, which ceased monetary operations in August 1997; Gov. MIRSAD KURTOVIĆ.

#### Selected Banks

**Export Banka a.d., Bijeljina:** Bijeljina, ul. Svetog Save br. 46; tel. (76) 401409; fax (76) 401410; f. 1992; Pres. JOVO STANKIĆ; Chair. SLAVKO ROGULJIĆ; Man. Dir MILADIN VIDIĆ.

**Glumina Banka d.d. Mostar:** Ljubuški, a Šimića b.b.; tel. (88) 835451; fax (88) 835450; e-mail glumba-ljubuski@int.tel.hr; f. 1996; cap. 41.0m., res 0.9m., dep. 305.8m. (Dec. 1997); Pres. ANTE ZDILAR; Gen. Man. LEON BEGIĆ.

**Hrvatska Banka d.d. Mostar:** 88000 Mostar, Kardinala Stepinca b.b.; tel.(88) 312123; fax (88) 312121; cap. 86.9m., res 0.1m., dep. 571.6m. (Dec. 1998); Pres. DRAGAN COVIĆ; Gen. Man. BERISLAV KUTLE.

**Investiciono-Komercijalna Banka d.d., Zenica:** 72000 Zenica, POB 62, trg Samoupravljača 1; tel. (72) 21804; fax (72) 417022; f. 1990; cap. 10.7m., res 24.4m., dep. 131.2m. (Dec. 1998); Gen. Man. UZEIR FETIĆ.

**Privredna Banka Brčko d.d.:** Brčko, Kralja Petra I Oslobodioca broj 1; tel. (76) 204222; fax (76) 204055; f. 1993; Pres. JOVICA SOPIĆ; Chair. MILAN KARANOVIĆ; Gen. Man. STOJAN MAJSTOROVIĆ.

**Privredna Banka Gradiška d.d.:** Gradiška, Vidovdanska bb; tel. (78) 813333; fax (78) 813205; f. 1953, registered as independent bank since 1992; cap. 5.9m., res 3.0m., dep. 53.2m. (Dec. 1998); Pres. STOJAN TODOROVIĆ.

**Privredna Banka Sarajevo a.d.:** ul. Srpskih Ratnika br. 14, Pale; tel. (71) 664852; fax (71) 663807; f. 1970 by merger of five banks; Man. Dir. MOMČILO MANDIĆ.

**Privredna Banka Sarajevo d.d., Sarajevo:** 71000 Sarajevo, Vojvode Stepe Obala 19, POB 160; tel. (71) 213144; fax (71) 218511; f. 1971; cap. 3,713.1m., res 1,131.1m., dep. 35,471.6m. (Dec. 1990); Pres. and Gen. Man. DJORDJE ZARIĆ; 14 brs.

**Razvojna Banka a.d.:** 78000 Banja Luka, Bana Milosavljevica 4; tel. (78) 12012; fax (78) 17575; e-mail sdb@inecco.net; f. 1996; cap. 18m., res 4.6m., dep. 3.9m.; Gen. Dir RANKO TRAVAR; 12 brs.

**Semberska Banka d.d., Bijeljina:** Bijeljina, Karadjordjeva 3; tel. (76) 471588; fax (76) 472247; Pres. MILAN MIHAJLOVIĆ; Chair. ARSEN TEŠIĆ; Man. Dir CVIJETIN NIKIĆ.

**Turkish Ziraat Bank Bosnia d.d.:** 71000 Sarajevo, Strossmayerova 10; tel. (71) 230619; fax (71) 441902; e-mail ziraat@bin.net.ba; f. 1996; cap. 10.3m., dep. 11.3m. (Dec. 1998); Pres. METIN ERTÜRK.

#### Banking Agency

**Agency for Banking of the Federation of Bosnia and Herzegovina** (Agencija za Bankarstvo Federacije Bosne i Hercegovine): 71000 Sarajevo, Ćemaluša 6/2; f. 1996; Dir ZLATKO BARŠ.

## Trade and Industry

### GOVERNMENT AGENCIES

**Privatization Agency of the Federation of Bosnia and Herzegovina:** Sarajevo, Alipašina 41; tel. (71) 212884; fax (71) 212883; e-mail apfbih@bih.net.ba; internet www.apf.com.ba; Dir ADNAD MUJAGIĆ.

### DEVELOPMENT ORGANIZATION

**Energoinvest—RO ITEN** (Institute for Thermal and Nuclear Technologies): 71000 Sarajevo, Bratstva Jedinstva; f. 1961; research and devt in the fields of thermal and nuclear technology.

### CHAMBERS OF COMMERCE

**Chamber of Economy of Bosnia and Herzegovina:** 71000 Sarajevo, Mis Irbina 13; tel. (71) 663631; fax (71) 663632; Pres. ANTE DOMAZET.

**Chamber of Commerce of the Serb Republic:** Banja Luka; Pres. BOZO ANTIĆ.

### UTILITIES

#### Electricity

**Elektroprivreda of Bosnia and Herzegovina Ltd:** 71000 Sarajevo, Vilsonovo šetalište 15; tel. (71) 472481; fax (71) 654266; generation, transmission and distribution of electric energy; Dir-Gen. MEHO OBRADOVIĆ.

#### Gas

**Bosnia and Herzegovina Gas:** Sarajevo; Dir MIRSAD HANOVIĆ.

### TRADE UNIONS

**Independent Trade Union Association of Bosnia and Herzegovina:** Sarajevo; Pres. SULEJMAN HRLE.

**Independent Union of Professional Journalists:** Sarajevo; f. Dec. 1994; Chair. MEHMED HALILOVIĆ; Vice-Pres. BORO KONTIĆ.

**Serb Republic Trade Union Federation:** Banja Luka; legalized 1996; Chair. CEDO GOLAS.

## Transport

### RAILWAYS

At the beginning of the 1990s the railway system consisted of some 1,030 km of track, of which 75% was electrified. Much of the system was damaged or destroyed during the civil war, but in July 1996 the Sarajevo–Mostar service was restored and in 1997 the Tuzla–Doboj and Tuzla–Brčko services were reopened. Following the outbreak of hostilities, the state railway company was divided into three regional state-owned companies: the **Bosnia and Herzegovina Railway Company (ZBH),** based in Sarajevo; the **Herzeg-Bosnia Railway Company (ZHB),** based in the Croat-majority part of the Federation; and the **Serb Republic Railway and Transport Company (ZTP),** based in Banja Luka.

## ROADS

The transport infrastructure in Bosnia and Herzegovina was badly damaged during the civil war of 1992–95. Some 35% of the country's roads and 40% of its bridges were affected by the conflict. A new Transportation Corporation was established (with its headquarters in Sarajevo), under the terms of the Dayton accords, in order to organize and operate roads, ports and railways on the territory of the two entities. The agreement also provided for the construction of a new road linking the Goražde enclave, in the east of Bosnia and Herzegovina, with the rest of the Federation.

**Transportation Corporation:** Sarajevo; public corporation.

## CIVIL AVIATION

The country has an international airport at Sarajevo, and three smaller civil airports, at Tuzla, Banja Luka and Mostar. Civil aviation was severely disrupted by the 1992–95 civil war. Commercial flights resumed to Sarajevo in August 1996, to Banja Luka in November 1997 and to Mostar in July 1998; negotiations to reopen the airport in Tuzla proved unsuccessful throughout 1997. In March 1997 a new airline (RS Airlines) was founded in the Serb Republic, and in June it was announced that a new airport at Dubrave, near Tuzla, was to be built.

**Air Bosna:** 71000 Sarajevo, 6 Cemalasa; tel. (71) 650794; fax (71) 667953; regular services to Croatia, Germany, Slovenia, Sweden, Turkey and the Federal Republic of Yugoslavia; Man. Dir MUSTAFA EMINEFENDIĆ.

**Air Commerce:** charter flights from Sarajevo to Turkey and Egypt, and scheduled service to Switzerland; Dir MOHAMED ABADŽIĆ.

**Air Srpska:** f. 1999; flights from Banja Luka airport to Yugoslavia.

**RS Airlines:** Pale; f. 1997; flights from Banja Luka airport to Yugoslavia, Greece, Hungary, Romania, Bulgaria and Russia; Dir JOVAN TINTOR.

# BOTSWANA

## Introductory Survey

### Location, Climate, Language, Religion, Flag, Capital

The Republic of Botswana is a land-locked country in southern Africa, with South Africa to the south and east, Zimbabwe to the north-east and Namibia to the west and north. A short section of the northern frontier adjoins Zambia. The climate is generally sub-tropical, with hot summers. Annual rainfall averages about 457 mm (18 ins), varying from 635 mm (25 ins) in the north to 228 mm (9 ins) or less in the western Kalahari desert. The country is largely near-desert, and most of its inhabitants live along the eastern border, close to the main railway line. English is the official language, and Setswana the national language. Most of the population follow traditional animist beliefs, but several Christian churches are also represented. The national flag (proportions 3 by 2) consists of a central horizontal stripe of black, edged with white, between two blue stripes. The capital is Gaborone.

### Recent History

Botswana was formerly Bechuanaland, which became a British protectorate, at the request of the local rulers, in 1885. It was administered as one of the High Commission Territories in southern Africa, the others being the colony of Basutoland (now Lesotho) and the protectorate of Swaziland. The British Act of Parliament that established the Union of South Africa in 1910 also allowed for the inclusion in South Africa of the three High Commission Territories, on condition that the local inhabitants were consulted. Until 1960 successive South African Governments asked for the transfer of the three territories, but the native chiefs always objected to such a scheme.

Within Bechuanaland, gradual progress was made towards self-government, mainly through nominated advisory bodies. A new Constitution was introduced in December 1960, and a Legislative Council (partly elected, partly appointed) first met in June 1961. Bechuanaland was made independent of High Commission rule in September 1963, and the office of High Commissioner was abolished in August 1964. The seat of government was transferred from Mafeking (now Mafikeng), in South Africa, to Gaberones (now Gaborone) in February 1965. On 1 March 1965 internal self-government was achieved, and the territory's first direct election, for a Legislative Assembly, was held on the basis of universal adult suffrage. Of the Assembly's 31 seats, 28 were won by the Bechuanaland Democratic Party (BDP or Domkrag), founded in 1962. The leader of the BDP, Seretse Khama, was sworn in as the territory's first Prime Minister. Bechuanaland became the independent Republic of Botswana, within the Commonwealth, on 30 September 1966, with Sir Seretse Khama (as he had become) taking office as the country's first President, while the Legislative Assembly was renamed the National Assembly. The BDP, restyled the Botswana Democratic Party at independence, won elections to the National Assembly, with little opposition, in 1969, 1974 and 1979.

Khama died in July 1980, and was succeeded as President by Dr Quett Masire (later Sir Ketumile Masire), hitherto Vice-President and Minister of Finance. Following elections to the National Assembly in September 1984, at which the BDP again achieved a decisive victory, Masire was re-elected President by the legislature. However, the BDP fared badly in local government elections which were held simultaneously with the parliamentary elections, apparently reflecting discontent at the country's high level of unemployment. An unprecedented outbreak of rioting, in March 1987, was similarly attributed by observers to popular dissatisfaction with the Government as a result of increasing unemployment; the Government accused the principal opposition party, the Botswana National Front (BNF), of fomenting the unrest. At a referendum in September a large majority endorsed amendments to the electoral system, as defined by the Constitution, although the BNF boycotted the vote.

Despite widespread labour unrest during 1989, in October the BDP received 65% of the votes cast at a general election to the National Assembly, winning 27 of the 30 elective seats (the remaining three seats were won by the BNF), and the new legislature re-elected Masire for a third term as President. In November 1991 the Government dismissed some 12,000 members of public-service trade unions who had been campaigning for wage increases.

In March 1992 the Vice-President and Chairman of the BDP, Peter Mmusi, resigned as Vice-President and Minister of Local Government and Lands, while the party's Secretary-General, Daniel Kwelagobe, resigned as Minister of Agriculture, having been accused of corruption involving the illegal transfer of land. Festus Mogae, the Minister of Finance and Development Planning, was appointed as the new Vice-President. In June Mmusi and Kwelagobe were suspended from the Central Committee of the BDP; both were, however, re-elected to their former positions within the party at the BDP congress in July 1993. In early 1993 the Deputy Minister of Finance and Development Planning was forced to resign, apparently implicated in allegations of improper financial transactions involving the Botswana Housing Corporation. In the same year it was revealed that seven government ministers were among the debtors of the National Development Bank, which was reported to be in financial difficulties.

For the general election of 15 October 1994 the number of directly-elective seats in the National Assembly was increased to 40. The BDP, which received 53.1% of the votes cast, won 26 seats (three government ministers failed to secure re-election, and several members were returned with considerably reduced majorities), while the BNF, which obtained 37.7% of the votes, increased its representation to 13 seats. More than 70% of registered voters participated in the election. In general, the BDP retained its dominance in rural areas, while the BNF received strong support in urban constituencies. The National Assembly re-elected Masire to the presidency on 17 October. One week later the Assembly elected four additional parliamentary members. The new Cabinet, the composition of which was announced on the same day, included two of these, as well as Kwelagobe, who had been acquitted by the High Court in connection with the 1992 allegations.

Rioting, which had begun in January 1995 in Mochudi (to the north of Gaborone) following the release without charge of three people who had been detained on suspicion of involvement in a ritual murder, spread to the capital in February. One person was killed during three days of violent confrontations; shops were looted and government vehicles damaged. The BNF denied government assertions that it had incited the unrest, countering that the demonstrations reflected frustrations at the high level of unemployment and other social problems.

In June 1995 the Governor of the central Bank of Botswana stated that the country's economic strategies had to be revised if growth were to be restored and social unrest and political instability avoided. In the following month a BNF motion expressing 'no confidence' in the Government—prompted by the alleged involvement of members of the Masire administration in the National Development Bank scandal and in other questionable financial affairs, as well as by the Government's apparent failure to address social concerns—was defeated in the National Assembly. Also in July the Minister of Presidential Affairs and Public Administration, Ponatshego Kedikilwe, was elected Chairman of the BDP (the post had remained vacant since the death of Mmusi prior to the 1994 elections).

A number of constitutional amendments, which had been proposed during 1995–96, were adopted in August and September 1997. In August the National Assembly formally approved revisions restricting the presidential mandate to two terms of office and providing for the automatic succession to the presidency of the Vice-President, in the event of the death or resignation of the President. Further amendments approved by the National Assembly, reforming aspects of the electoral system, were endorsed in a national referendum in September. The reforms reduced the age of eligibility to vote from 21 to 18 years and provided for the introduction of votes for Batswana resident abroad, and for the establishment of an independent electoral commission; opposition parties had hitherto been critical of the prevailing system, whereby the election supervisor was an appointee of the President's office.

In early November 1997 Masire formally announced his intention to retire from politics in March 1998; in accordance with the constitutional amendment adopted three months earlier, Vice-President Mogae was temporarily to assume the presidency pending the holding of elections in 1999. Mogae was inaugurated as President on 1 April 1998 and subsequently appointed a new Cabinet, in which the only new minister was Lt-Gen. Seretse Khama Ian Khama, son of Botswana's first President (the late Sir Seretse Khama) and hitherto Commander of the Botswana Defence Force (BDF). Ian Khama received the portfolio of presidential affairs and public administration, and was later designated as Mogae's Vice-President, subject to his election to the National Assembly. Kedikilwe, who had been favoured for the vice-presidency by certain prominent members of the BDP leadership, was appointed Minister of Finance and Development Planning. Ian Khama was elected to the National Assembly in July, and was sworn in as Vice-President in the same month.

Meanwhile, hostility between Kenneth Koma, the leader of the BNF, and his deputy, Michael Dingake, had led to a split in the party. At the BNF's annual congress in April 1998 relations deteriorated over the issue of dissident members who had been expelled from the party. Koma, supported by the dissidents, ordered the expulsion from the party of central committee members. His actions were upheld by the party's constitution, and ultimately on appeal by the High Court. In June members of the dissolved central committee formed the Botswana Congress Party (BCP), under the leadership of Dingake. The BCP was declared the official opposition in mid-July, after 11 of the BNF's 13 deputies joined the new party.

The Government's attempts to relocate Bushmen from their homeland within the Central Kalahari Game Reserve to a new settlement outside the reserve provoked international concern during 1996–98; it was claimed that officials had forced many Bushmen to move by disconnecting water supplies and threatening military intervention.

In late August 1999 President Mogae dissolved the National Assembly in preparation for the holding of a general election in mid-October. In early September, to the surprise and consternation of the opposition parties, Mogae declared a state of emergency, the purpose of which was to reconvene the legislature in order to amend the Electoral Act, thus permitting the Independent Electoral Commission (IEC) to complete its work and prevent the disenfranchisement of around 60,000 Batswana. The general election was held, as scheduled, on 16 October, despite opposition demands that it be postponed owing to the Government's apparent disregard for correct electoral procedure. The BDP, which received 57.2% of the votes, increased its representation in the National Assembly from 26 to 33 seats, while the number of seats held by the BNF (with 26.0% of the votes) fell significantly to only six seats, and the BCP (having received 11.9%) obtained just one seat. The IEC declared that the election had been conducted in a free and fair manner and recorded that 77.3% of the electorate had participated in the polls. Mogae was re-elected to the presidency by the new National Assembly on 20 October and announced the formation of a new Cabinet the following day. In December Mogae provoked outrage among the opposition parties when he granted Vice-President Khama an unprecedented one-year sabbatical leave, effective from 1 January 2000. The BCP subsequently announced that it would challenge the legality of Mogae's decision in the High Court.

Although, as one of the 'front-line' states, Botswana did not have diplomatic links with the apartheid regime in South Africa, it was (and remains) heavily dependent on its neighbour for trade and communications. Botswana is a member of the Southern African Development Community (SADC—see p. 263), which superseded the Southern African Development Co-ordination Conference (SADCC), in 1992. The SADC, of which South Africa became a member in 1994, has its headquarters in Gaborone.

From independence, it was the Botswana Government's stated policy not to permit any guerrilla groups to operate from Botswanan territory. Relations with South Africa deteriorated in May 1984, when Masire accused the South African Government of exerting pressure on Botswana to sign a non-aggression pact, aimed at preventing the alleged use of Botswana's territory by guerrilla forces of the (then outlawed) African National Congress of South Africa (ANC). In the second half of the 1980s South African forces launched a number of raids on alleged ANC bases in Botswana, causing several deaths. Owing to Botswana's vulnerable position, however, the Government did not commit itself to the imposition of economic sanctions against South Africa when this was recommended by the SADCC in August 1986. In 1988–89 Botswana took action against the extension onto its territory of hostilities between South African government and anti-apartheid forces. Two South African commandos, who had allegedly opened fire on Botswana security forces while engaged in a raid, were sentenced to 10 years' imprisonment; nine South Africans were expelled for 'security reasons', and five ANC members were convicted on firearms charges. It was reported in August 1989 that the South African army had erected an electrified fence along a 24-km section of the South Africa–Botswana border, in order to halt the reputed threat of guerrilla infiltration into South Africa via Botswana.

With the dismantling of apartheid in the first half of the 1990s, Botswana's relations with South Africa improved markedly and full diplomatic relations were established in June 1994. President Nelson Mandela of South Africa visited Botswana in September 1995; the need for the two countries to co-operate in combating crime was identified as a priority during discussions on issues of mutual concern. Meanwhile, in August 1994 it was announced that the 'front-line' states were to form a political and security wing within the SADC. In April 1999 Botswana and South Africa signed a bilateral agreement on the management of their adjacent national parks.

In August 1998 Botswana participated in attempts made by the SADC to resolve a political crisis in Lesotho, where opposition parties were demanding the annulment of elections held in May of that year. In August, as protests intensified, a commission of inquiry, composed of representatives from Botswana, South Africa and Zimbabwe, was charged with investigating allegations of electoral fraud. The publication of the commission's report in mid-September failed to ease the heightening tension; the commission concluded that, despite evidence of irregularities, there were insufficient grounds to declare the elections invalid. Following an increase in civil and military unrest and reports of an imminent coup attempt, on 22 September 200–300 members of the BDF and 600 South African troops entered Lesotho, in response to requests from the Prime Minister, Pakalitha Mosisili. The SADC-sponsored military intervention encountered strong resistance from dissident members of the Lesotho armed forces and civilians, who resented what was perceived as an unwarranted foreign invasion. After three days of heavy fighting and looting, in which more than 70 people died, relative calm was restored to the devastated capital, Maseru. In early 1999 the role of the BDF troops in Lesotho was the subject of debate in Botswana itself, and in May all the remaining SADC forces were withdrawn. A group of instructors from Botswana and South Africa remained in Lesotho in an advisory and training capacity and was to assist in dealing with any recurrence of internal unrest prior to the general election (scheduled to take place in 2000).

In 1983, following allegations that armed dissidents from Zimbabwe were being harboured among Zimbabwean refugees encamped in Botswana, the Botswana Government agreed to impose stricter restrictions on the refugees. In May Botswana and Zimbabwe established full diplomatic relations. The first meeting of the Botswana-Zimbabwe joint commission for co-operation was held in October 1984. A new influx of refugees, following the Zimbabwe general election in July 1985, threatened to strain relations between the two countries. In May 1988, however, Masire expressed confidence that the Zimbabwean refugees would return to their country as a result of an apparent improvement in the political climate in Zimbabwe. Nevertheless, in April 1989 about 600 Zimbabwean refugees remained in Botswana; at the end of that month the Botswana Government announced that refugee status for Zimbabwean nationals was to be revoked; by September almost all former Zimbabwean refugees had reportedly left Botswana. In the mid-1990s, however, the Government expressed concern at the growing number of illegal immigrants in the country, the majority of whom were from Zimbabwe; of more than 40,000 illegal immigrants repatriated during 1995, more than 14,000 were Zimbabwean.

Following Namibian independence, in July 1990 it was announced that a commission for bilateral co-operation was to be established by Botswana and Namibia. In 1992, however, a border dispute developed between the two countries regarding their rival territorial claims over a small island (Sedudu-Kasikili) in the Chobe river. In early 1995 the two states agreed to present the issue of the demarcation of their joint border for arbitration at the International Court of Justice (ICJ, in The Hague, Netherlands), and in February 1996 the two countries signed an agreement committing themselves in advance to the Court's eventual judgment. Meanwhile, Namibia appealed to Botswana to remove its troops—stated by the Botswana authorities to be anti-poaching patrols—and national flag from the island. In the following month the two countries agreed joint measures aimed at deterring smuggling and illegal border crossings. None the less, what were perceived as attempts by Botswana to extend the role and capabilities of its armed forces remained a source of friction between the two countries, although Botswana emphasized that a principal aim of such expansion was to enable its military to fulfil a wider regional and international peace-keeping role. Namibia's decision to construct a pipeline to take water from the Okavango river caused some concern in Botswana in 1996–97. (The river feeds the Okavango delta, which is an important habitat for Botswana's varied wildlife, and therefore of great importance to the tourist industry.) In early 1997 it was reported that Namibia had been angered by Botswana's erection of a fence along Namibia's Caprivi Strip, which separates the two countries to the north; Botswana insisted, however, that the fence was simply a measure to control the spread of livestock diseases. In January 1998 an emergency meeting of the Botswana-Namibia joint commission on defence and security was held to discuss ownership of another island (Situngu) in the Chobe river, following allegations by Namibia that the BDF had occupied the island and was stealing crops planted by Namibian farmers resident there. Representatives from both countries recommended that a joint technical commission be set up to demarcate the joint border; discussions regarding its establishment took place in mid-May. In late 1998 relations between the two countries were further strained by the arrival of refugees (a number of whom were reportedly leading political dissidents) in Botswana from the Caprivi Strip in Namibia. President Mogae rejected Namibian demands for the extradition of the refugees, whose number had increased to more than 2,000 by early 1999. In May, however, a formal agreement was signed by the two Governments under which prominent dissidents among the refugees would be allowed to leave Botswana for another country and an amnesty extended to other refugees returning to Namibia. At a meeting of the Botswana-Namibia joint commission on defence and security held in August, both countries reported that good progress was being made on the curbing of cross-border crime and stressed their commitment to strengthening ties and improving co-operation at all levels. In December the ICJ granted Botswana control over Sedudu-Kasikili.

## Government

Legislative power is vested in Parliament, consisting of the President and the National Assembly. The National Assembly is elected for a term of five years and comprises 40 members directly elected by universal adult suffrage, together with four members who are elected by the National Assembly from a list of candidates submitted by the President; the President and the Attorney-General are also *ex-officio* members of the Assembly. Executive power is vested in the President, elected by the Assembly for its duration. The President is restricted to two terms of office. He appoints and leads a Cabinet, which is responsible to the Assembly. The President has powers to delay implementation of legislation for six months, and certain matters also have to be referred to the 15-member House of Chiefs for approval, although this advisory body has no power of veto. Local government is effected through nine district councils and four town councils.

## Defence

Military service is voluntary. In August 1999 the total strength of the Botswana Defence Force was some 9,000, comprising an army of 8,500 and an air force of 500. In addition, there was a paramilitary police force of 1,000. There are plans to enlarge the strength of the army to 10,000 men. Projected budgetary expenditure on defence for 1999 was P990m.

## Economic Affairs

In 1997, according to estimates by the World Bank, Botswana's gross national product (GNP), measured at average 1995–97 prices, was US $5,070m., equivalent to $3,310 per head. During 1990–97, it was estimated, GNP per head increased, in real terms, at an average annual rate of 1.3%. Over the same period the population increased by an average of 2.6% per year. In 1998 GNP was estimated at $5,600m. ($3,653 per head). Botswana's gross domestic product (GDP) increased, in real terms, at an average annual rate of 10.3% during 1980–90 (one of the highest growth rates in the world), and by an average of 4.8% yearly in 1990–98. Real GDP growth in 1997/98 was 8.3%, and the government estimate for 1998/99 was 6.0%.

Agriculture (including hunting, forestry and fishing) contributed 3.0% of GDP in 1997/98, according to provisional figures, and engaged 15.6% of the employed labour force in 1996. The principal agricultural activity is cattle-raising (principally beef production), which supports about one-half of the population and contributes more than 80% of agricultural GDP. The main subsistence crops are vegetables, pulses and roots and tubers. Botswana, which is not self-sufficient in basic foods, imported some 133,000 metric tons of cereals in 1993. According to the World Bank, agricultural GDP rose at an average annual rate of 0.1% in 1990–98. The GDP of the sector decreased by 1.2% in 1997/98, according to provisional figures.

Industry (including mining, manufacturing, construction and power) engaged 25.6% of the employed labour force in 1996 and, according to provisional figures, provided 48.6% of GDP in 1997/98. According to the World Bank, industrial GDP increased at an average annual rate of 3.1% in 1990–98. Industrial GDP grew by 8.3% in 1997/98, according to provisional figures.

Mining contributed 36.6% of GDP in 1997/98, according to provisional figures, although the sector engaged only 4.3% of the employed labour force in 1996. In terms of value, Botswana is the world's largest producer of diamonds (which accounted for 73.8% of export earnings in 1997); copper-nickel matte and soda ash are also exported. In addition, coal, gold, cobalt and salt are mined, and there are known reserves of plutonium, asbestos, chromite, fluorspar, iron, manganese, potash, silver, talc and uranium. In 1998 a new mineral code included measures to encourage non-diamond mining projects. According to provisional figures, the GDP of the mining sector increased, in real terms, at an average rate of 3.3% per year in 1990/91–1996/97; growth of 9.5% was recorded in 1997/98.

Manufacturing engaged 8.5% of the employed labour force in 1996 and provided 4.7% of GDP in 1997/98, according to provisional figures. Based on the gross value of output, the principal branches of manufacturing in the year to June 1993 were food products (accounting for 38.7% of the total), beverages (13.2%) and textiles and clothing (10.9%). Car manufacturing has become increasingly important since 1994 (contributing 11.4% of the value of total exports in 1997). The GDP of the manufacturing sector increased at an average rate of 2.6% per year in 1990–96; growth of 4.7% was recorded in 1997/98, according to provisional figures.

The services sector contributed 48.4% of GDP in 1997/98, according to provisional figures, and engaged 58.7% of the employed labour force in 1996. Within the sector, tourism is of considerable importance, and the tourist industry is the third largest source of total foreign exchange. According to the World Bank, the GDP of the services sector increased at an average annual rate of 7.1% in 1990–98. Growth was 8.9% in 1997/98, according to provisional figures.

Energy is derived principally from fuel wood and coal; the use of solar power is currently being promoted as an alternative source of energy. According to provisional figures, imports of fuels accounted for 5.6% of the value of total imports in 1997.

In 1998 Botswana recorded a visible trade surplus of US $77.5m., and there was a surplus of $170.1m. on the current account of the balance of payments. In 1997 countries of the Southern African Customs Union (SACU—see below) provided 72.5% of imports; another major source was the Republic of Korea. European countries took 79.7% of exports in 1997; other important purchasers were the countries of SACU. The principal exports in that year were diamonds, vehicles and copper-nickel matte. The principal imports were vehicles and transport equipment, machinery and electrical equipment, food, beverages and tobacco, metals and metal products, chemicals and rubber products, textiles and footwear, wood and paper products, and fuels.

In the financial year to 31 March 1998 the central Government recorded a budgetary surplus of P664.9m. Botswana's external debt totalled US $562.0m. at the end of 1997, of which $522.0m. was long-term public debt. In 1996 the cost of debt-servicing was equivalent to 5.2% of the value of exports of goods and services. The average annual rate of inflation was 10.1% in 1992–98; consumer prices increased by an annual average of 10.1% in 1996, by 8.7% in 1997 and by 6.7% in 1998. About 21% of the labour force were unemployed in mid-1997.

Botswana is a member of the Southern African Development Community (see p. 263) and (with Lesotho, Namibia, South Africa and Swaziland) of SACU.

Botswana's high rate of growth during the 1980s was based predominantly on the successful exploitation of diamonds and other minerals. However, domestic factors, such as a vulnerability to drought, in conjunction with the world-wide economic recession of the early 1990s, depressed Botswana's economy and exemplified the need to reduce dependence on diamond-mining, to diversify agricultural production and to broaden the manufacturing base. By the mid-1990s, a return to growth had enabled the resumption of both public and private construction projects, which were expected to generate much-needed employment opportunities. Increased capacity at the Jwaneng diamond mine contributed to the strong performance of the economy in 1995/96. In the first half of 1998, however, diamond exports declined, as a result of the economic crisis in major Asian markets, most significantly Japan. The encouragement of private-sector growth, particularly in the manufacturing sector, was a key element of Botswana's eighth National Development Plan (1997/98–2002/03), which was presented in 1997 with the theme 'sustainable economic diversification'. Botswana's persistent dependence on the diamond sector in 1999, despite efforts to diversify its economic base, remained a source of potential weakness. The recovery of the diamond market in that year, together with an increase in diamond production, owing to the imminent completion of the Orapa mine expansion project, led to continued strong growth in the Botswana economy. In August the Botswana Government announced plans to establish the country as an international financial services centre for southern Africa; Botswana's proximity to South Africa, substantial tax incentives, and the stability of a well-established democratic system of government were all expected to aid the realization of these plans.

### Social Welfare

Compared with those of many other countries of the region, Botswana's health services are well-developed. In 1997 there were 14 primary hospitals, six district hospitals, three mission hospitals, three mine hospitals, two national referral hospitals, one private hospital and one mental hospital. In addition, there were 209 clinics, 314 health posts and 687 mobile health stops. In that year 94 registered medical specialists, 292 medical officers, 34 dentists and 3,866 nurses were working in the country. Medical treatment for children under 12 years of age is provided free of charge. Old-age pensions for all persons over 65 years of age were introduced in 1996. Acquired Immunodeficiency Syndrome (AIDS) had reached epidemic proportions in Botswana by the mid-1990s and, according to UN estimates released in 1998, was projected to reduce life expectancy from 61 years in 1990–95 to some 41 years by 2000–05. In early 1999 it was reported that nearly 60% of Bostwana's medical and paediatric wards were occupied by patients suffering from AIDS. Expenditure on health by the central Government in 1997/98 was estimated at P391.4m. (equivalent to 5.1% of total government spending).

### Education

Although education is not compulsory in Botswana, enrolment ratios are high. Primary education, which is provided free of charge, begins at six years of age and lasts for up to seven years. Secondary education, beginning at the age of 14, lasts for a further five years, comprising a first cycle of three years and a second of two years. As a proportion of the school-age population, the total enrolment at primary and secondary schools increased from 52% in 1975 to the equivalent of 94% (boys 93%; girls 96%) in 1996. Enrolment at primary schools in 1997 included 96.7% of children in the relevant age-group (boys 95.7%; girls 97.7%), while the comparable ratio for secondary enrolment was 53.3% (boys 51.0%; girls 55.5%). By the late 1990s the Government provided universal access to 10 years of basic education. Botswana has the highest teacher-pupil ratio in Africa, but continues to rely heavily on expatriate secondary school teachers. In 1999 tertiary education was provided by 30 technical and vocational training centres, including health institutes, four teacher-training colleges, two further education colleges and a university (which was attended by 8,007 students in 1997).

According to estimates by UNESCO, the average rate of adult illiteracy in 1995 was 30.2% (males 19.5%; females 40.1%). Budget estimates for 1997/98 allocated P1,842.0m. to education (representing 24.2% of total expenditure by the central Government).

### Public Holidays

**2000:** 1–2 January (New Year), 21–24 April (Easter), 1 May (Labour Day), 1 June (Ascension Day), 1 July (Sir Seretse Khama Day), 15–16 July (for President's Day), 30 September (Botswana Day), 25–26 December (Christmas).

**2001:** 1–2 January (New Year), 13–16 April (Easter), 1 May (Labour Day), 24 May (Ascension Day), 1 July (Sir Seretse Khama Day), 15–16 July (for President's Day), 30 September (Botswana Day), 25–26 December (Christmas).

### Weights and Measures

The metric system is in use.

# Statistical Survey

Source (unless otherwise stated): Central Statistics Office, Private Bag 0024, Gaborone; tel. 352200; fax 352201.

## Area and Population

**AREA, POPULATION AND DENSITY**

| | |
|---|---|
| Area (sq km) | 581,730* |
| Population (census results) | |
| 16 August 1981 | 941,027† |
| 21 August 1991 | |
| Males | 634,400 |
| Females | 692,396 |
| Total | 1,326,796 |
| Population (official estimates at 19 August) | |
| 1995 | 1,458,828 |
| 1996 | 1,495,993 |
| 1997 | 1,533,393 |
| Density (per sq km) at August 1997 | 2.6 |

* 224,607 sq miles.

† Excluding 42,069 citizens absent from the country during enumeration.

**POPULATION BY ADMINISTRATIVE DISTRICT**
(August 1997 estimates)

| | | | |
|---|---|---|---|
| Barolong | 19,837 | Lobatse | 29,872 |
| Central | 457,349 | Ngamiland | 62,403 |
| Chobe | 16,845 | Ngwaketse | 143,370 |
| Francistown | 88,195 | North-East | 47,312 |
| Gaborone | 183,487 | Okavango | 41,687 |
| Ghanzi | 27,099 | Orapa | 10,244 |
| Jwaneng | 14,866 | Selebi-Phikwe | 45,651 |
| Kgalagadi | 34,537 | South-East | 54,091 |
| Kgatleng | 63,712 | Sowa | 3,154 |
| Kweneng | 189,672 | | |

**PRINCIPAL TOWNS** (estimated population, August 1988)

| | | | |
|---|---|---|---|
| Gaborone (capital) | 110,973 | Kanye | 26,300 |
| Francistown | 49,396 | Mahalapye | 26,239 |
| Selebi-Phikwe | 46,490 | Lobatse | 25,689 |
| Molepolole | 29,212 | Maun | 18,470 |
| Serowe | 28,267 | Ramotswa | 17,961 |
| Mochudi | 26,320 | | |

**August 1991** (census results): Gaborone 133,468; Francistown 65,244; Selebi-Phikwe 39,772; Lobatse 26,052.

**BIRTHS AND DEATHS** (UN estimates, annual averages)

| | 1980–85 | 1985–90 | 1990–95 |
|---|---|---|---|
| Birth rate (per 1,000) | 44.1 | 40.2 | 36.8 |
| Death rate (per 1,000) | 9.5 | 7.7 | 8.0 |

**Expectation of life** (UN estimates, years at birth, 1990–95): 61.2 (males 59.5; females 62.9).

Source: UN, *World Population Prospects: The 1998 Revision*.

**ECONOMICALLY ACTIVE POPULATION***
(sample survey, persons aged 12 years and over, year ending August 1996)

| | Males | Females | Total |
|---|---|---|---|
| Agriculture, hunting, forestry and fishing | 37,050 | 16,729 | 53,779 |
| Mining and quarrying | 12,754 | 2,379 | 15,133 |
| Manufacturing | 14,157 | 15,373 | 29,530 |
| Electricity, gas and water supply | 2,633 | 172 | 2,805 |
| Construction | 28,096 | 12,929 | 41,025 |
| Wholesale and retail trade; repair of motor vehicles, motorcycles and personal and household goods | 19,526 | 24,615 | 44,141 |
| Hotels and restaurants | 2,524 | 7,491 | 10,015 |
| Transport, storage and communications | 5,778 | 1,937 | 7,715 |
| Financial intermediation | 1,781 | 2,315 | 4,096 |
| Real estate, renting and business services | 5,766 | 1,875 | 7,641 |
| Public administration and defence; compulsory social security | 37,928 | 22,029 | 59,957 |
| Education | 12,377 | 20,854 | 33,231 |
| Health and social work | 2,096 | 7,280 | 9,376 |
| Other community, social and personal service activities | 4,330 | 2,977 | 7,307 |
| Private households with employed persons | 1,957 | 16,997 | 18,954 |
| Extra-territorial organizations and bodies | 197 | 27 | 224 |
| Activities not adequately defined | 351 | 125 | 476 |
| **Total employed** | 189,301 | 156,104 | 345,405 |
| Unemployed | 45,461 | 49,067 | 94,528 |
| **Total labour force** | 234,762 | 205,171 | 439,933 |

* Excluding members of the armed forces and those not actively seeking work.

Source: Labour Statistics Unit, Central Statistics Office.

**Mid-1998** (estimates, '000 persons): Agriculture, etc. 309; Total labour force 689. (Source: FAO, *Production Yearbook*).

## Agriculture

**PRINCIPAL CROPS** ('000 metric tons)

| | 1996 | 1997 | 1998 |
|---|---|---|---|
| Wheat* | 1 | 1 | 1 |
| Maize | 23† | 12 | 1† |
| Millet* | 4 | 2 | 1 |
| Sorghum | 55* | 17 | 7* |
| Roots and tubers* | 9 | 10 | 10 |
| Pulses* | 16 | 15 | 12 |
| Cottonseed* | 2 | 2 | 1 |
| Cotton (lint)* | 1 | 1 | 1 |
| Vegetables* | 17 | 16 | 15 |
| Fruit* | 12 | 11 | 8 |

* FAO estimate(s). † Unofficial figure.

Source: FAO, *Production Yearbook*.

**LIVESTOCK** (FAO estimates, '000 head, year ending September)

| | 1996 | 1997 | 1998 |
|---|---|---|---|
| Cattle | 2,400 | 2,420 | 2,330 |
| Horses | 32 | 33 | 33 |
| Asses | 232 | 235 | 238 |
| Sheep | 240 | 250 | 240 |
| Goats | 1,850 | 1,870 | 1,820 |
| Pigs | 3 | 4 | 4 |

Poultry (FAO estimates, million): 2 in 1996; 2 in 1997; 2 in 1998.

Source: FAO, *Production Yearbook*.

**LIVESTOCK PRODUCTS** (FAO estimates, '000 metric tons)

| | 1996 | 1997 | 1998 |
|---|---|---|---|
| Beef and veal | 44 | 46 | 40 |
| Goat meat | 5 | 5 | 5 |
| Poultry meat | 7 | 7 | 7 |
| Other meat | 11 | 11 | 11 |
| Cows' milk | 102 | 102 | 98 |
| Goats' milk | 3 | 3 | 3 |
| Cheese | 2 | 2 | 2 |
| Butter and ghee | 1 | 1 | 1 |
| Hen eggs | 1 | 2 | 2 |
| Cattle hides | 6 | 6 | 5 |

Source: FAO, *Production Yearbook*.

# Forestry

**ROUNDWOOD REMOVALS** ('000 cubic metres, excl. bark)

| | 1995 | 1996 | 1997 |
|---|---|---|---|
| Industrial wood | 96 | 98 | 100 |
| Fuel wood | 1,450 | 1,484 | 1,518 |
| **Total** | 1,546 | 1,582 | 1,618 |

Source: FAO, *Yearbook of Forest Products*.

# Fishing

(FAO estimates, metric tons, live weight)

| | 1995 | 1996 | 1997 |
|---|---|---|---|
| Total catch (freshwater fishes) | 2,000 | 2,100 | 2,000 |

Source: FAO, *Yearbook of Fishery Statistics*.

# Mining

(metric tons, unless otherwise indicated)

| | 1996 | 1997 | 1998 |
|---|---|---|---|
| Diamonds ('000 carats) | 17,707 | 20,121 | 19,773 |
| Copper* | 20,979 | 18,350 | 19,432 |
| Nickel* | 17,461 | 14,996 | 15,593 |
| Cobalt* | 405 | 348 | 352 |
| Soda ash | 119,137 | 199,990 | 195,500 |
| Salt | 93,886 | 184,533 | 214,700 |
| Coal | 763,000 | 776,917 | 928,100 |
| Clay (cu metres) | 81,900 | 73,700 | 82,500 |
| Crushed stone (cu metres) | 845,526 | 1,091,877 | 997,244 |

* Figures refer to the metal content of ores.

Source: *Mining Journal*.

# Industry

**SELECTED PRODUCTS**

| | 1994 | 1995 | 1996 |
|---|---|---|---|
| Beer ('000 hectolitres) | 1,305 | 1,366 | 1,351 |
| Soft drinks ('000 hectolitres) | 278 | 293 | 308 |
| Electric energy (million kWh) | 1,088 | 1,070* | n.a. |

* Provisional or estimated figure.

Source: UN, *Industrial Commodity Statistics Yearbook*.

# Finance

**CURRENCY AND EXCHANGE RATES**

**Monetary Units**

100 thebe = 1 pula (P).

**Sterling, Dollar and Euro Equivalents** (30 September 1999)

£1 sterling = 7.464 pula;
US $1 = 4.533 pula;
€1 = 4.835 pula;
100 pula = £13.40 = $22.06 = €20.68.

**Average Exchange Rate** (pula per US $)

1996 3.3242
1997 3.6508
1998 4.2259

**BUDGET** (million pula, year ending 31 March)

| Revenue* | 1995/96 | 1996/97 | 1997/98 |
|---|---|---|---|
| Taxation | 4,016.2 | 5,198.5 | 6,762.7 |
| Mineral revenues | 2,591.4 | 3,640.1 | 4,681.1 |
| Customs pool revenues | 829.4 | 896.2 | 1,186.1 |
| Non-mineral income tax | 356.9 | 385.0 | 537.4 |
| General sales tax | 219.1 | 248.4 | 327.9 |
| Other current revenue | 1,411.1 | 2,113.3 | 1,406.5 |
| Interest | 231.6 | 235.4 | 257.1 |
| Other property income | 1,063.5 | 1,740.3 | 984.5 |
| Fees, charges, etc. | 102.7 | 111.6 | 137.9 |
| Sales of fixed assets and land | 13.2 | 26.0 | 32.5 |
| **Total** | 5,427.3 | 7,311.8 | 8,169.2 |

* Excluding grants received (million pula): 37.1 in 1995/96; 83.0 in 1996/97; 112.1 in 1997/98.

| Expenditure* | 1995/96 | 1996/97 | 1997/98† |
|---|---|---|---|
| General administration | 790.9 | 911.1 | 1,038.7 |
| Public order and safety | 185.7 | 253.3 | 305.7 |
| Defence | 462.3 | 468.9 | 638.6 |
| Education | 1,166.5 | 1,517.8 | 1,842.0 |
| Health | 256.6 | 299.2 | 391.4 |
| Housing, urban and regional development | 406.2 | 385.9 | 745.7 |
| Food and social welfare programme | 127.9 | 65.1 | 132.9 |
| Other community and social services | 82.1 | 96.0 | |
| Economic services | 1,147.4 | 1,459.5 | 1,815.2 |
| Agriculture, forestry and fishing | 283.2 | 514.3 | 333.1 |
| Mining | 246.7 | 59.9 | 85.3 |
| Electricity and water supply | 252.2 | 303.5 | 631.8 |
| Roads | 278.3 | 421.1 | 566.2 |
| Interest on public debt | 91.6 | 91.4 | 100.3 |
| Deficit grants to local authorities | 403.3 | 472.2 | 534.0 |
| Other grants | 72.0 | 72.0 | 72.0 |
| **Total** | 5,192.4 | 6,092.4 | 7,616.4 |

* Figures refer to recurrent and development expenditure, including net lending (million pula): 14.2 in 1995/96; −191.1 in 1996/97; −227.4 (estimate) in 1997/98.

† Estimates.

Sources: Bank of Botswana, Gaborone, and IMF, *Botswana: Selected Issues and Statistical Appendix* (April 1998).

**INTERNATIONAL RESERVES** (US $ million at 31 December)

| | 1996 | 1997 | 1998 |
|---|---|---|---|
| IMF special drawing rights | 41.28 | 40.96 | 45.63 |
| Reserve position in IMF | 28.63 | 24.46 | 38.87 |
| Foreign exchange | 5,027.66 | 5,675.00 | 5,940.67 |
| **Total** | 5,097.57 | 5,740.42 | 6,025.17 |

Source: IMF, *International Financial Statistics.*

**MONEY SUPPLY** (million pula at 31 December)

| | 1996 | 1997 | 1998 |
|---|---|---|---|
| Currency outside banks | 247 | 276 | 353 |
| Demand deposits at commercial banks | 704 | 762 | 1,160 |
| **Total money** | 951 | 1,038 | 1,513 |

Source: IMF, *International Financial Statistics.*

**COST OF LIVING** (Consumer Price Index; base: 1990 = 100)

| | 1995 | 1996 | 1997 |
|---|---|---|---|
| Food (incl. beverages) | 182.9 | 207.0 | 228.3 |
| Clothing (incl. footwear) | 198.0 | 219.1 | 239.9 |
| **All items** (incl. others) | 181.4 | 199.8 | 217.2 |

Source: ILO, *Yearbook of Labour Statistics.*

**1998:** Food 242.3; All items 231.4 (Source: UN, *Monthly Bulletin of Statistics*).

**NATIONAL ACCOUNTS**

(million pula at current prices, year ending 30 June)

**National Income and Product**

| | 1985/86 | 1986/87 | 1987/88 |
|---|---|---|---|
| Compensation of employees | 700.7 | 849.6 | 1,051.6 |
| Operating surplus | 1,216.7 | 1,312.3 | 1,936.3 |
| **Domestic factor incomes** | 1,917.4 | 2,161.9 | 2,987.9 |
| Consumption of fixed capital | 349.8 | 432.4 | 575.6 |
| **Gross domestic product (GDP) at factor cost** | 2,267.2 | 2,594.3 | 3,563.5 |
| Indirect taxes | 160.4 | 226.2 | 251.2 |
| *Less* Subsidies | 7.0 | 10.7 | 19.1 |
| **GDP in purchasers' values** | 2,420.6 | 2,809.8 | 3,795.6 |
| Factor income received from abroad | 173.0 | 225.9 | 308.7 |
| *Less* Factor income paid abroad | 495.8 | 477.9 | 773.8 |
| **Gross national product** | 2,097.8 | 2,557.8 | 3,330.5 |
| *Less* Consumption of fixed capital | 349.8 | 432.4 | 575.6 |
| **National income in market prices** | 1,748.0 | 2,125.4 | 2,754.9 |
| Other current transfers from abroad | 141.5 | 123.2 | 115.1 |
| *Less* Other current transfers paid abroad | 68.5 | 78.6 | 233.3 |
| **National disposable income** | 1,821.0 | 2,169.9 | 2,636.7 |

Source: UN, *National Accounts Statistics.*

**Expenditure on the Gross Domestic Product** (provisional figures)

| | 1995/96 | 1996/97 | 1997/98 |
|---|---|---|---|
| Government final consumption expenditure | 4,175.2 | 4,925.3 | 5,872.8 |
| Private final consumption expenditure | 4,036.9 | 4,368.0 | 5,774.2 |
| Increase in stocks | 101.6 | 512.3 | 699.5 |
| Gross fixed capital formation | 3,546.5 | 4,176.5 | 5,047.1 |
| **Total domestic expenditure** | 11,860.2 | 13,982.1 | 17,393.6 |
| Exports of goods and services | 7,509.6 | 10,110.8 | 11,484.7 |
| *Less* Imports of goods and services | 5,168.0 | 6,590.0 | 8,449.9 |
| **GDP in purchasers' values** | 14,201.8 | 17,502.9 | 20,428.4 |
| **GDP at constant 1985/86 prices** | 5,108.3 | 5,474.0 | 5,929.0 |

Sources: Bank of Botswana, Gaborone, and Central Statistics Office, Gaborone.

**Gross Domestic Product by Economic Activity** (provisional figures)

| | 1995/96 | 1996/97 | 1997/98 |
|---|---|---|---|
| Agriculture, hunting, forestry and fishing | 549.9 | 602.7 | 635.3 |
| Mining and quarrying | 4,845.7 | 6,469.1 | 7,682.2 |
| Manufacturing | 703.6 | 866.1 | 988.2 |
| Water and electricity | 272.0 | 316.0 | 366.3 |
| Construction | 883.1 | 1,016.5 | 1,152.7 |
| Trade, restaurants and hotels | 2,491.4 | 3,019.6 | 3,527.6 |
| Transport | 561.4 | 686.5 | 791.5 |
| Finance, insurance and business services | 1,553.6 | 1,816.1 | 2,068.6 |
| Government services | 2,117.1 | 2,490.3 | 2,969.6 |
| Social and personal services | 610.6 | 682.0 | 785.7 |
| **Sub-total** | 14,588.4 | 17,964.9 | 20,967.7 |
| *Less* Imputed bank service charge | 386.7 | 462.1 | 539.3 |
| **GDP in purchasers' values** | 14,201.8 | 17,502.9 | 20,428.3 |

Sources: Bank of Botswana, Gaborone, and Central Statistics Office, Gaborone.

**BALANCE OF PAYMENTS** (US $ million)

| | 1996 | 1997 | 1998 |
|---|---|---|---|
| Exports of goods f.o.b. | 2,217.5 | 2,819.8 | 2,060.6 |
| Imports of goods f.o.b. | −1,467.7 | −1,924.4 | −1,983.1 |
| **Trade balance** | 749.8 | 895.4 | 77.5 |
| Exports of services | 163.0 | 210.2 | 255.3 |
| Imports of services | −343.6 | −440.7 | −522.4 |
| **Balance on goods and services** | 569.2 | 664.9 | −189.6 |
| Other income received | 501.7 | 622.1 | 622.7 |
| Other income paid | −754.8 | −766.9 | −503.1 |
| **Balance on goods, services and income** | 316.1 | 520.1 | 70.0 |
| Current transfers received | 355.4 | 456.8 | 460.9 |
| Current transfers paid | −176.6 | −255.5 | −220.8 |
| **Current balance** | 495.0 | 721.5 | 170.1 |
| Capital account (net) | 6.2 | 16.9 | 31.8 |
| Direct investment abroad | 1.1 | −4.1 | −3.5 |
| Direct investment from abroad | 71.2 | 100.1 | 95.3 |
| Portfolio investment assets | −35.5 | −43.9 | −37.6 |
| Portfolio investment liabilities | 31.0 | 10.8 | −14.1 |
| Other investment assets | −95.6 | −166.5 | −310.8 |
| Other investment liabilities | 70.3 | 109.3 | 68.2 |
| Net errors and omissions | −32.9 | −108.9 | 63.0 |
| **Overall balance** | 510.7 | 635.1 | 62.6 |

Source: IMF, *International Financial Statistics.*

# External Trade

**PRINCIPAL COMMODITIES** (million pula)

| Imports c.i.f. | 1995 | 1996 | 1997 |
|---|---|---|---|
| Food, beverages and tobacco | 846.1 | 971.7 | 1,083.0 |
| Fuels | 270.5 | 366.3 | 464.8 |
| Chemicals and rubber products | 490.6 | 586.7 | 749.4 |
| Wood and paper products | 401.8 | 420.3 | 511.8 |
| Textiles and footwear | 399.8 | 427.3 | 533.3 |
| Metals and metal products | 460.9 | 506.4 | 880.7 |
| Machinery and electrical equipment | 831.6 | 923.7 | 1,453.2 |
| Vehicles and transport equipment | 988.8 | 809.2 | 1,648.5 |
| **Total** (incl. others) | 5,307.1 | 5,742.8 | 8,255.8 |

| Exports f.o.b. | 1995 | 1996 | 1997 |
|---|---|---|---|
| Meat and meat products | 179.2 | 207.1 | 231.4 |
| Diamonds | 3,983.7 | 5,721.9 | 7,670.0 |
| Copper-nickel matte | 328.4 | 446.5 | 480.6 |
| Textiles | 146.3 | 195.1 | 248.4 |
| Vehicles and parts | 957.1 | 1,147.6 | 1,182.7 |
| **Total** (incl. others) | 5,941.5 | 8,141.8 | 10,390.7 |

Source: Trade Statistics Unit, Gaborone.

**PRINCIPAL TRADING PARTNERS** (million pula)

| Imports c.i.f. | 1995 | 1996 | 1997 |
|---|---|---|---|
| SACU* | 3,925.0 | 4,480.7 | 5,981.6 |
| Zimbabwe | 293.0 | 329.3 | 368.1 |
| United Kingdom | 134.7 | 148.2 | 162.6 |
| Other Europe | 319.3 | 240.7 | 580.0 |
| Korea, Repub. | 377.5 | 250.2 | 785.4 |
| USA | 107.4 | 73.8 | 89.1 |
| **Total** (incl. others) | 5,307.1 | 5,742.8 | 8,255.8 |

| Exports f.o.b. | 1995 | 1996 | 1997 |
|---|---|---|---|
| SACU* | 1,276.9 | 1,489.7 | 1,485.2 |
| Zimbabwe | 181.6 | 250.5 | 382.5 |
| Other Africa | 49.3 | 50.5 | 113.6 |
| United Kingdom | 2,223.0 | 4,424.1 | 5,839.9 |
| Other Europe | 2,147.3 | 1,827.2 | 2,444.2 |
| USA | 52.4 | 77.9 | 101.8 |
| **Total** (incl. others) | 5,941.5 | 8,141.8 | 10,390.7 |

* Southern African Customs Union, of which Botswana is a member; also including Lesotho, Namibia, South Africa and Swaziland.

Source: Trade Statistics Unit, Gaborone.

# Transport

**RAILWAYS** (traffic)

| | 1994/95 | 1995/96 | 1996/97 |
|---|---|---|---|
| Number of passengers ('000) | 525 | 722 | 574 |
| Passenger-km (million) | 86 | 95 | 96 |
| Freight ('000 metric tons) | 1,759 | 1,745 | 1,967 |
| Freight net ton-km (million) | 626 | 672 | 795 |

Source: Botswana Railways.

**ROAD TRAFFIC** (vehicles registered at 31 December)

| | 1993 | 1994 | 1995 |
|---|---|---|---|
| Passenger cars | 26,320 | 27,058 | 30,517 |
| Lorries and vans | 51,352 | 57,235 | 59,710 |
| Others | 16,938 | 17,153 | 17,448 |
| **Total** | 94,610 | 101,446 | 107,675 |

**CIVIL AVIATION** (traffic on scheduled services)

| | 1993 | 1994 | 1995 |
|---|---|---|---|
| Kilometres flown (million) | 3 | 2 | 2 |
| Passengers carried ('000) | 123 | 101 | 100 |
| Passenger-km (million) | 75 | 58 | 53 |
| Total ton-km (million) | 8 | 6 | 5 |

Source: UN, *Statistical Yearbook*.

# Tourism

**FOREIGN TOURIST ARRIVALS** (incl. same-day visitors)*

| Country of origin | 1994 | 1995 | 1996 |
|---|---|---|---|
| South Africa | 491,000 | n.a. | 545,306 |
| United Kingdom and Ireland | 41,810 | n.a. | 42,275 |
| Zambia | 32,162 | n.a. | 34,975 |
| Zimbabwe | 337,697 | n.a. | 336,889 |
| **Total** (incl. others) | 991,000 | 1,020,000 | 1,052,000 |

* Figures refer to arrivals at frontiers of visitors from abroad.

**Receipts from tourism** (US $ million): 124 in 1994; 162 in 1995; 178 in 1996.

Source: World Tourism Organization, *Yearbook of Tourism Statistics*.

# Communications Media

| | 1994 | 1995 | 1996 |
|---|---|---|---|
| Radio receivers ('000 in use) | 180 | 190 | 230 |
| Television receivers ('000 in use) | 24 | 27 | 30 |
| Daily newspapers: | | | |
| Number | 1 | 1 | 1 |
| Average circulation ('000 copies) | 35 | 45 | 40 |
| Non-daily newspapers: | | | |
| Number | n.a. | 5 | 3 |
| Average circulation ('000 copies) | n.a. | 79 | 51 |

**Book production** (first editions only, 1991): 158 titles, including 61 pamphlets.

**Other periodicals** (1992): 14 titles (average circulation 177,000 copies).

Source: UNESCO, *Statistical Yearbook*.

**Telephones** ('000 main lines in use, year ending 31 March): 43 in 1993/94; 50 in 1994/95; 60 in 1995/96 (Source: UN, *Statistical Yearbook*).

**Telefax stations** (estimated number in use, year ending 31 March): 1,700 in 1993/94; 2,100 in 1994/95; 3,149 in 1995/96 (Source: UN, *Statistical Yearbook*).

# Education

(1997)

| | Institutions | Teachers | Students |
|---|---|---|---|
| Primary | 714 | 11,454 | 322,268 |
| Secondary | 274 | 6,772 | 116,076 |
| Brigades* | 31 | 456 | 3,828 |
| Teacher training | 4 | 167 | 999 |
| Technical education | 15 | 1,995 | 5,002 |
| Colleges of education | 2 | 194 | 1,261 |
| Agricultural college | 1 | 87 | 392 |
| University | 1 | 507† | 8,007 |

* Semi-autonomous units providing craft and practical training.

† 1994.

Source: Ministry of Education, Gaborone.

# Directory

## The Constitution

The Constitution of the Republic of Botswana took effect at independence on 30 September 1966; it was amended in August and September 1997.

### EXECUTIVE

**President**

Executive power lies with the President of Botswana, who is also Commander-in-Chief of the armed forces. Election for the office of President is linked with the election of members of the National Assembly. The President is restricted to two terms of office. Presidential candidates must be over 30 years of age and receive at least 1,000 nominations. If there is more than one candidate for the Presidency, each candidate for office in the Assembly must declare support for a presidential candidate. The candidate for President who commands the votes of more than one-half of the elected members of the Assembly will be declared President. In the event of the death or resignation of the President, the Vice-President will automatically assume the Presidency. The President, who is an *ex-officio* member of the National Assembly, holds office for the duration of Parliament. The President chooses four members of the National Assembly.

**Cabinet**

There is also a Vice-President, whose office is ministerial. The Vice-President is appointed by the President and deputizes in the absence of the President. The Cabinet consists of the President, the Vice-President and other Ministers, including Assistant Ministers, appointed by the President. The Cabinet is responsible to the National Assembly.

### LEGISLATURE

Legislative power is vested in Parliament, consisting of the President and the National Assembly, acting after consultation in certain cases with the House of Chiefs. The President may withhold assent to a Bill passed by the National Assembly. If the same Bill is again presented after six months, the President is required to assent to it or to dissolve Parliament within 21 days.

**House of Chiefs**

The House of Chiefs comprises the Chiefs of the eight principal tribes of Botswana as *ex-officio* members, four members elected by sub-chiefs from their own number, and three members elected by the other 12 members of the House. Bills and motions relating to chieftaincy matters and alterations of the Constitution must be referred to the House, which may also deliberate and make representations on any matter.

**National Assembly**

The National Assembly consists of 40 members directly elected by universal adult suffrage, together with four members who are elected by the National Assembly from a list of candidates submitted by the President; the President and the Attorney-General are also *ex-officio* members of the Assembly. The life of the Assembly is five years.

The Constitution contains a code of human rights, enforceable by the High Court.

## The Government

### HEAD OF STATE

**President:** FESTUS G. MOGAE (took office 1 April 1998; sworn in 20 October 1999).

**Vice-President:** Lt-Gen. SERETSE IAN KHAMA (sworn in 13 July 1998).

### CABINET
(January 2000)

**President:** FESTUS G. MOGAE.

**Vice-President and Minister of Presidential Affairs and Public Administration:** Lt-Gen. SERETSE IAN KHAMA.

**Minister of Health:** JOY PHUMAPHI.

**Minister of Agriculture:** JOHNNIE SWARTZ.

**Minister of Foreign Affairs:** Lt-Gen. MOMPATI MERAFHE.

**Minister of Minerals, Energy and Water Affairs:** BOOMETSWE MOKGOTHU.

**Minister of Commerce and Industry:** DANIEL KWELAGOBE.

**Minister of Local Government:** MARGARET NASHA.

**Minister of Transport and Communications:** DAVID MAGANG.

**Minister of Finance and Development Planning:** BALEDZI GAOLATHE.

**Minister of Education:** PONATSHEGO KEDIKILWE.

**Minister of Labour and Home Affairs:** THEBE MOGAMI.

**Minister of Lands and Housing:** JACOB NKATE.

In addition, there are four Assistant Ministers.

### MINISTRIES

**Office of the President:** Private Bag 001, Gaborone; tel. 350800.

**Ministry of Agriculture:** Private Bag 003, Gaborone; tel. 350581; fax 356027.

**Ministry of Commerce and Industry:** Private Bag 004, Gaborone; tel. 3601200; fax 371539.

**Ministry of Education:** Private Bag 005, Gaborone; tel. 3655400; fax 3655458.

**Ministry of Finance and Development Planning:** Private Bag 008, Gaborone; tel. 350100; fax 356086.

**Ministry of Foreign Affairs:** Private Bag 00368, Gaborone; tel. 3600700; fax 313366.

**Ministry of Health:** Private Bag 0038, Gaborone; tel. 352000.

**Ministry of Labour and Home Affairs:** Private Bag 002, Gaborone; tel. 3611100; fax 313584.

**Ministry of Lands and Housing:** Private Bag 006, Gaborone; tel. 354100; fax 352091.

**Ministry of Local Government:** Private Bag 006, Gaborone; tel. 354100; fax 352091.

**Ministry of Minerals, Energy and Water Affairs:** Khama Crescent, Private Bag 0018, Gaborone; tel. 3656600; fax 372738.

**Ministry of Presidential Affairs and Public Administration:** Private Bag 001, Gaborone; tel. 350800.

**Ministry of Transport and Communications:** Private Bag 007, Gaborone; tel. and fax 313303.

## Legislature

### HOUSE OF CHIEFS

The House has a total of 15 members.

**Chairman:** Chief SEEPAPITSO IV.

### NATIONAL ASSEMBLY

**Speaker:** MOUTAKGOLA P. K. NWAKO.

**General Election, 16 October 1999**

| Party | Votes | % | Seats |
|---|---|---|---|
| Botswana Democratic Party | 192,598 | 57.2 | 33 |
| Botswana National Front | 87,457 | 26.0 | 6 |
| Botswana Congress Party | 40,096 | 11.9 | 1 |
| Botswana Alliance Movement | 15,805 | 4.7 | — |
| Others | 1,026 | 0.3 | — |
| **Total** | 336,982 | 100.0 | 40* |

* The President and the Attorney-General are also *ex-officio* members of the National Assembly.

## Political Organizations

**Botswana Alliance Movement (BAM):** Private Bag BO 210, Gaborone; tel. 313476; fax 314634; f. 1998 as an alliance of three opposition parties to contest the 1999 general election; Leader LEPETU SETSHWAELO.

**Botswana People's Party (BPP):** POB 484, Francistown; f. 1960; Pres. Dr KNIGHT MARIPE; Chair. KENNETH MKHWA; Sec.-Gen. MATLHOMOLA MODISE.

**Independence Freedom Party (IFP):** POB 3, Maun; f. by merger of Botswana Freedom Party and Botswana Independence Party; Pres. MOTSAMAI K. MPHO.

**United Action Party (UAP):** Private Bag BO 210, Gaborone; f. 1998; Leader LEPETU SETSHWEALO.

**Botswana Congress Party (BCP):** POB 2918, Gaborone; tel. and fax 581805; f. 1998, following a split in the Botswana National Front; Leader MICHAEL DINGAKE.

**Botswana Democratic Party (BDP):** POB 28, Tsholetsa House, Gaborone; tel. 352564; fax 313911; e-mail domkrag@info.bw; f. 1962; Pres. FESTUS G. MOGAE; Chair. PONATSHEGO KEDIKILWE; Sec.-Gen. DANIEL K. KWELAGOBE.

**Botswana Labour Party:** POB 140, Mahalopye; f. 1989; Pres. LENYELETSE KOMA.

**Botswana National Front (BNF):** POB 1720, Gaborone; tel. 351789; fax 584970; f. 1966; Pres. Dr KENNETH KOMA; Sec.-Gen. JAMES PILANE.

**Botswana Progressive Union (BPU):** POB 328, Nkange; f. 1982; Leader G. KAELO.

**Botswana Workers' Front (BWF):** POB 597, Jweneng; tel. 380420; f. 1993; Leader M. M. AKANYANG.

**MELS Movement of Botswana:** POB 501818, Gaborone; tel. and fax 306005; f. 1993; Leader T. JOINA.

**Social Democratic Party (SDP):** POB 201818, Gaborone; tel. 356516; f. 1994; Leader Ms O. MARUMO.

**United Socialist Party (USP):** POB 233, Lobatse; f. 1994; Leader N. MODUBULE.

## Diplomatic Representation

### EMBASSIES AND HIGH COMMISSIONS IN BOTSWANA

**Angola:** 5131 Kopanyo House, Nelson Mandela Rd, Private Bag BR 111, Gaborone; tel. 300204; fax 375089; Ambassador: EVARISTO DOMINGOS KIMBA.

**China, People's Republic:** 3096 North Ring Rd, POB 1031, Gaborone; tel. 352209; fax 300156; Ambassador: ZHANG SHIHUA.

**Germany:** Professional House, Broadhurst, Segodithsane Way, POB 315, Gaborone; tel. 353143; fax 353038; Ambassador: Dr IRENE HINRICHSEN.

**India:** 5375 President's Dr., Private Bag 249, Gaborone; tel. 372676; fax 374636; e-mail hicomind@global.bw; High Commissioner: RAJEET MITTER.

**Libya:** POB 180, Plot 8851 (Government Enclave), Gaborone; tel. 352481; Ambassador: JUMA MOHAMED JUBAIL.

**Namibia:** POB 987, Gaborone; tel. 302181; fax 302248; High Commissioner: Dr JOSEPH HOEBEB.

**Nigeria:** POB 274, The Mall, Gaborone; tel. 313561; fax 313738; High Commissioner: Ms HARRISON-OBAFEMI.

**Russia:** Plot 4711 Tawana Close, POB 81, Gaborone; tel. 353389; fax 352930; e-mail embarus@info.bw; Ambassador: VALERIJ A. KALUGIN.

**South Africa:** Private Bag 00402, Kopanyo House, Plot 5131, Nelson Mandela Dr., Gaborone; tel. 304800; fax 305501; High Commissioner: (vacant).

**Sweden:** Development House, Private Bag 0017, Gaborone; tel. 353912; fax 353942; e-mail swembgab@global.co.za; Ambassador: CHRISTINA REHLEN.

**United Kingdom:** Private Bag 0023, Gaborone; tel. 352841; fax 356105; e-mail british@bc.bw; internet www.british.global.bw; High Commissioner: JOHN WILDE.

**USA:** POB 90, Gaborone; tel. 353982; fax 356947; Ambassador: Dr JOHN E. LANGE.

**Zambia:** POB 362, Gaborone; tel. 351951; fax 353952; High Commissioner: J. PHIRI.

**Zimbabwe:** Plot 8850, POB 1232, Gaborone; tel. 314495; fax 305863; High Commissioner: (vacant).

## Judicial System

There is a High Court at Lobatse and a branch at Francistown, and Magistrates' Courts in each district. Appeals lie to the Court of Appeal of Botswana. The Chief Justice and the President of the Court of Appeal are appointed by the President.

**High Court:** Private Bag 1, Lobatse; tel. 330396; fax 332317.

**Chief Justice:** JULIAN NGANUNU.

**President of the Court of Appeal:** A. N. E. AMISSAH.

**Justices of Appeal:** T. A. AGUDA, W. H. R. SCHREINER, J. STEYN, P. H. TEBBUTT, W. COWIE, G. G. HOEXTER, W. ALLANBRIDGE.

**Puisne Judges:** I. R. ABOAGYE, J. B. GITTINGS, M. DIBOTELO, M. GAEFELE, J. Z. MASOJANE, I. K. B. LESETEDI (acting).

**Registrar and Master:** W. G. GRANTE.

**Office of the Attorney-General:** Private Bag 009, Gaborone; tel. 354700; fax 357089.

**Attorney-General:** PHANDU SKELEMANI.

## Religion

The majority of the population hold animist beliefs; an estimated 30% are thought to be Christians. There are Islamic mosques in Gaborone and Lobatse. The Bahá'í Faith is also represented.

### CHRISTIANITY

**Lekgotla la Sekeresete la Botswana** (Botswana Christian Council): POB 355, Gaborone; tel. 351981; f. 1966; comprises 34 churches and organizations; Pres. Rev. K. F. MOKOBIJ; Gen. Sec. DAVID J. MODIEGA.

#### The Anglican Communion

Anglicans are adherents of the Church of the Province of Central Africa, comprising 12 dioceses and covering Botswana, Malawi, Zambia and Zimbabwe. The Province was established in 1955, and the diocese of Botswana was formed in 1972.

**Archbishop of the Province of Central Africa and Bishop of Botswana:** Most Rev. WALTER PAUL KHOTSO MAKHULU, POB 769, Gaborone; fax 313015; e-mail acenter@info.bw.

#### Protestant Churches

**African Methodist Episcopal Church:** POB 141, Lobatse; Rev. L. M. MBULAWA.

**Evangelical Lutheran Church in Botswana:** POB 1976, Gaborone; tel. 352227; fax 313966; Bishop Rev. PHILIP ROBINSON; 16,305 mems.

**Evangelical Lutheran Church in Southern Africa (Botswana Diocese):** POB 400, Gaborone; tel. 353976; Bishop Rev. M. NTUPING.

**Methodist Church in Botswana:** POB 260, Gaborone; Dist. Supt Rev. Z. S. M. MOSAI.

**United Congregational Church of Southern Africa (Synod of Botswana):** POB 1263, Gaborone; tel. 352491; Synod status since 1980; Chair. Rev. D. T. MAPITSE; Sec. Rev. M. P. P. DIBEELA; 24,000 mems.

Other denominations active in Botswana include the Church of God in Christ, the Dutch Reformed Church, the United Methodist Church and the Seventh-day Adventists.

#### The Roman Catholic Church

Botswana comprises one diocese and an apostolic vicariate. The metropolitan see is Bloemfontein, South Africa. The church was established in Botswana in 1928, and had an estimated 53,325 adherents (some 4.0% of the total population) in the country at 31 December 1997. The Bishop participates in the Southern African Catholic Bishops' Conference, currently based in Pretoria, South Africa.

**Bishop of Gaborone:** Rt Rev. BONIFACE TSHOSA SETLALEKGOSI, POB 218, Bishop's House, Gaborone; tel. 312958; fax 356970.

**Vicar Apostolic of Francistown:** Rt Rev. FRANKLYN NUBUASAH.

## The Press

### DAILY NEWSPAPER

**Dikgang tsa Gompieno** (Daily News): Private Bag 0060, Gaborone; tel. 352541. 1964; publ. by Dept of Information and Broadcasting; Setswana and English; Mon.–Fri.; Editor L. LESHAGA; circ. 50,000.

### PERIODICALS

**Agrinews:** Private Bag 003, Gaborone; f. 1971; monthly; agriculture and rural development; circ. 6,000.

**Botswana Advertiser:** POB 130, 5647 Nakedi Rd, Broadhurst, Gaborone; tel. 312844; weekly.

**The Botswana Gazette:** POB 1605, Gaborone; tel. 312833; fax 312833; weekly; circ. 16,000.

**Botswana Guardian:** POB 1641, Gaborone; tel. 308408; fax 308457; e-mail guardsun@info.bw; f. 1982; weekly; Editor OUTSA MOKONE; circ. 20,792.

**Government Gazette:** Private Bag 0081, Gaborone; tel. 314441; fax 312001; weekly.

**Kutlwano:** Private Bag 0060, Gaborone; tel. 352541; monthly; Setswana and English; publ. by Dept of Information and Broadcasting; circ. 24,000.

**The Midweek Sun:** POB 1641, Gaborone; tel. 308408; fax 308457; e-mail guardsun@info.bw; f. 1989; weekly; Editor MIKE MOTHIBI; circ. 18,108.

**Mmegi/The Reporter:** Private Bag BR50, Gaborone; tel. 374784; fax 305508; e-mail mmegi@info.bw; f. 1984; weekly; Setswana and English; publ. by Dikgang Publishing Co; circ. 24,000.

**Motswana Woman:** 686 Botswana Rd, Gaborone; tel. 375362; fax 375378; monthly; women's interests; circ. 4,000.

**Northern Advertiser:** POB 402, Francistown; tel. 212265; fax 213769; e-mail rsfish@global.bw; f. 1985; weekly; advertisements, local interest, sport; Editor GRACE FISH; circ. 5,500.

**The Zebra's Voice:** Private Bag 00114, National Museum, Independence Ave, Gaborone; tel. 374616; f. 1982; quarterly; cultural affairs; circ. 7,000.

### NEWS AGENCIES

**Botswana Press Agency (BOPA):** Private Bag 0060, Gaborone; tel. 313601. 1981.

#### Foreign Bureaux

**Deutsche Presse-Agentur** (Germany) and **Reuters** (UK) are represented in Botswana.

## Publishers

**A.C. Braby (Botswana) (Pty) Ltd:** POB 1549, Gaborone; tel. 371444; fax 373462; telephone directories.

**The Botswana Society:** POB 71, Gaborone; tel. 351500; fax 359321; f. 1968; archaeology, arts, history, law, sciences.

**Department of Information and Broadcasting:** Private Bag 0060, Gaborone; tel. 352541; fax 357138.

**Heinemann Educational Botswana (Pty) Ltd:** POB 10103, Gaborone; tel. 372305; fax 371832.

**Longman Botswana (Pty) Ltd:** POB 1083, Lobatse Rd, Gaborone; tel. 313969; fax 322682; e-mail joe@info.bw; f. 1981; educational; Man. Dir J. K. CHALASHIKA.

**Macmillan Botswana Publishing Co (Pty) Ltd:** POB 1155, Gaborone; tel. 314379; fax 374326; Gen. Man. W. UITERWIJK.

**Magnum Press (Pty) Ltd:** Gaborone; tel. 372852; fax 374558.

**Morula Press:** Business School of Botswana, POB 402492, Gaborone; tel. 353499; fax 304809; f. 1994; business, law.

**Printing and Publishing Co (Botswana) (Pty) Ltd:** POB 130, 5647 Nakedi Rd, Broadhurst, Gaborone; tel. 312844.

**Sygma Publishing:** POB 753, Gaborone; tel. 372532; fax 372531; e-mail sygma@info.bw.

#### Government Publishing House

**Department of Government Printing and Publishing Services:** Private Bag 0081, Gaborone; tel. 314441; fax 312001.

## Broadcasting and Communications

### TELECOMMUNICATIONS

In early 1998 two companies were granted licences to operate mobile cellular telephone networks.

**Botswana Telecommunications Corporation:** POB 700, Gaborone; tel. 358000; fax 313355; e-mail megaleng@btc.bw; internet www.btc.bw; f. 1980; state-owned; CEO M. T. CURRY.

### BROADCASTING

**Department of Information and Broadcasting:** Private Bag 0060, Gaborone; Dir TED MAKGEKENENE.

#### Radio

Botswana's first independent radio station, Yarona FM, was granted a licence in May 1999, and was expected to commence broadcasting later that year.

**Radio Botswana:** Private Bag 0060, Gaborone; tel. 352541; fax 357138; e-mail rbeng@info.bw; broadcasts in Setswana and English; govt-owned; f. 1965; Dir TED MAKGEKENENE; Chief Eng. HABUJI SOSOME.

**Radio Botswana II:** Private Bag 0060, Gaborone; tel. 352541; fax 371588; f. 1992; commercial service.

#### Television

**Botswana Television:** Department of Information & Broadcasting, Private Bag 0060, Gaborone; tel. 300050; fax 300051; e-mail kevin.hunt@btv.bw; govt-funded national TV service; scheduled to be launched in 2000; Dep. Dir KEVIN HUNT.

**TV Association of Botswana:** Gaborone; relays SABC-TV and BOP-TV programmes from South Africa.

## Finance

(cap. = capital; res = reserves; dep. = deposits; m. = million; brs = branches; amounts in pula)

### BANKING

#### Central Bank

**Bank of Botswana:** POB 712, Private Bag 154, Plot 1863, Khama Crescent, Gaborone; tel. 360600; fax 301100; f. 1975; bank of issue; cap. 25m., res 3,176m., dep. 22,436.3m. (Dec. 1998); Gov. LINAH MOHOHLO.

#### Commercial Banks

**Barclays Bank of Botswana Ltd:** POB 478, Barclays House, 6th Floor, Plot 8842, Khama Crescent, Gaborone; tel. 352041; fax 313672; f. 1975; 74.9% owned by Barclays Bank PLC (UK); cap. and res 136.5m., dep. 1,295.5m. (Dec. 1996); Chair. C. TIBONE; Man. Dir C. LOWE; 48 brs, etc.

**First National Bank of Botswana Ltd:** POB 1552, Finance House, 5th Floor, Plot 8843, Khama Crescent, Gaborone; tel. 311669; fax 306130; f. 1991; 70% owned by First National Bank Holdings Botswana Ltd; cap. and res 119m. (Sept. 1997), dep. 755.7m. (Dec. 1996); Chair. H. C. L. HERMANS; Man. Dir J. K. MACASKILL; 11 brs.

**Stanbic Bank Botswana Ltd:** Private Bag 00168, Travaglini House, Plot 1271, Old Lobatse Rd, Gaborone; tel. 301600; fax 300171; f. 1992 by merger; subsidiary of Standard Bank Investment Corpn Africa Holdings Ltd; cap. and res 54.3m., dep 571.6m. (March 1999); Chair. O. M. GABORONE; Man. Dir W. L. V. PRICE; 4 brs.

**Standard Chartered Bank Botswana Ltd:** POB 496, Standard House, 5th Floor, Plots 1124–1127, The Mall, Gaborone; tel. 3601500; fax 372933; f. 1975; 75% owned by Standard Chartered Holdings (Africa) BV, Amsterdam; cap. and res 109.9m. (Dec. 1997), dep. 881.7m. (Dec. 1995); Chair. P. L. STEENKAMP; Man. Dir D. N. T. KUWANA; 15 brs.

#### Other Banks

**Botswana Savings Bank:** POB 1150, Tshomarelo House, Gaborone; tel. 312555; fax 352608; cap. and res 45.8m. (Dec. 1997); Chair. F. MODISE; Man. Dir E. B. MATHE.

**Investec Bank:** Gaborone; f. 1998; merchant bank; Man. Dir KUMBULANI MUNAMTI.

**National Development Bank:** POB 225, Development House, Queens Rd, Gaborone; tel. 352801; fax 374446; f. 1964; cap. and res 94.8m. (March 1998), dep. 51.3m. (March 1997); priority given to agricultural credit for Botswana farmers, and co-operative credit and loans for local business ventures; Chair. F. MODISE; Gen. Man. J. HOWELL; 5 brs.

### STOCK EXCHANGE

**Botswana Stock Exchange:** Private Bag 00417, Barclays House, Ground Floor, Khama Crescent, Gaborone; tel. 357900; fax 357901; e-mail bse@info.bw; f. 1989; commenced formal functions of a stock exchange in 1995; Chair. LOUIS NCHINDO; CEO R. MCCAMMON.

### INSURANCE

**Botswana Co-operative Insurance Co Ltd:** POB 199, Gaborone; tel. 313654; fax 313654.

**Botswana Eagle Insurance Co Ltd:** POB 1221, 501 Botsalano House, Gaborone; tel. 212392; fax 213745; Gen. Man. JOHN MAIN.

**Botswana Insurance Co (Pty) Ltd:** POB 336, BIC House, Gaborone; tel. 351791; fax 313290; Gen. Man. P. B. SUMMER.

**Sedgwick James Insurance Brokers (Pty) Ltd:** POB 103, Plot 730, The Mall, Botswana Rd, Gaborone; tel. 314241; fax 373120.

**Tshireletso Insurance Brokers:** POB 1967, Gaborone; tel. 357064; fax 371558.

## Trade and Industry

### GOVERNMENT AGENCIES

**Botswana Housing Corporation:** POB 412, Gaborone; tel. 353341; fax 352070; f. 1971; provides housing for central govt and local authority needs and assists with private-sector housing schemes; Chair. Z. P. PITSO; Gen. Man. (vacant); 900 employees.

**Department of Food Resources:** POB 96, Gaborone; tel. 354124. 1982; procurement, storage and distribution of food commodities under the Drought Relief Programme; Admin. Officer M. S. SEHLULANE.

**Department of Town and Regional Planning:** Private Bag 0042, Gaborone; tel. 351935; e-mail infoterra@info.bw; f. 1972; responsible for physical planning matters throughout the country, including formulation of national physical planning policy; prepares devt plans

for settlements and regions and provides physical planning advice to govt and local authorities as well as private bodies.

### DEVELOPMENT ORGANIZATIONS

**Botswana Development Corporation Ltd:** Private Bag 160, Moedi, Plot 50380, Gaborone International Showgrounds, Off Machel Drive, Gaborone; tel. 3651300; fax 303114; f. 1970; Chair. S. S. G. Tumelo; Man. Dir O. K. Matambo.

**Botswana Enterprise Development Unit (BEDU):** Plot No. 1269, Lobatse Rd, POB 0014, Gaborone; f. 1974; promotes industrialization and rural devt; Dir J. Lindfors.

**Botswana Export Development and Investment Authority (BEDIA):** BIC House, 4th Floor, The Main Mall, POB 3122, Gaborone; tel. 581931; fax 581941; f. 1998; promotes and facilitates local and foreign investment.

**Department of Trade and Investment Promotion (TIPA), Ministry of Commerce and Industry:** Private Bag 00367, Gaborone; tel. 351790; fax 305375; e-mail tipa@info.bw; internet www.tipa.bw; promotes industrial and commercial investment, diversification and expansion; offers consultancy, liaison and information services; participates in overseas trade fairs and trade and investment missions; Dir D. Tsheko.

**Financial Services Co of Botswana (Pty) Ltd:** POB 1129, Finance House, Khama Crescent, Gaborone; tel. 351363; fax 357815; f. 1974; hire purchase, mortgages, industrial leasing and debt factoring; Chair. M. E. Hopkins; Man. Dir R. A. Pawson.

**Integrated Field Services:** Private Bag 004, Ministry of Commerce and Industry, Gaborone; tel. 353024; fax 371539; promotes industrialization and rural development; Dir B. T. Tibone.

### CHAMBER OF COMMERCE

**Botswana National Chamber of Commerce and Industry:** POB 20344, Gaborone; tel. 52677.

### INDUSTRIAL AND TRADE ASSOCIATIONS

**Botswana Agricultural Marketing Board (BAMB):** Private Bag 0053, 1227 Haile Selassie Rd, Gaborone; tel. 351341; fax 352926; Chair. the Perm. Sec., Ministry of Agriculture; Gen. Man. S. B. Taukobong.

**Botswana Meat Commission (BMC):** Private Bag 4, Lobatse; tel. 330321; fax 330530; f. 1966; slaughter of livestock, export of hides and skins, carcasses, frozen and chilled boneless beef; operates tannery and beef products cannery; Exec. Chair. Dr Martin M. Mannathoko.

### EMPLOYERS' ORGANIZATION

**Botswana Confederation of Commerce, Industry and Manpower (BOCCIM):** POB 432, BOCCIM House, Gaborone; f. 1971; Chair. D. N. Moroka; Dir Modiri J. Mbaakanyi; 1,478 affiliated mems.

### UTILITIES

#### Electricity

**Botswana Power Corporation:** POB 48, Motlakase House, Macheng Way, Gaborone; tel. 352211; fax 373563; f. 1971; operates power stations at Selebi-Phikwe (capacity 65 MW) and Moropule (132 MW); Chair. the Dep. Perm. Sec., Ministry of Minerals, Energy and Water Affairs; CEO K. Sithole.

#### Water

**Department of Water Affairs:** Gaborone; provides public water supplies for rural areas.

**Water Utilities Corporation:** Private Bag 00276, Gaborone; tel. 360400; fax 373852; e-mail botwucis@abaas.global.bw; f. 1970; 50% state-owned; provides public water supplies for principal townships; Chair. the Perm. Sec., Ministry of Minerals, Energy and Water Affairs; CEO B. Mpho.

### CO-OPERATIVES

**Department of Co-operative Development:** POB 86, Gaborone; f. 1964; promotes marketing and supply, consumer, dairy, horticultural and fisheries co-operatives, thrift and loan societies, credit societies, a co-operative union and a co-operative bank.

**Botswana Co-operative Union:** Gaborone. 1970; Dir Aaron Ramosako.

### TRADE UNIONS

**Botswana Federation of Trade Unions:** POB 440, Gaborone; tel. and fax 352534; f. 1977; Gen. Sec. Maranyane Kebitsang.

#### Affiliated Unions

**Air Botswana Employees' Union:** POB 92, Gaborone; Gen. Sec. Daniel Motsumi.

**Barclays Management Staff Union:** POB 478, Gaborone; Gen. Sec. Tefo Lionjanga.

**BCL Senior Staff Union:** POB 383, Selebi-Phikwe; Gen. Sec. Kabelo Matthews.

**Botswana Agricultural Marketing Board Workers' Union:** Private Bag 0053, Gaborone; Gen. Sec. M. E. Semathane.

**Botswana Bank Employees' Union:** POB 111, Gaborone; Gen. Sec. Keolopile Gaborone.

**Botswana Beverages and Allied Workers' Union:** POB 41358, Gaborone; Gen. Sec. S. Senwelo.

**Botswana Brigade Teachers' Union:** Private Bag 007, Molepolole; Gen. Sec. Sadike Kgokong.

**Botswana Commercial and General Workers' Union:** Gaborone; Gen. Sec. Kediretse Mpetang.

**Botswana Construction Workers' Union:** POB 1508, Gaborone; Gen. Sec. Joshua Kesiilwe.

**Botswana Diamond Sorters-Valuators' Union:** POB 1186, Gaborone; Gen. Sec. Felix T. Lesetedi.

**Botswana Housing Corporation Staff Union:** POB 412, Gaborone; Gen. Sec. Gorata Dingalo.

**Botswana Meat Industry Workers' Union:** POB 181, Lobatse; Gen. Sec. Johnson Bojosi.

**Botswana Mining Workers' Union:** Gaborone; Gen. Sec. Balekamang S. Ganasiane.

**Botswana Postal Services Workers' Union:** POB 87, Gaborone; Gen. Sec. Aaron Mosweu.

**Botswana Power Corporation Workers' Union:** Private Bag 0053, Gaborone; Gen. Sec. Molefe Modise.

**Botswana Railways and Artisan Employees' Union:** POB 1486, Gaborone; Gen. Sec. Patrick Magowe.

**Botswana Railways Senior Staff Union:** Mahalapye; Gen. Sec. Lentswe Letsweletse.

**Botswana Railways Workers' Union:** POB 181, Gaborone; Gen. Sec. Ernest T. G. Mohutsiwa.

**Botswana Telecommunications Employees' Union:** Gaborone; Gen. Sec. Sedibana Robert.

**Botswana Vaccine Institute Staff Union:** Private Bag 0031, Gaborone; Gen. Sec. Elliot Modise.

**Central Bank Union:** POB 712, Gaborone; Gen. Sec. Godfrey Ngidi.

**National Amalgamated Local and Central Government, Parastatal, Statutory Body and Manual Workers' Union:** POB 374, Gaborone; Gen. Sec. Dickson Kelatlhegetswe.

**National Development Bank Employees' Union:** POB 225, Gaborone; Sec.-Gen. Matshediso Fologang.

**Non-Academic Staff Union:** Private Bag 0022, Gaborone; Gen. Sec. Isaac Thothe.

## Transport

### RAILWAYS

The 960-km railway line from Mafikeng, South Africa, to Bulawayo, Zimbabwe, passes through Botswana and has been operated by Botswana Railways (BR) since 1987. In 1997 there were 888 km of 1,067-mm-gauge track within Botswana, including three branches serving the Selebi-Phikwe mining complex (56 km), the Morupule colliery (16 km) and the Sua Pan soda ash deposits (175 km). BR derives 85%–90% of its earnings from freight traffic, although passenger services do operate between Gaborone and Francistown, and Lobatse and Bulawayo. Through its links with Spoornet, which operates the South African railways system and the National Railways of Zimbabwe, BR provides connections with Namibia and Swaziland to the south, and an unbroken rail link to Zambia, the Democratic Republic of the Congo, Angola, Mozambique, Tanzania and Malawi to the north.

**Botswana Railways (BR):** Private Bag 0052, Mahalapye; tel. 411375; fax 411385; e-mail botrail@info.bw; f. 1987; Gen. Man. A. Ramji.

### ROADS

In 1996 there were 18,482 km of roads, including 4,350 km of main roads, and 4,566 km of secondary roads; some 23.5% of the road network was bituminized (including a main road from Gaborone, via Francistown, to Kazungula, where the borders of Botswana, Namibia, Zambia and Zimbabwe meet). The construction of a 340-km road between Nata and Maun is currently under way. Construction of the 600-km Trans-Kalahari Highway, from Jwaneng to the port of Walvis Bay on the Namibian coast, commenced in 1990 and was completed in 1998. A car-ferry service operates from Kazungula across the Zambezi river into Zambia.

**Roads Department:** Private Bag 0026, Gaborone; tel. 55515; responsible for national road network; responsible to the Ministry of Transport and Communications.

### CIVIL AVIATION

The main international airport is at Gaborone. Two other major airports are located at Kasane and Maun in northern Botswana. There are also airfiels at Francistown and Selebi-Phikwe, and there are numerous airstrips throughout the country. Scheduled services of Air Botswana are supplemented by an active charter and business sector.

**Air Botswana:** POB 92, Sir Seretse Khama Airport, Gaborone; tel. 352812; fax 375408; f. 1972; govt-owned; domestic services and regional services to countries in eastern and southern Africa.

## Tourism

There are five game reserves and three national parks, including Chobe, near Victoria Falls, on the Zambia–Zimbabwe border. Efforts to expand the tourist industry include plans for the construction of new hotels and the rehabilitation of existing hotel facilities. In 1996 tourist arrivals (including same-day visitors) totalled 1,052,000 and receipts from tourism amounted to US $178m.

**Department of Tourism:** Ministry of Commerce and Industry, Private Bag 0047, Standard House, 2nd Floor, Main Mall, Gaborone; tel. 353024; fax 308675; f. 1994; Dir GAYLARD KOMBANI.

**Department of Wildlife and National Parks:** POB 131, Gaborone; tel. 371405; fax 312354; e-mail dwnpbots@global.bw; Dir. S. MODISE.

**Hotel and Tourism Association of Botswana:** Gaborone; Dir MODISA MOTHOAGAE.

# BRAZIL

## Introductory Survey

### Location, Climate, Language, Religion, Flag, Capital

The Federative Republic of Brazil, the fifth largest country in the world, lies in central and north-eastern South America. To the north are Venezuela, Colombia, Guyana, Suriname and French Guiana, to the west Peru and Bolivia, and to the south Paraguay, Argentina and Uruguay. Brazil has a very long coastline on the Atlantic Ocean. Climatic conditions vary from hot and wet in the tropical rain forest of the Amazon basin to temperate in the savannah grasslands of the central and southern uplands, which have warm summers and mild winters. In Rio de Janeiro temperatures are generally between 17°C (63°F) and 29°C (85°F). The official language is Portuguese. Almost all of the inhabitants profess Christianity, and about 90% are adherents of the Roman Catholic Church. The national flag (proportions 10 by 7) is green, bearing, at the centre, a yellow diamond containing a blue celestial globe with 26 white five-pointed stars (one for each of Brazil's states), arranged in the pattern of the southern firmament, below an equatorial scroll with the motto 'Ordem e Progresso' ('Order and Progress'), and a single star above the scroll. The capital is Brasília.

### Recent History

Formerly a Portuguese possession, Brazil became an independent monarchy in 1822, and a republic in 1889. A federal constitution for the United States of Brazil was adopted in 1891. Following social unrest in the 1920s, the economic crisis of 1930 resulted in a major revolt, led by Dr Getúlio Vargas, who was installed as President. He governed the country as a benevolent dictator until forced to resign by the armed forces in December 1945. During Vargas's populist rule, Brazil enjoyed internal stability and steady economic progress. He established a strongly authoritarian corporate state, similar to fascist regimes in Europe, but in 1942 Brazil entered the Second World War on the side of the Allies.

A succession of ineffectual presidential terms (including another by Vargas, who was re-elected in 1950) failed to establish stable government in the late 1940s and early 1950s. President Jânio Quadros, elected in 1960, resigned after only seven months in office, and in September 1961 the Vice-President, João Goulart, was sworn in as President. Military leaders suspected Goulart, the leader of the Partido Trabalhista Brasileiro (PTB), of communist sympathies, and they were reluctant to let him succeed to the presidency. As a compromise, the Constitution was amended to restrict the powers of the President and to provide for a Prime Minister. However, following the appointment of three successive premiers during a 16-month period of mounting political crisis, the system was rejected when a referendum, conducted in January 1963, approved a return to the presidential system of government, whereupon President Goulart formed his own Cabinet.

Following a period of economic crisis, exacerbated by allegations of official corruption, the left-wing regime of President Goulart was overthrown in April 1964 by a bloodless right-wing military coup led by Gen. (later Marshal) Humberto Castelo Branco, the Army Chief of Staff, who was promptly elected President by the National Congress. In October 1965 President Castelo Branco assumed dictatorial powers, and all 13 existing political parties were banned. In December, however, two artificially-created parties, the pro-Government Aliança Renovadora Nacional (ARENA) and the opposition Movimento Democrático Brasileiro (MDB), were granted official recognition. President Castelo Branco nominated as his successor the Minister of War, Marshal Artur da Costa e Silva, who was elected in October 1966 and took office in March 1967 as President of the redesignated Federative Republic of Brazil (a new Constitution was introduced simultaneously). The ailing President da Costa e Silva was forced to resign in September 1969 and was replaced by a triumvirate of military leaders.

The military regime granted the President wide-ranging powers to rule by decree. In October 1969 the ruling junta introduced a revised Constitution, vesting executive authority in an indirectly-elected President. The Congress, suspended since December 1968, was recalled and elected Gen. Emílio Garrastazú Médici as President. Médici was succeeded as President by Gen. Ernesto Geisel and Gen. João Baptista de Figueiredo respectively. Despite the attempts of both Presidents to pursue a policy of *abertura*, or opening to democratization (legislation to end the controlled two-party system was approved in 1979), opposition to military rule intensified throughout the 1970s and early 1980s. In November 1982 the government-sponsored Partido Democrático Social (PDS) suffered significant losses at elections to the Chamber of Deputies, state governorships and municipal councils. However, the PDS secured a majority of seats in the Federal Senate and, owing to pre-election legislation, seemed likely to enjoy a guaranteed majority in the electoral college, scheduled to choose a successor to Gen. Figueiredo in 1985.

However, in July 1984 Vice-President Chaves de Mendonça and the influential Marco de Oliveira Maciel, a former Governor of Pernambuco State, announced the formation of an alliance of liberal PDS members with members of the Partido do Movimento Democrático Brasileiro (PMDB). This offered the opposition a genuine opportunity to defeat the PDS in the electoral college. In August Senator Tancredo Neves, the Governor of Minas Gerais State (who had been Prime Minister in 1961–62), was named presidential candidate for the liberal alliance, while the former President of the PDS, José Sarney, was declared vice-presidential candidate. In December the liberal alliance formed an official political party, the Partido Frente Liberal (PFL). At the presidential election, conducted in January 1985, Neves was elected as Brazil's first civilian President for 21 years, winning 480 of the 686 votes in the electoral college. Prior to the inauguration ceremony in March 1985, however, Neves was taken ill, and in April, following a series of operations, he died. José Sarney, who had assumed the role of Acting President in Neves' absence, took office as President in April. President Sarney made no alterations to the Cabinet selected by Neves, and he affirmed his commitment to fulfilling the objectives of the late President-designate. In May the Congress approved a constitutional amendment restoring direct elections by universal suffrage. The right to vote was also extended to illiterate adults. The first direct elections, to municipal councils in 31 cities, took place in November.

The introduction in February 1986 of an anti-inflation programme, the Cruzado Plan, proved, initially, to be successful and boosted the popularity of President Sarney. Support for the Government was further demonstrated in November 1986 at elections to the Congress, which was to operate as a Constitutional Assembly. The Constitutional Assembly was installed in February 1987, and the constitutional debate was dominated by the issue of the length of the presidential mandate. In June 1988 the Constitutional Assembly finally approved a presidential mandate of five years. The first round of voting for the presidential election was provisionally set for 15 November 1989, thereby enabling Sarney to remain in office until March 1990. This *de facto* victory for the President precipitated a series of resignations from the PMDB by some of its leading members, who subsequently formed a new centre-left party, the Partido da Social Democracia Brasileira (PSDB). The Constitution was approved by the Congress on 22 September 1988, and was promulgated on 5 October. Among its 245 articles were provisions transferring many hitherto presidential powers to the legislature. In addition, censorship was abolished; the National Security Law, whereby many political dissidents had been detained, was abolished; the minimum voting age was lowered to 16 years; and the principle of habeas corpus was recognized. However, the Constitution offered no guarantees of land reform, and was thought by many to be nationalistic and protectionist.

In April 1988 the Government revealed its commitment to drastic reductions in planned public-sector expenditure, primarily based on a 'freeze' on salary increases for state employees. The combination of industrial unrest and social tension which resulted was thought to have been a decisive factor in the PMDB's poor results at municipal elections held on 15 November, when the centre-left Partido Democrático Trabalhista

(PDT) and the left-wing Partido dos Trabalhadores (PT) made important gains at the expense of the ruling party.

Brazil's first presidential election by direct voting since 1960 took place on 15 November 1989. The main contenders were a young conservative, Fernando Collor de Mello of the newly-formed Partido de Reconstrução Nacional (PRN), Luiz Inácio (Lula) da Silva of the PT and Leonel Brizola of the PDT. Since no candidate received the required overall majority, a second round of voting was held on 17 December, contested by Collor de Mello and da Silva, who were first and second, respectively, in the November poll. Collor de Mello was declared the winner, with 53% of the votes cast. Following his inauguration as President on 15 March 1990, Collor de Mello announced an ambitious programme of economic reform, with the principal aim of reducing inflation, which had reached a monthly rate of more than 80%. Among the extraordinary provisions of the programme entitled 'New Brazil' (or, more commonly, the 'Collor Plan') was the immediate sequestration of an estimated US $115,000m. in personal savings and corporate assets for an 18-month period. A new currency, the cruzeiro (to replace, at par, the novo cruzado) was also introduced. The decision to rationalize the public sector, and the large number of redundancies involved, led to widespread labour unrest.

The results of elections to 31 senatorial seats, 503 seats in the Chamber of Deputies and 27 state governorships, conducted in October 1990, were interpreted as a rejection of extreme left- and right-wing parties in favour of familiar candidates from small, centre-right parties. Although the President would be forced to maintain a more delicate balance of political alliances in the Congress as a result, Collor de Mello was confident of securing sufficient support to continue to pursue a programme of radical economic reform. However, the results of a second round of voting to elect governors in those states where candidates had received less than the required 50% of the votes on 3 October, which was conducted on 25 November, represented a serious reversal for the Government. Few candidates associated with or supported by the Government were successful, and particularly damaging defeats were suffered by government-favoured candidates in the crucial states of São Paulo, Rio Grande do Sul, Rio de Janeiro and Espírito Santo.

The Government's dramatic loss of popularity was largely attributed to the severity and apparent failure of its economic austerity programme. A second economic plan, announced by the Minister of the Economy, Zélia Cardoso de Mello, and presented as a simple intensification of the first 'Collor Plan', had been implemented in February 1991. In March Collor de Mello announced a new Plan for National Reconstruction, which envisaged further deregulation and rationalization of many state-controlled areas, including the ports, and the communications and fuel sectors. By May 1991, despite a considerable decrease in the monthly rate of inflation, Cardoso de Mello's political popularity had been undermined by her confrontational style of negotiation, and she was forced to resign.

Collor de Mello's position became increasingly precarious towards the end of 1991, after allegations of mismanagement of federal funds were made against his wife and against several associates in the President's home state of Alagoas. In September 1991 the President embarked upon a series of informal multi-party negotiations in an attempt to achieve greater congressional consensus and to reinforce his own mandate. Following lengthy discussions at a specially-convened meeting of the emergency Council of the Republic in the same month, Collor de Mello presented a comprehensive series of proposals for constitutional amendment, before the Congress.

Allegations of high-level corruption persisted into 1992 and despite attempts, in January and April, to restore public confidence in the integrity of the Government with the implementation of comprehensive cabinet changes, the President failed to dispel suspicions sufficiently to attract the wider political participation in government which was considered necessary to facilitate the passage of legislation through an increasingly ineffectual Congress. In May, moreover, the President became the focus of further allegations, following a series of disclosures made by Collor de Mello's younger brother, Pedro, which appeared to implicate the President in a number of corrupt practices (including the misappropriation of federal funds) orchestrated by Paulo César Farias, Collor de Mello's 1989 election campaign treasurer. While the President dismissed the allegations as false, in late May the Congress approved the creation of a special commission of inquiry to investigate the affair. In early September, acting upon the report of the special commission of inquiry, and bolstered by massive popular support, a 49-member congressional committee authorized the initiation of impeachment proceedings against the President, within the Chamber of Deputies. On 29 September 1992 the Chamber voted to proceed with the impeachment of the President for abuses of authority and position, prompting the immediate resignation of the Cabinet. On 2 October Collor de Mello surrendered authority to Vice-President Itamar Franco for a six-month period, pending the final pronouncement regarding his future in office, to be decided by the Senate. Following lengthy negotiations, Franco announced the composition of a new Cabinet in October, representing a broad political base. A final round of municipal elections, conducted in November, revealed a significant resurgence of support for left-wing parties. In December the Minister of the Economy, Gustavo Krause, resigned, following Franco's unilateral decision to suspend, by presidential decree, the Government's privatization programme for a three-month period.

Meanwhile, in December 1992, the Senate had voted overwhelmingly to proceed with Collor de Mello's impeachment and to indict the President for 'crimes of responsibility'. Within minutes of the opening of the impeachment trial on 29 December, however, Collor de Mello announced his resignation from the presidency. Itamar Franco was immediately sworn in as President (to serve the remainder of Collor de Mello's term) at a specially convened session of the Congress. On the following day the Senate, which had agreed to continue with proceedings against Collor de Mello (despite his resignation), announced that the former President's political rights (including immunity from prosecution and the holding of public office for an eight-year period) were to be removed. In January 1993 Collor de Mello was notified by the Supreme Court that he was to stand trial, as an ordinary citizen, on charges of 'passive corruption and criminal association'. Proceedings against Collor de Mello were initiated in June, and in December the Supreme Federal Tribunal endorsed the Senate's eight-year ban on his holding public office. In December 1994, however, the Tribunal voted to acquit Collor de Mello of the charges, owing to insufficient evidence against him. In January 1998 the former President was cleared of charges of illegal enrichment.

At a referendum conducted in April 1993 voters overwhelmingly rejected the introduction of a parliamentary system of government or the restoration of the monarchy, opting instead to retain the presidential system.

In late 1992 and early 1993 several unsuccessful attempts, by three successive economic teams, to address the problems of burgeoning inflation and massive budget deficit largely failed to inspire the confidence of the business sector or of international finance organizations. In June 1993 the new Minister of the Economy, Fernando Henrique Cardoso, announced the terms of the Government's latest economic programme, the 'plano de verdade' (real plan). A new currency, the cruzeiro real, was introduced in August. A programme for economic stability, announced in December 1993, sought to regulate the flow of federal resources to states and municipalities. Congressional approval for the establishment of a Social Emergency Fund (providing for further centralization of control over the expenditures and revenue of states and government agencies) prompted the activation of a transitional index, the Unidade Real de Valor (URV), linked to the dollar, on 1 March 1994. On 1 July the new currency, the real, was introduced, at par with the dollar.

In April 1993 the PDT leader, Leonel Brizola, announced the party's withdrawal from the ruling coalition, following Franco's decision to proceed with the privatization of the prestigious National Steel Company (Companhia Siderúrgica Nacional—CSN). Minister of Justice and PDT member Maurício Corrêa Lima subsequently resigned from the party rather than relinquish the justice portfolio. In August the Partido Socialista Brasileiro (PSB) withdrew from the coalition, and in September the PMDB national council narrowly defeated a motion to end its association with the Government. The fragility of the Government was exacerbated by the emergence of a new corruption scandal in October, in which 22 deputies, four senators, two incumbent ministers, two former ministers and three governors were seemingly implicated in a fraudulent scheme in which political influence was allegedly exercised in order to secure state projects for individual construction companies, in exchange for bribes. A 44-member congressional committee of inquiry was established in October, and in January 1994 recommended the expulsion of 18 federal deputies, and the further investigation of 12 deputies, three governors and one senator. In mid-April the Chamber of Deputies voted to expel three of the 18 named deputies and to continue investigations into four deputies who had recently resigned, in order to prevent their participation in the October elections. In May, Ibsen Pinheiro, a prominent deputy who had been leader of the Chamber of Deputies when impeachment proceedings were initiated against Collor de Mello, was similarly expelled from the Congress.

In October 1993, as stipulated in the 1988 Constitution, a congressional review of the Constitution was initiated, despite the opposition of left-wing parties who feared the possible erosion of existing guarantees of civil and social rights. In May 1994 the Congress concluded its review of the Constitution, having adopted just six amendments, including a reduction in the length of the presidential term from five to four years.

A number of ministerial changes were made in late 1993 and early 1994, largely to enable ministers to seek election in the forthcoming polls. In March 1994 Cardoso resigned from the finance portfolio in order to meet the 2 April deadline for registration as presidential candidate of the PSDB. Lula da Silva was formally endorsed as presidential candidate of the PT-led Frente Popular (FP) on 1 May. Political events in the months preceding the election were dominated by numerous allegations of corruption and misconduct, which forced the replacement of the vice-presidential running mates of both Cardoso and da Silva, the withdrawal from the contest of the presidential candidate of the PL, Flávio Rocha, and the resignation of the Ministers of Finance and Mines and Energy, following two separate incidents in September 1994 in which they were accused of having abused their position.

Presidential, gubernatorial and legislative elections were conducted on 3 October 1994. Cardoso, whose candidacy was supported by the PFL, the PTB, the PL and the business community, won the presidential contest in the first round, with an overall majority of 54.3% of the votes, following a campaign that had focused largely on the success of his economic initiatives. The PT candidate, da Silva, with the support of the PSB, was second with 27.0% of the votes cast. The elections were notable for the high rate of voter abstention and for the large number of blank and spoiled ballots (almost 16% of total votes cast). The discovery of large-scale, organized electoral fraud in the State of Rio de Janeiro forced the annulment of elections for state and federal deputies there, which were reorganized (with a large military presence) to coincide with the 15 November run-off elections for governorships in states where no overall majority had been achieved in the October poll. PSDB candidates were also successful in the gubernatorial contests, securing six of the 27 state governorships, including the crucial industrial centres of São Paulo, Minas Gerais and Rio de Janeiro. While the PMDB increased its number of state governorships from seven to nine, and continued to boast the largest single-party representation in the Congress, the party's presidential candidate, Orestes Quércia, had attracted only 4.4% of the votes cast. The multi-party composition of Cardoso's Cabinet (with portfolios allocated not only to those parties that had supported his candidacy, but also to the PT and the PMDB), announced in late December 1994, demonstrated the new President's need to maintain a broad base of congressional support in order to secure prompt endorsement for proposed constitutional reform of the taxation and social security systems.

Cardoso was inaugurated as President on 1 January 1995 and a new Cabinet was installed on the following day. Cardoso immediately made clear his intention to continue the programme of economic reform in order to control public expenditure and reduce inflation. In February Cardoso employed the presidential veto to reject a draft congressional proposal to increase the minimum monthly wage. In March the currency was devalued, and the privatization programme, suspended by Franco during 1994, was reactivated (with the announcement of the future sale of the State's controlling interest in the Companhia Vale do Rio Doce—CVRD—mining concern); interest rates and tariffs on consumer durables were raised and the increase in the minimum wage, previously vetoed by the President, was approved. However, opposition to the programme of economic stabilization and to renewed efforts by the Government to introduce constitutional amendments, including those that would end state monopolies in the telecommunications and petroleum sectors, resulted in the organization, by the Central Unica dos Trabalhadores (CUT) trade union confederation, of a general strike in May 1995. The President's decision to order military intervention in a number of crucial petroleum refineries was widely interpreted as evidence of the Government's intent to undermine the concerted action of the political opposition and the trade unions. By early June, however, employees in the petroleum sector had begun to return to work, and on 20 June (despite vociferous congressional opposition) the Chamber of Deputies approved the proposal to open the sector to private participation. (The amendment relating to the petroleum sector was subsequently approved by the Senate in November; constitutional amendments providing for an end to state control of telecommunications, natural gas distribution and a number of shipping routes, were formally promulgated by the Congress in August.)

In September 1995, following presidential assurances that reforms to the tax and social security systems would not result in a reduction in state government revenues and that state debts to the Federal Government might be rescheduled, Cardoso's proposals for further constitutional reform attracted the support of the majority of state governors. In October the Congress approved the extension of the Social Emergency Fund for 18 months. In late May the Government had announced further economic adjustment, including plans to end the use of monetary correction indices in a broad rage of financial calculations and negotiations.

In September 1995 three existing right-wing parties, the Partido Progressista Reformador, the Partido Progressista and the Partido Republicano Progressista, merged to create the Partido Progressista Brasileiro (PPB), which expressed cautious support for the Government. By December, however, Cardoso's integrity had been seriously compromised by the alleged involvement of a number of his political associates in irregular financial transactions organized by the Banco Econômico in support of recent electoral campaigns, and by an influence-peddling scandal arising from the award to a US company, Raytheon, of the contract for development of an Amazon Regional Surveillance System (Sivam), which resulted in the resignation, in November, of the Minister of the Air Force. A congressional inquiry into the Sivam affair was initiated during November 1995. In February 1996 a special committee of the Senate made a recommendation, supported by Cardoso, that the Government should negotiate a substantial foreign loan to honour the Sivam contract with Raytheon, and in October 1996 the President was able to endorse the agreement.

Meanwhile, investigation of the so-called 'pink folder' of politicians, recovered from the ailing Banco Econômico, continued during 1996, as the banking sector was plunged into further crisis. In March it was revealed that the Government had withheld details of a US $5,000m.-fraud perpetrated at the Banco Nacional some 10 years earlier. Moreover, it emerged that the Government had extended a recent credit facility of US $5,800m. to the bank in order to facilitate its merger with UNIBANCO in November 1995. Also in March the Government announced emergency financing for the Banco do Brasil, which, in common with many Brazilian banks, had suffered huge losses during 1995.

During 1996 renewed attempts by the Government to secure congressional approval for constitutional reforms relating to taxation, public administration and social security were repeatedly obstructed, delayed or defeated in the Congresso, despite the adoption of a number of concessionary clauses and the successful negotiation of a compromise agreement on social security with trade union organizations in January.

A minor reorganization of the Cabinet was implemented in April 1996 to accommodate the introduction of the new Ministry of Political Co-ordination. In May José Serra resigned from the Planning, Budget and Co-ordination portfolio in order to contest the mayorship of São Paulo at municipal elections scheduled for October. Serra was replaced by Antônio Kandir, also a member of the PSDB. In August the Minister of Transport, Odacir Klein, resigned following his son's arraignment on charges relating to the death of a building worker as a result of a motor accident, and in November the Minister of Health, Abid Jatene, resigned in protest at inadequate levels of state funding for the health sector.

The results of municipal elections conducted on 3 October 1996 revealed a reduction in support for the PSDB; Serra was third in the contest for the São Paulo mayorship, with only 15.6% of the votes. Celso Pitta of the PPB was finally elected to the post at a second round of voting conducted on 15 November. The results of other run-off elections, conducted concurrently, also demonstrated a significant level of support for the PPB. The elections represented a disappointment for many veteran parties. The PPB, the PFL and the PSB, however, all made significant gains. None the less, Cardoso's own popularity continued to benefit from the success of the Government's attempts to control inflation. In January 1997 a legislative document, sponsored by the President, which sought to amend the Constitution in order to allow the incumbent head of state, state governors and mayors to seek re-election, received tentative endorsement from the Chamber of Deputies, despite vociferous opposition from the PMDB.

In mid-1996 the moderate Força Sindical trade union organization joined the CUT in urging workers to observe Brazil's first general strike in five years, to be organized on 21 June. Despite the Government's announcement, in April, of a job-creation programme to provide employment for 3m. Brazilians, the unions were dissatisfied with the Government's failure to halt rising levels of unemployment. However, the strike was only partially observed, and on the same day the Government announced details of the next phase of its massive divestment programme. Several companies in the power sector, 31 ports (including Santos and Rio de Janeiro) and the prestigious CVRD were among those state concerns to be offered for sale to the private sector. In July the Government announced that the divestment programme was to be accelerated, and that the state telecommunications company, Telebrás, together with large sections of the rail and power networks, would be privatized by the end of 1998. Further reductions in public spending were announced in August 1996. A new programme of economic measures designed to further reduce the fiscal deficit in 1997 was introduced, by executive decree, in October 1996. The Social Emergency Fund was again extended, to the end of 1999.

In February 1997 the Chamber of Deputies confirmed its approval of a constitutional amendment to permit the President to stand for re-election in 1998, Cardoso's position having been strengthened by the election of two of his supporters to the presidencies of both chambers of the Congress. Following the Senate vote in favour of the legislation in May (despite allegations of bribery relating to the passage through the lower house), the constitutional amendment received the upper house's final approval in June. The legislation was swiftly ratified by President Cardoso.

In March 1997, meanwhile, controversial legislation to end the long-standing monopoly of PETROBRÁS over the petroleum industry was approved by the Chamber of Deputies, which in the following month voted narrowly in favour of proposals to reform the civil service (thus to prepare for the dismissal of surplus employees). The Senate rejection of the latter item of legislation in June, however, was a major set-back to the Government's programme of economic reform and in particular to its attempts to reduce the budget deficit. Nevertheless, a series of compromises enabled the Government to renew its plans for reform of the civil service, and in July an opposition amendment to the proposed legislation was narrowly defeated in the Chamber of Deputies. In November the lower house gave its final approval to the legislation. In 1998, as the Government attempted to proceed with its reform programme, scrutiny of proposed legislation relating to amendments to the social security system continued.

As public confidence in the integrity of the country's police force continued to diminish, in mid-1997 thousands of troops were deployed in response to a strike by police officers protesting against low rates of pay. President Cardoso denounced as an 'uprising' the illegal strikes, which in some areas resulted in a complete breakdown of law and order.

In June 1997 the PT ordered an inquiry into allegations of corruption on the part of its presidential candidate, Lula da Silva. Although da Silva was exonerated by the investigation (thus permitting him to renew his candidacy for the 1998 election), other financial irregularities were uncovered, leading to a sharp decline in the PT's popularity. As the 1998 presidential election approached, various potential candidates announced changes in their party affiliation. In August 1997 Ciro Gomes, a former Minister of Finance, defected from the PSDB to the smaller Partido Popular Socialista (PPS), thereby exacerbating the internal crisis within the PSDB. (In the same month the Minister of Communications, Sérgio Vieira da Motta, announced his resignation from the party.) Former President Itamar Franco, meanwhile, declared his affiliation to the PMDB. In October 1997 the incumbent President Cardoso's candidacy was endorsed by the PMDB, and in November Lula da Silva officially declared his intention to stand as the PT's candidate.

In July 1997, meanwhile, an investigation by the Senate into a financial scandal arising from fraudulent bond issues concluded that 20 prominent politicians and senior officials (including three state governors and the mayor of São Paulo, Celso Pitta, along with his predecessor, Paulo Maluf), had been involved in a criminal operation. A total of 161 financial institutions, including Banco Bradesco, Brazil's largest private bank, were implicated in the scandal. In January 1998 Celso Pitta was found guilty of fraud, but remained in office pending an appeal.

In March 1998 three ministers, including the Minister of Planning, Budget and Co-ordination, were obliged to resign in order to permit their participation in the forthcoming elections. Kandir was replaced by Paulo Paiva of the PTB. President Cardoso announced the reallocation of several other cabinet portfolios in April. The deaths in rapid succession in April of two of the President's closest associates, however, was a major set-back to Cardoso's campaign for re-election. The loss of Sérgio Motta, the dynamic Minister of Communications and co-founder of the PSDB, followed by the demise of Luis Eduardo Magalhães, leader of government business in the Chamber of Deputies (and son of Antônio Carlos Magalhães, President of the Senate), obliged President Cardoso to curtail an official visit to Spain.

Despite his declared commitment to further economic austerity measures, at the presidential election held on 4 October 1998 Cardoso became the first President to be re-elected for a second consecutive term, securing almost 53.1% of the valid votes cast. Lula da Silva of the PT won 31.7% of the votes, while Ciro Gomes of the PPS received 11.0%. A high rate of abstention was recorded. At the concurrent legislative elections, the PSDB also performed well, securing 99 of the 513 seats in the lower chamber, while its electoral allies won a total of 278 seats (PFL 105, PMDB 82, PPB 60 and PTB 31), bringing the coalition's total representation to 377. Following the simultaneous first stage of the gubernatorial elections in 13 states, the second round was conducted where necessary on 25 October. Opposition candidates defeated the incumbent governors of the populous states of Rio de Janeiro, Rio do Sul and Minas Gerais (where Itamar Franco, the country's former President, was successful), although the São Paulo governorship was retained by Mário Covas, a close ally of President Cardoso.

In November 1998 the Minister of Communications, Luís Carlos Mendonça de Barros, and three other officials resigned as a result of the exposure of a scandal involving illegal tape recordings of telephone conversations detailing their alleged attempts to influence (through their support for the establishment of consortia) the sale to the private sector of Telebrás in July 1998.

Prior to formally resuming office on 1 January 1999, President Cardoso announced the composition of his Cabinet. Although most ministers, including Pedro Malan, the Minister of Finance, retained their portfolios, changes included the creation of a new development ministry (which assumed some of the functions of the Ministry of Industry and Trade, a separate tourism portfolio being established); the new Ministry, headed by Celso Lafer, was to be responsible for the co-ordination of all government policies relating to production, its initiation being regarded as necessary to improve relations with the business community. A civilian was appointed Minister of Defence.

In January 1999 Itamar Franco, the newly-elected Governor of Minas Gerais, declared that the state was defaulting on its debt to the federal Government, indirectly precipitating the devaluation of the Brazilian currency (see Economic Affairs). In the same month, however, having rejected the legislation on four occasions in the previous three years, the Chamber of Deputies finally endorsed the proposed reforms to the country's munificent pension system. The passage of the controversial legislation through the Senate in late January considerably enhanced the prospects of President Cardoso's programme of fiscal austerity.

In April 1999 Francisco Lopes, briefly President of the Central Bank until his removal in January 1999, was arrested, owing to his refusal to give evidence to a senate inquiry into allegations of corruption at the bank. He was acquitted of the charges of contempt, but remained under investigation with regard to allegations that officials of the Central Bank had accepted illicit payments in exchange for the disclosure of privileged information. In a separate inquiry, a senate committee continued its investigations into allegations of corruption within the country's judiciary.

Following the withdrawal of the PTB from the ruling coalition in March 1999, as a result of the unexpected removal from his post of the Minister of the Budget and Administration, Paulo

Paiva, the Government of President Cardoso came under further pressure in May when the PFL announced its intention to present its own candidate at the next presidential election, scheduled for 2002. In July 1999, in an attempt to promote unity within the administration and to give impetus to the programme of economic reform, President Cardoso announced a reorganization of the Cabinet. A new Ministry of National Integration was established. The administration's popularity continued to decline, however, and in August anti-Government demonstrations culminated in the arrival in Brasília of as many as 100,000 marchers, comprising political opponents led by the PT, trade unionists and landless individuals, all protesting against President Cardoso's economic and social policies. In early September, furthermore, Clovis Covilho, Minister of Development, Industry and Trade, was dismissed by the President, following a public disagreement over the policy of economic austerity. He was replaced by Alcides Tápias.

Meanwhile, in April 1999 a congressional commission had commenced investigations into allegations of organized criminal activities. In September 1999 Hildebrando Pascoal became the second member of the Chamber of Deputies that year to be expelled from the lower house as a result of accusations of murder. It was alleged that Pascoal had been the leader of a cocaine-trafficking gang involved in the torture and murder of numerous victims in the remote state of Acre. Moreover, in October the congressional commission exposed a nation-wide criminal network that allegedly encompassed politicians, government officials, judges, police officers, business executives and banking officials. Embarrassed by the scale of the revelations (which even extended to reports of drugs-trafficking within the National Congress building), in November President Cardoso announced the establishment of a new anti-corruption force to combat the growing problem of organized crime. In the following month, in an effort to improve accountability and to strengthen congressional powers of investigation, the Senate approved a constitutional amendment to restrict presidential use of provisional measures, to which successive governments had frequently resorted as a means to circumvent the cumbersome legislative process.

Meanwhile, in late February 1995, having announced an initiative to improve the quality of primary education earlier in the month, Cardoso launched a social improvement programme, Comunidade Solidária, with a consultative council comprising representatives of 10 ministries and headed by the President's wife, Ruth Cardoso, and with a budget of US $3,000m. In September the President announced a new programme for the defence of human rights and later in the month a government-sponsored bill was approved by the Chamber of Deputies, whereby responsibility for the deaths of more than 100 left-wing politicians and activists during the military regimes of the 1960s and 1970s was assumed by the State, which also approved financial compensation for the relatives of the victims. A National Plan for Human Rights, introduced in May 1996, contained 168 recommendations, including proposals to increase protection for the rights of children and workers. However, the absence of a financial or procedural framework for adoption of the plan prompted a cautious response to the document from human rights organizations. During 1995 the Government suffered from repeated criticism of its failure to address burgeoning urban crime (particularly in Rio de Janeiro) and the demands of the Landless Peasant Movement, the Movimento dos Sem-Terra (MST), which organized a number of illegal occupations of disputed land during the year in support of demands for an acceleration of the Government's programme of expropriation of uncultivated land for distribution to landless rural families.

Tensions arising from land ownership and reallocation disputes persisted. In January 1996 protests and land occupations were renewed following the enactment, by presidential decree, of a new law regulating the demarcation of Indian lands, which many indigenous groups interpreted as a serious erosion of the previously-existing land rights of the Indian population. Meanwhile, landless peasant groups challenged government claims that 100,000 itinerant families had been resettled during 1995 and 1996, and described the Government's reallocation programme as inadequate. (Official estimates of the number of landless families in Brazil were considerably lower than the figure of 4.8m. quoted by the MST.) Rapidly deteriorating relations between the authorities and the MST were further exacerbated in April 1996 by the violent intervention of the local military police in a demonstration, organized by the MST and supported by some 1,500 protesters at Eldorado de Carajás in the State of Pará, which resulted in the deaths of 19 demonstrators. (It was subsequently alleged that a number of those killed had been summarily executed.) Widespread public outrage prompted Cardoso to request immediate congressional priority for legislation relating to land expropriation, and to afford full cabinet status to the former agriculture ministry department responsible for executing the agrarian reform programme. Raúl Jungmann of the PPS was appointed to the new post of Minister of Agrarian Reform. José Eduardo de Andrade Vieira, who had attributed responsibility for the April massacre to the increasingly confrontational operations of the MST, was replaced as Minister of Agriculture and Supplies by Arlindo Porto of the PTB. However, Cardoso's attempts to propel land reform legislation through the Congress were promptly obstructed, and the emergence of a number of reports detailing the creation of close associations between local military police units and powerful rural landowners seemed likely to undermine efforts to bring to justice those responsible for the Eldorado de Carajás atrocity. Despite Jungmann's stated intention to facilitate dialogue amongst opposing groups in the dispute through the creation of a discussion council, by late 1996 the MST-sponsored campaign of illegal land seizures and occupations of federal and state government buildings had intensified, particularly in the States of São Paulo and Santa Catarina.

In April 1997, in response to the growing unrest and the arrival in Brasília of 1,500 MST members at the conclusion of a two-month march, the Government announced new measures to accelerate the process of land reform. At the end of April landless peasants threatened to occupy land belonging to the CVRD, in protest at the company's forthcoming transfer to the private sector. In May, however, despite various legal challenges, the sale of assets in this major producer of iron ore proceeded. In the following month José Rainha Júnior, an MST leader, was sentenced to more than 26 years' imprisonment for his involvement in the murder in 1989 of a landowner and of a police officer. In August 1997 a clash between riot police and illegal occupants of public land in Brasília resulted in 49 arrests and 20 persons injured. In the same month some 200 landless families seized two ranches in the state of São Paulo. In early 1998 the MST intensified its campaign for land reform. In March thousands of activists occupied government premises. In the same month Adelson Silva de Brito, an MST leader who had recently headed a land invasion, was shot dead in Barra Mansa. In September the head of the agrarian reform institute in São Paulo was obliged to suspend the state's land-expropriation proceedings when the organization's offices were occupied by 500 MST members.

In August 1999 the trial of 150 military policemen accused of participation in the 1996 killings in Eldorado de Carajás opened in Belém. Three commanding officers were promptly acquitted of the charges on the grounds of insufficient evidence. President Cardoso expressed regret at the ruling. The acquittal provoked outrage among the families of the victims of the massacre and led to rioting on the streets of Belém. Proceedings against the other 147 defendants were suspended.

Meanwhile, the murder of Francisco (Chico) Mendes, the leader of the rubber-tappers' union and a pioneering ecologist, in December 1988 brought Brazil's environmental problems to international attention. Widespread concern was expressed that large-scale development projects, together with the 'slash-and-burn' farming techniques of cattle ranchers, peasant smallholders and loggers, and the release of large amounts of mercury into the environment by an estimated 60,000 gold prospectors (or *garimpeiros*) in the Amazon region, presented a serious threat to the survival of both the indigenous Indians and the rain forest. Despite the appointment in March 1990 of internationally-acclaimed ecologist José Lutzemberger as Minister of the Environment, and the implementation of a number of initiatives to curb unauthorized gold prospecting in the Amazon region, international criticism of the Government's poor response to the threat to the environment persisted throughout the 1990s. Of particular concern to many international observers was the plight of the Yanomami Indian tribe in Roraima. It was estimated that, since the arrival of the *garimpeiros* in the region, some 10%–15% of the Yanomami's total population had been exterminated as a result of pollution and disease, introduced to the area by the gold prospectors. The National Indian Foundation (FUNAI) was heavily criticized for its role in the affair and was accused of failing to provide effective protection and support for Brazil's Indian population. In March 1992 Lutzemberger was dismissed following his repeated criticism of institutionalized opposition to his environmental programme. In June 1992, however, national prestige was heightened when Brazil successfully hosted the UN Conference on Environment and Development or 'Earth Summit'. In August 1993 international attention was again focused on the region, following the slaughter of 73 members of the Yanomami tribe by *garimpeiros,* in the context of the ongoing territorial dispute prompted by the miners' attempts to exploit the rich mineral deposits of the Yanomami land. A new cabinet post of Minister with Special Responsibility for the Brazilian Amazon was subsequently created. In March 1996 a US $5,700m.-rain forest protection programme (to be funded by the Brazilian Government, the European Union and the G-7 group of industrialized countries over a five-year period) was concluded between President Cardoso and the Secretary-General of the United Nations. At a meeting in Manaus in October 1997, the G-7 group pledged an additional US $68m. In July 1997 Júlio Gaiger, the head of FUNAI, resigned, claiming that the Government had failed to honour its commitment to assist indigenous people. Legislation to provide greater protection for Brazil's natural resources, through the establishment of criminal penalties for illegal activities, was approved by the President in February 1998. In early 1998, however, the federal Government's slow response to a series of forest fires (exacerbated by protracted drought) in the Yanomami reservation of Roraima drew some criticism.

In 1990 a series of bilateral trade agreements was signed with Argentina, representing the first stage in a process leading to the eventual establishment of a Southern Cone Common Market (Mercado Comum do Sul—Mercosul), also to include Paraguay and Uruguay. In March 1991, in Paraguay, the four nations signed the Asunción treaty whereby they reaffirmed their commitment to the creation of such a market by the end of 1994. Mercosul duly came into effect on 1 January 1995, following the signing, by the Presidents of the four member nations, of the Ouro Prêto Protocol, in Brazil, in December 1994. While a complete common external tariff was not expected until 2006, customs barriers on 80%–85% of mutually exchanged goods were removed immediately. In 1999, however, Brazil's commercial relations with Argentina, in particular, were severely strained by the devaluation of the real, which prompted the latter country to impose curbs on certain Brazilian exports.

In May 1994 Brazil declared its full adherence to the 1967 Tlatelolco Treaty for the non-proliferation of nuclear weapons in Latin America and the Caribbean. The Treaty was promulgated by presidential decree in September 1994. Brazil signed the international Treaty on the Non-Proliferation of Nuclear Weapons in June 1997. The Brazilian President ratified this and also the Comprehensive Test Ban Treaty (see p. 75) in July 1998.

## Government

Under the 1988 Constitution, the country is a federal republic comprising 26 States and a Federal District (Brasília). Legislative power is exercised by the bicameral Congresso Nacional (National Congress), comprising the Senado Federal (Federal Senate—members elected by a system of proportional representation for four years) and the Câmara dos Deputados (Chamber of Deputies—members elected by the majority principle in rotation for eight years). The number of deputies is based on the size of the population. Election is by universal adult suffrage. Executive power is exercised by the President, elected by direct ballot for four years. The President appoints and leads the Cabinet. Each State has a directly elected Governor and an elected legislature. For the purposes of local government, the States are divided into municipalities.

## Defence

Military service, lasting 12 months, is compulsory for men between 18 and 45 years of age. In August 1999 the armed forces totalled 291,000 (including 48,200 conscripts): army 189,000 (40,000 conscripts), navy 52,000 and air force 50,000. Public security forces number about 385,600. Defence expenditure for 1999 was budgeted at R$17,500m.

## Economic Affairs

In 1997, according to estimates by the World Bank, Brazil's gross national product (GNP), measured at average 1995–97 prices, was US $784,044m., equivalent to $4,790 per head. During 1990–97, it was estimated, GNP per head increased, in real terms, at an average rate of 1.9% per year. Over the same period, the population increased at an average annual rate of 1.4%. In 1998 GNP totalled about $758,000m. ($4,570 per head). Brazil's gross domestic product (GDP) increased, in real terms, at an average annual rate of 3.3% in 1990–98. According to the IMF, GDP increased by an estimated 0.1% in 1998, compared with a rise of 3.7% in 1997.

Agriculture (including hunting, forestry and fishing) engaged 23.4% of the employed labour force and contributed 8.0% of GDP in 1998. The principal cash crops are soya beans, coffee, tobacco, sugar cane and cocoa beans. Subsistence crops include wheat, maize, rice, potatoes, beans, cassava and sorghum. Beef and poultry production are also important, as is fishing (particularly tuna, crab and shrimp). During 1990–98, according to the World Bank, agricultural GDP increased at an average annual rate of 3.1%. Agricultural GDP increased by an estimated 2.7% in 1997 and by 0.2% in 1998. In late 1999 coffee production, in particular, was affected by drought.

Industry (including mining, manufacturing, construction and power) employed 20.1% of the working population and provided 32.3% of GDP in 1998. During 1990–98 industrial GDP increased at an average annual rate of 3.2%. Estimated growth of 5.5% was recorded in the sector in 1997. In 1998, however, industrial GDP declined by an estimated 0.9%.

Mining contributed 0.6% of GDP in 1998. The major mineral exports are iron ore (haematite—in terms of iron content, Brazil is the largest producer in the world), tin and aluminium (Brazil was the world's third largest producer of bauxite in 1997). Gold, phosphates, platinum, uranium, manganese, copper and coal are also mined. In 1990 deposits of niobium, thought to be the world's largest, were discovered in the state of Amazonas. Brazil's reserves of petroleum were estimated at 657m. metric tons in 1997.

Manufacturing contributed 19.3% of GDP in 1998. In the same year the sector engaged 11.8% of the total employed population. There is considerable state involvement in a broad range of manufacturing activity. While traditionally-dominant areas, including textiles and clothing, footwear and food- and beverage-processing, continue to contribute a large share to the sector, more recent developments in the sector have resulted in the emergence of machinery and transport equipment (including road vehicles and components, passenger jet aircraft and specialist machinery for the petroleum industry), construction materials (especially iron and steel), wood and sugar cane derivatives, and chemicals and petrochemicals as significant new manufacturing activities. According to the World Bank, manufacturing GDP increased at an average rate of 2.5% per year in 1990–97. The sector's production increased by 3.6% in 1997, but fell by 3.3% in 1998.

By the mid-1980s some 32% of total energy was derived from electricity (90% of which was hydroelectric), 30% from petroleum, 18% from wood and charcoal and 12% from fuel alcohol. Other energy sources, including coal and natural gas, accounted for some 8%. Attempts to exploit further the country's vast hydroelectric potential (estimated at 213,000 MW) were encouraged by the successful completion of preliminary stages of development of ambitious dam projects at Itaipú, on the border with Paraguay, and at Tucuruí, on the Tocantins river. The 12,600-MW Itaipú project is expected to produce as much as 35% of Brazil's total electricity requirements when fully operational. Plans to construct a 17,000-MW hydroelectric plant on the Xingu river, in the Amazon region, are also under consideration. By 1993 the share of electricity produced by hydroelectric sources had increased to 93.3%. The Angra I nuclear power plant, inaugurated in 1985, has subsequently operated only intermittently, while financial constraints have hindered the completion of the Angra II plant and have prevented further development of the country's nuclear programme. Imports of petroleum comprised 6.8% of the value of total merchandise imports in 1998.

The services sector contributed an estimated 59.7% of GDP and engaged 56.5% of the employed labour force in 1998. According to the World Bank, the GDP of the services sector increased at an average rate of 3.4% per year in 1990–98. Growth in the sector's GDP was estimated at 1.7% in 1997 and 0.7% in 1998.

In 1998 Brazil recorded a visible trade deficit of US $6,603m. There was a deficit of US $33,829m. on the current account of the balance of payments. In 1998 the principal source of imports (23.4%) was the USA, which was also the principal market for exports (19.1%). Other major trading partners were Germany, Japan, Italy, the Netherlands and Argentina. The principal exports in 1998 were food and food-processing products (notably coffee), iron ore and concentrates, iron and steel products, machinery, and road vehicles and parts. The principal imports were mineral fuels, machinery and mechanical appliances, road vehicles and parts, and chemical products.

The 1999 federal budget originally envisaged expenditure of R$187,800m. (subsequently reduced) and revenue of R$196,500m. (subsequently increased to R$199,900m.). Brazil's external debt was US $193,663m. at the end of 1997, of which $86,745m. was long-term public debt. In that year the cost of debt-servicing was equivalent to 57.4% of revenue from exports of goods and services. The annual rate of inflation averaged 289% in 1990–98. Consumer prices increased by an average of 3.2% in 1998 and by 7.5% in the year to October 1999. Official figures indicated an unemployment rate of 9.0% of the labour force in 1998, while other sources suggested that the figure was higher. (Unemployment in São Paulo was estimated at a record 16.3% in September 1997.)

Brazil is a member of ALADI (see. p. 292), Mercosul (p. 267), the Association of Tin Producing Countries (ATPC, p. 287) and the Cairns Group (p. 338). Brazil also joined the Comunidade dos Países de Língua Portuguesa (CPLP, p. 300), founded in 1996.

An economic stabilization programme, implemented during 1994 with the aim of balancing the budget and controlling inflation, was bolstered by the success of a new currency (the real), introduced on 1 July of that year, and by the reactivation of the privatization programme in early 1995. The auction of Telebrás, the state telecommunications company, to local and foreign private interests in July 1998 proved highly successful, yielding R$22,057m. (64% in excess of the reserve price). Upon his re-election to office in October 1998, President Cardoso immediately reiterated his pledge to reform the public sector and announced details of a three-year programme of fiscal adjustment. Drastic cuts in budgetary expenditure (a reduction of R$28,000m. for 1999 alone) and increases in taxes were envisaged. Civil servants' pension contributions were to be raised, in an attempt to curtail the state pension scheme's substantial deficit. As the rate of unemployment continued to rise, in November 1998 new measures included an improvement in benefits for the long-term unemployed and the introduction of greater flexibility into working contracts. In December, in support of the Government's programme, the IMF formally approved Brazil's request for a three-year stand-by credit equivalent to US$18,100m. In January 1999, however, the unexpected resignation of the President of the Central Bank and his successor's decision to devalue the Brazilian currency (thus abandoning the exchange-rate policy agreed with the IMF) precipitated a period of renewed capital flight, seriously depleting the country's reserves and leading to turmoil on international financial markets. By early March the Brazilian real had lost 40% of its value against the US dollar. In that month Brazil and the IMF reached agreement on a revised programme for 1999–2001, thus permitting lending to resume. Requirements included an increase in Brazil's budgetary surplus, which was to be raised from 2.6% of GDP (as agreed in late 1998) to 3.1%, a reduction of the country's public debt to a level below the original specification of 46.5% of GDP, the introduction of a new monetary policy, incorporating a formal target for the restriction of inflation, and the acceleration of the Government's privatization programme. Also in March 1999 the first reduction in interest rates, which had reached 45%, was made. By late 1999 the economy appeared to be recovering. Although there was no discernible growth in GDP in that year, expansion of 3.0% was envisaged for 2000. Meanwhile, fears of a return to high levels of inflation had proved unfounded, the rise in consumer prices being estimated at about 8% for 1999.

## Social Welfare

The social security system, in existence since 1923, was rationalized in 1960, and the Instituto Nacional de Previdência Social (INPS) was formed in 1966. All social welfare programmes were consolidated in 1977 under the National System of Social Insurance and Assistance (SINPAS). The INPS administers benefits to urban and rural employees and their dependants. Benefits include sickness benefit, invalidity, old age, length of service and widows' pensions, maternity and family allowances and grants. There are three government agencies: the Instituto de Administração Financeira da Previdência e Assistência Social collects contributions and revenue and supplies funds, the Instituto Nacional de Assistência Médica da Previdência Social is responsible for medical care, and CEME (Central Medicines) supplies medicines at a low price. According to official sources, the state social security budget for 2000 was projected at R $3,800m. In the early 1990s privatization of pension fund management, based on the Chilean model, was being implemented. By early 1997 it was estimated that some US $70,000m. were being managed by pension funds in Brazil (including US $17,600m. controlled by Previ—the pension fund for the Banco do Brasil, and US $7,000m. controlled by the 260 members of the private funds association—the Associação Brasileira das Entidades Fechadas de Previdência Privada). Total assets controlled by pension funds were expected to exceed US $400,000m. by 2010.

In 1984 there were 122,818 physicians working in Brazil; in the same year the country had 12,175 hospital establishments, with a total of 538,721 beds. The private medical sector controls 90% of Brazil's hospitals. Budget forecasts for 2000 envisaged expenditure on health services of R $14,100m.

The welfare of the dwindling population of indigenous American Indians is the responsibility of the Fundação Nacional do Indio (FUNAI), which was formed to assign homelands to the Indians, most of whom are landless and threatened by the exploitation of the Amazon forest.

## Education

Education is free in official pre-primary schools and is compulsory between the ages of seven and 14 years. Primary education begins at seven years of age and lasts for eight years. Secondary education, beginning at 15 years of age, lasts for three years and is also free in official schools. In 1998 95.8% of children in the relevant age-group were enrolled at primary schools, but only 30.7% of those aged 15 to 17 were enrolled at secondary schools. The Federal Government is responsible for higher education, and in 1997 there were 150 universities, of which 77 were state-administered. Numerous private institutions exist at all levels of education. Expenditure on education by the central Government was forecast at R $5,100m. for 2000.

Despite an anti-illiteracy campaign, initiated in 1971, according to official estimates in 1996 the adult illiteracy rate was 14.7%.

## Public Holidays

**2000:** 1 January (New Year's Day—Universal Confraternization Day), 6–7 March (Carnival), 21 April (Good Friday and Tiradentes Day—Discovery of Brazil), 1 May (Labour Day), 1 June (Ascension Day), 22 June (Corpus Christi), 7 September (Independence Day), 12 October (Our Lady Aparecida, Patron Saint of Brazil), 2 November (All Souls' Day), 15 November (Proclamation of the Republic), 25 December (Christmas Day).

**2001:** 1 January (New Year's Day—Universal Confraternization Day), 26–27 February (Carnival), 13 April (Good Friday), 21 April (Tiradentes Day—Discovery of Brazil) 1 May (Labour Day), 24 May (Ascension Day), 14 June (Corpus Christi), 7 September (Independence Day), 12 October (Our Lady Aparecida, Patron Saint of Brazil), 2 November (All Souls' Day), 15 November (Proclamation of the Republic), 25 December (Christmas Day).

Other local holidays include 20 January (Foundation of Rio de Janeiro) and 25 January (Foundation of São Paulo).

## Weights and Measures

The metric system is in force.

# Statistical Survey

Sources (unless otherwise stated): Economic Research Department, Banco Central do Brasil, SBS, Q 03, Bloco B, Brasília, DF; tel. (61) 414-1074; fax (61) 414-2036; e-mail coace.depec.@bcb.gov.br; internet www.bcb.gov.br/; Instituto Brasileiro de Geografia e Estatística (IBGE), Centro de Documentação e Disseminação de Informações (CDDI), Rua Gen. Canabarro 706, 4° andar, 20271-201 Maracanã, Rio de Janeiro, RJ; tel. (21) 569-2901; fax (21) 284-1959; internet www.ibge.gov.br.

## Area and Population

**AREA, POPULATION AND DENSITY**

| | |
|---|---|
| Area (sq km) | 8,547,403.5* |
| Population (census results)† | |
| 1 September 1980 | 119,002,706 |
| 1 September 1991 | |
| Males | 72,485,122 |
| Females | 74,340,353 |
| Total | 146,825,475 |
| 1 August 1996 | 157,070,163 |
| Population (official estimates at mid-year)† | |
| 1997 | 159,636,400 |
| 1998 | 161,790,300 |
| 1999 | 163,947,600 |
| Density (per sq km) at mid-1999 | 19.2 |

* 3,300,170.9 sq miles.

† Excluding Indian jungle population, numbering 45,429 in 1950.

**ADMINISTRATIVE DIVISIONS**
(population at census of 1 August 1996)

| State | Population | Capital |
|---|---|---|
| Acre (AC) | 483,593 | Rio Branco |
| Alagoas (AL) | 2,633,251 | Maceió |
| Amapá (AP) | 379,459 | Macapá |
| Amazonas (AM) | 2,389,279 | Manaus |
| Bahia (BA) | 12,541,675 | Salvador |
| Ceará (CE) | 6,809,290 | Fortaleza |
| Espírito Santo (ES) | 2,802,707 | Vitória |
| Goiás (GO) | 4,514,967 | Goiânia |
| Maranhão (MA) | 5,222,183 | São Luís |
| Mato Grosso (MT) | 2,235,832 | Cuiabá |
| Mato Grosso do Sul (MS) | 1,927,834 | Campo Grande |
| Minas Gerais (MG) | 16,672,613 | Belo Horizonte |
| Pará (PA) | 5,510,849 | Belém |
| Paraíba (PB) | 3,305,616 | João Pessoa |
| Paraná (PR) | 9,003,804 | Curitiba |
| Pernambuco (PE) | 7,399,071 | Recife |
| Piauí (PI) | 2,673,085 | Teresina |
| Rio de Janeiro (RJ) | 13,406,308 | Rio de Janeiro |
| Rio Grande do Norte (RN) | 2,558,660 | Natal |
| Rio Grande do Sul (RS) | 9,634,688 | Porto Alegre |
| Rondônia (RO) | 1,229,306 | Porto Velho |
| Roraima (RR) | 247,131 | Boa Vista |
| Santa Catarina (SC) | 4,875,244 | Florianópolis |
| São Paulo (SP) | 34,119,110 | São Paulo |
| Sergipe (SE) | 1,624,020 | Aracaju |
| Tocantins (TO) | 1,048,642 | Palmas |
| Distrito Federal (DF) | 1,821,946 | Brasília |
| **Total** | 157,070,163 | – |

**PRINCIPAL TOWNS** (population at census of 1 August 1996)*

| | | | |
|---|---|---|---|
| São Paulo | 9,839,066 | Campo Grande | 600,069 |
| Rio de Janeiro | 5,551,538 | João Pessoa | 549,363 |
| Salvador | 2,211,539 | Jaboatão | 529,966 |
| Belo Horizonte | 2,091,371 | Contagem | 492,214 |
| Fortaleza | 1,965,513 | São José dos Campos | 486,167 |
| Brasília (capital) | 1,821,946 | Ribeirão Preto | 456,252 |
| Curitiba | 1,476,253 | Feira de Santana | 450,487 |
| Recife | 1,346,045 | Niterói | 450,364 |
| Porto Alegre | 1,288,879 | São João de Meriti | 434,323 |
| Manaus | 1,157,357 | Cuiabá | 433,355 |
| Belém | 1,144,312 | Sorocaba | 431,561 |
| Goiânia | 1,003,477 | Aracaju | 428,194 |
| Guarulhos | 972,197 | Juíz de Fora | 424,479 |
| Campinas | 908,906 | Londrina | 421,343 |
| São Gonçalo | 833,379 | Uberlândia | 438,986 |
| Nova Iguaçu | 826,188 | Santos | 412,243 |
| São Luis | 780,833 | Joinville | 397,951 |
| Maceió | 723,142 | Campos dos Goytacazes | 389,547 |
| Duque de Caxias | 715,089 | Olinda | 349,380 |
| São Bernardo do Campo | 660,396 | Diadema | 323,116 |
| Natal | 656,037 | Porto Velho | 294,227 |
| Teresina | 655,473 | Jundiaí | 293,373 |
| Santo André | 624,820 | | |
| Osasco | 622,912 | | |

* Figures refer to *municípios*, which may contain rural districts.

**BIRTHS AND DEATHS** (official estimates)

| | Birth rate (per 1,000) | Death rate (per 1,000) |
|---|---|---|
| 1991 | 22.89 | 7.11 |
| 1992 | 22.09 | 7.04 |
| 1993 | 21.37 | 6.98 |
| 1994 | 20.75 | 6.92 |
| 1995 | 20.14 | 6.87 |
| 1996 | 19.69 | 6.82 |
| 1997 | 19.25 | 6.78 |
| 1998 | 20.30 | 6.75 |

**Expectation of life** (official estimates, years at birth, mid-1999): 66.97 (males 63.35; females 70.76).

**ECONOMICALLY ACTIVE POPULATION** (household surveys, September each year, '000 persons aged 10 years and over)*

| | 1996 | 1997 | 1998 |
|---|---|---|---|
| Agriculture, hunting, forestry and fishing | 16,647.0 | 16,770.7 | 16,338.1 |
| Manufacturing | 8,407.1 | 8,507.0 | 8,230.6 |
| Mining and quarrying; Electricity, gas and water | 770.5 | 774.3 | 861.6 |
| Construction | 4,335.6 | 4,583.5 | 4,980.0 |
| Wholesale and retail trade | 9,079.3 | 9,222.8 | 9,417.0 |
| Transport and communications | 2,554.9 | 2,759.0 | 2,786.6 |
| Community, social and personal services (incl. restaurants and hotels) | 24,940.2 | 25,436.4 | 26,040.5 |
| Financing, insurance, real estate and business services; Activities not adequately defined | 1,305.6 | 1,277.9 | 1,308.7 |
| **Total employed** | 68,040.2 | 69,331.5 | 69,963.1 |
| Unemployed | 5,079.9 | 5,881.8 | 6,922.6 |
| **Total labour force** | 73,120.1 | 75,213.3 | 76,885.7 |
| Males | 43,824.8 | 44,832.2 | 45,614.0 |
| Females | 29,295.3 | 30,381.1 | 31,271.7 |

* Figures exclude the rural population of the States of Rondônia, Acre, Amazonas, Roraima, Pará and Amapá.

# Agriculture

**PRINCIPAL CROPS** ('000 metric tons)

| | 1996 | 1997 | 1998 |
|---|---|---|---|
| Wheat | 3,359 | 2,441 | 2,222 |
| Rice (paddy) | 9,990 | 9,290 | 7,796 |
| Barley | 223 | 244 | 301 |
| Maize | 32,185 | 34,601 | 29,297 |
| Oats | 220 | 215 | 198 |
| Sorghum | 336 | 474 | 611 |
| Potatoes | 2,703 | 2,757 | 2,634 |
| Sweet potatoes* | 660 | 650 | 650 |
| Cassava (Manioc) | 24,584 | 24,305 | 19,809 |
| Yams* | 225 | 225 | 225 |
| Dry beans | 2,822 | 2,991 | 2,184 |
| Soybeans (Soya beans) | 23,562 | 26,431 | 31,357 |
| Groundnuts (in shell) | 154 | 140 | 186 |
| Castor beans | 43 | 96 | 14 |
| Cottonseed† | 636 | 526 | 754 |
| Coconuts | 660 | 660 | 649 |
| Babassu kernels* | 211 | 216 | 216 |
| Tomatoes | 2,675 | 2,641 | 2,692 |
| Onions (dry) | 963 | 884 | 835 |
| Other vegetables† | 2,160 | 2,209 | 2,204 |
| Water-melons* | 765 | 765 | 765 |
| Sugar cane | 325,929 | 337,195 | 338,348 |
| Grapes | 734 | 901 | 738 |
| Apples | 655 | 774 | 787 |
| Peaches and nectarines* | 126 | 136 | 146 |
| Oranges | 21,865 | 22,961 | 22,987 |
| Tangerines, mandarins, clementines and satsumas* | 749 | 749 | 749 |
| Lemons and limes* | 455 | 455 | 455 |
| Avocados* | 94 | 94 | 94 |
| Mangoes* | 456 | 456 | 456 |
| Pineapples | 1,623 | 1,807 | 1,607 |
| Bananas | 5,844 | 6,095 | 5,551 |
| Papayas* | 1,750 | 1,700 | 1,700 |
| Cashew nuts | 165 | 113 | 45 |
| Coffee beans (green)‡ | 1,343 | 1,171 | 1,690 |
| Cocoa beans | 257 | 285 | 282 |
| Tobacco (leaves) | 471 | 620 | 510 |
| Jute and allied fibres | 12 | 12 | 9 |
| Sisal | 129 | 145 | 127 |
| Cotton (lint) | 360* | 292† | 419† |
| Other fibre crops* | 88 | 88 | 88 |
| Natural rubber | 53 | 54* | 54* |

* FAO estimate(s).
† Unofficial figure(s).
‡ Official figures, reported in terms of dry cherries, have been converted into green coffee beans at 50%.

Source: FAO, *Production Yearbook*.

**LIVESTOCK** ('000 head, year ending September)

| | 1996 | 1997 | 1998 |
|---|---|---|---|
| Cattle* | 165,000 | 163,000 | 161,000 |
| Buffaloes* | 1,700 | 1,700 | 1,700 |
| Horses* | 6,400 | 6,400 | 6,400 |
| Asses* | 1,350 | 1,350 | 1,350 |
| Mules* | 2,000 | 2,000 | 2,000 |
| Pigs† | 32,068 | 31,369 | 31,427 |
| Sheep* | 18,000 | 18,300 | 18,300 |
| Goats* | 12,200 | 12,600 | 12,600 |

Chickens (FAO estimates, million): 810 in 1996; 892 in 1997; 900 in 1998.
Ducks (FAO estimates, million): 9 in 1996–98.
Turkeys (FAO estimates, million): 7 in 1996; 8 in 1997; 8 in 1998.

* FAO estimates.
† Unofficial figures.

Source: FAO, *Production Yearbook*.

**LIVESTOCK PRODUCTS** ('000 metric tons)

| | 1996 | 1997 | 1998 |
|---|---|---|---|
| Beef and veal* | 4,960 | 5,150 | 5,230 |
| Mutton and lamb† | 86 | 88 | 88 |
| Goat meat† | 42 | 43 | 43 |
| Pig meat* | 1,516 | 1,540 | 1,690 |
| Horse meat† | 14 | 14 | 14 |
| Poultry meat | 4,166 | 4,584 | 4,619 |
| Cows' milk* | 18,300 | 20,600 | 21,630 |
| Goats' milk† | 141 | 141 | 141 |
| Butter* | 70 | 72 | 70 |
| Cheese† | 33 | 34 | 39 |
| Dried milk* | 220 | 231 | 240 |
| Hen eggs† | 1,450 | 1,500 | 1,500 |
| Other poultry eggs† | 25 | 25 | 25 |
| Honey* | 18 | 18 | 18 |
| Wool: | | | |
| greasy* | 25 | 25† | 25 |
| scoured† | 16 | 16 | 16 |
| Cattle hides (fresh) | 496* | 515* | 527† |

* Unofficial figure(s). † FAO estimate(s).

Source: FAO, mainly *Production Yearbook*.

# Forestry

**ROUNDWOOD REMOVALS**
('000 cubic metres, excl. bark)

| | 1995 | 1996 | 1997 |
|---|---|---|---|
| Sawlogs, veneer logs and logs for sleepers | 47,779 | 47,779 | 47,779 |
| Pulpwood | 30,701 | 30,701 | 30,701 |
| Other industrial wood | 6,025 | 6,104 | 6,181 |
| Fuel wood | 135,652 | 135,652 | 135,652 |
| **Total** | 220,157 | 220,236 | 220,313 |

Source: FAO, *Yearbook of Forest Products*.

**SAWNWOOD PRODUCTION**
(FAO estimates, '000 cubic metres, incl. railway sleepers)

| | 1995 | 1996 | 1997 |
|---|---|---|---|
| Coniferous (softwood) | 8,591 | 8,591 | 8,591 |
| Broadleaved (hardwood) | 10,500* | 10,500 | 10,500 |
| **Total** | 19,091 | 19,091 | 19,091 |

* Unofficial figure.

Source: FAO, *Yearbook of Forest Products*.

# Fishing

('000 metric tons, live weight)

| | 1995 | 1996 | 1997 |
|---|---|---|---|
| Characins | 92.8 | 84.9 | 84.9* |
| Freshwater siluroids | 40.0 | 47.3 | 47.3* |
| Other freshwater fishes (incl. unspecified) | 58.8 | 75.4 | 75.2* |
| Sea catfishes | 10.3 | 16.9 | 16.7* |
| Weakfishes | 27.1 | 26.5 | 26.1* |
| Whitemouth croaker | 22.0 | 23.4 | 23.0* |
| Brazilian sardinella | 60.2 | 97.1 | 117.6 |
| Skipjack tuna | 16.6 | 22.1 | 26.6 |
| Other marine fishes (incl. unspecified) | 303.4 | 276.1 | 270.8* |
| **Total fish** | 631.2 | 669.6 | 688.1* |
| Penaeus shrimps | 33.7 | 23.8 | 23.4* |
| Other crustaceans | 33.8 | 34.7 | 34.2* |
| Molluscs | 8.0 | 4.4 | 4.3* |
| **Total catch** | 706.7 | 732.5 | 750.0* |
| Inland waters | 193.0 | 210.3 | 210.0* |
| Atlantic Ocean | 513.7 | 522.2 | 540.0* |

* FAO estimate.

Source: FAO, *Yearbook of Fishery Statistics*.

# Mining

('000 metric tons, unless otherwise indicated)

| | 1994 | 1995 | 1996 |
|---|---|---|---|
| Hard coal | 5,134 | 5,199 | 4,805 |
| Crude petroleum | 33,804 | 34,907 | 39,401 |
| Natural gas (petajoules) | 180 | 193 | 216 |
| Iron* | 108,800 | 115,050 | 117,000 |
| Copper* | 39.7 | 47.9 | 26.4 |
| Nickel† | 16.5 | 15.7 | 16.4 |
| Bauxite† | 8,673 | 10,214 | 10,998 |
| Lead† | 4.0 | 6.0 | 8.0 |
| Zinc† | 140.0 | 167.3 | 128.0 |
| Tin† | 19.6 | 19.4‡ | 20.3 |
| Manganese* | 819.0 | 821.0 | 858.0 |
| Chromium* | 108 | 134 | 135 |
| Tungsten (metric tons)* | 155 | 98 | 100 |
| Uranium (metric tons) | 106 | 110 | n.a. |
| Gold (kg)* | 70,535 | 62,424 | 62,500‡ |
| Limestone* | 60,000 | 60,000 | 60,000 |
| Salt (unrefined) | 6,043 | 5,800 | 5,900‡ |
| Diamonds (industrial, '000 carats)* | 600 | 600 | 600‡ |
| Crude gypsum* | 789 | 935 | 935‡ |
| Mica* | 7.2 | 7.0 | 7.0‡ |
| Talc* | 508 | 510 | 510‡ |
| Diamonds (gem, '000 carats)* | 300 | 700 | 700‡ |

Figures for metals refer to metal content of ores and concentrates; figures for gold refer to gold refined from domestic ores only.

* Source: US Bureau of Mines.

† Source: *World Metal Statistics* (London).

‡ Estimate.

Source: UN, *Industrial Commodity Statistics Yearbook*.

# Industry

**SELECTED PRODUCTS** ('000 metric tons, unless otherwise indicated)

| | 1996 | 1997 | 1998 |
|---|---|---|---|
| Asphalt | 1,358 | 1,454 | n.a. |
| Electric power (million kWh) | 310,853 | 330,358 | 341,826 |
| Coke* | 8,413 | n.a. | n.a. |
| Pig-iron | 23,978 | 25,013 | 25,111 |
| Crude steel | 25,237 | 26,153 | 25,760 |
| Cement† | 34,559 | 37,995 | 39,951 |
| Passenger cars ('000 units) | 1,459 | 1,679 | 1,254 |
| Commercial vehicles (units) | 345,752 | n.a. | n.a. |
| Tractors (units) | 17,088 | n.a. | n.a. |
| Newsprint | 277 | 265 | 273 |

* Source: UN, *Industrial Commodity Statistics Yearbook*.

† Portland cement only.

# Finance

**CURRENCY AND EXCHANGE RATES**

**Monetary Units**

100 centavos = 1 real (plural: reais).

**Sterling, Dollar and Euro Equivalents** (30 September 1999)

£1 sterling = 3.164 reais;
US $1 = 1.922 reais;
€1 = 2.049 reais;
100 reais = £31.61 = $52.04 = €48.80.

**Average Exchange Rates** (reais per US $)

| | |
|---|---|
| 1996 | 1.005 |
| 1997 | 1.078 |
| 1998 | 1.161 |

Note: In March 1986 the cruzeiro (CR $) was replaced by a new currency unit, the cruzado (CZ $), equivalent to 1,000 cruzeiros. In January 1989 the cruzado was, in turn, replaced by the new cruzado (NCZ $), equivalent to CZ $1,000 and initially at par with the US dollar (US $). In March 1990 the new cruzado was replaced by the cruzeiro (CR $), at an exchange rate of one new cruzado for one cruzeiro. In August 1993 the cruzeiro was replaced by the cruzeiro real, equivalent to CR $1,000. On 1 March 1994, in preparation for the introduction of a new currency, a transitional accounting unit, the Unidade Real de Valor (at par with the US $), came into operation, alongside the cruzeiro real. On 1 July 1994 the cruzeiro real was replaced by the real (R $), also at par with the US $ and thus equivalent to 2,750 cruzeiros reais.

**BUDGET** (R $ million)*

| Revenue | 1996 | 1997 | 1998 |
|---|---|---|---|
| Tax revenue | 91,878 | 108,731 | 130,681 |
| Income tax | 29,703 | 32,244 | 41,675 |
| Value-added tax on industrial products | 15,293 | 16,551 | 16,092 |
| Tax on financial operations | 2,835 | 3,769 | 3,514 |
| Import duty | 4,185 | 5,103 | 6,490 |
| Tax on financial and share transactions | −2 | 6,908 | 8,113 |
| Social security contributions | 17,241 | 18,405 | 17,732 |
| Tax on profits of legal entities | 7,157 | 7,241 | 7,183 |
| Contributions to Social Integration Programme and Financial Reserve Fund for Public Employees | 6,239 | 7,228 | 6,783 |
| Repayment of loans | 5,125 | 7,200 | 8,278 |
| Transfer of profits from Banco do Brasil | 129 | 103 | 127 |
| **Total** | 97,132 | 116,034 | 139,086 |

| Expenditure | 1996 | 1997 | 1998 |
|---|---|---|---|
| Earmarked expenditures | 27,187 | 32,193 | 38,468 |
| Transfers to state and local governments† | 20,830 | 25,042 | 29,166 |
| Other expenditures | 76,782 | 86,965 | 107,471 |
| Wages and social contributions | 40,505 | 42,848 | 47,296 |
| Interest payments | 15,992 | 17,975 | 27,706 |
| Funding and investment | 18,007 | 24,252 | 32,469 |
| Lending | 2,288 | 2,522 | 2,394 |
| **Total** | 106,257 | 121,680 | 148,333 |

* Figures refer to cash operations of the National Treasury, including the collection and transfer of earmarked revenues for social expenditure purposes. The data exclude the transactions of other funds and accounts controlled by the Federal Government.

† Constitutionally mandated participation funds.

Source: *Boletim do Banco Central do Brasil.*

**CENTRAL BANK RESERVES** (US $ million at 31 December)

| | 1996 | 1997 | 1998 |
|---|---|---|---|
| Gold* | 1,381 | 903 | 1,358 |
| IMF special drawing rights | 1 | 1 | 2 |
| Foreign exchange | 58,322 | 50,826 | 42,578 |
| **Total** | 59,704 | 51,730 | 43,938 |

* Valued at market-related prices.

Source: IMF, *International Financial Statistics.*

**MONEY SUPPLY** (R $ million at 31 December)

| | 1996 | 1997 | 1998 |
|---|---|---|---|
| Currency outside banks | 15,316 | 18,141 | 21,185 |
| Demand deposits at deposit money banks | 14,320 | 27,912 | 29,061 |
| **Total money** (incl. others) | 41,683 | 50,999 | 54,821 |

Source: IMF, *International Financial Statistics.*

**COST OF LIVING**
(Consumer Price Index at December; base: December 1992 = 100)

| | 1996 | 1997 | 1998 |
|---|---|---|---|
| Food | 31,831.6 | 32,214.0 | 32,842.0 |
| **All items** (incl. others) | 35,131.6 | 36,967.1 | 37,579.2 |

**NATIONAL ACCOUNTS** (R $ '000 at current prices)

**Composition of the Gross National Product**

| | 1996 | 1997 | 1998 |
|---|---|---|---|
| Compensation of employees | 300,207,553 | 318,785,117 | 328,210,516 |
| Operating surplus / Consumption of fixed capital | 363,442,828 | 419,503,163 | 445,594,317 |
| **Gross domestic product (GDP) at factor cost** | 663,650,381 | 738,288,280 | 773,804,833 |
| Indirect taxes | 118,651,934 | 129,541,930 | 129,464,334 |
| *Less* Subsidies | 3,415,588 | 3,719,184 | 3,455,035 |
| **GDP in purchasers' values** | 778,886,727 | 864,111,026 | 899,814,132 |
| Factor income received from abroad | 5,283,998 | 5,579,926 | 5,396,135 |
| *Less* Factor income paid abroad | 17,511,759 | 22,690,178 | 27,758,308 |
| **Gross national product** | 766,658,966 | 847,000,774 | 877,451,959 |

**Expenditure on the Gross Domestic Product**

| | 1996 | 1997 | 1998 |
|---|---|---|---|
| Government final consumption expenditure | 144,001,088 | 154,238,952 | 159,920,518 |
| Private final consumption expenditure | 486,812,616 | 545,113,309 | 572,390,773 |
| Increase in stocks | 12,903,180 | 15,342,520 | 12,271,254 |
| Gross fixed capital formation | 150,050,300 | 172,212,039 | 179,202,590 |
| **Total domestic expenditure** | 793,767,184 | 886,906,820 | 923,785,135 |
| Exports of goods and services | 54,430,127 | 65,490,952 | 66,862,010 |
| *Less* Imports of goods and services | 69,310,584 | 88,286,746 | 90,833,013 |
| **GDP in purchasers' values** | 778,886,727 | 864,111,026 | 899,814,132 |
| **GDP at constant 1998 prices** | 869,589,967 | 900,895,206 | 899,814,132 |

**Gross Domestic Product by Economic Activity** (at factor cost)

| | 1996 | 1997 | 1998 |
|---|---|---|---|
| Agriculture, hunting, forestry and fishing | 64,803,376 | 68,005,538 | 75,764,350 |
| Mining and quarrying | 7,399,424 | 7,776,999 | 5,758,810 |
| Manufacturing | 167,382,758 | 183,882,826 | 182,662,269 |
| Electricity, gas and water | 21,419,385 | 22,898,942 | 24,744,889 |
| Construction | 74,150,016 | 86,411,103 | 92,320,930 |
| Trade, restaurants and hotels | 60,675,276 | 66,363,727 | 65,236,525 |
| Transport, storage and communications | 38,165,450 | 43,724,018 | 50,389,591 |
| Finance, insurance, real estate and business services | 53,821,073 | 56,858,506 | 58,847,844 |
| Government services | 124,310,322 | 131,863,343 | 139,291,228 |
| Rents | 108,343,144 | 131,344,876 | 138,031,488 |
| Other community, social and personal services | 99,931,167 | 109,310,045 | 113,286,599 |
| **Sub-total** | 820,401,390 | 908,439,922 | 946,334,523 |
| *Less* Imputed bank service charge | 41,514,663 | 44,328,896 | 46,520,391 |
| **Total** | 778,886,727 | 864,111,026 | 899,814,132 |

**BALANCE OF PAYMENTS** (US $ million)

| | 1996 | 1997 | 1998 |
|---|---|---|---|
| Exports of goods f.o.b. | 47,851 | 53,189 | 51,136 |
| Imports of goods f.o.b. | -53,304 | -59,841 | -57,739 |
| **Trade balance** | -5,453 | -6,652 | -6,603 |
| Exports of services | 4,655 | 5,989 | 7,631 |
| Imports of services | -12,714 | -15,298 | -16,676 |
| **Balance on goods and services** | -13,512 | -15,961 | -15,648 |
| Other income received | 5,350 | 5,344 | 4,914 |
| Other income paid | -17,527 | -21,688 | -24,531 |
| **Balance on goods, services and income** | -25,689 | -32,305 | -35,265 |
| Current transfers received | 2,699 | 2,130 | 1,795 |
| Current transfers paid | -258 | -316 | -359 |
| **Current balance** | -23,248 | -30,491 | -33,829 |
| Capital account (net) | 494 | 482 | 375 |
| Direct investment abroad | 467 | -1,042 | -2,721 |
| Direct investment from abroad | 11,200 | 19,650 | 31,913 |
| Portfolio investment assets | -257 | -335 | -594 |
| Portfolio investment liabilities | 21,089 | 10,393 | 19,013 |
| Other investment assets | -3,327 | 2,251 | -5,992 |
| Other investment liabilities | 3,970 | -5,999 | -21,556 |
| Net errors and omissions | -1,992 | -3,160 | -2,911 |
| **Overall balance** | 8,396 | -8,251 | -16,302 |

Source: IMF, *International Financial Statistics.*

# External Trade

## PRINCIPAL COMMODITIES

(distribution by SITC, US $ million, excl. military goods)

| Imports f.o.b. | 1996 | 1997 | 1998 |
|---|---|---|---|
| **Food and live animals** | 4,784.5 | 4,226.2 | 4,626.7 |
| Cereals and cereal preparations | 2,177.4 | 1,569.3 | 1,939.8 |
| **Crude materials (inedible) except fuels** | 2,476.8 | 2,364.8 | 1,925.8 |
| **Mineral fuels, lubricants, etc.** | 6,928.1 | 6,783.1 | 5,109.0 |
| Petroleum, petroleum products, etc. | 5,729.1 | 5,549.2 | 3,923.2 |
| **Chemicals and related products** | 8,536.7 | 9,255.7 | 9,555.3 |
| Organic chemicals | 3,186.9 | 3,289.8 | 3,158.5 |
| Medicinal and pharmaceutical products | 1,247.4 | 1,410.6 | 1,582.0 |
| Plastics in primary forms | 1,050.8 | 1,091.0 | 1,117.1 |
| **Basic manufactures** | 5,360.6 | 6,257.8 | 6,171.4 |
| **Machinery and transport equipment** | 20,680.4 | 26,021.3 | 25,788.3 |
| Power-generating machinery and equipment | 1,443.4 | 1,979.8 | 2,332.4 |
| Machinery specialized for particular industries | 2,653.6 | 3,355.9 | 2,975.4 |
| General industrial machinery, equipment and parts | 2,830.0 | 3,582.5 | 3,621.2 |
| Office machines and automatic data-processing machines | 1,699.7 | 1,718.3 | 1,732.3 |
| Telecommunications and sound equipment | 2,578.5 | 3,277.4 | 2,787.9 |
| Other electrical machinery, apparatus, etc. | 4,186.6 | 4,877.0 | 4,745.5 |
| Road vehicles and parts* | 3,995.8 | 5,319.7 | 5,607.3 |
| Other transport equipment* | 472.6 | 1,018.9 | 1,125.1 |
| **Miscellaneous manufactured articles** | 3,980.0 | 4,238.8 | 3,903.2 |
| Professional, scientific and controlling instruments, etc. | 1,197.7 | 1,212.3 | 1,258.5 |
| **Total** (incl. others) | 53,345.8 | 59,757.7 | 57,726.9 |

* Excluding tyres, engines and electrical parts.

| Exports f.o.b. | 1996 | 1997 | 1998 |
|---|---|---|---|
| **Food and live animals** | 10,756.6 | 11,438.8 | 10,363.3 |
| Meat and meat preparations | 1,502.8 | 1,556.3 | 1,591.5 |
| Vegetables and fruit | 1,826.4 | 1,428.5 | 1,667.6 |
| Fruit juices and vegetable juices | 1,453.7 | n.a. | n.a. |
| Sugar, sugar preparations and honey | 1,690.0 | 1,863.6 | 2,030.7 |
| Coffee, tea, cocoa and spices | 2,461.5 | 3,426.3 | 2,939.3 |
| Coffee and coffee substitutes | 2,135.1 | n.a. | n.a. |
| Coffee (incl. husks and skins) and substitutes containing coffee | 1,718.6 | n.a. | n.a. |
| Unroasted coffee, husks and skins | 1,718.6 | n.a. | n.a. |
| Feeding-stuff for animals (excl. unmilled cereals) | 2,930.1 | 2,841.9 | 1,800.7 |
| **Beverages and tobacco** | 1,618.5 | 1,755.4 | 1,624.6 |
| Tobacco and tobacco manufactures | 1,515.4 | 1,664.8 | 1,559.0 |
| Tobacco, unmanufactured; tobacco refuse | 918.0 | n.a. | n.a. |
| **Crude materials (inedible) except fuels** | 5,953.1 | 7,700.8 | 7,949.0 |
| Oil seeds and oleaginous fruit | 1,020.1 | 2,453.6 | 2,180.4 |
| Oil seeds, etc., for 'soft' fixed vegetable oils | 1,019.6 | n.a. | n.a. |
| Soya beans | 1,017.9 | n.a. | n.a. |
| Pulp and waste paper | 999.5 | 1,024.2 | 1,049.4 |
| Metalliferous ores and metal scrap | 3,017.6 | 3,190.5 | 3,661.6 |
| Iron ore and concentrates | 2,695.2 | n.a. | n.a. |
| Iron ore and concentrates (not agglomerated) | 1,740.8 | n.a. | n.a. |
| **Chemicals and related products** | 3,160.4 | 3,402.7 | 3,195.6 |
| Organic chemicals | 1,064.6 | 1,155.1 | 1,054.7 |

| Exports f.o.b. — *continued* | 1996 | 1997 | 1998 |
|---|---|---|---|
| **Basic manufactures** | 11,164.2 | 11,223.0 | 10,184.4 |
| Textile yarn, fabrics, etc. | 1,006.8 | 1,021.9 | 891.0 |
| Iron and steel | 4,195.6 | 3,889.2 | 3,671.1 |
| Ingots and other primary forms | 1,329.8 | n.a. | n.a. |
| Non-ferrous metals | 1,636.7 | 1,668.0 | 1,276.0 |
| Aluminium and aluminium alloys | 1,296.4 | n.a. | n.a. |
| Unwrought aluminium and alloys | 1,102.8 | n.a. | n.a. |
| **Machinery and transport equipment** | 9,522.2 | 11,992.6 | 12,600.5 |
| Power-generating machinery and equipment | 1,403.2 | 1,488.6 | 1,550.2 |
| Internal combustion piston engines, and parts thereof | 1,029.4 | n.a. | n.a. |
| Machinery specialized for particular industries | 1,049.5 | 1,289.0 | 1,163.1 |
| General industrial machinery, equipment and parts | 1,521.7 | 1,595.3 | 1,508.4 |
| Electrical machinery, apparatus, etc. | 1,421.7 | 1,640.5 | 1,534.5 |
| Road vehicles and parts* | 2,929.4 | 4,453.3 | 4,827.8 |
| Parts and accessories for cars, buses, lorries, etc.* | 1,562.3 | n.a. | n.a. |
| Other transport equipment* | 659.8 | 1,000.1 | 1,481.3 |
| **Miscellaneous manufactured articles** | 3,049.4 | 3,084.1 | 2,869.0 |
| Footwear | 1,650.1 | 1,594.5 | 1,387.1 |
| **Total** (incl. others) | 47,746.7 | 52,994.3 | 51,139.9 |

* Excluding tyres, engines and electrical parts.

## PRINCIPAL TRADING PARTNERS (US $ million)*

| Imports f.o.b. | 1996 | 1997 | 1998 |
|---|---|---|---|
| Algeria | 668 | 768 | 624 |
| Argentina | 6,782 | 8,032 | 8,034 |
| Belgium-Luxembourg | 548 | 638 | 718 |
| Canada | 1,258 | 1,416 | 1,338 |
| Chile | 918 | 974 | 817 |
| China, People's Republic | 1,129 | 1,166 | 1,034 |
| France | 1,341 | 1,637 | 1,971 |
| Germany | 4,777 | 4,958 | 5,236 |
| Italy | 2,915 | 3,405 | 3,229 |
| Japan | 2,757 | 3,534 | 3,277 |
| Korea, Republic | 1,158 | 1,355 | 988 |
| Mexico | 947 | 1,173 | 983 |
| Netherlands | 572 | 576 | 697 |
| Paraguay | 551 | 518 | 350 |
| Saudi Arabia | 1,196 | 1,100 | 727 |
| Spain | 903 | 1,141 | 1,195 |
| Sweden | 684 | 857 | 1,104 |
| Switzerland | 768 | 849 | 896 |
| Taiwan | 707 | 801 | 699 |
| United Kingdom | 1,247 | 1,430 | 1,489 |
| USA | 11,700 | 13,706 | 13,512 |
| Uruguay | 932 | 967 | 1,042 |
| Venezuela | 969 | 1,006 | 756 |
| **Total** (incl. others) | 53,296 | 59,840 | 57,731 |

| Exports f.o.b. | 1996 | 1997 | 1998 |
|---|---|---|---|
| Argentina | 5,170 | 6,770 | 6,748 |
| Belgium-Luxembourg | 1,432 | 1,483 | 2,195 |
| Canada | 506 | 584 | 544 |
| Chile | 1,055 | 1,197 | 1,024 |
| China, People's Republic | 1,114 | 1,088 | 905 |
| France | 911 | 1,112 | 1,229 |
| Germany | 2,083 | 2,608 | 3,006 |
| Italy | 1,531 | 1,709 | 1,931 |
| Japan | 3,047 | 3,068 | 2,205 |
| Korea, Republic | 838 | 737 | 467 |

| Exports f.o.b. — *continued* | 1996 | 1997 | 1998 |
|---|---|---|---|
| Mexico | 679 | 828 | 1,002 |
| Netherlands | 3,549 | 3,998 | 2,745 |
| Paraguay | 1,325 | 1,407 | 1,249 |
| Russia | 466 | 761 | 647 |
| Spain | 937 | 1,056 | 1,055 |
| United Kingdom | 1,324 | 1,259 | 1,339 |
| USA | 9,312 | 9,276 | 9,747 |
| Uruguay | 811 | 870 | 881 |
| Venezuela | 454 | 768 | 706 |
| **Total** (incl. others) | 47,747 | 52,994 | 51,140 |

* Imports by country of purchase; exports by country of last consignment.

Source: Ministério do Desenvolvimento, Indústria e Comércio Exterior, Brasília, DF.

# Transport

**RAILWAYS***

| | 1996 | 1997 | 1998 |
|---|---|---|---|
| Passengers (million) | 1,257 | 1,221 | 1,255 |
| Passenger-km (million) | 13,999 | 12,688 | 12,667 |
| Freight ('000 metric tons) | 248,224 | 267,795 | 269,217 |
| Freight ton-km (million) | 128,976 | 138,724 | 141,239 |

* Including suburban and metro services.

Source: Empresa Brasileira de Planejamento de Transportes (GEIPOT), Brasília, DF.

**ROAD TRAFFIC** (motor vehicles in use at 31 December)

| | 1996 | 1997 | 1998 |
|---|---|---|---|
| Passenger cars | 19,354,083 | 20,194,882 | 21,313,351 |
| Buses and coaches | 331,796 | 348,168 | 430,062 |
| Light goods vehicles | 3,019,151 | 3,158,695 | 3,313,774 |
| Heavy goods vehicles | 1,675,400 | 1,699,338 | 1,755,877 |
| Motorcycles and mopeds | 2,924,227 | 3,365,121 | 3,854,646 |

Source: Empresa Brasileira de Planejamento de Transportes (GEIPOT), Brasília, DF.

**SHIPPING**

**Merchant Fleet** (registered at 31 December)

| | 1996 | 1997 | 1998 |
|---|---|---|---|
| Number of vessels | 539 | 536 | 504 |
| Total displacement ('000 grt) | 4,530 | 4,372 | 4,171 |

Source: Lloyd's Register of Shipping, *World Fleet Statistics*.

**International Sea-borne Freight Traffic** ('000 metric tons)

| | 1996 | 1997 | 1998 |
|---|---|---|---|
| Goods loaded | 239,932 | 259,238 | 269,935 |
| Goods unloaded | 146,452 | 155,002 | 173,070 |

Source: Empresa Brasileira de Planejamento de Transportes (GEIPOT), Brasília, DF.

**CIVIL AVIATION** (embarked passengers, mail and cargo)

| | 1996 | 1997 | 1998 |
|---|---|---|---|
| Number of passengers ('000) | 26,898 | 28,902 | 31,098 |
| Passenger-km (million) | 24,844 | 27,357 | 27,386 |
| Freight ('000 metric tons) | 618,605 | 572,909 | 602,743 |
| Freight ton-km ('000)* | 1,936,624 | 2,034,000 | 2,195,401 |

* Including mail.

Source: Empresa Brasileira de Planejamento de Transportes (GEIPOT), Brasília, DF.

# Tourism

**FOREIGN TOURIST ARRIVALS**

| Country of origin | 1996 | 1997 | 1998 |
|---|---|---|---|
| Argentina | 856,859 | 938,973 | 1,467,926 |
| Chile | 89,874 | 92,233 | 159,673 |
| France | 79,477 | 84,552 | 121,274 |
| Germany | 147,576 | 140,578 | 262,739 |
| Italy | 114,543 | 123,114 | 169,567 |
| Paraguay | 110,317 | 146,581 | 451,693 |
| Portugal | 66,592 | 63,315 | 105,593 |
| Spain | 70,087 | 63,809 | 91,969 |
| United Kingdom | 60,140 | 62,308 | 117,518 |
| USA | 350,086 | 402,200 | 524,093 |
| Uruguay | 204,274 | 206,468 | 359,188 |
| **Total** (incl. others) | 2,665,508 | n.a. | 4,818,084 |

**Receipts from tourism** (US$ million): 2,469.1 in 1996; 2,594.9 in 1997; 3,678 in 1998.

Source: Instituto Brasileiro de Turismo—EMBRATUR, Brasília, DF.

# Communications Media

| | 1994 | 1995 | 1996 |
|---|---|---|---|
| Radio receivers ('000 in use)* | 62,500 | 63,500 | 70,000 |
| Television receivers ('000 in use)* | 33,200 | 35,000 | 36,000 |
| Book production (excl. pamphlets)* | | | |
| Titles | 21,574† | n.a. | n.a. |
| Copies ('000) | 104,397 | n.a. | n.a. |
| Daily newspapers* | | | |
| Number | 317 | 352 | 380 |
| Average circulation ('000 copies) | n.a. | 6,551 | 6,472 |
| Non-daily newspapers (estimates)* | | | |
| Number | n.a. | 1,400 | n.a. |
| Average circulation ('000 copies) | n.a. | 5,000 | n.a. |
| Telephones in use ('000 main lines)‡ | 13,055 | 14,875 | 17,729 |
| Mobile cellular telephones (subscribers)§ | 574,009 | 1,285,533 | n.a. |

**Telefax stations** ('000 in use)§: 200 in 1993.

* Source: UNESCO, *Statistical Yearbook*.

† Including reprints.

‡ Source: Fundação Instituto Brasileiro de Geografia e Estatística (IBGE).

§ Source: UN, *Statistical Yearbook*.

**1998** ('000): Fixed telephone lines 22,599.9; Mobile cellular telephones 9,099.9 (Source: ANATEL, Ministério das Comunicações, Brasília, DF).

# Education

(1998)

| | Institutions | Teachers | Students |
|---|---|---|---|
| Pre-primary | 78,107 | 219,594 | 4,111,153 |
| Literacy classes (Classe de Alfabetização) | 34,064 | 46,126 | 806,288 |
| Primary | 187,497 | 1,460,469 | 35,845,742 |
| Secondary | 17,602 | 380,222 | 6,968,531 |
| Higher* | 900 | 173,705 | 1,948,200 |

* 1997 figures (preliminary).

Source: Ministério da Educação, Brasília, DF.

# Directory

## The Constitution

A new Constitution was promulgated on 5 October 1988. The following is a summary of the main provisions:

The Federative Republic of Brazil, formed by the indissoluble union of the States, the Municipalities and the Federal District, is constituted as a democratic state. All power emanates from the people. The Federative Republic of Brazil seeks the economic, political, social and cultural integration of the peoples of Latin America.

All are equal before the law. The inviolability of the right to life, freedom, equality, security and property is guaranteed. No one shall be subjected to torture. Freedom of thought, conscience, religious belief and expression are guaranteed, as is privacy. The principles of habeas corpus and 'habeas data' (the latter giving citizens access to personal information held in government data banks) are granted. There is freedom of association, and the right to strike is guaranteed.

There is universal suffrage by direct secret ballot. Voting is compulsory for literate persons between 18 and 69 years of age, and optional for those who are illiterate, those over 70 years of age and those aged 16 and 17.

Brasília is the federal capital. The Union's competence includes maintaining relations with foreign states, and taking part in international organizations; declaring war and making peace; guaranteeing national defence; decreeing a state of siege; issuing currency; supervising credits, etc.; formulating and implementing plans for economic and social development; maintaining national services, including communications, energy, the judiciary and the police; legislating on civil, commercial, penal, procedural, electoral, agrarian, maritime, aeronautical, spatial and labour law, etc. The Union, States, Federal District and Municipalities must protect the Constitution, laws and democratic institutions, and preserve national heritage.

The States are responsible for electing their Governors by universal suffrage and direct secret ballot for a four-year term. The organization of the Municipalities, the Federal District and the Territories is regulated by law.

The Union may intervene in the States and in the Federal District only in certain circumstances, such as a threat to national security or public order, and then only after reference to the National Congress.

### LEGISLATIVE POWER

The legislative power is exercised by the Congresso Nacional (National Congress), which is composed of the Câmara dos Deputados (Chamber of Deputies) and the Senado Federal (Federal Senate). Elections for deputies and senators take place simultaneously throughout the country; candidates for the Congresso must be Brazilian by birth and have full exercise of their political rights. They must be at least 21 years of age in the case of deputies and at least 35 years of age in the case of senators. The Congresso meets twice a year in ordinary sessions, and extraordinary sessions may be convened by the President of the Republic, the Presidents of the Câmara and the Senado, or at the request of the majority of the members of either house.

The Câmara is made up of representatives of the people, elected by a system of proportional representation in each State, Territory and the Federal District for a period of four years. The total number of deputies representing the States and the Federal District will be established in proportion to the population; each Territory will elect four deputies.

The Senado is composed of representatives of the States and the Federal District, elected according to the principle of majority. Each State and the Federal District will elect three senators with a mandate of eight years, with elections after four years for one-third of the members and after another four years for the remaining two-thirds. Each Senator is elected with two substitutes. The Senado approves, by secret ballot, the choice of Magistrates, when required by the Constitution; of the Attorney-General of the Republic, of the Ministers of the Accounts Tribunal, of the Territorial Governors, of the president and directors of the central bank and of the permanent heads of diplomatic missions.

The Congresso is responsible for deciding on all matters within the competence of the Union, especially fiscal and budgetary arrangements, national, regional and local plans and programmes, the strength of the armed forces and territorial limits. It is also responsible for making definitive resolutions on international treaties, and for authorizing the President to declare war.

The powers of the Câmara include authorizing the instigation of legal proceedings against the President and Vice-President of the Republic and Ministers of State. The Senado may indict and impose sentence on the President and Vice-President of the Republic and Ministers of State.

Constitutional amendments may be proposed by at least one-third of the members of either house, by the President or by more than one-half of the legislative assemblies of the units of the Federation. Amendments must be ratified by three-fifths of the members of each house. The Constitution may not be amended during times of national emergency, such as a state of siege.

### EXECUTIVE POWER

Executive power is exercised by the President of the Republic, aided by the Ministers of State. Candidates for the Presidency and Vice-Presidency must be Brazilian-born, be in full exercise of their political rights and be over 35 years of age. The candidate who obtains an absolute majority of votes will be elected President. If no candidate attains an absolute majority, the two candidates who have received the most votes proceed to a second round of voting, at which the candidate obtaining the majority of valid votes will be elected President. The President holds office for a term of four years and (under an amendment adopted in 1997) is eligible for re-election.

The Ministers of State are chosen by the President and their duties include countersigning acts and decrees signed by the President, expediting instructions for the enactment of laws, decrees and regulations, and presentation to the President of an annual report of their activities.

The Council of the Republic is the higher consultative organ of the President of the Republic. It comprises the Vice-President of the Republic, the Presidents of the Câmara and Senado, the leaders of the majority and of the minority in each house, the Minister of Justice, two members appointed by the President of the Republic, two elected by the Senado and two elected by the Câmara, the latter six having a mandate of three years.

The National Defence Council advises the President on matters relating to national sovereignty and defence. It comprises the Vice-President of the Republic, the Presidents of the Câmara and Senado, the Minister of Justice, military Ministers and the Ministers of Foreign Affairs and of Planning.

### JUDICIAL POWER

Judicial power in the Union is exercised by the Supreme Federal Tribunal; the Higher Tribunal of Justice; the Regional Federal Tribunals and federal judges; Labour Tribunals and judges; Electoral Tribunals and judges; Military Tribunals and judges; and the States' Tribunals and judges. Judges are appointed for life; they may not undertake any other employment. The Tribunals elect their own controlling organs and organize their own internal structure.

The Supreme Federal Tribunal, situated in the Union capital, has jurisdiction over the whole national territory and is composed of 11 ministers. The ministers are nominated by the President after approval by the Senado, from Brazilian-born citizens, between the ages of 35 and 65 years, of proved judicial knowledge and experience.

## The Government

### HEAD OF STATE

**President:** Fernando Henrique Cardoso (took office 1 January 1995, re-elected 4 October 1998).

**Vice-President:** Marco Antônio de O. Maciel.

### THE CABINET
(January 2000)

**Minister of Foreign Affairs:** Luiz Felipe Palmeira Lampreia.

**Minister of Justice:** José Carlos Dias.

**Minister of Finance:** Pedro Sampaio Malan.

**Minister of Defence:** Geraldo Magela da Cruz Quintão.

**Minister of Agriculture:** Marcus Vinicius Pratini de Moraes.

**Minister of Agrarian Reform:** Raúl Belens Jungmann Pinto.

**Minister of Civilian Household:** Pedro Parente.

**Minister of Military Household:** Gen. Alberto Cardoso.

**Minister of Labour and Employment:** Francisco Oswaldo Neves Dornelles.

**Minister of Transport:** Eliseu Lemos Padilha.

**Minister of Planning, Budget and Administration:** Martus Antônio Rodrigues Tavares.

**Minister of Mines and Energy:** Rodolpho Tourinho Neto.

**Minister of Culture:** Francisco Corrêa Weffort.

**Minister of the Environment:** José Sarney, Filho.

**Minister of Development, Industry and Trade:** Alcides Tápias.

**Minister of Education:** Paulo Renato de Souza.

**Minister of Health:** José Serra.

**Minister of National Integration:** Fernando Bezerra.

**Minister of Social Security and Assistance:** Waldeck Vieira Ornélas.

**Minister of Communications:** João Pimenta da Veiga, Filho.

**Minister of Science and Technology:** Ronaldo Sardenberg.

**Minister of Sport and Tourism:** Rafael Valdomiro Greca de Macedo.

**Minister of Urban Policies:** Ovídio Antônio de Angelis.

### MINISTRIES

**Office of the President:** Palácio do Planalto, Praça dos Três Poderes, 70150 Brasília, DF; tel. (61) 211-1221; fax (61) 226-7566; e-mail protocolo@planalto.gov.br; internet www.planalto.gov.br.

**Office of the Civilian Cabinet:** Palácio do Planalto, 4° andar, Praça dos Três Poderes, 70150 Brasílila, DF; tel. (61) 211-1034; fax (61) 321-5804.

**Ministry of Administration:** Esplanada dos Ministérios, Bloco C, 8° andar, Brasília, DF; tel. (61) 226-6432; fax (61) 226-3577.

**Ministry of Agrarian Reform:** Brasília, DF; tel. (61) 223-8852; fax (61) 226-3855.

**Ministry of Agriculture:** Esplanada dos Ministérios, Bloco D, 8° andar, 70043 Brasília, DF; tel. (61) 226-5161; fax (61) 218-2586.

**Ministry of the Budget:** Esplanada dos Ministérios, Bloco K, 70040-602 Brasília, DF; tel. (61) 215-4100; fax (61) 321-5292.

**Ministry of Communications:** Esplanada dos Ministérios, Bloco R, 8° andar, 70.000 Brasília, DF; tel. (61) 225-9446; fax (61) 226-3980.

**Ministry of Culture:** Esplanada dos Ministérios, Bloco B, 3° andar, 70068-900 Brasília, DF; tel. (61) 224-6114; fax (61) 225-9162.

**Ministry of Defence:** Esplanada dos Ministérios, Bloco Q, 70049-900 Brasília, DF; tel. (61) 223-5356; fax (61) 321-2477.

**Ministry of Development, Industry and Trade:** Esplanada dos Ministérios, Bloco J, 7° andar, Sala 700, 70056-900 Brasília, DF; tel. (61) 325-2056; fax (61) 325-2063.

**Ministry of Education:** Esplanada dos Ministérios, Bloco L, 8° andar, 70047-900 Brasília, DF; tel. (61) 225-6515; fax (61) 223-0564; e-mail acordabr@acb.mec.gov.br.

**Ministry of the Environment:** SAIN, Av. L4 Norte, Edif. Sede Terreo, 70800 Brasília, DF; tel. (61) 226-8221; fax (61) 322-1058.

**Ministry of Finance:** Esplanada dos Ministérios, Bloco P, 5° andar, 70048 Brasília, DF; tel. (61) 314-2000; fax (61) 223-5239.

**Ministry of Foreign Affairs:** Palácio do Itamaraty, Esplanada dos Ministérios, 70170 Brasília, DF; tel. (61) 224-2773; fax (61) 226-1762; internet www.mre.gov.br.

**Ministry of Health:** Esplanada dos Ministérios, Bloco G, 5° andar, 70058 Brasília, DF; tel. (61) 223-3169; fax (61) 224-8747.

**Ministry of Justice:** Esplanada dos Ministérios, Bloco T, 4° andar, 70064-900 Brasília, DF; tel. (61) 226-4404; fax (61) 322-6817.

**Ministry of Labour and Employment:** Esplanada dos Ministérios, Bloco F, 5° andar, 70059-900 Brasília, DF; tel. (61) 225-0041; fax (61) 226-3577; e-mail internacional@mtb.gov.br; internet www.mtb.gov.br.

**Ministry of Mines and Energy:** Esplanada dos Ministérios, Bloco U, 7° andar, 70000 Brasília, DF; tel. (61) 225-8106; fax (61) 225-5407; internet www.mme.gov.br.

**Ministry of National Integration:** Esplanada dos Ministérios, 70000 Brasília, DF.

**Ministry of Science and Technology:** Esplanada dos Ministérios, Bloco E, 4° andar, 70062-900 Brasília, DF; tel. (61) 224-4364; fax (61) 225-7496; internet www.mct.gov.br.

**Ministry of Social Security and Assistance:** Esplanada dos Ministérios, Bloco A, 6° andar, 70054-900 Brasília, DF; tel. (61) 224-7300; fax (61) 226-3861; internet www.mpas.gov.br.

**Ministry of Sport and Tourism:** Esplanada dos Ministérios, Brasília, DF.

**Ministry of Transport:** Esplanada dos Ministérios, Bloco R, 70000 Brasília, DF; tel. (61) 218-6335; fax (61) 218-6315.

## President and Legislature

### PRESIDENT

**Election, 4 October 1998**

| Candidate | Valid votes cast | % valid votes cast |
|---|---|---|
| Fernando Henrique Cardoso (PSDB) | 35,936,916 | 53.06 |
| Luiz Inácio 'Lula' da Silva (PT) | 21,475,348 | 31.71 |
| Ciro Gomes (PPS) | 7,426,235 | 10.97 |
| Others | 2,884,528 | 4.26 |
| **Total** | 67,723,027 | 100.00 |

### CONGRESSO NACIONAL
(National Congress)

#### Câmara dos Deputados
(Chamber of Deputies)

**President:** Michel Temer (PMDB).

The Chamber has 513 members who hold office for a four-year term.

**General Election, 4 October 1998**

| Party | Seats |
|---|---|
| Partido da Frente Liberal (PFL) | 106 |
| Partido da Social Democracia Brasileira (PSDB) | 99 |
| Partido do Movimento Democrático Brasileiro (PMDB) | 82 |
| Partido Progressista Brasileiro (PPB) | 60 |
| Partido dos Trabalhadores (PT) | 58 |
| Partido Trabalhista Brasileiro (PTB) | 31 |
| Partido Democrático Trabalhista (PDT) | 25 |
| Partido Socialista Brasileiro (PSB) | 19 |
| Partido Liberal (PL) | 12 |
| Partido Comunista do Brasil (PC do B) | 7 |
| Partido Popular Socialista (PPS) | 3 |
| Others | 11 |
| **Total** | 513 |

#### Senado Federal
(Federal Senate)

**President:** Antônio Carlos Magalhães (PFL).

The 81 members of the Senate are elected by the 26 States and the Federal District (three Senators for each) according to the principle of majority. The Senate's term of office is eight years, with elections after four years for one-third of the members and after another four years for the remaining two-thirds.

Following the elections of 4 October 1998, the PMDB was represented by 27 senators, the PFL by 19, the PSDB by 16, the PT by 7 and the PPB by 5. The PSB, the PDT, the PTB and the PPS were also represented.

## Governors

### STATES

**Acre:** Jorge Viana (PT).

**Alagoas:** Ronaldo Lessa (PSB).

**Amapá:** João Alberto Capiberibe (PSB).

**Amazonas:** Amazonino Mendes (PFL).

**Bahia:** César Borges (PFL).

**Ceará:** Tasso Ribeiro Jereissati (PSDB).

**Espírito Santo:** José Ignácio (PSDB).

**Goias:** Marconi Perillo (PSDB).

**Maranhão:** Roseana Sarney (PFL).

**Mato Grosso:** Dante Martins de Oliveira (PSDB).

**Mato Grosso do Sul:** Antônio Zeca (PT).

**Minas Gerais:** Itamar Franco (PMDB).

**Pará:** Almir de Oliveira Gabriel (PSDB).

**Paraíba:** José Targino Maranhão (PMDB).

**Paraná:** Jaime Lerner (PFL).

**Pernambuco:** Jarbas Vasconcelos (PMDB).

**Piauí:** Mão Santa (PMDB).

**Rio de Janeiro:** Antonio Garotinho (PDT).

**Rio Grande do Norte:** Garibaldi Alves, Filho (PMDB).

**Rio Grande do Sul:** Olívio Dutra (PT).

**Rondônia:** José Bianco (PFL).

**Roraima:** NEUDO RIBEIRO CAMPOS (PTB).

**Santa Catarina:** ESPERIDIÃO AMIN (PPB).

**São Paulo:** MÁRIO COVAS (PSDB).

**Sergipe:** ALBANO DO PRADO PIMENTEL FRANCO (PSDB).

**Tocantins:** SIQUEIRA CAMPOS (PFL).

**FEDERAL DISTRICT**

**Brasília:** JOAQUIM RORIZ (PMDB).

# Political Organizations

In May 1985 the National Congress approved a constitutional amendment providing for the free formation of political parties.

**Partido Comunista do Brasil (PC do B):** Rua Major Diogo 834, Bela Vista, São Paulo, SP; tel. (11) 232-1622; fax (11) 606-4104; e-mail pcdobcc@uol.com.br; internet www.pcdob.org.br; f. 1922; Leader ALDO REBELO ; Sec.-Gen. JOÃO AMAZONAS; 185,000 mems.

**Partido Democrático Trabalhista (PDT):** Rua 7 de Setembro 141, 4°, 20050 Rio de Janeiro, RJ; internet www.pdt.org.br; f. 1980; formerly the PTB (Partido Trabalhista Brasileiro), renamed 1980 when that name was awarded to a dissident group following controversial judicial proceedings; member of Socialist International; Pres. LEONEL BRIZOLA; Gen. Sec. VIVALDO BARBOSA.

**Partido da Frente Liberal (PFL):** Câmara dos Deputados, 70160-900 Brasília, DF; internet www.pfl.org.br; f. 1984 by moderate members of the PDS and PMDB; Pres. JORGE BORNHAUSEN; Gen. Sec. SAULO QUEIROZ.

**Partido Liberal (PL):** Câmara dos Deputados, 70160-900 Brasília, DF; internet www.pl.org.br; Pres. (vacant); Leader VALDEMAR COSTA NETO.

**Partido do Movimento Democrático Brasileiro (PMDB):** Câmara dos Deputados, Edif. Principal, 70160-900 Brasília, DF; e-mail pmdb@tba.com.br; internet www.pmdb.org.br; f. 1980; moderate elements of former MDB; merged with Partido Popular February 1982; Pres. JADER BARBALHO; Sec.-Gen. SARANA FELIPE; factions include: the **Históricos** and the **Movimento da Unidade Progressiva (MUP).**

**Partido Popular Socialista (PPS):** Rua Coronel Lisboa 260, Vila Mariana, 04020-040, São Paulo, SP; tel. (11) 570-2182; fax (11) 549-9841; internet www.pps.com.br; f. 1922; Pres. ROBERTO FREIRE.

**Partido Progressista Brasileiro (PPB):** Senado Federal, Anexo 1, 17° andar, 70165-900 Brasília, DF; tel. (61) 311-3041; fax (61) 226-8192; internet www.ppb.org.br; f. 1995 by merger of Partido Progressista Reformador (PPR), Partido Progressista (PP) and the Partido Republicano Progressista (PRP); right-wing; Pres. ESPIRIDIÃO AMIN.

**Partido de Reconstrução Nacional (PRN):** Brasília, DF; f. 1988; right-wing; Leader FERNANDO COLLOR DE MELLO.

**Partido da Social Democracia Brasileira (PSDB):** Câmara dos Deputados, 70160-900 Brasília, DF; e-mail lideranca@psdb.org.br; internet www.psdb.org.br; f. 1988; centre-left; formed by dissident members of the PMDB (incl. Históricos), PFL, PDS, PDT, PSB and PTB; Pres. ARTUR DE TAVOLA; Vice-Pres. LUIZ CARLOS MENDONÇA DE BARROS.

**Partido Socialista Brasileiro (PSB):** Brasília, DF; tel. (61) 318-6951; fax (61) 318-2104; internet www.psb.org.br; f. 1947; Pres. MIGUEL ARRAES; Sec.-Gen. RENATO SOARES.

**Partido dos Trabalhadores (PT):** Congresso Nacional, 70160, Brasília, DF; tel. (61) 224-1699; internet www.pt.org.br; f. 1980; first independent labour party; associated with the *autêntico* branch of the trade union movement; 350,000 mems; Pres. JOSÉ DIRCEU DE OLIVEIRA E SILVA; Vice-Pres. JACÓ BITTAR.

**Partido Trabalhista Brasileiro (PTB):** SCLN 303, Bloco C, Sala 105, Asa Norte, 70735-530 Brasília, DF; tel. (61) 226-0477; fax (61) 225-4757; e-mail ptb@ptb.org.br; internet www.ptb.org.br; f. 1980; Pres. JOSÉ EDUARDO ANDRADE VIEIRA; Sec.-Gen. RODRIGUES PALMA.

Other political parties represented in the Congresso Nacional include the Partido Social Cristão (PSC; internet www.psc.org.br), the Partido Social-Democrático (PSD), the Partido Verde (PV; internet www.pv.org.br) and the Partido da Mobilização Nacional (PMN).

# Diplomatic Representation

**EMBASSIES IN BRAZIL**

**Algeria:** SHIS, QI 09, Conj. 13, Casa 01, Lago Sul, 71625-010 Brasília, DF; tel. (61) 248-4039; fax (61) 248-4691; Ambassador: HOCINE MEGHALOUI.

**Angola:** SHIS, QI 07, Conj. 11, Casa 9, Brasília, DF; tel. (61) 248-4489; fax (61) 248-1567; Ambassador: OSWALD DE JESÚS VAN-DÚNEM.

**Argentina:** SHIS, QL 02, Conj. 1, Casa 19, Lago Sul, 70442-900 Brasília, DF; tel. (61) 356-3000; fax (61) 365-2109; Ambassador: JORGE HUGO HERRERA VEGAS.

**Australia:** SHIS, QI 09, Conj. 16, Casa 01, Lago Sul, 70469-900 Brasília, DF; tel. (61) 248-5569; fax (61) 248-1066; e-mail embaustr@nutecnet.com.br; Ambassador: GARY CONROY.

**Austria:** SES, Quadra 811, Av. das Nações, Quadra 811, Lote 40, 70426-900 Brasília, DF; tel. (61) 443-3111; fax (61) 443-5233; e-mail emb.austria@zaz.com.br; Ambassador: DANIEL KRUMHOLZ.

**Bangladesh:** SHIS, QI 15, Conj. 15, Casa 16, 71635-350 Brasília, DF; tel. (61) 248-4830; fax (61) 248-4609; e-mail bdoot.bz@nutecnet.com.br; Ambassador: SYED NOOR HOSSAIN.

**Belgium:** SES, Av. das Nações, Lote 32, 70422-900 Brasília, DF; tel. (61) 243-1133; fax (61) 243-1219; Ambassador: FRANZ MICHILS.

**Bolivia:** SHIS, QL 04, Bloco E, 70470-900 Brasília, DF; tel. (61) 322-4227; fax (61) 322-4148; e-mail embolivia.brasil@nutecnet.com.br; Ambassador: GONZALO MONTENEGRO IRIGOYEN.

**Bulgaria:** SEN, Av. das Nações, Lote 8, 70432-900 Brasília, DF; tel. (61) 223-6193; fax (61) 323-3285; e-mail tchavo@tba.com.br; Ambassador: TCHAVDAR MLADENOV NIKOLOV.

**Cameroon:** SHIS, QI 09, Conj. 07, Casa 01, Lago Sul, 71625-070 Brasília, DF; tel. (61) 248-4433; fax (61) 248-0443; Ambassador: MARTIN NGUELE MBARGA.

**Canada:** SES, Av. das Nações, Quadra 803, Lote 16, 70410-900 Brasília, DF; CP 00961, 70359-970 Brasília, DF; tel. (61) 321-2171; fax (61) 321-4529; e-mail brsla@dfait-maeci.gc.ca; Ambassador: RICHARD KOHLER.

**Cape Verde:** SHIS, QL 6, Conj. 4, Casa 15, 71260-045 Brasília, DF; tel. (61) 365-3190; fax (61) 365-3191; e-mail embcaboverde@rudah.com.br; Ambassador: MANUEL AUGUSTO AMANTE DE ROSA.

**Chile:** SES, Av. das Nações, Lote 11, 70407 Brasília, DF; tel. (61) 226-5762; fax (61) 225-5478; Ambassador: JUAN ANTONIO MARTABIT SCAFF.

**China, People's Republic:** SES, Av. das Nações, Lote 51, 70443-900 Brasília, DF; tel. (61) 346-4436; fax (61) 346-3299; Ambassador: LI GUOXIN.

**Colombia:** SES, Av. das Nações, Lote 10, 70444-900 Brasília, DF; tel. (61) 226-8997; fax (61) 224-4732; e-mail emb-col@zaz.com.br; Ambassador: MARIO GALOFRE CANO.

**Congo, Democratic Republic:** SHIS, QI 09, Conj. 8, Casa 20, Lago Sul, CP 07-0041, 71600 Brasília, DF; tel. (61) 248-3348; Chargé d'affaires: BOIDOMBE MANZIJI.

**Costa Rica:** SHIS, QL 10, Conj. 4, Casa 03, Lago Sul, 71630-045 Brasília, DF; tel. (61) 248-7656; fax (61) 248-6234; e-mail embrica@solar.com.br; Ambassador: JAVIER SANCHO BONILLA.

**Côte d'Ivoire:** SEN, Av. das Nações, Lote 9, 70473-900 Brasília, DF; tel. (61) 321-4656; fax (61) 321-1306; Ambassador: DJIBO FELICIEN ABDOULAYE.

**Croatia:** SHIS QI 9, Conj. 11, Casa 3, 71625-110 Brasília, DF; tel. (61) 248-0610; fax (61) 248-1708; Ambassador: ŽELIMIR URBAN.

**Cuba:** SHIS, QI 05, Conj. 18, Casa 01, Lago Sul, 70481-900 Brasília, DF; tel. (61) 248-4710; fax (61) 248-6778; Ambassador: RAMÓN SÁNCHEZ-PAROD.

**Czech Republic:** Via L-3/Sul, Q-805, Lote 21, 70414, CP 70414-900 Brasília, DF; tel. (61) 242-7785; fax (61) 242-7833; e-mail czech@brnet.com.br; Ambassador: LADISLAV SKERIK.

**Denmark:** SES, Av. das Nações, Lote 26, 70416-900 Brasília, DF; tel. (61) 443-8188; fax (61) 443-5154; e-mail danmark@tba.com.br; Ambassador: ANITA HUGAU.

**Dominican Republic:** SHIS, QL 8, Conj. 5, Casa 14, Lago Sul, 71620-255 Brasília, DF; tel. (61) 248-1405; fax (61) 248-1405; e-mail embajdargan@nutcnet.com.br; Ambassador: CIRO AMAURY DARGAM CRUZ.

**Ecuador:** SHIS, QI 11, Conj. 9, Casa 24, 71625-290 Brasília, DF; tel. (61) 248-5560; fax (61) 248-1290; e-mail embec@solar.com.br; Ambassador: DIEGO RIBADENEIRA ESPINOSA.

**Egypt:** SEN, Av. das Nações, Lote 12, 70435-900 Brasília, DF; tel. (61) 225-8517; fax (61) 223-5812; e-mail embegypt@brnet.com.br; Ambassador: EL SAYED RAMZI EZEDIM RAMZI.

**El Salvador:** SHIS, QI 07, Conj. 6, Casa 14, 71615-260 Brasília, DF; tel. (61) 248-3788; fax (61) 248-5636; e-mail embelsalvador@tba.com.br; Ambassador: MARTÍN ALBERTO RIVERA GÓMEZ.

**Finland:** SES, Av. das Nações, Lote 27, 70417-900 Brasília, DF; tel. (61) 248-0017; fax (61) 364-2251; e-mail suomi@tba.com.br; Ambassador: ASKO NUMMINEN.

**France:** SES, Av. das Nações, Lote 4, 70404-900 Brasília, DF; tel. (61) 312-9100; fax (61) 312-9108; Ambassador: ALAIN ROUQUIÉ.

**Gabon:** SHIS QI 9, Conji. 11, Casa 24, 71615-300, Brasília, DF; tel. (61) 248-3536; fax (61) 248-2241; e-mail mgabao@nutecnet.com.br; Ambassador: MARCEL ODONGUI-BONNARD.

**Germany:** SES, Av. das Nações, Lote 25, 70415-900 Brasília, DF; tel. (61) 443-7330; fax (61) 443-7508; Ambassador: HANS-BODO BERTRAM.

**Ghana:** SHIS, QL 10, Conj. 8, Casa 2, CP 07-0456, 70466-900 Brasília, DF; tel. (61) 248-6047; fax (61) 248-7913; Ambassador: (vacant).

**Greece:** SHIS, QL 04, Conj. 1, Casa 18, 70461-900 Brasília, DF; tel. (61) 365-3090; fax (61) 3653093; e-mail joul@ssopnutecnet.com.br; internet www.emb.gzecik.org; Ambassador: EMMANUEL WLANDIS.

**Guatemala:** SHIS, QL 08, Conj. 5, Casa 11, 70460-900 Brasília, DF; tel. (61) 248-3318; fax (61) 248-4383; Ambassador: HERBERT ESTUARDO MENESES CORONADO.

**Guyana:** SBN, Quadra 2, Bloco J, Edif. Paulo Maurício, 13° andar, salas 1310–1315, 70438-900 Brasília, DF; tel. (61) 224-9229; fax (61) 220-3022; e-mail embguyana@apis.com.br; Ambassador: MARILYN CHERYL MILES.

**Haiti:** SHIS, QI 17, Conj. 4, Casa 19, Lago Sul, 70465-900 Brasília, DF; tel. (61) 248-6860; fax (61) 248-7472; Chargé d'affaires: JEAN-BAPTISTE HARVEL.

**Holy See:** SES, Av. das Nações, Lote 1, CP 07-0153, 70359-970 Brasília, DF (Apostolic Nunciature); tel. (61) 223-0794; fax (61) 224-9365; e-mail nunapost@ucb.br; Apostolic Nuncio: Most Rev. ALFIO RAPISARDA, Titular Archbishop of Cannae.

**Honduras:** SHIS, QI 05, Conj. 13, Casa 1, 70464-900 Brasília, DF; tel. (61) 248-1200; fax (61) 248-1425; Ambassador: GERARDO MARTÍNEZ BLANCO.

**Hungary:** SES, Av. das Nações, Lote 19, Qd. 805, 70413-900 Brasília, DF; tel. (61) 443-0836; fax (61) 443-3434; e-mail embhung @uninet.com.br; Ambassador: GÁBOR TÓTH.

**India:** SHIS, QI 9, Conj. 9, Casa 7, 71625-090 Brasília, DF; tel. (61) 248-4006; fax (61) 248-7849; Ambassador: MUTHAL PUREDATH M. MENON.

**Indonesia:** SES, Av. das Nações, Lote 20, Q. 805, 70200 Brasília, DF; tel. (61) 243-0233; fax (61) 243-1713; Ambassador: SUTADI DJAJAKUSUMA.

**Iran:** SES, Av. das Nações, Lote 31, 70421 Brasília, DF; tel. (61) 242-5733; fax (61) 244-9640; Ambassador: BAHMAN TAHERIAN MOBAREKAH.

**Iraq:** SES, Av. das Nações, Lote 64, Brasília, DF; tel. (61) 346-2822; fax (61) 346-7034; Ambassador: OAIS TAWFIG ALMUKHFAR.

**Israel:** SES, Av. das Nações, Lote 38, 70424-900 Brasília, DF; tel. (61) 244-7675; fax (61) 244-6129; e-mail embisrae@solar.com.br; Ambassador: YAACOV KEINAN.

**Italy:** SES, Av. das Nações, Lote 30, 70420 Brasília, DF; tel. (61) 244-0044; fax (61) 244-0034; e-mail itu.org.br/itembassy/busit.html; Ambassador: MICHELANGELO JACOBUCCI.

**Japan:** SES, Av. das Nações, Lote 39, 70425-900 Brasília, DF; tel. (61) 242-6866; fax (61) 242-0738; Ambassador: KATSUNARI SUZUKI.

**Jordan:** SHIS, QI 9, Conj. 18, Casa 14, 70483-900 Brasília, DF; tel. (61) 248-5407; fax (61) 248-1698; Ambassador: FARIS SHAWKAT MUFTI.

**Korea, Republic:** SEN, Av. das Nações, Lote 14, 70436-900 Brasília, DF; tel. (61) 321-2500; fax (61) 321-2508; Ambassador: WON-YOUNG LEE.

**Kuwait:** SHIS, QI 05, Chácara 30, 71600-750 Brasília, DF; tel. (61) 248-1633; fax (61) 248-09691; Ambassador: NASSER SABEEH B. AL-SABEEH.

**Lebanon:** SES, Av. das Nações, Q- 805, Lote 17, 70411-900 Brasília, DF; tel. (61) 443-9837; fax (61) 443-8574; e-mail emblibano@uol .com.br; Ambassador: ISHAYA EL-KHOURY.

**Libya:** SHIS, QI 15, Chácara 26, CP 3505, 70462-900 Brasília, DF; tel. (61) 248-6710; fax (61) 248-0598; Head of People's Bureau: ALI SULEIMAN AL-AUJALI.

**Malaysia:** SHIS, QI 05, Chácara 62, Lago Sul, 70477-900 Brasília, DF; tel. (61) 248-5008; fax (61) 248-6307; Ambassador: S. THANARAJASINGAM.

**Mexico:** SES, Av. das Nações, Lote 18, 70412-900 Brasília, DF; tel. (61) 244-1011; fax (61) 244-1755; e-mail embamexbra@brnet.com.br; Ambassador: JORGE EDUARDO NAVARRETE.

**Morocco:** Av. das Nacões, Lote 2, 70432-900 Brasília, DF; tel. (61) 321-4487; fax (61) 321-0745; e-mail sifamabr@tba.com.br; internet www.mincom.gov.ma; Ambassador: ABDELMALEK CHARKAOUI GHAZOUANI.

**Mozambique:** SHIS, QL 12, Conj. 7, Casa 9, 71630-275 Brasília, DF; tel. (61) 248-4222; fax (61) 248-3917; Ambassador: FELIZARDA ISAURA MONTEIRO.

**Myanmar:** SHIS, QL 8, Conj. 4, Casa 5, 71620-245 Brasília, DF; tel. (61) 248-3747; fax (61) 248-1922; e-mail mebrsl@brnet.com.br; Ambassador: KYAR NYO CHIT PE.

**Netherlands:** SES, Av. das Nações, Quadra 801, Lote 05, 70359-970 Brasília, DF; tel. (61) 321-4769; fax (61) 321-1518; e-mail nlgovbra@pepz.brnet.com.br; Ambassador: FRANCISCUS B. A. M. VAN HAREN.

**Nicaragua:** SHIS, QI 15, Conj. 07, Casa 14, Lago Sul, 70365-270 Brasília, DF; tel. (61) 248-5366; fax (61) 248-3148; Ambassador: EDGARD SOLÍS MARTÍNEZ.

**Nigeria:** SEN, Av. das Nações, Lote 05, CP 11-1190, 70432 Brasília, DF; tel. (61) 226-1717; fax (61) 224-9830; Ambassador: Dr PATRICK DELE COLE.

**Norway:** SES, Av. das Nações, Lote 28, CP 07-0670, 70359-970 Brasília, DF; tel. (61) 243-8720; fax (61) 242-7989; e-mail embno@ tba.com.br; Ambassador: LIV A. KERR.

**Pakistan:** SHIS, QI 05, Conj. 14, Casa 21, 71615-140 Brasília, DF; tel. (61) 364-1632; fax (61) 248-3484; Ambassador: MUHAMMAD NASSER.

**Panama:** SHIS, QI 11, Conj. 6, Casa 6, 71625-260 Brasília, DF; tel. (61) 248-7309; fax (61) 248-2834; e-mail empanama@nettur.com.br; Ambassador: OLIMPO ANÍBAL SAEZ MARCUCCI.

**Paraguay:** SES, Av. das Nações, Lote 42, CP 14-2314, 70427-900 Brasília, DF; tel. (61) 242-3742; fax (61) 242-4605; Ambassador: CARLOS ALBERTO GONZÁLEZ GARABELLI.

**Peru:** SES, Av. das Nações, Lote 43, 70428-900 Brasília, DF; tel. (61) 242-9933; fax (61) 244-9344; e-mail emb-peru@nutecnet.com.br; Ambassador: EDUARDO PONCE VIVANCO.

**Philippines:** SEN, Av. das Nações, Lote 1, 70431 Brasília, DF; tel. (61) 223-5143; fax (61) 226-7411; e-mail pr@pop.persocom.com.br; Ambassador: ORCAR G. VALENZUELA.

**Poland:** SES, Av. das Nações, Lote 33, 70423-900 Brasília, DF; tel. (61) 243-3438; fax (61) 242-8543; Ambassador: BOGUSŁAW ZAKRZEWSKI.

**Portugal:** SES, Av. das Nações, Lote 2, 70402-900 Brasília, DF; tel. (61) 321-3434; fax (61) 224-7347; e-mail embporbr@abordo.com.br; Ambassador: FRANCISCO KNOPFLI.

**Romania:** SEN, Av. das Nações, Lote 6, 70456 Brasília, DF; tel. (61) 226-0746; fax (61) 226-6629; Ambassador: ION FLOROIU.

**Russia:** SES, Av. das Nações, Quadra 801, Lote A, 70476-900 Brasília, DF; tel. (61) 223-3094; fax (61) 223-7319; e-mail embrus@brnet.com.br; internet www.brnet.com.br/pages/embrus; Ambassador: VASSILII PETROVICH GROMOV.

**Saudi Arabia:** SHIS, QL 10, Conj. 9, Casa 20, 70471 Brasília, DF; tel. (61) 248-3523; fax (61) 284-2905; Ambassador: YAHYA AHMED AL YAHYA.

**Slovakia:** A/C, W/3 Sul 508, CP 880, 70359-970 Brasília, DF; tel. (61) 243-1263; fax (61) 243-1267; Ambassador: JOZEF ADAMEC.

**South Africa:** SES, Av. das Nações, Lote 6, CP 11-1170, 70406 Brasília, DF; tel. (61) 312-9500; fax (61) 322-8491; e-mail saemb@brnet.com.br; Ambassador: MBULELO RAKWENA.

**Spain:** SES, Av. das Nações, Lote 44, 70429-900 Brasília, DF; tel. (61) 244-2121; fax (61) 242-1781; Ambassador: CÉSAR ALBA Y FUSTER.

**Suriname:** SHIS, QI 09, Conj. 8, Casa 24, 70457-900 Brasília, DF; tel. (61) 248-6706; fax (61) 248-3791; e-mail sur.emb@persocom .com.br; Ambassador: RUPERT L. CHRISTOPHER.

**Sweden:** SES, Av. das Nações, Lote 29, 70419-900 Brasília, DF; tel. (61) 443-1444; fax (61) 443-1187; e-mail swebra@tba.com.br; Ambassador: CHRISTER MANHUSEN.

**Switzerland:** SES, Av. das Nações, Lote 41, 70448 Brasília, DF; CP 08671, 70312-970 Brasília, DF; tel. (61) 244-5500; fax (61) 244-5711; e-mail swissembra@brasilia.com.br; Ambassador: OSCAR KNAPP.

**Syria:** SEN, Av. das Nações, Lote 11, 70434-900 Brasília, DF; tel. (61) 226-0970; fax (61) 223-2595; Ambassador: MUHAMMAD TAUFIK JUHANI.

**Thailand:** SEN, Av. das Nações Norte, Lote 10, 70433-900 Brasília, DF; tel. (61) 224-6943; fax (61) 321-2994; Ambassador: SAMROENG LAKSANASUT.

**Togo:** SHIS, QI 11, Conj. 9, Casa 10, 70478-900 Brasília, DF; tel. (61) 248-4209; fax (61) 248-4752; Ambassador: LAMBANA TCHAOU.

**Trinidad and Tobago:** SHIS, QL 02, Conj. 02, Casa 01, 71665-028 Brasília, DF; tel. (61) 365-1132; fax (61) 365-1733; e-mail trinbago@tba.com.br; Ambassador: ROBERT M. TORRY.

**Tunisia:** SHIS, QI 19, Conj. 16, Casa 20, 71625-160 Brasília, DF; tel. (61) 248-3725; fax (61) 248-7355; Ambassador: ABBES MOHSEN.

**Turkey:** SES, Av. das Nações, Lote 23, 70452-900 Brasília, DF; tel. (61) 242-1850; fax (61) 242-1448; e-mail emb.turquia@nrp.com.br; Ambassador: DOGAN ALPAN.

**Ukraine:** SHIS, QL 6, Conj. 2, Casa 17, 71620-025 Brasília, DF; tel. (61) 365-3898; fax (61) 365-3898; e-mail brucemb@brnet.com.br; Ambassador: OLEKSANDR NIKONENKO.

**United Arab Emirates:** SHIS, QI 5, Chácara 18, 70486-901 Brasília, DF; tel. (61) 248-0717; fax (61) 248-7543; Ambassador: ALI MUBARAK AHMED AL-MANSOORI.

**United Kingdom:** SES, Quadra 801, Conj. K, Lote 8, CP 07-0586, 70408-900 Brasília, DF; tel. (61) 225-2710; fax (61) 225-1777; e-mail briteml@zaz.com.br; Ambassador: ROGER BONE.

**USA:** SES, Av. das Nações, Lote 3, 70403-900 Brasília, DF; tel. (61) 321-7272; fax (61) 225-9136; Ambassador: MELVYN LEVITSKY.

**Uruguay:** SES, Av. das Nações, Lote 14, 70450-900 Brasília, DF; tel. (61) 322-1200; fax (61) 322-6534; e-mail urubras@tba.com.br; Ambassador: MARIO C. FERNÁNDEZ.

**Venezuela:** SES, Av. das Nações, Lote 13, Q-803, 70451-900 Brasília, DF; tel. (61) 223-9325; fax (61) 226-5633; e-mail embvenbr@nutecnet.com.br; Ambassador: MILOS ALCALAY.

**Yugoslavia:** SES, Av. das Nações, Q-803, Lote 15, 70409-900 Brasília, DF; CP 1240, 70000 Brasília, DF; tel. (61) 223-7272; fax (61) 223-8462; e-mail embiugos@nutecnet.com.br; Chargé d'affaires a.i.: DRAGAN S. VUJNOVIĆ.

# Judicial System

The judiciary powers of the State are held by the following: the Supreme Federal Tribunal, the Higher Tribunal of Justice, the five Regional Federal Tribunals and Federal Judges, the Higher Labour Tribunal, the 24 Regional Labour Tribunals, the Conciliation and Judgment Councils and Labour Judges, the Higher Electoral Tribunal, the 27 Regional Electoral Tribunals, the Electoral Judges and Electoral Councils, the Higher Military Tribunal, the Military Tribunals and Military Judges, the Tribunals of the States and Judges of the States, the Tribunal of the Federal District and of the Territories and Judges of the Federal District and of the Territories.

The Supreme Federal Tribunal comprises 11 ministers, nominated by the President and approved by the Senate. Its most important role is to rule on the final interpretation of the Constitution. The Supreme Federal Tribunal has the power to declare an act of Congress void if it is unconstitutional. It judges offences committed by persons such as the President, the Vice-President, members of the Congresso Nacional, Ministers of State, its own members, the Attorney General, judges of other higher courts, and heads of permanent diplomatic missions. It also judges cases of litigation between the Union and the States, between the States, or between foreign nations and the Union or the States; disputes as to jurisdiction between higher Tribunals, or between the latter and any other court, in cases involving the extradition of criminals, and others related to the writs of habeas corpus and habeas data, and in other cases.

The Higher Tribunal of Justice comprises at least 33 members, appointed by the President and approved by the Senado. Its jurisdiction includes the judgment of offences committed by State Governors. The Regional Federal Tribunals comprise at least seven judges, recruited when possible in the respective region and appointed by the President of the Republic. The Higher Labour Tribunal comprises 27 members, appointed by the President and approved by the Senado. The judges of the Regional Labour Tribunals are also appointed by the President. The Higher Electoral Tribunal comprises at least seven members: three judges from among those of the Supreme Federal Tribunal, two from the Higher Tribunal of Justice (elected by secret ballot) and two lawyers appointed by the President. The Regional Electoral Tribunals are also composed of seven members. The Higher Military Tribunal comprises 15 life members, appointed by the President and approved by the Senate; three from the navy, four from the army, three from the air force and five civilian members. The States are responsible for the administration of their own justice, according to the principles established by the Constitution.

### SUPREME FEDERAL TRIBUNAL

**Supreme Federal Tribunal:** Praça dos Três Poderes, 70175-900 Brasília, DF; tel. (61) 316-5000; fax (61) 316-5483; internet www.stf.gov.br.

**President:** CARLOS MÁRIO DA SILVA VELLOSO.

**Vice-President:** MARCO AURÉLIO MENDES DE FARIAS MELLO.

**Justices:** JOSÉ CARLOS MOREIRA ALVES, JOSÉ NÉRI DA SILVEIRA, SYDNEY SANCHES, LUIZ OCTAVIO PIRES E ALBUQUERQUE GALLOTTI, JOSÉ PAULO SEPÚLVEDA PERTENCE, JOSÉ CELSO DE MELLO, Filho, ILMAR NASCIMENTO GALVÃO, MAURÍCIO JOSÉ CORRÊA, NELSON DE AZEVEDO JOBIM.

**Attorney-General:** GERALDO BRINDEIRO.

**Director-General (Secretariat):** JOSÉ GERALDO DE LANA TÔRRES.

# Religion

### CHRISTIANITY

**Conselho Nacional de Igrejas Cristãs do Brasil—CONIC** (National Council of Christian Churches in Brazil): SCS, Quadra 01, Bloco E, Edif. Ceará, Sala 713, 70303-900 Brasília, DF; tel. (61) 321-8341; fax (61) 321-4034; f. 1982; seven mem. churches; Pres. GLAUCO SOARES DE LIMA; Exec. Sec. P. ERVINO SCHMIDT.

### The Roman Catholic Church

Brazil comprises 38 archdioceses, 205 dioceses (including one each for Catholics of the Maronite, Melkite and Ukrainian Rites), 14 territorial prelatures and two territorial abbacies. The Archbishop of São Sebastião do Rio de Janeiro is also the Ordinary for Catholics of other Oriental Rites in Brazil (estimated at 10,000 in 1994). The great majority of Brazil's population are adherents of the Roman Catholic Church (around 106m. at the time of the 1980 census), although a report published by the Brazilian weekly, *Veja,* in July 1989 concluded that since 1950 the membership of non-Catholic Christian Churches had risen from 3% to 6% of the total population, while membership of the Roman Catholic Church had fallen from 93% to 89% of Brazilians.

**Bishops' Conference:** Conferência Nacional dos Bispos do Brasil, SE/Sul Q 801, Conj. B, CP 02067, 70259-970 Brasília, DF; tel. (61) 225-2955; fax (61) 225-4361; e-mail cnbb@cnbb.org.br; f. 1980 (statutes approved 1986); Pres. JAYME HENRIQUE CHEMELLO, Bishop of Pelotas, RS; Sec.-Gen. RAYMUNDO DAMASCENO ASSIS.

*Latin Rite*

**Archbishop of São Salvador da Bahia, BA:** GERALDO MAJELLA AGNELO, Primate of Brazil, Rua Martin Afonso de Souza 270, 40100-050 Salvador, BA; tel. and fax (71) 247-5987.

**Archbishop of Aparecida, SP:** Cardinal ALOÍSIO LORSCHEIDER.

**Archbishop of Aracajú, SE:** JOSÉ PALMEIRA LESSA.

**Archbishop of Belém do Pará, PA:** VICENTE JOAQUIM ZICO.

**Archbishop of Belo Horizonte, MG:** Cardinal SERAFIM FERNANDES DE ARAÚJO.

**Archbishop of Botucatú, SP:** ANTÔNIO MARIA MUCCIOLO.

**Archbishop of Brasília, DF:** Cardinal JOSÉ FREIRE FALCÃO.

**Archbishop of Campinas, SP:** GILBERTO PEREIRA LOPES.

**Archbishop of Campo Grande, MS:** VITÓRIO PAVANELLO.

**Archbishop of Cascavel, PR:** LÚCIO IGNÁCIO BAUMGAERTNER.

**Archbishop of Cuiabá, MT:** BONIFÁCIO PICCININI.

**Archbishop of Curitiba, PR:** PEDRO ANTÔNIO MARCHETTI FEDALTO.

**Archbishop of Diamantina, MG:** PAULO LOPES DE FARIA.

**Archbishop of Florianópolis, SC:** EUSÉBIO OSCAR SCHEID.

**Archbishop of Fortaleza, CE:** (vacant).

**Archbishop of Goiânia, GO:** ANTÔNIO RIBEIRO DE OLIVEIRA.

**Archbishop of Juiz de Fora, MG:** CLÓVIS FRAINER.

**Archbishop of Londrina, PR:** ALBANO BORTOLETTO CAVALLIN.

**Archbishop of Maceió, AL:** EDVALDO GONÇALVES AMARAL.

**Archbishop of Manaus, AM:** LUIZ SOARES VIEIRA.

**Archbishop of Mariana, MG:** LUCIANO P. MENDES DE ALMEIDA.

**Archbishop of Maringá, PR:** MURILO SEBASTIÃO RAMOS KRIEGER.

**Archbishop of Natal, RN:** HEITOR DE ARAÚJO SALES.

**Archbishop of Niterói, RJ:** CARLOS ALBERTO ETCHANDY GIMENO NAVARRO.

**Archbishop of Olinda e Recife, PE:** JOSÉ CARDOSO SOBRINHO.

**Archbishop of Palmas, PR:** ALBERTO TAVEIRA CORRÊA.

**Archbishop of Paraíba, PB:** MARCELO PINTO CARVALHEIRA.

**Archbishop of Porto Alegre, RS:** ALTAMIRO ROSSATO.

**Archbishop of Porto Velho, RO:** MOACYR GRECHI.

**Archbishop of Pouso Alegre, MG:** RICARDO PEDRO CHAVES PINTO, Filho.

**Archbishop of Ribeirão Prêto, SP:** ARNALDO RIBEIRO.

**Archbishop of São Luís do Maranhão, MA:** PAULO EDUARDO DE ANDRADE PONTE.

**Archbishop of São Paulo, SP:** CLAUDIO HUMMES.

**Archbishop of São Sebastião do Rio de Janeiro, RJ:** Cardinal EUGÊNIO DE ARAÚJO SALES.

**Archbishop of Sorocaba, SP:** JOSÉ LAMBERT.

**Archbishop of Teresina, PI:** MIGUEL FENELON CÂMARA, Filho.

**Archbishop of Uberaba, MG:** ALOÍSIO ROQUE OPPERMANN.

**Archbishop of Vitória, ES:** SILVESTRE LUÍS SCANDIAN.

*Maronite Rite*

**Bishop of Nossa Senhora do Líbano em São Paulo, SP:** JOSEPH MAHFOUZ.

*Melkite Rite*

**Bishop of Nossa Senhora do Paraíso em São Paulo, SP:** PIERRE MOUALLEM.

*Ukrainian Rite*

**Bishop of São João Batista em Curitiba, PR:** EFRAIM BASÍLIO KREVEY.

### The Anglican Communion

Anglicans form the Episcopal Anglican Church of Brazil (Igreja Episcopal Anglicana do Brasil), comprising seven dioceses.

**Igreja Episcopal Anglicana do Brasil:** CP 11-510, 90841-970 Porto Alegre, RS; tel. and fax (51) 318-6200; f. 1890; 103,021 mems (1997); Primate Most Rev. GLAUCO SOARES DE LIMA, Bishop of São Paulo-Brazil; Gen. Sec. Rev. MAURICIO J. A. DE ANDRADE; e-mail m_andrade@ieab.org.br.

### Protestant Churches

**Igreja Cristã Reformada do Brasil:** CP 2808, 01000 São Paulo, SP; Pres. Rev. JANOS APOSTOL.

**Igreja Evangélica de Confissão Luterana no Brasil (IECLB):** Rua Senhor dos Passos 202, 2° andar, CP 2876, 90020-180 Porto Alegre, RS; tel. (51) 221-3433; fax (51) 225-7244; e-mail secretariageral@ieclb.org.br; f. 1949; 870,000 mems; Pres. Pastor HUBERTO KIRCHHEIM.

**Igreja Evangélica Congregacional do Brasil:** CP 414, 98700 Ijuí, RS; tel. (55) 332-4656; f. 1942; 41,000 mems, 310 congregations; Pres. Rev. H. HARTMUT W. HACHTMANN.

**Igreja Evangélica Luterana do Brasil:** Rua Cel. Lucas de Oliveira 894, 90440-010 Porto Alegre, RS; tel. (51) 332-2111; fax (51) 332-8145; e-mail ielb@zaz.com.br; f. 1904; 207,000 mems; Pres. Rev. CARLOS WALTER WINTERLE.

**Igreja Metodista do Brasil:** General Communication Secretariat, Rua Artur Azevedo 1192, Apdo 81, Pinheiros, 05404 São Paulo, SP; Exec. Sec. Dr ONÉSIMO DE OLIVEIRA CARDOSO.

**Igreja Presbiteriana Unida do Brasil (IPU):** CP 01-212, 29001-970 Vitória, ES; tel. (27) 222-8024; f. 1978; Sec. PAULO RÜCKERT.

## BAHÁ'Í FAITH

**Bahá'í Community of Brazil:** SHIS, QL 08, Conj. 2, Casa 15, 71620-285, Brasília, DF; CP 7035, 71619-970 Brasília, DF; tel. (61) 364-3597; fax (61) 364-3470; e-mail bahai@ax.apc.org; f. 1921; Sec. GUITTY M. MILANI.

## BUDDHISM

**Federação das Seitas Budistas do Brasil:** Av. Paulo Ferreira 1133, 02915-100, São Paulo, SP; tel. (11) 876-5771; fax (11) 877-8687.

**Sociedade Budista do Brasil** (Rio Buddhist Vihara): Dom Joaquim Mamede 45, Lagoinha, Santa Tereza, 20241-390 Rio de Janeiro, RJ; tel. (21) 205-4400; f. 1972; Principal Dr PUHULWELLE VIPASSI.

# The Press

The most striking feature of the Brazilian press is the relatively small circulation of newspapers in comparison with the size of the population. The newspapers with the largest circulations are *O Día* (250,000), *O Globo* (350,000), *Fôlha de São Paulo* (560,000), and *O Estado de São Paulo* (242,000). The low circulation is mainly owing to high costs resulting from distribution difficulties. In consequence there are no national newspapers. In 1996 a total of 380 daily newspaper titles were published in Brazil.

## DAILY NEWSPAPERS

### Belém, PA

**O Liberal:** Rua Gaspar Viana 253, 66020 Belém, PA; tel. (91) 222-3000; fax (91) 224-1906; f. 1946; Pres. LUCIDEA MAIORANA; circ. 20,000.

### Belo Horizonte, MG

**Diário da Tarde:** Rua Goiás 36, 30190 Belo Horizonte, MG; tel. (31) 273-2322; fax (31) 273-4400; f. 1931; evening; Dir-Gen. PAULO C. DE ARAÚJO; total circ. 150,000.

**Diário de Minas:** Rua Francisco Salles 540, 30150-220 Belo Horizonte, MG; tel. (31) 222-5622; f. 1949; Pres. MARCO AURÍLIO F. CARONE; circ. 50,000.

**Diário do Comércio:** Av. Américo Vespúcio 1660, 31.230 Belo Horizonte, MG; tel. (31) 469-1011; fax (31) 469-1080; f. 1932; Pres. JOSÉ COSTA.

**Estado de Minas:** Rua Goiás 36, 30190 Belo Horizonte, MG; tel. (31) 273-2322; fax (31) 273-4400; f. 1928; morning; independent; Pres. PAULO C. DE ARAÚJO; circ. 65,000.

### Blumenau, SC

**Jornal de Santa Catarina:** Rua São Paulo 1120, 89010-000 Blumenau, SC; tel. (2147) 340-1400; e-mail redacao@santa.com.br; f. 1971; Dir ALVARO IAHNIG; circ. 25,000.

### Brasília, DF

**Correio Brasiliense:** SIG, Q2, Lotes 300/340, 70610-901 Brasília, DF; tel. (61) 321-1314; fax (61) 321-2856; f. 1960; Dir-Gen. PAULO C. DE ARAÚJO; circ. 30,000.

**Jornal de Brasília:** SIG, Trecho 1, Lotes 585/645, 70610-400 Brasília, DF; tel. (61) 225-2515; f. 1972; Dir-Gen. FERNANDO CÔMA; circ. 25,000.

### Campinas, SP

**Correio Popular:** Rua Conceição 124, 13010-902 Campinas, SP; tel. (192) 32-8588; fax (192) 31-8152; f. 1927; Pres. SYLVINO DE GODOY NETO; circ. 40,000.

### Curitiba, PR

**O Estado do Paraná:** Rua João Tschannerl 800, 80820-000 Curitiba, PR; tel. (41) 335-8811; fax (41) 335-2838; f. 1951; Pres. PAULO CRUZ PIMENTEL; circ. 15,000.

**Gazeta do Povo:** Praça Carlos Gomes 4, 80010 Curitiba, PR; tel. (41) 224-0522; fax (41) 225-6848; f. 1919; Pres. FRANCISCO CUNHA PEREIRA; circ. 40,000.

**Tribuna do Paraná:** Rua João Tschannerl 800, 80820-010 Curitiba PR; tel. (41) 335-8811; fax (41) 335-2838; f. 1956; Pres. PAULO CRUZ PIMENTEL; circ. 15,000.

### Florianópolis, SC

**O Estado:** Rodovia SC-401, Km 3, 88030 Florianópolis, SC; tel. (482) 388-8888; fax (482) 380-0711; f. 1915; Pres. JOSÉ MATUSALÉM COMELLI; circ. 20,000.

### Fortaleza, CE

**Jornal O Povo:** Av. Aguanambi 282, 60055 Fortaleza, CE; tel. (85) 211-9666; fax (85) 231-5792; f. 1928; evening; Pres. DEMÓCRITO ROCHA DUMMAR; circ. 20,000.

**Tribuna do Ceará:** Av. Desemb. Moreira 2900, 60170 Fortaleza, CE; tel. (85) 247-3066; fax (85) 272-2799; f. 1957; Dir JOSÉ A. SANCHO; circ. 12,000.

### Goiânia, GO

**Diário da Manhã:** Av. Anhanguera 2833, Setor Leste Universitário, 74000 Goiânia, GO; tel. (62) 261-7371; f. 1980; Pres. JULIO NASSER CUSTÓDIO DOS SANTOS; circ. 16,000.

**Jornal O Popular:** Rua Thómas Edson Q7, Setor Serrinha, 74835-130 Goiânia, GO; tel. (62) 250-1000; fax (62) 241-1018; f. 1938; Pres. JAIME CÂMARA JÚNIOR; circ. 65,000.

### Londrina, PR

**Fôlha de Londrina:** Rua Piauí 241, 86010 Londrina, PR; tel. (432) 24-2020; fax (432) 21-1051; f. 1948; Pres. JOÃO MILANEZ; circ. 40,000.

### Manaus, AM

**A Crítica:** Av. André Araújo, Km 3, 69060 Manaus; tel. (92) 642-2000; fax (92) 642-1501; f. 1949; Dir UMBERTO CADERARO; circ. 19,000.

### Niterói, RJ

**O Fluminense:** Rua Visconde de Itaboraí 184, 24030 Niterói, RJ; tel. (21) 719-3311; fax (21) 719-6344; f. 1978; Dir ALBERTO FRANCISCO TORRES; circ. 80,000.

**A Tribuna:** Rua Barão do Amazonas 31, 24210 Niterói, RJ; tel. (21) 719-1886; f. 1926; Dir-Gen. JOURDAN AMÓRA; circ. 18,000.

### Porto Alegre, RS

**Zero Hora:** Av. Ipiranga 1075, 90169-900 Porto Alegre, RS; tel. (51) 218-4101; fax (51) 218-4405; f. 1964; Pres. JAYME SIROTSKY; circ. 163,000 (Mon.), 115,000 weekdays, 250,000 Sunday.

### Recife, PE

**Diário de Pernambuco:** Praça da Independência 12, 2° andar, 50010-300 Recife, PE; tel. (81) 424-3666; fax (81) 424-2527; f. 1825; morning; independent; Pres. ANTÔNIO C. DA COSTA; circ. 31,000.

### Ribeirão Preto, SP

**Diário da Manhã:** Rua Duque de Caxias 179, 14015 Ribeirão Preto, SP; tel. (16) 634-0909; f. 1898; Dir PAULO M. SANT'ANNA; circ. 17,000.

### Rio de Janeiro, RJ

**O Dia:** Rua Riachuelo 359, 20235 Rio de Janeiro, RJ; tel. (21) 272-8000; fax (21) 507-1038; f. 1951; morning; centrist labour; Pres. ANTÔNIO ARY DE CARVALHO; circ. 250,000 weekdays, 500,000 Sundays.

**O Globo:** Rua Irineu Marinho 35, CP 1090, 20233-900 Rio de Janeiro, RJ; tel. (21) 534-5000; fax (21) 534-5510; f. 1925; morning; Dir FRANCISCO GRAELL; circ. 350,000 weekdays, 600,000 Sundays.

**Jornal do Brasil:** Av. Brasil 500, 6° andar, São Cristovão, 20949-900 Rio de Janeiro, RJ; tel. (21) 585-4422; f. 1891; morning; Catholic, liberal; Pres. M. F. DO NASCIMENTO BRITO; circ. 200,000 weekdays, 325,000 Sundays.

**Jornal do Comércio:** Rua do Livramento 189, 20221 Rio de Janeiro, RJ; tel. (21) 253-6675; f. 1827; morning; Pres. AUSTREGÉSILO DE ATHAYDE; circ. 31,000 weekdays.

**Jornal dos Sports:** Rua Tenente Possolo 15/25, Cruz Vermelha, 20230 Rio de Janeiro, RJ; tel. (21) 232-8010; f. 1931; morning; sporting daily; Dir VENÂNCIO P. VELLOSO; circ. 38,000.

**Ultima Hora:** Rua Equador 702, 20220 Rio de Janeiro, RJ; tel. (21) 223-2444; fax (21) 223-2444; f. 1951; evening; Dir K. NUNES; circ. 56,000.

### Salvador, BA

**Jornal da Bahia:** Rua Peruvia Carneiro 220, 41100 Salvador, BA; tel. (71) 384-2919; fax (71) 384-5726; f. 1958; Pres. MÁRIO KERTÉSZ; circ. 20,000.

**Jornal Correio da Bahia:** Av. Luis Viana Filho s/n, 41100 Salvador, BA; tel. (71) 371-2811; fax (71) 231-3944; f. 1979; Pres. ARMANDO GONÇALVES.

**Jornal da Tarde:** Av. Tancredo Neves 1092, 41820-020 Salvador, BA; tel. (71) 231-9683; fax (71) 231-1064; f. 1912; evening; Pres. REGINA SIMÕES DE MELLO LEITÃO; circ. 54,000.

### Santo André, SP

**Diário do Grande ABC:** Rua Catequese 562, 09090-900 Santo André, SP; tel. (11) 715-8112; fax (11) 715-8257; e-mail Maury Dotto@dgabc.com.br; internet www.dgabc.com.br; f. 1958; Pres. MAURY DE CAMPOS DOTTO; circ. 78,500.

### Santos, SP

**A Tribuna:** Rua General Câmara 90/94, 11010-903 Santos, SP; tel. (13) 211-7000; fax (13) 219-6783; f. 1984; Dir ROBERTO M. SANTINI; circ. 40,000.

### São Luís, MA

**O Imparcial:** Rua Afonso Pena 46, 65000 São Luís, MA; tel. (98) 222-5120; fax (98) 222-5120; f. 1926; Dir-Gen. PEDRO BATISTA FREIRE.

### São Paulo, SP

**Diário Comércio e Indústria:** Rua Alvaro de Carvalho 354, 01050-020 São Paulo, SP; tel. (11) 256-5011; fax (11) 258-1989; f. 1933; morning; Pres. HAMILTON LUCAS DE OLIVEIRA; circ. 50,000.

**Diário Popular:** Rua Major Quedinho 28, 1°-6° andares, 01050 São Paulo, SP; tel. (11) 258-2133; fax (11) 256-1627; f. 1884; evening; independent; Dir RICARDO GURAL DE SABEYA; circ. 90,000.

**O Estado de São Paulo:** Av. Eng. Caetano Álvares 55, 02550 São Paulo, SP; tel. (11) 856-2122; fax (11) 266-2206; f. 1875; morning; independent; Dir FRANCISCO MESQUITA NETO; circ. 242,000 weekdays, 460,000 Sundays.

**Fôlha de São Paulo:** Alameda Barão de Limeira 425, Campos Elíseos, 01202-900 São Paulo, SP; tel. (11) 224-3222; fax (11) 223-1644; f. 1921; morning; Editorial Dir OCTAVIO FRIAS, Filho; circ. 557,650 weekdays, 1,401,178 Sundays.

**Gazeta Mercantil:** Rua Major Quedinho 90, 5° andar, 01050 São Paulo, SP; tel. (11) 256-3133; fax (11) 258-5864; f. 1920; business paper; Pres. LUIZ FERREIRA LEVY; circ. 80,000.

**Jornal da Tarde:** Rua Peixoto Gomidi 671, 01409 São Paulo, SP; tel. (11) 284-1944; fax (11) 289-3548; f. 1966; evening; independent; Dir R. MESQUITA; circ. 120,000, 180,000 Mondays.

**Notícias Populares:** Alameda Barão de Limeira 425, 01202 São Paulo, SP; tel. (11) 874-2222; fax (11) 223-1644; f. 1963; Dir RENATO CASTANHARI; circ. 150,000.

### Vitória, ES

**A Gazeta:** Rua Charic Murad 902, 29050 Vitória, ES; tel. (27) 222-8333; fax (27) 223-1525; f. 1928; Pres. MARIO LINDENBERG; circ. 19,000.

## PERIODICALS

### Rio de Janeiro, RJ

**Amiga:** Rua do Russel 766/804, 22214 Rio de Janeiro, RJ; tel. (21) 285-0033; fax (21) 205-9998; weekly; women's interest; Pres. ADOLPHO BLOCH; circ. 83,000.

**Antenna-Eletrônica Popular:** Av. Marechal Floriano 143, CP 1131, 20080-005 Rio de Janeiro, RJ; tel. (21) 223-2442; fax (21) 263-8840; e-mail antenna@unisys.com.br; f. 1926; monthly; telecommunications and electronics, radio, TV, hi-fi, amateur and CB radio; Dir (vacant); circ. 15,000.

**Carinho:** Rua do Russel 766/804, 22214 Rio de Janeiro, RJ; tel. (21) 285-0033; fax (21) 205-9998; monthly; women's interest; Pres. ADOLPHO BLOCH; circ. 65,000.

**Conjuntura Econômica:** Praia de Botafogo 190, Sala 923, 22253-900 Rio de Janeiro, RJ; tel. (21) 536-9267; fax (21) 551-2799; f. 1947; monthly; economics and finance; published by Fundação Getúlio Vargas; Pres. JORGE OSCAR DE MELLO FLÔRES; Editor LAURO VIEIRA DE FARIA; circ. 20,000.

**Desfile:** Rua do Russel 766/804, 22214 Rio de Janeiro, RJ; tel. (21) 285-0033; fax (21) 205-9998; f. 1969; monthly; women's interest; Dir ADOLPHO BLOCH; circ. 120,000.

**Ele Ela:** Rua do Russel 766/804, 22214 Rio de Janeiro RJ; tel. (21) 285-0033; fax (21) 205-9998; f. 1969; monthly; men's interest; Dir ADOLPHO BLOCH; circ. 150,000.

**Manchete:** Rua do Russel 766/804, 20214 Rio de Janeiro, RJ; tel. (21) 285-0033; fax (21) 205-9998; f. 1952; weekly; general; Dir ADOLPHO BLOCH; circ. 110,000.

### São Paulo, SP

**Capricho:** Rua Geraldo Flausino Gomes 61, 6°, 04573-900 São Paulo, SP; tel. (11) 534-5231; monthly; youth interest; Dir ROBERTO CIVITA; circ. 250,000.

**Carícia:** Av. das Nações Unidas 5777, 05479-900 São Paulo, SP; tel. (11) 211-7866; fax (11) 813-9115; monthly; women's interest; Dir ANGELO ROSSI; circ. 210,000.

**Casa e Jardim:** B. Machado 82, 01230-010 São Paulo, SP; fax (11) 824-9079; f. 1953; monthly; homes and gardens, illustrated; Pres. LUCIANA JALONETSKY; circ. 120,000.

**Claudia:** Rua Geraldo Flausino Gomes 61, CP 2371, 04573-900 São Paulo, SP; tel. (11) 534-5130; fax (11) 534-5638; f. 1962; monthly; women's magazine; Dir ROBERTO CIVITA; circ. 460,000.

**Criativa:** Rua do Centúria 655, 05065-001, São Paulo, SP; tel. (11) 874-6003; fax (11) 864-0271; monthly; women's interest; Dir-Gen. RICARDO A. SÁNCHEZ; circ. 121,000.

**Digesto Econômico:** Associação Comercial de São Paulo, Rua Boa Vista 51, 01014-911 São Paulo, SP; tel. (11) 234-3322; fax (11) 239-0067; every 2 months; Pres. ELVIO ALIPRANDI; Chief Editor JOÃO DE SCANTIMBURGO.

**Disney Especial:** Av. das Nações Unidas 7221, 05477-000 São Paulo, SP; tel. (11) 3037-2000; fax (11) 3037-4124; every 2 months; children's magazine; Dir ROBERTO CIVITA; circ. 211,600.

**Elle:** Av. das Nações Unidas 7221, 05425-902 São Paulo; tel. (11) 3037-5197; fax (11) 3037-5451; internet www.uol.com.br/elle/; monthly; women's magazine; Editor CARLOS COSTA; circ. 100,000.

**Exame:** Av. Octaviano Alves de Lima, 4400, 02909-900 São Paulo, SP; tel. (11) 877-1421; fax (11) 877-1437; e-mail publicidade .exame@email.abril.com.br; two a week; business; Dir JOSÉ ROBERTO GUZZO; circ. 168,300.

**Iris, A Revista da Imagem:** Rua Brito Peixoto 322, Brooklin, 04582-020 São Paulo, SP; tel. (11) 531-1299; fax (11) 531-1627; e-mail irisfoto@totalnet.com.br; internet www.totalnet.com.br /irisfoto; f. 1947; monthly; photography and general pictures; Dirs BEATRIZ AZEVEDO MARQUES, HÉLIO M. VALENTONI; circ. 50,000.

**Manequim:** Rua Geraldo Flausino Gomes 61, 04573-900 São Paulo, SP; tel. (11) 534-5668; fax (11) 534-5632; monthly; fashion; Dir ROBERTO CIVITA; circ. 300,000.

**Máquinas e Metais:** Alameda Olga 315, 01155-900, São Paulo, SP; tel. (11) 826-4511; fax (11) 3666-9585; e-mail info@arandanet .com.br; internet www.arandanet.com.br; f. 1964; monthly; machine and metal industries; Editor JOSÉ ROBERTO GONÇALVES; circ. 15,000.

**Marie Claire:** Rua Dr Renato Paes Barros 613, 04530-000; tel. (11) 866-3373; monthly; women's magazine; Publr REGINA LEMUS; circ. 273,000.

**Mickey:** Av. das Nações Unidas 7221, 05477-000 São Paulo, SP; tel. (11) 3037-2000; fax (11) 3037-4124; monthly; children's magazine; Dir ROBERTO CIVITA; circ. 76,000.

**Micromundo-Computerworld do Brasil:** Rua Caçapava 79, 01408 São Paulo, SP; tel. (11) 289-1767; monthly; computers; Gen. Dir ERIC HIPPEAU; circ. 38,000.

**Nova:** Rua Geraldo Flausino Gomes 61, 04573-900 São Paulo, SP; tel. (11) 534-5712; fax (11) 534-5187; f. 1973; monthly; women's interest; Dir ROBERTO CIVITA; circ. 300,000.

**Pato Donald:** Av. das Nações Unidas 7221, 05477-000 São Paulo, SP; tel. (11) 3037-2000; fax (11) 3037-4124; every 2 weeks; children's magazine; Dir ROBERTO CIVITA; circ. 120,000.

**Placar:** Av. das Nações Unidas 7221, 14° andar, 05477-000 São Paulo, SP; tel. (11) 3037-5816; fax (11) 3037-5597; e-mail placar .leitor@email.abril.com.br; f. 1970; monthly; soccer magazine; Dir MARCELO DURATE; circ. 127,000.

**Quatro Rodas:** Rua Geraldo Flausino Gomes 61, Brooklin, 04573-900 São Paulo, SP; tel. (11) 534-5491; fax (11) 530-8549; f. 1960; monthly; motoring; Pres. ROBERTO CIVITA; circ. 250,000.

**Revista O Carreteiro:** Rua Palacete das Aguias 239, 04035-021 São Paulo, SP; tel. (11) 542-9311; monthly; transport; Dirs JOÃO ALBERTO ANTUNES DE FIGUEIREDO, EDSON PEREIRA COELHO; circ. 80,000.

**Saúde:** Av. das Nações Unidas 5777, 05479-900 São Paulo, SP; tel. (11) 211-7675; fax (11) 813-9115; monthly; health; Dir ANGELO ROSSI; circ. 180,000.

**Veja:** Rua do Copturno 571, 6°, São Paulo, SP; tel. (11) 877-1322; fax (11) 877-1640; internet www.veja.com.br; f. 1968; news weekly; Dirs JOSÉ ROBERTO GUZZO, TALES ALVARENGA, MÁRIO SERGIO CONTI; circ. 800,000.

**Visão:** São Paulo, SP; tel. (11) 549-4344. 1952; weekly; news magazine; Editor HENRY MAKSOUD; circ. 148,822.

### NEWS AGENCIES

**Editora Abril, SA:** Av. Otaviano Alves de Lima 4400, CP 2372, 02909-970 São Paulo, SP; tel. (11) 877-1322; fax (11) 877-1640; f. 1950; Pres. ROBERTO CIVITA.

**Agência ANDA:** Edif. Correio Brasiliense, Setor das Indústrias Gráficas 300/350, Brasília, DF; Dir EDILSON VARELA.

**Agência o Estado de São Paulo:** Av. Eng. Caetano Alvares 55, 02588-900 São Paulo, SP; tel. (11) 856-2122; Rep. SAMUEL DIRCEU F. BUENO.

**Agência Fôlha de São Paulo:** Alameda Barão de Limeira 425, 4° andar, 01290-900 São Paulo; tel. (11) 224-3790; fax (11) 221-0675; Dir MARION STRECKER.

**Agência Globo:** Rua Irineu Marinho 35, 2° andar, Centro, 20233-900 Rio de Janeiro, RJ; tel. (21) 292-2000; fax (21) 292-2000; Dir CARLOS LEMOS.

**Agência Jornal do Brasil:** Av. Brasil 500, 6° andar, São Cristóvão, 20949-900 Rio de Janeiro, RJ; tel. (21) 585-4453; fax (21) 580-9944; f. 1966; Exec. Dir. EDGAR LISBOA.

#### Foreign Bureaux

**Agence France-Presse (AFP)** (France): CP 2575-ZC-00, Rua México 21, 7° andar, 20031-144 Rio de Janeiro, RJ; tel. (21) 533-4555; fax (21) 262-7933; e-mail afprio@unisys.com.br; Bureau Chief (Brazil) ALAIN BOEBION.

**Agencia EFE** (Spain): Praia de Botafogo 228, Bloco B, Gr. 1106, 22359-900 Rio de Janeiro, RJ; tel. (21) 553-6355; fax (21) 553-4494; Bureau Chief ZOILO G. MARTÍNEZ DE LA VEGA.

**Agenzia Nazionale Stampa Associata (ANSA)** (Italy): Av. São Luís 258, 23° andar, Of. 1302, São Paulo, SP; tel. (11) 256-5835; Bureau Chief RICCARDO CARUCCI.

**Associated Press (AP)** (USA): Av. Brasil 500, sala 847, CP 72-ZC-00, 20001 Rio de Janeiro, RJ; tel. (21) 580-4422; Bureau Chief BRUCE HANDLER; Rua Major Quedinho Sala 707, CP 3815, 01050 São Paulo, SP; tel. (11) 256-0520; fax (11) 256-4135; Correspondent STAN LEHMAN; a/c Sucursal Folha de São Paulo, CLS 104 Bloco C Loja 41, CP 14-2260, 70343 Brasília, DF; tel. (61) 223-9492; Correspondent JORGE MEDEROS.

**Deutsche Presse-Agentur (dpa)** (Germany): Rua Abade Ramos 65, 22461-90 Rio de Janeiro, RJ; tel. (21) 266-5937; fax (21) 537-8273; Bureau Chief ESTEBAN ENGEL.

**Inter Press Service (IPS)** (Italy): Rua Vicente de Souza 29, 2° andar, 22251-070 Rio de Janeiro; tel. (21) 286-5605; fax (21) 286-5324; Correspondent MARIO CHIZUO OSAVA.

**Jiji Tsushin-Sha (Jiji Press)** (Japan): Av. Paulista 854, 13° andar, Conj. 133, Bela Vista, 01310-913 São Paulo, SP; tel. (11) 285-0025; fax (11) 285-3816; e-mail jijisp@nethall.com.br; f. 1958; Chief Correspondent MUTSUHIRO TAKABAYASHI.

**Kyodo Tsushin** (Japan): Praia do Flamengo 168-701, Flamengo, 22210 Rio de Janeiro, RJ; tel. (21) 285-2412; fax (21) 285-2270; Bureau Chief TAKAYOSHI MAKITA.

**Prensa Latina** (Cuba): Marechal Mascarenhas de Moraís 121, Apto 602, Copacabana, 22030-040 Rio de Janeiro, RJ; tel. and fax (21) 237-1766; Correspondent FRANCISCO FORTEZA.

**Reuters** (United Kingdom): Av. Nações Unidas 17891, 8° andar, 04795-100 São Paulo, SP; tel. (11) 232-4411; fax (11) 604-6538; Rua Sete de Setembro 99, 4° andar, sala 401, 20050-005 Rio de Janeiro, RJ; tel. (21) 507-4151; fax (21) 507-2120; Bureau Chief (News and Television): ADRIAN DICKSON.

**United Press International (UPI)** (USA): Rua Uruguaina 94, 18°, Centro, 20050 Rio de Janeiro, RJ; tel. (21) 224-4194; fax (21) 232-8293; Rua Sete de Abril 230, Bloco A, 816/817, 01044 São Paulo, SP; tel. (11) 258-6869; Edif. Gilberto Salamão, Sala 805/806, 70305 Brasília, DF; tel. (61) 224-6413. Man. ANTÔNIO PRAXEDES; Chief Correspondent H. E. COYA HONORES.

**Xinhua (New China) News Agency** (People's Republic of China): SHIS QI 15, Conj. 16, Casa 14, CP 7089; 71.600 Brasília, DF; tel. (61) 248-5489; Chief Correspondent WANG ZHIGEN.

Central News Agency (Taiwan) and Rossiyskoye Informatsionnoye Agentstvo—Novosti (Russia) are also represented in Brazil.

### PRESS ASSOCIATIONS

**Associação Brasileira de Imprensa:** Rua Araújo Pôrto Alegre 71, Castelo, 20030 Rio de Janeiro, RJ; f. 1908; 4,000 mems; Pres. BARBOSA LIMA SOBRINHO; Sec. JOSUÉ ALMEIDA.

**Associação Nacional de Editores de Revistas:** SCS, Edif. Bandeirantes 201/204, 70300-910 Brasília, DF; tel. (61) 322-5511; fax (61) 321-8348; e-mail redshoes@embratel.net.br; Pres. JOSÉ CARLOS SALLES NETO; Exec. Dir DR MURILLO DE ARAGÃO.

**Federação Nacional dos Jornalistas—FENAJ:** Higs 707, Bloco R, Casa 54, 70351-718 Brasília, DF; tel. (61) 244-0650; fax (61) 242-6616; f. 1946; represents 31 regional unions; Pres. AMÉRICO CÉSAR ANTUNES.

## Publishers

### Rio de Janeiro, RJ

**Ao Livro Técnico Indústria e Comércio Ltda:** Rua Sá Freire 36/40, São Cristovão, 20930-430 Rio de Janeiro, RJ; tel. (21) 580-1168; fax (21) 580-9955; internet www.editoraaolivrotécnico.com.br; f. 1933; textbooks, children's and teenagers' fiction and non-fiction, art books, dictionaries; Man. Dir REYNALDO MAX PAUL BLUHM.

**Bloch Editores, SA:** Rua do Russell 766/804, Glória, 22214 Rio de Janeiro, RJ; tel. (21) 265-2012; fax (21) 205-9998; f. 1966; general; Pres. ADOLPHO BLOCH.

**Distribuidora Record de Serviços de Imprensa, SA:** Rua Argentina 171, São Cristóvão, CP 884, 20921 Rio de Janeiro, RJ; tel. (21) 585-2000; fax (21) 580-4911; e-mail sacm@record.com.br; internet www.record.com.br; f. 1941; general fiction and non-fiction, education, textbooks, fine arts; Pres. SÉRGIO MACHADO.

**Ediouro Publicações, SA:** Rua Nova Jerusalém 345, CP 1880, Bonsucesso, 21042-230 Rio de Janeiro, RJ; tel. (21) 260-6122; fax (21) 280-2438; e-mail editoriallivros@ediouro.com.br; internet www.ediouro.com.br; f. 1939; general.

**Editora Artenova, SA:** Rua Pref. Olímpio de Mello 1774, Benfica, 20000 Rio de Janeiro, RJ; tel. (21) 264-9198; f. 1971; sociology, psychology, occultism, cinema, literature, politics and history; Man. Dir ALVARO PACHECO.

**Editora Brasil-América (EBAL), SA:** Rua Gen. Almério de Moura 302/320, São Cristóvão, 20921-060 Rio de Janeiro, RJ; tel. (21) 580-0303; fax (21) 580-1637; f. 1945; children's books; Dir PAULO ADOLFO AIZEN.

**Editora Campus:** Rua Sete de Setembro 111, 16° andar, 20050-002 Rio de Janeiro; tel. (21) 509-5340; fax (21) 507-1991; e-mail c.rothmuller@campus.com.br; business, computing, non-fiction; Man. Dir CLAUDIO ROTHMULLER.

**Editora Delta, SA:** Av. Almirante Barroso 63, 26° andar, CP 2226, 20031 Rio de Janeiro, RJ; tel. (21) 240-0072; f. 1958; reference books.

**Editora Expressão e Cultura—Exped Ltda:** Estrada dos Bandeirantes 1700, Bl. E, 22710-113, Rio de Janeiro, RJ; tel. (21) 444-0676; fax (21) 444-0700; e-mail exped@ggh.com.br; f. 1967; textbooks, literature, reference; Gen. Man. RICARDO AUGUSTO PAMPLONA VAZ.

**Editora e Gráfica Miguel Couto, SA:** Rua da Passagem 78, Loja A, Botafogo, 22290-030 Rio de Janeiro, RJ; tel. (21) 541-5145; f. 1969; engineering; Dir PAULO KOBLER PINTO LOPES SAMPAIO.

**Editora Nova Fronteira, SA:** Rua Bambina 25, Botafogo, 22251-050 Rio de Janeiro, RJ; tel. (21) 537-8770; fax (21) 286-6755; e-mail novafr2@embratel.net.br; f. 1965; fiction, psychology, history, politics, science fiction, poetry, leisure, reference; Pres. CARLOS AUGUSTO LACERDA.

**Editora Vozes, Ltda:** Rua Frei Luís 100, CP 90023, 25689-900 Petrópolis, RJ; tel. (242) 43-5112; fax (242) 31-4676; e-mail editorial@vozes.com.br; f. 1901; Catholic publishers; management, theology, anthropology, fine arts, history, linguistics, science, fiction, education, data processing, etc.; Dir DR GILBERTO M. S. PISCITELLI.

**Livraria Francisco Alves Editora, SA:** Rua Uruguaiana 94/13°, 20050-002 Rio de Janeiro, RJ; tel. (21) 221-3198; fax (21) 242-3438; f. 1854; textbooks, fiction, non-fiction; Pres. CARLOS LEAL.

**Livraria José Olympio Editora, SA:** Rua da Glória 344, 4° andar, Glória, 20241-180 Rio de Janeiro, RJ; tel. (21) 221-6939; fax (21) 242-0802; f. 1931; juvenile, science, history, philosophy, psychology, sociology, fiction; Dir MANOEL ROBERTO DOMINGUES.

### São Paulo, SP

**Atual Editora, Ltda:** Av. Gen. Valdomiro de Lima 833, Pq. Jabaquara, 04344-070 São Paulo, SP; tel. (11) 5071-2288; fax (11) 5071-3099; e-mail www.atualeditora.com.br; f. 1973; school and children's books, literature; Dirs GELSON IEZZI, OSVALDO DOLCE.

**Cia Editora Nacional:** Rua Joli 294, Brás, CP 5312, 03016 São Paulo, SP; tel. (11) 291-2355; fax (11) 291-8614; f. 1925; textbooks, history, science, social sciences, philosophy, fiction, juvenile; Dirs JORGE YUNES, PAULO C. MARTI.

**Cia Melhoramentos de São Paulo:** Rua Tito 479, 05051-000 São Paulo, SP; tel. (11) 873-2200; fax (11) 872-0556; f. 1890; general non-fiction; e-mail blerner@melhoramentos.com.br; internet www.melhoramentos.com.br; Dir BRENO LERNER.

**Ebid-Editora Páginas Amarelas Ltda:** Av. Liberdade 956, 5° andar, 01502-001 São Paulo, SP; tel. (11) 278-6622; fax (11) 279-8723; e-mail mail@guiaspaginasamarelas.com.br; f. 1947; commercial directories.

**Editora Abril, SA:** Av. Octaviano Alves de Lima 4400, 02909-900 São Paulo, SP; tel. (11) 877-1322; fax (11) 877-1640; f. 1950; Pres. ROBERTO CIVITA.

**Editora Atica, SA:** Rua Barão de Iguape 110, 01507-900 São Paulo, SP; tel. (11) 278-9322; fax (11) 279-2185; e-mail rpimazzoni@atica.com.br; f. 1965; textbooks, Brazilian and African literature; Pres. ANDERSON FERNANDES DIAS.

**Editora Atlas, SA:** Rua Conselheiro Nébias 1384, Campos Elíseos, 01203-904 São Paulo, SP; tel. 221-9144; fax (11) 220-7830; e-mail edatlas@editora-atlas.com.br; f. 1944; business administration, data-processing, economics, accounting, law, education, social sciences; Pres. LUIZ HERRMANN.

**Editora Brasiliense, SA:** Rua Atucuri 318, 03646 São Paulo, SP; tel. (11) 6942-0545; fax (11) 6942-0813; e-mail brasilse@uol.com.br; f. 1943; education, racism, gender studies, human rights, ecology, history, literature, social sciences; Man. YOLANDA C. DA SILVA PRADO.

**Editora do Brasil, SA:** Rua Conselheiro Nébias 887, Campos Elíseos, CP 4986, 01203-001 São Paulo, SP; tel. (11) 222-0211; fax (11) 222-9655; e-mail editora@editoradobrasil.com.be; internet www.editoradobrasil.com.br; f. 1943; education.

**Editora FTD, SA:** Rui Barbosa 156, 01328-010 São Paulo, SP; tel. (11) 253-5011; fax (11) 288-0132; e-mail ftd@dial&ta.com.br; f. 1897; textbooks; Pres. JOÃO TISSI.

**Editora Globo, SA:** Av. Jaguare 1485/1487, 05346-902 São Paolo, SP; tel. (11) 874-6000; fax (11) 836-7098; e-mail dflmkt@edglobo.com.br; f. 1957; fiction, engineering, agriculture, cookery, environmental studies; Gen. Man. RICARDO A. FISCHER.

**Editora Luzeiro Ltda:** Rua Almirante Barroso 730, Brás, 03025-001 São Paulo, SP; tel. (11) 292-3188; f. 1973; folklore and literature.

**Editora Michalany Ltda:** Rua Biobedas 321, Saúde, 04302-010 São Paulo, SP; tel. (11) 585-2012; fax (11) 276-8775; e-mail editora@editoramichalany.com.br; internet www.editoramichalany.com.br; f. 1965; biographies, economics, textbooks, geography, history, religion, maps; Dir DOUGLAS MICHALANY.

**Editora Moderna, Ltda:** Rua Padre Adelino 758, Belenzinho, 03303-904, São Paulo, SP; tel. (11) 6090-1316; fax (11) 6090-1369; e-mail valentim@moderna.com.br; internet www.moderna.com.br.

**Editora Pioneira:** Praça Dirceu de Lima 313, Casa Verde, 02515-050 São Paulo, SP; tel. (11) 858-3199; fax (11) 858-0443; e-mail pioneira@virtual-net.com.br; f. 1960; architecture, computers, political and social sciences, business studies, languages, children's books; Dirs ROBERTO GUAZZELLI, LILIANA GUAZZELLI.

**Editora Revista dos Tribunais Ltda:** Rua Conde do Pinhal 78, CP 8153, 01501 São Paulo, SP; tel. (11) 37-8689; f. 1955; law and jurisprudence, administration, economics and social sciences; Man. Dir NELSON PALMA TRAVASSOS.

**Editora Rideel Ltda:** Alameda Afonso Schmidt 879, Santa Terezinha, 02450-001 São Paulo, SP; tel. (11) 267-8344; fax (11) 290-7415; e-mail rideel@virtual-net.com.br; f. 1971; general; Dir ITALO AMADIO.

**Editora Scipione Ltda:** Praça Carlos Gomes 46, 01501-040 São Paulo, SP; tel. (11) 239-2255; fax (11) 239-1700; e-mail scipione@scipione.com.br; internet www.scipione.com.br; f. 1983; schoolbooks, literature, reference; Dir LUIZ ESTEVES SALLUM.

**Encyclopaedia Britannica do Brasil Publicações Ltda:** Rua Rego Freitas 192, Vila Buarque, CP 299, 01059-970 São Paulo, SP; tel. (11) 250-1900; fax (11) 250-1960; e-mail vicepresidencia@barsa.com.br; f. 1951; reference books.

**Instituto Brasileiro de Edições Pedagógicas, Ltda:** Rua Joli 294, Brás, CP 285, 03016-020 São Paulo, SP; tel. (11) 291-2355; fax (11) 264-5338; e-mail ibep@uol.com.br; f. 1972; textbooks, foreign languages, reference books and chemistry.

**Lex Editora, SA:** Rua Machado de Assis 47/57, Vila Mariana, 04106-900 São Paulo, SP; tel. (11) 549-0122; fax (11) 575-9138; e-mail adm@lexli.com.br; internet www.lexli.com.br; f. 1937; legislation and jurisprudence; Dir MILTON NICOLAU VITALE PATARA.

**Saraiva SA Livreiros Editores:** Av. Marquês de São Vicente 1697, CP 2362, 01139-904 São Paulo, SP; tel. (11) 861-3344; fax (11) 861-3308; f. 1914; education, textbooks, law, economics; Pres. JORGE EDUARDO SARAIVA.

**Belo Horizonte, MG**

**Editora Lê, SA:** Av. D. Pedro II, 4550 Jardin Montanhês, CP 2585, 30730 Belo Horizonte, MG; tel. (31) 462-6262. 1967; textbooks.

**Editora Lemi, SA:** Av. Nossa Senhora de Fátima 1945, CP 1890, 30000 Belo Horizonte, MG; tel. (31) 201-8044; f. 1967; administration, accounting, law, ecology, economics, textbooks, children's books and reference books.

**Editora Vigília, Ltda:** Rua Felipe dos Santos 508, Bairro de Lourdes, CP 1068, 30180-160 Belo Horizonte, MG; e-mail lerg@planetarium.com.br; tel. (31) 337-2744; fax (31) 337-2834; f. 1960; general.

**Curitiba, PR**

**Editora Educacional Brasileira, SA:** Rua XV de Novembro 178, salas 101/04, CP 7498, 80000 Curitiba, PR; tel. (41) 223-5012; f. 1963; biology, textbooks and reference books.

**PUBLISHERS' ASSOCIATIONS**

**Associação Brasileira do Livro:** Av. 13 de Maio 23, 16°, 20031-000 Rio de Janeiro, RJ; tel. (21) 240-9115; fax (21) 532-6678; e-mail abralivro@uol.com.br; Pres. MARCOS DAVID GOMES.

**Câmara Brasileira do Livro:** Av. Ipiranga 1267, 10° andar, 01039-907 São Paulo, SP; tel. (11) 3315-8277; fax (11) 229-7463; e-mail cbl@cbl.org.br; internet www.cbl.org.br; f. 1946; Pres. RAUL WASSERMANN.

**Sindicato Nacional dos Editores de Livros:** Av. Rio Branco 37, 1503/6 and 1510/12, 20090-003 Rio de Janeiro, RJ; tel. (21) 233-6481; fax (21) 253-8502; 200 mems; Pres. SÉRGIO ABREU DA CRUZ MACHADO; Man. NILSON LOPES DA SILVA.

There are also regional publishers' associations.

# Broadcasting and Communications

**TELECOMMUNICATIONS**

**BCP Telecomunicações:** São Paulo; internet www.bcp.com.br; f. 1997; mobile services in São Paulo area; Pres. ROBERTO PEÓN.

**Empresa Brasileira de Telecomunicações, SA (EMBRATEL):** Av. Pres. Vargas 1012, CP 2586, 20179-900 Rio de Janeiro, RJ; tel. (21) 519-8182; e-mail cmsocial@embratel.net.br; internet www.embratel.com.br; f. 1965; operates national and international telecommunications system; controlled by MCI WorldCom of USA; Chair. DANIEL CRAWFORD.

**Empresa Brasileira de Comunicação, SA (Radiobrás):** CP 04-0340, 70710 Brasília, DF; tel. (61) 321-3949; fax (61) 321-7602; internet www.radiobras.gov.br; f. 1988 following merger of Empresa Brasileira de Radiodifusão and Empresa Brasileira de Notícias; Pres. MARCELO AMORIM NETTO.

**Telecomunicações Brasileiras, SA (Telebrás):** SAS Quadra 6, Conjunto Sede, Brasília, DF; tel. (61) 215-2120; fax (61) 322-1213; internet www.telebras.com.br; f. 1972; transferred to the private sector in July 1998; 28 divisions.

**Telecomunicações de Rio de Janeiro (Telerj):** Rio de Janeiro; internet www.telerj.com.br.

**Telecomunicações de São Paulo, SA (Telesp):** Rua Martiniano de Carvalho 851, 01321-001 São Paulo; tel. (11) 285-8011; fax (11) 253-3050; e-mail webmaster@telesp.com.br; internet www.telesp.com.br; services operated by Telefónica, SA, of Spain; Pres. FERNANDO XAVIER FERREIRA; Chief Exec. SAMPAIO DORIA.

**Regulatory Authority**

**Agência Nacional de Telecomunicações (ANATEL):** SAS Quadra 06, Bloco H, 3° andar, 70313-900, Brasília, DF; tel. (61) 312-2336; fax (61) 312-2211; e-mail biblioteca@anatel.gov.br; internet www.anatel.gov.br/default.htm; f. 1998; Pres. RENATO GUERREIRO.

**RADIO**

In April 1992 there were 2,917 radio stations in Brazil, including 20 in Brasília, 38 in Rio de Janeiro, 32 in São Paulo, 24 in Curitiba, 24 in Porto Alegre and 23 in Belo Horizonte.

The main broadcasting stations in Rio de Janeiro are: Rádio Nacional, Rádio Globo, Rádio Eldorado, Rádio Jornal do Brasil, Rádio Tupi and Rádio Mundial. In São Paulo the main stations are Rádio Bandeirantes, Rádio Mulher, Rádio Eldorado, Rádio Gazeta and Rádio Excelsior; and in Brasília: Rádio Nacional, Rádio Alvorada, Rádio Planalto and Rádio Capital.

**TELEVISION**

In April 1992 there were 256 television stations in Brazil, of which 118 were in the state capitals and six in Brasília.

The main television networks are:

**TV Bandeirantes—Canal 13:** Rádio e Televisão Bandeirantes Ltda, Rua Radiantes 13, 05699 São Paulo, SP; tel. (11) 842-3011; fax (11) 842-3067; 65 TV stations and repeaters throughout Brazil; Pres. JOÃO JORGE SAAD.

**RBS TV-TV Gaúcha, SA:** Rua Rádio y TV Gaúcha 189, 90850-080 Porto Alegre, RS; tel. (51) 218-5002; fax (51) 218-5005; Vice-Pres WALMOR BERGESCH.

**TV Globo–Canal 4:** Rua Lopes Quintas 303, Jardim Botânico, 22460-010 Rio de Janeiro, RJ; tel. (21) 511-1711; fax (21) 511-4305; e-mail apm@domain.com.br; internet www.redeglobo.com.br; f. 1965; 8 stations; national network; Dir ADILSON PONTES MALTA.

**TV Manchete-Canal 6:** Rua do Russel 766, 20000 Rio de Janeiro, RJ; tel. (21) 265-2012; Dir-Gen. R. FURTADO.

**TV Record–Rede Record de Televisão–Radio Record, SA:** Rua de Várzea 240, Barra Funda, 01140-080 São Paulo, SP; tel. (11) 824-7000; Pres. JOÃO BATISTA R. SILVA; Exec. Vice-Pres. H. GONÇALVES.

**TVSBT–Canal 4 de São Paulo, SA:** Rua Dona Santa Veloso 535, Vila Guilherme, 02050 São Paulo, SP; tel. (11) 292-9044; fax (11) 264-6004; Vice-Pres. GUILHERME STOLIAR.

### BROADCASTING ASSOCIATIONS

**Associação Brasileira de Emissoras de Rádio e Televisão (ABERT):** Centro Empresarial Varig, SCN Quadra 04, Bloco B, Conjunto 501, Pétala A, 70710-500 Brasília, DF; tel. (61) 327-4600; fax (61) 327-3660; e-mail abert@nutecnet.com.br; f. 1962; mems: 32 shortwave, 1,275 FM, 1,574 medium-wave and 80 tropical-wave radio stations and 258 television stations (1997); Pres. JOAQUIM MENDONÇA; Exec. Dir OSCAR PICONEZ.

There are regional associations for Bahia, Ceará, Goiás, Minas Gerais, Grande do Sul, Santa Catarina, São Paulo, Amazonas, Distrito Federal, Mato Grosso and Mato Grosso do Sul (combined) and Sergipe.

## Finance

(cap. = capital; dep. = deposits; res = reserves; m. = million; brs = branches; amounts in reais, unless otherwise stated)

### BANKING

**Conselho Monetário Nacional:** SBS, Q.03, Bloco B, Edif. Sede do Banco do Brasil, 21° andar, 70074-900 Brasília, DF; tel. (61) 414-1945; fax (61) 414-2528; f. 1964 to formulate monetary policy and to supervise the banking system; Pres. Minister of Finance.

#### Central Bank

**Banco Central do Brasil:** SBS, Q 03, Bloco B, CP 04-0170, 70074-900 Brasília, DF; tel. (61) 414-1000; fax (61) 223-1033; e-mail secre.surel@bcb.gov.br; internet www.bcb.gov.br; f. 1965 to execute the decisions of the Conselho Monetário Nacional; bank of issue; Pres. ARMÍNIO FRAGA NETO; 10 brs.

#### State Commercial Banks

**Banco do Brasil, SA:** Setor Bancário Sul, SBS, Quadra 4, Bloco C, Lote 32, 70089-900 Brasília, DF; tel. (61) 310-3400; fax (61) 310-2563; internet www.bancobrasil.com.br; f. 1808; cap. 6,629.9m., dep. 78,743.8m. (Dec. 1998); Pres. PAOLO ZAGHEN; 2,778 brs.

**Banco do Estado do Paraná, SA:** Rua Máximo João Kopp 274, Santa Cândida, 82630-900 Curitiba, PR; tel. (41) 351-8745; fax (41) 351-7252; e-mail helphb@email.banestado.com.br; internet www.banestado.com.br; f. 1928; cap. 385.5m., res 65.2m., dep. 4,402.9m. (Dec. 1996); Pres. REINHOLD STEPHANES; 389 brs.*

**Banco do Estado do Rio Grande do Sul, SA:** Rua Capitão Montanha 177, CP 505, 90010-040 Porto Alegre, RS; tel. (51) 215-2501; fax (51) 215-1715; e-mail banrisul@banrisul.com.br; internet www.banrisul.com.br; f. 1928; cap. 267.2m., res 150.3m., dep. 2,832.2 (Dec. 1996); Pres. JOÃO ALCIR VERLE; 303 brs.*

**Banco do Estado de Santa Catarina SA:** Rua Padre Miguelinho 80, CEP 88010-550, Florianópolis, Santa Catarina; tel. (48) 224-2100; fax (48) 223-4962; e-mail decam/dinte@besc.com.br; internet www.besc.com.br; f. 1962; cap. 158.1m., res 104.3m., dep. 1,329.6m. (Dec. 1997); Pres. VITOR FONTANA.*

**Banco do Estado de São Paulo, SA (Banespa):** Praça Antônio Prado 6, 01010-010 São Paulo, SP; tel. (11) 259-7722; fax (11) 239-2409; f.1926; cap. 2,409.3m., res 1,733.9m., dep. 12,650.7m. (Dec. 1998); Chair. (vacant); 1,404 brs.*

**Banco do Nordeste do Brasil, SA:** Av. Paranjana 5700, Passaré, 60740-000 Fortaleza, CE; tel. (85) 299-3022; fax (85) 299-3585; e-mail banconordeste.gov.br; internet www.banconordeste.gov.br; f. 1954; cap. 624.0m., res 111.3m., dep. 1,610.4m. (Dec. 1997); Pres. and CEO BYRON COSTA DE QUEIROZ; 186 brs.

* Scheduled for transfer to private sector during 2000.

#### Private Banks

**Banco ABN AMRO SA:** Rua Verbo Divino 1711, 1°–4° andares, 04719-002 São Paulo, SP; tel. (11) 525-6000; fax (11) 525-6387.

**Banco da Amazônia, SA:** Av. Presidente Vargas 800, 66017-000 Belém, PA; tel. (91) 216-3000; fax (91) 223-5403; internet www.bancoamazonia.com.br; f. 1942; cap. 88,211m., res 78,957m., dep. 638,953m. (Dec. 1998); Pres. ANIVALDO JUVENIL VALE; 109 brs.

**Banco América do Sul, SA:** Av. Paulista 1000, 13100-100 São Paulo, SP; tel. (11) 3170-9251; fax (11) 3170-9564; e-mail bas@bas.com.br; internet www.bas.com.br; f. 1940; cap. 214.6m., dep. 2,832.8m. (Dec. 1997); CEO YVES L. J. LE JEUNE; 139 brs.

**Banco Barclays e Galicia, SA:** Av. Paulista 1842, Edif. Cetenco Plaza, Torre Norte 24°–25° andares, 01310-200 São Paulo, SP; tel. (11) 269-2700; fax (11) 283-3168; f. 1967 as Banco de Investimento; cap. 110.3m., res 60.9m., dep. 1,307.8m. (Dec. 1998); Pres. ADEMAR LINS DE ALBUQUERQUE.

**Banco BBA-Creditanstalt, SA:** Av. Paulista 37, 20°, 01311-902 São Paulo, SP; tel. (11) 281-8000; fax (11) 284-2158; e-mail bancobba@bba.com.br; internet www.bba.com.br; f. 1988; cap. 161.6m., res 488.8m., dep. 2,374.5m. (Dec. 1998); Pres. FERNÃO CARLOS BOTELHO BRACHER; 5 brs.

**Banco BMC, SA:** Av. das Nações Unidas 12.995, 24° andar, 04578-000 São Paulo, SP; tel. (11) 5503-7807; fax (11) 5503-7676; e-mail bancobmc@bmc.com.br; internet www.bmc.com.br; f.1939, adopted current name in 1990; cap. 159.8m., res 47.5m., dep. 723.4m. (Dec. 1998); Chair. FRANCISCO JAIME NOGUEIRA PINHEIRO; 9 brs.

**Banco BMG, SA:** Av. Alvares Cabral 1707, Santo Agostinho, 30170-001 Belo Horizonte, MG; tel. (31) 290-3000; fax (31) 290-3315; f. 1988; cap. 89.8m., res 50.9m., dep. 305.0m. (Dec. 1996); Pres. FLÁVIO PENTAGNA GUIMARÃES; 4 brs.

**Banco Bandeirantes, SA:** Rua Boa Vista 162, 01014-902 São Paulo, SP; tel. (11) 233-7155; fax (11) 233-7329; e-mail band@bandeirantes.com.br; f. 1944; cap. 196.4m., res 19.5m., dep. 3,071.0m. (Dec. 1997); assumed control of Banorte in Dec. 1995; Pres. Dr CARLOS TRAGUELHO; 167 brs.

**Banco Bilbao Vizcaya Brasil, SA:** Av. Antônio Carlos Magalhães 2728, 41840-000 Salvador, BA; tel. (71) 354-7000; fax (71) 354-7106; internet www.exceleconomico.com.br; f. 1996 as a result of merger of Excel Banco and Banco Econômico; name changed in 1998; cap. 535.9m., res 5.6m., dep. 8,933.4m. (Dec. 1997); Pres. EZEQUIEL NASSER; 232 brs.

**Banco Boavista Interatlântico, SA:** Praça Pio X 118, 20091-040 Rio de Janeiro, RJ; tel. (21) 849-1661; fax (21) 253-1579; e-mail boavista@ibm.net; internet www.boavista.com.br; f. 1997; cap. 542.9m., res –123.3m., dep. 3,237.6m. (Dec. 1998); Pres. and Gen. Man. JOSÉ LUIZ SILVEIRA MIRANDA.

**Banco Bozano, Simonsen, SA:** Av. Rio Branco 138-Centro, 20057-900 Rio de Janeiro, RJ; tel. (21) 508-4711; fax (21) 508-4479; e-mail info@bozano.com.br; f. 1967; cap. 248.2m., res 89.9m., dep. 355.5m. (June 1997); Pres. PAULO VEIGA FERRAZ PEREIRA; 4 brs.

**Banco Bradesco, SA:** Av. Ipiranga 282, 10° andar, 01046-920 São Paulo, SP; tel. (11) 235-9566; fax (11) 235-9161; internet www.bradesco.com.br; f. 1943; fmrly Banco Brasileiro de Descontos; cap. 3,464.3m., res 2,856.7m., dep. 39,296.4m. (June 1998); Chair. MARCIO CYPRIANO; Vice-Chair. DURVAL SILVÉRIO; 2,106 brs.

**Banco CCF Brasil SA:** Av. Brigadeiro Faria Lima 3064, 1°–4° andares, Itaim Bibi, 01451-000 São Paulo, SP; tel. (11) 827-5000; fax (11) 827-5299; internet www.ccfbrasil.com.br; f. 1980; cap. 409.0m., res 77.1m., dep. 418.1m. (Dec. 1998); Pres. BERNARD MENCIER.

**Banco Chase Manhattan, SA:** Rua Verbo Divino, 04719-002 São Paulo, SP; tel. (11) 546-4433; fax (11) 546-4624; f. 1925; fmrly Banco Lar Brasileiro, SA; Chair. PETER ANDERSON.

**Banco Cidade, SA:** Praça Dom José Gaspar 106, 01047-010 São Paulo, SP; tel. (11) 3150-5000; fax (11) 255-4176; f. 1965; cap. 75.0m., res 122.6m., dep. 1,259.3m. (Dec. 1997); Pres. EDMUNDO SAFDIÉ; 25 brs.

**Banco Credibanco, SA:** Av Paulista 1294, 21° andar, 01310-915 São Paulo, SP; tel. (11) 3150-5000; fax (11) 285-3431; e-mail crediban@credibanco.com.br; internet www.credibanco.com.br; f. 1967; cap. 120.0m., res 63.6m., dep. 458.1m. (Dec. 1997); CEO PETER ANDERSON; 2 brs.

**Banco de Crédito Nacional, SA (BCN):** Av. das Nações Unidas 12901, CENU-Torre Oeste, 04578-000 Vila Cordeiro, SP; tel. (11) 5509-2801; fax (11) 5509-2802; internet www.bcn.com.br; f. 1924; acquired by Banco Bradesco in 1997; cap. 579.7m., res 170.1m., dep. 7,834.7m. (Dec. 1998); Pres. JOSÉ LUIZ ACAR PEDRO; 122 brs.

**Banco Dibens, SA:** Alameda Santos 200, Cerqueira Cesar, 01418-000 São Paulo, SP; tel. (11) 253-2177; fax (11) 284-3132; f. 1989; cap. 81.7m., res 84.0m., dep. 760.9m. (Dec. 1996); Pres. MAURO SADDI; 23 brs.

**Banco do Estado de Minas Gerais, SA:** Rua Rio de Janeiro 471, Centro Belo Horizonte, 30160-910 Belo Horizonte, MG; tel. (31) 239-1211; fax (31) 239-1859; f. 1967; acquired by Banco de Crédito Nacional in 1997; cap. 240.8m., res –157.6m., dep. 2,450.3m. (Dec. 1997); Pres. JOSÉ AFONSO B. BELTRÃO DA SILVA; 755 brs.

**Banco Fibra:** Av. Brigadeiro Faria Lima 3064, 7° andar, Itaim Bibi, 01451-000, São Paulo, SP; tel. (11) 827-6700; fax (11) 827-6620; e-mail internacional@bancofibra.com.br; f. 1988; cap. 106.1m., res 111.4m., dep. 1,334.0m. (Dec. 1998); Pres. BENJAMIN STEINBRUCH; CEO JOÃO AYRES RABELLO, Filho.

**Banco Francês e Brasileiro, SA:** Av. Paulista 1294, 01310-915 São Paulo, SP; tel. (11) 238-8216; fax (11) 238-8622; e-mail bfb.international@itau.com.br; internet www.bfb.com.br; f. 1948; affiliated with Crédit Lyonnais; cap. 472.3m., res 29.5m., dep. 1,152.0m. (Dec. 1997); Pres. ROBERTO EGYDIO SETÚBAL; 32 brs.

**Banco Industrial e Comercial, SA:** Rua Boa Vista 192, 01014-030 São Paulo, SP; tel. (11) 237-6800; fax (11) 607-3204; e-mail bicdinte@uol.com.br; internet www.bicbanco.com.br; f. 1938; cap. 172.8m., res 55.2m., dep. 2,759.9m. (Dec. 1998); Pres. JOSÉ BEZERRA DE MENEZES; 38 brs.

**Banco Itaú, SA:** Rua Boa Vista 176, CP 30341, 01014-919 São Paulo, SP; tel. (11) 237-3000; fax (11) 277-1044; e-mail info@itau.com.br; internet www.itau.com.br; f. 1944; cap. 2,000.0m., res 2,651.3m., dep. 23,730.5m. (Dec. 1998); Chair. OLAVO EGYDIO SETÚBAL; Pres. and CEO ROBERTO EGYDIO SETÚBAL; 1,007 brs.

**Banco Mercantil Finasa SA São Paulo:** CP 4077, Av. Paulista 1450, 01310-917 São Paulo; tel. (11) 252-2121; fax (11) 284-3312; e-mail finasa@finasa.com.br; internet www.finasa.com.br; f. 1938; cap. 735.0m., res 305.5m., dep. 3,906.3m. (Dec. 1998); Pres. Dr GASTÃO EDUARDO DE BUENO VIDIGAL.

**Banco Meridional, SA:** Rua 7 de Setembro 1028, 3° andar, 90010-230 Porto Alegre, RS; tel. (51) 271-9666; fax (51) 271-9634; internet www.meridional.com.br; f. 1985, formerly Banco Sulbrasileiro, SA; taken over by the Government in Aug. 1985; acquired by Banco Bozano, Simonsen in 1997; cap. 1,200.5m., res –121.1m., dep. 5,782.5m. (Dec. 1998); Pres. JOSÉ CARLOS MIGUEL; 222 brs.

**Banco Santander Noroeste, SA:** Rua Amador Bueno 474, 3° andar, 04752-000 São Paulo, SP; tel. (11) 538-6892; fax (11) 538-6680; f. 1923; cap. 302.2m., dep. 3,366.6m. (Dec. 1998); Pres. ANTÔNIO MOTA DE SOUZA HORTA OSIORIO; 169 brs.

**Banco Pactual:** Av. República do Chile 230, 28°–29° andares, 20031-170 Rio de Janeiro, RJ; tel. (21) 272-1100; fax (21) 533-1661; internet www.pactual.com.br; f. 1983; cap. 175.9m., res 92.5m., dep. 1,767.0m. (Dec. 1998); Pres. LUÍS CEZAR FERNANDES.

**Banco Real, SA:** Av. Paulista 1374, 3° andar, CP 5766, 01310-916 São Paulo, SP; tel. (11) 3174-9507; fax (11) 3174-9557; e-mail direct@real.com.br; internet www.bancoreal.com.br; f. 1925; cap. 574.4m., res 1,190.6m., dep. 11,877.8m. (Dec. 1997); Pres. and CEO FABIO C. BARBOSA; 592 brs.

**Banco Safra, SA:** Av. Paulista 2100, 16° andar, 01310-930 São Paulo, SP; tel. (11) 3175-7575; fax (11) 3175-8605; f. 1940; cap. 277.1m., res 654.1m., dep. 8,180.8m. (Dec. 1998); Pres. CARLOS ALBERTO VIEIRA; 65 brs.

**Banco Sogeral, SA:** Rua Verbo Divino 1207, 3° e 4° andares, CP 8785, 04719-002 São Paulo, SP; tel. (11) 5180-5052; fax (11) 5180-5258; f. 1981; cap. 83.0m., res 18.7m., dep. 457.2m. (Dec. 1998); Pres. BERNARD SONNTAC; 6 brs.

**Banco Sudameris Brasil, SA:** Av. Paulista 1000, 2°, 10°–16° andares, 01310-100 São Paulo, SP; tel. (11) 3170-9899; fax (11) 289-1239; internet www.sudameris.com.br; f. 1910; cap. 742.6m., res 93.6m., dep. 4,803.3m. (Dec. 1998); Exec. Dirs GIOVANNI URIZIO, SEBASTIÃO G. T. CUNHA; 153 brs.

**BankBoston SA:** Rua Líbero Badaró 487-3°, 01009-000 São Paulo, SP; tel. (11) 3118-5622; fax (11) 3118-4438; internet www.bankboston.com.br; Pres. GERALDO JOSÉ CARBONE; 31 brs.

**HSBC Bank Brasil, SA, Banco Multiplo:** Travessa Oliveira Belo 34, Centro, 80020-030 Curitiba, PR; tel. (41) 321-6161; fax (41) 321-6081; internet www.hsbc.com.br; f. 1997; cap. 652.8m., res 684.3m., dep. 9,381.0m. (Dec. 1995); Pres. M. F. GEOGHEGAN; 1,214 brs.

**UNIBANCO—União de Bancos Brasileiros, SA:** Av. Eusébio Matoso 891, 22° andar, CP 8185, 05423-901 São Paulo, SP; tel. (11) 867-4461; fax (11) 814-0528; internet www.unibanco.com.br; f. 1924; cap. 1,574.1m., res 1,332.3m., dep. 10,331.1m. (Dec. 1998); Chair. PEDRO MOREIRA SALLES; 644 brs.

### Development Banks

**Banco de Desenvolvimento de Minas Gerais, SA—BDMG:** Rua da Bahia 1600, CP 1026, 30160-011 Belo Horizonte, MG; tel. (31) 226-3292; fax (31) 273-5084; f. 1962; long-term credit operations; cap. 250.5m., res –124.6m., dep. 3.3m. (Dec. 1997); Pres. MARCOS RAYMUNDO PESSÔA DUARTE.

**Banco de Desenvolvimento do Espírito Santo, SA:** Av. Princesa Isabel 54, Edif. Caparão, 12° andar, CP 1168, 29010-906 Vitoria, ES; tel. (27) 223-8333; fax (27) 223-6307; total assets US $12.5m. (Dec. 1993); Pres. SÉRGIO MANOEL NADER BORGES.

**Banco Nacional de Crédito Cooperativo, SA:** Brasília, DF; tel. (61) 224-5575; established in association with the Ministry of Agriculture and guaranteed by the Federal Government to provide co-operative credit; cap. 4.7m. (cruzeiros, July 1990); Pres. ESUPÉRIO S. DE CAMPOS AGUILAR (acting); 41 brs.

**Banco Nacional do Desenvolvimento Econômico e Social (BNDES):** Av. República do Chile 100, 20139-900 Rio de Janeiro, RJ; tel. (21) 277-7447; fax (21) 533-1665; internet www.bndes.gov.br; f. 1952 to act as main instrument for financing of development schemes sponsored by the Government and to support programmes for the development of the national economy; charged with supervision of privatization programme of the 1990s; Pres. ANDREA SANDRO CALABI; 2 brs.

**Banco Regional de Desenvolvimento do Extremo Sul (BRDE):** Rua Uruguai 155, 3°–4° andares, CP 139, 90010-140 Porto Alegre, RS; tel. (51) 121-9200. 1961; cap. 15m. (Dec. 1993); development bank for the states of Paraná, Rio Grande do Sul and Santa Catarina; finances small- and medium-sized enterprises; Dir-Pres. NELSON WEDEKIN; 3 brs.

### Investment Bank

**Banco de Investimentos Garantia, SA:** Av. Brigadeiro Faria Lima 3064, 13° andar, Itaim Bibi, 01451-020 São Paulo, SP; tel. (11) 821-6000; fax (11) 821-6900; f. 1969; cap. 956.6m., res 107.2m., dep. 1,794.7m. (Dec. 1996); Dir CLAUDIO LUIZ DA SILVA HADDED; 3 brs.

### State-owned Savings Bank

**Caixa Econômica Federal:** SBS, Q 04, Lote 3/4, Edif. Sede de Caixa Econômica, 70070-000 Brasília, DF; tel. (61) 321-9209; fax (61) 225-0215; f. 1860; cap. 60,247,000m. (cruzeiros, May 1993); dep. 796,113,000m. (April 1993); Pres. EMÍLIO CARRAZAI; 1,752 brs.

### Foreign Banks

**Banco de la Nación Argentina:** Av. Paulista 2319, Sobreloja, 01310 São Paulo, SP; tel. (11) 883-1555; fax (11) 881-4630; e-mail bnaspbb@dialdata.com.br; f. 1891; Dir-Gen. GERARDO LUIS PONCE; 2 brs.

**Banco Unión** (Venezuela): Av. Paulista 1708, 01310 São Paulo, SP; tel. (11) 283-3722; fax (11) 283-2434; f. 1892; Dir-Gen. DONALDISON MARQUES DA SILVA.

**The Chase Manhattan Bank** (USA): Rua Verbo Divino 1400, São Paulo, SP; tel. (11) 546-4433; fax (11) 546-44624.

**Dresdner Bank Lateinamerika AG** (Germany): Rua Verbo Divino 1488, Centro Empresarial Transatlântico, CP 3641, 01064-970 São Paulo, SP; fmrly Deutsch-Sudamerikanische Bank; tel. (11) 5188-6700; fax (11) 5188-6900; f. 1969; Chair. WINSTON FRITSCH; 3 brs.

**Lloyds TSB Bank PLC** (United Kingdom): Av. Jurubatuba 73, 4°–10° andares, 04583-900 São Paulo, SP; tel. (11) 534-6983; fax (11) 534-6373; e-mail lloyds.dmkt@lloyds.com.br; Gen. Man. DAVID V. THOMAS; 11 brs.

### Banking Associations

**Federação Brasileira das Associações de Bancos:** Rua Líbero Badaró 425, 17° andar, 01069-900 São Paulo, SP; tel. (11) 239-3000; fax (11) 607-8486; f. 1966; Pres. MAURÍCIO SCHULMAN; Vice-Pres ROBERTO EGYDIO SETÚBAL, JOSÉ AFONSO SANCHO.

**Sindicato dos Bancos dos Estados do Rio de Janeiro e Espírito Santo:** Av. Rio Branco 81, 19° andar, Rio de Janeiro, RJ; Pres. THEÓPHILO DE AZEREDO SANTOS; Vice-Pres. Dr NELSON MUFARREJ.

**Sindicato dos Bancos dos Estados de São Paulo, Paraná, Mato Grosso e Mato Grosso do Sul:** Rua Líbero Badaró 293, 13° andar, 01905 São Paulo, SP; f. 1924; Pres. PAULO DE QUEIROZ.

There are other banking associations in Maceió, Salvador, Fortaleza, Belo Horizonte, João Pessoa, Recife and Porto Alegre.

## STOCK EXCHANGES

**Comissão de Valores Mobiliários CVM:** Rua Sete de Setembro 111, 32° andar, 20159-900 Rio de Janeiro, RJ; tel. (21) 212-0200; fax (21) 212-0524; e-mail pte@cvm.gov.br; f. 1977 to supervise the operations of the stock exchanges and develop the Brazilian securities market; Chair. FRANCISCO AUGUSTO DA COSTA E SILVA.

**Bolsa de Valores do Rio de Janeiro:** Praça XV de Novembro 20, 20010-010 Rio de Janeiro, RJ; tel. (21) 271-1001; fax (21) 221-2151; f. 1845; 585 companies listed in 1997; Chair. FERNANDO OPITZ.*

**Bolsa de Valores de São Paulo (BOVESPA):** Rua XV de Novembro 275, 01013-001 São Paulo, SP; tel. (11) 233-2000; fax (11) 233-2099; e-mail bovespa@bovespa.com.br; f. 1890; 550 companies listed in 1997; CEO GILBERTO MIFANO.*

* To merge in early 2000.

There are commodity exchanges at Porto Alegre, Vitória, Recife, Santos and São Paulo.

## INSURANCE

### Supervisory Authorities

**Superintendência de Seguros Privados (SUSEP):** Rua Buenos Aires 256, 4° andar, 20061-000 Rio de Janeiro, RJ; tel. (21) 297-4415; fax (21) 221-6664; f. 1966; within Ministry of the Economy; Superintendent HELIO PORTOCARRERO.

**Conselho Nacional de Seguros Privados (CNSP):** Rua Buenos Aires 256, 20061-000 Rio de Janeiro, RJ; tel. (21) 297-4415; fax (21) 221-6664; f. 1966; Sec. THERESA CHRISTINA CUNHA MARTINS.

**Federação Nacional dos Corretores de Seguros e de Capitalização (FENACOR):** Av. Rio Branco 147, 6° andar, 20040-006 Rio de Janeiro, RJ; tel. (21) 507-0033; fax (21) 507-0041; e-mail fenacor@IBM.net; Pres. LEÔNCIO DE ARRUDA.

**Federação Nacional das Empresas de Seguros Privados e de Capitalização (FENASEG):** Rua Senador Dantas 74, 20031-200 Rio de Janeiro, RJ; tel. (21) 524-1204; fax (21) 220-0046; e-mail fenaseg@fenaseg.org.br; Pres. JOÃO ELISIO FERRAZ DE CAMPOS.

**IRB—Brasil Resseguros:** Av. Marechal Câmara 171, 20023-900 Rio de Janeiro, RJ; tel. (21) 272-0200; fax (21) 240-6261; e-mail info@irb-brasilre.com.br; f. 1939; fmrly Instituto de Resseguros do Brasil; reinsurance; Pres. DEMÓSTHENES MADUREIRA DE PINHO, Filho.

### Principal Companies

The following is a list of the principal national insurance companies, selected on the basis of assets.

**AGF Brasil Seguros, SA:** Rua Luís Coelho 26, 01309-000 São Paulo; tel. (11) 281-5572; fax (11) 283-1401; internet www.agf.com.br; Dir EUGÊNIO DE OLIVEIRA MELLO.

**Cia de Seguros Aliança da Bahia:** Rua Pinto Martins 11, 2° andar, 40015-020 Salvador, BA; tel. (71) 242-1055; fax (71) 242-8998; f. 1870; general; Pres. PAULO SÉRGIO FREIRE DE CARVALHO GONÇALVES TOURINHO.

**Cia de Seguros Aliança do Brasil:** Rua Senador Dantas 105, 32° andar, 20031-201 Rio de Janeiro; tel. (21) 533-1080; fax (21) 220-2105; Pres. KHALID MOHAMMED RAOUF.

**Allianz-Bradesco Seguros, SA:** Rua Barão de Itapagipe 225, 20269-900 Rio de Janeiro; tel. (21) 563-1101; fax (21) 293-9489.

**BCN Seguradora, SA:** Alameda Santos 1940, 9° andar, 01418-100 São Paulo; tel. (11) 283-2244; fax (11) 284-3415; internet www.bcn.com.br/seguro.htm; f. 1946; Pres. ANTÔNIO GRISI, Filho.

**Bradesco Previdência e Seguros, SA:** Av. Deputado Emílio Carlos 970, 06028-000 São Paulo; tel. (11) 704-4466; fax (11) 703-3063; internet www.bradesco.com.br/prodserv/bradprev.html; f. 1989; Pres. ANTÔNIO LOPES CRISTOVÃO.

**Bradesco Seguros, SA:** Rua Barão de Itapagipe 225, 20269-900 Rio de Janeiro, RJ; tel. (21) 563-1199; fax (21) 503-1466; internet www.bradesco.com.br/prodserv/bradseg.html; f. 1935; general; Pres. EDUARDO VIANNA.

**CGU Cia de Seguros:** Av. Almirante Barroso 52, 23°–24° andares, 20031-000 Rio de Janeiro; tel. (21) 292-1125; fax (21) 262-0291; internet www.york.com.br/york0700.html; Pres. ROBERT CHARLES WHEELER.

**Finasa Seguradora, SA:** Alameda Santos 1827, 6° andar, CJS 61, 01419-002 São Paulo; tel. (11) 253-8181; fax (11) 285-1994; internet www.finasa.com.br/ficoli02.html; f. 1939; Pres. MARCELLO DE CAMARGO VIDIGAL.

**Golden Cross Seguradora, SA:** Rua Maestro Cardim 1164, 013200-301; Rio de Janeiro, RJ; tel. (21) 283-4922; fax (21) 289-4624; e-mail comunica@goldencross.com.br; internet www.golden.com.br; f. 1971; Pres. ALBERT BULLUS.

**HSBC Seguros (Brasil), SA:** Travessa Oliveira Belo 11-B, 2° andar, 80020-030 Curitiba, PR; tel. (41) 321-6162; fax (41) 321-8800; f. 1938; all classes; Pres. SIMON LLOYD BRETT.

**Itaú Seguros, SA:** Praça Alfredo Egydio de Souza Aranha 100, Bloco A, 04344-920 São Paulo, SP; tel. (11) 5582-3322; fax (11) 5582-3514; e-mail itauseguros@itauseguros.com.br; internet www.itauseguros.com.br; f. 1921; all classes; Pres. LUIZ DE CAMPOS SALLES.

**Cia de Seguros Minas-Brasil:** Rua dos Caetés 745, 5° andar, 30120-080 Belo Horizonte, MG; tel. (31) 219-3882; fax (31) 219-3820; f. 1938; life and risk; Pres. JOSÉ CARNEIRO DE ARAÚJO.

**Cia Paulista de Seguros:** Rua Dr Geraldo Campos Moreira 110, 04571-020 São Paulo, SP; tel. (11) 5505-2010; fax (11) 5505-2122; internet www.pauliseg.com.br; f. 1906; general; Pres. PHILLIP NORTON MOORE.

**Porto Seguro Cia de Seguros Gerais:** Rua Guaianazes 1238, 01204-001 São Paulo, SP; tel. (11) 224-6129; fax (11) 222-6213; internet www.porto-seguro.com.br; f. 1945; life and risk; Pres. ROSA GARFINKEL.

**Sasse, Cia Nacional de Seguros Gerais:** SCN Qd. 01, Bl. A, 15°–17° andares, 70710-500 Brasília, DF; tel. (61) 329-2400; fax (61) 321-0600; internet www.sasse.com.br; f. 1967; general; Pres. PEDRO PEREIRA DE FREITAS.

**Sul América Aetna Seguros e Previdência, SA:** Rua Anchieta 35, 9° andar, 01016-030 São Paulo; tel. (11) 232-6131; fax (11) 606-8141; internet www.sulaamerica.com.br; f. 1996; Pres. RONY CASTRO DE OLIVEIRA LYRIO.

**Sul América, Cia Nacional de Seguros:** Rua da Quitanda 86, 20091-000 Rio de Janeiro, RJ; tel. (21) 276-8585; fax (21) 276-8317; f. 1895; life and risk; Pres. RONY CASTRO DE OLIVEIRA LYRIO.

**Sul América Santa Cruz Seguros, SA:** Tv. Franc. Leonardo Truda 98, 6° andar, 90010-050 Porto Alegre; tel. (51) 211-5455; fax (51) 225-5894; f. 1943; Pres. RONY CASTRO DE OLIVEIRA LYRIO.

**Unibanco Seguros, SA:** Av. Eusebio Matoso 1375, 13° andar, 05423-180 São Paulo, SP; tel. (11) 819-8000; fax (11) 3039-4005; internet www.unibancoseguros.com.br; f. 1946; life and risk; Pres. JOSÉ CASTRO ARAÚJO RUDGE.

**Vera Cruz Seguradora, SA:** Av. Maria Coelho Aguiar 215, Bloco D, 3° andar, 05804-906 São Paulo, SP; tel. (11) 3741-3815; fax (11) 3741-3827; internet www.veracruz.com.br; f. 1955; general; Pres. ALFREDO FERNANDEZ DE L. ORTIZ DE ZARATE.

## Trade and Industry

### GOVERNMENT AGENCIES

**Agência Nacional de Petróleo (ANP):** Brasília, DF; internet www.anp.gov.br; f. 1998; regulatory body of the petroleum industry; Chair. DAVID ZYLBERSTAJN.

**Comissão de Fusão e Incorporação de Empresa (COFIE):** Ministério da Fazenda, Edif. Sede, Ala B, 1° andar, Esplanada dos Ministérios, Brasília, DF; tel. (61) 225-3405; mergers commission; Pres. SEBASTIÃO MARCOS VITAL; Exec. Sec. EDGAR BEZERRA LEITE, Filho.

**Conselho de Desenvolvimento Comercial (CDC):** Bloco R, Esplanada dos Ministérios, 70044 Brasília, DF; tel. (61) 223-0308; commercial development council; Exec. Sec. Dr RUY COUTINHO DO NASCIMENTO.

**Conselho de Desenvolvimento Econômico (CDE):** Bloco K, 7° andar, Esplanada dos Ministérios, 70063 Brasília, DF; tel. (61) 215-4100; f. 1974; economic development council; Gen. Sec. JOÃO BATISTA DE ABREU.

**Conselho de Desenvolvimento Social (CDS):** Bloco K, 3° andar, 382, Esplanada dos Ministérios, 70063 Brasília, DF; tel. (61) 215-4477; social development council; Exec. Sec. JOÃO A. TELES.

**Conselho Nacional do Comércio Exterior (CONCEX):** Fazenda, 5° andar, Gabinete do Ministro, Bloco 6, Esplanada dos Ministérios, 70048 Brasília, DF; tel. (61) 223-4856; f. 1966; responsible for foreign exchange and trade policies and for the control of export activities; Exec. Sec. NAMIR SALEK.

**Conselho Nacional de Desenvolvimento Científico e Tecnológico (CNPq):** Brasília, DF; tel. (61) 348-9401; fax (61) 273-2955; f. 1951; scientific and technological development council; Pres. JOSÉ GALIZIA TUNDISI.

**Conselho Nacional de Desenvolvimento Pecuário (CONDEPE):** to promote livestock development.

**Conselho de Não-Ferrosos e de Siderurgia (CONSIDER):** Ministério da Indústria e Comércio, Esplanada dos Ministérios, Bloco 7, 7° andar, 70056-900 Brasília, DF; tel. (61) 224-6039; f. 1973; exercises a supervisory role over development policy in the non-ferrous and iron and steel industries; Exec. Sec. WILLIAM ROCHA CANTAL.

**Fundação Instituto Brasileiro de Geografia e Estatística (IBGE):** Centro de Documentação e Disseminação de Informações (CDDI), Rua Gen. Canabarro 706, 2° andar, Maracanã, 20271-201 Rio de Janeiro, RJ; tel. (21) 569-5997; fax (21) 569-1103; e-mail webmaster@ibge.gov.br; internet www.ibge.gov.br; f. 1936; produces and analyses statistical, geographical, cartographic, geodetic, demographic and socio-economic information; Pres. (IBGE) SÉRGIO BESSERMAN VIANNA; Superintendent (CDDI) DAVID WU TAI.

**Instituto Nacional de Metrologia, Normalização e Qualidade Industrial (INMETRO):** Rua Santa Alexandrina 416, Rio Comprido, 20261-232 Rio de Janeiro, RJ; tel. (21) 273-9002; fax (21) 293-0954; e-mail pusi@inmetro.gov.br; in 1981 INMETRO absorbed the Instituto Nacional de Pesos e Medidas (INPM), the weights and measures institute; Pres. Dr JÚLIO CESAR CARMO BUENO.

**Instituto de Planejamento Econômico e Social (IPEA):** SBS, Edif. BNDE, 6° andar, 70076 Brasília, DF; tel. (61) 225-4350; planning institute; Pres. RICARDO SANTIAGO.

**Secretaria Especial de Desenvolvimento Industrial:** Brasília, DF; tel. (61) 225-7556; fax (61) 224-5629; f. 1969; industrial development council; offers fiscal incentives for selected industries and for producers of manufactured goods under the Special Export Programme; Exec. Sec. Dr ERNESTO CARRARA.

### REGIONAL DEVELOPMENT ORGANIZATIONS

**Companhia de Desenvolvimento do Vale do São Francisco (CODEVASF):** SGAN, Q 601, Lote 1, Edif. Sede, 70830 Brasília, DF; tel. (61) 223-2797; fax (61) 226-2468; e-mail divulgacao@codevasf.gov.br; internet www.codevasf.gov.br/indice.html; f. 1974; promotes integrated development of resources of São Francisco Valley.

**Superintendência do Desenvolvimento da Amazônia (SUDAM):** Av. Almirante Barroso 426, Bairro do Marco, 66000

Belém, PA; tel. (91) 226-0044; f. 1966 to develop the Amazon regions of Brazil; supervises industrial, cattle breeding and basic services projects; Superintendent Eng. HENRY CHECRALLA KAYATH.

**Superintendência do Desenvolvimento do Nordeste (SUDENE):** Edif. SUDENE s/n, Praça Ministro João Gonçalves de Souza, Cidade Universitária, 50670-900 Recife, PE; tel. (81) 416-2880; fax (81) 453-1277; f. 1959; attached to the Ministry of Planning, Budget and Co-ordination; assists development of north-east Brazil; Superintendent NILTON MOREIRA RODRIGUES.

**Superintendência do Desenvolvimento da Região Centro Oeste (SUDECO):** SAS, Quadra 1, Bloco A, Lotes 9/10, 70070 Brasília, DF; tel. (61) 225-6111; f. 1967 to co-ordinate development projects in the states of Goiás, Mato Grosso, Mato Grosso do Sul, Rondônia and Distrito Federal; Superintendent RAMEZ TEBET.

**Superintendência da Zona Franca de Manaus (SUFRAMA):** Rua Ministro João Gonçalves de Souza s/n, Distrito Industrial, 69075-770 Manaus, AM; tel. (92) 237-1691; fax (92) 237-6549; e-mail 15dinf@internet.com.br; to assist in the development of the Manaus Free Zone; Superintendent MAURO RICARDO MACHADO COSTA.

## AGRICULTURAL, INDUSTRIAL AND TRADE ORGANIZATIONS

**ABRASSUCOS:** São Paulo, SP; association of orange juice industry; Pres. MÁRIO BRANCO PERES.

**Associação do Comércio Exterior do Brasil (AEB):** Av. General Justo 335, 4° andar, Rio de Janeiro, RJ; tel. (21) 240-5048; fax (21) 240-5463; e-mail aebbras@embratel.net.br; internet www.probrazil.com/aeb.html; exporters' association.

**Companhia de Pesquisa de Recursos Minerais (CPRM):** Esplanada dos Ministérios, Bloco U, 7° andar, 70055-900 Brasília, DF; mining research, attached to the Ministry of Mining and Energy; Pres. CARLOS BERBERT.

**Confederação das Associações Comerciais do Brasil:** Brasília, DF; confederation of chambers of commerce in each state; Pres. AMAURY TENPORAL.

**Confederação Nacional da Agricultura (CNA):** Brasília, DF; tel. (61) 225-3150; national agricultural confederation; Pres. ALYSSON PAULINELLI.

**Confederação Nacional do Comércio (CNC):** SCS, Edif. Presidente Dutra, 4° andar, Quadra 11, 70327 Brasília, DF; tel. (61) 223-0578; national confederation comprising 35 affiliated federations of commerce; Pres. ANTÔNIO JOSÉ DOMINGUES DE OLIVEIRA SANTOS.

**Confederação Nacional da Indústria (CNI):** Av. Nilo Peçanha 50, 34° andar, 20044 Rio de Janeiro, RJ; tel. (21) 292-7766; fax (21) 262-1495; f. 1938; national confederation of industry comprising 26 state industrial federations; Pres. DR ALBANO DO PRADO FRANCO; Vice-Pres. MÁRIO AMATO.

**Conselho dos Exportadores de Café Verde do Brasil (CECAFE):** internet www.coffee.com.br/cecafe/; in process of formation in 1999/2000 through merger of Federação Brasileira dos Exportadores de Café and Associação Brasileira dos Exportadores de Café; council of green coffee exporters.

**Departamento Nacional da Produção Mineral (DNPM):** SAN, Quadra 1, Bloco B, 3° andar, 70040-200 Brasília, DF; tel. (61) 224-7097; fax (61) 225-8274; e-mail webmaster@dnpm.gov.br; internet www.dnpm.gov.br; f. 1934; responsible for geological studies and control of exploration of mineral resources; Dir-Gen. JOÃO R. PIMENTEL.

**Empresa Brasileira de Pesquisa Agropecuária (EMBRAPA):** SAIN, Parque Rural, W/3 Norte, CP 040315, 70770-901 Brasília, DF; tel. (61) 348-4433; fax (61) 347-1041; f. 1973; attached to the Ministry of Agriculture; agricultural research; Pres. ALBERTO DUQUE PORTUGAL.

**Federação das Indústrias do Estado de São Paulo (FIESP):** Av. Paulista 1313, 01311-923 São Paulo, SP; tel. (11) 252-4200; fax (11) 284-3611; regional manufacturers' association; Pres. CARLOS EDUARDO MOREIRA FERREIRA.

**Instituto Brasileiro do Meio Ambiente e Recursos Naturais Renováveis (IBAMA):** Ed. Sede IBAMA, Av. SAIN, L4 Norte, Bloco C, Subsolo, 70800-200 Brasília, DF; tel. (61) 316-1205; fax (61) 226-5094; e-mail cnia@sede.ibama.gov.br; internet www.ibama.gov.br; f. 1967; responsible for the annual formulation of national environmental plans; merged with SEMA (National Environmental Agency) in 1988 and replaced the IBDF in 1989; Pres. EDUARDO MAILIUS.

**Instituto Brasileiro do Mineração (IBRAM):** Brasília, DF; Pres. JOÃO SÉRGIO MARINHO NUNES.

**Instituto Nacional da Propriedade Industrial (INPI):** Praça Mauá 7, 18° andar, 20081-240 Rio de Janeiro, RJ; tel. (21) 223-4182; fax (21) 263-2539; e-mail inpipres@inpi.gov.br; internet www.inpi.gov.br; f. 1970; intellectual property, etc.; Pres. JORGE MACHADO.

**Instituto Nacional de Tecnologia (INT):** Av. Venezuela 82, 8° andar, 20081-310 Rio de Janeiro, RJ; tel. (21) 206-1100; fax (21) 263-6552; e-mail int@ riosoft.softex.br; f. 1921; co-operates in national industrial development; Dir MARIA APARECIDA STALLIVIERI NEVES.

## UTILITIES

### Electricity

**Centrais Elétricas Brasileiras, SA (ELETROBRÁS):** Av. Pres. Vargas 642, 10° andar, 20079-900 Rio de Janeiro, RJ; tel. (21) 203-3137; fax (21) 233-3248; f. 1961; government holding company responsible for planning, financing and managing Brazil's electrical energy programme; scheduled for division into eight generating cos and privatization; Pres. FIRMINO SAMPAIO.

**Centrais Elétricas do Norte do Brasil, SA (ELETRONORTE):** SCN, Quadra 6, Conj. A, Blocos B E C, sala 602, Super Center Venâncio 3000, 70718-900 Brasília, DF; tel. (61) 212-6101; fax (61) 321-7798; f. 1973; Pres. RICARDO PINTO PINHEIRO.

**Centrais Elétricas do Sul do Brasil, SA (ELETROSUL):** Rua Deputado Antônio Edu Vieira 353, Pantanal, 88040-901 Florianópolis, SC; tel. (482) 31-7010; fax (81) 34-5678; Gerasul responsible for generating capacity; f. 1969; Pres. CLÁUDIO AVILA DA SILVA.

**Companhia Hidro Elétrica do São Francisco (CHESF):** 333 Edif. André Falcão, Bloco A, sala 313 Bongi, Rua Delmiro Golveia, 50761-901 Recife, PE; tel. (81) 228-3160; fax (81) 227-4970; e-mail chesf@cr.pe.rnp.br; f. 1945; Pres. JÚLIO SÉRGIO DE MAYA PEDROSA MOREIRA.

**Furnas Centrais Elétricas, SA:** Rua Real Grandeza 219, Bloco A, 16° andar, Botafogo, 22281-031 Rio de Janeiro, RJ; tel. (21) 536-3112; fax (21) 286-2249; f. 1957; Pres. LUIZ CARLOS SANTOS.

Associated companies included:

**Espírito Santo Centrais Elétricas, SA (ESCELSA):** Rua Sete de Setembro 362, Centro, CP 01-0452, 29015-000 Vitória, ES; tel. (27) 322-0155; fax (27) 222-8650; f. 1968; Pres. HENRIQUE MELLO DE MORÃES.

**Nuclebrás Engenharia, SA (NUCLEN):** Rua Visconde de Ouro Preto 5, 12° andar, Botafogo, 22250-180 Rio de Janeiro, RJ; tel. (21) 552-2345; fax (21) 552-1745; f. 1975; nuclear-power generation/distribution; Pres. EVALDO CÉSARI DE OLIVEIRA.

**Centrais Elétricas de Santa Catarina, SA (CELESC):** Rodovia SC 404, Km 3, Itacorubi, 88034-900 Florianópolis, SC; tel. (48) 231-5000; fax (48) 231-6530; production and distribution of electricity throughout state of Santa Catarina.

**Comissão Nacional de Energia Nuclear (CNEN):** Rua General Severiano 90, Botafogo, 22294-900 Rio de Janeiro, RJ; tel. (21) 546-2320; fax (21) 546-2282; e-mail corin@cnen.gov.br; internet www.cnen.gov.br; f. 1956; state organization responsible for management of nuclear power programme; Pres. JOSÉ MAURO ESTEVES DOS SANTOS.

**Companhia de Eletricidade do Estado da Bahia (COELBA):** Av. Edgard Santos 300, Cabula IV, 41186-900 Salvador, BA; tel. (71) 370-5130; fax (71) 370-5132; CEO E. LOPEZ-ARANGUREN MARCOS.

**Companhia de Eletricidade do Estado do Rio de Janeiro (CERJ):** Rua Luiz Leopoldo Pinheiro 517, 24016 Niterói, RJ; tel. (21) 719-7171; f. 1907; Man. HARI ALEXANDRE BRUST.

**Companhia Energética Ceará (COELCE):** Av. Barão de Studart 2917, 60120 Fortaleza, CE; tel. (85) 247-1444; fax (85) 272-4711; internet www.coelce.com.br; f. 1971; Pres. FRANCISCO DE QUEIROZ M. JÚNIOR.

**Companhia Energética de Minas Gerais (CEMIG):** Av. Barbacena 1200, 30123-970 Belo Horizonte; tel. (31) 349-2111; fax (31) 299-4691; fmrly state-owned, sold to a Brazilian-US consortium in May 1997; CEO CARVALHO GUIMARÃES.

**Companhia Energética de Pernambuco (CELPE):** Av. João de Barros 111, Sala 301, 50050-902 Recife, PE; tel. (81) 421-6074; fax (81) 421-2018; state distributor of electricity; CEO J. BOSCO DE ALMEIDA.

**Companhia Energética de São Paulo (CESP):** Al. Ministro Rocha Azevedo 25, 01410-900 São Paulo, SP; tel. (11) 287-1026; fax (11) 251-5028; e-mail inform@cesp.com.br; internet www.cesp.com.br; f. 1966; Pres. GUILHERME AUGUSTO CIRNE DE TOLEDO.

**Companhia Força Luz Cataguases Leopoldina:** Praça Rui Barbosa 80, 36770-000 Cataguases, MG; tel. (32) 422-4555; fax (32) 422-1701.

**Companhia Paranaense de Energia (COPEL):** Rua Coronel Dulcidio 800, 80420-170 Curitiba, PR; tel. (41) 322-3535; fax (41) 331-3136; state distributor of electricity and gas; CEO I. H. HUBERT.

**Companhia Paulista de Força e Luz:** Rodovia Campinas Mogi-Mirim Km 2.5, Campinas, SP; tel. (192) 253-8704; fax (192) 252-7644; provides electricity through govt concessions.

**Eletricidade de São Paulo (ELETROPAULO):** Av. Alfredo Egidio de Souza Aranha 100, 04791-900 São Paulo, SP; tel. (11) 546-

1319; fax (11) 546-1933; e-mail administracao@eletropaulo.com.br; internet www.eletropaulo.com.br; f. 1899; state-owned, but partially privatized in 1998; Pres. DAVID ZYLBERSTAJN.

**Itaipú Binacional:** Rua Comendador Araújo 551, 11° andar, 80420-000 Curitiba, PR; tel. (41) 321-4210; fax (41) 321-4474; e-mail itaipu@itaipu.gov.br; internet www.itaipu.gov.br; f. 1974; 1,490 employees (Itaipú Brasil–1998); Dir-Gen. (Brazil) EUCLIDES SCALCO.

**LIGHT—Serviços de Eletricidade, SA:** Av. Pres. Vargas 642, 19° andar, 20071-001 Rio de Janeiro, RJ; tel. (21) 211-2552; fax (21) 233-6823; f. 1899; electricity generation and distribution in Rio de Janeiro; formerly state-owned, in May 1996 it was sold to a Brazilian-French-US consortium; Pres. JOAQUIM ALFONSO MACDOWELL LEITE DE CASTRO.

Regulatory Agency

**Agência Nacional de Energia Elétrica (ANEEL):** SGAN 603, Módulo J, 70830-030 Brasília, DF; e-mail aneel@aneel.gov.br; internet www.aneel.gov.br; Dir JOSÉ MARIA ABDO.

**Gas**

**Companhia Estadual de Gás do Rio de Janeiro (CEG):** Av. Pres. Vargas 2610, 20210 Rio de Janeiro, RJ; tel. (21) 351-8852; gas distribution in the Rio de Janeiro region; privatized in July 1997.

**Companhia de Gás de São Paulo (COMGÁS):** Rua Augusta 1600, 01304 São Paulo, SP; tel. (11) 289-0344; distribution in São Paulo of gas; sold in April 1999 to consortium including British Gas PLC and Royal Dutch/Shell Group; Pres. OSCAR PRIETO.

**Water**

The first transfers to private ownership of state-owned water and sewerage companies were scheduled to commence in 2000, the sale of Compesa (Pernambuco) and of Embasa (Bahia) being the first disposals.

### TRADE UNIONS

**Central Unica dos Trabalhadores (CUT):** Rua São Bento 405, Edif. Martinelli, 7° andar, 01011 São Paulo, SP; tel. (11) 255-7500; fax (11) 37-5626; f. 1983; central union confederation; left-wing; Pres. VINCENTE PAULO DA SILVA; Gen. Sec. GILMAR CARNEIRO.

**Confederação General dos Trabalhadores (CGT):** São Paulo, SP; f. 1986; fmrly Coordenação Nacional das Classes Trabalhadoras; represents 1,258 labour organizations linked to PMDB; Pres. LUÍS ANTÔNIO MEDEIROS.

**Confederação Nacional dos Metalúrgicos** (Metal Workers): f. 1985; Pres. JOAQUIM DOS SANTOS ANDRADE.

**Confederação Nacional das Profissões Liberais (CNPL)** (Liberal Professions): SAU/SUL, Edif. Belvedere Gr. 202, 70070-000 Brasília, DF; tel. (61) 223-1683; fax (61) 223-1944; e-mail cnpliber@nutecnet.com.br; internet www.bsb.nutecut.com.br/web/cnpl; f. 1953; confederation of liberal professions; Pres. LUÍS EDUARDO GAUTÉRIO GALLO; Exec. Sec. JOSÉ ANTÔNIO BRITO ANDRADE.

**Confederação Nacional dos Trabalhadores na Indústria (CNTI)** (Industrial Workers): Av. W/3 Norte, Quadra 505, Lote 01, 70730-517 Brasília, DF; tel. (61) 274-4150; fax (61) 274-7001; f. 1946; Pres. JOSÉ CALIXTO RAMOS.

**Confederação Nacional dos Trabalhadores no Comércio (CNTC)** (Commercial Workers): Av. W/5 Sul, Quadra 902, Bloco C, 70390 Brasília, DF; tel. (61) 224-3511; f. 1946; Pres. ANTÔNIO DE OLIVEIRA SANTOS.

**Confederação Nacional dos Trabalhadores em Transportes Marítimos, Fluviais e Aéreos (CONTTMAF)** (Maritime, River and Air Transport Workers): Av. Pres. Vargas 446, gr. 2205, 20071 Rio de Janeiro, RJ; tel. (21) 233-8329; f. 1957; Pres. MAURÍCIO MONTEIRO SANT'ANNA.

**Confederação Nacional dos Trabalhadores em Comunicações e Publicidade (CONTCOP)** (Communications and Advertising Workers): SCS, Edif. Serra Dourada, 7° andar, gr. 705/709, Q 11, 70315 Brasília, DF; tel. (61) 224-7926; fax (61) 224-5686; f. 1964; 350,000 mems; Pres. ANTÔNIO MARIA THAUMATURGO CORTIZO.

**Confederação Nacional dos Trabalhadores nas Empresas de Crédito (CONTEC)** (Workers in Credit Institutions): SEP-SUL, Av. W4, EQ 707/907 Lote E, 70351 Brasília, DF; tel. (61) 244-5833; f. 1958; 814,532 mems (1988); Pres. LOURENÇO FERREIRA DO PRADO.

**Confederação Nacional dos Trabalhadores em Estabelecimentos de Educação e Cultura (CNTEEC)** (Workers in Education and Culture): SAS, Quadra 4, Bloco B, 70302 Brasília, DF; tel. (61) 226-2988; f. 1967; Pres. MIGUEL ABRAHÃO.

**Confederação Nacional dos Trabalhadores na Agricultura (CONTAG)** (Agricultural Workers): SDS Ed Venâncio VI, 1° andar, 70393-900 Brasília, DF; tel. (61) 321-2288; fax (61) 321-3229; f. 1964; Pres. FRANCISCO URBANO ARAÚJO, Filho.

**Força Sindical (FS):** São Paulo, SP; f. 1991; 6m. mems (1991); Pres. LUÍS ANTÔNIO MEDEIROS.

## Transport

**Ministério dos Transportes (MT):** Esplanada dos Ministérios, Bloco R, 70044-900 Brasília, DF; tel. (61) 224-0185; fax (61) 225-0915; f. 1990 to study, co-ordinate and execute government transport policy and reorganize railway, road and ports and waterways councils; Exec. Sec. PAULO RUBENS FONTENELE ALBUQUERQUE.

**Empresa Brasileira de Planejamento de Transportes (GEIPOT):** SAN, Quadra 3, Blocos N/O, Edif. Núcleo dos Transportes, 70040-902 Brasília, DF; tel. (61) 315-4890; fax (61) 315-4895; e-mail deind@geipot.gov.br; internet www.geipot.gov.br; f. 1973; agency for the promotion of an integrated modern transport system; advises the Minister of Transport on transport policy; Pres. CARLOS ALBERTO WANDERLEY NÓBREGA.

### RAILWAYS

**Rede Ferroviária Federal, SA (RFFSA)** (Federal Railway Corporation): Praça Procópio Ferreira 86, 20224-900 Rio de Janeiro, RJ; tel. (21) 291-2185; fax (21) 263-0420; f.1957; holding company for 18 railways grouped into regional networks, with total track length of 20,500 km in 1998; privatization of federal railways was completed in 1997; freight services; Pres. JOSÉ ALEXANDRE NOGUEIRA DE REZENDE.

**Companhia Brasileira de Trens Urbanos (CBTU):** Estrada Velha da Tijuca 77, Usina, 20531-080 Rio de Janeiro, RJ; tel. (21) 575-3399; fax (21) 571-6149; fmrly responsible for surburban networks and metro systems throughout Brazil; 252 km in 1998; the transfer of each city network to its respective local government is currently under way; Pres. LUIZ OTAVIO MOTA VALADARES.

**Belo Horizonte Metro (CBTU/STU/BH-Demetrô):** Av. Afonso Pena 1500, 11° andar, 30130-921 Belo Horizonte, MG; tel. (31) 250-4002; fax (31) 250-4004; e-mail metrobh@gold.horizontes.com.br; f. 1986; 21.2 km open in 1997; Gen. Man. M. L. L. SIQUEIRA.

**Trem Metropolitano de Recife:** Rua José Natário 478, Areias, 50900-000 Recife, PE; tel. (81) 455-4655; fax (81) 455-4422; f.1985; 53 km open in 1997; Supt FERNANDO ANTÔNIO C. DUEIRE.

There are also railways owned by state governments and several privately-owned railways:

**Companhia Fluminense de Trens Urbanos (Flumitrens):** Praça Cristiano Otoni, sala 445, 20221 Rio de Janeiro, RJ; tel. (21) 233-8594; fax (21) 253-3089; f. 1975 as operating division of RFFSA, current name adopted following takeover by state government in 1994; suburban services in Rio de Janeiro and its environs; 293 km open in 1998; Supt MURILO JUNQUEIRA.

**Companhia do Metropolitano do Rio de Janeiro:** Av. Nossa Senhora de Copacabana 493, 22021-031 Rio de Janeiro, RJ; tel. (21) 235-4041; fax (21) 235-4546; 2-line metro system, 42 km open in 1997; Pres. ALVARO J. M. SANTOS.

**Companhia do Metropolitano de São Paulo:** Rua Augusta 1626, 03310-200 São Paulo, SP; tel. (11) 283-7411; fax (11) 283-5228; f. 1974; 3-line metro system, 56 km open in 1998; Pres. PAULO CLARINDO GOLDSCHMIDT.

**Companhia Paulista de Trens Metropolitanos (CPTM):** Av. Paulista 402, 5° andar, 01310-903 São Paulo, SP; tel. (11) 281-6101; fax (11) 288-2224; f. 1993 to incorporate suburban lines fmrly operated by the CBTU and FEPASA; 286 km; Pres. Eng. OLIVER HOSSEPIAN SALLES DE LIMA.

**Departamento Metropolitano de Transportes Urbanos:** SES, Quadra 4, Lote 6, Brasília, DF; tel. (61) 317-4090; fax (61) 226-9546; the first section of the Brasília metro, linking the capital with the western suburb of Samambaia, was inaugurated in 1994; 38.5 km open in 1997; Dir LEONARDO DE FARIA E SILVA.

**Empresa de Trens Urbanos de Porto Alegre, SA:** Av. Ernesto Neugebauer 1985, 90250-140 Porto Alegre, RS; tel. (51) 371-5000; fax (51) 371-1219; e-mail secos@trensurb.com.br; internet www.trensurb.com.br; f. 1985; 31 km open in 1998; Pres. PEDRO BISCH NETO.

**Estrada de Ferro do Amapá:** Praia de Botafogo 300, 11° andar, ala A, 22250-050 Rio de Janeiro, RJ; tel. (21) 552-4422; f. 1957; operated by Indústria e Comércio de Minérios, SA; 194 km open in 1998; Pres. OSVALDO LUIZ SENRA PESSOA.

**Estrada de Ferro Campos do Jordão:** Rua Martin Cabral 87, CP 11, 12400-000 Pindamonhangaba, SP; tel. (22) 242-4233; fax (22) 242-2499; operated by the Tourism Secretariat of the State of São Paulo; 47 km open in 1998; Dir ARTHUR FERREIRA DOS SANTOS.

**Estrada de Ferro Carajás:** Av. dos Portugueses s/n, 65085-580 São Luís, MA; tel. (98) 218-4000; fax (98) 218-4530; f. 1985 for movement of minerals from the Serra do Carajás to the new port at Ponta da Madeira; operated by the Companhia Vale do Rio Doce; 955 km open in 1998; Supt JUARES SALIBRA.

**Estrada de Ferro do Jari:** Monte Dourado, 68230-000 Pará, PA; tel. (91) 735-1155; fax (91) 735-1475; transportation of timber and bauxite; 68 km open; Dir ARMINDO LUIZ BARETTA.

**Estrada de Ferro Mineração Rio do Norte, SA:** Praia do Flamengo 200, 5° e 6° andares, 22210-030 Rio de Janeiro, RJ; tel. (21) 205-9112; fax (21) 545-5717; 35 km open in 1998; Pres. ANTÔNIO JOÃO TORRES.

**Estrada de Ferro Paraná-Oeste, SA (Ferroeste):** Av. Iguaçu 420, 80230-902 Curitiba, PR; tel. (41) 243-5758; fax (41) 243-5482; f. 1988 to serve the grain-producing regions in Paraná and Mato Grosso do Sul; 248 km inaugurated in 1995; privatized in late 1996, South African company, Comazar, appointed as administrator; Pres. OSIRIS STENGHEL GUIMARÃES.

**Estrada de Ferro Vitória-Minas:** Av. Dante Michelini 5.500, 29090-900 Vitória, ES; tel. (27) 335-3666; fax (27) 226-0093; f. 1942; operated by Companhia Vale de Rio Doce; transport of iron ore, general cargo and passengers; 898 km open in 1998; Dir THIER BARSOTTI MANZANO.

**Ferrovia Bandeirante, SA (Ferroban):** Rua Mauá 51, 01018-900 São Paulo, SP; tel. (11) 222-3392; fax (11) 220-8852; f. 1971 by merger of five railways operated by São Paulo State; transferred to private ownership, Nov. 1998; fmrly Ferrovia Paulista; 4,235 km open in 1998.

## ROADS

In 1998 there were an estimated 1,659,000 km of roads in Brazil, of which 3,630 km were main roads. Brasília has been a focal point for inter-regional development, and paved roads link the capital with every region of Brazil. The building of completely new roads has taken place predominantly in the north. Roads are the principal mode of transport, accounting for 63% of freight and 96% of passenger traffic, including long-distance bus services, in 1998. Major projects include the 5,000-km Trans-Amazonian Highway, running from Recife and Cabedelo to the Peruvian border, the 4,138-km Cuibá–Santarém highway, which will run in a north–south direction, and the 3,555-km Trans-Brasiliana project, which will link Marabá, on the Trans-Amazonian highway, with Aceguá, on the Uruguayan frontier. A 20-year plan to construct a highway linking São Paulo with the Argentine and Chilean capitals was endorsed in 1992 within the context of the development of the Southern Cone Common Market (Mercosul).

**Departamento Nacional de Estradas de Rodagem (DNER)** (National Roads Development): SAN, Quadra 3, Blocos N/O, 4° andar, Edif. Núcleo dos Transportes, 70040-902 Brasília, DF; tel. (61) 315-4100; fax (61) 315-4050; f. 1945 to plan and execute federal road policy and to supervise state and municipal roads with the aim of integrating them into the national network; Dir GENÉSIO B. SOUZA.

## INLAND WATERWAYS

River transport plays only a minor part in the movement of goods. There are three major river systems, the Amazon, Paraná and the São Francisco. The Amazon is navigable for 3,680 km, as far as Iquitos in Peru, and ocean-going ships can reach Manaus, 1,600 km upstream. Plans have been drawn up to improve the inland waterway system and one plan is to link the Amazon and Upper Paraná to provide a navigable waterway across the centre of the country. In October 1993 the member governments of Mercosul, together with Bolivia, reaffirmed their commitment to a 10-year development programme (initiated in 1992) for the extension of the Tietê Paraná river network along the Paraguay and Paraná Rivers as far as Buenos Aires, improving access to Atlantic ports and creating a 3,442 km waterway system, navigable throughout the year.

**Secretaria de Transportes Aquaviários:** Ministério dos Transportes, SAN, Q.3, Blocos N/O, 70040-902 Brasília, DF; tel. (61) 315-8102; Sec. WILDJAN DA FONSECA MAGNO.

**Administração da Hidrovia do Paraguai (AHIPAR):** Rua Treze de Junho 960, Corumbá, MS; tel. (67) 231-2841; fax (67) 231-2661; Supt. PAULO CÉSAR C. GOMES DA SILVA.

**Administração da Hidrovia do Paraná (AHRANA):** Rua Vinte e Quatro de Maio 55, 9° andar, Conj. B, 01041-001 São Paulo, SP; tel. (11) 221-3230; fax (11) 220-8689; Supt LUIZ EDUARDO GARCIA.

**Administração da Hidrovia do São Francisco (AHSFRA):** Praça do Porto 70, Distrito Industrial, 39270-000 Pirapora, MG; tel. (38) 741-2555; fax (38) 741-2510; Supt JOSÉ H. BORATO JABUR JÚNIOR.

**Administração das Hidrovias do Sul (AHSUL):** Praça Oswaldo Cruz 15, 3° andar, 90030-160 Porto Alegre, RS; tel. (51) 228-3677; fax (51) 226-9068; Supt JOSÉ LUIZ F. DE AZAMBUJA.

**Empresa de Navegação da Amazônia, SA (ENASA):** Av. Pres. Vargas 41, 66000-000 Belém, PA; tel. (91) 223-3878; fax (91) 224-0528; f. 1967; cargo and passenger services on the Amazon river and its principal tributaries, connecting the port of Belém with all major river ports; Pres. ANTÔNIO DE SOUZA MENDONÇA; 48 vessels.

## SHIPPING

There are more than 40 deep-water ports in Brazil, all but two of which (Luis Correia and Imbituba) are directly or indirectly administered by the Government. The majority of ports are operated by eight state-owned concerns (Cia Docas do Pará, Maranhão, Ceará, Rio Grande do Norte, Bahia, Espírito Santo, Rio de Janeiro and Estado de São Paulo), while a smaller number (including Suape, Cabedelo, Barra dos Coqueiros, São Sebastião, Paranaguá, Antonina, São Francisco do Sul, Porto Alegre, Pelotas and Rio Grande) are administered by state governments. In late 1996 the Government announced plans to privatize 31 ports (including Santos and Rio de Janeiro).

The ports of Santos, Rio de Janeiro and Rio Grande have specialized container terminals handling more than 1,200,000 TEUs (20-ft equivalent units of containerized cargo) per year. Santos is the major container port in Brazil, accounting for 800,000 TEUs annually. The ports of Paranaguá, Itajaí, São Francisco do Sul, Salvador, Vitória and Imbituba cater for containerized cargo to a lesser extent.

Total cargo handled by Brazilian ports in 1998 amounted to 443m. tons, of which 250m. was bulk cargo, 148m. was liquid cargo and 45m. was general cargo. Some 43,000 vessels used Brazil's ports in 1998.

Brazil's merchant fleet comprised 504 vessels totalling 4,170,577 grt in December 1998.

**Departamento de Marinha Mercante:** Coordenação Geral de Transporte Maritimo, Av. Rio Branco 103, 6° e 8° andar, 20040-004 Rio de Janeiro, RJ; tel. (21) 221-4014; fax (21) 221-5929; Dir PAULO OCTÁVIO DE PAIVA ALMEIDA.

### Port Authorities

**Departamento de Portos:** SAN, Q3, Bl. N/O, CEP 70040-902, Brasília, DF; Dir PAULO ROBERTO K. TANNFNBAUM.

**Paranaguá:** Administração dos Portos de Paranaguá e Antonina (APPA), BR-277, km 0, 83206-380 Paranaguá, PR; tel. (41) 420-1102; fax (41) 423-4252; Port Admin. Eng. OSIRIS STENGHEL GUIMARÃES.

**Recife:** Administração do Porto do Recife, Praça Artur Oscar, 50030-370 Recife, PE; tel. (81) 424-4044; fax (81) 224-2848; Port Dir CARLOS DO REGO VILAR.

**Rio de Janeiro:** Companhia Docas do Rio de Janeiro (CDRJ), Rua do Acre 21, 20081-000 Rio de Janeiro, RJ; tel. (21) 296-5151; fax (21) 253-0528; CDRJ also administers the ports of Forno, Niterói, Sepetiba and Angra dos Reis; Pres. MAURO OROFINO CAMPOS.

**Rio Grande:** Administração do Porto de Rio Grande, Av. Honório Bicalho, CP 198, 96201-020 Rio Grande do Sul, RS; tel. (532) 31-1996; fax (532) 31-1857; Port Dir LUIZ FRANCISCO SPOTORNO.

**Santos:** Companhia Docas do Estado de São Paulo (CODESP), Av. Conselheiro Rodrigues Alves s/n, 11015-900 Santos, SP; tel. (13) 233-6565; fax (13) 233-3080; CODESP also administers the ports of Charqueadas, Estrela, Cáceres, Corumbá/Ladário, and the waterways of Paraná (AHRANA), Paraguai (AHIPAR) and the South (AHSUL); Pres. PAULO FERNANDES DO CARMO.

**São Francisco do Sul:** Administração do Porto de São Francisco do Sul, Av. Eng. Leite Ribeiro 782, CP 71, 89240-000 São Francisco do Sul, SC; tel. (474) 44-0200; fax (474) 44-0115; Dir-Gen. ARNALDO S. THIAGO.

**Tubarão:** Companhia Vale do Rio Doce, Porto de Tubarão, Vitória, ES; tel. (27) 335-5727; fax (27) 228-0612; Port Dir CANDIDO COTTA PACHECO.

**Vitória:** Companhia Docas do Espírito Santo (CODESA), Av. Getúlio Vargas 556, Centro, 29020-030 Vitória, ES; tel. (27) 321-1311; fax (27) 222-7360; e-mail assecs@codesa.com.br; internet www.codesa.com.br; f. 1983; Pres. FÁBIO NUNES FALCE.

Other ports are served by the following state-owned companies:

**Companhia Docas do Estado de Bahia:** Av. da França 1551, 40010-000 Salvador, BA; tel. (71) 243-5066; fax (71) 241-6712; administers the ports of Aracaju, Salvador, Aratu, Ilhéus and Pirapora, and the São Francisco waterway (AHSFRA); Pres. JORGE FRANCISCO MEDAUAR.

**Companhia Docas do Estado de Ceará (CDC):** Praça Amigos da Marinha s/n, 60182-640 Fortaleza, CE; tel. (85) 263-1551; fax (85) 263-2433; administers the port of Fortaleza; Dir MARCELO MOTA TEIXEIRA.

**Companhia Docas de Maranhão (CODOMAR):** Porto do Itaquí, Rua de Paz 561, 65085-370 São Luís, MA; tel. (98) 222-2412; fax (98) 221-1394; administers ports of Itaquí and Manaus, and waterways of the Western Amazon (AHIMOC) and the North-East (AHINOR); Dir WASHINGTON DE OLIVEIRA VIEGAS.

**Companhia Docas do Pará (CDP):** Av. Pres. Vargas 41, 2° andar, 66010-000 Belém, PA; tel. (91) 216-2011; fax (91) 241-1741; f. 1967; administers the ports of Belém, Macapá, Porto Velho, Santarém and Vila do Conde, and the waterways of the Eastern Amazon (AHIMOR) and Tocantins and Araguaia (AHITAR); Dir-Pres. CARLOS ACATAUSSÚ NUNES.

**Companhia Docas do Estado do Rio Grande do Norte (CODERN):** Av. Hildebrando de Góis 2220, Ribeira, 59010-700 Natal, RN; tel. (84) 211-5311; fax (84) 221-6072; administers the ports of Areia Branca, Natal, Recife and Maceió; Dir EMILSON MEDEIROS DOS SANTOS.

### Other State-owned Companies

**Companhia de Navegação do Estado de Rio de Janeiro:** Praça 15 de Novembro 21, 20010-010 Rio de Janeiro, RJ; tel (21) 533-6661; fax (21) 252-0524; Pres. MARCOS TEIXEIRA.

**Frota Nacional de Petroleiros—Fronape:** Rua Carlos Seidl 188, CP 51015, 20931, Rio de Janeiro, RJ; tel. (21) 580-9773; fleet of tankers operated by the state petroleum company, PETROBRÁS, and the Ministry of Transport; Chair. ALBANO DE SOUZA GONÇALVES.

### Private Companies

**Companhia Docas de Imbituba (CDI):** Porto de Imbituba, Av. Presidente Vargas s/n, 88780-000 Imbituba, SC; tel. (482) 55-0080; fax (482) 55-0701; administers the port of Imbituba; Exec. Dir. MANUEL ALVES DO VALE.

**Companhia de Navegação do Norte (CONAN):** Av. Rio Branco 23, 25° andar, 20090-003 Rio de Janeiro, RJ; tel. (21) 223-4155; fax (21) 253-7128; f. 1965; services to Brazil, Argentina, Uruguay and inland waterways; Chair. J. R. RIBEIRO SALOMÃO.

**Empresa de Navegação Aliança, SA:** Av. Pasteur 110, Botafogo, 22290-240 Rio de Janeiro, RJ; tel. (21) 546-1112; fax (21) 546-1161; f. 1950; cargo services to Argentina, Uruguay, Europe, Baltic, Atlantic and North Sea ports; Pres. CARLOS G. E. FISCHER.

**Companhia de Navegação do São Francisco:** Av. São Francisco 1517, 39270-000 Pirapora, MG; tel. (38) 741-1444; fax (38) 741-1164; Pres. JOSÉ HUMBERTO BARATA JABUR.

**Frota Oceânica Brasileira, SA:** Av. Venezuela 110, CP 21-020, 20081-310 Rio de Janeiro, RJ; tel. (21) 291-5153; fax (21) 263-1439; f. 1947; Pres. JOSÉ CARLOS FRAGOSO PIRES; Vice-Pres. LUIZ J. C. ALHANATI.

**Serviço de Navegação Bacia Prata:** Av. 14 de Março 1700, 79370-000 Ladário, MS; tel. (67) 231-4354; Dir LUIZ CARLOS DA SILVA ALEXANDRE.

**Vale do Rio Doce Navegação, SA (DOCENAVE):** Rua Voluntários da Pátria 143, Botafogo, 22279-900 Rio de Janeiro, RJ; tel. (21) 536-8002; fax (21) 536-8276; bulk carrier to Japan, Arabian Gulf, Europe, North America and Argentina; Pres. HENRIQUE SABÓIA.

### CIVIL AVIATION

There are about 1,500 airports and airstrips. Of the 67 principal airports 22 are international, although most international traffic is handled by the two airports at Rio de Janeiro and two at São Paulo.

**Empresa Brasileira de Infra-Estrutura Aeroportuária (INFRAERO):** SCS, Q 04, NR 58, Edif. Infraero, 6° andar, 70304-902 Brasília, DF; tel. (61) 312-3222; fax (61) 321-0512; e-mail fernandalima@infraero.gov.br; internet www.infraero.gov.br; Pres. EDUARDO BOGALHO PETTENGILL.

### Principal Airlines

**Lider Taxi Aéreo, SA:** Av. Santa Rosa 123, 31270 Belo Horizonte, MG; tel. (31) 448-4700; fax (31) 443-4179; Pres. JOSÉ AFONSO ASSUMPÇÃO.

**Nordeste Linhas Aéreas Regionais:** Av. Tancredo Neves 1672, Edif. Catabas Empresarial, 1° andar, Pituba, 41820-020 Salvador, BA; tel. (71) 341-7533; fax (71) 341-0393; e-mail nordeste@provider.com.br; internet www.nordeste.com.br; f. 1976; services to 26 destinations in north-east Brazil; Pres. PERCY LOURENÇO RODRIGUES.

**Pantanal Linhas Aéreas Sul-Matogrossenses, SA:** Av. das Nações Unidas 10989, 8° andar, São Paulo, SP; tel. (11) 3040-3900; fax (11) 866-3424; e-mail pantanal@uninet.com.br; internet www.pantanal-airlines.com.br; f. 1993; regional services; Pres. MARCOS FERREIRA SAMPAIO.

**Rio-Sul Serviços Aéreos Regionais, SA:** Av. Rio Branco 85, 11° andar, 20040-004 Rio de Janeiro, RJ; tel. (21) 263-4282; fax (21) 253-2044; internet www.rio-sul.com; f. 1976; subsidiary of VARIG; domestic passenger services to cities in southern Brazil; Pres. PAULO ENRIQUE MORÃES COCO.

**TAM—Transportes Aéreos Regionais (TAM):** Rua Monsenhor Antônio Pepe 94, Jardim Aeroporto, 04342-001 São Paulo, SP; tel. (11) 5582-8811; fax (11) 578-5946; e-mail tamimprensa@tam.com.br; f. 1976; scheduled passenger and cargo services from São Paulo to destinations throughout Brazil; Chair. Capt. ROLIM ADOLFO AMARO.

**Transbrasil SA Linhas Aéreas:** Rua Gen. Pantaleão Teles 40, Hangar Transbrasil, Aeroporto de Congonhas, 04355-900 São Paulo, SP; tel. (11) 533-5367; fax (11) 543-8048; internet www.transbrasil.com.br; f. 1955 as Sadia, renamed 1972; scheduled passenger and cargo services to major Brazilian cities and Orlando; cargo charter flights to the USA; Pres. CELSO CIPRIANI.

**Transportes Aéreos Regionais da Bacia Amazônica (TABA):** Rua João Balb 202, Nazaré, 66055-260 Belém, PA; tel. (91) 242-6300; fax (91) 222-0471; f. 1976; domestic passenger services throughout north-west Brazil; Chair. MARCÍLIO JACQUES GIBSON.

**VARIG, SA (Viação Aérea Rio Grandense):** Av. Almirante Sílvio de Noronha 365, Bloco A, sala 45, 20021-010 Rio de Janeiro, RJ; tel. (21) 272-5000; fax (21) 272-5700; internet www.varig.com.br; f. 1927; international services throughout North, Central and South America, Africa, Western Europe and Japan; domestic services to major Brazilian cities; cargo services; Chair. and Pres. FERNANDO PINTO.

**VASP, SA (Viação Aérea São Paulo):** Praça Comte-Lineu Gomes s/n, Aeroporto Congonhas, 04626-910 São Paulo, SP; tel. (11) 533-7011; fax (11) 542-0880; internet www.vasp.com.br; f. 1933; privatized in Sept. 1990; domestic services throughout Brazil; international services to Argentina, Belgium, the Caribbean, South Korea and the USA; Pres. WAGNER CANHEDO.

## Tourism

In 1998 some 4.8m. tourists visited Brazil. Receipts from tourism totalled US $3,678m. in 1998. Rio de Janeiro, with its famous beaches, is the centre of the tourist trade. Like Salvador, Recife and other towns, it has excellent examples of Portuguese colonial and modern architecture. The modern capital, Brasília, incorporates a new concept of city planning and is the nation's show-piece. Other attractions are the Iguaçu Falls, the seventh largest (by volume) in the world, the tropical forests of the Amazon basin and the wildlife of the Pantanal.

**Divisão de Feiras e Turismo/Departamento de Promoção Comercial:** Ministério das Relações Exteriores, Esplanada dos Ministérios, 5° andar, 70170-900 Brasília, DF; tel. (61) 211-6394; f. 1977; organizes Brazil's participation in trade fairs and commercial exhibitions abroad; Principal Officer JOÃO ALBERTO DOURADO QUINTÃES.

**Instituto Brasileiro de Turismo—EMBRATUR:** SCN, Q 02, Bloco G, 3° andar, 70710-500 Brasília, DF; tel. (61) 224-9100; fax (61) 223-9889; internet www.embratur.gov.br; f. 1966; Pres. CAIO LUIZ DE CARVALHO.

# BRUNEI

## Introductory Survey

### Location, Climate, Language, Religion, Flag, Capital

The Sultanate of Brunei (Negara Brunei Darussalam) lies in South-East Asia, on the north-west coast of the island of Borneo (most of which is comprised of the Indonesian territory of Kalimantan). It is surrounded and bisected on the landward side by Sarawak, one of the two eastern states of Malaysia. The country has a tropical climate, characterized by consistent temperature and humidity. Annual rainfall averages about 2,540 mm (100 ins) in coastal areas and about 3,300 mm (130 ins) in the interior. Temperatures are high, with average daily temperatures ranging from 24°C (75°F) to 32°C (90°F). The principal language is Malay, although Chinese is also spoken and English is widely used. The Malay population (an estimated 67.6% of the total in 1999) are mainly Sunni Muslims. Most of the Chinese in Brunei (14.9% of the population) are Buddhists, and some are adherents of Confucianism and Daoism. Europeans and Eurasians are predominantly Christians, and the majority of indigenous tribespeople (Iban, Dayak and Kelabit—5.9% of the population) adhere to various animist beliefs. The flag (proportions 2 by 1) is yellow, with two diagonal stripes, of white and black, running from the upper hoist to the lower fly; superimposed in the centre is the state emblem (in red, with yellow Arabic inscriptions). The capital is Bandar Seri Begawan (formerly called Brunei Town).

### Recent History

Brunei, a traditional Islamic monarchy, formerly included most of the coastal regions of North Borneo (now Sabah) and Sarawak, which later became states of Malaysia. During the 19th century the rulers of Brunei ceded large parts of their territory to the United Kingdom, reducing the sultanate to its present size. In 1888, when North Borneo became a British Protectorate, Brunei became a British Protected State. In accordance with an agreement made in 1906, a British Resident was appointed to the court of the ruling Sultan as an adviser on administration. Under this arrangement, a form of government that included an advisory body, the State Council, emerged.

Brunei was invaded by Japanese forces in December 1941, but reverted to its former status in 1945, when the Second World War ended. The British-appointed Governor of Sarawak was High Commissioner for Brunei from 1948 until the territory's first written Constitution was promulgated in September 1959, when a further agreement was made between the Sultan and the British Government. The United Kingdom continued to be responsible for Brunei's defence and external affairs until the Sultanate's declaration of independence in 1984.

In December 1962 a large-scale revolt broke out in Brunei and in parts of Sarawak and North Borneo. The rebellion was undertaken by the 'North Borneo Liberation Army', an organization linked with the Parti Rakyat Brunei (PRB—Brunei People's Party), led by Sheikh Ahmad Azahari, which was strongly opposed to the planned entry of Brunei into the Federation of Malaysia. The rebels proclaimed the 'revolutionary State of North Kalimantan', but the revolt was suppressed, after 10 days' fighting, with the aid of British forces from Singapore. A state of emergency was declared, the PRB was banned, and Azahari was given asylum in Malaya. In the event, the Sultan of Brunei, Sir Omar Ali Saifuddin III, decided in 1963 against joining the Federation. From 1962 he ruled by decree, and the state of emergency remained in force. In October 1967 Saifuddin, who had been Sultan since 1950, abdicated in favour of his son, Hassanal Bolkiah, who was then 21 years of age. Under an agreement signed in November 1971, Brunei was granted full internal self-government.

In December 1975 the UN General Assembly adopted a resolution advocating British withdrawal from Brunei, the return of political exiles and the holding of a general election. Negotiations in 1978, following assurances by Malaysia and Indonesia that they would respect Brunei's sovereignty, resulted in an agreement (signed in January 1979) that Brunei would become fully independent within five years. Independence was duly proclaimed on 1 January 1984, and the Sultan took office as Prime Minister and Minister of Finance and of Home Affairs, presiding over a Cabinet of six other ministers (including two of the Sultan's brothers and his father, the former Sultan).

The future of the Chinese population, who controlled much of Brunei's private commercial sector but had become stateless since independence, appeared threatened in 1985, when the Sultan indicated that Brunei would become an Islamic state in which the indigenous, mainly Malay, inhabitants, known as *bumiputras* ('sons of the soil'), would receive preferential treatment. Several Hong Kong and Taiwan Chinese, who were not permanent Brunei residents, were repatriated.

In May 1985 a new political party, the Parti Kebangsaan Demokratik Brunei (PKDB—Brunei National Democratic Party), was formed. The new party, which comprised business executives loyal to the Sultan, based its policies on Islam and a form of liberal nationalism. However, the Sultan forbade employees of the Government (about 40% of the country's working population) to join the party. Persons belonging to the Chinese community were also excluded from membership. Divisions within the new party led to the formation of a second group, the Parti Perpaduan Kebangsaan Brunei (PPKB—Brunei National Solidarity Party), in February 1986. This party, which also received the Sultan's official approval, placed greater emphasis on co-operation with the Government, and was open to both Muslim and non-Muslim ethnic groups.

Although the Sultan was not expected to allow any relaxation of restrictions on radical political activities, it became clear during 1985 and 1986 that a more progressive style of government was being adopted. The death of Sir Omar Ali Saifuddin, the Sultan's father, in September 1986 was expected to hasten modernization. In October the Cabinet was enlarged to 11 members, and commoners and aristocrats were assigned portfolios that had previously been given to members of the royal family. In February 1988, however, the PKDB was dissolved by the authorities after it had demanded the resignation of the Sultan as Head of Government (although not as Head of State), an end to the 26-year state of emergency and the holding of democratic elections. The official reason for the dissolution of the party was its connections with a foreign organization, the Pacific Democratic Union. The leaders of the PKDB, Abdul Latif Hamid and Abdul Latif Chuchu, were arrested, under provisions of the Internal Security Act, and detained until March 1990. Abdul Latif Hamid died in May. In January of that year the Government ordered the release of six political prisoners, who had been detained soon after the revolt in 1962.

In 1990 the Government encouraged the population to embrace *Melayu Islam Beraja* (Malay Islamic Monarchy) as the state ideology. This affirmation of traditional Bruneian values for Malay Muslims was widely believed to be a response to an increase in social problems, including the abuse of alcohol and mild narcotics. Muslims were encouraged to adhere more closely to the tenets of Islam, greater emphasis was laid on Islamic holiday celebrations, and the distribution of alcohol was discouraged.

Extremely moderate progress towards reform was apparent in subsequent years. In 1994 a constitutional committee, appointed by the Government and chaired by the Minister of Foreign Affairs, Prince Mohamad Bolkiah, submitted a recommendation that the Constitution be amended to provide for an elected legislature. In February 1995 the PPKB was given permission to convene a general assembly, at which Abdul Latif Chuchu, the former Secretary-General of the PKDB, was elected President. Latif Chuchu was, however, compelled to resign shortly afterwards, owing to a condition of his release from detention in 1990. In May 1998 the PKDB was permitted to hold a further annual general meeting, at which Hatta Zainal Abidin, the son of a former opposition leader, was elected party President.

In February 1997 the Sultan replaced his brother, Prince Jefri Bolkiah, as Minister of Finance. It was rumoured that the Sultan's assumption of the finance portfolio was due to alleged financial disagreements rather than Prince Jefri's frequently criticized extravagant lifestyle. In March the Sultan and Prince Jefri denied accusations of misconduct made by a former winner

of a US beauty contest, Shannon Marketic. A US court granted the Sultan immunity from legal action in August, owing to his status as a foreign head of state; this immunity was extended to Prince Jefri in March 1998. Similar allegations against Prince Jefri, submitted to a court in Hawaii, resulted in an undisclosed financial settlement, following the judge's rejection of Prince Jefri's claims to immunity. Marketic subsequently appealed against the granting of exemption from prosecution in her case. Further allegations concerning the extravagant lifestyle of Prince Jefri emerged in a court case in the United Kingdom in February, in which Jefri was being sued for £80m. by two former business associates, Watche (Bob) and Rafi Manoukian. The Manoukians claimed that Prince Jefri had reneged on two property agreements; Prince Jefri was counter-suing them for £100m., alleging that they had exploited their relationship with him to amass considerable wealth. The case, which was unreported in Brunei, was also settled out of court for an undisclosed sum.

Prince Jefri, who had left Brunei in April 1998, was removed as Chairman of the Brunei Investment Agency (BIA), which controls the country's overseas investments, at the end of July, following the collapse earlier in the month of his business conglomerate, the Amedeo Development Corporation. He was also removed from the boards of seven communications companies. Prince Jefri claimed that he was the victim of a conspiracy of conservative Islamists, led by his estranged brother, Prince Mohamad Bolkiah (the Minister of Foreign Affairs), and the Minister of Education, Pehin Dato' Haji Abdul Aziz bin Pehin Haji Umar; his removal from positions of authority took place amid more rigorous enforcement of the ban on alcohol and the confiscation from retailers of non-Islamic religious artefacts. Abdul Aziz, who replaced Prince Jefri as Chairman of the BIA, also headed an investigation (which was initiated in June) into the finances of the BIA. In September Abdul Aziz announced that large amounts of government funds had been misappropriated during Prince Jefri's tenure as Chairman. The Prince returned to Brunei in early October.

Abdul Aziz also assumed responsibility for the health portfolio, following the dismissal in March 1998, after 14 years in office, of Dato' Dr Haji Johar bin Dato' Haji Noordin, reportedly owing to the inadequacy of his response to the haze over Brunei caused by forest fires in Indonesia and Malaysia. The resignations of the Attorney-General, Pengiran Haji Bahrin bin Pengiran Haji Abbas (who was granted leave from his position as Minister of Law), and the Solicitor-General were accepted by the Sultan in June. An acting Attorney-General and Solicitor-General were appointed, while the Sultan assumed temporary responsibility for the law portfolio. On 10 August the Sultan's son, Prince Al-Muhtadee Billah Bolkiah, was installed as the heir to the throne.

Relations with the United Kingdom had become strained during 1983, following the Brunei Government's decision, in August, to transfer the management of its investment portfolio from the British Crown Agents to the newly-created BIA. However, normal relations were restored in September, when the British Government agreed that a battalion of Gurkha troops, stationed in Brunei since 1971, should remain in Brunei after independence, at the Sultanate's expense, specifically to guard the oil and gas fields.

Brunei has developed close relations with the members of the Association of South East Asian Nations (ASEAN—see p. 128), in particular Singapore, and became a full member of the organization immediately after independence. Brunei also joined the UN, the Commonwealth (see p. 144) and the Organization of the Islamic Conference (see p. 249) in 1984. In September 1991 Brunei applied for membership of the Non-aligned Movement (see p. 302), and was formally admitted to the organization in September 1992. In late 1991 Brunei established diplomatic relations with the People's Republic of China at ambassadorial level. As a member of ASEAN, Brunei's relations with Viet Nam improved during 1991 (following Viet Nam's withdrawal from Cambodia in September 1989). In February 1992 diplomatic relations were formally established with Viet Nam during a visit to Brunei of the Vietnamese Premier. In October 1993 the Brunei Government announced the establishment of diplomatic relations at ambassadorial level with Myanmar.

In July 1990, in response to the uncertainty over the future of US bases in the Philippines (see chapter on the Philippines, Vol. II), Brunei joined Singapore in offering the USA the option of operating its forces from Brunei. A bilateral memorandum of understanding was subsequently signed, providing for up to three visits a year to Brunei by US warships. Under the memorandum, Brunei forces were to train with US personnel.

Conflicting claims (from Brunei, Viet Nam, the People's Republic of China, the Philippines, Malaysia and Taiwan) to all, or some, of the uninhabited Spratly Islands, situated in the South China Sea, remained a source of tension in the region. Brunei is the only claimant not to have stationed troops on the islands, which are both strategically important and possess potentially large reserves of petroleum. Attempts through the 1990s to resolve the dispute through a negotiated settlement have resulted in little progress, and military activity in the area has increased.

### Government

The 1959 Constitution confers supreme executive authority on the Sultan. He is assisted and advised by four Constitutional Councils: the Religious Council, the Privy Council, the Council of Cabinet Ministers and the Council of Succession. Since the rebellion of 1962, certain provisions of the Constitution (including those pertaining to elections and to a fifth Council, the Legislative Council) have been suspended, and the Sultan has ruled by decree.

### Defence

At 1 August 1999 the Royal Brunei Malay Regiment numbered 5,000 (including 600 women): army 3,900; navy 700; air force 400. Military service is voluntary, but only Malays are eligible for service. Paramilitary forces comprised 1,750 Royal Brunei Police. Defence expenditure in 1998 was budgeted at B $614m., representing 14.3% of total expenditure. One Gurkha battalion of the British army, comprising about 1,050 men, has been stationed in Brunei since 1971. There are also about 500 troops from Singapore, operating a training school in Brunei.

### Economic Affairs

In 1994, according to estimates by the World Bank, Brunei's gross national product (GNP), measured at average 1992–94 prices, was US $3,975m., equivalent to US $14,240 per head. During 1985–94, it was estimated, GNP per head declined, in real terms, at an average rate of 1.5% per year. In 1990–97 the population increased by an average of 2.6% annually. According to preliminary World Bank data, GNP in 1997 was US $7,151m. Brunei's gross domestic product (GDP) increased at an estimated average annual rate of 2.3% during 1990–97. Real GDP growth in 1998 was estimated at 1.0%.

Agriculture (including forestry and fishing) employed an estimated 0.9% of the working population in 1998 and provided an estimated 2.8% of GDP in that year. In 1998 an estimated 1.2% of the total land area was cultivated; the principal crops include rice, cassava, bananas and pineapples. In the 1990s Brunei imported about 80% of its total food requirements. Owing to the increasing emphasis on Islamic values in Brunei, a severe shortage of meat was caused in 1999 following a decision to ensure that all food was *halal* (slaughtered in accordance with Islamic traditions) by either imposing supervisors in foreign abattoirs or by slaughtering imported livestock in Brunei. During 1990–97 agricultural GDP increased, in real terms, at an average annual rate of 2.7%. Agricultural GDP increased by an estimated 2.9% in 1998.

Industry (comprising mining, manufacturing, construction and utilities) employed 24.1% of the working population in 1991 and contributed an estimated 39.1% of GDP in 1998. Total industrial GDP declined at an average annual rate of 1.6% in 1985–95. Industrial GDP, including oil and gas services, increased by an average of 6.6% per year in 1993–97. Industrial GDP growth was estimated at 4.1% in 1998.

Brunei's economy depends almost entirely on its petroleum and natural gas resources. Mining and quarrying employed only 5.0% of the working population in 1991, but the petroleum sector provided an estimated 50.1% of GDP in 1998. Production of crude petroleum from the eight offshore and two onshore fields averaged 157,000 barrels per day in 1998. In that year output of natural gas totalled 10,751m. cu m. In the 1990s there were significant further discoveries of both petroleum and natural gas reserves. Crude petroleum, natural gas and petroleum products together accounted for an estimated 88.6% of total export earnings in 1998. Reserves of petroleum and natural gas were sufficient to enable production to be maintained at current levels until 2018 and 2033 respectively. The GDP of the mining sector declined at an average rate of 5.3% per year in 1985–89, but rose by 1.4% in 1990 and by 10.0% in

1991. The GDP of the petroleum and gas sector declined by an annual average of 0.3% in 1990–97 and by an estimated 1.6% in 1998.

Manufacturing is dominated by petroleum refining. The sector employed 3.8% of the working population in 1991 (increasing to 5.4% in 1995) and contributed an estimated 8.1% of GDP in 1991. Since the mid-1980s Brunei has attempted to expand its manufacturing base. In the mid-1990s the textile industry provided the largest non-oil and -gas revenue; other industries included cement, mineral water, canned food, dairy products, silica sands products, footwear and leather products, the design and manufacture of printed circuits, publishing and printing. Manufacturing GDP increased at an average annual rate of 4.8% in 1985–89 and by 5.3% in 1990, but fell by 22.6% in 1991.

Services employed 73.7% of the working population in 1991 and provided an estimated 58.1% of GDP in 1998. In 1998 the sector comprising wholesale and retail trade, restaurants and hotels contributed 12.6% of GDP, and the finance sector 8.3%. Plans are under way to develop Brunei as a regional centre for finance and banking. The GDP of the banking and finance sector increased by an annual average of 7.7% in 1993–97 and by an estimated 3.8% in 1998. The tourism sector is also being actively promoted as an important part of Brunei's policy of diversification away from its reliance on petroleum and natural gas; 2001 was designated 'Visit Brunei Year'. During 1985–96 the combined GDP of the service sectors increased, in real terms, at an average rate of 5.5% per year.

In 1998 Brunei recorded a visible trade surplus of US $175m., while, as a result of high investment income from abroad, there was a surplus of US $2,085m. on the current account of the balance of payments. In 1997 the principal source of imports (25.6%) was Singapore; other major suppliers were the USA, Malaysia, the United Kingdom and Japan. The principal market for exports in that year was Japan, which accounted for 53.1% of total exports (mainly natural gas on a long-term contract); other significant purchasers were the Republic of Korea (also a purchaser of natural gas), Thailand and Singapore. Principal imports comprised machinery and transport equipment, basic manufactures, food and live animals and chemicals; principal exports were crude petroleum and natural gas.

In 1997 there was a budgetary deficit of B $27m. (equivalent to 0.3% of GDP). Brunei has no external public debt. International reserves were unofficially estimated at US $38,000m. in 1997 but were estimated to have declined to US $20,000m. in late 1998. Consumer prices increased at an average rate of 2.7% per year in 1990–97, but declined by 0.4% in 1998. Foreign workers, principally from Malaysia and the Philippines, have helped to ease the labour shortage resulting from the small size of the population, and comprised about 30% of the labour force in 1998, compared with 41% in 1995, owing to an exodus of foreign workers in 1998. However, the rate of unemployment was estimated at 5.1% in 1998, reflecting a shortage of non-manual jobs for the well-educated Bruneians.

Brunei is a member of the Association of South East Asian Nations (ASEAN—see p. 128). In October 1991 the member states formally announced the establishment of the ASEAN Free Trade Area, which was to be implemented over 15 years (later reduced to 10), and, as a member of ASEAN, Brunei endorsed Malaysia's plan for an East Asia Economic Caucus. Brunei is also a member of the UN Economic and Social Commission for Asia and the Pacific (see p. 27), which aims to accelerate economic progress in the region. In 1994 the East ASEAN Growth Area (EAGA) was established, encompassing Mindanao, in the Philippines, Sarawak and Sabah, in Malaysia, Kalimantan and Sulawesi, in Indonesia, and Brunei. The EAGA was modelled on the Singapore-Johore-Riau 'growth triangle'. In October 1995 Brunei joined the International Monetary Fund (IMF—see p. 90) and the World Bank.

The seventh (1996–2000) National Development Plan continued the emphasis of the fifth (1986–1990) and sixth (1991–95) Plans on diversification of the economy to reduce the country's dependence on income from petroleum and natural gas. In 1996 the Government announced proposals to develop Brunei as a 'Service Hub for Trade and Tourism' by the year 2003, following earlier plans for the development of the private sector and the conversion of Brunei into a regional centre for banking and finance. Various measures were taken to accelerate the broadening of Brunei's economic base, which had been extremely slow, owing to the constraints of high labour costs, the small domestic market and a lack of entrepreneurial skills and motivation in the indigenous population. However, the regional financial crisis, which began in 1997, resulted in the depreciation of the Brunei dollar, reduced income from the stock market and a sharp reduction in tourist arrivals, owing to the recession in other Asian countries. The situation was compounded by a significant decline in the price of petroleum from mid-1997 and huge financial losses caused by alleged mismanagement of the Brunei Investment Agency (BIA) by the Sultan's brother, Prince Jefri Bolkiah. Another factor was the collapse of Prince Jefri's Amedeo Development Corporation, which was responsible for many building projects in Brunei. In an attempt to address the economic situation, budgetary allocations were drastically reduced, halting much government investment (although complaints from the business community caused the Government to reverse some decisions). Service industries were then also adversely affected by the exodus of thousands of unemployed foreign workers. Amedeo's liquidation in July 1999, without compensating its 25 creditors (mostly foreign construction companies), was expected to have an adverse effect on investor confidence in Brunei. However, a recovery in petroleum prices in 1999 offered the prospect of an economic revival. Analysts agreed that a principal problem for the Bruneian economy was a lack of transparency, particularly in the BIA, where there was little or no distinction between government funds and those of the royal family. However, these concerns seemed unlikely to be addressed in the foreseeable future.

## Social Welfare

Free medical services are provided by the Government. In 1996 there were 281 physicians working in the country and 961 hospital beds. In the same year there were 40 dentists, 15 pharmacists and 1,438 nurses. The main central referral hospital is in Bandar Seri Begawan, but there are three other hospitals (in Kuala Belait, Tutong and Temburong), as well as private facilities provided by Brunei Shell in Seria. For medical care not available in Brunei, citizens are sent abroad at the Government's expense. There is a 'flying doctor' service, as well as various clinics, travelling dispensaries and dental clinics. A non-contributory state pensions scheme for elderly and disabled persons came into operation in 1955. The State also provides financial assistance to the poor, the destitute and widows. Of total ordinary expenditure by the Government in 1995, B $154m. (6.5%) was for the Ministry of Health.

## Education

Education is free and is compulsory for 12 years from the age of five years. Islamic studies form an integral part of the school curriculum. Pupils who are Brunei citizens and reside more than 8 km (5 miles) from their schools are entitled to free accommodation in hostels, free transport or a subsistence allowance. Schools are classified according to the language of instruction, i.e. Malay, English or Chinese (Mandarin). In 1994 enrolment at pre-primary level was equivalent to 51% of children in the relevant age-group (males 51%; females 51%). Primary education lasts for six years from the age of six years. Secondary education, usually beginning at 12 years of age, lasts for seven years, comprising a first cycle of three years (lower secondary), a second of two years (upper secondary) and a third of two years (pre-tertiary). In 1994 enrolment in primary schools included 91% of children in the relevant age-group (males 91%; females 91%), while the comparable enrolment ratio at secondary level was 68% (males 64%; females 71%). In 1996 there was one teacher-training college, five colleges for vocational and technical education, three institutes of higher education and one university. The University of Brunei Darussalam was formally established in 1985, but many students continue to attend universities abroad, at government expense. In 1994 enrolment at tertiary level was equivalent to 6.6% of the relevant age-group (males 5.3%; females 8.0%). In 1995, according to UNESCO estimates, the adult illiteracy rate averaged 11.8% (males 7.4%; females 16.6%). Of total ordinary expenditure by the Government in 1995, B $311m. (13.1%) was for the Ministry of Education.

## Public Holidays

**2000:** 1 January (New Year's Day), 8 January†‡ (Hari Raya Puasa, end of Ramadan), 5–7 February* (Chinese New Year), 23 February (National Day), 16 March† (Hari Raya Haji, Feast of the Sacrifice), 6 April† (Hizrah, Islamic New Year), 31 May (Royal Brunei Armed Forces Day), 15 June† (Hari Mouloud, Birth of the Prophet), 15 July (Sultan's Birthday), 26 October† (Isra Meraj, Ascension of the Prophet Muhammad), 28 November† (Beginning of Ramadan), 14 December† (Memperingati Nuzul Al-Quran, Anniversary of the Revelation of the Koran), 25 December (Christmas), 28 December†‡ (Hari Raya Puasa, end of Ramadan).

**2001:** 1 January (New Year's Day), 23 February (National Day), 25–27 February* (Chinese New Year), 6 March† (Hari Raya Haji, Feast of the Sacrifice), 26 March† (Hizrah, Islamic New Year), 31 May (Royal Brunei Armed Forces Day), 4 June† (Hari Mouloud, Birth of the Prophet), 15 July (Sultan's Birthday), 15 October† (Isra Meraj, Ascension of the Prophet Muhammad), 17 November† (Beginning of Ramadan), 3 December† (Memperingati Nuzul Al-Quran, Anniversary of the Revelation of the Koran), 17 December† (Hari Raya Puasa, end of Ramadan), 25 December (Christmas).

* From the first to the third day of the first moon of the lunar calendar.

† These holidays are dependent on the Islamic lunar calendar and may vary by one or two days from the dates given.

‡ N.B. This festival will occur twice (in the Islamic years AH 1420 and 1421) within the same Gregorian year.

### Weights and Measures

The imperial system is in operation but local measures of weight and capacity are used. These include the gantang (1 gallon), the tahil (1⅓ oz) and the kati (1⅓ lb).

# Statistical Survey

Source (unless otherwise stated): Department of Economic Planning and Development, Ministry of Finance, Bandar Seri Begawan 2012; tel. (2) 241991; fax (2) 226132.

## AREA AND POPULATION

**Area:** 5,765 sq km (2,226 sq miles); *by district:* Brunei/Muara 570 sq km (220 sq miles), Seria/Belait 2,725 sq km (1,052 sq miles), Tutong 1,165 sq km (450 sq miles), Temburong 1,305 sq km (504 sq miles).

**Population** (excluding transients afloat): 192,832 (males 102,942, females 89,890) at census of 25 August 1981; 260,482 (males 137,616, females 122,866) at census of 7 August 1991. *By district* (official estimates at mid-1999): Brunei/Muara 218,800; Seria/Belait 66,800; Tutong 35,700; Temburong 9,400; Total 330,700 (males 175,200, females 155,500).

**Density** (mid-1999): 57.3 per sq km.

**Ethnic Groups** (1991 census): Malay 174,319, Chinese 40,621, Other indigenous 15,665, Others 29,877, Total 260,482; (official estimates at mid-1999): Malay 223,500, Chinese 49,300, Other indigenous 19,600, Others 38,300, Total 330,700.

**Principal Town:** Bandar Seri Begawan (capital), population 45,867 at 1991 census, 50,000 in 1995 (estimate).

**Births, Marriages and Deaths** (registrations, 1998): Live births 7,411 (birth rate 22.9 per 1,000), Deaths 928 (death rate 2.9 per 1,000); (1995): Marriages 1,793 (marriage rate 6.1 per 1,000).

**Expectation of Life** (years at birth, 1992): Males 72.4; Females 76.2.

**Economically Active Population** (1991 census): Agriculture, hunting, forestry and fishing 2,162; Mining and quarrying 5,327; Manufacturing 4,070; Electricity, gas and water 2,223; Construction 14,145; Trade, restaurants and hotels 15,404; Transport, storage and communications 5,392; Financing, insurance, real estate and business services 5,807; Community, social and personal services 52,121; Activities not adequately defined 95; *Total employed* 106,746 (males 72,338; females 34,408); Unemployed 5,209 (males 2,745; females 2,464); *Total labour force* 111,955 (males 75,083; females 36,872).

*1998* (estimate): Total labour force 132,390.

## AGRICULTURE, ETC.

**Principal Crops** ('000 metric tons, 1998): Rice (paddy) 0.1, Cassava (Manioc) 2 (FAO estimate), Vegetables (incl. arable crops) 6, Fruit 1.

**Livestock** ('000 head, 1998): Cattle 1.9, Buffaloes 5.9, Goats 5 (FAO estimate), Poultry 5,703.

**Livestock Products** (1998): Poultry meat 7,396 metric tons; Hen eggs ('000) 77,000.

**Forestry** ('000 cu m, 1998): *Roundwood removals:* Sawlogs, veneer logs and logs for sleepers 108.0; Other industrial wood 131.6; Fuel wood 66.2; Total 305.8.

*Sawnwood production:* Total (incl. railway sleepers) 90 in 1997 (Source: FAO, *Yearbook of Forest Products*).

**Fishing** (metric tons, live weight, 1998): Inland waters 21.1 (Giant river prawn 21.1); Pacific Ocean 1,925.2 (Marine fishes 1,473.2, Shrimps 367.7, Other crustaceans and molluscs 84.3); Total catch 1,946.3.

## MINING

**Production** (1998): Crude petroleum ('000 cu m) 8,329; Natural gas (million cu m) 10,751.

## INDUSTRY

**Production** ('000 metric tons, unless otherwise indicated, 1998): Motor spirit (petrol) 187.6; Distillate fuel oils 147.8; Kerosene 76.5; Electric energy (million kWh) 1,528.5.

## FINANCE

**Currency and Exchange Rates:** 100 sen (cents) = 1 Brunei dollar (B $). *Sterling, US Dollar and Euro Equivalents* (30 September 1999): £1 sterling = B $2.8032; US $1 = B $1.7025; €1 = B $1.8157; B $100 = £35.67 = US $58.74 = €55.07. *Average Exchange Rate* (Brunei dollars per US $): 1.4100 in 1996; 1.4848 in 1997; 1.6736 in 1998. Note: The Brunei dollar is at par with the Singapore dollar.

**Budget** (B $ million, 1997): *Revenue:* Tax revenue 1,561 (Import duty 224, Corporate income tax 1,333); Non-tax revenue 1,282 (Commercial receipts 303, Property income 957); Transfers from Brunei Investment Agency 1,146; Total 3,989. *Expenditure:* Ordinary expenditure 2,564 (Prime Minister's Office 183, Defence 548, Foreign Affairs 116, Finance 502, Home Affairs 94, Education 347, Industry and Primary Resources 43, Religious Affairs 113, Development 286, Health 178); Other current expenditure 36; Capital expenditure 1,350; Investment in public enterprises by Brunei Investment Agency 67; Total 4,016.

(B $ million, 1998, estimates): *Revenue:* 2,775 (excl. transfers from Brunei Investment Agency); *Expenditure:* 4,295 (excl. investment by Brunei Investment Agency).

Source: IMF, *Brunei Darussalam: Recent Economic Developments* (April 1999).

**Money Supply** (B $ million, 1998): Currency in circulation 627.2; Demand deposits of private sector 1,637.6; Total money 2,264.8.

**Cost of Living** (Consumer Price Index; base: 1990 = 100): All items 118.8 in 1996; 120.8 in 1997; 120.3 in 1998 (Food 118.0; Clothing and footwear 127.2; Rent, fuel and power 110.4).

**Gross Domestic Product by Economic Activity** (B $ million in current prices, 1998, provisional): Agriculture, hunting, forestry and fishing 231.9; Mining, quarrying and manufacturing 2,633.6; Electricity, gas and water 87.5; Construction 539.2; Trade, restaurants and hotels 1,049.0; Transport, storage and communications 422.4; Finance, insurance, real estate and business services 693.9; Community, social and personal services 2,673.1; *Sub-total* 8,330.7; *Less* Imputed bank service charge 219.7; *GDP in purchasers' values* 8,111.0.

**Balance of Payments** (US $ million, 1998, estimates): Exports of goods 1,894; Imports of goods –1,718; *Trade balance* 175; Exports of services 486; Imports of services –774; *Balance on goods and services* –112; Other income received 2,439; Other income paid –58; *Balance on goods, services and income* 2,269; Current transfers received 8; Current transfers paid –192; *Current balance* 2,085; Foreign investment (net) 151; Long-term capital (net) –2,610; Short-term capital (net) 376; *Overall balance* 3. Source: IMF, *Brunei Darussalam: Recent Economic Developments* (April 1999).

## EXTERNAL TRADE

**Principal Commodities** (B $ million, 1997, estimates): *Imports:* Food and live animals 352; Beverages and tobacco 62; Crude materials (inedible) except fuels 108; Chemicals 201; Basic manufactures 804; Machinery and transport equipment 1,229; Miscellaneous manufactured articles 364; Total (incl. others) 3,154. *Exports*: Mineral fuels and lubricants 3,620 (Crude petroleum 1,605, Petroleum products 110, Natural gas 1,860); Machinery and transport equipment 179; Miscellaneous manufactured articles 93; Total (incl. others) 3,973.

**Principal Trading Partners** (B $ million, 1997, estimates): *Imports:* Australia 83; People's Republic of China 78; France 37; Germany 189; Hong Kong 115; Indonesia 59; Italy 74, Japan 353; Republic of Korea 57; Malaysia 428; Netherlands 38; Singapore 807; Taiwan 42; Thailand 124; United Kingdom 192; USA 316; Total (incl. others) 3,154. *Exports:* Japan 2,108; Republic of Korea 721; Malaysia 111; Singapore 264; Taiwan 106; Thailand 446; USA 97; Total (incl. others) 3,973.

Source: IMF, *Brunei Darussalam: Recent Economic Developments* (April 1999).

### TRANSPORT

**Road Traffic** (registered vehicles, 1998): Private cars 170,247, Goods vehicles 17,091, Motorcycles and scooters 6,386, Buses and taxis 2,016, Others 4,432.

**Merchant Fleet** (displacement, '000 grt at 31 December): 368.9 in 1996; 368.6 in 1997; 361.9 in 1998. Source: Lloyd's Register of Shipping, *World Fleet Statistics*.

**International Sea-borne Shipping** (freight traffic, '000 metric tons, 1998): Goods loaded (excl. petroleum and gas) 25.9; Goods unloaded 1,195.2; Registered boats 249.

**Civil Aviation** (1998): Passenger arrivals 490,700, passenger departures 489,900; freight loaded 1,494.4 metric tons, freight unloaded 5,749.5 metric tons; mail loaded 24.6 metric tons, mail unloaded 175.2 metric tons.

### TOURISM

**Visitor Arrivals by Nationality** (1998): Australia 10,464; Cambodia 30,062; Japan 6,639; Malaysia 789,093; Nepal 5,939; Philippines 30,751; Singapore 23,718; Thailand 8,751; United Kingdom 31,500; USA 5,806; Total (incl. others) 964,080 (Source: Ministry of Industry and Primary Resources, Bandar Seri Begawan).

**Tourist Receipts** (US $ million): 36 in 1994; 37 in 1995; 38 in 1996 (Source: World Tourism Organization, *Yearbook of Tourism Statistics*).

### COMMUNICATIONS MEDIA

**Radio Receivers** (1998, estimate): 329,000 in use.

**Television Receivers** (1998, estimate): 201,900 in use.

**Telephones** (1998): 79,800 direct exchange lines in use.

**Telefax Stations** (1995, estimate): 2,000 in use (Source: UN, *Statistical Yearbook*).

**Mobile Cellular Telephones** (1995): 35,881 subscribers (Source: UN, *Statistical Yearbook*).

**Book Production** (1990): 25 titles; 56,000 copies.

**Daily Newspaper** (1998): 1 (estimated circulation 12,000 copies per issue).

**Non-daily Newspapers** (1998): 3 (estimated combined circulation 63,000 copies per issue).

**Other Periodicals** (1998): 15 (estimated combined circulation 132,000 copies per issue).

### EDUCATION

(1998)

**Pre-primary and Primary:** 184 schools; 3,858 teachers; 58,548 pupils.

**General Secondary:** 38 schools; 2,636 teachers; 30,956 pupils.

**Teacher Training:** 1 college; 46 teachers; 568 pupils.

**Vocational**: 8 colleges; 470 teachers; 1,985 pupils.

**Higher Education**: 4 institutes (incl. 1 university); 370 teachers; 2,080 students.

# Directory

## The Constitution

Note: Certain sections of the Constitution relating to elections and the Legislative Council have been in abeyance since 1962.

A new Constitution was promulgated on 29 September 1959 (and amended significantly in 1971 and 1984). Under its provisions, sovereign authority is vested in the Sultan and Yang Di-Pertuan, who is assisted and advised by five Councils: the Religious Council, the Privy Council, the Council of Cabinet Ministers, the (inactive) Legislative Council and the Council of Succession. Power of appointment to the Councils is exercised by the Sultan.

The 1959 Constitution established the Chief Minister as the most senior official, with the British High Commissioner as adviser to the Government on all matters except those relating to Muslim and Malay customs.

In 1971 amendments were introduced reducing the power of the British Government, which retained responsibility for foreign affairs, while defence became the joint responsibility of both countries.

In 1984 further amendments were adopted as Brunei acceded to full independence and assumed responsibility for defence and foreign affairs.

### THE RELIGIOUS COUNCIL

In his capacity as head of the Islamic faith in Brunei, the Sultan and Yang Di-Pertuan is advised on all Islamic matters by the Religious Council, whose members are appointed by the Sultan and Yang Di-Pertuan.

### THE PRIVY COUNCIL

This Council, presided over by the Sultan and Yang Di-Pertuan, is to advise the Sultan on matters concerning the Royal prerogative of mercy, the amendment of the Constitution and the conferment of ranks, titles and honours.

### THE COUNCIL OF CABINET MINISTERS

Presided over by the Sultan and Yang Di-Pertuan, the Council of Cabinet Ministers considers all executive matters.

### THE LEGISLATIVE COUNCIL

The role of the Legislative Council is to scrutinize legislation. However, following political unrest in 1962, provisions of the Constitution relating, *inter alia*, to the Legislative Council were amended, and the Legislative Council has not met since 1984. In the absence of the Legislative Council, legislation is enacted by royal proclamation.

### THE COUNCIL OF SUCCESSION

Subject to the Constitution, this Council is to determine the succession to the throne, should the need arise.

The State is divided into four administrative districts, in each of which is a District Officer responsible to the Prime Minister and Minister of Home Affairs.

## The Government

### HEAD OF STATE

**Sultan and Yang Di-Pertuan:** HM Sultan Haji HASSANAL BOLKIAH (succeeded 4 October 1967; crowned 1 August 1968).

### COUNCIL OF CABINET MINISTERS

(January 2000)

**Prime Minister, Minister of Defence, of Finance and of Law:** HM Sultan Haji HASSANAL BOLKIAH.

**Minister of Foreign Affairs:** HRH Prince MOHAMAD BOLKIAH.

**Minister of Home Affairs and Special Adviser to the Prime Minister:** Pehin Dato' Haji ISA BIN Pehin Haji IBRAHIM.

**Minister of Education and Acting Minister of Health:** Pehin Dato' Haji ABDUL AZIZ BIN Pehin Haji UMAR.

**Minister of Industry and Primary Resources:** Dato' Haji ABDUL RAHMAN TAIB.

**Minister of Religious Affairs:** Pehin Dato' Dr Haji MOHAMAD ZAIN BIN Haji SERUDIN.

**Minister of Development:** Pengiran Dato' Dr Haji ISMAIL BIN Haji DAMIT.

**Minister of Culture, Youth and Sports:** Pehin Dato' Haji HUSSEIN BIN Pehin Haji MOHAMAD YOSOF.

**Minister of Communications:** Pehin Dato' Haji ZAKARIA BIN Haji SULEIMAN.

There are, in addition, eight deputy ministers.

### MINISTRIES

**Office of the Prime Minister** (Jabatan Perdana Menteri): Istana Nurul Iman, Bandar Seri Begawan BA 1000; tel. (2) 229988; fax (2) 241717; e-mail pro@jpm.gov.bn.

**Ministry of Communications** (Kementerian Perhubungan): Old Airport, Jalan Berakas, Bandar Seri Begawan 1150; tel. (2) 383838; fax (2) 380127.

**Ministry of Culture, Youth and Sports** (Kementerian Kebudayaan, Belia dan Sukan): Jalan Residency, Bandar Seri Begawan 1200; tel. (2) 240585; fax (2) 241620.

**Ministry of Defence** (Kementerian Pertahanan): Bolkiah Garrison, Bandar Seri Begawan BB 3510; tel. (2) 386000; fax (2) 382110.

**Ministry of Development** (Kementerian Pembangunan): Old Airport, Jalan Berakas, Bandar Seri Begawan 1190; tel. (2) 241911.

**Ministry of Education** (Kementerian Pendidikan): Old Airport, Jalan Berakas, Bandar Seri Begawan 1170; tel. (2) 244233; fax (2) 240250.

**Ministry of Finance** (Kementerian Kewangan): Bandar Seri Begawan 1130; tel. (2) 241991; fax (2) 226132.

**Ministry of Foreign Affairs** (Kementerian Hal Ehwal Luar Negeri): Jalan Subuk, Bandar Seri Begawan BD 2710; tel. (2) 261177; fax (2) 261709.

**Ministry of Health** (Kementerian Kesihatan): Old Airport, Jalan Berakas, Bandar Seri Begawan 1210; tel. (2) 226640; fax (2) 240980; e-mail moh2@brunet.bn.

**Ministry of Home Affairs** (Kementerian Hal Ehwal Dalam Negeri): Bandar Seri Begawan 1140; tel. (2) 223225.

**Ministry of Industry and Primary Resources** (Kementerian Perindustrian dan Sumber-sumber Utama): Jalan Menteri Besar, Bandar Seri Begawan 2069; tel. (2) 382822; fax (2) 244811.

**Ministry of Religious Affairs** (Kementerian Hal Ehwal Ugama): Jalan Menteri Besar, Jalan Berakas, Bandar Seri Begawan BB 3910; tel. (2) 382525; fax (2) 382330.

## Political Organizations

**Parti Perpaduan Kebangsaan Brunei—PPKB** (Brunei National Solidarity Party—BNSP): Bandar Seri Begawan; f. 1986, after split in PKDB (see below); ceased political activity in 1988, but re-emerged in 1995; Pres. HATTA ZAINAL ABIDIN.

Former political organizations included: **Parti Rakyat Brunei—PRB** (Brunei People's Party), banned in 1962, leaders are all in exile; **Barisan Kemerdeka'an Rakyat—BAKER** (People's Independence Front), f. 1966 but no longer active; **Parti Perpaduan Kebangsaan Rakyat Brunei—PERKARA** (Brunei People's National United Party), f. 1968 but no longer active, and **Parti Kebangsaan Demokratik Brunei—PKDB** (Brunei National Democratic Party—BNDP), f. 1985 and dissolved by government order in 1988.

## Diplomatic Representation

### EMBASSIES AND HIGH COMMISSIONS IN BRUNEI

**Australia:** Teck Guan Plaza, 4th Floor, Jalan Sultan, Bandar Seri Begawan 2085; tel. (2) 229435; fax (2) 221652; High Commissioner: DOUG CHESTER.

**Bangladesh:** AAR Villa, 5 Simpang 308, Kampong Lambak Kanan, Jalan Berakas, Bandar Seri Begawan BB 1714; tel. (2) 394716; fax (2) 394715; High Commissioner: MUHAMMAD MUMDAZ HUSSAIN.

**Canada:** Suite 51, 5th Floor, Britannia House, Jalan Cator, Bandar Seri Begawan BS 8811; tel. (2) 220043; fax (2) 220040; High Commissioner: GARDINER WILSON.

**China, People's Republic:** Lot 23966, Simpang 612, Kampong Salambigar, Jalan Muara, Bandar Seri Begawan 3895; tel. (2) 334164; Ambassador: WANG JIANLI.

**France:** Jalan Sultan Complex, Units 301–306, 3rd Floor, Jalan Sultan, Bandar Seri Begawan BS 8811; tel. (2) 220960; fax (2) 243373; e-mail france@brunet.bn; Ambassador: JEAN-PIERRE LAFOSSE.

**Germany:** Bangunan Yayasan Sultan Haji Hassanal Bolkiah, 2nd Floor, Jalan Pretty, Bandar Seri Begawan BS 8711; POB 3050, Bandar Seri Begawan BS 8711; tel. (2) 225547; fax (2) 225583; e-mail prgerman@brunet.bn; Ambassador: KLAUS PETER BRANDES.

**India:** Simpang 337, Lot 14034, Kampong Manggis, Jalan Muara, Bandar Seri Begawan BC 3515; tel. (2) 339947; fax (2) 339783; e-mail hicomind@pso.brunei.bn; High Commissioner: DINESH K. JAIN.

**Indonesia:** Simpang 528, Jalan Sungai Hanching Baru, off Jalan Muara, Bandar Seri Begawan 3890; tel. (2) 330180; fax (2) 330646; Ambassador: KOESNADI POEDJIWINARTO.

**Iran:** 19 Simpang 477, Kg. Sg. Hanching, Jalan Muara, BC 2115 Bandar Seri Begawan; tel. (2) 330021; fax (2) 331744; Ambassador: JAVAD ANSARI.

**Japan:** Kampong Mabohai, 1–3 Jalan Jawatan Dalam, Bandar Seri Begawan 2092; tel. (2) 229265; fax (2) 229481; Ambassador: SHIGENOBI YOSHIDA.

**Korea, Republic:** No. 9, Lot 21652, Kampong Beribi, Jalan Gadong, Bandar Seri Begawan 3188; POB 2169, Bandar Seri Begawan 1921; tel. (2) 650471; fax (2) 650299; Ambassador: SA BOO-SUNG.

**Laos:** Lot 1982, 11 Simpang, 480 Jalan Kebangsaan Lama, off Jalan Muara, Bandar Seri Begawan BC 4115; tel. (2) 345666; fax (2) 345888; Ambassador: Dr AMMONE SINGHAVONG.

**Malaysia:** 27–29 Simpang 396–39, Lot 9075, Kampong Sungai Akar, Jalan Kebangsaan, POB 2826, Bandar Seri Begawan BS 8675; tel. (2) 345652; fax (2) 345654; High Commissioner: WAN YUSOF EMBONG.

**Myanmar:** 14 Lot 2185/46292, Simpang 212, Jalan Rimba, Bandar Seri Begawan BE 3119; tel. (2) 450506; fax (2) 451008; Ambassador: U THAN TUN.

**Oman:** 35, Simpang 100, Kampong Pengkalan, Jalan Tungku Link, Gadong, Bandar Seri Begawan; tel. (2) 446953; fax (2) 449646; Ambassador: AHMAD BIN MOHAMMED AL-RIYAMI.

**Pakistan:** No. 5, Simpang 396/128, Kampong Sungai Akar, Jalan Kebangsaan, POB 3026, Bandar Seri Begawan; tel. (2) 339797; fax (2) 334990; High Commissioner: Maj.-Gen. (retd) IRSHAD ULLAH TARAR.

**Philippines:** Badiah Bldg, 4th–5th Floors, Mile 1, Jalan Tutong, Bandar Seri Begawan 1930; tel. (2) 241465; fax (2) 237707; Ambassador: RAMON TIROL.

**Saudi Arabia:** 1, Simpang 570, Kampong Salar, Muara, Bandar Seri Begawan BT 2528; tel. (2) 792821; fax (2) 792826; Ambassador: (vacant).

**Singapore:** RBA Plaza, 5th Floor, Jalan Sultan, Bandar Seri Begawan 2085; tel. (2) 227583; fax (2) 220957; High Commissioner: ANTHONY CH'NG CHYE TONG.

**Thailand:** No. 13, Simpang 29, Kampong Kiarong, Jalan Elia Fatimah, Bandar Seri Begawan 3186; tel. (2) 429653; fax (2) 421775; Ambassador: MAITRI CHULADUL.

**United Kingdom:** Block D, Bangunan Yayasan Sultan Haji Hassanal Bolkiah, 2nd Floor, Jalan Pretty, POB 2197, Bandar Seri Begawan 1921; tel. (2) 222231; fax (2) 226002; High Commissioner: STUART LAING.

**USA:** Teck Guan Plaza, 3rd Floor, Jalan Sultan, Bandar Seri Begawan 2085; tel. (2) 229670; fax (2) 225293; Ambassador: GLEN ROBERT RASE.

**Viet Nam:** Lot 13489, Jalan Manggis Dua, off Jalan Muara, Bandar Seri Begawan; tel. (2) 343167; fax (2) 343169; Ambassador: NGUYEN NGOC DIEN.

## Judicial System

### SUPREME COURT

The Supreme Court consists of the Court of Appeal and the High Court. Syariah (Shari'a) courts coexist with the Supreme Court and deal with Islamic laws.

**Supreme Court:** Km 1½, Jalan Tutong, Bandar Seri Begawan BA 1910; tel. (2) 225853; fax (2) 241984; e-mail supcourt@brunet.bn.

**Chief Registrar:** HAYATI SALLEH.

**The Court of Appeal:** composed of the President and two Commissioners appointed by the Sultan. The Court of Appeal considers criminal and civil appeals against the decisions of the High Court and the Intermediate Court. The Court of Appeal is the highest appellate court for criminal cases. In civil cases an appeal may be referred to the Judicial Committee of Her Majesty's Privy Council in London if all parties agree to do so before the hearing of the appeal in the Brunei Court of Appeal.

**President:** KUTLU TEKIN FUAD.

**The High Court:** composed of the Chief Justice and judges sworn in by the Sultan as Commissioners of the Supreme Court. In its appellate jurisdiction, the High Court considers appeals in criminal and civil matters against the decisions of the Subordinate Courts. The High Court has unlimited original jurisdiction in criminal and civil matters.

**Chief Justice:** Dato' Seri Paduka Sir DENYS TUDOR EMIL ROBERTS.

### OTHER COURTS

**Intermediate Courts:** have jurisdiction to try all offences other than those punishable by the death sentence and civil jurisdiction to try all actions and suits of a civil nature where the amount in dispute or value of the subject/matter does not exceed B $100,000.

**The Subordinate Courts:** presided over by the Chief Magistrate and magistrates, with limited original jurisdiction in civil and criminal matters and civil jurisdiction to try all actions and suits of civil nature where the amount in dispute does not exceed B $50,000 (for Chief Magistrate) and B $30,000 (for magistrates).

**Chief Magistrate:** HAIROLARNI Haji ABDUL MAJID.

**The Courts of Kathis:** deal solely with questions concerning Islamic religion, marriage and divorce. Appeals lie from these courts to the Sultan in the Religious Council.

**Chief Kathi:** Dato' Seri Setia Haji SALIM BIN Haji BESAR.

**Attorney-General:** Attorney-General's Chambers, Office of the Prime Minister, Bandar Seri Begawan 1160; tel. (2) 244872; fax (2) 241428; KIFRAWI BIN Dato' Paduka Haji KIFLI.

**Solicitor-General:** MAGDELENE CHONG.

# Religion

The official religion of Brunei is Islam, and the Sultan is head of the Islamic community. The majority of the Malay population are Muslims of the Shafi'is school of the Sunni sect; at the 1991 census Muslims accounted for 67.2% of the total population. The Chinese population is either Buddhist (accounting for 12.8% of the total population at the 1991 census), Confucianist, Daoist or Christian. Large numbers of the indigenous ethnic groups practise traditional animist forms of religion. The remainder of the population are mostly Christians, generally Roman Catholics, Anglicans or members of the American Methodist Church of Southern Asia. At the 1991 census Christians accounted for 10.0% of the total population.

### ISLAM

**Supreme Head of Islam:** Sultan and Yang Di-Pertuan.

### CHRISTIANITY

#### The Anglican Communion

Within the Church of the Province of South East Asia, Brunei forms part of the diocese of Kuching (Malaysia).

#### The Roman Catholic Church

Brunei became an apostolic prefecture on 21 November 1997; in that year an estimated 10.2% of the population were adherents.

**Prefect Apostolic:** Rev. CORNELIUS SIM, St John's Church, POB 53, Kuala Belait 6000; tel. (3) 334207; fax (3) 342817.

# The Press

### NEWSPAPERS

**Borneo Bulletin:** Locked Bag No. 2, MPC (Old Airport Rd, Berakas), Bandar Seri Begawan 3799; tel. (2) 451468; fax (2) 451461; f. 1953; daily; English; independent; owned by QAF Group; Editor CHARLES REX DE SILVA; circ. 25,000.

**Brunei Darussalam Newsletter:** Dept of Information, Prime Minister's Office, Istana Nurul Iman, Bandar Seri Begawan 1100; tel. (2) 229988; monthly; English; circ. 14,000.

**News Express:** Bandar Seri Begawan; f. 1999; daily; English; Propr PETER WONG; Eidtor-in-Chief R. NADESWARAN.

**Pelita Brunei:** Dept of Information, Prime Minister's Office, Istana Nurul Iman, Bandar Seri Begawan 1100; tel. (2) 229988; fax (2) 225942; f. 1956; weekly (Wed.); Malay; govt newspaper; distributed free; Editor TIMBANG BIN BAKAR; circ. 45,000.

**Salam:** c/o Brunei Shell Petroleum Co Sdn Bhd, Seria 7082; tel. (3) 4184; fax (3) 4189; f. 1953; monthly; Malay and English; distributed free to employees of the Brunei Shell Petroleum Co Sdn Bhd; circ. 9,200.

# Publishers

**Borneo Printers & Trading Sdn Bhd:** POB 2211, Bandar Seri Begawan BS 8674; tel. (2) 651387; fax (2) 654342.

**Brunei Press Sdn Bhd:** Lots 8 and 11, Perindustrian Beribi II, Gadong, Bandar Seri Begawan BE 1118; tel. (2) 451468; fax (2) 451460; e-mail brupress@jtb.brunet.bn; internet http://web3.asia1.com.sg/borneo; f. 1953; Gen. Man. REGGIE SEE.

**Capital Trading & Printing Pte Ltd:** POB 1089, Bandar Seri Begawan; tel. (2) 244541.

**Leong Bros:** 52 Jalan Bunga Kuning, POB 164, Seria; tel. (3) 22381.

**Offset Printing House:** POB 1111, Bandar Seri Begawan; tel. (2) 224477.

**The Star Press:** Bandar Seri Begawan; f. 1963; Man. F. W. ZIMMERMAN.

#### Government Publishing House

**Government Printer:** Government Printing Department, Office of the Prime Minister, Bandar Seri Begawan BB 3510; tel. (2) 382541; fax (2) 381141; e-mail info@printing.gov.bn; Dir WAHID Haji SALLEH.

# Broadcasting and Communications

### TELECOMMUNICATIONS

**DST Communications Sdn Bhd:** Block D, Yayasan Sultan Haji Hassanal Bolkiah Complex, Bandar Seri Begawan; tel. (2) 232323; mobile service provider.

**Jabatan Telecom Brunei** (Department of Telecommunications of Brunei): Ministry of Communications, Berakas, Bandar Seri Begawan 2051; tel. (2) 382382; fax (2) 382445; Dir of Telecommunications BUNTAR BIN OSMAN.

### BROADCASTING

#### Radio

**Radio Television Brunei (RTB):** Jalan Elizabeth II, Bandar Seri Begawan 2042; tel. (2) 243111; fax (2) 241882; e-mail rtbeng@brunet.bn; internet www.brunet.bn/gov/rtb/rtbmain.htm; f. 1957; five radio networks: four broadcasting in Malay, the other in English, Chinese (Mandarin) and Gurkhali; Dir Pengiran Dato' Paduka Haji BADARUDDIN BIN Pengiran Haji GHANI.

The British Forces Broadcasting Service (Military) broadcasts a 24-hour radio service to a limited area.

#### Television

**Radio Television Brunei (RTB):** Jalan Elizabeth II, Bandar Seri Begawan 2042; tel. (2) 243111; fax (2) 227204; f. 1957; programmes in Malay and English; a satellite service relays RTB television programmes to the South-East Asian region for nine hours per day; Dir Pengiran Dato' Paduka Haji BADARUDDIN BIN Pengiran Haji GHANI.

# Finance

### BANKING

The Department of Financial Services (Treasury), the Brunei Currency Board and the Brunei Investment Agency (see Government Agencies, below), under the Ministry of Finance, perform most of the functions of a central bank.

#### Commercial Banks

**Baiduri Bank Bhd:** 145 Jalan Pemancha, POB 2220, Bandar Seri Begawan BS 8674; tel (2) 233233; fax (2) 237575; Gen. Man. LUC ROUSSELET; 5 brs.

**Development Bank of Brunei Bhd:** RBA Plaza, 1st Floor, Jalan Sultan, POB 3080, Bandar Seri Begawan BS 8811; tel. (2) 233430; fax (2) 233429; f. 1995; Man. Dir Datuk Hajah URAI Pengiran ALI; 1 br.

**Islamic Bank of Brunei Bhd:** Lot 159, Bangunan IBB, Jalan Pemancha, POB 2725, Bandar Seri Begawan BS 8711; tel. (2) 235686; fax (2) 235722; f. 1981 as Island Development Bank; name changed from International Bank of Brunei Bhd to present name in January 1993; practises Islamic banking principles; Chair. Haji ABDUL RAHMAN BIN Haji ABDUL KARIM; Man. Dir Haji ZAINASALLEHEN BIN Haji MOHAMED TAHIR; 10 brs.

#### Foreign Banks

**Citibank NA** (USA): Darussalam Complex 12–15, Jalan Sultan, Bandar Seri Begawan BS 8811; tel. (2) 243983; fax (2) 237344; e-mail glen.rase@citicorp.com; Vice-Pres. and Country Head GLEN R. RASE; 1 br.

**The Hongkong and Shanghai Banking Corpn Ltd** (Hong Kong): Jalan Sultan, cnr Jalan Pemancha, Bandar Seri Begawan BS 8811; POB 59, Bandar Seri Begawan BS 8670; tel. (2) 242305; fax (2) 241316; e-mail hsbc@brunet.bn; internet www.hsbc.com; f. 1947; acquired assets of National Bank of Brunei in 1986; CEO STUART R. BANNISTER; 10 brs.

**Malayan Banking Bhd** (Malaysia): 148 Jalan Pemancha, Bandar Seri Begawan BS 8811; tel. (2) 242494; fax (2) 226101; f. 1960; Branch Man. BURHAN BIN LASA; 2 brs.

**Overseas Union Bank Ltd** (Singapore): Unit G5, RBA Plaza, Jalan Sultan, Bandar Seri Begawan BS 8811; POB 2218, Bandar Seri Begawan BS 8674; tel. (2) 225477; fax (2) 240792; f. 1973; Vice-Pres. and Man. SAN BENG; 1 br.

**Sime Bank Bhd (Malaysia):** Unit G02, Block D, Bangunan Yayasan Sultan Haji Hassanal Bolkiah, Ground Floor, Jalan Pretty, Bandar Seri Begawan BS 8711; tel. (2) 222515; fax (2) 237487; fmrly

United Malayan Banking Corpn Bhd; Branch Man. SHAFIK YUSSOF; 1 br.

**Standard Chartered Bank** (United Kingdom): 51–55 Jalan Sultan, Bandar Seri Begawan BS 8811; POB 186, Bandar Seri Begawan BS 8670; tel. (2) 242386; fax (2) 242390; f. 1958; CEO DAVID KNIGHT; 10 brs.

### INSURANCE

In 1998 there were 18 general, three life and two composite (takaful) insurance companies operating in Brunei, including:

#### General Companies

**AGF Insurance (S) Pte Ltd:** c/o A&S Associates Sdn Bhd, Bangunan Gadong Properties, 03-01, Jalan Gadong, Bandar Seri Begawan BE 4119; tel. (2) 420766; fax (2) 440279; Man. SEBASTIAN TAN.

**The Asia Insurance Co Ltd:** 04A, Bangunan Gadong Properties, 1st Floor, Jalan Gadong, Bandar Seri Begawan BE 4119; tel. (2) 443663; fax (2) 443664; Man. DAVID WONG KOK MING.

**BALGI Insurance (B) Sdn Bhd:** Unit 13, Kompleks Haji Tahir II, 1st Floor, Jalan Gadong, Bandar Seri Begawan BE 4119; tel. (2) 422736; fax (2) 445204; Man. Dir PATRICK SIM SONG JUAY.

**Borneo Insurance Sdn Bhd:** Unit 103, Bangunan Kambang Pasang, Km 2, Jalan Gadong, Bandar Seri Begawan BE 4119; tel. (2) 420550; fax (2) 428550; Man. LIM TECK LEE.

**Citystate Insurance Pte Ltd:** c/o Dominic Choong & Sons, Bangunan Guru-Guru Melayu Brunei, 3rd Floor, Jalan Kianggeh, Bandar Seri Begawan BS 8711; tel. (2) 242361; fax (2) 226203; Man. BETTY CHOONG.

**Commercial Union Assurance (M) Sdn Bhd:** c/o Jasra Harrisons Sdn Bhd, Jalan McArthur, cnr Jalan Kianggeh, Bandar Seri Begawan BS 8711; tel. (2) 242361; fax (2) 226203; Man. WHITTY LIM.

**Cosmic Insurance Corpn Sdn Bhd:** Block J, Unit 11, Abdul Razak Complex, 1st Floor, Jalan Gadong, Bandar Seri Begawan BE 3919; tel. (2) 427112; fax (2) 427114; Man. RONNIE WONG.

**General Accident Fire & Life Assurance Corpn Ltd:** Unit 311, 3rd Floor, Mohamad Yussof Complex, Km 4, Jalan Tutong, Bandar Seri Begawan BA 2111; tel. (2) 223632; fax (2) 220965; Man. DOREEN CHUA.

**GRE Insurance (B) Sdn Bhd:** Unit 608, 6th Floor, Jalan Sultan Complex, 51-55 Jalan Sultan, Bandar Seri Begawan BS 8811; tel. (2) 226138; fax (2) 243474; Man. MOK HAI TONG.

**ING General Insurance International NV:** Shop Lot 86, 2nd Floor, Jalan Bunga Raya, Kuala Belait 6082; tel. (3) 335338; fax (3) 335338; Man. SHERRY SOON PECK ENG.

**MBA Insurance Co Sdn Bhd:** 7 Bangunan Hasbullah I, 1st Floor, Km 4, Jalan Gadong, Bandar Seri Begawan BE 3519; tel. (2) 441535; fax (2) 441534; Man. CHEAH LYE CHONG.

**Motor and General Insurance Sdn Bhd:** 6 Bangunan Hasbullah II, Km 4, Jalan Gadong, Bandar Seri Begawan BE 3919; tel. (2) 440797; fax (2) 420336; Man. Dir Haji ABDUL AZIZ BIN ABDUL LATIF.

**National Insurance Co Bhd:** Unit 604-606, Jalan Sultan Complex, 6th Floor, 51-55 Jalan Sultan, Bandar Seri Begawan BS 8811; tel. (2) 227493; fax (2) 227495; Man. Dir TIMOTHY ONG.

**The Royal Insurance (Global) Ltd:** c/o H C Lau & Sons, Khoon Foh Bldg, Bangunan Maju, Jalan Bunga Raya, Kuala Belait KA 1131; tel. (3) 334599; fax (3) 334671; Gen. Man. TOMMY LEONG TONG KAW.

**Sime AXA Assurance Bhd:** No 9, Bangunan Haji Mohd Salleh Simpang 103, 1st Floor, Jalan Gadong, Bandar Seri Begawan BE 4119; tel. (2) 443393; fax (2) 427451; Man. ROBERT LAI CHIN YIN.

**South East Asia Insurance (B) Sdn Bhd:** Unit 2, Block A, Abdul Razak Complex, 1st Floor, Jalan Gadong, Bandar Seri Begawan BE 3919; tel. (2) 443842; fax (2) 420860; Man. BILLINGS TEO.

**Standard Insurance (B) Sdn Bhd:** 11 Bangunan Hasbullah II, Ground Floor, Bandar Seri Begawan BE 3919; tel. and fax (2) 445348; Man. PAUL KONG.

**Winterthur Insurance (Far East) Pte Ltd:** c/o Borneo Co (B) Sdn Bhd, Lot 9771, Km 3½, Jalan Gadong, Bandar Seri Begawan BE 4119; tel. (2) 422561; fax (2) 424352; Man. HII CHANG WOO.

#### Life Companies

**American International Assurance Co Ltd:** Unit 509A, Wisma Jaya Building, 5th Floor, No 85/94, Jalan Pemancha, Bandar Seri Begawan BS 8511; tel. (2) 239112; fax (2) 221667; Man. PHILIP TAN.

**The Asia Life Assurance Society Ltd:** Unit 2, Block D, Abdul Razak Complex, Gadong, Bandar Seri Begawan; tel. (2) 8716189; fax (2) 225515; Exec. Officer PATRICIA CHIN YUNG YIN.

**The Great Eastern Life Assurance Co Ltd:** Suite 1, Badi'ah Complex, 2nd Floor, Jalan Tutong, Bandar Seri Begawan BA 2111; tel. (2) 243792; fax (2) 225754; Man. HELEN YEO.

#### Takaful (Composite Insurance) Companies

**Syarikat Insurans Islam TAIB Sdn Bhd:** Bangunan Pusat Komersil dan Perdagangan Bumiputera, Ground Floor, Jalan Cator, Bandar Seri Begawan BS 8811; tel. (2) 237724; fax (2) 237729; Man. Dir Haji MOHAMED ROSELAN BIN Haji MOHAMED DAUD.

**Takaful IBB Bhd:** Unit 5, Block A, Kiarong Complex, Lebuhraya Sultan Hassanal Bolkiah, Bandar Seri Begawan BE 1318; tel. (2) 451803; fax (2) 451808; Man. Dir Haji MUSIB Haji MOHD YUSOF.

## Trade and Industry

Trade in Brunei is largely conducted by Malay and Chinese agency houses and merchants.

### GOVERNMENT AGENCIES

**Brunei Currency Board:** c/o Ministry of Finance, Secretariat Bldg, POB 660, Bandar Seri Begawan BS 8670; tel. (2) 222095; fax (2) 241559; e-mail bcb@brunet.bn; f. 1967; maintains control of currency circulation; Dir Dato' YAAKUB BIN ABU BAKAR.

**Brunei Investment Agency:** Ministry of Finance, Bandar Seri Begawan; Chair. Pehin Dato' Haji ABDUL AZIZ BIN Pehin Haji UMAR.

**Brunei Oil and Gas Authority:** Bandar Seri Begawan; f. 1993 to oversee the hydrocarbons sector; Chair. Minister of Finance.

### DEVELOPMENT ORGANIZATIONS

**Brunei Industrial Development Authority (BINA):** Ministry of Industry and Primary Resources, Jalan Gadong, BE 1118 Bandar Seri Begawan; tel. (2) 444100; fax (2) 423300; e-mail binal1@brunet.bn; f. 1996.

**Brunei Islamic Trust Fund (Tabung Amanah Islam Brunei):** Bandar Seri Begawan; f. 1991; promotes trade and industry.

**Semaun Holdings Sdn Bhd:** Unit 2.02, Block D, 2nd Floor, Yayasan Sultan Haji Hassanal Bolkiah Complex, Jalan Pretty, Bandar Seri Begawan BS 8711; tel. (2) 232950; e-mail semaun@brunet.bn; internet www.semaun.gov.bn; promotes industrial and commercial development through direct investment in key industrial sectors; 100% govt-owned; the board of directors is composed of ministers and senior govt officials; Chair. Minister of Industry and Primary Resources; Man. Dir Haji KAMIS Haji TAMIN (acting).

### CHAMBERS OF COMMERCE

**Brunei Darussalam International Chamber of Commerce and Industry:** POB 2246, Bandar Seri Begawan 1922; tel. (2) 236601; fax (2) 228389; Chair. SULAIMAN Haji AHAI; Sec. Haji SHAZALI BIN Dato' Haji SULAIMAN; 108 mems.

**Brunei Malay Chamber of Commerce and Industry:** Bangunan Guru-Guru Melayu Brunei, Suite 301, 2nd Floor, Jalan Kianggeh, Bandar Seri Begawan 1910; tel. (2) 227297; fax (2) 227298; f. 1964; Pres. Dato' A. A. HAPIDZ; 160 mems.

**Chinese Chamber of Commerce:** Chinese Chamber of Commerce Bldg, 72 Jalan Roberts, Bandar Seri Begawan 2085; POB 281, Bandar Seri Begawan 1902; tel. (2) 235494; fax (2) 235492; Chair. LIM ENG MING.

**National Chamber of Commerce and Industry of Brunei Darussalam:** Rm 201, Bangunan Guru-Guru Melayu Brunei, Jalan Kianggeh, Bandar Seri Begawan 2086; POB 1099, Bandar Seri Begawan 1910; tel. (2) 227297; fax (2) 227298.

### HYDROCARBON COMPANIES

**Brunei LNG Sdn Bhd:** Lumut 7380, Seria; tel. (3) 378125; fax (3) 236919; f. 1969; natural gas liquefaction; owned jointly by the Brunei Govt, Shell and Mitsubishi Corpn; operates LNG plant at Lumut, which has a capacity of 7.2m. tons per year; merged with Brunei Coldgas Sdn Bhd in 1995; Man. H. A. W. HAMDILLAH.

**Brunei Shell Marketing Co Bhd:** Maya Puri Bldg, 36/37 Jalan Sultan, POB 385, Bandar Seri Begawan; tel. (2) 25739; fax (2) 240470; f. 1978 (from the Shell Marketing Co of Brunei Ltd), when the Govt became equal partner with Shell; markets petroleum and chemical products throughout Brunei; Marketing Man. HAMIDON Haji ABD LATIF.

**Brunei Shell Petroleum Co Sdn Bhd:** Seria 7082; tel. (3) 73999; fax (3) 72883; f. 1957; the largest industrial concern in the country; 50% state holding; petroleum output 150,000 barrels per day (1989); Man. Dir GEORGE INNES.

### TRADE UNIONS

**Brunei Government Junior Officers' Union:** Bandar Seri Begawan; tel. (2) 241911; Pres. Haji ALI BIN Haji NASAR; Gen. Sec. Haji OMARALI BIN Haji MOHIDDIN.

**Brunei Government Medical and Health Workers' Union:** Bandar Seri Begawan; Pres. Pengiran Haji MOHIDDIN BIN Pengiran TAJUDDIN; Gen. Sec. HANAFI BIN ANAI.

**Brunei Oilfield Workers' Union:** XDR/11, BSP Co Sdn Bhd, Seria KB 3534; f. 1964; 470 mems; Pres. SUHAINI Haji OTHMAN; Sec.-Gen. ABU TALIB BIN Haji MOHAMAD.

**Royal Brunei Custom Department Staff Union:** Badan Sukan dan Kebajikan Kastam, Royal Brunei Customs and Excise, Kuala Belait KA 1131; tel. (3) 334248; fax (3) 334626; Chair. Haji MOHD DELI BAKAR; Sec. HAMZAH Haji ABD. HAMID.

# Transport

### RAILWAYS

There are no public railways in Brunei. The Brunei Shell Petroleum Co Sdn Bhd maintains a 19.3-km section of light railway between Seria and Badas.

### ROADS

In 1995 there were an estimated 2,469.6 km of roads in Brunei (2,693.4 km in 1997), comprising 1,678.7 km with a bituminous or concrete surface, 593.8 km surfaced with gravel and 197.1 km passable only in dry conditions. The main highway connects Bandar Seri Begawan, Tutong and Kuala Belait. A 59-km coastal road links Muara and Tutong.

**Land Transport Department:** Ministry of Communications, Km 4, Jalan Gadong, Bandar Seri Begawan; tel. (2) 452300; fax (2) 424775; Dir Haji HAMIDON BIN Haji MOHD TAHIR.

### SHIPPING

Most sea traffic is handled by a deep-water port at Muara, 28 km from the capital, which has a 611-m wharf and a draught of 8 m. The port has a container terminal, warehousing, freezer facilities and cement silos. The original, smaller port at Bandar Seri Begawan itself is mainly used for local river-going vessels, for vessels to Malaysian ports in Sabah and Sarawak and for vessels under 30 m in length. There is a port at Kuala Belait, which takes shallow-draught vessels and serves mainly the Shell petroleum field and Seria. Owing to the shallow waters at Seria, tankers are unable to come up to the shore to load, and crude petroleum from the oil terminal is pumped through an underwater loading line to a single buoy mooring, to which the tankers are moored. At Lumut there is a 4.5-km jetty for liquefied natural gas (LNG) carriers.

Four main rivers, with numerous tributaries, are an important means of communication in the interior, and boats or water taxis the main form of transport for most residents of the water villages. Larger water taxis operate daily to the Temburong district.

**Bee Seng Shipping Co:** 7, Block D, Sufri Complex, Km 2, Jalan Tutong, POB 92, Bandar Seri Begawan; tel. (2) 220033; fax (2) 224495.

**Belait Shipping Co (B) Sdn Bhd:** B1, 2nd Floor, 94 Jalan McKerron, Kuala Belait 6081; POB 632, Kuala Belait; tel. (3) 335418; fax (3) 330239; f. 1977; Man. Dir Haji FATIMAH BINTE Haji ABDUL AZIZ.

**Brunei Shell Tankers Sdn Bhd:** Seria KB 3534; tel. (3) 373999; f. 1986; vessels operated by Shell Tankers (UK) Ltd; Man. Dir JOHN DARLEY.

**Harper Wira Sdn Bhd:** B2 Bangunan Haji Mohd Yussof, Jalan Gadong, Bandar Seri Begawan 3188; tel. (2) 448529; fax (2) 448529.

**Inchcape Borneo:** Bangunan Inchcape Borneo, Km 4, Jalan Gadong, Bandar Seri Begawan; tel. (2) 422561; fax (2) 424352; f. 1856; Dir LO FAN KEE.

**New Island Shipping:** Unit 5, 1st Floor, Block C, Kiarong Complex, Jalan Kiarong, Bandar Seri Begawan 3186; POB 850, Bandar Seri Begawan 1908; tel. (2) 451800; fax (2) 451480; f. 1975; Chair. TAN KOK VOON; Man. JIMMY VOON.

**Pansar Co Sdn Bhd:** Muara Port; tel. (2) 445246; fax (2) 445247.

**Seatrade Shipping Co:** Muara Port; tel. (2) 421457; fax (2) 421453.

**Silver Line (B) Sdn Bhd:** Muara Port; tel. (2) 445069; fax (2) 430276.

**Wei Tat Shipping and Trading Co:** Mile 4½, Jalan Tutong, POB 103, Bandar Seri Begawan; tel. 65215.

### CIVIL AVIATION

There is an international airport near Bandar Seri Begawan, which can handle up to 1.5m. passengers and 50,000 metric tons of cargo a year. The Brunei Shell Petroleum Co Sdn Bhd operates a private airfield at Anduki for helicopter services.

**Department of Civil Aviation:** Brunei International Airport, Bandar Seri Begawan BB 2513; tel. (2) 330142; fax (2) 331706; Dir Haji KASIM BIN Haji LATIP.

**Royal Brunei Airlines Ltd:** RBA Plaza, POB 737, Bandar Seri Begawan 1907; tel. (2) 240500; fax (2) 244737; f. 1974; operates services within the Far East and to the Middle East, Australasia and Europe; Chair. (vacant); Man. Dir (vacant).

# Tourism

Tourist attractions in Brunei include the flora and fauna of the rainforest and the national parks, as well as mosques and water villages. There were 964,080 foreign visitor arrivals (including same-day visitors) in 1998. In 1996 international tourist receipts totalled US $38m. The year 2001 has been designated 'Visit Brunei Year'.

**Brunei Tourism:** c/o Ministry of Industry and Primary Resources, Jalan Menteri Besar, Bandar Seri Begawan BB 3910; tel. (2) 382822; fax (2) 383811; Man. Sheikh JAMALUDDIN BIN Sheikh MOHAMED.

# BULGARIA

## Introductory Survey

### Location, Climate, Language, Religion, Flag, Capital

The Republic of Bulgaria lies in the eastern Balkans, in south-eastern Europe. It is bounded by Romania to the north, by Turkey and Greece to the south, by Yugoslavia (Serbia) to the west and by the former Yugoslav republic of Macedonia to the south-west. The country has an eastern coastline on the Black Sea. The climate is one of fairly sharp contrasts between winter and summer. Temperatures in Sofia are generally between −5°C (23°F) and 28°C (82°F). The official language is Bulgarian, a member of the Slavonic group, written in the Cyrillic alphabet. Minority languages include Turkish and Macedonian. The majority of the population are Christian, most of whom adhere to the Bulgarian Orthodox Church, while there is a substantial minority of Muslims. The national flag (proportions 3 by 2) has three equal horizontal stripes, of white, green and red. The capital is Sofia.

### Recent History

After almost 500 years of Ottoman rule, Bulgaria declared itself an independent kingdom in 1908. In both the First and Second World Wars Bulgaria allied itself with Germany, and in 1941 joined in the occupation of Yugoslavia. Soviet troops occupied Bulgaria in 1944. In September of that year the Fatherland Front, a left-wing alliance formed in 1942, seized power, with help from the USSR, and installed a Government, led by Kimon Georgiev. In September 1946 the monarchy was abolished, following a popular referendum, and a republic was proclaimed. The first post-war election was held in October, when the Fatherland Front received 70.8% of the votes and won 364 seats, of which 277 were held by the Bulgarian Communist Party (BCP), in the 465-member National Assembly. In November Georgi Dimitrov, the First Secretary of the BCP and a veteran international revolutionary, became Chairman of the Council of Ministers (Prime Minister) in a Government that comprised members of the Fatherland Front. All opposition parties were abolished, and a new Constitution, based on the Soviet model, was adopted in December 1947, when Bulgaria was designated a People's Republic. Dimitrov was replaced as Prime Minister by Vasil Kolarov in March 1949, but remained leader of the BCP until his death in July. His successor as party leader, Vulko Chervenkov, became Prime Minister in February 1950.

Todor Zhivkov succeeded Chervenkov as leader of the BCP in March 1954, although the latter remained Prime Minister until April 1956, when he was replaced by Anton Yugov. Following an ideological struggle within the BCP, Zhivkov became Prime Minister in November 1962. In May 1971 a new Constitution was adopted, and in July Zhivkov relinquished his position as Prime Minister to become the first President of the newly-formed State Council. He was re-elected in 1976, 1981 and 1986. At the twelfth BCP Congress, held in March and April 1981, the party's leader was restyled General Secretary. In June, following elections to the National Assembly, a new Government was formed, headed by Grisha Filipov, a member of the BCP's Political Bureau, succeeding Stanko Todorov, who had been Prime Minister since 1971. In March 1986 Filipov was replaced in this post by Georgi Atanasov, a former Vice-President of the State Council.

In local elections, held in March 1988, the nomination of candidates other than those endorsed by the BCP was permitted for the first time. Candidates presented by independent public organizations and workers' collectives obtained about one-quarter of the total votes cast. At a plenum of the BCP, held in July 1988, several prominent proponents of the Soviet-style programme of reform were dismissed from office.

On 10 November 1989 Zhivkov was unexpectedly removed from his post of General Secretary of the BCP (which he had held for 35 years) and from the Political Bureau. He was replaced as General Secretary by Petur Mladenov, who had been the Minister of Foreign Affairs since 1971 and a member of the BCP's Political Bureau since 1977. Mladenov also replaced Zhivkov as President of the State Council (while resigning as Minister of Foreign Affairs). In mid-November 1989 the National Assembly voted for the abolition of part of the penal code prohibiting 'anti-State propaganda', and for the granting of an amnesty to persons who had been convicted under the code's provisions. Zhivkov was subsequently denounced by the BCP and divested of his party membership, and an investigation into the extent of corruption during his tenure of power was initiated. In 1990 Zhivkov was arrested on charges of embezzlement of state funds.

In early December 1989 Angel Dimitrov became the new leader of the Bulgarian Agrarian People's Union (BAPU, the sole legal political party apart from the BCP, with which it was originally allied); the BAPU was subsequently reconstituted as an independent opposition party. In mid-December the BCP proposed amendments to the Constitution and the adoption of a new electoral law that would permit free and democratic elections to be held in the second quarter of 1990. In January 1990 the National Assembly voted overwhelmingly to remove from the Constitution the article guaranteeing the BCP's dominant role in society. It also approved legislation permitting citizens to form independent groups and to stage demonstrations.

A series of discussions regarding political and economic reforms was initiated in early January 1990 between the BCP, the BAPU and the Union of Democratic Forces (UDF), a co-ordinating organization (established in December 1989) which comprised several dissident and independent groups, including Ecoglasnost and the Podkrepa (Support) Trade Union Confederation. In early February the BCP adopted a new manifesto, pledging the party's commitment to extensive political and economic reforms, the separation of party and state, and the introduction of a multi-party system. It was stressed, however, that the BCP would retain its Marxist orientation. The party's Central Committee was replaced by a Supreme Council, chaired by Aleksandur Lilov, who was formerly head of the BCP's ideology department and who had been expelled from the party in 1983 for criticism of Zhivkov. The Political Bureau and Secretariat of the Central Committee were replaced by the Presidium of the Supreme Council, also with Lilov as Chairman. Mladenov (who remained as President of the State Council) proposed the formation of an interim coalition government, pending elections to the National Assembly (which were subsequently scheduled for June 1990). The UDF and the BAPU, however, rejected Mladenov's invitation to participate in such a coalition. Accordingly, the new Council of Ministers, which was appointed on 8 February 1990, was composed solely of BCP members, chaired by Andrei Lukanov, the former Minister of Foreign Economic Relations, who was regarded as an advocate of reform.

There was further unrest in mid-February 1990, when an estimated 200,000 supporters of the UDF gathered in Sofia to demand the end of BCP rule. Following discussions on reform in late March, with the participation of the BAPU and other political and public organizations, it was finally agreed that Mladenov was to be re-elected as President, pending elections to the National Assembly in June and the subsequent approval of a new constitution. The participants in the talks also decided to dissolve the State Council. In early April the National Assembly adopted an electoral law, together with legislation that provided for political pluralism, and guaranteed the right to form political parties. Also in early April the BCP voted overwhelmingly to rename itself the Bulgarian Socialist Party (BSP).

Following an electoral campaign which was marred by acts of intimidation and violence, elections to the 400-member Grand National Assembly were held in two rounds, on 10 and 17 June 1990. The BSP won 211 seats, but failed to gain the two-thirds majority of seats in the legislature necessary to secure support for the approval of constitutional and economic reforms. The UDF, which won the majority of votes in urban areas, obtained 144 seats in the Assembly. The Movement for Rights and Freedoms (MRF), which had been established earlier in 1990 to represent the country's Muslim minority, won a large percentage of the votes in areas populated by ethnic Turks, and secured 23 seats. The BAPU won 16 seats in the legislature, considerably fewer than had been expected. The UDF, after initial protests against alleged electoral fraud, accepted the validity of the result, although it again rejected the BSP's invitation to join a coalition government.

In July 1990 Mladenov announced his resignation as President, following a campaign of protests and strikes, led by students. Zhelyu Zhelev, the Chairman of the UDF, was elected to replace him in early August. Zhelev was succeeded as Chairman of the UDF by Petur Beron, hitherto the party's Secretary, and, following Beron's resignation in December, by Filip Dimitrov, a lawyer and the Vice-President of the Green Party.

Anti-Government demonstrations continued in late 1990, prompted, in particular, by the severe deterioration in the economy, which had resulted in widespread shortages of food and fuel. In October Lukanov proposed that the Grand National Assembly approve a programme of extensive economic reforms. The UDF (which held more than one-third of the seats in the legislature) refused to support the reforms, and proceeded to organize rallies in many parts of Bulgaria to demand the resignation of Lukanov's Government.

In mid-November 1990 the Grand National Assembly voted to rename the country the Republic of Bulgaria, and voted to remove from the national flag the state emblem, which included communist symbols.

Increasing division between conservative and reformist elements within the BSP became manifest in early November 1990, when 16 BSP delegates to the Grand National Assembly announced their decision to form a separate parliamentary group, as a result of which the party no longer held an absolute majority in the legislature. A motion expressing 'no confidence' in the Government, proposed by the UDF in late November, was defeated by 201 votes to 159. However, following a four-day general strike organized by the Podkrepa Trade Union Confederation, Lukanov and his Government resigned at the end of the month. Subsequent discussions between representatives of all the political forces in the Grand National Assembly resulted in the formation of a new 'government of national consensus' in mid-December, comprising members of the BSP, the UDF, the BAPU and four independents. Dimitur Popov, a lawyer with no party affiliation, had been elected in early December to chair the new Council of Ministers.

The new Constitution was adopted by the Grand National Assembly in mid-July 1991. The document stipulated, *inter alia,* a five-year residency qualification for presidential candidates, effectively disqualifying the candidacy of Simeon II, the pretender to the Bulgarian throne, who had lived in exile since 1946. Following its approval of the Constitution, the Grand National Assembly voted to dissolve itself, although it continued sessions in an interim capacity pending legislative elections. In the months preceding the elections, internal divisions occurred in many of the major parties, including the UDF. Nevertheless, at the elections to the new 240-seat National Assembly, which were held on 13 October, the majority UDF obtained the largest share of the vote (34.4%), defeating the BSP (which contested the election in alliance with a number of smaller parties) by a narrow margin of just over 1% of votes cast. The UDF won a total of 110 seats in the legislature, while the BSP obtained 106 seats. The ethnic Turkish MRF became the third strongest political force, securing a total of 24 seats. The new Council of Ministers, composed of UDF members and six independents, was announced in early November. Filip Dimitrov, the leader of the UDF, was elected Chairman of the new Government. A direct presidential election was held in January 1992. Following an inconclusive first round, a second ballot, involving the two leading candidates (the incumbent President Zhelev and Velko Valkanov, an independent supported by the BSP), took place. Zhelev was re-elected for a five-year term, receiving 53% of the votes cast.

In April 1992 a government programme of price liberalization, which had been adopted in early 1991 in fulfilment of IMF conditions, caused further trade union disaffection, and the main trade union federations, the Confederation of Independent Trade Unions in Bulgaria (CITUB) and Podkrepa, abandoned talks with the Government.

In March 1992 attempts by the Government to introduce legislation that would further reduce the power of former communists was opposed by the BSP with the support of President Zhelev, who maintained that the apparent restriction of political freedom could undermine Bulgaria's application for membership of the Council of Europe (see p. 158). In the same month a compromise solution was agreed by the Minister of Foreign Affairs, Stoyan Ganev, and President Zhelev, whereby the National Intelligence Service was eventually to be placed under the jurisdiction of the Government rather than the Office of the Presidency. In early April, despite BSP opposition, the Government adopted legislation restoring ownership of land and property that had been transferred to the state sector during 1947–62. This was followed in the same month by legislation approving the privatization of state-owned companies.

In May 1992 Dimitrov threatened to resign as Prime Minister unless the Minister of Defence, Dimitur Ludzhev, relinquished his post. This was widely believed to be indicative of a broader struggle for control of the increasingly factional UDF. Ludzhev resigned later that month, and Dimitrov implemented an extensive reorganization of the Council of Ministers. In July the former BCP Prime Minister, Lukanov (now a BSP deputy of the National Assembly), was arrested, prompting the BSP deputies to withdraw from a meeting of the National Assembly in protest. Legal proceedings were initiated against Lukanov and a further 60 senior officials (including two other former Prime Ministers, Grisha Filipov and Georgi Atanasov) on charges of misappropriating state funds. (Atanasov was officially pardoned by President Zhelev in August 1994 on the grounds of ill health.)

In mid-July 1992 there were further strikes, and miners were joined by other public-sector employees. Podkrepa continued to support the strike and to condemn the Government's economic policies. In early August the Chairman of Podkrepa, Konstantin Trenchev, was arrested with 37 others, and charged with incitement to destroy public property in 1990. Meanwhile, relations between President Zhelev and the UDF became increasingly strained. In late August 1992 Zhelev publicly criticized Dimitrov's Government and received support for his position from both the MRF and the CITUB. In September the UDF convened a national conference and agreed to initiate discussions with the President and the MRF, but reaffirmed its support for Dimitrov. In late September the MRF declared a lack of confidence in Dimitrov's leadership. At the end of October MRF and BSP deputies in the National Assembly defeated the Government by 121 votes to 111 in a motion of confidence, proposed by Dimitrov. The Government subsequently resigned.

In November 1992 President Zhelev invited Dimitrov (as the nominee of the party with the largest representation in the National Assembly) to form a new government. The MRF, however, declined to form a coalition with the UDF, and Dimitrov's nomination was thus defeated in the National Assembly. The BSP was then assigned a mandate to nominate a candidate for the premiership. President Zhelev, however, rejected the candidacy of the BSP nominee, Petur Boyadzhiev, on the grounds that he held dual nationality (Bulgarian and French) and his candidacy was thus disallowed under the terms of the Constitution. Following the failure of the UDF and the MRF to reach agreement for a coalition under the MRF mandate, in December the MRF nominated an academic, Prof. Lyuben Berov, hitherto an economic adviser to President Zhelev, to the office of Prime Minister. The UDF accused Berov of collaborating with the former communist regime and organized a large rally to protest against his candidacy, while threatening to expel members who voted in his favour in the National Assembly. In the event, the majority of UDF deputies abstained but Berov was approved as Prime Minister on 30 December by 124 votes to 25 in a secret ballot. Berov's proposed Council of Ministers, principally composed of 'experts' without party political allegiances, was also accepted by the National Assembly. On the same day, the BSP and the MRF voted in the National Assembly to discharge Lukanov from custody. It was widely speculated that BSP support for Berov's Government had been, in part, conditional on Lukanov's release.

In March 1993 internal divisions within the UDF became more apparent when a breakaway faction of the party formed a new organization, known as the New Union for Democracy (NUD). The UDF, in response to the formation of the pro-Berov NUD, intensified its campaign of opposition, claiming, in particular, that the Government was planning to reintroduce socialism. In May the former Speaker of the National Assembly, Stefan Savov, was injured by a policeman during a demonstration, organized by the UDF, outside the parliamentary building in Sofia; the UDF claimed that he had been attacked on government orders. In early June a UDF deputy, Edvin Sugarev, began a hunger strike to demand President Zhelev's resignation. In the same month large demonstrations were staged by the UDF in Sofia and several other cities to denounce Zhelev for allegedly attempting the restoration of communism and to demand immediate elections. The situation improved slightly later that month, when Sugarev ended his hunger strike. On 29 June, however, the Vice-President, Blaga Dimitrova, resigned from her post, claiming that she had been insufficiently consulted while in office. The crisis finally subsided when two votes expressing 'no confidence' in Berov's Government, which were proposed by the UDF in the National Assembly, proved unsuccessful. Political unrest continued, however, and in November the Berov administration survived another motion of 'no confidence', proposed by the UDF. In the same month Berov's National Security Adviser was dismissed from his post, and in December further allegations of government corruption were presented to the Chief Prosecutor.

In January 1994 Zhivkov was sentenced to seven years in prison for embezzlement of government funds. (In February 1996, however, the Supreme Court upheld his subsequent appeal against the sentence.) In mid-January the Minister of the Interior, Viktor Mihailov, resigned, following the accidental shooting of two policemen by their colleagues. In the following month the Berov Government survived a fifth motion of 'no confidence', proposed by the UDF in protest against the Government's apparent inability to control the dramatic increase in the crime rate. In early April Zhelev announced that he could no longer give his political support to Berov's administration, citing its failure to achieve certain objectives, such as the imposition of an accelerated privatization programme. Following the controversial introduction of value-added tax (VAT), unpopular rises in fuel prices and the dramatic fall of the lev, thousands of demonstrators protested in Sofia against government policies. In mid-May a proposal by Berov for the appointment of a new Council of Ministers was rejected by the National Assembly; it was claimed by certain political groups that Berov wished to install a BSP-dominated administration. Later that month Berov's Government survived a further vote of 'no confidence', again proposed by the UDF. In late May the Government narrowly won a vote of confidence presented in the National Assembly. The UDF deputies subsequently boycotted National Assembly sessions throughout June.

In late June 1994 the Government finally launched the delayed May privatization programme, whereby each Bulgarian citizen was offered a 500-leva voucher which could be invested either directly into state enterprises or into private investment funds. In early September, however, Berov's Government submitted its resignation, following increasing criticism of the poor organization of the privatization programme. Both the BSP and the UDF refused presidential mandates to form a new Government. In October President Zhelev dissolved the National Assembly and announced that a general election would take place on 18 December. Later in October Zhelev appointed an interim neutral Government, headed by Reneta Indzhova.

At the general election, which was held as scheduled on 18 December 1994, the BSP (in alliance, as the Democratic Left, with two small parties, the Aleksandur Stamboliyski Bulgarian Agrarian People's Union and the Ecoglasnost Political Club—the political wing of the Ecoglasnost National Movement) obtained an outright majority in the National Assembly, with 125 seats (43.5% of the total votes cast), while the UDF won 69 seats (24.2%). Other groups that gained more than the 4% of votes required for representation in the legislature were: the People's Union (an alliance of BAPU and the Democratic Party), the MRF and the Bulgarian Business Bloc (BBB). A new Government, headed by the Chairman of the BSP, Zhan Videnov, was appointed at the end of January 1995; the majority of the ministers were members of the BSP.

In February 1995 the National Assembly passed a bill that amended the 1992 property restitution law (see above), extending for a further three years the deadline by which certain properties had to be restored to their rightful owners. In March the National Assembly abolished a law, adopted by the UDF Government in 1992, prohibiting former communists from senior academic positions. In the same month the Government drafted a programme for mass privatization in 1995, which envisaged payment through a combination of cash, debt bonds and investment vouchers (the vouchers were made available from early January 1996). Mass demonstrations took place throughout March 1995, however, reflecting widespread dissatisfaction with government amendments to the Agricultural Land Tenure Act, on the grounds that they would restrict landowners' rights to dispose of their property and would encourage the restoration of communist-style collective farms. In late April President Zhelev exercised his right of veto against the highly unpopular amendments, which had been adopted by the National Assembly in mid-April; the President claimed that the amendments contravened the constitutional right of Bulgarian citizens to own private property. The case was subsequently examined by the Constitutional Court, which in June rejected the amendments as unconstitutional.

In late June 1995 the Government removed the heads of the state television and radio services and the Director-General of the national news agency; the opposition alleged that the dismissals represented an attempt by the BSP to control the state media. In August the Government also dismissed the Director of the Centre for Mass Privatization, Yosif Iliev, following a series of delays to the privatization process. In late September the Government survived a motion of 'no confidence' (by 130 votes to 102), which was introduced by the opposition in the National Assembly, in protest at the continued failure of Videnov's administration to control the rapid increase in levels of crime.

At municipal elections, which took place in late October and early November 1995, the ruling coalition won 195 of a total of 255 mayoralties, although the UDF secured the mayoralties in the country's three main cities. In mid-November President Zhelev announced that he would seek re-election in 1997.

On 10 January 1996 a further motion of 'no confidence' in the Videnov administration was proposed by the opposition, in protest at a severe shortage of grain, which had resulted from the Government's repeal of a ban on grain exports in July 1995. The motion was defeated, but the situation prompted the resignation of the Deputy Prime Minister and a further two ministers. In Febuary 1996 the MRF staged a demonstration in Sofia in protest at the annulment, owing to alleged irregularities, of the result of the municipal elections in the south-eastern town of Kurdzhali (where the MRF had narrowly secured a victory). In April, however, the Supreme Court upheld the election result. In May the Minister of the Interior resigned, following an incident in which three members of the security forces were killed by criminals. Meanwhile, a sharp devaluation of the lev (see Economic Affairs) resulted in further economic hardship, exacerbated by continuing shortages of grain. In June the UDF proposed a motion expressing 'no confidence' in the Government's management of the economy, which was, however, defeated by a large majority in the National Assembly.

In primary elections for a UDF presidential candidate, which were conducted in early June 1996, Petar Stoyanov, a lawyer and senior member of the opposition alliance, secured 66% of votes cast, defeating Zhelev. Zhelev subsequently announced that he would support Stoyanov's candidature for the presidency. In July the National Assembly scheduled the presidential election for 27 October. In the same month the Constitutional Court ruled that Georgi Pirinski, the candidate who had been nominated in June to contest the election on behalf of the BSP, was ineligible, on the grounds that he was not a Bulgarian citizen by birth, as stipulated in the Constitution. Pirinski (who had been considered to be the most popular of the nominated candidates) declared that political bias had influenced the decision, and initially insisted that he would contest the election. In September, following a ruling by the Supreme Court that confirmed the invalidity of Pirinski's candidature, the BSP selected the Minister of Culture, Ivan Marazov, as its presidential candidate; Marazov was to represent a newly-formed electoral alliance, known as Together for Bulgaria, which comprised the parties in the Democratic Left parliamentary coalition (the BSP, Aleksandur Stamboliyski and the Ecoglasnost Political Club).

In early October 1996 the former Prime Minister, Andrei Lukanov (who had remained an influential member of the BSP), was assassinated. Ensuing speculation regarding the motive for the killing focused, in particular, on Lukanov's critical stance towards the Videnov administration's slow implementation of economic reforms. Later that month CITUB and Podkrepa organized a demonstration in Sofia to demand the resignation of the Government. In the first round of the presidential election, which was contested by 14 political groups on 27 October (as scheduled), Stoyanov secured 44.1% of votes cast; Marazov received only 27.0% of the votes, while the candidate of the BBB, Georgi Ganchev, won 21.9%. Only 61% of the electorate voted in the second round of the presidential election, which took place on 3 November, reflecting increasing public disaffection with the Government's management of the critical economic situation. Stoyanov was elected to the presidency, with 59.7% of votes cast. Stoyanov (who was believed to favour Bulgaria's entry into NATO) subsequently announced that he was to establish a Council of National Salvation, which would devise measures to improve financial stability.

Following the election of Stoyanov, the political council of the UDF agreed to initiate a campaign to demand that parliamentary elections be conducted later that year (earlier than scheduled). The electoral defeat of the BSP in the presidential election aggravated existing divisions within the organization; in early November 1996 several senior members of the BSP accused Videnov of causing the party's unpopularity and demanded the resignation of the Government. However, a joint convention of the BSP and its allied parties subsequently rejected a motion of 'no confidence' in the Government. Later in November Pirinski, who was a leading opponent of Videnov within the BSP, submitted his resignation from the post of Minister of Foreign Affairs, on the grounds that the Government no longer commanded public support and that the party vote had failed to indicate sufficient confidence in Videnov.

In December 1996 the UDF staged a series of demonstrations to demand early legislative elections and the resignation of the Government. On 21 December, at an extraordinary congress of the BSP, Videnov unexpectedly tendered his resignation from the office of Prime Minister and the post of party leader. (The incumbent Council of Ministers was to remain in office, pending the formation of a new administration.) Georgi Purvanov, who was a supporter of Videnov, subsequently replaced him as Chairman of the BSP. At the end of December the National Assembly voted by a large majority to accept the resignation of Videnov's Government. In January 1997 the BSP designated the Minister of the Interior, Nikolai Dobrev, to replace Videnov as Prime Minister. The UDF, however, intensified its campaign of demonstrations; in early January an attempt by protesters to seize the parliamentary building was suppressed by security forces. Zhelev subsequently announced that he would not invite Dobrev to form a new government as expected. Later that month the UDF, with the support of Podkrepa, organized a series of one-hour strikes to demand early parliamentary elections. On 19 January Stoyanov was inaugurated as President. At the end of January the BSP accepted a proposal by Stoyanov that the party form a new government, pending legislative elections, which were expected to take place in the second half of 1997. In early February the BSP announced the appointment of a new Council of Ministers; following continued protests and strikes by supporters of the UDF, however, Dobrev agreed to relinquish the party's mandate to form a new government (owing to increasing concern that the disorder might escalate into civil conflict). The Consultative National Security Council adopted recommendations (which were approved by the National Assembly) that, in the absence of agreement between the political parties represented in the legislature on the formation of a government, the President should appoint an interim council of ministers, dissolve the incumbent National Assembly and schedule new legislative elections. Stoyanov subsequently nominated the mayor of Sofia, Stefan Sofianski, to the office of Prime Minister, and formed an interim Council of Ministers, pending elections, which were scheduled to be held on 19 April; the National Assembly was dissolved on 19 February. Following the resumption of negotiations between the new Government and the IMF, agreement was reached in March regarding the establishment of a currency control board, as a prerequisite to economic and financial stability. Later in March the interim Government announced that Videnov was to be charged with criminal negligence as a result of government policies that had caused the severe shortage of grain in 1995–96; the Minister of Agriculture in the Videnov administration and three of his deputies were also prosecuted.

At the elections to the National Assembly, which took place as scheduled on 19 April 1997, the UDF secured 137 seats, while the BSP (which again contested the elections in the Democratic Left alliance) obtained only 58 seats; the Alliance for National Salvation (a coalition comprising the MRF and other monarchist and centrist groups) won 19 seats, a newly-established left-wing organization, known as Euro-Left, gained 14 seats and the BBB 12 seats. Later in April the UDF formally nominated the party Chairman, Ivan Kostov, to the office of Prime Minister (subject to the approval of the National Assembly). At the first session of the new National Assembly, which was convened in early May, deputies adopted a seven-point declaration of national consensus, which had been proposed by the UDF; the stated policies included the implementation of economic reforms which had been agreed with the IMF, the acceleration of measures to restore agricultural land to rightful ownership, and support for Bulgaria's accession to the EU and NATO. (However, a number of the issues, particularly the proposed introduction of the currency control board in agreement with the IMF, were opposed by some groups in the National Assembly.) Later in May the National Assembly elected Kostov to the office of Prime Minister; only deputies belonging to the Democratic Left alliance opposed his nomination. The new Council of Ministers, which had been formed by Kostov, included five members of the outgoing interim administration.

Following its installation, the new Government replaced the President of the State Savings Bank. In June 1997 the National Assembly adopted legislation providing for the establishment of the currency control board, which was installed at the beginning of July. In a further effort to impose fiscal discipline, the Government replaced the senior officials of the Bulgarian National Bank; Svetoslav Gavriyski, who had served as Minister of Finance in the interim Council of Ministers, was appointed Governor. At the end of July the National Assembly voted in favour of declassifying security files on politicians and public officials, and adopted legislation to expedite the restoration of land to rightful ownership. In early September two parliamentary representatives of the BBB were expelled from the party after criticizing the leadership of Ganchev, who, they claimed, intended to establish links with the BSP; another deputy resigned in protest at their removal. The BBB was consequently obliged to dissolve its parliamentary group, which had been reduced to below the required minimum of 10 representatives. In October a government commission announced that 23 prominent public officials, including 14 members of the National Assembly, had been members of the security services of former communist governments. In early November, following protests from deputies belonging to the Democratic Left, the Constitutional Court ruled that the appointment of directors of the national radio and television stations by the National Assembly (rather than by an independent media council) was in contravention of the Constitution. In January 1998 the National Assembly rejected a motion expressing 'no confidence' in the Government, which had been proposed by Democratic Left deputies in protest at the Council of Ministers' policy on health care. In March Stoyanov replaced a senior army official, who (apparently with the support of many other army officers) had publicly opposed plans by the Government to reduce the size of the armed forces under structural reforms. The senior commanders of the armed forces were reorganized in May. At an annual congress of the BSP in the same month Purvanov was re-elected as Chairman of the party, obtaining 58% of the voters cast. In late September a Security Council, chaired by the Prime Minister, was established to advise on state security activities.

Local government elections took place on 16 and 23 October 1999: the UDF narrowly won, with 31.3% of votes cast (while the BSP secured 29.4%). In December Stoyanov accepted a reorganization of the Council of Ministers by Kostov.

Bulgaria maintained close links with other Eastern European countries through its membership of the Warsaw Pact and of the Council for Mutual Economic Assistance (CMEA). Following the political upheavals which took place in Eastern Europe in 1989 and 1990, both the Warsaw Pact and the CMEA were dissolved in mid-1991. Diplomatic relations with several Western nations were re-established in 1990 and 1991, and in mid-1992 Bulgaria became a member of the Council of Europe (see p. 158). In May 1994 Bulgaria was granted associate partnership status by the Western European Union (WEU—see p. 268). In June 1992 Bulgaria, together with 10 other countries (including six of the former Soviet republics), signed a pact to establish the Organization of the Black Sea Economic Co-operation (see p. 135), which envisaged the creation of a Black Sea economic zone that would complement the European Community (now European Union—EU, see p. 172). In 1996 Bulgaria submitted an official application for membership of the EU. In October of that year Bulgaria joined the World Trade Organization (see p. 274). Negotiations on Bulgaria's accession to the EU, which were conditional on the Government's fulfilment of certain criteria (see Economic Affairs), were due to begin in early 2000.

Bulgaria's establishment of formal relations with the former Yugoslav republic of Macedonia (FYRM) in January 1992 prompted harsh criticism from the Greek Government. Relations with Greece appeared to improve, however, after the visit of the Bulgarian Minister of Foreign Affairs to Athens in May 1992. In November 1993 the FYRM expressed its desire to establish full diplomatic relations with Bulgaria. In the following month Bulgaria announced that it was to open an embassy in the FYRM and relax border procedures between the two states.

In February 1999 Kostov and the Prime Minister of the FYRM, Ljubčo Georgievski, signed a declaration pledging that neither country had a territorial claim on the other. In March the Ministers of Defence of Bulgaria and the FYRM signed a joint declaration providing for increased military co-operation, including joint exercises and the supply of military equipment to the FYRM, in connection with the aim of both countries to join NATO. Public opposition in Bulgaria to the NATO air bombardment of Yugoslavia which commenced in late March 1999 (see chapter on Yugoslavia), increased, after a misdirected NATO missile damaged a private residence in the outskirts of Sofia in April. Nevertheless, the Bulgarian National Assembly approved a decision made by the Council of Ministers to allow NATO use of the country's airspace (despite opposition from the BSP). It was reported that public support for Bulgaria's proposed membership of NATO had declined in response to the bombardment.

Relations between Bulgaria and Russia improved in 1992, following the signing of co-operation agreements, and the visit of the Russian President, Boris Yeltsin, to Sofia in August of that year. Reciprocal visits by the premiers of Bulgaria and Russia in 1995 further improved relations between the two countries. In late 1996 a Russian parliamentary delegation visited Sofia to meet Bulgarian deputies; it was agreed that joint Bulgarian-Russian debates would be conducted on significant issues of mutual concern. In April 1998 the Bulgarian Government signed a significant agreement with the Russian national gas company, Gazprom, providing for the supply and transit of Russian gas (see Economic Affairs).

Relations with neighbouring Turkey have been intermittently strained since the mid-1980s, when the Zhivkov regime began a campaign of forced assimilation of Bulgaria's ethnic Turkish minority (which constitutes an estimated 10% of the total population). The ethnic Turks were forced to adopt Slavic names prior to the December 1985 census, and were banned from practising Islamic religious rites. In February 1988, on the eve of a conference of Ministers of Foreign Affairs of the six Balkan nations, Bulgaria and Turkey signed a protocol to further bilateral economic and social relations. However, the situation deteriorated in May 1989, when Bulgarian militia units violently suppressed demonstrations by an estimated 30,000 ethnic Turks in eastern Bulgaria against the continued assimilation campaign. In June more than 80,000 ethnic Turks were expelled from Bulgaria, although the Bulgarian authorities claimed that the Turks had chosen to settle in Turkey, following a relaxation in passport regulations to ease foreign travel. In response, the Turkish Government opened the border and declared its commitment to accepting all the ethnic Turks as refugees from Bulgaria. By mid-August an estimated 310,000 Bulgarian Turks had crossed into Turkey. In late August the Turkish Government, alarmed by the continued influx of refugees, closed the border. In the following month a substantial number of the Bulgarian Turks, disillusioned with conditions in Turkey, began to return to Bulgaria.

The Turkish Government repeatedly proposed that discussions with the Bulgarian Government be held, under the auspices of the UN High Commissioner for Refugees, to establish the rights of the Bulgarian Turks and to formulate a clear immigration policy. Finally, Bulgaria agreed to negotiations, and friendly relations between Bulgaria and Turkey had apparently been restored by late 1991. In March 1992 a bilateral defence agreement was signed. In May Prime Minister Dimitrov visited Turkey, and the two countries signed a treaty of friendship and co-operation.

Meanwhile, in December 1989, some 6,000 Pomaks (ethnic Bulgarian Muslims who form a community of about 300,000 people) held demonstrations to demand religious and cultural freedoms, as well as an official inquiry into alleged atrocities against Pomaks during Zhivkov's tenure of office. In January 1990 anti-Turkish demonstrations were held in the Kurdzhali district of southern Bulgaria, in protest at the Government's declared intention to restore civil and religious rights to the ethnic Turkish minority. Despite continuing demonstrations by Bulgarian nationalist protesters, in March the National Assembly approved legislation that permitted ethnic Turks and Pomaks to use their original Islamic names. This development was welcomed by the Turkish Government. Nevertheless, inter-ethnic disturbances continued, particulary in the Kurdzhali region, during 1990. Proposals in early 1991 to introduce the teaching of Turkish in schools in predominantly Turkish regions led to renewed inter-ethnic conflict. In November of that year the Government finally decreed that Turkish be taught as an optional subject four times weekly in the regions concerned, following which the MRF ended a boycott on school attendance, which it had imposed in mid-1991. By 1993 ethnic tensions had generally been contained in Bulgaria, although there were reports of some disturbances between ethnic Turks and ethnic Bulgarian Muslims in the south of the country in September. In July 1995 a visit by President Demirel of Turkey to Bulgaria, during which regional security and economic relations between the two countries were discussed, indicated a significant improvement in Bulgarian-Turkish relations. Following a visit to Bulgaria by the Turkish Minister of Foreign Affairs in May 1998, it was announced that a number of co-operation agreements had been signed. In June the National Assembly ratified an agreement demarcating the border between Bulgaria and Turkey (which had been signed during an official visit to Sofia by the Turkish Prime Minister, Mesut Yılmaz, in December 1997).

## Government

Legislative power is held by the unicameral National Assembly, comprising 240 members, who are elected for four years by universal adult suffrage. The President of the Republic (Head of State) is elected directly by the voters for a period of five years, and is also Supreme Commander-in-Chief of the Armed Forces. The Council of Ministers, the highest organ of state administration, is elected by the National Assembly. For local administration, Bulgaria comprises 29 regions (divided into a total of 259 municipalities).

## Defence

Military service is compulsory and lasts for 18 months. The total strength of the armed forces in August 1999 was 80,760 (including 49,800 conscripts), comprising an army of 43,400, an air force of 18,300, a navy of an estimated 5,260, 12,500 centrally-controlled staff and 1,300 Ministry of Defence staff. Paramilitary forces include an estimated 12,000 border guards, 18,000 railway and construction troops and 4,000 security police. The 2000 state budget proposals allocated 702,000m. leva to defence. Bulgaria joined NATO's 'partnership for peace' programme of military co-operation (see p. 228) in 1994. In late 1999 the Government announced plans to reduce the armed forces to number 45,000 by 2004.

## Economic Affairs

In 1997, according to estimates by the World Bank, Bulgaria's gross national product (GNP), measured at average 1995–97 prices, was US $9,750m., equivalent to $1,170 per head. During 1990–97, it was estimated, GNP per head decreased, in real terms, at an average annual rate of 2.0%. Over the same period the population decreased at an average rate of 0.7% per year. In 1998 GNP was estimated at $10,100m. ($1,230 per caput). According to the World Bank, Bulgaria's gross domestic product (GDP) declined, in real terms, by an average of 3.3% annually during 1990–97. According to official estimates, real GDP declined by 10.1% in 1996 and by 6.9% in 1997, but increased by 11.9% in 1998.

Agriculture (including forestry and fishing) contributed 26.2% of GDP in 1997. In that year the sector engaged 24.3% of the employed labour force. In 1990 private farming was legalized, and farmland was restituted, in its former physical boundaries, to former owners and their heirs. In 1996 privately-owned farms supplied 75.4% of total agricultural production. The principal crops are wheat, maize, barley, sunflower seeds, grapes, potatoes and tobacco. Bulgaria is a major exporter of wine. There is a large exportable surplus of processed agricultural products. During 1990–97, according to the World Bank, the real GDP of the agricultural sector declined at an average annual rate of 3.1%. According to official estimates, agricultural GDP declined by 7.4% in 1996, but rose by 26.2% in 1997, and by 8.0% in 1998.

Industry (including mining, manufacturing, construction and utilities) provided 29.4% of GDP and engaged 32.2% of the employed labour force in 1997. According to the World Bank, industrial GDP declined, in real terms, at an average annual rate of 5.5% in 1990–97. Industrial GDP declined, according to official estimates, by 11.8% in 1996 and by 13.1% in 1997, but increased by 19.5% in 1998.

In 1997 mining and quarrying engaged 1.9% of the employed labour force. Coal, iron ore, copper, manganese, lead and zinc are mined, while petroleum is extracted on the Black Sea coast. Bulgaria's annual output of coal (including brown coal) decreased from 31.3m. metric tons in 1996 to 29.7m. tons in 1997. In 1986 the construction of a gas pipeline, linking Bulgaria to the USSR, was completed. In April 1998 Bulgaria and Russia signed an agreement providing for Russia's delivery of natural gas to Bulgaria until the year 2010; the volume of gas transported across Bulgaria to neighbouring countries was to be increased, and the existing pipeline network upgraded.

The manufacturing sector engaged 23.6% of the employed labour force in 1997. Based on the value of output, the main branches of manufacturing in 1997 were food products, beverages and tobacco products, refined petroleum products, basic metals, and chemicals and chemical products. The output of the manufacturing sector has declined significantly in recent years.

Bulgaria's production of primary energy in 1996 was equivalent to 48.6% of gross consumption. Coal and nuclear power are the main domestic sources of energy. The country's sole nuclear power station, at Kozloduy, provided some 40% of electric energy in 1990. Imports of mineral fuels comprised 26.3% of the value of the merchandise imports in 1995.

The services sector contributed an estimated 44.4% of GDP and engaged 43.5% of the employed labour force in 1997. Trade represented an estimated 8.4% of GDP in that year. According to the World Bank, the real GDP of the services sector declined at an average rate of 0.6% per year in 1990–97. The sector's GDP declined, according to official estimates, by 9.3% in 1996 and by 23.6% in 1997, but increased by 4.8% in 1998.

In 1998 Bulgaria recorded a visible trade deficit of US $458m., while there was a deficit of $376m. on the current account of the balance of payments. In 1997 the principal source of imports was the Russian Federation, which provided 28.1% of the total; Germany and Italy were also major suppliers. The main market for exports was Italy (taking 11.7% of the total) in 1997; Germany, Greece and the Russian Federation were also significant purchasers. The principal exports in 1993 were basic manufactures, machinery and transport equipment, and chemicals and related products. The principal imports in that year were mineral fuels and lubricants (particularly petroleum and petroleum products), machinery and transport equipment and miscellaneous manufactured articles.

Bulgaria's overall budget surplus for 1998 was 599,300m. old leva (equivalent to 2.8% of GDP). Bulgaria's total external debt at the end of 1997 was US $9,858m., of which $7,721m. was long-term public debt. In that year the cost of debt-servicing was equivalent to 14.4% of revenue from exports of goods and services. The annual rate of inflation averaged 149% in 1990–98. Consumer prices increased by 1,082.3% in 1997, but by only 22.3% in 1998. An estimated 11.4% of the labour force were unemployed at the end of 1998.

Bulgaria is a member of the International Bank for Economic Co-operation (see p. 291), the UN Economic Commission for Europe (see p. 26) and the Organization of the Black Sea Economic Co-operation (see p. 135). In 1990 Bulgaria became a member of the IMF and the World Bank. Bulgaria made a formal application for membership of the European Union (EU, see p. 172) in 1996, and in 1999 was admitted to the Central European Free Trade Association (CEFTA, see p. 290). Bulgaria is a founding member of the European Bank for Reconstruction and Development (EBRD, established in 1990, see p. 168).

In the late 1980s the Bulgarian economy entered a severe decline. Output in most sectors was considerably reduced, and there was a sharp rise in the rates of unemployment and inflation. Bulgaria's economy was further affected by UN sanctions against Iraq, Libya and Yugoslavia in the early 1990s. In an effort to prevent total economic collapse, the Government introduced an extensive programme of privatization and restructuring of the banking system, under a planned transition to a market economy, and in 1991 adopted austerity measures in fulfilment of conditions stipulated by the IMF. In September 1996, however, the IMF suspended the disbursement of funds, pending progress in the implementation of the planned reforms. Following the resumption of negotiations between a new interim administration (see Recent History) and the IMF, agreement was reached in March 1997 regarding the adoption of structural reforms, which included the establishment of a currency control board, the acceleration of the privatization programme, the liberalization of trade and price controls, and the rationalization of state-sector employees in an effort to reduce government expenditure on loss-making companies. In April the IMF approved financial credit to support the government programme. At the beginning of July, in an effort to impose fiscal discipline, the Government established a currency control board which fixed the exchange rate of the lev to that of the Deutsche Mark. In May 1998 legislation ending state subsidies to the agricultural sector was approved. In July the Government signed an agreement providing for Bulgaria's accession to the CEFTA; following its admission to the organization in January 1999, Bulgaria was to remove gradually tariffs on industrial products traded with other CEFTA countries. In September 1998 the IMF supported a further three-year credit to finance debt-servicing repayments and to support further reforms. By the end of that year the currency board had achieved some success in establishing fiscal control, restraining the rate of inflation to below the target level. Considerable progress in the privatization programme was achieved in 1999; industrial privatization was due to be completed by mid-2000, with further restructuring planned for the energy and water sectors. Negotiations on Bulgaria's accession to the EU were conditional on the achievement of growth of 3.4%, greater progress in economic reform, and on agreement on closure dates for four of the six reactors of Kozloduy nuclear power installation (on the grounds that they were unsafe). Bulgaria pledged that the first two reactors would be closed by 2003, and the other two by 2010; the country was to be granted financial assistance from the EU for restructuring the energy sector, and upgrading the remaining two nuclear reactors. In 1999 Western donor Governments provided additional funds to compensate for the impact of the NATO bombardment of Yugoslavia in March–June of that year, which adversely affected trade and foreign investment in Bulgaria. Despite the Government's continued success at curbing the rate of inflation, lack of private investment (and consequently growth) remained major impediments to progress.

## Social Welfare

The Bulgarian health service is administered by the Ministry of Health, with the assistance of local government and the Bulgarian Red Cross; medical care is provided free of charge. The development of the private health sector is also encouraged (private medical and dentistry practices were banned between 1972 and November 1989). In 1997 there were 28,605 doctors and 5,227 dentists working in the country. In the same year there were 288 hospital establishments, with 83,219 beds, and 4,635 sanatoriums and other institutions, with 47,243 beds. State provision is made for social benefits, including sickness and unemployment allowances, maternity leave payments and pensions. The retirement age is 60 years for men and 55 years for women; many employees are entitled to early retirement.

State social insurance is directed by the Department of Public Insurance and the Directorate of Pensions. In 1997 there were 196 social welfare institutions. Of total government expenditure in 1997, 326,700m. old leva (5.7%) was for health, and a further 1,552,300m. old leva (27.1%) for social security and welfare. Social security expenditure for 1999 was projected at 2,436,200m. old leva, of which 1,999,600m. old leva was to finance pension reform.

## Education

Education is free and compulsory between the ages of seven and 16 years. Children between the ages of three and six years may attend kindergartens (in 1995 62% of pre-school age children attended). Primary education, beginning at seven years of age, lasts for four years. Secondary education, from 11 years of age, lasts for up to eight years, comprising two cycles of four years each. Secondary education is undertaken at general schools, which provide a general academic course, or vocational and technical schools, and art schools, which offer specialized training. In 1996 primary enrolment included 92% of children in the relevant age-group, while enrolment at secondary schools included 74% of those in the relevant age-group. In 1997/98 there were a total of 42 higher educational institutions, with a total enrolment of 236,740 students, and an additional 44 colleges.

In 1996 enrolment in higher education courses was equivalent to 41.2% of those in the relevant age-group (males 31.2%; females 51.6%). The 1997 state budget allocated 323,900m. old leva to education (representing 5.6% of total expenditure by the central Government). In 1995, according to UNESCO estimates, 1.7% of the adult population were illiterate (males 1.1%; females 2.3%).

## Public Holidays

**2000:** 1 January (New Year), 3 March (National Day), 24 April (Easter Monday), 1 May (Labour Day), 6 May (St George's

Day), 24 May (Education Day), 6 September (Union of Eastern Rumelia and the Bulgarian Principality), 22 September (Independence Day), 1 November (Commemoration of the Leaders of the Bulgarian National Revival), 24–25 December (Christmas).

**2001:** 1 January (New Year), 3 March (National Day), 16 April (Easter Monday), 1 May (Labour Day), 6 May (St George's

Day), 24 May (Education Day), 6 September (Union of Eastern Rumelia and the Bulgarian Principality), 22 September (Independence Day), 1 November (Commemoration of the Leaders of the Bulgarian National Revival), 24–25 December (Christmas).

**Weights and Measures**

The metric system is in force.

# Statistical Survey

Source (unless otherwise stated): National Statistical Institute, 1000 Sofia, ul. Shesti Septemvri 10; tel. (2) 98-57-27-27; fax (2) 98-57-20-02.

## Area and Population

**AREA, POPULATION AND DENSITY**

| | |
|---|---|
| Area (sq km)* | 110,994† |
| Population (census results) | |
| 4 December 1985 | 8,948,649 |
| 4 December 1992 | |
| Males | 4,170,622 |
| Females | 4,316,695 |
| Total | 8,487,317 |
| Population (official estimates at 31 December) | |
| 1995 | 8,384,715 |
| 1996 | 8,340,936 |
| 1997 | 8,283,200 |
| Density (per sq km) at 31 December 1997 | 74.6 |

* Including territorial waters of frontier rivers (261.4 sq km).

† 42,855 sq miles.

**ETHNIC GROUPS** (1992 census)

| | Number | % |
|---|---|---|
| Bulgarian | 7,271,185 | 85.67 |
| Turkish | 800,052 | 9.43 |
| Gypsy | 313,396 | 3.69 |
| Armenian | 13,677 | 0.16 |
| Others | 80,526 | 0.95 |
| Unknown | 8,481 | 0.10 |
| **Total** | 8,487,317 | 100.00 |

**ADMINISTRATIVE REGIONS** (31 December 1993)

| | Area (sq km) | Estimated population* | Density (per sq km) |
|---|---|---|---|
| Sofia (town)† | 1,310.8 | 1,188,556 | 906.7 |
| Burgas | 14,724.3 | 850,003 | 57.7 |
| Khaskovo | 13,824.1 | 903,928 | 65.4 |
| Lovech | 15,150.0 | 1,009,196 | 66.6 |
| Montana‡ | 10,606.8 | 626,205 | 59.0 |
| Plovdiv | 13,585.4 | 1,221,449 | 89.9 |
| Ruse | 10,842.5 | 765,719 | 70.6 |
| Sofia (region)† | 19,021.1 | 980,588 | 51.6 |
| Varna | 11,928.6 | 914,079 | 76.6 |
| **Total** | 110,993.6 | 8,459,723 | 76.2 |

* Figures are provisional. The revised total is 8,459,763.

† The city of Sofia, the national capital, has separate regional status. The area and population of the capital region are not included in the neighbouring Sofia region.

‡ Formerly Mikhailovgrad.

**PRINCIPAL TOWNS**

(estimated population at 31 December 1996)

| | | | |
|---|---|---|---|
| Sofia (capital) | 1,116,823 | Stara Zagora | 149,666 |
| Plovdiv | 344,326 | Pleven | 125,029 |
| Varna | 301,421 | Sliven | 107,011 |
| Burgas (Bourgas) | 199,470 | Dobrich* | 103,532 |
| Ruse (Roussé) | 168,051 | Shumen | 97,230 |

* Dobrich was renamed Tolbukhin in 1949, but its former name was restored in 1990.

Source: UN, *Demographic Yearbook*.

**BIRTHS, MARRIAGES AND DEATHS**

| | Registered live births | | Registered marriages* | | Registered deaths | |
|---|---|---|---|---|---|---|
| | Number | Rate (per 1,000) | Number | Rate (per 1,000) | Number | Rate (per 1,000) |
| 1991 | 95,910 | 11.1 | 48,820 | 5.6 | 110,423 | 12.8 |
| 1992 | 89,134 | 10.4 | 44,806 | 5.2 | 107,998 | 12.6 |
| 1993 | 84,987 | 10.0 | 40,022 | 4.7 | 109,540 | 12.9 |
| 1994 | 79,934 | 9.4 | 37,910 | 4.5 | 111,787 | 13.2 |
| 1995 | 72,428 | 8.6 | 36,795 | 4.4 | 114,670 | 13.6 |
| 1996 | 72,743 | 8.6 | n.a. | 4.3 | 117,056 | 14.0 |
| 1997 | 64,609 | 7.7 | n.a. | 4.2 | 121,861 | 14.7 |
| 1998 | 65,360 | 7.9 | n.a. | 4.3 | 118,193 | 14.3 |

* Including marriages of Bulgarian nationals outside the country but excluding those of aliens in Bulgaria.

**Expectation of life** (UN estimates, years at birth, 1990–95): 71.2 (males 67.8; females 74.9).

**ECONOMICALLY ACTIVE POPULATION** (1992 census)*

| | Males | Females | Total |
|---|---|---|---|
| Agriculture, hunting, forestry and fishing | 266,929 | 204,359 | 471,288 |
| Mining and quarrying | 61,897 | 19,898 | 81,795 |
| Manufacturing | 484,594 | 489,310 | 973,904 |
| Electricity, gas and water | 31,495 | 11,822 | 43,317 |
| Construction | 164,754 | 41,847 | 206,601 |
| Trade, restaurants and hotels | 182,688 | 218,269 | 400,957 |
| Transport, storage and communications | 178,483 | 69,814 | 248,297 |
| Financing, insurance, real estate and business services | 8,872 | 29,387 | 38,259 |
| Community, social and personal services | 326,987 | 494,489 | 821,476 |
| Activities not adequately defined | 479 | 282 | 761 |
| **Total employed** | 1,707,178 | 1,579,477 | 3,286,655 |
| Unemployed | 323,015 | 322,798 | 645,813 |
| **Total labour force** | 2,030,193 | 1,902,275 | 3,932,468 |

* Figures refer to employed persons aged 14 years and over and to unemployed persons aged 15 to 59 years.

Source: ILO, *Yearbook of Labour Statistics*.

**November 1997** ('000 persons): Total employed 3,030.1 (males 1,616.2, females 1,413.9); Unemployed 534.1 (males 278.7, females 255.4); Total labour force 3,564.2 (males 1,894.9, females 1,669.2).

**EMPLOYMENT**
(annual averages, excluding armed forces)

| | 1996 | 1997 |
|---|---|---|
| Agriculture, hunting, forestry and fishing | 800,290 | 776,822 |
| Mining and quarrying | 64,995 | 60,463 |
| Manufacturing | 782,292 | 755,647 |
| Electricity, gas and water supply | 57,196 | 57,906 |
| Construction | 166,075 | 157,291 |
| Wholesale and retail trade; repair of motor vehicles, motorcycles and personal and household goods | 321,377 | 319,435 |
| Hotels and restaurants | 76,455 | 76,255 |
| Transport, storage and communications | 252,076 | 245,972 |
| Financial intermediation | 42,881 | 40,055 |
| Real estate, renting and business activities | 102,046 | 96,086 |
| Public administration and defence; compulsory social security | 73,211 | 77,139 |
| Education | 255,820 | 247,551 |
| Health and social work | 187,204 | 183,787 |
| Other community, social and personal service activities | 103,959 | 103,725 |
| **Total employees** | 3,285,877 | 3,198,134 |

# Agriculture

**PRINCIPAL CROPS** ('000 metric tons)

| | 1996 | 1997 | 1998 |
|---|---|---|---|
| Wheat | 1,802 | 3,556 | 3,295* |
| Rice (paddy) | 9 | 12 | 12† |
| Barley | 457 | 809 | 749* |
| Maize | 1,042 | 1,696 | 1,340* |
| Rye | 16 | 18* | 18† |
| Oats | 40 | 44† | 44† |
| Potatoes | 319 | 463 | 463† |
| Dry beans | 20 | 25 | 25† |
| Dry peas | 11 | 12† | 12† |
| Soybeans | 10 | 19* | 19† |
| Sunflower seed | 526 | 446 | 477* |
| Seed cotton | 12 | 10 | 20† |
| Cabbages | 102 | 120† | 120† |
| Tomatoes | 324 | 244 | 244† |
| Pumpkins, squash and gourds† | 46 | 60 | 46 |
| Cucumbers and gherkins | 118 | 145 | 145† |
| Green peppers† | 15 | 15 | 15 |
| Dry onions | 52 | 71 | 71† |
| Green beans | 19 | 23† | 23† |
| Green peas† | 3 | 3 | 3 |
| Melons and watermelons | 227 | 246 | 246† |
| Grapes | 661 | 624 | 624† |
| Apples | 204 | 152 | 152† |
| Pears | 25 | 22† | 22† |
| Plums | 90 | 78† | 78† |
| Peaches and nectarines | 69 | 65† | 65† |
| Apricots | 24 | 20† | 20† |
| Strawberries | 5 | 5 | 5† |
| Sugar beets | 87 | 81 | 45* |
| Tobacco (leaves) | 40* | 52* | 52† |

* Unofficial figure. † FAO estimate(s).

Source: FAO, *Production Yearbook*.

**LIVESTOCK** ('000 head at 1 January each year)

| | 1996 | 1997 | 1998 |
|---|---|---|---|
| Horses | 151 | 170 | 170* |
| Asses | 281 | 287 | 287* |
| Cattle | 632 | 582 | 612 |
| Pigs | 2,140 | 1,500 | 1,480 |
| Sheep | 3,383 | 3,020 | 2,848 |
| Goats | 833 | 849 | 966 |
| Buffaloes | 14 | 11 | 11 |
| Poultry (million)† | 17 | 15 | 14 |

* FAO estimate. † Unofficial figures.

Source: FAO, *Production Yearbook*.

**LIVESTOCK PRODUCTS** ('000 metric tons)

| | 1996 | 1997 | 1998 |
|---|---|---|---|
| Beef and veal | 78* | 66* | 66† |
| Buffalo meat† | 2 | 2 | 2 |
| Mutton and lamb | 49* | 44* | 44† |
| Goat meat† | 7 | 6 | 6† |
| Pig meat | 252 | 225* | 225† |
| Poultry meat | 99 | 94 | 94† |
| Cows' milk | 1,163 | 1,197 | 1,200† |
| Buffaloes' milk | 12 | 12† | 12† |
| Sheeps' milk | 114 | 110 | 110† |
| Goats' milk | 143 | 162* | 162† |
| Butter | 2 | 2 | 2 |
| Cheese | 76 | 67 | 67† |
| Hen eggs | 96 | 87* | 87† |
| Other poultry eggs | 2 | 2* | 2† |
| Honey | 5 | 5 | 5† |
| Wool: | | | |
| greasy | 9 | 7 | 7† |
| scoured | 4* | 3* | 3† |
| Cattle and buffalo hides† | 13 | 11 | 11 |
| Sheepskins† | 20 | 18 | 18 |

* Unofficial figure(s). † FAO estimate(s).

Source: FAO, *Production Yearbook*.

# Forestry

**ROUNDWOOD REMOVALS** ('000 cubic metres, excl. bark)

| | 1995 | 1996 | 1997 |
|---|---|---|---|
| Sawlogs, veneer logs and logs for sleepers | 877 | 869 | 810 |
| Pulpwood | 934 | 1,001 | 927 |
| Other industrial wood | 159 | 150 | 125 |
| Fuel wood | 892 | 1,203 | 1,197 |
| **Total** | 2,862 | 3,223 | 3,059 |

Source: FAO, *Yearbook of Forest Products*.

**SAWNWOOD PRODUCTION** ('000 cubic metres, incl. sleepers)

| | 1995 | 1996 | 1997 |
|---|---|---|---|
| Coniferous (softwood)* | 186 | 186 | 186 |
| Broadleaved (hardwood)* | 67 | 67 | 67 |
| **Total** | 253 | 253 | 253 |

* FAO estimates.

Source: FAO, *Yearbook of Forest Products*.

# Fishing

('000 metric tons, live weight)

| | 1995 | 1996 | 1997 |
|---|---|---|---|
| Cyprinids | 0.4 | 0.5 | 0.5 |
| Gobies | 0.6 | 0.5 | 0.4 |
| European sprat | 2.9 | 3.5 | 3.6 |
| Other fishes (incl. unspecified)* | 1.0 | 1.1 | 1.8 |
| **Total fish** | 4.9 | 5.6 | 6.3 |
| Crustaceans | 3.3 | 3.3 | 4.9 |
| **Total catch** | 8.2 | 8.8 | 11.2 |
| Inland waters | 0.8 | 1.1 | 1.9 |
| Mediterranean and Black Seas | 7.2 | 7.7 | 9.4 |
| Atlantic Ocean | 0.2 | — | — |

Source: FAO, *Yearbook of Fishery Statistics*.

# Mining

('000 metric tons, unless otherwise indicated)

| | 1995 | 1996 | 1997 |
|---|---|---|---|
| Anthracite | 24 | 19 | 14 |
| Other hard coal | 170 | 119 | 88 |
| Lignite | 27,449 | 28,104 | 26,929 |
| Other brown coal | 3,187 | 3,060 | 2,677 |
| Iron ore* | 270 | 282 | 264 |
| Copper ore* | 75.5† | 84.8† | n.a. |
| Lead ore* | 32.5† | 28.5† | n.a. |
| Zinc ore* | 30.0† | 28.0† | n.a. |
| Manganese ore* | 5.6 | 13.1 | 14.2 |
| Crude petroleum | 43 | 32 | 28 |
| Natural gas (million cu metres) | 22.5 | 18.8 | 12.9 |

* Figures relate to the metal content of ores. Data for copper, lead and zinc are from *World Metal Statistics* (London).

† Source: UN, *Industrial Commodity Statistics Yearbook*.

# Industry

**SELECTED PRODUCTS**

('000 metric tons, unless otherwise indicated)

| | 1995 | 1996 | 1997 |
|---|---|---|---|
| Flour | 977 | 875 | 750 |
| Refined sugar | 237 | 292 | 235 |
| Wine ('000 hectolitres) | 2,481 | 2,264 | 1,361 |
| Beer ('000 hectolitres) | 4,331 | 4,402 | 3,300 |
| Cigarettes and cigars (metric tons) | 74,600 | 57,300 | 43,300 |
| Cotton yarn (metric tons)[1] | 27,600 | 26,000 | 28,000 |
| Woven cotton fabrics ('000 metres)[2] | 76,600 | 68,800 | 76,100 |
| Flax and hemp yarn (metric tons) | 800 | 800 | 500 |
| Wool yarn (metric tons)[1] | 14,000 | 12,900 | 11,200 |
| Woven woollen fabrics ('000 metres)[2] | 13,200 | 12,100 | 11,200 |
| Woven fabrics of man-made fibres ('000 metres)[3] | 19,200 | 19,300 | 16,000 |
| Leather footwear ('000 pairs) | 11,000 | 8,200 | 5,500 |
| Rubber footwear ('000 pairs) | 1,300 | 1,000 | 500 |
| Chemical wood pulp | 105.6 | 84.7 | 92.4 |
| Paper | 194.9 | 175.4 | 158.6 |
| Paperboard | 31.3 | 26.9 | 19.6 |
| Rubber tyres ('000)[4] | 642 | 532 | 391 |
| Sulphuric acid (100%) | 453.8 | 524.7 | 550.3 |
| Caustic soda (96%) | 70.4 | 81.0 | 79.5 |
| Soda ash (98%) | 796.0 | 866.1 | n.a. |
| Nitrogenous fertilizers[5] | 459.2 | 468.2 | 375.6 |
| Phosphate fertilizers[5] | 53.1 | 90.4 | 110.2 |
| Coke (gas and coke-oven) | 1,240 | 1,157 | 1,239 |
| Unworked glass—rectangles ('000 sq metres) | 12,000 | 12,300 | 10,500 |
| Clay building bricks (million) | 668 | 622 | 344 |
| Cement | 2,070 | 2,137 | 1,654 |
| Pig-iron and ferro-alloys | 1,614 | 1,513 | 1,654 |
| Crude steel | 2,724 | 2,457 | 2,628 |
| Refined copper—unwrought (metric tons) | 25,500 | 22,300 | 34,500 |
| Refined lead—unwrought (metric tons) | 60,100 | 74,700 | 72,600 |
| Zinc—unwrought (metric tons) | 68,800 | 68,000 | 70400 |
| Metal-working lathes (number) | 2,496 | 2,513 | 2,268 |
| Fork-lift trucks (number)[6] | 11,700 | 3,900 | 3,100 |
| Refrigerators—household (number) | 49,300 | 36,400 | 21,300 |
| Washing machines—household (number) | 26,500 | 23,700 | 4,900 |
| Radio receivers (number) | 1,800 | 300 | 30 |
| Television receivers (number) | 9,700 | 10,600 | 5,700 |
| Buses (number)[7] | 83 | 93 | n.a. |
| Lorries (number)[7] | 253 | 60 | n.a. |

| *— continued* | 1995 | 1996 | 1997 |
|---|---|---|---|
| Construction: dwellings completed (number)[8] | 6,815 | 8,099 | 7,452 |
| Electric energy (million kWh) | 41,790 | 42,716 | 42,720 |

[1] Pure and mixed yarn. Figures for wool include yarn of man-made staple.

[2] Pure and mixed fabrics, after undergoing finishing processes.

[3] Finished fabrics, including fabrics of natural silk.

[4] Tyres for road motor vehicles (passenger cars and commercial vehicles).

[5] Figures for nitrogenous fertilizers are in terms of nitrogen, and for phosphate fertilizers in terms of phosphoric acid. Data for nitrogenous fertilizers include urea.

[6] Including hoisting gears.

[7] Including vehicles assembled from imported parts.

[8] Including restorations and conversions.

# Finance

**CURRENCY AND EXCHANGE RATES**

**Monetary Units**

100 stotinki (singular: stotinka) = 1 new lev (plural: leva).

**Sterling, Dollar and Euro Equivalents** (30 September 1999)

£1 sterling = 3.020 new leva;
US $1 = 1.834 new leva;
€1 = 1.956 new leva;
100 new leva = £33.12 = $54.53 = €51.13.

**Average Exchange Rate** (old leva per US$)

1996 177.89
1997 1,681.88
1998 1,760.36

Note: On 5 July 1999 a new lev, equivalent to 1,000 old leva, was introduced. Most of the figures in this Survey are still in terms of old leva.

**STATE BUDGET** ('000 million old leva)*

| Revenue† | 1995 | 1996 | 1997 |
|---|---|---|---|
| Taxation | 243.0 | 424.4 | 4,303.4 |
| Taxes on income, profits, etc. | 52.7 | 107.7 | 1,222.0 |
| Social security contributions | 66.8 | 118.2 | 1,171.4 |
| From employers | 58.6 | 109.0 | 1,146.8 |
| Taxes on payroll or work-force | 9.4 | 12.4 | 116.7 |
| Domestic taxes on goods and services | 87.0 | 146.9 | 1,424.3 |
| Sales, turnover or value-added taxes | 62.9 | 118.8 | 1,050.0 |
| Excises | 24.1 | 28.0 | 374.3 |
| Taxes on international trade and transactions | 25.6 | 38.2 | 363.6 |
| Import duties | 19.5 | 29.1 | 351.4 |
| Other current revenue | 69.6 | 143.8 | 1,169.8 |
| Entrepreneurial and property income | 34.3 | 71.2 | 614.6 |
| Administrative fees and charges, non-industrial and incidental sales | 23.9 | 50.3 | 276.5 |
| Capital revenue | 2.0 | 1.2 | 84.9 |
| **Total revenue** | 314.6 | 569.4 | 5,558.0 |

| Expenditure‡ | 1995 | 1996 | 1997 |
|---|---|---|---|
| General public services | 13.2 | 19.7 | 327.6 |
| Defence | 22.8 | 41.4 | 460.3 |
| Public order and safety | 15.6 | 24.2 | 279.5 |
| Education | 14.3 | 28.6 | 323.9 |
| Health | 12.1 | 23.1 | 326.7 |
| Social security and welfare | 91.3 | 157.1 | 1,552.3 |
| Housing and community amenities | 3.9 | 4.3 | 24.5 |
| Recreational, cultural and religious affairs and services | 4.1 | 6.1 | 62.4 |
| Economic affairs and services | 25.6 | 127.4 | 934.6 |
| Fuel and energy | 3.5 | 6.1 | 184.1 |
| Agriculture, forestry, fishing and hunting | 7.0 | 10.7 | 146.2 |
| Mining, manufacturing and construction | 2.3 | 2.6 | 23.7 |
| Transport and communications | 10.3 | 13.4 | 167.1 |
| Other purposes | 157.7 | 408.8 | 1,441.5 |
| **Total expenditure** | 360.6 | 840.6 | 5,733.2 |
| Current§ | 347.0 | 818.3 | 5,284.0 |
| Capital | 13.6 | 22.3 | 449.2 |

* Figures refer to the consolidated accounts of the central Government (including social security funds and other extrabudgetary units).

† Excluding grants received ('000 million old leva): 0.9 in 1995; 4.1 in 1996; 104.1 in 1997.

‡ Excluding lending minus repayments ('000 million old leva): 1.1 in 1995; 2.6 in 1996; −424.4 in 1997.

§ Including interest payments ('000 million old leva): 128.7 in 1995; 353.3 in 1996; 1,439.3 in 1997.

Source: IMF, *Government Finance Statistics Yearbook*.

**INTERNATIONAL RESERVES** (US $ million at 31 December)

| | 1996 | 1997 | 1998 |
|---|---|---|---|
| Gold* | 309 | 290 | 296 |
| IMF special drawing rights | 12 | 11 | 30 |
| Reserve position in IMF | 47 | 44 | 45 |
| Foreign exchange | 425 | 2,193 | 2,755 |
| **Total** | 793 | 2,539 | 3,127 |

* Valued until 1997 at US $300 per troy ounce, and subsequently at market-related prices.

Source: IMF, *International Financial Statistics*.

**MONEY SUPPLY** ('000 million old leva at 31 December)

| | 1996 | 1997 | 1998 |
|---|---|---|---|
| Currency outside banks | 126.5 | 1,314.1 | 1,742.0 |
| Demand deposits at deposit money banks | 110.0 | 968.2 | 1,084.1 |
| **Total money** (incl. others) | 236.6 | 2,290.3 | 2,826.1 |

Source: IMF, *International Financial Statistics*.

**COST OF LIVING**
(Consumer Price Index; base: 1990=100)

| | 1995 | 1996 | 1997 |
|---|---|---|---|
| Food | 3,968.3 | 8,663.6 | 106,100 |
| Fuel and light | 4,026.1 | 12,299 | 145,080 |
| Clothing | 3,251.8 | 6,527.0 | 71,375 |
| Rent | 4,391.3 | 10,142 | 69,484 |
| **All items** (incl. others) | 3,722.0 | 8,300.2 | 98,132 |

Source: ILO, *Yearbook of Labour Statistics*.

**NATIONAL ACCOUNTS** (million old leva at current prices)

**Expenditure on the Gross Domestic Product**

| | 1995 | 1996 | 1997 |
|---|---|---|---|
| Government final consumption expenditure | 134,408 | 207,496 | 2,115,739 |
| Private final consumption expenditure | 622,139 | 1,373,622 | 12,521,201 |
| Increase in stocks | 3,538 | −91,607 | 93,443 |
| Gross fixed capital formation | 134,269 | 238,470 | 1,931,561 |
| Adjustment* | — | −33,388 | −247,116 |
| **Total domestic expenditure** | 894,354 | 1,694,593 | 16,154,619† |
| Exports of goods and services | 393.172 | 1,099,950 | 10,478,299 |
| *Less* Imports of goods and services | 407,204 | 1,045,842 | 9,529,485 |
| **GDP in purchasers' values** | 880,322 | 1,748,701 | 17,103,433 |

* Referring to consumption by Bulgarian residents abroad, less consumption by non-residents in Bulgaria.

† Including statistical discrepancy (million leva): −260,209.

**Gross Domestic Product by Economic Activity**

| | 1995 | 1996 | 1997 |
|---|---|---|---|
| Agriculture | 108,913 | 210,781 | 3,938,721 |
| Forestry | 2,503 | 5,217 | 48,591 |
| Industry* | 272,721 | 534,298 | 4,482,908 |
| Trade | 101,841 | 178,505 | 1,282,813 |
| Transport | 37,522 | 83,537 | 826,083 |
| Communications | 12,160 | 30,371 | 298,775 |
| Other services | 298,716 | 607,663 | 4,358,311 |
| **Sub-total** | 834,376 | 1,650,372 | 15,236,202 |
| Turnover tax and excises | 24,527 | 61,993 | 555,684 |
| Import duties and value-added tax<br>*Less* Imputed bank service charge | 21,419 | 36,336 | 1,311,547 |
| **GDP in purchasers' values** | 880,322 | 1,748,701 | 17,103,433 |

* Comprising mining and quarrying, manufacturing, construction, and electricity, gas and water.

**BALANCE OF PAYMENTS** (US $ million)

| | 1996 | 1997 | 1998 |
|---|---|---|---|
| Exports of goods f.o.b. | 4,890 | 4,940 | 4,299 |
| Imports of goods f.o.b. | −4,703 | −4,559 | −4,757 |
| **Trade balance** | 188 | 380 | −458 |
| Exports of services | 1,366 | 1,337 | 1,255 |
| Imports of services | −1,246 | −1,171 | −1,120 |
| **Balance on goods and services** | 308 | 547 | −322 |
| Other income received | 181 | 211 | 307 |
| Other income paid | −577 | −567 | −590 |
| **Balances on goods services and income** | −89 | 190 | −606 |
| Current transfers received | 232 | 276 | 261 |
| Current transfers paid | −128 | −39 | −32 |
| **Current balance** | 16 | 427 | −376 |
| Capital account (net) | 66 | — | — |
| Direct investment abroad | 29 | 2 | — |
| Direct investment from abroad | 109 | 505 | 401 |
| Portfolio investment assets | −7 | −14 | −69 |
| Portfolio investment liabilities | −122 | 147 | −112 |
| Other investment assets | −568 | −54 | 252 |
| Other investment liabilities | −155 | −123 | −251 |
| Net errors and omissions | −105 | 256 | 60 |
| **Overall balance** | −739 | 1,145 | −94 |

Source: IMF, *International Financial Statistics*.

# External Trade

**PRINCIPAL COMMODITIES** (US $ million)

| Imports c.i.f. | 1993 | 1994 | 1995 |
|---|---|---|---|
| **Food and live animals** | 295.0 | n.a. | n.a. |
| Sugar, sugar preparations and honey | 72.3 | 112.4 | 112.5 |
| Sugar and honey | n.a. | 98.9 | 105.4 |
| **Beverages and tobacco** | 117.8 | n.a. | n.a. |
| Tobacco and tobacco manufactures | 103.3 | 46.6 | 21.0 |
| **Crude materials (inedible) except fuels** | 203.8 | n.a. | n.a. |
| Textile fibres and wastes | 55.8 | n.a. | n.a. |
| Cotton | n.a. | 91.0 | 100.5 |
| Synthetic fibres | n.a. | 135.6 | 148.9 |
| **Mineral fuels, lubricants, etc.** | 1,743.2 | 1,242.7 | 1,350.2 |
| Petroleum, petroleum products, etc. | 1,249.0 | n.a. | n.a. |
| Crude petroleum oils, etc. | 994.7 | 636.9 | 720.0 |
| Gas (natural and manufactured) | 358.8 | n.a. | n.a. |
| **Chemicals and related products** | 454.8 | n.a. | n.a. |
| Organic chemicals | 64.3 | 121.4 | 133.2 |
| Inorganic chemicals | 114.0 | 28.1 | 103.5 |
| Artificial resins, plastic materials, etc. | 45.0 | 117.7 | 138.5 |
| **Basic manufactures** | 614.0 | n.a. | n.a. |
| Paper, paperboard, etc. | 76.1 | 111.7 | 175.3 |
| Textile yarn, fabrics, etc. | 173.7 | n.a. | n.a. |
| Iron and steel | 176.2 | 147.6 | 130.6 |
| **Machinery and transport equipment** | 934.6 | n.a. | n.a. |
| Power-generating machinery and equipment | 37.5 | 460.0 | 483.5 |
| Machinery specialized for particular industries | 170.6 | n.a. | n.a. |
| General industrial machinery, equipment and parts | 128.8 | n.a. | n.a. |
| Electrical machinery, apparatus, etc. (excl. telecommunications and sound equipment) | 126.3 | 218.4 | 250.5 |
| Road vehicles and parts (excl. tyres, engines and electrical parts) | 289.0 | 243.6 | 226.8 |
| Passenger motor cars (excl. buses) | 171.2 | 121.5 | 99.3 |
| **Miscellaneous manufactured articles** | 290.4 | n.a. | n.a. |
| **Total** (incl. others) | 4,962.3 | 4,593.0 | 5,125.0 |

| Exports f.o.b. | 1993 | 1994 | 1995 |
|---|---|---|---|
| **Food and live animals** | 598.7 | 300.5 | n.a. |
| Cereals and cereal preparations | 17.9 | n.a. | n.a. |
| Wheat and meslin (unmilled) | 5.0 | 1.4 | 100.7 |
| Vegetables and fruit | 89.7 | n.a. | n.a. |
| **Beverages and tobacco** | 331.6 | n.a. | n.a. |
| Beverages | 111.5 | 160.3 | 186.1 |
| Wine, etc. | 75.3 | 100.5 | 122.6 |
| Tobacco and tobacco manufactures | 220.1 | 241.1 | 301.3 |
| Manufactured tobacco | 167.0 | n.a. | n.a. |
| Cigarettes | 166.7 | 189.8 | 238.4 |
| **Crude materials (inedible) except fuels** | 199.7 | n.a. | n.a. |
| **Mineral fuels, lubricants, etc.** | 304.1 | 302.7 | 318.1 |
| Petroleum, petroleum products, etc. | 281.1 | 302.7 | 318.1 |
| **Chemicals and related products** | 510.4 | n.a. | n.a. |
| Organic chemicals | 68.0 | 148.4 | 185.1 |
| Medicinal and pharmaceutical products | 171.1 | 93.1 | 89.1 |
| Manufactured fertilizers | 92.6 | 140.6 | 236.0 |
| Artificial resins, plastic materials, etc. | 56.7 | 120.0 | 150.3 |

| Exports f.o.b. — *continued* | 1993 | 1994 | 1995 |
|---|---|---|---|
| **Basic manufactures** | 879.2 | n.a. | n.a. |
| Textile yarn, fabrics, etc. | 106.9 | n.a. | n.a. |
| Iron and steel | 340.9 | 479.2 | 528.5 |
| Universals, plates and sheets | 123.8 | 223.0 | 266.6 |
| Non-ferrous metals | 220.7 | n.a. | n.a. |
| Copper | 137.8 | 177.9 | 270.1 |
| **Machinery and transport equipment** | 603.4 | n.a. | n.a. |
| Power-generating machinery and equipment | 41.4 | 255.8 | 288.0 |
| General industrial machinery, equipment and parts | 250.2 | n.a. | n.a. |
| Electrical machinery, apparatus, etc. (excl. telecommunications and sound equipment) | 133.9 | 205.0 | 182.5 |
| **Miscellaneous manufactured articles** | 342.1 | n.a. | n.a. |
| Clothing and accessories (excl. footwear) | 166.5 | 195.0 | 230.5 |
| Footwear | 73.7 | 98.2 | 94.3 |
| **Total** (incl. others) | 3,500.4 | 4,446.7 | 5,184.4 |

Source: UN, *International Trade Statistics Yearbook*.

**Total trade** (US $ million): Imports c.i.f. 5,273 in 1996, 5,009 in 1997; Exports f.o.b. 5,062 in 1996, 5,005 in 1997 (Source: UN, *Monthly Bulletin of Statistics*).

**PRINCIPAL TRADING PARTNERS** (million old leva)*

| Imports c.i.f. | 1995 | 1996 | 1997 |
|---|---|---|---|
| Algeria | 5,126.0 | 2,140.2 | 3,982.8 |
| Austria | 10,570.3 | 21,662.2 | 197,857.7 |
| Belgium | 5,013.0 | 10,422.7 | 101,445.6 |
| Czech Republic | 5,105.0 | 11,593.7 | 105,592.8 |
| France | 10,596.4 | 28,606.5 | 262,311.6 |
| Germany | 46,983.5 | 101,121.3 | 944,187.0 |
| Greece | 16,729.9 | 34,469.6 | 345,999.8 |
| Italy | 22,018.6 | 56,042.2 | 581,847.9 |
| Macedonia, former Yugoslav republic | 11,826.0 | 5,558.9 | 44,156.6 |
| Netherlands | 7,471.3 | 16,062.3 | 152,524.5 |
| Poland | 2,068.5 | 5,880.5 | 95,636.3 |
| Romania | 4,101.1 | 12,388.5 | 96,638.1 |
| Russia† | 106,658.4 | 297,871.1 | 2,304,843.2 |
| Switzerland | 6,676.7 | 13,893.6 | 129,890.1 |
| Ukraine | 9,960.2 | 21,524.9 | 296,069.3 |
| United Kingdom | 9,960.2 | 18,470.0 | 212,729.8 |
| USA | 8,020.1 | 19,639.5 | 303,820.1 |
| **Total** (incl. others) | 380,012.1 | 892,101.2 | 8,190,980.8 |

| Exports f.o.b. | 1995 | 1996 | 1997 |
|---|---|---|---|
| Austria | 3,089.9 | 8,843.9 | 90,592.8 |
| Belgium | 5,526.7 | 12,469.2 | 127,762.1 |
| Egypt | 2,909.2 | 9,673.3 | 72,594.1 |
| France | 10,295.9 | 22,327.9 | 221,759.3 |
| Germany | 30,795,4 | 77,718.5 | 784,725.7 |
| Greece | 24,760.0 | 61,119.8 | 680,454.8 |
| Italy | 29,279.4 | 86,696.0 | 964,074.3 |
| Macedonia, former Yugoslav republic | 29,257.7 | 26,132.7 | 164,557.1 |
| Netherlands | 6,891.3 | 14,021.4 | 126,404.8 |
| Romania | 6,391.8 | 13,251.6 | 110,461.7 |
| Russia† | 36,110.0 | 84,400.8 | 656,867.6 |
| Syria | 4,760.1 | 13,079.9 | 51,129.2 |
| Ukraine | 12,869.5 | 29,235.0 | 245,583.4 |
| United Kingdom | 11,307.3 | 24,769.6 | 218,910.7 |
| USA | 10,939.0 | 19,879.9 | 215,869.9 |
| Yugoslavia, Federal Republic | 5,786.7 | 40,698.1 | 208,877.1 |
| **Total** (incl. others) | 359,663.6 | 859,796.5 | 8,238,160.6 |

* Imports by country of purchase; exports by country of sale.

† Including Azerbaijan, Kazakhstan, Kyrgyzstan, Tajikistan, Turkmenistan and Uzbekistan.

# Transport

**RAILWAYS** (traffic)

| | 1995 | 1996 | 1997 |
|---|---|---|---|
| Passengers carried ('000) | 58,940 | 66,097 | 82,656 |
| Passenger-kilometres (million) | 4,693 | 5,065 | 5,886 |
| Freight carried ('000 metric tons) | 32,916 | 30,118 | 29,220 |
| Freight net ton-kilometres (million) | 8,595 | 7,549 | 7,444 |

**ROAD TRAFFIC** (motor vehicles in use at 31 December)

| | 1995 | 1996 | 1997 |
|---|---|---|---|
| Passenger cars | 1,647,571 | 1,707,023 | 1,730,506 |
| Buses and coaches | 41,019 | 40,835 | 40,422 |
| Lorries and vans | 203,257 | 207,258 | 210,960 |
| Motorcycles and mopeds | 519,266 | 521,710 | 524,950 |

Source: International Road Federation, *World Road Statistics*.

**INLAND WATERWAYS** (traffic)

| | 1995 | 1996 | 1997 |
|---|---|---|---|
| Passengers carried ('000) | 10 | 11 | 10 |
| Passenger-kilometres (million) | 10 | 12 | 12 |
| Freight carried ('000 metric tons) | 1,121 | 999 | 919 |
| Freight ton-kilometres (million) | 733 | 627 | 677 |

**SHIPPING**

**Merchant Fleet** (registered at 31 December)

| | 1996 | 1997 | 1998 |
|---|---|---|---|
| Number of vessels | 192 | 187 | 181 |
| Total displacement ('000 grt) | 1,149.7 | 1,128.2 | 1,091.2 |

Source: Lloyd's Register of Shipping, *World Fleet Statistics*.

**Sea-borne Traffic** (international and coastal)

| | 1995 | 1996 | 1997 |
|---|---|---|---|
| Passengers carried ('000) | 18 | 20 | 21 |
| Freight ('000 metric tons) | 18,089 | 17,070 | 19,623 |

**CIVIL AVIATION** (traffic)

| | 1995 | 1996 | 1997 |
|---|---|---|---|
| Passengers carried ('000) | 1,297 | 1,216 | 1,209 |
| Passenger-kilometres (million) | 3,133 | 2,840 | 2,711 |
| Freight carried ('000 metric tons) | 14 | 10 | 13 |
| Freight ton-kilometres (million) | 46 | 35 | 41 |

# Tourism

**ARRIVALS OF FOREIGN VISITORS**

| Country of origin | 1995 | 1996 | 1997 |
|---|---|---|---|
| Czech Republic | 74,901 | 74,139 | 61,345 |
| Slovakia* | | 55,035 | 57,312 |
| Germany | 202,401 | 124,592 | 228,662 |
| Greece | 230,767 | 156,392 | 210,963 |
| Macedonia, former Yugoslav republic | n.a. | n.a. | 487,641 |
| Poland* | 37,324 | 83,084 | 70,511 |
| Romania* | 1,509,601 | 1,280,431 | 1,202,325 |
| Russia | n.a. | n.a. | 548,572 |
| Turkey* | 1,825,061 | 1,185,826 | 2,587,223 |
| Ukraine* | n.a. | n.a. | 846,005 |
| United Kingdom | 51,063 | 41,581 | 79,206 |
| Yugoslavia, Federal Republic | n.a. | n.a. | 601,134 |
| **Total** (incl. others) | 8,004,584 | 6,810,688 | 7,543,185 |

* Mainly visitors in transit, totalling 4,538,713 in 1995, 4,015,493 in 1996 and 4,562,948 in 1997.

**Receipts from tourism** (US $ million): 473 in 1995; 388 in 1996; 369 in 1997 (Source: mainly World Tourism Organization, *Yearbook of Tourism Statistics*).

# Communications Media

| | 1995 | 1996 | 1997 |
|---|---|---|---|
| Telephone subscribers | 3,030,300 | 3,107,400 | 3,118,800 |
| Telefax stations (number in use) | 15,000* | n.a. | n.a. |
| Mobile cellular telephones (subscribers) | 20,920 | n.a. | n.a. |
| Radio licences (at 31 December) | 1,448,000 | 1,390,700 | 1,329,900 |
| Television licences (at 31 December) | 1,479,100 | 1,470,700 | 1,462,500 |
| Book production:† | | | |
| Titles | 5,400 | 4,840 | 4,809 |
| Copies ('000) | 32,085 | 20,300 | 9,300 |
| Newspapers: | | | |
| Titles | 1,058 | 920 | 669 |
| Total circulation ('000 copies) | 505,000 | 470,800 | 416,400 |
| Magazines:‡ | | | |
| Titles | 659 | 722 | 595 |
| Total circulation ('000 copies) | 15,800 | 16,700 | 9,200 |

* Provisional data.
† Including pamphlets.
‡ Including bulletins.

Sources: partly UNESCO, *Statistical Yearbook*, and UN, *Statistical Yearbook*.

# Education

(1997/98)

| | Institutions | Teachers | Students |
|---|---|---|---|
| Kindergartens | 3,559 | 20,607 | 220,200 |
| General schools | 3,137 | 67,659 | 927,206 |
| Special | 121 | 2,201 | 13,588 |
| Vocational technical | 7 | 117 | 2,614 |
| Secondary vocational | 186 | 4,431 | 68,245 |
| Technical colleges and schools of arts | 352 | 14,015 | 131,752 |
| Semi-higher institutes* | 44 | 2,702 | 23,747 |
| Higher educational | 42 | 19,416 | 236,740† |

* Including technical, teacher-training, communications and librarians' institutes.
† Including post-graduate students.

# Directory

## The Constitution

The Constitution of the Republic of Bulgaria, summarized below, took effect upon its promulgation, on 13 July 1991, following its enactment on the previous day.

### FUNDAMENTAL PRINCIPLES

Chapter One declares that the Republic of Bulgaria is to have a parliamentary form of government, with all state power derived from the people. The rule of law and the life, dignity and freedom of the individual are guaranteed. The Constitution is the supreme law; the power of the State is shared between the legislature, the executive and the judiciary. The Constitution upholds principles such as political and religious freedom (although no party may be formed on separatist, ethnic or religious lines), free economic initiative and respect for international law.

### FUNDAMENTAL RIGHTS AND OBLIGATIONS OF CITIZENS

Chapter Two establishes the basic provisions for Bulgarian citizenship and fundamental human rights, such as the rights of privacy and movement, the freedoms of expression, assembly and association, and the enfranchisement of Bulgarian citizens aged over 18 years. The Constitution commits the State to the provision of basic social welfare and education and to the encouragement of culture, science and the health of the population. The study and use of the Bulgarian language is required. Other obligations of the citizenry include military service and the payment of taxes.

### THE NATIONAL ASSEMBLY

The National Assembly is the legislature of Bulgaria and exercises parliamentary control over the country. It consists of 240 members, elected for a four-year term. Only Bulgarian citizens aged over 21 years (who do not hold a state post or another citizenship and are not under judicial interdiction or in prison) are eligible for election to parliament. A member of the National Assembly ceases to serve as a deputy while holding ministerial office. The National Assembly is a permanently-acting body, which is free to determine its own recesses and elects its own Chairman and Deputy Chairmen. The Chairman represents and convenes the National Assembly, organizes its proceedings, attests its enactments and promulgates its resolutions.

The National Assembly may function when more than one-half of its members are present, and may pass legislation and other acts by a majority of more than one-half of the members present, except where a qualified majority is required by the Constitution. Ministers are free to, and can be obliged to, attend parliamentary sessions. The most important functions of the legislature are: the enactment of laws; the approval of the state budget; the scheduling of presidential elections; the election and dismissal of the Chairman of the Council of Ministers (Prime Minister) and of other members of the Council of Ministers; the declaration of war or conclusion of peace; the foreign deployment of troops; and the ratification of any fundamental international instruments to which the Republic of Bulgaria has agreed. The laws and resolutions of the National Assembly are binding on all state bodies and citizens. All enactments must be promulgated in the official gazette, *Durzhaven Vestnik*, within 15 days of their passage through the legislature.

### THE PRESIDENT OF THE REPUBLIC

Chapter Four concerns the Head of State, the President of the Republic of Bulgaria, who is assisted by a Vice-President. The President and Vice-President are elected jointly, directly by the voters, for a period of five years. A candidate must be eligible for election to the National Assembly, but also aged over 40 years and a resident of the country for the five years previous to the election. To be elected, a candidate must receive more than one-half of the valid votes cast, in an election in which more than one-half of the eligible electorate participate. If necessary, a second ballot must then be conducted, contested by the two candidates who received the most votes. The one who receives more votes becomes President. The President and Vice-President may hold the same office for only two terms and, during this time, may not engage in any unsuitable or potentially compromising activities. If the President resigns, is incapacitated, impeached or dies, the Vice-President carries out the presidential duties. If neither official can perform their duties, the Chairman of the National Assembly assumes the prerogatives of the Presidency, until new elections take place.

The President's main responsibilities include the scheduling of elections and referendums, the conclusion of international treaties and the promulgation of laws. The President is responsible for appointing a Prime Minister-designate (priority must be given to the leaders of the two largest parties represented in the National Assembly), who must then attempt to form a government.

The President is Supreme Commander-in-Chief of the Armed Forces of the Republic of Bulgaria and presides over the Consultative National Security Council. The President has certain emergency powers, usually subject to the later approval of the National Assembly. Many of the President's actions must be approved by the Chairman of the Council of Ministers. The President may return legislation to the National Assembly for further consideration, but can be over-ruled.

### THE COUNCIL OF MINISTERS

The principal organ of executive government is the Council of Ministers, which supervises the implementation of state policy and the state budget, the administration of the country and the Armed Forces, and the maintenance of law and order. The Council of Ministers is headed and co-ordinated by the Chairman (Prime Minister), who is responsible for the overall policy of government. The Council of Ministers, which also includes Deputy Chairmen and Ministers, must resign upon the death of the Chairman or if the National Assembly votes in favour of a motion of no confidence in the Council or in the Chairman.

### JUDICIAL POWER

The judicial branch of government is independent. All judicial power is exercised in the name of the people. Individuals and legal entities are guaranteed basic rights, such as the right to contest administrative acts and the right to legal counsel. One of the principal organs is the Supreme Court of Cassation, which exercises supreme judicial responsibility for the precise and equal application of the law by all courts. The Supreme Administrative Court rules on all challenges to the legality of acts of any organ of government. The Chief Prosecutor supervises all other prosecutors and ensures that the law is observed, by initiating court actions and ensuring the enforcement of penalties, etc.

The Supreme Judicial Council is responsible for appointments within the ranks of the justices, prosecutors and investigating magistrates, and recommends to the President of the Republic the appointment or dismissal of the Chairmen of the two Supreme Courts and of the Chief Prosecutor (they are each appointed for a single, seven-year term). These last three officials are, *ex officio,* members of the Supreme Judicial Council, together with 22 others, who must be practising lawyers of high integrity and at least 15 years of professional experience. These members are elected for a term of five years, 11 of them by the National Assembly and 11 by bodies of the judiciary. The Supreme Judicial Council is chaired by the Minister of Justice, who is not entitled to vote.

### LOCAL SELF-GOVERNMENT AND LOCAL ADMINISTRATION

Chapter Seven provides for the division of Bulgaria into regions and municipalities. Municipalities are the basic administrative territorial unit at which local self-government is practised; their principal organ is the municipal council, which is elected directly by the population for a term of four years. The council elects the mayor, who is the principal organ of executive power. Bulgaria is also divided into regions (nine in 1993, including the capital). Regional government, which is entrusted to regional governors (appointed by the Council of Ministers) and administrations, is responsible for regional policy, the implementation of state policy at a local level and the harmonization of local and national interests.

### THE CONSTITUTIONAL COURT

The Constitutional Court consists of 12 justices, four of whom are elected by the National Assembly, four appointed by the President of the Republic and four elected by the justices of the two Supreme Courts. Candidates must have the same eligibility as for membership of the Supreme Judicial Council. They serve a single term of nine years, but a part of the membership changes every three years. A chairman is elected by a secret ballot of the members.

The Constitutional Court provides binding interpretations of the Constitution. It rules on the constitutionality of: laws and decrees; competence suits between organs of government; international agreements; national and presidential elections; and impeachments. A ruling of the Court requires a majority of more than one-half of the votes of all the justices.

### CONSTITUTIONAL AMENDMENTS AND THE ADOPTION OF A NEW CONSTITUTION

Chapter Nine provides for constitutional changes. Except for those provisions reserved to the competence of a Grand National Assembly (see below), the National Assembly is empowered to amend the Constitution with a majority of three-quarters of all its Members, in three ballots on three different days. Amendments must be proposed by one-quarter of the parliamentary membership or by the President. In some cases, a majority of two-thirds of all the Members of the National Assembly will suffice.

**Grand National Assembly**

A Grand National Assembly consists of 400 members, elected by the generally-established procedure. It alone is empowered to adopt a new constitution, to sanction territorial changes to the Republic of Bulgaria, to resolve on any changes in the form of state structure or form of government, and to enact amendments to certain parts of the existing Constitution (concerning the direct application of the Constitution, the domestic application of international agreements, the irrevocable nature of fundamental civil rights and of certain basic individual rights even in times of emergency or war, and amendments to Chapter Nine itself).

Any bill requiring the convening of a Grand National Assembly must be introduced by the President of the Republic or by one-third of the members of the National Assembly. A decision to hold elections for a Grand National Assembly must be supported by two-thirds of the members of the National Assembly. Enactments of the Grand National Assembly require a majority of two-thirds of the votes of all the members, in three ballots on three different days. A Grand National Assembly may resolve only on the proposals for which it was elected, whereupon its prerogatives normally expire.

## The Government

(January 2000)

### HEAD OF STATE

**President:** PETAR STOYANOV (elected 3 November 1996; took office 19 January 1997).

### COUNCIL OF MINISTERS

**Prime Minister and Minister of State Administration:** IVAN KOSTOV.

**Deputy Prime Minister and Minister of Economy:** PETUR ZHOTEV.

**Minister without Portfolio:** ALEKSANDUR PRAMATARSKI.

**Minister of Transport and Communications:** ANTONI SLAVINSKI.

**Minister of Defence:** BOIKO NOEV.

**Minister of Education and Science:** Prof. DIMITER DIMITROV.

**Minister of the Interior:** EMANUIL YORDANOV.

**Minister of Culture:** EMMA MOSKOVA.

**Minister of the Environment and Waters:** EVDOKIA MANEVA.

**Minister of Regional and Urban Development:** EVGENI CHACHEV.

**Minister of Health:** ILKO SEMERDJIEV.

**Minister of Labour and Social Policy:** IVAN NEIKOV.

**Minister of Finance:** MOURAVEI RADEV.

**Minister of Foreign Affairs:** NADEZHDA MIHAILOVA.

**Minister of Justice:** TEODOSSIY SIMEONOV.

**Minister of Agriculture and Forestry:** VENTSISLAV VURBANOV.

### MINISTRIES

**Council of Ministers:** 1000 Sofia, Blvd Kniyas Dondukov 1; tel. (2) 85-01; fax (2) 87-08-78.

**Ministry of Agriculture and Forestry:** 1040 Sofia, Blvd Botev 55; tel. (2) 85-39; fax (2) 981-91-73 .

**Ministry of Culture:** 1040 Sofia, Blvd A. Stamboliiski 17; tel. (2) 861-11; fax (2) 987-89-71.

**Ministry of Defence:** 1000 Sofia, Aksakov St 1; tel. (2) 54-60-01; fax (2) 87-57-32.

**Ministry of the Economy:** 1000 Sofia, Slavyanska St 8; tel. (2) 87-07-41; fax (2) 980-26-90.

**Ministry of Education and Science:** 1540 Sofia, A. Stamboliiski 18; tel. (2) 84-81; fax (2) 988-26-93.

**Ministry of the Environment and Waters:** 1000 Sofia, William Gladstone St 67; tel. (2) 84-72-20; fax (2) 81-05-09 .

**Ministry of Finance:** 1000 Sofia, Rakovski St 102; tel. (2) 84-91; fax (2) 960-68-63.

**Ministry of Foreign Affairs:** 1113 Sofia, Al. Zhendov St 2; tel. (2) 27-14-41; fax (2) 80-38-34.

**Ministry of Health:** 1000 Sofia, Sveta Nedelya Sq. 5; tel. (2) 981-18-30; fax (2) 981-26-39.

**Ministry of the Interior:** 1000 Sofia, Shesti Septemvri St 29; tel. (2) 82-20-14; fax (2) 82-40-47.

**Ministry of Justice and European Legal Integration:** 1040 Sofia, 1 Slavyanska St; tel. (2) 91408; fax (2) 9879960; e-mail pr@mjeli.government.bg; internet www.mjeli.government.bg.

**Ministry of Labour and Social Policy:** 1000 Sofia, Triaditza St 2; tel. (2) 83-56-00; fax (2) 981-53-76; e-mail inter.coop@mlsp.government.bg.

**Ministry of Regional and Urban Development:** Sofia, Kirili Metodi 17–19; tel. (2) 8-38-41; fax (2) 987-25-17.

**Ministry of Transport and Communications:** 1000 Sofia, Levski St 9; tel. (2) 87-10-81; fax (2) 988-50-94.

## President and Legislature

### PRESIDENT

**Presidential Election, First Ballot, 27 October 1996**

| Candidates | % of votes |
|---|---|
| PETAR STOYANOV (Union of Democratic Forces) | 44.07 |
| IVAN MARAZOV (Together for Bulgaria)* | 27.01 |
| GEORGI GANCHEV (Bulgaria Business Bloc) | 21.87 |
| Others | 7.05 |
| **Total** | 100.00 |

**Second Ballot, 3 November 1996**

| Candidates | % of votes |
|---|---|
| PETAR STOYANOV | 59.73 |
| IVAN MARAZOV | 40.27 |
| **Total** | 100.00 |

* An electoral alliance, comprising the Bulgarian Socialist Party, the Aleksandur Stamboliyski Bulgarian Agrarian People's Union and the Ecoglasnost Political Club.

### NARODNO SOBRANIYE

(National Assembly)

**Chairman:** YORDAN SOKOLOV.

**General Election, 19 April 1997**

| Parties | % of votes | Seats |
|---|---|---|
| Union of Democratic Forces | 52.57 | 137 |
| Bulgarian Socialist Party* | 22.08 | 58 |
| Alliance for National Salvation† | 7.60 | 19 |
| Euro-Left | 5.50 | 14 |
| Bulgarian Business Bloc | 4.93 | 12 |
| Others | 7.32 | — |
| **Total** | 100.00 | 240 |

* The BSP contested the election in alliance (as the Democratic Left) with the Aleksandur Stamboliyski Bulgarian Agrarian People's Union and the Ecoglasnost Political Club.

† An alliance comprising the Movement for Rights and Freedoms and other groups.

## Political Organizations

There are over 80 registered political parties in Bulgaria, many of them incorporated into electoral alliances. The most significant political forces are listed below:

**Aleksandur Stamboliyski Bulgarian Agrarian People's Union** (Bulgarski Zemedelski Naroden Sayuz 'Aleksandur Stamboliyski'): c/o National Assembly, 1000 Sofia, Narodno Sobraniye Sq. 3; contested 1994 general election and 1996 presidential election in alliance with the Bulgarian Socialist Party and the Ecoglasnost Political Club.

**Alliance for National Salvation (ONS):** c/o National Assembly, 1000 Sofia, Narodno Sobraniye Sq. 3; f. 1997; electoral coalition of Movement for Rights and Freedoms and other monarchist and centrist groups; Leader AHMED DOGAN.

**Bulgarian Business Bloc—BBB:** 1000 Sofia, Shipka 13; tel. (2) 44-61-28; Leader GEORGI GANCHEV.

**Bulgarian Communist Party** (Bulgarska Komunisticheska Partiya): 1404 Sofia, Blvd P. J. Todorov; tel. and fax (2) 59-16-73; f. 1990 by conservative mems of the former, ruling Bulgarian Communist

Party (now the Bulgarian Socialist Party); First Sec. of the Central Cttee VLADIMIR SPASSOV.

**Bulgarian Socialist Party—BSP** (Bulgarska Sotsialisticheska Partiya): Sofia, 20 Positano St; POB 382; tel. (2) 980-12-91; fax (2) 980-52-91; e-mail BSP@mail.bol.bg; f. 1891 as the Bulgarian Social Democratic Party (BSDP); renamed the Bulgarian Communist Party (BCP) in 1919; renamed as above in 1990; 320,000 mems (Jan. 1996); Chair. GEORGI PURVANOV.

**Christian Republican Party:** 1606 Sofia; POB 113; tel. (2) 52-24-06; f. 1989; Chair. KONSTANTIN ADZHAROV.

**Confederation—Kingdom Bulgaria** (Tsarstvo Bulgaria): 7000 Ruse, Vassil Kolarov 45; tel. (82) 299-64; f. 1990; advocates the restoration of the former King, Simeon II; Chair. GEORGI BAKARDZHIEV.

**Democratic Alternative for the Republic—DAR:** c/o National Assembly, Sofia; left-of-centre coalition.

**Democratic Party of Justice:** Sofia; f. 1994; ethnic Turkish group; frmly part of the Movement for Rights and Freedoms; Chair. NEDIM GENDZHEV.

**Ecoglasnost National Movement:** 1000 Sofia, Blvd Kniyas Dondukov 9, 4th Floor, Rm 45; tel. (2) 986-22-21; fax (2) 88-15-30; e-mail ekogl@bulnet.bg; f. 1989; contested 1994 general election and 1996 presidential election in alliance with the BSP and Aleksandur Stamboliyski (BAPU); represented in more than 140 clubs and organizations in Bulgaria; Chair. IVAN SUNGARSKY; Sec. LUCHEZAR TOSHEV.

**Euro-Left:** c/o National Assembly, 1000 Sofia, Narodno Sobraniye Sq. 3; f. 1997 by the Civic Union of the Republic, the Movement for Social Humanism, and former mems of the Bulgarian Socialist Party; Leader ALEKSANDUR TOMOV.

**Fatherland Party of Labour:** 1000 Sofia, Slavyanska St 3, Hotel Slavyanska Beseda; tel. (2) 65-83-10; nationalist; Chair. RUMEN POPOV.

**Fatherland Union:** Sofia, Blvd Vitosha 18; tel. (2) 88-12-21; f. 1942 as the Fatherland Front (a mass organization unifying the BAPU, the BCP (now the BSP) and social organizations); named as above when restructured in 1990; a socio-political organization of independents and individuals belonging to different political parties; Chair. GINYO GANEV.

**Inner Macedonian Revolutionary Organization (IMRO):** 1301 Sofia, Pirotska St 5; tel. (2) 980-25-82; fax (2) 980-25-83; e-mail vmro@vmro.org; internet www.vmro.org; f. 1893; Chair. KRASSIMIR KARAKACHANOV.

**Liberal Congress Party:** 1000 Sofia, Blvd Kniyas Dondukov 39; tel. and fax (2) 39-00-18; f. 1989 as the Bulgarian Socialist Party, renamed Bulgarian Social Democratic Party (non-Marxist) in 1990 and as above in 1991; membership of the Union of Democratic Forces suspended 1993; c. 20,000 mems; Chair. YANKO N. YANKOV.

**Liberal Democratic Alliance:** f. July 1998; electoral alliance; Pres. ZHELYU ZHELEV.

**Free Radical Democratic Party:** Sofia.

**Liberal Democratic Alternative:** f. 1997; Leader ZHELYU ZHELEV.

**Movement for Rights and Freedoms—MRF** (Dvizhenie za Prava i Svobodi—DPS): 1408 Sofia, Ivan Vazov, Tzarigradsko Shosse 47/1; tel. (2) 88-18-23; f. 1990; represents the Muslim minority in Bulgaria; 95,000 mems (1991); Pres. AHMED DOGAN.

**New Choice Liberal Alliance:** f. 1994 by a former faction of the Union of Democratic Forces; Co-Chair. DIMITUR LUDZHEV, IVAN PUSHKAROV.

**National Movement for Rights and Freedoms:** f. 1999; breakaway faction of the Movement for Rights and Freedoms; Leader GYUNER TAHIR.

**New Union for Democracy—NUD:** Sofia; f. 1993; fmrly section of the Union of Democratic Forces.

**Party of Democratic Change:** Sofia; f. 1994 by a group from the MRF; Chair. MUKADDES NALBANT.

**Party of Free Democrats (Centre):** 6000 Stara Zagora; tel. (42) 2-70-42; f. 1989; Chair. Asst Prof. KHRISTO SANTULOV.

**Union of Democratic Forces—UDF** (Sayuz na Demokratichni Sili—SDS): 1000 Sofia, Blvd Rakovski 134; tel. (2) 88-25-01; f. 1989; Chair. IVAN KOSTOV; alliance of the following parties, organizations and movements:

**Bulgarian Agrarian People's Union—'Nikola Petkov'** (Bulgarski Zemedelski Naroden Sayuz—'Nikola Petkov'): 1000 Sofia, 1 Vrabtcha St; tel. (2) 87-80-81; fax (2) 981-09-49; f. 1899; in govt coalition from April 1997; Leader GEORGI PINCHEV.

**Bulgarian Democratic Forum:** 1505 Sofia; tel. (2) 89-022-85; Chair. VASSIL ZLATAREV.

**Bulgarian Social Democratic Party (United—BSDP):** 1504 Sofia, Ekzarkh Yosif St 37; tel. (2) 80-15-84; fax (2) 39-00-86; f. 1891; re-established 1989; Chair. PETUR DERTLIEV.

**Christian Democratic Union:** Sofia; Chair. JULIUS PAVLOV.

**Christian 'Salvation' Union:** Sofia; Chair. Bishop KHRISTOFOR SAHEV.

**Citizens' Initiative Movement:** 1000 Sofia; tel. (2) 39-01-93; Chair. TODOR GAGALOV.

**Conservative Ecological Party:** Sofia; Chair. KHRISTO BISSEROV.

**Democratic Party 1896:** f. 1994 by a former faction of the Democratic Party; Chair. STEFAN RAYCHEVSKI.

**Federation of Democracy Clubs:** 1000 Sofia, Blvd Kniyas Dondukov 39; tel. (2) 39-01-89; f. 1988 as Club for the Support of Glasnost and Perestroika; merged with other groups, as above in 1990; Chair. YORDAN VASSILEV.

**Federation of Independent Student Committees:** Sofia; Leader ANDREI NENOV.

**New Social Democratic Party:** 1504 Sofia; POB 14; tel. (2) 44-99-47; f. 1990; membership of UDF suspended 1991, resumed 1993; Chair. Dr VASSIL MIKHAILOV.

**New United Labour Bloc:** f. 1997; Chair. KRUSTYU PETKOV.

**People's Union:** c/o National Assembly, 1000 Sofia, Narodno Sobraniye Sq. 1; tel. (2) 987-90-32; fax (2) 981-09-49; f. 1994 as an electoral alliance between the following:

**Bulgarian Agrarian People's Union (BAPU)** (Bulgarski Zemedelski Naroden Sayuz—BZNS): 1000 Sofia, Yanko Zabunov St 1; tel. (2) 88-19-51; fax (2) 80-09-91; f. 1899; in ruling coalition 1946–89; Leader ANASTASIA MOSER.

**Democratic Party:** 1000 Sofia, Blvd Kniyas Dondukov 34; tel. (2) 80-01-87; re-formed 1990; Chair. STEFAN SAVOV.

**Radical Democratic Party:** 1000 Sofia, Blvd Kniyas Dondukov 8, 3rd Floor, Rms 6–8; tel. (2) 980-54-91; fax (2) 980-34-85; Chair. Dr KYRIL BOYADZHIEV.

**Real Reform Movement (DESIR):** f. 1997; Leader RENATA INDZHOVA.

**Republican Party:** Sofia; Chair. LENKO RUSSANOV.

**United Christian Democratic Centre:** 1000 Sofia, Blvd Kniyas Dondukov 34; tel. (2) 80-04-09; Chair. STEFAN SOFIANSKI.

The Independent Association for Human Rights in Bulgaria (Leader STEFAN VALKOV), the Union of Victims of Repression (Leader IVAN NEVROKOPSKY) and the Union of Non-Party Members (Leader BOYAN VELKOV) all enjoy observer status in the UDF.

# Diplomatic Representation

## EMBASSIES IN BULGARIA

**Afghanistan:** 1618 Sofia, Bl. 216A, Boryana St 61; tel. (2) 55-61-96; fax (2) 955-99-76; Chargé d'affaires: FAZEL SAIFI.

**Albania:** Sofia, Dimitur Polyanov St 10; tel. (2) 44-33-81; Ambassador: KOCO KOTE.

**Algeria:** Sofia, Slavyanska St 16; tel. (2) 87-56-83; Ambassador: ZINE EL-ABIDINE HACHICHI.

**Argentina:** Sofia, Dragan Tsankov 36, 2nd Floor; POB 635; tel. (2) 971-25-39; fax (2) 71-61-30-28; Ambassador: ARTURO HOTTON RISLER.

**Austria:** 1000 Sofia, Shipka St 4; tel. (2) 80-35-72; fax (2) 87-22-60; Ambassador: Dr ERICH KRISTEN.

**Belarus:** 1421 Sofia, Kokitche St 20; tel. (2) 65-28-43; fax (2) 963-40-23; Ambassador: ALYAKSANDR GERASIMENKA.

**Belgium:** 1126 Sofia, Velchova Zavera St 1; tel. (2) 963-36-22; fax (2) 963-36-38; e-mail ambabel@einet.bg; Ambassador: GUILLAUME SPELTINCX.

**Brazil:** 1113 Sofia, Fr. Joliot Curie St 19, Bl. 156/1; tel. (2) 72-35-27; fax (2) 971-28-18; e-mail sofbrem@main.infotel.bg; Ambassador: CARLOS ALBERTO PESSÔA PARDELLAS.

**Cambodia:** Sofia, Mladost 1, Blvd S. Allende, Res. 2; tel. (2) 75-71-35; fax (2) 75-40-09 Ambassador: BO RASSI.

**China, People's Republic:** Sofia, Blvd Ruski 18; tel. (2) 87-87-24; Ambassador: CHEN DELAI.

**Colombia:** 1113 Sofia, Aleksandur Zhendov St 1; POB 562; tel. (2) 971-31-03; fax (2) 72-76-60; e-mail emcolsof@mbox.digsys.bg; Ambassador: (vacant).

**Cuba:** 1113 Sofia, Mladezhka St 1; tel. (2) 72-09-96; fax (2) 72-07-94; Ambassador: LUIS FELIPE VÁZQUEZ.

**Czech Republic:** 1000 Sofia, ul. Yanko Sakazov 9; tel. (2) 946-11-10; fax (2) 946-18-00; Ambassador: ONDŘEJ HAVLÍN.

**Denmark:** 1000 Sofia, Blvd Tsar Osvoboditel 10; POB 1393; tel. (2) 980-08-30; fax (2) 980-08-31; Ambassador: CHRISTIAN FABER-ROD.

**Egypt:** 1000 Sofia, Shesti Septemvri St 5; tel. (2) 87-02-15; fax (2) 980-12-63; Ambassador: MAY ABOUL-DAHAB.

**Ethiopia:** Sofia, Vasil Kolarov St 28; tel. (2) 88-39-24; Chargé d'affaires a.i.: AYELLE MAKONEN.

**Finland:** 1126 Sofia, Simeonovsko 57, Res. 3; tel. (2) 962-58-70; fax (2) 962-51-70; Ambassador: Tapio Saarela.

**France:** 1505 Sofia, Oborishte St 29; tel. (2) 44-11-71; Ambassador: Dominique Chassard.

**Germany:** 1113 Sofia, Uliza Joliot Curie 25, POB 869; tel. (2) 918-38; fax (2) 963-16-58; e-mail gemb@ttm.bg; Ambassador: Ursula Seiler-Albring.

**Ghana:** Sofia; tel. (2) 70-65-09; Chargé d'affaires a.i.: Henry Andrew Anum Amah.

**Greece:** Sofia, Blvd Klement Gottwald 68; tel. (2) 44-37-70; Ambassador: Anastasios Sidheris.

**Holy See:** 1000 Sofia, 11 August 6, POB 9; tel. (2) 981-17-43; fax (2) 981-61-95; e-mail nuntius@mbox.digsys.bg; Apostolic Nuncio: Most Rev. Blasco Francisco Collaço, Titular Archbishop of Octava.

**Hungary:** Sofia, Shesti Septemvri St 57; tel. (2) 963-04-60; fax (2) 963-21-10; Ambassador: Ioan Talpes.

**India:** Sofia, Blvd Patriiarkh Evtimii 31; tel.(2) 981-17-02; fax 981-41-24; e-mail india@inet.bg; Ambassador: Nirupam Sen.

**Indonesia:** 1126 Sofia, Simeonovsko Shosse 53; tel. (2) 962-52-40; fax (2) 962-58-42; Ambassador: R. Suharjono.

**Iran:** Sofia, Blvd Vassil Levski 77; tel. (2) 44-10-13; Ambassador: Mohammad Ali Kormi-Nouri.

**Iraq:** 1113 Sofia, Anton Chekhov St 21; tel. (2) 973-33-48; fax (2) 971-11-91; e-mail iraqiyah@asico.net; internet www.bgnet.bg/~iraqiyah; Ambassador: Hassan Majid al-Saffar.

**Italy:** Sofia, Shipka St 2; tel. (2) 88-17-06; Ambassador: Agostino Mathis.

**Japan:** Sofia, Lyulyakova Gradina St 14; tel. (2) 72-39-84; fax (2) 49-210-95; Ambassador: Yoshihiro Jibiki.

**Korea, Democratic People's Republic:** Sofia, Mladost 1, Blvd S. Allende, Res. 4; tel. (2) 77-53-48; Ambassador: Kim Man-Ik.

**Korea, Republic:** 1414 Sofia, Bulgaria Sq. 1, National Palace of Culture; tel. (2) 650-162; Ambassador: Pill-Joo Sung.

**Kuwait:** Sofia, Blvd Klement Gottwald 47; tel. (2) 44-19-92; Ambassador: Talib Jalal ad-Din an-Naqib.

**Laos:** Sofia, Ovcha Kupel, Buket St 80; tel. (2) 56-55-08; Ambassador: Somsavat Lengsavad.

**Lebanon:** 1113 Sofia, Frédéric Joliot-Curie St 19; tel. (2) 971-31-69; fax (2) 973-32-56; e-mail amliban@bgnet.bg; Ambassador: Hussein Moussawi.

**Libya:** 1784 Sofia, Blvd Andrei Sakharov 1; tel. (2) 974-35-56; fax (2) 974-32-73; Secretary of People's Bureau: Farag Gibril.

**Macedonia, former Yugoslav republic:** Sofia; Ambassador: Nikola Todorchevski.

**Moldova:** Sofia; Ambassador: Mihai Coscodan.

**Morocco:** Sofia, Blvd Evlogui Gueorguiev 129; tel. (2) 44-27-94; fax (2) 946-10-43; e-mail sifmasof@bulnet.bg; Ambassador: Abdesselam Alem.

**Mozambique:** Sofia; Ambassador: Gonçalves Rafael Sengo.

**Netherlands:** 1126 Sofia, Galichitsa St 38; tel. (2) 962-57-90; fax (2) 962-59-88; e-mail nlgovsof@mbox.digsys.bg; Ambassador: W. Six.

**Nicaragua:** Sofia, Mladost 1, Blvd Allende, Res. 1; tel. (2) 75-41-57; Ambassador: Umberto Carión.

**Peru:** Sofia, Volokolamsko Shose 11; tel. (2) 68-32-43; Chargé d'affaires: Julio Vega Erausquín.

**Poland:** Sofia, Khan Krum St 46; tel. (2) 88-51-66; Ambassador: Jaroslaw Lindenberg.

**Portugal:** 1124 Sofia, Ivatz Voivoda St 6; tel. (2) 943-36-67; fax (2) 943-30-89; Ambassador: António Carvalho de Faria.

**Romania:** Sofia, Sitnyakovo St 4; tel. (2) 70-70-47; Ambassador: Ioan Talpes.

**Russian Federation:** Sofia, Blvd Dragan Tsankov 28; tel. (2) 963-44-58; fax (2) 963-41-03; Ambassador: Leonid Kerestedzhiyants.

**Slovakia:** Sofia, Blvd Janko Sakazov 9; tel. (2) 943-32-81; fax (2) 943-38-37; e-mail svkemba@mbox.ttm.bg; Ambassador: Ján Kováč.

**Spain:** Sofia, Sheinovo 27; tel. (2) 943-30-32; fax (2) 946-12-01; Ambassador: José Corderch.

**Sweden:** Sofia, Alfred Nobel Str. 4; tel. (2) 971-24-31; fax (2) 973-37-95; Ambassador: Sten Ask.

**Switzerland:** 1504 Sofia, Shipka St 33; tel. (2) 946-01-97; fax (2) 946-11-86; Ambassador: Gaudenz Ruf.

**Syria:** Sofia, Khristo Georgiev 10; tel. (2) 44-15-85; Chargé d'affaires: Saddik Saddikni.

**Turkey:** Sofia, Blvd Tolbukhin 23; tel. (2) 87-23-06; Ambassador: Mehmed Ali Irtemcelik.

**Ukraine:** Sofia; Ambassador: Oleksandr Vorobyov.

**United Kingdom:** Sofia, Blvd Vassil Levski 38; tel. (2) 980-12-20; fax (2) 980-12-29; e-mail britembsof@mbox.cit.bg; Ambassador: Richard Stagg.

**USA:** Sofia, Suborna St 1; tel. (2) 980-52-41; fax (2) 981-89-77; Ambassador: Avis T. Bohlen.

**Uruguay:** Sofia, Tsar Ivan Asen II St 91; POB 213; tel. (2) 943-45-45; fax (2) 943-40-40; e-mail urubulg@mbox.digsys.bg; Ambassador: Olga Barbarov.

**Venezuela:** 1504 Sofia, Tulovo St 1; tel. (2) 44-32-82; fax (2) 46-52-05; Ambassador: Gerardo E. Wills.

**Viet Nam:** Sofia, Ilya Petrov St 1; tel. (2) 65-83-34; Ambassador: Nguyen Tien Thong.

**Yemen:** Sofia, Blvd S. Allende, Res. 3; tel. (2) 75-61-63; Ambassador: Ali Munassar Muhammad.

**Yugoslavia:** Sofia, Veliko Turnovo St 3; tel. (2) 44-32-37; Ambassador: Rados Smilković.

# Judicial System

The 1991 Constitution provided for justice to be administered by the Supreme Court of Cassation, the Supreme Administrative Court, courts of appeal, courts of assizes, military courts and district courts. The main legal officials are the justices, or judges, of the higher courts, the prosecutors and investigating magistrates. The Chief Prosecutor is responsible for the precise and equal application of the law. The judicial system is independent, most appointments being made or recommended by the Supreme Judicial Council. The Ministry of Justice and Legal Euro-Integration co-ordinates the administration of the judicial system and the prisons. There is also the Constitutional Court, which is the final arbiter of constitutional issues. Under transitional arrangements attached to the 1991 Constitution, the existing Supreme Court of Bulgaria was to exercise the prerogatives of the two new Supreme Courts until the new judicial system was enacted and established.

**Supreme Court of Cassation:** 1000 Sofia, Blvd Vitosha 2, Sudebna Palata; tel. (2) 987-76-98; fax (2) 88-39-85; Chair. Rumen Yankov.

**Constitutional Court:** 1194 Sofia, Blvd Dondukov 1; tel. (2) 88-47-66; fax (2) 87-19-86; Pres. Zhivko Stalev; Sec.-Gen. Kiril A. Manov.

**Supreme Judicial Council:** Sofia; Head Vassill Gotsev, Minister of Justice and Legal Euro-integration.

**Ministry of Justice and Legal Euro-Integration:** see The Government (Ministries).

**Office of the Chief Prosecutor:** 1000 Sofia; tel. (2) 85-71; fax (2) 80-13-27; Chief Prosecutor Ivan Tatarchev; Military Prosecutor Milko Yotsov.

# Religion

Most of the population profess Christianity, the main denomination being the Bulgarian Orthodox Church, with a membership of more than 80% of the population. The 1991 Constitution guarantees freedom of religion, although Eastern Orthodox Christianity is declared to be the 'traditional religion in Bulgaria'. In accordance with the 1949 Bulgarian Law on Religious Faith, all new religious denominations must be registered by a governmental board before being allowed to operate freely. There is a significant Muslim minority (some 9% of the population), most of whom are ethnic Turks, although there are some ethnic Bulgarian Muslims, known as Pomaks. There is a small Jewish community.

**Directorate of Religious Affairs:** 1000 Sofia, Blvd Dondukov 1; tel. and fax (2) 88-04-88; a dept of the Council of Ministers; conducts relations between govt and religious organizations; Chair. Dr Khristo Matanov.

## CHRISTIANITY

In 1992 a schism occurred in the Bulgarian Orthodox Church, but it was resolved in October 1998 (the retirement of Patriarch Maksim was widely expected thereafter).

**Bulgarian Orthodox Church:** 1090 Sofia, Oborishte St 4, Synod Palace; tel. (2) 87-56-11; fax (2) 89-76-00; f. 865; autocephalous Exarchate 1870 (recognized 1945); administered by the Bulgarian Patriarchy; 11 dioceses in Bulgaria and two dioceses abroad (Diocese of North and South America and Australia, and Diocese of West Europe), each under a Metropolitan; Chair. of the Bulgarian Patriarchy His Holiness Patriarch Maksim.

**Armenian Apostolic Orthodox Church:** Sofia 1080, Nishka St 31; tel. (2) 88-02-08; 20,000 adherents (1996); administered by Bishop Dirayr Mardikiyan (resident in Bucharest, Romania); Chair. of the Diocesan Council in Bulgaria Owanes Kirazian.

### The Roman Catholic Church

Bulgarian Catholics may be adherents of either the Latin (Western) Rite, which is organized in two dioceses, or the Byzantine-Slav

(Eastern) Rite (one diocese). All three dioceses are directly responsible to the Holy See.

**Bishops' Conference** (Mejduritualnata Episcopska Konferenzia vâv Bâlgaria): 1606 Sofia, Liulin Plamina 5; tel. (2) 54-04-06; fax (2) 54-29-69; Pres. CHRISTO PROYKOV (Titular Bishop of Briula).

*Western Rite*

**Bishop of Nicopolis:** PETKO CHRISTOV; 7000 Ruse, Ivan Vazov St 26A; tel. (82) 22-52-45; fax (82) 82-28-81; e-mail dionicop@elits.rousse.bg; 30,000 adherents (1998).

**Diocese of Sofia and Plovdiv:** GEORGI IVANOV YOVCHEV (Apostolic Administrator); 4000 Plovdiv, Nezavisimost St 3; tel. and fax (32) 62-20-42; 35,000 adherents (1996).

*Eastern Rite*

**Apostolic Exarch of Sofia:** CHRISTO NIKOLOV PROYKOV (Titular Bishop of Briula), 1606 Sofia, Liulin Plamina 5; tel. (2) 54-04-06; fax (2) 54-29-69; e-mail cproikov@leff.bulnet.bg; 10,000 adherents (1998).

### The Protestant Churches

**Bulgarian Church of God:** Sofia 1408, Petko Karavelov St 1; tel. (2) 65-75-52; fax 51-91-31; 30,000 adherents (1992); Head Pastor PAVEL IGNATOV.

**Bulgarian Evangelical Church of God:** Plovdiv, Velbudge St 71; tel. (32) 43-72-92; 300 adherents (1992); Head Pastor BLAGOI ISEV.

**Bulgarian Evangelical Methodist Episcopal Church:** 1000 Sofia, Rakovski St 86; tel. and fax (2) 981-37-83; 1,000 adherents (1994); Gen. Superintendent Rev. BEDREA ALTUNIAN.

**Church of Jesus Christ of Latter-day Saints in Bulgaria:** Sofia, Drugba estate, Bl. 82/B/6, Flat 54; tel. (2) 74-08-06; f. 1991; 64 adherents (1992); Pres. VENTSESLAV LAZAROV.

**Open Biblical Confraternity:** 9300 Dobrich, Complex Dobrotiza, Bl. 27/A, Flat 17; f. 1991; Head Pastor ANTONIA POPOVA.

**Union of the Churches of the Seventh-day Adventists:** Sofia, Solunska St 10; tel. (2) 88-12-18; fax (2) 980-17-09; e-mail sda.bg@sbline.net; 6,700 adherents (1997); Head Pastor AGOP TACHMISSJAN.

**Union of Evangelical Baptist Churches:** 1303 Sofia, Ossogovo St 63; tel. and fax (2) 31-60-87; 2,500 adherents (1993); Pres. Dr TEODOR ANGELOV.

**Union of Evangelical Congregational Churches:** Sofia, Solunska St 49; tel. (2) 980-56-85; fax (2) 39-41-17; f. 1988; 4,000 adherents (1998); Head Pastor HRISTO KULICHEV.

**Union of Evangelical Pentecostal Churches:** 1557 Sofia, Bacho Kiro St 21; tel. (2) 83-51-69; f. 1928; 30,000 adherents (1991); Head Pastor VIKTOR VIRCHEV.

**Universal White Fraternity:** 1612 Sofia, Balshik St 8/B, Flat 27; tel. (2) 54-69-43; f. 1900; unifies the principles of Christianity with the arts and sciences; more than 6,000 adherents (1994); Chair. Dr ILIYAN STRATEV.

### ISLAM

**Supreme Muslim Theological Council:** Sofia, Bratya Miladinovi St 27; tel. (2) 87-73-20; fax (2) 39-00-23; adherents estimated at 9% of the actively religious population, with an estimated 708 acting regional imams; Chair. Hadzhi NEDIM GENDZHEV; Chief Mufti of the Muslims in Bulgaria HADZHIBASRI HADZHISHARIF.

### JUDAISM

**Central Jewish Theological Council:** 1000 Sofia, Eksarkh Yosif St 16; tel. 83-12-73; fax (2) 83-50-85; 5,000 adherents (1992); Head YOSSIF LEVI.

# The Press

### PRINCIPAL DAILIES

**24 Chasa** (24 Hours): 1000 Sofia, Blvd Tzarigradsko Shosse 47; tel. (2) 44-19-45; fax (2) 43-39-339; f. 1991; privately-owned; Editor-in-Chief VALERI NAIDENOV; circ. 330,000.

**Bulgarska Armiya** (Bulgarian Army): 1080 Sofia, Ivan Vasov St 12, POB 629; tel. (2) 87-47-93; fax (2) 987-91-26; f. 1944 as Narodna Armiya, name changed 1991; organ of the Ministry of Defence; Editor-in-Chief Col VLADI VLADKOV; circ. 30,000.

**Chernomorsky Far** (Black Sea Lighthouse): 8000 Burgas, Milin Kamak St 9; tel. and fax (56) 423-96; f. 1950; independent regional from 1988; Editor-in-Chief GALENTIN VLAHOV; circ. 37,000.

**Debati** (Debates): 1000 Sofia, Blvd Kniyas Korsakov 2; tel. (2) 887-25-04; fax (2) 80-05-10; f. 1990; independent; parliamentary issues, politics and diplomacy; Editor-in-Chief GEORGI INGILIROV; circ. 50,000.

**Demokratsiya** (Democracy): 1000 Sofia, Rakovski St 134; tel. (2) 981-29-79; fax (2) 980-73-42; f. 1990; newspaper of the Union of Democratic Forces; Editor-in-Chief NEVEN KOPANDANOVA; circ. 45,000.

**Duma** (Word): 1000 Sofia, Blvd Tzarigradsko Shosse 47; tel. (2) 43-431; fax (2) 87-50-73; f. 1927; fmrly *Rabotnichesko Delo*; organ of the Bulgarian Socialist Party; Editor-in-Chief STEFAN PRODEV ; circ. 130,000.

**Isik/Svetlina** (Light): 1000 Sofia, Blvd Tzarigradsko Shosse 47; tel. (2) 44-21-07; f. 1945; formerly *'Eni Isik' Nova Svetlina*; independent newspaper in Turkish and Bulgarian; Editor-in-Chief IVAN BADZHEV; circ. 30,000.

**Kontinent:** 1000 Sofia, Blvd Tzarigradsko Shosse 47A; tel. (2) 943-44-46; fax (2) 44-19-04; e-mail kont@bgnet.bg; f. 1992; independent; Editor-in-Chief BOIKO PANGELOV; circ. 12,000.

**Maritza:** 4000 Plovdiv, Bogomil St 59; POB 27 and 348; tel. (32) 26-84-34; fax (32) 27-47-60; f. 1991; Editor-in-Chief SPASS VASSILEV; circ. 40,000.

**Narodno Delo** (People's Cause): 9000 Varna, Blvd Khristo Botev 3; tel. (52) 23-10-71; fax (52) 23-90-67; f. 1944; 6 a week; regional independent; business, politics and sport; Editor-in-Chief DIMITUR KRASIMIROV; circ. 56,000.

**Noshten Trud** (Night Labour): 1000 Sofia, Blvd Kniyas Dondukov 52; tel. and fax (2) 87-70-63; f. 1992; 5 a week; Editor-in-Chief PLAMEN KAMENOV; circ. 332,000.

**Nov Glas** (New Voice): 5500 Lovech, G. Dimitrov St 24, 3rd Floor; tel. (68) 2-22-42; f. 1988; regional independent; Editor-in-Chief VENETSII GEORGIEV; circ. 50,000.

**Otechestven Vestnik** (Fatherland Newspaper): 1504 Sofia, Blvd Tzarigradsko Shosse 47; tel. (2) 43-431; fax (2) 46-31-08; f. 1942 as *Otechestven Front*; published by the journalists' co-operative 'Okchestvo'; Editor-in-Chief KONSTANCE ANSCHVA; total circ. 16,000.

**Pari** (Money): 1504 Sofia, Blvd Tzarigradsko Shosse 47; POB 46; tel. (2) 44-65-73; fax (2) 46-35-32; f. 1991; financial and economic news; Editor-in-Chief EVGENII PETROV; circ. 13,500.

**Pirinsko Delo** (Pirin's Cause): 2700 Blagoevgrad, Assen Khristove St 19; tel. 2-37-36; fax 2-31-06; f. 1945; independent regional daily from 1989; Editor-in-Chief KATYA Z. CATKOVA; circ. 20,000.

**Podkrepa** (Support): 1000 Sofia, Ekzarkh Yosif St 37; tel. (2) 83-12-27; fax (2) 46-73-74; f. 1991; organ of the Podkrepa (Support) Trade Union Confederation; Editor-in-Chief (vacant); circ. 18,000.

**Shipka:** 6300 Khaskovo, Georgi Dimitrov St 14; tel. (38) 12-52-52; fax (38) 3-76-28; f. 1988; independent regional newspaper; Editor-in-Chief DIMITUR DOBREV; circ. 25,000.

**Sport:** 1000 Sofia, National Stadium 'Vassil Levski', Sektor V; POB 88; tel. (2) 88-03-43; fax (2) 81-49-70; f. 1927; Editor-in-Chief IVAN NANKOV; circ. 80,000.

**Standart News Daily:** Sofia, Blvd Tzarigradsko Shosse 113A; tel. (2) 975-36-88; fax (2) 76-28-77; e-mail root@standart.news.com; f. 1992; Editor-in-Chief YULY MOSKOV; circ. 110,000.

**Telegraf:** 1113 Sofia, Blvd Tzarigradsko Shosse 72; POB 135; tel. (2) 75-11-22; fax (2) 77-04-11; f. 1990; privately-owned independent newspaper; Editor-in-Chief PLAMEN DIMITROV; circ. 30,000.

**Trud** (Labour): 1000 Sofia, Kniyas Dondukov 52; tel. (2) 987-98-05; fax (2) 80-11-40; f. 1923; organ of the Confederation of Independent Trade Unions in Bulgaria; Editor-in-Chief TOSHO TOSHEV; circ. 200,000.

**Vecherni Novini** (Evening News): 1000 Sofia; tel. (2) 44-14-69; fax (2) 46-73-65; f. 1951; independent newspaper; centre-left; publ. by the Vest Publishing House; Dir GEORGI GANCHEV; Editor-in-Chief LYUBOMIR KOLAROV; circ. 35,000.

**Vselena** (Universe): 34000 Montana, Geravitza Sq.; tel. (96) 2-25-06; fmrly *Delo*; Editor-in-Chief BOYAN MLADENOV.

**Zemedelsko Zname** (Agrarian Banner); Sofia, Yanko Zabunov St 23; tel. (2) 87-38-51; fax (2) 87-45-35; f. 1902; organ of the Bulgarian Agrarian People's Union; circ. 178,000.

**Zemya** (Earth): Sofia, 11 August St 18; tel. (2) 88-50-33; fax (2) 83-52-27; f. 1951 as *Kooperativno Selo*; renamed 1990; fmrly an organ of the Ministry of Agriculture, BSP daily; Editor-in-Chief KOSTA ANDREEV; circ. 53,000.

### PRINCIPAL PERIODICALS

**168 Chasa** (168 Hours): 1504 Sofia, Blvd Tzarigradsko Shosse 47; tel. (2) 43-39-288; fax (2) 43-39-315; f. 1990; weekly; business, politics, entertainments; Editor-in-Chief VASELKA VALILEVA; circ. 93,000.

**166 Politzeiski Vesti** (166 Police News): 1680 Sofia, J. K. Belite Brezi, Solun St bl. 25 and 26, Ground Floor; tel. (2) 82-30-30; fax 82-30-28; f. 1945; fmrly *Naroden Strazh*; weekly; criminology and public security; Editor-in-Chief PETUR VITANOV; circ. 22,000.

**Anti:** 1000 Sofia, Blvd Dondukov 9; tel. and fax (2) 80-43-03; f. 1991; weekly; Editor-in-Chief VASIL STANILOV; circ. 7,000.

**Avto-moto Svyat** (Automobile World): 1000 Sofia, Sveta Sofia St 6; POB 1348; tel. and fax (2) 88-08-08; f. 1957; monthly; illustrated publication on cars and motor sports; Editor-in-Chief ILJA SELIKTAR; circ. 33,600.

**Az Buki** (Alphabet): 1113 Sofia, Blvd Tzarigradsko Shosse 125; tel. (2) 71-65-73; f. 1991; weekly; education and culture; for schools; sponsored by the Ministry of Education and Science; Editor-in-Chief MILENA STRAKOVA; circ. 11,800.

**Bulgarski Biznes** (Bulgarian Business): 1505 Sofia, Oborishte St 44; POB 15; tel. (2) 46-70-23; fax (2) 44-63-61; weekly; organ of National Union of Employers; Editor-in-Chief DETELIN SERTOV; circ. 10,000–15,000.

**Bulgarski Fermer** (Bulgarian Farmer): 1797 Sofia, Blvd Dr G. M. Dimitrov 89; tel. (2) 71-04-48; fax (2) 73-10-08; f. 1990; weekly; Editor-in-Chief VASSIL ASPARUHOV; circ. 20,000.

**Businessman:** 1527 Sofia, Blvd Tzarigradsko Shosse 23; tel. and fax (2) 44-52-80; f. 1991; Editor-in-Chief GRIGOR SCHERNER.

**Computer World:** 1421 Sofia, Blvd Hr. Smirnenski 1, Block B, Flat 11; tel. (2) 81-42-70; fax (2) 80-26-52; f. 1990; weekly; US-Bulgarian joint venture; information technology; Editor-in-Chief SNEZHINA BADZHEVA; circ. 15,000.

**Domashen Maistor** (Household Manager): 1000 Sofia, Blvd Tolbukhin 51A; tel. (2) 87-09-14; f. 1991; monthly; magazine for household repairs; Editor-in-Chief GEORGI BALANSKI; circ. 12,000.

**Durzhaven Vestnik** (State Gazette): 1169 Sofia; tel. (2) 80-01-27; 2 a week; official organ of the National Assembly; 2 bulletin of parliamentary proceedings and the publication in which all legislation is promulgated; Editor-in-Chief PLAMEN MLADENOV; circ. 73,000.

**Edinstvo** (Unity): 1000 Sofia, Blvd Khristo Botev 48; tel. (2) 84-101 Ext. 218; f. 1991; weekly; Editor-in-Chief GENCHO BUCHVAROV.

**Ekho** (Echo): 1000 Sofia, 'Vasil Levski' St 75; tel. (2) 87-54-41; f. 1957; weekly; organ of the Bulgarian Tourist Union; tourism publication; Editor-in-Chief LUBOMIR GLIGOROV; circ. 7,000.

**Emigrant:** Sofia; tel. (2) 87-23-08; fax (2) 87-46-17; f. 1991 (to replace *Kontakti*); weekly; magazine for Bulgarians living abroad; Editor-in-Chief MANOL MANOV; circ. 20,000.

**Futbol** (Football): 1000 Sofia, Blvd Bulgaria 1, Vassil Levski Stadium; tel. (2) 87-19-51; fax (2) 65-72-57; f. 1988; weekly; independent soccer publication; Editor-in-Chief IVAN CHOMAKOV; circ. 132,500.

**Ikonomicheski Zhivot** (Economic Life): 1000 Sofia, Alabin St 33; tel. (2) 87-95-06; fax (2) 87-65-60; f. 1970; weekly; independent; marketing and advertising; Editor-in-Chief VASIL ALEKSIEV; circ. 21,000.

**Kompyutar** (Computer): 1142 Sofia, Blvd Vlevski 54; tel. (2) 87-50-45; e-mail newteck@ttm.bg; internet www.newteck.bg; f. 1985; monthly; hardware and software; Editor-in-Chief GEORGI BALANSKI; circ. 9,000.

**Komunistichesko Delo** (Communist Cause): 1000 Sofia, Central Post Office; POB 183; tel. (2) 59-16-73; organ of the Bulgarian Communist Party; Editor-in-Chief VLADIMIR SPASSOV; circ. 15,000–20,000.

**Krile** (Wings): 1184 Sofia, Blvd Tzarigradsko Shosse 111; tel. (2) 70-45-73; f. 1911; fmrly *Kam Nebeto*, renamed 1991; monthly; official organ; civil and military aviation; Editor-in-Chief TODOR ANDREEV; circ. 20,000.

**Kultura** (Culture): 1040 Sofia, Kniyas Aleksandur Battenberg St 4; tel. (2) 83-33-22; fax (2) 87-40-27; f. 1957; weekly; issue of the Ministry of Culture; arts, publicity and cultural affairs; Editor-in-Chief KOPRINKA CHERVENKOVA; circ. 3,300.

**Kurier 5** (Courier 5): 1000 Sofia, Blvd Tzarigradsko Shosse 47; tel. (2) 46-30-26; f. 1991; weekdays; advertising newspaper; Editor-in-Chief STEPAN ERAMIAN; circ. 30,000.

**Liberalen Kongres** (Liberal Congress): 1000 Sofia; tel. (2) 39-00-18; fax (2) 68-77-14; f. 1990; weekly; organ of the Liberal Congress Party; Editor-in-Chief ROSSEN ELEZOV; circ. 12,000.

**LIK:** Sofia, Blvd Tzarigradsko Shosse 49; weekly; publication of the Bulgarian Telegraph Agency; literature, art and culture; Editor-in-Chief SIRMA VELEVA; circ. 19,000.

**Literaturen Forum** (Literary Forum): 1000 Sofia, Aleksandur Battenberg Ave 4; tel. (2) 88-10-69; fax (2) 88-10-69; f. 1990; weekly; independent; Editor-in-Chief ATANAS SVILENOV; circ. 5,300.

**Makedonia** (Macedonia): 1301 Sofia, Pirotska St 5; tel. (2) 80-05-32; fax 87-46-64; e-mail mpress@virbus.bg; f. 1990; weekly; organ of the Inner Macedonian Revolutionary Organization (IMRO)—Union of Macedonian Societies; Editor-in-Chief DINKO DRAGANOV; circ. 22,000.

**Missul** (Thought): 1000 Sofia, Pozitano St 20; POB 382; tel. (2) 85-141; f. 1990; weekly; organ of the Marxist Alternative Movement; politics, culture; Editor-in-Chief GEORGI SVEZHIN; circ. 15,000.

**Napravi Sam** (Do It Yourself): 1164 Sofia; tel. (2) 87-50-45; e-mail newteck@einet.bg; internet www.newteck.bg; f. 1981; monthly; Editor-in-Chief GEORGI BALANSKI; circ. 8,000.

**Nie Zhenite** (We the Women): 1000 Sofia, Blvd Patriarch Evtimii 84; tel. (2) 52-31-98; f. 1990; weekly; organ of the Democratic Union of Women; Editor-in-Chief EVGINIA KIRANOVA; circ. 176,600.

**Nov Den** (New Day): 1000 Sofia, Blvd Vassil Levski 65, 3rd Floor; tel. (2) 80-02-05; f. 1990; weekly; organ of the Union of Free Democrats; Editor-in-Chief IVAN KALCHEV; circ. 25,000.

**Paraleli:** Sofia, Blvd Tzarigradsko Shosse 49; tel. (2) 87-40-35; f. 1964; weekly; illustrated publication of the Bulgarian Telegraph Agency; Editor-in-Chief KRASSIMIR DRUMEV; circ. 50,000.

**Pardon:** 1000 Sofia, Blvd Tzarigradsko Shosse 47; tel. (2) 43-431; f. 1991; weekly; satirical publication; Editor-in-Chief CHAVDAR SHINOV; circ. 8,560.

**Pogled** (Review): 1090 Sofia, Slaveikov Sq. 11; tel. (2) 87-70-97; fax (2) 65-80-23; f. 1930; weekly; organ of the Union of Bulgarian Journalists; Editor-in-Chief EVGENII STANCHEV; circ. 47,300.

**Prava i Svobodi** (Rights and Freedoms): 1504 Sofia, Blvd Tzarigradsko Shosse 47A, Alley 1; POB 208; tel. (2) 46-72-12; fax (2) 46-73-35; f. 1990; weekly; organ of the Movement for Rights and Freedoms; politics, culture; Editor-in-Chief (vacant); circ. 7,500.

**Progres** (Progress): 1000 Sofia, Gurko St 16; tel. (2) 89-06-24; fax (2) 89-59-98; f. 1894; fmrly *Tekhnichesko Delo*; weekly; organ of the Federation of Scientific and Technical Societies in Bulgaria; Editor-in-Chief PETKO TOMOV; circ. 35,000.

**Reporter 7:** 1184 Sofia, Blvd Tzarigradsko Shosse 113; tel. (2) 76-90-28; fax (2) 74-51-14; e-mail reporter@techno-link.com; f. 1990; weekly; private independent newspaper; Man. KRUM BLAGOV; circ. 60,000.

**Start:** 1000 Sofia, Vassil Levski Stadium; POB 797; tel. (2) 980-25-17; fax (2) 981-29-42; f. 1971; weekly; sports, illustrated; Editor-in-Chief NIKOLAY RANGELOV; circ. 21,300.

**Sturshel** (Hornet): 1504 Sofia, Blvd Tzarigradsko Shosse 47; tel. (2) 44-35-50; fax (2) 443-550; f. 1946; weekly; humour and satire; Editor-in-Chief YORDAN POPOV; circ. 45,200.

**Svoboden Narod** (Free People): 1000 Sofia, Ekzarkh Yosif St 37, 8th Floor; f. 1990; weekly; organ of the Bulgarian Social Democratic Party; Editor-in-Chief TEODOR DETCHEV; circ. 10,000.

**Televiziya i Radio** (Television and Radio): 1000 Sofia, Bulgarian National Television, San Stefano St 29; tel. (2) 44-32-94; f. 1964; weekly; broadcast listings; Editor-in-Chief LUBOMIR YANKOV; circ. 70,300.

**Tsarkoven Vestnik** (Church Newspaper): 1000 Sofia, Oborishte St 4; tel. (2) 87-56-11; f. 1900; weekly; organ of the Bulgarian Orthodox Church; Editor-in-Chief DIMITUR KIROV; circ. 4,000.

**Uchitelsko Delo** (Teachers' Cause): 1113 Sofia, Blvd Tzarigradsko Shosse 125, Studentski Obshtezhitiya, Blok 5; tel. (2) 70-00-12; f. 1905; weekly; organ of the Union of Bulgarian Teachers; Editor-in-Chief YORDAN YORDANOV; circ. 12,700.

**Vek 21** (21st Century): 1000 Sofia, Kaloyan St 10; tel. (2) 46-54-23; fax (2) 46-61-23; f. 1990; weekly; organ of the Radical Democratic Party; liberal politics and culture; Editor-in-Chief ALEKSANDUR YORDANOV; circ. 5,900.

**Zdrave** (Health): 1527 Sofia, Byalo More St 8; tel. (2) 44-30-26; fax (2) 44-17-59; f. 1936; monthly; published by Bulgarian Red Cross; Editor-in-Chief YAKOV YANAKIEV; circ. 55,000.

**Zhenata Dnes** (Women Today): 1000 Sofia, Narodno Sobraniye Sq. 12; tel. (2) 89-16-00; f. 1946; monthly; organ of Zhenata Dnes Ltd; Editor-in-Chief BOTIO ANGELOV; circ. 50,000.

**Zname** (Banner): 1184 Sofia, Blvd Kniyas Korsakov 34; tel. (2) 80-01-83; f. 1894, publ. until 1934 and 1945–49, resumed publishing 1990; weekly; Editor-in-Chief BOGDAN MORFOV; circ. 20,000.

**Zora** (Dawn): 1000 Sofia, Blvd Tzarigradsko Shosse 77; tel. (2) 71-41-826; f. 1990; weekly; independent; Editor-in-Chief MINCHO MINCHEV; circ. 20,000.

## NEWS AGENCIES

**Bulgarska Telegrafna Agentsia—BTA** (Bulgarian Telegraph Agency): 1024 Sofia, Blvd Tzarigradsko Shosse 49; tel. (2) 87-73-63; fax (2) 80-24-88; f. 1898; official news agency; publishes weekly surveys of science and technology, international affairs, literature and art; Gen. Dir MILEN VULKOV.

**Bulnet:** 1000 Sofia, Rakovski St 127; tel. (2) 987-11-22; fax (2) 980-30-71; e-mail support@bulnet.bg; f. 1994; provides on-line access, internet services, communications software, hardware and consultancy; photo service; Exec. Dir. R. MEVA.

**Sofia-Press Agency:** 1040 Sofia, Slavyanska St 29; tel. (2) 88-58-31; fax (2) 88-34-55; f. 1967 by the Union of Bulgarian Writers, the Union of Bulgarian Journalists, the Union of Bulgarian Artists and the Union of Bulgarian Composers; publishes socio-political and scientific literature, fiction, children's and tourist literature, publications on the arts, a newspaper, magazines and bulletins in foreign languages; also operates **Sofia-Press Info** (tel. (2) 87-66-80; Pres. ALEKSANDUR NIKOLOV), which provides up-to-date information on Bulgaria, in print and for broadcast; Dir-Gen. KOLIO GEORGIEV.

### Foreign Bureaux

**Agence France-Presse (AFP):** 1000 Sofia, Blvd Tolbukhin 16; tel. (2) 71-91-71; Correspondent VESSELA SERGEVA-PETROVA.

**Agencia EFE** (Spain): Sofia; tel. (2) 87-29-63; Correspondent SAMUEL FRANCES.

**Allgemeiner Deutscher Nachrichtendienst (ADN)** (Germany): 1000 Sofia, Moskovska 27A; tel. (2) 87-82-73; fax (2) 87-53-16; Correspondent HANS-PETKO TEUCHERT.

**Česká tisková kancelář (ČTK)** (Czech Republic): 1113 Sofia, Bl. 154A, Gagarin St, Apt 19; tel. (2) 70-91-36; Correspondent VĚRA IVANOVIČOVÁ.

**Deutsche Presse Agentur (dpa)** (Germany): Sofia; tel. (2) 72-02-02; Correspondent ELENA LALOVA.

**Informatsionnoye Telegrafnoye Agentstvo Rossii—Telegrafnoye Agentstvo Suverennykh Stran (ITAR—TASS)** (Russia): 1000 Sofia, A. Gendov St 1, Apt 29; tel. (2) 87-38-03; Correspondent ALEKSANDR STEPANENKO.

**Magyar Távirati Iroda (MTI)** (Hungary): Sofia, Frédéric Joliot-Curie St 15, blok 156/3, Apt 28; tel. (2) 70-18-12; Correspondent TIVADAR KELLER.

**Novinska Agencija Tanjug** (Yugoslavia): 1000 Sofia, L. Koshut St 33; tel. (2) 71-90-57; Correspondent PERO RAKOSEVIĆ.

**Polska Agencja Prasowa (PAP)** (Poland): Sofia; tel. (2) 44-14-39; Correspondent BOGDAN KORNEJUCK.

**Prensa Latina** (Cuba): 1113 Sofia, Yuri Gagarin St 22, Bl. 154B, Apt 22; tel. (2) 71-91-90; Correspondent SUSANA UGARTE SOLER.

**Reuters** (United Kingdom): 1000 Sofia, Ivan Vazov St 16; tel. (2) 911-88; fax (2) 980-91-31; e-mail sofia.newsroom@reuters.com; Correspondent THALIA GRIFFITHS.

**Rossiyskoye Informatsionnoye Agentstvo—Novosti (RIA—Novosti)** (Russia): Sofia; tel. and fax (2) 943-48-47; Bureau Man. YEVGENII VOROBYOV.

**United Press International (UPI)** (USA): Sofia; tel. (2) 62-24-65; Correspondent GUILLERMO ANGELOV.

**Xinhua (New China) News Agency** (People's Republic of China): Sofia; tel. (2) 88-49-41; Correspondent U. SIZIUN.

The following agencies are also represented: SANA (Syria) and Associated Press (USA).

### PRESS ASSOCIATIONS

**Union of Bulgarian Journalists:** 1000 Sofia, Graf Ignatiev St 4; tel. (2) 87-27-73; fax (2) 88-30-47; f. 1955; Pres. ALEKSANDUR ANGELOV; 5,600 mems.

**Union of Journalists in Bulgaria:** 1000 Sofia, Geneva St 3; tel. and fax (2) 65-18-49; Chair. CHAVDAR TONCHEV.

## Publishers

**Darzhavno Izdatelstvo 'Khristo G. Danov'** ('Khristo G. Danov' State Publishing House): 4005 Plovdiv, Stoyan Chalakov St 1; tel. (32) 23-12-01; fax (32) 26-05-60; f. 1855; fiction, poetry, literary criticism; Dir NACHO HRISTOSKOV.

**Darzhavno Izdatelstvo 'Meditsina i Fizkultura':** 1080 Sofia, Slaveikov Sq. 11; tel. (2) 87-13-08; fax (2) 987-99-75; f. 1948; medicine, physical culture and tourism; Dir PETKO PETKOV.

**Darzhavno Izdatelstvo 'Prosveta':** 1184 Sofia, Blvd Tzarigradsko Shosse 117; tel. (2) 76-06-51; fax (2) 76-44-51; f. 1948; educational publishing house; Man. Dir RUMEN EVTIMOV.

**Darzhavno Izdatelstvo 'Tekhnika':** 1000 Sofia, Slaveikov Sq. 1; tel. (2) 87-12-83; fax (2) 87-49-06; f. 1958; textbooks for technical and higher education and technical literature; Dir NINA DENEVA.

**Darzhavno Izdatelstvo 'Zemizdat':** 1504 Sofia, Blvd Tzarigradsko Shosse 47; tel. (2) 44-18-29; f. 1949; specializes in works on agriculture, shooting, fishing, forestry, livestock-breeding, veterinary medicine and popular scientific literature and textbooks; Dir PETUR ANGELOV.

**Galaktika:** 9000 Varna, Nezavissimost Sq. 6; tel. (52) 24-11-56; fax (52) 23-47-50; f. 1960; science fiction, economics, Bulgarian and foreign literature; Dir ASSYA KADREVA.

**Izdatelstvo na Bulgarskata Akademiya na Naukite 'Marin Drinov':** 1113 Sofia, Acad. Georgi Bonchev St, blok 6; tel. (2) 72-09-22; fax (2) 70-40-54; f. 1869; scientific works and periodicals of the Bulgarian Academy of Sciences; Dir TODOR RANGELOV.

**Izdatelstvo 'Bulgarski Houdozhnik':** 1504 Sofia, Shipka St 6; tel. (2) 46-72-85; fax (2) 946-02-12; f. 1952; art books, children's books; Dir BOUYAN FILCHEV.

**Izdatelstvo 'Bulgarsky Pisatel':** Sofia, Shesti Septemvri St 35; publishing house of the Union of Bulgarian Writers; Bulgarian fiction and poetry, criticism; Dir SIMEON SULTANOV.

**Izdatelstvo 'Khristo Botev':** 1504 Sofia, Blvd Tzarigradsko Shosse 47; tel. (2) 43-431; f. 1944; fmrly the Publishing House of the Bulgarian Communist Party, renamed as above 1990; Dir IVAN GRANITSKY.

**Izdatelstvo na Ministerstvo na Otbranta** (Ministry of Defence Publishing House): 1000 Sofia, Ivan Vazov St 12; tel. (2) 88-44-31; fax (2) 88-15-68; Head Maj. BOYAN SULTANOV.

**Izdatelstvo Mladezh,** (Youth Publishing House): 1000 Sofia, Tsar Kaloyan St 10; tel. (2) 88-21-37; fax (2) 87-61-35; art, history, original and translated fiction and original and translated poetry for children; Gen. Dir STANIMIR ILCHEV.

**Izdatelstvo 'Profizdat'** (Publishing House of the Central Council of Bulgarian Trade Unions): Sofia, Blvd Dondukov 82; specialized literature and fiction; Dir STOYAN POPOV.

**Knigoizdatelstvo 'Galaktika':** 9000 Varna, Deveti Septemvri Sq. 6; tel. (2) 22-50-77; fax (2) 22-50-77; f. 1960; popular science, science fiction, economics, Bulgarian and foreign literature; Dir PANKO ANCHEV.

**'Narodna Kultura' Publishers:** 1000 Sofia, Angel Kanchev St 1, tel. (2) 87-47-90; e-mail nauk-izk@sigma-bg.com; f. 1944; general; Dir PETAR MANOLOV.

**Nauka i Izkustvo:** 1000 Sofia, Slaveikov Sq. 11; tel. and fax (2) 87-24-96; f. 1948; general publishers; Man. LORETA PUCHKAROVA.

**Sinodalno Izdatelstvo:** Sofia, Oboriste St 4; tel. (2) 87-56-11; religious publishing house; Dir ANGEL VELITEHKOV.

### STATE ORGANIZATION

**Jusautor:** Sofia; tel. (2) 87-28-71; fax (2) 87-37-40; state organization of the Council of Ministers; Bulgarian copyright agency; represents Bulgarian authors of literary, scientific, dramatic and musical works, and deals with the grant of options, authorization for translations, and drawing up of contracts for the use of works by foreign publishers and producers; Dir-Gen. YANA MARKOVA.

### PUBLISHERS' ASSOCIATION

**Bulgarian Book Publishers' Association:** 1000 Sofia, Slaveikov Sq. 11, POB 1076; tel. and fax (2) 980-78-39; Chair. NIKOLA KITZERSKY.

### WRITERS' UNION

**Union of Bulgarian Writers:** Sofia, Slaveikov Sq. 2; tel. (2) 88-06-85; fax (2) 87-47-57; f. 1913; Chair. NIKOLAI HAITOV; 501 mems.

## Broadcasting and Communications

### TELECOMMUNICATIONS

In October 1997 there were 32 telephone lines for every 100 residents. Approximately 5% of the telephone network was digitized; there were 17 digital exchanges, with a total capacity of 107,000 subscribers.

**Committee of Posts and Telecommunications:** 1000 Sofia, Gourko St 6, POB 1352; tel. (2) 981-29-49; fax (2) 980-61-05; supervises and regulates the post and telecommunications systems; Pres. ANTONI SLAVINSKI.

**Bulgarian Telecommunications Company (BTC):** 1606 Sofia, Blvd Totleben 8; tel. (2) 88-94-38; fax (2) 87-58-85; e-mail central .office.@btc.bg; internet www.btc.bg; scheduled for privatization in 1999; provides telecommunications and information services; Pres. MARIAN DRAGOSTINOV; 23,000 employees.

### BROADCASTING

**National Radio and Television Council:** 1504 Sofia, San Stefano St 29, tel. (2) 46-81; Chair. (vacant).

#### Radio

An estimated nine private local radio stations were broadcasting in 1995.

**Bulgarsko Nationalno Radio:** 1040 Sofia, Blvd Dragan Tzankov 4; tel. (2) 985-24; fax (2) 65-72-98; e-mail bgintrel.nationalradio.bg; internet www.nationalradio.bg; f. 1929; two Home Service programmes; local stations at Blagoevgrad, Plovdiv, Shumen, Stara Zagora and Varna. The Foreign Service broadcasts in Bulgarian, Turkish, Greek, Serbo-Croat, French, Italian, German, English, Portuguese, Spanish, Albanian and Arabic; Dir-Gen. ALEKSANDUR VELEV.

**Radio Alma Mater:** 1000 Sofia, Moskovska St 49; tel. (2) 986-16-07; fax (2) 930-84-80; f. 1993; cable radio service introduced by Sofia Univ.; from July 1998 24-hour broadcasting at 87.7 MHz in Sofia; culture and science programmes; Editor-in-Chief DILIANA KIRKOVSKA.

#### Television

**Bulgarska Televiziya:** 1504 Sofia, San Stefano St 29; tel. (2) 44-63-29; fax (2) 946-12-10; f. 1952; daily transmission of programmes on two channels—Channel 1 and Efir 2; Dir.-Gen. LILYANA POPOVA; 3,000 employees.

**Nova Televiziya:** 1000 Sofia, Sveta Nedela Sq. 16; tel. (2) 80-50-25; fax (2) 87-02-98; f. 1994; first private television channel in Bulgaria; commercial news and entertainment.

# Finance

(cap. = capital; dep. = deposits; res = reserves;
m. = million; amounts in old leva, unless otherwise indicated)

## BANKING

The Bulgarian banking system was restructured during the 1990s as part of a comprehensive reform of the entire economic system, in order to establish a market economy. By late 1991 the transition to a two-tier banking sector had been achieved. In September 1992 almost 80 commercial banks were organized as self-managing joint-stock companies. However, only 16 of these were licensed for cross-border foreign-exchange operations, with most of the remainder less important in terms of size and activities. In late 1992 21 commercial banks merged to form the United Bulgarian Bank, which opened in 1993. In early 1993 two new banks emerged, Commercial Bank Expressbank (formed from the merger of 12 banks) and Hebrosbank (a merger of eight banks). In 1996 14 banks, including five state-owned banks, collapsed. In May 1996 the total number of banks was 47, and in October 1997 state-owned banks accounted for 73% of the total. A currency board was established in July 1997.

### Currency Board

**Currency Board of the Republic of Bulgaria:** Sofia; f. 1997; monetary supervision; Head MARTIN ZAIMOV.

### Central Bank

**Bulgarian National Bank** (Bulgarska Narodna Banka): 1000 Sofia, Aleksandur Battenberg Sq. 1; tel. (2) 886-12-03; fax (2) 980-24-25; e-mail press_office@bnbank.org; internet www.bnb.bg; f. 1879; bank of issue; cap. 20,000m., res 816,111m., dep. 2,498,540m. (Dec. 1998); Gov. SVETOSLAV GAVRIYSKI; 6 brs; 1,330 employees.

### State Savings Bank

**State Savings Bank:** 1000 Sofia, Moskovska St 19; tel. (2) 988-10-41; fax (2) 54-13-55; f. 1951; provides general retail banking services throughout the country; assets 881.2m. (1997); Pres. SPAS DIMITROV; 481 brs.

### Commercial Banks Licensed for Cross-border Foreign Exchange Operations

**BNP-Ak-Dresdner Bank:** 1000 Sofia, Narodno Sobraniye 1, POB 11; tel. (2) 980-12-37; fax (2) 981-69-91; cap. 16,000m., dep. 237,271.2m., res 8,651.7m. (Dec. 1998); f. 1994; Gen. Man. and Chief Exec. XAVIER DE BEAUSSE.

**BRIBANK AD:** 1000 Sofia, Saborna St 11A; tel. (2) 98-50-02-40; fax (2) 981-25-26; e-mail nkratchounoja@hg.bribank.bg; f. 1994; formerly Bulgarian Russian Investment Bank; cap. 10,000m., res 1,676.7m., dep. 80,031.4m. (Dec. 1998); Chair. KRASSIMIR ANGARSKI; 10 brs.

**Bulbank (Bulgarian Foreign Trade Bank):** 1000 Sofia, Sveta Nedelya Sq. 7; tel. (2) 98-41-11-11; fax (2) 988-46-36; e-mail info@sof.bulbank.bg; internet www.bulbank.bg; f. 1964; scheduled for privatization; cap. 166,370m., res 307,557m., dep. 1,428,047m. (1998); Chair. and Chief Exec. CHAVDAR KANTCHEV; 40 brs.

**Bulgarian Investment Bank plc:** 1000 Sofia, Serdika St 20; tel. (2) 981-65-25; fax (2) 981-41-02; e-mail icb@internet-bg.net; f. 1994; assets 28.5m. (1998); Chief Exec. STEPHEN B. STRAUSS.

**Bulgarian Post Bank:** 1414 Sofia, Bulgaria Sq. 1; tel. (2) 963-20-96; fax (2) 963-04-82; e-mail intldiv@postbank.bg; f. 1991; cap. 70,971m., dep. 361,865m. (Dec. 1998); Chair. VLADIMIR VLADIMIROV.

**CB Unionbank Ltd:** 1606 Sofia, 10–12 Damyan Gruev St; tel. (2) 988-46-39; fax (2) 980-20-04; e-mail mainmail@unionbank.erix.net; internet www.unionbank.bg; cap. 2,772.0m., res 21,339.9m., dep. 55,786.5m.; Exec. Dir IVAN TOTEV RADEV.

**Central Co-operative Bank Ltd:** 1000 Sofia, G. S. Rakovsky St 103; tel. (2) 98-44-32-50; fax (2) 987-19-48; e-mail centralccb@ccb.bg; f. 1991; cap. 15,000m., res 7,399.4m., dep. 198,733.2m. (Dec. 1998); Chair. and Chief Exec. TENCHO TENEV.

**Commercial Bank Biochim:** 1040 Sofia, Ivan Vazov St 1; tel. (2) 86-16-9; fax (2) 980-49-26; e-mail sstoev@biochim.com; internet www.biochim.com; f. 1987; scheduled for privatization; cap. 16,757.2m., res 23,709.8m. dep. 342,545.2m. (1997); Chief Exec. TSVETAN TSEKOV.

**Commercial Bank Bulgaria Invest Ltd:** 1202 Sofia, 65 Maria Louiza; tel. (2) 988-54-88; fax (2) 981-93-07; e-mail bgynvyd@maileryx.net; cap. 8,000m., res 201.2m., dep. 9,921.1m.; Chair. DIMITAR ZHELEV.

**Commercial Bank Expressbank AD:** 9000 Varna, Blvd Varnenchik 92; tel. (52) 60-04-80; fax (52) 60-16-81; f. 1993 through the merger of 12 banks; cap. 14,264m., res 34,542m., dep. 275,846m. (Dec. 1998); Chair. and CEO IVAN KONSTANTINOV; 26 brs.

**Corporate Commercial Bank:** 1000 Sofia, Ekzarkh Yosif St 65, POB 632; tel. (2) 980-93-62; fax (2) 980-89-48; f. 1989; cap. 10,000m., res 1,315.3m., dep. 2,282.6m. (Dec. 1998); Chair. VENTZISLAV ANTONOV.

**ELITBANK:** 1000 Sofia, Hristo Belchev St 7; tel. (2) 845-41-31; fax (2) 81-01-13; f. 1994; cap. 1,000m., res 346.5m., dep. 9,002.2m. (Dec. 1995); Chair. and Exec. Pres. IVO GEORGIEV.

**Eurobank:** 1407 Sofia, Cherni Vrach Blvd 43; tel. (2) 62-33-66; fax (2) 68-10-86; e-mail mariola@eurobank.bg; internet www.eurobank.bg; f. 1993 as Commercial Bank Mollov Ltd; cap. 36,348.9m., dep. 40,124.7m. (1998); Chief Exec. JAN TUSIM.

**Expressbank:** 9000 Varna, Blvd Vl. Varnenchik 92; tel. (52) 66-04-80; fax (52) 60-13-24; e-mail office@expressbank.bg; internet www.expressbank.bg; f. 1987 as Transport Bank, name changed following merger in 1993; scheduled for privatization; cap. 14,264.8m., res 56,345.0m., dep. 275,846.6m. (Dec. 1998); Chair. and Exec. Dir IVAN KONSTANTINOV; 26 brs; 1,313 employees.

**First East International Bank:** 1504 Sofia, 106 Vassil Levski Blvd; tel. (2) 946-16-82; fax (2) 946-16-83; e-mail feib@asico.net; cap. 7,100.2m., res 292.8m., dep. 67,346.4m. (1997); Pres. ANNA SABEVA; 100 brs; 1,200 employees.

**First Investment Bank Ltd:** 1000 Sofia, St Karadja St 10; tel. (2) 9-10-01; fax (2) 980-50-33; e-mail fib@fibank.bg; internet www.fibank.bg; f. 1993; cap. US $20m., dep. $113.4m. (Dec. 1998); Exec. Dir BOZHIDAR GRIGOROV.

**First Private Bank:** 1000 Sofia, Ivan Vazov St 16; tel. (2) 980-50-10; fax (2) 980-51-01; f. 1990; placed under supervision of the Bulgarian National Bank in May 1996; cap. 2,015.7m., res 36,444.7m., dep. 129,426.9m. (1996); Pres. VENTSISLAV YOSIFOV; 71 brs.

**Hebrosbank:** 4018 Plovdiv, Blvd Tsar Boris III Obedinitel 37; tel. (32) 56-26-68; fax (2) 62-39-64; f. 1993 following merger of eight banks; scheduled for privatization; cap. 154.9m., res 167,779.0m. (Dec. 1998); Chair. MARIN MARINOV; Chief Exec. IVAN ZLATAREV; 2,137 employees.

**International Bank for Trade and Development:** 1000 Sofia, Ivan Vazov St 2; tel. (2) 987-15-16; fax (2) 87-30-41; e-mail biededp@bsbg.net; cap. 13,000m. (1998); Chief Exec. PLAMEN BONEV; 8 brs.

**Municipal Bank plc:** 1000 Sofia, 6 Vrabcha St; tel. (2) 930-01-85; fax (2) 981-51-47; f. 1986 as Sofia Municipal Bank Plc; name changed Jan. 1998; cap. 20,767.2m., res 5,354.4m., dep. 140,280.0m. (Dec. 1998); Exec. Dir VANYA GEORGIEVA VASSILEVA.

**Neftinvestbank AD:** 1000 Sofia, 155 Rakovski St, POB 1138; tel. (2) 981-69-38; fax (2) 980-77-22; f. 1994 as International Orthodox Bank 'St Nikola'; cap. 32,200.0m., res 203.6m., dep. 39,675.4m. (Dec. 1997); Chair PETIA IVANOVA BARAKOVA-SLAVOVA.

**Raiffeisenbank (Bulgaria):** 1504 Sofia, Serdika St 18-20; tel. (2) 91-98-59; fax (2) 943-45-28; e-mail ibgaddg@rbb-sofia.raiffeisen.at; f. 1994; cap. 16,700m., dep. 81,400m. (June 1998); Exec. Gen. Mans DOUGLAS G. DRYDEN, MOMTCHIL ANDREEV.

**Rosexim Bank Plc:** 1000 Sofia, 15 Lege St; tel. (2) 98-44-61-21; fax (2) 980-26-23; cap. 33,618.3m., res 18,100.4m., dep. 78,265.2m.; Chair. and Exec. Dir DIANA MLADENOVA.

**Teximbank:** 1202 Sofia, Blvd Maria Luisa 107, Sredetz Municipality; tel. (2) 931-12-07; fax (2) 931-12-07; f. 1992; cap. 1,000m., res 1,421.5m., dep. 3,059.0m. (Dec. 1996); Pres GEORGI NAYDENOV, MARIA VIDOLOVA.

**United Bulgarian Bank Inc.:** 1000 Sofia, Sveta Sofia St 5; tel. (2) 84-70-90; fax (2) 988-08-22; e-mail info@sof.ubb.bg; internet www.ubb.bg; f. 1992 following a merger of 22 commercial banks; universal commercial bank; cap. 75,964.0m., res 33,935.0m., dep. 628,977.0m. (Dec. 1998); Chair. PIERRE MELLINGER; CEO STILIAN VATEV; 57 brs.

## STOCK EXCHANGE

**Bulgarian Stock Exchange:** 1040 Sofia, Makedonia Sq. 1; tel. (2) 986-59-15; fax (2) 986-58-63; e-mail bsemail@online; internet www.online.bg/bs; Chair. GEORGE PROHASKY; CEO APOSTOL APOSTOLOV.

## INSURANCE

In 1947 all insurance firms were nationalized, and reorganized into a single state insurance company (see below). In 1989 private insurance companies began to reappear.

**National Insurance Institute (DZI):** 1040 Sofia, Blvd Tzar Osvoboditel 6; tel. (2) 981-57-99; fax (2) 87-69-82; f. 1946; all areas of insurance; Pres. NIKOLAY NIKOLOV; 101 brs.

**Bulstrad Insurance and Reinsurance:** 1000 Sofia, Dunav St 5; POB 627; tel. (2) 8-51-91; fax (2) 80-12-03; f. 1961; all classes of insurance and reinsurance; Chief Exec. RUMEN YANCHEV.

# Trade and Industry

## GOVERNMENT AGENCIES

**Privatization Agency:** 1000 Sofia, Aksakov St 29; tel. (2) 897-75-79; fax (2) 981-62-01; e-mail bgpriv@mbox.digsys.bg; internet www.privatization.bg; f. 1992; organizes the privatization of state-owned enterprises whose assets exceed 70m. leva; Exec. Dir ZAKHARI ZHELYAZKOV.

## INTERNATIONAL FREE-TRADE ZONES

**Bourgas Free-Trade Zone:** 8000 Burgas, Trapezitza St 5; POB 154; tel. (56) 84-20-47; fax (56) 84-15-62; e-mail freezone@bse.bg; internet www.freetradezone-bourgas.com; f. 1989; Exec. Dirs ANGELIN POPOV, KRASIMIR GRUDOV.

**Dobrotitza Free-Trade Zone:** 4649 Kranevo, Dobrich District.

**Dragoman Free-Trade Zone:** 2210 Dragoman; tel. (9971) 72-20-14.

**Plovdiv Free-Trade Zone:** 4003 Plovdiv, V. Turnovo St 25; tel. (32) 65-02-85; fax (32) 65-08-33; f. 1990; CEO NEDELTCHO DRAGANOV.

**Rousse International Free-Trade Zone:** 7000 Ruse, Knyazheska St 5; POB 107; tel. (82) 27-22-47; fax (82) 27-00-84; e-mail freezone@elits.rousse.bg; f. 1988; Gen. Man. NIKOLAY KORFONOZOV.

**Svilengrad Free-Trade Zone:** 6500 Svilengrad; tel. (359) 379-74-45; fax (359) 379-75-41; e-mail sbz@svilengrad.spnet.net; internet www.svilengrad.spnet.net/sbz; f. 1990; Exec. Dir DIMO HARAKCHIEV.

**Vidin Free-Trade Zone:** 3700 Vidin; tel. (94) 228-37; fax (94) 309-47; f. 1988; Gen. Man. K. MARINOV.

## CHAMBER OF COMMERCE

**Bulgarian Chamber of Commerce and Industry:** 1000 Sofia, Parteviechi St 42; tel. (2) 87-26-31; fax (2) 87-32-09; f. 1895; promotes economic relations and business contacts between Bulgarian and foreign cos and orgs; organizes participation in international fairs and exhibitions; publishes economic publs in Bulgarian and foreign languages; organizes foreign trade advertising and publicity; provides legal and economic consultations, etc.; registers all Bulgarian cos trading internationally (more than 67,000 at mid-1994); Pres. BOJIDAR BOJINOV; 24 regional chambers.

## EMPLOYERS' ASSOCIATIONS

**Bulgarian Industrial Association (BISA):** 1000 Sofia, Alabin St 16–20; tel. (2) 980-99-14; fax (2) 87-26-04; e-mail office@bia.bol.bg; internet www.bia-bg.com; f. 1980; assists Bulgarian economic enterprises with promotion and foreign contacts; analyses economic situation; formulates policies for legislative and commercial projects; assists development of small-and medium-sized firms; organizes privatization and investment operations; Chair. and Pres. BOJIDAR DANEV.

**National Union of Employers:** 1505 Sofia, Oborishte St 44; POB 15; f. 1989; federation of businessmen in Bulgaria.

**Union of Private Owners in Bulgaria:** 1000 Sofia, Graf Ignatiev St 2; f. 1990; Chair. DIMITUR TODOROV.

**Vuzrazhdane Union of Bulgarian Private Manufacturers:** 1618 Sofia, Blvd Todor Kableshkov 2; tel. (2) 55-00-16; Chair. DRAGOMIR GUSHTEROV.

## UTILITIES

### Electricity

**Central Laboratory of Solar Energy and New Energy Sources:** 1784 Sofia, Blvd Tzarigradsko chaussée 72; tel. and fax (2) 75-40-16; e-mail solar@phys.bas.bg; research into alternative energy production; Dir Assoc. Prof. PETKO VITANOV.

**Committee on Energy:** 1000 Sofia, Blvd Knjaz Dondukov 1; Chair. KONSTANTIN ROSINOV.

**Committee on the Use of Atomic Energy for Peaceful Purposes:** 1574 Sofia, Blvd Shipchenski Prokhod 69; tel. (2) 72-02-17; fax (2) 70-21-43; f. 1957; Chair. LUCHEZAR KOSTOV.

**National Electricity Company:** 1040 Sofia, Vestlets St 5; tel. (2) 549-09; fax (2) 87-25-50; e-mail nek@nek.bg; internet www.nek.bg; f. 1991; scheduled for privatization; responsible for all thermal, nuclear and hydroelectric electricity production; Chair. K. SHUSHULOV; CEO D. TAFROV.

### Gas

**Bulgargaz:** Sofia; tel. (2) 25-90-74; Chair. KRASIMIR NIKOLOV; Dir KIRIL GEGOV.

**Topenergy Joint-Stock Co:** Sofia; f. 1995; owned by Gazprom of Russia; responsible for supply of Russian natural gas to Bulgaria; Chair. BOGDAN BUDZULIAK; Dir SERGEI PASHIN.

## CO-OPERATIVES

**Central Union of Workers' Productive Co-operatives:** 1000 Sofia, Blvd Dondukov 11; POB 55; tel. (2) 80-39-38; fax (2) 87-03-20; f. 1988; umbrella organization of 164 workers' productive co-operatives; Pres. STILIAN BALASSOPOULOV; 60,000 mems.

## TRADE UNIONS

**Confederation of Independent Trade Unions in Bulgaria (CITUB):** Sofia, D. Blagoev Sq. 1; tel. (2) 86-61; fax (2) 87-17-87; f. 1904; name changed from Bulgarian Professional Union and independence declared from all parties and state structures in 1990; in 1998 remained the main trade-union organization; approx. 75 mem. federations and four associate mems (principal mems listed below); Chair. Prof. Dr KRUSTYU PETKOV; Sec. MILADIN STOYNOV; some 3m. mems .

**Edinstvo (Unity) People's Trade Union:** 1000 Sofia, Moskovska St 5; tel. (2) 87-96-40; f. 1990; co-operative federation of Clubs, based on professional interests, grouped into 84 asscns, 2 prof. asscns and 14 regional groups; Chair. OGNYAN BONEV; 384,000 mems.

**Podkrepa (Support) Trade Union Confederation:** 1000 Sofia, Angel Kanchev St 2; tel. (2) 988-78-39; fax (2) 988-87-38; e-mail fciw@mail.techno-link.com; f. 1990 as an opposition trade union (affiliated to the Union of Democratic Forces); organized into territorial (31 regions) and professional asscns (33 syndicates); Pres. Dr KONSTANTIN TRENCHEV; Gen. Sec. PETUR GANCHEV; 15,000 mems (1997).

### Principal CITUB Trade Unions

**Federation of Independent Agricultural Trade Unions:** 1606 Sofia, Dimo Hadzhidimov St 29; tel. (2) 52-15-40; Pres. LYUBEN KHARALAMPIEV; 44,600 mems (mid-1994).

**Federation of Independent Trade Unions of Construction Workers:** 1000 Sofia, Sveta Nedelya Sq. 4; tel. (2) 80-16-003; Chair. NIKOLAI RASHKOV; 220,000 mems.

**Federation of the Independent Trade Unions of Employees of the State and Social Organizations:** 1000 Sofia, Alabin Sq. 52; tel. (2) 87-98-52; Chair. PETUR SUCHKOV; 144,900 mems.

**Federation of Independent Mining Trade Unions:** 1233 Sofia, 32 Veania St; tel. (2) 931-07-00; fax (2) 931-00-50; f. 1992; Pres. PENCHO TOKMAKCHIEV; 20,000 mems.

**Federation of Light Industry Trade Unions:** 1040 Sofia, Makedonia Sq. 1; tel. (2) 88-15-70; fax (2) 88-15-20; Chair. IORDAN VASSILEV IVANOV; 64,320 mems (1997).

**Federation of Metallurgical Trade Unions:** 1000 Sofia, 6 September St 4; tel. (2) 88-48-21; fax (2) 88-27-10; f. 1992; Pres. VASSIL YANACHKOV; 20,000 mems.

**Federation of Trade Unions in the Chemical Industry:** 1040 Sofia, Makedonia Sq. 1; tel. (2) 87-39-07; Pres. LYUBEN MAKOV; 60,000 mems (mid-1993).

**Federation of Trade Union Organizations in the Forestry and Woodworking Industries:** 1606 Sofia, Vladayska St 29; tel. (2) 52-31-21; fax (2) 51-73-97; Pres. PETER IVANOV ABRACHEV; 16,570 mems (mid-1999).

**Federation of Trade Unions of Health Services:** 1202 Sofia, Blvd Maria Louisa 45; tel. (2) 988-20-97; fax (2) 83-18-14; f. 1990; Pres. Dr IVAN KOKALOV; 31,580 mems (mid-1999).

**Independent Trade Union Federation of the Co-operatives:** 1000 Sofia, Rakovski St 99; tel. (2) 87-36-74; Chair. NIKOLAI NIKOLOV; 96,000 mems.

**Independent Trade Union Federation for Trade, Co-operatives, Services and Tourism:** 1000 Sofia, 6 September St 4; tel. (2) 88-02-51; Chair. PETUR TSEKOV; 212,221 mems.

**Independent Trade Union of Food Industry Workers:** 1606 Sofia, Dimo Hadzhidimov St 29; tel. (2) 52-30-72; fax (2) 52-16-70; Pres. SLAVCHO PETROV; 53,000 mems (mid-1994).

**'Metal-electro' National Trade Union Federation:** 1040 Sofia, Makedonia Sq. 1; POB 543; tel. (2) 87-48-06; fax (2) 87-75-38; Pres. ASSEN ASSENOV; 80,000 mems (1995).

**National Federation of Energy Workers:** 1040 Sofia, Makedonia Sq. 1; tel. (2) 88-48-22; f. 1927; Pres. BOJIL PETROV; 15,000 mems.

**Union of Bulgarian Teachers:** 1000 Sofia; tel. (2) 87-78-18; f. 1905; Chair. IVAN YORDANOV; 186,153 mems.

**Union of Transport Workers:** 1233 Sofia, Blvd Princess Maria Luiza 106; tel. (2) 31-51-24; fax (2) 31-71-24; f. 1911; Pres. IOROLANKA MILANOVA RADEVA; 70,000 mems (mid-1991).

### Other Principal Trade Unions

**Bulgarian Military Legion 'G. S. Rakovski':** 1000 Sofia, Blvd Ruski 9; tel. (2) 87-72-96; Chair. DOICHIN BOYADZHIEV.

**Ministry of Agriculture:** 03 BP 7005, Ouagadougou 03; tel. 32-49-63.

**Ministry of Animal Resources:** 03 BP 7026, Ouagadougou 03; tel. 32-46-51; fax 31-84-75.

**Ministry of the Civil Service and Institutional Development:** 03 BP 7006, Ouagadougou 03; tel. 32-40-10.

**Ministry of Communications:** 03 BP 7045, Ouagadougou 03; tel. 32-48-86; fax 31-55-99.

**Ministry of Culture and Arts:** 03 BP 7045, Ouagadougou 03; tel. 32-48-86; fax 31-55-99.

**Ministry of Defence:** 01 BP 496, Ouagadougou 01; tel. 30-72-14; fax 31-36-10.

**Ministry of the Economy and Finance:** 03 BP 7012, Ouagadougou 03; tel. 30-69-98; fax 31-27-15; e-mail finances@cenatrin.bf; internet www.finances.gov.bf.

**Ministry of Employment, Labour and Social Security:** 03 BP 7016, Ouagadougou 03; tel. 30-09-60; fax 31-88-01.

**Ministry of Energy and Mines:** 01 BP 644, Ouagadougou 01; tel. 31-84-29; fax 31-84-30.

**Ministry of the Environment and Water Resources:** 565 rue Agostino Neto, Secteur 4, Koulouba, 03 BP 7044, Ouagadougou 03; tel. 32-40-74; fax 31-46-05; e-mail diallo@ouaga.orstom.bf; internet www.ohraoc.orstom.bf/htmlf/partnat/mee.

**Ministry of Foreign Affairs:** 03 BP 7038, Ouagadougou 03; tel. 32-47-34; fax 30-87-92; e-mail mam@cenatrin.bf.

**Ministry of Health:** 03 BP 7009, Ouagadougou 03; tel. 32-41-71.

**Ministry of Infrastructure, Housing and Town Planning:** 03 BP 7011, Ouagadougou 03; tel. 32-49-54; fax 31-84-08.

**Ministry of Justice:** 01 BP 526, Ouagadougou 01; tel. 32-48-33.

**Ministry of Primary Education and Mass Literacy:** 03 BP 7032, Ouagadougou 03; tel. 32-48-70; fax 30-80-86.

**Ministry of Regional Integration:** 01 BP 06, Ouagadougou 01; tel. 32-48-33; fax 31-41-90.

**Ministry of Secondary and Higher Education and Scientific Research:** 03 BP 7047, Ouagadougou 03; tel. 32-48-68; fax 31-41-41.

**Ministry of Social Welfare and the Family:** 01 BP 515, Ouagadougou 01; tel. 30-68-75; fax 31-67-37.

**Ministry of Territorial Administration and Security:** 03 BP 7034, Ouagadougou 03; tel. 32-47-83; fax 30-84-17.

**Ministry of Trade, Industry and Crafts:** 01 BP 514, Ouagadougou 01; tel. 32-47-86; fax 32-48-28.

**Ministry of Transport and Tourism:** 03 BP 7048, Ouagadougou 03; tel. 30-62-11.

**Ministry of Women's Promotion:** Ouagadougou.

**Ministry of Youth and Sports:** 03 BP 7035, Ouagadougou 03; tel. 32-47-86.

# President and Legislature

### PRESIDENT

**Presidential Election, 15 November 1998**

| Candidate | Votes | % of votes |
|---|---|---|
| Blaise Compaoré | 1,996,151 | 87.53 |
| Ram Ouédraogo | 150,793 | 6.61 |
| Frédéric Guirma | 133,552 | 5.86 |
| **Total** | 2,280,496* | 100.00 |

* There were, in addition, 89,458 blank votes.

### PARLEMENT

#### Assemblée Nationale

**President:** Mélégué Maurice Traoré.

**General Election, 11 May 1997**

| Party | Seats |
|---|---|
| Congrès pour la démocratie et le progrès (CDP) | 101* |
| Parti pour la démocratie et le progrès (PDP) | 6 |
| Alliance pour la démocratie et la fédération (ADF) | 2 |
| Rassemblement démocratique africain (RDA) | 2 |
| **Total** | 111 |

* This total includes the results of voting in four constituencies won by the CDP at a further round of voting on 18 June, after the Supreme Court annulled the previous results.

#### Chambre des Représentants

**President:** Moussa Sanogo.

The second chamber comprises 178 members, nominated from among the 'active forces of the nation' for a three-year term. The Chambre des Représentants, which has advisory functions, was inaugurated in December 1995.

# Advisory Council

**Conseil Economique et Social:** 01 BP 6162, Ouagadougou 01; tel. 32-40-90; fax 31-06-54; f. 1985 as Conseil Révolutionnaire Economique et Social, present name adopted in 1992; 90 mems; Pres. Juliette Bonkougou.

# Political Organizations

There were about 30 political parties in late 1999. The following are amongst the most important.

**Alliance pour la démocratie et la fédération—Rassemblement démocratique africain (ADF—RDA):** 01 BP 2061 Ouagadougou 01; tel. 31-15-15; f. 1990 as Alliance pour la démocratie et la fédération, absorbed faction of Rassemblement démocratique africain in 1998; Pres. Me Herman Yaméogo.

**Congrès pour la démocratie et le progrès (CDP):** f. 1996, by merger of more than 10 parties, to succeed the Organisation pour la démocratie populaire/Mouvement du travail as the prin. political org. supporting Pres. Compaoré; social democratic; Exec. Sec. Roch Marc-Christian Kaboré.

**Convention des partis sankaristes (CPS):** f. 1999, by merger of four parties; promotes the policies of former president Sankara; Pres. Ernest Nongma Ouédraogo.

**Mouvement pour la tolérance et le progrès (MTP):** Nayabtigungou Congo Kaboré.

**Parti pour la démocratie et le progrès (PDP):** f. 1993, expanded in 1996 to include three other parties; Pres. Joseph Ki-Zerbo.

**Rassemblement démocratique africain (RDA):** pre-independence party; self-styled Front de refus du Rassemblement démocratique africain represented by Frédéric Guirma at 1998 presidential election; Leader Gérard Kango Ouédraogo.

**Union des verts pour le développement du Burkina (UVDB):** Ouagadougou; ecologist party; Leader Ram Ouédraogo.

The **Groupe du 14 février (G-14f)**, an alliance of some eight opposition parties including the PDP and the ADF—RDA, boycotted the 1998 presidential election.

# Diplomatic Representation

### EMBASSIES IN BURKINA FASO

**Algeria:** 01 BP 3893, Ouagadougou 01; tel. 30-64-01; Ambassador: Ahcene Boukhelfa.

**Canada:** 01 BP 548, Ouagadougou 01; tel. 31-18-94; fax 31-18-00.

**China (Taiwan):** 01 BP 5563, Ouagadougou 01; tel. 31-61-95; fax 31-61-97; Ambassador: Sainting Kung.

**Côte d'Ivoire:** 01 BP 20, Ouagadougou 01; tel. 31-82-28; fax 31-82-30; Ambassador: Georges Bakayoko.

**Cuba:** 01 BP 3422, Ouagadougou 06; tel. 30-64-91; Ambassador: Miguel Alberto Otero López.

**Denmark:** rue Agostino Neto, 01 BP 1760, Ouagadougou 01; tel. 31-31-92; fax 31-31-89; e-mail ambadane@fasonet.bf; Chargé d'affaires: Hans Henrik Liljeborg.

**Egypt:** Zone du Conseil de L'Entente, Secteur 4, 03 BP 3893, Ouagadougou 03; tel. 30-66-37; Ambassador: Dr Mohamed Said Abdel Hamid.

**France:** 902 ave de l'Indépendance, 01 BP 504, Ouagadougou 01; tel. 30-67-70; fax 31-41-66; Ambassador: Maurice Portiche.

**Germany:** 01 BP 600, Ouagadougou 01; tel. 30-67-31; fax 31-39-91; e-mail amb.allemagne@fasonet.bf; Ambassador: Dr Helmut Rau.

**Ghana:** 22 ave d'Oubritenga, 01 BP 212, Ouagadougou 01; tel. 30-76-35; Ambassador: Baffour Assasie-Gyimah.

**India:** 167 rue Joseph Badoua, BP 6648, Ouagadougou; tel. 31-20-09.

**Italy:** 01 BP 3432, Ouagadougou 01; tel. 30-86-94; fax 31-04-77.

**Libya:** 01 BP 1601, Ouagadougou 01; tel. 30-67-53; fax 31-34-70; Secretary of People's Bureau: Muhammad Madani al-Azari.

**Mali:** 01 BP 1911, Ouagadougou 01; tel. 38-19-22.

**Netherlands:** 415 ave du Dr Kwamé N'Krumah, 01 BP 1302, Ouagadougou 01; tel. 30-61-34; fax 30-76-95; Ambassador: Alphons J. M. G. Hennekens.

**Nigeria:** 01 BP 132, Ouagadougou 01; tel. 30-66-67; Ambassador: LAWAL MOHAMMED MUNIR.

**USA:** 01 BP 35, Ouagadougou 01; tel. 30-67-23; fax 31-23-68; Ambassador: JIMMY KOLKER (designate).

# Judicial System

The Constitution provides for the independence of the judiciary. Judges are to be accountable to a Higher Council, under the chairmanship of the President of the Republic.

**Supreme Court:** 01 BP 5577, Ouagadougou 01; tel. 31-08-35; fax 31-08-96; Pres. SAMBO ANTOINE KOMI.

# Religion

More than 50% of the population follow animist beliefs.

### ISLAM

An estimated 30% of the population are Muslims.

### CHRISTIANITY

#### The Roman Catholic Church

Burkina comprises one archdiocese and ten dioceses. At 31 December 1997 Roman Catholics comprised an estimated 10.5% of the total population.

**Bishops' Conference:** Conférence des Evêques de Burkina Faso et du Niger, BP 1195, Ouagadougou; tel. 30-60-26; f. 1966, legally recognized 1978; Pres. Rt Rev. JEAN-BAPTISTE SOMÉ, Bishop of Diébougou.

**Archbishop of Ouagadougou:** Most Rev. JEAN-MARIE UNTAANI COMPAORÉ, Archevêché, 01 BP 1472, Ouagadougou 01; tel. 30-67-04; fax 30-72-75.

#### Protestant Churches

At 31 December 1986 there were an estimated 106,467 adherents.

# The Press

**Direction de la presse écrite:** Ouagadougou; govt body responsible for press direction.

### DAILIES

**Le Journal du Soir:** 02 BP 5468, Ouagadougou 02; tel. 31-59-20; fax 31-59-22; Dir ISSA TAPSOBA.

**L'Observateur Paalga** (New Observer): 01 BP 584, Ouagadougou 01; tel. 33-27-05; fax 31-45-79; f. 1974; Dir EDOUARD OUÉDRAOGO; circ. 8,000.

**Le Pays:** 01 BP 4577, Ouagadougou 01; tel. 31-35-46; fax 31-45-50; f. 1991; Dir SIGUÉ JÉRÉMIE BOUREIMA; circ. 4,000.

**Sidwaya** (Truth): 5 rue du Marché, 01 BP 507, Ouagadougou 01; tel. 30-63-07; fax 31-03-62; f. 1984; state-owned; Mossi; Editor-in-Chief ISSAKA SOURWEMA; circ. 3,000.

### PERIODICALS

**Bendré:** Ouagadougou; weekly; Dir CHERIFF SY.

**Le Berger:** Zone commerciale, ave Binger, BP 2581, Bobo-Dioulasso; f. 1992; weekly; Dir KOULIGA BLAISE YAMÉOGO.

**Bulletin de l'Agence d'Information du Burkina:** 01 BP 2507, Ouagadougou 01; tel. 30-70-52; fax 30-70-56; 2 a week; Editor-in-Chief JAMES DABIRÉ; circ. 200.

**La Clef:** Ouagadougou; tel. 31-38-27; f. 1992; weekly; Dir KY SATURNIN; circ. 3,000.

**L'Indépendant:** 01 BP 4809, Ouagadougou 01; tel. 30-74-93; fax 31-44-58; weekly.

**L'Intrus:** 01 BP 2009, Ouagadougou 01; f. 1985; weekly; satirical; Dir JEAN HUBERT BAZIÉ; circ. 3,000.

**Le Journal du Jeudi:** 01 BP 4707, Ouagadougou 01; tel. 31-41-08; fax 31-38-74; e-mail jj@fasonet.bf; internet altern.org/journaldujeudi; f. 1991; weekly; Dir BOUBACAR DIALLO; circ. 9,000.

**Le Matin:** Bobo-Dioulasso; tel. 97-16-93; f. 1992; weekly; Dir DOFINITA FLAURENT BONZI.

**Nekr Wagati:** Ouagadougou; six a year; Dir SIMON COMPAORÉ.

**La Nouvelle Tribune:** Ouagadougou; weekly; Dir KYALBABOUÉ BAYILI.

**L'Opinion:** Ouagadougou; weekly; Editor ISSAKA LINGANI.

**L'Ouragan:** Ouagadougou; weekly; Dir LOHÉ ISSA KONATÉ.

**Regard:** 01 BP 4707, Ouagadougou 01; tel. 31-16-70; fax 31-57-47; weekly; Dir CHRIS VALÉA.

**San Finna:** Ouagadougou; privately owned; weekly; Editor-in-Chief PAULIN YAMÉOGO.

**Sidwaya Magazine:** 5 rue du Marché, 01 BP 507, Ouagadougou 01; state-owned; Mossi; monthly; Editor-in-Chief BONIFACE COULIBALY; circ. 2,500.

**Yeelen** (Light): Ouagadougou; monthly; pro-Govt.

### NEWS AGENCIES

**Agence d'Information du Burkina (AIB):** 03 BP 2507, Ouagadougou 03; tel. 32-46-39; fax 32-46-40; f. 1963; fmrly Agence Burkinabè de Presse; state-controlled; Dir JAMES DABIRÉ.

#### Foreign Bureaux

**Agence France-Presse (AFP):** BP 391, Ouagadougou; tel. 33-56-56; Bureau Chief KIDA TAPSOBA.

Reuters (UK) is also represented in Burkina Faso.

### PRESS ASSOCIATION

**Association des Journalistes du Burkina:** 01 BP 507, Ouagadougou 01; tel. 31-01-14; fax 31-62-03; Pres. JEAN-CALUDE MÉDA.

# Publishers

**Presses Africaines SA:** BP 1471, Ouagadougou; tel. 33-43-07; general fiction, religion, primary and secondary textbooks; Man. Dir A. WININGA.

**Société Nationale d'Edition et de Presse (SONEPRESS):** BP 810, Ouagadougou; f. 1972; general, periodicals; Pres. MARTIAL OUÉDRAOGO.

#### Government Publishing House

**Imprimerie Nationale du Burkina Faso (INBF):** route de l'Hôpital Yalgado, BP 7040, Ouagadougou; tel. 33-52-92; f. 1963; Dir LATY SOULEYMANE TRAORÉ.

# Broadcasting and Communications

### TELECOMMUNICATIONS

The introduction of a regulatory framework for the telecommunications industry is ongoing.

**Office National des Télécommunications (ONATEL):** ave Nelson Mandela, 01 BP 10000, Ouagadougou 01; tel. 33-40-01; fax 31-03-31; internet www.onatel.bf; privatization pending; Dir-Gen. JUSTIN T. THIOMBIANO.

### BROADCASTING

#### Regulatory Authority

**Conseil Supérieur de l'Information (CSI):** 290 ave Ho Chi Minh, 01 BP 6618, Ouagadougou 01; tel. 30-11-24; fax 30-11-33; internet www.primature.gov.bf/republic/acc_csi.htm; f. 1995; Pres. ADAMA FOFANA.

#### Radio

**Radiodiffusion Nationale du Burkina:** 03 BP 7029, Ouagadougou 03; tel. 32-40-55; fax 31-04-41; f. 1959; state radio service; Dir RODRIGUE BARRY.

**Canal Arc-en-Ciel:** Ouagadougou; tel. 32-41-41.

**Fréquence Espoir:** Dédougou.

**Radio ABGA (Radio Energie):** Ouagadougou; tel. 31-61-69.

**Radio Bobo-Dioulasso:** BP 392, Bobo-Dioulasso; tel. 97-14-13; daily programmes in French and vernacular languages; Dir of Programmes SITA KAM.

**Radio Evangile:** Ouagadougou; tel. 34-08-38.

**Radio Horizon FM:** 01 BP 2714, Ouagadougou 01; tel. 31-28-58; fax 31-39-34; private commercial station; broadcasts in French, English and eight vernacular languages; Dir MOUSTAPHA LAABLI THIOMBIANO.

**Radio Maria:** Ouagadougou; tel. 31-70-70.

**Radio Palabre:** Kougoudou; tel. 44-00-81.

**Radio Toamba:** Fada N'Gourma; tel. 77-02-33.

**Radio Vive le Paysan:** Saponé; tel. 40-56-21.

#### Television

**Télévision Nationale du Burkina:** 29 blvd de la Révolution, 01 BP 2530, Ouagadougou 01; tel. 31-83-53; fax 32-48-50; internet www.tnb.bf; f. 1963; Dir AINÉE KOALA.

# Finance

(cap. = capital; res = reserves; m. = million; brs = branches; amounts in francs CFA)

## BANKING

### Central Bank

**Banque Centrale des Etats de l'Afrique de l'Ouest (BCEAO):** ave Gamel-Abdel-Nasser, BP 356, Ouagadougou; tel. 30-60-15; fax 31-01-22; HQ in Dakar, Senegal; f. 1962; bank of issue for the mem. states of the Union économique et monétaire ouest-africaine (UEMOA, comprising Benin, Burkina Faso, Côte d'Ivoire, Guinea-Bissau, Mali, Niger, Senegal and Togo); cap. and res 806,918m., total assets 4,084,464m. (December 1998); Gov. CHARLES KONAN BANNY; Dir in Burkina Faso MOUSSA KONÉ; br. in Bobo-Dioulasso.

### Other Banks

**Bank of Africa—Burkina (BOA—Burkina):** 01 BP 1319, Ouagadougou 01; tel. 31-79-83; fax 31-26-73; commenced activities 1998; cap. 1,250m.; Pres. LASSINÉ DIAWARA; Man. Dir PHILIPPE NADAUD.

**Banque Commerciale du Burkina (BCB):** ave Nelson Mandela, 01 BP 1336, Ouagadougou 01; tel. 30-79-00; fax 31-06-28; e-mail bcb@fasonet.bf; f. 1988; 50% state-owned, 50% owned by Libyan Arab Foreign Bank; cap. and res 613m., total assets 7,456m. (Dec. 1996); Pres. IBRAHIM OUATTARA; Man. Dir MAHMUD HAMMUDA.

**Banque Internationale du Burkina (BIB):** ave Dimdolobsom, 01 BP 362, Ouagadougou 01; tel. 30-61-69; fax 31-00-94; e-mail bib.ouaga@fasonet.bf; f. 1974; 25% owned by Banque Belgolaise SA (Belgium), 23% state-owned; cap. and res 8,837m. (Dec. 1997); Pres. and Man. Dir GASPARD OUÉDRAOGO; 21 brs.

**Banque Internationale pour le Commerce, l'Industrie et l'Agriculture du Burkina (BICIA—B):** ave Dr Kwamé N'Krumah, 01 BP 8, Ouagadougou 01; tel. 30-62-26; fax 31-19-55; e-mail biciadg@fasonet.bf; f. 1973; 25% state-owned; cap. and res 6,892m., total assets 115,258m. (Dec. 1996); Pres. AMADOU TRAORÉ; Dir-Gen. AMADÉ OUÉDRAOGO; 11 brs.

**Caisse Nationale de Crédit Agricole du Burkina (CNCAB):** 2 ave Gamal-Abdel-Nasser, 01 BP 1644, Ouagadougou 01; tel. 30-24-88; fax 31-43-52; e-mail cncabf@cenatrin.bf; f. 1979; 26% state-owned; cap. and res 8,440m., total assets 31,498m. (Dec. 1996); Pres. ANGÈLE SOUDRE; Man. Dir NOËL KABORÉ; 4 brs.

**Ecobank—Burkina SA:** 633 rue Maurice Bishop, 01 BP 145, Ouagadougou 01; operations commenced 1997; 80% owned by Ecobank Transnational Inc (operating under the auspices of the Economic Community of West African States); cap. 1,250m.; Pres. PAUL BALKOUMA; Man. Dir OLAYEMI ALAMU AKAPO.

**Société Générale des Banques du Burkina (SGBB):** 5 rue du Marché, 01 BP 585, Ouagadougou 01; tel. 30-60-34; fax 31-05-61; f. 1998 by restructuring of Banque pour le Financement du Commerce et des Investissements du Burkina; cap. and res 1,917m., total assets 24,106m. (Dec. 1996); Pres. and Man. Dir EMILE PARÉ.

### Credit Institution

**Burkina Bail SA:** Immeuble CGP, 1ère étage BIB CGB, Ouagadougou 01; tel. 30-69-87; 52% owned by BIB; cap. 500m.

## STOCK EXCHANGE

**Bourse Régionale des Valeurs Mobilières (BRVM):** Ouagadougou; tel. 30-87-73; fax 30-61-16; f. 1998; national branch of BRVM (regional stock exchange based in Abidjan, Côte d'Ivoire, serving the member states of UEMOA); Man. LÉOPOLD OUÉDRAOGO.

## INSURANCE

**Fonci-Assurances (FONCIAS):** ave Léo Frobénius, 01 BP 398, Ouagadougou 01; tel. 30-62-04; fax 31-01-53; f. 1978; 51% owned by Athena Afrique (France), 20% state-owned; cap. 140m.; Pres. El Hadj OUMAROU KANAZOE; Man. Dir GÉRARD G. MANTOUX.

**Société Nationale d'Assurances et de Réassurances (SONAR):** 01 BP 406, Ouagadougou 01; tel. 33-46-66; fax 30-89-75; e-mail sonar@cenatrin.bf; f. 1973; 25% state-owned; cap. 240m.; Man. Dir ANDRÉ BAYALA.

**Union des Assurances du Burkina (UAB):** 08 BP 11041, Ouagadougou 08; tel. 31-26-15; fax 31-26-20; f. 1991; 20% owned by l'Union Africaine—IARD (Côte d'Ivoire); cap. 270m.; Man. Dir J. V. ALFRED YARÉOGO.

# Trade and Industry

## GOVERNMENT AGENCIES

**Bureau des Mines et de la Géologie du Burkina (BUMIGEB):** 01 BP 601, Ouagadougou 01; tel. 30-01-94; fax 30-01-87; f. 1978, restructured 1997; research into geological and mineral resources; Pres. MODESTE DABIRA; Man. Dir JEAN-LÉONARD COMPAORÉ.

**Caisse de Stabilisation des Prix des Produits Agricoles du Burkina (CSPPAB):** 01 BP 1453, Ouagadougou 01; tel. 30-62-17; fax 31-06-14; f. 1964; responsible for purchase and marketing of shea-nuts (karité nuts), sesame seeds, cashew nuts and groundnuts; transfer pending to private ownership; Admin. DIANGO CHARLY HEBIE (acting); br. at Bobo-Dioulasso, representation at Boromo, Fada N'Gourma and Gaoua.

**Comptoir Burkinabè des Métaux Précieux (CBMP):** Ouagadougou; promotes gold sector, liaises with artisanal producers.

**Office National d'Aménagement des Terroirs (ONAT):** 01 BP 524, Ouagadougou 01; tel. 30-61-10; fax 30-61-12; f. 1974; fmrly Autorité des Aménagements des Vallées des Voltas; integrated rural development, including economic and social planning; Man. Dir ZACHARIE OUÉDRAOGO.

**Office National du Commerce Exterieur (ONAC):** ave Léo Frobénius, 01 BP 389, Ouagadougou 01; tel. 31-13-00; fax 31-14-69; f. 1974; promotes and supervises external trade; Man. Dir SÉRIBA OUATTARA (acting).

## DEVELOPMENT ORGANIZATIONS

**Agence Française de Développement (AFD):** ave Binger, BP 529, Ouagadougou; tel. 30-68-26; fmrly Caisse Française de Développement; Dir M. GLEIZES.

**Mission Française de Coopération:** 01 BP 510, Ouagadougou 01; tel. 30-67-71; fax 30-89-00; centre for administering bilateral aid from France under co-operation agreements signed in 1961; Dir PIERRE JACQUEMOT.

## CHAMBER OF COMMERCE

**Chambre de Commerce, d'Industrie et d'Artisanat du Burkina:** 180/220 rue 3-119, 01 BP 502, Ouagadougou 01; tel. 31-12-66; fax 30-61-16; f. 1948; Pres. El Hadj OUMAROU KANAZOÉ; Dir.-Gen. SALIF LAMOUSSA KABORÉ; br. in Bobo-Dioulasso.

## EMPLOYERS' ORGANIZATIONS

**Association Professionnelle des Banques et Établissements Financiers (APBEF):** Ouagadougou; Pres. HAMADÉ OUÉDRAOGO.

**Conseil National du Patronat Burkinabè:** Ouagadougou; Pres. BRUNO ILBOUDO.

**Groupement Professionnel des Industriels:** BP 810, Ouagadougou; tel. 30-28-19; f. 1974; Pres. MARTIAL OUÉDRAOGO.

**Syndicat des Commerçants Importateurs et Exportateurs (SCIMPEX):** 01 BP 552, Ouagadougou 01; tel. 31-18-70; fax 31-30-36; e-mail scimpex@cenatrin.bf; Pres. OLE KAM.

## UTILITIES

### Electricity

**Société Nationale Burkinabè d'Electricité (SONABEL):** ave Nelson Mandela, BP 54, Ouagadougou; tel. 33-62-05; f. 1968; cap. 963m. francs CFA; production and distribution of electricity; Dir-Gen. M. BARRO.

### Water

**Office National de l'Eau et de l'Assainissement (ONEA):** 01 BP 170, Ouagadougou 01; tel. 30-60-73; fax 30-33-60; f. 1977; storage, purification and distribution of water; Dir ALY CONGO.

## CO-OPERATIVES

**Société de Commercialisation du Burkina 'Faso Yaar':** ave du Loudun, BP 531, Ouagadougou; tel. 30-61-28; f. 1967; 99% state-owned; transfer pending to private ownership; import-export and domestic trade; Pres. Minister of Trade, Industry and Crafts.

**Union des Coopératives Agricoles et Maraîchères du Burkina (UCOBAM):** 01 BP 277, Ouagadougou 01; tel. 30-65-27; fax 30-65-28; e-mail ucobam@cenatrin.bf; f. 1968; comprises 8 regional co-operative unions (20,000 mems); production and marketing of fruit, vegetables, jams and conserves.

## TRADE UNIONS

There are more than 20 autonomous trade unions. The five trade union syndicates are:

**Confédération Générale du Travail Burkinabè (CGTB):** Ouagadougou; f. 1988; confed. of several autonomous trade unions; Sec.-Gen. TOLE SAGNON.

**Confédération Nationale des Travailleurs Burkinabè (CNTB):** BP 445, Ouagadougou; f. 1972; Leader of Governing Directorate ABDOULAYE BÂ.

**Confédération Syndicale Burkinabè (CSB):** Ouagadougou; f. 1974; mainly public service unions; Sec.-Gen. YACINTHE OUÉDRAOGO.

**Organisation Nationale des Syndicats Libres (ONSL):** BP 99, Ouagadougou; f. 1960; 6,000 mems.

**Union Syndicale des Travailleurs Burkinabè (USTB):** BP 381, Ouagadougou; f. 1958; Sec.-Gen. BONIFACE SOMDAH; 35,000 mems in 45 affiliated orgs.

# Transport

### RAILWAY

At the end of 1991 there were some 622 km of track in Burkina Faso. A 105-km extension from Donsin to Ouagadougou was inaugurated in December of that year. Plans exist for the construction of an extension to the manganese deposits at Tambao. Responsibility for operations on the railway line linking Abidjan (Côte d'Ivoire) and Kaya, via Ouagadougou, was transferred to SITARAIL (a consortium of French, Belgian, Ivorian and Burkinabè interests) in May 1995.

**SITARAIL—Transport Ferroviaire de Personnes et de Marchandises:** 01 BP 1192, Ouagadougou 01; tel. 30-60-50; fax 30-85-21; national branch of SITARAIL (based in Abidjan, Côte d'Ivoire); Rep. in Burkina S. YAMÉOGO.

### ROADS

In 1996 there were an estimated 12,100 km of roads, including 5,720 km of main roads and 3,030 km of secondary roads; about 16% of the road network was paved in 1995. A major aim of current road projects is to improve transport links with other countries of the region. In 1999 a US $37m. project was begun to upgrade the road linking Ouagadougou with the Ghanaian border via the more isolated southern provinces.

**Burkina Transit:** 01 BP 1947, Ouagadougou 01; tel. 30-79-88; fax 31-05-15; passenger transport.

**Interafricaine de Transport et de Transit (IATT):** 04 BP 8242, Ouagadougou 04; tel. 30-25-12; fax 30-37-04.

**Régie Nationale des Transports en Commun (RNTC X9):** 01 BP 2991, Ouagadougou 01; tel. 30-42-96; f. 1984; urban, national and international public transport co; Dir FRANÇOIS KONSEIBO.

**Société Africaine de Transit (SAT):** 01 BP 4249, Ouagadougou 01; tel. 31-09-16.

**Société Africaine de Transports Routiers (SATR):** 01 BP 5298, Ouagadougou 01; tel. 34-08-62.

**Société Nationale du Transit du Burkina (SNTB):** 474 ave Bishop, 01 BP 1192, Ouagadougou 01; tel. 30-60-54; fax 30-85-21.

### CIVIL AVIATION

There are international airports at Ouagadougou and Bobo-Dioulasso, 49 small airfields and 13 private airstrips. Ouagadougou airport handled an estimated 176,400 passengers and 7,000 metric tons of freight in 1997.

**Air Afrique:** BP 141, Ouagadougou; tel. 30-60-20; see under Côte d'Ivoire.

**Air Burkina:** ave Loudun, 01 BP 1459, Ouagadougou 01; tel. 30-76-76; fax 31-48-80; f. 1967 as Air Volta; 25% state-owned; operates domestic and regional services; Man. Dir MATHIEU BOUDA.

**Air Inter-Burkina:** Ouagadougou; f. 1994; operates domestic passenger and postal services.

# Tourism

Among the principal tourist activities is big game hunting in the east and south-west, and along the banks of the Mouhoun (Black Volta) river. There is a wide variety of wild animals in the game reserves. Important cultural events, notably the pan-African film festival held biennially in Ouagadougou, attract many visitors. In 1996 there were 131,113 tourist arrivals, and receipts from tourism totalled US $23m.

**Direction de l'Administration Touristique et Hôtelière:** 01 BP 624, Ouagadougou 01; tel. 30-63-96; Dir-Gen. MOUSSA DIALLO.

**Office National du Tourisme Burkinabè:** BP 1318, Ouagadougou; tel. 3-19-59; fax 31-44-34; Dir-Gen. ABDOULAYE SANKARA.

# BURUNDI

## Introductory Survey

**Location, Climate, Language, Religion, Flag, Capital**

The Republic of Burundi is a land-locked country lying on the eastern shore of Lake Tanganyika, in central Africa, a little south of the Equator. It is bordered by Rwanda to the north, by Tanzania to the south and east, and by the Democratic Republic of the Congo (formerly Zaire) to the west. The climate is tropical (hot and humid) in the lowlands, and cool in the highlands, with an irregular rainfall. The population is composed of three ethnic groups: the Hutu (85%), the Tutsi (14%) and the Twa (1%). The official languages are French and Kirundi, while Swahili is used, in addition to French, in commercial circles. More than 65% of the inhabitants profess Christianity, with the great majority of the Christians being Roman Catholics. A large minority still adhere to traditional animist beliefs. The national flag (proportions 5 by 3) consists of a white diagonal cross on a background of red (above and below) and green (hoist and fly), with a white circle, containing three green-edged red stars, in the centre. The capital is Bujumbura.

**Recent History**

Burundi (formerly Urundi) became part of German East Africa in 1899. In 1916, during the First World War, the territory was occupied by Belgian forces from the Congo (now the Democratic Republic of the Congo). Subsequently, as part of Ruanda-Urundi, it was administered by Belgium under a League of Nations mandate and later as a UN Trust Territory. Elections in September 1961, conducted under UN supervision, were won by the Union pour le progrès national (UPRONA), which had been formed in 1958 by Ganwa (Prince) Louis Rwagasore, son of the reigning Mwami (King), Mwambutsa IV. As leader of UPRONA, Prince Rwagasore became Prime Minister later in the month, but was assassinated after only two weeks in office. He was succeeded by his brother-in-law, André Muhirwa. Internal self-government was granted in January 1962 and full independence on 1 July, when the two parts of the Trust Territory became separate states, as Burundi and Rwanda. Tensions between Burundi's two main ethnic groups, the Tutsi (traditionally the dominant tribe, despite representing a minority of the overall population) and the Hutu, escalated during 1965. Following an unsuccessful attempt by the Hutu to overthrow the Tutsi-dominated Government in October, virtually the entire Hutu political élite was executed, eliminating any significant participation by the Hutu in Burundi's political life until the late 1980s (see below). In July 1966 the Mwami was deposed, after a reign of more than 50 years, by his son Charles, and the Constitution was suspended. In November Charles, now Mwami Ntare V, was himself deposed by his Prime Minister, Capt. (later Lt-Gen.) Michel Micombero, who declared Burundi a republic.

Several alleged plots against the Government in 1969 and 1971 were followed, in 1972, by an abortive coup during which Ntare V was killed. Hutu activists were held responsible for the attempted coup, and this served as a pretext for the Tutsi to conduct a series of large-scale massacres of the rival tribe, with the final death-toll estimated at around 100,000. Large numbers of the Hutu fled to neighbouring countries.

In 1972 Micombero began a prolonged restructuring of the executive, which resulted in 1973 in an appointed seven-member Presidential Bureau, with Micombero as President and Prime Minister. In July 1974 the Government introduced a new republican Constitution which vested sovereignty in UPRONA, the sole legal political party. Micombero was elected Secretary-General of the party and re-elected for a seven-year presidential term.

On 1 November 1976 an army coup deposed Micombero, who died in exile in July 1983. The leader of the coup, Lt-Col (later Col) Jean-Baptiste Bagaza, was appointed President by the Supreme Revolutionary Council (composed of army officers), and a new Council of Ministers was formed. In October 1978 Bagaza announced a ministerial reorganization in which he abolished the post of Prime Minister. The first national congress of UPRONA was held in December 1979, and a party Central Committee, headed by Bagaza, was elected to take over the functions of the Supreme Revolutionary Council in January 1980. A new Constitution, adopted by national referendum in November 1981, provided for the establishment of a national assembly, to be elected by universal adult suffrage. The first legislative elections were held in October 1982. Having been re-elected President of UPRONA at the party's second national congress in July 1984, Bagaza, the sole candidate, was elected President of Burundi by direct suffrage in August, winning 99.63% of the votes cast.

On 3 September 1987 a military coup deposed Bagaza while he was attending a conference in Canada. The coup was led by Maj. Pierre Buyoya, who accused Bagaza of corruption and immediately formed a Military Committee for National Salvation (CMSN) to administer the country, pending the appointment of a new President. The Constitution was suspended, and the National Assembly was dissolved. On 2 October Buyoya was sworn in as President of the Third Republic. His Council of Ministers included mostly civilians, retaining no minister from the previous regime.

In August 1988 tribal tensions erupted into violence in the north of the country when groups of Hutus, claiming Tutsi provocation, slaughtered hundreds of Tutsis in the towns of Ntega and Marangara. The Tutsi-dominated army was immediately dispatched to the region to restore order, and large-scale tribal massacres occurred. In October Buyoya announced changes to the Council of Ministers, including the appointment of a Hutu, Adrien Sibomana, to the newly-restored post of Prime Minister. For the first time the Council included a majority of Hutu representatives. Buyoya subsequently established a Committee for National Unity (comprising an equal number of Tutsis and Hutus) to investigate the massacres and make recommendations for national reconciliation. Following the publication of the Committee's report, Buyoya announced plans to combat all forms of discrimination against the Hutu and to introduce new regulations to ensure equal opportunities in education, employment and in the armed forces. Notwithstanding Buyoya's efforts to achieve ethnic reconciliation, political tension remained at a high level in 1989.

In May 1990, in response to a new draft charter on national unity, Buyoya announced plans to introduce a 'democratic constitution under a one-party government' in place of military rule. A charter designed to reconcile the Tutsi and the Hutu was to be the subject of a referendum. In December, at an extraordinary national congress of UPRONA, the CMSN was abolished and its functions transferred to an 80-member Central Committee, with Buyoya as Chairman and with a Hutu, Nicolas Mayugi, as Secretary-General. At a referendum conducted in February 1991 the draft charter on national unity was overwhelmingly approved, despite vociferous criticism from opposition groups. Later in the month a ministerial reorganization, whereby Hutus were appointed to 12 of the 23 government portfolios, was viewed with scepticism by political opponents. In March a commission was established to prepare a report on the democratization of national institutions and political structures, in preparation for the drafting of a new constitution. The commission's report, presented in September, recommended the establishment of a parliamentary system to operate in conjunction with a presidential system of government, a renewable five-year presidential mandate, the introduction of proportional representation, freedom of the press, the compilation of a declaration of human rights and a system of 'controlled multipartyism' whereby political groupings seeking legal recognition would be forced to fulfil specific requirements, including subscription to the Charter of Unity (adopted in February). The proposals received the support of more than 90% of the voters in a referendum held on 9 March 1992, and the new Constitution was promulgated on 13 March.

In an extensive ministerial reshuffle in April 1992, seven ministers left the Government, Buyoya relinquished the defence portfolio, and Hutus were appointed to 15 of the 25 portfolios. In the same month Buyoya approved legislation relating to the creation of new political parties in accordance with the provisions of the new Constitution. New political parties were to be obliged to demonstrate impartiality with regard to ethnic or regional origin, gender and religion, and were to refrain from militarization. In October Buyoya announced the creation of the National Electoral Preparatory Commission (NEPC), a 33-member body comprising representatives of the eight recognized political parties, together with administrative, judicial, religious and military officials. The NEPC was convened for the first time at the end of November. By early December Buyoya had appointed a new 12-member technical commission, charged with drafting an electoral code and a communal law.

Presidential elections, held on 1 June 1993, were won, with 64.8% of the votes cast, by Melchior Ndadaye, the candidate of the Front pour la démocratie au Burundi (FRODEBU), with the support of the Rassemblement du peuple burundien (RPB), the Parti du peuple and the Parti libéral; Buyoya received 32.4% of the vote as the UPRONA candidate, with support from the Rassemblement pour la démocratie et le développement économique et social (RADDES) and the Parti social démocrate. Legislative elections for 81 seats in the National Assembly were conducted on 29 June. Once again, FRODEBU emerged as the most successful party, with 71% of the votes and 65 of the seats in the new legislature. UPRONA, with 21.4% of the votes, secured the remaining 16 seats. None of the other four parties contesting the elections secured the minimum 5% of votes needed for representation in the legislature. Ndadaye, Burundi's first Hutu Head of State, assumed the presidency on 10 July. A new Council of Ministers was subsequently announced. The new Prime Minister, Sylvie Kinigi, was one of seven newly-appointed Tutsi ministers.

On 21 October 1993 more than 100 army paratroopers, supported by armoured vehicles, swiftly overwhelmed supporters of the Government and occupied the presidential palace and the headquarters of the national broadcasting company. Ndadaye and several other prominent Hutu politicians and officials were detained and subsequently killed by the insurgents, who later proclaimed François Ngeze, one of the few Hutu members of UPRONA and a minister in the Government of former President Buyoya, as head of a National Committee for Public Salvation (CPSN). While members of the Government sought refuge abroad and in the offices of foreign diplomatic missions in Bujumbura, the armed forces declared a state of emergency, closing national borders and the capital's airport. However, immediate and unanimous international condemnation of the coup, together with the scale and ferocity of renewed tribal violence (fuelled by reports of Tutsi-dominated army units seeking out and eliminating Hutu intellectuals), undermined support for the insurgents from within the armed forces, and precipitated the collapse of the CPSN, which was disbanded on 25 October. The Prime Minister, Kinigi, announced the ending of the curfew, but remained in hiding and urged the deployment of an international force in Burundi to protect the civilian Government. Communications were restored on 27 October, and on the following day the UN confirmed that the Government had resumed control of the country. Ngeze and 10 coup leaders were arrested, while some 40 other insurgents were thought to have fled to Zaire (now the Democratic Republic of the Congo). In December a commission of judicial inquiry was created to investigate the insurgency.

Meanwhile, in early November 1993 several members of the Government, including the Prime Minister, had left the French Embassy (where they had remained throughout the uprising) with a small escort of French troops, and on 8 November Kinigi met with 15 of the 17 surviving ministers in an attempt to address the humanitarian crisis arising from the massacre and displacement of hundreds of thousands of Burundians following the failed coup. On the same day the Constitutional Court officially recognized the presidential vacancy resulting from the murder of both Ndadaye and his constitutional successor, Giles Bimazubute, the Speaker of the National Assembly, and stated that presidential power should be exercised by the Council of Ministers, acting in a collegiate capacity, pending a presidential election which was to be conducted within three months. However, the Minister of External Relations and Co-operation, Sylvestre Ntibantunganya (who succeeded Ndadaye as leader of FRODEBU), suggested that no electoral timetable should be considered before the resolution of internal security difficulties and the initiation of a comprehensive programme for the repatriation of refugees. In December Ntibantunganya was elected Speaker of the National Assembly. The foreign affairs portfolio was assumed by Jean-Marie Ngendahayo, previously Minister of Communications and Government Spokesman.

Meanwhile, in November 1993, following repeated requests by the Government for an international contribution to the protection of government ministers in Burundi, the Organization of African Unity (OAU, see p. 240) agreed to the deployment of a 200-strong protection force (MIPROBU), to be composed of civilian and military personnel, for a period of six months. In December opposition parties, including UPRONA and the RADDES, organized demonstrations in protest at the arrival of the 180-strong military contingent, scheduled for January 1994, claiming that Burundi's sovereignty and territorial integrity were being infringed. As a compromise, in mid-March the Government secured a significant reduction in the size of the force. The mandate of the mission (comprising a military contingent of 47 and 20 civilian observers) was subsequently extended at three-monthly intervals.

In early January 1994 FRODEBU deputies in the National Assembly approved a draft amendment to the Constitution, allowing a President of the Republic to be elected by the National Assembly, in the event of the Constitutional Court's recognition of a presidential vacancy. UPRONA deputies, who had boycotted the vote, challenged the constitutionality of the amendment, and expressed concern that such a procedure represented election by indirect suffrage, in direct contravention of the terms of the Constitution. The continued boycott of the National Assembly by UPRONA deputies, together with procedural impediments to the immediate ratification of the amendment, forced the postponement on 10 January of an attempt by FRODEBU deputies to elect their presidential candidate, the Minister of Agriculture and Livestock, Cyprien Ntaryamira. Three days later, none the less, following the successful negotiation of a political truce with opposition parties, Ntaryamira was elected President by the National Assembly (with 78 of the 79 votes cast). He assumed the post on 5 February; a Tutsi Prime Minister, Anatole Kanyenkiko, was appointed two days later, while the composition of a new multi-party Council of Ministers was finally agreed in mid-February. During that month ethnic tension was renewed as armed Hutu and Tutsi extremist factions attempted to establish territorial strongholds.

On 6 April 1994, returning from a regional summit meeting in Dar es Salaam, Tanzania, Ntaryamira was killed (together with the Ministers of Development, Planning and Reconstruction and of Communications) when the aircraft of Rwandan President Juvénal Habyarimana, in which he was travelling at Habyarimana's invitation, was the target of a rocket attack above Kigali airport, Rwanda, and crashed on landing. Habyarimana was also killed, and was widely acknowledged to have been the intended victim of the attack. In contrast to the violent political and tribal chaos that erupted in Rwanda (q.v.) in the aftermath of the death of Habyarimana, Burundians responded positively to appeals for calm issued by Ntibantunganya, the Speaker of the National Assembly, who, on 8 April, was confirmed (in accordance with the Constitution) as interim President for a three-month period. However, violent exchanges between Hutu extremist rebels and factions of the armed forces continued in April, claiming numerous victims. The failure of the warring militias to respond to an ultimatum, issued by the interim President, Ntibantunganya, in late April, to surrender all illegal arms by 1 May, resulted in the military bombardment of several rebel strongholds, forcing the withdrawal and surrender of a number of insurgents. Relations between the Government and the armed forces subsequently improved, and were further cemented by the Prime Minister's announcement, in early May, that the Minister of State for the Interior and Public Security, Léonard Nyangoma, had forfeited his position in the Council of Ministers, having failed to return from official business abroad; he had earlier been accused of attempting to provoke large-scale civil confrontation.

Having discounted the possibility of organizing a general election, owing to security considerations, in June 1994 all major political parties joined lengthy negotiations to establish a procedure for the restoration of the presidency. The mandate of the interim President was extended for three months by the Constitutional Court in July, and by the end of August it had been decided that a new President would be elected by a broadly representative commission, with a composition yet to be decided. A new agreement on power-sharing was announced on 10 September. This Convention of Government, which detailed the terms of government for a four-year transitional period (including the allocation of 45% of cabinet posts to opposition parties), was incorporated into the Constitution on 22 September. The Convention also provided for the creation of a

National Security Council (Conseil de sécurité nationale, CSN), which was formally inaugurated on 10 October to address the national security crisis. On 30 September the Convention elected Ntibantunganya to the presidency from a list of six candidates including Charles Mukasi, the UPRONA leader. Ntibantunganya's appointment was endorsed by the National Assembly, and he was formally inaugurated on 1 October. Anatole Kanyenkiko was reappointed as Prime Minister, and a coalition Government was announced with a composition reflecting the terms of the September Convention. In December, however, UPRONA announced its intention to withdraw from the Government and from the legislature, following the election, in early December, of Jean Minani (a prominent FRODEBU member) to the post of Speaker of the National Assembly. UPRONA members accused Minani of having incited Hutu attacks against Tutsis in the aftermath of the October 1993 attempted coup. In January 1995 the political crisis was averted by agreement on a compromise FRODEBU candidate, Léonce Ngendakumana. Minani subsequently assumed the FRODEBU party leadership. UPRONA then declared its willingness to rejoin the Government, but later in January Kanyenkiko resisted attempts by the UPRONA leadership to expel him from the party for having failed to comply with party demands for the withdrawal from the Government of all party members over the Minani affair. Two UPRONA ministers were subsequently dismissed from the Council of Ministers, in apparent retaliation, prompting Mukasi, in mid-February, to demand the resignation of the Prime Minister and to declare an indefinite general strike in support of this demand. Increased political opposition to Kanyenkiko forced the Prime Minister to acknowledge that he no longer commanded the necessary mandate to continue in office, and on 22 February Antoine Nduwayo, a UPRONA candidate selected in consultation with other opposition parties, was appointed Prime Minister by presidential decree. A new coalition Council of Ministers was announced on 1 March, but political stability was undermined immediately by the murder, in early March, of the Hutu Minister of Energy and Mines, Ernest Kabushemeye.

Ethnic tension persisted in the second half of 1994, exacerbated by the scale and proximity of the violence in Rwanda and by the presence in Burundi of an estimated 200,000 Rwandan Hutu refugees. Ethnically-motivated atrocities became a daily occurrence in parts of the country (several prominent politicians and government officials were murdered), resulting in the imposition of a partial curfew in the capital in December. Fears that the security crisis in Burundi would develop into civil war were aggravated, in late 1994, by reports that the 30,000-strong Force pour la défense de la démocratie (FDD), the armed wing of Nyangoma's extremist Conseil national pour la défense de la démocratie (CNDD), were making preparations for an armed struggle against the armed forces in Burundi. In early November the CSN had urged all political and civilian groups to dissociate themselves from Nyangoma, who was believed to be co-ordinating party activities from Zaire.

An escalation in the scale and frequency of incidents of politically- and ethnically-motivated violence during 1995 prompted renewed concern that the security crisis would precipitate a large-scale campaign of ethnic massacres similar to that in Rwanda during 1994. Government-sponsored military initiatives were concentrated in Hutu-dominated suburbs of Bujumbura and in the north-east, where an aggressive campaign was waged against the alleged insurgent activities of the Parti de libération du peuple hutu (PALIPEHUTU—a small, proscribed, Hutu opposition group based in Tanzania), resulting in the deaths of hundreds of Hutu civilians. The Government accused Hutu extremist militias of conducting an intimidating and violent programme of recruitment of Hutu males in the region. In May 1995 humanitarian organizations suspended their activities in Burundi for one week, in an attempt to draw international attention to the deteriorating security situation and the increasingly dangerous position of relief workers in the area. Anti-insurgency operations were intensified in June in several suburbs of the capital, where an estimated 2,000 heavily-armed troops sought to apprehend members of the FDD. It was reported that as many as 130 civilians were killed (many of them women and children) in the ensuing hostilities, which also forced thousands of Hutus to flee into the surrounding countryside. (In October the armed forces claimed to have destroyed the FDD headquarters.) Also in June a report published by the human rights organization, Amnesty International, claimed that national security forces in Burundi had collaborated with extremist Tutsi factions in the murder of thousands of Hutus since 1993. Increased security measures announced by Ntibantunganya in the same month included restrictions on a number of civil liberties and the regrouping of many communes into administrative sectors to be administered jointly by civilian and military personnel. Notwithstanding the latest security initiative, in late June the Minister of State in charge of External Relations and Co-operation, Jean-Marie Ngendahayo, announced his resignation, expressing dissatisfaction at the Government's inability to guarantee the safety and basic rights of the population. Later in the month a meeting of the OAU, convened in Addis Ababa, Ethiopia, concluded that some degree of military intervention in Burundi would be necessary should ethnic violence continue to escalate. (In April the Burundian Government had declined an OAU offer of military intervention in favour of increasing the number of MIPROBU personnel to 67.)

By early 1996 reports of atrocities perpetrated against both Hutu and Tutsi civilians by rogue elements of the Tutsi-led armed forces (including militias known as the *Sans Echecs*), and by extremist Hutu rebel groups had become almost commonplace in rural areas. It was believed that the capital had been effectively 'cleansed' of any significant Hutu presence by the end of 1995. In late December the UN Secretary-General had petitioned the Security Council to sanction some form of international military intervention in Burundi to address the crisis, and in February 1996 these efforts were renewed after the UN Special Rapporteur on Human Rights concluded that no discernible improvement had been made in the protection of human rights since mid-1995 and that a state of near civil war existed in many areas of the country. However, the Burundian Government (and the weight of political opinion in Burundi) remained vehemently opposed to a foreign military presence, claiming that reports of the severity of the security crisis had been exaggerated, and persuading the UN Security Council that a negotiated settlement to the conflict was still attainable.

In early April 1996 representatives of the US Agency for International Development and the Humanitarian Office of the European Union (EU, see p. 172) visited Burundi. Their findings—which were severely critical of the administration's failure to reconcile the country's various ethnic and political interests within government, and expressed doubts that effective power-sharing could be achieved within the terms of the 1994 Convention of Government and under the leadership of a Tutsi premier with considerable executive power—prompted the USA and the EU to announce the immediate suspension of aid to Burundi. Despite an undertaking by Ntibantunganya in late April 1996 that a human rights commission was to be established and a comprehensive reform of the security forces and the judiciary was to be undertaken, violence continued to escalate, prompting the suspension of French military co-operation with Burundi at the end of May. In early June the International Committee of the Red Cross (ICRC) suspended all activities in Burundi, following the murder of three ICRC workers in the north-west of the country; other aid agencies announced that future operations would be restricted to the capital.

In November 1995 the Presidents of Burundi, Rwanda, Uganda and Zaire, together with a Tanzanian presidential envoy, met in Cairo, Egypt, to discuss the crises in Burundi and Rwanda. The Great Lakes' representatives announced a sub-regional peace initiative for Burundi, to be led by the former President of Tanzania, Julius Nyerere. A further Great Lakes summit took place in Tunisia in mid-March 1996, at which Ntibantunganya reiterated his commitment to the restoration of internal security and the organization of democratic, multi-party elections in 1998. Representatives of some 13 political parties (including FRODEBU and UPRONA) participated in inter-party discussions conducted in Mwanza, Tanzania, in April 1996. Talks resumed in Mwanza in early June, but political polarization appeared to have been intensified by the negotiating process. The leader of UPRONA, Charles Mukasi, with support from an informal coalition of seven smaller, predominantly Tutsi parties (the Rassemblement unitaire), accused FRODEBU deputies of seeking to abrogate the Convention of Government, a charge which was strenuously denied by FRODEBU spokesmen following the talks. At a conference of regional powers in Arusha, Tanzania, in late June, it was reported that Ntibantunganya and Nduwayo had requested foreign intervention to protect politicians, civil servants and strategic installations. By early July a regional technical commission to examine the request for 'security assistance' (comprising regional defence ministers, but not representatives of the Burundian armed forces) had convened in Arusha and had reached preliminary agreement, with the support of the UN, for an intervention force to be composed of units of the Ugandan and Tanzanian armed forces and police officers from Kenya. Meanwhile, significant differences of interpretation with regard to the purpose and mandate of such a force had emerged between Ntibantunganya and Nduwayo (who suggested that the President was attempting to neutralize the country's military capability). At a mass rally in Bujumbura of Tutsi-dominated opposition parties, the Prime Minister joined Mukasi and other anti-Government figures in rejecting foreign military intervention and condemning what they regarded as Ntibantunganya's encouragement of external interference in domestic affairs. Some days later, however, full endorsement of the Arusha proposal for intervention was recorded by member nations of the OAU at a summit meeting convened in Yaoundé, Cameroon.

Political and ethnic enmities intensified still further when reports of a massacre of more than 300 Tutsi civilians at Bugendana, allegedly committed by Hutu extremists including heavily-armed Rwandan Hutu refugees, emerged just hours after the UN accused the Burundian authorities of collaborating with the Rwandan administration in a new initiative of (largely enforced) repatriation of Rwandan refugees in Burundi. While FRODEBU members made an urgent appeal for foreign military intervention to contain the increasingly violent civil and military reaction to these events, the former President, Bagaza, urged civil resistance to foreign intervention; his appeal for a general strike in Bujumbura was partially observed. Meanwhile, students (with the support of the political opposition) began a second week of protests against regional military intervention, and demonstrated in support of demands for the removal of the country's leadership. On 23 July 1996 Ntibantunganya was forced to abandon an attempt to attend the funeral of the victims of the Bugendana massacre when mourners stoned the presidential helicopter. The following day, amid strong indications that UPRONA intended to join a number of smaller opposition parties that had already withdrawn from the Convention of Government, it was reported that Ntibantunganya had sought refuge in the US embassy building. Several government Ministers and the Speaker of the National Assembly similarly sought refuge within the German embassy compound, while the FRODEBU Chairman, Jean Minani, fled the country.

On 25 July 1996, in a bloodless military coup, the armed forces were extensively deployed in the capital. A statement made by the Minister of National Defence, Lt-Col Firmin Sinzoyiheba, criticized the failure of the administration to safeguard national security, and announced the suspension of the National Assembly and all political activity, the imposition of a nationwide curfew and the closure of national borders and the airport at Bujumbura. Former President Buyoya was declared to be interim President of a transitional republic. In an address to the nation, delivered on the same day, Buyoya defined his immediate aim as the restoration of peace and national security, and sought to reassure former ministers and government officials that their safety would be guaranteed by the new regime. Ntibantunganya conveyed his refusal to relinquish office, but Nduwayo immediately resigned, attributing his failure to effect national reconciliation principally to Ntibantunganya's ineffective leadership. In response to widespread external condemnation of the coup, Buyoya announced that a largely civilian, broadly-based government of national unity would be promptly installed, and that future negotiations with all Hutu groups would be considered. The forced repatriation of Rwandan Hutu refugees was halted with immediate effect.

Despite the appointment, at the end of July 1996, of Pascal-Firmin Ndimira, a Hutu member of UPRONA, as Prime Minister, and an urgent attempt by Buyoya to obtain regional support, the leaders of Ethiopia, Kenya, Rwanda, Tanzania, Uganda and Zaire met in Arusha, under OAU auspices, the same day, and declared their intention to impose stringent economic sanctions against the new regime unless constitutional government was restored immediately. In early August the composition of a new 23-member, multi-ethnic Cabinet was announced. In mid-August Buyoya announced that an expanded transitional national assembly, incorporating existing elected deputies, would be inaugurated during September for a three-year period. A consultative council of elders was also to be established to oversee a period of broad political debate, during which time formal political activity would remain proscribed. Buyoya was formally inaugurated as President on 27 September.

Despite some evidence of violations, the regional sanctions that were imposed in early August 1996 resulted in the suspension of all significant trade and in Burundi's virtual economic isolation. However, the threat of a humanitarian crisis, particularly among children and the Rwandan refugee population, prompted the sanctions co-ordinating committee, meeting in Arusha in September, to authorize a relaxation of the embargo to facilitate the distribution of food and medical aid. An attempt, later in the month, by Buyoya to secure the repeal of all sanctions, by announcing an end to the ban on political parties and the restoration of the National Assembly, was received with scepticism by opponents, given the continued suspension of the Constitution and Buyoya's refusal to address preconditions to the ending of sanctions that required the organization of unconditional peace negotiations. In early October Buyoya agreed to enter into negotiations with the CNDD, but a subsequent meeting, in Arusha, of regional leaders decided that sanctions should be maintained until evidence emerged of constructive progress in the negotiations. This prompted the Burundian Government to denounce the actions and motives of the group, and to withdraw the offer of unconditional dialogue with the CNDD as long as sanctions remained in place. Meanwhile, in early October 1996, some 37 deputies had attended the formal reopening of the National Assembly, which was boycotted by the majority of FRODEBU legislators. According to the Speaker, Léonce Ngendakumana, who had been sheltering in the German embassy since the military coup that had returned Buyoya to power, 22 of the Assembly's original 81 deputies had been murdered during the recent hostilities, and a large number remained in exile or in hiding.

Reports emerged that the armed forces were targeting Hutus (thousands were estimated to have been killed since the coup), in an attempt to safeguard rural and border regions for Tutsi communities, to which the CNDD and other Hutu militia retaliated with attacks against military installations near Bujumbura as well as against Tutsi civilians. A UN report on the causes of the 1993 coup, published in mid-August, implicated two of Buyoya's military leaders, who were subsequently dismissed. By late 1996 the military action in eastern Zaire had led to the repatriation of 30,000 Burundians and had severely weakened FDD fighting capacity, although some activists continued the fight from Tanzania. A report issued by the office of the UN High Commissioner for Refugees (UNHCR) in December estimated that more than 1,100 individuals (predominantly Hutu refugees) had been killed by the armed forces during October and November alone. Also in December Amnesty International denounced what it termed a 'policy of systematic extermination of a section of population' on the part of the armed forces, alleging that the army had massacred as many as 500 Hutu civilians in Butaganza, in the north-west, earlier in the month. Such reports were denied by the Burundian Government. In January 1997 UNHCR reported that the army had, over a period of seven weeks, massed more than 100,000 (mainly Hutu) civilians in camps—in a 'regroupment' scheme stated by the authorities to protect villagers in areas of rebel activity—and that some 1,000 civilians had been killed by the armed forces. Although the authorities asserted that the 'regroupment' programme was voluntary, and that members of all ethnic groups were seeking the protection of the camps, it was widely believed that Hutu civilians were being coerced into regroupment centres by the armed forces, under threat that they would be treated as guerrillas should they fail to comply. Furthermore, the policy was frequently interpreted as a means of isolating rebel militia from their support base within the civilian population. By mid-1997, according to government figures, some 200,000 civilians had been 'regrouped' in about 50 camps, while non-governmental organizations variously estimated the number of civilians affected at 350,000–500,000. Concern was expressed regarding poor living conditions in the camps, but, despite clear evidence of disease and malnutrition, the reluctance of humanitarian organizations to intervene apparently reflected concerns that to do so might be interpreted as a tacit endorsement of the regroupment policy.

The security situation was, meanwhile, further troubled by the return of CNDD fighters among large numbers of Hutu refugees effectively expelled by the Tutsi-led rebellion in eastern Zaire, as well as by the enforced repatriation of refugees from Tanzania. In mid-January 1997 Buyoya condemned the killing of some 120 Hutu refugees who had apparently been expelled from Tanzania, accused of fomenting unrest in camps there. In late May UNHCR appealed to bordering countries to cease repatriating Burundian refugees, owing to renewed massacres notably in the regroupment centres. (Confrontations between the army and Hutu fighters had intensified in recent weeks, and there were frequent reports of massacres of civilians as fighting neared the capital.) A further report by Amnesty International, issued in mid-July, denounced extrajudicial executions as a result of regroupment, and appealed to the Buyoya regime to end the policy and ensure the protection of the displaced population.

The trial began in mid-May 1997 of some 79 military officers accused of involvement in the October 1993 coup attempt—an earlier hearing, scheduled for March, having been postponed. (Of those charged, 22 were reportedly at large, while four of the accused had died.) A number of senior officers, including Lt-Col Jean Bikomagu, who had been Chief of Staff of the Army prior to Ndadaye's assassination, were indicted. In May 1999 five of those accused were sentenced to death and a number of others received prison terms; however, all of the senior officers, including Bikomagu, were acquitted. Meanwhile, at the end of July 1997 it was reported that six people convicted of involvement in acts of genocide perpetrated in 1993 had been executed. In all during July–August 1997, the Burundian courts issued 30 death sentences in relation to such crimes; 10 defendants were sentenced to life imprisonment, and 19 to 20 years' custody.

Six ministers were replaced in a reorganization of Ndimira's Government in early May 1997, and in August Ambroise Niyonsaba was allocated the new post of Minister of the Peace Process. Meanwhile, the introduction of a new law regulating the press was denounced by opposition groups, human rights activists and journalists' representatives as seeking to curb the freedom of the media.

Civil unrest continued in late 1997, and on 1 January 1998 an attack on Bujumbura airport by more than 1,000 Hutu rebels resulted in at least 250 deaths. Similar attacks, although on a smaller scale, continued during early 1998. On 18 February the second stage of the inter-Burundian peace talks was held. The talks, which had been delayed following the death of the Minister of Defence in a helicopter crash, were attended by representatives of the Government, the political parties and the National Assembly, and prominent civilians. The CNDD, however, suspended its participation, calling on the Government publicly to renounce the massacre of innocent civilians, the imposition of death sentences and executions. Following the announcement in late February that a regional summit, held in Kampala, had voted to maintain the sanctions on Burundi, President Buyoya announced the impending repeal of travel restrictions which had been applied to former Presidents Bagaza and Ntibantunganya, and to the Speaker of the National Assembly, Ngendakumana; this was regarded as a significant step towards fulfilling the conditions necessary for the removal of sanctions. In mid-March the courts dismissed a case against Ngendakumana, on charges of genocide.

Following negotiations between the Government and the National Assembly concerning the expiry of FRODEBU's electoral mandate in June 1998, Buyoya and Ngendakumana publicly signed a political accord, and a new Transitional Constitution was promulgated on 6 June, replacing the law (enabling him to rule by decree) enacted by Buyoya after he took power in July 1996. The new charter provided for institutional reforms, including the creation of two vice-presidencies to replace the office of Prime Minister, the enlargement of the National Assembly from 81 to 121 seats, and the creation of a seven-member Constitutional Court, which was sworn in on 24 June 1998. In accordance with the Transitional Constitution, Buyoya was inaugurated as President on 11 June. On the following day the two Vice-Presidents were appointed: Frédérique Bavuginyumvira, a senior member of FRODEBU, who was allocated responsibility for political and administrative affairs, and Mathias Sinamenye (a Tutsi and hitherto the Governor of the Central Bank), with responsibility for economic and social issues. A new 22-member Council of Ministers, sworn in on 13 June, included 13 Hutus and eight Tutsis. The newly-enlarged National Assembly was inaugurated on 18 July, incorporating nine representatives from smaller political parties (with four further seats remaining vacant, owing to internal party disputes or the lack of a candidate) as well as 27 civilian representatives and 21 new representatives of FRODEBU to replace those who had been killed or gone into exile. On 22 July the inter-Burundian peace talks were adjourned at the request of the Government, as the parties were unable to reach agreement on the structure of the negotiations.

Meanwhile, little substantive progress was made in regional efforts to bring about direct peace talks between the Buyoya Government and its opponents. Consultations in Arusha in mid-December 1996 were attended by representatives of the Buyoya administration, FRODEBU, the CNDD, PALIPEHUTU and other organizations. However, the Government's stipulation that fighting must be brought to a formal halt prior to any negotiations effectively precluded direct contacts. The first of a series of national seminars on the peace process began in late January 1997, attended by academics, religious leaders, politicians and representatives of civil society. However, prominent political organizations, notably FRODEBU, refused to attend the talks, and the seminars' credibility was undermined when the UN Development Programme, which had initially agreed to finance the negotiations, withdrew its support, on the grounds that all parties were not represented. Buyoya attended the fourth Arusha summit meeting on the Burundi conflict, in mid-April, in his capacity as Head of State. The leaders of the Great Lakes countries agreed to an easing of the economic sanctions in the interests of alleviating conditions for the civilian population. The summit made the full revocation of sanctions dependent on the opening of direct, unconditional peace talks between the Burundian Government and opposition, and, in its final communiqué, urged the Government to dismantle the regroupment camps and to assure the freedom and facilitate the work of the Speaker of the National Assembly. The CNDD pronounced itself 'greatly disappointed' by the outcome of the meeting.

In May 1997 it was disclosed that the Burundian Government and CNDD had been participating in discreet talks in Rome, Italy. A meeting of OAU Heads of State, held in early June in the Zimbabwean capital, Harare, was attended by Buyoya and also by a representative of the CNDD. Also in early June Ntibantunganya left the US embassy for the first time since July 1996, stating that he was prepared to contribute to the peace process. However, initial optimism that planned inter-party talks, scheduled to take place in Arusha in August 1997, would achieve progress in ending the political crisis diminished as the Buyoya Government became increasingly vociferous in its opposition to Nyerere as mediator, denouncing the latter as biased in favour of the opposition. After it became clear that the sanctions would not be revoked immediately upon the opening of negotiations (a decision for which the Burundian authorities appeared to hold Nyerere personally responsible), the Buyoya Government announced that it would not be attending the Arusha talks, stating that it required more time to prepare. The session was effectively abandoned after the Burundian authorities refused to allow an aircraft that had been sent to carry other delegates from Burundi to the meeting to land at Bujumbura. Nyerere openly condemned the stance of the Buyoya regime, announcing that the peace process had reached a stalemate and appealing for wider international assistance in resolving the crisis. A meeting of regional leaders, convened (in Buyoya's absence) in the Tanzanian capital in early September, reaffirmed its support for Nyerere's mediation, castigated the Burundian Government for its intransigence, and resolved to maintain all existing sanctions. The Government was represented at informal discussions between parties involved in the Burundian conflict, organized under UNESCO auspices in Paris, France, in late September; the conference, described as positive by the government delegation, urged the UNESCO directorate to pursue dialogue between the Government and CNDD.

In May 1998 Nyerere held talks with Burundian political leaders, in preparation for the peace negotiations which opened on 15 June in Arusha. At the Arusha talks, which were attended by all the interested parties, it was agreed that the next round of talks would be held on 20 July, and that all factions would suspend hostilities as of that date. The Government, however, expressed reservations concerning the cease-fire, citing the need to maintain state security; the FDD, which had rebelled against the political leadership of the CNDD and was represented by its own delegates at the conference (but not accorded a vote), rejected the cease-fire as unrealistic. The talks set the length of the negotiations at three months, and it was agreed that commissions would be established to negotiate each of the main issues of contention: the nature of the Burundian conflict, genocide, crimes against humanity and political exclusion; democracy and good governance; the judicial system and the defence and security forces; and the return of refugees and displaced people and reconstruction and economic development. At the

July talks, however, little progress was made. After 10 days of negotiations, no procedural framework had been established, and the composition of the proposed commissions had not been decided. Western donors, who were financing the talks, were concerned about the lack of progress, and, following reports of continued violent incidents in Burundi, about the implementation of the cease-fire. Prior to the third round of negotiations, a split emerged in UPRONA between those who supported the Chairman, Mukasi's, opposition to the Arusha talks and those who were prepared to negotiate with the Hutu opposition. In October some moderate members of the UPRONA central committee elected a rival Chairman, Dr Luc Rukingama, the Minister of Information and a supporter of Buyoya. Mukasi was arrested in August, following outspoken criticism of the Government. At the third round of talks, which took place in October, three of the envisaged commissions were established. The commissions convened in mid-December prior to the fourth round of talks, which took place in January 1999. At the January talks a further commission was constituted, but no substantive progress was achieved.

At a regional summit meeting, held in Arusha in January 1999, following an appeal from the UN Security Council earlier in the month, regional Heads of State voted to suspend the economic sanctions, in recognition of the progress made in the peace negotiations, although they emphasized that the eventual lifting of the sanctions would be dependent on the progress made at the peace talks. The Arusha commissions continued their work in March in preparation for the fifth round of talks, which were held in July, although they again ended without agreement. Nyerere expressed his unhappiness with the slow progress made at the talks and criticized the commissions for being unwilling to reach a consensus. Western donors, who were funding the talks, also expressed concern at the apparent lack of progress. In May the 18 parties represented at the peace talks had formed three broad groups—one Hutu, one Tutsi and a third comprising Buyoya's supporters—which it was hoped would facilitate the talks. At that time Buyoya unveiled his plan for reconciliation, under which he proposed a 10-year transition period during which he would occupy the presidency for the first five years and a Hutu representative would assume the post for the second five years. The plan also envisaged the extension of the National Assembly to include Hutu rebel factions, the creation of a senate, the establishment of communal police forces, to resolve the issue of Tutsi-dominated defence and security forces, and the establishment of a national truth commission. Buyoya's opponents dismissed the proposals, citing his failure to honour his commitment to return the country swiftly to civilian rule in 1996 and the absence of any reference to elections in his plan. It was reported in July that the Tutsi and Hutu groupings were uniting in opposition to Buyoya, led by Jean Minani of FRODEBU and the former President, Bagaza. Progress at Arusha talks held in September were impeded by the escalation of violence throughout the country but particularly around the capital, Bujumbura. The Government complained that the issue of a cease-fire was not even under discussion at the negotiations and the rebel Hutu faction, the FDD, which was largely responsible for insurgent activity, was excluded from discussions. None the less facilitators still aimed to have an agreement signed by the end of the year. However, further talks were postponed owing to the death of Nyerere in mid-October. All the parties involved in the talks expressed their commitment to the process and nine political parties, including FRODEBU and and UPRONA created a movement for peace and solidarity, the Convergence nationale pour la paix et réconciliation (CNPR), which proposed that negotiations continue on neutral territory, owing to the alleged role of Tanzania in sheltering Hutu rebels. In December the former President of South Africa, Nelson Mandela, whose candidature had been supported by Buyoya, was appointed mediator.

In June 1999 a new penal code was adopted by the National Assembly, to come into effect from 1 January 2000. This new code was to provide protection for civil rights and liberties and also introduced controls to reduce torture and arbitrary, lengthy and preventive detention. In mid-August 169 suspects, who had been detained for two years, were released pending their court appearance under the terms of this new code which reduced preventive detention to a maximum of one year. It was hoped that this measure would reduce the number of prison inmates in Burundi (some 10,000 at that time), up to three-quarters of whom were in preventive detention.

Unrest continued throughout 1999 and increased in the second half of the year. Rebel attacks, including an ambush during which a World Food Programme (WFP) aid worker was injured, resulted in the restriction of WFP staff movement in early July. Further clashes were reported between rebel and government forces in August and September. Several hundred people were killed in an attack on a market in Kanyosha, on the outskirts of Bujumbura; the armed forces were accused of the massacre of 147 civilians whilst the army claimed that the massacre had been perpetrated by rebel forces. Human rights groups accused both government and rebel forces of killing civilians in the continuing violence. The escalation of Hutu-led attacks around the capital led to the alleged rearming of Tutsi militias by the Tutsi-dominated security forces. A further response to increased Hutu rebel activity was the enforced relocation of more than 320,000 Hutus into regroupment camps. The Government claimed that the camps provided protection for the civilian population and would prevent members from seeking shelter in the community. However, the camps had not been adequately prepared and lacked basic accommodation, supplies of food and water and medical assistance. The UN, the USA and the EU all expressed their concern at the Government's enforced regroupment of Hutu civilians in these camps. In mid-October following an ambush in which two UN aid workers were killed attempting to inspect a regroupment camp, the UN announced that it was to restrict its operations and confine its staff to Bujumbura. Insecurity continued during October and November with further clashes between government and rebel forces. A UN human rights report, issued in October, criticized Burundi for its regroupment policy and for the insecurity and prevalence of massacres. At this time it was estimated that more than 200,000 people, mainly civilians, had been killed since the outbreak of hostilities in 1993 and 1.1m. people displaced. The Government agreed that human rights were being violated but claimed that this was inevitable in a country affected by civil war. In November the aid agency, Médecins sans Frontières, announced that it was suspending its programme in the camps and Amnesty International issued a warning that conditions in Burundi now resembled those that had preceded the genocide in Rwanda in 1994.

In January 2000 a cabinet reorganization was effected in which five new ministers were appointed, including Col Cyrille Ndayirukiye as Minister of National Defence and Charles Nihangaza as Minister of Finance.

The cross-border movement of vast numbers of refugees, provoked by regional ethnic and political violence, has dominated recent relations with Rwanda, Tanzania and the Democratic Republic of the Congo (DRC, formerly Zaire), and has long been a matter of considerable concern to the international aid community. In October and November 1993, following the abortive coup by factions of the Tutsi-dominated armed forces (see above), ethnic violence erupted on a massive scale throughout the country, claiming an estimated 150,000 lives and displacing an estimated 800,000 people, including 500,000 who fled into Tanzania, Rwanda and Zaire. Limited relief resources were overburdened in April 1994 by the exodus into Burundi of thousands of Rwandans, and by the repatriation of vast numbers of Burundians from refugee camps in Rwanda, as a result of the political violence and accompanying massacres following the death of President Habyarimana. In July 1995 UNHCR estimated that some 50,000 Rwandan refugees had been repatriated since the beginning of the year. By 31 December 1996, following a programme of forced repatriation in July of that year, the refugee population in Burundi had declined to less than 1,000 (although this estimate excluded Zairean refugees, the number of whom was unknown to UNHCR). At that time some 882,900 internally displaced Burundians and 71,031 returnees from Tanzania were of concern to UNHCR. In early 1999 UNHCR estimated that there was a total of 299,400 Burundian refugees, although this figure excluded some 200,000 long-term Burundian residents in Tanzania, who were increasingly vulnerable to expulsion. According to UNHCR, some 5,000 refugees were repatriated to Burundi between January and April 1999.

The uprising by Laurent-Désiré Kabila's Alliance des forces démocratiques pour la libération du Congo-Zaïre (AFDL) in eastern Zaire resulted in the return of large numbers of refugees: an estimated 300,000 returned to Burundi from late 1996, severely undermining the operations from Zaire of large numbers of FDD fighters who were believed to have been massed in refugee camps there. Moreover, the seizure of power by the

AFDL in May 1997 was welcomed by the Buyoya regime, which moved to forge close relations with Kabila's Democratic Republic of the Congo (DRC). The DRC remained a party to the continuing regional sanctions against Burundi, although a bilateral trade co-operation agreement was concluded in mid-1997. In April 1998 Burundi, the DRC and Uganda agreed to establish a combined police force to provide security along their common borders. Burundi initially denied any involvement in the civil war which began in the DRC in August, but by May 1999 some 3,000 Burundian troops were believed to be stationed there with the aim of destroying FDD camps in the eastern DRC. The FDD has supported the DRC Government in the civil war and has used the conflict as an opportunity to regroup and rearm despite the insistence of its political leadership that it supports the continuing peace talks in Tanzania. In June the DRC instituted proceedings against Burundi, together with Rwanda and Uganda, at the ICJ, accusing them of acts of armed aggression in contravention of the terms of both the UN Charter and the Charter of the OAU.

Meanwhile, the Buyoya regime's relations with Tanzania were characterized not only by the continued presence of large numbers of Burundian refugees but also by increasingly vociferous accusations on the part of the Buyoya Government that Tanzania was supporting the Hutu rebellion. Such allegations were strenuously denied by the Tanzanian Government, which stated that it would never allow the use of refugee camps on its territory for military training. Mutual suspicion was exacerbated by Tanzania's refusal to allow a representative of the Buyoya regime to take up the position of chargé d'affaires at the Burundian embassy in Dar es Salaam. In late August Tanzania announced that it had placed its armed forces on alert, stating that Burundian forces were mobilizing near the border in preparation for an invasion of the refugee camps. Meanwhile, the Buyoya Government's assertions that Nyerere was unduly biased in his role as mediator in the Burundian conflict further strained bilateral ties. In late 1997 Burundian allegations that the Tanzanian Government was involved in cross-border raids by Hutu militias, based in Tanzania, adversely affected relations, and in November there were reports of clashes between troops on the Tanzanian-Burundian border. In the same month Burundi's ambassador-designate to Tanzania, Clavera Mayegara, was sent to assume control of the Burundian embassy in Dar es Salaam, which was occupied by members of the CNDD and FRODEBU. She was, however, arrested by the Tanzanian authorities and subsequently expelled. In 1998 bilateral relations improved slightly, and in July Tanzania agreed to the reopening of the Burundian embassy. Relations appeared to improve further in early 1999 and, following a meeting of the Burundian and Tanzanian ministers of foreign affairs, it was announced that a tripartite commission was to be established (with representatives from Burundi, Tanzania and UNHCR) to investigate allegations that armed milita groups had used Tanzania as a base from which to launch attacks on Burundi. However, the commission's first meeting, scheduled for March, was cancelled without explanation by Tanzania, and relations remained tense.

## Government

Under the Constitution of March 1992, executive power is vested in the President, who is elected directly, by universal adult suffrage, for a five-year term, renewable only once. Statutory power is shared with the Prime Minister, who appoints a Council of Ministers. Legislative power is exercised by the National Assembly, whose members are elected directly, by universal adult suffrage, for a five-year renewable mandate. A Convention of Government, concluded among the major political parties in September 1994, detailed the terms of government for a four-year transitional period, and was incorporated into the Constitution in the same month. Following the *coup d'état* of 25 July 1996, the terms of the Constitution and the Convention of Government were suspended.

On 6 June 1998 a Transitional Constitution was promulgated. The membership of the National Assembly was increased from 81 to 121, and two vice-presidencies were created to replace the post of Prime Minister.

For the purposes of local government, Burundi comprises 15 provinces (administered by civilian governors), each of which is divided into districts and further subdivided into communes.

## Defence

The total strength of the armed forces in August 1999 was 45,500, comprising an army of an estimated 40,000 (including an air wing of 200), and a paramilitary force of an estimated 5,500 gendarmes (including a 50-strong marine police force). Defence expenditure for 1999 was budgeted at 35,000m. Burundian francs.

## Economic Affairs

In 1997, according to estimates by the World Bank, Burundi's gross national product (GNP), measured at average 1995–97 prices, was US $924m., equivalent to $140 per head. During 1990–97, it was estimated, GNP per head decreased, in real terms, at an average rate of 5.9% per year. Over the same period the population increased by an average of 2.4% annually. GNP totalled an estimated $900m. in 1998, equivalent to $140 per head. Burundi's gross domestic product (GDP) increased, in real terms, at an average rate of 4.4% per year in 1980–90, but declined at an average annual rate of 3.2% in 1990–98; GDP showed a marginal increase, of 0.4% in 1997, and registered growth of 4.5% in 1998.

Agriculture (including forestry and fishing) contributed an estimated 53.3% of GDP in 1997. An estimated 90.6% of the labour force were employed in the sector at mid-1998. The principal cash crops are coffee (which accounted for 87.7% of export earnings in 1997) and tea. Hides and skins are also exported. The main subsistence crops are cassava and sweet potatoes. Although Burundi is traditionally self-sufficient in food crops, population displacement as a result of the political crisis has resulted in considerable disruption in the sector, while the economic sanctions imposed following the 1996 coup further affected production, owing to a shortage of inputs. Moreover, an army-imposed ban on fishing on Lake Tanganyika has entailed the loss of an important source of food supply. The livestock-rearing sector was also severely affected by the civil war. During 1990–98, according to the World Bank, agricultural GDP decreased at an average annual rate of 2.4%. Over the same period agricultural output declined by 1.7% per year.

Industry (comprising mining, manufacturing, construction and utilities) engaged only 2.1% of the employed labour force in 1990, but contributed an estimated 16.7% of GDP in 1997. Industrial GDP decreased at an average annual rate of 7.8% in 1990–98, according to the World Bank.

Mining and power engaged 0.1% of the employed labour force in 1990 and contributed an estimated 0.8% of GDP in 1997. Gold (alluvial), tin, tungsten and columbo-tantalite are mined in small quantities, although much activity has hitherto been outside the formal sector. Burundi has important deposits of nickel (estimated at 5% of world reserves), vanadium and uranium. In addition, petroleum deposits have been detected.

Manufacturing engaged 1.2% of the employed labour force in 1990 and contributed an estimated 9.7% of GDP in 1997. The sector consists largely of the processing of agricultural products (coffee, cotton, tea and the extraction of vegetable oils). A number of small enterprises also produce beer, flour, cement, flootwear and textiles. According to the World Bank, manufacturing GDP decreased at an average annual rate of 9.9% in 1990–97.

Energy is derived principally from hydroelectric power (51.3% of electricity consumed in 1994 was imported, but the proportion declined to 4.2% in 1996, owing to the imposition of economic sanctions). Peat is also exploited as an additional source of energy. Imports of fuel and energy comprised 32% of the value of merchandise imports in 1995, prior to the imposition of sanctions.

The services sector contributed an estimated 30.0% of GDP in 1997 but engaged just 4.4% of the employed labour force in 1990. According to the World Bank, the GDP of the services sector decreased at an average annual rate of 2.9% in 1990–98.

In 1997 Burundi recorded a visible trade deficit of US $10.6m., but there was a surplus of $4.0m. on the current account of the balance of payments. In 1997 the principal source of imports (18.2%) was Belgium; other important suppliers in that year were France, Germany, Japan and Zambia. The principal market for exports in 1997 (27.0%) was the United Kingdom; other important markets were Germany and Belgium. Significant trade was also conducted with Kenya and Tanzania prior to the regional sanctions imposed between 1996 and early 1999. The main imports in 1993 were machinery and transport equipment, basic manufactures, chemicals, mineral fuels and food. The principal exports in 1997 were coffee, tea and hides and skins.

In 1997 the budget deficit, after adjustment, was 18,555m. Burundian francs, equivalent to 5.4% of GDP. Burundi's external debt at the end of 1997 was US $1,066m., of which

$1,022m. was long-term public debt. In that year the cost of debt-servicing was equivalent to 29.0% of revenue from the export of goods and services. The annual rate of inflation averaged 15.2% in 1990–98. Consumer prices increased by 31.1% in 1997, although the inflation rate slowed to an average of 12.5% in 1998.

Burundi, with its neighbours Rwanda and the Democratic Republic of the Congo, is a member of the Economic Community of the Great Lakes Countries (CEPGL, see p. 291). Burundi is also a member of the Common Market for Eastern and Southern Africa (COMESA, see p. 142), and of the International Coffee Organization (see p. 287).

Burundi's acute economic decline after 1993, owing to the severe political upheaval and accompanying population displacement, was further exacerbated by the regional economic sanctions imposed following the *coup d'état* of July 1996. By early 1999, when the sanctions were revoked, a sustained decline in government revenue had resulted in the depletion of official reserves; capital expenditure was minimal, and the Government was borrowing heavily in order to meet its financing requirements. As a result, domestic and foreign debts had accumulated at an unsustainable level, and Burundi was defaulting on its debt-servicing obligations. Meanwhile, smuggling and tax evasion were largely unchecked, and a 'black market' for both goods and currency was flourishing. The ending of the regional blockade had little positive impact during 1999, as aid inflows and international co-operation, on which the Burundian economy depends, remained at a very low level compared with that of the early 1990s. The recovery especially of agricultural activity was, furthermore, effectively prevented by the degree of population displacement: an estimated 800,000 people were internally displaced, and the prevailing climate of insecurity meant that the distribution of food supplies most notably to some 300,000 people forcibly relocated under the military's encampment programme could not be guaranteed. Despite the reopening of regional trading links, Burundi's principal export commodity, coffee, remained uncompetitive at a time of low international prices, although a 15% devaluation of the Burundian franc in August 1999 was intended partially to offset this impediment to trade. Currency controls were relaxed in late 1999, by means of new regulations allowing the operation of private bureaux de change and permitting private individuals to hold foreign-currency accounts, with the aim of discouraging capital flight from the country. Meanwhile, the revival of plans to exploit important nickel reserves at Musongati, in the south of the country, was accompanied by prospects for much-needed investment and infrastructural development. However, the normalization of economic activity, and thus the eventual return of sustained growth, continues to depend on the success of efforts to bring about lasting peace not only for Burundi, but for the Great Lakes region as a whole.

### Social Welfare

Wage-earners are protected by insurance against accidents and occupational diseases, and can draw on a pension fund. Medical facilities are, however, limited. In the mid-1990s there were 34 hospitals, with one bed for every 1,526 inhabitants. There were 329 physicians in hospitals (1 per 17,210 inhabitants) and one nurse for every 4,800 inhabitants. Of total expenditure by the central Government in 1997, 2,085m. Burundian francs (2.6%) was for health, and a further 4,718m. Burundian francs (5.8%) for social security and welfare.

### Education

Education is provided free of charge. Kirundi is the language of instruction in primary schools, while French is used in secondary schools. Primary education, which is officially compulsory, begins at seven years of age and lasts for six years. Secondary education begins at the age of 13 and lasts for up to seven years, comprising a first cycle of four years and a second of three years. In 1995 the total enrolment at primary schools included 51% of children in the relevant age-group (males 55%; females 46%). Enrolment at secondary schools included only 7% of the population in the appropriate age-group (males 9%; females 5%). There is one university, in Bujumbura; some 4,256 students were enrolled at university-level institutions in 1992/93. In 1996 there were 4,379 students in higher education. According to UNESCO estimates, the average rate of illiteracy among the population aged 15 years and over was 64.7% (males 50.7%; females 77.5%) in 1995. Expenditure on education by the central Government in 1997 was 11,204m. Burundian francs (13.9% of total government expenditure).

### Public Holidays

**2000:** 1 January (New Year's Day), 24 April (Easter Monday), 1 May (Labour Day), 1 June (Ascension Day), 1 July (Independence Day), 15 August (Assumption), 18 September (Victory of UPRONA Party), 1 November (All Saints' Day), 25 December (Christmas).

**2001:** 1 January (New Year's Day), 16 April (Easter Monday), 1 May (Labour Day), 24 May (Ascension Day), 1 July (Independence Day), 15 August (Assumption), 18 September (Victory of UPRONA Party), 1 November (All Saints' Day), 25 December (Christmas).

### Weights and Measures

The metric system is in force.

# Statistical Survey

## Area and Population

**AREA, POPULATION AND DENSITY**

| | |
|---|---|
| Area (sq km) | 27,834* |
| Population (census results)† | |
| 15–16 August 1979 | 4,028,420 |
| 16–30 August 1990 | |
| Males | 2,473,599 |
| Females | 2,665,474 |
| Total | 5,139,073 |
| Population (official estimates at mid-year) | |
| 1996 | 6,088,000 |
| 1997 | 6,194,000 |
| 1998 | 6,300,000 |
| Density (per sq km) at mid-1998 | 226.3 |

* 10,747 sq miles.

† Excluding adjustment for underenumeration.

**PRINCIPAL TOWNS**

Bujumbura (capital), population 235,440 (census result, August 1990); Gitega 15,943 (1978).

Source: Banque de la République du Burundi.

**BIRTHS AND DEATHS** (UN estimates, annual averages)

| | 1980–85 | 1985–90 | 1990–95 |
|---|---|---|---|
| Birth rate (per 1,000) | 46.2 | 46.7 | 46.2 |
| Death rate (per 1,000) | 17.9 | 18.1 | 21.5 |

**Expectation of life** (UN estimates, years at birth, 1990–95): 41.6 (males 40.1; females 43.0).

Source: UN, *World Population Prospects: The 1998 Revision.*

**ECONOMICALLY ACTIVE POPULATION***
(persons aged 10 years and over, 1990 census)

| | Males | Females | Total |
|---|---|---|---|
| Agriculture, hunting, forestry and fishing | 1,153,890 | 1,420,553 | 2,574,443 |
| Mining and quarrying | 1,146 | 39 | 1,185 |
| Manufacturing | 24,120 | 9,747 | 33,867 |
| Electricity, gas and water | 1,847 | 74 | 1,921 |
| Construction | 19,447 | 290 | 19,737 |
| Trade, restaurants and hotels | 19,667 | 6,155 | 25,822 |
| Transport, storage and communications | 8,193 | 311 | 8,504 |
| Financing, insurance, real estate and business services | 1,387 | 618 | 2,005 |
| Community, social and personal services | 68,905 | 16,286 | 85,191 |
| Activities not adequately defined | 8,653 | 4,617 | 13,270 |
| **Total labour force** | 1,307,255 | 1,458,690 | 2,765,945 |

* Figures exclude persons seeking work for the first time, totalling 13,832 (males 9,608; females 4,224).

Source: UN, *Demographic Yearbook*.

**Mid-1998** (estimates in '000): Agriculture, etc. 3,132; Total 3,458 (Source: FAO, *Production Yearbook*).

# Agriculture

**PRINCIPAL CROPS** ('000 metric tons)

| | 1996 | 1997 | 1998 |
|---|---|---|---|
| Wheat | 9* | 10* | 10 |
| Rice (paddy) | 42* | 65* | 41 |
| Maize | 144* | 145* | 132 |
| Millet | 11* | 17* | 11 |
| Sorghum | 66* | 68* | 67 |
| Potatoes | 42* | 49* | 23 |
| Sweet potatoes | 670* | 681* | 590 |
| Cassava (Manioc) | 549* | 603* | 622 |
| Yams | 8* | 11* | 11 |
| Taro (Coco yam) | 95* | 105* | 76 |
| Dry beans | 288* | 271* | 275 |
| Dry peas | 36* | 37* | 36 |
| Groundnuts (in shell) | 10† | 11† | 9* |
| Cottonseed | 2* | 1* | 2 |
| Palm kernels† | 2 | 2 | 2 |
| Vegetables and melons† | 215 | 220 | 215 |
| Sugar cane | 158† | 178† | 190 |
| Bananas and plantains | 1,544* | 1,543* | 1,399 |
| Other fruits (excl. melons) | 85 | 86 | 85 |
| Coffee (green) | 25 | 20* | 17 |
| Tea (made) | 6 | 4 | 6 |
| Cotton (lint) | 1 | 1* | 1* |

* Unofficial figure. † FAO estimate(s).

Source: FAO, *Production Yearbook*.

**LIVESTOCK** ('000 head, year ending September)

| | 1996 | 1997 | 1998 |
|---|---|---|---|
| Cattle | 449* | 311* | 346 |
| Pigs | 75† | 70† | 73 |
| Sheep† | 320 | 310 | 320 |
| Goats† | 900 | 890 | 900 |

Poultry (million): 5† in 1996; 4† in 1997; 5 in 1998.

* Unofficial figure. † FAO estimate(s).

Source: FAO, *Production Yearbook*.

**LIVESTOCK PRODUCTS** (FAO estimates, '000 metric tons)

| | 1996 | 1997 | 1998 |
|---|---|---|---|
| Beef and veal | 13 | 9 | 10 |
| Mutton and lamb | 1 | 1 | 1 |
| Goat meat | 3 | 3 | 3 |
| Pig meat | 5 | 4 | 4 |
| Poultry meat | 6 | 6 | 6 |
| Cows' milk | 35 | 24 | 27 |
| Sheep's milk | 1 | 1 | 1 |
| Goats' milk | 9 | 9 | 9 |
| Poultry eggs | 3 | 3 | 3 |
| Cattle hides | 3 | 2 | 2 |
| Goatskins | 1 | 1 | 1 |

Source: FAO, *Production Yearbook*.

# Forestry

**ROUNDWOOD REMOVALS** ('000 cubic metres, excl. bark)

| | 1995 | 1996 | 1997 |
|---|---|---|---|
| Sawlogs, veneer logs and logs for sleepers | 43 | 33 | 33 |
| Other industrial wood | 72 | 10 | 10 |
| Fuel wood | 4,616 | 4,734 | 4,866 |
| **Total** | 4,731 | 4,777 | 4,909 |

Source: FAO, *Yearbook of Forest Products*.

**SAWNWOOD PRODUCTION** ('000 cubic metres, incl. railway sleepers)

| | 1995 | 1996 | 1997 |
|---|---|---|---|
| Coniferous (softwood) | 21 | 7 | 7* |
| Broadleaved (hardwood) | 22 | 26 | 26* |
| **Total** | 43 | 33 | 33 |

* FAO estimate.

Source: FAO, *Yearbook of Forest Products*.

# Fishing

('000 metric tons, live weight)

| | 1995 | 1996 | 1997 |
|---|---|---|---|
| Dagaas | 18.2 | 1.5 | 17.9 |
| Freshwater perches | 2.9 | 1.2 | 2.4 |
| **Total catch** (incl. others) | 21.1 | 3.0 | 20.3 |

Source: FAO, *Yearbook of Fishery Statistics*.

# Mining

| | 1994 | 1995 | 1996 |
|---|---|---|---|
| Gold (kilograms)*† | 20 | 10 | 10 |
| Tin ore (metric tons)*† | 10 | 0 | 0 |
| Kaolin ('000 metric tons)*† | 5 | 1 | 1 |
| Peat ('000 metric tons)* | 10 | 10 | 10 |

* Data from US Bureau of Mines.

† Estimate(s). Figures for gold and tin refer to the metal content of ores.

Source: UN, *Industrial Commodity Statistics Yearbook*.

# Industry

**SELECTED PRODUCTS** ('000 metric tons, unless otherwise indicated)

| | 1995 | 1996 | 1997* |
|---|---|---|---|
| Flour | 0.5 | 0.4 | n.a. |
| Beer ('000 hectolitres) | 1,404.2 | 1,227.9 | 1,161.2 |
| Soft drinks ('000 hectolitres) | 219.7 | 179.1 | 146.6 |
| Cottonseed oil ('000 hectolitres) | 211.5 | 234.6 | 199.7 |
| Sugar | 15.3 | 17.8 | 19.6 |
| Paint | 0.5 | 0.4 | 0.4 |
| Insecticides | 2.4 | 2.4 | 2.4 |
| Soap | 5.6 | 3.4 | 2.8 |
| Bottles | 3.7 | 2.5 | 2.1 |
| Blankets ('000) | 137.7 | 116.2 | 21.7 |
| Footwear ('000 pairs) | 10.0 | n.a. | n.a. |
| Fibro-cement products | 0.6 | 0.2 | 0.7 |
| Steel rods | 0.3 | 0.1 | 0.1 |
| Batteries ('000 cartons)† | n.a. | 14.5 | n.a. |
| Electric energy (million kWh) | 97.2 | 99.3 | 87.8 |

* Estimates.

† Cartons of 240 batteries.

Source: IMF, *Burundi: Statistical Annex* (February 1999).

# Finance

**CURRENCY AND EXCHANGE RATES**

**Monetary Units**

100 centimes = 1 Burundian franc.

**Sterling, Dollar and Euro Equivalents** (30 September 1999)

£1 sterling = 1,001.7 francs;
US $1 = 608.4 francs;
€1 = 648.8 francs;
10,000 Burundian francs = £9.983 = $16.437 = €15.412.

**Average Exchange Rate** (Burundian francs per US dollar)

1996 302.75
1997 352.35
1998 447.77

**BUDGET** (million Burundian francs)*

| Revenue† | 1995 | 1996 | 1997 |
|---|---|---|---|
| Tax revenue | 44,816 | 38,646 | 42,880 |
| Taxes on income and profits | 9,039 | 9,712 | 10,322 |
| Social security contributions | 3,143 | 3,288 | 3,731 |
| Domestic taxes on goods and services | 19,512 | 16,316 | 20,744 |
| Transaction tax | 7,107 | 5,845 | 7,281 |
| Excise tax | 11,852 | 10,236 | 13,155 |
| Taxes on international trade | 12,647 | 7,988 | 7,229 |
| Import duties | 7,727 | 6,688 | 6,527 |
| Export tax | 4,919 | 1,298 | 702 |
| Entrepreneurial and property income | 2,113 | 6,190 | 1,920 |
| Other current revenue | 1,229 | 1,509 | 1,345 |
| Capital revenue | 239 | 56 | 108 |
| **Total** | 48,397 | 46,401 | 46,253 |

| Expenditure‡ | 1995 | 1996 | 1997 |
|---|---|---|---|
| General public services | 18,851 | 12,788 | 18,154 |
| Defence | 10,517 | 15,408 | 21,100 |
| Public order and safety | 648 | 4,464 | 1,334 |
| Education | 10,763 | 11,502 | 11,204 |
| Health | 2,688 | 2,647 | 2,085 |
| Social security and welfare | 5,547 | 4,925 | 4,718 |
| Housing and community amenities | 136 | — | — |
| Recreational, cultural and religious affairs and services | 441 | 349 | 334 |
| Economic affairs and services | 13,007 | 12,900 | n.a. |
| Fuel and energy | 1,309 | 3,176 | n.a. |
| Agriculture, forestry, fishing and hunting | 3,897 | 3,597 | n.a. |
| Mining, manufacturing and construction | 3,313 | 3,198 | n.a. |
| Transport and communications | 1,754 | 1,683 | n.a. |
| Other purposes | 12,524 | 10,422 | n.a. |
| Interest payments | 3,722 | 4,422 | 6,071 |
| **Sub-total** | 75,122 | 75,405 | 80,800 |
| Adjustment to total expenditure | 1,281 | — | — |
| **Total** | 76,403 | 75,405 | 80,800 |
| Current | 42,957 | 48,358 | 58,207 |
| Capital | 31,867 | 21,047 | 12,322 |
| Adjustment to total expenditure | 1,579 | 6,000 | 10,271 |

* Figures refer to the consolidated operations of the central Government, comprising the general budget, social security funds and extrabudgetary accounts (covering transactions undertaken through foreign borrowing arrangements and grants not recorded in treasury accounts). The data exclude the operations of other central government units with individual budgets.

† Excluding grants received (million Burundian francs): 16,286 in 1995; 6,148 in 1996; 10,271 in 1997.

‡ Excluding lending minus repayments (million Burundian francs): −452 in 1995; −447 in 1996; −2,583 in 1997.

Source: IMF, *Government Finance Statistics Yearbook*.

**CENTRAL BANK RESERVES** (US $ million at 31 December)

| | 1996 | 1997 | 1998 |
|---|---|---|---|
| Gold* | 6.36 | 4.99 | 4.95 |
| IMF special drawing rights | 0.11 | 0.06 | 0.09 |
| Reserve position in IMF | 8.43 | 7.91 | 8.25 |
| Foreign exchange | 131.06 | 105.07 | 57.18 |
| **Total** | 145.96 | 118.03 | 70.47 |

* Valued at market-related prices.

Source: IMF, *International Financial Statistics*.

**MONEY SUPPLY** (million Burundian francs at 31 December)

| | 1996 | 1997 | 1998 |
|---|---|---|---|
| Currency outside banks | 23,974 | 23,693 | n.a. |
| Deposits at central bank | 371 | 749 | 860 |
| Demand deposits at commercial banks | 18,038 | 22,235 | 22,180 |
| Demand deposits at other monetary institutions | 1,259 | 1,527 | n.a. |
| **Total money** | 43,642 | 48,203 | n.a. |

Source: IMF, *International Financial Statistics*.

**COST OF LIVING**

(Consumer Price Index for Bujumbura; base: January 1991 = 100)

| | 1995 | 1996 | 1997 |
|---|---|---|---|
| Food | 160.4 | 199.0 | 268.7 |
| Clothing | 157.0 | 199.3 | 308.7 |
| Housing, heating and light | 148.0 | 192.1 | 235.4 |
| Transport | 102.0 | 176.4 | 229.1 |
| **All items** (incl. others) | 153.0 | 193.4 | 253.6 |

Source: IMF, *Burundi: Statistical Annex* (February 1999).

**1998** (base: 1995 = 100): All items 186.5 (Source: IMF, *International Financial Statistics*).

**NATIONAL ACCOUNTS** (million Burundian francs at current prices)

**Composition of the Gross National Product**

| | 1996 | 1997 | 1998 |
|---|---|---|---|
| **GDP in purchasers' values** | 265,414 | 346,099 | 404,383 |
| Net factor income from abroad | −4,223 | −4,416 | −3,699 |
| **Gross national product** | 261,191 | 341,683 | 400,684 |

Source: IMF, *International Financial Statistics.*

**Expenditure on the Gross Domestic Product**

| | 1996 | 1997 | 1998 |
|---|---|---|---|
| Government final consumption expenditure | 45,412 | 52,068 | 59,761 |
| Private final consumption expenditure | 216,390 | 282,564 | 376,907 |
| Increase in stocks | −2,935 | 5,205 | −10,529 |
| Gross fixed capital formation | 32,712 | 21,976 | 24,000 |
| **Total domestic expenditure** | 291,579 | 361,812 | 450,139 |
| Exports of goods and services | 15,289 | 33,760 | 32,019 |
| *Less* Imports of goods and services | −41,454 | −49,473 | −77,775 |
| **GDP in purchasers' values** | 265,414 | 346,099 | 404,383 |
| **GDP at constant 1980 prices** | 105,113 | 105,512 | 110,249 |

Source: IMF, *International Financial Statistics.*

**Gross Domestic Product by Economic Activity (estimates)**

| | 1995 | 1996 | 1997 |
|---|---|---|---|
| Agriculture, hunting, forestry and fishing | 105,035 | 136,018 | 163,354 |
| Mining and quarrying } Electricity, gas and water } | 1,296 | 1,487 | 2,432 |
| Manufacturing* | 26,344 | 22,682 | 29,592 |
| Construction | 14,339 | 13,970 | 19,193 |
| Trade, restaurants and hotels | 12,957 | 10,884 | 13,165 |
| Transport, storage and communications | 10,440 | 12,598 | 13,593 |
| Government services | 41,728 | 43,706 | 57,757 |
| Other services | 5,998 | 6,837 | 7,347 |
| **GDP at factor cost** | 218,137 | 248,182 | 306,432 |
| Indirect taxes, *less* subsidies | 31,728 | 24,400 | 30,900 |
| **GDP in purchasers' values** | 249,865 | 272,582 | 337,332 |

* Including handicrafts (million francs): 5,709 in 1995; 6,182 in 1996; 9,302 in 1997.

Source: IMF, *Burundi: Statistical Annex* (February 1999).

**BALANCE OF PAYMENTS** (US $ million)

| | 1995 | 1996 | 1997 |
|---|---|---|---|
| Exports of goods f.o.b. | 112.5 | 40.1 | 87.3 |
| Imports of goods f.o.b. | −175.6 | −100.0 | −97.9 |
| **Trade balance** | −63.1 | −59.9 | −10.6 |
| Exports of services | 16.4 | 10.5 | 8.7 |
| Imports of services | −101.2 | −38.4 | −41.3 |
| **Balance on goods and services** | −147.8 | −87.7 | −43.3 |
| Other income received | 10.4 | 6.4 | 4.3 |
| Other income paid | −22.9 | −20.4 | −16.8 |
| **Balance on goods, services and income** | −160.3 | −101.6 | −55.8 |
| Current transfers received | 154.7 | 62.5 | 61.3 |
| Current transfers paid | −2.1 | −1.1 | −1.6 |
| **Current balance** | −7.8 | −40.3 | 4.0 |
| Capital account (net) | −0.8 | −0.3 | −0.1 |
| Direct investment abroad | −0.6 | — | — |
| Direct investment from abroad | 2.0 | — | — |
| Other investment assets | 8.2 | 6.6 | 15.4 |
| Other investment liabilities | 11.4 | 7.6 | −1.4 |
| Net errors and omissions | 24.2 | −8.9 | −7.1 |
| **Overall balance** | 36.7 | −35.3 | 10.8 |

Source: IMF, *International Financial Statistics.*

# External Trade

**PRINCIPAL COMMODITIES** (distribution by SITC, US $ '000)

| Imports c.i.f. | 1991 | 1992 | 1993 |
|---|---|---|---|
| **Food and live animals** | 22,675 | 19,706 | 20,312 |
| Cereals and cereal preparations | 14,424 | 12,520 | 13,341 |
| Wheat meal and flour of wheat and meslin | 6,453 | 3,904 | 3,859 |
| Flour of wheat or meslin | 6,445 | 3,835 | 3,859 |
| Cereal preparations, etc. | 6,447 | 7,116 | 7,480 |
| Malt (incl. malt flour) | 6,290 | 6,962 | 7,365 |
| **Crude materials (inedible) except fuels** | 8,081 | 4,915 | 5,478 |
| **Mineral fuels, lubricants, etc.** | 31,183 | 27,992 | 25,387 |
| Petroleum, petroleum products, etc. | 31,044 | 27,888 | 25,346 |
| Refined petroleum products | 29,603 | 27,248 | 24,538 |
| Motor spirit (gasoline) and other light oils | 12,511 | 10,570 | 8,630 |
| Gas oils | 9,893 | 8,966 | 7,993 |
| **Chemicals and related products** | 33,890 | 32,475 | 28,807 |
| Medicinal and pharmaceutical products | 10,289 | 11,554 | 8,523 |
| Manufactured fertilizers | 3,228 | 4,865 | 4,562 |
| Artificial resins, plastic materials, etc. | 4,774 | 4,721 | 5,401 |
| Disinfectants, insecticides, fungicides, weed-killers, etc., for retail sale | 5,809 | 3,581 | 2,785 |
| Insecticides | 5,713 | 3,451 | 2,635 |
| **Basic manufactures** | 52,433 | 48,948 | 42,868 |
| Rubber manufactures | 6,641 | 5,383 | 7,077 |
| Rubber tyres, tubes, etc. | 5,334 | 4,059 | 5,215 |
| Paper, paperboard and manufactures | 6,062 | 5,777 | 5,556 |
| Non-metallic mineral manufactures | 13,512 | 12,898 | 9,445 |
| Lime, cement, etc. | 11,093 | 10,896 | 7,145 |
| Cement | 10,481 | 10,226 | 6,820 |
| **Machinery and transport equipment** | 70,144 | 63,206 | 43,603 |
| General industrial machinery, equipment and parts | 29,926 | 23,147 | 20,484 |
| Electrical machinery, apparatus and appliances | 12,351 | 14,437 | 3,894 |
| Road vehicles and parts (excl. tyres, engines and electrical parts) | 26,388 | 23,999 | 18,265 |
| Passenger motor cars (excl. buses) | 9,687 | 8,202 | 5,350 |
| Motor vehicles for the transport of goods or materials | 9,557 | 7,530 | 5,984 |
| Parts and accessories for cars, buses, lorries, etc. | 4,326 | 5,543 | 4,194 |
| **Miscellaneous manufactured articles** | 12,105 | 16,798 | 8,188 |
| Photographic apparatus, optical goods, watches and clocks | 6,725 | 10,154 | 4,182 |
| **Special transactions and commodities not classified according to kind** | 14,291 | 13,406 | 19,877 |
| **Total** (incl. others) | 247,087 | 229,508 | 204,525 |

Source: UN, *International Trade Statistics Yearbook.*

**1994** (US $ million): *Imports c.i.f.:* Capital goods 80.9; Intermediate goods 55.3 (Petroleum products 29.0); Consumption goods 87.4 (Food 30.0); Total 223.6.

**1995** (US $ million): *Imports c.i.f.:* Capital goods 87.6; Intermediate goods 62.4 (Petroleum products 26.6); Consumption goods 82.9 (Food 28.8); Total 232.9.

**1996** (US $ million): *Imports c.i.f.:* Capital goods 48.5; Intermediate goods 38.1 (Petroleum products 18.2); Consumption goods 36.8 (Food 10.9); Total 123.4.

**1997** (estimates, US $ million): *Imports c.i.f.:* Capital goods 45.3; Intermediate goods 33.3 (Petroleum products 13.8); Consumption goods 44.1 (Food 11.2); Total 122.7.

Source (for 1994, 1995, 1996 and 1997): IMF, *Burundi: Statistical Annex* (February 1999).

| Exports f.o.b. | 1995 | 1996 | 1997 |
|---|---|---|---|
| **Food and live animals** | 92,088 | 34,526 | 86,094 |
| Coffee, tea, cocoa and spices | 90,386 | 30,663 | 85,583 |
| Coffee (incl. husks and skins) | 80,778 | 25,243 | 76,567 |
| Tea and maté | 9,608 | 5,420 | 9,015 |
| Tea | 9,608 | 5,420 | 9,015 |
| **Beverages and tobacco** | 3,241 | 289 | 36 |
| **Crude materials (inedible) except fuels** | 3,806 | 713 | 127 |
| Raw hides, skins and furskins | 2,103 | 713 | 127 |
| **Special transactions and commodities not classified according to kind** | 3,730 | 1,230 | 897 |
| **Total** (incl. others) | 104,026 | 37,300 | 87,320 |

Source: Banque de la République du Burundi.

**PRINCIPAL TRADING PARTNERS**

| Imports c.i.f. (US $ '000) | 1995 | 1996 | 1997 |
|---|---|---|---|
| Belgium | 35,885 | 18,929 | 22,358 |
| China, People's Repub. | 9,379 | 4,234 | 2,812 |
| France | 23,426 | 10,555 | 11,545 |
| Germany | 18,968 | 10,886 | 8,042 |
| Iran | 2,958 | 134 | 900 |
| Italy | 9,194 | 4,865 | 4,220 |
| Japan | 13,392 | 8,230 | 7,567 |
| Kenya | 9,606 | 4,596 | 5,305 |
| Korea, Repub. | 2,501 | 1,070 | 768 |
| Netherlands | 12,461 | 5,980 | 5,234 |
| Tanzania | 6,334 | 3,895 | 3,057 |
| United Arab Emirates | 2,279 | 956 | 5,445 |
| United Kingdom | 9,149 | 2,019 | 2,041 |
| USA | 11,436 | 5,705 | 2,281 |
| Zambia | 7,734 | 4,287 | 6,761 |
| Zimbabwe | 4,142 | 1,625 | 2,806 |
| **Total** (incl. others) | 232,968 | 123,309 | 122,745 |

| Exports (million Burundian Francs) | 1995 | 1996 | 1997 |
|---|---|---|---|
| Belgium-Luxembourg | 542.3 | 284.7 | 4,929.3 |
| France | 465.2 | 3.2 | 37.3 |
| Germany | 1,013.7 | 236.0 | 6,579.5 |
| Italy | 311.8 | 85.9 | 72.0 |
| United Kingdom | 7,383.7 | 1,511.0 | 8,305.7 |
| **Total** (incl. others) | 25,982.4 | 11,292.7 | 30,767.2 |

Source: Banque de la République du Burundi.

# Transport

**ROAD TRAFFIC** (estimates, '000 motor vehicles in use)

| | 1992 | 1993 | 1994 |
|---|---|---|---|
| Passenger cars | 17.5 | 18.5 | 17.5 |
| Commercial vehicles | 11.8 | 12.3 | 10.2 |

Source: UN, *Statistical Yearbook*.

**LAKE TRAFFIC** (Bujumbura—'000 metric tons)

| | 1989 | 1990 | 1991 |
|---|---|---|---|
| Goods: | | | |
| Arrivals | 150.4 | 152.9 | 188.4 |
| Departures | 33.0 | 32.5 | 35.1 |

Source: Banque de la République du Burundi.

**CIVIL AVIATION** (traffic on scheduled services)

| | 1993 | 1994 | 1995 |
|---|---|---|---|
| Passengers carried ('000) | 9 | 9 | 9 |
| Passenger-km (million) | 2 | 2 | 2 |

Source: UN, *Statistical Yearbook*.

# Tourism

**TOURIST ARRIVALS BY REGION***

| | 1994† | 1995 | 1996 |
|---|---|---|---|
| Africa | 14,072 | 16,066 | 12,798 |
| Americas | 2,052 | 2,343 | 1,870 |
| Asia | 2,345 | 2,678 | 2,134 |
| Europe | 10,847 | 12,385 | 9,868 |
| **Total** | 29,316 | 33,472 | 26,670 |

* Including Burundian nationals residing abroad.

† Arrivals at Bujumbura International Airport only.

**Tourism receipts** (US $ million): 2 in 1994; 1 in 1995; 1 in 1996.

Source: World Tourism Organization, *Yearbook of Tourism Statistics*.

# Communications Media

| | 1994 | 1995 | 1996 |
|---|---|---|---|
| Radio receivers ('000 in use) | 400 | 410 | 425 |
| Television receivers ('000 in use) | 9 | 12 | 20 |
| Telephones ('000 main lines in use) | 16 | 17 | n.a. |
| Mobile cellular telephones (subscribers) | 343 | n.a. | n.a. |
| Daily newspapers: | | | |
| Number | 1 | 1 | 1 |
| Circulation ('000 copies) | 20 | 20 | 20 |

**Telefax stations** (number in use): 78 in 1993.

Sources: UNESCO, *Statistical Yearbook*, and UN, *Statistical Yearbook*.

# Education

(1992/93, unless otherwise indicated)

| | Teachers | Students: Males | Students: Females | Students: Total |
|---|---|---|---|---|
| Pre-primary* | 49 | 1,220 | 1,161 | 2,381 |
| Primary | 10,400 | 358,180 | 292,906 | 651,086 |
| Secondary: | | | | |
| General | 2,060 | 28,706 | 17,675 | 46,381 |
| Teacher-training | | 1,237 | 1,233 | 2,470 |
| Vocational | 502 | 4,170 | 2,692 | 6,862 |
| Higher | 556 | 3,129 | 1,127 | 4,256 |

* Figures refer to 1988/89.

**Primary schools:** 1,418 in 1992/93.

Source: UNESCO, *Statistical Yearbook*.

**1996** (students): *Primary* 453,746; *Secondary (General)* 56,887; *Secondary (Teacher-training and Vocational)* 5,712; *Higher* 4,379 (Source: IMF, *Burundi: Statistical Annex* (February 1999)).

# Directory

## The Constitution

The Constitution was promulgated on 13 March 1992 and provided for the establishment of a plural political system. The Constitution seeks to guarantee human rights and basic freedoms for all citizens, together with the freedom of the press. Executive powers are vested in the President, who (under normal circumstances—see below) is elected directly, by universal adult suffrage, for a five-year term, renewable only once. Statutory power is shared with the Prime Minister, who appoints a Council of Ministers. Legislative power is exercised by a National Assembly, whose members are elected directly, by universal adult suffrage, for a five-year renewable mandate. In September 1994 a Convention of Government was agreed among the country's major political parties. The Convention, which defines the terms of government for a four-year transitional period, provides for the establishment of a National Security Council whose members include the President, the Prime Minister and the Ministers of State with responsibility for External Affairs, Interior and Public Security, and National Defence. The Convention was incorporated into the Constitution on 22 September 1994. However, the Convention disintegrated in July 1996, prompting the military coup which returned Maj. Pierre Buyoya to power.

On 6 June 1998 a Transitional Constitution was promulgated. It combined elements of the 1992 Constitution and the terms of office introduced by Buyoya in 1996, and provided for the enlargement of the National Assembly from 81 to 121 seats and the creation of two vice-presidencies to replace the post of Prime Minister.

## The Government

### HEAD OF STATE

**President:** Maj. PIERRE BUYOYA (assumed power 25 July 1996).

### COUNCIL OF MINISTERS

(January 2000)

**Vice-President responsible for Political and Administrative Affairs:** FRÉDÉRIQUE BAVUGINYUMVIRA.

**Vice-President responsible for Economic and Social Affairs:** MATHIAS SINAMENYE.

**Minister of External Relations and Co-operation:** SÉVÉRIN NTAHOMVUKIYE.

**Minister of the Interior and Public Security:** Col ASCENSION TWAGIRAMUNGU.

**Minister of Justice:** TÉRENCE SINUNGURUZA.

**Minister of National Defence:** Col CYRILLE NDAYIRUKIYE.

**Minister of Development, Planning and Reconstruction:** LÉON NIMBONA.

**Minister of Communal Development and Handicrafts:** DENIS NSHIMIRIMANA.

**Minister of Relocation and Resettlement of Displaced and Repatriated Persons:** PASCAL NKURUNZIZA.

**Minister of the Peace Process:** AMBROISE NIYONSABA.

**Minister of Territorial Development and the Environment:** JEAN-PACIFIQUE NSENGIYUMVA.

**Minister of Agriculture and Livestock:** SALVATOR NTIHABOSE.

**Minister of Labour, the Public Service and Professional Training:** EMMANUEL TUNGAMWESE.

**Minister of Finance:** CHARLES NIHANGAZA.

**Minister of Commerce, Industry and Tourism:** JOSEPH NTANYOTORA.

**Minister of Education:** PROSPER MPAWENAYO.

**Minister of Social Action and Women's Affairs:** ROMAINE NDORIMANA.

**Minister of Culture, Youth and Sport:** GÉRARD NYAMWIZA.

**Minister of Public Health:** Dr STANISLAS NTAHOBARI.

**Minister of Information and Government Spokesman:** Dr LUC RUKINGAMA.

**Minister of Public Works and Housing:** GASPARD NTIRAMPEBA.

**Minister of Transport, Posts and Telecommunications:** CYPRIEN MBONIGABA.

**Minister of Energy and Mines:** BERNARD BARANDEREKA.

**Minister of Human Rights, Institutional Reforms and Relations with the National Assembly:** EUGÈNE NINDORERA.

There are also two Secretaries of State.

### MINISTRIES

**Office of the President:** Bujumbura; tel. 226063.

**Ministry of Agriculture and Livestock:** Bujumbura; tel. 222087.

**Ministry of Commerce, Industry and Tourism:** Bujumbura; tel. 225330.

**Ministry of Communal Development:** Bujumbura.

**Ministry of Culture, Youth and Sport:** Bujumbura; tel. 226822.

**Ministry of Development, Planning and Reconstruction:** BP 1830, Bujumbura; tel. 223988.

**Ministry of Education:** Bujumbura.

**Ministry of Energy and Mines:** BP 745, Bujumbura; tel. 225909; fax 223337.

**Ministry of External Relations and Co-operation:** Bujumbura; tel. 222150.

**Ministry of Finance:** BP 1830, Bujumbura; tel. 225142; fax 223128.

**Ministry of Human Rights, Institutional Reforms and Relations with the National Assembly:** Bujumbura.

**Ministry of Information:** BP 2870, Bujumbura.

**Ministry of the Interior and Public Security:** Bujumbura.

**Ministry of Justice:** Bujumbura; tel. 222148.

**Ministry of Labour, the Public Service and Professional Training:** BP 1480, Bujumbura; tel. 223514; fax 228715.

**Ministry of National Defence:** Bujumbura.

**Ministry of the Peace Process:** Bujumbura.

**Ministry of Public Health:** Bujumbura.

**Ministry of Public Works and Housing:** BP 1860, Bujumbura; tel. 226841; fax 226840.

**Ministry of Relocation and Resettlement of Displaced and Repatriated Persons:** Bujumbura.

**Ministry of Social Action and Women's Affairs:** Bujumbura; tel. 225039.

**Ministry of Territorial Development and the Environment:** Bujumbura.

**Ministry of Transport, Posts and Telecommunications:** BP 2000, Bujumbura; tel. 222923; fax 226900.

## President and Legislature

### PRESIDENT

Following the assassination of President Melchior Ndadaye and his constitutional successor in October 1993, a constitutional amendment was adopted whereby a successor was to be elected by the National Assembly. On 13 January 1994 Cyprien Ntaryamira, a member of FRODEBU, was elected President by 78 of the 79 votes cast by the National Assembly. Following Ntaryamira's death in April 1994, the Speaker of the National Assembly, Sylvestre Ntibantunganya, assumed the presidency for an interim, three-month period (subsequently extended for a further three months), in accordance with the Constitution. Ntibantunganya was subsequently appointed to the presidency for a four-year transitional term, by broad consensus in accordance with the Convention of Government adopted in September 1994. In July 1996 Ntibantunganya was deposed by a military coup and replaced by Maj. Pierre Buyoya.

**NATIONAL ASSEMBLY***

**Speaker:** LÉONCE NGENDAKUMANA (FRODEBU).

**Legislative Elections, 29 June 1993**

| Party | Votes cast | % of votes cast | Seats |
|---|---|---|---|
| FRODEBU | 1,532,107 | 71.04 | 65 |
| UPRONA | 462,324 | 21.44 | 16 |
| RPB | 35,932 | 1.67 | – |
| PRP | 29,966 | 1.39 | – |
| RADDES | 26,631 | 1.23 | – |
| PP | 24,372 | 1.13 | – |
| Independents | 853 | 0.04 | – |
| Invalid votes | 44,474 | 2.06 | – |
| **Total** | 2,156,659 | 100.00 | 81 |

* The National Assembly was suspended following the July 1996 coup, but was reconvened in October. Under the Transitional Constitution promulgated in June 1998, the membership of the National Assembly was enlarged from 81 to 121 members in order to incorporate representatives of smaller parties and the civilian population. The composition of the new National Assembly, which was inaugurated on 18 July, was as follows: FRODEBU controlled 65 seats, UPRONA 16, other political parties 13 seats (although four remained vacant, owing to internal party problems) and civilians 27 seats.

**PROVINCIAL GOVERNORS**
(January 2000)

**Bubanza:** GILBERT KAYONDE.

**Bujumbura (Rural):** Maj. BALTHAZAR NTAMAHUNGIRO.

**Bururi:** ANDRÉ NDAYIZAMBA.

**Cankuzo:** HENRI TUZAGI.

**Cibitoke:** Lt-Col ANTOINE NIMBESHA.

**Gitega:** Lt-Col LOUIS MURENGERA.

**Karuzi:** (vacant).

**Kayanza:** Lt-Col DANIEL MENGERI.

**Kirundo:** DEOGRATIAS BIZIMANA.

**Makamba:** Lt-Col GABRIEL GUNUNGU.

**Muramvya:** (vacant).

**Muyinga:** Col ALEXIS BANUMA.

**Mwaro:** NESTOR NIYUNGEKO.

**Ngozi:** (vacant).

**Rutana:** LÉONIDAS HAKIZIMANA.

**Ruyigi:** ISAAC BUJABA.

# Political Organizations

Political parties are required to demonstrate firm commitment to national unity, and impartiality with regard to ethnic or regional origin, gender and religion, in order to receive legal recognition.

There were 14 officially recognized political parties at the beginning of 2000.

**Alliance burundaise-africaine pour le salut (ABASA):** Bujumbura.

**Alliance nationale pour les droits et le développement economique (ANADDE):** Bujumbura; f. 1992.

**AV–Intware (Alliance of the Brave):** Bujumbura.

**Front pour la démocratie au Burundi (FRODEBU):** Bujumbura; f. 1992; Chair. JEAN MINANI; Sec.-Gen. AUGUSTIN NZOJIBWAMI.

**Inkinzo y'Ijambo Ry'abarundi (Inkinzo)** (Guarantor of Freedom of Speech in Burundi): Bujumbura; f. 1993; Pres. Dr ALPHONSE RUGAMBARARA.

**Parti indépendant des travailleurs (PIT):** Bujumbura.

**Parti libéral (PL):** Bujumbura; f. 1992; Sec.-Gen. JOSEPH NTIDENDEREZA.

**Parti du peuple (PP):** Bujumbura; f. 1992; Leader SHADRAK NIYONKURU.

**Parti de réconciliation du peuple (PRP):** Bujumbura; f. 1992.

**Parti pour le redressement national (PARENA):** Bujumbura; f. 1994; Leader JEAN-BAPTISTE BAGAZA.

**Parti social démocrate (PSD):** Bujumbura; f. 1993.

**Rassemblement pour le démocratie et le développement économique et social (RADDES):** Bujumbura; f. 1992; Chair. JOSEPH NZENZIMANA.

**Rassemblement du peuple burundien (RPB):** Bujumbura; f. 1992; Leader PHILIPPE NZOGBO.

**Union pour le progrès national (UPRONA):** BP 1810, Bujumbura; tel. 225028; f. 1958; following the 1961 elections, the numerous small parties which had been defeated merged with UPRONA, which became the sole legal political party in 1966; party activities were suspended following the coup of Sept. 1987, but resumed in 1989; Chair. CHARLES MUKASI; in Oct. 1999 moderate mems of the cen. cttee who opposed Mukasi's rejection of the Arusha talks elected Dr LUC RUKINGAMA as a rival Chair.

The exclusion of political organizations advocating 'tribalism, divisionalism or violence' and the requirement that party leaderships be equally representative of Hutu and Tutsi ethnic groups have been opposed by some externally-based opposition parties. These include the **Parti de libération du peuple hutu (PALIPEHUTU**, f. 1980 and based in Tanzania), which seeks to advance the interests of the Hutu ethnic group. An armed dissident wing of PALIPEHUTU, known as the **Force nationale de libération (FNL)**, led by KABORA KHOSSAN, is based in southern Rwanda. Another grouping representing the interests of Hutu extremists, the **Conseil national pour la défense de la démocratie (CNDD)** is led by LÉONARD NYANGOMA, who was in exile in Zaire (now the Democratic Republic of the Congo) prior to Tutsi-led rebellion of 1996–97. The 30,000-strong armed wing of the CNDD, the **Force pour la défence de la démocratie (FDD)**, rebelled against the political leadership of the CNDD in 1998 and was led by its Commander-in-Chief, JEAN-BOSCO NDYIKENGURUKIYE.

# Diplomatic Representation

**EMBASSIES IN BURUNDI**

**Belgium:** 9 ave de l'Industrie, BP 1920, Bujumbura; tel. 223676; Ambassador: JAN MUTTON.

**China, People's Republic:** BP 2550, Bujumbura; tel. 224307; Ambassador: SHI TONGNING.

**Egypt:** 31 ave de la Liberté, BP 1520, Bujumbura; tel. 223161; Ambassador: MUHAMMAD MOUSA.

**France:** 60 ave de l'UPRONA, BP 1740, Bujumbura; tel. 226767; fax 227443; Ambassador: CHRISTIAN DAZIANO.

**Germany:** 22 rue 18 septembre, BP 480, Bujumbura; tel. 226412; Ambassador: Dr BERND MORAST.

**Holy See:** 46 chaussée Prince Louis-Rwagasore, BP 1068, Bujumbura (Apostolic Nunciature); tel. 222326; fax 223176; Apostolic Nuncio: Most Rev. EMIL PAUL TSCHERRIG, Titular Archbishop of Voli.

**Korea, Democratic People's Republic:** BP 1620, Bujumbura; tel. 222881; Ambassador: PAE SOK JUN.

**Russia:** 78 blvd de l'UPRONA, BP 1034, Bujumbura; tel. 226098; fax 222984; Ambassador: IGOR S. LIAKIN-FROLOV.

**Rwanda:** 24 ave du Zaïre, BP 400, Bujumbura; tel. 223140; Ambassador: SYLVESTRE UWIBAJIJE.

**Tanzania:** BP 1653, Bujumbura; Ambassador: ANTHONY NYAKYI.

**USA:** ave des Etats-Unis, BP 1720, Bujumbura; tel. 223454; fax 222926; Ambassador: MARY CARLIN YATES.

# Judicial System

**Constitutional Court:** Bujumbura.

**Supreme Court:** BP 1460, Bujumbura; tel. 222571; fax 222148. Court of final instance; four divisions: ordinary, cassation, constitutional and administrative.

**Courts of Appeal:** Bujumbura, Gitega and Ngozi.

**Tribunals of First Instance:** There are 17 provincial tribunals and 123 smaller resident tribunals in other areas.

**Tribunal of Trade:** Bujumbura.

**Tribunals of Labour:** Bujumbura and Gitega.

**Administrative Courts:** Bujumbura and Gitega.

# Religion

More than 65% of the population are Christians, the majority of whom (an estimated 61%) are Roman Catholics. Anglicans number about 60,000. There are about 200,000 other Protestant adherents, of whom about 160,000 are Pentecostalists. Fewer than 40% of the population adhere to traditional beliefs, which include the worship of the God 'Imana'. About 1% of the population are Muslims. The Bahá'í Faith is also active in Burundi.

**CHRISTIANITY**

**Conseil National des Eglises protestantes du Burundi (CNEB):** BP 17, Bujumbura; tel. 224216; fax 227941; f. 1970; five mem. churches; Pres. Rt. Rev. JEAN NDUWAYO (Anglican Bishop of Gitega); Gen. Sec. Rev. OSIAS HABINGABWA.

### The Anglican Communion

The Church of the Province of Burundi, established in 1992, comprises five dioceses.

**Archbishop of Burundi and Bishop of Buye:** Most Rev. SAMUEL NDAYISENGA, BP 94, Ngozi; fax 302317.

**Provincial Secretary:** (vacant), BP 2098, Bujumbura.

### The Roman Catholic Church

Burundi comprises one archdiocese and six dioceses. At 31 December 1997 there were an estimated 4,502,660 adherents.

**Bishops' Conference:** Conférence des Evêques Catholiques du Burundi, 5 blvd de l'UPRONA, BP 1390, Bujumbura; tel. 223263; fax 223270; e-mail cecab@cbinf.com; f. 1980; Pres. Most Rev. SIMON NTAMWANA, Archbishop of Gitega.

**Archbishop of Gitega:** Most Rev. SIMON NTAMWANA, Archevêché, BP 118, Gitega; tel. 402160; fax 402620.

### Other Christian Churches

**Union of Baptist Churches of Burundi:** Rubura, DS 117, Bujumbura 1; Pres. PAUL BARUHENAMWO.

Other denominations active in the country include the Evangelical Christian Brotherhood of Burundi, the Free Methodist Church of Burundi and the United Methodist Church of Burundi.

### BAHÁ'Í FAITH

**National Spiritual Assembly:** BP 1578, Bujumbura.

## The Press

### NEWSPAPERS

**Burundi chrétien:** BP 232, Bujumbura; Roman Catholic weekly; French.

**Le Renouveau du Burundi:** Ministry of Information, BP 2870, Bujumbura; f. 1978; publ. by UPRONA; daily; French; circ. 20,000; Dir JEAN NZEYIMANA.

**Ubumwe:** BP 1400, Bujumbura; tel. 223929; f. 1971; weekly; Kirundi; circ. 20,000.

### PERIODICALS

**Au Coeur de l'Afrique:** Association des conférences des ordinaires du Rwanda et Burundi, BP 1390, Bujumbura; fax 223027; e-mail cnid@cbinf.com; bimonthly; education; circ. 1,000.

**Bulletin économique et financier:** BP 482, Bujumbura; bimonthly.

**Bulletin mensuel:** Banque de la République du Burundi, Service des études, BP 705, Bujumbura; tel. 225142; monthly.

**Bulletin officiel du Burundi:** Bujumbura; monthly.

**Le Burundi en Images:** BP 1400, Bujumbura; f. 1979; monthly.

**Culture et Sociétés:** BP 1400, Bujumbura; f. 1978; quarterly.

**Ndongozi Y'uburundi:** Catholic Mission, BP 690, Bujumbura; tel. 222762; fax 228907; fortnightly; Kirundi.

**Revue administration et juridique:** Association d'études administratives et juridiques du Burundi, BP 1613, Bujumbura; quarterly; French.

### PRESS ASSOCIATION

**Burundian Association of Journalists (BAJ):** Bujumbura; Pres. FRANÇOIS SENDAZIRASA.

### NEWS AGENCY

**Agence burundaise de Presse (ABP):** ave Nicolas Mayugi, BP 2870, Bujumbura; tel. 225793; fax (2) 22282; e-mail abp@cbinf.com; internet cni.cbinf.com/abp.htm; publ. daily bulletin.

## Publishers

**BURSTA:** BP 1908, Bujumbura; tel. 231796; fax 232842; f. 1986; Dir RICHARD KASHIRAHAMWE.

**Editions Intore:** 14 ave Patrice Emery Lumumba, BP 2524, Bujumbura; tel. 223499; f. 1992; philosophy, history, journalism, literature, social sciences; Dir Dr ANDRÉ BIRABUZA.

**GRAVIMPORT:** BP 156, Bujumbura; tel. 222285; fax 226953.

**IMPARUDI:** ave du 18 septembre 3, BP 3010, Bujumbura; tel. 223125; fax 222572; f. 1982; Dir THÉONESTE MUTAMBUKA.

**Imprimerie la Licorne:** 29 ave de la Mission, BP 2942, Bujumbura; tel. 223503; fax 227225; f. 1991.

**Imprimerie MAHI:** BP 673, Bujumbura.

**MICROBU:** BP 645, Bujumbura.

**Imprimerie Moderne:** BP 2555, Bujumbura.

**Imprimerie du Parti:** BP 1810, Bujumbura.

**Les Presses Lavigerie:** 5 ave de l'UPRONA, BP 1640, Bujumbura; tel. 222368; fax 220318.

**Régie de Productions Pédagogiques:** BP 3118, Bujumbura; tel. 226111; fax 222631; f. 1984; school textbooks; Dir LÉONARD BIZONGWAKO.

**SASCO:** BP 204, Bujumbura.

### Government Publishing House

**Imprimerie nationale du Burundi (INABU):** BP 991, Bujumbura; tel. 224046; fax 225399; f. 1978; Dir NICOLAS NIJIMBERE.

## Broadcasting and Communications

### TELECOMMUNICATIONS

**Direction générale des transports, postes et télécommunications:** BP 2390, Bujumbura; tel. 225422; fax 226900; govt telecommunications authority; Dir-Gen. APOLLINAIRE NDAYIZEYE.

**Office nationale des télécommunications (ONATEL):** BP 60, Bujumbura; tel. 223196; fax 226917; service provider; privatization pending; Dir-Gen. Lt-Col NESTOR MISIGARO.

**Téléphonie Cellulaire du Burundi (TELECEL):** Bujumbura; 40% govt-owned; mobile telephone service provider.

### BROADCASTING

#### Radio

**Radio Umwizero/Radio Hope:** BP 5314, Bujumbura; tel. 217068; e-mail umwizero@cbinf.com; f. 1996; EU-funded, private station promoting national reconciliation, peace and development projects; broadcasts nine hours daily in Kirundi, Swahili and French; Dir. HUBERT VIEILLE.

**Voix de la Révolution/La Radiodiffusion et Télévision Nationale du Burundi (RTNB):** BP 1900, Bujumbura; tel. 223742; fax 226547; f. 1960; govt-controlled; daily radio broadcasts in Kirundi, Swahili, French and English; Dir-Gen. LOUIS-MARIE NINDORERA; Dir (Radio) GÉRARD MFURANZIMA.

#### Television

**Voix de la Révolution/La Radiodiffusion et Télévision Nationale du Burundi (RTNB):** BP 1900, Bujumbura; tel. 223742; fax 226547; f. 1960; govt-controlled; television service in Kirundi, Swahili, French and English; Dir (Television) CLÉMENT KIRAHAGAZWI.

## Finance

(cap. = capital; res = reserves; dep. = deposits; m. = million; brs = branches; amounts in Burundian francs)

### BANKING

#### Central Bank

**Banque de la République du Burundi (BRB):** BP 705, Bujumbura; tel. 225142; fax 223128; f. 1964 as Banque du Royaume du Burundi; state-owned; bank of issue; cap. and res 14,378.3m., dep. 10,473.9m. (Dec. 1997); Gov. GRÉGOIRE BANYIYEZAKO; Vice-Gov. CYPRIEN SINZOBAHAMVYA; 2 brs.

#### Commercial Banks

**Banque Burundaise pour le Commerce et l'Investissement SARL (BBCI):** blvd du Peuple Murundi, BP 2320, Bujumbura; tel. 223328; fax 223339; f. 1988; cap. and res 507.4m., total assets 3,451.0m. (Dec. 1998); Pres. ZACHARIE GASABANYA; Vice-Pres. CLÔTILDE NIZIGAMA.

**Banque Commerciale du Burundi SARL (BANCOBU):** 84 chaussée Prince Louis-Rwagasore, BP 990, Bujumbura; tel. 222317; fax 221018; e-mail bancobu@cbinf.com; f. 1988 by merger; cap. and res 2,914.6m., total assets 27,155.4m. (Sept. 1999); Pres. N. BARUTWANAYO; Dir-Gen. LIBÈRE NDABAKWAJE; 6 brs.

**Banque de Commerce et de Développement (BCD):** ave de Grèce, BP 2020, Bujumbura;; tel. 210950; fax 210952; e-mail bcd@cbinf.com; f. 1999; cap. and res 1,016.0m., total assets 5,024.7m. (June 1999); Pres. FRANÇOIS BUTOKE; Man. Dir ANTOINE NDUWAYO.

**Banque de Crédit de Bujumbura SMei:** ave Patrice Emery Lumumba, BP 300, Bujumbura; tel. 222091; fax 223007; f. 1964; cap. and res 3,282.4m., total assets 22,546.8m. (Dec. 1998); Pres. CHARLES NIHANGAZA; Man. ATHANASE GAHUNGU; 6 brs.

**Banque de Gestion et de Financement:** 1 blvd de la Liberté, BP 1035, Bujumbura; tel. 221352; fax 221351; e-mail bgf@cbinf.com;

f. 1992; cap. and res 760.1m., total assets 3,847.8m. (Dec. 1998); Pres. DIDACE NZOHABONAYO; Dir-Gen. MATHIAS NDIKUMANA.

**Banque Populaire du Burundi (BPB):** 10 ave du 18 Septembre, BP 1780, Bujumbura; tel. 221257; fax 221256; e-mail bpb@cbinf.com; internet www.cbinf.com; f. 1992; cap. and res 685.4m., total assets 5,328.3m. (Dec. 1998); Pres. THÉODORE KAMWENUBUSA; Dir-Gen. D. BUKOBERO.

**Interbank Burundi SARL:** 15 ave de l'Industrie, BP 2970, Bujumbura; tel. 220629; fax 220461; e-mail interb@cbinf.com; cap. and res 1,623.6m., total assets 14,545.7m. (Dec. 1997); Pres. GEORGES COUCOULIS.

### Development Bank

**Banque Nationale pour le Développement Economique SARL (BNDE):** 3 ave du Marché, BP 1620, Bujumbura; tel. 222888; fax 223775; e-mail bndc@cbinf.com; f. 1966; cap. and res 2,112m., total assets 12,533m. (Dec. 1998); Pres. and Dir-Gen. GASPARD SINDIYIGAYA; Gen. Sec. FRANÇOIS BARWENDERE.

### Co-operative Bank

**Banque Coopérative d'Epargne et de Crédit Mutuel (BCM):** BP 1340, Bujumbura; operating licence granted in April 1995; Vice-Pres. JULIEN MUSARAGANY.

## INSURANCE

**Burundi Insurance Corporation (BICOR):** BP 2377, Bujumbura.

**Société d'Assurances du Burundi (SOCABU):** 14–18 rue de l'Amitié, BP 2440, Bujumbura; tel. 226520; fax 226803; e-mail socabu@cbinf.com; f. 1977; partly state-owned; cap. 180m.; Man. SÉRAPHINE RUVAHAFI.

**Société Générale d'Assurances et de Réassurance (SOGEAR):** BP 2432, Bujumbura; tel. 222345; fax 229338; f. 1991; Pres. B. NDORIMANA; Dir-Gen. L. SAUSSEZ.

**Union Commerciale d'Assurances et de Réassurance (UCAR):** BP 3012, Bujumbura; tel. 223638; fax 223695; f. 1986; cap. 150m.; Chair. Lt-Col EDOUARD NZAMBIMANA; Man. Dir HENRY TARMO.

# Trade and Industry

## GOVERNMENT AGENCIES

**Agences de Promotion des Echanges Extérieurs (APEE):** Bujumbura; promotes and supervises foreign exchanges.

**Office des Cultures Industrielles du Burundi (Office du Café du Burundi) (OCIBU):** BP 450, Bujumbura; tel. 224017; fax 225532; e-mail ocibu3@cbinf.com; f. 1964; supervises coffee plantations and coffee exports; Dir-Gen. BARTHÉLÉMY NIYIKIZA.

**Office du Thé du Burundi (OTB):** 52 blvd de l'UPRONA, Bujumbura; tel. 224228; fax 224657; f. 1979 supervises production and marketing of tea; Dir REMY NIBIGARA.

**Office National du Commerce (ONC):** Bujumbura; f. 1973; supervises international commercial operations between the Govt of Burundi and other states or private orgs; also organizes the import of essential materials; subsidiary offices in each province.

**Office National du Logement (ONL):** BP 2480, Bujumbura; tel. 226074; f. 1974 to supervise housing construction.

## DEVELOPMENT ORGANIZATIONS

**Compagnie de Gérance du Coton (COGERCO):** BP 2571, Bujumbura; tel. 222208; fax 224370; e-mail cogerco@cbinf.com; f. 1947; promotion and development of cotton industry; Dir FRANÇOIS KABURA.

**Fonds de Développement Communal (FDC):** Bujumbura; funds local development.

**Institut des Sciences Agronomiques du Burundi (ISABU):** BP 795, Bujumbura; tel. 223390; fax 225798; e-mail isabu@cni.cbinf.com.; f. 1962 for the scientific development of agriculture and livestock.

**Office National de la Tourbe (ONATOUR):** BP 2360, Bujumbura; tel. 226480; fax 226709; f. 1977 to promote the exploitation of peat deposits.

**Société d'Exploitation du Quinquina du Burundi (SOKINABU):** 16 blvd Mwezi Gisabo, BP 1783, Bujumbura; tel. 223469; f. 1975 to develop and exploit cinchona trees, the source of quinine; Dir RAPHAËL REMEZO.

**Société de Financement et Développement de l'Habitat Urbain (SOFIDHAR):** Bujumbura; urban development.

**Société Régionale de Développement de l'IMBO (SRDI):** Bujumbura; promotes development of IMBO region.

**Société Régionale de Développement de Kayanza (SRD KAYANZA):** Kayanza; promotes development of Kayanza region.

**Société Régionale de Développement de Kirimiro (SRD KIRIMIRO):** Bujumbura; promotes development of Kirimiro region.

**Société Régionale de Développement de Kirundo (SRD KIRUNDO):** Bujumbura; promotes development of Kirundo region.

**Société Régionale de Développement de Mumirwa (SRD MUMIRWA):** Bujumbura; promotes development of Mumirwa region.

**Société Régionale de Développement de Rumonge (SRD RUMONGE):** Bujumbura; promotes development of Rumonge region.

**Société Sucrière du Mosso (SOSUMO):** BP 835, Bujumbura; tel. 275002; fax 275004; e-mail sosumo@cbinf.com; f. 1982 to develop and manage sugar cane plantations.

## CHAMBER OF COMMERCE

**Chambre de Commerce et de l'Industrie du Burundi:** BP 313, Bujumbura; tel. 222280; f. 1923; Chair. DONATIEN BIHUTE; 130 mems.

## UTILITIES

**Régie de Distribution d'Eau et d'Electricité (REGIDESCO):** Bujumbura; state-owned distributor of water and electricity services.

## TRADE UNIONS

**Confédération des Syndicats du Burundi (COSIBU):** Bujumbura; Chair. CHARLES NDAMIRAWE.

**Union des Travailleurs du Burundi (UTB):** BP 1340, Bujumbura; tel. 223884; f. 1967 by merger of all existing unions; closely allied with UPRONA; sole authorized trade union prior to 1994, with 18 affiliated nat. professional feds; Sec.-Gen. MARIUS RURAHENYE.

# Transport

## RAILWAYS

There are no railways in Burundi. Plans have been under consideration since 1987 for the construction of a line passing through Uganda, Rwanda and Burundi, to connect with the Kigoma–Dar es Salaam line in Tanzania. This rail link would relieve Burundi's isolated trade position.

## ROADS

The road network is very dense and in 1996 there was a total of 14,480 km of roads, of which 1,950 km were national highways and 2,530 km secondary roads. A new crossing of the Ruzizi River, the Bridge of Concord (Burundi's longest bridge), was opened in early 1992.

**Office des Transports en Commun (OTRACO):** Bujumbura; 100% govt-owned; operates public transport.

## INLAND WATERWAYS

Bujumbura is the principal port for both passenger and freight traffic on Lake Tanganyika, and the greater part of Burundi's external trade is dependent on the shipping services between Bujumbura and lake ports in Tanzania, Zambia and the Democratic Republic of the Congo.

**Exploitation du Port de Bujumbura (EPB):** Bujumbura; 43% state-owned; controls Bujumbura port.

## CIVIL AVIATION

The international airport at Bujumbura is equipped to take large jet-engined aircraft.

**Air Burundi:** 40 ave du Commerce, BP 2460, Bujumbura; tel. 224609; fax 223452; f. 1971 as Société de Transports Aériens du Burundi; state-owned; operates charter and scheduled passenger services to destinations throughout central Africa; CEO Maj. ISAAC GAFURERO.

# Tourism

Tourism is relatively undeveloped. The annual total of tourist arrivals declined from 125,000 in 1991 (with receipts amounting to US $4m.) to only 26,670 in 1996 (receipts $1m.).

**Office National du Tourisme (ONT):** 2 ave des Euphorbes, BP 902, Bujumbura; tel. 224208; fax 229390; f. 1972; responsible for the promotion and supervision of tourism; Dir HERMENEGILDE NIMBONA (acting).

# CAMBODIA

## Introductory Survey

### Location, Climate, Language, Religion, Flag, Capital

The Kingdom of Cambodia occupies part of the Indochinese peninsula in South-East Asia. It is bordered by Thailand and Laos to the north, by Viet Nam to the east and by the Gulf of Thailand to the south. The climate is tropical and humid. There is a rainy season from June to November, with the heaviest rainfall in September. The temperature is generally between 20°C and 36°C (68°F to 97°F), with March and April generally the hottest months; and the annual average temperature in Phnom-Penh is 27°C (81°F). The official language is Khmer, which is spoken by everybody except the Vietnamese and Chinese minorities. The state religion is Theravada Buddhism. The national flag (proportions 3 by 2) consists of three horizontal stripes, of dark blue, red (half the depth) and dark blue, with a stylized representation (in white) of the temple of Angkor Wat, with three towers, in the centre. The capital is Phnom-Penh.

### Recent History

The Kingdom of Cambodia became a French protectorate in the 19th century and was incorporated into French Indo-China. In April 1941 Norodom Sihanouk, then aged 18, succeeded his grandfather as King. In May 1947 he promulgated a Constitution which provided for a bicameral Parliament, including an elected National Assembly. Cambodia became an Associate State of the French Union in November 1949 and attained independence on 9 November 1953. In order to become a political leader, King Sihanouk abdicated in March 1955 in favour of his father, Norodom Suramarit, and became known as Prince Sihanouk. He founded a mass movement, the Sangkum Reastr Niyum (Popular Socialist Community), which won all the seats in elections to the National Assembly in 1955, 1958, 1962 and 1966. King Suramarit died in April 1960, and in June Parliament elected Prince Sihanouk as Head of State. Prince Sihanouk's Government developed good relations with the People's Republic of China and with North Viet Nam, but it was highly critical of the USA's role in Asia. From 1964, however, the Government was confronted by an underground Marxist insurgency movement, the Khmers Rouges, while it also became increasingly difficult to isolate Cambodia from the war in Viet Nam.

In March 1970 Prince Sihanouk was deposed by a right-wing coup, led by the Prime Minister, Lt-Gen. (later Marshal) Lon Nol. The new Government pledged itself to the removal of foreign communist forces and appealed to the USA for military aid. Sihanouk went into exile and formed the Royal Government of National Union of Cambodia (GRUNC), supported by the Khmers Rouges. Sihanoukists and the Khmers Rouges formed the National United Front of Cambodia (FUNC). Their combined forces, aided by South Viet Nam's National Liberation Front and North Vietnamese troops, posed a serious threat to the new regime, but in October 1970 Marshal Lon Nol proclaimed the Khmer Republic. In June 1972 he was elected the first President. During 1973 several foreign states recognized GRUNC as the rightful government of Cambodia. In 1974 the republican regime's control was limited to a few urban enclaves, besieged by GRUNC forces, mainly Khmers Rouges, who gained control of Phnom-Penh on 17 April 1975. Prince Sihanouk became Head of State again but did not return from exile until September. The country was subjected to a pre-arranged programme of radical social deconstruction immediately after the Khmers Rouges' assumption of power; towns were largely evacuated, and their inhabitants forced to work in rural areas. During the following three years an estimated 1.7m. people died as a result of ill-treatment, hunger, disease and executions.

A new Constitution, promulgated in January 1976, renamed the country Democratic Kampuchea, and established a republican form of government; elections for a 250-member People's Representative Assembly were held in March 1976. In April Prince Sihanouk resigned as Head of State and GRUNC was dissolved. The Assembly elected Khieu Samphan, formerly Deputy Prime Minister, to be President of the State Presidium (Head of State). The little-known Pol Pot (formerly Saloth Sar) became Prime Minister. In September 1977 it was officially disclosed that the ruling organization was the Communist Party of Kampuchea (CPK), with Pol Pot as the Secretary of its Central Committee.

After 1975 close links with the People's Republic of China developed, while relations with Viet Nam deteriorated. In 1978, following a two-year campaign of raids across the Vietnamese border by the Khmers Rouges, the Vietnamese army launched a series of offensives into Kampuchean territory. In December the establishment of the Kampuchean National United Front for National Salvation (KNUFNS, renamed Kampuchean United Front for National Construction and Defence—KUFNCD—in December 1981, and United Front for the Construction and Defence of the Kampuchean Fatherland—UFCDKF—in 1989), a communist-led movement opposed to Pol Pot and supported by Viet Nam, was announced. Later in the month, Viet Nam invaded Kampuchea, supported by the KNUFNS.

On 7 January 1979 Phnom-Penh was captured by Vietnamese forces, and three days later the People's Republic of Kampuchea was proclaimed. A People's Revolutionary Council was established, with Heng Samrin, leader of the KNUFNS, as President. It pledged to restore freedom of movement, freedom of association and of religion, and to restore the family unit. The CPK was replaced as the governing party by the Kampuchean People's Revolutionary Party (KPRP). The Khmer Rouge forces, however, remained active in the western provinces, near the border with Thailand, and conducted sporadic guerrilla activities elsewhere in the country. Several groups opposing both the Khmers Rouges and the Heng Samrin regime were established, including the Khmer People's National Liberation Front (KPNLF), headed by a former Prime Minister, Son Sann. In July, claiming that Pol Pot's regime had been responsible for 3m. deaths, the KPRP administration sentenced Pol Pot and his former Minister of Foreign Affairs, Ieng Sary, to death *in absentia*. In January 1980 Khieu Samphan assumed the premiership of the deposed Khmer Rouge regime, while Pol Pot became Commander-in-Chief of the armed forces. In 1981 the CPK was reportedly dissolved and was replaced by the Party of Democratic Kampuchea (PDK).

During the first few years of the KPRP regime Viet Nam launched regular offensives on the Thai-Kampuchean border against the united armed forces of Democratic Kampuchea, the coalition Government-in-exile of anti-Vietnamese resistance groups formed in June 1982. As a result of the fighting, and the prevalence of starvation and disease, thousands of Kampuchean refugees crossed the border into Thailand; in turn, a large number of Vietnamese citizens subsequently settled on Kampuchean territory. The coalition Government-in-exile, of which Prince Sihanouk became President, Khieu Samphan (PDK) Vice-President and Son Sann (KPLNF) Prime Minister, received the support of the People's Republic of China and of member states of the Association of South East Asian Nations (ASEAN—see p. 128), whilst retaining the Kampuchean seat in the UN General Assembly.

In the mid-1980s an increasingly conciliatory attitude between the USSR and the People's Republic of China led to a number of diplomatic exchanges, aimed at reconciling the coalition Government-in-exile with the Government in Phnom-Penh, led by the General Secretary of the KPRP, Heng Samrin. Largely, however, because of mistrust of the PDK (due to Pol Pot's continuing influence), the Heng Samrin Government rejected peace proposals from ASEAN and the coalition Government-in-exile in 1985 and 1986. In September 1987 the Government of the People's Republic of China stated that it would accept a Kampuchean 'government of national reconciliation' under Prince Sihanouk, but that the presence of Vietnamese troops in Kampuchea remained a major obstacle. In the same month the USSR also declared that it was 'prepared to facilitate a political settlement' in Kampuchea. In October, after having announced its readiness to conduct negotiations with some PDK leaders (but not Pol Pot), the Heng Samrin Government offered Prince Sihanouk a government post and issued a set of peace proposals which included the complete withdrawal of Vietnamese troops, internationally-observed elections and the form-

As timber industries benefited from increased (multilateral) governmental support and favourable unit prices, new technologies were introduced that increased harvesting rates and milling capacities, spurring further demand for a larger commercial timber estate (Vink, 1970; Viera, 1980). The introduction of tractors, open-bed trucks and eventually bulldozers and skidders increased hauling rates and capacities tremendously. Larger, more marketable logs (e.g. square pilings) could be hauled intact along roads built for timber extraction. The introduction of the chainsaw to industries in Suriname and Guyana in the late 1960s further transformed timber production methods as both felling and haulage rates increased. Downstream processing facilities began to employ gang saws and band-saw riggings, increasing milling capacities and reducing machine-borne wastage associated with the traditional use of circular saws. Installation of plywood and particle board manufacturing facilities, first in Suriname during the 1950s, then in Guyana during the early 1990s, opened up tremendous processing capacities for low-density peeler species that previously had contributed little to annual production (Vink, 1970; Guyana Forestry Commission, 1980–2002). The presence of large, relatively modern mill facilities spawned booms in timber extraction and led to expansion of the area of forest under consideration (e.g. Suriname: Sizer and Rice, 1995), or eventually allocated (e.g. Guyana) to timber production. Recent improvements in forest operational technologies and methods (e.g. GPS, GIS, sonar distance measuring) now offer opportunities to further increase production efficiencies through preharvest planning, better road alignment and residual stand protection measures that form part of the reduced-impact logging basket of selective logging techniques.

### *Cataracts, wood density, market prices and costs of commercial extraction*

The role of the river cataracts in checking the rapid penetration of timber production into the interior cannot be overstated. Unlike extraction industries along the Amazon *varzéa* or selective mahogany extraction from western Amazonia, the timber industry across the Guiana Shield was faced with limited river navigability combined with a confounding, but ultimately profitable, abundance of extremely dense tropical timber species.

The density of these timbers spurred demand during the early 20th century, in part based on a reputation established during the 18th and 19th centuries (Bancroft, 1769; Schomburgk, 1840; Walker, 1878; McTurk, 1882; Rodway, 1912) and, later, through research assessments of their physical and structural properties (e.g. Findley, 1938; Horn, 1948; Edmondson, 1949). The few alternative materials, mainly temperate hardwoods, had been depleted to such an extent that they could no longer satisfy growing industrial demand (e.g. oak), did not exist at the time (e.g. composites) or were not competitively priced against the unusually high volumes of heavy hardwoods found in the forests of the Guiana Shield (e.g. steel).

A series of inventories and assessments were undertaken to establish and promote the commercial wood production potential of the shield region during the first half of the 20th century by highlighting the abundance of dense tropical timbers (Benoist, 1931; Williams, 1939; Ducke, 1943; Hughes, 1946; Corothie, 1948; Detienne and Chanson, 1996).

Large-scale, commercial timber production in the Guiana Shield was ultimately formed around the wholesale extraction of these heavy hardwoods as post-war conditions, combined with favourable government subsidies and large urban-industrial developments (Ciudad Bolivar) led to the final depletion of most major timber species from the forests of the near interior. Road construction offered the only feasible solution to the river navigability problem, but would create a serious challenge to profitability.

As early as the 1920s, foresters in (British) Guiana recognized the relationship between the uncommonly high wood density of commercial species in the region and the rising costs of transporting this over long distances without the use of river currents (Hohenkerk, 1922). Kiln drying was prescribed as a means of minimizing the higher cost of transporting dense timber products by reducing water content prior to transport and reducing incidence of warping and staining. Prices for structural timbers, unlike those used in joinery such as true mahogany, were more exposed to fluctuating market prices as competing materials were more readily adopted and high variable costs attached to poor operational decision-making quickly eroded profit margins. Ultimately, the commercial extraction of the region's heavy hardwoods above the falls in Suriname, French Guiana, North Pará and Roraima had yet to take place by the end of the 20th century. Transport costs associated with accessing commercial forests of the shield's interior continue to quell investment and (unsubsidized) profit in heavy hardwood extraction at modern market prices and only government-financed road-building and other incentives maintain industrial expansion. Growing concerns over the negative environmental and socio-economic impacts of large-scale, commercial forestry operations in the region (Colchester, 1997b; Miranda *et al.*, 1998) and the wider tropics (e.g. Fimbel *et al.*, 2001) has also had a significant effect on both short-term costs of extraction and demand in traditional export markets, a challenge that is reviewed in Chapter 9 of this book.

### Production and consumption of energy

The production and consumption of energy play a fundamental role in the way and extent forest lands are used worldwide and how they contribute to national economic growth. Hydrocarbon extraction facilities create new road networks and require localized production facilities that are potential point sources of environmental contamination. The production of hydrocarbons also plays an important role in offsetting the costs and exposure of importing economies to the vagaries of the international energy markets and provides a measure of national security. Even without refinement capabilities, hydrocarbon production can, if rationally invested, provide a foundation for economic expansion and diversification, alleviate pressure to liquidate short-term forest land values, and drive social development through better education, health care and law enforcement. The transformation of value derived from liquidation of hydrocarbon reserves into broader socio-economic benefits has historically experienced substantive leakages or dominant capture by a very small group.

Installation and development of non-thermal, electricity-generating sources can also create a stable national energy economy, but with different costs and benefits. Hydroelectric generation offers an indigenous source of power independent of commodity markets, but also entirely dependent on regional climate patterns. Large areas of prime forest land are submerged and the cost to local residents of accruing economic benefit for distant economies remains a prominent challenge in achieving sustainable development in tropical lowland areas. Non-traditional renewables, such as wind, tidal and solar power, hardly register on the world energy map and tropical forest regions globally show virtually no installed capacity (US Energy Information Administration, 2003), despite clear opportunities to profitably generate electricity using these sources.

#### *Fossil hydrocarbon reserves*

The Guiana Shield sits as a geological island surrounded by rivers of oil (Fig. 8.18). To the north, the largest exploitable oil fields in the neotropics dominate the sedimentary basins from Lake Maracaibo to Trinidad and Tobago. South and west of the shield, oil fields run along the upper Amazon Downwarp and throughout the Sub-Andean Foredeep. The relationship between continental-scale geomorphic features and the proven or prospective location of fossil hydrocarbon deposits precludes any significant finds within the interior of the Guiana Shield. The only prospective line of exploration follows the sediment-filled fault of the Takutu Graben and the along-shore and offshore extension of the Berbice Basin (the Tamboredjo field) (Fig. 8.18). Several drilling attempts to locate commercial deposits in the Rupununi area of the Takutu Graben have met with only marginal success (Gibbs and Barron, 1993). Berrangé (1977) suggests that the shallowing of the graben westward would make any hydrocarbon find of marginal commercial prospect. While the use of modern exploration techniques may alter this view, the poor performance of previous drilling efforts and lack of any further exploration in the area since the early 1990s would seem to support this assessment.

Efforts to procure commercial-scale production offshore have met with substantially greater success, most significantly along the south rim of Trinidad and seaward of the mouth of the Courantyne River in the Guyana–Suriname Basin (Fig. 8.18). Both the Guyana–Suriname and Tacutu Basins rank as two of the smallest proven petroleum reserves assessed in the USGS's World Energy Survey, with less than 100 million and 10 million barrels of estimated reserves, respectively. By comparison, the eastern Venezuela Basin immediately north of the shield region and embracing the eastern Venezuelan llanos and Trinidad and Tobago is ranked 13th globally, with a reserve estimate of 52.6 billion barrels, albeit based in a large part on heavy-grade oils (US Energy Information Administration, 2003).

However, the prospects for future oil production from the Guyana–Suriname Basin are good. An analysis of the basin as part of the USGS World Petroleum Assessment ascribes a 95% probability of an actual reserve measuring at least 2.793 billion barrels of oil (Schenk *et al.*, 2000), one of the largest undiscovered reserve estimates in South America.

### Petroleum production

The potential for oil production in the Cretaceous sedimentaries off the Guyana–Suriname coast was suspected since the 1960s (Lawrence and Coster, 1965), but physical exploration didn't begin until the mid-1970s, when several multinational oil companies began to drill wildcat wells and conduct geophysical and seismic assessments (Theofilos, 1975). Exploratory work and wildcatting continued until production began from a shallow heavy-oil deposit near Groningen on the Suriname coast in 1984, producing around 1000 barrels per day (Velasco and Ensminger, 1984). By 1990, activation of the Tambaredjo oil field raised this production rate to over 4000 barrels (Table 8.5). By 2002, production reached 14,000 barrels per day and further exploration was undertaken to expand facilities in both Guyanese and Surinamese territorial waters. The initiation of oil production from Guyana is expected before 2010. Estimated undiscovered reserves off the French Guiana coast are of marginal prospect (Schenk *et al.*, 2000). In addition to low gas and oil production, the three Guianas had little or no refinement capacity during the later 20th century and imported all of their gasoline and other products. Venezuela, Brazil, Trinidad and Tobago and Colombia all had significant and growing domestic refineries by 2000.

### Hydroelectricity

Without any significant petroleum reserves in the shield region, but many cataracts and ample rainfall, water power dominates the regional energy economies. Hydroelectric power in the region is generated through five main installations: (i) Guri dam (and smaller Macagua complex), south of Ciudad Bolivar on the Caroni River in Bolivar state, Venezuela; (ii) Afobakka Dam south of Paramaribo on the Suriname River in Suriname; (iii) Petit Saut, southwest of the Kourou Space Centre on the Sinnamary River in French Guiana; (iv) Alto Jatapu, in Roraima state; and (v) Balbina dam on the Uatumã River in northeast Amazonas state. There are two smaller Brazilian hydroelectric facilities, on the Araguari River in Amapá (Couracy Nunes) and on the Pitinga River in Amazonas (Pitinga). Several other

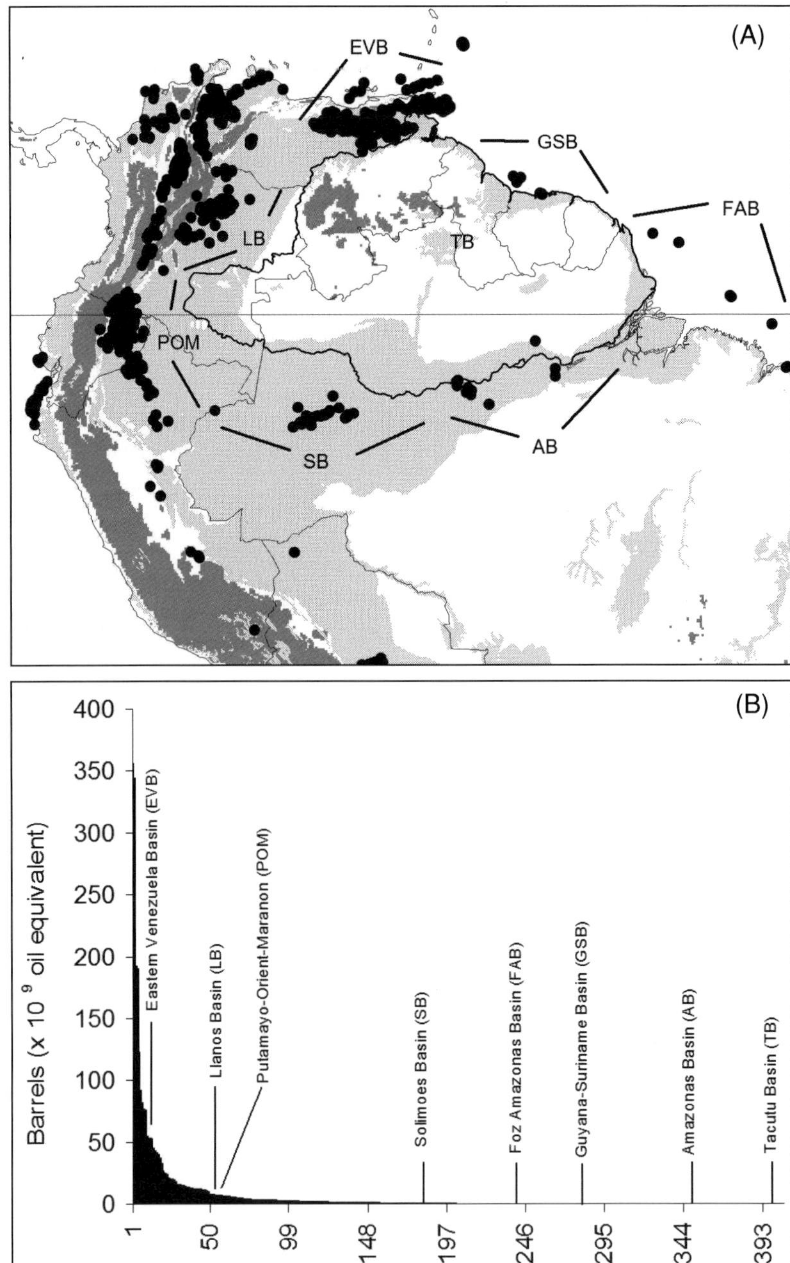


**Fig. 8.18.** (A) Ring of oil and natural gas fields (filled circles) circumscribing the Guiana Shield. Stippled area demarcates Phanerozoic sediment cover in the shield area based on Gibbs and Barron (1993). Filled grey areas >1100 m asl. Acronyms represent basin nomenclature used in Fig. 8.18B. Source: Schenk *et al.* (1999). (B) Ranked hydrocarbon reserves of 406 basins assessed in USGS World Energy Assessment Team (2000) with position of main basins surrounding and intersecting Guiana Shield identified. Assessed basins account for >99% of known global deposits.

## Diplomatic Representation

### EMBASSIES IN CAMBODIA

**Australia:** Villa 11 R. V., Senei Vinnavaut Oum (rue 254), Chartaumuk, Khan Daun Penh, Phnom-Penh; tel. (23) 213470; fax (23) 213413; Ambassador: MALCOLM LEADER.

**Brunei:** Office 5, Hotel Sofitel Cambodiana, Ground Floor, 313 quai Sisowath, Phnom-Penh; tel. (23) 363331; fax (23) 363332; Ambassador: Pengiran Haji SALLEHUDDIN.

**Bulgaria:** 177/227 blvd Norodom, Phnom-Penh; tel. (23) 723181; fax (23) 426491; Chargé d'affaires a.i.: STOYAN DAVIDOV.

**Canada:** Villa 9, R.V. Senei Vinnavaut Oum, Chartaumuk, Khan Daun Penh, Phnom-Penh; tel. (23) 426001; fax (23) 211389; e-mail cdnemb@camnet.com.kh; Ambassador: D. GORDON LONGMUIR.

**China, People's Republic:** 256 blvd Mao Tse Toung, Phnom-Penh; tel. (15) 911062; fax (23) 426271; Ambassador: YAN TINGAI.

**Cuba:** 98 route 214, Phnom-Penh; tel. (23) 724181; fax (23) 427428; Ambassador: RUBÉN PÉREZ VALDÉS.

**France:** 1 blvd Monivong, Phnom-Penh; tel. (23) 430020; fax (23) 430037; Ambassador: ANDRÉ-JEAN LIBOUREL.

**Germany:** 76–78 route 214, BP 60, Phnom-Penh; tel. (23) 216381; fax (23) 427746; Ambassador: Dr HARALD LOESCHNER.

**Hungary:** 463 blvd Monivong, Phnom-Penh; tel. (23) 722781; fax (23) 426216; Ambassador: (vacant).

**India:** Villa 777, blvd Monivong, Phnom-Penh; tel. (23) 210912; fax (23) 364489; Ambassador: JASJIT SINGH RANDHAWA.

**Indonesia:** 90 blvd Norodom, Phnom-Penh; tel. (23) 216148; fax (23) 217566; Ambassador: HAMID ALHADAD.

**Japan:** 75 blvd Norodom, Phnom-Penh; tel. (23) 217161; fax (23) 216162; Ambassador: MASAKI SAITO.

**Korea, Democratic People's Republic:** 39 rue 268, Phnom-Penh; tel. (15) 912567; fax (23) 426230; Ambassador: KIM YOUNG SOP.

**Korea, Republic:** 64 rue 214, Phnom-Penh; tel. (23) 211901; fax (23) 211903; Ambassador: KIM WON-TAE.

**Laos:** 15–17 blvd Mao Tse Toung, Phnom-Penh; tel. (23) 982632; fax (23) 720907; Ambassador: LY SOUTHAVILAY.

**Malaysia:** Villa 161, rue 51, Khan Daun Penh, Phnom-Penh; tel. (23) 216176; fax (23) 216004; Ambassador: MOHD KAMAL ISMAUN.

**Myanmar:** 181 blvd Norodom, Phnom-Penh; tel. (23) 213664; fax (23) 213665; Chargé d'affaires a.i.: U MAUNG WAI.

**Philippines:** 33 rue 294, Phnom-Penh; tel. (23) 428592; fax (23) 428048; Ambassador: FRANCISCO E. ATAYDE.

**Poland:** 767 blvd Monivong, Phnom-Penh; tel. (23) 217782; fax (23) 217781; e-mail emb.pol.pp@bigpond.com.kh; Chargé d'affaires a.i.: KAZIMIERZ A. DUCHOWSKI.

**Russia:** 73 blvd Sothearos, Phnom-Penh; tel. (23) 210931; fax (23) 216776; e-mail russemba@forum.org.kh; Ambassador: VIKTOR V. SAMOILENKO.

**Singapore:** 92 blvd Norodom, Phnom-Penh; tel. (23) 360855; fax (23) 360850; Ambassador: MUSHAHID ALI.

**Thailand:** blvd Norodom, Phnom-Penh; tel. (23) 363869; fax (18) 810860; e-mail thaipnp@mfa.go.th; Ambassador: ASIPHOL CHABCHITRCHAIDOL.

**United Kingdom:** 27–29 rue 75, Phnom-Penh; tel. (23) 427124; fax (23) 427125; Ambassador: CHRISTOPHER GEORGE EDGAR.

**USA:** 27 rue 240, Phnom-Penh; tel. (23) 216436; fax (23) 216437; Ambassador: KENT WIEDEMANN.

**Viet Nam:** 436 blvd Monivong, Phnom-Penh; tel. (23) 725481; fax (23) 427385; Ambassador: NGUYEN DU HONG.

## Judicial System

An independent judiciary was established under the 1993 Constitution.

**Supreme Court:** rue 134, cnr rue 63, Phnom-Penh; tel. 17816663; Chair. DID MONTY.

## Religion

### BUDDHISM

The principal religion of Cambodia is Theravada Buddhism (Buddhism of the 'Tradition of the Elders'), the sacred language of which is Pali. A ban was imposed on all religious activity in 1975. By a constitutional amendment, which was adopted in April 1989, Buddhism was reinstated as the national religion and was retained as such under the 1993 Constitution. By 1992 2,800 monasteries (of a total of 3,369) had been restored and there were 21,800 Buddhist monks. In 1992 about 90% of the population were Buddhists.

**Supreme Patriarchs:** Ven. Patriarch TEP VONG, Ven. Patriarch BOU KRI.

**Patriotic Kampuchean Buddhists' Association:** Phnom-Penh; mem. of UFCDKF; Pres. LONG SIM.

### CHRISTIANITY

#### The Roman Catholic Church

Cambodia comprises the Apostolic Vicariate of Phnom-Penh and the Apostolic Prefectures of Battambang and Kompong-Cham. In 1994 there were an estimated 20,000 adherents (6,000 Cambodians and 14,000 ethnic Vietnamese) in the country. An Episcopal Conference of Laos and Kampuchea was established in 1971. In 1975 the Government of Democratic Kampuchea banned all religious practice in Cambodia, and the right of Christians to meet to worship was not restored until 1990.

**Vicar Apostolic of Phnom-Penh:** Rt Rev. YVES-GEORGES-RENÉ RAMOUSSE (Titular Bishop of Pisita), 787 blvd Monivong (rue 93), BP 123, Phnom-Penh; tel. and fax (23) 720552.

### ISLAM

Islam is practised by a minority in Cambodia. Islamic worship was also banned in 1975, but it was legalized in 1979, following the defeat of the Democratic Kampuchean regime.

## The Press

### NEWSPAPERS

Newspapers are not widely available outside Phnom-Penh.

**Areyathor** (Civilization): Phnom-Penh; tel. (23) 913662; Editor CHIN CHAN MONTY.

**Bayon Pearnik:** POB 2279, Phnom-Penh); tel. (23) 219189; fax (23) 213401; English; monthly; Editor CRAIG MAPLESTON.

**Cambodia Daily:** Villa 50B, rue 240, Phnom-Penh; tel. (23) 426602; fax (23) 426573; e-mail cambodia.daily@camnet.com.kh; f. 1993; in English and Khmer; Mon.–Sat.; Editor-in-Chief CHRIS DECHERD; Publr BERNARD KRISHER.

**Cambodia Times:** 252A blvd Monivong, Phnom-Penh; tel. (23) 723405; fax (23) 426647; f. 1992 (in Kuala Lumpur, Malaysia); English-language weekly.

**Chakraval:** Phnom-Penh; tel. (23) 720410; fax (23) 720141; Editor SO SOVAN RITH.

**Commercial News:** 75 rue 134, Phnom-Penh; tel. (23) 725506; fax (23) 725135; f. 1993; Chinese; Chief Editor EANG SOVAN; circ. 3,000.

**Construction** (Kasang): Phnom-Penh; tel. 18818292; Khmer; Editor CHHEA VARY.

**Equality Voice:** Phnom-Penh; tel. 12842471; Khmer; Publr HUON MARA.

**Intervention:** Phnom-Penh; tel. 12843285; Khmer; Editor NGUON THAI DAY.

**Kampuchea:** 158 blvd Norodom, Phnom-Penh; tel. (23) 725559; f. 1979; weekly; Chief Editor KEO PRASAT; circ. 55,000.

**Khmer Wisdom:** Phnom-Penh; tel. 12850690; Khmer; CHUM SOPHAL.

**Khmer Youth Voice:** Phnom-Penh; tel. 15917153; Khmer; Editor KEO SOKHA.

**Koh Santepheap** (Island of Peace): Phnom-Penh; tel. (23) 801149; fax (23) 364515; Khmer.

**Moneaksekar Khmer:** Phnom-Penh; tel. (23) 16880389; Editor DAM SITHIK.

**Neak Chea:** 1 rue 158, Daun Penh, Phnom-Penh; tel. (23) 428653; fax (23) 427229; e-mail adhoc@forum.org.kh.

**Phnom Penh:** Phnom-Penh; tel. 15917682; Khmer; Editor VA DANE.

**Phnom Penh Post:** 10A rue 264, Phnom-Penh; tel. (23) 83312811; fax (23) 426568; e-mail michael.pppost@bigpond.com.kh; internet www.newspapers.com.kh/phnompenhpost; f. 1992; English; fortnightly; Editor-in-Chief MICHAEL HAYES; Publrs MICHAEL HAYES, KATHLEEN HAYES.

**Pracheachon** (The People): 101 blvd Norodom, Phnom-Penh; f. 1985; 2 a week; organ of the CPP; Editor-in-Chief SOM KIMSUOR; circ. 50,000.

**Reaksmei Kampuchea:** 476 blvd Monivong, Phnom-Penh; tel. (23) 362881; fax (23) 362472; daily; local newspaper in northern Cambodia; Editor PEN PHENG.

**Samleng Thmei** (New Voice): Phnom-Penh; tel. 15920589; Khmer; Editor KHUN NGOR.

### NEWS AGENCIES

**Agence Khmere de Presse (AKP):** 62 blvd Monivong, Phnom-Penh; tel. (23) 723469; f. 1978; Dir-Gen. SUM MEAN.

### Foreign Bureaux

**Agence France-Presse (AFP)** (France): 18 rue 214, Phnom-Penh; tel. (23) 426227; fax (23) 426226; Correspondent STEFAN SMITH.

**Associated Press (AP)** (USA): 18C rue 19, BP 870, Phnom-Penh; tel. (23) 426607; e-mail ap@bigpond.com.kh; Correspondent CHRIS FONTAINE.

**Deutsche Presse-Agentur (dpa):** 5E rue 178, Phnom-Penh; tel. (23) 427846; fax (23) 427846; Correspondent JOE COCHRANE.

**Reuters** (UK): 15 rue 246, Phnom-Penh; tel. (23) 427854; fax (23) 723405; Bureau Chief ROBERT BIRSEL.

**Xinhua (New China) News Agency** (People's Republic of China): 19 rue 294, Phnom-Penh; tel. (23) 211608; fax (23) 426613; Correspondent LEI BOSONG.

### ASSOCIATIONS

**Khmer Journalists' Association:** 101 blvd Preah Norodom, Phnom-Penh; tel. (23) 725459; f. 1979; mem. of UFCDKF; Pres. PIN SAMKHON.

**League of Cambodian Journalists (LCJ):** Phnom-Penh; tel. 15917682; fax (23) 360612; Pres. CHUM KANAL.

# Broadcasting and Communications

### TELECOMMUNICATIONS

**Camintel:** 1 quai Sisowath, Phnom-Penh; tel. (23) 981234; fax (23) 981277; a jt venture between the Ministry of Post and Telecommunications and the Indonesian co, Indosat; operates domestic telephone network; Chair. STEVE YANUAN.

**Telstra Corpn:** 58 blvd Norodom, Phnom-Penh; tel. (23) 426022; fax (23) 426023; e-mail ahankins@oibucbg1.telstra.com.au; Australian corpn contracted to manage the international calls system until Oct. 2000; Man. ANDREW HANKINS.

### BROADCASTING

#### Radio

**Apsara:** 69 rue 360, Phnom-Penh; tel. (23) 361197; fax (23) 721888; Head of Admin. KEO SOPHEAP; News Editor SIN SO CHEAT.

**Bayon:** c/o Bayon Media Group, 954 rue 2, Takhmau, Kandal Province; tel. (23) 983435; fax (23) 363895; Dir-Gen. KEM KUNNAVATH.

**Bee Hive Radio:** 41 rue 214, Phnom-Penh; tel. (23) 720401; Dir-Gen. MAM SONANDO.

**FM 90 MHZ:** 65 rue 178, Phnom-Penh; tel. (23) 363699; fax (23) 368623; Dir-Gen. NHIM BUN THON; Dep. Dir-Gen. TUM VANN DET.

**FM 99 MHZ:** 41 rue 360, Phnom-Penh; tel. (23) 426794; Gen. Man. SOM CHHAYA.

**FM 107 MHZ:** 81 rue 562, Phnom-Penh; tel. (23) 428047; fax (23) 368212; Dir-Gen. KHUN HANG.

**Phnom-Penh Municipality Radio:** 131–132 blvd Pochentong, Phnom-Penh; tel. (23) 725205; fax (23) 360800; Gen. Man. KHAMPUN KEOMONY.

**RCAF Radio:** c/o Borei Keila, rue 169, Phnom-Penh; tel. (23) 366061; fax (23) 366063; f. 1994; Royal Cambodian Armed Forces radio station; Dir THA TANA; News Editor SENG KATEKA.

**Vithyu Cheat Kampuchea** (National Radio of Cambodia): rue Preah Kossamak, Phnom-Penh; tel. (23) 368140; fax (23) 427319; f. 1978; fmrly Vithyu Samleng Pracheachon Kampuchea (Voice of the Cambodian People); controlled by the Ministry of Information and the Press; home service in Khmer; daily external services in English, French, Lao, Vietnamese and Thai; Dir-Gen. VANN SENG LY; Dep. Dir Gen. TAN YAN.

There are also eight private local radio stations based in Phnom-Penh, Battambang Province, Sihanoukville, and Stung Treng Province.

#### Television

**Apsara Television (TV11):** 69 rue 360, Phnom-Penh; tel. (23) 724402; fax (23) 724302; Dir-Gen. TEN SIMAN.

**Bayon Television (TV27):** 954 rue 2, Takhmau, Kandal Province; tel. (23) 983435; fax (23) 982232; Dir-Gen. KEM KUNNAVATH.

**National Television of Cambodia (Channel 7):** 19 rue 242, Phnom-Penh; tel. (23) 722983; fax (23) 426407; opened 1983; broadcasts for 10 hours per day in Khmer; Dir-Gen. (Head of Television) MAO AYUTH.

**Phnom-Penh Television (TV3):** 131–132 blvd Pochentong, Phnom-Penh; tel. (23) 725205; fax (23) 360800; Dir-Gen. KHAMPHUN KEOMONY.

**RCAF Television (TV5):** 165 rue 169, Phnom-Penh; tel. (23) 366061; fax (23) 366063; Editor-in-Chief PRUM KIM.

**TV Khmer (TV9):** 81 rue 562, Phnom-Penh; tel. (23) 428047; fax (23) 368212; Dir-Gen. KHUN HANG; News Editor PHAN TITH.

# Finance

### BANKING

The National Bank of Cambodia, which was established as the sole authorized bank in 1980 (following the abolition of the monetary system by the Government of Democratic Kampuchea in 1975), is the central bank, and assumed its present name in February 1992. The adoption of a market economy led to the licensing of privately-owned and joint-venture banks from July 1991. At June 1999 there were a further 32 banks operating in Cambodia, including two state-owned banks, 22 locally-incorporated private banks and eight branches of foreign banks. Rural financing was often provided by a decentralized system of non-governmental organizations. Plans were confirmed in early 1998 to establish a Rural Development Bank to supervise these institutions.

#### Central Bank

**National Bank of Cambodia:** 22–24 blvd Norodom, BP 25, Phnom-Penh; tel. (23) 428105; fax (23) 426117; f. 1980; cap. 1,550m. riels; Gov. CHEA CHANTO; Dep. Gov. SUM NIPHA.

#### State Banks

**Foreign Trade Bank:** 24–26 blvd Norodom, Phnom-Penh; tel. (23) 525866; scheduled for privatization; Man. TIM BO PHOL.

**Rural Development Bank:** Phnom-Penh.

#### Private Banks

**Advanced Bank of Asia Ltd:** 97–99 blvd Norodom, Khan Daun Penh, Phnom-Penh; tel. (23) 720434; fax (23) 720435; Dir CHAE WAN CHO.

**Agriculture and Commercial Bank of Cambodia (ACBC) Ltd:** 49 rue 214, Samdach Pann, Phnom-Penh; tel. (23) 722272; fax (23) 426683; e-mail 012812428@mobitel.com.kh; Man. THAI SOVANA.

**Cambodia Agriculture, Industrial and Merchant Bank:** 87 blvd Norodom, Phnom-Penh; tel. 366856; Man. CHHOR SANG.

**Cambodia Asia Bank Ltd:** 252 blvd Monivong, Phnom-Penh; tel. (23) 426628; Man. WONG TOW FOCK.

**Cambodia Farmers Bank:** 45 rue Kampuchea Viet Nam, Phnom-Penh; tel. (23) 426183; fax (23) 426801; f. 1992; joint venture by Thai business executives and the National Bank of Cambodia; Man. PHOT PUNYARATABANDHU; Dep. Man. NORODOM ARUNRASMY; 2 brs.

**Cambodia International Bank Ltd:** 21 rue 128, 107 S. Monorom, Khan 7 Makara, Phnom-Penh; tel. (23) 725920; Man. CHIEE YOON CHENG.

**Cambodia Mekong Bank:** 1 rue Kramuonsar, Khan Daun Penh, Phnom-Penh; tel. (23) 430518; fax (23) 426525; Man. KHOV BOUN CHHAY.

**Cambodian Commercial Bank Ltd:** 26 blvd Monivong, Phnom-Penh; tel. (23) 25644; fax (23) 426116; f. 1991; Man. BHENGBHASANG KRISHMMSA; 4 brs.

**Cambodian Public Bank (Campu Bank):** Villa 23, rue 114, BP 899, Phnom-Penh; tel. (23) 426067; fax (23) 426068; e-mail campu@bigpond.com.kh; Man. CHAN KOK CHOY.

**Canadia Bank Ltd:** 265–269 rue Ang Duong, Sangkat Wat Phnom, Khan Daun Penh, Phnom-Penh; tel. (23) 725548; fax (23) 427064; e-mail canadia@camnet.com.kh; internet www.camnet.com.kh/canadia/; Man. PUNG KHEAV SE; 6 brs.

**Chansavangwong Bank:** 145A–145B rue 154–51, Khan Daun Penh, Phnom-Penh; tel. (23) 427464; fax (23) 427461; Man. TAING LI PHENG.

**Emperor International Bank Ltd:** 230–232 blvd Monivong, Phnom-Penh; tel. (23) 426254; fax (23) 426417; e-mail ciba@bigpond.com.kh; Man. VAN SOU IENG.

**First Overseas Bank Ltd:** 20 rue 114, Phnom-Penh; tel. (23) 213023; fax (23) 427439; e-mail drskchoy@mol.net.my; Man. CHOY SOOK KUEN; 3 brs.

**Global Commercial Bank Ltd:** 337 blvd Monivong, Sangkat Orassey 4, Khan 7 Makara, Phnom-Penh; tel. (23) 364258; fax (23) 426612; Man. WELLSON HSIEH.

**Great International Bank Ltd:** 320A–320B blvd Monivong, Khan Daun Penh, Phnom-Penh; tel. (23) 427282; Man. LY TAK BOUALAY.

**Khmer Bank (Thaneakar Khmer):** 116 rue Sihanouk, Phnom-Penh; tel. (23) 724853; Man. HÉNG KIM Y.

**Pacific Commercial Bank Ltd:** 350 rue 217, Sangkat Orassey 2, Khan 7 Makara, Phnom-Penh; tel. (23) 426896; Man. TENG DANNY.

**Phnom-Penh City Bank Ltd:** 101 blvd Norodom, rue 214, Phnom-Penh; tel. (23) 62885; fax (23) 427353; Man. THEERAYUT SEANG AROON.

**Rich Nation Bank Ltd:** 272–278 Charles de Gaulle, Sangkat Orassey 2, Khan 7 Makara, Phnom-Penh; tel. (23) 720100; fax (23) 720118; Man. HENRY SHI CALLE; Dep. Man. DANIEL CHAN.

**Singapore Banking Corporation Ltd:** 68 rue 214, Sangkat Boeung Reang, Khan Daun Penh, Phnom-Penh; tel. (23) 723366; fax (23) 427277; f. 1993; Exec. Dir ANDY KUN.

**Singapore Commercial Bank Ltd:** 316 blvd Monivong, Khan Daun Penh, BP 1199, Phnom-Penh; tel. and fax (23) 427471; cap. US $5m.; Pres. KONG LOOK SEN; Gen. Man. TEOH SAM MING; 1 br.

**Union Commercial Bank Ltd:** 61 rue 130, Khan Daun Penh, Phnom-Penh; tel. (23) 427995; fax (23) 427997; CEO YUM SUI SANG.

#### Foreign Banks

**Bangkok Bank Ltd** (Thailand): 26 blvd Norodom, Phnom-Penh; tel. (23) 426593; Man. NICOM PHONGSOIPETCH.

**Crédit Agricole Indosuez** (France): 70 blvd Norodom, Khan Daun Penh, Phnom-Penh; tel. (23) 724772; fax (23) 427235; Man. GEORGES LOUBEYRE.

**Krung Thai Bank PLC** (Thailand): 149 rue 215 Jawaharlal Nehru, Depot Market 1, Tuolkok Division, Phnom-Penh; tel. (23) 5519076; fax (23) 5519325; Man. WICHITR XOMNUEK.

**Lippo Bank** (Indonesia): 273 Preah Andoung, S.K. Wat Phnom, Khan Daun Penh, Phnom-Penh; Man. MARKUS PARMADI.

**Maybank Bhd** (Malaysia): 2 blvd Norodom, Phnom-Penh; tel. (23) 427590; Man. CHAN KIN CHOY.

**Siam City Bank Ltd** (Thailand): 79 rue Kampuchea Viet Nam, Khan Makara, Phnom-Penh; tel. (23) 427199; Man. TOSACHAI SOPHAKALIN.

**Standard Chartered Bank:** 89 blvd Norodom, Phnom-Penh; tel. (23) 216685; fax (23) 216687; CEO PAUL FREER; 1 br.

**Thai Farmers Bank** (Thailand): 2 rue 118, Khan Daun Penh, Phnom-Penh; tel. (23) 724035; Man. PERAWAP SING TONG.

### INSURANCE

**Commercial Union:** 28 rue 47, Phnom-Penh; tel. (23) 426694; fax (23) 427171; general insurance; Gen. Man. PAUL CABLE.

**Indochine Insurance Ltd:** 55 rue 178, BP 808, Phnom-Penh; tel. (23) 210761; fax (23) 210501; e-mail insurance@indochine.com.kh; internet www.indochine.net; Dir PHILIPPE LENAIN.

## Trade and Industry

### DEVELOPMENT ORGANIZATIONS

**Cambodian Development Council (CDC):** Government Palace, quai Sisowath, Wat Phnom, Phnom-Penh; tel. (23) 981156; fax (23) 361516; f. 1993; sole body responsible for approving foreign investment in Cambodia, also grants exemptions from customs duties and other taxes, and provides other facilities for investors; Chair. HUN SEN; Sec.-Gen. SOK CHENDA.

**Cambodian Investment Board:** Phnom-Penh; Sec.-Gen. ITH VICHIT.

### CHAMBER OF COMMERCE

**Phnom-Penh Chamber of Commerce:** 22 rue Kramuon Sar, Psar Thmei 2, Phnom-Penh; tel. (23) 722744; fax (23) 427207; Pres. SOK KONG.

### INDUSTRIAL AND TRADE ASSOCIATION

**Garment Manufacturers' Association:** Phnom-Penh; tel. 12888222; fax (23) 427983; Pres. VAN SOU IENG; Sec. ROGER TAN.

### UTILITIES

#### Electricity

**Electricité du Cambodge:** rue 19, Wat Phnom, Phnom-Penh; tel. (23) 811327; fax (23) 426018; Dir-Gen. TAN KIM VIN.

#### Water

**Phnom-Penh Water Supply Authority:** nr Railway Station, Phnom-Penh; tel. (23) 427657; fax (23) 428969; e-mail ppwsa@bigpond.com.kh; f. 1996 as an autonomous public enterprise; Dir-Gen. EK SONN CHAN.

### TRADE UNIONS

**Cambodian Federation of Trade Unions (CAFTU):** Phnom-Penh; f. 1979; affiliated to WFTU; Chair. MEN SAM-AN; Vice-Chair. LAY SAMON.

**Cambodian Union Federation:** f. 1997 with the support of the CPP in response to the formation of the FTUWKC.

**Free Trade Union of Workers of the Kingdom of Cambodia (FTUWKC):** f. 1997 with the assistance of Sam Rainsy; Leader CHEA VICHEA.

## Transport

### RAILWAYS

**Royal Railway of Cambodia:** Moha Vithei Pracheathippatay, Phnom-Penh; tel. (23) 725156; comprises two 1,000 mm-gauge single track main lines with a total length of 649 km: the 385-km Phnom-Penh to Poipet line, the 264-km Phnom-Penh to Sihanoukville line and branch lines and special purpose sidings; the condition of the lines is very poor, with many temporary repairs, owing to mine damage, and the service also suffers from other operational difficulties, such as a shortage of rolling stock; there are 14 'Gares' (main stations), 19 stations and 38 halts; Dir PICH KIMSREANG.

### ROADS

In 1996 the total road network was 35,769 km in length, of which 4,165 km were highways and 3,604 km were secondary roads; about 7.5% of the road network was paved.

### INLAND WATERWAYS

The major routes are along the Mekong river, and up the Tonlé Sap river into the Tonlé Sap (Great Lake), covering, in all, about 2,400 km. The inland ports of Neak Luong, Kompong Cham and Prek Kdam have been supplied with motor ferries and the ferry crossings have been improved.

### SHIPPING

The main port is Sihanoukville, on the Gulf of Thailand, which has 11 berths and can accommodate vessels of 10,000–15,000 tons. Phnom-Penh port lies some distance inland. Steamers of up to 4,000 tons can be accommodated.

### CIVIL AVIATION

There is an international airport at Pochentong, near Phnom-Penh. In August 1997 the Government announced the formation of a second state-owned airline, Kampuchea Airlines. Prince Norodom Chakkrapong established a new airline named Phnom-Penh Airline in 1999.

**State Secretariat of Civil Aviation (SSCA):** 62 blvd Norodom, Phnom-Penh; tel. (23) 724167; fax (23) 426169; Gen. Dir KEO SAPHAL.

**Royal Air Cambodge (RAC):** 24 ave Kramuonsar, blvd Monivong, Phnom-Penh; tel. (23) 428831; fax (17) 428895; e-mail flights@royalaircambodge.com.kh; re-established 1994; national airline; joint venture between the Govt (60%) and Malaysian Helicopter Services (now known as Naluri Bhd, 40%); operates flights to six domestic destinations and routes to Malaysia, Singapore, Thailand, Viet Nam, Hong Kong and the People's Republic of China; Chair. and CEO PAN CHANTRA.

## Tourism

Visitor arrivals reached 260,489 in 1996, but declined to 213,910 in 1997, as a result of the political violence in July of that year. Tourism continued to be adversely affected by civil unrest in 1998, with arrivals declining to 186,333. However, arrivals were projected to increase to 210,000 in 1999, owing to the improvement in the security situation caused by the establishment of a potentially stable coalition Government in November 1998 and the cessation of official armed resistance by the Khmers Rouges.

**General Directorate for Tourism:** 3 blvd Monivong, Phnom-Penh; tel. (23) 427130; fax (23) 426107; e-mail tourism@camnet.com.kh; f. 1988; Dir SO MARA.

# CAMEROON

## Introductory Survey

### Location, Climate, Language, Religion, Flag, Capital

The Republic of Cameroon lies on the west coast of Africa, with Nigeria to the west, Chad and the Central African Republic to the east, and the Republic of the Congo, Equatorial Guinea and Gabon to the south. The climate is hot and humid in the south and west, with average temperatures of 26°C (80°F). Annual rainfall in Yaoundé averages 4,030 mm (159 ins). The north is drier, with more extreme temperatures. The official languages are French and English; many local languages are also spoken, including Fang, Bamileke and Duala. Approximately 53% of Cameroonians profess Christianity, 25% adhere to traditional religious beliefs, and about 22%, mostly in the north, are Muslims. The national flag (proportions 3 by 2) has three equal vertical stripes, of green, red and yellow, with a five-pointed gold star in the centre of the red stripe. The capital is Yaoundé.

### Recent History

In 1884 a German protectorate was established in Cameroon (Kamerun). In 1916, during the First World War, the German administration was overthrown by invading British and French forces. Under an agreement reached between the occupying powers in 1919, Cameroon was divided into two zones: a French-ruled area in the east and south, and a smaller British-administered area in the west. In 1922 both zones became subject to mandates of the League of Nations, with France and the United Kingdom as the administering powers. In 1946 the zones were transformed into UN Trust Territories, with British and French rule continuing in their respective areas.

French Cameroons became an autonomous state within the French Community in 1957. Under the leadership of Ahmadou Ahidjo, a northerner who became Prime Minister in 1958, the territory became independent, as the Republic of Cameroon, on 1 January 1960. The first election for the country's National Assembly, held in April 1960, was won by Ahidjo's party, the Union camerounaise. In May the new National Assembly elected Ahidjo to be the country's first President.

British Cameroons, comprising a northern and a southern region, was attached to neighbouring Nigeria, for administrative purposes, prior to Nigeria's independence in October 1960. Plebiscites were held, under UN auspices, in the two regions of British Cameroons in February 1961. The northern area voted to merge with Nigeria (becoming the province of Sardauna), while the south voted for union with the Republic of Cameroon, which took place on 1 October 1961.

The enlarged country was named the Federal Republic of Cameroon, with French and English as joint official languages. It comprised two states: the former French zone became East Cameroon, while the former British portion became West Cameroon. John Ngu Foncha, the Prime Minister of West Cameroon and leader of the Kamerun National Democratic Party, became Vice-President of the Federal Republic. Under the continuing leadership of Ahidjo, who (as the sole candidate) was re-elected President in May 1965, the two states became increasingly integrated. In September 1966 the two governing parties and several opposition groups combined to form a single party, the Union nationale camerounaise (UNC). The only significant opposition party, the extreme left-wing Union des populations camerounaises (UPC), was suppressed in 1971 (although it was allowed to operate again when multi-party politics was reintroduced in the early 1990s). Meanwhile, Ahidjo was re-elected as President in March 1970, and Solomon Muna (who had replaced Foncha as Prime Minister of West Cameroon in 1968) became Vice-President.

In June 1972, following the approval by referendum of a new Constitution, the federal system was ended and the country was officially renamed the United Republic of Cameroon. The office of Vice-President was abolished. A centralized political and administrative system was rapidly introduced, and in May 1973 a new National Assembly was elected for a five-year term. After the re-election of Ahidjo as President in April 1975, the Constitution was revised, and a Prime Minister, Paul Biya (a bilingual Christian southerner), was appointed in June. In April 1980 Ahidjo was unanimously re-elected to the presidency for a fifth five-year term of office.

Ahidjo announced his resignation as President in November 1982, and nominated Biya as his successor. In subsequent cabinet reorganizations Biya removed a number of supporters of the former President. In August 1983 Biya announced the discovery of a conspiracy to overthrow his Government, and simultaneously dismissed the Prime Minister and the Minister of the Armed Forces, both northern Muslims. Later in August Ahidjo resigned as President of the UNC and strongly criticized Biya's regime. In September Biya was elected President of the ruling party, and in January 1984 he was re-elected as President of the Republic, reportedly obtaining 99.98% of the votes cast. In a subsequent reorganization of the Cabinet the post of Prime Minister was abolished, and it was announced that the country's name was to revert from the United Republic of Cameroon to the Republic of Cameroon.

In February 1984 Ahidjo and two of his close military advisers were tried (Ahidjo *in absentia*) for their alleged complicity in the coup plot of August 1983, and received death sentences, which were, however, commuted to life imprisonment. On 6 April 1984 rebel elements in the presidential guard, led by Col Saleh Ibrahim (a northerner), attempted to overthrow the Biya Government. After three days of intense fighting, in which hundreds of people were reported to have been killed, the rebellion was suppressed by forces loyal to the President; a total of 51 defendants received death sentences at trials held in May and November. Following extensive changes within the military hierarchy, the UNC Central Committee and the leadership of state-controlled companies, Biya reorganized his Government in July and introduced more stringent press censorship.

In March 1985 the UNC was renamed the Rassemblement démocratique du peuple camerounais (RDPC). In January 1986 members of the exiled UPC movement claimed that 200–300 opponents of the Biya Government (most of whom were anglophones or members of clandestine opposition movements) had been arrested in the preceding months, and that some of those in detention were being subjected to torture. A number of detainees were subsequently released. In July 1987 the National Assembly approved a new electoral code providing for multiple candidacy in public elections, and in October voters had a choice of RDPC-approved candidates in local government elections.

Ostensibly for reasons of economy, the presidential election, originally scheduled for January 1989, was brought forward to coincide with elections to the National Assembly in April 1988. In the presidential poll Biya was re-elected unopposed, securing 98.75% of the votes cast. In the concurrent legislative elections voters were presented with a choice of RDPC-approved candidates; 153 of those elected to the National Assembly were new members. (In accordance with constitutional amendments agreed in March 1988, the number of members in the National Assembly was increased from 150 to 180.)

In February 1990 11 people, including the former President of the Cameroonian Bar Association, Yondo Black, were arrested in connection with their alleged involvement in an unofficial opposition organization, the Social Democratic Front (SDF). In April Black was sentenced to three years' imprisonment on charges of 'subversion'. Later in the same month, however, Biya announced that all the prisoners who had been detained in connection with the 1984 coup attempt were to be released. In May 1990 a demonstration organized by the SDF was violently suppressed by security forces, and six deaths were subsequently reported. In the same month the Government suspended the publication of an independent newspaper, the *Cameroon Post*, which had implied support for the SDF. In June the Vice-President of the RDPC, John Ngu Foncha, resigned, alleging corruption and human rights violations on the part of the Government. In the same month the Congress of the RDPC re-elected Biya as President of the party. In response to continued civil unrest, Biya stated that he envisaged the future adoption of a multi-party system and announced a series of reforms, including the abolition of laws governing subversion, the revision of the law on political associations, and the reinforcement of press freedom. In the same month a committee was established to revise legislation on human rights. In August several political prisoners, including Yondo Black, were released.

In September 1990 Biya announced an extensive cabinet reshuffle, in which a new ministry to implement the Government's economic stabilization programme was created. In early December the National Assembly adopted legislation whereby Cameroon officially became a multi-party state. Under the new legislation, the Government was required to provide an official response within three months to any political organization seeking legal recognition. However, the recruitment of party activists on an ethnic or regional basis and the financing of political parties from external sources remained illegal. Legislative elections, which were due in April 1993, were rescheduled to take place by the end of 1991 (but were later postponed).

In January 1991 anti-Government demonstrators protested at Biya's failure (despite previous undertakings) to grant an amnesty to prisoners implicated in the 1984 coup attempt. In the same month the trial of two journalists, who had criticized Biya in an independent publication, *Le Messager,* provoked violent rioting. Meanwhile, opposition leaders reiterated demands for Biya's resignation and the convening of a national conference to formulate a timetable for multi-party elections. Biya's continued opposition to the holding of a conference provoked a series of demonstrations, which were violently suppressed by the security forces. In April the principal anti-Government groups created an informal alliance, the National Co-ordination Committee of Opposition Parties (NCCOP), which organized a widely-observed general strike. Later in April, in response to increasing pressure for political reform, the National Assembly approved legislation granting a general amnesty for political prisoners and reintroducing the post of Prime Minister. Biya subsequently appointed Sadou Hayatou, hitherto Secretary-General at the Presidency, to the position. Hayatou named a 32-member transitional Government, principally composed of members of the former Cabinet. The Government's refusal to comply with demands issued by the NCCOP for an unconditional amnesty for all political prisoners (the existing provisions for an amnesty excluded an estimated 400 political prisoners jailed for allegedly non-political crimes) and for the convening of a national conference prompted the alliance to organize a campaign of civil disobedience, culminating in a general strike in June, which halted commercial activity in most towns. The Government subsequently placed seven of Cameroon's 10 provinces under military rule, prohibited opposition gatherings, and later in June, following continued civil disturbances, banned the NCCOP and several opposition parties, alleging that the opposition alliance was responsible for terrorist activities. Although opposition leaders announced that the campaign of civil disobedience would continue, the effect of the general strike declined in subsequent months. In September several opposition leaders were temporarily detained, following renewed violent demonstrations in Douala.

In October 1991 Biya announced that legislative elections were to be held in February 1992, and that a Prime Minister would be appointed from the party that secured a majority in the National Assembly. Tripartite negotiations between the Government, opposition parties and independent officials commenced at the end of October 1991; however, progress was impeded by opposition demands that the agenda of the meeting be extended to include a review of the Constitution. In mid-November, however, the Government and about 40 of the 47 registered opposition parties (including some parties belonging to the NCCOP) signed an agreement providing for the establishment of a committee to draft constitutional reforms. The opposition undertook to suspend the campaign of civil disobedience, while the Government agreed to end the ban on opposition meetings and to release all prisoners who had been arrested during anti-Government demonstrations. However, several principal opposition parties belonging to the NCCOP, including the SDF, subsequently declared the agreement to be invalid, and stated that the campaign of civil disobedience would continue. The Government revoked the ban on opposition gatherings later in November, and in December ended the military rule that had been imposed in seven provinces.

In January 1992 the Government announced that the legislative elections were to be postponed until March (opposition leaders had demanded that the elections take place in May), in order to allow parties sufficient time for preparation. However, several opposition movements, including two of the principal parties, the SDF and the Union démocratique du Cameroun (UDC), refused to contest the elections, on the grounds that the scheduled date was too early and therefore benefited the RDPC. In February more than 100 people were killed in the northern town of Kousseri, following violent clashes between the Kokoto and Arab Choa ethnic groups, which occurred during the registration of voters. In the same month those opposition parties that had not accepted the tripartite agreement in November 1991 formed the Alliance pour le redressement du Cameroun (ARC), and announced that they were to boycott the elections.

The legislative elections, which took place on 1 March 1992, were contested by 32 political parties; the RDPC won 88 of the National Assembly's 180 seats, while the Union nationale pour la démocratie et le progrès (UNDP) obtained 68, the UPC 18, and the Mouvement pour la défense de la République (MDR) six seats. The RDPC subsequently formed an alliance with the MDR, thereby securing an absolute majority in the National Assembly. In early April Biya formed a 25-member Cabinet, principally comprising members of the previous Government; Simon Achidi Achu, an anglophone member of the RDPC who had served in the Ahidjo administration, was appointed Prime Minister. Five members of the MDR, including the party leader, Dakolle Daissala, also received ministerial portfolios.

In August 1992 Biya announced that the forthcoming presidential election, scheduled for May 1993, was to be brought forward to 11 October 1992. In September Biya promulgated legislation regulating the election of the President which prohibited the formation of electoral alliances. Shortly before the election two of the seven opposition candidates withdrew in favour of the Chairman of the SDF, John Fru Ndi, who received the support of the ARC alliance. The presidential election, which took place as scheduled, immediately provoked opposition allegations of malpractice on the part of the Government. In mid-October Fru Ndi proclaimed himself President, following unconfirmed reports that he had won the election. Later that month, however, the Government announced that Biya had been re-elected by 39.9% of the votes cast, while Fru Ndi had secured 35.9%, prompting violent demonstrations by opposition supporters in many areas, particularly in the north-west and in Douala. The Supreme Court rejected a subsequent appeal by Fru Ndi that the results of the election be declared invalid. At the end of October, in response to the continued unrest, the Government placed Fru Ndi and several of his supporters under house arrest, and imposed a state of emergency in North-West Province for a period of three months. Biya was inaugurated as President on 3 November, and pledged to implement further constitutional reforms. Later that month international condemnation of the Government increased, following the death by torture of a detained opposition member; the USA and Germany suspended economic aid to Cameroon in protest at the continued enforcement of the state of emergency. At the end of November Biya announced the appointment of a new 30-member Cabinet, which, in addition to three members of the MDR, included representatives of the UPC, the UNDP and the Parti national du progrès. In late December the state of emergency was revoked in North-West Province. In January 1993 the Government granted an amnesty to a number of political prisoners who had been arrested in October 1992.

In March 1993 an informal alliance of opposition parties (led by the SDF), the Union pour le changement, organized a series of demonstrations and a boycott of French consumer goods (in protest at the French Government's involvement with Biya), in support of demands for a new presidential election. The Government accused the alliance of incitement to civil disorder, and continued efforts to suppress opposition activity. Later in March three people were killed in clashes between members of the armed forces and opposition supporters in Bamenda, in North-West Province, while a number of members of a prominent opposition movement, the Union des forces démocratiques du Cameroun, were arrested shortly before a demonstration was due to take place. In response to international pressure, however, the Government announced its intention to conduct a national debate on constitutional reform. In April a gathering organized by the Cameroon Anglophone Movement (CAM) in Buéa, in South-West Province, demanded the restoration of a federal system of government, in response to the traditional dominance of the French-speaking section of the population. In the following month the Government promulgated draft constitutional amendments which provided for the installation of a democratic political system, with the establishment of new organs of government, including an upper legislative chamber, to be known as the Senate, and restricted the power vested in the President (who was to serve a maximum of two five-year terms of office). The draft legislation retained a unitary state, but, in recognition of demands by supporters of federalism, envisaged a more decentralized system of local government.

During the second half of 1993 the opposition organized a series of anti-Government strikes and demonstrations; consequently, many opposition activists were either arrested or detained. In December public-sector workers initiated a general strike, with the support of the opposition, after the Government announced substantial reductions in state-sector salaries. In early 1994, however, strike action in protest at the devaluation of the CFA franc subsided, following the imposition of sanctions against striking civil servants.

Meanwhile, in September 1993 a peace agreement was signed between the Kokoto and Arab Choa ethnic groups in Kousseri; however, further clashes were reported later in the year. In February 1994 security forces killed some 50 members of the Arab Choa ethnic group at the village of Karena in northern Cameroon, apparently in retaliation for acts of armed banditry in the region, which were, however, widely attributed to former Chadian rebels. In March some 1,200 citizens took refuge in Chad, in response to continuing clashes between security forces and bandits in northern Cameroon.

In July 1994, in accordance with the Government's aim of promoting economic recovery, a new ministerial department with responsibility for the economy and finance was created as part of an extensive cabinet reorganization. In September an informal alliance of 16 opposition movements, the Front des alliés pour le changement (FAC), was established, effectively replacing the Union pour le changement; the FAC denounced what it alleged to be human rights violations on the part of the authorities, together with the indefinite postponement of municipal elections and the transfer of state-owned enterprises to the private sector. Two prominent opposition parties, the UNDP and the UDC refused to join the alliance, however, on the grounds that it was dominated by the SDF. (In February 1995 the leader of the Mouvement pour la démocratie et le progrès (MDP), Samuel Eboua, was elected President of the FAC, replacing Fru Ndi of the SDF.) In November 1994 Biya announced that discussions on the revision of the Constitution were to resume, following the establishment of a Consultative Constitutional Review Committee, and that municipal elections were to take place in 1995. Constitutional discussions commenced in mid-December 1994, but were boycotted by the opposition, which cited limitations in the agenda of the debate. In early 1995, however, the Consultative Constitutional Review Committee submitted revised constitutional amendments to Biya for consideration.

In early July 1995 members of a newly-emerged anglophone organization, the Southern Cameroons National Council (SCNC, which demanded that the former portion of the British Cameroons that had amalgamated with the Republic of Cameroon in 1961 be granted autonomy), staged a demonstration in Bamenda, at which they clashed with security forces. In the same month a number of independently-owned newspapers temporarily suspended publication in protest at alleged increasing press censorship and intimidation of journalists. In August representatives of anglophone movements, including the SCNC and the CAM, officially presented their demands for the establishment of an independent, English-speaking republic of Southern Cameroons at the UN, and urged the international community to assist in resolving the issue in order to avert civil conflict in Cameroon; the organizations claimed that the plebiscite of 1961, whereby the former southern portion of British Cameroons had voted to merge with the Republic of Cameroon on terms of equal status, had been rendered invalid by subsequent francophone domination.

In October 1995 a special congress of the RDPC re-elected Biya as leader of the party for a further term of five years. Meanwhile, Cameroon's pending application for membership of the Commonwealth (which had been accepted, in principle, in 1993, subject to the Government's fulfilment of certain democratic conditions) prompted further controversy; opposition movements urged the Commonwealth to refuse admission to Cameroon on the grounds that no progress had been achieved with regard to human rights and the democratic process, while the SCNC submitted a rival application for membership on behalf of the proposed independent republic of Southern Cameroons. In early November, however, Cameroon was formally admitted to the Commonwealth. In the same month Biya announced that the long-awaited municipal elections were to take place in January 1996 (although both opposition movements and parties belonging to the government coalition had demanded that the elections be preceded by constitutional reform and the establishment of an independent electoral commission). In December 1995 the National Assembly adopted the revised constitutional amendments, submitted by Biya earlier that month, which increased the presidential mandate from five to seven years (while restricting the maximum tenure of office to two terms) and provided for the establishment of a Senate. Municipal elections, in which some 38 political parties participated, duly took place in January 1996; the RDPC won the majority of seats in 56% of local councils, and the SDF in 27%, while the UNDP received popular support in the north of the country. (The two main opposition parties performed well in the elections, despite having both suffered internal division during 1994–95.) In March 1996 the SDF and the UNDP urged a campaign of civil disobedience in protest at the Government's appointment by decree of representatives to replace the elected mayors in principal towns (following the municipal elections, the opposition had gained control of 13 towns). At the beginning of that month at least two people were killed in a demonstration which had been organized by the SDF in the south-western town of Limbe as part of the campaign. In April the Government imposed a total ban on all media reports of the SDF/UNDP campaign of civil disobedience. In May–June the two parties organized general strikes, which were principally observed in western and northern regions. In September Simon Achidi Achu was replaced as Prime Minister by Peter Mafany Musonge, the General Manager of the Cameroon Development Corporation, and a new Cabinet was appointed.

At the end of January 1997 the Government announced the postponement of the legislative elections (which had been scheduled to take place in early March) owing to organizational difficulties, following opposition complaints that its supporters had been allowed insufficient time for registration; Biya's subsequent failure to extend the mandate of the incumbent National Assembly (which expired in early March), however, prompted criticism from a number of opposition deputies. At the end of March some 10 people were killed when unidentified armed groups staged attacks against government and security buildings in Bamenda and other towns in North-West Province; the violence was generally attributed to members of the SCNC. In April the Government announced that the legislative elections were to take place on 17 May. Pre-election violence, in which some five people were killed, prompted the imposition of increased security measures, including the closure of the country's borders. The elections, which were contested by 46 political parties, were monitored by a Commonwealth observer mission. The announcement of provisional election results (which attributed a large majority of seats to the RDPC) prompted claims from the opposition parties of widespread electoral malpractice; the observer group also expressed general dissatisfaction with the election process. The Supreme Court, however, rejected opposition appeals against RDPC victories. Three people were killed in clashes between RDPC and SDF members in South-West Province in the second half of May, where the election result was disputed by the two parties. In early June the Supreme Court announced the official election results: the RDPC had secured 109 of the 180 seats in the legislature, while the SDF had obtained 43, the UNDP 13 and the UDC five seats; the Mouvement pour la jeunesse du Cameroun (MLJC), the UPC and the MDR obtained one seat each. The Cabinet remained virtually unchanged from the previous administration and Musonge was retained as Prime Minister. In August further polls were conducted in seven constituencies, where the results had been annulled, owing to alleged irregularities; the RDPC won all of the seats, thus increasing its level of representation in the National Assembly to 116 seats.

In July 1997 it was reported that the former Minister of Public Health, Titus Edzoa, who in April had resigned from the Cabinet in order to contest the presidential election later that year, had been arrested and charged with embezzlement; his supporters claimed, however, that Edzoa (a leading figure in the RDPC) was being held as a political prisoner at a 'torture centre'. It was announced in September that the election would be held on 12 October. Shortly afterwards, the three major opposition parties, the SDF, UNDP and UDC, declared a boycott of all elections, including the imminent presidential election, in protest against the absence of an independent electoral commission; a fourth opposition party, the Union du peuple africain, later joined the boycott. In mid-September Biya was officially elected as the RDPC presidential candidate. At the election, which was contested by seven candidates, Biya was re-elected, winning 92.6% of the votes cast. The level of voter participation in the election was much-disputed, with official sources asserting that a record 81.4% of the electorate took part, while opposition leaders rejected this figure, claiming that the abstention rate was higher than 80%, and dismissed the poll on various grounds as an 'electoral masquerade'. Biya, however, was formally inaugurated on 3 November, beginning, in accordance with the revised Constitution, a seven-year term in presidential office. Following talks with various opposition groups in November and December, the RDPC reached an agreement with the UNDP on the creation of a coalition government; the SDF, however, refused to co-operate with the ruling party. In December, after having reappointed Musonge as Prime Minister, Biya effected a major cabinet reshuffle. The new Government included representatives from four of the country's many political groups, although the RDPC retained 45 of the 50 ministerial posts.

At the end of December 1997 the editor of *Le Messager*, Pius Njawe, was arrested, following the publication of an article in which he alleged that President Biya had suffered a heart attack. In January 1998 Njawe was fined and sentenced to two years' imprisonment; this was widely condemned, as were the convictions of three other journalists for similar offences. In April, as a result of an appeal, Njawe's prison sentence was reduced to one year, and, following reports that the editor had been denied medical attention, he was granted presidential clemency and released in October.

In March 1998 renewed communal clashes were reported in Bamenda. In July 10 of the 43 SDF parliamentary deputies resigned from the party, in protest at the perceived tribalism and authoritarianism of its leadership. In October the SDF expelled its First National Vice-President, Soulaimane Mahamad, following the latter's criticism of Fru Ndi as authoritarian. In January 1999 Fru Ndi announced that he was prepared to initiate direct dialogue with President Biya. It was, however, alleged that the leader of the SDF had announced this radical change of policy in the hope of securing a favourable verdict in his imminent court appearance on charges of defamation. In April Fru Ndi was none the less, found guilty and was fined and given a three-year suspended sentence. At the SDF party conference in the same month Fru Ndi was re-elected Chairman of the party by an overwhelming majority of delegates, despite accusations made by opponents that he had presided over the disintegration of the SDF as a political force. The conference also voted not to enter into dialogue with the Government until an independent electoral commission had been established, and to improve internal party discipline.

Meanwhile, in September 1998 it was reported that some 60 English-speaking Cameroonians, who were alleged to be secessionists campaigning for the independence of Southern Cameroons, were being detained and tortured in Yaoundé, following attacks on police premises. There were counter-accusations made by the opposition, however, that the raids had been staged by government agents as a pretext for further suppression of demands for increased decentralization. In January 1999 the opposition condemned the Government for the alleged marginalization of the anglophone minority in Cameroon, noting that only three of the 2,000 soldiers recently recruited by the armed forces were English-speaking. In June the trial of the alleged anglophone secessionists (the majority of whom had been arrested in 1997) began in Yaoundé. The trial was notable for frequent adjournments and complaints by defence lawyers relating to the competence of the military tribunal to hear the case. In mid-July several of the defendants claimed that confessions that they were members of the separatist SCNC had been extracted under torture and threats of summary execution. The human rights organization Amnesty International later claimed that, prior to the start of the trial, several of the detainees had died in prison either from torture or from lack of medical care. In late August the accused formally denied all the charges against them, although several individuals admitted to being members of a cultural association linked to the SCNC. In October three of the defendants were sentenced to life imprisonment, others received lengthy prison sentences, while 29 were acquitted. Amnesty International criticized the verdicts, alluding to the alleged bias of the military court and the reported torture of detainees, and in November the United Nations Human Rights Committee criticized Cameroon for its alleged failure to protect and to respect fundamental human rights.

In September 1999 Mounchipou Seydou was dismissed from his post as Minister of Posts and Telecommunications and was subsequently arrested on charges of embezzlement of public funds. In October a report by a German non-governmental organization, Transparency International (see p. 303), rated Cameroon as the most corrupt country in the world. The Government strenuously denied the allegations of Transparency International; none the less, a meeting was held in November of the National Commission on Corruption, which had met infrequently since its creation in 1997, at which senior government officials outlined strategies to curb corruption in their areas of responsibility.

Relations with Nigeria, which had become strained as a result of a series of border disputes, showed signs of improvement following a state visit by the Nigerian President in late 1987, when it was announced that joint border controls were to be established. In 1991, however, the Nigerian Government claimed that Cameroon had annexed nine Nigerian fishing settlements, following a long-standing border dispute, based on a 1913 agreement between Germany and the United Kingdom that ceded the Bakassi peninsula in the Gulf of Guinea to Cameroon. Subsequent negotiations between the Governments of Nigeria and Cameroon, in an effort to resolve the dispute, achieved little progress. In December 1993 some 500 Nigerian troops were dispatched to the region, in response to a number of incidents in which Nigerian nationals had been killed by Cameroonian security forces. Later that month the two nations agreed to establish a joint patrol in the disputed area, and to investigate the incidents. In February 1994, however, Cameroon announced that it was to submit the dispute for adjudication by the UN, the Organization of African Unity (OAU—see p. 240) and the International Court of Justice (ICJ), and requested military assistance from France. Subsequent reports of clashes between Cameroonian and Nigerian forces in the region prompted fears of a full-scale conflict between the two nations. In March Cameroon agreed to enter into negotiations with Nigeria (without the involvement of international mediators) to resolve the issue. In the same month the OAU issued a resolution urging the withdrawal of troops from the disputed region. In May negotiations between the two nations, with mediation by the Togolese Government, resumed in Yaoundé. In September the Cameroonian Government submitted additional claims to territory in north-eastern Nigeria to the ICJ.

In February 1996 renewed hostilities between Nigerian and Cameroonian forces in the Bakassi region resulted in several casualties. Later that month, however, Cameroon and Nigeria agreed to refrain from further military action, and delegations from the two countries resumed discussions, with Togolese mediation, in an attempt to resolve the dispute. In March the ICJ ruled that Cameroon had failed to provide sufficient evidence to substantiate its contention that Nigeria had instigated the border dispute, and ordered both nations to cease military operations in the region, to withdraw troops to former positions, and to co-operate with a UN investigative mission, which was to be dispatched to the area. In April, however, clashes continued, with each Government accusing the other of initiating the attacks. Claims by Nigeria that the Cameroonian forces were supported by troops from France were denied by the French Government. Diplomatic efforts to avoid further conflict increased. Nevertheless, both nations continued to reinforce their contingents in the region (where some 5,000 Cameroonian and 3,000 Nigerian troops were deployed at the end of May). Further tension arose in July, when Nigeria accused Cameroon of substantially increasing troops and artillery on the Bakassi peninsula. In September both countries assured the UN investigative mission of their commitment to a peaceful settlement of the dispute. In December and again in May 1997, however, the Nigerian authorities claimed that Cameroonian troops had resumed attacks in the region. In May 1997 the UN requested that the Togolese Government continue efforts to mediate in the dispute. Further clashes were reported in late 1997 and early 1998.

In March 1998, at the preliminary ICJ hearing on the dispute, Nigeria argued that the ICJ did not have jurisdiction in the matter since the two countries had agreed to settle the dispute through bilateral discussion. In June, however, the ICJ declared itself competent to examine the case. In May, and again in September, Cameroon denied reports that it was massing troops on the peninsula. In October further contention arose when

Nigeria alleged that Cameroon had awarded a Canadian company a concession to prospect for petroleum in the disputed area. Cameroon insisted that no such concession had been granted.

From late 1998 relations between Cameroon and Nigeria began to improve, and in November the International Committee of the Red Cross organized an exchange of prisoners between the two sides. In April 1999 the President-elect of Nigeria, Gen. Olusegun Obasanjo, visited Cameroon, the first such since the beginning of the border conflict in 1994, and in May 1999 the outgoing Nigerian Head of State, Gen. Abdulsalami Abubakar, held further talks with President Biya in Yaoundé. The two countries reportedly agreed to resolve the dispute 'in a fraternal way'. It was, however, announced that ICJ proceedings would be continued, and in late May Nigeria filed its defence. In July the ICJ ruled that it would allow counter-claims from Nigeria relating to the apportioning of responsibility for border incidents; the counter-claims were to be examined alongside Cameroonian complaints.

## Government

Under the amended 1972 Constitution, the Republic of Cameroon is a multi-party state. Executive power is vested in the President, as Head of State, who is elected by universal adult suffrage for a term of seven years, and may serve a maximum of two terms. Legislative power is held by the National Assembly, which comprises 180 members and is elected for a term of five years. In December 1995 constitutional amendments provided for the establishment of an upper legislative chamber (to be known as the Senate). The Cabinet is appointed by the President. Local administration is based on 10 provinces, each with a governor who is appointed by the President.

## Defence

In August 1999 Cameroon's armed forces were estimated to total 22,100 men, including 9,000 in paramilitary forces. The army numbered 11,500, the navy about 1,300 and the air force 300. Cameroon has a bilateral defence agreement with France. The defence budget for 1999 was estimated at US $156m.

## Economic Affairs

In 1997, according to estimates by the World Bank, Cameroon's gross national product (GNP), measured at average 1995–97 prices, was US $8,610m., equivalent to $620 per head. During 1990–97, it was estimated, GNP per head declined, in real terms, at an average annual rate of 3.3%. Over the same period the population increased at an average annual rate of 2.8%. In 1998 estimated GNP totalled $8,700m. (equivalent to $610 per head). Cameroon's gross domestic product (GDP) increased, in real terms, at an average annual rate of 0.6% in 1990–98. Real GDP rose by 5.1% in the year to June 1997 and by an estimated 5.0% in 1997/98.

Agriculture (including forestry and fishing) contributed an estimated 42.4% of GDP in 1997/98. An estimated 61.6% of the labour force were employed in agriculture in 1998. The principal cash crops are cocoa beans (which accounted for 13.4% of export earnings in 1997/98), coffee and cotton. The principal subsistence crops are roots and tubers (mainly cassava), maize and sorghum; Cameroon is not, however, self-sufficient in cereals. In 1995 an estimated 42% of the country's land area was covered by forest, but an inadequate transport infrastructure has impeded the development of the forestry sector. Livestock-rearing makes a significant contribution to the food supply. During 1990–98, according to the World Bank, the real GDP of the agricultural sector increased at an average annual rate of 5.0%. Agricultural GDP rose by 7.6% in 1996/97 and by an estimated 6.8% in 1997/98.

Industry (including mining, manufacturing, construction and power) employed 6.7% of the working population in 1985, and contributed an estimated 21.6% of GDP in 1997/98. During 1990–98, according to the World Bank, industrial GDP declined at an average annual rate of 3.3%. Industrial GDP rose by 7.7% in 1996/97 and again by an estimated 7.7% in 1997/98.

Mining contributed 5.7% of GDP in 1997/98, but employed only 0.05% of Cameroon's working population in 1985. Receipts from the exploitation of the country's petroleum reserves constitute a principal source of government revenue. Deposits of limestone are also quarried. Significant reserves of natural gas, bauxite, iron ore, uranium and tin remain largely undeveloped. According to the IMF, the GDP of the mining sector increased by 6.7% in 1996/97 and by an estimated 6.6% in 1997/98.

Manufacturing contributed 10.7% of GDP in 1997/98, and employed an estimated 7% of the working population in 1995. The sector is based on the processing of both indigenous primary products (petroleum-refining, agro-industrial activities) and of imported raw materials (an aluminium-smelter uses alumina imported from Guinea). In the financial year ending June 1996, according to a survey of industrial enterprises in the modern sector, the main branches of manufacturing, based on the value of output, were food products (accounting for 16.2% of the total), beverages (13.1%), petroleum and coal products (13.0%) and wood products (12.6%). Manufacturing GDP declined by an average of 2.3% per year in 1990–97, according to the World Bank. However, the GDP of the sector increased by 8.0% per year in 1996/97 and 1997/98.

In the early 1990s about 95% of Cameroon's energy was derived from hydroelectric power installations. Imports of fuel products accounted for only an estimated 0.6% of the value of total imports in 1995.

Services contributed 35.9% of GDP in 1997/98. During 1990–98, according to the World Bank, the GDP of the services sector remained at a constant level. It rose by 1.8% in 1996/97 and by an estimated 9.1% in 1997/98.

In 1997/98 Cameroon recorded a visible trade surplus of an estimated 297,000m. francs CFA, but there was a deficit of 132,600m. francs CFA on the current account of the balance of payments. In 1997 the principal source of imports (24.4%) was France; other major suppliers were the USA, Nigeria and Germany. The principal market for exports in that year (26.9%) was Italy; other significant purchasers were Spain, France and the Netherlands. The principal exports in 1997/98 were petroleum and petroleum products (accounting for 31.7% of the total), cocoa, coffee and timber and timber products. The principal imports in 1997/98 were enterprise consumption goods (accounting for 17.7% of the total), semi-finished goods and mineral and other raw materials.

In the financial year ending June 1997 there was a budget deficit of 24,900m. francs CFA (equivalent to 0.5% of GDP). Cameroon's total external debt at the end of 1997 was US $9,293m., of which $7,688m. was long-term public debt. In that year the cost of debt-servicing was equivalent to 20.4% of revenue from exports of goods and services. The annual rate of inflation averaged 6.4% in 1990–97; consumer prices increased by an average of 13.9% in 1995, by 4.7% in 1996 and by 1.5% in 1997. In the year to March 1998 average prices declined by 1.2%. An estimated 5.8% of the labour force were unemployed in mid-1985.

Cameroon is a member of the Central African organs of the Franc Zone (see p. 200), of the Communauté économique des états de l'Afrique centrale (CEEAC, see p. 290), of the International Cocoa Organization (see p. 287) and of the International Coffee Organization (see p. 287).

The devaluation of the CFA franc in January 1994 (by 50% in relation to the French franc) resulted in an immediate increase in economic hardship, but also in an increase in real growth. An increase in international prices for Cameroon's major export commodities contributed to an improvement in economic conditions in 1995–96, while a number of structural reforms were implemented in compliance with IMF requirements. In August 1997 the IMF approved a three-year loan for Cameroon, equivalent to about US $221m., as an Enhanced Structural Adjustment Facility (ESAF). The 1997/98 and 1998/99 programmes supported a series of macroeconomic reforms, which contributed to increased economic activity and reduced inflation rates. The 1999/2000 programme, supported by the third of the three annual loans, sought to continue the process of reform, to limit the annual rate of inflation to 2% and to contain the external current account deficit to 3.5% of GDP. Cameroon's key budgetary objectives were to achieve a primary surplus equivalent to 5.2% of GDP and to reduce the overall fiscal deficit to 2.9% of GDP. It was hoped that higher economic growth would permit increased spending on the priority sectors of health, education and poverty alleviation. None the less, fraud and corruption remained a hindrance to the development of Cameroon, as did the country's poor physical infrastructure.

## Social Welfare

The Government and Christian missions maintain hospitals and medical centres. In the early 1990s there were three central hospitals in Cameroon, 73 general hospitals, 46 private hospitals and 792 health centres (112 of which were privately owned). There were also 49 maternal and child health centres, and 11 centres for the treatment of leprosy. At that time Cameroon had 28,000 hospital beds, 618 physicians and 135 pharmacists. A long-term national health development plan was inaugurated in April 1999 for the period 1999–2008. The main aims of the plan were to rehabilitate Cameroon's 135 health districts and to secure their financing, and to curb the infection rate of the human immunodeficiency virus (HIV). Expenditure on health by the central Government in 1996/97 was an estimated 30,100m. francs CFA (3.8% of total spending).

### Education

Since independence, Cameroon has achieved one of the highest rates of school attendance in Africa, but provision of educational facilities varies according to region. Education, which is bilingual, is provided by the Government, missionary societies and private concerns. Education in state schools is available free of charge, and the Government provides financial assistance for other schools.

Primary education begins at six years of age. It lasts for six years in Eastern Cameroon (where it is officially compulsory), and for seven years in Western Cameroon. Secondary education, beginning at the age of 12 or 13, lasts for a further seven years, comprising two cycles of four years and three years in Eastern Cameroon and five years and two years in Western Cameroon. In 1994 primary enrolment was equivalent to 88% of children in the appropriate age-group (males 93%; females 84%), while enrolment at secondary schools was equivalent to only 27% (males 32%; females 22%). In 1995, according to estimates by UNESCO, the average rate of adult illiteracy was 36.6% (males 25.0%; females 47.9%). Expenditure on education by the central Government in 1996/97 was an estimated 93,600m. francs CFA (11.8% of total spending).

### Public Holidays

**2000:** 1 January (New Year), 8 January*† (Djoulde Soumae, end of Ramadan), 11 February (Youth Day), 16 March* (Festival of Sheep), 21 April (Good Friday), 24 April (Easter Monday), 1 May (Labour Day), 20 May (National Day), 1 June (Ascension Day), 15 August (Assumption), 25 December (Christmas), 28 December*† (Djoulde Soumae, end of Ramadan).

**2001:** 1 January (New Year), 11 February (Youth Day), 6 March* (Festival of Sheep), 13 April (Good Friday), 16 April (Easter Monday), 1 May (Labour Day), 20 May (National Day), 24 May (Ascension Day), 15 August (Assumption), 17 December* (Djoulde Soumae, end of Ramadan), 25 December (Christmas).

* These holidays are dependent on the Islamic lunar calendar and may vary by one or two days from the dates given.

† This festival will occur twice (in the Islamic years AH 1420 and AH 1421) within the same Gregorian year.

### Weights and Measures

The metric system is in force.

# Statistical Survey

Source (unless otherwise stated): Direction de la Prévision, Ministère de l'Economie et des Finances, BP 18, Yaoundé; tel. 23-40-40; fax 23-21-50.

## Area and Population

**AREA, POPULATION AND DENSITY**

| | |
|---|---|
| Area (sq km) | 475,442* |
| Population (census results) | |
| 9 April 1976† | 7,663,246 |
| 9 April 1987 | |
| Males | 5,162,878 |
| Females | 5,330,777 |
| Total | 10,493,655 |
| Population (official estimates at mid-year) | |
| 1997 | 14,044,000 |
| 1998 | 14,439,000 |
| 1999 | 14,859,000 |
| Density (per sq km) at mid-1999 | 31.3 |

* 183,569 sq miles.

† Including an adjustment for underenumeration, estimated at 7.4%. The enumerated total was 7,090,115.

**PROVINCES** (population at 1987 census)

| | Urban | Rural | Total |
|---|---|---|---|
| Centre | 877,481 | 774,119 | 1,651,600 |
| Littoral | 1,093,323 | 259,510 | 1,352,833 |
| West | 431,337 | 908,454 | 1,339,791 |
| South-West | 258,940 | 579,102 | 838,042 |
| North-West | 271,114 | 966,234 | 1,237,348 |
| North | 234,572 | 597,593 | 832,165 |
| East | 152,787 | 364,411 | 517,198 |
| South | 104,023 | 269,775 | 373,798 |
| Adamaoua | 178,644 | 316,541 | 495,185 |
| Far North | 366,698 | 1,488,997 | 1,855,695 |
| **Total** | 3,968,919 | 6,524,736 | 10,493,655 |

**PRINCIPAL TOWNS** (population at 1987 census)

| | | | |
|---|---|---|---|
| Douala | 810,000 | Bamenda | 110,000 |
| Yaoundé (capital) | 649,000 | Nkongsamba | 85,420 |
| Garoua | 142,000 | Kumba | 70,112 |
| Maroua | 123,000 | Limbé | 44,561 |
| Bafoussam | 113,000 | | |

**1999** (estimated population, '000): Douala 1,448.3; Yaoundé 1,372.8 (Source: MINPAT, *Indicateurs démographiques sur le Cameroun*).

**BIRTHS AND DEATHS** (official estimates, annual averages)

| | 1987–92 | 1993–97 | 1998–2000 |
|---|---|---|---|
| Birth rate (per 1,000) | 41.7 | 39.7 | 38.2 |
| Death rate (per 1,000) | 12.8 | 11.4 | 10.1 |

**Expectation of life** (official estimates, years at birth, 1998–2000): 59.0 (males 56.7; females 61.3).

Source: MINPAT, *Indicateurs démographiques sur le Cameroun.*

**ECONOMICALLY ACTIVE POPULATION**
(official estimates, persons aged six years and over, mid-1985)

| | Males | Females | Total |
|---|---|---|---|
| Agriculture, hunting, forestry and fishing | 1,574,946 | 1,325,925 | 2,900,871 |
| Mining and quarrying | 1,693 | 100 | 1,793 |
| Manufacturing | 137,671 | 36,827 | 174,498 |
| Electricity, gas and water | 3,373 | 149 | 3,522 |
| Construction | 65,666 | 1,018 | 66,684 |
| Trade, restaurants and hotels | 115,269 | 38,745 | 154,014 |
| Transport, storage and communications | 50,664 | 1,024 | 51,688 |
| Financing, insurance, real estate and business services | 7,447 | 562 | 8,009 |
| Community, social and personal services | 255,076 | 37,846 | 292,922 |
| Activities not adequately defined | 18,515 | 17,444 | 35,959 |
| **Total in employment** | 2,230,320 | 1,459,640 | 3,689,960 |
| Unemployed | 180,016 | 47,659 | 227,675 |
| **Total labour force** | 2,410,336 | 1,507,299 | 3,917,635 |

Source: ILO, *Yearbook of Labour Statistics*.

**Mid-1998** (estimates in '000): Agriculture, etc. 3,585; Total labour force 5,816 (Source: FAO, *Production Yearbook*).

# Agriculture

**PRINCIPAL CROPS** ('000 metric tons)

| | 1996 | 1997 | 1998 |
|---|---|---|---|
| Rice (paddy) | 54 | 55† | 55† |
| Maize | 750 | 600† | 600† |
| Millet | 71 | 71† | 71† |
| Sorghum | 439 | 400* | 500* |
| Potatoes | 35 | 35† | 35† |
| Sweet potatoes† | 250 | 250 | 220 |
| Cassava (Manioc)† | 1,700 | 1,700 | 1,500 |
| Yams† | 130 | 130 | 130 |
| Other roots and tubers | 600 | 600† | 550† |
| Dry beans† | 95 | 91 | 91 |
| Groundnuts (in shell) | 171 | 90* | 170† |
| Sesame seed† | 16 | 16 | 16 |
| Cottonseed | 72* | 48* | 80† |
| Palm kernels* | 62 | 58 | 58 |
| Tomatoes | 60 | 60† | 60† |
| Onions (dry) | 20 | 20† | 20† |
| Other vegetables | 413 | 423† | 433† |
| Sugar cane† | 1,350 | 1,350 | 1,350 |
| Avocados† | 45 | 45 | 45 |
| Pineapples | 48 | 48† | 48† |
| Bananas | 986 | 986† | 986† |
| Plantains† | 1,000 | 1,030 | 1,030 |
| Other fruit | 105 | 105† | 105† |
| Coffee (green) | 53 | 92* | 102* |
| Cocoa beans | 126 | 127* | 130* |
| Tea (made) | 4 | 4† | 4† |
| Tobacco (leaves) | 2 | 2† | 2† |
| Cotton lint | 79 | 75* | 61* |
| Natural rubber | 53 | 54† | 54† |

* Unofficial figure(s). † FAO estimate(s).

Source: FAO, *Production Yearbook*.

**LIVESTOCK** (FAO estimates, '000 head, year ending September)

| | 1996 | 1997 | 1998 |
|---|---|---|---|
| Horses | 15 | 15 | 15 |
| Asses | 36 | 36 | 36 |
| Cattle | 5,500 | 5,700 | 5,900 |
| Pigs | 1,410 | 1,410 | 1,410 |
| Sheep | 3,800 | 3,800 | 3,800 |
| Goats | 3,800 | 3,800 | 3,800 |

Poultry (FAO estimates, million): 20 in 1996; 20 in 1997; 20 in 1998.

Source: FAO, *Production Yearbook*.

**LIVESTOCK PRODUCTS** (FAO estimates, '000 metric tons)

| | 1996 | 1997 | 1998 |
|---|---|---|---|
| Beef and veal | 85 | 88 | 90 |
| Mutton and lamb | 16 | 16 | 16 |
| Goat meat | 14 | 14 | 14 |
| Pig meat | 18 | 18 | 18 |
| Poultry meat | 20 | 20 | 20 |
| Other meat | 47 | 46 | 46 |
| Cows' milk | 125 | 125 | 125 |
| Sheep's milk | 17 | 17 | 17 |
| Goats' milk | 42 | 42 | 42 |
| Poultry eggs | 13 | 13 | 13 |
| Honey | 3 | 3 | 3 |
| Cattle hides | 12 | 13 | 13 |
| Sheepskins | 3 | 3 | 3 |
| Goatskins | 1 | 1 | 1 |

Source: FAO, *Production Yearbook*.

# Forestry

**ROUNDWOOD REMOVALS** ('000 cubic metres, excl. bark)

| | 1995 | 1996 | 1997 |
|---|---|---|---|
| Sawlogs, veneer logs and logs for sleepers | 2,447 | 2,447 | 2,447 |
| Other industrial wood | 889 | 913 | 939 |
| Fuel wood | 12,335 | 12,648 | 12,970 |
| **Total** | 15,671 | 16,008 | 16,356 |

Source: FAO, *Yearbook of Forest Products*.

**SAWNWOOD PRODUCTION**
(FAO estimates, '000 cubic metres, incl. railway sleepers)

| | 1995 | 1996 | 1997 |
|---|---|---|---|
| **Total** (all broadleaved) | 1,400 | 1,400 | 1,400 |

Source: FAO, *Yearbook of Forest Products*.

# Fishing

('000 metric tons, live weight)

| | 1995 | 1996 | 1997* |
|---|---|---|---|
| Freshwater fishes* | 21.0 | 23.0 | 25.0 |
| Croakers and drums | 10.8 | 10.5 | 10.5 |
| Threadfins and tasselfishes | 2.2 | 2.0 | 2.0 |
| Sardinellas | 24.0 | 24.0 | 24.0 |
| Bonga shad | 24.0 | 24.0 | 24.0 |
| Other marine fishes (incl. unspecified) | 3.2 | 3.0 | 3.1 |
| **Total fish*** | 85.2 | 86.5 | 88.5 |
| Crustaceans and molluscs | 0.5 | 0.5 | 0.5 |
| **Total catch*** | 85.7 | 87.0 | 89.0 |

* FAO estimates.

Source: FAO, *Yearbook of Fishery Statistics*.

Affairs left the Government, following his admission of a 'technical breach' of ethical guidelines in the conduct of government business. In the same month, the Chief of Staff of the Armed Forces relinquished his post, following an inquiry into alleged attempts to suppress information concerning the maltreatment of a Somalian civilian by Canadian troops participating in the United Nations peace-keeping mission in Somalia in 1993.

The question of land treaty claims by Canada's indigenous peoples came to prominence during the early 1990s, when disputes over land rights arose in Ontario, Manitoba and, most notably, Québec, where armed confrontations took place in 1990 between the civil authorities and militant indigenous groups. During the 1980s debate began to intensify in the formulation of a new constitutional status for the NWT, in which a population of only 58,000 (of which Inuit and other indigenous peoples comprised about one-half) occupied an area comprising one-third of Canada's land mass. In November 1982 the Federal Government agreed in principle to implement the decision of a territorial referendum held in April, in which 56% of the voters approved a division of the NWT. Proposals to replace the NWT with two self-governing units: Nunavut (to the east of a proposed boundary running northwards from the Saskatchewan-Manitoba border), and a second newly-constituted territory to the west), were approved by the NWT legislature in January 1987 and were endorsed in May 1992 by a plebiscite among NWT residents. In December 1991 specific terms for the creation of a semi-autonomous Nunavut Territory, covering an area of 2.2m. sq km, were agreed by Inuit representatives and the Federal Government. In September 1988, following 13 years of negotiations, the Federal Government formally transferred to indigenous ownership an area covering 673,000 sq km in the NWT. In the Yukon Territory, an area of 41,000 sq km (representing 8.6% of the Territory's land) was transferred to indigenous control.

In April 1991 the Federal Government undertook that all outstanding land treaty claims would be resolved by the year 2000. A formal agreement to this effect was finalized in May 1993, providing for Nunavut and a second territory, as yet unnamed, to come into official existence on 1 April 1999. In October 1997 the NWT Government recommended that the Federal Government approve the establishment of a 17-seat Legislature for Nunavut, to be located at Iqaluit. Elections to the new Legislature were held in February 1999, and the new Territorial Government took office in April. It was announced in November that inhabitants of the residual area of the NWT would be balloted on the choice of a new name for the territory.

In November 1996 an official inquiry into the social and economic condition of Canada's indigenous peoples recommended the creation of a new chamber of the Federal Parliament to function as a permanent commission to review issues affecting the indigenous groups, and that these communities receive increased powers of self-government. In December 1997 the Supreme Court awarded legal title to 57,000 sq km of ancestral land to two native groups in British Columbia, and in the following month the Federal Government offered a formal apology to all native groups for past mistreatment and injustices. The principle of 'aboriginal title', established by the Supreme Court ruling, was again exercised in April 1999 with the transfer, together with substantial powers of self-government, of a further 2,000 sq km of land to native ownership in British Columbia.

During his period in office, Mulroney sought to re-establish Canada's traditional 'special relationship' with the USA, which had operated until the Trudeau period. There was considerable support in Canada for efforts by the Government to secure effective control by the USA of the emission of gases from industrial plants, which move northwards into Canada to produce environmentally destructive 'acid rain'. In 1986 a joint US-Canadian governmental commission recommended the implementation of a US $5,000m. anti-pollution programme, to be financed jointly by the US Government and the relevant industries. The Canadian Government itself proceeded with a programme costing an estimated C $128,000m. to achieve the reduction by 20% of acid-pollution emissions from domestic sources by the year 2005. These aims were extended by a new environmental programme announced in December 1990, under which the Government was to spend a total of C $3,000m. on a range of environmental improvement measures. These sought to reduce air pollution by 40% over a 10-year period, while stabilizing carbon dioxide emissions at 1990 levels by the end of the century. In addition, work was to be undertaken to eliminate industrial pollution from the Great Lakes and other waterways. Financial provision was also made for contributions to projects seeking to stem global warming, and to reduce emissions of carbon dioxide and other gases that have a warming effect on the atmosphere ('greenhouse gases'). In March 1991 the US and Canadian Governments reached a formal agreement under which US industries were to contribute financially to measures reducing acid rain pollution. In the same year, Canada, with the USA and 23 European countries, signed an international treaty on cross-border pollution control, under which the signatories undertook to prevent, reduce and control environmental degradation caused by industrial activity. In June 1994 Canada joined 25 European countries in signing a UN protocol on the reduction of sulphur emissions, which the Canadian Government undertook to reduce by 30% over a six-year period. A further agreement with the USA on the reduction of industrial pollution was signed in April 1997. In December, at the third Conference of the Parties to the Framework Convention on Climate Change (see UN Environment Programme, p. 47), held in Kyoto, Japan, Canada undertook to implement reductions of its emissions of 'greenhouse gases' to 6% below 1990 levels by the year 2012. Canada assumed a leading role in the establishment, with seven other circumpolar countries, of the Arctic Council (see p. 290), which commenced operation in September 1996. The aims of the Council include the protection of the environment of the polar region, the formation of co-ordinated policies governing its future, and the safeguarding of the interests of its indigenous population groups.

Relations between the USA and Canada came under strain in August and September 1985, when a US coastguard ice-breaker traversed the Northwest Passage without seeking prior permission from Canada, in assertion of long-standing US claims that the channels within this 1.6m. sq km tract of ice-bound islands are international waters. The Canadian Government declared sovereignty of this area as from 1 January 1986, and in January 1988 the USA recognized Canadian jurisdiction over the Arctic islands (but not over their waters) and undertook to notify the Canadian Government in advance of all Arctic passages by US surface vessels. There have also been recurrent disagreements between Canada and France concerning the boundary of disputed waters near the French-controlled islands of St Pierre and Miquelon, off the southern coast of Newfoundland. In June 1992 an international arbitration tribunal presented its report, generally regarded as favourable to Canada, on this dispute. It was reported in December 1994 that the two countries had agreed a 10-year accord on the allocation of fishing rights around the islands.

In December 1992 Canada and the EC (European Community, now European Union—EU) announced the resolution of a seven-year disagreement over the allocation of fishing rights to European commercial fleets in the north-west Atlantic Ocean. In 1994, however, the EU unilaterally awarded itself almost 70% of the internationally agreed quota of Greenland halibut (also sometimes known as turbot) caught in the north-west Atlantic fishing grounds. This action was not recognized by other members of the Northwest Atlantic Fishing Organization (NAFO), and was vigorously contested by the Canadian Government, which declared that it would act to prevent EU fishing trawlers (principally from Spain and Portugal) from overfishing the already seriously depleted stocks of Greenland halibut. It was also announced that Canada was extending its maritime jurisdiction beyond its Exclusive Economic Zone (EEZ), already extending 200 nautical miles (370 km) from the coastline. This action was rejected by the EU as contrary to international law.

In February 1995 the Canadian Government formally notified the EU that its fishing fleets would not be permitted to increase their Greenland halibut catches in the Grand Banks, off the eastern coast of Canada, and warned that force would be used if necessary to ensure that total catches by EU vessels did not exceed 3,400 tons of the NAFO-agreed world Greenland halibut quota of 27,000 tons. On 6 March the Canadian Government declared a 60-day moratorium on all trawling for this fish in the north-west Atlantic, and three days later its enforcement vessels fired on and impounded a Spanish trawler fishing in international waters. The EU responded by suspending all official political contacts with Canada, pending the release of the trawler, and the Spanish Government responded by instituting proceedings against Canada in the International Court of Justice (ICJ). The impasse was eased by the release of the trawler on 15 March, when it was agreed to initiate quota allocation negotiations. In late March, however, a further three

Spanish vessels were prevented by the Canadian coast guard from fishing in international waters. Divisions began to emerge within the EU when the British Government refused to endorse an EU protest against these interceptions, and declared its support of Canada's desire to conserve north-west Atlantic fishing stocks. The progress of negotiations was impeded by further confrontations in April between Spanish trawlers and Canadian enforcement vessels, and by dissident views expressed within the EU by Britain and Denmark. A resolution was eventually reached in mid-April, under which Canada and EU countries each agreed to accept 41% of the 1996 Greenland halibut quota. Canada undertook to cease further seizures of vessels in international waters, and it was agreed that independent observers would monitor the activities of trawlers in the north-west Atlantic fishing zone. However, during the negotiation of an accord in June 1996 governing bilateral relations between Canada and the EU, the Canadian Government rejected a request by Spain that it suspend the enforcement of its fishing regulations outside Canadian territorial waters. In December 1998 the ICJ accepted the contention by Canada that it had no jurisdiction to deal with the complaint by Spain over the trawler incident in 1995.

Canada, which maintains significant economic and commercial links with Cuba and operates a policy of 'constructive engagement' in its relations with that country, adopted a prominent role in international opposition to efforts, initiated by the US Government in March 1996, to penalize investors whose business in any way involves property in Cuba that was confiscated from US citizens following the 1959 revolution. The imposition of these measures, known as the Helms-Burton Act, led in July 1996 to the exclusion from the USA of nine Canadian businessmen involved in nickel-mining operations in Cuba. The Canadian Government responded by introducing legislation prohibiting Canadian companies from compliance with the Helms-Burton Act, and refused to recognize foreign court rulings arising from the Act, or to assist in the enforcement of judgments obtained against Canadian businesses under the Act. With Mexico, which also conducts significant trade with Cuba, Canada co-ordinated a joint challenge to the US Government through NAFTA dispute procedures. In November 1996 Canada actively promoted a resolution by the UN General Assembly condemning the US trade sanctions against Cuba, and in the same month joined the EU in a complaint against the embargo to the World Trade Organization. In late 1997 the Canadian Government protested to the USA over its penalization of a Canadian petroleum company with business interests in Iran. In April 1998, following an official visit to Cuba by Chrétien, the Canadian Government signed a series of co-operation agreements with Cuba. However, relations between the two countries subsequently experienced a sharp decline, owing to increasing official and public concern in Canada at the Cuban Government's human rights record, particularly in relation to the treatment of political prisoners. In July 1999 the Canadian Government stated that it would implement no further assistance programmes to Cuba that did not clearly further the protection of human rights, and it was indicated that Canada would not support, or encourage other countries to support, the admission of Cuba to the Organization of American States (see p. 245). In June 1999, however, relations with the USA were improved following the resolution of a long-standing disagreement over the demarcation of salmon-fishing rights off the Pacific coast.

During the mid-1990s Canada actively sought to obtain an international ban on the manufacture and use of land-mines. At a conference held in Ottawa in December 1997, Canada became the first signatory of a treaty, agreed by 121 countries, undertaking to discontinue the use of these armaments and providing for the destruction of existing stockpiles. However, by early 2000 the USA, Russia and the People's Republic of China had not become parties to the agreement. Humanitarian concerns remained at the forefront of Canadian foreign policy during 1999: in May the Government contributed forces to the NATO peace-keeping operations in Kosovo, and a contingent of troops was sent to East Timor in September. In October the Canadian Minister of Foreign Affairs led a Commonwealth delegation to Pakistan to seek the restoration of democratic government following a military coup.

## Government

Canada is a federal parliamentary state. Under the Constitution Act 1982, executive power is vested in the British monarch, as Head of State, and exercisable by her representative, the Governor-General, whom she appoints on the advice of the Canadian Prime Minister. The Federal Parliament comprises the Head of State, a nominated Senate (a maximum of 112 members, appointed on a regional basis) and a House of Commons (301 members, elected by universal adult suffrage for single-member constituencies). A Parliament may last no longer than five years. The Governor-General appoints the Prime Minister and, on the latter's recommendation, other ministers to form the Cabinet. The Prime Minister should have the confidence of the House of Commons, to which the Cabinet is responsible. Canada comprises 10 provinces (each with a Lieutenant-Governor and a legislature, which may last no longer than five years, from which a Premier is chosen), and three territories constituted by Act of Parliament.

## Defence

Canada co-operates with the USA in the defence of North America and is a member of NATO. Military service is voluntary. In August 1999 the armed forces numbered 60,600: army 20,900, navy 9,000, air force 15,000, and 15,700 not identified by service. The Federal Government's defence expenditure for 1998/99 was budgeted at C $9,700m.

## Economic Affairs

In 1997, according to estimates by the World Bank, Canada's gross national product (GNP), measured at average 1995–97 prices, was US $594,976m., equivalent to US $19,640 per head. Between 1990 and 1997, it was estimated, GNP per head increased, in real terms, at an average rate of 0.8% per year. Over the same period, the population increased at an average annual rate of 1.2%. According to preliminary estimates, GNP in 1998 was about US $612,200m. (US $20,020 per head). Canada's gross domestic product (GDP) increased, in real terms, at an average rate of 2.2% per year in 1990–98; GDP increased by 1.7% in 1996, by 4.0% in 1997 and by 3.1% in 1998.

Agriculture (including forestry and fishing) contributed 2.4% of GDP (in constant 1992 prices), and engaged 3.7% of the labour force, in 1998. The principal crops are wheat, barley and other cereals, which, together with livestock production (chiefly cattle and pigs) and timber, provide an important source of export earnings. Canada is a leading world exporter of forest products and of fish and seafood. The production of furs is also important. In real terms, the GDP of the agricultural sector increased at an average annual rate of 1.5% in 1980–90, but declined by 4.4% in 1991 and by 5.0% in 1992. It rose, however, by 6.7% in 1993 and by 3.9% in 1994. Agricultural GDP declined by 0.3% in 1997 and by 0.4% in 1998.

Industry (including mining, manufacturing, construction and power) provided 30.5% of GDP (in constant 1992 prices), and employed 22.2% of the labour force, in 1998. Industrial GDP increased, in real terms, at an average annual rate of 2.9% during 1980–90, but declined by 4.8% in 1991 and by 0.1% in 1992. It rose by 3.3% in 1993 and by 6.3% in 1994. Industrial GDP increased by 5.4% in 1997 and by 2.2% in 1998.

Mining provided 3.9% of GDP (in constant 1992 prices), but employed only 1.3% of the labour force, in 1998. Canada is a major world producer of zinc, asbestos, nickel, potash and uranium. Gold, silver, iron, copper, cobalt and lead are also exploited. There are considerable reserves of petroleum and natural gas in Alberta, off the Atlantic coast and in the Canadian Arctic islands. The GDP of the mining sector increased, in real terms, at an average rate of 1.3% per year during 1980–90, and by 3.8% per year in 1990–94. It rose by 6.3% in 1994. Mining GDP increased by 4.1% in 1997, but declined by 0.3% in 1998.

Manufacturing contributed 17.8% of GDP (in constant 1992 prices), and employed 14.6% of the labour force, in 1998. The principal branches of manufacturing in 1995, measured by the value of output, were transport equipment (accounting for 22.9% of the total), food products (11.6%), paper and allied products (7.0%), chemical products (7.0%), electrical and electronic products (6.8%) and primary metal industries (6.5%). The GDP of the sector increased, in real terms, at an average rate of 2.1% per year in 1980–90, but declined by 7.1% in 1991. It rose by 1.3% in 1992, by 4.8% in 1993 and by 7.0% in 1994. Manufacturing GDP increased by 6.5% in 1997 and by 3.9% in 1998.

Energy is derived principally from hydroelectric power (which provided 67% of the electricity supply in 1985) and from coal-fired and nuclear power stations. Canada is an important source of US energy supplies, accounting in 1989 for 7.0% of the USA's requirements of natural gas and for 5.0% of its petroleum imports. In 1998 energy products accounted for 7.4% of Canada's exports and 2.9% of imports.

Services engaged 71.1% of the labour force, and provided 67.1% of GDP (in constant 1992 prices), in 1998. The combined GDP of the service sectors increased, in real terms, at an average rate of 3.1% per year in 1980–90, but declined by 0.2% in 1991. It rose by 1.2% in 1992, by 2.1% in 1993 and by 3.2% in 1994. Services GDP increased by 3.6% in 1997 and by 3.2% in 1998.

In 1998 Canada recorded a visible trade surplus of US $12,625m., but there was a deficit of US $11,213m. on the current account of the balance of payments. In 1998 the USA accounted for 85.1% of Canada's total exports and 68.2% of total imports; the European Union (EU, see p. 172) and Japan were also important trading partners. The principal exports in that year were machinery and equipment, motor vehicles and parts and industrial goods. The principal imports were motor vehicle parts, passenger vehicles and computers. In January 1989 a free-trade agreement with the USA entered into force, whereby virtually all remaining trade tariffs imposed between the two countries were to be eliminated over a 10-year period. Negotiations with the USA and Mexico, aimed at the eventual creation of a full North American free-trade area, began in 1991 and concluded in December 1992 with the signing of an agreement. Following its formal ratification in December 1993, the North American Free Trade Agreement (NAFTA, see p. 225) entered into operation on 1 January 1994. Since the implementation of NAFTA, however, disagreements have persisted between Canada and the USA over alleged violations of the Agreement by the US Government in relation to bilateral trade in softwood lumber, wheat and other commodities. Since the mid-1990s the Canadian Government has implemented measures aimed at expanding trade in the Far East, notably with the People's Republic of China, the Republic of Korea, Indonesia and Viet Nam. In November 1996 Canada finalized a trade agreement with Chile, which will, with effect from June 1997, phase out most customs duties by 2002. In October 1998 negotiations began with the members of the European Free Trade Association (EFTA, see p. 291) for the creation of a free-trade area, while Canada has also pursued efforts to develop similar arrangements with the EU.

In the financial year ending 31 March 1998 there was a federal budget surplus of C $5,339m. The annual rate of inflation averaged 1.9% in 1990–98. Consumer prices increased by an average of 1.6% in 1997 and by 1.0% in 1998. The rate of unemployment exceeded 10% of the labour force in each of the years between 1991 and 1994, declining to 9.5% in 1995 and rising to 9.7% in 1996. It averaged 9.1% in 1997 and 8.3% in 1998. The rate of unemployment stood at 6.9% in November 1999, its lowest rate since March 1990.

Many sectors of Canadian industry rely heavily on foreign investment. Following the international recession of the mid-1970s, Canada's economy experienced inflationary pressures and, despite anti-inflationary measures (including the imposition of high interest rates), the average annual rate of inflation remained above 4% throughout the 1980s. A series of budgetary deficits were attributable largely to high interest rates, which continued into the early 1990s, to the detriment of a sustained economic recovery. The persistence of substantial budgetary deficits both at federal and provincial level, together with political uncertainties surrounding the future of Québec, necessitated further rises in interest levels during 1994, despite the achievement at mid-year of a negative rate of inflation. Deflationary measures in the 1995/96 budget included a decrease of 4% in federal government allocations to provincial governments for the provision of social and welfare services. The 1996/97 budget imposed additional restraints on government spending and imposed further reductions on foreign borrowing, which were retained as government policy in the budget for 1997/98. However, following the economy's strong revival in 1997/98 and 1998/99, proposals for the 1999/2000 budget, announced in February 1999, included provisions for increased expenditure on health care and for reductions in personal rates of taxation, while achieving a budgetary surplus for the second successive year. The Government indicated that it intended to retain a target annual inflation rate of 1%–3%, announced in February 1998, to December 2001. The Government's emphasis on fiscal stringency led, in part, in August 1996 to the country's first current-account surplus in the balance of payments since 1984. This recovery was further aided by low rates of domestic inflation and by the beneficial effects of NAFTA on Canadian export sales to the USA. The Canadian economy, however, remains vulnerable to adverse movements in world prices for its major exports of raw materials.

### Social Welfare

The Federal Government administers family allowances, unemployment insurance and pensions. Other services are provided by the provinces. A federal medical care insurance programme covers all Canadians against medical expenses, and a federal-provincial hospital insurance programme covers over 99% of the insurable population. In 1994/95 there were 978 hospitals, with a total of 156,547 beds. Of total budgetary expenditure by the Federal Government in the financial year 1998/99, C $1,607m. (1.0%) was for health, and a further C $49,570m. (30.0%) for social services. In addition, substantial welfare payments are made by social security funds under federal government control. Expenditure by the governments of the provinces and territories in 1994/95 included C $45,987m. (25.9% of the total) for health services.

### Education

Education policy is a provincial responsibility, and the period of compulsory school attendance varies. French-speaking students are entitled by law, in some provinces, to instruction in French. Primary education is from the age of five or six years to 13–14, followed by three to five years at secondary or high school. In 1994 an estimated 95% of children aged six to 11 years (males 96%; females 94%) attended primary schools, while 92% of those aged 12 to 17 (males 92%; females 91%) were enrolled at secondary schools. In 1997/98 there were 76 universities and 195 other institutions of post-secondary education. Federal government budgetary expenditure on education totalled C $3,731m. (2.3% of total spending) in 1998/99, compared with C $3,366m. (2.1%) in 1997/98. Expenditure on education by provincial and territorial governments was C $31,284m. (17.6% of total spending) in 1994/95.

### Public Holidays*

**2000:** 1 January (New Year's Day), 21 April (Good Friday), 24 April (Easter Monday), 22 May (Victoria Day), 1 July (Canada Day), 4 September (Labour Day), 9 October (Thanksgiving Day), 11 November (Remembrance Day), 25 December (Christmas Day), 26 December (Boxing Day).

**2001:** 1 January (New Year's Day), 13 April (Good Friday), 16 April (Easter Monday), 21 May (Victoria Day), 1 July (Canada Day), 3 September (Labour Day), 8 October (Thanksgiving Day), 11 November (Remembrance Day), 25 December (Christmas Day), 26 December (Boxing Day).

*Standard public holidays comprise the listed days, together with any other day so proclaimed by individual provinces.

### Weights and Measures

The metric system is in force.

# Statistical Survey

Source (unless otherwise stated): Statistics Canada, Ottawa, ON K1A 0T6; tel. (613) 951-8116; fax (613) 951-0581; internet www.statcan.ca.

## Area and Population

**AREA, POPULATION AND DENSITY**

| | |
|---|---|
| Area (sq km) | |
| Land | 9,203,210 |
| Inland water | 755,109 |
| Total | 9,958,319* |
| Population (census results)† | |
| 4 June 1991 | 27,296,860 |
| 14 May 1996 | |
| Males | 14,170,030 |
| Females | 14,676,735 |
| Total | 28,846,761 |
| Population (official estimates at 1 July) | |
| 1996 | 29,671,892 |
| 1997 | 30,010,974 |
| 1998 | 30,301,185 |
| Density (per sq km) at 1 July 1998 | 3.0 |

* 3,844,928 sq miles.

† Excluding census data for one or more incompletely enumerated Indian reserves or Indian settlements. The overall extent of underenumeration at the 1991 census was estimated to be 2.8%.

**PROVINCES AND TERRITORIES** (census results, 14 May 1996)

| | Land area (sq km) | Population* | Capital |
|---|---|---|---|
| Provinces: | | | |
| Alberta | 638,233 | 2,696,826 | Edmonton |
| British Columbia | 892,677 | 3,724,500 | Victoria |
| Manitoba | 547,704 | 1,113,898 | Winnipeg |
| New Brunswick | 71,569 | 738,133 | Fredericton |
| Newfoundland | 371,635 | 551,792 | St John's |
| Nova Scotia | 52,841 | 909,282 | Halifax |
| Ontario | 916,734 | 10,753,573 | Toronto |
| Prince Edward Island | 5,660 | 134,557 | Charlottetown |
| Québec | 1,357,812 | 7,138,795 | Québec |
| Saskatchewan | 570,113 | 990,237 | Regina |
| Territories: | | | |
| Northwest Territories | 1,004,471 | 39,672 | Yellowknife |
| Nunavut Territory† | 2,241,919 | 24,730 | Iqaluit |
| Yukon Territory | 531,844 | 30,766 | Whitehorse |
| **Total** | 9,203,210 | 28,846,761 | — |

* Excluding census data for one or more incompletely enumerated Indian reserves or Indian settlements.

† Formerly part of Northwest Territories. Constituted as a separate Territory with effect from 1 April 1999.

**PRINCIPAL METROPOLITAN AREAS** (census results, 14 May 1996)

| | | | |
|---|---|---|---|
| Toronto | 4,263,757 | London | 398,616 |
| Montréal* | 3,326,510 | Kitchener | 382,940 |
| Vancouver | 1,831,665 | St Catharines-Niagara | 372,406 |
| Ottawa (capital) | 1,010,498† | Halifax | 332,518 |
| Edmonton* | 862,597 | Victoria* | 304,287 |
| Calgary* | 821,628 | Windsor | 278,685 |
| Québec | 671,889 | Oshawa | 268,773 |
| Winnipeg | 667,209 | Saskatoon | 219,056 |
| Hamilton | 624,360 | | |

* Excluding census data for one or more incompletely enumerated Indian reserves or Indian settlements.

† Including Hull.

**BIRTHS, MARRIAGES AND DEATHS**

| | Registered live births* | | Registered marriages | | Registered deaths* | |
|---|---|---|---|---|---|---|
| | Number | Rate (per 1,000) | Number | Rate (per 1,000) | Number | Rate (per 1,000) |
| 1990 | 405,486 | 14.6 | 187,737 | 6.8 | 191,973 | 6.9 |
| 1991 | 402,258 | 14.4 | 172,251 | 6.1 | 195,568 | 7.0 |
| 1992 | 398,642 | 14.0 | 164,573 | 5.8 | 196,535 | 6.8 |
| 1993 | 388,394 | 13.5 | 159,316 | 5.6 | 204,912 | 7.1 |
| 1994 | 385,112 | 13.3 | 159,959 | 5.5 | 207,077 | 7.1 |
| 1995 | 378,011 | 12.9 | 160,256 | 5.5 | 210,733 | 7.2 |
| 1996 | 366,189 | 12.3 | 156,691 | 5.3 | 212,859 | 7.2 |
| 1997 | 361,785 | 12.1 | 159,350 | 5.3 | 216,970 | 7.2 |

* Including Canadian residents temporarily in the USA but excluding US residents temporarily in Canada.

**Expectation of life** (years at birth, 1992): Males 74.6; Females 80.9 (Source: UN, *Demographic Yearbook*).

**IMMIGRATION**

| Country of Origin | 1996 | 1997 | 1998* |
|---|---|---|---|
| United Kingdom | 5,837 | 4,872 | 4,047 |
| USA | 5,846 | 5,069 | 4,550 |
| Other | 214,391 | 206,122 | 165,445 |
| **Total** | 226,074 | 216,063 | 174,042 |

* Preliminary.

**ECONOMICALLY ACTIVE POPULATION***
(annual averages, '000 persons aged 15 years and over)

| | 1996 | 1997 | 1998 |
|---|---|---|---|
| Agriculture, hunting, forestry and fishing | 597.0 | 572.2 | 585.7 |
| Mining and quarrying | 194.0 | 197.4 | 197.0 |
| Manufacturing | 2,134.8 | 2,190.6 | 2,282.6 |
| Utilities | 126.6 | 119.6 | 120.9 |
| Construction | 831.0 | 843.5 | 862.0 |
| Trade, restaurants and hotels | 3,244.9 | 3,254.9 | 3,297.3 |
| Transport and storage | 723.5 | 746.9 | 735.6 |
| Financing, insurance, real estate and business services | 2,132.5 | 2,223.9 | 2,341.0 |
| Community, social and personal services | 4,645.8 | 4,662.5 | 4,741.8 |
| Unclassified† | 515.3 | 542.6 | 467.6 |
| **Total labour force** | 15,145.4 | 15,354.0 | 15,631.5 |
| Males | 8,301.4 | 8,428.0 | 8,530.0 |
| Females | 6,844.0 | 6,926.0 | 7,101.5 |

* Figures exclude military personnel, inmates of institutions, residents of the Yukon and Northwest Territories, and Indian reserves. The data include unemployed persons, totalling (in '000): 1,469.2 in 1996; 1,413.5 in 1997; 1,305.1 in 1998.

† Referring to unemployed persons without previous work experience or those whose last activity was not adequately defined.

# Agriculture

**PRINCIPAL CROPS** ('000 metric tons)

| | 1996 | 1997 | 1998* |
|---|---|---|---|
| Wheat | 29,801.4 | 24,280.3 | 24,393.2 |
| Barley | 15,562.0 | 13,527.3 | 12,698.7 |
| Maize (Corn)† | 7,541.7 | 7,179.8 | 8,912.4 |
| Rye | 309.4 | 320.0 | 398.1 |
| Oats | 4,361.1 | 3,484.7 | 3,957.5 |
| Buckwheat | 22.2 | 16.5 | 14.8 |
| Mixed grain | 581.9 | 602.8 | 540.0 |
| Potatoes | 4,084.6 | 4,166.3 | 4,292.9 |
| Beans (dry) | 61.2 | 82.6 | 73.9 |
| Peas (dry) | 1,173.0 | 1,762.2 | 2,336.9 |
| Soybeans | 2,169.5 | 2,737.7 | 2,736.9 |
| Sunflower seed | 54.9 | 65.1 | 111.8 |
| Rapeseed (Canola) | 5,062.3 | 6,393.1 | 7,587.8 |
| Linseed | 851.0 | 895.4 | 1,106.2 |
| Mustard seed | 230.8 | 243.3 | 238.6 |
| Sugar beets | 1,034.2 | 635.0 | 880.6 |
| Tame hay | 28,025.0 | 20,865.0 | 21,436.6 |

* Preliminary.

† Maize for grain only, excluding fodder maize.

**LIVESTOCK** ('000 head at 1 July)

| | 1996 | 1997 | 1998* |
|---|---|---|---|
| Milch cows | 1,219.6 | 1,215.3 | 1,202.0 |
| Beef cattle | 4,763.2 | 4,638.4 | 4,555.1 |
| Sheep | 846.7 | 821.5 | 827.5 |
| Pigs | 11,543.0 | 11,668.0 | 12,445.0 |

* Preliminary.

**LIVESTOCK PRODUCTS**

| | 1996 | 1997 | 1998* |
|---|---|---|---|
| Beef and veal (metric tons) | 1,016,333 | 1,076,279 | 1,150,687 |
| Mutton and lamb (metric tons) | 10,671 | 10,031 | 9,813 |
| Pig meat (metric tons) | 1,227,763 | 1,256,696 | 1,338,236 |
| Poultry meat (metric tons) | 892,222 | 917,053 | 962,654 |
| Milk (kilolitres)† | 7,172,203 | 7,421,376 | 7,456,000 |
| Creamery butter (metric tons) | 93,174 | 89,537 | 85,935 |
| Cheddar cheese (metric tons) | 115,562 | 129,220 | 127,466 |
| Ice-cream mix (kilolitres) | 166,296 | 154,974 | 154,802 |
| Eggs ('000 dozen) | 484,914 | 494,269 | 498,847 |

* Preliminary. † Farm sales of milk and cream.

# Forestry

**ROUNDWOOD REMOVALS** (1995, '000 cubic metres)

| | Softwoods | Hard-woods | Total |
|---|---|---|---|
| Alberta | 14,068 | 6,219 | 20,287 |
| British Columbia | 72,331 | 2,129 | 74,460 |
| Manitoba | 1,695 | 292 | 1,987 |
| New Brunswick | 7,750 | 2,305 | 10,055 |
| Newfoundland | 2,824 | 160 | 2,983 |
| Nova Scotia | 4,858 | 625 | 5,483 |
| Ontario | 19,511 | 6,750 | 26,261 |
| Prince Edward Island | 490 | 148 | 638 |
| Québec | 31,719 | 9,961 | 41,680 |
| Saskatchewan | 2,724 | 1,534 | 4,258 |
| **Total** (incl. others) | 158,311 | 30,122 | 188,433 |

**SAWNWOOD PRODUCTION**
('000 cubic metres, incl. railway sleepers)

| | 1996 | 1997 | 1998 |
|---|---|---|---|
| Coniferous (softwood) | 63,898 | 65,008 | 65,090 |
| Broadleaved (hardwood) | 883 | 951 | 1,038 |
| **Total** | 64,781 | 65,959 | 66,129 |

# Fur Industry

**NUMBER OF PELTS PRODUCED**

| | 1995 | 1996 | 1997 |
|---|---|---|---|
| Newfoundland | 21,438 | 21,258 | n.a. |
| Prince Edward Island | 40,548 | 34,033 | 36,203 |
| Nova Scotia | 316,611 | 358,129 | 376,660 |
| New Brunswick | 61,272 | 72,809 | n.a. |
| Québec | 297,467 | 309,665 | 342,242 |
| Ontario | 596,385 | 724,021 | 695,895 |
| Manitoba | 169,206 | 238,427 | 250,786 |
| Saskatchewan | 136,764 | 204,123 | 189,594 |
| Alberta | 189,015 | 218,522 | n.a. |
| British Columbia | 206,667 | 188,122 | 228,378 |
| Northwest Territories | 33,800 | 46,801 | 55,429 |
| Yukon | 9,072 | 12,217 | 9,179 |
| **Total*** | 2,078,245 | 2,433,912 | 2,557,105 |

* Including ranch-raised.

# Fishing*

('000 metric tons, live weight)

| | 1995 | 1996 | 1997 |
|---|---|---|---|
| Pink salmon | 19.7 | 8.4 | 12.2 |
| Sockeye salmon | 10.5 | 10.5 | 25.3 |
| Atlantic cod | 12.4 | 15.5 | 29.8 |
| Atlantic redfishes | 18.0 | 21.6 | 18.8 |
| Capelin | 0.3 | 32.6 | 21.8 |
| Atlantic herring | 193.3 | 188.8 | 186.2 |
| Pacific herring | 27.0 | 22.1 | 31.6 |
| Atlantic mackerel | 17.8 | 21.0 | 21.3 |
| Queen crab | 65.4 | 65.8 | 71.4 |
| American lobster | 41.1 | 39.4 | 39.5 |
| Northern prawn | 30.2 | 31.3 | 48.3 |
| Pink shrimps | 24.4 | 24.1 | 28.6 |
| American sea scallop | 58.6 | 47.6 | 53.6 |
| Clams | 33.0 | 33.5 | 32.6 |
| **Total catch** (incl. others) | 868.0 | 901.2 | 944.6 |
| Inland waters | 38.2 | 39.6 | 39.1 |
| Atlantic Ocean | 591.2 | 630.0 | 679.3 |
| Pacific Ocean | 238.6 | 231.6 | 226.2 |

* Figures exclude aquatic mammals (whales, seals, etc.), aquatic plants and the products of fish-farming.

Source: FAO, *Yearbook of Fishery Statistics*.

# Mining

('000 metric tons, unless otherwise indicated)

| | 1996 | 1997 | 1998* |
|---|---|---|---|
| Metallic | | | |
| Bismuth (metric tons) | 150 | 196 | 217 |
| Cadmium (metric tons) | 1,540 | 1,272 | 1,384 |
| Cobalt (metric tons) | 2,150 | 2,168 | 2,324 |
| Copper (metric tons) | 652,499 | 647,779 | 688,576 |
| Gold (kilograms) | 164,660 | 171,479 | 166,089 |
| Iron ore | 34,400 | 38,928 | 38,908 |
| Lead (metric tons) | 241,751 | 170,847 | 151,708 |
| Molybdenum (metric tons) | 8,789 | 7,594 | 7,563 |
| Nickel (metric tons) | 182,404 | 180,624 | 200,908 |
| Platinum group (kilograms) | 13,934 | 11,836 | 14,522 |
| Selenium (metric tons) | 694 | 592 | 384 |
| Silver (metric tons) | 1,243 | 1,194 | 1,115 |
| Uranium (metric tons) | 11,348 | 11,127 | 9,984 |
| Zinc (metric tons) | 1,162,720 | 1,026,864 | 987,361 |

| *— continued* | 1996 | 1997 | 1998* |
|---|---|---|---|
| Non-metallic | | | |
| Asbestos | 506 | 420 | 320 |
| Gypsum | 8,202 | 8,628 | 8,095 |
| Nepheline syenite | 606 | 648 | 617 |
| Potash ($K_2O$) | 8,120 | 9,235 | 8,969 |
| Salt | 12,248 | 13,497 | 13,192 |
| Sulphur, in smelter gas | 789 | 800 | 838 |
| Sulphur, elemental | 8,327 | 8,272 | 8,410 |
| Fuels | | | |
| Coal | 75,860 | 78,670 | 74,370 |
| Natural gas (million cubic metres)† | 153,578 | 156,171 | 161,015 |
| Natural gas by-products ('000 cubic metres)†‡ | 26,657 | 26,427 | 26,612 |
| Petroleum, crude ('000 cubic metres)† | 117,621 | 123,827 | 128,769 |
| Structural materials | | | |
| Cement | 11,587 | 11,736 | 12,064 |
| Sand and gravel§ | 213,831 | 225,495 | 217,650 |
| Stone | 92,449 | 99,265 | 95,998 |

* Preliminary.
† Marketable production.
‡ Excludes sulphur.
§ Includes quartz.

# Industry

**VALUE OF SHIPMENTS** (preliminary figures, C $ million)

| | 1996 | 1997 | 1998 |
|---|---|---|---|
| Food industries | 48,298 | 50,279 | 51,681 |
| Beverage industries | 6,928 | 7,180 | 7,505 |
| Tobacco products industries | 2,784 | 2,831 | 2,956 |
| Rubber products industries | 3,922 | 4,157 | 4,430 |
| Plastic products industries | 8,804 | 9,348 | 9,886 |
| Leather and allied products industries | 909 | 975 | 901 |
| Primary textile industries | 3,655 | 4,021 | 3,980 |
| Textiles products industries | 3,307 | 3,603 | 3,631 |
| Clothing industries | 6,325 | 6,761 | 7,527 |
| Wood industries | 24,531 | 26,917 | 26,330 |
| Furniture and fixture industries | 5,375 | 6,298 | 7,527 |
| Paper and allied products industries | 31,018 | 30,556 | 31,617 |
| Printing, publishing and allied industries | 14,817 | 15,563 | 16,191 |
| Primary metal industries | 26,380 | 28,373 | 27,811 |
| Fabricated metal products industries | 21,016 | 22,820 | 24,564 |
| Machinery industries (excl. electrical machinery) | 15,547 | 17,837 | 17,989 |
| Transportation equipment industries | 89,581 | 99,565 | 107,272 |
| Electrical and electronic products industries | 27,926 | 29,364 | 32,591 |
| Non-metallic mineral products industries | 7,497 | 7,968 | 8,510 |
| Refined petroleum and coal products industries | 21,807 | 21,925 | 17,473 |
| Chemical and chemical products industries | 28,490 | 30,447 | 30,573 |
| Other manufacturing industries | 7,659 | 7,959 | 8,232 |
| **Total** | 406,575 | 434,746 | 448,496 |

**Electric Energy** (net production, million kWh): 549,000 in 1996; 553,800 in 1997; 543,100 in 1998.

# Finance

**CURRENCY AND EXCHANGE RATES**

**Monetary Units**

100 cents = 1 Canadian dollar (C $).

**Sterling, US Dollar and Euro Equivalents** (30 September 1999)

£1 sterling = C $2.420;
US $1 = C $1.470;
€1 = C $1.568;
C $100 = £41.32 = US $68.03 = €63.79.

**Average Exchange Rate** (C $ per US $)

1996 1.3635
1997 1.3846
1998 1.4835

**FEDERAL BUDGET** (C $ million, year ending 31 March)

| Revenue | 1996/97 | 1997/98 | 1998/99 |
|---|---|---|---|
| Taxes on income and profits | 87,513 | 100,275 | 103,284 |
| Personal income tax | 68,521 | 76,139 | 79,416 |
| Corporation income tax | 16,855 | 22,152 | 22,000 |
| Taxes on payments to non-residents | 2,138 | 1,983 | 1,868 |
| Taxes on goods and services | 32,007 | 33,807 | 34,379 |
| General sales taxes | 20,923 | 22,324 | 23,461 |
| Gasoline and motive fuel tax | 4,439 | 4,626 | 4,674 |
| Alcoholic beverages and tobacco taxes | 3,038 | 3,119 | 3,203 |
| Custom duties | 2,677 | 2,766 | 2,500 |
| Contributions to social security plans | 19,846 | 18,831 | 19,283 |
| Sales of goods and services | 6,253 | 4,049 | 5,471 |
| Investment income | 4,536 | 4,517 | 5,000 |
| **Total** | 152,541 | 164,240 | 170,416 |

| Expenditure | 1996/97 | 1997/98 | 1998/99 |
|---|---|---|---|
| General services | 5,785 | 5,760 | 5,827 |
| Protection of persons and property | 16,094 | 15,612 | 15,819 |
| Transport and communications | 3,306 | 3,141 | 1,906 |
| Health | 1,177 | 1,328 | 1,607 |
| Hospital care | −44 | 26 | 17 |
| Social services | 48,459 | 47,757 | 49,570 |
| Social assistance | 46,280 | 45,427 | 47,017 |
| Education | 3,355 | 3,366 | 3,731 |
| Resource conservation and industrial development | 6,013 | 5,979 | 6,352 |
| Foreign affairs and international assistance | 3,837 | 3,690 | 3,687 |
| General purpose transfers to other levels of government | 23,834 | 20,204 | 21,924 |
| Debt charges | 44,916 | 43,443 | 44,100 |
| **Total** (incl. others) | 166,041 | 159,745 | 165,077 |

**INTERNATIONAL RESERVES** (US $ million at 31 December)

| | 1996 | 1997 | 1998 |
|---|---|---|---|
| Gold* | 155 | 146 | 122 |
| IMF special drawing rights | 1,168 | 1,126 | 1,098 |
| Reserve position in IMF | 1,226 | 1,575 | 2,299 |
| Foreign exchange | 18,028 | 15,122 | 19,911 |
| **Total** | 20,577 | 17,969 | 23,430 |

* National valuation.

Source: IMF, *International Financial Statistics.*

**MONEY SUPPLY** (C $ '000 million at 31 December)

| | 1996 | 1997 | 1998 |
|---|---|---|---|
| Currency outside banks | 28.78 | 30.15 | 32.32 |
| Demand deposits at chartered banks | 127.94 | 141.60 | 149.61 |
| **Total money** (incl. others) | 156.89 | 171.91 | 182.14 |

Source: IMF, *International Financial Statistics.*

**COST OF LIVING** (Consumer Price Index; base: 1992 = 100)

| | 1996 | 1997 | 1998 |
|---|---|---|---|
| Food | 105.9 | 107.6 | 109.3 |
| Housing | 103.1 | 103.3 | 103.7 |
| Household expenses and furnishings | 105.3 | 106.6 | 108.2 |
| Clothing | 101.4 | 102.7 | 103.9 |
| Transport | 117.8 | 121.5 | 120.5 |
| Health and personal care | 104.1 | 105.9 | 108.1 |
| Recreation, education and reading | 112.1 | 114.9 | 117.5 |
| Tobacco and alcohol | 86.6 | 89.3 | 92.6 |
| **All items** | 105.9 | 107.6 | 108.6 |

## NATIONAL ACCOUNTS

**National Income and Product** (C $ million at current prices)

| | 1993 | 1994 | 1995* |
|---|---|---|---|
| Compensation of employees | 398,163 | 409,085 | 422,110 |
| Operating surplus | 128,521 | 143,317 | 154,216 |
| **Domestic factor incomes** | 526,684 | 552,402 | 576,326 |
| Consumption of fixed capital | 87,904 | 92,925 | 96,234 |
| **Gross domestic product at factor cost** | 614,588 | 645,327 | 672,560 |
| Indirect taxes, *less* subsidies | 88,731 | 92,492 | 95,113 |
| Statistical discrepancy | 2,668 | 2,310 | 906 |
| **GDP at market prices** | 705,987 | 740,129 | 768,580 |
| Factor income from abroad† | 10,624 | 11,516 | 14,613 |
| *Less* Factor income paid abroad† | 34,615 | 38,615 | 41,070 |
| **Gross national product** | 681,996 | 713,030 | 742,123 |
| *Less* Consumption of fixed capital | 87,904 | 92,925 | 96,234 |
| Statistical discrepancy | −2,668 | −2,310 | −906 |
| **National income at market prices** | 591,424 | 617,795 | 644,983 |
| Other current transfers from abroad‡ | 2,944 | 3,081 | 3,184 |
| *Less* Other current transfers paid abroad‡ | 3,836 | 3,563 | 3,698 |
| **National disposable income** | 590,532 | 617,313 | 644,469 |

* Preliminary.

† Remitted profits, dividends and interest only.

‡ Transfers to and from persons and governments.

**Expenditure on the Gross Domestic Product**
(C $ '000 million at current prices)

| | 1996 | 1997 | 1998* |
|---|---|---|---|
| Government final consumption expenditure | 169.5 | 173.3 | 177.0 |
| Private final consumption expenditure | 479.4 | 511.2 | 530.3 |
| Increase in stocks | 1.4 | 8.8 | 4.7 |
| Gross fixed capital formation | 142.7 | 165.2 | 171.2 |
| **Total domestic expenditure** | 793.0 | 858.4 | 883.2 |
| Exports of goods and services | 320.7 | 345.1 | 370.0 |
| *Less* Imports of goods and services | 288.4 | 329.9 | 357.3 |
| Statistical discrepancy | 8.6 | 0.4 | −0.2 |
| **GDP at market prices** | 833.9 | 874.0 | 895.7 |
| **GDP at constant 1992 prices** | 782.1 | 813.0 | 838.3 |

* Preliminary.

Source: IMF, *International Financial Statistics*.

**Gross Domestic Product by Economic Activity**
(C $ million at constant 1992 prices)

| | 1996 | 1997 | 1998 |
|---|---|---|---|
| Agriculture, hunting, forestry and fishing | 17,358 | 17,307 | 17,243 |
| Mining and quarrying | 26,837 | 27,935 | 27,858 |
| Manufacturing | 115,658 | 123,155 | 127,901 |
| Electricity, gas and water | 24,645 | 24,728 | 24,209 |
| Construction | 36,060 | 38,270 | 38,727 |
| Trade, restaurants and hotels | 94,020 | 100,243 | 105,559 |
| Transport, storage and communications | 51,300 | 54,146 | 56,649 |
| Finance, insurance, real estate and business services* | 146,837 | 153,778 | 159,543 |
| Other services | 158,676 | 158,697 | 159,863 |
| **GDP at factor cost** | 671,391 | 698,259 | 717,552 |

* Including imputed rents of owner-occupied dwellings.

**BALANCE OF PAYMENTS** (US $ million)

| | 1996 | 1997 | 1998 |
|---|---|---|---|
| Exports of goods f.o.b. | 205,306 | 217,620 | 217,238 |
| Imports of goods f.o.b. | −174,520 | −200,485 | −204,614 |
| **Trade balance** | 30,786 | 17,135 | 12,625 |
| Exports of services | 29,189 | 30,478 | 30,922 |
| Imports of services | −35,622 | −37,041 | −35,677 |
| **Balance on goods and services** | 24,353 | 10,573 | 7,870 |
| Other income received | 19,212 | 21,832 | 20,599 |
| Other income paid | −40,761 | −43,285 | −40,217 |
| **Balance on goods, services and income** | 2,804 | −10,880 | −11,748 |
| Current transfers received | 3,528 | 3,580 | 3,352 |
| Current transfers paid | −3,006 | −3,004 | −2,817 |
| **Current balance** | 3,327 | −10,304 | −11,213 |
| Capital account (net) | 5,845 | 5,453 | 3,363 |
| Direct investment abroad | −12,890 | −22,057 | −26,411 |
| Direct investment from abroad | 9,408 | 11,466 | 16,515 |
| Portfolio investment assets | −14,062 | −8,121 | −14,928 |
| Portfolio investment liabilities | 13,413 | 11,859 | 16,757 |
| Other investment assets | −21,169 | −16,031 | 12,256 |
| Other investment liabilities | 16,336 | 27,954 | 7,355 |
| Net errors and omissions | 5,290 | −2,612 | 1,303 |
| **Overall balance** | 5,498 | −2,393 | 4,996 |

Source: IMF, *International Financial Statistics*.

# External Trade

**PRINCIPAL COMMODITIES** (C $ million)

| Imports f.o.b. | 1996 | 1997 | 1998 |
|---|---|---|---|
| Agricultural and fishing products | 14,137.9 | 15,645.6 | 17,262.1 |
| Fruits and vegetables | 4,012.2 | 4,354.1 | 4,717.5 |
| Other agricultural and fishing products | 10,125.7 | 11,291.4 | 12,544.6 |
| Energy products | 9,605.1 | 10,628.8 | 8,678.6 |
| Crude petroleum | 6,707.8 | 7,189.4 | 5,217.6 |
| Forestry products | 1,913.7 | 2,386.2 | 2,498.2 |
| Industrial goods and materials | 46,482.5 | 54,559.1 | 60,286.2 |
| Metals and metal ores | 11,752.5 | 14,396.1 | 15,328.4 |
| Chemicals and plastics | 17,377.9 | 19,606.8 | 21,516.4 |
| Other industrial goods and materials | 17,352.1 | 20,556.2 | 23,441.4 |
| Machinery and equipment (excl. automotive products) | 76,613.3 | 91,314.9 | 101,302.6 |
| Industrial and agricultural machinery | 19,989.9 | 25,622.2 | 28,217.0 |
| Aircraft and other transportation equipment | 8,212.3 | 10,983.6 | 12,663.0 |
| Office machines and equipment | 13,369.3 | 14,883.2 | 15,738.9 |
| Other machinery and equipment | 35,041.8 | 39,825.9 | 44,683.7 |
| Automotive products | 51,106.5 | 60,825.8 | 66,762.5 |
| Passenger automobiles and chassis | 13,538.2 | 17,687.5 | 17,630.7 |
| Trucks and other motor vehicles | 7,092.4 | 8,598.4 | 9,656.3 |
| Motor vehicle parts | 30,475.9 | 34,539.9 | 39,475.5 |
| Other consumer goods | 25,840.1 | 29,726.1 | 34,574.2 |
| Apparel and footwear | 4,869.3 | 5,818.0 | 6,621.7 |
| Miscellaneous consumer goods | 20,970.8 | 23,908.1 | 27,952.5 |
| Special transactions trade | 7,075.5 | 6,936.4 | 6,298.0 |
| Unallocated adjustments | 5,142.2 | 5,684.8 | 5,737.1 |
| **Total** | 237,917.2 | 277,707.8 | 303,399.7 |

| Exports f.o.b. | 1996 | 1997 | 1998 |
|---|---|---|---|
| Agricultural and fishing products | 23,167.7 | 24,963.0 | 25,142.7 |
| Wheat | 4,658.6 | 5,093.7 | 3,677.4 |
| Other agricultural and fishing products | 18,509.1 | 19,869.3 | 21,465.3 |
| Energy products | 26,009.6 | 27,089.4 | 23,901.0 |
| Crude petroleum | 10,453.7 | 10,334.9 | 7,827.2 |
| Natural gas | 7,432.8 | 8,625.6 | 8,987.5 |
| Other energy products | 8,123.1 | 8,128.9 | 7,086.3 |
| Forestry products | 34,470.8 | 34,852.7 | 35,174.1 |
| Lumber and sawmill products | 15,802.7 | 16,804.1 | 16,564.7 |
| Wood pulp and other wood products | 6,471.9 | 6,509.6 | 6,222.8 |
| Newsprint and other paper and paperboard products | 12,196.2 | 11,539.0 | 12,386.6 |
| Industrial goods and materials | 52,283.2 | 56,066.2 | 57,453.5 |
| Metals and metal ores | 5,915.8 | 5,960.9 | 5,423.3 |
| Chemicals, plastics and fertilizers | 15,358.0 | 17,095.2 | 17,531.8 |
| Metals and alloys | 19,662.8 | 20,048.6 | 19,756.7 |
| Other industrial goods and materials | 11,346.8 | 12,961.5 | 14,741.7 |
| Machinery and equipment (excl. automotive products) | 61,895.8 | 68,218.7 | 78,822.9 |
| Industrial and agricultural machinery | 13,220.8 | 14,811.4 | 16,611.7 |
| Aircraft and other transportation equipment | 12,467.4 | 12,961.3 | 16,404.3 |
| Other machinery and equipment | 36,207.6 | 40,446.0 | 45,806.9 |
| Automotive products | 63,369.7 | 69,008.8 | 77,414.9 |
| Passenger automobiles and chassis | 33,737.9 | 35,492.6 | 41,841.0 |
| Trucks and other motor vehicles | 12,467.8 | 14,476.9 | 13,993.6 |
| Motor vehicle parts | 17,164.0 | 19,039.3 | 21,580.3 |
| Other consumer goods | 9,501.5 | 10,667.4 | 12,424.4 |
| Special transactions trade | 3,154.5 | 4,074.5 | 5,563.3 |
| Unallocated adjustments | 6,039.0 | 6,440.4 | 6,365.6 |
| **Total** | 279,891.8 | 301,381.4 | 322,262.4 |

**PRINCIPAL TRADING PARTNERS** (C $ million)

| Imports f.o.b. | 1996 | 1997 | 1998 |
|---|---|---|---|
| China, People's Repub. | 4,925 | 6,342 | 7,650 |
| France | 3,339 | 5,137 | 4,903 |
| Germany | 4,820 | 5,410 | 6,134 |
| Italy | 2,718 | 3,069 | 3,470 |
| Japan | 10,439 | 12,555 | 13,987 |
| Korea, Repub. | 2,727 | 2,838 | 3,315 |
| Mexico | 6,012 | 7,019 | 7,645 |
| Norway | 2,777 | 3,317 | 2,534 |
| Taiwan | 2,863 | 3,475 | 4,034 |
| United Kingdom | 5,908 | 6,502 | 6,229 |
| USA | 157,344 | 184,344 | 203,347 |
| **Total** (incl. others) | 232,937 | 272,856 | 298,317 |

| Exports f.o.b. | 1996 | 1997 | 1998 |
|---|---|---|---|
| China, People's Repub. | 2,706 | 2,355 | 2,121 |
| Germany | 3,149 | 2,625 | 2,486 |
| Japan | 10,377 | 11,043 | 8,173 |
| Korea, Repub. | 2,676 | 2,986 | 1,744 |
| United Kingdom | 3,808 | 3,641 | 4,100 |
| USA | 210,071 | 229,279 | 252,350 |
| **Total** (incl. others) | 258,418 | 281,226 | 296,700 |

# Transport

**RAILWAYS** (revenue traffic)*

| | 1995 | 1996 | 1997 |
|---|---|---|---|
| Passenger-km (million) | 1,473 | 1,517 | 1,515 |
| Freight ton-km (million) | 280,466 | 282,482 | 306,943 |

* Seven major rail carriers only.

**ROAD TRAFFIC** ('000 vehicles registered at 31 December)

| | 1995 | 1996 | 1997 |
|---|---|---|---|
| Passenger cars (incl. taxis and for car hire) | 13,131 | 13,251 | 13,487 |
| Trucks and truck tractors (commercial and non-commercial) | 3,411 | 3,476 | 3,527 |
| Buses (school and other) | 64 | 65 | 64 |
| Motorcycles | 298 | 291 | 299 |
| Other (ambulances, fire trucks, etc.) | 60 | 79 | 80 |

**INLAND WATER TRAFFIC** (St Lawrence Seaway, '000 metric tons)

| | 1996 | 1997 | 1998 |
|---|---|---|---|
| Montréal—Lake Ontario | n.a. | 36,901 | 39,246 |
| Welland Canal | n.a. | 40,902 | 40,657 |

Source: St Lawrence Seaway Management Corporation.

**SHIPPING**

**Merchant Fleet** (registered at 31 December)

| | 1996 | 1997 | 1998 |
|---|---|---|---|
| Number of vessels | 872 | 852 | 835 |
| Total displacement ('000 grt) | 2,406.2 | 2,526.6 | 2,501.3 |

Source: Lloyd's Register of Shipping, *World Fleet Statistics*.

**International Sea-borne Freight Traffic**

| | 1996 | 1997 | 1998* |
|---|---|---|---|
| Goods ('000 metric tons) | | | |
| Loaded | 174,305 | 188,019 | 179,049 |
| Unloaded | 85,792 | 94,799 | 100,532 |
| Vessels (number) | | | |
| Arrived | 26,252 | 27,520 | n.a. |
| Departed | 25,297 | 27,438 | n.a. |

* Preliminary.

**CIVIL AVIATION** (Canadian carriers—revenue traffic, '000)*

| | 1996 | 1997 | 1998 |
|---|---|---|---|
| Passengers | 23,164 | 24,363 | 24,571 |
| Passenger-km | 57,015,549 | 62,479,410 | 64,426,065 |
| Goods ton-km | 1,882,803 | 2,058,953 | 2,340,594 |

* Figures refer to the operations of 'Level I' air carriers.

## Tourism

| | 1996 | 1997 | 1998 |
|---|---|---|---|
| Travellers from the USA: | | | |
| Number ('000) | 12,909 | 13,401 | 14,823 |
| Expenditure (C $ million) | 5,150 | 5,355 | 6,702 |
| Travellers from other countries: | | | |
| Number ('000) | 4,377 | 4,234 | 3,935 |
| Expenditure (C $ million) | 4,520 | 4,516 | 4,462 |

## Communications Media

('000)

| | 1995 | 1996 | 1997 |
|---|---|---|---|
| Total households | 10,247 | 11,412 | 11,580 |
| Homes with radio | 10,134 | 11,268 | 11,425 |
| Homes with television | 10,147 | 11,258 | 11,482 |
| Homes with telephone | 10,141 | 11,305 | 11,423 |

Daily newspapers in French and English 105 (1996); total circulation 5,200,000.

**Telefax stations** (1993): 525,000 in use (Source: UN, *Statistical Yearbook*).

**Mobile cellular telephones** (1995): 2,589,780 subscribers (Source: UN, *Statistical Yearbook*).

**Book production** (titles): 17,931 in 1995; 19,900 in 1996 (Source: UNESCO, *Statistical Yearbook*).

**Non-daily newspapers** (1996, provisional): 1,071; average circulation 21,235,000 copies (Source: UNESCO, *Statistical Yearbook*).

## Education

(1997/98)

| | Institutions | Teachers* | Pupils* |
|---|---|---|---|
| Primary and secondary | 16,465 | 303,743 | 5,042,094† |
| Post-secondary colleges | 195† | n.a. | 398,062† |
| Universities | 76 | 35,000† | 582,190† |

* Full-time only.
† Estimates.

# Directory

## The Constitution

Under the Constitution Act 1982, which entered into force on 17 April 1982, executive authority is vested in the Sovereign, and exercised in her name by a Governor-General and Privy Council. Legislative power is exercised by a Parliament of two Houses, the Senate and the House of Commons. The Constitution includes a Charter of Rights and Freedoms, and provisions which recognize the nation's multicultural heritage, affirm the existing rights of native peoples, confirm the principle of equalization of benefits among the provinces and strengthen provincial ownership of natural resources.

### THE GOVERNMENT

The national government operates through three main agencies: Parliament (consisting of the Sovereign as represented by the Governor-General, the Senate and the House of Commons), which makes the laws; the Executive (the Cabinet or Ministry), which applies the laws; and the Judiciary, which interprets the laws.

The Prime Minister is appointed by the Governor-General and is habitually the leader of the political party commanding the confidence of the House of Commons. He chooses the members of his Cabinet from members of his party in Parliament, principally from those in the House of Commons. Each Minister or member of the Cabinet is usually responsible for the administration of a department, although there may be Ministers without portfolio whose experience and counsel are drawn upon to strengthen the Cabinet, but who are not at the head of departments. Each Minister of a department is responsible to Parliament for that department, and the Cabinet is collectively responsible before Parliament for government policy and administration generally.

Meetings of the Cabinet are presided over by the Prime Minister. From the Cabinet signed orders and recommendations go to the Governor-General for his or her approval, and the Crown acts only on the advice of its responsible Ministers. The Cabinet takes the responsibility for its advice being in accordance with the support of Parliament and is held strictly accountable.

### THE FEDERAL PARLIAMENT

Parliament must meet at least once a year, so that 12 months do not elapse between the last meeting in one session and the first meeting in the next. The duration of Parliament may not be longer than five years from the date of election of a House of Commons. Senators (normally a maximum of 104 in number) are appointed until age 75 by the Governor-General in Council. They must be at least 30 years of age, residents of the province they represent and in possession of C $4,000 of real property over and above their liabilities. Members of the House of Commons are elected by universal adult suffrage for the duration of a Parliament.

Under the Constitution, the Federal Parliament has exclusive legislative authority in all matters relating to public debt and property; regulation of trade and commerce; raising of money by any mode of taxation; borrowing of money on the public credit; postal service, census and statistics; militia, military and naval service and defence; fixing and providing for salaries and allowances of the officers of the Government; beacons, buoys and lighthouses; navigation and shipping; quarantine and the establishment and maintenance of marine hospitals; sea-coast and inland fisheries; ferries on an international or interprovincial frontier; currency and coinage; banking, incorporation of banks, and issue of paper money; savings banks; weights and measures; bills of exchange and promissory notes; interest; legal tender; bankruptcy and insolvency; patents of invention and discovery; copyrights; Indians and lands reserved for Indians; naturalization and aliens; marriage and divorce; the criminal law, except the constitution of courts of criminal jurisdiction but including the procedure in criminal matters; the establishment, maintenance and management of penitentiaries; such classes of subjects as are expressly excepted in the enumeration of the classes of subjects exclusively assigned to the Legislatures of the provinces by the Act. Judicial interpretation and later amendment have, in certain cases, modified or clearly defined the respective powers of the Federal Government and provincial governments.

Both the Parliament of Canada and the legislatures of the provinces may legislate with respect to agriculture and immigration, but provincial legislation shall have effect in and for the provinces as long and as far only as it is not repugnant to any Act of Parliament. Both Parliament and the provincial legislatures may legislate with respect to old age pensions and supplementary benefits, but no federal law shall affect the operation of any present or future law of a province in relation to these matters.

### PROVINCIAL AND MUNICIPAL GOVERNMENT

In each of the 10 provinces the Sovereign is represented by a Lieutenant-Governor, appointed by the Governor-General in Council, and acting on the advice of the Ministry or Executive Council, which is responsible to the Legislature and resigns office when it ceases to enjoy the confidence of that body. The Legislatures are unicameral, consisting of an elected Legislative Assembly and the Lieutenant-Governor. The duration of a Legislature may not exceed five years from the date of the election of its members.

The Legislature in each province may exclusively make laws in relation to: amendment of the constitution of the province, except as regards the Lieutenant-Governor; direct taxation within the province; borrowing of money on the credit of the province; establishment and tenure of provincial offices and appointment and payment of provincial officers; the management and sale of public lands belonging to the province and of the timber and wood thereon; the establishment, maintenance and management of public and reformatory prisons in and for the province; the establishment, maintenance and management of hospitals, asylums, charities and charitable institutions in and for the province other than marine hospitals; municipal institutions in the province; shop, saloon, tavern, auctioneer and other licences issued for the raising of provincial or municipal revenue; local works and undertakings other than interprovincial or international lines of ships, railways, canals, telegraphs, etc., or works which, though wholly situtated within the province are declared by the Federal Parliament to be for the general advantage either of Canada or two or more provinces; the incorporation of companies with provincial objects; the solemnization of marriage in the province; property and civil rights in the province; the administration of justice in the province, including the constitution, maintenance and organization of provincial courts both in civil and criminal jurisdiction, and including procedure in civil matters in these courts; the imposition of punishment by fine, penalty or imprisonment for enforcing any law of the province relating to any of the aforesaid subjects; generally all matters of a merely local or private nature in the province. Further, provincial Legislatures may exclusively make laws in relation to education, subject to the protection of religious minorities; and to non-renewable natural resources, forestry resources and electrical energy, including their export from one province to another, and to the right to impose any mode or system of taxation thereon, subject in both cases to such laws not being discriminatory.

Under the Constitution Act, the municipalities are the creations of the provincial governments. Their bases of organization and the extent of their authority vary in different provinces, but almost everywhere they have very considerable powers of local self-government.

## The Government

**Head of State:** HM Queen ELIZABETH II (succeeded to the throne 6 February 1952).

**Governor-General:** ADRIENNE CLARKSON (took office 7 October 1999).

### FEDERAL MINISTRY
(January 2000)

**Prime Minister:** JEAN CHRÉTIEN.

**Deputy Prime Minister:** HERBERT GRAY.

**Minister of Foreign Affairs:** LLOYD AXWORTHY.

**Minister of Transport:** DAVID COLLENETTE.

**Minister of the Environment:** DAVID ANDERSON.

**Minister of Natural Resources and Minister responsible for the Canadian Wheat Board:** RALPH GOODALE.

**Minister of Canadian Heritage:** SHEILA COPPS.

**Minister of Industry:** JOHN MANLEY.

**Minister of Finance:** PAUL MARTIN.

**Minister of National Defence:** ARTHUR EGGLETON.

**Minister of Justice and Attorney-General:** ANNE MCLELLAN.

**Minister of Health:** ALLAN ROCK.

**Solicitor-General:** LAWRENCE MACAULAY.

**Minister of Public Works and Government Services:** ALFONSO GAGLIANO.

**President of the Treasury Board and Minister responsible for Infrastructure:** LUCIENNE ROBILLARD.

**Minister of National Revenue and Secretary of State (Economic Development Agency of Canada for the Regions of Québec):** MARTIN CACHON.

**Minister of Human Resources Development:** JANE STEWART.

**President of the Queen's Privy Council for Canada and Minister of Intergovernmental Affairs:** STÉPHANE DION.

**Minister for International Trade:** PIERRE PETTIGREW.

**Leader of the Government in the House of Commons:** DON BOUDRIA.

**Minister of Agriculture and Agri-Food:** LYLE VANCLIEF.

**Minister of Fisheries and Oceans:** HERB DHALIWAL.

**Minister of Labour:** CLAUDETTE BRADSHAW.

**Minister of Veterans' Affairs and Secretary of State (Atlantic Canada Opportunities Agency):** GEORGE BAKER.

**Minister of Indian Affairs and Northern Development:** ROBERT NAULT.

**Minister for International Co-operation:** MARIA MINNA.

**Minister of Citizenship and Immigration:** ELINOR CAPLAN.

**Leader of the Government in the Senate:** J. BERNARD BOUDREAU.

**Secretary of State (Children and Youth):** ETHEL BLONDIN-ANDREW.

**Secretary of State (Asia–Pacific):** RAYMOND CHAN.

**Secretary of State (Multiculturalism and Status of Women):** HEDY FRY.

**Secretary of State (Latin America and Africa):** DAVID KILGOUR.

**Secretary of State (International Financial Institutions):** JAMES PETERSON.

**Secretary of State (Western Economic Diversification and Francophonie):** RONALD DUHAMEL.

**Secretary of State (Rural Developments and Federal Economic Development Initiative for Northern Ontario):** ANDREW MITCHELL.

**Secretary of State (Science, Research and Development):** GILBERT NORMAND.

**Secretary of State (Amateur Sport):** DENIS CODERRE.

### MINISTRIES

**Office of the Prime Minister:** Langevin Block, 80 Wellington St, Ottawa, ON K1A 0A3; tel. (613) 992-4211; fax (613) 941-6900; e-mail pm@pm.gc.ca; internet www.pm.gc.ca.

**Agriculture and Agri-Food Canada:** Sir John Carling Bldg, 930 Carling Ave, Ottawa, ON K1A 0C5; tel. (613) 759-1000; fax (613) 759-6726; e-mail PIRS@em.agr.ca; internet www.agr.ca.

**Canadian Heritage:** Immeuble Jules Léger, 25 rue Eddy, Hull, QC K1A 0M5; tel. (819) 997-0055; fax (819) 953-5382; internet www.pch.gc.ca.

**Citizenship and Immigration Canada:** Jean Edmonds Towers, 365 ave Laurier ouest, Hull, QC K1A 1L1; tel. (613) 954-9019; fax (613) 954-2221; internet www.cicnet.ingenia.com/english/index.html.

**Department of Justice Canada:** East Memorial Bldg, 284 Wellington St, Ottawa, ON K1A 0H8; tel. (613) 957-4222; fax (613) 954-0811; internet www.canada.justice.gc.ca.

**Environment Canada:** Ottawa, ON K1A 0H3; tel. (819) 997-2800; fax (819) 953-2225; e-mail enviroinfo@ec.gc.ca; internet www.ec.ga.ca.

**Finance Canada:** L'Esplanade Laurier, 140 O'Connor St, Ottawa, ON K1A 0G5; tel. (613) 992-1573; fax (613) 996-8404; internet www.fin.gc.ca.

**Fisheries and Oceans Canada:** 200 Kent St, Ottawa, ON K1A 0E6; tel. (613) 993-0999; fax (613) 990-1866; e-mail info@www.ncr.dfo.ca; internet www.dfo-mpo.gc.ca.

**Foreign Affairs and International Trade Canada:** Lester B. Pearson Bldg, 125 Sussex Drive, Ottawa, ON K1A 0G2; tel. (613) 996-9134; fax (613) 952-3904; e-mail infotech@dfait-maeci.gc.ca; internet www.dfait-maeci.gc.ca.

**Health Canada:** Brooke Claxton Bldg, Tunney's Pasture, Ottawa, ON K1A 0K9; tel. (613) 957-2991; fax (613) 941-5366; internet www.hwc.ca/links/english/html.

**Human Resources Development Canada:** 140 promenade du Portage, Hull, QC K1A 0J9; tel. (819) 994-6013; fax (819) 953-3981; internet www.hrdc-drhc.gc.ca.

**Indian and Northern Affairs Canada:** Les Terrasses de la Chaudière, Bureau 1400, 10 rue Wellington, Hull, QC K1A 0H4; tel. (819) 997-0811; fax (819) 953-5491; e-mail reference@inac.gc.ca; internet www.inac.gc.ca.

**Industry Canada:** C. D. Howe Bldg, 235 Queen St, Ottawa, ON K1A 0H5; tel. (613) 954-2788; fax (613) 954-2303; internet www.info.ic.gc.ca.

**National Defence (Canada):** Maj.-Gen. George R. Pearkes Bldg, 101 Colonel By Drive, Ottawa, ON K1A 0K2; tel. (613) 992-4581; fax (613) 992-4241; internet www.dnd.ca.

**Natural Resources Canada:** 580 Booth St, Ottawa, ON K1A 0E4; tel. (613) 995-0947; fax (613) 996-9094; internet www.NRCan.gc.ca/.

**Public Works and Government Services Canada:** place du Portage, rue Laurier, Hull, QC K1A 0S5; tel. (819) 956-3115; internet www.pwgsc.gc.ca.

**Revenue Canada:** 871 Heron Rd, Ottawa, ON K1A 0L8; tel. (613) 952-0384; internet www.rc.gc.ca.

**Solicitor-General Canada:** Sir Wilfrid Laurier Bldg, 340 Laurier Ave West, Ottawa, ON K1A 0P8; tel. (613) 991-3283; fax (613) 993-7062; internet www.sgc.gc.ca.

**Transport Canada:** Transport Canada Bldg, 330 Sparks St, Ottawa, ON K1A 0N5; tel. (613) 990-2309; fax (613) 954-4731; e-mail mintc@tc.gc.ca; internet www.tc.gc.ca.

**Treasury Board:** East Tower, L'Esplanade Laurier, 140 O'Connor St, Ottawa, ON K1A 0R5; tel. (613) 957-2400; fax (613) 952-3658; internet www.tbs-sct.gc.ca.

**Veterans Affairs Canada:** 161 Grafton St, POB 7700, Charlottetown, PE C1A 8M9; tel. (902) 566-8888; fax (902) 566-8508; internet www.vac-acc.gc.ca.

**Western Economic Diversification Canada:** Canada Place, 9700 Jasper Ave, Suite 1500, Edmonton, AB T5J 4H7; tel. (780) 495-4164; fax (403) 495-6876; internet www.wd.gc.ca.

# Federal Legislature

### THE SENATE

**Speaker:** GILDAS MOLGAT.

**Seats at November 1999**

| | |
|---|---|
| Liberal | 55 |
| Progressive Conservative | 42 |
| Independent | 5 |
| Vacant | 3 |
| **Total** | 105 |

### HOUSE OF COMMONS

**Speaker:** GILBERT PARENT.

**General Election, 2 June 1997**

| | % of votes at election | Seats at election | Seats at Nov. 1999 |
|---|---|---|---|
| Liberal | 38.4 | 155 | 157 |
| Reform Party | 19.4 | 60 | 58 |
| Bloc Québécois | 10.7 | 44 | 44 |
| New Democratic Party | 11.0 | 21 | 20 |
| Progressive Conservative | 18.9 | 20 | 19 |
| Independent | 1.6 | 1 | 3 |
| **Total** | 100.0 | 301 | 301 |

# Provincial Legislatures

### ALBERTA

**Lieutenant-Governor:** LOIS HOLE.

**Premier:** RALPH KLEIN.

**Election, March 1997**

| | Seats at election | Seats at Oct. 1999 |
|---|---|---|
| Progressive Conservative | 63 | 64 |
| Liberal | 18 | 17 |
| New Democratic Party | 2 | 2 |
| **Total** | 83 | 83 |

### BRITISH COLUMBIA

**Lieutenant-Governor:** GARDE B. GARDOM.

**Premier:** DAN MILLER.

**Election, May 1996**

| | Seats at election | Seats at Oct. 1999 |
|---|---|---|
| New Democratic Party | 39 | 40 |
| Liberal | 33 | 33 |
| Reform Party | 2 | — |
| Progressive Democratic Alliance | 1 | — |
| Independent | — | 1 |
| Vacant | — | 1 |
| **Total** | 75 | 75 |

### MANITOBA

**Lieutenant-Governor:** PETER LIBA.

**Premier:** GARY DOER.

**Election, September 1999**

| | Seats at election |
|---|---|
| New Democratic Party | 31 |
| Progressive Conservative | 25 |
| Liberal | 1 |
| **Total** | 57 |

### NEW BRUNSWICK

**Lieutenant-Governor:** MARILYN TRENHOLME COUNSELL.

**Premier:** BERNARD LORD.

**Election, June 1999**

| | Seats at election | Seats at Oct. 1999 |
|---|---|---|
| Progressive Conservative | 44 | 44 |
| Liberal | 10 | 10 |
| New Democratic Party | 1 | 1 |
| **Total** | 55 | 55 |

### NEWFOUNDLAND AND LABRADOR

**Lieutenant-Governor:** DR A. M. (MAX) HOUSE.

**Premier:** BRIAN TOBIN.

**Election, February 1999**

| | Seats at election | Seats at Oct. 1999 |
|---|---|---|
| Liberal | 32 | 32 |
| Progressive Conservative | 14 | 14 |
| New Democratic Party | 2 | 2 |
| **Total** | 48 | 48 |

### NOVA SCOTIA

**Lieutenant-Governor:** J. JAMES KINLEY.

**Premier:** JOHN F. HAMM.

**Election, July 1999**

| | Seats at election |
|---|---|
| Progressive Conservative | 29 |
| New Democratic Party | 12 |
| Liberal | 11 |
| **Total** | 52 |

### ONTARIO

**Lieutenant-Governor:** HILARY WESTON.

**Premier:** MICHAEL D. HARRIS.

**Election, June 1999**

| | Seats at election | Seats at Oct. 1999 |
|---|---|---|
| Progressive Conservative | 59 | 59 |
| Liberal | 35 | 35 |
| New Democratic Party | 9 | 9 |
| **Total** | 103 | 103 |

### PRINCE EDWARD ISLAND

**Lieutenant-Governor:** GILBERT R. CLEMENTS.

**Premier:** PAT BINNS.

**Election, November 1996**

| | Seats at election | Seats at Oct. 1999 |
|---|---|---|
| Progressive Conservative | 18 | 18 |
| Liberal | 8 | 8 |
| New Democratic Party | 1 | 1 |
| **Total** | 27 | 27 |

### QUÉBEC

**Lieutenant-Governor:** LISE THIBAULT.

**Premier:** LUCIEN BOUCHARD.

**Election, November 1998**

| | Seats at election | Seats at Oct. 1999 |
|---|---|---|
| Parti Québécois | 76 | 76 |
| Liberal | 48 | 48 |
| Action Démocratique du Québec | 1 | 1 |
| **Total** | 125 | 125 |

### SASKATCHEWAN

**Lieutenant-Governor:** LYNDA HAVERSTOCK.

**Premier:** ROY ROMANOW.

**Election, September 1999**

| | Seats at election |
|---|---|
| New Democratic Party | 29 |
| Saskatchewan Party | 26 |
| Liberal | 3 |
| **Total** | 58 |

## Territorial Legislatures

### NORTHWEST TERRITORIES

**Commissioner:** DANIEL J. MARION.

**Premier and Minister of the Executive Department:** JIM ANTOINE.

The Legislative Assembly, elected in December 1999, consists of 19 independent members without formal party affiliation.

### NUNAVUT TERRITORY

**Commissioner:** HELEN MAGSAGAK.

**Premier:** PAUL OKALIK.

The Legislative Assembly, elected in February 1999, consists of 19 independent members without formal party affiliation.

### YUKON TERRITORY

**Commissioner:** JUDY GINGELL.

**Government Leader and Minister of the Executive Council Office:** PIERS MCDONALD.

**Election, September 1996**

| | Seats at election | Seats at Oct. 1999 |
|---|---|---|
| New Democratic Party | 11 | 10 |
| Yukon Party | 3 | 3 |
| Liberal | 3 | 3 |
| Vacant | — | 1 |
| **Total** | 17 | 17 |

## Political Organizations

**Action Démocratique du Québec:** 1050 rue de la Montagne, 3e étage, Montréal, QC H3G 1Y7; tel. (514) 932-5505; internet www.adq.qc.ca; f. 1994; provincial nationalist; Leader MARIO DUMONT; Pres. RÉAL BARETTE.

**Bloc Québécois:** 1200 ave Papineau, Montréal, QC H2K 4R5; tel. (514) 526-3000; fax (514) 526-2868; e-mail infobloc@bloc.org; internet www.blocquebecois.org; f. 1990 by group of seven Progressive Conservative MPs representing Québec constituencies in fed. parl.; subsequently attracted Liberal support; main opposition party in Federal House of Commons during 1993–97; seeks negotiated sovereignty for Québec; Leader GILLES DUCEPPE; Dir-Gen. YVES DUFOUR.

**Canadian Action Party:** 99 Atlantic Ave, Suite 302, Toronto ON M6K 3J8; tel. (416) 535-4144; fax (416) 535-6325; e-mail cap-pac@istar.ca; internet www.canadianactionparty.ca; Leader PAUL HELLYER.

**Christian Heritage Party of Canada:** 155 Queen St, Suite 200, Ottawa, ON K1P 6L1; tel. (613) 788-3716; fax (613) 457-9242; f. 1986; Pres. THOMAS KROESBERGEN; Leader RONALD O. GRAY.

**Communist Party of Canada (Marxist-Leninist):** 171 Dalhousie St, Ottawa, ON K1N 7C7; tel. (613) 241-7052; e-mail cpc-ml@fox.nstn.ca; f. 1970; Nat. Leader (vacant).

**Confederation of Regions Party:** 6155 99th St, Edmonton, AB T6E 3P1; tel. (780) 435-4185; fax (780) 437-2297; Nat. Leader ELMER S. KNUTSON.

**COR (Confederation of Regions) Party of New Brunswick:** POB 3322,Station B, Fredericton, NB E3A 5H1; tel. (506) 444-4040; fax (506) 444-4053; e-mail cor@nbnet.nb.ca; f. 1989 to promote populist democratic principles; opposes legislation and govt subsidies relating to linguistic and cultural matters; Leader JAMES A. WEBB (acting); Pres. DOLORES COOK.

**Equality Party:** Box 21, Station NDG, Montréal, QC H4A 3P4; tel. (514) 488-7586; fax (514) 488-7306; e-mail canadian@equality.qc.ca; internet www.equality.qc.ca; f. 1989; represents interests of federalists in Québec; Leader KEITH HENDERSON.

**Green Party of Canada:** POB 397, London, ON N6A 4W1; tel. (519) 474-3294; fax (519) 474-3294; f. 1983; environmentalist; Leader JOAN RUSSOW.

**Liberal Party of Canada:** 81 Metcalfe St, Suite 400, Ottawa, ON K1P 6M8; tel. (613) 237-0740; fax (613) 235-7208; e-mail info@liberal.ca; internet www.liberal.ca; supports comprehensive social security, economic growth and a balanced economy; Leader JEAN CHRÉTIEN; Pres. DAN HAYS; Nat. Dir GEORGE YOUNG.

**New Democratic Party of Canada:** 81 Metcalfe St, Suite 900, Ottawa, ON K1P 6K7; tel. (613) 236-3613; fax (613) 230-9950; e-mail ndpadmin@fed.ndp.ca; internet www.ndp.ca; f. 1961; social democratic; Leader ALEXA MCDONOUGH; Pres. DAVE MACKINNON; Sec. JILL MARZETTI; 100,000 mems. (1996).

**Parti Québécois:** 1200 ave Papineau, Bureau 150, Montréal, QC H2K 4R5; tel. (514) 526-0200; fax (514) 526-0272; e-mail info@pq.org; f. 1968; social democratic; seeks political sovereignty for Québec; governing party of Québec in 1976–85 and since Sept. 1994; Pres. LUCIEN BOUCHARD; 200,000 mems (1999).

**Progressive Conservative Party of Canada:** 275 Slater St, Suite 501, Ottawa, ON K1P 5H9; tel. (613) 238-6111; fax (613) 238-7429; e-mail pcinfo@pcparty.ca; f. 1854; advocates individualism and free enterprise; Leader C. JOSEPH CLARK; Pres. PETER VAN LOAN; Nat. Dir SUSAN ELLIOTT.

**Reform Party of Canada:** 833 4th Ave, SW, Suite 600, Calgary, AB T2P 0K5; tel. (403) 269-1990; fax (403) 269-4077; e-mail info@reform.ca; internet www.reform.ca; f. 1987; supports decentralization of fed. govt, with provincial jurisdiction over language and culture; advocates fiscal reform; main opposition party in Federal House of Commons since June 1997; Leader E. PRESTON MANNING; Exec. Dir GLEN MCMURRAY; 97,000 mems (1997).

**Saskatchewan Party:** Legislative Bldg, Rm 265, Regina, SK S4S 0B3; tel. (306) 787-4300; fax (306) 787-3174; e-mail skcaucus@sk.sympatico.ca; internet www.skcaucus.ca; Leader ELWIN HERMANSON.

**Socialist Party of Canada:** POB 4280, Victoria, BC V8X 3X8; tel. (250) 595-2144; fax (250) 676-7417; e-mail spc@iname.com; internet www.worldsocialism.org/canada/; Gen. Sec. STEVE SZALAI.

**Yukon Party:** POB 2703, Whitehorse, YT Y1A 2C6; fax (867) 393-6252; Leader JOHN OSTASHEK.

## Diplomatic Representation

### EMBASSIES AND HIGH COMMISSIONS IN CANADA

**Algeria:** 435 Daly Ave, Ottawa, ON K1N 6H3; tel. (613) 789-8505; fax (613) 789-1406; e-mail aao@docuweb.ca; Ambassador: ABDESSELAIM BEDRANE.

**Angola:** 75 Albert St, Suite 900, Ottawa, ON K1P 5E7; tel. (613) 234-1152; fax (613) 234-1179; Chargé d'affaires a.i.: ANDRÉ PANZO.

**Antigua and Barbuda, Dominica, Grenada, Montserrat, Saint Christopher and Nevis, Saint Lucia and Saint Vincent and the Grenadines:** 130 Albert St, Suite 700, Ottawa, ON K1P 5G4; tel. (613) 236-8952; fax (613) 236-3042; e-mail echcc@travel-net.com; High Commissioner: GEORGE R. E. BULLEN.

**Argentina:** Royal Bank Centre, 90 Sparks St, Suite 910, Ottawa, ON K1P 5B4; tel. (613) 236-2351; fax (613) 235-2659; Ambassador: SUSANA M. RUIZ CERUTTI.

**Armenia:** 7 Delaware Ave, Ottawa, ON K2P 0Z2; tel. (613) 234-3710; fax (613) 234-3444; Ambassador: LEVON BARKHUDARYAN.

**Australia:** 50 O'Connor St, Suite 710, Ottawa, ON K1P 6L2; tel. (613) 236-0841; fax (613) 236-4376; High Commissioner: GREGORY S. R. WOOD.

**Austria:** 445 Wilbrod St, Ottawa, ON K1N 6M7; tel. (613) 789-1444; fax (613) 789-3431; e-mail embassy@austro.org; internet www.austro.org; Ambassador: Dr WENDELIN ETTMAYER.

**Bahamas:** 50 O'Connor St, Suite 1313, Ottawa, ON K1P 6L2; tel. (613) 232-1724; fax (613) 232-0097; e-mail ottawa-mission@bahighco.com; Chargé d'affaires a.i.: JULIE ANN CAMPBELL.

**Bangladesh:** 275 Bank St, Suite 302, Ottawa, ON K2P 2L6; tel. (613) 236-0138; fax (613) 567-3213; e-mail bdootcanda@iosphere.net; High Commissioner: M. AMINUL ISLAM.

**Barbados:** 130 Albert St, Suite 302, Ottawa, ON K1P 5G4; tel. (613) 236-9517; fax (613) 230-4362; e-mail barhcott@travel-net.com; High Commissioner: VICTOR LEROY JOHNSON.

**Belgium:** 80 Elgin St, 4th Floor, Ottawa, ON K1P 1B7; tel. (613) 236-7267; fax (613) 236-7882; Ambassador: LUC CARBONEZ.

**Benin:** 58 Glebe Ave, Ottawa, ON K1S 2C3; tel. (613) 233-4429; fax (613) 233-8952; Ambassador: LÉOPOLD DAVID-GNAHOUI.

**Bolivia:** 130 Albert St, Suite 416, Ottawa, ON K1P 5G4; tel. (613) 236-5730; fax (613) 236-8237; e-mail bolcan@iosphere.net; internet www.iosphere.net/~bolcan/; Ambassador: RENÉ A. SORIA GALVARRO HAENSEL.

**Bosnia and Herzegovina:** 130 Albert St, Suite 805, Ottawa, ON K1P 5G4; tel. (613) 236-0028; fax (613) 236-1139; Ambassador: KRUNOSLAV VASILJ.

**Brazil:** 450 Wilbrod St, Ottawa, ON K1N 6M8; tel. (613) 237-1090; fax (613) 237-6144; e-mail brasemb@ottawa.net; Ambassador: HENRIQUE RODRIGUES VALLE JÚNIOR.

**Brunei:** Hongkong Bank Bldg, 395 Laurier Ave East, Suite 400, Ottawa, ON K1N 6R4; tel. (603) 234-5656; fax (603) 234-4397; High Commissioner: Dato' JOCKLIN KONG PAW.

**Bulgaria:** 325 Stewart St, Ottawa, ON K1N 6K5; tel. (613) 789-3215; fax (613) 789-3524; Ambassador: SLAV DANEV.

**Burkina Faso:** 48 Range Rd, Ottawa, ON K1N 8J4; tel. (613) 238-4796; fax (613) 238-3812; e-mail burkina.faso@sympatico.ca; internet www.amba.burkina_canada.org; Ambassador: MOUHOUSSINE NACRO.

**Burundi:** Ottawa; Ambassador: EDONIAS NIYONGABO.

**Cameroon:** 170 Clemow Ave, Ottawa, ON K1S 2B4; tel. (613) 236-1522; fax (613) 238-3885; High Commissioner: PHILÉMON YUNJI YANG.

**Chile:** 50 O'Connor St, Suite 1413, Ottawa, ON K1N 6L2; tel. (613) 235-4402; fax (613) 235-1176; e-mail echileca@istar.ca; Ambassador: JOSÉ THOMAS LETELIER.

**China, People's Republic:** 515 St Patrick St, Ottawa, ON K1N 5H3; tel. (613) 789-3434; fax (613) 789-1911; Ambassador: PING MEI.

**Colombia:** 360 Albert St, Suite 1002, Ottawa, ON K1R 7X7; tel. (613) 230-3760; fax (613) 230-4416; e-mail embcolot@travel-net.com; internet www.travel-net.com/~embcolot; Ambassador: JOSÉ MARÍA DE GUZMÁN MORA.

**Congo, Democratic Republic:** 18 Range Rd, Ottawa, ON K1N 8J3; tel. (613) 236-7103; fax (613) 567-1404; Chargé d'affaires a.i.: LEYAN' SIMBI M'FUMU KANUNU.

**Costa Rica:** 135 York St, Suite 208, Ottawa, ON K1N 5T4; tel. (613) 562-2855; fax (613) 562-2582; e-mail embcrica@travel-net.com; Ambassador: CARLOS MIRANDA.

**Côte d'Ivoire:** 9 Marlborough Ave, Ottawa, ON K1N 8E6; tel. (613) 236-9919; fax (613) 563-8287; Ambassador: JEAN OBÉO-COULIBALY.

**Croatia:** 229 Chapel St, Ottawa, ON K1N 7Y6; tel. (613) 562-7820; fax (613) 562-7821; Ambassador: ANDRIJA JAKOČEVIĆ.

**Cuba:** 388 Main St, Ottawa, ON K1S 1E3; tel. (613) 563-0141; fax (613) 563-0068; e-mail cuba@idirect.com; Ambassador: CARLOS FERNÁNDEZ DE COSSIO DOMÍNGUEZ.

**Czech Republic:** 541 Sussex Drive, Ottawa, ON K1N 6Z6; tel. (613) 562-3875; fax (613) 562-3878; e-mail ottawa@embassy.mzv.cz; Ambassador: VLADIMÍR KOTZY.

**Denmark:** 47 Clarence St, Suite 450, Ottawa, ON K1N 9K1; tel. (613) 562-1811; fax (613) 562-1812; e-mail danemb@cyberus.ca; internet www.danish-embassy-canada.com; Ambassador: JØRGEN M. BEHNKE.

**Ecuador:** 50 O'Connor St, Suite 316, Ottawa, ON K1P 6L2; tel. (613) 563-8206; fax (613) 235-5776; e-mail mecucan@inasec.ca; Ambassador: MANUEL A. PESANTES.

**Egypt:** 454 Laurier Ave East, Ottawa, ON K1N 6R3; tel. (613) 234-4931; fax (613) 234-9347; Ambassador: HAMDY NADA.

**El Salvador:** 209 Kent St, Suite 504, Ottawa, ON K2P 1Z8; tel. (613) 238-2939; fax (613) 238-6940; e-mail 103234.607@compuserve.com; Ambassador: Dr MAURICIO ROSALES RIVERA.

**Ethiopia:** 151 Slater St, Suite 210, Ottawa, ON K1P 5H3; tel. (613) 235-6637; fax (613) 235-4638; e-mail infoethi@magi.com; internet www.ethiopia.ottawa.on.ca; Ambassador: Dr FECADU GADAMU.

**Finland:** 55 Metcalfe St, Suite 850, Ottawa, ON K1P 6L5; tel. (613) 236-2389; fax (613) 238-1474; e-mail finembott@synapse.net; internet www.finemb.com; Ambassador: VEIJO SAMPOVAARA.

**France:** 42 Sussex Drive, Ottawa, ON K1M 2C9; tel. (613) 789-1795; fax (613) 562-3735; e-mail presse@amba-ottawa.fr; internet www.amba-ottawa.fr; Ambassador: DENIS BAUCHARD.

**Gabon:** 4 Range Rd, Ottawa, ON K1N 8J5; tel. (613) 232-5301; fax (613) 232-6916; Ambassador: ALPHONSE OYABI-GNALA.

**Germany:** 1 Waverley St, Ottawa, ON K2P 0T8; tel. (613) 232-1101; fax (613) 594-9330; e-mail 100566.2620@compuserve.com; Ambassador: Dr ERNST JÜRGEN PÖHLMANN.

**Ghana:** 1 Clemow Ave, Ottawa, ON K1S 2A9; tel. (613) 236-0871; fax (613) 236-0874; High Commissioner: OLIVER K. K. LAWLUVI.

**Greece:** 76–80 MacLaren St, Ottawa, ON K2P 0K6; tel. (613) 238-6271; fax (613) 238-5676; e-mail greekembott@travel-net.com; Ambassador: JOHN-ALEXANDER THOMOGLOU.

**Guatemala:** 130 Albert St, Suite 1010, Ottawa, ON K1P 5G4; tel. (613) 233-7237; fax (613) 233-0135; e-mail embguate@webruler.com; Ambassador: JORGE SKINNER-KLEE.

**Guinea:** 483 Wilbrod St, Ottawa, ON K1N 6N1; tel. (613) 789-8444; fax (613) 789-7560; Ambassador: THIERNO DIALLO.

**Guyana:** Burnside Bldg, 151 Slater St, Suite 309, Ottawa, ON K1P 5H3; tel. (613) 235-7249; fax (613) 235-1447; High Commissioner: RAJNARINE SINGH.

**Haiti:** Place de Ville, Tower B, 112 Kent St, Suite 205, Ottawa, ON K1P 5P2; tel. (613) 238-1628; fax (613) 238-2986; e-mail bohio@sympatico.ca; Chargé d'affaires a.i.: LHANDE HENRIQUEZ.

**Holy See:** Apostolic Nunciature, 724 Manor Ave, Rockcliffe Park, Ottawa, ON K1M 0E3; tel. (613) 746-4914; fax (613) 746-4786; e-mail nuncioap@istar.ca; Nuncio: Most Rev. PAOLO ROMEO, Titular Archbishop of Vulturia.

**Honduras:** 151 Slater St, Suite 805, Ottawa, ON K1P 5H3; tel. (613) 233-8900; fax (613) 232-0193; e-mail scastell@magmacom.com; Ambassador: SALOMÉ CASTELLANOS-DELGADO.

**Hungary:** 299 Waverley St, Ottawa, ON K2P 0V9; tel. (613) 230-2717; fax (613) 230-7560; e-mail h2embott@docuweb.ca; internet www.docuweb.ca/hungary/; Ambassador: SÁNDOR PAPP.

**India:** 10 Springfield Rd, Ottawa, ON K1M 1C9; tel. (613) 744-3751; fax (613) 744-0913; e-mail hicomind@ottawa.net; internet www.docuweb.ca/india; High Commissioner: RAJANIKANTA VERMA.

**Indonesia:** 55 Parkdale Ave, Ottawa, ON K1Y 1E5; tel. (613) 724-1100; fax (613) 724-1105; e-mail jupiter@prica.org; internet www.prica.org; Ambassador: BUDIMAN DARMOSUTANTO.

**Iran:** 245 Metcalfe St, Ottawa, ON K2P 2K2; tel. (613) 235-4726; fax (613) 232-5712; e-mail iranemb@sonetis.com; Chargé d'affaires a.i.: REZA SHAKER.

**Iraq:** 215 McLeod St, Ottawa, ON K2P 0Z8; tel. (613) 236-9177; fax (613) 567-1101; Chargé d'affaires a.i.: MOHAMMAD H. RADHI AL-SAFAR.

**Ireland:** 130 Albert St, Suite 1105, Ottawa, ON K1P 5G4; tel. (613) 233-6281; fax (613) 233-5835; Ambassador: PAUL DEMPSEY.

**Israel:** 50 O'Connor St, Suite 1005, Ottawa, ON K1P 6L2; tel. (613) 567-6450; fax (613) 237-8865; e-mail embisrott@cyberus.ca; internet www.israelca.org; Ambassador: DAVID SULTAN.

**Italy:** 275 Slater St, 21st Floor, Ottawa, ON K1P 5H9; tel. (613) 232-2401; fax (613) 233-1484; Ambassador: ROBERTO NIGIDO.

**Jamaica:** 275 Slater St, Suite 800, Ottawa, ON K1P 5H9; tel. (613) 233-9311; fax (613) 233-0611; High Commissioner: RAYMOND WOLFE.

**Japan:** 255 Sussex Drive, Ottawa, ON K1N 9E6; tel. (613) 241-8541; fax (613) 241-7415; e-mail infocul@embjapan.can.org; Ambassador: KATSUHISA UCHIDA.

**Jordan:** 100 Bronson Ave, Suite 701, Ottawa, ON K1R 6G8; tel. (613) 238-8090; fax (613) 232-3341; Ambassador: SAMIR M. KHALIFEH.

**Kenya:** 415 Laurier Ave East, Ottawa, ON K1N 6R4; tel. (613) 563-1773; fax (613) 233-6599; e-mail kenrep@on.aibn.com; Chargé d'affaires a.i.: JOSEPH O. O. KISEREMA.

**Korea, Republic:** 150 Boteler St, Ottawa, ON K1N 5A6; tel. (613) 244-5010; fax (613) 244-5043; Ambassador: SAM HOON KIM.

**Kuwait:** 80 Elgin St, Ottawa, ON K1P 1C6; tel. (613) 780-9999; fax (613) 780-9905; e-mail 75057.2763@compuserve.com; Ambassador: MAJDI AHMAD E. AL-DAFIRI.

**Latvia:** Place de Ville, Tower B, 112 Kent St, Suite 208, Ottawa, ON K1P 5P2; tel. (613) 238-6014; fax (613) 238-7044; internet www.2.magmacom.com//~latemb; Ambassador: JĀNIS LŪSIS.

**Lebanon:** 640 Lyon St, Ottawa, ON K1S 3Z5; tel. (613) 236-5825; fax (613) 232-1609; Ambassador: Dr ASSEM SALMAN JABER.

**Lithuania:** 130 Albert St, Suite 204, Ottawa, ON K1P 5G4; tel. (613) 567-5458; fax (613) 567-5315; Ambassador: Dr ALFONSAS EIDINTAS.

**Macedonia, former Yugoslav republic:** 130 Albert St, Suite 1006, Ottawa, ON K1P 5G4; tel. (613) 234-3882; fax (613) 233-1852; Ambassador: JORDAN VESELINOV.

**Madagascar:** 649 Blair Rd, Gloucester, ON K1J 7M4; tel. (613) 744-7995; fax (613) 744-2530; e-mail ambamadott@on.aibn.com; Ambassador: RENÉ FIDÈLE RAJAONAH.

**Malawi:** 7 Clemow Ave, Ottawa, ON K1S 2A9; tel. (613) 236-8931; fax (613) 236-1054; e-mail malawihighcommission@sympatico.ca; High Commissioner: HENRY R. CHIRWA.

**Malaysia:** 60 Boteler St, Ottawa, ON K1N 8Y7; tel. (613) 241-5182; fax (613) 241-5214; e-mail malott@istar.ca; High Commissioner: Datuk A. W. OMARDIN.

**Mali:** 50 Goulburn Ave, Ottawa, ON K1N 8C8; tel. (613) 232-1501; fax (613) 232-7429; Ambassador: MANASSA DANIOKO DIAKITÉ.

**Mauritania:** 249 McLeod St, Ottawa, ON KZP 1A1; tel. (613) 237-3283; fax (613) 237-3287; Ambassador: ABDEL MAJID KAMIL.

**Mexico:** 45 O'Connor St, Suite 1500, Ottawa, ON K1P 1A4; tel. (613) 233-8988; fax (613) 235-9123; e-mail press@embamexcan.com; Ambassador: EZEQUIEL PADILLA.

**Morocco:** 38 Range Rd, Ottawa, ON K1N 8J4; tel. (613) 236-7391; fax (613) 236-6164; Ambassador: ABDELKADER LECHEHEB.

**Myanmar:** 85 Range Rd, Suite 902, Ottawa, ON K1N 8J6; tel. (613) 232-6434; fax (613) 232-6435; Chargé d'affaires a.i.: Mme YIN YIN OO.

**Netherlands:** 350 Albert St, Suite 2020, Ottawa, ON K1R 1A4; tel. (613) 237-5030; fax (613) 237-6471; Ambassador: D. J. VAN HOUTEN.

**New Zealand:** Metlife Centre, 99 Bank St, Suite 727, Ottawa, ON K1P 6G3; tel. (613) 238-5991; fax (613) 238-5707; e-mail nzhcott@istar.ca; internet www.nzhcottawa.org; High Commissioner: RICHARD JAMES GERARD.

**Niger:** 38 Blackburn Ave, Ottawa, ON K1N 8A3; tel. (613) 232-4291; fax (613) 230-9808; Ambassador: RAKIATOU MAYAKI.

**Nigeria:** 295 Metcalfe St, Ottawa, ON K2P 1R9; tel. (613) 236-0522; fax (613) 236-0529; High Commissioner: ABDUL-AZIZ GARUBA.

**Norway:** 90 Sparks St, Suite 532, Ottawa, ON K1P 5B4; tel. (613) 238-6571; fax (613) 238-2765; e-mail nor-emb-ott@intranet.ca; Ambassador: JOHAN L. LOVALD.

**Pakistan:** Burnside Bldg, 151 Slater St, Suite 608, Ottawa, ON K1P 5H3; tel. (613) 238-7881; fax (613) 238-7296; e-mail hcpak@sprint.com; High Commissioner: RAFAT MAHDI.

**Panama:** 130 Albert St, Suite 300, Ottawa, ON K1P 5G4; tel. (613) 236-7177; fax (613) 236-5775; e-mail pancanem@travel-net.com; Chargé d'affaires a.i.: GUILLERMO A. VILORIA AROSEMENA.

**Papua New Guinea:** 130 Albert St, Suite 300, Ottawa, ON K1A 5G4; fax (613) 236-5775; High Commissioner: NAGORA Y. BOGAN.

**Paraguay:** 151 Slater St, Suite 501, Ottawa, ON K1P 5H3; tel. (613) 567-1283; fax (613) 567-1679; e-mail embapar@magmacom.com; internet www.magmacom.com/~embapar; Chargé d'affaires a.i.: VICTOR HUGO AQUINO FORNERA.

**Peru:** 130 Albert St, Suite 1901, Ottawa, ON K1P 5G4; tel. (613) 238-1777; fax (613) 232-3062; e-mail emperuca@magi.com; Ambassador: HERNÁN COUTURIER-MARIATEGUI.

**Philippines:** 130 Albert St, Suite 606, Ottawa, ON K1P 5G4; tel. (613) 233-1121; fax (613) 233-4165; e-mail ottawape@istar.ca; internet www.geocities.com/capitolhill/senate/3551; Ambassador: FRANCISCO L. BENEDICTO.

**Poland:** 443 Daly Ave, Ottawa, ON K1N 6H3; tel. (613) 789-0468; fax (613) 789-1218; e-mail polamb@hookup.net; Ambassador: BOGDAN GRZELONSKI.

**Portugal:** 645 Island Park Drive, Ottawa, ON K1Y 0B8; tel. (613) 729-0883; fax (613) 729-4236; Ambassador: JOSÉ MANUEL DUARTE DE JESUS.

**Romania:** 655 Rideau St, Ottawa, ON K1N 6A3; tel. (613) 789-3709; fax (613) 789-4365; e-mail romania@cyberus.ca; internet www.cyberus.ca/~romania; Ambassador: GABRIEL GAFIȚA.

**Russia:** 285 Charlotte St, Ottawa, ON K1N 8L5; tel. (613) 235-4341; fax (613) 236-6342; e-mail rusemb@intranet.ca; Ambassador: VITALY CHURKIN.

**Rwanda:** 121 Sherwood Drive, Ottawa, ON K1Y 3V1; tel. (613) 722-5835; fax (613) 722-4052; e-mail embarwa@travel-net.com; Ambassador: LAURENT NKONGOLI.

**Saudi Arabia:** 99 Bank St, Suite 901, Ottawa, ON K1P 6B9; tel. (613) 237-4100; fax (613) 237-0567; Ambassador: Dr MOHAMMED R. AL-HUSANI AL-SHARIF.

**Senegal:** 57 Marlborough Ave, Ottawa, ON K1N 8E8; tel. (613) 238-6392; fax (613) 238-2695; Ambassador: PIERRE DIOUF.

**Slovakia:** 50 Rideau Terrace, Ottawa, ON K1M 2A1; tel. (613) 749-4442; fax (613) 749-4989; Ambassador: Dr MIROSLAV MIKOLÁŠIK.

**Slovenia:** 150 Metcalfe St, Suite 2101, Ottawa, ON K2P 1P1; tel. (613) 565-5781; fax (613) 565-5783; Ambassador: Dr BOŽO CERAR.

**South Africa:** 15 Sussex Drive, Ottawa, ON K1M 1M8; tel. (613) 744-0330; fax (613) 741-1639; e-mail rsafrica@sympatico.ca; internet www.docuweb.ca/SouthAfrica; High Commissioner: ANDRÉ JAQUET.

**Spain:** 74 Stanley Ave, Ottawa, ON K1M 1P4; tel. (613) 747-2252; fax (613) 744-1224; e-mail spain@docuweb.ca; internet www.DocuWeb.ca/SpainInCanada/; Abassador: JOSÉ CUENCA ANAYA.

**Sri Lanka:** 333 Laurier Ave West, Suite 1204, Ottawa, ON K1P 1C1; tel. (613) 233-8449; fax (613) 238-8448; e-mail lankacom@magi.com; High Commissioner: A. C. GOONASEKERA.

**Sudan:** 85 Range Rd, Suite 507, Ottawa, ON K1N 8J6; tel. (613) 235-4000; fax (613) 235-6880; Chargé d'affaires a.i.: ABD EL-HANI E. AWAD EL-KARIM.

**Swaziland:** 130 Albert St, Suite 1204, Ottawa, ON K1P 5G4; tel. (613) 567-1480; fax (613) 567-1058; High Commissioner: BREMER M. NXUMALO.

**Sweden:** Mercury Court, 377 Dalhousie St, Ottawa, ON K1N 9N8; tel. (613) 241-8553; fax (613) 241-2277; e-mail sweden@cyberus.ca; Ambassador: JAN STÅHL.

**Switzerland:** 5 Marlborough Ave, Ottawa, ON K1N 8E6; tel. (613) 235-1837; fax (613) 563-1394; e-mail vertretung@ott.rep.admin.ch; Ambassador: URS ZISWEILER.

**Syria:** 151 Slater St, Suite 1000, Ottawa, ON K1P 5H3; tel. (613) 569 5556; fax (613) 569-3800; Chargé d'affaires a.i.: AHMAD FAROUK ARNOUS.

**Tanzania:** 50 Range Rd, Ottawa, ON K1N 8J4; tel. (613) 232-1500; fax (613) 232-5184; High Commissioner: FADHIL D. MBAGA.

**Thailand:** 180 Island Park Drive, Ottawa, ON K1Y 0A2; tel. (613) 722-4444; fax (613) 722-6624; e-mail thaiott@magma.ca; Ambassador: SUNAI BUNYASIRIPHANT.

**Togo:** 12 Range Rd, Ottawa, ON K1N 8J3; tel. (613) 238-5916; fax (613) 235-6425; Ambassador: (vacant).

**Trinidad and Tobago:** 75 Albert St, Suite 508, Ottawa, ON K1P 5E7; tel. (613) 232-2418; fax (613) 232-4349; e-mail ottawa@ttmissions.com; internet www.ttmissions.com; High Commissioner: ROBERT M. SABGA.

**Tunisia:** 515 O'Connor St, Ottawa, ON K1S 3P8; tel. (613) 237-0330; fax (613) 237-7939; Ambassador: HABIB LAZREG.

**Turkey:** 197 Wurtemburg St, Ottawa, ON K1N 8L9; tel. (613) 789-4044; fax (613) 789-3442; Ambassador: ERHAN ÖĞÜT.

**Ukraine:** 310 Somerset St West, Ottawa, ON K2P 0J9; tel. (613) 230-2961; fax (613) 230-2400; Ambassador: VOLODYMYR KHANDOGIY.

**United Arab Emirates:** World Exchange Plaza, 45 O'Connor St, Suite 1800, Ottawa, ON K1P 1A4; tel. (613) 565-7272; fax (613) 565-8007; Ambassador: MOHAMMAD J. SAMHAN.

**United Kingdom:** 80 Elgin St, Ottawa, ON K1P 5K7; tel. (613) 237-1530; fax (613) 237-7980; High Commissioner: Sir ANTHONY GOODENOUGH.

**USA:** 490 Sussex Drive, POB 866, Station B, Ottawa, ON K1N 1G8; tel. (613) 238-5335; Ambassador: GORDON D. GIFFIN.

**Uruguay:** 130 Albert St, Suite 1905, Ottawa, ON K1P 5G4; tel. (613) 234-2727; fax (613) 233-4670; e-mail urott@iosphere.net; internet www.iosphere.net/~uruott/; Ambassador: GASTON LASARTE.

**Venezuela:** 32 Range Rd, Ottawa, ON K1N 8J4; tel. (613) 235-5151; fax (613) 235-3205; e-mail embavene@travel-net.com; Ambassador: JORGE OSORIO.

**Viet Nam:** 470 Wilbrod St, Ottawa, ON K1M 6M8; tel. (613) 236-0772; fax (613) 236-2704; Ambassador: THANH QUANG TRINH.

**Yemen:** 788 Island Park Drive, Ottawa, ON K1Y 0C2; tel. (613) 729-6627; fax (613) 729-8915; Chargé d'affaires a.i.: ABDULMALEK ABDULGHANI SALEH.

**Yugoslavia:** 17 Blackburn Ave, Ottawa, ON K1N 8A2; tel. (613) 233-6289; fax (613) 233-7850; e-mail embotava@capitalnet.com; Ambassador: Dr PAVLE TODOROVIĆ.

**Zimbabwe:** 332 Somerset St West, Ottawa, ON K2P 0J9; tel. (613) 237-4388; fax (613) 563-8269; e-mail zim.highcomm@sympatico.ca; internet www.docuweb.ca/zimbabwe; High Commissioner: LILLIE CHITAURO.

# Judicial System

### FEDERAL COURTS

**The Supreme Court of Canada:** Supreme Court Bldg, 301 Wellington St, Ottawa, ON K1A 0J1; tel. (613) 995-4330; fax (613) 996-3063; e-mail reception@scc-csc.gov.ca; ultimate court of appeal in both civil and criminal cases throughout Canada. The Supreme Court is also required to advise on questions referred to it by the Governor-General in Council. Important questions concerning the interpretation of the Constitution Act, the constitutionality or interpretation of any federal or provincial law, the powers of Parliament or of the provincial legislatures, among other matters, may be referred by the Government to the Supreme Court for consideration.

In civil cases, appeals may be brought from any final judgment of the highest court of last resort in a province, or of the Federal Court of Appeal. The Supreme Court will grant permission to appeal if it is of the opinion that a question of public importance is involved, one that transcends the immediate concerns of the parties to the litigation. In criminal cases, the Court will hear appeals as of right concerning indictable offences where an acquittal has been set aside or where there has been a dissenting judgment on a point of law in a provincial court of appeal. The Supreme Court may, in addition, consent to hear appeals on questions of law concerning both summary conviction and all other indictable offences.

**Chief Justice of Canada:** BEVERLEY MCLACHLIN.

**Puisne Judges:** CLAIRE L'HEUREUX-DUBÉ, CHARLES DOHERTY GONTHIER, FRANK IACOBUCCI, JOHN C. MAJOR, MICHEL BASTARACHE, W. IAN BINNIE, LOUISE ARBOUR, LOUIS LEBEL.

**The Federal Court of Canada:** Supreme Court Bldg, Wellington St, Ottawa, ON K1A 0H9; tel. (613) 992-4238; has jurisdiction in claims against the Crown, claims by the Crown, miscellaneous cases involving the Crown, claims against or concerning crown officers and servants, relief against Federal Boards, Commissions, and other tribunals, interprovincial and federal-provincial disputes, industrial or industrial property matters, admiralty, income tax and estate tax appeals, citizenship appeals, aeronautics, interprovincial works and undertakings, residuary jurisdiction for relief if there is no other Canadian court that has such jurisdiction, jurisdiction in specific matters conferred by federal statutes.

**The Federal Court of Appeal:** Supreme Court Bldg, Wellington St, Ottawa, ON K1A 0H9; tel. (613) 996-6795; has jurisdiction on appeals from the Trial Division, appeals from Federal Tribunals, review of decisions of Federal Boards and Commissions, appeals from Tribunals and Reviews under Section 28 of the Federal Court Act, and references by Federal Boards and Commissions. The Court has one central registry and consists of the principal office in Ottawa and local offices in major centres throughout Canada.

**Chief Justice:** JOHN D. RICHARD.

**Associate Chief Justice:** (vacant).

**Court of Appeal Judges:** LOUIS PRATTE, LOUIS MARCEAU, ARTHUR STONE, BARRY STRAYER, ALICE DESJARDINS, ROBERT DÉCARY, ALLEN LINDEN, GILLES LÉTOURNEAU, JOSEPH ROBERTSON, MARC NOËL, F. JOSEPH MCDONALD, J. EDGAR SEXTON.

**Trial Division Judges:** J.-E. DUBÉ, PAUL ROULEAU, FRANCIS MULDOON, BARBARA REED, PIERRE DENAULT, YVON PINARD, L. MARCEL JOYAL, BUD CULLEN, MAX TEITELBAUM, WILLIAM MACKAY, DONNA MCGILLIS, MARSHALL ROTHSTEIN, WILLIAM MCKEOWN, FREDERICK GIBSON, SANDRA SIMPSON, MARC NADON, HOWARD WETSTON, DANIÈLE TREMBLAY-LAMER, DOUGLAS CAMPBELL, ALLAN LUTFY, PIERRE BLAIS, JOHN M. EVANS.

## PROVINCIAL COURTS

### Alberta

Court of Appeal

**Chief Justice of Alberta:** CATHERINE A. FRASER.

Court of Queen's Bench

**Chief Justice:** WILLIAM K. MOORE.

**Associate Chief Justice:** ALLAN H. J. WACHOWICH.

### British Columbia

Court of Appeal

**Chief Justice of British Columbia:** ALLAN MCEACHERN.

Supreme Court

**Chief Justice:** BRYAN WILLIAMS.

**Associate Chief Justice:** P. D. DOHM.

### Manitoba

Court of Appeal

**Chief Justice of Manitoba:** R. J. SCOTT.

Court of Queen's Bench

**Chief Justice:** B. HEWAK.

**Associate Chief Justice:** J. J. OLIPHANT.

**Associate Chief Justice (Family Division):** G. W. J. MERCIER.

### New Brunswick

Court of Appeal

**Chief Justice of New Brunswick:** JOSEPH Z. DAIGLE.

Court of Queen's Bench

**Chief Justice:** D. D. SMITH.

### Newfoundland

Supreme Court—Court of Appeal

**Chief Justice:** CLYDE K. WELLS.

Trial Division

**Chief Justice:** T. A. HICKMAN.

### Nova Scotia

Court of Appeal

**Chief Justice of Nova Scotia:** CONSTANCE R. GLUBE.

Supreme Court

**Chief Justice:** J. P. KENNEDY.

**Associate Chief Justice:** J. M. MACDONALD.

Supreme Court (Family Division)

**Associate Chief Justice:** R. F. FERGUSON.

### Ontario

Court of Appeal

**Chief Justice of Ontario:** ROY R. MCMURTRY.

**Associate Chief Justice of Ontario:** COULTER A. OSBORNE.

Court of Justice

**Chief Justice:** P. J. LESAGE.

**Associate Chief Justice:** Madam H. J. SMITH.

### Prince Edward Island

Supreme Court—Appeal Division

**Chief Justice:** NORMAN H. CARRUTHERS.

Supreme Court—Trial Division

**Chief Justice:** KENNETH R. MACDONALD.

### Québec

Court of Appeal

**Chief Justice of Québec:** PIERRE A. MICHAUD.

Superior Court

**Chief Justice:** LYSE LEMIEUX.

**Senior Associate Chief Justice:** RENÉ W. DIONNE.

**Associate Chief Justice:** ANDRÉ DESLONGCHAMPS.

### Saskatchewan

Court of Appeal

**Chief Justice of Saskatchewan:** E. D. BAYDA.

Court of Queen's Bench

**Chief Justice:** D. K. MACPHERSON.

### Northwest Territories

Court of Appeal

**Chief Justice:** CATHERINE A. FRASER (Alberta).

Supreme Court

**Judges of the Supreme Court:** B. A. BROWNE, R. G. KILPATRICK.

### Nunavut Territory

Court of Appeal

**Chief Justice:** CATHERINE A. FRASER (Alberta).

### Yukon Territory

Court of Appeal

**Chief Justice:** ALLAN MCEACHERN (British Columbia).

Supreme Court

**Judges of the Supreme Court:** RALPH E. HUDSON, HARRY C. B. MADDISON.

# Religion

## CHRISTIANITY

About 75% of the population belong to the three main Christian churches: Roman Catholic, United and Anglican. Numerous other religious denominations are active in Canada.

**Canadian Council of Churches/Conseil canadien des Eglises:** 3250 Bloor St West, 2nd Floor, Etobicoke, ON M8X 2Y4; tel. (416) 232-6070; fax (416) 236-4532; e-mail ccadmin@web.net; internet www.web.net/~ccchurch; f. 1944; 18 mem. churches, one assoc. mem; Pres. Most Rev. J. BARRY CURTIS (Anglican Archbishop of Calgary); Gen. Sec. JANET SOMERVILLE.

### The Anglican Communion

The Anglican Church of Canada (L'Eglise anglicane du Canada) comprises 30 dioceses in four ecclesiastical provinces (each with a Metropolitan archbishop). The Church had 780,897 members in 1,740 parishes in 1997.

**General Synod of the Anglican Church of Canada:** Church House, 600 Jarvis St, Toronto, ON M4Y 2J6; tel. (416) 924-9192; fax (416) 968-7983; e-mail info@national.anglican.ca; internet www.anglican.ca; Gen. Sec. Archdeacon JAMES BOYLES.

**Primate of the Anglican Church of Canada:** Most Rev. MICHAEL G. PEERS.

**Province of British Columbia and Yukon:** Metropolitan Most Rev. DAVID P. CRAWLEY, Archbishop of Kootenay.

**Province of Canada:** Metropolitan Most Rev. ARTHUR PETERS, Archbishop of Nova Scotia.

**Province of Ontario:** Metropolitan Most Rev. PERCY R. O'DRISCOLL, Archbishop of Huron.

**Province of Rupert's Land:** Acting Metropolitan Rt Rev. THOMAS O. MORGAN, Bishop of Saskatoon.

### The Orthodox Churches

**Greek Orthodox Metropolis of Toronto (Canada):** 1 Patriarch Bartholomew Way, Toronto, ON M4H 1C6; tel. (416) 429-5757; fax (416) 429-4588; e-mail gocanada@total.net; 350,000 mems (1997); Metropolitan Archbishop SOTIRIOS ATHANASSOULAS.

**Ukrainian Orthodox Church of Canada:** 9 St John's Ave, Winnipeg, MB R2W 1G8; tel. (204) 586-3093; fax (204) 582-5241; e-mail consistory@uocc.ca; internet www.uocc.ca; f. 1918; 281 parishes, 120,000 mems (1998); Metropolitan of Winnipeg and of all Canada His Beatitude WASYLY (FEDAK); Chancellor Rt Rev Dr OLEH KRAWCHENKO.

The Romanian, Serbian, Coptic, Antiochian and Armenian Churches are also represented in Canada.

### The Roman Catholic Church

For Catholics of the Latin rite, Canada comprises 18 archdioceses (including one directly responsible to the Holy See), 46 dioceses and one territorial abbacy. There are also one archdiocese and four dioceses of the Ukrainian rite. In addition, the Maronite, Melkite and Slovak rites are each represented by one diocese (all directly responsible to the Holy See). In October 1997 the Roman Catholic Church had about 7.2m. adherents in Canada.

**Canadian Conference of Catholic Bishops/Conférence des évêques catholiques du Canada:** 90 Parent Ave, Ottawa, ON K1N 7B1; tel. (613) 241-9461; fax (613) 241-8117; e-mail cecc@cccb.ca; internet www.cccb.ca; Pres. Rt Rev. GERALD WIESNER, Bishop of Prince George; Vice-Pres. Rt Rev. JACQUES BERTHELET, Bishop of St-Jean-Longueuil.

*Latin Rite*

**Archbishop of Edmonton:** THOMAS COLLINS.

**Archbishop of Gatineau-Hull:** ROGER ÉBACHER.

**Archbishop of Grouard-McLennan:** (vacant).

**Archbishop of Halifax:** TERRENCE PRENDERGAST.

**Archbishop of Keewatin-Le Pas:** PETER ALFRED SUTTON.

**Archbishop of Kingston:** FRANCIS J. SPENCE.

**Archbishop of Moncton:** ERNEST LÉGER.

**Archbishop of Montréal:** Cardinal JEAN-CLAUDE TURCOTTE.

**Archbishop of Ottawa:** MARCEL A. GERVAIS.

**Archbishop of Québec:** MAURICE COUTURE.

**Archbishop of Regina:** PETER J. MALLON.

**Archbishop of Rimouski:** BERTRAND BLANCHET.

**Archbishop of St Boniface:** ANTOINE HACAULT.

**Archbishop of St John's, Nfld:** JAMES H. MACDONALD.

**Archbishop of Sherbrooke:** ANDRÉ GAUMOND.

**Archbishop of Toronto:** Cardinal ALOYSIUS M. AMBROZIC.

**Archbishop of Vancouver:** ADAM J. EXNER.

**Archbishop of Winnipeg:** LEONARD J. WALL.

*Ukrainian Rite*

**Ukrainian Catholic Church in Canada:** 233 Scotia St, Winnipeg, MB R2V 1V7; tel. (204) 338-7801; fax (204) 339-4006; 133,490 mems (1991 census); Archeparch-Metropolitan of Winnipeg Most Rev. MICHAEL BZDEL; Auxiliary Bishop STEFAN SOROKA, Titular Bishop of Acarasso.

### The United Church of Canada

The United Church of Canada (L'Eglise unie du Canada) was founded in 1925 with the union of Methodist, Congregational and Presbyterian churches in Canada. The Evangelical United Brethren of Canada joined in 1968. In 1997 there were 3,872 congregations and 1,835,215 mems.

**Moderator:** WILLIAM F. PHIPPS.

**General Secretary:** VIRGINIA COLEMAN, 3250 Bloor St West, Suite 300, Toronto, ON M8X 2Y4; tel. (416) 231-5931; fax (416) 231-3103; e-mail info@uccan.org; internet www.uccan.org.

### Other Christian Churches

**Canadian Baptist Ministries:** 7185 Millcreek Drive, Mississauga, ON L5N 5R4; tel. (905) 821-3533; fax (905) 826-3441; e-mail dphillips@cbmin.org; internet www.cbmin.org; 1,133 churches; 129,000 mems (1996); Pres. Dr BRUCE MILNE; Gen. Sec. Rev. DAVID PHILLIPS.

**Christian Reformed Church in North America (Canadian Council):** 3475 Mainway, POB 5070, Burlington, ON L7R 3Y8; tel. (905) 336-2920; fax (905) 336-8344; internet www.crcna.org; f. 1857; 236 congregations; 81,000 mems (1998); Dir in Canada RAY ELGERSMA.

**Church of Jesus Christ of Latter-day Saints (Mormon):** 1185 Eglinton Ave East, POB 116, Toronto, ON M3C 3C6; tel. (416) 424-2485; fax (416) 424-3326; 391 congregations; 130,000 mems in Canada (1996).

**Evangelical Lutheran Church in Canada:** 393 Portage Ave, Suite 302, Winnipeg, MB R3B 3H6; tel. (204) 984-9150; fax (204) 984-9185; e-mail sartison@elcic.ca; internet www.elcic.ca/; f. 1967; 640 congregations, 196,000 mems (1997); Bishop Rev. TELMOR G. SARTISON.

**Lutheran Church–Canada:** 3074 Portage Ave, Winnipeg, MB R3K 0Y2; tel. (204) 895-3433; fax (204) 897-4319; e-mail lcc@mts.net; internet www.lutheranchurch-canada.ca; f. 1988; 325 congregations; 80,000 mems (1997); Pres. Rev. RALPH MAYAN.

**Mennonite Central Committee–Canada:** 134 Plaza Drive, Winnipeg, MB R3T 5K9; tel. (204) 261-6381; fax (204) 269-9875; e-mail mcc@mennonitecc.ca; f. 1963; 120,000 mems in 600 congregations; Exec. Dir MARVIN FREY.

**Pentecostal Assemblies of Canada:** 6745 Century Ave, Mississauga, ON L5N 6P7; tel. (905) 542-7400; fax (905) 542-7313; e-mail info@paoc.org; internet www.paoc.org; 1,938 congregations, 237,000 mems (1998); Gen. Supt Dr WILLIAM D. MORROW.

**Presbyterian Church in Canada:** 50 Wynford Drive, North York, ON M3C 1J7; tel. (416) 441-1111; fax (416) 441-2825; internet www.presbycan.ca; f. 1875; 1,010 congregations; 211,000 mems (1997); Moderator Dr ALAN M. MCPHERSON; Prin. Clerk Rev. THOMAS GEMMELL.

**Religious Society of Friends:** 91A Fourth Ave, Ottawa, ON K1S 2L1; tel. (613) 235-8553; fax (613) 235-1753; e-mail cym@web.net; internet www.web.net/~cym; Clerk of Canadian Yearly Meeting GORDON MCCLURE.

**Seventh-day Adventists:** 1148 King St East, Oshawa, ON L1H 1H8; tel. (905) 433-0011; fax (905) 433-0982; internet www.sdacc.org; 332 congregations; 48,000 mems (1998); Pres. ORVILLE PARCHMENT; Sec. CLAUDE SABOT.

## BAHÁ'Í FAITH

**Bahá'í Community of Canada:** 7200 Leslie St, Thornhill, ON L3T 6L8; tel. (905) 889-8168; fax (905) 889-8184; e-mail secretariat@cdnbnc.org; internet www.bahai.org; f. 1902; 29,000 mems (1998); Sec. JUDY FILSON.

## BUDDHISM

**Buddhist Churches of Canada:** 11786 Fentiman Place, Richmond, BC V7E 6M6; tel. (604) 272-3330; fax (604) 272-6865; internet www.bcc.ca; Jodo Shinshu Hongwanji-ha of Mahayana Buddhism; Bishop KYOJO IKUTA.

## ISLAM

There are an estimated 260,000 Muslims in Canada.

**Ahmadiyya Movement in Islam (Canada):** 10610 Jane St, Maple, ON L6A 1S1; tel. (416) 832-2669; fax (416) 832-3220; e-mail info@islam.ahmadiyya.org; Pres. and Missionary-in-Charge NASEEM MAHDI.

**Canadian Islamic Organization Inc:** 2069 Kempton Park Drive, Mississauga, ON L5M 2Z4; tel. (905) 820-4655; fax (905) 820-0832; Gen. Sec. FAREED AHMAD KHAN.

**Council of Muslim Communities of Canada:** 1250 Ramsey View Court, Suite 504, Sudbury, ON P3E 2E7; co-ordinating agency; Dir MIR IQBAL ALI.

**Federation of Islamic Associations:** 73 Patricia Ave, North York, ON M2M 1J1; tel. (416) 222-2794; fax (416) 674-8168; Pres. AYUBE ALLY.

**Organization of North American Shi'a Itha-Asheri Muslim Communities (NASIMCO):** 300 John St, POB 87629, Thornhill, ON L3T 5W0; tel. (905) 763-7512; fax (905) 763-7509; e-mail nasimco@idirect.com; f. 1980; Pres. GHULAM ABBAS SAJAN.

## JUDAISM

The Jews of Canada are estimated to number 320,000.

**Canadian Council for Conservative Judaism:** 1250 Steeles Ave, Suite 112, Concord, ON L4K 3B9; tel. (905) 738-1717; fax (905) 738-1331; e-mail 71263.302@compuserve.com; Pres. DAVID GREENBERG; Exec. Sec. RHONDA SCHILD.

**Canadian Council for Reform Judaism:** 36 Atkinson Ave, Thornhill, ON L4J 8C9; tel. (905) 709-2275; fax (905) 709-1895; Pres. CHARLES ROTHSCHILD.

**Canadian Jewish Congress:** 100 Sparks St, Suite 650, Ottawa, ON K1P 5B7; tel. (613) 233-8703; fax (613) 233-8748; e-mail canadianjewishcongress@cjc.ca; f. 1919; 10 regional offices; Exec. Vice-Pres. JACK SILVERSTONE.

### SIKHISM

There are an estimated 250,000 Sikhs in Canada.

**Federation of Sikh Societies of Canada:** POB 91, Station B, Ottawa, ON K1P 6C3; tel. (613) 737-7296; fax (613) 739-7153; f. 1981; Pres. MOHINDER SINGH GOSAL.

## The Press

The daily press in Canada is essentially local and regional in coverage, influence and distribution. Chain ownership is predominant: in 1998 48.6% of daily newspaper circulation was represented by two major groups: Southam Inc (32.2% of daily newspaper circulation) and Sun Media (16.4%). In 1998 the Thomson Corporation (which announced in February 2000 that it was to divest itself of all its newspaper interests except the Toronto *Globe and Mail*), accounted for 10.7% of the total circulation. In 1998 Torstar (which owns the *Toronto Star*) accounted for 10.6% of total circulation, while Hollinger and Québecor each had between 8%–9%. There are also six smaller groups. In October 1998 Southam Inc launched Canada's first national daily newspaper, the *National Post*, based in Toronto.

In late 1998 there were 105 daily newspapers with a combined circulation exceeding 5m., and about 1,100 weekly and twice-weekly community newspapers serving mainly the more remote areas of the country. A significant feature of the Canadian press is the number of newspapers catering for immigrant groups: there are over 80 of these daily and weekly publications appearing in over 20 languages.

There are numerous periodicals for business, trade, professional, recreational and special interest readership, although periodical publishing, particularly, encounters substantial competition from publications originating in the USA.

The following are among the principal newspaper publishing groups:

**Québécor Inc:** 612 rue St-Jacques, Montréal, QC H3C 1C8; tel. (514) 877-9777; fax (514) 877-9790; f. 1965; Pres. and CEO PIERRE PELADIEU.

**Southam Inc:** 1450 Don Mills Rd, Don Mills, ON M3B 2X7; tel. (416) 445-6641; fax (416) 442-2077; Pres. DON BABICK.

**Thomson Corporation:** POB 24, Toronto-Dominion Centre/Bank Tower, Toronto, ON M5K 1A1; tel. (416) 360-8700; fax (416) 360-8812; Chair. K. R. THOMSON; Pres. and CEO RICHARD HARRINGTON.

### PRINCIPAL DAILY NEWSPAPERS

(D = all day; E = evening; M = morning; S = Sunday)

#### Alberta

**Calgary Herald:** 215 16th St, SE, POB 2400, Station M, Calgary, AB T2P 0W8; tel. (403) 235-7100; internet www.calgaryherald.com; f. 1883; Publr DAN GAYNOR; Editor-in-Chief PETER MENZIES; circ. 123,000 (M); 113,000 (S).

**Calgary Sun:** 2615 12th St, NE, Calgary, AB T2E 7W9; tel. (403) 250-4200; fax (403) 250-4180; e-mail calpromo@sunpub.com; internet www.canoe.ca; f. 1980; Publr GUY HUNTINGFORD; Editor-in-Chief CHRIS NELSON; circ. 72,000 (M), 101,000 (S).

**Daily Herald–Tribune:** 10604 100th St, Postal Bag 3000, Grande Prairie, AB T8V 6V4; tel. (403) 532-1110; fax (403) 532-2120; e-mail bowes@telusplanet.net; internet www.bowesnet.com/dht; f. 1913; Publr PETER J. WOOLSEY; Man. Editor DAVID LASSNER; circ. 12,000 (E).

**Edmonton Journal:** POB 2421, Edmonton, AB T5J 2S6; tel. (780) 429-5100; fax (780) 429-5536; e-mail bcox@the-journal.southam.ca; internet www.edmontonjournal.com; f. 1903; Publr LINDA HUGHES; Editor-in-Chief MURDOCH DAVIS; circ. 198,000 (M); 138,000 (S).

**Edmonton Sun:** 4990 92nd Ave, Suite 250, Edmonton, AB T6B 3A1; tel. (780) 468-0100; fax (780) 468-0128; e-mail edmonton .sun@ccinet.ab.ca; internet www.canoe.ca/; f. 1978; Publr CRAIG MARTIN; Editor PAUL STANWAY; circ. 86,000 (M), 113,000 (S).

**Fort McMurray Today:** 8550 Franklin Ave, Fort McMurray, AB T9H 3G1; tel. (403) 743-8186; fax (403) 790-1006; e-mail today@ ccinet.ab.ca; Publr TIM O'ROURKE; Editor DARRELL SKIDNUK; circ. 5,000 (E).

**Lethbridge Herald:** 504 Seventh St South, POB 670, Lethbridge, AB T1J 3Z7; tel. (403) 328-4411; fax (403) 328-4536; internet www .lis.ab.ca/lherald/; f. 1907; Publr GREG LUTES; Man. Editor BILL WHITELAW; circ. 22,000 (E), 19,000 (S).

**Medicine Hat News:** 3257 Dunmore Rd, SE, POB 10, Medicine Hat, AB T1A 7E6; tel. (403) 527-1101; fax (403) 527-6029; internet www.medicinehatnews.com; f. 1887; Publr MICHAEL J. HERTZ; Man. Editor GORDON WRIGHT; circ. 14,000 (E).

**Red Deer Advocate:** 2950 Bremner Ave, Bag 5200, Red Deer, AB T4N 5G3; tel. (403) 343-2400; fax (403) 341-4772; e-mail editorial@ advocate.red-deer.ab.ca; Editor JOE MCLAUGHLIN; circ. 21,000 (M).

#### British Columbia

**Alaska Highway News:** 9916 89th St, Fort St John, BC V1J 3T8; tel. (250) 785-5631; fax (250) 785-3522; Publr BRUCE LANTZ; Editor JOE PAVLIN; circ. 4,000 (E).

**Alberini Valley Times:** 4918 Napier St, POB 400, Port Alberini, BC V9Y 7N1; tel. (250) 723-8171; fax (250) 723-0586; e-mail avtimes @arrowsmith.net; internet www.arrowsmith.net/~avtimes; Publr NIGEL E. HANNAFORD; circ. 7,000 (M).

**Daily Bulletin:** 335 Spokane St, Kimberley, BC V1A 1Y9; tel. (250) 427-5333; fax (250) 427-5336; e-mail bulletin@cyberlink.bc.ca; f. 1932; Publr STEEN JORGENSEN; Editor CHRIS DOUAN; circ. 2,000 (E).

**Daily Courier:** 550 Doyle Ave, Kelowna, BC V1Y 7V1; tel. (250) 762-4445; fax (250) 763-0194; e-mail pkapyrka@ok.bc.ca; internet www.ok.bc.ca; f. 1904; Publr PETER KAPYRKA; Man. Editor GORD SMILEY; circ. 18,000 (E); 16,000 (S).

**Daily News:** 2575 McCullough Rd, Nanaimo, BC V9S 5W5; tel. (250) 758-4917; fax (250) 758-4513; f. 1874; Publr NIGEL LARK; Man. Editor DOYLE MACKINNON; circ. 11,000 (E).

**Daily Townsman:** 822 Cranbrook St North, Cranbrook, BC V1C 3R9; tel. (250) 426-5201; fax (250) 426-5003; e-mail townsman@ cyberlink.bc.ca; Publr STEEN JORGENSEN; Editor DAVID SANDS; circ. 4,000 (E).

**Kamloops Daily News:** 393 Seymour St, Kamloops, BC V2C 6P6; tel. (250) 372-2331; fax (250) 374-3884; e-mail kamnews@ wkpowerlink.com; internet www.southam.com/kamloopsdailynews/; f. 1930; Publr DALE BRIN; Editor MEL ROTHENBURGER; circ. 17,000 (E).

**Nelson Daily News:** 266 Baker St, Nelson, BC V1L 4H3; tel. (250) 352-3552; fax (250) 352-2418; e-mail adnews@netidea.com; internet www.nelsondailynews.com; f. 1902; Publr JOHN A. SMITH; Editor DREW EDWARDS; circ. 4,000 (E).

**Peace River Block News:** 901 100th Ave, Dawson Creek, BC V1G 1W2; tel. (250) 782-4888; fax (250) 782-6770; e-mail prbnews@ pris.bc.ca; f. 1930; Publr MARGARET FORBES; Editor JEREMY HAINSWORTH; circ. 3,000 (E), 11,000 (S).

**Penticton Herald:** 186 Nanaimo Ave West, Suite 101, Penticton, BC V2A 1N4; tel. (250) 492-4002; fax (250) 492-2403; e-mail jhcoady@ok.bc.ca; internet www.ok.bc.ca/ph; Publr JANE HOWARD COADY; Editor MIKE TURNER; circ. 9,000 (E).

**Prince George Citizen:** 150 Brunswick St, POB 5700, Prince George, BC V2L 5K9; tel. (250) 562-2441; fax (250) 562-7453; e-mail pgcnews@prg.southam.ca; internet www.princegeorgecitizen.com; f. 1957; Publr BOB MCKENZIE; Editor ROY K. NAGEL; circ. 18,000 (E).

**The Province:** 200 Granville St, Suite 1, Vancouver, BC V6C 3N3; tel. (604) 605-2222; fax (604) 605-2720; e-mail mcooke@pacpress .southam.ca; f. 1898; Publr DONALD BABICK; Editor-in-Chief MICHAEL COOKE; circ. 216,000 (M), 185,000 (S).

**Sing Tao Daily News:** 8874 Hudson St, Vancouver, BC V6A 2V1; tel. (604) 261-5066; fax (604) 261-7093; Chinese; Editor PAUL TSANG; circ. 15,000 (M).

**Times Colonist:** 2621 Douglas St, POB 300, Victoria, BC V8T 4M2; tel. (250) 380-5211; fax (250) 380-5353; e-mail timesc@ interlink.bc.ca; f. 1858; Publr PETER BAILLIE; Editor-in-Chief BOB POOLE; circ. 79,000 (M), 73,000 (S).

**Trail Daily Times:** 1163 Cedar Ave, Trail, BC V1R 4B8; tel. (250) 368-8551; fax (250) 368-8550; e-mail konschuk@wkpowerlink.com; Publr JON JARRETT; Editor TRACY KONSCHUK; circ. 7,000 (E).

**The Vancouver Sun:** 200 Granville St, Suite 1, Vancouver, BC V6C 3N3; tel. (604) 732-2111; fax (604) 732-2323; e-mail jcruickshank@ pacpress.southam.ca; f. 1886; Publr KEN KING; Editor-in-Chief JOHN CRUICKSHANK; circ. 252,000 (M), 254,000 (Sat.).

**World Journal (Vancouver):** 2288 Clark Drive, Vancouver, BC V5N 3G8; tel. (604) 876-1338; fax (604) 876-9191; Chinese; Publr WILSON CHIEN; circ. 10,000 (M).

#### Manitoba

**Brandon Sun:** 501 Rosser Ave, Brandon, MB R7A 0K4; tel. (204) 727-2451; fax (204) 727-0385; e-mail bmarshall@brandonsun.com; internet www.netreader.com; f. 1882; Publr RUDY REDEKOP; Man. Editor BRIAN D. MARSHALL; circ. 18,000 (E), 24,000 (S).

**Daily Graphic:** 1941 Saskatchewan Ave West, POB 130, Portage La Prairie, MB R1N 3B4; tel. (204) 857-3427; fax (204) 239-1270;

e-mail plpnews@mb.sympatico.ca; Publr W. J. HAMILTON; Editor IAN R. WHITE; circ. 4,000 (E).

**Flin Flon Reminder:** 10 North Ave, Flin Flon, MB R8A 0T2; tel. (204) 687-3454; fax (204) 687-4473; e-mail reminder@mb.sympatico.ca; f. 1946; Publr RANDY DANELIUK; Editor RICH BILLY; circ. 4,000 (E).

**Winnipeg Free Press:** 1355 Mountain Ave, Winnipeg, MB R2X 3B6; tel. (204) 697-7000; fax (204) 697-7375; internet www.mbnet.mb.ca/freepress/; f. 1874; Publr H. R. REDEKOP; Editor NICHOLAS HIRST; circ. 146,000 (E), 149,000 (Sat.).

**Winnipeg Sun:** 1700 Church Ave, Winnipeg, MB R2X 3A2; tel. (204) 694-2022; fax (204) 632-8709; e-mail wpgsuned@wpgsun.com; f. 1980; Publr RICHARD BOYER; Man. Editor GLEN CHEATER; circ. 47,000 (M), 63,000 (S).

### New Brunswick

**L'Acadie Nouvelle:** 476 blvd St-Pierre ouest, CP 5536, Caraquet, NB E1W 1B7; tel. (506) 727-4444; fax (506) 727-7620; e-mail nouvelle@nbnet.nb.ca; f. 1984; Publr GILLES GAGNÉ; Editor LORIO ROY; circ. 19,000 (M).

**Daily Gleaner:** POB 3370, Fredericton, NB E3B 5A2; tel. (506) 452-6671; fax (506) 452-7405; e-mail dgnews@nbnet.nb.ca; f. 1880; Publr BRIAN BUTTERS; Editor-in-Chief HAL WOOD; circ. 30,000 (E).

**Telegraph–Journal** (M), **St John Times–Globe** (E): 210 Crown St, POB 2350, Saint John, NB E2L 3V8; tel. (506) 632-8888; fax (506) 648-2654; e-mail tjetg@nbnet.nb.ca; Publr JONATHAN FRANKIN (Telegraph–Journal), VICTOR MLODECKI (Times–Globe); circ. 33,000 (M), 29,000 (E).

**Times–Transcript:** 939 Main St, POB 1001, Moncton, NB E1C 8P3; tel. (506) 859-4900; fax (506) 859-4899; e-mail news@timestranscript.com; f. 1983; Publr JONATHAN FRANKLIN; Man. Editor MIKE BEMBRIDGE; circ. 43,000 (E), 53,000 (Sat.).

### Newfoundland

**Telegram:** Columbus Drive, POB 5970, St John's, NF A1C 5X7; tel. (709) 364-6300; fax (709) 364-9333; e-mail telegram@thetelegram.com; internet www.thetelegram.com; f. 1879; Publr MILLER H. AYRE; Man. Editor BRETTON LONEY; circ. 44,000 (E), 62,000 (Sat.).

**Western Star:** 106 West St, POB 460, Corner Brook, NF A2H 6E7; tel. (709) 634-4348; fax (709) 634-9824; e-mail star@thezone.net; f. 1900; Publr IAN BAIRD; Editor RICHARD WILLIAMS; circ. 12,000 (M).

### Nova Scotia

**Amherst Daily News:** POB 280, Amherst, NS B4H 3Z2; tel. (902) 667-5102; fax (902) 667-0419; e-mail cumbpub@istar.ca; f. 1893; Publr EARL J. GOUCHIE; Editor JOHN CONRAD; circ. 5,000 (M).

**Cape Breton Post:** 255 George St, POB 1500, Sydney, NS B1P 6K6; tel. (902) 564-5451; fax (902) 562-7077; e-mail maned@cbpost.com; internet www.capebretonpost.com; f. 1900; Publr MILTON ELLIS; Man. Editor FRED JACKSON; circ. 28,000 (M).

**Chronicle–Herald** (M), **Mail–Star** (E): 1650 Argyle St, POB 610, Halifax, NS B3J 2T2; tel. (902) 426-2811; fax (902) 426-3014; e-mail iscott@herald.ns.ca; internet www.herald.ns.ca; Publr GRAHAM W. DENNIS; Man. Editor JANE PURVES; circ. 100,000 (M), 42,000 (E).

**Daily News:** POB 8330, Station A, Halifax, NS B3K 5M1; tel. (902) 468-1222; fax (902) 468-3609; e-mail citydesk@hfxnews.southam.ca; internet www.hfxnews.southam.ca/; f. 1974; Publr. MARK RICHARDSON; Editor-in-Chief BILL TURPIN; circ. 29,000 (M), 42,000 (S).

**Evening News:** 352 East River Rd, POB 159, New Glasgow, NS B2H 5E2; tel. (902) 752-3000; fax (902) 752-1945; f. 1910; Publr RICHARD RUSSELL; Man. Editor DOUG MACNEIL; circ. 10,000 (E).

**Truro Daily News:** 6 Louise St, POB 220, Truro, NS B2N 5C3; tel. (902) 893-9405; fax (902) 893-0518; e-mail editor.news@north.nsis.com; internet www.truro.canada.com; f. 1891; Publr LEITH ORR; Man. Editor BILL MCGUIRE; circ. 8,000 (E).

### Ontario

**Barrie Examiner:** 16 Bayfield St, Barrie, ON L4M 4T6; tel. (705) 726-6537; fax (705) 726-7706; e-mail examiner@sympatico.ca; f. 1864; Publr RON LAURIN; Man. Editor JOANNE KUSHNIER; circ. 12,000 (E).

**Beacon–Herald:** 108 Ontario St, POB 430, Stratford, ON N5A 6T6; tel. (519) 271-2220; fax (519) 271-1026; e-mail beacan@cyg.net; f. 1854; Publr CHARLES W. DINGMAN; Man. Editor JOHN KASTNER; circ. 12,000 (E).

**Brockville Recorder and Times:** 23 King St West, POB 10, Brockville, ON K6V 5T8; tel. (613) 342-4441; fax (613) 342-4456; e-mail editor@recorder.ca; internet www.recorder.ca; f. 1821; Publr PHILIP MCLEOD; Editor-in-Chief DAVID TAYLOR; circ. 15,000 (E).

**Cambridge Reporter:** 26 Ainslie St South, POB 1510, Cambridge, ON N1R 5T2; tel. (519) 621-3810; fax (519) 621-8239; e-mail news@cambridge-reporter.com; f. 1846; Publr L. R. (VERNE) SHAULL; Man. Editor CLYDE WARRINGTON; circ. 11,000 (E).

**Chatham Daily News:** 45 Fourth St, POB 2007, Chatham, ON N7M 5M6; tel. (519) 354-2000; fax (519) 436-0949; e-mail chathamnews@cha.southam.ca; f. 1862; Publr JOHN CHEEK; Man. Editor JIM BLAKE; circ. 16,000 (E).

**Chronicle–Journal:** 75 Cumberland St South, Thunder Bay, ON P7B 1A3; tel. (807) 343-6200; fax (807) 345-5991; e-mail cj-editorial@cwconnect.ca; Publr COLIN BRUCE; Man. Editor PETER HAGGERT; circ. 28,000 (M).

**Cobourg Daily Star:** 415 King St West, POB 400, Cobourg, ON K9A 4L1; tel. (905) 372-0131; fax (905) 372-4966; e-mail starletters@eagle.ca; internet www.eagle.ca/cobourgstar; Publr MIKE WALSH; Editorial Dir JIM GROSSMITH; circ. 6,000 (E).

**Daily Observer:** 186 Alexander St, Pembroke, ON K8A 4L9; tel. (613) 732-3691; fax (613) 732-2645; e-mail observer@webhart.net; f. 1855; Publr STEVE GLOSTER; Man. Editor PETER LAPINSKIE; circ. 8,000 (E).

**Daily Press:** 187 Cedar St South, POB 560, Timmins, ON P4N 2G9; tel. (705) 268-5050; fax (705) 268-7373; e-mail tdp@nt.net; internet www.timminspress.com; f. 1933; Publr SYL BÉLISLE; Man. Editor DAVE MCGEE; circ. 14,000 (M).

**Le Droit:** 47 rue Clarence, Pièce 222, CP 8860, succursale Terminus, Ottawa, ON K1G 3J9; tel. (613) 562-0111; fax (613) 562-6280; e-mail publicite@ledroit.com; internet www.ledroit.com; f. 1913; Publr PIERRE BERGERON; Man. Editor FRANÇOIS ROY; circ. 35,000 (M), 42,000 (Sat.).

**The Expositor:** 53 Dalhousie St, POB 965, Brantford, ON N3T 5S8; tel. (519) 756-2020; fax (519) 756-4911; e-mail brtexp@southam.ca; internet www.southam.com/brantfordexpositor/; f. 1852; Publr MICHAEL PEARCE; Editor DAVID SCHULTZ; circ. 33,000 (E).

**Financial Post:** 333 King St East, Toronto, ON M5A 4N2; tel. (416) 350-6300; fax (416) 350-6301; e-mail letters@finpost.com; f. 1907; Publr and CEO WILLIAM NEILL; Editor DIANE FRANCIS; circ. 91,000 (M).

**The Globe and Mail:** 444 Front St West, Toronto, ON M5V 2S9; tel. (416) 585-5000; fax (416) 585-5085; e-mail newsroom@globeandmail.ca; internet www.globeandmail.com; f. 1844; Publr PHILIP CRAWLEY; Editor RICHARD ADDIS; circ. 318,000 (M), 395,000 (Sat.).

**Guelph Mercury:** 14 Macdonnell St, POB 3604, Guelph, ON N1H 6P7; tel. (519) 822-4310; fax (519) 767-1681; e-mail mercury@in.on.ca; f. 1854; Publr STEPHEN RHODES; Editor ED CASSAVOY; circ. 17,000 (E).

**Hamilton Spectator:** 44 Frid St, POB 300, Hamilton, ON L8N 3G3; tel. (905) 526-3333; fax (905) 526-1139; internet www.hamiltonspectator.com; f. 1846; Publr PATRICK J. COLLINS; Editor-in-Chief MARYANNE MCNELLIS; circ. 104,000 (E).

**Intelligencer:** 45 Bridge St East, POB 5600, Belleville, ON K8N 5C7; tel. (613) 962-9171; fax (613) 962-9652; e-mail intel@intranet.on.ca; f. 1870; Publr MICHAEL A. POWER; Man. Editor NICK PALMER; circ. 17,000 (E).

**Kingston Whig–Standard:** 6 Cataraqui St, POB 2300, Kingston, ON K7L 1Z7; tel. (613) 544-5000; fax (613) 530-4119; e-mail kinwig@seldom.ca; internet www.seldom.com/kingstonwhig-standard; f. 1834; Publr FRED LAFLAMME; Man. Editor LYNN MESSERSCHMIDT; circ. 28,000 (D).

**Lindsay Daily Post:** 15 William St North, Lindsay, ON K9V 3Z8; tel. (705) 324-2114; fax (705) 324-0174; e-mail lindsay.post.sympatico.ca; Publr JIM AMBROSE; Editor STEPHANIE WALSH; circ. 9,000 (E).

**London Free Press:** 369 York St, POB 2280, London, ON N6A 4G1; tel. (519) 679-1111; fax (519) 667-5520; e-mail letters@lfpress.com; internet www.lfpress.com; f. 1849; Publr JOHN PATON; Editor PHILIP MCLEOD; circ. 109,000 (M); 132,000 (Sat.).

**Ming Pao Daily News:** 1355 Huntingwood Drive, Scarborough, ON M1S 3J1; tel. (416) 321-0093; fax (416) 321-3499; Chinese; Editor-in-Chief K. M. LUI; circ. 33,000 (M), 51,000 (S).

**National Post:** 1450 Don Mills Rd, Suite 300, Don Mills, ON M3B 2X7; tel. (416) 510-6748; fax (416) 510-6743; f. 1998; internet www.nationalpost.com; Publr DON BABICK; Editor-in-Chief KEN WHYTE; national newspaper with printing centres in nine cities; circ. 325,000 (M).

**Niagara Falls Review:** 4801 Valley Way, POB 270, Niagara Falls, ON L2E 6T6; tel. (905) 358-5711; fax (905) 356-0785; e-mail review@nfreview.com; internet www.nfreview.com; f. 1879; Publr DAVID A. BEATTIE; Man. Editor MICHAEL BROWN; circ. 18,000 (E).

**North Bay Nugget:** 259 Worthington St, POB 570, North Bay, ON P1B 8J6; tel. (705) 472-3200; fax (705) 472-5128; e-mail nugnews@onlink.net; f. 1909; Publr ROBERT HULL; Man. Editor BRUCE COWAN; circ. 27,000 (E).

**Northern Daily News:** 8 Duncan Ave, POB 1030, Kirkland Lake, ON P2N 3L4; tel. (705) 567-5321; fax (705) 567-6162; f. 1922; Publr SYL BELISLE; Editor TOM PERRY; circ. 6,000 (E).

**Ottawa Citizen:** 1101 Baxter Rd, POB 5020, Ottawa, ON K2C 3M4; tel. (613) 829-9100; fax (613) 596-3755; internet www.ottawacitizen.com; f. 1845; Publr RUSSELL A. MILLS; Editor NEIL REYNOLDS; circ. 148,000 (M), 192,000 (Sat.).

**Ottawa Sun:** 380 Hunt Club Rd, POB 9729, Station T, Ottawa, ON K1G 5H7; tel. (613) 739-7000; fax (613) 739-9383; internet www.canoe.com/OttawaSun/home.html; Publr JUDY BULLIS; circ. 57,000 (M), 59,000 (S).

**The Packet and Times:** 31 Colborne St East, Orillia, ON L3V 1T4; tel. (705) 325-1355; fax (705) 325-7691; e-mail packet@barint.on.ca; f. 1953; Publr KEN KOYAMA; Man. Editor MARK BISSET; circ. 10,000 (E), 9,000 (S).

**Peterborough Examiner:** 730 Kingsway, Peterborough, ON K9J 8L4; tel. (705) 745-4641; fax (705) 743-4581; e-mail news1@ptbo.igs.net; f. 1884; Publr JIM AMBROSE; Man. Editor ED ARNOLD; circ. 25,000 (E).

**The Record:** 225 Fairway Rd, Kitchener, ON N2G 4E5; tel. (519) 894-2231; fax (519) 894-3912; internet www.therecord.com; f. 1878; Publr WAYNE MACDONALD; Editor CAROLYNE RITTINGER; circ. 82,000 (E).

**St Catharines Standard:** 17 Queen St, St Catharines, ON L2R 5G5; tel. (905) 684-7251; fax (905) 684-6670; e-mail akrulik@scs.southam.ca; internet www.scstandard.com; f. 1891; Publr DAN GAYNOR; Man. Editor DOUG FIRBY; circ. 47,000 (E).

**St Thomas Times–Journal:** 16 Hincks St, St Thomas, ON N5R 5Z2; tel. (519) 631-2790; fax (519) 631-5653; e-mail tj—mail@st.thomas.on.ca; internet www.bowesnet.com/timesjournal; f. 1882; Publr AMBER OGILVIE; Man. Editor ROSS PORTER; circ. 9,000 (E).

**Sarnia Observer:** 140 Front St South, POB 3009, Sarnia, ON N7T 7M8; tel. (519) 344-3641; fax (519) 332-2951; e-mail observer@xcelco.on.ca; f. 1917; Publr DARYL C. SMITH; Man. Editor TERRY SHAW; circ. 24,000 (E).

**Sault Star:** 145 Old Garden River Rd, POB 460, Sault Ste Marie, ON P6A 5M5; tel. (705) 759-3035; fax (705) 759-0102; ssmstar@southam.ca; internet www.southam.com/saultstar; f. 1912; Publr ROBERT W. RICHARDSON; Man. Editor JOHN HALUCHA; circ. 25,000 (E).

**Sentinel–Review:** 18 Brock St, POB 1000, Woodstock, ON N4S 8A5; tel. (519) 537-2341; fax (519) 537-3049; e-mail sentinel@annexweb.com; internet www.annexweb.com; f. 1886; Publr PAT LOGAN; Man. Editor ALISON DOWNIE; circ. 10,000 (E).

**Simcoe Reformer:** 105 Donly Drive South, POB 370, Simcoe, ON N3Y 4L2; tel. (519) 426-5710; fax (519) 426-9255; e-mail refedit@swopp.com; internet www.annexweb.com/reformernet; f. 1858; Publr MICHAEL FREDERICKS; Man. Editor KIM NOVAK; circ. 10,000 (E).

**Sing Tao Daily News:** 417 Dundas St West, Toronto, ON M5T 1G6; tel. (416) 596-8168; fax (416) 861-8169; Chinese; Editor-in-Chief TONY KU; circ. 38,000 (M).

**Standard–Freeholder:** 44 Pitt St, Cornwall, ON K6J 3P3; tel. (613) 933-3160; fax (613) 933-7168; e-mail johnf@standard-freeholder.southam.ca; Publr JOHN A. FARRINGTON; Editor ALF LAFAVE; circ. 15,000 (M).

**Sudbury Star:** 33 MacKenzie St, Sudbury, ON P3C 4Y1; tel. (705) 674-5271; fax (705) 674-0624; e-mail editorial@sightseer.ca; f. 1909; Publr KEN D. SEGUIN; Man. Editor ROGER CAZABON; circ. 26,000 (E).

**Sun Times:** 290 9th St East, POB 200, Owen Sound, ON N4K 5P2; tel. (519) 376-2250; fax (519) 376-7190; e-mail owtimes@southam.ca; internet www.southam.com/owensoundsuntimes; f. 1853; Publr CLYDE T. WICKS; Editor JIM MERRIAM; circ. 24,000 (E).

**Toronto Star:** One Yonge St, Toronto, ON M5E 1E6; tel. (416) 367-2000; fax (416) 869-4328; e-mail newsroom@webramp.net; internet www.thestar.com; f. 1892; Publr JOHN A. HONDERICH; circ. 463,000 (M), 786,000 (Sat.), 470,000 (S).

**Toronto Sun:** 333 King St East, Toronto, ON M5A 3X5; tel. (416) 947-2221; fax (416) 361-1205; internet www.canoe.ca; ; f. 1971; Publr DOUG KNIGHT; Exec. Editor PETER O'SULLIVAN; circ. 247,000 (M), 430,000 (S).

**Welland-Port Colborne Tribune:** 228 East Main St, POB 278, Welland, ON L3B 5P5; tel. (905) 732-2411; fax (905) 732-4883; e-mail tribune@iaw.on.ca; f. 1863; Publr L. R. (VERNE) SHAULL; Editor GARY MANNING; circ. 18,000 (M).

**Windsor Star:** 167 Ferry St, Windsor, ON N9A 4M5; tel. (519) 256-5533; fax (519) 255-5515; e-mail letters@win.southam.ca; internet www.southam.com/windsorstar; f. 1918; Publr JIM MCCORMACK; Editor GERRY NOTT; circ. 82,000 (E).

**World Journal (Toronto):** 415 Eastern Ave, Toronto, ON M4M 1B7; tel. (416) 778-0889; fax (416) 778-4889; Chinese; Editor-in-Chief LOUIS CHU; circ. 38,000 (M).

### Prince Edward Island

**Guardian:** 165 Prince St, POB 760, Charlottetown, PE C1A 4R7; tel. (902) 629-6000; fax (902) 566-3808; f. 1887; Publr DON BRANDER; Editor G. MACDOUGALL; circ. 22,000 (M).

**Journal–Pioneer:** 4 Queen St, POB 2480, Summerside, PE C1N 4K5; tel. (902) 436-2121; fax (902) 436-0784; e-mail dshea@itas.net; f. 1865; Publr SANDY RUNDLE; Editor DARLENE SHEA; circ. 11,000 (E).

### Québec

**Le Devoir:** 2050 rue de Bleury, 9e étage, Montréal, QC H3A 3M9; tel. (514) 985-3333; fax (514) 985-3360; e-mail redaction@ledevoir.com; Publr BERNARD DESCÔTEAUX; circ. 30,000 (M), 38,000 (Sat.).

**The Gazette:** 250 rue St-Antoine ouest, Montréal, QC H2Y 3R7; tel. (514) 987-2222; fax (514) 987-2270; internet www.montrealgazette.com; f. 1778; Publr MICHAEL GOLDBLOOM; Editor-in-Chief ALAN ALLNUTT; circ. 143,000 (M), 195,000 (Sat.).

**Le Journal de Montréal:** 4545 rue Frontenac, Montréal, QC H2H 2R7; tel. (514) 521-4545; fax (514) 525-542; internet www.ledevoir.com-tirage; f. 1964; Publr and Editor PIERRE FRANCOEUR; circ. 278,000 (M), 336,000 (Sat.).

**Le Journal de Québec:** 450 ave Béchard, Vanier, QC G1M 2E9; tel. (418) 683-1573; fax (418) 683-1027; f. 1967; Publr JEAN-CLAUDE L'ABBÉE; Chief Editor SERGE CÔTÉ; circ. 102,000 (M), 119,000 (Sat.).

**Le Nouvelliste:** 1920 rue Bellefeuille, CP 668, Trois Rivières, QC G9A 5J6; tel. (819) 376-2501; fax (819) 376-0946; e-mail noured@lenouvelliste.qc.ca; f. 1920; Pres. and Editor JEAN SISTO; circ. 46,000 (M).

**La Presse:** 7 rue St-Jacques, Montréal, QC H2Y 1K9; tel. (514) 285-7272; fax (514) 285-6808; f. 1884; Pres. and Editor ROGER D. LANDRY; circ. 191,000 (M), 331,000 (Sat.).

**Le Quotidien du Saguenay-Lac-St-Jean:** 1051 blvd Talbot, Chicoutimi, QC G7H 5C1; tel. (418) 545-4474; fax (418) 690-8824; f. 1973; Pres. and Editor CLAUDE GAGNON; circ. 33,000 (M).

**The Record:** CP 1200, Sherbrooke, QC J1H 5L6; tel. (819) 569-9525; fax (819) 569-3945; e-mail record@interlinx.qc.ca; internet www.sherbrookerecord.com; f. 1837; Publr RANDY KINNEAR; Editor SHARON MCCULLY; circ. 6,000 (M).

**Le Soleil:** 925 chemin St-Louis, CP 1547, succursale Terminus, Québec, QC G1K 7J6; tel. (418) 686-3394; fax (418) 686-3374; internet www.lesoleil.com; f. 1896; Pres. and Editor GILBERT LACASSE; circ. 102,000 (M), 131,000 (Sat.).

**La Tribune:** 1950 rue Roy, Sherbrooke, QC J1K 2X8; tel. (819) 564-5454; fax (819) 564-8098; e-mail redaction@latribune.qc.ca; internet www.latribune.qc.caf. 1910; Pres. and Editor RAYMOND TARDIF; circ. 36,000 (M), 48,000 (Sat.).

**La Voix de L'Est:** 76 rue Dufferin, Granby, QC J2G 9L4; tel. (450) 375-4555; fax (450) 777-4865; e-mail vde@indirect.qc.ca; internet www.endirect.qc.ca; f. 1945; Pres. and Editor PIERRE GOBEIL; circ. 16,000 (M).

### Saskatchewan

**Daily Herald:** 30 10th St East, POB 550, Prince Albert, SK S6V 5R9; tel. (306) 764-4276; fax (306) 763-3331; e-mail pa@dailyherald@sk.sympatico.ca; internet www.paherald.sk.ca; f. 1894; Publr and Gen. Man. ROBERT W. GIBB; Man. Editor BARB GUSTAFSON; circ. 10,000 (M).

**Leader–Post:** 1964 Park St, POB 2020, Regina, SK S4P 3G4; tel. (306) 565-8211; fax (306) 565-2588; e-mail leader-post.sk.ca; f. 1883; Publr BOB CALVERT; Editor BOB HUGHES; circ. 65,000 (M).

**StarPhoenix:** 204 5th Ave North, Saskatoon, SK S7K 2P1; tel. (306) 652-9200; fax (306) 664-0433; e-mail spnews@TheSP.com; internet www.The StarPhoenix.com; f. 1902; Publr LYLE SINKEWICZ; Editor STEVE GIBB; circ. 62,000 (M).

**Times–Herald:** 44 Fairford St West, POB 3000, Moose Jaw, SK S6H 6E4; tel. (306) 692-6441; fax (306) 692-2101; e-mail moose.jaw.times@sasknet.sk.ca; f. 1889; Publr AB CALVERT; Editor CARL DEGURSE; circ. 11,000 (E).

### Yukon Territory

**Whitehorse Star:** 2149 2nd Ave, Whitehorse, Yukon, YT Y1A 1C5; tel. (867) 667-4481; fax (867) 668-7130; e-mail star@hypertech.yk.ca; internet www.whitehorsestar.com; f. 1985; Publr ROBERT ERLAM; Editor JIM BUTLER; circ. 3,000 (E).

## SELECTED PERIODICALS

(W = weekly; F = fortnightly; M = monthly; Q = quarterly)

### Alberta

**Alberta FarmLIFE:** 250 Shawville Blvd, SE, Calgary, AB T2Y 2Z7; tel. (403) 274-4002; fax (403) 274-4116; e-mail farmlife@cadvision.com; Man. BRUCE TUNNICLIFFE; circ. 65,000; 24 a year.

**Ukrainski Visti** (Ukrainian News): 12227 107th Ave, Suite 1, Edmonton, AB T5M 1Y9; tel. (780) 488-3693; fax (780) 488-3859; e-mail ukrnews@compusmart.ab.ca; f. 1929; Ukrainian and English; Editor Marco Levytsky; circ. 4,000 (f).

### British Columbia

**BC Outdoors:** 780 Beatty St, Suite 300, Vancouver, BC V6B 2M1; tel. (604) 687-1581; fax (604) 687-1925; e-mail oppubl@istar.ca; internet www.oppub.com; f. 1945; Editor George Gruenefeld; circ. 37,000; 8 a year.

**Pacific Yachting:** 780 Beatty St, Suite 300, Vancouver, BC V6B 2M1; tel. (604) 606-4644; fax (604) 687-1925; e-mail oppubl@istar.ca; f. 1968; Editor Duart Snow; circ. 15,000 (m).

**Vancouver Magazine:** 555 West 12th Ave, SE Tower, Suite 300, Vancouver, BC V5Z 4L4; tel. (604) 877-7732; fax (604) 877-4823; e-mail vanmag@vanmag.com; internet www.vanmag.com; f. 1957; Editor Jim Sutherland; circ. 60,000; 9 a year.

**Western Living:** 555 West 12th Ave, SE Tower, Suite 300, Vancouver, BC V5Z 4L4; tel. (604) 877-7732; fax (604) 877-4849; e-mail westernliving@ican.net; f. 1971; Editor Carolann Rule; circ. 253,000 (m).

**WestWorld BC:** 4180 Lougheed Hwy, 4th Floor, Burnaby, BC V5C 6A7; tel. (604) 299-7311; fax (604) 299-9188; f. 1974; Editor Pat Price; circ. 495,000; (q).

### Manitoba

**The Beaver: Exploring Canada's History:** 167 Lombard Ave, Suite 478, Winnipeg, MB R3B 0T6; tel. (204) 988-9300; fax (204) 988-9309; e-mail beaver@cyberspc.mb.ca; f. 1920; Canadian social history; Editor Annalee Greenberg; circ. 40,000; 6 a year.

**Cattlemen:** 201 Portage Ave, Suite 2500, Winnipeg, MB R3C 3A7; tel. (204) 944-5750; fax (204) 942-8463; e-mail gwinslow@fbc.unitedgrain.ca; internet www.agcanada.com; f. 1938; animal husbandry; Editor Gren Winslow; circ. 27,000 (m).

**Country Guide:** 201 Portage Ave, Suite 2500, Winnipeg, MB R3C 3A7; tel. (204) 944-5750; fax (204) 942-8463; internet www.agcanada.com; f. 1882; agriculture; Editor David Wreford; circ. 61,000; 11 a year.

**Grainews:** 201 Portage Ave, Suite 2500, POB 6600, Winnipeg, MB R3C 3A7; tel. (204) 944-5587; fax (204) 944-5416; e-mail jham@fbc/unitedgrain.ca; f. 1975; grain and cattle farming; Editor Andy Sirski; circ. 50,000; 16 a year.

**Kanada Kurier:** 955 Alexander Ave, POB 1054, Winnipeg, MB R3C 2X8; tel. (204) 774-1883; fax (204) 783-5740; f. 1889; German; Editor Renate Achenbach; circ. 25,000 (w).

**The Manitoba Co-operator:** 220 Portage Ave, POB 9800, Main Station, Winnipeg, MB R3C 3K7; tel. (204) 954-1400; fax (204) 954-1422; e-mail news@co-operator.mb.ca; f. 1925; farming; Editor John W. Morriss; circ. 17,000 (w).

### Northwest Territories

**L'Aquilon:** POB 1325, Yellowknife, NT X1A 2N9; tel. (403) 873-6603; fax (403) 873-2158; e-mail aquilon@internorth.com; f. 1985; Editor Alain Bessette; circ. 1,000 (w).

**The Hub:** 3 Capital Drive, Suite 105, MacKenzie Hwy, Hay River, NT X0E 1Q2; tel. (867) 874-8577; fax (867) 874-2679; e-mail hub@cancom.net; f. 1973; Editor Chris Brodeur; circ. 3,000 (w).

**News/North:** 5108 50th St, Yellowknife, NT X1A 2R1; tel. (403) 873-4031; fax (403) 873-8507; e-mail newsnorth@nnsl.yk.ca; f. 1945; Editor Jack Sigvaldason; circ. 11,000 (w).

**Slave River Journal:** 207 McDougal Rd, POB 990, Fort Smith, NT X0E 0P0; tel. (867) 872-2784; fax (867) 872-2754; e-mail srj@aurora.net.nt.ca; Publr Don Jaque; Editor Brent Kerrigan; circ. 2,000 (w).

**Yellowknifer:** 5108 50th St, Yellowknife, NT X1A 2R1; tel. (403) 873-4031; fax (403) 873-8507; e-mail yellowknifer@nnsl.yk.com; Editor Bruce Valpy; circ. 5,000 (w).

### Nova Scotia

**Atlantic Progress Magazine:** 1660 Hollis St, Suite 603, Halifax, NS B3J 1V7; tel. (902) 494-0999; fax (902) 494-0997; f. 1993; regional business; Editor David Holt; circ. 22,000; 8 a year.

**Canadian Forum:** 5502 Atlantic St, Halifax, NS B3H 1G4; tel. (902) 421-7022; fax (902) 425-0166; f. 1920; political, literary and economic; Editor Robert Cludos; circ. 9,000; 10 a year.

### Nunavut

**Nunatsiaq News:** POB 8, Iqaluit, NT X0A 0H0; tel. (867) 979-5357; fax (867) 979-4763; e-mail nunat@nunanet.com; internet www.nunatsiaq.com; f. 1972; English and Inuktitut; Publr Steven Roberts; Editor Jim Bell; circ. 9,000 (w).

### Ontario

**Anglican Journal:** 600 Jarvis St, Toronto, ON M4Y 2J6; tel. (416) 924-9199; fax (416) 921-4452; e-mail editor@national.anglican.ca; internet www.anglicanjournal.com; f. 1871; official publ. of the Anglican Church of Canada; Editor Rev. David Harris; circ. 250,000; 10 a year.

**Books in Canada:** 50 St Clair Ave East, 3rd Floor, Toronto, ON M4T 1M9; tel. (416) 924-2777; fax (416) 924-8682; e-mail binc@istar.ca; f. 1971; Editor Diana Kuprel; circ. 8,000; 9 a year.

**CA magazine:** The Canadian Institute of Chartered Accountants, 277 Wellington St West, Toronto, ON M5V 3H2; tel. (416) 977-3222; fax (416) 204-3409; e-mail christian.bellavance@cica.ca; f. 1911; Editor-in-Chief Christian Bellavance; circ. 69,000 (m).

**Campus Canada:** 287 MacPherson Ave, Toronto, ON M4V 1A4; tel. (416) 928-2909; fax (416) 966-1181; f. 1983; 30 campus edns; Man. Editor Sarah Moore; circ. 125,000 (q).

**Canada Gazette:** Canada Gazette Division, Public Works and Government Services, 350 Albert St, Ottawa, ON K1A 0S5; tel. (613) 991-1347; fax (613) 991-3540; f. 1867; official bulletin of the Govt of Canada; (w).

**Canadian Architect:** 1450 Don Mills Rd, Don Mills, ON M3B 2X7; tel. (416) 442-3390; fax (416) 442-2213; e-mail cdnarchitect@southam.ca; internet www.cdnarchitect.com; f. 1955; Man. Editor Marco Polo; circ. 11,000 (m).

**Canadian Art:** 70 The Esplanade, 2nd Floor, Toronto, ON M5E 1R2; tel. (416) 368-8854; fax (416) 368-6135; e-mail canart@istar.ca; Editor Richard Rhodes; circ. 24,000 (q).

**Canadian Aviation & Aircraft for Sale:** POB 47555, Hamilton, ON L8H 7S7; tel. (909) 544-0560; fax (909) 544-8121; e-mail jhminc@cml.com; f. 1928; Editor Garth Wallace; circ. 10,000; 6 a year.

**Canadian Banker:** Commerce Court West, Box 348, Toronto, ON M5L 1G2; tel. (416) 362-6092; fax (416) 362-5658; e-mail shally@cba.ca; internet www.cba.ca; f. 1893; Editor Simon Hally; circ. 34,000; 6 a year.

**Canadian Bar Review:** Canadian Bar Asscn, 50 O'Connor St, Suite 902, Ottawa, ON K1P 6L2; tel. (613) 237-2925; fax (613) 237-0185; e-mail CBA:info@cba.org; internet www.cba.org; f. 1923; Editor Prof. Edward Veitch; circ. 36,000 (q).

**Canadian Business:** 777 Bay St, 5th Floor, Toronto, ON M5W 1A7; tel. (416) 596-5100; fax (416) 596-5152; internet www.canbus.com; f. 1927; Editor Arthur Johnson; circ. 81,000; 21 a year.

**Canadian Chemical News:** 130 Slater St, Suite 550, Ottawa, ON K1P 6E2; tel. (613) 232-6252; fax (613) 232-5862; e-mail cic_publ@fox.nstn.ca; internet www.accn.ca; f. 1949; Editor Nola Haddadian; circ. 7,000; 10 a year.

**Canadian Defence Quarterly:** 310 Dupont St, Toronto, ON M5R 1V9; tel. (416) 968-7252; fax (416) 968-2377; e-mail cdq@baxter.net; Editor Martin Shadwick; circ. 6,000.

**Canadian Dental Association Journal:** 1815 Alta Vista Drive, Ottawa, ON K1G 3Y6; tel. (613) 523-1770; fax (613) 523-7736; e-mail reception@cda–adc.ca; internet www.cda_adc.ca; f. 1935; Editor Dr John O'Keefe; (m).

**Canadian Electronics:** 135 Spy Court, Markham, ON L3R 5H6; tel. (905) 447-3222; fax (905) 477-4320; e-mail ce@actionaction.com.com; f. 1986; Editor Tim Gouldson; circ. 22,000; 6 a year.

**Canadian Geographic:** 39 McArthur Ave, Ottawa, ON K1L 8L7; tel. (613) 745-4629; fax (613) 744-0947; e-mail editorial@cangeo.ca; internet www.canadiangeographic.ca; f. 1930; publ. of the Royal Canadian Geographical Soc.; Editor Rick Boychuk; circ. 227,000; 7 a year.

**Canadian Home Workshop:** 340 Ferrier St, Suite 210, Markham, ON L3R 2Z5; tel. (905) 475-8440; fax (905) 475-9246; e-mail letters@canadianworkshop.ca; f. 1977; do-it-yourself; Editorial Dir Tom Hopkins; circ. 104,000 (m).

**Canadian House & Home:** 511 King St West, Suite 120, Toronto, ON M5V 2Z4; tel. (416) 593-0204; fax (416) 591-1630; e-mail exec@canhomepub.com; internet www.canadianhouseandhome.com; f. 1982; Editor Cobi Ladner; circ. 142,000; 9 a year.

**Canadian Jewish News:** 1500 Don Mills Rd, Suite 205, North York, ON M3B 3KY; tel. (416) 391-1836; fax (416) 391-0829; e-mail torcjn1@aol.com; Editor Mordechai Ben-Dat; circ. 44,000; 50 a year.

**Canadian Journal of Economics:** c/o University of Toronto Press, 5201 Dufferin St, North York, ON M3H 5T8; tel. (416) 667-7782; fax (416) 667-7881; e-mail journals@gpw.utcc.utoronto.ca; f. 1968; Editor B. Curtis Eaton; circ. 3,000 (q).

**Canadian Medical Association Journal:** 1867 Alta Vista Drive, Ottawa, ON K1G 3Y6; tel. (613) 731-8610; fax (613) 565-5471; e-mail murrej@cma.ca; internet www.cma.ca; f. 1911; Scientific Editor Dr John Hoey; circ. 59,000; 24 a year.

**Canadian Musician:** 23 Hannover Drive, Suite 7, St Catharines, ON L2W 1A3; tel. (905) 641-1512; fax (905) 641-1648; e-mail info@nor.com; internet www.canadianmusician.com; f. 1979; Man. Editor JIM NORRIS; circ. 30,000; 6 a year.

**Canadian Nurse/L'infirmière canadienne:** 50 Driveway, Ottawa, ON K2P 1E2; tel. (613) 237-2133; fax (613) 237-3520; e-mail cnj@cna-nurses.ca; f. 1905; journal of the Canadian Nurses' Asscn; Editor-in-Chief JUDITH HAINES; circ. 111,000; 10 a year.

**Canadian Pharmaceutical Journal:** c/o C. K. Goodman, Inc, 1382 Hurontario St, Mississauga, ON L5G 3H4; tel. (905) 278-6700; fax (905) 278-4850; f. 1868; Editor ANDREW REINBOLDT; circ. 13,000; 10 a year.

**Canadian Public Policy/Analyse de Politiques:** School of Policy Studies, Rm 409, Queen's University, Kingston, ON K7L 3N6; tel. (613) 545-6644; fax (613) 545-6960; e-mail cpp@qsilver.queensu.ca; internet www.qsilver.queensu.ca/~cpp/; Editor CHARLES M. BEACH; circ. 2,000 (Q).

**Canadian Travel Press Weekly:** 310 Dupont St, Toronto, ON M5R 1V9; tel. (416) 968-7252; fax (416) 968-2377; e-mail ctp@baxter.net; Editor-in-Chief EDITH BAXTER; circ. 13,000; 46 a year.

**Chatelaine:** 777 Bay St, Suite 405, Toronto, ON M5W 1A7; tel. (416) 596-5891; fax (416) 596-5158; e-mail chatcour@maclean.hunter-quebec.qc.ca; f. 1928; women's journal; Editor RONA MAYNARD; circ. 803,000 (M).

**ComputerWorld Canada:** 55 Town Centre Court, Scarborough, ON M1P 4X4; tel. (416) 290-0240; fax (416) 290-0238; internet www.lti.on.ca; f. 1984; Editor-in-Chief NORMAN TOLLINSKY; circ. 47,000; 25 a year.

**Elm Street:** 665 Bay St, Suite 1100, Toronto, ON M5G 2K4; tel. (416) 595-9944; fax (416) 595-7217; e-mail elmstreet@m-v-p.com; f. 1996; women's interest; Editor-in-Chief STEVIE CAMERON; circ. 701,000; 8 a year.

**Farm & Country:** One Yonge St, Suite 1504, Toronto, ON M5E 1E5; tel. (416) 364-5324; fax (416) 364-5857; e-mail agpub@inforamp.net; f. 1936; Editor RICHARD CHARTERIS; circ. 43,000; 23 a year.

**Flare:** 777 Bay St, Suite 405, Toronto, ON M5W 1A7; tel. (416) 596-5891; fax (416) 596-5158; e-mail editors@flare.com; f. 1964; women's interest; Editor-in-Chief SUZANNE BOYD; cir. 174,000 (M).

**Hockey News:** 777 Bay St, Suite 2700, Toronto, ON M5G 2N1; tel. (416) 340-8000; fax (416) 340-2786; e-mail amosb@pathcom.com; f. 1947; Editor-in-Chief STEVE DRYDEN; circ. 205,000; 42 a year.

**Holstein Journal:** 9120 Leslie St, Unit 105, Richmond Hill, ON L4B 3J9; tel. (905) 886-4222; fax (905) 886-0037; internet www.holsteinjournal.com; f. 1938; Editor BONNIE COOPER; circ. 10,000 (M).

**Kanadai Magyarsag** (Canadian Hungarians): 74 Advance Rd, Etobicoke, ON M8Z 2T7; tel. (416) 233-3131; fax (416) 233-5964; circ. 10,000 (W).

**Legion Magazine:** 359 Kent St, Suite 407, Ottawa, ON K2P 0R6; tel. (613) 235-8741; fax (613) 233-7159; e-mail magazine@legion.ca; f. 1926; Editor MAC JOHNSTON; circ. 394,000; 5 a year.

**Maclean's Canada's Weekly Newsmazagine:** 777 Bay St, Suite 405, Toronto, ON M5W 1A7; tel. (416) 596-5891; fax (416) 596-5158; e-mail letters@macleans.ca; f. 1905; Editor-in-Chief ROBERT LEWIS; circ. 500,000.

**Northern Miner:** 1450 Don Mills Rd, Don Mills, ON M3B 2X7; tel. (416) 510-6744; fax (416) 442-2181; e-mail tnm@southam.ca; internet www.northernminer.com; f. 1915; Editor VIVIAN DANIELSON; circ. 23,000 (W).

**Ontario Medical Review:** 525 University Ave, Suite 300, Toronto, ON M5G 2K7; tel. (416) 599-2580; fax (416) 340-2232; e-mail jeff_henry@oma.org; internet www.oma.org; f. 1922; Editor JEFF HENRY; circ. 23,000 (M).

**Oral Health:** 1450 Don Mills Rd, Don Mills, ON M3B 2X7; tel. (416) 442-2193; fax (416) 442-2214; e-mail cwilson@corporate.southam.ca; f. 1911; dentistry; Man. Editor CATHERINE WILSON; circ. 17,000 (M).

**Photo Life:** 1 Dundas St West, Suite 2500, POB 84, Toronto, ON M5G 1G3; tel. (800) 905-7468; fax (800) 664-2739; internet www.photolife.com; f. 1976; Editor-in-Chief SUZY KETENE; circ. 74,000; 6 a year.

**Quill & Quire:** 70 The Esplanade, Suite 210, Toronto, ON M5E 1R2; tel. (416) 360-0044; fax (416) 955-0794; e-mail quill@idirect.com; f. 1935; book-publishing industry; Editor SCOTT ANDERSON; circ. 7,000 (M).

**Saturday Night:** 184 Front St East, Suite 400, Toronto, ON M5A 4N3; tel. (416) 368-7237; fax (416) 368-5112; e-mail editorial@saturdaynight.ca; internet www.saturdaynight.ca; f. 1887; Editor PAUL TOUGH; circ. 400,000; 10 a year.

**Style:** 1448 Lawrence Ave East, Suite 302, Toronto, ON M4A 2V6; tel. (416) 755-5199; fax (416) 755-9123; e-mail style@style.ca; internet www.style.ca; f. 1888; Editor DORIS MONTANERA; circ. 12,000 (M).

**Style at Home:** 25 Sheppard Ave West, Suite 100, Toronto, ON M2N 6S7; tel. (416) 733-7600; fax (416) 218-3632; f. 1997; e-mail letters@styleathome.com; Editor GAIL JOHNSTON HABS; circ. 204,000; 8 a year.

**Sympatico Netlife:** 25 Sheppard Ave West, Suite 100, North York, ON M2N 6S7; tel. (416) 733-7600; fax (416) 733-8272; e-mail giffen@sympatico.ca; internet www.sympatico.ca/mags/netlife; computer technology; Editor PETER GIFFEN; circ. 450,000; 6 a year.

**Toronto Life Magazine:** 59 Front St East, 3rd Floor, Toronto, ON M5E 1B3; tel. (416) 364-3333; fax (416) 861-1169; internet www.torontolife.com; f. 1966; Editor JOHN MACFARLANE; circ. 97,000 (M).

**Tribute Magazine:** 71 Barber Greene Rd, Don Mills, ON M3C 2A2; tel. (416) 445-0544; fax (416) 445-2894; f. 1984; entertainment; Publr and Editor SANDRA STEWART; circ. 653,000; 7 a year.

**TV Guide:** 25 Sheppard Ave West, Suite 100, North York, ON M2N 6S7; tel. (416) 733-7600; fax (416) 733-3632; e-mail tvguide@telemedia.org; f. 1976; Editor CHRISTOPHER LOUDON; circ. 838,000 (W).

**TV Times:** 1450 Don Mills Rd, Don Mills, ON M3B 2X7; tel. (416) 442-3444; fax (416) 442-2088; f. 1969; 14 regional edns; circ. 1,941,000 (W).

### Québec

**L'Actualité:** 1001 blvd de Maisonneuve ouest, Montréal, QC H3A 3E1; tel. (514) 845-2543; fax (514) 845-7503; e-mail ucteour@maclean-hunter-quebec.qc.ca; f. 1976; current affairs; Editor DAVID A. LADKIN; circ. 191,000 (M).

**Affaires Plus:** 1100 blvd René-Lévesque ouest, 24e étage, Montréal, QC H3B 4X9; tel. (514) 392-9000; fax (514) 392-4726; e-mail aplus@transcontinental.ca; internet www.transcontinental-gtc.com; f. 1978; Editor-in-Chief MARIE-AGNÈS THELLIER; circ. 96,000 (M).

**Le Bulletin des Agriculteurs:** 1001 blvd de Maisonneuve ouest, Montréal, QC H3A 3E1; tel. (514) 843-2100; fax (514) 845-6261; e-mail simon@lebulletin.com; internet www.lebulletin.com; f. 1918; Editor SIMON M. GUERTIN; circ. 36,000 (M).

**Canadian Forest Industries:** 1 rue Pacifique, Ste-Anne-de-Bellevue, QC H9X 1C5; tel. (514) 457-2211; fax (514) 457-2558; e-mail jcft@aei.ca; f. 1880; Editor SCOTT JAMIESON; circ. 13,000; 8 a year.

**Châtelaine:** 1001 blvd de Maisonneuve ouest, 11e étage, Montréal, QC H3A 3E1; tel. (514) 843-2504; fax (514) 845-4302; e-mail lettres@chatelaine-quebec.com; f. 1960; Editor CATHERINE ELIE; circ. 207,000 (M).

**CIM Bulletin:** 3400 blvd de Maisonneuve ouest, Bureau 1210, Montréal, QC H3Z 3B8; tel. (514) 939-2710; fax (514) 939-2714; internet www.cim.org; publ. by the Canadian Inst. of Mining, Metallurgy and Petroleum; Editor PERLA GANTZ; circ. 9,000 (M).

**Il Cittadino Canadese:** 5960 Jean-Talon est, Bureau 209, Montréal, QC H1S 1M2; tel. (514) 253-2332; fax (514) 253-6574; f. 1941; Italian; Editor BASILIO GIORDANO; circ. 46,000 (W).

**Equinox:** 11450 blvd Albert-Hudon, Montréal-Nord, QC H1G 3J9; tel. (514) 327-4464; fax (514) 327-7592; e-mail eqxmag@globetrotter.net; internet www.equinox.ca; f. 1982; Editor ALAN MORANTZ; circ. 130,000; 6 a year.

**Harrowsmith Country Life:** 11450 blvd Albert-Hudon, Montréal-Nord, QC H1G 3J9; tel. (514) 327-4464; fax (514) 327-0514; e-mail hclmag@globetrotter.net; f. 1986; Editor TOM CRUICKSHANK; circ. 190,000; 6 a year.

**Le Lundi:** 7 chemin Bates, Outrement, QC H2V 1A6; tel. (514) 270-1100; fax (514) 270-4810; f. 1976; Editor MICHAEL CHOINIÈRE; circ. 62,000 (W).

**Le Producteur de Lait Québécois:** 555 blvd Roland-Thérrien, Longueuil, QC J4H 3Y9; tel. (514) 679-0530; fax (514) 670-4788; e-mail rioiseau@tcn.upa.qc.ca; f. 1980; dairy farming; Editor-in-Chief JEAN VIGNEAULT; circ. 12,000 (M).

**Progrès-Dimanche:** 1051 blvd Talbot, Chicoutimi, QC G7H 5C1; tel. (418) 545-4474; fax (418) 690-8805; f. 1964; Pres. and Editor CLAUDE GAGNON; circ. 45,000 (W).

**Québec Science:** 3430 rue St-Denis, Bureau 300, Montréal, QC H2X 3L3; tel. (514) 843-6888; fax (514) 843-4897; e-mail courrier@QuebecScience.qc.ca; internet www.cybersciences.com; f. 1969; Editor-in-Chief RAYMOND LEMIEUX; circ. 22,000; 10 a year.

**Rénovation Bricolage:** 7 chemin Bates, Outremont, QC H2V 1A6; tel. (514) 270-1100; fax (514) 270-6900; f. 1976; Editor YVES MOQUIN; circ. 35,000; 10 a year.

**Revue Commerce:** 1100 blvd René-Lévesque ouest, 24e étage, Montréal, QC H3B 4X9; tel. (514) 392-9000; fax (514) 392-4726; e-mail commerce@transcontinental.ca; internet www.transcontinental-gtc.com; f. 1898; Editor-in-Chief PIERRE DUHAMEL; circ. 44,000 (M).

**Sélection du Reader's Digest:** 1100 blvd Réne-Lévesque ouest, Montréal, QC H3B 5H5; tel. (514) 940-7328; fax (514) 940-7340;

## Diplomatic Representation

### EMBASSIES IN CAPE VERDE

**Brazil:** Chã de Areia, CP 93, Praia, Santiago; tel. 61-56-07; fax 61-56-09; Ambassador: ROMEO ZERO.

**China, People's Republic:** Achada de Santo António, Praia, Santiago; tel. 61-55-86; Ambassador: JIANG YUANDE.

**Cuba:** Prainha, Praia, Santiago; tel. 61-55-97; fax 61-55-90; Ambassador: PABLO REYES.

**France:** CP 192, Praia, Santiago; tel. 61-55-89; fax 61-55-90; Ambassador: ANDRÉ BARBE.

**Portugal:** Achada de Santo António, CP 160, Praia, Santiago; tel. 61-56-02; fax 61-40-58; Ambassador: EUGÉNIO ANACORETA CORREIA.

**Russia:** Achada de Santo António, CP 31, Praia, Santiago; tel. 62-27-39; fax 62-27-38; Ambassador: VLADIMIR E. PETUKHOV.

**Senegal:** Prainha, Praia, Santiago; tel. 61-56-21; Ambassador: AMADOU MOUSTAPHA DIOP.

**USA:** Rua Hoji Ya Yenna 81, CP 201, Praia, Santiago; tel. 61-56-16; fax 61-13-55; Ambassador: MICHAEL METELITS.

## Judicial System

**Supremo Tribunal da Justiça:** Rua Cesário de Lacerda, CP 117, Praia, Santiago; tel. 61-58-10; fax 61-17-51; established 1975; the highest court.

**President:** Dr OSCAR GOMES.

**Attorney-General:** Dr HENRIQUE MONTEIRO.

## Religion

### CHRISTIANITY

At 31 December 1997 there were an estimated 419,825 adherents of the Roman Catholic Church, representing 95.6% of the total population. Protestant churches, among which the Church of the Nazarene is prominent, represent about 1% of the population.

#### The Roman Catholic Church

Cape Verde comprises the single diocese of Santiago de Cabo Verde, directly responsible to the Holy See. The Bishop participates in the Episcopal Conference of Senegal, Mauritania, Cape Verde and Guinea-Bissau, currently based in Senegal.

**Bishop of Santiago de Cabo Verde:** Rt Rev. PAULINO DO LIVRAMENTO EVORA, Avda Amílcar Cabral, Largo 5 de Outubro, CP 46, Praia, Santiago; tel. 61-11-19; fax 61-45-99.

#### The Anglican Communion

Cape Verde forms part of the diocese of The Gambia, within the Church of the Province of West Africa. The Bishop is resident in Banjul, The Gambia.

## The Press

**Agaviva:** Mindelo, São Vicente; tel. 31-21-21; f. 1991; monthly; Editor GERMANO ALMEIDA; circ. 4,000.

**Boletim Informativo:** CP 126, Praia, Santiago; f. 1976; weekly; publ. by the Ministry of Foreign Affairs; circ. 1,500.

**Boletim Oficial da República de Cabo Verde:** Imprensa Nacional, CP 113, Praia, Santiago; tel. 61-41-50; weekly; official announcements.

**Contacto:** CP 89C, Praia, Santiago; tel. 61-57-52; fax 61-14-42; f. 1993; quarterly; economic bulletin publ. by Centro de Promoção Turística, do Investimento Externo e das Exportações (PROMEX); circ. 1,500.

**Novo Jornal Cabo Verde:** Largo do Hospital Dr Agostinho Neto, CP 118, Praia, Santiago; tel. 61-39-89; fax 61-38-29; f. 1993; two a week; Editor LÚCIA DIAS; circ. 5,000.

**Perspectiva:** Achada de Santo António, CP 89C, Praia, Santiago; tel. 62-27-41; fax 62-27-37; f. 1995; annual; economic bulletin publ. by Centro de Promoção Turística, do Investimento Externo e das Exportações (PROMEX); Editor Dr AGUINALDO MARÇAL; circ. 5,000.

**Raízes:** CP 98, Praia, Santiago; tel. 319; f. 1977; quarterly; cultural review; Editor ARNALDO FRANÇA; circ. 1,500.

**A Semana:** CP 36C, Avda Cidade de Lisboa, Praia, Santiago; tel. 61-39-50; fax 61-52-91; e-mail asemana@mail.cvtelecom.cv; weekly; independent; Editor FILOMENA SILVA; circ. 5,000.

**Terra Nova:** CP 166, São Vicente; tel. 32-24-42; fax 32-14-75; f. 1975; monthly; Roman Catholic; Editor P. FIDALGO BARROS; circ. 3,000.

### NEWS AGENCIES

**Cabopress:** Achada de Santo António, CP 40/A, Praia, Santiago; tel. 62-30-21; fax 62-30-23; f. 1988.

#### Foreign Bureaux

**Agence France-Presse (AFP):** CP 26/118 Praia, Santiago; tel. 61-38-89; Rep. FÁTIMA AZEVEDO.

**Agência Portuguesa de Notícias (LUSA):** Prainha, Praia, Santiago; tel. 61-35-19.

**Inter Press Service (IPS)** (Italy): CP 14, Mindelo, São Vicente; tel. 31-45-50; Rep. JUAN A. COLOMA.

## Publisher

#### Government Publishing House

**Imprensa Nacional:** CP 113, Praia, Santiago; tel. 61-42-09; Admin. JOÃO DE PINA.

## Broadcasting and Communications

### TELECOMMUNICATIONS

**Cabo Verde Telecom:** Praia, Santiago.

### BROADCASTING

**Rádio Televisão de Cabo Verde (RTC):** Praça Albuquerque, CP 26, Praia, Santiago; tel. 61-57-55; fax 61-57-54; govt-controlled; five radio transmitters and five solar relay radio transmitters; FM transmission only; radio broadcasts in Portuguese and Creole for 18 hours daily; one television transmitter and seven relay television transmitters; television broadcasts in Portuguese and Creole for eight hours daily with co-operation of RTPI (Portugal); Dir MANUELA FONSECA SOARES.

**Rádio Educativa de Cabo Verde:** Achada de Santo António, Praia, Santiago; tel. 61-11-61.

**Rádio Nova—Emissora Cristã/Cabo Verde:** CP 426, Mindelo, São Vicente; tel. 32-20-83; fax 32-14-75; Dir ANTONIO FIDALGO BARROS.

**Voz de São Vicente:** CP 29, Mindelo, São Vicente; fax 31-10-06; f. 1974; govt-controlled; Dir JOSÉ FONSECA SOARES.

## Finance

(cap. = capital; res = reserves; dep. = deposits; m. = million; †brs = branches; amounts in Cape Verde escudos)

### BANKING

#### Central Bank

**Banco de Cabo Verde (BCV):** 117 Avda Amílcar Cabral, CP 101, Praia, Santiago; tel. 61-55-29; fax 61-19-14; f. 1976; bank of issue; cap. and res 2,501.4m., dep. 5,097.7m. (Dec. 1995); Gov. OLAVO CORREIA.

#### Other Banks

**Banco Comercial do Atlântico (BCA):** 117 Avda Amílcar Cabral, CP 214, Praia, Santiago; tel. 61-55-35; fax 61-31-00; f. 1993; commercial and development bank; cap. 1,728m. (1995); Gov. AMÉLIA FIGUEIREDO; 17 brs.

**Banco Totta e Açores (BTA)** (Portugal): 1 Rua Justino Lopes, CP 593, Praia, Santiago; tel. 61-16-62; fax 61-40-06; Gen. Man. RODRIGO NASCIMENTO; 1 br.

**Caixa de Crédito Rural:** Praia, Santiago; f. 1995; rural credit bank.

**Caixa Económica de Cabo Verde (CECV):** Avda Cidade de Lisboa, CP 193, Praia, Santiago; tel. 61-55-61; fax 61-55-60; f. 1928; commercial and development bank; cap. 348m. (Aug. 1993).

The **Fundo de Solidariedade Nacional** is the main savings institution; the **Fundo de Desenvolvimento Nacional** channels public investment resources; and the **Instituto Caboverdiano** administers international aid.

### STOCK EXCHANGE

A stock exchange opened in Praia in April 1998.

### INSURANCE

**Companhia Caboverdiana de Seguros (IMPAR):** Avda Amílcar Cabral, CP 469, Praia, Santiago; tel. 61-14-05; fax 61-37-65; f. 1991; Pres. Dr CORSINO FORTES.

**Garantia Companhia de Seguros:** CP 138, Praia, Santiago; tel. 61-35-32; fax 61-25-55; f. 1991.

## Trade and Industry

### GOVERNMENT AGENCIES

**Centro de Promoção Turística, do Investimento Externo e das Exportações (PROMEX):** CP 89C, Achada de Santo António, Praia, Santiago; tel. 62-27-41; fax 62-27-37; f. 1990; promotes tourism, foreign investment and exports; Pres. Dr PEDRO BARROS.

**Gabinete de Apoio à Reestruturação do Sector Empresarial do Estado (GARSEE):** Praia; bureau in charge of planning and supervising restructuring and divestment of public enterprises.

### DEVELOPMENT ORGANIZATION

**Instituto Nacional de Investigação e Desenvolvimento Agrário:** CP 84, Praia, Santiago; tel. 71-11-47; fax 71-11-33; e-mail inida@mail.cvtelecom.cv; f. 1979; under the supervision of the Ministry of Agriculture, Food and the Environment; research and training on agricultural issues.

### CHAMBERS OF COMMERCE

**Associação Comercial Industrial e Agrícola de Barlavento (ACIAB):** CP 62, Mindelo, São Vicente; tel. 31-32-81; fax 32-36-58; f. 1918.

**Associação Comercial de Sotavento (ACAS):** Rua Serpa Pinto 23, 1°, CP 78, Praia, Santiago; tel. 61-29-91; fax 61-29-64; e-mail acs@milton.cvtelecom.cv.

### STATE INDUSTRIAL ENTERPRISES

**Correios de Cabo Verde, SARL:** CP 92, Praia, Santiago; tel. 61-10-49; fax 61-34-78.

**Empresa de Comercialização de Produtos do Mar—INTERBASE, EP:** CP 59, Mindelo, São Vicente; tel. 32-66-89; fax 32-66-91; e-mail interbase-sv@mail.cvtelecom.sv; supervises marketing of seafood; shipping agency and ship chandler; Man. Dir CARLOS ALBERTO RAMOS FARIA.

**Empresa Nacional de Conservação e Reparação de Equipamentos (SONACOR):** Praia, Santiago; tel. 61-25-57.

**Empresa Nacional de Produtos Farmacêuticos (EMPROFAC):** CP 59, Praia, Santiago; tel. 62-78-95; fax 62-78-99; f. 1979; state monopoly of pharmaceuticals and medical imports.

**Empresa Pública de Abastecimento (EMPA):** CP 107, Praia, Santiago; tel. 63-39-69; fax 63-39-22; e-mail empa@mail.cvtelecom.cv; f. 1975; state provisioning enterprise, supervising imports, exports and domestic distribution; Dir-Gen. NASOLINO SILVA DOS SANTOS.

### UTILITIES

#### Electricity and Water

**Empresa de Electricidade e Água (ELECTRA):** 10 Avda Baltazar Lopes Silva, CP 137, Mindelo, São Vicente; tel. 32-44-48; fax 32-44-46; e-mail dg-electra@mail.cvtelecom.cv; f. 1982.

### CO-OPERATIVES

**Instituto Nacional das Cooperativas:** Fazenda, CP 218, Praia, Santiago; tel. 61-41-12; fax 61-39-59; central co-operative organization.

### TRADE UNIONS

**Confederação Cabo-Verdiana dos Sindicatos Livres (CCSL):** Rua Dr Júlio Abreu, Praia, Santiago; tel. 61-63-19; Sec.-Gen. JOSÉ MANUEL VAZ.

**Sindicato da Indústria, Agricultura e Pesca (SIAP):** Plateau, Praia, Santiago; tel. 61-63-19.

**Sindicato dos Transportes, Comunicações e Turismo (STCT):** Praia, Santiago; tel. 61-63-38.

**União Nacional dos Trabalhadores de Cabo Verde—Central Sindical (UNTC—CS):** Estrada do Aeroporto, Praia, Santiago; tel. 61-43-05; fax 61-36-29; f. 1978; Chair. JÚLIO ASCENSÃO SILVA.

## Transport

### ROADS

In 1996 there were an estimated 1,100 km of roads, of which 858 km were paved.

### SHIPPING

Cargo-passenger ships call regularly at Porto Grande, Mindelo, on São Vicente, and Praia, on Santiago. In 1993 plans were announced for the upgrading of Porto Grande, and for the re-establishment of the port of Vale dos Cavaleiros, on Fogo island. There are small ports on the other inhabited islands.

**Comissão de Gestão dos Transportes Marítimos de Cabo Verde:** CP 153, São Vicente; tel. 31-49-79; fax 31-20-55.

**Empresa Nacional de Administração dos Portos, EP (ENAPOR):** Avda Marginal, CP 82, Mindelo, São Vicente; tel. 31-44-14; fax 31-46-61.

**Companhia Cabo-Verdiana de Transportes Marítimos:** CP 150, Praia, Santiago; tel. 61-22-84; fax 61-60-95.

**Companhia Nacional de Navegação Arca Verde:** Rua 5 de Julho, CP 41, Praia, Santiago; tel. 61-10-60; fax 61-54-96; f. 1975.

**Companhia de Navegação Estrela Negra:** Avda 5 de Julho 17, CP 91, São Vicente; tel. 31-54-23; fax 31-53-82.

**Companhia Portuguesa de Transportes Marítimos:** Agent in Santiago: João Benoliel de Carvalho, Lda, CP 56, Praia, Santiago.

**CS Line:** Praia, Santiago.

**Linhas Marítimas Caboverdianas (LINMAC):** Dr João Battista Ferreira Medina, CP 357, Praia, Santiago; tel. 61-43-52; fax 61-37-15.

**Mare Verde:** Mindelo, São Vicente.

**Seage Agência de Navegação de Cabo Verde:** Avda Cidade de Lisboa, CP 232, Praia, Santiago; tel. 61-57-58; fax 61-25-24; Chair. CÉSAR MANUEL SEMEDO LOPES.

### CIVIL AVIATION

The Amílcar Cabral international airport, at Espargos, on Sal island, can accommodate aircraft of up to 50 tons and 1m. passengers per year. The airport's facilities were expanded during the 1990s. A second international airport, under construction on Santiago, capable of accommodating Airbus 310 aircraft, was due for completion in late 1999. There is also a small airport on each of the other inhabited islands. Work was begun in 1998, with financing of US $7m. from France, to upgrade the airport on São Vicente to international capacity. Plans were also under way for the construction of an international airport on Boa Vista island.

**Empresa Nacional de Aeroportos e Segurança Aérea, EP (ASA):** Aeroporto Amílcar Cabral, CP 58, Ilha do Sal; tel. 41-13-94; fax 41-15-70; airports and aircraft security.

**CABOVIMO:** 32 Avda Unidade Guiné-Cabo Verde, Praia, Santiago; tel. 61-33-14; fax 61-55-59; f. 1992; internal flights; Gen. Man. JORGE DANIEL SPENCER LIMA.

**Transportes Aéreos de Cabo Verde (TACV):** Avda Amílcar Cabral, CP 1, Praia, Santiago; tel. 61-58-13; fax 61-35-85; f. 1958; internal services connecting the nine inhabited islands; also operates regional services to Senegal, Guinea, the Gambia and Guinea-Bissau, and long-distance services to Europe and the USA; Dir ALFREDO CARVALHO.

## Tourism

The islands of Santiago, Santo Antão, Fogo and Brava offer attractive mountain scenery. There are extensive beaches on the islands of Santiago, Sal, Boa Vista and Maio. There are six hotels on Sal, one on Boa Vista, two on São Vicente, and four on Santiago. Some 57,000 tourists visited Cape Verde during 1998, mainly from Italy (32%), Portugal (30%), Germany, Austria, France, the Netherlands, Belgium and Spain. In 1996 tourism receipts totalled US $11m. The sector is undergoing rapid expansion, with tourist arrivals projected to increase to about 400,000 annually by 2008.

**Centro de Promocão Turística, do Investimento Externo e das Exportações (PROMEX):** CP 89c, Achada de Santo António, Praia, Santiago; tel. 62-27-41; fax 62-27-37; f. 1990; promotes tourism, foreign investment and exports; Dir of Tourism AIDA DUARTE SILVA.

# THE CENTRAL AFRICAN REPUBLIC

## Introductory Survey

### Location, Climate, Language, Religion, Flag, Capital

The Central African Republic is a land-locked country in the heart of equatorial Africa. It is bordered by Chad to the north, by Sudan to the east, by the Democratic Republic of the Congo (formerly Zaire) and the Republic of the Congo to the south and by Cameroon to the west. The climate is tropical, with an average annual temperature of 26°C (79°F) and heavy rainfall in the south-western forest areas. The national language is Sango, but French is the official language and another 68 languages and dialects have been identified. It is estimated that about one-half of the population are Christian; another 15% are Muslims, while animist beliefs are held by an estimated 24%. The national flag (proportions 5 by 3) has four equal horizontal stripes, of blue, white, green and yellow, divided vertically by a central red stripe, with a five-pointed yellow star in the hoist corner of the blue stripe. The capital is Bangui.

### Recent History

The former territory of Ubangi-Shari (Oubangui-Chari), within French Equatorial Africa, became the Central African Republic (CAR) on achieving self-government in December 1958. Barthélemy Boganda, the first Prime Minister, died in March 1959. He was succeeded by his nephew, David Dacko, who led the country to full independence, and became the first President, on 13 August 1960. In 1962 a one-party state was established, with the ruling Mouvement d'évolution sociale de l'Afrique noire (MESAN) as the sole authorized party. President Dacko was overthrown on 31 December 1965 by a military coup which brought to power his cousin, Col (later Marshal) Jean-Bédel Bokassa, Commander-in-Chief of the armed forces.

In January 1966 Bokassa formed a new Government, rescinded the Constitution and dissolved the National Assembly. Bokassa, who became Life President in March 1972 and Marshal of the Republic in May 1974, forestalled several alleged coup attempts and employed increasingly repressive measures against dissidents. From January 1975 to April 1976 Elisabeth Domitien, the Vice-President of MESAN, was Prime Minister; she was the first woman to hold this position in any African country.

In September 1976 the Council of Ministers was replaced by the Council for the Central African Revolution, and the former President, Dacko, was appointed personal adviser to the President. In December the Republic was renamed the Central African Empire (CAE), and a new Constitution was instituted. Bokassa was proclaimed the first Emperor, and Dacko became his Personal Counsellor. The Imperial Constitution provided for the establishment of a national assembly, but no elections were held. The elaborate preparations for Bokassa's coronation in December 1977 were estimated to have consumed about one-quarter of the country's income. In May 1978 Bokassa reorganized the army leadership and strengthened its powers. In July he appointed a new Council of Ministers, headed by a former Deputy Prime Minister, Henri Maidou. In January 1979 violent protests, led by students, were suppressed, reportedly with the help of Zairean troops. Following a protest by schoolchildren against compulsory school uniforms (made by a company owned by the Bokassa family), many children were arrested in April. About 100 were killed in prison, and Bokassa himself allegedly participated in the massacre. On 20 September, while Bokassa was in Libya, Dacko deposed him in a bloodless coup, which received considerable support from France. The country was again designated a republic, with Dacko as its President and Maidou as Vice-President.

President Dacko's principal concern was to establish order and economic stability, but his Government encountered opposition, particularly from students who objected to the continuation in office of CAE ministers. In August 1980 Dacko accepted demands for the dismissal of both Maidou and the Prime Minister, Bernard Christian Ayandho. Bokassa, at that time in exile in Côte d'Ivoire (and subsequently in Paris), was sentenced to death *in absentia* in December. In February 1981 a new Constitution, providing for a multi-party system, was approved by referendum and promulgated by President Dacko. He won a presidential election in March, amid allegations of electoral malpractice, and was sworn in for a six-year term in April. Political tension intensified in subsequent months, and on 1 September the Chief of Staff of the Armed Forces, Gen. André Kolingba, deposed Dacko in a bloodless coup. Kolingba was declared President, and a ruling Comité militaire pour le redressement national (CMRN) and an all-military Government were formed. All political activity was suspended.

In March 1982 the exiled leader of the banned Mouvement pour la libération du peuple centrafricain (MLPC), Ange-Félix Patassé, returned to Bangui and was implicated in an unsuccessful coup attempt. Patassé, who had been the Prime Minister under Bokassa in 1976–78 and who had contested the 1981 presidential election, sought asylum in the French embassy in Bangui, from where he was transported to exile in Togo. A visit by President Mitterrand of France to the CAR in October 1982 normalized bilateral relations, which had been strained by French support for Patassé. Domestic opposition to Kolingba's regime continued, and in August 1983 elements of the three main opposition parties formed a united front. In September 1984 Kolingba announced an amnesty for the leaders of banned political parties, who had been under house arrest since January.

In September 1985 the CMRN was dissolved and, for the first time since Kolingba's assumption of power, civilians were appointed to the Council of Ministers. In early 1986 a specially-convened commission drafted a new Constitution, which provided for the creation of a sole legal political party, the Rassemblement démocratique centrafricain (RDC), and conferred extensive executive powers on the President, while defining a predominantly advisory role for the legislature. At a referendum in November some 91.17% of voters approved the draft Constitution and granted Kolingba a mandate to serve a further six-year term as President. The Council of Ministers was reorganized in December to include a majority of civilians. The RDC was officially established in February 1987, with Kolingba as founding President, and elections to the new Assemblée nationale took place in July, at which 142 candidates, all nominated by the RDC, contested the 52 seats.

In October 1986 Bokassa returned unexpectedly to the CAR and was immediately arrested. His new trial opened in November and continued until June 1987, when the former Emperor was sentenced to death, having been convicted on charges of murder, conspiracy to murder, the illegal detention of prisoners and embezzlement. In February 1988 Kolingba commuted the sentence to one of life imprisonment with hard labour.

The appointment during 1988 of former associates of Bokassa, Dacko and Patassé to prominent public offices appeared to represent an attempt by Kolingba to consolidate national unity. In August 1989, however, 12 opponents of his regime, including members of the Front patriotique oubanguien-Parti du travail and the leader of the Rassemblement populaire pour la reconstruction de la Centrafrique, Brig.-Gen. (later Gen.) François Bozize, were arrested in Benin, where they had been living in exile, and extradited to the CAR. Bozize was subsequently found guilty of complicity in the 1982 coup attempt.

During 1990 demands for higher salaries, improved working conditions and the payment of salary arrears owed to public-sector workers created unrest, which escalated into a general strike in November. In the same year opposition movements exerted pressure on the Government to introduce a plural political system, and in October violent anti-Government demonstrations were suppressed by the security forces. In December the Executive Council of the RDC recommended a review of the Constitution and the re-establishment of the premiership. Accordingly, in March 1991 Edouard Franck, a former Minister of State at the Presidency, was appointed Prime Minister, and in July the Assemblée nationale approved legislation to revise the Constitution to provide for the establishment of a multi-party political system. Kolingba announced his resignation from the presidency of the RDC in the following month, in order to remain 'above parties'. In October the Kolingba administration agreed to convene a national debate on the country's political future, with representatives of opposition movements invited to attend. In December Kolingba pardoned Brig.-Gen. Bozize.

The Grand National Debate took place in August 1992. It was, however, boycotted by the influential Concertation des forces démocratiques (CFD), an alliance of opposition groupings, which announced that it would only participate in a multi-party national conference with sovereign powers. At the end of August the Assemblée nationale approved legislation in accordance with decisions taken by the Grand National Debate: constitutional amendments provided for the strict separation of executive, legislative and judicial powers and Kolingba was granted temporary powers to rule by decree until the election of a new multi-party legislature. Concurrent legislative and presidential elections commenced in October, but were suspended by decree of the President and subsequently annulled by order of the Supreme Court, owing to alleged sabotage of the electoral process. In December Franck resigned as Prime Minister and was replaced by Gen. Timothée Malendoma, the leader of the Forum civique.

In February 1993 Malendoma, who had accused Kolingba of curtailing his powers, was dismissed from the premiership and replaced by Enoch Derant Lakoué, the leader of the Parti social-démocrate. In June, in response to mounting pressure from both the opposition and the French Government, Kolingba announced that elections would commence in August. Accordingly, two rounds of concurrent legislative and presidential elections were held in late August and mid-September. At the legislative elections the MLPC won 34 of the 85 seats in the Assemblée nationale while the RDC, in second place, secured 13 seats. Patassé, the MLPC leader and former Prime Minister, was elected President, winning 52.47% of the votes cast at the second round of presidential elections. The seven other presidential candidates included Kolingba, Prof. Abel Goumba (the leader of the CFD) and former President Dacko. In late August Kolingba, who had been defeated at the first round of presidential elections, attempted to delay the publication of the election results by issuing two decrees which modified the electoral code and altered the composition of the Supreme Court; however, the decrees were revoked, after the French Government threatened to suspend all co-operation with the CAR in protest.

In September 1993 Bokassa was released from prison under a general amnesty for convicts; however, the former Emperor was banned for life from participating in elections and demoted from the military rank of marshal. He died in November 1996.

In October 1993 Patassé was inaugurated as President. Soon afterwards he appointed Jean-Luc Mandaba, Vice-President of the MLPC, as Prime Minister; Mandaba formed a coalition Government, which had a working majority of 53 seats in the Assemblée nationale. In December the Government announced the establishment of a commission of inquiry into the conduct of Kolingba during his 12-year presidency, which was to include an audit of government finances during this period. In March 1994, following the arrest of two senior members of the RDC on charges of provoking popular discontent, Kolingba was stripped of his army rank.

In December 1994 a draft Constitution was approved by 82% of voters in a national referendum. The new Constitution, which was adopted in January 1995, included provisions empowering the President to nominate senior military, civil service and judicial officials, and requiring the Prime Minister to implement policies decided by the President. In addition, provision was made for the creation of directly-elected regional assemblies and for the establishment of an advisory State Council, which was to deliberate on administrative issues. Several groups in the governing coalition (notably the Mouvement pour la démocratie et le développement—MDD, led by Dacko) expressed concern at the powers afforded to the President.

In April 1995 Mandaba resigned as Prime Minister, pre-empting a threatened vote of 'no confidence' in his administration (initiated by his own party, the MLPC), following accusations of corruption and incompetence. Immediately afterwards Patassé appointed Gabriel Koyambounou, formerly a civil servant, as the new Prime Minister. Koyambounou subsequently nominated a new Council of Ministers, with an enlarged membership. In August supporters of the RDC staged a peaceful demonstration in protest at perceived abuses of power by the Government, such as the imposition of a two-year term of imprisonment on the editor of the RDC newspaper, who had been found guilty of treason following the publication of an article critical of Patassé. In December several opposition movements (including the MDD, but excluding the RDC) united to form the Conseil démocratique des partis politiques de l'opposition (CODEPO), which aimed to campaign against alleged corruption and mismanagement by the Patassé regime.

In the mid-1990s the Government repeatedly failed to pay the salaries of public-sector employees and members of the security forces, prompting frequent strikes and mounting political unrest. In mid-April 1996 CODEPO staged an anti-Government rally in Bangui. Shortly afterwards part of the national army mutinied in the capital and demanded the immediate settlement of all salary arrears. Patassé promised that part of the overdue salaries would be paid and that the mutineers would not be subject to prosecution. The presence of French troops (the Elements français d'assistance opérationelle—EFAO) in Bangui, with a mandate to secure the safety of foreign nationals and (in accordance with a bilateral military accord) to protect the presidential palace and other key installations, contributed to the swift collapse of the rebellion. About nine people, including civilians, were reported to have died in the uprising. In late April Patassé appointed a new Chief of Staff of the Armed Forces, Col Maurice Regonessa, and banned all public demonstrations. In mid-May, however, discontent again resurfaced and CODEPO organized another rally in Bangui, at which it demanded the resignation of the Government. Soon afterwards, in an attempt to tighten his hold on power, the President ordered that control of the national armoury should be transferred from the regular army to the presidential guard. However, adverse reaction to this move within the ranks of the armed forces rapidly escalated into a second, more determined insurrection. Once again EFAO troops were deployed to protect the Patassé administration; some 500 reinforcements were brought in from Chad and Gabon to consolidate the resident French military presence (numbering 1,400). Five hostages were taken by the mutineers, including Col Regonessa, together with a government minister and the President of the Assemblée nationale. After five days of fierce fighting between dissident and loyalist troops, the French forces intervened to suppress the rebellion. France's military action (which allegedly resulted in civilian deaths) prompted intense scrutiny of the role of the former colonial power, and precipitated large pro- and anti-French demonstrations in Bangui. In total, 11 soldiers and 32 civilians were reported to have been killed in the second army mutiny. Following extended negotiations between the mutineers and government representatives, the two sides eventually signed an accord, providing for an amnesty for the rebels (who were to return to barracks under EFAO guard), the immediate release of hostages, and the installation of a new Government of National Unity. The political opposition now became active in the debate, rejecting the proposed Government of National Unity and demanding instead a transitional government leading to fresh legislative and presidential elections. The opposition also requested a revision of the Constitution to remove some executive powers from the President and enhance the role of the Prime Minister.

In early June 1996 the Government and the opposition signed a protocol providing for the establishment of a Government of National Unity led by a civilian Prime Minister with no official party ties. Although the Constitution was not to be amended to alter the balance of power between the President and the Prime Minister, Patassé agreed to permit 'some room for manoeuvre'. Meanwhile, France agreed to assist the CAR authorities with the payment of salary arrears. Following the publication of the protocol, Koyambounou's Government resigned. Jean-Paul Ngoupandé, hitherto Ambassador to France and with no official political affiliation (although he had been Secretary-General of the RDC in the late 1980s), was appointed as the new Prime Minister. Ngoupandé immediately nominated a new Council of Ministers. National co-operation, however, remained elusive, as CODEPO, dissatisfied with the level of its ministerial representation, immediately withdrew from the Government of National Unity. Moreover, a growing animosity was reported between Patassé and Ngoupandé, with the former refusing to transfer any effective power to the latter.

At a conference on national defence held in August/September 1996, several resolutions were adopted regarding restructuring and improving conditions within the army. In late October, however, it was reported that troops who had been involved in the insurrections of April and May were refusing to be transferred from their barracks in the capital to a more remote location; Patassé insisted that their departure would take place none the less. However, in mid-November a further mutiny erupted among these troops. A substantial part of Bangui was occupied by the rebels, and a number of hostages were taken. The latest uprising appeared to have a strong tribal and political motivation: the mutineers, who demanded the resignation of Patassé, belonged to the Yakoma ethnic group of Kolingba. EFAO troops were deployed once again, ostensibly to maintain order and protect foreign residents; however, by guarding key installations and government buildings they also effectively prevented the overthrow of the Patassé administration. More than 100 people were killed in the unrest during late November and early December.

In December 1996 the Presidents of Burkina Faso, Chad, Gabon and Mali negotiated a 15-day truce, which was supervised by the former transitional President of Mali, Brig.-Gen. Amadou Toumani Touré; a one-month extension to the cease-fire was subsequently agreed. In January 1997, following the killing of two French soldiers in Bangui (reportedly by mutineers), EFAO troops retaliated by killing at least 10 members of the rebel forces; French military involvement in the CAR was condemned by the opposition, which also sought (without success) to initiate impeachment proceedings against Patassé. Subsequent to the renewal of violence, Touré again came to Bangui as mediator and helped to create a cross-party Committee of Consultation and Dialogue. The 'Bangui Accords', drawn up by this committee, were signed towards the end of January; these, as well as offering an amnesty to the mutineers, agreed upon the formation of a new Government of National Unity and on the replacement of the EFAO troops by peace-keeping forces from African nations. The opposition at first threatened to boycott the new Government, largely owing to the appointment of Michel Gbezera-Bria (a close associate of Patassé and hitherto the Minister of Foreign Affairs) as Prime Minister. However, with the creation of new ministerial posts for opposition politicians, a 'Government of Action' (which did not include Ngoupandé) was formed on 18 February; soon afterwards, Gen. Bozize replaced Gen. Regonessa as Chief of Staff of the Armed Forces.

In early February 1997 responsibility for peace-keeping operations was transferred from the EFAO to forces of the newly-formed Mission interafricaine de surveillance des accords de Bangui (MISAB), comprising some 700 soldiers from Burkina Faso, Chad, Gabon, Mali, Senegal and Togo (with logistical support from 50 French military personnel). MISAB soldiers were also to assist in disarming the former mutineers; however, when in late March they attempted to do so, fighting broke out in which some 20 MISAB soldiers were killed. A spokesman for the rebels, Capt. Anicet Saulet, claimed that the lack of representation of the former mutineers in the new Government constituted a breach of the Bangui Accords. Following a meeting between Saulet and Patassé in early April, the Council of Ministers was expanded to include two military officers as representatives of the rebels. Later that month several hundred former mutineers attended a ceremony marking their reintegration into the regular armed forces.

In mid-April 1997 a curfew was imposed on Bangui, owing to a serious escalation in violent crime, much of which was allegedly perpetrated by groups of former mutineers. In early May, following the deaths in police custody of three former rebels suspected of criminal activities, nine ministers representing the G11 (a grouping of 11 opposition parties, including the MDD—which had left CODEPO in November 1996—and the RDC), as well as the two representatives of the former mutineers, suspended participation in the Government. In late June violent clashes erupted once again between MISAB forces and former mutineers. In response to several attacks on the French embassy by the rebels, several hundred EFAO troops were redeployed on the streets of Bangui, and MISAB forces launched a major offensive in the capital, capturing most of the rebel-controlled districts. This assault led to the arrest of more than 80 former mutineers, but also to some 100 deaths, both of soldiers and of civilians, while numerous homes and business premises were destroyed. Soon afterwards some 500 demonstrators gathered outside the French embassy to protest against alleged abuses of human rights by MISAB troops; MISAB officials claimed that criminals were impersonating their soldiers in order to perpetrate atrocities. On the same day Touré returned to Bangui in his capacity as Chairman of MISAB, and negotiated a four-day truce, which took effect at the end of June, followed by a 10-day cease-fire agreement, signed at the beginning of July; all of the former mutineers were to be reintegrated into the regular armed forces, and their safety and that of the people living in the districts under their control was guaranteed; the rebels, for their part, were to relinquish their weaponry. Towards the end of July many of the people who had been held in custody in relation to the previous month's violence were released by the authorities, and the curfew in Bangui was eased, while it was reported that almost all of the former mutineers had rejoined the regular armed forces. In early September the nine representatives of opposition parties in the Council of Ministers resumed their vacant posts.

In July 1997, in accordance with a foreign policy decision to disengage forces from its former African colonies, France announced its intention to withdraw its troops from the CAR by April 1998; the first troops left the country in October 1997. France campaigned vigorously for the formation of a UN force, but encountered initial resistance from the USA. A National Reconciliation Conference, held in Bangui, in February 1998 led to the signing on 5 March of a National Reconciliation Pact by President Patassé and 40 representatives of all the country's political and social groups. The accord was countersigned by Brig.-Gen. Touré and witnessed by many other African Heads of State. The Pact restated the main provisions of the Bangui Accords and of the political protocol of June 1996. It provided for military and political restructuring, to be implemented by a civilian Prime Minister, supported by all of the country's social and political groups. The powers and position of the President were, however, guaranteed, and a presidential election was scheduled for late 1999.

The signature of the Pact facilitated the authorization later in March 1998 by the UN Security Council of the establishment of a peacekeeping mission, the UN Mission in the Central African Republic (MINURCA), to replace MISAB. MINURCA comprised 1,345 troops from Benin, Burkina Faso, Canada, Chad, Côte d'Ivoire, Egypt, France, Gabon, Mali, Portugal, Senegal and Togo, and was granted a mandate to remain in the country for an initial period of three months. MINURCA's initial mandate was to maintain security and stability around Bangui, to supervise the final disposition of weapons retrieved under the disarmament programme, to assist in efforts to train a national police force, and to provide advice and technical assistance for the legislative elections. The mission was subsequently extended until the end of February 1999 in order to support and verify the legislative elections.

There was substantial support for the new political solution and, significantly, when in April 1998 the principal trade union, the Union Syndicale des Travailleurs de la Centrafrique, called for a 48-hour general strike to protest against outstanding pay arrears, their action received little support. However, preparations for the legislative elections were marked by disagreement between the Government and the G11 group of opposition parties over electoral procedure. When the authorities announced in August that the elections were to be postponed, owing to the difficulties of registering rural voters, the opposition claimed that there was little political will for the elections in government circles. Demonstrations took place outside the Assemblée nationale in September to protest against the indefinite postponement of the legislative elections and the subsequent extension of the term of office of deputies.

Elections to the newly-reorganized Assemblée nationale finally took place on 22 November and 13 December 1998. A reportedly large number of the electorate participated in the polls, which were contested by 29 parties. The MPLC won 47 of the 109 seats in the legislature, but secured the co-operation of seven independent members. The opposition won 55 seats; however, the defection, amidst allegations of bribery, of a newly-elected deputy belonging to the Parti social-démocrate (PSD) gave the ruling MPLC a majority in the Assemblée. The opposition called for the defector to give up his seat, and the opening of the Assemblée nationale was delayed. Most of the opposition representatives boycotted the opening of the legislature, which was eventually held on 4 January 1999, and MINURCA troops were deployed to protect deputeis from anti-Government protesters gathered outside. Patassé's decision to call on a close associate, the nominally independent erstwhile Minister of Finance, Anicet Georges Dologuele, to form a new Government provoked public demonstrations, and caused the opposition formally to withdraw from the legislature (the boycott lasted until March). Dologuele announced the composition of a new coalition Council of Ministers in early January, but 10 opposition ministers immediately resigned in protest at the MPLC's alleged disregard for the results of the election. In mid-January Dologuele announced the formation of another Council of Ministers, which included four members of the MDD, despite an earlier agreement made by the opposition not to accept posts in the new Government. The MDD leadership subsequently ordered its members to resign from their government positions; three of the four ministers did so, but Armand Sama, the nominated Minister of Town Planning, Housing and Public Buildings, defied his party's directives and retained his portfolio. In March two PSD deputies resigned from the party, announcing their intention to retain their seats in the Assemblée nationale as independents.

In February 1999 the UN Security Council extended MINURCA's mandate until mid-November in order that it might assist in the preparations and conduct of the presidential election, which was scheduled to be held on 29 August. It was simultaneously agreed, however, that the force would gradually be reduced after the successful conclusion of the election with the aim of withdrawing all troops prior to the end of MINURCA's mandate. France was reported to have opposed an extension of the mandate, and in February the French contingent withdrew from MINURCA (as did the troops from Côte d'Ivoire in April). The UN Secretary-General, Kofi Annan, called on all factions in the CAR to co-operate in preparations for the presidential election. In particular, Annan criticized delays in the appointment of the independent electoral commission, the Commission électorale mixte indépendante (CEMI), the 27 members of which were finally approved in May. In July the Constitutional Court authorized 10 candidates to stand in the presidential election. President Patassé was to seek re-election, while other candidates included two former presidents, Gen. André Kolingba and David Dacko, two former prime ministers, Jean-Paul Ngoupandé and Enoch Derant Lakoué, as well as Prof. Abel Goumba, the opposition candidate in the 1993 presidential election. In the same month MINURCA supervised the destruction in Bangui of hundreds of weapons collected under the disarmament programme. In early August a 45-member body was established, at the request of bilateral creditors and the UN, in order to supervise the activities of the CEMI. It comprised members of both opposition and pro-Patassé parties, and was intended to ensure transparency in the conduct of the election. In mid-August the opposition grouping, the Union des forces acquises à la paix (UFAP), requested that voting be postponed until late September becuase of the delay in the appointment of the CEMI. Patassé later announced that the election would be postponed until 12 September. In the event, the election was not held until 19 September, owing to organizational problems. The voting procedure was conducted in a peaceful manner and international observers reported that, despite some attempts at fraud by a number of individuals, no widespread irregularities had been discovered. On 2 October the Constitutional Court announced that Patassé had won 517,993 votes, equivalent to 51.6% of the total votes cast, and had, therefore, by attaining more than 50% of the vote, been re-elected President without the need for a second round of voting. Patassé's nearest rivals were Kolingba, who won 194,486 votes (19.4%), Dacko, who received 111,886 votes (11.2%), and Goumba, who obtained 60,778 votes (6.1%). The nine defeated candidates subsequently demanded the annulment of the election results, which they claimed had been manipulated; however, they asked their supporters to remain calm, and on 22 October Patassé was sworn in as president for a further six-year term. In early November the recently-reappointed Prime Minister Dologuele announced the formation of a new Council of Ministers, which included members of parties loyal to Patassé as well as independents, three opposition representatives and two members of the armed forces. In late November the Government stated that its main priorities were to improve human development in the CAR and to combat poverty; particular emphasis was also laid on the restructuring of the public sector and of the armed forces.

In late November 1999 it was reported that several members of the MLPC, who were allegedly dissatisfied at the party's level of representation in the Council of Ministers, had threatened to assassinate Patassé; security was consequently reinforced at the presidential residence. In the same month two bombs were found near the Ministry of Foreign Affairs and Francophone Affairs; they were successfully defused by a MINURCA unit, and it remained unclear whether they had been lying there undiscovered since the 1997 mutinies. Also in November, numerous disturbances, a number of which allegedly involved members of the security forces, were reported in the south-east of the country. At the end of the month, accounts that armed insurgents had erected barricades in the streets of Kembe and the neighbouring town of Bimbi led the authorities to dispatch troops and police reinforcements to the region in order to restore order and to initiate a judical enquiry into the recent events.

In October 1999 Kofi Annan requested the UN Security Council to authorize the gradual withdrawal of MINURCA from the CAR over a three-month period following the end of its mandate on 15 November. Annan highlighted the important role of MINURCA in guaranteeing stability in the post-electoral period, while he also noted that a delayed withdrawal would enable MINURCA units to complete a training course for local police recruits. In mid-December the UN announced proposals to establish a Bureau de soutien à la consolidation de la paix en Centrafrique (BONUCA), in Bangui, the role of which would be to monitor developments in the CAR in the areas of politics, socio-economics, human rights and security issues, as well as to facilitiate dialogue between political figures. It was intended that BONUCA should be created before the final withdrawal of MINURCA (scheduled for 15 February 2000), and that it should be operational initially for a one-year period.

In May 1997 the CAR recognized the administration of President Laurent Kabila in the Democratic Republic of the Congo (DRC, formerly Zaire). In the same month the CAR and the DRC signed a mutual assistance pact, which provided for permanent consultation on internal security and defence. The pact also sought to guarantee border security; however, during mid-1997 armed soldiers of what had been the Zairean army were reported to be fleeing troops loyal to Kabila and crossing the Oubangui river into the CAR. In 1998 the CAR authorities blamed the country's rapidly escalating AIDS problem on the continuing influx of refugees from the DRC, the Republic of the Congo, Rwanda, Chad and Sudan, and in January 1999 there was a further influx of DRC civilians to the CAR. The refugees crossed the Oubangui river to escape the fighting between government and rebel soldiers, who were occupying the northern part of the DRC. DRC troops also entered the CAR, with the agreement of the CAR authorities, to try to halt the rebel advance in the northern part of the DRC. By early August, following significant rebel advances, it was reckoned that as many as 20,000 DRC refugees had entered the CAR, including around 6,000 members of the DRC armed forces, prompting fears of a humanitarian disaster. In mid-August the regional office of the UN High Commissioner for Refugees estimated that the CAR was sheltering about 54,000 refugees from the DRC, Chad and Sudan.

In late 1994 the CAR and Chad agreed to establish a bilateral security structure to ensure mutual border security. In 1994 the CAR also became the fifth member of the Lake Chad Basin Commission (see p. 292). Attacks on Chadian nationals resident in Bangui and on the Chadian contingent of the MISAB forces in late 1996 and early 1997 led the Chadian Government to issue a communiqué in March 1997 warning that further incidences of such aggression would not be tolerated. In June 1999 President Patassé issued an official apology to Chad following a disturbance at a market in Bangui in which five Chadian nationals were killed by members of the CAR security forces. In August the CAR Government agreed to pay compensation to the families of the victims. None the less, in December it was reported that some 1,500 Chadian refugees were preparing to leave the CAR, allegedly owing to fears for their security following the scheduled departure of MINURCA forces.

The CAR maintains amicable relations with Nigeria, and in June 1999 the two countries signed a bilateral trade agreement. The CAR is also a close ally of Libya, and in April 1999 joined the Libyan-sponsored Community of Sahel–Saharan States (COMESSA, see p. 290).

## Government

Executive power is vested in the President of the Republic, and legislative power in the Congress. The Congress consists of a 109-seat Assemblée nationale, sessions of which are held at the summons of the President, an advisory Economic and Regional Council, one-half of the members of which are elected by the Assembly and one-half appointed by the President, and an advisory State Council, which deliberates on matters that are referred to it by the President of the Assemblée nationale. Both the President and the Assemblée nationale are elected by direct universal suffrage, the former for a six-year term and the latter for a five-year term. The Prime Minister, who presides over a Council of Ministers, is appointed by the President.

For administrative purposes, the country is divided into 14 prefectures, two economic prefectures (Gribingui and Sangha), and one commune (Bangui). It is further divided into 67 sub-prefectures and two postes de contrôle administratif. At community level there are 65 communes urbaines, 102 communes rurales and seven communes d'élevage. The 1995 Constitution provided for the election of new regional assemblies by universal suffrage.

### Defence

In August 1999 the armed forces numbered about 2,650 men (army 2,500; air force 150), with a further 2,300 men in paramilitary forces. Military service is selective and lasts for two years. The full withdrawal of the 1,345 troops of the United Nations Mission in the Central African Republic (MINURCA) was scheduled to be completed by mid-February 2000. Government expenditure on defence in 1999 was estimated at 28,000m. francs CFA.

### Economic Affairs

In 1997, according to estimates by the World Bank, the CAR's gross national product (GNP), measured at average 1995–97 prices, was US $1,104m., equivalent to $320 per head. During 1990–97, it was estimated, GNP per head declined, in real terms, at an average rate of 1.0% per year. Over the same period, the population increased at an average annual rate of 2.1%. GNP in 1998 was estimated at $1,000m., equivalent to $300 per head. The country's gross domestic product (GDP) increased, in real terms, at an average annual rate of 1.5% in 1990–98. Real GDP rose by 6.0% in 1995, declined by an estimated 1.5% in 1996 and increased by 5.2% in 1997 and by 4.7% in 1998.

Agriculture (including forestry and fishing) contributed 54.5% of GDP in 1998. About 74.4% of the economically active population were employed in the sector in that year. The principal cash crops are coffee (which accounted for 28.7% of export earnings in 1989 and an estimated 5.8% in 1998) and cotton (19.4% of total exports in 1996). Livestock and tobacco are also exported. The major subsistence crops are cassava (manioc) and yams. The Government is encouraging the cultivation of horticultural produce for export. The exploitation of the country's large forest resources represents a significant source of export revenue (exports of wood accounted for an estimated 25.4% of the total in 1997); however, the full potential of this sector has yet to be realized, owing to the inadequacy of the transport infrastructure. Rare butterflies are also exported. Agricultural GDP increased at an average annual rate of 3.5% during 1990–98, and by an estimated 4.1% in 1998.

Industry (including mining, manufacturing, construction and power) engaged 3.3% of the employed labour force in 1988 and provided 18.0% of GDP in 1998. Industrial GDP increased at an average annual rate of 0.2% in 1990–98, but declined by an estimated 3.6% in 1997. It increased, however, by 3.4% in 1998.

Mining and quarrying engaged a labour force estimated at between 40,000 and 80,000 in the late 1990s, and contributed 3.9% of GDP in 1997. The principal activity is the extraction of predominantly gem diamonds (exports of diamonds provided an estimated 42.8% of total export revenue in 1998). The introduction of gem-cutting facilities and the eradication of widespread 'black market' smuggling operations would substantially increase revenue from diamond-mining. The reopening in 1997 of the Bangui diamond bourse, which had been established in 1996, was intended to increase revenue by levying a 10% sales tax on transactions. Deposits of gold are also exploited. The development of uranium resources may proceed. Reserves of iron ore, copper, tin and zinc have also been located. The GDP of the mining sector increased at an average rate of 7.0% per year during 1992–94, but declined by 2.4% per year in 1994–97.

The manufacturing sector engaged 1.6% of the employed labour force in 1988. Manufacturing, which contributed 8.8% of GDP in 1998, is based upon the processing of primary products. In 1997 the major activities were the processing of foods, beverages and tobacco, furniture, fixtures and paper and textiles. In real terms, the GDP of the manufacturing sector increased at an average annual rate of 6.5% in 1992–95, but declined by an average of 10.0% per year in 1995–97, before recording an increase of 4.7% in 1998.

In 1997 an estimated 99.7% of electrical energy generated within the CAR was derived from the country's two hydroelectric power installations. Imports of fuel products comprised an estimated 8.9% of the cost of merchandise imports in 1997.

Services engaged 15.5% of the employed labour force in 1988 and provided 27.5% of GDP in 1998. In real terms, the GDP of the services sector decreased at an average rate of 1.3% per year during 1990–98. It increased, however, by 7.2% in 1997 and by 6.4% in 1998.

In 1997 the CAR recorded a visible trade surplus of an estimated 27,000m. francs CFA and a surplus of an estimated 3,600m. francs CFA on the current account of the balance of payments. In 1996 the principal source of imports was France (providing 39.5% of the total), while the principal markets for exports were the Belgo-Luxembourg Economic Union (accounting for 60.1% of the total) and France (30.9%). Other major trading partners in that year were Cameroon, Japan and the United Kingdom. The principal exports in 1997 were diamonds, wood products, coffee and cotton. The principal imports in 1996 were road vehicles, machinery, basic manufactures, cotton, mineral fuels and lubricants, chemical products and food.

In 1997 there was an estimated budget deficit of 16,600m. francs CFA. At the end of 1997 the CAR's external debt was US $885.3m., of which $803.7m. was long-term public debt. In that year the cost of debt-servicing was equivalent to 6.1% of revenue from exports of goods and services. Consumer prices rose by 24.5% in 1994, following the devaluation of the currency, and by 19.2% in 1995. In 1996 and 1997 the annual rate of inflation averaged 4.4% and 0.6% respectively. According to the IMF, prices declined by an average of 1.9% in 1998 and by 0.6% in the year to August 1999. At the December 1988 census 7.5% of the labour force were unemployed.

The CAR is a member of the Central African organs of the Franc Zone (see p. 200) and of the Communauté economique des états de l'Afrique centrale (CEEAC, see p. 290).

The CAR's land-locked position, the inadequacy of the transport infrastructure and the country's vulnerability to adverse climatic conditions and to fluctuations in international prices for its main agricultural exports have impeded sustained economic growth. The January 1994 devaluation of the CFA franc had a profound effect on the CAR economy, increasing export competitiveness, but also increasing consumer prices. Economic growth recovered in 1994–95, partly reflecting an improvement in prices for the CAR's agricultural exports. By late 1995, however, the Government was unable to control its mounting budgetary deficit and failed to pay the salaries of public-sector employees and the armed forces, thereby precipitating serious political instability during 1996–97, which, in turn, badly disrupted economic activity, destroying much of Bangui's industry. In mid-1998, following the signing of the National Reconciliation Pact and the appointment of an economist, Anicet Georges Dologuele, as Prime Minister, the IMF approved a three-year Enhanced Structural Adjustment Facility (ESAF), valued at US $66m., to support the CAR's economic programme for 1998–2000. The objectives of the programme were to reduce the fiscal deficit, lessen the country's debt burden, stabilize inflation, improve tax collection, reform the financial sector, privatize non-financial public enterprises within a reformed regulatory framework, and continue the restructuring of the civil service. In order to normalize relations with external creditors, the CAR undertook to eliminate arrears on external payments in 1998 and to make regular payments on all external obligations. In September 1998 the 'Paris Club' of creditor nations expressed its approval of these plans by rescheduling and reducing the CAR's external debt. Despite its high levels of external indebtedness, the CAR's debt-service ratio remains relatively modest, as much of its debt is on concessional terms and is owed to official creditors. In July 1999 the IMF noted that, while progress had been less than envisaged under the terms of the ongoing economic programme, the CAR had succeeded in significantly improving budgetary receipts, from 6.1% of GDP in 1996 to an estimated 9.0% of GDP in mid-1999; the IMF subsequently agreed to the early release of the second tranche of ESAF funding. Hopes were expressed that increases in state revenue would permit the Government to fulfil its external obligations, as well as allowing higher rates of investment in priority sectors such as education and health.

### Social Welfare

The Government's commitments to the social welfare and health sectors were neglected during the 1990s, owing to a severe lack of funds. The provision of health-care facilities in rural areas is minimal. In 1991 there were three hospitals in Bangui, four regional hospitals and 11 prefectoral hospitals, of which four were privately operated. In addition, there were 413 other health centres and five leper hospitals. An estimated 4,030 beds were available in that year, equivalent to a ratio of 718 inhabitants per bed. In the early 1990s there were only 6 physicians and 45 nurses per 100,000 population working in the country. Government expenditure on health was estimated at an average annual rate of 1.9% of GDP in 1990–95.

### Education

Education is officially compulsory for eight years between six and 14 years of age. Primary education begins at the age of six and lasts for six years. Secondary education begins at the age of 12 and lasts for up to seven years, comprising a first cycle of four years and a second of three years. In 1991 an estimated 58% of children in the relevant age-group (71% of boys; 46% of girls) attended primary schools, while secondary enrolment was equivalent to only 10% (boys 15%; girls 6%). According to estimates by the World Bank, the adult illiteracy rate in 1997 averaged 44% among males and 70% among females. Current expenditure by the Ministry of Education in 1995 totalled 8,820m. francs CFA, equivalent to 1.6% of GNP. The provision of state-funded education was severely disrupted during the 1990s, owing to the inadequacy of the Government's resources.

### Public Holidays

**2000:** 1 January (New Year), 29 March (Anniversary of death of Barthélemy Boganda), 24 April (Easter Monday), 1 May (May Day), 1 June (Ascension Day), 12 June (Whit Monday), 30 June (National Day of Prayer), 13 August (Independence Day), 15 August (Assumption), 1 November (All Saints' Day), 1 December (National Day), 25 December (Christmas).

**2001:** 1 January (New Year), 29 March (Anniversary of death of Barthélemy Boganda), 16 April (Easter Monday), 1 May (May Day), 24 May (Ascension Day), 4 June (Whit Monday), 30 June (National Day of Prayer), 13 August (Independence Day), 15 August (Assumption), 1 November (All Saints' Day), 1 December (National Day), 25 December (Christmas).

### Weights and Measures

The metric system is officially in force.

# Statistical Survey

Source (unless otherwise stated): Division des Statistiques et des Etudes Economiques, Ministère de l'Economie, du Plan et de la Coopération Internationale, Bangui.

## Area and Population

**AREA, POPULATION AND DENSITY**

| | |
|---|---|
| Area (sq km) | 622,984* |
| Population (census results) | |
| 8 December 1975 | 2,054,610 |
| 8 December 1988 | |
| Males | 1,210,734 |
| Females | 1,252,882 |
| Total | 2,463,616 |
| Population (official estimate at mid-year) | |
| 1997 | 3,245,000 |
| Density (per sq km) at mid-1997 | 5.2 |

* 240,535 sq miles.

**PRINCIPAL TOWNS** (population, 1988 census)

| | | | |
|---|---|---|---|
| Bangui (capital) | 451,690 | Bambari | 38,633 |
| Berbérati | 41,891 | Bossangoa | 31,502 |
| Bouar | 39,676 | Carnot | 31,324 |

**1996:** Bangui 524,000 (estimate).

**BIRTHS AND DEATHS** (UN estimates, annual averages)

| | 1980–85 | 1985–90 | 1990–95 |
|---|---|---|---|
| Birth rate (per 1,000) | 42.4 | 42.1 | 39.6 |
| Death rate (per 1,000) | 18.5 | 17.9 | 17.4 |

Source: UN, *World Population Prospects: The 1998 Revision*.

**1994:** Registered live births 124,707 (birth rate 41.6 per 1,000); Registered deaths 50,063 (death rate 16.7 per 1,000) (Source: UN, *Population and Vital Statistics Report*).

**Expectation of life** (UN estimates, years at birth, 1990–95): 47.5 (males 45.9; females 49.3) (Source: UN, *World Population Prospects: The 1998 Revision*).

**ECONOMICALLY ACTIVE POPULATION**
(persons aged 6 years and over, 1988 census)

| | Males | Females | Total |
|---|---|---|---|
| Agriculture, hunting, forestry and fishing | 417,630 | 463,007 | 880,637 |
| Mining and quarrying | 11,823 | 586 | 12,409 |
| Manufacturing | 16,096 | 1,250 | 17,346 |
| Electricity, gas and water | 751 | 58 | 809 |
| Construction | 5,583 | 49 | 5,632 |
| Trade, restaurants and hotels | 37,435 | 54,563 | 91,998 |
| Transport, storage and communications | 6,601 | 150 | 6,751 |
| Financing, insurance, real estate and business services | 505 | 147 | 652 |
| Community, social and personal services | 61,764 | 8,537 | 70,301 |
| Activities not adequately defined | 7,042 | 4,627 | 11,669 |
| **Total employed** | 565,230 | 532,974 | 1,098,204 |
| Unemployed | 66,624 | 22,144 | 88,768 |
| **Total labour force** | 631,854 | 555,118 | 1,186,972 |

Source: International Labour Office, *Yearbook of Labour Statistics*.

**Mid-1998** (estimates in '000): Agriculture, etc. 1,238; Total labour force 1,665 (Source: FAO, *Production Yearbook*).

# Agriculture

**PRINCIPAL CROPS** ('000 metric tons)

| | 1996 | 1997 | 1998 |
|---|---|---|---|
| Rice (paddy) | 15 | 17 | 17* |
| Maize | 76 | 82 | 82* |
| Millet | 12* | 12† | 10* |
| Sorghum | 35 | 38 | 38* |
| Cassava (Manioc) | 526 | 579 | 579* |
| Yams* | 340 | 340 | 360 |
| Taro (Coco yam)* | 90 | 90 | 100 |
| Pulses* | 28 | 28 | 28 |
| Groundnuts (in shell) | 91 | 97 | 100† |
| Sesame seed | 31 | 32 | 32* |
| Cottonseed* | 21 | 26 | 22 |
| Palm kernels* | 5 | 5 | 5 |
| Pumpkins, squash and gourds | 17† | 18 | 18* |
| Other vegetables (incl. melons) | 55 | 57 | 57* |
| Sugar cane | 79 | 80* | 80* |
| Oranges* | 20 | 22 | 22 |
| Mangoes* | 9 | 9 | 9 |
| Pineapples* | 13 | 13 | 13 |
| Bananas* | 105 | 110 | 110 |
| Plantains* | 78 | 80 | 80 |
| Other fruits (excl. melons)* | 10 | 11 | 11 |
| Coffee (green) | 18 | 15 | 14† |
| Cotton (lint) | 18 | 22 | 19† |

* FAO estimate(s). † Unofficial figure.

Source: FAO, *Production Yearbook*.

**LIVESTOCK** ('000 head, year ending September)

| | 1996 | 1997 | 1998* |
|---|---|---|---|
| Cattle | 2,861 | 2,926 | 2,992 |
| Goats | 2,093 | 2,213 | 2,339 |
| Sheep | 181 | 191 | 201 |
| Pigs | 571 | 596 | 622 |

Poultry (million): 4 in 1996; 4* in 1997; 4* in 1998.

* Unofficial figure(s).

Source: FAO, *Production Yearbook*.

**LIVESTOCK PRODUCTS** ('000 metric tons)

| | 1996 | 1997 | 1998 |
|---|---|---|---|
| Beef and veal† | 61 | 50 | 51 |
| Mutton and lamb* | 1 | 1 | 1 |
| Goat meat | 7 | 8 | 8* |
| Pig meat | 11 | 12 | 12* |
| Poultry meat | 3 | 3 | 3† |
| Other meat* | 9 | 7 | 7 |
| Cows' milk | 58 | 60* | 60* |
| Cattle hides (fresh)* | 8 | 7 | 8 |
| Goatskins (fresh)* | 1 | 1 | 1 |
| Hen eggs* | 1 | 1 | 1 |
| Honey* | 11 | 11 | 11 |

* FAO estimate(s). † Unofficial figure(s).

Source: FAO, *Production Yearbook*.

# Forestry

**ROUNDWOOD REMOVALS** ('000 cubic metres, excluding bark)

| | 1995 | 1996 | 1997 |
|---|---|---|---|
| Sawlogs, veneer logs and logs for sleepers | 326 | 305 | 461 |
| Other industrial wood | 284 | 290 | 296 |
| Fuel wood | 3,000 | 2,804 | 2,915 |
| **Total** | 3,610 | 3,399 | 3,672 |

Source: FAO, *Yearbook of Forest Products*.

**SAWNWOOD PRODUCTION**
('000 cubic metres, including railway sleepers)

| | 1995 | 1996 | 1997 |
|---|---|---|---|
| **Total** (all broadleaved) | 70 | 61 | 72 |

Source: FAO, *Yearbook of Forest Products*.

# Fishing

(FAO estimates, '000 metric tons, live weight)

| | 1995 | 1996 | 1997 |
|---|---|---|---|
| **Total catch** (freshwater fish) | 12.9 | 12.7 | 12.5 |

Source: FAO, *Yearbook of Fishery Statistics*.

# Mining

| | 1996 | 1997 | 1998 |
|---|---|---|---|
| Gold (kg, metal content of ore) | 38.7 | 35.1 | 23.8 |
| Diamonds ('000 carats) | 487.4 | 486.8 | 419.8 |

Source: Banque des Etats de l'Afrique Centrale, *Etudes et Statistiques*.

# Industry

**SELECTED PRODUCTS**

| | 1995 | 1996 | 1997* |
|---|---|---|---|
| Beer ('000 hectolitres) | 268.9 | 156.4 | 130.2 |
| Soft drinks and syrups ('000 hectolitres) | 52.8 | 60.6 | 42.1 |
| Cigarettes (million packets) | 18.6 | 7.8 | n.a. |
| Palm oil ('000 metric tons) | 3.2 | 2.3 | 2.5 |
| Plywood ('000 cubic metres) | 2.4 | 1.5 | 1.4 |
| Motor cycles (number) | 338 | n.a. | n.a. |
| Bicycles (number) | 647 | n.a. | n.a. |
| Electric energy (million kWh) | 101.4 | 98.7 | 100.7 |

* Figures are provisional.

Source: IMF, *Central African Republic: Statistical Annex* (September 1998).

Raw sugar (FAO estimates, '000 metric tons): 10 in 1995; 10 in 1996; 11 in 1997; 11 in 1998 (Source: mainly FAO, *Production Yearbook*).

# Finance

**CURRENCY AND EXCHANGE RATES**

**Monetary Units**

100 centimes = 1 franc de la Coopération financière en Afrique centrale (CFA).

**Sterling, Dollar and Euro Equivalents** (30 September 1999)

£1 sterling = 1,012.69 francs CFA;
US $1 = 615.06 francs CFA;
€1 = 655.96 francs CFA;
10,000 francs CFA = £9.875 = $16.259 = €15.245.

**Average Exchange Rate** (francs CFA per US $)

1996 511.55
1997 583.67
1998 589.95

Note: The exchange rate of 1 French franc = 50 francs CFA, established in 1948, remained in force until January 1994, when the CFA franc was devalued by 50%, with the exchange rate adjusted to 1 French franc = 100 francs CFA.

**BUDGET** (million francs CFA)

| Revenue | 1995 | 1996 | 1997* |
|---|---|---|---|
| Tax revenue | 49,300 | 32,900 | 42,400 |
| Taxes on income and profits | 10,600 | 8,100 | 8,700 |
| Domestic taxes on goods and services | 16,800 | 11,900 | 16,500 |
| Taxes on international trade | 21,900 | 12,900 | 17,100 |
| Import duties and taxes | 17,900 | 9,700 | 15,400 |
| Other receipts | 2,200 | 300 | 2,600 |
| **Total** | 51,500 | 33,200 | 45,000 |

| Expenditure | 1995 | 1996 | 1997* |
|---|---|---|---|
| Current expenditure | 57,400 | 47,400 | 52,200† |
| Wages and salaries | 26,000 | 25,300 | 26,600 |
| Other goods and services | 11,500 | 7,600 | 10,200 |
| Transfers and subsidies | 7,200 | 4,100 | 3,800 |
| Interest payments | 12,800 | 10,500 | 7,900 |
| Capital expenditure | 57,900 | 13,200 | 30,700 |
| **Sub-total** | 115,300 | 60,600 | 82,900 |
| Adjustment for payments arrears‡ | −25,700 | 22,800 | −21,300 |
| **Total** | 89,600 | 83,400 | 61,600 |

* Estimates.

† Including extrabudgetary expenditure (million francs CFA): 3,600.

‡ Minus sign indicates an increase in arrears.

Source: IMF, *Central African Republic: Statistical Annex* (September 1998).

**INTERNATIONAL RESERVES** (US $ million at 31 December)

| | 1996 | 1997 | 1998 |
|---|---|---|---|
| Gold* | 4.10 | 3.24 | 3.20 |
| IMF special drawing rights | 0.01 | — | 0.01 |
| Reserve position in IMF | 0.14 | 0.13 | 0.13 |
| Foreign exchange | 232.09 | 178.43 | 145.56 |
| **Total** | 236.34 | 181.80 | 148.90 |

* National valuation.

Source: IMF, *International Financial Statistics.*

**MONEY SUPPLY** (million francs CFA at 31 December)

| | 1996 | 1997 | 1998 |
|---|---|---|---|
| Currency outside banks | 104,000 | 92,963 | 75,247 |
| Demand deposits at commercial and development banks | 12,644 | 14,223 | 12,332 |
| **Total money** | 116,644 | 107,186 | 87,579 |

Source: Banque des Etats de l'Afrique Centrale, *Etudes et Statistiques.*

**COST OF LIVING**
(Consumer Price Index for Bangui; base: 1981 = 100)

| | 1995 | 1996 | 1997 |
|---|---|---|---|
| Food | 179.9 | 193.2 | 188.1 |
| Fuel and light | 151.5 | 153.4 | 161.7 |
| Clothing | 238.7 | 223.5 | 252.6 |
| **All items** (incl. others)* | 187.5 | 195.7 | 196.8 |

* Excluding rent.

Source: IMF, *Central African Republic: Statistical Annex* (September 1998).

**NATIONAL ACCOUNTS**
(IMF estimates, million francs CFA at current prices)

**Expenditure on the Gross Domestic Product**

| | 1995 | 1996 | 1997 |
|---|---|---|---|
| Government final consumption expenditure | 73,700 | 41,700 | 55,300 |
| Private final consumption expenditure | 453,100 | 41,700 | 55,300 |
| Increase in stocks<br>Gross fixed capital formation } | 83,500 | 19,100 | 53,400 |
| **Total domestic expenditure** | 610,300 | 596,900 | 608,400 |
| Exports of goods and services | 114,200 | 97,400 | 124,100 |
| *Less* Imports of goods and services | 155,100 | 117,700 | 137,800 |
| **GDP in purchasers' values** | 569,400 | 556,600 | 594,600 |
| **GDP at constant 1985 prices** | 403,100 | 397,200 | 417,600 |

Source: IMF, *Central African Republic: Statistical Annex* (September 1998).

**Gross Domestic Product by Economic Activity**

| | 1995 | 1996 | 1997 |
|---|---|---|---|
| Agriculture, hunting, forestry and fishing | 257,600 | 277,800 | 303,700 |
| Mining and quarrying | 23,000 | 21,900 | 21,600 |
| Manufacturing | 55,400 | 53,100 | 48,000 |
| Electricity, gas and water | 5,000 | 5,000 | 4,800 |
| Construction | 30,100 | 23,800 | 26,600 |
| Trade, restaurants and hotels | 72,200 | 77,500 | 79,900 |
| Transport, storage and communications | 13,900 | 14,400 | 14,700 |
| Other private services | 25,900 | 27,600 | 27,800 |
| Government services | 47,700 | 30,800 | 33,800 |
| **GDP at factor cost** | 530,700 | 531,800 | 561,000 |
| Indirect taxes | 38,700 | 24,800 | 33,600 |
| **GDP in purchasers' values** | 569,400 | 556,600 | 594,600 |

Source: IMF, *Central African Republic: Statistical Annex* (September 1998).

**BALANCE OF PAYMENTS** ('000 million francs CFA)

| | 1995 | 1996 | 1997* |
|---|---|---|---|
| Exports of goods | 89.3 | 74.5 | 101.2 |
| Imports of goods | −89.2 | −60.6 | −74.2 |
| **Trade balance** | 0.1 | 13.9 | 27.0 |
| Services and other income (net) | −51.3 | −39.6 | −47.0 |
| **Balance on goods, services and income** | −51.2 | −25.7 | −20.0 |
| Private unrequited transfers (net) | −5.4 | −5.1 | −5.8 |
| Public unrequited transfers (net) | 51.9 | 25.2 | 29.4 |
| **Current balance** | −4.7 | −5.6 | 3.6 |
| Long-term capital (net) | 5.3 | −5.4 | −11.8 |
| Short-term capital (net) | 3.1 | 7.8 | −5.8 |
| Net errors and omissions | −8.4 | −4.7 | −8.9 |
| **Overall balance** | −4.7 | −7.9 | −22.9 |

* Estimates.

Source: La Zone Franc, *Rapport Annuel 1997.*

# External Trade

**PRINCIPAL COMMODITIES** (distribution by SITC, US $'000)

| Imports c.i.f. | 1994 | 1995 | 1996 |
|---|---|---|---|
| **Food and live animals** | 24,635 | 27,587 | 12,585 |
| Cereals and cereal preparations | 17,183 | 15,010 | 5,915 |
| Flour of wheat or meslin | 13,990 | 7,999 | 3,442 |
| **Beverages and tobacco** | 14,238 | 12,128 | 8,977 |
| Tobacco and tobacco manufactures | 12,216 | 9,244 | 6,709 |
| Unmanufactured tobacco and tobacco refuse | 4,417 | 8,510 | 3,632 |
| Cigarettes | 7,799 | 734 | 3,077 |
| **Crude materials (inedible) except fuels** | 10,353 | 27,184 | 25,177 |
| Cork and wood | 97 | 2,466 | 4,365 |
| Coniferous sawlogs and veneer logs | 90 | 1,921 | 3,901 |
| Textile fibres (excl. wool tops) and waste | 9,361 | 22,443 | 19,132 |
| Cotton | 7,951 | 20,547 | 17,501 |
| **Mineral fuels, lubricants, etc.** | 11,606 | 23,063 | 14,594 |
| Petroleum, petroleum products, etc. | 11,374 | 22,755 | 14,550 |
| Refined petroleum products | 11,223 | 22,715 | 14,447 |
| Motor spirit (gasoline) and other light oils | 3,223 | 8,364 | 4,756 |
| Kerosene and other medium oils | 3,948 | 4,239 | 2,973 |
| Gas oils (distillate fuels) | 2,242 | 7,651 | 4,809 |
| **Chemicals and related products** | 25,037 | 20,721 | 14,056 |
| Medicinal and pharmaceutical products | 16,759 | 9,522 | 6,416 |
| Medicaments | 15,912 | 8,300 | 5,960 |
| Disinfectants, insecticides, fungicides, etc. | 2,824 | 3,760 | 4,039 |
| **Basic manufactures** | 21,404 | 29,201 | 19,118 |
| Paper, paperboard and manufactures | 3,483 | 4,169 | 3,970 |
| Non-ferrous metals | 4,685 | 3,548 | 1,812 |
| Aluminium and aluminium alloys | 4,393 | 3,204 | 1,210 |
| Plates, sheets and strip | 3,985 | 2,575 | 1,066 |
| **Machinery and transport equipment** | 36,668 | 112,122 | 67,289 |
| Power-generating machinery and equipment | 1,424 | 3,897 | 3,704 |
| Machinery specialized for particular industries | 2,809 | 26,240 | 7,912 |
| Civil engineering and contractors' plant and equipment | 876 | 23,753 | 4,939 |
| Construction and mining machinery | 460 | 20,437 | 3,685 |
| Self-propelled bulldozers, angledozers and levellers | 366 | 14,872 | 472 |
| General industrial machinery, equipment and parts | 5,969 | 9,441 | 5,042 |
| Telecommunications and sound equipment | 3,131 | 12,119 | 4,777 |
| Television and radio transmitters, etc. | 983 | 6,170 | 2,496 |
| Other electrical machinery, apparatus, etc. | 4,120 | 5,494 | 4,180 |
| Road vehicles and parts* | 16,456 | 49,770 | 33,043 |
| Passenger motor cars (excl. buses) | 2,948 | 8,935 | 5,473 |
| Motor vehicles for goods transport and special purposes | 4,847 | 17,160 | 13,314 |
| Goods vehicles (lorries and trucks) | 4,500 | 11,006 | 11,387 |
| Special-purpose motor lorries and vans | 347 | 6,154 | 1,927 |
| Public-service passenger motor vehicles (buses, etc.) | 1,071 | 5,987 | 2,815 |
| Parts and accessories for cars, buses, lorries, etc.* | 4,204 | 9,836 | 7,056 |
| Other transport equipment* | 557 | 1,963 | 5,771 |
| Aircraft, associated equipment and parts* | 548 | 1,791 | 5,771 |
| **Miscellaneous manufactured articles** | 7,040 | 12,019 | 10,386 |
| Printed matter | 1,544 | 2,582 | 3,890 |
| **Armoured fighting vehicles, arms of war and ammunition** | 17 | 6 | 7,152 |
| Tanks and other armoured fighting vehicles, motorized, and parts | — | — | 6,830 |
| **Total** (incl. others) | 154,162 | 265,499 | 179,942 |

* Excluding tyres, engines and electrical parts.

| Exports f.o.b. | 1994 | 1995 | 1996 |
|---|---|---|---|
| **Food and live animals** | 2,605 | 4,142 | 1,295 |
| Coffee, tea, cocoa and spices | 2,054 | 3,109 | 872 |
| Coffee and coffee substitutes | 2,049 | 3,103 | 872 |
| Unroasted coffee, husks and skins | 2,049 | 3,103 | 872 |
| **Crude materials (inedible) except fuels** | 42,858 | 59,829 | 57,334 |
| Cork and wood | 1,299 | 2,790 | 4,756 |
| Coniferous sawlogs and veneer logs | 142 | 1,736 | 3,883 |
| Textile fibres (excl. wool tops) and waste | 7,531 | 20,351 | 22,379 |
| Cotton | 7,528 | 20,309 | 22,379 |
| Crude fertilizers and crude minerals (excl. coal, petroleum and precious stones) | 33,545 | 35,998 | 29,437 |
| Industrial diamonds (sorted) | 33,545 | 35,998 | 29,435 |
| **Basic manufactures** | 31,114 | 41,776 | 40,107 |
| Non-metallic mineral manufactures | 30,839 | 39,887 | 39,725 |
| Diamonds (excl. sorted industrial diamonds), unmounted | 30,836 | 39,880 | 39,715 |
| Sorted non-industrial diamonds, rough or simply worked | 29,877 | 39,812 | 39,663 |
| **Machinery and transport equipment** | 2,239 | 10,543 | 8,663 |
| Road vehicles and parts* | 2,008 | 9,259 | 7,119 |
| Public-service passenger motor vehicles (buses, etc.) | 74 | 3,277 | 823 |
| Parts and accessories for cars, buses, lorries, etc.* | 1,237 | 3,351 | 4,141 |
| **Armoured fighting vehicles, arms of war and ammunition** | 692 | — | 6,992 |
| Tanks and other armoured fighting vehicles, motorized, and parts | — | — | 6,829 |
| **Total** (incl. others) | 81,451 | 119,522 | 115,128 |

* Excluding tyres, engines and electrical parts.

Source: UN, *International Trade Statistics Yearbook*.

**PRINCIPAL TRADING PARTNERS** (US $'000)*

| Imports c.i.f. | 1994 | 1995 | 1996 |
|---|---|---|---|
| Belgium-Luxembourg | 2,675 | 6,589 | 2,805 |
| Cameroon | 8,448 | 12,880 | 7,103 |
| Congo, Dem. Repub. | 1,386 | 1,841 | 1,938 |
| Congo, Repub. | 18,047 | 4,738 | 3,371 |
| France (incl. Monaco) | 59,149 | 90,739 | 71,137 |
| Germany | 3,213 | 7,626 | 2,792 |
| Italy | 1,332 | 2,921 | 1,674 |
| Japan | 8,586 | 52,303 | 15,676 |
| Netherlands | 1,685 | 2,815 | 1,845 |
| United Kingdom | 1,437 | 1,563 | 3,148 |
| USA | 2,447 | 4,871 | 2,971 |
| **Total** (incl. others) | 154,162 | 265,499 | 179,942 |

**LIVESTOCK PRODUCTS** (FAO estimates, '000 metric tons)

| | 1996 | 1997 | 1998 |
|---|---|---|---|
| Beef and veal | 38 | 39 | 40 |
| Mutton and lamb | 12 | 12 | 12 |
| Goat meat | 13 | 13 | 14 |
| Poultry meat | 4 | 4 | 5 |
| Other meat | 5 | 6 | 4 |
| Cows' milk | 123 | 123 | 123 |
| Sheep's milk | 10 | 10 | 10 |
| Goats' milk | 22 | 23 | 23 |
| Poultry eggs | 4 | 4 | 4 |
| Cattle hides | 6 | 6 | 6 |
| Sheepskins | 2 | 2 | 2 |
| Goatskins | 2 | 2 | 2 |

Source: FAO, *Production Yearbook*.

## Forestry

**ROUNDWOOD REMOVALS** ('000 cubic metres, excl. bark)

| | 1995 | 1996 | 1997 |
|---|---|---|---|
| Sawlogs, veneer logs and logs for sleepers | 14 | 14 | 14 |
| Other industrial wood | 634 | 652 | 671 |
| Fuel wood | 3,864 | 3,977 | 4,091 |
| **Total** | 4,512 | 4,643 | 4,776 |

Source: FAO, *Yearbook of Forest Products*.

**SAWNWOOD PRODUCTION** ('000 cubic metres, incl. railway sleepers)

| | 1995 | 1996 | 1997 |
|---|---|---|---|
| **Total** (all broadleaved) | 2 | 2 | 2* |

* FAO estimate.

Source: FAO, *Yearbook of Forest Products*.

## Fishing

('000 metric tons, live weight)

| | 1995 | 1996 | 1997 |
|---|---|---|---|
| **Total catch** (freshwater fishes) | 90.0 | 100.0 | 85.0 |

Source: FAO, *Yearbook of Fishery Statistics*.

## Industry

**SELECTED PRODUCTS**

| | 1996 | 1997 | 1998 |
|---|---|---|---|
| Edible oil ('000 hectolitres) | 114.1 | 156.1 | 160.0 |
| Sugar ('000 metric tons) | 35.0 | 33.0 | 29.0 |
| Beer ('000 hectolitres) | 118.2 | 123.0 | 135.0 |
| Cigarettes (million) | 700 | 780 | 860 |
| Woven cotton fabrics (million metres) | 0.8 | 1.0 | 1.1 |
| Electric energy (million kWh) | 92.1 | 81.2 | 74.9 |

Source: IMF, *Chad—Recent Economic Developments* (May 1999).

## Finance

**CURRENCY AND EXCHANGE RATES**

**Monetary Units**

100 centimes = 1 franc de la Coopération financière en Afrique centrale (CFA).

**Sterling, Dollar and Euro Equivalents** (30 September 1999)

£1 sterling = 1,012.69 francs CFA;
US $1 = 615.06 francs CFA;
€1 = 655.96 francs CFA;
10,000 francs CFA = £9.875 = $16.259 = €15.245.

**Average Exchange Rate** (francs CFA per US $)

1996 511.55
1997 583.67
1998 589.95

Note: An exchange rate of 1 French franc = 50 francs CFA, established in 1948, remained in force until January 1994, when the CFA franc was devalued by 50%, with the exchange rate adjusted to 1 French franc = 100 francs CFA.

**BUDGET** ('000 million francs CFA)

| Revenue* | 1996 | 1997 | 1998† |
|---|---|---|---|
| Tax revenue | 53.0 | 61.3 | 69.8 |
| Taxes on income and profits | 21.5 | 21.6 | 22.6 |
| Companies | 11.9 | 9.7 | 10.7 |
| Individuals | 8.5 | 10.8 | 10.6 |
| Employers' payroll tax | 1.1 | 1.0 | 1.4 |
| Taxes on goods and services | 11.1 | 17.0 | 14.4 |
| Turnover tax | 6.5 | 10.8 | 8.5 |
| Tax on petroleum products | 2.9 | 3.4 | 3.5 |
| Taxes on international trade | 18.6 | 20.7 | 27.4 |
| Import taxes | 17.0 | 18.7 | 25.7 |
| Export taxes | 0.9 | 1.4 | 1.3 |
| Other tax revenues | 1.9 | 2.1 | 5.4 |
| Other revenue | 6.5 | 7.1 | 6.5 |
| Property income | 0.4 | 1.3 | 1.3 |
| **Total** | 59.6 | 68.4 | 76.2 |

| Expenditure‡ | 1996 | 1997 | 1998† |
|---|---|---|---|
| Current expenditure | 77.2 | 73.5 | 75.4 |
| Primary current expenditure | 64.4 | 61.3 | 65.7 |
| Wages and salaries | 30.8 | 30.8 | 31.5 |
| Materials and supplies | 17.1 | 14.6 | 16.1 |
| Transfers | 3.9 | 6.1 | 8.6 |
| Defence | 12.7 | 9.7 | 9.5 |
| Salaries | 10.7 | 8.4 | 8.3 |
| Elections | 3.8 | 0.3 | 0.0 |
| Interest | 8.4 | 8.5 | 8.9 |
| External | 7.1 | 7.0 | 7.5 |
| Investment expenditure | 74.6 | 85.4 | 78.4 |
| Foreign-financed | 74.0 | 81.4 | 73.3 |
| **Total** | 151.8 | 158.9 | 153.8 |

* Excluding grants received ('000 million francs CFA): 50.6 in 1996; 56.4 in 1997; 50.9 (provisional) in 1998.

† Preliminary figures.

‡ Excluding adjustment for payments arrears.

Source: IMF, *Chad: Recent Economic Developments* (May 1999).

**INTERNATIONAL RESERVES** (US $ million at 31 December)

| | 1996 | 1997 | 1998 |
|---|---|---|---|
| Gold* | n.a. | n.a. | 3.20 |
| IMF special drawing rights | 0.24 | 0.01 | 0.01 |
| Reserve position in IMF | 0.40 | 0.38 | 0.40 |
| Foreign exchange | 163.84 | 135.44 | 119.68 |
| **Total** | n.a. | n.a. | 123.29 |

* Valued at market-related prices.

Source: IMF, *International Financial Statistics*.

**MONEY SUPPLY** ('000 million francs CFA at 31 December)

| | 1996 | 1997 | 1998 |
|---|---|---|---|
| Currency outside banks | 89.36 | 78.81 | 73.62 |
| Demand deposits at commercial and development banks | 22.98 | 27.11 | 25.38 |
| **Total money** (incl. others) | 113.88 | 108.47 | 98.99 |

Source: IMF, *International Financial Statistics*.

**COST OF LIVING** (Consumer Price Index for African households in N'Djamena; base: 1995 = 100)

| | 1996 | 1997 | 1998 |
|---|---|---|---|
| **All items** | 112.4 | 118.7 | 126.4 |

Source: IMF, *International Financial Statistics*.

**NATIONAL ACCOUNTS**

('000 million francs CFA at current prices)

**Expenditure on the Gross Domestic Product**

| | 1996 | 1997 | 1998 |
|---|---|---|---|
| Government final consumption expenditure | 100.4 | 97.0 | 94.1 |
| Private final consumption expenditure | 752.9 | 803.9 | 887.8 |
| Increase in stocks | 13.0 | 16.8 | 5.0 |
| Gross fixed capital formation | 98.8 | 128.0 | 144.6 |
| **Total domestic expenditure** | 965.2 | 1,045.7 | 1,131.5 |
| Exports of goods and services | 144.7 | 155.7 | 180.5 |
| *Less* Imports of goods and services | 279.2 | 313.5 | 327.8 |
| **GDP in purchasers' values** | 830.7 | 887.9 | 984.2 |

**Gross Domestic Product by Economic Activity**

| | 1996 | 1997 | 1998 |
|---|---|---|---|
| Agriculture* | 285.0 | 306.1 | 348.6 |
| Mining and quarrying† | 23.5 | 25.8 | 28.1 |
| Electricity, gas and water | 5.4 | 5.5 | 5.4 |
| Manufacturing | 92.5 | 110.6 | 117.8 |
| Construction | 13.8 | 14.4 | 15.4 |
| Wholesale and retail trade, restaurants and hotels; Transport and communications | 204.2 | 214.2 | 239.9 |
| Public administration | 98.6 | 95.0 | 104.7 |
| Other services | 85.2 | 91.0 | 92.1 |
| **GDP at factor cost** | 808.2 | 862.6 | 951.9 |
| Indirect taxes, *less* subsidies | 22.5 | 25.3 | 32.3 |
| **GDP in purchasers' values** | 830.7 | 887.9 | 984.2 |

* Excluding fishing. † Including fishing.

Source: IMF, *Chad: Recent Economic Developments* (May 1999).

**BALANCE OF PAYMENTS** ('000 million francs CFA)

| | 1996 | 1997 | 1998 |
|---|---|---|---|
| Exports of goods f.o.b. | 113.1 | 123.2 | 145.3 |
| Imports of goods f.o.b. | −148.0 | −165.5 | −175.0 |
| **Trade balance** | −34.9 | −42.3 | −29.7 |
| Exports of services | 31.6 | 32.5 | 35.2 |
| Imports of services | −131.2 | −148.0 | −152.8 |
| **Balance on goods and services** | −134.4 | −157.8 | −147.2 |
| Other income (net) | −16.6 | −17.0 | −17.9 |
| **Balance on goods, services and income** | −151.0 | −174.8 | −165.1 |
| Current transfers (net) | 50.0 | 41.6 | 43.5 |
| **Current balance** | −101.0 | −133.2 | −121.6 |
| Capital account | 36.4 | 36.1 | 28.4 |
| Direct investment (net) | 7.6 | 9.2 | 15.8 |
| Other investment (net) | 64.1 | 75.4 | 81.9 |
| Net errors and omissions | 13.7 | 6.3 | −9.6 |
| **Overall balance** | 20.7 | −6.2 | −5.1 |

Source: IMF, *Chad: Recent Economic Developments* (May 1999).

# External Trade

**PRINCIPAL COMMODITIES**

| Imports c.i.f. (US $'000) | 1995 |
|---|---|
| **Food and live animals** | 41,182 |
| Cereals and cereal preparations | 16,028 |
| Rice (semi- or wholly-milled) | 4,589 |
| Wheat and meslin (unmilled) | 8,945 |
| Sugar, sugar preparations and honey | 17,078 |
| Sugar and honey | 16,970 |
| Refined sugars, etc. | 16,825 |
| **Beverages and tobacco** | 7,175 |
| Beverages | 4,526 |
| **Mineral fuels, lubricants, etc.** | 38,592 |
| Petroleum, petroleum products, etc. | 38,574 |
| Refined petroleum products | 38,551 |
| Motor spirit (gasoline) and other light oils | 6,490 |
| Kerosene and other medium oils | 8,456 |
| Gas oils | 23,318 |
| **Chemicals and related products** | 15,507 |
| Medicinal and pharmaceutical products | 7,789 |
| Medicaments (incl. veterinary medicaments) | 6,351 |
| **Basic manufactures** | 26,190 |
| Non-metallic mineral manufactures | 7,654 |
| Lime, cement and fabricated construction materials | 6,394 |
| Cement | 6,247 |
| Metal manufactures | 8,804 |
| **Machinery and transport equipment** | 51,246 |
| General industrial machinery, equipment and parts | 8,175 |
| Telecommunications and sound recording and reproducing equipment and parts | 4,572 |
| Telecommunications equipment and parts | 4,375 |
| Road vehicles (incl. air-cushion vehicles) and parts* | 17,873 |
| Motor vehicles for the transport of goods or materials, etc. | 4,444 |
| Lorries and trucks | 4,338 |
| Parts and accessories for cars, lorries, buses, etc.* | 8,253 |
| **Miscellaneous manufactured articles** | 27,335 |
| Professional, scientific and controlling instruments and apparatus | 5,073 |
| Printed matter | 13,565 |
| Postage stamps, banknotes, etc. | 11,622 |
| **Total** (incl. others) | 215,171 |

* Excluding tyres, engines and electrical parts.

Source: UN, *International Trade Statistics Yearbook*.

| Exports (million francs CFA) | 1983 |
|---|---|
| Live cattle | 49.5 |
| Meat | 23.5 |
| Fish | 2.0 |
| Oil-cake | 8.1 |
| Natron | 8.1 |
| Gums and resins | 0.4 |
| Hides and skins | 16.6 |
| Raw cotton | 3,753.7 |
| **Total** (incl. others) | 4,120.0 |

**Total exports** (million francs CFA): 27,781 in 1985; 34,145 in 1986; 32,892 in 1987; 42,900 in 1988; 49,570 in 1989; 51,202 in 1990; 54,600 in 1991; 48,250 in 1992; 37,330 in 1993; 82,160 in 1994; 125,600 in 1995; 117,230 in 1996; 138,100 in 1997. (Source: Banque des Etats de l'Afrique Centrale).

**Cotton exports** ('000 million francs CFA): 26.8 in 1991; 25.3 in 1992.

**PRINCIPAL TRADING PARTNERS**

| Imports c.i.f. (US $'000) | 1995 |
|---|---|
| Belgium-Luxembourg | 4,771 |
| Cameroon | 33,911 |
| Central African Repub. | 3,010 |
| China, People's Repub. | 6,251 |
| France | 88,887 |
| Germany | 2,988 |
| Italy | 6,452 |
| Japan | 5,121 |
| Malaysia | 2,234 |
| Netherlands | 2,843 |
| Nigeria | 25,269 |
| Spain | 3,402 |
| USA | 13,966 |
| **Total** (incl. others) | 215,171 |

Source: UN, *International Trade Statistics Yearbook*.

| Exports (million francs CFA) | 1984 | 1985 | 1986 |
|---|---|---|---|
| Cameroon | 929 | 1,711 | 2,661 |
| Central African Repub. | 64 | 1,219 | 321 |
| France | 6,950 | 1,432 | 1,774 |
| Nigeria | 113 | 1,981 | 425 |
| Sudan | 8 | 47 | 101 |
| Congo, Democratic Repub. | 125 | 5 | n.a. |
| **Total** (incl. others) | 8,231 | 6,446 | 5,374 |

# Transport

**ROAD TRAFFIC** (motor vehicles in use at 31 December)

| | 1994 | 1995* | 1996* |
|---|---|---|---|
| Passenger cars | 8,720 | 9,700 | 10,560 |
| Buses and coaches | 708 | 760 | 820 |
| Lorries and vans | 12,650 | 13,720 | 14,550 |
| Tractors | 1,413 | 1,500 | 1,580 |
| Motorcycles and mopeds | 1,855 | 2,730 | 3,640 |

* Estimates.

Source: International Road Federation, *World Road Statistics*.

**CIVIL AVIATION** (traffic on scheduled services*)

| | 1993 | 1994 | 1995 |
|---|---|---|---|
| Kilometres flown (million) | 2 | 2 | 3 |
| Passengers carried ('000) | 85 | 86 | 92 |
| Passengers-km (million) | 214 | 222 | 231 |
| Total ton-km (million) | 34 | 35 | 37 |

* Including an apportionment of the traffic of Air Afrique.

Source: UN, *Statistical Yearbook*.

# Tourism

| | 1994 | 1995 | 1996 |
|---|---|---|---|
| Tourist arrivals ('000) | 19 | 7 | 8 |
| Tourism receipts (US $ million) | 12 | 10 | 10 |

Source: World Tourism Organization, *Yearbook of Tourism Statistics*.

# Communications Media

| | 1994 | 1995 | 1996 |
|---|---|---|---|
| Radio receivers ('000 in use) | 1,520 | 1,570 | 1,620 |
| Television receivers ('000 in use) | 9 | 9 | 9 |
| Telephones ('000 main lines in use) | 5 | 5 | n.a. |
| Telefax stations (number in use) | 140 | 174 | n.a. |
| Daily newspapers: | | | |
| Number | 1 | 1 | 1 |
| Average circulation ('000 copies) | 2 | 2 | 6 |
| Non-daily newspapers: | | | |
| Number | n.a. | 2 | n.a. |
| Average circulation ('000 copies) | n.a. | 10 | n.a. |

Sources: UNESCO, *Statistical Yearbook*; UN *Statistical Yearbook*.

# Education

(1996/97, unless otherwise indicated)

| | Institutions | Teachers | Students: Males | Females | Total |
|---|---|---|---|---|---|
| Pre-primary* | 24 | 67 | 938 | 735 | 1,673 |
| Primary | 2,660† | 10,151 | 447,685 | 233,224 | 680,909 |
| Secondary: | | | | | |
| General | 153† | 2,598 | 77,622 | 19,389 | 97,011 |
| Teacher training | 6† | 46 | 360 | 265 | 625 |
| Vocational | 12† | 148 | 1,506 | 647 | 2,153 |
| University-level† | n.a. | 288 | 8 | 406 | 3,274 |

* 1994/95 figures; public education only.

† 1995/96 figures.

Source: mainly UNESCO, *Statistical Yearbook*.

# Directory

## The Constitution

The Constitution of the Republic of Chad, which was adopted by national referendum on 31 March 1996, enshrines a unitary state. The President is elected for a term of five years by direct universal adult suffrage, and is restricted to a maximum of two terms in office. The Prime Minister, who is appointed by the President, nominates the Council of Ministers. The bicameral legislature includes a 125-member Assemblée nationale, which is elected by direct universal adult suffrage for a term of four years. Provision is also made for an upper legislative chamber, the Sénat, with one-third of members renewed every two years. The Constitution provides for an independent judicial system, with a High Court of Justice, and the establishment of a Constitutional Court and a High Council for Communication.

## The Government

**HEAD OF STATE**

**President and Commander-in-Chief of the Armed Forces:** IDRISS DEBY (assumed office 4 December 1990; elected President 3 August 1996).

**COUNCIL OF MINISTERS**
(January 2000)

**Prime Minister:** NAGOUM YAMASSOUM.

**Minister of State, Minister of Agriculture:** SALEH KEBZABO.

**Minister of the Economy, Territorial Development and Co-operation:** MAHAMAT ALI HASSANE.

**Minister of Foreign Affairs and Co-operation:** MAHAMAT SALEH ANNADIF.

**Minister of Mines, Energy and Petroleum:** MOCTAR MOUSSA.

**Minister of Finance:** BICHARA CHÉRIF DAOUSSA.

**Minister of National Defence and Reintegration:** WEIDING ASSI-ASSOUE.

**Minister of the Interior, Security and Decentralization:** ABDERAHMANE MOUSSA.

**Minister of Justice, Keeper of the Seals:** ROUTOUANG YOMA GOLOM.

**Minister of Livestock:** MAHAMAT NOURI.

**Minister of Public Health:** ABDOULAYE LAMANA.

**Minister of Higher Education:** ABDERAHIM BREME HAMID.

**Minister of Industrial and Commercial Development and Crafts:** ASSANA DINGAMADJI.

**Minister of Communications, Delegate to the Parliament, Spokesperson for the Government:** MAHAMAT AHMAT CHOUKOU.

**Minister of Social Welfare and the Family:** FATIME KIMTO.

**Minister of the Environment and Water Resources:** NADJO ABDEL KERIM.

**Minister of Tourism Development:** SALIBOU GARBA.

**Minister of Civil Service, Labour, Employment Promotion and Modernization:** ABBA KOI DJOUASSAB.

**Minister of Public Works, Transport, Housing and Town Planning:** AHMAT LAMINE ALI.

**Minister of Posts and Telecommunications:** OUMAR KADJALLAMI BOUKAR.

**Minister of Culture, Youth and Sports:** LAOUKISSAM NISSALA.

**Minister, Secretary-General of the Government:** DAVID HOUDEINGAR.

**MINISTRIES**

**Office of the President:** N'Djamena; tel. 51-44-37.

**Office of the Prime Minister:** N'Djamena.

**Ministry of Agriculture:** N'Djamena.

**Ministry of the Civil Service, Labour, Employment Promotion and Modernization:** BP 437, N'Djamena; tel. and fax 52-21-98.

**Ministry of Communications:** BP 154, N'Djamena; tel. 51-41-64; fax 51-60-94.

**Ministry of Culture, Youth and Sports:** N'Djamena.

**Ministry of Education:** N'Djamena.

**Ministry of the Environment and Water Resources:** N'Djamena.

**Ministry of Finance and the Economy:** BP 144, N'Djamena; tel. 52-21-61.

**Ministry of Foreign Affairs and Co-operation:** N'Djamena; tel. 51-50-82.

**Ministry of the Interior, Security and Decentralization:** N'Djamena.

**Ministry of Justice:** N'Djamena; tel. 51-56-56.

**Ministry of Livestock:** N'Djamena; tel. 51-59-07.

**Ministry of Mines, Energy and Petroleum:** N'Djamena; tel. 51-56-03; fax 51-25-65.

**Ministry of National Defence:** N'Djamena; tel. 51-58-89.

**Ministry of Posts and Telecommunications:** BP 154, N'Djamena; tel. 51-41-64; fax 51-28-35.

**Ministry of Public Health:** N'Djamena; tel. 51-39-60.

**Ministry of Public Works, Transport, Housing and Town Planning:** BP 436, N'Djamena; tel. 51-20-96.

**Ministry of Social Welfare and the Family:** N'Djamena.

**Ministry of Tourism Development:** N'Djamena.

# President and Legislature

**PRESIDENT**

In a first round of voting, which took place on 2 June 1996, none of the 15 candidates secured the requisite 50% of total votes cast. A second round of voting took place on 3 July: the incumbent, President IDRISS DEBY, was elected by 69.1% of the votes, while the other candidate, Gen. WADAL ABDELKADER KAMOUGUÉ, received 30.9%.

**ASSEMBLÉE NATIONALE**

**President:** Gen. WADAL ABDELKADER KAMOUGUÉ.

**General Election, 5 January and 23 February 1997**

| Party | Seats |
|---|---|
| Mouvement patriotique du salut | 65 |
| Union pour le renouveau et la démocratie | 29 |
| Union nationale pour le développement et le renouveau | 15 |
| Union pour la démocratie et la République | 4 |
| Parti pour la liberté et le développement | 3 |
| Rassemblement pour la démocratie et le progrès | 3 |
| Other opposition parties | 6 |
| **Total** | 125 |

Note: The Constitution also makes provision for an upper house of the legislature, the Sénat.

# Political Organizations

Legislation permitting the operation of political associations, subject to official registration, took effect in October 1991. In late 1999 there were about 60 active political organizations, of which the most important are listed below.

**Action pour l'unité et le socialisme (ACTUS):** N'Djamena; f. 1992; Leader Dr FIDÈLE MOUNGAR.

**Alliance nationale pour la démocratie et le développement (ANDD):** BP 4066, N'Djamena; tel. 51-46-72; f. 1992; Leader SALIBOU GARBA.

**Comité de sursaut national pour la paix et la démocratie (CSNPD):** fmr dissident faction; obtained legal recognition in Sept. 1994; Leader Col MOÏSE NODJI KETTE.

**Concertation nationale pour la démocratie sociale (CNDS):** N'Djamena; Leader ADOUM MOUSSA SEIF.

**Front des forces d'action pour la République (FAR):** Leader NGARLEDJY YORONGAR (sentenced to three years' imprisonment in July 1998).

**Mouvement patriotique du salut (MPS):** N'Djamena; f. 1990 as a coalition of several opposition movements; other opposition groups joined during the Nov. 1990 offensive against the regime of Hissène Habré, and following the movement's accession to power in Dec. 1990; Chair. MALDOM BADA ABBAS; Sec.-Gen. MAHAMAT SALEH AHMAT.

**Mouvement pour la démocratie et le socialisme du Tchad (MDST):** N'Djamena; Leader Dr SALOMON NGARBAYE TOMBALBAYE.

**Parti pour la liberté et le développement (PLD):** N'Djamena; f. 1993; Leader IBN OUMAR MAHAMAT SALEH.

**Rassemblement pour la démocratie et le progrès (RDP):** N'Djamena; f. 1992; Leader LOL MAHAMAT CHOUA.

**Rassemblement pour le développement et le progrès:** f. 1992; Leader MAMADOU BISSO.

**Rassemblement national pour la démocratie et le progrès (RNDP):** N'Djamena; f. 1992; Pres. KASSIRE DELWA KOUMAKOYE.

**Union pour la démocratie et la République (UDR):** N'Djamena; f. 1992; Leader Dr JEAN ALINGUE BAWOYEU.

**Union nationale pour le développement et le renouveau (UNDR):** Leader SALEH KEBZABO.

**Union pour le renouveau et la démocratie (URD):** BP 92, N'Djamena; tel. 51-44-23; fax 51-41-87; f. 1992; Leader Gen. WADAL ABDELKADER KAMOUGUÉ.

A number of unregistered dissident groups (some based abroad) are also active. These 'politico-military' organizations include the **Conseil démocratique révolutionnaire (CDR)**, led by ACHEIKH IBN OUMAR; the **Front de libération nationale du Tchad (FROLINAT)**, based in Algeria and led by GOUKOUNI OUEDDEI; the **Front national du Tchad (FNT)**, based in Sudan and led by Dr FARIS BACHAR; the **Front national du Tchad renové (FNTR)**, led by AHMAT YACOUB; the **Mouvement pour la démocratie et le développement (MDD)**, led by ISSA FAKI MAHAMAT and GAILETH GATOUL BOURKOUMANDAH; the **Mouvement pour la démocratie et la justice au Tchad (MDJT)**, led by YOUSSOUF TOGOIMI; the **Résistance armée contre les forces antidémocratiques (RAFAD)**, based in northern Nigeria, under the chairmanship of ADOUM MOUSSA SEIF; and the **Union des forces démocratiques (UFD)**, led by Dr MAHAMAT NAHOUR.

Under the terms of a peace agreement signed by the Chadian Government and the **Forces armées pour la République fédérale (FARF)** in April 1997 (the terms of which were renewed in

May 1998), the FARF was to cease armed activities and was to be legalized as a political organization. The FARF, reportedly under the leadership of Dienambaye Barde, rallied to the MPS in November 1998. The former MDD leader, MOUSSA MEDELLA MAHAMAT, signed a reconciliation document, on behalf of the movement, with the Government in July 1999, but the accord was denounced by the present MDD leadership.

# Diplomatic Representation

### EMBASSIES IN CHAD

**Algeria:** N'Djamena; tel. 51-38-15; Ambassador: MOHAMED CHELLALI KHOURI.

**Central African Republic:** BP 115, N'Djamena; tel. 51-32-06; Ambassador: DAVID NGUINDO.

**Congo, Democratic Republic:** ave du 20 août, BP 910, N'Djamena; tel. 51-59-35; Ambassador: (vacant).

**Egypt:** BP 1094, N'Djamena; tel. 51-36-60; Ambassador: AZIZ M. NOUR EL-DIN.

**France:** BP 431, N'Djamena; tel. 52-25-75; fax 52-28-55; Ambassador: ALAIN DU BOISPÉAN.

**Germany:** ave Félix Eboué, BP 893, N'Djamena; tel. 51-62-02; fax 51-48-00; Chargé d'affaires a.i.: DIETER FREUND.

**Holy See:** BP 490, N'Djamena; tel. 52-31-15; fax 52-38-27; Apostolic Nuncio: Most Rev. DIEGO CAUSERO, Titular Archbishop of Meta.

**Libya:** N'Djamena; Sec. of People's Bureau: GHAYTH SALIM.

**Nigeria:** 35 ave Charles de Gaulle, BP 752, N'Djamena; tel. 51-24-98; Chargé d'affaires a.i.: A. M. ALIYU BIU.

**Sudan:** BP 45, N'Djamena; tel. 51-34-97; Ambassador: TAHA MAKKAWI.

**USA:** ave Félix Eboué, BP 413, N'Djamena; tel. 51-40-09; fax 51-33-72; Ambassador: CHRISTOPHER GOLDTHWAITE.

# Judicial System

The highest judicial authority is the Supreme Court. There is also a Constitutional Council, with final jurisdiction in matters of state. The legal structure also comprises the Court of Appeal, and Magistrate and Criminal Courts. Under the terms of the Constitution adopted in 1996, a High Court of Justice was to be established.

**President of the Supreme Court:** AHMAT BATCHIRET.

**President of the Constitutional Council:** ÑAGOUM YAMASSOUM.

# Religion

It is estimated that some 50% of the population are Muslims and about 30% Christians. Most of the remainder follow animist beliefs.

### ISLAM

**Conseil Suprême des Affaires Islamiques:** POB 1101, N'Djamena; tel. 51-81-80; fax 52-58-84.

**Head of the Islamic Community:** Imam MOUSSA IBRAHIM.

### CHRISTIANITY

#### The Roman Catholic Church

Chad comprises one archdiocese and six dioceses. At 31 December 1997 Roman Catholics numbered an estimated 512,331 (about 8.4% of the total population).

**Bishops' Conference:** Conférence Episcopale du Tchad, BP 456, N'Djamena; tel. 51-44-43; fax 51-28-60; Pres. Most Rev. CHARLES VANDAME, Archbishop of N'Djamena.

**Archbishop of N'Djamena:** Most Rev. CHARLES VANDAME, Archevêché, BP 456, N'Djamena; tel. 51-74-44; fax 52-28-60.

#### Protestant Churches

**Entente des Eglises et Missions Evangéliques au Tchad:** BP 2006, N'Djamena; tel. and fax 51-53-93; an asscn of churches and missions working in Chad; includes Assemblées Chrétiennes au Tchad (ACT), Eglise Evangélique des Frères au Tchad (EEFT), Eglise Evangélique au Tchad (EET), Eglise Fraternelle Luthérienne au Tchad (EFLT); also five assoc. mems.

### BAHÁ'Í FAITH

**National Spiritual Assembly:** BP 181, N'Djamena; tel. 51-47-05; mems in 1,125 localities.

# The Press

**Al-Watan:** BP 407, N'Djamena; tel. 51-57-96; weekly; Editor-in-Chief MOUSSA NDORKOÏ.

**Bulletin Mensuel de Statistiques du Tchad:** BP 453, N'Djamena; monthly.

**Comnat:** BP 731, N'Djamena; tel. 51-46-75; fax 51-46-71; quarterly; publ. by Commission Nationale Tchadienne for UNESCO.

**Contact:** N'Djamena; f. 1989; current affairs; Dir KOULAMALO SOURADJ.

**Info-Tchad:** BP 670, N'Djamena; tel. 515867; news bulletin issued by Agence Tchadienne de Presse; daily; French.

**Informations Economiques:** BP 458, N'Djamena; publ. by the Chambre de Commerce, d'Agriculture et d'Industrie; weekly.

**N'Djamena Hebdo:** BP 760, N'Djamena; tel. 515314; fax 521498; weekly; Editor-in-Chief DIEUDONNÉ DJONABAYE.

**L'Observateur:** N'Djamena; fortnightly; Editor-in-Chief SINGA GALI KOUMBA.

**Le Progrès:** N'Djamena; daily.

### NEWS AGENCIES

**Agence Tchadienne de Presse (ATP):** BP 670, N'Djamena; tel. 51-58-67.

#### Foreign Bureaux

**Agence France-Presse (AFP):** N'Djamena; tel. 51-54-71; Correspondent ALDOM NADJI TITO.

# Publisher

**Government Publishing House:** BP 453, N'Djamena.

# Broadcasting and Communications

### TELECOMMUNICATIONS

**Office Nationale des Postes et des Télécommunications (ONPT):** BP 154, N'Djamena; tel. 52-14-28; fax 51-28-35; state-owned; Dir-Gen. ALHOKI BLAMKAKOU.

The ONPT was to be reorganized into two structures, the **Société des Télécommunications du Tchad (SOTE–TCHAD)** and the **Société Tchadienne des Postes et de l'Epargne (STPE)**, prior to the privatization of the telecommunications sector. A tender was issued in late 1998 for a licence to operate the country's first cellular telephone network.

### BROADCASTING

#### Radio

**Radiodiffusion Nationale Tchadienne:** BP 892, N'Djamena; tel. 51-60-71; state-controlled; programmes in French, Arabic and eight vernacular languages; there are four transmitters; Dir KHAMIS TOGOÏ.

**Radio Abéché:** BP 105, Abéché; tel. 69-81-49; Dir SANOUSSI SAÏD.

**Radio Moundou:** BP 122, Moundou; tel. 69-13-22; daily programmes in French, Sara and Arabic; Dir DIMANANGAR DJAÏNTA.

**Radio Sarh:** BP 270, Sarh; tel. 68-13-61; daily programmes in French, Sara and Arabic; Dir BIANA FOUDA NACTOUANDI.

#### Television

**Télé-Chad:** Commission for Information and Culture, BP 748, N'Djamena; tel. 51-29-23; state-controlled; broadcasts c. 12 hours per week in French and Arabic; Dir HOURMADJI HOUSSA DOUMGOR.

# Finance

(cap. = capital; res = reserves; m. = million; br. = branch; amounts in francs CFA)

### BANKING

#### Central Bank

**Banque des Etats de l'Afrique Centrale (BEAC):** BP 50, N'Djamena; tel. 52-41-76; fax 52-44-87; HQ in Yaoundé, Cameroon; f. 1973; bank of issue for mem. states of the Communauté économique et monétaire de l'Afrique centrale (CEMAC, fmrly Union douanière et économique de l'Afrique centrale), comprising Cameroon, the Central African Repub., Chad, the Repub. of the Congo, Equatorial Guinea and Gabon); cap. and res 218,644m., total assets 1,303,372m. (June 1998); Gov. JEAN-FÉLIX MAMALEPOT; Dir in Chad MAHAMAD AMINE BEN BARKA; 2 brs.

#### Other Banks

**Banque de Développement du Tchad (BDT):** rue Capitaine Ohrel, BP 19, N'Djamena; tel. 52-28-29; fax 52-33-18; f. 1962; 25.9% state-owned; transfer to private ownership pending; cap. and res

3,386m., total assets 13,536m. (Dec. 1998); Pres. MAHAMAT AHMAT SALEH; Dir-Gen. ABDESSIT MAHAMAT.

**Banque Internationale pour l'Afrique au Tchad:** ave Charles de Gaulle, BP 87, N'Djamena; tel. 51-43-14; fax 51-23-45; f. 1980; fmrly Banque Meridien BIAO Tchad.

**Financial Bank Tchad:** ave Charles de Gaulle, BP 804; tel. 52-33-89; fax 52-29-05; f. 1992; 97.9% owned by Financial BC SA (Switzerland); cap. and res 1,000m., total assets 9,675m. (Dec. 1998); Pres. RÉMY BAYSSET; Dir-Gen. PIERRE LECLAIRE.

**Société Générale Tchadienne de Banque (SGBT):** 2–6 rue Robert Lévy, BP 461, N'Djamena; tel. 52-28-76; fax 52-37-13; f. 1963; fmrly Banque Tchadienne de Crédit et de Dépôtes; 30% owned by Société Générale, SA (France), 20% state-owned, cap. and res 2,189m., total assets 33,233m. (Dec. 1998); Pres. and Dir-Gen. CHEMI KOGRIMI; br. at Moundou.

#### Bankers' Organizations

**Association Professionnelle des Banques au Tchad:** 2–6 rue Robert Lévy, BP 461, N'Djamena; tel. 52-41-90; fax 52-17-13; Pres. CHEMI KOGRIMI.

**Conseil National de Crédit:** N'Djamena; f. 1965 to formulate a national credit policy and to organize the banking profession.

### INSURANCE

**Assureurs Conseils Tchadiens Cécar & Jutheau:** BP 139, N'Djamena; tel. 52-21-15; fax 52-35-39; e-mail biliou.alikeke@intnet.td; Dir BILIOU ALI-KEKE.

**Société de Représentation d'Assurances et de Réassurances Africaines (SORARAF):** N'Djamena; Dir Mme FOURNIER.

**Société Tchadienne d'Assurances et de Réassurances (STAR):** BP 914, N'Djamena; tel. 51-56-77; Dir PHILIPPE SABIT.

## Trade and Industry

### DEVELOPMENT ORGANIZATIONS

**Agence Française de Développement:** BP 478, N'Djamena; tel. 51-40-71; fax 51-28-31; fmrly Caisse Française de Développement; Dir JACBIE BATHANY.

**Mission Française de Coopération et d'Action Culturelle:** BP 898, N'Djamena; tel. 52-42-87; fax 52-44-38; administers bilateral aid from France; Dir EDOUARD LAPORTE.

**Office National de Développement Rural (ONDR):** BP 896, N'Djamena; tel. 51-48-64; f. 1968; Dir MICKAEL DJIBRAEL.

**Société pour le Développement de la Région du Lac (SODELAC):** BP 782, N'Djamena; tel. 51-35-03; f. 1967; cap. 180m. francs CFA; Pres. CHERIF ABDELWAHAB; Dir-Gen. MAHAMAT MOCTAR ALI.

### CHAMBER OF COMMERCE

**Chambre Consulaire:** BP 458, N'Djamena; tel. 51-52-64; f. 1938; Pres. ELIE ROMBA; Sec.-Gen. SALEH MAHAMAT RAHMA; brs at Sarh, Moundou, Bol and Abéché.

### TRADE ASSOCIATIONS

**Office National des Céréales (ONC):** BP 21, N'Djamena; tel. 51-37-31; f. 1978; production and marketing of cereals; Dir YBRAHIM MAHAMAT TIDEI; 11 regional offices.

**Société Nationale de Commercialisation du Tchad (SONACOT):** N'Djamena; f. 1965; cap. 150m. francs CFA; 76% state-owned; nat. marketing, distribution and import-export co; Man. Dir MARBROUCK NATROUD.

### UTILITIES

#### Electricity and Water

**Société Tchadienne d'Eau et d'Electricité (STEE):** 11 rue du Colonel Largeau, BP 44, N'Djamena; tel. 51-28-81; fax 51-21-34; f. 1968; state-owned; transfer to private ownership pending; production and distribution of electricity and water; Pres. GOMON MAWATA WAKAG; Dir-Gen. ISMAEL MAHAMAT ADOUM.

### TRADE UNION

**Union Syndicale du Tchad (UST):** BP 1143, N'Djamena; tel. 51-42-75; f. 1988 by merger; Pres. DOMBAL DJIMBAGUE; Sec.-Gen. DJIBRINE ASSALI HAMDALLAH.

## Transport

### RAILWAYS

There are no railways in Chad. In 1962 the Governments of Chad and Cameroon signed an agreement to extend the Transcameroon railway from Ngaoundéré to Sarh, a distance of 500 km. Although the Transcameroon reached Ngaoundéré in 1974, its proposed extension into Chad remains indefinitely postponed.

### ROADS

The total length of the road network in 1996 was an estimated 33,400 km, of which 7,880 km were principal roads and 5,380 km were secondary roads. There are also some 20,000 km of tracks suitable for motor traffic during the October–July dry season. The European Union is contributing to the construction of a highway connecting N'Djamena with Sarh and Léré, on the Cameroon border, and of a 400-km highway linking Moundou and Ngaoundéré.

**Coopérative des Transportateurs Tchadiens (CTT):** BP 336, N'Djamena; tel. 51-43-55; road haulage; Pres. SALEH KHALIFA; brs at Sarh, Moundou, Bangui (CAR), Douala and Ngaoundéré (Cameroon).

### INLAND WATERWAYS

The Chari and Logone rivers, which converge to the south of N'Djamena, are navigable. These waterways connect Sarh with N'Djamena on the Chari and Bongor and Moundou with N'Djamena on the Logone.

### CIVIL AVIATION

The international airport is at N'Djamena. There are also more than 40 smaller airfields.

**Air Afrique:** BP 466, N'Djamena; tel. 51-40-20; see under Côte d'Ivoire.

**Air Tchad:** 27 ave du Président Tombalbaye, BP 168, N'Djamena; tel. 51-50-90; f. 1966; 98% govt-owned; liquidation pending; international charters and domestic passenger, freight and charter services; Chair. DJIBANGAR MADJIREBAYE; Man. Dir MAHAMAT NOURI.

## Tourism

Chad's potential attractions for tourists include a variety of scenery from the dense forests of the south to the deserts of the north. Receipts from tourism in 1996 totalled an estimated US $10m. An estimated 8,000 tourists visited Chad in 1996.

**Direction de la Promotion Touristique:** BP 86, N'Djamena; tel. 52-44-16; fax 52-44-19; Dir ANTOINETTE MEKONDENE.

# CHILE

## Introductory Survey

### Location, Climate, Language, Religion, Flag, Capital

The Republic of Chile is a long, narrow country lying along the Pacific coast of South America, extending from Peru and Bolivia in the north to Cape Horn in the far south. Isla de Pascua (Rapa Nui or Easter Island), about 3,780 km (2,350 miles) off shore, and several other small islands form part of Chile. To the east, Chile is separated from Argentina by the high Andes mountains. Both the mountains and the cold Humboldt Current influence the climate; between Arica in the north and Punta Arenas in the extreme south, a distance of about 4,000 km (2,500 miles), the average maximum temperature varies by no more than 13°C. Rainfall varies widely between the arid desert in the north and the rainy south. The language is Spanish. There is no state religion but the great majority of the inhabitants profess Christianity, and some 79% are adherents of the Roman Catholic Church. The national flag (proportions 3 by 2) is divided horizontally: the lower half is red, while the upper half has a five-pointed white star on a blue square, at the hoist, with the remainder white. The capital is Santiago.

### Recent History

Chile was ruled by Spain from the 16th century until its independence in 1818. For most of the 19th century it was governed by a small oligarchy of landowners. Chile won the War of the Pacific (1879–83) against Peru and Bolivia. The greater part of the 20th century was characterized by the struggle for power between right- and left-wing forces.

In September 1970 Dr Salvador Allende Gossens, the Marxist candidate of Unidad Popular (a coalition of five left-wing parties, including the Partido Comunista de Chile), was elected to succeed Eduardo Frei Montalva, a Christian Democrat who was President between 1964 and 1970. Allende promised to transform Chilean society by constitutional means, and imposed an extensive programme of nationalization. The Government failed to obtain a congressional majority in the elections of March 1973 and encountered a deteriorating economic situation as well as an intensification of violent opposition to its policies. Accelerated inflation led to food shortages and there were repeated clashes between pro- and anti-Government activists. The armed forces finally intervened in September 1973. President Allende died during the coup. The Congreso (Congress) was subsequently dissolved, all political activity banned and strict censorship introduced. The military Junta dedicated itself to the eradication of Marxism and the reconstruction of Chile, and its leader, Gen. Augusto Pinochet Ugarte, became Supreme Chief of State in June 1974 and President in December. The Junta was widely criticized abroad for its repressive policies and violations of human rights. Critics of the regime were tortured and imprisoned, and several thousand were abducted or 'disappeared'. Some of those who had been imprisoned were released, as a result of international pressure, and sent into exile.

In September 1976 three constitutional acts were promulgated with the aim of creating an 'authoritarian democracy'. All political parties were banned in March 1977, when the state of siege was extended. Following a UN General Assembly resolution, adopted in December 1977, which condemned the Government for violating human rights, President Pinochet organized a referendum in January 1978 to seek endorsement of the regime's policies. Since more than 75% of the voters supported the President in his defence of Chile 'in the face of international aggression', the state of siege (in force since 1973) was ended and was replaced by a state of emergency.

At a plebiscite held in September 1980, 67% of voters endorsed a new Constitution, drafted by the Government, although dubious electoral practices were allegedly employed. The new Constitution was described as providing a 'transition to democracy' but, although President Pinochet ceased to be head of the armed forces, additional clauses allowed him to maintain his firm hold on power until 1989. The new Constitution became effective from March 1981. Political parties, which were still officially outlawed, began to re-emerge, and in July 1983 five moderate parties formed a coalition, the 'Alianza Democrática', which advocated a return to democratic rule within 18 months. A left-wing coalition was also created.

In February 1984 the Council of State, a government-appointed consultative body, began drafting a law to legalize political parties and to prepare for elections in 1989. Despite the Government's strenuous attempts to eradicate internal opposition through the introduction of anti-terrorist legislation and extensive security measures, a campaign of explosions and public protests continued throughout 1984 and 1985. A number of protesters were killed in violent clashes with security forces during this period, and many opposition leaders and trade unionists were detained and sent into internal exile.

Throughout 1986 President Pinochet's regime came under increasing attack from the Roman Catholic Church, guerrilla organizations (principally the Frente Patriótico Manuel Rodríguez—FPMR) and international critics, including the US administration, which had previously refrained from condemning the regime's notorious record of violations of human rights. In September the FPMR made an unsuccessful attempt to assassinate President Pinochet. The regime's immediate response was to impose a state of siege throughout Chile, under which leading members of the opposition were detained and strict censorship was introduced. One consequence of the state of siege was the reappearance of right-wing 'death squads', which were implicated in a series of murders following the assassination attempt.

By mid-1987 President Pinochet had clearly indicated his intention to remain in office beyond 1989 by securing the presidential candidacy to be rejected or approved by the same plebiscite which would decide the future electoral timetable; a cabinet reshuffle in July enabled him to appoint staunch supporters of his policies. By mid-1988 several political parties and opposition groups had established the Comando por el No to co-ordinate the campaign for the anti-Government vote at the forthcoming referendum. The hopes of the opposition were encouraged by the high level of popular registration for the plebiscite and by the Government's repeal, in August, of the states of exception, which had prohibited opposition groups from organizing public rallies. Later in the month, Pinochet was named by the Junta as the single candidate at the plebiscite, which was scheduled for 5 October. Despite some reports of electoral malpractice, the plebiscite took place without major incident. The official result recorded 54.7% of the votes cast for the anti-Pinochet campaign, and 43.1% for President Pinochet. Following the plebiscite, the opposition made repeated demands for changes to the Constitution, in order to accelerate the democratic process, and sought to initiate discussions with the armed forces. However, President Pinochet rejected the opposition's proposals, and affirmed his intention to remain in office until March 1990.

In mid-1989 Patricio Aylwin Azócar, a lawyer and former senator who had been a vociferous supporter of the 'no' vote in the October 1988 plebiscite, emerged as the sole presidential candidate for the centre-left Concertación de los Partidos de la Democracia (CPD, formerly the Comando por el No), an alliance of 17 parties, including the Partido Demócrata Cristiano (PDC), of which Aylwin had hitherto been President, and several socialist parties. Throughout 1989 the election campaign was dominated by demands from both the CPD and right-wing parties for constitutional reform, and by the ensuing lengthy negotiations with Carlos Cáceres Contreras, the Minister of the Interior. A document detailing 54 amendments (including the legalization of Marxist political parties) ratified by the Junta was finally accepted by the opposition, with some reservations, and the constitutional reforms (see p. 938) were approved by 85.7% of voters in a national referendum in July 1989.

The electoral campaign was conducted amidst intermittent outbursts of political violence and government intervention. Uncertainty regarding President Pinochet's own intentions concerning the forthcoming elections was finally dispelled in mid-1989, when he dismissed the possibility of his candidacy as unconstitutional, but reiterated his intention to continue as Commander-in-Chief of the Army for at least four years. Opposition leaders interpreted subsequent actions by the Government (including the implementation of a law providing for the autonomy of the Banco Central de Chile, the appointment of directors to state-owned companies with mandates of up to 10 years and curbs on the Government's power to remove state officials from their posts) as an attempt by the President to retain a degree of influence beyond his term of office.

The presidential and congressional elections were conducted on 14 December 1989. Patricio Aylwin Azócar of the centre-left CPD secured 55.2% of the valid votes cast in the presidential election, thus achieving a clear victory over the former Minister of Finance, Hernán Büchi Buc, who was supported by the Government and won 29.4%. In January 1990 President-Elect Aylwin announced the composition of his Cabinet, and asked two members of the outgoing Junta to remain as commanders of the air force and police. The transfer of power took place on 11 March.

Having failed to obtain the support of the two-thirds' majority in the Congreso necessary to amend the 1981 Constitution significantly (owing partly to an electoral system weighted heavily in favour of pro-regime candidates and the power of the outgoing Junta to nominate almost one-fifth of the Senado—Senate), Aylwin's new CPD administration was forced to reconcile attempts to fulfil campaign promises as quickly as possible with the need to adopt a conciliatory approach towards more right-wing parties in the Congreso, whose support was essential for the enactment of new legislation. Agreement was reached almost immediately, however, on a series of modifications to the tax laws, which were expected to generate sufficient surplus revenue for the implementation of several new initiatives for social welfare. Attempts to amend existing articles of law considered repressive by the new administration (including the death penalty and provisions for the censorship of the press) were less successful. In October 1990 military courts were continuing to initiate proceedings against journalists for alleged defamation of the armed forces, and in November a draft law proposing the abolition of the death penalty was finally defeated in the Senado, the sentence being retained for some 30 offences.

In April 1990 the Government created the National Commission for Truth and Reconciliation (Comisión Nacional de Verdad y Reconciliación—CNVR) to document and investigate alleged violations of human rights during the previous administration. Although Pinochet, before leaving office, had provided for the impunity of the former military Junta with regard to abuses of human rights, it was suggested by human rights organizations that such safeguards might be circumvented by indicting known perpetrators of atrocities on charges of 'crimes against humanity', a provision which gained considerable public support following the discovery, during 1990, of a number of mass graves containing the remains of political opponents of the 1973–90 military regime. The army High Command openly condemned the Commission for undermining the prestige of the armed forces and attempting to contravene the terms of a comprehensive amnesty declared in 1978. Although a new accord between military leaders and the Government-Elect had been negotiated in January 1990 (whereby the Junta of Commanders-in-Chief was abolished and the role of the armed forces redefined as essentially subservient to the Ministry of Defence), relations between the new Government and the army High Command remained tense throughout the year. Pinochet, who had warned, in early 1990, that attempted reprisals against members of the armed forces would imperil a peaceful transition to democracy, became the focus for widespread disaffection with the military élite, but resisted repeated demands for his resignation, reiterating his intention to continue as Commander-in-Chief of the Army until 1997.

Throughout 1990 and 1991 escalating public and political antagonism towards the former military leadership was fuelled by further revelations of abuses of human rights and financial corruption, and erupted into widespread popular outrage and renewed political violence following the publication, in March 1991, of the findings of the CNVR The report documented the deaths of 2,279 alleged political opponents of the former regime who were executed, died as a result of torture or disappeared (and were presumed to be dead) in 1973–90. In accordance with President Aylwin's recommendation that the report should foster national reconciliation and fulfil an expositionary rather than judicial function, those responsible for the deaths were identified only by the institutions to which they belonged. However, President Aylwin pledged full government co-operation for families wishing to pursue private prosecutions. The report concluded that the military Government had embarked upon a 'systematic policy of extermination' of its opponents through the illegal activities of the covert military intelligence agency, Dirección de Inteligencia Nacional (Dina), and was also highly critical of the Chilean judiciary for failing to protect the rights of individuals by refusing thousands of petitions for habeas corpus submitted by human rights lawyers. Later in the month, Pinochet publicly denounced the document, claiming that it contained no 'historical or juridical validity', and declared his opposition to plans, previously announced by President Aylwin, to make material reparation to the families of the victims named in the report.

In November 1992, following a prolonged investigation, former Dina officials Gen. Manuel Contreras and Col. Pedro Espinoza were charged with the murder of Orlando Letelier, a former cabinet minister (and Chile's ambassador to the USA during the government of Salvador Allende in the early 1970s), who was assassinated, together with an associate, by a car bomb in Washington, DC, in 1976. (In November 1993 Contreras and Espinoza received prison sentences of seven and six years respectively. An appeal against the sentences was rejected by the Supreme Court in May 1995, although their sentences were reduced by 15 months as a result of a Supreme Court ruling on technicalities.) In October 1999 the Supreme Court granted an Italian court permission to pursue the extradition of Contreras—on completion of his sentence in Chile—on charges connected to the murders of Chilean politician Bernardo Leighton and his wife in Italy in 1975. Hopes that this development might herald an end to the apparent impunity of the former military regime were somewhat frustrated, however, following the decision of the Supreme Court, announced later in the month, to withdraw charges, recently brought against former police chief and Junta member, César Mendoza Durán, of complicity in the kidnap and murder of three members of the Partido Comunista de Chile (PCCh) in 1985. (In March 1994 15 former members of the subsequently-disbanded paramilitary police intelligence unit, Dicomcar, were sentenced to varying terms of imprisonment, having been convicted on charges connected with the murders in July 1993. However, Gen. Rodolfo Stange Oelckers, head of the military police since 1985, refused a request, made by President Frei in April 1994, that he should resign the post, refuting formal allegations made during the hearing, that he had impeded the investigation and was therefore guilty of serious dereliction of duty. In October 1995, however, Stange announced his resignation, denying that his decision had been influenced by continued pressure from the Government, but was rather in protest at Government attempts to undermine the autonomy of the armed forces.)

Notwithstanding increasing frustration at the Government's reluctance or inability to bring to justice the perpetrators of the atrocities documented in the report, the conclusions of the CNVR were widely welcomed. However, following the publication of the report, a series of terrorist attacks by left-wing extremists against right-wing opponents threatened to undermine the process of national reconciliation. Fears of an escalation in extremist violence were partially dispelled, however, by the announcement, in late May 1991, of the FPMR's intention to renounce its armed struggle and join the political mainstream as the Movimiento Patriótico Manuel Rodríguez.

Throughout 1991 President Aylwin reaffirmed his commitment to dismantling the apparatus of political centralization that was embodied in the 1981 Constitution. In November the Congreso approved constitutional amendments to local government statutes, which provided for the replacement of centrally-appointed local officials with directly-elected representatives. Elections to the 326 municipalities were conducted in June 1992, and the results demonstrated clear public endorsement of the ruling coalition, which received some 53% of the votes, compared with 29% for the right-wing opposition. However, constitutional amendments envisaged by the President (including plans to restore presidential power to remove Commanders-in-Chief of the armed forces, to counter right-wing bias in the electoral system, to balance politically the composition of the constitutional tribunal and to abolish government-appointed senators) continued to encounter considerable right-wing opposition in the Senado during 1992.

During 1993 the delicate political balance within the Government and within the Congreso continued to frustrate Aylwin's attempts to enact legislation. Proposals to accelerate the prosecution of military personnel accused of human rights abuses, while safeguarding their anonymity, put forward by the President in August 1993, were rejected by the right as ill-considered and precipitate, while left-wing groups challenged the concessionary nature of the legislation, with regard to the military. In September Aylwin was forced to withdraw the proposals from the

Congreso, following a declaration of opposition to the legislation, made by two member parties of the ruling coalition, in response to the petitions of human rights organizations.

A presidential election, held on 11 December 1993, was won by the CPD candidate Eduardo Frei Ruiz-Tagle, a PDC senator, with 58% of the votes cast, ahead of Arturo Alessandri Besa, the candidate of the right-wing coalition, the Unión para el Progreso de Chile (UPC), who received 24% of the votes. However, the ruling coalition failed to make significant gains at concurrently conducted congressional elections, attributing the disappointing results to the binomial electoral system, which requires each party to secure two-thirds of the votes in each district for the successful election of its two candidates to the legislature. Frei, whose electoral campaign had identified the need for increased spending on health and education, the consolidation of municipalities, and greater support for small businesses, announced the composition of a new Cabinet in December 1993 and January 1994. In February 1994 formal congressional endorsement was secured for constitutional reform whereby the length of the non-renewable presidential term would be henceforth fixed at six years.

On 11 March 1994 Frei assumed the presidency. Some days later he identified the immediate aims of his presidency as the alleviation of poverty, the elimination of corrupt government, and the fostering of significant economic growth. However, the President's affirmation of Pinochet's right to remain in office until 1997, appeared to compromise his pre-election demands for greater powers for the executive to nominate and remove the military High Command. In August 1994 Frei presented several consitutional reform proposals to the Congreso, including the abolition of the nine appointed senators (installed by the former military regime) and the introduction of an electoral system based on proportional representation (to replace the unrepresentative binomial system). However, Frei encountered the same level of opposition to constitutional reform (particularly from the right and from the upper house), that had undermined most attempts at constitutional amendment made by the previous administration.

In August 1995 a number of congressional bills, presented by the President as a crucial step towards national reconciliation, sought once again to remove the institutionalized influence of the military High Command (implemented by the outgoing military regime) and to accelerate the prosecution of armed forces personnel implicated in abuses of human rights by the report of the CNVR.

In November 1995 the Government secured the support of the opposition Renovación Nacional (RN) for revised proposals for new legislation relating to human rights and constitutional reform (see above). However, the compromised nature of the agreement provoked considerable disaffection within the RN, and within the opposition UPC alliance in general, which was effectively dissolved following the departure of the Unión Demócrata Independiente (UDI) and the Unión de Centro-Centro (UCC) in protest at the actions of the RN. Concern was also expressed by members of the Partido Socialista (PS—within the ruling coalition) that the legislation relating to human rights had been severely compromised.

At municipal elections conducted in late October 1996 the ruling coalition increased its share of the total votes cast to 56.2%, compared with some 53% of the votes in 1992. Jaime Ravinet, the PDC Mayor of Santiago, was re-elected with an overwhelming majority. However, the UDI and the RN, who in July had announced their intention to contest the municipal elections (and legislative elections scheduled for December) as a right-wing alliance (Unión por Chile), also recorded a significant increase in support. In May 1997 a group of disaffected PDC deputies announced the formation of a new centrist party, the Partido Popular Cristiano (PPC), to be led by Ramón Elizalde and Samuel Venegas.

During 1997 efforts by the Government to abolish the designated seats in the Senado were intensified, in response to Pinochet's stated intention to assume one of the seats assigned to former Presidents on retirement as Commander-in-Chief of the Army in March 1998, and by speculation that Pinochet would seek to exert considerable influence over future legislation by installing close military associates in other designated seats. In July 1997 the Senado rejected the Government's latest petition for reform to the system of appointments to the Senado.

In October 1997 it was announced that Maj.-Gen. Ricardo Izurieta, previously chief of defence staff, was to succeed Pinochet as Commander-in-Chief of the Army. The announcement was made amid a number of changes in the military High Command, which appeared to confirm earlier predictions that military influence was henceforth to be concentrated in the Senado, where it would bolster the political right wing.

Legislative elections to renew all 120 seats in the Cámara de Diputados and 20 of the elective seats in the Senado were conducted on 11 December 1997. The Government expressed satisfaction with the performance of parties within the governing Concertación, which secured 50.5% of the votes for deputies and retained (with 70 seats) a comfortable majority in the lower house. However, political analysts noted an erosion of support for the centre-left alliance (which had attracted 55.4% of votes for the lower house at the 1993 elections) and observed that the group's disappointing showing at elections to the Senado (where one seat was lost to the UDI) would make future attempts to effect constitutional reform as problematic as those undertaken in the past, particularly given the predominance of right-wing sympathizers among the nine designated senators (three nominated by the Supreme Court, four by the National Security Council—from a list of former chiefs of the armed forces—and two by the President), named later in December, who were scheduled to take their seats, together with the newly-elected senators, in March 1998. The elections revealed a shifting balance of power within the two major political groupings (support for the UDI, in particular, appeared to have superseded that for the RN within the Unión por Chile), and prompted renewed criticism of the country's binomial system of voting, the PCCh having failed to secure congressional representation despite attracting 8.4% and 6.9% of the votes to the upper and lower houses respectively.

During December 1997 Pinochet reiterated his intention to assert his constitutional right, on retirement, to assume an *ex-officio* seat (for life) in the Senado (in addition to the nine designated senators). Expressing the opinion that to extend such an opportunity to Pinochet, who had headed an administration that had suspended all legislative processes for many years, would be wholly inappropriate, a number of centre-left politicians pledged to obstruct Pinochet's accession to the Senado. During January 1998 separate attempts were made by junior members of the Concertación (despite the declarations of senior members of the Government—anxious to ensure a peaceful exchange of offices in March—that such action was untimely and politically inconvenient) and by the leadership of the PCCh to begin judicial proceedings against Pinochet on charges related to gross abuses of human rights. Pinochet responded by announcing that he would not retire as Commander-in-Chief of the Army on 26 January, as previously suggested, but would continue in office until 10 March, thereby preserving the immunity from prosecution provided by the position for as long as possible. Pinochet's announcement and a perceived entrenchment of the divergent interests of the Government and the armed forces prompted the resignation of the Minister of National Defence, Edmundo Pérez Yoma, who was immediately replaced by Raúl Troncoso. In early March the Minister of Planning and Co-operation, Roberto Pizarro Hofer, resigned following disagreement over responsibility for President Frei's social programme. Pizarro Hofer was replaced by Antonio Lara.

On 6 March 1998 the military High Command announced that Pinochet had been named an honorary commander-in-chief—a position with no historical precedent. On 11 March Pinochet assumed his seat in the Senado. A largely symbolic attempt by 11 Concertación deputies to instigate a formal impeachment action against Pinochet was initiated in the Cámara in mid-March. The motion was defeated by 62 votes to 52 in early April. The result prompted a crisis within the Concertación—the majority of PDC deputies having voted against the motion.

In July and August 1998 a substantial cabinet reshuffle was implemented, partly in order to facilitate the campaign preparations of a number of politicians (in particular the outgoing Minister of Public Works, Ricardo Lagos Escobas—who hoped to secure the Concertación presidential nomination) who were seeking election at a presidential poll scheduled for 1999.

Preparations for the December presidential poll dominated domestic affairs during 1999. In January the RN and the UDI announced that they would present a joint presidential candidate to represent a new political alliance, the Alianza por Chile. In April Joaquín Lavín of the UDI was chosen as its candidate. In May a primary election to select the presidential candidate of the ruling Concertación was won by Ricardo Lagos of the PS, with 71.3% of the estimated 1.4m. votes. The poor showing of the candidate of the PDC, Andrés Zaldívar, prompted a crisis in that party and resulted in the adoption of a new reformist manifesto and the selection of a new national executive in July. Meanwhile, in June a minor cabinet reshuffle had been implemented, in which the recall to government of Eduardo Pérez Yoma as Minister of National Defence was widely interpreted as an attempt to foster improved relations with the armed forces.

Although it was widely expected that a clear margin favouring Lagos would emerge in the presidential poll held on 12 December 1999, he received 47.96% of the total votes cast, with Lavín obtaining 47.52%. Four minor candidates, among whom only Gladys Marín (representing the PCCh) received more than 3.0% of the poll, were eliminated. At the second round of voting, which took place on 16 January 2000, Lagos emerged victorious with 51.3% of the total votes, while Lavín received 48.7%.

As the controversy surrounding the detention of former President Pinochet in the United Kingdom continued (see below), domestic attentions were once again focused on the actions of the security forces during the post-1973 military regime. In June 1999 the arrest of five retired army officers (former commanders of a notorious élite army unit popularly referred to as the 'caravan of death') was ordered by an appeal court judge following renewed investigation into the disappearance of 72 political prisoners in the immediate aftermath of the 1973 military coup. The decision to arrest and prosecute the five men on charges of aggravated kidnapping was considered a breakthrough in Chilean judical practice, since the absence of physical or documented evidence of the deaths of the prisoners meant that the crimes were technically in continuance, and that the accused men were not protected by the 1978 amnesty which guaranteed the impunity of military personnel for crimes committed before that year. In July 1999 the legality of the arrests was confirmed by the Supreme Court, and the indictment (and extradition from the USA) of a sixth former army officer was sought in connection with the case in August. Attempts by the Government to stem the resurgence of popular resentment of the past actions of the armed forces included, in August, the first direct discussions of the fate of the 'disappeared' between representatives of the armed forces and human rights organizations. However, tensions were exacerbated by the US National Security Council's declassification, in June, of some 5,800 CIA documents which recorded abuses of human rights during 1973–78, and appeared to support claims that the Chilean armed forces had falsified evidence purporting to demonstrate the threat posed by the Allende administration in order to justify the 1973 coup. A further 1,100 US documents were declassified in October 1999, and later in the same month a Chilean court issued an arrest warrant against Gen. (retd) Hugo Salas Wendel, a former Director of the National Intelligence Agency, on charges of complicity in the killings in 1987 of 12 alleged members of a left-wing guerrilla group. Meanwhile, in September 1999 the Supreme Court had ruled in favour of criminal proceedings brought against two retired generals, Humberto Gordon Rubio and Roberto Schmied, earlier in the month for their alleged involvement in the murder of trade union leader Tucapel Jiménez in 1982. (Gordon Rubio, a former head of covert national intelligence operations, was the most senior military officer to date to face prosecution in Chile for crimes committed during the period of military rule.)

On 16 October 1998 former President Pinochet was arrested at a private clinic in London (United Kingdom), where he was receiving medical treatment for a back injury. The arrest was prompted by a preliminary request, made to the British authorities by Spanish magistrates, that Pinochet should be extradited to Spain to answer charges of 'genocide and terrorism' committed against some 4,000 individuals, including Spanish nationals, by his administration during 1973–90. A second Spanish request for Pinochet's extradition, received on 23 October 1998, cited his alleged involvement in institutionalized torture, conspiracy and the taking of hostages. On 28 October, however, a unanimous judgment of the British High Court rejected the Spanish petitions (presented by the British Crown Prosecution Service—CPS), largely on the ground that Pinochet enjoyed the 'sovereign immunity' of a former head of state. However, leave to appeal to the British House of Lords (the upper house of parliament and the supreme judicial authority) was granted to those wishing to pursue the extradition. In early November a formal request for extradition was made, although the Spanish Government (like the British Government) was anxious to emphasize its neutrality in what it considered to be a purely judicial affair.

In Chile the Frei Government protested that Pinochet's diplomatic immunity had been infringed by the British authorities, while the British Government denied Pinochet's status as an accredited diplomat. This issue was complicated by subsequent revelations that Pinochet had been invited to visit the Royal Ordnance arms subsidiary of British Aerospace during his visit, and had been welcomed by an officially-sanctioned reception committee on arrival in the United Kingdom on 21 September 1998. (However, in May 1999, the Chilean Government admitted that Pinochet's diplomatic passport for the visit had been issued erroneously.) Meanwhile, supporters and opponents of Pinochet clashed during demonstrations in Santiago, and political commentators expressed concerns that Pinochet's detention was threatening to polarize popular opinion, to splinter the ruling coalition and to undermine the country's delicate political and military balance.

The House of Lords' hearing of the extradition appeal began on 4 November 1998. The case for extradition was once again presented by the CPS, and was supported by lawyers representing the London-based human rights organization Amnesty International and testimonies from Chilean nationals with first-hand experience of the crimes under discussion. The hearing ended dramatically on 25 November with a 3–2 majority judgment by the panel of five senior law lords overturning the October ruling of the High Court on the basis that Pinochet's sovereign immunity did not extend to functions of office deemed unacceptable under international law. Despite the remonstrances of the Chilean Minister of Foreign Affairs, José Miguel Insulza, who travelled to London in late November to meet British cabinet ministers, and pressure from the US Secretary of State, Madeleine Albright, to allow Pinochet to return to Chile, on 9 December the British Secretary of State for the Home Department, Jack Straw, authorized the start of formal extradition proceedings.

President Frei reacted angrily to Straw's decision, recalling the Chilean ambassador in London for consultations, and suspending travel permits to London and Madrid for Chilean nationals. Pinochet appeared in a British court in person for the first time on 11 December 1998, where initially he refused to recognize the competence of any court outside of Chile to try him with the 'lies of Spain'. Prior to the announcement of Straw's decision, meanwhile, it had emerged that Lord Hoffmann, one of the three law lords who had rejected Pinochet's immunity in the November ruling, had failed to declare potentially compromising personal links to Amnesty International. A submission made by Pinochet's lawyers to the House of Lords, for a review of the November ruling in the light of this revelation, was accepted, and on 17 December a new panel of five senior judges unanimously suspended the November pronouncement and ordered the case to be re-submitted to a new appellate committee of seven law lords. Meanwhile, Pinochet remained under effective house arrest in the United Kingdom.

The new House of Lords' hearing began on 18 January 1999. In a change of defence strategy, the Chilean Government announced that it would be arguing that Pinochet's detention amounted to an infringement of Chilean sovereignty. The hearing ended on 4 February. The ruling of the appellate committee, announced on 24 March, supported the November 1998 pronouncement overturning Pinochet's claims to immunity, by a majority of six to one. However, the committee also found that only charges relating to events subsequent to December 1988 (at which time the 1984 UN Convention against Torture and Other Cruel, Inhuman or Degrading Treatment or Punishment had entered into British law) should be considered relevant, thus reducing the number of draft charges brought by Spain from 33 to three. In the light of this diminution of evidence, the commitee urged Jack Straw to reconsider his December 1998 decision to allow extradition proceedings to continue. In response to the ruling, the Spanish magistrate responsible for the prosecution attempt, Baltasar Garzón, announced that additional pertinent charges, relating to crimes committed after December 1988 were being prepared. On 15 April 1999 Jack Straw confirmed his decision to allow the petition for extradition to proceed. Straw contended that the serious nature of the three remaining charges from the original draft petition was sufficient to justify the extradition. At the end of April Pinochet's legal representatives announced that they would challenge Straw's decision in the High Court, but this challenge was rejected on 27 May. Formal extradition proceedings were initiated in a London magistrates' court on 27 September. On 8 October the court found that Pinochet could be lawfully extradited to Spain to answer some 35 charges. Pinochet's lawyers made a formal appeal against the decision on 22 October.

Attempts by the Chilean Government to persuade Spain to allow international arbitration in the case against Pinochet had been dismissed by the Spanish judiciary in September, prompting the Chilean Minister of Foreign Affairs, Juan Gabriel Valdés, to announce that Chile would ask the International Court of Justice in The Hague (Netherlands) to examine Spain's claims to jurisdiction in the matter. Meanwhile, international media attention was riveted to the affair by the succession of prominent political figures (including George Bush, Margaret Thatcher and Dr Henry Kissinger) who expressed support for Pinochet's return to Chile, by the involvement of the Roman Catholic Church (in response to petitions from the Chilean Government, in November 1999 the Vatican had written to the British authorities requesting Pinochet's release in the interest of humanitarianism and of national reconciliation in Chile) and by widespread discussion of the advisability and profitability of continuing with prolonged legal proceedings, given Pinochet's advanced years and failing health. In January 2000, having considered the contents of an independent doctors' report stating the opinion that Pinochet was medically unfit to undergo further legal proceedings, Straw indicated that he was inclined to order Pinochet's release, although he agreed to defer his final decision pending further representations from those seeking Pinochet's extradition. Such representations swiftly followed from legal authorities in Belgium, France, Spain and Switzerland, and from six human rights organizations. However, on 2 March Straw announced that Pinochet was to be released, and on the following day the former President returned by air to Chile.

In August 1991 Argentina and Chile reached a settlement regarding disputed territory in the Antarctic region. Responsibility for the contentious Laguna del Desierto region, however, was to be decided by international arbitration. In October 1994 Argentina's claim to the territory was upheld by a five-member international arbitration panel. In July 1997 it was announced unexpectedly that the two countries were to conduct joint military exercises in 1998, and in September it was agreed to proceed with the creation of a conciliation commission, originally envisaged within the terms of a peace and friendship treaty concluded in 1984. Joint naval exercises began in August 1998. In December agreement on border demarcation of the still contentious 'continental glaciers' territory in the Antarctic region was reached by the Presidents of the two countries.

Prospects for renewed diplomatic relations with Bolivia (which severed relations with Chile in 1978 over the issue of Bolivian access to the Pacific Ocean) were encouraged during 1993 by the successful conclusion of a comprehensive trade agreement in April, and by a series of bilateral co-operation treaties, negotiated in July. By 1997, however, relations had deteriorated again. The Bolivian Government made repeated requests during the year for the renewal of discussions on Bolivian access to the sea, and sought Peru's assistance in the dispute. Relations between the two countries deteriorated further in late 1997 when the Bolivian Government made an official protest to Chile regarding its failure to remove land-mines (planted during the 1970s) from the two countries' border. Subsequent ministerial discussions have failed to produce an effective formula for the restoration of diplomatic relations. In November 1999, following an Iberio-American summit meeting in Havana, Cuba, at which Bolivia sought to initiate a regional discussion of the dispute, Chile stated that the issue was a matter for bilateral, rather than international, negotiation. In the same month it was announced that Chile was to take immediate action to remove land-mines on its borders with Bolivia, Peru and Argentina.

A free-trade agreement, the Acuerdo de Complementación Económica (ACE), concluded with Colombia in December 1993, took effect from 1 January 1994, and was expected to have eliminated tariffs on most goods by the time of its full implementation on 1 January 1999. A free-trade agreement was negotiated with Ecuador in late 1994, and came into effect on 1 January 1995. In December 1994 the signatory nations to the North American Free Trade Agreement (NAFTA) issued a formal invitation to Chile to join the group. Formal discussions on Chile's accession to the Agreement by late 1996, began in June 1995. However, despite the removal of contentious clauses relating to labour and the environment, US President Bill Clinton failed to secure US congressional support for 'fast track' authorization for Chile's accession to the Agreement, and Chile seemed unlikely to achieve full member status until 2000. In the context of this delay, Chile intensified attempts to negotiate a bilateral free-trade agreement with Canada and a formal trade agreement with the Mercado Común del Sur (Mercosur—see p. 267). In November 1996 agreement was reached with Canada on the imminent removal of tariffs on three-quarters of bilateral trade, with the gradual removal of remaining duties over a five-year period. The agreement received formal congressional approval in mid-1997 and came into effect in July of that year; the terms of the agreement were modified and expanded in early 1998. Meanwhile, in June 1996, at a summit meeting of Mercosur member nations in San Luis (Argentina), Chile had secured associate membership of the group following negotiations which established the immediate reduction of tariffs on 90% of Chilean goods, and the subsequent elimination of tariffs on 'sensitive' goods including meat, sugar, edible oils and wheat, over an 18-year period. Chile's associate membership became effective from 1 October.

In April 1998 Chile and Mexico signed a free-trade agreement, expanding the terms of an Acuerdo de Complementación Económica (ACE) in force since 1992. In June 1998 Chile signed an ACE agreement with Peru, whereby cutoms duties were to be abolished on 2,500 products passing between the two countries from 1 July. The agreement also envisaged the free passage of 50% of all products by 2003 and the creation of a free-trade area within 18 years. With the exception of Bolivia, Chile has now negotiated free-trade agreements throughout the South American continent. During 1998 agreements to facilitate and increase trade between Chile and the countries of Central America were also signed. A second 'Summit of the Americas' was convened in Santiago on 18–19 April 1998, and was attended by representatives of all nations in the region (with the exception of Cuba), who reiterated commitments to establishing a 'Free-Trade Area of the Americas' by 2005.

In January 1994 Chile declared its full adherence to the 1967 Tlatelolco Treaty, which proscribes nuclear weapons in Latin America and the Caribbean. In April 1995 full diplomatic relations with Cuba, severed as a result of the 1973 military coup in Chile, were restored. From late 1998 Chile's relations with both the United Kingdom and Spain came under strain as a result of the detention of former President Pinochet (see above).

## Government

Chile is a republic, divided into 12 regions and a metropolitan area. Under the terms of the Constitution, executive power is vested in the President, who is directly elected for a six-year term. The President is assisted by a Cabinet. Legislative power is vested in the bicameral Congreso Nacional (National Congress), comprising the 47-member Senado (Senate) and the 120-member Cámara de Diputados (Chamber of Deputies).

## Defence

Military service is for one year (army) or 22 months (navy and air force) and is compulsory for men at 19 years of age. In August 1999 the army had a strength of 51,000, the navy 29,000 and the air force 13,000. Paramilitary security forces numbered about 29,500 carabineros. Defence expenditure for 1999 was budgeted at 1,033,000m. pesos.

## Economic Affairs

In 1997, according to estimates by the World Bank, Chile's gross national product (GNP), measured at average 1995–97 prices, was US $70,510m., equivalent to $4,820 per head. Total GNP for 1998 was estimated at $71,300m. ($4,810 per head). During 1990–97, it was estimated, GNP per head increased, in real terms, at an average annual rate of 6.4%. Over the same period, the population increased by an average of 1.6% per year. Chile's gross domestic product (GDP) increased, in real terms, by an average of 7.9% per year in 1990–98; real GDP growth was estimated at 7.6% in 1997 and 3.4% in 1998.

Agriculture (including forestry and fishing) contributed an estimated 8.1% of GDP in 1998. About 14.4% of the employed labour force were engaged in this sector in that year. Important subsistence crops include wheat, oats, barley, rice, beans, lentils, maize and chick-peas. Industrial crops include sugar beet, sunflower seed and rapeseed. Fruit and vegetables are also important export commodities (together contributing 10.2% of total export revenues in 1996), particularly, beans, asparagus, onions, garlic, grapes, citrus fruits, avocados, pears, peaches, plums and nuts. The production and export of wine has increased significantly in recent years. Forestry and fishing, and derivatives from both activities, also make important contributions to the sector. During 1990–98 agricultural GDP increased, in real terms, by an average of 5.2% per year. Agricultural GDP declined by 1.8% in 1997, but increased by 3.0% in 1998.

Industry (including mining, manufacturing, construction and power) contributed an estimated 34.4% of GDP in 1998 and accounted for 25.5% of the employed labour force in the same year. During 1990–98 industrial GDP increased by an annual average of 6.8% per year. GDP growth in all industrial sectors was an estimated 7.3% in 1997 and just 0.6% in 1998.

Mining contributed an estimated 9.7% of GDP in 1998 and engaged 1.6% of the employed labour force in that year. Chile, with some 28% of the world's known reserves, is the world's largest producer and exporter of copper. Copper accounted for 87.5% of Chile's total export earnings in 1970, but the proportion had decreased to around 42% by 1997. Gold, silver, iron ore, nitrates, molybdenum, manganese, lead and coal are also mined, and the whole sector contributed some 50% of total export earnings in 1997. In real terms, the sector's GDP increased by an estimated 9.8% in 1997, and by some 4.1% in 1998. Petroleum and natural gas deposits have been located in the south, and plans to exploit significant reserves of lithium are under consideration.

Manufacturing contributed an estimated 16.4% of GDP in 1998, and engaged 15.1% of the employed labour force in that year. The most important branches of manufacturing, measured by gross value of output, are food (22.3% of the total) and non-ferrous metals (15.4%). Manufacturing GDP increased by an average of 6.3% per year in 1990–97. The sector's GDP increased by some 5.4% in 1997, but declined by an estimated 1.5% in 1998.

Energy is derived mainly from petroleum and natural gas (some 55%), hydroelectric power (26%) and coal (18%). Chile produces some 40% of its national energy requirements. Plans are under consideration to develop Chile's vast hydroelectric potential (estimated at 18,700 MW—the largest in the world). Meanwhile, Chile imported fuel and energy products equivalent to some 10% of the value of total merchandise imports in 1997.

The services sector contributed an estimated 57.5% of GDP in 1998 and engaged some 60.0% of the employed labour force in that year. The financial sector continued to expand in the 1990s, fuelled, in part, by the success of private pension funds (AFPs—see section on Social Welfare). During 1990–98 services GDP increased by an average of 7.7% per year. The sector's GDP increased, in real terms, by some 8.2% in 1997 and by an estimated 5.3% in 1998.

In 1998 Chile recorded a visible trade deficit of US $2,516m., and there was a deficit of $4,139m. on the current account of the balance of payments. In 1997 the principal source of imports (22.9%) was the USA, which was also the principal market for exports (15.9%). Other major trading partners were Japan, the Belgo-Luxembourg Economic Union, Brazil, Germany, Argentina and the United Kingdom. The principal exports in 1997 were copper and copper manufactures (42.3% of total export revenue), fruit (6.7%), fish (6.0%) and wood pulp (4.0%). The principal imports in that year were machinery and transport equipment, and chemical and mineral products.

In 1997 there was a budgetary surplus of some 623,210m. pesos (equivalent to 2.0% of GDP). Chile's external debt totalled US $31,440m. at the end of 1997, of which $4,364m. was long-term public debt. Debt-servicing costs in that year were equivalent to some 20.4% of the value of exports of goods and services. The annual rate of inflation averaged 11.0% in 1990–98, and stood at 5.1% in 1998. An average 6.1% of the labour force were unemployed in 1997.

Chile is a member of the Latin American Integration Association (ALADI—see p. 292) and was admitted to the Rio Group (see p. 302) in 1990 and to the Asia-Pacific Economic Co-operation group (APEC—see p. 122) in 1994. Chile is also among the founding members of the World Trade Organization (see p. 274).

Owing to the relaxation of import duties in the early 1980s, Chile's potential in the agricultural and manufacturing sectors was stifled by cheaper imported goods. Exports of fruit, seafoods and wines, however, have expanded considerably, yet Chile remains heavily dependent on exports of copper and on the stability of the world copper market. The 1990–94 Aylwin administration successfully maintained significant economic growth while reducing inflation from 26% in 1990 to 12.7% in 1993. In September 1997 a report published by the World Trade Organization praised the economic achievements of the previous two decades in liberalizing trade and reducing inflation, but warned that recent preoccupation with the creation of regional trade associations was leading to the perpetuation of serious imbalances in the structure of Chile's trade. As a result of the 1997–98 economic crisis in Asia (one of Chile's principal markets), economic forecasts were revised during 1998; GDP growth was expected to reach only 5.5%, while the current-account deficit was predicted to amount to 6% of GDP. The average rate of inflation was expected to be some 4.5% in 1998. Chile entered a period of recession during 1999, largely as a result of depressed world prices for copper; the economy contracted by some 6% in April, and forecasts of overall growth for the year were revised to just 0.5%. In June President Frei announced a number of new initiatives to reactivate the economy, including the immediate creation of 150,000 jobs; these measures were supported by a reduction in interest rates. In September, in an attempt to stimulate exports, the Central Bank abandoned its strict regulation of the peso, allowing the currency to float agaist the US dollar. The draft budget for 2000, announced in September 1999, was based on growth predictions of 5% for that year.

## Social Welfare

Employees, including agricultural workers, may receive benefits for sickness, unemployment, accidents at work, maternity and retirement, and there are dependants' allowances, including family allowances. In May 1981 the management of social security was opened to the private sector. By the mid-1990s some 90% of Chile's 5m. pensions contributors were participating in the private pension system operated by Administradoras de Fondos de Pensiones (AFPs), while responsibility for the remainder was assumed by the Instituto de Normalización Previsional, a transitional state organization. In late 1997 it was estimated that Chile's AFPs were managing more than US $30,000m. of funds. However, the Government retains ultimate control of the sector, monitoring the performance of AFP managers and regulating the proportion of assets to be invested at home and abroad. A National Health Service (Sistema Nacional de Servicios de Salud—SNSS) was established in 1952. In March 1998 President Frei announced an ambitious two-year social reform programme. There were 17,467 medical personnel in 1998; in 1997 there were 182 hospital establishments, with a total of 42,222 beds. In 1993 there were an estimated 108 doctors and 42 nurses for every 100,000 Chileans. Of total expenditure by the central Government in 1997, about 806,540m. pesos (11.7%) was for health services, and a further 2,237,910m. pesos (32.4%) for social security and welfare.

## Education

Pre-primary education is widely available for all children from five years of age. Primary education is officially compulsory, and is provided free of charge, for eight years, beginning at six or seven years of age. It is divided into two cycles: the first lasts for four years and provides a general education; the second cycle offers more specialized schooling. Secondary education, beginning at 13 or 14 years of age, is divided into the humanities-science programme (lasting for four years), with the emphasis on general education and possible entrance to university, and the technical-professional programme (lasting for between four and six years), designed to fulfil the requirements of specialist training. In 1996 the total enrolment at primary schools included an estimated 88% of children in the relevant age-group, while the comparable ratio for secondary enrolment was 58%. Higher education is provided by three kinds of institution: universities, professional institutes and centres of technical information. An intensive national literacy campaign, launched in 1980, reduced the rate of adult illiteracy from 11% in 1970 to an estimated 4.8% (males 4.6%; females 5.0%) in 1995. Expenditure on education by the central Government in 1997 was about 1,069,650m. pesos (15.5% of total spending).

## Public Holidays

**2000:** 1 January (New Year's Day), 21–22 April (Good Friday and Easter Saturday), 1 May (Labour Day), 21 May (Battle of Iquique), 15 August (Assumption), 4 September (National Unity Day), 18 September (Independence Day), 12 October (Day of the Race, anniversary of the discovery of America), 1 November (All Saints' Day), 8 December (Immaculate Conception), 25 December (Christmas Day).

**2001:** 1 January (New Year's Day), 13–14 April (Good Friday and Easter Saturday), 1 May (Labour Day), 21 May (Battle of Iquique), 15 August (Assumption), 4 September (National Unity Day), 18 September (Independence Day), 12 October (Day of the Race, anniversary of the discovery of America), 1 November (All Saints' Day), 8 December (Immaculate Conception), 25 December (Christmas).

## Weights and Measures

The metric system is officially in force.

# Statistical Survey

Source (unless otherwise stated): Instituto Nacional de Estadísticas, Avda Bulnes 418, Casilla 498-3, Correo 3, Santiago; tel. (2) 366-7777; fax (2) 671-2169; e-mail inesdadm@reuna.cl; internet www.ine.cl; and Banco Central de Chile, Agustinas 1180, Santiago; tel. (2) 696-2281; fax (2) 698-4847.

## Area and Population

**AREA, POPULATION AND DENSITY***

| | |
|---|---|
| Area (sq km) | 756,096† |
| Population (census results)‡ | |
| 21 April 1982 | 11,329,736 |
| 22 April 1992 | |
| Males | 6,553,254 |
| Females | 6,795,147 |
| Total | 13,348,401 |
| Population (official estimates at mid-year) | |
| 1997 | 14,622,354 |
| 1998 | 14,821,714 |
| 1999 | 15,017,760 |
| Density (per sq km) at mid-1999 | 19.9 |

* Excluding Chilean Antarctic Territory (approximately 1,250,000 sq km).
† 291,930 sq miles.
‡ Excluding adjustment for underenumeration.

**REGIONS** (30 June 1999)

| | | Area (sq km) | Population ('000) | Capital |
|---|---|---|---|---|
| I | De Tarapacá | 59,099.1 | 392.6 | Iquique |
| II | De Antofagasta | 126,049.1 | 462.3 | Antofagasta |
| III | De Atacama | 75,176.2 | 269.1 | Copiapó |
| IV | De Coquimbo | 40,579.9 | 569.8 | La Serena |
| V | De Valparaíso | 16,396.1 | 1,543.6 | Valparaíso |
| VI | Del Libertador Gen. Bernardo O'Higgins | 16,387.0 | 778.8 | Rancagua |
| VII | Del Maule | 30,296.1 | 906.9 | Talca |
| VIII | Del Bíobío | 37,062.6 | 1,915.8 | Concepción |
| IX | De la Araucanía | 31,842.3 | 865.0 | Temuco |
| X | De Los Lagos | 67,013.1 | 1,050.6 | Puerto Montt |
| XI | Aisén del Gen. Carlos Ibáñez del Campo | 108,494.4 | 93.6 | Coihaique |
| XII | De Magallanes y Antártica Chilena | 132,297.2 | 156.5 | Punta Arenas |
| | Metropolitan Region (Santiago) | 15,403.2 | 6,013.2 | — |
| | **Total** | 756,096.3 | 15,017.8 | — |

**PRINCIPAL TOWNS** (provisional figures, population at 30 June 1997)

| | | | |
|---|---|---|---|
| Gran Santiago (capital) | 4,640,635 | Arica | 178,457 |
| Puente Alto | 363,012 | Talca | 174,858 |
| Concepción | 362,589 | Chillán | 162,969 |
| Viña del Mar | 330,736 | Iquique | 159,815 |
| Valparaíso | 283,489 | Puerto Montt | 128,945 |
| Talcahuano | 269,265 | Coquimbo | 126,886 |
| Temuco | 253,451 | Osorno | 126,645 |
| Antofagasta | 243,038 | La Serena | 123,166 |
| San Bernardo | 223,055 | Valdivia | 122,166 |
| Rancagua | 202,067 | Calama | 121,326 |
| | | Punta Arenas | 120,148 |

Source: UN, *Demographic Yearbook*.

**BIRTHS, MARRIAGES AND DEATHS**

| | Registered live births | | Registered marriages | | Registered deaths | |
|---|---|---|---|---|---|---|
| | Number | Rate (per 1,000) | Number | Rate (per 1,000) | Number | Rate (per 1,000) |
| 1990 | 307,522 | 23.5 | 98,702 | 7.5 | 78,434 | 6.0 |
| 1991 | 299,456 | 22.5 | 91,732 | 6.9 | 74,862 | 5.6 |
| 1992 | 293,787 | 21.7 | 89,370 | 6.6 | 74,090 | 5.5 |
| 1993 | 290,438 | 21.1 | 92,821 | 6.7 | 76,261 | 5.5 |
| 1994 | 288,175 | 20.6 | 91,555 | 6.5 | 75,445 | 5.4 |
| 1995 | 279,928 | 19.7 | 87,205 | 6.1 | 78,531 | 5.5 |
| 1996 | 264,793 | 18.4 | 83,547 | 5.8 | 79,123 | 5.5 |
| 1997 | 259,959 | 17.8 | 78,077 | 5.3 | 78,472 | 5.4 |

**Expectation of Life** (official estimates, years at birth, 1997): Males 72.13; Females 78.10.

Source: partly UN, *Demographic Yearbook*.

**ECONOMICALLY ACTIVE POPULATION***

('000 persons aged 15 years and over, October–December)

| | 1996 | 1997 | 1998 |
|---|---|---|---|
| Agriculture, hunting, forestry and fishing | 816.4 | 775.9 | 784.4 |
| Mining and quarrying | 90.6 | 87.9 | 81.8 |
| Manufacturing | 859.6 | 860.8 | 818.6 |
| Electricity, gas and water | 41.7 | 31.1 | 37.6 |
| Construction | 417.0 | 488.8 | 448.5 |
| Trade, restaurants and hotels | 931.9 | 975.9 | 1,005.5 |
| Transport, storage and communications | 393.9 | 401.0 | 432.7 |
| Financing, insurance, real estate and business services | 369.4 | 376.5 | 405.7 |
| Community, social and personal services | 1,377.9 | 1,382.4 | 1,417.7 |
| Activities not adequately defined | 0.2 | — | — |
| **Total employed** | 5,298.7 | 5,380.2 | 5,432.3 |
| Unemployed | 302.0 | 303.6 | 419.2 |
| **Total labour force** | 5,600.7 | 5,683.8 | 5,851.5 |
| Males | 3,789.9 | 3,812.5 | n.a. |
| Females | 1,811.2 | 1,871.3 | n.a. |

* Figures are based on sample surveys, covering 36,000 households, and exclude members of the armed forces. Estimates are made independently, therefore totals are not always the sum of the component parts.

# Agriculture

**PRINCIPAL CROPS** ('000 metric tons)

| | 1996 | 1997 | 1998 |
|---|---|---|---|
| Wheat | 1,227 | 1,677 | 1,400 |
| Rice (paddy) | 153 | 88 | 104 |
| Barley | 64 | 81 | 115 |
| Oats | 200 | 347 | 250 |
| Rye | 2 | 4 | 3 |
| Maize | 932 | 881 | 943 |
| Dry beans | 66 | 42 | 55 |
| Dry peas | 3 | 2 | 3 |
| Chick-peas | 10 | 6 | 4 |
| Lentils | 10 | 5 | 4 |
| Potatoes | 828 | 1,114 | 792 |
| Sunflower seed | 3 | 3 | 3 |
| Sugar beet | 3,109 | 2,707 | 3,085 |
| Rapeseed | 34 | 30 | 52 |
| Tomatoes | 1,370 | 1,121† | 1,197 |
| Pumpkins, etc. | 155* | 160 | 111 |
| Onions (dry) | 390 | 200 | 219 |
| Watermelons | 85* | 70* | 63 |
| Melons* | 77 | 77 | 77 |
| Grapes | 1,515 | 1,517 | 1,665 |
| Apples | 860 | 850 | 880 |
| Peaches and nectarines | 280 | 270 | 285 |

* FAO estimate(s). † Unofficial figure.

Source: FAO, *Production Yearbook*.

**LIVESTOCK** ('000 head, year ending September)

| | 1996 | 1997 | 1998 |
|---|---|---|---|
| Horses* | 580 | 590 | 590 |
| Cattle | 3,858 | 3,914 | 3,755 |
| Pigs | 1,486 | 1,655 | 1,771 |
| Sheep | 4,516 | 3,835 | 3,754 |
| Goats | 600* | 738 | 738* |

* FAO estimate(s).

Poultry (FAO estimates, million): 68 in 1996; 68 in 1997; 70 in 1998.

Source: FAO, *Production Yearbook*.

**LIVESTOCK PRODUCTS** ('000 metric tons)

| | 1996 | 1997 | 1998 |
|---|---|---|---|
| Beef and veal | 259 | 262 | 256 |
| Mutton and lamb | 9 | 10 | 11 |
| Pig meat | 185 | 209 | 235 |
| Horse meat | 12 | 12 | 12 |
| Poultry meat | 305 | 314 | 339 |
| Cows' milk | 1,924 | 2,050 | 2,080 |
| Goats' milk* | 10 | 10 | 10 |
| Butter | 6 | 10 | 12 |
| Cheese | 49 | 50 | 53 |
| Hen eggs* | 95 | 95 | 95 |
| Wool: | | | |
| greasy | 19 | 16 | 15 |
| clean | 9 | 8 | 8 |

* FAO estimates.

Source: FAO, *Production Yearbook*.

# Forestry

**ROUNDWOOD REMOVALS** ('000 cubic metres, excluding bark)

| | 1995 | 1996 | 1997 |
|---|---|---|---|
| Sawlogs, veneer logs and logs for sleepers | 11,645 | 11,024 | 12,132 |
| Pulpwood | 12,591 | 7,765 | 7,063 |
| Other industrial wood | 644 | 593 | 593 |
| Fuel wood | 10,356 | 10,767 | 10,773 |
| **Total** | 35,236 | 30,149 | 30,561 |

Source: FAO, *Yearbook of Forest Products*.

**SAWNWOOD PRODUCTION**
('000 cubic metres, including railway sleepers).

| | 1995 | 1996 | 1997 |
|---|---|---|---|
| Coniferous (softwood) | 3,394 | 3,744 | 4,274 |
| Broadleaved (hardwood) | 408 | 396 | 387 |
| **Total** | 3,802 | 4,140 | 4,661 |

Source: FAO, *Yearbook of Forest Products*.

# Fishing*

('000 metric tons, live weight)

| | 1995 | 1996 | 1997 |
|---|---|---|---|
| Patagonian grenadier | 206.7 | 379.0 | 71.5 |
| Chilean jack mackerel | 4,404.2 | 3,883.3 | 2,917.1 |
| South American pilchard (sardine) | 161.6 | 81.0 | 40.5 |
| Araucanian herring | 126.7 | 446.7 | 441.2 |
| Anchoveta (Peruvian anchovy) | 2,086.5 | 1,400.6 | 1,757.5 |
| Chub mackerel | 110.2 | 146.6 | 211.6 |
| Other marine fishes (incl. unspecified) | 174.1 | 187.6 | 217.0 |
| **Total fish** | 7,270.0 | 6,524.8 | 5,656.3 |
| Crustaceans | 31.0 | 32.6 | 37.3 |
| Molluscs | 74.9 | 77.5 | 69.2 |
| Other aquatic animals | 58.0 | 56.1 | 48.7 |
| **Total catch** | 7,433.9 | 6,691.0 | 5,811.6 |

* Excluding aquatic plants but including quantities landed by foreign fishing craft in Chilean ports.

Source: FAO, *Yearbook of Fishery Statistics*.

# Mining

('000 metric tons, unless otherwise indicated)

| | 1996 | 1997 | 1998* |
|---|---|---|---|
| Copper (metal content) | 3,144 | 3,512 | 3,707 |
| Coal | 1,446 | 1,431 | 379 |
| Iron ore† | 9,082 | 8,738 | 9,112 |
| Zinc—metal content (metric tons) | 36,004 | 34,350 | 16,166 |
| Molybdenum—metal content (kilograms) | 17,415 | 21,337 | 25,517 |
| Manganese (kilograms)‡ | 62,887 | 62,750 | 48,159 |
| Gold (kilograms) | 53,098 | 49,486 | 43,824 |
| Silver (kilograms) | 1,147,002 | 1,091,490 | 1,336,841 |
| Petroleum ('000 cubic metres)§ | 532.7 | 490.0 | n.a. |

* Figures are provisional.

† Gross weight. The estimated iron content is 61%.

‡ Gross weight. The estimated metal content is 32%.

§ Data from UN Economic Commission for Latin America and the Caribbean, *Statistical Yearbook for Latin America and the Caribbean*.

Source: mainly Servicio Nacional de Geología y Minería.

**Natural Gas** (petajoules): 67 in 1993; 73 in 1994; 70 in 1995. Source: UN, *Industrial Commodity Statistics Yearbook*.

# Industry

**SELECTED PRODUCTS** ('000 metric tons, unless otherwise indicated)

| | 1994 | 1995 | 1996 |
|---|---|---|---|
| Refined sugar | 463 | 549 | 423 |
| Beer (million litres) | 330 | 355 | 346 |
| Soft drinks (million litres) | 936 | 1,021 | 1,112 |
| Cigarettes (million) | 10,801 | 10,891 | 11,569 |
| Non-rubber footwear ('000 pairs) | 8,317 | 7,410 | 7,134 |
| Particle board ('000 cu metres) | 299 | 348 | 348 |
| Mattresses ('000) | 948 | 1,063 | 1,081 |
| Sulphuric acid | 1,174 | 1,427 | 1,518 |
| Motor spirit (petrol) | 1,746 | 1,849 | 2,106 |
| Aviation gasoline | 16 | 11 | |
| Jet fuels | 360 | 359 | 649 |
| Kerosene | 266 | 273 | |
| Distillate fuel oils | 2,450 | 2,698 | 3,074 |
| Residual fuel oils | 1,601 | 1,737 | 2,017 |
| Cement | 3,001 | 3,304 | 3,627 |
| Tyres ('000) | 2,285 | 2,330 | 2,269 |
| Sanitary ceramic fittings | 22.6 | 22.9 | n.a. |
| Glass sheets ('000 sq metres) | 7,089 | 6,536 | 10,659 |
| Blister copper*† | 1,148.3 | 1,322.8 | 1,589.6 |
| Refined copper (unwrought) | 1,080.0 | 1,288.8 | 1,518.0 |

* Data from *World Metal Statistics* (London).

† Including some production at refined stage.

Source: UN, *Industrial Commodity Statistics Yearbook* and *Monthly Bulletin of Statistics*.

**Electric Energy:** (million kWh): 30,261 in 1996; 32,549 in 1997; 34,886 (provisional) in 1998.

# Finance

**CURRENCY AND EXCHANGE RATES**

**Monetary Units**

100 centavos = 1 Chilean peso.

**Sterling, Dollar and Euro Equivalents** (30 September 1999)

£1 sterling = 874.5 pesos;
US $1 = 531.1 pesos;
€1 = 566.4 pesos;
1,000 Chilean pesos = £1.144 = $1.883 = €1.765.

**Average Exchange Rate** (pesos per US $)

| | |
|---|---|
| 1996 | 412.27 |
| 1997 | 419.30 |
| 1998 | 460.29 |

**BUDGET** ('000 million pesos)

| Revenue | 1995 | 1996 | 1997 |
|---|---|---|---|
| Current revenue* | 5,738.45 | 6,624.71 | 7,342.12 |
| Taxation | 4,749.72 | 5,605.68 | 6,122.30 |
| Taxes on income, profits and capital gains | 998.18 | 1,227.49 | 1,302.36 |
| Social security contributions | 349.12 | 403.05 | 449.47 |
| Domestic taxes on goods and services | 2,604.81 | 3,066.43 | 3,377.00 |
| Sales or turnover taxes | 2,128.19 | 2,492.12 | 2,707.94 |
| Excises | 476.62 | 574.31 | 669.06 |
| Taxes on international trade and transactions | 535.55 | 616.67 | 604.80 |
| Other taxes | 262.06 | 292.04 | 388.67 |
| Administrative fees and charges, non-industrial and incidental sales | 399.59 | 440.44 | 470.91 |
| Other current revenue* | 589.14 | 578.59 | 748.09 |
| Capital revenue | 15.59 | 9.16 | 24.52 |
| **Total revenue** | 5,754.04 | 6,633.87 | 7,366.64 |

| Expenditure† | 1995 | 1996 | 1997 |
|---|---|---|---|
| General public services | 203.70 | 233.28 | 269.23 |
| Defence | 439.01 | 489.05 | 564.64 |
| Public order and safety | 271.03 | 327.16 | 375.53 |
| Education | 754.39 | 914.57 | 1,069.65 |
| Health | 614.68 | 716.88 | 806.54 |
| Social security and welfare | 1,735.77 | 2,014.25 | 2,237.91 |
| Housing | 288.61 | 345.79 | 351.39 |
| Economic services | 765.52 | 931.08 | 1,094.31 |
| Other expenditures | 192.36 | 165.94 | 140.78 |
| **Sub-total** | 5,265.07 | 6,138.00 | 6,909.98 |
| *Less* Lending included in expenditure | 128.01 | 155.23 | 214.63 |
| **Total expenditure** | 5,137.06 | 5,982.77 | 6,695.35 |
| Current | 4,331.18 | 4,972.08 | 5,575.82 |
| Capital | 805.88 | 1,010.69 | 1,119.53 |

* Including unclassified current revenue ('000 million pesos): 261.46 in 1995; 213.00 in 1996; 305.89 in 1997.

† Excluding lending minus repayments ('000 million pesos): –50.62 in 1995; –6.71 in 1996; 48.08 in 1997.

Source: IMF, *Government Finance Statistics Yearbook*.

**CENTRAL BANK RESERVES** (US $ million at 31 December)

| | 1996 | 1997 | 1998 |
|---|---|---|---|
| Gold* | 637.4 | 533.0 | 321.9 |
| IMF special drawing rights | 1.9 | 1.3 | 8.3 |
| Reserve position in IMF | 50.4 | 313.1 | 604.9 |
| Foreign exchange | 14,780.9 | 16,991.4 | 15,049.4 |
| **Total** | 15,470.6 | 17,838.8 | 15,984.5 |

* National valuation.

Source: IMF, *International Financial Statistics*.

**MONEY SUPPLY** ('000 million pesos at 31 December)

| | 1996 | 1997 | 1998 |
|---|---|---|---|
| Currency outside banks | 859.5 | 985.3 | 977.3 |
| Demand deposits at commercial banks | 1,826.6 | 2,242.6 | 1,821.9 |
| **Total money** (incl. others) | 2,312.9 | 2,686.7 | 2,799.4 |

Source: IMF, *International Financial Statistics*.

**COST OF LIVING**

(Consumer Price Index for Santiago; base: 1990 = 100)

| | 1995 | 1996 | 1997 |
|---|---|---|---|
| Food (incl. beverages) | 195.6 | 207.5 | 222.3 |
| Rent, fuel and light | 189.5 | 204.2 | 216.3 |
| Clothing (incl. footwear) | 154.2 | 143.2 | 136.4 |
| **All items** (incl. others) | 191.1 | 205.2 | 217.8 |

Source: ILO, *Yearbook of Labour Statistics*.

**1998:** Food 230.6; All items 228.9 (Source: UN, *Monthly Bulletin of Statistics*).

Agustinas 1817, Santiago; tel. (2) 672-1622; affiliated to CDT; Pres. Luis Hernán Alegría; Sec. Luis Vives Gallardo.

**Confederación Nacional de Sindicatos de Trabajadores Textiles de la Confección, Vestuario y Ramos Conexos de Chile (CONTEVECH):** Agustinas 2349, Santiago; tel. (2) 699-3442; affiliated to CUT; Pres. Miguel Vega; Sec.-Gen. Miguel Cabrera.

**Confederación Nacional Sindical Campesina Provincias Agrarias Unidas de Chile:** Santo Domingo 1083, Of. 504, Santiago; tel. (2) 696-2797; Pres. Raúl Orrego Escanilla; Sec.-Gen. Miguel Arellano Torres.

**Confederación Nacional Unitaria de Trabajadores del Transporte Y Afines de Chile (CONUTT):** Almirante Latorre 93, 2°, Santiago; tel. (2) 698-1004; fax (2) 697-1321; Pres. Ricardo I. Maldonado Olivares; Gen. Sec. Ramón Becerra.

**Confederación de Sindicatos y Federaciones de Trabajadores Electrometalúrgicos, Mineros, Automotrices y Ramos Conexos (CONSFETEMA):** Vicuña Mackenna 3101, Casilla 1803, Correo Central, Santiago; tel. (2) 238-1732; Pres. Raúl Ponce de León; Sec. Arnoldo Montoya.

**Confederación de Sindicatos y Federaciones de Trabajadores de la Industria Metalúrgica y Ramos Similares y Conexos (CONSTRAMET):** Brasil 43, 2°, Santiago; tel. (2) 672-5803; affiliated to CUT; Pres. José Ortiz; Sec.-Gen. Miguel Chávez Soazo.

**Confederación de Trabajadores del Cobre (CTC):** MacIver 283, 5°, Casilla 9094, Santiago; tel. (2) 38-0835; fax (2) 33-1449; comprises 21 unions; Pres. Darwin Bustamente; Sec.-Gen. Jorge Sepúlveda Segovia; 20,000 mems.

**Confederación de Trabajadores Molineros de Chile:** Santiago; tel. (2) 698-6538; Pres. Luis Cordero Leiva; Sec. Daniel Miranda.

**Confederación de Trabajadores de Santiago:** Miguel León Prado 135, Santiago; tel. (2) 556-7759; Pres. Manuel Oyaneder Cárdenas; Sec.-Gen. Luis González Sepúlveda.

The trade unions include:

**Central Democrática de Trabajadores:** Erasmo Escala 2170, Santiago; tel. (2) 699-4756; 20 affiliated organizations; Pres. Eduardo Ríos Arias.

**Central Democrática de Trabajadores (CDT):** Avda B. O'Higgins 1603, Santiago; tel. (2) 696-2957; nine affiliated organizations; Pres. Hernol Flores Opazo; Sec.-Gen. Milenko Mihovilovich Eterovic.

**Central de Trabajadores de Chile (CTCH):** Teatinos 20, Of. 75, Santiago; tel. (2) 697-0171; Pres. Pedro Briceño Molina; Sec.-Gen. Mario Delannays Avalos.

**Central Unitaria de Trabajadores de Chile (CUT–Chile):** Avda B. O'Higgins 1346, Santiago; tel. (2) 695-8053; fax (2) 695-8055; f. 1988; two associations, 27 confederations, 49 federations; 36 regional headquarters; Pres. Manuel Bustos Huerta; Sec.-Gen. Guillermo Cortés; 411,000 mems.

**Comisión Nacional Campesina (CNC):** Dieciocho 390, Santiago; tel. (2) 698-8407; fax (2) 695-1093; five affiliated organizations; Pres. Osvaldo Valladares.

**Consejo Coordinador de Trabajadores de Chile:** Sazié 1761, Santiago; tel. (2) 698-7318; fax (2) 695-3388; Pres. Hernán Baeza Jara; Sec.-Gen. Santiago Pereira Becerra.

**Frente Nacional de Organizaciones Autónomas–FRENAO:** Santa Lucía 162, Santiago; tel. (2) 38-2354; seven affiliated organizations; Pres. Manuel Contreras Loyola; Sec.-Gen. Julieta Provoste Sepúlveda.

**Movimiento Unitario Campesino y Etnias de Chile (MUCECH):** Lira 220, Santiago; tel. (2) 222-1677; Pres. Francisco León Tobar; Sec.-Gen. Ramón Velásquez.

# Transport

## RAILWAYS

### State Railways

**Empresa de los Ferrocarriles del Estado:** Avda B. O'Higgins 3322, 3°, Casilla 124-D, Santiago; tel. (2) 779-0707; fax (2) 776-2052; f. 1851; 3,427 km of track (1997); the State Railways are divided between the Ferrocarril Regional de Arica (formerly Ferrocarril Arica–La Paz), Ferrocarriles del Pacífico (cargo division), Metro Regional de Valparaíso (passenger service only) and Ferrovía (formerly the Ferrocarril del Sur); several lines scheduled for privatization; Pres. H. Trivelli; Gen. Man. J. Mondaca.

### Parastatal Railways

**Ferrocarriles del Pacífico (FEPASA):** Alfredo Barros Errázuriz 1960, 6°, Providencia, Santiago; tel. (2) 330-4900; fax (2) 330-4905; e-mail fepasa@chilnet.cl; f. 1993; freight services; scheduled for privatization; Gen. Man. F. Langer.

**Metro de Santiago:** Empresa de Transporte de Pasajeros Metro, SA, Avda B. O'Higgins 1414, Santiago; tel. (2) 698-8218; fax (2) 699-2475; e-mail mstgo@entelchile.net; started operations 1975; 37.7 km (1997); 3 lines; Pres. Daniel Fernández Koprich; Gen. Man. R. Azócar Hidalgo.

### Private Railways

**Antofagasta (Chile) and Bolivia Railway PLC:** Bolívar 255, Casillas ST, Antofagasta; tel. (55) 20-6700; fax (55) 20-6220; e-mail webmaster@fcab.cl; internet www.fcab.com; f. 1888; British-owned; operates an internat. railway to Bolivia and Argentina; cargo forwarding services; total track length 934 km; Chair. Andrónico Luksic Abaroa; Gen. Man. M. V. Sepúlveda.

**Empresa de Transporte Ferroviario, SA (Ferronor):** Avda Alessandri 042, Coquimbo; tel. (51) 31-2442; fax (51) 31-3460; 2,200 km of track (1995); established as a public/private concern, following the transfer of the Ferrocarril Regional del Norte de Chile to the Ministry of Production Development (CORFO) as a *Sociedad Anónima* in 1989; controlling interest purchased by RailAmerica of the USA in 1997; operates cargo services only; Pres. G. Marino; Gen. Man. P. Espy.

**Ferrocarril Codelco-Chile:** Barquito, Region III, Atacama; tel. (52) 48-8521; fax (52) 48-8522; Gen. Man. B. Behn Theune.

**Diego de Almagro a Potrerillos:** transport of forest products, minerals and manufactures; 99 km.

**Ferrocarril Rancagua–Teniente:** transport of forest products, livestock, minerals and manufactures; 68 km.

**Ferrocarril Tocopilla–Toco:** Calle Arturo Prat 1060, Casilla 2098, Tocopilla; tel. (55) 81-2139; fax (55) 81-2650; owned by Sociedad Química y Minera de Chile, SA; 117 km (1995); Gen. Man. Segisfredo Hurtado Guerrero.

### Association

**Asociación Chilena de Conservación de Patrimonio Ferroviario (Chilean Railway Society–ACCPF):** Casilla 179-D, Santiago; tel. (2) 210-2280; fax (2) 280-0252; Pres. H. Venegas.

## ROADS

The total length of roads in Chile in 1996 was an estimated 79,800 km, of which some 6,350 km were highways and some 16,700 km were secondary roads. The road system includes the completely paved Pan American Highway extending 3,455 km from north to south. Toll gates exist on major motorways. The 1,200 km-Carretera Austral (Southern Highway), linking Puerto Montt and Puerto Yungay, was completed in March 1996, at an estimated total cost of US $200m.

## SHIPPING

As a consequence of Chile's difficult topography, maritime transport is of particular importance. In 1997 90% of the country's foreign trade was carried by sea (51m. metric tons). The principal ports are Valparaíso, Talcahuano, Antofagasta, San Antonio, Arica, Iquique, Coquimbo, San Vicente, Puerto Montt and Punta Arenas.

Chile's merchant fleet amounted to 753,432 grt (comprising 472 vessels) at December 1998.

### Supervisory Authorities

**Asociación Nacional de Armadores:** Blanco 869, 3°, Valparaíso; tel. (32) 21-2057; fax (32) 21-2017; e-mail armadore@entelchile.net; f. 1931; shipowners' association; Pres. Juan Fernando Waidele; Gen. Man. Arturo Sierra Merino.

**Cámara Marítima y Portuaria de Chile, AG:** Blanco 869, Valparaíso; tel. (32) 25-3443; fax (32) 25-0231; e-mail camport@entelchile.net; Pres. Jaime Barahona Vargas; Vice-Pres. Rodolfo García Sánchez.

**Dirección General de Territorio Marítimo y Marina Mercante:** Errázuriz 537, 4°, Valparaíso; tel. (32) 25-8061; fax (32) 25-2539; maritime admin. of the coast and national waters, control of the merchant navy; Dir Rear Adm. Fernando Lazcano.

**Empresa Portuaria Antofagasta:** Grecia s/n, Antofagasta; tel. (55) 25-1737; fax (55) 22-3171; e-mail epa@puertoantofagasta.cl; Pres. Blas Enrique Espinoza Sepúlveda; Dir Eduardo Salvador Abedrapo Bustos.

**Empresa Portuaria Arica:** Máximo Lira 389, Arica; tel. (58) 25-5078; fax (58) 23-2284; e-mail puertoarica@entelchile.net; Pres. Carlos Eduardo Mena Keymer; Dir Raúl Ricardo Balbontín Fernández.

**Empresa Portuaria Austral:** B. O'Higgins 1385, Punta Arenas; tel. (61) 24-1760; fax (61) 24-1822; e-mail portspug@ctc-mundo.net; Pres. Lautaro Hernán Poblete Knudtzon-Trampe; Dir Fernando Arturo Jofré Weiss.

**Empresa Portuaria Chacabuco:** B. O'Higgins s/n, Puerto Chacabuco; tel. (67) 35-1198; fax (67) 35-1174; e-mail ptochb@entelchile.net; Pres. Luis Musalem Musalem; Dir Raimundo Cristi Saavedra.

**Empresa Portuaria Coquimbo:** Melgareja 676, Coquimbo; tel. (51) 31-3606; fax (51) 32-6146; e-mail ptoqq@entelchile.net; Pres. ARMANDO ARANCIBIA CALDERÓN; Gen. Man. MIGUEL ZUVIC MUJICA.

**Empresa Portuaria Iquique:** Jorge Barrera 62, Iquique; tel. (57) 40-0100; fax (57) 41-3176; e-mail pdavila@port-iquique.cl; Pres. PATRICIO ARRAU PONS; Gen. Man. PEDRO DÁVILA PINO.

**Empresa Portuaria Puerto Montt:** Angelmó 1673, Puerto Montt; tel. (65) 25-2247; e-mail puertomont@telsur.cl; Pres. JOSÉ DANIEL BARRETA SÁEZ; Gen. Man. RICARDO GHIORZI CARCEY.

**Empresa Portuaria San Antonio:** Alan Macowan 0245, San Antonio; tel.(35) 21-2159; fax (35) 21-2114; e-mail fcrisost@saiport.cl; Pres. JOSÉ MANUEL MORALES TALLAR; Gen. Man. FERNANDO CRISÓSTOMO BURGOS.

**Empresa Portuaria Talcahuano-San Vicente:** Latorre 1590, Talcahuano; tel. (41) 54-1419; fax (41) 54-1807; e-mail eportuaria@ptotalsve.co.cl; Pres. JUAN ENRIQUE COEYMANS AVARIA; Gen. Man. PATRICIO CAMPAÑA CUELLO.

**Empresa Portuaria Valparaíso:** Errázuriz 25, 4°, Of. 1, Valparaíso; tel. (32) 25-7167; fax (32) 23-4427; e-mail hjaeger@vap.cl; Pres. JORGE NAVARRETE MARTÍNEZ; Gen. Man. HARALD JAEGER KARL.

### Principal Shipping Companies

Santiago

**Cía Chilena de Navegación Interoceánica, SA:** B. O'Higgins 949, 22°, Casilla 4246, Santiago; tel. (2) 696-8147; fax (2) 203-9060; f. 1930; regular sailings to Japan, Republic of Korea, Taiwan, Hong Kong, USA, Mexico, South Pacific, South Africa and Europe; bulk and dry cargo services; Pres. ALEJANDRO PINO TORCHE; Man. Dir ANTONIO JABAT ALONSO.

**Marítima Antares, SA:** MacIver 225, Of. 2001, 2°, Santiago; tel. (2) 38-3036; Pres. ALFONSO GARCÍA-MIÑAUR G.; Gen. Man. LUIS BEDRIÑANA RODRÍGUEZ.

**Naviera Magallanes, SA (NAVIMAG):** Avda El Bosque, Norte 0440, 11°, Of. 1103/1104, Las Condes, Santiago; tel. (2) 203-5180; fax (2) 203-5191; f. 1979; Chair. PEDRO LECAROS MENÉNDEZ; Gen. Man. EDUARDO SALAZAR RETAMALES.

**Nisa Navegación, SA:** Avda El Bosque Norte 0440, 11°, Casilla 2829, Santiago; tel.(2) 203-5180; fax (2) 203-5190; Chair. PEDRO LECAROS MENÉNDEZ; Gen. Man. SERGIO VIAL.

Valparaíso

**A. J. Broom y Cía, SAC:** Blanco 951, Casilla 910, Valparaíso and MacIver 225, 10°, Casilla 448, Santiago; e-mail genmanager@ajbroom.cl; f. 1920; Pres. GASTÓN ANRÍQUEZ; Man. Dir JAMES C. WELLS M.

**Agencias Universales, SA (AGUNSA):** Urriola 87, 3°, Valparaíso; tel. (32) 21-7333; fax (32) 25-4261; maritime transportation and shipping, port and docking services; Dir J. M. U. SALAMANCA.

**Cía Sud-Americana de Vapores:** Plaza Sotomayor 50, Casilla 49-V, Valparaíso; tel. (32) 20-3000; fax (32) 20-3333; also Hendaya 60, 12°, Santiago; tel. (2) 330-7000; fax (2) 330-7700; f. 1872; regular service between South America and US/Canadian ports, US Gulf ports, North European, Mediterranean, Scandinavian and Far East ports; bulk carriers, tramp and reefer services; Pres. RICARDO CLARO VALDÉS; Gen. Man. FRANCISCO SILVA DONOSO.

**Empresa Marítima, SA (Empremar Chile):** Almirante Gómez Carreño 49, Casilla 105-V, Valparaíso; tel. (32) 25-0563; fax (32) 21-3904; f. 1953; international and coastal services; Chair. LORENZO CAGLEVIC.

**Naviera Chilena del Pacífico, SA:** Almirante Señoret 70, 6°, Casilla 370, Valparaíso; tel. (32) 25-0563; fax (32) 25-3869; e-mail nachipav@entelchile.net; also Serrano 14, Of. 502, Casilla 2290, Santiago; tel. (2) 633-3063; fax (2) 639-2069; e-mail nachipa@entelchile.net; cargo; Pres. ARTURO FERNÁNDEZ ZEGERS; Gen. Man. PABLO SIMIAN ZAMORANO.

**Sociedad Anónima de Navegación Petrolera (SONAP):** Cochrane 813, 6°, Casilla 1870, Valparaíso; tel. (32) 25-9476; fax (32) 25-1325; e-mail jthomsen@sonap.cl; f. 1954; tanker services; Chair. FELIPE VIAL C.; Gen. Man. JOSÉ THOMSEN Q.

**Transmares Naviera Chilena Ltda:** Moneda 970, 20°, Edif. Eurocentro, Casilla 193-D, Santiago; tel. (2) 630-1000; fax (2) 698-9205; e-mail transmares@transmares.cl; also Cochrane 813, 8°, Casilla 52-V, Valparaíso; tel. (32) 20-2000; fax (32) 25-6607; f. 1969; dry cargo service Chile–Uruguay–Brazil; Chair. WOLF VON APPEN; CEO RICARDO SCHLECHTER.

Several foreign shipping companies operate services to Valparaíso.

Punta Arenas

**Cía Marítima de Punta Arenas, SA:** Avda Independencia 830, Casilla 337, Punta Arenas; tel. (61) 24-1702; fax (61) 24-7514; also Casilla 2829, Santiago; tel. (2) 203-5180; fax (2) 203-5191; f. 1949; shipping agents and owners operating in the Magellan Straits; Pres. PEDRO LECAROS MENÉNDEZ; Gen. Man. ARTURO STORAKER MOLINA.

Pucrto Montt

**Transporte Marítimo Chiloé-Aysén, SA:** Angelmo 2187, Puerto Monttjel. (65) 27-0419; Deputy Man. PEDRO HERNÁNDEZ LEHMAN.

San Antonio

**Naviera Aysén Ltda:** San Antonio; tel. (35) 32578; also Huérfanos 1147, Of. 542, Santiago; tel. (2) 698-8680; Man. RAÚL QUINTANA A.

**Naviera Paschold Ltda:** Centenario 9, San Antonio; tel. (35) 31654; also Huérfanos 1147, Santiago; tel. (2) 698-8680; Gen. Man. PATRICIO JARA RAMOS.

### CIVIL AVIATION

There are 325 airfields in the country, of which eight have long runways. Arturo Merino Benítez, 20 km north-east of Santiago, and Chacalluta, 14 km north-east of Arica, are the principal international airports.

**Aerocardal:** José Arrieta 7808, Casilla 9630, La Reina, Santiago; tel. (2) 279-3535; fax (2) 279-4272; f. 1989; charter services; Chair. ALEX CASASEMPERE.

**Aerovías DAP:** Casilla 633, Punta Arenas; tel. (61) 22-3340; fax (61) 22-1693; f. 1980; domestic services; CEO ALEX PISCEVIC.

**Lineas Aéreas Chilenas:** B. O'Higgins 107, 7°, Santiago; tel. (2) 290-5140; fax (2) 290-5144; Man. RICARDO MARDONES.

**Línea Aérea Nacional de Chile (LAN-Chile):** Américo Vespucio 901, Renca, Santiago; tel. (2) 565-2525; fax (2) 565-2817; internet www.lanchile.com; f. 1929; operates scheduled domestic passenger and cargo services, also Santiago–Easter Island; international services to French Polynesia, Spain, and throughout North and South America; under the Govt's privatization programme, 99% of LAN-Chile shares have been sold to private interests since 1989; Chair. JORGE AWAD; CEO ENRIQUE CUETO.

**Línea Aérea del Cobre SA—LADECO:** Américo Vespucio 901, Renca, Santiago; tel. (2) 565-2862; fax (2) 565-2689; f. 1958; affiliated to LAN-Chile in 1996; internal passenger and cargo services; international passenger and cargo services to the USA and throughout South America; Chair. JOSÉ COX; CEO SERGIO PURCELL.

## Tourism

Chile has a wide variety of attractions for the tourist, including fine beaches, ski resorts in the Andes, lakes, rivers and desert scenery. There are many opportunities for hunting and fishing in the southern archipelago, where there are plans to make an integrated tourist area with Argentina, requiring investment of US $120m. Isla de Pascua (Easter Island) may also be visited by tourists. In 1998 there were an estimated 1.76m. tourist arrivals, and receipts from tourism totalled US $1,062m.

**Servicio Nacional de Turismo—SERNATUR:** Avda Providencia 1550, Casilla 14082, Santiago; tel. (2) 236-1420; fax (2) 236-1417; e-mail sernatur@ctc-mundo.net; internet www.segegob.cl/sernatur/; f. 1975; Pres. MARÍA EUGENIA CASTRO; Man. ISABEL BACHLER.

**Asociación Chilena de Empresas de Turismo—ACHET:** Moneda 973, Of. 647, Casilla 3402, Santiago; tel. (2) 696-5677; fax (2) 699-4245; f. 1945; 240 mems; Pres. IVONNE LAHAYE DE MONTES MARDONES; Man. CARLOS MESCHI MONTALDO.

# THE PEOPLE'S REPUBLIC OF CHINA

## Introductory Survey

**Location, Climate, Language, Religion, Flag, Capital**

The People's Republic of China covers a vast area of eastern Asia, with Mongolia and Russia to the north, Tajikistan, Kyrgyzstan and Kazakhstan to the north-west, Afghanistan and Pakistan to the west, and India, Nepal, Bhutan, Myanmar (formerly Burma), Laos and Viet Nam to the south. The country borders the Democratic People's Republic of Korea in the north-east, and has a long coastline on the Pacific Ocean. The climate ranges from subtropical in the far south to an annual average temperature of below 10°C (50°F) in the north, and from the monsoon climate of eastern China to the aridity of the north-west. The principal language is Northern Chinese (Mandarin); in the south and south-east local dialects are spoken. The Xizangzu (Tibetans), Wei Wuer (Uygurs), Menggus (Mongols) and other groups have their own languages. The traditional religions and philosophies of life are Confucianism, Buddhism and Daoism. There are also Muslim and Christian minorities. The national flag (proportions 3 by 2) is plain red, with one large five-pointed gold star and four similar but smaller stars, arranged in an arc, in the upper hoist. The capital is Beijing (Peking).

**Recent History**

The People's Republic of China was proclaimed on 1 October 1949, following the victory of Communist forces over the Kuomintang Government, which fled to the island province of Taiwan. The new Communist regime received widespread international recognition, but it was not until 1971 that the People's Republic was admitted to the United Nations, in place of the Kuomintang regime, as the representative of China. Most countries now recognize the People's Republic.

With the establishment of the People's Republic, the leading political figure was Mao Zedong, who was Chairman of the Chinese Communist Party (CCP) from 1935 until his death in 1976. Chairman Mao, as he was known, also became Head of State in October 1949, but he relinquished this post in December 1958. His successor was Liu Shaoqi, First Vice-Chairman of the CCP, who was elected Head of State in April 1959. Liu was dismissed in October 1968, during the Cultural Revolution (see below), and died in prison in 1969. The post of Head of State was left vacant, and was formally abolished in January 1975, when a new Constitution was adopted. The first Premier (Head of Government) of the People's Republic was Zhou Enlai, who held this office from October 1949 until his death in 1976. Zhou was also Minister of Foreign Affairs from 1949 to 1958.

The economic progress of the early years of Communist rule enabled China to withstand the effects of the industrialization programmes of the late 1950s (called the 'Great Leap Forward'), the drought of 1960–62 and the withdrawal of Soviet aid in 1960. To prevent the establishment of a ruling class, Chairman Mao launched the Great Proletarian Cultural Revolution in 1966. The ensuing excesses of the Red Guards caused the army to intervene; Liu Shaoqi and Deng Xiaoping, General Secretary of the CCP, were disgraced. In 1971 an attempted coup by the Defence Minister, Marshal Lin Biao, was unsuccessful, and by 1973 it was apparent that Chairman Mao and Premier Zhou Enlai had retained power. In 1975 Deng Xiaoping re-emerged as first Vice-Premier and Chief of the General Staff. Zhou Enlai died in January 1976. Hua Guofeng, hitherto Minister of Public Security, was appointed Premier, and Deng was dismissed. Mao died in September 1976. His widow, Jiang Qing, tried unsuccessfully to seize power, with the help of three radical members of the CCP's Politburo. The 'gang of four' and six associates of Lin Biao were tried in November 1980. All were found guilty and were given lengthy terms of imprisonment. (Jiang Qing committed suicide in May 1991.) The 10th anniversary of Mao's death was marked in September 1986 by an official reassessment of his life; while his accomplishments were praised, it was now acknowledged that he had made mistakes, although most of the criticism was directed at the 'gang of four'.

In October 1976 Hua Guofeng succeeded Mao as Chairman of the CCP and Commander-in-Chief of the People's Liberation Army. The 11th National Congress of the CCP, held in August 1977, restored Deng Xiaoping to his former posts. In September 1980 Hua Guofeng resigned as Premier, but retained his chairmanship of the CCP. The appointment of Zhao Ziyang, a Vice-Premier since April 1980, to succeed Hua as Premier confirmed the dominance of the moderate faction of Deng Xiaoping. In June 1981 Hua Guofeng was replaced as Chairman of the CCP by Hu Yaobang, former Secretary-General of the Politburo, and as Chairman of the party's Central Military Commission by Deng Xiaoping. A sustained campaign by Deng to purge the Politburo of leftist elements led to Hua's demotion to a Vice-Chairman of the CCP and, in September 1982, to his exclusion from the Politburo.

In September 1982 the CCP was reorganized and the post of Party Chairman abolished. Hu Yaobang became, instead, General Secretary of the CCP. A year later a 'rectification' (purge) of the CCP was launched, aimed at expelling 'Maoists', who had risen to power during the Cultural Revolution, and those opposed to the pragmatic policies of Deng. China's new Constitution, adopted in December 1982, restored the office of Head of State, and in June 1983 Li Xiannian, a former Minister of Finance, became President of China.

In late 1983, following the reported execution of thousands of people in an alleged operation to combat crime, a campaign was launched against 'spiritual pollution' and stricter censorship was introduced to limit the effects of Western cultural influences. The reorganization of the CCP and of the Government continued. During 1984–85 a programme of modernization for the armed forces was undertaken. In September 1986 the sixth plenary session of the 12th CCP Central Committee adopted a detailed resolution on the 'guiding principles for building a socialist society', which redefined the general ideology of the CCP, to provide a theoretical basis for the programme of modernization and the 'open door' policy of economic reform.

In January 1986 a high-level 'anti-corruption' campaign was launched, to investigate reports that many officials had exploited the programme of economic reform for their own gain. The field of culture and the arts underwent significant liberalization in 1986, with a revival of the 'Hundred Flowers' movement of 1956–57, which had encouraged the development of intellectual debate. However, a series of student demonstrations in major cities in late 1986 was regarded by China's leaders as an indication of excessive 'bourgeois liberalization'. In January 1987 Hu Yaobang unexpectedly resigned as CCP General Secretary, being accused of 'mistakes on major issues of political principles'. Zhao Ziyang became acting General Secretary.

The campaign against 'bourgeois liberalization' was widely regarded as part of a broader, ideological struggle between those Chinese leaders who sought to extend Deng's reforms and those, generally elderly, 'conservative' leaders who opposed the reforms and the 'open door' policy. At the 13th National Congress of the CCP, which opened in October 1987, it became clear that the 'reformist' faction within the Chinese leadership had prevailed. Deng Xiaoping retired from the Central Committee, but amendments to the Constitution of the CCP permitted him to retain the influential positions of Chairman of the State and of the CCP Central Military Commissions.

A new Politburo was appointed by the Central Committee in November 1987. The majority of its 18 members were relatively young officials, who supported Deng Xiaoping's policies. The membership of the new Politburo also indicated a decline in military influence in Chinese politics. The newly-appointed Standing Committee of the Politburo was regarded, on balance, as being 'pro-reform'. In late November Li Peng was appointed Acting Premier of the State Council, in place of Zhao Ziyang. At the first session of the Seventh National People's Congress (NPC), held in March–April 1988, Li Peng was confirmed as Premier, and Yang Shangkun (a member of the CCP Politburo) was elected President.

The death of Hu Yaobang in April 1989 led to the most serious student demonstrations ever seen in the People's Republic. The students criticized the alleged prevalence of corruption and nepotism within the Government, and sought a limited degree of Soviet-style *glasnost* in public life. When negotiations between government officials and the students' leaders had failed to satisfy the protesters' demands, workers from various professions joined the demonstrations in Tiananmen Square, Beijing, which had now become the focal point of the protests. At one stage more than 1m. people congregated in the Square, as demonstrations spread to more than 20 other Chinese cities. In mid-May some 3,000 students began a hunger strike in Tiananmen Square, while protesters demanded the resignation of both Deng Xiaoping and Li Peng, and invited President Gorbachev of the USSR, who was visiting Beijing, to address them. The students ended their hunger strike at the request of Zhao Ziyang, who was generally regarded as being sympathetic to the students' demands. On 20 May a state of martial law was declared in Beijing. Within days, some 300,000 troops had assembled. At the end of May the students erected a 30-m high replica of the US Statue of Liberty in the Square.

On 3 June 1989 a further unsuccessful attempt was made to dislodge the demonstrators, but on the following day troops of the People's Liberation Army (PLA) attacked protesters on and around Tiananmen Square, killing an unspecified number of people. Television evidence and eye-witness accounts estimated the total dead at between 1,000 and 5,000. The Government immediately rejected these figures and claimed, furthermore, that the larger part of the casualties had been soldiers and that a counter-revolutionary rebellion had been taking place. Arrests and executions ensued, although some student leaders eluded capture and fled to Hong Kong. Zhao Ziyang was dismissed from all his party posts and replaced as General Secretary of the CCP by Jiang Zemin, hitherto the secretary of the Shanghai municipal party committee. Zhao was accused of participating in a conspiracy to overthrow the CCP and placed under house arrest. In November Deng resigned as Chairman of the CCP Central Military Commission, his sole remaining party position, and was succeeded by Jiang Zemin, who was hailed as the first of China's 'third generation' of communist leaders (Mao being representative of the first, and Deng of the second). In January 1990 martial law was lifted in Beijing, and it was announced that a total of 573 prisoners, detained following the pro-democracy demonstrations, had been freed. Further groups of detainees were released subsequently. In March Deng Xiaoping resigned from his last official post, that of Chairman of the State Central Military Commission, and was succeeded by Jiang Zemin. An extensive military reshuffle ensued.

In January 1992 Deng Xiaoping emphasized the importance of reform, thus initiating a period of intense debate between reformists and 'hard-liners' within the CCP. In March, at a session of the NPC, Premier Li Peng affirmed China's commitment to rapid economic reform, but stressed the need for stability. At the CCP's 14th National Congress, held in October 1992, a new 319-member Central Committee was elected. The Politburo was expanded and a new Secretariat was chosen by the incoming Central Committee. Many opponents of Deng Xiaoping's support for a 'socialist market economy' were replaced.

At the first session of the Eighth NPC, convened in March 1993, Jiang Zemin was elected as the country's President, remaining CCP General Secretary. Li Peng was reappointed as Premier, and an extensive reorganization of the State Council was announced. The Congress also approved amendments to the 1982 Constitution. Changes included confirmation of the State's practice of a 'socialist market economy'. During 1993, however, the Government became concerned at the growing disparity between urban and rural incomes (exacerbated by the heavy taxes imposed on farmers) and the resultant problems of rural migration, and the decline in support for the CCP in the countryside. In June thousands of peasants took part in demonstrations in Sichuan Province to protest against excessive official levies. In response to the ensuing riots, the central Government banned the imposition of additional local taxes.

In March 1995, at the third session of the Eighth NPC, the appointment of Wu Bangguo and of Jiang Chunyun as Vice-Premiers of the State Council was approved. In an unprecedented display of opposition, however, neither nominee received the NPC's full endorsement. Nevertheless, the position of Jiang Zemin, now regarded by many as the eventual successor to the 'paramount' leadership of the ailing Deng Xiaoping, appeared to have been strengthened. Personnel changes in the military hierarchy later in the year were also viewed as favourable to Jiang Zemin.

The death of Deng Xiaoping, at the age of 92, on 19 February 1997, precipitated a period of uncertainty regarding China's future direction. President Jiang Zemin, however, declared that the economic reforms would continue and this was reiterated in Premier Li Peng's address to the fifth session of the Eighth NPC in March 1997, during which he emphasized the urgent need to restructure state-owned enterprises (SOEs). Delegates at the Congress approved legislation reinforcing the CCP's control over the PLA, and revisions to the criminal code were also promulgated, whereby statutes concerning 'counter-revolutionary' acts (under which many of the pro-democracy demonstrators had been charged in 1989) were removed from the code, but were replaced by 11 crimes of 'endangering state security'. Financial offences, such as money laundering, were also included for the first time, an indication of the rapidly-evolving economic situation. The Procurator-General's annual report to the NPC, detailing the Government's progress in addressing the rising levels of criminal activity, was rejected by some 40% of delegates, in an unprecedented vote of protest.

The 15th National Congress of the CCP convened in mid-September 1997. Emphasis on radical reform of the 370,000 SOEs formed the central theme of the Congress. The economic restructuring measures, however, were not matched by any substantial commitment to political reform. Delegates approved amendments to the party Constitution, enshrining the 'Deng Xiaoping Theory' of socialism with Chinese characteristics alongside 'Mao Zedong Thought' as the guiding ideology of the CCP. The Congress elected a new 344-member Central Committee, which re-elected Jiang Zemin as General Secretary of the CCP, and appointed a 22-member Politburo. The composition of the new Politburo appeared to confirm Jiang Zemin's enhanced authority: Qiao Shi, a reformist and Jiang's most influential rival, who was ranked third in the party hierarchy, was excluded, reportedly because of his age, as was Gen. Liu Huaqing, China's most senior military figure. Zhu Rongji, a former mayor of Shanghai, replaced Qiao Shi, and was also widely regarded as the likely successor to Li Peng, on Li's retirement as Premier of the State Council in March 1998. Gen. Liu was replaced by a civilian, Wei Jinxiang, who was responsible for combating corruption within the CCP. The absence of the military from the Politburo, and the composition of the new Central Military Commission, confirmed Jiang's increased authority over the PLA.

At the first session of the Ninth NPC, which commenced in early March 1998, a bureaucratic restructuring was approved, in which the number of ministry-level bodies was reduced from 40 to 29, mainly through mergers. On 16 March Jiang Zemin was re-elected President of the State Council, and Hu Jintao was elected Vice-President. Li Peng resigned as Premier and was replaced by Zhu Rongji, who received overwhelming support from the NPC delegates. Li Peng replaced Qiao Shi as Chairman of the NPC. However, showing unusual defiance, more than 10% of delegates voted against him or abstained. Zhu's appointments to a new 39-member State Council included the replacement of Qian Qichen as Minister of Foreign Affairs (although he retained his position as a Vice-Premier) by Tang Jiaxuan, formerly a Vice-Minister of Foreign Affairs. Tang was reportedly close to Jiang Zemin, whose associates also assumed responsibility for the defence and state security portfolios. Zhu also promoted a number of technocrats who were supportive of his own policies, most notably Xiang Huaicheng, hitherto a Vice-Minister of Finance, who was allocated the finance portfolio.

At the second session of the Ninth NPC, held in March 1999, a number of constitutional amendments were ratified, including the elevation in status of private-sector and other non-state enterprises to 'important components of the socialist market economy', a recommendation for adherence to the rule of law, and the incorporation of Deng Xiaoping's ideology into the Constitution alongside Marxism-Leninism and 'Mao Zedong thought'. In October Hu Jintao was appointed a Vice-Chairman of the Central Military Commission, and in December Zeng Qinghong became a full member of the Politburo, replacing Xie Fei, who had died in September.

Public disquiet over corruption within the CCP, the state bureaucracy and economic enterprises was acknowledged in August 1993, when the Party initiated an anti-corruption campaign. Hundreds of executions of officials were subsequently reported, and in April 1995, following allegations of corruption, Wang Baosen, a deputy mayor of Beijing, committed suicide. In the same month Chen Xitong, Secretary of the Beijing Municipality Committee, was arrested. An extensive inquiry concluded that Wang Baosen, a protégé of Chen Xitong, had been responsible for serious irregularities, including the embezzlement of the equivalent of millions of US dollars. In September, having been similarly disgraced, Chen Xitong was expelled from the Politburo and from the Central Committee of the CCP. In April 1996 it was announced that proceedings against 18 (unidentified) associates of Wang Baosen were to be instigated. Owing to his implication in the scandal, the mayor of Beijing, Li Qiyan, finally resigned in October 1996. The campaign against corruption intensified in 1997 with the sentencing in August of Chen Xiaotong, son of Chen Xitong, to 12 years' imprisonment for the misappropriation of public funds. Lengthy prison terms were also conferred on two former senior officials in the Beijing administration for accepting bribes. In September Chen Xitong was expelled from the CCP. In August 1998 he was sentenced to 16 years' imprisonment for corruption and dereliction of duty; a subsequent appeal was rejected by the Supreme People's Court. It was reported that between October 1992 and June 1997 121,000 people had been expelled from the CCP for corruption, while 37,500 others had faced criminal charges.

In an attempt to eradicate illicit trade, in July 1998 President Jiang Zemin ordered the closure of all the business interests of the PLA, comprising some 15,000 companies across all sections of the economy. The divestment of all the PLA's enterprises to a state body, styled the Takeover Office for Military, Armed Police, Government and Judiciary Businesses, was completed by mid-December.

The number of labour disputes increased significantly in 1996 and 1997. In March 1997, in the worst unrest since 1949, more than 20,000 workers at a silk factory in Sichuan Province took part in a demonstration to demand payment of substantial wage arrears. Further protests by disaffected workers in a variety of sectors took place throughout the year. Grievances ranged from dismissal and reductions in wages and benefits to allegations of fraud against local party officials. Labour unrest intensified in 1998, as the restructuring of the SOEs led to massive redundancies.

An extensive operation to counter the sharp increase in crimes such as drugs-trafficking, prostitution and the distribution of pornography continued, resulting in hundreds of executions. In April 1996 the Government initiated 'Strike Hard', a new campaign against crime, executing hundreds of people. In September 1998 Amnesty International released a report stating that China had executed 1,876 people in 1997, more than the rest of the world combined. This represented, however, a considerable reduction compared with the 4,367 executions documented in 1996.

China's treatment of political dissidents attracted international attention in November 1997, with the release on medical grounds into exile in the USA of Wei Jingsheng. Wei had been imprisoned in 1979, but was released on parole in September 1993 (shortly before the International Olympic Committee was due to vote upon the venue for the 2000 Games, for which Beijing was bidding). He was rearrested, however, in April 1994, and detained incommunicado until December 1995, when he was convicted of conspiring to overthrow the Government. His sentencing to 14 years' imprisonment provoked an international outcry, and he was released shortly after Jiang Zemin's visit to the USA in October 1997 (see below). Bao Ge, a prominent Shanghai dissident and campaigner for compensation for Chinese victims of Japanese war aggression, was released from three years' imprisonment without trial in June. He left for the USA in November.

In June 1990 Fang Lizhi, the prominent astrophysicist and dissident, was permitted to leave the country for the United Kingdom. In October Wang Ruowang, the eminent writer and dissident, was released from prison after 13 months in detention. In January 1991 the trials of many of those arrested during the pro-democracy protests of 1989 commenced. Most activists received relatively short prison sentences. In July 1992 Bao Tong, a senior aide of Zhao Ziyang, the former General Secretary of the CCP, was found guilty of involvement in the pro-democracy unrest of mid-1989. At the end of his seven-year prison sentence, Bao Tong was released in May 1996 and placed under house arrest. He was freed from house arrest in May 1997, but remained under constant police surveillance.

In September 1992, following his return to China from exile in the USA, Shen Tong, a leader of the pro-democracy movement, was arrested and later deported. In February 1994 Asia Watch, an independent New York-based human rights organization, issued a highly critical report of the situation in China, which detailed the cases of more than 1,700 detainees, imprisoned for their political, ethnic or religious views. In April, shortly before the USA was due to decide upon a renewal of China's favourable trading status, Wang Juntao, imprisoned for his part in the 1989 protests, was unexpectedly released and permitted to travel to the USA for medical treatment. Other releases followed. In July, however, the trial on charges of counter-revolutionary activity of 14 members of a dissident group, in detention since 1992, commenced. In December 1994 nine of the defendants received heavy prison sentences. A university lecturer, Hu Shigen, was sentenced to 20 years' imprisonment.

In February 1993 Wang Dan and Guo Haifeng, leading student activists in the 1989 demonstrations, were freed. In late 1994, however, complaining of police harassment, Wang Dan filed a lawsuit against the authorities. He was rearrested in May 1995. The imposition of an 11-year sentence on Wang Dan at the conclusion of his cursory trial on charges of conspiracy, in October 1996, received international condemnation. Appeals for his release on medical grounds in 1997 were rejected, but in April 1998 he was released on medical parole and was sent into exile in the USA on the following day. In May 1993, having served 12 years of a 15-year sentence, Xu Wenli was released from prison. He was rearrested in April 1994, but released shortly afterwards. In August 1993 the arrest and expulsion from China of Han Dongfang, a trade union activist who had attempted to return to his homeland after a year in the USA, attracted much international attention.

In June 1995 Liu Gang, a leader of the 1989 uprising, was released from prison, and in May 1996 he was granted temporary asylum in the USA. Two further dissidents, Ren Wanding and Zhang Xianliang, were freed upon completion of their prison terms in June 1996. Having been released in the same month, Wang Xizhe escaped from Guangzhou and was permitted to enter the USA in October. His fellow activist, Liu Xiaobo, was arrested in Beijing, however, and ordered to serve three years in a labour camp. In November, shortly before a visit to China by the US Secretary of State, Chen Zeming, another alleged leader of the 1989 pro-democracy demonstrations, was released on medical parole.

In 1997 there was increasing pressure on the CCP to reconsider its assessment of the 1989 Tiananmen Square pro-democracy demonstrations as a 'counter-revolutionary rebellion'. In June 1997, in an unprecedented decision, a court in Liaoning Province overturned convictions of 'counter-revolution' against four dissidents imprisoned for their role in the 1989 pro-democracy movement. However, an appeal to the CCP National Congress by Zhao Ziyang, who remained under house arrest, to reassess the official verdict, was dismissed. During Jiang's visit to the USA, in October 1997, having first described the brutal treatment of the 1989 demonstrators as a 'necessary measure', a subsequent acknowledgement that mistakes may have been made was not, according to the Chinese authorities, to be regarded as an apology. Amnesty International reported that in mid-1997 some 303 people remained in prison for their part in the pro-democracy movement. Beijing, however, declared that there were no political prisoners in China, classifying as criminals the estimated 2,000 people imprisoned on charges of 'counter-revolution'.

The UN Commissioner for Human Rights, Mary Robinson, made an unprecedented official visit to China and Hong Kong in September 1998. Following the visit, on 5 October China signed the International Covenant on Civil and Political Rights in New York, guaranteeing freedom of expression, a fair trial and protection against arbitrary arrest. Although the Government's signing of the Covenant was hailed as a great advance in its attitude towards human rights, the treaty would only come into force once ratified by the NPC. No date was set for ratification.

In 1998 attempts by dissidents in Beijing and the provinces to create an opposition party, the Chinese Democratic Party (CDP), with the principal aim of democratic elections, were suppressed by the Government. The exiled dissident, Wang Binzhang, was deported to the USA in February after entering the country to meet fellow opposition activists. Attempts to register the party in 14 provinces resulted in numerous arrests and detentions throughout the year. In November the Government published a judicial interpretation of the crimes of political subversion (thereby expanding existing punishable offences), specifying that 'incitement to subvert state power' would result in imprisonment for between three years and life for any publisher, musician, author, artist or filmmaker found guilty of the charge. In December at least 30 members of the CDP were detained, and three veteran activists, Xu Wenli, Qin Yongmin and Wang Youcai, were sentenced to 13, 12 and 11 years' imprisonment, respectively, provoking strong international condemnation. Human rights groups declared the release on medical parole and subsequent exile to the USA of the prominent dissident, Liu Nianchun, shortly before the conviction of the CDP activists, to be an attempt to deflect criticism of their trials. A speech by President Jiang Zemin in December appeared to confirm the end of a period of relative tolerance of political dissent. By November 1999 a further 18 CDP leaders had been convicted of subverting state power and sentenced to lengthy terms of imprisonment.

At the first Sino-US discussions on human rights for four years in Washington DC in January 1999 the US delegation urged their Chinese counterparts to halt their harsh treatment of dissidents. In February of that year two dissidents, Gao Yu (a journalist) and Sun Weibang, who had received substantial sentences, were released ahead of schedule, prompting speculation that Beijing was attempting to counter criticism before the imminent visit to the People's Republic by the US Secretary of State and the forthcoming meeting of the UN Commission on Human Rights in Geneva. None the less, China continued its suppression of dissent. In late April, however, a US-sponsored resolution at the aforementioned UN Commission meeting, condemning China's human rights record, was defeated. A number of activists were detained in advance of the 10th anniversary of the killings in Tiananmen Square in June 1999; despite official fears, the day passed without major incident in Beijing (in Hong Kong, however, thousands attended a commemorative rally). The Square had been closed for some time, ostensibly for repairs before the 50th anniversary of the founding of the People's Republic in October, and did not reopen until late June.

The CCP's desire to protect its supremacy became increasingly apparent when it banned the popular Falun Gong religious cult in July 1999, on the grounds that it constituted a threat to society. The ban was prompted by demonstrations, attended by tens of thousands of supporters in numerous towns and cities, in protest at the arrest of more than 100 adherents of the sect. The authorities embarked on a campaign of harsh persecution of both leaders and followers who refused to renounce their faith, and by the end of the month more than 6,000 arrests had been made in connection with the sect. The authorities had been initially alarmed by a peaceful protest in central Beijing, attended by some 10,000 practitioners in April. Four members of the sect were imprisoned in December, with sentences ranging from seven to 18 years, for their part in organizing the demonstration. This followed the conviction and imprisonment of four of Falun Gong's provincial leaders in November. The authorities were also concerned by the high level of Falun Gong membership among CCP and PLA officials. The CCP took the opportunity to demonstrate its continuing power on 1 October 1999, with lavish but strictly controlled celebrations of the 50th anniversary of the foundation of the People's Republic of China. In a highly symbolic gesture, a picture of Jiang Zemin was paraded alongside portraits of Mao Zedong and Deng Xiaoping: the first time that the current President had been publicly placed on a par with his predecessors. In January 2000 five Catholic bishops were ordained in a show of strength by the state-controlled Chinese Catholic Church, impeding any improvement in relations with the Vatican, which opposed the ordination. In August 1999 Beijing had refused to grant permission for the Pope to visit Hong Kong later in the year, owing to the Vatican's links with Taiwan.

Tibet (Xizang), a semi-independent region of western China, was occupied in October 1950 by Chinese Communist forces. In March 1959 there was an unsuccessful armed uprising by Tibetans opposed to Chinese rule. The Dalai Lama, the head of Tibet's Buddhist clergy and thus the region's spiritual leader, fled with some 100,000 supporters to Dharamsala, northern India, where a government-in-exile was established. The Chinese ended the former dominance of the lamas (Buddhist monks) and destroyed many monasteries. Tibet became an 'Autonomous Region' of China in September 1965, but the majority of Tibetans have continued to regard the Dalai Lama as their 'god-king', and to resent the Chinese presence. In October 1987 violent clashes occurred in Lhasa (the regional capital) between the Chinese authorities and Tibetans seeking independence. Further demonstrations during a religious festival in March 1988 resulted in a riot and several deaths, and a number of Tibetan separatists were arrested and detained without trial. The Dalai Lama, however, renounced demands for complete independence, and in 1988 proposed that Tibet become a self-governing Chinese territory, in all respects except foreign affairs. In December 1988 an offer from the Dalai Lama to meet Chinese representatives in Geneva was rejected, and later that month two more demonstrators were killed by security forces during a march to commemorate the 40th anniversary of the UN General Assembly's adoption of the Universal Declaration of Human Rights.

On 7 March 1989 martial law was imposed in Lhasa for the first time since 1959, after further violent clashes between separatists and the Chinese police, which resulted in the deaths of 16 protesters. In October 1989 the Chinese Government condemned as an interference in its internal affairs the award of the Nobel Peace Prize to the Dalai Lama. In November several Tibetan Buddhist nuns claimed to have been severely tortured for their part in the demonstrations in March of that year. In early May 1990 martial law was lifted in Lhasa. Human rights groups claimed that during the last six months of the period of martial law as many as 2,000 persons had been executed. Furthermore, political and religious repression and torture were reported to be continuing throughout 1990. Renewed anti-Chinese protests were reported in October 1991 and in March 1992. In May a report issued by Amnesty International was critical of the Chinese authorities' violations of the human rights of the monks and nuns of Tibet. A document entitled *Tibet—Its Ownership and Human Rights Situation* was published by the Chinese Government in September, attempting to prove that historically the region is part of China. In May 1993 several thousand Tibetans were reported to have demonstrated in Lhasa against Chinese rule. A number of protesters were believed to have been killed by the security forces. In January 1994 two prominent Tibetan activists were released from detention. In July, however, five secessionists were found guilty of counter-revolutionary acts and received prison sentences of up to 15 years.

In March 1994 the Dalai Lama, who had continued to demand only limited autonomy for Tibet, acknowledged that he had made no progress in his attempts to negotiate with the Chinese authorities and, recognizing the disillusionment of many Tibetans, indicated that his moderate approach might be reviewed. In the following month China condemned the Dalai Lama's meeting with President Clinton during the former's lecture tour of the USA. In September the Dalai Lama warned China that Tibet might resort to armed uprising if oppression continued to worsen. In late 1994 the construction of new monasteries and temples in Tibet was banned. In March 1995 regulations restricting the number of Buddhist monks were announced, and in the same month the Dalai Lama's proposal that a referendum be held on the future of Tibet was dismissed by China. In May the Dalai Lama's nomination of the 11th incarnation of the Panchen Lama (the second position in the spiritual hierarchy, the 10th incumbent having died in 1989) was condemned by the Chinese authorities, which stated that the six-year old boy would not be allowed to travel to Dharamsala. In early September 1995, as the 30th anniversary of the imposition of Chinese rule approached, it was reported that independence activists had carried out two bombings in Lhasa.

In September 1995, during the UN World Conference on Women and the Non-Governmental Organizations' Forum held concurrently in China, a silent protest by a group of female Tibetan exiles attracted much attention. Following an informal meeting between the Dalai Lama and President Clinton in Washington in mid-September, China lodged a strong protest. In November the Chinese Government announced its own nomination of a new Panchen Lama. The boy was enthroned at a ceremony in Lhasa in December, the whereabouts of the Dalai Lama's choice remaining unknown until mid-1996, when China's ambassador to the UN in Geneva admitted that the boy was in detention in Beijing. There were violent confrontations in Tibet in May 1996, following the banning of any public display of images of the Dalai Lama. During a visit to the United Kingdom in July the Dalai Lama urged democratic countries to put pressure on China to improve the human rights situation in his homeland. In September the Dalai Lama's visit to Australia and his reception by the Prime Minister aroused further protests from the Chinese Government. A series of minor explosions during 1996 culminated in late December with the detonation of a powerful bomb outside a government office in Lhasa. The attack, which injured several people and caused extensive damage, was denounced by the Dalai Lama, who warned of the likelihood of an increase in repression by the Chinese authorities. In an unprecedented admission, the Chinese Government acknowledged the existence of a terrorist problem in Tibet.

The Chinese leadership condemned the Dalai Lama's visit to Taiwan in March 1997, despite assurances that he was visiting in his capacity as a spiritual leader. In May it was reported that Chatral Rinpoche, an official in the Tibetan administration, and one of Tibet's most senior monks, had been sentenced to six years' imprisonment for allegedly revealing information to the Dalai Lama about Beijing's search for the new Panchen Lama. The USA's decision in mid-1997 to appoint a special co-ordinator for Tibet was criticized by the Chinese authorities. In October the Dalai Lama appealed to the Chinese Government to reopen negotiations over the status of Tibet, confirming that he did not seek full independence for the region. In December the Geneva-based International Commission of Jurists (see p. 306) published a report accusing China of suppressing nationalist dissent in Tibet and attempting to extinguish Tibetan culture, and appealed for a referendum, under the auspices of the UN, to decide the territory's future status.

In April 1998 China agreed to allow EU envoys to make a one-week investigatory visit to Tibet. Later that month in New Delhi, India, Thupten Ngodup, one of six Tibetan exiles, who had been engaged in a hunger strike for 49 days, died after setting himself alight as security forces attempted forcibly to transport the protesters to hospital to end their hunger strike. The hunger strikers had declared their intention of starving themselves to death unless the UN agreed to debate Tibet in the UN General Assembly, appoint a special rapporteur to investigate human rights violations and oversee a referendum on independence. The protest was arranged by the Tibetan Youth Congress (TYC), a movement advocating independence for Tibet. In May 1998 the EU adopted two resolutions relating to China, condemning the sale of organs of prisoners awaiting execution and calling for a UN committee to investigate the issue and urging the UN to appoint a rapporteur for Tibet issues. During her visit to China in September (see above), the UN Commissioner for Human Rights, Mary Robinson, visited Tibet.

During his visit to China and Hong Kong in late June 1998 (see below), the US President, Bill Clinton, discussed Tibet with Chinese leaders, with the Dalai Lama's support. Beijing proclaimed its readiness to open negotiations if the Dalai Lama first declared both Tibet and Taiwan to be inalienable parts of China. This statement was repeated regularly during 1998. In October the Dalai Lama admitted that since the 1960s he had received US $1.7m. annually from the CIA to support the Tibetan separatist movement. Whilst visiting the USA in early November the Dalai Lama had an unofficial meeting with Bill Clinton, thereby angering the Chinese authorities. Later that month the Dalai Lama requested informal talks with the Chinese leadership before he would make any unilateral statement. In December he was presented with a human rights prize by the French Prime Minister, Lionel Jospin, in Paris.

In January 1999 a new US special co-ordinator for Tibetan affairs was appointed, amid opposition from China, which declared that no other country had the right to interfere in Tibet's affairs, the territory being an inalienable part of the People's Republic. Earlier in the month TYC activists had attempted to storm the Chinese embassy in New Delhi and had burnt Chinese flags outside the building to protest against China's occupation of Tibet. In May of that year the Dalai Lama visited the United Kingdom and met the British Prime Minister, Tony Blair. In order to avoid criticism from Beijing, it was reported that Blair had received the religious leader in a spiritual capacity. The World Bank provoked US anger in the following month, when it approved a loan to settle 58,000 Chinese farmers on land in western China considered by Tibetans to be their own. Tibetan support groups feared that the project would aid China's policy of diluting the minority Tibetan population living in the region. It was agreed that no funds would be disbursed until an independent panel had ensured that the plan conformed to World Bank rules. In August Sino-US relations deteriorated further following the injury in police custody of a US academic and human rights activist who had been detained whilst conducting an unofficial investigation into the project; he was reportedly released and repatriated in September. In January 2000 the Chinese Government was embarrassed by the flight of Tibet's second most important Lama, the Karmapa, from Tibet to Dharamsala. Frequent requests by him to be permitted to visit his guru in India had been ignored. The Karmapa, who had, unusually, been recognized both by the Dalai Lama and by Beijing, had previously been rewarded by the latter for his perceived loyalty to the Chinese regime.

Anti-Chinese sentiment in the Xinjiang Uygur Autonomous Region intensified in early 1990, and in April as many as 60 people were reported to have been killed when government troops opened fire on Muslim protesters. A new campaign to repress the Islamic separatist movement was initiated and in October 1993 protests by thousands of Muslims in Qinghai Province were brutally suppressed by the authorities. Suppression of separatism intensified in 1996, following a number of violent incidents. Hundreds of people were detained for their part in rioting and bomb attacks, and many were subsequently executed or given lengthy terms of imprisonment. Reports in late 1997 indicated that there had been a renewal of armed separatist activity, prior to the Chinese national day, in which more than 300 people had been killed. In January 1998 13 people were executed in Xinjiang, allegedly for robbery and murder, although unofficial reports suggested that those executed were Muslim separatist demonstrators. Muslim separatists were believed to be responsible for an incendiary device on a bus in Wuhan in February, which killed 16 people. Two leading Muslim separatists, Yibulayin Simayi and Abudureyimu Aisha, were executed in January 1999. Detentions continued during the year, and a further 10 separatists were allegedly executed at the end of May. Three Muslims were sentenced to death in September for participating in the separatist campaign, whilst six others received lengthy prison sentences.

In September 1984, following protracted negotiations, China reached agreement with the British Government over the terms of Chinese administration of Hong Kong, following its return to Chinese sovereignty on 1 July 1997. In 1985 a Basic Law Drafting Committee (BLDC), including 25 representatives from Hong Kong, was established in Beijing to prepare a new Basic Law (Constitution) for Hong Kong. The Basic Law for Hong Kong was approved by the NPC in April 1990. High-level consultations on the future of Hong Kong were held in 1990 and 1991. In September 1991, during a visit to China by the British Prime Minister, a Memorandum of Understanding on the construction of a new airport in Hong Kong was signed. Relations between China and the United Kingdom were strained in 1992 by the announcement of ambitious plans for democratic reform in Hong Kong prior to 1997. In January 1993 a senior Chinese official warned that Hong Kong would experience 'hardship' if the programme of political reform were pursued. China and the United Kingdom resumed negotiations in April on the future of the territory, thus ending an impasse of several months. By the end of the year, however, no progress had been made, and in December, following Hong Kong's decision to press ahead with electoral reform, China declared that it would regard as null and void any laws enacted by the territory's Legislative Council. In December 1994 Lu Ping, the director of the mainland Hong Kong and Macau Affairs Office, formally confirmed that the Legislative Council of Hong Kong would be disbanded in 1997. A detailed accord on the financing of Hong Kong's new airport was signed in June 1995. In the same month China and the United Kingdom also reached agreement on the contentious issue of the establishment in Hong Kong (in 1997) of the Court of Final Appeal. In early July the Chief Secretary of Hong Kong, Anson Chan, confirmed that she had had clandestine meetings with Chinese officials during a three-day visit to Beijing. The improvement in Sino-British relations was confirmed in October when Qian Qichen, the Chinese Vice-Premier and Minister of Foreign Affairs, visited London for discussions with the British Prime Minister and his Foreign Secretary. In November 1995, however, the Governor of Hong Kong warned the Chinese Government that its repudiation of the territory's Bill of Rights, enacted in June 1991, would be detrimental to international confidence. China's disclosure of a plan to establish a parallel administration six months prior to the transfer of sovereignty aroused further controversy.

In January 1996 the 150-member Preparatory Committee of the Hong Kong Special Administrative Region (SAR) was formally established in Beijing, in succession to the Preliminary Working Committee (PWC), which had been formed in July 1993 to study issues relating to the transfer of sovereignty. Chaired by Qian Qichen and comprising 56 mainland and 94 Hong Kong delegates, including representatives of the territory's business and academic communities, the new body was to appoint a 400-member Selection Committee responsible for the choice of Hong Kong's future Chief Executive. In March 1996 the Preparatory Committee approved a resolution to appoint a provisional body to replace Hong Kong's Legislative Council. In September China and the United Kingdom finally reached agreement on the contentious issue of arrangements for the ceremony to mark the transfer of sovereignty on 30 June 1997. In December 1996 the Selection Committee chose Tung Chee-hwa as the Hong Kong SAR's first Chief Executive and elected the 60 members of the Provisional Legislative Council (PLC). The PLC held its first meeting in January 1997. Objections from the United Kingdom and the USA to Chinese proposals to abolish the Legislative Council, and to repeal human rights legislation, were dismissed by China. In May the PLC approved its first bill, despite previous assurances that no legislation would be passed before the handover. However, following objections from democracy campaigners, it was declared that the legislation would only become effective on 1 July.

The handover of Hong Kong from British to Chinese sovereignty was effected at midnight on 30 June 1997. Shortly afterwards some 4,000 PLA troops were deployed in Hong Kong, joining two smaller contingents that had arrived earlier, following protracted negotiations with the United Kingdom. The Government of the new SAR announced that elections to a new Legislative Council would be held in 1998. The elections took place on 24 May, following revisions to the SAR's electoral law, introduced in September 1997, which disenfranchised many voters. (For further information, see chapter on Hong Kong.) On 8 December 1997 36 deputies from Hong Kong were directly elected to the Ninth NPC. Protests ensued because no member of the Democratic Party managed to obtain the 10 nominations from the election conference needed to stand in the election. The question of the right of abode in the territory for mainland-born children (see chapter on Hong Kong) caused problems in 1999. Beijing's assistance was sought by the SAR Chief Executive in restricting the influx of mainland immigrants by a reinterpretation of the Basic Law, following a ruling in January by the SAR Court of Final Appeal that effectively revoked restrictive immigration legislation. There was much opposition in Hong Kong to this undermining of the SAR's autonomy. However, in December the SAR Court of Final Appeal confirmed the NPC's supremacy over the SAR, by ruling that the Government of mainland China had a right to interpret the Basic Law and to overturn judgments by the Court of Final Appeal. The second anniversary of the resumption of Chinese sovereignty prompted a pro-democracy protest against the administration in June by 2,000 demonstrators in Hong Kong. Meanwhile, following the NATO bombing of the Chinese embassy in Yugoslavia (see below), US military aircraft and ships were denied access to Hong Kong. The ban was revoked in July.

Taiwan has repeatedly rejected China's proposals for reunification, whereby the island would become a 'special administrative region' along the lines of Hong Kong, and has sought reunification under its own terms. China threatened military intervention, should Taiwan declare itself independent of the mainland. Trade and reciprocal visits greatly increased in 1988, as relations improved. Reconciliation initiatives were abruptly halted, however, by the violent suppression of the pro-democracy movement in June 1989.

In May 1990 President Lee of Taiwan suggested the opening of direct dialogue on a government-to-government basis with the People's Republic. Beijing, however, maintained that it would negotiate only on a party-to-party basis with the Kuomintang. In April 1991 a delegation from the Straits Exchange Foundation (SEF) of Taiwan, established in late 1990 to handle bilateral issues, travelled to China for discussions, the first such delegation ever to visit the People's Republic. The Association for Relations across the Taiwan Straits (ARATS) was established in Beijing in December 1991. In May 1992 the People's Republic rejected Taiwan's proposal for a non-aggression pact. Nevertheless, in April 1993 historic talks between the Chairmen of the ARATS and SEF took place in Singapore, where a formal structure for future negotiations on economic and social issues was agreed. In August, however, the People's Republic issued a document entitled *The Taiwan Question and the Reunification of China,* reaffirming its claim to sovereignty over the island. Relations were further strained by a series of aircraft hijackings from the mainland to Taiwan, and they deteriorated sharply in April 1994, when 24 Taiwanese tourists were among those robbed and murdered on board a pleasure boat on Qiandao Lake, Zhejiang Province. In June three men were convicted of the murders and promptly executed. In August Tang Shubei, the Vice-Chairman and Secretary-General of the ARATS, travelled to Taipei for discussions, the most senior CCP official ever to visit the island. In mid-November relations were strained once again when, in an apparent accident during a training exercise, Taiwanese anti-aircraft shells landed on a mainland village, injuring several people. Nevertheless, in late November a further round of ARATS-SEF talks took place in Nanjing, at which agreement in principle on the procedure for the repatriation of hijackers and illegal immigrants was confirmed.

Discussions were resumed in Beijing in January 1995. At the end of that month President Jiang Zemin announced an 'eight-point' policy for Taiwan's peaceful reunification with the mainland. In response, in April, President Lee proposed a 'six-point' programme for cross-Straits relations (see p. 1021). Following President Lee's controversial visit to the USA in June, however, the ARATS postponed the forthcoming second session of SEF discussions at senior level. Cross-Straits relations deteriorated further in July upon the People's Republic's announcement that it was to conduct a series of guided missile and artillery-firing tests off the northern coast of Taiwan. In the following month President Jiang Zemin confirmed that the People's Republic would not renounce the use of force against Taiwan, and President Lee reaffirmed the island's commitment to reunification.

In early 1996 unconfirmed reports suggested that 400,000 mainland troops had been mobilized around Fujian Province. A new series of missile tests began in March, arousing international concern. Live artillery exercises were conducted in the Taiwan Strait. Tension subsequently eased, however, and at the end of April the SEF urged that bilateral discussions be resumed. Cross-Straits co-operation was renewed from mid-1996: mainland executives from the transport, petroleum, trade and finance sectors travelled to Taiwan. In November President Lee's renewed offer to visit the mainland was rebuffed. In January 1997, however, as the reversion of the entrepôt of Hong Kong to Chinese sovereignty approached, representatives of the People's Republic and Taiwan reached a preliminary consensus on the issue of direct shipping links. Limited services resumed in April, thus ending a ban of 48 years.

Major military exercises were carried out in Taiwan in June 1997. In August the deputy secretary-general of the ARATS, the highest-ranking Chinese official to visit Taiwan since 1995, held talks with members of the SEF. However, in the following month President Lee's assertion of Taiwan's independence threatened the renewal of negotiations. An invitation for the resumption of more formal talks, on the basis of the 'one China' principle, was made by Jiang Zemin in October. Following the success of the pro-independence Democratic Progressive Party in the Taiwanese mayoral elections in November, divisions within Taiwan over its relationship with the People's Republic were becoming apparent. Support for reunification with China was weakening, although many in the business community were opposed to President Lee's continued ban on direct links with the mainland. In July 1998 Lee reaffirmed his commitment to reunification with the People's Republic under a system of democracy for all.

Following preliminary visits by members of the ARATS and SEF, Koo Chen-fu, Chairman of the SEF, visited China for cross-straits talks in October 1998. He held several meetings with his ARATS counterpart, Wang Daohan, as well as an historic meeting with Jiang Zemin and Qian Qichen on 18 October. A four-point agreement was reached, allowing for increased communications between the two sides. In response to Taiwanese concerns over the widely publicized killings of its citizens on the mainland (see chapter on Taiwan for further information), the two sides also agreed to improve co-operation in order to protect the lives and property of each other's citizens. Wang accepted an invitation for a reciprocal visit to Taiwan in March 1999.

In January 1999 the ARATS invited the SEF Deputy Secretary-General to visit the People's Republic for talks in order to prepare for Wang Daohan's visit. The SEF made a counter-proposal that ARATS officials visit Taiwan to discuss preparations. In the following month, during a flight to the island of Kinmen, an SEF official was attacked by four Chinese convicted aircraft hijackers, who were part of a group being transferred to the nearby island prior to their repatriation to the mainland. During the following months Taiwan repatriated several hundred Chinese illegal immigrants. In March an ARATS delegation, led by Deputy Secretary-General Lin Yafei, visited Taiwan. It was agreed that Wang Daohan's visit would take place later in the year, but no date was set. In April President Lee reaffirmed that Beijing should recognize Taiwan as being of equal status. An SEF group went to Beijing in March, and a preliminary agreement was reached that Wang Daohan would visit Taiwan in either mid-September or mid-October. In August, however, the ARATS suspended contacts with the SEF, following President Lee's insistence on the 'two-state theory' (see below), and it was confirmed in October that Wang Daohan would not visit Taiwan as long as it adhered to the theory.

Meanwhile, China was becoming increasingly demonstrative in its opposition to Taiwan's inclusion in the US-led Theater Missile Defence anti-missile system. Ballistic missiles were deployed in mainland coastal regions facing Taiwan, and fears were heightened within the international community in July 1999, when the People's Republic announced that it had developed a neutron bomb, after declaring itself ready for war should Taiwan attempt to gain independence. This declaration was prompted by an interview given by President Lee to a German radio station, during which he asserted that relations with the People's Republic were 'state-to-state'. Chinese military exercises took place in the Taiwan Strait later that month, allegedly to intimidate Taiwan. Faced with this aggression and a lack of US support, Taiwan promised that it would not amend its Constitution to enshrine its claim to statehood in law. In August the USA reaffirmed its readiness to defend Taiwan against Chinese military action. Shortly afterwards the Taiwanese Government refused a request by Beijing that it retract the 'state-to-state' theory with regard to cross-Straits relations, and tension increased in late August when the KMT incorporated the 'two-state theory' into the party resolution, claiming that this would henceforth become the administrative guideline and priority of the Taiwanese authorities. Later that month the Mainland Affairs Council announced that former Taiwan government officials involved in affairs related to national intelligence or secrets were not to be permitted to travel to China within three years of leaving their posts. In September, however, following a severe earthquake in Taiwan that killed or injured several thousand people, China was among the many countries to offer emergency assistance to the island. Taiwan, however, accused the People's Republic of contravening humanitarian principles by trying to force other countries to seek its approval before offering help.

In June 1986 China and Portugal opened formal negotiations for the return of the Portuguese overseas territory of Macau to full Chinese sovereignty. In January 1987 Portugal agreed that withdrawal from Macau should take place in December 1999. The agreement is based upon the 'one country, two systems' principle, which formed the basis of China's negotiated settlement regarding the return of Hong Kong. In March 1993 the final draft of the Basic Law for Macau was approved by the NPC. In May 1995 China proposed the swift establishment of a preparatory working committee to facilitate the transfer of sovereignty. Cordial relations were maintained, and the Portuguese Minister of Foreign Affairs visited Beijing in February 1996. The two sides agreed to accelerate the pace of work of the Sino-Portuguese Joint Liaison Group (JLG). In January 1997 Qian Qichen travelled to Portugal for discussions. Confidence in the future of Macau was reiterated. Following a wave of murders, bombings and arson attacks in Macau, Qian Qichen announced that China would station an 'appropriate' number of troops in Macau to help combat organized crime and ensure public security when it resumed sovereignty in December 1999.

In April 1999 the 200-member Selection Committee, which was comprised entirely of residents of the territory and which was to be responsible for the appointment of members to Macau's post-1999 government, was established in Beijing. In the following month Edmund Ho, a banker and a member of the legislature since 1988, was elected first Chief Executive of Macau. China resumed sovereignty of the territory at midnight on 19–20 December 1999, and on the following day Ho was inaugurated and the PLA garrison was established. In general, local reaction was favourable, as it was hoped that China would succeed, where Portugal had failed, in restoring public security.

In the early years of the People's Republic, China was dependent on the USSR for economic and military aid, and Chinese planning was based on the Soviet model, with highly centralized control. From 1955 onwards, however, Mao Zedong set out to develop a distinctively Chinese form of socialism. As a result, the USSR withdrew all technical aid to China in August 1960. Chinese hostility to the USSR increased, and was aggravated by territorial disputes, and by the Soviet invasion of Afghanistan and the Soviet-supported Vietnamese invasion of Cambodia. Sino-Soviet relations remained strained until 1987, when representatives of the two countries signed a partial agreement concerning the exact demarcation of the disputed Sino-Soviet border at the Amur river. The withdrawal of Soviet troops from Afghanistan (completed in February 1989) and Viet Nam's assurance that it would end its military presence in Cambodia by September 1989 resulted in a further *rapprochement*.

In May 1989 the Soviet President, Mikhail Gorbachev, attended a full summit meeting with Deng Xiaoping in Beijing, at which normal state and party relations between the two countries were formally restored. In April 1990 Li Peng paid an official visit to the USSR, the first by a Chinese Premier for 26 years. Jiang Zemin, CCP General Secretary, visited Moscow in May 1991. In December, upon the dissolution of the USSR, China recognized the newly-independent states of the former union. The President of Russia, Boris Yeltsin, visited China in December 1992. In May 1994, in Beijing, Premier Li Peng and his Russian counterpart signed various co-operation agreements relating to the border issue, trade, agriculture and environmental protection. In September President Jiang Zemin travelled to Moscow, the first visit to Russia by a Chinese head of state since 1957. The two sides reached agreement on the formal demarcation of the western section of the border (the eastern section having been delimited in May 1991), and each pledged not to aim nuclear missiles at the other. In June 1995 the Chinese Premier paid an official visit to Russia, where several bilateral agreements were signed.

Sino-Russian relations continued to improve, and in April 1996 in Beijing Presidents Jiang and Yeltsin signed a series of agreements, envisaging the development of closer co-operation in areas such as energy, space research, environmental protection, and the combating of organized crime. Together with their counterparts from Kazakhstan, Kyrgyzstan and Tajikistan, the two Presidents also signed a treaty aimed at reducing tension along their respective borders. Progress on the Sino-Russian border question, and also on matters such as trade, was made during the Chinese Premier's visit to Moscow in December 1996.

A further treaty on military co-operation and border demilitarization was signed by the Presidents of China, Russia, Kazakhstan, Kyrgyzstan and Tajikistan in April 1997, during a visit by President Jiang Zemin to Russia. Presidents Jiang and Yeltsin affirmed their commitment to building a strategic, co-operative partnership, and a Sino-Russian committee on friendship, peace and development was established. Measures to increase bilateral trade were the focus of the Russian Prime Minister's visit to Beijing in June. Progress on the Sino-Russian border issue culminated in the signing of an agreement, during President Yeltsin's visit to Beijing in November, which formally ended the territorial dispute.

In May 1998 a direct telephone link was established between Jiang Zemin and President Yeltsin of Russia, the first between a Chinese leader and a foreign counterpart. In November Jiang visited Yeltsin in Moscow in an informal summit meeting to promote rapidly improving political and economic relations between the two countries. Earlier that month, in Moscow, representatives from Russia, China and the Democratic People's Republic of Korea had signed an inter-governmental agreement on the delimitation of their borders along the Tumannaya River. Relations continued to improve between China and Russia in 1999. In February 11 agreements on bilateral economic and trade co-operation were signed during a visit to Russia by Zhu Rongji. In June, following a visit to China by the Russian Minister of Foreign Affairs, it was announced that a final accord on the demarcation of a common border between the two countries had been agreed after seven years of negotiations. The relevant legal documents were signed in December. During a summit meeting of China, Russia, Kazakhstan, Kyrgyzstan and Tajikistan in the Kyrgyz capital, Bishkek, agreements were signed on the China-Kazakhstan-Kyrgyzstan and the Chinese-Kyrgyz borders. In November it was announced that all Chinese-Kazakh border issues had been completely resolved.

During the 1970s there was an improvement in China's relations with the West and Japan. Almost all Western countries had recognized the Government of the People's Republic as the sole legitimate government of China, and had consequently withdrawn recognition from the 'Republic of China', which had been confined to Taiwan since 1949. For many years, however, the USA refused to recognize the People's Republic, regarding the Taiwan administration as the legitimate Chinese government. In February 1972 President Richard Nixon of the USA visited the People's Republic and acknowledged that 'Taiwan is a part of China'. In January 1979 the USA recognized the People's Republic and severed diplomatic relations with Taiwan.

China's relations with the USA improved steadily throughout the 1980s. Following the suppression of the pro-democracy movement in 1989, however, all high-level government exchanges were suspended and the export of weapons to China was prohibited. In November 1990 President Bush received the Chinese Minister of Foreign Affairs in Washington, thereby resuming contact at the most senior level. In August 1993 the USA imposed sanctions on China, in response to the latter's sales of technology for nuclear-capable missiles to Pakistan, in alleged violation of international non-proliferation guidelines. The sanctions remained in force until October 1994. In October 1995 Sino-US relations appeared to improve when, at a meeting in New York, Presidents Jiang Zemin and Bill Clinton agreed to resume dialogue on various issues, the USA reaffirming its commitment to a 'one China' policy. In November the two countries reached agreement on the resumption of bilateral military contacts.

In February 1996 Sino-US tension was renewed over the issue of China's exports of nuclear-capable technology to Pakistan. Further areas of dispute included China's record on human rights, US import quotas for Chinese textiles, intellectual property rights and the issue of China's membership of the World Trade Organization (WTO).

Another obstacle to good relations between China and the USA is the question of Taiwan, and, in particular, the continued sale of US armaments to Taiwan. Sino-US relations deteriorated in September 1992, upon President Bush's announcement of the sale of 150 F-16 fighter aircraft to Taiwan. China condemned the USA's decision, in September 1994, to expand its official links with Taiwan. In June 1995, following President Clinton's highly controversial decision to grant him a visa, President Lee of Taiwan embarked upon an unofficial visit to the USA, where he met members of the US Congress. The visit provoked outrage in Beijing, and led to the withdrawal of the Chinese ambassador to Washington. In March 1996, as China began a new series of missile tests, the USA stationed two naval convoys east of Taiwan, its largest deployment in Asia since 1975. President Clinton's decision to sell anti-aircraft missiles and other defensive weapons to Taiwan was condemned by China.

Negotiations on the issue of human rights, the USA's growing trade deficit with China, and China's proposed entry into the WTO were the focus of Sino-US relations in 1997. President Jiang Zemin visited the USA in October 1997, the first such visit by a Chinese Head of State since 1985. Discussions centred on trade, human rights and the issue of Chinese exports of nuclear material. Vocal public criticism of China's failure to observe human rights, particularly with regard to Tibet, was widespread in the USA, but the Clinton administration defended its policy of engagement with China, warning of the dangers of isolation. Measures to reduce the trade deficit with China and to hasten China's entry into the WTO were negotiated. In addition, the Chinese Government agreed to control the export of nuclear-related materials, in return for the removal of sanctions on the sale of nuclear-reactor technology to the People's Republic. Increased military co-operation and the holding of annual summit meetings were also agreed.

In April 1998 the US Secretary of State, Madeleine Albright, visited China to prepare for an official visit by President Clinton in late June and early July. Prior to his visit it was announced that China's most favoured nation (subsequently restyled normal trading relations) status would be renewed for a further year. Before the visit Clinton was criticized for his constructive engagement policy, owing to persistent human rights abuses in China. It was also alleged that the PLA had illegally funded Clinton's re-election campaign in 1996. The visit was a diplomatic success, notable for an unprecedented live broadcast in which Clinton and Jiang debated such generally taboo issues as human rights, freedom of speech and the 1989 events in Tiananmen Square. In response to China's pledge in March 1998 to sign the International Covenant on Civil and Political Rights, the USA announced that it would abandon its sponsorship of an annual resolution of the UN Commission on Human Rights condemning China for human rights abuses. The decision, which followed a similar commitment by the EU in February, was deplored by human rights organizations.

Sino-US relations deteriorated significantly during 1999, owing to continued differences over China's human rights record, Tibet, trade relations, espionage and US plans for a missile defence system for Asia. During an official visit by Albright to the People's Republic at the end of February, she reiterated US disapproval at the suppression of organized dissent in China and urged the release of a number of political prisoners (although emphasizing that the USA would continue its policy of separating human rights issues from trade relations). Further acrimonious exchanges took place concerning demands from the US Congress that the proposed US theater missile defence system, which was principally designed to protect Japan and the Republic of Korea, be extended to include Taiwan. During an important visit to the USA by Zhu Rongji in April, despite Zhu's offer of a number of economic concessions in return for a bilateral trade agreement to facilitate WTO entry, no agreement was reached. At a final press conference, however, the two sides affirmed their commitment to signing an agreement by the end of 1999. Although China suspended bilateral negotiations in May, following the NATO bombing of the Chinese embassy in Yugoslavia (see below), China's normal trade relations status was renewed in July. China agreed to resume talks in September, and in November (following 13 years of negotiations) a bilateral trade agreement was concluded, which would allow for China's eventual accession to the WTO. The agreement with the USA was expected to facilitate the conclusion of bilateral trade agreements with the EU and 23 WTO members in 2000.

It was widely believed that the failure to reach a trade agreement in April 1999 was, in part, due to popular US anti-Chinese sentiment, which had been exacerbated by US claims in March that a Chinese spy had stolen important nuclear data during the 1980s. A further disclosure of Chinese espionage (which had allegedly taken place in 1995), involving information relevant to the construction of a 'neutron' bomb emerged during Zhu's visit to the USA. Beijing dismissed the reports as unfounded. The findings of a select committee of the US House of Representatives, which were released in May, confirmed that Chinese spies had systematically stolen US nuclear technology from the late 1970s until the mid-1990s. China denounced the document as a plot to encourage anti-Chinese sentiment and to deflect attention from the bombing of the Chinese embassy in Yugoslavia, which had occurred earlier that month. China had vigorously opposed the NATO bombing of Yugoslavia, during which the Chinese embassy had been severely damaged, leading to the deaths of three people and injuring 20 others. US apologies and explanations were rejected, and violent popular attacks on the US and British diplomatic missions in Beijing, allegedly encouraged by the Government, ensued. Bilateral relations improved slightly in July, when the USA agreed to pay US $4.5m. in compensation to the families of those killed and injured by the bombing, leading to the lifting of a ban imposed on US military access to Hong Kong. In December compensation of US $28m. was agreed for damage caused to the Chinese embassy building.

China's relations with Japan began to deteriorate in 1982, after China complained that passages in Japanese school textbooks sought to justify the Japanese invasion of China in 1937. In June 1989 the Japanese Government criticized the Chinese Government's suppression of the pro-democracy movement and suspended (until late 1990) a five-year aid programme to China. The Prime Minister of Japan visited Beijing for discussions with his Chinese counterpart in August 1991. In April 1992 Jiang Zemin travelled to Japan, the first visit by the General Secretary of the CCP for nine years. In October Emperor Akihito made the first ever imperial visit to the People's Republic. Japan was one of many countries to criticize China's resumption of underground nuclear testing, at Lop Nor in Xinjiang Province, in October 1993. In March 1994 the Japanese Prime Minister paid a visit to China. Relations were seriously strained in May, however, when the Japanese Minister of Justice referred to the 1937 Nanjing massacre (in which more than 300,000 Chinese citizens were killed by Japanese soldiers) as a 'fabrication', and again in August, when a second Japanese minister was obliged to resign, following further controversial remarks about his country's war record. In May 1995, during a visit to Beijing, the Japanese Prime Minister expressed his deep remorse for the wartime atrocities, but offered no formal apology.

China's continuation of its nuclear-testing programme, in defiance of international opinion, prompted Japan to announce a reduction in financial aid to China. In August 1995, after a further test, Japan suspended most of its grant aid to China. Following China's conduct of its 'final' nuclear test in July 1996, and its declaration of a moratorium, Japan resumed grant aid in March 1997. (China signed the Comprehensive Nuclear Test Ban Treaty in September 1996). In July 1996, however, Sino-

Japanese relations were affected by a territorial dispute relating to the Diaoyu (or Senkaku) Islands, a group of uninhabited islets in the East China Sea, to which Taiwan also laid claim. The construction of a lighthouse on one of the islands by a group of Japanese nationalists led to strong protests from the Governments of both the People's Republic and Taiwan. The Japanese Government sought to defuse the tension by withholding recognition of the lighthouse, but did not condemn the right-wing activists responsible. A further incursion in September prompted China to warn of damage to bilateral relations if Japan failed to take action.

At a meeting with President Jiang Zemin during the Asia-Pacific Economic Co-operation (APEC) conference, in November 1996, the Japanese Prime Minister, Ryutaro Hashimoto, apologized for Japanese aggression during the Second World War, and emphasized his desire to resolve the dispute over the Diaoyu Islands. In May 1997, following the landing on one of the Islands by a member of the Japanese Diet, the Japanese Government distanced itself from the incident. The US-Japanese agreement on expanded military co-operation caused further tension in Sino-Japanese relations. Nevertheless, Japan's support for China's entry into the WTO remained firm, while China backed Japanese proposals for a permanent seat on the UN Security Council. Hashimoto visited China in September, when measures to dispose of the thousands of chemical weapons deployed in China by the Japanese troops during the Second World War were discussed. Premier Li Peng visited Japan in November.

Following the normalization of ties between the Japanese Communist Party (JCP) and its Chinese equivalent after a period of more than 30 years, the Chairman of the JCP, Tetsuzo Fuwa, paid an official visit to China in July 1998. The Japanese Minister of Foreign Affairs, Masahiko Komura, visited China in August to prepare for President Jiang's proposed visit to Japan, which was postponed until November, owing to the floods in China. During this visit, the first of its kind by a Chinese Head of State, relations were strained when Japan failed to issue an unequivocal apology for its invasion and occupation of China during 1937–45. The summit meeting between Jiang and the Japanese Prime Minister, Keizo Obuchi, was, nevertheless, deemed to have been successful. Keizo Obuchi paid a reciprocal visit to the People's Republic, intended to repair ties, in July 1999, during which he held summit talks with Zhu Rongji and Jiang Zemin. Tensions remained, but a number of co-operation agreements were reached, including a bilateral accord on terms for China's WTO entry. The People's Republic, however, opposed the new US-Japan defence co-operation guidelines, as it suspected that they could be invoked to defend Taiwan. Obuchi refused to guarantee that Taiwan be excluded from the security arrangements.

The long-standing border dispute with India, which gave rise to a short military conflict in 1962, remained unresolved (see chapter on India). Discussions on the issue were held in 1988 and in 1991, and in September 1993 the two countries signed an agreement to reduce their troops along the frontier and to resolve the dispute by peaceful means. Discussions continued in 1994. In December China and India agreed to hold joint military exercises in mid-1995. In August 1995 it was confirmed that the two countries were to disengage their troops from four border posts in Arunachal Pradesh. Further progress was made at the ninth round of Sino-Indian border discussions, held in October 1996, and during the visit of President Jiang Zemin to India (the first by a Chinese Head of State) in November. Negotiations continued in August 1997. The question of China's nuclear co-operation with Pakistan, however, remained a contentious issue.

The question of the sovereignty of the Spratly (Nansha) Islands, situated in the South China Sea and claimed by six countries (including China and Viet Nam), remained unresolved. By 1994 both China and Viet Nam had awarded petroleum exploration concessions to US companies, leading to increased tension among the claimants. In February 1995 it emerged that Chinese forces had occupied a reef to which the Philippines laid claim, resulting in a formal diplomatic protest from Manila. More than 60 Chinese fishermen and several vessels were subsequently detained by the Philippine authorities. Discussions between the two countries, held in Beijing in March, ended without agreement. After two days of consultations in August, however, China and the Philippines declared their intention to resolve peacefully their claims to the Spratly Islands. In January 1996 the Chinese Government denied any involvement in a naval skirmish in Philippine waters, during which a ship flying the Chinese flag and a Philippine patrol boat exchanged gunfire. In March China and the Philippines agreed to co-operate in combating piracy in the region.

In November 1998 China angered the Philippine Government by building permanent structures on the disputed Mischief Reef. In late November 20 Chinese fishermen were arrested near Mischief Reef by the Philippine navy. Following Chinese protests, the men were released. In December China reiterated both its claim to sovereignty over the Spratly Islands and surrounding water and its commitment to pursuing a peaceful solution through negotiation. Following unsuccessful discussions between the two countries in April 1999, relations deteriorated further in May, when a Chinese fishing vessel sank following a collision with a Philippine navy boat, which was claimed to be accidental by the Philippines but deliberate by the People's Republic. A further Chinese fishing vessel sank in a collision with a Philippine navy vessel in July. A code of conduct for claimants of the Spratly Islands, drafted by members of the Association of South East Asian Nations (ASEAN, see p.128) in late 1999, had not been fully agreed by the organization or signed by China in early 2000.

In 1996 China's application to become a full dialogue partner of the ASEAN Regional Forum (ARF, see p. 129) was approved. It was hoped that this would facilitate discussions on the question of the Spratly Islands. A similar territorial dispute relating to the Paracel (Xisha) Islands, which had been seized by China from South Vietnamese forces in 1974, also remained unresolved. In May 1996, despite having agreed to abide by the UN Convention on the Law of the Sea, China declared an extension of its maritime boundaries in the South China Sea. Other claimants to the Paracel Islands, in particular Indonesia, the Philippines and Viet Nam, expressed grave concern at China's apparent expansionism.

In August and October 1990 diplomatic relations were established with Indonesia and Singapore respectively. During 1992 China established diplomatic relations with Israel and with the Republic of Korea. China remained committed to the achievement of peace on the Korean peninsula, and in June 1996 it was reported that secret discussions between representatives of the Republic and of the Democratic People's Republic of Korea had been held in Beijing. In late 1997 China participated in quadripartite negotiations, together with the USA, the Democratic People's Republic of Korea and the Republic of Korea, to resolve the Korean issue. The Republic of Korea remained a major trading partner, and was one of the largest investors in China. Further quadripartite negotiations took place throughout 1999.

Relations between China and the United Kingdom improved significantly in 1998. The British Secretary of State for Foreign and Commonwealth Affairs, Robin Cook, paid a visit to China and Hong Kong in January. The first China-EU summit, which was scheduled to become an annual event, took place in London in April, prior to the Asia-Europe Meeting (ASEM). China and the EU, presided over at the time by the United Kingdom, committed themselves to greater mutual co-operation in the area of trade and economic relations. The Chinese Premier, Zhu Rongji, also had talks with his British counterpart, Tony Blair, on Sino-British relations, apparently consolidating an improved relationship between the two countries, following the disagreements leading up to the return of Hong Kong. Blair visited China and Hong Kong in October 1998. He declared his intention to broach the issue of human rights through 'persuasion and dialogue' rather than 'confrontation and empty rhetoric'. Following the visit, the two sides pledged to increase co-operation in a number of areas, and it was announced that in 1999 Jiang Zemin would become the first Chinese Head of State to visit the United Kingdom. This visit took place in October 1999, as part of a six-nation tour, which also included France, Portugal, Morocco, Algeria and Saudi Arabia. The visit was the first by a Chinese Head of State to the latter three countries. In the United Kingdom and France Jiang's visit prompted protests by supporters of human rights, resulting in complaints from the Chinese authorities that more should have been done to suppress demonstrations in London. In December, during a China-EU summit in Beijing, the Chinese Goverment rejected criticism of human rights abuses, reiterating its previous position that economic development would precede an improvement in human rights and defending its use of the death penalty, citing social stability.

### Government

China is a unitary state. Directly under the Central Government there are 22 provinces, five autonomous regions, including Xizang (Tibet), and four municipalities (Beijing, Chongqing, Shanghai and Tianjin). The highest organ of state power is the National People's Congress (NPC). In March 1993 the first session of the Eighth NPC was attended by 2,921 deputies, indirectly elected for five years by the people's congresses of the provinces, autonomous regions, municipalities directly under the Central Government, and the People's Liberation Army. The NPC elects a Standing Committee to be its permanent organ. The current Constitution, adopted by the NPC in December 1982 and amended in 1993, was China's fourth since 1949. It restored the office of Head of State (President of the Republic). Executive power is exercised by the State Council (Cabinet), comprising the Premier, Vice-Premiers and other ministers heading ministries and commissions. The State Council is appointed by, and accountable to, the NPC.

Political power is held by the Chinese Communist Party (CCP). The CCP's highest authority is the Party Congress, convened every five years. In September 1997 the CCP's 15th National Congress elected a Central Committee of 193 full members and 151 alternate members. To direct policy, the Central Committee elected a 22-member Politburo.

Provincial people's congresses are the local organs of state power. Local revolutionary committees, created during the Cultural Revolution, were abolished in January 1980 and replaced by provincial people's governments.

### Defence

China is divided into seven major military units. All armed services are grouped in the People's Liberation Army (PLA). In August 1999, according to Western estimates, the regular forces totalled 2,480,000, of whom 1,275,000 were conscripts: the army numbered 1,830,000, the navy 230,000 (including a naval air force of 26,000), and the air force 420,000 (including 220,000 air defence personnel). Reserves number about 1.2m., and the People's Armed Police comprises an estimated 1m. Military service is by selective conscription, and lasts for three years in the army and marines, and for four years in the air force and navy. In September 1997 it was announced that the number of forces in the PLA was to be reduced by some 500,000 over the next three years. Defence expenditure for 1999 was budgeted at 104,700m. yuan.

### Economic Affairs

In 1997, according to estimates by the World Bank, China's gross national product (GNP), measured at average 1995–97 prices, was US $1,055,372m., equivalent to some $860 per head. During 1990–97, it was estimated, GNP per head increased, in real terms, at an average annual rate of 10.0%, one of the highest growth rates in the world. Over the same period, the population grew at an average annual rate of 1.1%. GNP in 1998 was $928,900m., equivalent to $750 per head. China's gross domestic product (GDP) increased, in real terms, at an average annual rate of 11.1% in 1990–98. According to official sources, GDP increased by 7.8% in 1998 and by an estimated 7.1% in 1999.

Agriculture (including forestry and fishing) contributed 18.4% of GDP in 1998, and employed 49.8% of the working population in that year. China's principal crops are rice (production of which accounted for an estimated 34.7% of the total world harvest in 1997), sweet potatoes, wheat, maize, soybeans, sugar cane, tobacco, cotton and jute. Devastating floods in July and August 1998 had a significant adverse effect on agricultural production in that year. The floods were partly attributed to massive deforestation and prompted the introduction of a forest conservation programme and restrictions on logging. According to the World Bank, agricultural GDP increased at an average annual rate of 4.3%, in real terms, in 1990–98. According to official figures, growth in agricultural GDP was 3.5% in 1998.

Industry (including mining, manufacturing, construction and power) contributed 48.7% of GDP and engaged 23.5% of the employed labour force in 1998. According to the World Bank, industrial GDP increased at an average annual rate of 15.4%, in real terms, in 1990–98. According to official figures, growth in industrial GDP was 9.2% in 1998.

The mining sector accounted for 1.2% of total employment in 1998, and output in the sector accounted for some 6% of total industrial output, in 1996. China has enormous mineral reserves and is the world's largest producer of coal, natural graphite, antimony, tungsten, iron ore and zinc. Other important minerals include molybdenum, tin, lead, mercury, bauxite, phosphate rock, diamonds, gold, manganese, crude petroleum and natural gas. In 1999 a joint venture was established between China National Petroleum Company (CNPC) and Shell to exploit reserves of natural gas in China. A move to increase competitiveness, and to reduce air pollution caused by the burning of coal, resulted in the closure of some 14 major coal mines in 1999, with the loss of 400,000 jobs.

The manufacturing sector contributed an estimated 37.6% of GDP in 1995, and the sector accounted for 13.3% of total employment in 1998. China is the world's leading producer of cotton cloth and cement, with output in 1998 totalling an estimated 24,100m. and 536.0m. metric tons, respectively. With output of more than 101m. metric tons in 1996, China also became the world's largest producer of steel; production increased to 116m. metric tons in 1998. The GDP of the manufacturing sector increased at an average annual rate of 15.5%, in real terms, during 1990–97, according to the World Bank.

Energy is derived principally from coal (72.0% in 1998); other sources are petroleum, hydroelectric power and natural gas. China became a net importer of crude petroleum in 1993. By December 1999 the People's Republic's largest hydroelectric power station, at Ertan, was fully functioning. The 18,200-MW Three Gorges hydropower scheme on the Chanjiang (River Yangtze), the world's largest civil engineering project, is scheduled for completion in 2009 and will have a potential annual output of 84,700m. kWh. China's national grid was also scheduled for completion in that year. Imports of mineral fuels comprised 5.0% of the cost of total imports in 1996.

Services contributed 32.9% of GDP in 1998 and engaged 26.7% of the employed labour force in that year. Tourism and retail and wholesale trade are expanding rapidly. During 1990–98, according to the World Bank, the GDP of the services sector increased at an average annual rate of 9.3% in real terms. According to official figures, growth in services GDP was 7.6% in 1998.

In 1998 China recorded a trade surplus of US $46,613m., and there was a surplus of $29,325m. on the current account of the balance of payments. In 1998 the principal source of imports was Japan (which provided 20.1% of total imports). Other important suppliers were the USA (12.1%), Taiwan (11.9%), and the Republic of Korea (10.7%). The principal markets for exports in 1998 were Hong Kong (21.1% of total exports), the USA (20.7%) and Japan (16.2%). Most of the goods exported to Hong Kong are subsequently re-exported. The principal imports in 1998 were machinery and transport equipment, chemicals and related products, and textiles and textile articles. The principal exports in that year were machinery and transport equipment, textiles and clothing, and footwear, headgear and umbrellas.

In 1998 China's overall budget deficit was 92,223m. yuan, equivalent to 1.2% of GDP. China's total external debt at the end of 1997 was estimated to be US $146,697m., of which $115,233m. was long-term public debt. In 1997 the cost of debt-servicing was equivalent to 8.6% of the value of exports of goods and services. The annual rate of inflation averaged 9.2% in 1990–98. The average rise in consumer prices was 8.3% in 1996 and 2.8% in 1997, but in 1998 prices declined by 0.8%. According to a sample survey, the number of unemployed persons in December 1998 was officially estimated at 14.5m. (2.0% of the total labour force). The scale of rural surplus labour in May 1997, however, was estimated at 130m., equivalent to 25% of the total rural labour force; unofficial estimates put the total as high as 300m. In December 1998 the total number of registered unemployed in urban areas was some 5,710,000 (3.1% of the urban labour force).

China joined the Asian Development Bank (ADB, see p. 125) in 1986 and the Asia-Pacific Economic Co-operation forum (APEC, see p. 122) in 1991. In 1994 China became a member of the Association of Tin Producing Countries (ATPC, see p. 287). China failed to become a founder-member of the World Trade Organization (WTO, see p. 274), which succeeded GATT in January 1995. In July of that year, however, China was granted observer status. Negotiations on full membership continued, and by late 1999 substantial progress had been made towards entry in 2000. China joined the Bank for International Settlements (BIS, see p. 133) in 1996. In the same year the secretariat of the Tumen River Economic Development Area (TREDA) was established in Beijing by the Governments of China, North and South Korea, Mongolia and Russia.

In 1978 Deng Xiaoping introduced the 'open door' reform policy, which aimed to decentralize the economic system and to attract overseas investment to China. The state monopoly on foreign trade was gradually relinquished, commercial links with foreign contries were diversified, several Special Economic Zones were established, and the planned economy was combined with market regulation. In 1997, following several years of high economic growth, the Government announced a three-year plan for the revitalization of the state-owned enterprises (SOEs) and the reform of the weak banking sector. The performance of the SOEs had suffered a significant decline in the 1990s, and failing SOEs were often supported by credit from the banking sector; around 25% of all bank loans were believed to be non-performing. However, concerns about possible social unrest slowed SOE reform in 1999, to minimize the number of workers being made redundant. A massive government spending programme (mostly on infrastructure projects), initiated in 1998, promoted GDP growth but failed to achieve a recovery from the problems of low domestic demand, a decline in consumer prices and a reduction in foreign investment. The increased government expenditure, which was funded by state borrowing and bond issues, caused a significant rise in the fiscal deficit. The economy failed to respond to measures to stimulate consumption, including interest rate reduction and the imposition of a tax on savings, owing to employment insecurity, caused by state-sector reform. In September 1999 the salaries of urban residents and allowances for the unemployed were increased significantly, whilst new tax incentives, introduced in August, were expected to stimulate activity in the property market. Export growth slowed in 1999 (as a result of the effects of the Asian economic crisis and the strength of the yuan), reducing the record trade surplus of 1998. However, following an apparent regional recovery from the financial crisis, an increase in exports to Asian countries was expected to relieve the pressure to devalue the currency during 2000. The most significant development in 1999 was the signing of a bilateral trade agreement with the USA in November, relating to China's future accession to the WTO. The principal concessions gained by the People's Republic comprised the recognition of China's status as a developing economy on entry to the WTO (which exempted it from certain penalties and sanctions) and the ending of US quotas on China's textile exports by 2005 (the USA had previously insisted on 2010). WTO accession would help to overcome the political obstacles to the restructuring of SOEs and banks, as they would have to become competitive in external markets, and was expected to generate increased investment in China in the longer term. In the short term, however, it was likely to cause a consolidation of domestic industries, which would exert negative pressures on the economy.

## Social Welfare

In mid-1997 five extrabudgetary funds (pension, unemployment, medical, injury and maternity) financed social welfare provisions in China. Large enterprises also provided social services for their employees. However, a programme of comprehensive social security reforms was being devised, in recognition of the increasing levels of expenditure required to provide for an ageing population (it was estimated that by 2050 the number of people aged over 65 will have reached 300m., compared with 76m. in 1995) and the rising rate of unemployment. The Chinese authorities have implemented a variety of social welfare schemes, in order to determine how best to structure and finance the new social security system. These include a health care programme in several cities, where medical costs are financed by the State, the employer and the employee. A medical insurance system, announced in December 1996, was to cover all urban employees by the year 2000. Western and traditional medical care, for which a fee is charged, is available in the cities and, to a lesser extent, in rural areas. Semi-professional peasant physicians assist with simple cures, treatment and the distribution of contraceptives. In December 1998 there were 2.0m. physicians, more than 1.2m. nurses and over 2.9m. hospital beds. In that year there were 314,097 health establishments, including 67,081 hospitals. Budgetary expenditure on pensions and social welfare in 1998 was 17,126m. yuan (1.6% of total government spending). In 1996 it was announced that a unified, nation-wide pension scheme was to be implemented by the year 2000, to provide pensions to all categories of worker (the current pension system is limited to urban areas and state-owned enterprises). Individual pension accounts, financed by contributions from the State, the employer and the employee, were to be established. The provision of social insurance for the rural population was also to be expanded.

Unemployment-insurance funds, established in cities in 1986, were also undergoing revision. It was reported that by September 1999 some 94.8m. people had registered with an unemployment insurance system.

## Education

The education system expanded rapidly after 1949. Fees are charged at all levels. Much importance is attached to kindergartens. Primary education begins for most children at seven years of age and lasts for five years. Secondary education usually begins at 12 years of age and lasts for a further five years, comprising a first cycle of three years and a second cycle of two years. Free higher education was abolished in 1985; instead, college students have to compete for scholarships, which are awarded according to academic ability. As a result of the student disturbances in 1989, college students were required to complete one year's political education, prior to entering college. In November 1989 it was announced that postgraduate students were to be selected on the basis of assessments of moral and physical fitness, as well as academic ability. Since 1979 education has been included as one of the main priorities for modernization. The whole educational system was to be reformed, with the aim of introducing nine-year compulsory education in 85% of the country by the year 2000. The establishment of private schools has been permitted since the early 1980s. As a proportion of the total school-age population, enrolment at primary and secondary schools in 1996 was equivalent to 97% (boys 99%; girls 95%). In that year 100% of both boys and girls in the relevant age-group were enrolled at primary schools. Total enrolment at secondary schools in 1996 was equivalent to 71% of the relevant age-group (males 74%; females 67%). In 1996 enrolment at tertiary level schools was equivalent to 5.7% of the relevant age-group (males 7.3%; females 3.9%). According to census results, the average rate of adult illiteracy in 1990 was 22.2% (males 13.0%; females 31.9%). In 1998, according to a sample survey, the rate had declined to 15.8% (males 9.0%, females 22.6%). Budgetary expenditure on education by all levels of government was 135,770m. yuan in 1997.

## Public Holidays

**2000:** 1 January (Solar New Year), 4–7 February* (Lunar New Year), 8 March (International Women's Day, women only), 1 May (Labour Day), 1 August (Army Day), 9 September (Teachers' Day), 1–2 October (National Days).

**2001:** 1 January (Solar New Year), 24–27 January* (Lunar New Year), 8 March (International Women's Day, women only), 1 May (Labour Day), 1 August (Army Day), 9 September (Teachers' Day), 1–2 October (National Days).

* From the first to the fourth day of the first moon of the lunar calendar.

## Weights and Measures

The metric system is officially in force, but some traditional Chinese units are still used.

# Statistical Survey

Source (unless otherwise stated): State Statistical Bureau, 38 Yuetan Nan Jie, Sanlihe, Beijing 100826; tel. (10) 68515074; fax (10) 68515078.

Note: Wherever possible, figures in this Survey exclude Taiwan. In the case of unofficial estimates for China, it is not always clear if Taiwan is included or excluded. Where a Taiwan component is known, either it has been deducted from the all-China figure or its inclusion is noted. Figures for the Hong Kong Special Administrative Region (SAR — incorporated into the People's Republic of China on 1 July 1997) and for the Macau SAR (incorporated on 20 December 1999) are listed separately (pp. 996–1000 and p. 1015 respectively). Transactions between the SARs and the rest of the People's Republic continue to be treated as external transactions.

## Area and Population

**AREA, POPULATION AND DENSITY**

| | |
|---|---|
| Area (sq km) | 9,571,300* |
| Population (census results) | |
| 1 July 1982 | 1,008,180,738 |
| 1 July 1990 | |
| Males | 581,820,407 |
| Females | 548,690,231 |
| Total | 1,130,510,638 |
| Population (official estimates at 31 December) | |
| 1996 | 1,223,890,000 |
| 1997 | 1,236,260,000 |
| 1998 | 1,248,100,000 |
| Density (per sq km) at 31 December 1998 | 130.4 |

* 3,695,500 sq miles.

**PRINCIPAL ETHNIC GROUPS** (at census of 1 July 1990)

| | Number | % |
|---|---|---|
| Han (Chinese) | 1,039,187,548 | 91.92 |
| Zhuang | 15,555,820 | 1.38 |
| Manchu | 9,846,776 | 0.87 |
| Hui | 8,612,001 | 0.76 |
| Miao | 7,383,622 | 0.65 |
| Uygur (Uigur) | 7,207,024 | 0.64 |
| Yi | 6,578,524 | 0.58 |
| Tujia | 5,725,049 | 0.51 |
| Mongolian | 4,802,407 | 0.42 |
| Tibetan | 4,593,072 | 0.41 |
| Bouyei | 2,548,294 | 0.23 |
| Dong | 2,508,624 | 0.22 |
| Yao | 2,137,033 | 0.19 |
| Korean | 1,923,361 | 0.17 |
| Bai | 1,598,052 | 0.14 |
| Hani | 1,254,800 | 0.11 |
| Li | 1,112,498 | 0.10 |
| Kazakh | 1,110,758 | 0.10 |
| Dai | 1,025,402 | 0.09 |
| She | 634,700 | 0.06 |
| Lisu | 574,589 | 0.05 |
| Others | 3,838,337 | 0.34 |
| Unknown | 752,347 | 0.07 |
| **Total** | 1,130,510,638 | 100.00 |

**BIRTHS AND DEATHS** (sample surveys)

| | 1996 | 1997 | 1998 |
|---|---|---|---|
| Birth rate (per 1,000) | 16.98 | 16.57 | 16.03 |
| Death rate (per 1,000) | 6.56 | 6.51 | 6.50 |

**Marriages** (number registered): 9,339,615 in 1996; 9,090,571 in 1997, 8,866,593 in 1998.

**Expectation of life** (official estimates, years at birth, 1996): 70.80 (males 68.71; females 73.04).

**PRINCIPAL TOWNS**

(Wade-Giles or other spellings in brackets)

**Population at 31 December 1990** (official estimates in '000)*

| | |
|---|---|
| Shanghai (Shang-hai) | 7,830 |
| Beijing (Pei-ching or Peking, the capital) | 7,000 |
| Tianjin (T'ien-chin or Tientsin) | 5,770 |
| Shenyang (Shen-yang or Mukden) | 4,540 |
| Wuhan (Wu-han or Hankow) | 3,750 |
| Guangzhou (Kuang-chou or Canton) | 3,580 |
| Chongqing (Ch'ung-ch'ing or Chungking) | 2,980 |
| Harbin (Ha-erh-pin) | 2,830 |
| Chengdu (Ch'eng-tu) | 2,810 |
| Xian (Hsi-an or Sian) | 2,760 |
| Nanjing (Nan-ching or Nanking) | 2,500 |
| Zibo (Tzu-po or Tzepo) | 2,460 |
| Dalian (Ta-lien or Dairen) | 2,400 |
| Jinan (Chi-nan or Tsinan) | 2,320 |
| Changchun (Ch'ang-ch'un) | 2,110 |
| Qingdao (Ch'ing-tao or Tsingtao) | 2,060 |
| Taiyuan (T'ai-yüan) | 1,960 |
| Zhengzhou (Cheng-chou or Chengchow) | 1,710 |
| Guiyang (Kuei-yang or Kweiyang) | 1,530 |
| Kunming (K'un-ming) | 1,520 |
| Lanzhou (Lan-chou or Lanchow) | 1,510 |
| Tangshan (T'ang-shan) | 1,500 |
| Anshan (An-shan) | 1,390 |
| Qiqihar (Ch'i-ch'i-ha-erh or Tsitsihar) | 1,380 |
| Fushun (F'u-shun) | 1,350 |
| Nanchang (Nan-ch'ang) | 1,350 |
| Hangzhou (Hang-chou or Hangchow) | 1,340 |
| Changsha (Chang-sha) | 1,330 |
| Shijiazhuang (Shih-chia-chuang or Shihkiachwang) | 1,320 |
| Fuzhou (Fu-chou or Foochow) | 1,290 |
| Jilin (Chi-lin or Kirin) | 1,270 |
| Baotau (Pao-t'ou or Paotow) | 1,200 |
| Huainan (Huai-nan or Hwainan) | 1,200 |
| Luoyang (Lo-yang) | 1,190 |
| Urumqi (Urumchi) | 1,160 |
| Datong (Ta-t'ung or Tatung) | 1,110 |
| Handan (Han-tan) | 1,110 |
| Ningbo (Ning-po) | 1,090 |
| Nanning (Nan-ning) | 1,070 |
| Hefei (Hofei) | 1,000 |

* Data refer to municipalities, which may include large rural areas as well as an urban centre. The listed towns comprise those with a total population of more than 1,000,000 and a non-agricultural population of more than 500,000.

**Peru:** 2-82 San Li Tun, Bangonglou, Beijing 100600; tel. (10) 65323477; fax (10) 65322178; e-mail embperu@public.bta.net.cn; internet www.embperu.cn.net; Ambassador: LUZMILA ZANABRIA ISHIKAWA.

**Philippines:** 23 Xiu Shui Bei Jie, Jian Guo Men Wai, Beijing 100600; tel. (10) 65321872; fax (10) 65323761; Ambassador: ROMUALDO A. ONG.

**Poland:** 1 Ri Tan Lu, Jian Guo Men Wai, Beijing 100600; tel. (10) 65321235; fax (10) 65321745; Ambassador: ZDZISŁAW GÓRALCZYK.

**Portugal:** 2-15-1 Tayuan Diplomatic Office Bldg, Beijing 100600; tel. (10) 65323497; fax (10) 65324637; Ambassador: PEDRO CATARINO.

**Qatar:** 2-9-2 Tayuan Diplomatic Office Bldg, 14 Liang Ma He Nan Lu, Beijing 100600; tel. (10) 65322231; fax (10) 65325274; Ambassador: MOHAMMED ABDUL-GHANI.

**Romania:** Ri Tan Lu, Dong Er Jie, Beijing 100600; tel. (10) 65323442; fax (10) 65325728; Ambassador: IOAN DONCA.

**Russia:** 4 Dong Zhi Men Nei, Bei Zhong Jie, Beijing 100600; tel. (10) 65321291; fax (10) 65324853; e-mail rusemb@public3.bta.net.cn; Ambassador: IGOR ROGACHEV.

**Rwanda:** 30 Xiu Shui Bei Jie, Jian Guo Men Wai, Beijing 100600; tel. (10) 65322193; fax (10) 65322006; Ambassador: VALENS MUNYABAGISHA.

**Saudi Arabia:** 1 Bei Xiao Jie, San Li Tun, Beijing 100600; tel. (10) 65324825; fax (10) 65325324; Ambassador: Mr YUSEF.

**Sierra Leone:** 7 Dong Zhi Men Wai Dajie, Beijing 100600; tel. (10) 65321222; fax (10) 65323752; Ambassador: ALHUSIN DEEN.

**Singapore:** 1 Xiu Shui Bei Jie, Jian Guo Men Wai, Beijing 100600; tel. (10) 65323926; fax (10) 65322215; Ambassador: CHIN SIAT YOON.

**Slovakia:** Ri Tan Lu, Jian Guo Men Wai, Beijing 100600; tel. (10) 65321531; fax (10) 65324814; Ambassador: (vacant).

**Slovenia:** 23 Jian Guo Men Wai Dajie, 3-53 Jian Guo Men Wai Diplomatic Residence, Beijing 100600; tel. (10) 65326356; fax (10) 65326358; Ambassador: TIT TURNSEK.

**Somalia:** 2 San Li Tun Lu, Beijing 100600; tel. (10) 65321752; Ambassador: MOHAMED HASSAN SAID.

**South Africa:** 5 Dongzhimen Wai Dajie, Chaoyang Qu, Beijing 100016; tel. (10) 65320175; fax (10) 65320177; e-mail safrican@homeway.com.cn; Ambassador: CHRISTOPHER DLAMINI.

**Spain:** 9 San Li Tun Lu, Beijing 100600; tel. (10) 65321986; fax (10) 65323401; Ambassador: EUGENIO BREGOLAT.

**Sri Lanka:** 3 Jian Hua Lu, Jian Guo Men Wai, Beijing 100600; tel. (10) 65321861; fax (10) 65325426; e-mail lkembj@public.east.cn.net; Ambassador: R. C. A. VANDERGERT.

**Sudan:** 1 Dong Er Jie, San Li Tun, Beijing 100600; tel. (10) 65323715; fax (10) 65321280; Ambassador: ABDELHAMEED ABDEEN MOHAMMED.

**Sweden:** 3 Dong Zhi Men Wai Dajie, San Li Tun, Beijing 100600; tel. (10) 65323331; fax (10) 65325008; Ambassador: KJELL ANNELING.

**Switzerland:** 3 Dong Wu Jie, San Li Tun, Beijing 100600; tel. (10) 65322736; fax (10) 65324353; Ambassador: DOMINIQUE DREYER.

**Syria:** 6 Dong Si Jie, San Li Tun, Beijing 100600; tel. (10) 65321563; fax (10) 65321575; Ambassador: LOUTOF ALLAH HAYDAR.

**Tanzania:** 8 Liang Ma He Nan Lu, San Li Tun, Beijing 100600; tel. (10) 65321408; fax (10) 65324985; Ambassador: SEIF ALI IDDI.

**Thailand:** 40 Guang Hua Lu, Jian Guo Men Wai, Beijing 100600; tel. (10) 65321903; fax (10) 65321748; Ambassador: NIKHOM TANTEMSAPYA.

**Togo:** 11 Dong Zhi Men Wai Dajie, Beijing 100600; tel. (10) 65322202; Ambassador: NOLANA TA-AMA.

**Tunisia:** 1 Dong Jie, San Li Tun, Beijing 100600; tel. (10) 65322435; fax (10) 65325818; e-mail ambtun@public.netchina.com.cn; Ambassador: MOHAMED MONGI LAHBIB.

**Turkey:** 9 Dong Wu Jie, San Li Tun, Beijing 100600; tel. (10) 65322650; fax (10) 65325480; e-mail trkelcn@public.bta.net.cn; Ambassador: DARYAL BATIBAY.

**Turkmenistan:** 5-2-131/5-2-132 Tayuan Diplomatic Compound, Beijing 100600; tel. (10) 65326975; fax (10) 65326976; Ambassador: AMANGELDY RAKHMANOV.

**Uganda:** 5 Dong Jie, San Li Tun, Beijing 100600; tel. (10) 65322370; fax (10) 65322242; e-mail ugembssy@public.bta.net.cn; Ambassador: PHILIP IDRO.

**Ukraine:** 11 Dong Liu Jie, San Li Tun, Beijing 100600; tel. (10) 65326359; fax (10) 65326765; Ambassador: IGOR A. LITVIN.

**United Arab Emirates:** 1-9-1 Tayuan Diplomatic Office Bldg, Beijing 100600; tel. (10) 65322112; fax (10) 65325089; Ambassador: ISMIAIL OBAID YOUSEF OBAID.

**United Kingdom:** 11 Guang Hua Lu, Jian Guo Men Wai, Beijing 100600; tel. (10) 65321961; fax (10) 65321937; e-mail beinfo@public.bta.net.cn; Ambassador: Sir ANTHONY GALSWORTHY.

**USA:** 3 Xiu Shui Bei Jie, Beijing 100600; tel. (10) 65323831; fax (10) 65323178; internet www.usembassy-china.org.cn; Ambassador: Adm. JOSEPH PRUEHER.

**Uruguay:** 2-7-2 Tayuan Diplomatic Office Bldg, Beijing 100600; tel. (10) 65324445; fax (10) 65324357; e-mail urubei@public.bta.net.cn; Ambassador: ALVARO ALVAREZ.

**Uzbekistan:** 11 Bei Xiao Jie, San Li Tun, Beijing 100600; tel. (10) 65326305; fax (10) 65326304; Ambassador: I. R. IRGASHEV.

**Venezuela:** 14 San Li Tun Lu, Beijing 100600; tel. (10) 65321295; fax (10) 65323817; e-mail embvenez@public.bta.net.cn; Ambassador: JOCELYN HENRÍQUEZ.

**Viet Nam:** 32 Guang Hua Lu, Jian Guo Men Wai, Beijing 100600; tel. (10) 65321155; fax (10) 65325720; Ambassador: BUI HONG PHUC.

**Yemen:** 5 Dong San Jie, San Li Tun, Beijing 100600; tel. (10) 65321558; fax (10) 65324305; Ambassador: MOHAMMED HADI AWAD.

**Yugoslavia:** 1 Dong Liu Jie, San Li Tun, Beijing 100600; tel. (10) 65323516; fax (10) 65321207; Ambassador: Dr SLOBODAN UNKOVIĆ.

**Zambia:** 5 Dong Si Jie, San Li Tun, Beijing 100600; tel. (10) 65321554; fax (10) 65321891; Ambassador: JACOB MWANSA KABINGA.

**Zimbabwe:** 7 Dong San Jie, San Li Tun, Beijing 100600; tel. (10) 65323795; fax (10) 65325383; Ambassador: LUCAS PANDE TAVAYA.

# Judicial System

The general principles of the Chinese judicial system are laid down in Articles 123–135 of the December 1982 Constitution (q.v.).

### PEOPLE'S COURTS

**Supreme People's Court:** 27 Dongjiaomin Xiang, Beijing 100745; tel. (10) 65136195; f. 1949; the highest judicial organ of the State; handles first instance cases of national importance; handles cases of appeals and protests lodged against judgments and orders of higher people's courts and special people's courts, and cases of protests lodged by the Supreme People's Procuratorate in accordance with the procedures of judicial supervision; reviews death sentences meted out by local courts, supervises the administration of justice by local people's courts; interprets issues concerning specific applications of laws in judicial proceedings; its judgments and rulings are final; Pres. XIAO YANG (five-year term of office coincides with that of National People's Congress, by which the President is elected).

**Local People's Courts:** comprise higher courts, intermediate courts and basic courts.

**Special People's Courts:** include military courts, maritime courts and railway transport courts.

### PEOPLE'S PROCURATORATES

**Supreme People's Procuratorate:** 147 Beiheyan Dajie, Beijing 100726; tel. (10) 65126655; acts for the National People's Congress in examining govt depts, civil servants and citizens, to ensure observance of the law; prosecutes in criminal cases. Procurator-Gen. HAN ZHUBIN (elected by the National People's Congress for five years).

**Local People's Procuratorates:** undertake the same duties at the local level. Ensure that the judicial activities of the people's courts, the execution of sentences in criminal cases and the activities of departments in charge of reform through labour conform to the law; institute, or intervene in, important civil cases which affect the interest of the State and the people.

# Religion

During the 'Cultural Revolution' places of worship were closed. After 1977 the Government adopted a policy of religious tolerance, and the 1982 Constitution states that citizens enjoy freedom of religious belief and that legitimate religious activities are protected. Many temples, churches and mosques have reopened. Since 1994 all religious organizations have been required to register with the Bureau of Religious Affairs.

**Bureau of Religious Affairs:** Beijing; tel. (10) 652625; Dir YE XIAOWEN.

### ANCESTOR WORSHIP

Ancestor worship is believed to have originated with the deification and worship of all important natural phenomena. The divine and human were not clearly defined; all the dead became gods and were worshipped by their descendants. The practice has no code or dogma and the ritual is limited to sacrifices made during festivals and on birth and death anniversaries.

### BUDDHISM

Buddhism was introduced into China from India in AD 67, and flourished during the Sui and Tang dynasties (6th–8th century), when eight sects were established. The Chan and Pure Land sects are the most popular. According to official sources, in 1998 there were 9,500 Buddhist temples in China. There were 100m. believers in 1997.

**Buddhist Association of China (BAC):** f. 1953; Pres. ZHAO PUCHU; Sec.-Gen. DAO SHUREN.

**Tibetan Institute of Lamaism:** Pres. BUMI JANGBALUOZHU; Vice-Pres. CEMOLIN DANZENGCHILIE.

**14th Dalai Lama:** His Holiness the Dalai Lama TENZIN GYATSO, Thekchen Choeling, McLeod Ganj, Dharamsala 176 219, Himachal Pradesh, India; tel. (91) 1892-21343; fax (91) 1892-21813; e-mail ohhdl@cta.unv.ernet.ind; spiritual and temporal leader of Tibet; fled to India after failure of Tibetan national uprising in 1959.

### CHRISTIANITY

During the 19th century and the first half of the 20th century large numbers of foreign Christian missionaries worked in China. According to official sources, there were 6.5m. Protestants and 4m. Catholics in China in 1998, although unofficial sources estimate that the Christian total could be as high as 90m. The Catholic Church in China operates independently of the Vatican.

**Three-Self Patriotic Movement Committee of Protestant Churches of China:** Chair. LUO GUANZONG; Sec.-Gen. DENG FUCUN.

**China Christian Council:** 169 Yuan Ming Yuan Lu, Shanghai 200002; tel. (21) 63210806; fax (21) 63232605; e-mail ban9sb@online.sh.cn; f. 1980; comprises provincial Christian councils; Pres. Dr HAN WENZAO; Sec.-Gen. Rev. SU DECI.

**The Roman Catholic Church:** Catholic Mission, Si-She-Ku, Beijing; Bishop of Beijing MICHAEL FU TIESHAN (not recognized by the Vatican).

**Chinese Patriotic Catholic Association:** Chair. MICHAEL FU TIESHAN; Sec.-Gen. LIU BAINIAN; c. 3m. mems (1988).

### CONFUCIANISM

Confucianism is a philosophy and a system of ethics, without ritual or priesthood. The respects that adherents accord to Confucius are not bestowed on a prophet or god, but on a great sage whose teachings promote peace and good order in society and whose philosophy encourages moral living.

### DAOISM

Daoism was founded by Zhang Daoling during the Eastern Han dynasty (AD 125–144). Lao Zi, a philosopher of the Zhou dynasty (born 604 BC), is its principal inspiration, and is honoured as Lord the Most High by Daoists. According to official sources, there were 600 Daoist temples in China in 1998.

**China Daoist Association:** Temple of the White Cloud, Xi Bian Men, Beijing 100045; tel. (10) 6367179; f. 1957; Pres. (vacant); Sec.-Gen. LI WENCHENG.

### ISLAM

According to Muslim history, Islam was introduced into China in AD 651. There were some 18m. adherents in China in 1997, chiefly among the Wei Wuer (Uygur) and Hui people.

**Beijing Islamic Association:** Dongsi Mosque, Beijing; f. 1979; Chair. Imam Al-Hadji SALAH AN SHIWEI.

**China Islamic Association:** Beijing 100053; tel. (10) 63546384; fax (10) 63529483; f. 1953; Chair. Imam Al-Hadji SALAH AN SHIWEI; Sec.-Gen. WAN YAOBIN.

## The Press

In mid-1998 China had 2,045 newspaper titles (including those below provincial level) and 7,927 periodicals. Each province publishes its own daily. Only the major newspapers and periodicals are listed below. In late 1999 the Government announced its intention to merge or close down a number of newspapers, leaving a single publication in each province.

### PRINCIPAL NEWSPAPERS

**Anhui Ribao** (Anhui Daily): 206 Jinzhai Lu, Hefei, Anhui 230061; tel. (551) 2827842; fax (551) 2847302; Editor-in-Chief WANG HONG.

**Beijing Ribao** (Beijing Daily): 34 Xi Biaobei Hutong, Dongdan, Beijing 100743; tel. (10) 65131071; fax (10) 65136522; f. 1952; organ of the Beijing municipal cttee of the CCP; Dir WAN YUNLAI; Editor-in-Chief LIU HUSHAN; circ. 700,000.

**Beijing Wanbao** (Beijing Evening News): 34 Xi Biaobei Hutong, Dongdan, Beijing 100743; tel. (10) 65132233; fax (10) 65126581; f. 1958; Editor LI BINGREN; circ. 800,000.

**Beijing Youth Daily:** Beijing; national and local news; promotes ethics and social service; circ. 3m.–4m.

**Changsha Wanbao** (Changsha Evening News): 161 Caie Zhong Lu, Changsha, Hunan 410005; tel. (731) 4424457; fax (731) 4445167.

**Chengdu Wanbao** (Chengdu Evening News): Qingyun Nan Jie, Chengdu 610017; tel. (28) 664501; fax (28) 666597; circ. 700,000.

**China Business Times:** Beijing; f. 1989; Editor HUANG WENFU; circ. 500,000.

**Chungcheng Wanbao** (Chungcheng Evening News): 51 Xinwen Lu, Kunming, Yunnan 650032; tel. (871) 4144642; fax (871) 4154192.

**Dazhong Ribao** (Masses Daily): 46 Jinshi Lu, Jinan, Shandong 250014; tel. (531) 2968911; fax (531) 2962450; f. 1939; Dir XU XIYU; Editor-in-Chief LIU GUANGDONG; circ. 550,000.

**Economic News:** Editor-in-Chief DU ZULIANG.

**Fujian Ribao** (Fujian Daily): Hualin Lu, Fuzhou, Fujian; tel. (591) 57756; daily; Dir HUANG SHIYUN; Editor-in-Chief HUANG ZHONGSHENG.

**Gongren Ribao** (Workers' Daily): Liupukang, Andingmen Wai, Beijing 100718; tel. (10) 64211561; fax (10) 64214890; f. 1949; trade union activities and workers' lives; also major home and overseas news; Dir and Editor-in-Chief QU ZUGENG; circ. 2.5m.

**Guangming Ribao** (Guangming Daily): 106 Yongan Lu, Beijing 100050; tel. (10) 63017788; fax (10) 63039387; f. 1949; literature, art, science, education, history, economics, philosophy; Editor-in-Chief WANG CHEN; circ. 920,000.

**Guangxi Ribao** (Guangxi Daily): Guangxi Region; Dir and Editor-in-Chief LI MINGDE.

**Guangzhou Ribao** (Canton Daily): 10 Dongle Lu, Renmin Zhonglu, Guangzhou, Guangdong; tel. (20) 81887294; fax (20) 81862022; f. 1952; daily; social, economic and current affairs; Editor-in-Chief LI YUANJIANG; circ. 600,000.

**Guizhou Ribao** (Guizhou Daily): Guiyang, Guizhou; tel. (851) 627779; f. 1949; Dir and Editor-in-Chief GAO ZONGWEN; circ. 300,000.

**Hainan Ribao** (Hainan Daily): 7 Xinhua Nan Lu, Haikou, Hainan 570001; tel. (898) 6222021.

**Hebei Ribao** (Hebei Daily): 210 Yuhuazhong Lu, Shijiazhuang, Hebei 050013; tel. (311) 6048901; fax (311) 6046969; f. 1949; Dir LIU HAIQUAN; Editor-in-Chief YE ZHEN; circ. 500,000.

**Heilongjiang Ribao** (Heilongjiang Daily): Heilongjiang Province; Editor-in-Chief JIA SHIXIANG.

**Henan Ribao** (Henan Daily): 1 Weiyi Lu, Zhengzhou, Henan; tel. (371) 5958319; fax (371) 5955636; f. 1949; Editor-in-Chief GUO ZHENGLING; circ. 390,000.

**Huadong Xinwen** (Eastern China News): f. 1995; published by Renmin Ribao.

**Huanan Xinwen** (South China News): Guangzhou; f. 1997; published by Renmin Ribao.

**Hubei Ribao** (Hubei Daily): 65 Huangli Lu, Wuhan, Hubei 430077; tel. (27) 6833522; fax (27) 6813989; f. 1949; Dir LU JIAN; Editor-in-Chief SONG HANYAN; circ. 800,000.

**Hunan Ribao** (Hunan Daily): 18 Furong Zhong Lu, Changsha, Hunan 410071; tel. (731) 4312999; fax (731) 4314029; Dir and Editor-in-Chief JIANG XIANLI.

**Jiangxi Ribao** (Jiangxi Daily): 175 Yangming Jie, Nanchang, Jiangxi; tel. (791) 6849888; fax (791) 6772590; f. 1949; Dir ZHOU JINGUANG; Editor-in-Chief DUAN FURUI; circ. 300,000.

**Jiefang Ribao** (Liberation Daily): 300 Han Kou Lu, Shanghai 200001; tel. (21) 63521111; fax (21) 63516517; f. 1949; Editor-in-Chief ZHAO KAI; circ. 1m.

**Jiefangjun Bao** (Liberation Army Daily): Beijing; f. 1956; official organ of the Central Military Comm.; Dir Maj.-Gen. SUN ZHONGTONG; Editor-in-Chief YU SHUNCHANG; circ. 800,000.

**Jilin Ribao** (Jilin Daily): Jilin Province; Dir and Editor-in-Chief YI HONGBIN.

**Jingji Ribao** (Economic Daily): 2 Bai Zhi Fang Dong Jie, Beijing 100054; tel. (10) 63559988; fax (10) 63539408; f. 1983; financial affairs, domestic and foreign trade; administered by the State Council; Editor-in-Chief AI FENG; circ. 1.2m.

**Jinrong Shibao** (Financial News): 44 Taipingqiao Fengtaiqu, Beijing 100073; tel. (10) 63269233; fax (10) 68424931.

**Liaoning Ribao** (Liaoning Daily): Liaoning Province; Dir ZHU SHILIANG; Editor-in-Chief XIE ZHENGQIAN.

**Nanfang Ribao** (Nanfang Daily): 289 Guangzhou Da Lu, Guangzhou, Guangdong 510601; tel. (20) 87373998; fax (20) 87375203; f. 1949; Dir LI MENGYU; Editor-in-Chief FAN YIJIN; circ. 1m.

**Nanjing Ribao** (Nanjing Daily): 53 Jiefang Lu, Nanjing, Jiangsu 210016; tel. (25) 4496564; fax (25) 4496544.

**Nongmin Ribao** (Farmers' Daily): Shilipu Beili, Chao Yang Qu, Beijing 100025; tel. (10) 65005522; fax (10) 65071154; f. 1980; 6 a week; circulates in rural areas nation-wide; Dir SUN YONGREN; Editor-in-Chief ZHANG DEXIU; circ. 1m.

**Renmin Ribao** (People's Daily): 2 Jin Tai Xi Lu, Chao Yang Men Wai, Beijing 100733; tel. (10) 65092121; fax (10) 65091982; f. 1948; organ of the CCP; also publishes overseas edn; Dir SHAO HUAZE; Editor-in-Chief XU ZHONGTIAN; circ. 2.15m.

**Shaanxi Ribao** (Shaanxi Daily): Shaanxi Province; Pres. YIN WEIZU; Editor-in-Chief LI DONGSHENG.

**Shanxi Ribao** (Shanxi Daily): 24 Shuangtasi Jie, Taiyuan, Shanxi; tel. (351) 446561; fax (351) 441771; Dir WANG XIYI; Editor-in-Chief LI DONGXI; circ. 300,000.

**Shenzhen Commercial Press:** Shenzhen; Editor-in-Chief GAO XINGLIE.

**Shenzhen Tequ Bao** (Shenzhen Special Economic Zone Daily): 4 Shennan Zhonglu, Shenzhen 518009; tel. (755) 3902688; fax (755) 3906900; f. 1982; reports on special economic zones, as well as mainland, Hong Kong and Macau; Pres. and Editor-in-Chief WU SONGYING.

**Sichuan Ribao** (Sichuan Daily): 70 Hongxing Zhong Lu, Erduan, Chengdu, Sichuan 610012; tel. (28) 6758900; fax (28) 6745035; f. 1952; Editor-in-Chief TANG XIAOQIANG; circ. 8m.

**Tianjin Ribao** (Tianjin Daily): 873 Dagu Nan Lu, Heri Qu, Tianjin 300211; tel. (22) 7301024; fax (22) 7305803; f. 1949; Dir QIU YUNSHENG; Editor-in-Chief WU BINGJING; circ. 600,000.

**Wenhui Bao** (Wenhui Daily): 50 Huqiu Lu, Shanghai 200002; tel. (21) 63211410; fax (21) 63230198; f. 1938; Editor-in-Chief SHI JUNSHENG; circ. 500,000m.

**Xin Min Wan Bao** (Xin Min Evening News): 839 Yan An Zhong Lu, Shanghai 200040; tel. (21) 62791234; fax (21) 62473220; f. 1929; specializes in public policy, education and social affairs; Editor-in-Chief DING FAZHANG; circ. 1.8m.

**Xinhua Ribao** (New China Daily): 55 Zhongshan Lu, Nanjing, Jiangsu 210005; tel. (21) 741757; fax (21) 741023; Editor-in-Chief ZHOU ZHENGRONG; circ. 900,000.

**Xinjiang Ribao** (Xinjiang Daily): Xinjiang Region; Dir TIAN YUMIAN; Editor-in-Chief HUANG YANCAI.

**Xizang Ribao** (Tibet Daily): Tibet; Editor-in-Chief LI CHANGWEN.

**Yangcheng Wanbao** (Yangcheng Evening News): 733 Dongfeng Dong Lu, Guangzhou, Guangdong 510085; tel. (20) 87776211; fax (20) 87765103; e-mail ycwbic@ycwb.com.cn; internet www.ycwb.com.cn; f. 1957; Pres. CAO CHUNLIANG; Editor-in-Chief PAN WEI WEN; circ. 1.3m.

**Yunnan Ribao** (Yunnan Daily): Yunnan Province; Editor-in-Chief WANG ZIMING.

**Zhejiang Ribao** (Zhejiang Daily): Zhejiang Province; Editor-in-Chief ZHANG XI.

**Zhongguo Qingnian Bao** (China Youth News): 2 Haiyuncang, Dong Zhi Men Nei, Beijing 100702; tel. (10) 64032233; fax (10) 64033792; f. 1951; daily; aimed at 14–40 age-group; Dir and Editor-in-Chief XU ZHUQING; circ. 1.0m.

**Zhongguo Ribao** (China Daily): 15 Huixin Dongjie, Chao Yang Qu, Beijing 100029; tel. (10) 64918633; fax (10) 64918377; internet www.chinadaily.com.cn; f. 1981; English; China's political, economic and cultural developments; world, financial and sports news; also publishes *Business Weekly* (f. 1985), *Beijing Weekend* (f. 1991), *Shanghai Star* (f. 1992), *Reports from China* (f. 1992), *21st Century* (f. 1993); Editor-in-Chief ZHU YINGHUANG; circ. 300,000.

**Zhongguo Xinwen** (China News): 12 Baiwanzhuang Nanjie, Beijing; tel. (10) 68315012; f. 1952; daily; Editor-in-Chief WANG XIJIN; current affairs.

### SELECTED PERIODICALS

**Ban Yue Tan** (Fortnightly Review): Beijing; tel. (10) 6668521; f. 1980; in Chinese and Wei Wuer (Uygur); Editor-in-Chief YU YOUHAI; circ. 6m.

**Beijing Review:** 24 Baiwanzhuang Lu, Beijing 100037; tel. (10) 68328115; fax (10) 68326628; e-mail bjreview@public3.bta.net.cn; weekly; edns in English, French, Spanish, Japanese and German; also **Chinafrica** (monthly in English and French); Dir LIN LIANGQI; Editor-in-Chief GENG YUXIN.

**BJ TV Weekly:** 2 Fu Xing Men Wai Zhenwumiao Jie, Beijing 100045; tel. (10) 6366036; fax (10) 63262388; circ. 1m.

**China TV Weekly:** 15 Huixin Dong Jie, Chao Yang Qu, Beijing 100013; tel. (10) 64214197; circ. 1.7m.

**Chinese Literature Press:** 24 Baiwanzhuang Lu, Beijing 100037; tel. (10) 68326010; fax (10) 68326678; Editor-in-Chief chinalit@public.east.cn.net; f. 1951; monthly (bilingual in English); quarterly (bilingual in French); contemporary and classical writing, poetry, literary criticism and arts; Exec. Editor LING YUAN.

**Chinese Science Abstracts:** Science Press, 16 Donghuangchenggen Beijie, Beijing 100717; tel. (10) 64018833, ext. 391; fax (10) 64019810; f. 1982; monthly; in English; science and technology; Chief Editor LI RUIXU.

**Dianying Xinzuo** (New Films): 796 Huaihai Zhong Lu, Shanghai; tel. (21) 64379710; f. 1979; bi-monthly; introduces new films.

**Dianzi yu Diannao** (Electronics and Computers): Beijing; f. 1985; popularized information on computers and microcomputers.

**Elle (China):** 14 Lane 955, Yan'an Zhong Lu, Shanghai; tel. (21) 62790974; fax (21) 62479056; f. 1988; monthly; fashion; Pres. YANG XINCI; Chief Editor WU YING; circ. 300,000.

**Family Magazine:** 14 Siheng Lu, Xinhepu, Dongshan Qu, Guangzhou 510080; tel. (20) 7777718; fax (20) 7185670; monthly; circ. 2.5m.

**Feitian** (Fly Skywards): 50 Donggan Xilu, Lanzhou, Gansu; tel. (931) 25803; f. 1961; monthly.

**Guoji Xin Jishu** (New International Technology): Zhanwang Publishing House, Beijing; f. 1984; also publ. in Hong Kong; international technology, scientific and technical information.

**Guowai Keji Dongtai** (Recent Developments in Science and Technology Abroad): Institute of Scientific and Technical Information of China, 15 Fuxing Lu, Beijing 100038; tel. (10) 68515544, ext. 2954; fax (10) 68514027; e-mail baiyr@istic.ac.cn; internet www.chinainfo.gov.cn/periodical; f. 1962; monthly; scientific journal; Editor-in-Chief LI YANYAN; circ. 100,100.

**Hai Xia** (The Strait): 27 De Gui Xiang, Fuzhou, Fujian; tel. (10) 33656; f. 1981; quarterly; literary journal; CEOs YANG YU, JWO JONG LIN.

**Huasheng Monthly** (Voice for Overseas Chinese): 12 Bai Wan Zhuang Nan Jie, Beijing 100037; tel. (10) 68311578; fax (10) 68315039; f. 1995; monthly; intended mainly for overseas Chinese and Chinese nationals resident abroad; Editor-in-Chief FAN DONGSHENG.

**Jianzhu** (Construction): Baiwanzhuang, Beijing; tel. (10) 68992849; f. 1956; monthly; Editor FANG YUEGUANG; circ. 500,000.

**Jinri Zhongguo** (China Today): 24 Baiwanzhuang Lu, Beijing 100037; tel. (10) 68326037; fax (10) 68328338; internet www.china.org.cn; f. 1952; fmrly *China Reconstructs*; monthly; edns in English, Spanish, French, Arabic, German, Chinese and English braille; economic, social and cultural affairs; illustrated; Pres. and Editor-in-Chief HUANG ZU'AN.

**Liaowang** (Outlook): 57 Xuanwumen Xijie, Beijing; tel. (10) 63073049; f. 1981; weekly; current affairs; Gen. Man. ZHOU YICHANG; Editor CHEN DABIN; circ. 500,000.

**Luxingjia** (Traveller): Beijing; tel. (10) 6552631; f. 1955; monthly; Chinese scenery, customs, culture.

**Meishu Zhi You** (Friends of Art): 32 Beizongbu Hutong, East City Region, Beijing; tel. (10) 65122583. 1982; every 2 months; art review journal, also providing information on fine arts publs in China and abroad; Editors PENG SHEN, BAOLUN WU.

**Nianqingren** (Young People): 169 Mayuanlin, Changsha, Hunan; tel. (731) 23610; f. 1981; monthly; general interest for young people.

**Nongye Zhishi** (Agricultural Knowledge): 21 Ming Zi Qian Lu, Jinan, Shandong 250100; tel. (531) 8932238; e-mail sdnyzs@jn-public.sd.cninfo.net; internet www.sd.cninfo.net/nongye; f. 1950; fortnightly; popular agricultural science; Dir YANG LIJIAN; circ. 410,000.

**Qiushi** (Seeking Truth): 2 Shatan Beijie, Beijing 100727; tel. (10) 64037005; fax (10) 64018174; f. 1988 to succeed *Hong Qi* (Red Flag); 2 a month; theoretical journal of the CCP; Editor-in-Chief DAI ZHOU; circ. 1.83m.

**Renmin Huabao** (China Pictorial): Huayuancun, West Suburbs, Beijing 100044; tel. (10) 68411144; fax (10) 68413023; f. 1950; monthly; edns: 2 in Chinese, 1 in Tibetan and 12 in foreign languages; Dir and Editor-in-Chief ZHANG JIAHUA.

**Shichang Zhoubao** (Market Weekly): 2 Duan, Sanhao Jie, Heping Qu, Shenyang, Liaoning; tel. (24) 482983; f. 1979; weekly in Chinese; trade, commodities, and financial and economic affairs; circ. 1m.

**Shufa** (Calligraphy): 81 Qingzhou Nan Lu, Shanghai 200233; tel. (21) 64519008; fax (21) 64519015; f. 1977; every 2 months; journal on ancient and modern calligraphy; Chief Editor LU FUSHENG.

**Tiyu Kexue** (Sports Science): 8 Tiyuguan Lu, Beijing 100763; tel. (10) 67112233. 1981; sponsored by the China Sports Science Soc.; every 2 months; summary in English; Chief Officer YUAN WEIMIN; in Chinese; circ. 20,000.

**Wenxue Qingnian** (Youth Literature Journal): 27 Mu Tse Fang, Wenzhou, Zhejiang; tel. (577) 3578; f. 1981; monthly; Editor-in-Chief CHEN YUSHEN; circ. 80,000.

**Xian Dai Faxue** (Modern Law Science): Chongqing, Sichuan 630031; tel. (811) 961671; f. 1979; bi-monthly; with summaries in English; Dirs XU JINGCUN, XIE XOUPING.

**Yinyue Aihaozhe** (Music Lovers): 74 Shaoxing Lu, Shanghai 200020; tel. (21) 64372608; fax (21) 64332019; f. 1979; every 2 months; music knowledge; illustrated; Editor-in-Chief CHEN XUEYA; circ. 50,000.

**Zhongguo Duiwai Maoyi Ming Lu** (Directory of China's Foreign Trade): CCPIT Bldg, 1 Fuxingmen Wai Da Jie, Beijing 100860; tel. (10) 68022948; fax (10) 68510201; e-mail inform@press-media.com; f. 1974; monthly; edns in Chinese and English; information on Chinese imports and exports, foreign trade and economic policies; Editor-in-Chief YANG HAIQING.

**Zhongguo Ertong** (Chinese Children): 21 Xiang 12, Dongsi, Beijing; tel. (10) 6444761. 1980; monthly; illustrated journal for elementary school pupils.

**Zhongguo Funu** (Women of China): 15 Jian Guo Men Dajie, Beijing 100730; tel. (10) 65134616; fax (10) 65225380; f. 1956; monthly; in English; administered by All-China Women's Federation; women's rights and status, marriage and family, education, family planning, arts, cookery, etc.; Editor-in-Chief Ms WANG XIULIN.

**Zhongguo Guangbo Dianshi** (China Radio and Television): 12 Fucheng Lu, Beijing; tel. (10) 6896217; f. 1982; monthly; reports and comments.

**Zhongguo Jin Rong Xin Xi:** Beijing; f. 1991; monthly; economic news.

**Zhongguo Sheying** (Chinese Photography): 61 Hongxing Hutong, Dongdan, Beijing 100005; tel. (10) 65252277; fax (10) 65253197; e-mail cphoto@public.bta.net.cn; internet www.cphoto.com.cn; f. 1957; monthly; photographs and comments; Editor LIU BANG.

**Zhongguo Zhenjiu** (Chinese Acupuncture and Moxibustion): China Academy of Traditional Chinese Medicine, Dongzhimen Nei, Beijing 100700; tel. (10) 84014607; fax (10) 64013968; e-mail weihongliu@263.net; f. 1981; monthly; publ. by Chinese Soc. of Acupuncture and Moxibustion; abstract in English; Editor-in-Chief Prof. DENG LIANGYUE.

**Zijing** (Bauhinia): Pres. and Editor-in-Chief CHEN HONG.

Other popular magazines include **Gongchandang Yuan** (Communists, circ. 1.63m.) and **Nongmin Wenzhai** (Peasants' Digest, circ. 3.54m.).

### NEWS AGENCIES

**Xinhua (New China) News Agency:** 57 Xuanwumen Xidajie, Beijing 100803; tel. (10) 63071114; fax (10) 63071210; f. 1931; offices in all Chinese provincial capitals, and about 100 overseas bureaux; news service in Chinese, English, French, Spanish, Portuguese, Arabic and Russian, feature and photographic services; Pres. GUO CHAOREN; Editor-in-Chief NAN ZHENZHONG.

**Zhongguo Xinwen She** (China News Agency): POB 1114, Beijing; f. 1952; office in Hong Kong; supplies news features, special articles and photographs for newspapers and magazines in Chinese printed overseas; services in Chinese; Dir WANG SHIGU.

#### Foreign Bureaux

**Agence France-Presse (AFP)** (France): 11-11 Jian Guo Men Wai, Diplomatic Apts, Beijing 100600; tel. (10) 65321409; fax (10) 65322371; e-mail afppek@afp.com; Bureau Chief ELIZABETH ZINGO.

**Agencia EFE** (Spain): 2-2-132 Jian Guo Men Wai, Beijing 100600; tel. (10) 65323449; fax (10) 65323688; Rep. CARLOS REDONDO.

**Agenzia Nazionale Stampa Associata (ANSA)** (Italy): 1-11 Ban Gong Lu, San Li Tun, Beijing 100600; tel. (10) 65323651; fax (10) 65321954; e-mail barbara@public3.bta.net.cn; Bureau Chief BARBARA ALIGHIERO.

**Allgemeiner Deutscher Nachrichtendienst (ADN)** (Germany): 7-2-61, Jian Guo Men Wai, Qi Jia Yuan Gong Yu, Beijing 100600; tel. and fax (10) 65321115; Correspondent Dr LUTZ POHLE.

**Associated Press (AP)** (USA): 6-2-22 Jian Guo Men Wai, Diplomatic Quarters, Beijing 100600; tel. (10) 65326650; fax (10) 65323419; Bureau Chief ELAINE KURTENBACH.

**Deutsche Presse-Agentur (dpa)** (Germany): Ban Gong Lou, Apt 1-31, San Li Tun, Beijing 100600; tel. (10) 65321473; fax (10) 65321615; e-mail dpa@public3.bta.net.cn; Bureau Chief ANDREAS LANDWEHR.

**Informatsionnoye Telegrafnoye Agentstvo Rossii—Telegrafnoye Agentstvo Suverennykh Stran (ITAR—TASS)** (Russia): 6-1-41 Tayuan Diplomatic Office Bldg, Beijing 100600; tel. (10) 65324821; fax (10) 65324820; Bureau Chief GRIGORII KURBANOVICH ARSLANOV.

**Inter Press Service (TIPS)** (Italy): 15 Fuxing Lu, POB 3811, Beijing 100038; tel. (10) 68514046; fax (10) 68518210; e-mail tipscn@istic.ac.cn; internet www.tips.org.cn; Dir WANG XIAOYING.

**Jiji Tsushin** (Japan): 9-1-13 Jian Guo Men Wai, Waijiao, Beijing; tel. (10) 65322924; fax (10) 65323413; Correspondents YOSHIHISA MURAYAMA, TETSUYA NISHIMURA.

**Korean Central News Agency** (Democratic People's Republic of Korea): Beijing; Bureau Chief SONG YONG SONG.

**Kyodo News Service** (Japan): 3-91 Jian Guo Men Wai, Beijing; tel. (10) 6532680; fax (10) 65322273; e-mail kyodob@ccnet.cn.net; Bureau Chief YASUHIRO MORI.

**Magyar Távirati Iroda (MTI)** (Hungary): 1-42 Ban Gong Lu, San Li Tun, Beijing 100600; tel. (10) 65321744; Correspondent GYÖRGY BARTA.

**Prensa Latina** (Cuba): 4-1-23 Jianguomenwai, Beijing 100600; tel. and fax (10) 65321914; e-mail prelatin@public.bta.net.cn; Correspondent ILSA RODRÍGUEZ SANTANA.

**Press Trust of India:** 5-131 Diplomatic Apts, Jian Guo Men Wai, Beijing 100600; tel. and fax (10) 65322221.

**Reuters** (UK): Hilton Beijing, 1 Dong Fang Lu/Bei Dong Sanhuan Lu, Chaoyang Qu, Beijing; tel. (10) 64662288; fax (10) 64653052; Bureau Man. RICHARD PASCOE.

**Tanjug News Agency** (Yugoslavia): Qijayuan Diplomatic Apt, Beijing 100600; tel. (10) 65324821.

**United Press International (UPI)** (USA): 7-1-11 Qi Jia Yuan, Beijing; tel. (10) 65323271; Bureau Chief CHRISTIAAN VIRANT.

The following are also represented: Rompres (Romania) and VNA (Viet Nam).

### PRESS ORGANIZATIONS

**All China Journalists' Association:** Xijiaominxiang, Beijing 100031; tel. (10) 66023981; fax (10) 66014658; Exec. Chair. WU LENGXI.

**China Newspapers Association:** Beijing; Chair. XU ZHONGTIAN.

**The Press and Publication Administration of the People's Republic of China:** 85 Dongsi Nan Dajie, East District, Beijing 100703; tel. (10) 65124433; fax (10) 65127875; Dir YU YOUXIAN.

## Publishers

In 1998 there were 530 publishing houses in China. A total of 130,613 titles (and 7,238.6m. copies) were published in that year.

**Beijing Chubanshe** (Beijing Publishing House): 6 Bei Sanhuan Zhong Lu, Beijing 100011; tel. (10) 62016699; fax (10) 62012339; e-mail geo@bph.com.cn; f. 1956; politics, history, law, economics, geography, science, literature, art, etc.; Dir ZHU SHUXIN; Editor-in-Chief TAO XINCHENG.

**Beijing Daxue Chubanshe** (Beijing University Publishing House): Beijing University, Haidian Qu, Beijing 100871; tel. (10) 62502024; fax (10) 62556201; f. 1979; academic and general.

**China International Book Trading Corpn:** POB 399, 35 Chegongzhuang Xilu, Beijing 100044; tel. (10) 68412255; fax (10) 68412023; e-mail cibtc@www.cibtc.co.cn; internet www.cibtc.com.cn; f. 1949; foreign trade org. specializing in publs, including books, periodicals, art and crafts, microfilms, etc.; import and export distributors; Pres. LIU ZHIBIN.

**CITIC Publishing House:** Beijing; Pres. WANG MINGHUI.

**Dianzi Gongye Chubanshe** (Publishing House of the Electronics Industry—PHEI): POB 173, Wan Shou Lu, Beijing 100036; tel. (10) 68159028; fax (10) 68159025; f. 1982; electronic sciences and technology; Pres. LIANG XIANGFENG; Vice-Pres. WANG MINGJUN.

**Dolphin Books:** 24 Baiwanzhuang Lu, Beijing 100037; tel. (10) 68326332; fax (10) 68326642; f. 1986; children's books in Chinese and foreign languages; Dir WANG YANRONG.

**Falü Chubanshe** (Law Publishing House): POB 111, Beijing 100036; tel. (10) 6815325; f. 1980; current laws and decrees, legal textbooks, translations of important foreign legal works; Dir LAN MINGLIANG.

**Foreign Languages Press:** 19 Chegongzhuang Xi Lu, Fu Xing Men Wai, Beijing 100044; tel. (10) 68413344; fax (10) 68424931; e-mail info@flp.com.cn; internet www.flp.com.cn; f. 1952; books in 20 foreign languages reflecting political and economic developments in People's Republic of China and features of Chinese culture; Dir GUO JIEXIN; Editor-in-Chief XU MINGQIANG.

**Gaodeng Jiaoyu Chubanshe** (Higher Education Press): 55 Shatan Houjie, Beijing 100009; tel. (10) 64014043; fax (10) 64054602; e-mail linm@public.bta.net.cn; f. 1954; academic, textbooks; Pres. YU GUOHUA; Editor-in-Chief ZHANG ZENGSHUN.

**Gongren Chubanshe** (Workers' Publishing House): Liupukeng, Andingmen Wai, Beijing; tel. (10) 64215278; f. 1949; labour movement, trade unions, science and technology related to industrial production.

**Guangdong Keji Chubanshe** (Guangdong Science and Technology Press): 11 Shuiyin Lu, Huanshidong Lu, Guangzhou, Guangdong 510075; tel. (20) 87768688; fax (20) 87769412; f. 1978; natural sciences, technology, agriculture, medicine, computing, English language teaching; Dir OUYANG LIAN.

**Heilongjiang Kexue Jishu Chubanshe:** (Heilongjiang Science and Technology Press): 41 Jianshe Jie, Nangang Qu, Harbin 150001, Heilongjiang; tel. and fax (451) 3642127; f. 1979; industrial and agricultural technology, natural sciences, economics and management, popular science, children's and general.

**Huashan Wenyi Chubanshe** (Huashan Literature and Art Publishing House): 45 Bei Malu, Shijiazhuang, Hebei; tel. 22501; f. 1982; novels, poetry, drama, etc.

**Kexue Chubanshe** (Science Press): 16 Donghuangchenggen Beijie, Beijing 100717; tel. (10) 64034205; fax (10) 64010642; f. 1954; books and journals on science and technology; Dir of Int. Sales & Marketing ZHAO SHIXIONG.

**Lingnan Meishu Chubanshe** (Lingnan Art Publishing House): 11 Shuiyin Lu, Guangzhou, Guangdong 510075; tel. (20) 87771044; fax (20) 87771049; f. 1981; works on classical and modern painting, picture albums, photographic, painting techniques; Pres. CAO LIXIANG.

**Minzu Chubanshe** (Nationalities Publishing House): 14 Hepingli Beijie, Beijing 100013; tel. (10) 64211261; f. 1953; books and periodicals in minority languages, e.g. Mongolian, Tibetan, Uygur, Korean, Kazakh, etc.; Editor-in-Chief ZHU YINGWU.

**Qunzhong Chubanshe** (Masses Publishing House): Bldg 15, Part 3, Fangxingyuan, Fangzhuan Lu, Beijing 100078; tel. (10) 67633344; f. 1956; politics, law, judicial affairs, criminology, public security, etc.

**Renmin Chubanshe** (People's Publishing House): 8 Hepinglidongjie, Andingmenwai, Beijing; tel. (10) 4213713; managed by the Ministry of Communications; science and technology, textbooks, laws and specifications of communications; Dir and Editor-in-Chief XUE DEZHEN.

**Renmin Jiaoyu Chubanshe** (People's Education Press): 55 Sha Tan Hou Jie, Beijing 100009; tel. (10) 64035745; fax (10) 64010370; f. 1950; school textbooks, guidebooks, teaching materials, etc.

**Renmin Meishu Chubanshe** (People's Fine Arts Publishing House): Beijing; tel. (10) 65122371; fax (10) 65122370; f. 1951; works by Chinese and foreign painters, sculptors and other artists, picture albums, photographic, painting techniques; Dir CHEN YUNHE; Editor-in-Chief LIU YUSHAN.

**Renmin Weisheng Chubanshe** (People's Medical Publishing House): Beijing; tel. (01) 67617283; fax (01) 645143; f. 1953; medicine (Western and traditional Chinese), pharmacology, dentistry, public health; Pres. LIU YIQING.

**Renmin Wenxue Chubanshe** (People's Literature Publishing House): 166 Chaoyangmen Nei Dajie, Beijing 100705; tel. (10) 65138394; f. 1951; largest publr of literary works and translations into Chinese; Dir NIE ZHENNING; Editor-in-Chief CHEN ZAOCHUN.

**Shanghai Guji Chubanshe** (Shanghai Classics Publishing House): 272 Ruijin Erlu, Shanghai 200020; tel. (21) 64370011; fax (21) 64339287; f. 1956; classical Chinese literature, history, philosophy, geography, linguistics, science and technology.

**Shanghai Jiaoyu Chubanshe** (Shanghai Educational Publishing House): 123 Yongfu Lu, Shanghai 200031; tel. (21) 64377165; fax (21) 64339995; f. 1958; academic; Dir and Editor-in-Chief CHEN HE.

**Shanghai Yiwen Chubanshe** (Shanghai Translation Publishing House): 14 Xiang 955, Yanan Zhonglu, Shanghai 200040; tel. (21) 62472890; fax (21) 62475100; e-mail cpbq@bj.cal.com.cn; internet www.cp.com.cn; f. 1978; translations of foreign classic and modern literature; philosophy, social sciences, dictionaries, etc.

**Shangwu Yinshuguan** (The Commercial Press): 36 Wangfujing Dajie, Beijing; tel. (10) 65252026; f. 1897; dictionaries and reference books in Chinese and foreign languages, translations of foreign works on social sciences; Pres. YANG DEYAN.

**Shaonian Ertong Chubanshe** (Juvenile and Children's Publishing House): 1538 Yan An Xi Lu, Shanghai 200052; tel. (21) 62823025; fax (21) 62821726; f. 1952; children's educational and literary works, teaching aids and periodicals; Gen. Man. ZHOU SHUNPEI.

**Shijie Wenhua Chubanshe** (World Culture Publishing House): Dir ZHU LIE.

**Wenwu Chubanshe** (Cultural Relics Publishing House): 29 Wusi Dajie, Beijing 100009; tel. (10) 64048057; fax (10) 64010698; e-mail web@wenwu.com; internet www.wenwu.com; f. 1956; books and catalogues of Chinese relics in museums and those recently discovered; Dir XU AIXIAN.

**Wuhan Daxue Chubanshe** (Wuhan University Press): Suojia Hill, Wuhan, Hubei; tel. (27) 7820651; fax (27) 7812661; f. 1981; reference books, academic works, etc.; Pres. and Editor-in-Chief Prof. NIU TAICHEN.

**Xiandai Chubanshe** (Modern Press): 504 Anhua Li, Andingmenwai, Beijing 100011; tel. (10) 64263515; fax (10) 64214540; f. 1981; directories, reference books, etc.; Dir ZHOU HONGLI.

**Xinhua Chubanshe** (Xinhua Publishing House): 57 Xuanwumen Xidajie, Beijing 100803; tel. (10) 63074022; fax (10) 63073880; e-mail rdzhou@public.bta.net.cn; f. 1979; social sciences, economy, politics, history, geography, directories, dictionaries, etc.; Dir and Editor-in-Chief QIU YONGSHENG.

**Xuelin Chubanshe** (Scholar Books Publishing House): 120 Wenmiao Lu, Shanghai 200010; tel. and fax (21) 63768540; f. 1981; academic, including personal academic works at authors' own expense; Dir LEI QUNMING.

**Zhongguo Caizheng Jingji Chubanshe** (China Financial and Economic Publishing House): 8 Dafosi Dongjie, Dongcheng Qu, Beijing; tel. (10) 64011805; f. 1961; finance, economics, commerce and accounting.

**Zhongguo Dabaike Quanshu Chubanshe** (Encyclopaedia of China Publishing House): 17 Fu Cheng Men Bei Dajie, Beijing 100037; tel. (10) 68315610; fax (10) 68316510; e-mail ygh@bj.col.com.cn; f. 1978; specializes in encyclopaedias; Dir SHAN JIFU.

**Zhongguo Ditu Chubanshe** (China Cartographic Publishing House): 3 Baizhifang Xijie, Beijing 100054; tel. and fax (10) 63014136; f. 1954; cartographic publr; Dir ZHANG XUELIANG.

**Zhongguo Funü Chubanshe** (China Women Publishing House): 24A Shijia Hutong, 100010 Beijing; tel. (10) 65126986; f. 1981; women's movement, marriage and family, child-care, etc.; Dir LI ZHONGXIU.

**Zhongguo Qingnian Chubanshe** (China Youth Press): 21 Dongsi Shiertiao, Beijing 100708; tel. (10) 84015396; fax (10) 64031803; e-mail cyph@eastnet.co.cn; f. 1950; literature, social and natural sciences, youth work, autobiography; also periodicals; Editor-in-Chief CHEN HAOZENG.

**Zhongguo Shehui Kexue Chubanshe** (China Social Sciences Publishing House): 158A Gulou Xidajie, Beijing 100720; tel. (10) 64073837; fax (10) 64074509; f. 1978; Dir ZHENG WENLIN.

**Zhongguo Xiju Chubanshe** (China Theatrical Publishing House): 52 Dongsi Batiao Hutong, Beijing; tel. (10) 64015815. 1957; traditional and modern Chinese drama.

**Zhongguo Youyi Chuban Gongsi** (China Friendship Publishing Corpn): e-mail tmdoxu@public.east.cn.net; Dir YANG WEI.

**Zhonghua Shuju** (Zhonghua Book Co): 38 Taipingqiao Xili, Fenglai Qu, Beijing; tel. (10) 63458226; f. 1912; general; Pres. SONG YIFU.

### PUBLISHERS' ASSOCIATION

**Publishers' Association of China:** Beijing; f. 1979; arranges academic exchanges with foreign publrs; Chair. SONG MUWEN; Sec.-Gen. FANG ZHENJIANG.

# Broadcasting and Communications

### TELECOMMUNICATIONS

**Ministry of Information Industry:** 13 Xichangan Jie, Beijing 100804; tel. (10) 66014249; fax (10) 66034248; internet www.mii.gov.cn; regulates all issues concerning the telecommunications sector.

**China Telecom:** internet www.chinatelecom.com.cn; f. 1997 as a vehicle for foreign investment in telecommunications sector; Dir.-Gen. LI LIGUI.

**China Netcom Corpn:** Beijing; f. 1999; internet telephone service provider; CEO EDWARD TIAN.

**China United Telecommunications Corpn (UNICOM):** 1/F, Hongji Centre Office Bldg, 18 Jianguomenei Dajie, Beijing; tel. (10) 65181800; fax (10) 65183405; internet www.chinaunicom.com.cn; f. 1994; cellular telecommunications; Chair. ZHAO WEICHEN; Pres. LI HUIFEN.

### BROADCASTING

At the end of 1997 there were 1,363 radio broadcasting stations, 747 medium- and short-wave radio transmitting and relay stations (covering 86.0% of the population), 923 television stations and 41,205 television transmitting and relay stations with a capacity of over 1,000 watts (covering 87.6% of the population).

#### Regulatory Authorities

**State Administration of Radio, Film and Television (SARFT):** 2 Fu Xing Men Wai Dajie, POB 4501, Beijing 100866; tel. (10) 68513409; fax (10) 68512174; internet www.dns.incmrft.gov.cn; controls the Central People's Broadcasting Station, the Central TV Station, Radio Beijing, China Record Co., Beijing Broadcasting Institute, Broadcasting Research Institute, the China Broadcasting Art Troupe, etc.; Chair. TIAN CONGMING.

**State Radio Regulatory Authority:** Beijing; operates under the State Council; Chair. ZOU JIAHUA.

#### Radio

**China National Radio (CNR):** 2 Fu Xing Men Wai Dajie, Beijing 100866; tel. (10) 68515522; f. 1945; domestic service in Chinese, Zang Wen (Tibetan), Min Nan Hua (Amoy), Ke Jia (Hakka), Hasaka (Kazakh), Wei Wuer (Uygur), Menggu Hua (Mongolian) and Chaoxian (Korean); Dir TONG XIANGRONG.

**Zhongguo Guoji Guangbo Diantai** (China Radio International): 16A Shijingshan Lu, Beijing 100039; tel. (10) 68891001; fax (10) 68891582; e-mail crieng@public.bta.net.cn; internet www.cri.com.cn; f. 1941; fmrly Radio Beijing; foreign service in 38 languages incl. Arabic, Burmese, Czech, English, Esperanto, French, German, Indonesian, Italian, Japanese, Lao, Polish, Portuguese, Russian, Spanish, Turkish and Vietnamese; Dir ZHANG ZHENHUA.

### Television

**China Central Television (CCTV):** 11 Fuxing Lu, Haidian, Beijing 100859; tel. (10) 8500000; fax (10) 8513025; internet www.wtdb.com/CCTV/about.htm; operates under Bureau of Broadcasting Affairs of the State Council, Beijing; f. 1958; operates eight networks; 24-hour global satellite service commenced in 1996; Pres. YANG WEIGWANG.

In April 1994 foreign companies were prohibited from establishing or operating cable TV stations in China. By mid-1996 there were more than 3,000 cable television stations in operation, with networks covering 45m. households. The largest subscriber service is Beijing Cable TV (Dir GUO JUNJIN). Satellite services are available in some areas: millions of satellite receivers are in use. In October 1993 the Government approved new regulations, attempting to restrict access to foreign satellite broadcasts.

# Finance

(cap. = capital; auth. = authorized; p.u. = paid up; res = reserves; dep. = deposits; m. = million; amounts in yuan unless otherwise stated)

## BANKING

Radical economic reforms, introduced in 1994, included the strengthening of the role of the central bank and the establishment of new commercial banks. The Commercial Bank Law took effect in July 1995. The establishment of private banks was to be permitted.

### Central Bank

**People's Bank of China:** 32 Chengfang Jie, Xicheng Qu, Beijing 100800; tel. (10) 66194114; fax (10) 66015346; e-mail master@pbc.gov.cn; internet www.pbc.gov.cn; f. 1948; bank of issue; decides and implements China's monetary policies; Gov. DAI XIANGLONG; 2,204 brs.

### Other Banks

**Agricultural Bank of China:** 23A Fuxing Lu, Haidian Qu, Beijing 100036; tel. (10) 68216807; fax (10) 68297160; e-mail webmaster@intl.abocn.com; internet www.abocn.com; f. 1951; serves mainly China's rural financial operations, providing services for agriculture, industry, commerce, transport, etc. in rural areas; cap. 35,926m., res 2,915m., dep. 901,905m. (Dec. 1995); Pres. SHANG FULIN; 2,500 brs.

**Agricultural Development Bank of China:** 2A Ritanbei Jie, Xicheng Qu, Beijing 100645; tel. (10) 68081556; fax (10) 65235059; cap. 20,000m.; Pres. HE LINXIANG.

**Bank of China:** Bank of China Bldg, 410 Fu Cheng Men Nei Dajie, Beijing 100818; tel. (10) 66016688; fax (10) 66016869; e-mail webmaster@bank-of-china.com; internet www.bank-of-china.com; f. 1912; handles foreign exchange and international settlements; cap. 104,500m., res 32,690m., dep. 2,228,572m. (Dec. 1998); Chair. LIU MINGKANG; 116 domestic, 74 overseas brs.

**Bank of Communications Ltd:** 18 Xian Xia Lu, Shanghai 200335; tel. (21) 62756784; fax (21) 62756874; internet www.bankcomm.com; f. 1908; commercial bank; cap. 11,710.7m., res 10,156.0m., dep. 457,074.0m. (Dec. 1998); Chair. YIN JIEYAN; Pres. WANG MINGQUAN; 90 brs.

**Beijing City Co-op Bank:** 65 You An Men Nei Lu, Xuanwu Qu, Beijing 100054; tel. and fax (10) 63520159; f. 1996; cap. 1,000m., res 3,466m., dep. 26,660m. (Dec. 1996); 90 brs.

**Bengbu House Saving Bank:** 85 Zhong Rong Jie, Bengbu 233000; tel. (552) 2042069.

**China and South Sea Bank Ltd:** 410 Fu Cheng Men Nei Dajie, Beijing; f. 1921; cap. 1,200m., res 2,815m., dep. 37,760m. (Dec. 1997); Chair. CUI PING.

**China Construction Bank (CCB):** 25 Jinrong Jie, Beijing 100032; tel. (10) 67597114; fax (10) 66212863; e-mail ccb@bj.china.com; internet www.ccb.com.cn; f. 1954; fmrly People's Construction Bank of China; makes payments for capital construction projects in accordance with state plans and budgets; issues medium- and long-term loans to enterprises and short-term loans to construction enterprises and others; also handles foreign exchange business; housing loans; cap. 35,922m., res 12,524m., dep. 1,456,347m. (Dec. 1997); Pres. WANG XUEBING; 49 brs.

**China International Capital Corporation (CICC):** 23rd Floor, Everbright Bldg, 6 Fu Xing Men Wai Dajie, Beijing 100045; tel. (10) 68561166; fax (10) 68561145; f. 1995; international investment bank; 42.5% owned by China Construction Bank; registered cap. US $100m.; CEO EDWIN LIM.

**China International Trust and Investment Corporation (CITIC):** Capital Mansion, 6 Xianyuannan Lu, Chaoyang Qu, Beijing 100004; tel. (10) 64661105; fax (10) 64662137; f. 1979; economic and technological co-operation; finance, banking, investment and trade; registered cap. 3,000m.; Chair. WANG JUN; Pres. QIN XIAO.

**China Merchants Bank:** News Centre Bldg, 2 Shennan Lu, Shenzhen 518001; tel. (755) 2290000; fax (755) 2243666; internet www.cmbchina.com; f. 1987; cap. 2,807m., res 3,858m., dep. 119,768m. (Dec. 1998); Chair. JIANG BO; Pres. WANG SHIZHEN; 12 brs.

**China Minsheng Banking Corporation:** 4 Zhengyi Lu, Dongcheng Qu, Beijing 100006; tel. (10) 65269610; fax (10) 68588570; e-mail msbgs@cmbc.com.cn; internet www.cmbc.com.cn; first non-state national commercial bank, opened Jan. 1996; registered cap. 1,380m., res 112m., dep. 22,477m. (Dec. 1998); Chair. JING SHUPING; Pres. CAI LULUN; 5 brs.

**China State Bank Ltd:** 17 Xi Jiao Min Xiang, Beijing 100031; f. 1927; cap. 1,100m., res 3,365m., dep. 46,825m. (Dec. 1998); Gen. Man. LI PINZHOU.

**Chinese Mercantile Bank:** Ground and 23rd Floors, Dongfeng Bldg, 2 Yannan Lu, Futian Qu, Shenzhen 518031; tel. (755) 3257880; fax (755) 3257801; e-mail szcmbank@public.szptt.net.cn; f. 1993; cap. US $55.3m., res US $3.2m., dep. US $227.0m. (Dec. 1998); Pres. HUANG MINGXIANG.

**CITIC Industrial Bank:** Block C, Fuhua Bldg, 8 Chao Yang Men Bei Dajie, Dongcheng Qu, Beijing 100027; f. 1987; tel. (10) 65541658; fax (10) 65541671; cap. 5,307m., res 282m., dep. 102,174m. (Dec. 1997); Chair. QIN YIAO; Pres. DOU JIANZHONG; 17 brs.

**Everbright Bank of China:** Everbright Tower, 6 Fu Xing Men Wai Lu, Beijing 100045; tel. (10) 58565577; fax (10) 68561260; e-mail EBBC@public.bta.net.cn; internet www.ebeb.com.cn/bank/index.html; f. 1992; acquired China Investment Bank in 1999; cap. 2,800m., res 2,179.6m., dep. 65,343.8m. (Dec. 1998); Chair. ZHU XIAOHUA; Pres. XU BIN; 10 brs.

**Export and Import Bank of China:** 1 Dingandongli, Yongdingmenwai, Beijing; tel. (10) 67626688; fax (10) 67638940; f. 1994; provides trade credits for export of large machinery, electronics, ships, etc.; Chair. DONG ZHIGUANG; Pres. YANG ZILIN.

**Fujian Asia Bank Ltd:** 2nd Floor, Yuan Hong Bldg, 32 Wuyi Lu, Fuzhou, Fujian 350005; tel. (591) 3330788; fax (591) 3330843; f. 1993; cap. US $27.0m., res US $1.1m., dep. US $4.8m. (Dec. 1997); Chair. YAN JIANGUO; Gen. Man. DENNIS H. LAM.

**Fujian Industrial Bank:** Zhong Shang Bldg, 154 Hudong Lu, Hualin, Fuzhou, Fujian 350003; tel. (591) 7844196; fax (591) 7841932; internet www.fujian-window.com/Fujian_w/ad/xy/xy.html; f. 1982; cap. 1,500m., res 1,658m., dep. 29,912m. (Dec. 1998); Pres. CHEN YI; 11 brs.

**Guangdong Development Bank:** 83 Nonglinxia Lu, Dongshan Qu, Guangzhou, Guangdong 518001; tel. (20) 87310888; fax (20) 83349194; internet www.gdb.com.cn; f. 1988; cap. 2,292m., res 1,443.3m., dep. 77,244.1m. (Dec. 1998); Pres. LI RUOHONG; Chair. and Gen. Man. WU CHIXIN; 32 brs.

**Guangdong (Kwangtung) Provincial Bank:** 410 Fu Cheng Men Nei Dajie, Beijing 100818; f. 1924; cap. 1,500m., res 4,900m., dep. 71,470m. (Dec. 1997).

**Hua Xia Bank:** 9th–12th Floors, Xidan International Mansion, 111 Xidan Bei Dajie, Beijing 100032; tel. (10) 66151199; fax (10) 66188484; internet www.serve.cei.gov/so1/007/huaxia; f. 1992 as part of Shougang Corpn; registered cap. 2,500m., res 249m., dep. 28,287m. (Dec. 1998); Chair. LU YUCHENG.

**Industrial and Commercial Bank of China:** 55 Fuxingmennai Dajie, Xicheng Qu, Beijing 100031; tel. (10) 66106114; fax (10) 66106053; internet www.icbc.com.cn; f. 1984; handles industrial and commercial credits and international business; cap. 86,024m., res 4,288m. (Dec. 1996), dep. 2,251,100m. (Dec. 1997); Pres. JIANG JIANQING; 38,219 brs.

**International Bank of Paris and Shanghai:** 13th Floor, North Tower, Shanghai Stock Exchange Bldg, 528 Pudong Nan Lu, Shanghai 200120; tel. (21) 58405500; fax (21) 58889232; f. 1992; cap. US $33.6m., res US $824,000, dep. US $111m. (Dec. 1998); Chair. and Dir JIANG JIANQING.

**Kincheng Banking Corporation:** 410 Fu Cheng Men Nei Dajie, Beijing; f. 1917; cap. 2,200m., res 4,434m., dep. 58,934m. (Dec. 1997); Chair. ZHANG GUOWEN.

**National Commercial Bank Ltd:** 410 Fu Cheng Men Nei Dajie, Beijing; e-mail hkbrmain@natcombank.com; f. 1907; cap. 1,200m., res 3,390m., dep. 47,458m. (Dec. 1997); 27 brs.

**Qingdao International Bank:** Full Hope Mansion C, 12 Hong Kong Middle Rd, Qingdao, Shandong 266071; tel. (532) 5026211; fax (532) 5026221; e-mail qibankc@public.qd.sd.cn; f. 1996; joint venture between Industrial and Commercial Bank of China and Korea First Bank; cap. US $166m., res US $5.6m., dep. US $61.4m. (Dec. 1998); Pres. DUCK SUNG YUN.

**Shanghai Pudong Development Bank:** 12 Zongshan Lu, Shanghai 200002; tel. (21) 63296188; fax (21) 63232036; internet www.spdb.com.cn; f. 1993; cap. 2,010m., res 695m., dep. 78,623m. (Dec. 1997); Pres. JIN YUN.

**Shenzhen Development Bank Co Ltd:** Shenzhen Development Bank Tower, 178 Shen Nan Dong Lu, Shenzhen 518001; tel. (755) 2080387; fax (755) 2080386; f. 1987; cap. 1,552m., res 1,139m., dep. 32,482m. (Dec. 1998); Pres. ZHOU LIN.

**Sin Hua Bank Ltd:** 17 Xi Jiao Min Xiang, Beijing 100031; subsidiary of Bank of China; cap. 2,200m., res 6,343m., dep. 78,418m. (Dec. 1997); Chair. JIANG ZU QI.

**State Development Bank (SDB):** 29 Fuchengmenwai Lu, Xicheng Qu, Beijing 100037; tel. (10) 68306557; fax (10) 68306541; f. 1994; merged with China Investment Bank 1998; handles low-interest loans for infrastructural projects and basic industries; Gov. CHEN YUAN.

**Xiamen International Bank:** 10 Hu Bin Bei Lu, Xiamen, Fujian 361012; tel. (592) 5310686; fax (592) 5310685; e-mail xib@public.xm.fi.cn; f. 1985; cap. HK $620m., res HK $513m., dep. HK $7,356m. (Dec. 1998); Chair. LI LIHUI; 3 brs.

**Yantai House Saving Bank:** 248 Nan Da Jie, Yantai 264001; tel. (535) 6207047.

**Yien Yieh Commercial Bank Ltd:** 17 Xi Jiao Min Xiang, Beijing 100031; f. 1915; cap. 800m., res 3,716m., dep. 41,942m. (Dec. 1998); Chair. ZHAO AN GE; Gen. Man. WU GUO RUI; 29 brs.

**Zhejiang Commercial Bank Ltd:** 88 Xi Zhongshan Lu, Ningbo 315010; tel. (574) 7245678; fax (574) 7245409; f. 1993; cap. US $40m., dep. US $86m. (Dec. 1997); Pres. and Chair. SHEN SONGJUN.

Zhongxin Shiye Bank is a nation-wide commercial bank. Other commercial banks include the Fujian Commercial Bank and Zhaoshang Bank.

#### Foreign Banks

Before mid-1995 foreign banks were permitted only to open representative offices in China. The first foreign bank established a full branch in Beijing in mid-1995, and by March 1998 there were 51 foreign banks in China. In March 1997 foreign banks were allowed for the first time to conduct business in yuan. However, they are only entitled to accept yuan deposits from joint-venture companies. Representative offices totalled 519 in December 1996. In March 1999 the Government announced that foreign banks, hitherto restricted to 23 cities and Hainan province, were to be permitted to open branches in all major cities.

### STOCK EXCHANGES

Several stock exchanges were in the process of development in the mid-1990s, and by early 1995 the number of shareholders had reached 38m. By 1995 a total of 15 futures exchanges were in operation, dealing in various commodities, building materials and currencies. By the end of 1997 the number of companies listed on the Shanghai and Shenzhen Stock Exchanges had reached 745. In August 1997, in response to unruly conditions, the Government ordered the China Securities Regulatory Commission (see below) to assume direct control of the Shanghai and Shenzhen exchanges.

**Stock Exchange Executive Council (SEEC):** Beijing; tel. (10) 64935210; f. 1989 to oversee the development of financial markets in China; mems comprise leading non-bank financial institutions authorized to handle securities; Vice-Pres. WANG BOMING.

**Securities Association of China (SAC):** Olympic Hotel, 52 Baishiqiao Lu, Beijing 100081; tel. (10) 68316688; fax (10) 68318390; f. 1991; non-governmental organization comprising 122 mems (stock exchanges and securities cos) and 35 individual mems; Pres. GUO ZHENQIAN.

**Beijing Securities Exchange:** 5 Anding Lu, Chao Yang Qu, Beijing 100029; tel. (10) 64939366; fax (10) 64936233.

**Shanghai Stock Exchange:** 528 Pudong Nan Lu, Shanghai 200120; f. 1990; tel. (21) 68808888; fax (21) 68807813; e-mail webmaster@sse.com.cn; internet www.sse.com.cn; Chair. YANG XIANGHAI; Pres. TU GUANGSHAO.

**Shenzhen Stock Exchange:** 2nd Floor, The Grand Theatre, Shenzhen, Guangdong 518001; tel. and fax (755) 5564330. 1991; Chair. LUO XIANRONG.

#### Regulatory Authorities

Operations are regulated by the State Council Securities Policy Committee and by the following:

**China Securities Regulatory Commission (CSRC):** Bldg 3, Area 3, Fangqunyuan, Fangzhuang, Beijing 100078; tel. (10) 67617343; fax (10) 67653117; f. 1993; Chair. ZHOU XIAOCHUAN; Sec.-Gen. WANG YI.

### INSURANCE

A new Insurance Law, formulated to standardize activities and to strengthen the supervision and administration of the industry, took effect in October 1995. Changes included the separation of life insurance and property insurance businesses. By late 1998 the number of insurance companies totalled 25. Total premiums rose from 44,000m. yuan in 1994 to 108,740m. yuan in Dec. 1997, of which 60,000m. yuan were life insurance premiums.

**AXA-Minmetals Assurance Co:** f. 1999; joint venture by Groupe AXA (France) and China Minmetals Group; Gen. Man. JOSEPH SIN.

**China Insurance Co Ltd:** 22 Xi Jiao Min Xiang, POB 20, Beijing 100032; tel. (10) 6654231; fax (10) 66011869; f. 1931; cargo, hull, freight, fire, life, personal accident, industrial injury, motor insurance, reinsurance, etc.; Man. SONG GUO HUA.

**China Insurance Group:** 410 Fu Cheng Men Nei Dajie, Beijing; tel. (10) 66016688; fax (10) 66011869; f. 1996 (fmrly People's Insurance Co of China (PICC), f. 1949); hull, marine cargo, aviation, motor, life, fire, accident, liability and reinsurance, etc.; in process of division into three subsidiaries (life insurance (China Life Insurance Co—CLIC), property-casualty insurance and reinsurance) by mid-1996, in preparation for transformation into joint-stock cos; 1996 300m. policy-holders; Chair. and Pres. MA YONGWEI.

**China Pacific Insurance Co Ltd (CPIC):** 12 Zhongshan Lu (Dong 1), Shanghai 200001; tel. (21) 63232488; fax (21) 63218398; internet www.cpic.com.cn.; f. 1991; joint-stock co; Chair. WANG MINGQUAN; Pres. WANG GUOLIANG.

**China Ping An Insurance Co:** Ping An Bldg, Bagua San Lu, Bagualing, Shenzhen 518029; tel. (755) 2262888; fax (755) 2431019; f. 1988.

**Hua Tai Insurance Co of China Ltd:** Beijing; tel. (10) 68565588; fax (10) 68561750; f. 1996 by 63 industrial cos.

**Pacific-Aetna Life Insurance Co:** Shanghai; f. 1998 by CPIC and Aetna Life Insurance Co.; China's first Sino-US insurance co.

**Tai Ping Insurance Co Ltd:** 410 Fu Cheng Men Nei Dajie, Beijing 100034; tel. (10) 66016688; fax (10) 66011869; marine freight, hull, cargo, fire, personal accident, industrial injury, motor insurance, reinsurance, etc.; Pres. SUN XIYUE.

**Taikang Life Insurance Co Ltd:** Beijing; f. 1996; Chair. CHEN DONGSHENG.

Joint-stock companies include the Xinhua (New China) Life Insurance Co Ltd (Gen. Man. SUN BING). By April 1998 a total of 84 foreign insurance companies had established some 150 offices in China, being permitted to operate in Shanghai and Guangzhou only.

#### Regulatory Authority

**China Insurance Regulatory Commission (CIRC):** Beijing; f. 1998; Vice-Chair. MA YONGWEI.

## Trade and Industry

### GOVERNMENT AGENCIES

**China Council for the Promotion of International Trade (CCPIT):** 1 Fuxingmenwai Dajie, Beijing 100860; tel. (10) 68013344; fax (10) 68011370; e-mail ccpitweb@public.bta.net.cn; internet www.ccpit.org; f. 1952; encourages foreign trade and economic co-operation; sponsors and arranges Chinese exhbns abroad and foreign exhbns in China; helps foreigners to apply for patent rights and trade-mark registration in China; promotes foreign investment and organizes tech. exchanges with other countries; provides legal services; publishes trade periodicals; Chair. YU XIAOSONG; Sec.-Gen. ZHONG MIN.

**Chinese General Association of Light Industry:** 22B Fuwai Dajie, Beijing 100833; tel. (10) 68396114; under supervision of State Council; Chair. YU CHEN.

**Chinese General Association of Textile Industry:** 12 Dong Chang An Jie, Beijing 100742; tel. (10) 65129545; under supervision of State Council; Chair. SHI WANPENG.

**Ministry of Foreign Trade and Economic Co-operation:** (see under Ministries).

**National Administration of State Property:** Dir ZHANG YOUCAI.

**State Administration for Industry and Commerce:** 8 San Li He Dong Lu, Xicheng Qu, Beijing 100820; tel. (10) 68010463; fax (10) 68020848; responsible for market supervision and administrative execution of industrial and commercial laws; functions under the direct supervision of the State Council; Dir WANG ZHONGFU.

**Takeover Office for Military, Armed Police, Government and Judiciary Businesses:** Beijing; f. 1998 to assume control of enterprises formerly operated by the People's Liberation Army.

## CHAMBERS OF COMMERCE

**All-China Federation of Industry and Commerce:** 93 Beiheyan Dajie, Beijing 100006; tel. (10) 65136677; fax (10) 65122631; f. 1953; promotes overseas trade relations; Chair. JING SHUPING; Sec.-Gen. HUAN YUSHAN.

**China Chamber of International Commerce—Shanghai:** Jinling Mansions, 28 Jinling Lu, Shanghai 200021; tel. (21) 53060228; fax (21) 63869915; e-mail ccpitllb@online.sh.cn; Chair. YANG ZHIHUA.

**China Chamber of International Commerce—Zhuhai:** 127 Xinguangli, Zhuhai, Guangdong 519000; tel. (756) 2218954; fax (756) 2228640.

## TRADE AND INDUSTRIAL ORGANIZATIONS

**Anshan Iron and Steel Co:** Huangang Lu, Tiexi Qu, Anshan 114021; tel. and fax(412) 6723090; Pres. LIU JIE.

**Aviation Industries of China:** 67 Nan Dajie, Jiaodaokou, Dongcheng Qu, Beijing; tel. (10) 64013322; fax (10) 64013648; Pres. ZHU YULI.

**Baoshan Iron and Steel Complex Corpn (Group):** 2 Mudangjiang Lu, Shanghai 201900; tel. (21) 5646944; fax (21) 56600260; proposals for merger with Shanghai Metallurgical announced late 1997; registered cap. 100m. yuan; Chair. LI MING; Pres. XIE QIHUA.

**Baotou Iron and Steel Co:** Gangtie Dajie, Kundulun Qu, Baotou 014010, Inner Mongolia; tel. (472) 2125619; fax (472) 2183708; Pres. ZENG GUOAN.

**China Aviation Supplies Corpn:** 155 Xi Dongsi Jie, Beijing 100013; tel. (10) 64012233; fax (10) 64016392; f.1980; Pres. LIU YUANFAN.

**China Civil Engineering Construction Corpn (CCECC):** 4 Beifeng Wo, Haidian Qu, Beijing 100038; tel. (10) 63263392; fax (10) 63263864; e-mail zongban@ccecc.com.cn; f. 1953; general contracting, provision of technical and labour services, consulting and design, etc.; Pres. WANG GUOQING.

**China Construction International Inc:** 9 Sanlihe Lu, Haidian Qu, Beijing; tel. (10) 68394086; fax (10) 68394097; Pres. FU RENZHANG.

**China Electronics Corpn:** 27 Wanshou Lu, Haidian Qu, Beijing 100846; tel. (10) 68218529; fax (10) 68213745; e-mail cec@public.gb.com.cn; internet www.cec.com.cn; Pres. LIU XUEHONG.

**China Garment Industry Corpn:** 9A Taiyanggong Beisanhuandong Lu, Chao Yang Qu, Beijing 100028; tel. (10) 64216660; fax (10) 64239134; Pres. DONG BINGGEN.

**China General Technology (Group) Holding Ltd:** f. 1998 through merger of China National Technical Import and Export Corpn, China National Machinery Import and Export Corpn, China National Instruments Import and Export Corpn and China National Corpn for Overseas Economic Co-operation; total assets 16,000m. yuan; Chair. TONG CHANGYIN.

**China Gold Co:** 1 Bei Jie, Qingnianhu, Andingmenwai, Beijing; tel. (10) 64214831; Pres. CUI LAN.

**China Great Wall Computer Group:** 38A Xueyuan Lu, Haidian Qu, Beijing 100083; tel. (10) 68342714; fax (10) 62011240; internet www.gwssi.com.cn; Pres. LU MING.

**China Great Wall Industry Corpn:** Hangtian Changcheng Bldg, 30 Haidian Nanlu, Haidian Qu, Beijing 100080; tel. (10) 68748737; fax (10) 68748865; e-mail cgwic@cgwic.com; internet www.cgwic.com.cn; registered cap. 200m. yuan; Pres. ZHANG XINXIA.

**China International Book Trading Corpn:** (see under Publishers).

**China International Contractors Association:** 28 Donghouxiang, Andingmenwai, Beijing 100710; tel. (10) 64211159; fax (10) 64213959; Chair. LI RONGMIN.

**China International Futures Trading Corpn:** 24th Floor, Capital Mansion, 6 Xinyuan Nan Lu, Chao Yang Qu, Beijing 100004; tel. (10) 64665388; fax (10) 64665140; Chair. TIAN YUAN; Pres. LU JIAN.

**China International Telecommunications Construction Corpn (CITCC):** 22 Yuyou Lane, Xicheng Qu, Beijing 100035; tel. (10) 66012244; fax (10) 66024103; Pres. QI FUSHENG.

**China International Water and Electric Corpn:** 3 Liupukang Yiqu Zhongjie, Xicheng Qu, Beijing 100011; tel. (10) 64015511; fax (10) 64014075; e-mail cwe@mx.cei.go.cn; f. 1956 as China Water and Electric International Corpn, name changed 1983; imports and exports equipment for projects in the field of water and electrical engineering; undertakes such projects; provides technical and labour services; Pres. WANG SHUOHAO.

**China Iron and Steel Industry and Trade Group Corpn:** 17B Xichangan Jie, Beijing 100031; tel. (10) 66067733; fax (10) 66078450; e-mail support@sinosteel.com.cn; internet www.sinosteel. com; f. 1999 by merger of China National Metallurgical Import and Export Corpn, China Materials Corpn and China Metallurgical Steel Products Processing Corpn.; Pres. BAI BAOHUA.

**China National Aerotechnology Import and Export Corpn:** 5 Liangguochang, Dongcheng Qu, Beijing 100010; tel. (10) 64017722; fax (10) 64015381; f.1952; exports signal flares, electric detonators, tachometers, parachutes, general purpose aircraft, etc.; Pres. YANG CHUNSHU; Gen. Man. LIU GUOMIN.

**China National Animal Breeding Stock Import and Export Corpn (CABS):** 10 Yangyi Hutong Jia, Dongdan, Beijing 100005; tel. (10) 65131107; fax (10) 65128694; sole agency for import and export of stud animals including cattle, sheep, goats, swine, horses, donkeys, camels, rabbits, poultry, etc., as well as pasture and turf grass seeds, feed additives, medicines, etc.; Pres. YANG CHENGSHAN.

**China National Arts and Crafts Import and Export Corpn:** Arts and Crafts Bldg, 103 Jixiangli, Chao Yang Men Wai, Chao Yang Qu, Beijing 100020; tel. (10) 65931075; fax (10) 65931036; e-mail po@mbox.cnart.com.cn; internet www.cnart-group.com; deals in jewellery, ceramics, handicrafts, embroidery, pottery, wicker, bamboo, etc.; Pres. CHEN KUN.

**China National Automotive Industry Corpn (CNAIC):** 46 Fucheng Lu, Haidian Qu, Beijing 100036; tel. (10) 88123968; fax (10) 68125556; Pres. GU YAOTIAN.

**China National Automotive Industry Import and Export Corpn (CAIEC):** 5 Beisihuan Xi Lu, Beijing 100083; tel. (10) 62310650; fax (10) 62310688; e-mail info@chinacaiec.com; internet www.chinacaiec.com; sales US $540m. (1995); Pres. CHEN XULIN; 1,100 employees.

**China National Cereals, Oils and Foodstuffs Import and Export Corpn:** 7th–13th Floors, Tower A, COFCO Plaza, Jian Guo Men Wai Dajie, Beijing 100005; tel. (10) 65268888; fax (10) 65278612; e-mail minnie@cofco.com.cn; internet www.cofco.com.cn; imports and exports grains, etc.; Pres. ZHOU MINGCHEN.

**China National Chartering Corpn (SINOCHART):** Rm 1601/1602, 1607/1608, Jiu Ling Bldg, 21 Xisanhuan Bei Lu, Beijing 100081; tel. (10) 68405601; fax (10) 68405628; e-mail sinochrt@public.intercom.co.cn; f. 1950; functions under Ministry of Foreign Trade and Economic Co-operation; subsidiary of SINOTRANS (see below); arranges chartering of ships, reservation of space, managing and operating chartered vessels; Pres. LIU SHUNLONG; Gen. Man. ZHANG JIANWEI.

**China National Chemical Construction Corpn:** Block 7, 16 Hepingli, Dongcheng Qu, Beijing 100013; tel. (10) 64214043; fax (10) 64215982; e-mail infolegal@cncccc.cnnet.sic.gov.cn; internet www.cnccc.com; registered cap. 50m.; Pres. CHEN LIHUA.

**China National Chemicals Import and Export Corpn (SINOCHEM):** Sinochem Tower, 2A Fuxingmenwai Jie, Beijing 100045; tel. (10) 68568888; fax (10) 685868890; internet www.sinochem.com; deals in rubber products, crude petroleum, petroleum products, chemicals, etc.; Pres. LIU DESHU.

**China National Coal Industry Import and Export Corpn (CNCIEC):** 88B Andingmenwai, Dongcheng Qu, Beijing 100011; tel. (10) 64287188; fax (10) 64287166; e-mail cnciec@chinacoal.com; internet www.chinacoal.com; f. 1982; sales US $800m. (1992); imports and exports coal and tech. equipment for coal industry, joint coal development and compensation trade; Chair. and Pres. WANG CHANGCHUN.

**China National Coal Mine Corpn:** 21 Bei Jie, Heipingli, Beijing 100013; tel. (10) 64217766; Pres. WANG SENHAO.

**China National Complete Plant Import and Export Corpn (Group):** 9 Xi Bin He Lu, An Ding Men, Beijing; tel. (10) 64253388; fax (10) 64211382; Chair. HU ZHAOFING; Pres. LI ZHIMIN.

**China National Electronics Import and Export Corpn:** 8th Floor, Electronics Bldg, 23A Fuxing Lu, Beijing 100036; tel. (10) 68219550; fax (10) 68212352; e-mail ceiec@ceiec.com.cn; internet www.ceiec.com.cn; imports and exports electronics equipment, light industrial products, ferrous and non-ferrous metals; advertising; consultancy; Pres. QIAN BENYUAN.

**China National Export Bases Development Corpn:** Bldg 16–17, District 3, Fang Xing Yuan, Fang Zhuang Xiaoqu, Fengtai Qu, Beijing 100078; tel. (10) 67628899; fax (10) 67628803; Pres. XUE ZHAO.

**China National Foreign Trade Transportation Corpn (Group) (SINOTRANS):** Sinotrans Plaza, A43, Xizhimen Beidajie, Beijing 100044; tel. (10) 62295900; fax (10) 62295901; e-mail office@sinotrans.com; internet www.sinotrans.com; f. 1950; agents for Ministry's import and export corpns; arranges customs clearance, deliveries, forwarding and insurance for sea, land and air transportation; registered cap. 150m. yuan; Pres. LUO KAIFU.

**China National Import and Export Commodities Inspection Corpn:** 15 Fanghuadi Xi Jie, Chaoyang Qu, Beijing 100020; tel. (10) 65013951; fax (10) 65004625; internet www.ccic.com; inspects, tests and surveys import and export commodities for overseas trade, transport, insurance and manufacturing firms; Pres. ZHOU WENHUI.

**China National Instruments Import and Export Corpn (Instrimpex):** Instrimpex bldg, 6 Xizhimenwai Jie, Beijing 100044; tel. (10) 68330618; fax (10) 68330528; e-mail zcb@instrimpex.com.cn; internet www.instrimpex.com.cn; f. 1955; imports and exports; technical service, real estate, manufacturing, information service, etc.; Pres. ZHANG RUEN.

**China National Light Industrial Products Import and Export Corpn:** 910, 9th Section, Jin Song, Chao Yang Qu, Beijing 100021; tel. (10) 67766688; fax (10) 67747246; e-mail info@chinalight.com.cn; internet www.chinalight.com.cn; imports and exports household electrical appliances, audio equipment, photographic equipment, films, paper goods, building materials, bicycles, sewing machines, enamelware, glassware, stainless steel goods, footwear, leather goods, watches and clocks, cosmetics, stationery, sporting goods, etc.; Pres. XU LIEJUN.

**China National Machine Tool Corpn:** 19 Fang Jia Xiaoxiang, An Nei, Beijing 100007; tel. (10) 64033767; fax (10) 64015657; f. 1979; imports and exports machine tools and tool products, components and equipment; supplies apparatus for machine building industry; Pres. QUAN YILU.

**China National Machinery and Equipment Import and Export Corpn (Group):** 6 Xisanhuannan Lu, Liuliqiao, Beijing 100073; tel. (10) 63271392; fax (10) 63261865; f. 1978; imports and exports machine tools, all kinds of machinery, automobiles, hoisting and transport equipment, electric motors, photographic equipment, etc.; Pres. XI JIACHENG.

**China National Machinery Import and Export Corpn:** Sichuan Mansion, West Wing, 1 Fu Xing Men Wai Jie, Xicheng Qu, Beijing 100037; tel. (10) 68991188; fax (10) 68991000; e-mail cmc@cmc.com.cn; internet www.cmc.com.cn; f. 1950; imports and exports machine tools, diesel engines and boilers and all kinds of machinery; imports aeroplanes, ships, etc.; Pres. CHEN WEIGUN.

**China National Medicine and Health Products Import and Export Corpn:** Meheco Plaza, 18 Guangming Zhong Jie, Chongwen Qu, Beijing 100061; tel. (10) 67116688; fax (10) 67021579; e-mail webmaster@meheco.com.cn; internet www.meheco.com.cn; Pres. SHEN YINFA.

**China National Metals and Minerals Import and Export Corpn:** Bldg 15, Block 4, Anhuili, Chao Yang Qu, Beijing 100101; tel. (10) 64916666; fax (10) 64916421; e-mail support@minmetals.com.cn; internet www.minmetals.com.cn; f. 1950; principal imports and exports include steel, antimony, tungsten concentrates and ferrotungsten, zinc ingots, tin, mercury, pig iron, cement, etc.; Pres. MIAO GENGSHU.

**China National Native Produce and Animal By-Products Import and Export Corpn (TUHSU):** Sanli Bldg, 208 Andingmenwai Jie, Beijing 100011; tel. (10) 64248899; fax (10) 64204099; e-mail info@china-tuhsu.com; internet www.china-tuhsu.com; f. 1949; imports and exports include tea, coffee, cocoa, fibres, etc.; 13 subsidiary enterprises; 18 tea brs; 19 overseas subsidiaries; Pres. ZHANG ZHENMING.

**China National Non-Ferrous Metals Import and Export Corpn (CNIEC):** 12B Fuxing Lu, Beijing 100814; tel. (10) 63975588; fax (10) 63964424; Chair. WU JIANCHANG; Pres. XIAO JUNQING.

**China National Nuclear Corpn:** 1 Nansanxiang, Sanlihe, Beijing; tel. (10) 68512211; fax (10) 68533989; internet www.cnnc.com.cn; Pres. LI DINGFAN.

**China National Offshore Oil Corpn (CNOOC):** PO Box 4705, Jingxin Bldg, 2A North Dongsanhuan Lu, Chao Yang Qu, Beijing 100027; tel. (10) 64662993; fax (10) 64669007; e-mail webinfo@cnooc.com.cn; internet www.cnooc.com.cn; sales 2,039m.; Pres. WEN LIUCHENG.

**China National Oil Development Corpn:** Liupukang, Beijing 100006; tel. (10) 6444313; Pres. CHENG SHOULI.

**China National Packaging Import and Export Corpn:** Xinfu Bldg B, 3 Dong San Huan Bei Lu, Chao Yang Qu, Beijing 100027; tel. (10) 64611166; fax (10) 64616437; e-mail info@chinapack.net; internet www.chinapack.net; handles import and export of packaging materials, containers, machines and tools; contracts for the processing and converting of packaging machines and materials supplied by foreign customers; registered cap. US $30m.; Pres. ZHENG CHONGXIANG.

**China National Petro-Chemical Corpn (SINOPEC):** Jia 6, Dong Huixin Lu, Chao Yang Qu, Beijing 100029; tel. (10) 64225533; fax (10) 64212429; f. 1983; restructured mid-1998; responsible for petroleum extraction and refining in northern and western China, and for setting retail prices of petroleum products.

**China National Petroleum Corpn:** 6 Liupukang Jie, Xicheng Qu, Beijing 100724; tel. (10) 62094538; fax (10) 62094806; e-mail admin@hq.cnpc.com.cn; internet www.cnpc.com.cn; restructured mid-1998; responsible for petroleum extraction and refining in southern and eastern China, and for setting retail prices of petroleum products; Pres. MA FUCAI.

**China National Publications Import and Export Corpn:** 16 Gongrentiyuguandong Lu, Chao Yang Qu, Beijing; tel. (10) 65066688; fax (10) 65063101; internet www.cnpiec.com.cn; imports principally foreign books, newspapers and periodicals, records, CD-ROMs, etc., exports principally Chinese scientific and technical journals published in foreign languages; Pres. GAN SHIJUN.

**China National Publishing Industry Trading Corpn:** POB 782, 504 An Hua Li, Andingmenwai, Beijing 100011; tel. (10) 64215031; fax (10) 64214540; f. 1981; imports and exports publications, printing equipment technology; holds book fairs abroad; undertakes joint publication; Pres. ZHOU HONGLI.

**China National Seed Group Corpn:** 16A Xibahe, Chao Yang Qu, Beijing 100028; tel. (10) 64201817; fax (10) 64201820; imports and exports crop seeds, including cereals, cotton, oil-bearing crops, teas, flowers and vegetables; seed production for foreign seed companies etc.; Pres. HE ZHONGHUA.

**China National Silk Import and Export Corpn:** 105 Bei He Yan Jie, Dongcheng Qu, Beijing 100006; tel. (10) 65123338; fax (10) 65125125; e-mail cnsiec@public.bta.net.cn; internet www.chinasilk.com; Pres. XU HONGXIN.

**China National Star Petroleum Corpn:** Beijing; e-mail jf@mail.cnspc.com.cn; internet www.cnspc.com.cn; f. 1997; Pres. ZHU JIAZHEN.

**China National Technical Import and Export Corpn:** Jiuling Bldg, 21 Xisanhuan Beilu, Beijing 100081; tel. (10) 68404000; fax (10) 68414877; e-mail info@cntic.com.cn; internet www.cntic.com.cn; f. 1952; imports all kinds of complete plant and equipment, acquires modern technology and expertise from abroad, undertakes co-production and jt ventures, and technical consultation and updating of existing enterprises; registered cap. 200m.; Pres. WANG HUIHENG.

**China National Textiles Import and Export Corpn:** 82 Donganmen Jie, Beijing 100747; tel. (10) 65123844; fax (10) 65124711; e-mail webmaster@chinatex.com; internet www.chinatex-group.com; imports synthetic fibres, raw cotton, wool, garment accessories, etc.; exports cotton yarn, cotton fabric, knitwear, woven garments, etc.; Pres. WANG RUIXIANG.

**China National Tobacco Import and Export Corpn:** 11 Hufang Lu, Xuanwu Qu, Beijing 100052; tel. (10) 63533399; fax (10) 63015331; Pres. XUN XINGHUA.

**China National United Oil Corpn:** 57 Wangfujing Jie, Dongcheng Qu, Beijing 100006; tel. (10) 65223828; fax (10) 65223817; Chair. ZHANG JIAREN; Pres. ZHU YAOBIN.

**China No. 1 Automobile Group:** 63 Dongfeng Jie, Chao Yang Qu, Changchun, Jilin; tel. (431) 5003030; fax (431) 5001309; f. 1953; mfr of passenger cars; Gen. Man. GENG ZHAOJIE.

**China North Industries Group:** 46 Sanlihe Lu, Beijing 100821; tel. (10) 68594210; fax (10) 68594232; internet www.corincogroup.com.cn; exports vehicles and mechanical products, light industrial products, chemical products, opto-electronic products, building materials, military products, etc.; Pres. MA ZHIGENG.

**China Nuclear Energy Industry Corpn (CNEIC):** 1A Yuetan Bei Jie, Xicheng Qu, Beijing 100037; tel. (10) 68013395; fax (10) 68512393; internet www.cnnc.com.cn; exports air filters, vacuum valves, dosimeters, radioactive detection elements and optical instruments; Pres. ZHANG ZHIFENG.

**China Petro-Chemical International Co:** 2 Ofc Bldg, 6A Huixin Dongjie, Chao Yang Qu, Beijing 100029; tel. (10) 64916672; fax (10) 64218351; f. 1983; registered cap. 120m.; Pres. YANG SHUSHAN.

**China Road and Bridge Corpn:** Zhonglu Bldg, 88C, An Ding Men Wai Dajie, Beijing 100011; tel. (10) 64285616; fax (10) 64285686; e-mail crbc@crbc.com; internet www.crbc.com; overseas and domestic building of highways, urban roads, bridges, tunnels, industrial and residential buildings, airport runways and parking areas; contracts to do surveying, designing, pipe-laying, water supply and sewerage, building, etc., and/or to provide technical or labour services; Chair. ZHOU JICHANG.

**China Shipbuilding Trading Corpn Ltd:** 10 Yue Tan Bei Xiao Jie, Beijing 100861; tel. (10) 68032560; fax (10) 68033380; e-mail webmaster@cstc.com.cn; internet www.ctsc.com.cn; Pres. LI ZHUSHI.

**China State Construction Engineering Corpn:** Baiwanzhuang, Xicheng Qu, Beijing 100835; tel. (10) 68347766; fax (10) 68314326; e-mail cscec-us@worldnet.att.net; internet www.cscec.com; Pres. MA TINGGUI.

**China State Shipbuilding Corpn:** 5 Yuetan Beijie, Beijing; tel. (10) 68030208; fax (10) 68031579; Pres. CHEN XIAOJIN; Gen. Man. XU PENGHANG.

**China Tea Import and Export Corpn:** Zhongtuchu Bldg, 208 Andingmenwai Jie, Beijing 100011; tel. (10) 64204123; fax (10) 64204101; e-mail info@teachina.com; internet www.chinatea.com.cn; Pres. LI JIAZHI.

**China Xinshidai (New Era) Corpn:** 40 Xie Zuo Hu Tong, Dongcheng Qu, Beijing 100007; tel. (10) 64017384; fax (10) 64032935; Pres. QIN ZHONGXING.

**China Xinxing Corpn (Group):** 17 Xisanhuan Zhong Lu, Beijing 100036; tel. (10) 685166688; fax (10) 68514669; e-mail black-lily@nihao.com; internet www.black-lily.com; Pres. FAN YINGJUN.

**Chinese General Co of Astronautics Industry (State Aerospace Bureau):** 8 Fucheng Lu, Haidian Qu, Beijing 100712; tel. (10) 68586047; fax (10) 68370080; Pres. LIU JIYUAN.

**Daqing Petroleum Administration Bureau:** Sartu Qu, Daqing, Heilongjiang; tel. (459) 814649; fax (459) 322845; Gen. Man. WANG ZHIWU.

**Maanshan Iron and Steel Co:** 8 Hongqibei Lu, Maanshan 243003, Anhui; tel. (555) 2883492; fax (555) 2324350; Chair. HANG YONGYI; Pres. LI ZONGBI.

**Shanghai Automobile Industry Sales Corpn:** 548 Caoyang Lu, Shanghai 200063; tel. and fax (21) 62443223; Gen. Man. XU JIANYU.

**Shanghai Foreign Trade Corpn:** 27 Zhongshan Dong Yi Lu, Shanghai 200002; tel. (21) 63217350; fax (21) 63290044; f. 1988; handles import-export trade, foreign trade transportation, chartering, export commodity packaging, storage and advertising for Shanghai municipality; Gen. Man. WANG MEIJUN.

**Shanghai International Trust Trading Corpn:** 201 Zhaojiabang Lu, Shanghai 200032; tel. (21) 64033866; fax (21) 64034722; f. 1979, present name adopted 1988; handles import and export business, international mail orders, processing, assembling, compensation trade etc.

**Shougang Corpn:** Shijingshan, Beijing 100041; tel. and fax (10) 68293532; e-mail webmaster@shougang.com.cn; internet www.shougang.com.cn; Chair. BI QUN; Gen. Man. LUO BINGSHENG.

**State Bureau of Non-Ferrous Metals Industry:** 12B Fuxing Lu, Beijing 100814; tel. (10) 68514477; fax (10) 68515360; under supervision of State Economic and Trade Commission; Dir ZHANG WULE.

**Wuhan Iron and Steel (Group) Co:** Qingshan Qu, Wuhan, Hubei Province; tel. (27) 6892004; fax (27) 6862325; proposals for merger with two other steel producers in Hubei announced late 1997; Pres. LIU BENREN.

**Xinxing Oil Co (XOC):** Beijing; f. 1997; exploration, development and production of domestic and overseas petroleum and gas resources; Gen. Man. ZHU JIAZHEN.

**Yuxi Cigarette Factory:** Yujiang Lu, Yuxi, Yunnan Province; tel. and fax (877) 2052343; Gen. Man. CHU SHIJIAN.

**Zhongjiang Group:** Nanjing, Jiansu; f. 1998; multi-national operation mainly in imports and exports, contract projects and real estate; group consists of 126 subsidiaries incl. 25 foreign ventures.

## UTILITIES

### Electricity

**Beijing Power Supply Co:** Qianmen Xidajie, Beijing 100031; tel. (10) 63129201.

**Beijing Datang Power Generation:** one of China's largest independent power producers.

**Central China Electric Power Group Co:** 47 Xudong Lu, Wuchang, Wuhan 430077; tel. (27) 6813398.

**Changsha Electric Power Bureau:** 162 Jiefang Sicun, Changsha 410002; tel. (731) 5912121; fax (731) 5523240.

**China Atomic Energy Authority:** Chair. ZHANG HUAZHU.

**China Northwest Electric Power Group Co:** 57 Shangde Lu, Xian 710004; tel. (29) 7215016; fax (29) 7212451.

**China Power Grid Development (CPG):** f. to manage transmission and transformation lines for the Three Gorges hydroelectric scheme; Pres. ZHOU XIAOQIAN.

**China Yangtze Three Gorges Project Development Corpn:** 1 Jianshe Dajie, Yichang, Hubei Province; tel. (717) 6762212; fax (717) 6731787; Pres. LU YOUMEI.

**Dalian Electric Power Bureau:** 102 Zhongshan Lu, Dalian 116001; tel. (411) 2612222; fax (411) 2803515.

**Fujian Electric Power Bureau:** 264 Wusi Lu, Fuzhou 350003; tel. (591) 7023279; fax (591) 7023871.

**Gansu Bureau of Electric Power:** 306 Xijin Dong Lu, Lanzhou 730050; tel. (931) 2334311; fax (93) 2331042.

**Guangdong Electric Power Bureau:** 757 Dongfeng Dong Lu, Guangzhou 510600; tel. (20) 87767888; fax (20) 87770307.

**Guangdong Shantou Electric Power Bureau:** Jinsha Zhong Lu, Shantou 515041; tel. (754) 8257606.

**Guangxi Electric Power Bureau:** 6 Minzhu Lu, Nanning 530023; tel. (771) 2801123; fax (771) 2803414.

**Guangzhou Electric Power Co:** 9th Floor, Huale Bldg, 53 Huale Lu, Guangzhou 510060; tel. (20) 83821111; fax (20) 83808559.

**Hainan Electric Power Industry Bureau:** 34 Haifu Dadao, Haikou 570203; tel. (898) 5334777; fax (898) 5333230.

**Heilongjiang Electric Power Co:** 63 Hongjun Jie, Nangang Qu, Harbin 150001; tel. (451) 3682350; fax (451) 3682331.

**Huadong Electric Power Group Corpn:** 201 Nanjing Dong Lu, Shanghai; tel. (21) 63290000; fax (21) 63290727; power supply.

**Huazhong Electric Power Group Corpn:** Liyuan, Donghu, Wuhan, Hubei Province; tel. (27) 6813398; fax (27) 6813143; electrical engineering; Gen. Man. LIN KONGXING.

**Inner Mongolia Electric Power Co:** 28 Xilin Nan Lu, Huhehaose 010021; tel. (471) 6942222; fax (471) 6924863

**Jiangmen Electric Power Supply Bureau:** 87 Gangkou Lu, Jiangmen 529030; tel. and fax (750) 3360133.

**Jiangxi Electric Power Bureau:** 13 Yongwai Zheng Jie, Nanchang 330006; tel. (791) 6224701; fax (791) 6224830.

**National Grid Construction Co:** established to oversee completion of the National Grid by 2009.

**North China Electric Power Group Corpn:** 32 Zulinqianjie, Xuanwu Qu, Beijing 100053; tel. (10) 63543377.

**Northeast China Electric Power Group:** 11 Shiyiwei Lu, Heping Qu, Shenyang 110003; tel. (24) 3114382; fax (24)3872665.

**Shandong Electric Power Group Corpn:** 150 Jinger Lu, Jinan 250001; tel. (531) 6911919.

**Shandong Rizhao Power Co Ltd:** 1st Floor, Bldg 29, 30 Northern Section, Shunyu Xiaoqu, Jinan 250002; tel. (531) 2952462; fax (531) 2942561.

**Shanghai Electric Power Co:** 181 Nanjing Dong Lu, Shanghai 200002; tel. (21) 63291010; fax (21) 63291440.

**Shenzhen Power Supply Co:** 2 Yanhe Xi Lu, Luohu Qu, Shenzhen 518000; tel. (755) 5561920.

**Sichuan Electric Power Co:** Room 1, Waishi Bldg, Dongfeng Lu, Chengdu 610061; tel. (28) 444321; fax (28) 6661888.

**State Power Corpn:** Pres. GAO YAN.

**Tianjin Electric Power Industry Bureau:** 29 Jinbu Dao, Hebei Qu, Tianjin 300010; tel. (22) 24406326; fax (22) 22346965.

**Wenergy Co Ltd:** 81 Wuhu Lu, Hefei 230001; tel. (551) 2626906; fax (551) 2648061.

**Wuhan Power Supply Bureau:** 981 Jiefang Dadao, Hankou, Wuhan 430013; tel. (27) 2426455; fax (27) 2415605.

**Wuxi Power Supply Bureau:** 8 Houxixi, Wuxi 214001; tel. (510) 2717678; fax (510) 2719182.

**Xiamen Power Transformation and Transmission Engineering Co:** 67 Wenyuan Lu, Xiamen 361004; tel. (592) 2046763.

**Xian Power Supply Bureau:** Huancheng Dong Lu, Xian 710032; tel. (29) 7271483.

### Gas

**Beijing Gas Co:** 30 Dongsanhuan Zhong Lu, Beijing 100020; tel. (10) 65024131; fax (10) 65023815.

**Beijing Natural Gas Co:** Bldg 5, Dixingju, An Ding Men wai, Beijing 100011; tel. (10) 64262244.

**Changchun Gas Co:** 30 Tongzhi Jie, Changchun 130021; tel. (431) 8926479.

**Changsha Gas Co:** 18 Shoshan Lu, Changsha 410011; tel. (731) 4427246.

**Qingdao Gas Co:** 399A Renmin Lu, Qingdao 266032; tel. (532) 4851461; fax (532) 4858653.

**Shanghai Gas Supply Co:** 656 Xizang Zhong Lu, Shanghai 200003; tel. (21) 63222333.

**Wuhan Gas Co:** Qingnian Lu, Hankou, Wuhan 430015; tel. (27) 5866223.

**Xiamen Gas Corpn:** Ming Gong Bldg, Douxi Lukou, Hubin Nan Lu, Xiamen 361004; tel. (592) 2025937; fax (592) 2033290.

### Water

**Beijing District Heating Co:** 1 Xidawang Lu, Hongmiao, Chao Yang Qu, Beijing 100026; tel. (10) 65060066; fax (10) 65678891.

**Beijing Municipal Water Works Co:** 19 Yangrou Hutong, Xicheng Qu, Beijing 100034; tel. (10) 66167744; fax (10) 66168028.

**Changchun Water Co:** 53 Dajing Lu, Changchun 130000; tel. (431) 8968366.

**Chengdu Water Co:** 16 Shierqiao Jie, Shudu Dadao, Chengdu 610072; tel. (28) 77663122; fax (28) 7776876.

**The China Water Company:** f. to develop investment opportunities for water projects.

**Guangzhou Water Supply Co:** 5 Huanshi Xi Lu, Guangzhou 510010; tel. (20) 81816951.

**Haikou Water Co:** 31 Datong Lu, Haikou 570001; tel.(898) 6774412.

**Harbin Water Co:** 49 Xi Shidao Jie, Daoli Qu, Harbin 150010; tel. (451) 4610522; fax (451) 4611726.

**Jiangmen Water Co:** 44 Jianshe Lu, Jiangmen 529000; tel. (750) 3300138; fax (750) 3353704.

**Qinhuangdao Pacific Water Co:** Hebei; Sino-US water supply project; f. 1998.

**Shanghai Municipal Waterworks Co:** 484 Jiangxi Zhong Lu, Shanghai 200002; tel. (21) 63215577; fax (21) 63231346; service provider for municipality of Shanghai.

**Shenzhen Water Supply Group Co:** Water Bldg, 1019 M. Shennan Lu, Shenzhen 518031; tel. (755) 2137888; fax (755) 2137882, internet www.waterchina.com.

**Tianjin Waterworks Group:** 54 Jianshe Lu, Heping Qu, Tianjin 300040; tel. (22) 3393887; fax (22) 3306720.

**Xian Water Co:** Huancheng Xi Lu, Xian 710082; tel. (29) 4244881.

**Zhanjiang Water Co:** 20 Renmin Dadaonan, Zhanjiang 524001; tel. (759) 2286394.

**Zhongshan Water Supply Co:** 23 Yinzhu Jie, Zhuyuan Lu, Zhongshan 528403; tel. (760) 8312969; fax (760) 6326429.

**Zhuhai Water Supply General Corpn:** Yuehai Zhong Lu, Gongbei, Zhuhai 519020; tel. (756) 8881160; fax (756) 8884405

### TRADE UNIONS

**All-China Federation of Trade Unions (ACFTU):** 10 Fu Xing Men Wai Jie, Beijing 100865; tel. (10) 68592114; fax (10) 68562030; f. 1925; organized on an industrial basis; 15 affiliated national industrial unions, 30 affiliated local trade union councils; membership is voluntary; trade unionists enjoy extensive benefits; 103,996,000m. mems (1995); Pres. WEI JIANXING; First Sec. ZHANG DINGHUA.

Principal affiliated unions:

**All-China Federation of Railway Workers' Unions:** Chair. CHEN XIAODA.

**Architectural Workers' Trade Union:** Sec. SONG ANRU.

**China Self-Employed Workers' Association:** Pres. REN ZHONGLIN.

**Educational Workers' Trade Union:** Chair. JIANG WENLIANG.

**Light Industrial Workers' Trade Union:** Chair. LI SHUYING.

**Machinery Metallurgical Workers' Union:** Chair. ZHANG CUNEN.

**National Defence Workers' Union:** Chair. GUAN HENGCAI.

**Postal and Telecommunications Workers' Trade Union of China:** Chair. LUO SHUZHEN.

**Seamen's Trade Union of China:** Chair. ZHANG SHIHUI.

**Water Resources and Electric Power Workers' Trade Union:** Chair. DONG YUNQI.

**Workers' Autonomous Federation (WAF):** f. 1989; aims to create new trade union movement in China, independent of the All-China Federation of Trade Unions.

## Transport

### RAILWAYS

**Ministry of Railways:** 10 Fuxing Lu, Haidian Qu, Beijing 100844; tel. (10) 63246915; fax (10) 63981065; controls all railways through regional divisions. The railway network has been extended to all provinces and regions except Tibet (Xizang), where construction is in progress. Total length in operation in December 1998 was 57,584 km, of which 12,984 km were electrified. The major routes include Beijing–Guangzhou, Tianjin–Shanghai, Manzhouli–Vladivostok, Jiaozuo–Zhicheng and Lanzhou–Badou. In addition, special railways serve factories and mines. A new 2,536-km line from Beijing to Kowloon (Hong Kong) was completed in late 1995. Plans for a 1,300-km high-speed link between Beijing and Shanghai, to be completed by the year 2000, were announced in 1994. China's first high-speed service, linking Guangzhou and Shenzhen, commenced in December 1994. A direct service between Shanghai and Hong Kong commenced in 1997.

An extensive programme to develop the rail network was announced in early 1998, which aimed to increase the total network to 68,000 km by the year 2000, and to more than 70,000 km by 2002. Railways were to be constructed along the Changjiang valley, starting at Sichuan, and along China's east coast, originating at Harbin. In December 1999 plans were announced for a railway to Kazakhstan.

#### City Underground Railways

**Beijing Metro Corpn:** 2 Beiheyan Lu, Xicheng, Beijing 100044; tel. (10) 68024566; f. 1969; total length 54 km, with 64 km of further lines to be built by the year 2010; Gen. Man. FENG SHUANGSHENG.

**Guangzhou Metro:** 204 Huanshi Lu, Guangzhou 510010; tel. (20) 6665287; fax (20) 6678232; opened June 1997; total network of 35.9 km planned; Gen. Man. CHEN QINGQUAN.

**Shanghai Metro Corpn:** 12 Heng Shan Lu, Shanghai 200031; tel. (21) 64312460; fax (21) 64339598; f. 1995; 21 km open, with a further 41.1 km under construction; Pres. SHI LIAN.

**Tianjin Metro:** 97 Jiefangbei Lu, Heping, Tianjin 300041; tel. (22) 23395410; fax (22) 23396194; f. 1984; total planned network 154 km; Gen. Man. WANG YUJI.

Underground systems were planned for Chongqing and Qingdao.

### ROADS

At the end of 1998 China had 1,278,474 km of highways (of which at least 1,190,086 km were paved). Four major highways link Lhasa (Tibet) with Sichuan, Xinjiang, Qinghai Hu and Kathmandu (Nepal). A programme of expressway construction began in the mid-1980s. By 1998 there were 4,735 km of expressways (1,313 km of which were constructed in 1997), routes including the following: Shenyang–Dalian, Beijing–Tanggu, Shanghai–Jiading, Guangzhou–Foshan and Xian–Lintong. A new 123-km highway linking Shenzhen (near the border with Hong Kong) to Guangzhou opened in 1994. A 58-km road between Guangzhou and Zhongshan connects with Zhuhai, near the border with Macau. Construction of a bridge, linking Zhuhai with Macau, began in June 1998 and was scheduled for completion by late 1999. A bridge connecting the mainland with Hong Kong was to be built, with completion scheduled for the year 2004. In 1997 some 20% of villages in China were not connected to the road infrastructure.

### INLAND WATERWAYS

At the end of 1998 there were some 110,263 km of navigable inland waterways in China. The main navigable rivers are the Changjiang (Yangtze River), the Zhujiang (Pearl River), the Heilongjiang, the Grand Canal and the Xiangjiang. The Changjiang is navigable by vessels of 10,000 tons as far as Wuhan, more than 1,000 km from the coast. Vessels of 1,000 tons can continue to Chongqing upstream. There were 5,142 river ports at the end of 1996. In 1997 there were some 5,100 companies involved in inland waterway shipping.

### SHIPPING

China has a network of more than 2,000 ports, of which more than 130 are open to foreign vessels. The main ports include Dalian, Qinhuangdao, Tianjin, Yantai, Qingdao, Rizhao, Lianyungang, Shanghai, Ningbo, Guangzhou and Zhanjiang. In 1998 the main coastal ports handled 922m. tons of cargo. In December 1998 China's merchant fleet comprised 3,214 ships, totalling 16.5m. grt.

**Bureau of Water Transportation:** Beijing; controls rivers and coastal traffic.

**China National Chartering Corpn (SINOCHART):** see p. 986.

**China Ocean Shipping (Group) Co (COSCO):** 3 Dongsanhuan Bei Lu, Chaoyang Qu, Beijing 100027; tel. (10) 64661188; fax (10) 64669859; reorg. 1993, re-established 1997; head office transferred to Tianjin late 1997; br. offices: Shanghai, Guangzhou, Tianjin, Qingdao, Dalian; 200 subsidiaries (incl. China Ocean Shipping Agency—PENAVIC) and joint ventures in China and abroad, engaged in ship-repair, container-manufacturing, warehousing, insurance, etc.; merchant fleet of 600 vessels; 47 routes; Pres. CHEN ZHONGBIAO.

**China Shipping Group:** f. 1997; Pres. LI KELIN.

**Minsheng Shipping Co Ltd:** Minsheng Bldg, 83 Xinhua Lu, Chongqing 400011; tel. (23) 63833121 fax (23) 63832359; f. 1984; Gen. Man. LU GUOJI.

### CIVIL AVIATION

Air travel is expanding very rapidly. In 1998 106 airports were equipped to handle Boeing-737 and larger aircraft. Chinese airlines carried a total of 57.6m. passengers in 1998. In that year there were 34 airlines, including numerous private companies, operating in China.

**General Administration of Civil Aviation of China (CAAC):** POB 644, 155 Dongsixi Jie, Beijing 100710; tel. (10) 64014104; fax (10) 64016918; f. 1949 as Civil Aviation Administration of China; restructured in 1988 as a purely supervisory agency, its operational functions being transferred to new, semi-autonomous airlines (see below; also China United Airlines (division of Air Force) and China Capital Helicopter Service); domestic flights throughout China; external services are mostly operated by **Air China, China Eastern** and **China Southern Airlines**; Dir LIU JIANFENG.

**Air China:** Beijing International Airport, POB 644, Beijing 100621; tel. (10) 64663366; fax (10) 64563831; e-mail webmaster@airchina.com.cn; internet www.airchina.com.cn; international and domestic scheduled passenger and cargo services; Pres. WANG LIAN.

**China Eastern Airlines:** 2550 Hongqiao Rd, Hongqiao Airport, Shanghai 200335; tel. (21) 62688558; fax (21) 62688107; e-mail webmaster@cea.online.sh.cn; internet www.cea.online.sh.cn; f. 1987; domestic services; overseas destinations include USA, Europe, Japan, Singapore, Seoul and Bangkok; Pres. LI ZHONGMING.

**China Northern Airlines:** 3-1 Xiaoheyan Lu, Dadong Qu, Shenyang, Liaoning 110043; tel. (24) 23198405; fax (24) 23198410; e-mail northern_air@163.net; internet www.cna.ln.cninfo.net; f. 1990; scheduled flights to the Democratic People's Republic of Korea, the Republic of Korea, Russia, Hong Kong, Macau and Japan; Pres. JIANG LIANYING.

**China Northwest Airlines:** Laodong Nan Lu, Xian, Shaanxi 710082; tel. (29) 8702021; fax (29) 4207040; e-mail cnwadzz@pub.xa-online.sn.cn; internet www.cnwa.com; f. 1992; domestic services and flights to Macau, Singapore and Nagoya; Pres. NIE SHENGLI.

**China Southern Airlines:** Baiyuan International Airport, Guangzhou, Guangdong 510406; tel. (20) 86122528; fax (20) 86644623; e-mail webmaster@cs-air.com; internet www.csair.com; f. 1991; domestic services; overseas destinations include Bangkok, Hanoi, Ho Chi Minh City, Kuala Lumpur, Penang, Singapore, Manila, Vientiane, Jakarta and Surabaya; Chair. YU YANEN; Pres. YAN SHIQING.

**China Southwest Airlines:** Shuangliu Airport, Chengdu, Sichuan 610202; tel. (28) 5814466; fax (28) 5582630; e-mail szmaster@cswa.com; internet www.cswa.com; f. 1987; 70 domestic routes; international services to Singapore and Bangkok; also Lhasa (Tibet) to Kathmandu (Nepal); Pres. WANG RUCEN.

**Changan Airlines:** 6 Dong Feng Hao Lu, Xian, Shaanxi 710082; tel. and fax (29) 4263432; e-mail caair@pub.baonline; internet www.changanair.com.cn; f. 1992; local passenger and cargo services; Pres. SHE YINING.

**China General Aviation Corpn:** Wusu Airport, Taiyuan, Shanxi 030031, tel. (351) 7040600; fax (351) 7040094; f. 1989; 34 domestic routes; Pres. ZHANG CHANGJING.

**China Xinhua Airlines:** 1 Jinsong Nan Lu, Chaoyang Qu, Beijing 100021; tel. (10) 67739754; fax (10) 67740126; e-mail infoxh@homeway.com.cn; internet www.chinaxinhuaair.com; f. 1992; Pres. LAN SHILIANG.

**Fujian Airlines:** 228A Fuxing East Road, Fuzhou 350014; tel. (591) 3674504; fax (591) 3674304; f. 1993; domestic services; Man. Dir HU JIANNAN.

**Guizhou Airlines:** 20 Shengfu Lu, Guiyang, Guizhou 550001; tel. (851) 525626; f. 1991; regional passenger and cargo services; Pres. MA YONGXING.

**Hainan Airlines:** Haihang Devt Bldg, 29 Haixiu Lu, Haikou, Hainan 570206; tel. (898) 6709602; fax (898) 6798976; f. 1993; domestic services; Chair. CHENG FENG.

**Nanjing Airlines:** Dajiaochang Airport, Nanjing 210000; tel. (25) 4602629; fax (25) 4494461; f. 1994; local services; Pres. JIANG HEPING.

**Shandong Airlines:** Yaoqiang Airport, Jinan, Shandong 250011; tel. (531) 7966043; fax (531) 7966020; f. 1991; domestic services; Pres. SUN DEHAN.

**Shanghai Air Lines:** North Gate of Hongqiao International Airport, Shanghai 200335; tel. (21) 62688558; fax (21) 62688107; internet www.shanghai-air.com; f. 1985; domestic services; Chair. HE PENGNIAN; Pres. ZHOU CHI.

**Shanxi Airlines:** 36 Yingze Jie, Taiyun 030001; tel. and fax (351) 447178; f. 1991; domestic services; Pres. QIN JIANMING.

**Shenzhen Airlines:** Lingtian Tian, Lingxiao Garden, Shenzhen Airport, Shenzhen, Guangdong 518128; tel. (755) 7777243; fax (755) 7777242; f. 1993; domestic services; Pres. DUAN DAYANG.

**Sichuan Airlines:** Chengdu Shuangliu International Airport, Chengdu, Sichuan 610202; tel. (28) 5393114; fax (28) 5393888; e-mail scaloffice@mail.sc.cninfo.net; f. 1986; domestic services; Pres. LAN XINCLIO.

**Wuhan Air Lines:** 435 Jianshe Dajie, Wuhan 430030; tel. (87) 83624600; fax (87) 83625693; e-mail wuhanair@public.wh.hb.cn; f. 1986; domestic services; Pres. CHENG YAOKUN.

**Xiamen Airlines:** Gaoqi Airport, Xiamen, Fujian 361009; tel. (592) 6022961; fax (592) 6028263; f. 1992; domestic services; Pres. WU RONGNAN.

**Zhejiang Airlines:** Jian Qiao Airport, 78 Shiqiao Lu, Hangzhou, Zhejiang 310021; tel. (571) 6400888; fax (571) 6400777; e-mail zjair@public.hz.zj.cn; f. 1990; domestic services; Pres. LUO QIANG.

**Zhong Yuan Airlines:** 143 Minggong Lu, Zhengzhou, Henan 450000; tel. and fax (371) 6222542; f. 1986; domestic services; CEO XIE YONGLIANG.

## Tourism

China has enormous potential for tourism, and the sector is developing rapidly. Attractions include dramatic scenery and places of historical interest such as the Temple of Heaven and the Forbidden City in Beijing, the Great Wall, the Ming Tombs, and also the terracotta warriors at Xian. Tibet (Xizang), with its monasteries and temples, has also been opened to tourists. Tours of China are organized for groups of visitors, and Western-style hotels have been built as joint ventures in many areas. By 1998 5,782 tourist hotels were in operation. A total of 63.5m. tourists visited China in 1998. In that year receipts from tourism totalled US $12,602m.

**China International Travel Service (CITS):** 103 Fu Xing Men Nei Dajie, Beijing 100800; tel. (10) 66011122; fax (10) 66012013; e-mail mktng@cits.com.cn; internet www.cits.net; makes travel arrangements for foreign tourists; general agency in Hong Kong, business offices in London, Paris, New York, Los Angeles, Frankfurt, Sydney and Tokyo; Pres. LI LUAN.

**China National Tourism Administration (CNTA):** 9A Jian Guo Men Nei Dajie, Beijing 100740; tel. (10) 65138866; fax (10) 65122096; Dir HE GUANGWEI.

**Chinese People's Association for Friendship with Foreign Countries:** 1 Tai Ji Chang Dajie, Beijing 100740; tel. (10) 65122474; fax (10) 65128354; f. 1954; Pres. QI HUAIYUAN; Sec.-Gen. BIAN QINGZU.

**State Bureau of Tourism:** Jie 3, Jian Guo Men Nei Dajie, Beijing 100740; tel. (10) 65122847; fax (10) 65122095; Dir LIU YI.

# CHINESE SPECIAL ADMINISTRATIVE REGIONS

## HONG KONG

### Introductory Survey

**Location, Climate, Language, Religion, Flag, Capital**

The Special Administrative Region (SAR) of Hong Kong, as the territory became on 1 July 1997, lies in east Asia, off the south coast of the People's Republic of China, and consists of the island of Hong Kong, Stonecutters Island, the Kowloon Peninsula and the New Territories, which are partly on the mainland. The climate is sunny and dry in winter, and hot and humid in summer. The average annual rainfall is 2,214 mm (87 ins), of which about 80% falls between May and September. The official languages are English and Chinese: Cantonese is spoken by the majority of the Chinese community, while Putonghua (Mandarin) is widely understood and of increasing significance. The main religion is Buddhism. Confucianism, Islam, Hinduism and Daoism are also practised, and there are about 500,000 Christians. The flag of the Hong Kong SAR (proportions 3 by 2), introduced in July 1997 and flown subordinate to the flag of the People's Republic of China, displays a bauhinia flower consisting of five white petals, each bearing a red line and a red five-pointed star, at the centre of a red field. The capital is Victoria.

**Recent History**

Hong Kong Island was ceded to the United Kingdom under the terms of the Treaty of Nanking (Nanjing) in 1842. The Kowloon Peninsula was acquired by the Convention of Peking (Beijing) in 1860. The New Territories were leased from China in 1898 for a period of 99 years. From the establishment of the People's Republic in 1949, the Chinese Government asserted that the 'unequal' treaties giving Britain control over Hong Kong were no longer valid.

Japanese forces invaded Hong Kong in December 1941, forcing the British administration to surrender. In August 1945, at the end of the Second World War, the territory was recaptured by British forces. Colonial rule was restored, with a British military administration until May 1946. With the restoration of civilian rule, the territory was again administered in accordance with the 1917 Constitution, which vested full powers in the British-appointed Governor. In 1946 the returning Governor promised a greater measure of self-government but, after the communist revolution in China in 1949, plans for constitutional reform were abandoned. Thus, unlike most other British colonies, Hong Kong did not proceed, through stages, to democratic rule. The essential features of the colonial regime remained unaltered until 1985, when, following the Sino-British Joint Declaration (see below), the first changes were introduced into the administrative system. Prior to 1985 the Executive and Legislative Councils consisted entirely of nominated members, including many civil servants in the colonial administration. There were, however, direct elections for one-half of the seats on the Urban Council, responsible for public health and other amenities, but participation was low.

Between 1949 and 1964 an estimated 1m. refugees crossed from the People's Republic to Hong Kong, imposing serious strains on Hong Kong's housing and other social services. More than 460,000 Chinese immigrants arrived, many of them illegally, between 1975 and 1980. Strict measures, introduced in October 1980, reduced the continuous flow of refugees from China (at one time averaging 150 per day), but the number of legal immigrants remained at a high level—more than 50,000 per year in 1980 and 1981, although by 1984 the figure had declined to around 27,700.

In 1981–82 a new problem arose with the arrival of Vietnamese refugees: by January 1987 there were 8,254 in Hong Kong, of whom 62% had spent more than three years living in camps, and refugees continued to arrive in increasing numbers. The Hong Kong authorities, meanwhile, exerted pressure on the British Government to end its policy of granting first asylum to the refugees. In response, legislation was introduced in June 1988 to distinguish between political refugees and 'economic migrants'. The latter were to be denied refugee status, and in October the British and Vietnamese Governments agreed terms for their voluntary repatriation. In March 1989 the first group of co-operative 'economic migrants' flew back to Viet Nam.

More than 18,000 Vietnamese arrived in Hong Kong between June 1988 and May 1989, despite the extremely unpleasant conditions in the detention camps where they were confined on arrival, and the restricting of the definition of refugee status. The relative paucity of those who agreed to return to Viet Nam (totalling 1,225 by February 1990) caused the British Government to claim that the policy of voluntary repatriation was not effective. After the United Kingdom had failed on a number of occasions to gain general international endorsement for a policy of compulsory repatriation (which, it was claimed, would discourage further large-scale immigration), the Vietnamese Government announced in December 1989 that an agreement had been concluded between the United Kingdom and Viet Nam on a programme of 'involuntary' repatriation. Under the agreement, 'economic migrants' could be returned to Viet Nam against their will, on condition that no physical force were used. Reports that a group of 51 Vietnamese had been forcibly repatriated led to violent disturbances in many of the camps. The programme of involuntary repatriation was halted, in anticipation of a meeting in January 1990 of the UN steering committee for the Comprehensive Plan of Action on Indochinese refugees. The 29-nation committee failed to agree upon a policy, the USA and Viet Nam each adhering to the principle of a moratorium on involuntary repatriation, in order to allow more time to persuade 'economic migrants' to return voluntarily. By May 1990 no further cases of the repatriation of Vietnamese against their will had been reported. At an international conference held in that month, Hong Kong and the member countries of ASEAN threatened to refuse asylum to Vietnamese refugees altogether, unless the USA and Viet Nam gave approval to the policy of involuntary repatriation. In September Hong Kong, Viet Nam and the United Kingdom reached an agreement, supported by the UNHCR, to allow the repatriation of a new category of refugees—those who were not volunteering to return but who had indicated that they would not actively resist repatriation. By mid-1991, however, very few refugees had returned to Viet Nam, and the number of those arriving in Hong Kong had increased considerably. By June more than 60,000 Vietnamese were accommodated in permanent camps. In October, following protracted negotiations, it was announced that Viet Nam had agreed to the mandatory repatriation of refugees from Hong Kong. The first forcible deportation (mainly of recent arrivals) under the agreement was carried out in November. Tension in the camps continued, and in February 1992 23 refugees were burned to death and almost 130 were injured in rioting at one of the detention centres. In May the United Kingdom and Viet Nam signed an agreement providing for the forcible repatriation of all economic migrants. By the end of 1995 the detention camp population had been reduced to 21,704, of whom 1,479 were classified as refugees. Demonstrations and riots in the camps continued intermittently. Almost 200 people were injured during clashes in May 1995, when security officers attempted to transfer 1,500 inmates from a detention centre to a transit camp prior to repatriation. In May 1996 more than 100 asylum-seekers escaped from Whitehead Detention Centre following rioting during which 50 security officers were injured. In June there was an attempted mass escape from High Island Detention Centre in the New Territories. The People's Republic of China, meanwhile, continued to insist that all camps be cleared prior to the transfer of sovereignty in mid-1997. The Whitehead Detention Centre was closed in January 1997, and the refugees were transferred to other detention centres. Despite an acceleration in the repatriation programme, some 1,200 Vietnamese migrants remained in Hong Kong in December 1997. In January 1998 the SAR administration (see below) announced that it was abolishing the 'port of asylum' policy which had been applied to Vietnamese refugees. Those arriving illegally would no longer be given time to apply for asylum.

Following a visit to Hong Kong by the British Prime Minister in September 1982, talks between the United Kingdom and China were held at diplomatic level about the territory's future status. In 1984 the United Kingdom conceded that in mid-1997, upon the expiry of the lease on the New Territories, China would regain sovereignty over the whole of Hong Kong. In September 1984 British and Chinese representatives met in Beijing and initialled a legally-binding agreement, the Sino-British Joint Declaration, containing detailed assurances on the future of Hong Kong. China guaranteed the continuation of the territory's capitalist economy and life-style for 50 years after 1997. The territory, as a special administrative region of the People's Republic, would be designated 'Hong Kong, China', and would continue to enjoy a high degree of autonomy, except in matters of defence and foreign affairs. It was agreed that Hong Kong would retain its identity as a free port and separate customs territory, and its citizens would be guaranteed freedom of speech, of assembly, of association, of travel and of religious belief. In December 1984, after being approved by the National People's Congress (Chinese legislature) and the British Parliament, the agreement was signed in Beijing by the British and Chinese Prime Ministers, and in May 1985 the two Governments exchanged documents ratifying the agreement. A Joint Liaison Group (JLG), comprising British and Chinese representatives, was established to monitor the provisions of the agreement, and this group held its first meeting in July 1985. A 58-member Basic Law Drafting Committee (BLDC), including 23 representatives from Hong Kong, was formed in Beijing in June, with the aim of drawing up a new Basic Law (Constitution) for Hong Kong, in accordance with Article 31 of the Chinese Constitution, which provides for special administrative regions within the People's Republic.

A special office, which had been established in Hong Kong to assess the views of the people of the territory, reported that the majority of the population accepted the terms of the Joint Declaration, but the sensitive issue of the future nationality of Hong Kong residents proved controversial. The 1981 British Nationality Act had already caused alarm in the territory, where the reclassification of 2.3m. citizens was seen as a downgrading of their status. As holders of Hong Kong residents' permits, they had no citizenship status under British law. Following the approval of the Hong Kong agreement, the British Government announced a new form of nationality, to be effective from 1997, designated 'British National (Overseas)', which would not be transferable to descendants and would confer no right of abode in the United Kingdom.

In September 1985 indirect elections were held for 24 new members of an expanded Legislative Council, to replace the former appointees and government officials. The turn-out for the elections was low (less than 1% of the total population was eligible to vote, and only 35% of these participated). In March 1986 municipal elections were held for the urban and regional councils, which were thus, for the first time, wholly directly-elected. In December the Governor, Sir Edward Youde, died unexpectedly while on a visit to Beijing. The new Governor, Sir David Wilson (who had played a prominent part in the Sino-British negotiations on the territory's future), formally assumed office in April 1987. In May the Hong Kong Government published proposals regarding the development of representative government during the final decade of British rule. Among the options that it proposed was the introduction, in 1988, of direct elections to the Legislative Council, based upon universal adult franchise. In spite of the disapproval of the Chinese Government with regard to the introduction of direct elections before the new Constitution was promulgated in 1990, a survey, held in 1987, found the majority of people to be in favour of the introduction of direct elections before 1990. In February 1988 the Hong Kong Government published a policy document on the development of representative government; the principal proposal was the introduction, in 1991, of 10 (subsequently increased) directly-elected members of the Legislative Council.

In April 1988 the first draft of the Basic Law for Hong Kong was published, and a Basic Law Consultative Committee (BLCC) was established in Hong Kong, initially with 176 members, to collect public comments on its provisions, over a five-month period; the draft was to be debated by the Legislative Council and by the Parliament of the United Kingdom, but no referendum was to be held in Hong Kong, and final approval of the Basic Law rested with the National People's Congress (NPC) of China. The draft offered five options for the election of a chief executive and four options were presented regarding the composition of the future Legislative Council, none of which, however, proposed that the Council should be elected entirely by universal suffrage. Although the legislature would be empowered to impeach the chief executive for wrongdoing, the Chinese Government would have final responsibility for his removal. Critics of the draft Basic Law complained that it failed to offer democratic representation or to guarantee basic human rights; they argued that Hong Kong's autonomy was not clearly defined, and would be threatened by the fact that power to interpret those parts of the Basic Law relating to defence, foreign affairs and China's 'executive acts' would be granted to the NPC in Beijing and not to the Hong Kong judiciary.

In November 1988 the UN Commission on Human Rights criticized the British attitude to the transfer of Hong Kong, with particular reference to the lack of direct elections. A second draft of the Basic Law was approved by China's National People's Congress in February 1989, which ignored all five options previously proposed for the election of a chief executive. In May there were massive demonstrations in Hong Kong in support of the anti-Government protests taking place in China. In June, following the killing of thousands of protesters by the Chinese armed forces in Tiananmen Square in Beijing, further demonstrations and a general strike took place in Hong Kong, expressing the inhabitants' revulsion at the massacres and their doubts as to whether the Basic Law would, in practice, be honoured by the Chinese Government after 1997. The British Government refused to consider renegotiating the Sino-British Joint Declaration, but, in response to demands that the British nationality laws should be changed to allow Hong Kong residents the right to settle in the United Kingdom after 1997, it announced in December 1989 that the British Parliament would be asked to enact legislation enabling as many as 50,000 Hong Kong residents (chosen on a 'points system', which was expected to favour leading civil servants, business executives and professional workers), and an estimated 175,000 dependants, to be given the right of abode in the United Kingdom. The measure was intended to 'maintain confidence' in the colony during the transition to Chinese sovereignty, by stemming the emigration of skilled personnel (42,000 Hong Kong residents having left the colony in 1989). The announcement received a cautious welcome from the Hong Kong authorities. However, China warned prospective applicants that their British nationality would not be recognized by the Chinese Government after 1997. There were also widespread popular protests in Hong Kong itself over the unfairness of a scheme which was perceived as elitist. The bill containing the measures received approval at its second reading in the United Kingdom House of Commons in April 1990. (It was estimated that a record 66,000 Hong Kong residents left the colony in 1992, the number of emigrants fluctuating thereafter and declining to 43,100 in 1995.)

Among other recommendations made by the parliamentary select committee were the introduction of a Bill of Rights for Hong Kong and an increase in the number of seats subject to direct election in the Hong Kong Legislative Council, to one-half of the total in 1991, leading to full direct elections in 1995. A draft Bill of Rights, based on the UN International Covenant on Civil and Political Rights, was published by the Hong Kong Government in March 1990. The draft was criticized in principle because its provisions would have been subordinate, in the case of conflict, to the provisions of the Basic Law. Nevertheless, the Bill of Rights entered into law in June 1991, its enactment immediately being deemed unnecessary by the Government of China.

China's NPC approved a final draft of the Basic Law for Hong Kong in April 1990. In the approved version, 24 of the 60 seats in the Legislative Council would be subject to direct election in 1999, and 30 seats in 2003; a referendum, to be held after 2007, would consult public opinion on the future composition of the Council, although the ultimate authority to make any changes would rest with China's National People's Congress. The British Government had agreed to co-operate with these measures by offering 18 seats for direct election in 1991 and 20 seats in 1995. Under the Basic Law, the Chief Executive of the Hong Kong Special Administrative Region (SAR), as the territory was to be designated in 1997, would initially be elected for a five-year term by a special 800-member election committee; a referendum was to be held during the third term of office in order to help to determine whether the post should be subject to a general election. However, no person with the right of residence in another country would be permitted to hold an important government post. Particular concern was expressed over a clause in the Law which would 'prohibit political organizations and groups in the Hong Kong SAR from establishing contacts with foreign political organizations or groups'. The British Government and the Hong Kong authorities expressed disappointment that the Basic Law did not allow the development of democratic government at a more rapid pace.

In April 1990 liberal groups formed Hong Kong's first formal political party, the United Democrats of Hong Kong (UDHK), with Martin Lee as its Chairman. The party subsequently became the main opposition to the conservatives, and achieved considerable success in local elections in March and May 1991, and in the territory's first direct legislative elections in September. Of the 18 seats in the Legislative Council subject to election by universal suffrage, 17 were won by members of the UDHK and like-minded liberal and independent candidates. Only 39% of registered electors, however, were reported to have voted. Despite the party's electoral success, the Governor nominated only one of the UDHK's 20 suggested candidates when selecting his direct appointees to the Legislative Council. Changes in the membership of the Executive Council were announced in October, liberal citizens again being excluded by the Governor.

In September 1991 the Sino-British JLG announced the future composition of the Hong Kong Court of Appeal, which in 1993 was to assume the function hitherto performed by the British Privy Council in London. Local lawyers, however, denounced the proposed membership, arguing that the new body would lack independence and flexibility. In December the Legislative Council voted overwhelmingly to reject the proposed composition of the Court.

Sir David Wilson was to retire in 1992. Months of speculation over the Governor's replacement were ended in April, with the appointment of Christopher Patten, hitherto Chairman of the Conservative Party in the United Kingdom, who took office in July. In the following month Patten held discussions with Zhou Nan, director of the Xinhua News Agency and China's most senior representative in Hong Kong. Ambitious plans for democratic reform in the territory, announced by the Governor in October, included the separation of the Executive Council from the Legislative Council. The former was reorganized to include prominent lawyers and academics. At the 1995 elections to the latter, the number of directly-elected members was to be increased to the maximum permissible of 20; the franchise for the existing 21 'functional constituencies', representing occupational and professional groups, was to be widened and nine additional constituencies were to be established, in order to encompass all categories of workers. Various social and economic reforms were also announced. In the same month Patten paid his first visit to China.

The proposed electoral changes were denounced by China as a contravention of the Basic Law and of the 1984 Joint Declaration. Although Patten's programme received the general support of the Legislative Council, many conservative business leaders were opposed to the proposals. In November 1992, following Hong Kong's announcement that it was to proceed with the next stage of preparations for the disputed construction of a new airport (without, as yet, the Chinese Government's agreement to the revised financing of the project), China threatened to cancel, in 1997, all commercial contracts, leases and agreements between the Hong Kong Government and the private sector that had been signed without its full approval. The dispute continued in early 1993, China's criticism of the territory's Governor becoming increasingly acrimonious. In February China announced plans to establish a 'second stove', or alternative administration for Hong Kong, if the Governor's proposed reforms were implemented. In April, however, the impasse was broken when the United Kingdom and China agreed to resume negotiations. In July the 57-member Preliminary Working Committee (PWC), established to study issues relating to the transfer of sovereignty in 1997 and chaired by the Chinese Minister of Foreign Affairs, held its inaugural meeting in Beijing. Negotiations between the United Kingdom and China continued intermittently throughout the year. In December, however, no progress having been made, proposed electoral reforms were submitted to the Legislative Council. The Governor's decision to proceed unilaterally was denounced by China, which declared that it would regard as null and void any laws enacted in Hong Kong.

In January 1994, during a visit to London for consultations, Patten urged China to resume negotiations. In the following month the Legislative Council approved the first stage of the reform programme, which included the lowering of the voting age from 21 to 18 years. China confirmed that all recently-elected bodies would be disbanded in 1997. The second stage was presented to the Legislative Council in March. Relations with China deteriorated further in April, upon the publication of a British parliamentary report endorsing Patten's democratic reforms. In the same month the UDHK and Meeting Point, a smaller party, announced their intention to merge and form the Democratic Party of Hong Kong. In April the trial in camera of a Beijing journalist (who worked for a respected Hong Kong newspaper) on imprecise charges of 'stealing state secrets' and his subsequent severe prison sentence aroused widespread concern in the territory over future press freedom. Hundreds of journalists took part in a protest march through the streets of Hong Kong.

In June 1994, in an unprecedented development that reflected growing unease with Patten's style of government, the Legislative Council passed a motion of censure formally rebuking the Governor for refusing to permit a debate on an amendment to the budget. Nevertheless, at the end of the month the Legislative Council approved further constitutional reforms, entailing an increase in the number of its directly-elected members and an extension of the franchise. Despite China's strong opposition to these reforms, shortly afterwards the People's Republic and the United Kingdom concluded an agreement on the transfer of defence sites, some of which were to be retained for military purposes and upgraded prior to 1997, while others were to be released for redevelopment. At the end of August, following the issuing of a report by the PWC in the previous month, the Standing Committee of the National People's Congress in Beijing approved a decision on the abolition, in 1997, of the current political structure of Hong Kong. . In September, during a visit to the territory, the British Foreign Secretary was accused by members of the Legislative Council of failing to give adequate support to Hong Kong, and was urged to permit the establishment of an independent commission to protect human rights in the territory after 1997.

In September 1994, at elections to the 18 District Boards (the first to be held on a fully democratic basis), 75 of the 346 seats were won by the Democratic Party. The pro-Beijing Democratic Alliance for the Betterment of Hong Kong (DAB) won 37 seats, the progressive Association for Democracy and People's Livelihood (ADPL) 29 seats, and the pro-Beijing Liberal Party and Liberal Democratic Foundation 18 seats and 11 seats, respectively. Independent candidates secured 167 seats. The level of voter participation was a record 33.1%.

In early October 1994 the Governor of Hong Kong offered his full co-operation with China during the 1,000 remaining days of British sovereignty. In December the director of the State Council's Hong Kong and Macau Affairs Office and secretary-general of the PWC, Lu Ping, formally confirmed that the Legislative Council would be disbanded in 1997.

A new dispute with China, relating to the personal files of Hong Kong civil servants, arose in January 1995. China's demand for immediate access to these confidential files, ostensibly for the purposes of verifying integrity and of determining nationality (and thus eligibility for senior posts), was rejected by the Governor.

Elections for the 32 seats on the Urban Council and the 27 seats on the Regional Council took place in March 1995. The Democratic Party took 23 seats, the DAB eight seats and the ADPL also eight seats. Fewer than 26% of those eligible voted in the polls. In the same month Donald Tsang was nominated as Financial Secretary; his predecessor, along with other expatriate senior officials, had been requested to take early retirement to allow for the appointment of a local civil servant. Tsang took office in September.

Following a redrafting of the legislation, in June 1995 the United Kingdom and China reached agreement on the establishment of the Court of Final Appeal. Contrary to the Governor's original wishes, this new body would not now be constituted until after the transfer of sovereignty in mid-1997. The agreement was approved by the Legislative Council in July 1995. In the same month an unprecedented motion of 'no confidence' in the Governor was defeated at a session of the Legislative Council. Also in July the territory's Chief Secretary, Anson Chan, confirmed that she had had clandestine meetings with senior Chinese officials during a three-day visit to Beijing.

At elections to the Legislative Council in September 1995, for the first time all 60 seats were determined by election. The Democratic Party won 12 of the 20 seats open to direct election on the basis of geographical constituencies and two of the 10 chosen by an electoral committee, bringing the party's total representation to 19. The Liberal Party took nine of the 60 seats, the pro-Beijing DAB six seats and the ADPL four seats. Independent candidates won 17 seats. The level of participation in the geographical constituencies was 35.8%.

The Governor aroused much controversy in September 1995, when he urged the United Kingdom to grant the right of abode to more than 3m. citizens of Hong Kong. The proposals were rebuffed by the British Home Secretary. In October, however, an improvement in Sino-British relations was confirmed by the visit of the Chinese Minister of Foreign Affairs to London. The two sides reached agreement on the establishment of a liaison office to improve bilateral contacts between civil servants. China's disclosure of a plan to establish a parallel administration six months prior to the transfer of sovereignty provoked outrage in Hong Kong.

In January 1996 the 150-member Preparatory Committee of the Hong Kong SAR was formally established in Beijing to succeed the PWC. The 94 Hong Kong delegates included representatives of the territory's business and academic communities. The Democratic Party was excluded from the new body, which was to appoint a 400-member Selection Committee responsible for the choice of the territory's future Chief Executive.

In March 1996, during a visit to the territory, the British Prime Minister announced that more than 2m. holders of the forthcoming Hong Kong SAR passports would be granted visa-free access to (but not residency in) the United Kingdom. He also declared that China had a legal obligation to maintain the Legislative Council and to uphold basic rights in the territory. The Preparatory Committee in Beijing, however, approved a resolution to appoint a provisional body to replace the Legislative Council. Towards the end of March, as the final deadline approached, there were chaotic scenes in Hong Kong as thousands of residents rushed to submit applications for British Dependent Territories Citizenship (BDTC) which, although conferring no right of abode in the United Kingdom, would provide an alternative travel document to the new SAR passports. As tension continued to rise, in April the Chief Secretary of Hong Kong travelled to Beijing for discussions with Lu Ping. A visit to Hong Kong by Lu Ping earlier in the month had been disrupted by pro-democracy demonstrators. In early July eight pro-democracy politicians, including five members of the Legislative Council, were refused entry to China, having flown from Hong Kong in an attempt to deliver a petition of 60,000 signatures criticizing the proposed establishment of a provisional legislative body for Hong Kong. In mid-August nominations opened for candidacy for the 400-member Selection Committee. In the same month a new pro-democracy movement, The Frontier, comprising teachers, students and trade unionists, was established.

In September 1996 the United Kingdom and China finally reached agreement on the ceremonial arrangements to commemorate the transfer of sovereignty on 30 June 1997. In October 1996 the Chinese Minister of Foreign Affairs declared that from mid-1997 the annual protests against the Tiananmen Square massacre of 1989 (and similar demonstrations) would not be tolerated in Hong Kong; furthermore, criticism of the Chinese leadership by the territory's press would not be permitted.

In December 1996 the second ballot for the selection of Hong Kong's Chief Executive (the first having been held in November) resulted in the choice of Tung Chee-hwa, a shipping magnate and former member of the territory's Executive Council, who obtained 320 of the 400 votes, defeating the former Chief Justice, (Sir) Yang Ti-Liang, and a business executive, Peter Woo. Later in the month the Selection Committee reassembled to choose the 60 members of the SAR's controversial Provisional Legislative Council (PLC). More than 30 of the new appointees were members of the existing Legislative Council, belonging mainly to the DAB and to the Liberal Party. Despite much criticism of the PLC's establishment, the new body held its inaugural meeting in Shenzhen in January 1997, and elected Rita Fan as its President.

In early 1997 the Chief Executive-designate announced the composition of the Executive Council, which was to comprise three ex-officio members (as previously) and 11 non-official members. The latter included two members of the outgoing Executive Council. Anson Chan was to remain as Chief Secretary, while Donald Tsang was to continue as Financial Secretary; Elsie Leung was to become Justice Secretary, replacing the incumbent Attorney General. China's approval of Tung Chee-hwa's recommendations that senior civil servants be retained did much to enhance confidence in the territory's future. In February, however, relations with the outgoing administration deteriorated when the Preparatory Committee voted overwhelmingly in favour of proposals to repeal or amend 25 laws, thereby reducing the territory's civil liberties. The British Foreign Secretary reiterated concerns regarding the establishment of the PLC and the proposed curbs on civil liberties.

Meanwhile, Lawrence Leung had abruptly resigned as Director of Immigration in July 1996 for 'personal reasons'. In January 1997 he cast doubt on the integrity of the Hong Kong Government when he appeared before a hearing of the Legislative Council and claimed that he had in fact been dismissed, thus denying the official version of his departure from office. The scandal deepened with the revelation that Leung had been found to possess undisclosed business interests. Newspaper reports alleged that Leung had passed sensitive information to unauthorized parties, leading to speculation that the security of mainland dissidents in the territory, of civil servants who held foreign passports, and of others who had been granted British nationality, had been severely compromised. The Government finally admitted that Leung had indeed been dismissed, but denied that he had been involved in any espionage activities on behalf of China.

In May 1997 the PLC approved its first legislation (a bill on public holidays), despite protests from the British Government and pro-democracy groups in Hong Kong that the PLC was not entitled to pass laws during the transition period. However, the PLC declared that the legislation would come into effect only on 1 July. Following the circulation in April of a public consultation document on proposed legislation governing civil liberties and social order, a series of amendments, relating to the holding of public demonstrations and the funding of political organizations, was announced in May. Pro-democracy groups and the outgoing administration remained dissatisfied with the legislation.

Shortly after the transfer of Hong Kong from British to Chinese sovereignty at midnight on 30 June 1997, the inauguration of the SAR Executive Council, the PLC and members of the judiciary was held. Some 4,000 dignitaries attended the ceremonies, although the British Prime Minister and Foreign Secretary, and the US Secretary of State, did not attend the inauguration of the PLC, to register their disapproval at the undemocratic nature of its formation. Pro-democracy groups and members of the former legislature staged peaceful demonstrations in protest at the abolition of the Legislative Council. More than 4,000 Chinese People's Liberation Army troops entered Hong Kong shortly after the handover ceremony, joining the small number of Chinese military personnel that had been deployed in the territory in April, following protracted negotiations with the British Government; a further 500 had entered the territory on 30 June, immediately prior to the handover.

Details of the procedure for elections to a new Legislative Council, which would replace the PLC, were announced by the SAR Government in early July 1997. The elections were scheduled to take place in May 1998, and were to be conducted under a new system of voting. Of the 60 seats in the legislature, 20 were to be directly elected by means of a revised system of proportional representation, 30 were to be elected by 'functional constituencies' (comprising professional and special interest groups) and 10 by an 800-member electoral college. Legislative amendments governing the electoral arrangements were approved by the PLC in late September 1997. The significant reduction of the franchise, by comparison with the 1995 legislative elections, was condemned by the Democratic Party. The appointment by indirect election of 36 Hong Kong delegates to the Chinese National People's Congress, in December 1997, also attracted criticism from pro-democracy activists. Nevertheless, the arrangements were defended by Anson Chan, who maintained that democracy and the rule of law were being upheld in Hong Kong.

Following the transfer of power to China, concerns continued about freedom of expression in the SAR. In March 1998 a prominent publisher and a member of the Chinese People's Political Consultative Conference (CPPCC), Xu Simin, challenged the right of the public broadcaster, Radio Television Hong Kong, to criticize government policy, while Tung stated on the same day that government policies should be positively presented by the media. Following expressions of popular discontent, Tung issued a denial that Xu's position reflected government policy. In the same month the Secretary of Justice, Elsie Leung, was forced to defend the independence of the Justice Department, following the Government's decision not to prosecute another prominent publisher, CPPCC member and a friend of Tung's, Sally Aw Sian, for corruption, despite a ruling against her by the Independent Commission Against Corruption. Pro-democracy groups expressed fears that people with connections to the Chinese Government were above the law. This occurred two weeks after Leung had declined to prosecute the official Chinese news agency, Xinhua, for an alleged breach of privacy laws, following its failure to respond adequately to a disclosure request from Emily Lau, the leader of the pro-democracy movement, The Frontier. Xinhua took 10 months (despite a legal 40-day limit) to issue a denial that it possessed information pertaining to Lau. (In March 1999 a motion of 'no confidence' in Elsie Leung, prompted by these controversial legal decisions, was defeated in the Legislative Council.) In May 1998 two pro-democracy activists were found guilty of defacing flags of China and the Hong Kong SAR at a rally in January, the first such conviction since Hong Kong's transfer to Chinese sovereignty. In March 1999 the Court of Final Appeal ruled that the law prohibiting the defacing of the SAR flag was an unconstitutional restriction of freedom of expression. The Court, however, overturned its own decision in December of that year, under pressure from Beijing, and the conviction stood, provoking protests from civil rights organizations. In January 1998 a demonstration was staged to coincide with the visit of the former Chinese President, Yang Shangkun, who was regarded as one of those responsible for the Tiananmen Square massacre in 1989. Similar protests were conducted during a visit by Qiao Shi, the Chairman of the Standing Committee of the Eighth Chinese National People's Congress, in February 1998, and in June a peaceful commemoration of the 1989 massacre took place without incident. In the following year, the 10th anniversary of the massacre was marked by a peaceful demonstration, attended by 70,000 protesters. On the second anniversary of the resumption of Chinese sovereignty, on 1 July 1999, more than 2,000 pro-democracy demonstrators protested against Chinese control.

In October 1999 the SAR administration announced the sudden transfer of Cheung Man-yee, Director of Broadcasting of the government-owned Radio Television Hong Kong, to a post as senior economic and trade representative in Tokyo, Japan. It was suspected that Cheung's defence of the broadcaster's editorial independence had made her unpopular with the pro-China establishment, resulting in her removal for political reasons. Shortly afterwards Emily Lau announced that she would report the transfer to the UN Committee on Human Rights, citing it as an example of the erosion of freedom of expression in Hong Kong.

Fears concerning the SAR's autonomy were exacerbated by the rapid adoption by the PLC in April 1998 of the Adaptation of Laws Bill. The Bill was ostensibly just to replace references to the British crown in existing legislation but in practice it exempted Xinhua, the office of the Chinese Ministry of Foreign Affairs and the garrison of the People's Liberation Army from all laws unless otherwise stated. Concerns about the territory's legal autonomy were also raised by the conviction and execution, in November and December respectively, of five criminals from Hong Kong in the People's Republic.

At the elections to the first Legislative Council (Legco) of the SAR on 24 May 1998, participation (53.3% of registered voters) was the highest since the introduction of direct elections in Hong Kong. The Democratic Party and other pro-democracy parties suffered a reduction in their overall political strength in the legislature, despite the fact that they won 14 of the 20 directly elective seats. A total of 19 seats were secured by pro-democracy candidates, including 13 by the Democratic Party (nine directly-elected), led by Martin Lee, which became the largest party in the Legislative Council. Lee advocated direct elections by universal suffrage for all 60 seats in the next poll, to be held in 2000. Pro-Beijing supporters dominated the functional constituencies and the election committee ballot. The pro-business Liberal Party, led by Allen Lee, failed to win a single seat in the direct elections but obtained nine in the other constituencies. The Democratic Alliance for the Betterment of Hong Kong also won nine seats, five of which were directly elective.

The powers of the new legislature have been curbed by the Basic Law. Legislative Councillors are not permitted to introduce bills related to political expenditure, the political structure or the opera-

between the Kowloon Peninsula and Central, the main business district of Hong Kong; between Central and Hung Hom; between Tsimshatsui and Wanchai; between Tsimshatsui and Central; and between Wanchai and Hung Hom; Man. JOHNNY LEUNG.

### SHIPPING

Hong Kong is one of the world's largest shipping centres and was among the world's busiest container ports in 1998. Hong Kong was a British port of registry until the inauguration of a new and independent shipping register in December 1990. Following Hong Kong's reunification with the People's Republic of China, Hong Kong maintains full autonomy in its maritime policy. At the end of 1998 the register comprised a fleet of 391 vessels, totalling 6.2m. grt. The eight container terminals at Kwai Chung, which are privately-owned and operated, comprised 18 berths in 1998. The construction of a ninth terminal (CT9) commenced in 1998 and was expected to be operational by 2001. Lantau Island has been designated as the site for any future expansion.

**Hong Kong Government Marine Department:** Harbour Bldg, 22/F, 38 Pier Rd, Central, GPOB 4155; tel. 28523001; fax 25449241; e-mail webmaster@mardep.gen.gov.hk; Dir of Marine S. Y. TSUI.

#### Shipping Companies

**Anglo-Eastern Ship Management Ltd:** Universal Trade Centre, 14/F, 3 Arbuthnot Rd, Central, POB 11400; tel. 28636111; fax 28612419; e-mail allhx470@gncomtext.com; internet www.webhk.com/angloeastern/; Chair. PETER CREMERS; Man. Dir MARCEL LIEDTS.

**Chung Gai Ship Management Co Ltd:** Admiralty Centre Tower 1, 31/F, 18 Harcourt Rd; tel. 25295541; fax 28656206; Chair. S. KODA; Man. Dir K. ICHIHARA.

**Fairmont Shipping (HK) Ltd:** Fairmont House, 21/F, 8 Cotton Tree Drive; tel. 25218338; fax 28104560; Man. CHARLES LEUNG.

**Far East Enterprising Co (HK) Ltd:** China Resources Bldg, 18–19/F, 26 Harbour Rd, Wanchai; tel. 28283668; fax 28275584; f. 1949; shipping, chartering, brokering; Gen. Man. WEI KUAN.

**Gulfeast Shipmanagement Ltd:** Great Eagle Centre, 9/F, 23 Harbour Rd, Wanchai; tel. 28313344; Finance Dir A. T. MIRMOHAMMADI.

**Hong Kong Borneo Shipping Co Ltd:** 815 International Bldg, 141 Des Voeux Rd, Central; tel. 25413797; fax 28153473; Pres. Datuk LAI FOOK KIM.

**Hong Kong Ming Wah Shipping Co:** Unit 3701, China Merchants Tower, 37/F, Shun Tak Centre, 168–200 Connaught Rd, Central; tel. 25172128; fax 25473482; e-mail mwins@cmhk.com; Chair. CHEUNG KING WA; Man. Dir and Vice-Chair. Capt. MAO SHI JIAN.

**Island Navigation Corpn International Ltd:** Harbour Centre, 28–29/F, 25 Harbour Rd, Wanchai; tel. 28333222; fax 28270001; Man. Dir F. S. SHIH.

**Jardine Ship Management Ltd:** Jardine Engineering House, 11/F, 260 King's Rd, North Point; tel. 28074101; fax 28073351; e-mail jsmhk@ibm.net; Man. Dir Capt. PAUL UNDERHILL.

**Oak Maritime (HK) Inc Ltd:** 2301 China Resources Bldg, 26 Harbour Rd, Wanchai; tel. 25063866; fax 25063563; Chair. STEVE G. K. HSU; Pres. FRED C. P. TSAI.

**Ocean Tramping Co Ltd:** Hongkong Shipping Centre, 24–29/F, 167 Connaught Rd West; tel. 25892645; fax 25461041; Chair. Z. M. GAO.

**Orient Overseas Container Line Ltd:** Harbour Centre, 31/F, 25 Harbour Rd, Wanchai; tel. 28333888; fax 25318122; internet www.oocl.com; member of the Grand Alliance of shipping cos (five partners); Chair. C. C. TUNG.

**Teh-Hu Cargocean Management Co Ltd:** Unit B, Belgian Bank Tower, 15/F, 77–79 Gloucester Rd, Wanchai; tel. 25988688; fax 28249339; f. 1974; Man. Dir KENNETH K. W. LO.

**Wah Kwong Shipping Agency Co Ltd:** Shanghai Industrial Investment Bldg, 26/F, 48–62 Hennessy Rd, POB 283; tel. 25279227; fax 28656544; internet www.allhx118@gncomtext.com; Chair. ANTHONY T. C. GAW.

**Wah Tung Shipping Agency Co Ltd:** China Resources Bldg, Rooms 2101–5, 21/F, 26 Harbour Rd, Wanchai; tel. 28272818; fax 28275361; e-mail mgr@watunship.com.hk; f. 1981; Dir and Gen. Man. B. L. LIU.

**Wallem Shipmanagement Ltd:** Hopewell Centre, 46/F, 183 Queen's Rd East; tel. 28768200; fax 28761234; e-mail rgb@wallem.com; Man. Dir R. G. BUCHANAN.

**Worldwide Shipping Agency Ltd:** Wheelock House, 6–7/F, 20 Pedder St; tel. 28423888; fax 28100617; Man. J. WONG.

#### Associations

**Hong Kong Cargo-Vessel Traders' Association:** 21–23 Man Wai Bldg, 2/F, Ferry Point, Kowloon; tel. 23847102; fax 27820342; 978 mems; Chair. CHOW YAT-TAK; Sec. CHAN BAK.

**Hong Kong Shipowners' Association:** Queen's Centre, 12/F, 58–64 Queen's Rd East, Wanchai; tel. 25200206; fax 25298246; e-mail hksoa@hksoa.org.hk; internet www.hksoa.org.hk; 220 mems; Chair. ANDREW Y. CHEN; Dir ARTHUR BOWRING.

**Hong Kong Shippers' Council:** Wu Chung House, 31/F, 213 Queen's Rd East; tel. 28340010; fax 28919787; e-mail hksc@hk.super.net; 63 mems; Chair. CHAN WING-KEE; Exec. Dir CLEMENT YEUNG.

### CIVIL AVIATION

By the end of 1998 Hong Kong was served by 62 foreign airlines. The planned construction of a new international airport, on the island of Chek Lap Kok, near Lantau Island, was announced in 1989. Opening of the new airport, to replace that at Kai Tak and initially scheduled for April 1998, was postponed to July, following delays in the construction of a connecting high-speed rail-link. The airport has two runways, with the capacity to handle 35m. passengers and 3m. metric tons of cargo per year. The second runway commenced operations in May 1999. A helicopter link with Macau was established in 1990.

**Airport Authority of Hong Kong:** Hong Kong International Airport, 8 Chun Yue Rd, Lantau; tel. 28247111; fax 28240717; f. 1995; Chair. FUNG KWOK-KING; CEO BILLY C. L. LAM.

**Civil Aviation Department:** Queensway Government Offices, 46/F, 66 Queensway; tel. 28674332; fax 28690093; e-mail cadeng@cad.gcn.gov.hk; internet www.info.gov.hk/cad/; Dir ALBERT K. Y. LAM.

**AHK Air Hong Kong Ltd:** Units 3601–8, 36/F, Tower 1, Millennium City, 388 Kwun Tong Rd, Kowloon; tel. 27618588; fax 27618586; e-mail ahk.hq@airhongkong.com.hk; f. 1986; international cargo carrier; Chief Operating Officer KENNY TANG.

**Cathay Pacific Airways Ltd:** Swire House, 9 Connaught Rd, Central; tel. 27475000; fax 28106563; f. 1946; services to more than 40 major cities in the Far East, Middle East, North America, Europe, South Africa, Australia and New Zealand; Chair. PETER D. A. SUTCH; Man. Dir DAVID TURNBULL.

**Hong Kong Dragon Airlines Ltd (Dragonair):** Devon House, 22/F, Taikoo Place, 979 King's Rd, Quarry Bay; tel. 25901328; fax 25901333; internet www.dragonair.com; f. 1985; scheduled and charter flights to 25 destinations in Asia, 16 of which are in mainland China; scheduled regional services include Phuket (Thailand), Hiroshima and Sendai (Japan), Kaohsiung (Taiwan), Phnom-Penh (Cambodia), Dhaka (Bangladesh), Bandar Seri Begawan (Brunei), and Kota Kinabalu (Malaysia); Chair. WANG GUIXIANG; Dir and CEO STANLEY HUI.

## Tourism

Tourism is a major source of foreign exchange, contributing revenue of HK $72,641m. (including receipts from visitors from mainland China) in 1998. Of this, HK $55,251m. were tourism receipts and HK $17,390m. were from related passenger services. Some 9.5m. people visited Hong Kong in 1998 and there were 8.7m. visitors between January and October 1999. In October 1999 there were some 91 hotels, and the number of rooms available totalled 35,102. The number of rooms was to be increased to 38,550 in 97 hotels by December 2000. In November 1999 it was agreed that a new Disneyland theme park would be constructed in Hong Kong, to be opened in 2005. The Government expected the park to create a huge influx of tourists to the territory.

**Hong Kong Tourist Association:** Citicorp Centre, 9–11/F, 18 Whitfield Rd, North Point; tel. 28076543; fax 28076595; e-mail plr@hkta.org; internet www.hkta.org; f. 1957; co-ordinates and promotes the tourist industry; has govt support and financial assistance; 11 mems of the Board represent the Govt, the private sector and the tourism industry; Chair. Y. S. LO; Exec. Dir AMY CHAN.

# MACAU

## Introductory Survey

### Location, Climate, Language, Religion, Flag, Capital

The Special Administrative Region (SAR) of Macau comprises the peninsula of Macau, an enclave on the mainland of southern China, and two nearby islands, Taipa, which is linked to the mainland by two bridges, and Coloane, which is connected to Taipa by a causeway. The territory lies opposite Hong Kong on the western side of the mouth of the Xijiang (Sikiang) river. The climate is subtropical, with temperatures averaging 15°C in January and 29°C in July. There are two official languages, Chinese (Cantonese being the principal dialect) and Portuguese. English is also widely spoken. The predominant religions are Roman Catholicism, Chinese Buddhism, Daoism and Confucianism. The flag of the Macau SAR (proportions 3 by 2), introduced upon the territory's reversion to Chinese sovereignty in December 1999 and flown subordinate to the flag of the People's Republic of China, displays a stylized white flower below an arc of one large and four small yellow stars, above five white lines, on a green background. The capital, the city of Macau, is situated on the peninsula.

### Recent History

Established by the Portuguese in 1557 as a trading post with China, Macau became a Portuguese Overseas Province in 1951. After the military coup in Portugal in April 1974, Col José Garcia Leandro was appointed Governor of the province. A new statute, promulgated in February 1976, redefined Macau as a 'Special Territory' under Portuguese jurisdiction, but with a great measure of administrative and economic independence (see Government, below). Proposals to enlarge the Legislative Assembly from 17 to 21 members, thus giving the Chinese population an increased role in the administration of Macau, were abandoned when they did not receive the approval of the Government of the People's Republic of China in March 1980. China and Portugal established diplomatic relations in February 1979.

In February 1979 Col Leandro was replaced as Governor by Gen. Nuno de Melo Egídio, deputy chief of staff of Portugal's armed forces. In June 1981 Gen. Egídio was, in turn, replaced by Cdre (later Rear-Adm.) Vasco Almeida e Costa, a Portuguese former minister and naval commander. Following a constitutional dispute in March 1984 over the Governor's plans for electoral reform (extending the franchise to the ethnic Chinese majority), the Legislative Assembly was dissolved. Elections for a new Assembly were held in August, at which the Chinese majority were allowed to vote for the first time, regardless of their length of residence in the territory. Four of the six directly-elected seats were won by the Electoral Union, a coalition of pro-Beijing and conservative Macanese (lusophone Eurasian) groups, while the six indirectly-elected members, all Chinese, were returned unopposed. The Governor appointed four government officials and a Chinese business executive to complete the Assembly, which was then for the first time dominated by ethnic Chinese deputies.

In January 1986 Governor Almeida e Costa resigned. In May he was replaced by Joaquim Pinto Machado, who had hitherto been a professor of medicine. Pinto Machado's appointment represented a break in the tradition of military governors for Macau, but his political inexperience placed him at a disadvantage. In May 1987 he resigned, citing 'reasons of institutional dignity' (apparently referring to the problem of corruption in the Macau administration). He was replaced in August by Carlos Melancia, a former Socialist deputy in the Portuguese legislature, who had held ministerial posts in several Portuguese governments.

In May 1985, meanwhile, President Eanes visited Beijing and Macau, and it was announced that the Portuguese and Chinese Governments would negotiate the future of Macau during 1986. Portugal's acceptance of China's sovereignty greatly simplified the issue. The first round of negotiations took place in June 1986 in Beijing. On 13 April 1987, following the conclusion of the fourth round of negotiations, a joint declaration was formally signed in Beijing by the Portuguese and Chinese Governments, during an official visit to China by the Prime Minister of Portugal. According to the agreement (which was formally ratified in January 1988), Macau was to become a 'special administrative region' (SAR) of the People's Republic (to be known as Macau, China) on 20 December 1999. Macau was thus to have the same status as that agreed (with effect from 1997) for Hong Kong, and was to enjoy autonomy in most matters except defence and foreign policy. A Sino-Portuguese Joint Liaison Group (JLG), established to oversee the transfer of power, held its inaugural meeting in Lisbon in April 1988. In 1999 a Chief Executive for Macau was to be appointed by the Chinese Government, following 'elections or consultations to be held in Macau', and the territory's legislature was to contain 'a majority of elected members'. The inhabitants of Macau were to become citizens of the People's Republic of China. The Chinese Government refused to allow the possibility of dual Sino-Portuguese citizenship, although Macau residents in possession of Portuguese passports were apparently to be permitted to retain them for travel purposes. The agreement guaranteed a 50-year period during which Macau would be permitted to retain its free capitalist economy, and to be financially independent of China.

In August 1988 the establishment of a Macau Basic Law Drafting Committee was announced by the Chinese Government. Comprising 30 Chinese members and 19 representatives from Macau, the Committee was to draft a law determining the territory's future constitutional status within the People's Republic of China. Elections to the Legislative Assembly were held in October 1988. Low participation (fewer than 30% of the electorate) was recorded, and a 'liberal' grouping secured three of the seats reserved for directly-elected candidates, while the Electoral Union won the other three.

In January 1989 it was announced that Portuguese passports were to be issued to about 100,000 ethnic Chinese inhabitants, born in Macau before October 1981, and it was anticipated that as many as a further 100,000 would be granted before 1999. Unlike their counterparts in the neighbouring British dependent territory of Hong Kong, therefore, these Macau residents (but not all) were to be granted the full rights of a citizen of the European Community (EC, now European Union—EU). In February 1989 President Mário Soares of Portugal visited Macau, in order to discuss the transfer of the territory's administration to China.

Following the violent suppression of the pro-democracy movement in China in June 1989, as many as 100,000 residents of Macau participated in demonstrations in the enclave to protest against the Chinese Government's action. The events in the People's Republic caused great concern in Macau, and it was feared that many residents would wish to leave the territory prior to 1999. In August 1989, however, China assured Portugal that it would honour the agreement to maintain the capitalist system of the territory after 1999.

In March 1990 the implementation of a programme to grant permanent registration to parents of 4,200 Chinese residents, the latter having already secured the right of abode in Macau, developed into chaos when other illegal immigrants demanded a similar concession. The authorities decided to declare a general amnesty, but were unprepared for the numbers of illegal residents who rushed to take advantage of the scheme, thereby revealing the true extent of previous immigration from China. In the ensuing stampede by 50,000 illegal immigrants, desperate to obtain residency rights, about 200 persons were injured and 1,500 arrested. Border security was increased, in an effort to prevent any further illegal immigration from China.

In late March 1990 the Legislative Assembly approved the final draft of the territory's revised Organic Law. The Law was approved by the Portuguese Assembly of the Republic in mid-April, and granted Macau greater administrative, economic, financial and legislative autonomy, in advance of 1999. The powers of the Governor and of the Legislative Assembly, where six additional seats were to be created, were therefore increased. The post of military commander of the security forces was abolished, responsibility for the territory's security being assumed by a civilian Under-Secretary.

In June 1990 the Under-Secretary for Justice, Dr Manuel Magalhães e Silva, resigned, owing to differences of opinion on the issues of Macau's political structure and Sino-Portuguese relations. In the same month, while on a visit to Lisbon for consultations with the President and Prime Minister, Carlos Melancia rebuked the Chinese authorities for attempting to interfere in the internal affairs of Macau. This unprecedented reproach followed criticism of the Governor's compromising attitude towards the People's Republic of China.

Meanwhile, in February 1990, Carlos Melancia had been implicated in a financial scandal. It was alleged that the Governor had accepted 50m. escudos from a Federal German company which hoped to be awarded a consultancy contract for the construction of the new airport in Macau. In September Melancia was served with a summons in connection with the alleged bribery. Although he denied any involvement in the affair, the Governor resigned, and was replaced on an acting basis by the Under-Secretary for Economic Affairs, Dr Francisco Murteira Nabo. In September 1991 it was announced that Melancia and five others were to stand trial on charges of corruption. Melancia's trial opened in April 1993. At its conclusion in August the former Governor was acquitted on the grounds of insufficient evidence. In February 1994, however, it was announced that Melancia was to be retried, owing to irregularities in his defence case.

The ability of Portugal to maintain a stable administration in the territory had once again been called into question. Many observers believed that the enclave was being adversely affected by the political situation in Lisbon, as differences between the socialist President and centre-right Prime Minister were being reflected in rivalries between officials in Macau. In an attempt to restore confidence, therefore, President Soares visited the territory in November 1990. In January 1991, upon his re-election as Head of State, the President appointed Gen. Vasco Rocha Vieira (who had served as the territory's Chief of Staff in 1973/74 and as Under-Secretary for Public Works and Transport in 1974/75) to be the new Governor of Macau. In March 1991 the Legislative Assembly was expanded from 17 to 23 members. All seven Under-Secretaries were replaced in May.

Following his arrival in Macau, Gen. Rocha Vieira announced that China would be consulted on all future developments in the territory. The 10th meeting of the Sino-Portuguese JLG took place in Beijing in April 1991. Topics under regular discussion included the participation of Macau in international organizations, progress towards an increase in the number of local officials employed in the civil service (hitherto dominated by Portuguese and Macanese personnel) and the status of the Chinese language. The progress of the working group on the translation of local laws from Portuguese into Chinese was also examined, a particular problem being the lack of suitably-qualified bilingual legal personnel. It was agreed that Portuguese was to remain an official language after 1999. The two sides also reached agreement on the exchange of identity cards for those Macau residents who would require them in 1999. Regular meetings of the JLG continued.

In July 1991 the Macau Draft Basic Law was published by the authorities of the People's Republic of China. Confidence in the territory's future was enhanced by China's apparent flexibility on a number of issues. Unlike the Hong Kong Basic Law, that of Macau did not impose restrictions on holders of foreign passports assuming senior posts in the territory's administration after 1999, the only exception being the future Chief Executive. Furthermore, the draft contained no provision for the stationing of troops from China in Macau after the territory's return to Chinese administration.

In November 1991 the Governor of Macau visited the People's Republic of China, where it was confirmed that the 'one country, two systems' policy would operate in Macau from 1999. Following a visit to Portugal by the Chinese Premier in February 1992, the Governor of Macau stated that the territory was to retain 'great autonomy' after 1999. In March 1993 the final draft of the Basic Law of the Macau SAR was ratified by the National People's Congress in Beijing, which also approved the design of the future SAR's flag. The adoption of the legislation was welcomed by the Governor of Macau, who reiterated his desire for a smooth transfer of power in 1999. The Chief Executive of the SAR was to be selected by local representatives. The SAR's first Legislative Council was to comprise 23 members, of whom eight would be directly elected. Its term of office would expire in October 2001, when it would be expanded to 27 members, of whom 10 would be directly elected.

Meanwhile, elections to the Legislative Assembly were held in September 1992. The level of participation was higher than on previous occasions, with 59% of the registered electorate (albeit only 13.5% of the population) attending the polls. Fifty candidates contested the eight directly-elective seats, four of which were won by members of the main pro-Beijing parties, the União Promotora para o Progresso and the União para o Desenvolvimento.

Relations between Portugal and China remained cordial. In June 1993 the two countries reached agreement on all outstanding issues regarding the construction of the territory's airport and the future use of Chinese air space. Furthermore, Macau was to be permitted to negotiate air traffic agreements with other countries. In October, upon the conclusion of a three-day visit to Macau, President Soares expressed optimism regarding the territory's smooth transition to Chinese administration. In November President Jiang Zemin of China was warmly received in Lisbon, where he had discussions with both the Portuguese President and Prime Minister. In February 1994 the Chinese Minister of Communications visited Macau to discuss with the Governor the progress of the airport project.

In April 1994, during a visit to China, the Portuguese Prime Minister received an assurance that Chinese nationality would not be imposed on Macanese people of Portuguese descent, who would be able to retain their Portuguese passports. Speaking in Macau itself, the Prime Minister expressed confidence in the territory's future. Regarding the issue as increasingly one of foreign policy, he stated his desire to transfer jurisdiction over Macau from the Presidency of the Republic to the Government, despite the necessity for a constitutional amendment.

In July 1994 a group of local journalists dispatched a letter, alleging intimidation and persecution in Macau, to President Soares, urging him to intervene to defend the territory's press freedom. The journalists' appeal followed an incident involving the director of the daily *Gazeta Macaense*, who had been obliged to pay 300,000 escudos for reproducing an article from *Semanário*, a Lisbon weekly newspaper, and now faced trial. The territory's press had been critical of the Macau Supreme Court's decision to extradite ethnic Chinese to the mainland (despite the absence of any extradition treaty) to face criminal charges and the possibility of a death sentence.

Gen. Rocha Vieira embarked upon a second visit to China in August 1994. The Governor of Macau had discussions with the Chinese Minister of Foreign Affairs, who declared Sino-Portuguese relations to be sound but, as a result of a gaffe relating to the delegation's distribution to the press of a biography of Premier Li Peng containing uncomplimentary remarks, stressed the need for vigilance.

The draft of the new penal code for Macau did not incorporate the death penalty. In January 1995, during a visit to Portugal, Vice-Premier Zhu Rongji of China confirmed that the People's Republic would not impose the death penalty in Macau after 1999, regarding the question as a matter for the authorities of the future SAR. The new penal code, prohibiting capital punishment, took effect in January 1996.

On another visit to the territory in April 1995, President Soares emphasized the need for Macau to assert its identity, and stressed the importance of three issues: the modification of the territory's legislation; the rights of the individual; and the preservation of the Portuguese language. Travelling on to Beijing, accompanied by Gen. Rocha Vieira, the Portuguese President had successful discussions with his Chinese counterpart on various matters relating to the transition.

In May 1995, during a four-day visit to the territory, Lu Ping, the director of the mainland Hong Kong and Macau Affairs Office, proposed the swift establishment of a preparatory working committee (PWC) to facilitate the transfer of sovereignty. He urged that faster progress be made on the issues of the localization of civil servants and of the law, and on the use of Chinese as the official language. Lu Ping also expressed his desire that the reorganized legislative and municipal bodies to be elected in 1996–97 conform with the Basic Law.

In November 1995, following the change of government in Lisbon, the incoming Portuguese Minister of Foreign Affairs, Jaime Gama, urged that the rights and aspirations of the people of Macau be protected. In December, while attending the celebrations to mark the inauguration of the territory's new airport, President Soares had discussions with the Chinese Vice-President, Rong Yiren. During a four-day visit to Beijing in February 1996, Jaime Gama met President Jiang Zemin and other senior officials, describing the discussions as positive. While acknowledging the sound progress of recent years, Gama and the Chinese Minister of Foreign Affairs agreed on an acceleration in the pace of work of the Sino-Portuguese JLG. In the same month Gen. Rocha Vieira was reappointed Governor of Macau by the newly-elected President of Portugal, Jorge Sampaio. António Guterres, the new Portuguese Prime Minister, confirmed his desire for constitutional consensus regarding the transition of Macau.

At elections to the Legislative Assembly in September 1996, a total of 62 candidates from 12 electoral groupings contested the eight directly-elective seats. The pro-Beijing União Promotora para o Progresso received 15.2% of the votes and won two seats, while the União para o Desenvolvimento won 14.5% and retained one of its two seats. The business-orientated groups were more successful: the Associação Promotora para a Economia de Macau took 16.6% of the votes and secured two seats; the Convergência para o Desenvolvimento and the União Geral para o Desenvolvimento de Macau each won one seat. The pro-democracy Associação de Novo Macau Democrático also won one seat. The level of voter participation was 64%. The 23-member legislature was to remain in place beyond the transfer of sovereignty in 1999.

In October 1996 Portugal and China announced the establishment of a mechanism for regular consultation on matters pertaining to international relations. In the same month citizens of Macau joined a flotilla of small boats carrying activists from Taiwan and Hong Kong to protest against a right-wing Japanese group's construction of a lighthouse on the disputed Daioyu (or Senkaku) Islands, situated in the East China Sea (see People's Republic of China, p. 959). Having successfully evaded Japanese patrol vessels, the protesters raised the flags of China and Taiwan on the disputed islands. In November activists from around the world attended a three-day conference in Macau, in order to discuss their strategy for the protection of the islands.

During 1996 the rising level of violent criminal activity became a cause of increasing concern. Between January and December there were 14 bomb attacks, in addition to numerous brutal assaults. In November a Portuguese gambling inspector narrowly survived an attempt on his life by an unidentified gunman and, as attacks on local casino staff continued, three people were killed and three wounded in six separate incidents. Violent attacks continued in 1997, giving rise to fears for the future of the territory's vital tourism industry. Many attributed the alarming increase in organized crime to the opening of the airport in Macau, which was believed to have facilitated the entry of rival gangsters from mainland China, Taiwan and Hong Kong. In May, following the murder of three men believed to have associations with one such group of gangsters, the Chinese Government expressed its concern at the deterioration of public order in Macau and urged Portugal to observe its responsibility, as undertaken in the Sino-Portuguese joint declaration of 1987, to maintain the enclave's social stability during the transitional period, whilst pledging the enhanced co-operation of the Chinese security forces in the effort to curb organized crime in Macau.

The freedom of Macau's press was jeopardized in June 1997, when several Chinese-language newspapers, along with a television station, received threats instructing them to cease reporting on the activities of the notorious 14K triad, a 10,000-member secret society to which much of the violence had been attributed. In July, during a night of arson and shooting, an explosive device was detonated in the grounds of the Governor's palace, although it caused no serious damage. In the following month China deployed 500 armed police-officers to reinforce the border with Macau in order to intensify its efforts to combat illegal immigration, contraband and the smuggling of arms into the enclave. Despite the approval in July of a law further to restrict activities such as extortion and 'protection rackets', organized crime continued unabated. In early October the police forces of Macau and China initiated a joint campaign against illegal immigration. In late October Leong Kwok-hong, an alleged leader of the 14K triad, was shot dead.

Meanwhile, the slow progress of the 'three localizations' (civil service, laws and the implementation of Chinese as an official language) continued to concern the Government of China. In mid-1996 almost 50% of senior government posts were still held by Portuguese expatriates. In January 1997 the Governor pledged to accelerate the process with regard to local legislation, the priority being the training of the requisite personnel. In the same month, during a visit to Portugal, the Chinese Minister of Foreign Affairs reiterated his confidence in the future of Macau. In February President Sampaio travelled to both Macau and China, where he urged respect for Macau's identity and for the Luso-Chinese declaration regarding the transfer of sovereignty. In December 1997 details of the establishment in Macau of the office of the Chinese Ministry of Foreign Affairs, which was to commence operations in December 1999, were announced. In January 1998 the Macau Government declared that 76.5% of 'leading and directing' posts in the civil service were now held by local officials.

In March 1998 the murder of a Portuguese gambling official, followed by the killing of a marine police-officer, prompted the Chinese authorities to reiterate their concern at the deteriorating situation in Macau. In the following month the driver of the territory's Under-Secretary for Public Security was shot dead. In April, by which month none of the 34 triad-related murders committed since January 1997 had been solved, the Portuguese and Chinese Governments agreed to co-operate in the exchange of information about organized criminal activities. Also in April 1998 the trial, on charges of breaching the gaming laws, of the head of the 14K triad, Wan Kuok-koi ('Broken Tooth'), was adjourned for two months, owing to the apparent reluctance of witnesses to appear in court. Following an attempted car-bomb attack on Macau's chief of police, António Marques Baptista, in early May Wan Kuok-koi was rearrested. The charge of the attempted murder of Marques Baptista, however, was dismissed by a judge three days later on the grounds of insufficient evidence. Wan Kuok-koi remained in prison, charged with other serious offences. The renewed detention of Wan Kuok-koi led to a spate of arson attacks. The Portuguese Government was reported to have dispatched intelligence officers to the enclave to reinforce the local security forces. In June Marques Baptista travelled to Beijing and Guangzhou for discussions on the problems of cross-border criminal activity and drugs-trafficking.

In April 1998 the Portuguese Prime Minister, accompanied by his Minister of Foreign Affairs and a business delegation, paid an official visit to Macau, where he expressed confidence that after 1999 China would respect the civil rights and liberties of the territory. The delegation travelled on to China, where the Prime Minister had cordial discussions with both President Jiang Zemin and Premier Zhu Rongji.

The Preparatory Committee for the Establishment of the Macau SAR, which was to oversee the territory's transfer to Chinese sovereignty and was to comprise representatives from both the People's Republic and Macau, was inaugurated in Beijing in May 1998. Four subordinate working groups (supervising administrative, legal, economic, and social and cultural affairs) were subsequently established. The second plenary session of the Preparatory Committee was convened in July 1998, discussions encompassing issues such as the 'localization' of civil servants, public security and the drafting of the territory's fiscal budget for the year 2000. In July 1998, during a meeting with the Chinese Premier, the Governor of Macau requested an increase in the mainland's investment in the territory prior to the 1999 transfer of sovereignty.

In July 1998, as abductions continued and as it was revealed, furthermore, that the victims of kidnapping and ransom had included two serving members of the Legislative Assembly, President Jiang Zemin of China urged the triads of Macau to cease their campaign of intimidation. The police forces of Macau, Hong Kong and Guangdong Province launched 'S Plan', an operation aiming to curb the activities of rival criminal gangs. In August, in an apparent attempt to intimidate the judiciary, the territory's Attorney-General and his pregnant wife were shot and slightly wounded. In the following month five police-officers and 10 journalists who were investigating a bomb attack were injured when a second bomb exploded.

In August 1998 representatives of the JLG agreed to intensify Luso-Chinese consultations on matters relating to the transitional period. In September, in response to the increasing security problems, China unexpectedly announced that, upon the transfer of sovereignty, it was to station troops in the territory. This abandonment of a previous assurance to the contrary caused much disquiet in Portugal, where the proposed deployment was deemed unnecessary. Although the Basic Law made no specific provision for the stationing of a mainland garrison, China asserted that it was to be ultimately responsible for the enclave's defence. By October, furthermore, about 4,000 soldiers of the People's Liberation Army (PLA) were on duty at various Chinese border posts adjacent to Macau. During a one-week visit to Beijing, the territory's Under-Secretary for Public Security had discussions with senior officials, including the Chinese Minister of Public Security. In mid-October the detention without bail of four alleged members of the 14K triad in connection with the May car-bombing and other incidents led, later in the day, to an outburst of automatic gunfire outside the courthouse.

In November 1998 procedures for the election of the 200 members of the Selection Committee were established by the Preparatory Committee. Responsible for the appointment of the members of Macau's post-1999 Government, the delegates of the Selection Committee were required to be permanent residents of the territory: 60 members were to be drawn from the business and financial communities, 50 from cultural, educational and professional spheres, 50 from labour, social service and religious circles and the remaining 40 were to be former political personages.

About 70 people were arrested in November 1998, when the authorities conducted raids on casinos believed to be engaged in illegal activities. In December an off-duty Portuguese prison warder was shot dead and a colleague wounded by a gunman, the pair having formed part of a contingent recently dispatched from Lisbon to improve security at the prison where Wan Kuok-koi was being held. At the end of December it was confirmed that Macau residents of wholly Chinese origin would be entitled to full mainland citizenship, while those of mixed Chinese and Portuguese descent would be obliged to decide between the two nationalities. In January 1999 protesters clashed with police during demonstrations to draw attention to the plight of numerous immigrant children, who had been brought illegally from China to Macau to join their legitimately-resident parents. Several arrests were made. The problem had first emerged in 1996 when, owing to inadequate conditions, the authorities had closed down an unofficial school attended by 200 children, who because of their irregular status were not entitled to the territory's education, health and social services.

In January 1999 a grenade attack killed one person, and the proprietor of a casino and suspected member of 14K was shot dead. In that month details of the composition of the future PLA garrison were disclosed. The troops were to comprise solely ground forces, totalling fewer than 1,000 soldiers and directly responsible to the Commander of the Guangzhou Military Unit. They would be permitted to intervene to maintain social order in the enclave only if the local police were unable to control major triad-related violence or if street demonstrations posed a threat of serious unrest. In March, during a trip to Macau (where he had discussions with the visiting Portuguese President), Qian Qichen, a Chinese Vice-Premier, indicated that an advance contingent of PLA soldiers would be deployed in Macau prior to the transfer of sovereignty. Other sources of contention between China and Portugal remained the unresolved question of the post-1999 status of those Macau residents who had been granted Portuguese nationality and also the issue of the court of final appeal.

In April 1999 an alleged member of the 14 Carats triad was shot dead by a gunman on a motor cycle. Also in April, at the first plenary meeting of the Selection Committee, candidates for the post of the SAR's Chief Executive were elected. Edmund Ho received 125 of the 200 votes, while Stanley Au garnered 65 votes. Three other candidates failed to secure the requisite minimum of 20 votes. Edmund Ho and Stanley Au, both bankers and regarded as moderate pro-business candidates, thus proceeded to the second round of voting by secret ballot, held in May. The successful contender, Edmund Ho, received 163 of the 199 votes cast, and confirmed his intention to address the problems of law and order, security and the economy. The Chief Executive-designate also fully endorsed China's decision to deploy troops in Macau.

During 1999, in co-operation with the Macau authorities, the police forces of Guangdong Province, and of Zhuhai in particular, initiated a new offensive against the criminal activities of the triads.

China's desire to deploy an advance contingent of troops prior to December 1999, however, reportedly continued to be obstructed by Portugal. Furthermore, the announcement that, subject to certain conditions, the future garrison was to be granted law-enforcement powers raised various constitutional issues. Some observers feared the imposition of martial law, if organized crime were to continue unabated. Many Macau residents, however, appeared to welcome the mainland's decision to station troops in the enclave. In a further effort to address the deteriorating security situation, from December 1999 Macau's 5,800-member police force was to be restructured.

In July 1999 the penultimate meeting of the JLG took place in Lisbon. In August, in accordance with the nominations of the Chief Executive-designate, the composition of the Government of the future SAR was announced by the State Council in Beijing. Appointments included that of Florinda da Rosa Silva Chan as Secretary for Administration and Justice. Also in August an outspoken pro-Chinese member of the Legislative Assembly was attacked and injured by a group of unidentified assailants. This apparently random assault on a serving politician again focused attention on the decline in law and order in the enclave. In September the Governor urged improved co-operation with the authorities of Guangdong Province in order to combat organized crime, revealing that more than one-half of the inmates of Macau's prisons were not residents of the territory. In the same month it was reported that 90 former Gurkhas of the British army were being drafted in as prison warders, following the intimidation of local officers. In September the Chief Executive-designate announced the appointment of seven new members of the Legislative Council, which was to succeed the Legislative Assembly in December 1999. While the seven nominees of the Governor in the existing Legislative Assembly were thus to be replaced, 15 of the 16 elected members (one having resigned) were to remain in office as members of the successor Legislative Council. The composition of the 10-member Executive Council was also announced.

In October 1999 President Jiang Zemin paid a two-day visit to Portugal, following which it was declared that the outstanding question of the deployment of an advance contingent of Chinese troops in Macau had been resolved. The advance party was to be restricted to a technical mission, which entered the territory in early December. In November the 37th and last session of the JLG took place in Beijing, where in the same month the Governor of Macau held final discussions with President Jiang Zemin.

Meanwhile, in April 1999 Wan Kuok-koi had been acquitted of charges of coercing croupiers. In November the trial of Wan Kuok-koi on other serious charges concluded: he was found guilty of criminal association and other illegal gambling-related activities and sentenced to 15 years' imprisonment. Eight co-defendants, including Wan Kuok-koi's brother, received lesser sentences. In a separate trial Artur Chiang Calderon, a former police officer alleged to be Wan Kuok-koi's military adviser, received a prison sentence of 10 years and six months for involvement in organized crime. While two other defendants were also imprisoned, 19 were released on the grounds of insufficient evidence. As the transfer of the territory's sovereignty approached, by mid-December almost 40 people had been murdered in triad-related violence on the streets of Macau since January 1999.

In late November 1999 representatives of the JLG reached agreement on details regarding the deployment of Chinese troops in Macau and on the retention of Portuguese as an official language. At midnight on 19 December 1999, therefore, in a ceremony attended by the Presidents and heads of government of Portugal and China, the sovereignty of Macau was duly transferred; 12 hours later (only after the departure from the newly-inaugurated SAR of the Portuguese delegation), 500 soldiers of the 1,000-strong force of the PLA, in a convoy of armoured vehicles, crossed the border into Macau, where they were installed in a makeshift barracks in a vacant apartment building. Prior to the ceremony, however, it was reported that the authorities of Guangdong Province had detained almost 3,000 persons, including 15 residents of Macau, suspected of association with criminal gangs. The celebrations in Macau were also marred by the authorities' handling of demonstrations by members of Falun Gong, a religious movement recently outlawed in China. The expulsion from Macau of several members of the sect in the days preceding the territory's transfer and the arrest of 30 adherents on the final day of Portuguese sovereignty prompted strong criticism from President Jorge Sampaio of Portugal.

### Government

The Macau Special Administrative Region (SAR) is governed by a Chief Executive, who was chosen by a 200-member Selection Committee in May 1999. The Chief Executive is assisted by a number of Secretaries and is accountable to the State Council of China, the term of office being five years, with a limit of two consecutive terms. Upon the territory's transfer to Chinese sovereignty in December 1999, a 10-member Executive Council, appointed by the Chief Executive to assist in policy-making, assumed office. The 23-member Legislative Assembly, which included eight deputies elected by direct, universal suffrage and eight chosen by indirect election, was superseded by the Legislative Council: 15 of the 16 elected deputies remained in office (one representative having failed to request continued membership), while the seven members appointed by the Governor were replaced by nominees of the new Chief Executive. The term of office of the SAR's transitional Legislative Council was to expire in 2001, when it was to be expanded to 27 members, of whom 10 would be directly elected, 10 indirectly elected and seven appointed, all with a mandate of four years. In 2005 the membership of the Legislative Council was to be increased to 29, to incorporate two additional deputies to be chosen by direct election. For the purposes of local government, the islands of Taipa and Colane are administered separately.

### Defence

The 1998 budget allocated 1,200m. patacas to Macau's security. Upon the territory's transfer of sovereignty in December 1999, troops of the People's Liberation Army (PLA) were stationed in Macau. The force comprises around 1,000 troops: a maximum of 500 soldiers are stationed in Macau, the remainder being positioned in China, on the border with the SAR. The unit is directly responsible to the Commander of the Guangzhou Military Region and to the Central Military Commission. The Macau garrison is composed mainly of ground troops. Naval and air defence tasks are performed by the naval vessel unit of the PLA garrison in Hong Kong and by the airforce unit in Huizhou. Subject to certain conditions, the garrison was granted law-enforcement powers, to assist the maintenance of public security.

### Economic Affairs

In 1998, according to official estimates, Macau's gross domestic product (GDP), measured at current prices, was 54,609m. patacas (about US $6,845m.), equivalent to 128,500 patacas ($16,100) per head. During 1990–95 the territory's GDP increased, in real terms, at an average annual rate of 6.0%. Compared with the previous year, real GDP contracted by 0.5% in 1996. In 1997 and 1998, in real terms, negative growth rates of 0.1% and 3.3% respectively were recorded. Between 1990 and 1997 the population increased at an average annual rate of 2.6%.

Agriculture is of minor importance. In 1989 only 0.6% of the economically active population were employed in agriculture and fishing. The main crops are rice and vegetables. Cattle, buffaloes and pigs are reared.

Industry (including manufacturing, construction and public utilities) employed 27.2% of the economically active population in 1998. Mining is negligible.

The manufacturing sector engaged 20.6% of the economically active population in 1998. The most important manufacturing industry is the production of textiles and garments. Exports of textiles and garments in 1998 reached 14,441.6m. patacas, compared with 14,564.9m. in 1997. Other industries include toys, footwear, furniture and electronics.

Macau possesses few natural resources. Energy is derived principally from imported petroleum. Imports of fuels and lubricants accounted for 6.3% of total import costs in 1998. The territory receives some electricity and water supplies from the People's Republic of China.

The services sector employed 72.5% of the economically active population in 1998. Tourism makes a substantial contribution to the territory's economy, the licensed casinos' gambling receipts totalling US $2,300m. in 1997. In 1997 the tourism and gambling industries employed an estimated 25% of the labour force and contributed an estimated 43% of GDP. The number of visitor arrivals, however, declined from 7.0m. in 1997, when arrivals from Hong Kong accounted for almost 63% of the total, to 6.9m. in 1998. In 1997 the number of visitors from the People's Republic of China decreased to 527,927, compared with 604,227 in 1996. Visitors from China, including Hong Kong, accounted for 75.7% of the total in 1998. In 1996 the Government's receipts from gambling decreased to 4,954m. patacas, before rising to 6,013m. in 1997. In 1998, however, provisional estimates indicated that direct taxes from gambling yielded only 4,886m.patacas, contributing 55.0% to the Government's revenue. Legislation regulating 'offshore' banking was introduced in 1987. It was hoped that the territory would develop as an international financial centre. The Financial System Act, which took effect in September 1993, aimed to improve the reputation of Macau's banks by curbing the unauthorized acceptance of deposits. A law enacted in April 1995 aimed to attract overseas investment by offering the right of abode in Macau to entrepreneurs with substantial funds (at least US $250,000) at their disposal.

In 1998 Macau recorded a trade surplus of 1,487.2m. patacas, compared with a surplus of 525.8m. patacas in 1997. The trade surplus continued to increase during 1999. The principal sources of imports in 1998 were the People's Republic of China (which supplied 32.6% of the total), Hong Kong (23.7%), and Japan (7.7%). The principal market for exports was the USA (which purchased 47.7%), followed by Germany, Hong Kong, France and the People's Republic of China. The main exports were textiles and garments (which accounted for 84.5% of the total), toys and electronic equipment. The principal imports were raw materials for industry, fuels, foodstuffs and other consumer goods. Following the territory's reversion to Chinese sovereignty in December 1999, Macau retained its status as a free port, and remained a separate customs territory. The pataca was retained, remaining freely convertible.

In 1998 the budget was projected to balance (for the second consecutive year) at 14,831.1m. patacas. Revenue was lower than anticipated, however, owing to a shortfall in receipts from gambling and from land leases (95% of land in Macau being owned by the Government). A budgetary deficit, equivalent to an estimated 1.5% of GDP, thus resulted. The average annual rate of inflation (excluding rents) between 1990 and 1997 was 6.7%. The rate of inflation declined from 3.5% in 1997 to only 0.2% in 1998. The level of unemployment increased from 3.2% of the labour force in 1997 to an estimated 7.0% in 1999. There is a shortage of skilled labour in Macau.

In 1991 Macau became a party to the General Agreement on Tariffs and Trade (GATT, now superseded by the World Trade Organization—WTO, see p. 274) and an associate member of the Economic and Social Commission for Asia and the Pacific (ESCAP, see p. 27). In June 1992 Macau and the European Community (now the European Union) signed a five-year trade and economic co-operation agreement, granting mutual preferential treatment on tariffs and other commercial matters.The agreement was extended in December 1997. Macau was to remain a 'privileged partner' of the EU after December 1999. Macau was also to retain its membership of WTO after December 1999.

The opening of an airport in 1995 afforded the enclave access to international transport networks. In the airport's first year of operation, however, passenger numbers proved disappointing. Furthermore, compared with 1996, tourist arrivals decreased by 14.1% in 1997, as a result of the Asian currency crisis and the upsurge of casino-related crime in the territory. The sharpest decline, of 43.6%, was in the number of Japanese visitors, the Government of Japan being among those to warn citizens not to visit Macau. Tourist arrivals continued to decrease in 1998, as the security situation worsened. During 1998 many garment manufacturers reported a substantial decrease in export orders for Japan (Macau's leading non-quota market), owing to that country's economic recession. Attempts to diversify the economy, in order to reduce dependence on tourism and the textile industry, have been made. During the 1990s, however, many non-textile operations were relocated to China and to South-East Asia, where labour costs were lower. From mid-1997 Macau's position was further weakened by the relative appreciation of the pataca against the currencies of its South-East Asian competitors. A major land reclamation programme continued to progress. The completion of the Nam Van Lakes project, scheduled for 2001, will enlarge the territory's peninsular area by 20%. The development was to incorporate residential and business accommodation for 60,000 people. Owing to a sharp decline in the property market, however, by late 1996 the number of unsold apartments (mainly on the island of Taipa) was estimated at 30,000–50,000, thus casting some doubt on the viability of the Nam Van Lakes scheme. Competition between Macau and the neighbouring Chinese Special Economic Zone of Zhuhai continued to increase, the latter's lower labour costs having encouraged many factories to relocate from Macau. It was hoped that a series of reductions in interest rates in 1998/99 would stimulate the housing market. As in Hong Kong, many skilled personnel were expected to leave Macau before its return to Chinese administration in December 1999. Following the transfer of sovereignty, doubts surrounded the forthcoming renewal of the franchise of the gambling and entertainment syndicate, STDM (see p. 1019). The company's concession was due to expire in 2001, leading to much speculation that, owing to the recent sharp increase in casino-related crime, STDM would lose its long-standing monopoly. Nevertheless, further development of the hotel and tourism sector was envisaged. The Chinese authorities also planned greater integration of Macau within the Zhujiang (Pearl River) Delta region, particularly with regard to infrastructural development.

## Social Welfare

In addition to the network of health centres, Macau has two major hospitals (one public and one private). In 1997 there were 491 inhabitants per physician and 466 per nurse. There were 438 inhabitants per hospital bed. The elderly have access to free medicines. Certain others receive subsidized medicines. In 1998 the sum of 1,400m. patacas, or 13% of the territory's total budget, was allocated to public health and social affairs.

## Education

The education system in Macau comprises: pre-school education (lasting two years); primary preparatory year (one year); primary education (six years); secondary education (five–six years, divided into lower secondary of three years and higher secondary of two–three years). Schooling normally lasts from the ages of three to 17. In the school year 1998/99 the 114 schools enrolled a total of 95,768 pupils (pre-school education 11,033; primary preparatory year 6,059; primary 46,587; secondary 31,612; and special education 477). From 1995/96 free education was extended from government schools to private schools. Private schools provide education for more than 90% of children. Of these schools more than 60% have joined the free education system, and together with the official schools they form the public school system, in which all pupils from primary preparatory year up to the junior secondary level (10 years) are not required to pay tuition fees. Based on the four years of free education, compulsory education was implemented from 1999/2000. In 1997/98 the enrolment rate was as follows: pre-school education and primary preparatory year 93.2% (some families leave their children in China); primary education 100%; and secondary education 74.7%. In higher learning, there are eight public and private universities, polytechnic institutes and research centres. Around 8,000 students attended courses offered by those institutions in the academic year 1997/98, ranging from the bacharelato (three-year courses) to doctorate programmes. The University of Macau was inaugurated, as the University of East Asia, in 1981 (passing from private to government control in 1988), and had 3,281 students, with 300 full-time and 19 part-time teachers, in 1997/98. The languages of instruction are primarily English, Cantonese and Portuguese. The rate of illiteracy in Macau is very low, being confined mainly to elderly women. The 1998 budget allocated 1,910.8m. patacas to education and training (13.7% of total government expenditure).

## Public Holidays

**2000:** 1 January (New Year), 5–7 February (Chinese Lunar New Year), 4 April (Ching Ming), 21–22 April (Easter), 1 May (Labour Day), 11 May (Feast of Buddha), 6 June (Dragon Boat Festival), 13 September (day following Chinese Mid-Autumn Festival), 1–2 October (National Day of the People's Republic of China and day following), 6 October (Festival of Ancestors—Chung Yeung), 2 November (All Souls' Day), 8 December (Immaculate Conception), 20 December (SAR Establishment Day), 21 December (Winter Solstice), 24–25 December (Christmas).

**2001** (provisional): 1 January (New Year), 25–27 January (Chinese Lunar New Year), 5 April (Ching Ming), 13–15 April (Easter), 1 May (Labour Day), May (Feast of Buddha), May/June (Dragon Boat Festival), September (day following Chinese Mid-Autumn Festival), 1–2 October (National Day of the People's Republic of China and day following), October (Festival of Ancestors—day following Chung Yeung), 2 November (All Souls' Day), 8 December (Immaculate Conception), 20 December (SAR Establishment Day), 21 December (Winter Solstice), 24–25 December (Christmas).

## Weights and Measures

The metric system is in force.

# Statistical Survey

Source (unless otherwise indicated): Direcção dos Serviços de Estatística e Censos, Alameda Dr Carlos d'Assumpcão 411–417, Dynasty Plaza, 17° andar, Macau; tel. 728188; fax 307825; fax 307825; e-mail info@dsec.gov.mo; internet www.dsec.gov.mo.

## AREA AND POPULATION

**Area** (1998): 23.60 sq km (9.11 sq miles).

**Population:** 414,128 (males 199,257, females 214,871) at census of 30 August 1996; 112,706 inhabitants were of Portuguese nationality; 430,549 at 31 December 1998 (estimate).

**Density** (at 31 December 1998): 18,244 per sq km.

**Births, Marriages and Deaths** (1998): Registered live births 4,434 (birth rate 10.4 per 1,000); Registered marriages 1,451 (marriage rate 3.4 per 1,000); Registered deaths 1,356 (death rate 3.2 per 1,000).

**Expectation of Life** (years at birth, 1993–96): 76.57 (males 75.11; females 79.98).

**Economically Active Population** (1998): Manufacturing 41,497; Electricity, gas and water 1,395; Construction and public works 11,810; Trade, restaurants and hotels 54,563; Transport and communications 13,697; Finance, insurance and services 13,567; Personal and social services 64,014; Others 504; Total employed 201,047.

## AGRICULTURE, ETC.

**Meat Production** (1996, metric tons, slaughter weight): Buffaloes 1,246.5, Pigs 10,938.5.

**Fishing** ('000 metric tons, live weight): Total catch 1.9 in 1994; 1.6 in 1995; 0.6 in Jan.–June 1996 (fishing suspended in July 1996).

## INDUSTRY

**Production** (1997): Wine 542,499 litres; Knitwear 23.87m. units; Footwear 3.75m. pairs; Clothing 181.15m. units (of which Children's clothing 21.52m. units); Furniture 21,665 units; Explosives and pyrotechnic products (1995) 1,363.1 metric tons; Electric energy (1998) 1,520.6m. kWh.

## FINANCE

**Currency and Exchange Rates:** 100 avos = 1 pataca. *Sterling, Dollar and Euro Equivalents* (30 September 1999): £1 sterling = 13.170 patacas; US $1 = 7.999 patacas; €1 = 8.531 patacas; 1,000 patacas = £75.93 = $125.02 = €117.22. *Average Exchange Rate* (patacas per US dollar): 7.966 in 1996; 7.974 in 1997; 7.978 in 1998. Note: The pataca has a fixed link with the value of the Hong Kong dollar (HK $1 = 1.030 patacas).

**Budget** (million patacas, 1998): *Total revenue:* 14,831.1 (direct taxes 7,313.3; indirect taxes 551.6; others 6,966.2). *Total expenditure:* 14,831.1.

**Money Supply** (million patacas at 31 December): *Total money:* 20,438.3 in 1996; 18,953.1 in 1997; 20,164.1 in 1998.

**Cost of Living** (Consumer Price Index; base: July 1995/June 1996 = 100): 99.35 in 1996; 102.82 in 1997; 103.00 in 1998.

**Gross Domestic Product** (million patacas at current prices): 58,256 in 1996; 58,620 in 1997; 54,609 in 1998.

## EXTERNAL TRADE

**Principal Commodities** (million patacas, 1998): *Imports:* Foodstuffs, beverages and tobacco 1,118.2; Raw materials 9,067.6; Fuels and lubricants 989.3; Capital goods 1,515.4; Other consumer goods 2,905.9; Total 15,596.4. *Exports:* Textiles and garments 14,441.6; Radios, television sets, etc. 15.0; Toys 95.4; Total (incl. others) 17,083.6.

**Principal Trading Partners** (million patacas, 1998): *Imports:* China, People's Republic 5,091.5; EU 1,641.3 (France 306.8, Germany 266.9); Hong Kong 3,697.0; Japan 1,208.2; Total (incl. others) 15,596.4. *Exports:* China, People's Republic 1,157.1; EU 5,210.0 (France 1,046.2, Germany 1,495.3); Hong Kong 1,300.7; Japan 114.0; USA 8,140.7; Total (incl. others) 17,083.6.

## TRANSPORT

**Road Traffic** (motor vehicles in use, Dec. 1998): Light vehicles 48,920; Heavy vehicles 3,990; Motor cycles 53,373.

**Shipping** (international sea-borne freight traffic, '000 metric tons, 1990): Goods loaded 755; Goods unloaded 3,935. Source: UN, *Monthly Bulletin of Statistics.*

## COMMUNICATIONS MEDIA

**Radio receivers** (1996): 155,000 in use.

**Television receivers** (1996): 47,000 in use.

Source: UNESCO, *Statistical Yearbook.*

**Daily newspapers** (1998): 12.

**Telephones** (Dec. 1998): 240,935 in use.

## TOURISM

**Visitor arrivals** (1998): China, People's Republic (incl. Hong Kong) 5,263,237; Japan 167,164; Taiwan 822,194; Thailand 28,057; United Kingdom (incl. British passport holders resident in Hong Kong) 228,915; USA 77,531; Total (incl. others) 6,948,535.

## EDUCATION
(1997/98)

**Kindergarten:** 65 schools; 715 teachers; 18,291 pupils.

**Primary:** 81 schools; 1,744 teachers; 47,235 pupils.

**Secondary** (incl. technical colleges): 47 schools; 1,577 teachers; 28,280 pupils.

**Higher:** 10 institutes; 865 teachers; 8,381 students (of which Teacher-Training: 2 institutes; 47 teachers; 699 students; Nurse-Training: 2 institutes; 110 teachers; 227 students).

Notes: Figures for schools and teachers refer to all those for which the category is applicable. Some schools and teachers provide education at more than one level. There was no teaching activity at one of the higher institutes in 1997/98.

# Directory

## The Constitution

Under the terms of the Basic Law of the Macau Special Administrative Region (SAR), which was to take effect on 20 December 1999, the Macau SAR is an inalienable part of the People's Republic of China. The Macau SAR, which comprises the Macau peninsula and the islands of Taipa and Coloane, exercises a high degree of autonomy and enjoys executive, legislative and independent judicial power, including that of final adjudication. The executive authorities and legislature are composed of permanent residents of Macau. The socialist system and policies shall not be practised in the Macau SAR, and the existing capitalist system and way of life shall not be changed for 50 years. In addition to the Chinese language, the Portuguese language may also be used by the executive, legislative and judicial organs.

The central people's Government is responsible for foreign affairs and for defence. The Government of Macau is responsible for maintaining social order in the SAR. The central people's Government appoints and dismisses the Chief Executive, principal executive officials and Procurator-General.

The Chief Executive of the Macau SAR is accountable to the central people's Government. The Chief Executive shall be a Chinese national of no less than 40 years of age, who is a permanent resident of the region and who has resided in Macau for a continuous period of 20 years. He or she is elected locally by a broadly-representative Selection Committee and appointed by the central people's Government.

The 200-member Selection Committee serves a four-year term and is comprised of the following: 60 representatives of business and financial circles; 50 from cultural, educational and professional circles; 50 from labour, social welfare and religious circles; and 40 former politicians. The term of office of the Chief Executive of the Macau SAR is five years; he or she may serve two consecutive terms. The Chief Executive's functions include the appointment of a portion of the legislative councillors and the appointment or removal of members of the Executive Council.

With the exception of the first term (which expires on 15 October 2001), the term of office of members of the Legislative Council shall be four years. The second Legislative Council shall be composed of 27 members, of whom 10 shall be returned by direct election, 10 by indirect election and seven by appointment. The third and subsequent Legislative Councils shall comprise 29 members, of whom 12 shall be returned by direct election, 10 by indirect election and seven by appointment.

The Macau SAR shall maintain independent finances. The central people's Government shall not levy taxes in the SAR, which shall practise an independent taxation system. The Macau pataca will remain the legal currency. The Macau SAR shall retain its status as a free port and as a separate customs territory.

# The Government

(January 2000)

**Chief Executive:** EDMUND H. W. HO.

**Secretary for Administration and Justice:** FLORINDA DA ROSA SILVA CHAN.

**Secretary for Economy and Finance:** FRANCIS TAM PAK YUEN.

**Secretary for Security:** CHEONG KUOK VA.

**Secretary for Social and Cultural Affairs:** FERNANDO CHUI SAI ON.

**Secretary for Transport and Public Works:** AO MAN LONG.

## GOVERNMENT OFFICES

**Office of the Chief Executive:** Alameda Dr Carlos d'Assumpção, NAPE; tel. 7978111; fax 725468.

The offices of the following Secretaries and of the Executive Council are also located at the above address.

**Office of the Secretary for Administration and Justice:** tel. 7978133; fax 726880.

**Office of the Secretary for Economy and Finance:** tel. 7978160; fax 726665.

**Office of the Secretary for Security:** tel. 7978169; fax 725778.

**Office of the Secretary for Social and Cultural Affairs:** tel. 7978197; fax 725778.

**Office of the Secretary for Transport and Public Works:** tel. 7978218; fax 727566.

**Macau Government Information Services:** Gabinete de Comunicação Social do Governo de Macau, Rua de S. Domingos 1, POB 706; tel. 332886; fax 336372; e-mail info@macau.gov.mo; internet www.macau.gov.mo; Dir AFONSO CAMÕES.

**Economic Services:** Direcção dos Serviços de Economia, Rua Dr Pedro José Lobo 1–3, Edif. Luso Internacional, 25/F; tel. 386937; fax 590310; e-mail cdidse@economia.gov.mo; internet www.economia.gov.mo.

## EXECUTIVE COUNCIL

VICTOR NG, MA IAO LAI, TONG CHI KIN, LEONG HENG TENG, FERNANDO CHUI SAI ON, FLORINDA DA ROSA SILVA CHAN, CHEONG KUOC VA, LIU CHAK WAN, AO MAN LONG, FRANCIS TAM PAK UN.

# Legislature

## LEGISLATIVE COUNCIL

Alameda Dr Carlos d'Assumpção 411–417, Edif. Dynasty Plaza, 8° andar; tel. 728377; fax 727857.

Following the revision of Macau's Organic Law in 1990, the then Legislative Assembly comprised 23 members: seven appointed by the Governor, eight elected directly and eight indirectly. Members served for four years. The Assembly chose its President from among its members, by secret vote. The most recent elections were held in September 1996. The business-orientated Associação Promotora para a Economia de Macau won two of the eight directly-elective seats, while the Convergência para o Desenvolvimento and União Geral para o Desenvolvimento de Macau each won one seat. The pro-Beijing candidates of the União Promotora para o Progresso and of the União para o Desenvolvimento won two seats and one seat respectively. The pro-democracy Associação de Novo Macau Democrático took one seat. Fifteen of the 16 elected members of the above Legislative Assembly remained in office beyond Macau's transfer of sovereignty in December 1999 (one deputy having resigned). Vacancies were to be filled by nominees chosen by the 200-member Selection Committee. The seven members appointed by the Governor were replaced by nominees of the new Chief Executive, the Legislative Assembly being superseded by the Legislative Council.

**President:** SUSANA CHOU.

# Political Organizations

There are no formal political parties, but a number of civic associations exist. Those contesting the 1996 Legislative Assembly elections included the União Promotora para o Progresso (UNIPRO), Associação Promotora para a Economia de Macau (APPEM), União para o Desenvolvimento (UPD), Associação de Novo Macau Democrático (ANMD), Convergência para o Desenvolvimento (CODEM), União para o Desenvolvimento (UPD), União Geral para o Desenvolvimento de Macau (UDM), Associação de Amizade (AMI), Aliança para o Desenvolvimento da Economia (ADE), Associação dos Empregados e Assalariados (AEA) and Associação pela Democracia e Bem-Estar Social de Macau (ADBSM).

# Judicial System

The judicial system was administered directly from Portugal until 1993, when formal autonomy was granted to the territory's judiciary. A new penal code took effect in January 1996. In March 1999 the authority of final appeal was granted to the supreme court of Macau, effective from June. By August 1999, two of the five major codes, namely the Penal Code and the Code of Criminal Procedure, had been revised, and along with the revisions to the Commercial Code and the Civic Code, were to took effect in October 1999.

**Court of Final Appeal:** Praçeta 25 de Abril, Edif. dos Tribunais de Segunda e Ultima Instâncias; Pres. SAM HOU FAI.

**Procurator-General:** HO CHIO MENG.

# Religion

The majority of the Chinese residents profess Buddhism, and there are numerous Chinese places of worship, Daoism and Confucianism also being widely practised. The Protestant community numbers about 2,500. There are small Muslim and Hindu communities.

## CHRISTIANITY

### The Roman Catholic Church

Macau forms a single diocese, directly responsible to the Holy See. At 31 December 1997 there were 20,138 adherents in the territory.

**Bishop of Macau:** Rt Rev. DOMINGOS LAM KA TSEUNG, Paço Episcopal, Largo da Sé s/n, POB 324; tel. 3975228; fax 309861.

### The Anglican Communion

Macau forms part of the Anglican diocese of Hong Kong (q.v.).

# The Press

A new Press Law, prescribing journalists' rights and obligations, was enacted in August 1990.

## PORTUGUESE LANGUAGE

**Boletim Oficial:** Rua da Imprensa Nacional, POB 33; tel. 573822; fax 596802; e-mail iom@macau.ctm.net; f. 1838; govt weekly; Dir Dr EDUARDO RIBEIRO.

**O Clarim:** Rua Central 26-A; tel. 573860; fax 307867; e-mail clarim@macau.ctm.net; f. 1948; weekly; Editor ALBINO BENTO PAIS; circ. 1,500.

**Jornal Tribuna de Macau:** Calçada do Tronco Velho 4–6, POB 945; tel. 329270; fax 573277; f. 1998 through merger of Jornal de Macau (f. 1982) and Tribuna de Macau (f. 1982); daily; Editor JOÃO FERNANDES; circ. 2,000.

**Macau Hoje:** Rua do Chunambeiro, Edif. Keng Fai 5° D; tel. 371950; fax 976575; e-mail hoje@macau.ctm.net; internet www.macauhoje.ctm.net/; daily; Dir JOÃO SEVERINO; circ. 1,000.

**Ponto Final:** Rua da Praia Grande 763, Edif. Lun Pon, 11/F–D; tel. 339566; fax 339563; e-mail pontofin@macau.ctm.net; internet www.unitel.net/pontofinal; Dir RICARDO PINTO; circ. 2,000.

## CHINESE LANGUAGE

**Cheng Pou:** Rua da Praia Grande 57–63, Edif. Hang Cheong, E–F; tel. 965972; fax 965741; daily; Dir KUNG SU KAN; Editor-in-Chief CHENG PUI; circ. 5,000.

**Correio Sino-Macaense:** Av. Venseslau de Morais 221, Edif. Ind. Nam Fong, 2a Fase, 15°, Bloco E; tel. 717569; fax 717572; daily; Dir LAM CHONG; circ. 1,500.

**Jornal 'Si-Si':** Rua do Padre António 26, R/C; tel. 974354; weekly; Dir and Editor-in-Chief CHEANG VENG PENG; circ. 3,000.

**Jornal Son Pou:** Rua de Fran António 22, 1° C, Edif. Mei Fun; tel. 561557; fax 566575; weekly; Dir CHAO CHONG PENG; circ. 8,000.

**Ou Mun Iat Pou** (Macau Daily News): Rua Pedro Nolasco da Silva 37; tel. 371688; fax 331998; f. 1958; daily; Dir LEI SENG CHUN; Editor-in-Chief LEI PANG CHU; circ. 100,000.

**Macau Tempo:** Macau; f. 1999; weekly.

**Semanário Desportivo:** Estrada D. Maria II, Edif. Kin Chit Garden, 2 G–H; tel. 718259; fax 718285; weekly; sport; Dir FONG SIO LON; Editor-in-Chief FONG LIN LAM; circ. 2,000.

**Seng Pou** (Star): Travessa da Caldeira 9; tel. 938387; fax 388192; f. 1963; daily; Dir KUOK KAM SENG; Editor-in-Chief TOU MAN KAM; circ. 6,000.

**Si Man Pou** (Jornal do Cidadão): Rua dos Pescadores, Edif. Ind. Oceano, Bl. 11, 2/F–B; tel. 722111; fax 722133; f. 1944; daily; Dir KONG MAN; Editor LEI FOC LON; circ. 12,000.

**Tai Chung Pou:** Rua Dr Lourenço P. Marques 7A, 2/F; tel. 939888; fax 934114; f. 1933; daily; Dir VONG U. KONG; Editor-in-Chief SOU KIM KEONG; circ. 8,000.

**Today Macau Journal:** Pátio da Barca 20, R/C; tel. 215050; fax 210478; daily; Dir LAM VO I; circ. 6,000.

**Va Kio Pou:** Rua da Alfândega 7–9; tel. 345888; fax 580638; f. 1937; daily; Dir CHIANG SAU MENG; Editor-in-Chief TANG CHOU KEI; circ. 48,000.

### NEWS AGENCIES

**Agência Noticiosa Lusa (Asia Pacific):** Av. da República 72, Edif. Bela Jardim, 2/F; tel. 967601; fax 967605; Dir GONÇALO CÉSAR DE SÁ.

**Associated Press (AP)** (USA): POB 221; tel. 361204; fax 343220; Correspondent ADAM LEE.

**Reuters** (United Kingdom): Rua da Alfândega 69; tel. 345888; fax 930076; Correspondent HARALD BRUNING.

**Xinhua (New China) News Agency** (People's Republic of China): Av. da Amizade 823, Edif. Xinhua; tel. 700222; fax 701378; Dir CHEN BOLIANG.

### PRESS ASSOCIATION

**Associação dos Jornalistas de Macau:** Macau; f. 1999.

**Associação dos Trabalhadores da Imprensa de Macau:** Travessa do Auto Novo 301–303, Edif. Cheng Peng; tel. 375245; Pres. TANG CHOU KEI.

**Clube de Jornalistas de Macau:** Travessa dos Alfaiates 8–10; tel. 921395; fax 921315; Pres. VICTOR CHAN.

## Publisher

**Instituto Cultural de Macau:** see under Tourism; publishes literature, social sciences and history.

## Broadcasting and Communications

## Finance

(cap. = capital; res = reserves; dep. = deposits; m. = million; brs = branches; amounts in patacas unless otherwise indicated)

### BANKING

Macau has no foreign-exchange controls, its external payments system being fully liberalized on current and capital transactions. The Financial System Act, aiming to improve the reputation of the territory's banks and to comply with international standards, took effect in September 1993.

#### Issuing Authority

**Autoridade Monetária e Cambial de Macau—AMCM** (Monetary and Foreign Exchange Authority of Macau): POB 3017; tel. 325416; fax 325433; e-mail amcm@macau.ctm.net; internet www.amcm.macau.gov.mo; f. 1989, to replace the Instituto Emissor de Macau; govt-owned; Pres. ANSELMO L. S. TENG; Exec. Dirs ANTÓNIO FÉLIX PONTES, ANTÓNIO DOS SANTOS RAMOS.

#### Banks of Issue

**Banco Nacional Ultramarino, SA:** Av. Almeida Ribeiro 2, POB 465; tel. 376644; fax 355653; e-mail jmorgado@bnu.com.mo; f. 1864, est. in Macau 1902; Head Office in Lisbon; agent of Macau Government; Gen. Man. HERCULANO J. SOUSA.

**Bank of China:** Bank of China Bldg, Av. Dr Mário Soares; tel. 781828; fax 781833; f. 1950 as Nan Tung Bank, name changed 1987; authorized to issue banknotes from Oct. 1995; Gen. Man. WANG ZHENJUN 23 brs.

#### Other Commercial Banks

**Banco da América (Macau), SARL:** Av. Almeida Ribeiro 70–76, 2F–2G, POB 165; tel. 568821; fax 570386; f. 1937; fmrly Security Pacific Asian Bank (Banco de Cantão); Chair. SAMUEL NG TSIEN; Man. Dir and Gen. Man. ALFRED LAU.

**Banco Comercial de Macau, SARL:** Av. da Praia Grande 572, POB 545; tel. 7910000; fax 595817; f. 1995; cap. 225m., res 101m., dep. 5,640m. (Nov. 1999); Chair. JARDIM GONÇALVES; CEO Dr MANUEL MARECOS DUARTE; 18 brs.

**Banco Delta Asia, SARL:** Av. Conselheiro Ferreira de Almeida 79; tel. 559898; fax 570068; e-mail deltasia@deltasia.com; internet www.deltasia.com; f. 1935; fmrly Banco Hang Sang; cap. 150m., res 52m., dep. 2,324m. (Dec. 1997); Chair. STANLEY AU; Gen. Man. MOISES BERNARDO; 8 brs.

**Banco Seng Heng, SARL:** Seng Heng Bank Tower, 18/F, Macau Landmark, Av. da Amizade; tel. 555222; fax 338064; e-mail sengheng@macau.ctm.net; internet www.senghengbank.com; f. 1972; cap. 150m., dep. 9,387m. (Dec. 1998); Gen. Man. ALEX LI; 6 brs.

**Banco Tai Fung, SARL:** Tai Fung Bank Bldg, Av. Alameda Dr Carlos d'Assumpção 418; tel. 322323; fax 570737; e-mail tfbsecr@taifungbank.com; internet www.taifungbank.com; f. 1971; cap. 1,000m., dep. 15,183m. (Dec. 1998); Chair. FUNG KA YORK; Gen. Man. LONG RONGSHEN; 20 brs.

**Banco Totta e Açores, SA** (Portugal): Av. da Praia Grande 429, 21/F, POB 912; tel. 573299; fax 563852; e-mail totta@macau.ctm.net; f. 1843; est. in Macau 1982; Gen. Man. Dr CARLOS DE CASTRO.

**Banco Weng Hang, SARL:** Av. Almeida Ribeiro 241; tel. 335678; fax 576527; e-mail wenghang@macau.ctm.net; f. 1973; subsidiary of Wing Hang Bank Ltd, Hong Kong; cap. 120m., dep. 6,056m. (Dec. 1998); Chair. PATRICK FUNG YUK-BUN; Gen. Man. and Dir TAM MAN-KUEN; 12 brs.

**Finibanco (Macau), SARL:** Av. da Praia Grande 111–111B, Edif. Centro Comercial Talento, R/C; tel. 3226789; fax 322680; Gen. Man. JÚLIO CEIRÃO.

**Guangdong Development Bank:** Av. da Praia Grande 269; tel. 323628; fax 323668; Gen. Man. LI RUO-HONG.

**Luso International Banking Ltd:** Av. Dr Mário Soares 47; tel. 378977; fax 578517; e-mail lusobank@lusobank.com.mo; internet www.lusobank.com.mo; f. 1974; cap. 151.5m., res 196.9m., dep. 6,183.4m. (Dec. 1998); Chair. EUGENE HO; Gen. Man. IP KAI MING; 13 brs.

#### Foreign Banks

**Banco Comercial Português** (Portugal): Av. Dr Mário Soares, BOC Bldg, 21/F; tel. 786769; fax 786772; Gen. Man. Dr MANUEL MARECOS DUARTE.

**Banco Espírito Santo do Oriente** (Portugal): Av. Dr Mário Soares 323, Bank of China Bldg, 28/F, E–F; tel. 785222; fax 785228; e-mail besor@macau.ctm.net; f. 1996; subsidiary of Banco Espírito Santo, SA (Portugal); Exec. Dir Dr LUÍS DE ALMEIDA CAPELA; Man. JOÃO MANUEL AMBRÓSIO.

**Banque Nationale de Paris** (France): Av. da Praia Grande 219; tel. 562777; fax 560626; f. 1979; Gen. Man. MOY CHIN KUAN.

**Citibank NA** (USA): Rua da Praia Grande 31B–C; tel. 378188; fax 578451; Man. ALEX LI.

**Deutsche Bank AG** (Germany): Av. Almeida Ribeiro, Nam Wah Commercial Bldg, 7/F, 1L-1LB; tel. 378440; fax 304939; Man. KENNETH CHEONG.

**The Hongkong and Shanghai Banking Corporation Ltd** (Hong Kong): Av. da Praia Grande 639, POB 476; tel. 553669; fax 322716; f. 1972; CEO DAVID R. D. HUTCHESON.

**International Bank of Taipei** (Taiwan): Av. Infante D. Henrique 52–58; tel. 715175; fax 715035; e-mail tpbbmomx@macau.ctm.net; f. 1996; fmrly Taipei Business Bank; Gen. Man. CLIFF CHANG.

**Liu Chong Hing Bank Ltd** (Hong Kong): Av. da Praia Grande 693, Edif. Tai Wah, R/C; tel. 339982; fax 339990; Gen. Man. LAM MAN KING.

**Overseas Trust Bank Limited** (Hong Kong): Rua de Santa Clara 5–7E, Edif. Ribeiro, Loja C e D; tel. 329338; fax 323711; Senior Man. CYRIL F. T. LING.

**Standard Chartered Bank** (UK): Av. Infante D. Henrique 60–64, Edif. Centro Comercial Central, 16/F–17/F; tel. 378271; fax 594134; f. 1982; Gen. Man. IRVING LAW.

#### Banking Association

**Associação de Bancos de Macau—ABM** (The Macau Association of Banks): Av. da Praia Grande 575, Edif. 'Finanças', 15/F; tel. 511921; fax 346049; Pres. SIO NG KAN.

### INSURANCE

**AIA Co (Bermuda):** Centro Comercial Praia Grande, 26/F; tel. 5999111; fax 335940; Rep. KENNETH LEI.

**Asia Insurance Co Ltd:** Av. da Amizade 11, Luso International Bank Bldg, Rm 1103; tel. 563166; fax 570438; Rep. S. T. CHAN.

**China Insurance Co Ltd:** Av. Dr Rodrigo Rodrigues, Edif. do Grupo de Seguros da China, 19/F; tel. 785578; fax 787216; Rep. JIANG JIDONG.

**China Life Insurance Co Ltd:** Centro Comercial Praia Grande, 24/F; tel. 558918; fax 559348; Rep. CHAN MAN LONG.

**Companhia de Seguros de Macau, SARL:** Centro Comercial Praia Grande 57, 18/F; tel. 555078; fax 551074; Gen. Man. MANUEL BALCÃO REIS.

**Crown Life Insurance Co:** Rua da Praia Grande 37, Nam Yue Commercial Centre, Bl. B, 8/F; tel. 570828; fax 570844; Rep. STEVEN SIU.

**Forex Insurance Co Ltd:** Av. da Praia Grande 51, Edif. Keng Ou, 13/F–D, tel. 337036; fax 337037; Rep. STUART LUI.

**HSBC Insurance Co Ltd:** Av. Horta e Costa 122–124, 4/F, Rm A; tel. 212323; fax 217162; Rep. JOHNNY HO.

**Insurance Co of North America:** Av. Almeida Ribeiro, Tai Fung Bank Bldg, Rm 806–7; tel. 557191; fax 570188; Rep. JAMES HO.

**Luen Fung Hang Insurance Co Ltd:** Rua de Pequim 202A–246, Macau Finance Centre, 6/F–A; tel. 700033; fax 700088; Rep. SI CHI HOK.

**Macau Life Insurance:** Centro Comercial Praia Grande 57, 18/F; tel. 555078; fax 551074.

**Manulife (International) Ltd:** Av. Almeida Ribeiro 61, Central Plaza D & E, 12/F; tel. 3980388; fax 323312; internet www.manulife.com.hk; Rep. CARMEN LEONG.

**Min Xin Insurance Co Ltd:** Av. da Amizade 11, Luso International Bank Bldg, 27/F, Rm 2704; tel. 305684; fax 305600; Rep. ALFRED LO.

**National Mutual Ins. Co (Bermuda) Ltd:** Rua de Xang Hai 175, Commercial Union Ass. Bldg; tel. 781188; fax 780022; Rep. PHOEBE TSOI.

**QBE Insurance (International) Ltd:** Rua Dr Pedro José Lobo 11, Luso International Bank Bldg, Rm 2003; tel. 567214; fax 580948; Rep. SALLY SIU.

**Royal Sun Alliance Insurance (Hong Kong) Ltd:** 12B Central Plaza, 1D–1K Av. de Almeida Ribeiro; tel. 920909; fax 920922; fmrly Taikoo Royal; Rep. PIERRE FONG.

**Sumitomo Marine and Fire Insurance Co, Ltd:** Av. Almeida Ribeiro 32, Tai Fung Bank Bldg, Rm 802; tel. 385917; fax 596667; Rep. CARMEN PANG.

**The Wing On Fire & Marine Insurance Co Ltd:** Centro Comercial de Praia Grande, 11/F; tel. 550233; fax 333710; Rep. HAZEL AO.

#### Insurers' Association

**Macau Insurers' Association:** Av. da Praia Grande 575, Edif. 'Finanças', 15/F; tel. 511923; fax 337531; Pres. JIANG JIDONG.

## Trade and Industry

### CHAMBER OF COMMERCE

**Associação Comercial de Macau:** Rua de Xangai 175, Edif. ACM, 5/F; tel. 576833; fax 594513; Pres. MA MAN KEI.

### INDUSTRIAL AND TRADE ASSOCIATIONS

**Associação dos Construtores Civis** (Association of Building Development Cos): Rua do Campo 9–11; tel. 323854; fax 345710; Pres. CHUI TAK KEI.

**Associação dos Exportadores e Importadores de Macau:** Av. Infante D. Henrique 60–62, Centro Comercial 'Central', 3/F; tel. 375859; fax 512174; e-mail aeim@macau.ctm.net; exporters' and importers' asscn; Pres. VÍTOR NG.

**Associação dos Industriais de Tecelagem e Fiação de Lã de Macau** (Macau Weaving and Spinning of Wool Manufacturers' Asscn): Av. da Amizade 271, Edif. Kam Wa Kok, 6/F–A; tel. 553378; fax 511105; Pres. WONG SHOO KEE; Dir SUSANA CHOU.

**Associação Industrial de Macau:** Rua Dr Pedro José Lobo 34–36, Edif. AIM, 17/F, POB 70; tel. 574125; fax 578305; f. 1959; Pres. PETER PAN.

**Centro de Produtividade e Transferência de Tecnologia de Macau** (Macau Productivity and Technology Transfer Centre): Rua de Xangai 175, Edif. ACM, 6/F; tel. 781313; fax 788233; e-mail cpttm@cpttm.org.mo; internet www.cpttm.org.mo; Dir ERIC YEUNG.

**Euro-Info Centre Macau:** Av. Sidónio Pais 1A, Edif. Tung Hei Kok, R/C; tel. 713338; fax 713339; e-mail eic@macau.ctm.net; internet www.ieem.org.mo/eic/eicmacau.html; promotes trade with EU; Man. SAM LEI.

**Instituto de Promocão do Comércio e do Investimento de Macau** (Macau Trade and Investment Promotion Institute): Av. da Amizade 918, World Trade Center Bldg, 4/F–5/F; tel. 710300; fax 590309; e-mail ipim@ipim.gov.mo; internet www.ipim.gov.mo; Pres. LEE PENG HONG.

**Investimentos, Comércio e Turismo de Portugal (ICEP):** Av. da Amizade 918, Edif. World Trade Center, 17/F–D; tel. 728300; fax 728303; Dir JOAQUIM MENDONÇA MOREIRA.

**World Trade Center Macau, SARL:** Av. da Amizade 918, Edif. World Trade Center, 16/F–19/F; tel. 727666; fax 727633; e-mail wtcmc@macau.ctm.net; internet www.wtc-macau.com; f. 1995; trade information and business services, office rentals, exhibition and conference facilities; Man. Dir Dr ANTÓNIO LEÇA DA VEIGA PAZ.

### UTILITIES

#### Electricity

**Companhia de Electricidade de Macau, SARL—CEM:** Estrada D. Maria II 32–36, Edif. CEM; tel. 339933; fax 719760; f. 1972; sole distributor; Pres. Eng. CUSTÓDIO MIGUENS.

#### Water

**Sociedade de Abastecimento de Aguas de Macau, SARL—SAAM:** Av. do Conselheiro Borja 718; tel. 233332; fax 234658; f. 1984 as jt venture with Suez Lyonnaise des Eaux; Dir-Gen. JIM CONLON.

### TRADE UNIONS

**Macau Federation of Trade Unions:** Rua Ribeira do Patane 2; tel. 576231; fax 553110; Pres. TONG SENG CHUN.

## Transport

### RAILWAYS

There are no railways in Macau. A plan to connect Macau with Guangzhou (People's Republic of China) is under consideration.

### ROADS

In January 1995 there were 130 km of roads. The peninsula of Macau is linked to the islands of Taipa and Coloane by two bridges and by a 2.2-km causeway respectively. The first bridge (2.6 km) opened in 1974. In conjunction with the construction of an airport on Taipa (see below), a new 4.4-km four-lane bridge to the mainland was opened in April 1994. Construction work on a 1.3-km six-lane road bridge (the Lotus Bridge) linking Macau with Zhuhai's Hengqin Island was completed in October 1999. In 1997 plans for a 37.9-km bridge linking the enclave with Hong Kong, which was to take four years to complete, were announced.

### SHIPPING

There are representatives of shipping agencies for international lines in Macau. There are passenger and cargo services to the People's Republic of China. Catamarans, jetfoils and high-speed ferries operate regular services between Macau and Hong Kong. The principal services carried 7.4m. passengers in 1997. A new terminal opened in late 1993. The new port of Kao-ho (on the island of Coloane), which handles cargo and operates container services, entered into service in 1991.

**CTS Parkview Holdings Ltd:** Av. Amizade, Porto Exterior, Terminal Marítimo de Macau, Sala 2006B; tel. 726789; fax 727112; purchased by STDM in 1998.

**Hongkong Macao Hydrofoil Co Ltd:** Av. Amizade Porto Exterior, Terminal Marítimo de Macau, 2/F, Sala 2011B; tel. 726266; fax 726277.

**STDM Shipping Dept:** Av. da Amizade Terminal Marítimo do Porto Exterior; tel. 726111; fax 726234; affiliated to Sociedade de Turismo e Diversões de Macau; Gen. Man. ALAN HO; Exec. Man. Capt. AUGUSTO LIZARDO.

#### Association

**Associação de Agências de Navegação e Congêneres de Macau:** Av. Horta e Costa 7D–E, POB 6133; tel. 528207; fax 302667; Pres. VONG KOK SENG.

#### Port Authority

**Capitania dos Portos de Macau:** Quartel dos Mouros; tel. 559922; fax 511986.

### CIVIL AVIATION

In August 1987 plans were approved for the construction of an international airport, on reclaimed land near the island of Taipa, and work began in 1989. The final cost of the project was 8,900m. patacas. Macau International Airport was officially opened in December 1995. In 1998 the airport handled a total of 2,214,487 passengers. The terminal has the capacity to handle 6m. passengers a year. Between January and December 1998 65,167 tons of cargo were processed. In December 1998 Air Macau and 11 other scheduled airlines were using the airport, while regular charter services were provided by other carriers. By the end of 1998 AACM had negotiated

34 air service agreements. A helicopter service between Hong Kong and Macau commenced in 1990: East Asia Airlines transported a total of 52,149 helicopter passengers in 1998.

**AACM—Macau Civil Aviation Authority:** Rua Dr Pedro José Lobo 1–3, Luso International Bldg, 26/F; tel. 511213; fax 338089; e-mail aacm@macau.ctm.net; internet www.macau-airport.gov.mo; f. 1991; Pres. RUI ALFREDO BALACO MOREIRA.

**Administração de Aeroportos, Lda—ADA:** Av. de João IV, Centro Comercial Iat Teng Hou, 5/F; tel. 711808; fax 711803; e-mail adamkt@macau.ctm.net; internet www.ada.com.mo; airport administration; Dir CARLOS SERUCA SALGADO.

**CAM—Sociedade do Aeroporto Internacional de Macau, SARL:** Av. Dr Mário Soares, Bank of China Bldg, 29/F; tel. 785448; fax 785465; e-mail cam@macau.ctm.net; internet www.macau-airport.gov.mo; f. 1989; airport owner, responsible for design, construction, development and international marketing of Macau International Airport; Chair. Eng. JOÃO MANUEL DE SOUSA MOREIRA.

**Air Macau:** Av. da Praia Grande 693, Edif. Tai Wah, 9/F–12/F, POB 1910; tel. 3966888; fax 3966866; e-mail airmacau@airmacau.com.mo; internet www.airmacau.com.mo; f. 1994; controlled by China National Aviation Corporation (Group) Macau Co Ltd; services to several cities in the People's Republic of China, the Republic of Korea, the Philippines, Taiwan and Thailand; other destinations planned; Chair. WANG GUIXIANG; Pres. LI KELI.

## Tourism

Tourism is now a major industry, a substantial portion of the Government's revenue being derived from the territory's casinos. The other attractions are the cultural heritage and museums, dog-racing, horse-racing, and annual events such as Chinese New Year (January/February), the Macau Arts Festival (February/March), Dragon Boat Festival (May/June), the Macau International Fireworks Festival (September/October), the International Music Festival, (October) the Macau Grand Prix for racing cars and motorcycles (November) and the Macau International Marathon (December). Hotel capacity totalled 8,970 rooms at the end of 1998. In 1998 total visitor arrivals reached 6.95m., of whom 4.01m. were arrivals from Hong Kong. Per caput visitor spending (excluding expenditure by mainland Chinese visitors) decreased from 980.3 patacas in 1997 to 977.9 patacas in 1998. In the latter year per caput expenditure by visitors from the People's Republic of China reached 2,821.7 patacas, compared with 2,373.8 in 1997.

**Macau Government Tourist Office (MGTO):** Direcção dos Serviços de Turismo, Largo do Senado 9, Edif. Ritz, POB 3006; tel. 315566; fax 510104; e-mail mgto@macautourism.gov.mo; internet www.macautourism.gov.mo; Dir MARIA HELENA DE SENNA FERNANDES (acting).

**Instituto Cultural de Macau:** Praceta de Miramar 87U, Edif. San On; tel. 700391; fax 700405; e-mail icmctm11@macau.ctm.net; internet www.icm.gov.mo; f. 1982; organizes performances concerts, exhibitions, festivals, etc.; library facilities; Pres. WANG ZENG YANG.

**Macau Hotels Association:** Rua Luís Gonzaga Gomes s/n, Bl. IV, r/c, Centro de Actividades Turísticas, Cabinet A; tel. 703416; fax 703415.

**Sociedade de Turismo e Diversões de Macau (STDM), SARL:** Macau; tel. 566065; fax 371981; e-mail stdmmdof@macau.ctm.net; operates 10 casinos, five hotels, tour companies, helicopter and jetfoil services from Hong Kong, etc.; Man. Dir Dr STANLEY HO.

## Tourism

**TOURIST ARRIVALS BY COUNTRY OF ORIGIN**

| | 1996 | 1997 | 1998 |
|---|---|---|---|
| Japan | 911,777 | 900,714 | 822,817 |
| Korea, Republic | 121,399 | 94,632 | 59,766 |
| Malaysia | 55,430 | 54,022 | 48,904 |
| Philippines | 104,525 | 112,844 | 120,543 |
| Singapore | 77,642 | 81,356 | 86,695 |
| Thailand | 120,089 | 121,534 | 127,987 |
| USA | 277,236 | 293,681 | 300,753 |
| Overseas Chinese* | 269,682 | 256,591 | 266,895 |
| **Total** (incl. others) | 2,358,221 | 2,372,232 | 2,298,706 |

* i.e. those bearing Taiwan passports.

**Tourism receipts** (US $ million): 3,636 in 1996; 3,403 in 1997; 3,372 in 1998.

## Communications Media

| | 1996 | 1997 | 1998 |
|---|---|---|---|
| Book production (titles) | 24,876 | 23,801 | 30,868 |
| Newspapers | 361 | 344 | 360 |
| Magazines | 5,480 | 5,676 | 5,888 |
| Telephone subscribers ('000) | 10,011 | 10,862 | 11,500 |
| Mobile telephones ('000 in use) | 970 | 1,492 | 2,180 |

Radio receivers (1994): more than 16 million in use.
Television receivers (1994): 5,050,000 in use.

## Education

(1998/99)

| | Schools | Full-time teachers | Pupils/ Students |
|---|---|---|---|
| Pre-school | 2,874 | 17,795 | 238,787 |
| Primary | 2,557 | 95,029 | 1,910,681 |
| Secondary (incl. vocational) | 1,158 | 98,857 | 1,814,202 |
| Higher | 137 | 40,149 | 915,921 |
| Special | 20 | 1,532 | 5,588 |
| Supplementary | 981 | 3,460 | 285,135 |
| **Total** (incl. others) | 7,731 | 256,916 | 5,215,773 |

# Directory

## The Constitution

On 1 January 1947 a new Constitution was promulgated for the Republic of China (confined to Taiwan since 1949). The form of government that was incorporated in the Constitution is based on a five-power system and has the major features of both cabinet and presidential government. A process of constitutional reform, initiated in 1991, continued in 1999. The following is a summary of the Constitution, as subsequently amended:

### PRESIDENT

The President shall be directly elected by popular vote for a term of four years. Both the President and Vice-President are eligible for re-election to a second term. The President represents the country at all state functions, including foreign relations; commands land, sea and air forces, promulgates laws, issues mandates, concludes treaties, declares war, makes peace, declares martial law, grants amnesties, appoints and removes civil and military officers, and confers honours and decorations. The President convenes the National Assembly and, subject to certain limitations, may issue emergency orders to deal with national calamities and ensure national security; may dissolve the Legislative Yuan; also nominates the Premier (who may be appointed without the Legislative Yuan's confirmation), and the officials of the Judicial Yuan, the Examination Yuan and the Control Yuan.

### NATIONAL ASSEMBLY

The National Assembly is elected by popular vote for a four-year term, and shall comprise 334 members: 228 regional representatives; six aboriginal delegates; 20 overseas Chinese delegates; and 80 delegates from one national constituency. The functions of the National Assembly are: to amend the Constitution; to vote on proposed constitutional amendments submitted by the Legislative Yuan; to confirm the appointment of personnel nominated by the President; to hear a report on the state of the nation by the President, to discuss national affairs and to offer counsel; to elect a new Vice-President should the office become vacant; to recall the President and the Vice-President; and to pass a resolution on the impeachment of the President or Vice-President instituted by the Control Yuan.

### EXECUTIVE YUAN

The Executive Yuan is the highest administrative organ of the nation and is responsible to the Legislative Yuan; has three categories of subordinate organization:

Executive Yuan Council (policy-making organization)
Ministries and Commissions (executive organization)
Subordinate organization (19 bodies, including the Secretariat, Government Information Office, Directorate-General of Budget, Accounting and Statistics, Council for Economic Planning and Development, and Environmental Protection Administration).

### LEGISLATIVE YUAN

The Legislative Yuan is the highest legislative organ of the State, empowered to hear administrative reports of the Executive Yuan, and to change government policy. It may hold a binding vote of 'no confidence' in the Executive Yuan. It comprises 225 members, 176 chosen by direct election, the remaining delegates being appointed on the basis of proportional representation. Members serve for three years and are eligible for re-election.

### JUDICIAL YUAN

The Judicial Yuan is the highest judicial organ of state and has charge of civil, criminal and administrative cases, and of cases concerning disciplinary measures against public functionaries (see Judicial System).

### EXAMINATION YUAN

The Examination Yuan supervises examinations for entry into public offices, and deals with personnel questions of the civil service.

### CONTROL YUAN

The Control Yuan is the highest control organ of the State, exercising powers of impeachment, censure and audit. Comprising 29 members serving a six-year term, nominated and (with the consent of the National Assembly) appointed by the President, the Control Yuan may impeach or censure a public functionary at central or local level, who is deemed guilty of violation of law or dereliction of duty, and shall refer the matter to the law courts for action in cases involving a criminal offence; may propose corrective measures to the Executive Yuan or to its subordinate organs.

# The Government

### HEAD OF STATE

**President:** LEE TENG-HUI (took office 13 January 1988, re-elected by the National Assembly 20 March 1990, directly elected by popular vote 23 March 1996).

**Vice-President:** LIEN CHAN.

**Secretary-General:** DING MOU-SHIH.

### THE EXECUTIVE YUAN
(February 2000)

**Premier:** VINCENT C. SIEW (HSIAO WAN-CHANG).

**Vice-Premier and Chairman of the Consumer Protection Commission:** LIU CHAO-SHIUAN.

**Minister without Portfolio and Director-General of the Council for Economic Planning and Development:** CHIANG PIN-KUNG.

**Ministers without Portfolio:** WU JUNG-MIN, HUANG TA-CHOU, CHEN CHIENG-MING, CHAO SHU-PO, SHIRLEY W. Y. KUO, YANG SHIH-CHIEN.

**Secretary-General:** SHIEH SHEN-SAN.

**Minister of the Interior:** HUANG CHU-WEN.

**Minister of Foreign Affairs:** CHANG CHE-SHEN.

**Minister of National Defense:** TANG FEI.

**Minister of Finance:** YANG KUO-CI.

**Minister of Education:** KIRBY C. YUNG.

**Minister of Economic Affairs:** WANG CHIH-KANG.

**Minister of Justice:** YEH CHIN-FONG.

**Minister of Transportation and Communications:** LIN FENG-CHENG.

**Chairman of the Mainland Affairs Council:** SU CHI.

**Chairman of the Overseas Chinese Affairs Commission:** CHIAO JEN-HO.

**Chairman of the Mongolian and Tibetan Affairs Commission:** KAO KOONG-TIAN.

**Director-General of the Government Information Office:** CHAO YI.

**Director-General of Directorate-General of Budget, Accounting and Statistics:** WEI TUAN.

**Director-General of Central Personnel Administration:** CHANG CHE-SHEN.

**Director-General of the Department of Health:** CHAN CHI-SHEAN.

**Director-General of the Environmental Protection Administration:** TSAI HSUNG-HSIUNG.

**Chairman of the National Science Council:** HWANG JENN-TAI.

**Chairman of the Council of Agriculture:** LIN HSIANG-NUNG.

**Chairwoman of the Council for Cultural Affairs:** LIN CHEN-CHI.

**Chairman of the Research, Development and Evaluation Commission:** WEA CHI-LIN.

**Chairman of Veterans' Affairs Commission:** Gen. LEE CHEN-LIN.

**Chairwoman of the National Youth Commission:** LEE JIH-CHU.

**Chairman of the Atomic Energy Council:** HU CHING-PIAO.

**Chairman of the Council of Labor Affairs:** CHAN HUO-SHENG.

**Chairman of the Fair Trade Commission:** CHAO YANG-CHING.

**Chairman of the Public Construction Commission:** TSAY JAW-YANG.

**Chairman of the Council of Aboriginal Affairs:** HUA CHIA-CHIH.

**Chairwoman of the National Sports Council:** CHAO LI-YUN.

### MINISTRIES, COMMISSIONS, ETC.

**Office of the President:** Chiehshou Hall, 122 Chungking South Rd, Sec. 1, Taipei 100; tel. (2) 23718889; fax (2) 23611604; e-mail public@mail.oop.gov.tw; internet www.oop.gov.tw.

**Ministry of Economic Affairs:** 15 Foo Chou St, Taipei; tel. (2) 23212200; fax (2) 23919398; e-mail service@moea.gov.tw; internet www.moea.gov.tw.

**Ministry of Education:** 5 Chung Shan South Rd, Taipei 10040; tel. (2) 23566051; fax (2) 23976978; internet www.moe.gov.tw.

**Ministry of Finance:** 2 Ai Kuo West Rd, Taipei; tel. (2) 23228000; fax (2) 23965829; e-mail root@www.mof.gov.tw; internet www.mof.gov.tw.

**Ministry of Foreign Affairs:** 2 Chiehshou Rd, Taipei 10016; tel. (2) 23119292; fax (2) 23144972; internet www.mofa.gov.tw.

**Ministry of the Interior:** 5th–9th Floors, 5 Hsu Chou Rd, Taipei; tel. (2) 23565005; fax (2) 23566201; e-mail gethics@mail.moi.gov.tw; internet www.moi.gov.tw.

**Ministry of Justice:** 130 Chungking South Rd, Sec. 1, Taipei 10036; tel. (2) 23146871; fax (2) 23896759; internet www.moj.gov.tw.

**Ministry of National Defense:** 2nd Floor, 164 PoAi Rd, Taipei; tel. (2) 23116117; fax (2) 23144221; internet www.ndmc.edu.tw.

**Ministry of Transportation and Communications:** 2 Chang Sha St, Sec. 1, Taipei; tel. (2) 23492900; fax (2) 23118587; e-mail motceyes@motc.gov.tw; internet www.motc.gov.tw.

**Mongolian and Tibetan Affairs Commission:** 4th Floor, 5 Hsu Chou Rd, Sec. 1, Taipei; tel. (2) 23566166; fax (2) 23566432; internet gopher://serv.hinet.net//11/government/department/EY/mtac.

**Overseas Chinese Affairs Commission:** 4th Floor, 5 Hsu Chou Rd, Taipei; tel. (2) 23566166; fax (2) 23566323; e-mail ocacinfo@mail.ocac.gov.tw; internet www.ocac.gov.tw.

**Directorate-General of Budget, Accounting and Statistics:** 2 Kwang Chow St, Taipei 100; tel. (2) 23823899; fax (2) 23319925; e-mail sicbs@emc.dgbasey.gov.tw; internet www.dgbasey.gov.tw.

**Government Information Office:** 2 Tientsin St, Taipei; tel. (2) 23228888; fax (2) 23568733; e-mail service@mail.gio.gov.tw; internet www.gio.gov.tw.

**Council of Aboriginal Affairs:** 16-17th Floors, 4 Chung Hsiao West Rd, Sec. 1, Taipei; tel. (2) 23882122; fax (2) 23891967.

**Council of Agriculture:** see p. 1041.

**Atomic Energy Council:** 67 Lane 144, Kee Lung Rd, Sec. 4, Taipei; tel. (2) 23634180; fax (2) 23635377; internet www.aec.gov.tw.

**Central Personnel Administration:** 109 Huai Ning St, Taipei; tel. (2) 23111720; fax (2) 23715252; internet www.cpa.gov.tw.

**Consumer Protection Commission:** 1 Chung Hsiao East Rd, Sec. 1, Taipei; tel. (2) 23566600; fax (2) 23214538; e-mail tcpc@ms1.hinet.net; internet www.cpc.gov.tw.

**Council for Cultural Affairs:** 102 Ai Kuo East Rd, Taipei; tel. (2) 25225300; fax (2) 25519011; e-mail wwwadm@ccpdunx.ccpd.gov.tw; internet expo96.org.tw/cca/welcome_c.html.

**Council for Economic Planning and Development:** 9th Floor, 87 Nanking East Rd, Sec. 2, Taipei; tel. (2) 25225300; fax (2) 25519011; internet www.cepd.gov.tw.

**Environmental Protection Administration:** 41 Chung Hua Rd, Sec. 1, Taipei; tel. (2) 23228751; fax (2) 23516227; e-mail www@sun.epa.gov.tw; internet www.epa.gov.tw.

**Fair Trade Commission:** 12–14th Floor, 2-2 Chi Nan Rd, Sec. 2, Taipei; tel. (2) 23517588; fax (2) 23974997; e-mail ftcse@ftc.gov.tw; internet www.ftc.gov.tw.

**Department of Health:** 100 Ai Kuo East Rd, Taipei; tel. (2) 23210151; fax (2) 23122907; internet www.doh.gov.tw.

**Council of Labor Affairs:** 5th–15th Floors, 132 Min Sheng East Rd, Sec. 3, Taipei; tel. (2) 27182512; fax (2) 25149240; internet gopher://192.192.46.131.

**Mainland Affairs Council:** 5th–13th Floors, 2-2 Chi-nan Rd, Sec. 1, Taipei; tel. (2) 23975589; fax (2) 23975700; e-mail macst@mac.gov.tw; internet www.mac.gov.tw.

**National Science Council:** 17th–22nd Floors, 106 Ho Ping East Rd, Sec. 2, Taipei; tel. (2) 27377501; fax (2) 27377668; e-mail nsc@nsc.gov.tw; internet www.nsc.gov.tw.

**National Youth Commission:** 14th Floor, 5 Hsu Chou Rd, Taipei; tel. (2) 23566271; fax (2) 23566290; internet www.nyc.gov.tw.

**Research, Development and Evaluation Commission:** 7th Floor, 2-2 Chi-nan Rd, Sec. 1, Taipei; tel. (2) 23419066; fax (2) 23928133; e-mail service@rdec.gov.tw; internet rdec.gov.tw.

**Veterans' Affairs Commission:** 222 Chung Hsiao East Rd, Sec. 5, Taipei; tel. (2) 27255700; fax (2) 27253578; e-mail hsc@www.vac.gov.tw; internet vac.gov.tw.

# President and Legislature

## PRESIDENT

**Election, 23 March 1996**

| Candidate | Votes | % of votes |
|---|---|---|
| LEE TENG-HUI (Kuomintang—KMT) | 5,813,699 | 54.0 |
| PENG MING-MIN (Democratic Progressive Party—DPP) | 2,274,586 | 21.1 |
| LIN YANG-KANG (Independent) | 1,603,790 | 14.9 |
| CHEN LI-AN (Independent) | 1,074,044 | 10.0 |

Note: the next presidential election was scheduled for 18 March 2000.

## KUO-MIN TA-HUI
(National Assembly)

The National Assembly comprises 334 members: 228 regional representatives, three mountain aborigines, three plains aborigines, 20 overseas Chinese and 80 representatives of a national constituency. Members serve a four-year term. In 1999 18 seats were vacant.

**Speaker:** (vacant).

**Election, 23 March 1996**

| Party | % of votes | Seats |
|---|---|---|
| Kuomintang (KMT) | 54.8 | 183 |
| Democratic Progressive Party (DPP) | 29.6 | 99 |
| New Party (NP) | 13.8 | 46 |
| Independents | 1.8 | 5 |
| Green Party | | 1 |
| **Total** | 100.0 | 334 |

## LI-FA YUAN
(Legislative Yuan)

The Legislative Yuan is the highest legislative organ of the State. It comprises 225 seats. The 176 directly-elected members include eight representatives of aboriginal communities. The remaining delegates are appointed on a proportional basis according to the parties' share of the popular vote, with eight seats reserved for overseas Chinese communities. Members serve a three-year term.

**President:** WANG JIN-PYNG.

**General Election, 5 December 1998**

| Party | % of votes | Seats |
|---|---|---|
| Kuomintang (KMT) | 46.4 | 125 |
| Democratic Progressive Party (DPP) | 29.6 | 72 |
| New Party (NP) | 7.1 | 11 |
| Democratic Union of Taiwan (DUT) | 3.7 | 4 |
| Nationwide Democratic Non-Partisan Union (NDNU) | 0.7 | 2 |
| New Nation Alliance (NNA) | 1.6 | 1 |
| Jiann Gwo (Taiwan Independence) Party (TAIP) | 1.5 | 1 |
| Independents | 9.4 | 9 |
| **Total** | 100.0 | 225 |

# Political Organizations

Legislation adopted in 1989 permitted political parties other than the KMT to function. By June 1999 a total of 88 parties had registered with the Ministry of the Interior.

**China Democratic Socialist Party (CDSP):** 1/F, 6 Lane 7, Ho Ping East Rd, Sec. 2, Taipei; tel. (2) 27072883; f. 1932 by merger of National Socialists and Democratic Constitutionalists; aims to promote democracy, to protect fundamental freedoms, and to improve public welfare and social security; Chair. SHIEH HANN-RU; Sec.-Gen. KAO SHAO-CHUNG.

**China Young Party:** 12th Floor, 2 Shin Sheng South Rd, Sec. 3, Taipei; tel. (2) 23626715; f. 1923; aims to recover sovereignty over mainland China, to safeguard the Constitution and democracy, and to foster understanding between Taiwan and the non-communist world; Chair. JAW CHWEN-SHIAW.

**Chinese Republican Party (CRP):** 3rd Floor, 26 Lane 90, Jong Shuenn St, Sec. 2, Taipei; tel. (2) 29366572; f. 1988; advocates peaceful struggle for the salvation of China and the promotion of world peace; Chair. WANG YING-CHYUN.

**Democratic Liberal Party (DLP):** 4th Floor, 20 Lane 5, Ching Tyan, Taipei; tel. (2) 23121595; f. 1989; aims to promote political democracy and economic liberty for the people of Taiwan; Chair. HER WEI-KANG.

**Democratic Progressive Party (DPP):** 8th Floor, 30 Pei Ping East Rd, Taipei; tel. and fax (2) 23929989; f. 1986; advocates 'self-determination' for the people of Taiwan and UN membership; supports establishment of independent Taiwan following plebiscite; 140,000 mems; Chair. LIN YI-HSIUNG; Sec.-Gen. YOU HSI-KUN.

**Democratic Union of Taiwan (DUT):** 16th Floor, 15-1 Harng Joe South Rd, Sec. 1, Taipei; tel. (2) 23211531; f. 1998; Chair. HSU CHERNG-KUEN.

**Green Party:** 11th Floor, 273 Roosevelt Rd, Sec. 3, Taipei; tel. (2) 23621362; f. 1996 by breakaway faction of the DPP; Chair. CHEN GUANG-YEU.

**Jiann Gwo Party** (Taiwan Independence Party—TAIP): 8-1 Hsu Chou Rd, Taipei; tel. (2) 23958545; f. 1996 by dissident mems of DPP; Chair. JENG BANG-JENN; Sec.-Gen. LI SHENG-HSIUNG.

**Kungtang (KT)** (Labour Party): 2nd Floor, 22 Kai Feng St, Sec. 2, Taipei; tel. (2) 23118248; fax (2) 23719687; e-mail no1hsieh@eagle.seed.net.tw; f. 1987; aims to become the main political movement of Taiwan's industrial work-force; 10,000 mems; Chair. JENG JAU-MING; Sec.-Gen. HSIEH CHENG-YI.

**Kuomintang (KMT)** (Nationalist Party of China): 11 Chung Shan South Rd, Taipei 100; tel. (2) 23121472; fax (2) 23434524; f. 1894; ruling party; aims to supplant communist rule in mainland China; supports democratic, constitutional government, and advocates the unification of China under the 'Three Principles of the People'; aims to promote market economy and equitable distribution of wealth; 2,523,984 mems; Chair. LEE TENG-HUI; Sec.-Gen. HUANG KUN-HUEI.

**Nationwide Democratic Non-Partisan Union (NDNU):** Taipei.

**New Nation Alliance:** 14th Floor, 9 Song Jiang Rd, Taipei; tel. (2) 23585643; f. 1998; promotes independence for Taiwan and the establishment of a 'new nation, new society and new culture'; Chair. PERNG BAE-SHEAN.

**New Party (NP):** 4th Floor, 65 Guang Fuh South Rd, Taipei; tel. (2) 27562222; fax (2) 27565750; e-mail npncs@ms2.hinet.net; f. 1993 by dissident KMT legislators (hitherto mems of New Kuomintang Alliance faction); merged with China Social Democratic Party in late 1993; advocates co-operation with the KMT and DPP in negotiations with the People's Republic, the maintenance of security in the Taiwan Straits, the modernization of the island's defence systems, measures to combat government corruption, the support of small and medium businesses and the establishment of a universal social security system; 80,000 mems; Chair. LI CHING-HWA; Sec.-Gen. LI BING-NAN.

**Workers' Party:** 2nd Floor, 181 Fu-hsing South Rd, Taipei; tel. (2) 27555868; f. 1989 by breakaway faction of the Kungtang; radical; Leader LOU MEIWEN.

Various pro-independence groups (some based overseas and, until 1992, banned in Taiwan) are in operation. These include the **World United Formosans for Independence** (WUFI—4,000 mems world-wide; Chair. GEORGE CHANG) and the **Organization for Taiwan Nation-Building**.

# Diplomatic Representation

## EMBASSIES IN THE REPUBLIC OF CHINA

**Burkina Faso:** 6/F, 9-1, Lane 62, Tien Mou West Rd, Taipei 111; tel. (2) 28383776; fax (2) 28342701; Ambassador: JACQUES Y. SAWADOGO.

**Chad:** 8/F, 9 Lane 62, Tien Mou West Rd, Taipei; tel. (2) 28742943; fax (2) 28732971; Ambassador: SALIM ABDERAMAN TAHA.

**Costa Rica:** 5/F, 9-1, Lane 62, Tien Mou West Rd, Taipei 111; tel. (2) 28752964; fax (2) 28753151; Ambassador: OSCAR ALVAREZ.

**Dominican Republic:** 6/F, 9 Lane 62, Tien Mou West Rd, Taipei 111; tel. (2) 28751357; fax (2) 28752661; Ambassador: VÍCTOR MANUEL SÁNCHEZ PEÑA.

**El Salvador:** 2/F, 9 Lane 62, Tien Mou West Rd, Shih Lin, Taipei 111; tel. (2) 28763509; fax (2) 28763514; e-mail embasal@netvigator.com.tw; Ambassador: FRANCISCO RICARDO SANTANA BERRÍOS.

**The Gambia:** 9/F, 9-1 Lane 62, Tien Mou West Rd, Taipei 111; tel. (2) 28753911; fax (2) 28752775; Ambassador: MAMBURY NJIE.

**Guatemala:** 2/F, 334 Shihpai Rd, Sec. 2, Taipei 112; tel. (2) 28756952; fax (2) 28740699; Ambassador: LUIS ALBERTO NORIEGA MORALES.

**Haiti:** 8/F, 9-1 Lane 62, Tien Mou West Rd, Taipei 111; tel. (2) 28384945; fax (2) 28317086; Ambassador: (vacant).

**Holy See:** 87 Ai Kuo East Rd, Taipei 106 (Apostolic Nunciature); tel. (2) 23216847; fax (2) 23911926; e-mail aposnunc@tptsl.seed.net.tw; Chargé d'affaires a.i.: Mgr ADOLFO TITO C. YLLANA.

**Honduras:** 9/F, 9 Lane 62, Tien Mou West Rd, Taipei 111; tel. (2) 28755507; fax (2) 28755726; Ambassador: MARGARITA DURÓN DE GÁLVEZ.

**Liberia:** 11/F, 9-1 Lane 62, Tien Mou West Rd, Taipei 111; tel. (2) 28730505; fax (2) 28745768; e-mail libemb@tpts5.seed.net.tw; Ambassador: JOHN CUMMINGS.

**Macedonia, former Yugoslav republic:** 5/F, 9 Lane 62, Tien Mou West Road, Taipei 111; tel. (2) 28760189; fax (2) 28729254; Envoy: VERA MODANU.

**Nicaragua:** 3/F, 9 Lane 62, Tien Mou West Rd, Taipei 111; tel. (2) 28749034; fax (2) 28749080; Ambassador: SALVADOR STADTHAGEN.

**Panama:** 6th Floor, 111 Sung Kiang Rd, Taipei 104; tel. (2) 25099189; fax (2) 25099801; Ambassador: JOSÉ ANTONIO DOMÍNGUEZ.

**Paraguay:** 7/F, 9-1 Lane 62, Tien Mou West Rd, Taipei 111; tel. (2) 28736310; fax (2) 28736312; Ambassador: CEFERINO ADRIÁN VÁLDEZ PERALTA.

**Senegal:** 10/F, 9-1 Lane 62, Tien Mou West Rd, Taipei 111, tel. (2) 28310661; fax (2) 28319397; Ambassador: AHMED TIJANE KANE.

# Judicial System

The power of judicial review is exercised by the Judicial Yuan's Grand Justices nominated and appointed for nine years by the President of Taiwan with the consent of the National Assembly. The President of the Judicial Yuan is also the *ex-officio* chairman for the Plenary Session of the Grand Justices. The Ministry of Justice is under the jurisdiction of the Executive Yuan.

**Judicial Yuan:** 124 Chungking South Rd, Sec. 1, Taipei; tel. (2) 23618577; fax (2) 23821739; Pres. WENG YUEH-SHENG; Sec.-Gen. YANG JEN-SHOU; the highest judicial organ, and the interpreter of the constitution and national laws and ordinances; supervises the following:

**Supreme Court:** 6 Chang Sha St, Sec. 1, Taipei; tel. (2) 23141160; fax (2) 23114246; Court of third and final instance for civil and criminal cases; Pres. LIN MING-TEH.

**High Courts:** Courts of second instance for appeals of civil and criminal cases.

**District Courts:** Courts of first instance in civil, criminal and non-contentious cases.

**Administrative Court:** 1 Lane 126, Chungking South Rd, Sec. 1, Taipei; tel. (2) 23113691; fax (2) 23111791; e-mail jessie@judicial.gov.tw; Court of final resort in cases brought against govt agencies; Pres. JONG YAW-TANG.

**Committee on the Discipline of Public Functionaries:** 124 Chungking South Rd, 3rd Floor, Sec. 1, Taipei 10036; tel. (2) 23619375; fax (2) 23311934; decides on disciplinary measures against public functionaries impeached by the Control Yuan; Chair. LIN KUO-HSIEN.

# Religion

According to the Ministry of the Interior, in 1998 41% of the population were adherents of Buddhism, 38% of Daoism (Taoism), 8% of I-Kuan Tao and 3.6% of Christianity.

### BUDDHISM

**Buddhist Association of Taiwan:** Mahayana and Theravada schools; 1,613 group mems and more than 9.61m. adherents; Leader Ven. CHIN-HSIN.

### CHRISTIANITY

#### The Roman Catholic Church

Taiwan comprises one archdiocese, six dioceses and one apostolic administrative area. In December 1998 there were 304,000 adherents.

**Bishops' Conference:** Regional Episcopal Conference of China, 34 Lane 32, Kuangfu South Rd, Taipei 10552; tel. (2) 25782355; fax (2) 25773874; f. 1967; Pres. Cardinal PAUL SHAN KUO-HSI, Bishop of Kaohsiung.

**Archbishop of Taipei:** Most Rev. JOSEPH TI-KANG, Archbishop's House, 94 Loli Rd, Taipei 10668; tel. (2) 27371311; fax (2) 27373710.

#### The Anglican Communion

Anglicans in Taiwan are adherents of the Protestant Episcopal Church. In 1998 the Church had 2,000 members.

**Bishop of Taiwan:** Rt Rev. JOHN CHIH-TSUNG CHIEN, 7 Lane 105, Hangchow South Rd, Sec. 1, Taipei 100; tel. (2) 23411265; fax (2) 23962014; e-mail skhtpe@ms12.hinet.net.

#### Presbyterian Church

**Tai-oan Ki-tok Tiu-Lo Kau-Hoe** (Presbyterian Church in Taiwan): No. 3, Lane 269, Roosevelt Rd, Sec. 3, Taipei 106; tel. (2) 23625282; fax (2) 23628096; f. 1865; Gen. Sec. Rev. L. K. LO; 224,819 mems (1997).

### DAOISM (TAOISM)

In 1998 there were about 4.32m. adherents. Temples numbered 8,557, and clergy totalled 33,200.

### I-KUAN TAO

Introduced to Taiwan in the 1950s, this 'Religion of One Unity' is a modern, syncretic religion, drawn mainly from Confucian, Buddhist and Daoist principles and incorporating ancestor worship. In 1998 there were 87 temples and 18,000 family shrines. Adherents totalled 983,000.

### ISLAM

Leader MOHAMMED MA CHA-JENG; 52,000 adherents in 1998.

# The Press

By mid-1997 the number of registered newspapers had increased to 367. The majority of newspapers are privately owned.

### PRINCIPAL DAILIES

#### Taipei

**Central Daily News:** 260 Pa Teh Rd, Sec. 2, Taipei; tel. (2) 27765368; fax (2) 27775835; f. 1928; morning; Chinese; official Kuomintang organ; Publr and Editor-in-Chief CHAN TIEN-SHING; circ. 600,000.

**The China Post:** 8 Fu Shun St, Taipei 104; tel. (2) 25969971; fax (2) 25957962; e-mail cpost@msl.hinet.net; f. 1952; morning; English; Publr and Editor JACK HUANG; circ. 200,000.

**China Times:** 132 Da Li St, Taipei; tel. (2) 23087111; fax (2) 23063312; f. 1950; morning; Chinese; Chair. YU CHI-CHUNG; Publr YU ALBERT CHIEN-HSIN; circ. 1.2m.

**China Times Express:** 132 Da Li St, Taipei; tel. (2) 23087111; fax (2) 23048138; e-mail chinaexpress@mail.chinatimes.com.tw; f. 1988; evening; Chinese; Publr S. F. LIN; Editor C. L. HUANG; circ. 400,000.

**Commercial Times:** 132 Da Li St, Taipei; tel. (2) 23087111; fax (2) 23069456; e-mail commercialtimes@mail.chinatimes.com.tw; f. 1978; morning; Chinese; Publr CHOU SHENG-YUAN; Editor-in-Chief PHILLIP CHEN; circ. 300,000.

**Economic Daily News:** 555 Chung Hsiao East Rd, Sec. 4, Taipei; tel. (2) 27681234; fax (2) 27656613; f. 1967; morning; Chinese; Publr WANG PI-LY.

**The Great News:** 216 Chen Teh Rd, Sec. 3, Taipei; tel. (2) 25973111; f. 1988; morning; also *The Great News Daily-Entertainment* (circ. 460,000) and *The Great News Daily-Sport* (circ. 410,000); Publr CHEN CHI-CHIA.

**Independence Evening Post:** 15 Chi Nan Rd, Sec. 2, Taipei; tel. (2) 23519621; fax (2) 23215211; f. 1947; afternoon; Chinese; Publr CHEN TSEN-HUEI; Editor LEE SEN-HONG; circ. 307,071.

**Liberty Times:** 137 Nanking East Rd, 11th Floor, Sec. 2, Taipei; tel. (2) 25042828; fax (2) 25042212; f. 1988; Publr WU A-MING; Editor-in-Chief LIN JIAN-LIAN.

**Mandarin Daily News:** 4 Foo Chou St, Taipei; tel. (2) 23213479; fax (2) 23410203; f. 1948; morning; Publr LIN LIANG.

**Min Sheng Daily:** 555 Chung Hsiao East Rd, Sec. 4, Taipei; tel. (2) 27681234; fax (2) 27560955; f. 1978; sport and leisure; Publr WANG SHAW-LAN.

**Taiwan Hsin Sheng Pao:** 12th Floor, 110 Yengping South Rd, Taipei; tel. (2) 23117000; fax (2) 23825093; f. 1945; morning; Chinese; also southern edn publ. in Kaohsiung; Publr CHAO LIE-NIAN.

**Taiwan News:** 10th Floor, 41 Tung Hsing St, Taipei; tel. (2) 27686002; fax (2) 27686773; f. 1949; morning; English; Chair. and Publr LING WEI.

**United Daily News:** 555 Chung Hsiao East Rd, Sec. 4, Taipei; tel. (2) 27681234; fax (2) 27632303; e-mail udnid@eagle.seed.net.tw; f. 1951; morning; Publr WANG SHAW-LAN; Editor SHUANG KUO-NING; circ. 1.2m.

**Youth Daily News:** 3 Hsinyi Rd, Sec. 1, Taipei; tel. (2) 23222722; fax (2) 2322245; f. 1984; morning; Chinese; armed forces; Publr TIEN TUAN.

#### Provincial

**China Daily News** (Southern Edn): 57 Hsi Hwa St, Tainan; tel. (6) 2296381; fax (6) 2201804; f. 1946; morning; Publr LIN SHE-CHI; Man. Dir and Editor TIEN SHING CHAN; circ. 670,000.

**Keng Sheng Daily News:** 36 Wuchuan St, Hualien; tel. (38) 340131; fax (38) 329664; f. 1947; morning; Publr HSIEH YING-YIN; Editor CHEN HSING; circ. 50,000.

**Min Chung Daily News:** 180 Min Chuan 2 Rd, Kaohsiung; tel. (7) 3363131; fax (7) 3363604; f. 1950; morning; Publr LEE JER-LANG; Editor LEE WANG-TAI; circ. 148,000.

**Taiwan Daily News:** 361 Wen Shin Rd, Sec. 3, Taichung; tel. (4) 2958511; fax (4) 2958950; f. 1964; morning; Publr TEN WEN-SHUAN; Editor CHAO LI-NAIN; circ. 250,000.

**Taiwan Hsin Wen Daily News:** 249 Chung Cheng 4 Rd, Kaohsiung; tel. (7) 2958951; f. 1949; morning; southern edn of *Hsin Sheng Pao*; Publr CHAO LI-NIEN; Editor HSIEH TSUNG-MIN.

**Taiwan Times:** 110 Chung Shan 1 Rd, Kaohsiung; tel. (7) 2155666; fax (7) 2150264; f. 1971; Publr WANG YUH-CHEN; Editor HWANG DONG-LIEH.

## SELECTED PERIODICALS

**Artist Magazine:** 6th Floor, 147 Chung Ching South Rd, Sec. 1, Taipei; tel. (2) 23719692; fax (2) 23317096; f. 1975; monthly; Publr HO CHENG KUANG; circ. 28,000.

**Better Life Monthly:** 11 Lane 199, Hsin-yih Rd, Sec. 4, Taipei; tel. (2) 27549588; fax (2) 27016068; f. 1987; Publr JACK S. LIN.

**Biographical Literature:** 4th Floor-1, 230 Jen Ai Rd, Sec. 2, Taipei; tel. (2) 23410213; fax (2) 23960057; f. 1962; monthly; Publr LIU SHAW-TANG.

**Brain:** 9th Floor, 47 Nanking East Rd, Sec. 4, Taipei; tel. (2) 27132644; fax (2) 27137318; f. 1977; f. 1977; monthly; Publr JOHNSON WU.

**Business Weekly:** 5th Floor, 62 Tun Hwa North Rd, Taipei; tel. (2) 27736611; fax (2) 27110833; f. 1987; Publr JIN WEI-TSUN.

**Car Magazine:** 1st Floor, 3 Lane 3, Tun-Shan St, Taipei; tel. (2) 23218128; fax (2) 23935614; e-mail carguide@ms13.hinet.net; f. 1982; monthly; Publr H. K. LIN; Editor-in-Chief TA-WEI LIN; circ. 85,000.

**Central Monthly:** 7th Floor, 11 Chung Shan South Rd, Taipei; tel. (2) 23433140; fax (2) 23433139; f. 1950; Publr HUANG HUI-TSEN.

**China Times Weekly:** 5th Floor, 25 Min Chuan East Rd, Sec. 6, Taipei; tel. (2) 27929688; fax (2) 27929568; f. 1978; weekly; Chinese; Editor CHANG KUO-LI; Publr CHUANG SHU-MING; circ. 180,000.

**Continent Magazine:** 3rd Floor, 11-6 Foo Chou St, Taipei; tel. (2) 23518310; f. 1950; monthly; archaeology, history and literature; Publr HSU CHO-YU.

**Cosmopolitan:** 14th Floor, 51 Keelung Rd, Sec. 2, Taipei; tel. (2) 23777968; fax (2) 23777966; f. 1992; monthly; Publr LING WEN-RONG.

**Country Road:** 14 Wenchow St, Taipei; tel. (2) 23628148; fax (2) 23636724; e-mail h3628148@ms15.hinet.net; internet www.coa.gov.tw/ch/fst/index.htm; f. 1975; monthly; Editor CHRISTINE S. L. YU; Publr HONG PI-FENG.

**Crown Magazine:** 50 Lane 120, Tun Hua North Rd, Taipei; tel. (2) 27168888; fax (2) 27133422; f. 1954; monthly; literature and arts; Publr PING HSIN TAO; Editor CHEN LIH-HWA; circ. 76,000.

**Defense Technology Monthly:** 10th Floor, 74 Song Der Rd, Taipei; tel. (2) 27204568; fax (2) 27581335; f. 1894; Publr J. D. BIH.

**Earth Geographic Monthly:** 2nd Floor, 130 Min Chuan Rd, Hsin-Tien, Taipei; tel. (2) 22182218; fax (2) 22185418; f. 1988; Publr HSU CHEN ERH-HONG.

**Elle-Taipei:** 9/F, 9 Lane 30, Sec. 3, Minsheng East Rd, Taipei; tel. (2) 27522425; fax (2) 27514583; e-mail jdewitt@hft.com.tw; f. 1991; monthly; women's magazine; Publr JEAN DE WITT; Editor-in-Chief LENA YANG; circ. 50,000.

**Evergreen Monthly:** 11th Floor, 2 Pa Teh Rd, Sec. 3, Taipei; tel. (2) 25785078; fax (2) 25786838; f. 1983; health care knowledge; Publr LIANG GUANG-MING; circ. 50,000.

**Excellence Magazine:** 2nd Floor, 15 Lane 3, Sec. 2, Chien Kuo North Rd, Taipei; tel. (2) 25093578; fax (2) 25173607; f. 1984; monthly; business; Man. WU SHIEN-ER; Editor-in-Chief LIU JEN; circ. 70,000.

**Families Monthly:** 11th Floor, 2 Pa Teh Rd, Sec. 3, Taipei; tel. (2) 25785078; fax (2) 25786838; f. 1976; family life; Editor-in-Chief THELMA KU; circ. 155,000.

**Foresight Investment Weekly:** 7th Floor, 52 Nanking East Rd, Sec. 1, Taipei; tel. (2) 25512561; fax (2) 25681999; f. 1980; weekly; Dir and Publr SUN WUN HSIUNG; Editor-in-Chief WU WEN SHIN; circ. 55,000.

**Free China Journal:** 2 Tientsin St, Taipei 10041; tel. (2) 23970180; fax (2) 23568233; f. 1964 (fmrly Free China Weekly); weekly; English; news review; Publr C. J. CHEN; Exec. Editor VANCE CHANG; circ. 37,000.

**Free China Review:** 2 Tientsin St, Taipei 100; tel. (2) 23516419; fax (2) 23510829; e-mail fcr@gio.gov.tw; f. 1951; monthly; English; illustrated; Publr CHIEN-JEN CHEN; Editor-in-Chief JIANG PING-LUN.

**The Gleaner:** 7th Floor, 7 Chung Ching South Rd, Sec. 1, Taipei; tel. (2) 23813781; fax (2) 23899801; Publr CHIN KAI-YIN.

**Global Views Monthly:** 7th Floor, 87 Sung Chiang Rd, Taipei; tel. (2) 25078627; fax (2) 25079011; f. 1986; Pres. CHARLES H. C. KAO; Publr and Editor-in-Chief WANG LI-HSING.

**Gourmet World:** 4th Floor, 52 Hang Chou South Rd, Taipei; tel. (2) 23972215; fax (2) 23412184; f. 1990; Publr HSU TANG-JEN.

**Harvest Farm Magazine:** 14 Wenchow St, Taipei; tel. (2) 23628148; fax (2) 23636724; e-mail h3628148@ms15.hinet.net; internet www.coa.gov.tw/ch/fst/index.htm; f. 1951; every 2 weeks; Publr HONG PI-FENG; Editor KAO MING-TANG.

**Information and Computer:** 6th Floor, 153 Hsinyi Rd, Sec. 3, Taipei; tel. (2) 23255750; fax (2) 23255749; f. 1980; monthly; Chinese; Publr FANG HSIEN-CHI; Editor JENNIFER CHIU; circ. 28,000.

**Issues and Studies:** Institute of International Relations, 64 Wan Shou Rd, Wenshan, Taipei 116; tel. (2) 29394921; fax (2) 29397352; e-mail scchang@nccu.edu.tw; f. 1965; bimonthly; English; Chinese studies and international affairs; Publr HO SZU-YIN; Editor JAUSHIEH JOSEPH WU.

**Jade Biweekly Magazine:** 7th Floor, 222 Sung Chiang Rd, Taipei; tel. (2) 25811665; fax (2) 25210586; f. 1982; economics, social affairs, leisure; Publr HSU CHIA-CHUNG; circ. 98,000.

**Journalist:** 4th Floor-6, 79 Hsin Tai Wu Rd, Hsi Chin, Taipei; tel. (2) 26981898; fax (2) 26981086; f. 1987; weekly; Publr WANG SHIN-CHING.

**Ladies Magazine:** 11F-3, 187 Shin Yi Rd, Sec. 4, Taipei; tel. (2) 27026908; fax (2) 27014090; f. 1978; monthly; Publr CHENG CHIN-SHAN; Editor-in-Chief THERESA LEE; circ. 60,000.

**Living:** 7th Floor, 2531-1 Chung Cheng Rd, Hsin Tien, Taipei; tel. (2) 21181828; fax (2) 22181081; f. 1997; monthly; Publr LISA WU.

**Management Magazine:** 3rd Floor, 143 Sim-Yi Rd, Sec. 4, Hsichih, Taipei; tel. (2) 26485828; fax (2) 26484666; e-mail flhung@email.gcn.net.tw; internet www.harment.com; monthly; Chinese; Publr and Editor FRANK L. HUNG; circ. 65,000.

**Marie Claire:** 5th Floor, 25 Min Chuan East Rd, Sec. 6, Taipei; tel. (2) 27921898; fax (2) 27928838; f. 1993; Publr YANG REN-KAE.

**Money Monthly:** 12th Floor, 102 Tun Hua North Rd, Taipei; tel. (2) 25149822; fax (2) 27154657; f. 1986; monthly; personal financial management; Publr PATRICK SUN; Man. Editor JENNIE SHUE; circ. 55,000.

**Music and Audiophile:** 2nd Floor, 2 Kingshan South Rd, Sec. 1, Taipei; tel. (2) 25684607; fax (2) 23958654; f. 1973; Publr CHANG KUO-CHING; Editor-in-Chief CHARLES HUANG.

**National Palace Museum Bulletin:** Wai Shuang Hsi, Shih Lin, Taipei 11102; tel. (2) 28812021; fax (2) 28821440; e-mail bulletin@npm.gov.tw; f. 1966; every 2 months; Chinese art history research in English; Publr and Dir CHIN HSIAO-YI; Editor-in-Chief LIN PO-TING; circ. 1,000.

**National Palace Museum Monthly of Chinese Art:** Wai Shuang Hsi, Shih Lin, Taipei 11102; tel. (2) 28821230; fax (2) 28821440; f. 1983; monthly in Chinese; Publr CHIN HSIAO-YI; Editor-in-Chief CHANG YUEH-YUN; circ. 10,000.

**Nong Nong Magazine:** 7th Floor, 531-1 Chung Cheng Rd, Hsin Tien, Taipei; tel. (2) 22181828; fax (2) 22181081; e-mail group@nongnong.com.tw; f. 1984; monthly; women's interest; Publr LISA WU; Editor DIANA LIU; circ. 70,000.

**PC Home:** 3rd Floor-1, 64 Tun Hwa North Rd, Taipei; tel. (2) 27739858; fax (2) 27116527; f. 1996; monthly; Publr HUNG-TZE JANG.

**PC Office:** 11th Floor, 8 Tun Hwa North Rd, Taipei; tel. (2) 27815390; fax (2) 27780899; f. 1997; monthly; Publr HUNG-TZE JANG.

**Reader's Digest** (Chinese Edn): 2nd Floor, 2 Ming Sheng East Rd, Taipei; tel. (2) 27607262; fax (2) 27461588; monthly; Editor-in-Chief ANNIE CHENG.

**Sinorama:** 8th Floor, 15-1 Hangchow South Rd, Sec. 1, Taipei 100; tel. (2) 23922256; fax (2) 23970655; f. 1976; monthly; cultural; bilingual magazine with edns in Chinese with Japanese, Spanish and English; Publr CHIEN-JEN CHEN; Editor-in-Chief ANNA Y. WANG; circ. 110,000.

**Sinwen Tienti** (Newsdom): 10th Floor, 207 Fuh Hsing North Rd, Taipei; tel. (2) 27139668; fax (2) 27131763; f. 1945; weekly; Chinese; Dir PU SHAO-FU.

**Studio Classroom:** 10 Lane 62, Ta-Chih St, Taipei; tel. (2) 25339123; fax (2) 25331811; f. 1962; monthly; Publr DORIS BROUGHAM.

**Tien Hsia** (CommonWealth Monthly): 4th Floor, 87 Sung Chiang Rd, Taipei; tel. (2) 25078627; fax (2) 25079011; f. 1981; monthly; business; Pres. CHARLES H. C. KAO; Publr and Editor DIANE YING; circ. 83,000.

**Time Express:** 7th Floor-2, 76 Tun Hwa South Rd, Sec. 2, Taipei; tel. (2) 27084410; fax (2) 27084420; f. 1973; monthly; Publr RICHARD C. C. HUANG.

**TV Weekly:** 11th Floor, 2 Pa Teh Rd, Taipei; tel. (2) 25785078; fax (2) 25786838; f. 1962; Publr LIANG GUANG-MING; circ. 160,000.

**Unitas:** 7th Floor, 180 Keelung Rd, Sec. 1, Taipei; tel. (2) 27666759; fax (2) 27567914; monthly; Chinese; literary journal; Publr CHANG PAO-CHING; Editor-in-Chief CHU AN-MIN.

**Vi Vi Magazine:** 7th Floor, 550 Chung Hsiao East Rd, Sec. 5, Taipei; tel. (2) 27275336; fax (2) 27592031; f. 1984; monthly; women's interest; Pres. TSENG CHING-TANG; circ. 60,000.

**Vogue:** 5th Floor, 232 Tun Hwa North Rd, Taipei; tel. (2) 27172000; fax (2) 27172004; f. 1996; monthly; Publr BENTHAM LIU.

**Wealth Magazine:** 7th Floor, 52 Nanking East Rd, Sec. 1, Taipei; tel. (2) 25512561; fax (2) 25816196; f. 1974; monthly; finance; Pres. TSHAI YEN-KUEN; Editor ANDY LIAN; circ. 75,000.

**Win Win Weekly:** 7th Floor, 52 Nanking East Rd, Taipei; tel. (2) 25816196; fax (2) 25119596; f. 1996; Publr GIN-HO HSHIE.

**Youth Literary:** 3rd Floor, 66-1 Chung Cheng South Rd, Sec. 1, Taipei; tel. (2) 23146181; fax (2) 23612239; f. 1954; Publr LEE CHUNG-GUAI.

### NEWS AGENCIES

**Central News Agency Inc. (CNA):** 209 Sung Chiang Rd, Taipei; tel. (2) 25051180; fax (2) 25014806; f. 1924; news service in Chinese, English and Spanish; feature and photographic services; 7 domestic and 28 overseas bureaux; Pres. KERMIN SHIH; Editor-in-Chief W. L. LEE.

**Chiao Kwang News Agency:** 4th Floor, 58 Chinsan South Rd, Sec. 1, Taipei; tel. (2) 23214803; fax (2) 23516416; Dir HUANG HER.

#### Foreign Bureaux

**Agence France-Presse (AFP):** Room 617, 6th Floor, 209 Sung Chiang Rd, Taipei; tel. (2) 25016395; fax (2) 25011881; Bureau Chief YANG HSIN-HSIN.

**Associated Press (AP)** (USA): Room 630, 6th Floor, 209 Sung Chiang Rd, Taipei; tel. (2) 25015109; fax (2) 25007133; Bureau Chief PAN YUEH-KA.

**Reuters** (UK): 8th Floor, 196 Chien Kuo North Rd, Sec. 2, Taipei; tel. (2) 25004881; fax (2) 25080204; Bureau Chief JEFFREY PARKER.

## Publishers

There are 6,388 publishing houses. In 1998 a total of 28,000 titles were published.

**Art Book Co:** 4th Floor, 18 Lane 283, Roosevelt Rd, Sec. 3, Taipei; tel. (2) 23620578; fax (2) 23623594; Publr HO KUNG SHANG.

**Cheng Wen Publishing Co:** 3rd Floor, 277 Roosevelt Rd, Sec. 3, Taipei; tel. (2) 23628032; fax (2) 23660806; e-mail ccicncwp@ms17.hinet.net; Publr LARRY C. HUANG.

**China Economic News Service (CENS):** 555 Chung Hsiao East Rd, Sec. 4, Taipei 110; tel. (2) 26422629; fax (2) 26427422; e-mail webmaster@www.cens.com; internet www.cens.com; f. 1974; trade magazines.

**China Times Publishing Co:** 5th Floor, 240 Hoping West Rd, Sec. 3, Taipei; tel. (2) 23027845; fax (2) 23027844; e-mail ctpc@mse.hinet.net; internet www.publish.chinatimes.com.tw; f. 1975; Pres. MO CHAO-PING.

**Chinese Culture University Press:** 55 Hua Kang Rd, Yangming-shan, Taipei; tel. (2) 28611861; fax (2) 28617164; e-mail ccup@ccuo16.pccu.edu.tw; Publr LEE FU-CHEN.

**Chung Hwa Book Co Ltd:** 14th Floor, 51 Keelung Rd, Sec. 2, Taipei; tel. (2) 23780215; fax (2) 27355887; e-mail du13@ms29.hinet.net; humanities, social sciences, medicine, fine arts, school books, reference books; Publr LIN WIN-RONG.

**The Commercial Press Ltd:** 37 Chungking South Rd, Sec. 1, Taipei; tel. (2) 23116118; fax (2) 23710274; e-mail cptw@ms12.hinet.net; Publr REX HOW.

**Crown Publishing Co:** 50 Lane 120, Tun Hua North Rd, Taipei; tel. (2) 27168888; fax (2) 27161793; e-mail magazine@crown.com.tw; internet www.crown.crown.com.tw; Publr PHILIP PING.

**The Eastern Publishing Co Ltd:** 121 Chungking South Rd, Sec. 1, Taipei; tel. (2) 23114514; fax (2) 23317402; Publr CHENG LI-TSU.

**Elite Publishing Co:** 1st Floor, 33-1 Lane 113, Hsiamen St, Taipei 100; tel. (2) 23671021; fax (2) 23657047; e-mail elite113@ms12.hinet.net; f. 1975; Publr KO CHING-HWA.

**Far East Book Co:** 10th Floor, 66-1 Chungking South Rd, Sec. 1, Taipei; tel. (2) 23118740; fax (2) 23114184; e-mail webmaster@mail.fareast.com.tw; internet www.fareast.com.tw; art, education, history, physics, mathematics, law, literature, dictionaries, textbooks, language tapes, Chinese-English dictionary; Publr GEORGE C. L. PU.

**Hilit Publishing Co Ltd:** 11th Floor, 79 Hsin Tai Wu Rd, Sec. 1, Hsichih Town, Taipei County; tel. (2) 26984565; fax (2) 26984980; e-mail hilit@tpts5.seed.net.tw; internet www.ptri.org.tw/hilit/; Publr DIXON D. S. SUNG.

**Hua Hsin Culture and Publications Center:** 2nd Floor, 133 Kuang Fu North Rd, Taipei; tel. (2) 27658190; fax (2) 27694980; f. 1960; Dir CHENG CHI.

**International Cultural Enterprises:** 5th Floor, 25 Po Ai Rd, Taipei 100; tel. (2) 23318080; fax (2) 23318090; e-mail itstpeh@MS8.hinet.net; internet www.itstpeh.com.tw; Publr LAKE HU.

**Kwang Fu Book Enterprises Co Ltd:** 6th Floor, 38 Fu Hsing North Rd, Taipei; tel. (2) 27716622; fax (2) 27218230; e-mail lolatiao@kfgroup.com.tw; internet www.kfgroup.com.tw; Publr LIN CHUN-HUI.

**Kwang Hwa Publishing Co:** 8th Floor, 15-1 Hangchow South Rd, Sec. 1, Taipei; tel. (2) 23516419; fax (2) 23510821; e-mail fcr@mail.gio.gov.tw; Publr CHEN CHIEN-JEN.

**Li-Ming Cultural Enterprise Co:** 3rd Floor, 49 Chungking South Rd, Sec. 1, Taipei 100; tel. (2) 23821233; fax (2) 23821244; e-mail liming2f@ms15.hinet.net; internet www.limingco.com.tw; Pres. HSU MING-SHIUNG.

**Linking Publishing Co Ltd:** 555 Chung Hsiao East Rd, Sec. 4, Taipei; tel. (2) 27683708; fax (2) 27634590; e-mail linkingp@ms9.hinet.net; internet www.udngroup.com.tw/linkingp; Publr LIU KUO-JUEI.

**San Min Book Co Ltd:** 5th Floor, 386 Fushing North Rd, Taipei; tel. (2) 25006600; fax (2) 25064000; e-mail sanmin@ms2.hinet.net; internet www.sanmin.com.tw; f. 1953; literature, history, philosophy, social sciences, dictionaries, art, politics, law; Publr LIU CHEN-CHIANG.

**Senseio Business Group:** 259 Tun Hwa South Rd, Sec. 1, Taipei; tel. (2) 27037777; fax (2) 27049948; f. 1966; Publr LIAW SUSHI-IGU.

**Sitak Publishing Group:** 10th Floor, 15 Lane 174, Hsin Ming Rd, Neihu Dist, Taipei; tel. (2) 27911197; fax (2) 27955824; e-mail cryco@ms27.hinet.net; Publr CHU PAO-LOUNG; Dir KELLY CHU.

**Taiwan Kaiming Book Co:** 77 Chung Shan North Rd, Sec. 1, Taipei; tel. (2) 25415369; fax (2) 25212894; Publr LUCY CHOH LIU.

**Tung Hua Book Co Ltd:** 105 Ermei St, Taipei; tel. (2) 23114027; fax (2) 23116615; Publr CHARLES CHOH.

**The World Book Co:** 99 Chungking South Rd, Sec. 1, Taipei; tel. (2) 23311616; fax (2) 23317963; e-mail wbc@ms2.hinet.net; internet www.worldbook.com.tw; f. 1921; literature, textbooks; Chair. YEN FENG-CHANG; Publr YEN ANGELA CHU.

**Youth Cultural Enterprise Co Ltd:** 3rd Floor, 66-1 Chungking South Rd, Sec. 1, Taipei; tel. (2) 23112837; fax (2) 23711736; e-mail youth@ms2.hinet.net; internet www.youth.com.tw; Publr LEE CHUNG-KUEI.

**Yuan Liou Publishing Co Ltd:** 7F/5, 184 Ding Chou Rd, Sec. 3, Taipei 100; tel. (2) 23651212; fax (2) 23657979; e-mail ylib@yuanliou.ylib.com.tw; internet www.ylib.com.tw; f. 1975; fiction, non-fiction, children's; Publr WANG JUNG-WEN.

## Broadcasting and Communications

### TELECOMMUNICATIONS

**Directorate-General of Telecommunications:** Taipei; regulatory authority.

**Chunghwa Telecommunications Co Ltd:** 21 Hsinyi Rd, Sec. 1, Taipei; tel. (2) 23445385; fax (2) 23972254; internet www.cht.com.tw; f. 1996; state-controlled company, scheduled for privatization; sole provider of telecommunications services, fixed-line competition scheduled to begin 2001.

### BROADCASTING

Broadcasting stations are mostly commercial. The Ministry of Transportation and Communications determines power and frequencies, and the Government Information Office supervises the operation of all stations, whether private or governmental.

#### Radio

In 1999 there were 143 radio broadcasting corporations in operation, and permission for the establishment of a further 11 radio stations had been given.

**Broadcasting Corpn of China (BCC):** 375 Sung Chiang Rd, Taipei 10647; tel. (2) 25019688; fax (2) 25018793; e-mail pr@mailbcc.com.tw; internet www.bcc.com.tw; f. 1928; domestic (6 networks and 1 channel) and external services in 13 languages and dialects; 9 local stations, 117 transmitters; Pres. LEE CHING-PING; Chair. CHIEN HAN-SEN.

**Central Broadcasting System (CBS):** 55 Pei An Rd, Tachih, Taipei 104; tel. (2) 25918161; fax (2) 25850741; e-mail rtm@cbs.org.tw; internet www.cbs.org.tw; domestic and international service; Dir. HUANG SZE-CHUAN.

**Cheng Sheng Broadcasting Corpn Ltd:** 7th Floor, 66-1 Chung-king South Rd, Sec. 1, Taipei; tel. (2) 23617231; fax (2) 23715665; f. 1950; 6 stations, 3 relay stations; Chair. YANG HSUEH-YENN; Pres. CHEN SHENG-CHUAN.

**International Community Radio Taipei (ICRT):** 8-1 Chung-yung 2 Rd, Shantzehou, Yangmingshan, Taipei; tel. (2) 28612280; fax (2) 28613863; internet www.icrt.com.tw; predominantly English-language broadcaster; Station Man. GEORGE CHU.

**Kiss Radio:** 34th Floor, 6 Min Chuan 2 Rd, Kaohsiung; tel. (7) 3365888; fax (7) 3364931; Chair. IVAN YUAN; Pres. HELENA YUAN.

**M-radio Broadcasting Corpn:** 8th Floor, 1-18 Taichung Kang Rd, Sec. 2, Taichung City; tel. (4) 3235656; fax (4) 3231199; e-mail jason@taichungnet.com.tw; internet www.taichungnet .com.tw; Pres. SHEN CHIN-HWEI; Gen. Man. JASON C. LIN.

**UFO Broadcasting Co Ltd:** 25th Floor, 102 Roosevelt Rd, Sec. 2, Taipei; tel. (2) 23636600; fax (2) 23673083; Pres. JAW SHAU-KONG.

**Voice of Taipei Broadcasting Co Ltd:** 10th Floor, B Rm, 15-1 Han Chou South Rd, Sec. 1, Taipei; tel. (2) 23957255; fax (2) 27724370; Pres. WEI-CHUNG WANG; Man. HSU LU.

### Television

Legislation to place cable broadcasting on a legal basis was adopted in mid-1993, and by June 1999 123 cable television companies were in operation. A non-commercial station, Public Television (PTV), went on air in July 1998.

**China Television Co (CTV):** 120 Chung Yang Rd, Nan Kang District, Taipei; tel. (2) 27838308; fax (2) 27826007; e-mail pubr@mail.chinatv.com.tw; internet www.chinatv.com.tw; f. 1969; Pres. JIANG FENG-CHYI; Chair. SUMING CHENG.

**Chinese Television System (CTS):** 100 Kuang Fu South Rd, Taipei 10658; tel. (2) 27510321; fax (2) 27775414; e-mail public@ mail.cts.com.tw; internet www.cts.com.tw; f. 1971; cultural and educational; Chair. YEE CHIEN-CHIU; Pres. WU SHIH-SHUNG.

**Formosa Television Co (FTV):** 14th Floor, 30 Pa Teh Rd, Sec. 3, Taipei; tel. (2) 25702570; fax (2) 25773170; internet www.ftv.com.tw; f. 1997; Chair. TSAI TUNG-RONG: Pres. LEE GUANG-HUEI.

**Public Television Service Foundation (PTS):** 90, Lane 95, Sec. 9, Kang Ning Rd, Neihu, Taipei; tel. (2) 26349122; fax (2) 26338124; e-mail pts@mail.pts.org.tw; internet www.pts.org.tw; Chair. FRANK WU; Pres. YUNG-PE LEE.

**Taiwan Television Enterprise (TTV):** 10 Pa Teh Rd, Sec. 3, Taipei 10560; tel. (2) 25781515; fax (2) 25799626; internet www.ttv.com.tw; f. 1962; Chair. HSU CHING-TEH; Pres. WALTER C. H. YANG.

# Finance

(cap. = capital; dep. = deposits; m. = million; brs = branches; amounts in New Taiwan dollars unless otherwise stated)

## BANKING

In June 1991 the Ministry of Finance granted 15 new banking licences to private banks. A 16th bank was authorized in May 1992; further authorizations followed. Restrictions on the establishment of offshore banking units were relaxed in 1994.

### Central Bank

**Central Bank of China:** 2 Roosevelt Rd, Sec. 1, Taipei 100; tel. (2) 23936161; fax (2) 23571974; e-mail adminrol@mail.cbc.gov.tw; internet www.cbc.gov.tw; f. 1928; bank of issue; cap. 80,000m., dep. 2,539,626m. (May 1999); Gov. PERNG FAI-NAN.

### Domestic Banks

**Bank of Taiwan:** 120 Chungking South Rd, Sec. 1, Taipei 10036; tel. (2) 23493456; fax (2) 23613203; e-mail bot076@mail.bot.com.tw; internet www.bot.com.tw; f. 1899; cap. 32,000m., dep. 1,535,168m. (Dec. 1998); Chair. JAMES C. T. LO; Pres. HO KUO-HWA; 102 brs, incl. 5 overseas.

**Chiao Tung Bank:** 91 Heng Yang Rd, Taipei 100; tel. (2) 23613000; fax (2) 23612046; e-mail dp092@ctnbank.com.tw; internet www .cntbank.com.tw; f. 1907; fmrly Bank of Communications; 60.4% govt-owned; cap. 18,000m., dep. 212,070m. (June 1999); Chair. PATRICK C. J. LIANG; Pres. Dr CHAO CHIEH-CHIEN; 34 brs, incl. 2 overseas.

**Export-Import Bank:** 8th Floor, 3 Nan Hai Rd, Taipei 100; tel. (2) 23210511; fax (2) 23940630; e-mail eximbank@eximbank.com.tw; internet www.eximbank.com.tw; f. 1979; cap. 10,000m., dep. 8,487m. (Dec. 1998); Chair. WEN LIN-CHEN; Pres. PAULINE FU; 2 brs.

**Farmers Bank of China:** 85 Nanking East Rd, Sec. 2, Taipei 10408; tel. (2) 25517141; fax (2) 25622162; internet www .farmerbank.com.tw; f. 1933; cap. 9,000m., dep. 389,294m. (June 1999); Chair. MU-TSAI CHEN; Pres. C. C. HUANG; 74 brs.

**International Commercial Bank of China:** 100 Chi Lin Rd, Taipei 10424; tel. (2) 25633156; fax (2) 25632614; e-mail service@ icbc.com.tw; internet www.icbc.com.tw/; f. 1912; cap. 27,334m., dep. 383,847m. (May 1999); Chair. LEE YUNG-SAM; Pres. SHUE-SHENG WANG; 82 brs, incl. 18 overseas.

**Land Bank of Taiwan:** 46 Kuan Chien Rd, Taipei 10038; tel. (2) 23483456; fax (2) 23819548; e-mail lbot@mail.landbank.com.tw; internet www.landbank.com.tw; f. 1946; cap. 25,000m., dep. 1,216,411m. (June 1999); Chair. DONALD T. CHEN; Pres. LIN PONG-LONG; 108 brs.

**Taiwan Co-operative Bank:** POB 33, 77 Kuan Chien Rd, Taipei 10038; tel. (2) 23118811; fax (2) 23316567; e-mail tacbid01@14 .hinet.net; internet www.tcb-bank.com.tw; f. 1946; acts as central bank for co-operatives, and as major agricultural credit institution; cap. 18,900m., dep. 1,414,949m. (June 1998); Chair. W. H. LEE; Pres. MCKINNEY Y. C. TSAI; 142 brs.

### Commercial Banks

**Asia Pacific Bank:** 66 Minchuan Rd, Taichung; tel. (4) 2272458; fax (4) 2265110; e-mail service@apacbank.com.tw; internet www .apacbank.com.tw; f. 1992; cap. 11,366m., dep. 107,181m. (May 1999); Chair. CHIOU JIA-SHYONG; Pres. CHARNG GENG-HWANG; 35 brs.

**Bank of Kaohsiung:** 168 Po Ai 2nd Rd, Kaohsiung; tel. (7) 3480583; fax (7) 3478392; e-mail service@mail.bok.com.tw; internet www .bok.com.tw; f. 1982; cap. 4,487m., dep. 109,289m. (May 1999); Chair. JEROME J. CHEN; Pres. WAYNE CHEN; 32 brs.

**Bank of Overseas Chinese:** 8 Hsiang Yang Rd, Taipei 10014; tel. (2) 23715181; fax (2) 23814056; internet www.booc.com.tw; f. 1961; cap. 16,752m., dep. 216,104m. (May 1999); Chair. LININ DAY; Pres. RICHARD L. C. CHERN; 52 brs.

**Bank of Panhsin:** 18 Cheng Tu St, Pan Chiao City, Taipei; tel. (2) 29629170; fax (2) 29572011; f. 1997; cap. 6,000m., dep. 71,444m. (June 1999); Chair. L. P. HUI; Pres. JAMES J. C. CHEN; 27 brs.

**Bank SinoPac:** 9-1, Chien Kuo North Rd, Sec. 2, Taipei; tel. (2) 25082288; fax (2) 25083456; f. 1992; cap. 15,189m., dep. 144,235m. (March 1999); Chair. L. S. LIN; Pres. PAUL C. Y. LO; 25 brs.

**Bao-Dao Commercial Bank:** 10 Chung King S. Rd, Sec. 1, Taipei; tel. (2) 25615888; fax (2) 25219889; f. 1992; cap. 10,815m., dep. 136,896m. (May 1999); Chair. CHEN CHUN-KUAN; Pres. T. H. CHUNG; 24 brs.

**Central Trust of China:** 49 Wu Chang St, Sec. 1, Taipei 10006; tel. (2) 23111511; fax (2) 23118107; e-mail ctc17001@ctc.com.tw; internet www.ctoc.com.tw; f. 1935; cap. 8,000m., dep. 136,694m. (May 1999); Chair. CHANG YU-HUI; Pres. LIN CHING-HSIEN; 20 brs.

**Chang Hwa Commercial Bank Ltd:** 38 Tsuyu Rd, Sec. 2, Taichung 40010; tel. (4) 2222001; fax (4) 2231170; e-mail ChangBK@ms8.Hinetnet; internet www.ccb.com.tw; f. 1905; 27.7% govt-owned; cap. 29,492m., dep. 732,455m. (April 1999); Chair. MOU HSING-TSAI; Pres. CHIUNG SHIN-WU; 155 brs, 7 overseas.

**Chinatrust Commercial Bank:** 3 Sung Shou Rd, Taipei; tel. (2) 27222002; fax (2) 27233872; internet www.chinatrust.com.tw; f. 1966; cap. 34,002m., dep. 435,137m. (Sept. 1999); Chair. JEFFREY L. S. KOO; 35 brs, 13 overseas.

**The Chinese Bank:** 68 Nanking East Rd, Sec. 3, Taipei; tel. (2) 25168686; fax (2) 25170797; internet www.chinesebank.com.tw; f. 1992; dep. 151,620m. (Dec. 1998); Chair. WANG YOU-THENG; Pres. CHEN FEN; 33 brs.

**Chinfon Commercial Bank:** 1 Nanyang St, Taipei 100; tel. (2) 23114881; fax (2) 23141068; f. 1971; cap 11,128m., dep. 134,307m. (May 1999); Chair. HUANG SHI-HUI; Pres HOWARD J. S. LIN; 34 brs, 2 overseas.

**Chung Shing Bank:** 228–230 Sung Chiang Rd, Taipei; tel. (2) 25616601; fax (2) 25114389; internet www.csbank.com.tw; f. 1992; cap. 15,096m., dep. 154,083m. (May 1999); Chair. Y. Y. WANG; Pres. ABEL S. WANG; 25 brs.

**Cosmos Bank:** 39 Tun Hua South Rd, Sec. 2, Taipei; tel. (2) 27011777; fax (2) 27541742; e-mail ibd@cosmosbank.com.tw; internet www.cosmosbank.com.tw; f. 1992; cap. 13,375m., dep. 158,451m. (May 1999); Chair. HSUI SHENG-FA; Pres. C. C. HU; 35 brs.

**COTA Commercial Bank:** 32-1 Kung Yuan Rd, Taichung; tel. (4) 2245161; fax (4) 2275237; f. 1999; cap. 3,183m., dep. 51,844m. (June 1999); Chair. CHUN TZE-LIAO; Pres JUN-CHUN WANG; 15 brs.

**Da Chong Bank:** 58 Chungcheng 2nd Rd, Kaohsiung; tel. (7) 2242220; fax (7) 2241620; f. 1992; cap. 13,563m., dep. 139,459m. (May 1999); Chair. CHEN TIEN-MAO; Pres. P. W. CHANG; 38 brs.

**Dah An Commercial Bank:** 117 Ming Sheng East Rd, Sec. 3, Taipei; tel. (2) 27126666; fax (2) 27197415; e-mail A804@mail.dab .com.tw; internet www.dab.com.tw; f. 1992; cap. 14,664m., dep. 142,222m. (Dec. 1998); Chair. J. K. LOH; Pres. KENG PING; 35 brs.

**E. Sun Commercial Bank:** 77 Wuchang St, Sec. 1, Taipei; tel. (2) 23891313; fax (2) 23125182; internet www.esunbank.com.tw;

f. 1992; cap. 15,610m., dep. 179,970m. (Oct. 1999); Chair. LIN JONG-SHONG; Pres. HUANG YUNG-JEN; 41 brs.

**En Tie Commercial Bank:** 3rd Floor, 158 Ming Sheng East Rd, Sec. 3, Taipei; tel. (2) 27189999; fax (2) 27175940; f. 1993; cap. 13,377m., dep. 143,567m. (Dec. 1998); Chair. YU-LIN LIN; Pres. CHENG-DER LIU; 39 brs.

**Far Eastern International Bank:** 27th Floor, 207 Tun Hua South Rd, Sec. 2, Taipei; tel. (2) 23786868; fax (2) 23765691; e-mail 800@mail.feib.com.tw; internet www.feib.com.tw; f. 1992; cap. 14,797m., dep. 114,200m. (June 1999); Chair. DOUGLAS T. HSU; Pres. ELI HONG; 33 brs.

**First Commercial Bank:** POB 395, 30 Chungking South Rd, Sec. 1, Taipei; tel. (2) 23481111; fax (2) 23610036; e-mail io77a@mail.firstbank.com.tw; internet www.firstbank.com.tw; f. 1899; 39.50% govt-owned; cap. 27,367m., dep. 968,313m. (June 1998); Chair. T. L. HUANG; Pres. A. C. CHEN; 150 brs, 10 overseas.

**Fubon Commercial Bank:** 2nd Floor, 169 Jen Ai Rd, Sec. 4, Taipei; tel. (2) 27716699; fax (2) 27730763; internet www.fubonbank.com.tw; f. 1992; cap. 18,481m., dep. 164,112m. (Dec. 1998); Chair. CHUN S. YU; Pres. WANG CHUAN-HSI; 33 brs.

**Grand Commercial Bank:** 17 Chengteh Rd, Sec. 1, Taipei; tel. (2) 25562088; fax (2) 25561579; e-mail gcb8405@ms2.hinet.net; internet www.grandbank.com.tw; f. 1991; cap. 14,222m., dep. 130,356m. (May 1999); Chair. KAO CHIH-YEN; Pres. and Man. Dir ALEXANDER T. Y. DEAN; 34 brs.

**Hsinchu International Bank:** 106 Chung Yang Rd, Hsinchu 300; tel. (3) 5245131; fax (3) 5250977; f. 1948; cap. 11,514m., dep. 240,252m. (June 1999); Chair. S. Y. CHAN; Pres C. W. WU; 74 brs.

**Hua Nan Commercial Bank Ltd:** POB 989, 38 Chungking South Rd, Sec. 1, Taipei; tel. (2) 23713111; fax (2) 23711972; e-mail service@ms.hncb.com.tw; internet www.hncb.com.tw; f. 1919; cap. 25,605m., dep. 671,894m. (May 1998); Chair. EDWARD H. T. CHIEN; Pres. BSU THE-NAN; 154 brs, 5 overseas.

**Hwa Tai Commercial Bank:** 246 Chang An E. Rd, Sec. 2, Taipei; tel. (2) 27525252; fax (2) 27711495; f. 1999; cap. 3,300m., dep. 49,212m. (June 1999); Chair. M. H. LIN; Pres. S. Y. WU: 20 brs.

**International Bank of Taipei:** 36 Nanking East Rd, Sec. 3, Taipei; tel. (2) 25063333; fax (2) 25062462; e-mail 630@ibtpe.com.tw; internet www.ibtpe.com.tw; f. 1948; cap. 13,900m., dep. 233,207m. (April 1999); Chair. S. C. HO; Pres. K. C. YU; 82 brs.

**Kao Shin Commercial Bank:** 75 Lih Wen Rd, Kaohsiung; tel. (7) 3460711; fax (7) 3502980; f. 1997; cap. 2,300m., dep. 50,254m. (June 1999); Chair. C. N. HUANG; Pres. F. T. CHAO; 29 brs.

**Lucky Bank:** 35 Chung Hua Rd, Sec. 1, Taichung 403; tel. (4) 2259111; fax (4) 2232652; f. 1997; cap. 3,000m., dep. 69,578m. (June 1999); Chair. C. C. CHANG; Pres. T. Y. SU; 27 brs.

**Makoto Bank:** 134 Hsi Chang St, Taipei; tel. (2) 23812160; fax (2) 23880828; f. 1997; cap. 4,118m., dep. 111,531m. (June 1999); Chair. C. I. LIN; Pres. SHERMAN CHUANG; 49 brs.

**Pan Asia Bank:** 3rd–4th Floors, 60-8 Chungkang Rd, Taichung; tel. (4) 3171234; fax (4) 3147934; e-mail pabkdbu@ms4.hinet.net; internet www.panasiabank.com.tw; f. 1992; cap. 14,700m., dep. 136,174m. (May 1999); Chair. KOH FEI-LO; Pres. YIN YI-NA; 39 brs.

**Shanghai Commercial and Savings Bank Ltd:** 2 Min Chuan East Rd, Sec. 1, Taipei 104; tel. (2) 25817111; fax (2) 25671921; internet www.scsb.com.tw; f. 1915; cap. 9,000m., dep. 228,653m. (May 1999); Chair. H. C. YUNG; Pres. C. S. CHOU; 51 brs.

**Sunny Bank:** 88 Shin Pai Rd, Sec. 1, Taipei 112; tel. (2) 28208166; fax (2) 28233414; f. 1997; cap. 3,000m., dep. 77,827m. (June 1999); Chair. S. H. CHEN; Pres. C. W. CHEN; 23 brs.

**Taichung Commercial Bank:** 45 Min Tsu Rd, POB 108, Taichung 400; tel. (4) 22360021; fax (4) 2240748; e-mail webmaster@ms1.tcbbank.com.tw; internet www.tcbbank.com.tw; f. 1953; cap. 15,380m., dep. 191,919m. (June 1999); Chair. Y. F. TSAI; Pres. Y. C. TSAI; 78 brs.

**Taipeibank:** 50 Chung Shan North Rd, Sec. 2, Taipei 10419; tel. (2) 25425656; fax (2) 25428870; e-mail 0180@mail.taipeibank.com.tw; internet www.taipeibank.com.tw; f. 1969; fmrly City Bank of Taipei; cap. 14,000m., dep. 466,765m. (June 1999); Chair. C. C. LIAO; Pres. JESSE Y. DING ; 71 brs, 1 overseas.

**Taishin International Bank:** 44 Chung Shan North Rd, Sec. 2, Taipei; tel. (2) 25683988; fax (2) 25234564; internet www.taishinbank.com.tw; f. 1992; cap. 13,680m., dep. 162,934m. (May 1999); Chair. THOMAS T. L. WU; Pres. JULIUS H. C. CHEN; 24 brs.

**Union Bank of Taiwan:** 109 Ming Sheng East Rd, Sec. 3, Taipei; tel. (2) 27180001; fax (2) 27137515; e-mail 014_0199@email.ubot.com.tw; internet www.ubot.com.tw; f. 1992; cap. 13,615m., dep. 134,133m. (May 1999); Chair. C. C. HUANG; Pres. S. C. LEE; 29 brs.

**United World Chinese Commercial Bank:** 65 Kuan Chien Rd, POB 1670, Taipei 10038; tel. (2) 23125555; fax (2) 23311093; e-mail ho8p@uwccb.com.tw; internet www.uwccb.com.tw; f. 1975; cap. 27,052m., dep. 439,510m. (May 1999); Chair. IRWINE W. HO; Pres. GREGORY K. H. WANG; 66 brs.

There are also a number of Medium Business Banks throughout the country.

### Community Financial System

The community financial institutions include both credit co-operatives and credit departments of farmers' and fishermen's associations. These local financial institutions focus upon providing savings and loan services for the community. At the end of 1998 there were 54 credit co-operatives, 287 credit departments of farmers' associations and 27 credit departments of fishermen's associations, with a combined total deposit balance of NT $2,414,001m., or 14.95% of the market share, while outstanding loans amounted to NT $1,160,137m., or 10.57% of the market share.

### Foreign Banks

In April 1998 45 foreign banks maintained 72 branches in Taiwan.

## STOCK EXCHANGE

In January 1991 the stock exchange was opened to direct investment by foreign institutions, and in March 1996 it was also opened to direct investment by foreign individuals. By the end of June 1999 404 foreign institutional investors had been approved to invest in the local securities market. Various liberalization measures have been introduced since 1994. In March 1999 the limits on both single and aggregate foreign investment in domestic shares were raised to 50% of the outstanding shares of a listed company.

**Taiwan Stock Exchange Corpn:** 13th Floor, 17 Po Ai Rd, Taipei 100; tel. (2) 23485678; fax (2) 23485324; f. 1962; Chair. C. Y. LEE.

### Supervisory Body

**Securities and Futures Commission:** 85 Hsin Sheng South Rd, Sec. 1, Taipei; tel. (2) 287734202; fax (2) 28734134; Chair. LIN TZONG-YEONG; Sec.-Gen. NING KOU-HUEI.

## INSURANCE

In 1993 the Ministry of Finance issued eight new insurance licences, the first for more than 30 years. Two more were issued in 1994.

**Allianz President Life Insurance Co Ltd:** 12–14/F, 69 Ming-Sheng East Rd, Sec. 3, Taipei; tel. (2) 25151888; fax (2) 25151777; e-mail azpl@ms2.seeder.net; internet www.espl.com.tw; f. 1995; Chair. NAN-TEN CHUNG; Gen. Man. NICHOLAS CHANG.

**Cathay Life Insurance Co Ltd:** 296 Jen Ai Rd, Sec. 4, Taipei 10650; tel. (2) 27551399; fax (2) 27551322; f. 1962; Chair. TSAI HONG-TU; Gen. Man. DAVID K. H. FAN.

**Central Insurance Co Ltd:** 6 Chung Hsiao West Rd, Sec. 1, Taipei; tel. (2) 23819910; fax (2) 23116901; f. 1962; Chair. H. K. SHE; Gen. Man. C. C. HUANG.

**Central Reinsurance Corpn:** 53 Nanking East Rd, Sec. 2, Taipei; tel. (2) 25115211; fax (2) 25235350; f. 1968; Chair. C. K. LIU; Pres. C. T. YANG.

**Central Trust of China, Life Insurance Dept:** 3rd–8th Floors, 69 Tun Hua South Rd, Sec. 2, Taipei; tel. (2) 27849151; fax (2) 27052214; f. 1941; life insurance; Pres. EDWARD LO; Man. S. TSAU.

**China Life Insurance Co Ltd:** Taipei; tel. (2) 27196678; fax (2) 27125966; f. 1963; Chair. C. F. KOO; Gen. Man. CHESTER C. Y. KOO.

**China Mariners' Assurance Corpn Ltd:** 11th Floor, 2 Kuan Chien Rd, Taipei; tel. (2) 23757676; fax (2) 23756363; f. 1948; Chair. K. S. FAN; Gen. Man. VINCENT M. S. FAN.

**Chinfon Life Insurance Co Ltd:** 12th Floor, 550 Chung Hsiao East Rd, Sec. 4, Taipei; tel. (2) 27582727; fax (2) 27586758; f. 1962; fmrly First Life Insurance Co; 57.8% interest bought by Prudential Corpn 1999; Chair. C. Y. CHENG; Gen. Man. C. S. TU.

**Chung Kuo Insurance Co Ltd:** 10th–12th Floors, ICBC Bldg, 100 Chilin Rd, Taipei 10424; tel. (2) 25513345; fax (2) 25414046; f. 1931; fmrly China Insurance Co Ltd; Chair. J. T. LEE; Pres. S. N. TAUNG.

**Chung Shing Life Insurance Co Ltd:** 18th Floor, 200 Keelung Rd, Sec. 1, Taipei 110; tel. (2) 27583099; fax (2) 23451635; f. 1993; Chair. T. H. CHAO; Gen. Man. TERRY W. Y. CHEN.

**The First Insurance Co Ltd:** 54 Chung Hsiao East Rd, Sec. 1, Taipei; tel. (2) 23913271; fax (2) 23930685; f. 1962; Chair. C. H. LEE; Gen. Man. M. C. CHEN.

**Fubon Insurance Co Ltd:** 237 Chien Kuo South Rd, Sec. 1, Taipei; tel. (2) 27067890; fax (2) 27042915; f. 1961; Chair. TSAI MING-CHUNG; Gen. Man. T. M. SHIH.

**Fubon Life Insurance Co Ltd:** 237 Chien Kuo South Rd, Sec. 1, Ta-an District, Taipei; tel. (2) 27067890; fax (2) 27042915; f. 1993; Chair. RICHARD M. TSAI; Gen. Man. Y. Y. HO.

**Global Life Insurance Co Ltd:** 502 San Ho St, Sec. 2, Peitou, Taipei 11235; tel. (2) 8967899; fax (2) 8958312; f. 1993; Chair. JOHN TSENG; Gen. Man. ROBERT KUO.

**Hung Fu Life Insurance Co Ltd:** 7th Floor, 70 Cheng Teh Rd, Sec. 1, Taipei; tel. (2) 25595151; fax (2) 25562840; f. 1994; Chair. ROBERT CHEN; Gen. Man. HIRO TSEN.

**Kuo Hua Insurance Co Ltd:** 166 Chang An East Rd, Sec. 2, Taipei; tel. (2) 27514225; fax (2) 27819388; e-mail kh11601@kuohua.com.tw; internet www.kuohua.com.tw; f. 1962; Chair. and Gen. Man. J. B. WANG.

**Kuo Hua Life Insurance Co Ltd:** 42 Chung Shan North Rd, Sec. 2, Taipei; tel. (2) 25621101; fax (2) 25374083; internet www.khl.com.tw; f. 1963; Chair. JASON CHANG; Gen. Man. CHEN TUNG-CHENG.

**Mercuries Life Insurance Co Ltd:** 6th Floor, 2 Lane 150, Sin-Yi Rd, Sec. 5, Taipei; tel. (2) 23455511; fax (2) 23456616; f. 1993; Chair. GEORGE C. S. WONG; Gen. Man. STEVE WANG.

**Mingtai Fire and Marine Insurance Co Ltd:** 1 Jen Ai Rd, Sec. 4, Taipei; tel. (2) 27725678; fax (2) 27729932; f. 1961; Chair. LARRY P. C. LIN; Pres. H. T. CHEN.

**Nan Shan Life Insurance Co Ltd:** 144 Min Chuan East Rd, Sec. 2, Taipei 104; tel. (2) 25013333; fax (2) 25012555; internet www.nanshanlife.com.tw; f. 1963; Chair. EDMUND TSE; Pres. SUNNY LIN.

**Shin Fu Life Insurance Co Ltd:** 6th Floor, 123 Chung Hsiao East Rd, Sec. 2, Taipei; tel. (2) 23563921; fax (2) 23563927; f. 1993; Chair. M. H. KAO; Gen. Man. NING HAI JIN.

**Shin Kong Fire and Marine Insurance Co Ltd:** 7th–12th Floors, 13 Chien Kuo North Rd, Sec. 2, Taipei; tel. (2) 25075335; fax (2) 25074580; f. 1963; Chair. ANTHONY T. S. WU; Pres. Y. H. CHANG.

**Shin Kong Life Insurance Co Ltd:** 66 Chung Hsiao West Rd, Sec. 1, Taipei; tel. (2) 23895858; fax (2) 23758688; f. 1963; Chair. EUGENE T. C. WU; Gen. Man. C. M. SU.

**Shinung Life Insurance Co Ltd:** 11-2F, 155 Tsu Chih St, Taichung; tel. (4) 3721653; fax (4) 3722008; f. 1993; Chair. YANG WEN-BEN; Gen. Man. P. T. LAI.

**South China Insurance Co Ltd:** 5th Floor, 560 Chung Hsiao East Rd, Sec. 4, Taipei; tel. and fax (2) 27298022. 1963; Chair. C. F. LIAO; Pres. ALLAN I. R. HUANG.

**Tai Ping Insurance Co Ltd:** 3rd–5th Floors, 550 Chung Hsiao East Rd, Sec. 4, Taipei; tel. (2) 27582700; fax (2) 27295681; f. 1929; Chair. T. C. CHEN; Gen. Man. T. Y. TUNG.

**Taian Insurance Co Ltd:** 59 Kwantsien Rd, Taipei; tel. (2) 23819678; fax (2) 23315332; f. 1961; Chair. C. H. CHEN; Gen. Man. PATRICK S. LEE.

**Taiwan Fire and Marine Insurance Co Ltd:** 49 Kuan Chien Rd, Taipei; tel. (2) 23317261; fax (2) 23145287; f. 1946; Chair. HSU HUNG-CHIH; Gen. Man. JOHN F. KAO.

**Taiwan Life Insurance Co Ltd:** 16th–19th Floors, 17 Hsu Chang St, Taipei; tel. (2) 23116411; fax (2) 23710854; e-mail tlib411@ms2.hinet.net; internet www.tpg.gov.tw/tli/defaulthtm; f. 1947; Chair. CHUNG-HSIUNG TSAI; Pres. CHENG-TAO LIN.

**Union Insurance Co Ltd:** 12th Floor, 219 Chung Hsiao East Rd, Sec. 4, Taipei; tel. (2) 27765567; fax (2) 27737199; f. 1963; Chair. S. H. CHIN; Gen. Man. FRANK S. WANG.

**Zurich Insurance Taiwan Ltd:** 56 Tun Hua North Rd, Taipei; tel. (2) 27752888; fax (2) 27416004; f. 1961; Chair. and Gen. Man. CHARLES C. T. WANG.

In 1995 there were 26 foreign insurance companies operating in Taiwan.

# Trade and Industry

## GOVERNMENT AGENCIES

**Board of Foreign Trade (Ministry of Economic Affairs):** 1 Houkow St, Taipei; tel. (2) 23510271; fax (2) 23513603; Dir-Gen. CHEN RUEY-LONG.

**Council of Agriculture (COA):** 37 Nan Hai Rd, Taipei 100; tel. (2) 23812991; fax (2) 23310341; e-mail webmaster@www.coa.gov.tw; f. 1984; govt agency directly under the Executive Yuan, with ministerial status; a policy-making body in charge of national agriculture, forestry, fisheries, the animal industry and food administration; promotes technology and provides external assistance; Chair. Dr PENG TSO-KWEI; Sec.-Gen. Dr HUANG CHIN-RONG.

**Industrial Development Bureau (Ministry of Economic Affairs):** 41-3 Hsin Yi Rd, Sec. 3, Taipei; tel. (2) 27541255; fax (2) 27043784; Dir-Gen. WANG YA-KANG.

**Industrial Development and Investment Center (Ministry of Economic Affairs):** 19th Floor, 4 Chung Hsiao West Rd, Sec. 1, Taipei; tel. (2) 23892111; fax (2) 23820497; e-mail njlin@mail.idic.gov.tw; internet www.idic.gov.tw; f. 1959 to assist investment and planning; Dir-Gen. LIN NENG-JONG.

## CHAMBER OF COMMERCE

**General Chamber of Commerce of the Republic of China:** 6th Floor, 390 Fu Hsing South Rd, Sec. 1, Taipei; tel. (2) 27012671; fax (2) 27542107; f. 1946; 39 mems, incl. 14 nat. feds of trade asscns, 22 district export asscns and 3 district chambers of commerce; Chair. Dr Y. T. WANG; Sec.-Gen. CHIU JAW-SHIN.

## INDUSTRIAL AND TRADE ASSOCIATIONS

**China External Trade Development Council:** 4th–8th Floors, CETRA Tower, 333 Keelung Rd, Sec. 1, Taipei 110; tel. (2) 27255200; fax (2) 27576653; trade promotion body; Sec.-Gen. RICKY Y. S. KAO.

**China Productivity Center:** 2nd Floor, 79 Hsin Tai 5 Rd, Sec. 1, Hsichih, Taipei County; tel. (2) 26982989; fax (2) 26982976; f. 1956; management, technology, training, etc.; Pres. CHEN MING-CHANG.

**Chinese National Association of Industry and Commerce:** 13th Floor, 390 Fu Hsing South Rd, Sec. 1, Taipei; tel. (2) 27070111; fax (2) 27017601; Chair. JEFFREY L. S. KOO.

**Chinese National Federation of Industries (CNFI):** 12th Floor, 390 Fu Hsing South Rd, Sec. 1, Taipei; tel. (2) 27033500; fax (2) 27033982; f. 1948; 136 mem. asscns; Chair. KAO CHIN-YUAN; Sec.-Gen. HO CHUN-YIH.

**Taiwan Handicraft Promotion Centre:** 1 Hsu Chou Rd, Taipei; tel. (2) 23933655; fax (2) 23937330; f. 1956; Pres. Y. C. WANG.

**Trading Department of Central Trust of China:** 49 Wuchang St, Sec. 1, Taipei 10006; tel. (2) 23111511; fax (2) 23821047; f. 1935; export and import agent for private and govt-owned enterprises.

## UTILITIES

### Electricity

**Taiwan Power Co (Taipower):** 242 Roosevelt Rd, Sec. 3, Taipei 100; tel. (2) 3967777; fax (2) 3968593; e-mail service@taipower.com.tw; internet www.taipower.com.tw; f. 1946; electricity generation; scheduled for privatization from 2001; Chair. S. C. HSI; Pres. J. H. KUO.

### Gas

**The Great Taipei Gas Corpn:** 5th Floor, 35 Kwang Fu North Rd, Taipei; tel. (2) 27684999; fax (2) 27630480; supply of gas and gas equipment.

### Water

**Taipei Water Dept:** 131 Changxing St, Taipei; tel. (2) 7352141; fax (2) 7353185; f. 1907; responsible for water supply in Taipei and suburban areas; Commr LIN WEN-YUAN.

## CO-OPERATIVES

In December 1998 there were 5,375 co-operatives, with a total membership of 5,956,014 and total capital of NT $46,000m. Of the specialized co-operatives the most important was the consumers' co-operative (4,482 co-ops).

The Co-operative League (f. 1940) is a national organization responsible for co-ordination, education and training and the movement's national and international interests (Chair. K. L. CHEN).

## TRADE UNIONS

**Chinese Federation of Labour:** 11th Floor, Back Bldg, 201–18 Tun Hua North Rd, Taipei; tel. (2) 27135111; fax (2) 27135116; e-mail cfllabor@ms10.hinet.net; f. 1958; mems: c. 3,154 unions representing 2,938,446 workers; Pres. LEE CHENG-CHONG.

### National Federations

**Chinese Federation of Postal Workers:** 9th Floor, 45 Chungking South Rd, Sec. 2, Taipei 100; tel. (2) 23921380; fax (2) 23414510; e-mail cfpw@ms16.hinet.net; f. 1930; 27,957 mems; Pres. CHEN SHIAN-JUH.

**Chinese Federation of Railway Workers Union:** Room 6048, 6th Floor, 3 Peiping West Rd, Taipei; tel. (2) 23815226; fax (2) 23831523; f. 1947; 17,129 mems; Pres. LIN HUI-KUAN.

**National Chinese Seamen's Union:** 8th Floor, 25 Nanking East Rd, Sec. 3, Taipei; tel. (2) 25150259; fax (2) 25078211; f. 1913; 22,588 mems; Pres. CHANG KAI-FENG.

### Regional Federations

**Taiwan Federation of Textile and Dyeing Industry Workers' Unions (TFTDWU):** 2 Lane 64, Chung Hsiao East Rd, Sec. 2, Taipei; tel. (2) 23415627; f. 1958; 11,906 mems; Chair. CHANG MING-KEN.

**Taiwan Provincial Federation of Labour:** 11th Floor, 44 Roosevelt Rd, Sec. 2, Taipei; tel. and fax (2) 23938080; f. 1948; 81 mem. unions and 1,571,826 mems; Pres. WU HAI-RAY; Sec.-Gen. HUANG YAO-TUNG.

# Transport

## RAILWAYS

**Taiwan Railway Administration (TRA):** 3 Peiping West Rd, Taipei 10026; tel. (2) 23815226; fax (2) 23831367; f. 1891; a public utility under the provincial govt of Taiwan; operates both the west line and east line systems, with a route length of 1,103.7 km, of which 497.5 km are electrified; the west line is the main trunk line from Keelung, in the north, to Fangliao, in the south, with several branches; electrification of the main trunk line was completed in 1979; the east line runs along the east coast, linking Hualien with Taitung; the north link line, with a length of 79.2 km from Suao Sing to Hualien, connecting Suao and Hualien, was opened in 1980; the south link line, with a length of 98.2 km from Taitung Shin to Fangliao, opened in late 1991, completing the round-the-island system; construction of a high-speed link between Taipei and Kaohsiung (345 km) was scheduled for completion in 2003; Man. Dir T. P. CHEN.

There are also 1,440 km of private narrow-gauge track, operated by the Taiwan Sugar Corpn in conjunction with the Taiwan Forestry Bureau and other organizations. These railroads are mostly used for freight, but they also offer a limited public passenger service.

Construction of a five-line, 86.8-km, mass rapid-transit system (MRTS) in Taipei, incorporating links to the airport, began in 1987. The first 10.9km section of the Mucha line opened in March 1996 and the Tamshui line (22.8 km) opened in December 1997. The remainder of the network was scheduled for completion by 2005. A 42.7-km system is planned for Kaohsiung, scheduled for completion in the year 2006. MRT systems are also projected for Taoyuan, Hsinchu, Taichung and Tainan.

## ROADS

There were 20,222 km of highways in 1998, most of them asphalt-paved. The Sun Yat-sen (North–South) Freeway was completed in 1978. Construction of a 505-km Second Freeway, which is to extend to Pingtung, in southern Taiwan, began in July 1987 and was scheduled to be completed by the end of 2003. Work on the Taipei–Ilan freeway began in 1991.

**Taiwan Area National Expressway Bureau:** 1 Lane 1, Hoping East Rd, Sec. 3, Taipei; tel. (2) 27078808; fax (2) 27017818; f. 1946; responsible for planning, design, construction and maintenance of provincial and county highways and administration of motor vehicles and drivers; Dir-Gen. CHENG WEN-LON.

**Taiwan Area National Freeway Bureau:** POB 75, Sinchwang, Taipei 242; tel. (2) 29096141; fax (2) 29093218; internet www.freeway.gov.tw; f. 1970; Dir-Gen. HO NUAN-HSUAN.

**Taiwan Motor Transport Co Ltd:** 5th Floor, 17 Hsu Chang St, Taipei; tel. (2) 23715364; fax (2) 23820664; f. 1980; operates national bus service; Gen. Man. CHEN WU-SHIUNG.

## SHIPPING

Taiwan has five international ports: Kaohsiung, Keelung, Taichung, Hualien and Suao. In 1998 the merchant fleet comprised 686 vessels, with a total displacement of 5,491,718 grt.

**Evergreen Marine Corpn:** 166 Ming Sheng East Rd, Sec. 2, Taipei 104; tel. (2) 25057766; fax (2) 25055256; f. 1968; world-wide container liner services; Indian subcontinent feeder service; two-way round-the-world services; Chair. LING SENG-SAN; Pres. GEORGE HSU.

**Taiwan Navigation Co Ltd:** 29, Chi Nan Rd, Sec. 2, Taipei; tel. (2) 23941769; Chair. J. M. MA; Pres. I. Y. CHANG.

**U-Ming Marine Transport Corpn:** 29th Floor, Taipei Metro Tower, 207 Tun Hua South Rd, Sec. 2, Taipei; tel. (2) 27338000; fax (2) 27359900; world-wide tramp services; Chair. D. T. HSU; Pres. C. S. CHEN.

**Uniglory Marine Corpn:** 6th Floor, 172 Ming Sheng East Rd, Sec. 2, Taipei; tel. (2) 25016711; fax (2) 25017592; Chair. LOH YAO-FON; Pres. LEE MUN-CHI.

**Wan Hai Lines Ltd:** 10th Floor, 136 Sung Chiang Rd, Taipei; tel. (2) 25677961; fax (2) 25216000; f. 1965; regional container liner services; Chair. CHAO CHUAN CHEN; Pres. T. S. CHEN.

**Yang Ming Marine Transport Corpn (Yang Ming Line):** 271 Ming de 1st Rd, Chidu, Keelung 206; tel. (2) 24559988; fax (2) 24559958; e-mail winsor@imail.yml.com.tw; internet www.yml.com.tw; f. 1972; world-wide container liner services, bulk carrier and supertanker services; Chair. T. H. CHEN; Pres. FRANK F. H. LU.

## CIVIL AVIATION

There are two international airports, Chiang Kai-shek at Taoyuan, near Taipei, which opened in 1979 (a second passenger terminal and expansion of freight facilities being scheduled for completion by 2000), and Hsiaokang, in Kaohsiung (where an international terminal building was inaugurated in 1997). There are also 14 domestic airports.

**Civil Aeronautics Administration:** 340 Tun Hua North Rd, Taipei; tel. (2) 23496000; fax (2) 23496277; e-mail gencaa@ms31.hinet.net; Dir-Gen. Dr CHANG YU-HERN.

**China Air Lines Ltd (CAL):** 131 Nanking East Rd, Sec. 3, Taipei; tel. (2) 25062345; fax (2) 25145786; internet www.chinaairlines.com.tw; f. 1959; international services to destinations in the Far East, Europe, the Middle East and the USA; Chair. CHIANG HUNG-I.

**EVA Airways:** Eva Air Bldg, 376 Hsin-nan Rd, Sec. 1, Luchu, Taoyuan Hsien; tel. (3) 3515151; fax (3) 3510005; internet www.evaair.com.tw; f. 1989; subsidiary of Evergreen Group; commenced flights in 1991; services to destinations in Asia (incl. Hong Kong and Macau), the Middle East, Europe, North America, Australia and New Zealand; Pres. FRANK HSU.

**Far Eastern Air Transport Corpn (FAT):** 5, Alley 123, Lane 405, Tun Hua North Rd, Taipei 10592; tel. (2) 7121555; fax (2) 7122428; f. 1957; domestic services and international services to Palau and Subic Bay (Philippines); Chair. Capt. Y. L. LEE.

**Mandarin Airlines (AE):** 13th Floor, 134 Ming Sheng East Rd, Sec. 3, Taipei; tel. (2) 7171188; fax (2) 7170716; e-mail mandarin@mandarin-airlines.com; internet www.mandarin-airlines.com; f. 1991; subsidiary of CAL; merged with Formosa Airlines 1998; domestic and Asian services; Chair. CHIANG HUNG-I; Pres. MICHAEL LO.

**TransAsia Airways:** 9th Floor, 139 Chengchou Rd, Taipei; tel. (2) 25575767; fax (2) 25570631; internet www.tna.com.tw; f. 1989; fmrly Foshing Airlines; domestic flights and international services to Macau; Chair. CHARLES C. LIN; Pres. ITOY WANG.

**U-Land Airlines:** 340 Tun Hua North Rd, Taipei; tel. (2) 26981280; fax (2) 26982890; fmrly China Asia Airlines; domestic services; Chair. WANG KER-GER; Pres. TING ZEAN.

**UNI Airways Corpn:** 2-6 Chung Shan 4th Rd, Kaohsiung; tel. (7) 7917611; fax (7) 7917511; internet www.uniair.com.tw; f. 1989; fmrly Makung Airlines; merged with Great China Airlines and Taiwan Airlines 1998; domestic flights and international services (to Kota Kinabalu, Malaysia); Pres. JOSEPH LIN.

# Tourism

The principal tourist attractions are the cuisine, the cultural artefacts and the island scenery. In 1998 there were 2,298,706 visitor arrivals (including 266,895 overseas Chinese) in Taiwan. Receipts from tourism in that year totalled US $3,372m.

**Tourism Bureau, Ministry of Transportation and Communications:** 9th Floor, 290 Chung Hsiao East Rd, Sec. 4, Taipei 106; tel. (2) 23491635; fax (2) 27735487; f. 1966; Dir-Gen. CHANG SHUO-LAO.

**Taiwan Visitors' Association:** 5th Floor, 9 Min Chuan East Rd, Sec. 2, Taipei; tel. (2) 25943261; fax (2) 25943265; f. 1956; promotes domestic and international tourism; Chair. STANLEY C. YEN.

# COLOMBIA

## Introductory Survey

### Location, Climate, Language, Religion, Flag, Capital

The Republic of Colombia lies in the north-west of South America, with the Caribbean Sea to the north and the Pacific Ocean to the west. Its continental neighbours are Venezuela and Brazil to the east, and Peru and Ecuador to the south, while Panama connects it with Central America. The coastal areas have a tropical rain forest climate, the plateaux are temperate, and in the Andes mountains there are areas of permanent snow. The language is Spanish. Almost all of the inhabitants profess Christianity, and about 95% are Roman Catholics. There are small Protestant and Jewish minorities. The national flag (proportions 3 by 2) has three horizontal stripes, of yellow (one-half of the depth) over dark blue over red. The capital is Santafé de Bogotá (formerly Bogotá).

### Recent History

Colombia was under Spanish rule from the 16th century until 1819, when it achieved independence as part of Gran Colombia, which included Ecuador, Panama and Venezuela. Ecuador and Venezuela seceded in 1830, when Colombia (then including Panama) became a separate republic. In 1903 the province of Panama successfully rebelled and became an independent country. For more than a century, ruling power in Colombia has been shared between two political parties, the Conservatives (Partido Conservador Colombiano, PCC) and the Liberals (Partido Liberal Colombiano, PL), whose rivalry has often led to violence. President Laureano Gómez of the PCC, who was elected 'unopposed' in November 1949, ruled as a dictator until his overthrow by a coup in June 1953, when power was seized by Gen. Gustavo Rojas Pinilla. President Rojas established a right-wing dictatorship but, following widespread rioting, he was deposed in May 1957, when a five-man military junta took power. According to official estimates, lawlessness during 1949–58, known as 'La Violencia', caused the deaths of about 280,000 people.

In an attempt to restore peace and stability, the PCC and the PL agreed to co-operate in a National Front. Under this arrangement, the presidency was to be held by the PCC and the PL in rotation, while cabinet portfolios would be divided equally between the two parties and both would have an equal number of seats in each house of the bicameral Congress. In December 1957, in Colombia's first vote on the basis of universal adult suffrage, this agreement was overwhelmingly approved by a referendum and was subsequently incorporated in Colombia's Constitution, dating from 1886.

In May 1958 the first presidential election under the amended Constitution was won by the National Front candidate, Dr Alberto Lleras Camargo, a PL member who had been President in 1945–46. He took office in August 1958, when the ruling junta relinquished power. As provided by the 1957 agreement, he was succeeded by a member of the PCC, Dr Guillermo León Valencia, who was, in turn, succeeded by a PL candidate, Dr Carlos Lleras Restrepo, in 1966.

At the presidential election in April 1970, the National Front candidate, Dr Misael Pastrana Borrero (PCC) narrowly defeated Gen. Rojas, the former dictator, who campaigned as leader of the Alianza Nacional Popular (ANAPO), with policies that had considerable appeal for the poorer sections of the population. At elections to Congress, held simultaneously, the National Front lost its majority in each of the two houses, while ANAPO became the main opposition group in each. The result of the presidential election was challenged by supporters of ANAPO, and an armed wing of the party, the Movimiento 19 de Abril (M-19), began to organize guerrilla activity against the Government. It was joined by dissident members of a pro-Soviet guerrilla group, the Fuerzas Armadas Revolucionarias de Colombia (FARC), established in 1966.

The bipartisan form of government ended formally with the presidential and legislative elections of April 1974, although the 1974–78 Cabinet remained subject to the parity agreement. The PCC and the PL together won an overwhelming majority of seats in Congress, and support for ANAPO was greatly reduced. The presidential election was won by the PL candidate, Dr Alfonso López Michelsen.

At elections to Congress in February 1978, the PL won a clear majority in both houses, and in June the PL candidate, Dr Julio César Turbay Ayala, won the presidential election. President Turbay continued to observe the National Front agreement, and attempted to address the problems of urban terrorism and drugs-trafficking. In 1982 the guerrillas suffered heavy losses after successful counter-insurgency operations, combined with the activities of a new anti-guerrilla group which was associated with drugs-smuggling enterprises, the Muerte a Secuestradores (MAS, Death to Kidnappers), whose targets later became trade union leaders, academics and human rights activists.

At congressional elections in March 1982, the PL maintained its majority in both houses. In May the PCC candidate, Dr Belisario Betancur Cuartas, won the presidential election, benefiting from a division within the PL. President Betancur, who took office in August, declared a broad amnesty for guerrillas in November, reconvened the Peace Commission (first established in 1981) and ordered an investigation into the MAS. An internal pacification campaign, which was begun in November, met with only moderate success. Despite the Peace Commission's successful negotiation of cease-fire agreements with the FARC, the M-19 (now operating as a left-wing guerrilla movement) and the Ejército Popular de Liberación (EPL) during 1984, factions of all three groups which were opposed to the truce continued to conduct guerrilla warfare against the authorities. In May 1984 the Government's campaign for internal peace was severely hampered by the assassination of the Minister of Justice. His murder was regarded as a consequence of his energetic attempts to eradicate the flourishing drugs industry, and Colombia's leading drugs dealers were implicated in the killing. The Government declared a nation-wide state of siege and announced its intention to enforce its hitherto unobserved extradition treaty with the USA.

Relations between the M-19 and the armed forces deteriorated during 1985, and in June the M-19 formally withdrew from the cease-fire agreement. In November a dramatic siege by the M-19 at the Palace of Justice in the capital, during which more than 100 people were killed, resulted in severe public criticism of the Government and the armed forces for their handling of events. Negotiations with the M-19 were suspended indefinitely.

At congressional elections in March 1986, the traditional wing of the PL secured a clear victory over the PCC and obtained 49% of the votes cast. The Unión Patriótica (UP), formed by the FARC in 1985, won seats in both houses. At the presidential election in May, Dr Virgilio Barco Vargas of the PL was elected President, with 58% of the votes cast. The large majority secured by the PL at both elections obliged the PCC to form the first formal opposition to a government for 30 years.

Attempts by the new administration to address the problems of political violence and the cultivation and trafficking of illicit drugs enjoyed little success during 1986–87. Hopes that an indefinite cease-fire agreement, concluded between the FARC and the Government in March 1986, would facilitate the full participation of the UP in the political process were largely frustrated by the Government's failure to respond effectively to a campaign of assassinations of UP members, conducted by paramilitary 'death squads' during 1985–87, which resulted in an estimated 450 deaths. The crisis was compounded in October 1987 by the decision of six guerrilla groups, including the FARC, the Ejército de Liberación Nacional (ELN) and the M-19, to form a joint front, the Coordinadora Guerrillera Simón Bolívar (CGSB). Although in 1987 the Government extended police powers against drugs dealers, its efforts were severely hampered by the Supreme Court's rulings that Colombia's extradition treaty with the USA was unconstitutional.

In mid-1988 the Comisión de Convivencia Democrática (Commission of Democratic Cohabitation) was established, with the aim of holding further meetings between all sides in the internal conflict in Colombia. Moreover, in September President Barco announced a peace initiative, composed of three phases: pacification; transition; and definitive reintegration into the democratic system. Under the plan, the Government was committed to entering into a dialogue with those guerrilla groups that renounced violence and intended to resume civilian life. However, violence continued to escalate, and in December it was estimated that some 18,000 murders had occurred in Colombia in 1988, of which at least 3,600 were attributed to political motives or related to drugs-trafficking.

In January 1989 the Government and the M-19 concluded an agreement to initiate direct dialogue between the Government, all political parties in Congress and the CGSB. In March the M-19 and the Government signed a document providing for the reintegration of the guerrillas into society. In the same month, the ELN, the EPL and the FARC publicly confirmed their willingness to participate in peace talks with the Government; in July the leading guerrilla groups (including the M-19) held a summit meeting, at which they agreed to the formation of a commission, which was to draft proposals for a peace dialogue with the Government. In September the M-19 announced that it had reached agreement with the Government on a peace treaty, under which its members were to demobilize and disarm in exchange for a full pardon. In addition, the movement was to enter the political mainstream; in October the M-19 was formally constituted as a political party, and its leader, Carlos Pizarro León Gómez, was named presidential candidate for the movement. By March 1990 all M-19 guerrilla forces had surrendered their weapons. In exchange for firm commitments from the Barco administration that a referendum would be held to decide the question of constitutional reform and that proposals for comprehensive changes to the electoral law would be introduced in Congress, members of the M-19 were guaranteed a general amnesty, reintegration into civilian life and full political participation in forthcoming elections.

The increasingly destabilizing influence of the drugs cartels, meanwhile, continued to undermine government initiatives. The murder, in August 1989, of a popular PL politician who had been an outspoken critic of the drugs-traffickers, was the latest in a series of assassinations of prominent citizens, ascribed to the drugs cartels of Cali and Medellín, and was widely deplored, prompting President Barco to introduce emergency measures, including the reactivation of Colombia's extradition treaty with the USA. The US administration requested the arrest by the Colombian authorities of 12 leading drugs-traffickers, popularly known as the 'Extraditables', who responded to the USA's request by issuing a declaration of 'total war' against the Government and all journalists, judges and trade unionists opposed to their activities.

At the congressional and municipal elections in March 1990 the PL won 72 of the 114 seats in the Senate and an estimated 60% of the 199 contested seats in the House of Representatives, as well as regaining the important mayorships of Bogotá and Medellín. Ballot papers had also presented the opportunity to vote for the convening of a National Constituent Assembly (a measure which was heavily endorsed) and the selection procedure for the PL's presidential candidate, from which César Gaviria Trujillo emerged as a clear winner.

Bernardo Jaramillo, the presidential candidate of the UP (who had secured the only left-wing seat in the Senate), was assassinated later in March 1990, and in April Carlos Pizarro became the third presidential candidate to be killed by hired assassins since August 1989. Pizarro was replaced by Antonio Navarro Wolff as presidential candidate for the M-19, in conjunction with the recently established Convergencia Democrática (later Alianza Democrática—AD), an alliance of 13 (mainly left-wing) groups and factions. Although responsibility for the murder of Pizarro was officially ascribed to the Medellín drugs cartels (as in the case of Jaramillo), spokesmen representing the cartels strenuously denied the allegations, leading to further speculation that both men had been the victims of political extremists.

A presidential election was held on 27 May 1990. César Gaviria Trujillo of the PL, who had been the most vociferous opponent of the drugs cartels among the surviving candidates, was proclaimed the winner, with 47% of the votes cast, ahead of Alvaro Gómez Hurtado of the conservative Movimiento de Salvación Nacional (MSN), with 24%. Antonio Navarro Wolff of the AD—M-19 received 13% of the votes. Voters were also required to indicate support for, or opposition to, more detailed proposals for the creation of a National Constituent Assembly in a *de facto* referendum held simultaneously. Some 90% of voters indicated their approval of the proposal.

Gaviria's Cabinet, which was announced shortly before his inauguration on 7 August 1990, was described as a cabinet of 'national unity' and comprised seven members of the PL, four of the PCC and, most surprisingly, Navarro Wolff, who was appointed Minister of Public Health. President Gaviria emphasized, however, that the diversity in composition of the Cabinet did not represent the installation of a coalition government. In his inaugural address, Gaviria confirmed his commitment to continuing the strenuous efforts to combat drugs-trafficking, having previously made comprehensive changes to police and military personnel in an apparent attempt to strengthen the Government's resistance to infiltration by the cartels. In October the Government proposed an initiative by which some articles of law would be relaxed and others not invoked (including the extradition treaty) for suspected drugs-traffickers who were prepared to surrender to the authorities. By early 1991 Jorge Luis Ochoa (who narrowly avoided extradition in 1987) and two brothers, members of one of Medellín's most notorious cartels and all sought by US courts for drugs-related offences, had surrendered. In January 1991 the deaths of two hostages, who had been held by the 'Extraditables', threatened to undermine the recent success of the Government's latest initiative.

In October 1990 the creation of the National Constituent Assembly was declared constitutionally acceptable by the Supreme Court, and later in the month Navarro Wolff resigned the health portfolio in order to head the list of candidates representing the AD—M-19 in elections to the Assembly which took place in December. Candidates for the AD—M-19 secured around 27% of the votes cast and 19 of the 70 contested Assembly seats, forcing the ruling PL (with a total of 24 seats) and the Conservatives (with a combined total of 20 seats) to seek support from the AD—M-19 members and seven elected independents for the successful enactment of reform proposals.

In February 1991 the five-month session of the National Constituent Assembly was inaugurated. The composition of the Assembly had been expanded from 70 to 73 members in order to incorporate three invited members of former guerrilla groupings (two from the EPL and one from the Partido Revolucionario de Trabajadores—PRT) and was later expanded further to accommodate a representative of the Comando Quintín Lame. By June a political pact had been negotiated between President Gaviria and representatives of the PL, the AD—M-19 and the MSN, and an agreement was reached that, in order to facilitate the process of political and constitutional renovation, Congress should be dissolved prematurely. The Assembly subsequently voted to dismiss Congress in July, pending new congressional and gubernatorial elections, to be conducted in October 1991 (although congressional elections had not been scheduled to take place until 1994). Incumbent government ministers and members of the National Constituent Assembly, which was itself to be dissolved on 5 July, were declared to be ineligible for congressional office.

At midnight on 5–6 July 1991 the new Constitution became effective. At the same time, the state of siege, which had been imposed in 1984 in response to the escalation in political and drugs-related violence, was ended. Although the new Constitution preserved the existing institutional framework of a president and a bicameral legislature (reduced in size to a 102-seat Senate and a 161-seat House of Representatives), considerable emphasis was placed upon provisions to encourage greater political participation and to restrict electoral corruption and misrepresentation. The Constitution also identified and sought to protect a comprehensive list of civil liberties. The duration of the state of siege was to be restricted to 90 days (only to be extended with the approval of the Senate). The judiciary was to be restructured with the creation of the posts of Prosecutor-General and Defender of the People (Defensor del Pueblo). All marriages were to be placed under civil jurisdiction, with the guaranteed right to divorce. Most controversially, extradition of Colombian nationals was to be prohibited (see below). While the Constitution was welcomed enthusiastically by the majority of the population, reservations were expressed that clauses relating to the armed forces remained largely unchanged and that provisions which recognized the democratic rights of indigenous groups did not extend to their territorial claims.

Relations with the Medellín cartel improved considerably following the release, in May 1991, of two remaining hostages, and in June, following the decision to prohibit constitutionally the practice of extradition, the Government's efforts were rewarded with the surrender of Pablo Escobar, the supposed head of the Medellín cartel. Charges later brought against

Escobar included several of murder, kidnapping and terrorism. In July spokesmen for the Medellín drugs cartel announced that its military operations were to be suspended and that the 'Extraditables' were to be disbanded. Hopes that Escobar's surrender might precipitate a decline in drugs-related violence were frustrated by reports that Escobar was continuing to direct the operations of the Medellín cocaine cartels from his purpose-built prison at Envigado, and by the emergence of the powerful Cali drugs cartel, which was expected to compensate for any shortfall in the supply of illicit drugs resulting from the demise of the Medellín cartel.

Congressional and gubernatorial elections, conducted in October 1991, were distinguished by a high level of voter apathy, attributed to the busy electoral schedule of the previous 18 months. The Liberals, who presented a confusing number of electoral lists, were most successful, with a clear majority of seats in both chambers, and victory in the gubernatorial elections in 18 of the 27 contested departments. The traditional Conservative opposition suffered from a division in their support between the PCC, the MSN and the Nueva Fuerza Democrática, securing around one-quarter of the seats in both houses between them. The AD—M-19 received only 10% of the votes cast, equivalent to nine seats in the Senate and 15 seats in the House of Representatives.

Meanwhile, in February 1990 the Government had established the National Council for Normalization, in an attempt to repeat the success of recent peace initiatives with the M-19 in negotiations with other revolutionary groups. The EPL announced the end of its armed struggle in August and joined the political mainstream (retaining the Spanish acronym EPL as the Partido de Esperanza, Paz y Libertad), along with the Comando Quintín Lame and the PRT, in early to mid-1991. Attempts to negotiate with the FARC and the ELN, however, proved fruitless, and violent clashes between the remaining guerrilla groups (now co-ordinating actions as the Coordinadora Nacional Guerrillera Simón Bolívar—CNGSB) and security forces persisted in the early 1990s.

The results of municipal elections, conducted in March 1992, represented a significant reversal for the PL and for the M-19. In the capital, support for candidates for council seats, from both parties, was undermined by the popularity of two former PL ministers who had campaigned as vociferous opponents of recent government policy regarding drugs-trafficking and urban terrorism. Coalition candidates proved most successful in mayoral contests to several major cities including Medellín, Cali and Barranquilla. In June President Gaviria effected a comprehensive reorganization of the Cabinet, while maintaining a multi-party composition.

An escalation in guerrilla activity during May and September 1992 prompted the Government to intensify anti-insurgency measures. In October Congress approved government proposals for an increased counterinsurgency budget and for the creation of new armed units to combat terrorism. The Government's rejection of any agenda for renewed negotiations provoked an intensification of the conflict, and this, together with a resurgence of drugs-related violent incidents following the death of the supposed military commander of the Medellín cartel, prompted Gaviria, in November, to declare a 90-day state of emergency or 'internal disturbance', thereby extending wide-ranging powers to the security forces and imposing restrictions on media coverage. In late November the M-19 announced that, in view of the Government's uncompromising armed response to recent internal disturbances, the party was to withdraw from the Government and resume an active opposition role.

The security situation continued to deteriorate during 1993, following increased activity from guerrilla groups in response to the capture of several prominent rebel leaders in January and February, and the internecine activities of the drugs cartels (see below). In February the Government announced a significant increase in its budget allocation for security, and in April it was revealed that the duration of terms of imprisonment awarded for acts of terrorism resulting in death or injury was to be doubled. The state of internal disturbance was extended for 90 days in February, and again in November. Attempts by the Government and the ELN to negotiate a truce were frustrated by a perceived lack of commitment to compromise on both sides, and the prospects for future successful discussions were severely undermined by the insistence of security forces that ELN members were responsible for the murder of the Vice-President of the Senate in November. In December negotiations with the Corriente de Renovación Socialista (CRS), a dissident faction of the ELN more disposed to political assimilation, produced an agreement for the guerrillas' reincorporation into civilian life and transformation into a legitimate political force. However, agreement had been reached somewhat tentatively, owing to the experience of other former guerrilla groups which had effected a similar move to the political mainstream only to be persecuted by less compromising guerrilla factions. (In January 1994 more than 30 EPL members were murdered, allegedly by FARC activists, during a demonstration in the Urabá region.) However, in April 1994, under the supervision of international observers, the CRS duly surrendered its weapons, and was subsequently awarded two seats in the newly-elected House of Representatives (see below).

An intensification of drugs-related violence in the capital during early 1993 was attributed to an attempt by Pablo Escobar (who had escaped from prison in mid-1992) to force the Government to negotiate more favourable conditions for his surrender, and prompted the formation of a vigilante group, Pepe (Perseguidos por Pablo Escobar—those Persecuted by Pablo Escobar), which launched a campaign of retaliatory violence against Escobar's family, associates and property. Pepe was thought to number among its members several of Escobar's disgruntled rivals from the Medellín cartel. A simultaneous and sustained assault by Pepe and by the security forces against the remnants of the Medellín cartel resulted in the death and surrender of many notable cartel members, culminating in the death of Escobar himself, in December, during an exchange of fire with security forces attempting to effect his arrest. In late December it was reported that the Government was again considering the negotiation of a rehabilitation programme for prominent members of the Cali cartel, following their offer to dismantle all illicit operations in return for lenient prison sentences and negligible financial penalties.

The dispatch of a contingent of US troops to the Valle del Cauca region in December 1993, described as a humanitarian mission to improve communications and health and education facilities, aroused widespread political outrage from the Government's opponents, who interpreted the accommodation of the troops as capitulation to US demands for military participation in the region, in order to ensure the destruction of the Cali cartel. By late February 1994, however, the troops had been withdrawn, the Council of State having ruled earlier in the month that President Gaviria had abused his authority by endorsing their deployment prior to consultation with the Senate. Relations with the USA deteriorated further in March following US criticism of the lenient terms of surrender being offered to leaders of the Cali cartel. A suspension of co-operation with regard to the exchange of evidence relating to drugs offences ensued. The situation was exacerbated in May following a Constitutional Court ruling which recognized the legal right of the individual to possess small quantities of drugs (including cocaine) for personal use. An unsuccessful attempt by Gaviria to amend the ruling by emergency decree, together with his statement of intent to revoke the decision by means of a referendum, did little to allay US fears that the Colombian judiciary was attempting to destroy the wealth of the cartels by legalizing the trade in illicit drugs.

The results of congressional and local elections conducted in March 1994 represented a serious reversal for the political left in Colombia and re-established the traditional two-party dominance of the PL and the PCC. The elections were particularly disappointing for the AD—M-19, whose representation was reduced from 13 seats to two in the House of Representatives and from nine seats to just one in the Senate. The PL retained a comfortable congressional majority. No candidate secured the margin of victory necessary to be declared outright winner in the presidential election conducted on 29 May, and a second poll was contested on 19 June between Ernesto Samper Pizano (PL) and Andrés Pastrana Arango (PCC), who had been placed first and second respectively in the first round. The similarity in the two contestants' campaign manifestos (advocating economic liberalization, job creation and improved social welfare) resulted in a second close contest. Samper was eventually declared President-elect, with 50.9% of the valid votes cast. Samper was inaugurated on 7 August and a new Cabinet was installed simultaneously. PL candidates were also successful in departmental and municipal elections conducted in October, securing 22 of the 32 contested governorships. However, the PL lost control of a number of crucial cities including Cali, Medellín and the capital.

Shortly after President Samper's inauguration, allegations emerged that his election campaign had been partly funded by contributions from the Cali cartel. Tape-recordings of conversations which appeared to provide evidence that contact had at least been made with the cartels were subsequently dismissed by the Prosecutor-General as insufficient proof of such contributions actually having been made. In July 1994 a similar recording, which appeared to implicate the Colombian Chief of National Police in the payment of a bribe by the Cali cartel, prompted the US Senate to vote to make the disbursement of future aid to Colombia dependent on an assessment of the level of its co-operation in anti-drugs programmes. The existence of the tape-recordings was widely attributed to the US Drugs Enforcement Agency (DEA) which the Colombian media accused of fomenting mistrust in an attempt to ensure that the new administration would pursue an uncompromising anti-drugs policy. Restrictions were subsequently imposed on DEA operations and access to information in Colombia. However, it was hoped that bilateral relations would improve following the appointment of a new Prosecutor-General and a new Chief of the National Police in late 1994, and the House of Representatives' rejection, in December, of the 'narco bill' which sought to limit the powers of the authorities to confiscate funds and assets proceeding from illicit activities.

CNGSB offensives during 1994 were launched to coincide with campaigning for the March legislative elections, and to disrupt the weeks preceding the transfer of power from Gaviria to Samper in early August. Fighting between guerrillas and the security forces resulted in numerous deaths on both sides and considerable damage was inflicted on power installations and the transport infrastructure. Prospects for the swift negotiation of a peace agreement between the new administration and the CNGSB were immediately undermined by the murder of the UP's Manuel Cepeda Vargas (the only left-wing member of the Senate) and deteriorated as guerrilla activities intensified in late 1994. However, in November Samper complied with a guerrilla request that rebel leaders currently in detention should be moved from military installations to civilian prisons, and also declared the Government's willingness to enter into unconditional dialogue with the guerrillas, preferably outside of Colombia.

During 1994 the Government was subject to intense international pressure to formalize a greater commitment to respect for human rights, following a series of revelations in which members of the security forces were implicated in abuses of human rights, and the publication of a report by Amnesty International in which it was claimed that the vast majority of infringements of human rights in Colombia were perpetrated by the armed forces and associated paramilitary groups. In September the Minister of the Interior, Horacio Serpa Uribe, announced an initiative to address the human rights crisis, including plans to reform the National Police and to disband all paramilitary units. In September 1995 Brig.-Gen. Alvaro Velandia Hurtado was removed from active duty by the Government, after a report by the office of the Prosecutor for Human Rights had pronounced him responsible for the detention and murder of a prominent M-19 member in 1987. Velandia's dismissal marked the first such action undertaken by the Government against senior army personnel in response to abuses of human rights.

In February 1995, in the context of the US Government's persistence in attaching preconditions to the disbursement of financial aid to Colombia, President Samper reiterated his commitment to the eradication of all illegal drugs-related activities in the country. A number of initiatives to address the problem were launched in Cali, resulting in the capture of the head of the Cali drugs cartel, Gilberto Rodríguez Orejuela, and four other cartel leaders in mid-1995. Meanwhile, in April nine prominent PL politicians were suspended from the party pending their investigation by the office of the Prosecutor-General, following allegations of their maintaining links with the Cali cartel. In the following months it was confirmed that the Comptroller-General and the Attorney-General were also to be the subject of investigation as a result of similar allegations, while Samper's former election campaign treasurer, Santiago Medina, was arrested on charges related to the processing of drugs cartel contributions through Samper's election fund. In August the Minister of National Defence, Fernando Botero Zea, resigned, having been implicated in the affair by evidence submitted to the authorities by Medina. Medina also insisted that Samper had been fully aware of the origin of the funds, prompting opposition demands for the President's resignation. Samper's former campaign manager was arrested in September, in which month Samper protested his own innocence before a congressional accusations committee. In October the Constitutional Court confirmed the jurisdiction of the congressional committee to conduct further investigations into the allegations.

In May 1995 the Government extended an offer of participation in legislative and consultative processes to the FARC, in the hope of securing their commitment to surrender arms. While the FARC responded positively to the initial proposal, further progress was to be dependent on the Government's successful execution of its stated intention to demilitarize the sensitive north-eastern region of La Uribe. A Government proposal for the exchange of armed struggle for a political agenda, issued to the ELN and dissident groups of the EPL and the M-19 at the same time, received a more cautious response from the guerrillas. However, all negotiations were severely hampered by renewed FARC and ELN offensives in late May. An escalation in the number of acts of violence perpetrated by guerrilla forces and by paramilitary defence groups in the north-western Urabá region resulted in the deaths during 1995 of some 600 civilians by August, prompting Samper to declare a state of internal disturbance for a 90-day period. In October, however, the Constitutional Court rejected the terms of the state of emergency, forcing the President to seek immediate congressional approval for alternative powers to extend the period of detention of some 3,500 suspected insurgents. Following the assassination, in November, of a prominent Conservative politician, the President declared a new 90-day state of internal disturbance. Responsibility for the assassination was claimed by the little-known Movimiento por la Dignidad de Colombia. (In April 1996 the group kidnapped the brother of former President Gaviria and demanded that the latter resign as Secretary-General of the Organization of American States—OAS; the hostage was released in June, even though the demand was not met.) However, negotiations between the President and Andrés Pastrana of the PCC, for a 'national agreement against violence', were frustrated by the latter's insistence that the establishment of an independent commission of inquiry into the allegations of Samper's campaign funding by the Cali cartel should be a precondition to any political negotiation. Increased emergency powers for regional evacuations were assumed by the President in November as part of an initiative to re-establish the military supremacy of the armed forces in all regions.

In December 1995 the congressional accusations committee voted against the initiation of a full-scale inquiry into allegations of Samper's impropriety in the use of funds proceeding from drugs cartels, on the grounds of insufficient evidence at that time. The repercussions of the scandal, however, were considered to have severely undermined the political integrity of the Government, both at home and abroad. Relations between the US Government and the Samper administration deteriorated dramatically during 1995, culminating in allegations—made by official sources in Colombia—that the US Government was attempting to destabilize the administration through the covert actions of the DEA.

In January 1996 Botero reiterated Medina's claim that Samper had been in full possession of the facts regarding the cartel's funding of his election campaign, prompting the PCC to announce an immediate suspension of co-operation with the Government and the resignation of two of the four incumbent PCC members of the Cabinet. (The PL Minister of Public Health also resigned, in protest at the Government's failure to refute the mounting evidence of widespread corruption which had been presented.) Samper subsequently urged Congress to reopen investigations into his involvement in the affair, seeking to demonstrate his innocence. Evidence collected by the Prosecutor-General, Alfonso Valdivieso, was submitted to the accusations committee in February, together with four formal charges to be brought against the President, including that of illegal enrichment. Later in the month congressional commissions of both parliamentary chambers decided to launch a new and public investigation into the funding of Samper's election campaign. In March Samper testified before the accusations committee and denied allegations that he had contrived the plan to solicit funding from the Cali cartel; however, he did concede that the cartel had part-financed the campaign, albeit without his knowledge.

In March 1996, in the context of the Supreme Court's investigation into the financing of Samper's election campaign, the Ministers of the Interior, Foreign Affairs and Communications were summoned to face charges of illegal enrichment. In the following month Rodrigo Pardo García-Peña (who had since announced his temporary retirement as Minister of Foreign Affairs) admitted that he had been aware of the Cali cartel's role in the financing of the campaign. In May the charges of illegal enrichment against the three ministers were abandoned, although they were formally accused of the lesser charge of deliberately concealing the use of illicit funds in the campaign. Meanwhile, in April the Supreme Court took the unprecedented step of requesting that the Senate suspend the Attorney-General, Orlando Vásquez Velásquez, in order that he face charges of obstructing the course of justice (he had allegedly fabricated evidence to discredit the Prosecutor-General). In October Vásquez Velásquez was found guilty of the charges; he was dismissed as Attorney-General and banned from holding public office for a five-year period. Moreover, in December 1997 he was sentenced to eight years' imprisonment on drugs charges. During 1996 Botero, Medina and María Izquierdo, a former PL Senator, were all sentenced to terms of imprisonment for their involvement in the Samper affair.

In June 1996 Congress voted to acquit Samper of charges of having been aware of the part-financing of his election campaign by drugs-traffickers. The US administration condemned the result and threatened to impose trade sanctions against Colombia. (In March the US Congress had refused to 'certify' Colombia as a co-operating nation with regard to US anti-drugs activities after a leading Cali cartel member escaped from prison.) In July, following the release of a prominent Medellín cartel member after only five-and-a-half years in prison, the US Government accused Samper of failing to take appropriate measures to deter drugs-trafficking and revoked his visa to travel to the USA.

Meanwhile, civil unrest and guerrilla activity continued during 1996. The state of internal disturbance was extended for a further 90 days in January, and then again in April following a CNGSB-organized nation-wide 'armed industrial strike', which had resulted in as many as 40 deaths. In March a FARC attack on a drugs-control police unit had renewed speculation of links between guerrilla groups and the drugs cartels. Moreover, it was suggested that a major offensive launched in August by FARC and ELN rebels (resulting in as many as 100 fatalities) had been deliberately timed to coincide with large-scale protests by coca growers demanding a review of the coca eradication programme, particularly the use of aerial spraying. Serious clashes between guerrillas and the security forces continued in September, prompting the Government to announce the imminent mobilization of thousands of reserves. Although 26 members of the FARC and some 250 dissident EPL rebels surrendered to the authorities during September and October, violent skirmishes continued unabated, and disaffected members of the ELN were reported to have regrouped as the Ejército Revolucionario del Pueblo. Some 780 guerrillas and 500 members of the armed forces were estimated to have been killed during 1996.

In September 1996 Samper's credibility was undermined by the resignation of the Vice-President, Humberto de la Calle, who appealed to the President to renounce his office in order to prevent the country from descending into 'total chaos'. (Congress subsequently elected Carlos Lemos-Simmonds as the new Vice-President.) Later in September Samper was again humiliated by the discovery of 3.7 kg of heroin aboard the aircraft in which he had been scheduled to fly to the USA (using a diplomat visa) to attend a meeting of the UN General Assembly. (A subsequent investigation into the drugs seizure did not implicate the President in any way.) In an apparent attempt to appease the US administration, Samper announced that Colombia's Congress would debate whether to amend the Constitution in order to permit the extradition of Colombian nationals. Moreover, in December Congress approved controversial legislation to allow for the confiscation of drugs-traffickers' assets. (Many members of the congressional constitutional committees had been reluctant to adopt or even debate the law for fear of reprisals from the drugs cartels.) In addition, the authorities arrested six prominent Cali cartel members during 1996.

In early 1997 the Samper administration encountered increasing pressure from the USA to address the issues of drugs-trafficking and corruption. The appointment of Guillermo Alberto González as Colombia's Minister of National Defence was condemned by the USA, which alleged that he had maintained links with drugs-traffickers, notably with Justo Pastor Perafán. In March González resigned as a result of the allegations; in the same month Perafán was arrested in Venezuela. In February, meanwhile, the USA again refused to 'certify' Colombia, claiming that there had been a substantial increase in the production of illicit drugs in that country during 1996. The US administration had also been critical of the lenient prison sentences imposed on two notorious drugs-traffickers in January. In response, Samper announced the temporary suspension of Colombia's drugs-crop eradication programme. The programme was resumed shortly afterwards, but relations with the USA remained strained. Although legislation permitting the extradition of Colombian nationals sought for criminal offences abroad was approved in November, it was strongly criticized by the US administration as it would not have retroactive effect. Nevertheless, in February 1998 the USA waived sanctions on Colombia, although it did not fully 'certify' the country.

Meanwhile, in January 1997 President Samper risked civil unrest by decreeing a state of economic emergency. In the following month, after an eight-day nation-wide strike, the Government agreed to substantial pay awards for public-sector employees and to the establishment of a joint commission with labour unions to analyze the effects of its privatization plans. In March the Constitutional Court legally annulled the economic emergency, obliging Samper to seek congressional approval for the measures announced in January.

The activities of guerrilla and paramilitary groups in Colombia intensified during 1997. In May the Government agreed to the temporary demilitarization of part of the Caquetá department in order to secure the release of 70 members of the armed forces captured by the FARC in August 1996 and January 1997. The release of the captives in June received widespread media coverage and led to speculation that a peace agreement might be imminent. Notably, President Samper acknowledged that paramilitary groups had increasingly instigated violent attacks (sometimes with the tacit support of the security forces) and agreed that they should be included in peace negotiations. In the following month, after a series of assaults on the security forces by FARC and ELN rebels, Samper reorganized the military and police command, replacing the Commander-in-Chief of the Armed Forces, Gen. Harold Bedoya Pizzaro, who had vehemently opposed negotiating with the guerrillas. In addition, Samper presented legislation to Congress that would lead to the establishment of a national peace commission.

In mid-1997 there was a marked increase in violent attacks by guerrilla and paramilitary groups, apparently intent on sabotaging departmental and municipal elections which were scheduled to be held in October. In the months preceding the elections more than 40 candidates were killed, some 200 were kidnapped and as many as 1,900 were persuaded to withdraw after receiving death threats. Voting was cancelled in numerous municipalities, while in August the vulnerability of the Government to rebel attacks was emphasized by the assassination (most probably by the ELN) of a PL senator who was a close ally of Samper. Meanwhile, reports of secret preliminary peace negotiations between government representatives and the FARC were undermined by a major military offensive in September, in which 652 FARC guerrillas were killed and a further 1,600 were captured. The Government's subsequent conciliatory gestures to the guerrillas, including a promise by the President to submit legislation to Congress granting an amnesty in return for the signing of a peace accord, were met with little enthusiasm by the FARC and the ELN.

Departmental and municipal elections took place in October 1997, despite the campaign of intimidation by guerrilla and paramilitary groups. The PL won 19 of the 32 contested governorships (the PCC obtained four) and took control of 412 local councils (compared with 301 by the PCC). An independent Liberal won the mayorship of the capital, while a PCC candidate became mayor of Medellín. Meanwhile, in early November the ELN secured significant concessions from the Government in return for the release of two OAS election observers abducted in October. During November there was a sharp increase in attacks by paramilitary groups; some 47 people were killed in an eight-day period.

Changes to the Cabinet took place on numerous occasions during 1997 and early 1998, affecting most of the principal ministries. Horacio Serpa Uribe, a close ally of President Samper, resigned as Minister of the Interior in May 1997 and was selected as the official PL presidential candidate in January 1998. His candidature was strongly opposed by the US administration as he was alleged to have links with drugs-traffickers and was implicated in the affair regarding the illegal funding of Samper's 1994 election campaign. (In December 1997 Serpa was cleared of criminal charges relating to the affair.) Also in May 1997, Alfonso Valdivieso, whose vigorous investigations into corruption and drugs-trafficking had bolstered his popularity, resigned as Prosecutor-General in order to contest the presidency. In March 1998, however, Valdivieso withdrew his candidacy and pledged support for Pastrana, who had been selected again as the PCC nominee.

At congressional elections, conducted on 8 March 1998, the PL retained a narrow overall majority in the legislature, obtaining 53 of the 102 seats in the Senate, and 84 of the 161 seats in the House of Representatives. The PCC secured 27 and 28 seats in each chamber, respectively. An estimated 54% of the electorate participated in the elections, which were preceded by a period of violent attacks on the security forces by the FARC and the ELN; in one incident 80 counter-insurgency troops were killed by the FARC, and a further 43 were taken prisoner. In May tens of thousands of Colombians staged a demonstration to protest at the escalation of violence by guerrillas and paramilitary groups.

In the first round of the presidential election, held on 31 May 1998, Serpa secured 34.6% of the valid votes cast, followed by Pastrana (34.3%), Noemí Sanín Posada—an independent candidate who performed particularly well in Medellín, Cali and the capital—(26.9%), and Gen. (rtd) Bedoya (1.8%). Nine other candidates contested the election. A second ballot was held on 21 June, at which Pastrana defeated Serpa, winning 50.4% of the valid votes cast. Pastrana was inaugurated as President on 7 August and a new Cabinet was installed simultaneously. Shortly afterwards the military leadership was reorganized and Gen. Fernando Tapias Stahelín, a moderate, was appointed Commander-in-Chief of the Armed Forces. Pastrana's immediate declared priorities included reaching a peace settlement with the guerrillas, eliminating corruption and strengthening the ailing economy.

In July 1998 President-elect Pastrana announced that he had held secret talks with Manuel Marulanda Vélez (alias 'Tirofijo'), the FARC leader, and that he had agreed to demilitarize five southern municipalities for a 90-day period (commencing in November) in order to facilitate negotiations with the guerrillas. Pastrana subsequently recognized the political status of the FARC, thereby allowing the Government to negotiate with an outlawed group. Notwithstanding, FARC attacks on the security forces continued, increasing significantly in August, before Pastrana's inauguration, and also in November, prior to the completion of the demilitarization of the five districts in the departments of Caquetá and Meta. Despite the demilitarization, negotiations with the FARC were stalled owing to the group's objection to the continued presence of some 100 soldiers in a barracks in San Vicente del Caguán, Caquetá. The soldiers were evacuated in December, and in January 1999 peace negotiations between the Government and the FARC began in San Vicente. Shortly before the negotiations began, it was revealed that in December the FARC had held informal talks in Costa Rica with government officials from the USA and Colombia. The FARC was reported to have invited the US officials to visit illegal crop plantations in Colombia and to consider possible substitution programmes. (Relations between Colombia and the USA had improved notably under the Pastrana administration: in October Pastrana made an official visit to the USA—the first by a Colombian Head of State in 23 years—and in December the two countries agreed on measures to improve military co-operation in the fight against the drugs trade.) In mid-January 1999 the FARC suspended talks with the Government until the authorities provided evidence that they were taking action against paramilitary groups, which claimed responsibility for the massacre of more than 130 civilians earlier in the month. In February Pastrana announced the extension of the period of demilitarization by three months, in order to facilitate negotiations.

The ELN, meanwhile, made tentative moves to negotiate a peace settlement during 1998. In February the group signed an accord with government peace negotiators in Madrid, Spain, on the holding of preliminary peace talks. In April the ELN disclosed that its leader, Gregorio Manuel Pérez Martínez, had died shortly afterwards; a collective leadership was appointed subsequently, with José Nicolás Rodríguez Bautista as the group's political commander. In July, at a meeting in Mainz, Germany, between the ELN and representatives of Colombian 'civil society' (grouped in the National Peace Council—Consejo Nacional de Paz—CNP), the ELN made concessions on the 'humanization' of the war and agreed to facilitate talks between its members and the Government. The guerrillas subsequently postponed a meeting with the CNP in protest at its signing of an agreement with the Autodefensas Unidas de Colombia (AUC), an organization representing most of Colombia's paramilitary groups, to hold parallel peace talks. Nevertheless, in October representatives of the ELN, the CNP and the Government agreed on a timetable for preliminary peace talks, beginning in February 1999, which would culminate in the assembling of a national convention. The Government recognized the political status of the ELN, but the group did not cease hostilities. Later in October 1998 an ELN attack on an oil pipeline in the department of Antioquia resulted in the deaths of at least 66 civilians. The planned peace negotiations failed to begin in February 1999, not least because of the Government's refusal to agree to the ELN's request that four districts in the department of Bolívar be demilitarized. The ELN subsequently intensified its operations, in an apparent attempt to increase pressure on the Government to accede to its demands. The guerrillas hijacked a domestic flight in April, kidnapping all 46 people on board, and abducted some 140 members of the congregation of a church in Cali in May. In June Pastrana withdrew political recognition of the ELN and made the release of hostages a precondition for future peace talks. A civilian commission was subsequently appointed by the Government to negotiate towards this end. The ELN gradually freed hostages throughout 1999, although by late November the guerrillas still held 16 hostages from the church raid and nine from the seizure of the aircraft. Following several unofficial meetings between Colombian government representatives and the ELN, which reportedly took place in Cuba and Venezuela in late 1999, it was hoped that a national convention, as demanded by the guerrilla movement, would be held in early 2000.

Little progress was achieved in negotiations with the FARC until April 1999, as the guerrillas continued to insist that the Government demonstrate some success in its actions against paramilitary groups prior to a resumption of talks. The enforced resignation in that month of two senior army officers, alleged to have collaborated with paramilitary groups, appeared to appease the FARC, however, and in early May talks between Marulanda and Pastrana resulted in an agreement on a comprehensive agenda for future peace negotiations; the period of demilitarization was again extended. Shortly afterwards a police offensive against a cocaine-production complex operated by paramilitaries in the central department of Magdalena was perceived as further evidence of a change in the attitude of the authorities towards paramilitary groups. However, Pastrana's strategy was not entirely supported by his administration, and at the end of May Rodrigo Lloreda, the Minister of National Defence, resigned in protest at concessions granted to the FARC. Meanwhile, the AUC was demanding to be granted political status and included in the peace negotiations. Pastrana's position was further undermined by Congress's rejection of legislation aimed at increasing the President's power concerning the peace process, as independent deputies voted with the opposition PL for the first time. Furthermore, the FARC continued to pursue its military campaign. The postponement of talks in early July, owing to a failure to agree on the role of international observers, was followed by a nation-wide guerrilla offensive which resulted in more than 200 deaths. The proximity of the fighting to the capital was of particular concern. The talks were subsequently postponed indefinitely, with the Government insisting that international monitors be allowed to investigate abuses allegedly committed by the FARC in the demilitarized zone. As negotiations resumed on 24 October in La Uribe, after Pastrana had apparently withdrawn his demand for international observers, demonstrations for peace were attended by some 10m. people throughout the country. Further talks were held in early and mid-November, at which it was agreed public hearings on the peace process would be held from late December. However, the FARC's commitment to the process was questioned by the military when, prior to the second round of November talks, the guerrillas launched attacks against 13 towns in several departments, amid renewed claims that they were using the demilitarized zone as a recruitment and training base from which to mount offensives. Guerrilla violence continued, although, following two weeks of heavy fighting with the security forces, in which more than 200 people were killed, on 19 December the FARC declared a 22-day unilateral ceasefire.

Relations between the US Government and the Pastrana administration continued to improve in 1999, most notably regarding anti-drugs activities, and in March the USA decided to 'certify' Colombia's efforts to combat drugs-trafficking. In September Pastrana announced the establishment of a new anti-narcotics battalion, which was to be trained and financed by the USA. Furthermore, collaboration between the Colombian and US authorities led to the arrest of more than 60 suspected drugs-traffickers in two major operations conducted in October and December. A car bomb that exploded in northern Santafé de Bogotá, in November, killing at least eight people and injuring some 45, was believed to have been a reaction to the Government's decision to resume the extradition of suspected drugs-traffickers to stand trial in the USA. The first extraditions were effected later in November. In late 1999 the Government was disappointed by the failure of the US Congress to approve the disbursement of some US $1,500m. of aid that Colombia had been hoping to receive in support of anti-drugs programmes. Further proposals regarding aid for Colombia were being considered by the US Congress in February 2000.

Colombia has a long-standing border dispute with Venezuela. However, relations between the countries improved following the signing, in October 1989, of a border integration agreement, which included a provision on joint co-operation in the campaign to eradicate drugs-trafficking. (A permanent reconciliation commission to investigate the border dispute had been established in March 1989.) In March 1990 the San Pedro Alejandrino agreement, signed by the two countries, sought to initiate the implementation of recommendations made by existing bilateral border commissions and to establish a number of new commissions, including one to examine the territorial claims of both sides. Colombia's efforts to improve relations with Venezuela were hampered by the activities of FARC guerrillas in the border region, leading the two countries to sign an agreement to improve border co-operation in February 1997; however, in April Venezuela deployed 5,000 troops along its frontier with Colombia in an attempt to halt repeated incursions by Colombian guerrillas. Agreements were subsequently signed by the two countries to strengthen military co-operation and intelligence sharing. In June Panama also announced its intention to station 1,200 soldiers along its border with Colombia to counter an increase in the activities of Colombian guerrilla and paramilitary groups in the country, and, following the death of a member of Panama's security forces during an attack by the FARC in November, the Heads of State of the two countries agreed to improve border co-operation. In 1999 increasing concern regarding the threat posed to regional stability by Colombia's internal conflict prompted neighbouring countries to increase security measures on the common border.

In 1980 Nicaragua laid claim to the Colombian-controlled islands of Providencia and San Andrés. Colombia has a territorial dispute with Honduras over cays in the San Andrés and Providencia archipelago. In October 1986 the Colombian Senate approved a delimitation treaty of marine and submarine waters in the Caribbean Sea, which had been signed by the Governments of Colombia and Honduras in August. In late 1999 the Honduran National Assembly finally ratified the treaty, strengthening Colombia's claim to the islands of Providencia and San Andrés, and thus angering Nicaragua, which filed a complaint with the International Court of Justice.

In April 1991 the ministers with responsibility for foreign affairs of Colombia, Mexico and Venezuela (known as the Group of Three) announced their intention to create a free-trade zone by mid-1994. In October 1993 the Group of Three announced the implementation, as of 1 January 1994, of a 10-year trade liberalization programme.

In December 1991 the leaders of the countries of the Andean Pact agreed to remove trade barriers between their countries in early 1992 and to adopt unified external tariffs by 1993. However, subsequent negotiations failed to produce agreement on a common external tariff. In February 1995 a three-level tariff system was implemented to cover 90% of imports (the remainder to be incorporated by 1999). In March 1996 the Presidents of the member nations of the Pact signed the Reform Protocol of the Cartagena Agreement, whereby the Pact was superseded by the Andean Community.

A free trade agreement, the Acuerdo de Complementación Económica (ACE), concluded with Chile in December 1993, took effect from 1 January 1994, and was expected to have eliminated tariffs on most goods by the time of its full implementation on 1 January 1999.

## Government

Executive power is exercised by the President (assisted by a Cabinet), who is elected for a four-year term by universal adult suffrage. Legislative power is vested in the bicameral Congress, consisting of the Senate (102 members elected for four years) and the House of Representatives (161 members elected for four years). The country is divided into 32 Departments and one Capital District.

## Defence

At 18 years of age, every male (with the exception of students) must present himself as a candidate for military service of between one and two years. In August 1999 the strength of the army was 121,000 (including 63,800 conscripts), the navy 15,000 (including 8,500 marines) and the air force 8,000. The paramilitary police force numbers about 87,000 men. Some 3,700,000m. pesos were allocated to defence expenditure as part of the state budget for 1999.

## Economic Affairs

In 1997, according to estimates by the World Bank, Colombia's gross national product (GNP), measured at average 1995–97 prices, was US $87,125m., equivalent to $2,180 per head. During 1990–97, it was estimated, GNP per head increased, in real terms, by an average of 2.6% per year. Over the same period, the population increased at an average annual rate of 1.9%. Estimated GNP in 1998 was $106,100m. ($2,600 per head). Colombia's gross domestic product (GDP) increased, in real terms, by an average of 4.2% per year in 1990–98; GDP increased by 3.4% in 1997 and by 0.6% in 1998.

Agriculture (including hunting, forestry and fishing) contributed 12.9% of GDP in 1997, and employed some 21.6% of the labour force in 1998. The principal cash crops are coffee (which accounted for 17.4% of official export earnings in 1998), cocoa, sugar cane, bananas, tobacco, cotton and cut flowers. Rice, cassava, plantains and potatoes are the principal food crops. Timber and beef production are also important. During 1990–98 agricultural GDP increased at an average annual rate of 1.6%. Growth in agricultural GDP was 0.8% in 1998.

Industry (including mining, manufacturing, construction and power) employed 19.9% of the labour force in 1997, and contributed 27.6% of GDP in that year. During 1990–98 industrial GDP increased at an average annual rate of 2.9%. Industrial GDP declined by 2.7% in 1996, but increased by 1.3% in 1997.

Mining contributed 3.6% of GDP in 1997, and employed 0.7% of the labour force in that year. Petroleum, natural gas, coal, nickel, emeralds and gold are the principal minerals exploited. Silver, platinum, iron, lead, zinc, copper, mercury, limestone and phosphates are also mined. Growth in mining GDP was 3.7% in 1997 and 10.0% in 1998.

Manufacturing contributed 14.1% of GDP in 1997, and employed 13.1% of the labour force in that year. During 1990–97 manufacturing GDP increased at an average annual rate of 1.5%. Manufacturing GDP increased by 0.4% in 1997, although it declined by 0.5% in 1998. Based on the value of output, the most important branches of manufacturing in 1995 were food products (accounting for 25.3% of the total), chemical products (14.8%), beverages, textiles and transport equipment.

In 1987 hydroelectricity provided about 75% of Colombia's electricity requirements. The country is self-sufficient in petroleum and coal, and minerals accounted for 29.8% of export revenues in 1998.

The services sector contributed 59.5% of GDP in 1997, and engaged 56.7% of the labour force in that year. During 1990–98 the combined GDP of the service sectors increased, in real terms, at an estimated average rate of 4.9% per year. Growth in services GDP was 5.1% in 1997.

In 1998 Colombia recorded a visible trade deficit of US $2,635m. and there was a deficit of $5,866m. on the current account of the balance of payments. The country's principal trading partner in 1997 was the USA, which (together with Puerto Rico) provided 41.5% of imports and took 37.8% of exports. Other important trading partners in that year were Venezuela and Germany. The principal exports in 1998 were minerals (particularly petroleum and its derivatives and coal), coffee, other agricultural products (chiefly cut flowers and bananas), chemicals, textiles and leather products, and foodstuffs, beverages and tobacco. The principal imports in 1997 were machinery and transport equipment, chemicals, vegetables and vegetable products, minerals, metals, and foodstuffs, beverages and tobacco. A significant amount of foreign exchange is believed to be obtained from illegal trade in gold, emeralds and, particularly, the drug cocaine: in 1995 it was estimated that some $3,500m. (equivalent to around 4% of GDP) was entering Colombia each year as the proceeds of drugs-trafficking activities.

In 1998 there was a budgetary deficit of 6,940,600m. pesos in central government spending, equivalent to 5.3% of GDP. Colombia's external debt amounted to US $31,777m. at the end of 1997, of which $15,273m. was long-term public debt. In that year the cost of debt-servicing was equivalent to 26.6% of the value of exports of goods and services. In 1990–98 the average annual rate of inflation was 22.9%; consumer prices increased by an annual average of 20.4% in 1998. Some 19.8% of the labour force were unemployed in June 1999.

Colombia is a member of ALADI (see p. 292) and of the Andean Community (see p. 119). Both organizations attempt to increase trade and economic co-operation within the region.

Colombia's principal export commodities are petroleum and coffee, although the export of other agricultural products and manufactured goods has become increasingly important. Unlike most Latin American countries, Colombia avoided the need to reschedule its foreign debt during the 1980s. A programme of structural reform was adopted in 1990–94, resulting in the liberalization of trade and the reorganization of the public sector. Strong economic growth was recorded during this period, not least because of the discovery of significant petroleum reserves. However, during the Samper administration (1994–98) GDP slowed, unemployment soared and the fiscal deficit widened. In the late 1990s economic problems in Colombia were compounded by a fall in the international price of the country's principal export commodities, and by high interest rates, which had led to a rise in the cost of debt-servicing. Despite the attempts of newly-inaugurated President Pastrana to prevent further decline, the economy continued to contract in late 1998 and throughout 1999. Real GDP decreased by some 6.6% in the first half of 1999, while domestic demand fell substantially, largely as a result of fiscal adjustments, and the rate of unemployment continued to increase. Meanwhile, efforts were made to attract foreign investment to the country, although the continued sabotage of petroleum installations by guerrilla groups did little to inspire investor confidence. In September 1999 the central bank allowed the flotation of the peso, the value of which had depreciated by 23% since the beginning of the year. Also in September the Government secured some US $6,900m. in financial assistance from international donors, including an IMF credit worth some $2,700m. (which was approved in December) in support of its economic programme for 1999–2002, which emphasized further fiscal reform, the restructuring of the financial sector and a reduction in public spending, as well as the introduction of new social welfare programmes to alleviate the effects of austerity measures.

## Social Welfare

There is compulsory social security, paid for by the Government, employers and employees, and administered by the Institute of Social Security. It provides benefits for disability, old age, death, sickness, maternity, industrial accidents and unemployment. Large enterprises are required to provide life insurance schemes for their employees, and there is a comprehensive system of pensions. Implementation of a system of private pension funds (modelled on the AFP system in Chile) was under consideration in the late 1990s. In 1980 the country had 849 hospital establishments, with a total of 44,495 beds. In the early 1990s there were 105 physicians per 100,000 people and 49 nurses per 100,000 people working in Colombia. Of total expenditure by the central Government in 1998, 1,862,700m. pesos (9.3%) was for health.

## Education

Primary education is free and compulsory for five years, to be undertaken by children between six and 12 years of age. No child may be admitted to secondary school unless these five years have been successfully completed. Secondary education, beginning at the age of 11, lasts for up to six years. Following completion of a first cycle of four years, pupils may pursue a further two years of vocational study, leading to the Bachiller examination. In 1996 the total enrolment at primary schools included 89% of pupils in the relevant age-group, while the comparable ratio for secondary education in 1995 was 50%. In the late 1990s there were 25 public universities in Colombia. Government expenditure on education in the 1998 budget was 4,706,900m. pesos, representing 23.6% of total spending. The rate of adult illiteracy averaged 19.2% in 1973, but, according to estimates by UNESCO, had declined to 8.7% (males 8.8%; females 8.6%) by 1995.

## Public Holidays

**2000:** 1 January (New Year's Day), 10 January (for Epiphany), 20 March (for St Joseph's Day), 20 April (Maundy Thursday), 21 April (Good Friday), 1 May (Labour Day), 5 June (for Ascension Day), 26 June (for Corpus Christi), 3 July (for SS Peter and Paul and Sacred Heart of Jesus), 20 July (Independence), 7 August (Battle of Boyacá), 21 August (for Assumption), 16 October (for Discovery of America), 6 November (for All Saints' Day), 13 November (for Independence of Cartagena), 8 December (Immaculate Conception), 25 December (Christmas Day).

**2001:** 1 January (New Year's Day), 8 January (for Epiphany), 19 March (St Joseph's Day), 12 April (Maundy Thursday), 13 April (Good Friday), 1 May (Labour Day), 28 May (for Ascension Day), 18 June (for Corpus Christi), 25 June (for SS Peter and Paul), 2 July (for Sacred Heart of Jesus), 20 July (Independence), 7 August (Battle of Boyacá), 20 August (for Assumption), 15 October (for Discovery of America), 5 November (for All Saints' Day), 12 November (for Independence of Cartagena), 8 December (Immaculate Conception), 25 December (Christmas Day).

## Weights and Measures

The metric system is in force.

Santafé de Bogotá, DC; tel. (1) 345-6600; fax (1) 217-1021; f. 1927; totally responsible for fostering and regulating the coffee economy; Gen. Man. JORGE CÁRDENAS GUTIÉRREZ; 203,000 mems.

**Federación Nacional de Cultivadores de Cereales (FENALCE):** Carrera 14, No 97-62, Apdo Aéreo 8694, Santafé de Bogotá, DC; tel. (1) 218-9366; fax (1) 218-9463; f. 1960; fed. of grain growers; Gen. Man. ADRIANO QUINTANA SILVA; 12,000 mems.

**Federación Nacional de Comerciantes (FENALCO):** Carrera 4, No 19-85, 7°, Santafé de Bogotá, DC; tel. (1) 286-0600; fax (1) 282-7573; fed. of businessmen; Pres. SABAS PRETELT DE LA VEGA.

**Sociedad de Agricultores de Colombia (SAC)** (Colombian Farmers' Society): Carrera 7A, No 24-89, 44°, Apdo Aéreo 3638, Santafé de Bogotá, DC; tel. (1) 281-0263; fax (1) 284-4572; e-mail socdeagr@impsat.net.co; f. 1871; Pres. JUAN MANUEL OSPINA RESTREPO; Sec.-Gen. Dr GABRIEL MARTÍNEZ TELÁEZ.

There are several other organizations, including those for rice growers, engineers and financiers.

### UTILITIES

#### Electricity

**Corporación Eléctrica de la Costa Atlántica (Corelca):** Calle 55, No 72-109, 9°, Barranquilla, Atlántico; tel. (5) 56-0247; fax (5) 56-2370; responsible for supplying electricity to the Atlantic departments; generates more than 2,000m. kWh annually from thermal power-stations; Man. Dir ENRIQUE JAVIER PACHECO.

**Empresa de Energía Eléctrica de Bogotá, SA (EEB):** Avda El Dorado, No 55-51, Santafé de Bogotá, DC; tel. (1) 221-1665; fax (1) 221-6858; internet www.eeb.com.co; provides electricity for Bogotá area by generating capacity of 680 MW, mainly hydroelectric; Man. Dir FABIO CHAPARRO.

**Instituto Colombiano de Energía Eléctrica ICEL:** Carrera 13, No 27-00, 3°, Apdo Aéreo 16243, Santafé de Bogotá, DC; tel. (1) 342-0181; fax (1) 286-2934; formulates policy for the devt of electrical energy; constructs systems for the generation, transmission and distribution of electrical energy; Man. DOUGLAS VELÁSQUEZ JACOME; Sec.-Gen. PATRICIA OLIVEROS LAVERDE.

**Interconexión Eléctrica, SA (ISA):** Calle 12 Sur, No 18-168, Apdo Aéreo 8915, Medellín, Antioquia; tel. (4) 317-1331; fax (4) 317-0848; f. 1967; created by Colombia's principal electricity production and distribution cos to form a national network; installed capacity of 2,641m. kWh; operates major power-stations at Chivor and San Carlos; Man. Dir JAVIER GUTIÉRREZ.

**Isagen:** Medellín, Antioquia; e-mail isagen@isagen.com.co; internet www.isagen.com.co; generates electricity from three hydraulic and two thermal power plants.

#### Gas

**Gas Natural ESP:** Avda 40A, No 13-09, 9°, Santafé de Bogotá, DC; tel. (1) 338-1199; fax (1) 288-0807; f. 1987; private gas corpn; Pres. ANTONI PERIS MINGOT.

**Gasoriente:** distributes gas to 8 municipalities in northeastern Colombia.

### TRADE UNIONS

According to official figures, an estimated 900 of Colombia's 2,000 trade unions are independent.

**Central Unitaria de Trabajadores (CUT):** Calle 35, No 7-25, 9°, Apdo Aéreo 221, Santafé de Bogotá, DC; tel. (1) 288-8577; fax (1) 287-5769; f. 1986; comprises 50 feds and 80% of all trade union members; Pres. LUIS EDUARDO GARZÓN; Sec.-Gen. MIGUEL ANTONIO CARO.

**Frente Sindical Democrática (FSD):** f. 1984; centre-right trade union alliance; comprises:

**Confederación de Trabajadores de Colombia (CTC)** (Colombian Confederation of Workers): Calle 39, No 26A-23, 5°, Apdo Aéreo 4780, Santafé de Bogotá, DC; tel. (1) 269-7119; f. 1934; mainly Liberal; 600 affiliates, including 6 national orgs and 20 regional feds; admitted to ICFTU; Pres. ALVIS FERNÁNDEZ; 400,000 mems.

**Confederación de Trabajadores Democráticos de Colombia (CTDC):** Carrera 13, No 59-52, Of. 303, Santafé de Bogotá, DC; tel. (1) 255-3146; fax (1) 484-581; f. 1988; comprises 23 industrial feds and 22 national unions; Pres. MARIO DE J. VALDERRAMA.

**Confederación General de Trabajadores Democráticos (CGTD):** Calle 39A, No 14-48, Apdo Aéreo 5415, Santafé de Bogotá, DC; tel. (1) 288-1560; fax (1) 288-1504; Christian Democrat; Sec.-Gen. JULIO ROBERTO GÓMEZ ESGUERRA.

## Transport

Land transport in Colombia is rendered difficult by high mountains, so the principal means of long-distance transport is by air. As a result of the development of the El Cerrejón coal field, Colombia's first deep-water port was constructed at Bahía de Portete and a 150 km rail link between El Cerrejón and the port became operational in 1989.

**Instituto Nacional del Transporte (INTRA):** Edif. Minobras (CAN), 6°, Apdo Aéreo 24990, Santafé de Bogotá, DC; tel. (1) 222-4100; govt body; Dir Dr GUILLERMO ANZOLA LIZARAZO.

### RAILWAYS

In 1989, following the entry into liquidation of the Ferrocarriles Nacionales de Colombia (FNC), the Government created three new companies, which assumed responsibility for the rail network in 1992. However, the new companies were beset by financial difficulties, and many rail services were subsequently suspended.

**Empresa Colombiana de Vías Férreas (Ferrovías):** Calle 31, No 6-41, 20°, Santafé de Bogotá, DC; tel. (1) 287-9888; fax (1) 287-2515; responsible for the maintenance and devt of the national rail network; Pres. L. B. VILLEGAS GIRALDO.

**Ferroviario Atlántico, SA:** Calle 72, No 13-23, 2°, Santafé de Bogotá, DC; tel. (1) 255-8684; fax (1) 255-8704; operated on a 30-year concession, awarded in 1998 to Asociación Futura Ferrocarriles de la Paz (Fepaz); 1,490 km (1993).

**Fondo de Pasivo Social de Ferrocarriles Nacionales de Colombia:** Santafé de Bogotá, DC; administers welfare services for existing and former employees of the FNC.

**El Cerrejón Mine Railway:** International Colombia Resources Corpn, Carrera 54, No 72-80, Apdo Aéreo 52499, Barranquilla, Atlántico; tel. (5) 350-5389; fax (5) 350-2249; f. 1989 to link the mine and the port at Bahía de Portete; 150 km (1996); Supt M. MENDOZA.

**Metro de Medellín Ltda:** Calle 44, No 46-001, Apdo Aéreo 9128, Medellín, Antioquia; tel. (4) 452-6000; fax (4) 452-4450; e-mail emetro@col3.telecom.com.co; two-line metro with 25 stations opened in stages in 1995–96; 29 km; Gen. Man. LUIS GUILLERMO GÓMEZ A.

### ROADS

In 1996 there were an estimated 107,000 km of roads, of which 25,600 km were highways and main roads and 43,900 km were secondary roads. About 12% of the total road network was paved in the same year. The country's main highways are the Caribbean Trunk Highway, the Eastern and Western Trunk Highways, the Central Trunk Highway and there are also roads into the interior. There are plans to construct a Jungle Edge highway to give access to the interior, a link road between Turbo, Bahía Solano and Medellín, a highway between Bogotá and Villavicencio and to complete the short section of the Pan-American highway between Panama and Colombia. In 1992 the World Bank granted a loan of US $266m. to Colombia for the construction of 400 km of new roads and the completion of 2,000 km of roads begun under an earlier programme.

There are a number of national bus companies and road haulage companies.

**Instituto Nacional de Vías:** Transversal 45, Entrada 2, Santafé de Bogotá, DC; tel. (1) 315-0400; fax (1) 315-6713; e-mail director@latino.net.co; f. 1966, reorganized 1994; wholly state-owned; responsible to the Ministry of Transport; maintenance and construction of national road network; Gen. Man. GUILLERMO GAVIRIA CORREA.

### INLAND WATERWAYS

The Magdalena–Cauca river system is the centre of river traffic and is navigable for 1,500 km, while the Atrato is navigable for 687 km. The Orinoco system has more than five navigable rivers, which total more than 4,000 km of potential navigation (mainly through Venezuela); the Amazonas system has four main rivers, which total 3,000 navigable km (mainly through Brazil). There are plans to connect the Arauca with the Meta, and the Putamayo with the Amazon, and also to construct an Atrato–Truandó inter-oceanic canal.

**Dirección de Navegación y Puertos:** Edif. Minobras (CAN), Of. 562, Santafé de Bogotá, DC; tel. (1) 222-1248; responsible for river works and transport; the waterways system is divided into four sectors: Magdalena, Atrato, Orinoquia, and Amazonia; Dir ALBERTO RODRÍGUEZ ROJAS.

### SHIPPING

The four most important ocean terminals are Buenaventura on the Pacific coast and Santa Marta, Barranquilla and Cartagena on the Atlantic coast. The port of Tumaco on the Pacific coast is gaining in importance and there are plans for construction of a deep-water port at Bahía Solano.

In 1998 Colombia's merchant fleet totalled 111,686 grt.

#### Port Authorities

**Port of Barranquilla:** Sociedad Portuaria Regional de Barranquilla, Carrera 38, Calle 1A, Barranquilla, Atlántico; tel. (5) 379-

9555; fax (5) 379-9557; e-mail sportuaria@rednet.net.co; internet www.colombiaexport.com/baqport.htm; privatized in 1993; Port Man. MARTÍN VÁSQUEZ LEBOLO.

**Port of Buenaventura:** Empresa Puertos de Colombia, Edif. El Café, Of. 1, Buenaventura; tel. (224) 22543; fax (224) 34447; Port Man. VÍCTOR GONZÁLEZ.

**Port of Cartagena:** Sociedad Portuaria Regional de Cartagena, SA, Manga, Terminal Marítimo, Cartagena, Bolívar; tel. (5) 660-7781; fax (5) 650-2239; e-mail comercial@sprc.com.co; internet www.sprc.com.co; f. 1959; Port Man. ALFONSO SALAS TRUJILLO; Harbour Master Capt. GONZALO PARRA.

**Port of Santa Marta:** Empresa Puertos de Colombia, Calle 15, No 3-25, 11°, Santa Marta, Magdalena; tel. (54) 210739; fax (54) 210711; Port Man. JULIÁN PALACIOS.

### Principal Shipping Companies

**Flota Mercante Grancolombiana, SA:** Edif. Grancolombiana, Carrera 13, No 27-75, Apdo Aéreo 4482, Santafé de Bogotá, DC; tel. (1) 286-0200; fax (1) 286-9028; f. 1946; owned by the Colombian Coffee Growers' Federation (80%) and Ecuador Development Bank (20%); f. 1946; one of Latin America's leading cargo carriers serving 45 countries world-wide; Pres. ENRIQUE VARGAS.

**Colombiana Internacional de Vapores, Ltda (Colvapores):** Avda Caracas, No 35-02, Apdo Aéreo 17227, Santafé de Bogotá, DC; cargo services mainly to the USA.

**Líneas Agromar, Ltda:** Calle 73, Vía 40-350, Apdo Aéreo 3256, Barranquilla, Atlántico; tel. (5) 353-1049; fax (5) 353-1042; Pres. MANUEL DEL DAGO FERNÁNDEZ.

**Petromar Ltda:** Bosque, Diagonal 23, No 56-152, Apdo Aéreo 505, Cartagena, Bolívar; tel. (5) 662-7208; fax (5) 662-7592; Chair. SAVERIO MINERVINI S.

**Transportadora Colombiana de Graneles, SA (NAVESCO, SA):** Avda 19, No 118-95, Of. 214-301, Santafé de Bogotá, DC; tel. (1) 620-9035; fax (1) 620-8801; e-mail navesco@colomsat.net.co; Gen. Man. GUILLERMO SOLANO VARELA.

Several foreign shipping lines call at Colombian ports.

## CIVIL AVIATION

Colombia has more than 100 airports, including 11 international airports: Santafé de Bogotá, DC (El Dorado International Airport), Medellín, Cali, Barranquilla, Bucaramanga, Cartagena, Cúcuta, Leticia, Pereira, San Andrés and Santa Marta.

### Airports Authority

**Unidad Administrativa Especial de Aeronáutica Civil:** Aeropuerto Internacional El Dorado, 4°, Santafé de Bogotá, DC; tel. (1) 413-9500; fax (1) 413-9878; f. 1967 as Departamento Administrativo de Aeronáutica Civil, reorganized 1993; wholly state-owned; Dir ABEL ENRIQUE JIMÉNEZ.

### National Airlines

**Aerolíneas Centrales de Colombia, SA (ACES):** Edif. del Café, Calle 49, No 50-21, 34°, Apdo Aéreo 6503, Medellín, Antioquia; tel. (4) 251-7500; fax (4) 251-1677; e-mail gusuga@acescolombia.com.co; internet www.acescolombia.com; f. 1971; operates scheduled domestic passenger services throughout Colombia, and charter and scheduled flights to the USA and the Caribbean; Pres. JUAN E. POSADA.

**Aerotaca, SA (Aerotransportes Casanare):** Avda El Dorado, Entrada 1, Interior 20, Santafé de Bogotá, DC; tel. (1) 413-9040; fax (1) 413-5256; f. 1965; scheduled regional and domestic passenger services; Gen. Man. RAFAEL URDANETA.

**AVIANCA (Aerovías Nacionales de Colombia, SA):** Avda El Dorado, No 93-30, 5°, Santafé de Bogotá, DC; tel. (1) 413-9511; fax (1) 269-9131; internet www.avianca.com; f. 1940; operates domestic services to all cities in Colombia and international services to the USA, France, Spain and throughout Central and Southern America; Chair. ANDRÉS OBREGÓN SANTO DOMINGO; Pres. GUSTAVO A. LENIS.

**Intercontinental de Aviación:** Avda El Dorado, Entrada 2, Interior 6, Santafé de Bogotá, DC; tel. (1) 413-9700; fax (1) 413-8458; internet www.insite-network.com/inter; f. 1965 as Aeropesca Colombia (Aerovías de Pesca y Colonización del Suroeste Colombiano): operates scheduled domestic, regional and international passenger and cargo services: Pres. Capt. LUIS HERNÁNDEZ ZIA.

**Servicio de Aeronavegación a Territorios Nacionales (Satena):** Avda El Dorado, Entrada 1, Interior 11, Apdo Aéreo 11163, Santafé de Bogotá, DC; tel. (1) 413-8438; fax (1) 413-8178; f. 1962; commercial enterprise attached to the Ministry of National Defence; internal services; CEO and Gen. Man. Brig.-Gen. ALFREDO GARCÍA ROJAS.

**Sociedad Aeronáutica de Medellín Consolidada, SA (SAM):** Edif. SAM, Calle 53, No 45-211, 21°, Apdo Aéreo 1085, Medellín, Antioquia; tel. (4) 251-5544; fax (4) 251-0711; f. 1945; subsidiary of AVIANCA; internal services; and international cargo services to Central America and the Caribbean; Pres JULIO MARIO SANTO DOMINGO, GUSTAVO LENIS.

**Transportes Aéreos Mercantiles Panamericanos (Tampa):** Carrera 76, No 34A-61, Apdo Aéreo 494, Medellín, Antioquia; tel. (4) 250-2939; fax (4) 250-5639; e-mail tampa@ticsanet.net; f. 1973; operates international cargo services to destinations throughout South America, also to Puerto Rico and the USA; Chair. GUSTAVO MORENO; Pres. FREDERICK JACOBSEN.

In addition, the following airlines operate international and domestic charter cargo services: Aerosucre Colombia, Aero Transcolombiana de Carga (ATC), Aerovías Colombianas (ARCA), Líneas Aéreas del Caribe (LAC Airlines Colombia), and Líneas Aéreas Suraméricanas (LAS).

# Tourism

The principal tourist attractions are the Caribbean coast (including the island of San Andrés), the 16th-century walled city of Cartagena, the Amazonian town of Leticia, the Andes mountains rising to 5,700 m above sea-level, the extensive forests and jungles, pre-Columbian relics and monuments of colonial art. In 1996 there were 1,253,916 visitors (compared with an estimated 1,400,000 in 1995), most of whom came from Venezuela, Ecuador and the USA. Tourism receipts in 1996 were estimated to be US $909m.

**Viceministerio de Turismo:** Calle 28, No 13A-15, 17°, Edif. Centro de Comercio Internacional, Santafé de Bogotá, DC; tel. (1) 283-9558; fax (1) 286-4492; Vice-Minister of Tourism MARÍA PAULINA ESPINOSA DE LÓPEZ.

**Asociación Colombiana de Agencias de Viajes y Turismo—ANATO:** Carrera 21, No 83-63/71, Santafé de Bogotá, DC; tel. (1) 610-7099; fax (1) 218-7103; e-mail presidencia@anato.com.co; internet www.anato.com.co; f. 1949; Pres. Dr OSCAR RUEDA GARCÍA.

# THE COMOROS*

## Introductory Survey

### Location, Climate, Language, Religion, Flag, Capital

The Federal Islamic Republic of the Comoros is an archipelago in the Mozambique Channel, between the island of Madagascar and the east coast of the African mainland. The group comprises four main islands (Njazidja, Nzwani and Mwali, formerly Grande-Comore, Anjouan and Mohéli respectively, and Mayotte) and numerous islets and coral reefs. The climate is tropical, with average temperatures ranging from 23°C (73.4°F) to 28°C (82.4°F). Average annual rainfall is between 1,500 mm (59 ins) and 5,000 mm (197 ins). The official languages are Comorian (a blend of Swahili and Arabic), French and Arabic. Islam is the state religion. The flag is green, with a white crescent moon and four five-pointed white stars in the centre; the white Arabic inscriptions 'Allah' and 'Muhammad' appear respectively in the upper fly and lower hoist corners of the flag. The capital, which is situated on Njazidja, is Moroni.

### Recent History

Formerly attached to Madagascar, the Comoros became a separate French Overseas Territory in 1947. The islands achieved internal self-government in December 1961, with a Chamber of Deputies and a Government Council responsible for local administration.

Elections in December 1972 resulted in a large majority for parties advocating independence, and Ahmed Abdallah became President of the Government Council. In June 1973 he was restyled President of the Government. At a referendum in December 1974 96% of the voters expressed support for independence, despite the opposition of the Mayotte Party, which sought the status of a French Department for the island of Mayotte. On 6 July 1975, despite French insistence that any constitutional settlement should be ratified by all the islands voting separately, the Chamber of Deputies voted for immediate independence, elected Abdallah to be first President of the Comoros and reconstituted itself as the National Assembly. Although France made no attempt to intervene, it maintained control of Mayotte. Abdallah was deposed in August, and the National Assembly was abolished. A National Executive Council was established, with Prince Saïd Mohammed Jaffar, leader of the opposition party, the Front national uni, as its head, and Ali Soilih, leader of the coup, among its members. In November the Comoros was admitted to the UN, as a unified state comprising the whole archipelago. In December France officially recognized the independence of Njazidja, Nzwani and Mwali, but all relations between France and the Comoros were effectively suspended. In February 1976 Mayotte voted overwhelmingly to retain its links with France.

In January 1976 Ali Soilih was elected Head of State, and adopted extended powers under the terms of a new Constitution. In May 1978 Soilih was killed, following a coup by a group of about 50 European mercenaries, led by a Frenchman, Bob Denard, on behalf of the exiled former President, Ahmed Abdallah, and the Comoros was proclaimed a Federal Islamic Republic. Shortly afterwards, diplomatic relations with France were restored. In July the Comoran delegation was expelled from the Organization of African Unity (OAU, see p. 240) as a result of the continued presence of the mercenaries (but was readmitted in February 1979).

In October 1978 a new Constitution was approved in a referendum, on the three islands excluding Mayotte, by 99.3% of the votes cast. Abdallah was elected President in the same month, and in December elections for a new legislature, the Federal Assembly, took place. In January 1979 the Federal Assembly approved the formation of a one-party state. Unofficial opposition groups, however, continued to exist, and 150 people were arrested in February 1981, following reports (which were officially denied) of an attempted coup. Ali Mroudjae, hitherto Minister of Foreign Affairs and Co-operation, was appointed Prime Minister in February 1982, and legislative elections took place in March. Constitutional amendments, which were adopted in October, vested additional powers in the President. Abdallah was the sole candidate at a presidential election in September 1984. Despite appeals by the opposition for voters to boycott the election, 98% of the electorate participated. Abdallah was re-elected President for a further six-year term by 99.4% of the votes cast. In January 1985, following further amendments to the Constitution, the position of Prime Minister was abolished, and Abdallah assumed the office of Head of Government.

In March 1985 an attempt by members of the presidential guard to overthrow Abdallah, while he was in France, failed. In November 17 people, including Moustoifa Saïd Cheikh, the Secretary-General of the banned opposition movement, Front démocratique (FD), were sentenced to forced labour for life for their involvement in the coup attempt. In February 1987 Abdallah indicated that independent opposition candidates would be permitted to contest legislative elections scheduled for March. In the event, however, opposition candidates were only allowed to contest 20 seats on Njazidja, where they received 35% of the total votes, and pro-Government candidates retained full control of the 42-seat Federal Assembly. There were allegations of widespread fraud and intimidation of opposition candidates, and, according to Comoran dissidents in Réunion, about 400 people were arrested, 200–300 of whom were later imprisoned. In November a further coup attempt by a left-wing group was suppressed by the authorities.

In early November 1989 a constitutional amendment, which permitted Abdallah to remain in office for a third six-year term, was approved by 92.5% of votes cast in a popular referendum. The result of the referendum, however, was disputed by the President's opponents. Violent demonstrations followed, and opposition leaders were detained.

On the night of 26–27 November 1989 Abdallah was assassinated by members of the presidential guard (which included a number of European advisers), under the command of Bob Denard. Under the terms of the Constitution, the President of the Supreme Court, Saïd Mohamed Djohar, was appointed interim Head of State, pending a presidential election. Denard, however, staged a coup, in which 27 members of the security forces were reportedly killed, and the regular army was defeated by Denard and his supporters. The mercenaries' action provoked international condemnation, despite denials by Denard of complicity in Abdallah's death. (In May 1999 Denard stood trial in Paris, France, in connection with the assassination. Both Denard and his co-defendant, Dominique Malacrino, were acquitted of the murder charge by the French court.) A French naval force was sent to the area, ostensibly to prepare for the evacuation of French citizens from the Comoros. In mid-December Denard finally agreed to relinquish power, and, following the arrival of French paratroops in Moroni, was transported to South Africa, together with the remaining mercenaries. Djohar subsequently announced that the French Government's troops were to remain in the Comoros for up to two years in order to train local security forces.

At the end of December 1989 the main political groups formed a provisional Government of National Unity. An amnesty for all political prisoners was proclaimed, and an inquiry into the death of Abdallah was instigated. It was announced that a multi-candidate presidential election, which was to end the system of single-party rule, was to take place in January 1990. Following delays caused by alleged widespread irregularities and after an inconclusive first round held on 4 March, Djohar, the official candidate for the Union comorienne pour le progrès (Udzima), was elected President on 11 March, with 55.3% of the votes cast, while Mohamed Taki Abdulkarim, the leader of the Union nationale pour la démocratie aux Comores (UNDC), secured 44.7% of the votes. In late March Djohar appointed a new Government, in which the eight political parties that had

* Some of the information contained in this chapter refers to the whole Comoros archipelago, which the independent Comoran state claims as its national territory. However, the island of Mayotte (Mahoré) is, in fact, administered by France. Separate information on Mayotte may be found in the chapter on French Overseas Possessions.

supported his presidential candidacy were represented. In April Djohar announced plans for the formal constitutional restoration of a multi-party political system.

In August 1990 an attempted coup was staged by armed rebels, who attacked various French installations on Njazidja. The revolt was allegedly organized by a small group of European mercenaries, who intended to provoke Djohar's resignation through the enforced removal of French forces from the islands; however, supporters of Mohamed Taki were also implicated in the conspiracy. In September the Minister of the Interior and Administrative Reforms was dismissed for his alleged involvement in the attempted coup, and more than 20 arrests were made. In October it was reported that the leader of the conspirators had been killed by Comoran security forces. In the same month Djohar implemented an extensive ministerial reorganization.

In March 1991 the Government announced that a conference, comprising three representatives of each political association, was to be convened to discuss constitutional reform. The conference took place in May, but several principal opposition parties, which objected to arrangements whereby Djohar reserved the right to modify the conference's recommendations, refused to attend. However, the conference presented draft constitutional amendments, which were to be submitted for endorsement by a national referendum.

On 3 August 1991 the President of the Supreme Court, Ibrahim Ahmed Halidi, announced the dismissal of Djohar, on the grounds of negligence, and proclaimed himself interim President with the support of the Supreme Court. Opposition leaders declared the seizure of power to be legitimate under the terms of the Constitution. However, the Government condemned the coup attempt, and Halidi and several other members of the Supreme Court were arrested. A state of emergency was imposed, and remained in force until early September. A number of demonstrations in favour of Djohar took place in early August, although members of Udzima did not express support for the Government. Later that month, however, the Government banned all public demonstrations, following clashes between members of the opposition and pro-Government demonstrators.

In late August 1991 Djohar established a new coalition Government, which included two members of the FD and, in an attempt to appease increasing discontent on Mwali, two members of the Mwalian opposition. However, the two leading political associations represented in the coalition Government, Udzima and the Parti comorien pour la démocratie et le progrès (PCDP), objected to the ministerial reshuffle, and accused Djohar of attempting to reduce their power; shortly afterwards the ministers belonging to the two parties resigned. In November Udzima (which had been officially renamed Parti Udzima—Udzima) withdrew its support for Djohar and joined the opposition. It also condemned the proposed constitutional amendments that had been drafted in May. Opposition leaders demanded the dissolution of the Federal Assembly, which was declared to be invalid on the grounds that it had been elected under the former one-party system. In the same month, despite efforts at appeasement by Djohar, Mwali announced plans to conduct a referendum on self-determination for the island. Later in November, agreement was reached between Djohar and the principal opposition leaders to initiate a process of national reconciliation, which would include the formation of a government of national unity and the convening of a constitutional conference. The accord also guaranteed the legitimacy of Djohar's election as President. In January 1992 a new transitional Government of National Unity was formed, under the leadership of Mohamed Taki, who was named as its Co-ordinator, pending legislative elections, which were originally scheduled for April. Later in January a national conference, comprising representatives of political parties and other organizations, was convened to draft a new constitution. (Mwalian representatives, however, refused to attend the conference.)

In May 1992 opposition parties demanded the resignation of Djohar's son-in-law, Mohamed Saïd Abdallah M'Changama, as Minister of Finance, Commerce and Planning, following allegations of irregularities in the negotiation of government contracts. Djohar subsequently formed a new interim Council of Ministers, in which, however, M'Changama retained his portfolio. At a constitutional referendum, held on 7 June, the reform proposals, which had been submitted in April, were approved by 74.3% of the votes cast, despite opposition from eight parties, notably Udzima and the FD. The new Constitution limited the presidential tenure to a maximum of two five-year terms of office, and provided for a bicameral legislature, comprising a Federal Assembly, elected for a term of four years, and a 15-member Senate, selected for a six-year term by the regional Councils. In early July Djohar dismissed Mohamed Taki, following the latter's appointment of a former mercenary to a financial advisory post in the Government. Later that month Djohar formed a new Government, although the post of Co-ordinator remained vacant.

In mid-1992 social and economic conditions on the Comoros deteriorated, following renewed strikes in a number of sectors. In early September Djohar announced that legislative elections were to commence in late October, contrary to the recommendation of an electoral commission that they take place in December. Opposition parties claimed that the schedule allowed insufficient time for preparation, and indicated that they would boycott the elections. Later that month a demonstration, organized by Udzima, the UNDC and the FD, in support of demands for Djohar's resignation, was suppressed by security forces. In an apparent attempt to restore order, Djohar subsequently anounced a new electoral schedule, whereby legislative elections would take place in early November, and local government elections in December.

In late September 1992 an abortive coup attempt was staged by disaffected members of the armed forces, who seized the radio station at Moroni and announced that the Government had been overthrown. Six opposition leaders and six members of the armed forces, including two sons of the former President, Ahmed Abdallah, were subsequently arrested, and, in October, were charged with involvement in the attempted coup. In mid-October some 100 rebel troops, led by a former member of Abdallah's presidential guard, attacked the military garrison of Kandani, in an attempt to release the detainees. Shortly afterwards government forces attacked the rebels at Mbeni, to the north-east of Moroni; fighting was also reported on Nzwani. Later in October a demonstration was staged in protest at the French Government's support of Djohar, following French consignments of food rations to government forces, which prompted speculation that armaments had also been dispatched. By the end of October some 25 people had been killed in clashes between rebels and government forces in Moroni.

In October 1992 Djohar agreed to reschedule the legislative elections for late November, although opposition parties demanded a further postponement, and Udzima and the UNDC continued to support an electoral boycott. The first round of the legislative elections, which took place on 22 November, was contested by some 320 candidates representing 21 political parties. Numerous electoral irregularities and violent incidents were reported, however, and several opposition parties demanded that the results be declared invalid, and joined the boycott. Election results in six constituencies were subsequently annulled, while the second round of voting on 29 November took place in only 34 of the 42 constituencies. Following partial elections on 13 and 30 December, reports indicated that candidates supporting Djohar—including seven members of the Union des démocrates pour la démocratie (UDD), a pro-Government organization based on Nzwani—had secured a narrow majority in the Federal Assembly. The leader of the UDD, Ibrahim Abdérémane Halidi, was appointed Prime Minister on 1 January 1993, and formed a new Council of Ministers. Later in January a Mwalian, Amir Attoumane, was elected as Speaker of the Federal Assembly in response to demands by Mwalian deputies in the Assembly.

Shortly after the new Government took office, however, disagreement between Djohar and Halidi was reported, while the presidential majority in the Federal Assembly fragmented into three dissenting factions. In mid-February 1993 a vote of censure against the Government, which was proposed by representatives of several pro-Djohar parties, was rejected. Later that month Halidi effected an extensive reorganization of the Council of Ministers, although the political parties that supported Djohar remained dissatisfied with its composition.

In April 1993 nine people, including Abdallah's sons and two prominent members of Udzima, were convicted on charges of involvement in the coup attempt of September 1992, and sentenced to death. Following considerable domestic and international pressure, however, Djohar commuted the sentences to terms of imprisonment. In May 1993 eight supporters of M'Changama, allied with a number of opposition deputies, proposed a motion of 'no confidence' in the Government (apparently with the tacit support of Djohar), which was approved by 23 of the 42 deputies in the Federal Assembly. Shortly afterwards,

Djohar appointed an associate of M'Changama, Saïd Ali Mohamed, as Prime Minister and a new Council of Ministers was formed. In mid-June an alliance of pro-Halidi parliamentary deputies proposed a motion of censure against the new Government, on the grounds that the Prime Minister had not been appointed from a party that commanded a majority in the Federal Assembly. Djohar, however, declared the motion to be unconstitutional, and, in view of the continued absence of a viable parliamentary majority, dissolved the Federal Assembly, and announced legislative elections. He subsequently dismissed Mohamed, and appointed a former presidential adviser, Ahmed Ben Cheikh Attoumane, as Prime Minister. Shortly afterwards, an interim Council of Ministers was formed (although two of the newly-appointed ministers immediately resigned).

Following the dissolution of the Federal Assembly, opposition parties declared Djohar to be unfit to hold office, in view of the increasing political confusion, and demanded that legislative elections take place within the period of 40 days stipulated in the Constitution. In early July 1993, however, Djohar announced that the legislative elections (which were to take place concurrently with local government elections), were to be postponed until October. In response, opposition parties organized a one-day strike, in support of demands that Djohar bring forward the date of the legislative elections or resign. In early September a number of opposition movements, notably Udzima and the UNDC, established an informal electoral alliance, known as the Union pour la République et le progrès, while the FD, the PCDP, CHUMA (Islands' Fraternity and Unity Party), and the Mouvement pour la démocratie et le progrès (MDP) agreed to present joint candidates. Later in September Djohar postponed the legislative elections until November, officially on financial grounds. In October Djohar (who had failed to induce the political parties that supported him to form an electoral alliance, owing to their hostility towards M'Changama) established a political organization, known as Rassemblement pour la démocratie et le renouveau (RDR), principally comprising supporters of M'Changama and several prominent members of the Government. In November the legislative elections were rescheduled for December, while the local government elections were postponed indefinitely. Later in November Djohar reorganized the Council of Ministers, and established a new National Electoral Commission, in compliance with the demands of the opposition (which had objected to the composition of the former commission).

In the first round of the legislative elections, which took place on 12 December 1993, four opposition candidates secured seats in the Federal Assembly, apparently prompting concern in the Government. Following the second round of the polls on 20 December, it was reported that three people had been killed in violent incidents in Nzwani, where the authorities had assumed control of the electoral process. The National Electoral Commission subsequently declared the results in several constituencies to be invalid. Opposition candidates refused to participate in further elections in these constituencies, on the grounds that voting was again to be conducted under the supervision of the authorities, rather than that of the National Electoral Commission; RDR candidates consequently secured all 10 contested seats, and 22 seats overall, thereby securing a narrow majority in the Federal Assembly. In early January 1994 Djohar appointed the Secretary-General of the RDR, Mohamed Abdou Madi, as Prime Minister. The new Council of Ministers included several supporters of M'Changama, who was elected Speaker of the Federal Assembly. Later in January 12 principal opposition parties, which claimed that the RDR had assumed power illegally, formed a new alliance, known as the Forum pour le redressement national (FRN).

In February 1994 security forces seized the transmitters of a private radio station, owned by Udzima, which had broadcast independent news coverage. In March the Comoran authorities protested to the French Government after a French periodical published an article claiming that M'Changama was implicated in a number of fraudulent business transactions. At a religious ceremony later that month, which was attended by Djohar, a former bodyguard of an RDR candidate was arrested by security forces and discovered to be in possession of a firearm. A former Governor of Njazidja and member of the FRN, Mohamed Abdérémane, was subsequently arrested on suspicion of involvement in an assassination attempt against Djohar, while two other prominent opposition leaders were also questioned in connection with the incident. Abdérémane was later released, however, and there was speculation that the Government had arranged the episode in an attempt to discredit the opposition.

In April 1994 pressure increased from both the Comoran opposition and the French Government in support of an amnesty for political prisoners. In the same month division emerged between M'Changama and Abdou Madi regarding the appointment of a number of prominent government officials. At the end of May teachers initiated strike action (which was later joined by health workers) in support of demands for an increase in salaries and the reorganization of the public sector. In early June a motion of censure against Abdou Madi, which was proposed by supporters of the FRN in the Federal Assembly, was rejected. In mid-June it was reported that five people had been killed on Mwali, following an opposition demonstration in support of the public-sector strike, which was violently suppressed by the security forces. Later that month legislation (which had been approved by Djohar) providing for the sale of the state-owned airline, Air Comores, to an alleged international financier, known as Rowland Ashley, was rescinded, following protests from both opposition and government supporters in the Federal Assembly. Under a compromise arrangement, Ashley's privately-owned company was granted management of the airline's operations. In August, however, Ashley's background was proved to be fraudulent, and the existence of his company fabricated. Ashley subsequently claimed that prominent members of the Government had accepted financial inducements in connection with the proposed sale of the airline. Later that month the political management committee of the RDR, which was headed by M'Changama, criticized Abdou Madi's involvement in the affair.

In early September 1994 public-sector workers initiated further strike action; union officials refused to enter into negotiations with the authorities while Abdou Madi's Government remained in power. In the same month the French national airline, Air France, threatened to suspend flights to the Comoros, in protest at debts incurred by Air Comores under Ashley's management. Despite previous expressions of support for Abdou Madi, in October Djohar dismissed him from the office of Prime Minister (apparently owing to his involvement in the Air Comores affair), and appointed Halifa Houmadi to the post. A new Council of Ministers included only two members of the former administration.

In December 1994 Djohar failed to accede to a request by the Federal Assembly that political prisoners who had been implicated in the abortive coup attempt in September 1992 be granted amnesty. In January 1995 public-sector workers suspended strike action, after the Government agreed to a number of union demands. In the same month Djohar condemned a decision by the French Government to reimpose visa requirements for Comoran nationals entering Mayotte (which further undermined the Comoros' claim of sovereignty over the territory). A demonstration at the French embassy in Moroni, which was staged in protest at the measure, was suppressed by security forces, after degenerating into violence. It was subsequently reported that threats had been issued against French nationals resident in the Comoros. Later in January division emerged within the RDR, after the party Chairman and Secretary-General (Abdou Madi) both criticized the Government's failure to contain the hostility towards French citizens. At a congress of the RDR in early February the two officials were removed from the party, and Houmadi became Chairman. In the same month the Government announced that elections to the regional councils were to take place in April, and were to be followed by the establishment of a Senate and a Constitutional Council (in accordance with the terms of the Constitution). The opposition, however, accused Djohar of acting unconstitutionally in the preparation for elections, and claimed that he planned to assume control of the electoral process. In March Djohar announced that the forthcoming elections to the regional councils were to be rescheduled for July, ostensibly owing to lack of finance; it was widely speculated, however, that the postponement had been decided in response to an opposition campaign in support of an electoral boycott.

In April 1995 reports emerged of a widening rift between Djohar and Houmadi, after the Prime Minister apparently claimed that Djohar and M'Changama had engaged in financial malpractice. At the end of that month Djohar dismissed Houmadi from the premiership and appointed a former Minister of Finance, Mohamed Caabi El Yachroutu, as his successor. A 13-member Council of Ministers, which included only five members of the previous administration, was established. In May three former Prime Ministers (Mohamed, Abdou Madi and Houmadi) conducted a series of political meetings urging public support for the removal of M'Changama (who, they claimed, exerted undue influence over Djohar), and demanded the dissolution of the Federal Assembly. In July further tension developed within the Government over an agreement whereby Air Comores was to be transferred to the joint management of an airline based in the United Arab Emirates; M'Changama and the Minister of Transport and Tourism, Ahmed Saïd Issilame, claimed that the agreement was technically invalid on the grounds that it had been signed by Djohar before legislation providing for the privatization of Air Comores had been approved in the Federal Assembly. Meanwhile, it was feared that the further postponement of elections to the regional councils would delay the presidential election. In an effort to facilitate the organization of the presidential election, the Government introduced minor constitutional amendments, including the relaxation of regulations governing the registration of political candidates and a provision empowering the Prime Minister to act as interim Head of State. At the end of July Djohar removed Issilame and a further three associates of M'Changama from the Council of Ministers.

In late September 1995 about 30 European mercenaries, led by Denard, staged a military coup, seizing control of the garrison at Kandani and capturing Djohar. The mercenaries, who were joined by some 300 members of the Comoran armed forces, released a number of prisoners (including those detained for involvement in the failed coup attempt in September 1992), and installed a former associate of Denard, Capt. Ayouba Combo, as leader of a Transitional Military Committee. The French Government denounced the coup and suspended economic aid to the Comoros, but initially refused to take military action, despite requests for assistance from El Yachroutu, who had taken refuge in the French embassy. In early October Combo announced that he had transferred authority to Mohamed Taki and the leader of CHUMA, Saïd Ali Kemal (who had both welcomed the coup), as joint civilian Presidents, apparently in an attempt to avert military repercussions by the French Government. The FRN, however, rejected the new leadership and entered into negotiations with El Yachroutu. Following a further appeal for intervention from El Yachroutu, who invoked a defence co-operation agreement that had been established between the two countries in 1978, some 900 French military personnel landed on the Comoros and surrounded the mercenaries at Kandani. Shortly afterwards, Denard and his associates, together with the disaffected members of the Comoran armed forces, surrendered to the French troops. The mercenaries were subsequently placed under arrest and transported to France. (In October 1996, following his release from imprisonment in France in July, Denard claimed that the coup attempt had been planned at the request of several Comoran officials, including Mohamed Taki.)

Following the French military intervention, El Yachroutu declared himself interim President in accordance with the Constitution and announced the formation of a Government of National Unity, which included members of the constituent parties of the FRN. Djohar (who had been transported to Réunion by the French in order to receive medical treatment) rejected El Yachroutu's assumption of power and announced the reappointment of Saïd Ali Mohamed as Prime Minister. Later in October 1995 a National Reconciliation Conference decided that El Yachroutu would remain interim President, pending the forthcoming election, which was provisionally scheduled for early 1996. The incumbent administration opposed Djohar's stated intention to return to the Comoros and announced that measures would be taken to prevent him from entering the country. At the end of October El Yachroutu granted an amnesty to all Comorans involved in the coup attempt and appointed representatives of the UNDC and Udzima (which had supported the coup) to the new Council of Ministers. In early November Djohar announced the formation of a rival Government, headed by Mohamed. El Yachroutu, who was supported by the Comoran armed forces, refused to recognize the legitimacy of Djohar's appointments, while opposition parties equally opposed his return to power; only elements of the RDR continued to support Djohar's authority. It was reported that representatives of the OAU, who visited the Comoros and Réunion in mid-November in an effort to resolve the situation, had unofficially concluded that only El Yachroutu's administration was capable of governing. There was also widespread speculation that the French Government had believed Djohar's authority to be untenable and had tacitly supported his removal from power. Later that month, however, supporters of Djohar, including M'Changama, organized a political gathering to demand the resignation of El Yachroutu's administration. Meanwhile, political leaders on Mwali rejected the authority of both rival Governments, urged a campaign of civil disobedience and established a 'citizens' committee' to govern the island; discontent with the central administration also emerged on Nzwani.

In December 1995 a decision by El Yachroutu's Government to schedule the presidential election for the end of January 1996 was opposed by a number of political leaders, who demanded a postponement until March, ostensibly on the grounds that the stipulated date would coincide with the Islamic festival of Ramadan; the Government subsequently agreed to reschedule the presidential election for March. Later in January Djohar returned to the Comoros, after apparently signing an agreement stipulating that he would retain only symbolic presidential powers. In February it was reported that the island of Mwali had unilaterally proclaimed itself a democratic republic. In the first round of the presidential election, which took place on 6 March and was contested by some 15 candidates, Mohamed Taki obtained the highest number of votes, with 21%, while the leader of the FRN, Abbas Djoussouf, secured about 15% of votes; it was subsequently reported that 12 of the 13 unsuccessful candidates had urged support for Mohamed Taki in the second round of the election. Taki was duly elected to the presidency on 16 March, obtaining 64% of the vote. International observers, including delegates from the UN and OAU, were satisfied with the electoral process; officials reported that 62% of the electorate had participated in the second round. The new Head of State was sworn in on 25 March. Taki appointed a new Council of Ministers, which included five of the presidential candidates who had supported him in the second round of the election.

In early April 1996 Taki dissolved the Federal Assembly and announced that legislative elections would take place in October, despite the constitutional requirement that elections be held within a period of 40 days following the dissolution of the legislature. New Governors, all belonging to the UNDC, were appointed to each of the three islands. In mid-August Taki issued a decree awarding himself absolute powers. This measure was widely criticized in the media, and by opposition groups, notably CHUMA, the Forces pour l'action républicaine (FAR) and the FRN, as being in violation of the Constitution. In a government reorganization later in August, Saïd Ali Kemal and a representative of FAR were dismissed, following their parties' refusal to disband in order to join the single pro-presidential party that Taki intended to establish.

In September 1996 Taki established a constitutional consultative committee, comprising 42 representatives of political parties and other organizations, which was to provide advice concerning the drawing up of a new constitution; the FRN refused to participate in the committee. Also in that month the forthcoming legislative elections were postponed until November. At the beginning of October a national referendum to endorse a new draft Constitution was scheduled for 20 October. In order to comply with a constitutional proposal, which effectively restricted the number of political parties to a maximum of three, 24 pro-Taki political organizations merged to form one presidential party, the Rassemblement national pour le développement (RND). The opposition condemned the extensive powers that the draft Constitution vested in the President, and the rapidity with which it was to be installed, and urged a boycott of the constitutional referendum. On 20 October, however, the new Constitution was approved by 85% of votes cast; according to official estimates, about 64% of the electorate voted. The new Constitution vested legislative power in a unicameral parliament, the Federal Assembly (thereby abolishing the Senate), and extended the presidential term to six years, with an unrestricted number of consecutive mandates. Political parties were required to have two parliamentary deputies from each island (following legislative elections) to be considered legal; organizations that did not fulfil these stipulations were to be dissolved. Extensive executive powers were vested in the President, who was to appoint the Governors of the islands, and gained the right to initiate constitutional amendments. The opposition parties disputed the official result of the referendum, insisting that only about 20% of the electorate had voted.

Following unsuccessful negotiations with the Government, which rejected demands for the creation of an independent electoral commission and the revision of electoral lists, the opposition parties (having formed a new alliance) refused to participate in the electoral process. Consequently, the legislative elections, which took place after a further delay, in two rounds, in early December 1996, were only contested by the RND and the Front national pour la justice (FNJ), a fundamentalist Islamic organization, together with 23 independent candidates (in apparent contravention of a stipulation in the new Constitution that only legally-created political parties were entitled to participate in national elections). The RND secured 36 of the 43 seats in the Federal Assembly, while the FNJ won three, with four seats taken by independent candidates. In late December Taki nominated Ahmed Abdou, who had served in the administration of the former President Ahmed Abdallah, as Prime Minister to head a new Council of Ministers.

In late December 1996 industrial action in the public sector in support of demands by civil servants for the payment of salary arrears resulted in severe disruption in government services. A grouping of teachers' and hospital workers' unions joined the strike action in January 1997, and up to 30 people were injured when the security forces violently suppressed a demonstration organized by trade unions in Moroni. Civil unrest, exacerbated by severe shortages of water and electricity, continued, and in mid-February a one-day general strike, organized by the opposition, was widely supported. Meanwhile, discontent with the Government intensified on Nzwani; in mid-March a general strike escalated into riots, during which four people were killed, when some 3,000 demonstrators (reported to be secessionists) clashed with the security forces in Mutsamudu, the main town. Taki replaced the Governor of Nzwani and other senior island officials and carried out a government reshuffle. In late May it was reported that, in an attempt to alleviate the crisis, Taki and Djoussouf had agreed to establish a joint commission to define terms for the participation of the FRN in the governing of internal affairs. However, sympathy for the separatist movements on both Nzwani and Mwali continued to increase, amid claims that the Government had consistently ignored their political and economic interests, and on 14 July (France's national day) two people were killed in skirmishes between the security forces and demonstrators. Separatist leaders declared their intention to seek the restoration of French rule and established a 'political directorate' on Nzwani, chaired by Abdallah Ibrahim, the leader of the Mouvement populaire anjouanais, a grouping of separatist movements on Nzwani. (The relative prosperity of neighbouring Mayotte appeared to have prompted the demand for a return to French rule; it was reported that up to 200 illegal migrants a day attempted to enter Mayotte from Nzwani.) Military reinforcements were sent to Nzwani and the Governor of the island was replaced once again. The French Government denounced the separatist actions and insisted on its respect for the 'territorial integrity' of the Comoros.

On 3 August 1997 the 'political directorate' unilaterally declared Nzwani's secession from the Comoros. The separatists subsequently elected Ibrahim as president of a 13-member 'politico-administrative co-ordination', which included Abdou Madi, a former Prime Minister during Djohar's presidency, as spokesperson. The declaration of independence was condemned by Djoussouf who appealed for French mediation in the crisis. However, France, while denouncing the secession, declared itself in favour of the intervention of the OAU. The OAU responded by sending a special envoy, Pierre Yéré, to the Comoros. Meanwhile, separatist agitation intensified on Mwali, culminating on 11 August when secessionists declared Mwali's independence from the Comoros, appointed a president and a prime minister to head a 12-member government, and called for reattachment to France.

As OAU mediation efforts continued, it was announced in mid-August 1997 that secessionist leaders on Mwali and Nzwani had agreed to negotiate with the authorities in Moroni, although those on Nzwani had insisted on the immediate withdrawal of the military reinforcements that had been sent to the island in July. By late August the Government had complied with this demand and the OAU announced its intention to hold a reconciliation conference in mid-September in Addis Ababa, Ethiopia; the organization maintained its position, however, that secession was unacceptable. Nzwani's Governor, who had been appointed in July, resigned and was not replaced. At the end of August Yéré returned to the Comoros in order to prepare for the forthcoming conference. However, in early September, despite OAU and French opposition to military intervention, Taki despatched some 300 troops to Nzwani in an attempt forcibly to suppress the separatist insurrection. After two days of heavy fighting between secessionist and government forces, the OAU declared that the government troops had failed to quash the rebellion. The Government claimed that the separatists had been aided by foreign elements and expressed regret at France's refusal to support the military operation. As it emerged that some 40 Comoran soldiers and 16 Nzwani residents had been killed in the fighting, with many more injured, demonstrators demanding Taki's resignation clashed violently with the security forces in Moroni. The separatists on Nzwani reaffirmed their independence and empowered Ibrahim to rule by decree. Taki subsequently declared a state of emergency, assumed absolute power and dismissed the Government of Ahmed Abdou and his military and civilian advisers. (Abdou, from Mutsamudu, had reportedly resigned his position in late August, although this had not been announced publicly.) Shortly afterwards, Taki established a State Transition Commission, which included representatives from Nzwani and Mwali. The reconciliation conference was postponed indefinitely by the OAU. The League of Arab States (Arab League) agreed to a request from Taki for assistance, and following talks with the OAU regarding the co-ordination of the mediation effort, all three islands hosted discussions in late September, which were convened by envoys from both organizations. The opposition continued to call for Taki's resignation, the decentralization of power through constitutional reform and the organization of new elections.

In late September 1997, despite the misgivings of some members of the 'politico-administrative co-ordination', notably Abdou Madi, Ibrahim announced his decision to hold a referendum on self-determination for Nzwani on 26 October, prior to a reconciliation conference sponsored by both the OAU and the Arab League, which all parties had agreed to attend. Despite international opposition, the referendum was conducted as scheduled; according to separatist officials, 99.9% of the electorate voted in favour of independence for Nzwani, with a turnout of 94%. The following day Ibrahim dissolved the 'politico-administrative co-ordination' and appointed a temporary government, which was charged with preparing a constitution and organizing a presidential election, although it did not receive international recognition. Taki responded by severing Nzwani's telephone lines, suspending air and maritime links and establishing a commission to liaise with opposition leaders prior to the appointment of a government of national unity. However, the opposition refused to participate in such a government before the reconciliation conference had taken place. The conference had been postponed several times, largely owing to disagreements regarding the composition and strength of the delegations. In mid-November the OAU announced plans to deploy a force of military observers in the Comoros, despite the separatists' insistence that the force would not be allowed to land on Nzwani; an initial eight-member contingent, which arrived later that month, was subsequently to be increased to 25 and was to receive logistical support from France. Meanwhile, amid reports of dissension within the separatist government on Nzwani, it was reported that Abdou Madi (believed to hold more moderate views than Ibrahim) was in Moroni, having fled Nzwani.

In early December 1997 Taki formed a new Council of Ministers, appointing Nourdine Bourhane as Prime Minister. The inter-Comoran reconciliation conference was held later that month; some agreement was reached on proposals for the establishment of an international commission of inquiry to investigate September's military intervention and on the holding of a Comoran inter-island conference to discuss institutional reform. In late January 1998, following the first meeting in Fomboni, Mwali, of a committee charged with pursuing negotiations on the crisis, the OAU announced that both the Comoran Government and the Nzwani separatists had agreed to a number of conciliatory measures, including the restoration of air and maritime links and the release of 18 federal soldiers still detained on Nzwani. However, Ibrahim subsequently rejected all the agreements that his delegation had signed in Fomboni, with the exception of the release of detainees.

In early February 1998 tension increased further on Nzwani, where several rival separatist factions had emerged; fighting broke out between Ibrahim's supporters and followers of Abdou Madi, who had returned to the island, with the apparent support of both Taki and the OAU, in an abortive attempt to mount resistance to the secessionists. Later in February a separatist constitution was approved by a reported 99.5% of voters in a referendum on Nzwani. Ibrahim subsequently appointed a new separatist government. OAU mediation efforts effectively broke down in late March, following an unsuccessful visit to Nzwani by a ministerial delegation.

In Moroni public discontent intensified in May 1998, when a 48-hour strike was widely supported by civil servants (who claimed to be owed some 15 months of salary); at least three people were reported to have been killed in violent anti-Government protests. Later that month Taki, who appeared to be moderating his stance, acted to break the political deadlock, forming a committee to re-establish dialogue with the opposition, appointing a new Council of Ministers, and releasing a prominent separatist from detention in Moroni. Abdou Madi returned to federal government and, seemingly as a conciliatory gesture to the secessionists, the premiership (a position traditionally held by a Nzwanian) was left vacant. In late June Taki held discussions with a number of opposition leaders, although the FRN refused to participate.

In early July 1998, as social unrest on Nzwani escalated, a dispute over the future aims of the secessionist movement led to the dismissal of the island's government, provoking violent clashes between islanders loyal to Ibrahim, who favoured independence within the framework of an association of the Comoran islands, and supporters of the outgoing prime minister of the island, Chamassi Saïd Omar, who continued to advocate re-attachment to France. It was subsequently reported that Ahmed Mohamed Hazi, a former Comoran army Chief of Staff and ally of Omar, had failed in an attempt to depose Ibrahim.

Meanwhile, as social and economic conditions deteriorated further, with salaries still unpaid and strike action ongoing, Taki sought overseas assistance in resolving the crisis. In August 1998 the Government provisionally suspended transport links with both Nzwani and Mayotte. France later refused the Government's request for a suspension of links between Mayotte and Nzwani, thus worsening the already fragile relations between the two countries. As industrial action continued into September, it was reported that the Government had banned news broadcasts by privately-owned radio and television stations. In October, in a renewed effort to find a solution to the Comoran crisis, the OAU suggested that a meeting be held in South Africa between Taki and Ibrahim, and also encouraged dialogue between Taki and opposition leaders. At subsequent meetings with Djoussouf and the leadership of his own party, Taki proposed the establishment of a government of public salvation, an idea opposed by many members of the RND and several government ministers.

On 6 November 1998 President Taki died unexpectedly. It was reported that he had suffered a heart attack, although several senior officials expressed serious doubts about the cause of death. Tadjidine Ben Saïd Massoundi, the President of the High Council of the Republic and a former Prime Minister (March–December 1996), was designated acting President, in accordance with the Constitution, pending an election, which would be held after 30–90 days. Massoundi immediately revoked the ban on the movement of people and goods to Nzwani and, despite the continued opposition of several government ministers, proceeded with Taki's project for the formation of a government of public salvation. Djoussouf, the main opposition leader, was subsequently appointed Prime Minister, to head a Council of Ministers composed of members of the FRN and the RND. Divisions within the RND over its participation in the new Government led to a split in the party. In late January 1999 Massoundi extended his presidential mandate, which was soon to expire, pending a resolution of the crisis dividing the islands. In February an agreement was signed by the acting President and political parties opposed to the FRN-RND Government, which provided for the formation of a new federal administration to be supported by up to three technical commissions. However, the FRN refused to participate in the agreement, declaring its intention to remain in power until a Comoran inter-island conference had been held.

Meanwhile, renewed tension within the separatist administration on Nzwani escalated in December 1998, provoking eight days of armed clashes between rival militias, which reportedly resulted in at least 60 deaths before a cease-fire agreement was signed. In January 1999 Ibrahim agreed to relinquish some of his powers to a five-member 'politico-administrative directorate', as meetings commenced between the rival separatist factions. No consensus was reached in the following months, however, and when Ibrahim replaced the directorate with a 'committee of national security' in March, the new administration was immediately rejected by rival leaders. In Moroni there were further protests against the ruling federal administration, during which President Massoundi was vehemently denounced. Several anti-Government demonstrators were injured in clashes with the security forces.

An OAU-sponsored inter-island conference was held in Antananarivo, Madagascar, on 19–23 April 1999, at which an agreement was reached which envisaged substantial autonomy for Nzwani and Mwali, the changing of the country's name to the Union of the Comoran Islands, the rotation of the presidency among the three islands, and which also provided for a transitional period of one year until the new presidential and legislative structures were fully implemented. However, the delegates from Nzwani refused to sign the agreement, insisting on the need to consult the Nzwani population prior to a full endorsement. There followed several days of rioting in Moroni, as demonstrators protested against Nzwani's failure to ratify the accord, and more than 1,000 Nzwanians were reportedly forced from their homes before order was restored. On 30 April the Chief of Staff of the Comoran armed forces, Col Assoumani Azzali, seized power in a bloodless coup, deposing Massoundi and dissolving the Government, the Federal Assembly and all other constitutional institutions. Azzali promulgated a new constitutional charter, in which he proclaimed himself head of state and of government and Commander-in-Chief of the armed forces, and sought to justify the coup (the nineteenth in 25 years) by claiming that the authorities had not taken the political measures necessary to control the security situation in the Comoros. Full legislative functions were also vested in Azzali, who announced his intention to stay in power for one year only, during which time he pledged to oversee the creation of the new institutions provided for in the Antananarivo accord. The appointment of a State Committee (composed of six members from Njazidja, four from Mwali and two from Nzwani) was followed by that of a State Council, which was to supervise the activities of the State Committee and comprised eight civilians and 11 army officers. The coup was condemned by the OAU, which withdrew its military observers from the Comoros and urged the international community not to recognize the new regime; the UN, however, sent representatives to Azzali's inauguration.

In early June 1999 Azzali created five technical commissions which were charged with directing the implementation of the Antananarivo accord, including the drafting of new constitutions for the proposed union and its component parts. However, against the background of increasing discontent with the new administration, the main political parties boycotted a meeting at which they were to have nominated representatives to serve on the new commissions. In mid-June Lt-Col Adérémane Saïd Abeid, who had previously held the role of 'national mediator' on Nzwani, formed a government of national unity on the island and assumed the role of 'national co-ordinator'. At the beginning of July delegates from the three islands, including Azzali and Abeid, met on Mwali for talks aimed at resolving the political crisis. The negotiations represented the most senior-level contact between the islands since the secessions of August 1997.

In mid-August 1999 elections to establish a 25-member national assembly on Nzwani were held. No official results were released, but reports indicated that the most staunch separatists won the majority of seats. In the same month the OAU Secretary-General's newly-appointed special envoy for the Comoros, Francisco Caetano José Madeira, visited the islands in an attempt to persuade the separatists on Nzwani to sign the Antananarivo accord. By the end of August the growing divisions between Njazidja and Nzwani became more apparent when Azzali refused to allow 500 Nzwanian secondary-school students to sit an exam on Njazidja. Furthermore, several senior civil servants from Nzwani were dismissed from their jobs in Moroni and many more were threatened with transfers back to their island. In mid-September the Nzwani executive council announced its decision not to sign the Antananarivo peace agreement; Abeid stated that the signature of the accord would not be in accordance with the aspirations of the island's population. In late October Madeira once again visited the Comoros in an attempt to convince the separatists to sign the Antananarivo peace agreement. The separatist leaders, however, refused to relent, citing their fear of social unrest if they signed the agreement. In response, Madeira suggested that an OAU peacekeeping force be dispatched to Nzwani to prevent possible trouble; this offer led the separatist leaders to request further time to reconsider their position. In December the OAU adopted a tougher stance towards the Nzwani separatists by threatening the imposition of sanctions on the island should its leaders not have signed the peace accord by 1 February 2000. In retaliation, Abeid announced that a referendum would be held on Nzwani on 23 January 2000 regarding the signing of the Antananarivo accord. According to the separatist authorities of Nzwani, the results of the referendum revealed an overwhelming majority in favour of full independence for the island; the OAU, however, announced that it did not recognize the outcome of the ballot.

Meanwhile, following a series of meetings between Azzali and a number of political parties from all three islands regarding the establishment of a more representative and decentralized government in Moroni, the State Committee underwent an extensive reorganization in early December 1999, including the appointment of a Prime Minister, namely Bianrifi Tarmidi (from Mwali). Although Mwali was well represented in the new executive, only one Nzwani minister was appointed.

On 1 February 2000, as earlier threatened, the OAU imposed economic sanctions on Nzwani and demanded the co-operation of all countries in the region in implementing the sanctions; the overseas assets of the separatist leaders were 'frozen' and they themselves were confined to the island. There were, however, subsequent reports that Azzali, who had declared his intention to remain in power until the signature of the Antananarivo agreement by the Nzwanian leaders, advocated military intervention on the island. In mid-February, as part of the OAU sanctions, the federal Government suspended sea and air transport links with Nzwani.

Diplomatic relations between the Comoros and France, suspended in December 1975, were restored in July 1978; in November of that year the two countries signed agreements on military and economic co-operation, apparently deferring any decision on the future of Mayotte. In subsequent years, however, member countries of the UN General Assembly repeatedly voted in favour of a resolution affirming the Comoros' sovereignty over Mayotte, with only France dissenting. Following Djohar's accession to power, diplomatic relations were established with the USA in June 1990. In September 1993 the Arab League (see p. 218) accepted an application for membership from the Comoros. In mid-1999, following the military coup headed by Col Azzali, France and the USA suspended all military co-operation with the Comoros.

## Government

Under the Constitution of 20 October 1996, each of the islands in the Comoros has a Council and Governor, who is appointed by the President. The Head of State is the President, who is elected by direct universal suffrage for an unlimited number of six-year terms. The President appoints the Prime Minister, who heads the Council of Ministers. The Constitution provides for a unicameral legislature, a 43-member Federal Assembly, which is directly-elected for a term of five years.

On 6 May 1999, following the coup of 30 April, Col Assoumani Azzali promulgated a new constitutional charter, pending the introduction of new constitutional arrangements which were to take effect within one year. According to the charter, Col Azzali was the Head of State and held full legislative and executive power. He also appointed and headed an executive body known as the State Committee.

## Defence

In mid-1997 the national army, the Force Comorienne de Défense (FCD), numbered about 1,500 men. Government expenditure on defence in 1994 was an estimated US $3m. In December 1996 an agreement was ratified with France, which provided for the permanent presence of a French military contingent in the Comoros, which was to be renewed by rotation. In July 1997, however, it was reported that the rotations had ceased several months previously.

## Economic Affairs

In 1997, according to estimates from the World Bank, the gross national product (GNP) of the Comoros (excluding Mayotte), measured at average 1995–97 prices, was US $209m., equivalent to $400 per head. During 1990–97, it was estimated, GNP per head declined, in real terms, at an average rate of 3.1% per year. Over the same period, the population increased at an average annual rate of 2.6%. Estimated GNP in 1998 was $196m. ($370 per head). According to the IMF, the Comoros' gross domestic product (GDP) declined, in real terms, at an average annual rate of 0.7% in 1990–96; real GDP declined by 3.9% in 1995 and by 0.4% in 1996. It was officially estimated that GDP declined by 0.1% in 1997, but increased, according to provisional figures, by more than 1% in 1998.

Agriculture (including hunting, forestry and fishing) contributed 40.6% of GDP in 1998. Approximately 74.4% of the labour force were employed in the agricultural sector in that year. In 1989 the sector accounted for more than 98% of total export earnings. The principal cash crops are vanilla, ylang-lang, cloves and basil. Cassava, taro, rice, maize, pulses, coconuts and bananas are also cultivated. According to the IMF, the real GDP of the agricultural sector declined at an average annual rate of 0.7% in 1990–96; agricultural GDP declined by 1.2% in 1995 and by 0.4% in 1996.

Industry (including manufacturing, construction and power) contributed 11.2% of GDP in 1998. About 6% of the labour force were employed in the industrial sector at mid-1980. According to the IMF, the Comoros' industrial GDP increased at an average annual rate of 5.7% in 1990–96 (owing mainly to a sharp rise in construction activity), although it declined by 9.1% in 1995 and by 0.4% in 1996.

The manufacturing sector contributed 3.8% of GDP in 1998. The sector consists primarily of the processing of agricultural produce, particularly of vanilla and essential oils. According to the IMF, manufacturing GDP declined at an average annual rate of 0.5% in 1990–96; it declined by 14.2% in 1995 and by 0.4% in 1996.

Electrical energy is derived from wood (78%), and from thermal installations. Imports of fuel and energy comprised an estimated 11.8% of the total cost of imports in 1995.

The services sector contributed 48.2% of GDP in 1998. Strong growth in tourism from 1991 led to a significant expansion in trade, restaurant and hotel activities, although political instability has inhibited subsequent growth. According to the IMF, the GDP of the services sector declined at an average rate of 1.9% per year in 1990–96; it declined by 4.6% in 1995 and by 0.4% in 1996.

In 1998 the Comoros recorded a visible trade deficit of 16,064m. Comoros francs, and there was a deficit of 2,601.5m. Comoros francs on the current account of the balance of payments. In that year the principal source of imports was France (accounting for 36.2% of the total), which was also the principal market for exports (54.7%). Pakistan, South Africa, Germany and Madagascar were also major trading partners. The leading exports in 1997 were vanilla (providing 42.6% of the total), ylang-ylang and clove buds. The principal imports in 1998 were rice (14.3%), vehicles and petroleum products.

The overall budget deficit in 1998 was estimated at 5,493m. Comoros francs (equivalent to 6.4% of GDP). The Comoros' external public debt at the end of 1997 totalled US $197.4m., of which $181.1m. was long-term public debt. In that year the cost of debt-servicing was equivalent to 1.3% of the value of exports of goods and services. The annual rate of inflation averaged 4.6% during 1990–98. The rate rose to 25.3% in 1994, following the 33.3% devaluation of the Comoros franc in January 1994, but slowed to 5.5% in 1995, to 2.4% in 1996 and to 1.6% in 1997. Consumer prices increased by an average of 1.8% in 1998. About 20% of the labour force were unemployed at the 1991 census.

In 1985 the Comoros joined the Indian Ocean Commission (IOC, see p. 291). The country is also a member of the Common Market for Eastern and Southern Africa (COMESA, see p. 142) and of the Franc Zone (see p. 200).

The Comoros has a relatively undeveloped economy, with high unemployment, a limited transport system, a severe shortage of natural resources and heavy dependence on foreign aid, particularly from France. In January 1994 the devaluation of the Comoros franc by 33.3% in relation to the French franc resulted in a dramatic increase in the price of imported goods. In mid-1995, in response to a further deterioration in the fiscal situation, the Government introduced measures to limit budgetary expenditure under a public finance recovery programme. However, political instability continued to impede economic progress. Falling prices and increased competition on the international market for the Comoros' principal export products contributed to economic decline in 1996–97. In February 1997 the Government agreed a six-month surveillance programme with the IMF and the World Bank, which laid emphasis on fiscal reform, greater control of public-sector wage costs and the effective privatization of state-owned enterprises. Following a six-month extension of the programme, in February 1998 the IMF concluded that insufficient progress had been achieved. In August mounting arrears on loan repayments led the World Bank to suspend the disbursement of funds to the Comoros.

The European Union (EU) suspended all aid to the islands in early 1999. An intensification of political instability on the islands, following the seizure of power by the army in April 1999, had a particularly adverse effect on maritime trade and tourism. According to official figures, the decrease in the number of tourists visiting the archipelago led to a loss of revenue of 200m. Comoros francs in the first half of 1999. Government figures, released in September, showed a 21% decline in the value of exports in the first half of 1999, compared with the previous year. Despite this decline, the trade deficit narrowed over the six-month period, owing to a decrease in the cost of imports. In addition, largely owing to tax reform and improved methods of trade revenue collection, a budgetary surplus of 886m. Comoros francs was announced for the period January–June 1999. In January 2000, following the required repayment of arrears by the Comoran authorities, the World Bank resumed the disbursement of funds to the Comoros (the EU was expected to follow suit). Nevertheless, the ongoing political unrest appeared certain to continue to hinder the prospects of urgently-required economic reforms.

### Social Welfare

In 1978 the Government administered six hospital establishments, with a total of 698 beds, and in 1984 there were 31 physicians working in the country. In 1989 it was estimated that there was one hospital bed per 342 inhabitants, and in the early 1990s there were an estimated 10 physicians per 100,000 inhabitants in the country and 33 nurses per 100,000 inhabitants.

### Education

Education is officially compulsory for nine years between seven and 16 years of age. Primary education begins at the age of six and lasts for six years. Secondary education, beginning at 12 years of age, lasts for seven years, comprising a first cycle of four years and a second of three years. Enrolment at primary schools in 1995 was equivalent to 74% of children in the relevant age-group. Children may also receive a basic education through traditional Koranic schools, which are staffed by Comoran teachers. Enrolment at secondary schools in 1995 was equivalent to 22% of children in the relevant age-group. Current expenditure by the Ministry of Education in 1995 was 3,381m. Comoros francs, representing 21.1% of total current government expenditure. In 1995, according to estimates by UNESCO, the average rate of adult illiteracy was 42.7% (males 35.8%; females 49.6%).

### Public Holidays

**2000:** 8 January*† (Id al-Fitr, end of Ramadan), 16 March* (Id al-Adha, Feast of the Sacrifice), 6 April* (Muharram, Islamic New Year), 15 April* (Ashoura), 15 June* (Mouloud, Birth of the Prophet), 6 July (Independence Day), 26 October* (Leilat al-Meiraj, Ascension of the Prophet), 27 November (Anniversary of President Abdallah's assassination), 28 November* (Ramadan begins), 28 December*† (Id al-Fitr, end of Ramadan).

**2001:** 6 March* (Id al-Adha, Feast of the Sacrifice), 26 March* (Muharram, Islamic New Year), 4 April* (Ashoura), 4 June* (Mouloud, Birth of the Prophet), 6 July (Independence Day), 15 October* (Leilat al-Meiraj, Ascension of the Prophet, 27 November (Anniversary of President Abdallah's assassination), 17 November* (Ramadan begins), 17 December* (Id al-Fitr, end of Ramadan).

* Religious holidays, which are dependent on the Islamic lunar calendar, may differ by one or two days from the dates given.

† This festival will occur twice (in the Islamic years AH 1420 and 1421) within the same Gregorian year.

### Weights and Measures

The metric system is in force.

# Statistical Survey

Source (unless otherwise stated): Ministry of Finance, the Budget and the Economy, BP 324, Moroni; tel. (73) 2767.

Note: Unless otherwise indicated, figures in this Statistical Survey exclude data for Mayotte.

## AREA AND POPULATION

**Area:** 1,862 sq km (719 sq miles) *By island:* Njazidja (Grande-Comore) 1,146 sq km, Nzwani (Anjouan) 424 sq km, Mwali (Mohéli) 290 sq km.

**Population:** 335,150 (males 167,089; females 168,061), excluding Mayotte (estimated population 50,740), at census of 15 September 1980; 484,000 (official estimate), including Mayotte, at 31 December 1986; 446,817 (males 221,152; females 225,665), excluding Mayotte, at census of 15 September 1991. *By island* (1991 census): Njazidja (Grande-Comore) 233,533, Nzwani (Anjouan) 188,953, Mwali (Mohéli) 24,331.

**Density** (per sq km, 1991 census): 240.0 (Njazidja 203.8; Nzwani 445.6; Mwali 83.9).

**Principal Towns** (population at 1980 census): Moroni (capital) 17,267; Mutsamudu 13,000; Fomboni 5,400.

**Births and Deaths** (including figures for Mayotte, UN estimates): Average annual birth rate 48.5 per 1,000 in 1980–85, 42.4 per 1,000 in 1985–90, 38.2 per 1,000 in 1990–95; average annual death rate 13.8 per 1,000 in 1980–85, 11.9 per 1,000 in 1985–90, 10.2 per 1,000 in 1990–95. Source: UN, *World Population Prospects: The 1998 Revision.*

**Expectation of Life** (UN estimates, years at birth, including Mayotte, 1990–95): 57.2 (males 55.4; females 59.2). Source: UN, *World Population Prospects: The 1998 Revision.*

**Economically Active Population** (ILO estimates, '000 persons at mid-1980, including figures for Mayotte): Agriculture, forestry and fishing 150; Industry 10; Services 20; Total 181 (males 104, females 77). Source: ILO, *Economically Active Population Estimates and Projections, 1950–2025.*

*1991 census* (persons aged 12 years and over, excluding Mayotte): Total labour force 126,510 (males 88,034; females 38,476). Source: UN, *Demographic Yearbook.*

## AGRICULTURE, ETC.

**Principal Crops** (estimates, '000 metric tons, unless otherwise indicated, 1998): Rice (paddy) 2.9; Maize 4.0; Potatoes 1.0; Cassava (Manioc) 51.9; Taro 8.7; Other tubers 5.3; Pulses 0.8; Groundnuts 0.2; Coconuts (million) 75; Tomatoes 0.5; Other vegetables 5.6; Bananas 58.9; Other fruits 3.3; Vanilla (dried, metric tons) 180; Clove buds (metric tons) 1,700; Ylang-ylang essence (metric tons) 67. Source: Banque Centrale des Comores, *Rapport Annuel.*

**Livestock** (FAO estimates, '000 head, year ending September 1998): Asses 5, Cattle 50, Sheep 20, Goats 128. Source: FAO, *Production Yearbook.*

**Livestock Products** (estimates, metric tons, unless otherwise indicated, 1998): Beef and veal 950; Mutton, lamb and goat meat 170; Poultry meat 210; Milk ('000 litres) 970; Eggs ('000) 4,700. Source: Banque Centrale des Comores, *Rapport Annuel.*

**Fishing** (FAO estimates, '000 metric tons, live weight): Total catch 13.2 in 1995; 13.0 in 1996; 12.5 in 1997. Source: FAO, *Yearbook of Fishery Statistics.*

*1998* ('000 metric tons): Total catch 14.3. Source: Banque Centrale des Comores, *Rapport Annuel.*

## INDUSTRY

**Electric energy** (million kWh): 30.9 in 1996; 12.3 in 1997; 28.5 in 1998. Source: Banque Centrale des Comores, *Rapport Annuel.*

## FINANCE

**Currency and Exchange Rates:** 100 centimes = 1 Comoros franc. *Sterling, Dollar and Euro Equivalents* (30 September 1999): £1 sterling = 759.52 Comoros francs; US $1 = 461.29 Comoros francs; €1 = 491.97 Comoros francs; 1,000 Comoros francs = £1.317 = $2.168 = €2.033. *Average Exchange Rate* (Comoros francs per US $): 383.66 in 1996; 437.75 in 1997; 442.46 in 1998. Note: The Comoros franc was introduced in 1981, replacing (at par) the CFA franc. The fixed link to French currency was retained, with the exchange rate set at 1 French franc = 50 Comoros francs. This remained in effect until

January 1994, when the Comoros franc was devalued by 33.3%, with the exchange rate adjusted to 1 French franc = 75 Comoros francs.

**Budget** (provisional, million Comoros francs, 1998): *Revenue:* Tax revenue 9,172; Other revenue 959; Total 10,131, excluding grants received (7,144). *Expenditure:* Budgetary current expenditure 12,683 (Wages and salaries 7,100; Goods and services 4,100; Transfers 561; Interest payments 922); Current expenditure under technical assistance programmes 4,658; Budgetary capital expenditure 360; Capital expenditure financed with external resources 5,067; Total 22,768. Source: Banque Centrale des Comores, *Rapport Annuel.*

**International Reserves** (US $ million at 31 December 1998): Gold 0.17; IMF special drawing rights 0.01; Reserve position in IMF 0.76; Foreign exchange 38.37; Total 39,31. Source: IMF, *International Financial Statistics.*

**Money Supply** (million Comoros francs at 31 December 1998): Currency outside deposit money banks 5,418; Demand deposits at deposit money banks 4,250; Total money (incl. others) 10,015. Source: IMF, *International Financial Statistics.*

**Cost of Living** (Consumer Price Index; base: 1993 = 100): All items 135 in 1996; 137 in 1997; 139 in 1998. Source: Banque Centrale des Comores, *Rapport Annuel.*

**Expenditure on the Gross Domestic Product** (million Comoros francs at current prices, 1996): Government final consumption expenditure 12,434; Private final consumption expenditure 74,366; Increase in stocks 104; Gross fixed capital formation 15,333; *Total domestic expenditure* 102,237; Exports of goods and services 16,204; *Less* Imports of goods and services 36,594; *GDP in purchasers' values* 81,847. Source: IMF, *Comoros—Statistical Annex* (November 1997).

**Gross Domestic Product by Economic Activity** (million Comoros francs at current prices, 1998, provisional figures): Agriculture, hunting, forestry and fishing 35,387; Manufacturing 3,276; Electricity, gas and water 1,299; Construction 5,179; Trade, restaurants and hotels 21,864; Transport and communications 4,457; Finance, insurance, real estate and business services 3,034; Government services 12,196; Other services 426; *Sub-total* 87,116; *Less* Imputed bank service charge 1,448; *GDP in purchasers' values* 85,668. Source: Banque Centrale des Comores, *Rapport Annuel.*

**Balance of Payments** (US $ million, 1995): Exports of goods f.o.b. 11.32; Imports of goods f.o.b. –53.50; *Trade balance* –42.18; Exports of services 34.51; Imports of services –49.85; *Balance on goods and services* –57.53; Other income received 3.40; Other income paid –2.39; *Balance on goods, services and income* –56.51; Current transfers received 41.06; Current transfers paid –3.50; *Current balance* –18.96; Direct investment from abroad 0.89; Other investment assets –1.83; Other investment liabilities 11.81; Net errors and omissions –1.77; *Overall balance* -9.86. Source: IMF, *International Financial Statistics.*

### EXTERNAL TRADE

**Principal Commodities** (million Comoros francs, 1998): *Imports c.i.f.:* Rice 3,184; Meat and fish 1,786; Flour 597; Sugar 699; Dairy products 639; Petroleum products 2,253; Cement 1,131; Vehicles 2,459; Iron and steel 794; Total (incl. others) 22,241. *Exports f.o.b.:* Vanilla 1,058; Ylang-ylang 566; Total (incl. others) 1,967. Note: Figures for exports exclude shipments of cloves from Nzwani (Anjouan). Source: Banque Centrale des Comores, *Rapport Annuel.*

**Principal Trading Partners** (US $'000, 1995): *Imports:* France 20,040; India 10,834; Saudi Arabia 5,887; Total (incl. others) 62,625. *Exports:* France 4,150; Germany 913; USA 3,222; Total (incl. others) 11,361. Source: UN, *International Trade Statistics Yearbook.*

*1996* (percentage of trade): *Imports:* Belgium/Luxembourg 2.0%; France 41.6%; Germany 1.2%; Kenya 7.0%; Madagascar 1.4%; Mauritius 1.2%; Pakistan 8.2%; Réunion 2.9%; Romania 1.5%; Saudi Arabia 3.2%; Singapore 1.7%; South Africa 7.0%; Switzerland 1.1%; Viet Nam 6.1%. *Exports:* France 48.9%; Germany 13.6%; Netherlands 2.3%; USA 11.8%. Source: IMF, *Comoros—Statistical Annex* (November 1997).

*1998* (percentage of trade): *Imports:* France 36.2%; Pakistan 11.8%; South Africa 9.1%; United Arab Emirates 7.5%. *Exports:* France 54.7%. Source: Banque Centrale des Comores, *Rapport Annuel.*

### TRANSPORT

**Road Traffic** (estimates, motor vehicles in use, 1996): Passenger cars 9,100; Lorries and vans 4,950. Source: International Road Federation, *World Road Statistics.*

**International Shipping** (estimated sea-borne freight traffic, '000 metric tons, 1991): Goods loaded 12; Goods unloaded 107. Source: UN Economic Commission for Africa, *African Statistical Yearbook.*

**Civil Aviation** (traffic on scheduled services, 1995): Passengers carried ('000) 27; Passenger-km (million) 3. Source: UN, *Statistical Yearbook.*

### TOURISM

**Tourist Arrivals** 23,775 in 1996; 26,219 in 1997; 28,840 in 1998. Source: Banque Centrale des Comores, *Rapport Annuel.*

**Receipts from Tourism** (million Comoros francs): 3,900 in 1994; 3,600 in 1995; 3,500 in 1996. Source: IMF, *Comoros—Statistical Annex* (November 1997).

### COMMUNICATIONS MEDIA

**Radio Receivers** (1996): 87,000 in use. Source: UNESCO, *Statistical Yearbook.*

**Television Receivers** (1996): 1,000 in use. Source: UNESCO, *Statistical Yearbook.*

**Telephones** (1998): 6,226 main lines in use. Source: Banque Centrale des Comores, *Rapport Annuel.*

**Telefax Stations** (1993): 98 in use. Source: UN, *Statistical Yearbook.*

### EDUCATION

**Pre-primary** (1980/81): 600 teachers; 17,778 pupils.

**Primary** (1995/96): 327 schools; 1,508 teachers (public education only); 78,527 pupils.

**Secondary:** Teachers: general education 591 (1995/96, public education only); teacher training 11 (1991/92); vocational 31 (1986/87). Pupils: general education 21,192 (1995/96); teacher training 37 (1993/94); vocational 126 (1993/94).

**Higher:** 32 teachers (1989/90); 348 pupils (1995/96).

Source: UNESCO, *Statistical Yearbook.*

# Directory

## The Constitution

On 6 May 1999, following the coup of 30 April, Col Assoumani Azzali promulgated a new constitutional charter, pending the introduction of new constitutional arrangements which were to take effect within one year. According to the charter, Col Azzali is the Head of State and leader of a State Committee and the Armed Forces, and holds full legislative and executive power. Prior to their revocation, the following constitutional provisions had been in effect since their approval by referendum on 20 October 1996.

### PREAMBLE

The preamble affirms the will of the Comoran people to derive from the state religion, Islam, inspiration for the principles and laws that the State and its institutions govern, to adhere to the principles laid down by the Charters of the UN, the Organization of African Unity and the Organization of the Islamic Conference and by the Treaty of the League of Arab States, and to guarantee the rights of all citizens, without discrimination, in accordance with the UN Declaration of Human Rights and the African Charter of Human Rights.

### GENERAL PROVISIONS

The Comoros archipelago constitutes a federal Islamic republic. Sovereignty belongs to the people, and is exercised through their elected representatives or by the process of referendum. There is universal secret suffrage, which can be direct or indirect, for all citizens who are over the age of 18 and in full possession of their civil and political rights. Political parties and groups operate freely, respecting national sovereignty, democracy and territorial integrity. However, political parties which are not represented by at least two deputies from each island, as a result of the first legislative election to follow the adoption of the Constitution, will be dissolved, unless those parties merge with others which are legitimately represented in the Federal Assembly. If only one political party has representation in the Federal Assembly, the party which has obtained the second highest number of votes will continue to operate freely. Only political parties and groups active throughout the Republic may participate in national elections. Political parties must be democratic both in their internal structure and their activities.

### PRESIDENT OF THE REPUBLIC

The President is the Head of State and is elected by direct universal suffrage for a six-year term, which is renewable for an unrestricted number of mandates. He is also Head of the Armed Forces and ensures the legitimate functioning of public powers and the continuation of the State. He is the guarantor of national independence, the unity of the Republic, the autonomy of the islands, territorial integrity and adherence to international agreements. Candidates for the presidency must be aged between 40 and 75 years, of Comoran nationality by birth, and resident in the archipelago for at least 12 consecutive months prior to elections. The President presides over the Council of Ministers. He is empowered to ask the Federal Assembly to reconsider a Bill. The President can, having consulted with the Prime Minister and the Presidents of the Federal Assembly and the High Council of the Republic in writing, dissolve the Federal Assembly. The President determines and implements the Republic's foreign policy.

### THE GOVERNMENT

The President appoints the Prime Minister, and on his recommendations, the other members of the Government. Under the authority of the President of the Republic, the Council of Ministers determines and implements domestic policy.

### LEGISLATIVE POWER

Legislative power is vested in the Federal Assembly, which represents the Comoran nation. Deputies in the Federal Assembly are elected for five years by direct suffrage. Legislative elections take place between 30 and 90 days after the expiry of the mandate of the incumbent Federal Assembly. The electoral law dictates the number of members of the Federal Assembly, but there is a minimum of five deputies from each island. The deputies elect the President of the Federal Assembly at the beginning of their mandate. The Federal Assembly sits for two sessions each year and, if necessary, for extraordinary sessions. Matters covered by federal legislation include constitutional institutions, defence, posts and telecommunications, transport, civil and penal law, public finance, external trade, federal taxation, long-term economic planning, education and health.

### JUDICIAL POWER

Judicial power is independent of executive and legislative power. The President is the guarantor of the independence of the judicial system and chairs the Higher Council of the Magistracy (Conseil Supérieur de la Magistrature), of which the Minister of Justice is Vice-President.

### HIGH COUNCIL OF THE REPUBLIC

The High Council of the Republic considers constitutional matters and the control of public finance, and acts as a High Court of Justice. It has a renewable mandate of seven years and is composed of four members appointed by the President, three members elected by the Federal Assembly and one member elected by the Council of each island. The High Council oversees and proclaims the results of presidential and legislative elections and referendums.

### COUNCIL OF THE ULÉMAS

The Council of the Ulémas offers opinions on projects for laws, ordinances and decrees. The President of the Republic, the Prime Minister, the President of the Federal Assembly, the Presidents of the Councils and the Governors of the islands may consult the Council of the Ulémas on any religious issue. The Council of the Ulémas may submit recommendations to the Federal Assembly, the Government or the Governors of the islands if it considers legislation to be in contravention of the principles of Islam.

### ISLAND INSTITUTIONS

While respecting the unity of the Republic, each island is an autonomous territorial entity which freely controls its own administration through a Governor and a Council. The Governor of each island is appointed by the President of the Republic, from three candidates proposed by the Council of the island. The Council of each island is composed of the mayors of the communes and sits for not more than 15 days at a time, in March and December, and, if necessary, for extraordinary sessions. The Council is responsible for such matters as the budget of the island, taxes, culture, health, primary education and the environment.

### REVISION OF THE CONSTITUTION

The power to initiate constitutional revision is vested in the President of the Republic. However, one-third of the members of the Federal Assembly may propose amendments to the President. Constitutional revision must be approved by a majority of two-thirds of the deputies in the Federal Assembly, and is subject to approval by national referendum. However, the President of the Republic may decide to promulgate a constitutional project, without submitting it to a referendum, if it has been adopted at a congress of deputies and the councillors of the islands, by a majority of two-thirds. The Republican and Islamic nature of the State cannot be revised.

## The Government

### HEAD OF STATE

**Head of State and Minister of Defence:** Col ASSOUMANI AZZALI (assumed power 30 April 1999, inaugurated 6 May 1999).

### STATE COMMITTEE
(February 2000)

**Head of State and Minister of Defence:** Col ASSOUMANI AZZALI.

**Prime Minister:** BIANRIFI TARMIDI.

**Minister of Finance, the Budget and Planning:** SOUNDI ABDOU TOUBOU.

**Minister of the Interior and the Implementation of Institutions:** MOHAMED ABDOU SOIMADOU.

**Minister of Justice and Islamic Affairs:** ABDOULBAR YOUSSOUF.

**Minister of Production and the Environment:** CHARIF ABDALLAH.

**Minister of National Education, Professional and Vocational Training, and Francophone Affairs:** MOINAECHA YAHAYA CHEIKH.

**Minister of Foreign Affairs and Co-operation:** SOUEFOU MOHAMED ELAMINE.

**Minister of Public Health, Population and the Status of Women:** MIAHAILI MISTOIHI.

**Minister of Civil Service, Employment and Labour:** MILISSANI HAMDIYA.

**Minister of the Economy, Trade, Industry and Crafts:** ASSOUMANY ABOUDOU.

**Minister of Information, Youth and Sports:** Capt. AHMED SIDI.

**Minister of Tourism, Transport, and Posts and Telecommunications:** SAÏD DHOIFIR BOUNOU.

**Minister of Facilities and Energy:** DJAFFAR M'MADI.

**Governor of National Defence:** AHMADI MADI (BOLERO).

### MINISTRIES

**Office of the Head of State:** BP 521, Moroni; tel. (74) 4814; fax (74) 4829.

**Ministry of the Civil Service, Employment and Labour:** Moroni; tel. (74) 4277.

**Ministry of Defence:** Moroni; tel. (74) 4862.

**Ministry of the Economy, Trade, Industry and Crafts:** Moroni; tel. (74) 4235.

**Ministry of Facilities and Energy:** Moroni.

**Ministry of Finance, the Budget and Planning:** BP 324, Moroni; tel. (74) 4145; fax (74) 4140.

**Ministry of Foreign Affairs and Co-operation:** BP 482, Moroni; tel. (74) 4100; fax (74) 4111.

**Ministry of Information, Youth and Sports:** BP 421, Moroni.

**Ministry of the Interior and the Implementation of Institutions:** BP 520, Moroni; tel. (74) 4666.

**Ministry of Justice and Islamic Affairs:** Moroni; tel. (74) 4200.

**Ministry of National Education, Professional and Vocational Training, and Francophone Affairs:** BP 421, Moroni; tel. (74) 4185; fax (74) 4180.

**Ministry of Production and the Environment:** Moroni.

**Ministry of Public Health, Population and the Status of Women:** Moroni.

**Ministry of Tourism, Transport and Posts and Telecommunications:** Moroni; tel. (73) 2098.

## President and Legislature

### PRESIDENT

In the first round of voting, which took place on 6 March 1996, none of the 15 candidates received 50% of the total votes cast. A second round of voting took place on 16 March, when voters chose between the two leading candidates. MOHAMED TAKI ABDOULKARIM received 64.3% of the votes, while ABBAS DJOUSSOUF obtained 35.7%. Following the death of MOHAMED TAKI ABDOULKARIM on 6 November 1998, TADJIDINE BEN SAÏD MASSOUNDI was designated acting President, pending

**Minister of the Civil Service and Labour:** PAUL-GABRIEL KAPITA SHABANGI.

**Minister of Land Affairs, the Environment, Fisheries and Forests:** BISHIKWABO TSHUBAKA.

**Minister of Agriculture and Animal Husbandry:** KITANGA ESHIMA MUSEBO ETIENNE.

**Minister of Finance:** FERDINAND MAWAPANGA MWANA NANGA.

**Minister of Health:** DR MASHAKO MAMBA.

**Minister of Transport and Communications:** BABANDOA ETOA ODETTE.

**Minister of Youth, Sports and Leisure:** VINCENT MUTOMB TSHIBAL.

**Minister of Education:** KAMARA RWAKAÏHARA.

**Minister of Public Works:** YAGI SITOLO.

**Minister of Mines:** FRÉDÉRIC KIBASA MALIBA.

**Minister of Post, Telephones and Telecommunications:** PROSPER KIBUEY MOLAMBO DG.

**Minister of Social Affairs:** DR MOLEKO MOLIWA.

**Minister of Energy:** BABI MBAYI.

**Minister of Culture and the Arts:** JULIANA LUMUMBA.

**Minister of Human Rights:** LÉONARD SHE OKITUNDU.

**Minister of Reconstruction:** DENIS KALUME NUMBI.

### MINISTRIES

All ministries are in Kinshasa.

**Office of the President:** Hôtel du Conseil Exécutif, ave de Lemera, Kinshasa-Gombe; tel. (12) 30892.

**Ministry of Agriculture and Animal Husbandry:** Immeuble SOZACOM, 3rd floor, blvd du 30 juin, BP 8722 KIN I, Kinshasa-Gombe; tel. (12) 31821.

**Ministry of the Civil Service:** ave des Ambassadeurs, BP 3, Kinshasa-Gombe; tel. (12) 30209.

**Ministry of Culture and the Arts:** BP 8541, Kinshasa 1; tel. (12) 31005.

**Ministry of Defence:** BP 4111, Kinshasa-Gombe; tel. (12) 59375.

**Ministry of the Economy, Industry and Commerce:** Immeuble ONATRA, blvd du 30 juin, BP 8500 KIN I, Kinshasa-Gombe.

**Ministry of Energy:** Immeuble SNEL, 239 ave de la Justice, BP 5137 KIN I, Kinshasa-Gombe; tel. (12) 22570.

**Ministry of the Environment, Fisheries and Forests:** 15 ave des Cliniques, BP 12348 KIN I, Kinshasa-Gombe; tel. (12) 31252.

**Ministry of Finance and the Budget:** blvd du 30 juin, BP 12998 KIN I, Kinshasa-Gombe; tel. (12) 31197.

**Ministry of Foreign Affairs:** place de l'Indépendance, BP 7100, Kinshasa-Gombe; tel. (12) 32450.

**Ministry of Health:** blvd du 30 juin, BP 3088 KIN I, Kinshasa-Gombe; tel. (12) 31750.

**Ministry of Information and the Press:** ave du 24 novembre, BP 3171 KIN I, Kinshasa-Kabinda; tel. (12) 23171.

**Ministry of Internal Affairs:** ave de Lemera, Kinshasa-Gombe; tel. (12) 23171.

**Ministry of International Co-operation:** ave de Lemera, Enceinte SNEL, ave de la Justice, Kinshasa-Gombe; tel. (12) 23171.

**Ministry of Justice:** 228 ave de Lemera, BP 3137, Kinshasa-Gombe; tel. (12) 32432.

**Ministry of Labour and Social Security:** blvd du 30 juin, BP 3840, Kinshasa.

**Ministry of Mines:** Immeuble SNEL, 239 ave de la Justice, BP 5137 KIN I, Kinshasa-Gombe; tel. (12) 30336.

**Ministry of National Education:** Enceinte de l'Institut de la Gombe, BP 3163, Kinshasa-Gombe; tel. (12) 30098.

**Ministry of Planning:** 4155 ave des Côteaux, BP 9378, Kinshasa-Gombe 1; tel. (12) 31346.

**Ministry of Post and Telecommunications:** Immeuble KILOU, 4484 ave des Huiles, BP 800 KIN I, Kinshasa-Gombe; tel. (12) 24854.

**Ministry of Public Works:** Immeuble TRAVAUX PUBLICS, Kinshasa-Gombe.

**Ministry of Transport:** Immeuble ONATRA, blvd du 30 juin, BP 3304, Kinshasa-Gombe; tel. (12) 23660.

**Ministry of Youth and Sports:** 77 ave de la Justice, BP 8541 KIN I, Kinshasa-Gombe.

## President

Laurent-Désiré Kabila declared himself President on 17 May 1997,and was inaugurated on 29 May 1997. Presidential elections were scheduled to take place in 1999.

## Legislature

The Head of State legislates by decree. Legislative elections were scheduled to take place in 1999.

### PROVINCIAL GOVERNORS

(February 2000)

**Bandundu:** MARC KATSHUNGA.

**Bas-Congo:** DR SÉRAPHIN BAVUIDI BABINGI.

**Equateur:** GABRIEL MOLA MOTYA.

**Kasaï Occidental:** CLAUDEL ANDRÉ LUBAYA.

**Kasaï Oriental:** JEAN-CHARLES OKOTO LOLAKOMBE.

**Katanga:** AUGUSTIN KATUMBA MWANKE.

***Kivu-Maniema:** (vacant).

***Nord-Kivu:** (vacant).

***Province Orientale:** (vacant).

***Sud-Kivu:** (vacant).

**Kinshasa (City):** THÉOPHILE MBEMBA FUNDU.

* These provinces were under rebel control in February 2000.

## Political Organizations

**Comités du pouvoir populaire (CPP):** f. 1999 as successor to **Alliance des forces démocratiques pour la libération du Congo-Zaïre** (AFDL, Leader LAURENT-DÉSIRÉ KABILA); committees formed in each village to devolve power to the people; to debate political policy.

Political parties reported to be active in late 1999 included:

**Forces novatrices pour l'union et la solidarité (FONUS):** Kinshasa; advocates political pluralism; Pres. JOSEPH OLENGHANKOY; Sec.-Gen. JOHN KWET.

**Forces politiques du conclave (FPC):** Kinshasa; f. 1993; alliance of pro-Mobutu groups, incl the UFERI, led by MPR; Chair. JEAN NGUZA KARL-I-BOND.

**Mouvement national du Congo–Lumumba (MNC–Lumumba):** Kinshasa; f. 1994; coalition of seven parties, incl. the Parti lumumbiste unifié (PALU), led by ANTOINE GIZENGA; supports the aims of the late Patrice Lumumba; Co-ordinating Cttee PASCAL TABU, MBALO MEKA, OTOKO OKITASOMBO.

**Mouvement populaire de la révolution (MPR):** f. 1966 by Pres. Mobutu; sole legal political party until Nov. 1990; advocates national unity and opposes tribalism; Leader (vacant); Sec.-Gen. KITHIMA BIN RAMAZANI.

**Mouvement pour la libération du Congo (MLC):** Equateur; f. 1998; rebel movement; Head JEAN-PIERRE BEMBA.

**Parti démocrate et social chrétien (PDSC):** 32B ave Tombalbaye, Kinshasa-Gombe; tel. (12) 21211; f. 1990; centrist; Pres. ANDRÉ BO-BOLIKO; Sec. Gen. TUYABA LEWULA.

**Rassemblement congolais démocratique (RCD):** e-mail rcd_98@hotmail.com; f. 1998; advocates introduction of a democratic political system; split into two factions in 1999: Ilunga faction: Goma; supported by Rwanda; Pres. Dr EMILE ILUNGA; Wamba dia Wamba faction: Bunia; supported by Uganda; Pres. ERNEST WAMBA DIA WAMBA.

**Union des fédéralistes et républicains indépendants (UFERI):** Kinshasa; f. 1990; seeks autonomy for province of Katanga; dominant party in the USOR; Pres. JEAN NGUZA KARL-I-BOND; Leader KOUYOUMBA MUCHULI MULEMBE.

**Union pour la démocratie et le progrès social (UDPS):** Twelfth St, Limete Zone, Kinshasa; internet www.udps.org/udps.html; f. 1982; Leader ETIENNE TSHISEKEDI WA MULUMBA; Sec.-Gen. Dr ADRIEN PHONGO KUNDA.

**Union pour la République (UPR):** Kinshasa; f. 1997 by fmr mems of the MPR; Leader CHARLES NDAYWEL.

**Union sacrée de l'opposition radicale (USOR):** Kinshasa; f. 1991, comprising c. 130 movements and factions opposed to Pres. Mobutu, in which the UDPS was the dominant party; a radical internal faction, known as the **Union sacrée de l'opposition radicale et ses alliés (USORAL)** (Pres. FRÉDÉRIC KIBASSA MALIBA), emerged in 1994.

**Union sacrée rénovée (USR):** Kinshasa; f. 1993 by several ministers in fmr Govt of Nat. Salvation; Leader KIRO KIMATE.

## Diplomatic Representation

### EMBASSIES IN THE DEMOCRATIC REPUBLIC OF THE CONGO

**Angola:** 4413–4429 blvd du 30 juin, BP 8625, Kinshasa; tel. (12) 32415; Ambassador: MAWETE JOÃO BAPTISTA.

**Belgium:** Immeuble Le Cinquantenaire, place du 27 octobre, BP 899, Kinshasa; tel. (12) 20110; fax 22120; Ambassador: FRANK DE CONINCK.

**Benin:** 3990 ave des Cliniques, BP 3265, Kinshasa-Gombe; tel. (12) 33156; Ambassador: ANDRÉ GUY OLOGOUDOU.

**Cameroon:** 171 blvd du 30 juin, BP 10998, Kinshasa; tel. (12) 34787; Chargé d'affaires a.i.: DOMINIQUE AWONO ESSAMA.

**Canada:** BP 8341, Kinshasa 1; tel. (88) 41276; Ambassador: VERONA EDELSTEIN.

**Central African Republic:** 11 ave Pumbu, BP 7769, Kinshasa; tel. (12) 30417; Ambassador: SISSA LE BERNARD.

**Chad:** 67–69 ave du Cercle, BP 9097, Kinshasa; tel. (12) 22358; Ambassador: MAITINE DJOUMBE.

**China, People's Republic:** 49 ave du Commerce, BP 9098, Kinshasa; tel. (12) 21207; Ambassador: SUN KUNSHAN.

**Congo, Republic:** 179 blvd du 30 juin, BP 9516, Kinshasa; tel. (12) 30220; Ambassador: MAURICE OGNAMY.

**Côte d'Ivoire:** 68 ave de la Justice, BP 9197, Kinshasa; tel. (12) 30440; Ambassador: GILBERT DOH.

**Cuba:** 4660 ave Cateam, BP 10699, Kinshasa; Ambassador: ENRIQUE MONTERO.

**Egypt:** 519 ave de l'Ouganda, BP 8838, Kinshasa; tel. (12) 34368; Ambassador: AZIZ ABDEL HAMID HAMZA.

**Ethiopia:** BP 8435, Kinshasa; tel. (12) 23327; Ambassador: DIEUDEONNE A. GANGA.

**France:** 97 ave de la République du Tchad, BP 3093, Kinshasa; tel. (12) 30513; Ambassador: GILDAS LE LIDEC.

**Gabon:** ave du 24 novembre, BP 9592, Kinshasa; tel. (12) 68325; Ambassador: MICHEL MADOUNGOU.

**Germany:** 82 ave de Lemera, BP 8400, Kinshasa-Gombe; tel. (12) 33399; fax (satellite) 871-112-0323; Ambassador: HELMUT OHBRAUN.

**Greece:** Immeuble de la Communauté Hellénique, 3ème étage, blvd du 30 juin, BP 478, Kinshasa; tel. (88) 44862; fax (12) 21561; e-mail grembkin@ic.cd; Ambassador: PANAYOTIS TH. BAIZOS.

**Holy See:** 81 ave Goma, BP 3091, Kinshasa; tel. (12) 33128; fax (12) 33346; Apostolic Nuncio: Most Rev. FAUSTINO SAINZ MUÑOZ, Titular Archbishop of Novaliciana.

**Iran:** 76 blvd du 30 juin, BP 16599, Kinshasa; tel. (12) 31052.

**Israel:** 12 ave des Aviateurs, BP 8343, Kinshasa; tel. (12) 21955; Ambassador: JAMAR F. GOLAN.

**Italy:** 8 ave de la Mongala, BP 1000, Kinshasa; tel. (88) 46106; e-mail ambitalykin@raga.net; Ambassador: PIETRO BALLERO.

**Japan:** Immeuble Citibank, 2e étage, ave Colonel Lukusa, BP 1810, Kinshasa; tel. (88) 45305; fax (satellite) 871-761-21-41-42; e-mail ambj@ic.cd; Ambassador YASUO TAKANO.

**Kenya:** 5002 ave de l'Ouganda, BP 9667, Kinshasa; tel. (12) 30117; Ambassador: MWABILI KISAKA.

**Korea, Democratic People's Republic:** 168 ave de l'Ouganda, BP 16597, Kinshasa; tel. (12) 31566; Ambassador: HAN PON CHUN.

**Korea, Republic:** 2A ave des Orangers, BP 628, Kinshasa; tel. (88) 20722; Ambassador: CHUN SOON-KYU.

**Lebanon:** 3 ave de l'Ouganda, Kinshasa; tel. (12) 82469; Chargé d'affaires a.i.: CHEHADE MOUALLEM.

**Liberia:** 3 ave de l'Okapi, BP 8940, Kinshasa; tel. (12) 82289; Ambassador: JALLA D. LANSANAH.

**Mauritania:** BP 16397, Kinshasa; tel. (12) 59575; Ambassador: Lt-Col M'BARECK OULD BOUNA MOKHTAR.

**Morocco:** 4497 ave Lubefu, BP 912, Kinshasa; tel. (12) 34794; Ambassador: ABDELAZIZ BENNIS.

**Netherlands:** 11 ave Zongo Ntolo, BP 10299, Kinshasa; tel (12) 30733; Ambassador: F. RACKE.

**Nigeria:** 141 blvd du 30 juin, BP 1700, Kinshasa; tel. (12) 43272; Ambassador: DAG S. CLAUDE-WILCOX.

**Portugal:** 270 ave des Aviateurs, BP 7775, Kinshasa; tel. (12) 21335; Ambassador: LUÍS DE VASCONCELOS PIMENTEL QUARTIN BASTOS.

**Russia:** 80 ave de la Justice, BP 1143, Kinshasa 1; tel. (12) 33157; fax (12) 45575; Ambassador: VALERII GAMAIVNE.

**South Africa:** 17 ave Pumbu, BP 7829, Kinshasa-Gombe; tel. (88) 48287; fax (satellite) 1-212-3723510; Ambassador: (vacant).

**Sudan:** 83 ave des Treis, BP 7347, Kinshasa; tel. (12) 33200; Ambassador: MUBARAK ADAM HADI.

**Sweden:** 89 ave de Lemera, BP 11096, Kinshasa; tel. (12) 34084; fax (12) 33683; e-mail ambasuede@ic.cd; Chargé d'affaires a.i.: EVA EMNÉUS.

**Togo:** 3 ave de la Vallée, BP 10117, Kinshasa; tel. (12) 30666; Ambassador: MAMA GNOFAM.

**Tunisia:** 67–69 ave du Cercle, BP 1498, Kinshasa; tel. and fax (88) 03901; Chargé d'affaires a.i.: FARHAT BAROUN.

**Turkey:** 18 ave Pumbu, BP 7817, Kinshasa; tel. (88) 01207; fax (88) 04740; Ambassador: DENIZ UZMEN.

**United Kingdom:** ave de Lemera, BP 8049, Kinshasa; tel. (88) 46102; fax (satellite) 871-144-7753; e-mail ambrit@ic.cd; Ambassador: DOUGLAS SCRAFTON.

**USA:** 310 ave des Aviateurs, BP 697, Kinshasa; tel. (12) 21532; fax 21232; Ambassador: WILLIAM L. SWING.

**Zambia:** 54–58 ave de l'Ecole, BP 1144, Kinshasa; tel. (12) 23038; Ambassador: IAN SIKAZWE.

# Judicial System

The Minister of Justice is responsible for the organization and definition of competence of the judiciary; civil, penal and commercial law and civil and penal procedures; the status of persons and property; the system of obligations and questions pertaining to nationality; international private law; status of magistrates; organization of the legal profession, counsels for the defence, notaries and of judicial auxiliaries; supervision of cemeteries, non-profit-making organizations, cults and institutions working in the public interest; the operation of prisons; confiscated property.

There is a Supreme Court in Kinshasa, and there are also nine Courts of Appeal and 36 County Courts.

The Head of State is empowered to appoint and dismiss magistrates.

**Supreme Court:** cnr ave de la Justice and ave de Lemera, BP 3382, Kinshasa-Gombe; tel. (12) 25104.

**President of the Supreme Court:** BIYANGO KETESE.

**Procurator-General of the Republic:** MONGULU T'APANGANE.

# Religion

Many of the country's inhabitants follow traditional beliefs, which are mostly animistic. A large proportion of the population is Christian, predominantly Roman Catholic, and there are small Muslim, Jewish and Greek Orthodox communities.

## CHRISTIANITY

### The Roman Catholic Church

The Democratic Republic of the Congo comprises six archdioceses and 41 dioceses. An estimated 51% of the population are Roman Catholics.

**Bishops' Conference:** Conférence Episcopale de la République Démocratique du Congo, BP 3258, Kinshasa-Gombe; tel. (12) 30082; f. 1981; Pres. Rt Rev. FAUSTIN NGABU, Bishop of Goma.

**Archbishop of Bukavu:** Most Rev. EMMANUEL KATALIKO, Archevêché, BP 3324, Bukavu; tel. 2707; fax (16) 82060067.

**Archbishop of Kananga:** Most Rev. GODEFROID MUKENG'A KALOND, Archevêché, BP 70, Kananga; tel. 2477.

**Archbishop of Kinshasa:** Cardinal FRÉDÉRIC ETSOU-NZABI-BAMUNGWABI, Archevêché, ave de l'Université, BP 8431, Kinshasa 1; tel. (12) 3723-546.

**Archbishop of Kisangani:** Most Rev. LAURENT MONSENGWO PASINYA, Archevêché, ave Mpolo 10B, BP 505, Kisangani; tel. (761) 608334; fax (761) 3132898.

**Archbishop of Lubumbashi:** Most Rev. FLORIBERT SONGASONGA MWITWA, Archevêché, BP 72, Lubumbashi; tel. (2) 34-1442.

**Archbishop of Mbandaka-Bikoro:** Most Rev. JOSEPH KUMUONDALA MBIMBA, Archevêché, BP 1064, Mbandaka; tel. 2234.

### The Anglican Communion

The Church of the Province of the Congo comprises six dioceses.

**Archbishop of the Province of the Congo and Bishop of Boga:** Most Rev. PATRICE BYANKYA NJOJO, CAC-Boga, POB 21285, Nairobi, Kenya.

**Bishop of Bukavu:** Rt Rev. FIDÈLE BALUFUGA DIROKPA, CAC-Bukavu, POB 53435, Nairobi, Kenya.

**Bishop of Katanga:** Rt Rev. ISINGOMA KAHWA, CAZ-Lubumbashi, c/o United Methodist Church, POB 22037, Kitwe, Zambia.

**Bishop of Kindu:** Rt Rev. ZACHARIA MASIMANGE KATANDA, CAC-Kindu, POB 53435, Nairobi, Kenya; e-mail angkindu@antenna.nl.

**Bishop of Kisangani:** Rt Rev. SYLVESTRE MUGERA TIBAFA, CAC-Kisangani, BP 861, Kisangani.

**Bishop of Nord Kivu:** Rt Rev. METHUSELA MUNZENDA MUSUBAHO, CAC-Butembo, POB 21285, Nairobi, Kenya; fax (satellite) 871-166-1121.

### Kimbanguist

**Eglise de Jésus Christ sur la Terre par le Prophète Simon Kimbangu:** BP 7069, Kinshasa; tel. (12) 68944; f. 1921 (officially est.

1959); c. 5m. mems (1985); Spiritual Head HE SALOMON DIALUNGANA KIANGANI; Sec.-Gen. Rev. LUNTADILLA.

### Protestant Churches

**Eglise du Christ au Congo (ECC):** ave de la Justice (face no. 75), BP 4938, Kinshasa-Gombe; f. 1902; a co-ordinating agency for all the Protestant churches, with the exception of the Kimbanguist Church; 62 mem. communities and a provincial org. in each province; c. 10m. mems (1982); Pres. Bishop MARINI BODHO; includes:

**Communauté Baptiste du Congo-Ouest:** BP 4728, Kinshasa 2; f. 1970; 450 parishes; 170,000 mems (1985); Gen. Sec. Rev. LUSAKWENO-VANGU.

**Communauté des Disciples du Christ:** BP 178, Mbandaka; tel. 31062; f. 1964; 250 parishes; 650,000 mems (1985); Gen. Sec. Rev. Dr ELONDA EFEFE.

**Communauté Episcopale Baptiste en Afrique:** 2 ave Jason Sendwe, BP 3866, Lubumbashi 1; tel. (2) 24724; f. 1956; 1,300 episcopal communions and parishes; 150,000 mems (1993); Pres. Bishop KITOBO KABWEKA-LEZA.

**Communauté Evangélique:** BP 36, Luozi; f. 1961; 50 parishes; 33,750 mems (1985); Pres. Rev. K. LUKOMBO NTONTOLO.

**Communauté Lumière:** BP 10498, Kinshasa 1; f. 1931; 150 parishes; 220,000 mems (1985); Patriarch KAYUWA TSHIBUMBU WA KAHINGA.

**Communauté Mennonite:** BP 18, Tshikapa; f. 1960; 40,000 mems (1985); Gen. Sec. Rev. KABANGY DJEKE SHAPASA.

**Communauté Presbytérienne:** BP 117, Kananga; f. 1959; 150,000 mems (1985); Gen. Sec. Dr M. L. TSHIHAMBA.

**Eglise Missionaire Apostolique:** BP 15859, Kinshasa 1; f. 1986; 3 parishes; 1,000 mems.; Apostle for Africa L. A. NANANDANA.

## The Press

### DAILIES

**L'Analyste:** 129 ave du Bas-Congo, BP 91, Kinshasa-Gombe; tel. (12) 80987; Dir and Editor-in-Chief BONGOMA KONI BOTAHE.

**Boyoma:** 31 blvd Mobutu, BP 982, Kisangani, Dir and Editor BADRIYO ROVA ROVATU.

**Elima:** 1 ave de la Révolution, BP 11498, Kinshasa; tel. (12) 77332; f. 1928; evening; Dir and Editor-in-Chief ESSOLOMWA NKOY EA LINGANGA.

**Mjumbe:** BP 2474, Lubumbashi; tel. (2) 25348; f. 1963; Dir and Editor TSHIMANGA KOYA KAKONA.

**Le Palmarès:** Kinshasa; supports Union pour la démocratie et le progrès social; Editor MICHEL LADELUYA.

**Le Potentiel:** Kinshasa; Chief Ed. MODESTE LITUNGA.

**La Référence Plus:** Kinshasa; Dir ANDRÉ IPAKALA.

**Le Soft:** Kinshasa; Man. KINKIEY MALUMBA; Chief Editor AWASI KHAROMON.

### PERIODICALS

**Allo Kinshasa:** 3 rue Kayange, BP 20271, Kinshasa-Lemba; monthly; Editor MBUYU WA KABILA.

**L'Aurore Protestante:** Eglise du Christ au Congo, BP 4938, Kinshasa-Gombe; French; religion; monthly; circ. 1,000.

**BEA Magazine de la Femme:** 2 ave Masimanimba, BP 113380, Kinshasa 1; every 2 weeks; Editor MUTINGA MUTWISHAYI.

**Bingwa:** ave du 30 juin, zone Lubumbashi no 4334; weekly; sport; Dir and Editor MATEKE WA MULAMBA.

**Cahiers Economiques et Sociaux:** BP 257, Kinshasa XI, (National University of the Congo); sociological, political and economic review; quarterly; Dir Prof. NDONGALA TADI LEWA; circ. 2,000.

**Cahiers des Religions Africaines:** Faculté de Théologie Catholique de Kinshasa, BP 712, Kinshasa/Limete; tel. (12) 78476; f. 1967; English and French; religion; 2 a year; circ. 1,000.

**Le Canard Libre:** Kinshasa; f. 1991; Editor JOSEPH CASTRO MULEBE.

**Circulaire d'Information:** Association Nationale des Entreprises du Congo, 10 ave des Aviateurs, BP 7247, Kinshasa 1; tel. (12) 22565; f. 1959; French; legal and statutory texts for the business community; monthly.

**La Colombe:** 32B ave Tombalbaye, Kinshasa-Gombe; tel. (12) 21211; organ of Parti démocrate et social chrétien; circ. 5,000.

**Congo-Afrique:** Centre d'Etudes pour l'Action Sociale, 9 ave Père Boka, BP 3375, Kinshasa-Gombe; tel. (12) 34682; f. 1961; economic, social and cultural; monthly; Editors FRANCIS KIKASSA MWANALESSA, RENÉ BEECKMANS; circ. 2,500.

**Le Conseiller Comptable:** 51 rue du Grand Séminaire, Quartier Nganda, BP 308, Kinshasa; tel. (88) 01216; fax (88) 00075; f 1974; French; public finance and taxation; quarterly; Editor TOMENA FOKO; circ. 2,000.

**Le Courrier du Zaïre:** aut. no 04/DIMOPAP 0018/84, 101 Lukolela, Kinshasa; weekly; Editor NZONZILA NDONZUAU.

**Cultures au Zaïre et en Afrique:** BP 16706, Kinshasa; f. 1973; French and English; quarterly.

**Dionga:** Immeuble Amassio, 2 rue Dirna, BP 8031, Kinshasa; monthly.

**Documentation et Information Protestante (DIP):** Eglise du Christ au Congo, BP 4938, Kinshasa-Gombe; tel. and fax (88) 46387; e-mail eccm@ic.cd; French and English; religion.

**Documentation et Informations Africaines (DIA):** BP 2598, Kinshasa 1; tel. (12) 33197; fax (12) 33196; Roman Catholic news agency reports; 3 a week; Dir Rev. Père VATA DIAMBANZA.

**L'Entrepreneur Flash:** Association Nationale des Entreprises du Congo, 10 ave des Aviateurs, BP 7247, Kinshasa 1; tel. (12) 22565; f. 1978; business news; monthly; circ. 1,000.

**Etudes d'Histoire Africaine:** National University of the Congo, BP 1825, Lubumbashi; f. 1970; French and English; history; annually; circ. 1,000.

**Horizons 80:** Société Congolaise d'Edition et d'Information, BP 9839, Kinshasa; economic affairs; weekly.

**Les Kasaï:** 161 9e rue, BP 575, Kinshasa/Limete; weekly; Editor NSENGA NDOMBA.

**Kin-Média:** BP 15808, Kinshasa 1; monthly; Editor ILUNGA KASAMBAY.

**KYA:** 24 ave de l'Equateur, BP 7853, Kinshasa-Gombe; tel. (12) 27502; f. 1984; weekly for Bas-Congo; Editor SASSA KASSA YI KIBOBA.

**Libération:** Kinshasa; f. 1997; politics; supports the AFDL; weekly; Man. NGOYI KABUYA DIKATETA M'MIANA.

**Mambenga 2000:** BP 477, Mbandaka; Editor BOSANGE YEMA BOF.

**Le Moniteur de l'Economie** (Economic Monitor): Kinshasa; Man. Ed. FÉLIX NZUZI.

**Mwana Shaba:** Générale des Carrières et des Mines, BP 450, Lubumbashi; monthly; circ. 25,000.

**Ngabu:** Société Nationale d'Assurances, Immeuble Sonas Sankuru, blvd du 30 juin, BP 3443, Kinshasa-Gombe; tel. (12) 23051; f. 1973; insurance news; quarterly.

**Njanja:** Société Nationale des Chemins de Fer Congolais, 115 place de la Gare, BP 297, Lubumbashi; tel. (2) 23430; fax (2) 61321; railways and transportation; annually; circ. 10,000.

**NUKTA:** 14 chaussée de Kasenga, BP 3805, Lubumbashi; weekly; agriculture; Editor NGOY BUNDUKI.

**L'Opinion:** BP 15394, Kinshasa; weekly; Editor SABLE FWAMBA KIEPENDA.

**Problèmes Sociaux Zaïrois:** Centre d'Exécution de Programmes Sociaux et Economiques, Université de Lubumbashi, 208 ave Kasavubu, BP 1873, Lubumbashi; f. 1946; quarterly; Editor N'KASHAMA KADIMA.

**Promoteur Congolais:** Centre du Commerce International du Congo, 119 ave Colonel Tshatshi, BP 13, Kinshasa; f. 1979; international trade news; six a year.

**Sciences, Techniques, Informations:** Centre de Recherches Industrielles en Afrique Centrale (CRIAC), BP 54, Lubumbashi.

**Le Sport Africain:** 13è niveau Tour adm., Cité de la Voix du Congo, BP 3356, Kinshasa-Gombe; monthly; Pres. TSHIMPUMPU WA TSHIMPUMPU.

**Taifa:** 536 ave Lubumba, BP 884, Lubumbashi; weekly; Editor LWAMBWA MILAMBU.

**Telema:** Faculté Canisius, Kimwenza, BP 3724, Kinshasa-Gombe; f. 1974; religious; quarterly; edited by the Central Africa Jesuits; circ. 1,200.

**Umoja:** Kinshasa; weekly.

**Vision:** Kinshasa; Man. Ed. THIERRY TIALUMBA KABUMGA.

**Zaïre Business:** Immeuble Amasco, 3968 rue ex-Belgika, BP 9839, Kinshasa; f. 1973; French; weekly.

**Zaïre Informatique:** Conseil Permanent de l'Informatique au Zaïre, Kinshasa 1; f. 1978; quarterly.

**Zaïre Ya Sita:** Direction Générale et Administration, 1 rue Luozi Kasavubu, BP 8246, Kinshasa; f. 1968; Lingala; political science; 6 a year.

### NEWS AGENCIES

**Agence Congolaise de Presse (ACP):** 44–48 ave Tombalbaye, BP 1595, Kinshasa 1; tel. (12) 22035; f. 1957; state-controlled; Dir-Gen. ALI KALONGA.

**Documentation et Informations Africaines (DIA):** BP 2598, Kinshasa 1; tel. (12) 34528; f. 1957; Roman Catholic news agency; Dir Rev. Père VATA DIAMBANZA.

#### Foreign Bureaux

**Agence France-Presse (AFP):** Immeuble Wenge 3227, ave Wenge, Zone de la Gombe, BP 726, Kinshasa 1; tel. (12) 27009; Bureau Chief JEAN-PIERRE REJETTE.

**Agencia EFE** (Spain): BP 2653, Lubumbashi; Correspondent KANKU SANGA.

**Agência Lusa de Informação** (Portugal): BP 4941, Kinshasa; tel. (12) 24437.

**Agenzia Nazionale Stampa Associata (ANSA)** (Italy): BP 2790, Kinshasa 15; tel. (12) 30315; Bureau Chief (vacant).

**Pan-African News Agency (PANA)** (Senegal): BP 1400, Kinshasa; tel. (12) 23290; f. 1983; Bureau Chief ADRIEN HONORÉ MBEYET.

**Xinhua (New China) News Agency** (People's Republic of China): 293 ave Mfumu Lutunu, BP 8939, Kinshasa; tel. (12) 25647; Correspondent CHEN WEIBIN.

### PRESS ASSOCIATIONS

**Médias Libres—Médias pour Tous:** Kinshasa; org. representing Kinshasa newspapers.

**Union de la Presse du Congo:** BP 4941, Kinshasa 1; tel. (12) 24437.

## Publishers

**Aequatoria Centre:** BP 276, Mbandaka; f. 1980; anthropology, biography, ethnicity, history, language and linguistics, social sciences; Dir HONORÉ VINCK.

**CEEBA Publications:** BP 246, Bandundu; f. 1965; humanities, languages, fiction; Man. Dir (Editorial) Dr HERMANN HOCHEGGER.

**CELTA (Centre de Linguistique Théorique et Appliquée):** BP 4956, Kinshasa-Gombe; tel. (2) 30503; fax (2) 21394; f 1971; language arts and linguistics; Gen. Man. N. KIKO; Dir NTITA NYEMBWE.

**Centre de Documentation Agricole:** BP 7537, Kinshasa 1; tel. (12) 32498; agriculture, science; Dir PIERTE MBAYAKABUYI; Chief Editor J. MARCELLIN KAPUKUNGESA.

**Centre de Recherches Pédagogiques:** BP 8815, Kinshasa 1; f. 1959; accounting, education, geography, language, science; Dir P. DETIENNE.

**Centre de Vulgarisation Agricole:** BP 4008, Kinshasa 2; tel. (12) 71165; fax (12) 21351; agriculture, environment, health; Dir-Gen. KIMPIANGA MAHANIAH.

**Centre International de Semiologie:** 109 ave Pruniers, BP 1825, Lubumbashi.

**Centre Protestant d'Editions et de Diffusion (CEDI):** 209 ave Kalémie, BP 11398, Kinshasa 1; tel. (12) 22202; fax (12) 26730; f. 1935; fiction, poetry, biography, religious, juvenile; Christian tracts, works in French, Lingala, Kikongo, etc.; Dir-Gen. HENRY DIRKS.

**Commission de l'Education Chrétienne:** BP 3258, Kinshasa-Gombe; tel. (12) 30086; education, religion; Man. Dir Abbé MUGADJA LEHANI.

**Connaissance et Pratique du Droit Congolais Editions (CDPC):** BP 5502, Kinshasa-Gombe; f. 1987; law; Editor DIBUNDA KABUINJI.

**Facultés Catholiques de Kinshasa:** BP 1534, Kinshasa-Limete; tel. and fax (12) 46965; f. 1957; anthropology, art, economics, history, politics, computer science; five titles in 1994; Dir Mgr LUDIONGO NDOMBASI.

**Editions Lokole:** BP 5085, Kinshasa 10; state org. for the promotion of literature; Dir BOKEME SHANE MOLOBAY.

**Editions Saint Paul:** BP 8505, Kinshasa; tel. (12) 77726; fiction, general non-fiction, poetry, religion; Dir Sister FRANKA PERONA.

**Les Editions du Trottoir:** BP 629, Kinshasa; f. 1989; communications, fiction, literature, drama; Pres. CHARLES DJUNJU-SIMBA.

**Librarie les Volcans:** 22 ave Pres. Mobutu, BP 400, Goma, Nord-Kivu; f. 1995; social sciences; Man. Dir RUHAMA MUKANDOLI.

**Presses Universitaires du Congo (PUC):** 290 rue d'Aketi, BP 1682, Kinshasa 1; tel. (12) 30652; f. 1972; scientific publs; Dir Prof. MUMBANZA MWA BAWELE.

### Government Publishing House

**Imprimerie du Gouvernement Central:** BP 3021, Kinshasa-Kalina.

## Broadcasting and Communications

### TELECOMMUNICATIONS

**Comcell:** Kinshasa; provides satellite communications network; 4,000 subscribers.

**Office Congolais des Postes et des Télécommunications (OCPT):** Hôtel des postes, blvd du 30 juin, BP 13798, Kinshasa; tel. (12) 21871; fax (88) 45010; state-owned; 13,000 lines; 40,000 subscribers; Dir-Gen. KAPITAO MAMBWENI.

**Telecel-Congo:** Kinshasa; provides satellite communications network; largest private operator; 45% nationalized in 1998; 12,000 subscribers.

### BROADCASTING

**Radio-Télévision Nationale Congolaise (RTNC):** BP 3171, Kinshasa-Gombe; tel. (12) 23171; state radio terrestrial and satellite television broadcasts; Dir-Gen. JOSE KAJANGUA.

#### Radio

Several private radio broadcasters operate in Kinshasa.

**Radio Candip:** Centre d'Animation et de Diffusion Pedagogique, BP 373, Bunia; state-controlled; under rebel control in late 1998.

**La Voix du Congo:** Station Nationale, BP 3164, Kinshasa-Gombe; tel. (12) 23175; state-controlled; operated by RTNC; broadcasts in French, Swahili, Lingala, Tshiluba, Kikongo; regional stations at Kisangani, Lubumbashi, Bukavu, Bandundu, Kananga, Mbuji-Mayi, Matadi, Mbandaka and Bunia.

#### Television

Several private television broadcasters operate in Kinshasa.

**Antenne A:** Immeuble Forescom, 2e étage, ave du Port 4, POB 2581, Kinshasa 1; tel. (243) 21736; private and commercial station; Dir-Gen. IGAL AVIVI NEIRSON.

**Canal Z:** ave du Port 6, POB 614, Kinshasa 1; tel. (243) 20239; commercial station; Dir-Gen. FRÉDÉRIC FLASSE.

**Tele Kin Malebo (TKM):** Kinshasa; private television station; nationalization announced 1997; Dir-Gen. NGONGO LUWOWO.

**Télévision Congolais:** BP 3171, Kinshasa-Gombe: tel. (12) 23171; govt commercial station; operated by RTNC; broadcasts for 5 hours daily on weekdays and 10 hours daily at weekends.

## Finance

(cap. = capital; res = reserves; dep. = deposits; m. = million; brs = branches; amounts in old zaires unless otherwise indicated)

### BANKING

A reorganization of the banking sector was expected to follow the introduction as legal tender of a new currency unit, the Congolese franc (CF), which was completed on 30 June 1999.

#### Central Bank

**Banque Centrale du Congo:** blvd Colonel Tshatshi au nord, BP 2697, Kinshasa; tel. (12) 20701; f. 1964; cap. and res 50,088.4m. (Dec. 1988); Gov. JEAN-CLAUDE MASANGU MULONGO; 8 brs.

#### Commercial Banks

**African Trade Bank (ATB):** ave Lemarinel, BP 3459, Kinshasa-Gombe; tel. (12) 33845; fax (12) 8846991; cap. and res NZ 67,893.3m., total assets NZ 406,946.6m. (Dec. 1996); Pres. ABDALLAH HASSAN WAZNI; Gen. Man. GHAZI ABDALLAH WAZNI.

**BANCOR SARL:** Immeuble Régidesco-DG, BP 7997, Kinshasa; tel. (12) 20635; fax (satellite) 1-212-3769207; f. 1998.

**Banque de Commerce et de Développement (BCD):** 87 blvd du 30 juin, Kinshasa; tel. (12) 20106; fax (satellite) 1-703-3902716; e-mail bcd-kin@ic.cd; cap. and res CF 5.2m., total assets CF 29.1m. (Dec. 1998).

**Banque Commerciale du Congo SARL (BCDC):** blvd du 30 juin, BP 488, Kinshasa; tel. (12) 21693; fax (12) 21770; e-mail bcdc@raga.cd; f. 1909 as Banque du Congo Belge, name changed as above 1997; cap. and res CF 98.6m., total assets CF 240.9m. (Dec. 1998); Pres. NKEMA LILOO; Gen. Man. KASONGO TAIBU; 29 brs.

**Banque Congolaise du Commerce Extérieur SARL:** blvd du 30 juin, BP 400, Kinshasa 1; tel. (12) 20393; fax (12) 27947; f. 1947, reorg. 1987; state-owned; in liquidation in 1999; cap. and res NZ 19,303.1m., dep. NZ 27,419.9m. (Dec. 1994); Chair. and Gen. Man. GBENDO NDEWA TETE; Dirs MAKUMA NDESEKE, ZIKONDOLO BIWABEKI; 31 brs.

**Banque Continentale Africaine (Congo) SCARL:** 4 ave de la Justice, BP 7613, Kinshasa-Gombe; tel. (12) 24388; fax (12) 21237; f. 1983; total assets 28,786.5m. (Dec. 1994); Pres. NASIR ABID; Dir-Gen. M. A. DOCHY.

**Banque de Crédit Agricole:** angle ave Kasa-Vubu et ave M'Polo, BP 8837, Kinshasa-Gombe; tel. (12) 21800; fax (12) 27221; f. 1982 to expand and modernize enterprises in agriculture, livestock and fishing, and generally to improve the quality of rural life; state-owned; in liquidation in 1999; cap. 5m. (Dec. 1991); Pres. MOLOTO MWA LOPANZA.

**Banque Internationale de Crédit SCARL (BIC):** 191 ave de l'Equateur, BP 1299, Kinshasa 1; tel. (88) 41940; fax (12) 123769600; f. 1994; cap. and res NZ 8,355.4m., total assets NZ 35,077.9m. (Dec.

1995); Pres. PASCAL KINDUELO LUMBU; Man. Dir THARCISSE K. M. MILEMBWE.

**Banque Internationale pour l'Afrique au Congo (BIAC):** Immeuble Nioki, ave de la Douane, Kinshasa 1; tel. (88) 20612; fax (12) 20120; e-mail biac-rj@raga.net; cap. and res US $1.4m., total assets US $17.4m. (Dec. 1998); Pres. ROBERT JONCHERAY.

**Caisse Générale d'Epargne du Congo:** 38 ave de la Caisse d'Epargne, BP 8147, Kinshasa-Gombe; tel. (12) 33701; f. 1950; state-owned; Chair. and Man. Dir NSIMBA M'VUEDI; 45 brs.

**Citibank NA Congo:** Immeuble Citibank Congo, angle aves Col Lukusa et Ngongo Lutete, BP 9999, Kinshasa 1; tel. (12) 20554; fax (12) 21064; f. 1971; cap. and res NZ 199,425.2m., total assets NZ 1,928,804.9m. (Dec. 1996); Pres. ROBERT THORNTON; 1 br.

**Fransabank (Congo) SARL:** Immeuble Flavica 14/16, ave du Port, BP 9497, Kinshasa 1; tel. (88) 00445376; fax (88) 0046423; f. 1989; cap. and res NZ 7,351.7m., total assets NZ 174,809.7m. (Dec. 1996); Pres. ADNAN WAFIC KASSAR.

**Nouvelle Banque de Kinshasa:** 1 place du Marché, BP 8033, Kinshasa 1; tel. (12) 26361; fax (12) 20587; f. 1969, nationalized 1975; control transferred to National Union of Congolese Workers in 1989; in liquidation in 1999; cap. NZ 2,000 (1990), res NZ 92,179.4m., dep. NZ 25,396.8m. (Dec. 1994); Pres. MANTOMINA KIALA; 15 brs.

**Société Financière de Développement SCARL (SOFIDE):** Immeuble SOFIDE, 9–11 angle aves Ngabu et Kisangani, BP 1148, Kinshasa 1; tel. (12) 20676; fax (12) 20788; f. 1970; partly state-owned; provides tech. and financial aid, primarily for agricultural devt; cap. and res NZ 44,610.4m., total assets NZ 519,789.7m. (Dec. 1997); Pres. and Dir-Gen. KIYANGA KI-N'LOMBI; 4 brs.

**Stanbic Bank Congo SARL:** 12 ave de Mongala, BP 16297, Kinshasa 1; tel. (12) 20028; fax (12) 46216; f. 1973; subsidiary of Standard Bank Investment Corpn (South Africa); cap. and res CF 1.2m., total assets CF 21.3m. (Dec. 1998); Chair. J. N. LEGGETT; Man. Dir NICOLAS CLAVEL; 1 br.

**Union de Banques Congolaises (UBC) SARL:** angle ave de la Nation et ave des Aviateurs 19, BP 197, Kinshasa 1; tel. (88) 41333; fax (88) 46628; e-mail ubc@ic.cd; f. 1929, renamed as above in 1997; total assets US $ 59.3m. (Dec. 1997); Man. Dir LUC DELVA; 8 brs.

### INSURANCE

**Société Nationale d'Assurances (SONAS):** 3473 blvd du 30 juin, Kinshasa-Gombe; tel. (12) 23051; f. 1966; state-owned; cap. 23m.; 9 brs.

## Trade and Industry

At November 1994 the Government's portfolio of state enterprises numbered 116, of which 56 were wholly owned by the Government. The heads of all state-owned enterprises were suspended by decree in June 1997.

### DEVELOPMENT ORGANIZATIONS

**Caisse de Stabilisation Cotonnière (CSCo):** BP 3058, Kinshasa-Gombe; tel. (12) 31206; f. 1978 to replace Office National des Fibres Textiles; acts as an intermediary between the Govt, cotton ginners and textile factories, and co-ordinates international financing of cotton sector.

**La Générale des Carrières et des Mines (GÉCAMINES):** BP 450, Lubumbashi; tel. (2) 6768105; fax (2) 6768041; f. 1967 to acquire assets of Union Minière du Haut-Katanga; state-owned corpn engaged in mining and marketing of copper, cobalt, zinc and coal; also has interests in agriculture; privatization announced in 1994, subsequently delayed; Exec. Chair. BILLY RAUTENBACH; operates the following enterprise:

**GÉCAMINES—Exploitation:** mining operations.

**Institut National pour l'Etude et la Recherche Agronomiques:** BP 1513, Kisangani; f. 1933; agricultural research.

**Office Congolais du Café:** ave Général Bobozo, BP 8931, Kinshasa 1; tel. (12) 77144; f. 1979; state agency for coffee and also cocoa, tea, quinquina and pyrethrum.

**Pêcherie Maritime Congolaise:** Kinshasa; DRC's only sea-fishing enterprise.

### CHAMBERS OF COMMERCE

**Chambre de Commerce, d'Industrie et d'Agriculture du Congo:** 10 ave des Aviateurs, BP 7247, Kinshasa 1; tel. (12) 22286.

### INDUSTRIAL AND TRADE ASSOCIATIONS

**Association Nationale des Entreprises du Congo:** 10 ave des Aviateurs, BP 7247, Kinshasa; tel. (12) 24623; f. 1972; represents business interests for both domestic and foreign institutions; Man. Dir EDOUARD LUBOYA DIYOKA; Gen. Sec. ATHANASE MATENDA KYELU.

### EMPLOYERS' ASSOCIATION

**Fédération des Entreprises du Congo (FEC):** Kinshasa; Head JOSE ENDUNDO.

### UTILITIES

#### Electricity

**Société Nationale d'Electricité (SNEL):** 2831 ave de la Justice, BP 500, Kinshasa; tel. (12) 26893; fax (12) 33735; f. 1970; state-owned; Dir-Gen. PASCAL KUNDA PAKA (acting).

#### Water

**Régie de Distribution d'Eau (REGIDESCO):** 65 blvd du 30 juin, BP 12599, Kinshasa; tel. (12) 22792; water supply admin; Dir-Gen. EALE BOMBOLE (acting).

### TRADE UNIONS

The Union Nationale des Travailleurs was founded in 1967 as the sole trade union organization. In 1990 the establishment of independent trade unions was legalized, and by early 1991 there were 12 officially recognized trade union organizations.

**Union Nationale des Travailleurs du Congo:** BP 8814, Kinshasa; f. 1967; comprises 16 unions; Pres. KATALAY MOLELI SANGOL.

## Transport

**Office National des Transports (ONATRA):** BP 98, Kinshasa 1; tel. (12) 24761; fax (12) 24892; operates 12,174 km of waterways, 366 km of railways and road and air transport; administers ports of Kinshasa, Matadi, Boma and Banana; Pres. and Gen. Man. JACQUES MBELOLO BITWEMI.

### RAILWAYS

The main line runs from Lubumbashi to Ilebo. International services run to Dar es Salaam (Tanzania) and Lobito (Angola), and also connect with the Zambian, Zimbabwean, Mozambican and South African systems. In 1994 an agreement was concluded with the South African Government for the provision of locomotives, rolling stock and fuel, to help rehabilitate the rail system. In May 1997 the railway system was nationalized.

**Kinshasa–Matadi Railway:** BP 98, Kinshasa 1; 366 km operated by ONATRA; Pres. JACQUES MBELOLO BITWEMI.

**Société Nationale des Chemins de Fer du Congo (SNCC):** 115 place de la Gare, BP 297, Lubumbashi; tel. (2) 23430; f. 1974; 4,772 km (including 858 km electrified); administers all internal railway sections as well as river transport and transport on Lakes Tanganyika and Kivu; man. contract concluded with a Belgian-South African corpn, Sizarail, in 1995 for the man. of the Office des Chemins de Fer du Sud (OCS) and the Société des Chemins de Fer de l'Est (SFE) subsidiaries, with rail networks of 2,835 km and 1,286 km respectively; assets of Sizarail nationalized and returned to SNCC control in May 1997; Dir-Gen. R. DIFAND.

### ROADS

In 1996 there were approximately 157,000 km of roads, of which some 33,100 km were main roads. In general road conditions are poor, owing to inadequate maintenance. In August 1997 a rehabilitation plan was announced by the Government under which 28,664 km of roads were to be built or repaired. The project was to be partly financed by external sources.

**Office des Routes:** Direction Générale, ave Ex-Descamp, BP 10899, Kinshasa-Gombe; tel. (12) 32036; construction and maintenance of roads.

### INLAND WATERWAYS

The River Congo is navigable for more than 1,600 km. Above the Stanley Falls the Congo becomes the Lualaba, and is navigable along a 965-km stretch from Ubundu to Kindu and Kongolo to Bukama. The River Kasai, a tributary of the River Congo, is navigable by shipping as far as Ilebo, at which the line from Lubumbashi terminates. The total length of inland waterways is 13,700 km.

**Régie des voies fluviales:** 109 ave Lumpungu, Kinshasa-Gombe, BP 11697, Kinshasa 1; administers river navigation; Gen. Man. NGIAM KIPOY.

**Société Congolaise des Chemins de Fer des Grands Lacs:** River Lualaba services: Bubundu–Kindu and Kongolo–Malemba N'kula; Lake Tanganyika services: Kamina–Kigoma–Kalundu–Moba–Mpulungu.

### SHIPPING

The principal seaports are Matadi, Boma and Banana on the lower Congo. The port of Matadi has more than 1.6 km of quays and can accommodate up to 10 deep-water vessels. Matadi is linked by rail with Kinshasa. The country's merchant fleet numbered 20 vessels and amounted to 12,918 gross registered tons at 31 December 1998.

**Compagnie Maritime du Congo SARL:** USB Centre, place de la Poste, BP 9496, Kinshasa; tel. (12) 21031; fax (12) 26234; f. 1946; services: North Africa, Europe, North America and Asia to West Africa, East Africa to North Africa; Chair. MAYILUKILA LUSIASIA; Pres. Gen. A. I. JEAN-FAUSTIN MASSAMBA ASHINGA MBIANSHU.

### CIVIL AVIATION

International airports are located at Ndjili (for Kinshasa), Luano (for Lubumbashi), Bukavu, Goma and Kisangani. There are smaller airports and airstrips dispersed throughout the country.

**Blue Airlines:** BP 1115, Kinshasa 1; tel. (12) 20455; f. 1991; regional and domestic charter services for passengers and cargo; Man. T. MAYANI.

**Compagnie Africaine d'Aviation:** Edifice du GAP, blvd du 30 juin, Kinshasa; f. 1992.

**Congo Airlines:** 1928 ave Kabambare, N'dolo-Kinshasa, BP 12847, Kinshasa; tel. (88) 43947; fax (88) 00235; e-mail cal-fih-dg@ic.cd; f.1994 as Express Cargo, assumed present name in 1997; international, regional and domestic scheduled services for passengers and cargo; Pres. JOSE ENDUNO; CEO STAVROS PAPAIOANNOU.

**Eastern Congo Airlines:** Bukavu; f. 1997; 60% state-owned, 40% by Belgian interests; Chair. Chief NAKAZIBA CIMANYE.

**Filair:** BP 14671, Kinshasa; tel. (88) 45702; fax (88) 45702; f. 1987; regional and domestic charter services; Pres. DANY PHILEMOTTE.

**Lignes Aériennes du Congo (LAC):** 3555-3560 blvd du 30 juin, BP 2111, Kinshasa; tel. (12) 24624; relaunched 1997; national carrier.

**Scibe Airlift:** BP 614, Kinshasa; tel. (12) 26237; fax (12) 24386; f. 1979; domestic and international passenger and cargo charter services between Kinshasa, Lubumbashi, Bujumbura (Burundi) and Brussels; Pres. BEMBA SAOLONA; Dir-Gen. BEMBA GOMBO.

**Zairean Airlines (Congo):** 3555–3560 blvd du 30 juin, BP 2111, Kinshasa; tel. (88) 48103; f. 1981; international, regional and domestic services for passengers and cargo; Dir-Gen. Capt. ALFRED SOMMERAUER.

Local charter services are also provided by Trans Service Airlift, Transair Cargo and Wetrafa Airlift.

## Tourism

The country offers extensive lake and mountain scenery, although tourism remains largely undeveloped. In 1996 tourist arrivals totalled some 37,000 and receipts from tourism amounted to an estimated US $5m.

**Office National du Tourisme:** 2A/2B ave des Orangers, BP 9502, Kinshasa-Gombe; tel. (12) 30070; f. 1959; Man. Dir BOTOLO MAGOZA.

**Société Congolaise de l'Hôtellerie:** Immeuble Memling, BP 1076, Kinshasa; tel. (12) 23260; Man. N'JOLI BALANGA.

# THE REPUBLIC OF THE CONGO

## Introductory Survey

**Location, Climate, Language, Religion, Flag, Capital**

The Republic of the Congo is an equatorial country on the west coast of Africa. It has a coastline of about 170 km on the Atlantic Ocean, from which the country extends northward to Cameroon and the Central African Republic. The Republic of the Congo is bordered by Gabon to the west and the Democratic Republic of the Congo (formerly Zaire) to the east, while in the south there is a short frontier with the Cabinda exclave of Angola. The climate is tropical, with temperatures averaging 21°C–27°C (70°F–80°F) throughout the year. The average annual rainfall is about 1,200 mm (47 ins). The official language is French; Kikongo, Lingala and other African languages are also used. At least one-half of the population follow traditional animist beliefs and about 45% are Roman Catholics. There are small Protestant and Muslim minorities. The national flag (proportions 3 by 2) comprises a yellow stripe running diagonally from lower hoist to upper fly, separating a green triangle at the hoist from a red triangle in the fly. The capital is Brazzaville.

**Recent History**

Formerly part of French Equatorial Africa, Middle Congo became the autonomous Republic of the Congo, within the French Community, in November 1958, with Abbé Fulbert Youlou as the first Prime Minister, and subsequently as President when the Congo became fully independent on 15 August 1960. Youlou was compelled to relinquish office in August 1963, following a period of ethnic tensions and internal unrest, and was succeeded by Alphonse Massamba-Débat, initially as Prime Minister, and from December as President. In the following July the Mouvement national de la révolution (MNR) was established as the sole political party. In August 1968 Massamba-Débat was overthrown in a military coup, led by Capt. (later Maj.) Marien Ngouabi, who was proclaimed President in January 1969. A new Marxist-Leninist party, the Parti congolais du travail (PCT), replaced the MNR, and in January 1970 the country was renamed the People's Republic of the Congo. In March 1977 Ngouabi was assassinated by supporters of ex-President Massamba-Débat, and in the following month Col (later Brig.-Gen.) Jacques-Joachim Yhombi-Opango, the head of the armed forces, became the new Head of State. In February 1979, faced with a collapse in support, Yhombi-Opango surrendered his powers to a Provisional Committee appointed by the PCT. In the following month the head of the Provisional Committee, Col (later Gen.) Denis Sassou-Nguesso, became Chairman of the PCT Central Committee and President of the Republic.

Persistent ethnic rivalries, together with disillusionment with the Government's response to the country's worsening economic situation, resulted in an increase in opposition to the Sassou-Nguesso regime during the late 1980s. In July 1987 some 20 army officers were arrested for alleged complicity in a coup plot. Shortly afterwards fighting broke out in the north between government forces and troops led by Pierre Anga, a supporter of Yhombi-Opango. In September government troops suppressed the rebellion with French military assistance. Yhombi-Opango was transferred from house arrest to prison. Anga was subsequently killed by Congolese security forces.

At the PCT Congress in July 1989 Sassou-Nguesso, the sole candidate, was re-elected Chairman of the party and President of the Republic for a third five-year term. In August Alphonse Mouissou Poaty-Souchalaty, formerly the Minister of Trade and Small and Medium-sized Enterprises, was appointed Prime Minister. At legislative elections in September the PCT-approved single list of 133 candidates was endorsed by 99.2% of voters. The list included, for the first time, candidates who were not members of the party. In November Sassou-Nguesso announced plans for economic reform, signifying a departure from socialist policies.

Progress towards political reform dominated the latter half of 1990. In July the Government announced that an extraordinary Congress of the PCT would be convened to formulate legislation enabling the introduction of a multi-party system. The regime also approved measures that would limit the role of the ruling party in the country's mass and social organizations. In August, on the occasion of the 30th anniversary of the country's independence, several political prisoners were released, among them Yhombi-Opango. In September the Confederation of Congolese Trade Unions (CSC) was refused permission by the Government to disaffiliate itself from the ruling PCT. The CSC had also demanded the immediate implementation of a multi-party system and increased salaries for workers in the public sector. Following a two-day general strike, Sassou-Nguesso assented to free elections to the leadership of the trade union organization, and in late September the Central Committee of the PCT agreed to the immediate registration of new political parties. In early December Poaty-Souchalaty resigned. On the following day the extraordinary Congress of the PCT commenced. The party abandoned Marxism-Leninism as its official ideology, and formulated constitutional amendments legalizing a multi-party system, which took effect in January 1991. Gen. Louis Sylvain Goma was appointed Prime Minister (a position he had previously held between December 1975 and August 1984), and shortly afterwards an interim Government was installed.

A National Conference on the country's future was convened in February 1991. Opposition movements were allocated seven of the 11 seats on the Conference's governing body, and were represented by 700 of the 1,100 delegates attending the Conference. The Roman Catholic Bishop of Owando, Ernest N'Kombo, was elected as Chairman. The Conference voted to establish itself as a sovereign body, the decisions of which were to be binding and not subject to approval by the transitional Government. In April the Conference announced proposals to draft legislation providing for the abrogation of the Constitution and the abolition of the National People's Assembly, several national institutions and regional councils. In June, prior to the dissolution of the Conference, a 153-member legislative Higher Council of the Republic was established, under the chairmanship of N'Kombo; this was empowered to supervise the implementation of the resolutions made by the National Conference, pending the adoption of a new constitution and the holding of legislative and presidential elections in 1992. From June 1991 the President was replaced as Chairman of the Council of Ministers by the Prime Minister, and the country reverted to its previous official name, the Republic of the Congo. A new Prime Minister, André Milongo (a former World Bank official), was appointed in June, and during that month the Government agreed to permit workers to form independent trade unions. In December the Higher Council of the Republic adopted a draft Constitution, which provided for legislative power to be vested in an elected Assemblée nationale and Senate and for executive power to be held by an elected President.

In January 1992, following a reallocation of senior army posts by the Prime Minister, members of the army occupied strategic positions in Brazzaville and demanded the reinstatement of military personnel who had allegedly been dismissed because of their ethnic allegiances, the removal of the newly-appointed Secretary of State for Defence and the immediate payment of overdue salaries. Milongo refused to comply with these demands, whereupon the mutineers demanded his resignation as Prime Minister, and he was temporarily forced to go into hiding. The crisis was eventually resolved by the resignation of the Secretary of State for Defence and the installation of a candidate acceptable to the army as Minister of Defence. Milongo appointed himself Chief of the Armed Forces.

The draft Constitution was approved by 96.3% of voters at a national referendum in March 1992. In May Milongo appointed a new Council of Ministers, membership of which was drawn from each of the country's regions, in order to avoid accusations of domination by any one ethnic group. Following two rounds of elections to the new Assemblée nationale, in late June and mid-July, the Union panafricaine pour la démocratie social (UPADS) became the major party, winning 39 of the 125 contested seats; the Mouvement congolais pour la démocratie et le développement intégral (MCDDI) took 29 seats and the PCT secured 18 seats. At elections to the Senate, held in late July, the UPADS again won the largest share (23) of the 60 contested seats, followed by the MCDDI, with 13 seats. At the first round of presidential voting, in early August, Pascal Lissouba, the leader of the UPADS (who had been Prime Minister in 1963–66), won the largest share of the votes cast (35.9%); of the 15 other candidates, his closest rival was Bernard Kolelas of the MCDDI (22.9%). Sassou-Nguesso took 16.9% of the votes cast. Lissouba and Kolelas thus proceeded to a second round of voting, held two weeks later, at which Lissouba won 61.3% of the votes cast.

Lissouba took office as President at the end of August 1992. Maurice-Stéphane Bongho-Nouarra (a member of the UPADS) was appointed as Prime Minister at the head of a new Council of Ministers. Meanwhile, the Union pour le renouveau démocratique (URD), a new alliance of seven parties, including the MCDDI, formed a coalition with the PCT, thereby establishing a parliamentary majority. In October the URD-PCT coalition won a vote of 'no confidence' in the Government, on the grounds that the Prime Minister no longer commanded a parliamentary majority. In November Bongho-Nouarra announced the resignation of his Government, and shortly afterwards Lissouba dissolved the Assemblée nationale and announced that fresh legislative elections would be held in 1993. The URD-PCT coalition, which demanded the right to form the Government, commenced a protest campaign of civil disobedience. In December Claude Antoine Dacosta, a former FAO and World Bank official, was appointed Prime Minister and formed a transitional Government, comprising members of all the main political parties.

At the first round of legislative elections, which took place in early May 1993, the Mouvance présidentielle (MP), an electoral coalition of the UPADS and its allies, won 62 of the 125 seats in the Assemblée nationale, while the URD-PCT coalition secured 49. Protesting that serious electoral irregularities had occurred, the URD-PCT refused to contest the second round of elections in early June (for seats where a clear majority had not been achieved in the first round) and demanded that some of the first-round polls should be repeated. At the second round the MP secured an absolute majority (69) of seats in the Assemblée nationale. In late June President Lissouba appointed a new Council of Ministers, with ex-President Yhombi-Opango as Prime Minister. During June Bernard Kolelas, the leader of the MCDDI and of the URD-PCT coalition, urged his supporters to compel the Government to organize new elections by means of a campaign of civil disobedience. The ensuing political crisis soon led to violent conflict between armed militiamen, representing party political and ethnic interests, and the security forces. At the end of June the Supreme Court ruled that electoral irregularities had occurred at the first round of elections. In mid-July Lissouba declared a state of emergency, but by the end of the month the Government and the opposition had negotiated a truce, and in early August, following mediation by the Organization of African Unity (OAU—see p. 240), France and President Bongo of Gabon, the two sides agreed to refer the disputed first-round election results to impartial international arbitration and that the second round of elections should be rerun. The state of emergency was repealed in mid-August.

In the repeated second round of legislative elections, which took place in October 1993, the MP secured 65 seats and retained its overall majority in the Assemblée nationale. Yhombi-Opango remained as Prime Minister in an unchanged Council of Ministers. The URD-PCT coalition, which had taken 57 seats, agreed to participate in the new Assemblée. In November, however, confrontations erupted once again between armed militia affiliated to political parties and the security forces. During the second half of 1993 militia activity caused serious social and economic disruption and, reportedly, at least 2,000 deaths. Although a cease-fire was agreed at the end of January 1994, sporadic fighting continued.

In February 1994 the committee of international arbitrators, which had been investigating the conduct of the first round of legislative elections held in May 1993, ruled that the results in eight constituencies were unlawful. In September 1994 six opposition parties formed an alliance, the Forces démocratiques unies (FDU), headed by the leader of the PCT, Sassou-Nguesso, and affiliated with the URD. In early December the Government announced its intention to re-form as a coalition administration, including members of the opposition, in the near future. At the end of the month, following the holding of reconciliation talks between the Government and the opposition, a co-ordinating body was established to oversee the disarmament of the party militia and the restoration of judicial authority. Meanwhile, Lissouba and the two main opposition leaders—Sassou-Nguesso and Kolelas—signed an agreement seeking a permanent end to hostilities between their respective supporters. In January 1995 it was announced that 2,000 places would be set aside in the national army for former militiamen once their units had disbanded.

In mid-January 1995 the Government resigned, and a new coalition Council of Ministers was appointed later in the month, including members of the MCDDI and headed by Yhombi-Opango. The FDU, however, refused to participate in the new administration. Some 12 parliamentary deputies defected from the majority UPADS in protest at the lack of representation for south-western Congolese in the newly-appointed Council of Ministers; they subsequently established a new party, the Union pour la République, which affiliated itself with the MP.

During early 1995 by-elections were contested for seven seats in the Assemblée nationale (unfilled since the partially annulled elections of May 1993): five were won by opposition parties and two by the UPADS. In March 1995 the Government announced the introduction of measures to restrain state expenditure, including significant reductions in the number of civil service personnel, in order to secure continued assistance from the IMF. The Lissouba administration banned all public demonstrations in August, in order to restrict protests by trade unions. In the following month the Assemblée nationale approved legislation to restrict the freedom of the press.

In October 1995 the Government announced the impending restructuring of the armed forces, with the aim of achieving a more balanced representation of ethnic and regional interests. In late December political parties from the MP and opposition groupings signed a peace pact that required the disarmament of all party militia and the integration into the national security forces of 1,200 former militia members. In February 1996 about 100 soldiers who had previously belonged to militias staged a short-lived mutiny, in order to demand improved pay and conditions; five people were reportedly killed during the unrest. Later in that month the FDU suspended the integration of its militia associates into the national armed forces, claiming that the peace pact favoured pro-Government militias. In March the Government agreed to increase the quota of opposition recruits into the security forces and, consequently, the integration of FDU-affiliated militia members resumed. During 1994–96 some 4,000 militiamen were integrated into the defence and security forces. Nevertheless, activities by armed militia groups continued to be reported.

In late August 1996 Yhombi-Opango resigned as Prime Minister; he was replaced shortly afterwards by David Charles Ganao, the leader of the Union des forces démocratiques and a former Minister of Foreign Affairs. In early September Ganao appointed an expanded Council of Ministers, including representatives of the URD. The Ganao administration undertook to continue with the implementation of the economic reform programme agreed with the IMF. In early October elections were held for 23 of the 60 seats in the Senate. The MP retained its majority, winning 12 of the seats, while opposition organizations took 10 seats and one seat was secured by an independent candidate.

Factional divisions remained apparent in early 1997. Opposition politicians accused Lissouba of political and ethnic partiality when, on several occasions, he was perceived to grant preferential treatment to army members from his native southern Congo, while, during April and May, dismissing several high-ranking northern officers installed under the Sassou-Nguesso administration. In February 19 opposition parties demanded the expedited establishment of republican institutions, the free movement of people and goods, and more equitable access to the media and to public funds; in the short term they also requested, as matters of urgency, the creation of an independent electoral commission, the disarmament of civilians and the deployment of a multinational peace-keeping force, on the basis that the continued existence of armed militias was otherwise likely to lead to a resumption of large-scale factional violence. During May inter-militia unrest did erupt once again, and in early June an attempt by the Government forceably to disarm the militia group associated with Sassou-Nguesso's Forces démocratiques et patriotiques (as the FDU had been renamed), in preparation for legislative and presidential elections scheduled for July and August, precipitated a fierce national conflict along ethnic and political lines, involving the militias and also opposing factions within the regular armed forces. Barricades were erected in Brazzaville, and the capital was divided into three zones, controlled by supporters of Lissouba, Sassou-Nguesso and Kolelas. The conflict soon became polarized between troops loyal to the Lissouba administration and the rebel forces of Sassou-Nguesso; both sides were allegedly reinforced by mercenaries and by foreign troops. Despite efforts to mediate—led by Kolelas at a national level and, on behalf of the international community, President Bongo of Gabon and Muhammad Sahnoun, the joint UN-OAU special representative to the Great Lakes region—none of the numerous cease-fires signed during mid-1997 led to more than a brief lull in hostilities. An attempt by Lissouba to postpone the impending elections and prolong his presidential mandate beyond the end of August was strongly opposed by Sassou-Nguesso, and both sides were unable to agree on the nature or composition of a proposed government of national unity. In early June French troops assisted in the evacuation of foreign residents from Brazzaville; in mid-June they themselves departed, despite mediators' requests that they remain to protect the civilian population and to attempt to forestall further hostilities. Fighting intensified in August, spreading to the north. In early September Lissouba appointed a Government of National Unity, under the premiership of Kolelas, thereby compromising the latter's role as a national mediator and impeding negotiations. Sassou-Nguesso refused to accept the offer of five seats for his allies in the Council of Ministers. In September political organizations loyal to Lissouba formed the Espace républicain pour la défense de la démocratie et l'unité nationale.

In mid-October 1997 Sassou-Nguesso's forces, assisted by Angolan government troops, won control of Brazzaville and the strategic port of Pointe-Noire. Lissouba was ousted from the presidential palace, and, with Kolelas, found refuge in Burkina Faso. In late October Sassou-Nguesso was inaugurated as President, having retaken by force the office which he lost at the 1992 presidential election. He appointed a new transitional Government in early November.

It was reported that some 10,000 people were killed during the civil war and that about 800,000 people were displaced. Brazzaville was ransacked and largely destroyed, while the national infrastructure and institutions were severely disrupted.

A Forum for Unity and National Reconciliation was established in January 1998. Subsequently, a National Transitional Council was to hold legislative power, pending the creation of a new constitution, to be approved by a referendum scheduled for 2001, and the organization of legislative elections. Upon his accession to power, President Sassou-Nguesso decreed that party militias would be disarmed and outlawed as a matter of priority. This proved difficult to enforce. In January 1998 the Director-General of the judicial police was assassinated during arms seizures in Gambona, and in February members of Sassou-Nguesso's militia looted businesses in Brazzaville, in protest at their exclusion from the armed forces. In April militiamen loyal to former President Lissouba took control of the Moukoukoulou hydroelectric dam, only surrendering to the army in May. In the same month, Sassou-Nguesso rejected an appeal from the country's Roman Catholic bishops for the removal of political and civil rights from the leaders of private militias, declaring that this would further jeopardize the reconciliation process. Throughout 1998 clashes continued in the southern Pool region, a stronghold of the militia loyal to Kolelas, causing thousands of refugees to flee the area. Warrants were issued in November for the arrests of Lissouba, Kolelas and Yhombi-Opango, on charges of genocide and crimes against humanity, allegedly commited during 1997.

In November 1998 President Sassou-Nguesso appointed a constitutional committee to draft proposals for a new constitution, to be submitted to a national forum scheduled for January 1999 and then to a public referendum later in 1999. These plans were stalled by the spread of violence in December 1998 from the Pool region to the outskirts of Brazzaville. In late December a full-scale battle for control of Brazzaville broke out between pro-Kolelas forces, allegedly supported by Angolan rebel groups, and Congolese government forces, augmented by Sassou-Nguesso's militia and Angolan government troops. Both sides claimed victory; Kolelas, speaking from the USA, suggested that he might return to take power, while the Congolese authorities denied that there had been a concerted attack on the city, blaming looters and bandits for the eruption of violence. Brazzaville was severely damaged in the fighting, and more than 8,000 refugees were reported to have fled into the neighbouring Democratic Republic of the Congo (DRC). In late December government forces, aided by Angolan troops, launched offensives against Kolelas' forces in the south and west of the country.

On 12 January 1999 Sassou-Nguesso appointed a new Council of Ministers, with the responsibility of restoring security and peace in the south. Itihi Ossetoumba Lekoundzou, the former Minister of State for Reconstruction and Urban Development, was appointed Minister of Defence, a portfolio previously held by Sassou-Nguesso. In mid-January rebels again seized the Moukoukoulou hydroelectric dam, while in Brazzaville sporadic fighting continued as government forces sought to suppress insurgents in the southern districts. Fighting was also reported in the south-west of the country, where the militia loyal to former President Lissouba were involved in skirmishes with government forces around the strategically important city of Dolisie. In February the military commander of Dolisie was killed in a militia attack on the city's airport, and the struggle for control of the city continued throughout February and March.

In late February 1999 the conflict in the area immediately south of Brazzaville intensified, and a further 10,000 people were estimated to have taken refuge in the DRC. By early March, however, the rebel militias had been obliged to withdraw to the Pool region, where clashes continued, and residents began to return to the south of Brazzaville. Many returning refugees later alleged that their properties had been looted by the security forces and by militiamen loyal to Sassou-Nguesso. In early April refugees also began to return to Dolisie, although the city's water, electricity and health services had been destroyed in the fighting. In May the army secured the city of Kinkala, capital of the Pool region, and captured the main rebel base in the south-west, while an insurgent attack to the north of Brazzaville was also repulsed. In June and July government forces continued their advances in the south and west of the country; a number of pro-Lissouba rebels were reported to have surrendered to the armed forces. At the same time, in an attempt to secure the railway line between Brazzaville and Pointe-Noire, the armed forces regained control of several railway stations and strategic towns. In late July government forces dismantled a major road-block to the south of Brazzaville, and in August it was reported that residents of the southern districts of Brazzaville had begun to return to their homes in large numbers. In late August the armed forces announced that they had succeeded in regaining control of the railway line between Brazzaville and Pointe-Noire.

In mid-August 1999, during an address marking the 39th anniversary of the Congo's independence, Sassou-Nguesso offered to grant an amnesty to any militiamen prepared to renounce violence and to surrender their weapons. It was also announced that the Government had begun talks with the exiled opposition, although it was reported that the authorities had demanded an end to factional violence as a precondition for further discussions. In September it was reported that some 600 militiamen loyal to Kolelas had surrendered to the authorities under the terms of the amnesty proposed by Sassou-Nguesso. In the same month several prominent opposition members, including four former ministers, voluntarily returned to the Congo from exile, and in mid-October 12 senior officers, who had been imprisoned for supporting Lissouba, were released at a public ceremony; it was announced that they were to be reintegrated into the armed forces. In early October, however, the Government rejected an appeal for a cease-fire made by Congolese bishops, suggesting that the refusal of Lissouba and Kolelas to renounce violence excluded them from participation in any negotiations. In the same month the authorities announced that the armed forces had regained control of all the towns in the Pool region.

On 17 November 1999, following intensive negotiations with local militia leaders, the Government announced that it had reached agreement with the militias loyal to Lissouba and Kolelas. The agreement, which included provision for a cease-fire and for a general amnesty, was, however, rejected by Lissouba and Kolelas themselves, who described it as 'a complete fabrication'. Sassou-Nguesso claimed, however, that the militias had decided for themselves to respond to the Government's calls for peace. In mid-December the National Transitional Council adopted legislation providing for an amnesty for those militiamen who surrendered their weapons to the authorities before 15 January 2000. The amnesty excluded the opposition leaders in exile, in particular Lissouba and Kolelas, and the Government announced its intention to continue to seek their prosecution for alleged war crimes. In December 1999 President Bongo of Gabon was designated the official mediator between the Government and the militias, and at the end of the month he hosted further discussions in Libreville. These discussions led to the signing of a second peace agreement, in the presence of Presidents Bongo and Sassou-Nguesso, by representatives of the armed forces and of the rebel militias. The new agreement provided for further dialogue, for the integration of militiamen into the armed forces and for the opening of a humanitarian corridor to enable displaced persons to return to their homes. Militia leaders continued, however, to demand the withdrawal of Angolan troops from the Congo. None the less, in late December a ceremony of reconciliation was held in Brazzaville between senior government figures and members of the previous Lissouba administration.

Since the 1997 civil war, the principal aim of Congolese foreign policy has been to gain international recognition of the legitimacy of the Sassou-Nguesso Government, and to ensure the continued support of the country's bilateral and multilateral donors. Sassou-Nguesso's exiled political opponents have, however, appealed for international support for their efforts to overthrow the regime.

During the 1997 civil war President Lissouba accused France of favouring the rebel forces of Sassou-Nguesso (who was reported to have allied himself with French petroleum interests) over the elected administration. In April 1998 Lissouba and Kolelas unsuccessfully sought to prosecute a French petroleum company, Elf Aquitaine, claiming that it had provided support for Sassou-Nguesso. In May France extended its formal recognition to the Sassou-Nguesso Government, and in the following month resumed aid payments that had been suspended since the 1997 conflict. France granted further economic assistance in July, and in September French military advisers were sent to Brazzaville to train the Congolese gendarmerie.

In the 1997 conflict Angolan government troops facilitated Sassou-Nguesso's victory by providing tactical support, including the occupation of Pointe-Noire, the Congo's main seaport and focus of the petroleum industry. Angola had accused the Lissouba Government of providing assistance both to rebels of the União Nacional para a Independência Total de Angola and to Cabindan separatist guerrillas. In May 1998 Sassou-Nguesso visited Angola to express his gratitude for the Angolan Government's support. In response to international criticism of his role, President dos Santos of Angola announced that the majority of his forces had departed the Congo, and that the role of the remaining troops was merely to help rebuild and train the Congolese army. None the less, Angolan troops reportedly played an important role in the defeat of the rebel militia's attack on Brazzaville in December 1998.

Relations between the Republic of the Congo and the DRC steadily improved during 1998. In May a bilateral meeting was held to discuss the prevention of the clandestine movement of armed groups across the two countries' common border. In August Sassou-Nguesso reaffirmed that he would not allow any military force to use his territory to launch attacks on the DRC, and agreed to return fugitive rebels to the DRC. At a further meeting held in Kinshasa in September, it was decided to establish a joint commission to examine border security and the free flow of travellers and trade. Relations were, however, undermined later that month when the DRC alleged that the Congo had turned back a DRC naval vessel seeking to enlist the services of Rwandan Hutu refugees in the Congo, and in December relations were strained by Congolese claims that a training camp for anti-Government militiamen existed in the DRC. This accusation was strongly denied by the DRC, and later in the month the two countries signed a non-aggression pact (ratified in August 1999) and agreed to establish a joint force to guarantee border security. In December 1999 further discussions on border security were held in Kinshasa.

## Government

The 1992 Constitution, providing for an elected President, Assemblée nationale and Senate, was suspended following the assumption of power by Gen. Denis Sassou-Nguesso on 15 October 1997. A Forum for Unity and National Reconciliation was established in January 1998. Subsequently a National Transitional Council was appointed, with 75 designated members, to act as a legislative body pending the organization of national elections in 2001. In November 1998 a Constitutional Committee was appointed, with responsibility for formulating proposals for a new Constitution.

For administrative purposes the country is divided into nine regions and one commune (Brazzaville).

## Defence

In August 1999 the army numbered 8,000, the navy about 800 and the air force 1,200. There were 5,000 men in paramilitary forces (Gendamerie and People's Militia). National service is voluntary for men and women, and lasts for two years. The estimated defence budget for 1999 was 45,000m. francs CFA.

## Economic Affairs

In 1997, according to estimates by the World Bank, the Congo's gross national product (GNP), measured at average 1995–97 prices, was US $1,827m., equivalent to $670 per head. During 1990–97, it was estimated, GNP per head declined, in real terms, at an average rate of 2.9% annually. Over the same period, the population increased at an average annual rate of 2.8%. According to preliminary World Bank data, GNP in 1998 was about $1,900m. ($690 per head). The Congo's gross domestic product (GDP) increased, in real terms, at an average annual rate of of 1.0% in 1990–98. GDP increased by 2.2% in 1995. An estimated 6.8% increase in GDP in 1996 was attributed to a substantial rise in petroleum production. GDP declined by 1.9% in 1997, but grew by 4.0% in 1998.

Agriculture (including forestry and fishing) contributed an estimated 11.5% of GDP in 1998 and employed about 42.3% of the total labour force in that year. The staple crops are cassava and plantains, while the major cash crops are sugar cane, oil palm, cocoa and coffee. Forests cover about 57% of the country's total land area, and forestry is a major economic activity. Sales of timber provided an estimated 8.4% of export earnings in 1995, but in February 1998, to encourage local processing of wood, forestry companies were banned from exporting rough timber. During 1990–98 agricultural GDP increased at an average annual rate of 1.6%.

Industry (including mining, manufacturing, construction and power) contributed 49.9% of GDP in 1998, and employed an estimated 12.7% of the labour force in 1984. During 1990–98 industrial GDP increased at an average annual rate of 0.2%.

Mining contributed 28.6% of GDP in 1989. The hydrocarbons sector is the only significant mining activity. In 1995 sales of petroleum and petroleum products provided an estimated 84.6% of export earnings. The real GDP of the petroleum sector (extraction and refining) declined by 1.4% in 1994 and by an estimated 1.8% in 1995. However, annual petroleum production (11.6m. metric tons in 1997, according to the Banque des Etats de l'Afrique Centrale—BEAC) was expected to continue to grow, as a result of major exploration and development planned at various offshore deposits. Deposits of natural gas are also exploited. Lead, zinc, gold and copper are produced in small quantities, and the large-scale mining of magnesium was expected to commence by 2000. There are also exploitable reserves of diamonds, phosphate, iron ore, bauxite and potash.

Manufacturing contributed an estimated 7.5% of GDP in 1998. The most important industries are the processing of agricultural and forest products. The textile, chemical and construction materials industries are also important. During 1988–98 manufacturing GDP decreased at an average annual rate of 1.7%.

Energy is derived principally from hydroelectric power. Imports of fuel and energy comprised an estimated 26.1% of the value of total imports in 1995.

The services sector contributed an estimated 38.6% of GDP in 1998. During 1990–98, it was estimated, the GDP of the services sector increased at an average annual rate of 1.4%. The sector's GDP increased by 6.1% in 1997, and by 4.7% in 1998.

In 1998, according to the BEAC, the Congo recorded a visible trade surplus of 318,200m. francs CFA, but there was a deficit of 377,300m. francs CFA on the current account of the balance of payments. In 1995 the principal source of imports (32.0%) was France, while the USA was the principal market for exports (22.6%). Italy and the Netherlands are also important trading partners. The principal exports in 1996 were petroleum and petroleum products. The principal imports were machinery, chemical products, iron and steel and transport equipment.

The budget deficit for 1999 was estimated at 179,050m. francs CFA. The country's external debt totalled US $5,071m. at the end of 1997, of which $4,284m. was long-term public debt. In that year the cost of debt-servicing was equivalent to 6.2% of the value of exports of goods and services. The annual rate of inflation averaged 8.6% in 1990–98. The rate rose to 42.5% in 1994, following the 50% devaluation of the currency in January of that year, but declined to 9.4% in 1995. Consumer prices increased by an average of 10.0% in 1996 and by 19.2% in 1997, but fell by 4.1% in 1998.

The Republic of the Congo is a member of the Central African organs of the Franc Zone (see p. 200) and of the Communauté économique des Etats de l'Afrique centrale (CEEAC, see p. 290).

From 1985 the decline in international petroleum prices significantly reduced government revenue, leading to a decline in industrial investment and growth, and to unsustainable levels of external borrowing. In January 1994 the devaluation by 50% of the CFA franc resulted in an immediate sharp increase in the prices of consumer goods. In May the Government agreed a programme of economic measures with the IMF, which aimed to stimulate growth in non-petroleum GDP and to control inflation, and in July the Government obtained an agreement on debt rescheduling with the 'Paris Club' of official creditors. In June 1996 the IMF agreed to support an economic reform programme for 1996–99, which aimed to consolidate reforms introduced in 1994. This programme was, however, halted by the debilitating 1997 civil war, and in November 1997 the World Bank suspended relations with the Congo in protest at the non-payment of debt arrears. In June 1998 a meeting of the Congo's international creditors agreed to co-ordinate action to support reconstruction. The World Bank subsequently approved an emergency post-conflict loan and also agreed to negotiate a new three-year programme, dependent on successful privatizations, a reduction of external debt, and a return to democratic institutions. However, the outbreak in December 1998 of further hostilities led to the suspension of all donor activity, and in June 1999 the World Bank suspended the disbursement of the remaining funds accorded to the Congo under the June 1998 agreement. The Government's economic objectives for the 2000 budget were to ensure sustainable economic growth and to continue the rehabilitation of state infrastructure, the cost of which was estimated at some US $1,000m., while the strengthening of the non-petroleum sectors of the economy remained an essential long-term goal.

### Social Welfare

There is a state pension scheme and a system of family allowances and other welfare services. Both social welfare and health provision have, however, been seriously impeded by a lack of government funds and by the devastating effects of the 1997 civil war. The breakdown in water supplies and sanitation, caused by the civil war, was blamed for the 1998 cholera epidemic in Pointe-Noire. In 1987 there were 43 hospitals, providing a total of 7,917 hospital beds. In the early 1990s there were an estimated 27 physicians per 100,000 inhabitants, and 49 nurses per 100,000 inhabitants, working in the country. Since the late 1980s rising numbers of AIDS cases have placed considerable strain on resources. Average annual health expenditure per caput was estimated at US $77 during 1990–97.

### Education

Education is officially compulsory for 10 years between six and 16 years of age. Primary education begins at the age of six and lasts for six years. Secondary education, from 12 years of age, lasts for seven years, comprising a first cycle of four years and a second of three years. In 1996 there were 489,546 pupils enrolled at primary schools, while 190,409 pupils were receiving general secondary education. In addition, 23,606 students were attending vocational institutions. The Marien Ngouabi University, at Brazzaville, was founded in 1971. In 1999 there were some 16,000 students at university level, with 1,100 lecturers. The provision of education has been severely disrupted by the ongoing conflict in the Congo. In 1995, according to estimates by UNESCO, the average rate of adult illiteracy was 25.1% (males 16.9%, females 32.8%), one of the lowest in Africa. Expenditure on education by all levels of government was 52,274m. francs CFA in 1995, equivalent to 6.2% of GNP.

### Public Holidays

**2000:** 1 January (New Year's Day), 21 April (Good Friday), 24 April (Easter Monday), 1 May (Labour Day), 12 June (Whit Monday), 15 August (Independence Day), 25 December (Christmas).

**2001:** 1 January (New Year's Day), 13 April (Good Friday), 16 April (Easter Monday), 1 May (Labour Day), 4 June (Whit Monday), 15 August (Independence Day), 25 December (Christmas).

### Weights and Measures

The metric system is in force.

# Statistical Survey

Source (unless otherwise stated): Centre National de la Statistique et des Etudes Economiques, BP 2031, Brazzaville; tel. 81-59-09; fax 81-41-45.

## Area and Population

**AREA, POPULATION AND DENSITY**

| | |
|---|---|
| Area (sq km) | 342,000* |
| Population (census results) | |
| 7 February 1974 | 1,319,790 |
| 22 December 1984 | 1,843,421 |
| Population (UN estimates at mid-year)† | |
| 1996 | 2,634,000 |
| 1997 | 2,709,000 |
| 1998 | 2,785,000 |
| Density (per sq km) at mid-1998 | 8.1 |

* 132,047 sq miles.

† Source: UN, *World Population Prospects: The 1998 Revision*.

**REGIONS** (estimated population at 1 January 1983)*

| | | | |
|---|---|---|---|
| Brazzaville | 456,383 | Kouilou | 78,738 |
| Pool | 219,329 | Lékoumou | 67,568 |
| Pointe-Noire | 214,466 | Sangha | 42,106 |
| Bouenza | 135,999 | Nkayi | 40,419 |
| Cuvette | 127,558 | Likouala | 34,302 |
| Niari | 114,229 | Loubomo | 33,591 |
| Plateaux | 110,379 | **Total** | 1,675,067 |

* Figures have not been revised to take account of the 1984 census results.

**PRINCIPAL TOWNS** (estimated population in 1997)

| | |
|---|---|
| Brazzaville (capital) | 950,000 |
| Pointe-Noire | 500,000 |
| Loubomo | 83,000 |

Source: La Zone Franc, *Rapport Annuel*.

**BIRTHS AND DEATHS** (UN estimates, annual averages)

| | 1980–85 | 1985–90 | 1990–95 |
|---|---|---|---|
| Birth rate (per 1,000) | 43.9 | 44.3 | 44.7 |
| Death rate (per 1,000) | 15.7 | 15.6 | 16.1 |

**Expectation of life** (UN estimates, years at birth, 1990-95): 48.9 (males 46.6; females 51.3).

Source: UN, *World Population Prospects: The 1998 Revision*.

**EMPLOYMENT** ('000 persons at 1984 census)

| | Males | Females | Total |
|---|---|---|---|
| Agriculture, etc. | 105 | 186 | 291 |
| Industry | 61 | 8 | 69 |
| Services | 123 | 60 | 183 |
| **Total** | 289 | 254 | 543 |

**Mid-1998** (FAO estimates, '000 persons): Agriculture, etc. 483; Total labour force 1,141 (Source: FAO, *Production Yearbook*).

 

# Agriculture

**PRINCIPAL CROPS**
('000 metric tons)

| | 1996 | 1997 | 1998 |
|---|---|---|---|
| Maize† | 5 | 4 | 2 |
| Sugar cane* | 465 | 480 | 470 |
| Potatoes* | 2 | 2 | 2 |
| Sweet potatoes* | 25 | 23 | 24 |
| Cassava (Manioc) | 791† | 780 | 791 |
| Yams* | 13 | 12 | 13 |
| Other roots and tubers* | 36 | 34 | 34 |
| Dry beans* | 6 | 6 | 6 |
| Tomatoes* | 10 | 10 | 10 |
| Other vegetables (incl. melons)* | 37 | 35 | 34 |
| Oranges* | 4 | 3 | 3 |
| Avocados* | 26 | 25 | 24 |
| Pineapples* | 13 | 13 | 12 |
| Bananas* | 39 | 38 | 37 |
| Plantains | 76† | 76 | 76* |
| Palm kernels* | 3 | 3 | 3 |
| Palm oil* | 17 | 16 | 15 |
| Groundnuts (in shell) | 25* | 23 | 22* |
| Coffee (green) | 1* | 1 | 1* |
| Cocoa beans | 2* | 2 | 2* |
| Natural rubber* | 1 | 1 | 1 |

* FAO estimate(s). † Unofficial figure(s).

Source: FAO, *Production Yearbook*.

**LIVESTOCK** ('000 head, year ending September)

| | 1996* | 1997 | 1998 |
|---|---|---|---|
| Cattle | 72 | 75 | 72 |
| Pigs | 46 | 45 | 44* |
| Sheep | 114 | 115 | 114 |
| Goats | 295 | 286 | 280* |

* FAO estimate(s).

Poultry (FAO estimates, million): 2 in 1996; 2 in 1997; 2 in 1998.

Source: FAO, *Production Yearbook*.

**LIVESTOCK PRODUCTS** (FAO estimates, '000 metric tons)

| | 1996 | 1997 | 1998 |
|---|---|---|---|
| Beef and veal | 2 | 2 | 2 |
| Pig meat | 2 | 2 | 2 |
| Poultry meat | 6 | 6 | 6 |
| Other meat | 13 | 14 | 15 |
| Cows' milk | 1 | 1 | 1 |
| Hen eggs | 1 | 1 | 1 |

Source: FAO, *Production Yearbook*.

# Forestry

**ROUNDWOOD REMOVALS** ('000 cubic metres, excluding bark)

| | 1995 | 1996 | 1997 |
|---|---|---|---|
| Sawlogs, veneer logs and logs for sleepers | 636 | 704 | 969 |
| Pulpwood | 505 | 120 | 373 |
| Other industrial wood | 334 | 344 | 354 |
| Fuel wood | 2,358 | 2,426 | 2,496 |
| **Total** | 3,833 | 3,594 | 4,192 |

Source: FAO, *Yearbook of Forest Products*.

**SAWNWOOD PRODUCTION**
('000 cubic metres, including railway sleepers)

| | 1995 | 1996 | 1997 |
|---|---|---|---|
| **Total** (all broadleaved) | 62 | 59 | 60 |

Source: FAO, *Yearbook of Forest Products*.

# Fishing

('000 metric tons, live weight)

| | 1995 | 1996 | 1997 |
|---|---|---|---|
| Freshwater fishes | 26.8 | 25.9 | 19.0 |
| Boe drum | 0.6 | 0.7* | 0.6* |
| West African croakers* | 0.6 | 0.6 | 0.6 |
| Sardinellas | 11.9 | 12.1 | 11.8 |
| Other clupeoids* | 1.7 | 1.7 | 1.7 |
| Other marine fishes (incl. unspecified)* | 3.9 | 3.9 | 3.8 |
| Crustaceans | 0.3 | 0.6 | 0.6* |
| **Total catch** | 45.8 | 45.5 | 38.1 |

* FAO estimate(s).

Source: FAO, *Yearbook of Fishery Statistics*.

# Mining

('000 metric tons, unless otherwise indicated)

| | 1995 | 1996 | 1997 |
|---|---|---|---|
| Crude petroleum | 9,267 | 10,359 | 11,586 |
| Gold (kg)* | 5 | 5 | n.a. |

* Estimates from the US Bureau of Mines, referring to the metal content of ores.

Sources: UN, *Industrial Commodity Statistics Yearbook*; Banque des Etats de l'Afrique Centrale, *Etudes et Statistiques*.

# Industry

**SELECTED PRODUCTS** ('000 metric tons, unless otherwise indicated)

| | 1994 | 1995 | 1996 |
|---|---|---|---|
| Raw sugar* | 28 | 41 | 42 |
| Veneer sheets ('000 cu metres)* | 47 | 49 | 50 |
| Jet fuels† | 15 | 16 | 16 |
| Motor spirit (petrol)† | 55 | 55 | 56 |
| Kerosene† | 50 | 48 | 50 |
| Distillate fuel oils† | 92 | 90 | 92 |
| Residual fuel oils† | 268 | 258 | 260 |
| Cement | 114‡ | 100‡ | n.a. |
| Electric energy (million kWh)† | 431 | 435 | 438 |

**1997:** Raw sugar ('000 metric tons) 45*; Veneer sheets ('000 cu metres) 50*.
**1998:** Raw sugar ('000 metric tons) 44*.

* Data from the FAO.
† Provisional figures.
‡ Estimate from the US Bureau of Mines.

Source: mainly UN, *Industrial Commodity Statistics Yearbook*.

# Finance

**CURRENCY AND EXCHANGE RATES**

**Monetary Units**

100 centimes = 1 franc de la Coopération financière en Afrique centrale (CFA).

**Sterling, Dollar and Euro Equivalents** (30 September 1999)

£1 sterling = 1,012.69 francs CFA;
US $1 = 615.06 francs CFA;
€1 = 655.96 francs CFA;
10,000 francs CFA = £9.875 = $16.259 = €15.245.

**Average Exchange Rate** (francs CFA per US $)

1996 511.55
1997 583.67
1998 589.95

Note: The exchange rate of 1 French franc = 50 francs CFA, established in 1948, remained in force until January 1994, when the CFA franc was devalued by 50%, with the exchange rate adjusted to 1 French franc = 100 francs CFA.

**BUDGET** ('000 million francs CFA)

| Revenue* | 1993 | 1994 | 1995† |
|---|---|---|---|
| Petroleum revenue | 93.9 | 138.9 | 131.0 |
| Royalties | 44.1 | 74.4 | 78.5 |
| Profits tax | 0.8 | 0.2 | 13.1 |
| Dividends | 49.0 | 64.3 | 39.4 |
| Tax revenue | 83.8 | 77.8 | 116.9 |
| Taxes on income and profits | 31.8 | 34.1 | 31.4 |
| Excise duty | 36.6 | 30.6 | 47.8 |
| Domestic petroleum tax | 0.1 | 10.3 | 13.0 |
| Other indirect taxes | 15.3 | 2.8 | 24.7 |
| Other revenue | 5.4 | 3.4 | 1.5 |
| **Total** | 183.1 | 220.1 | 249.4 |

| Expenditure | 1993 | 1994 | 1995† |
|---|---|---|---|
| Current expenditure | 266.4 | 333.3 | 315.0 |
| Wages and salaries | 136.2 | 130.8 | 111.1 |
| Local authority subsidies | 7.3 | 11.1 | 4.4 |
| Interest payments | 56.1 | 119.0 | 148.9 |
| Other current expenditure | 66.8 | 72.3 | 50.6 |
| Capital expenditure | 12.7 | 27.3 | 31.6 |
| **Sub-total** | 279.1 | 360.6 | 346.6 |
| *Less* Adjustment for payment arrears | 37.9 | 95.1 | 71.9 |
| **Total** (cash basis) | 241.2 | 265.5 | 274.7 |

* Excluding grants received ('000 million francs CFA): 0.1 in 1993; 10.4 in 1994; 10.7 in 1995.

† Provisional figures.

Source: IMF, *Republic of Congo—Statistical Annex* (August 1996).

**CENTRAL BANK RESERVES** (US $ million at 31 December)

| | 1996 | 1997 | 1998 |
|---|---|---|---|
| Gold* | 4.10 | 3.24 | 3.20 |
| IMF special drawing rights | 0.02 | 0.01 | 0.01 |
| Reserve position in IMF | 0.77 | 0.72 | 0.75 |
| Foreign exchange | 90.20 | 59.19 | 0.08 |
| **Total** | 95.09 | 63.16 | 4.04 |

* National valuation.

Source: IMF, *International Financial Statistics.*

**MONEY SUPPLY** ('000 million francs CFA at 31 December)

| | 1996 | 1997 | 1998 |
|---|---|---|---|
| Currency outside banks | 87.35 | 93.26 | 73.26 |
| Demand deposits at commercial and development banks | 61.08 | 68.85 | 68.39 |
| **Total money** (incl. others) | 153.18 | 166.56 | 143.98 |

Source: IMF, *International Financial Statistics.*

**COST OF LIVING**

(Consumer Price Index for Africans in Brazzaville; base: 1990 = 100)

| | 1994 | 1995 | 1996 |
|---|---|---|---|
| Food (incl. beverages) | 139.2 | 148.6 | 159.4 |
| **All items** (incl. others) | 141.1 | 153.8 | 169.5 |

Source: ILO, *Yearbook of Labour Statistics.*

**All items** (base: 1977 = 100): 353.5 in 1996; 421.2 in 1997; 403.7 in 1998 (Source: Banque des Etats de l'Afrique Centrale, *Etudes et Statistiques*).

**NATIONAL ACCOUNTS** (million francs CFA at current prices)

**National Income and Product**

| | 1986 | 1987 | 1988 |
|---|---|---|---|
| Compensation of employees | 264,296 | 253,198 | 245,033 |
| Operating surplus | 133,347 | 183,843 | 188,612 |
| **Domestic factor incomes** | 397,643 | 437,041 | 433,645 |
| Consumption of fixed capital | 156,074 | 164,360 | 144,647 |
| **Gross domestic product (GDP) at factor cost** | 553,717 | 601,401 | 578,292 |
| Indirect taxes | 91,444 | 90,790 | 82,358 |
| *Less* Subsidies | 4,754 | 1,668 | 1,686 |
| **GDP in purchasers' values** | 640,407 | 690,523 | 658,964 |
| Factor income from abroad | 2,781 | 9,333 | 3,112 |
| *Less* Factor income paid abroad | 44,717 | 86,030 | 93,328 |
| **Gross national product** | 598,471 | 613,826 | 568,748 |
| *Less* Consumption of fixed capital | 156,074 | 164,360 | 144,647 |
| **National income in market prices** | 442,397 | 449,466 | 424,101 |
| Other current transfers from abroad | 17,470 | 25,403 | 24,100 |
| *Less* Other current transfers paid abroad | 25,512 | 36,255 | 36,264 |
| **National disposable income** | 434,355 | 438,614 | 411,937 |

Source: UN, *National Accounts Statistics.*

**Expenditure on the Gross Domestic Product**

| | 1996 | 1997 | 1998 |
|---|---|---|---|
| Government final consumption expenditure | 189,100 | 337,400 | 199,100 |
| Private final consumption expenditure | 582,000 | 552,900 | 572,300 |
| Increase in stocks | 25,600 | 4,100 | — |
| Gross fixed capital formation | 337,000 | 299,000 | 322,900 |
| Statistical discrepancy | -59,100 | -500 | — |
| **Total domestic expenditure** | 1,074,600 | 1,192,900 | 1,094,300 |
| Exports of goods and services | 829,400 | 976,000 | 835,300 |
| *Less* Imports of goods and services | 669,300 | 834,300 | 685,900 |
| **GDP in purchasers' values** | 1,234,700 | 1,334,600 | 1,243,700 |

Source: IMF, *International Financial Statistics.*

**Gross Domestic Product by Economic Activity**

| | 1993 | 1994 | 1995* |
|---|---|---|---|
| Agriculture, hunting, forestry and fishing | 85,500 | 101,300 | 107,800 |
| Mining and quarrying† } Manufacturing† } | 245,400 | 397,900 | 410,900 |
| Electricity, gas and water | 14,900 | 14,200 | 14,800 |
| Construction | 8,000 | 16,800 | 16,100 |
| Trade, restaurants and hotels | 104,300 | 113,000 | 119,000 |
| Transport, storage and communication | 71,300 | 76,900 | 87,300 |
| Government services | 133,800 | 135,000 | 130,300 |
| Other services | 68,200 | 80,300 | 78,700 |
| **Sub-total** | 731,400 | 935,400 | 964,900 |
| Import duties | 28,700 | 29,000 | 39,100 |
| **GDP in purchasers' values** | 760,100 | 964,400 | 1,003,900 |

* Provisional figures.

† Including petroleum sector (million francs CFA): 184,700 in 1993; 322,400 in 1994; 329,400 (provisional figure) in 1995.

Source: IMF, *Republic of Congo—Statistical Annex* (August 1996).

# Diplomatic Representation

### EMBASSIES IN COSTA RICA

**Argentina:** Calle 27, Avda Central, Apdo 1.963, San José; tel. 221-3438; Chargé d'affaires a.i.: BERNARDO JUAN OCHOA.

**Belgium:** Los Yoses, 4a entrada, 25 metros sur, Apdo 3.725, 1000 San José; tel. 225-6255; fax 225-0351; Ambassador: WILLY J. STEVENS.

**Brazil:** Paseo Colón frente a Nissan Lachner y Sáenz, San José; tel. 233-1544; fax 223-4325; Ambassador: LUIZ JORGE RANGEL DE CASTRO.

**Bulgaria:** Edif. Delcoré, 3°, 100 metros sur Hotel Balmoral, Apdo 4.752, San José; Ambassador: KIRIL ZLATKOV NIKOLOV.

**Canada:** Oficentro Ejecutivo La Sabana, Edif. 5, 3°, detrás de la Contracoría, Centro Colón, Apdo 351, 1007 San José; tel. 296-4149; fax 296-4270; Ambassador: DAN GOODLEAF.

**Chile:** De la Pulpería La Luz 125 metros norte, Casa 116, Apdo 10.102, San José; tel. 224-4243; Ambassador: PEDRO PALACIOS CAMERÓN.

**China (Taiwan):** 500 metros al sur del ICE en San Pedro, Apdo 907, San José; tel. 224-8180; fax 253-8333; Ambassador: KAO-WEN MAO.

**Colombia:** Apdo 3.154, 1000 San José; tel. 221-0725; fax 255-1705; Ambassador: MARÍA CRISTINA ZULETA DE PATÍN.

**Czech Republic:** 75 metros oeste de la entrada principal del Colegio Humboldt, Apdo 12041, 1000 San José; tel. 296-5671; fax 296-5595; Ambassador: Ing. VÍT KORSELT.

**Dominican Republic:** Lomas de Ayarco, Curridabat, de la Embajada de Rusia 100 metros oeste, 300 metros sur, 300 metros oeste y 150 metros norte, Apdo 4.746, San José; tel. and fax 272-2398; Ambassador: ALFONSO ARIA JIMÉNEZ.

**Ecuador:** Edif. de la esquina sureste del Museo Nacional, 125 metros al este, Avda 2, Calles 19 y 21, Apdo 1.374, 1000 San José; tel. 223-6281; Ambassador: Lic. ANDRÉS CÓRDOVA GALARZA.

**El Salvador:** Edif. Trianón, 3°, Avda Central y Calle 5, Apdo 1.378, San José; tel. 222-5536; Ambassador: CARLOS MATAMOROS GUIROLA.

**France:** Carretera a Curridabat, del Indoor Club 200 metros sur y 25 metros oeste, Apdo 10.177, San José; tel. 234-4187; fax 234-4197; e-mail sjfrance@sol.racsa.co.cr; Ambassador: NICOLE TRAMOND.

**Germany:** Barrio Rohrmoser, de la Embajada de España 200 metros norte, 50 metros oeste, Apdo 4.017, San José; tel. 232-5533; fax 231-6403; Ambassador Dr WILFRIED RUPPRECHT.

**Guatemala:** De Pops Curridabat 500 metros sur y 30 metros este, 2ª Casa Izquierda, Apdo 328, 1000 San José; tel. 283-2290; fax 231-6645; Ambassador: GUILLERMO ARGUETA VILLAGRÁN.

**Holy See:** Urbanización Rohrmoser, Sabana Oeste, Centro Colón, Apdo 992, 1007 San José (Apostolic Nunciature); tel. 232-2128; fax 231-2557; e-mail nuapcr@sol.racsa.co.cr; Apostolic Nuncio: Most Rev. ANTONIO SOZZO, Titular Archbishop of Concordia.

**Honduras:** Los Yoses sur, del ITAN hacia la Presidencia la primera entrada a la izquierda, 200 metros norte y 100 metros este, Apdo 2.239, San José; tel. 234-9502; fax 253-2209; Ambassador: EDGARDO SEVILLA IDIÁQUEZ.

**Hungary:** Los Yoses, 5a entrada, 50 metros sur, No 1099, Apdo 765, 2010 San José; tel. 225-0908; fax 225-9741; Ambassador: Dr ZSOLT HORVÁTH.

**Israel:** Edif. Centro Colón, 11°, Calle 2, Avdas 2 y 4, Apdo 5.147, San José; tel. 221-6444; fax 257-0867; Ambassador: YAACOV BRAKHA.

**Italy:** Los Yoses, 5a entrada, Apdo 1.729, San José; tel. 224-6574; fax 225-8200; Ambassador: FRANCO MICIELI DE BIASE.

**Japan:** De la primera entrada del Barrio Rohrmoser (Sabana Oeste) 500 metros oeste y 100 metros norte, Apdos 501 y 10.145, San José; tel. 232-1255; fax 231-3140; Ambassador: AKIMOTO KENSHIRO.

**Korea, Republic:** Calle 28, Avda 2, Barrio San Bosco, Apdo 3.150, San José; tel. 221-2398; Ambassador: JAE HOON KIM.

**Mexico:** Avda 7, No 1371, Apdo 10.107, San José; tel. 257-0633; fax 222-6080; Ambassador: ENRIQUE BERRUGA FILLOY.

**Netherlands:** Los Yoses, Avda 8, Calles 35 y 37, Apdo 10.285, 1000 San José; tel. 296-1490; fax 296-2933; Ambassador: F. B. A. M. VAN HAREN.

**Nicaragua:** Edif. Trianón, Calles 25 y 27, Avda Central, San José; tel. 222-4749; Ambassador: CLAUDIA CHAMORRO BARRIOS.

**Panama:** 200 metros sur, 25 metros este de Higuerón, La Granja, San Pedro, Montes de Oca, San José; tel. 225-3401; Ambassador: WALTER MYERS.

**Peru:** Barrio Pops de Curridabat, del Indoor Club 100 metros sur y 75 metros oeste, Apdo 4.248, 1000 San José; tel. 225-9145; fax 253-0457; Ambassador: ALBERTO VARILLAS MONTENEGRO.

**Romania:** Urbanización Rohrmoser, al costado norte de la Nunciatura Apostólica, Sabana Oeste, Centro Colón, Apdo 10.321, San José; tel. 231-0741; fax 232-6461; Ambassador: NICOLAE TURTUREA.

**Russia:** Apdo 6.340, San José; tel. 272-1021; Ambassador: VLADIMIR N. KAZIMIROV.

**Slovakia:** 200 metros sur de McDonald's en Plaza del Sol, Residencial El Prado, Curridabat, Apdo 3.910, San José; tel. 224-6467; fax 224-9184; Chargé d'affaires a.i.: VLADIMIR GRÁCZ.

**Spain:** Calle 32, Paseo Colón, Avda 2, Apdo 10.150, San José; tel. 221-1933; Ambassador: J. A. ORTIZ RAMOS.

**Switzerland:** Paseo Colón, Centro Colón, Apdo 895, San José; tel. 221-4829; Ambassador: Dr JOHANN BUCHER.

**United Kingdom:** Edif. Centro Colón, 11°, Apdo 815, 1007 San José; tel. 258-2025; fax 233-9938; e-mail britemb@sol.racsa.co.cr; Ambassador: PETER SPICELEY.

**USA:** Pavas San José; tel. 220-3939; fax 220-2305; Ambassador: PETER JON DE VOS.

**Uruguay:** Calle 2, Avda 1, San José; tel. 223-2512; Ambassador: JORGE JUSTO BOERO-BRIAN.

**Venezuela:** Avda Central, Los Yoses, 5a entrada, Apdo 10.230, San José; tel. 225-5813; Ambassador: Dr FRANCISCO SALAZAR MARTÍNEZ.

# Judicial System

Ultimate judicial power is vested in the Supreme Court, the 22 justices of which are elected by the Assembly for a term of eight years, and are automatically re-elected for an equal period, unless the Assembly decides to the contrary by a two-thirds vote. Judges of the lower courts are appointed by the Supreme Court's five-member Supreme Council.

The Supreme Court may also meet as the Corte Plena, with power to declare laws and decrees unconstitutional. There are, in addition, four appellate courts, criminal courts, civil courts and special courts. The jury system is not used.

**La Corte Suprema:** San José; tel. 295-3000; fax 257-0801.

**President of the Supreme Court:** EDGAR CERVANTES VILLALTA.

# Religion

Under the Constitution, all forms of worship are tolerated. Roman Catholicism is the official religion of the country. Various Protestant Churches are represented. There are an estimated 7,000 members of the Methodist Church.

### CHRISTIANITY

#### The Roman Catholic Church

Costa Rica comprises one archdiocese and six dioceses. At 31 December 1998 Roman Catholics represented some 88% of the total population.

**Bishops' Conference:** Conferencia Episcopal de Costa Rica, Arzobispado, Apdo 497, 1000 San José; tel. 221-3053; fax 221-6662; f. 1977; Pres. Most Rev. ROMÁN ARRIETA VILLALOBOS, Archbishop of San José de Costa Rica.

**Archbishop of San José de Costa Rica:** Most Rev. ROMÁN ARRIETA VILLALOBOS, Arzobispado, Apdo 497, 1000 San José; tel. 258-1015; fax 221-2427; e-mail curiam@sol.racsa.co.cr.

#### The Anglican Communion

Costa Rica comprises one of the five dioceses of the Iglesia Anglicana de la Región Central de América.

**Bishop of Costa Rica:** Rt Rev. CORNELIUS JOSHUA WILSON, Apdo 2.773, 1000 San José; tel. 225-0209; fax 253-8331; e-mail amiecr@sol.racsa.co.cr.

#### Other Churches

**Federación de Asociaciones Bautistas de Costa Rica:** Apdo 1.631, 2100 Guadalupe; tel. 253-5820; fax 253-4723; f. 1946; represents Baptist churches; Pres. CARLOS MANUEL UMAÑA ROJAS.

**Iglesia Evangélica Metodista de Costa Rica** (Evangelical Methodist Church of Costa Rica): Apdo 5.481, 1000 San José; tel. 236-2171; fax 236-5921; autonomous since 1973; 6,000 mems; Pres. Bishop LUIS F. PALOMO.

### BAHÁ'Í FAITH

**Bahá'í Information Centre:** Apdo 553, 1150 San José; tel. 231-0647; fax 296-1033; adherents resident in 242 localities.

**National Spiritual Assembly of the Bahá'ís of Costa Rica:** Apdo 553, 1150 La Uruca; tel. 231-0647; fax 296-1033; e-mail bahaiscr@sol.racsa.co.cr.

# The Press

### DAILIES

**Al Día:** Llorente de Tibás, Apdo 7.0270, San José; tel. 247-4647; fax 247-4665; e-mail aldia@nacion.co.cr; f. 1992; morning; independent; Dir ARMANDO M. GONZÁLEZ RODICIO; circ. 60,000.

**Boletín Judicial:** La Uruca, Apdo 5.024, San José; tel. 231-5222; f. 1878; journal of the judiciary; Dir ISAÍAS CASTRO VARGAS; circ. 2,500.

**Diario Extra:** Edif. Borrasé, 2°, Calle 4, Avda 4, Apdo 177, 1009 San José; tel. 223-9505; fax 223-5921; f. 1978; morning; independent; Dir WILLIAM GÓMEZ VARGAS; circ. 120,000.

**La Gaceta:** La Uruca, Apdo 5.024, San José; tel. 231-5222; f. 1878; official gazette; Dir ISAÍAS CASTRO VARGAS; circ. 5,300.

**El Heraldo:** 400 metros al este de las oficinas centrales, Apdo 1500, San José; tel. 222-6665; fax 222-3039; e-mail info@elheraldo.net; internet www.elheraldo.net; f. 1994; morning; independent; Dir ERWIN KNOHR R.; circ. 30,000.

**La Nación:** Llorente de Tibás, Apdo 10.138, San José; tel. 247-4747; fax 240-6485; e-mail webmaster@nacion.co.cr; internet www.nacion.co.cr; f. 1946; morning; independent; Dir EDUARDO ULIBARRI BILBAO; circ. 107,000.

**La Prensa Libre:** Calle 4, Avda 4, Apdo 10.121, San José; tel. 223-6666; fax 233-6831; e-mail plibre@prensalibre.co.cr; internet www.prensalibre.co.cr; f. 1889; evening; independent; Dir ANDRÉS BORRASÉ SANOU; circ. 56,000.

**La República:** Barrio Tournón, Guadalupe, Apdo 2.130, San José; tel. 223-0266; fax 255-3950; e-mail larazon@sol.racsa.co.cr; internet www.larepublica.cr; f. 1950, reorganized 1967; morning; independent; Dir JULIO SUÑOL; circ. 60,000.

### PERIODICALS

**Abanico:** Calle 4, esq. Avda 4, Apdo 10.121, San José; tel. 223-6666; fax 223-4671; weekly supplement of *La Prensa Libre*; women's interests; Editor MARÍA DEL CARMEN POZO C.; circ. 50,000.

**Acta Médica:** Sabana Sur, Apdo 548, San José; tel. 232-3433; f. 1954; organ of the Colegio de Médicos; 3 issues per year; Editor Dr BAUDILIO MORA MORA; circ. 2,000.

**Contrapunto:** La Uruca, Apdo 7-1.980, San José; tel. 231-3333; f. 1978; fortnightly; publication of Sistema Nacional de Radio y Televisión; Dir FABIO MUÑOZ CAMPOS; circ. 10,000.

**Eco Católico:** Calle 22, Avdas 3 y 5, Apdo 1.064, San José; tel. 222-6156; fax 256-0407; f. 1931; Catholic weekly; Dir ARMANDO ALFARO; circ. 20,000.

**Mujer y Hogar:** San José; tel. 236-3128; f. 1943; weekly; women's journal; Editor and Gen. Man. CARMEN CORNEJO MÉNDEZ; circ. 15,000.

**Noticiero del Café:** Calle 1, Avdas 18 y 20, Apdo 37, San José; tel. 222-6411; f. 1964; bi-monthly; coffee journal; owned by the Instituto del Café de Costa Rica; Dir MELVYN ALVARADO SOTO; circ. 5,000.

**Perfil:** Llorente de Tibás, Apdo 10.138, San José, 1000; tel. 247-4355; fax 247-4477; fortnightly; women's interest; Dir GRETTEL ALFARO CAMACHO; circ. 20,000.

**Polémica:** Icadis, Paseo de los Estudiantes, Apdo 1.006, San José; tel. 233-3964; f. 1981; every 4 months; left-wing; Dir GABRIEL AGUILERA PERALTA.

**Primera Plana:** Sabana Este, San José; tel. 255-1590.

**Rumbo:** Llorente de Tibás, Apdo 10.138, 1000 San José; tel. 240-4848; fax 240-6480; f. 1984; weekly; general; Dir ROXANA ZÚÑIGA; circ. 15,000.

**San José News:** Apdo 7-2.730, San José; 2 a week; Dir CHRISTIAN RODRÍGUEZ.

**Semanario Libertad:** Calle 4, Avdas 8 y 10, Apdo 6.613, 1000 San José; tel. 225-5857; f. 1962; weekly; organ of the Partido del Pueblo Costarricense; Dir RODOLFO ULLOA B.; Editor JOSÉ A. ZÚÑIGA; circ. 10,000.

**Semanario Universidad:** Ciudad Universitaria Rodrigo Facio, San Pedro, Montes de Oca, Apdo 21, San José; tel. 207-5355; fax 207-4774; internet cariari.ucr.ac.cr/-semana/univ.html; f. 1970; weekly; general; Dir EDUARDO AMADOR HERNÁNDEZ; circ. 15,000.

**The Tico Times:** Calle 15, Avda 8, Apdo 4.632, San José; tel. 258-1558; fax 223-6378; e-mail ttimes@sol.racsa.co.cr; internet www.ticotimes.co.cr; weekly; in English; Dir DERY DYER; circ. 15,210.

### PRESS ASSOCIATIONS

**Colegio de Periodistas de Costa Rica:** Sabana Este, Calle 42, Avda 4, Apdo 5.416, San José; tel. 233-5850; fax 223-8669; f. 1969; 550 mems; Exec. Dir Licda ADRIANA NÚÑEZ.

**Sindicato Nacional de Periodistas:** Sabana Este, Calle 42, Avda 4, Apdo 5.416, San José; tel. 222-7589; f. 1970; 200 mems; Sec.-Gen. ADRIÁN ROJAS JAÉN.

### FOREIGN NEWS BUREAUX

**ACAN-EFE** (Central America): Costado Sur, Casa Matute Gómez, Casa 1912, Apdo 84.930, San José; tel. 222-6785; Correspondent WILFREDO CHACÓN SERRANO.

**Agence France-Presse** (France): Calle 13, Avdas 9 y 11 bis, Apdo 5.276, San José; tel. 233-0757; Correspondent DOMINIQUE PETTIT.

**Agencia EFE** (Spain): Avda 10, Calles 19 y 21, No 1912, Apdo 84.930, San José; tel. 222-6785.

**Agenzia Nazionale Stampa Associata (ANSA)** (Italy): c/o Diario La República, Barrio Tournón, Guadalupe, Apdo 545-1200, San José; tel. 231-1140; fax 231-1140; Correspondent LUIS CARTÍN S.

**Associated Press (AP)** (USA): San José; tel. 221-6146; Correspondent REID MILLER.

**Deutsche Presse-Agentur (dpa)** (Germany): Edif. 152, 3°, Calle 11, Avdas 1 y 3, Apdo 7.156, San José; tel. 233-0604; fax 233-0604; Correspondent ERNESTO RAMÍREZ.

**Informatsionnoye Telegrafnoye Agentstvo Rossii—Telegrafnoye Agentstvo Suverennykh Stran (ITAR—TASS)** (Russia): De la Casa Italia 1000 metros este, 50 metros norte, Casa 675, Apdo 1.011, San José; tel. 224-1560; Correspondent ENRIQUE MORA.

**Inter Press Service (IPS)** (Italy): Latin American Regional Center, Calle 11, Avdas 1 y 3, No 152, Paseo de los Estudiantes, Apdo 70, 1002 San José; tel. 255-3861; fax 233-8583; Regional Dir GONZALO ORTIZ-CRESPO.

**Prensa Latina** (Cuba): Avda 11, No 3185, Calles 31 y 33, Barrio Escalante (de la parrillada 25 metros al oeste), San José; tel. 253-1457; Correspondent FRANCISCO A. URIZARRI TAMAYO.

**Rossiyskoye Informatsionnoye Agentstvo—Novosti (RIA—Novosti)** (Russia): De la Casa Italiana 100 metros este, 50 metros norte, San José; tel. 224-1560.

**United Press International (UPI)** (USA): Calle 15, Avda 2, Radioperiódicos Reloj, Apdo 4.334, San José; tel. 222-2644; Correspondent WILLIAM CESPEDES CHAVARRÍA.

**Xinhua (New China) News Agency** (People's Republic of China): Apdo 4.774, San José; tel. 231-3497; Correspondent XU BIHUA.

## Publishers

**Alfalit Internacional:** Apdo 292, 4050 Alajuela; f. 1961; educational; Dirs GILBERTO BERNAL, OSMUNDO PONCE.

**Antonio Lehmann Librería, Imprenta y Litografía, Ltda:** Calles 1 y 3, Avda Central, Apdo 10.011, San José; tel. 223-1212; f. 1896; general fiction, educational, textbooks; Man. Dir ANTONIO LEHMANN STRUVE.

**Editorial Caribe:** Apdo 1.307, San José; tel. 222-7244; f. 1949; religious textbooks; Dir JOHN STROWEL.

**Editorial Costa Rica:** 100 metros sur y 50 metros este del Supermercado Periféricos en San Francisco de Dos Ríos, Apdo 10.010, San José; tel. 286-1817; f. 1959; government-owned; cultural; Gen. Man. SHEILA DI PALMA GAMBOA.

**Editorial Fernández Arce:** Apdo 6.523, 1000 San José; tel. 224-5201; fax 234-1300; f. 1967; textbooks for primary, secondary and university education; Dir Dr MARIO FERNÁNDEZ LOBO.

**Editorial de la Universidad Autónoma de Centroamérica (UACA):** Apdo 7.637, 1000 San José; tel. 234-0701; fax 224-0391; e-mail lauaca@sol.racsa.co.cr; f. 1981; Editor ALBERTO DI MARE.

**Editorial de la Universidad Estatal a Distancia (EUNED):** Paseo de los Estudiantes, Apdo 597, 1002 San José; tel. 223-5430; fax 257-5042; f. 1979; Dir AUXILIADORA PROTTI QUESADA.

**Editorial Universitaria Centroamericana (EDUCA):** Ciudad Universitaria Rodrigo Facio, San Pedro, Montes de Oca, Apdo 64, 2060 San José; tel. 224-3727; fax 253-9141; e-mail educacr@sol.racsa.co.cr; f. 1969; organ of the CSUCA; science, literature, philosophy; Dir ANITA DE FORMOSO.

**Mesén Editores:** Urbanización El Cedral, 52, Cedros de Montes de Oca, Apdo 6.306, 1000 San José; tel. 253-5203; fax 283-0681; f. 1978; general; Dir DENNIS MESÉN SEGURA.

**Trejos Hermanos Sucs, SA:** Curridabat, Apdo 10.096, San José; tel. 224-2411; f. 1912; general and reference; Man. ALVARO TREJOS.

### PUBLISHING ASSOCIATION

**Cámara Costarricense del Libro:** San José; Pres. LUIS FERNANDO CALVO FALLAS.

## Broadcasting and Communications

### TELECOMMUNICATIONS

**Cámara Costarricense de Telecomunicaciones:** Edif. Centro Colón, Apdo 591-1007, 1000 San José; tel. and fax 255-3422; Pres. EVITA ARGUEDAS MAKLOUF.

**Cámara Nacional de Medios de Comunicación Colectiva (CANAMECC):** Apdo 6.574, 1000 San José; tel. 222-4820; f. 1954; Pres. ANDRÉS QUINTANA CAVALLINI.

**Instituto Costarricense de Electricidad (ICE):** govt agency for power and telecommunications (see Trade and Industry: Utilities, below).

**Radiográfica Costarricense, SA (RACSA):** Avda 5, Calle 1, Frente al Edif. Numar, Apdo 54, 1000 San José; tel. 287-0087; fax 287-0379; e-mail mcruz@sol.sacsa.co.cr; f. 1921; state telecommunications co.; Dir-Gen. MARCO A. CRUZ MIRANDA.

### RADIO

**Asociación Costarricense de Información y Cultura (ACIC):** Apdo 365, 1009 San José; f. 1983; independent body; controls private radio stations; Pres. JUAN FCO. MONTEALEGRE MARTÍN.

**Cámara Nacional de Radio (CANARA):** Paseo de los Estudiantes, Apdo 1.583, 1002 San José; tel. 233-1845; fax 255-4483; e-mail canara@sol.racsa.co.cr; internet www.elparaiso.com/canara; f. 1947; Exec. Dir LUZMILDA VARGAS GONZÁLEZ.

**Control Nacional de Radio (CNR):** Dirección Nacional de Comunicaciones, Ministerio de Gobernación y Policia, Apdo 10.006, 1000 San José; tel. 221-0992; fax 283-0741; f. 1954; governmental supervisory department; Dir MELVIN MURILLO ALVAREZ.

#### Non-commercial

**Faro del Caribe:** Apdo 2.710, 1000 San José; tel. 226-2573; fax 227-1725; f. 1948; religious and cultural programmes in Spanish and English; Man. CARLOS ROZOTTO PIEDRASANTA.

**Radio Costa Rica:** De Autos Bohío, en barrio Córdoba, 100 metros sur y 100 metros este, Apdo 6.462, 1000 San José; tel. 227-4690; fax 231-3408; e-mail canalcr@sol.racsa.co.cr; f. 1988; broadcasts Voice of America news bulletins (in Spanish) and locally-produced educational and entertainment programmes; Gen. Man. ANTONIO ALEXANDRE GARCÍA.

**Radio Fides:** Avda 4, Curia Metropolitana, Apdo 5.079, 1000 San José; tel. 233-4546; fax 233-2387; f. 1952; Roman Catholic station; Dir Rev. ROMÁN ARRIETA VILLALOBOS.

**Radio Nacional:** 1km oeste del Parque Nacional de Diversiones, La Uruca, Apdo 7-1980, San José; tel. 231-7983; fax 220-0070; e-mail sinart@sol.racsa.co.cr; f. 1978; Dir RODOLFO RODRÍGUEZ.

**Radio Santa Clara:** Santa Clara, San Carlos, Apdo 221, Ciudad Quesada, Alajuela; tel. 479-1264; f. 1986; Roman Catholic station; Dir Rev. MARCO A. SOLÍS V.

**Radio Universidad:** Ciudad Universitaria Rodrigo Facio, San Pedro, Montes de Oca, Apdo 2060, 1000 San José; tel. 207-5356; fax 207-5459; f. 1949; classical music; Dir CARLOS MORALES.

#### Commercial

There are about 40 commercial radio stations, including:

**89 Ya!:** Costado sur del Parque Desamparados, Apdo 301, San José; tel. 259-3657; fax 250-2376; f. 1995; Dir ALEXANDER RAMOS RODRÍGUEZ.

**Cadena de Emisoras Columbia:** Apdo 708, 1002 San José; tel. 234-0355; fax 225-9275; operates Radio Columbia, Radio Uno, Radio Sabrosa, Radio Puntarenas; Dir C. ARNOLDO ALFARO CHAVARRA.

**Cadena Musical:** Apdo 854, 1000, San José; tel. 257-2789; fax 233-9975; f. 1954; operates Radio Musical, Radio Emperador; Gen. Man. JORGE JAVIER CASTRO.

**Grupo Centro:** Apdo 6.133, San José; tel. 240-7591; fax 236-3672; operates Radio Centro 96.3 FM, Radio 820 AM, Televisora Guanacasteca Channels 16 and 28; Dir ROBERTO HERNÁNDEZ RAMÍREZ.

**Radio Chorotega:** Apdo 92, 5175 Santa Cruz de Guanacaste; tel. 663-2757; fax 663-0183; f. 1983; Roman Catholic station; Dir Rev. EMILIO MONTES DE OCA CORDERO.

**Radio Emaus:** San Vito de Coto Brus; tel. and fax 773-3101; f. 1962; Roman Catholic station; Dir Rev. LUIS PAULINO CABRERA SOTO.

**Radio Monumental:** Avda Central y 2, Calle 2, Apdo 800, 1000 San José; tel. 222-0000; fax 222-8237; e-mail monument@sol.racsa.co.cr; internet www.novanet.co.cr/monumental; f. 1929; all news station; Gen. Man. TERESA MARÍA CHÁVES ZAMORA.

**Radio Sinaí:** Apdo 262, 8000 San Isidro de El General; tel. 771-0367; f. 1957; Roman Catholic station; Dir Mgr ALVARO COTO OROZCO.

**Sistema Radiofónico:** Edif. Galería La Paz, 3°, Avda 2, Calles 2 y 4, Apdo 341, 1000 San José; tel. 222-4344; fax 255-0587; operates Radio Reloj; Dir Dr HERNÁN BARQUERO MONTES DE OCA.

### TELEVISION

#### Government-owned

**Sistema Nacional de Radio y Televisión Cultural (SINART):** 1 km al oeste del Parque Nacional de Diversiones La Uruca, Apdo 7-1.980, San José; tel. 231-0839; fax 231-6604; e-mail sinart@racsa .co.cr; f. 1977; cultural; Dir-Gen. GUIDO SÁENZ GONZÁLEZ.

#### Commercial

**Alphavisión (Canal 19):** Detrás Iglesia de Santa María y Griega, Carretera a Desamparados, Apdo 1490, San José; tel. 226-9333; fax 226-9095; f. 1987; Gen. Man. CECILIA RAMÍREZ.

**Canal 2:** Del Hospital México 300 metros oeste, Antiguo Hotel Cristal, Apdo 2.860, San José; tel. 231-2222; fax 231-0791; f. 1983; Pres. RAMÓN COLL MONTERO.

**Canal 54:** De Plaza Mayot, en Rohrmoser, 50 metros oeste, 50 metros sur, Apdo 640, San José; tel. 232-6337; fax 231-3408; e-mail canalcr@sol.racsa.co.cr; f. 1996; Pres. ANTONIO ALEXANDRE GARCÍA.

**Corporación Costarricense de Televisión, SA (Canal 6):** Apdo 2.860, 1000 San José; tel. 232-9255; fax 232-6087; Gen. Man. MARIO SOTELA BLEN.

**Multivisión de Costa Rica, Ltda (Canales 4 y 9):** 150 metros oeste del Centro Comercial de Guadelupe, Apdo 4.666, 1000 San José; tel. 233-4444; fax 221-1734; f. 1961; operates Radio Sistema Universal A.M. (f. 1956), Channel 9 (f. 1962) and Channel 4 (f. 1964) and FM (f. 1980); Gen. Man. ARNOLD VARGAS V.

**Televisora de Costa Rica (Canal 7), SA (Teletica):** Costado oeste Estadio Nacional, Apdo 3.876, San José; tel. 232-2222; fax 231-6258; f. 1960; operates Channel 7; Pres. OLGA COZZA DE PICADO; Gen. Man. RENÉ PICADO COZZA.

**Televisora Sur y Norte (Canal 11):** Apdo 99, 1000 San José; tel. 233-4988; Gen. Man. FEDERICO ZAMORA.

## Finance

(cap. = capital; p.u. = paid up; res = reserves; dep. = deposits; m. = million; brs = branches; amounts in colones, unless otherwise indicated)

### BANKING

**Banco Central de Costa Rica:** Avdas Central y Primera, Calles 2 y 4, Apdo 10.058, 1000 San José; tel. 233-4233; fax 233-5930; internet www.sugef.fi.cr; f. 1950; cap. 5.0m., res 10.0m., total resources 1,078,058.4m. (Dec. 1997); Pres. EDUARDO LIZANO FAIT; Man. CARLOS MUÑOZ V.

#### State-owned Banks

**Banco de Costa Rica:** Avdas Central y 2, Calles 4 y 6, Apdo 10.035, 1000 San José; tel. 255-1100; fax 255-0911; f. 1877; responsible for industry; cap. 2,385.4m., surplus and res 5,995.9m., dep. 86,080.3m. (Dec. 1993); Pres. JORGE ELÍAS RAMÍREZ R.; Gen. Man. RODOLFO MONTERO B.; 44 brs and agencies.

**Banco Crédito Agrícola de Cartago:** Avda 2, Calles 3 y 5, Apdo 297, Cartago; tel. 550-0202; fax 552-0364; f. 1918; responsible for housing; cap. and res 1,056m., dep. 8,966m. (Aug. 1991); Pres. BERNARDO GARCÍA UMAÑA; Gen. Man. VALENTÍN FONSECA MENA; 10 brs.

**Banco Nacional de Costa Rica:** Calles 2 y 4, Avda Primera, Apdo 10.015, 1000 San José; tel. 221-2223; fax 233-3875; f. 1914; responsible for the agricultural sector; cap. 3,546.6m., surplus, profit and reserves 6,935.0m., dep. 143,295.2m. (Dec. 1992); Gen. Man. Lic. OMAR GARRO V.; 125 brs and agencies.

**Banco Popular y de Desarrollo Comunal:** Calle 1, Avdas 2 y 4, Apdo 10.190, San José; tel. 257-5797; fax 255-1966; f. 1969; cap. 260m., res 6m., dep. 940m. (June 1981); Pres. Ing. RODOLFO NAVAS ALVARADO; Gen. Man. ALVARO UREÑA ALVAREZ.

#### Private Banks

**Banco BANEX, SA:** Avda Primera y Calle Central, Apdo 7.893, 1000 San José; tel. 257-0522; fax 257-5967; f. 1981 as Banco Agro Industrial y de Exportaciones, SA; adopted present name 1987; cap. 1,300.0m., res 889.6m., dep. 24,003.7m. (Dec. 1997); Pres. RICHARD BECK; Gen. Man. Ing. OSCAR RODRÍGUEZ ULLOA; 3 brs.

**Banco BCT, SA:** Calle Central No. 160, Apdo 7.698, San José; tel. 257-0544; fax 233-6833; f. 1984; cap. and res 279m. (Aug. 1991); Pres. ANTONIO BURGUÉS; Gen. Man. Lic. LEONEL BARUCH.

**Banco BFA, SA:** Centro Comercial CAFESA, La Uruca, Apdo 6.531, 1000 San José; tel. 231-4444; fax 232-7476; f. 1984 as Banco de Fomento Agrícola; present name adopted 1994; cap. US $3.9m.; res $4.5m.; dep. $16.0m. (Dec. 1996); Pres. ERNESTO ROHRMOSER; Gen. Man. and CEO MANUEL PÉREZ LARA.

**Banco de COFISA, SA:** Barrio Tournón, San Francisco de Goicoechea, Apdo 10.067, San José; tel. 257-6363; fax 223-4594; f. 1986; cap. and res 378m. (Aug. 1991); Pres. Lic. OMAR DENGO; Gen. Man. WILLIAM J. PHELPS.

**Banco del Comercio, SA:** 150 metros norte de la Catedral Metropolitana, Apdo 1.106, 1000 San José; tel. 257-6010; fax 222-3706; e-mail bancomer@bancomer.fi.cr; internet www.bancomer.fi.cr; f. 1978; cap. 1,216.3m., res 191.3m., dep. 9,426.0m. (Dec. 1997); Pres. JAVIER QUIRÓS RAMOS DE ANAYA; Gen. Man. RAFAEL ANGEL MORA BADILLA.

**Banco Continental, SA:** Edif. LAICA, Barrio Tournón, Apdo 7.969, San José; tel. 257-1155; fax 257-1169; f. 1984; cap. and res 782m. (Oct. 1993); Pres. RODOLFO SALAS; Gen. Man. Ing. JUAN J. FLÓREZ.

**Banco Cooperativo Costarricense, RL:** Avda 7, Calles 3 y 5, Apdo 8.593, 1000 San José; tel. 233-5044; fax 233-9661; f. 1982;

cap. 602.7m., res 104.1m., dep. 4,000.9m. (Dec. 1997); Pres. MARIO CARVAJAL HERRERA; Gen. Man. Dr DENNIS MELÉNDEZ HOWELL.

**Banco de Crédito Centroamericano, SA (Bancentro):** Calles 26 y 38, Paseo Colón, de la Mercedes Benz 200 metros norte y 150 metros oeste, Apdo 5.099, 1000 San José; tel. 280-5555; fax 280-5090; f. 1974; cap. 492m. (1996); Pres. ROBERTO J. ZAMORA LLANES; Gen. Man GILBERTO SERRANO GUTIÉRREZ.

**Banco FINCOMER, SA:** Calles 7 y 9, Avda 2, Apdo 1.002, Paseo de los Estudiantes, San José; tel. 551-1351; fax 552-0667; f. 1977; cap. 600m., dep. 2,300m. (Sept. 1993); Pres. Lic. DANIEL CASAFONT FLORES; Gen. Man. Lic. RAFAEL A. MORA BADILLA.

**Banco Federado, RL:** 200 metros sur Autos Subarú, Los Yoses, San Pedro, Apdo 806, 1000 San José; tel. 283-5050; fax 253-4803; f. 1987; cap. and res 505m. (Aug. 1991); Pres. CARLOS BONILLA AYUB; Gen. Man. PABLO CRUZ MONGE.

**Banco de la Industria, SA:** Calle 9, Avdas Central y Primera, Apdo 4.254, 1000 San José; tel. 221-3355; fax 233-8383; f. 1985; cap. and res 200m. (Aug. 1993); Pres. Lic. ALBÁN BRENES IBARRA; Gen. Man. Dr ABELARDO BRENES IBARRA.

**Banco Interfin, SA:** Calle 3, Avdas 2 y 4, Apdo 6.899, San José; tel. 287-4000; fax 233-4823; f. 1982; cap. and res 2,198.6m. (Dec. 1996); Pres. Ing. LUIS LUKOWIECKI; Gen. Man. Dr LUIS LIBERMAN.

**Banco Internacional de Costa Rica, SA:** Edif. Inmobiliaria BICSA, Barrio Tournón, Apdo 6.116, San José; tel. 243-1000; fax 257-2378; f. 1987; cap. and res 1,625m. (Nov. 1994); Pres. Lic. FERNANDO SUÑOL PREGO; Gen. Man. MARCO ALFARO CHAVARRÍA.

**Banco Internacional de Exportación, SA:** Calle Central, Avda 3, Apdo 5.384, San José; tel. 222-3033; f. 1981; Pres. HOJABAR YAZDANI; Gen. Man. HERNÁN VOLIO.

**Banco del Istmo, SA:** Calle 2, Avdas Primera y Central, Apdo 10.184, 1000 San José; tel. 257-9011; fax 221-6795; f. 1871; frmly Banco Lyon, SA, name changed as above 1996; cap. 592.5m., res 78.4m., dep. 636.5m. (Dec. 1993); Pres. ALBERTO VALLARINO CLEMENT; Gen. Man. MARCIAL DÍAZ DEL VALLE.

**Banco Latinoamericano (Costa Rica), SA:** San José; f. 1974; cap. 5m.; Pres. FERNANDO BERROCAL S.; Man. FRED O'NEILL G.

**Banco Mercantil de Costa Rica, SA:** Avda Primera, Calles Central y 2, Apdo 5.395, San José; tel. 257-6868; fax 255-3076; f. 1987; cap. and res 750m. (Sept. 1994); Pres. IGNACIO AIZENMAN; Gen. Man. JACOBO AIZENMAN.

**Banco Metropolitano, SA:** Calle Central, Avda 2, Apdo 6.714, 1000 San José; tel. 290-6900; fax 296-9665; f. 1985; cap. 386.0m., res 610.1m., dep. 3,828.9m. (Dec. 1996); Pres. ABRAHAM MELTZER SPIGEL; Gen. Man. FRANCISCO LAY SOLANO; 3 brs.

**Banco de San José, SA:** Calle Central, Avdas 3 y 5, Apdo 5.445, 1000 San José; tel. 256-9911; fax 223-3063; f. 1968; fmrly Bank of America, SA; cap. 405.0m., surplus, profits and reserves 1,606m., dep. 15,234.3m. (Dec. 1994); Pres. ERNESTO CASTEGNARO ODIO; Gen. Man. MARIO MONTEALEGRE-SABORÍO.

**Banco de Santander (Costa Rica), SA:** Avda 2, Calle Central, Apdo 6.714, San José; tel. 222-8066; fax 222-8840; f. 1977; cap. 60m. (1986); Pres. ABRAHAM WAIESLEDER; Gen. Man. LUIS MIER ABANS.

**Citibank (Costa Rica), SA:** Oficentro ejecutivo la Sabana, distrito Mata Redonda, Apdo 10.277, San José; tel. 296-1494; fax 296-2458.

### Credit Co-operatives

**Federación Nacional de Cooperativas de Ahorro y Crédito (Fedecrédito, RL):** Calle 20, Avdas 8 y 10, Apdo 4.748, 1000 San José; tel. 233-5666; fax 257-1724; f. 1963; 55 co-operatives, with 150,000 mems; combined cap. US $82m.; Pres. Lic. CARLOS BONILLA AYUB; Gen. Man. Lic. MARIO VARGAS ALVARADO.

## STOCK EXCHANGE

**Bolsa Nacional de Valores, SA:** Edif. Cartagena, 4°, Calle Central, Avda Primera, Apdo 1.736, 1000 San José; tel. 256-1180; fax 255-0131; e-mail bnv@internet.bnv.co.cr; f. 1976; Chair. RODRIGO ARIAS SÁNCHEZ; CEO ROBERTO VENEGAS RENAULD.

## INSURANCE

In mid-1998 the Legislative Assembly approved legislative reform effectively terminating the state monopoly of all insurance activities.

**Instituto Nacional de Seguros:** Calles 9 y 9 bis, Avda 7, Apdo 10.061, 1000 San José; tel. 223-5800; fax 255-3381; internet www.ins.go.cr; f. 1924; administers the state monopoly of insurance; services of foreign insurance companies may be used only by authorization of the Ministry of the Economy, Industry and Commerce, and only after the Instituto has certified that it will not accept the risk; Exec. Pres. JORGE A. HERNÁNDEZ CASTAÑEDA; Gen. Man. ANA ROSS SALAZAR.

# Trade and Industry

## GOVERNMENT AGENCIES

**Instituto Nacional de Vivienda y Urbanismo (INVU):** Apdo 2.534, San José; tel. 221-5266; fax 223-4006; housing and town planning institute; Exec. Pres. Ing. Lic. VICTOR EVELIO CASTRO; Gen. Man. Lic. PEDRO HERNÁNDEZ RUIZ.

**Ministry of Planning:** Avdas 3 y 5, Calle 4, Apdo 10.127, 1000 San José; tel. 221-9524; fax 253-6243; f. 1963; formulates and supervises execution of the National Development Plan; main aims: to increase national productivity; to improve distribution of income and social services; to increase citizen participation in solution of socio-economic problems; Pres. Dr LEONARDO GARNIER.

**Promotora de Comercio Exterior de Costa Rica (PROCOMER):** Calle 40, Avdas Central y 3, Centro Colón, Apdo 1.278, 1007 San José; tel. 256-7111; fax 233-5755; e-mail info@procomer.com; internet www.procomer.com; f. 1968 to improve international competitiveness by providing services aimed at increasing, diversifying and expediting international trade.

## DEVELOPMENT ORGANIZATIONS

**Cámara de Azucareros:** Calle 3, Avda Fernández Güell, Apdo 1.577, 1000 San José; tel. 221-2103; fax 222-1358; f. 1949; sugar growers; Pres. RODRIGO ARIAS SÁNCHEZ.

**Cámara Nacional de Bananeros:** Edif. Urcha, 3°, Calle 11, Avda 6, Apdo 10.273, 1000 San José; tel. 222-7891; fax 233-1268; f. 1967; banana growers; Pres. Lic. JOSÉ ALVARO SANDOVAL; Exec. Dir Lic. JORGE MADRIGAL.

**Cámara Nacional de Cafetaleros:** Calle 3, Avdas 6 y 8, No. 652, Apdo 1.310, San José; tel. 221-8207; fax 257-5381; f. 1948; 70 mems; coffee millers and growers; Pres. CARLOS R. AUBERT Z.; Exec. Dir JOAQUÍN VALVERDE B.

**Cámara Nacional de Ganaderos:** Edif. Ilifilán, 4°, Calles 4 y 6, Avda Central, Apdo 5.539, 1000 San José; tel. 222-1652; cattle farmers; Pres. Ing. ALBERTO JOSÉ AMADOR ZAMORA.

**Cámara Nacional de Artesanía y Pequeña Industria de Costa Rica (CANAPI):** Calle 17, Avda 10, detrás estatua de San Martín, Apdo 1.783-2.100 Goicoechea, San José; tel. 223-2763; fax 255-4873; f. 1963; development, marketing and export of small-scale industries and handicrafts; Pres. and Exec. Dir RODRIGO GONZÁLEZ.

**CINDE (Costa Rican Investment and Development Board):** Apdo 7.170, 1000 San José; tel. 220-0366; fax 220-4750; e-mail cindes.m@sol.racsa.co.cr; internet www.cinde.co.cr; f. 1983; coalition for development of initiatives to attract foreign investment for production and export of new products; Chair. EMILIO BRUCE; CEO ENRIQUE EGLOFF.

**Instituto del Café de Costa Rica:** Calle 1, Avdas 18 y 20, Apdo 37, San José; tel. 222-6411; fax 222-2838; f. 1948 to develop the coffee industry, to control production and to regulate marketing; Pres. Lic. LUIS DIEGO ESCALANTE; Exec. Dir GUILLERMO CANET.

## CHAMBERS OF COMMERCE

**Cámara de Comercio de Costa Rica:** Urbanización Tournón, 150 metros noroeste del parqueo del Centro Comercial El Pueblo, Apdo 1.114, 1000 San José; tel. 221-0005; fax 233-7091; e-mail biofair@sol.racsa.co.cr; f. 1915; 1,200 mems; Pres. CARLOS A. FEDERSPIEL PINTO; Exec. Dir Lic. JULIO UGARTE TATÚM.

**Cámara de Industrias de Costa Rica:** Calles 13–15, Avda 6, Apdo 10.003, 1000 San José; tel. 223-2411; fax 222-1007; f. 1943; Pres. Ing. MIGUEL SCHYFTER LEPAR; Exec. Dir HELIO FALLAS V.

**Unión Costarricense de Cámaras y Asociaciones de la Empresa Privada (UCCAEP):** 1002 Paseo de los Estudiantes, Apdo 539, San José; tel. 290-5595; fax 290-5596; f. 1974; business federation; Pres. Ing. SAMUEL YANKELEWITZ BERGER; Exec. Dir ALVARO RAMÍREZ BOGANTES.

## INDUSTRIAL AND TRADE ASSOCIATIONS

**Cámara Nacional de Agricultura:** Avda 10-10 bis, Cv. 23, Apdo 1.671, 1000 San José; tel. 221-6864; fax 233-8658; f. 1947; Pres. Ing. LEONEL PERALTA; Exec. Dir Lic. JOSÉ CARLOS BARQUERO ARCE.

**Consejo Nacional de Producción:** Calle 36 a 12, Apdo 2.205, San José; tel. 223-6033; fax 233-9660; f. 1948 to encourage agricultural and fish production and to regulate production and distribution of basic commodities; Pres. Ing. JAVIER FLORES GALAGARZA; Man. Lic. VIRGINIA VALVERDE DE MOLINA.

**Instituto de Desarrollo Agrícola (IDA):** Apdo 5.054, 1000 San José; tel. 224-6066; Exec. Pres. Ing. ROBERTO SOLÓRZANO SANABRIA; Gen. Man. Ing. JORGE ANGEL JIMÉNEZ CALDERÓN.

**Instituto Mixto de Ayuda Social (IMAS):** Calle 29, Avdas 2 y 4, Apdo 6.213, San José; tel. 225-5555; fax 224-8783; Pres. CLOTILDE FONSECA QUESADA.

**Instituto Nacional de Fomento Cooperativo:** Apdo 10.103, 1000 San José; tel. 223-4355; fax 255-3835; f. 1973; to encourage the establishment of co-operatives and to provide technical assistance and credit facilities; Pres. Lic. RAFAEL ANGEL ROJAS JIMÉNEZ; Exec. Dir Lic. LUIS ANTONIO MONGE ROMÁN.

### UTILITIES

#### Electricity

**Instituto Costarricense de Electricidad—ICE** (Costa Rican Electricity Institute): Apdo 10.032, 1000 San José; tel. 220-7720; fax 220-1555; govt agency for power and telecommunications; Exec. Pres. ROBERTO DOBLES M.; Gen. Man. INGRID HERRMAN.

**Servicio Nacional de Electricidad:** Apdo 936, 1000 San José; tel. 220-0102; fax 220-0374; co-ordinates the development of the electricity industry; Chair. LEONEL FONSECA.

#### Water

**Instituto Costarricense de Acueductos y Alcantarillados:** Avda Central, Calle 5, Apdo 5.120, 1000 San José; tel. 233-2155; fax 222-2259; water and sewerage; Pres. MARIO FERNÁNDEZ ORTIZ.

### TRADE UNIONS

By the end of 1987 there were only 19 unions, with a total of 4,313 members nation-wide; membership of 'solidarista' associations had risen to 16,229. A new labour code, adopted in 1988, encouraged the further growth of these associations (in which employers' interests tend to predominate) at the expense of the trade unions.

**Central del Movimiento de Trabajadores Costarricenses—CMTC** (Costa Rican Workers' Union): Calle 20, Avdas 3 y 5, Apdo 4.137, 1000 San José; tel. 221-7701; fax 222-6519; Pres. DENNIS CABEZAS BADILLA.

**Confederación Auténtica de Trabajadores Democráticos** (Democratic Workers' Union): Calle 13, Avdas 10 y 12, Solera; tel. 253-2971; Pres. LUIS ARMANDO GUTIÉRREZ; Sec.-Gen. Prof. CARLOS VARGAS.

**Confederación Costarricense de Trabajadores Democráticos** (Costa Rican Confederation of Democratic Workers): Calles 3 y 5, Avda 12, Apdo 2.167, San José; tel. 222-1981; f. 1966; mem. ICFTU and ORIT; Sec.-Gen. LUIS ARMANDO GUTIÉRREZ R.; 50,000 mems.

**Confederación Unitaria de Trabajadores—CUT:** Calles 1 y 3, Avda 12, Casa 142, Apdo 186, 1009 San José; tel. 233-4188; f. 1980 from a merger of the Federación Nacional de Trabajadores Públicos and the Confederación General de Trabajadores; 53 affiliated unions; Sec.-Gen. GILBER BERMÚDEZ UMAÑA; c. 75,000 mems.

**Federación Sindical Agraria Nacional—FESIAN** (National Agrarian Confederation): Apdo 2.167, 1000 San José; tel. 233-5897; 20,000 member families; Sec.-Gen. JUAN MEJÍA VILLALOBOS.

The **Consejo Permanente de los Trabajadores,** formed in 1986, comprises six union organizations and two teachers' unions.

## Transport

**Ministry of Public Works and Transport:** Apdo 10.176, 1000 San José; tel. 226-7311; fax 227-1434; the ministry is responsible for setting tariffs, allocating funds, maintaining existing systems and constructing new ones.

**Cámara Nacional de Transportes:** Calle 20, Avda 7, San José; tel. 222-5394; national chamber of transport.

### RAILWAYS

**Instituto Costarricense de Ferrocarriles (INCOFER):** Calle 2, Avda 20, Apdo 1-1009, San José; tel. 221-0777; fax 222-3458; e-mail incofer@sol.racsa.co.cr; f. 1985; government-owned; 471 km, of which 388 km are electrified; Exec. Pres. Lic. JOSÉ FRANCISCO BOLAÑOS ARQUÍN.

INCOFER comprises:

**División I:** Atlantic sector running between Limón, Río Frío, Valle la Estrella and Siquirres. Main line of 109 km, with additional 120 km of branch lines, almost exclusively for transport of bananas.

**División II:** Pacific sector running from San José to Puntarenas and Caldera; 116 km of track, principally for transport of cargo.

Plans for the introduction of a third division of the rail network, comprising 43 km linking Alajuela, Heredia, San José and Cartago, were being pursued in 1997.

Note: In 1995 INCOFER suspended operations, pending privatization.

### ROADS

In 1997 there were 35,597 km of roads, of which 7,405 km were main roads and 28,192 km were secondary roads. An estimated 17% of the total road network was paved.

### SHIPPING

Local services operate between the Costa Rican ports of Puntarenas and Limón and those of Colón and Cristóbal in Panama and other Central American ports. The multi-million dollar project at Caldera on the Gulf of Nicoya is now in operation as the main Pacific port; Puntarenas is being used as the second port. The Caribbean coast is served by the port complex of Limón/Moín. International services are operated by various foreign shipping lines.

**Junta de Administración Portuaria y de Desarrollo Económico de la Vertiente Atlántica (JAPDEVA):** Calle 17, Avda 7, Apdo 8-5.330, 1000 San José; tel. 233-5301; state agency for the development of Atlantic ports; Exec. Pres. Ing. JORGE ARTURO CASTRO HERRERA.

**Instituto Costarricense de Puertos del Pacífico (INCOP):** Calle 36, Avda 3, Apdo 543, 1000 San José; tel. 223-7111; fax 223-9685; state agency for the development of Pacific ports; Exec. Pres. GERARDO MEDINA MADRIZ.

### CIVIL AVIATION

Costa Rica's main international airport is the Juan Santamaría Airport, 16 km from San José at El Coco. A US $180m. expansion of the airport was expected to begin in January 2000. There is a second international airport, the Daniel Oduber Quirós Airport, at Liberia and there are regional airports at Limón and Pavas (Tobías Bolaños Airport).

**Aero Costa Rica:** San Pedro, Montes de Oca, Apdo 1.328, San José; tel. 296-1111; fax 232-1815; regional carrier; Chair. CALIXTO CHAVEL; Gen. Man. JUAN FERNÁNDEZ.

**Líneas Aéreas Costarricenses, SA—LACSA** (Costa Rican Airlines): Edif. Lacsa, La Uruca, Apdo 1.531, San José; tel. 290-2727; fax 232-4178; internet www.flylatinamerica.com; f. 1945; operates international services within Latin America and to North America; Chair. ALONSO LARA; Pres. JOSÉ G. ROJAS.

**Servicios Aéreos Nacionales, SA (SANSA):** Paseo Colón, Centro Colón, Apdo 999, 1.007 San José; tel. 233-2714; fax 255-2176; subsidiary of LACSA; international, regional and domestic scheduled passenger and cargo services; Man. Dir CARLOS MANUEL DELGADO AGUILAR.

**Servicios de Carga Aérea (SERCA):** Aeropuerto Internacional Juan Santamaría, Apdo 6.855, San José; f. 1982; operates cargo service from San José.

## Tourism

Costa Rica boasts a system of nature reserves and national parks unique in the world, which cover one-third of the country. The main tourist features are the Irazú and Poás volcanoes, the Orosí valley and the ruins of the colonial church at Ujarras. Tourists also visit San José, the capital, the Pacific beaches of Guanacaste and Puntarenas, and the Caribbean beaches of Limón. In 1995 plans were being pursued for the construction of a US $2,300m.-tourism development at Papagayo Gulf in Guanacaste province. The project, for which the majority concession was held by the Mexican development company, Situr, envisaged the construction of a marina and as many as 25,000 hotel rooms. According to preliminary figures, a total of 805,300 tourists visited Costa Rica in 1997, when tourism receipts totalled an estimated $731.2m. In 1996 most visitors came from the USA (34.7% of the total) and Nicaragua (15.4%). There were 11,650 hotel rooms in Costa Rica in 1993.

**Instituto Costarricense de Turismo:** Edif. Genaro Valverde, Calles 5 y 7, Avda 4, Apdo 777, 1000 San José; tel. 223-1733; fax 223-5107; f. 1955; Exec. Pres. Ing. CARLOS ROESCH CARRANZA.

# CÔTE D'IVOIRE

## (THE IVORY COAST)

# Introductory Survey

### Location, Climate, Language, Religion, Flag, Capital

The Republic of Côte d'Ivoire lies on the west coast of Africa, between Ghana to the east and Liberia to the west, with Guinea, Mali and Burkina Faso to the north. Average temperatures vary between 21°C and 30°C (70°F and 86°F). The main rainy season, from May to July, is followed by a shorter wet season in October–November. The official language is French, and a large number of African languages are also spoken. At the time of the 1988 census some 39% of the population were Muslims, 26% Christians (mainly Roman Catholics), and about 17% followed traditional beliefs. The national flag (proportions 3 by 2) has three equal vertical stripes, of orange, white and green. The political and administrative capital is Yamoussoukro, although most government ministries and offices remain in the former capital, Abidjan, which is the major centre for economic activity.

### Recent History

Formerly a province of French West Africa, Côte d'Ivoire achieved self-government, within the French Community, in December 1958. Dr Félix Houphouët-Boigny, leader of the Parti démocratique de la Côte d'Ivoire—Rassemblement démocratique africain (PDCI—RDA), became Prime Minister in 1959. The country became fully independent on 7 August 1960; a new Constitution was adopted in October 1960, and Houphouët-Boigny became President in November.

Until 1990 the PDCI—RDA, founded in 1946, was Côte d'Ivoire's only legal political party. Despite constitutional provision for the existence of other political organizations, no opposition party was granted official recognition (although from November 1980 more than one candidate was permitted to contest each seat in the legislature, the Assemblée nationale), since Houphouët-Boigny maintained that a multi-party system would impede progress towards national unity. A high rate of economic growth (particularly during the 1970s), together with strong support from France, contributed, until the late 1980s, to the stability of the regime, and sporadic political unrest was without strong leadership. (A number of plots against the Government in the 1960s were later admitted by Houphouët-Boigny to have been fabricated as a means of strengthening support for the regime and removing potential rivals from positions of influence.)

In October 1985 the PDCI—RDA voted to amend Article 11 of the Constitution, thereby abolishing the post of Vice-President of the Republic and allowing for the President of the Assemblée nationale to succeed the Head of State, on an interim basis, in the event of a vacancy. Later that month Houphouët-Boigny was re-elected President for a sixth five-year term. Municipal and legislative elections took place in November, and in January 1986 Henri Konan Bédié was re-elected to the presidency of the legislature.

In April 1986 it was announced that the country wished to be known internationally by its French name of Côte d'Ivoire, rather than by translations of it. The request was subsequently endorsed by the UN.

The announcement in early 1990 of austerity measures, in compliance with an IMF-sponsored economic revival programme, precipitated an unprecedented level of student and labour unrest, particularly following the announcement of reductions in salaries for all state employees and of a 'solidarity tax' on private-sector incomes. In April, as it became clear that the measures would, in any case, fail to generate the revenue necessary to reduce Côte d'Ivoire's increasingly burdensome foreign debt, Houphouët-Boigny appointed Alassane Ouattara, the Governor of the Banque centrale des états de l'Afrique de l'ouest (the regional central bank), to chair a special commission whose task would be to formulate new measures that would be both more economically effective and politically acceptable. Economic reform was accompanied by political change, and in May it was announced that Article 7 of the Constitution was to be implemented. Hitherto unofficial political organizations were formally recognized, and many new parties were formed. A new Minister of the Economy and Finance, Daniel Kablan Duncan, was appointed in July. Pope John Paul II visited Côte d'Ivoire in September, in order to consecrate a basilica in Yamoussoukro (Houphouët-Boigny's birthplace), constructed, officially at the President's own expense, at a cost of some 40,000m. francs CFA.

Côte d'Ivoire's first contested presidential election was held on 28 October 1990. During the campaign period security forces had intervened at several opposition rallies and demonstrations, and Houphouët-Boigny's opponents had frequently accused the Government of impeding democratization. Houphouët-Boigny—challenged by Laurent Gbagbo, the candidate of the Front populaire ivoirien (FPI)—was re-elected for a seventh term with the support of 81.7% of those who voted. The FPI and its allies alleged malpractice, and appealed unsuccessfully to the Supreme Court to declare the election invalid. In November the legislature approved two constitutional amendments. The first concerned the procedure to be adopted should the presidency become vacant: Article 11 was again amended to the effect that the President of the Assemblée nationale would assume the functions of the President of the Republic until the expiry of the previous incumbent's mandate. Secondly, provision was made for the appointment of a Prime Minister, who would be accountable to the President; Ouattara was subsequently designated premier.

Almost 500 candidates, representing some 17 political parties, contested legislative elections on 25 November 1990. Opposition parties again accused the PDCI—RDA of electoral fraud. The PDCI—RDA returned 163 deputies to the 175-member Assemblée nationale; Gbagbo and eight other members of the FPI were elected, along with the leader of the Parti ivoirien des travailleurs (PIT), Francis Wodié, and two independent candidates. Bédié was subsequently re-elected President of the legislature. Ouattara's first Council of Ministers was named following the elections, in which the Prime Minister—assisted by Duncan—assumed personal responsibility for the economy and finance.

Tensions between the authorities and the education sector were revived in May 1991, after security forces used violent methods to disperse a students' meeting at the University of Abidjan; about 180 students were said to have been arrested. Subsequent protests by students and academic staff were disrupted by the security forces. In June Houphouët-Boigny announced that a commission would be established to investigate the campus violence, but the crisis deepened when the death of a student who had defied an order to boycott classes, following an attack by members of the Fédération estudiantine et scolaire de Côte d'Ivoire (FESCI), prompted the Government to order that FESCI be disbanded, and that security forces be deployed at the university. Academic staff began an indefinite strike, and further protests resulted in the arrest, in July, of 11 FESCI activists suspected of involvement in the student's death. The situation was temporarily resolved in August, when the Government withdrew security forces, suspended legal proceedings against FESCI members and restored the right of 'non-academic assembly' at the university (although the ban on FESCI remained in force). The commission of inquiry's report, published in January 1992, held the armed forces Chief of the General Staff, Brig.-Gen. Robert Gueï, ultimately responsible for violent acts perpetrated by forces under his command. However, Houphouët-Boigny made it clear that neither Gueï nor any member of the security forces would be subject to disciplinary proceedings. Demonstrations erupted at the university, prompting the arrest of FESCI activists, and in February Gbagbo and the President of the Ligue ivoirienne des droits de l'homme (LIDHO), René Degny-Segui, were among more than 100 people arrested during a violent anti-Government demonstration in Abidjan. It was subsequently announced that Gbagbo and other opposition leaders were to be prosecuted under the terms of a new presidential ordinance that rendered political leaders responsible for violent acts committed by their supporters during demonstrations. Later in the month the leader of FESCI was fined and sentenced to three years' imprisonment, convicted of reconstituting a banned organization and of responsibility for offences committed by students. The trials of other opposition activists followed: among those convicted were Gbagbo and Degny-Segui, who each received two-year prison sentences. In April FPI deputies began a boycott of the Assemblée nationale, in protest against the imprisonment of Gbagbo and another FPI member of parliament; the PIT leader joined the boycott in May.

In July 1992 Houphouët-Boigny proclaimed an amnesty for all political offences committed since the time of the 1990 disturbances. PDCI—RDA deputies approved the amnesty later in the month, but opposition deputies maintained their boycott of the legislature, protesting that the amnesty not only prevented detainees from pursuing the right of appeal, but also exempted members of the security forces from charges relating to alleged offences committed during this period.

Houphouët-Boigny left Côte d'Ivoire in May 1993, and spent the following six months receiving medical treatment in France and Switzerland. As his health failed, controversy intensified concerning the presidential succession. Many senior politicians, including Ouattara and Gbagbo (both of whom were known to have presidential aspirations), asserted that the process defined in the Constitution effectively endorsed an 'hereditary presidency' (since Bédié, like Houphouët-Boigny, was a member of the Baoulé ethnic group) and demanded that Article 11 again be revised to permit the President of the Assemblée nationale to assume the post of President of the Republic on an interim basis only, pending new elections. Houphouët-Boigny died, officially aged 88, in Yamoussoukro on 7 December. Later the same day Henri Konan Bédié made a television broadcast announcing that, in accordance with the Constitution, he was assuming the duties of President of the Republic with immediate effect. Ouattara initially refused to recognize Bédié's right of succession, but tendered his resignation two days later. Duncan was subsequently designated Prime Minister and Minister of the Economy, Finance and Planning. Senior members of the previous administration were retained in charge of defence, foreign affairs, the interior and raw materials. In January 1994 Charles Donwahi (the Vice-President of the legislature since 1991) was elected President of the Assemblée nationale.

Several months of sporadic labour unrest were brought to an end by Houphouët-Boigny's death, and, largely owing to a two-month period of national mourning, reactions to the 50% devaluation, in January 1994, of the CFA franc were generally more muted in Côte d'Ivoire than in other countries of the Franc Zone in Africa. In subsequent months President Bédié appointed close associates to positions of influence in government, the judiciary and in the state-owned media. The new regime also used far-reaching legislation (introduced under Houphouët-Boigny) governing the press to bring charges against several journalists deemed to have been disrespectful to Bédié or to other state officials.

Bédié's position was further consolidated by his election to the chairmanship of the PDCI—RDA in April 1994, and by Ouattara's departure for the USA following his appointment, in May, to the post of Deputy Managing Director of the IMF. Disaffected members of the PDCI—RDA left the party in June to form what they termed a moderate, centrist organization, the Rassemblement des républicains (RDR); Ouattara formally announced his membership of the RDR in early 1995.

In June 1995 the Assemblée nationale approved proposals for legislation permitting the extension of the death penalty (already in existence for murder convictions, although there was no record of its implementation since independence) to cases of robbery with violence. Security operations accompanying the new administration's anti-crime measures, which frequently targeted non-Ivorian groups, were denounced by Bédié's opponents as indicative of xenophobic tendencies within the new regime.

Meanwhile, a new electoral code, adopted by parliament in December 1994, imposed new restrictions on eligibility for public office, notably stipulating that candidates for the Presidency or for the Assemblée nationale must be of direct Ivorian descent. The RDR in particular protested that these restrictions might prevent Ouattara from contesting the presidency, since the former Prime Minister was of Burkinabè descent and would also be affected by the code's requirement that candidates have been continuously resident in Côte d'Ivoire for five years prior to seeking election. Opposition parties, grouped in a Front républicain (FR), organized a series of mass demonstrations in Abidjan to demand the withdrawal of the electoral code, the establishment of an independent electoral commission and a revision of voters' lists. Ouattara, who had been invited by the RDR to be the party's presidential candidate, subsequently announced that, while he wished to contest the presidency, he would not attempt to do so in violation of the law. In September, citing the need to ensure the continuation of economic activity, the Government imposed a three-month ban on political demonstrations. The FR countered that the ban was in violation of constitutional recognition of the right to demonstrate, emphasizing that it would continue to hold protest marches.

In early October 1995 the FPI (which was to have been represented by Gbagbo) and the RDR (whose Secretary-General, Djény Kobina, was to have replaced Ouattara as the party's candidate) stated that they would not contest the presidential election as long as the conditions were not 'clear and open'. An eruption of violence in Abidjan and in other major towns coincided with the opening of an international investment forum in Abidjan. Subsequent negotiations involving Bédié and opposition groups made no effective progress, as the FR refused to accept a government offer to include opposition representatives on the commission responsible for scrutinizing voters' lists and election results as sufficient guarantee of the commission's autonomy, while the Government rejected the opposition's demand that the elections be postponed.

The presidential election took place on 22 October 1995, following a week of violence in several towns. The FR claimed that its campaign for an 'active boycott' of the poll had been largely successful (despite appeals by Wodié, Bédié's sole challenger, for the support of opposition sympathizers), while the Government claimed that voters had participated peacefully and in large numbers. Troops were deployed, ostensibly to prevent the disruption of voting by the opposition, although it was reported that polling had proceeded in only one of 60 designated centres in the FPI stronghold of Gagnoa, in the Centre-Ouest region. Bédié's overwhelming victory, with 95.25% of the valid votes cast, was confirmed by the Constitutional Council five days after the poll. While most areas remained generally calm following the election, there were reports of the persecution of Baoulé around Gagnoa by members of the local majority Bété ethnic group.

In early November 1995 it was announced that the FR had agreed to abandon its threatened boycott of the legislative elections, which were scheduled for 26 November, in return for government concessions regarding the revision of voters' lists; representatives of both the FPI and the RDR were subsequently appointed to the electoral commission. The opposition suffered a considerable reverse when the authorities announced that voting in three of Gagnoa's four constituencies (including the constituency that was to have been contested by Gbagbo) was to be postponed, owing to the disruption arising from the recent disturbances; moreover, Kobina's candidacy (in Abidjan's Adjamé constituency) was disallowed, on the grounds that he had been unable to prove direct Ivorian descent. Voting none the less proceeded generally without incident, and the earliest indications were that the PDCI—RDA had retained a decisive majority—despite a notable loss of support for the party in the Nord region, in favour of the RDR. The FPI secured strong representation in the Centre-Ouest region, while the PDCI—RDA secured overwhelming victories in the Centre, Ouest and Sud-Ouest regions, and registered strong support in Abidjan and other major towns. Wodié failed to secure re-election to the Assemblée nationale. In late December the Constitutional Council annulled the results of the elections in three constituencies, including the one seat in Gagnoa for which voting had been permitted. The PDCI—RDA thus held 146 seats, the RDR 14, and the FPI nine. Also in December Donwahi was re-elected President of the Assemblée nationale. (By-elections for eight parliamentary seats, including those for which voting did not take place or was cancelled in 1995, took place in December 1996: the FPI won five seats, and the PDCI—RDA three.)

In October 1995, shortly before the presidential election, Brig.-Gen. Gueï was replaced in his armed forces command by Cdre Lassana Timité, and appointed to the Government as Minister of Employment and the Civil Service. In a reorganization of the Government in January 1996 Léon Konan Koffi was transferred from the post of Minister of Defence to that of Minister of

State responsible for Religious Affairs and Dialogue with the Opposition, while Gueï became Minister of Sports. In May 1996 reports emerged in the independent press of a coup attempt by disaffected members of the armed forces at the time of the civil unrest that preceded the 1995 presidential election. Gueï's appointment, prior to the election, to a relatively minor government post was thus interpreted as a reaction to unrest in the forces under his command. In a televised statement, the Minister of Defence, Bandama N'Gatta, confirmed that members of the military high command had recently sought an audience with Bédié, at which they had affirmed their loyalty to the Head of State and had demanded that 'exemplary sanctions' be taken against armed forces personnel involved in 'disloyal' actions in September and October 1995. Also in May 1996 a prominent human rights organization, Amnesty International, alleged that opposition activists in Côte d'Ivoire were, notably since the 1995 election campaign, the target of systematic repression: particular concern was expressed regarding detentions (many without trial) under anti-riot legislation.

A reorganization of government portfolios in August 1996, as a result of which Gueï and Koffi left the Government, apparently demonstrated Bédié's concern both to remove from positions of influence figures connected with the insecurity prior to the 1995 elections and to strengthen national security. A new Minister of Justice and Public Freedom was appointed, and the Secretary-General of the country's new National Security Council (intended to co-ordinate all issues of national security) took the rank of Minister-delegate to the Presidency. In November the Government announced the dismissal of seven members of the armed forces and the suspension of several other members of the military, in accordance with investigations into what was now apparently confirmed as a coup plot. In January 1997 Gueï was dismissed from the army, having been found to have committed 'serious disciplinary offences' in the discharge of his duties. It was announced in March that Bédié had instructed N'Gatta to effect the release from custody of military personnel detained in connection with the events of late 1995.

A congress of the PDCI—RDA held in October 1996 re-elected Bédié as party Chairman and Laurent Dona-Fologo (also Minister of State with responsibility for National Solidarity) as Secretary-General. At the conference, Bédié advocated the opening of government to the parliamentary and non-parliamentary opposition, stating that, to this end, the process of bringing to trial detained members of the military and opposition activists must be expedited. A commission of inquiry into the 1995 pre-election unrest was inaugurated in December 1996. The RDR and the FPI refused to take up their allotted seats, however, protesting that the opposition had been judged responsible in advance of the inquiry.

In December 1996 university students in Abidjan began a protest against the late payment of grants and to demand changes to the examinations system. Four members of FESCI (which remained outlawed) were arrested in connection with a disturbance outside the Ministry of Security. Three of the students were fined and sentenced to two years' imprisonment in January 1997, provoking further disturbances at the university. Later in the month a student died while fleeing police who had stormed a FESCI meeting, and shortly afterwards two students were seriously injured in clashes with security forces at the Yopougon campus in Abidjan. Further protests followed the arrest, in February, of the Secretary-General and other leading members of FESCI. At the end of the month, Bédié issued a decree pardoning the three students who had been sentenced in January, and ordered the release of all detained student activists. This, together with the proposed establishment of a permanent committee to mediate or arbitrate in future disputes, served briefly to restore calm, but in April disturbances at the University of Bouaké prompted the Government to announce the closure of the university and its halls of residence. FESCI gave notice of a five-day strike, and in May the authorities ordered the closure of university residences in Abidjan, in an effort to curb persistent disturbances. (Lectures were to continue, and the resumption of classes at Bouaké was announced by the Government at the end of the month.) The university year was extended until December, in view of the disruption of recent months, but many students failed to resume classes at the beginning of a new term in September. National consultations on higher education began at the end of that month, apparently at Bédié's instigation, as a result of which the ban on FESCI was revoked, and, in response, the students' union announced an end to the boycott of classes.

Inaugurating the National Security Council in August 1997, Bédié announced that a general audit of the military, paramilitary and national police was to be undertaken, with a view to their restructuring, and that the armed forces were to be given additional responsibilities in countering illegal immigration, smuggling and organized crime, as well as in areas such as humanitarian assistance. Opponents of the Government denounced the Council, which was to be directly responsible to the Head of State, as a means of supporting the Bédié regime through espionage, intelligence and propaganda.

A reorganization of the Council of Ministers in March 1998 included the appointment of Adama Coulibaly, the Deputy Secretary-General of the RDR (also the Mayor of Korhogo and the leader of the RDR group of deputies in the Assemblée nationale), to the post of Minister of Transport. Coulibaly's acceptance of this post was denounced by the RDR, and he was subsequently expelled from the party. Further government changes were implemented in August. Amara Essy, the Minister of Foreign Affairs, was promoted to the rank of Minister of State, while Guy Alain Emmanuel Gauze, the long-serving Minister of Raw Materials, was redesignated Minister of Foreign Trade Promotion; Wodié, the PIT leader, was appointed to the Government as Minister of Higher Education and Scientific Research.

Constitutional amendments were approved by the Assemblée nationale in June 1998. The vote was taken in the absence of deputies of the RDR and FPI, who objected, in particular, to provisions conferring wider powers on the Head of State, specifically a clause allowing the President of the Republic to delay elections, or the proclamation of election results, on the grounds of 'events, serious troubles or *force majeure*'. The presidential mandate was, furthermore, to be extended to seven years. Conditions of eligibility to seek office as President were for the first time to be enshrined in the Constitution: candidates would be required to be Ivorian by birth, of direct Ivorian descent, and continuously resident in Côte d'Ivoire for 10 years. The amendments also included provisions for the establishment of an upper legislative chamber, the Sénat. The opposition denounced the arrangements for its composition, whereby two-thirds of its members were to be indirectly elected and the remainder appointed by the Head of State, as a retreat for democracy. (An earlier series of draft amendments, presented by Bédié to the Assemblée nationale in August 1997, had been broadly welcomed by the main opposition parties, but had been overwhelmingly rejected by the PDCI—RDA.) In September 1998 Gbagbo and Kobina led a demonstration in Abidjan to denounce the amendments. The Government denied foreign radio reports of 15,000 protesters, citing estimates by the security forces of 3,500–4,000 participants. Kobina died in October. Attending his funeral, Ouattara (who earlier in the year had announced that he would return to Côte d'Ivoire in 1999, upon the expiry of his contract with the IMF) confirmed his intention to contest the presidency at the election due in 2000. The former Prime Minister expressed confidence that laws of filiation, nationality and residency which might prevent his candidacy would be altered.

Meanwhile, it was reported in September 1998 that Bédié was preparing to declare an amnesty for the remainder of those detained in connection with the 1995 'active boycott'. This was expected to apply to 26 detainees, including 13 sentenced to life imprisonment. The President subsequently sought contacts with the opposition, with the expressed aim of promoting national reconciliation. In December 1998 the PDCI—RDA and the FPI reached an agreement on democracy and good governance, whereby the authorities agreed to an amnesty in respect of the 1995 'active boycott' together with new legislation relating to the funding of political parties during elections and the establishment of a national electoral commission. Consultations between the Government and the RDR (now led by Henriette Dagri Diabaté, who had assumed the post of party Secretary-General following the death of Kobina) began in March 1999, but ended in failure after several sessions.

There was renewed unrest involving FESCI from April 1999, as students and school pupils boycotted classes in support of demands regarding tuition fees and the disbursement of scholarships and other allowances. Progress apparently made at meetings between the ministers responsible for secondary and higher education in May was undermined when a number of students were sentenced to five years' imprisonment for disrupting law and order. FESCI ordered renewed protests, and police subsequently used batons and tear gas to disperse a group of activists intending to hold a news conference at the Cocody campus in Abidjan. At the end of May the Government ordered the closure of all university campuses, asserting that accommodation was, with the collusion of FESCI, being occupied by non-students, and that stockpiles of weapons had been found on campus. FESCI denied these allegations, and strike action proceeded, despite a government ban, from the beginning of June. The boycott of classes was suspended later in the month following a meeting between Bédié and FESCI, pending efforts to secure a lasting settlement of the education crisis. In early August, in his address to commemorate the country's National Day, Bédié spoke of appeasement measures for the education sector. However, tensions swiftly escalated following the arrest, in mid-August, of Charles Blé Goudé, the FESCI leader, on charges arising from the murder of a trader, forced entry into the Prime Minister's residence, destruction of property and looting. It was reported that more than 200 students had hitherto been given custodial sentences in connection with these events. In early October, however, prior to the opening of the new academic year, Bédié signed a decree granting amnesty to school pupils and students detained in relation to the FESCI boycott.

Meanwhile, there were persistent allegations of corruption at all levels in the Bédié regime. A reorganization of the Council of Ministers in mid-August 1999 followed the dismissal of the ministers responsible for national education, employment and health. The departure of the Minister of Public Health, Maurice Kakou Guikahue, was apparently in connection with the misappropriation, revealed in an audit conducted within the European Union (EU), of aid allocated for health care projects. The discovery of the apparent fraud resulted in the suspension of much EU assistance, which, combined with the withholding of IMF funding as a result, *inter alia*, of suspicions of fraud at the state marketing body for cocoa and coffee, resulting in a loss of much external budgetary support and a severe depletion of the country's capital reserves. Bédié, who earlier in August had announced renewed efforts to counter corruption in public life, undertook to ensure the repayment of the missing funds.

The return of Alassane Ouattara to Côte d'Ivoire in late July 1999 apparently opened a critical phase in advance of the 2000 presidential election. At the beginning of August 1999 an extraordinary congress of the RDR overwhelmingly appointed Ouattara to the newly created post of party Chairman, and Ouattara again announced his intention to contest the forthcoming presidential election. However, the authorities, who had persisted in their assertions that Ouattara was not an Ivorian national, questioned the validity of his appointment as party Chairman, and in early September the office of the public prosecutor ordered an investigation into the validity of documents submitted by Ouattara as proof of his Ivorian citizenship. Ouattara in turn announced his intention to file a defamation suit against the Government. In mid-September a reported 388 RDR militants were briefly detained, after a police-officer who had been attempting to deliver an interrogation notice to Outtara was seriously injured by activists who were protecting their leader's residence. One person was killed in ensuing protests.

At the end of September 1999 an extraordinary session of the Assemblée nationale approved an amnesty for those members of the military implicated in the events surrounding the 1995 presidential election. However, there were few signs of any relaxation of political tensions, as the Minister of Justice and Human Rights, Jean Kouacou Brou, announced his decision to instruct the appropriate authorities to begin proceedings with a view to the annulment, on the grounds of apparent irregularities, of Ouattara's certificate of nationality, which had been issued by a court in Dimbokro in late September 1999 and presented to the Minister of State for the Interior and Decentralization as evidence of the former Prime Minister's eligibility to become Chairman of an Ivorian political party. In mid-October there were clashes in Abidjan as police used force to disperse supporters of Ouattara who were protesting against the perceived 'demonization' of the RDR leader by the state-owned media. Shortly afterwards the public prosecutor submitted a request to the legislature to revoke the parliamentary immunity of an RDR deputy, Amadou Gon Coulibaly (also the RDR deputy Secretary-General), in respect of widely broadcast remarks that he had made during an RDR rally in late September that were judged to be insulting to Bédié and likely to disturb public order and discredit the institutions of the Republic. At the end of October clashes erupted between RDR activists and security forces, who had intervened to disperse a protest march and planned blockade of the offices of the state broadcasting company, resulting in the arrest under anti-riot legislation of some 20 RDR activists, among them Diabaté and Coulibaly. (The protest had been banned at short notice by the authorities.) Demonstrations in Korhogo also culminated in clashes between RDR supporters and the security forces. On the same day it was announced that Ouattara's nationality certificate had been annulled. In mid-November Diabaté and Coulibaly, together with three further RDR deputies and six other party activists, were each sentenced to two years' imprisonment, convicted on charges related to the Abidjan protest in late October; five others received a one-year custodial sentence. Compensation was also ordered to be paid to the transport company SOTRA, and to the government newspaper *Fraternité Matin*, for damage to property resulting from the rioting. An opposition daily, *Le Patriote*, subsequently reported that 11 RDR members, arrested in protests as the trial began, had been found guilty of violence, assault and battery and sentenced to 12 months' imprisonment. Shortly afterwards, Ouattara, who had spent much of the previous two months in France, announced that he would not, as previously intended, shortly return to Côte d'Ivoire, since his party judged it more useful for him to remain abroad to keep the international community appraised of the political situation in Côte d'Ivoire. (Ouattara frequently asserted that one of his first actions, if elected to the presidency in 2000, would be to repeal the anti-riot legislation, introduced under his premiership in 1992, which had brought about the prosecution of his party colleagues.)

The deterioration in the political situation in Côte d'Ivoire attracted considerable concern among the country's regional and international allies. In mid-November 1999 the French Minister-delegate responsible for Co-operation, Charles Josselin, commenting on events in the border region with Burkina Faso, where migrant workers were being systematically expelled by indigenous Krou militants, stated that the atmosphere in Abidjan was not conducive to a climate of calm in the interior. Such comments, together with expressions of concern already made by the US Department of State and the French Parti socialiste, were denounced by Bédié as unwarranted interference in Côte d'Ivoire's internal affairs. French protests were renewed in early December, when it was revealed that a mandate had been issued for the arrest of Ouattara, should he return to Côte d'Ivoire, on charges of fraud and use of fraud in procuring identity papers.

Bédié was overthrown on 24 December 1999, after a mutiny by soldiers demanding salary increases and the payment of outstanding arrears escalated into a *coup d'état*. Brig.-Gen. Robert Gueï, the former armed forces Commander-in-Chief, announced that he had assumed power at the head of a Comité national de salut public (CNSP), and that the Constitution and its institutions had been suspended. Constitutional review and fresh legislative elections were promised, and the country's opposition parties were invited to submit nominations for an interim government, pending the restoration of constitutional order. Bédié sought refuge in his native town of Daoukro, leaving in early January 2000 for Togo and subsequently for France.

The unexpected coup was, initially, condemned internationally, but apparently largely welcomed within Côte d'Ivoire, where the Bédié regime had been increasingly regarded as authoritarian and corrupt. None the less, despite intensive contacts with representatives of Côte d'Ivoire's diverse political and civilian organizations, Gueï encountered considerable difficulty in achieving his early objective of constituting a broadly-based government, as the FPI, perceiving the coalition appointed in early January 2000 to be unduly dominated by the RDR and its associates, withdrew its nominees; the PDCI—RDA had declined to propose ministers, and the two representatives of the former ruling party selected by Gueï were not regarded as influential. In mid-January, however, the FPI agreed to join the Government, having been allocated two additional portfolios. A constitutional review body was inaugurated at the end of the month. Meanwhile, Gueï announced that elections leading to the installation of new organs of government would have been completed by 31 October. While the response of the international community to the military takeover had become increasingly positive in the weeks following the coup, both the Organization of African Unity and the Economic Community of West African States (ECOWAS, see p. 163) continued to demand a return to constitutional government by the end of June. Also in January an amnesty was proclaimed for all those convicted of political offences under the Bédié regime. (Henrietta Dagri Diabaté had been among RDR leaders released following the coup, and she had been appointed to the interim Government as Minister of Francophone Affairs and Culture.)

President Houphouët-Boigny was widely respected as an active participant in regional and international affairs, although his commitment to a policy of dialogue between black Africa and the apartheid regime in South Africa prompted frequent criticism. In April 1992 (once the process of dismantling apartheid had begun) Côte d'Ivoire became the first black African country to establish diplomatic relations with South Africa. Moreover, in the final years of his life Houphouët-Boigny's role in the civil conflict in Liberia (see below) was a focus of considerable external scrutiny.

Côte d'Ivoire's foreign policy orientation remained largely unaltered under Bédié. Relations with France, the country's principal trading partner and provider of bilateral assistance, which have been close since independence, were apparently enhanced following the election of the Gaullist Jacques Chirac to the presidency in May 1995—Chirac's predecessor, François Mitterrand, having latterly shown considerable support for Gbagbo and the FPI. The Bédié administration sought assurances from France that its programme of armed forces restructuring would not entail any significant reduction of French military commitments in Côte d'Ivoire. Details of the intended reduction of French forces in Africa, announced in August 1997, apparently confirmed that a military base would be maintained at Port-Bouët. Visiting Côte d'Ivoire in October, the French Minister of Defence, Alain Richard, announced that France would assist Côte d'Ivoire both in restructuring its armed forces and in establishing a centre for the training of African military personnel for peace-keeping operations. Ivorian troops joined the UN peace-keeping mission in the Central African Republic in April 1998 (see p. 61); this was Côte d'Ivoire's first involvement in such an operation.

Despite evidence to the contrary, Houphouët-Boigny consistently denied suggestions that his Government was supporting Charles Taylor's rebel National Patriotic Front of Liberia (NPFL), which was instrumental in the overthrow of President Samuel Doe of that country in mid-1990. (The Doe administration had maintained that rebel forces had entered Liberia via Côte d'Ivoire.) Although Côte d'Ivoire did not contribute troops to the ECOMOG force that was dispatched to Liberia by ECOWAS in August 1990 (see p. 164), the Ivorian authorities assumed an active role in attempts to achieve a peaceful dialogue between opposing forces in Liberia during 1991. In December, none the less, the Liberian interim President, Dr Amos Sawyer, accused Côte d'Ivoire of providing the NPFL with arms and training facilities. Relations with other ECOWAS members deteriorated in February 1993, when (following recent allegations that NPFL units were operating from Ivorian territory) aircraft under ECOMOG command bombed the Ivorian border region of Danané. (ECOWAS officials claimed that the area attacked had been mistaken for Liberian territory.) Rumours persisted that Ivorian authorities were violating the international economic and military blockade of Liberia by (either actively or passively) allowing the NPFL access to the sea via the port of San Pedro in south-western Côte d'Ivoire, and there were reports that several of Taylor's associates had taken up residence in Abidjan.

The presence in Côte d'Ivoire of a large number of refugees from Liberia was increasingly cited by the Ivorian authorities as a cause of the perceived escalation in insecurity in the country, and periodic incursions on to Ivorian territory by members of armed factions in the Liberian conflict provoked considerable disquiet. In July 1995 Côte d'Ivoire, which had hitherto promoted the full integration of refugees into Ivorian society, announced the establishment of the first reception centre for Liberian refugees at Guiglo. Côte d'Ivoire expressed support for the Liberian peace agreement that was signed in Abuja in August, and Taylor was a member of a high-level Liberian delegation that visited Côte d'Ivoire in October, where discussions took place with the Ivorian authorities on joint concerns including border security and the repatriation of refugees. In mid-1996 the Ivorian Government announced that security measures were to be increased in the west (in an effort to stem rebel incursions and the infiltration of refugee groups by Liberian fighters, and in July the Government proclaimed western Côte d'Ivoire to be a military 'operational zone', extending the powers of the armed forces to act in response to rebel activity. The installation of elected institutions in Liberia in 1997 facilitated the repatriation of refugees. The office of the UN High Commissioner for Refugees put the total number of refugees in Côte d'Ivoire at 119,900 at the end of 1998, compared with 208,500 in 1997.

## Government

Following the *coup d'état* of 24 December 1999, the Constitution that had been in force since 1960 was suspended, and its institutions dissolved. A commission was installed in January 2000 to draft a new Constitution. The military Comité national de salut public, which had assumed power, announced that elections leading to the installation of new organs of government would be completed by 31 October. The country is divided into 16 Regions, and further sub-divided into 49 Departments, each with its own elected Council.

## Defence

In August 1999 Côte d'Ivoire's active armed forces comprised an army of 6,800 men, a navy of about 900, an air force of 700, a presidential guard of 1,100 and a gendarmerie of 4,400. There was also a 1,500-strong militia. Reserve forces numbered 12,000 men. Military service is by selective conscription and lasts for six months. France supplies equipment and training, and maintains a military presence in Côte d'Ivoire (570 men in 1999). The defence budget for 1999 was 109,000m. francs CFA.

## Economic Affairs

In 1997, according to estimates by the World Bank, Côte d'Ivoire's gross national product (GNP), measured at average 1995–97 prices, was US $10,152m., equivalent to $710 per head. During 1990–97, it was estimated, GNP per head increased at an average annual rate of 0.9% in real terms, while the population increased by an average of 2.9% per year. GNP in 1998 was estimated at $10,100m., equivalent to $700 per head. During 1990–98 Côte d'Ivoire's gross domestic product (GDP) increased by an average of 3.5% per year, in real terms. According to data published by the IMF, GDP increased by 6.0% in 1997 and by an estimated 5.4% in 1998.

Agriculture (including forestry and fishing) contributed an estimated 27.2% of GDP in 1998, and employed about 51.4% of the labour force in that year. Côte d'Ivoire is the world's foremost producer of cocoa, and exports of cocoa and related products contributed an estimated 37.2% of total export earnings in 1998. Côte d'Ivoire is also among the world's largest producers and exporters of coffee. Other major cash crops include cotton, rubber, bananas and pineapples. The principal subsistence crops are maize, yams, cassava, plantains and, increasingly, rice (although large quantities of the last are still imported). Excessive exploitation of the country's forest resources has led to a decline in the importance of this sector, although measures have now been instigated to preserve remaining forests. Abidjan is among sub-Saharan Africa's principal fishing ports; however, the participation of Ivorian fishing fleets is minimal. During 1990–98 agricultural GDP increased by an average of 2.4% per year.

Industry (including mining, manufacturing, construction and power) contributed an estimated 23.7% of GDP in 1998. According to UN estimates, 11.5% of the labour force were employed in the sector in 1994. During 1990–98 industrial GDP increased by an average of 5.1% per year.

Mining contributed only an estimated 0.3% of GDP in 1998. The sector's contribution was, however, expected to increase considerably following the commencement, in the mid-1990s, of commercial exploitation of important offshore reserves of petroleum and natural gas. Gold and diamonds are also mined, although illicit production of the latter has greatly exceeded commercial output. There is believed to be significant potential for the development of nickel deposits, and there are also notable reserves of manganese, iron ore and bauxite.

The manufacturing sector, which contributed an estimated 14.6% of GDP in 1998, is dominated by agro-industrial activities (such as the processing of cocoa, coffee, cotton, palm kernels, pineapples and fish). Crude petroleum is refined at Abidjan, while the tobacco industry uses mostly imported tobacco.

Almost two-thirds of Côte d'Ivoire's electricity generation in 1998 was derived from thermal sources, the remainder being derived mainly from hydroelectric installations. Through the exploitation, from 1995, of indigenous reserves of natural gas, the country expected to generate sufficient energy for its own requirements by 2000, and for regional export thereafter. Imports of petroleum products (including crude oil for refining) accounted for 14.9% of the value of total imports in 1998.

An important aim of economic policy in the late 1990s was the expansion of the services sector, which contributed an estimated 49.1% of GDP in 1998, and (according to UN estimates) employed 37.4% of the labour force in 1994. The transformation of Abidjan's stock market into a regional exchange for the member states of the Union économique et monétaire ouest-africaine (UEMOA, see p. 201) was expected to enhance the city's status as a centre for financial services. In addition, emphasis was placed on the revival of tourism as a major source of foreign exchange. Abidjan is also central to regional communications and trade. The GDP of the sector increased by an average of 3.5% per year in 1990–98.

In 1998 Côte d'Ivoire recorded a visible trade surplus of US $1,870.0m., although there was a deficit of $312.6m. on the current account of the balance of payments. In that year the principal source of imports was France (which supplied 28.6% of total imports); Italy and the USA were also notable suppliers. France was the principal market for exports in 1998 (taking 17.1% of total exports), followed by the Netherlands, the USA, Italy and Ghana. The principal exports in 1998 were cocoa, coffee, petroleum products, and fish products. The principal imports in the same year were petroleum products, machinery and transport equipment, cereals, and fish and shellfish.

Côte d'Ivoire's overall budget deficit in 1998 was 118,400m. francs CFA (equivalent to 1.8% of GDP). The country's total external debt was US $15,609m. at the end of 1997, of which $12,498m. was long-term public debt. In that year the cost of debt-servicing was equivalent to 27.4% of the value of exports of goods and services. The annual rate of inflation averaged 2.7% in 1990–93. Consumer prices increased by an average of 26.1% in 1994 (following the devaluation of the currency at the beginning of the year); the inflation rate slowed to an annual average of 14.3% in 1995, and averaged 4.4% in 1996–98. Some 114,880 persons were registered as unemployed at the end of 1992.

Côte d'Ivoire is a member of numerous regional and international organizations, including the Economic Community of West African States (ECOWAS, see p. 163), the west African organs of the Franc Zone (see p. 200), the African Petroleum Producers' Association (APPA, see p. 287), the Association of Coffee Producing Countries (ACPC, see p. 287), the International Cocoa Organization (ICCO, see p. 287), the International Coffee Organization (see p. 287) and the Conseil de l'Entente (see p. 291). The African Development Bank (see p. 117) has its headquarters in Abidjan.

Côte d'Ivoire's return to GDP growth from 1994, after seven years of recession, was in large part attributable to the 50% devaluation of the CFA franc, which increased demand for traditional exports and stimulated growth in the non-traditional agricultural sector and in manufacturing. A further cause of optimism was the self-sufficiency in hydrocarbons expected to result from the exploitation of new petroleum and natural gas reserves. Annual GDP growth in 1995–98 was in excess of the rate of population increase. Policies of economic liberalization sought to reduce vulnerability to fluctuations in world prices for cocoa and coffee, with IMF support, under its Enhanced Structural Adjustment Facility (ESAF), in particular stipulating the dismantling of marketing monopolies and removal of price controls, together with efforts to foster domestic and foreign private investment. However, the total liberalization of the coffee and cocoa sectors and the restructuring of the former monopoly Caisse de stabilisation et de soutien des prix des productions agricoles (Caistab), as Nouvelle Caistab, which was completed in August 1999, coincided with a sharp fall in international prices for cocoa. This clearly illustrated the economy's continuing dependence on this sector, as projected revenue declined steeply and cocoa producers demanded government support for the newly deregulated sector. Furthermore, IMF funding was suspended from late 1998, as a result of Côte d'Ivoire's failure to comply notably with ESAF targets for spending restraint and the elimination of tax fraud, and also pending the satisfactory outcome of an independent audit of Caistab's finances. This, compounded by the suspension of assistance by the European Union, following revelations of the misappropriation of aid, meant that actual receipts of foreign budgetary assistance for 1999 stood at about 10% of the level originally forecast. As a consequence, expectations diminished that Côte d'Ivoire would fulfil the criteria necessary for concessionary debt relief, under the Bretton Woods' institutions' Heavily Indebted Poor Countries Initiative, on its burdensome foreign debt (some 39% of expenditure under the draft budget for 2000 was allocated to debt-servicing). Thus, by the time of the *coup d'état* of late December 1999, Côte d'Ivoire's financial situation was precarious. Gen. Robert Gueï undertook to meet all debt-servicing commitments, to improve conditions particularly for farmers, and to accommodate the demands of the military—whose protests had precipitated the overthrow of the Bédié regime. He further pledged to eliminate the institutionalized corruption which had apparently flourished under the ousted regime. However, in the continued absence of support from the country's principal international creditors, such commitments would be difficult to achieve, while the erosion of the country's long-standing reputation for political stability prompted concerns that the private investment on which the progress of the Ivorian economy depends would in future be less assured.

### Social Welfare

Medical services are organized by the State. In 1994 the country had 7,928 hospital beds, 4,971 nurses and 1,592 midwives. There were some 700 physicians in the mid-1990s. There is a minimum wage for workers in industry and commerce. Total government expenditure on health in 1997 was estimated at 69,700m. francs CFA, equivalent to 5.8% of total spending (excluding expenditure on the external debt). Expenditure by the Caisse nationale de prévoyance sociale and the Caisse générale de retraite des agents de l'Etat was estimated at 85,500m. francs CFA in 1997, and at 94,900m. francs CFA in 1998.

### Education

At the time of the 1988 census adult illiteracy averaged 65.9% (males 55.6%; females 76.6%); UNESCO estimated the average in 1995 to be 59.9% (males 50.1%; females 70.0%). Education at all levels is available free of charge. Primary education, which is officially compulsory for six years between the ages of seven and 13 years, begins at six years of age and lasts for six years. Total enrolment at primary schools in 1996/97 included 55% of children in the relevant age-group (males 63%; females 47%). The Ivorian Government's long-term objective is to provide primary education for all children by 2010. Secondary education, from the age of 12, lasts for up to seven years, comprising a first cycle of four years and a second cycle of three years. In 1996/97 total enrolment at secondary schools was equivalent to 24% of children in the relevant age-group (males 33%; females 16%). The National University at Abidjan has six faculties, and university-level facilities have been constructed in Yamoussoukro. Some 43,147 students were enrolled at university-level institutions in 1994/95. Expenditure on education in 1997 was estimated at 302,400m. francs CFA, equivalent to 25.3% of total government expenditure (excluding spending on the public debt).

### Public Holidays

**2000:** 1 January (New Year's Day), 8 January*† (Id al-Fitr, end of Ramadan), 16 March* (Id al-Adha, Feast of the Sacrifice), 21 April (Good Friday), 24 April (Easter Monday), 1 May (Labour Day), 1 June (Ascension Day), 12 June (Whit Monday), 7 August (National Day), 15 August (Assumption), 1 November (All Saints' Day), 7 December (Félix Houphouët-Boigny Remembrance Day), 25 December (Christmas), 28 December*† (Id al-Fitr, end of Ramadan).

**2001:** 1 January (New Year's Day), 6 March* (Id al-Adha, Feast of the Sacrifice), 13 April (Good Friday), 16 April (Easter Monday), 1 May (Labour Day), 24 May (Ascension Day), 4 June (Whit Monday), 7 August (National Day), 15 August (Assumption), 1 November (All Saints' Day), 7 December (Félix Houphouët-Boigny Remembrance Day), 17 December (Id al-Fitr, end of Ramadan), 25 December (Christmas).

* These holidays are dependent on the Islamic lunar calendar and may vary by one or two days from the dates given.

† This festival will occur twice (in the Islamic years AH 1420 and 1421) within the same Gregorian year.

### Weights and Measures

The metric system is in force.

# Statistical Survey

Source (unless otherwise stated): Institut National de la Statistique, BP V55, Abidjan; tel. 21-05-38.

## Area and Population

**AREA, POPULATION AND DENSITY**

| | |
|---|---|
| Area (sq km) | 322,462* |
| Population (census results) | |
| 30 April 1975 | 6,702,866 |
| 1 March 1988 | |
| Males | 5,527,343 |
| Females | 5,288,351 |
| Total | 10,815,694 |
| Population (official estimates at mid-year) | |
| 1994 | 13,695,000 |
| 1995 | 14,230,000 |
| 1996 | 14,781,000 |
| Density (per sq km) at mid-1996 | 45.8 |

* 124,503 sq miles.

**POPULATION BY ETHNIC GROUP** (1988 census)

| Ethnic group | Number | % |
|---|---|---|
| Akan | 3,251,227 | 30.1 |
| Voltaïque | 1,266,235 | 11.7 |
| Mane Nord | 1,236,129 | 11.4 |
| Krou | 1,136,291 | 10.5 |
| Mane Sud | 831,840 | 7.7 |
| Naturalized Ivorians | 51,146 | 0.5 |
| Others | 3,039,035 | 28.1 |
| Unknown | 3,791 | 0.0 |
| **Total** | 10,815,694 | 100.0 |

Source: UN, *Demographic Yearbook*.

**POPULATION BY REGION** (1988 census)

| Region | Population |
|---|---|
| Centre | 815,664 |
| Centre-Est | 300,407 |
| Centre-Nord | 915,269 |
| Centre-Ouest | 1,542,945 |
| Nord | 745,816 |
| Nord-Est | 514,134 |
| Nord-Ouest | 522,247 |
| Ouest | 968,267 |
| Sud | 3,843,249 |
| Sud-Ouest | 647,696 |
| **Total** | 10,815,694 |

Source: UN, *Demographic Yearbook*.

Note: In January 1997 the Government adopted legislation whereby Côte d'Ivoire's regions were to be renamed. The new regions (with their regional capitals) were to be: Lagoon (Abidjan), Upper Sassandra (Daloa), Savannah (Korhogo), Bandama Valley (Bouaké), Lakes (Yamoussoukro), Middle Comoé (Abengourou), Mountains (Man), Zanzan (Bondoukou), Lower Cavally (San Pedro), Denguélé (Odienné), Marahoué (Bouaflé), Nzi Comoé (Dimbroko), South Comoé (Aboisso), Worodougou (Seguéla), South Bandama (Divo), Agneby (Agboville).

**PRINCIPAL TOWNS** (population at 1988 census)

| | | | |
|---|---|---|---|
| Abidjan* | 1,929,079 | Korhogo | 109,445 |
| Bouaké | 329,850 | Yamoussoukro* | 106,786 |
| Daloa | 121,842 | | |

* The process of transferring the official capital from Abidjan to Yamoussoukro began in 1983.

Source: UN, *Demographic Yearbook*.

**BIRTHS AND DEATHS** (UN estimates, annual averages)

| | 1980–85 | 1985–90 | 1990–95 |
|---|---|---|---|
| Birth rate (per 1,000) | 50.1 | 45.6 | 38.9 |
| Death rate (per 1,000) | 16.0 | 14.8 | 14.9 |

**Expectation of life** (UN estimates, years at birth, 1990–95): 48.9 (males 47.9; females 50.2).

Source: UN, *World Population Prospects: The 1998 Revision*.

**ECONOMICALLY ACTIVE POPULATION**

**Mid-1998** (estimates in '000): Agriculture, etc. 2,892; Total 5,623 (Source: FAO, *Production Yearbook*).

## Agriculture

**PRINCIPAL CROPS** ('000 metric tons)

| | 1996 | 1997 | 1998 |
|---|---|---|---|
| Maize | 569 | 576 | 547 |
| Millet | 60* | 65 | 65* |
| Sorghum | 19† | 19 | 19* |
| Rice (paddy) | 833 | 1,287 | 1,223 |
| Sweet potatoes | 36* | 36 | 36 |
| Cassava (Manioc) | 1,653 | 1,699 | 1,700 |
| Yams | 2,924 | 2,986 | 2,800 |
| Taro (Coco yam) | 361 | 374 | 355 |
| Pulses* | 8 | 8 | 8 |
| Tree nuts | 33* | 27 | 27* |
| Sugar cane* | 1,320 | 1,350 | 1,155 |
| Palm kernels | 30 | 28* | 28* |
| Groundnuts (in shell) | 147 | 143 | 136 |
| Cottonseed | 112 | 142 | 140* |
| Coconuts* | 205 | 221 | 221 |
| Copra* | 30 | 34 | 34 |
| Tomatoes | 130* | 137 | 130 |
| Aubergines (Eggplants)* | 40 | 40 | 40 |
| Chillies and peppers (green)* | 20* | 21 | 21* |
| Other vegetables* | 341 | 343 | 343 |
| Oranges | 28* | 29 | 29* |
| Other citrus fruit* | 28 | 28 | 28 |
| Bananas | 219 | 304 | 222 |
| Plantains | 1,400* | 1,441 | 1,200 |
| Mangoes | 6† | 9 | 9* |
| Pineapples | 251 | 261 | 227 |
| Other fruit* | 13 | 14 | 14 |
| Coffee (green) | 165 | 279 | 332 |
| Cocoa beans | 1,254 | 1,119 | 1,120 |
| Tobacco (leaves)* | 10 | 10 | 10 |
| Cotton (lint) | 96 | 114 | 130 |
| Natural rubber (dry weight) | 91 | 108 | 116 |

* FAO estimate(s). † Unofficial figure.

Source: FAO, *Production Yearbook*.

**LIVESTOCK** ('000 head, year ending September)

| | 1996 | 1997 | 1998* |
|---|---|---|---|
| Cattle | 1,286 | 1,312 | 1,312 |
| Pigs | 290 | 271 | 271 |
| Sheep | 1,314 | 1,347 | 1,347 |
| Goats | 1,027 | 1,053 | 1,053 |

Poultry (million): 27 in 1996; 31 in 1997; 31* in 1998.

* FAO estimate(s).

Source: FAO, *Production Yearbook*.

**LIVESTOCK PRODUCTS**
(FAO estimates unless otherwise indicated, '000 metric tons)

| | 1996 | 1997 | 1998 |
|---|---|---|---|
| Beef and veal | 40 | 42 | 46 |
| Mutton and lamb | 5 | 5 | 5 |
| Goat meat | 4 | 5 | 5 |
| Pig meat | 14 | 13 | 13 |
| Poultry meat | 49 | 50 | 51 |
| Other meat | 28 | 28 | 28 |
| Cows' milk | 23* | 23* | 23 |
| Poultry eggs | 16* | 16 | 16 |
| Cattle hides | 5 | 6 | 6 |
| Sheepskins | 1 | 1 | 1 |
| Goatskins | 1 | 1 | 1 |

* Official figure.

Source: FAO, *Production Yearbook*.

# Forestry

**ROUNDWOOD REMOVALS** ('000 cubic metres, excluding bark)

| | 1995 | 1996 | 1997 |
|---|---|---|---|
| Sawlogs, veneer logs and logs for sleepers | 2,297 | 2,081 | 2,054 |
| Other industrial wood | 864 | 884 | 902 |
| Fuel wood | 11,128 | 11,392 | 11,624 |
| **Total** | 14,289 | 14,357 | 14,580 |

Source: FAO, *Yearbook of Forest Products*.

**SAWNWOOD PRODUCTION**
('000 cubic metres, including railway sleepers)

| | 1995 | 1996 | 1997 |
|---|---|---|---|
| Coniferous (softwood) | 10* | — | — |
| Broadleaved (hardwood) | 696 | 596 | 613 |
| **Total** | 706 | 596 | 613 |

* FAO estimate.

Source: FAO, *Yearbook of Forest Products*.

# Fishing

('000 metric tons, live weight)

| | 1995 | 1996 | 1997 |
|---|---|---|---|
| Freshwater fishes | 10.8 | 11.5 | 11.5 |
| Bigeye grunt | 4.8 | 4.6* | 4.5* |
| Sardinellas | 14.4 | 13.7* | 13.4* |
| Bonga shad* | 10.0 | 9.5 | 9.3 |
| Other marine fishes (incl. unspecified)* | 29.4 | 28.0 | 27.5 |
| **Total fish** | 69.5 | 67.2 | 66.2 |
| Crustaceans | 0.7 | 0.7 | 0.9 |
| **Total catch** | 70.2 | 67.9 | 67.2 |
| Inland waters | 11.3 | 12.0 | 12.0 |
| Atlantic Ocean | 58.9 | 55.9 | 55.1 |

* FAO estimate(s).

Source: FAO, *Yearbook of Fishery Statistics*.

# Mining

**Diamonds** ('000 carats): 117.3 in 1992; 98.4 in 1993; 84.3 in 1994.

**Gold** (metal content of ore, metric tons): 3.6 in 1996; 4.0 in 1997; 3.4 in 1998 (Source: Gold Fields Mineral Services Ltd, *Gold Survey 1999*).

**Crude Petroleum** ('000 metric tons): 348 (estimate) in 1994; 314 in 1995; 1,263 in 1996 (Source: UN, *Industrial Commodity Statistics Yearbook*).

# Industry

**SELECTED PRODUCTS** ('000 metric tons, unless otherwise indicated)

| | 1994 | 1995 | 1996 |
|---|---|---|---|
| Salted, dried or smoked fish* | 15.0 | 0.0 | n.a. |
| Canned fish* | 43.6 | 49.9 | n.a. |
| Palm oil—unrefined* | 259 | 249 | n.a. |
| Raw sugar* | 125 | 119 | 121 |
| Plywood ('000 cubic metres) | 41 | 58 | 57 |
| Jet fuel† | 61 | 62 | 62 |
| Motor gasolene (Petrol)† | 425 | 428 | 432 |
| Kerosene† | 488 | 490 | 491 |
| Gas-diesel (Distillate fuel) oils† | 685 | 705 | 710 |
| Residual fuel oils† | 474 | 477 | 479 |
| Cement†‡ | 500 | 500 | n.a. |

Cocoa powder (exports, '000 metric tons): 22.1*† in 1988.
Cocoa butter (exports, '000 metric tons): 28.2*† in 1988.
Cotton yarn (pure and mixed, '000 metric tons): 24.7† in 1989.

* Data from FAO.
† Provisional or estimated figure(s).
‡ Data from the US Bureau of Mines.

Source: UN, *Industrial Commodity Statistics Yearbook*.

**Electric energy** (million kWh): 2,355 in 1994; 2,489 in 1995; 2,502 in 1996; 2,753 in 1997; 3,957 (estimate) in 1998 (Source: IMF, *Côte d'Ivoire: Statistical Appendix*, August 1999).

# Finance

**CURRENCY AND EXCHANGE RATES**

**Monetary Units**

100 centimes = 1 franc de la Communauté financière africaine (CFA).

**Sterling, Dollar and Euro Equivalents** (30 September 1999)

£1 sterling = 1,012.69 francs CFA;
US $1 = 615.06 francs CFA;
€1 = 655.96 francs CFA;
10,000 francs CFA = £9.875 = $16.259 = €15.245.

**Average Exchange Rate** (francs CFA per US $)

1996 511.55
1997 583.67
1998 589.95

Note: An exchange rate of 1 French franc = 50 francs CFA, established in 1948, remained in force until January 1994, when the CFA franc was devalued by 50%, with the exchange rate adjusted to 1 French franc = 100 francs CFA.

**BUDGET** ('000 million francs CFA)

| Revenue* | 1996 | 1997 | 1998 |
|---|---|---|---|
| Tax revenue | 1,040.7 | 1,112.9 | 1,142.0 |
| Direct taxes | 252.2 | 303.5 | 327.7 |
| Taxes on profits | 126.5 | 147.2 | 166.2 |
| Individual income taxes | 77.0 | 97.8 | 104.8 |
| Employers' contributions | 19.4 | 22.4 | 26.0 |
| Taxes on petroleum products | 100.1 | 96.9 | 96.2 |
| Excise taxes | 62.4 | 61.2 | 62.8 |
| Value-added tax (VAT) | 28.8 | 30.5 | 28.3 |
| Other indirect taxes | 200.1 | 227.3 | 240.0 |
| VAT and withholding tax | 136.8 | 145.6 | 146.8 |
| Registration and stamp taxes | 24.7 | 30.6 | 33.5 |
| Other taxes on imports | 282.5 | 311.9 | 320.2 |
| Customs, fiscal and statistical duties | 128.6 | 153.0 | 162.2 |
| Other import charges | 23.4 | 20.6 | 83.3 |
| VAT | 130.5 | 138.4 | 170.9 |
| Taxes on exports | 205.7 | 173.2 | 158.0 |
| Coffee and cocoa | 196.4 | 165.9 | 150.2 |
| Other revenue | 191.2 | 215.1 | 246.5 |
| Stabilization fund surplus | 70.1 | 84.0 | 131.6 |
| Social security contributions | 74.3 | 83.1 | 79.2 |
| Petroleum revenue | 27.8 | 29.1 | 17.3 |
| **Total** | 1,231.9 | 1,328.0 | 1,388.5 |

| Expenditure | 1996 | 1997 | 1998 |
|---|---|---|---|
| Wages and salaries | 389.6 | 408.1 | 415.2 |
| Social security benefits | 68.8 | 73.6 | 76.5 |
| Subsidies and other current transfers | 40.6 | 54.9 | 55.9 |
| Other current expenditure | 260.0 | 285.3 | 267.6 |
| Investment expenditure | 304.0 | 372.3 | 455.9 |
| Interest due on public debt | 322.2 | 303.2 | 286.3 |
| **Total** | 1,385.1 | 1,497.4 | 1,557.4 |

* Excluding grants received ('000 million francs CFA): 40.5 in 1996; 44.1 in 1997; 50.5 in 1998.

Source: IMF, *Côte d'Ivoire: Statistical Appendix* (August 1999).

**INTERNATIONAL RESERVES** (US $ million at 31 December)

| | 1995 | 1996 | 1997 |
|---|---|---|---|
| Gold* | 17.1 | 16.7 | 13.6 |
| IMF special drawing rights | 1.8 | 1.2 | — |
| Reserve position in IMF | 0.1 | 0.2 | 0.2 |
| Foreign exchange | 527.0 | 604.4 | 618.1 |
| **Total** | 546.1 | 622.5 | 632.0 |

* Valued at market-related prices.

Source: IMF, *International Financial Statistics.*

**MONEY SUPPLY** ('000 million francs CFA at 31 December)

| | 1996 | 1997 | 1998 |
|---|---|---|---|
| Currency outside banks | 473.2 | 571.8 | 667.2 |
| Demand deposits at deposit money banks* | 489.0 | 502.8 | 562.0 |
| Checking deposits at post office | 2.4 | 3.6 | n.a. |
| **Total money** (incl. others) | 966.4 | 1,080.0 | 1,236.0 |

* Excluding the deposits of public establishments of an administrative or social nature.

Source: IMF, *International Financial Statistics.*

**COST OF LIVING** (Consumer Price Index for African households in Abidjan; base: 1995 = 100)

| | 1996 | 1997 | 1998 |
|---|---|---|---|
| **All items** | 102.5 | 108.2 | 113.3 |

Source: IMF, *International Financial Statistics.*

**NATIONAL ACCOUNTS**

('000 million francs CFA at current prices)

**Expenditure on the Gross Domestic Product**

| | 1996 | 1997 | 1998* |
|---|---|---|---|
| Government final consumption expenditure | 661.6 | 695.1 | 690.9 |
| Private final consumption expenditure | 3,592.1 | 3,928.3 | 4,207.9 |
| Increase in stocks | –25.0 | 0.0 | 0.0 |
| Gross fixed capital formation | 760.3 | 957.5 | 1,181.6 |
| **Total domestic expenditure** | 4,989.0 | 5,580.8 | 6,080.5 |
| Exports of goods and services | 2,565.0 | 2,788.4 | 2,870.6 |
| *Less* Imports of goods and services | 2,142.5 | 2,384.8 | 2,458.5 |
| Statistical discrepancy | 62.1 | — | — |
| **GDP in purchasers' values** | 5,473.6 | 5,984.4 | 6,492.6 |

**Gross Domestic Product by Economic Activity**

| | 1996 | 1997 | 1998* |
|---|---|---|---|
| Agriculture, livestock-rearing, forestry and fishing | 1,512.0 | 1,587.7 | 1,688.2 |
| Mining and quarrying | 19.7 | 19.6 | 19.5 |
| Manufacturing | 704.9 | 799.3 | 906.1 |
| Electricity, gas and water | 249.6 | 291.2 | 314.5 |
| Construction and public works | 156.3 | 199.8 | 231.6 |
| Transport, storage and communications | 514.4 | 561.3 | 623.8 |
| Trade | 929.5 | 1,030.3 | 1,128.5 |
| Public administration | 438.3 | 459.5 | 462.2 |
| Other services | 693.1 | 759.2 | 836.6 |
| **Sub-total** | 5,217.8 | 5,708.0 | 6,211.0 |
| Import duties and taxes | 255.8 | 276.4 | 281.6 |
| **GDP in purchasers' values** | 5,473.6 | 5,984.4 | 6,492.6 |

* Estimates.

Source: IMF, *Côte d'Ivoire: Statistical Appendix* (August 1997).

**BALANCE OF PAYMENTS** (US $ million)

| | 1996 | 1997 | 1998 |
|---|---|---|---|
| Exports of goods f.o.b. | 4,446.1 | 4,298.7 | 4,575.1 |
| Imports of goods f.o.b. | –2,622.4 | –2,479.5 | –2,705.1 |
| **Trade balance** | 1,823.7 | 1,819.2 | 1,870.0 |
| Exports of services | 565.9 | 532.3 | 549.9 |
| Imports of services | –1,443.4 | –1,367.7 | –1,474.4 |
| **Balance on goods and services** | 946.1 | 983.8 | 945.5 |
| Other income received | 171.0 | 167.4 | 169.8 |
| Other income paid | –939.5 | –895.4 | –879.6 |
| **Balance on goods, services and income** | 177.7 | 255.8 | 235.8 |
| Current transfers received | 55.5 | 50.0 | 50.9 |
| Current transfers paid | –546.6 | –547.6 | –599.2 |
| **Current balance** | –313.4 | –241.7 | –312.6 |
| Capital account (net) | 49.8 | 39.7 | 36.3 |
| Direct investment abroad | –0.4 | — | |
| Direct investment from abroad | 269.2 | 341.3 | 435.3 |
| Portfolio investment assets | –19.2 | –15.4 | –14.2 |
| Portfolio investment liabilities | 26.6 | 30.7 | 38.5 |
| Other investment assets | –254.1 | –278.4 | –324.3 |
| Other investment liabilities | –719.4 | –533.7 | –669.2 |
| Net errors and omissions | –36.2 | 64.8 | 171.3 |
| **Overall balance** | –997.0 | –592.8 | –638.9 |

Source: IMF, *International Financial Statistics.*

# External Trade

**PRINCIPAL COMMODITIES** ('000 million francs CFA)

| Imports c.i.f. | 1996 | 1997 | 1998 |
|---|---|---|---|
| Foodstuffs, beverages and tobacco | 256.1 | 311.3 | 369.1 |
| Dairy products | 27.8 | 28.1 | 32.3 |
| Fish and shellfish (fresh) | 75.2 | 90.5 | 112.6 |
| Cereals | 81.5 | 104.4 | 119.0 |
| Rice | 44.7 | 64.6 | 81.9 |
| Wheat | 25.8 | 29.7 | 35.3 |
| Other consumer goods | 305.7 | 346.4 | 379.9 |
| Pharmaceutical products | 61.2 | 63.3 | 67.6 |
| Plastic products | 60.9 | 73.1 | 84.9 |
| Passenger cars | 56.3 | 59.4 | 55.0 |
| Raw materials and semi-finished products | 556.8 | 547.3 | 542.6 |
| Petroleum products | 333.1 | 296.1 | 262.1 |
| Crude petroleum | 242.5 | 254.1 | 195.0 |
| Chemical products | 40.9 | 45.5 | 45.2 |
| Fertilizers | 22.1 | 30.9 | 41.5 |
| Construction materials | 30.4 | 35.7 | 36.6 |
| Clinker | 25.5 | 29.9 | 29.6 |
| Paper and paperboard | 41.8 | 43.6 | 48.0 |
| Capital goods | 324.8 | 393.0 | 472.9 |
| Mechanical | 119.0 | 156.2 | 160.6 |
| Electrical | 55.7 | 75.7 | 116.9 |
| Transport equipment | 68.1 | 66.2 | 80.9 |
| Iron and steel products | 61.6 | 69.9 | 94.6 |
| **Total** (incl. others) | 1,443.4 | 1,598.1 | 1,746.6 |

| Exports f.o.b. | 1996 | 1997 | 1998* |
|---|---|---|---|
| Coffee beans | 119.8 | 174.3 | 176.9 |
| Cocoa beans | 720.3 | 707.8 | 735.5 |
| Cotton fibre | 58.7 | 76.9 | 67.1 |
| Bananas | 44.7 | 39.9 | 40.8 |
| Natural rubber | 59.6 | 63.2 | 48.5 |
| Processed cocoa | 95.7 | 120.0 | 162.9 |
| Processed coffee | 32.0 | 33.7 | 45.3 |
| Sawnwood | 141.1 | 152.3 | 119.6 |
| Fish products | 110.7 | 126.0 | 148.6 |
| Crude petroleum | 73.0 | 98.0 | 62.2 |
| Petroleum products | 251.6 | 215.8 | 155.3 |
| **Total** (incl. others) | 2,190.2 | 2,378.9 | 2,414.1 |

* Estimates.

Source: IMF, *Côte d'Ivoire: Statistical Appendix* (August 1999).

**PRINCIPAL TRADING PARTNERS** (percentage of trade)

| Imports | 1996 | 1997 | 1998 |
|---|---|---|---|
| Belgium-Luxembourg | 3.0 | 3.3 | 3.1 |
| Brazil | 1.1 | 0.8 | 1.2 |
| China, People's Repub. | 1.8 | 2.4 | 2.2 |
| France | 25.1 | 26.7 | 28.6 |
| Germany | 5.7 | 4.7 | 4.6 |
| Italy | 4.7 | 4.3 | 5.2 |
| Japan | 4.1 | 4.3 | 3.4 |
| Netherlands | 3.4 | 3.7 | 3.7 |
| Pakistan | 0.1 | 1.1 | 0.6 |
| Spain | 2.8 | 3.2 | 3.6 |
| Taiwan | 6.6 | 0.4 | 0.4 |
| United Kingdom | 2.9 | 2.9 | 2.7 |
| USA | 5.9 | 6.1 | 5.0 |

| Exports | 1996 | 1997 | 1998* |
|---|---|---|---|
| Belgium-Luxembourg | 2.8 | 4.2 | 2.5 |
| Benin | 0.9 | 1.2 | 1.2 |
| Burkina Faso | 2.4 | 3.0 | 3.6 |
| Cameroon | 0.6 | 1.2 | 0.8 |
| France | 16.9 | 17.3 | 17.1 |
| Germany | 5.0 | 4.8 | 4.9 |
| Ghana | 2.9 | 3.7 | 5.7 |
| Italy | 5.7 | 5.3 | 5.9 |
| Mali | 4.3 | 4.9 | 4.8 |
| Netherlands | 16.7 | 13.2 | 12.2 |
| Niger | 0.8 | 1.0 | 1.1 |
| Senegal | 1.3 | 1.1 | 1.1 |
| Spain | 4.0 | 4.0 | 3.7 |
| Taiwan | 0.5 | 0.6 | 1.3 |
| Togo | 1.6 | 1.6 | 1.4 |
| United Kingdom | 2.9 | 2.6 | 2.4 |
| USA | 8.2 | 7.5 | 9.0 |

* Estimates.

Source: IMF, *Direction of Trade Statistics*, in IMF, *Côte d'Ivoire: Statistical Appendix* (August 1999).

# Transport

**RAILWAYS** (traffic)

| | 1991 | 1992 | 1993 |
|---|---|---|---|
| Passengers ('000) | 926 | 820 | 744 |
| Passenger-km (million) | 199 | 189 | 173 |
| Freight ('000 metric tons) | 488 | 484 | 292 |
| Freight (million net ton-km) | 272 | 266 | 168 |

Source: Société Ivoirienne des Chemins de Fer, Abidjan.

**ROAD TRAFFIC** (estimates, '000 motor vehicles in use)

| | 1994 | 1995 | 1996 |
|---|---|---|---|
| Passenger cars | 255 | 271 | 293 |
| Lorries and vans | 140 | 150 | 163 |

Source: IRF, *World Road Statistics*.

**SHIPPING**

**Merchant Fleet** (registered at 31 December)

| | 1996 | 1997 | 1998 |
|---|---|---|---|
| Number of vessels | 45 | 43 | 35 |
| Total displacement ('000 grt) | 12.7 | 11.4 | 9.5 |

Source: Lloyd's Register of Shipping, *World Fleet Statistics*.

**International Sea-borne Freight Traffic**
(freight traffic at Abidjan, '000 metric tons)

| | 1993 | 1994 | 1995 |
|---|---|---|---|
| Goods loaded | 3,882.4 | 3,702.3 | 4,172.9 |
| Goods unloaded | 5,936.4 | 6,183.9 | 7,227.8 |

**Freight Traffic at San Pedro** ('000 metric tons, 1994): Goods loaded 883.8; Goods unloaded 184.9.

Source: Banque centrale des états de l'Afrique de l'ouest.

air force of 5,000. There were, in addition, 40,000 armed military police. In 1998 the UN Mission of Observers in Prevlaka, comprising 28 military monitors, was deployed in Croatia, with responsibility for supervising the demilitarization of the Prevlaka peninsula. Projected budgetary expenditure on defence by the central Government was estimated at 5,801.7m. kuna (12.0% of total spending) in 1999.

## Economic Affairs

In 1997, according to estimates by the World Bank, Croatia's gross national product (GNP), measured at average 1995–97 prices, was US $19,343m., equivalent to $4,060 per head. During 1990–97, according to estimates by the World Bank, Croatia's population neither increased nor declined. In 1998 estimated GNP was $20,700m. ($4,520 per head). Croatia's gross domestic product (GDP) declined, in real terms, at an average annual rate of 2.8% during 1990–97; however, GDP increased by 6.5% in 1997 and by an estimated 2.7% in 1998.

Agriculture (including forestry and fishing) contributed an estimated 8.5% of GDP in 1998. About 16.7% of the employed labour force were engaged in the sector in that year. The principal crops are maize, wheat and sugar beet. (However, the civil conflict, which began in 1991, destroyed much arable land.) The GDP of the agricultural sector declined, in real terms, at an average annual rate of 6.5% in 1990–95. Agricultural production declined by 7.9% in 1997, but increased by 6.1% in 1998.

Industry (including mining, manufacturing, construction and power) contributed an estimated 31.0% of GDP, and engaged 29.8% of the employed labour force, in 1998. In real terms, industrial GDP declined at an average rate of 13.3% per year during 1990–95. Industrial production (excluding construction) increased by 6.8% in 1997 and by 3.7% in 1998.

The mining sector contributed an estimated 0.5% of GDP, and engaged only 0.6% of the employed labour force, in 1998. Croatia has many exploitable mineral resources, including petroleum, coal and natural gas.

The manufacturing sector contributed an estimated 24.0% of GDP, and engaged 20.9% of the employed labour force, in 1998. In 1992 the principal branches of the manufacturing sector, measured by the value of output, were food products (accounting for 19.2% of the total), chemicals (12.8%), textiles and clothing (8.5%), transport equipment and electrical machinery. The output of the manufacturing sector declined at an average rate of 6.6% per year during 1990–98. However, it increased by 3.9% in 1997 and by 3.2% in 1998.

Approximately 30% of Croatia's electricity-generating capacity was destroyed in the civil conflict. Production of electricity declined by 21.3% in 1997, but increased by 13.5% in 1998. However, the country remains dependent on imported fuel, which accounted for some 7.1% of total imports in 1998.

Services provided an estimated 60.5% of GDP, and engaged 53.5% of the employed labour force, in 1998. The virtual elimination of tourism in Croatia (which in the late 1980s accounted for some 82% of Yugoslavia's total tourism trade) represented the largest war-related economic loss for Croatia. However, there was a significant recovery in the tourism sector in the 1990s, with total arrivals increasing by 100.2% in 1996, and by 44.7% in 1997. However, the conflict in the FRY in March–June 1999 severely disrupted regional tourism. In real terms, the GDP of services declined at an average annual rate of 3.3% in 1990–95 (but increased by 7.8% in 1995).

In 1998 Croatia recorded a visible trade deficit of US $4,160.7m., while there was a deficit of $1,543.4m. on the current account of the balance of payments. In 1998 the principal source of imports was Germany (19.3%); other major sources were Italy, Slovenia and Austria. The principal market for exports in that year was Italy (17.7%); other important purchasers were Germany, Bosnia and Herzegovina and Slovenia. The principal exports in 1998 were machinery and transport equipment, miscellaneous manufactured articles (particularly clothing and accessories), basic manufactures, and chemical products. The main imports in that year were machinery and transport equipment (most notably road vehicles), basic manufactures, miscellaneous manufactured articles, chemical products, foodstuffs and fuels (particularly petroleum and petroleum products).

Croatia's overall budget surplus for 1998 was 1,256.7m. kuna. The country's total external debt was US $6,842m. at the end of 1997, of which $4,217m. was long-term public debt. In that year the cost of debt-servicing was equivalent to 11.9% of the value of exports of goods and services. Consumer prices increased by an average of 124.7% per year in 1990–98. However, the average rate of inflation was only 6.4% in 1998 and 3.5% in 1999. At the end of 1999 the rate of unemployment was estimated at 20.2% of the labour force.

Croatia was admitted to the IMF in Janury 1993, and became a member of the European Bank for Reconstruction and Development (EBRD, see p. 168) in April of that year.

The outbreak of civil conflict in Croatia in the early 1990s resulted in a rapid deterioration of the economy. In 1993 the Government initiated a macro-economic programme, which achieved some success in slowing the rate of inflation and controlling public expenditure. The introduction of a new national currency, the kuna, in May 1994 rapidly restrained the rate of inflation. In October of that year the IMF extended its first stand-by loan to Croatia. The Government subsequently received reconstruction loans from other official creditors and concluded a rescheduling agreement with the 'Paris Club' of donor nations. In April 1996 an agreement was reached with the 'London Club' of commercial creditor banks, establishing Croatia's share of the foreign commercial bank debt incurred by the former Yugoslavia. In March 1997 the IMF approved a further three-year credit arrangement to support the Government's programme of economic reform. The introduction of a value-added tax system at the beginning of 1998 resulted in a substantial increase in government revenue, but contributed to a slowing in the rate of economic growth in that year (following a significant recovery in 1995–97). The conflict in Yugoslavia in March–June 1999 adversely affected Croatia's economy, particularly trade and tourism, and impeded efforts to attract foreign investment. Despite an acceleration of the privatization process in an attempt to increase budgetary revenue, industrial production declined by about 2% in 1999, while external debt remained high (with large instalments of repayments due over the subsequent three years). In addition, a severe lack of liquidity in the economy resulted in the failure of several banks in that year. Following the death of President Tudjman in December, however, a new coalition Government was elected (see Recent History), prompting expectations of economic reforms and improved relations with the US and Western European Governments (and consequently increased financial aid). In January 2000 the new Prime Minister announced plans to introduce measures for economic reconstruction, including a 17% reduction in budgetary expenditure, greater transparency in the privatization of state enterprises and banks, and further efforts to restrain the high rate of unemployment; he also pledged to reduce substantially salaries in government administration.

## Social Welfare

A state health service is available to all citizens. In 1992 there were 9,446 physicians, about 2,500 dentists and 1,747 pharmacists working in Croatia. Of total projected expenditure by the central Government in 1999, 9,862m. kuna (14.0%) was for health, and a further 26,599m. kuna (37.8%) for social security and welfare. Most government spending on social services is disbursed through extrabudgetary funds, principally the Health Insurance Fund and the Pension Fund.

## Education

Pre-school education, for children aged from three to six years, is available free of charge. Education is officially compulsory for eight years, between seven and 15 years of age. Primary education, which is provided free, begins at the age of seven and (since the 1995/96 academic year) lasts for four years. Enrolment at primary schools in 1996 was equivalent to 87% of children in the appropriate age-group (boys 87%; girls 86%). Special education in foreign languages is provided for children of non-Croat ethnic origin, since all national minorities in Croatia have the right to learn their minority language. Secondary education is available free (although private schools also exist) and lasts for up to eight years, comprising two cycles of four years each. There are various types of secondary school: grammar, technical and specialized schools and mixed-curriculum schools. Enrolment at secondary schools in 1995 was equivalent to 82% of the relevant age-group (boys 81%; girls 83%). In 1995 there were four universities in Croatia—in Zagreb, Rijeka, Osijek and Split. In 1998/99 a total of 91,874 students were enrolled in higher education establishments.

Projected budgetary expenditure on education by the central Government in 1999 was 5,743.2m. kuna (11.9% of total spending).

**Public Holidays**

**2000:** 1 January (New Year's Day), 6 January (Epiphany), 21 April (Good Friday), 24 April (Easter Monday), 1 May (Labour Day), 30 May (Independence Day), 22 June (Anti-Fascism Day), 5 August (National Day), 15 August (Assumption), 1 November (All Saints' Day), 25–26 December (Christmas).

**2001:** 1 January (New Year's Day), 6 January (Epiphany), 13 April (Good Friday), 16 April (Easter Monday), 1 May (Labour Day), 30 May (Independence Day), 22 June (Anti-Fascism Day), 5 August (National Day), 15 August (Assumption), 1 November (All Saints' Day), 25–26 December (Christmas).

**Weights and Measures**

The metric system is in force.

# Statistical Survey

Source (unless otherwise stated): Central Bureau of Statistics of the Republic of Croatia, 10000 Zagreb, Ilica 3; tel. (1) 4806111; fax (1) 4806148; e-mail ured@dzs.hr; internet www.dzs.hr.

## Area and Population

**AREA, POPULATION AND DENSITY**

| | |
|---|---|
| Area (sq km) | 56,542* |
| Population (census results) | |
| 31 March 1981 | 4,601,469 |
| 31 March 1991 | |
| Males | 2,318,623 |
| Females | 2,465,642 |
| Total | 4,784,265 |
| Population (official estimates at mid-year) | |
| 1996 | 4,494,000 |
| 1997 | 4,572,000 |
| 1998 | 4,501,000 |
| Density (per sq km) at mid-1998 | 79.6 |

* 21,831 sq miles.

**POPULATION BY ETHNIC GROUP** (census of 31 March 1991)

| | Number ('000) | % |
|---|---|---|
| Croat | 3,736.4 | 78.1 |
| Serb | 581.7 | 12.2 |
| Muslim | 43.5 | 0.9 |
| Slovene | 22.4 | 0.5 |
| Hungarian | 22.3 | 0.5 |
| Italian | 21.3 | 0.4 |
| Czech | 13.1 | 0.3 |
| Albanian | 12.0 | 0.3 |
| Montenegrin | 9.7 | 0.2 |
| Gypsy | 6.7 | 0.1 |
| Macedonian | 6.3 | 0.1 |
| Slovak | 5.6 | 0.1 |
| Others* | 303.3 | 6.3 |
| **Total** | 4,784.3 | 100.0 |

* Including (in '000) persons who declared themselves to be Yugoslav (106.0), persons with a regional affiliation (45.5), persons of unknown nationality (62.9) and persons who refused to reply (73.4).

**PRINCIPAL TOWNS** (population at 1991 census)

| | | | |
|---|---|---|---|
| Zagreb (capital) | 706,770 | Vukovar | 44,639 |
| Split | 189,388 | Varaždin | 41,846 |
| Rijeka | 167,964 | Šibenik | 41,012 |
| Osijek | 104,761 | Vinkovci | 35,347 |
| Zadar | 76,343 | Sesvete | 35,337 |
| Pula | 62,378 | Velika Gorica | 31,614 |
| Karlovac | 59,999 | Bjelovar | 26,926 |
| Slavonski Brod | 55,683 | Koprivnica | 24,238 |
| Dubrovnik | 49,728 | Požega | 21,046 |
| Sisak | 45,792 | Djakovo | 20,317 |

**BIRTHS, MARRIAGES AND DEATHS**

| | Registered live births | | Registered marriages | | Registered deaths | |
|---|---|---|---|---|---|---|
| | Number | Rate (per 1,000) | Number | Rate (per 1,000) | Number | Rate (per 1,000) |
| 1991 | 51,829 | 10.8 | 21,583 | 4.5 | 54,832 | 11.5 |
| 1992 | 46,970 | 10.5 | 22,169 | 4.9 | 51,800 | 11.6 |
| 1993 | 48,535 | 10.8 | 23,021 | 5.1 | 50,846 | 11.4 |
| 1994 | 48,584 | 10.9 | 23,966 | 5.3 | 49,482 | 11.1 |
| 1995 | 50,182 | 11.2 | 24,385 | 5.1 | 50,536 | 11.3 |
| 1996 | 53,811 | 12.0 | 24,596 | 5.5 | 50,636 | 11.3 |
| 1997 | 55,501 | 12.1 | 24,517 | 5.4 | 51,964 | 11.4 |
| 1998 | 47,068 | 10.5 | 24,243 | 5.4 | 52,311 | 11.6 |

**Expectation of life** (years at birth, 1991): Males 68.6; Females 76.0.

**EMPLOYMENT** (labour force surveys, '000 persons)

| | 1996* | 1997† | 1998‡ |
|---|---|---|---|
| Agriculture, hunting and forestry | 303.3 | 280.0 | 255.0 |
| Fishing | 2.7 | 3.1 | 2.7 |
| Mining and quarrying | 7.9 | 7.2 | 8.6 |
| Manufacturing | 318.5 | 343.1 | 323.3 |
| Electricity, gas and water supply | 26.3 | 29.8 | 28.6 |
| Construction | 95.7 | 90.5 | 98.9 |
| Wholesale and retail trade; repair of motor vehicles, motorcycles and personal and household goods | 204.5 | 210.5 | 206.1 |
| Hotels and restaurants | 74.1 | 81.3 | 82.4 |
| Transport, storage and communications | 98.8 | 108.1 | 110.5 |
| Financial intermediation | 35.0 | 32.5 | 32.8 |
| Real estate, renting and business activities | 49.2 | 55.2 | 60.5 |
| Public administration and defence; compulsory social security | 111.2 | 123.2 | 108.4 |
| Education | 74.4 | 78.6 | 75.3 |
| Health and social work | 85.0 | 89.3 | 92.5 |
| Other community, social and personal service activities | 49.0 | 49.8 | 52.0 |
| Private households with employed persons | 2.9 | 4.6 | 4.2 |
| Extra-territorial organizations and bodies | 1.8 | 6.2 | 2.0 |
| **Total employed** | 1,540.3 | 1,593.0 | 1,543.8 |
| Males | n.a. | 863.6 | 832.2 |
| Females | n.a. | 729.4 | 711.6 |

* November. † June. ‡ Annual average.

**Unemployed** (sample surveys, '000 persons): 170.2 in November 1996; 175.2 in June 1997; 193.5 in January–June 1998.

**Registered unemployed** (annual averages, '000 persons): 261.0 in 1996; 277.7 in 1997; 287.8 in 1998.

# Agriculture

**PRINCIPAL CROPS** ('000 metric tons)

| | 1996 | 1997 | 1998 |
|---|---|---|---|
| Wheat | 741 | 834 | 1,020 |
| Barley | 88 | 108 | 144 |
| Maize | 1,886 | 2,183 | 1,983 |
| Rye | 6 | 5 | 6 |
| Oats | 40 | 47 | 56 |
| Potatoes | 666 | 620 | 665 |
| Dry beans | 20 | 21 | 21 |
| Soybeans (Soya beans) | 36 | 39 | 77 |
| Sunflower seed | 29 | 36 | 62 |
| Rapeseed | 12 | 11 | 22 |
| Cabbages | 123 | 134 | 127 |
| Tomatoes | 49 | 48 | 81 |
| Cucumbers and gherkins* | 19 | 19 | 19 |
| Onions (fresh) | 39 | 44 | 50 |
| Garlic | 9* | 9 | 10 |
| Carrots | 20 | 20 | 27 |
| Watermelons and melons | 27 | 25 | 60 |
| Grapes | 373 | 406 | 421 |
| Sugar beet | 906 | 931 | 1,233 |
| Apples | 75 | 58 | 72 |
| Pears | 12 | 10 | 12 |
| Peaches and nectarines | 8 | 7 | 8 |
| Plums | 72 | 47 | 83 |
| Tobacco (leaves) | 11 | 11 | 12 |

* FAO estimate(s).

**LIVESTOCK** ('000 head, year ending September)

| | 1996 | 1997 | 1998 |
|---|---|---|---|
| Horses | 21 | 19 | 16 |
| Asses and mules* | 4 | 4 | 4 |
| Cattle | 462 | 451 | 443 |
| Pigs | 1,196 | 1,175 | 1,166 |
| Sheep | 427 | 453 | 427 |
| Goats | 105 | 100 | 100* |
| Chickens (million)† | 11 | 11 | 10 |

* FAO estimate(s). † Unofficial figure(s).

**LIVESTOCK PRODUCTS** ('000 metric tons)

| | 1996 | 1997 | 1998 |
|---|---|---|---|
| Beef and veal | 26 | 26 | 21 |
| Mutton and lamb | 2* | 2* | 2† |
| Pigmeat | 46 | 44 | 40 |
| Poultry meat | 36 | 36 | 30 |
| Cows' milk | 594 | 622 | 205 |
| Butter | 3 | 3 | 2 |
| Cheese (all kinds) | 20 | 22 | 19 |
| Hen eggs | 47 | 45 | 45† |
| Honey | 1 | 1 | 1† |

* Unofficial figures.

Source: mainly FAO, *Production Yearbook*.

# Forestry

**ROUNDWOOD REMOVALS** ('000 cubic metres)*

| | 1996 | 1997 | 1998 |
|---|---|---|---|
| Sawlogs and veneer logs | 1,326 | 1,404 | 2,105 |
| Pulpwood | 221 | 227 | |
| Other industrial wood | 162 | 203 | |
| Fuel wood | 831 | 900 | 874 |
| **Total** | 2,540 | 2,734 | 2,979 |

* From state-owned forests only.

**SAWNWOOD PRODUCTION** ('000 cubic metres)

| | 1996 | 1997 | 1998 |
|---|---|---|---|
| Coniferous (softwood) | 114 | 99 | 106 |
| Broadleaved (hardwood) | 483 | 462 | 424 |
| **Total** | 597 | 561 | 530 |

# Fishing

('000 metric tons, live weight)

| | 1996 | 1997 | 1998 |
|---|---|---|---|
| Freshwater fishes | 3.0 | 3.6 | 3.2 |
| Marine fishes | 15.5 | 14.5 | 21.6 |
| Crustaceans and molluscs | 1.8 | 2.2 | 3.1 |
| **Total catch** | 20.3 | 20.3 | 27.9 |

# Mining

('000 metric tons, unless otherwise indicated)

| | 1996 | 1997 | 1998 |
|---|---|---|---|
| Coal | 64 | 49 | 51 |
| Crude petroleum | 1,469 | 1,496 | 1,389 |
| Natural gas (million cu m) | 1,786 | 1,717 | 1,570 |

# Industry

**SELECTED PRODUCTS** ('000 metric tons, unless otherwise indicated)

| | 1996 | 1997 | 1998 |
|---|---|---|---|
| Beer ('000 hectolitres) | 3,292 | 3,607 | 3,759 |
| Spirits ('000 hectolitres) | 262 | 260 | 241 |
| Cigarettes (million) | 11,548 | 11,416 | 11,987 |
| Cotton fabric blankets ('000 sq metres) | 18,941 | 15,797 | 16,749 |
| Household linen ('000 sq metres) | 7,758 | 7,677 | 8,088 |
| Ready-to-wear clothing ('000 sq metres) | 28,597 | 26,643 | 26,640 |
| Leather footwear ('000 pairs) | 5,882 | 6,161 | 5,685 |
| Paper and cardboard | 134 | 171 | 158 |
| Cardboard packaging | 130 | 141 | 156 |
| Motor spirit (petrol) | 1,057 | 1,097 | 1,117 |
| Gas oil (distillate fuels) | 832 | 811 | 906 |
| Compound fertilizers | 516 | 537 | 458 |
| Synthetic materials and resin | 118 | 121 | 123 |
| Cement | 1,842 | 2,134 | 2,294 |
| Tractors (number) | 607 | 2,978 | 3,755 |
| Tankers ('000 gross registered tons) | 144 | 113 | 209 |
| Cargo ships ('000 gross registered tons) | 51 | 54 | 53 |
| Chairs ('000) | 793 | 668 | 675 |
| Electric energy (million kWh) | 11,465 | 9,028 | 10,244 |

# Finance

## CURRENCY AND EXCHANGE RATES

**Monetary Unit**
100 lipa = 1 kuna.

**Sterling, Dollar and Euro Equivalents** (30 September 1999)
£1 sterling = 11.936 kuna;
US $1 = 7.249 kuna;
€1 = 7.731 kuna;
1,000 kuna = £83.78 = $137.95 = €129.35.

**Average Exchange Rate** (kuna per US $)
1996 5.434
1997 6.101
1998 6.362

Note: The Croatian dinar was introduced on 23 December 1991, replacing (and initially at par with) the Yugoslav dinar. On 30 May 1994 the kuna, equivalent to 1,000 dinars, was introduced.

## STATE BUDGET (million kuna)

| Revenue | 1997 | 1998 | 1999* |
|---|---|---|---|
| Tax revenue | 31,775.5 | 40,327.5 | 38,317.6 |
| Taxes on personal income | 4,102.2 | 4,915.1 | 4,571.1 |
| Taxes on corporate income | 1,785.3 | 2,461.1 | 2,366.0 |
| General sales, turnover or value-added taxes | 15,133.2 | 22,200.3 | 20,217.9 |
| Excises | 5,369.3 | 5,768.0 | 6,011.3 |
| Excises on petroleum products | 2,728.3 | 3,169.8 | 3,433.0 |
| Excises on tobacco products | 2,000.0 | 1,983.4 | 1,969.9 |
| Customs duties | 4,640.0 | 4,127.5 | 4,287.9 |
| Other current revenue | 1,609.5 | 1,691.9 | 1,693.9 |
| Capital revenue | 461.1 | 1,789.2 | 6,268.3 |
| Proceeds of privatization | 143.8 | 1,432.4 | 6,036.4 |
| **Total** | 33,846.1 | 43,808.6 | 46,279.8 |

| Expenditure† | 1997 | 1998 | 1999‡ |
|---|---|---|---|
| General public services | 2,182.8 | 3,411.4 | 3,551.7 |
| Defence | 6,990.7 | 7,373.2 | 5,801.7 |
| Public order and safety | 4,169.9 | 4,251.5 | 4,431.1 |
| Education | 4,050.8 | 4,668.8 | 5,743.2 |
| Health | 184.8 | 816.8 | 802.7 |
| Social security and welfare | 6,452.0 | 8,024.6 | 10,815.7 |
| Housing and community amenities | 2,069.5 | 2,620.4 | 2,527.0 |
| Recreational, cultural and religious affairs | 539.5 | 576.6 | 835.4 |
| Agriculture, forestry and fisheries | 616.3 | 1,103.2 | 1,115.8 |
| Mining and mineral resources, manufacturing and construction | 692.8 | 728.9 | 2,639.0 |
| Transport and communications | 3,433.5 | 4,126.9 | 4,747.6 |
| Other economic affairs and services | 648.4 | 548.4 | 688.0 |
| Other purposes | 2,364.4 | 3,222.4 | 4,523.8 |
| **Total** | 34,395.2 | 41,473.2 | 48,223.4 |

* Preliminary figures.
† Excluding lending minus repayments (million kuna): 611.1 in 1997; 1,078.7 in 1998; 1,110.6 (projected) in 1999.
‡ Projected figures.
Source: Ministry of Finance.

## INTERNATIONAL RESERVES (US $ million at 31 December)

| | 1996 | 1997 | 1998 |
|---|---|---|---|
| IMF special drawing rights | 125.6 | 147.1 | 231.2 |
| Reserve position in IMF | — | 0.1 | 0.2 |
| Foreign exchange | 2,188.4 | 2,391.9 | 2,584.4 |
| **Total** | 2,314.0 | 2,539.1 | 2,815.7 |

Source: IMF, *International Financial Statistics*.

## MONEY SUPPLY (million kuna at 31 December)

| | 1996 | 1997 | 1998 |
|---|---|---|---|
| Currency outside banks | 4,366.2 | 5,319.6 | 5,730.1 |
| Demand deposits at deposit money banks | 6,997.2 | 8,404.8 | 7,782.8 |
| **Total** (incl. others) | 11,409.3 | 13,795.3 | 13,595.0 |

Source: IMF, *International Financial Statistics*.

## COST OF LIVING (Consumer price index; base: 1990 = 100)

| | 1997 | 1998 | 1999 |
|---|---|---|---|
| Food | 58,330.4 | 62,296.9 | 62,359.2 |
| Fuel and light | 55,319.2 | 56,646.9 | 57,949.8 |
| Clothing (incl. footwear) | 60,988.4 | 64,525.7 | 69,816.8 |
| Housing | 51,188.5 | 54,669.3 | 56,473.4 |
| **All items** (incl. others) | 61,075.7 | 64,984.5 | 67,259.0 |

## NATIONAL ACCOUNTS

**Gross Domestic Product by Economic Activity**
(million kuna at current prices)

| | 1996 | 1997 | 1998* |
|---|---|---|---|
| Agriculture, hunting and forestry | 8,887.4 | 9,471.2 | 9,673.6 |
| Fishing | 171.4 | 216.5 | 167.2 |
| Mining and quarrying | 234.9 | 645.9 | 616.3 |
| Manufacturing | 19,660.2 | 22,791.4 | 22,980.8 |
| Electricity, gas and water supply | 3,411.3 | 3,675.5 | 4,438.7 |
| Construction | 5,965.1 | 7,439.0 | 7,807.2 |
| Wholesale and retail trade; repair of motor vehicles, motorcycles and personal and household goods | 11,121.6 | 13,050.9 | 13,250.7 |
| Hotels and restaurants | 2,731.8 | 3,266.3 | 3,421.0 |
| Transport, storage and communications | 8,022.3 | 9,091.7 | 10,608.0 |
| Financial intermediation | 3,952.3 | 4,043.7 | 5,428.1 |
| Real estate, renting and business activities | 9,362.5 | 10,649.9 | 12,211.1 |
| Public administration and defence; compulsory social security | 8,241.9 | 9,548.7 | 11,877.7 |
| Education | 3,433.8 | 3,864.6 | 4,870.2 |
| Health and social work | 3,522.2 | 4,441.4 | 5,398.8 |
| Other community, social and personal service activities | 2,140.8 | 2,487.9 | 2,802.2 |
| Private households with employed persons | 20.7 | 24.7 | 37.2 |
| **Sub-total** | 90,880.4 | 104,707.2 | 115,588.9 |
| *Less* Financial intermediation services indirectly measured | 2,793.7 | 3,788.2 | 5,056.2 |
| **GDP at basic prices** | 88,086.7 | 100,918.9 | 110,532.7 |
| Taxes, *less* subsidies, on products | 19,893.9 | 22,891.8 | 27,859.0 |
| **GDP in purchasers' values** | 107,980.6 | 123,810.7 | 138,391.7 |

* Preliminary figures.

**BALANCE OF PAYMENTS** (US $ million)

| | 1996 | 1997 | 1998 |
|---|---|---|---|
| Exports of goods f.o.b. | 4,545.9 | 4,210.4 | 4,612.8 |
| Imports of goods f.o.b. | -8,235.7 | -9,434.7 | -8,773.5 |
| **Trade balance** | -3,689.8 | -5,224.3 | -4,160.7 |
| Exports of services | 3,296.8 | 4,010.9 | 3,964.0 |
| Imports of services | -1,717.1 | -1,979.9 | -1,889.2 |
| **Balance on goods and services** | -2,110.1 | -3,193.3 | -2,085.9 |
| Other income received | 269.9 | 364.9 | 394.9 |
| Other income paid | -339.5 | -385.9 | -560.2 |
| **Balance on goods, services and income** | -2,179.7 | -3,214.3 | -2,251.2 |
| Current transfers received | 1,183.2 | 966.1 | 921.1 |
| Current transfers paid | -150.8 | -94.5 | -213.3 |
| **Current balance** | -1,147.3 | -2,342.7 | -1,543.4 |
| Capital account (net) | 16.2 | 21.3 | 19.1 |
| Direct investment abroad | -24.4 | -185.3 | -92.4 |
| Direct investment from abroad | 533.3 | 486.9 | 872.9 |
| Portfolio investment assets | 6.2 | 11.2 | -0.1 |
| Portfolio investment liabilities | 625.2 | 653.4 | 25.3 |
| Other investment assets | 850.8 | 190.3 | 368.3 |
| Other investment liabilities | 1,081.3 | 1,942.2 | 458.0 |
| Net errors and omissions | -983.6 | -390.3 | 47.0 |
| **Overall balance** | 957.7 | 387.0 | 154.7 |

Source: IMF, *International Financial Statistics*.

# External Trade

**PRINCIPAL COMMODITIES** (distribution by SITC, US $ million)

| Imports c.i.f. | 1996 | 1997 | 1998 |
|---|---|---|---|
| **Food and live animals** | 767 | 832 | 675 |
| Vegetables and fruit | 194 | 178 | 151 |
| **Crude materials (inedible) except fuels** | 220 | 274 | 223 |
| **Mineral fuels, lubricants, etc.** | 857 | 850 | 596 |
| Petroleum and petroleum products | 707 | 672 | 394 |
| **Chemicals and related products** | 848 | 965 | 961 |
| Medicinal and pharmaceutical products | 188 | 185 | 200 |
| **Basic manufactures** | 1,384 | 1,515 | 1,398 |
| Paper, paperboard, etc. | 249 | 251 | 242 |
| Textile yarn, fabrics, etc. | 203 | 212 | 194 |
| Non-metallic mineral manufactures | 142 | 188 | 173 |
| Iron and steel | 257 | 285 | 247 |
| **Machinery and transport equipment** | 2,129 | 3,062 | 2,952 |
| Machinery specialized for particular industries | 318 | 381 | 324 |
| General industrial machinery, equipment and parts | 370 | 455 | 393 |
| Office machines and automatic data-processing equipment | 185 | 247 | 175 |
| Telecommunications and sound equipment | 162 | 251 | 171 |
| Other electrical machinery, apparatus, etc. | 399 | 427 | 380 |
| Road vehicles and parts (excl. tyres, engines and electrical parts) | 478 | 947 | 853 |
| **Miscellaneous manufactured articles** | 1,117 | 1,178 | 1,068 |
| Clothing and accessories (excl. footwear) | 286 | 271 | 257 |
| Footwear | 240 | 246 | 208 |
| **Total** (incl. others) | 7,788 | 9,104 | 8,383 |

| Exports f.o.b. | 1996 | 1997 | 1998 |
|---|---|---|---|
| **Food and live animals** | 411 | 385 | 385 |
| **Beverages and tobacco** | 92 | 121 | 111 |
| **Crude materials (inedible) except fuels** | 247 | 261 | 231 |
| Wood, lumber and cork | 166 | 168 | 157 |
| **Mineral fuels, lubricants, etc.** | 416 | 426 | 264 |
| Petroleum and petroleum products | 371 | 385 | 232 |
| **Chemicals and related products** | 643 | 570 | 545 |
| Medicinal and pharmaceutical products | 139 | 157 | 149 |
| Fertilizers (other than crude) | 118 | 87 | 76 |
| Plastics in primary forms | 209 | 171 | 176 |
| **Basic manufactures** | 594 | 589 | 584 |
| Paper, paperboard, etc. | 62 | 72 | 63 |
| Textile yarn, fabrics, etc. | 110 | 91 | 89 |
| Non-metallic mineral manufactures | 135 | 133 | 131 |
| **Machinery and transport equipment** | 964 | 752 | 1,380 |
| Telecommunications and sound equipment | 80 | 93 | 80 |
| Other electrical machinery, apparatus, etc. | 219 | 227 | 234 |
| Transport equipment (excl. road vehicles) | 410 | 165 | 771 |
| **Miscellaneous manufactured articles** | 1,133 | 1,049 | 1,023 |
| Furniture and parts | 120 | 125 | 107 |
| Clothing and accessories (excl. footwear) | 633 | 555 | 556 |
| Footwear | 235 | 226 | 199 |
| **Total** (incl. others) | 4,512 | 4,171 | 4,541 |

**PRINCIPAL TRADING PARTNERS** (US $ million)

| Imports c.i.f. | 1996 | 1997 | 1998 |
|---|---|---|---|
| Austria | 597 | 709 | 612 |
| Belgium | 100 | 96 | 110 |
| Bosnia and Herzegovina | 63 | 137 | 156 |
| Czech Republic | 207 | 208 | 181 |
| France | 199 | 293 | 401 |
| Germany | 1,602 | 1,841 | 1,616 |
| Hungary | 193 | 239 | 212 |
| Iran | 165 | 12 | 18 |
| Italy | 1,421 | 1,705 | 1,500 |
| Japan | 104 | 139 | 146 |
| Libya | 242 | 133 | 64 |
| Netherlands | 176 | 170 | 161 |
| Russia | 214 | 457 | 564 |
| Slovakia | 84 | 81 | 65 |
| Slovenia | 769 | 756 | 722 |
| Spain | 62 | 94 | 110 |
| Sweden | 117 | 147 | 109 |
| Switzerland | 144 | 213 | 181 |
| United Kingdom | 225 | 189 | 176 |
| USA | 213 | 266 | 278 |
| **Total** (incl. others) | 7,788 | 9,104 | 8,383 |

| Exports f.o.b. | 1996 | 1997 | 1998 |
|---|---|---|---|
| Austria | 198 | 223 | 247 |
| Bosnia and Herzegovina | 549 | 649 | 654 |
| France | 84 | 79 | 102 |
| Germany | 839 | 746 | 767 |
| Hungary | 55 | 48 | 52 |
| Italy | 949 | 787 | 802 |
| Liberia | 266 | 124 | 336 |
| Macedonia, former Yugoslav republic | 59 | 77 | 64 |
| Netherlands | 69 | 62 | 53 |
| Poland | 56 | 47 | 46 |
| Russia | 131 | 164 | 164 |
| Slovenia | 611 | 506 | 432 |
| United Kingdom | 70 | 67 | 71 |
| USA | 89 | 97 | 89 |
| **Total** (incl. others) | 4,512 | 4,171 | 4,541 |

# Transport

**RAILWAYS** (traffic)

| | 1996 | 1997 | 1998 |
|---|---|---|---|
| Passenger journeys ('000) | 17,375 | 17,003 | 17,102 |
| Passenger-kilometres (million) | 1,029 | 981 | 921 |
| Freight carried ('000 metric tons) | 11,061 | 12,168 | 12,643 |
| Freight net ton-km (million) | 1,717 | 1,876 | 2,001 |

**ROAD TRAFFIC** (registered motor vehicles at 31 December)

| | 1996 | 1997 | 1998 |
|---|---|---|---|
| Passenger cars | 835,714 | 932,278 | 1,000,052 |
| Buses | 4,596 | 4,771 | 4,814 |
| Lorries / Special vehicles | 87,028 | 101,051 | 106,634 |
| Motorcycles and mopeds | 31,917 | 42,178 | 50,538 |

**INLAND WATERWAYS** (vessels and traffic)

| | 1996 | 1997 | 1998 |
|---|---|---|---|
| Tugs | 25 | 25 | 27 |
| Motor barges | 2 | 3 | 3 |
| Barges | 105 | 101 | 95 |
| Goods unloaded (million metric tons) | 1 | 1 | 1 |

**SHIPPING**

**Merchant Fleet** (registered at 31 December)

| | 1996 | 1997 | 1998 |
|---|---|---|---|
| Number of vessels | 232 | 245 | 260 |
| Total displacement ('000 grt) | 579.8 | 871.0 | 896.4 |

Source: Lloyd's Register of Shipping, *World Fleet Statistics*.

**International Sea-borne Freight Traffic**

| | 1996 | 1997 | 1998 |
|---|---|---|---|
| Vessels entered (million gross reg. tons) | 18.1 | 21.5 | 24.4 |
| Goods loaded ('000 metric tons) | 2,543 | 2,458 | 2,373 |
| Goods unloaded ('000 metric tons) | 6,474 | 6,782 | 6,666 |
| Goods in transit ('000 metric tons) | 1,947 | 3,180 | 3,578 |

**CIVIL AVIATION**

| | 1996 | 1997 | 1998 |
|---|---|---|---|
| Kilometres flown ('000) | 11,092 | 11,083 | 12,100 |
| Passengers carried ('000) | 824 | 866 | 920 |
| Passenger-kilometres (million) | 597 | 546 | 624 |
| Freight carried (metric tons) | 5,167 | 4,696 | 5,215 |
| Ton-kilometres ('000) | 3,676 | 2,997 | 3,374 |

# Tourism

**FOREIGN TOURIST ARRIVALS BY COUNTRY OF ORIGIN** ('000)

| | 1996 | 1997 | 1998 |
|---|---|---|---|
| Austria | 342 | 447 | 457 |
| Czech Republic | 546 | 579 | 499 |
| France | 27 | 35 | 42 |
| Germany | 449 | 640 | 721 |
| Hungary | 85 | 127 | 138 |
| Italy | 467 | 688 | 751 |
| Netherlands | 42 | 65 | 88 |
| Slovakia | 84 | 154 | 162 |
| Slovenia | 438 | 578 | 638 |
| United Kingdom | 31 | 51 | 68 |
| **Total** (incl. others) | 2,650 | 3,834 | 4,112 |

**Receipts from tourism** (US $ million): 2,014 in 1996; 2,530 in 1997; 2,733 in 1998.

# Communications Media

| | 1996 | 1997 | 1998 |
|---|---|---|---|
| Radio licences ('000) | 999 | 1,032 | 1,098 |
| Television licences ('000) | 948 | 989 | 1,056 |
| Telephone subscribers ('000) | 1,358 | 1,477 | 1,573 |
| Book production: titles | 1,718 | 3,500 | 3,150 |
| Daily newspapers: Number | 8 | 10 | 11 |

**Non-daily newspapers** (1996): 767 (average circulation 584,000 copies).
**Other periodicals** (1990): 352 (average circulation 6,357,000 copies).
**Telefax stations** (number in use): 14,322 in 1993; 28,350 in 1994; 38,272 in 1995 (Source: UN, *Statistical Yearbook*).
**Mobile cellular telephones** (subscribers): 11,382 in 1993; 21,664 in 1994; 33,688 in 1995 (Source: UN, *Statistical Yearbook*).

# Education

(1998/99)

| | Institutions | Teachers | Students: Males | Students: Females | Students: Total |
|---|---|---|---|---|---|
| Pre-primary | 1,003 | 6,359 | 36,121 | 33,221 | 69,342 |
| Primary | 2,140 | 10,353 | 104,513 | 98,486 | 202,999 |
| Secondary: general | 1,120 | 19,821 | 129,283 | 135,980 | 265,263 |
| Secondary: vocational | 474 | 13,732 | 81,677 | 69,448 | 151,125 |
| University level* | 85 | 6,748 | 43,170 | 48,704 | 91,874 |

* Excluding post-graduate students.

# Directory

## The Constitution

The Constitution of the Republic of Croatia was promulgated on 21 December 1990. Croatia issued a declaration of dissociation from the Socialist Federal Republic of Yugoslavia in June 1991, and formal independence was proclaimed on 8 October 1991. Constitutional amendments, which were adopted in November 1997, included a prohibition on the re-establishment of a union of Yugoslav states.

The following is a summary of the main provisions of the Constitution:

### GENERAL PROVISIONS

The Republic of Croatia is a democratic, constitutional state where power belongs to the people and is exercised directly and through the elected representatives of popular sovereignty.

The Republic of Croatia is an integral state, while its sovereignty is inalienable, indivisible and non-transferable. State power in the Republic of Croatia is divided into legislative, executive and judicial power.

All citizens of the Republic of Croatia over the age of 18 years have the right to vote and to be candidates for election to public office. The right to vote is realized through direct elections, by secret ballot. Citizens of the Republic living outside its borders have the right to vote in elections for the Assembly and the President of the Republic.

In a state of war or when there is a direct threat to the independence and unity of the Republic, as well as in the case of serious natural disasters, some freedoms and rights that are guaranteed by the Constitution may be restricted. This is decided by the Assembly of the Republic of Croatia by a two-thirds majority of its deputies and, if the Assembly cannot be convened, by the President of the Republic.

### BASIC RIGHTS

The following rights are guaranteed and protected in the Republic: the right to life (the death sentence has been abolished), fundamental freedoms and privacy, equality before the law, the right to be presumed innocent until proven guilty and the principle of legality, the right to receive legal aid, the right to freedom of movement and residence, the right to seek asylum, inviolability of the home, freedom and secrecy of correspondence, safety and secrecy of personal data, freedom of thought and expression of opinion, freedom of conscience and religion (all religious communities are equal before the law and are separated from the State), the right of assembly and peaceful association, the right of ownership, entrepreneurship and free trade (monopolies are forbidden), the right to work and freedom of labour, the right to a nationality, the right to strike, and the right to a healthy environment.

Members of all peoples and minorities in the Republic enjoy equal rights. They are guaranteed the freedom to express their nationality, to use their language and alphabet and to enjoy cultural autonomy.

### GOVERNMENT

#### Legislature

Legislative power resides with the Assembly (Sabor), which consists of the 151-member Chamber of Representatives (Zastupnički dom), and the 68-member Chamber of Counties (Županijski dom).

The Chamber of Representatives decides on the adoption and amendment of the Constitution, approves laws, adopts the state budgets, decides on war and peace, decides on the alteration of the borders of the Republic, calls referendums, supervises the work of the Government and other public officials responsible to the Assembly, in accordance with the Constitution and the law, and deals with other matters determined by the Constitution.

The Chamber of Counties proposes laws and gives opinions on issues within the competence of the Chamber of Representatives; however, after the adoption of a law in the Chamber of Representatives, the Chamber of Counties may return the same law to the former for reconsideration. The citizens of each district elect, by direct and secret ballot, three deputies to the Chamber of Counties. A further five deputies are appointed by the President.

Members of the Chambers of the Assembly are elected by universal, direct and secret ballot for a term of four years, and their term is not mandatory. The Chambers of the Assembly may be dissolved, if the majority of all the deputies decides so, while the President of the Republic may, in accordance with the Constitution, dissolve the Chamber of Representatives.

#### President of the Republic

The President of the Republic is the Head of State of Croatia. The President represents the country at home and abroad and is responsible for ensuring respect for the Constitution, guaranteeing the existence and unity of the Republic and the regular functioning of state power. The President is elected directly for a term of five years.

The President determines elections for the Chambers of the Assembly, orders referendums, appoints and dismisses the Prime Minister, the Deputy Prime Ministers and members of the Government, appoints and recalls diplomatic representatives of the Republic and is the Supreme Commander of the Armed Forces of the Republic of Croatia. In the event of war or immediate danger, the President issues decrees having the force of law. The President may convene a meeting of the Government and place on its agenda items which, in his opinion, should be discussed. The President attends the Government's meetings and presides over them.

The President may dissolve the Chamber of Representatives, if it approves a vote of 'no confidence' in the Government or if it does not approve the state budget within a specified period.

#### Ministers

Executive power in the Republic resides with the President, the Prime Minister and the Ministers. The Government of the Republic consists of the Ministers and the Prime Minister. The Government issues decrees, proposes laws and the budget, and implements laws and regulations that have been adopted by the Assembly. In its work, the Government is responsible to the President of the Republic and the Chamber of Representatives.

### JUDICATURE

Judicial power is vested in the courts and is autonomous and independent. The courts issue judgments on the basis of the Constitution and the law. The Supreme Court is the highest court and is responsible for the uniform implementation of laws and equal rights of citizens. Judges and state public prosecutors are appointed and relieved of duty by the Judicial Council of the Republic, which is elected, from among distinguished lawyers, by the Chamber of Representatives for a term of eight years.

## The Government

(February 2000)

### HEAD OF STATE

**President of the Republic:** STIPE MESIĆ (elected 7 February 2000; inaugurated 18 February 2000).

**Office of the President:** 10000 Zagreb, Banski Dvori.

### GOVERNMENT

(February 2000)

A coalition of the Social Democratic Party (SDP), the Croatian Social-Liberal Party (CSLP), the Croatian People's Party (CPP), the Liberal Party (LP), the Croatian Peasants' Party and the Istrian Democratic Assembly (IDA).

**Prime Minister:** IVICA RAČAN (SDP).

**Deputy Prime Ministers:** GORAN GRANIĆ (CSLP), SLAVKO LINIĆ (SDP), ZELJKA ANTUNOVIĆ (SDP).

**Minister of Finance:** MATO CRKVENAC (SDP).

**Minister of Defence:** JOZO RADOS (CSLP).

**Minister of the Interior:** SIME LUCIN (SDP).

**Minister of Foreign Affairs:** TONINO PICULA (SDP).

**Minister of Immigration, Development and Reconstruction:** RADIMIR ČAČIĆ (Independent).

**Minister of the Economy:** GORANKO FIZULIĆ (CSLP).

**Minister of Croatian Homeland War Defenders:** IVICA PANDIĆ.

**Minister of Agriculture and Forestry:** BOZIDAR PANKRETIĆ (Croatian Peasants' Party).

**Minister of Transport and Telecommunications:** ALOJZ TUSEK (CSLP).

**Minister of Justice:** STJEPAN IVANISEVIĆ (SDP).

**Minister of Urban Development, Construction and Housing:** BOZO KOVACEVIĆ (LP).

**Minister of Education and Sport:** VLADIMIR STRUGAR (Croatian Peasants' Party).

**Minister of Labour and Social Welfare:** DAVORKO VIDOVIĆ (SDP).

**Minister of Tourism:** PAVE ZUPAN RUSKOVIĆ (Independent).

**Minister of Health:** MAJA STAVLJEVIĆ-RUKAVINA (Independent).

**Minister of Science and Technology:** HRVOJE KRALJEVIĆ (CSLP).

**Minister of Culture:** ANTUN VUJIĆ (SDP).

**Minister of European Integration:** IVAN JAKOVČIĆ (IDA).

**Minister of Small and Medium Businesses:** ZELJKO PECEK (CSLP).

### MINISTRIES

**Office of the Prime Minister:** Government of the Republic of Croatia, 10000 Zagreb, trg sv. Marka 2; tel. (1) 4569201; fax (1) 432041.

**Ministry of Agriculture and Forestry:** 10000 Zagreb, Ave. Vukovar 78; tel. (1) 6133444; fax (1) 442070.

**Ministry of Croatian Homeland War Defenders:** Zagreb.

**Ministry of Culture:** 10000 Zagreb, trg Burze 6; tel. (1) 4569000; fax (1) 410487.

**Ministry of Defence:** 10000 Zagreb, trg kralja Petra Krešimira IV 1; tel. (1) 4567111.

**Ministry of the Economy:** 10000 Zagreb, trg sv. Marka 2; tel. (1) 4569207; fax (1) 4550606.

**Ministry of Education and Sport:** 10000 Zagreb, trg Burze 6; tel. (1) 4569000; fax (1) 4569087.

**Ministry of European Integration:** 10000 Zagreb, trg sv. Marka 2; tel. (1) 4569222; fax (1) 432041.

**Ministry of Finance:** 10000 Zagreb, ul. Katančićeva 5; tel. (1) 4591333; fax (1) 432789; internet www.mfin.hr.

**Ministry of Foreign Affairs:** 10000 Zagreb, trg Nikole Šubića Zrinskog 7-8; tel. (1) 4569964; fax (1) 4569977.

**Ministry of Health:** 10000 Zagreb, ul. Baruna Tranka 6; tel. (1) 431068; fax (1) 431067.

**Ministry of Immigration, Development and Reconstruction:** Zagreb, Savska Cesta 41/12; tel. (1) 6176011; fax (1) 6176161; e-mail mpu@mpu.hr.

**Ministry of the Interior:** 10000 Zagreb, Savska cesta 39; tel. (1) 6122129.

**Ministry of Justice:** 10000 Zagreb, Savska cesta 41; tel. (1) 535935; fax (1) 536321.

**Ministry of Labour and Social Welfare:** 10000 Zagreb, Prisavlje 14; tel. (1) 6113337; fax (1) 6113593.

**Ministry of Small and Medium Businesses:** 10000 Zagreb, Gajeva 30A; tel. (1) 4569103; fax (1) 4569133.

**Ministry of Tourism:** 10000 Zagreb, Ave. Vukovar 78; tel. (1) 6106300; fax (1) 6109300; e-mail mthcei@mint.hr; internet www.mint.hr.

**Ministry of Transport and Telecommunications:** 10000 Zagreb, Prisavlje 14; tel. (1) 6169100; fax (1) 6196519.

**Ministry of Urban Development, Construction and Housing:** 10000 Zagreb, Republike Austrije 20; tel. (1) 3782444; fax (1) 3772822.

# President and Legislature

### PRESIDENT

**Presidential Election, First Ballot, 24 January 2000**

| | Votes | % of votes |
|---|---|---|
| STIPE MESIĆ* | 1,100,671 | 41.11 |
| DRAŽEN BUDIŠA† | 741,837 | 27.71 |
| DR MATE GRANIĆ (Croatian Democratic Union) | 601,588 | 22.47 |
| SLAVEN LETICA (Independent) | 110,782 | 4.14 |
| ANTE DJAPIĆ (Croatian Party of Rights) | 49,288 | 1.84 |
| ANTE LEDIĆ (Independent) | 22,875 | 0.85 |
| TOMISLAV MERCEP (Croatian People's Party) | 22,672 | 0.85 |
| ANTE PRKACIN (New Croatia) | 7,401 | 0.28 |
| DR ZVONIMIR ŠEPAROVIĆ (Independent) | 7,235 | 0.27 |
| **Total** | 2,664,349‡ | 100.00 |

* Candidate of the Croatian Peasants' Party, the Liberal Party, the Croatian People's Party and the Istrian Democratic Assembly.
† Candidate of the Social Democratic Party and the Croatian Social-Liberal Party.
‡ Excluding 13,212 invalid votes (0.49% of the total votes).

**Presidential Election, Second Ballot, 7 February 2000***

| | % of votes |
|---|---|
| STIPE MESIĆ† | 56.21 |
| DRAŽEN BUDIŠA‡ | 43.79 |
| **Total** | 100.00 |

* Preliminary results.
† Candidate of the Croatian Peasants' Party, the Liberal Party, the Croatian People's Party and the Istrian Democratic Assembly.
‡ Candidate of the Social Democratic Party and the Croatian Social-Liberal Party.

### SABOR
(Assembly)

**President:** ZLATKO TOMČIĆ; 10000 Zagreb, trg sv. Marka 617; tel. (1) 4569222; fax (1) 276483.

**Vice-Presidents:** MATO ARLOVIĆ, ZDRAVKO TOMAC, BALTAZAR JALSOVEC, VLATKO PAVLETIĆ, IVIĆ PASALIĆ.

#### Zastupnički dom
(Chamber of Representatives)

**President:** ZLATKO TOMČIĆ.

**Election, 3 January 2000**

| | % of votes | Seats |
|---|---|---|
| Social Democratic Party | 47.0 | 44 |
| Croatian Social-Liberal Party | | 24 |
| Primorian-Goranian Union | | 2 |
| Slavonian-Baranian Croatian Party | | 1 |
| Croatian Democratic Union | 30.5 | 45 |
| Croatian Peasants' Party | 15.9 | 16 |
| Istrian Democratic Assembly | | 4 |
| Liberal Party | | 2 |
| Croatian People's Party | | 2 |
| Croatian Social Democrats' Action | | 1 |
| Croatian Party of Rights | 3.3 | 5 |
| Croatian Christian Democratic Union | | 1 |
| **Total*** | 100.0 | 151 |

* Includes one representative of the Serbian National Party, one representative of the Hungarian Democratic Community of Croatia and two independent representatives of minorities.

#### Županijski dom
(Chamber of Counties)

**President:** KATICA IVANEŠEVIĆ.

**Election, 13 April 1997**

| Party | Seats |
|---|---|
| Croatian Democratic Union (CDU) | 41 |
| Croatian Peasants' Party (HSS) | 9 |
| Croatian Social-Liberal Party (CSLP) | 7 |
| Social Democratic Party (SDP) | 4 |
| Istrian Democratic Assembly (IDA) | 2 |
| **Total** | 63* |

* An additional five deputies, of whom two were members of the Serb community, were appointed by the President.

# Political Organizations

**Christian People's Party (CPP)** (Kršćanska Narodna Stranka—KNS): 10000 Zagreb, Degenova 7; tel. (1) 427258; fax (1) 273595; Pres. ZDRAVKO MRŠIĆ.

**Croatian Christian Democratic Union (CCDU)** (Hrvatska Kršćanska Demokratska Unija—HKDU): 10000 Zagreb; tel. (1) 327233; fax (1) 325190; Pres. IVAN CESAR.

**Croatian Democratic Party (CDP)** (Hrvatska Demokratska Stranka—HDS): 10000 Zagreb; tel. (1) 431837; Pres. MARKO VESELICA.

**Croatian Democratic Union (CDU)** (Hrvatska Demokratska Zajednica—HDZ): 10000 Zagreb, trg hrvatskih velikana 4; tel. (1) 4553000; fax (1) 4552600; f. 1989; Christian Democrat; Chair. VLADIMIR SEKS (acting); Sec.-Gen. JOSO SKARA.

**Croatian Independent Democrats (CID)** (Hrvatski Nezavisni Demokrati—HND): 10000 Zagreb; f. 1994 by a faction from the CDU.

**Croatian Muslim Democratic Party (CMDP)** (Hrvatska Muslimanska Demokratska Stranka—HMDS): 10000 Zagreb; tel. (1) 421562.

**Croatian Party of Rights (CPR)** (Hrvatska Stranka Prava—HSP): 10000 Zagreb, ul. Šenoina 13; tel. and fax (1) 4839938; e-mail hsp1861@hsp1861.hr; internet www.hsp1861.hr; f. 1861, re-established 1990; right-wing, nationalist; armed br. was the Croatian Defence Asscn or Hrvatske Obrambene Snage (HOS); Pres. DOBROSLAV PARAGA.

**Croatian Party of Slavonia and Baranja (CPSB)** (Slavonsko–Baranjska Hrvatska Stranka—SBHS): Osijek.

**Croatian Peasants' Party** (Hrvatska Seljačka Stranka—HSS): 10000 Zagreb, Trsnkoga 8; tel. (1) 212325; fax (1) 217411; Pres. ZLATKO TOMČIĆ.

**Croatian People's Party (CPP)** (Hrvatska Narodna Stranka—HNS): 10000 Zagreb, Ilica 61; tel. (1) 427888; fax (1) 273552; Pres. TOMISLAV MERCEP.

**Croatian Republican Party (CRP)** (Hrvatska Republikanska Stranka—HRS): 10000 Zagreb, Nalješkovićeva 11; tel. (1) 6153532; Pres. BORKO JURIN.

**Croatian Social Democrats' Action** (Akcija socijaldemokrata Hrvatske—ASH): Zagreb.

**Croatian Social-Liberal Party (CSLP)** (Hrvatska Socijalno-Liberalna Stranka—HSLS): 10000 Zagreb, trg N. Š. Zrinskog 17; tel. (1) 4810401; fax (1) 4810404; e-mail hsls@hsls.hr; internet www.hsls.hr; f. 1989; Pres. DRAŽEN BUDIŠA; Gen. Sec. JOZO RADOŠ.

**Dalmatian Action (DA)** (Dalmatinska Akcija): 21000 Split, Ulica bana Jelačića 4/I; tel. (21) 344322; f. 1990; Pres. Dr MIRA LJUBIĆ-LORGER.

**Independent Democratic Serb Party** (Samostalne Demokratska Srpska Stranka—SDSS): 32000 Vukovar, Radnički dom 1-3; tel. and fax (32) 665116; f. 1997 by Serbs in Eastern Slavonia; Pres. Dr VOJISLAV STANIMIROVIĆ.

**Istrian Democratic Assembly (IDA)** (Istarski Demokratski Sabor—IDS): Pula, Splitska 3; tel. (52) 223316; fax (52) 213702; e-mail ids-ddi@pu.tel.hr; internet www.ids-ddi.com; Pres. IVAN JAKOVČIĆ.

**Istrian People's Party (IPP)** (Istarska Pučka Stranka—IPS): Pula, trg revolucije 3; tel. (52) 23863; fax (52) 23832; Pres. JOSIP FABRIS.

**Liberal Party:** 10000 Zagreb; f. 1998 by a breakaway faction of the Croatian Social-Liberal Party; Pres. VLADO GOTOVAC.

**New Croatia:** Zagreb; Pres. ANTE PRKACIN.

**Party of Serbs:** 10000 Zagreb; f. 1993 by mems of Serb cultural asscn Prosveta (Enlightenment) and Serb Democratic Forum; promotes liberal, democratic values; Leader MILORAD PUPOVAĆ.

**Primorian-Goranian Union** (Primorski-Goranski Savez): Zagreb; regionalist.

**Rijeka Democratic Alliance (RDA)** (Riječki Demokratski Savez—RDS): 51000 Rijeka, Žrtava fašizma 29; tel. (51) 423713; Pres. NIKOLA IVANIŠ; Sec. FRANJO BUTORAC.

**Serb People's Party (SPP)** (Srpska Narodna Stranka—SNS): 10000 Zagreb, Mažuranića trg 3; tel. and fax (1) 451090; promotes cultural and individual rights for ethnic Serbs in Croatia; 4,500–5,000 mems; Pres. MILAN DUKIĆ.

**Slavonian-Baranian Croatian Party** (Slavonsko-baranjska hrvatska stranka): Zagreb.

**Social Democratic Party (SDP)** (Socijaldemokratska Partija Hrvatske—SPH): 10000 Zagreb, Iblerov trg 9; tel. (1) 519490; fax (1) 518249; formerly the ruling League of Communists of Croatia (Party of Democratic Reform), renamed as above in 1993; 20,000 mems; Chair. IVICA RAČAN.

**Social Democratic Union of Croatia (SDUC)** (Socijalno Demokratska Unija Hrvatske—SDUH): 10000 Zagreb, Tratinska 27; tel. and fax (1) 394055; f. 1992; Pres. VLADIMIR BEBIĆ.

**Socialist Party of Croatia (SPC)** (Socijalistička Stranka Hrvatske—SSH): 10000 Zagreb, Prisavlje 14; tel. (1) 517835; fax (1) 510235; Pres. ŽELJKO MAŽAR.

**Socialist Workers' Party of Croatia (SRPH):** 10000 Zagreb; f. 1997; Leader STIPE SUVAR.

# Diplomatic Representation

### EMBASSIES IN CROATIA

**Australia:** 10000 Zagreb, Kralja Zvonimira 43; tel. (1) 442885; fax (1) 410071.

**Austria:** 10000 Zagreb, Jabukovać 39; tel. (1) 427359; fax (1) 424065; e-mail austrijsko-veleposlanstvo@alf.tel.hr; Ambassador: RUDOLF BOGNER.

**Bosnia and Herzegovina:** 10000 Zagreb, Torbarova 9; tel. (1) 425899; fax (1) 4556177; Ambassador: HASAN MURATOVIĆ.

**Bulgaria:** 10000 Zagreb, Novi Gajeva 19; Chargé d'affaires: LYUBCHO TROHAROV.

**Canada:** 10000 Zagreb, Prilaz Djure Deželića; tel. (1) 4573223; fax (1) 4577913; e-mail canada@zg.tel.hr; Ambassador: GRAHAM N. GREEN.

**China, People's Republic:** 10000 Zagreb, Kvaternikova 111; tel. (1) 197277; Chargé d'affaires: GUAN YUSEN.

**Czech Republic:** 10000 Zagreb, Prilaz Djure Deželića 10; tel. (1) 430099; fax (1) 430121.

**Denmark:** 10000 Zagreb, Pantovčak 35; tel. (1) 3760536; fax (1) 3760535; e-mail danski-konzulat@zg.tel.hr.

**France:** 10000 Zagreb, Schlosserove stube 5; tel. (1) 272985; fax (1) 274923; Ambassador: JEAN-JACQUES GAILLARDE.

**Germany:** 10000 Zagreb, Ulica grada Vukovara 64; tel. (1) 6158105; fax (1) 6158103; Ambassador: VOLKER HAAK.

**Holy See:** 10000 Zagreb, Ksaverska cesta bb; tel. (1) 4554995; fax (1) 4554997; Apostolic Delegate: Most Rev. GIULIO EINAUDI, Titular Archbishop of Villamagna in Tripolitania.

**Hungary:** 10000 Zagreb, Krležin gvozd 11A; tel. (1) 4834990; fax (1) 4834998; Ambassador: GYÖRGY CSÓTI.

**Iran:** 10000 Zagreb, Pantovčak 125C; tel. (1) 4578981; fax (1) 4578987; Ambassador: KEYVAN IMANI.

**Israel:** 10000 Zagreb; Ambassador: NATAN MERON.

**Italy:** 10000 Zagreb, Medulićeva 22; tel. (1) 4846386; fax (1) 4846384; e-mail veleposlanstvo_italije@zg.tel.hr; Ambassador: FABIO PIGLIAPOCO.

**Korea, Republic:** 10000 Zagreb, III, Cvjetno naselje 7; tel. (1) 516662.

**Netherlands:** 10000 Zagreb, Medvečsak 56; tel. (1) 423959; fax (1) 424205; internet www.nlgovzag@zg.tel.hr; Chargé d'affaires: IDA L. VAN VELDHUIZEN ROTHENBÜCHER.

**Norway:** 10000 Zagreb, Petrinjska 9; Ambassador: KNUT MØRKVED.

**Panama:** 10000 Zagreb, Tribaljska 11/I; tel. (1) 325159.

**Poland:** 10000 Zagreb, Krležin Gvozd 3; tel. (1) 427759; fax (1) 420305; Ambassador: JERZY CHMIELEWSKI.

**Portugal:** 10000 Zagreb, trg hrvatskih velikana 3; tel. (1) 413921.

**Romania:** 10000 Zagreb, Becićeve 2; tel. (1) 436754; Ambassador: Dr VASILE LECA.

**Russia:** 10000 Zagreb, Bosanska 44; tel. (1) 3755038; fax (1) 3755040; Ambassador: (vacant).

**Slovakia:** 10000 Zagreb, Prilaz Djure Deželića 10; tel. (1) 4848941; fax (1) 4848942; e-mail velep-rep-slovacke-u-rh@zg.tel.hr; Ambassador JÁN PETRÍK.

**Slovenia:** 10000 Zagreb, Savska cesta 41/II; tel. (1) 517401; fax (1) 517837; Ambassador: MATIJA MALEŠIĆ.

**Sri Lanka:** 10000 Zagreb, trg Burze 1/I; tel. (1) 442687; fax (1) 442878.

**Sudan:** 10000 Zagreb, Andrlievićeva 21; tel. (1) 3777808; fax (1) 3777809; e-mail veleposlanstvo.republike-sudan@zg.tel.hr; Chargé d'affaires a.i.: OSAMA MOHAMED YASSAIN.

**Sweden:** 10000 Zagreb, Frankopanska 22; tel. (1) 422116; fax (1) 428244; Ambassador: INGEMAR BÖRJESSON.

**Switzerland:** 10000 Zagreb, Bogovićeva 3; tel. (1) 4810891; fax (1) 4810890; e-mail swiemzag@zg.tel.hr; Ambassador: PAUL WIDMER.

**Turkey:** 10000 Zagreb, Masarykova 3/II; tel. (1) 4855200; fax (1) 4855606; e-mail turembzag@zg.tel.hr; Ambassador: SELAHATTIN ALPAR.

**United Kingdom:** 10000 Zagreb, Vlaska 121; tel. (1) 4555310; fax (1) 4551685; e-mail british-embassy@zg.tel.hr; Ambassador: COLIN MUNRO.

**USA:** 10000 Zagreb, Andrije Hebranga 2; tel. (1) 4555500; fax (1) 440235; Ambassador: WILLIAM MONTGOMERY.

**Venezuela:** 10000 Zagreb, Strossmayera trg 11; tel. and fax (1) 423651.

**Yugoslavia:** 10000 Zagreb; Chargé d'affaires: VELJKO KNEZEVIĆ.

# Judicial System

The judicial system of Croatia is administered by the Ministry of Justice. The Supreme Court is the highest judicial body in the country, comprising 26 judges who are elected for a period of eight years by the Chamber of Municipalities at the proposal of the Chamber of Representatives. The Constitutional Court consists of 11 judges, elected for a period of eight years by the House of Representatives, on the proposal of the House of Counties.

**Public Prosecutor:** PETAR ŠALE.

**Public Attorney:** BERISLAV ŽIVKOVIĆ.

**Ombudsman:** 10000 Zagreb, Opatička 4; tel. (1) 4814893.

**Constitutional Court of Croatia:** 10000 Zagreb, Marka trg 4; tel. (1) 4851276; fax (1) 4550908; Pres. SMILJO SOKOL.

**Supreme Court:** 10000 Zagreb, trg Nikole Zrinskog 3; tel. (1) 4810036; fax (1) 4810035; Pres. MARIJAN HRANJSKI.

**Office of the Public Prosecutor:** 10000 Zagreb, Ulica Grada Vukovara 84; tel. (1) 6159042; fax (1) 6159055.

# Religion

Most of the population are Christian, the largest denomination being the Roman Catholic Church, of which most ethnic Croats are adherents. The Archbishop of Zagreb is the most senior Roman Catholic prelate in Croatia. The Croatian Old Catholic Church does not acknowledge the authority of Rome or the papal reforms of the 19th century. There is a significant Serbian Orthodox minority. According to the 1991 census, 76.5% of the population of Croatia were Roman Catholics, 11.1% were Serbian Orthodox, 1.2% Muslims and there were small communities of Protestants and Jews.

## CHRISTIANITY

### The Roman Catholic Church

For ecclesiastical purposes, Croatia comprises four archdioceses (including one, Zadar, directly responsible to the Holy See) and nine dioceses (including one for Catholics of the Byzantine rite). At 31 December 1997 there were an estimated 3.8m. adherents.

*Latin Rite*

**Bishops' Conference:** 10000 Zagreb, Kaptol 22; tel. (1) 4811893; fax (1) 4811894; f. 1993; Pres. Mgr JOSIP BOZANIĆ, Archbishop of Zagreb.

**Archbishop of Rijeka-Senj:** Dr ANTON TAMARUT, Nadbiskupski Ordinarijat, 51000 Rijeka, Slaviše Vajnera Čiče 2; tel. (51) 337999; fax (51) 215287.

**Archbishop of Split-Makarska:** ANTE JURIĆ, 21001 Split, pp 328, ul. Zrinjsko-Frankopanska 14; tel. (21) 319515; fax (21) 319522.

**Archbishop of Zadar:** IVAN PRENDJA, Nadbiskupski Ordinarijat, 23000 Zadar, Zeleni trg 1; tel. (23) 315712; fax (23) 316299.

**Archbishop of Zagreb:** JOSIP BOZANIĆ, 10001 Zagreb, pp 553, Kaptol 31; tel. (1) 4894802; fax (1) 4816094.

*Byzantine Rite*

**Bishop of Križevci:** SLAVOMIR MIKLOVŠ, Ordinarijat Križevačke Eparhije, 10000 Zagreb, Kaptol 20; tel. (1) 270767; 48,975 adherents (1993).

### Old Catholic Church

**Croatian Catholic Church:** Hrvatska Katolička Crkva Ordinariat, 10000 Zagreb, ul. Kneza Branimirova 11; tel. (1) 275224; f. 894, re-established 1923; Archbishop MIHOVIL DUBRAVČIĆ.

### Serbian Orthodox Church

**Metropolitan of Zagreb and Ljubljana:** Bishop JOVAN, Srpska Biskupija, 10000 Zagreb.

# The Press

## PRINCIPAL DAILIES

### Osijek

**Glas Slavonije:** 31000 Osijek, Hrvatske Republike 20; tel. (31) 223200; fax (31) 223203; e-mail glas@glas-slavonije.tel.hr; morning; independent; Editor SANJA MARKETIĆ; circ. 25,000.

### Pula

**Glas Istre:** 52100 Pula, Riva 10; tel. (52) 212969; fax (52) 211434; morning; Dir ŽELJKO ŽMAK; circ. 20,000.

### Rijeka

**Novi List:** 51000 Rijeka, POB 130, Zvonimirova 20A; tel. (51) 32122; fax (51) 213654; morning; Editor VELJKO VICEVIĆ; circ. 60,000.

**La Voce del Popolo:** 51000 Rijeka, Zvonimirova 20A; tel. (51) 211154; fax (51) 213528; f. 1944; morning; Italian; Editor RODOLFO SEGNAN; circ. 4,000.

### Split

**Nedjeljna Dalmacija:** 21000 Split, Gundulićeva 23; tel. (21) 362821; fax (21) 362526; f. 1972; weekly; politics and culture; Editor DRAŽEN GUDIĆ; circ. 45,000.

**Slobodna Dalmacija:** 21000 Split, ul. Hrvatske mornarice 4; tel. (21) 513888; fax (21) 551220; morning; Editor JOSIP JOVIĆ; circ. 102,000.

### Zagreb

**Nedjeljna Dalmacija:** 10000 Zagreb, Ilica 24/II; tel. (1) 433716; fax (1) 433916; f. 1972; weekly; politics and culture; Editor-in-chief DUBRAVKO GRAKALIĆ; circ. 45,000.

**Novi Vjesnik:** 10000 Zagreb, Slavonska Ave. 4; tel. (1) 333333; fax (1) 341650; f. 1940; morning; Editor RADOVAN STIPETIĆ; circ. 45,000.

**Sportske novosti:** 10000 Zagreb, Slavonska Ave. 4; tel. (1) 341920; fax (1) 341950; morning; Editor DARKO TIRONI; circ. 55,000.

**Večernji list:** 10000 Zagreb, Slavonska Ave. 4; tel. (1) 6500600; fax (1) 6500676; evening; Editor BRANKO TUDEN; circ. 200,000.

**Vjesnik:** 10000 Zagreb, Slavonska Ave. 4, POB 104; tel. (1) 342760; fax (1) 341602; morning; Editor IGOR MANDIĆ; circ. 50,000.

## PERIODICALS

**Arena:** 10000 Zagreb, Slavonska Ave. 4; tel. (1) 6162795; fax (1) 6161572; e-mail arena@eph.hr; f. 1957; illustrated weekly; Editor MLADEN GEROVAĆ; circ. 135,000.

**Feral Tribune:** 21000 Split; weekly; satirical; Editor VIKTOR IVANCIĆ.

**Glasnik:** 10000 Zagreb, trg hrvatskih velikana 4; tel. (1) 453000; fax (1) 453752; fortnightly; Editor ZDRAVKO GAVRAN; circ. 9,000.

**Globus:** 10000 Zagreb, Slavonska Ave. 4; tel. (1) 6162057; fax (1) 6162058; e-mail globus@eph.hr; f. 1990; political weekly; Editor MIRKO GALIĆ; circ. 110,000.

**Gloria:** 10000 Zagreb, Slavonska Ave. 4; tel. (1) 6161288; fax (1) 6182042; e-mail gloria@eph.hr; weekly; Editor DUBRAVKA TOMEKOVIĆ-ARALICA: circ. 110,000.

**Informator:** 10000 Zagreb, Masarykova 1; tel. (1) 429222; fax (1) 424904; f. 1950; economic and legal matters; Dir Dr IVO BURIĆ.

**Mila:** 10000 Zagreb, Slavonska Ave. 4; tel. (1) 6161982; fax (1) 6162021; e-mail mila@eph.hr; weekly; Editor ZOJA PADOVAN; circ. 110,000.

**Nacionalni Oglasnik:** 10000 Zagreb, Slavonska Ave. 4; tel. (1) 6162061; fax (1) 6161541; weekly; Editor IVO PUKANIĆ; circ. 55,000.

**OK: Croatia:** 10000 Zagreb, Slavonska Ave. 4; tel. 6162127; fax (1) 6162125; e-mail ok@eph.hr; f. 1989; illustrated monthly; Editor NEVEN KEPESKI; circ. 55,000.

**Privredni vjesnik:** 10000 Zagreb, Kačićeva 9A; tel. (1) 422182; fax (1) 422100; f. 1953; weekly; economic; Man. ANTE GAVRANOVIĆ; Editor-in-Chief FRANJO ŽILIĆ; circ. 10,000.

**Republika:** 10000 Zagreb, trg bana Josipa Jelačića; tel. (1) 274211; fax (1) 434790; f. 1945; monthly; published by Društvo hrvatskih književnika; literary review; Editor-in-Chief VELIMIR VISKOVIĆ.

**Studio:** 10000 Zagreb, Slavonska Ave. 4; tel. (1) 6162085; fax (1) 6162031; e-mail studio@eph.hr; f.1964; illustrated weekly; Editor ROBERT NAPRTA; circ. 45,000.

**Vikend:** 10000 Zagreb, Slavonska Ave. 4; tel. and fax (1) 6162064; 2 a week; Editor JOSIP MUŠNJAK; circ. 50,000.

## NEWS AGENCIES

**HINA News Agency:** 10000 Zagreb, Marulićev trg 16; tel. (1) 4808700; fax (1) 4808820; e-mail newsline@hina.hr; internet www.hina.hr; f. 1990; Man. LJUBOMIR ANTIĆ.

**IKA** (Catholic Information Agency): 10000 Zagreb, Kaptol 4; tel. (1) 4814951; fax (1) 4814957; e-mail ika-zg@zg.tel.hr; internet www.ofm.hr; Man. Editor ANTON ŠULJIĆ.

# Publishers

**AGM Publisher:** 10000 Zagreb, Mihanovićeva 28; tel. (1) 4856307; fax (1) 4856316; Croatian and foreign literature, arts, economics, science; Gen. Dir BOŽE ČOVIĆ.

**Algoritam:** 10000 Zagreb, Gajeva 12; tel. (1) 4803333; fax (1) 271541; e-mail mm@algoritam.hr; international bestsellers; Pres. NEVEN ANTIČEVIĆ.

**August Cesarec:** 10000 Zagreb, Prilaz Gjure Deželića 57; tel. (1) 171071; fax (1) 573695; Croatian and foreign literature.

**Books Trade and Services (BTS)—Knjiga Trgovina:** 10000 Zagreb, Donji prečac 19; tel. (1) 4554921; fax (1) 4554924; e-mail bts@zg.tel.hr; imports and exports publications; Gen. Man. BRANKO VUKOVIĆ.

**Ceres:** 10000 Zagreb, Tomašićeva 13; tel. (1) 4558501; fax (1) 4550387; e-mail ceres@zg.tel.hr; internet www.ceres.hr; poetry, fiction, and philosophical and scientific writings; Gen. Dir DRAGUTIN DUMANČIĆ.

**Erasmus Publishing:** 10000 Zagreb, Rakušina 4; tel. and fax (1) 433114; Croatian literature; Gen. Dir SREĆKO LIPOVČAN.

**Europa Press:** 10000 Zagreb, Slavonska Ave. 4; tel. (1) 6190011; fax (1) 6190033; Dir MARJAN JURLEKA.

**Hena Com:** 10000 Zagreb, Horvaćanska 65; tel. and fax (1) 3694136; childrens' books; Gen. Man. UZEIR HUSKOVIĆ.

**Hrvatska Akademija Znanosti i Umjetnosti:** 10000 Zagreb, Zrinski trg 11; tel. (1) 4819983; fax (1) 4819979; e-mail kabpred@ mahazu.hazu.hr; f. 1861; publishing dept of the Croatian Academy of Sciences and Arts; Pres. Dr Ivo Padovan.

**Izvori:** 10000 Zagreb, Trnjanska 64; tel. and fax (1) 6112576; e-mail izvori@iname.com; internet www.bakal.hr/izvori; scientific journalism, literature, comic books.

**Kršćanska Sadašnjost:** 10001 Zagreb, PB 434, Marulićev trg 14; tel. (1) 4828219; fax (1) 4828227; e-mail ks@zg.tel.hr; internet www.ks.hr; theological publications.

**Leksikografski zavod 'Miroslav Krleža' (Miroslav Krleža Lexicographic Institute):** 10000 Zagreb, Frankopanska 26; tel. (1) 4800333; fax (1) 4800399; f. 1951; encyclopedias, bibliographies and dictionaries; Pres. Dalibor Brozović.

**Masmedia:** 10000 Zagreb, Ulica baruna Trenka 13; tel. (1) 4577400; fax (1) 4577769; e-mail masmedia@zg.tel.hr; business and professional literature; Gen. Dir Stjepan Andrašić.

**Matica Hrvatska** (Matrix Croatica): 10000 Zagreb, Strossmayerov trg 2; tel. (1) 4819310; fax (1) 4819319; arts and science; Pres. Prof. Josip Bratulić.

**Mladost:** 10000 Zagreb, Ilica 30; tel. (1) 453222; fax (1) 434878; f. 1947; fiction, science, art, children's books; Gen. Dir Branko Vuković.

**Mosta:** 10000 Zagreb, Majevička 12a; tel. (1) 325196; fax (1) 327898; popular fiction; Gen. Dir Nladimir Vućur.

**Mozaik Knjiga:** 10000 Zagreb, Tomićeva 5a; tel. (1) 425011; fax (11) 431291; educational books; Gen. Dir Nives Tomašević.

**Nakladni zavod Matice hrvatske:** 10000 Zagreb, Nova ves 5; tel. (1) 4812422; fax (1) 4819317; e-mail nzm@zg.tel.hr; f. 1960; fiction, popular science, politics, economics, sociology, history; Dir Niko Vidović.

**Naprijed:** 10000 Zagreb, POB 1029, trg bana Jelacica 17; tel. (1) 432026; fax (1) 426897; e-mail naklada-napried@zg.tel.hr; f. 1946; philosophy, psychology, religion, sociology, medicine, dictionaries, children's books, art, politics, economics, tourist guides; Dir Zdenko Ljevak.

**Naša Djeca:** 10000 Zagreb, Gundulićeva 40; tel. (1) 423046; fax (1) 430613; picture books, postcards, etc.; Dir Prof. Drago Kozina.

**Nip Školske Novine:** 10000 Zagreb, Hebranga 40; tel. (1) 4855709; fax (1) 4855712; education, religion, poetry, textbooks; Gen. Man. Ivan Rodić.

**Sims:** 10000 Zagreb, Ive Tijardovića 4; tel. (1) 3880500; fax (1) 3880731; e-mail info@sims-hr.com; internet www.simshr .com; exports Croatian and foreign language books; Gen. Man. Ivan Matijević.

**Školska Knjiga:** 10001 Zagreb, POB 1039, Masarykova 28; tel. (1) 420784; fax (1) 430260; e-mail skolska@skolskaknjiga.hr; education, textbooks, art; Dir Dr Dragomir Maderić.

**Tehnička Knjiga:** 10000 Zagreb, Jurišičeva 10; tel. (1) 278172; fax (1) 423611; f. 1947; technical literature, popular science, reference books; Gen. Man. Zvonimir Vistrička.

**Verbum:** 21000 Split, Kraj zlatnih vrata 1; tel. and fax (21) 356770; e-mail verbum@st.tel.hr; religion, philosophy and humanism; Gen. Man. Miro Radalj.

**Znanje:** 10000 Zagreb, Zvonimirova 17; tel. (1) 4551500; fax (1) 4553652; e-mail znanje@zg.tel.hr; f. 1946; popular science, agriculture, fiction, poetry, essays; Pres. Žarko Šepetavić; Dir Branko Jazbec.

### PUBLISHERS' ASSOCIATION

**Croatian Publishers' and Authors' Business Union** (Poslovna Zajednica Izdavača i Knjižara Hrvatske): 10000 Zagreb, Klaićeva 7; fax (1) 171624.

## Broadcasting and Communications

### TELECOMMUNICATIONS

**Croatian Telecommunications (Hrvatske Telekomunikacije—HT):** 10000 Zagreb, Jurišićeva 13; tel. (1) 435435; fax (1) 429000; f. 1987; 35% owned by Deutsche Telekom (Germany); Pres. Ivica Mudrinić.

### BROADCASTING

**Croatian Radio and Television** (Hrvatska Radiotelevizija—HRT): 10000 Zagreb, Dezmanova 10; tel. (1) 276338; fax (1) 424654; govt-owned; Chair. Zacko Canjuga.

#### Radio

**Croatian Radio:** 10000 Zagreb, HRT House, Prisavlje 3; tel. (1) 6163280; fax (1) 6163285; f. 1926; 3 radio stations; 7 regional stations (Sljeme, Osijek, Pula, Rijeka, Split, Zadar and Dubrovnik); broadcasts in Serbo-Croat; Dir Tomislav Bakarić.

**Radio 101:** Zagreb; independent radio station; Editor-in-Chief Zrinka Vrabec-Mojzes.

**Radio Baranja:** Beli Manastir; independent radio station; Dir Karolj Janesi.

**Vaš Otvoreni Radio:** 10000 Zagreb, Radnička cesta 27; tel. (1) 6154805; fax (1) 6154802; broadcasts nationwide.

#### Television

**Croatian Television:** 10000 Zagreb, Prisavlje bb; tel. (1) 6163366; fax (1) 6163692; internet www.hrt.hr; f. 1956; 3 channels; broadcasts in Serbo-Croat; Head of TV Ivan Vrkić; Editor-in-Chief Obrad Kosovac.

## Finance

A new currency, the kuna (equivalent to 1,000 Croatian dinars), was introduced on 30 May 1994.

(d.d. = dioničko društvo (joint-stock company); cap. = capital; res = reserves; dep. = deposits; m. = million; amounts in kuna, unless otherwise indicated; HRD = Croatian dinars; brs = branches)

### BANKING

#### Central Bank

**National Bank of Croatia:** 10000 Zagreb, trg burze 3; tel. (1) 4564555; fax (1) 4550726; e-mail webmaster@hnb.hr; internet www.hnb.hr; in 1991 it assumed the responsibilities of a central bank empowered as the republic's bank of issue; cap. and res 2,898.2m., dep. 8,449.3m. (Dec. 1998); Gov. Marko Škreb.

#### Selected Banks

**Bjelovarska Banka d.d., Bjelovar:** 43000 Bjelovar, POB 68, Jurja Haulika 19a; tel. (43) 275101; fax 242361; e-mail bjelovarska-banka @bj.tel.hr; f. 1961; cap. 176.2m., res 51.5m., dep. 606.6m. (Dec. 1998); Pres. Petar Radaković.

**Croatia Banka d.d.:** 10000 Zagreb, Kvaternikov trg 9; tel. (1) 2391111; fax (1) 2332470; internet www.open.hr/com/crobanka/; f. 1989; cap. 171.7m., res 31.1m., dep. 1,814.8m. (Sept. 1997); Chair. Ivan Tarle; 29 brs.

**Croatian Bank for Reconstruction and Development** (Hrvatska Banka za Obnovu i Razvoj—HBOR): 10000 Zagreb, Gajeva 30a; tel. (1) 4569106; fax (1) 5569166; f. 1995; Dir Anton Kovačev.

**Dalmatinska Banka d.d., Zadar:** 23000 Zadar, trg sv. Stošije 3; tel. (23) 311311; fax (23) 437867; e-mail dbz@dbz.hr; internet www.dbz.hr; f. 1957; 79% privately-owned; cap. 208.0m., res 69.8m., dep. 1,917.0m. (1998); Chair. Zdravko Bubalo; 2 brs.

**Dubrovačka Banka d.d., Dubrovnik** (Bank of Dubrovnik): 20000 Dubrovnik, put Republike 9; tel. (20) 356333; fax (20) 356778; e-mail dubank@dubank.hr; internet www.dubank.hr; f. 1955; cap. US $29.6m., res $5.3m., dep. $332.0m. (Dec. 1998); CEO Niko Koncul.

**Glumina Banka d.d., Zagreb:** 10000 Zagreb, POB 215, Trpinjska 9; tel. (1) 2394444; fax (1) 2395706; e-mail gpries@open.hr; f. 1994; cap. 185.1m., res 3.0m., dep. 1,064.4m. (Dec. 1996); Chair. Marko Marčinko.

**Hrvatska Gospodarska Banka d.d., Zagreb:** 10000 Zagreb, Metalčeva 5; tel. (1) 3651888; fax (1) 3651819; e-mail sanja .zagajsek@hgb.tel.hr; f. 1992; cap. 65.0m., res 4.1m., dep. 610.3m. (Dec. 1997); Chair. Željko Šupe.

**Istarska Kreditna Banka Umag d.d.:** 52470 Umag, Ernesta Miloša 1; tel. (52) 741622; fax (52) 741275; e-mail ikb-marketing @ikb-umag.tel.hr; f. 1956; commercial and joint-stock bank; cap. 64.9m., res 15.6m., dep. 445.3m. (Dec. 1998); Chair. Miro Dodić; 14 brs.

**Kreditna Banka Zagreb d.d.:** 10000 Zagreb, Ulica grada Vukovara 74; tel. (1) 6167333; fax (1) 6117666; e-mail kbz-forex@kbz.hr; internet www.kbz.hr/kbz; f. 1994; cap. 156.5m., res 20.6m. (Dec. 1997); Pres. Ante Todorić.

**Medimurska Banka d.d., Čakovec;** 40000 Čakovec, Valenta Morandinija 37; tel. (40) 370676; fax (40) 314610; e-mail ljhorvst@ open.hr; internet www.open.hr/com.mb; f. 1954; cap. 125.1m., res 24.9m., dep. 893.9m. (June 1999); Gen. Man Mašan Sredanović.

**Podravska Banka dd:** 48000 Koprivnica, Opaticka la; tel. (48) 622193; fax (48) 622542; e-mail podravska-banka1@podravska -banka.tel.hr; cap. 62.9m., res 49.9m., dep. 342.8m. (Dec. 1998); Pres. Julio Kurac.

**Privredna Banka Zagreb d.d.:** 10000 Zagreb, POB 1032, Račkoga 6; tel. (1) 4550822; fax (1) 4610447; e-mail pbz@pbz.hr; internet www.pbz.hr; f. 1966; commercial bank; cap. 1,666m., res 33m., dep. 7,713m. (Dec. 1997); CEO Bozo Prka; 28 brs.

**Raiffeisenbank Austria d.d.:** 10000 Zagreb, POB 651, Petrinjska ulica 59; tel. (1) 4566466; fax (1) 4811624; e-mail ihrakud@rba-zagreb.raiffeisen.at; internet www.tel.hr/ba; cap. 215.0m., res 3.8m., dep. 1,008.8m. (Dec. 1998); Chair. ZDENKO ADROVIĆ.

**Riječka Banka d.d.:** 51000 Rijeka, POB 300, trg Jadranski 3A; tel. (51) 208211; fax (51) 330525; e-mail dkurpis1@alf.tel.hr; internet www.multilink.hr/ribri; f. 1954 as Komunalna banka i štedionica, renamed 1967; cap. 305.4m., res 140.5m., dep. 4,013.5m. (Dec. 1998); Chair. IVAN ŠTOKIĆ; 18 brs.

**Sisačka Banka d.d.:** 44000 Sisak, trg Ljudevita Posavskog 1; tel. (44) 549100; fax (44) 549101; e-mail savia@sibank.hr; internet www.sibank.hr/sibank; f. 1957; cap. 93.1m., res 23.4m., dep. 341.5m. (Dec. 1998); Pres. DINKO PINTARIĆ.

**Slavonska Banka d.d., Osijek** (Bank of Slavonia): 31000 Osijek, POB 108, Kapucinska 29; tel. (31) 231231; fax (31) 127125; e-mail sbo@slavonska-banka.tel.hr; internet www.slbo.hr; f. 1989; cap. 149.2m., res 110.4m., dep. 1,011.9m. (Dec. 1998); Pres. IVAN MIHALJEVIĆ; 9 brs.

**Splitska Banka dd. Split:** 21000 Split, Boškovića 16; tel. (21) 370516; fax (21) 370541; internet www.splitskabanka.hr; f. 1966; cap. 320.0m., res 64.9m., dep. 4,769.1m. (Dec. 1998); Man. Dir TOMO BOLOTIN.

**Trgovačka Banka d.d.:** 10000 Zagreb, Varšavska 3–5; tel. (1) 4561999; fax (1) 4561900; e-mail trg-banka@trg-banka.hr; internet www.trg-banka.hr; f. 1990; cap. 71.6m., res 35.6m., dep. 209.3m. (Dec. 1998); Pres. BRANKO KONDIĆ; CEO BORIS NINIĆ.

**Varaždinska Banka d.d.:** 42000 Varaždin, POB 95, Kapucinski trg 5; tel. (42) 106200; fax (42) 106146; internet www.banka.hr; f. 1869, adopted current name 1981; cap. 177.6m., res 14.5m., dep. 1,671.7m. (Dec. 1998); Pres. MATO LUKINIĆ; 17 brs.

**Zagrebačka Banka Zagreb d.d.** (Bank of Zagreb): 10000 Zagreb, Paromlinska 2; tel. (1) 6104000; fax (1) 536626; e-mail hrvoje.poljak@zaba.hr; internet www.zaba.hr; f. 1913; 1,096.2m., res 322.2m., dep. 17,536.9m. (June 1999); Chair. FRANJO LUKOVIĆ; 139 brs.

**Zagrebačka Banka—Pomorska Banka d.d., Split:** 21000 Split, Ivana Gundulića 26a; tel. (21) 352222; fax (21) 380190; f. 1992; cap. 65.0m., res 1.2m., dep. 1,220.4m. (Dec. 1998); Pres. Dr MLADEN RAKELIĆ.

### STOCK EXCHANGE

**Zagreb Stock Exchange:** 10000 Zagreb, Ksaver 208; tel. (1) 428455; fax (1) 420293; f. 1990; Gen. Man. MARINKO PAPUGA.

## Trade and Industry

### GOVERNMENT AGENCY

**Croatian Privatization Fund:** 10000 Zagreb, Gajeva 30A; tel. (1) 469168; fax (1) 469138; f. 1994 by merger of the Croatian Fund for Development and the Restructuring and Development Agency; Chair. TOMISLAV DRUZAK.

### CHAMBERS OF COMMERCE

**Croatian Chamber of Economy** (Hrvatska Gospodarska Komora): 10000 Zagreb, Rooseveltov trg 2; tel. (1) 4561555; fax (1) 4828380; e-mail hgk@alf.hr; internet www.hgk.hr; Pres. NADAN VIDOŠEVIĆ.

**Zagreb Chamber of Commerce:** 10000 Zagreb, Draškovićeva 45; tel. (1) 4606777; fax (1) 4606813; e-mail hgk-zagreb@hgk.hr; internet www.hgk.hr; f. 1852.

### UTILITIES

#### Electricity

**HEP—Hrvatska Elektroprivreda d.d.:** 10000 Zagreb, Ave. Vukovar 37; tel. (1) 625111; fax (1) 511612; f. 1990; production and distribution of electricity; Dir DAMIR BEGOVIĆ.

#### Gas

**Gradska Plinara:** 10000 Zagreb, Radnička 1; tel. (1) 6302333; fax (1) 6184653; f. 1862; municipal and regional distribution of natural gas; Dir IVAN VULAS.

**INA—Naftaplin:** 10000 Zagreb, Subičeva 29; tel. (1) 418011; fax (1) 440604; subsidiary of Industrija Nafte d.d.; exploration of petroleum, natural-gas and geothermal energy.

#### Water

**Hrvatske Vode:** 10000 Zagreb, Ulica grada Vukovara 220; tel. (1) 6151779; fax (1) 6151793; water management organization.

### TRADE UNIONS

**Association of Autonomous Trade Unions of Croatia:** 10000 Zagreb; f. 1990; 26 branch unions with some 500,000 mems; Pres. DRAGUTIN LESAR.

**Confederation of Independent Trade Unions of Croatia:** 10000 Zagreb; f. 1990; 40,000 mems; Pres. DAVOR JURIĆ.

**Croatian Association of Trade Unions:** Zagreb; f. 1990; 200,000 mems. Pres. BERISLAV BELEC.

**Croatian Union of Posts and Telecommunications:** Zagreb; Pres. JOSIP PUPIĆ.

## Transport

### RAILWAYS

In 1995 there were 2,452 km of railway lines in Croatia, of which 36% were electrified. In mid-1996 railway links between Croatia and Serbia, via Eastern Slavonia, were reopened.

**Croatian Railways Ltd** (Hrvatske Željeznice p.o.): 10000 Zagreb, Mihanovićeva 12; tel. (1) 4577111; fax (1) 4577730; f. 1990 as Hrvatsko željezničko poduzeće, renamed 1992; state-owned; public railway transport, construction, modernization and maintenance of railway vehicles; Pres. DAVOR ŠTERN; Gen. Dir DRAGUTIN ŠUBAT.

### ROADS

The Road Fund was responsible for the planning, construction, maintenance and rehabilitation of all interurban roads in Croatia. As of 1 January 1995 the Fund was under the control of the budgetary central Government. In 1996 there were 27,247 km of roads in Croatia, of which 318 km were motorways, 4,740 km were main roads and 7,588 km were secondary roads. In late 1995 a US $705m.-project was announced to build a 75-km. motorway linking Dragonje, near the Slovenian border, with Pula in southern Istria. The construction of the road was to be undertaken by a French company, Bouygues, and was to be financed by World Bank loans, tolls and a domestic debt. In 1996 plans were announced to build a further 1,200 km of new roads over a period of 10 years. In May 1996 the motorway between Zagreb and Belgrade (Yugoslavia) was reopened.

**Croatian Roads Authority** (Hrvatske Ceste): 10000 Zagreb, Vončinina 3; tel. (1) 445422; fax (1) 445215; f. 1991; state-owned; maintenance, construction and reconstruction of public roads; Pres. J. ZAVOREO; Man. Dir ALEKSANDAR ČAKLOVIĆ.

### SHIPPING

**Atlantska Plovidba d.d.:** 20000 Dubrovnik, od sv. Mihajla 1; tel. (20) 412666; fax (20) 20384; f. 1974; Dir ANTE JERKOVIĆ.

**Croatia Line:** 51000 Rijeka, POB 379, Riva 18; tel. (51) 205111; fax (51) 331915; f. 1986; cargo and passenger services; chartering and tramp service; Gen. Man. DARIO VUKIĆ; 377 employees.

**Jadrolinija** (Adriatic Shipping Line): 51000 Rijeka, Riva 16; tel. (51) 330899; fax (51) 213116; f. 1872; regular passenger and carferry services between Italian, Greek and Croatian ports; Pres. M. RUŽIĆ.

**Jadroplov:** 21000 Split, Obala kneza Branimira 16; tel. (21) 302666; fax (21) 342198; f. 1984; fleet of 17 vessels and 1,500 containers engaged in linear and tramp service; Gen. Man. NIKŠA GIOVANELLI.

**Lošinjska Plovidba—Brodarstvo:** 51550 Mali Lošinj, Privlaka bb; tel. (51) 231832; fax (51) 231811; f. 1980; Dir DUMANČIĆ MARINKO.

**Slobodna Plovidba:** 22000 Šibenik, Drage 2; tel. (22) 23755; fax (22) 27860; f. 1976; transport of goods by sea; tourism services; Dir VITOMIR JURAGA.

**Tankerska Plovidba d.d.:** 23000 Zadar, Božidara Petranovića 4; tel. (23) 311132; fax (23) 314375; f. 1976; Dir STANKO BANIĆ; 420 employees.

### CIVIL AVIATION

There are 10 international airports in Croatia.

**Croatia Airlines:** 10000 Zagreb, Teslina 5; tel. (1) 427752; fax (1) 427935; internet www.ctn.tel.hr/ctn; f. 1989 as Zagreb Airlines; name changed 1990; operates domestic services and 24 international routes to European destinations; Pres. MATIJA KATIČIĆ.

**Anić Airways:** Zagreb; tel. (1) 200200; fax (1) 204253; f. 1992; first private airline company in Croatia; domestic and international flights; Pres. DAMIR ANIĆ.

## Tourism

The attractive Adriatic coast and the country's 1,185 islands made Croatia a very popular tourist destination before the 1990s. However, the civil conflict, which began in mid-1991, greatly reduced tourist activity in the country. The industry showed signs of recovery after 1992, however, with foreign tourist arrivals reaching some 4.1m. in 1998. Receipts from tourism in 1998 were US $2,733m.

**Croatian National Tourist Board:** 10000 Zagreb, Ilica 1a; tel. (1) 4556455; fax (1) 4816757; e-mail info@htz.hr; internet www.htz.hr/text_e/htz.htm.

# CUBA

## Introductory Survey

**Location, Climate, Language, Religion, Flag, Capital**

The Republic of Cuba is an archipelago of two main islands, Cuba and the Isla de la Juventud (Isle of Youth), formerly the Isla de Pinos (Isle of Pines), and about 1,600 keys and islets. It lies in the Caribbean Sea, 145 km (90 miles) south of Florida, USA. Other nearby countries are the Bahamas, Mexico, Jamaica and Haiti. The climate is tropical, with the annual rainy season from May to October. The average annual temperature is 25°C (77°F) and hurricanes are frequent. The language spoken is Spanish. Most of the inhabitants are Christians, of whom the great majority are Roman Catholics. The national flag (proportions 2 by 1) has five equal horizontal stripes, of blue, white, blue, white and blue, with a red triangle, enclosing a five-pointed white star, at the hoist. The capital is Havana (La Habana).

**Recent History**

Cuba was ruled by Spain from the 16th century until 1898, when the island was ceded to the USA following Spain's defeat in the Spanish–American War. Cuba became an independent republic on 20 May 1902, but the USA retained its naval bases on the island and, until 1934, reserved the right to intervene in Cuba's internal affairs. In 1933 an army sergeant, Fulgencio Batista Zaldivar, came to power at the head of a military revolt. Batista ruled the country, directly or indirectly, until 1944, when he retired after serving a four-year term as elected President.

In March 1952, however, Gen. Batista (as he had become) seized power again, deposing President Carlos Prío Socarrás in a bloodless coup. Batista's new regime soon proved to be unpopular and became harshly repressive. In July 1953 a radical opposition group, led by Dr Fidel Castro Ruz, attacked the Moncada army barracks in Santiago de Cuba. Castro was captured, with many of his supporters, but was later released. He went into exile and formed a revolutionary movement which was committed to Batista's overthrow. In December 1956 Castro landed in Cuba with a small group of followers, most of whom were captured or killed. However, 12 survivors, including Castro and the Argentine-born Dr Ernesto ('Che') Guevara, escaped into the hills of the Sierra Maestra, where they formed the nucleus of the guerrilla forces which, after a prolonged struggle, forced Batista to flee from Cuba on 1 January 1959. The Batista regime collapsed, and Castro's forces occupied Havana.

The assumption of power by the victorious rebels was initially met with great popular acclaim. The 1940 Constitution was suspended in January 1959 and replaced by a new 'Fundamental Law'. Executive and legislative power was vested in the Council of Ministers, with Fidel Castro as Prime Minister and his brother Raúl as his deputy. Guevara reportedly ranked third in importance. The new regime ruled by decree but promised to hold elections within 18 months. When it was firmly established, the Castro Government adopted a radical economic programme, including agrarian reform and the nationalization of industrial and commercial enterprises. These drastic reforms, combined with the regime's authoritarian nature, provoked opposition from some sectors of the population, including former supporters of Castro, and many Cubans went into exile.

All US business interests in Cuba were expropriated, without compensation, in October 1960, and the USA severed diplomatic relations in January 1961. A US-sponsored force of anti-Castro Cuban émigrés landed in April 1961 at the Bahía de Cochinos (Bay of Pigs), in southern Cuba, but the invasion was thwarted by Castro's troops. Later in the year, all pro-Government groups were merged to form the Organizaciones Revolucionarias Integradas (ORI). In December 1961 Fidel Castro publicly announced that Cuba had become a communist state, and he proclaimed a 'Marxist-Leninist' programme for the country's future development. In January 1962 Cuba was excluded from active participation in the Organization of American States (OAS). The USA instituted a full economic and political blockade of Cuba. Hostility to the USA was accompanied by increasingly close relations between Cuba and the USSR. In October 1962 the USA revealed the presence of Soviet missiles in Cuba but, after the imposition of a US naval blockade, the weapons were withdrawn. The missile bases, capable of launching nuclear weapons against the USA, were dismantled, thus resolving one of the most serious international crises since the Second World War. In 1964 the OAS imposed diplomatic and commercial sanctions against Cuba.

The ORI was replaced in 1962 by a new Partido Unido de la Revolución Socialista Cubana (PURSC), which was established, under Fidel Castro's leadership, as the country's sole legal party. Guevara resigned his military and government posts in April 1965, subsequently leaving Cuba to pursue revolutionary activities abroad. In October 1965 the PURSC was renamed the Partido Comunista de Cuba (PCC). Although ostracized by most other Latin American countries, the PCC Government maintained and consolidated its internal authority, with little effective opposition. Supported by considerable aid from the USSR, the regime made significant progress in social and economic development, including improvements in education and public health. At the same time, Cuba continued to give active support to left-wing revolutionary movements in Latin America and in many other parts of the world. Guevara was killed in Bolivia, following an unsuccessful guerrilla uprising under his leadership, in October 1967.

In July 1972 Cuba's links with the Eastern bloc were strengthened when the country became a full member of the Council for Mutual Economic Assistance (CMEA—dissolved in 1991), a Moscow-based organization linking the USSR and other communist states. As a result of its admission to the CMEA, Cuba received preferential trade terms and more technical advisers from the USSR and East European countries.

In June 1974 the country's first elections since the revolution were held for municipal offices in Matanzas province. Cuba's first 'socialist' Constitution was submitted to the First Congress of the PCC, held in December 1975, and came into force in February 1976, after being approved by popular referendum. As envisaged by the new Constitution, elections for 169 municipal assemblies were held in October 1976. These assemblies later elected delegates to provincial assemblies and deputies to the National Assembly of People's Power, inaugurated in December 1976 as 'the supreme organ of state'. The National Assembly chose the members of a new Council of State, with Fidel Castro as President. The Second Congress of the PCC was held in December 1980, when Fidel and Raúl Castro were re-elected First and Second Secretaries respectively. In December 1981 Fidel Castro was re-elected by the Assembly as President of the Council of State, and Raúl Castro re-elected as First Vice-President.

Cuba continued to be excluded from the activities of the OAS, although the Organization voted in favour of allowing members to normalize their relations with Cuba in 1975. Relations with the USA deteriorated because of Cuban involvement in Angola in 1976 and in Ethiopia in 1977. The relaxation of restrictions on emigration in April 1980 resulted in the departure of more than 125,000 Cubans for Florida, USA. Antagonism continued as Cuba's military and political presence abroad increased, threatening US spheres of influence.

In 1981 Cuba expressed interest in discussing foreign policy with the USA, and declared that the shipment of arms to guerrilla groups in Central America had ceased. High-level talks between the two countries took place in November 1981 but US hostility increased. Economic sanctions were strengthened, the major air link was closed, and tourism and investment by US nationals was prohibited in April 1982. Cuba's support of Argentina during the 1982 crisis concerning the Falkland Islands improved relations with the rest of Latin America, and the country's legitimacy was finally acknowledged when it was elected to the chair of the UN General Assembly Committee on Decolonization in September 1982, while continuing to play a leading role in the Non-Aligned Movement (despite its firm alliance with the Soviet bloc).

An increase in US military activity in Honduras and the Caribbean region led President Castro to declare a 'state of national alert' in August 1983. The US invasion of Grenada in October, and the ensuing short-lived confrontation between US forces and Cuban personnel on the island, severely damaged hopes that the two countries might reach an agreement over the problems in Central America, and left Cuba isolated in the Caribbean, following the weakening of its diplomatic and military ties with Suriname in November.

In July 1984 official negotiations were begun with the USA on the issues of immigration and repatriation. In December agreement was reached on the resumption of Cuban immigration to the USA and the repatriation of 2,746 Cuban 'undesirables', who had accompanied other Cuban refugees to the USA in 1980. The repatriation of Cuban 'undesirables' began in February 1985, but, following the inauguration of Radio Martí (a radio station sponsored by the 'Voice of America' radio network, which began to broadcast Western-style news and other programmes to Cuba from Florida, USA), the Cuban Government suspended its immigration accord with the USA. Subsequently, all visits to Cuba by US residents of Cuban origin were banned. The US Government responded by restricting visits to the USA by PCC members and Cuban government officials. In September 1986, as a result of mediation by the Roman Catholic Church, more than 100 political prisoners and their families were permitted to leave Cuba for the USA.

In 1987 relations with the USA continued to deteriorate when, in February, the US Government launched a campaign to direct public attention to violations of human rights in Cuba. A resolution to condemn Cuba's record on human rights was narrowly defeated at a meeting of the UN Commission on Human Rights in March. The Cuban Government subsequently allowed 348 current and former political prisoners to return to the USA. The restoration of the 1984 immigration accord, in October 1987, provoked rioting by Cuban exiles detained in US prisons lasting several days until the US Government assured the exiles that their return to Cuba would be suspended indefinitely and that their cases would be studied individually. The accord allowed for the repatriation of 2,500 Cuban 'undesirables' in exchange for a US agreement to allow 23,000 Cubans to enter the USA annually. In 1988 the Government released some 250 political prisoners, and in the following January President Castro pledged to release the remaining 225 political prisoners acknowledged by the regime. In 1989 human rights activists formed a co-ordinating body and increased their operations. The Government responded in August by imprisoning leading activists for up to two years for having published allegedly false information. In September 1991 eight Cuban dissident organizations united to form a single democratic opposition group, the Concertación Democrática Cubana—CDC (Cuban Democratic Convergence), to campaign for political pluralism and economic reform.

At the Third Congress of the PCC in February 1986 drastic changes were made within the Central Committee; almost one-third of the 146 full members were replaced. A new Council of State was elected in December.

In June 1989 President Castro was confronted by Cuba's most serious political crisis since the 1959 Revolution. It was discovered that a number of senior military personnel were not only involved in smuggling operations in Angola but were also aiding Colombian drugs-traffickers from the infamous Medellín cartel, by enabling them to use Cuban airstrips as refuelling points (en route from Colombia to the USA) in return for bribes. Following court-martial proceedings, Gen. Arnaldo Ochoa Sánchez, who had led the military campaign in Angola, was found guilty of high treason and was executed. Three other officers were also executed. A further purge led to the imposition of harsh sentences on 14 senior officials, including the head of civil aviation and the Ministers of the Interior and of Transport, who had been found guilty of corruption. President Castro insisted that the bureaucracy in Cuba needed to undergo a process of 'purification' but not reform. However, the scandal had clearly undermined the regime's credibility at the international, as well as the domestic, level.

In Angola, where Cuban troops numbered an estimated 50,000, the peace process gathered momentum in 1988. In May a large Cuban offensive almost succeeded in expelling South African forces from Angola and lent new impetus to the peace negotiations. A cease-fire was implemented, and at discussions held in New York, USA, in October, agreement was reached on a phased withdrawal of Cuban troops over a period of 24–30 months. By December a timetable had been agreed, and withdrawal began in April 1989 and was completed in May 1991.

In April 1989 President Gorbachev of the USSR undertook the first official visit to Cuba by a Soviet leader since 1974. The two Heads of State discussed ways in which Cuba's dependence on Soviet aid might be reduced and Central American issues, and the talks culminated in the signing of a treaty of friendship and economic co-operation. Although, ostensibly, relations remained good, tensions had arisen, owing to Castro's resistance to Soviet-style reforms. Gorbachev made it clear that, in future, general financial aid would be replaced by assistance for specific projects, thus giving the USSR greater power to influence policy decisions in Cuba. In July President Castro strongly attacked the ideas of *perestroika* and *glasnost*, which he blamed for the 'crisis in socialism'. He pledged to eradicate all market forms of economic activity, despite the fact that Cuba's failure to integrate into the new supply-and-demand system of many Eastern European factories had led to delays in imports and acute shortages.

In early October 1990 President Castro announced plans to reduce the PCC's bureaucracy by as much as 50%, including the reassignment of thousands of employees to more productive sectors. In November rationing was extended to all products. Cubans were told to prepare for the possibility of a 'special wartime period' by the Minister of the Revolutionary Armed Forces, Gen. Raúl Castro, who warned of a possible US military attack if the currently intensified US economic blockade should fail. In spite of the gravity of Cuba's political and economic situation, President Castro was defiant in his rejection of recommendations that, as a condition for the removal of the blockade, Cuba should adopt a market economy and political pluralism.

In September 1991 the USSR announced that it intended to withdraw the majority of its military personnel (some 3,000 troops and advisers) from Cuba. The decision, which was condemned by Cuba as presenting a major threat to its national security, came as the result of US demands that the USSR reduce its aid to Cuba as a precondition to the provision of US aid to the USSR. Cuba's subsequent demands that the USA withdraw its troops from the naval base at Guantánamo were rejected. The Soviet withdrawal was completed in June 1993.

At the Fourth Congress of the PCC, held in October 1991, the structure of the party underwent a series of reforms. However, the party excluded the possibility of political pluralism and remained defiant in its rejection of capitalism, despite the developments in the USSR that had led to Cuba's virtual isolation.

In early 1992 President Castro's efforts to quiet internal dissent and bolster the country against the perceived US threat revealed an increasingly militant attitude, as several death sentences were imposed on Cuban dissidents. In the same year the USA began to implement a series of measures tightening its economic blockade against Cuba. In April US President Bush issued an executive order barring ships that were engaged in trade with Cuba from entering US ports. In October the Cuban Democracy Act, also known as the 'Torricelli Law', was adopted, making it illegal for foreign subsidiaries of US companies to trade with Cuba. These measures encountered widespread international criticism, including protests by the European Community (EC, later European Union—EU) that they violated international law. In November the UN General Assembly adopted a non-binding resolution demanding the cessation of the trade embargo.

In July 1992 the National Assembly approved a number of amendments to the Constitution. Under the reforms, President Castro was granted the authority to declare a state of emergency and, in such an event, to assume full control of the armed forces at the head of a National Defence Council. An electoral reform, which had originally been proposed at the Fourth Congress of the PCC in October 1991, was formally adopted, providing for elections to the National Assembly to be conducted by direct vote. The constitutional revisions also included an updating of the business law, legitimizing foreign investment in approved state enterprises and recognizing foreign ownership of property in joint ventures.

On 24 February 1993 elections to the National Assembly and the 14 provincial assemblies were, for the first time, conducted by direct secret ballot. Only candidates nominated by the PCC were permitted to contest the elections. According to official results, there was an abstention rate of only 1.2%, and 87.3% of the electorate cast a 'united' ballot (a vote for the entire list of candidates). Only 7.2% of votes cast were blank or spoilt. All 589 deputies of the National Assembly were elected with more than the requisite 50% of the votes. In the following month Fidel Castro and Gen. Raúl Castro were unanimously re-elected by the National Assembly to their respective posts as President and First Vice-President of the Council of State.

In July 1993, with the economic crisis deepening and international reserves exhausted, Castro announced that a 30-year ban on Cuban citizens' possessing foreign currency was to be lifted. The measure, which represented a significant departure from the country's centrally-planned socialist economy, was intended to attract the large sums of foreign currency (principally US dollars) in circulation on the black market into the economy, and to encourage remittances from Cuban exiles. Restrictions on Cuban exiles travelling to Cuba were also to be relaxed. Concerns that the measures were socially divisive, affording privileges to those receiving currency from relatives abroad, were acknowledged by the Government. In September, in a further move away from traditional economic policy, the Government authorized limited individual private enterprise in a range of 117 occupations. In the same month plans were announced for the introduction of agricultural reforms allowing for the decentralization and reorganization of state farms into 'Units of Basic Co-operative Production', to be managed and financed by the workers themselves.

In April 1994, in a reorganization of the Government, four new ministries were created and a number of state committees and institutes dissolved. The creation of the new ministries (of economy and planning, finance and prices, foreign investment and economic co-operation, and tourism) reflected a significant change in the economic management of the country. In early August, however, increasing discontent at deteriorating economic conditions resulted in rioting in the capital, precipitated by a confrontation between police and a large number of Cubans attempting to commandeer a ferry in order to take the vessel to the USA. In a public speech broadcast on the following day Castro indicated that, if the USA failed to halt the promotion of such illegal departures, Cuba would suspend its travel restrictions. The resultant surge of Cubans attempting to reach the USA by sea reached crisis proportions, and President Clinton was forced to adopt measures to deter them. The automatic refugee status conferred on Cubans under the 1966 Cuban Adjustment Act was revoked, and Cubans were warned that those intercepted by the US Coast Guard would be transported to Guantánamo naval base and would not be allowed entry into the USA. Further measures imposed included the halting of cash remittances from Cuban exiles in the USA. However, these measures failed to stem the flow of Cubans seeking refuge in the USA, and in late August the US Government agreed to hold bilateral talks with Cuba to seek a resolution to the crisis. The talks concluded in September with an agreement providing a commitment by the USA to grant visas allowing for the migration of a minimum of 20,000 Cubans annually (despite the 1984 immigration accord, a total of only 11,222 US entry visas had been granted to Cubans between December 1984 and July 1994). An additional 4,000–6,000 Cubans already on waiting lists for US visas would be granted them. In return, Cuba reintroduced border restrictions. More than 30,000 Cubans were estimated to have left the country during the period when travel restrictions were suspended, although the majority of these were detained by the US authorities and transported to camps in Guantánamo and the Panama Canal Zone. Talks continued with the USA throughout 1995. In May a further immigration accord was signed, bringing to an official end the automatic refugee status which had been revoked in August 1994. The accord also stated that all Cuban refugees intercepted at sea by the USA would thenceforth be repatriated. In addition, the USA agreed to grant visas to the majority of the approximately 20,000 Cuban refugees detained at Guantánamo, although the figure was to be deducted, over a period of four years, from the annual quota of visas granted under the September 1994 accord.

In early 1995 legislative proposals seeking to tighten the US embargo against Cuba were introduced to the US Congress by the Chairman of the Senate Foreign Relations Committee, Jesse Helms, and the Chairman of the House of Representatives Sub-Committee on the Western Hemisphere, Dan Burton. The proposals, referred to as the Helms-Burton bill, sought to impose sanctions on countries trading with or investing in Cuba, and threatened to reduce US aid to countries providing Cuba with financial assistance, notably Russia. The bill provoked international criticism, and a formal complaint was registered by the EU, which claimed that the legislation would be in violation of international law and the rules of the World Trade Organization (WTO). The bill was approved by the House of Representatives in September but was considerably modified by the Senate.

In February 1996 Cuban MiG fighters shot down two US light aircraft piloted by members of the Cuban-American exile group Brothers to the Rescue, killing all four crew members. The action was vigorously condemned by the USA, which rejected Cuban claims that the aircraft had violated Cuban airspace. Further US sanctions were immediately implemented, including the indefinite suspension of charter flights to Cuba. In June, following an investigation, the International Civil Aviation Organization issued a report confirming US claims that the aircraft had been shot down over international waters. As a result of the incident, President Clinton reversed his previous opposition to certain controversial elements of the Helms-Burton bill, and on 12 March he signed the legislation, officially entitled the Cuban Liberty and Solidarity Act, thus making it law. However, Clinton was empowered to issue executive orders, at six-monthly intervals, postponing the implementation of a section of the law, Title III, which allowed US citizens, including naturalized Cuban exiles, to prosecute through US courts any foreign corporation or investor with business dealings involving property that had been expropriated during the Castro regime. Approval of the Helms-Burton bill prompted strenuous criticism from Cuba's major trading partners. The EU announced its intention to challenge the extra-territorial provisions of the Act through the WTO, while Mexico and Canada sought to dispute the law under the provisions of the North American Free Trade Agreement. International opposition to the Helms-Burton bill increased following the issue, in May, by the US State Department of letters to companies in Canada, Mexico and Italy, warning of possible prosecution. In June Canada initiated a series of legal measures to protect Canadian companies against the Act. Similar legislation was subsequently adopted by Mexico and the EU. In July Clinton imposed a six-month moratorium on Title III of the Act, which had been due to come into force in August. In November, in its annual vote on the US embargo, the UN General Assembly voted for its repeal with the largest majority to date. Notably, the United Kingdom, Germany and the Netherlands, which had all previously abstained on this question, voted in favour of a repeal. In the same month the WTO adopted a resolution to establish a disputes panel to rule on the legality of the Helms-Burton-sponsored Act.

In December 1996 agreement was reached by the members of the EU to make the extent of economic co-operation with Cuba contingent upon progress towards democracy in the country. In that month the Cuban Government adopted legislation to counteract the application of the Cuban Liberty and Solidarity (Helms-Burton) Act in an attempt to protect foreign investment in the country. The Government also expressed its readiness to negotiate with the USA regarding the compensation of US citizens with property claims in Cuba. In January 1997 Clinton suspended Title III for a further six-month period. In early February the EU requested that the WTO postpone the appointment of a disputes panel in order that further discussions be conducted with the USA in an effort to reach a negotiated settlement. However, these efforts were not successful, and on 20 February a disputes panel was appointed and given six months to reach a decision on whether the extra-territorial provisions of the Act contravened WTO rules on multilateral trade, or whether, as the USA maintained, the Act was a matter of national security and therefore not within the jurisdiction of the WTO. In March, in a futher attempt to avoid confrontation, the EU and the USA resumed discussions concerning the Act, and in the following month agreement was reached in principle on a resolution of the dispute. Under the terms of the agreement, the USA was to continue deferring the implementation of Title III indefinitely, while the EU was to withdraw its petition to the WTO until October. In the interim, negotiations were to continue towards a multilateral accord defining investment principles, with particular emphasis on expropriated foreign assets. In a move widely interpreted as a concession to mounting domestic pressure to end restrictions on exports of food and medicines from the USA to Cuba, in March 1998 it was agreed that shipments of both commodities, via non-governmental organizations, were to be permitted. In addition, President Clinton announced an end to the ban on direct flights between the USA and Cuba (imposed in 1996) and on the transfer of cash remittances from the USA to Cuba. Henceforth, Cuban residents in the USA were to be permitted to send up to US $300 quarterly to relatives in Cuba. The process whereby applications for licences to sell medicines to Cuba were considered was also to be examined, with a view to accelerating procedures. However, the Cuban Government was extremely critical of a further outline agreement on extraterritorial legislation drafted by the US Government and the EU in May, which it considered to be highly concessionary on the part of the EU, at the expense of Cuban interests. Under the terms of the agreement, in return for a commitment from President Clinton to seek congressional consensus for a relaxation of the application of the Cuban Liberty and Solidarity (Helms-Burton) Act, EU member states would participate in the compilation of a register of former US assets in Cuba (considered to have been illegally expropriated) and would observe firm US recommendations regarding their exclusivity.

Support for the annual UN General Assembly resolution urging an end to the US embargo against Cuba increased once again in October 1998. The resolution received the support of 157 member nations. Twelve members abstained from the vote, while only two (the USA and Israel) voted against the resolution.

Despite a further easing of restrictions relating to the US embargo in August 1999, and well-publicized vists to Cuba by the head of the US Chamber of Commerce in July, by two prominent US senators in August and by George Ryan, Governor of the US State of Illinois in October, attempts by the US Government to appease the increasingly influential anti-embargo lobby were largely frustrated by an exchange of legal challenges. In March a US judge ruled that payments owed to the Cuban national telecommunications company, which were currently being withheld by a number of US telecommunications companies by judicial request, could be used to help honour a compensation award of US $187m. against the Cuban authorities, made in the USA in 1997 to benefit relatives of four pilots shot down by the Cuban air force in 1996 (see above). The US Government had made known its objection to the ruling, claiming that the decision amounted to interference in foreign policy. In response, in early June a new lawsuit was brought to the Cuban courts by a number of government-sponsored organizations which were seeking some $181,100m. in compensation for more than 3,000 deaths and more than 2,000 injuries allegedly inflicted on Cuban nationals since the 1959 Revolution by the 'aggressive' policies of the US Government. In September a unanimous declaration of the National Assembly condemned the US trade embargo as an act of 'genocide'.

In May 1995, following the first visit to Cuba by an international human rights mission since the 1959 Revolution, the Government authorized the release of six political prisoners. The mission had been co-ordinated by the human rights organization France-Libertés. According to Cuban human rights groups, however, more than 1,000 political prisoners remained in detention in the country.

In November 1996, following a meeting in the Vatican between President Castro and Pope John Paul II, it was announced that Cuba was to receive its first ever papal visit. During 21–25 January 1998 John Paul II conducted four large-scale open-air masses throughout Cuba, and attended a private meeting with President Castro. During the visit the Pope was critical of the 'unjust and ethically unacceptable' US embargo against Cuba, and urged the reintegration of Cuba into the international community. In response, in late January, the Guatemalan Government announced that diplomatic relations were to be restored with Cuba, prompting a rebuke from the US Department of State. During February, moreover, it was announced that almost 300 Cuban prisoners were to be released, many as a result of a petition for clemency made by the papal delegation. In April, at a meeting of the UN Commission on Human Rights the annual US-sponsored vote of censure against the Cuban Government for alleged abuses of human rights was defeated for the first time since 1991; the motion was supported by 16 countries and opposed by 19, while 18 abstained.

In mid-March 1999 the Provincial Court in Havana sentenced four prominent political dissidents to prison terms of between three and a half and five years' duration. The decision followed the introduction, in February, of uncompromising new legislation to combat increasing criminal activity and to curb subversion and dissent. The incarceration of the dissidents, together with the imposition of death sentences in March on two Salvadorean nationals (see below), drew criticism of Cuba's respect for human rights from the international community in general, and resulted in a significant deterioration in relations with Canada (Cuba's largest trading partner) and Spain in particular.

In mid-1997 a spate of bombings directed against hotels and tourist locations began in the capital. In September an Italian businessman was killed by an explosion in a Havana hotel. The Government maintained that the campaign, designed to undermine the country's vital tourism industry, had been organized by the anti-Castro Cuban-American National Foundation (CANF) from its base in Florida, USA. In March 1999 two Salvadorean nationals were convicted on terrorism charges relating to the bomb attacks; death sentences were imposed on both men. Meanwhile, in August 1998 the US Department of Justice had brought charges against seven Cuban exiles, including a member of the CANF executive, relating to a plot to assassinate President Castro in Venezuela in 1997. During a televised interview in October 1998 President Castro admitted that Cuban nationals had been deployed in the USA on espionage duties, charged with infiltrating counter-revolutionary organizations there. These remarks followed an announcement by the US Government in the previous month that 10 Cubans had been arrested on charges of spying for the Cuban Government.

On 11 January 1998 elections to the National Assembly (enlarged from 589 to 601 seats) and to the 14 provincial assemblies were conducted. All 601 candidates who contested the legislative ballot were elected. Of the 7.8m. registered voters, 98.35% participated in the elections. Only 5% of votes cast were blank or spoilt. At the first meeting of the newly-constituted National Assembly on 24 February, the new Council of State was announced, confirming Fidel and Raúl Castro, and the five incumbent Vice-Presidents in their positions for a further five-year term. Of the remaining 23 ordinary members of the Council, 14 were new appointments. Minor cabinet reorganizations were implemented in March, May, August and October 1999.

Since 1985 Cuba has succeeded in establishing strong ties throughout Latin America and the Caribbean. Full diplomatic relations were restored with Colombia (suspended in 1981) in 1993, with Chile in 1995 and with Guatemala in 1998. Diplomatic relations were also re-established with the Dominican Republic in 1998. In August of that year, during President Castro's first visit to the Dominican Republic, he attended a summit meeting of the Cariforum grouping of CARICOM (see p. 136) states and the Dominican Republic, at which the Statement of Santo Domingo was endorsed, envisaging full Cuban participation in any successor arrangement to Lomé IV (see p. 196). (Recent statements by the US and British Governments had indicated that pressure might be applied to EU member states to attach preconditions relating to human rights and democratic processes to Cuban participation in such an arrangement.) Earlier in the month Castro had completed a successful tour of Jamaica, Barbados and Grenada. Cuba was afforded observer status at a meeting of the Council of Ministers of the Africa, Caribbean and Pacific (ACP) signatory nations to the Lomé Convention (see p. 196) convened in Barbados in early May 1998. At the meeting representatives of the ACP group expressed support for Cuba's eventual admission as a full member. In November 1998 Cuba became the 12th full member of the Latin American Integration Association (LAIA—see p. 292), having enjoyed observer status since 1986.

In September 1988 diplomatic relations were established with the EC (restyled the European Union—EU—in late 1993). Since 1993 Spain has played a significant role in advising Cuba on economic affairs and mediating in negotiations with the IMF, with a view to future co-operation. In 1994 Cuba and Spain concluded an agreement providing for the compensation of Spanish citizens whose property was expropriated during the Cuban Revolution of 1959. In 1996, following the transfer of power in Spain from a socialist government to the centre-right administration of José María Aznar, relations between Spain and Cuba began to deteriorate. In October Spain suspended its programme of aid to Cuba, and in the following month Cuba revoked its approval of a newly-appointed Spanish ambassador who had expressed his intention to maintain contacts with and assist Cuban dissidents. Improved relations between Cuba and Spain resulted in the Cuban Government's approval of a new Spanish ambassador to Havana in April 1998. In the same month the Cuban Minister of Foreign Relations, Roberto Robaina, visited Madrid, where he received assurances that Spain would promote Cuban interests (including its application to join the ACP group) at the EU.

In 1992 Cuba signed a number of accords and protocols establishing diplomatic relations with republics of the former Soviet Union, including Belarus, Georgia, Kyrgyzstan and Ukraine.

In October 1989 Cuba was elected to the UN Security Council (for a two-year term from January 1990) for the first time in the 30 years of President Castro's rule.

### Government

Under the 1976 Constitution (the first since the 1959 Revolution, amended in July 1992), the supreme organ of state, and the sole legislative authority, is the National Assembly of People's Power (Asamblea Nacional del Poder Popular), with 601 deputies elected for five years by direct vote. The National Assembly elects 31 of its members to form the Council of State, the Assembly's permanent organ. The Council of State is the highest representative of the State, and its President is both Head of State and Head of Government. Executive and administrative authority is vested in the Council of Ministers, appointed by the National Assembly on the proposal of the Head of State. Municipal, regional and provincial assemblies have also been established. The Partido Comunista de Cuba (PCC), the only authorized political party, is 'the leading force of society and the State'. The PCC's highest authority is the Party Congress, which elects a Central Committee (150 members in December 1997) to supervise the Party's work. To direct its policy, the Central Committee elects a Politburo (24 members in 1997).

### Defence

Conscription for military service is for a two-year period, and conscripts also work on the land. In August 1999, according to Western estimates, the armed forces totalled 65,000 (including ready reserves serving 45 days per year to complete active and reserve units): the army numbered 45,000, the navy 5,000 and the air force 10,000. Army reserves were estimated to total 39,000. Paramilitary forces include 20,000 State Security troops, 6,500 border guards, a civil defence force of 50,000 and a Youth Labour Army of 65,000. A local militia organization (Milicias de Tropas Territoriales—MTT), comprising an estimated 1m. men and women, was formed in 1980. Expenditure on defence and internal security for 1998 was estimated at US $750m. Despite Cuban hostility, the USA maintains a base at Guantánamo Bay, with 590 naval and 490 marine personnel in 1999. In June 1993, in accordance with the unilateral decision of the Soviet Union in September 1991, the 3,000-strong military unit of the former Soviet Union, which had been stationed in Cuba since 1962, was withdrawn. A number of Russian military personnel remained to operate military intelligence facilities. Following the political changes in eastern Europe, previously high levels of military aid to Cuba were dramatically reduced in the early 1990s, and the size of the army has been reduced by some 60,000 personnel.

### Economic Affairs

In 1997, according to UN estimates, Cuba's gross domestic product (GDP), measured at constant 1981 prices, was 14,572.4m. pesos. During 1990–97, it was estimated, GDP declined, in real terms, at an average annual rate of 3.7%. However, GDP increased by 2.5% in 1995, by an estimated 7.8% in 1996 and by 2.5% in 1997. During 1990–97 the population increased by an average of 0.6% per year.

Agriculture (including forestry and fishing) contributed 7.4% of GDP in 1997. About 14.9% of the labour force were employed in this sector in 1998. The principal cash crop is sugar cane, with sugar and its derivatives accounting for 73.2% of export earnings in 1989. Other important crops are tobacco, rice, citrus fruits, plantains and bananas. In real terms, the GDP of the agricultural sector declined at an average rate of 14.5% per year during 1989–94, but increased at an average annual rate of 6.9% in 1994–97. Agricultural GDP increased by 17.5% in 1996, but decreased by 0.2% in 1997.

Industry (including mining, manufacturing, construction and power) contributed 36.5% of GDP in 1997. The sector employed 27.7% of the labour force in 1981. Industrial GDP decreased, in real terms, at an average rate of 12.9% per year in 1989–93, but increased by an average of 8.4% per year during 1994–97. The sector's GDP increased by an estimated 7.4% in 1997.

Mining contributed 1.2% of GDP in 1997. Nickel is the principal mineral export. In 1996 nickel output reached a record level of 53,600 metric tons, an increase of some 30% compared with the previous year. Cuba also produces considerable amounts of chromium, cobalt and copper, and there are workable deposits of gold and silver. In the late 1990s Cuba produced approximately 30,000 b/d of crude petroleum.

Manufacturing contributed 28.5% of GDP in 1997. Measured by the value of output, the principal branches of manufacturing in 1989 were food products (34.3% of the total), beverages and tobacco, machinery and industrial chemicals. During 1990–97 manufacturing GDP declined, in real terms, at an average annual rate of 1.6%. The sector's GDP increased by 7.8% in 1996, and by 8.3% in 1997.

Energy is derived principally from petroleum and natural gas. Current levels of production of crude petroleum satisfy approximately 20% of domestic demand. Imports of mineral fuels accounted for 32.4% of the total cost of imports in 1989.

Services employed 46.3% of the total labour force in 1981 and accounted for 56.2% of GDP in 1997. Tourism is one of the country's principal sources of foreign exchange, earning an estimated US $1,500m. in 1997, and development of the sector remains a priority of the Government. In real terms, the GDP of the service sectors decreased at an average rate of 3.6% per year during 1990–97. The GDP of services increased by 5.5% in 1996, but decreased by 0.1% in 1997.

In 1996 Cuba recorded a trade deficit of US $1,190m., and in 1995 there was a deficit of $41m. on the current account of the balance of payments. In 1989 the principal source of imports (68.0%) was the USSR, which was also the principal market for exports (59.9%). Other major trading partners were the German Democratic Republic, the People's Republic of China, Czechoslovakia and Bulgaria. The principal imports in 1989 were mineral fuels, machinery and transport equipment. The principal exports in the same year were sugar, minerals and concentrates, and agricultural produce. The re-export of mineral fuels was a major source of convertible currency, earning Cuba an estimated US $500m. in 1989. In 1990, however, imports of subsidized petroleum from the USSR, which had, hitherto, provided 95% of Cuba's total petroleum requirements, were dramatically reduced.

In 1997 Cuba recorded an estimated budget deficit of 459m. pesos (equivalent to 2.0% of GDP). Cuba's external debt to Western creditor nations was estimated to be between US $9,000m. and $11,000m. in 1997. Cuba's debt to the USSR was estimated to be $24,780m. at mid-1990. According to official figures, some 6.9% of the labour force were unemployed at the end of 1997. No index of consumer prices is published.

Cuba is a member of the Latin American Economic System (see p. 292) and of the Group of Latin American and Caribbean Sugar Exporting Countries (see p. 287).

In the early 1990s Cuba suffered severe economic decline, prompted by the collapse of the Soviet Union and by the consequent termination of the favourable aid and trade arrangements that had supported the Cuban economy. Resultant shortages, particularly of petroleum and basic raw materials, seriously affected production in all sectors and necessitated wide-ranging austerity measures. In 1994, in a significant departure from the country's traditional command economy, a series of adjustment measures was introduced in an attempt to reduce the budget deficit and to address the problem of excess liquidity. The measures included the introduction of new taxes and a drastic reduction (by some 40%) of subsidies to loss-making state enterprises. In December 1994 a new 'convertible peso' was introduced to regulate the circulation of foreign currency. A new investment law, approved in September 1995, opened all sectors of the economy, with the exception of defence, health and education, to foreign participation and introduced the possibility of 100% foreign ownership (in February 1999 it was reported that such an investment project—for a Panamanian-Lebanese diesel-electric power station—had been approved, although ownership would revert to the Cuban authorities within five years).

In 1996 the USA intensified its sanctions against Cuba with the introduction of the Cuban Liberty and Solidarity (Helms-Burton) Act. Denied access to medium- and long-term loans, Cuba's indebtedness increased substantially as high-interest short-term loans were contracted in order to finance production, most notably in the sugar industry. Despite reports of a shortage of foreign exchange in mid-1998 resulting from a poor sugar harvest (an estimated 3.2m. tons for 1997/98, compared with 4.2m. in the previous season) and a decline in world prices for nickel, other sectors of the economy performed sufficiently well to encourage forecasts of economic growth of 2.5%–3.0% for 1998, compared with 2.1% in 1997. During 1999 the Central Bank made known its intention henceforth to prefer to conduct international transactions in euros, hoping thus to weaken the stranglehold of the US dollar on the Cuban economy. In September the Central Bank announced a debt-rescheduling agreement involving £17m. of short-term debt with the United Kingdom Government's export credits guarantee department. It was hoped that the move would signal a reactivation of British investor interest in Cuba.

### Social Welfare

Through the State Social Security System, employees receive benefits for sickness, accidents, maternity, disability, retirement and unemployment. Health services are available free of charge. In 1997 there were 82,037 hospital beds, and there were 62,624 physicians working in the country. In 1997 the infant mortality rate was only 7.2 per 1,000 live births. The 1996 budget allocation for public health, was some 1,200m. pesos, equivalent to 9.3% of total expenditure.

### Education

Education is universal and free at all levels. Education is based on Marxist-Leninist principles and combines study with manual work. Day nurseries are available for all children after their 45th day, and national schools at the pre-primary level are operated by the State for children of five years of age. Primary education, from six to 11 years of age, is compulsory, and secondary education lasts from 12 to 17 years of age, comprising two cycles of three years each. In 1996 total enrolment at primary and secondary schools was equivalent to 93% of the school-age population (males 92%; females 94%). In that year primary enrolment included almost 100% of children in the relevant age-group, while secondary enrolment was equivalent to 77% of the population in the appropriate age-group (males 73%; females 82%). In 1996/97 there were 111,587 students in higher education. Workers attending university courses receive a state subsidy to provide for their dependants. Courses at intermediate and higher levels lay an emphasis on technology, agriculture and teacher training. In 1995, according to estimates by UNESCO, the illiteracy rate among persons aged 15 years and over was 4.3% (males 3.8%; females 4.7%). In 1996 budgetary expenditure on education was estimated at 1,535m. pesos (12.6% of total spending).

### Public Holidays

**2000:** 1 January (Liberation Day), 1 May (Labour Day), 25–27 July (Anniversary of the 1953 Revolution), 10 October (Wars of Independence Day), 25 December (Christmas Day).

**2001:** 1 January (Liberation Day), 1 May (Labour Day), 25–27 July (Anniversary of the 1953 Revolution), 10 October (Wars of Independence Day), 25 December (Christmas Day).

### Weights and Measures

The metric system is in force.

# Statistical Survey

Source (unless otherwise stated): Cámara de Comercio de la República de Cuba, Calle 21, No 661/701, esq. Calle A, Apdo 4237, Vedado, Havana; tel. (7) 30-3356; fax (7) 33-3042; Comité Estatal de Estadísticas, Calle Sta y Paseo, Vedado, Havana; tel. (7) 31-5171.

## Area and Population

### AREA, POPULATION AND DENSITY

| | |
|---|---|
| Area (sq km) | 110,860* |
| Population (census results) | |
| 6 September 1970 | 8,569,121 |
| 11 September 1981 | |
| Males | 4,914,873 |
| Females | 4,808,732 |
| Total | 9,723,605 |
| Population (official estimates at mid-year) | |
| 1995 | 10,980,000 |
| 1996 | 11,019,000 |
| 1997 | 11,059,000 |
| Density (per sq km) at mid-1997 | 99.8 |

* 42,803 sq miles.

### PRINCIPAL TOWNS

(estimated population at 31 December 1995)

| | | | |
|---|---|---|---|
| La Habana (Havana, the capital) | 2,184,990 | Santa Clara | 206,900 |
| Santiago de Cuba | 432,396 | Guantánamo | 204,903 |
| Las Tunas | 324,011 | Bayamo | 140,900 |
| Camagüey | 296,601 | Pinar del Río | 137,200 |
| Holguín | 243,240 | Cienfuegos | 132,000 |
| | | Matanzas | 122,886 |

### BIRTHS, MARRIAGES AND DEATHS*

| | Registered live births† | | Registered marriages‡ | | Registered deaths | |
|---|---|---|---|---|---|---|
| | Number | Rate (per 1,000) | Number | Rate (per 1,000) | Number | Rate (per 1,000) |
| 1989 | 184,891 | 17.6 | 85,535 | 8.1 | 67,356 | 6.4 |
| 1990 | 186,658 | 17.6 | 101,515 | 9.5 | 72,144 | 6.8 |
| 1991 | 173,896 | 16.2 | 162,020 | 15.1 | 71,709 | 6.7 |
| 1992 | 157,349 | 14.5 | 191,837 | 17.7 | 75,457 | 7.0 |
| 1993 | 152,238 | 14.0 | 135,138 | 12.4 | 78,531 | 7.2 |
| 1994 | 147,265 | 13.4 | 116,935 | 10.7 | 78,648 | 7.2 |
| 1995 | 147,170 | 13.4 | 70,413 | 6.4 | 77,937 | 7.1 |
| 1996 | 148,276 | 13.5 | 65,009 | 5.9 | 79,654 | 7.2 |

**1997** (provisional): Registered live births 152,000 (birth rate 13.7 per 1,000); Registered marriages 60,220 (marriage rate 5.4 per 1,000).

* Data are tabulated by year of registration rather than by year of occurrence.

† Births registered in the National Consumers Register, established on 31 December 1964.

‡ Including consensual unions formalized in response to special legislation.

**Expectation of life** (UN estimates, years at birth, 1990–95): 74.9 (males 73.5; females 77.3). Source: UN, *World Population Prospects: The 1998 Revision*.

**ECONOMICALLY ACTIVE POPULATION** (1981 census)

| | Males | Females | Total |
|---|---|---|---|
| Agriculture, hunting, forestry and fishing | 677,565 | 113,304 | 790,869 |
| Mining and quarrying<br>Manufacturing<br>Electricity, gas and water | 472,399 | 195,941 | 668,340 |
| Construction | 279,327 | 33,913 | 313,240 |
| Trade, restaurants and hotels | 170,192 | 135,438 | 305,630 |
| Transport, storage and communications | 205,421 | 43,223 | 248,644 |
| Financing, insurance, real estate and business services<br>Community, social and personal services | 541,387 | 544,665 | 1,086,052 |
| Activities not adequately defined | 87,778 | 40,139 | 127,917 |
| **Total labour force** | 2,434,069 | 1,106,623 | 3,540,692 |

**1988** (sample survey, persons aged 15 years and over): Total employed labour force 4,570,236 (males 2,920,698; females 1,649,538).

Source: ILO, *Yearbook of Labour Statistics*.

**CIVILIAN EMPLOYMENT IN THE STATE SECTOR**
(annual averages, '000 persons)

| | 1987 | 1988 | 1989 |
|---|---|---|---|
| Industry* | 726.9 | 742.8 | 767.5 |
| Construction | 314.1 | 339.4 | 344.3 |
| Agriculture | 602.7 | 653.2 | 690.3 |
| Forestry | 30.1 | 26.8 | 30.8 |
| Transport | 196.9 | 199.9 | 204.4 |
| Communications | 28.4 | 30.1 | 31.5 |
| Trade | 376.2 | 387.3 | 395.3 |
| Social services | 116.5 | 121.5 | 124.5 |
| Science and technology | 28.7 | 27.5 | 27.4 |
| Education | 383.0 | 388.2 | 396.4 |
| Arts and culture | 42.2 | 42.1 | 43.9 |
| Public health | 222.4 | 232.5 | 243.5 |
| Finance and insurance | 20.6 | 20.9 | 21.7 |
| Administration | 161.4 | 155.1 | 151.7 |
| **Total** (incl. others) | 3,299.2 | 3,408.4 | 3,526.6 |

* Fishing, mining, manufacturing, electricity, gas and water.

# Agriculture

**PRINCIPAL CROPS** ('000 metric tons)

| | 1996 | 1997 | 1998 |
|---|---|---|---|
| Rice (paddy) | 369 | 388 | 388* |
| Maize | 104 | 126 | 126* |
| Potatoes | 365 | 326 | 326* |
| Sweet potatoes* | 220 | 220 | 220 |
| Cassava (Manioc)* | 250 | 250 | 250 |
| Dry beans | 14 | 16 | 16* |
| Groundnuts (in shell)* | 15 | 15 | 15 |
| Coconuts* | 26 | 26 | 26 |
| Cabbages* | 26 | 26 | 26 |
| Tomatoes | 163 | 164 | 164* |
| Pumpkins, squash and gourds* | 45 | 45 | 45 |
| Cucumbers and gherkins* | 35 | 35 | 35 |
| Other vegetables | 85 | 85 | 85* |
| Melons* | 30 | 30 | 30 |
| Sugar cane | 41,300 | 43,000* | 35,000* |
| Oranges | 283 | 340† | 340* |
| Tangerines, mandarins, clementines and satsumas* | 15 | 15 | 15 |
| Lemons and limes | 20 | 30† | 30* |
| Grapefruit and pomelos | 350 | 420† | 420* |
| Mangoes | 50 | 50* | 50* |
| Pineapples* | 19 | 19 | 19 |
| Bananas | 323† | 325* | 325* |
| Plantains | 216† | 216* | 216* |
| Other fruits and berries | 78 | 78 | 78* |
| Coffee (green)† | 17 | 20 | 21 |
| Tobacco (leaves) | 31 | 31 | 31* |

* FAO estimate(s). † Unofficial figure(s).

Source: FAO, *Production Yearbook*.

**LIVESTOCK** ('000 head, year ending September)

| | 1996 | 1997 | 1998 |
|---|---|---|---|
| Cattle | 4,601 | 4,600* | 4,650† |
| Horses* | 620 | 620 | 620 |
| Mules* | 32 | 32 | 32 |
| Pigs* | 1,500 | 1,500 | 1,500 |
| Sheep* | 310 | 310 | 310 |
| Goats | 119 | 118* | 118* |

* FAO estimate(s). † Unofficial figure.

Poultry (million): 12 in 1996; 12 (FAO estimate) in 1997; 12 (FAO estimate) in 1998.

Source: FAO, *Production Yearbook*.

**LIVESTOCK PRODUCTS** ('000 metric tons)

| | 1996 | 1997 | 1998 |
|---|---|---|---|
| Beef and veal | 68 | 68 | 75* |
| Pig meat | 74 | 71 | 71* |
| Poultry meat | 62 | 60* | 60* |
| Cows' milk | 640 | 660* | 660* |
| Butter* | 8 | 8 | 8 |
| Cheese* | 15 | 15 | 15 |
| Hen eggs | 58 | 56* | 56* |

* FAO estimate(s).

Source: FAO, *Production Yearbook*.

# Forestry

**ROUNDWOOD REMOVALS**
('000 cubic metres, excl. bark)

| | 1995 | 1996 | 1997 |
|---|---|---|---|
| Sawlogs, veneer logs and logs for sleepers | 193 | 193 | 193 |
| Other industrial wood | 418 | 418 | 418 |
| Fuel wood | 2,535 | 2,541 | 2,541 |
| **Total** | 3,146 | 3,152 | 3,152 |

Source: FAO, *Yearbook of Forest Products*.

**SAWNWOOD PRODUCTION**
('000 cubic metres, incl. railway sleepers)

| | 1987 | 1988 | 1989 |
|---|---|---|---|
| Coniferous (softwood) | 40 | 46 | 59 |
| Broadleaved (hardwood) | 75 | 73 | 72 |
| **Total** | 114 | 118 | 130 |

**1990–97:** Annual production as in 1989.

Source: FAO, *Yearbook of Forest Products*.

# Fishing

(metric tons, live weight)

| | 1995 | 1996 | 1997 |
|---|---|---|---|
| Freshwater fishes | 348 | 450 | 200 |
| Silver hake | 16,785 | 22,279 | 12,697 |
| Lane snapper | 1,943 | 1,848 | 2,472 |
| Ponyfishes | 2,221 | 1,719 | 1,346 |
| Grunts and sweetlips | 2,128 | 1,723 | 1,451 |
| Atlantic thread herring | 2,005 | 2,361 | 1,900 |
| Sharks, rays and skates | 3,061 | 3,415 | 3,285 |
| Other marine fishes | 26,489 | 24,737 | 31,165 |
| Caribbean spiny lobster | 9,405 | 9,375 | 9,034 |
| Northern pink shrimp | 1,851 | 1,710 | 2,003 |
| Other crustaceans | 1,113 | 1,304 | 1,666 |
| Mangrove cupped oyster | 1,408 | 1,409 | 1,535 |
| Ark clams | 1,905 | 1,963 | 2,989 |
| Northern shortfin squid | 959 | 493 | 2,979 |
| Other molluscs | 78 | 851 | 1,685 |
| Frogs and turtles | 161 | 140 | 94 |
| **Total catch** | 71,860 | 75,777 | 76,501 |
| Atlantic Ocean | 71,166 | 74,905 | 75,329 |
| Inland waters | 694 | 872 | 1,172 |

Source: FAO, *Yearbook of Fishery Statistics*.

# Mining

('000 metric tons, unless otherwise indicated)

| | 1987 | 1988 | 1989 |
|---|---|---|---|
| Crude petroleum | 894.5 | 716.8 | 718.4 |
| Natural gas (million cu metres) | 23.9 | 21.9 | 33.6 |
| Copper concentrates* | 3.5 | 3.0 | 2.8 |
| Nickel and cobalt* | 36.8 | 43.9 | 46.6 |
| Refractory chromium | 52.4 | 52.2 | 50.6 |
| Salt (unrefined) | 230.5 | 200.3 | 206.1 |
| Silica and sand ('000 cu metres) | 5,826.3 | 6,467.7 | 6,396.7 |
| Crushed stone ('000 cu metres) | 11,102.3 | 12,676.6 | 12,510.1 |

**1990:** Crude petroleum 726,000 metric tons; Nickel and cobalt 40,000* metric tons; Salt (unrefined) 200,000 metric tons.

**1991:** Crude petroleum 748,000 metric tons; Nickel and cobalt 36,500* metric tons; Salt (unrefined) 200,000 metric tons.

**1992:** Crude petroleum 936,000 metric tons; Nickel and cobalt 33,400* metric tons.

**1993:** Crude petroleum 975,000 metric tons; Nickel and cobalt 29,900* metric tons.

**1994:** Crude petroleum 1,258,000 metric tons; Nickel and cobalt 32,000* metric tons.

**1995:** Crude petroleum 1,449,000 metric tons; Nickel and cobalt 42,800* metric tons.

**1996:** Crude petroleum 1,454,000 metric tons; Nickel and cobalt 55,600* metric tons.

* Figures refer to the metal content of ores and concentrates.

Source (for 1990–96): UN, *Industrial Commodity Statistics Yearbook*.

# Industry

**SELECTED PRODUCTS**
('000 metric tons, unless otherwise indicated)

| | 1987 | 1988 | 1989 |
|---|---|---|---|
| Crude steel | 401.5 | 320.5 | 314.2 |
| Corrugated steel bars | 312.9 | 359.7 | 367.1 |
| Grey cement | 3,535.3 | 3,565.8 | 3,758.8 |
| Mosaics ('000 sq metres) | 3,443.8 | 3,987.9 | 4,478.1 |
| Motor spirit (gasoline) | 960.3 | 1,011.8 | 1,025.7 |
| Kerosene | 546.5 | 558.5 | 640.1 |
| Sulphuric acid (98%) | 372.0 | 392.7 | 381.1 |
| Fertilizers | 996.3 | 840.4 | 898.6 |
| Tyres ('000) | 324.7 | 428.1 | 315.0 |
| Woven textile fabrics ('000 sq metres) | 258,400 | 260,400 | 220,300 |
| Cigarettes (million) | 15,397.6 | 16,885.2 | 16,500 |
| Cigars (million) | 278.6 | 270.2 | 308.5 |
| Raw sugar* | 6,961.5 | 7,815.6 | 7,328.8 |
| Leather footwear ('000 pairs) | 14,200 | 13,300 | 11,000 |
| Electric energy (million kWh) | 13,593.5 | 14,542.3 | 15,239.8 |

* Corresponding to calendar year.

**1990:** Crude steel 270,000 metric tons; Grey cement 3,696,000 metric tons; Motor spirit (gasoline) 1,306,000 metric tons; Kerosene 575,000 metric tons; Raw sugar 8,050,000 metric tons; Leather footwear 13,400,000 pairs; Electric energy 14,678m. kWh.

**1991:** Crude steel 270,000 metric tons; Motor spirit (gasoline) 880,000 metric tons; Kerosene 510,000 metric tons; Raw sugar 7,233,000 metric tons; Leather footwear 13,000,000 pairs; Electric energy 12,741m. kWh.

**1992:** Crude steel 134,000 metric tons (estimate); Motor spirit (gasoline) 940,000 metric tons (estimate); Kerosene 500,000 metric tons (estimate); Raw sugar 7,104,000 metric tons (FAO figure); Leather footwear 13,400,000 pairs; Electric energy 11,127m. kWh.

**1993:** Crude steel 90,000 metric tons (estimate); Motor spirit (gasoline) 939,000 metric tons (estimate); Kerosene 490,000 metric tons (estimate); Raw sugar 4,365,000 metric tons (FAO figure); Electric energy 10,552m. kWh.

**1994:** Crude steel 131,000 metric tons (estimate); Motor spirit (gasoline) 939,000 metric tons (estimate); Kerosene 500,000 metric tons (estimate); Raw sugar 4,024,000 metric tons (FAO figure); Electric energy 11,685m. kWh.

**1995:** Crude steel 207,000 metric tons (estimate); Motor spirit (gasoline) 958,000 metric tons; Kerosene 515,000 metric tons (estimate); Raw sugar 3,300,000 metric tons (FAO figure); Electric energy 12,458m. kWh.

**1996:** Crude steel 231,000 metric tons; Motor spirit (gasoline) 978,000 metric tons; Kerosene 517,000 metric tons (estimate); Raw sugar 4,400,000 metric tons (FAO figure); Electric energy 13,236m. kWh.

Source: UN, *Industrial Commodity Statistics Yearbook*.

**Tyres** ('000): 373.1 in 1990; 87.5 in 1991; 126.0 in 1992; 62.6 in 1993; 111.6 in 1994; 193.6 in 1995; 212.4 in 1996.

**Grey cement** ('000 metric tons): 1,850.5 in 1991; 1,340.0 in 1992; 1,048.5 in 1993; 1,085.2 in 1994; 1,456.4 in 1995; 1,437.9 in 1996.

Source: UN Economic Commission for Latin America and the Caribbean, *Statistical Yearbook*.

# Finance

**CURRENCY AND EXCHANGE RATES**

**Monetary Units:**
100 centavos = 1 Cuban peso.

**Sterling, Dollar and Euro Equivalents** (30 September 1999)
£1 sterling = 1.6465 pesos;
US $1 = 1.0000 pesos;
€1 = 1.0665 pesos;
100 Cuban pesos = £60.73 = $100.00 = €93.76.

Note: The foregoing information relates to official exchange rates. For the purposes of foreign trade, the peso was at par with the US dollar during each of the 10 years 1987–96. A 'convertible peso' was introduced in December 1994. The free market rate of exchange in September 1998 was US $1 = 23 Cuban pesos.

**STATE BUDGET** (million pesos)

| | 1987 | 1988* | 1989* |
|---|---|---|---|
| Total revenue | 11,272 | 11,386 | 11,903.5 |
| Total expenditure | 11,881 | 12,532 | 13,527.5 |
| Productive sector | 4,575 | 4,713 | 4,975.1 |
| Housing and community services | 680 | 787 | 859.8 |
| Education and public health | 2,725 | 2,857 | 2,906.2 |
| Other social, cultural and scientific activities | 1,850 | 2,060 | 2,300.8 |
| Government administration and judicial bodies | 565 | 561 | 524.5 |
| Defence and public order | 1,242 | 1,274 | 1,377.4 |
| Other | 244 | 280 | 583.7 |

* Preliminary.

Source: State Committee for Finance, Havana.

**INTERNATIONAL RESERVES** (million pesos at 31 December)

| | 1987 | 1988 |
|---|---|---|
| Gold and other precious metals | 17.5 | 19.5 |
| Cash and deposits in foreign banks (convertible currency) | 36.5 | 78.0 |
| **Sub-total** | 54.0 | 97.5 |
| Deposits in foreign banks (in transferable roubles) | 142.5 | 137.0 |
| **Total** | 196.5 | 234.5 |

**NATIONAL ACCOUNTS**

**Composition of Gross National Product**
(million pesos at current prices)

| | 1994 | 1995 | 1996 |
|---|---|---|---|
| Compensation of employees | 9,614.5 | 9,860.7 | 10,181.9 |
| Operating surplus<br>Consumption of fixed capital | 3,712.1 | 4,283.6 | 5,671.2 |
| **Gross domestic product (GDP) at factor cost** | 13,326.6 | 14,144.3 | 15,853.1 |
| Indirect taxes *less* subsidies | 5,871.7 | 7,592.8 | 6,961.6 |
| **GDP in purchasers' values** | 19,198.3 | 21,737.1 | 22,814.7 |
| *Less* Factor income from abroad (net) | 340.4 | 524.8 | 492.6 |
| **Gross national product** | 18,857.9 | 21,212.3 | 22,322.1 |

**Expenditure on the Gross Domestic Product**
(million pesos at current prices)

| | 1994 | 1995 | 1996 |
|---|---|---|---|
| Government final consumption expenditure | 5,234.6 | 5,302.5 | 5,521.8 |
| Private final consumption expenditure | 13,206.2 | 15,454.5 | 16,281.7 |
| Increase in stocks | −566.7 | −160.8 | −637.4 |
| Gross fixed capital formation | 1,573.1 | 1,685.5 | 2,258.2 |
| **Total domestic expenditure** | 19,447.2 | 22,281.7 | 23,424.3 |
| Exports of goods and services | 2,541.8 | 2,913.1 | 3,563.6 |
| *Less* Imports of goods and services | 2,790.7 | 3,457.7 | 4,173.2 |
| **GDP in purchasers' values** | 19,198.3 | 21,737.1 | 22,814.7 |
| **GDP at constant 1981 prices** | 12,868.3 | 13,184.5 | 14,218.0 |

**Gross Domestic Product by Economic Activity**
(million pesos at constant 1981 prices)

| | 1995 | 1996 | 1997 |
|---|---|---|---|
| Agriculture, hunting, forestry and fishing | 915.5 | 1,075.4 | 1,073.7 |
| Mining and quarrying | 152.1 | 177.3 | 181.9 |
| Manufacturing | 3,555.2 | 3,835.4 | 4,154.5 |
| Electricity, gas and water | 384.2 | 398.0 | 421.8 |
| Construction | 412.1 | 538.5 | 556.0 |
| Wholesale and retail trade, restaurants and hotels | 2,984.8 | 3,250.8 | 3,175.8 |
| Transport, storage and communications | 748.4 | 813.4 | 845.4 |
| Finance, insurance, real estate and business services | 483.8 | 518.6 | 544.5 |
| Community, social and personal services | 3,548.4 | 3,610.6 | 3,618.8 |
| **Total** | 13,184.5 | 14,218.0 | 14,572.4 |

Source: UN Economic Commission for Latin America and the Caribbean, *Statistical Yearbook*.

# External Trade

**PRINCIPAL COMMODITIES** (million pesos)

| Imports | 1987 | 1988 | 1989 |
|---|---|---|---|
| Food and live animals | 716.2 | 730.4 | 925.3 |
| Crude materials (inedible) except fuels | 301.5 | 281.1 | 307.2 |
| Mineral fuels, lubricants, etc. | 2,621.0 | 2,589.0 | 2,629.9 |
| Chemicals and related products | 447.2 | 433.8 | 530.2 |
| Basic manufactures | 821.1 | 816.3 | 838.0 |
| Machinery and transport equipment | 2,353.7 | 2,409.5 | 2,530.7 |
| Miscellaneous manufactured articles | 244.7 | 233.8 | 276.5 |
| **Total** (incl. others) | 7,583.6 | 7,579.8 | 8,124.2 |

| Exports | 1987 | 1988 | 1989 |
|---|---|---|---|
| Sugar and sugar products | 4,012.6 | 4,116.5 | 3,948.5 |
| Minerals and concentrates | 332.2 | 455.0 | 497.7 |
| Tobacco and tobacco products | 90.5 | 98.4 | 83.6 |
| Fish and fish preparations | 144.3 | 149.0 | 128.8 |
| Other agricultural products | 250.9 | 248.2 | 211.3 |
| **Total** (incl. others) | 5,402.1 | 5,518.3 | 5,392.0 |

**1990** (million pesos): Total imports c.i.f. 6,745; Total exports f.o.b. 4,910.
**1991** (million pesos): Total imports c.i.f. 3,690; Total exports f.o.b. 3,550.
**1992** (million pesos): Total imports c.i.f. 2,185; Total exports f.o.b. 2,050.
**1993** (million pesos): Total imports c.i.f. 1,990; Total exports f.o.b. 1,275.
**1994** (million pesos): Total imports c.i.f. 2,055; Total exports f.o.b. 1,385.
**1995** (million pesos): Total imports c.i.f. 2,825; Total exports f.o.b. 1,600.
**1996** (million pesos): Total imports c.i.f. 3,205; Total exports f.o.b. 2,015.

Source (for 1990–96): UN, *Monthly Bulletin of Statistics*.

**PRINCIPAL TRADING PARTNERS** ('000 pesos)

| Imports c.i.f. | 1987 | 1988 | 1989 |
|---|---|---|---|
| Argentina | 124,339 | 127,506 | 179,198 |
| Bulgaria | 183,980 | 171,797 | 177,501 |
| China, People's Republic | 100,750 | 175,886 | 255,483 |
| Czechoslovakia | 200,134 | 219,453 | 216,283 |
| German Democratic Republic | 338,836 | 340,950 | 358,688 |
| Italy | 45,825 | 75,850 | 62,577 |
| Japan | 106,503 | 88,563 | 49,456 |
| Mexico | 72,064 | 108,022 | 79,954 |
| Poland | 81,481 | 64,027 | 57,795 |
| Romania | 182,112 | 179,918 | 155,970 |
| Spain | 165,405 | 146,139 | 184,865 |
| USSR | 5,445,979 | 5,364,418 | 5,522,391 |
| United Kingdom | 70,195 | 59,746 | 81,769 |
| **Total** (incl. others) | 7,583,600 | 7,579,800 | 8,124,200 |

| Exports f.o.b. | 1987 | 1988 | 1989 |
|---|---|---|---|
| Bulgaria | 169,073 | 164,339 | 176,940 |
| Canada | 36,848 | 38,490 | 54,835 |
| China, People's Republic | 85,468 | 226,253 | 216,071 |
| Czechoslovakia | 143,998 | 183,542 | 136,026 |
| France | 57,585 | 66,854 | 54,429 |
| German Democratic Republic | 281,597 | 311,430 | 285,913 |
| Germany, Federal Republic | 28,360 | 73,015 | 71,395 |
| Hungary | 66,710 | 35,533 | 55,437 |
| Japan | 77,171 | 109,206 | 104,074 |
| Poland | 43,849 | 37,569 | 54,122 |
| Romania | 108,953 | 96,663 | 121,986 |
| Spain | 84,903 | 81,521 | 86,031 |
| Switzerland | 48,746 | 12,163 | 72,615 |
| USSR | 3,868,736 | 3,683,073 | 3,231,222 |
| United Kingdom | 13,365 | 42,491 | 113,782 |
| **Total** (incl. others) | 5,402,060 | 5,518,316 | 5,392,004 |

# Transport

**RAILWAYS**

| | 1994 | 1995 | 1996 |
|---|---|---|---|
| Passenger-kilometres (million) | 2,353.3 | 2,188.2 | 2,159.5 |
| Freight ton-kilometres (million) | 798.7 | 886.4 | n.a. |

Source: UN Economic Commission for Latin America and the Caribbean, *Statistical Yearbook*.

**Passengers** ('000): 23,600 in 1987; 25,200 in 1988; 26,400 in 1989.

**ROAD TRAFFIC** ('000 motor vehicles in use)

| | 1986 | 1987 | 1988 |
|---|---|---|---|
| Passenger cars | 217.2 | 229.5 | 241.3 |
| Commercial vehicles | 184.2 | 194.9 | 208.4 |

Source: UN, *Statistical Yearbook*.

**1997** (estimates, motor vehicles in use): 172,574 passenger cars; 185,495 commercial vehicles (Source: IRF, *World Road Statistics*).

**SHIPPING**

**Merchant Fleet** (registered at 31 December)

| | 1996 | 1997 | 1998 |
|---|---|---|---|
| Number of vessels | 324 | 148 | 105 |
| Total displacement ('000 grt) | 291 | 203 | 158 |

Source: Lloyd's Register of Shipping, *World Fleet Statistics*.

**International Sea-borne Freight Traffic** ('000 metric tons)

| | 1988 | 1989 | 1990 |
|---|---|---|---|
| Goods loaded | 8,600 | 8,517 | 8,092 |
| Goods unloaded | 15,500 | 15,595 | 15,440 |

Source: UN, *Monthly Bulletin of Statistics*.

**CIVIL AVIATION** (traffic on scheduled services)

| | 1994 | 1995 | 1996 |
|---|---|---|---|
| Kilometres flown (million) | 13.2 | 15.6 | 19.8 |
| Passengers carried ('000) | 731 | 824 | 929 |
| Passenger-kilometres (million) | 1,556 | 2,006 | 2,649 |
| Total ton-kilometres (million) | 29.8 | 33.2 | 44.4 |

Source: UN Economic Commission for Latin America and the Caribbean, *Statistical Yearbook*.

# Tourism

**ARRIVALS BY NATIONALITY**

| | 1994 | 1995 | 1996 |
|---|---|---|---|
| Argentina | 36,414 | 32,583 | 31,331 |
| Canada | 109,731 | 143,541 | 162,766 |
| Chile | 6,814 | 13,747 | 12,416 |
| Colombia | 7,310 | 21,035 | 25,251 |
| France | 33,910 | 34,332 | 62,742 |
| Germany | 60,598 | 57,487 | 80,185 |
| Italy | 66,367 | 114,767 | 192,297 |
| Mexico | 49,096 | 32,069 | 37,229 |
| Spain | 62,179 | 89,501 | 117,957 |
| United Kingdom | n.a. | 19,614 | 28,077 |
| USA | 17,937 | 20,672 | 27,113 |
| **Total** (incl. others) | 619,218 | 745,495 | 1,004,336 |

* Figures refer to arrivals at frontiers of visitors from abroad. Excluding same-day visitors (excursionists), the total number of tourist arrivals (in '000) was: 617 in 1994; 742 in 1995; 999 in 1996.

**Tourism receipts** (US $ million): 763 in 1994; 977 in 1995; 1,231 in 1996.

Source: World Tourism Organization, *Yearbook of Tourism Statistics*.

# Communications Media

| | 1993 | 1994 | 1995 |
|---|---|---|---|
| Radio receivers ('000 in use) | 3,768 | 3,800 | 3,850 |
| Television receivers ('000 in use) | n.a. | n.a. | 2,500 |
| Telephones ('000 main lines in use) | 349 | 350 | 353 |
| Mobile cellular telephones (subscribers) | 500 | 1,152 | 1,939 |
| Book production (titles) | 568 | 932 | 698 |

Telefax stations (number in use): 392 in 1992.
Radio receivers ('000 in use): 3,870 in 1996.
Television receivers ('000 in use): 2,600 in 1996.
Book production (titles): 679 in 1996.

Sources: UNESCO, *Statistical Yearbook*, and UN, *Statistical Yearbook*.

# Education

(1996/97)

| | Institutions | Teachers | Students: Males | Females | Total |
|---|---|---|---|---|---|
| Pre-primary | n.a. | 6,970 | 79,674 | 74,846 | 154,520 |
| Primary* | 9,926 | 92,820 | 570,290 | 524,578 | 1,094,868 |
| Secondary: | | | | | |
| General* | n.a. | 46,629 | 233,465 | 266,874 | 500,339 |
| Teacher training | n.a. | 193 | 115 | 391 | 506 |
| Vocational | n.a. | 23,806 | 111,374 | 100,678 | 212,052 |
| Universities and equivalent institutions | n.a. | 22,574 | 44,453 | 67,134 | 111,587 |

* Figures include special education.

Source: UNESCO, *Statistical Yearbook*.

# Directory

## The Constitution

Following the assumption of power by the Castro regime, on 1 January 1959, the Constitution was suspended and a Fundamental Law of the Republic was instituted, with effect from 7 February 1959. In February 1976 Cuba's first socialist Constitution came into force after being submitted to the first Congress of the Communist Party of Cuba, in December 1975, and to popular referendum, in February 1976; it was amended in July 1992. The main provisions of the Constitution, as amended, are summarized below:

### POLITICAL, SOCIAL AND ECONOMIC PRINCIPLES

The Republic of Cuba is a socialist, independent, and sovereign state, organized with all and for the sake of all as a unitary and democratic republic for the enjoyment of political freedom, social justice, collective and individual well-being and human solidarity. Sovereignty rests with the people, from whom originates the power of the State. The Communist Party of Cuba is the leading force of society and the State. The State recognizes, respects and guarantees freedom of religion. Religious institutions are separate from the State. The socialist State carries out the will of the working people and guarantees work, medical care, education, food, clothing and housing. The Republic of Cuba bases its relations with other socialist countries on socialist internationalism, friendship, co-operation and mutual assistance. It reaffirms its willingness to integrate with and co-operate with the countries of Latin America and the Caribbean.

The State organizes and directs the economic life of the nation in accordance with a central social and economic development plan. The State directs and controls foreign trade. The State recognizes the right of small farmers to own their lands and other means of production and to sell that land. The State guarantees the right of citizens to ownership of personal property in the form of earnings, savings, place of residence and other possessions and objects which serve to satisfy their material and cultural needs. The State also guarantees the right of inheritance.

Cuban citizenship is acquired by birth or through naturalization.

The State protects the family, motherhood and matrimony.

The State directs and encourages all aspects of education, culture and science.

All citizens have equal rights and are subject to equal duties.

The State guarantees the right to medical care, education, freedom of speech and press, assembly, demonstration, association and privacy. In the socialist society work is the right and duty, and a source of pride for every citizen.

### GOVERNMENT

**National Assembly of People's Power**

The National Assembly of People's Power (Asamblea Nacional del Poder Popular) is the supreme organ of the State and is the only organ with constituent and legislative authority. It is composed of deputies, over the age of 18, elected by free, direct and secret ballot, for a period of five years. All Cuban citizens aged 16 years or more, except those who are mentally incapacitated or who have committed a crime, are eligible to vote. The National Assembly of People's Power holds two ordinary sessions a year and a special session when requested by one-third of the deputies or by the Council of State. More than one-half of the total number of deputies must be present for a session to be held.

All decisions made by the Assembly, except those relating to constitutional reforms, are adopted by a simple majority of votes. The deputies may be recalled by their electors at any time.

The National Assembly of People's Power has the following functions:

to reform the Constitution;

to approve, modify and annul laws;

to supervise all organs of the State and government;

to decide on the constitutionality of laws and decrees;

to revoke decree-laws issued by the Council of State and the Council of Ministers;

to discuss and approve economic and social development plans, the state budget, monetary and credit systems;

to approve the general outlines of foreign and domestic policy, to ratify and annul international treaties, to declare war and approve peace treaties;

to approve the administrative division of the country;

to elect the President, First Vice-President, the Vice-Presidents and other members of the Council of State;

to elect the President, Vice-President and Secretary of the National Assembly;

to appoint the members of the Council of Ministers on the proposal of the President of the Council of State;

to elect the President, Vice-President and other judges of the People's Supreme Court;

to elect the Attorney-General and the Deputy Attorney-Generals;

to grant amnesty;

to call referendums.

The President of the National Assembly presides over sessions of the Assembly, calls ordinary sessions, proposes the draft agenda, signs the Official Gazette, organizes the work of the commissions appointed by the Assembly and attends the meetings of the Council of State.

**Council of State**

The Council of State is elected from the members of the National Assembly and represents that Assembly in the period between sessions. It comprises a President, one First Vice-President, five Vice-Presidents, one Secretary and 23 other members. Its mandate ends when a new Assembly meets. All decisions are adopted by a simple majority of votes. It is accountable for its actions to the National Assembly.

The Council of State has the following functions:

to call special sessions of the National Assembly;

to set the date for the election of a new Assembly;

to issue decree-laws in the period between the sessions of the National Assembly;

to decree mobilization in the event of war and to approve peace treaties when the Assembly is in recess;

to issue instructions to the courts and the Office of the Attorney-General of the Republic;

to appoint and remove ambassadors of Cuba abroad on the proposal of its President, to grant or refuse recognition to diplomatic representatives of other countries to Cuba;

to suspend those provisions of the Council of Ministers that are not in accordance with the Constitution;

to revoke the resolutions of the Executive Committee of the local organs of People's Power which are contrary to the Constitution or laws and decrees formulated by other higher organs.

The President of the Council of State is Head of State and Head of Government and for all purposes the Council of State is the highest representative of the Cuban state.

**Head of State**

The President of the Council of State is the Head of State and the Head of Government and has the following powers:

to represent the State and Government and conduct general policy;

to convene and preside over the sessions of the Council of State and the Council of Ministers;

to supervise the ministries and other administrative bodies;

to propose the members of the Council of Ministers to the National Assembly of People's Power;

to receive the credentials of the heads of foreign diplomatic missions;

to sign the decree-laws and other resolutions of the Council of State;

to exercise the Supreme Command of all armed institutions and determine their general organization;

to preside over the National Defence Council;

to declare a state of emergency in the cases outlined in the Constitution.

In the case of absence, illness or death of the President of the Council of State, the First Vice-President assumes the President's duties.

**The Council of Ministers**

The Council of Ministers is the highest-ranking executive and administrative organ. It is composed of the Head of State and Government, as its President, the First Vice-President, the Vice-Presidents, the Ministers, the Secretary and other members determined by law. Its Executive Committee is composed of the President, the First Vice-President, the Vice-Presidents and other members of the Council of Ministers determined by the President.

The Council of Ministers has the following powers:

to conduct political, economic, cultural, scientific, social and defence policy as outlined by the National Assembly;

to approve international treaties;

to propose projects for the general development plan and, if they are approved by the National Assembly, to supervise their implementation;

to conduct foreign policy and trade;

to draw up bills and submit them to the National Assembly;

to draw up the draft state budget;

to conduct general administration, implement laws, issue decrees and supervise defence and national security.

The Council of Ministers is accountable to the National Assembly of People's Power.

### LOCAL GOVERNMENT

The country is divided into 14 provinces and 169 municipalities. The provinces are: Pinar del Río, Habana, Ciudad de la Habana, Matanzas, Villa Clara, Cienfuegos, Sancti Spíritus, Ciego de Avila, Camagüey, Las Tunas, Holguín, Granma, Santiago de Cuba and Guantánamo.

Voting for delegates to the municipal assemblies is direct, secret and voluntary. All citizens over 16 years of age are eligible to vote. The number of delegates to each assembly is proportionate to the number of people living in that area. A delegate must obtain more than one-half of the total number of votes cast in the constituency in order to be elected. The Municipal and Provincial Assemblies of People's Power are elected by free, direct and secret ballot. Nominations for Municipal and Provincial Executive Committees of People's Power are submitted to the relevant assembly by a commission presided over by a representative of the Communist Party's leading organ and consisting of representatives of youth, workers', farmers', revolutionary and women's organizations. The President and Secretary of each of the regional and the provincial assemblies are the only full-time members, the other delegates carrying out their functions in addition to their normal employment.

The regular and extraordinary sessions of the local Assemblies of People's Power are public. More than one-half of the total number of members must be present in order for agreements made to be valid. Agreements are adopted by simple majority.

### JUDICIARY

Judicial power is exercised by the People's Supreme Court and all other competent tribunals and courts. The People's Supreme Court is the supreme judicial authority and is accountable only to the National Assembly of People's Power. It can propose laws and issue regulations through its Council of Government. Judges are independent but the courts must inform the electorate of their activities at least once a year. Every accused person has the right to a defence and can be tried only by a tribunal.

The Office of the Attorney-General is subordinate only to the National Assembly and the Council of State and is responsible for ensuring that the law is properly obeyed.

The Constitution may be totally or partially modified only by a two-thirds majority vote in the National Assembly of People's Power. If the modification is total, or if it concerns the composition and powers of the National Assembly of People's Power or the Council of State, or the rights and duties contained in the Constitution, it also requires a positive vote by referendum.

## The Government

(February 2000)

**Head of State:** Dr FIDEL CASTRO RUZ (took office 2 December 1976; re-elected December 1981, December 1986, March 1993 and February 1998).

### COUNCIL OF STATE

**President:** Dr FIDEL CASTRO RUZ.

**First Vice-President:** Gen. RAÚL CASTRO RUZ.

**Vice-Presidents:**
JUAN ALMEIDA BOSQUE.
Gen. ABELARDO COLOMÉ IBARRA.
CARLOS LAGE DÁVILA.
JUAN ESTEBAN LAZO HERNÁNDEZ.
JOSÉ RAMÓN MACHADO VENTURA.

**Secretary:** Dr JOSÉ M. MIYAR BARRUECOS.

**Members:**
JOSÉ RAMÓN BALAGUER CABRERA.
VILMA ESPÍN GUILLOIS DE CASTRO.
Dr ARMANDO HART DÁVALOS.
ORLANDO LUGO FONTE.
REGLA MARTÍNEZ HERRERA.
MAÍA CARIDAD ABREUS RUIZ.
CONRADO MARTÍNEZ CORONA.
Gen. JULIO CASAS REGUEIRO.
MARCOS RAÚL AGUILERA GUETÓN.
JOSÉ LUIS RODRÍGUEZ GARCÍA.
SALVADOR VALDÉS MESA.
PEDRO MIRET PRIETO.
ROBERTO DÍAZ SOTOLONGO.
SERGIO CORRIERI HERNÁNDEZ.
ROBERTO FERNÁNDEZ RETAMAR.
FELIPE PÉREZ ROQUE.
MARCOS J. PORTAL LEÓN.
CARIDAD DIEGO BELLO.
JUAN CONTINO ASLÁN.
PEDRO ROSS LEAL.
OTTO RIVERO TORRES.
CARLOS MANUEL VALENCIAGA DÍAZ.

### COUNCIL OF MINISTERS

**President:** Dr FIDEL CASTRO RUZ.

**First Vice-President:** Gen. RAÚL CASTRO RUZ.

**Vice-Presidents:**
JOSÉ RAMÓN FERNÁNDEZ ALVAREZ.
ADOLFO DÍAZ SUÁREZ.
OSMANY CIENFUEGOS GORRIARÁN.
PEDRO MIRET PRIETO.
JAIME CROMBET HERNÁNDEZ BAQUERO.

**Secretary:** CARLOS LAGE DÁVILA.

**Minister of Agriculture:** ALFREDO JORDÁN MORALES.

**Minister of Foreign Trade:** RICARDO CABRISAS RUIZ.

**Minister of Internal Trade:** BÁRBARA CASTILLO CUESTA.

**Minister of Communications:** Gen. SILVANO COLÁS SÁNCHEZ.

**Minister of Construction:** JUAN MARIO JUNCO DEL PINO.

**Minister of Culture:** ABEL ENRIQUE PRIETO JIMÉNEZ.

**Minister of Economy and Planning:** JOSÉ LUIS RODRÍGUEZ GARCÍA.

**Minister of Education:** LUIS IGNACIO GÓMEZ GUTIÉRREZ.

**Minister of Higher Education:** FERNANDO VECINO ALEGRET.

**Minister of the Revolutionary Armed Forces:** Gen. RAÚL CASTRO RUZ.

**Minister of Finance and Prices:** MANUEL MILLARES RODRÍGUEZ.

**Minister of the Food Industry:** ALEJANDRO ROCA IGLESIAS.

**Minister of Foreign Investment and Economic Co-operation:** MARTA LOMAS MORALES.

**Minister of Sugar:** Gen. ULISES ROSALES DEL TORO.

**Minister of the Construction Materials Industry:** (vacant).

**Minister of Light Industry:** JESÚS PÉREZ OTHÓN.

**Minister of the Fishing Industry:** ORLANDO FELIPE RODRÍGUEZ ROMAY.

**Minister of the Iron and Steel, Metallurgical and Electronic Industries:** ROBERTO IGNACIO GONZÁLEZ PLANAS.

**Minister of Basic Industries:** MARCOS J. PORTAL LEÓN.

**Minister of the Interior:** Gen. ABELARDO COLOMÉ IBARRA.

**Minister of Justice:** ROBERTO DÍAZ SOTOLONGO.

**Minister of Foreign Affairs:** FELIPE PÉREZ ROQUE.

**Minister of Labour and Social Security:** ALFREDO MORALES CARTAYA.

**Minister of Public Health:** CARLOS DOTRES MARTÍNEZ.

**Minister of Science, Technology and the Environment:** Dra ROSA ELENA SIMEÓN NEGRÍN.

**Minister of Transport:** ALVARO PÉREZ MORALES.

**Minister of Tourism:** IBRAHÍM FERRADAZ GARCÍA.

**Minister, President of the State Committee for Technical and Material Supplies:** SONIA RODRÍGUEZ CARDONA.

**Minister, President of the State Committee for Statistics:** FIDEL EMILIO VASCOS GONZÁLEZ.

**Minister, President of the State Committee for Standardization:** RAMÓN DARIAS RODÉS.

**Minister, President of the Banco Central de Cuba:** FRANCISCO SOBERÓN VALDEZ.

**Minister without Portfolio:** WILFREDO LÓPEZ RODRÍGUEZ.

### MINISTRIES

**Ministry of Agriculture:** Avda Independencia, entre Conill y Sta Ana, Havana; tel. (7) 84-5770; fax (7) 33-5086.

**Ministry of Basic Industries:** Avda Salvador Allende 666, Havana; tel. (7) 70-7711.

**Ministry of Communications:** Plaza de la Revolución 'José Martí', CP 10600, Havana; tel. (7) 81-7654.

**Ministry of Construction:** Avda Carlos M. de Céspedes y Calle 35, Havana; tel. (7) 81-8385; fax (7) 33-5585; e-mail dirinter@ceniai.inf.cu.

**Ministry of the Construction Materials Industry:** Calle 17, esq. 0, Vedado, Havana; tel. (7) 32-2541; fax (7) 33-3176.

**Ministry of Culture:** Calle 2, No 258, entre 11 y 13, Vedado, Havana; tel. (7) 55-2228; fax (7) 66-2053; e-mail rinter@ceisic.cult.cu.

**Ministry of Economy and Planning:** 20 de Mayo y Ayestarán, Plaza de la Revolución, Havana; fax (7) 33-3387.

**Ministry of Education:** Obispo 160, Havana; tel. (7) 61-4888.

**Ministry of Finance and Prices:** Obispo 211, esq. Cuba, Havana; tel. (7) 60-4111; fax (7) 62-0252.

**Ministry of the Fishing Industry:** Avda 5 y 248 Jaimanitas, Santa Fe, Havana; tel. (7) 29-7034; fax (7) 24-9168; e-mail cubafish@ceniai.inf.cu.

**Ministry of the Food Industry:** Avda 41, No 4455, Playa, Havana; tel. (7) 23-6801; fax (7) 23-4052; e-mail minalvm1@ceniai.inf.cu.

**Ministry of Foreign Affairs:** Calzada 360, Vedado, Havana; tel. (7) 32-4074.

**Ministry of Foreign Investment and Economic Co-operation:** Calle 1, No 201, Vedado, Havana; tel. (7) 3-6661.

**Ministry of Foreign Trade:** Infanta 16, esquina 23, Vedado, Havana; tel. (7) 55-0428; fax (7) 55-0376; e-mail cepecdir@infocex.cu; internet www.infocex.cu/cepec/.

**Ministry of Higher Education:** Calle 23, No 565, esq. a F, Vedado, Havana; tel. (7) 3-6655; fax (7) 33-3090; e-mail dri@reduniv.edu.cu.

**Ministry of the Interior:** Plaza de la Revolución, Havana.

**Ministry of Internal Trade:** Calle Habana 258, Havana; tel. (7) 62-5790.

**Ministry of the Iron and Steel, Metallurgical and Electronic Industries:** Avda Rancho Boyeros y Calle 100, Havana; tel. (7) 20-4861.

**Ministry of Justice:** Calle 0, No 216, entre 23 y Humboldt, Vedado, CP 10400, Havana 4; tel. (7) 32-6319.

**Ministry of Labour and Social Security:** Calle 23, esq. Calle P, Vedado, Havana; tel. (7) 70-4571; fax (7) 33-5816.

**Ministry of Light Industry:** Empedrado 302, Havana; tel. (7) 62-4041.

**Ministry of Public Health:** Calle 23, No 301, Vedado, Havana; tel. (7) 32-2561.

**Ministry of the Revolutionary Armed Forces:** Plaza de la Revolución, Havana.

**Ministry of Science, Technology and the Environment:** Havana.

**Ministry of Sugar:** Calle 23, No 171, Vedado, Havana; tel. (7) 30-5061.

**Ministry of Tourism:** Havana.

**Ministry of Transport:** Avda Independencia y Tulipán, Havana; tel. (7) 81-2076.

# Legislature

### ASAMBLEA NACIONAL DEL PODER POPULAR

The National Assembly of People's Power was constituted on 2 December 1976. In July 1992 the National Assembly adopted a constitutional amendment providing for legislative elections by direct vote. Only candidates nominated by the PCC were permitted to contest the elections. At elections to the National Assembly conducted on 11 January 1998 all 601 candidates were elected. Of the 7.8m. registered voters, 98.35% participated in the elections. Only 5% of votes cast were blank or spoilt.

**President:** Ricardo Alarcón de Quesada.

**Vice-President:** Jaime Crombet Hernández Maurell.

**Secretary:** Dr Ernesto Suárez Méndez.

# Political Organizations

**Partido Comunista de Cuba (PCC)** (Communist Party of Cuba): Havana; f. 1961 as the Organizaciones Revolucionarias Integradas (ORI) from a fusion of the Partido Socialista Popular (Communist), Fidel Castro's Movimiento 26 de Julio and the Directorio Revolucionario 13 de Marzo; became the Partido Unido de la Revolución Socialista Cubana (PURSC) in 1962; renamed as the Partido Comunista de Cuba in 1965; 150-member Central Committee, Political Bureau (24 mems in 1997), and five Commissions; 706,132 mems (1994).

Political Bureau: Dr Fidel Castro Ruz, Gen. Raúl Castro Ruz, Juan Almeida Bosque, José Ramón Machado Ventura, Juan Esteban Lazo Hernández, Gen. Abelardo Colomé Ibarra, Pedro Ross Leal, Carlos Lage Dávila, Roberto Robaína González, Alfredo Jordán Morales, Gen. Ulises Rosales del Toro, Concepción Campa Huergo, Yadira García Vera, Abel Enrique Prieto Jiménez, Gen. Julio Casas Regueiro, Gen. Leopoldo Cintra Frías, Ricardo Alarcón de Quesada, José Ramón Balaguer Cabrera, Misael Enamorado Dager, Gen. Ramón Espinosa Martín, Marcos J. Portal León, Juan Carlos Robinson Agramonte, Pedro Sáez Montejo, Jorge Luis Sierra Cruz.

There are a number of dissident groups operating in Cuba. These include:

**Concertación Democrática Cubana—CDC:** f. 1991; alliance of eight dissident organizations campaigning for political pluralism and economic reform.

**Partido Cubano Ortodoxo:** f. 1999; Leader Nelson Aguiar.

**Partido pro-Derechos Humanos:** f. 1988 to defend human rights in Cuba; Pres. Hiram Abi Cobas; Sec.-Gen. Tania Díaz.

# Diplomatic Representation

### EMBASSIES IN CUBA

**Afghanistan:** Calle 24, No 106, entre 1 y 3, Miramar, Havana; tel. (7) 22-1145; Ambassador: Nur Ahmad Nur.

**Albania:** Calle 13, No 851, Vedado, Havana; tel. (7) 30-2788; Ambassador: Clirim Cepani.

**Algeria:** Avda 5, No 2802, esq. 28, Miramar, Havana; tel. (7) 2-6538; Ambassador: Abdelhamid Latreche.

**Angola:** Avda 5, No 1012, entre 10 y 12, Miramar, Havana; tel. (7) 33-2474; fax (7) 33-2117; Ambassador: António Burity da Silva Neto.

**Argentina:** Calle 36, No 511, entre 5 y 7, Miramar, Havana; tel. (7) 33-2972; fax (7) 33-2140; Ambassador: Juan Carlos Olima.

**Austria:** Calle 4, No 101, entre 1 y 3, Miramar, Havana; tel. (7) 24-2824; fax (7) 24-1235; Ambassador: Dr Yuri Standenat.

**Belgium:** Avda 5, No 7408, esq. 76, Miramar, Havana; tel. (7) 33-2410; fax (7) 33-1318; Ambassador: Count Louis Cornet d'Elzius du Chenoy.

**Benin:** Calle 20, No 119, entre 1 y 3, Miramar, Havana; tel. (7) 24-2179; fax (7) 24-2334; Ambassador: Joseph Victor Menard.

**Bolivia:** Calle 26, No 113, entre 1 y 3, Miramar, Havana; tel. (7) 33-2426; fax (7) 33-2739; Ambassador: Óscar Peña Franco.

**Brazil:** Calle 16, No 503, entre 5 y 7, Miramar, Havana; tel. (7) 33-2917; fax (7) 33-2328; Ambassador: José Nogueira Filho.

**Bulgaria:** Calle B, No 252, entre 11 y 13, Vedado, Havana; tel. (7) 33-3125; fax (7) 33-3297; Chargé d'affaires a.i.: Kiril Kotzaliev.

**Burkina Faso:** Calle 7, No 8401, entre 84 y 84a, Miramar; tel. (7) 24-2895; fax (7) 24-1942; Ambassador: Salif Nebie.

**Cambodia:** Avda 6, No 7001, esq. 70, Miramar, Havana; tel. (7) 33-6151; fax (7) 33-6400; Ambassador: Ros Kong.

**Canada:** Calle 30, No 518, esq. 7, Miramar, Havana; tel. (7) 33-2516; fax (7) 33-2044; Ambassador: Keith Christie.

**Cape Verde:** Calle 98, No 508, entre 5 y 5b, Miramar, Havana; tel. (7) 33-2979; fax (7) 33-1072; Chargé d'affaires a.i.: Arnaldo Delgado.

**Chile:** Avda 33, No 1423, entre 16 y 18, Mitamar, Havana.

**China, People's Republic:** Calle 13, No 551, Vedado, Havana; tel. (7) 32-5205; Ambassador: Liu Peigen.

**Colombia:** Calle 14, No 515, entre 5 y 7, Miramar, Havana; tel. (7) 33-1246; fax (7) 33-1249; Ambassador: Alberto Villamizar Cardenas.

**Congo, Democratic Republic:** Calle 36, No 716, entre 7 y 9, Miramar, Havana; tel. (7) 29-1580; Ambassador: Simba Ndombe.

**Congo, Republic:** Avda 5, No 1003, Miramar, Havana; tel. (7) 2-6513; Ambassador: Marcel Touanga.

**Czech Republic:** Avda Kohly 259, entre 41 y 43, Nuevo Vedado, Havana; tel. (7) 33-3201; fax (7) 33-3596; Chargé d'affaires a.i.: Petr Mikyska.

**Ecuador:** Avda 5-a, No 4407, entre 44 y 46, Miramar, Havana; tel. (7) 33-2820; fax (7) 33-2868; Ambassador: Gustavo Jarrín Ampudia.

**Egypt:** Avda 5, No 1801, esq. 18, Miramar, Havana; tel. (7) 24-2441; fax (7) 24-0905; Ambassador: Hazem Muhammad Taher.

**Ethiopia:** Calle 6, No 318, Miramar, Havana; tel. (7) 22-1260; Ambassador: Abebe Belayneh.

**Finland:** Havana; tel. (7) 33-2698; Ambassador: Heikki Puurunen.

**France:** Calle 14, No 312, entre 3 y 5, Miramar, Havana; tel. (7) 33-2132; fax (7) 33-1439; Ambassador: Yvon Roe d'Albert.

**Germany:** Calle 28, No 313, entre 3 y 5, Miramar, Havana; tel. (7) 33-2539; fax (7) 33-1586; Ambassador: Dr GEORG TREFFTZ.

**Ghana:** Avda 5, No 1808, esq. Calle 20, Miramar, Havana; tel. (7) 24-2153; Ambassador: Dr KWAKU DANSO-BOAFO.

**Greece:** Avda 5, No 7802, esq. 78, Miramar, Havana; tel. (7) 33-2995; Ambassador: MARINOS RAFTOPOULOS.

**Guinea:** Calle 20, No 504, Miramar, Havana; tel. (7) 2-6428; Ambassador: LAMINE SOUGOULÉ.

**Guinea-Bissau:** Calle 14, No 313, entre 3 y 5, Miramar, Havana; tel. (7) 33-2689; fax (7) 33-2794; Ambassador: CONSTANTINO LOPES DA COSTA.

**Guyana:** Calle 18, No 506, Miramar, Havana; tel. (7) 24-2094; fax (7) 24 2867; Chargé d'affaires: RITA R. RAMLALL.

**Holy See:** Calle 12, No 514, Miramar, Havana (Apostolic Nunciature); tel. (7) 24-2296; fax (7) 24-2257; e-mail csa@pcn.net; Apostolic Nuncio: Most Rev. LUIS ROBLES DÍAZ, Titular Archbishop of Stephaniacum.

**Hungary:** Avda de los Presidentes 458, entre 19 y 21, Vedado, Havana; tel. (7) 33-3365; fax (7) 33-3286; e-mail embhuncu@ceniai.inf.cu; Ambassador: Dr JÓZSEF NÉMETH.

**India:** Calle 21, No 202, esq. a K, Vedado, Havana; tel. (7) 33-3777; fax (7) 33-3287; Ambassador: RAMIAH RAJAGOPALAN.

**Indonesia:** Avda 5, No 1607, esq. 18, Miramar, Havana; tel. (7) 33-9618; fax (7) 80-5517.

**Iran:** Avda 5, No 3002, esq. 30, Miramar, Havana; tel. (7) 33-2675; fax (7) 33-2770; Ambassador: MASUD EDRISI-KERMANSHAHI.

**Iraq:** Avda 5, No 8201, entre 82 y 84, Miramar, Havana; tel. (7) 33-2326; fax (7) 33-2157; Ambassador: WALEED A. ABBASS.

**Italy:** Paseo 606, No 54, entre 25 y 27, Vedado, Havana; tel. (7) 33-3334; fax (7) 33-3416; Ambassador: GIUSEPPE MOSCATO.

**Jamaica:** Avda 5, No 3608, entre 36 y 36A, Miramar, Havana; tel. (7) 24-2908; fax (7) 24-2531; e-mail embjmcub@mail.infocom.etecsa.cu; Ambassador: CARLYLE DUNKLEY.

**Japan:** Havana; tel. (7) 33-3598; fax (7) 33-3172; Ambassador: RYO KAWADE.

**Korea, Democratic People's Republic:** Calle 17, No 752, Vedado, Havana; tel. (7) 30-5132; Ambassador: KIM GIL HWAN.

**Laos:** Avda 5, No 2808, esq. 30, Miramar, Havana; tel. (7) 33-1057; Ambassador: PONMEK DELALOY.

**Lebanon:** Calle 174, No 1707, entre 17 y 17A, Sihoney, Havana; tel. (7) 21-8974; Chargé d'affaires a.i.: ZOUHAIR KAZZAZ.

**Libya:** Calle 8, No 309, Miramar, Havana; tel. (7) 2-4892; Ambassador: ALI MUHAMMAD AL-EJILI.

**Mexico:** Calle 12, No 518, Miramar, Playa, Havana; tel. (7) 24-2553; fax (7) 24-2217; Ambassador: PEDRO JOAQUÍN COLDWELL.

**Mongolia:** Calle 66, No 505, Miramar, Havana; tel. (7) 33-2763; fax (7) 33-0639; Ambassador: PUNTSAG DARIIN.

**Mozambique:** Avda 7, No 2203, entre 22 y 24, Miramar, Havana; tel. (7) 26445; Ambassador: JULIO BRAGA.

**Namibia:** Hotel Neptuno, Apdo 92, Miramar, Havana; tel. (7) 33-1430; fax (7) 33-1431.

**Netherlands:** Calle 8, No 307, Miramar, Havana; tel. (7) 33-2511; Ambassador: GERHARD JOHAN VAN HATTUM.

**Nicaragua:** Calle 20, No 709, entre 7 y 9, Miramar, Havana; tel. (7) 33-1025; fax (7) 33-6323; Chargé d'affaires a.i.: AURA ESTELA CANO ARAGÓN.

**Nigeria:** Avda 5, No 1401, Apdo 6232, Miramar, Havana; tel. (7) 29-1091; Ambassador: SOLOMON KIKIOWO OMOJOKUN.

**Panama:** Calle 26, No 109, entre 1 y 3, Miramar, Havana; tel. (7) 33-1673; fax (7) 33-1674; Ambassador: RAFAEL MORENO SAAVEDRA.

**Peru:** Calle 36, No 109, entre 3 y 5, Miramar, Havana; tel. (7) 33-2477; fax (7) 33-2636; Ambassador: JOSÉ TORRES MURGA.

**Philippines:** Avda 5, No 2207, esq. 24, Miramar, Havana; tel. (7) 24-2915; fax (7) 33-2915; e-mail philhav@ip.etecsa.cu; Chargé d'affaires: MARIA LETICIA C. RAMOS.

**Poland:** Avda 5, No 4407, esq. a 46, Miramar, Havana; tel. and fax (7) 33-1323; Chargé d'affaires a.i.: SLAWOMIR KLIMKIEWICZ.

**Portugal:** Avda 5, No 6604, entre 66 y 68, Miramar, Havana; tel. (7) 24-2871; fax (7) 24-2593; Ambassador: MANUEL SILVA DUARTE COSTA.

**Romania:** Calle 21, No 307, Vedado, Havana; tel. (7) 32-4303; Ambassador: ION SIMINICEANU.

**Russia:** Avda 5, No 6402, entre 62 y 66, Miramar, Havana; tel. (7) 33-1749; fax (7) 33-1038; Ambassador: YURII VLADIMIROVICH PETROV.

**Slovakia:** Calle 66, No 521, entre 5 y 7, Miramar, Havana; tel. (7) 33-1884; fax (7) 33-1883; Chargé d'affaires a.i.: BETER SULOVSKY.

**Spain:** Cárcel No 51, esq. Zulueta, Havana; tel. (7) 33-8025; fax (7) 33-8006; Ambassador: EDUARDO JUNCO.

**Sri Lanka:** Calle 32, No 307, entre 3 y 5, Miramar, Havana; tel. (7) 24-2562; fax (7) 24-2183; e-mail sri.lanka@ip.erecsa.cu; Chargé d'affaires a.i. DON BERNARD KALIDASA WITHANAGE.

**Sweden:** Avda 31, No 1411, entre 14 y 18, Miramar, Havana; tel. (7) 33-2831; fax (7) 33-1194; Ambassador: MICHAEL FRÜHLING.

**Switzerland:** Avda 5, No 2005, entre 20 y 22, Miramar, Havana; tel. (7) 33-2729; fax (7) 33-1148; Ambassador: MARCUS KAISER.

**Syria:** Avda 5, No 7402, Miramar, Havana; tel. (7) 22-5266; Chargé d'affaires: R. F. JAJHAI.

**Turkey:** Avda 1-A, No 4215, entre 42 y 44, Miramar, Havana; tel. (7) 22-3933; Ambassador: MEHMET GÜNEY.

**United Kingdom:** Calle 34, No 702/4, entre 7 y 17, Miramar, Havana; tel. (7) 24-1771; fax (7) 24-8104; e-mail embrit@ceniai.inf.cu; Ambassador: DAVID RIDGWAY.

**USA:** (Relations broken off in 1961); Interests Section: Calzada, entre L y M, Vedado, Havana; tel. (7) 33-3543; Counsellor and Principal Officer: ALAN H. FLANIGAN.

**Uruguay:** Calle 14, No 506, entre 5 y 7, Miramar, Havana; tel. (7) 24-2311; fax (7) 24-2246; e-mail urucub@ceniai.inf.cu; Ambassador: ENRIQUE ESTRÁZULAS.

**Venezuela:** Calle 36-A, No 704, entre 7 y 42, Miramar, Havana; tel. (7) 33-2612; fax (7) 33-2773; e-mail vencuba@ceniai.cu; Ambassador: M. C. LÓPEZ.

**Viet Nam:** Avda 5, No 1802, Miramar, Havana; tel. (7) 2-5214; Ambassador: DO VAN TAI.

**Yemen:** Avda 7, No 2207, esq. 24, Miramar, Havana; tel. (7) 22-2594; Ambassador: MUHAMMAD ABDULRAHMAN HUSSEIN.

**Yugoslavia:** Calle 42, No 115, Miramar, Havana; tel. (7) 2-4982; Ambassador: MIHAJLO POPOVIĆ.

**Zimbabwe:** Avda 3, No 1001, esq. a 10, Miramar, Havana; tel. (7) 24-2857; Ambassador: AGRIPPAH MUJERE MUTAMBARA.

## Judicial System

The judicial system comprises the People's Supreme Court, the People's Provincial Courts and the People's Municipal Courts. The People's Supreme Court exercises the highest judicial authority.

### PEOPLE'S SUPREME COURT

The People's Supreme Court comprises the Plenum, the six Courts of Justice in joint session and the Council of Government. When the Courts of Justice are in joint session they comprise all the professional and lay judges, the Attorney-General and the Minister of Justice. The Council of Government comprises the President and Vice-President of the People's Supreme Court, the Presidents of each Court of Justice and the Attorney-General of the Republic. The Minister of Justice may participate in its meetings.

**President:** Dr RUBÉN REMIGIO FERRO.

**Vice-Presidents:** Dr MANUEL DE JESÚS PÉREZ PÉREZ, Dra GRACIELA PRIETO MARTÍN.

**Criminal Court:**
**President:** Dr JORGE L. BODES TORRES.

**Civil and Administrative Court:**
**President:** ANDRÉS BOLAÑOS GASSÓ.

**Labour Court:**
**President:** Dr ANTONIO R. MARTÍN SÁNCHEZ.

**Court for State Security:**
**President:** Dr GUILLERMO HERNÁNDEZ INFANTE.

**Economic Court:**
**President:** Dr ELPIDIO PÉREZ SUÁREZ.

**Military Court:**
**President:** Col JUAN MARINO FUENTES CALZADO.

**Attorney-General:** JUAN ESCALONA REGUERA.

## Religion

There is no established Church, and all religions are permitted, though Roman Catholicism predominates. The Afro-Cuban religions of Regla de Ocha (Santéria) and Regla Conga (Palo Monte) also have numerous adherents.

### CHRISTIANITY

**Consejo Ecuménico de Cuba** (Ecumenical Council of Cuba): Calle 14, No 304, entre 3 y 5, Miramar, Playa, Havana; tel. (7) 33-1792; fax (7) 33-178820; f. 1941; 11 mem. churches; Pres. Rev. ORESTES GONZÁLEZ; Exec. Sec. Rev. JOSÉ LÓPEZ.

### The Roman Catholic Church

Cuba comprises three archdioceses and eight dioceses. At 31 December 1997 adherents represented about 40% of the total population.

**Conferencia de Obispos Católicos de Cuba—COCC (Bishops' Conference):** Calle 26, No 314, entre 3 y 5, Miramar, Apdo 594, Havana; tel. (7) 22-3868; fax (7) 33-2168; e-mail cocc@brigadoon.com; f. 1983; Pres. ADOLFO RODRÍGUEZ HERRERA, Archbishop of Camagüey.

**Archbishop of Camagüey:** ADOLFO RODRÍGUEZ HERRERA, Calle Luaces, No 55, Apdo 105, Camagüey 70100; tel. (322) 92268; fax (322) 33-5372.

**Archbishop of San Cristóbal de la Habana:** Cardinal JAIME LUCAS ORTEGA Y ALAMINO, Calle Habana 152, esq. a Chacón, Apdo 594, Havana 10100; tel. (7) 62-4000; fax (7) 33-8109.

**Archbishop of Santiago de Cuba:** PEDRO CLARO MEURICE ESTIÚ, Sánchez Hechevarría 607, Apdo 26, Santiago de Cuba 90100; tel. (226) 25480; fax (226) 86186.

### The Anglican Communion

Anglicans are adherents of the Iglesia Episcopal de Cuba (Episcopal Church of Cuba).

**Bishop of Cuba:** Rt Rev. JORGE PERERA HURTADO, Calle 6, No 273, Vedado, Havana 10400; fax (7) 33-3293.

### Protestant Churches

**Convención Bautista de Cuba Oriental** (Baptist Convention of Eastern Cuba): San Jerónimo, No 467, entre Calvario y Carnicería, Santiago; tel. 2-0173; f. 1905; Pres. Rev. Dr ROY ACOSTA; Sec. RAFAEL MUSTELIER.

**Iglesia Metodista en Cuba** (Methodist Church in Cuba): Calle K, No 502, 25 y 27, Vedado, Apdo 10400, Havana; tel. (7) 32-2991; fax (7) 33-3135; autonomous since 1968; 6,000 mems; Bishop FRANCISCO GUSTAVO CRUZ DÍAZ.

**Iglesia Presbiteriana-Reformada en Cuba** (Presbyterian-Reformed Church in Cuba): Apdo 154, Matanzas; autonomous since 1967; 8,000 mems; Gen. Sec. Rev. Dr SERGIO ARCE.

Other denominations active in Cuba include the Apostolic Church of Jesus Christ, the Bethel Evangelical Church, the Christian Pentecostal Church, the Church of God, the Church of the Nazarene, the Free Baptist Convention, the Holy Pentecost Church, the Pentecostal Congregational Church and the Salvation Army.

# The Press

### DAILY

In October 1990 President Castro announced that, in accordance with other wide-ranging economic austerity measures, only one newspaper, *Granma*, would henceforth be published as a nationwide daily. The other national dailies were to become weeklies or were to cease publication.

**Granma:** Avda Gen. Suárez y Territorial, Plaza de la Revolución, Apdo 6187, Havana; tel. (7) 81-3333; fax (7) 33-5176; e-mail redac@granmai.get.cma.net; internet www.granma.cubaweb.cu; f. 1965 to replace *Hoy* and *Revolución*; official Communist Party organ; Dir FRANK AGÜERO GÓMEZ; circ. 400,000.

### PERIODICALS

**Adelante:** Avda A, Rpto Jayamá, Camagüey; f. 1959; morning; Dir EVARISTO SARDIÑAS VERA; circ. 42,000.

**Ahora:** Salida a San Germán y Circunvalación, Holguín; f. 1962; Dir RADOBALDO MARTÍNEZ PÉREZ; circ. 50,000.

**ANAP:** Línea 206, entre H e I, Vedado, Havana; f. 1961; monthly; information for small farmers; Dir LEONEL VÁLDEZ ALONSO; circ. 30,000.

**Bastión:** Territorial esq. a Gen. Suárez, Plaza de la Revolución, Havana; tel. (7) 79-3361; organ of the Revolutionary Armed Forces; Dir FRANK AGÜERO GÓMEZ; circ. 65,000.

**Bohemia:** Avda Independencia y San Pedro, Apdo 6000, Havana; tel. (7) 81-9213; fax (7) 33-5511; f. 1908; weekly; politics; Dir CARIDAD MIRANDA MARTÍNEZ; circ. 100,000.

**Boletín Alimentaria de Cuba:** Amargura 103, 10100 Havana; tel. (7) 62-9245. 1996; quarterly; food industry; Dir ANTONIO CAMPOS; circ. 10,000.

**El Caimán Barbudo:** Paseo 613, Vedado, Havana; f. 1966; monthly; cultural; Dir ALEX PAUSIDES; circ. 47,000.

**Cinco de Septiembre:** Calle 35, No 5609, entre 56 y 58, Cienfuegos; f. 1980; Dir FRANCISCO VALDÉS PETITÓN; circ. 18,000.

**Cómicos:** Calle 28, No 112, entre 1 y 3, Miramar, Havana; tel. (7) 22-5892; monthly; humorous; circ. 70,000.

**Con la Guardia en Alto:** Avda Salvador Allende 601, Havana; tel. (7) 79-4443; f. 1961; monthly; for mems of the Committees for the Defence of the Revolution; Dir OMELIA GUERRA PÉREZ; circ. 60,000.

**Cuba Internacional:** Calle 21, No 406, Vedado, Havana 4, Apdo 3603 Havana 3; tel. (7) 32-3578; fax (7) 32-3268; f. 1959; monthly; political; Dir FÉLIX ALBISÚ; circ. 30,000.

**Dedeté:** Territorial y Gen. Suárez, Plaza de la Revolución, Apdo 6344, Havana; tel. (7) 82-0134; fax (7) 81-8621; e-mail jrebelde@teleda.get.cma.net; f. 1969; monthly; Dir ALEN LAUZÁN; circ. 70,000.

**La Demajagua:** Amado Estévez, esq. Calle 10, Rpto R. Reyes, Bayamo; f. 1977; Dir PEDRO MORA ESTRADA; circ. 21,000.

**El Deporte, Derecho del Pueblo:** Vía Blanca y Boyeros, Havana; tel. (7) 40-6838; f. 1968; monthly; sport; Dir MANUEL VAILLANT CARPENTE; circ. 15,000.

**Escambray:** Adolfo del Castillo 10, Sancti Spíritus; tel. (41) 23003; e-mail escambray@esiss.colombus.cu; internet www.escambray.islagrande.cu; f. 1979; Dir JUAN ANTONIO BORREGO DÍAZ; circ. 21,000.

**Girón:** Avda Camilo Cienfuegos No 10505, P. Nuero, Matanzas; f. 1960; Dir OTHONIEL GONZÁLEZ QUEVEDO; circ. 25,000.

**Guerrillero:** Colón esq. Delicias y Adela Azcuy, Pinar del Río; f. 1969; Dir RONALD SUÁREZ; circ. 33,000.

**El Habanero:** Gen. Suárez y Territorial, Plaza de la Revolución, Apdo 6269, Havana; tel. (7) 6160; f. 1987; Dir TUBAL PÁEZ HERNÁNDEZ; circ. 21,000.

**Invasor:** Marcial Gómez 401, esq. Estrada Palma, Ciego de Avila; f. 1979; Dir MIGDALIA UTRERA PEÑA; circ. 10,500.

**Juventud Rebelde:** Territorial esq. Gen. Suárez, Plaza de la Revolución, Apdo 6344, Havana; tel. (7) 81-9087; fax (7) 81-8621; e-mail jrebelde@teleda.get.cma.net; internet www.cubaweb.cu/jrebelde/index.html; f. 1965; organ of the Young Communist League; Dir ROGELIO POLANCO FUENTES; circ. 250,000.

**Juventud Técnica:** Prado 553, esq. Teniente Rey, Habana Vieja, Havana; tel. (7) 31-1825; f. 1965; monthly; scientific-technical; Dir GERMÁN FERNÁNDEZ BURGUET; circ. 100,000.

**Mar y Pesca:** San Ignacio 303, Havana; tel. (7) 61-5518; fax 33-8438; f. 1965; quarterly; fishing; Dir GUSTAVO LÓPEZ; circ. 20,000.

**El Militante Comunista:** Calle 11, No 160, Vedado, Havana; tel. (7) 32-7581; f. 1967; monthly; Communist Party publication; Dir MANUEL MENÉNDEZ; circ. 200,000.

**Moncada:** Belascoaín esq. Zanja, Havana; tel. (7) 79-7109; f. 1966; monthly; Dir RICARDO MARTÍNEZ; circ. 70,000.

**Muchacha:** Galiano 264, esq. Neptuno, Havana; tel. (7) 61-5919; f. 1980; monthly; young women's magazine; Dir SILVIA MARTÍNEZ; circ. 120,000.

**Mujeres:** Galiano 264, esq. Neptuno, Havana; tel. (7) 61-5919; f. 1961; monthly; women's magazine; Dir REGLA ZULUETA; circ. 270,000.

**El Muñe:** Calle 28, No 112, entre 1 y 3, Mirimar, Havana; tel. (7) 22-5892; weekly; circ. 50,000.

**Opciones:** Territorial esq. Gen. Suárez, Plaza de la Revolucíon, Havana; e-mail jrebelde@teleda.get.cma.net; internet www.cubaweb.cu/jrebelde/index.html; weekly; finance, commerce and tourism.

**Opina:** Edif. Focsa, M entre 17 y 19, Havana; f. 1979; 2 a month; consumer-orientated; published by Institute of Internal Demand; Dir EUGENIO RODRÍGUEZ BALARI; circ. 250,000.

**Pablo:** Calle 28, No 112, entre 1 y 3, Mirimar, Havana; tel. (7) 22-5892; 16 a year; circ. 53,000.

**Palante:** Calle 21, No 954, entre 8 y 10, Vedado, Havana; tel. (7) 3-5098; f. 1961; weekly; humorous; Dir ROSENDO GUTIÉRREZ ROMÁN; circ. 235,000.

**Pionero:** Calle 17, No 354, Havana 4; tel. (7) 32-4571; f. 1961; weekly; children's magazine; Dir PEDRO GONZÁLEZ (PÉGLEZ); circ. 210,000.

**Prisma:** Calle 21 y Avda G, No 406, Vedado, Havana; tel. (7) 8-7995; f. 1979; bimonthly; international news; Man. Dir LUIS MANUEL ARCE; circ. 15,000 (Spanish), 10,000 (English).

**RIL:** O'Reilly 358, Havana; tel. (7) 62-0777; f. 1972; 2 a month; technical; Dir Exec. Council of Publicity Dept, Ministry of Light Industry; Chief Officer MIREYA CRESPO; circ. 8,000.

**Sierra Maestra:** Avda de Los Desfiles, Santiago de Cuba; tel. (7) 2-2813; f. 1957; weekly; Dir ARNALDO CLAVEL CARMENATY; circ. 45,000.

**Sol de Cuba:** Calle 19, No 60, entre M y N, Vedado, Havana 4; tel. (7) 32-9881; f. 1983; every 3 months; Spanish, English and French editions; Gen. Dir ALCIDES GIRO MITJANS; Editorial Dir DORIS VÉLEZ; circ. 200,000.

**Somos Jóvenes:** Calle 17, No 354, esq. H, Vedado, Havana; tel. (7) 32-4571; f. 1977; monthly; Dir GUILLERMO CABRERA; circ. 200,000.

**Trabajadores:** Territorial esq. Gen. Suárez, Plaza de la Revolución, Havana; tel. (7) 79-0819; f. 1970; organ of the trade-union movement; Dir JORGE LUIS CANELA CIURANA; circ. 150,000.

**Tribuna de la Habana:** Territorial esq. Gen. Suárez, Plaza de la Revolución, Havana; tel. (7) 81-5932; f. 1980; weekly; Dir ANGEL ZÚÑIGA SUÁREZ; circ. 90,000.

**Vanguardia:** Céspedes 5 (altos), Santa Clara, Matanzas; f. 1962; Dir PEDRO HERNÁNDEZ SOTO; circ. 24,000.

**Venceremos:** Carretera Jamaica, Km 1½, Guantánamo; tel. (7) 35980; f. 1962; Dir HAYDÉE LEÓN MOYA; circ. 28,000.

**Ventiseis:** Avda Carlos J. Finley, Las Tunas; f. 1977; Dir JOSÉ INFANTES REYES; circ. 21,000.

**Verde Olivo:** Avda de Rancho Boyeros y San Pedro, Havana; tel. (7) 79-8373; f. 1959; monthly; organ of the Revolutionary Armed Forces; Dir EUGENIO SUÁREZ PÉREZ; circ. 100,000.

**Victoria:** Carretera de la Fe, Km 1½, Plaza de la Revolución, Nueva Gerona, Isla de la Juventud; f. 1967; Dir NIEVE VARONA PUENTE; circ. 9,200.

### PRESS ASSOCIATIONS

**Unión de Periodistas de Cuba:** Calle 23, No 452, esq. I, Vedado, 10400 Havana; tel. (7) 32-7098; fax (7) 33-3079; e-mail upec@jcce.org.cu; f. 1963; Pres. TUBAL PÁEZ HERNÁNDEZ.

**Unión de Escritores y Artistas de Cuba:** Calle 17, No 351, Vedado, Havana; tel. (7) 32-4571; fax (7) 33-3158; Pres. ABEL E. PRIETO JIMÉNEZ; Exec. Vice-Pres. LISANDRO OTERO.

### NEWS AGENCIES

**Agencia de Información Nacional (AIN):** Calle 23, No 358, esq. a J, Vedado, Havana; tel. (7) 32-5541; fax (7) 66-2049; e-mail RPT@ain.sld.cu; national news agency; Dir ROBERTO PAVÓN TAMAYO.

**Prensa Latina (Agencia Informativa Latinoamericana, SA):** Calle 23, No 201, esq. a N, Vedado, Havana; tel. (7) 32-5561; fax (7) 33-3069; f. 1959; Dir PEDRO MARGOLLES VILLANUEVA.

#### Foreign Bureaux

**Agence France-Presse (AFP):** Calle 17, No 4, 13°, entre N y 0, Vedado, Havana; tel. (7) 33-3503; fax (7) 33-3034; Bureau Chief DENIS ROUSSEAU.

**Agencia EFE** (Spain): Calle 36, No 110, entre 1 y 3, Miramar, Apdo 5, Havana; tel. (7) 33-2293; fax (7) 33-2272; Bureau Chief SOLEDAD MARÍN MARTÍN.

**Agenzia Nazionale Stampa Associata (ANSA)** (Italy): Edif. Fomeillán, Línea 5, Dpt 12, Vedado, Havana; tel. (7) 33-3542; Correspondent KATTY SALERNO.

**Bulgarska Telegrafna Agentsia (BTA)** (Bulgaria): Edif. Focsa, Calle 17, esq. M, Vedado, Apdo 22-E, Havana; tel. (7) 32-4779; Bureau Chief VASIL MIKOULACH.

**Česká tisková kancelář (ČTK)** (Czech Republic): Edif. Fajardo, Calle 17 y M, Vedado, Apdo 3-A, Vedado, Havana; tel. (7) 32-6101; Bureau Chief PAVEL ZOVADIL.

**Deutsche Presse-Agentur (dpa)** (Germany): Edif. Focsa, Calle 17 y M, Vedado, Apdo 2-K, Havana; tel. (7) 33-3501; Bureau Chief VICTORIO COPA.

**Informatsionnoye Telegrafnoye Agentstvo Rossii–Telegrafnoye Agentstvo Suverennykh Stran (ITAR–TASS)** (Russia): Calle 96, No 317, entre 3 y 5, Miramar, Havana 4; tel. (7) 29-2528; Bureau Chief ALEKSANDR KANICHEV.

**Inter Press Service (IPS)** (Italy): Calle 36-A, No 121 Bajos, esq. a 3, Miramar, Apdo 1, Havana; tel. (7) 22-1981; Bureau Chief CLAUDE JOSEPH HACKIN; Correspondent CARLOS BASTISTA MORENO.

**Korean Central News Agency** (Democratic People's Republic of Korea): Calle 10, No 613, esq. 25, Vedado, Apdo 6, Havana; tel. (7) 31-4201; Bureau Chief CHANG YON CHOL.

**Magyar Távirati Iroda (MTI)** (Hungary): Edif. Fajardo, Calle 17 y M, Apdo 2-C, Havana; tel. (7) 32-8353; Bureau Chief: ZOLTÁN TAKACS; Correspondent TIBOR CSÁSZÁR.

**Novinska Agencija Tanjug** (Yugoslavia): Calle 5-F, No 9801, esq. 98, Miramar, Havana; tel. (7) 22-7671; Bureau Chief DUŠAN DAKOVIĆ.

**Polska Agencja Prasowa (PAP)** (Poland): Calle 6, No 702, Apdo 5, entre 7 y 9, Miramar; Havana; tel. (7) 20-7067; Bureau Chief PIOTR SOMMERFED.

**Reuters** (United Kingdom): Edif. Someillán, Linea 5, 9°, Vedado, Havana 4; tel. (7) 33-3145; Bureau Chief FRANCES KERRY.

**Rossiyskoye Informatsionnoye Agentstvo—Novosti (RIA—Novosti)** (Russia): Calle 28, No 510, entre 5 y 7, Miramar, Havana; tel. (7) 22-4129; Bureau Chief YURII GOLOVIATENKO.

**Viet Nam Agency (VNA):** Calle 16, No 514, 1°, entre 5 y 7, Miramar, Havana; tel. (7) 2-4455; Bureau Chief PHAM DINH LOI.

**Xinhua (New China) News Agency** (People's Republic of China): Calle G, No 259, esq. 13, Vedado, Havana; tel. (7) 32-4616; Bureau Chief GAO YONGHUA.

## Publishers

**Casa de las Américas:** Calle 3 y Avda G, Vedado, Havana; tel. (7) 32-3587; fax (7) 32-7272; e-mail casa@arsoft.cult.cu; f. 1960; Latin American literature and social sciences; Dir ROBERTO FERNÁNDEZ RETAMAR.

**Ediciones Unión:** Calle 17, No 354 esq. a H, Vedado, Havana; tel. (7) 55-3112; fax (7) 33-3158; f.1962; publishing arm of the Unión de Escritores y Artistas de Cuba; Cuban literature, art; Dir MERCY RUIZ.

**Editora Abril:** Prado 553, esq. Teniente Rey, Habana Vieja, Havana; tel. (7) 62-7871; fax (7) 62-7871; e-mail eabril@tinored.cu; f. 1980; attached to the Union of Young Communists; children's literature; Dir IROEL SÁNCHEZ ESPINOSA.

**Editora Política:** Belascoaín No 864, esq. a Desagüe y Peñalver, Havana; tel. (7) 79-8553; fax (7) 81-1024; f. 1963; publishing institution of the Communist Party of Cuba; Dir HUGO CHINEA CABRERA.

**Editorial Academia:** Industria No 452, esq. a San José, Habana Vieja, Havana; tel. (7) 62-9501; f. 1963; attached to the Ministry of Science, Technology and the Environment; scientific and technical; Dir MIRIAM RAYA HERNÁNDEZ.

**Editorial de Ciencias Médicas y Centro Nacional de Información de Ciencias Médicas:** Calle E, No 452, entre 19 y 21, Vedado, Apdo 6520, Havana 10400; tel. (7) 32-4519; fax (7) 32-5008; attached to the Ministry of Public Health; books and magazines specializing in the medical sciences; Dir AUGUSTO HERNÁNDEZ BATISTA.

**Editorial Ciencias Sociales:** Calle 14, No 4104, entre 41 y 43, Miramar, Playa, Havana; tel. (7) 23-3959; f. 1967; attached to the Cuban Book Institute; social and political literature, history, philosophy, juridical sciences and economics; Dir RICARDO GARCÍA PAMPÍN.

**Editorial Científico-Técnica:** Calle 2, No 58, entre 3 y 5, Vedado, Havana; tel. (7) 3-9417; f. 1967; attached to the Ministry of Culture; technical and scientific literature; Dir ISIDRO FERNÁNDEZ RODRÍGUEZ.

**Editorial Gente Nueva:** Palacio del Segundo Cabo, Calle O'Reilly, No 4, esq. a Tacón, Havana; tel. (7) 62-4753; f. 1967; books for children; Dir RUBÉN DEL VALLE LANTARÓN.

**Editorial José Martí/Arte y Literatura:** Calzada 259, entre I y J, Apdo 4208, Havana; tel. (7) 33-3541; fax (7) 33-8187; f. 1983; attached to the Ministry of Culture; foreign-language publishing; Dir CECILIA INFANTE GUERRERO.

**Editorial Letras Cubanas:** Calle O'Reilly, No 4, esq. Tacón, Habana Vieja, Havana; tel. (7) 62-4378; fax (7) 33-8187; e-mail prolibro@artsof.cult.cu; f. 1977; attached to the Ministry of Culture; general, particularly classic and contemporary Cuban literature and arts; Dir DANIEL GARCÍA SANTOS.

**Editorial Oriente:** Santa Lucía 356, Santiago de Cuba; tel. (226) 22496; fax (226) 23715; f. 1971; publishes works from the Eastern provinces; general; Dir AIDA BAHR.

**Editorial Pueblo y Educación:** Avda 3A, No 4601, entre 46 y 60, Playa, Havana; tel. (7) 22-1490; fax (7) 24-0844; e-mail epe@ceniai.inf.cu; f. 1967; textbooks; Dir CATALINA LAJUD HERRERO.

#### Government Publishing Houses

**Instituto Cubano del Libro:** Palacio del Segundo Cabo, Calle O'Reilly, No 4, esq. a Tacón, Havana; tel. (7) 62-4789; fax (7) 33-8187; e-mail cclfilh@artsoft.cult.cu; printing and publishing organization attached to the Ministry of Culture which combines several publishing houses and has direct links with others; presides over the National Editorial Council (CEN); Pres. OMAR GONZÁLEZ JIMÉNEZ.

**Oficina de Publicaciones:** Calle 17, No 552, esq. a D, Vedado, Havana; tel. (7) 32-1883; fax (7) 33-5106; attached to the Council of State; books, pamphlets and other printed media on historical and political matters; Dir PEDRO ALVAREZ TABÍO.

## Broadcasting and Communications

### TELECOMMUNICATIONS

**Empresa de Telecomunicaciones de Cuba, SA (ETECSA):** Calle Egido, No 610, entre Gloria y Apodaca, Habana Vieja, Havana; tel. (7) 33-4848; fax (7) 33-5144; Exec. Pres. RAFAEL MARRERO GÓMEZ.

**Empresa de Telecomunicaciones Internacionales (EMTELCUBA):** Zanja, No 855, 6°, Havana; tel. (7) 70-8794; fax (7) 78-3722; Dir REGINO GONZÁLEZ TOLEDO.

**Instituto de Investigación y Desarrollo de las Telecomunicaciones (LACETEL):** Rancho Boyeros, Km 14½, Santiago de las Vegas, Rancho Boyeros, Havana; tel. (7) 20-2929; fax (7) 33-5812; Dir EDUARDO TRUFFÍN TRIANA.

**Ministerio de Comunicaciones (Dirección General de Telecomunicaciones):** Plaza de la Revolución, Havana: Dir CARLOS MARTÍNEZ ALBUERNE.

**Teléfonos Celulares de Cuba, SA (CUBACEL):** Calle 28, No 10, entre 5 y 7, Playa, Havana; tel. (7) 33-2222; fax (7) 33-1737; Dir-Gen. RAFAEL GALINDO MIER.

### BROADCASTING

**Ministerio de Comunicaciones (Dirección de Frecuencias Radioeléctricas):** Plaza de la Revolución, CP 10600, Havana; tel. (7) 70-6932; Dir CARLOS MARTÍNEZ ALBUERNE.

**Empresa Cubana de Radio y Televisión (INTERTV):** Avda 23, No 156, entre N y O, Vedado, Havana; tel. (7) 32-7571; fax (7) 33-3939; Dir ANDRÉS SALCEDO GANCEDO.

**Instituto Cubano de Radio y Televisión (ICRT):** Edif. Radiocentro, Avda 23, No 258, entre L y M, Vedado, Havana 4; tel. (7) 32-1568; fax (7) 33-3107; e-mail icrt@cecm.get.tur.cu; f. 1962; Pres. ENRIQUE ROMÁN HERNÁNDEZ.

#### Radio

In 1997 there were 5 national networks and 1 international network, 14 provincial radio stations and 31 municipal radio stations, with a total of some 170 transmitters.

**Radio Enciclopedia:** Calle N, No 266, entre 21 y 23, Vedado, Havana; tel. (7) 81-2809; national network; instrumental music programmes; 24 hours daily; Dir EDELSA PALACIOS GORDO.

**Radio Habana Cuba:** Infanta 105 esq. a 25, 6°, Apdo 6240, Havana; tel. (7) 78-4954; fax (7) 79-5810; e-mail cartas@radiohc.org; f. 1961; shortwave station; broadcasts in Spanish, English, French, Portuguese, Arabic, Esperanto, Quechua, Guaraní and Creole; Dir MILAGRO HERNÁNDEZ CUBA.

**CMBF—Radio Musical Nacional:** Avda 23, No 258, Vedado, Havana; tel. (7) 70-4561; f. 1948; national network; classical music programmes; 17 hours daily; Dir PEDRO PABLO RODRÍGUEZ.

**Radio Progreso:** Infanta 105, Apdo 3042, Havana; tel. (7) 70-4561; f. 1929; national network; mainly entertainment and music; 24 hours daily; Dir MANUEL E. ANDRÉS MAZORRA.

**Radio Rebelde:** Edif. Radiocentro, Avda 23, No 258, entre L y M, Vedado, Apdo 6277, Havana; tel. (7) 31-3514; fax (7) 33-4270; e-mail rebelde@ceniai.inf.cu; internet www.ceniai.rebelde.inf.cu; f. 1984 (after merger of former Radio Rebelde and Radio Liberación); national network; 24-hour news programmes, music and sports; Dir MARIO ROBAINA DÍAZ.

**Radio Reloj:** Edif. Radiocentro, Avda 23, No 258, entre L y M, Vedado, Havana; tel. (7) 32-9689; f. 1947; national network; 24-hour news service; Dir OSVALDO RODRÍGUEZ MARTÍNEZ.

#### Television

**Instituto Cubano de Radiodifusión (Televisión Nacional):** Calle M, No 313, entre 21 y 23, Vedado, Havana; tel. (7) 32-5000; broadcasts in colour on channel 2 and channel 6; Vice-Pres. JOSEFA BRACERO TORRES, OVIDIO CABRERA, ERNESTO LÓPEZ.

**Cubavisión:** Calle M, No 313, Vedado, Havana.

**Tele Rebelde:** Mazón, No 52, Vedado, Havana; tel. (7) 32-3369; Vice-Pres. GARY GONZÁLEZ.

**CHTV:** Habana Libre Hotel, Havana; f. 1990; subsidiary station of Tele-Rebelde.

## Finance

### BANKING

All banks were nationalized in 1960. Legislation establishing the national banking system was approved by the Council of State in 1984. A restructuring of the banking system, initiated in 1995, to accommodate Cuba's transformation to a more market-orientated economy was proceeding in 1999. A new central bank, the Banco Central de Cuba (BCC), was created in 1997 to supersede the Banco Nacional de Cuba (BNC). The BCC was to be responsible for issuing currency, proposing and implementing monetary policy and the regulation of financial institutions. The BNC was to continue functioning as a commercial bank and servicing the country's foreign debt. Also envisaged in the restructuring of the banking system was the creation of an investment bank, the Banco de Inversiones, to provide medium- and long-term financing for investment, and the Banco Financiero Internacional, SA, to offer short-term financing. A new agro-industrial and commercial bank was also to be created to provide services for farmers and co-operatives. The new banking system is under the control of Grupo Nueva Banca, which holds a majority share in each institution.

#### Central Bank

**Banco Central de Cuba (BCC):** Havana; f. 1997; sole bank of issue; Pres. FRANCISCO SOBERÓN VALDEZ.

#### Commercial Banks

**Banco Financiero Internacional, SA:** Edif. Someillán, Calle Línea, y 0, Vedado, Havana; tel. (7) 32-1518; fax (7) 33-3006; f. 1984; autonomous; capital US $10m. (1985); mainly short-term financing; Chair. EDUARDO BENCOMO ZURDOS; Gen. Man. ARNALDO ALAYÓN.

**Banco Internacional de Comercio, SA:** 20 de Mayo y Ayestarán, Apdo 6113, Havana; tel. (7) 55-5482; fax (7) 33-5112; e-mail bicsa@bicsa.colombus.cu; f. 1993; cap. and res US $45.5m., dep. $212.7m. (Dec. 1997); Chair. ERNESTO MEDINA.

**Banco Metropolitano:** Línea, No 63, esq. Calle M, Vedado, Havana; tel. (7) 55-3116; fax (7) 33-4241; e-mail banmet@nbbm.colombus.cu; f. 1996; offers foreign currency and deposit account facilities; Pres. IVANIOSKY MATOS TORRES.

**Banco Nacional de Cuba (BNC):** Aguiar 456, entre Amargura y Lamparillla, Habana Vieja, Havana; tel. (7) 62-8896; fax (7) 66-9514; f. 1950, reorganized 1997; Chair. HÉCTOR RODRÍGUEZ LLOMPART.

#### Savings Bank

**Banco Popular del Ahorro:** Calle 16, No 306, entre 3 y 5, Playa, Havana; tel. (7) 22-2545; f. 1983; savings bank; cap. 30m. pesos; dep. 5,363.7m. pesos; Pres. MARISELA FERREYRA DE LA GÁNDARA; 520 brs.

### INSURANCE

#### State Organizations

**Empresa del Seguro Estatal Nacional (ESEN):** Obispo No 211, 3°, Apdo 109, 10100 Havana; tel. (7) 60-4111; f. 1978; motor and agricultural insurance; Man. Dir PEDRO MANUEL ROCHE ALVAREZ.

**Seguros Internacionales de Cuba, SA—Esicuba:** Cuba No 314, Apdo 79, Havana; tel. (7) 62-5051; fax (7) 33-8038; f. 1963, reorganized 1986; all classes of insurance except life; Pres. RAMÓN MARTÍNEZ CARRERA.

## Trade and Industry

### GOVERNMENT AGENCIES

**Ministry of Foreign Investment and Economic Co-operation:** Primera No 1404, entre 14 y 16, Miramar, Havana; tel. (7) 22-3873; fax (7) 24-0797; e-mail cecupi@ceniai.cu.

**Free-Trade Zones National Office:** Calie 22, No 528, entre 3 y 5, Miramar, Havana; tel. (7) 24-7636; fax (7) 24-7637.

### CHAMBER OF COMMERCE

**Cámara de Comercio de la República de Cuba:** Calle 21, No 661/701, esq. Calle A, Apdo 4237, Vedado, Havana; tel. (7) 30-3356; fax (7) 33-3042; f. 1963; mems include all Cuban foreign trade enterprises and the most important agricultural and industrial enterprises; Pres. CARLOS MARTÍNEZ SALSAMENDI; Sec.-Gen. MARTA CAMACHO FUNDORA.

### AGRICULTURAL ORGANIZATION

**Asociación Nacional de Agricultores Pequeños—ANAP** (National Association of Small Farmers): Calle I, No 206, entre Linea y 13, Vedado, Havana; tel. (7) 32-4541; fax (7) 33-4244; f. 1961; 220,000 mems; Pres. ORLANDO LUGO FONTE; Vice-Pres. EVELIO PAUSA BELLO.

### STATE IMPORT-EXPORT BOARDS

**Alimport** (Empresa Cubana Importadora de Alimentos): Infanta 16, 3°, Apdo 7006, Havana; tel. (7) 54-2501; fax (7) 33-3151; e-mail precios@alimport.com.cu; controls import of foodstuffs and liquors; Man. Dir PEDRO ALVAREZ.

**Autoimport** (Empresa Central de Abastecimiento y Venta de Equipos de Transporte Ligero): Galiano 213, entre Concordia y Virtudes, Havana; tel. (7) 62-8180; imports cars, light vehicles, motor cycles and spare parts; Man. Dir EDELIO VERA RODRÍGUEZ.

**Aviaimport** (Empresa Cubana Importadora y Exportadora de Aviación): Calle 182, No 126, entre 1 y 5, Reparto Flores, Playa, Havana; tel. (7) 21-7687; fax (7) 33-6234; import and export of aircraft and components; Man. Dir MARCOS LAGO MARTÍNEZ.

**Caribex** (Empresa Exportadora del Caribe): Havana; tel. (7) 22-7889; fax (7) 22-8452; import and export of seafood and marine products; Dir PEDRO SUÁREZ GAMBE.

**Construimport** (Empresa Central de Abastecimiento y Venta de Equipos de Construcción y sus Piezas): Carretera de Varona, Km 1.5, Capdevila, Havana; tel. (7) 45-2567; fax (7) 66-6180; e-mail construimport@colombus.cu; f. 1969; controls the import and export of construction machinery and equipment; Man. Dir JESÚS SERRANO RODRÍGUEZ.

**Consumimport** (Empresa Cubana Importadora de Artículos de Consumo General): Calle 23, No 55, 9°, Apdo 6427, Vedado, Havana;

tel. (7) 55-0554; fax (7) 79-2584; e-mail consumim@infocex-cu; f. 1962; imports and exports general consumer goods; Dir BERTHA DELGADO-GUANCHE.

**Copextel** (Corporación Productora y Exportadora de Tecnología Electrónica): Calle 194 y 7A, Siboney, Havana; tel. (7) 21-8400; fax (7) 33-1414; f. 1986; exports LTEL personal computers and microcomputer software; Man. Dir LUIS J. CARRASCO.

**Coprefil** (Empresa Comercial y de Producciones Filatélicas): Zanja No 855, 2°, esq. San Francisco e Infanta, Havana 1; tel. (7) 7-8812; fax (7) 33-5077; imports and exports postage stamps, postcards, calendars, handicrafts, communications equipment, electronics, watches, etc.; Dir NELSON IGLESIAS FERNÁNDEZ.

**Cubaelectrónica** (Empresa Importadora y Exportadora de Productos de la Electrónica): Calle 22, No 510, entre 5 y 7, Miramar, Havana; tel. (7) 22-7316; fax (7) 33-1233; f. 1986; imports and exports electronic equipment and devices; Man. LUIS BLANCA.

**Cubaequipos** (Empresa Cubana Importadora de Productos Mecánicos y Equipos Varios): Calle 23, No 55, Vedado, Apdo 6052, Havana; tel. (7) 70-6985; fax (7) 7-1350; f. 1982; imports of mechanical goods and equipment; Dir VÍCTOR MENÉNDEZ MORALES.

**Cubaexport** (Empresa Cubana Exportadora de Alimentos y Productos Varios): Calle 23, No 55, entre Infanta y P, 8°, Vedado, Apdo 6719, Havana; tel. (7) 54-3130; fax (7) 33-3587; export of foodstuffs and industrial products; Man. Dir MILDA PICOS RIVERS.

**Cubafrutas** (Empresa Cubana Exportadora de Frutas Tropicales): Calle 23, No 55, Apdo 6683, Vedado, Havana; tel. and fax (7) 79-5653; f. 1979; controls export of fruits, vegetables and canned foodstuffs; Dir JORGE AMARO MOREJÓN.

**Cubalse** (Empresa para Prestación de Servicios al Cuerpo Diplomático): Avda 3ra y Final, Miramar, Havana; tel. (7) 24-2284; fax (7) 24-2282; e-mail cubalse@ceniai.inf.cu; f. 1974; imports consumer goods for the diplomatic corps and foreign technicians residing in Cuba; exports beverages and tobacco, leather goods and foodstuffs; other operations include real estate, retail trade, restaurants, clubs, automobile business, state-of-the-art equipment and household appliances, construction, investments, wholesale, road transport, freight transit, shipping, publicity, photography and video, financing, legal matters; Pres. REIDAL RONCOURT FONT.

**Cubametales** (Empresa Cubana Importadora de Metales, Combustibles y Lubricantes): Infanta 16, 4°, Apdo 6917, Vedado, Havana; tel. (7) 70-4225; fax (7) 33-3477; controls import of metals (ferrous and non-ferrous), crude petroleum and petroleum products; also engaged in the export of petroleum products and ferrous and non-ferrous scrap; Dir RAFAEL PRIEDE GONZÁLEZ.

**Cubaniquel** (Empresa Cubana Exportadora de Minerales y Metales): Calle 23, No 55, 8°, Apdo 6128, Havana; tel. (7) 33-5334; fax (7) 33-3332; f. 1961; sole exporter of minerals and metals; Man. Dir ARIEL MASÓ MARZAL.

**Cubatabaco** (Empresa Cubana del Tabaco): Calle O'Reilly, No 104, Apdo 6557, Havana; tel. (7) 61-5759; fax (7) 33-8214; f. 1962; controls export of leaf tobacco, cigars and cigarettes to France; Dir JUAN MANUEL DÍAZ TENORIO.

**Cubatécnica** (Empresa de Contratación de Asistencia Técnica): Calle 12, No 513, entre 5 y 7, Miramar, Havana; tel. (7) 22-7455; fax (7) 24-0923; e-mail cubatec@ceniai.inf.cu; controls export and import of technical assistance; Dir RAFAEL JIMENO LÓPEZ.

**Cubatex** (Empresa Cubana Importadora de Fibras, Tejidos, Cueros y sus Productos): Calle 23, No 55, Apdo 7115, Vedado, Havana; tel. (7) 70-3269; fax (7) 33-3321; controls import of fibres, textiles, hides and by-products and export of fabric and clothing; Dir LUISA AMPARO SESÍN VIDAL.

**Cubazúcar** (Empresa Cubana Exportadora de Azúcar y sus Derivados): Calle 23, No 55, 7°, Vedado, Apdo 6647, Havana; tel. (7) 54-2175; fax (7) 33-3482; e-mail cubazucar@infocex.cu; f. 1962; controls export of sugar, molasses and alcohol; Dir ALEJANDRO GUTÍERREZ MAIRIGAL.

**Ecimact** (Empresa Comercial de Industrias de Materiales, Construcción y Turismo): Calle 1aC, entre 152 y 154, Miramar, Havana; tel. (7) 21-9783; controls import and export of engineering services and plant for industrial construction and tourist complexes; Dir OCTAVIO CASTILLA CANGAS.

**Ecimetal** (Empresa Importadora y Exportadora de Objetivos Industriales): Calle 23, No 55, esq. Plaza, Vedado, Havana; tel. (7) 55-0548; fax (7) 33-4737; e-mail ecimetal@infocex.cu; f. 1977; controls import and export of plant, equipment and raw materials for all major industrial sectors; Dir ADALBERTO DUMÉNIGO CABRERA.

**Ediciones Cubanas** (Empresa de Comercio Exterior de Publicaciones): Obispo 527, Apdo 43, Havana; tel. (7) 63-1989; fax (7) 33-8943; e-mail edicuba@artsoft.cult.cu; controls import and export of books and periodicals; Dir JORGE PAZ CRUZ.

**Egrem** (Estudios de Grabaciones y Ediciones Musicales): San Miguel 410, Havana; tel. (7) 62-9762; fax (7) 33-8043; f. 1964; controls the import and export of records, tapes, printed music and musical instruments; Dir Gen. JULIO BALLESTER GUZMÁN.

**Emexcon** (Empresa Importadora y Exportadora de la Construcción): Calle 25, No 2602, Miramar, Havana; tel. (7) 22-3694; f. 1978; consulting engineer services, contracting, import and export of building materials and equipment; Dir ELEODORO PÉREZ.

**Emiat** (Empresa Importadora y Exportadora de Suministros Técnicos): Calle 20, No 519, entre 5 y 7, Miramar, Havana; tel. (7) 22-1163; fax (7) 22-5176; f. 1983; imports technical materials, equipment and special products; exports furniture, kitchen utensils and accessories; Dir MARTA ALFONSO SÁNCHEZ.

**Emidict** (Empresa Especializada Importadora, Exportadora y Distribuidora para la Ciencia y la Técnica): Calle 16, No 102, esq. Avda 1, Miramar, Playa, 13000 Havana; tel. (7) 22-8452; fax (7) 24-1768; e-mail emidict@ceniai.inf.cu; f. 1982; controls import and export of scientific and technical products and equipment, live animals; scientific information; Dir MIGUEL JULIO PÉREZ FLEITAS.

**Energoimport** (Empresa Importadora de Objetivos Electro-energéticos): Calle 7, No 2602, esq. a 26, Miramar, Havana; tel. (7) 23-8156; fax (7) 33-0147; f. 1977; controls import of equipment for electricity generation; Man. LÁZARO HERNÁNDEZ

**Eprob** (Empresa de Proyectos para las Industrias de la Básica): Avda 31-A, entre 18 y 20, Miramar, Playa, Apdo 12100, Havana; tel. (7) 33-2146; fax (7) 33-2146; f. 1967; exports consulting services and processing of engineering construction projects, consulting services and supplies of complete industrial plants and turn-key projects; Man. Dir RAÚL RIVERO MARTÍNEZ.

**Eproyiv** (Empresa de Proyectos para Industrias Varias): Calle 33, No 1815, entre 18 y 20, Playa, Havana; tel. (7) 24-2149; e-mail eproyiv@ceniai.inf.cu; f. 1967; consulting services, feasibility studies, development of basic and detailed engineering models, project management and turn-key projects; Dir MARTA ELENA HERNÁNDEZ DÍAZ.

**Esi** (Empresa de Suministros Industriales): Calle Aguiar, No 556, entre Teniente Rey y Muralla, Havana; tel. (7) 62-0696; fax (7) 33-8951; f. 1985; imports machinery, equipment and components for industrial plants; Dir-Gen. FRANCISCO DÍAZ CABRERA.

**Fecuimport** (Empresa Cubana Importadora y Exportadora de Ferrocarriles): Avda 7, No 6209, entre 62 y 66, Miramar, Apdo 6003, Havana; tel. (7) 79-7678; f. 1968; imports and exports railway equipment; Pres. DOMINGO HERRERA.

**Ferrimport** (Empresa Cubana Importadora de Artículos de Ferretería): Calle 23, No 55, 2°, Vedado, Apdo 6258, Havana; tel. (7) 70-6678; fax (7) 79-4417; importers of industrial hardware; Dir.-Gen. ALEJANDRO MUSTELIER.

**Fondo Cubano de Bienes Culturales:** Calle 36, esq. 47, Reparto Kohly, Playa, Havana; tel. (7) 23-6523; fax (7) 24-0391; f. 1978; controls export of fine handicraft and works of art; Dir ANGEL ARCOS.

**Habanos, S.A.:** Mercaderes 21, Havana; tel. 33-8998; fax 33-8946; e-mail habanos@infocex.cu; f. 1994; controls export of leaf tobacco, cigars and cigarettes (except to France—see Cubatabaco).

**ICAIC** (Instituto Cubano del Arte e Industria Cinematográficos): Calle 23, No 1155, Vedado, Havana 4; tel. (7) 55-3128; fax (7) 33-3032; f. 1959; production, import and export of films and newsreel; Dir ANTONIO RODRÍGUEZ RODRÍGUEZ.

**Imexin** (Empresa Importadora y Exportadora de Infraestructura): Avda 5, No 1007, esq. a 12, Miramar, Havana; tel. (7) 23-9293; f. 1977; controls import and export of infrastructure; Man. Dir RAÚL BENCE VIJANDE.

**Imexpal** (Empresa Importadora y Exportadora de Plantas Alimentarias, sus Complementos y Derivados): Calle 22, No 313, entre 3 y 5, Miramar, Havana; tel. (7) 29-1671; controls import and export of food-processing plants and related items; Man. Dir Ing. CONCEPCIÓN BUENO CAMPOS.

**Maprinter** (Empresa Cubana Importadora y Exportadora de Materias Primas y Productos Intermedios): Infanta 16, 2ä, Apdo 2110, Havana; tel. (7) 74-2971; fax (7) 33-3535; f. 1962; controls import and export of raw materials and intermediate products; Dir ENRIQUE DÍAZ DE VILLEGAS OTERO.

**Maquimport** (Empresa Cubana Importadora de Maquinarias y Equipos): Calle 23, No 55, Vedado, Apdo 6052, Havana; tel. (7) 66-2217; fax (7) 33-5443; e-mail maquimport@infocex-cu; controls import of machinery and equipment; Dir ERNESTO GUERRERO PAZ.

**Marpesca** (Empresa Cubana Importadora y Exportadora de Buques Mercantes y de Pesca): Conill No 580, esq. Avda 26, Nuevo Vedado, Havana; tel. (7) 81-1300; f. 1978; imports and exports ships and port and fishing equipment; Dir JOSÉ CEREIJO CASAS.

**Medicuba** (Empresa Cubana Importadora y Exportadora de Productos Médicos): Máximo Gómez 1, esq. a Egido, Havana; tel. (7) 62-3983; fax (7) 61-7995; enterprise for the export and import of medical and pharmaceutical products; Dir ALFONSO SÁNCHEZ DÍAZ.

**Produimport** (Empresa Central de Abastecimiento y Venta de Productos Químicos y de la Goma): Calle Consulado 262, entre

Animas y Virtudes, Havana; tel. (7) 62-0581; fax (7) 62-9588; f. 1977; imports and exports spare parts for motor vehicles; Dir José Guerra Matos.

**Quimimport** (Empresa Cubana Importadora y Exportadora de Productos Químicos): Calle 23, No 55, Apdo 6088, Vedado, Havana; tel. (7) 33-3394; fax (7) 33-3190; controls import and export of chemical products; Dir Armando Barrera Martínez.

**Suchel** (Empresa de Jabonería y Perfumería): Calzada de Buenos Aires 353, esq. a Durege, Apdo 6359, Havana; tel. (7) 33-8008; fax (7) 33-5311; f. 1985; exports and imports materials for the detergent, perfumery and cosmetics industry, exports cosmetics, perfumes, hotel amenities and household products; Dir José García Díaz.

**Tecnoazúcar** (Empresa de Servicios Técnicos e Ingeniería para la Agro-industria Azucarera): Calle 12, No 310, entre 3 y 5, Miramar, Playa, Havana; tel. (7) 29-5441; fax (7) 33-1218; imports machinery and equipment for the sugar industry, provides technical and engineering assistance for the sugar industry; exports sugar-machinery equipment and spare parts; provides engineering and technical assistance services for sugar-cane by-product industry; Gen. Man. Victor R. Hernández Martínez.

**Tecnoimport** (Empresa Importadora y Exportadora de Productos Técnicos): Edif. La Marina, Avda del Puerto 102, entre Justiz y Obrapía, Habana Vieja, Havana; tel. (7) 61-5552; fax (7) 66-9777; f. 1968; imports technical products; Dir Adel Izquierdo Rodríguez.

**Tecnotex** (Empresa Cubana Exportadora e Importadora de Servicios, Artículos y Productos Técnicos Especializados): Avda 47, No 3419, Playa, Havana; tel. (7) 81-3989; fax (7) 33-1682; f. 1983; imports specialized technical and radiocommunications equipment, exports outdoor equipment and geodetic networks; Dir Adel Izquierdo Rodríguez.

**Tractoimport** (Empresa Central de Abastecimiento y Venta de Maquinaria Agrícola y sus Piezas de Repuesto): Avda Rancho Boyeros y Calle 100, Apdo 7007, Havana; tel. (7) 20-3474; fax (7) 33-8786; f. 1960 for the import of tractors and agricultural equipment; also exports pumps and agricultural implements; Dir Manuel Castro del Aguila.

**Transimport** (Empresa Central de Abastecimiento y Venta de Equipos de Transporte Pesados y sus Piezas): Calle 102 y Avda 63, Marianao, Apdo 6665, 11500 Havana; tel. (7) 20-0325; fax (7) 33-5338; f. 1962; controls import and export of vehicles and transportation equipment; Dir Jesús Dinis Rivero.

### UTILITIES

#### Electricity

**Empresa Consolidada de Electricidad:** Avda Salvador Allende 666, Havana; public utility.

### TRADE UNIONS

All workers have the right to become members of a national trade union according to their industry and economic branch.

The following industries and labour branches have their own unions: Agriculture, Chemistry and Energetics, Civil Workers of the Revolutionary Armed Forces, Commerce and Gastronomy, Communications, Construction, Culture, Education and Science, Food, Forestry, Health, Light Industry, Merchant Marine, Mining and Metallurgy, Ports and Fishing, Public Administration, Sugar, Tobacco and Transport.

**Central de Tradajadores de Cuba—CTC** (Confederation of Cuban Workers): Palacio de los Trabajadores, San Carlos y Peñalver, Havana; tel. (7) 78-4901; f. 1939; affiliated to WFTU and CPUSTAL; 19 national trade unions affiliated; Gen. Sec. Pedro Ross Leal; 2,767,806 mems (1996).

## Transport

The Ministry of Transport controls all public transport.

### RAILWAYS

The total length of railways in 1990 was 14,519 km, of which 9,638 km were used by the sugar industry. The remaining 4,881 km were public service railways operated by Ferrocarriles de Cuba (reduced to 4,693 km in 1997). All railways were nationalized in 1960.

**Ferrocarriles de Cuba:** Edif. Estación Central, Egido y Arsenal, Havana; tel. (7) 62-1530; fax (7) 33-8628; f. 1960; operates public services; Dir Gen. P. Pérez Fleites; divided as follows:

**División Occidente:** serves Pinar del Río, Ciudad de la Habana, Havana Province and Matanzas.

**División Centro:** serves Villa Clara, Cienfuegos and Sancti Spíritus.

**División Centro-Este:** serves Camagüey, Ciego de Avila and Tunas.

**División Oriente:** serves Santiago de Cuba, Granma, Guantánamo and Holguín.

**División Camilo Cienfuegos:** serves part of Havana Province and Matanzas.

### ROADS

In 1997 there were an estimated 60,858 km of roads, of which 4,353 km were highways or main roads. The Central Highway runs from Pinar del Río in the west to Santiago, for a length of 1,144 km. In addition to this paved highway, there are a number of secondary and 'farm-to-market' roads. A small proportion of these secondary roads is paved but many can be used by motor vehicles only during the dry season.

### SHIPPING

Cuba's principal ports are Havana (which handles 60% of all cargo), Santiago de Cuba, Cienfuegos, Nuevitas, Matanzas, Antilla, Guayabal and Mariel. Maritime transport has developed rapidly since 1959, and at 31 December 1998 Cuba had a merchant fleet of 105 ships (with a total displacement of 157,847 grt).

**Coral Container Lines, SA:** Oficios 170, 1°, Habana Vieja, Havana; tel. (7) 33-8549; fax (7) 62-1867; e-mail bfdez@coral.com.cu; f. 1994; liner services to Europe, Canada, Brazil and Mexico; 11 containers; Chair. and Man. Dir Luis Rodríguez Hernández.

**Empresa Consignataria Mambisa:** San José No 65, entre Prado y Zulueta, Habana Vieja, Havana; tel. (7) 62-2061; fax (7) 33-8111; e-mail denis@mambisas.com.cu; shipping agent, bunker suppliers; Man. Dir Eduardo Denis Valcárcel.

**Empresa Cubana de Fletes (Cuflet):** Calle Oficios No 170, entre Teniente Rey y Amargura, Apdo 6755, Havana; tel. (7) 61-2604; freight agents for Cuban cargo; Man. Dir Carlos Sánchez Perdomo.

**Empresa de Navegación Caribe (Navecaribe):** San Martín, 4°, Agramonte y Pasco de Martí, Habana Vieja, Havana; tel. (7) 62-5878; fax (7) 33-8564; f. 1966; operates Cuban coastal fleet; Dir Ramón Durán Suárez.

**Empresa de Navegación Mambisa:** San Ignacio No 104, Apdo 543, Havana; tel. (7) 62-7031; fax (7) 61-0044; operates dry cargo, reefer and bulk carrier vessels; Gen. Man. Gumersindo González Feliú.

**Naviera Frigorífica Marítima:** Havana; tel. (7) 35743; fax (7) 33-5185.

**Naviera Mar América:** Calle de San Ignacio 104, Havana; tel. (7) 62-3560; fax (7) 61044.

**Naviera Poseidon:** Altos de la Aduana, San Pedro 1, Habana Vieja, Havana; tel. (7) 62-5618; fax (7) 33-8627.

**Nexus Reefer:** Avda de la Pesquera y Atarés, Puerto Pesquero de la Habana, Habana Vieja, Havana 1; tel. (7) 33-8478; fax (7) 33-8046; merchant reefer ships; Gen. Dir Quirino L. Gutiérrez López.

### CIVIL AVIATION

There are a total of 16 civilian airports, with international airports at Havana, Santiago de Cuba, Camagüey, Varadero and Holguín.

**Aerocaribbean:** Calle 23, No 64 esq. a P. Vedado, Havana; tel. (7) 33-4543; fax (7) 33-5016; e-mail aerocarvpcr@iacc3.6ct.cma.net; f. 1982; international and domestic charter services; Chair. Julián Infiesta.

**Aerogaviota:** Avda 47, No 2814, Reparto Kolhy, Havana; tel. (7) 81-3068; fax (7) 33-2621; f. 1994; operated by Cuban air force.

**Empresa Consolidada Cubana de Aviación (Cubana):** Calle 23, Pt 64 Vedado, La Rampa, Havana 4; tel. (7) 78-4961; fax (7) 79-3333; internet www.cubana.cu; f. 1929; international services to North America, Central America, the Caribbean, South America and Europe; internal services from Havana to 14 other cities; Gen. Dir Heriberto Prieto.

**Instituto de Aeronáutica Civil de Cuba (IACC):** Calle 23, No 64, La Rampa, Vedado, Havana; tel. (7) 33-4471; fax (7) 33-3082; f. 1985; Pres. Rogelio Acevedo González.

## Tourism

Tourism began to develop after 1977, with the easing of travel restrictions by the USA, and Cuba subsequently attracted European tourists. At the Fourth Congress of the PCC, held in 1991, emphasis was placed on the importance of expanding the tourism industry, and, in particular, on its promotion within Latin America. Receipts totalled an estimated US $1,500m. in 1997, when there were some 1,180,000 visitors. In that year there were more than 26,800 hotel rooms. The Government planned to increase the number of hotel rooms to some 50,000 and annual visitor arrivals to 2.5m. by 2000.

**Cubanacán:** Calle 148, entre 11 y 13, Playa, Apdo 16046, Havana; tel. (7) 22-5512; fax (7) 22-8382; f. 1987; Pres. ABRAHAM MACIQUES MACIQUES.

**Empresa de Turismo Internacional (Cubatur):** Calle 23, No 156, entre N y O, Apdo 6560, Vedado, Havana; tel. (7) 35-4521; fax (7) 32-3157; f. 1968; Dir JOSÉ PADILLA.

**Empresa de Turismo Nacional (Viajes Cuba):** Calle 20, No 352, entre 21 y 23, Vedado, Havana; tel. (7) 30-0587; f. 1981; Dir ANA ELIS DE LA CRUZ GARCÍA.

# CYPRUS

## Introductory Survey

### Location, Climate, Language, Religion, Flag, Capital

The Republic of Cyprus is an island in the eastern Mediterranean Sea, about 100 km south of Turkey. The climate is mild, although snow falls in the mountainous south-west between December and March. Temperatures in Nicosia are generally between 5°C (41°F) and 36°C (97°F). About 75% of the population speak Greek and almost all of the remainder speak Turkish. The Greek-speaking community is overwhelmingly Christian, and nearly all Greek Cypriots adhere to the Orthodox Church of Cyprus, while most of the Turks are Muslims. The national flag (proportions 5 by 3) is white, with a gold map of Cyprus, above two crossed green olive branches, in the centre. The capital is Nicosia.

### Recent History

A guerrilla war against British rule in Cyprus was begun in 1955 by Greek Cypriots seeking unification (*Enosis)* with Greece. Their movement, the National Organization of Cypriot Combatants (EOKA), was led politically by Archbishop Makarios III, head of the Greek Orthodox Church in Cyprus, and militarily by Gen. George Grivas. Archbishop Makarios was suspected by the British authorities of being involved in EOKA's campaign of violence, and in March 1956 he and three other leaders of the *Enosis* movement were deported. After a compromise agreement between the Greek and Turkish communities, a constitution for an independent Cyprus was finalized in 1959. Following his return from exile, Makarios was elected the country's first President in December 1959. Cyprus became independent on 16 August 1960, although the United Kingdom retained sovereignty over two military base areas.

Following a constitutional dispute, the Turks withdrew from the central Government in December 1963 and serious intercommunal fighting occurred. In March 1964 the UN Peacekeeping Force in Cyprus (UNFICYP, see p. 62) was established to prevent a recurrence of fighting between the Greek and Turkish Cypriot communities. The effective exclusion of the Turks from political power led to the creation of separate administrative, judicial and legislative organs for the Turkish community. Discussions concerning the establishment of a more equitable constitutional arrangement began in 1968, and continued sporadically for six years, without achieving any agreement, as the Turks favoured some form of federation, while the Greeks advocated a unitary state. Each community received military aid from its mother country, and the Greek Cypriot National Guard was controlled by officers of the Greek Army.

In 1971 Gen. Grivas returned to Cyprus, revived EOKA, and began a terrorist campaign for *Enosis,* directed against the Makarios Government and apparently supported by the military regime in Greece. Gen. Grivas died in January 1974, and in June Makarios ordered a purge of EOKA sympathizers from the police, National Guard and civil service, accusing the Greek regime of subversion. On 15 July President Makarios was deposed by a military coup, led by Greek officers of the National Guard, who appointed Nikos Sampson, an extremist Greek Cypriot politician and former EOKA terrorist, to be President. Makarios escaped from the island on the following day and travelled to the United Kingdom. At the invitation of Rauf Denktaş, the Turkish Cypriot leader, the Turkish army intervened to protect the Turkish community and to prevent Greece from using its control of the National Guard to take over Cyprus. Turkish troops landed on 20 July and rapidly occupied the northern third of Cyprus, dividing the island along what became the Attila Line, which runs from Morphou through Nicosia to Famagusta. President Sampson resigned on 23 July, and Glavkos Klerides, the President of the House of Representatives, became acting Head of State. The military regime in Greece collapsed on the same day. In December Makarios returned to Cyprus and resumed the presidency. However, the Turkish Cypriots' effective control of northern Cyprus enabled them to establish a *de facto* Government, and in February 1975 to declare the establishment of the 'Turkish Federated State of Cyprus' ('TFSC'), with Denktaş as President.

President Makarios died in August 1977. He was succeeded by Spyros Kyprianou, a former Minister of Foreign Affairs, who had been President of the House of Representatives since 1976. In September 1980 a ministerial reshuffle by President Kyprianou caused the powerful communist party, the Anorthotiko Komma Ergazomenou Laou (AKEL—Progressive Party of the Working People), to withdraw its support from the ruling Dimokratiko Komma (DIKO—Democratic Party). Kyprianou therefore lost his overall majority in the House of Representatives. At the next general election, held in May 1981, the AKEL and the Dimokratikos Synagermos (DISY—Democratic Rally) each won 12 seats in the House. The DIKO, however, won only eight seats, so the President remained dependent on the support of the AKEL.

In the 'TFSC' a new Council of Ministers was formed in December 1978 under a former minister belonging to the Ulusal Bırlık Partisi (UBP—National Unity Party), Mustafa Çağatay. At the elections held in June 1981, President Denktaş was returned to office, but his party, the UBP, lost its majority, and the Government that was subsequently formed by Çağatay was defeated in December. In March 1982 a coalition Government, comprising the UBP, the Demokratik Halk Partisi (Democratic People's Party) and the Türkiye Bırlık Partisi (Turkish Unity Party), was formed by Çağatay.

In September 1980 the intermittent UN-sponsored intercommunal peace talks were resumed. The constitutional issue remained the main problem: the Turkish Cypriots demanded equal status for the two communities, with equal representation in government and strong links with the mother country, while the Greeks, although accepting the principle of an alternating presidency, favoured a strong central government, and objected to any disproportionate representation for the Turkish community, who formed less than 20% of the population. In November 1981 a UN plan (involving a federal council, an alternating presidency and the allocation of 70% of the island to the Greek community) was presented, but discussions faltered in February 1982, when the Greek Prime Minister, Andreas Papandreou, proposed the withdrawal of all Greek and Turkish troops and the convening of an international conference, rather than the continuation of intercommunal talks.

In February 1983 Kyprianou was re-elected President, with the support of the AKEL, gaining 56.5% of the votes. In May the UN General Assembly voted in favour of the withdrawal of Turkish troops from Cyprus, whereupon Denktaş threatened to boycott any further intercommunal talks and to seek recognition for the 'TFSC' as a sovereign state; simultaneously it was announced that the Turkish lira was to replace the Cyprus pound as legal tender in the 'TFSC'.

On 15 November 1983 the 'TFSC' made a unilateral declaration of independence as the 'Turkish Republic of Northern Cyprus' ('TRNC'), with Denktaş continuing as President. An interim Government was formed in December, led by Nejat Konuk (Prime Minister of the 'TFSC' from 1976 to 1978 and President of the Legislative Assembly from 1981), pending elections in 1984. Like the 'TFSC', the 'TRNC' was recognized only by Turkey, and the declaration of independence was condemned by the UN Security Council. Following the establishment of diplomatic links between the 'TRNC' and Turkey in April 1984, the 'TRNC' formally rejected UN proposals for a suspension of its declaration of independence prior to further talks.

During 1984 a 'TRNC' Constituent Assembly, comprising the members of the Legislative Assembly and 30 nominated members, drafted a new Constitution, which was approved by a referendum in May 1985. At the 'TRNC' presidential election on 9 June, Denktaş was returned to office with over 70% of the vote. A general election followed on 23 June, with the UBP, led by Dr Derviş Eroğlu, winning 24 of the 50 seats in the Legislative Assembly. In July Dr Eroğlu became Prime Minister of the 'TRNC', leading a coalition Government formed by the UBP and the Toplumcu Kurtuluş Partisi (TKP—Communal Liberation Party).

In November 1985, following a debate on President Kyprianou's leadership, the House of Representatives was dissolved.

A general election for an enlarged House was held in December. The DISY won 19 seats, President Kyprianou's DIKO won 16 seats and the AKEL won 15 seats. The AKEL and the DISY therefore failed to secure the two-thirds majority required to amend the Constitution and thus challenge the President's tenure of power. The election result was regarded as a vindication of President Kyprianou's policies.

Settlement plans proposed by the UN Secretary-General in July 1985 and in April 1986 were rejected by the Turkish Cypriots and the Greek Cypriots, respectively. Further measures concerning the demilitarization of the island, reportedly proposed by the Greek Cypriot Government, were rejected by Denktaş, who maintained that negotiations on the establishment of a two-zone, federal republic should precede any demilitarization.

A presidential election, held in the Greek Cypriot zone in February 1988, was won by Georghios Vassiliou, an economist, who presented himself as an independent, but who was unofficially supported by the AKEL. He took office later in February and promised to re-establish the National Council (originally convened by President Makarios), which was to include representatives of all the main Greek Cypriot political parties, to discuss the resolution of the Cyprus problem.

In April 1988 the Prime Minister of the 'TRNC', Dr Eroğlu, and the other members of the Council of Ministers resigned from their posts, following a disagreement between the UBP and its coalition partner (since September 1986), the Yeni Doğuş Partisi (New Dawn Party), which was demanding greater representation in the Government. At the request of President Denktaş, however, Dr Eroğlu resumed his post and formed a new Council of Ministers in May, comprising mainly UBP members but also including independents.

In March 1988 President Vassiliou rejected various proposals that had been submitted, via the UN, by President Denktaş of the 'TRNC', and which included a plan to form committees to study the possibilities of intercommunal co-operation. Following a meeting with the newly-revived National Council in June, however, President Vassiliou agreed to a proposal by the UN Secretary-General to resume intercommunal talks, without preconditions, with President Denktaş, in their capacity as the leaders of two communities. After consulting the Turkish Government in July, Denktaş also approved the proposal. Accordingly, a summit meeting, under UN auspices, took place in Geneva in August, the first such meeting between Greek and Turkish Cypriot leaders since January 1985. As a result of this meeting, Vassiliou and Denktaş began direct negotiations, under UN auspices, in September 1988. No real progress was made and, although Vassiliou and Denktaş resumed negotiations at the UN in February 1990, the talks were abandoned in March, chiefly because Denktaş demanded recognition of the right to self-determination for Turkish Cypriots.

In April 1990 Denktaş was the successful candidate in an early presidential election in the 'TRNC', securing nearly 67% of the votes cast. In May, at the elections to the 'TRNC' Legislative Assembly, the UBP won 34 of the 50 seats, and its leader, Dr Eroğlu, retained the office of Prime Minister.

In July 1990 the Government of Cyprus formally applied to join the European Community (EC, now European Union—EU). Denktaş condemned the application, on the grounds that the Turkish Cypriots had not been consulted, and stated that the action would prevent the resumption of intercommunal talks. However, in June 1993 the European Commission approved the eligibility of Cyprus for EC membership, although it insisted that the application be linked to progress in the latest UN-sponsored talks concerning the island. The Commission's recommendation was endorsed by the EC Council of Ministers in October.

At the Greek Cypriot general election held on 19 May 1991, the conservative DISY, in alliance with the Komma Phileleftheron (Liberal Party), received 35.8% of the votes cast, thereby securing 20 seats in the House of Representatives. The AKEL, contrary to pre-election predictions, made the most significant gains, obtaining 30.6% of the votes and 18 seats.

At by-elections to 12 seats in the Turkish Cypriot Legislative Assembly, conducted in October 1991, the UBP increased its representation in the 50-seat Assembly to 45 members.

Following unsuccessful attempts to promote the resumption of discussions between Vassiliou and Denktaş by the UN, the EC and the USA during 1990 and 1991, the new UN Secretary-General, Dr Boutros Boutros-Ghali, made the resolution of the Cyprus problem one of his priorities in 1992. In February UN envoys visited Cyprus, Turkey and Greece, and in January and March Dr Boutros-Ghali himself held separate meetings in New York, USA, with Vassiliou and Denktaş. However, in his report to the UN Security Council in April, Dr Boutros-Ghali was unable to announce any progress on the basic differences between the two sides concerning territory and displaced persons.

In mid-1992 Dr Boutros-Ghali held a second round of talks with Vassiliou and Denktaş in New York, initially separately, but subsequently involving direct discussions between the two leaders. The talks aimed to arrive at a draft settlement based on a 'set of ideas', compiled by Dr Boutros-Ghali and endorsed by a UN Security Council resolution, which advocated 'uninterrupted negotiations' until a settlement was reached. Discussions centred on UN proposals for the demarcation of Greek Cypriot and Turkish Cypriot areas of administration under a federal structure. However, following the publication of what was described as a 'non-map' in the Turkish Cypriot press, which showed the proposed area of Turkish administration about 25% smaller than the 'TRNC', Denktaş asserted that the UN's territorial proposals were totally unacceptable to the 'TRNC' Government, while political opinion in the Greek Cypriot area was divided. The five weeks of talks in New York came to an end in August, again without having achieved significant progress. A third round of UN-sponsored talks opened in New York in late October 1992. The talks were suspended in the following month with no discernible progress having been made in the main areas of discussion, i.e. refugees, constitutional and territorial issues. The UN Security Council held Denktaş responsible for the lack of progress, and adjourned the talks.

In February 1993 a presidential election was held in two rounds in the Greek Cypriot zone. In the second round of voting, which was held on 14 February, Glavkos Klerides, the leader of the DISY, defeated the incumbent President, Georghios Vassiliou, by a margin of less than 1%, to become the new President. Following his defeat, Vassiliou founded a new party called the Kinema ton Eleftheron Dimokraton (KED—Movement of Free Democrats).

Negotiations were reconvened in May 1993 under UN auspices in New York, concerning the Secretary-General's plan to introduce a series of 'confidence-building measures' (CBMs). These included the proposed reopening, under UN administration, of the international airport at Nicosia, and the resettlement, also under UN directives, of a fenced suburb of Famagusta. Denktaş presented separate demands at the talks, which included the removal of the embargo against 'TRNC' airports, ports and sporting activities. The talks were abandoned in June, when the Turkish Cypriot negotiators declined to respond to the UN proposals. In December the Council of Ministers of the EU decided to appoint an observer to monitor and report on the UN talks. Negotiations between the Greek Cypriots and Turkish Cypriots were to be resumed following the holding of the general election in the 'TRNC'.

In November 1993 Klerides and the newly-appointed Prime Minister of Greece, Andreas Papandreou, agreed at a meeting in Athens that their countries would take joint decisions in negotiations for the settlement of the Cyprus problem. The two leaders also agreed on a common defence doctrine, whereby Greece was to provide Cyprus with a guarantee of air, land and naval protection. In October 1994 the Greek airforce participated for the first time in an exercise of the Cypriot National Guard.

In December 1993 an early general election was held in the 'TRNC', partly in response to increasing conflict between President Denktaş and Prime Minister Eroğlu over the handling of the UN-sponsored peace talks. The UBP lost its majority in the Legislative Assembly, winning only 17 of the 50 seats, and at the end of the month a coalition Government was formed by the Demokrat Parti (DP—Democrat Party), which had been supported by Denktaş, and the left-wing Cumhuriyetçi Türk Partisi (CTP—Republican Turkish Party). Together, the DP and the CTP won 53.4% of the votes cast and 28 seats. The leader of the DP, Hakkı Atun (hitherto the Speaker of the Assembly), was appointed as Prime Minister of the new administration.

In February 1994, following the confirmation by both authorities of their acceptance, in principle, of the CBMs, UN officials began conducting so-called 'proximity talks' separately with the two leaders. The negotiations focused on practical arrangements for the implementation of the CBMs. Denktaş insisted, however, that the proposals under discussion differed from the intention of the original measures that had been agreed upon, and therefore refused to accept the document that was presented to both sides in March. At the end of May a report issued by the UN Secretary-General for consideration by the Security Council placed responsibility for the breakdown of the peace efforts on the 'TRNC' authorities. In the following month the UN conducted negotiations to reclarify the CBM package. Denktaş accepted certain UN requests on the implementation of the measures, including the withdrawal of Turkish Cypriot troops from the access road to Nicosia international airport, but no substantive progress was made.

In July 1994 the UN Security Council adopted resolution 939, which advocated a new initiative on the part of the Secretary-General to formulate a solution for peace, but one that should be based on a single nationality, international identity and sovereignty. The 'TRNC' Legislative Assembly responded to the resolution by approving a policy, in August, establishing principles of future foreign policy. It stated that no peace solution based on the concept of a federation would be acceptable, and urged greater integration with Turkey. During October five UN-sponsored informal meetings between Klerides and Denktaş failed to achieve any progress towards an agreement on issues of the peace settlement.

The issue of Cyprus's bid to accede to the EU had greatly unsettled the progress of peace negotiations. In June 1994 EU heads of government, meeting in Corfu, Greece, confirmed that Cyprus (together with Malta) would be included in the next round of expansion of the Union. Denktaş remained adamant that any approach by the Greek Cypriots to the EU would prompt the 'TRNC' to seek further integration with Turkey. In early 1995 US officials commenced discussions with the two sides in an attempt to break the existing deadlock: while Denktaş insisted that the 'TRNC' would oppose Cyprus's EU membership application until a settlement for the island had been reached, the Greek Cypriot Government demanded 'TRNC' acceptance of the application as a pre-condition to pursuing the talks. In March the Council of Ministers of the EU agreed to consider Cyprus's membership application without discrimination based on the progress (or otherwise) of settlement talks.

In February 1995 the 'TRNC' Prime Minister and his coalition Government resigned as a result of serious disagreements with Denktaş, concerning the redistribution of Greek Cypriot-owned housing and land. However, in the following month, after the UBP failed to negotiate the formation of a new government, Atun was reappointed as Prime Minister. At a presidential election, held in April, Denktaş achieved conclusive victory only in the second round of voting (having obtained 40.4% of votes cast in the first poll), when he obtained 62.5% of the votes, compared with 37.5% for his opponent, Dr Eroğlu. In early June, following protracted inter-party negotiations, a new coalition of the DP and CTP, under Atun's premiership, took office, having concluded a joint protocol agreement on economic and foreign policy.

In May 1995 so-called 'secret' negotiations between representatives of the two Cypriot communities, held in London on the initiative of the USA and the United Kingdom, achieved little apparent progress in furthering agreement on the island's future or in securing agreement for direct talks between Denktaş and Klerides. In June a meeting of the EU-Cyprus Association Council ratified the conclusions of the EU Council of Ministers in March regarding the Greek Cypriot membership application and agreed to commence pre-accession 'structured dialogue' talks. In late June Klerides, for the first time, attended a summit meeting of EU heads of government. In July a new political obstacle to inter-communal negotiations emerged over allegations that Turkish Cypriot construction work in the capital was, in fact, part of efforts to fortify the buffer zone.

In August 1995 the 'TRNC' Legislative Assembly adopted new legislation concerning compensation for Greek-owned property in the north (the issue which had provoked Atun's resignation earlier in the year). At the end of October Özker Özgür resigned as Deputy Prime Minister, reportedly owing to his disapproval of Denktaş's uncompromising attitude to the Cyprus issue. In early November Denktaş rejected a new list of CTP ministers, which Atun subsequently refused to amend since it had been approved by both parties in the coalition administration. Temporary appointments were made to replace three ministers who resigned. On 11 November, however, Atun submitted the resignation of his entire Government. A new DP-CTP coalition, again under Atun's leadership with Mehmet Ali Talat replacing Özgür as Deputy Prime Minister, took office in early December.

In December 1995 the US administration declared its intention to strengthen efforts in Cyprus, led by the Assistant Secretary of State with responsibility for Europe, Richard Holbrooke, with the aim of achieving significant progress towards a final settlement during 1996. Early in the new year, however, Holbrooke postponed a visit to the region, owing to renewed tension between Greece and Turkey in the Aegean and the absence of a Turkish Government following elections in that country in December 1995. Representatives of the British Government and of the EU did hold discussions with both sides in late February 1996 to assess the potential success of a new political initiative to achieve a peaceful settlement.

In May 1996 the results of elections for the Greek Cypriot House of Representatives produced little change in the composition of the legislature. DISY retained its 20 seats, obtaining 34.5% of the votes cast, while AKEL took 19 seats, an increase of one, with 33.0% of the votes. DIKO secured 10 seats (16.4%), EDEK five (8.1%) and KED two (3.7%). In December KED and Ananeotiko Dimokratiko Sosialistiko Kinema (ADISOK—Democratic Socialist Reform Movement) merged to form the Enomeni Demokrates (EDE—United Democrats).

In May 1996 the 'TRNC' governing party, the DP, elected Serdar Denktaş, the President's son, as its new leader, although Atun, now honorary party leader, was to continue to serve as Prime Minister. However, persisting policy differences between the two coalition parties undermined the stability of the Government, which resigned in early July. Negotiations to establish a new administration were undertaken by the DP and the UBP. A protocol coalition agreement, whereby UBP leader Dr Eroğlu would become Prime Minister, was finally signed by the leaders of the two parties in mid-August and the Government secured a confidence motion in the Legislative Assembly later in that month.

In April 1996 the UN Security Council endorsed a US initiative to promote a settlement in Cyprus, based on a federal arrangement. The Cyprus issue subsequently assumed a higher profile. In May the United Kingdom appointed Sir David Hannay, a former Permanent Representative to the UN, as its first special representative to Cyprus. In June Dr Boutros-Ghali held discussions, separately, with Presidents Denktaş and Klerides, with the intention of generating support for future direct bilateral negotiations. The meetings preceded a visit to the island by the UN Secretary-General's newly-appointed Special Representative in Cyprus, Han Sung-Joo. However, all efforts towards international mediation were diminished by a sharp escalation in intercommunal hostilities. Amid the tension, Sir David Hannay made a scheduled visit to revive the possibility of a meeting of the two Cypriot leaders in 1997. At the end of October 1996 a military dialogue, involving senior commanders of both armies on the island, commenced under UN mediation. The talks were to consider the following UN proposals for reducing intercommunal tension: the prohibition of loaded weapons along the buffer zone; the removal of military personnel from the most volatile parts of the demarcation line; and the formulation of a code of conduct to specify permissible activities in the border area. In November further efforts at mediation, including a visit by a high-level US official, were undermined by allegations of violations of Greek Cypriot airspace by Turkish military aircraft, efforts by the Greek Cypriot community to prevent tourists from visiting the 'TRNC' and the continued opposition of the 'TRNC' to the Cypriot application to join the EU.

In December 1996 the European Court of Human Rights ruled that Turkey was in breach of the European Convention on Human Rights by, as a result of its occupation in the north, denying a woman access to her property. The ruling implicated Turkey as fully responsible for activities in the 'TRNC' and for the consequences of the military action in 1974.

In January 1997 the purchase of an advanced anti-aircraft missile system by the Greek Cypriot authorities became the focus of political hostilities between the two sides and the cause of considerable international concern. The purchase agreement, which had been an issue of contention in the previous year and which was condemned by the 'TRNC' as an 'act of aggression', was reportedly concluded between the Cypriot authorities and the Russian Government at the beginning of the month, in order to secure Greek Cypriot defences. Deployment of the missiles would have the effect of challenging the air superiority that Turkish forces had enjoyed since 1974. The potential for conflict over the issue increased when the Turkish Government declared its willingness to use military force to prevent the deployment of the system. The Greek Government, in turn, insisted that it would defend Cyprus against any Turkish attack. US mediators sought urgent meetings with the Cypriot leaders, and were assured by the Greek Cypriot Government that the system would not be deployed until, at the earliest, May 1998, and that its deployment would be dependent upon the progress made in talks. In addition, both sides approved measures, supported by the UN, to reduce tension along the border area, although a US proposal for a ban on all military flights over the island was rejected by the Greek Cypriots. Later in January Turkey threatened to establish air and naval bases in the 'TRNC' if Greece continued to promote plans for the establishment of military facilities in the south, and at the end of the month Turkish warships arrived in the 'TRNC' port of Famagusta. Turkey and the 'TRNC' also declared their commitment to a joint military concept, whereby any attack on the 'TRNC' would be deemed a violation against Turkey.

In April 1997 Klerides announced a reorganization of the Council of Ministers, in which Yiannakis Kasoulides, a government spokesman, was appointed Minister of Foreign Affairs. In June, following proximity talks between Klerides and Denktaş that had begun in March, the Cypriot leaders agreed to take part in direct UN-sponsored negotiations in the USA in July, under the chairmanship of the UN Special Envoy for Cyprus, Dr Diego Córdovez. The talks took place under the auspices of the UN Secretary-General, Kofi Annan, and with the participation of Richard Holbrooke, whose appointment as the US Special Envoy to Cyprus in June had been welcomed by both Klerides and Denktaş. Further private direct talks took place in Nicosia at the end of July, when agreement was reached to co-operate in efforts to trace persons missing since the hostilities in 1974.

A second formal round of UN-sponsored peace negotiations in Switzerland in August 1997 collapsed without agreement, as Denktaş demanded the suspension of Cyprus's application for EU membership. The EU had formally agreed that Cyprus would be included in the next phase of the organization's enlargement at an EU summit in July. Denktaş opposed the application on the grounds that the negotiations, scheduled to begin in 1998, were to be conducted with the Greek Cypriot Government, ignoring the issue of Turkish Cypriot sovereignty. Prior to the UN-sponsored meeting in August 1997, the 'TRNC' and Turkey agreed to create a joint committee to co-ordinate the partial integration of the 'TRNC' into Turkey. This was widely regarded as a response to the EU's decision to negotiate with the Greek Cypriot Government concerning future membership of the EU while excluding Turkey. Despite Denktaş's threat to suspend discussions pending the resolution of the EU dispute, further UN-sponsored peace negotiations concerning security issues were held in September.

During October and November 1997 US and UN efforts to promote progress in the talks, including visits to Cyprus by both Holbrooke and Córdovez, achieved little success, partly owing to the imminence of the Greek Cypriot presidential election. Denktaş rejected Holbrooke's attempts to persuade the 'TRNC' to join the Greek Cypriot Government at EU accession talks in 1998, insisting on EU recognition of the 'TRNC' and the simultaneous admission of Turkey to EU membership. Tension between the two sides remained high, as Turkish fighter aircraft violated Cyprus's airspace in October 1997, in retaliation for Greek participation in Greek Cypriot military manoeuvres.

In November 1997 DIKO voted to leave the Greek Cypriot ruling coalition in advance of the presidential election; the five DIKO ministers resigned from their government positions and were subsequently replaced by members of the business community and civil servants. On 15 February 1998, in the second round of voting in the presidential election, Glavkos Klerides defeated Georghios Iacovou, an independent candidate (supported by AKEL and DIKO), by a margin of 1.6%, thus retaining the presidency. A new coalition Government, composed of members of the DISY, EDEK, EDE and independents, was sworn in at the end of the month.

The Greek Cypriot Government began accession talks with the EU in March 1998, and, in an effort to expand relations with the EU, Cyprus confirmed its application for associate membership of the Western European Union (WEU, see p. 268) the following month. In early May Holbrooke visited Cyprus and held talks with Klerides and Denktaş, with the aim of relaunching the peace negotiations. However, no progress was made; Holbrooke cited the principal obstacles as Denktaş' demands for the recognition of the 'TRNC' and for the withdrawal of the Cypriot application to join the EU, and the decision of the EU to delay further Turkey's application for membership. Russian efforts to facilitate the peace process at that time were also unsuccessful.

In June 1998 a number of Greek military aircraft landed at the Paphos airfield in southern Cyprus; this was the first such visit by Greek aircraft since the airfield's completion in January. A few days later, in response, Turkish warplanes landed in the 'TRNC'. During 1998 Turkish aircraft were accused of violating Greek Cypriot airspace on a number of occasions. In mid-July the Greek Cypriot Government condemned the arrival of Turkish warships and aircraft in the 'TRNC' for the celebrations of the anniversary of the Turkish invasion of the island.

In late August 1998 Denktaş rejected a UN plan to reunify Cyprus and, in a letter to the UN, proposed instead a confederation of equal status; this proposal was rejected by Klerides, on the grounds that it would legitimize the status of the 'TRNC'. In early October Holbrooke held a meeting in New York, USA, with the Greek Cypriot Deputy Minister of Foreign Affairs, Ioannis Kranidhiotis, to discuss the peace process. The UN Special Envoy also held individual meetings with Klerides and Denktaş in Cyprus that month, although no progress was made.

In mid-October 1998 Denktaş proposed a non-aggression treaty between the two sides. At the end of the month, however, Turkish fighter planes harassed Greek aircraft, which were present in Cyprus for joint Greek-Cypriot military exercises. In early November the Israeli President, Ezer Weizman, visited Cyprus in an effort to promote co-operation, and to assure Klerides that Israel's military agreement with Turkey was not directed against Cyprus. Shortly afterwards two Israelis were arrested in Cyprus on suspicion of spying; Israel later denied that the two men had acted either against Cyprus or on behalf of Turkey, but there was speculation that they were Mossad agents. (The two men were subsequently sentenced to three years' imprisonment for approaching a prohibited military area, although they were pardoned in August 1999.) Joint Turkish-'TRNC' military exercises were held in November 1998.

At the end of December 1998, following diplomatic pressure from Greece, the EU (which threatened to suspend Cypriot accession talks if the weapons were deployed in Cyprus), the USA and the UN, it was announced officially that the Russian missile system would not be deployed in Cyprus and that, instead, negotiations would be held with a view to their installation on Crete, Greece. The decision was influenced by the adoption earlier in December of two resolutions by the UN Security Council (both of which were dismissed by Denktaş): the first renewed the UNFICYP mandate and appealed for the resumption of negotiations on reunification as a single sovereign state (apparently rejecting the 'TRNC' Government's proposals for a confederation) and the second expressed concern at the lack of progress toward a political settlement and advocated the initiation of a phased reduction of troop and armament levels on the island. Both Turkey and the 'TRNC' welcomed the Cypriot decision, although Turkey warned that the deployment of the missiles in Greece would still be seen as a threat to its security. Klerides' decision provoked intense domestic criticism, and EDEK withdrew from the Greek Cypriot governing coalition in protest at the decision, precipitating the resignations of the Minister of Defence, Yiannakis Omirou, and the Minister of Education and Culture, Lykourgos Kappas. Their replacements were appointed in early January 1999.

On 6 December 1998 legislative elections were held in the 'TRNC'. The UBP increased its representation to 24 seats (from 16 in 1993), while the DP obtained only 13 seats. The TKP won seven of the 50 seats and the CTP took the remaining six. On 30 December the new Council of Ministers, a UBP-TKP coalition, received presidential approval. Eroğlu remained as Prime Minister, and the TKP leader, Mustafa Akıncı, was appointed Minister of State and Deputy Prime Minister. The missiles were reportedly deployed in Crete in March 1999, following the signature in February of an agreement with the Greek Government, confirming that Cyprus would own the missiles although they would be under Greek operational control.

The Greek Cypriot Minister of the Interior, Dinos Michaelides, resigned in March 1999, following allegations of corruption against him (strenuously denied), which had emerged in November 1998. A further government reorganization was effected in late August 1999, in which the defence, health and communications and works portfolios were reallocated.

In June 1999 the UN Security Council adopted two new resolutions on Cyprus. The first extended the mandate of

UNFICYP for a further six months and the second urged the two sides to participate in UN-sponsored negotiations in late 1999 without preconditions or proscribed issues. In November, despite his earlier reluctance to attend the proposed meeting, Denktaş confirmed that he would attend talks with Klerides in New York that month under the auspices of the UN. The UN Secretary-General acted as a mediator in the indirect talks, which aimed to facilitate meaningful negotiations leading to a comprehensive settlement in Cyprus. The negotiations were undermined by the results of the EU summit meeting in Helsinki, Finland, where it was announced that a political settlement in Cyprus was not a precondition to the accession of the Greek Cypriot Government to the EU. This decision was widely acknowledged to be a response to Greece's reversal of its opposition to Turkey's EU membership application; Turkey thus gained formal status as a candidate for EU membership in Helsinki. Denktaş criticized the EU decision on Cyprus's accession, but did not leave early from the discussions in New York and agreed to resume negotiations in 2000. Further UN-sponsored indirect talks between the two Presidents were held in Geneva, Switzerland, in January/February 2000; another round of negotiations was expected to take place in May.

Meanwhile, in mid-1999 both Denktaş and Eroğlu had announced that they were to stand as candidates in the 'TRNC' presidential election, scheduled to be held in April 2000.

## Government

The 1960 Constitution provided for a system of government in which power would be shared by the Greek and Turkish communities in proportion to their numbers. This Constitution officially remains in force, but since the ending of Turkish participation in the Government in 1963, and particularly since the creation of a separate Turkish area in northern Cyprus in 1974, each community has administered its own affairs, refusing to recognize the authority of the other's Government. The Greek Cypriot administration claims to be the Government of all Cyprus, and is generally recognized as such, although it has no Turkish participation. The northern area is under the *de facto* control of the 'Turkish Republic of Northern Cyprus' (for which a new Constitution was approved by a referendum in May 1985). Each community has its own President, Council of Ministers, legislature and judicial system.

## Defence

The formation of the National Guard was authorized by the House of Representatives in 1964, after the withdrawal of the Turkish members. Men between 18 and 50 years of age are liable to 26 months' conscription. At 1 August 1999 the National Guard comprised an army of 10,000 regulars, mainly composed of Cypriot conscripts but with an additional 200 seconded Greek Army officers and NCOs, and 88,000 reserves. A further 950 Greek army personnel were stationed in Cyprus at that time. There is also a Greek Cypriot paramilitary police force of 750. In 1999 the defence budget for the Greek Cypriot area was C£300m.

At 1 August 1999 the 'TRNC' had an army of about 4,500 regulars and 26,000 reserves. Men between 18 and 50 years of age are liable to 24 months' conscription. It was estimated that the 'TRNC' forces were being supported by 30,000–33,000 Turkish troops. In 1998 defence expenditure in the 'TRNC' was an estimated US $700m.

The UN Peace-keeping Force in Cyprus (UNFICYP) consisted of 1,263 military and police personnel at 30 September 1999 (see p. 62). There are British military bases (with personnel numbering 3,200 in August 1999) at Akrotiri, Episkopi and Dhekelia.

## Economic Affairs

In 1993, according to estimates by the World Bank, Cyprus's gross national product (GNP), measured at average 1991–93 prices, was US $7,539m., equivalent to $10,380 per head. During 1985–94, it was estimated, GNP per head increased, in real terms, by an average of 5.2% per year. In 1990–97 the population increased by an average of 1.3% per year. In 1997 estimated GNP was $10,839m., equivalent to $14,930 per head. Cyprus's gross domestic product (GDP), according to IMF figures, increased, in real terms, by an annual average of 4.0% in 1990–96. In the 'TRNC' GNP per head was valued at $3,093 in 1994. In 1997 the region's GNP was TL 118,227,300m. In 1991–97 real GDP increased at an average annual rate of 3.3%. However, in 1992 GDP per head in the 'TRNC' remained less than one-half that of the remainder of the island.

Agriculture (including forestry and fishing) contributed approximately 4.3% of GDP in 1998. In the government-controlled area 9.5% of the employed labour force were engaged in this sector in 1998. The principal crops of the government-controlled area are barley, potatoes (which accounted for 8.6% of domestic export earnings in 1998), grapes and citrus fruit. The agricultural sector was adversely affected by an increasing water shortage, which the Government was addressing through the granting of concessions to companies to build and operate several desalination plants. The area's agricultural output increased by an average of 2.2% per year in 1990–95, but declined by 4.5% in 1996 and by an estimated 2.5% in 1997. In the 'TRNC' 22.7% of the working population were employed in agriculture (mainly in the production of citrus fruit), forestry and fishing in 1995, and the sector contributed an estimated 7.7% of GDP in 1997. The principal crops of the 'TRNC' are wheat, barley, potatoes and citrus fruit. In order to address the water shortage in the 'TRNC', which was adversely affecting crop production, the Government has resorted to importing water from Turkey.

Industry (comprising mining, manufacturing, construction and utilities) engaged 23.0% of the employed labour force in the government-controlled area in 1998, and accounted for 22.0% of GDP. In the 'TRNC' the industrial sector contributed 19.4% of GDP in 1997, and engaged 23.5% of the working labour force in 1995.

Mining provided only 0.3% of GDP and engaged a mere 0.2% of the employed labour force in the government-controlled area in 1998. Minerals accounted for less than 2% of domestic exports (by value) from the government-controlled sector in 1989. In the 'TRNC' mining and quarrying contributed 0.8% of GDP in 1997.

Manufacturing accounted for 11.4% of GDP in the government-controlled area in 1998, and engaged 13.8% of the employed labour force. Clothing represents the southern sector's main export commodity, yielding C£29.0m., or 13.1% of total export earnings (excluding re-exports), in 1998. In the 'TRNC' the manufacturing sector provided 8.8% of GDP in 1997.

Energy is derived principally from imported petroleum, which comprised 4.0% of total imports in the government-controlled area in 1997. Mineral fuels, lubricants, etc. comprised 8.7% of total imports in the 'TRNC' in 1997.

The services sector in the government-controlled area contributed an estimated 73.7% of GDP and engaged 67.6% of the employed labour force in 1998. Within the sector, financial and business services provided an estimated 19.5% of GDP and generated 8.5% of employment in that year. By 1998 the government-controlled area supported 29 'offshore' banking units; an estimated 26,000 'offshore' enterprises had been registered in the sector since incentives were introduced in 1975. In the 'TRNC' the services sector contributed 72.9% of GDP in 1997, and engaged 53.8% of the employed labour force in 1995. Both Cypriot communities have undertaken measures to expand their tourism industries, which are important sources of revenue and employment. Tourist arrivals to the government-controlled area increased from 1,950,000 in 1996, to 2,088,000 in 1997 and to 2,222,706 in 1998. Receipts from tourism in 1998 amounted to C£878m. In 1997 a total of 399,364 tourists (326,364 of whom were from the Turkish mainland) visited the 'TRNC', and net tourism receipts in that year totalled US $192.2m.

In 1998 the government-controlled area recorded a visible trade deficit of US $2,425.7m. and a current account deficit of $560.6m. The trade deficit in the 'TRNC' in 1997 was $316.5m., while the current account deficit was $42.2m. In 1998 the principal sources of imports to the government-controlled area were the United Kingdom (11.2%) and the USA (12.5%); the former was also the principal market for domestic exports (20.1%). Other major trading partners were Greece, Germany, Japan and Italy. The principal domestic exports in 1998 were clothing, potatoes and pharmaceutical products. The principal imports were textiles, vehicles, minerals, metals and foodstuffs (including beverages, spirits and vinegar and tobacco and manufactured tobacco substitutes). In 1997 the principal imports of the 'TRNC' were machinery and transport equipment, basic manufactures, and food and live animals; the principal exports were citrus fruit and clothing. In 1997 the Turkish Cypriot area's main source of imports was Turkey (56.4%), which was also the principal destination for exports (47.0%).

In 1997 there was a budget deficit of C£231m. in the government-controlled area. External debt totalled C£1,199.7m. at the end of 1994, of which C£694.7m. was medium- and long-term public debt. In that year the cost of debt-servicing was equivalent to 12.9% of the value of exports of goods and services. The annual rate of inflation averaged 4.1% in 1990–98. Consumer prices increased by an average of 3.0% in 1996, by 3.6% in 1997 and by 2.2% in 1998. The average level of unemployment in the government-controlled area was 3.5% of the labour force in 1997.

The 1997 budget of the 'TRNC' recorded expenditure of TL 50,160,862.0m. and revenue of TL 46,666,566.3m. (with aid from Turkey contributing TL 12,171,847.1m. to revenue), resulting in a deficit of TL 3,494,295.7m. (equivalent to 3.0% of GDP). The annual average rate of inflation in the 'TRNC' was 81.7% in 1997. According to census figures, 6.5% of the labour force were unemployed in December 1996.

In 1972 Cyprus concluded an association agreement with the European Community (EC, now European Union—EU), and in 1987 an agreement was signed on the progressive establishment of a customs union with the EC, with effect from 1 January 1988. An application to become a full member of the EC was submitted by the Greek Cypriot Government in July 1990; accession negotiations commenced in March 1998. The 'TRNC' is a member of the Economic Co-operation Organization (ECO, see p. 167).

In the 1990s the failure of efforts to conclude a political settlement continued to affect the economy and future prospects of the island. The Greek Cypriot Government's principal concern was to develop further relations with the EU and to achieve the necessary economic criteria to secure accession to the grouping. Economic growth in the Greek Cypriot part of the island has been dominated by the service sectors, in particular tourism, banking and the 'offshore' sector. Following rapid growth, Cyprus's shipping registry, by the end of 1998, was ranked as the sixth largest in the world. The introduction of measures designed to help Cyprus to achieve convergence with EU economic indicators posed a number of problems, as the need to reduce taxation levels resulted in a decline in government revenues, thus increasing both the budget deficit and the level of public debt. In 1999 optimism concerning Cyprus's progress towards membership of the EU, and relative political stability following the decision taken in December not to deploy Russian missiles in Cyprus, resulted in enhanced business confidence and contributed to a rapid increase in the value of shares on the Nicosia stock exchange. The tourism sector also experienced rapid growth and, together with a recovery in manufacturing, this expansion led to projected GDP growth of 4% in 1999. Financial transactions have been facilitated by the central bank's decision to link the value of the Cyprus pound to the euro in January 1999. The significant demand for trade finance and consumer loans in 1999 prompted the imposition of restrictions aimed at limiting credit expansion in the private sector. However, although the economy is benefiting from sustained economic growth, low rates of inflation and unemployment, the Government has struggled to gain acceptance for vital fiscal reforms to reduce the growing budget deficit. Structural reforms have also been impeded by the trade unions. Cyprus had initially hoped to join the EU by 2002, but bureaucratic and political delays could postpone its entry until 2004. However, the EU's decision in December 1999 to dissociate Cyprus's accession to the EU from the achievement of a political settlement with the 'TRNC' prompted considerable optimism. Cyprus is also currently attempting to enhance the island's position as an entrepôt for shipping and trade throughout the Eastern Mediterranean.

The economy of the 'TRNC', although substantially less prosperous and affected by diplomatic isolation, has also achieved significant growth since the 1980s, with considerable assistance from Turkey. The close linkage with the Turkish economy, including the use of the Turkish lira as currency in the 'TRNC', has, however, resulted in persistently high levels of inflation. In July 1994 the 'TRNC' economy suffered a potential setback with a ruling by the Court of Justice of the European Communities that effectively prohibited EU member states from importing agricultural goods (unless certified by the recognized Cypriot authorities) and ended preferential treatment of textiles. In the late 1990s higher education became the territory's most significant economic sector. In 1999 20,000 students, mostly from Turkey, attended six private universities in the 'TRNC' and revenue was projected at US $250m. The rapid expansion in higher education was expected to lead to GDP growth of 5% in 1999. The tourism sector was also significant, but remained hampered by an international ban on direct flights to the 'TRNC' (visitors must land in Turkey). While there was little prospect of an imminent resolution of the political issue in Cyprus, the economic divergence of the two communities remained evident, with GNP per head estimated at US $13,300 in the government-controlled area in 1995, more than three times the estimated 'TRNC' figure of $4,000.

## Social Welfare

A comprehensive social insurance scheme, covering every working male and female and their dependants, is in operation in the government-controlled area. It includes provisions for protection against arbitrary and unjustified dismissal, for industrial welfare and for tripartite co-operation in the formulation and implementation of labour policies and objectives. Benefits and pensions from the social insurance scheme cover unemployment, sickness, maternity, widows, orphans, injury at work, old age and death. In 1996, in the government-controlled area, there was one doctor for every 404 inhabitants and a hospital bed for every 195 inhabitants. In 1994 there was a nurse for every 233 inhabitants. Of total expenditure by the central Government in the Greek Cypriot area in 1997, C£101.3m. (6.9%) was for health services, and a further C£392.7m. (26.6%) for social security and welfare. In 1997 the state health service in the Turkish Cypriot zone included nine hospital establishments, with a total of 814 beds, while there were 287 private establishments, with 263 beds. In that year there were 467 physicians and dentists, of whom 178 worked in the state health service.

## Education

In the Greek Cypriot sector elementary education, which is compulsory and available free of charge, is provided in six grades for children between five-and-a-half and 12 years of age. Enrolment at primary level included 97% of children in the relevant age-group in 1996 (males 96%; females 97%). Secondary education is free for all years of study and lasts six years, with three compulsory years at the Gymnasium being followed by three non-compulsory years at a technical school or a Lyceum. In 1995 comprehensive secondary schools were also introduced. There are five options of specialization at the Lyceums: classical, science, economics, commercial/secretarial and foreign languages. In 1996 enrolment in secondary education included 92% of school-age children (males 90%; females 95%). There are 11 three-year technical schools. Higher education for teachers, technicians, engineers, hoteliers and caterers, foresters, nurses and health inspectors is provided by technical and vocational colleges. The University of Cyprus was inaugurated in September 1992, and there were a further 31 post-secondary institutions in 1994/95. In 1997/98 a total of 10,815 students from the Greek Cypriot area were studying in universities abroad. In 1994 enrolment at tertiary level was equivalent to 17.0% of the relevant age-group (males 15.0%; females 19.0%). Budgetary expenditure on education by the central Government in the Greek Cypriot area was C£190.3m. (12.9% of total spending) in 1997. In 1992, according to census results, 5.6%. of the adult population (males 2.2%; females 8.9%) were illiterate.

Education in the Turkish Cypriot zone is controlled by the 'TRNC'. Pre-primary education is provided by kindergartens for children of 5 and 6 years of age. Primary education is free and compulsory: it comprises elementary schools for the 7–11 age group, and secondary-junior schools for the 12–14 age group. Secondary education, for the 15–17 age group, is provided by high schools (Lycées) and vocational schools, including colleges of agriculture, nursing and hotel management. It is free, but not compulsory. In 1997/98 21,117 students proceeded to higher education in the 'TRNC', which is provided by seven institutions: the Eastern Mediterranean University in Gazi Mağusa (Famagusta); the Near East University College in Lefkoşa (Nicosia); the Girne (Kyrenia) American University; Lefke (Levka) University; the International American University; the Open University; and a Teachers' Training College in Lefkoşa (Nicosia). In 1996, according to census figures, the rate of adult illiteracy in the 'TRNC' was 6.5%.

## Public Holidays

**2000:** 1 January (New Year's Day), 6 January (Epiphany)*, 7–9 January (Ramazam Bayram—end of Ramadan)†‡, 13 March (Green Monday)*, 15–17 March (Kurban Bayram—Feast of the Sacrifice)†, 25 March (Greek Independence Day)*, 1 April (Anniversary of Cyprus Liberation Struggle), 23 April (National Sovereignty and Children's Day)†, 28 April–1 May (Easter)*, 1 May (May Day), 19 May (Youth and Sports Day)†, 15 June (Birth of the Prophet)†, 19 June (Pentecost)*, 20 July (Peace and Freedom Day, anniversary of the Turkish invasion in 1974)†, 1

August (Communal Resistance Day)†, 15 August (Assumption)*, 30 August (Victory Day)†, 1 October (Independence Day)*, 28 October (Greek National Day)*, 29 October (Turkish Republic Day)†, 15 November (TRNC Day)†, 25–26 December (Christmas)*, 27–29 December (Ramazam Bayram—end of Ramadan)†‡.

**2001:** 1 January (New Year's Day), 6 January (Epiphany)*, 26 February (Green Monday)*, 5–7 March (Kurban Bayram—Feast of the Sacrifice)†, 25 March (Greek Independence Day)*, 1 April (Anniversary of Cyprus Liberation Struggle), 13–16 April (Easter)*, 23 April (National Sovereignty and Children's Day)†, 1 May (May Day), 19 May (Youth and Sports Day)†, 4 June (Pentecost* and Birth of the Prophet†), 20 July (Peace and Freedom Day, anniversary of the Turkish invasion in 1974)†, 1 August (Communal Resistance Day)†, 15 August (Assumption)*. 30 August (Victory Day)†, 1 October (Independence Day)*, 28 October (Greek National Day)*, 29 October (Turkish Republic Day)†, 15 November (TRNC Day)†, 16–18 December (Ramazam Bayram—end of Ramadan)†, 25–26 December (Christmas)*.

* Greek and Greek Orthodox.

† Turkish and Turkish Muslim.

‡ This festival will occur twice (in the Islamic years AH 1420 and AH 1421) within the same Gregorian year.

### Weights and Measures

Although the imperial and the metric systems are understood, Cyprus has a special internal system:

*Weights:* 400 drams = 1 oke = 2.8 lb (1.27 kg.).
44 okes = 1 Cyprus kantar.
180 okes = 1 Aleppo kantar.

*Capacity:* 1 liquid oke = 2.25 pints (1.28 litres).
1 Cyprus litre = 5.6 pints (3.18 litres).

*Length and Area:* 1 pic = 2 feet (61 cm).

*Area:* 1 donum = 14,400 sq ft (1,338 sq m).

# Statistical Survey

Source (unless otherwise indicated): Department of Statistics and Research, Ministry of Finance, Nicosia; tel. (2) 309301; fax (2) 374830.

Note: Since July 1974 the northern part of Cyprus has been under Turkish occupation. As a result, some of the statistics relating to subsequent periods do not cover the whole island. Some separate figures for the 'TRNC' are given on pp. 1188–1189.

## AREA AND POPULATION

**Area:** 9,251 sq km (3,572 sq miles), incl. Turkish-occupied region.

**Population:** 602,025 (males 299,614; females 302,411), excl. Turkish-occupied region, at census of 1 October 1992; 751,500 (males 374,600; females 376,900), incl. 88,200 in Turkish-occupied region, at 31 December 1998 (official estimate). Note: Figures for the Turkish-occupied region exclude settlers from Turkey, estimated at 114,000 in 1998.

**Ethnic Groups** (estimates, 31 December 1998): Greeks 639,200 (85.1%), Turks 88,200 (11.7%), others 24,100 (3.2%); Total 751,500.

**Principal Towns** (population at 1 October 1992): Nicosia (capital) 181,234 (excl. Turkish-occupied portion); Limassol 139,424; Larnaca 62,178; Famagusta (Gazi Mağusa) 39,500 (mid-1974); Paphos 33,246; (estimated population at 31 December 1998): Nicosia 195,000 (excl. Turkish-occupied portion); Limassol 154,400; Larnaca 68,500; Paphos 38,800.

**Births, Marriages and Deaths** (government-controlled area, 1998): Registered live births 8,879 (birth rate 13.4 per 1,000); Registered marriages 7,738 (marriage rate 11.7 per 1,000); Registered deaths 5,432 (death rate 8.2 per 1,000).

**Expectation of Life** (government-controlled area, years at birth, 1996–97): Males 75.0; Females 80.0.

**Employment** (government-controlled area, provisional figures, '000 persons aged 15 years and over, excl. armed forces, 1998): Agriculture, hunting, forestry and fishing 27.5; Mining and quarrying 0.6; Manufacturing 40.0; Electricity, gas and water 1.6; Construction 24.5; Trade, restaurants and hotels 77.6; Transport, storage and communications 19.6; Financing, insurance, real estate and business services 24.8; Community, social and personal services 71.3; Employment on British sovereign bases 2.9; Total 290.4 (males 176.1, females 114.3).

## AGRICULTURE, ETC.

**Principal Crops** (government-controlled area, '000 metric tons, 1998): Wheat 11.5; Barley 54.0; Potatoes 138.1; Olives 10.7; Tomatoes 38.0; Watermelons 37.0; Melons 10.5; Grapes 124.0; Apples 11.0; Oranges 44.5; Tangerines, mandarins, etc. 22.0; Lemons and limes 21.5; Grapefruit 27.5.

**Livestock** (government-controlled area, '000 head, 1998): Cattle 55.8; Sheep 240.0; Goats 322.0; Pigs 31.3; Chickens 3,600.

**Livestock Products** (government-controlled area, '000 metric tons, 1998): Beef and veal 5.4; Mutton and lamb 4.6; Goat meat 5.4; Pig meat 47.3; Poultry meat 31.0; Cows' milk 134.0; Sheep's milk 17.5; Goats' milk 26.4; Cheese 3.2; Hen eggs 10.6.

**Forestry** (government-controlled area, '000 cubic metres, 1998): Roundwood removals (excl. bark) 29; Sawnwood production (incl. railway sleepers) 11.

**Fishing** (metric tons, live weight, government-controlled area): Total catch (excl. fish-farming) 2,593 in 1995; 2,639 in 1996; 2,389 in 1997. Source: FAO, *Yearbook of Fishery Statistics*.

## MINING AND QUARRYING

**Selected Products** (metric tons, government-controlled area, 1998): Sand and gravel 8,300,000; Marble 6,750; Gypsum 297,600; Bentonite 121,850.

## INDUSTRY

**Selected Products** (government-controlled area, 1998): Cement 1,206,674 metric tons; Bricks 44.4 million; Mosaic tiles 1.0 million sq metres; Cigarettes 4,362 million; Footwear (excluding plastic and semi-finished shoes) 2.1 million pairs; Beer 35.1 million litres; Wines 31.6 million litres; Carbonated soft drinks 58.9 million litres.

## FINANCE

**Currency and Exchange Rates:** 100 cents = 1 Cyprus pound (Cyprus £). *Sterling, Dollar and Euro Equivalents* (30 September 1999): £1 sterling = 89.28 Cyprus cents; US $1 = 54.23 Cyprus cents; €1 = 57.83 Cyprus cents; Cyprus £100 = £112.00 sterling = $184.41 = €172.91. *Average Exchange Rate* (US $ per Cyprus £): 2.1446 in 1996; 1.9476 in 1997; 1.9342 in 1998.

**Budget** (Cyprus £ million, government-controlled area, 1997): *Revenue:* Taxation 1,072.36 (Taxes on income 268.73, Social security contributions 206.41, Taxes on payroll 22.09, Taxes on property 24.31, Excises 107.67, Value-added tax 206.40, Other domestic taxes on goods and services 52.69, Import duties 76.54, Other taxes 107.53); Entrepreneurial and property income 204.66; Administrative fees and charges, non-industrial and incidental sales 65.42; Other current revenue 30.33; Capital revenue 0.58; Total 1,373.36, excl. grants from abroad (1.64). *Expenditure:* General public services 101.82; Defence 61.46; Public order and safety 89.55; Education 190.32; Health 101.34; Social security and welfare 392.67; Housing and community amenities 64.91; Recreational, cultural and religious affairs and services 27.47; Economic affairs and services 207.17 (Agriculture, forestry, fishing and hunting 90.04, Mining 0.15, Road transport 42.84, Other transport and communication 29.09, Other economic affairs 45.05); Other purposes 240.00; Sub-total 1,476.71 (Current 1,315.81, Capital 160.90); Adjustment 126.82; Total 1,603.53, excl. lending minus repayments (2.72).

**International Reserves** (US $ million at 31 December 1998): Gold (national valuation) 132.9; IMF special drawing rights 0.3; Reserve position in IMF 35.8; Foreign exchange 1,343.6; Total 1,512.6.

**Money Supply** (Cyprus £ million at 31 December 1998, government-controlled area): Currency outside banks 290.1, Demand deposits at deposit money banks 439.9; Total money 730.0.

**Cost of Living** (Retail Price Index, government-controlled area; base: 1992 = 100): 116.0 in 1996; 120.2 in 1997; 122.9 in 1998.

**Gross Domestic Product in Purchasers' Values** (Cyprus £ million at current prices, government-controlled area): 4,134.6 in 1996; 4,337.1 in 1997; 4,637.7 in 1998.

**Expenditure on the Gross Domestic Product** (Cyprus £ million at current prices, government-controlled area, 1998): Government final consumption expenditure 895.7; Private final consumption expenditure 2,944.5; Increase in stocks 310.2; Gross fixed capital formation 836.0; Statistical discrepancy 8.5; *Total domestic expenditure* 4,994.9; Exports of goods and services 2,041.1; *Less* Imports of goods and services 2,398.3; *GDP in purchasers' values* 4,637.7.

**Gross Domestic Product by Economic Activity** (provisional, Cyprus £ million at current prices, government-controlled area, 1998): Agriculture, hunting, forestry and fishing 190.8; Mining and quarrying 13.0; Manufacturing 506.7; Electricity, gas and water 97.2; Construction 360.0; Wholesale and retail trade, restaurants and hotels 926.2; Transport, storage and communications 395.7; Finance, insurance, real estate and business services 866.0; Government services 635.6; Other community, social and personal services 400.9; Other services 45.9; *Sub-total* 4,438.0; Import duties 137.3; Value-added tax 225.8; *Less* Imputed bank service charges 163.4; *GDP in purchasers' values* 4,637.7.

**Balance of Payments** (US $ million, government-controlled area, 1998): Exports of goods f.o.b. 1,064.6, Imports of goods f.o.b. –3,490.4; *Trade balance* –2,425.7; Exports of services 2,957.0; Imports of services –1,137.6; *Balance on goods and services* –606.4; Other income received 368.3; Other income paid –434.9; *Balance on goods, services and income* –673.0; Current transfers received 132.7; Current transfers paid –20.3; *Current balance* –560.6; Direct investment (net) –41.9; Portfolio investment (net) 215.5; Other investment (net) 398.6; Net errors and omissions –94.1; *Overall balance* –82.5.

### EXTERNAL TRADE

**Total Trade** (Cyprus £ '000, government-controlled area): *Imports c.i.f.:* 1,857,509 in 1996; 1,899,339 in 1997; 1,904,738 in 1998. *Exports f.o.b.* (incl. re-exports): 649,027 in 1996; 640,015 in 1997; 551,134 in 1998.

**Principal Commodities** (Cyprus £ '000, government-controlled area, 1998): *Imports c.i.f.:* Prepared foodstuffs, beverages, spirits and tobacco 287,297; Mineral products 129,397; Products of chemical or allied industries 144,617; Textiles and textile articles 143,540; Base metal and articles of base metal 132,726; Machinery and electrical equipment (incl. household appliances) 343,579; Vehicles and associated transport equipment 213,881; Total (incl. others) 1,904,738. *Exports f.o.b.:* Clothing 29,031; Potatoes 18,998; Cigarettes 12,179; Cement 8,970; Pharmaceutical products 20,281; Alcoholic beverages 7,575 (Wines 6,786); Fruit and vegetable juices 4,663; Total (incl. others) 221,337. Figures for exports exclude re-exports (Cyprus £ '000): 329,797.

**Principal Trading Partners** (Cyprus £ '000, government-controlled area, 1998): *Imports c.i.f.:* France 94,927; Germany 161,191; Greece 155,525; Italy 178,380; Japan 141,202; United Kingdom 214,906; USA 238,620; Total (incl. others) 1,904,738. *Exports f.o.b.* (excl. re-exports): Germany 20,425; Greece 15,797; Lebanon 18,286; Saudi Arabia 6,677; United Kingdom 44,398; USA 7,779; Total (incl. others) 221,337.

### TRANSPORT

**Road Traffic** (licensed motor vehicles, government-controlled area, 31 December 1998): Private passenger cars 241,800; Taxis and self-drive cars 7,425; Buses and coaches 2,754; Lorries and vans 109,294; Motorcycles 44,337; Total (incl. others) 419,446.

**Shipping** (freight traffic, '000 metric tons, government-controlled area, 1998): Goods loaded 1,418, Goods unloaded 5,080. At 31 December 1998 a total of 1,602 merchant vessels (combined displacement 23,301,517 grt) were registered in Cyprus (Source: Lloyd's Register of Shipping, *World Fleet Statistics*).

**Civil Aviation** (government-controlled area, 1998): Overall passenger traffic 5,091,990; Total freight transported 35,614 metric tons.

### TOURISM

**Tourist Arrivals** (government-controlled area): 1,950,000 in 1996; 2,088,000 in 1997; 2,222,706 in 1998.

**Tourism Receipts** (Cyprus £ million, government-controlled area): 780 in 1996; 843 in 1997; 878 in 1998.

### COMMUNICATIONS MEDIA

**Radio Receivers** (government-controlled area, 1996): 300,000 in use.

**Television Receivers** (government-controlled area, 1996): 244,000 in use.

**Telephones** (main lines in use, 1998): 404,710.

**Telefax Stations** (number in use, 1993): 7,000.

**Mobile Telephones** (subscribers, 1995): 44,453.

**Book Production** (government-controlled area, 1996): 930 titles and 1,776,000 copies.

**Newspapers** (1996): 9 daily (circulation 84,000 copies); 31 non-daily (circulation 185,000 copies).

Sources: mainly UNESCO, *Statistical Yearbook*, and UN, *Statistical Yearbook*.

### EDUCATION

**1997/98** (government-controlled area): Kindergarten: 665 institutions, 1,461 teachers, 26,517 pupils; Primary schools: 372 institutions, 3,521 teachers, 64,592 pupils; Secondary schools (Gymnasia and Lyceums): 114 institutions, 4,438 teachers, 56,872 pupils; Technical colleges: 11 institutions, 594 teachers, 4,831 pupils; University of Cyprus: 196 teachers, 2,311 students; Other post-secondary: 33 institutions, 639 teachers, 8,216 students.

## 'Turkish Republic of Northern Cyprus'

Source: Office of the London Representative of the 'Turkish Republic of Northern Cyprus', 29 Bedford Sq., London WC1B 3EG; tel. (20) 7631-1920; fax (20) 7631-1948.

### AREA AND POPULATION

**Area:** 3,355 sq km (1,295 sq miles).

**Population** (census, 15 December 1996): 200,587 (males 105,978; females 94,609).

**Ethnic Groups** (census, 15 December 1996): Turks 197,264, English 627, Greeks 384, Maronites 173, Russians 130, Germans 106, Others 1,903; Total 200,587.

**Principal Towns** (estimated population within the municipal boundary, 1996): Lefkoşa (Nicosia) 42,767 (Turkish-occupied area only); Gazi Mağusa (Famagusta) 22,216; Girne (Kyrenia) 7,893.

**Births, Marriages and Deaths** (registered, 1997): Live births 2,404 (birth rate 11.8 per 1,000); Marriages 1,141 (marriage rate 5.6 per 1,000); Deaths 638 (death rate 3.1 per 1,000).

**Expectation of life** (years at birth, 1985–90): Males 72.8; Females 76.4.

**Employment** (1995): Agriculture, forestry and fishing 17,383; Industry 8,348; Construction 9,584; Trade and tourism 8,367; Transport and communications 6,510; Financial institutions 2,397; Business and personal services 7,276; Public Services 16,589; *Total employed* 76,454. Total unemployed 567; *Total labour force* 77,021.

### AGRICULTURE, ETC.

**Principal Crops** ('000 metric tons, 1997): Wheat 6.9; Barley 16.5; Potatoes 8.3; Legumes 1.8; Tomatoes 2.4; Onions 2.3; Artichokes 0.4; Watermelons 4.6; Melons 0.8; Cucumbers 0.6; Carobs 3.2; Olives 0.8; Lemons 8.5; Grapefruit 38.0; Oranges 81.4; Tangerines 1.0.

**Livestock** ('000 head, 1997): Cattle 25.5; Sheep 226.8; Goats 63.7; Chickens 3,801.6.

**Livestock Products** ('000 metric tons, unless otherwise indicated, 1997): Sheep's and goats' milk 12.2; Cows' milk 44.1; Mutton and lamb 3.4; Goat meat 0.9; Beef 1.8; Poultry meat 5.6; Wool 0.3; Eggs (million) 24.5.

**Fishing** (metric tons, 1994): Total catch 400.

### FINANCE

**Currency and Exchange Rates:** Turkish currency: 100 kuruş = 1 Turkish lira (TL) or pound. *Sterling, Dollar and Euro Equivalents* (30 September 1999): £1 sterling = 756,562 liras; US $1 = 459,497 liras; €1 = 490,054 liras; 1,000,000 Turkish liras = £1.322 = $2.176 = €2.041. *Average Exchange Rate* (liras per US dollar): 81,405 in 1996; 151,865 in 1997; 260,724 in 1998.

**Budget** (million Turkish liras, 1997): *Revenue:* Internal revenue 34,385,089.9 (Direct taxes 14,161,807.2, Indirect taxes 10,939,145.2, Non-tax revenue 6,551,492.3); Aid from Turkey 12,171,847.1; Aid from other countries 109,629.3; Loans 3,494,295.7; Total 50,160,862.0. *Expenditure:* Personnel 17,756,985.3; Other goods and services 2,618,188.3; Transfers 19,359,870.8; Investments 6,100,817.6; Defence 4,325,000.0; Total 50,160,862.0.

**Cost of Living** (Retail Price Index at December; base: December of previous year = 100): 172.1 in 1995; 187.5 in 1996; 181.7 in 1997.

**Expenditure on the Gross Domestic Product** ('000 million Turkish liras at current prices, 1997): Government final consumption expenditure 29,112.5; Private final consumption expenditure 71,571.9; Increase in stocks 2,236.4; Gross fixed capital formation 21,890.8; *Total domestic expenditure* 124,811.6; Exports of goods and services, *less* Imports of goods and services –6,922.8; *GDP in purchasers' values* 117,888.8; *GDP at constant 1977 prices* (million liras) 7,943.4.

**Gross Domestic Product (GDP) by Economic Activity** (million Turkish liras, 1997): Agriculture, forestry and fishing 8,278,463.5; Industry 15,701,934.1 (Mining and quarrying 838,624.4; Manufacturing 9,499,365.3; Electricity and water 5,363,944.4); Construction 5,132,410.1; Wholesale and retail trade 14,550,666.2; Restaurants and hotels 5,352,079.4; Transport and communications 12,329,887.7; Finance 11,043,010.0; Ownership of dwellings 3,102,953.7; Business and personal services 9,457,990.4; Government services 22,577,205.8; *Sub-total* 107,526,600.9; Import duties 10,362,183.0; *GDP in purchasers' values* 117,888,783.9.

**Balance of Payments** (US $ million, 1997): Merchandise exports f.o.b. 57.7; Merchandise imports c.i.f. –374.2; *Trade balance* –316.5; Services and unrequited transfers (net) 274.3; *Current balance* –42.2; Capital movements (net) 49.3; Net errors and omissions –8.0; *Total* (net monetary movements) –0.9.

### EXTERNAL TRADE

**Principal Commodities** (US $ million, 1997): *Imports c.i.f.:* Food and live animals 76.6; Beverages and tobacco 25.9; Mineral fuels, lubricants, etc. 32.6; Chemicals 30.8; Basic manufactures 84.1; Machinery and transport equipment 89.7; Miscellaneous manufactured articles 25.6; Total (incl. others) 374.2. *Exports f.o.b.:* Food and live animals 23.4 (Citrus fruit 15.2, Concentrated citrus 1.4); Beverages and tobacco 5.5; Crude materials (inedible) except fuels 2.6; Clothing 24.0; Total (incl. others) 57.7.

**Principal Trading Partners** (US $ million, 1997): *Imports c.i.f:* Belgium 4.6; France 4.2; Germany 12.5; Hong Kong 8.3; Italy 9.9; Japan 6.9; Netherlands 5.8; Sri Lanka 25.0; Sweden 5.4; Turkey 211.0; United Kingdom 50.5; Total (incl. others) 374.2. *Exports f.o.b.:* Germany 6.2; Kuwait 1.4; Netherlands 2.2; Russia 2.9; Turkey 27.1; United Kingdom 15.0; USA 0.7; Total (incl. others) 57.7.

### TRANSPORT

**Road Traffic** (registered motor vehicles, 1997): Saloon cars 60,436; Estate cars 7,372; Pick-ups 3,054; Vans 7,139; Buses 1,672; Trucks 773; Lorries 5,009; Motor cycles 14,226; Agricultural tractors 5,966; Total (incl. others) 107,416.

**Shipping** (1997): Freight traffic ('000 metric tons): Goods loaded 253.9, Goods unloaded 931.2; Vessels entered 3,193.

**Civil Aviation:** Kilometres flown (Turkish Cypriot Airlines) 1,126,848 (1985); Passenger arrivals and departures 624,189 (1994); Freight landed and cleared (metric tons) 3,303 (1994).

### TOURISM

**Visitors** (1997): 399,364 (including 326,364 Turkish); **Accommodation** (1997): Hotels 43, Tourist beds (in all tourist accommodation, including pensions and hotel-apartments) 8,940; **Net Receipts** (US $ million, 1997): 192.2.

### COMMUNICATIONS MEDIA

**Radio Receivers** (1994, provisional): 56,450 in use.

**Television Receivers** (1994, provisional): 52,300 in use.

**Telephones** (31 December 1997): 77,023 subscribers.

### EDUCATION

**1997/98:** *Primary and pre-primary education:* 113 institutions, 1,829 teachers, 23,317 pupils; *High schools:* 14 institutions, 715 teachers, 8,022 students; *Vocational schools:* 10 institutions, 396 teachers, 2,428 students; *Higher education:* 8 institutions, 21,117 students.

# Directory

## The Constitution

The Constitution, summarized below, entered into force on 16 August 1960, when Cyprus became an independent republic.

### THE STATE OF CYPRUS

The State of Cyprus is an independent and sovereign Republic with a presidential regime.

The Greek Community comprises all citizens of the Republic who are of Greek origin and whose mother tongue is Greek or who share the Greek cultural traditions or who are members of the Greek Orthodox Church.

The Turkish Community comprises all citizens of the Republic who are of Turkish origin and whose mother tongue is Turkish or who share the Turkish cultural traditions or who are Muslims.

The official languages of the Republic are Greek and Turkish.

The Republic shall have its own flag of neutral design and colour, chosen jointly by the President and the Vice-President of the Republic.

The Greek and the Turkish Communities shall have the right to celebrate respectively the Greek and the Turkish national holidays.

### THE PRESIDENT AND VICE-PRESIDENT

Executive power is vested in the President and the Vice-President, who are members of the Greek and Turkish Communities respectively, and are elected by their respective communities to hold office for five years.

The President of the Republic as Head of the State represents the Republic in all its official functions; signs the credentials of diplomatic envoys and receives the credentials of foreign diplomatic envoys; signs the credentials of delegates for the negotiation of international treaties, conventions or other agreements; signs the letter relating to the transmission of the instruments of ratification of any international treaties, conventions or agreements; confers the honours of the Republic.

The Vice-President of the Republic, as Vice-Head of the State, has the right to be present at all official functions; at the presentation of the credentials of foreign diplomatic envoys; to recommend to the President the conferment of honours on members of the Turkish Community, which recommendation the President shall accept unless there are grave reasons to the contrary.

The election of the President and the Vice-President of the Republic shall be direct, by universal suffrage and secret ballot, and shall, except in the case of a by-election, take place on the same day but separately.

The office of the President and of the Vice-President shall be incompatible with that of a Minister or of a Representative or of a member of a Communal Chamber or of a member of any municipal council including a Mayor or of a member of the armed or security forces of the Republic or with a public or municipal office.

The President and Vice-President of the Republic are invested by the House of Representatives.

The President and the Vice-President of the Republic in order to ensure the executive power shall have a Council of Ministers composed of seven Greek Ministers and three Turkish Ministers. The Ministers shall be designated respectively by the President and the Vice-President of the Republic who shall appoint them by an instrument signed by them both. The President convenes and presides over the meetings of the Council of Ministers, while the Vice-President may ask the President to convene the Council and may take part in the discussions.

The decisions of the Council of Ministers shall be taken by an absolute majority and shall, unless the right of final veto or return is exercised by the President or the Vice-President of the Republic or both, be promulgated immediately by them.

The executive power exercised by the President and the Vice-President of the Republic conjointly consists of:

Determining the design and colour of the flag.

Creation or establishment of honours.

Appointment of the members of the Council of Ministers.

Promulgation by publication of the decisions of the Council of Ministers.

Promulgation by publication of any law or decision passed by the House of Representatives.

Appointments and termination of appointments as in Articles provided.

Institution of compulsory military service.

Reduction or increase of the security forces.

Exercise of the prerogative of mercy in capital cases.

Remission, suspension and commutation of sentences.

# THE CZECH REPUBLIC

## Introductory Survey

### Location, Climate, Language, Religion, Flag, Capital

The Czech Republic lies in central Europe. It comprises the Czech Lands of Bohemia and Moravia and part of Silesia. Its neighbours are Poland to the north, Germany to the north-west and west, Austria to the south and Slovakia to the east. The climate is continental, with warm summers and cold winters. The average mean temperature is 9°C (49°F). The official language is Czech, a member of the west Slavonic group. There is a sizeable Slovak minority and also small Polish, German, Silesian, Romany, Hungarian and other minorities. The major religion is Christianity (about 39% of the population are Roman Catholics). The national flag (proportions 3 by 2) has two equal horizontal stripes, of white and red, on which is superimposed a blue triangle (half the length) at the hoist. The capital is Prague (Praha).

### Recent History

In October 1918, following the collapse of the Austro-Hungarian Empire at the end of the First World War, the Republic of Czechoslovakia was established. The new state united the Czech Lands of Bohemia and Moravia, which had been incorporated into the Austrian Empire in the 16th and 17th centuries, and Slovakia, which had been under Hungarian rule for almost 1,000 years. In the inter-war period (1918–39) a stable democratic system of government flourished in Czechoslovakia, and the country's economy was considered to be the most industrialized and prosperous in eastern Europe. After the Nazis, led by Adolf Hitler, came to power in Germany in 1933, there was increased agitation in the Sudetenland (an area in northern Bohemia that was inhabited by about 3m. German-speaking people) for autonomy within, and later secession from, Czechoslovakia. In 1938, to appease German demands, the British, French and Italian Prime Ministers concluded an agreement with Hitler, whereby the Sudetenland was ceded to Germany, while other parts of Czechoslovakia were transferred to Hungary and Poland. The remainder of Czechoslovakia was invaded and occupied by Nazi armed forces in March 1939, and a German protectorate was established in Bohemia and Moravia. In Slovakia, which had been granted self-government in late 1938, a separate Slovak state was formed, under the pro-Nazi 'puppet' regime of Jozef Tiso.

After Germany's defeat in the Second World War (1939–45), the pre-1938 frontiers of Czechoslovakia were restored, although a small area in the east was ceded to the USSR in June 1945. Almost all of the German-speaking inhabitants of Czechoslovakia were expelled, and the Sudetenland was settled by Czechs from other parts of Bohemia. In response to Slovak demands for greater autonomy, a legislature (the Slovak National Council) and an executive Board of Commissioners were established in Bratislava, the Slovak capital. At elections in 1946 the Communist Party of Czechoslovakia (CPCz) emerged as the leading party, winning 38% of the votes. The CPCz's leader, Klement Gottwald, became Prime Minister in a coalition Government. After ministers of other parties resigned, communist control became complete on 25 February 1948. A People's Republic was established on 9 June 1948. Gottwald replaced Edvard Beneš as President, a position that he held until his death in 1953. The country aligned itself with the Soviet-led eastern European bloc, joining the Council for Mutual Economic Assistance (CMEA) and the Warsaw Pact.

Under Gottwald, government followed a rigid Stalinist pattern, and in the early 1950s there were many political trials. Although these ended under Gottwald's successors, Antonín Zápotocký and, from 1956, Antonín Novotný, 'de-Stalinization' was late in coming to Czechoslovakia, and there was no relaxation until 1963, when a new Government, with Jozef Lenárt as Prime Minister, was formed. Meanwhile, the country was renamed the Czechoslovak Socialist Republic, under a new Constitution, proclaimed in July 1960.

In January 1968 Alexander Dubček succeeded Novotný as CPCz Secretary, and in March Gen. Ludvík Svoboda succeeded Novotný as President. Oldřich Černík became Prime Minister in April. The policies of the new Government were more independent and liberal, and envisaged widespread reforms, including the introduction of more genuine elections, a greater freedom of expression and a greater degree of separation between party and state. A federal system of government was also to be introduced. The Government's reformist policies were regarded by other members of the eastern European bloc as endangering their unity, and in August Warsaw Pact forces (numbering an estimated 600,000 men) invaded Czechoslovakia, occupying Prague and other major cities. Mass demonstrations in protest at the invasion were held throughout the country, and many people were killed in clashes with occupation troops. The Soviet Government exerted heavy pressure on the Czechoslovak leaders to suppress their reformist policies, and in April 1969 Dubček was replaced by a fellow Slovak, Dr Gustáv Husák, as First (subsequently General) Secretary of the Central Committee of the CPCz. Under Husák's leadership, there was a severe purge of CPCz membership, and most of Dubček's supporters were removed from the Government. All the reforms of the so-called 'Prague Spring' of 1968 were duly abandoned, with the exception of the federalization programme. This was implemented in January 1969, when the unitary Czechoslovak state was transformed into a federation, with separate Czech and Slovak Republics, each having its own National Council (legislature) and Government. A Federal Government was established as the supreme executive organ of state power, while the country's existing legislature, the National Assembly, was transformed into a bicameral Federal Assembly. The first legislative elections since 1964 were held in November 1971 and produced a 99.81% vote in favour of candidates of the National Front (the communist-dominated organization embracing all the legal political parties in Czechoslovakia).

In May 1975 Husák was appointed to the largely ceremonial post of President of Czechoslovakia, while still holding the positions of Chairman of the National Front and General Secretary of the CPCz. He held the latter post until December 1987, when he was replaced by Miloš Jakeš, an economist and member of the Presidium of the party's Central Committee. However, Husák remained as President of the Republic.

Although Jakeš affirmed his commitment to the moderate programme of reform, initiated by his predecessor, there was little indication of a policy more liberal than that of Husák, as repressive measures against the Roman Catholic Church and dissident groups continued. Of the latter, the most influential was Charter 77, which had been established in January 1977 by intellectuals, former politicians and others to campaign for the observance of civil and political rights. Despite the regime's continued attempts to suppress it, the movement's sphere of influence broadened, and it played a leading role in anti-Government demonstrations, which began in 1988. In February 1989, following one such demonstration, the Czech playwright, Václav Havel (a leader of Charter 77), was sentenced to nine months' imprisonment. (He was released in May, following international condemnation.) Anti-Government demonstrations followed in May, August and October 1989.

In November 1989 the protest actions of preceding months evolved into a process of dramatic, yet largely peaceful, political change, which subsequently became known as the 'velvet revolution'. On 17 November some 50,000 people, mainly students, participated in an anti-Government demonstration in Prague, the largest public protest for 20 years. The demonstration was violently dispersed by the police, and more than 500 people were injured. Following rumours (which later proved to be unfounded) that a student had been killed, a series of demonstrations of escalating size took place, culminating in gatherings of as many as 500,000 people in Prague, while large-scale demonstrations took place in other towns throughout the country.

A new opposition group, Civic Forum, was established in November 1989 as an informal alliance embracing several existing opposition and human rights organizations, including Charter 77, and rapidly gained widespread popular support. Meanwhile, Alexander Dubček addressed mass rallies in Bratislava and Prague, expressing his support for the opposition's demands for reform. On 24 November it was announced that Jakeš and the entire membership of the Presidium of the Central Committee had resigned. Karel Urbánek, a member of the Presidium, replaced Jakeš as General Secretary of the party, and a new Presidium was elected.

The increasing strength of Civic Forum and its Slovak counterpart, Public Against Violence (PAV), was demonstrated during discussions on reform with the Federal Prime Minister, Ladislav Adamec. The opposition's demands for the ending of censorship and the release of all political prisoners were fulfilled, and, in late November 1989, the articles guaranteeing the CPCz's predominance were deleted from the Constitution. In the following month the CPCz condemned the invasion of Czechoslovakia by Warsaw Pact forces in 1968 as 'unjustified and mistaken'. Shortly afterwards, the Governments of the five countries that had invaded Czechoslovakia issued a joint statement condemning their action.

In early December 1989 a reshuffle of the Federal Government took place. Civic Forum and PAV denounced the new Government, as the majority of its ministers had been members of the previous administration, and it included only five non-communists. Adamec subsequently resigned as Prime Minister, and was replaced by Marián Čalfa, the newly-appointed First Deputy Prime Minister. In the following week a new, interim Federal Government was formed, with a majority of non-communist members, including seven non-party supporters of Civic Forum. Husák resigned as President of the Republic and, at the end of December, was replaced by Václav Havel. Alexander Dubček was elected Chairman of the Federal Assembly. At an emergency congress of the CPCz, held in December, Urbánek was dismissed from the post of General Secretary of the Central Committee and this position was abolished. Adamec was appointed to the new post of Chairman of the party.

In April 1990 the Federal Assembly voted to rename the country the Czech and Slovak Federative Republic (CzSFR). The decision, which followed intense controversy between Czech and Slovak deputies, satisfied Slovak demands that the new title should reflect the equal status of Slovakia within the federation.

On 8–9 June 1990 the first free legislative elections since 1946 were held in Czechoslovakia. About 97% of the electorate voted for a total of 27 parties and movements for representation in the Federal Assembly (now numbering 300 seats) and in the National Councils of each republic. In the elections at federal level, the largest share of the total votes cast (about 46%) was won by Civic Forum, in the Czech Lands, and by PAV, in Slovakia. The CPCz won a larger proportion of the total votes (about 14%) than had been expected, obtaining the second largest representation in the Federal Assembly. The Christian Democratic Union—a coalition of the Czechoslovak People's Party, the Christian Democratic Party (Chr.DP) and the Slovak-based Christian Democratic Movement (CDM)—obtained approximately 12% of the total votes. Contrary to expectations, two parties which had campaigned for regional autonomy or secession secured more than the 5% of the vote required for representation in the legislature: the Movement for Autonomous Democracy–Society for Moravia and Silesia (MAD–SMS), and the separatist Slovak National Party (SNP). The newly-elected Federal Assembly was to serve a transitional two-year term until the holding of fresh legislative elections in 1992, before which time it was to have drafted new federal and republican constitutions and elected a new President of the Republic. In late June 1990 Alexander Dubček was re-elected Chairman of the Federal Assembly. A new Federal Government, announced in that month, comprised 16 members: four from Civic Forum, three from PAV, one from the CDM and eight independents. In early July Václav Havel was re-elected to the post of President.

In the latter half of 1990 there was increasing unrest in Slovakia, as several newly-established parties and groups, most prominently the SNP, organized demonstrations and rallies as part of a campaign for Slovak autonomy. In an attempt to alleviate the increasing ethnic tension in the country, the Federal Assembly voted overwhelmingly, in December, to transfer broader powers to the Czech and Slovak Governments, while the Federal Government was to retain jurisdiction over defence, foreign affairs and monetary policy. None the less, the Slovak question remained the dominant topic of political debate during 1991 and 1992. A widening division appeared between the more moderate Slovak movements, such as PAV and the CDM (which advocated the preservation of the federation, albeit in a looser form), and a minority of more radical parties, which campaigned for full independence. In early March 1991 Vladimír Mečiar, the Slovak Prime Minister and a founding member of PAV, announced the formation of a minority faction within PAV—the Movement for a Democratic Slovakia (MDS)—in support of greater Slovak autonomy. However, leading officials in PAV and some of its representatives in the Slovak Government viewed Mečiar's policies and aggressive style of leadership as detrimental to the future of Czech–Slovak relations, and in April the Slovak National Council voted to remove Mečiar from the Slovak premiership. He was replaced by Ján Čarnogurský, the Chairman of the CDM. In response, Mečiar and his supporters left PAV, and the MDS was established as a separate political group.

Meanwhile, disagreement over the direction of post-communist politics and economic management had led to a split within Civic Forum. Two main groups emerged in February 1991—the conservative Civic Democratic Party (CDP), led by Václav Klaus, and the liberal Civic Movement (CM), led by Jiří Dienstbier. However, it was announced that, in the interests of national unity, the two new groups were to remain as coalition partners in the Federal Government until the holding of the next legislative elections, due in June 1992.

In March 1991 representatives of all political forces in Czechoslovakia reached agreement on the framework of a new federal Constitution. This stipulated, *inter alia,* that the country would remain a federative state comprising two 'sovereign and equal republics, linked voluntarily and by the free will of their citizens'. However, by late 1991, the Federal Assembly's discussions on the new Constitution had reached an impasse, as deputies failed to agree on the status of the two republics within any future federation. President Havel repeatedly proposed the holding of a referendum on the possible division of Czechoslovakia into two separate states, as the only democratic means of resolving the issue. His proposals, however, were rejected by the Federal Assembly. The constitutional debate continued in the first half of 1992, with increasing Slovak support for the loosest possible confederation, comprising two nominally independent states. The majority of Czech politicians, however, were in favour of preserving the existing state structure, and rejected Slovak proposals as impracticable. In March it was agreed to postpone the constitutional talks until after the legislative elections at federal and republican level, in June. Meanwhile, the results of public opinion polls indicated that the majority of Czechoslovaks favoured a continued federation.

The legislative elections of 5–6 June 1992 proved to be decisive in the eventual dismantling of Czechoslovakia, particularly as the MDS, led by Mečiar, emerged clearly as the dominant political force in Slovakia. With about 34% of the total Slovak votes, the party obtained 57 seats (the second largest representation) in the 300-member Federal Assembly. The leading party in the Slovak Government, the CDM (which advocated a continued federation), won only 9% of the Slovak votes, securing 14 seats in the Federal Assembly, one seat less than the separatist SNP. As had been expected, Václav Klaus's party, the CDP (in coalition with the Chr.DP), won the largest share (about 34%) of the total votes in the Czech Lands. The CDP was one of only two parties to contest the elections in both republics, and in Slovakia it received 4% of the votes cast. In total, the CDP won 85 seats in the Federal Assembly, thus becoming the largest party in the legislature. Two other splinter groups of the former Civic Forum—Dienstbier's CM and the Civic Democratic Alliance (CDA)—failed to win representation in the Federal Assembly, as did the Civic Democratic Union (formerly PAV), in Slovakia. The successor organizations to the communist parties of the two republics achieved considerable success: the Left Bloc (which included the Communist Party of Bohemia and Moravia, CPBM) won a total of 34 seats in the Federal Assembly, while the Slovak-based Party of the Democratic Left secured 23 seats. The representation of parties in the new republican legislatures did not differ greatly from that of the Federal Assembly, although the CDA and the MAD–SMS succeeded in winning seats in the Czech National Council.

Negotiations on the formation of a new federal government were initiated forthwith by the CDP and the MDS, but only served to emphasize the two leading parties' fundamental divergence of opinion on the future of the CzSFR. Nevertheless, a transitional Federal Government, dominated by members of the CDP and the MDS, was appointed in early July 1992. The new Prime Minister was Jan Stráský of the CDP, who had served as a Deputy Prime Minister in the outgoing Czech Government. There was now increasing recognition by Czech politicians that the constitutional talks on the future of Czechoslovakia were no longer viable and that a complete separation was preferable to the compromise measures that most Slovak parties favoured. The principal task of the new Federal Government, it was acknowledged, was to supervise the eventual dissolution of the CzSFR. Meanwhile, in late June, the new Slovak Government was announced, with Mečiar as Prime Minister. All but one of the ministers were members of the MDS. A new coalition Czech Government, dominated by the CDP and with Klaus as Prime Minister, was appointed in early July. In three rounds of presidential elections, held in the same month, the Federal Assembly failed to elect any of the candidates. Havel's re-election as President had effectively been blocked by the MDS and the SNP, and in mid-July he resigned from the post. Further rounds of voting, in August and October, were aborted, as no candidates presented themselves.

The events of June and July 1992 had ensured that the emergence of two independent states was now inevitable. On 17 July the Slovak National Council overwhelmingly approved a (symbolic) declaration of Slovak sovereignty, and in the following week the Czech and Slovak Prime Ministers agreed, in principle, to the dissolution of the CzSFR, the terms of which were to be settled shortly. In the following months extensive negotiations were conducted to determine the modalities of the division, which was to take effect from 1 January 1993. International observers expressed surprise not only that the dissolution of Czechoslovakia should be effected in so short a time, but also that the majority of Czechs and Slovaks (more than 60%, according to the results of public opinion polls) were still opposed to the country's division. Moreover, it now appeared that Slovak leaders were less intent to leave the federation. Indeed, the Federal Assembly's failure, in early October 1992 and again in mid-November, to adopt legislation permitting the dissolution of the CzSFR was due to opposition by (mainly) MDS deputies. However, the two republican Prime Ministers, supported by their respective governments, stressed that the process of partition was now irreversible. In late October the Czech and Slovak Governments ratified a number of accords, including a customs union treaty to abolish trade restrictions between the two republics following their independence. Finally, on 25 November, the Federal Assembly adopted legislation providing for the constitutional disbanding of the federation, having secured the necessary three-fifths majority by a margin of only three votes. Accordingly, the Federal Government accelerated the process of dividing the country's assets and liabilities as well as its armed forces, applying, in as far as was practically possible, a ratio of 2 to 1, to reflect the relative size of the Czech and Slovak populations. In most cases federal property was divided territorially (according to its location in either of the republics). It was agreed, however, that the two states would continue to share some federal infrastructure and would retain a single currency for the immediate future, although respective central banks were established. (Two separate currencies, the Czech and the Slovak koruna, were introduced in February 1993.)

On 17 December 1992 a treaty of good-neighbourliness, friendly relations and co-operation was signed, followed by the exchange of diplomatic relations between the two republics. At midnight on 31 December all federal structures were dissolved and the Czech Republic and the Slovak Republic came into being. The dissolution of the CzSFR, like the 'velvet revolution' of 1989, had thus been effected in an entirely peaceful fashion. As legal successors to Czechoslovakia, the two republics were quickly recognized by the states that had maintained diplomatic relations with the CzSFR, as well as by those international bodies of which the CzSFR had been a member. Existing treaties and agreements, to which the CzSFR had been a party, were to be honoured by both republics.

In anticipation of the establishment of the Czech Republic as an independent state, the existing legislature was replaced by a bicameral body, in accordance with the Czech Constitution (adopted in mid-December 1992); the Czech National Council was transformed into a Chamber of Deputies (lower house), which retained the Council's 200 members, while an upper house, or Senate, was due to be elected at a later date. In late January 1993 the Chamber of Deputies elected Václav Havel to be the Czech Republic's first President. The composition of the Government remained largely unchanged. It included among its principal objectives the pursuance of the former Federal Government's economic reforms, including its programme of large-scale privatization. Another of its priorities was to curb the recent rise in organized crime.

Relations between the Czech Republic and Slovakia were troubled in early 1993 by a number of disagreements over former Czechoslovak assets and property that still remained to be divided. In late 1993 the Czech Government was divided over the issue of the restitution of property that had been expropriated from Czech Jews during the period of Nazi occupation (1938–45). There were fears that any such restitution would lead to claims for compensation by those surviving Sudeten Germans who were expelled from Czechoslovakia in 1945 (see below). (The country's existing legislation on restitution of property covered only the communist period, 1948–89.) Nevertheless, in April 1994 the Chamber of Deputies adopted legislation permitting the restitution of Jewish property.

In November 1994 local elections were held, at which the CDP was confirmed as the party with the broadest support (receiving some 31% of the total votes), followed by the CPBM (with 13%). The electoral turn-out was about 60%.

There was renewed controversy in 1995 over the so-called 'lustration' or screening law, which had been adopted by the Czechoslovak Federal Assembly in October 1991. The law effectively banned former communist functionaries as well as members of the former state security service and the People's Militia (the CPCz's paramilitary force) from holding senior political, economic and judicial posts. In September 1995 the Chamber of Deputies voted to extend until the year 2000 the legislation on screening (which had been due to expire in late 1996). In the following month President Havel rejected the decision, but the Chamber approved it for a second time, and the extension of the screening law entered into force.

The first general election to be held since the dissolution of the CzSFR took place on 31 May and 1 June 1996. The CDP (which had merged with the Chr.DP in April) won 68 of the 200 seats in the Chamber of Deputies (with 29.6% of the total votes), while the Czech Social Democratic Party (CSDP), which had become a major force of the centre-left under the leadership of Miloš Zeman, almost quadrupled its parliamentary representation, winning 61 seats (26.4%). As a result, the coalition of the CDP, the Christian Democratic Union–Czechoslovak People's Party (CDU–CPP, which obtained 18 seats) and the CDA (13 seats) lost its overall majority, achieving a total of 99 seats. The CPBM and the Association for the Republic–Republican Party of Czechoslovakia were the only other parties to exceed the 5% threshold required for representation in the legislature, securing 22 seats and 18 seats, respectively. Despite losing its parliamentary majority, the governing coalition remained intact. The CSDP ruled out the possibility of joining the coalition, but agreed to give tacit support on most issues to a minority government. In early July Václav Klaus formed a new Government; in a major concession to the CSDP, Miloš Zeman was appointed Chairman of the Chamber of Deputies. The Government survived a vote of confidence in late July, despite CSDP opposition to government proposals to return some 175,000 ha of land, confiscated by the communists, to the Catholic Church, without seeking the approval of the legislature.

The turn-out for the elections to the 81-seat Senate, which were held in mid-November 1996, was low (35%), but the ruling coalition gained a majority of the votes, winning 52 seats. The CSDP won 25 seats, and the CPBM won two, while the remaining two seats went to the Democratic Union (DU) and an independent candidate. At the first meeting of the Senate (whose main role would be to scrutinize legislation), held in December, Petr Pithart was elected Chairman.

Economic problems and growing divisions within the ruling coalition created considerable pressure for government change in May 1997. Consequently, three senior ministers, including Jan Ruml, the Minister of the Interior, resigned, although Ruml's resignation was later rejected by Havel. In June the Government narrowly won a vote of confidence in the Chamber of Deputies, relying on the vote of one independent deputy.

In August 1997 the Government was forced to address the problems of the Romany population (unofficially estimated at some 300,000) as hundreds of Romanies, claiming to have suffered persecution in the Czech Republic, attempted to gain political asylum in Canada (which subsequently reimposed visa requirements for Czech visitors) and the United Kingdom. The Government established an interministerial commission for Romany community affairs in October and outlined further measures aimed at improving the situation of Romanies in the Czech Republic. In early 1998 the Government formed a second commission, headed by Romanies, to address issues affecting the Romany population, and a 40-year law restricting their nomadic way of life was revoked. None the less, large number of Romanies continued to seek political asylum abroad during 1998–99.

Tension within the CDP and between the coalition parties intensified in October 1997. Josef Zieleniec resigned from his position as Minister of Foreign Relations and as Deputy Chairman of the CDP, citing a lack of consultation on important party decisions as the reason for his departure. In early November, while coalition leaders failed to reach agreement on a solution to the political and economic situation, at least 60,000 trade-union members demonstrated in Prague against the Government's social welfare and economic policies. At the end of that month, allegations of impropriety in the funding of the CDP led to the resignation of the Klaus administration, following the withdrawal of the CDU–CPP and the CDA from the coalition, and appeals from both the President and senior members of the CDP for the Government to stand down. Klaus denied all allegations of corruption. In December Josef Lux, Chairman of the CDU–CPP, was asked to lead talks on the formation of a new government. Klaus was re-elected Chairman of the CDP at the party's national conference later that month, defeating Jan Ruml, who subsequently formed a new faction within the party. Josef Tošovský, hitherto Governor of the Czech National Bank, was designated Prime Minister in December, and a new temporary Government, comprising seven non-political ministers, four CDP members, three CDU–CPP members and three CDA members, was appointed in January 1998. The CDP was divided over its participation in the new administration, and the party's four ministers subsequently defected to the Freedom Union (FU), a newly-established breakaway party, which had 31 seats in the Chamber of Deputies by mid-February.

In the presidential election, which took place on 20 January 1998, Havel was narrowly re-elected in a second round of voting. At the end of that month the Government won a vote of confidence when its policy statement was adopted in the Chamber of Deputies. In February Jiří Skalický resigned as Deputy Prime Minister and Minister of the Environment, and as Chairman of the CDA, after admitting that, prior to the 1996 elections (when the CDA controlled the ministries responsible for privatization and industry), the party had received donations from a number of companies. A further two ministers were among a number of CDA deputies who subsequently resigned from the party, although they retained their positions in the Government. In April 1998 the Czech Republic's proposed membership of NATO was formally approved by the legislature; the CSDP had earlier withdrawn its demand for a referendum on the issue.

Early elections to the Chamber of Deputies were held on 19–20 June 1998. The CSDP retained its position (held since the defection of the CDP deputies to the FU earlier in the year) as the largest party in the Chamber of Deputies, winning 74 seats (with 32.3% of the votes cast), while the CDP secured 63 seats (with 27.7%). The remaining seats were divided between the CPBM (with 24 seats), the CDU—CPP (20 seats) and the FU (19 seats). The rate of voter participation was 74%. As leader of the CSDP, Zeman was given the difficult task of attempting to form a government. The parliamentary parties failed to reach agreement on a coalition grouping. In July Zeman and Klaus signed an agreement whereby the CDP pledged not to initiate or support a motion expressing 'no confidence' in a minority CSDP government, in exchange for a number of senior parliamentary posts, including the chairmanship of the Chamber of Deputies (to which Klaus was later elected), and a commitment to early constitutional reform. On 17 July Zeman was formally appointed Prime Minister, and a new Council of Ministers was subsequently named. Political observers doubted the ability of the new Government to survive a full electoral term, reliant as it was on the co-operation of the CDP in order to implement its policies. Later that year the new administration encountered strong opposition, particularly from the CDP, regarding its plan for a large budgetary deficit for 1999, a proposal that had already caused some dissent within the Government itself. In late September Josef Lux resigned as Chairman of the CDU—CPP, owing to serious health problems.

Elections to renew one-third of the seats in the Senate were held in two rounds in November 1998. The CSDP performed poorly, winning only three of the 27 seats contested, while the CDP secured nine seats, and a four-party informal alliance, comprising the CDU—CPP, the CDA, the DU and the FU, won 13 seats. The CPBM doubled its representation to four seats. The electoral turn-out was very low, reaching only 20.4% in the second round. In local elections, also held in November, independent candidates, followed by the CDU—CPP, gained the largest number of seats on municipal councils, owing to strong support in smaller, rural communities. In terms of votes, however, the CDP received the greatest endorsement, with 24.3% of the total votes cast, although the party secured only 9.2% of seats, mainly in urban areas. The CSDP won 17.5% of the total votes (6.8% of seats). Observers largely attributed the CSDP's poor performance in the November elections to its agreement with the CDP, which was deemed to be unpopular with the electorate.

The reputation of the Czech counter-intelligence service was badly damaged in early 1999 by revelations surrounding the dismissal of its head, Karel Vulterin, for committing unspecified professional errors which had allegedly endangered state security. Media reports speculated that Vulterin's dismissal had been provoked by the service's failure to inform the Government about a planned terrorist attack on Prague-based Radio Free Europe/Radio Liberty, a US-funded station which had commenced broadcasts to Iran and Iraq in late 1998. A commercial television station, Nova TV, subsequently revealed the identity and the address of the head of the Prague station of the British intelligence agency, MI6, claiming that the information had been leaked to the media by disaffected members of the Czech counter-intelligence service who had been angered by a letter that the agent had apparently sent to the Government criticizing the service's work. The Government later announced that it was considering restructuring and reducing the number of Czech intelligence services.

A decision by the Czech Council of Ministers to complete the construction of the controversial Temelín nuclear power plant in southern Bohemia provoked international concern in May 1999. The decision, which followed a resolution by the European Parliament opposing the completion of the plant, was also strongly criticized by President Havel, environmentalist groups and the Austrian Government.

In June 1999 the Chamber of Deputies rejected a government proposal for constitutional amendments that would have enabled the Council of Ministers to issue decrees with the effect of law, but without the approval of the legislature. As feared, the CSDP Government had encountered difficulties in enacting new legislation, owing to its minority status. In July Ivo Svoboda was dismissed from the post of Minister of Finance after it was announced that he was to be prosecuted for allegedly harming creditors of a bankrupt company of which he had been on the management board. In September the Council of Ministers approved a number of proposals for constitutional change that had been drafted by a joint CSDP-CDP commission. The amendments aimed to restrict presidential powers, including the right to appoint the Prime Minister and the heads of principal state institutions, and the right to grant amnesty. (The Chamber of Deputies approved the changes in January 2000, despite an opposition boycott of the vote; the amendments were still to be considered by the Senate at the end of February.)

Amid signs of growing dissatisfaction with the current political impasse, including a series of opinion polls identifying the CPBM as the most popular party, the formation of a new majority coalition government was under consideration in late 1999. On 17 November celebrations held to commemorate the 10th anniversary of the 'velvet revolution' were attended by Western leaders who had been in power at the time. On the same day, however, a group of former student leaders who had participated in the events of November 1989 staged a protest initiative against the current political system, urging the leaders of all the main parties to withdraw from political life. Their appeal, known as 'thank you, now go!', had been signed by some 150,000 people by early December 1999, when more than 50,000 demonstrators attended a rally in Prague. Jan Ruml subsequently resigned as Chairman of the FU, explaining that he felt a sense of responsibility for the current political situation. Meanwhile, Egon Lánský resigned as Deputy Prime Minister for European Integration in December 1999, citing ill health, although opposition parties had been demanding his resignation for several months, owing to dissatisfaction with preparations for EU entry, and also in connection with an Austrian bank account that he had opened in 1996 without authorization from the Czech central bank. The Minister of Foreign Affairs, Jan Kavan, was subsequently elevated to the position of Deputy Prime Minister. Ivan David, the Minister of Health, also resigned from the Government in December. No progress had been achieved by the end of 1999 regarding attempts to form a majority coalition government; the CDU—CPP and the FU had refused to enter talks with the CDP until it withdrew from its agreement with the ruling CSDP. In late January 2000, however, the CSDP and the CDP extended their agreement on bilateral co-operation; the CSDP promised to reshuffle the Council of Ministers and to propose electoral reform measures in return for the CDP's continued tolerance of the CSDP minority Government and its budgetary proposals for 2000.

During 1999 the Government sought to reverse a decision by the local authorities in Ústí nad Labem to proceed with a controversial plan (first proposed in May 1998) to erect a fence to separate municipal housing mainly inhabited by Romany rent-defaulters from private residences opposite. Despite condemnation from the President, human rights organizations and the EU, the construction of the fence was completed in October 1999. In November, however, the city council in Ústí nad Labem agreed to dismantle the fence after the Government pledged a subsidy of 10m. koruny, some of which was to be used to purchase the houses of the non-Romany families whose complaints had originally prompted the move towards segregation.

An important focus of the Czech Republic's foreign policy is to maintain close relations with Slovakia and other neighbouring eastern European states. It is a member, with Slovakia, Hungary and Poland, of the Visegrad Group (established, following the collapse of communist rule, to promote economic, defence and other co-operation in the region). The Governments of the Czech Republic, Hungary and Poland have agreed to co-ordinate preparations for accession to NATO and the EU (see below). Relations with Slovakia have been strained in recent years, mainly because of disagreements over the division of former federal property. In mid-September 1998, however, following talks between Miloš Zeman and Vladimír Mečiar, the Slovak Prime Minister, it was announced that a joint Czech-Slovak committee would meet shortly in an attempt to further discussions on unresolved issues. The success of opposition parties in Slovak elections held at the end of that month, and the subsequent change of government, led to a further improvement in bilateral relations. Measures providing for dual Czech-Slovak citizenship became fully effective in October 1999, and in November an agreement on the division of former federal property was signed in Bratislava by Zeman and Mikuláš Dzurinda, the Slovak Prime Minister. The agreement provided for the exchange of shares between the Czech Republic's Komerční banka and Slovakia's Všeobecná úverová banka and the restitution of gold reserves to Slovakia. The gold had been held by the Czech central bank as collateral for debts owed by Slovakia to the Czech Republic. These debts, totalling some 26,000m. koruny, had proved to be a major obstacle during negotiations, as they had never been recognized by Slovakia. The Czech Government consequently opted effectively to relieve Slovakia of its debts by buying the cental bank's claim for a symbolic one koruna, despite the opposition of several Czech politicians. The agreement awaited approval by both countries' legislatures in early 2000.

The Czech Republic actively pursues a policy of European integration and co-operation, and envisages early full membership of the EU (for which it officially applied in January 1996). In this connection, the Czech Government has emphasized the importance of close ties with western European states, particularly neighbouring Germany (the Czech Republic's most important trading partner). The Czech Republic was one of a number of central and eastern European states invited to begin negotiations in March 1998 on possible entry to the EU. In November more substantive talks commenced regarding the compliance of potential EU entrants with membership regulations. Earlier that month, however, the European Commission (EC) had criticized the slow pace of legislative reform in the Czech Republic. Preparations for accession to the EU continued to advance very slowly during 1999, and in October the EC was again critical of the Czech Republic's lack of progress in adopting necessary EU legislation and expressed concern regarding the situation of the country's Romany minority. Formal admittance to the EU was envisaged for 2003.

Since the end of the Second World War Czech-German relations have been dominated by two issues: the question of compensation for Czech victims of Nazism, and demands for the restitution of property to the Sudeten Germans who were driven from Czechoslovakia in 1945. From 1993 negotiations were held to formulate a declaration on bilateral relations, but progress was hampered by these two outstanding issues. However, a joint declaration was finally signed by both Ministers of Foreign Affairs on 20 December 1996, and by Václav Klaus of the Czech Republic and Chancellor Kohl of Germany on 21 January 1997. In the declaration, Germany admitted that it was to blame for the Nazi occupation and the partition of Czechoslovakia in 1939, while the Czech Republic apologized for the abuses of human rights that were committed during the deportation of ethnic Germans in 1945–46. The declaration did not, however, condemn the expulsion of the Sudeten Germans as a crime, which would have meant that those people expelled could have made claims for compensation. A joint Czech-German fund was established in January 1998 to finance joint projects, in particular benefiting victims of the Nazis. Relations were strained somewhat in February and August 1998, however, when the nomination of Sudeten Germans to a Czech-German advisory council was rejected by Miloš Zeman, who claimed that the nominees had opposed the January 1997 declaration that had provided for the establishment of the council.

In August 1993 the Czech Republic and the Russian Federation signed a treaty of friendship and co-operation (replacing the Russian-Czechoslovak treaty of 1992). In March 1994, despite Russia's apparent opposition, the Czech Republic joined NATO's 'Partnership for Peace' programme of military co-operation. In 1996 the Chamber of Deputies approved legislation prohibiting the storage of nuclear weapons on Czech territory, except where international treaties are concerned, thereby allowing for full membership of NATO. In July 1997 the Czech Republic, together with Hungary and Poland, was invited to commence NATO membership negotiations. A protocol providing for the accession of the three states to NATO was signed in December 1997 and was subsequently ratified by the legislatures of member states. In March 1999 the Czech Republic, Hungary and Poland became full members of NATO. Associate membership of the Western European Union (see p. 268) was subsequently granted. The Czech Republic is a member of the Council of Europe (see p. 158) and the Organization for Security and Co-operation in Europe (OSCE, see p. 237).

## Government

Legislative power is held by two chambers, the 200-member Chamber of Deputies (lower house) and the 81-member Senate. Members of the Chamber of Deputies and the Senate are elected for four and six years, respectively, by universal adult suffrage. The President of the Republic (Head of State) is elected for a term of five years by a joint session of the legislature. The President, who is also Commander of the Armed Forces, may be re-elected for a second consecutive term. He/she appoints the Prime Minister and, on the latter's recommendation, the other members of the Council of Ministers (the highest organ of executive power). For administrative purposes, the Czech Republic is divided into 72 districts.

## Defence

In August 1999 total armed forces numbered 58,200 (including 25,000 conscripts): an army of 25,300 and an air force of 15,400; there were also some 17,500 troops attached to the Ministry of Defence and centrally-controlled formations. In addition, there were 4,000 border guards and 1,600 internal security forces. Military service is compulsory and lasts for 12 months. The defence budget for 2000 was projected at 44,900m. koruny. In March 1994 the Czech Republic joined NATO's 'Partnership for Peace' programme of military co-operation (see p. 228), and in March 1999 it was formally admitted to NATO.

## Economic Affairs

In 1997, according to estimates by the World Bank, the Czech Republic's gross national product (GNP), measured at average 1995–97 prices, was US $53,952m., equivalent to $5,240 per head. During 1990–97, it was estimated, GNP per head declined, in real terms, at an average annual rate of 0.3%. Over the same period the population was estimated to have decreased by an average of 0.1% per year. In 1998 GNP was estimated at $51,800m., equivalent to $5,040 per head. Gross domestic product (GDP) declined, in real terms, by an average of 2.6% annually during 1990–95. Real GDP increased by 3.8% in 1996, and by 0.3% in 1997, but declined by 2.3% in 1998.

Agriculture (including forestry and fishing) contributed 4.5% of GDP in 1998, and provided 5.5% of employment in that year, according to preliminary figures. The principal crops are wheat, sugar beet, barley, potatoes and hops (the Czech Republic is a major beer producer and exporter). Agricultural GDP increased by 2.5% in 1997, and by 8.1% in 1998.

Industry (including manufacturing, mining, construction and power) contributed 41.8% of GDP in 1998, and provided 40.9% of employment in that year, according to preliminary figures. Industrial GDP increased by 6.5% in 1997, but declined by 4.7% in 1998. According to preliminary figures, the manufacturing sector provided 29.6% of employment in 1998. Based on the value of output, the most important branches of manufacturing in 1996 were food products and beverages (accounting for 16.3% of the total), basic metals (12.7%), non-electric machinery and domestic appliances (9.0%), and metal products (7.6%).

The principal minerals extracted are coal and lignite. In 1998 the mining sector provided 1.5% of employment, according to preliminary figures. In 1996 mining production increased by 1.4%, compared with the previous year.

In 1997 thermal power provided 77.4% of total electricity production, nuclear power 19.3% and hydroelectric power 3.2%. Imports of mineral fuels comprised 6.5% of the value of total imports in 1998, according to preliminary figures.

The services sector contributed 53.7% of GDP in 1998, and engaged 53.6% of the employed labour force in that year, according to preliminary figures. Tourism is an important source of revenue, providing receipts of US $3,792m. in 1998; the sector accounted for some 5.5% of GDP in 1994. The GDP of the services sector declined by 3.7% in 1997, and by 1.7% in 1998.

In 1998 the Czech Republic recorded a visible trade deficit of US $2,595m. and there was a deficit of US $1,110m. on the current account of the balance of payments. In 1998, according to preliminary figures, the principal source of imports (34.5%) was Germany; other major sources were Slovakia, Austria, Russia and Italy. Germany was also the principal market for exports (38.5%) in that year; other important purchasers were Slovakia, Austria and Poland. The principal exports were machinery and transport equipment, basic manufactures and miscellaneous manufactured articles. The principal imports were machinery and transport equipment, basic manufactures, chemicals and related products, and miscellaneous manufactured articles.

In 1998 there was a budgetary deficit of 29,200m. koruny (equivalent to 1.6% of GDP). The Czech Republic's total external debt was US $21,456m. at the end of 1997, of which $12,275m. was long-term public debt. In that year the cost of debt-servicing was equivalent to 14.1% of the value of exports of goods and services. The annual rate of inflation averaged 16.1% in 1990–98 the annual average rate in 1998 was 10.7%. About 9% of the labour force were unemployed in November 1999.

The Czech Republic is a member of the IMF and the World Bank and an associate member of the EU. It is also a member of the European Bank for Reconstruction and Development (EBRD, see p. 168) and, in late 1995, became the first post-communist state in eastern Europe to be admitted to the Organisation for Economic Co-operation and Development (OECD, see p. 232).

Of all the post-communist states of eastern Europe, for much of the 1990s the Czech Republic was considered to have undertaken the transition to a market economic system with greatest success. The country's programme of rapid privatization, price and currency stabilization and the establishment of a new banking system, while preserving a low level of unemployment, won strong popular support during 1992–95, attracting widespread foreign investment. In 1996, however, economic growth decelerated and the first budgetary deficit since the transition to a market economy was recorded. Difficulties were experienced in the banking sector, with several banks forced to cease operations. Economic performance deteriorated in 1997, and investor confidence was weakened by cases of embezzlement of investment funds. In May a series of speculative attacks on the koruna prompted the introduction of a floating exchange rate. In early 1998 the interim Government made some progress with economic reform, overseeing the establishment of a new securities commission and the privatization of Investiční a Pŏstovní banka. In August, however, it emerged that the economy had entered recession. As the economy declined further, with the rate of inflation slowing and unemployment rising, the central bank reduced interest rates some seven times in the second half of 1998. Despite the easing of fiscal and monetary policies, real GDP continued to contract, with a decline of 4.5% recorded in the first quarter of 1999. As levels of corporate debt increased, in April the Government announced that some 30 private-sector companies were to be placed temporarily under state control to avert the threat of bankruptcy. Additional funds were also allocated to measures designed to reduce unemployment. By October 1999 there was some evidence of economic recovery, with a slight return to growth in GDP and increases in export demand and household consumption. The two remaining state-owned banks, which had been heavily burdened by non-performing loans, were to be privatized in 2000. Further financial and industrial restructuring would be required, however, to ensure long-term sustainable growth.

## Social Welfare

A single and universal system of social security was established in Czechoslovakia after the Second World War. Protection of health was stipulated by law, and medical care, treatment, medicines, etc., were, in most cases, available free of charge to the entire Czechoslovak population. Following the dissolution of Czechoslovakia in January 1993, the two successor states announced plans to introduce changes to the existing social welfare system. In the Czech Republic the privatization programme was to extend to the health-care system, although at a slower rate than in many other parts of the economy. By September 1994 the Government had approved the privatization of 11 hospitals. In 1992 there were 31 physicians (in the state sector) per 10,000 inhabitants, and 82.4 hospital beds per 10,000 inhabitants. Of total expenditure by the central Government in 1997, 105,551m. koruny (17.7%) was for health, and a further 216,848m. koruny (36.3%) for social security and welfare. A new pensions insurance law was to come into effect in the late 1990s, which would gradually increase the retirement age for men to 65 years (from 60) and for women to 57–61 (from 53–57, according to the number of children born) by 2007.

## Education

Almost 90% of children between the ages of three and six years attend kindergarten. From the age of six children attend basic school, which covers both primary (grades 1–5) and lower secondary (grades 6–9) levels, and is attended by almost 97% of pupils aged between six and 15, when education is compulsory. Most children (almost 97%) continue their education at an upper secondary school, of which there were three types in 1999: gymnasia (providing general education and preparing students mainly for university entry), secondary vocational schools and secondary technical schools. Students follow three- to four-year courses. Tertiary education consists of non-university schools, which offer three-year courses, and universities, at which most courses last from five to six years. Since 1990 many private schools, particularly at upper secondary level, have been established.

In the 1998/99 academic year 1,194,824 children attended basic schools, while 449,426 attended the different types of upper secondary school. In the same year there were 236,207 students in higher education. Of total expenditure by the central Government in 1997, 67,166m. koruny (11.3%) was for education.

## Public Holidays

**2000:** 1 January (New Year's Day), 24 April (Easter Monday), 1 May (Labour Day), 8 May (Liberation Day), 5 July (Day of the Apostles St Cyril and St Methodius), 6 July (Anniversary of the Martyrdom of Jan Hus), 28 October (Independence Day), 24–25 December (Christmas), 26 December (St Stephen's Day).

**2001:** 1 January (New Year's Day), 16 April (Easter Monday), 1 May (Labour Day), 8 May (Liberation Day), 5 July (Day of the Apostles St Cyril and St Methodius), 6 July (Anniversary of the Martyrdom of Jan Hus), 28 October (Independence Day), 24–25 December (Christmas), 26 December (St Stephen's Day).

## Weights and Measures

The metric system is in force.

# Statistical Survey

Source: mainly Czech Statistical Office, Sokolovská 142, 186 04 Prague 8; tel. (2) 66042451; fax (2) 66310429.

## Area and Population

### AREA, POPULATION AND DENSITY

| | |
|---|---|
| Area (sq km) | 78,866* |
| Population (census results) | |
| 1 November 1980 | 10,291,927 |
| 3 March 1991 | |
| Males | 4,999,935 |
| Females | 5,302,280 |
| Total | 10,302,215 |
| Population (official estimates at 31 December) | |
| 1996 | 10,309,137 |
| 1997 | 10,299,125 |
| 1998 | 10,289,621 |
| Density (per sq km) at 31 December 1998 | 130.5 |

* 30,450 sq miles.

### POPULATION BY NATIONALITY (census of 3 March 1991)

| | Number | % |
|---|---|---|
| Czech (Bohemian) | 8,363,768 | 81.2 |
| Moravian | 1,362,313 | 13.2 |
| Slovak | 314,877 | 3.1 |
| Polish | 59,383 | 0.6 |
| German | 48,556 | 0.5 |
| Silesian | 44,446 | 0.4 |
| Roma (Gypsy) | 32,903 | 0.3 |
| Hungarian | 19,932 | 0.2 |
| Others | 34,020 | 0.3 |
| Unknown | 22,017 | 0.2 |
| **Total** | 10,302,215 | 100.0 |

### REGIONS (estimates, 1 January 1999)

| | Area (sq km) | Population | Density (per sq km) |
|---|---|---|---|
| Central Bohemia | 11,014 | 1,108,465 | 101 |
| Southern Bohemia | 11,346 | 700,685 | 62 |
| Western Bohemia | 10,875 | 857,384 | 79 |
| Northern Bohemia | 7,799 | 1,180,325 | 151 |
| Eastern Bohemia | 11,240 | 1,233,215 | 110 |
| Southern Moravia | 15,028 | 2,051,389 | 137 |
| Northern Moravia | 11,068 | 1,964,888 | 178 |
| Prague (city) | 496 | 1,193,270 | 2,406 |
| **Total** | 78,866 | 10,289,621 | 130 |

### PRINCIPAL TOWNS (estimated population, 1 January 1999)

| | | | |
|---|---|---|---|
| Praha (Prague, capital) | 1,193,270 | České Budějovice (Budweis) | 99,347 |
| Brno | 384,727 | Hradec Králové | 99,323 |
| Ostrava | 322,111 | Ústí nad Labem | 96,493 |
| Plzeň (Pilsen) | 168,422 | Pardubice | 92,495 |
| Olomouc | 103,372 | Havířov | 87,363 |
| Liberec | 99,794 | Zlín* | 81,851 |
| | | Kladno | 71,680 |
| | | Most | 70,283 |

* During the period of communist rule this town was renamed Gottwaldov, but it has since reverted to its former name.

### BIRTHS, MARRIAGES AND DEATHS

| | Registered live births | | Registered marriages | | Registered deaths | |
|---|---|---|---|---|---|---|
| | Number | Rate (per 1,000) | Number | Rate (per 1,000) | Number | Rate (per 1,000) |
| 1991 | 129,354 | 12.5 | 71,973 | 7.0 | 124,290 | 12.1 |
| 1992 | 121,705 | 11.8 | 74,060 | 7.2 | 120,337 | 11.7 |
| 1993 | 121,025 | 11.7 | 66,033 | 6.4 | 118,185 | 11.4 |
| 1994 | 106,579 | 10.3 | 58,440 | 5.7 | 117,373 | 11.4 |
| 1995 | 96,097 | 9.3 | 54,956 | 5.3 | 117,913 | 11.4 |
| 1996 | 90,446 | 8.8 | 53,896 | 5.2 | 112,782 | 10.9 |
| 1997 | 90,657 | 8.8 | 57,804 | 5.6 | 112,744 | 10.9 |
| 1998 | 90,535 | 8.8 | 55,027 | 5.3 | 109,527 | 10.6 |

### EMPLOYMENT (annual averages)*

| | 1996 | 1997† | 1998† |
|---|---|---|---|
| Agriculture, forestry and fishing | 303,233 | 278,185 | 266,405 |
| Mining and quarrying | 86,451 | 79,671 | 73,829 |
| Manufacturing | 1,440,618 | 1,441,239 | 1,440,162 |
| Electricity, gas and water | 87,601 | 84,553 | 81,596 |
| Construction | 451,654 | 435,401 | 399,308 |
| Trade, restaurants and hotels | 930,644 | 900,908 | 901,628 |
| Transport, storage and communications | 363,113 | 345,760 | 335,632 |
| Finance, insurance, real estate and business services | 471,147 | 480,753 | 484,041 |
| Public administration, defence and compulsory social security | 167,917 | 175,478 | 177,066 |
| Education | 321,839 | 308,612 | 304,403 |
| Health and social welfare | 268,202 | 267,173 | 262,729 |
| Other community, social and personal services | 151,997 | 148,841 | 146,612 |
| **Total** | 5,044,416 | 4,946,574 | 4,873,411 |

* Excluding women on maternity leave.
† Preliminary figures.

## Agriculture

### PRINCIPAL CROPS ('000 metric tons)

| | 1996 | 1997 | 1998 |
|---|---|---|---|
| Wheat | 3,727 | 3,640 | 3,845 |
| Barley | 2,262 | 2,485 | 2,093 |
| Maize | 169 | 285 | 201 |
| Rye* | 204 | 259 | 261 |
| Oats | 214 | 247 | 180 |
| Potatoes | 1,800 | 1,402 | 1,520 |
| Peas (dry) | 120 | 93 | 122 |
| Rapeseed | 521 | 561 | 680 |
| Cabbages | 175 | 154 | 157 |
| Tomatoes | 28 | 23 | 30 |
| Cauliflowers | 36 | 34 | 35 |
| Cucumbers and gherkins | 53 | 56 | 49 |
| Onions (dry) | 100 | 83 | 88 |
| Carrots | 91 | 74 | 76 |
| Other vegetables | 112 | 112 | 101 |
| Grapes | 70 | 36 | 55 |
| Sugar beet | 4,316 | 3,722 | 3,479 |
| Apples | 251 | 291 | 283 |
| Pears | 19 | 20 | 25 |
| Peaches and nectarines | 8 | 7 | 7 |
| Plums | 32 | 39 | 24 |
| Hops | 10 | 7 | 5 |

* Including mixed crops of wheat and rye.

**LIVESTOCK** ('000 head at 1 March)

| | 1996 | 1997 | 1998 |
|---|---|---|---|
| Horses | 19 | 21 | 23 |
| Cattle | 1,866 | 1,701 | 1,657 |
| Pigs | 4,080 | 4,013 | 4,001 |
| Sheep | 121 | 94 | 86 |
| Goats | 38 | 35 | 34 |
| Poultry | 27,573 | 29,035 | 30,222 |

**LIVESTOCK PRODUCTS**
('000 metric tons, unless otherwise indicated)

| | 1996 | 1997 | 1998 |
|---|---|---|---|
| Beef and veal* | 310.4 | 293.6 | 246.6 |
| Pig meat* | 727.0 | 679.9 | 669.9 |
| Poultry meat* | 172.1 | 206.1 | 240.9 |
| Milk (million litres) | 3,039 | 2,703 | 2,716 |
| Eggs (million) | 2,948 | 3,322 | 3,615 |

* Slaughter weight.

## Forestry

**LOGGING** ('000 cubic metres)

| | 1996 | 1997 | 1998 |
|---|---|---|---|
| Coniferous (softwood) | 11,259.9 | 11,942.1 | 12,250.1 |
| Broadleaved (hardwood) | 1,324.0 | 1,548.9 | 1,741.2 |
| **Total** | 12,583.9 | 13,491.0 | 13,991.3 |

## Fishing*

(metric tons)

| | 1996 | 1997 | 1998 |
|---|---|---|---|
| Common carp | 18,462 | 17,482 | 17,960 |
| Others | 3,262 | 3,339 | 3,223 |
| **Total catch** | 21,724 | 20,881 | 21,183 |

* Figures refer only to fish caught by the Fishing Association (formerly State Fisheries) and members of the Czech and Moravian Fishing Union.

## Mining

('000 metric tons)

| | 1996 | 1997 | 1998 |
|---|---|---|---|
| Hard coal | 16,532 | 16,069 | 16,112 |
| Brown coal and lignite | 59,692 | 57,446 | 51,419 |
| Kaolin | 742 | 822 | 879 |

**Crude petroleum** ('000 metric tons): 350 in 1996; 350 in 1997; 415 in 1998 (Source: Institute of Petroleum, London).

## Industry

**SELECTED PRODUCTS**
('000 metric tons, unless otherwise indicated)

| | 1996 | 1997 | 1998 |
|---|---|---|---|
| Wheat flour and meal | 893 | 858 | 826 |
| Refined sugar | 602 | 598 | 492 |
| Wine ('000 hectolitres) | 542.5 | 564.8 | 560.5 |
| Beer ('000 hectolitres) | 18,056.8 | 18,558.3 | 18,289.2 |
| Cotton yarn (metric tons) | 57,839 | 62,373 | 64,594 |
| Woven cotton fabrics ('000 metres) | 330,237 | 345,605 | 336,702 |
| Woollen fabrics ('000 metres) | 29,586 | 28,454 | 28,601 |
| Linen fabrics ('000 metres) | 27,329 | 27,504 | 28,453 |
| Paper and paperboard | 152.3 | 171.2 | 191.6 |
| Footwear ('000 pairs) | 23,652 | 15,682 | 11,110 |
| Nitrogenous fertilizers* | 253 | 245 | 247 |
| Soap | 44.4 | 34.0 | 34.1 |
| Motor spirit (petrol) | 1,243† | n.a. | n.a. |
| Gas-diesel (distillate fuel) oil | 2,581† | n.a. | n.a. |
| Residual fuel oils | 1,634† | n.a. | n.a. |
| Coke | 4,836 | 4,290 | 4,007 |
| Cement | 5,016 | 4,874 | 4,604 |
| Pig-iron | 4,898 | 5,276 | 5,165 |
| Crude steel | 6,500 | 6,749† | 6,525† |
| Trucks (number) | 27,036 | 39,537 | 38,983 |
| Motorcycles and mopeds (number) | 8,608 | 9,645 | 5,096 |
| Bicycles (number) | 500,525 | 473,505 | 346,830 |
| Tractors (number) | 1,910 | n.a. | n.a. |
| Electric energy (million kWh) | 64,257 | 64,598 | 65,112 |

* Production in terms of nitrogen.
† Source: UN, *Monthly Bulletin of Statistics*.

## Finance

**CURRENCY AND EXCHANGE RATES**

**Monetary Units**
100 haléřů (singular: haléř—heller) = 1 Czech koruna (Czech crown or Kč.; plural: koruny).

**Sterling, Dollar and Euro Equivalents** (30 September 1999)
£1 sterling = 55.72 koruny;
US $1 = 33.84 koruny;
€1 = 36.09 koruny;
1,000 koruny = £17.95 = $29.55 = €27.71.

**Average Exchange Rate** (koruny per US $)
1996 27.145
1997 31.698
1998 32.281

Note: In February 1993 the Czech Republic introduced its own currency, the Czech koruna, to replace (at par) the Czechoslovak koruna.

**BUDGET** (million koruny)*

| Revenue | 1995 | 1996 | 1997 |
|---|---|---|---|
| Taxation | 446,233 | 508,201 | 540,078 |
| Taxes on income, profits and capital gains | 71,828 | 77,396 | 75,580 |
| Individual | 8,491 | 29,726 | 33,378 |
| Corporate | 63,337 | 47,670 | 42,202 |
| Social security contributions | 195,652 | 226,013 | 249,863 |
| From employees | 54,785 | 63,272 | 67,297 |
| From employers | 140,867 | 162,741 | 170,903 |
| Domestic taxes on goods and services | 155,434 | 174,827 | 194,542 |
| Value-added tax | 94,801 | 109,313 | 117,656 |
| Excises | 56,650 | 61,170 | 64,171 |
| Taxes on international trade and transactions | 17,410 | 19,676 | 14,931 |
| Import duties | 17,410 | 19,676 | 14,931 |
| Other current revenue | 39,964 | 27,467 | 19,879 |
| Entrepreneurial and property income | 11,035 | 10,417 | 9,934 |
| Administrative fees and charges, non-industrial and incidental sales | 14,659 | 7,335 | 3,654 |
| Capital revenue | 150 | 257 | 350 |
| **Total** | 486,347 | 535,925 | 560,307 |

| Expenditure† | 1995 | 1996 | 1997 |
|---|---|---|---|
| General public services | 31,333 | 37,956 | 18,800 |
| Defence | 28,390 | 30,604 | 27,596 |
| Public order and safety | 29,733 | 34,825 | 32,316 |
| Education | 57,836 | 64,964 | 67,166 |
| Health | 84,319 | 95,416 | 105,551 |
| Social security and welfare | 144,059 | 139,433 | 216,848 |
| Housing and community amenities | 2,707 | 3,938 | 23,599 |
| Recreational, cultural and religious affairs and services | 5,019 | 5,547 | 6,515 |
| Economic affairs and services | 68,809 | 69,922 | 73,100 |
| Fuel and energy | 3,583 | 11,043 | 3,322 |
| Agriculture, forestry, fishing and hunting | 9,000 | 9,117 | 14,572 |
| Mining and mineral resources, manufacturing and construction | 2,560 | 2,029 | 1,429 |
| Transport and communications | 26,033 | 26,507 | 32,255 |
| Other purposes | 51,841 | 79,912 | 25,153 |
| **Sub-total** | 504,046 | 562,517 | 596,644 |
| Adjustment‡ | –3,937 | –4,509 | –4,574 |
| **Total** | 500,109 | 558,008 | 592,070 |
| Current§ | 439,352 | 496,837 | 538,378 |
| Capital | 60,757 | 61,171 | 53,692 |

* Figures represent a consolidation of transactions by the central Government, including the operations of the Central Budget, social security funds (controlled by the General Health Insurance Organization) and extrabudgetary accounts.

† Excluding lending minus repayments (million koruny): –18,584 in 1995; –21,510 in 1996; –12,582 in 1997.

‡ Relating to employer's contributions to social security schemes at the same level of government.

§ Including interest payments (million koruny): 15,366 in 1995; 16,612 in 1996; 18,307 in 1997.

Source: IMF, *Government Finance Statistics Yearbook.*

**1998** (Central Budget only, million koruny): Revenue 537,411; Expenditure 566,741.

**INTERNATIONAL RESERVES** (US $ million at 31 December)

| | 1996 | 1997 | 1998 |
|---|---|---|---|
| Gold* | 137 | 57 | 18 |
| Foreign exchange | 12,352 | 9,734 | 12,542 |
| **Total** | 12,489 | 9,791 | 12,560 |

* Valued at 60.61 koruny per gram.

Source: IMF, *International Financial Statistics.*

**MONEY SUPPLY** ('000 million koruny at 31 December)

| | 1996 | 1997 | 1998 |
|---|---|---|---|
| Currency outside banks | 118.90 | 118.74 | 127.16 |
| Demand deposits at deposit money banks | 317.46 | 297.24 | 275.68 |
| **Total money** (incl. others) | 451.55 | 418.39 | 404.00 |

Source: IMF, *International Financial Statistics.*

**COST OF LIVING**
(Consumer Price Index; base: 1994 = 100)

| | 1996 | 1997 | 1998 |
|---|---|---|---|
| Food, beverages and tobacco | 119.4 | 125.2 | 132.0 |
| Clothing and footwear | 121.7 | 132.4 | 140.6 |
| Housing, water, fuel and light | 123.5 | 146.6 | 190.9 |
| Furnishings, household equipment and maintenance | 110.1 | 116.0 | 123.0 |
| **All items** (incl. others) | 118.8 | 128.8 | 142.6 |

**NATIONAL ACCOUNTS** ('000 million koruny at current prices)

**Expenditure on the Gross Domestic Product**

| | 1996 | 1997 | 1998 |
|---|---|---|---|
| Government final consumption expenditure | 312.5 | 331.3 | 351.8 |
| Private final consumption expenditure | 810.7 | 891.5 | 949.8 |
| Increase in stocks | 48.9 | 50.2 | 43.4 |
| Gross fixed capital formation | 500.6 | 506.9 | 501.4 |
| **Total domestic expenditure** | 1,672.7 | 1,779.9 | 1,846.3 |
| Exports of goods and services | 831.3 | 949.7 | 1,092.1 |
| *Less* Imports of goods and services | 931.7 | 1,049.6 | 1,117.7 |
| **GDP in purchasers' values** | 1,572.3 | 1,680.0 | 1,820.7 |
| **GDP at constant 1995 prices** | 1,433.9 | 1,438.5 | 1,405.0 |

**Gross Domestic Product by Economic Activity**

| | 1996 | 1997 | 1998 |
|---|---|---|---|
| Agriculture, hunting, forestry and fishing | 68.1 | 69.2 | 76.4 |
| Mining and quarrying; Manufacturing; Electricity, gas and water | 470.1 | 526.7 | 586.0 |
| Construction | 121.4 | 129.7 | 127.7 |
| Trade, restaurants and hotels | 236.7 | 231.7 | 223.3 |
| Transport, storage and communications | 116.5 | 120.1 | 160.0 |
| Financial services | 59.1 | 74.7 | 84.7 |
| Business services* | 168.6 | 198.4 | 220.4 |
| Public administration, education and health | 210.5 | 213.9 | 228.5 |
| **Sub-total** | 1,451.0 | 1,564.4 | 1,707.0 |
| *Less* Imputed bank service charge | 60.4 | 67.1 | 73.6 |
| **GDP at basic prices** | 1,390.6 | 1,497.3 | 1,633.4 |
| Taxes on products; *Less* Subsidies on products | 181.7 | 182.7 | 187.3 |
| **GDP in purchasers' values** | 1,572.3 | 1,680.0 | 1,820.7 |

* Including real estate, renting and business activities.

Source: IMF, *Czech Republic: Statistical Appendix* (August 1999).

**BALANCE OF PAYMENTS** (US $ million)

| | 1996 | 1997 | 1998 |
|---|---|---|---|
| Exports of goods f.o.b. | 21,693 | 22,737 | 26,395 |
| Imports of goods f.o.b. | –27,571 | –27,325 | –28,989 |
| **Trade balance** | –5,877 | –4,588 | –2,595 |
| Exports of services | 8,181 | 7,132 | 7,513 |
| Imports of services | –6,264 | –5,389 | –5,724 |
| **Balance on goods and services** | –3,961 | –2,845 | –806 |
| Other income received | 1,170 | 1,405 | 1,525 |
| Other income paid | –1,892 | –2,197 | –2,237 |
| **Balance on goods, services and income** | –4,683 | –3,636 | –1,517 |
| Current transfers received | 617 | 866 | 781 |
| Current transfers paid | –233 | –501 | –373 |
| **Current balance** | –4,299 | –3,271 | –1,110 |
| Capital account (net) | 1 | 11 | 2 |
| Direct investment abroad | –155 | –28 | –55 |
| Direct investment from abroad | 1,435 | 1,286 | 2,554 |
| Portfolio investment assets | –50 | –159 | –44 |
| Portfolio investment liabilities | 771 | 1,152 | 1,146 |
| Other investment assets | –2,370 | –4,427 | –1,600 |
| Other investment liabilities | 4,571 | 3,298 | 749 |
| Net errors and omissions | –729 | 379 | 249 |
| **Overall balance** | –825 | –1,758 | 1,890 |

Source: IMF, *International Financial Statistics.*

# External Trade

**COMMODITY GROUPS** (distribution by SITC, million koruny)

| Imports f.o.b. | 1996 | 1997* | 1998* |
|---|---|---|---|
| Food and live animals | 43,039 | 44,584 | 45,974 |
| Crude materials (inedible) except fuels | 27,694 | 32,112 | 36,201 |
| Mineral fuels, lubricants, etc. | 65,570 | 74,493 | 60,227 |
| Chemicals and related products | 88,765 | 105,340 | 112,663 |
| Basic manufactures | 145,102 | 166,551 | 193,963 |
| Machinery and transport equipment | 286,969 | 327,496 | 367,085 |
| Miscellaneous manufactured articles | 86,198 | 99,699 | 102,547 |
| **Total** (incl. others) | 752,344 | 861,770 | 929,979 |

* Preliminary figures.

| Exports f.o.b. | 1996 | 1997* | 1998* |
|---|---|---|---|
| Food and live animals | 23,960 | 26,417 | 28,382 |
| Crude materials (inedible) except fuels | 28,862 | 29,137 | 29,416 |
| Mineral fuels, lubricants, etc. | 26,924 | 27,137 | 27,086 |
| Chemicals and related products | 53,671 | 63,593 | 65,515 |
| Basic manufactures | 171,278 | 193,380 | 225,033 |
| Machinery and transport equipment | 194,582 | 272,501 | 350,820 |
| Miscellaneous manufactured articles | 87,458 | 99,176 | 112,320 |
| **Total** (incl. others) | 594,629 | 722,501 | 850,240 |

* Preliminary figures.

**SELECTED TRADING PARTNERS** (million koruny)

| Imports f.o.b. | 1996 | 1997* | 1998* |
|---|---|---|---|
| Austria | 43,273 | 52,238 | 54,466 |
| China, People's Republic | 8,096 | 11,971 | 16,083 |
| France | 31,513 | 35,505 | 41,589 |
| Germany | 224,224 | 274,908 | 330,732 |
| Hungary | 7,481 | 11,255 | 13,493 |
| Italy | 44,335 | 47,390 | 48,610 |
| Japan | 12,856 | 16,613 | 17,200 |
| Netherlands | 17,105 | 20,786 | 22,272 |
| Poland | 21,901 | 27,609 | 31,325 |
| Russia | 55,907 | 57,435 | 51,186 |
| Slovakia | 71,946 | 72,081 | 66,897 |
| Switzerland | 13,257 | 14,251 | 16,568 |
| United Kingdom | 28,277 | 33,439 | 35,413 |
| USA | 25,502 | 32,637 | 34,675 |
| **Total** (incl. others) | 752,344 | 861,770 | 929,979 |

* Preliminary figures.

| Exports f.o.b. | 1996 | 1997* | 1998* |
|---|---|---|---|
| Austria | 38,312 | 46,420 | 53,500 |
| France | 17,003 | 22,980 | 28,684 |
| Germany | 214,163 | 258,251 | 327,554 |
| Hungary | 10,604 | 13,564 | 16,181 |
| Italy | 19,541 | 26,454 | 31,960 |
| Netherlands | 12,337 | 17,481 | 19,236 |
| Poland | 32,713 | 41,447 | 48,074 |
| Russia | 18,802 | 24,498 | 21,195 |
| Slovakia | 84,694 | 93,304 | 90,549 |
| Switzerland | 7,054 | 8,761 | 10,610 |
| United Kingdom | 14,975 | 21,876 | 28,884 |
| USA | 12,629 | 18,602 | 18,981 |
| **Total** (incl. others) | 594,629 | 722,501 | 850,240 |

* Preliminary figures.

# Transport

**RAILWAYS** (traffic)

| | 1996 | 1997 | 1998 |
|---|---|---|---|
| Passenger-km (million) | 8,111 | 7,710 | 7,001 |
| Freight net ton-km (million) | 24,174 | 22,173 | 19,529 |

**ROAD TRAFFIC** (motor vehicles in use at 31 December)

| | 1996 | 1997 | 1998 |
|---|---|---|---|
| Passenger cars* | 3,349,008 | 3,547,745 | 3,687,451 |
| Buses and coaches | 21,460 | 20,916 | 20,505 |
| Goods vehicles† | 235,114 | 265,598 | 312,404 |
| Motorcycles | 439,247 | 438,484 | 446,350 |

* Including vans.
† Excluding special-purpose lorries.

**INLAND WATERWAYS** (freight carried, '000 metric tons)

| | 1996 | 1997 | 1998 |
|---|---|---|---|
| Imports | 627 | 488 | 583 |
| Exports | 1,077 | 834 | 717 |
| Internal | 1,513 | 428 | 223 |
| **Total** (incl. others) | 3,252 | 1,828 | 1,678 |

**AIR TRANSPORT**

| | 1996 | 1997 | 1998 |
|---|---|---|---|
| Kilometres flown ('000) | 37,767 | 41,473 | 45,842 |
| Passengers carried ('000) | 1,982 | 2,166 | 2,377 |
| Freight carried (metric tons) | 13,959 | 13,585 | 13,168 |
| Passenger-km ('000) | 3,170,030 | 3,522,649 | 3,680,215 |
| Freight ton-km ('000) | 25,920 | 27,233 | 55,782 |

# Tourism

**FOREIGN TOURIST ARRIVALS***

| Country of origin | 1996 | 1997 | 1998 |
|---|---|---|---|
| Austria | 199,355 | 197,358 | 203,723 |
| Denmark | 95,112 | 106,631 | 133,600 |
| France | 149,295 | 161,427 | 178,772 |
| Germany | 1,668,849 | 1,753,858 | 1,731,103 |
| Italy | 250,237 | 282,220 | 287,183 |
| Netherlands | 312,043 | 267,240 | 296,100 |
| Poland | 213,543 | 247,030 | 346,843 |
| Russia | 149,462 | 211,639 | 273,658 |
| Slovakia | 207,714 | 243,308 | 266,425 |
| Spain | 134,730 | 139,742 | 139,581 |
| United Kingdom | 188,312 | 234,212 | 256,553 |
| USA | 185,691 | 201,827 | 246,392 |
| **Total** (incl. others) | 4,558,322 | 4,975,658 | 5,482,080 |

* Figures refer to visitors staying for at least one night at registered accommodation facilities.

**Tourism receipts** (US $ million): 4,075 in 1996; 3,647 in 1997; 3,792 in 1998 (Source: partly IMF, *Czech Republic: Statistical Appendix*, August 1999).

## Communications Media

| | 1996 | 1997 | 1998 |
|---|---|---|---|
| Radio receivers ('000 in use) | 8,261 | n.a. | n.a. |
| Television receivers ('000 in use) | 5,469 | n.a. | n.a. |
| Telephones (main lines in use) | 3,017,530 | 3,806,112 | 4,693,042 |
| Mobile cellular telephones (subscribers) | 203,180 | 524,641 | 968,760 |
| Book production: titles | 10,244 | 11,519 | 11,738 |
| Daily newspapers (number) | 90 | 99 | 103 |
| Other periodicals (number) | 4,938 | 5,164 | 5,337 |

Telefax stations: 73,552 in use in 1995.

Source: partly UNESCO, *Statistical Yearbook*, and UN, *Statistical Yearbook*.

## Education

(1998/99)

| | Institutions | Teachers | Students |
|---|---|---|---|
| Pre-primary | 7,037 | 26,559 | 311,755 |
| Basic: | | | |
| Primary | 4,948 | 52,047 | 654,513 |
| Lower secondary | 3,796 | 39,193 | 540,311 |
| Upper secondary: | | | |
| General | 350 | 7,088 | 77,636 |
| Technical and vocational schools | 1,674 | 48,126 | 371,790 |
| Tertiary: | | | |
| Universities | 23 | 15,763 | 206,641 |
| Higher professional schools | 168 | 5,904 | 29,566 |

Source: Institute for Information on Education, Prague.

# Directory

## The Constitution

The following is a summary of the main provisions of the Constitution of the Czech Republic, which was adopted on 16 December 1992 and entered into force on 1 January 1993:

### GENERAL PROVISIONS

The Czech Republic is a sovereign, unified and democratic law-abiding state, founded on the respect for the rights and freedoms of the individual and citizen. All state power belongs to the people, who exercise this power through the intermediary of legislative, executive and judicial bodies. The fundamental rights and freedoms of the people are under the protection of the judiciary.

The political system is founded on the free and voluntary operation of political parties respecting fundamental democratic principles and rejecting force as a means to assert their interests. Political decisions derive from the will of the majority, expressed through the free ballot. Minorities are protected in decision-making by the majority.

The territory of the Czech Republic encompasses an indivisible whole, whose state border may be changed only by constitutional law. Procedures covering the acquisition and loss of Czech citizenship are determined by law. No one may be deprived of his or her citizenship against his or her will.

### GOVERNMENT

**Legislative Power**

Legislative power in the Czech Republic is vested in two chambers, the Chamber of Deputies and the Senate. The Chamber of Deputies has 200 members, elected for a term of four years. The Senate has 81 members, elected for a term of six years. Every two years one-third of the senators are elected. Both chambers elect their respective Chairman and Deputy Chairmen from among their members. Members of both chambers of the legislature are elected on the basis of universal, equal and direct suffrage by secret ballot. All citizens of 18 years and over are eligible to vote.

The legislature enacts the Constitution and laws; approves the state budget and the state final account; and approves the electoral law and international agreements. It elects the President of the Republic (at a joint session of both chambers), supervises the activities of the Government, and decides upon the declaration of war.

**President of the Republic**

The President of the Republic is Head of State. He/she is elected for a term of five years by a joint session of both chambers of the legislature. The President may not be elected for more than two consecutive terms.

The President appoints, dismisses and accepts the resignation of the Prime Minister and other members of the Government, dismisses the Government and accepts its resignation; convenes sessions of the Chamber of Deputies; may dissolve the Chamber of Deputies; names the judges of the Constitutional Court, its Chairman and Deputy Chairmen; appoints the Chairman and Deputy Chairmen of the Supreme Court; has the right to return adopted constitutional laws to the legislature; initials laws; and appoints members of the Council of the Czech National Bank. The President also represents the State in external affairs; is the Supreme Commander of the Armed Forces; receives heads of diplomatic missions; calls elections to the Chamber of Deputies and to the Senate; and has the right to grant amnesty.

**Council of Ministers**

The Council of Ministers is the highest organ of executive power. It is composed of the Prime Minister, the Deputy Prime Ministers and Ministers. It is answerable to the Chamber of Deputies. The President of the Republic appoints the Prime Minister, on whose recommendation he/she appoints the remaining members of the Council of Ministers and entrusts them with directing the ministries or other offices.

### JUDICIAL SYSTEM

Judicial power is exercised on behalf of the Republic by independent courts. Judges are independent in the exercise of their function. The judiciary consists of the Supreme Court, the Supreme Administrative Court, high, regional and district courts.

The Constitutional Court is a judicial body protecting constitutionality. It consists of 15 judges appointed for a 10-year term by the President of the Republic with the consent of the Senate.

## The Government

### HEAD OF STATE

**President:** VÁCLAV HAVEL (elected 26 January 1993; re-elected 20 January 1998).

### COUNCIL OF MINISTERS

(February 2000)

A minority Government of the Czech Social Democratic Party (CSDP). All ministers are from the CSDP, except the Minister of Justice, Otakar Motejl, who is an Independent.

**Prime Minister:** MILOŠ ZEMAN.

**Deputy Prime Minister for Economic Policies and Minister of Finance:** PAVEL MERTLIK.

**Deputy Prime Minister responsible for Legislation:** PAVEL RYCHETSKÝ.

**Deputy Prime Minister and Minister of Employment and Social Affairs:** VLADIMIR ŠPIDLA.

**Deputy Prime Minister and Minister of Foreign Affairs:** JAN KAVAN.

**Minister of Defence:** VLADIMIR VETCHÝ.

**Minister of the Interior:** VÁCLAV GRULICH.

**Minister of Agriculture:** JAN FENCL.

**Minister of the Environment:** MILOŠ KUŽVART.

**Minister of Health:** Bohumil Fišer.

**Minister of Education, Youth and Sport:** Eduard Zeman.

**Minister of Transport and Communications:** Antonín Peltrám.

**Minister of Justice:** Otakar Motejl.

**Minister of Culture:** Pavel Dostál.

**Minister for Regional Development:** Jaromír Cisař.

**Minister of Trade and Industry:** Miroslav Grégr .

**Minister without Portfolio:** Jaroslav Bašta.

### MINISTRIES

**Office of the Government of the Czech Republic:** nábř. E. Beneše 4, 118 01 Prague 1; tel. (2) 24002111; fax (2) 24810231; e-mail www@vlada.cz; internet www.vlada.cz.

**Ministry of Agriculture:** Těšnov 17, 117 05 Prague 1; tel. (2) 2181111; fax (2) 24810478; e-mail vicenova@mze.cz.

**Ministry of Culture:** Milady Horákové 220/139, 160 41 Prague 6; tel. (2) 57085111; fax (2) 24318155.

**Ministry of Defence:** Tychonova 1, 160 01 Prague 6; tel. (2) 20201111; fax (2) 3116238.

**Ministry of Education, Youth and Sport:** Karmelitská 8, 118 12 Prague 1; tel. (2) 57193111; fax (2) 57193790; e-mail kastan@msmt.cz; internet www.msmt.cz.

**Ministry of Employment and Social Affairs:** Na poříčním právu 1, 128 01 Prague 2; tel. (2) 21921111; fax (2) 21922664.

**Ministry of the Environment:** Vršovická 65, 100 10 Prague 10; tel. (2) 67121111; fax (2) 67310308; e-mail info@env.cz.

**Ministry of Finance:** Letenská 15, 118 00 Prague 1; tel. (2) 57041111; fax (2) 57042788.

**Ministry of Foreign Affairs:** Loretánské nám. 5, 118 00 Prague 1; tel. (2) 24181111; fax (2) 24310017.

**Ministry of Health:** Palackého nám. 4, POB 81, 128 01 Prague 2; tel. (2) 24971111; fax (2) 24972111; e-mail mzcr@mzcr.cz.

**Ministry of the Interior:** Nad štolou 3, 170 34 Prague 7; tel. (2) 61432972; fax (2) 61433552; e-mail public@mvcr.cz.

**Ministry of Justice:** Vyšehradská 16, 128 10 Prague 2; tel. (2) 219977111; fax (2) 291720.

**Ministry of Regional Development:** Staroměstskě nám. 6, 110 15 Prague 1; tel. (2) 24861111; fax (2) 24861333.

**Ministry of Trade and Industry:** Na Františku 32, 110 15 Prague 1; tel. (2) 24851111; fax (2) 24811089.

**Ministry of Transport and Communications:** nábř. L. Svobody 12, 110 15 Prague 1; tel. (2) 23031111; fax (2) 24810596.

## Legislature

The Czech Constitution, which was adopted in December 1992, provided for the creation of a bicameral legislature as the highest organ of state authority in the Czech Republic (which was established as an independent state on 1 January 1993, following the dissolution of the Czech and Slovak Federative Republic). The lower house, the Chamber of Deputies, retained the structure of the Czech National Council (the former republican legislature). The upper chamber, or Senate, was first elected in November 1996.

### CHAMBER OF DEPUTIES
(Poslanecká sněmovna)

**Chairman:** Václav Klaus.

**General election, 19–20 June 1998**

| Party | % of votes | Seats |
|---|---|---|
| Czech Social Democratic Party | 32.3 | 74 |
| Civic Democratic Party | 27.7 | 63 |
| Communist Party of Bohemia and Moravia | 11.0 | 24 |
| Christian Democratic Union–Czechoslovak People's Party | 9.0 | 20 |
| Freedom Union | 8.6 | 19 |
| Others | 11.4 | — |
| **Total** | 100.0 | 200 |

### SENATE
(Senát)

**Chairman:** Libuse Benesova.

| Party | Seats after elections* November 1996 | November 1998 |
|---|---|---|
| Civic Democratic Party | 32 | 27 |
| Czech Social Democratic Party | 25 | 20 |
| Christian Democratic Union–Czechoslovak People's Party† | 13 | 12 |
| Civic Democratic Alliance† | 7 | 5 |
| Communist Party of Bohemia and Moravia | 2 | 4 |
| Freedom Union† | — | 1 |
| Independents | — | 12 |
| Others | 2 | — |
| **Total** | 81 | 81 |

* One-third of the 81 seats are renewable every two years.

† Contested the 1998 elections as an informal electoral alliance, together with the Democratic Union.

## Political Organizations

**Alternative 2000** (Alternativa 2000): POB 154, 718 00 Ostrava 18; e-mail kvazar@telecom.cz; f. 1998.

**Association for the Republic–Republican Party of Czechoslovakia** (Sdružení pro republiku–Republikánská strana Československa): Gerstnerova 5, 170 00 Prague 7; tel. (2) 20571450; fax (2) 20570075; f. 1989; extreme right-wing; Chair. Miroslav Sládek; Vice-Chair. Martin Smetana.

**Christian Democratic Union–Czechoslovak People's Party** (Křesťanská a demokratická unie–Československá strana lidová): Revoluční 5, 110 15 Prague 1; tel. (2) 2328086; fax (2) 24812114; f. 1992; Chair. Jan Kasal.

**Civic Democratic Alliance (CDA)** (Občanská demokratická aliance): Štefánikova 21, 150 00 Prague 5; tel. (2) 57329855; fax (2) 57327072; e-mail usek@oda.cz; internet www.oda.cz; f. 1991 as a formal political party, following a split in Civic Forum (f. 1989); fmrly an informal group within Civic Forum; conservative; Chair. Daniel Kroupa.

**Civic Democratic Party (CDP)** (Občanská demokratická strana): Sněmovní 3, 110 00 Prague 1; tel. (2) 3114809; fax (2) 24510731; e-mail foreign@ods.cz; f. 1991 following a split in Civic Forum (f. 1989); merged with Christian Democratic Party in 1996; liberal-conservative; c.17,000 mems (March 1998); Chair. Václav Klaus.

**Communist Party of Bohemia and Moravia** (Komunistická strana Čech a Moravy): Politických vězňů 9, 111 21 Prague 1; tel. (2) 24210172; fax 24264572; e-mail leftnews@kscm.cz; internet www.ksm.cz; f. 1991 as a result of the reorganization of the fmr Communist Party of Czechoslovakia; c. 200,000 mems; Leader Miroslav Grebeníček.

**Communist Party of Czechoslovakia:** f. 1995 as Party of Czechoslovak Communists; renamed as above 1999; 19,980 mems; Sec.-Gen. Miroslav Stepan.

**Conservative Consensus Party** (Strana konzervativní smlouvy): Címská 26, 120 00 Prague 2; tel. (2) 250223; fax (2) 259424; e-mail skos@skos.cz; f. 1998 by fmr mems of right-wing faction in CDA.

**Countryside Party:** f. 1996 to promote interests of rural areas; c. 3,000 mems; Chair. Jan Veleba.

**Czech Right** (Česká pravice): Pod Dívínem 34, 150 00 Prague 5; e-mail cp-praha@ceskapravice.cz; f. 1994; conservative.

**Czech Social Democratic Party (CSDP)** (Česká strana sociálně demokratická): Lidový dům, Hybernská 7, 110 00 Prague 1; tel. and fax (2) 24226222; f. 1878; prohibited 1948; re-established 1989; formerly the Czechoslovak Social Democratic Party; Chair. Ing. Miloš Zeman.

**Democratic Left** (Strana demokratická levice): Čitná 49, 110 00 Prague 1; tel. (2) 24221313; fax (2) 24221506; Chair. Josef Meěl.

**Democratic Socialist Party** (Strana demokratického socialismu): e-mail mailto:secret@sds.cz; f. 1997 by merger of Left Bloc and Party of the Democratic Left; c. 9,000 mems; Chair. Marie Stiborová.

**Democratic Union** (Demokratická unie): Revoluční 5, POB 3, 110 15 Prague 1; tel. and fax (2) 2323996; e-mail deu@login.cz; internet www.deu.cz; right-wing; c. 2,000 mems; Chair. Ratibor Majzlík.

**Free Democrats–Liberal National Social Party** (Svobodní demokraté–Liberální strana národně sociální): Republiky nám. 7, 111 49 Prague 1; tel. (2) 24223443; fax (2) 21618554; e-mail sdlsns@mbox.vol.cz; f. 1995 by merger of Free Democrats (fmrly Civic Movement) and Liberal National Social Party (fmrly Czechoslovak Socialist Party); Chair. Jiří Dienstbier .

**Freedom Union** (Unie svobody): Legerova 72, 120 00 Prague 2; tel. (2) 24221291; fax (2) 24221215; e-mail info@unie.cz; internet www.uniesvobody.cz; f. 1998, following a split in the Civic Democratic Party; c.2,500 mems (March 1998); Chair. KAREL KÜHNL.

**Green Party** (Strana zelených): Murmanská 13, Prague 10; tel. and fax (2) 736580; f. 1989; Chair. JAROSLAV VLČEK.

**Moravian Democratic Party:** Brno; f. 1997 by merger of Bohemian–Moravian Union of the Centre and Moravian National Party; Chair. IVAN DRIMAL.

# Diplomatic Representation

### EMBASSIES IN THE CZECH REPUBLIC

**Afghanistan:** V tišině 6, 160 00 Prague 6; tel. and fax (2) 372417; Chargé d'affaires a.i.: WAZIR AHMAD FAIZI.

**Albania:** Pod kaštany 22, 160 00 Prague 6; tel. (2) 379329; fax (2) 371742; Ambassador: PIRO MIBICANI.

**Algeria:** V tišině 10/483, POB 021, 225 21 Prague 025; tel. (2) 33371142; fax (2) 33371144; Ambassador: ABDERRAHMANE MEZIANE-CHERIF.

**Argentina:** Washingtonova 25, 225 22 Prague 1; tel. (2) 24212448; fax (2) 22241246; Ambassador: HORACIO ADOLFO BASABE.

**Austria:** Viktora Huga 10, 151 15 Prague 5; tel. (2) 57321282; fax (2) 57316045; Ambassador: PETER NIESNER.

**Belarus:** Sádky 626, 171 00 Prague 7; tel. (2) 6888216; fax (2) 6888217; Ambassador: ULADZIMIR PETROVIČ BELSKY.

**Belgium:** Valdštejnská 6, 118 01 Prague 1; tel. (2) 57320389; fax (2) 57320753; Ambassador: BERNARD PIERRE.

**Brazil:** Sušická 12, POB 79, 160 41 Prague 6; tel. (2) 3116694; fax (2) 3118274; Ambassador: SERGIO PAULO ROUANET.

**Bulgaria:** Krakovská 6, 125 25 Prague 1; tel. (2) 22211259; fax (2) 22211728; e-mail bulvelv@mbox.vol.cz; Ambassador: MARTIN TOMOV.

**Cambodia:** Na Hubálce 1, 169 00 Prague 6; tel. (2) 352603; fax (2) 351078; Chargé d'affaires a.i.: MAKANA YOUS.

**Canada:** Mickiewiczova 6, 125 33 Prague 6; tel. (2) 24311108; fax (2) 24310294; internet www.dfait-maeci.gc.ca/~prague/; Ambassador: RONALD HALPIN.

**Chile:** U Vorlíků 4/623, 160 00 Prague 6; tel. (2) 24315064; fax (2) 24316069; e-mail echilecz@mbox.vol.cz; internet www.eol.cz/CHILE; Ambassador: RICARDO CONCHA GAZMURI.

**China, People's Republic:** Pelléova 22, 160 00 Prague 6; tel. (2) 24311323; fax (2) 324902; Ambassador: YAN PENG.

**Colombia:** Washingtonova 25, 110 00 Prague 1; tel. (2) 21674200; fax (2) 24225538; Ambassador: ENRIQUE GAVIRIA LIEVANO.

**Costa Rica:** Eliášova 21, 160 00 Prague 6; tel. and fax (2) 3123750; Chargé d'affaires a.i.: JOHNNY JOSÉ SUÁREZ SANDÍ.

**Croatia:** V Průhledu 9, 162 00 Prague 6; tel. (2) 3120479; fax (2) 3123464; Ambassador: ZORAN PIČULJAN.

**Cuba:** Na Kazance 7/634, apts. 18 až 19, 177 00 Prague 7; tel. (2) 8544228; fax (2) 8544227; Chargé d'affaires a.i.: ALCIDES DE LA ROSA DEL TORO.

**Cyprus:** Eliasova 21, 160 00 Prague 6; tel. (2) 3124111; fax (2) 4314225; e-mail cyprusembass@mbox.vol.cz; Ambassador: ATHENA MAVRONICOLA.

**Denmark:** Maltézské nám. č. 5, POB 25, 118 01 Prague 1; tel. (2) 57316630; fax (2) 57316640; e-mail danemb@terminal.cz; internet www.denmark.cz; Ambassador: ULRIK HELWEG-LARSEN.

**Egypt:** Pelléova 14, 160 00 Prague 6; tel. (2) 24311516; fax (2) 24311157; Ambassador: ASSEM A. MEGAHED.

**Estonia:** Na Kampě 1, 118 00 Prague 1; tel. (2) 57317791; fax (2) 57317792; e-mail sekretar@estemb.cz; Chargé d'affaires a.i.: RIHO LAANEMÄE.

**Finland:** Hellichova 1, Chotkův palác, 110 00 Prague 1; tel. (2) 57007130; fax (2) 57007132; Ambassador: RISTO RÄNNÄLI.

**France:** Velkopřevorské nám. 2, POB 102, 118 01 Prague 1; tel. (2) 57532756; fax (2) 57532757; e-mail ambafrcz@mbox.vol.cz; Ambassador: PHILIPPE COSTE.

**Germany:** Vlašská 19, 118 01 Prague 1; tel. (2) 57113111; fax (2) 57320043; Ambassador: MICHAEL STEINER.

**Ghana:** V tišině 4, 160 00 Prague 6; tel. (2) 33377236; fax (2) 33375647; e-mail ghanaemb@mbox.vol.cz; Ambassador: S. VALIS-AKYIANU.

**Greece:** Na Ořechovce 19, 162 00 Prague 6; tel. (2) 3121702; fax (2) 24311235; Ambassador: GEORGES LINARDOS.

**Holy See:** Voršilská 12, 110 00 Prague 1; tel. (2) 24912192; fax (2) 24914160; e-mail nunciatgc@mbox.vol.cz; Apostolic Nuncio: Most Rev. GIOVANNI COPPA, Titular Archbishop of Serta.

**Hungary:** Badeniho 1, 225 37 Prague 6; tel. (2) 365041; fax (2) 329425; Ambassador: ZOLTÁN VEZÉR.

**India:** Valdštejnská 6, Malastrana, 118 00 Prague 1; tel. (2) 57320255; fax (2) 57314432; e-mail Indembprague@bohem-net.cz; Ambassador: GIRISH DHUME.

**Indonesia:** Nad Bud'ánkami II/7, 150 00 Prague 5; tel. (2) 57214388; fax (2) 57212105; e-mail informace@indoneske-velvyslanectvi.cz; internet www.indoneske-velvyslanectvi.cz; Ambassador: SOENARTO SOEDARNO.

**Iran:** Na Zátorce 18, 160 00 Prague 6; tel. (2) 20570454; fax (2) 371468; Ambassador: SEYED-JAFAR HASHEMI (recalled Nov. 1998).

**Iraq:** Na Zátorce 10, 160 00 Prague 6; tel. (2) 24321715; fax (2) 24315748; Ambassador: SADIQ KH. R. AHMED.

**Ireland:** Tržiště 13, 118 00 Prague 1; tel. (2) 57530061; fax (2) 57311492; Ambassador: MICHAEL COLLINS.

**Israel:** Badeniho 2, 170 06 Prague 7; tel. (2) 33325109; fax (2) 33320092; e-mail israemba@bohem-net.cz; Ambassador: ERELLA HADAR.

**Italy:** Nerudova 20, 118 00 Prague 1; tel. (2) 33080111; fax (2) 57531522; e-mail italemba@mbox.vol.cz; internet www.italianembassy.cz; Ambassador: PAOLO FAIOLA.

**Japan:** Maltézské nám. 6, 118 01 Prague 1; tel. (2) 57320561; fax (2) 539997; Ambassador: SHUNJI MARUYAMA.

**Kazakhstan:** Fetrovská 15, 160 00 Prague 6; tel. (2) 3114596; fax (2) 3112124; Ambassador: TULEUTAI SULEIMENOV.

**Korea, Democratic People's Republic:** Na Zátorce 6, 160 00 Prague 6; tel. (2) 24320783; fax (2) 24318817; Chargé d'affaires a.i.: KIM JONG NAM.

**Korea, Republic:** Slavíčkova 5, 160 00 Prague 6; tel. (2) 24318100; fax (2) 24320538; Ambassador: CHO CHANG-BEOM.

**Kuwait:** Pod kaštany 2, 160 00 Prague 6; tel. (2) 24311966; fax (2) 24311972; Ambassador: AHMAD BU-ZUOBAR.

**Latvia:** Hradešínská 3, POB 54, 101 00 Prague 10; tel. (2) 24252454; fax (2) 24255099; Ambassador: AIJA ODINA.

**Lebanon:** Masarykovo nábřeží 14, 110 00 Prague 1; tel. (2) 293633; fax (2) 293406; Ambassador: SLEIMAN YOUNES.

**Libya:** Na baště sv. Jiří 5–7, 160 00 Prague 6; tel. (2) 323410; fax (2) 329119; Chargé d'affaires a.i.: MILUD MOHAMED JADID.

**Lithuania:** Pod Klikovkou 1916/2, 150 00 Prague 5; tel. (2) 57210122; fax (2) 57210124; e-mail ltembcz@mbox.vol.cz; internet www.ltembassycz.urrn.lt; Ambassador: VYGINTAS GRINIS.

**Mexico:** Nad Kazankou 8, 171 00 Prague 7; tel. (2) 8555554; fax (2) 8550477; Ambassador: GONZALO AGUIRRE ENRILE.

**Mongolia:** Na Marně 5, 160 00 Prague 6; tel. (2) 24311198; fax (2) 24314827; Chargé d'affaires: NAIDANSUREN JARGALSAIKHAN.

**Morocco:** Ke starému Bubenči 4, 160 00 Prague 6; tel. (2) 329404; fax (2) 321758; Ambassador: ABDESSELEM OUAZZANI.

**Netherlands:** Gotthardská 6/27, 225 40 Prague 6; tel. (2) 24312190; fax (2) 24312160; Ambassador: PETER F. C. KOCH.

**Nigeria:** Před bateriemi 18, 162 01 Prague 6; tel. (2) 24312065; fax (2) 24312072; e-mail embassy@nigeria.cz; Chargé d'affaires a.i.: ABBA A. TIJJANT.

**Norway:** Na Ořechovce 69, 162 00 Prague 6; tel. (2) 3111411; fax (2) 3123797; Ambassador: LASSE SEIM.

**Pakistan:** Šmolíkova 1009, 161 00 Prague 6; tel. (2) 33312421; fax (2) 33311369; Ambassador: SAMUEL THOMAS JOSHUA.

**Peru:** Muchova 9, 160 00 Prague 6; tel. (2) 24316210; fax (2) 24314749; e-mail emba.peru.praga@ms.anat.cz; Ambassador: A. RAÚL PATIÑO-ALVÍSTUR.

**Philippines:** Karolíny Světlé 34, 110 00 Prague 1; tel. (2) 21635301; fax (2) 21635302; Ambassador: CARMELITA RODRÍGUEZ SALAS.

**Poland:** Valdštejnská 8, 118 01 Prague 1; tel. (2) 5732068; fax (2) 57320764; e-mail ambpolcz@mbox.vol.cz; Ambassador: MAREK PERNAL.

**Portugal:** Kinských nám. 7, 150 00 Prague 5; tel. (2) 57311230; fax (2) 57311234; Ambassador: ANTÓNIO CASCAIS.

**Romania:** Nerudova 5, POB 87, 118 10 Prague 1; tel. (2) 57320494; fax (2) 534393; Ambassador: NICOLAE VULPAŞIN.

**Russia:** Pod kaštany 1, 160 00 Prague 6; tel. (2) 33374100; fax (2) 373800; e-mail rusembas@bohem-net.cz; Ambassador: NIKOLAI T. RYABOV.

**Slovakia:** Pod hradbami 1, 160 00 Prague 6; tel. (2) 320521; fax (2) 320401; Ambassador: IVAN MJARTAN.

**Slovenia:** Pod hradbami 15, 160 41 Prague 6; tel. (2) 24315106; fax (2) 24314106; Ambassador: DAMJAN PRELOVŠEK.

**South Africa:** Ruská 65, POB 133, 100 00 Prague 10; tel. (2) 67311114; fax (2) 67311395; e-mail saprague@terminal.cz; Ambassador: THOMAS LANGLEY.

**Spain:** Pevnostní 9, 162 00 Prague 6; tel. (2) 24311222; fax (2) 3121770; Ambassador: JUAN M. DE BARANDICA Y LUXÁN.

**Sweden:** Úvoz 13-Hradčany, POB 35, 160 12 Prague 612; tel. (2) 20313200; fax (2) 20313240; e-mail ambassaden.prag@foreign.ministry.se; Ambassador: INGMAR KARLSSON.

**Switzerland:** Pevnostní 7, POB 84, 162 01 Prague 6; tel. (2) 24311228; fax (2) 24311312; Ambassador: WALTER FETSCHERIN.

**Syria:** Pod kaštany 16, 160 00 Prague 6; tel. (2) 24310952; fax (2) 24317911; Chargé d'affaires a.i.: HAYSSAM MASHFEJ.

**Thailand:** Romaina Rollanda 3, 160 00 Prague 6; tel. (2) 20571435; fax (2) 20570049; e-mail thai@thaiemb.cz; internet www.thaiemb.cz; Ambassador: NARIM PONTHAM.

**Tunisia:** Nad Kostelem 8, 147 00 Prague 4; tel. (2) 44460652; fax (2) 44460825; e-mail atprague@vol.cz; Ambassador: MONDHER MAMI.

**Turkey:** Pevnostní 3, 162 00 Prague 6; tel. (2) 24311402; fax (2) 24311279; Ambassador: TEMEL ISKIT.

**Ukraine:** Charlese de Gaulla 29, 160 00 Prague 6; tel. (2) 3122000; fax (2) 3124366; e-mail kosak@mbox.vol.cz; Ambassador: SERHII USTYCH.

**United Kingdom:** Thunovská 14, 118 00 Prague 1; tel. (2) 57320355; fax (2) 57321023; e-mail info@britain.cz; internet www.britain.cz; Ambassador: DAVID BROUCHER.

**USA:** Tržiště 15, 118 01 Prague 1; tel. (2) 57530663; fax (2) 57530583; Ambassador: JOHN SHATTUCK.

**Uruguay:** Malátova 12, 150 00 Prague 5; tel. (2) 545455; fax (2) 548852; Ambassador: Dr JOSÉ LUIS REMEDI.

**Venezuela:** Jánský vršek 2/350, 118 00 Prague 1; tel. (2) 57313740; fax (2) 57313742; e-mail embaven@mbox.vol.cz; internet www.vol.cz/embavenezuela; Chargé d'affaires a.i.: OSWALDO A. NIÑO H.

**Viet Nam:** Plzeňská 214, 150 00 Prague 5; tel. (2) 57211540; fax (2) 57211792; Ambassador: NGUYEN VAN KHIEU.

**Yemen:** Pod hradbami 5, 160 00 Prague 6; tel. (2) 3111598; Ambassador: ALI ABDULLAH ABO-LOHOM.

**Yugoslavia:** Mostecká 15, 118 00 Prague 1; tel. (2) 57320031; fax (2) 57320491; Ambassador: DJOKO STOJIČIĆ.

# Judicial System

The judicial system comprises the Supreme Court, the Supreme Administrative Court, chief, regional and district courts. There is also a 15-member Constitutional Court.

**Supreme Court:** Buresova 20, 657 37 Brno; tel. (5) 41321237; fax (5) 412134932; Chair. ELISKA WAGNEROVA.

**Office of the Attorney-General:** Jezuitska 4, 660 55 Brno; tel. (5) 42512111; fax (5) 42219621; Attorney-Gen. MARIE BENESOVA.

**Constitutional Court:** Jostova 8, 660 83 Brno; tel. (5) 42161111; fax (5) 42218326; Chair. ZDENĚK KESSLER.

# Religion

The principal religion in the Czech Republic is Christianity. The largest denomination in 1995 was the Roman Catholic Church. About 30% of the population profess no religious belief.

## CHRISTIANITY

**Ecumenical Council of Churches in the Czech Republic** (Ekumenická rada církví v České republice): Donská 5/370, 101 00 Prague 10; tel. and fax (2) 71742128; e-mail erc@anet.cz; f. 1955; 11 mem. churches; Pres. Rev. PAVEL SMETANA; Gen. Sec. NADĚJE MANDYSOVÁ.

### The Roman Catholic Church

*Latin Rite*

The Czech Republic comprises two archdioceses and six dioceses. At 31 December 1997 there were 4.1m. adherents in the country, representing about 39% of the population.

**Czech Bishops' Conference** (Česká biskupská konference): Thákurova 3, 160 00 Prague 6; tel. (2) 20181421; fax (2) 24310144; e-mail cbk2@ktf.cuni.cz; f. 1990; Pres. Cardinal Dr MILOSLAV VLK, Archbishop of Prague.

**Archbishop of Olomouc:** Most Rev. JAN GRAUBNER, Wurmova 9, 771 01 Olomouc; tel. (68) 5500211; fax (68) 5224840.

**Archbishop of Prague:** Cardinal Dr MILOSLAV VLK, Hradčanské nám. 16, 119 02 Prague 1; tel. (2) 20510615; fax (2) 20514647.

*Byzantine Rite*

**Apostolic Exarch in the Czech Republic:** Rt Rev. IVAN LJAVINEC (Titular Bishop of Acalissus), Haštalské nám. 4, 110 00 Prague 1; tel. and fax (2) 2312817.

### The Eastern Orthodox Church

**Orthodox Church** (Pravoslavná církev): V jámě 6, 111 21 Prague 1; divided into two eparchies: Prague and Olomouc; Head of the Orthodox Church, Metropolitan of Prague and of all Czechoslovakia His Holiness Patriarch DOROTEJ.

### Protestant Churches

**Baptist Union in the Czech Republic:** Na Topolce 14, 140 00 Prague 4; tel. and fax (2) 41434256; e-mail czechbaptist@iol.cz; f. 1994; 2,395 mems; Pres. Rev. MILOŠ SOLA; Sec. Rev. JAN TITERA.

**Brethren Church:** Soukenická 15, 110 00 Prague 1; tel. and fax (2) 2318131; e-mail pavel.cerny@cb.cz; internet www.cbchurch.cz; f. 1880; 8,331 mems, 46 churches; Pres. PAVEL ČERNÝ; Sec. KAREL FOJTÍK.

**Christian Corps:** nám. Konečného 5, 602 00 Brno; tel. (5) 756365; 3,200 mems; 123 brs; Rep. Ing. PETR ZEMAN.

**Evangelical Church of Czech Brethren** (Presbyterian): Jungmannova 9, 111 21 Prague 1; tel. (2) 24947503; fax (2) 24948556; f. 1781; united since 1918; activities extend over Bohemia, Moravia and Silesia; 138,616 adherents (1997) and 264 parishes (1995); Pres. Rev. PAVEL SMETANA; Synodal Curator Dr LYDIE ROSKOVCOVÁ.

**Silesian Evangelical Church of the Augsburg Confession in the Czech Republic** (Silesian Lutheran Church): Na nivách 7, 737 01 Český Těšín; tel. (659) 731804; fax (659) 731815; founded in the 16th century during the Lutheran Reformation, reorganized in 1948; 49,588 mems (1994); Bishop VLADISLAV VOLNÝ.

**United Methodist Church:** Ječná 19, 120 00 Prague 2; tel. (2) 290623; fax (2) 290167; e-mail ecmradacz@mbox.vol.cz; 1,890 mems; 17 parishes; Supt JOSEF ČERVEŇÁK.

**Unity of Brethren** (Moravian Church): Kollárova 456, 509 01 Nová Paka; tel. and fax (434) 621258; e-mail jbmb@iol.cz; internet www.moravian.cz; f. 1457; 2,447 mems; 21 parishes; Pres. Rev. JAROSLAV PLEVA.

### Other Christian Churches

**Apostolic Church in the Czech Republic:** V Zídkách 402, 280 02 Kolín; tel. (321) 720457; fax (321) 727668; e-mail hqbishopac@clever.cz; f. 1989; 3,356 mems; Bishop RUDOLF BUBÍK.

**Church of the Seventh-day Adventists:** Zálesí 50, 142 00 Prague 4; tel. (2) 4723745; fax (2) 4728222; e-mail unie@casd.cz; f. 1919; 10,000 mems; 184 churches; Pres. KAREL NOWAK.

**Czechoslovak Hussite Church:** Wuchterlova 5, 166 26 Prague 6; tel. (2) 20398109; fax (2) 24320308: f. 1920; 131,000 mems; five dioceses, divided into 310 parishes; Bishop-Patriarch JOSEF ŠPAK.

**Old Catholic Church:** Hládkov 3, 169 00 Prague 6; tel. and fax (2) 33353547; e-mail stkat@comp.cz; f. 3,900; 3,900 mems, 12 parishes; Bishop Mgr DUŠAN HEJBAL.

## JUDAISM

**Federation of Jewish Communities in the Czech Republic** (Federace židovských obcí v České republice): Maiselova 18, 110 01 Prague 1; tel. (2) 24811090; fax (2) 24810912; 3,000 mems; Pres. Dr JAN MUNK; Chief Rabbi KAROL SIDON.

# The Press

## PRINCIPAL DAILIES

### Brno

**Brněnský večerník** (Brno Evening Paper): Jakubské nám. 7, 658 44 Brno; tel. (5) 42321227; fax (5) 45215150; f. 1968; Editor-in-Chief PETR HOSKOVEC; circ. 16,000.

**Rovnost** (Equality): M. Horákové 9, 658 22 Brno; tel. (5) 45321121; fax (5) 45212873; f. 1885; morning; Editor-in-Chief LUBOMÍR SELINGER; circ. 62,000.

### České Budějovice

**Jihočeské listy** (South Bohemia Paper): Vrbenská 23, 370 45 České Budějovice; tel. (38) 22081; f. 1991; morning; Editor-in-Chief VLADIMÍR MAJER; circ. 53,000.

### Hradec Králové

**Hradecké noviny** (Hradec News): Škroupova 695, 501 72 Hradec Králové; tel. (49) 613511; fax (49) 615681; Editor-in-Chief JAROMÍR FRIDRICH; circ. 30,000.

### Karlovy Vary

**Karlovarské noviny** (Karlovy Vary News): třída TGM 32, 360 21 Karlovy Vary; tel. (17) 3224496; fax (17) 3225115; f. 1991; Editor-in-Chief JIŘÍ LINHART; circ. 15,000.

### Ostrava

**Moravskoslezský den** (Moravia-Silesia Daily): Novinářská 7, 700 00 Ostrava 1; tel. (69) 55134; fax (69) 57021; f. 1991; Editor-in-Chief VLADIMÍR VAVRDA; circ. 130,000.

**Svoboda** (Freedom): Mlýnská 10, 701 11 Ostrava; tel. (69) 2472311; fax (69) 2472312; f. 1991; morning; Editor-in-Chief JOSEF LYS; circ. 100,000.

### Pardubice

**Pardubické noviny** (Pardubice News): Tříd Míru 60, 530 02 Pardubice; tel. (40) 517366; fax (40) 517156; f. 1991; Editor-in-Chief ROMAN MARČÁK; circ. 15,000.

### Plzeň

**Plzeňský deník** (Plzeň Daily): Husova 15, 304 83 Plzeň; tel. (19) 551111; fax (19) 551234; f. 1991 (fmrly *Pravda*, f. 1919); Editor-in-Chief JAN PERTL; circ. 50,000.

### Prague

**Hospodářské noviny** (Economic News): Dobrovského 25, 170 55 Prague 7; tel. (2) 33071111; fax (2) 33072307; e-mail data@hn.economia.cz; f. 1957; morning; Editor-in-Chief PETR ŠTĚPÁNEK; circ. 130,000.

**Lidové noviny** (People's News): Pobřežni 20/224, 186 21 Prague 8; tel. (2) 67098700; fax (2) 67098799; e-mail inzerce@lidovky.cz; internet www.lidovenoviny.cz; f. 1893, re-established 1988; morning; Editor-in-Chief PAVEL ŠAFR; circ. 83,728.

**Mladá fronta Dnes** (Youth Front Today): Senovážná 4, 110 00 Prague 1; tel. (2) 22062111; fax (2) 22062229; e-mail mfdnes@mafra.cz; f. 1990; morning; independent; Editor-in-Chief PETR ŠABATA; circ. 350,000.

**Právo** (Right): Slezská 13, 120 00 Prague 2; tel. (2) 21001111; fax (2) 21001361; f. 1920, as *Rudé právo*: name changed as above 1995; morning; Editor-in-Chief ZDENĚK PORYBNÝ; circ. 250,000.

**Slovo** (Word): Václavské nám. 36, 112 12 Prague 1; tel. (2) 24227258; fax (2) 24229477; f. 1945; Editor-in-Chief LIBOR ŠEVČÍK; circ. 95,000.

**Večerník Praha** (Evening Prague): Na Florenci 19, 111 21 Prague 1; tel. (2) 24227625; fax (2) 2327361; f. 1991 (fmrly *Večerní Praha*, f. 1955); evening; Editor-in-Chief IVAN ČERVENKA; circ. 130,000.

### Ústí nad Labem

**Severočeský deník** (North Bohemia Daily): Ústí nad Labem; tel. (47) 5220525; fax (47) 5220587; f. 1920; Editor-in-Chief MARIE SRPOVÁ; circ. 95,000.

## PRINCIPAL PERIODICALS

### Czech Language

**100+1 ZZ:** Karlovo nám. 5, 120 00 Prague 2; tel. (2) 293291; fax (2) 299824; f. 1964; fortnightly foreign press digest; Editor-in-Chief VÁCLAV DUŠEK; circ. 85,000.

**Ateliér** (Studio): Masarykovo nábř. 250, 110 00 Prague 1; tel. and fax (2) 291884; e-mail atelier@auclionsarl.cz; f. 1988; visual arts; fortnightly; Editor-in-Chief BLANKA JIRÁČKOVÁ.

**Auto Tip:** Střelnična 1680/8, 182 21 Prague 8; tel. (2) 66193173; fax (2) 66193172; e-mail autotip@automedia.cz; f. 1990; fortnightly for motorists; Editor-in-Chief VLADIMÍR ŠULC; circ. 60,000.

**Českomoravský profit** (Czech–Moravia Profit): Domažlická 3, 130 00 Prague 3; tel. (2) 277084; fax (2) 278514; weekly; Editor-in-Chief JAN BALTUS.

**Divadelní noviny** (Theatre News): c/o Divadelní ústav, Celetná 17, 110 00 Prague 1; tel. and fax (2) 2315912; e-mail divadelni.noviny@czech-theatre.cz; internet www.divadlo.cz/noviny; fortnightly; Editor-in-Chief JAN KOLÁŘ.

**Ekonom** (Economist): Dobrovského 25, 170 55 Prague 7; tel. (2) 33071301; fax (2) 33072002; e-mail ekonom@economia.cz; weekly; Editor-in-Chief EVA KLVAČOVÁ.

**Katolický týdeník** (Catholic Weekly): Londýnská 44, 120 00 Prague 2; tel. (2) 24250385; fax (2) 24257041; e-mail tydenik@mbox.vol.cz; f. 1989; weekly; Editor-in-Chief NORBERT BADAL; circ. 70,000.

**Květy** (Flowers): Na Florenci 3, 117 14 Prague 1; tel. and fax (2) 24219549; f. 1834; illustrated family weekly; Editor-in-Chief JINDŘICH MAŘAN; circ. 320,000.

**Mladý svět** (Young World): Na Poříčí 30, 112 86 Prague 1; tel. (2) 24229087; fax (2) 24210211; f. 1956; illustrated weekly; Editor-in-Chief OLGA DOUBRAVOVÁ; circ. 110,000.

**Obchod-Kontakt-Marketing** (Trade-Contact-Marketing): Korunní 87, 130 00 Prague 3; tel. and fax (2) 255440; monthly; Editor-in-Chief MARCELA NOVÁKOVÁ.

**Reflex:** Jeseniova 51, 130 00 Prague 3; tel. (2) 67097542; fax (2) 61216239; f. 1990; social weekly; Editor-in-Chief PETR BÍLEK; circ. 220,000.

**Respekt:** Sokolská 66, 120 00 Prague 2; tel. (2) 24941962; fax (2) 24941965; e-mail redakce@respekt.cz; f. 1990; political weekly; Editor-in-Chief MARTIN FENDRYCH; circ. 30,000.

**Romano Hangos** (Romany Voice): f. 1999; bi-weekly; Editor-in-Chief KAREL HOLOMEK.

**Romano Kurko** (Romany Week): Černovické nábř. 7, 618 00 Brno; tel. and fax (5) 330785; f. 1991; weekly; in Czech with Romany vocabulary; Dir M. SMOLEŇ; circ. 8,000.

**Sondy** (Soundings): W. Churchilla 2, 130 00 Prague 3; tel. (2) 24462328; fax (2) 24462313; f. 1990; weekly; Editor-in-Chief JANA KAŠPAROVÁ; circ. 40,000.

**Týdeník Rozhlas** (Radio Weekly): Na Florenci 3, 112 86 Prague 1; tel. and fax (2) 2323261; f. 1923; Editor-in-Chief AGÁTA PILÁTOVÁ; circ. 170,000.

**Vesmír** (Universe): Národní 3, 111 42 Prague 1; tel. (2) 24229181; fax (2) 24240513; e-mail vesmir@mbox.cesnet.cz; f. 1871; monthly; popular science magazine; Editor IVAN M. HAVEL; circ. 8,000–10,000.

**Vlasta:** Žitná 18, 120 00 Prague 2; tel. (2) 298641; fax (2) 294535; f. 1947; weekly; illustrated magazine for women; Editor-in-Chief MARIE FORMÁČKOVÁ; circ. 380,000.

**Zahrádkář** (Gardener): Prague; tel. (2) 766346; fax (2) 768042; monthly; Editor-in-Chief ANTONÍN DOLEJŠÍ; circ. 200,000.

**Zora:** Krakovská 21, 115 17 Prague 1; tel. (2) 24228126; fax (2) 24228120; f. 1917; bimonthly; for the visually handicapped; Editor-in-Chief JIŘÍ REICHEL.

### Other Languages

**Amaro Lav** (Our Word): Černovické nábř. 7, 618 00 Brno; tel. and fax (5) 330785; f. 1990; monthly; in Romany and Czech; Dir M. SMOLEŇ; circ. 3,000.

**Czech Business and Trade:** V jirchářích 8, 110 00 Prague 1; tel. (2) 24912185; fax (2) 24912355; e-mail journal@ppagency.cz; internet www.ppagency.cz; f. 1960; monthly; publ. in English, German, Spanish, Russian and French; Editor-in-Chief Dr PAVLA PODSKALSKÁ; circ. 15,000.

**Prager Wochenblatt** (Prague Weekly): Vítkovická 373, 199 00 Prague 9; tel. (2) 6282029; weekly; politics, culture, economy; in German; Editor-in-Chief FELIX SEEBAUER; circ. 30,000.

**Prague Post:** Štěpánská 20 Prague 1; tel. (2) 96334400; fax (2) 96334450; e-mail office@praguepost.cz; f. 1991; political, economic and cultural weekly; in English; Editor-in-Chief ALAN LEVY; circ. 15,000.

**Prognosis:** Prague; tel. (2) 3167007; fax (2) 368139; f. 1991; political, economic and cultural fortnightly; in English; Editor-in-Chief BEN SULLIVAN; circ. 10,000.

## NEWS AGENCIES

**Česká tisková kancelář (ČTK)** (Czech News Agency): Opletalova 5–7, 111 44 Prague 1; tel. (2) 22098111; fax (2) 24220553; e-mail ctk@mail.ctk.cz; internet www.ctk.cz; f. Nov. 1992, assuming control of all property and activities (in the Czech Lands) of the former Czechoslovak News Agency; news and photo exchange service with all international and many national news agencies; maintains network of foreign correspondents; Czech and English general and economic news service; publishes daily bulletins in Czech and English; Gen. Dir Dr MILAN STIBRAL.

### Foreign Bureaux

**Agence France-Presse (AFP):** Ječná 15, 120 00 Prague 2; tel. (2) 24921155; fax (2) 24919155; e-mail afp@mbox.vol.cz; Bureau Chief RENÉ PASCAL BIAGI.

**Agencia EFE** (Spain): Ubrinivenka 65, 100 00 Prague 1; tel. (2) 67313620; fax (2) 67313975; Bureau Chief MIGUEL FERNÁNDEZ.

**Agenzia Nazionale Stampa Associata (ANSA)** (Italy): Prague; tel. and fax (2) 24222793; Bureau Chief LUCIO ATTILIO LEANTE.

**Allgemeiner Deutscher Nachrichtendienst (ADN)** (Germany): Milevská 835, 140 00 Prague 4; tel. (2) 6921911; fax (2) 6921627; Bureau Chief STEFFI GENSICKE.

**Associated Press (AP)** (USA): Prague; tel. (2) 24224346; fax (2) 24227445; Correspondent ONDŘEJ HEJMA.

**Deutsche Presse-Agentur (dpa)** (Germany): Petrské nám. 1, 110 00 Prague 1; tel. (2) 24810290; fax (2) 2315196; Bureau Chief WOLFGANG JUNG.

**Informatsionnoye Telegrafnoye Agentstvo Rossii—Telegrafnoye Agentstvo Suverennykh Stran (ITAR—TASS)** (Russia): Pevnostní 5, 162 00 Prague 6; tel. (2) 328307; fax (2) 327527; Bureau Chief ALEKSANDR YAKOVLEV.

**Magyar Távirati Iroda (MTI)** (Hungary): Prague; tel. and fax (2) 66710131; Bureau Chief GYÖRGY HARSÁNYI.

**Novinska Agencija Tanjug** (Yugoslavia): Prague; tel. (2) 2674401; Correspondent BRANKO STOŠIĆ.

**Polska Agencja Prasowa (PAP)** (Poland): Petrské nám. 1, 110 00 Prague 1; tel. and fax (2) 24812205; Correspondent ZBYGNIEW KRZYSTYNJAK.

**Rossiiskoye Informatsionnoye Agentstvo—Novosti (RIA—Novosti)** (Russia): Italská 36, 130 00 Prague 3; tel. (2) 22253088; fax (2) 22253084; e-mail riapraha@bohem-net.cz; Bureau Chief VALERIJ ENIN.

**Tlačová agentúra Slovenskej republiky (TASR)** (Slovakia): Šmeralova 7, 170 00 Prague 7; tel. (2) 33372617; fax (2) 33379663; e-mail bkopcak@iol.cz; internet www.tasr.sk; Correspondent BOHDAN KOPČÁK.

**Xinhua (New China) News Agency** (People's Republic of China): Pelléova 22, 169 00 Prague 6; tel. and fax (2) 24311325; Correspondent SAN XI-YOU.

### PRESS ASSOCIATION

**Syndicate of Journalists of the Czech Republic:** Pařížská 9, 116 30 Prague 1; tel. (2) 2325109; fax (2) 2327782; e-mail sncr@mbox.vol.cz; f. 1877; reorganized in 1990; 5,000 mems; Chair. IRENA VÁLOVÁ.

## Publishers

**Academia:** Legerova 61, 120 00 Prague 2; tel. (2) 24942584; fax (2) 24941982; f. 1953; scientific books, periodicals; Dir ALEXANDER TOMSKÝ.

**Akcent–Blok:** Rooseveltova 4, 657 00 Brno; tel. and fax (5) 42214516; f. 1957; regional literature, fiction, general; Dir JAROSLAV NOVÁK.

**Albatros:** Truhlářská 9, 110 01 Prague 1; tel. (2) 24810704; fax (2) 24810850; internet www.albatros.cz; f. 1949; literature for children and young people; Dir MARTIN SLAVÍK.

**Kalich, evangelické nakladatelství** (Evangelical Publishing House): Jungmannova 9, 111 21 Prague 1; tel. (2) 2350342; fax (2) 2357594; f. 1920; Dir Ing. JAN RYBÁŘ.

**Kartografie Praha, a.s.:** Fr. Křížka 1, 170 30 Prague 7; tel. (2) 375541; fax (2) 375555; f. 1954; cartographic publishing and printing house; Dir Ing. JIŘÍ KUČERA.

**Kruh** (Circle): Dlouhá 108, 500 21 Hradec Králové; tel. (49) 22076; f. 1966; regional literature, fiction and general; Dir Dr JAN DVOŘÁK.

**Melantrich:** Václavské nám. 36, 112 12 Prague 1; tel. (2) 22093215; fax (2) 24213176; f. 1919; general, fiction, humanities, newspapers and magazines; Dir MILAN HORSKÝ.

**Mladá fronta** (Young Front): Radlická 61, 150 02 Prague 5; tel. (2) 51550008; fax (2) 51554014; e-mail prodej@mfnakl.cz; f. 1945; fiction, history, poetry, popular science, magazines; Dir VLADIMÍR PISTORIUS.

**Nakladatelství dopravy a spojů** (Transport and Communications): Hybernská 5, 115 78 Prague 1; tel. (2) 2365774; fax (2) 2356772; Dir Ing. ALOIS HOUDEK.

**Nakladatelství Svoboda** (Freedom): Na Florenci 3, POB 704, 113 03 Prague 1; tel. (2) 24224705; fax (2) 24226026; f. 1945 as the publishing house of the Communist Party; restructured in 1992–94 as a limited company; in voluntary liquidation since Sept. 1997; politics, history, philosophy, fiction, general; Dir STEFAN SZERYŃSKI.

**Odeon:** Prague; tel. (2) 24225248; fax (2) 24225262; f. 1953; literature, poetry, fiction (classical and modern), literary theory, art books, reproductions; Dir MILUŠE SLAPNIČKOVÁ.

**Olympia:** Klimentská 1, 110 15 Prague 1; tel. (2) 24819491; fax (2) 2315192; e-mail olympia@mbox.vol.cz; f. 1954; sports, tourism, encyclopaedias, fiction, illustrated books; Dir Ing. KAREL ZELNÍČEK.

**Panton:** Radlická 99, 150 00 Prague 5; tel. and fax (2) 548627; f. 1958; publishing house of the Czech Musical Fund; books on music, sheet music, records; Dir KAREL ČERNÝ.

**Práce** (Labour): Václavské nám. 17, 112 58 Prague 1; tel. (2) 24009100; fax (2) 2320989; f. 1945; trade union movement, fiction, general, periodicals; Dir JANA SCHMIDTOVÁ.

**Rapid, a.s.:** 28. října 13, 112 79 Prague 1; tel. (2) 24195111; fax (2) 2327520; advertising; Dir-Gen. ČESTMÍR ČEJKA.

**Severočeské nakladatelství** (North Bohemian Publishing House): Ústí nad Labem; tel. (47) 28581; regional literature, fiction and general; Dir JIŘÍ ŠVEJDA.

**SNTL—Nakladatelství technické literatury** (Technical Literature): Prague; tel. (2) 297670; fax (2) 203774; f. 1953; technology, applied sciences, dictionaries, periodicals; Dir Dr KAREL ČERNÝ (acting).

**Státní pedagogické nakladatelství:** Ostrovní 30, 113 01 Prague 1; tel. and fax (2) 24912206; f. 1775; state publishing house; school and university textbooks, dictionaries, literature; Dir MILAN KOVÁŘ.

**Vyšehrad:** Bartolomějská 9, 110 00 Prague 1; tel. (2) 2326851; fax (2) 268390; e-mail vysehrad@login.cz; f. 1934; religion, philosophy, history, fiction; Dir PRAVOMIL NOVÁK; Chief Editor VLASTA HESOUNOVÁ.

### PUBLISHERS' ASSOCIATION

**Association of Czech Booksellers and Publishers:** Jana Masaryka 56, 120 00 Prague 2; tel. (2) 90030150; fax (2) 22513198; e-mail sckn@mbox.vol.cz; internet www.sckn.knihy.cz; f.1879; Chair. VLADIMÍR PISTORIUS.

### WRITERS' UNION

**Society of Writers** (Obec spisovatelů): POB 669, 111 21 Prague 1; tel. and fax (2) 269072; f. 1989; 700 mems; Dir ANTONÍN JELÍNEK.

## Broadcasting and Communications

### TELECOMMUNICATIONS

**Český Telecom:** Olsanska 5, 130 00 Prague 3; tel. (2) 67142500; fax (2) 67142526; e-mail jindrich.trpisovsky@ct.cz; fmrly SPT Telecom, renamed 2000; partially privatized 1995; 33%-owned by Dutch/Swiss consortium; scheduled for full privatization in 2000; monopoly operator of long-distance and international services; Chair. of Bd ANDRÉ FRANS BESSEL KOK.

**EuroTel:** Sokolovská 225, POB 49, 190 00 Prague 9; tel. (2) 67011111; fax (2) 2327383; f. 1991; mobile telephone communications; launched GSM service July 1996; owned by SPT Telecom (51%) and West Atlantic (49%—consortium of US West and Bell Atlantic); CEO and Man. Dir EDWARD KINGMAN.

**Český Mobil:** Prague; 51% owned by Telesystem International Wireless (Canada); awarded licence to operate mobile telephone network in October 1999; Dir-Gen. ALEXANDER TOLSLTOY.

**České Radiokomunikace, a.s.:** U nákladového nádraži 4, 130 00 Prague 3; tel. (2) 67005119; fax (2) 6919292; e-mail l.stary@cra.cz; internet www.cra. cz; f. 1994; 51% state-owned; scheduled for privatization in 2000; Dir.-Gen. MIROSLAV CURÍN.

**Czech RadioMobil, a.s.:** Prague; owned by České Radiokomunikace, a.s. (51%) and an international consortium, C-Mobil (49%); awarded 20-year licence to operate mobile telephone network in April 1996; launched GSM service September 1996; Gen. Dir KLAUS TEBBE.

### RADIO

The national networks include Radio Prague (medium wave and VHF), Radio Vltava (VHF from Prague—programmes on Czech and world culture), Radio Regina (medium and VHF—programme of regional studios), and Interprogramme (medium and VHF—for foreign visitors to the Czech Republic, in English, German and French).

Local stations broadcast from Prague (Central Bohemian Studio), Brno, České Budějovice, Hradec Králové, Ostrava, Plzeň, Ústí nad Labem and other towns. By August 1993 44 private stations had been licensed, 37 of which were in operation (14 in Prague).

**Český rozhlas** (Czech Radio): Vinohradská 12, 120 99 Prague 2; tel. (2) 24094111; fax (2) 24222223; 4 nation-wide stations; Dir-Gen. VÁCLAV KASÍK.

**Country Radio:** Zenklová 34, 180 00 Prague 8; tel. (2) 5102411; fax (2) 51024224; e-mail country@ecn.cz; internet www.ecn.cz/country; commercial station; Man. Dir ZDENĚK PETERA.

**Evropa 2:** Nádrazní 56, 150 05 Prague 5, tel. (2) 57001808; fax (2) 57001807; e-mail info@evropa2.cz; internet www.evropa2.cz; commercial station; Pres. MICHAEL FLEISCHMANN.

**Frekvence 1:** Nádrazní 56, 150 05 Prague 5; tel. (2) 57001900; fax (2) 57314186; e-mail info@frekvence1.cz; internet www.frekvence1.cz; commercial station; Pres. MICHAEL FLEISCHMANN.

**Radio Alfa:** Na Poříčí 12, 110 00 Prague 1; tel. (2) 24872822; fax (2) 24872823; commercial station; Man. Dir V. KASÍK.

**Radio FM Plus:** POB 40, 320 90 Plzeň; tel. (19) 276666; fax (19) 7422221; e-mail info@fmplus.cz; internet www.fmplus.cz; commercial station; Dir ZBYNĚK SUCHÝ.

**Radio Free Europe/Radio Liberty:** Vinohradská 1, 110 00 Prague 1; fax (2) 21123420; internet www.rferl.org; broadcasts in 23 languages.

### TELEVISION

In 1995 there were four main television stations: the two state-run channels, ČT1 and ČT2, reached 98% and 71% of the population, respectively, while the two private commercial stations, Nova TV and Prima TV, were received by 99% and approximately 50%, respectively.

**Česká televize** (Czech Television): Kavčí hory, 140 70 Prague 4; tel. (2) 61131111; fax (2) 6927202; e-mail jakub.puchalsky@czech-tv.cz; internet www.czech-tv.cz; f. 1992; state-owned; two channels; studios in Prague, Brno and Ostrava; Dir-Gen. DUŠAN CHMELÍČEK.

**Nova TV:** Vladislavova 20, 113 13 Prague 1; tel. (2) 21100111; fax (2) 21100565; f. 1994; 93.5%-owned by Central European Media Enterprises; the first independent commercial station; Dir-Gen. VLADIMÍR ŽELEZNÝ.

**Prima TV:** Na Žertvách 24, 180 00 Prague 8; tel. (2) 66100111; fax (2) 66100201; e-mail kvizova@prima-televize.cz; internet www.prima-televize.cz; f. 1993; Gen. Dir. KATEŘINA FRIČOVÁ.

# Finance

(cap. = capital; res = reserves; dep. = deposits; m. = million; brs = branches; amounts in Czech koruny)

## BANKING

With the establishment of independent Czech and Slovak Republics on 1 January 1993, the State Bank of Czechoslovakia was divided and its functions were transferred to the newly-created Czech National Bank and National Bank of Slovakia. The Czech National Bank is independent of the Government.

At 31 December 1998 there were 45 banks actively operating in the Czech Republic, with combined total assets of 2,437,915m. Czech koruny.

### Central Bank

**Czech National Bank** (Česká národní banka): Na Příkopě 28, 115 03 Prague 1; tel. (2) 24411111; fax (2) 24413708; e-mail milan .tomanek@cnb.cz; internet www.cnb.cz; f. 1993; bank of issue, the central authority of the Czech Republic in the monetary sphere, legislation and foreign exchange permission; central bank for directing and securing monetary policy, supervision of activities of other banks and savings banks; cap. 1,400m., res 62,604m., clients' dep. 31,812m. (Dec. 1998); Gov. JOSEF TOŠOVSKÝ; 7 brs.

### Commercial Banks

**Banka Haná, a.s.:** Rooseveltova 10, POB 58, 601 58 Brno; tel. (5) 42219548; fax (5) 42215681; internet www.bhan.cz; f. 1990; cap. 2,701m., res 601m., dep. 19,742m. (Dec. 1997); Chair. of Bd VLADIMÍR OHLÍDAL; 2 brs.

**Československá obchodní banka, a.s.** (Czechoslovak Commercial Bank): Na Příkopě 14, 115 20 Prague 1; tel. (2) 24111111; fax (2) 24225049; f. 1965; 66% state holding purchased by KBC Bank (Belgium) May 1999; commercial and foreign trade transactions; cap. 5,105m., res 15,190m., dep. 200,420m. (Dec. 1998); Chair. and Gen. Man. PAVEL KAVÁNEK; 34 brs.

**Investiční a Poštovní banka, a.s.:** Senovážné nám. 32, POB 819, 114 03 Prague 1; tel. (2) 22041111; fax (2) 24244035; e-mail info@ipb.cz; internet www.ipb.cz; f. 1990; 36% state holding purchased by Nomura (Japan) March 1998; cap. 13,383m., res 1,755m., dep. 231,135m. (Dec. 1998); Chair. and Gen. Man. JAN KLACEK; 157 brs.

**Komerční banka, a.s.:** Na Příkopě 33, POB 839, 114 07 Prague 1; tel. (2) 22433020; fax (2) 24243020; e-mail group_strategy@koba.cz; internet www.koba.cz; f. 1990; 49% state-owned; scheduled for privatization in 2000; cap. 9,502m., res 5,971m., dep. 10,956m. (Dec. 1998); Chair. and CEO (vacant); 354 brs.

**Konsolidační banka Praha, s.p.ú.:** Janovského 438/2, 170 06 Prague 7; tel. (2) 20141111; fax (2) 33370033; e-mail kobp@ms.aned.cz; internet www.kopb.cz; f. 1991; cap. 5,950m., res 31,485m., dep. 92,766m. (Dec. 1997); Chair. and Gen. Man. LIBOR LÖFLER.

**Union banka, a.s.:** ul. 30. dubna č. 35, 702 00 Ostrava; tel. (69) 6108111; fax (69) 211586; e-mail union@union.cz; internet www.union.cz; f. 1991; cap. 2,134m., res –569m., dep. 26,624m. (Dec. 1998); Pres., Chair. and Gen. Man. JIŘÍ BABIS; 101 brs.

### Foreign and Joint-Venture Banks

**Bank Austria Creditanstalt Czech Republic, a.s.:** Revoluční 7, 110 15 Prague 1; tel. (2) 21102111; fax (2) 24827337; e-mail cabra@creditanstalt.co.at; internet www.ba-ca.cz; f. 1998 by merger of Bank Austria, a.s. and Creditanstalt, a.s.; shareholders: Bank Austria Creditanstalt International AG, Vienna (89.1%), CARIPLO SpA, Milan (10.9%); cap. 1,997m., res 1,016m., dep. 41,405m. (Dec. 1998); Chair. of Bd MANFRED MEIER; 15 brs.

**BNP–Dresdner Bank (ČR), a.s.:** Vítězná 1, POB 229, 150 00 Prague 5; tel. (2) 57006111; fax (2) 57006200; internet www .bnp-dresdner-bank.cz; f. 1991; ownership: Banque Nationale de Paris (50%), Dresdner Bank (50%); cap. and res 1,448m., dep. 5,479m. (Dec. 1997); Chair. and Gen. Man. ROLF D. BECK.

**Citibank, a.s.:** Evropská 178, 166 40 Prague 6; tel. (2) 24304111; fax (2) 24304613; f. 1991; wholly-owned subsidiary of Citibank Overseas Investment Corpn (Delaware, USA); cap. 1,825m., res 1,597m., dep. 31,149m. (Dec. 1998); Gen. Man. AKSHAYA BHARGAVA; 6 brs.

**Crédit Lyonnais Bank Praha, a.s.:** Ovocný trh 8, 117 19 Prague 1; tel. (2) 22076111; fax (2) 22076119; wholly-owned subsidiary of Crédit Lyonnais Global Banking, Paris; cap. 500m., res 416m., dep. 32,495m. (Dec. 1997); Chair. and Gen. Man. HEINRICH SITTLER.

**Erste Bank Sparkassen (ČR), a.s.:** Václavské nám. 56, POB 749, 110 00 Prague 1; tel. (2) 21010202; fax (2) 21010406; e-mail erste@erstebank.cz; internet www.erstebank.cz; f. 1993; fmrly Girocredit-Sparkassen Banka Praha, a.s.; cap. 700m., res 397m., dep. 23,075m. (Dec. 1998); Chair. and Gen. Man. Dr WILHELM REICHMANN; 6 brs.

**GE Capital bank, a.s.:** Hybernská 18, 110 00 Prague 1; tel. (2) 24442000; fax (2) 24219995; f. 1998 from purchase of Agrobanka Praha, a.s.; wholly-owned by GE Capital International Holdings Corpn, Wilmington; cap. 510m., res 21,208m., dep. 37,878m. (Dec. 1998); Chair. and Gen. Man. PETR ŠMÍDA; 81 brs.

**HypoVereinsbank CZ, a.s.:** Italská 24, POB 70, Prague 2; tel. (2) 22091111; fax (2) 22251158; f. 1999 by merger of HYPO-BANK CZ, as and Vereinsbank CZ, as; wholly-owned subsidiary of Bayerische Hypo-und Vereinsbank AG, Munich; Exec. Mems of Bd HANS-PETER HORSTER, Dr KAREL KRATINA, DAVID SVOJITKA.

**Interbanka, a.s.:** Václavské nám. 40, 110 00 Prague 1; tel. (2) 24406215; fax (2) 24227333; f. 1991; cap. 1,359m., res 22m., dep. 5,897m. (Dec. 1998); Chair. and CEO VLADIMÍR KOLMAN.

**Raiffeisenbank, as:** Vodičkova 38, 111 21 Prague 1; tel. (2) 24231270; fax (2) 24231278; e-mail raiffeisenbank@rb.cz; internet www.rb.cz; f. 1993; cap. 1,000m., res –7m., dep. 24,428m. (Dec. 1998); Chair. and Gen. Man. Ing. JAN VLACHÝ.

**Živnostenská banka, a.s.:** Na Příkopě 20, POB 421, 113 80 Prague 1; tel. (2) 24121111; fax (2) 24125555; e-mail info@ziba.cz; internet www.ziba.cz; f. 1868; cap. 1,360m., res 1,270m., dep. 24,816m. (Dec. 1998); Chair. of Bd and Gen. Man. JIŘÍ KUNERT; 8 brs.

### Savings Bank

**Czech Savings Bank** (Česká spořitelna, a.s.): Na Příkopě 29, POB 838, 113 98 Prague 1; tel. (2) 61071111; fax (2) 61073006; e-mail csas@csas.cz; internet www.csas.cz; f. 1825; 52% state-owned; scheduled for privatization in 2000; accepts deposits and issues loans; 12,374,657 depositors (Sept. 1998); cap. 7,600., res 14,671m., dep. 355,603m. (Dec. 1998); Chair. and CEO DUŠAN BARAN; 876 brs.

### Bankers' Organization

**Association of Banks, Prague:** Vodičkova 30, 110 00 Prague 1; tel. (2) 24225926; fax (2) 24225957; e-mail bank.asociace@mbox.vol.cz.

## STOCK EXCHANGE

**Prague Stock Exchange** (Burza cenných papírů Praha, a.s.): Rybná 14, 110 00 Prague 1; tel. (2) 21832116; fax (2) 21833040; f. 1992; Man. Dir JIŘÍ HUEBNER.

### Regulatory Authority

**Czech Securities Commission:** Prague; f. 1998; Chair. JAN MÜLLER.

## INSURANCE

**Czech Association of Insurers:** f. 1994; 27 members.

**Co-operative Insurance Company** (Kooperativa, pojišťovna, a.s.): Templová 5, 110 01 Prague 1; tel. (2) 21000111; fax (2) 2322633; e-mail info@koop.cz; internet www.koop.cz; f. 1993; Chair. and Gen. Man. Ing. VLADIMÍR MRÁZ.

**Czech Insurance and Reinsurance Corporation** (Česká pojišťovna, a.s.): Spálená 16, 113 04 Prague 1; tel. (2) 24051111; fax (2) 24052200; e-mail murban@cpoj.cz; internet www.cpoj.cz; f. 1827; many home brs and some agencies abroad; issues life, accident, fire, aviation, industrial and marine policies, all classes of reinsurance; Lloyd's agency; Chair. of the Bd. IVAN KOČÁRNÍK; Gen. Man. LADISLAV BARTONÍČEK.

# Trade and Industry

## GOVERNMENT AGENCIES

**Česká agentura pro zahraniční investice (CzechInvest):** Štěpánská 15, 120 00 Prague 2; tel. (2) 96342500; fax (2) 96342501; e-mail marketing@czechinvest.com; internet www.czechinvest.com; f. 1992; foreign investment agency; Dir Ing. MARTIN JAHN.

**National Property Fund:** Rašínovo nábřeží 42, 128 00 Prague 2; tel. (2) 24991285; fax (2) 24991379; responsible for state property and state-owned companies in the period up to their privatization; Chair. JAN STIESS.

## CHAMBER OF COMMERCE

**Economic Chamber of the Czech Republic** (Hospodářská komora České republiky): Argentinská 38, 170 05 Prague 7; tel. (2) 66794939; fax (2) 875438; f. 1850; has almost 20,000 members (trading corporations, industrial enterprises, banks and private enterprises); Chair. Dr ZDENĚK SOMR.

## EMPLOYERS' ORGANIZATIONS

**Association of Entrepreneurs of the Czech Republic** (Sdružení podnikatelů České republiky): Škrétova 6/44, 120 59 Prague 2; tel. and fax (2) 24230572; Chair. RUDOLF BARÁNEK.

**Confederation of Industry of the Czech Republic** (Svaz průmyslu a dopravy České republiky): Mikulandská 7, 113 61

internet www.bibelselskabet.dk; religious and liturgical books, children's books; Sec.-Gen. MORTEN M. AAGAARD.

**Christian Ejlers' Forlag ApS:** Brolæggerstræde 4, POB 2228, 1018 Copenhagen K; tel. 33-12-21-14; fax 33-12-28-84; e-mail liber@ce-publishers.dk; internet www.ce-publishers.dk; f. 1967; art, cultural, educational and academic; Publr CHRISTIAN EJLERS.

**Forlaget for Faglitteratur A/S:** Vandkunsten 6, 1467 Copenhagen K; tel. 33-13-79-00; fax 33-14-51-56; medicine, technology.

**FinansSupport:** Hovedvejen 9, POB 70, 2600 Glostrup; tel. 43-44-04-44; fax 43-44-07-44; educational books; Pres. ERLING JENSEN.

**Flachs:** Øverødvej 98, 2840 Holte; tel. 45-42-48-30; fax 45-42-48-29; fiction, non-fiction, reference, educational and children's books; Publrs ALLAN FLACHS, ANETTE FLACHS.

**Palle Fogtdal A/S:** Østergade 22, 1100 Copenhagen K; tel. 33-15-39-15; fax 33-93-35-05; Danish history; Man. Dir PALLE FOGTDAL.

**Forum:** Snaregade 4, 1205 Copenhagen K; tel. 33-14-77-14; fax 33-14-77-91; f. 1940; history, fiction, biographies, quality paperbacks and children's books; Man. Dir WERNER SVENDSEN.

**Fremad:** Klareboderne 3, POB 2252, 1019 Copenhagen K; tel. 33-11-50-40; fax 33-11-50-82; f. 1912; general trade, fiction, non-fiction, juveniles, reference, children's books; Man. Dir NIELS KØLLE.

**Forlaget FSR:** Nytorv 5, 1450 Copenhagen K; tel. 33-74-07-74; fax 33-93-30-77; textbooks, legal, economic, financial, management, business, accounting; Editorial Dir VIBEKE CHRISTIANSEN.

**G.E.C. Gad Publishers Ltd:** Vimmelskaftet 32, 1161 Copenhagen K; tel. 33-15-05-58; fax 33-11-08-00; e-mail sekr@gads-forlag.dk; biographies, natural science, history, reference, fiction, educational materials, food and drink, travel guides; Man. Dir AXEL KIELLAND.

**Gyldendalske Boghandel, Nordisk Forlag A/S:** Klareboderne 3, 1001 Copenhagen K; tel. 33-11-07-75; fax 33-11-03-23; e-mail gyldendal@gyldendal.dk; internet www.gyldendal.dk; f. 1770; fiction, non-fiction, reference books, paperbacks, children's books, textbooks; Man. Dir STIG ANDERSEN.

**P. Haase & Søns Forlag A/S:** Løvstræde 8, 1152 Copenhagen K; tel. 33-14-41-75; fax 33-11-59-59; e-mail haase@haase.dk; internet www.haase.dk; f. 1877; educational books, audio-visual aids, children's books, humour, fiction, non-fiction; imprints: Natur og Harmoni, Rasmus Navers Forlag; Man. Dir MICHAEL HAASE.

**Edition Wilhelm Hansen A/S:** Bornholmsgade 1, 1266 Copenhagen K; tel. 33-11-78-88; fax 33-14-81-78; e-mail ewh@ewh.dk; internet www.ewh.dk; f. 1857; music books, school and educational books; Man. Dir TINE BIRGER CHRISTENSEN.

**Hernovs Publishing:** Siljangade 6, 4, 2300 Copenhagen S; tel. 32-96-33-14; fax 32-96-04-46; e-mail admin@hernov.dk; internet www.hernov.dk; f. 1941; fiction, non-fiction, children's; Publr ELSE HERNOV.

**Holkenfeldt 3:** Fuglevadsvej 71, 2800 Lyngby; tel. 45-93-12-21; fax 45-93-82-41; fiction, non-fiction, reference, sport, humour; Publr KAY HOLKENFELDT.

**Høst & Søns Forlag:** Købmagergade 62, POB 2212, 1018 Copenhagen K; tel. 33-15-30-31; fax 33-15-51-55; e-mail host@euroconnect.dk; f. 1836; crafts and hobbies, languages, books on Denmark, children's books; Skarv imprint (travel, ecology, etc.); Man. Dir ERIK C. LINDGREN.

**Forlaget Hovedland:** Stenvej 21, 8270 Højbjerg; tel. 86-27-65-00; fax 86-27-65-37; e-mail hovedland@isa.dknet.dk; internet www.hovedland.dk; fiction, non-fiction, environment, sport, health, crafts; Publr STEEN PIPER.

**Forlaget Klematis A/S:** Østre Skovvej 1, 8240 Risskov; tel. 86-17-54-55; fax 86-17-59-59; fiction, non-fiction, crafts, children's books; Dir CLAUS DALBY.

**Forlaget Per Kofod ApS:** Faksegade 5, 2100 Copenhagen Ø; tel. 35-43-50-27; fax 35-43-90-27; fiction, non-fiction, art and culture; Publr PER KOFOD.

**Krak:** Virumgaardsvej 21, 2830 Virum; tel. 45-95-65-00; fax 45-95-65-65; e-mail krak@krak.dk; internet www.krak.dk; f. 1770; reference works, maps and yearbooks; Dir IB LE ROY TOPHOLM.

**Egmont Lademann A/S:** Gerdasgade 37, 2500 Valby; tel. 36-15-66-00; fax 36-44-11-62; internet www.lademann.dk; f. 1954; non-fiction, reference; Man. Dir SØREN FOGTDAL; Editor-in-Chief LISELOTTE NELSON.

**Lindhardt og Ringhof A/S:** Frederiksborggade 1, 1360 Copenhagen K; tel. 33-69-50-00; fax 33-69-50-01; e-mail lr@lindhardt-og-ringhof.dk; general fiction and non-fiction.

**L & R FAKTA:** tel. 33-69-50-70; fax 33-69-50-01; e-mail bonnier@inet.uni-c.dk; f. 1997; non-fiction, reference; Man. Dir HENRIK HJORTH; Publr ANNEMARIE ELKJÆR.

**Lohses Forlag (incl. Forlaget Korskaer):** Korskærvej 25, 7000 Fredericia; tel. 75-93-44-55; fax 75-92-42-75; e-mail finn@lohse.imh.dk; f. 1868; religion, children's, biographies, devotional novels; Man. Dir FINN ANDERSEN.

**Forlaget Lotus:** Industrikrogen 4, 2635 Ishøj; tel. 43-45-78-74; fax 43-45-97-71; e-mail fiolotus@post7.tele.dk; management, health, religion, the occult, educational; Publr FINN ANDERSEN.

**Forlaget Magnus A/S Skattekartoteket:** Informationskontor, Palægade 4, 1261 Copenhagen K; tel. 33-11-78-74; fax 33-93-80-09; e-mail magnus@cddk.dk; f. 1962; guidebooks, journals, law; Man. Dirs PETER TAARNHØJ, HANNE TOMMERUP.

**Medicinsk Forlag ApS:** Tranevej 2, 3650 Ølstykke; tel. and fax 47-17-65-92; astrology, medical and scientific books; Man. Dir ANNI LINDELØV.

**Modtryk AmbA:** Anholtsgade 4, 8000 Århus C; tel. 87-31-76-00; fax 87-13-76-01; e-mail modtryk@ibm.net; internet www.modtryk.dk; f. 1972; children's and school books, fiction, thrillers and non-fiction; Man. Dir ILSE NØRR.

**Munksgaard International Publishers Ltd:** Nørre Søgade 35, POB 2148, 1016 Copenhagen K; tel. 77-33-33-33; fax 77-33-33-77; e-mail headoffice@munksgaard.dk; internet www.munksgaard.dk; f. 1917; medicine, nursing, dentistry, social science, psychology, scientific journals; Man. Dir ANDERS GEERTSEN.

**Nyt Nordisk Forlag-Arnold Busck A/S:** Købmagergade 49, 1150 Copenhagen K; tel. 33-73-35-75; fax 33-73-35-76; e-mail nnf@nytnordiskforlag.dk; internet www.nytnordiskforlag.dk; f. 1896; textbooks, school books, guidebooks, fiction and non-fiction; Man. Dir OLE ARNOLD BUSCK.

**Jørgen Paludans Forlag ApS:** 4 Straedet, 3100 Hornbaek; tel. 49-75-15-36; fax 49-75-15-37; language teaching, non-fiction, psychology, history, politics, economics, reference; Man. Dir JØRGEN PALUDAN.

**Politikens Forlag A/S:** Vestergade 26, 1456 Copenhagen K; tel. 33-47-07-07; fax 33-47-07-08; f. 1946; non-fiction, reference, history, family, health, biography, travel; Ekstra Bladets imprint; Man. Dir JOHANNES RAVN.

**C.A. Reitzels Boghandel og Forlag A/S:** Nørregade 20, 1165 Copenhagen K; tel. 33-12-24-00; fax 33-14-02-70; f. 1819; reference books, philosophy, educational and academic books, Hans Christian Andersen, Kierkegaard; Dir SVEND OLUFSEN.

**Hans Reitzels Forlag A/S:** Købmagergade 62, POB 1073, 1008 Copenhagen K; tel. 33-14-04-51; fax 33-15-51-55; e-mail reitzel@euroconnect.dk; f. 1949; education, philosophy, psychology, sociology, Hans Christian Andersen; Man. Dir ERIK C. LINDGREN.

**Rhodos, International Science and Art Publishers:** Niels Brocks Gård, Strandgade 36, 1401 Copenhagen K; tel. 32-54-30-20; fax 32-95-47-42; e-mail rhodos@rhodos.dk; internet www.rhodos.dk; f. 1959; university books, art, science, fiction, poetry; Man. Dir NIELS BLAEDEL; Dir RUBEN BLAEDEL.

**Samlerens Forlag A/S:** Snaregade 4, 1205 Copenhagen K; tel. 33-13-10-23; fax 33-14-43-14; Danish and foreign fiction, contemporary history and politics, biographies; Man. Dir PETER HOLST.

**Scandinavia Publishing House:** Drejervej 11–12, 2400 Copenhagen NV; tel. 33-14-00-91; fax 33-32-00-91; e-mail jvo@scanpublishing.dk; internet www.scanpublishing.dk; f. 1973; children's books, religion, Hans Christian Andersen; Dir JØRGEN VIUM OLESEN.

**Det Schønbergske Forlag A/S:** Landemærket 5, 1119 Copenhagen K; tel. 33-11-30-66; fax 33-33-00-45; f. 1857; fiction, humour, psychology, biography, children's books, paperbacks, textbooks; Dir JOAKIM WERNER; Editor ARVID HONORÉ.

**Spektrum:** Snaregade 4, 1205 Copenhagen K; tel. 33-14-77-14; fax 33-14-77-91; non-fiction, history, biographies, science, psychology, religion, philosophy, arts; Man. Dir WERNER SVENDSEN.

**Strandbergs Forlag ApS:** Vedbæk Strandvej 475, 2950 Vedbæk; tel. 42-89-47-60; fax 42-89-47-01; cultural history, travel; Publr HANS JØRGEN STRANDBERG.

**Strubes Forlag og Boghandel ApS:** Dag Hammerskjølds Allé 36, 2100 Copenhagen Ø; tel. 35-42-07-16; fax 35-42-23-98; health, astrology, philosophy, the occult; Man. Dir JONNA STRUBE.

**Teknisk Forlag A/S:** Skelbækgade 4, 1780 Copenhagen V; tel. 33-26-54-54; fax 33-26-55-95; e-mail bogredaktion@tekniskforlag.dk; internet www.tekniskforlag.dk; f. 1948; computing, technical books, reference, business, educational, science; Man. Dir PETER MÜLLER.

**Tiderne Skifter:** Pilestræde 51, 1001 Copenhagen K; tel. 33-32-57-72; fax 33-14-42-05; fiction, sexual and cultural politics, psychology, science, religion, arts; Man. Dir CLAUS CLAUSEN.

**Unitas Forlag:** Valby Langgade 19, 2500 Valby; tel. 36-16-64-81; fax 36-16-08-18; e-mail forlag@unitas.dk; internet www.unitas.dk; religion, fiction, education, children's books; Man. PEDER GUNDERSEN.

**Forlaget Vindrose A/S:** Valbygaardsvej 33, 2500 Valby; tel. 36-46-21-00; fax 36-44-14-88; f. 1980; general trade, fiction and non-fiction; Man. Dir NIELS BORGEN.

**Vitafakta ApS:** Kohavevej 28, 2950 Vedbæk; tel. and fax 45-16-11-50; health books, nutrition, school books; Dir INGER MARIE HAUT.

**Wisby & Wilkens:** Vestergade 6, POB 98, 8464 Galten; tel. 86-94-46-22; fax 86-94-47-22; e-mail mail@bogshop.dk; internet www.bogshop.dk; f. 1986; children's books, crafts, fiction, health, humour, science, religion; imprints: Mikro (drama, poetry, humour), Falkenlöwe (debate, gay literature, contemporary history); Publr JACOB WISBY.

### Government Publishing House

**Statens Information** (State Information Service): Nørre Farimagsgade 65, POB 1103, 1009 Copenhagen K; tel. 33-37-92-00; fax 33-37-92-99; e-mail si@si.dk; f. 1975; acts under the purview of the Ministry of Research and Information Technology, as public relations and information body for the public sector; publishes Statstidende (Official Gazette), etc.; Dir LEON ØSTERGAARD.

### PUBLISHERS' ASSOCIATION

**Den danske Forlæggerforening:** Købmagergade 11, 1150 Copenhagen K; tel. 33-15-66-88; fax 33-15-65-88; e-mail publassn@webpartner.dk; f. 1837; 75 mems; Chair. ERIK C. LINDGREN; Man. Dir IB TUNE OLSEN.

# Broadcasting and Communications

### TELECOMMUNICATIONS

Telecommunications services are administered by the Post- og Telegrafvæsenet (the general directorate of posts and telecommunications) and the National Telecom Agency.

Denmark participates in the Nordic Mobile Telephone (NMT) system, an integrated cellular-radio network which is compatible throughout Scandinavia.

Telecommunications links with the Faroe Islands are provided by satellite ground stations at Tórshavn and Herstedvester. The latter also provides international data communication links via the EUTELSAT system and the French Telecom 1 satellite system, while a station at Blåvand receives signals from INTELSAT.

#### Regulatory Organization

**National Telecom Agency:** Holsteinsgade 63, 2100 Copenhagen Ø; tel. 35-43-03-33; fax 35-43-14-34; e-mail tst@tst.dk; internet www.tst.dk; f. 1991; under the Ministry of Research and Information Technology, in charge of administration and regulation of the telecommunications sector as laid down in telecommunications legislation; works on legislation; government's centre of expertise in telecommunications; Dir-Gen. JØRGAN ABILD ANDERSEN; Deputy Dir-Generals FINN PETERSEN, VICTOR KJÆER.

#### Major Service Providers

**GN Store Nordiske Telegraf-Selskab as** (GN Great Northern Telegraph Co Ltd): Kongens Nytorv 26, POB 2167, 1016 Copenhagen; tel. 33-95-09-09; fax 33-95-09-09; e-mail info@gn.dk; Pres. and CEO JORGEN LINDEGAARD.

**LASAT Networks A/S:** Skalhuse 13, 9240 Nibe; tel. 96-71-10-00; fax 96-71-10-99; e-mail lasat@lasat.com; internet www.lasat.com; f. 1982; CEO CLAUS CHRISTENSEN.

**Telecom A/S:** Telegade 2, 2630 Tåstrup; tel. 42-52-91-11; fax 42-52-93-31; Man. Dir GREGERS MOGENSEN.

**Tele Danmark A/S:** Norregade 21, 0900 Copenhagen; tel. 33-43-77-77; fax 33-43-73-89; e-mail teledanmark@tdk.dk; internet www.teledanmark.dk; fmrly state-owned telecommunications company; transferred to private ownership in 1998; CEO HENNING DYREMOSE.

### RADIO

**DR RADIO:** Radio House, Rosenørns Alle 22, 1999 Frederiksberg C; tel. 35-20-30-40; fax 35-20-26-44; e-mail webmaster@dr.dk; internet www.dr.dk; fmrly Danmarks Radio; independent statutory corpn; Dir-Gen. CHR. S. NISSEN; Dir of Radio Programmes LEIF LØNSMANN; operates a foreign service (Radio Denmark), nine regional stations and four national channels:

Channel 1 broadcasts for 110 hours per week on FM, in Danish (Greenlandic programmes weekly); Head FINN SLUMSTRUP.

Channel 2, a music channel, broadcasts on FM, for 45 hours per week nationally, in Danish, as well as regional and special (for foreign workers) programmes; Head STEEN FREDERIKSEN.

Channel 3 broadcasts on FM for 24 hours per day, in Danish; primarily a popular music channel, there is news in Greenlandic, Faroese and in English; Head JESPER GRUNWALD.

Channel 4 broadcasts on FM for about 97 hours per week; news, entertainment and regional progs.

There are also some 250 operators licensed for low-power FM transmissions of local and community radio, etc.

### TELEVISION

**DR TV:** TV-Byen, 2860 Søborg; tel. 35-20-30-40; fax 35-20-26-44; e-mail dr-kontakten@dr.dk; internet www.dr.dk; operates two services, DR 1 and DR 2; Dir-Gen. CHR. S. NISSEN; Man. Dir BJØRN ERICHSEN.

**DR 1:** terrestrial television channel; Controller JØRGEN RAMSKOV.

**DR 2:** satellite television channel; Controller TORBEN FRØLICH.

**TV 2/DANMARK:** Rugaardsvej 25, 5100 Odense C; tel. 65-91-12-44; fax 65-91-33-22; e-mail tv2@tv2;.dk; internet www.tv2.dk; began broadcasts in 1988; Denmark's first national commercial and public service TV station; 20% of its finances come from licence fees, the rest from advertising and sponsorship; Dir-Gen. TØGER SEIDENFADEN; Head of Programmes JØRGEN STEEN NIELSEN.

**Viasat Broadcasting/TV 3:** Wildersgade 8, 1408 Copenhagen K; tel. 35-25-90-00; fax 35-25-90-10; e-mail viasat@viasat.dk; internet www.tv3.dk; reaches 71% of the country via cable and satellite; Man. Dir LARS BO ANDERSEN; Dir of Programmes HENRIK RAVN.

There are some 50 operators licensed for local television transmission.

# Finance

The first Danish commercial bank was founded in 1846. In 1975 restrictions on savings banks were lifted, giving commercial and savings banks equal rights and status, and restrictions on the establishment of full branches of foreign banks were removed. In 1988 all remaining restrictions on capital movements were ended. In 1998 there were some 187 banks and savings banks in operation. All banks are under government supervision, and public representation is obligatory on all bank supervisory boards.

### BANKING

(cap. = capital; p.u. = paid up; res = reserves; dep. = deposits; m. = million; brs = branches; amounts in kroner)

#### Supervisory Authority

**Finanstilsynet** (Danish Financial Supervisory Authority): Gammel Kongevej 74A, 1850 Frederiksberg C; tel. 33-55-82-82; fax 33-55-82-00; e-mail finanstilsynet@ftnet.dk; internet www.ftnet.dk; agency of the Ministry of Economic Affairs; Man. Dir HENRIK BJERRE-NIELSEN.

#### Central Bank

**Danmarks Nationalbank:** Havnegade 5, 1093 Copenhagen K; tel. 33-63-63-63; fax 33-63-71-06; internet www.nationalbanken.dk; f. 1818; self-governing; sole right of issue; conducts monetary policy; administers reserves of foreign exchange; cap. 50m., res 43,424m., dep. 93,114m. (Dec. 1998); Govs BODIL NYBOE ANDERSEN (Chair.), TORBEN NIELSEN, JENS THOMSEN.

#### Commercial Banks

**Alm. Brand Bank:** Jarmers Plads 7, 1551 Copenhagen V; tel. 33-30-70-30; fax 33-93-15-88; internet www.almbrand-bank.dk; f. 1988; cap. 350m., res 25m., dep. 9,688m. (Dec. 1998); Chair. CHRISTIAN N. B. ULRICH; Man. Dir HENRIK NORDAM; 24 brs.

**Amagerbanken A/S:** Amagerbrogade 25, 2300 Copenhagen S; tel. 32-66-66-66; fax 32-54-45-34; e-mail info@amagerbanken.dk; internet www.amagerbanken.dk; f. 1903; cap.195m., res 45m., dep. 7,555m. (Dec. 1998); Chair. N. E. NIELSEN; Man. Dirs KNUD CHRISTENSEN, BENT SCHØN HANSEN; 26 brs.

**Arbejdernes Landsbank A/S:** Vesterbrogade 5, 1502 Copenhagen V; tel. 33-38-80-00; fax 33-38-89-60; e-mail info@al-bank.dk; internet www.albank.dk; f. 1919; cap. 300m., res 78m., dep. 12,005m. (Dec. 1998); Chair. ANTON JOHANNSEN; Gen. Mans E. MIDTGAARD, P. E. LETH, E. CASTELLA; 14 brs.

**Bikuben Girobank A/S:** Højbro Plads 10, 1200 Copenhagen K; tel. 43-30-30-30; fax 33-15-90-33; e-mail info@bgbank.dk; internet www.bgbank.dk; f. 1996 by merger of Sparekassen Bikuben A/S (f. 1857) and Girobank A/S (f. 1990); cap. 3,000m., res 4,722m., dep. 150,844m. (Dec. 1998); Chair. HENRIK THUFASON; Vice-Chair. BJARNE WIND; 256 brs.

**Codan Bank A/S:** Borgergade 24, 1790 Copenhagen V; tel. 33-66-66-66; fax 33-66-66-67; e-mail codanbank@codanbank.dk; internet www.codanbank.dk; f. 1993 by merger of Alliance Bank of Copenhagen, Hafnia Bank A/S and Hafnia Börs-Börsmaeglerselskab; cap. 500m., res 127m., dep. 4,865m. (Dec. 1998); CEO JENS OLE PEDERSEN; Gen. Man. THORKILD KOKHOLM.

**Den Danske Bank A/S:** Holmens Kanal 2–12, 1092 Copenhagen K; tel. 33-44-00-00; fax 39-18-58-73; internet www.danskebank.dk; f. 1871 as Danske Landmandsbank; merged with Copenhagen Handelsbank and Provinsbanken in 1990 to form Den Danske Bank A/S; in 1995 the bank acquired the insurance group, Danica, and the Norwegian Fokus Bank in 1999; cap. 5,293m., res 52m., dep. 461,416m. (Dec. 1998); Chair. PETER STRAARUP; 430 brs.

**Egnsbank Nord A/S:** Jernbanegade 4–6, POB 701, 9900 Frederikshavn; tel. 99-21-22-23; fax 99-21-22-67; e-mail email@egnsbanknord.dk; internet www.egnsbanknord.dk; f. 1979; cap. 50m., res 347m., dep. 2,588m. (Dec. 1998); Chair. HANS JOERGEN KAPTAIN; Gen. Mans JENS OLE JENSEN, OLE KRISTENSEN; 26 brs.

**Forstædernes Bank A/S:** Malervangen 1, 2600 Glostrup; tel. 43-96-17-20; fax 43-63-32-36; e-mail finans@forbank.dk; internet www.forbank.dk; f. 1902; cap. 250m., res 3m., dep. 3,992m. (Dec. 1998); subsidiary, Den Fri Bank, f. 1994, provides telephone banking service to individual customers; Chair. HELMER OLSEN; Chief Exec. KJELD MOSEBO CHRISTENSEN; 19 brs.

**A/S Jyske Bank:** Vestergade 8–16, 8600 Silkeborg; tel. 89-22-22-22; fax 89-22-24-96; e-mail jyskebank@jyskebank.dk; internet www.jyskebank.dk; f. 1855, established in 1967; cap. 900m., res 4,208m., dep. 57,539m. (Dec. 1998); Chair. ANDERS DAM; Chief Exec. LEIF E. LARSEN; 133 brs.

**Midtbank A/S:** Østergade 2, 7400 Herning; tel. 96-26-26-26; fax 96-26-28-98; e-mail udland@midtbank.dk; internet www.midtbank.dk; f. 1965; cap. 282m., res 406m., dep. 5,768m. (Dec. 1998); Chair. GUNNAR PEDERSEN; Gen. Man. STEEN HOVE; 23 brs.

**Nørresundby Bank A/S:** Torvet 4, 9400 Nørresundby; tel. 98-17-33-33; fax 98-19-18-78; e-mail nbcentral@nrsbank.dk; internet www.nrsbank.dk; f. 1898; cap. 50m., res 11m., dep. 3,734m. (Dec. 1998); Chair. KJELD KOLIND JENSEN; Gen. Mans ANDREAS RASMUSSEN, FINN ØST ANDERSSON; 16 brs.

**Nykredit Bank A/S:** Bredgade 40, POB 3033, 1021 Copenhagen K; tel. 33-42-18-00; fax 33-42-18-01; e-mail nykredit-bank@nykredit.dk; internet www.nykredit.dk/bank;f. 1986; cap. 1,300m., res 915m., dep. 26,168m. (Dec. 1998); Chair. HENNING KRUSE PETERSEN; Chief Exec., Man. Dir HANS MØLLER CHRISTENSEN.

**Ringkjøbing Landbobank A/S:** Torvet 1, 6950 Ringkøbing; tel. 97-32-11-66; fax 97-32-18-18; e-mail post@landbobanken.dk; internet www.landbobanken.dk; f. 1886; res 560m., dep. 2,890m. (Dec. 1998); Chair. KR. OLE KRISTENSEN; Gen. Man. BENT NAUR KRISTENSEN; 12 brs.

**Roskilde Bank A/S:** Algade 14, POB 39, 4000 Roskilde; tel. 46-35-17-00; fax 46-34-83-52; f. 1884; cap. 100m., res 119m., dep. 4,087m. (Dec. 1998); Chair. JØRØGEN WESTERGAARD; Man. NIELS VALENTIN HANSEN; 17 brs.

**Sparbank Vest:** Adelgade 8, POB 505, 7800 Skive; tel. 97-52-33-11; fax 97-52-73-11; e-mail sparbank@inet.uni-c.dk; internet www.sparbankvest.dk; f. 1857; cap. 121m., res 576m., dep. 4,758m. (Dec. 1998); Chair. OLE BROENDUM JENSEN; CEO PREBEN RASMUSSEN; 35 brs.

**Sydbank A/S:** Peberlyk 4, POB 169, 6200 Åbenrå; tel. 74-36-36-36; fax 74-36-35-49; e-mail intl@sydbank.dk; internet www .sydbank.com; f. 1970; cap. 871m., res 953m., dep. 39,195m. (Dec. 1998); Chair. VAGN JACOBSEN; CEO CARSTEN ANDERSEN; 120 brs.

**Unibank A/S:** Strandegade 3, 1401 Copenhagen V; tel. 33-33-33-33; fax 33-33-63-63; internet www.unibank.dk; f. 1990 by merger of Andelsbanken, Privatbanken and SDS; in June 1999 the bank merged with Tryg-Baltica Forsikring A/S, the insurance company, but remained part of the Unidanmark A/S group; res 14,057m., dep. 377,437m. (Dec. 1998); Man. Dir THORLEIF KRARUP; 369 brs.

### Savings Banks

**Amtssparekassen Fyn A/S:** Vestre Stationsvej 7, POB 189, 5100 Odense C; tel. 66-14-04-74; fax 65-91-01-10; e-mail udland@amtssparekassen.dk; f. 1974; cap. 194m., res 718m., dep. 12,847m. (Dec. 1998); Chair. CLAUS HANSEN; Man. Dirs POUL BALLE, FINN B. SORENSEN; 39 brs.

**Lån & Spar Bank:** Højbro Plads 9-11, POB 2117, 1014 Copenhagen K; tel. 33-14-87-48; fax 33-14-18-48; e-mail laan.spar@laan-spar.dk; internet www.laan-spar.dk; f. 1880 (present name 1990); cap. 281m., res 264m., dep. 6,099m. (Dec. 1998); Chair. TOMMY AGERSKOV THOMSEN; Man. Dir, CEO PETER SCHOU; 12 brs.

**Spar Nord Bankaktieselskab:** Karlskogavej 4, POB 162, 9100 Ålborg; tel. 96-34-40-00; fax 96-34-45-75; e-mail int_div@sparnord.dk; internet www.sparnord.dk; f. 1967; cap. 519m., res 41m., dep. 19,695m. (Dec. 1998); Chair. POUL LAURITSEN; Man. Dirs OLE JØRGENSEN, LASSE NYBY; 70 brs.

**Sparekassen Kronjylland:** Middelgade 1, POB 162, 8900 Randers; tel. 89-12-12-12; fax 86-41-00-23; Dir JAKOB LETH; 30 brs.

**Sparekassen Vestsjælland:** POB 70, Ahlgade 51, 4300 Holboek; tel. 59-43-15-15; fax 59-44-25-15; e-mail sv@sparekassen-vestsjaelland.dk; f. 1825; cap. 91m., res 289m., dep. 2,294m. (Dec. 1998); Pres. FLEMMING HANSEN; 15 brs.

### Bankers' Organization

**Finansrådet:** Finansrådets Hus, Amaliegade 7, 1256 Copenhagen K; tel. 33-12-02-00; fax 33-93-02-60; e-mail f@finansraadet.dk; internet www.finansraadet.dk; f. 1990; 173 mems; Chair. PETER STRAARUP; Man. Dir LARS BARFOED.

## STOCK EXCHANGE

**Københavns Fondsbørs** (Copenhagen Stock Exchange): Nikolaj Plads 6, POB 1040, 1007 Copenhagen K; tel. 33-93-33-66; fax 33-12-86-13; e-mail xcse@xcse.dk; internet www.xcse.dk; f. 1861; part of the Norex Alliance (launched June 1999) with direct access to the Stockholm Stock Exchange in Sweden; Pres. HANS-OLE JOCHUMSEN; Chair. HANS EJVIND HANSEN.

## INSURANCE

### Principal Companies

**Alm. Brand af 1792:** Lyngby Hovedgade 4, POB 1792, 2800 Lyngby; tel. 45-96-70-00; fax 45-87-17-92; f. 1792; subsidiaries: finance, life, non-life and reinsurance; Chief Gen. Man. BENT KNIE-ANDERSEN.

**Forsikringsselskabet Codan A/S:** Codanhus, Gl. Kongevej 60, 1790 Copenhagen V; tel. 31-21-21-21; fax 31-21-21-22; f. 1915; controlled by Royal and Sun Alliance Group Ltd (UK); acquired insurance operations of Hafnia Holdings in 1993; accident, life; CEO PETER ZOBEL.

**Danica Liv I, Livsforsikringsaktieselskab:** Parallelvej 17, 2800 Lyngby; tel. 45-23-23-23; fax 45-23-20-20; e-mail servicecentre@danica.dk; internet www.danica.dk; f. 1842 as state insurance co; privatized in 1990; pensions, life and non-life.

**ERC Frankona Reinsurance A/S:** Grønningen 25, 1270 Copenhagen K; tel. 33-97-95-93; fax 33-97-94-41; f. 1894; reinsurance, life and non-life, international; Gen. Mans WALTHER HAMMERSTROEM, ANNETTE SADOLIN, AAGE LYTT JENSEN.

**A/S Det Kjøbenhavnske Reassurance-Compagni:** Lyngby Hovedgade 4, POB 325, 2800 Lyngby; tel. 45-96-75-75; fax 45-96-72-72; f. 1915; reinsurance; Gen. Man. LEIF CORINTH-HANSEN.

**Købstædernes almindelige Brandforsikring:** Grønningen 1, 1270 Copenhagen K; tel. 33-14-37-48; fax 33-32-06-66; e-mail kab@kab.dk; f. 1761; fire; Chair. SVENDE E. CHRISTENSEN; CEO MOGENS N. SKOV.

**Kompas Rejseforsikring A/S:** Klausdalsbrovej 601, 2750 Ballerup; tel. 44-68-81-00; fax 44-68-84-00; e-mail kompas@kompas.dk; internet www.kompas.dk; travel, health; Chief Gen. Man. PETER BOESEN.

**Kgl. Brand A/S** (The Royal Chartered General Fire Insurance Co. Ltd): Stamholmen 159, 2650 Hvidovre; tel. 36-87-47-47; fax 36-87-47-87; f. 1798; all branches; subsidiaries: workers' liability, life; Gen. Man. JØRN OLE JØRGENSEN.

**Max Levig & Cos Eft. A/S:** Vesterbrogade 2B, 1620 Copenhagen V; tel. 33-14-67-00; fax 33-93-67-01; f. 1890; Gen. Man. ERNST KAAS WILHJELM.

**PFA Pension:** Marina Park, Sundkrogsgade 4, 2100 Copenhagen Ø; tel. 39-17-50-00; fax 39-17-59-50; f. 1917; life; non-life, property; Gen. Mans ANDRÉ LUBLIN, A. KÜHLE.

**Top Danmark A/S:** Borupvang 4, 2750 Ballerup; tel. 44-68-33-11; fax 44-68-12-64; f. 1985; all classes, with subsidiaries; Man. Dir MICHAEL PRAM RASMUSSEN.

**Tryg-Baltica Forsikring A/S:** Klausdalsbrovej 601, 2750 Ballerup; tel. 44-20-20-20; fax 44-20-66-00; f. 1995 by merger of Tryg Forsikring A/S and Baltica Forsikring A/S; in June 1999 merged with Unibank A/S under the Unidanmark group; all classes, with subsidiaries; Group Chief Exec. HUGO ANDERSEN.

### Insurance Association

**Raadet For Dansk Forsikring og Pension:** Amaliegade 10, 1256 Copenhagen K; tel. 33-13-75-55; fax 33-11-23-53; e-mail dfp@forsikringenshus.dk; internet www.forsikringenshus.dk; f. 1918; Chair. BENT KNIE-ANDERSEN; Dir STEEN LETH JEPPESEN; 201 mems.

# Trade and Industry

## GOVERNMENT AGENCY

**Dansk Industri** (Confederation of Danish Industries): 1787 Copenhagen V; tel. 33-77-33-77; fax 33-77-33-00; e-mail di@di.dk; f. 1992; Dir HANS SKOV CHRISTENSEN.

## DEVELOPMENT ORGANIZATION

**Det Økonomiske Råd** (Danish Economic Council): Adelgade 13, 1304 Copenhagen K; tel. 33-13-51-28; fax 33-32-90-29; e-mail dors@dors.dk; f. 1962 to supervise national economic development and help to co-ordinate the actions of economic interest groups; 26 members representing both sides of industry, the Government and independent economic experts; Co-Chairs Prof. NIELS KIERGAARD, Prof. PETER BIRCH SØRENSEN, Prof. JØRGEN BIRK MORTENSEN; Sec.-Gen. PEDER ANDERSEN.

## CHAMBER OF COMMERCE

**Det Danske Handelskammer** (Danish Chamber of Commerce): Børsen, 1217 Copenhagen K; tel. 33-95-05-00; fax 33-32-52-16; e-mail handelskammeret@commerce.dk; internet www.commerce.dk; f. 1742; approx. 2,000 mems; Man. Dir LARS KROBAEK; Pres. BENT LARSEN.

## INDUSTRIAL AND TRADE ASSOCIATIONS

**Dansk Elvaerkers Forening** (Association of Danish Electric Utilities): Rosenørns Allé 9, 1970 Frederiksberg C; tel. 31-39-01-11f. 1923; promotes the interests of Danish producers and suppliers of electricity; 105 mem. companies.

**Det Kgl. Danske Landhusholdningsselskab** (The Royal Danish Agricultural Society): Mariendalsvej 27, 2, 2000 Frederiksberg; tel. 38-88-66-88; fax 38-88-66-11; e-mail jordbrugsforlaget@bogpost.dk; internet www.jordbrugsforlaget.dk; f. 1769 to promote agricultural progress; Pres JON KRABBE, SCHALL HOLBERG, NIELS KÆRGÅRD, KIRSTEN JAKOBSEN, IVER TESDORPF; Dir GRETHE ERSKOV; 1,400 mems.

**Landbrugsrådet** (Agricultural Council): Axelborg, Axeltorv 3, 1609 Copenhagen V; tel. 33-14-56-72; fax 33-14-95-74; f. 1919; Pres. (vacant); Dir KLAUS BUSTRUP; 38 mems.

**Mejeriforeningen** (Danish Dairy Board): Frederiks Allé 22, 8000 Århus; tel. 87-31-20-00; fax 87-31-20-01; e-mail ddb@mejeri.dk; f. 1912; Chair. KAJ OLE PEDERSEN; Man. Dir K. THAYSEN; 30 mems.

**Oliebranchens Fællesrepræsentation—OFR** (Danish Petroleum Industry Association): Vognmagergade 7, POB 120, 1004 Copenhagen K; tel. (01) 33-11-30-77; fax (01) 33-32-16-18; e-mail ofr@oil-forum.dk; internet www.oil-forum.dk; representative organization for petroleum industry; Chair. K. M. OLESEN; Sec.-Gen. J. STARBAEK CHRISTENSEN.

## EMPLOYERS' ORGANIZATIONS

**Bryggeriforeningen** (Danish Brewers' Association): Frederiksberggade 11, 1459 Copenhagen K; tel. 33-12-62-41; fax 33-14-25-13; e-mail info@bryggeriforeningen.dk; internet www.bryggeriforeningen.dk; f. 1899; Chair. FLEMMING LINDELØV; Dir NIELS HALD; 10 mems.

**Dansk Arbejdsgiverforening** (Danish Employers' Confederation): Vester Voldgade 113, 1790 Copenhagen V; tel. 33-93-40-00; fax 33-12-29-76; e-mail da@da.dk; internet www.da.dk; f. 1896; Chair. NIELS FOG; Dir-Gen. JØRN NEERGAARD LARSEN; 18 mem. orgs.

**Dansk Pelsdyravlerforening (DPF)** (Danish Fur Breeders' Association): Langagervej 60, POB 1479, 2600 Glostrup; tel. 43-26-10-00; fax 43-26-11-26; e-mail cfc@cfc.dk; internet www.cfc.dk; co-operative of 3,000 mems.

**Danske Husmandsforeninger** (Danish Family Farmers' Association): Landbrugsmagasinet, Vester Farimagsgade 6, 1606 Copenhagen V; tel. 33-12-99-50; fax 33-93-63-62; f. 1906; Chair. CHR. SØRENSEN; Sec.-Gen. OLAV POVLSGÅRD; 30,000 mems.

**Danske Landboforeninger** (Danish Farmers' Union): Axelborg, Vesterbrogade 4A, 1620 Copenhagen V; tel. 33-12-75-61; fax 33-32-76-62; e-mail ddl@ddl.dk; internet www.ddl.dk; f. 1893; Pres. PETER GÆMELKE; Dir CARL AAGE DAHL; 59,000 mems.

**Håndværksrådet** (Danish Federation of Small- and Medium-Sized Enterprises): Amaliegade 31, 1256 Copenhagen K; tel. 33-93-20-00; fax 33-32-01-74; e-mail hvr@hvr.dk; internet www.hvr.dk; f. 1879; Chair. POUL ULSØE; Man. LARS JØRGEN NIELSEN; 110 asscns with 26,000 mems.

**Industriens Arbejdsgivere i København** (The Copenhagen Employers' Federation): 1787 Copenhagen V; tel. 33-77-33-77; fax 33-77-33-00; e-mail di@di.dk; internet www.di.dk; Chair. GERHARD ALBRECHTSEN; Sec. H. ENGELHARDT; 475 mems.

**Provinsindustriens Arbejdsgiverforening** (Federation of Employers in the Provincial Industry): 1787 Copenhagen V; tel. 33-77-33-77; fax 33-77-33-00; e-mail di@di.dk; internet www.di.dk; f. 1895; Chair. SVEND-AAGE NIELSEN; Sec. GLENN SØGÅARD.

**Sammenslutningen af Landbrugets Arbejdsgiverforeninger (SALA)** (Danish Confederation of Employers' Associations in Agriculture): Vester Farimagsgade 1, 1606 Copenhagen V; tel. 33-13-46-55; fax 33-11-89-53.

**Skibsværftsforeningen** (Association of Danish Shipbuilders): St. Kongensgade 128, 1264 Copenhagen K; tel. 33-13-24-16; fax 33-11-10-96; e-mail association@shipbuilders.dk; internet www.shipbuilders.dk.

## UTILITIES

**Danish Energy Agency:** Amaliegade 44, 1256 Copenhagen K; tel. 33-92-67-00; fax 33-11-47-43; e-mail ens@ens.dk; internet www.ens.dk; f. 1976; department of the Ministry of the Environment and Energy; Dir IB LARSEN.

### Electricity

**Elektricitetsrådet** (Electricity Council): Gothersgade 160, 1123 Copenhagen K; tel. 33-73-20-00; fax 33-73-20-99; e-mail er@elraadet.dk; internet www.elraadet.dk; f. 1907; responsible for the general planning, operation and safety of the electricity-supply industry in Denmark; Pres. TAGE DRAEBYE; Man. Dir HR. JARBY.

**Elkraft Power Company Ltd:** Lautruphøj 5, 2750 Ballerup; tel. 44-66-00-22; fax 44-65-61-04; e-mail elkraft@elkraft.dk; f. 1978; co-ordinates supply of electricity and co-generated heat to eastern Denmark; Man. Dir BENT AGERHOLM.

**Københavns Belyningsvaesen** (The Copenhagen Energy Department): Vognmagergade 8, 1149 Copenhagen K; tel. 33-12-72-90; fax 33-12-72-91; one of the largest distributors of electricity in Denmark; also supplier of gas, district-heating and public-lighting systems.

**NESA A/S:** Strandvejen 102, 2900 Hellerup; tel. 72-10-10-10; fax 72-10-10-11; e-mail nesa@nesa.dk; internet www.nesa.dk; f. 1902; largest distributor of electricity in Denmark; Man. Dir PAUL LIND.

**SK Power Company, Denmark:** Strandvejen 102, 2900 Hellerup; tel. 39-47-39-47; fax 39-47-35-33; e-mail skpower@skpower.dk; internet www.skpower.dk; f. 1992; power production; owns and operates Asnæs, Avedøre, Kyndby, Masnedø and Stigsnæs power stations and a number of local stations.

### Gas

**Dansk Gasteknisk Forening** (Danish Technical Gas Association): Rønnehaven 12, 5320 Agedrup; f. 1911; promotes the use of gas; 680 mems.

**DONG** (Dansk Olie og Naturgas A/S): Agern Allé 24-26, 2970 Hørsholm; tel. 45-57-10-22; fax 45-17-10-44; e-maildong@dong.dk; internet www.dong.dk; f. 1972; petroleum and natural gas exploration, production and distribution; acts as consultant in other countries; Chair. SVEN RISKÆR.

## CO-OPERATIVE

**Fællesforeningen for Danmarks Brugsforeninger** (Co-operative of Denmark): Roskildevej 65, 2620 Albertslund; f. 1896; Chair. EBBE LUNDGAARD; 1,113,506 mems.

## TRADE UNIONS

**Landsorganisationen i Danmark (LO)** (Danish Confederation of Trade Unions): Rosenørns Allé 12, 1634 Copenhagen V; tel. 35-24-60-00; fax 35-24-63-00; e-mail lo@lo.dk; internet www.lo.dk; Pres. HANS JENSEN; Vice-Pres. TINE A. BRØNDUM; 1,483,828 mems (Jan. 1998); 1,031 brs.

### Principal Affiliated Unions

**Blik- og Rørarbejderforbundet i Danmark** (Metal and Steel Workers): Alholmvej 55, 2500 Valby; tel. 38-71-30-22; fax 38-71-29-97; Pres. PER FREDERIKSEN; 9,237 mems.

**Dansk Artist Forbund:** Vendersgade 24, 1363 Copenhagen K; tel. 33-32-66-77; fax 33-33-73-30; e-mail artisten@artisten.dk; internet www.artisten.dk; f. 1918; Pres. NICK OLANDER; Gen. Sec. ANDY FILIPSEN; 1,600 mems.

**Dansk Beklædnings- og Textilarbejderforbund** (Textile and Garment Workers): Copenhagen; tel. 33-11-67-65; fax 33-32-99-94; Pres. ANNE M. PEDERSEN; 18,450 mems.

**Dansk El-Forbund** (Electricians' Union): Vodroffsvej 26, 1900 Frederiksberg C; tel. 33-29-70-00; fax 33-29-70-70; e-mail def@def.dk; internet www.def.dk; Pres. ERIK ANDERSSON; 30,000 mems.

**Dansk Funktionærforbund—Serviceforbundet** (Danish Federation of Salaried Employees): Upsalagade 20, 2100 Copenhagen Ø; tel. 70-15-04-00; fax 70-15-04-05; Pres. KARSTEN HANSEN; 22,071 mems.

**Dansk Jernbaneforbund** (Railway Workers): Svanemøllevej 65, 2900 Hellerup; tel. 39-40-11-66; fax 39-40-17-71; f. 1899; Pres. KURT CHRISTIANSEN; 8,567 mems.

**Dansk Metalarbejderforbund** (Metalworkers): Nyropsgade 38, 1780 Copenhagen V; tel. 33-63-20-00; fax 33-63-21-50; f. 1888; Pres. MAX BAHRING; 143,808 mems.

**Dansk Postforbund** (Postal Workers): Vodroffsvej 13A, Frederiksberg C; tel. 33-21-41-24; fax 33-21-06-42; e-mail dpf@postforbundet.dk; f. 1908; Pres. JAN SVENDSEN; 11,916 mems.

**Forbundet af Offentligt Ansatte** (Public Employees): POB 11, Staunings Plads 1–3, 1790 Copenhagen V; tel. 33-13-40-00; fax 33-13-40-42; Pres. POUL WINCKLER; 202,479 mems.

**Forbundet Trae-Industri-Byg i Danmark** (Timber Industry and Construction Workers): Mimersgade 41, 2200 Copenhagen N; tel. 35-31-95-99; fax 35-31-94-52; Pres. ARNE JOHANSEN; 72,000 mems.

**Frisør- og Kosmetiker Forbund** (Hairdressers and Beauticians): Lersø Park Allé 21, 2100 Copenhagen Ø; tel. 31-83-18-80; fax 35-82-14-62; Pres. POUL MONGGAARD; 5,288 mems.

**Grafisk Forbund** (Printing Workers): Lygten 16, 2400 Copenhagen NV; tel. 31-81-44-89; fax 31-81-24-25; f. 1993 by merger; Pres. TOM DURBING; 24,025 mems.

**Hærens Konstabel- og Korporal-Forening:** Kronprinsensgade 8, 1114 Copenhagen K; tel. 33-93-65-22; fax 33-93-65-23; e-mail hkkf@hkkf.dk; Pres. SVEND-ERIK LARSEN; 4,586 mems.

**Handels- og Kontorfunktionærernes Forbund i Danmark** (Commercial and Clerical Employees): H. C. Andersens Blvd 50, POB 268, 1780 Copenhagen V; tel. 33-30-43-43; fax 33-30-40-99; f. 1900; Pres. JOHN DAHL; 370,000 mems.

**Kvindeligt Arbejderforbund i Danmark** (Female Workers): Applebys Plads 5, 1411 Copenhagen K; tel. 32-83-83-83; fax 32-83-86-67; f. 1901; Pres. LILLIAN KNUDSEN; 90,000 mems.

**Malerforbundet i Danmark** (Housepainters): Copenhagen; tel. 38-34-75-22; fax 38-33-75-22; f. 1890; Pres. JØRN ERIK NIELSEN; 14,042 mems.

**Nærings- og Nydelsesmiddelarbejder Forbundet** (Food, Sugar Confectionery, Chocolate, Dairy Produce and Tobacco Workers): C.F. Richsvej 103, POB 1479, 2000 Frederiksberg; tel. 38-18-72-72; fax 38-18-72-00; Pres. ANTON JOHANNSEN; 43,307 mems.

**Pædagogisk Medhjælper Forbund** (Nursery and Child-care Assistants): St. Kongensgade 79, 1017 Copenhagen K; tel. 33-11-03-43; fax 33-11-31-36; f. 1974; Pres. JAKOB BANG; 32,162 mems.

**Restaurations Branchens Forbund** (Restaurant Workers): Thoravej 29-33, 2400 Copenhagen NV; tel. 38-33-89-00; fax 38-33-67-91; e-mail postmaster@rbf.dk; Chair. PREBEN RASMUSSEN; 30,770 mems.

**Socialpædagogernes Landsforbund** (National Federation of Social Educators in Denmark): Brolæggerstræde 9, 1211 Copenhagen K; tel. 33-96-28-00; fax 33-96-29-96; e-mail sl@sl-dk.dk; Pres. KIRSTEN NISSEN; 21,864 mems.

**Specialarbejderforbundet i Danmark** (General Workers' Union in Denmark): Kampmannsgade 4, POB 392, 1790 Copenhagen V; tel. 33-14-21-40; fax 33-97-24-60; e-mail sid@sid.dk; internet www.sid.dk; Pres. POUL ERIK SKOV CHRISTENSEN; Int. Sec. SUNE BOEGH; 336,110 mems.

**Teknisk Landsforbund** (Technical Workers): Nørre Voldgade 12, 1358 Copenhagen K; tel. 33-12-22-00; fax 33-11-42-72; f. 1919; Pres. ESKE PEDERSEN; 33,915 mems.

**Telekommunikations Forbundet** (Telecommunications): Rolfsvej 37, 2000 Frederiksberg; tel. 38-88-00-55; fax 38-88-15-11; Pres. BO STENØR LARSEN; 11,500 mems.

### Other Unions

**Akademikernes Centralorganisation** (Danish Confederation of Professional Associations): Nørre Voldgade 29, 1358 Copenhagen K; tel. 33-69-40-40; fax 33-93-85-40; e-mail ac@ac.dk.

**Den Almindelige Danske Lægeforening** (Danish Medical Association): Trondhjemsgade 9, 2100 Copenhagen Ø; tel. 35-44-85-00; fax 35-44-85-05; e-mail dadl@dadl.dk.

**Dansk Journalistforbund** (Journalists): Gammel Strand 46, 1202 Copenhagen K; tel. 33-42-80-00; fax 33-42-80-03; e-mail dj@journalistforbundet.dk; internet www.journalistforbundet.dk; f. 1961; Pres. MOGENS BLICHER BJERREGAARD; 13,000 mems.

**Funktionærernes og Tjenestemændenes Fællesråd** (Civil Servants' and Salaried Employees' Confederation): Niels Hemmingsens Gade 12, POB 1169, 1010 Copenhagen K; tel. 33-36-88-00; fax 33-36-88-80; f. 1952; Chair. ANKER CHRISTOFFERSEN; 400,000 mems.

# Transport

In June 1998 an 18-km combined tunnel-and-bridge road and rail link across the Great Belt, linking the islands of Zealand and Funen, was completed, at a cost of US $6,500m.; the project incorporated the world's second longest suspension bridge. In August 1991 Denmark and Sweden signed an agreement on the construction of a 15.9-km road and rail link across the Oresund strait, between Copenhagen and Malmö. Although reservations expressed in the parliaments of both countries, on financial and environmental grounds, initially delayed the project, it was subsequently announced that construction was expected to be completed by July 2000. In October 1992 the Danish, German and Swedish state railways announced a plan to develop a high-speed rail system linking Stockholm and Oslo with Copenhagen, and Copenhagen with Berlin, Hamburg and Köln. The plan, which was estimated to cost 40,000m.–50,000m. kroner, would include the bridge over the Oresund and would require new track between Copenhagen and Hamburg and the construction of a tunnel under the Fehmern Belt. In 1996 contracts were signed for the construction of a 22-km underground light railway system in Copenhagen.

## RAILWAYS

**Banestyrelsen** (Danish National Railway Agency): Solvgade 40, 1349 Copenhagen; tel. 33-14-04-00; fax 33-11-20-38; f. 1997 to assume, from the DSB (see below), responsibility for the maintenance and development of the national rail network; controls 2,349 km of line, of which 602 km are electrified; also manages signalling and train control; CEO E. ELSBORG.

**DSB** (Danish State Railways): Sølvgade 40, 1349 Copenhagen K; tel. 33-14-04-00; fax 33-14-04-40; e-mail dsb@dsb.dk; internet www.dsb.dk; became an independent public corporation in Jan. 1999; operates passenger and freight services; Man. Dir HENRIK HASSENKAM.

A total of 526 km, mostly branch lines, is run by 15 private companies.

## ROADS

At 31 December 1996 Denmark had an estimated 71,600 km of paved roads, including 880 km of motorways, 3,690 km of national roads and 7,090 km of secondary roads.

## SHIPPING

The Port of Copenhagen is the largest port in Denmark and the only one including a Free Port Zone. The other major ports are Århus, Fredericia, Ålborg and Esbjerg, all situated in Jutland. There are oil terminals, with adjacent refineries, at Kalundborg, Stigsnæs and Fredericia. Ferry services are provided by DSB (see above) and by private companies.

**Farvandsvæsenet** (Royal Danish Administration of Navigation and Hydrography): Overgaden oven Vandet 62B, POB 1919, 1023 Copenhagen K; tel. 32-68-95-00; fax 31-57-43-41.

### Port Authorities

**Århus:** Port Authority of Århus, Mindet 2, POB 130, 8100 Århus; tel. 86-13-32-66; fax 86-12-76-62; e-mail port@aarhus.dk; Gen. Man. KAJ SCHMIDT.

**Copenhagen:** Port of Copenhagen Authority, Nordre Tolbod 7, POB 2083, 1013 Copenhagen K; tel. 33-47-99-99; fax 33-47-99-33; e-mail cphport@cphport.dk; internet www.cphport.dk; Gen. Man. H. HUMMELMOSE; Port captain S. ANDERSEN.

**Esbjerg:** Port of Esbjerg Authority, Hulvejen 1, POB 2, 6701 Esbjerg; tel. 75-12-41-44; fax 75-13-40-50; e-mail shae@shae.dk; internet www.esbjerg-info.dk; Gen. Man. V. V. LEISNER; Harbour Master IB MOLLER NIELSEN.

**Fredericia:** Port Authority of Fredericia, Vesthavnsvej 33, 7000 Fredericia; tel. 75-92-02-55; fax 75-92-51-04; e-mail fredericiahaven@fredericiaport.dk; internet www.fredericiaport.com; Harbour Dir P. E. SKOTT.

**Frederikshavn:** Frederikshavn Havnekontor, Oliepieren 7, POB 129, 9900 Frederikshavn; tel. 98-42-19-88; fax 96-20-09-88; e-mail info@frederikshavnhavn.dk; internet www.frederikshavnhavn.dk; Man. BOERGE MORTENSEN; Harbour Master JESPER THOMSEN.

**Kalundborg:** Kalundborg Port Authority, POB 50, 4400 Kalundborg; tel. 53-51-33-11; fax 53-51-00-89.

**Sønderborg:** Sønderborg Havn, Norrebro 1, 6400 Sønderborg; tel. 74-42-27-65; fax 74-43-30-19; internet www.sonderborg.dk; Harbour Master LASS ANDERSEN.

### Principal Shipping Companies

**Rederiet Otto Danielsen:** Kongevejen 272A, 2830 Virum; tel. 45-83-25-55; fax 45-83-50-55; f. 1944; 6 general cargo vessels, totalling 16,400 grt, under foreign flags; general tramp trade, chartering, ship sales; Fleet Man. JØRN STAUREBY.

**Dannebrog Rederi A/S:** Rungsted Strandvej 113, 2960 Rungsted Kyst; tel. 45-17-77-77; fax 45-17-77-70; e-mail dbrog@dannebrog.com; f. 1883; 3 ro-ro vessels, product chemical tanker services; liner service US–Europe, US Gulf–Caribbean, Mediterranean–Caribbean; CEO DITLEV WEDELL-WEDELLSBORG.

**DFDS A/S:** Skt Annæ Plads 30, 1295 Copenhagen K; tel. 33-42-33-42; fax 33-42-33-41; e-mail dfds@dfds.dk; internet www.dfds.com; f. 1866; 7 car/passenger ships of 166,233 grt and 21 ro-ro vessels of 390,812 grt (incl. Swedish and German subsidiaries); passenger and car ferry services between Denmark, Sweden, the UK, the Netherlands, Germany and Norway, liner trade between Denmark, Sweden, Norway, the UK, the Netherlands, eastern Europe and Belgium; J. Lauritzen Holding owns majority share; Pres. and CEO THORLEIF BLOK.

**The East Asiatic Co Ltd A/S:** Nikolai Plads 34, 1067 Copenhagen K; tel. 33-75-00-00; fax 33-75-00-11; e-mail eac@eac.dk; f. 1897; trading, industry, food processing, plantations, shipping; totally owned and managed tonnage: 4 bulk/log carriers of 94,400 grt and 2 tankers of 33,700 grt under foreign flags; world-wide services; Chair. JAN ERLUND; Man. Dir MICHAEL FIORINI.

**Elite Shipping A/S:** H.C. Andersens Blvd 12, 3rd floor, 1553 Copenhagen V; tel. 33-15-32-33; fax 33-15-32-06; internet www.elite-shipping.dk; 29 dry cargo vessels of 80,200 grt; tramp, world-wide; Man. Dirs RINO LANGE, TORBEN PALLE HANSEN.

**H. Folmer & Co:** Fredericiagade 57, 1310 Copenhagen K; tel. 33-13-25-10; fax 33-13-54-64; f. 1955; 14 general cargo vessels of 14,100 grt; world-wide tramping; Man. Owners J. J. FOLMER, UFFE MARTIN JENSEN.

**KIL Shipping A/S:** 8 Smakkedalen, 2820 Gentofte; tel. 39-77-03-00; fax 39-76-03-99; e-mail kil@kil.dk; f. 1998; 13 container vessels totalling 121,800 dwt, 4 under the Danish Flag and 9 under a foreign flag, 16 chemical carriers totalling 130,400 dwt under foreign flags, and 6 gas carriers totalling 18,056 dwt under foreign flags; Man. Dir BJARNE TUILDE.

**J. Lauritzen A/S:** Skt Annæ Plads 28, POB 2147, 1291 Copenhagen K; tel. 33-11-12-22; fax 33-11-85-13; e-mail info@j-lauritzen.com; internet www.j-lauritzen.com; f. 1884; operates reefer ships, LPG/C Carriers and bulk ships; Pres. TORBEN JANHOLT.

**Lauritzen Kosan Tankers:** Skt Annæ Plads 28, 1291 Copenhagen K; tel. 33-14-34-00; fax 33-91-00-39; e-mail cphkos@j-lauritzen.com; internet www.j-lauritzen.com; f. 1951; 26 gas carriers of 94,546 grt; Man. Dir TORBEN MEJNERTSEN.

**Mercandia Rederierne:** Amaliegade 27, 1256 Copenhagen K; tel. 33-12-01-55; fax 33-32-55-47; f. 1964; 24 ro-ro vessels and car ferries totalling 238,200 grt; tramp and liner services; Man. Owner PER HENRIKSEN.

**A. P. Møller:** Esplanaden 50, 1098 Copenhagen K; tel. 33-63-33-63; fax 33-14-15-15; internet www.maersk.com; f. 1904; fleet of 38 container vessels, 13 products tankers, 5 crude oil tankers, 13 gas carriers, 26 offshore vessels and 7 drilling rigs, totalling 3,081,900 grt under the Danish flag; further tonnage owned by subsidiary cos in Singapore and the UK; world-wide liner and feeder services under the name of **Maersk Line**, and world-wide tanker, bulk, offshore and rig services; Man. Owner JESS SØDERBERG.

**A/S Em. Z. Svitzer:** Park Allé 350B, 2605 Brøndby; tel. 43-43-43-71; fax 43-43-60-22; f. 1833; wholly-owned subsidiary of A. P. Møller; 22 tugs and salvage vessels and a barge fleet; salvage, towage and barge services; Gen. Man. KELD BALLE-MORTENSEN.

**Mortensen & Lange A/S:** Kongevejen 2, 2480 Fredensborg; tel. 48-40-85-85; fax 42-28-00-57; f. 1961; general cargo vessels of 13,800 grt and 6 reefer vessels of 8,000 grt; world-wide tramping; Man. Dir (vacant).

**Dampskibsselskabet Norden A/S:** Amaliegade 49, 1256 Copenhagen K; tel. 33-15-04-51; fax 33-15-61-99; e-mail mail@ds-norden.dk; internet www.ds-norden.com; f. 1871; 5 bulk carriers of 224,600 grt, 1 product tanker of 43,700 grt and 1 oil tanker of 55,000 grt; world-wide tramping; Man. Dir STEEN KRABBE.

**Sønderborg Rederiaktieselskab:** Havnevej 18, POB 20, 6320 Egernsund; tel. 74-44-14-35; fax 74-44-14-75; 6 livestock carriers of 5,700 grt; shipowners, managers, chartering agents; world-wide; Chair. B. CLAUSEN.

**Terkol-Rederierne:** Jægergårdsvej 107, 8000 Århus C; tel. 86-13-36-88; fax 86-18-15-10; 2 container vessels of 21,100 grt and 17 chemical tankers of 42,400 grt; world-wide tanker services; Gen. Man. N. B. TERKILDSEN.

**A/S D/S Torm:** Marina Park, Sundkrogsgade 10, 2100 Copenhagen Ø; tel. 39-17-92-00; fax 39-17-93-93; f. 1889; 15 product carriers of 560,741 grt, 6 bulk carriers of 163,322 grt, 2 multipurpose vessels of 27,376 grt and 2 AHTs (1999); operator of a time-chartered fleet; liner services USA–West Africa; Man. Dir ERIK BEHN.

### Shipping Association

**Danmarks Rederiforening** (Danish Shipowners' Assen): Amaliegade 33, 1256 Copenhagen K; tel. 33-11-40-88; fax 33-11-62-10; e-mail info@danmarksrederiforening.dk; internet www.danmarksrederiforening.dk; f. 1884; 21 members, representing 4,841,000 grt (July 1998); Chair. of the Board STEEN R. KRABBE; Man. Dir PETER BJERREGAARD.

## CIVIL AVIATION

The main international airport is Copenhagen Airport, situated about 10 km from the centre of the capital. The following domestic airports have scheduled flights to European and Scandinavian destinations: Ålborg, Århus and Billund in Jutland. Other domestic airports include Roskilde (30 km south-west of Copenhagen); Esbjerg, Karup, Skrydstrup, Stauning, Sønderborg and Thisted in Jutland; Odense in Funen; and Bornholm Airport on the island of Bornholm.

**Statens Luftfartsvæsen** (Civil Aviation Administration): Luftfartshuset, POB 744, 2450 Copenhagen SV; tel. 36-44-48-48; fax 36-44-03-03; e-mail dcaa@slv.dk; Dir-Gen. OLE ASMUSSEN.

**Det Danske Luftfartselskab A/S—DDL** (Danish Airlines): Industriens Hus, H. C. Andersens Blvd 18, 1553 Copenhagen V; tel. 33-14-13-33; fax 33-14-28-28; f. 1918; 50% govt-owned; Danish parent company of the designated national carrier, Scandinavian Airlines System—SAS (see under Sweden), SAS Commuter; Chair. HUGO SCHRØDER; Man. Dir GUNNAR TIETZ.

### National Airlines

**Cimber Air Denmark:** Sønderborg Airport, Lufthavnsvej 2, 6400 Sønderborg; tel. 74-42-22-77; fax 74-42-65-11; f. 1950; operates domestic service in co-operation with Lufthansa and SAS; operates charter flights and total route systems for other cos throughout Europe; markets electronic data systems for airlines and industry; Pres., CEO JORGEN NIELSEN; Vice-Pres. (Airline Division) HANS I. NIELSEN.

**Maersk Air:** Copenhagen Airport South, 2791 Dragør; tel. 32-31-44-44; fax 32-31-44-90; e-mail mail@maersk-air.dk; internet www.maersk-air.com; f. 1969; provides charter flights for Scandinavian tour operators, operates domestic services and international flights to Belgium, Germany, Sweden, the Netherlands, Norway, Italy, Greece and the UK; owned by Møller Group (see under Shipping); subsidiary: Maersk Air Cargo; Chair. BJARNE HANSEN; Pres. OLE DIETZ.

**Muk Air:** Copenhagen Airport South, 2791 Dragør; tel. 32-82-00-00; fax 32-82-00-78; f. 1979; operates scheduled services to destinations in Scandinavia and Germany; Pres. Capt. KNUT LINDAU; Vice-Pres. FRANK HOLTON.

**Premiair:** Copenhagen Airport South, Hangar 276, 2791 Dragør; tel. 32-47-72-00; fax 32-45-12-20; f. 1994 by merger of Conair A/S (Denmark) and Scanair (Sweden); controlling stake acquired by Airtours (United Kingdom) in 1996; flights to major destinations in Europe; Pres. TOM CLAUSEN.

**Star Air:** Copenhagen Airport South, 2791 Dragør; tel. 32-31-43-43; fax 32-31-43-90; f. 1987; operates cargo services in Europe; Pres. OLE DIETZ.

# Tourism

There were 43.2m. overnight stays in all types of accommodation in 1998, 60% of which were made by foreign visitors.

**Danmarks Turistråd** (The Danish Tourist Board): Vesterbrogade 6D, 1620 Copenhagen V; tel. 33-11-14-15; fax 33-93-14-16; e-mail dt@dt.dk; internet www.visitdenmark.com; f. 1967; Dir BJARNE EKLUND.

# DANISH EXTERNAL TERRITORIES

## THE FAROE ISLANDS

### Introductory Survey

**Location, Climate, Language, Religion, Flag, Capital**

The Faroe Islands are a group of 18 islands (of which 17 are inhabited) in the Atlantic Ocean, between Scotland and Iceland. The main island is Streymoy, where more than one-third of the population resides. The climate is mild in winter and cool in summer, with a mean temperature of 7°C (45°F). Most of the inhabitants profess Christianity: the majority of Faroese belong to the Evangelical Lutheran Church of Denmark. The principal language is Faroese, but Danish is a compulsory subject in all schools. The flag (proportions 22 by 16) displays a red cross, bordered with blue, on a white background, the upright of the cross being to the left of centre. The capital is Tórshavn, which is situated on Streymoy.

**History and Government**

The Faroe Islands have been under Danish administration since Queen Margrethe I of Denmark inherited Norway in 1380. The islands were occupied by the United Kingdom while Denmark was under German occupation during the Second World War, but they were restored to Danish control immediately after the war. The Home Rule Act of 1948 gave the Faroese control over all their internal affairs. The Faroe Islands did not join the European Community (EC) with Denmark in 1973. There is a local parliament (the Løgting), but the Danish Folketing, to which the Faroese send two members, is responsible for defence and foreign policy, constitutional matters and the judicial and monetary systems. The Faroes control fishing resources within their fisheries zone, and in September 1992 a long-standing dispute between Denmark and the Faroes was settled when the Danish Government agreed to give the Faroese authorities legislative and administrative power over mineral resources, including those beneath the bed of the sea in the area adjacent to the islands. This agreement removed one of the major obstacles to exploration for hydrocarbons off the Faroe Islands, where geologists consider that prospects for discovering reserves of petroleum and natural gas are favourable. In 1994 the Faroe Islands accordingly awarded a US company a licence to begin exploratory surveys, despite the existence of a long-standing dispute between Denmark and the United Kingdom over the demarcation of the continental shelf west of the Shetland Islands and south-east of the Faroe Islands, which had threatened to delay prospecting. This dispute was resolved in May 1999, however, when representatives of the Faroese Government signed an agreement with the Danish and UK Governments regarding the location of the boundaries of the area concerned. The area, known as the White Zone, was believed to be potentially rich in petroleum reserves, and it was anticipated that drilling would commence in 2001.

The centre-left coalition Government of the Social Democratic Party (SDP), Republicans and the People's Party, formed in 1975, collapsed in 1980 over a plan, opposed by the conservative People's Party, to extend through the winter months a government-owned ferry service linking the islands with Denmark, Norway and Scotland. At a general election, held in November, conservative political groups slightly increased their share of the popular vote. Although there was no material change in the balance of party representation in the Løgting, the Union Party formed a centre-right coalition with the People's Party and the Home Rule Party in January 1981. A general election was held in November 1984, and in December a four-party, centre-left coalition government was formed under the premiership of Atli Dam, comprising his SDP, the Home Rule Party, the Republican Party and the Christian People's Party combined with the Progressive and Fishing Industry Party (CPP-PFIP).

Elections in 1988 demonstrated a shift to the right in the Faroes, to the benefit of the People's Party. Its one member in the Danish Folketing increased his support in the national elections of September 1987 and May 1988. At a Faroese general election in November 1988 the incumbent Government lost its majority, and the People's Party became the largest party in the Løgting. In January 1989, after 10 weeks of negotiations, a centre-right coalition comprising the People's Party, the Republican Party, the Home Rule Party and the CPP-PFIP, and led by Jógvan Sundstein (Chairman of the People's Party), was formed. The coalition was committed to economic austerity and support for the fishing industry. In June 1989, however, the CPP-PFIP and the Home Rule Party withdrew their support for the Government. After three weeks a new coalition was formed. Sundstein remained Løgmaður (Prime Minister), and his People's Party was supported by the Republican and Union Parties. In October 1990, however, these two parties withdrew their support for the coalition Government. As a result, an early general election was held in November. The SDP obtained the largest share of the vote, winning 10 seats (an increase of three), while the People's Party, which led the outgoing coalition, won seven seats (a loss of one seat). In January 1991 a coalition between the SDP and the People's Party was formed, under the leadership of Atli Dam. He was replaced in January 1993 by Marita Petersen (also of the SDP). In April the People's Party withdrew from the coalition, and was replaced by the Republican Party and the Home Rule Party. At a general election, held in July 1994, the Union Party became the largest party in the Løgting, winning eight seats (an increase of two), while the SDP's allocation of seats was reduced from 10 to five. In September a coalition of the Union Party, the SDP, the Home Rule Party and the newly-formed Labour Front took office. Edmund Joensen replaced Petersen as Prime Minister. In 1996 the People's Party replaced the SDP in the governing coalition. Joensen remained Prime Minister, while Anfinn Kallsberg succeeded Jóannes Eidesgaard as Minister of Finance and Economics. A general election was held on 30 April 1998, at which both the Republican Party and the People's Party each increased their allocation of seats to eight, while the number of seats secured by the SDP rose from five to seven; the parliamentary representation of the Union Party was reduced from eight seats to six. In mid-May a coalition Government was formed by members of the People's Party, the Republican Party and the Home Rule Party, under the premiership of Anfinn Kallsberg. In October the Løgting adopted a resolution in support of the Government's intention (announced earlier that year) to seek status for the Faroe Islands as a 'sovereign nation' under the Danish monarchy, having a common monetary system with Denmark; it was envisaged by the Faroese Government that sovereignty for the islands would be most appropriately achieved through continued co-operation with Denmark within a new constitutional framework, based on a bilateral treaty between the two countries as equal, independent partners. A commission charged with the development of a proposal for a Faroese constitution was established by the Government in February 1999, and was to submit its conclusions to the Løgting by 1 June 2000. In the event of a satisfactory agreement being reached with Denmark on the proposal for a treaty establishing the Faroe Islands as a sovereign nation, and following the approval of the proposal by both the Danish and Faroese Governments, the Faroese Government stated that the issue would be submitted to approval by referendum on the islands in 2000.

In international affairs, the Faroe Islanders earned opprobrium for their traditional slaughter of pilot whales, an important source of food. After foreign journalists publicized the whaling in 1986, stricter regulations were imposed on whaling operations. In July 1992 the Faroes Government threatened to leave the International Whaling Commission (IWC, see p. 284), following the latter's criticism of whaling methods practised in the Faroe Islands. It was, however, claimed that the Faroese did not have the legal right to withdraw from the Commission independently of Denmark. In September the Faroe Islands, Greenland, Norway and Iceland agreed to establish the North Atlantic Marine Mammal Commission, in protest at what they viewed as the IWC's preoccupation with conservation.

Responsibility for foreign policy lies in Copenhagen, but in 1983 the Løgting unanimously declared the Faroe Islands a 'nuclear-free zone', and in 1987, as a consequence of this policy, requested the Danish Government to curtail a US naval visit. There have also been several declarations of 'non-aligned' status, notwithstanding NATO membership as part of the Kingdom of Denmark. When the People's Party changed its policy, however, to advocate closer co-operation with the NATO alliance, the party ended political unanimity on the issue and made gains in the elections of 1987 and 1988.

**Economic Affairs**

In 1995 gross national product (GNP), estimated at 1990 prices, was US $829m., equivalent to $19,000 per head. Between 1973 and 1988, it was estimated, GNP increased, in real terms, at an average rate of 4.5% per year, with real GNP per head rising by 3.3% annually. Between 1989 and 1993, however, real GNP decreased dramatically, at an average rate of 9.4% per year. During 1994–95 real GNP increased by 4.2%. The average annual rate of population growth between 1977 and 1988 was 1.2%. Since then, however, the population has decreased at an average annual rate of 1.3%, although it was expected to increase by some 2% in 1996.

Agriculture (principally sheep-farming) and fishing contributed 14.5% of gross domestic product (GDP) in 1996. Potatoes and other vegetables are the main crops. Only about 6% of the land surface is cultivated.

Fishing is the dominant industry. In 1994 fishing and fish-processing accounted for 18% of GDP and employed 23% of the labour force; in 1998 the sector accounted for 96.5% of exports. Most fishing takes place within the 200-nautical-mile (370-km) fisheries zone imposed around the Faroes in 1977, and in the 1980s there was massive investment in developing the fishing fleet and the processing plants on the islands. The fishing industry has considerably declined, however, since 1991. In the 1980s fish farming began to be encouraged, and in 1994 farmed fish amounted to about 12,400 metric tons and earned some 363m. kroner. The traditional hunting of whales (see Recent History) is an important source of meat.

Industry (including mining, manufacturing, construction and power) contributed 18.7% of GDP in 1996. The dominant sector is fish-processing. Coal is mined on Suðuroy, and a small textile industry exports traditional Faroese woollens. Manufacturing alone accounted for 13.1% of GDP in 1996. The export of sea-going vessels accounted for 2.6% of total exports in 1998. About 48% of the islands' energy requirements are provided by a hydroelectric power plant. The potential for petroleum production around the islands is believed to be significant.

In 1998 the Faroe Islands recorded a trade surplus of 316m. kroner, and there was a surplus of 887m. kroner on the current account of the balance of payments. Denmark remains the Faroes' principal trading partner, supplying 33.4% of imports and receiving 30.7% of exports in 1996. In 1995 the European Union (EU, as the EC was restyled in 1993) as a whole took 79% of exports, the UK receiving 26% and Germany 10%. Norway is also a major source of imports, supplying about 17.8% of the total in 1996. The principal imports from Norway are animal food and live animals, and machinery and transport equipment.

Danish subsidies are an important source of income to the islands, and accounted for about 24% of total government revenue in 1996. In that year, including the central government grant of 867m. kroner as revenue, the Faroese Government recorded a budget surplus of 926m. kroner. At the end of 1998 the net foreign debt was estimated at 2,190m. kroner. The annual rate of inflation averaged 3.2% between 1990 and 1996. In the 1980s there was an acute labour shortage in the Faroes, but by mid-1995 unemployment had increased to 3,200, equivalent to some 16% of the labour force. By the end of 1999, however, unemployment had declined to some 5% of the labour force.

The Faroe Islands did not join the EC with Denmark in 1973, but did secure favourable terms of trade with Community members and special concessions in Denmark and the United Kingdom. Agreements on free trade were concluded between the Faroe Islands and Iceland, Norway, Sweden, Finland and Austria in 1992 and 1993. In international fisheries organizations, where Denmark is represented by the EU, the Kingdom maintains separate membership in respect of the Faroe Islands (and Greenland). The Faroe Islands is also a member of the Nordic Council (see p. 222).

During the 1980s the Faroes' principal source of income, the fishing industry, was expanded with the help of substantial investment and official subsidies, financed by external borrowing. However, depletion of stocks and the resulting decline in catches, together with a fall in export prices, led to a reduction in export earnings and a financial crisis in the early 1990s (GDP was estimated to have declined by some 20% in 1993). The Danish Government attempted to stabilize the economy by restructuring the banking sector and by extending significant loans (by the end of 1997 it was estimated that the Faroes owed some 5,500m. kroner to the Danish Government, equivalent to 140,000 kroner per head). The report of an independent commission of inquiry into Denmark's response to the crisis in the Faroes, which had been established by the islanders in 1995, was published in early 1998 and levelled accusations of serious mismanagement at Danish government officials, and at the Danish Den Danske Bank. In June 1998 an agreement was reached by the Faroese and Danish Governments regarding a reduction of Faroese debt to Denmark as a form of compensation.

### Education and Social Welfare

The education system is similar to that of Denmark, except that Faroese is the language of instruction. Danish is, however, a compulsory subject in all schools. The Faroese Academy was upgraded to the University of the Faroe Islands in May 1990.

In 1995 government medical services included three hospitals, with a total of 297 beds. In 1998 there were 1.94 physicians and 0.84 dentist for every 1,000 of the population.

In 1995 government expenditure on social welfare represented 28% of total budget spending, while education received a further 13% of the total.

## Statistical Survey

Sources (unless otherwise stated): Statistical Bureau of the Faroe Islands, POB 355, 110 Tórshavn; tel. 314636; fax 318696; e-mail farostat@olivant.fo; Statistics Faroe Islands, Traðagøta 39, POB 2068, 165 Argir; tel 352028; fax 352038; e-mail hagstova@hagstova.fo; internet www.hagstova.fo; Faroese Government Office, Hovedvagtsgade 8, 2, 1103 Copenhagen K; tel. 33-14-08-66; fax 33-93-85-75; *Yearbook of Nordic Statistics*.

### AREA AND POPULATION

**Area:** 1,398.9 sq km (540.1 sq miles).

**Population:** 43,784 (males 22,578, females 21,206) at 31 December 1996; 44,300 (provisional) at 31 December 1997; 44,800 (provisional) at 31 December 1998.

**Density** (1998, provisional): 32.0 per sq km.

**Principal Town:** Tórshavn (capital), population 15,800 at 31 December 1997.

**Births and Deaths** (1996): Registered live births 672 (birth rate 15.4 per 1,000); Deaths 391 (death rate 9.0 per 1,000). *1997* (rates per 1,000): Births 15.0; Deaths 8.4. *1998* (rates per 1,000): Births 14.1; Deaths 8.4.

**Expectation of Life** (years at birth, 1998): Males 74.1; Females 80.8.

**Employed Labour Force** (1998): Total 23,890 (males 13,325, females 10,565).

### AGRICULTURE AND FISHING

**Principal Crop** (FAO estimate, 1998): Potatoes 2,000 metric tons. Source: FAO, *Production Yearbook*.

**Livestock** (FAO estimates, '000 head, year ending September 1998): Cattle 2; Sheep 68. Source: FAO, *Production Yearbook*.

**Fishing** ('000 metric tons, live weight, 1997): Atlantic cod 57.9; Haddock 21.4; Saithe (Pollock) 22.6; Redfish 11.4; Blue whiting (Poutassou) 28.8; Norway pout 8.7; Atlantic herring 65.9; Mackerel 11.5; Capelin 44.8; Northern prawn 10.9; Argentines 8.4; Sandeels (Sandlances) 11.2; Total catch (incl. others) 329.7. Source: FAO, *Yearbook of Fishery Statistics*.

### INDUSTRY

**Selected Products** ('000 metric tons, unless otherwise indicated, 1996): Frozen or chilled fish 123; Salted and processed fish products 15; Aquamarine products 13; Oils, fats and meal of aquatic animals 124; Electric energy (million kWh) 182.

### FINANCE

Danish currency is in use.

**Government Accounts** ('000 kroner, 1996): Revenue 2,781,000; Danish state subsidy 867,000; Expenditure 2,722,000.

**Cost of Living** (Consumer Price Index; base: 1983 = 100): *1997:* Food 22.1; Fuel and power 81; Clothing 169; Dwellings 142; Other 152; All items 166.

**Gross Domestic Product by Economic Activity** (million kroner at current factor cost, 1996): Agriculture, fishing, etc. 763; Mining and quarrying 10; Manufacturing 689; Electricity, gas and water 100; Construction 188; Trade, restaurants and hotels 610; Transport, storage and communications 378; Financing 341; Dwellings 689; Business services, etc. 126; Domestic services 13; Government services 1,301; Sub-total (incl. adjustment) 5,273; *Less* imputed bank service charges 412; Gross domestic product at factor cost 4,861.

**Balance of Payments** (US $ million, 1995): Merchandise exports f.o.b. 362; Merchandise imports c.i.f. –315; *Trade balance* 46; Services, other income and private unrequited transfers (net) –114; Official unrequited transfers (net) 193; *Current balance* 125.

### EXTERNAL TRADE

**Principal Commodities** (million kroner, 1995): *Imports c.i.f.:* Food and live animals 111; Mineral fuels, lubricants, etc. 202 (Petroleum products 190); Chemicals and related products 69; Commodities for final consumption 625; Machinery and transport equipment 248 (Machinery specialized for particular industries 45, General industrial machinery, equipment and parts 64, Electric machinery, apparatus, etc. 37, Road vehicles and parts 91); Total (incl. others) 1,766. *Exports f.o.b.:* Food and live animals 1,874; Machinery and transport equipment 35; Total (incl. others) 2,026.

**Principal Trading Partners** (million kroner, 1996): *Imports c.i.f.:* Denmark 707; Germany 199; Iceland 47; Japan 65; Norway 377; Sweden 108; United Kingdom 180; USA 48; Total (incl. others) 2,118. *Exports f.o.b.:* Denmark 737; France (incl. Monaco) 168; Germany 205; Italy 69; Japan 31; Spain 133; United Kingdom 589; USA 49; Total (incl. others) 2,398.

### TRANSPORT

**Road Traffic** (registered motor vehicles, 31 December 1997): Private motor cars 12,748; Goods vehicles 2,867; Buses 111; Coaches 107; Trailers 1,078; Motor cycles 148.

**Shipping:** Merchant fleet (31 December 1998): 141 vessels (fishing vessels 113), Total displacemet 103,478 grt (fishing vessels 70,789 grt); International sea-borne freight traffic (1996, '000 metric tons): Goods loaded 223, Goods unloaded 443.

### COMMUNICATIONS MEDIA

**Radio Receivers** (1996): 24,000 registered.

**Television Receivers** (1997): 13,000 registered.

**Book Production** (1998): 129 titles.

**Newspapers** (1996): 5 titles (average circulation 7,000 copies per issue).

**Telephones** ('000 main lines in use, 1995): 22 (Source: UN, *Statistical Yearbook*).

**Telefax Stations** (1993): 1,400 in use (Source: UN, *Statistical Yearbook*).

**Mobile Cellular Telephones** (subscribers, 1995): 2,558 (Source: UN, *Statistical Yearbook*).

# Directory

## The Government

The legislative body is the Løgting (Lagting in Danish) which consists of 27 members, elected on a basis of proportional representation in seven constituencies, with up to five supplementary seats dependent upon the discrepancy between the distribution of seats among the parties and the numbers of people voting. All Faroese over the age of 18 years have the right to vote. Based on the strength of the parties in the Løgting, a Government, the Landsstýri, is formed. This is the administrative body in certain spheres, chiefly relating to Faroese economic affairs. The Løgmaður (Prime Minister) has to ratify all Løgting laws. Power is decentralized and there are about 50 local authorities. The Ríkisumboðsmaður, or High Commissioner, represents the Danish Government, and has the right to address the Løgting and to advise on joint affairs. All Danish legislation must be submitted to the Landsstýri before becoming law in the Faroe Islands.

### LANDSSTÝRI
(February 2000)

A coalition of the People's Party (PP), the Republican Party (RP) and the Home Rule Party (HRP).

**Prime Minister (with responsibility for Constitutional Affairs, Foreign Affairs and Municipal Affairs):** ANFINN KALLSBERG (PP).

**Minister of Self-governmental and Judicial Affairs and of Nordic Affairs:** HØGNI HOYDAL (RP).

**Minister of Education and Cultural Affairs:** SIGAR Á BRÚNNI (RP).

**Minister of Finance:** KARSTIN HANSEN (RP).

**Minister of Industry, Transport and Communications:** FINNBOGI ARGE (PP).

**Minister of Oil-related Matters and Environmental Affairs:** EYÐUN ELTTØR (HRP).

**Minister of Health and Social Affairs:** HELENA DAM Á NEYSTABØ (HRP).

**Minister of Fisheries:** JØRGEN NICLASEN (PP).

### Government Offices

**Ríkisumboðsmaðurin** (Danish High Commission): POB 12, Amtmansbrekkan 4, 110 Tórshavn; tel. 311040; fax 310864; High Commissioner VIBEKE LARSEN.

**Løgtingsskrivstovan** (Parliament Office): POB 208, 110 Tórshavn; tel. 310850; fax 310686; Leader SÚSANNA DANIELSEN.

**Faroese Government Office:** Hovedvagtsgade 8, 2, 1103 Copenhagen K; tel. 33-14-08-66; fax 33-93-85-75; e-mail focph@faroff.dk.

### LØGTING

The Løgting has between 27 and 32 members, elected by universal adult suffrage.

**Speaker:** FINNBOGI ISAKSON (Republican Party).

**Election, 30 April 1998**

| | Votes | % of votes | Seats |
|---|---|---|---|
| Tjóðveldisflokkurin (Republican Party) | 6,583 | 23.8 | 8 |
| Fólkaflokkurin (People's Party) | 5,887 | 21.3 | 8 |
| Javnaðarflokkurin (Social Democratic Party) | 6,062 | 21.9 | 7 |
| Sambandsflokkurin (Union Party) | 4,992 | 18.0 | 6 |
| Sjálvstýrisflokkurin (Home Rule Party) | 2,116 | 7.7 | 2 |
| Miðflokkurin (Centre Party) | 1,123 | 4.1 | 1 |
| Kristiligi Fólkaflokkurin (Christian People's Party) | 682 | 2.5 | – |
| Verkmannafylkingin (Labour Front) | 215 | 0.8 | – |
| **Total** | 27,660 | 100.0 | 32 |

## Political Organizations

Unless otherwise indicated, the address of each of the following organizations is: Áarvegur, POB 208, 110 Tórshavn; tel. 310850; fax 310686.

**Fólkaflokkurin** (People's Party): f. 1940; conservative-liberal party, favours free enterprise and wider political and economic autonomy for the Faroes; Chair. ÓLI BRECKMANN.

**Hin Føroyski Flokkurin** (The Faroese Party): f. 1994; seeks to abolish Home Rule and fully to re-integrate the Faroes into the Kingdom of Denmark; Chair. ÓLAVUR CHRISTIANSEN.

**Javnaðarflokkurin** (Social Democratic Party—SDP): Argjavegur 26, 160 Argir; tel. 311820; fax 314720; f. 1928; Chair. JÓANNES EIDESGAARD.

**Kristiligi Fólkaflokkurin, Føroya Framburðs- og Fiskivinnuflokkurin** (Christian People's Party, Progressive and Fishing Industry Party—CPP-PFIP): à Brekku 5, 700 Klaksvík; tel. 457580; fax 457581; f. 1954; centre party; Chair. NIELS PAULI DANIELSEN; Parliamentary Chair. LASSE KLEIN.

**Miðflokkurin** (Centre Party): POB 3237, 110 Tórshavn; f. 1991; Chair. TORDUR NICLASEN.

**Sambandsflokkurin** (Union Party): f. 1906; favours the maintenance of close relations between the Faroes and the Kingdom of Denmark; conservative in internal affairs; Chair. EDMUND JOENSEN.

**Sjálvstýrisflokkurin** (Home Rule Party): f. 1906; social-liberal party advocating eventual political independence for the Faroes within the Kingdom of Denmark; Chair. HELENA DAM Á NEYSTABØ.

**Tjóðveldisflokkurin** (Republican Party): Villingadalsvegi, 100 Tórshavn; tel. 314412; f. 1948; left-wing party, advocates the secession of the Faroes from Denmark; Chair. FINNBOGI ÍSAKSON.

**Verkmannafylkingin** (Labour Front): f. 1994 by Union leaders and former members of the SDP.

## Religion

### CHRISTIANITY

The Faroes Church (Evangelical Lutheran Church of Denmark) regained its diocese in November 1990, and the suffragan bishop became Bishop of the Faroe Islands. The largest independent group is the 'Plymouth Brethren'. There is also a small Roman Catholic community.

### Evangelical Lutheran Church

**Føroya Biskupur** (Bishop of the Faroe Islands): HANS J. JOENSEN, J. Paturssonargøta 20, POB 8, 110 Tórshavn; tel. 311995; fax 315889.

## The Press

In 1996 there were six general interest newspapers in the Faroe Islands.

**Dagblaðið:** Reynagøta 9, 100 Tórshavn; tel. 319833; fax 319823; weekly; People's Party.

**Dimmalætting:** Smyrilsvegur, POB 19, 110 Tórshavn; tel. 311212; fax 310941; 4 a week; Union Party; circ. 11,000.

**FF/FA-Blaðið:** Vágsbotnur, POB 58, 110 Tórshavn; tel. 312169; fax 318769; weekly; Editor VILMUND JACOBSEN; circ. 2,500.

**Norðlýsið:** á Hædd, POB 58, 700 Klaksvík; tel. 456285; fax 456498; weekly; circ. 1,200.

**Oyggjatíðindi:** R. C. Effersøesgøta 7, POB 3312, 110 Tórshavn; tel. 314411; fax 316410; 2 a week; circ. 4,500.

**Tíðindablaðið Sosialurin:** POB 76, 110 Tórshavn; tel. 311820; fax 314720; e-mail post@sosialurin.fo; internet www.sosialurin.fo; f. 1927; 5 a week; Editor JAN MÜLLER; Social Democratic Party; circ. 7,000.

### NEWS AGENCY

**Ritzaus Bureau:** Gamli Vegur 3; tel. 316366; f. 1980; Man. RANDI MOHR.

## Broadcasting and Communications

### RADIO

**Útvarp Føroya** (Radio Faroe Islands): Norðari Ringvegur, POB 328, 110 Tórshavn; tel. 316566; fax 310471; e-mail uf@uf.fo; internet www.uf.fo; f. 1957; Man. JÓGVAN JESPERSEN.

### TELEVISION

**Sjónvarp Føroya** (Faroese Television): M. A. Winthersgøta, POB 21, 110 Tórshavn; tel. 317780; fax 318815; e-mail svf@svf.fo; f. 1984; Gen. Man. TRÓNDUR DJURHUUS.

## Finance

### BANKS

(cap. = capital; res = reserves; dep. = deposits; m. = million; amounts in kroner; brs = branches)

**Føroya Banki P/f:** Húsagøta 3, POB 3048, 110 Tórshavn; tel. 311350; fax 315850; e-mail fbk@post.olivant.fo; internet www .foroyabanki.fo; f. 1994 following merger of Føroya Banki (f. 1906) and Sjóvinnubankin (f. 1932); cap. 100m., res 861m., dep. 3,138m., total assets 4,437m. (Dec. 1998); Chair. JÓHAN PÁLL JOENSEN; Mans JØRN ASTRUP HANSEN, JANUS PETERSEN; 25 brs.

**Føroya Sparikassi** (Faroese Savings Bank): Sverrisgøta 3, POB 34, 110 Tórshavn; tel. 314800; fax 310048; e-mail spak@post.olivant.fo; internet www.sparikassin.fo; f. 1832; cap. 10.6m., res 6.7m., dep. 2,937.8m. (Dec. 1998); Chair. PETER ZACHARIASSEN; Chief Man. Dir MARNER JACOBSEN.

**Landsbanki Føroya:** Müllers Hús – Gongin, POB 229, 110 Tórshavn; tel. 318305; fax 318537; e-mail landsbankin@lbk.olivant.fo; Man. SIGURÐ POULSEN.

**Norðoya Sparikassi:** Ósávegur 1, POB 149, 700 Klaksvík; tel. 456366; fax 456761.

**Suðuroya Sparikassi:** POB 2, 900 Vágur; tel. 373064; fax 373340; e-mail sparsu@post.olivant.fo.

### INSURANCE

**Tryggingarfelagio Føroyar:** Kongabrúgvin, POB 329, 110 Tórshavn; tel. 314590; fax 315590; marine, fire, accident and life; sole insurance co in islands; Man. JENS PETUR ARGE.

## Trade and Industry

### GOVERNMENT AGENCY

**Fiskivinnuumsitingin** (Fisheries Administration): POB 87, 110 Tórshavn; tel. 313068; fax 314942.

### INDUSTRIAL AND TRADE ASSOCIATIONS

**L/F Føroya Fiskasøla—Faroe Seafood Prime P/F:** POB 68, 110 Tórshavn; tel. 345345; fax 345300; e-mail faroe@faroe.com; f. 1948, restructured 1995; joint stock company of fish producers; exports all seafood products; Man. Dir POUL MICHELSEN.

**Føroya Reiðarafelag** (Faroe Fishing Vessel-Owners' Association): R.C. Effersøesgøta, POB 179, 110 Tórshavn; tel. 311864; fax 317278.

### TRADE UNION

**Føroya Arbeiðarafelag** (Faroese Labour Organization): Tjarnðeild 5, POB 56, 110 Tórshavn; tel. 312101; fax 315374.

## Transport

There are about 458 km of roads in the Faroe Islands. In 1999 proposals were being considered for the construction of a 4.7-km-tunnel running under the sea, linking Vágar to Streymoy.

The main harbour is at Tórshavn; the other ports are at Fuglafjørður, Klaksvík, Skálafjorður, Tvøroyri, Vágur and Vestmanna. Between mid-May and mid-September, a summer roll-on, roll-off ferry service links the Faroe Islands with Iceland, Shetland (United Kingdom), Denmark and Norway.

There is an airport on Vágar.

**Atlantic Airways Faroe Islands:** Vágar Airport, 380 Sørvágur; tel. 333344; fax 333380; f. 1987; owned by Faroese Govt; scheduled and charter passenger and cargo services to Copenhagen; Pres. MAGNI ARGE.

## Tourism

**Ferðaráð Føroya** (Faroe Islands Tourist Board): Gongin, POB 118, 100 Tórshavn; tel. 316055; fax 310858; e-mail tourist@tourist.fo; internet www.tourist.fo; f. 1984; Man. ANNIKA W. JOENSEN.

# GREENLAND

## Introductory Survey

**Location, Climate, Language, Religion, Flag, Capital**

Greenland (Kalaallit Nunaat) is the world's largest island, with a total area of 2,166,086 sq km, and lies in the North Atlantic Ocean, east of Canada. Most of it is permanently covered by ice, but 410,449 sq km of coastland are habitable. Greenlandic, an Inuit (Eskimo) language, and Danish are the official languages. The majority of the population profess Christianity and belong mainly to the Evangelical Lutheran Church of Denmark. There are also small communities of other Protestant groups and of Roman Catholics. The flag (proportions 3 by 2) consists of two equal horizontal stripes (white above red), on which is superimposed a representation of the rising sun (a disc divided horizontally, red above white) to the left of centre. Nuuk (Godthåb) is the capital.

**Recent History**

Greenland first came under Danish rule in 1380. In the revision of the Danish Constitution in 1953, Greenland became part of the Kingdom and acquired the representation of two members in the Danish Folketing. In October 1972 the Greenlanders voted, by 9,658 to 3,990, against joining the European Community (EC) but, as part of Denmark, were bound by the Danish decision to join. Resentment of Danish domination of the economy, education and the professions continued, taking expression when, in 1977, the nationalist Siumut movement formed a left-wing party. In 1975 the Minister for Greenland appointed a commission to devise terms for Greenland home rule, and its proposals were approved, by 73.1% to 26.9%, in a referendum among the Greenland electorate in January 1979. Siumut, led by a Lutheran pastor, Jonathan Motzfeldt, secured 13 seats in the 21-member Landsting (the local legislature) at a general election in April, and a five-member Landsstyre (Home Rule Government), with Motzfeldt as Prime Minister, took office in May. From 1979 the island gradually assumed full administration of its internal affairs.

In February 1982 a referendum was held to decide Greenland's continued membership of the EC. This resulted in a 53% majority in favour of withdrawal. Negotiations were begun in May, with the Danish Government acting on Greenland's behalf, and were concluded in March 1984 (with effect from 1 February 1985): Greenland was accorded the status of an overseas territory in association with the Community, with preferential access to EC markets.

At the April 1983 general election to the Landsting (enlarged, by measures adopted in 1982, to between 23 and 26 seats, depending on the proportion of votes cast), Siumut and the conservative Atassut party won 12 seats each, while the Inuit Ataqatigiit (IA) won two seats. Siumut once again formed a Government, led by Motzfeldt, dependent on the support of the IA members in the Landsting: this support was withdrawn in March 1984, when the IA members voted against the terms of withdrawal from the EC, and Motzfeldt resigned. In the ensuing general election, held in June, Siumut and Atassut won 11 seats each, while the IA won three. Motzfeldt again formed a coalition Government, comprising Siumut and the IA.

In March 1987 the coalition Government collapsed, following a dispute between Siumut and the IA over policy towards the modernization of the US radar facility at Thule, which was claimed by the IA to be in breach of the 1972 US-Soviet Anti-Ballistic Missile Treaty. A general election was held in May. Siumut and Atassut retained 11 seats each in the Landsting (which had been enlarged in 1986, to 27 seats—23 of which were to be obtained by election in multi-member constituencies, while four were to be supplementary seats); the IA won four seats, and the remaining seat was won by the newly-formed Issittup Partiia, which was demanding the privatization of the trawler fleet. Motzfeldt eventually formed a new coalition Government with the IA. In May 1988, at elections to the Danish Folketing, Siumut was the most successful party. In June the coalition between Siumut and the IA collapsed, and Motzfeldt formed a new Siumut Government, with support from Atassut. In December 1990, when Atassut withdrew its support for the Siumut administration (following allegations that government ministers had misused public funds), Motzfeldt organized an early general election for March 1991, at which both Siumut and Atassut obtained a reduced share of the vote, while the IA's share rose. Accordingly, Siumut retained 11 seats in the Landsting, while Atassut's representation decreased to eight seats and the IA's increased to five. A new party, the liberal Akulliit Partiiaat, won two seats, and the remaining place was taken by the Issittup Partiia. Siumut and the IA formed a coalition Government and elected the Chairman of Siumut, Lars Emil Johansen, as Prime Minister.

At the general election held in March 1995 Siumut increased its representation in the Landsting (enlarged to 31 seats) to 12 seats, while Atassut won 10 seats and the IA obtained six seats. A coalition Government was formed between Siumut and Atassut, following the withdrawal from negotiations of the IA, which failed to reach agreement with Siumut on the question of independence. Johansen retained the premiership, while Daniel Skifte, the leader of Atassut, was appointed Minister of Finance and Housing. In early 1997 Johansen asserted that Greenland could achieve economic independence from Denmark on the basis of its unexploited mineral resources. In September Motzfeldt replaced Johansen as Prime Minister at the head of the coalition. Johansen was reported to have taken a senior position with the Royal Greenland fishing group.

At the general election held on 16 February 1999 Siumut received 35.3% of the votes cast, securing 11 seats in the Landsting. Atassut obtained 25.3% of the votes (eight seats), while the IA received 22.1% (seven seats). On 22 February a coalition Government was formed between Siumut and the IA; the two parties were to be represented in the Landsstyre by five and two ministers respectively. Jonathan Motzfeldt retained the premiership, while Josef Motzfeldt, the Chairman of the IA, was appointed Minister of Economy and Trade and of Taxation.

Denmark remains responsible for Greenland's foreign relations. Greenland does, however, have separate representation on the Nordic Council (see p. 222), and is a member of the Inuit Circumpolar Conference (see p. 301). Denmark, a member of NATO, retains its responsibility for defence, and Danish-US military co-operation in Greenland began in 1951. Under a 1981 agreement on the defence of Greenland, two US radar bases were established on the island, at Thule and at Kangerlussuaq (Søndre Strømfjord). An agreement between the USA and Denmark for the reduction of the bases from 325,000 ha to 160,000 ha took effect from October 1986, and the land thus becoming available was returned to the Inuit. In March 1991 the USA agreed to transfer ownership and control of the base at Kangerlussuaq to the Greenland Government in September 1992, in exchange for the right to use it again in the future. In July 1996 it was announced that the base at Thule would be opened to aircraft. In August 1999 it was reported that the Danish Court of Appeal had ordered the Danish Government to pay compensation to Inuits who had been forced to leave their land in 1953 to allow for the expansion of the base at Thule.

In June 1980 the Danish Government declared an economic zone extending 200 nautical miles (370 km) off the east coast of Greenland. This, however, caused a dispute with Norway over territorial waters, owing to the existence of the small Norwegian island of Jan Mayen, 460 km off the east coast of Greenland. In 1988 Denmark requested the International Court of Justice (ICJ), based in The Hague, the Netherlands, to arbitrate on the issue of conflicting economic zones. A delimitation line was established by the ICJ in June 1993. A subsequent accord on maritime delimitation, agreed between the Governments of Norway, Greenland and Iceland in November 1997, established the boundaries of a 1,934-sq km area of Arctic sea that had been excluded from the terms of the 1993 settlement.

## Government

Greenland is part of the Kingdom of Denmark, and the Danish Government, which remains responsible for foreign affairs, defence and justice, is represented by the Rigsombudsmand, or High Commissioner, in Nuuk (Godthåb). Most functions of government are administered by the 'Home Rule Government', the Landsstyre. The formation of this executive is dependent upon support in the local legislature, the Landsting. The Landsting has 31 members elected for a maximum term of four years, on a basis of proportional representation. Greenland also elects two members to the Danish Folketing. For administration purposes, Greenland is divided into 18 municipalities, of which the largest is Nuuk.

## Defence

The Danish Government, which is responsible for Greenland's defence, co-ordinates military activities through its Greenland Command. The Greenland Command, which also undertakes fisheries control and sea rescues, is based at the Grønnedal naval base, in south-west Greenland. Greenlanders are not liable for military service. As part of the Kingdom of Denmark, Greenland belongs to NATO. The USA operates an air base, at Pituffik in Thule (see Recent History). In 1998 the Danish Government spent 353m. kroner (11.1% of total central government expenditure on Greenland) on the territory's defence (including the Fisheries Inspectorate).

## Economic Affairs

In 1994, according to preliminary official estimates, Greenland's gross national product (GNP) was 6,381m. kroner, equivalent to some 114,800 kroner per head. The economy enjoyed overall growth during the 1970s and 1980s, but gross domestic product (GDP) declined by 9%, in real terms, in 1990, and continued to decline significantly (owing to depleted fish stocks and the discontinuation of lead and zinc mining) until 1994 and 1995, when real growth rates of 5% and 3%, respectively, were recorded. The population increased at an average annual rate of 0.1% in 1990–97.

Fishing dominates the commercial economy, as well as being important to the traditional way of life. In 1998 the fishing industry accounted for almost all of Greenland's total export revenue. It was estimated that the industry, including the processing of the catch, employed about one-sixth of the paid labour force in the late 1980s. The cod catch has declined substantially, however, since 1989. The traditional occupation of the Greenlanders is seal-hunting, which remains important in the north. The only feasible agricultural activity in the harsh climate is livestock-rearing, and only sheep-farming has proved to be of any commercial significance. There are also herds of domesticated reindeer.

Industry (including mining, manufacturing, construction and public works) employed some 25% of those in paid employment in March 1987. Mining earned 13.0% of total export revenue in 1990. A Swedish company extracted lead, zinc and some silver at the important mine at Marmorilik in the north-west. The mine was closed, however, in 1990. In recent years there have been several discoveries of petroleum, natural gas and other mineral deposits (including gold), which, it is hoped, can be exploited.

Manufacturing is mainly dependent upon the fishing industry. Water power (meltwater from the ice-cap and glaciers) is an important potential source of electricity. All mineral fuels are imported. Mineral fuels accounted for 8.5% of total imports in 1998.

In 1998 Greenland recorded a trade deficit of 1,038m. kroner. The principal trading partner remains Denmark, although its monopoly on trade ceased in 1950. Denmark supplied 69.6% of imports and received 65.5% of exports in 1998. Trade is still dominated by companies owned by the Home Rule Government. The principal exports are fish and fish products, and the principal imports are machinery and transport equipment.

Greenland is dependent upon large grants from the central Danish Government. In 1998 central government expenditure on Greenland included some 2,575m. kroner in the form of a direct grant to the Home Rule Government. Greenland has few debts, and also receives valuable revenue from the European Union (EU, as the EC was restyled in 1993) (see below) for fishing licences. The annual rate of inflation averaged 1.6% in 1990–97, and stood at 0.6% in 1997. In August 1997 8.4% of the urban labour force were unemployed.

Greenland, although a part of the Kingdom of Denmark, withdrew from the EC in 1985 (see Recent History). It remains a territory in association with the EU, however, and has preferential access to European markets. The loss of EU development aid has been offset by the annual payment (ECU 37.7m. during 1995–2000) for member countries to retain fishing rights in Greenlandic waters.

Greenland's economy is dominated by the fishing industry, but remains a subsistence, barter economy for a large part of the population. Migration to the towns and the rejection of a traditional life-style by many young people have, however, created new social and economic problems. Dependence on a single commodity leaves the economy vulnerable to the effects of depletion of fish stocks and fluctuating international prices. Any development or progress is possible only with Danish aid, which is already fundamental to Greenlandic finances. In an effort to generate revenue from the tourist industry, the Home Rule Government undertook, in 1990, to achieve a target of 35,000 tourist arrivals (equivalent to 500m. kroner) annually by 2005; by 1994 the campaign was showing positive results and tourist arrivals had doubled compared with levels in previous years.

the House of Assembly, was appointed to the presidency and assumed office in October.

At a general election in June 1995 the DFP's 15-year tenure was finally ended, with the party winning only five seats. The LPD also won five seats, while the UWP secured a narrow victory, with 11 seats and 34.5% of total votes cast (compared with 35.8% for the DFP). Some observers attributed the DFP's poor performance in the election to Charles's failure to give full support to her successor, Brian Alleyne, upon her retirement. The leader of the UWP, Edison James, was subsequently appointed as Prime Minister, and the LPD and DFP leaders agreed to occupy the position of Leader of the Opposition in alternate years, commencing with Brian Alleyne. In July a legal dispute arose concerning the eligibility to serve in the House of Assembly of one of the DFP's members, Charles Savarin, owing to a potential conflict of interests. As a result of the dispute, the position of Leader of the Opposition was transferred to the LPD leader, Rosie Douglas. In April 1996, however, Savarin was elected leader of the DFP following Alleyne's resignation, which had been prompted by his appointment as a judge in Grenada. In August a by-election for Alleyne's seat was won by the UWP candidate, thus increasing the Government's representation in the House of Assembly to 12 seats. Government support for a long-term programme to privatize several state-owned enterprises and to implement structural adjustment measures (recommended by the IMF) attracted criticism from the opposition in 1996–97, as well as from the Civil Service Association, which pledged its resistance to any retrenchment in the sector.

In April 1997 an investigation of the police force was conducted, following allegations of corruption. In November the Prime Minister announced that the Police Commissioner, Desmond Blanchard, his deputy and five other officers had been sent on leave, owing to the findings of the report. In April 1998 Rosie Douglas announced that he was taking legal action against the Government, on the grounds that it had acted unconstitutionally by failing to give him a copy of the report. Meanwhile, in 1997 the Government established a Constitutional Commission to examine several issues, including civil rights, standards in public service, the responsibility of politicians and public involvement in government. In late 1997 the Ministries of Trade and Marketing and of Foreign Affairs were merged, although responsibility for the respective portfolios was retained by Norris Charles and the Prime Minister.

In December 1997 the Government's citizenship programme (see above) again provoked controversy. *The Independent Newspaper* reported that, under the scheme, passports were being sold by agents for between US $15,000 and $20,000, and claimed that about 400 people (including 80 Russians and 50 Chinese) had acquired citizenship in 1997. The opposition LPD accused the Government of undermining the credibility of Dominican citizenship, and in August 1998 Rosie Douglas demanded an inquiry into the programme, following an administrative error which had allowed an Australian, who was sought by investigators in connection with a business collapse, to acquire citizenship. In late 1999 it was announced that the Dominican Government had stopped granting citizenship to Russians, following reports that up to 300 Russians had paid US $50,000 each to obtain a Dominican passport. In addition, there were complaints from the US Government that the trade in passports had increased 'suspicions of money-laundering' in Dominica.

In early 1998 the LPD complained to the Electoral Boundaries Commission, accusing the Government of proposing changes to the boundaries of six electoral constituencies (four of which were regarded as LPD strongholds) purely for political gain. In November the High Court upheld the opposition's complaint, ruling that the proposed alterations were unconstitutional. (This judgment was endorsed by the Eastern Caribbean Court of Appeal in May 1999.)

In early October 1998 President Sorhaindo's five-year term in office ended. Following the failure of the Prime Minister and the Leader of the Opposition to agree on a joint nominee, the House of Assembly held a secret ballot to elect the new President. Vernon Shaw, a former cabinet secretary in the previous administration of Eugenia Charles, was duly elected and assumed the presidency on 6 October.

In mid-1999 it was reported that the former Prime Minister, Patrick John, had demanded an inquiry into the 15-year administration of Eugenia Charles, accusing her of 'corruption, nepotism, financial mismanagement and violence'.

On 1 January 2000 the Prime Minister unexpectedly called a general election, to be held on 31 January. The DFP accused James of breaking a 1995 undertaking to give at least 90 days' notice of an election (which was not due constitutionally until June), and formed an electoral alliance with the LPD. The UWP was widely predicted to win a second term, but, in the event, it suffered a narrow electoral defeat, while the LPD was returned to power after two decades in opposition, winning 10 of the 21 elective seats in the House of Assembly and receiving 42.9% of total votes cast. The UWP secured nine seats (with 43.4% of the votes), and the DFP won two. The leader of the LPD, Rosie Douglas, was named as Prime Minister and formed a coalition Government with the DFP (which was allocated two ministerial portfolios).

In foreign policy, Dominica has close links with France and the USA. France helped in suppressing the coup attempts against the DFP Government in 1981, and Dominica was the first Commonwealth country to benefit from the French aid agency FAC. In October 1983 Dominica, as a member of the Organisation of Eastern Caribbean States (OECS—see p. 292), contributed forces to the US-backed invasion of Grenada. In 1988 four countries of the Windward group (Dominica, Grenada, Saint Lucia and Saint Vincent and the Grenadines) decided to proceed with plans for the formation of a political union. In 1990 the four countries decided to convene a constituent assembly, which in early 1992 agreed a draft constitution, including provision for the election of an executive president by universal suffrage. Following its election in mid-1995, the Government of Edison James stated its commitment to further economic integration of the Windward Islands, leading to political union.

## Government

Legislative power is vested in the unicameral House of Assembly, comprising 30 members (nine nominated and 21 elected for five years by universal adult suffrage). Executive authority is vested in the President, who is elected by the House, but in most matters the President is guided by the advice of the Cabinet and acts as the constitutional Head of State. He appoints the Prime Minister, who must be able to command a majority in the House, and (on the Prime Minister's recommendation) other ministers. The Cabinet is responsible to the House. The island is divided into 10 administrative divisions, known as parishes, and there is limited local government in Roseau, the capital, and in the Carib Territory.

## Defence

The Dominican Defence Force was officially disbanded in 1981. There is a police force of about 300, which includes a coastguard service. The country participates in the US-sponsored Regional Security System.

## Economic Affairs

In 1997, according to estimates by the World Bank, Dominica's gross national product (GNP), measured at average 1995–97 prices, was US $225m., equivalent to US $3,040 per head. Between 1990 and 1997, it was estimated, GNP per head increased, in real terms, at an average rate of 0.7% per year. Over the same period, the population increased by an average of 0.3% per year. Estimated GNP in 1998 was US $222m. (US $3,010 per head). Gross domestic product (GDP), in real terms, increased by an average of 2.2% per year in 1990–97. Real GDP growth was 2.0% in 1997 and an estimated 3.5% in 1998.

Agriculture (including forestry and fishing) is the principal economic activity, accounting for an estimated 18.9% of GDP in 1997. In 1995/96 the sector engaged 30.8% of the employed labour force. The principal cash crop is bananas. The banana industry, which was already experiencing difficulties (owing to a decline in prices), has been adversely affected by a September 1997 ruling of the World Trade Organization (WTO—see p. 274) against Dominica's preferential access to the European (particularly the British) market. In 1998 banana production decreased by some 18%, to an estimated 28,640 metric tons, while receipts from banana exports fell by 8.9% to EC $42.2m. (some 24.8% of total domestic exports). Other important crops include coconuts (which provide copra for export as well as edible oil and soap), mangoes, avocados, papayas, ginger, citrus fruits and, mainly for domestic consumption, vegetables. Livestock-rearing and fishing are also practised for local purposes. In mid-1997 construction of a fishing port and market in Roseau was completed. Dominica has extensive timber reserves (more than 40% of the island's total land area is forest and woodland), and international aid agencies are encouraging the development of a balanced timber industry. The GDP of the agricultural sector decreased at an average annual rate of 0.8% in 1990–97. In real terms, agricultural GDP contracted by 8.1% in 1995 (largely as a result of hurricane damage), increased by 5.5% in 1996, but then declined by 1.5% in 1997 and by an estimated 1.2% in 1998.

Industry (comprising mining, manufacturing, construction and utilities) provided 19.5% of GDP in 1997, and employed 21.6% of the labour force in 1991. Industrial GDP increased at an average rate of 2.9% per year during 1990–97; however, industrial GDP contracted by 0.2% in 1997, owing to a decline in the manufacturing sector. Manufacturing activity is mainly small-scale and dependent upon agriculture. The mining sector contributed only 0.8% of GDP in 1997, and employed 0.3% of the labour force in 1991. There is some quarrying of pumice, and there are extensive reserves of limestone and clay. In 1996 an Australian mining company began investigations into the possible exploitation of extensive copper deposits in north-eastern Dominica. Pumice is useful to the construction industry, which accounted for 8.5% of GDP in 1997, and employed 11.8% of the labour force in 1991. Extensive infrastructure development by the Government has maintained high levels of activity in the construction sector in recent years. The GDP of the construction sector increased at an average annual rate of 4.0% in 1990–97; however, the sector's GDP contracted by 1.7% in 1997 and by an estimated 2.0% in 1998. The Government has also encouraged the manufacturing sector in an attempt to diversify the economy. In 1997 manufacturing contributed 5.9% of GDP. Manufacturing GDP increased at an average rate of 0.1% per year during 1990–97, but rose by 2.5% in 1997 and by an estimated 21.1% in 1998. This considerable increase was largely due to an 18.8% increase in the output of soap products, but also to the production of toothpaste, which began in November 1997. The manufacturing sector employed 8.2% of the labour force in 1991. There is a banana-packaging plant and factories for the manufacturing and refining of crude and edible vegetable oils and for the production of soap, canned juices and cigarettes. A brewery was established in 1995 to supply domestic requirements. Furniture, paint, cardboard boxes and candles are also significant manufactures.

In 1996 60% of Dominica's energy requirements were supplied by hydroelectric power. Investment in a hydroelectric development scheme and in the water supply system has been partially financed by the export of water, from Dominica's extensive reserves, to drier Caribbean islands such as Aruba. A hydroelectric power station, with a generating capacity of 1.24 MW, began operation at Laudat in 1990. By 1991 Dominica had reduced imports of mineral fuels to 7.9% of the cost of total imports. In 1995 a US company announced that it would invest EC $25m. in a geothermal energy project in Soufrière, which began producing electricity in 1998. In December 1996 the state-owned Dominica Electricity Services (DOMLEC) was privatized, with the British Government's overseas private finance institution, the Commonwealth Development Corporation (CDC), buying 73% of the company. The CDC outlined plans to increase electricity generation by 80% by the year 2000. Construction of a new 20-MW electric power plant, at an estimated cost of EC $80m., was scheduled to begin in mid-1999 and was due for completion by early 2001.

Services engaged 44.7% of the employed labour force in 1991, and provided 61.6% of GDP in 1997. The combined GDP of the service sectors increased at an average rate of 3.4% per year during 1990–97, although the growth rate slowed to 2.5% in 1997. The tourist industry is of increasing importance to the economy and exploits Dominica's natural history and scenery. During 1998 the Government placed considerable emphasis on the country's potential as an 'eco-tourism' destination, pursuing a development programme funded by the European Union (EU). The majority of tourists are cruise-ship passengers. Arrivals from cruise ships increased from 6,777 in 1990 to 64,762 in the following year, and by 1998 totalled an estimated 240,905. In 1990 the Government decided to proceed with the construction of an international airport. However, in late 1999 the administration was still experiencing problems in securing the necessary finance for the project, although the Republic of China (Taiwan) had pledged US $35m. The 1999/2000 budget proposals allocated capital expenditure of US $28m. to the construction of the airport and related infrastructure, estimated to cost a total of US $110m.

In 1996 Dominica recorded a visible trade deficit of US $47.75m. and a deficit of US $39.92m. on the current account of the balance of payments. The principal source of imports in 1997 was the USA, which accounted for 38.3% of total imports, followed by Trinidad and Tobago (13.9%) and the United Kingdom (10.4%). The principal market for exports is the United Kingdom, which receives virtually all Dominica's banana production. In 1997 the United Kingdom received 32.8% of total domestic exports, while Jamaica received 22.3%. The principal imports are food and live animals, basic manufactures (such as paper), and machinery and transport equipment. The principal exports are bananas and soap.

In 1998 there was an estimated budget deficit of EC $18.7m. Recurrent expenditure for the financial year ending 30 June 2000 was projected to increase by 18.3%, to EC $223.3m., while a 31.4% increase in capital expenditure, to total EC $322.0m., was forecast. At the end of 1997 Dominica's total external debt was US $98.4m., of which US $86.2m. was long-term public debt. In that year the cost of debt-servicing was equivalent to 8.3% of the value of exports of goods and services. The annual rate of inflation averaged 2.4% in 1990–98; consumer prices increased by an average of 2.5% in 1997, but by only 1.0% in 1998. An estimated 23% of the labour force were unemployed in 1994. Labour shortages have occurred in the agricultural and construction sectors.

Dominica is a member of the Organization of American States (OAS—see p. 245), the Caribbean Community and Common Market (CARICOM, see p. 136), the OECS, and is a signatory of the Lomé Conventions with the EU (see p. 196). Under the Charles administration, the island received considerable aid from the United Kingdom, France, the USA and various international aid agencies.

The Dominican economy is heavily dependent on the production of coconut-based products and bananas, and their export to a limited market, and is thus vulnerable to adverse weather conditions, price fluctuations and economic conditions in its principal markets. In the 1990s growth in the economy slowed, owing to the uncertainty surrounding Dominica's preferential access to the European market and the devastation of the 1995 banana crop by a hurricane. Efforts to expand the country's economic base have been impeded by poor infrastructure and, in terms of tourism, a paucity of desirable beaches. However, by the late 1990s the tourist sector was expanding steadily, aided by an 'eco-tourism' development programme with EU funding. In 1998 the pace of economic activity increased, largely owing to strong growth in the manufacturing and services sectors. Banana exports decreased in that year, owing to a mid-year drought, a fall in producer prices and uncertainties caused by the WTO's ruling in September 1997 against the EU's banana import regime. Exports and foreign investment were, however, expected to increase, as OECS members prepared for a planned single market and economy in 1998, prior to the creation of a CARICOM single market in 2000. In the 1998/99 budget, in an effort to make the tax system more efficient, the Government announced the implementation of value-added tax (VAT), which was to be introduced over two years, and changes to income tax. Budget proposals for 1999/2000 focused on the planned construction of an international airport, which was expected to expedite further expansion of the tourism industry.

### Social Welfare

There are main hospitals at Roseau and Portsmouth, with 136 and 50 beds respectively, and two cottage hospitals, at Marigot and Grand Bay. There is a polyclinic at the Princess Margaret Hospital, Roseau. There are 51 health centres, located throughout the island. In 1996 Dominica had one hospital bed for every 88 citizens, and one physician for every 225 inhabitants.

### Education

Education is free and is provided by both government and denominational schools. There are also a number of schools for the mentally and physically handicapped. Education is compulsory for 10 years between five and 15 years of age. Primary education begins at the age of five and lasts for seven years. Enrolment of children in the primary age-group was 70.7% in 1992. Secondary education, beginning at 12 years of age, lasts for five years. A teacher-training college and nursing school provide further education, and there is also a branch of the University of the West Indies on the island. In 1997 the Government announced plans to invest EC $17.9m. in a Basic Education Reform project. The rate of adult illiteracy was only 5.6% in 1986.

### Public Holidays

**2000:** 1 January (New Year's Day), 14–15 February (Masquerade, Carnival), 21 April (Good Friday), 24 April (Easter

Monday), 1 May (May or Labour Day), 12 June (Whit Monday), 7 August (Emancipation, August Monday), 3 November (Independence Day), 4 November (Community Service Day), 25–26 December (Christmas).

**2001:** 1 January (New Year's Day), 12–13 February (Masquerade, Carnival), 13 April (Good Friday), 16 April (Easter Monday), 1 May (May or Labour Day), 4 June (Whit Monday), 6 August (Emancipation, August Monday), 3 November (Independence Day), 4 November (Community Service Day), 25–26 December (Christmas).

**Weights and Measures**

The imperial system is in use, although the metric system is to be introduced.

# Statistical Survey

Sources (unless otherwise stated): Ministry of Finance, Roseau; OECS Economic Affairs Secretariat, *Annual Digest of Statistics*.

## AREA AND POPULATION

**Area:** 751 sq km (290 sq miles).

**Population:** 69,548 at census of 7 April 1970; 73,795 at census of 7 April 1981; 71,183 (males 35,471, females 35,712) at census of 12 May 1991; 74,000 (official estimate) at mid-1996.

**Density** (mid-1996): 98.5 per sq km.

**Population by Ethnic Group** (*de jure* population, excl. those resident in institutions, 1981): Negro 67,272; Mixed race 4,433; Amerindian (Carib) 1,111; White 341; Total (incl. others) 73,795 (males 36,754, females 37,041). Source: UN, *Demographic Yearbook*.

**Principal Town** (population at 1991 census): Roseau (capital) 15,853.

**Births, Marriages and Deaths** (1996): Live births 1,419 (birth rate 19.1 per 1,000); Marriages 230 (marriage rate 3.1 per 1,000); Deaths 575 (death rate 7.7 per 1,000).

**Expectation of Life** (UN estimates, years at birth, 1990–95): 67.8 (males 64.1; females 71.4). Source: ECLAC Demography Unit.

**Economically Active Population** (persons aged 15 years and over, excl. institutional population, at census of May 1991): Agriculture, hunting, forestry and fishing 7,344; Mining and quarrying 65; Manufacturing 1,947; Electricity, gas and water 304; Construction 2,819; Trade, restaurants and hotels 3,658; Transport, storage and communications 1,202; Financing, insurance and real estate 810; Public administration, defence and social security 1,520; Community services 2,400; Other services 1,046; Activities not adequately defined 699; Total employed 23,814; Unemployed 2,541; Total labour force 26,355 (males 17,275; females 9,080).

## AGRICULTURE, ETC.

**Principal Crops** ('000 metric tons, 1998): Sweet potatoes 2*; Cassava 1*; Yams 8*; Taro (Dasheen) 11*; Other roots and tubers 4*; Coconuts 17*; Cabbages 1*; Pumpkins 1*; Cucumbers 2*; Carrots 1*; Other vegetables 1*; Sugar cane 5*; Oranges 8*; Lemons and limes 1*; Grapefruit 21*; Mangoes 2*; Bananas 30; Plantains 22*.

* FAO estimate.

Source: FAO, *Production Yearbook*.

**Livestock** (FAO estimates, '000 head, year ending September 1998): Cattle 13; Pigs 5; Sheep 8; Goats 10. Source: FAO, *Production Yearbook*.

**Livestock Products** (FAO estimates, '000 metric tons, 1998): Beef and veal 1; Cows' milk 6. Source: FAO, *Production Yearbook*.

**Fishing** (metric tons, live weight): Total catch 838 in 1995; 840 in 1996; 850 in 1997. Source: FAO, *Yearbook of Fishery Statistics*.

## MINING

**Pumice** ('000 metric tons): Estimated production 100 per year in 1988–95 (Source: US Bureau of Mines).

## INDUSTRY

**Production** (1996, metric tons, unless otherwise indicated): Soap 14,815; Crude coconut oil 753 (estimate); Edible coconut oil 82 (estimate); Coconut meal 350 (estimate); Electricity 52.4 million kWh (1994).

## FINANCE

**Currency and Exchange Rates:** 100 cents = 1 Eastern Caribbean dollar (EC $). *Sterling, US Dollar and Euro Equivalents* (30 September 1999): £1 sterling = EC $4.446; US $1 = EC $2.700; €1 = EC $2.880; EC $100 = £22.49 = US $37.04 = €34.73. *Exchange Rate:* Fixed at US $1 = EC $2.70 since July 1976.

**Budget** (estimates, EC $ million, 1998): *Revenue:* Tax revenue 173.9; Other current revenue 30.7; Capital revenue 3.9; Total 208.5, excl. grants received (7.2). *Expenditure:* Current expenditure 195.8 (Wages and salaries 108.3); Capital expenditure and net lending 38.5; Total 234.3. Source: Eastern Caribbean Central Bank, *Report and Statement of Accounts* (1999).

**International Reserves** (US $ million at 31 December 1998): Reserve position in IMF 0.01; Foreign exchange 27.65; Total 27.67. Source: IMF, *International Financial Statistics*.

**Money Supply** (EC $ million at 31 December 1998): Currency outside banks 29.13; Demand deposits at commercial banks 74.09; Total money (incl. others) 104.21. Source: IMF, *International Financial Statistics*.

**Cost of Living** (Retail Price Index, base: 1995 = 100): All items 101.7 in 1996; 104.2 in 1997; 105.2 in 1998. Source: IMF, *International Financial Statistics*.

**National Accounts** (EC $ million at current prices): Gross domestic product in purchasers' values 601.2 in 1995; 638.4 in 1996; 655.3 in 1997. Source: IMF, *International Financial Statistics*.

**Expenditure on the Gross Domestic Product** (EC $ million at current prices, 1996): Government final consumption expenditure 126.9; Private final consumption expenditure 422.4; Increase in stocks 10.7; Gross fixed capital formation 166.1; Statistical discrepancy –10.7; *Total domestic expenditure* 715.4; Exports of goods and services 307.9; *Less* Imports of goods and services 392.4; GDP in purchasers' values 630.9. Source: IMF, *International Financial Statistics*.

**Gross Domestic Product by Economic Activity** (EC $ million at current prices, 1997): Agriculture, hunting, forestry and fishing 114.0; Mining and quarrying 5.1; Manufacturing 35.5; Electricity and water 25.7; Construction 50.9; Wholesale and retail trade 65.4; Restaurants and hotels 14.5; Transport 54.9; Communications 44.0; Finance and insurance 60.3; Real estate and housing 19.3; Government services 104.1; Other services 8.5; Sub-total 602.2; *Less* imputed bank service charge 45.0; GDP at factor cost 557.1. Source: Eastern Caribbean Central Bank, *Statistical Digest* (December 1998).

**Balance of Payments** (US $ million, 1996): Exports of goods f.o.b. 52.74; Imports of goods f.o.b. –100.50; *Trade balance* –47.75; Exports of services 61.29; Imports of services –44.83; *Balance on goods and services* –31.30; Other income received 2.85; Other income paid –21.64; *Balance on goods, services and income* –50.09; Current transfers received 17.83; Current transfers paid –7.66; *Current balance* –39.92; Capital account (net) 25.30; Direct investment from abroad 17.79; Portfolio investment assets 0.48; Portfolio investment liabilities –0.02; Other investment assets –9.76; Other investment liabilities 1.24; Net errors and omissions 7.13; *Overall balance* 2.24. Source: IMF, *International Financial Statistics*.

## EXTERNAL TRADE

**Principal Commodities** (EC $ '000, 1997): *Imports c.i.f.:* Meat and meat preparation 15,379; Butter, milk and cheese 10,213; Alcoholic beverages 7,582; Wood and lumber 11,171; Motor spirit (petrol) 9,449; Diesel oil 8,656; Metals and metal products 22,038; Machinery (non-electric) 33,738; Electric machinery 24,364; Transport equipment 24,734; Total (incl. others) 363,142. *Exports f.o.b.:* Bananas 46,331; Plantains 5,111; Paints, varnishes and lacquers 3,949; Toothpaste 2,947; Soap 44,289; Disinfectant 3,985; Total (incl. others) 138,652, excl. re-exports (2,606).

**Principal Trading Partners** (EC $ '000, 1997): *Imports c.i.f.:* Barbados 13,865; Canada 7,490; China, People's Republic 3,524; France 4,092; Germany 4,843; Guadeloupe 4,328; Japan 15,884; Jamaica 5,323; Netherlands 5,497; Puerto Rico 11,850; Saint Lucia 6,574; Saint Vincent and the Grenadines 7,377; Trinidad and Tobago 50,475; United Kingdom 37,852; USA 138,973; Venezuela 5,332; Total (incl. others) 363,143. *Exports f.o.b.:* Antigua and Barbuda 8,502; Barbados 7,754; Guadeloupe 8,143; Guyana 7,473; Jamaica

30,860; Puerto Rico 2,107; Saint Kitts and Nevis 3,167; Saint Lucia 4,813; Sint Maarten 3,127; Trinidad and Tobago 6,022; United Kingdom 45,489; USA 4,984; Total (incl. others) 138,652.

### TRANSPORT

**Road Traffic** (motor vehicles licensed in 1994): Private cars 6,491; Taxis 90; Buses 559; Motorcycles 94; Trucks 2,266; Jeeps 461; Tractors 24; Total 9,985.

**Shipping:** *Merchant Fleet* (registered at 31 December 1998): 8 vessels (total displacement 2,522 grt) (Source: Lloyd's Register of Shipping, *World Fleet Statistics*); *International freight traffic* ('000 metric tons, estimates, 1993): Goods loaded 103.2; Goods unloaded 181.2.

**Civil Aviation** (1997): Aircraft arrivals and departures 18,672; Freight loaded 363 metric tons; Freight unloaded 575 metric tons.

### TOURISM

**Tourist Arrivals:** *Stop-overs:* 63,259 in 1996; 65,446 in 1997; 65,501 in 1998. *Cruise-ship passengers:* 193,484 in 1996; 230,581 in 1997; 240,905 in 1998. *Excursionists:* 5,389 in 1996; 3,310 in 1997; 1,447 in 1998. Source: Eastern Caribbean Central Bank, *Report and Statement of Accounts* (1999).

**Tourism Receipts** (EC $ million): 92.1 in 1995; 98.8 in 1996; 106.8 in 1997. Source: Eastern Caribbean Central Bank, *Balance of Payments* (1998).

### COMMUNICATIONS MEDIA

**Radio Receivers** (1996): 45,000 in use.

**Television Receivers** (1996): 5,000 in use.

**Telephones** (1995): 18,000 main lines in use.

**Telefax Stations** (1992): 290 in use.

**Non-daily Newspapers** (1993): 3.

Source: mainly UNESCO, *Statistical Yearbook.*

### EDUCATION

**Institutions** (1994/95): Pre-primary 72 (1992/93); Primary 64; Secondary 14; Tertiary 2.

**Teachers** (1994/95): Pre-primary 131 (1992/93); Primary 641; Secondary 269; Tertiary 34 (1992/93).

**Pupils** (1994/95): Pre-primary 3,000 (1992/93); Primary 12,627; Secondary 6,493; Tertiary 484.

# Directory

## The Constitution

The Constitution came into effect at the independence of Dominica on 3 November 1978. Its main provisions are summarized below:

### FUNDAMENTAL RIGHTS AND FREEDOMS

The Constitution guarantees the rights of life, liberty, security of the person, the protection of the law and respect for private property. The individual is entitled to freedom of conscience, of expression and assembly and has the right to an existence free from slavery, forced labour and torture. Protection against discrimination on the grounds of sex, race, place of origin, political opinion, colour or creed is assured.

### THE PRESIDENT

The President is elected by the House of Assembly for a term of five years. A presidential candidate is nominated jointly by the Prime Minister and the Leader of the Opposition and on their concurrence is declared elected without any vote being taken; in the case of disagreement the choice will be made by secret ballot in the House of Assembly. Candidates must be citizens of Dominica aged at least 40 who have been resident in Dominica for five years prior to their nomination. A President may not hold office for more than two terms.

### PARLIAMENT

Parliament consists of the President and the House of Assembly, composed of 21 elected Representatives and nine Senators. According to the wishes of Parliament, the latter may be appointed by the President—five on the advice of the Prime Minister and four on the advice of the Leader of the Opposition—or elected. The life of Parliament is five years.

Parliament has the power to amend the Constitution. Each constituency returns one Representative to the House who is directly elected in accordance with the Constitution. Every citizen over the age of 18 is eligible to vote.

### THE EXECUTIVE

Executive authority is vested in the President. The President appoints as Prime Minister the elected member of the House who commands the support of a majority of its elected members, and other ministers on the advice of the Prime Minister. Not more than three ministers may be from among the appointed Senators. The President has the power to remove the Prime Minister from office if a resolution expressing 'no confidence' in the Government is adopted by the House and the Prime Minister does not resign within three days or advise the President to dissolve Parliament.

The Cabinet consists of the Prime Minister, other ministers and the Attorney-General in an ex officio capacity.

The Leader of the Opposition is appointed by the President as that elected member of the House who, in the President's judgement, is best able to command the support of a majority of the elected members who do not support the Government.

## The Government

### HEAD OF STATE

**President:** VERNON LORDEN SHAW (assumed office 6 October 1998).

### CABINET
(February 2000)

A coalition of the Labour Party of Dominica (LPD) and the Dominica Freedom Party (DFP).

**Prime Minister and Minister of Foreign Affairs, Legal Affairs, Labour and Carib Affairs:** ROOSEVELT (ROSIE) DOUGLAS (LPD).

**Minister of Communications and Works:** PIERRE CHARLES (LPD).

**Minister of Finance:** AMBROSE GEORGE (LPD).

**Minister of Trade, Industry and Marketing:** OSBORNE RIVIERE (LPD).

**Minister of Community Development and Women's Affairs:** MATTHEW WALTER (LPD).

**Minister of Housing:** VINCE HENDERSON (LPD).

**Minister of Sports and Youth Affairs:** ROOSEVELT SKERRIT (LPD).

**Minister of Tourism:** CHARLES SAVARIN (DFP).

**Minister of Health and Social Security:** Sen. JOHN TOUSSAINT (LPD).

**Minister of Education, Science and Technology:** Sen. HERBERT SABROACHE (DFP).

**Minister of Agriculture, Planning and the Environment:** Sen. ATHERTON MARTIN (LPD).

**Attorney-General:** BERNARD WILTSHIRE (LPD).

### MINISTRIES

**Office of the President:** Morne Bruce, Roseau; tel. 4482054; fax 4498366.

**Office of the Prime Minister:** Government Headquarters, Kennedy Ave, Roseau; tel. 4482401; fax 4485200.

All other ministries are at Government Headquarters, Kennedy Ave, Roseau; tel. 4482401.

### CARIB TERRITORY

This reserve of the remaining Amerindian population is located on the central east coast of the island. The Caribs enjoy a measure of local government and elect their chief.

**Chief:** GARNET JOSEPH.

**Waitukubuli Karifuna Development Committee:** Salybia, Carib Territory; tel. 4457336.

## Legislature

### HOUSE OF ASSEMBLY

**Speaker:** F. OSBORNE G. SYMES.

**Clerk:** Mrs ALEX F. PHILLIP.

**Senators:** 9.

**Elected Members:** 21.

**General Election, 31 January 2000**

| Party | Votes cast | % | Seats |
|---|---|---|---|
| Labour Party of Dominica | 15,362 | 42.9 | 10 |
| Dominica United Workers' Party | 15,555 | 43.4 | 9 |
| Dominica Freedom Party | 4,858 | 13.6 | 2 |
| Independents | 29 | 0.1 | — |
| **Total** | 35,804 | 100.0 | 21 |

# Political Organizations

**Dominica Freedom Party (DFP):** Great George St, Roseau; tel. 4482104; Leader CHARLES SAVARIN.

**Dominica United Workers' Party (UWP):** 37 Cork St, Roseau; tel. 4485051; f. 1988; Leader EDISON JAMES; Chair. GARNET L. DIDIER.

**Labour Party of Dominica (LPD):** Cork St, Roseau; tel. 4488511; f. 1985 as a merger and reunification of left-wing groups, incl. the Dominica Labour Party (DLP; f. 1961); Leader ROOSEVELT (ROSIE) DOUGLAS; Deputy Leader PIERRE CHARLES.

# Diplomatic Representation

### EMBASSIES IN DOMINICA

**China (Taiwan):** Checkhall, Massacre, POB 56, Roseau; tel. 4491385; fax 4492085; e-mail rocemb@cwdom.dom; Chargé d'affaires: R. C. WU.

**Venezuela:** 37 Cork St, 3rd Floor, POB 770, Roseau; tel. 4483348; fax 4486198; Ambassador: HERNANI ESCOBAR.

# Judicial System

Justice is administered by the Eastern Caribbean Supreme Court (based in Saint Lucia), consisting of the Court of Appeal and the High Court. One of the six puisne judges of the High Court is resident in Dominica and presides over the Court of Summary Jurisdiction. The District Magistrate Courts deal with summary offences and civil offences involving limited sums of money (specified by law).

# Religion

Most of the population profess Christianity, but there are some Muslims, Bahá'ís and Jews. The largest denomination is the Roman Catholic Church (with some 80% of the inhabitants in 1991).

### CHRISTIANITY

#### The Roman Catholic Church

Dominica comprises the single diocese of Roseau, suffragan to the archdiocese of Castries (Saint Lucia). At 31 December 1997 there were an estimated 59,707 adherents in the country, representing a large majority of the inhabitants. The Bishop participates in the Antilles Episcopal Conference (currently based in Port of Spain, Trinidad).

**Bishop of Roseau:** Rt Rev. EDWARD J. GILBERT; Bishop's House, 20 Virgin Lane, POB 790, Roseau; tel. 4482837; fax 4483404; e-mail bishop@tod.dm.

#### The Anglican Communion

Anglicans in Dominica are adherents of the Church in the Province of the West Indies. The country forms part of the diocese of the North Eastern Caribbean and Aruba. The Bishop is resident in Antigua, and Archbishop of the Province is the Bishop of the Bahamas and the Turks and Caicos Islands.

#### Other Christian Churches

**Christian Union Church of the West Indies:** District 1, Rose St, Goodwill; tel. 4482725.

Other denominations include Methodist, Pentecostal, Baptist, Church of God, Presbyterian, the Assemblies of Brethren, Moravian and Seventh-day Adventist groups, and the Jehovah's Witnesses.

### BAHÁ'Í FAITH

**National Spiritual Assembly:** 9 James Lane, POB 136, Roseau; tel. 4484269; fax 4483881; e-mail coolesp@cwdom.dm.

# The Press

**The Chronicle:** Wallhouse, POB 1724, Roseau; tel. 4487887; fax 4480047; e-mail thechronicle@cwdom.dm; internet www.delphis.dm.chron.htm; f. 1996; Friday; progressive independent; Editor CHARLES HARDING; Gen. Man. J. ANTHONY WHITE; circ. 3,500.

**The Independent Newspaper:** POB 462, 9 Great Marlborough St, Roseau; tel. 4480221; fax 4484368; internet www.delphis.dm/indpub; weekly.

**Official Gazette:** Government Printery, Roseau; tel. 4482401, ext. 330; weekly; circ. 550.

**The Sun:** Sun Inc., POB 2255, Roseau; tel. 4484744; fax 4484764; e-mail acsun@cwdom.dm; f. 1998; Editor CHARLES JAMES.

**The Tropical Star:** Roseau; tel. 4484634; fax 4485984; weekly; circ. 3,000.

# Broadcasting and Communications

### TELECOMMUNICATIONS

**Telecommunications of Dominica (TOD):** Mercury House, Hanover St, Roseau.

### BROADCASTING

#### Radio

**Dominica Broadcasting Corporation:** Victoria St, POB 1, Roseau; tel. 4483283; fax 4482918; e-mail dbsradio@dbsradio.com; internet www.dbsradio.com; government station; daily broadcasts in English; 2 hrs daily in French patois; 10 kW transmitter on the medium wave band; FM service; programmes received throughout Caribbean excluding Jamaica and Guyana; Gen. Man. DENNIS JOSEPH; Programme Dir SHERMAINE GREEN-BROWN.

**Kairi FM:** Island Communications Corporation, Great George St, POB 931, Roseau; tel. 4487330; fax 4487332; e-mail kairfm@tod.dm; internet www.delphis.dm/kairi.htm; f. 1994.

**Radio Enba Mango:** Grand Bay; tel. 4463207.

**Voice of Life Radio—ZGBC:** Gospel Broadcasting Corpn, Loubiere, POB 205, Roseau; tel. 4487017; fax 4487094; e-mail volradio@tod.dm; linked to the US Christian Reformed Church; 112 hrs weekly AM, 24 hrs daily FM; Man. Dir GRANT HOEPPNER.

#### Television

There is no national television service, although there is a cable television network serving one-third of the island.

**Marpin Telecom and Broadcasting:** POB 2381, Roseau; tel. 4484107; fax 4482965; e-mail manager@marpin.dm; internet www.marpin.dm; commercial; cable service; Programme Man. RON ABRAHAM.

# Finance

(cap. = capital; res = reserves; dep. = deposits; m. = million; amounts in East Caribbean dollars)

The Eastern Caribbean Central Bank (see p. 294), based in Saint Christopher, is the central issuing and monetary authority for Dominica.

### BANKS

**Agricultural, Industrial and Development (AID) Bank:** cnr Charles Avenue and Rawles Lane, Goodwill, POB 215, Roseau; tel. 4482853; fax 4484903; e-mail aidbank@cwdom.dm; f. 1971; responsible to Ministry of Finance, Industry and Planning; planned privatization suspended in 1997; cap. 9.5m. (1991); Man PATRICIA CHARLES.

**Bank of Nova Scotia—Scotiabank** (Canada): 28 Hillsborough St, POB 520, Roseau; tel. 4485800; fax 4485805; Man. C. M. SMITH.

**Banque Française Commerciale** (France): Independent St, Roseau; tel. 4484040; fax 4485335; e-mail bfc@cwd.dom.dm; Man. THIERRY FREY.

**Barclays Bank PLC** (United Kingdom): 2 Old St, POB 4, Roseau; tel. 4482571; fax 4483471; Man. LEROY L. DANGLAR; sub-br. in Portsmouth.

**National Commercial Bank of Dominica:** 64 Hillsborough St, POB 271, Roseau; tel. 4484401; fax 4483982; e-mail ncbdom@cwdom.dm; f. 1976; cap. 10.0m., res 10.0m., dep. 224.5m. (June 1998); 51% govt-owned; Chair. CELINE BURTON-LARONDE; Gen. Man. JULIUS CORBETT; 2 brs.

**Royal Bank of Canada:** Bay Front, POB 19, Roseau; tel. 4482771; fax 4485398; Man. H. PINARD.

### INSURANCE

Several British, regional and US companies have agents in Roseau. Local companies include the following:

**First Domestic Insurance Co Ltd.** 19–21 King George V St, POB 1931, Roseau; tel. 4488337; fax 4485778; e-mail: insurance@cwdom.dm.

**Insurance Specialists and Consultants:** 19–21 King George V St, POB 20, Roseau; tel. 4482022; fax 4485778.

**J. B. Charles and Co Ltd:** Old St, POB 121, Roseau; tel. 4482876.

**Tonge Inc Ltd:** 19–21 King George V St, POB 20, Roseau; tel. 4484027; fax 4485778.

**Windward Islands Crop Insurance Co (Wincrop):** Vanoulst House, Goodwill, POB 469, Roseau; tel. 4483955; fax 4484197; f. 1987; regional; coverage for weather destruction of, mainly, banana crops; Man. KERWIN FERREIRA; brs in Grenada, Saint Lucia and Saint Vincent.

# Trade and Industry

### DEVELOPMENT ORGANIZATIONS

**National Development Corporation (NDC):** Valley Rd, POB 293, Roseau; tel. 4482045; fax 4485840; e-mail ndc@cwdom.dm; internet www.dominica.dm; f. 1988 by merger of Industrial Development Corpn (f. 1974) and Tourist Board; promotes local and foreign investment to increase employment, production and exports; promotes and co-ordinates tourism development; Chair. ISAAC BAPTISTE; Gen. Man. SHERIDAN G. GREGOIRE.

**Eastern Caribbean States Export Development and Agricultural Diversification Unit (EDADU):** POB 769, Roseau; tel. 4486655; fax 4485554; e-mail oecsundp@cwdom.dm; internet www.oecs-edadu.org; f. 1990 as Eastern Caribbean States Export Development Agency; reformed as above in 1997; OECS regional development org.; Exec. Dir COLIN BULLY.

### INDUSTRIAL AND TRADE ASSOCIATIONS

**Dominica Association of Industry and Commerce (DAIC):** POB 85, cnr Old St and Fields Lane, Roseau; tel. 4482874; fax 4486868; e-mail daic@marpin.dm; internet www.delphis.dm/daic.htm; f. 1972 by a merger of the Manufacturers' Association and the Chamber of Commerce; represents the business sector, liaises with the Government, and stimulates commerce and industry; 100 mems; Pres. MICHAEL ASTAPHAN; CEO JEANILIA R. V. DE SMET.

**Dominica Banana Marketing Corporation (DBMC):** Vanoulst House, POB 1620, Roseau; tel. 4482671; fax 4486445; internet www.delphis.dm/dbmc.htm; f. 1934 as Dominica Banana Growers' Association; restructured 1984; state-supported; Chair. GARNET DIDIER; Gen. Man. GREGORY SHILLINGFORD.

**Dominica Export-Import Agency (Dexia):** Bay Front, POB 173, Roseau; tel. 4483494; fax 4486308; e-mail dexia@cwdom.dm; internet www.delphis.dm/dexia/trade.htm; f. 1986; replaced the Dominica Agricultural Marketing Board and the External Trade Bureau; exporter of Dominican agricultural products, trade facilitator and importer of bulk rice, sugar and other essential commodities.

### EMPLOYERS' ORGANIZATION

**Dominica Employers' Federation:** 14 Church St, POB 1783, Roseau; tel. 4482314; fax 4484474; e-mail def@cwdom.dm; Pres. LAMBERT LEWIS.

### UTILITIES

#### Electricity

**Dominica Electricity Services Ltd (DOMLEC):** 18 Castle St, POB 1593, Roseau; tel. 4482681; fax 4485397; e-mail mandomlec@cwdom.dm; national electricity service; 72%-owned by the Commonwealth Development Corporation (UK); Chair. JUSTIN BRAITHWAITE.

#### Water

**Dominica Water and Sewerage Co Ltd (DOWASCO):** 3 High St, POB 185, Roseau; tel. 4484811; fax 4485813; Chair. CLEVELAND ROYER; Gen. Man. DAMIEN SHILLINGFORD.

### TRADE UNIONS

**Dominica Amalgamated Workers' Union (DAWU):** 18 King George V St, POB 137, Roseau; tel. 4483048; fax 4485787; f. 1960; Gen. Sec. FEDELINE MOULON; 950 mems.

**Dominica Teachers' Union:** Roseau.

**Dominica Trade Union:** 70–71 Independence St, Roseau; tel. and fax 4498139; f. 1945; Pres. HAROLD SEALEY; Gen. Sec. LEO J. BERNARD NICHOLAS; 800 mems.

**Media Workers' Association:** Roseau; Pres. MATTHIAS PELTIER.

**National Workers' Union:** 69 Queen Mary St, Roseau; tel. 4484465; f. 1977; Pres. RAWLINS JERMOTT; Gen. Sec. PATRICK JOHN; 800 mems.

**Public Service Union:** cnr Valley Rd and Windsor Lane, Roseau; tel. 4482102; fax 4488060; f. 1940 and registered as a trade union in 1960; representing all grades of civil servants, including firemen, prison officers, nurses, teachers and postal workers; Pres. SONIA D. WILLIAMS; Gen. Sec. THOMAS LETANG; 1,400 mems.

**Waterfront and Allied Workers' Union:** 43 Hillsborough St, Roseau; tel. 4482343; f. 1965; Pres. LOUIS BENOIT; Gen. Sec. NEVILLE LEE; 1,500 mems.

# Transport

### ROADS

In 1996 there were an estimated 780 km (485 miles) of roads, of which about 50.4% was paved; there were also numerous tracks. A road and bridge reconstruction project, costing an estimated EC $33m., was announced by the Government in 1997.

### SHIPPING

A deep-water harbour at Woodbridge Bay serves Roseau, which is the principal port. Several foreign shipping lines call at Roseau, and there is a high-speed ferry service between Martinique and Guadeloupe which calls at Roseau eight times a week. Ships of the Geest Line call at Prince Rupert's Bay, Portsmouth, to collect bananas, and cruise-ship facilities were constructed there during 1990. There are other specialized berthing facilities on the west coast.

**Dominica Ports Authority:** POB 243, Roseau; tel. 4484431; fax 4486131; f. 1972; responsible to the Ministry of Tourism, Ports and Employment; pilotage and cargo handling.

### CIVIL AVIATION

Melville Hall Airport, 64 km (40 miles) from Roseau, and Canefield Airport, 5 km (3 miles) from Roseau, are the two airports on the island. In 1990 it was decided to proceed with the construction of an international airport in the north-east of the island, although the project still lacked sufficient funding in late 1999. Work on the airport was, however, scheduled to commence in January 2000. A feasibility study on the expansion and upgrading of Melville Hall Airport was completed in 1998. The construction of a new runway at the nearby village of Wesley was chosen in preference to an earlier plan to realign Melville Hall's existing runway. The EC $78m.-project was due to begin in late 1998. Canefield Airport was also to be improved. The regional airline, LIAT (based in Antigua and Barbuda, and in which Dominica is a shareholder), provides daily services and, with Air Caraibe, Air Guadeloupe and Air BVI, connects Dominica with all the islands of the Eastern Caribbean, including the international airports of Puerto Rico, Antigua, Guadeloupe and Martinique.

# Tourism

The Government has designated areas of the island as nature reserves, to preserve the beautiful, lush scenery and the rich, natural heritage that constitute Dominica's main tourist attractions. Birdlife is particularly prolific, and includes several rare and endangered species, such as the Imperial parrot. There are also two marine reserves. Tourism is not as developed as it is among Dominica's neighbours, but the country is being promoted as an 'eco-tourism' and cruise destination. There were an estimated 307,853 visitors in 1998 (of whom 240,905 were cruise-ship passengers), and in 1996 there were 764 hotel rooms. Receipts from tourism increased by 8.1% from EC $98.8m. in 1996 to EC $106.8m. in 1997.

**National Development Corporation (NDC)—Division of Tourism:** Valley Rd, POB 73, Roseau; tel. 4482045; fax 4485840; e-mail ndc@cwdom.dm; internet www.dominica.dm; f. 1988, when Tourist Board merged with Industrial Development Corpn; Dir of Tourism STANTON CARTER.

**Dominica Hotel and Tourism Association:** POB 384, Roseau; tel. 4486565; fax 4480299; Pres. ATHERTON MARTIN.

# THE DOMINICAN REPUBLIC

## Introductory Survey

**Location, Climate, Language, Religion, Flag, Capital**

The Dominican Republic occupies the eastern part of the island of Hispaniola, which lies between Cuba and Puerto Rico in the Caribbean Sea. The country's only international frontier is with Haiti, to the west. The climate is sub-tropical, with an average annual temperature of 27°C (80°F). In Santo Domingo, temperatures are generally between 19°C (66°F) and 31°C (88°F). The west and south-west of the country are arid. Hispaniola lies in the path of tropical cyclones. The official language is Spanish. Almost all of the inhabitants profess Christianity, and some 88% are Roman Catholics. There are small Protestant and Jewish communities. The national flag (proportions 8 by 5) is blue (upper hoist and lower fly) and red (lower hoist and upper fly), quartered by a white cross. The state flag has, in addition, the national coat of arms, showing a quartered shield in the colours of the flag (on which are superimposed national banners, a cross and an open Bible) between scrolls above and below, at the centre of the cross. The capital is Santo Domingo.

**Recent History**

The Dominican Republic became independent in 1844, although it was occupied by US military forces between 1916 and 1924. General Rafael Leónidas Trujillo Molina overthrew the elected President, Horacio Vázquez, in 1930 and dominated the country until his assassination in May 1961. The dictator ruled personally from 1930 to 1947 and indirectly thereafter. His brother, Héctor Trujillo, was President from 1947 until August 1960, when he was replaced by Dr Joaquín Balaguer Ricardo, hitherto Vice-President. After Rafael Trujillo's death, President Balaguer remained in office, but in December 1961 he permitted moderate opposition groups to participate in a Council of State, which exercised legislative and executive powers. Balaguer resigned in January 1962, when the Council of State became the Provisional Government. A presidential election in December 1962, the country's first free election for 38 years, was won by Dr Juan Bosch Gaviño, the founder and leader of the Partido Revolucionario Dominicano (PRD), who had been in exile since 1930. President Bosch, a left-of-centre democrat, took office in February 1963 but was overthrown in the following September by a military coup. The leaders of the armed forces transferred power to a civilian triumvirate, led by Emilio de los Santos. In April 1965 a revolt by supporters of ex-President Bosch overthrew the triumvirate. Civil war broke out between pro-Bosch forces and military units headed by Gen. Elías Wessin y Wessin, who had played a leading role in the 1963 coup. The violence was eventually suppressed by the intervention of some 23,000 US troops, who were formally incorporated into an Inter-American peace force by the Organization of American States (OAS). The peace force withdrew in September 1965.

Following a period of provisional government under Héctor García Godoy, a presidential election in June 1966 was won by Balaguer, the candidate of the Partido Reformista Social Cristiano (PRSC), who won 57% of the votes cast, while Bosch won 39%. The PRSC, founded in 1964, also won a majority of seats in both houses of the new National Congress. Balaguer took office in July. A new Constitution was promulgated in November. Despite his association with the Trujillo dictatorship, Balaguer initially proved to be a popular leader, and in May 1970 he was re-elected for a further four years. In February 1973 a state of emergency was declared when guerrilla forces landed on the coast. Captain Francisco Caamaño Deño, the leader of the 1965 revolt, and his followers were killed. Bosch and other opposition figures went into hiding. Bosch later resigned as leader of the PRD (founding the Partido de la Liberación Dominicana—PLD), undermining hopes of a united opposition in the May 1974 elections, when Balaguer was re-elected with a large majority.

In the May 1978 presidential election, Balaguer was defeated by the PRD candidate, Silvestre Antonio Guzmán Fernández. This was the first occasion in the country's history when an elected President yielded power to an elected successor. An attempted military coup in favour of Balaguer was prevented by pressure from the US Government. On assuming office in August, President Guzmán undertook to professionalize the armed forces by removing politically ambitious high-ranking officers. In June 1981 he declared his support for Jacobo Majluta Azar, his Vice-President, as his successor, but in November the PRD rejected Majluta's candidacy in favour of Dr Salvador Jorge Blanco, a left-wing senator, who was elected President in May 1982. In the congressional elections, held at the same time, the PRD gained a majority in both the Senate and the Chamber of Deputies. Guzmán committed suicide in July after allegations of fraud were made against his Government and members of his family. Vice-President Majluta was immediately sworn in as interim President until Blanco assumed office in August. Although a member of the Socialist International, Blanco maintained good relations with the USA (on which the country is economically dependent) and declared that he would not resume relations with Cuba.

In April 1984 a series of public protests against substantial increases in the cost of essential items erupted into violent confrontations between the security forces and demonstrators in Santo Domingo and four other cities, which lasted for three days. In the course of the protests, more than 50 people were killed. The Government held opposition groups of the extreme right and left responsible for the unrest. In May the Government responded to the prospect of further demonstrations by ordering the arrest of more than 100 trade union and left-wing leaders. In August, in anticipation of civil unrest at the announcement of new price increases, more arrests were made among trade union and opposition leaders. Further demonstrations, including one attended by 40,000 people in Santo Domingo, were held in protest at the continuing economic decline.

In February 1985 a further series of substantial price increases led to violent clashes between demonstrators and the security forces, during which four people died. Public unrest was exacerbated by the Government's decision, in April, to accept the IMF's terms for further financial aid. In June a 24-hour general strike was organized by trade unions, in protest at the Government's economic policy and its refusal to increase the minimum wage. In July, however, the threat of a 48-hour general strike prompted the Government to order an immediate increase in the minimum wage.

Further violence preceded the presidential and legislative elections of May 1986. Several people were killed in clashes between rival political supporters. The three principal candidates in the presidential election were all former Presidents: Balaguer of the PRSC; Majluta, who, having registered La Estructura, his right-wing faction of the PRD, as a separate political party in July 1985, nevertheless secured the candidacy of the ruling PRD; and Bosch of the PLD. The counting of votes was suspended twice, following allegations by Majluta of fraud by the PRSC and by the Junta Central Electoral (JCE—Central Electoral Board). Balaguer was finally declared the winner by a narrow margin of votes over Majluta, his closest rival. In the simultaneous legislative elections, the PRSC won 21 of the 30 seats in the Senate and 56 of the 120 seats in the Chamber of Deputies.

Upon taking office as President (for the fifth time) in August 1986, Balaguer initiated an investigation into alleged corrupt practices by members of the outgoing administration. Blanco, the outgoing President, was charged with embezzlement and the illegal purchase of military vehicles. (In August 1991 he was finally convicted of 'abuse of power' and misappropriation of public funds, and sentenced to 20 years' imprisonment. However, in September 1994 legislation granting him amnesty was approved by the Chamber of Deputies.) The financial accounts of the armed forces were examined, and the former Secretary of State for the Armed Forces was subsequently imprisoned. In September 1987 the Cabinet resigned, at the request of the President, to enable him to restructure the Government. Some 35,000 government posts were abolished, in an attempt to reduce public spending, and expenditure was to be redirected to a programme of public works projects which were expected to create almost 100,000 new jobs. Nevertheless, strike action continued. The situation deteriorated in February 1988, when demonstrations took place throughout the country, to protest against the high cost of living, following an increase in the price of staple foods. Six people were killed as the security forces intervened to quell the protests. Subsequently, the Roman Catholic Church mediated between the opposing sides, and Balaguer agreed to stabilize prices of staple foods and to increase the minimum wage by 33%. However, prices continued to rise, provoking a new wave of strikes in June.

In 1989 opposition to the Government's economic policies intensified. Popular discontent was aggravated by the deterioration of public utilities, particularly water and electricity. In June a national strike committee called a 48-hour general strike. More than 300 organizations supported the action, which reportedly paralysed the country for two days. The major demands included the doubling of the minimum wage, a reduction in the prices of staple commodities, and the ending of interruptions in the supplies of water and electricity. Four people were killed and an estimated 3,000 were arrested during the protests. Despite mediation efforts by the Roman Catholic Church, the Government made no concessions to union demands. In October, following a 66% rise in fuel prices, there were further violent demonstrations.

With presidential and legislative elections due to take place in May 1990, Balaguer's prospects for re-election were hampered considerably by the continuing deterioration of the economy (particularly rapid inflation), the worsening energy crisis, and criticism of government spending on expansive public works programmes which had resulted in a severe depletion of the country's reserves of foreign exchange. The principal contender for the presidency was the PLD candidate, Bosch, who concentrated his election campaign on seeking support from the private sector, promising privatization of state-owned companies. In opinion polls conducted in the period preceding the presidential election, Bosch appeared to have a clear advantage. When the initial results indicated a narrow victory for Balaguer, Bosch accused the ruling PRSC and the JCE of fraud, necessitating a re-count, supervised by monitors from the OAS. Almost two months after the election, Balaguer was declared the official winner. The PRSC secured a narrow majority in the Senate, with 16 of the 30 seats; the PLD won 12 and the PRD two. At elections to the Chamber of Deputies the PLD obtained 44 of the 120 seats, while the PRSC won 42, the PRD 32 and the Partido Revolucionario Independiente (PRI) two. However, the lack of an outright majority in the Chamber of Deputies did not threaten seriously to impede government policies, in view of Balaguer's extensive powers to govern by decree.

In August 1990, in an attempt to reduce inflation by cutting government subsidies, the Government announced a programme of austerity measures, including substantial increases in the cost of fuel and food. Petrol and essential foodstuffs were almost doubled in price. The trade unions reacted angrily to the austerity measures, calling a 48-hour general strike. This action was violently suppressed by the security forces, and the ensuing conflict resulted in as many as 14 deaths. The price increases were partially offset by an increase of 30% in the salaries of army personnel and civilian employees in the public sector. The trade unions, however, rejected an identical offer by the private sector and threatened further strike action if their demands for basic food subsidies and considerable wage increases were not satisfied. In September a three-day general strike, organized by the Organizaciones Colectivas Populares (OCP), led to further arrests, injuries and at least one death. In the following month another general strike was called by the OCP and the Central General de Trabajadores (CGT), with the stated aim of ousting Balaguer from power. Violent clashes with the security forces in Santo Domingo resulted in a further four deaths.

In July 1991 a government announcement that a stand-by agreement had been concluded with the IMF prompted a series of general strikes in opposition to the accord and its concomitant economic guidelines. The strikes, called by the Confederación de Trabajadores Unitaria (CTU), also supported demands for a 100% rise in the minimum wage for state employees. Despite the adverse public response, the IMF agreement was formally signed in August.

In April 1992 evidence emerged of a serious rift within the PLD. Following the expulsion from the party, by the PLD's predominantly right-wing political committee, of Nélsida Marmolejos, a deputy and trade unionist who had criticized the party's position on a new labour code under discussion in Congress, 47 high-ranking, and mainly left-wing, members announced their resignation from the PLD. Those resigning included 10 deputies and one Senate representative, Max Puig. In June more than 400 former PLD members held a 'national assembly' to form a new political movement, the Alianza por la Democracia (APD), which was officially established in August. The APD was represented by all 11 former PLD deputies in the Chamber of Deputies, and by Max Puig in the Senate.

In late September 1992 a Dominican human rights leader, Rafael Efraín Ortiz, was shot dead by police during a demonstration in Santo Domingo, protesting at government plans to celebrate the 500th anniversary of the arrival in the Caribbean of Christopher Columbus. The demonstrations were the result of increasing public anger at the inordinate expense of the construction of the commemorative Columbus Lighthouse (estimated to have cost in excess of US $25m.). Protesters also denounced the celebration of the Spanish conquest, which had led to the enslavement and destruction of the indigenous Taino Indian population. In response to the death of Efraín, general strikes were called in several cities, and violent protests broke out, resulting in a further death as rioters clashed with the security forces.

In April 1993 the APD split into two factions, led, respectively, by Max Puig and Nélsida Marmolejos. In January 1994 the PLD announced that it had formed an alliance with the right-wing Fuerza Nacional Progresista (FNP) in order to contest the forthcoming general election in May. At a special convention of the PRSC held that month, Balaguer officially announced his intention to contest the forthcoming presidential election, and his nomination received the support of the majority of the party delegates. However, his decision prompted 20 members of the PRSC executive to withdraw from the party in order to support the presidential candidate of the Unidad Democrática (UD), Fernando Alvarez Bogaert, himself a defecting member of the PRSC. The UD subsequently signed an electoral pact with the PRD, with Alvarez to contest the vice-presidency and José Francisco Peña Gómez, of the PRD, the presidency.

The official results of the presidential and legislative elections of 16 May 1994 were delayed, amid accusations of widespread voting irregularities. Interim results, announced on 24 May, indicated a narrow victory for Balaguer in the presidential election. However, the PRD claimed that polling stations had been issued with abbreviated electoral rolls and that the PRSC, which had effective control of the JCE, had removed the names of some 200,000 PRD supporters from the lists. A full recount began on 25 May. In June the JCE rejected a request, made by the US Department of State, that fresh elections be conducted wherever voting irregularities had been detected. In the same month Bosch resigned as leader of the PLD. In July an investigative commission confirmed that, as a result of serious irregularities, some 73,000 of the registered electorate had been denied a vote. Despite an atmosphere of growing political instability, Balaguer rejected opposition demands for the formation of a provisional government. Strike action in protest at the electoral irregularities was reported to have seriously affected several regions, including the capital, during that month. On 2 August the JCE announced the final election results, having apparently overlooked the findings of the electoral investigative commission. Balaguer was proclaimed the winner of the presidential election by a margin of less than 1% of the votes cast, with 43.6%. Peña Gómez received 42.9% of the votes and Bosch obtained the remaining 13.5%. In the Senate the alliance of the PRD and the UD secured 15 seats, while the PRSC won 14 and the PLD one seat. In the Chamber of Deputies the PRD/UD alliance obtained 57 seats, while the PRSC gained 50 and the PLD 13 seats.

Talks aimed at ending the political crisis caused by the election were held in early August 1994, with the mediation of the OAS and the Roman Catholic Church, and resulted in the signing of the Pact for Democracy. Under the terms of the accord (agreed by all the major parties), a fresh presidential election was to be held in November 1995 and a series of constitutional reforms would be adopted, providing for the prohibition of the re-election of a president to a consecutive term, the replacement of the JCE, and the reorganization of the judiciary. As a result of the accord, Peña Gómez cancelled a series of planned strikes and demonstrations organized by the PRD. However, at a session of the National Congress, held on 14 August, the deputies of the PRSC, with the support of those of the PLD, voted to extend Balaguer's mandate from 18 months to two years. The PRD withdrew from the legislature in protest, and Peña Gómez announced that his party would boycott Congress and resume strike action. The OAS also criticized Congress for violating the terms of the Pact for Democracy. The constitutional amendments that the Pact envisaged were, however, approved by Congress. On 16 August Balaguer was inaugurated as President for a seventh term, and a new Cabinet was appointed over the following days.

The year 1995 was marked by a series of protests and disturbances, largely provoked by the deteriorating standards of public services. In March four people were killed when protest at increases in public transport fares erupted into violence and the security forces were dispatched to restore order. The fare increases, which had been imposed unilaterally by certain transport companies, were declared illegal by the Government. In April, following the most severe electricity shortages since the energy crisis of 1990, the administrator of the state electricity company, the Corporación Dominicana de Electricidad (CDE), was dismissed. In May a 24-hour general strike was conducted in protest at increases in food prices and at the deterioration of electricity and transport services, although it received only partial support. During the following month there were renewed disturbances in Santo Domingo and in towns to the north of the capital, as protesters demanding the provision of basic services clashed with the security forces. Protests continued in August, following the implementation by the Government of a 25% increase in public transport fares. In September as many as three people were killed during violent confrontations between the security forces and workers at a sugar plantation in San Luis, east of the capital. The workers had been protesting at the decision of the state sugar council, the Consejo Estatal de Azúcar, to dismiss some 12,700 of its work-force.

In April 1996 the energy shortfall again reached crisis proportions, with power cuts averaging between 14 and 20 hours per day, following the decision by a major private power station, owned by the US consortium Smith-Enron, to withdraw from the national grid pending the settlement of a debt of US $4.5m. owed to it by the CDE. Although the dispute was resolved later that month, the crisis prompted renewed demands for Congress to expedite legislation enabling the privatization of CDE, which, owing largely to inefficiency and corruption, operated at a considerable loss.

The presidential election of 16 May 1996, the first for some 30 years in which Balaguer was not a candidate, was conducted according to a new system, introduced since 1994, whereby a second round of voting would be conducted between the two leading candidates should no candidate secure an absolute majority in the initial ballot. In the first round Peña Gómez won 45.9% of the votes, while the candidate of the PLD, Leonel Fernández Reyna, obtained 38.9%. The candidate of the PRSC, Jacinto Peynado (who had received only nominal support from Balaguer), obtained just 15.0% of the votes. At the second round of the presidential election, conducted on 30 June, Fernández secured a narrow victory, winning 51.25% of the votes, while Peña Gómez obtained 48.75%. The establishment, earlier in the month, of an electoral alliance between the PLD and PRSC, entitled the Frente Nacional Patriótico, had ensured Fernández the support of the PRSC voters. While the PRSC failed to retain the presidency, Balaguer appeared to have succeeded in retaining considerable influence in the new administration, since the PLD had only minority representation in Congress and would be dependent on the support of the PRSC to implement planned institutional reforms. However, in early August relations between Fernández and Balaguer appeared to have deteriorated when the PRSC signed an unexpected agreement with the PRD, which guaranteed the PRSC the presidency of the Senate while the PRD obtained that of the Chamber of Deputies. On 16 August Fernández was inaugurated, and the Cabinet, consisting almost exclusively of PLD members, was sworn in.

In 1997, as part of a campaign to eliminate deep-seated corruption in the country's institutions (which was estimated to cost the State some 30,000m. pesos per year), Fernández restructured both the police and the judiciary. In May several senior police-officers, including the head of the Dirección Nacional de Control de Drogas (National Drug Control Directorate), Julio César Ventura Bayonet, were dismissed. Ventura's dismissal reflected concern that assets seized from imprisoned drugs-traffickers were being misappropriated. In the same month a new body, under the direct control of the Consejo Nacional de Drogas (National Drug Council), was created to deal with such confiscated assets. In August Fernández, in his role as Chairman of the Consejo Nacional de la Magistratura (National Judiciary Council), oversaw a restructuring of the Supreme Court, including the appointment of 15 new judges. Responsibility for appointing judges at all other levels of the judicial system was transferred from the Senate to the Supreme Court, principally to avoid appointments being influenced by political considerations.

Growing dissatisfaction with the continuing deterioration of public services and Fernández's failure to honour promises made during his election campaign provoked widespread disturbances and strike action throughout the country in 1997. Between July and September numerous violent confrontations between demonstrators and the security forces resulted in several deaths. In October, in an effort to defuse the volatile social and political climate, Fernández introduced a recovery plan aimed at overcoming electricity and food shortages. However, in the following month a two-day general strike was organized by an 'umbrella' protest group, the Coordinadora de Organizaciones Populares, in support of demands for pay increases, reductions in the price of fuel and basic foodstuffs and improved public services. In February 1998 the continuing deterioration of public utilities and popular discontent regarding unfulfilled government promises provoked renewed violent protest in Santo Domingo and in the north of the country.

At legislative elections held on 16 May 1998 the PRD won 83 seats in the 149-seat Chamber of Deputies (enlarged from 120 seats), while the PLD obtained 49 seats and the PRSC secured the remaining 17 seats. In the Senate the PRD gained 24 seats, while the PLD won four and the PRSC two seats. The number of registered voters who abstained from participating in the poll was, at some 48%, the highest on record. As a result of the success of the opposition PRD, and the considerable losses incurred by the PRSC (on whom the PLD Government had hitherto depended for support in the legislature), it was considered likely that Fernández would encounter considerable difficulty in implementing his legislative programme for the remainder of his term of office, due to end in 2000. In July 1998 the outgoing Congress approved controversial legislation granting an amnesty to all public officials accused of corruption since 1978. The new legislature was inaugurated in August 1998. However, the PRD failed to secure the presidency of the Chamber of Deputies when a dissident group of PRD deputies joined forces with the PLD and the PRSC to re-elect the outgoing President of the Chamber, Héctor Rafael Peguero Méndez, to the post. Peguero had been expelled from the PRD in July, after refusing to accept the party's choice of candidate for the position.

In January 1999 conflict within the legislature threatened to jeopardize the disbursement of some US $216m. in reconstruction loans from the World Bank and the Inter-American Development Bank, which had been made available following the destruction caused by 'Hurricane Georges' in September 1998. The dispute concerned the election for the post of Secretary-General of the Liga Municipal Dominicana (LMD), an association of local government bodies with significant financial powers, which directed local government expenditure amounting to some 4% of the national budget. In the event, two separate elections were held independently of one another: the PRD, which controlled the legislature, elected its own candidate. However, the governing PLD and its ally, the PRSC, elected and swore in the candidate of the PRSC. In February the PRD initiated legal proceedings to contest the Government's claim to control the LMD, while also signalling its intention to use its legislative majority to prevent the ratification of the reconstruction loans until agreement had been reached on the dispute. An accord was finally achieved in April, when it was agreed to appoint an impartial commission to manage the LMD pending a judicial ruling on the election.

Violent protest against electricity and water shortages and declining living standards continued in late 1998 and throughout 1999. In March 1999 protests in Salcedo and Licey al Medio, north of the capital, resulted in four deaths. In October a general strike was organized in protest against the introduction of fuel price increases of up to 34% and a concomitant rise in transport fares. The protest, which resulted in a further death, effectively paralysed the public transport sector before being abandoned on its second day.

In January 1989 a traffic accident, in which 47 Haitian sugar workers were killed, focused attention on the continuing illegal import of plantation labour into the Dominican Republic from Haiti. In June 1991, in reaction to increasing criticism of the Dominican Republic's human rights record (and, in particular, the Government's apparent acquiescence in the exploitation of Haitian child labourers), President Balaguer ordered the repatriation of all Haitian residents aged under 16 or over 60 years. Protests made by the Haitian Government that such a unilateral measure contravened normal diplomatic procedure were rejected by Balaguer. Following the army coup of September 1991 in Haiti, tens of thousands of Haitians were estimated to have fled to the Dominican Republic. However, only some 700 had been granted refugee status by mid-1993, according to the United Nations High Commissioner for Refugees. In mid-1994 reports of smuggling on a large scale from the Dominican Republic to Haiti, in defiance of UN sanctions against the Haitian military dictatorship, prompted the UN to seek assurances of co-operation from Balaguer. In June an agreement was reached, providing for the UN to send a monitoring mission to observe the enforcement of the embargo on the Dominican border with Haiti. The first contingent of UN observers arrived in August. The border remained closed after the US occupation of Haiti in mid-September and was reopened in mid-October, following the lifting of UN sanctions. In early 1997 relations with Haiti became strained following the expulsion from the Dominican Republic over a three-month period of some 20,000 Haitians who had been residing illegally in the country. In late February Fernández and his Haitian counterpart met in Antigua to discuss the situation, and agreement was reached to put an immediate end to large-scale repatriations. Accord was also achieved providing for the repatriation process to be monitored by an international body to ensure the observance of human rights. In June 1998 Fernández became the first Dominican Head of State to visit Haiti since 1936. Fernández and the Haitian President met in Port-au-Prince, where they reached agreement on the establishment of joint border patrols to combat the traffic of drugs, arms and other contraband across the countries' joint border.

### Government

The Dominican Republic comprises 26 provinces, each administered by an appointed governor, and a Distrito Nacional (DN) containing the capital. Under the 1966 Constitution (as amended in 1994), legislative power is exercised by the bicameral National Congress, with a Senate of 30 members and a Chamber of Deputies (149 members). Members of both houses are elected for four years by universal adult suffrage. Executive power lies with the President, who is also elected by direct popular vote for four years. He is assisted by a Vice-President and a Cabinet comprising Secretaries of State.

### Defence

Military service is voluntary and lasts for four years. In August 1999 the armed forces totalled 24,500 men: army 15,000, air force 5,500 and navy 4,000. Paramilitary forces number 15,000. The defence budget for 1999 was an estimated RD $1,200m.

### Economic Affairs

In 1997, according to estimates by the World Bank, the Dominican Republic's gross national product (GNP), measured at average 1995–97 prices, was US $14,148m., equivalent to $1,750 per head. During 1990–97, it was estimated, GNP per head increased, in real terms, at an average rate of 3.5% annually. Over the same period, the population increased by an average of 1.9% per year. In 1998 GNP was estimated at $14,600m. ($1,770 per head). The Dominican Republic's gross domestic product (GDP) increased, in real terms, by an average of 5.5% per year in 1990–98. Real GDP increased by 7.3% in 1998.

Agriculture, including forestry and fishing, contributed an estimated 11.6% of GDP, at constant 1970 prices, and employed an estimated 18.1% of the labour force in 1998. The principal cash crops are sugar cane (sugar and sugar derivatives accounted for 19.7% of total export earnings in 1997), coffee and cocoa beans. Agricultural GDP increased, in real terms, by an average of 3.6% per year during 1990–98, and by 1.0% in 1998.

Industry (including mining, manufacturing, construction and power) employed 25.1% of the economically active population in 1997, and contributed an estimated 32.8% of GDP, at constant prices, in 1998. Industrial GDP increased, in real terms, by an average of 6.1% per year during 1990–98, and by 8.8% in 1998.

Mining contributed an estimated 2.0% of GDP, at constant prices, in 1998, but employed only 0.3% of the economically active population in 1997. The major mineral export is ferronickel (providing 30.0% of total export earnings in 1995). Gold and silver are also exploited, and there are workable deposits of gypsum, limestone and mercury. The GDP of the mining sector increased, in real terms, by an average of 1.1% per year during 1990–97, but declined by 15.9% in 1998.

Manufacturing contributed an estimated 16.6% of GDP, at constant prices, in 1998, and employed 18.2% of the economically active population in 1997. Based on the value of sales, the most important branches of manufacturing in 1984 were food products (accounting for 38.9% of the total), petroleum refineries (11.3%), beverages (11.3%) and chemicals (8.4%). The GDP of the manufacturing sector increased, in real terms, at an average rate of 4.4% per year during 1990–97, and by 5.0% in 1998.

Energy is derived principally from petroleum. Imports of mineral fuels accounted for an estimated 13.2% of the total cost of imports in 1996.

The services sector contributed an estimated 55.6% of GDP, at constant prices, in 1998, and employed 54.9% of the economically active population in 1997. The GDP of the services sector expanded at an average annual rate of 5.6% during 1990–98, and by 7.7% in 1998. Tourism accounted for approximately 13.3% of GDP in 1995.

In 1997 the Dominican Republic recorded a visible trade deficit of US $1,995.0m., and there was a deficit of $163.0m. on the current account of the balance of payments. In 1986 the principal source of imports (37.9%) was the USA; other major suppliers were Venezuela, Mexico and Japan. In 1995 the USA was the principal market for exports (51.1% of the total, excluding exports from free-trade zones); other significant purchasers were the Netherlands and Belgium. The principal exports in 1997 were minerals (principally ferro-nickel) and sugar and sugar derivatives. The principal imports in 1986 were petroleum and petroleum products, and machinery.

In 1998 there was an estimated budgetary surplus of RD $2,109.8m. (equivalent to 0.9% of GDP). The Dominican Republic's total external debt at the end of 1997 was US $4,239m., of which $3,460m. was long-term public debt. In that year the cost of debt-servicing was equivalent to 6.2% of total revenue from exports of goods and services. In 1990–98 the average annual rate of inflation was 11.2%. Consumer prices increased by an average of 4.6% in 1998. An estimated 14.3% of the economically active population were unemployed in 1998.

In July 1984 the Dominican Republic was granted observer status in CARICOM (see p. 136). In December 1989 the country was accepted as a member of the ACP nations covered by the Lomé Convention (see p. 196). In 1990 the Dominican Republic's application for full membership of CARICOM was threatened when ACP nations accused the Dominican Republic of breaking an agreement made under the Lomé Convention concerning the export of bananas to countries of the European Community (now the European Union).

In the 1990s the economy of the Dominican Republic was severely affected by the unstable nature of the country's electricity supply. The situation reached crisis proportions in 1990 and again in 1995–98, when interruptions in the supply of electricity lasted up to 20 hours per day. A plan for the restructuring of the state electricity company (Corporación Dominicana de Electricidad—CDE) was agreed in principle in 1993. However, implementation of the plan was repeatedly delayed, while the CDE continued to operate at a significant loss. In May 1999 the generating and distribution operations of the CDE were partially privatized, with the divestment of 50%-shares producing revenue of US $644m. and saving the Government some $147m. per year in subsidies. In 1996 an emergency plan was introduced to revive the ailing sugar company, the Consejo Estatal de Azúcar (CEA). By 1999 the CEA had accumulated debts totalling more than $250m. In September four private consortiums were granted 30-year contracts to manage the CEA's operations, providing the Government with a further $11m. per year in revenue. Despite the structural difficulties in the state power and sugar sectors, the economy continued to record significant growth in the late 1990s, based on expansion in tourism and the free-trade zones. Damages resulting from the impact of 'Hurricane Georges' in September 1998 were estimated by the Government at $1,200m. In October the Government announced a 3,500m. pesos-emergency programme for reconstruction, which was to be partly financed by foreign grants. The Government also sought a rescheduling of debt-servicing obligations with the 'Paris Club' of creditors. In June 1999 the Government and the opposition agreed to sign a pact committing them to expedite delayed economic and financial legislation, including measures to reform the system of tariffs and taxation. GDP growth of 7% was forecast for 1999, while inflation of 5% was envisaged. Progress in the privatization process was expected to prompt the release of increased multilateral funds for development.

### Social Welfare

A voluntary national contributory scheme, introduced in 1947, provides insurance cover for sickness, unemployment, accidental injury, maternity, old age and death. Only 42% of the population are thought to benefit from the system. In 1980 there were 571 hospitals and clinics, 2,142 physicians and 8,953 hospital beds under the auspices of the public health and welfare department and the Institute of Social Security. In the early 1990s there were an estimated 10 physicians per 100,000 inhabitants and 33 nurses per 100,000 inhabitants. The central Government's 1996 budget allocated 3,197.4m. pesos (11.6% of total expenditure) to the health sector.

### Education

Education is, where possible, compulsory for children between the ages of six and 14 years. Primary education begins at the age of six and lasts for eight years. Secondary education, starting at 14 years of age, lasts for four years. In 1994 the total enrolment at primary and secondary schools was equivalent to 84% of the school-age population (males 81%; females 86%). In that year primary enrolment included an estimated 81% of children in the relevant age-group (males 79%; females 83%), while secondary enrolment included an estimated 22% of children in the relevant age-group (males 18%; females 26%). In 1994/95 there were 4,001 primary schools, and in 1983/84 there were an estimated 1,664 secondary schools. There are eight universities. Budgetary expenditure on education by the Secretariat of State for Education and Culture in 1996 was 3,610m. pesos, representing 13.2% of total government spending. In 1995, according to UNESCO estimates, the average rate of adult illiteracy was 17.9% (males 18.0%; females 17.8%).

### Public Holidays

**2000:** 1 January (New Year's Day), 6 January (Epiphany), 21 January (Our Lady of Altagracia), 26 January (Duarte), 27 February (Independence), 14 April (Pan-American Day), 21 April (Good Friday), 1 May (Labour Day), 16 July (Foundation of Sociedad la Trinitaria), 16 August (Restoration Day), 24 September (Our Lady of Mercedes), 12 October (Columbus Day), 24 October (United Nations Day), 1 November (All Saints' Day), 25 December (Christmas Day).

**2001:** 1 January (New Year's Day), 6 January (Epiphany), 21 January (Our Lady of Altagracia), 26 January (Duarte), 27 February (Independence), 13 April (Good Friday), 14 April (Pan-American Day), 1 May (Labour Day), 16 July (Foundation of Sociedad la Trinitaria), 16 August (Restoration Day), 24 September (Our Lady of Mercedes), 12 October (Columbus Day), 24 October (United Nations Day), 1 November (All Saints' Day), 25 December (Christmas Day).

### Weights and Measures

The metric system is officially in force but the imperial system is often used.

# Statistical Survey

Source (unless otherwise stated): Oficina Nacional de Estadísticas, Edif. de Oficinas Públicas, Avda México esq. Leopoldo Navarro, Santo Domingo; Banco Central de la República Dominicana, Calle Pedro Henríquez Ureña, esq. Leopoldo Navarro, Apdo 1347, Santo Domingo; tel. 689-7121; fax 687-7488.

## Area and Population

**AREA, POPULATION AND DENSITY**

| | |
|---|---|
| Area (sq km) | |
| Land | 48,072 |
| Inland water | 350 |
| Total | 48,422* |
| Population (census results)† | |
| 12 December 1981 | 5,647,977 |
| 24 September 1993 | |
| Males | 3,550,797 |
| Females | 3,742,593 |
| Total | 7,293,390 |
| Population (official estimates at mid-year)‡ | |
| 1995 | 7,915,321 |
| 1996 | 8,052,000 |
| 1997 | 8,190,000 |
| Density (per sq km) at mid-1997 | 169.1 |

* 18,696 sq miles.
† Excluding adjustment for underenumeration.
‡ Not adjusted to take account of the results of the 1993 census.

**PRINCIPAL TOWNS** (population at 1993 census)

| | |
|---|---|
| Santo Domingo, DN (capital) | 2,138,262 |
| Santiago de los Caballeros | 364,447 |
| La Romana | 132,693 |
| San Pedro de Macorís | 123,855 |

**Births and deaths** (1994): Registered live births 135,056 (birth rate 17.4 per 1,000); Registered deaths 10,103 (death rate 1.3 per 1,000). Note: Registration is incomplete. According to UN estimates, the average annual rates per 1,000 in 1990–95 were: Births 27.0; Deaths 5.6.

**Expectation of life** (UN estimates, years at birth, 1990–95): 69.3 (males 67.6; females 71.7) (Source: UN, *World Population Prospects: The 1998 Revision*).

**ECONOMICALLY ACTIVE POPULATION**
(ISIC Major Divisions, '000 persons aged 10 years and over, official estimates, 1997)

| | Males | Females | Total |
|---|---|---|---|
| Agriculture, hunting and forestry; Fishing | 512.5 | 16.5 | 529.0 |
| Mining and quarrying | 7.5 | 0.9 | 8.4 |
| Manufacturing | 332.7 | 150.7 | 483.3 |
| Electricity, gas and water supply | 13.7 | 6.6 | 20.3 |
| Construction | 150.4 | 3.1 | 153.6 |
| Wholesale and retail trade | 356.1 | 176.1 | 532.3 |
| Hotels and restaurants | 59.5 | 55.8 | 115.3 |
| Transport, storage and communications | 190.0 | 12.9 | 202.7 |
| Financial intermediation; Real estate, renting and business activities | 17.3 | 16.8 | 34.0 |
| Public administration and defence | 99.5 | 25.9 | 125.4 |
| Education; Health and social work; Other community, social and personal service activities | 152.2 | 295.3 | 447.5 |
| **Total employed** | 1,891.4 | 760.6 | 2,652.0 |
| Unemployed | 199.0 | 304.7 | 503.7 |
| **Total labour force** | 2,090.4 | 1,065.3 | 3,155.7 |

Source: ILO, *Yearbook of Labour Statistics*.

**Mid-1998** (estimates in '000): Agriculture, etc. 644. Total labour force 3,553 (Source: FAO, *Production Yearbook*).

# Agriculture

**PRINCIPAL CROPS** ('000 metric tons)

| | 1996 | 1997 | 1998 |
|---|---|---|---|
| Rice (paddy) | 466 | 521 | 475 |
| Maize | 40 | 32 | 37 |
| Sorghum | 18 | 22 | 22* |
| Potatoes | 24 | 22 | 17 |
| Sweet potatoes | 44 | 29 | 44 |
| Cassava (Manioc) | 130 | 97 | 126 |
| Yams | 9 | 11 | 13 |
| Other roots and tubers | 40 | 41 | 42 |
| Dry beans | 35 | 28 | 24 |
| Groundnuts (in shell) | 1 | 2 | 2* |
| Coconuts | 171* | 155 | 160 |
| Copra† | 12 | 11 | 11 |
| Tomatoes | 202 | 264 | 198 |
| Sugar cane | 6,131 | 6,294 | 5,097 |
| Oranges | 98 | 107 | 136 |
| Lemons and limes | 8* | 8* | 9 |
| Avocados* | 155 | 155 | 155 |
| Mangoes | 190* | 185* | 185 |
| Pineapples | 109 | 112 | 108 |
| Bananas | 383 | 389 | 359 |
| Plantains | 317 | 327 | 341 |
| Coffee (green) | 42 | 42 | 57 |
| Cocoa beans | 60 | 55 | 59 |
| Tobacco (leaves) | 30 | 39 | 43 |

* FAO estimate(s). † Unofficial figures.

Source: FAO, *Production Yearbook*.

**LIVESTOCK** ('000 head, year ending September)

| | 1996 | 1997 | 1998 |
|---|---|---|---|
| Horses* | 329 | 329 | 329 |
| Mules* | 135 | 135 | 135 |
| Asses* | 145 | 145 | 145 |
| Cattle | 2,435 | 2,481 | 2,528 |
| Pigs* | 950 | 960 | 960 |
| Sheep | 135* | 135 | 135* |
| Goats | 570* | 570 | 570* |

* FAO estimate(s).

Chickens (million): 43 in 1996; 43 in 1997; 38 in 1998.

Source: FAO, *Production Yearbook*.

**LIVESTOCK PRODUCTS** ('000 metric tons)

| | 1996 | 1997 | 1998 |
|---|---|---|---|
| Beef and veal | 80 | 79 | 77 |
| Poultry meat | 149 | 156 | 169 |
| Cows' milk | 393 | 390 | 358 |
| Butter | 2* | 2* | 2† |
| Cheese | 3† | 3 | 3† |
| Hen eggs | 47 | 48 | 50 |
| Cattle hides (fresh)† | 8 | 9 | 9 |

* Unofficial figure. † FAO estimate(s).

Source: FAO, *Production Yearbook*.

# Forestry

**ROUNDWOOD REMOVALS** ('000 cubic metres, excl. bark)

| | 1983 | 1984 | 1985 |
|---|---|---|---|
| Industrial wood | 6 | 6 | 6 |
| Fuel wood | 951 | 963 | 976 |
| **Total** | 957 | 969 | 982 |

**1986–97:** Annual output as in 1985 (FAO estimates).

Source: FAO, *Yearbook of Forest Products*.

# Fishing

('000 metric tons, live weight)

| | 1995 | 1996 | 1997 |
|---|---|---|---|
| Inland waters | 2.2 | 1.2 | 1.1 |
| Atlantic Ocean | 15.8 | 12.6 | 13.5 |
| **Total catch** | 18.0 | 13.8 | 14.5 |

Source: FAO, *Yearbook of Fishery Statistics*.

# Mining

| | 1996 | 1997 | 1998 |
|---|---|---|---|
| Ferro-nickel ('000 metric tons)* | 78 | n.a. | n.a. |
| Gold (metric tons) | 3.3 | 3.5 | 3.5 |
| Silver (million troy ounces) | 0.5 | 0.4 | 0.2 |

* Source: US Bureau of Mines (Washington, DC).

# Industry

**SELECTED PRODUCTS**

| | 1994 | 1995 | 1996 |
|---|---|---|---|
| Refined sugar ('000 metric tons) | 101* | 285† | 330† |
| Cement ('000 metric tons)‡ | 1,276 | 1,293 | n.a. |
| Beer ('000 hectolitres)* | 2,200 | n.a. | n.a. |
| Cigarettes (million)* | 4,446 | n.a. | n.a. |
| Electricity (million kWh)* | 6,182 | 6,506 | 6,847 |

* Estimate(s).

† FAO figure.

‡ Data from the UN Economic Commission for Latin America and the Caribbean.

Source: UN, *Industrial Commodity Statistics Yearbook*.

# Finance

**CURRENCY AND EXCHANGE RATES**

**Monetary Units**

100 centavos = 1 Dominican Republic peso (RD $ or peso oro)

**Sterling, Dollar and Euro Equivalents** (30 September 1999)

£1 sterling = 26.43 pesos;
US $1 = 16.05 pesos;
€1 = 17.12 pesos;
1,000 Dominican Republic pesos = £37.84 = US $62.30 = €58.41.

**Average Exchange Rate** (RD $ per US $)

1996 13.775
1997 14.265
1998 15.267

**BUDGET** (RD $ million)

| Revenue* | 1994 | 1995 | 1996 |
|---|---|---|---|
| Tax revenue | 20,357.6 | 23,624.5 | 25,474.8 |
| Taxes on income and profits | 3,171.8 | 4,074.9 | 4,566.7 |
| Taxes on goods and services | 7,543.4 | 8,823.4 | 9,345.8 |
| Taxes on international trade and transactions | 8,565.3 | 9,521.9 | 10,183.2 |
| Other current revenue | 1,819.2 | 2,395.0 | 2,171.2 |
| Property income | 889.2 | 1,119.8 | 944.9 |
| Fees and charges | 787.9 | 1,082.5 | 1,032.9 |
| Capital revenue | 82.0 | 77.1 | 299.0 |
| **Total** | 22,258.8 | 26,096.6 | 27,945.0 |

| Expenditure† | 1994 | 1995 | 1996 |
|---|---|---|---|
| General public services | 1,544.5 | 1,654.9 | 1,739.6 |
| Defence | 1,105.7 | 940.3 | 1,149.0 |
| Public order and safety | 771.9 | 692.6 | 815.4 |
| Education | 2,731.0 | 3,150.0 | 3,610.3 |
| Health | 2,440.4 | 2,701.6 | 3,197.4 |
| Social security and welfare | 904.5 | 937.2 | 1,313.0 |
| Housing and community amenities | 3,722.5 | 3,619.8 | 3,783.3 |
| Recreational, cultural and religious affairs and services | 295.3 | 222.2 | 327.2 |
| Economic affairs and services | 8,088.3 | 8,629.7 | 10,482.3 |
| Fuel and energy | 595.3 | 1,216.2 | 1,343.0 |
| Agriculture, forestry and fishing | 2,125.7 | 1,956.2 | 2,555.9 |
| Mining and mineral resources, manufacturing and construction | 2,004.6 | 2,221.3 | 2,206.1 |
| Transport and communications | 2,690.1 | 3,043.2 | 3,871.0 |
| Other purposes | 1,417.9 | 1,511.6 | 1,038.9 |
| **Sub-total** | 23,022.0 | 24,059.9 | 27,456.4 |
| Adjustment | 475.1 | 924.2 | 1,196.7 |
| **Total** | 23,497.1 | 24,984.1 | 28,653.1 |
| Current‡ | 11,248.9 | 14,090.4 | 16,446.2 |
| Capital | 11,840.4 | 10,510.9 | 11,613.6 |
| Adjustment | 407.8 | 382.8 | 593.3 |

* Excluding grants received (RD $ million): 301.3 in 1994; 152.5 in 1995; 213.7 in 1996.

† Excluding lending minus repayments (RD $ million): 13.8 in 1994; 18.5 in 1995; 23.8 in 1996.

‡ Including interest payments (RD $ million): 1,300.6 in 1994; 1,511.6 in 1995; 1,054.1 in 1996.

Source: IMF, *Government Finance Statistics Yearbook*.

**INTERNATIONAL RESERVES** (US $ million at 31 December)

| | 1996 | 1997 | 1998 |
|---|---|---|---|
| Gold* | 6.7 | 5.5 | 5.3 |
| IMF special drawing rights | 0.4 | 0.3 | 0.3 |
| Foreign exchange | 349.8 | 390.7 | 501.6 |
| **Total** | 356.9 | 396.5 | 507.2 |

* Valued at market-related prices.

Source: IMF, *International Financial Statistics*.

**MONEY SUPPLY** (RD $ million at 31 December)

| | 1996 | 1997 | 1998 |
|---|---|---|---|
| Currency outside banks | 9,635 | 11,534 | 12,568 |
| Demand deposits at commercial banks | 13,540 | 16,081 | 16,782 |
| **Total money** (incl. others) | 23,225 | 27,703 | 29,416 |

Source: IMF, *International Financial Statistics*.

**COST OF LIVING**

(Consumer Price Index; base: year ending April 1977 = 100)

| | 1990 | 1991 | 1992* |
|---|---|---|---|
| Food, beverages and tobacco | 1,376.6 | 2,048.0 | 2,048.8 |
| Housing | 948.2 | 1,388.7 | 1,581.7 |
| Clothing, shoes and accessories | 1,871.8 | 2,982.0 | 3,196.9 |
| Others | 975.8 | 1,778.2 | 1,929.3 |
| **All items** | 1,231.7 | 1,895.2 | 1,892.3 |

* Provisional figures.

**All items** (base: 1995 = 100): 82.1 in 1993; 88.9 in 1994; 100.0 in 1995; 105.4 in 1996; 114.1 in 1997; 119.3 in 1998 (Source: IMF, *International Financial Statistics*).

**NATIONAL ACCOUNTS**

**National Income and Product** (RD $ million at current prices)

| | 1996 | 1997 | 1998 |
|---|---|---|---|
| **GDP in purchasers' values** | 183,532 | 215,064 | 241,910 |
| Net factor income from abroad | −9,966 | −11,342 | −14,265 |
| **Gross national product (GNP)** | 173,566 | 203,722 | 227,645 |
| *Less* Consumption of fixed capital | 11,012 | 12,904 | 14,514 |
| **National income in market prices** | 162,554 | 190,818 | 213,131 |

Source: IMF, *International Financial Statistics*.

**Expenditure on the Gross Domestic Product**

(RD $ million at current prices)

| | 1996 | 1997 | 1998 |
|---|---|---|---|
| Government final consumption expenditure | 9,559 | 16,669 | 19,736 |
| Private final consumption expenditure | 143,743 | 161,234 | 181,217 |
| Increase in stocks | 240 | 293 | 330 |
| Gross fixed capital formation | 38,507 | 47,095 | 62,188 |
| **Total domestic expenditure** | 192,049 | 225,291 | 263,471 |
| Exports of goods and services | 84,485 | 100,513 | 113,595 |
| *Less* Imports of goods and services | 93,002 | 110,739 | 135,155 |
| **GDP in purchasers' values** | 183,532 | 215,064 | 241,910 |
| **GDP at constant 1970 prices** | 4,925 | 5,326 | 5,713 |

Source: IMF, *International Financial Statistics*.

**Gross Domestic Product by Economic Activity**

(RD $ million at constant 1970 prices)

| | 1996 | 1997 | 1998* |
|---|---|---|---|
| Agriculture, hunting, forestry and fishing | 636.7 | 658.5 | 665.3 |
| Mining and quarrying | 128.6 | 132.6 | 111.5 |
| Manufacturing | 838.6 | 904.6 | 949.7 |
| Electricity, gas and water† | 96.3 | 106.0 | 120.6 |
| Construction | 494.0 | 578.7 | 692.1 |
| Wholesale and retail trade, restaurants and hotels | 932.6 | 1,040.9 | 1,135.1 |
| Transport, storage and communications | 521.2 | 584.1 | 662.6 |
| Finance, insurance and real estate | 471.3 | 484.9 | 500.0 |
| Community, social, personal and business services‡ | 805.5 | 836.0 | 876.0 |
| **Total** | 4,925.0 | 5,326.4 | 5,712.9 |

* Preliminary figures.

† Refers to electricity and water only.

‡ Including gas.

across the political spectrum to surrender their weapons. The Government agreed to guarantee the civil rights of AVC members and promised to initiate a national dialogue in return for the group's demobilization. In the same month the MPL dissociated itself from the agreement between the Government and the AVC and pledged to continue violent opposition.

In October 1989 a plot to organize a coup to overthrow the President and replace him with the Vice-President was revealed. The alleged conspirators were based in the Guayaquil municipality, where the local business community resented the perceived growing centralization of power in Quito. Radical right-wing groups, headed by former President Febres Cordero, led the movement. In January 1990 Febres Cordero was detained and charged with embezzlement of public funds.

At mid-term legislative elections in June 1990, the ID lost 16 seats and conceded control of Congress to an informal alliance of the PSC and the PRE. In October a serious conflict arose between the Government and Congress when the newly-elected President of Congress, Dr Averroes Bucaram, attempted to stage a legislative coup against President Borja. Bucaram initially impeached several ministers, who were subsequently dismissed by Congress. Congress then dismissed the Supreme Court justices and other high-ranking members of the judiciary, and appointed new courts with shortened mandates. Both the Government and the judiciary refused to recognize these actions, on the grounds that Congress had exceeded its constitutional powers. Bucaram then announced that Congress would initiate impeachment proceedings against Borja himself. However, this move was averted when three opposition deputies transferred their allegiance, so restoring Borja's congressional majority. Bucaram was subsequently dismissed as President of Congress. None the less, impeachment proceedings against government ministers continued into 1991, and by August of that year a total of six ministers had been dismissed. The Government accused the opposition of using the proceedings as part of a deliberate campaign to undermine the prospects of the ID in the forthcoming elections.

In May 1990 about 1,000 indigenous Indians marched into Quito to demand official recognition of land rights for the indigenous population. In the following month the Confederación Nacional de Indígenas del Ecuador (CONAIE) (National Confederation of the Indigenous Population of Ecuador) organized an uprising covering seven Andean provinces. Roads were blockaded, *haciendas* occupied, and supplies to the cities interrupted. Following the arrest of 30 Indians by the army, the rebels took military hostages. The Government offered to hold conciliatory negotiations with CONAIE, in return for the release of the hostages. Among the demands made by the Indians were the return of traditional community-held lands, recognition of Quechua as an official language and compensation from petroleum companies for environmental damage. Discussions between CONAIE and President Borja collapsed in August. In January 1991 the FUT announced a joint anti-Government campaign with CONAIE. The FUT was protesting against the Government's decision on the level of increase of the minimum monthly wage. In February discussions between CONAIE and the Government were resumed, following the seizure by Indian groups in the Oriente of eight oil wells. The protest was halted two weeks later, when the Government promised to consider the Indians' demands for stricter controls on the operations of the petroleum industry, and for financial compensation.

In September 1991 the British Embassy in Quito was occupied by eight members of a dissident faction of the AVC. The siege, which ended peacefully after two days, formed part of a campaign to win the release of the dissidents' leader from prison. In February 1991 the AVC had concluded the process of demobilization that it had begun in February 1989. In October 1991 the party was absorbed by the ID.

In April 1992 several thousand Amazon Indians marched from the Oriente to Quito to demand that their historical rights to their homelands be recognized. In mid-May President Borja agreed to grant legal title to more than 1m. ha of land in the province of Pastaza to the Indians.

At legislative elections in May 1992 the PSC gained the highest number of seats in the enlarged National Congress, winning 21 of the 77 seats, while the PRE secured 13. The Partido Unidad Republicano (PUR) was formed prior to the elections by the former PSC presidential candidate, Sixto Durán Ballén, in order to contest the presidential election (since the PSC had nominated the President of the party, Jaime Nebot Saadi, as its candidate). The PUR won 12 seats, the ID only seven and the Partido Conservador (PC) six seats. In the presidential election no candidate secured an absolute majority of the votes. The two leading contenders, Durán and Nebot, who secured 32.9% and 25.2% of the votes respectively, proceeded to a second round of voting, at which Durán secured 58% of the votes cast, defeating Nebot, who won 38%. The PUR was to govern with its ally, the PC. However, as the two parties' seats did not constitute a majority in Congress, support from other centre-right parties, particularly the PSC, was sought.

In September 1992 the Government's announcement of a programme of economic austerity measures, including the restructuring of the public sector, prompted widespread protest. Following violent demonstrations and several bomb attacks in Quito and Guayaquil, the Government dispatched units of the armed forces to restore order. Widespread opposition to the Government's policies continued to manifest itself, however, in demonstrations and protests, and a general strike in May 1993. The 'Modernization Law', a crucial part of the controversial austerity programme (which was to provide for the privatization of some 160 state-owned companies and the reduction in the number of employees in the public sector by 100,000), was approved by Congress in August. In November striking teachers organized demonstrations throughout the country, demanding wage increases and reforms in the education system. During the protests two demonstrators were killed and many injured.

Environmental concerns regarding the exploitation of the Oriente by the petroleum industry continued to be expressed by national and international groups during 1993. In November five Amazon Indian tribes initiated legal proceedings against the international company Texaco to claim compensation totalling US $1,500m. for its part in polluting the rain forest. (It was estimated that some 17m. barrels of oil had been spilt during the company's 25 years of operations in the region.) Protests intensified in January 1994, when the Government initiated a round of bidding for petroleum-exploration licences for 10 hydrocarbon regions, including sites in the eastern Oriente, previously withheld because of opposition from environmentalists and indigenous communities. During the demonstrations, Indian groups occupied the Ministry of Energy and Mines and CONAIE renewed its demand for a 15-year moratorium on further bidding. In mid-1997 a US court provoked outrage among indigenous organizations by rejecting their claim for compensation from Texaco. The organizations announced their intention to pursue the matter.

Meanwhile, the Government's economic programme continued to arouse widespread hostility, and its decision in January 1994 to increase the price of fuel by more than 70% provoked violent demonstrations throughout the country and a general strike. In the following month the Tribunal of Constitutional Guarantees declared the rise to be unconstitutional, although Durán refused to recognize the ruling.

At mid-term congressional elections in May 1994 President Durán's PUR-PC governing alliance suffered a serious defeat, winning only nine of the 77 seats. The PSC secured 26 seats, while the PRE remained the second-largest party in Congress, winning 11 seats. Despite the fact that voting is compulsory in Ecuador, only some 70% of eligible voters participated in the poll, and of these 18% returned void ballot papers, reflecting a widespread disillusionment among the electorate with the democratic process.

In June 1994 the increasingly vociferous indigenous movement organized large-scale demonstrations across the country, in protest at a recently-approved Land Development Law. The law, which allowed for the commercialization of Amerindian lands for farming and resource extraction, provoked serious unrest and a general strike, during which a state of emergency was declared and the army mobilized. Seven protesters were killed, and many injured, in clashes with the security forces. The law was subsequently judged to be unconstitutional by the Tribunal of Constitutional Guarantees, although Durán refused to accept the ruling. In early July, however, the law was modified to extend the rights of landowners and those employed to work on the land.

In August 1994 a national referendum on constitutional reform finally took place, at President Durán's instigation, following much disagreement between the Government and the judiciary and opposition parties. All but one of the eight proposed reforms (which included measures to alter the electoral system and the role of Congress and the establishment of a bicameral legislature) were approved; however, only some 50% of eligible voters participated, of whom some 20% returned void ballot papers.

Protests against the Government's economic programme of austerity measures and privatizations in January 1995 resulted in the deaths of two students in Quito during clashes with riot police. In March the Minister of Finance resigned (the third to do so since the Government came to power), apparently because of differences within the Cabinet concerning economic policy. Industrial unrest continued during May and June, when the FUT launched a national strike against a new series of 'corrective' economic measures, introduced by the Government in an attempt to reduce the impact of the financial crisis caused by the border conflict with Peru (see below). Continued industrial unrest was compounded in July, when oil workers initiated a strike in protest at the impact of government policy on the petroleum industry. Later in the month, however, the country was plunged into a serious political crisis when Vice-President Alberto Dahik admitted giving funds from the state budget to opposition deputies (allegedly for use in local public-works projects) in return for their support for the Government's economic reform programme. Dahik refused to resign, despite the initiation of impeachment proceedings, and rejected the criminal charges against him. In a further development (believed by some observers to be an attempt to obstruct the case against Dahik) the President of the Supreme Court and two other justices were dismissed. Critics of the Government's action claimed that the dismissals themselves were unconstitutional, as they did not respect the separation of powers of the judiciary from the legislature and executive. In September impeachment proceedings began against the new Minister of Finance, Mauricio Pinto, for his role in various alleged financial irregularities. Meanwhile, the Superintendent of Banks resigned his post, following accusations that he had attempted to hinder the case against Dahik in the Supreme Court. Impeachment proceedings against Dahik began on 2 October, and on 11 October, following an appeal by Durán, the Vice-President resigned. A former Minister of Education, Dr Eduardo Peña Triviño, was subsequently elected as Vice-President by Congress. A further two cabinet ministers offered their resignations in support of Dahik, and on 13 October the entire Cabinet resigned in order that a reorganization of portfolios could take place.

In addition to the political crisis provoked by the scandal surrounding the Vice-President during mid-1995, the administration continued to be troubled by various industrial disputes and strikes. In September troops were dispatched to the Galápagos Islands, following disturbances among the islanders. The protesters were demanding the Government's acceptance of a special law granting increased political and financial autonomy to the islands, in addition to some US $16m. in priority economic aid. Concerned about the potentially disastrous effect of the protests on the country's important tourist industry, the Government quickly withdrew its opposition to the proposed legislation and agreed to establish a specialist commission to draft a new law acceptable to all parties. Moreover, in October petroleum workers resumed strike action in protest at the Government's privatization plans, and in one incident occupied the PETROECUADOR building, taking two cabinet ministers hostage for several hours, in order to prevent the signing of a contract to sell the Trans-Ecuadorean oil pipeline. The dispute ended following the resignation of the Minister of Energy and Mines at the end of the month. The strike, however, together with a severe drought, which halted production at the Paute hydroelectric plant (which, under normal circumstances, provided 60%–70% of the country's electricity), resulted in serious energy shortages in late 1995, which further exacerbated the country's troubled political and economic situation.

A referendum on government proposals for constitutional reform was held in November 1995. All of the proposed changes were rejected in the plebiscite, which was widely regarded as a reflection of the Government's continued unpopularity. Despite its decisive defeat, the Government announced its intention to pursue its programme of reforms. Widespread strikes and demonstrations by teachers and students in the same month, in which one student was killed in clashes with police, led to the resignation of the Minister of Education. The initiation of impeachment proceedings against one cabinet minister, and the resignation of another, further weakened the President's position, and pressure for him to resign intensified. Industrial action among employees in the energy sector continued, and in January 1996 army units were deployed at prominent sites throughout the country in order to prevent further unrest and a worsening of the energy crisis. Furthermore, an industrial dispute by transport workers in March resulted in serious disruption in the capital and prompted a series of strikes in other sectors.

A presidential election, held in May 1996, failed to produce an outright winner, thus necessitating a second round of voting for the two leading contenders. The PSC candidate, Jaime Nebot Saadi, secured 27.1% of the votes in the first round, while Abdalá Bucaram Ortiz of the PRE won 25.6%. An increasingly vocal and politically-organized indigenous movement resulted in the strong performance of Freddy Ehlers, a former journalist, who was the candidate for the newly-formed Movimiento Nuevo País-Pachakutik (MNPP), a coalition organization composed of Amerindian and labour groups. Ehlers secured 21% of the votes. At legislative elections held concurrently the PSC won 27 of the 82 seats in the enlarged National Congress, while the PRE secured 19 and Democracia Popular (DP—formerly DP-UDC) won 12. The MNPP emerged as a significant new force in Congress, with a total of eight seats. At the second round of voting in the presidential election in July, Bucaram was the unexpected victor, receiving 54.5% of total votes. The success of Bucaram, a populist figure and former Olympic athlete, was widely interpreted as a rejection of the policies of the outgoing Government (which Nebot had promised to continue) and an expression of disenchantment with established party politics. Following his inauguration in August, Bucaram sought to allay the fears of the business community (prompted by his proposals for costly social reform, put forward during his electoral campaign) stating that existing economic arrangements would be maintained. Moreover, a team of prominent businessmen was assigned the role of advising the President on economic policy.

A scandal at the Ministry of Finance in September 1996, which resulted in the arrest of seven senior officials on charges of embezzlement (estimated at more than US $300m.) was claimed by Bucaram as a victory for his anti-corruption policies. However, concern at the President's idiosyncratic style of leadership and increasingly eccentric behaviour began to intensify in late 1996. Moreover, a perceived inconsistency in many of Bucaram's policies and the apparently arbitrary nature of his decisions, together with his use of undiplomatic language, contributed to a rapid decline in his popularity.

A 48-hour general strike took place in early January 1997, prompted by increases of up to 600% in the price of certain commodities and a climate of considerable dissatisfaction with the President's leadership. Demonstrations in the capital continued throughout January and trade union leaders announced an indefinite extension of the general strike. Protests intensified in early February when several hundred thousand demonstrators marched through the streets of Quito demanding Bucaram's resignation. The President responded by declaring a national holiday and a one-week closure of schools across the country, and stated his support for the strike. Meanwhile, troops were deployed throughout the capital as violent clashes erupted between protesters and security personnel and Bucaram was barricaded inside the presidential palace. On 6 February, at an emergency session, Congress voted by 44 votes to 34 to dismiss the President on the grounds of mental incapacity; by questioning the President's sanity, Congress was able to evade the normal impeachment requirements of a two-thirds' majority. A state of emergency was declared, and the erstwhile Speaker, Fabián Alarcón Rivera, who had assumed the presidency in an acting capacity, urged demonstrators to storm the presidential palace. Bucaram, however, refused to leave office and claimed that he would retain power by force if necessary. The situation was further complicated by the claim of the Vice-President, Rosalia Arteaga, to be the legitimate constitutional successor to Bucaram. Political confusion over the correct procedure prompted fears of a military coup, despite a declaration of neutrality by the armed forces. Bucaram reportedly fled from the presidential palace on 9 February, and on the following day Arteaga was declared interim President after narrowly winning a congressional vote. However, by 11 February Arteaga had resigned, amid continued constitutional uncertainty, and Alarcón was reinstated as President following a congressional vote on the same day, at which 57 members indicated their support for him. Alaracón, who stated that his priorities as President were political reform and the restoration of economic confidence, announced a reorganization of cabinet portfolios (which included no members of the two largest parties in Congress, the PSC and the PRE) and the creation of a commission to investigate allegations of corruption against Bucaram and his administration. In March Bucaram's extradition from Panama (where he had fled and successfully sought political asylum) was requested in order that he face charges of misappropriating some US $90m. of government funds. Bucaram responded by stating that if he were fit to face criminal charges he could not be insane and should, therefore, be reinstated as President. He also reiterated his view that his removal from office constituted a *coup d'état*. In the following month the President of the Supreme Court announced that extradition would only be possible once a prison sentence had been issued. Furthermore, in May Bucaram declared his intention to present himself as a presidential candidate at Ecuador's next elections. The announcement prompted Congress to vote almost unanimously in favour of a motion to impose an indefinite ban on Bucaram's candidacy in any future presidential election in the country. The legislature similarly voted to curtail the term of office of the Vice-President, Rosalia Arteaga, such that it would terminate, along with that of the interim President, in August 1998 when elections would take place. Arteaga, however, who had urged that fresh elections be held immediately, criticized the decision as unconstitutional, claiming that, as she had been elected legitimately and not appointed by Congress following the dismissal of Bucaram, she was entitled to remain in office for the full term. However, the Minister of Government insisted that all senior positions should be renewed simultaneously in order to maintain institutional stability.

On 25 May 1997 a national referendum sought public opinion on a variety of matters, including electoral reform, the modernization of the judiciary and the authenticity of Alarcón's position. Although some 40.7% of the electorate did not participate, the vote revealed considerable support for the decision to remove Bucaram from office (75.7%) and for the appointment of Alarcón as interim President (68.3%). Some 64.5% of voters also favoured the creation of a national assembly to consider constitutional reform. Alarcón's apparent success in the referendum, however, was undermined in early June by a scandal which threatened the stability of the administration. Allegations that leading drugs-traffickers in the country had contributed to political party funds, and, particularly, to Alarcón's Frente Radical Alfarista (FRA), were to be investigated in an official inquiry launched by Congress.

In July 1997 Congress dismissed all 31 judges of the Supreme Court, claiming that its action was in accordance with the views on the depoliticization of the judiciary (which is nominated by the legislature) expressed in the recent referendum. The President of the Supreme Court condemned the action as unconstitutional.

The announcement in August 1997 that a national assembly to review the Constitution (as proposed in the referendum of May 1997) would not be installed until August 1998 was widely opposed, and provoked a 48-hour strike in demand of the earlier establishment of the assembly. The strike led by CONAIE, which virtually paralyzed the country by means of numerous roadblocks, was supported most strongly by Indian and peasant organizations, who insisted that an assembly should be convened as soon as possible in order to discuss indigenous rights and the proposed privatization of key areas of the economy. In response to the apparent strength of public opinion, it was announced in September that elections for the 70 representatives to the assembly would take place in late November. However, 11 indigenous organizations demonstrated their lack of confidence in the Government to address their concerns by convening a mass rally in Quito to establish guidelines for their own constitution.

Criticism of the Government increased during the second half of 1997, with both the Roman Catholic Church and ex-President Borja urging Alarcón to resign. The uneasy relationship between Alarcón and Arteaga also became more apparent in August when the Vice-President publicly expressed support for the striking indigenous groups, and when Alarcón refused to transfer power to Arteaga while he left the country on a brief foreign tour. Alarcón's problems in office were further exacerbated by charges of embezzlement filed against him in the Supreme Court by a former FRA colleague. In January 1998 the Supreme Court issued a four-year prison sentence to Bucaram for libel. Numerous other legal suits against the ex-President remained pending.

In January 1998, following persistent pleas from international environmental and scientific organizations for greater protection of the Galápagos Islands, Congress approved a law which aimed to preserve the islands' unique environment more effectively. An element of the law, providing for an extension of the marine reserve around the islands from 15 to 40 nautical miles, attracted intense criticism from powerful fishing interests in the country and was, consequently, vetoed by Alarcón, prompting condemnation by environmentalists and small-scale fishing concerns, who claimed that the President had acceded to commercial pressures.

In February 1998 the recently-established National Constituent Assembly (convened to review the Constitution) announced a number of institutional reforms, including the enlargement of Congress from 82 to 121 seats, the extension of the presidential term (for Alarcón's successor) from four years to four years, five months and five days, the abolition of mid-term elections and the completion of a presidential term by the Vice-President in the case of the indefinite absence of the President. The new Constitution, which retained the majority of the provisions of the 1979 Constitution, officially came into force on 10 August.

At a presidential election on 31 May 1998 the DP candidate and mayor of Quito, Jamil Mahuad Witt, emerged as the strongest contender, securing 35.2% of total votes cast. Alvaro Noboa Pontón for the PRE, whose popularity was concentrated in Guayaquil and the coastal regions, received 26.5% of votes, while ex-President Borja and Freddy Ehlers won 15.6% and 14.3% respectively. At concurrent elections to the newly-enlarged Congress the DP secured 32 of the 121 seats, the PSC won 27, the PRE 24 and the ID 18 seats. At the second round of voting in the presidential election on 12 July, Mahuad narrowly defeated Noboa with 51.2% of total votes. Noboa rejected the result, alleging widespread voting irregularities, none of which was upheld by the Supreme Electoral Tribunal or the international observers present in the country. Mahuad was consequently sworn in on 10 August and appointed a Cabinet consisting predominantly of independent members. Mahuad's stated objectives as President focused on the stimulation of economic recovery, following a series of serious reversals, including a decrease in world petroleum prices and the infrastructural and sociological damage caused by El Niño (a periodic warming of the tropical Pacific Ocean—see below). In addition, Mahuad proposed a number of social programmes (involving the creation of new jobs and the construction of low-cost homes), which prompted scepticism amongst observers, who doubted the feasibility of such plans.

A programme of severe adjustment measures, which included huge rises in the cost of domestic gas and electricity, as well as substantial increases in public transport fares and fuel prices, was introduced in September 1998. The FUT and CONAIE organized a general strike in protest at the measures in the following month. Subsequent rioting and violent confrontation between demonstrators and security personnel resulted in the deaths of four people. Disagreement over economic policy led to the resignation of the Minister of Finance, Fidel Jaramillo Buendia, in February 1999. Serious social unrest continued in early 1999, as a result of ongoing economic hardship caused by the Government's adherence to adjustment measures. Severe disruption arising from extensive fuel shortages prompted the resignation of the Minister of Energy and Mines, Patricio Rivadeneira García, in February. In the same month the leader of the left-wing Movimiento Popular Democrático and member of Congress, Jaime Hurtado González, was assassinated in Quito. A number of people were subsequently arrested, and the killing was linked to a right-wing Colombian paramilitary group. In March former interim President Alarcón was arrested on charges of illegally hiring personnel during his term in office as Speaker of Congress.

In early March 1999 a substantial decrease in the value of the sucre led President Mahuad to declare a week-long bank holiday in an attempt to prevent the withdrawal of deposits and reduce the pressure on the currency. A few days later a 60-day state of emergency was declared by the Government in response to a two-day strike, organized by leaders of the main trade unions and Indian groups. In addition, the Government announced an economic retrenchment programme in an attempt to restore investor confidence and prevent economic collapse. Measures included an increase in fuel prices of up to 160%, a number of tax reforms (notably an increase in value-added tax), the partial 'freezing' of bank accounts, and the planned privatization of certain state-owned companies. These prompted a further series of protests, demands for Mahuad's resignation, and the resignation of four of the five members of the board of the central bank (citing differences over government financial policies). The main opposition party, the PSC, similarly refused to endorse the austerity programme, thus compelling the President to compromise with the proposal of less severe economic measures, which were narrowly approved by Congress. The new measures included a partial reduction of fuel price increases, and the reinstatement of income tax; following their approval, Mahuad lifted the state of emergency. However, a further rise in prices and the collapse of a major bank (the Guayaquil-based Banco del Progreso) later in March led to renewed protests.

In April 1999 the Government announced an emergency plan entitled 'Ecuador 2000', which aimed to revive the economy and which included a number of requisite measures to gain the support of the IMF. The plan incorporated numerous social and public works development schemes, tax reforms and moves towards less centralized government. The plan was approved by the IMF, and, following the appointment of four new board members of the central bank in June, hopes were renewed that the IMF would provide an estimated US $400m. in initial funding. However, in July taxi drivers and public transport workers took nation-wide industrial action in protest at increases in fuel prices and at the new economic retrenchment plan proposed by the IMF. In response to the ensuing massive disruption, the Government imposed a further state of emergency and called in the military. An agreement between transport officials and the Government was reached in mid-July, when Mahuad agreed to 'freeze' fuel prices and to allow co-operatives and transport companies access to 'frozen' bank deposits. The state of emergency was then lifted.

In late August 1999 the Government announced its intention to default on US $96m. in interest payments on $6,000m. in outstanding foreign debt repayments (on so-called Brady bonds—restructured commercial bank loans) for a period of 30 days, and to attempt to restructure its large external debts. The move, which was supported by the IMF, was implemented owing to the country's inability to honour repayments on its foreign debt (which, at a total of more than $13,000m., was equivalent to some 90% of GDP). In early September the Minister of Finance, Ana Lucia Armijos, resigned, prompted by the unpopularity of the recent economic measures (her successor, however, remained in the post only six weeks before himself resigning). Nevertheless, at the end of September, the IMF signed a preliminary agreement with Ecuador which was expected to provide up to $1,250m. in funding (comprising a $400m. stand-by loan from the IMF and $850m. in loans from other multilateral agencies).

In early January 2000 President Mahuad imposed a state of emergency in an attempt to curb increasing unrest, amid indications that the economic crisis was deteriorating. On 21 January President Mahuad was forced to flee from the presidential palace, following large-scale protests by thousands of Indian demonstrators, who were supported by sections of the armed forces, in Quito over the President's perceived mismanagement of the economic crisis (including his controversial decision to replace the sucre with the US dollar). A three-man council was established to oversee the country. However, Gen. Carlos Mendoza, the Chief of Staff of the Armed Forces, disbanded the council within only 24 hours of its creation, and announced the appointment of former Vice-President Gustavo Noboa Bejerano as President. This move followed talks with US officials, who had warned that foreign aid to Ecuador would be curtailed if power were not restored to the elected Government. The coup was widely condemned by governments around the world and by international organizations. Noboa, whose appointment as Head of State was endorsed by a large majority in Congress, promised to restore economic stability to the country. However, Indian activists who had supported the short-lived three-member council (one of whose members had been the leader of CONAIE, Antonio Vargas) continued to demonstrate against the assumption of the presidency by Noboa, whom they viewed as ideologically similar to Mahuad. Noboa appointed Pedro Pinto Rubianes as the new Vice-President on 27 January and began the process of forming a new Cabinet.

In early February 2000 four members of the armed forces, who allegedly participated in the events leading up to Mahuad's removal from office, were apprehended on charges of insurrection. It was later announced that as many as 113 army officers were to be charged in connection with the previous month's events. Protesters demanded the release of the four detainees, and threatened further action if the deteriorating economic situation were not resolved.

In April 1999 the World Trade Organization (WTO) upheld the complaint, put forward by the USA, Ecuador and four other Latin American countries, that the EU unfairly favoured Caribbean banana producers, and authorized the USA to impose trade sanctions against EU goods. A two-tier tariff rate quota arrangement was subsequently agreed at a meeting between Ecuadorean government officials and leaders of Caribbean banana-producing countries in November 1999, easing restrictions on Latin American banana exporters and consequently assisting Ecuadorean producers.

The long-standing border dispute with Peru over the Cordillera del Cóndor erupted into war in January 1981. A cease-fire was declared a few days later under the auspices of the guarantors of the Rio Protocol of 1942 (Argentina, Brazil, Chile and the USA). The Protocol was not recognized by Ecuador as it awarded the area, which affords access to the Amazon river system, to Peru. Further clashes occurred along the border with Peru in December 1982 and January 1983. In January 1992 discussions on the border dispute were resumed. A number of minor incidents along the border were reported during 1994. However, in January 1995 serious fighting broke out between the two sides, following reports of Peruvian incursions into Ecuadorean territory. Both Governments denied responsibility for initiating hostilities and issued contradictory reports concerning subsequent clashes. Following offers from the Organization of American States (OAS) and the four guarantor nations of the Rio Protocol, representatives of the two Governments met for negotiations in Rio de Janeiro, Brazil. A cease-fire agreement was eventually concluded in late February, and an observer mission, representing the four guarantor nations, was dispatched to the border, to oversee the separation of forces and demilitarization of the border area. Despite mutual accusations of the cease-fire having been broken, the separation of forces continued and both Governments ordered the release of a number of prisoners taken during the conflict. Intensive negotiations continued to take place in Brazil, and, as a result, agreement on the delimitation of the demilitarized zone in the disputed area was reached in July. In October Ecuador finally repealed the state of emergency. Official discussions between the Ministers of Foreign Affairs of Peru and Ecuador began in January 1996, amid renewed controversy that the two countries were engaged in a campaign to strengthen their military capability by negotiating contracts for the supply of weapons from a number of foreign countries. A resumption of negotiations in September resulted in the signing of the Santiago Agreement by both sides in the following month, which was to provide a framework for a definitive solution on the border issue. In March 1997 Ecuador lodged an official complaint against the Peruvian army's use of land-mines along the border. A new round of talks (which had been postponed twice as a result of the Japanese embassy hostage crisis in Lima and the political crisis in Ecuador) began in Brasilia in April. In August the two countries signed an agreement aimed at ensuring transparent mechanisms in arms procurement. The agreement, however, failed to prevent a series of rumours that Ecuador had secretly purchased considerable quantities of armaments from Israel. Negotiations continued in Brasilia during 1997, although Ecuador's insistence on including the issue of a sovereign outlet to the Amazon river threatened the progress of the talks.

Following further negotiations in early 1998 a number of commissions were established to examine specific aspects of a potential agreement between Ecuador and Peru, including a trade and navigation treaty and the fixing of frontier markers on the ground in the Cordillera del Cóndor. Talks continued during 1998 and culminated in the signing of an accord in Brasilia on 26 October by the Ministers of Foreign Affairs of Ecuador and Peru in the presence of the two countries' Presidents and of six other regional leaders. The accord confirmed Peru's claim regarding the delineation of the border, but granted Ecuador navigation and trading rights on the Amazon and its tributaries and the opportunity to establish two trading centres in Peru (although this was not to constitute sovereign access). Moreover, Ecuador was given 1 sq km of territory, as private property, at Tiwintza in Peru where many Ecuadorean soldiers, killed during the conflict in 1995, were buried. Both countries were committed to establish ecological parks along the border where military personnel would not be allowed access. Although considerable opposition to the accord was expressed in Peru, international reaction was very favourable and resulted in several offers of finance from multilateral agencies for cross-border development projects.

An official ceremony in May 1999 marked the transfer of Tiwintza from Peru to Ecuador, and both parties confirmed that two ecological parks were to be created along the common border. Presidents Mahuad and Alberto Fujimori reiterated their intention to seek US $3,000m. in funding, over a 10-year period, to finance a number of development projects (including the construction of new roads and health and education centres) and to organize the removal of land mines in the border area.

Following the suspected involvement of Colombian guerrillas in the murder of an Ecuadorean politician in Quito in March 1999 (see above) and reports (denied by the Ecuadorean Government) of the presence of Colombian paramilitary troops in the country, Ecuador's military presence was strengthened at its border with Colombia. In September 12 foreigners, several of whom were employees of a petroleum company operating in the region, were kidnapped by suspected Colombian guerillas in the jungle near the Colombian border. In November an explosion which damaged an oil pipeline in the same area was linked to a Colombian rebel group, although any foreign involvement in the incident was denied by the Ecuadorean Government.

## Government

Executive power is vested in the President, who is directly elected by universal adult suffrage for a four-year term (starting from 15 January of the year following his election). The President is not eligible for re-election. Legislative power is held by the 121-member unicameral Congress, which is also directly elected for a four-year term: 12 members are elected on a national basis and serve a four-year term, while 65 members are elected on a provincial basis. Ecuador comprises 21 provinces, composed of 193 cantons, 322 urban parishes and 757 rural parishes. Each province has a Governor, who is appointed by the President.

## Defence

Military service, which lasts one year, is selective for men at the age of 20. In August 1999 there were 57,100 men in the armed forces: army 50,000, navy 4,100 (including 1,500 marines) and air force 3,000. Defence expenditure in 1998 was estimated to be 2,900,000m. sucres.

## Economic Affairs

In 1997, according to estimates by the World Bank, Ecuador's gross national product (GNP), measured at average 1995–97 prices, was US $18,785m., equivalent to $1,570 per head. During 1990–97, it was estimated, GNP per head increased, in real terms, at an average annual rate of 0.9%. Over the same period, the population increased at an average annual rate of 2.2%. In 1998, according to preliminary World Bank data, GNP was about $18,600m. ($1,530 per head). Ecuador's gross domestic product (GDP) increased, in real terms, at an average annual rate of 2.9% in 1990–98. Real GDP rose by 3.4% in 1997 and by 0.4% in 1998.

Agriculture (including forestry and fishing) contributed 17.4% of GDP (at constant 1975 prices) in 1998. An estimated 27.2% of the economically active population were employed in the agricultural sector in 1998. The principal cash crops are bananas, coffee and cocoa. The seafood sector, particularly the shrimp industry, expanded rapidly in the 1980s, and in 1995 Ecuador was the second largest producer of shrimps in the world. Ecuador's extensive forests yield valuable hardwoods, and the country is a leading producer of balsawood. Exports of cut flowers increased from US $0.5m. in 1985 to $99m. in 1996. During 1990–98 agricultural GDP increased at an average annual rate of 2.6%. It rose by 4.1% in 1997, but declined by 1.4% in 1998.

Industry (including mining, manufacturing, construction and power) employed 18.1% of the labour force in 1990, and provided 33.2% of GDP (at constant 1975 prices) in 1998. During 1990–98 industrial GDP increased at an average annual rate of 3.4%. It rose by 3.4% in 1997, but fell by 0.6% in 1998.

Mining contributed 13.6% of GDP (at constant 1975 prices) in 1998, although the mining sector employed only 0.6% of the labour force in 1990. Petroleum and its derivatives remained the major exports in the late 1990s. In 1998 some 388,000 barrels of crude petroleum were produced per day, of which 40% was exported. Earnings from petroleum exports amounted to some US $1,400m. in 1997, but declined to $791m. in 1998. Natural gas is extracted, but only a small proportion is retained. Gold, silver, copper, antimony and zinc are also mined. In real terms, the GDP of the mining sector increased at an average rate of 4.6% per year during 1990–98. Mining GDP rose by 3.5% in 1997, but declined by 3.3% in 1998.

Manufacturing contributed 15.6% of GDP (at constant 1975 prices) in 1998, and employed 11.2% of the labour force in 1990. Measured by the value of output, the most important branches of manufacturing in 1996 were food products (accounting for 33.1% of the total), petroleum refineries (16.5%), chemicals (7.3%) and pulp and paper products (6.0%). During 1990–98 manufacturing GDP increased at an average annual rate of 2.9%. It rose by 3.5% in 1997 and by 0.4% in 1998.

Energy is derived principally from thermoelectric and hydroelectric plants. Imports of mineral fuels and lubricants comprised 4.4% of the value of total imports in 1996.

The services sector contributed 49.4% of GDP (at constant 1975 prices) in 1998. Around 46% of the active population were employed in services in 1990. The sector's GDP increased at an average annual rate of 2.8% during 1990–98. It rose by 2.6% in 1997 and by 0.8% in 1998.

In 1998 Ecuador recorded a visible trade deficit of US $995m., and a deficit of $2,169m. on the current account of the balance of payments. In 1996 the principal source of imports was the USA (accounting for 31.5% of the total), which was also the principal market for exports (37.9%). Other major trading partners were Colombia, Japan, Germany, Italy and the Republic of Korea. The principal exports in 1996 were petroleum and petroleum derivatives (36.3%), bananas (19.9%) and seafood and seafood products (18.9%). The principal imports in 1996 were machinery and transport equipment (35.4%), chemicals (18.8%) and basic manufactures (19.8%).

In 1998 there was a budgetary surplus of about 374,300m. sucres. In 1996 some 40% of government expenditure was financed by revenue from petroleum. Ecuador's total external debt was US $14,918m. at the end of 1997, of which $12,376m. was long-term public debt. In that year the cost of debt-servicing was equivalent to 31.0% of the total value of exports of goods and services. Official development assistance was equivalent to 1.4% of GNP in 1994. The average annual rate of inflation in 1990–98 was 35.7%; the rate averaged 36.1% in 1998. An estimated 13.8% of the labour force were unemployed in mid-1998.

Ecuador is a member of the Andean Community (see p. 119), the Organization of American States (OAS—see p. 245) and of the Asociación Latinoamericana de Integración (ALADI—p. 292). In 1992 Ecuador withdrew from the Organization of the Petroleum Exporting Countries (OPEC—p. 252) and announced its intention of seeking associate status. In 1995 Ecuador joined the World Trade Organization (WTO—p. 274).

In the mid-1990s Ecuador's proven petroleum reserves almost tripled, following discoveries in the Amazon region, and the Government signed contracts with numerous companies for further exploration and drilling. In late 1997 work to expand the capacity of the trans-Ecuadorean pipeline from 330,000 b/d to 410,000 b/d began. Construction of a new pipeline, financed by a consortium of private companies at a cost of US $500m., was also expected to begin in early 1999. Flooding of the coastal lowlands in mid-1997, caused by El Niño (a periodic warming of the tropical Pacific Ocean), adversely affected various cash crops (notably bananas) and fishing catches, and cost the country an estimated US $250m. in lost agricultural income. In 1998 Ecuador's economy was adversely affected by a significant decrease in world petroleum prices, a decrease in foreign investment and the depreciation of the sucre by 35.1%. The implementation of a privatization programme, first proposed in 1992, was repeatedly impeded by political turmoil and trade union opposition (including several general strikes). In 1999 a further decline in revenue from petroleum exports, another substantial depreciation in the value of the sucre and the resultant rise in inflation (to 36.1%), as well as the partial 'freezing' of bank accounts and a series of strikes and violent protests, contributed to a worsening of the economic crisis (with Ecuador unable to honour its massive external debt repayments) and had serious political repercussions (see Recent history). It was estimated that GDP declined by as much 7% in 1999 and, according to government sources, there was a budgetary deficit of approximately US $700m. Gradual economic recovery in 2000 appeared dependent upon the approval of an IMF agreement, which would provide as much as $1,250m. in funding. The signing of this agreement was itself conditional on the successful implementation of a series of stringent economic measures (including tax reforms and decentralization), as outlined in the 'Ecuador 2000' plan.

### Social Welfare

Social insurance is compulsory for all employees. Benefits are available for sickness, industrial accidents, disability, maternity, old age, widowhood and orphanhood. Hospitals and welfare institutions are administered by Central Public Assistance Boards. Budgetary expenditure on social welfare and labour was 134,697m. sucres (2.4% of total spending) in 1994. In 1993 there were 433 hospitals, and in 1997 there were 18,510 hospital beds and 15,866 physicians in the country. Budgetary expenditure on health and community development by the central Government was 319,470m. sucres (5.8% of total spending) in 1994.

### Education

Education is compulsory for 10 years, to be undertaken between five and 15 years of age, and all state schools are free. Private schools continue to play a vital role in the educational system. Primary education begins at six years of age and lasts for six years. Secondary education, in general and specialized technical or humanities schools, begins at the age of 12 and lasts for up to six years, comprising two equal cycles of three years each. In 1997 the total enrolment at primary and secondary schools was equivalent to 89.5% of the school-age population (122% in primary schools and 57% in secondary schools). In 1993/94 there were 2,868 secondary schools and in 1994/95 there were 17,194 primary schools. University courses extend for up to six years, and include programmes for teacher training. A number of adult schools and literacy centres have been built, aimed at reducing the rate of adult illiteracy, which averaged an estimated 4.1% of the urban population (males 3.4%; females 4.8%) in 1997. Total expenditure on education by the central Government was estimated at 1,957,051m. sucres (equivalent to 3.5% of GNP) in 1996. In many rural areas, Quechua and other indigenous Indian languages are used in education.

### Public Holidays

**2000:** 1 January (New Year's Day), 6 January (Epiphany), 6–7 March (Carnival), 20 April (Holy Thursday), 21 April (Good Friday), 22 April (Easter Saturday), 1 May (Labour Day), 24 May (Battle of Pichincha), 22 June (Corpus Christi), 24 July (Birth of Simón Bolívar), 10 August (Independence of Quito), 9 October (Independence of Guayaquil), 12 October (Discovery of America), 1 November (All Saints' Day), 2 November (All Souls' Day), 3 November (Independence of Cuenca), 6 December (Foundation of Quito), 25 December (Christmas Day).

**2001:** 1 January (New Year's Day), 6 January (Epiphany), 26–27 February (Carnival), 12 April (Holy Thursday), 13 April (Good Friday), 14 April (Easter Saturday), 1 May (Labour Day), 24 May (Battle of Pichincha), 14 June (Corpus Christi), 24 July (Birth of Simón Bolívar), 10 August (Independence of Quito), 9 October (Independence of Guayaquil), 12 October (Discovery of America), 1 November (All Saints' Day), 2 November (All Souls' Day), 3 November (Independence of Cuenca), 6 December (Foundation of Quito), 25 December (Christmas Day).

### Weights and Measures

The metric system is in force.

# Statistical Survey

Sources (unless otherwise stated): Banco Central del Ecuador, Quito; Ministerio de Industrias, Comercio, Integración y Pesquería, Quito; Instituto Nacional de Estadística y Censos, 10 de Agosto 229, Quito; tel. (2) 519-320.

## Area and Population

**AREA, POPULATION AND DENSITY**

| | |
|---|---|
| Area (sq km) | 272,045* |
| Population (census results)† | |
| 28 November 1982 | 8,060,712 |
| 25 November 1990 | |
| Males | 4,796,412 |
| Females | 4,851,777 |
| Total | 9,648,189 |
| Population (official estimates at mid-year)† | |
| 1996 | 11,698,496 |
| 1997 | 11,936,858 |
| 1998 | 12,174,628 |
| Density (per sq km) at mid-1998 | 44.8 |

* 105,037 sq miles.

† Figures exclude nomadic tribes of indigenous Indians. Census results also exclude any adjustment for underenumeration, estimated to have been 5.6% in 1982 and 6.3% in 1990.

**PROVINCES** (official estimates, mid-1995)*

| | Population | Capital |
|---|---|---|
| Azuay | 578,229 | Cuenca |
| Bolívar | 175,342 | Guaranda |
| Cañar | 205,818 | Azogues |
| Carchi | 156,803 | Tulcán |
| Cotopaxi | 296,647 | Latacunga |
| Chimborazo | 402,914 | Riobamba |
| El Oro | 500,707 | Machala |
| Esmeraldas | 372,303 | Esmeraldas |
| Guayas | 3,055,907 | Guayaquil |
| Imbabura | 308,047 | Ibarra |
| Loja | 411,010 | Loja |
| Los Ríos | 608,402 | Babahoyo |
| Manabí | 1,172,814 | Portoviejo |
| Morona Santiago | 124,133 | Macas |
| Napo | 137,234 | Tena |
| Pastaza | 54,139 | Puyo |
| Pichincha | 2,181,315 | Quito |
| Sucumbíos | 117,629 | Nueva Loja |
| Tungurahua | 415,372 | Ambato |
| Zamora Chinchipe | 83,379 | Zamora |
| Archipiélago de Colón (Galápagos) | 13,239 | Puerto Baquerizo (Isla San Cristóbal) |
| **Total** | 11,371,383 | |

* Figures exclude persons in unspecified areas, totalling 88,734.

**PRINCIPAL TOWNS** (estimated population at mid-1997)

| | | | |
|---|---|---|---|
| Guayaquil | 1,973,880 | Manta | 156,981 |
| Quito (capital) | 1,444,363* | Eloy Alfaro | 127,832* |
| Cuenca | 255,028 | Quevedo | 120,640 |
| Machala | 197,350 | Milagro | 119,371 |
| Santo Domingo de los Colorados | 183,219 | Esmeraldas | 117,722 |
| | | Loja | 117,365 |
| Portoviejo | 167,956 | Riobamba | 114,322* |
| Ambato | 160,302 | Ibarra | 113,791* |

* Population at mid 1996.

Source: UN, *Demographic Yearbook*.

**BIRTHS, MARRIAGES AND DEATHS**
(excluding nomadic Indian tribes)

| | Registered live births | | Registered marriages | | Registered deaths | |
|---|---|---|---|---|---|---|
| | Number | Rate (per 1,000) | Number | Rate (per 1,000) | Number | Rate (per 1,000) |
| 1993 | 314,522 | 28.6 | 68,193 | 6.2 | 52,453 | 4.8 |
| 1994 | 350,838 | 31.3 | 71,289 | 6.4 | 51,165 | 4.6 |
| 1995 | 408,983 | 35.7 | 70,480 | 6.2 | 50,867 | 4.4 |
| 1996 | 302,217 | 25.8 | 72,094 | 6.2 | 52,300 | 4.5 |
| 1997 | 288,803 | 24.2 | 66,967 | 5.6 | 52,089 | 4.4 |

Sources: Instituto Nacional de Estadística y Censos; UN, *Demographic Yearbook*.

**Expectation of life** (UN estimates, years at birth, 1990-95): 68.5 (males 66.4, females 71.4) (Source: UN, *World Population Prospects: The 1998 Revision*).

**ECONOMICALLY ACTIVE POPULATION***
(ISIC Major Divisions, 1990 census)

| | Males | Females | Total |
|---|---|---|---|
| Agriculture, hunting, forestry and fishing | 904,701 | 131,011 | 1,035,712 |
| Mining and quarrying | 18,849 | 2,021 | 20,870 |
| Manufacturing | 248,157 | 122,181 | 370,338 |
| Electricity, gas and water | 10,741 | 1,919 | 12,660 |
| Construction | 192,034 | 4,682 | 196,716 |
| Trade, restaurants and hotels | 295,855 | 180,875 | 476,730 |
| Transport, storage and communications | 123,807 | 7,277 | 131,084 |
| Financing, insurance, real estate and business services | 54,043 | 27,314 | 81,357 |
| Community, social and personal services | 483,821 | 354,308 | 838,129 |
| Activities not adequately defined | 111,919 | 45,811 | 157,730 |
| **Total labour force** | 2,443,927 | 877,399 | 3,321,326 |

* Figures refer to persons aged 8 years and over, excluding those seeking work for the first time, totalling 38,441 (males 27,506; females 10,935).

**1997:** Total employed 3,062,185; Total unemployed 311,625; Total labour force 3,373,810.

# Agriculture

**PRINCIPAL CROPS** ('000 metric tons)

| | 1996 | 1997 | 1998 |
|---|---|---|---|
| Wheat | 28 | 20 | 15† |
| Rice (paddy) | 1,270 | 1,072 | 1,072* |
| Barley | 46 | 35 | 35* |
| Maize | 598 | 688 | 688* |
| Potatoes | 454 | 602 | 602* |
| Cassava (Manioc) | 77 | 138 | 138* |
| Dry beans | 42 | 41 | 41* |
| Soybeans (Soya beans) | 78 | 9 | 61† |
| Seed cotton | 18 | 15 | 14* |
| Coconuts | 42 | 31 | 31* |
| Palm kernels | 31 | 41 | 41* |
| Tomatoes | 65 | 45 | 45* |
| Pumpkins, squash and gourds* | 40 | 40 | 40 |
| Sugar cane* | 6,700 | 5,000 | 4,800 |
| Apples | 43 | 25 | 25* |
| Oranges | 91 | 217 | 217* |
| Other citrus fruits | 83 | 106 | 106* |
| Pineapples | 58 | 30 | 30* |
| Mangoes | 54 | 3 | 3* |
| Avocados | 32 | 44 | 44* |
| Bananas | 5,727 | 7,494 | 7,494* |
| Plantains | 870 | 894 | 894* |
| Papayas | 13 | 69 | 69* |
| Coffee (green) | 191 | 87 | 120* |
| Cocoa beans | 94 | 83 | 35† |

* FAO estimate(s). † Unofficial figure.

Source: FAO, *Production Yearbook*.

**LIVESTOCK** ('000 head)

| | 1996 | 1997 | 1998 |
|---|---|---|---|
| Cattle | 5,105 | 5,150 | 5,329 |
| Sheep | 1,709 | 1,933 | 2,056 |
| Pigs | 2,621 | 2,708 | 2,795 |
| Horses* | 520 | 520 | 520 |
| Goats | 309 | 310 | 310* |
| Asses* | 266 | 267 | 268 |
| Mules* | 155 | 156 | 157 |
| Poultry | 63,000 | 65,000 | 65,000* |

* FAO estimate(s).

Source: FAO, *Production Yearbook*.

**LIVESTOCK PRODUCTS** ('000 metric tons)

| | 1996 | 1997 | 1998 |
|---|---|---|---|
| Beef and veal | 153 | 156 | 153 |
| Mutton and lamb* | 6 | 6 | 6 |
| Pig meat* | 103 | 107 | 110 |
| Goat meat* | 1 | 1 | 2 |
| Poultry meat* | 150 | 177 | 135 |
| Cows' milk | 1,951 | 1,929 | 1,950* |
| Sheep's milk* | 5 | 6 | 6 |
| Goats' milk* | 2 | 2 | 2 |
| Butter* | 5 | 5 | 5 |
| Cheese* | 7 | 7 | 7 |
| Hen eggs | 54 | 58 | 58* |
| Wool: | | | |
| greasy | 2 | 2 | 2* |
| clean* | 1 | 1 | 1 |
| Cattle hides (fresh)* | 31 | 31 | 31 |

* FAO estimate(s).

Source: FAO, *Production Yearbook*.

# Forestry

**ROUNDWOOD REMOVALS** ('000 cubic metres, excluding bark)

| | 1995 | 1996 | 1997 |
|---|---|---|---|
| Sawlogs, veneer logs and logs for sleepers | 4,491 | 4,814 | 5,168 |
| Pulpwood | 599 | 635 | 682 |
| Other industrial wood | 60 | 65 | 70 |
| Fuel wood | 5,258 | 5,474 | 5,888 |
| **Total** | 10,408 | 10,988 | 11,808 |

Source: FAO, *Yearbook of Forest Products*.

**SAWNWOOD PRODUCTION**
('000 cubic metres, including railway sleepers)

| | 1995 | 1996 | 1997 |
|---|---|---|---|
| Coniferous (softwood) | 340 | 377 | 416 |
| Broadleaved (hardwood) | 1,356 | 1,509 | 1,663 |
| **Total** | 1,696 | 1,886 | 2,079 |

Source: FAO, *Yearbook of Forest Products*.

made a joint declaration in support of the Palestinians' right to declare an independent state after the expiry of the Oslo agreements on 4 May. However, owing to an increasingly volatile security situation in the Israeli-Occupied Territories and the forthcoming Israeli general election, Egypt and Jordan subsequently joined other countries in urging Yasser Arafat to postpone his planned 4 May declaration of statehood. The election of the leader of the One Israel alliance, Ehud Barak, to the Israeli premiership was generally welcomed in Egypt. In July, however, the Egyptian Minister of Foreign Affairs, Amr Moussa, stressed that there could be no normalization of Egyptian–Israeli relations prior to the resumption of comprehensive peace talks. In early July President Mubarak became the first Arab leader to meet the Israeli Prime Minister and expressed optimism that Barak could revitalize the stalled peace process. Egyptian mediation was influential in discussions between Israeli and Palestinian negotiators that led to the signing of the Sharm esh-Sheikh Memorandum by Barak and Arafat in early September 1999 (see chapter on Israel). Nevertheless, relations between the Egyptian and Israeli Governments remained strained in late 1999.

Relations with the USA have remained tense. The US Secretary of Defense, William Perry, visited Cairo in April 1996 and denied rumours that the USA had signed a secret defence agreement with Israel. Perry announced that the USA would supply advanced military equipment to Egypt, including 21 F-16 fighter aircraft, in acknowledgement of its key role in the peace process. In August 1998 Egypt was highly critical of US military air-strikes against alleged terrorist strongholds in Afghanistan, and a pharmaceuticals factory in Khartoum, Sudan, which the US Government insisted was being used by associates of the Saudi militant Islamist Osama bin Laden (in exile in Afghanistan) to manufacture chemical weapons' components. Moreover, air-strikes against Iraq, undertaken by US and British forces in the Persian (Arabian) Gulf in December 1998, exacerbated existing tensions between Egypt and the USA, since Mubarak had consistently urged a diplomatic solution to the crisis (see chapter on Iraq). Tensions persisted as the US Secretary of Defense, William Cohen, visited Cairo and other regional capitals in March 1999 to seek support for a renewed air campaign against Iraq. During his visit to Egypt, Cohen agreed to supply Egypt with US $3,200m. of US weaponry, including a further 24 F-16 fighter jets. President Mubarak visited Washington in late June and the two countries made significant progress on proposals for the resumption of Middle East peace talks; differences remained, however, over the issue of sanctions imposed against Iraq and Libya. The US Government also expressed its opposition to a proposed Egyptian-Libyan initiative aimed at securing an end to Sudan's civil war.

In late October 1999 an EgyptAir plane, travelling from New York to Cairo, crashed into the Atlantic Ocean, killing all 217 passengers. Allegations made by US investigators that the crash had been caused by the suicide of the flight's Egyptian co-pilot were dismissed by Egypt's state-owned media; nevertheless, mutual accusations that the other country was seeking to absolve its nationals from blame continued into late 1999.

Egypt's relations with Libya have been dominated by the repercussions of the Lockerbie affair (see chapter on Libya) and allegations, by the USA and its western allies, of Libya's involvement in the incident. As there are more than 1m. Egyptian expatriate workers in Libya, Egypt has used its diplomacy to seek to avert a confrontation between Libya and the West, which could threaten not only the livelihood of its workers there, but also a steadily growing market for its exports.

Egypt has a long-standing border dispute with Sudan. In September 1994 Sudan alleged that Egyptian troops had entered the disputed border area of Halaib. Relations deteriorated sharply in June 1995, after the attempted assassination of President Mubarak in Addis Ababa (see above). Egypt accused Sudan of complicity in the attack and immediately strengthened its control of the Halaib triangle. In July, in contravention of an agreement concluded with Sudan in 1978, Egypt imposed visa and permit requirements on Sudanese nationals visiting or resident in Egypt. Bilateral relations deteriorated further in September 1995, when the OAU accused Sudan of direct involvement in the assassination attempt, and in December, when it demanded that Sudan should immediately extradite three individuals who were sought in connection with the attack. (It was reported in July 1999 that one of the suspects had been extradited to Cairo.) In February 1996 Sudan introduced permit requirements for Egyptian nationals resident in Sudan. Presidents Mubarak and al-Bashir met at the Arab League summit meeting in Cairo in May. In July, however, Egypt accused Sudan of harbouring Egyptian terrorists, contrary to an agreement concluded at the summit meeting. None the less, Egypt opposed the imposition of more stringent economic sanctions against Sudan by the UN (in addition to diplomatic sanctions and an embargo on international flights operated by Sudan Airways), on the grounds that they would harm the Sudanese people more than the regime. In January 1997 Egypt refused to provide the Sudanese Government with military support in its struggle against rebel advances in southern Sudan. In June Sudan accused Egypt of providing the opposition with military training, and in October the Sudanese press reported that Egypt was obstructing the import of medical supplies to Halaib. Despite such accusations,and claims made by members of the Sudanese opposition in January 1998 that the Sudanese Government was supporting Egypt's armed Islamist groups, there was evidence of attempts to normalize bilateral relations. In August 1997 security talks between the two countries restarted after a year-long suspension. In February 1998 river transport resumed between the Egyptian port of Aswan and the Sudanese port of Wadi Halfa. In April the two countries agreed to the establishment of a joint ministerial committee (involving the Ministers of Higher Education, Defence and Irrigation). Although Sudan considered the presence of Sudanese opposition leaders in Egypt an obstacle to the normalization process, a meeting in Cairo, in May 1999, between Sudan's former President Nimeri and a Sudanese government delegation, to discuss arrangements for his return from exile, represented significant progress on this issue. In December Egypt and Sudan agreed to a full normalization of relations and agreed to co-operate to resolve the dispute over the border area of Halaib.

## Government

Legislative power is held by the unicameral Majlis ash-Sha'ab (People's Assembly), which has 454 members: 10 nominated by the President and 444 directly elected for five years from 222 constituencies. The Assembly nominates the President, who is elected by popular referendum for six years (renewable). The President has executive powers and appoints one or more Vice-Presidents, a Prime Minister and a Council of Ministers. There is also a 210-member advisory body, the Shura Council. The country is divided into 27 governorates.

## Defence

In August 1999 Egypt had total armed forces of 450,000 (army 320,000, air defence command 80,000, navy an estimated 20,000, air force 30,000), with 254,000 reserves. There is a selective three-year period of national service. Defence expenditure for 1999 was budgeted at £E7,600m. ($2,200m.).

## Economic Affairs

In 1997, according to estimates by the World Bank, Egypt's gross national product (GNP), measured at average 1995–97 prices, was US $72,164m., equivalent to $1,200 per head. During 1990–97, it was estimated, GNP per head increased, in real terms, by an average of 2.8% per year. Over the same period, the population increased by an average of 2.0% per year. Total GNP for 1998 was estimated at $79,200m., equivalent to $1,290 per head. The average annual rate of growth of overall gross domestic product (GDP), measured in constant prices, was 5.4% in 1980–90 and 4.2% in 1990–98. According to the IMF, GDP increased, in real terms, by 5.0% in 1996, by 5.5% in 1997 and by an estimated 5.6% in 1998.

Agriculture (including forestry and fishing) contributed 17.3% of GDP in 1997/98 and employed an estimated 34.7% of the economically active population in 1998. The principal crops include cotton, rice, wheat, sugar cane, maize and tomatoes. Exports of food and live animals accounted for 10.2% of total exports in 1996. During 1990–98 agricultural GDP increased at an average annual rate of 2.9%. Agricultural GDP grew by 3.7% in 1997/98.

Industry (including mining, manufacturing, construction and power) employed 21.9% of the working population in 1995, and provided 32.5% of GDP in 1997/98. During 1990–98 industrial GDP rose at an average annual rate of 4.2%. Industrial GDP grew by 8.0% in 1997/98.

Mineral resources include petroleum, natural gas, phosphates, manganese, uranium, coal, iron ore and gold. The petroleum industry contributed an estimated 6.0% of GDP in 1998/99, and petroleum and petroleum products accounted for 43.9%

of total export earnings in 1997. However, the mining sector employed only 0.3% of the working population in 1995.

Manufacturing contributed some 25% of GDP in 1997 and employed 14.2% of the working population in 1995. Based on the value of output, the main branches of manufacturing in 1994/95 were food products (accounting for 20.5% of the total), petroleum refineries (16.5%) and textiles (11.4%). In 1990–97 the real GDP of the manufacturing sector grew by an average of 4.8% per year.

Energy is derived principally from hydroelectric power and coal. Petroleum production averaged an estimated 842,000 barrels per day in 1998, and at the end of that year Egypt's proven published petroleum reserves totalled 3,500m. barrels, sufficient to sustain production at 1998 levels for some 11.4 years. At the end of 1998 Egypt's proven natural gas reserves totalled 890,000m. cu m. In 1998 all the natural gas produced (about 1,600m. cu ft per day) was consumed locally. Levels of gas production are expected to double by the year 2000, and the Government plans to begin exporting in 2001. In 1996 imports of fuel and energy accounted for about 4% of the value of all imports.

Services contributed 50.1% of GDP in 1997/98 and employed 44.1% of the working population in 1995. In the late 1980s tourism became one of the most dynamic sectors of the Egyptian economy. However, the sector's prospects have been damaged by a campaign of Islamic fundamentalist violence aimed at tourists. In 1998 the number of visitors to Egypt and tourism revenues were significantly lower than in 1997. By 1999, however, there were signs of a recovery in the sector. In 1990–98 the real GDP of the service sector grew by an average of 4.1% per year. The service sector grew by 4.9% in 1997/98.

In 1998 Egypt recorded a visible trade deficit of US $10,214m., while there was a deficit of $2,566m. on the current account of the balance of payments. In 1996 the principal source of imports (20.0%) was the USA, which was also the principal market for exports (13.0%). Other major trading partners were Germany, France, the Netherlands and Italy. Egypt's principal exports in 1996 were petroleum and petroleum products, textiles, food, non-ferrous metals and clothing. The principal imports were cereals, chemicals, machinery and transport equipment, and basic manufactures.

For the financial year ending 30 June 1995 there was a consolidated budget surplus of £E1,828m., equivalent to 0.9% of GDP. For 1999/2000 there was a projected deficit of £E8,860m. in the state public budget. Egypt's external debt totalled US $29,849m. at the end of 1997, of which $26,804m. was long-term public debt. In that year the cost of servicing the foreign debt was equivalent to 9.0% of the value of exports of goods and services. The annual rate of inflation averaged 9.6% in 1990–98. Consumer prices increased by an average of 4.6% in 1997, by some 3.6% in 1998 and by a reported 2.9% in 1999. In 1999 an estimated 7.9% of the total labour force were unemployed.

Egypt is a member of the Arab League (see p. 218), the Organization of Arab Petroleum Exporting Countries (see p. 248), the Arab Co-operation Council (see p. 290) and the Organization of the Islamic Conference (see p. 249). In mid-1998 Egypt was admitted to the Common Market for Eastern and Southern Africa (COMESA, see p. 142).

Since 1990 Egypt's economic difficulties, including over-reliance on an inflexible public sector and unwieldy public debt, have resulted in a decline in investment and high levels of inflation and unemployment. In 1991 the Government initiated an economic reform programme which sought to increase production and reduce unemployment, partly through a comprehensive rationalization of public enterprises. Although some success was achieved in reducing inflation and narrowing the fiscal deficit, buyers could not be found for many inefficient state-owned companies. In mid-1999 the public sector still accounted for almost 70% of GDP; however, the scheduled privatization of a major state-owned bank, as well as Telecom Egypt and insurance and electricity companies, was expected to reactivate the divestment programme. In 1999 the annual rate of inflation was reportedly at its lowest level for 30 years, while unemployment was also falling. In 1997 the Government provided tax incentives to new businesses, particularly those established in rural areas, as part of a long-term strategy to encourage investment and population away from the congested Nile Valley. The loss of tourism revenue resulting from international reaction to attacks on tourists by militant Islamist groups, together with the unstable world price of petroleum, have made it difficult to maintain the levels of growth necessary to create jobs for Egypt's burgeoning population, and attracting greater levels of foreign investment and encouraging domestic savings remain economic priorities for the Government.

## Social Welfare

Substantial progress has been made in social welfare services in recent years. There are comprehensive state schemes for sickness benefits, pensions, health insurance and training. In 1982 Egypt had 1,521 hospital establishments, with a total of 87,685 beds. (The number of hospital beds had increased to an estimated 126,097 by 1998, while, in the same year, there were an estimated 7,411 medical treatment units, including 331 general and district hospitals.) There were 9,495 physicians working in the country in 1985. Government expenditure on health in the year 1998/99 was projected to be some £E4,600m. (an estimated 5.0% of total spending).

## Education

Education is officially compulsory for eight years between six and 14 years of age. Primary education, beginning at six years of age, lasts for five years. Secondary education, beginning at 11 years of age, lasts for a further six years, comprising two cycles (the first being preparatory) of three years each. In 1996 total enrolment at primary and secondary schools was equivalent to 88% of the school-age population (males 94%; females 82%). In that year primary enrolment included 80% of children in the relevant age-group (males 86%; females 74%), while the comparable ratio for secondary enrolment was 68% (males 71%; females 64%). More than 13.8m. people were receiving state education in 1993. There are 14 universities. The Al-Azhar University and its various preparatory and associated institutes provide instruction and training in various disciplines, with emphasis on adherence to Islamic principles and teachings. In 1996/97 some 166,000 students were enrolled at the University. Education at all levels is available free of charge. Expenditure on education by the central Government in the financial year 1996/97 was £E11,590m. (14.8% of total spending). Allocations for education increased significantly from 1991 (largely as a result of an extensive school building programme). In 1998 the Government allocated an estimated £E13,700m. (19% of total spending) for education. In 1995, according to UNESCO estimates, the rate of adult illiteracy stood at 48.6% (males 36.4%; females 61.2%). However, by 1998 the rate of adult illiteracy was believed to have decreased to 37.8%, as a direct result of a government initiative to expand education.

## Public Holidays

**2000:** 1 January (New Year), 8 January (Id al-Fitr, end of Ramadan)*, 16 March (Id al-Adha, Feast of the Sacrifice), 6 April (Muharram, Islamic New Year), 25 April (Sinai Day), 1 May (Sham an-Nessim, Coptic Easter Monday), 15 June (Mouloud/Yum an-Nabi, Birth of Muhammad), 23 July (Revolution Day), 6 October (Armed Forces Day), 24 October (Popular Resistance Day), 26 October (Leilat al-Meiraj, Ascension of Muhammad), 23 December (Victory Day), 28 December (Id al-Fitr, end of Ramadan)*.

**2001:** 1 January (New Year), 6 March (Id al-Adha, Feast of the Sacrifice), 26 March (Muharram, Islamic New Year), 16 April (Sham an-Nessim, Coptic Easter Monday), 25 April (Sinai Day), 4 June (Mouloud/Yum an-Nabi, Birth of Muhammad), 23 July (Revolution Day), 6 October (Armed Forces Day), 15 October (Leilat al-Meiraj, Ascension of Muhammad), 24 October (Popular Resistance Day), 17 December (Id al-Fitr, end of Ramadan), 23 December (Victory Day).

* This festival will occur twice (in the Islamic years AH 1420 and 1421) in the same Gregorian year.

Coptic Christian holidays include: Christmas (7 January), Palm Sunday and Easter Sunday.

## Weights and Measures

The metric system is in force, but some Egyptian measurements are still in use.

# Statistical Survey

Sources (unless otherwise stated): Central Agency for Public Mobilization and Statistics, POB 2086, Cairo (Nasr City); tel. (2) 604632; Research Department, National Bank of Egypt, Cairo.

## Area and Population

**AREA, POPULATION AND DENSITY**

| | |
|---|---|
| Area (sq km) | 1,002,000* |
| Population (census results)† | |
| 17–18 November 1986 | 48,254,238 |
| 31 December 1996 | |
| Males | 30,351,390 |
| Females | 28,961,524 |
| Total | 59,312,914 |
| Density (per sq km) at 31 December 1996 | 59.2 |

* 386,874 sq miles. Inhabited and cultivated territory accounts for 55,039 sq km (21,251 sq miles).

† Excluding Egyptian nationals abroad, totalling an estimated 2,250,000 in 1986 and an estimated 2,180,000 in 1996.

**Population** (official estimates at December): 60,839,000 in 1997 (excluding Egyptian nationals abroad); 62,056,000 in 1998.

**GOVERNORATES** (population at 1996 census*)

| Governorate | Area (sq km)† | Population ('000) | Capital |
|---|---|---|---|
| Cairo | 214.20 | 6,801.0 | Cairo |
| Alexandria | 2,679.36 | 3,339.1 | Alexandria |
| Port Said | 72.07 | 472.3 | Port Said |
| Ismailia | 1,441.59 | 714.8 | Ismailia |
| Suez | 17,840.42 | 417.5 | Suez |
| Damietta | 589.17 | 913.6 | Damietta |
| Dakahlia | 3,470.90 | 4,223.9 | El-Mansoura |
| Sharkia | 4,179.55 | 4,281.1 | Zagazig |
| Kalyoubia | 1,001.09 | 3,301.2 | Banha |
| Kafr esh-Sheikh | 3,437.12 | 2,223.7 | Kafr esh-Sheikh |
| Gharbia | 1,942.21 | 3,406.0 | Tanta |
| Menoufia | 1,532.13 | 2,760.4 | Shebien el-Kom |
| Behera | 10,129.48 | 3,994.3 | Damanhour |
| Giza | 85,153.56 | 4,784.1 | Giza |
| Beni-Suef | 1,321.50 | 1,859.2 | Beni-Suef |
| Fayoum | 1,827.10 | 1,989.8 | El-Fayoum |
| Menia | 2,261.70 | 3,310.1 | El-Menia |
| Asyout | 1,553.00 | 2,802.3 | Asyout |
| Suhag | 1,547.20 | 3,123.1 | Suhag |
| Qena | 1,850.60 | 2,442.0 | Qena |
| Aswan | 678.45 | 974.1 | Aswan |
| Red Sea | 203,685.00 | 157.3 | Hurghada |
| El-Wadi el-Gidid | 376,505.00 | 141.8 | El-Kharga |
| Matruh | 212,112.00 | 212.0 | Matruh |
| North Sinai | } 60,714.00 | 252.2 | El-Areesh |
| South Sinai | | 54.8 | Et-Tour |

* Figures exclude data for the recently-created governorate of Luxor City, with an area of 55 sq km and a population (in '000) of 361.1.

† The sum of these figures is 997,738.40 sq km, compared with the official national total of 1,002,000 sq km.

**PRINCIPAL TOWNS** (estimated population at 1 July 1992)

| | | | |
|---|---|---|---|
| Cairo (Al-Qahirah, the capital)* | 6,800,992 | Asyout (Asyut) | 321,000 |
| Alexandria (Al-Iskandariyah)* | 3,339,076 | Zagazig (Az-Zaqaziq) | 287,000 |
| Giza (Al-Jizah)* | 4,784,099 | Ismailia (Al-Ismailiyah) | 255,000 |
| Shoubra el-Kheima (Shubra al-Khaymah) | 834,000 | El-Fayum (Al-Fayyum) | 250,000 |
| Port Said (Bur Sa'id)* | 472,335 | Kafr ed-Dawar (Kafr ad-Dawwar) | 226,000 |
| Suez (As-Suways)* | 417,527 | Damanhour (Damanhur) | 222,000 |
| El-Mahalla el-Koubra (Al-Mahallah al-Kubra) | 408,000 | Aswan | 220,000 |
| Tanta | 380,000 | El-Menia (Al-Minya) | 208,000 |
| El-Mansoura (Al-Mansurah) | 371,000 | Beni-Suef (Bani-Suwayf) | 179,000 |
| | | Shebien el-Kom (Shibin al-Kawn) | 158,000 |
| | | Suhag (Sawhaj) | 156,000 |

* At census of December 1996.

Source: mainly UN, *Demographic Yearbook*.

**BIRTHS, MARRIAGES AND DEATHS**

| | Registered live births | | Registered marriages | | Registered deaths | |
|---|---|---|---|---|---|---|
| | Number | Rate (per 1,000) | Number | Rate (per 1,000) | Number | Rate (per 1,000) |
| 1991 | 1,662,000 | 31.4 | 400,000 | 7.5 | 393,000 | 7.4 |
| 1992 | 1,521,000 | 28.1 | 397,000 | 7.3 | 385,000 | 7.1 |
| 1993 | 1,622,000 | 29.4 | 432,000 | 7.8 | 382,000 | 6.9 |
| 1994 | 1,636,000 | 29.0 | 452,000 | 8.0 | 388,000 | 6.9 |
| 1995 | 1,605,000 | 27.9 | 471,000 | 8.2 | 385,000 | 6.7 |
| 1996 | 1,662,000 | 28.3 | 489,000 | 8.3 | 380,000 | 6.5 |
| 1997 | 1,655,000 | 27.5 | 493,000 | 8.2 | 389,000 | 6.5 |
| 1998* | 1,687,000 | 27.5 | 562,000 | 9.2 | 399,000 | 6.5 |

* Provisional figures.

**Expectation of life** (years at birth, 1996): males 65.1; females 69.0.

**ECONOMICALLY ACTIVE POPULATION*** (sample surveys, '000 persons aged 12 to 64 years)

| | 1993 | 1994 | 1995 |
|---|---|---|---|
| Agriculture, hunting, forestry and fishing | 5,188.4 | 5,360.5 | 5,215.6 |
| Mining and quarrying | 45.4 | 47.3 | 40.7 |
| Manufacturing | 2,045.2 | 2,055.1 | 2,183.5 |
| Electricity, gas and water | 147.6 | 154.1 | 166.8 |
| Construction | 949.5 | 1,019.4 | 967.6 |
| Trade, restaurants and hotels | 1,437.0 | 1,561.1 | 1,587.7 |
| Transport, storage and communications | 806.5 | 843.3 | 907.6 |
| Finance, insurance, real estate and business services | 276.4 | 295.3 | 282.7 |
| Community, social and personal services | 3,805.4 | 3,903.1 | 3,990.8 |
| Activities not adequately defined | 1.9 | 2.1 | 1.2 |
| **Total employed** | 14,703.4 | 15,241.4 | 15,344.2 |
| Unemployed | 1,800.6 | 1,877.4 | 1,917.0 |
| **Total labour force** | 16,504.0 | 17,118.8 | 17,261.2 |
| Males | 12,718.6 | 13,107.3 | 13,393.2 |
| Females | 3,785.4 | 4,011.5 | 3,868.0 |

* Figures for each year represent the average of two surveys, conducted in May and November.

# Agriculture

**PRINCIPAL CROPS** ('000 metric tons)

| | 1996 | 1997 | 1998 |
|---|---|---|---|
| Wheat | 5,735 | 5,849 | 6,093 |
| Rice (paddy) | 4,895 | 5,580 | 5,585* |
| Barley | 120 | 126 | 148 |
| Maize | 5,165 | 5,147 | 5,330* |
| Sorghum | 604 | 766 | 770* |
| Potatoes | 2,626 | 1,803 | 2,000* |
| Sweet potatoes | 148† | 150* | 155* |
| Taro (Coco yam) | 148† | 136* | 140* |
| Dry broad beans | 442 | 476 | 523 |
| Other pulses | 67 | 61 | 66 |
| Soybeans (Soya beans) | 40 | 35 | 25* |
| Groundnuts (in shell) | 125 | 125† | 126* |
| Sunflower seed | 49 | 50† | 55* |
| Cottonseed | 590† | 580* | 390† |
| Cotton (lint) | 346 | 342 | 227* |
| Olives | 208 | 180 | 200* |
| Cabbages | 463† | 490 | 495* |
| Tomatoes | 5,995 | 5,873 | 5,980* |
| Cauliflowers | 103 | 93 | 110* |
| Pumpkins, squash and gourds | 498† | 568 | 570* |
| Cucumbers and gherkins* | 253 | 255 | 258 |
| Aubergines | 550† | 555* | 560* |
| Green chillies and peppers | 323 | 363 | 365* |
| Onions (dry) | 448 | 396 | 405* |
| Garlic | 255 | 159 | 200* |
| Green beans | 202 | 205* | 210* |
| Green peas | 127 | 123 | 125* |
| Carrots | 109 | 138 | 135* |
| Other vegetables | 722 | 751 | 766* |
| Watermelons | 1,127 | 1,735 | 1,650* |
| Melons | 526† | 547 | 550* |
| Grapes | 944 | 868 | 870* |
| Dates | 738 | 741 | 750* |
| Sugar cane | 13,958 | 13,726 | 13,850* |
| Sugar beets | 842 | 1,143 | 1,951 |
| Apples | 412 | 403 | 410* |
| Pears | 58 | 57 | 60* |
| Peaches and nectarines* | 60 | 62 | 65 |
| Plums | 47 | 35 | 4* |
| Oranges | 1,613 | 1,522 | 1,525* |
| Tangerines, mandarins, clementines and satsumas | 449 | 435 | 435* |
| Lemons and limes | 312 | 264 | 300* |
| Apricots | 51 | 41 | 45* |
| Mangoes | 203 | 231 | 231* |
| Bananas | 570 | 635 | 600* |
| Other fruits and berries* | 591 | 615 | 613 |

* FAO estimate(s). † Unofficial figure.

Source: FAO, *Production Yearbook*.

**LIVESTOCK** ('000 head, year ending September)

| | 1996 | 1997 | 1998 |
|---|---|---|---|
| Cattle | 3,107* | 3,117 | 3,022† |
| Buffaloes | 2,907* | 3,096 | 3,150† |
| Sheep | 4,220* | 4,260 | 4,300† |
| Goats | 3,131* | 3,187 | 3,200† |
| Pigs | 27 | 28 | 29 |
| Horses | 41* | 43† | 45† |
| Asses† | 2,980 | 2,990 | 2,995 |
| Camels | 131* | 133† | 135† |

* Unofficial figure. † FAO estimate(s).

Chickens (FAO estimates, million): 82 in 1996; 85 in 1997; 86 in 1998.

Ducks (FAO estimates, million): 9 in 1996; 9 in 1997; 9 in 1998.

Source: FAO, *Production Yearbook*.

**LIVESTOCK PRODUCTS** ('000 metric tons)

| | 1996 | 1997 | 1998 |
|---|---|---|---|
| Beef and veal | 244 | 311 | 318* |
| Buffalo meat | 208 | 225* | 231* |
| Mutton and lamb | 61 | 64* | 66* |
| Goat meat | 56 | 56* | 57* |
| Pig meat* | 3 | 3 | 3 |
| Poultry meat | 448 | 535 | 494* |
| Other meat | 108 | 108* | 113* |
| Cows' milk | 1,298 | 1,324 | 1,350* |
| Buffaloes' milk | 1,624 | 1,890 | 1,890* |
| Sheep's milk* | 90 | 91 | 93 |
| Goats' milk* | 14 | 15 | 15 |
| Butter and ghee* | 84 | 91 | 91 |
| Cheese* | 371 | 400 | 402 |
| Hen eggs | 162 | 168 | 165* |
| Honey | 9 | 9 | 10* |
| Wool: greasy | 7 | 7 | 7* |
| Cattle and buffalo hides* | 43 | 49 | 50 |
| Sheepskins* | 7 | 8 | 8 |
| Goatskins* | 7 | 7 | 7 |

* FAO estimate(s).

Source: FAO, mainly *Production Yearbook*.

# Forestry

**ROUNDWOOD REMOVALS**
('000 cubic metres, excluding bark)

| | 1995 | 1996 | 1997 |
|---|---|---|---|
| Industrial wood | 124 | 126 | 128 |
| Fuel wood | 2,539 | 2,587 | 2,636 |
| **Total** | 2,663 | 2,713 | 2,764 |

Source: FAO, *Yearbook of Forest Products*.

# Fishing

('000 metric tons, live weight)

| | 1995 | 1996 | 1997 |
|---|---|---|---|
| Common carp | 11.1 | 16.6 | 16.6 |
| Nile tilapia | 100.2 | 97.5 | 131.0 |
| Mudfish | 17.6 | 18.4 | 22.4 |
| Other torpedo-shaped catfishes | — | — | 8.9 |
| Other freshwater fishes | 78.6 | 81.8 | 40.3 |
| Flathead grey mullet | 9.9 | 4.9 | 8.0 |
| Other mullets | 8.2 | 9.9 | 8.6 |
| Silversides (Sand smelts) | 3.8 | 6.6 | 5.3 |
| Jacks and crevalles | 1.8 | 10.0 | 6.4 |
| Sardinellas | 11.9 | 15.1 | 16.3 |
| Narrow-barred Spanish mackerel | 1.4 | 2.0 | 8.5 |
| **Total fish** (incl. others) | 299.4 | 310.6 | 333.1 |
| Crustaceans and molluscs | 11.6 | 9.5 | 12.2 |
| **Total catch** | 311.0 | 320.1 | 345.2 |
| Inland waters | 229.0 | 230.7 | 246.1 |
| Mediterranean and Black Sea | 39.4 | 45.9 | 47.5 |
| Indian Ocean | 42.6 | 43.5 | 51.7 |

Source: FAO, *Yearbook of Fishery Statistics*.

# Mining

('000 metric tons, year ending 30 June)

| | 1995/96 | 1996/97 | 1997/98* |
|---|---|---|---|
| Crude petroleum | 44,000 | 42,000 | 40,000 |
| Iron ore† | 2,098 | 2,744 | 3,001 |
| Salt (unrefined) | 1,632 | 2,024 | 2,588 |
| Phosphate rock | 1,238 | 1,428 | 1,059 |
| Gypsum (crude) | 2,092 | 1,839 | 2,423 |
| Kaolin | 293 | 259 | 286 |

* Figures are provisional.

† Figures refer to gross weight. The estimated iron content is 50%.

Natural gas (estimates, petajoules): 411 in 1994; 530 in 1995 (Source: UN, *Industrial Commodity Statistics Yearbook*).

# Industry

**SELECTED PRODUCTS** ('000 metric tons, unless otherwise indicated)

| | 1994 | 1995 | 1996 |
|---|---|---|---|
| Wheat flour | 3,662 | 3,767 | 4,657 |
| Raw sugar* | 1,099 | 1,132 | 1,222 |
| Cottonseed oil (refined) | 318 | 305 | 288 |
| Beer ('000 hectolitres) | 360 | 360 | 380 |
| Cigarettes (million) | 39,145 | 42,469 | 49,959 |
| Cotton yarn (pure)† | 251.0 | 250.3 | 211.6 |
| Jute yarn | 20.8 | 19.8 | 15.3 |
| Jute fabrics | 17.0 | 19.0 | 20.0 |
| Wool yarn | 15.2 | 14.1 | 14.1 |
| Paper and paperboard* | 219 | 221 | 221 |
| Rubber tyres and tubes ('000)‡ | 3,858 | 3,690 | 3,046 |
| Sulphuric acid (100%) | 112 | 133 | 299 |
| Caustic soda (Sodium hydroxide) | 49 | 48 | 38 |
| Nitrogenous fertilizers†§ | 5,918 | 6,136 | 3,337 |
| Phosphate fertilizers‖ | 765 | 913 | 418 |
| Jet fuels | 780 | 860 | n.a. |
| Motor spirit (petrol) | 4,356 | 4,520 | 4,784 |
| Kerosene | 1,405 | 1,169 | n.a. |
| Distillate fuel oils | 5,246 | 5,792 | 5,663 |
| Residual fuel oil (Mazout) | 12,071 | 12,044 | 12,745 |
| Petroleum bitumen (asphalt) | 683 | 740 | n.a. |
| Cement | 13,554 | 14,237 | 15,569 |
| Pig-iron | 109 | 69 | 15 |
| Radio receivers ('000) | 52 | n.a. | n.a. |
| Television receivers ('000) | 234 | 243 | 336 |
| Passenger motor cars—assembly (number) | 6,000 | 9,000 | 13,000 |
| Electric energy (million kWh)†¶ | 49,500 | 48,864 | n.a. |

* Data from the FAO.

† Figures refer to the year ending 30 June.

‡ Tyres and inner tubes for road motor vehicles (including motorcycles) and bicycles.

§ Production in terms of nitrogen.

‖ Production in terms of phosphoric acid.

¶ UN estimates.

Source: mainly UN, *Industrial Commodity Statistics Yearbook*.

# Finance

**CURRENCY AND EXCHANGE RATES**

**Monetary Units**

1,000 millièmes = 100 piastres = 5 tallaris = 1 Egyptian pound (£E).

**Sterling, Dollar and Euro Equivalents** (30 September 1999)

£1 sterling = £E5.592;
US $1 = £E3.396;
€1 = £E3.622;
£E100 = £17.88 sterling = $29.45 = €27.61.

Note: From February 1991 foreign exchange transactions were conducted through only two markets, the primary market and the free market. With effect from 8 October 1991, the primary market was eliminated, and all foreign exchange transactions are effected through the free market. For external trade purposes, the average value of the Egyptian pound was 29.486 US cents in 1996, 29.509 US cents in 1997 and 29.516 US cents in 1998.

**STATE PUBLIC BUDGET** (£E million, year ending 30 June)

| Revenue | 1996/97 | 1997/98 | 1998/99 |
|---|---|---|---|
| Current revenue | 61,189 | 63,970 | 66,849 |
| Central Government | 57,641 | 60,148 | 62,488 |
| Tax revenue | 40,835 | 43,576 | 46,400 |
| Taxes on income and profits | 14,660 | 15,292 | 15,800 |
| Domestic taxes on goods and services | 11,250 | 12,647 | 14,200 |
| Customs duties | 8,330 | 8,834 | 9,200 |
| Stamp duties | 3,290 | 3,204 | 3,300 |
| Other current revenue | 16,806 | 16,572 | 16,088 |
| Profit transfers | 11,450 | 11,195 | 10,642 |
| Petroleum Authority | 4,749 | 4,220 | 3,300 |
| Suez Canal Authority | 2,814 | 2,960 | 2,950 |
| Central Bank of Egypt | 2,558 | 2,617 | 2,900 |
| Local government | 2,388 | 2,460 | 2,704 |
| Service authorities | 1,160 | 1,362 | 1,657 |
| Capital revenue | 3,734 | 4,078 | 4,600 |
| **Total** | 64,923 | 68,048 | 71,449 |

| Expenditure | 1996/97 | 1997/98 | 1998/99 |
|---|---|---|---|
| Current expenditure | 53,423 | 55,817 | 58,932 |
| Wages | 15,311 | 17,073 | 18,700 |
| Pensions | 4,300 | 4,600 | 4,809 |
| Goods and services | 3,543 | 3,707 | 3,951 |
| Defence | 7,377 | 7,740 | 8,200 |
| Public debt interest | 15,264 | 14,915 | 15,396 |
| Local | 12,154 | 12,200 | 12,772 |
| Foreign | 3,110 | 2,715 | 2,624 |
| Subsidies | 4,313 | 4,416 | 4,300 |
| Capital expenditure (net) | 13,417 | 14,985 | 15,517 |
| **Total** | 66,840 | 70,802 | 74,449 |

**1999/2000** (projections, £E million, year ending 30 June): Revenue 90,593 (current 79,108, capital 11,485); Expenditure 99,453 (current 77,110, capital 22,343).

**INTERNATIONAL RESERVES** (US $ million at 31 December)

| | 1996 | 1997 | 1998 |
|---|---|---|---|
| Gold* | 695 | 609 | 541 |
| IMF special drawing rights | 123 | 113 | 160 |
| Reserve position in IMF | 77 | 73 | 76 |
| Foreign exchange | 17,198 | 18,479 | 17,888 |
| **Total** | 18,093 | 19,274 | 18,665 |

* Valued at market-related prices.

Source: IMF, *International Financial Statistics*.

**MONEY SUPPLY** (£E million at 31 December)

| | 1996 | 1997 | 1998 |
|---|---|---|---|
| Currency outside banks | 24,954 | 28,215 | 31,502 |
| Demand deposits at deposit money banks | 18,026 | 18,920 | 19,335 |
| **Total money** (incl. others) | 44,521 | 48,708 | 58,577 |

Source: IMF, *International Financial Statistics*.

**COST OF LIVING** (Consumer Price Index; base: 1990 = 100)

| | 1995 | 1996 | 1997 |
|---|---|---|---|
| Food, beverages and tobacco | 164.0 | 176.5 | 183.8 |
| Clothing and footwear | 179.0 | 197.9 | 209.3 |
| Rent, fuel and light | 218.0 | 224.1 | 226.7 |
| **All items** (incl. others) | 178.7 | 191.6 | 200.4 |

Source: ILO, *Yearbook of Labour Statistics*.

**1998:** Food, beverages and tobacco 190.9; All items 207.5 (Source: UN, *Monthly Bulletin of Statistics*).

**NATIONAL ACCOUNTS**
(£E million, year ending 30 June)

**Expenditure on the Gross Domestic Product** (at current prices)

| | 1995/96 | 1996/97 | 1997/98 |
|---|---|---|---|
| Government final consumption expenditure | 23,600 | 26,050 | 28,250 |
| Private final consumption expenditure | 171,700 | 192,700 | 207,740 |
| Increase in stocks | 1,550 | 200 | 2,730 |
| Gross fixed capital formation | 42,100 | 49,400 | 59,600 |
| **Total domestic expenditure** | 238,950 | 268,350 | 298,320 |
| Exports of goods and services | 48,450 | 51,700 | 47,200 |
| *Less* Imports of goods and services | 59,100 | 63,800 | 65,300 |
| **GDP in purchasers' values** | 228,300 | 256,250 | 280,220 |

Source: IMF, *International Financial Statistics.*

**Gross Domestic Product by Economic Activity**
(at constant 1996/97 factor cost)

| | 1996/97 | 1997/98* |
|---|---|---|
| Agriculture, hunting, forestry and fishing | 42,325 | 43,905 |
| Mining and quarrying<br>Manufacturing | 59,237 | 63,734 |
| Electricity | 4,220 | 4,470 |
| Construction | 12,750 | 14,100 |
| Trade, restaurants and hotels | 45,275 | 46,898 |
| Transport and communications | 22,695 | 23,802 |
| Finance, insurance and real estate | 13,957 | 15,187 |
| Government services | 18,900 | 19,853 |
| Other services | 20,141 | 21,141 |
| **Total** | 239,500 | 253,090 |

* Figures are provisional.

**BALANCE OF PAYMENTS** (US $ million)

| | 1996 | 1997 | 1998 |
|---|---|---|---|
| Exports of goods f.o.b. | 4,779 | 5,525 | 4,403 |
| Imports of goods f.o.b. | −13,169 | −14,157 | −14,617 |
| **Trade balance** | −8,390 | −8,632 | −10,214 |
| Exports of services | 9,271 | 9,380 | 8,141 |
| Imports of services | −5,084 | −6,770 | −6,492 |
| **Balance on goods and services** | −4,203 | −6,021 | −8,565 |
| Other income received | 1,901 | 2,122 | 2,030 |
| Other income paid | −1,556 | −1,185 | −1,075 |
| **Balance on goods, services and income** | −3,858 | −5,085 | −7,610 |
| Current transfers received | 3,888 | 4,738 | 5,166 |
| Current transfers paid | −222 | −363 | −122 |
| **Current balance** | −192 | −711 | −2,566 |
| Direct investment abroad | −5 | −129 | 1,901 |
| Direct investment from abroad | 636 | 891 | −45 |
| Portfolio investment assets | — | n.a. | −63 |
| Portfolio investment liabilities | 545 | 816 | −537 |
| Other investment assets | −565 | −170 | 39 |
| Other investment liabilities | −2,070 | 551 | 1,431 |
| Net errors and omissions | −74 | −1,882 | −722 |
| **Overall balance** | −1,725 | −635 | −1,387 |

Source: IMF, *International Financial Statistics.*

# External Trade

Note: Figures exclude trade in military goods.

**PRINCIPAL COMMODITIES** (distribution by SITC, US $ million)

| Imports c.i.f. | 1994 | 1995 | 1996 |
|---|---|---|---|
| **Food and live animals** | 2,263.3 | 2,611.7 | 3,056.6 |
| Cereals and cereal preparations | 1,126.6 | 1,299.2 | 1,705.1 |
| Wheat and meslin (unmilled) | 766.6 | 875.7 | 1,231.3 |
| Maize (unmilled) | 263.8 | 349.3 | 435.2 |
| **Crude materials (inedible) except fuels** | 716.3 | 1,059.3 | 1,142.4 |
| Cork and wood | 377.4 | 551.0 | 501.9 |
| Simply worked wood and railway sleepers | 344.8 | 522.3 | 452.3 |
| Simply worked coniferous wood | 256.2 | 445.6 | 346.5 |
| Sawn coniferous wood | 256.1 | 445.6 | 346.5 |
| **Animal and vegetable oils, fats and waxes** | 193.4 | 510.3 | 512.8 |
| Fixed vegetable oils and fats | 172.4 | 466.7 | 481.7 |
| **Chemicals and related products** | 1,154.5 | 1,550.8 | 1,617.0 |
| Organic chemicals | 190.7 | 289.1 | 277.1 |
| Artificial resins, plastic materials, etc. | 358.3 | 448.4 | 496.2 |
| Products of polymerization, etc. | 288.3 | n.a. | n.a. |
| **Basic manufactures** | 1,821.4 | 2,360.3 | 2,580.6 |
| Paper, paperboard and manufactures | 282.6 | 530.1 | 406.6 |
| Paper and paperboard (not cut to size or shape) | 261.8 | 504.3 | 367.5 |
| Textile yarn, fabrics, etc. | 242.3 | 279.7 | 288.8 |
| Iron and steel | 546.1 | 777.5 | 1,007.5 |
| **Machinery and transport equipment** | 2,784.3 | 2,967.8 | 3,313.1 |
| Machinery specialized for particular industries | 439.1 | 481.4 | 613.4 |
| General industrial machinery, equipment and parts | 657.5 | 790.6 | 846.0 |
| Telecommunications and sound equipment | 201.4 | 212.0 | 237.8 |
| Other electrical machinery, apparatus, etc. | 444.7 | n.a. | n.a. |
| Road vehicles and parts* | 667.3 | 623.2 | 598.2 |
| Passenger motor cars (excl. buses) | 213.5 | 216.7 | 201.1 |
| Parts and accessories for cars, buses, lorries, etc.* | 228.1 | 228.4 | 201.5 |
| **Miscellaneous manufactured articles** | 370.6 | 392.1 | 427.7 |
| **Total** (incl. others) | 9,592.1 | 11,738.8 | 13,012.1 |

* Excluding tyres, engines and electrical parts.

| Exports f.o.b. | 1994 | 1995 | 1996 |
|---|---|---|---|
| **Food and live animals** | 266.3 | 324.2 | 359.2 |
| Cereals and cereal preparations | 86.0 | 60.3 | 122.7 |
| Rice | 79.2 | 56.7 | 117.7 |
| Vegetables and fruit | 121.0 | 206.8 | 169.9 |
| Fresh or simply preserved vegetables | 75.5 | 152.7 | 120.6 |
| **Crude materials (inedible) except fuels** | 305.2 | 241.3 | 180.0 |
| Textile fibres (excl. wool tops) and waste | 250.4 | 169.4 | 102.4 |
| Cotton | 237.6 | 157.8 | 92.3 |
| Raw cotton (excl. linters) | 233.8 | 152.2 | 91.8 |
| **Mineral fuels, lubricants, etc.** | 1,360.9 | 1,282.9 | 1,681.1 |
| Petroleum, petroleum products, etc. | 1,321.2 | 1,231.7 | 1,633.9 |
| Crude petroleum oils, etc. | 793.4 | 719.2 | 861.1 |
| Refined petroleum products | 503.8 | 496.3 | 809.6 |
| Residual fuel oils | 486.7 | n.a. | n.a. |
| **Chemicals and related products** | 159.3 | 201.4 | 176.5 |
| **Basic manufactures** | 1,047.4 | 1,033.2 | 785.4 |
| Textile yarn, fabrics, etc. | 619.2 | 570.1 | 425.3 |
| Textile yarn | 387.1 | 322.2 | 204.0 |
| Cotton yarn | 378.1 | 304.8 | 192.5 |
| Woven cotton fabrics (excl. narrow or special fabrics) | 121.3 | 109.2 | 88.7 |
| Unbleached fabrics (not mercerized) | 111.7 | 105.9 | 83.8 |
| Iron and steel | 134.8 | 159.8 | 68.8 |
| Non-ferrous metals | 168.3 | 199.8 | n.a. |
| Aluminium and aluminium alloys | 167.3 | n.a. | n.a. |
| Unwrought aluminium and alloys | 27.9 | 149.7 | 164.7 |
| Worked aluminium and alloys | 139.4 | 47.8 | 20.3 |
| Aluminium bars, wire, etc. | 125.6 | 9.2 | 6.7 |
| Other metal manufactures | 70.7 | 47.5 | 44.0 |
| **Miscellaneous manufactured articles** | 305.4 | 331.4 | 325.9 |
| Clothing and accessories (excl. footwear) | 230.7 | 252.5 | 239.2 |
| Knitted or crocheted undergarments (incl. foundation garments of non-knitted fabrics) | 73.0 | n.a. | n.a. |
| Cotton undergarments, non-elastic | 72.9 | n.a. | n.a. |
| **Total** (incl. others) | 3,474.5 | 3,444.1 | 3,532.5 |

**PRINCIPAL TRADING PARTNERS**
(countries of consignment, US $ million)

| Imports c.i.f. | 1994 | 1995 | 1996 |
|---|---|---|---|
| Argentina | 93.5 | 115.1 | 237.5 |
| Australia | 403.3 | 82.4 | 386.0 |
| Belgium-Luxembourg | 214.6 | 236.8 | 211.8 |
| Brazil | 158.2 | 189.9 | 265.5 |
| China, People's Repub. | 194.5 | 295.9 | 283.4 |
| Denmark | 96.3 | 95.0 | 94.1 |
| Finland | 135.7 | 183.0 | 166.3 |
| France (incl. Monaco) | 592.6 | 685.2 | 576.6 |
| Germany | 913.9 | 1,044.6 | 1,088.6 |
| India | 123.9 | 170.6 | 184.3 |
| Ireland | 200.3 | 217.9 | 131.7 |
| Italy | 614.0 | 731.1 | 870.4 |
| Japan | 401.2 | 314.0 | 344.7 |
| Korea, Republic | 107.1 | 2.0 | 0.2 |
| Malaysia | 93.7 | 220.4 | 240.9 |
| Netherlands | 285.7 | 381.4 | 363.3 |
| Romania | 121.5 | 160.4 | 197.0 |
| Russia | 273.9 | 405.3 | 370.5 |
| Saudi Arabia | 194.2 | 249.0 | 290.4 |
| Spain | 143.1 | 184.4 | 210.7 |
| Sweden | 157.6 | 259.6 | 306.5 |
| Switzerland-Liechtenstein | 211.6 | 311.9 | 333.9 |
| Turkey | 143.4 | 179.6 | 352.7 |
| United Kingdom | 349.8 | 379.8 | 441.1 |
| USA | 1,616.9 | 2,211.0 | 2,607.2 |
| **Total** (incl. others) | 9,592.0 | 11,738.8 | 13,012.1 |

| Exports f.o.b. | 1994 | 1995 | 1996 |
|---|---|---|---|
| Belgium-Luxembourg | 71.3 | 110.4 | 50.5 |
| France (incl. Monaco) | 138.3 | 144.2 | 144.0 |
| Germany | 209.8 | 207.0 | 162.8 |
| Greece | 117.2 | 137.3 | 142.3 |
| India | 66.1 | 53.0 | 14.1 |
| Israel | 188.3 | 173.6 | 343.4 |
| Italy | 426.7 | 458.8 | 438.1 |
| Japan | 49.8 | 43.7 | 41.3 |
| Jordan | 21.0 | 30.9 | 44.6 |
| Korea, Republic | 106.3 | 0.0 | 0.2 |
| Lebanon | 35.1 | 43.4 | 33.0 |
| Libya | 44.1 | 52.9 | 51.7 |
| Netherlands | 207.2 | 166.7 | 364.6 |
| Romania | 43.4 | 41.3 | 36.9 |
| Russia | 41.0 | 31.9 | 37.7 |
| Saudi Arabia | 155.1 | 113.1 | 122.7 |
| Singapore | 146.7 | 92.8 | 90.0 |
| Spain | 149.1 | 157.1 | 98.2 |
| Syria | 57.5 | 56.1 | 55.0 |
| Turkey | 71.5 | 82.7 | 115.2 |
| United Arab Emirates | 40.8 | 41.0 | 44.4 |
| United Kingdom | 144.0 | 142.4 | 165.3 |
| USA | 364.6 | 521.8 | 459.7 |
| **Total** (incl. others) | 3,474.5 | 3,444.1 | 3,532.5 |

Source: partly UN, *International Trade Statistics Yearbook*.

# Transport

**RAILWAYS** (traffic, year ending 30 June)

| | 1995/96 | 1996/97 | 1997/98* |
|---|---|---|---|
| Passenger-km (million) | 50,665 | 52,929 | 56,667 |

* Estimate.

**1993/94:** Freight ton-km (million): 3,621 (Source: UN, *Statistical Yearbook*).

**ROAD TRAFFIC** (licensed motor vehicles in use at 31 December)

| | 1995* | 1996 | 1997 |
|---|---|---|---|
| Passenger cars | 1,280,000 | 1,099,583 | 1,154,753 |
| Buses and coaches | 36,630 | 39,781 | 43,740 |
| Lorries and vans | 387,000 | 489,542 | 510,766 |
| Motorcycles and mopeds | 397,000 | 427,864 | 439,756 |

* Estimates from IRF, *World Road Statistics*.

**SHIPPING**

**Merchant Fleet** (registered at 31 December)

| | 1996 | 1997 | 1998 |
|---|---|---|---|
| Number of vessels | 375 | 378 | 379 |
| Displacement ('000 grt) | 1,230 | 1,288 | 1,368 |

Source: Lloyd's Register of Shipping, *World Fleet Statistics*.

**International sea-borne freight traffic** ('000 metric tons, incl. ships' stores, 1997): Goods loaded 12,411; Goods unloaded 39,963 (Source: UN, *Monthly Bulletin of Statistics*).

**Suez Canal Traffic**

| | 1996 | 1997 | 1998 |
|---|---|---|---|
| Transits (number) | 14,731 | 14,430 | 13,472 |
| Displacement ('000 net tons) | 354,974 | 368,720 | 386,099 |
| Northbound goods traffic ('000 metric tons) | 136,092 | 144,448 | 160,368 |
| Southbound goods traffic ('000 metric tons) | 145,923 | 151,456 | 118,107 |
| Net tonnage of tankers ('000) | 80,895 | 78,012 | 89,976 |

Source: Suez Canal Authority.

**CIVIL AVIATION** (traffic on scheduled services)

| | 1993 | 1994 | 1995 |
|---|---|---|---|
| Kilometres flown (million) | 44 | 54 | 55 |
| Passengers carried ('000) | 2,881 | 3,538 | 3,897 |
| Passenger-km (million) | 5,277 | 6,324 | 7,678 |
| Total ton-km (million) | 606 | 763 | 864 |

Source: UN, *Statistical Yearbook.*

# Tourism

**ARRIVALS BY NATIONALITY** ('000)*

| | 1994 | 1995 | 1996 |
|---|---|---|---|
| Belgium, Luxembourg and Netherlands | 53.1 | 84.4 | 133.1 |
| France | 77.2 | 122.2 | 242.2 |
| Germany | 242.1 | 319.3 | 436.8 |
| Israel | 213.2 | 295.9 | 321.1 |
| Italy | 145.7 | 257.3 | 366.3 |
| Japan | 58.7 | 69.3 | 89.8 |
| Kuwait | 75.7 | 70.8 | 76.2 |
| Libya | 146.8 | 156.9 | 150.9 |
| Palestine | 138.0 | 99.3 | 143.0 |
| Saudi Arabia | 234.8 | 179.5 | 216.2 |
| Sudan | 73.0 | 46.1 | 27.1 |
| Switzerland | 45.2 | 72.2 | 98.3 |
| Syria | 67.7 | 72.6 | 68.5 |
| USSR (former) | 67.2 | 111.8 | 124.9 |
| United Kingdom | 231.8 | 292.2 | 328.2 |
| USA | 125.5 | 154.9 | 174.7 |
| **Total** (incl. others) | 2,581.8 | 3,133.5 | 3,895.9 |

* Figures refer to arrivals at frontiers of visitors from abroad. Excluding same-day visitors (excursionists), the total number of tourist arrivals (in '000) was: 2,356 in 1994; 2,872 in 1995; 3,528 in 1996.

Source: World Tourism Organization, *Yearbook of Tourism Statistics.*

**Total arrivals** ('000): 3,961.4 in 1997; 3,453.8 in 1998.
**Tourism receipts** (£E million): 4,614.3 in 1994; 4,262.8 in 1995; 5,043.4 in 1996; 5,837.8 in 1997; 4,062.9 in 1998.

# Communications Media

| | 1994 | 1995 | 1996 |
|---|---|---|---|
| Radio receivers ('000 in use) | 18,950 | 19,400 | 20,000 |
| Television receivers ('000 in use) | 6,700 | 6,850 | 7,500 |
| Daily newspapers: | | | |
| Number | 17 | 15 | 17 |
| Average circulation ('000 copies) | 3,949 | 2,373 | 2,400 |
| Telephones ('000 main lines in use)* | 2,456 | 2,716 | n.a. |
| Telefax stations (number in use) | 21,591 | n.a. | n.a. |
| Mobile cellular telephones (subscribers) | 7,371 | 7,368 | n.a. |

* Year ending 30 June.

**Book production** (1995): 2,215 titles; 92,353,000 copies.

Sources: UNESCO, *Statistical Yearbook*; UN, *Statistical Yearbook.*

# Education

(1998/99)

| | Schools | Teachers | Students* |
|---|---|---|---|
| Pre-primary | 3,172 | 14,894 | 289,995 |
| Primary | 15,566 | 314,528 | 8,243,137 |
| Prepatory | 7,325 | 193,469 | 3,679,325 |
| Secondary | | | |
| General | 1,562 | 79,218 | 830,562 |
| Technical | 1,767 | 145,050 | 1,659,035 |
| Higher† | 356 | n.a. | 1,316,491 |

* 1996/97 figures. Source: partly UNESCO, *Statistical Yearbook.*
† Official estimates.

Source: Ministry of Education.

**Al-Azhar** (1996/97): *Primary:* 2,370 schools; 701,398 students. *Preparatory:* 1,408 schools; 274,300 students. *Secondary:* 742 schools; 154,157 students.

# Directory

## The Constitution

A new Constitution for the Arab Republic of Egypt was approved by referendum on 11 September 1971.

### THE STATE

Egypt is an Arab Republic with a democratic, socialist system based on the alliance of the working people and derived from the country's historical heritage and the spirit of Islam.

The Egyptian people are part of the Arab nation, who work towards total Arab unity.

Islam is the religion of the State; Arabic is its official language and the Islamic code is a principal source of legislation. The State safeguards the freedom of worship and of performing rites for all religions.

Sovereignty is of the people alone which is the source of all powers.

The protection, consolidation and preservation of the socialist gains is a national duty: the sovereignty of law is the basis of the country's rule, and the independence of immunity of the judiciary are basic guarantees for the protection of rights and liberties.

### THE FUNDAMENTAL ELEMENTS OF SOCIETY

Social solidarity is the basis of Egyptian society, and the family is its nucleus.

The State ensures the equality of men and women in both political and social rights in line with the provisions of Muslim legislation.

Work is a right, an honour and a duty which the State guarantees together with the services of social and health insurance, pensions for incapacity and unemployment.

The economic basis of the Republic is a socialist democratic system based on sufficiency and justice in a manner preventing exploitation.

Ownership is of three kinds: public, co-operative and private. The public sector assumes the main responsibility for the regulation and growth of the national economy under the development plan.

Property is subject to the people's control.

Private ownership is safeguarded and may not be sequestrated except in cases specified in law nor expropriated except for the general good against fair legal compensation. The right of inheritance is guaranteed in it.

Nationalization shall only be allowed for considerations of public interest in accordance with the law and against compensation.

Agricultural holding may be limited by law.

The State follows a comprehensive central planning and compulsory planning approach based on quinquennial socio-economic and cultural development plans whereby the society's resources are mobilized and put to the best use.

The public sector assumes the leading role in the development of the national economy. The State provides absolute protection of this sector as well as the property of co-operative societies and trade unions against all attempts to tamper with them.

### PUBLIC LIBERTIES, RIGHTS AND DUTIES

All citizens are equal before the law. Personal liberty is a natural right and no one may be arrested, searched, imprisoned or restricted in any way without a court order.

Houses have sanctity, and shall not be placed under surveillance or searched without a court order with reasons given for such action.

The law safeguards the sanctities of the private lives of all citizens; so have all postal, telegraphic, telephonic and other means of communication which may not therefore be confiscated, or perused except by a court order giving the reasons, and only for a specified period.

Public rights and freedoms are also inviolate and all calls for atheism and anything that reflects adversely on divine religions are prohibited.

The freedom of opinion, the Press, printing and publications and all information media are safeguarded.

Press censorship is forbidden, so are warnings, suspensions or cancellations through administrative channels. Under exceptional circumstances, as in cases of emergency or in wartime, censorship may be imposed on information media for a definite period.

Egyptians have the right to permanent or provisional emigration and no Egyptian may be deported or prevented from returning to the country.

Citizens have the right to private meetings in peace provided they bear no arms. Egyptians also have the right to form societies which have no secret activities. Public meetings are also allowed within the limits of the law.

### SOVEREIGNTY OF THE LAW

All acts of crime should be specified together with the penalties for the acts.

Recourse to justice is a right of all citizens. Those who are financially unable will be assured of means to defend their rights.

Except in cases of *flagrante delicto,* no person may be arrested or their freedom restricted unless an order authorizing arrest has been given by the competent judge or the public prosecution in accordance with the provisions of law.

### SYSTEM OF GOVERNMENT

The President, who must be of Egyptian parentage and at least 40 years old, is nominated by at least one-third of the members of the People's Assembly, approved by at least two-thirds, and elected by popular referendum. His term is for six years and he 'may be re-elected for another subsequent term'. He may take emergency measures in the interests of the State but these measures must be approved by referendum within 60 days.

The People's Assembly, elected for five years, is the legislative body and approves general policy, the budget and the development plan. It shall have 'not less than 350' elected members, at least half of whom shall be workers or farmers, and the President may appoint up to 10 additional members. In exceptional circumstances the Assembly, by a two-thirds vote, may authorize the President to rule by decree for a specified period but these decrees must be approved by the Assembly at its next meeting. The law governing the composition of the People's Assembly was amended in May 1979 (see People's Assembly, below).

The Assembly may pass a vote of no confidence in a Deputy Prime Minister, a Minister or a Deputy Minister, provided three days' notice of the vote is given, and the Minister must then resign. In the case of the Prime Minister, the Assembly may 'prescribe' his responsibility and submit a report to the President: if the President disagrees with the report but the Assembly persists, then the matter is put to a referendum: if the people support the President the Assembly is dissolved; if they support the Assembly the President must accept the resignation of the Government. The President may dissolve the Assembly prematurely, but his action must be approved by a referendum and elections must be held within 60 days.

Executive Authority is vested in the President, who may appoint one or more Vice-Presidents and appoints all Ministers. He may also dismiss the Vice-Presidents and Ministers. The President has 'the right to refer to the people in connection with important matters related to the country's higher interests.' The Government is described as 'the supreme executive and administrative organ of the state'. Its members, whether full Ministers or Deputy Ministers, must be at least 35 years old. Further sections define the roles of Local Government, Specialized National Councils, the Judiciary, the Higher Constitutional Court, the Socialist Prosecutor-General, the Armed Forces and National Defence Council and the Police.

### POLITICAL PARTIES

In June 1977 the People's Assembly adopted a new law on political parties, which, subject to certain conditions, permitted the formation of political parties for the first time since 1953. The law was passed in accordance with Article Five of the Constitution which describes the political system as 'a multi-party one' with four main parties: 'the ruling National Democratic Party, the Socialist Workers (the official opposition), the Liberal Socialists and the Unionist Progressive'. (The legality of the re-formed New Wafd Party was established by the courts in January 1984.)

### 1980 AMENDMENTS

On 30 April 1980 the People's Assembly passed a number of amendments, which were subsequently massively approved at a referendum the following month. A summary of the amendments follows:

(i) the regime in Egypt is socialist-democratic, based on the alliance of working people's forces.

(ii) the political system depends on multiple political parties; the Arab Socialist Union is therefore abolished.

(iii) the President is elected for a six-year term and can be elected for 'other terms'.

(iv) the President shall appoint a Consultative Council to preserve the principles of the revolutions of 23 July 1952 and 15 May 1971.

(v) a Supreme Press Council shall safeguard the freedom of the press, check government censorship and look after the interests of journalists.

(vi) Egypt's adherence to Islamic jurisprudence is affirmed. Christians and Jews are subject to their own jurisdiction in personal status affairs.

(vii) there will be no distinction of race or religion.

# The Government

### THE PRESIDENCY

**President:** MUHAMMAD HOSNI MUBARAK (confirmed as President by referendum, 13 October 1981, after assassination of President Sadat; re-elected and confirmed by referendum, 5 October 1987, 4 October 1993 and 26 September 1999).

### COUNCIL OF MINISTERS
(February 2000)

**Prime Minister:** Dr ATIF MUHAMMAD OBEID.

**Deputy Prime Minister and Minister of Agriculture and Land Reclamation:** Dr YOUSUF AMIN WALI.

**Minister of Defence and of Military Production:** Field Marshal MUHAMMAD HUSSAIN TANTAWI.

**Minister of Information:** MUHAMMAD SAFWAT MUHAMMAD YOUSUF ASH-SHARIF.

**Minister of Foreign Affairs:** AMR MUHAMMAD MOUSSA.

**Minister of Justice:** FAROUK MAHMOUD SAYF AN-NASR.

**Minister of Culture:** FAROUK ABD AL-AZIZ HOSNI.

**Minister of Education:** Dr HUSSAIN KAMAL BAHA ED-DIN.

**Minister of Economy and Foreign Trade:** Dr YOUSUF BOUTROS-GHALI.

**Minister of Tourism:** Dr MUHAMMAD MAMDOUH AHMAD EL-BELTAGI.

**Minister of Construction, Housing and New Urban Communities:** Dr Eng. MUHAMMAD IBRAHIM SULAYMAN.

**Minister of Labour and Migration:** AHMAD AHMAD EL-AMAWI.

**Minister of Awqaf (Islamic Endowments):** Dr MAHMOUD HAMDI ZAKZOUK.

**Minister of Health and Population:** Dr ISMAIL AWADALLAH SALAM.

**Minister of Higher Education and Scientific Research:** Dr MUFID MAHMOUD SHEHAB.

**Minister of Public Works and Water Resources:** Dr MAHMOUD ABD AL-HALIM ABU ZEID.

**Minister of the Interior:** Maj.-Gen. HABIB IBRAHIM EL-ADLI.

**Minister of Insurance and Social Affairs:** Dr AMINAH HAMZEH MAHMOUD AL-JUNDI.

**Minister of Industry and Technological Development:** Dr MOUSTAFA MUHAMMAD OSMAN AR-RIFA'I.

**Minister of Electricity and Energy:** Dr ALI FAHMI IBRAHIM AS-SA'IDI.

**Minister of Transport:** Dr IBRAHIM MUHAMMAD MUTAWALLI AD-DUMEIRI.

**Minister of Youth:** Dr ALI AD-DIN HELAL AD-DASUQI.

**Minister of Supply and Internal Trade:** Dr HASSAN ALI KHIDR.

**Minister of Planning and Minister of State for International Co-operation:** Dr AHMAD MAHRUS AD-DARSH.

**Minister of the Public Enterprise Sector:** Dr MUKHTAR ABD AL-MUN'IM KHATTAB.

**Minister of Finance:** Dr MUHAMMAD MIDHAT ABD AL-ATTI HASANAYN.

**Minister of Communications and Information Technology:** Dr AHMAD MAHMOUD MUHAMMAD NAZIF.

**Minister of Petroleum:** Dr AMIN SAMIH SAMIR FAHMI.

**Minister of State for Parliamentary Affairs:** KAMAL MUHAMMAD ASH-SHAZLI.

**Minister of State for Administrative Development:** Dr MUHAMMAD ZAKI ABU AMER.

**Minister of State for Environmental Affairs:** Dr NADIA RIAD MAKRAM OBEID.

**Minister of State for Local Development:** MOUSTAFA MUHAMMAD ABD AL-QADIR.

**Minister of State for Military Production:** Dr SAID ABDUH MOUSTAFA MASH'AL.

**Cabinet Secretary:** AHMAD HASSAN ABU TALEB.

### MINISTRIES

**Office of the Prime Minister:** Sharia Majlis ash-Sha'ab, Cairo; tel. (2) 3553192; fax (2) 3558016.

**Ministry of Administrative Development:** Sharia Salah Salem, Cairo (Nasr City); tel. (2) 4022910; fax (2) 2614126.

**Ministry of Agriculture and Land Reclamation:** Sharia Nadi es-Sayed, Dokki, Giza; tel. (2) 3772566; fax (2) 3498128; internet www.agri.gov.eg.

**Ministry of Awqaf (Islamic Endowments):** Sharia Sabri Abu Alam, Bab el-Louk, Cairo; tel. (2) 3929403; fax 3900362; e-mail mawkaf@idsc1.gov.eg.

**Ministry of Communications and Information Technology:** Ramses Sq., Cairo; tel. (2) 5770000; fax (2) 5744215.

**Ministry of Construction, Housing and New Urban Communities:** 1 Ismail Abaza, Sharia Qasr el-Eini, Cairo; tel. (2) 3553468; fax (2) 3557836; e-mail mhuuc@idsc1.gov.eg.

**Ministry of Culture:** 2 Sharia Shagaret ed-Dor, Cairo (Zamalek); tel. (2) 3320761; fax (2) 3406449; e-mail mculture@idsc.gov.eg.

**Ministry of Defence:** Sharia 23 July, Kobri el-Kobra, Cairo; tel. (2) 2602566; fax (2) 2916227; e-mail mod@idsc1.gov.eg.

**Ministry of Economy and Foreign Trade:** 8 Sharia Adly, Cairo; tel. (2) 3919661; fax (2) 3903029; e-mail mineco@idsc.gov.eg; internet www.economy.gov.eg.

**Ministry of Education:** 4 Sharia Ibrahim Nagiv, Cairo (Garden City); tel. (2) 5787643; fax (2) 3562952; e-mail moe@idsc.gov.eg.

**Ministry of Electricity and Energy:** Sharia Ramses, Abbassia, Cairo (Nasr City); tel. (2) 2616317; fax (2) 2616302; e-mail mee@idsc.gov.eg.

**Ministry of the Environment:** 30 Sharia Helwan, Cairo; tel. (2) 5256463; fax (2) 5256461.

**Ministry of Finance:** Justice and Finance Bldg, Sharia Majlis ash-Sha'ab, Lazoughli Sq., Cairo; tel. (2) 3541055; fax (2) 3551537; e-mail mofinance@idsc1.gov.eg.

**Ministry of Foreign Affairs:** Corniche en-Nil, Cairo (Maspiro); tel. (2) 5749816; fax (2) 5749533; e-mail minexter@idsc1.gov.eg; internet www.mfa.gov.eg.

**Ministry of Health and Population:** Sharia Majlis ash-Sha'ab, Lazoughli Sq., Cairo; tel. (2) 3541507; fax (2) 3553966; e-mail moh@idsc.gov.eg.

**Ministry of Higher Education and Scientific Research:** 101 Sharia Qasr el-Eini, Cairo; tel. (2) 3556962; fax (2) 3541005; e-mail mheducat@idsc.gov.eg.

**Ministry of Industry and Technological Development:** 2 Sharia Latin America, Cairo (Garden City); tel. (2) 3557034; fax (2) 3555025; e-mail moimw@idsc1.gov.eg.

**Ministry of Information:** Radio and TV Bldg, Corniche en-Nil, Cairo (Maspiro); tel. (2) 5748984; fax (2) 5748981; e-mail rtu@idsc.gov.eg.

**Ministry of Insurance and Social Affairs:** Sharia Sheikh Rihan, Bab el-Louk, Cairo; tel. (2) 3370039; fax (2) 3375390; e-mail msi@idsc.gov.eg.

**Ministry of the Interior:** Sharia Sheikh Rihan, Bab el-Louk, Cairo; tel. (2) 3557500; fax (2) 5792031; e-mail moi2@idsc.gov.eg.

**Ministry of Justice:** Justice and Finance Bldg, Sharia Majlis ash-Sha'ab, Lazoughli Sq., Cairo; tel. (2) 3551176; fax (2) 3555700; e-mail mojeb@idsc1.gov.eg.

**Ministry of Labour and Migration:** 3 Sharia Yousuf Abbas, Abbassia, Cairo (Nasr City); tel. (2) 4042910; fax (2) 2609891; e-mail mwlabor@idsc1.gov.eg; internet www.emigration.gov.eg.

**Ministry of Local Development:** Sharia Nadi es-Seid, Cairo (Dokki); tel. (2) 3497470; fax (2) 3497788.

**Ministry of Maritime Transport:** 4 Sharia Ptolemy, Alexandria; tel. (3) 4842119; fax (3) 4842096.

**Ministry of Military Production:** 5 Sharia Ismail Abaza, Qasr el-Eini, Cairo; tel. (2) 3552428; fax (2) 3548739.

**Ministry of Parliamentary Affairs:** Sharia Majlis ash-Sha'ab, Lazoughli Sq., Cairo; tel. (2) 3557750; fax (2) 3557681.

**Ministry of Petroleum:** Sharia el-Mokhayem ed-Dayem, Cairo (Nasr City); tel. (2) 2631010; fax (2) 2636060; e-mail mopm@idsc1.gov.eg.

**Ministry of Planning:** Sharia Salah Salem, Cairo (Nasr City); tel. (2) 4014615; fax (2) 4014733.

**Ministry of the Public Enterprise Sector:** Sharia Majlis ash-Sha'ab, Lazoughli Sq., Cairo; tel. (2) 3558026; fax (2) 3555882; e-mail mops@idsc.gov.eg.

**Ministry of Public Works and Water Resources:** Sharia Corniche en-Nil, Imbaba, Cairo; tel. (2) 3123304; fax (2) 3123357; e-mail mpwwr@idsc.gov.eg; internet www.starnet.com.eg/mpwwr.

**Ministry of Supply and Internal Trade:** 99 Sharia Qasr el-Eini, Cairo; tel. (2) 3557598; fax (2) 3544973; e-mail msit@idsc.gov.eg.

**Ministry of Tourism:** Misr Travel Tower, Abbassia Sq., Cairo; tel. (2) 2828439; fax (2) 2859551; e-mail mol@idsc.gov.eg; internet www.touregypt.net.

**Ministry of Transport:** 105 Sharia Qasr el-Eini, Cairo; tel. (2) 3555566; fax (2) 3555564; e-mail garb@idsc.gov.eg.

## Legislature

### MAJLIS ASH-SHA'AB

(People's Assembly)

There are 222 constituencies, which each elect two deputies to the Assembly. Ten deputies are appointed by the President, giving a total of 454 seats.

**Speaker:** Dr AHMAD FATHI SURUR.

**Deputy Speakers:** Dr ABD AL-AHAD GAMAL AD-DIN, AHMAD ABU ZEID, Dr AMAL UTHMAN.

**Elections, 29 November and 6 December 1995**

| | Seats |
|---|---|
| National Democratic Party* | 316 |
| New Wafd Party | 6 |
| National Progressive Unionist Party | 5 |
| Liberal Socialist Party | 1 |
| Nasserist Party | 1 |
| Independents | 115 |
| **Total†** | 444 |

* Official candidates of the National Democratic Party (NDP) gained 316 seats in the two rounds of voting. However, after the elections it was reported that 99 of the 115 candidates who had successfully contested the elections as independents had either joined or rejoined the NDP.

† There are, in addition, 10 deputies appointed by the President.

### MAJLIS ASH-SHURA

(Advisory Council)

In September 1980 elections were held for a 210-member **Shura (Advisory) Council**, which replaced the former Central Committee of the Arab Socialist Union. Of the total number of members, 140 are elected and the remaining 70 are appointed by the President. The opposition parties boycotted elections to the Council in October 1983, and again in October 1986, in protest against the 8% electoral threshold. In June 1989 elections to 153 of the Council's 210 seats were contested by opposition parties (the 'Islamic Alliance', consisting of the Muslim Brotherhood, the LSP and the SLP). However, all of the seats in which voting produced a result (143) were won by the NDP. NDP candidates won 88 of the 90 seats on the Council to which mid-term elections were held in June 1995. The remaining two elective seats were gained by independent candidates. On 21 June new appointments were made to 47 vacant, non-elective seats. Mid-term elections to the Council were held again in June 1998. The NDP won 85 of the 88 contested seats, while independent candidates won the remaining three seats. Most opposition parties chose not to contest the elections.

**Speaker:** Dr MUSTAFA KAMAL HELMI.

**Deputy Speakers:** THARWAT ABAZAH, AHMAD AL-IMADI.

## Political Organizations

**Democratic People's Party:** f. 1992; Chair. ANWAR AFIFI.

**Democratic Unionist Party:** f. 1990; Pres. IBRAHIM ABD AL-MONEIM TURK.

**Et-Takaful (Solidarity):** f. 1995; advocates imposition of 'solidarity' tax on the rich in order to provide needs of the poor; Chair. Dr USAMA MUHAMMAD SHALTOUT.

**Green Party:** f. 1990; Chair. Dr ABD AL-MONEIM EL-AASAR.

**Ikhwan** (Brotherhood): f. 1928; officially illegal, the (Muslim) Brotherhood advocates the adoption of the *Shari'a*, or Islamic law, as the sole basis of the Egyptian legal system; Sec.-Gen. MAAMOUN AL-HODAIBY.

**Liberal Socialist Party (LSP):** Cairo; f. 1976; advocates expansion of 'open door' economic policy and greater freedom for private enterprise and the press; Leader (vacant).

**Misr el-Fatah** (Young Egypt Party): f. 1990; Chair. GAMAL RABIE.

**Nasserist Party:** Cairo; f. 1991; Chair. DIAA ED-DIN DAOUD.

**National Democratic Party (NDP):** Cairo; f. 1978; government party established by Anwar Sadat; has absorbed Arab Socialist

Party; Leader MUHAMMAD HOSNI MUBARAK; Sec.-Gen. Dr YOUSUF AMIN WALI; Political Bureau: Chair. MUHAMMAD HOSNI MUBARAK.

**National Progressive Unionist Party** (Tagammu): 1 Sharia Karim ed-Dawlah, Cairo; f. 1976; left-wing; Leader KHALED MOHI ED-DIN; Sec. Dr RIFA'AT ES-SAID; 160,000 mems.

**New Wafd Party** (The Delegation): Cairo; original Wafd Party f. 1919; banned 1952; re-formed as New Wafd Party Feb. 1978; disbanded June 1978; re-formed 1983; Leader MUHAMMAD FOUAD SERAG ED-DIN; Sec.-Gen. IBRAHIM FARAG.

**Social Justice Party:** f. 1993; Chair. MUHAMMAD ABD AL-AAL.

**Socialist Labour Party (SLP):** 12 Sharia Awali el-Ahd, Cairo; f. 1978; official opposition party; Leader IBRAHIM SHUKRI; Dep. Chair. ADIL HUSSEIN.

The following organizations are proscribed by the Government:

**Islamic Jihad** (Holy Struggle): militant Islamist grouping established following the imposition of a ban on the Muslim Brotherhood.

**Jama'ah al-Islamiyah** (Islamic Group): militant Islamist group founded following the imposition of a ban on the Muslim Brotherhood; declared a cease-fire in March 1999; Spiritual Leader Sheikh OMAR ABD AR-RAHMAN; Chair. of the Shura Council RIFA'I AHMAD TAHA; Mil. Cmmdr ALA ABD AR-RAQIL.

**Muslim Brotherhood:** f. 1928 with the aim of establishing an Islamic society; banned in 1954; moderate; Dep. Supreme Guide MA'MUN AL-HUDA BI.

**Vanguards of Conquest:** militant Islamist grouping; breakaway group from Islamic Jihad; Leader YASIR AS-SIRRI.

# Diplomatic Representation

## EMBASSIES IN EGYPT

**Afghanistan:** 59 Sharia el-Orouba, Cairo (Heliopolis); tel. and fax (2) 417728; Ambassador: SAYED FAZLULLAH FAZIL.

**Albania:** 29 Sharia Ismail Muhammad, Cairo (Zamalek); tel. (2) 3415651; Ambassador: ARBEN PANDI CICI.

**Algeria:** 14 Sharia Bresil, Cairo (Zamalek); tel. (2) 3418527; Ambassador: MUHAMMAD ABRAHIMI EL-MILY.

**Angola:** 12 Fouad Mohi ed-Din Sq., Mohandessin, Cairo; tel. (2) 3498259; fax (2) 3378683; Ambassador: HERMINO JOAQUIM ESCORCIO.

**Argentina:** 8 Sharia es-Saleh Ayoub, Cairo (Zamalek); tel. (2) 3401501; fax (2) 3414355; e-mail argemb@idsc.gov.eg; Ambassador: DOMINGO CULLEN.

**Armenia:** 20 Sharia Muhammad Mazhar, Cairo (Zamalek); tel. (2) 3424157; fax (2) 3424158; e-mail armenemb@idsc.gov.eg; Ambassador: Dr EDWARD NALBANDIAN.

**Australia:** 11th Floor, World Trade Centre, Corniche en-Nil, Cairo 11111 (Boulac); tel. (2) 5750444; fax (2) 5781638; e-mail cairo .austremb@dfat.gov.au; Ambassador: VICTORIA OWEN.

**Austria:** 5th Floor, Riyadh Tower, 5 Sharia Wissa Wassef, cnr of Sharia en-Nil, Cairo 11111 (Giza); tel. (2) 5702975; fax (2) 5702979; e-mail aec@gega.net; Ambassador: FERDINAND TRAUTTMANSDORFF.

**Bahrain:** 8 Sharia Gamiet an-Nisr, Cairo (Dokki); tel. (2) 3407996; Ambassador: EBRAHIM AL-MAJED.

**Bangladesh:** 47 Sharia Ahmad Heshmat, Cairo (Zamalek); tel. (2) 3412645; fax (2) 3402401; e-mail bdoot@wnet1.worldnet.com.eg; Ambassador: RUHUL AMIN.

**Belarus:** 12–49 Misakha Sq., Cairo (Dokki); tel. and fax (2) 3493743; Chargé d'affaires: IGOR LESCHENYA.

**Belgium:** 20 Sharia Kamal esh-Shennawi, Cairo (Garden City); tel. (2) 3547494; Ambassador: ALAIN RENS.

**Bolivia:** Cairo; tel. and fax (2) 3546390; Ambassador: HERNANDO VELASCO.

**Bosnia and Herzegovina:** 26 July Square, Cairo (Agouza); tel. (2) 3474514; fax (2) 3456029; e-mail ebihebosnia@isdc.gov.eg; Chargé d'affaires a.i.: AVDIJA HADROVIĆ.

**Brazil:** 1125 Corniche en-Nil, Cairo 11561 (Maspiro); tel. (2) 5756938; fax (2) 761040; e-mail brazemb@idsc.gov.eg; Ambassador: VIRGILIO MORETZSOHN DE ANDRADE.

**Brunei:** 24 Sharia Hassan Assem, Cairo (Dokki); tel. (2) 3406656; Ambassador: (vacant).

**Bulgaria:** 6 Sharia el-Malek el-Ajdal, Cairo (Dokki); tel. (2) 3413025; fax (2) 3413826; Ambassador: PETKO DIMITROV.

**Burkina Faso:** POB 306, Ramses Centre, 9 Sharia el-Fawakeh, Mohandessin, Cairo; tel. (2) 3379098; fax (2) 3495310; Ambassador: AMADÉ OUÉDRAOGO.

**Burundi:** 22 Sharia en-Nakhil, Madinet ed-Dobbat, Cairo (Dokki); tel. (2) 3373078; Ambassador: GERVAIS NDIKUMAGNEGE.

**Cambodia:** 2 Sharia Tahawia, Cairo (Giza); tel. (2) 3489966; Ambassador: IN SOPHEAP.

**Cameroon:** POB 2061, 15 Sharia Israa, Madinet el-Mohandessin, Cairo; tel. (2) 3441101; fax (2) 3459208; Ambassador: MOUCHILI NJI MFOUAYO.

**Canada:** POB 1667, 5 Midan es-Saraya el-Kobra, Cairo (Garden City); tel. (2) 3543110; fax (2) 3563548; e-mail cairo@cairo01.x400.gc.ca; Ambassador: MARIE-ANDRÉE BEAUCHEMIN.

**Central African Republic:** 41 Sharia Mahmoud Azmy, Mohandessin, Cairo (Dokki); tel. (2) 3446873; Ambassador: HENRY KOBA.

**Chad:** POB 1869, 12 Midan ar-Refaï, Cairo 11511 (Dokki); tel. (2) 3373379; fax (2) 3373232; Ambassador: ADOUM ATTIMER.

**Chile:** 5 Sharia Shagaret ed-Dor, Cairo (Zamalek); tel. (2) 3408711; fax (2) 3403716; e-mail chilemb@idsc.gov.eg; Ambassador: NELSON HADAD HERESI.

**China, People's Republic:** 14 Sharia Bahgat Aly, Cairo (Zamalek); tel. (2) 3417691; e-mail chinaemb@idsc.gov.eg; Ambassador: AN HUIHOU.

**Colombia:** 6 Sharia Gueriza, Cairo (Zamalek); tel. (2) 3414203; fax (2) 3407429; e-mail colombemb@idsc.gov.eg; Ambassador: JAIME GIRÓN DUARTE.

**Congo, Democratic Republic:** 5 Sharia Mansour Muhammad, Cairo (Zamalek); tel. (2) 3403662; Ambassador: KAMIMBAYA WA DJONDO.

**Côte d'Ivoire:** 39 Sharia el-Kods esh-Sherif, Madinet el-Mohandessin, Cairo (Dokki); tel. (2) 699009; Ambassador: Gen. FÉLIX ORY.

**Croatia:** 3 Abou el-Feda, Cairo (Zamalek); tel. (2) 3405815; fax (2) 3405812; Ambassador: Dr DRAGO ŠLAMBUK.

**Cuba:** 6 Sharia el-Fawakeh, Madinet el-Mohandessin, Cairo (Dokki); tel. (2) 3350564; fax (2) 3612739; e-mail cubaemb@idsc.gov.eg; Ambassador: ORLANDO MARINO LANCIS SUÁREZ.

**Cyprus:** 23A Sharia Ismail Muhammad, Cairo (Zamalek); tel. (2) 3411288; fax (2) 3415299; Ambassador: CHARALAMBOS KAPSOS.

**Czech Republic:** 4 Sharia Dokki, Cairo 12511 (Giza); tel. (2) 3485531; fax (2) 3485892; e-mail caiembcz@intouch.com; Ambassador: DANA HUŇÁTOVÁ.

**Denmark:** 12 Sharia Hassan Sabri, Cairo 11211 (Zamalek); tel. (2) 3407411; fax (2) 3411780; e-mail rdemb@idsc.gov.eg; internet www.danemb.org.eg/cairo-dk.html; Ambassador: ERLING HARILD NIELSEN.

**Djibouti:** 11 Sharia el-Gazaer, Aswan Sq., Cairo (Agouza); tel. (2) 709787; Ambassador: Sheikh ADEN HASSEN.

**Ecuador:** Suez Canal Bldg, 4 Sharia Ibn Kasir, Cairo (Giza); tel. (2) 3496782; fax (2) 3609327; e-mail ecuademb@idsc.gov.eg; Ambassador: FRANKLIN BAHAMONDE.

**Ethiopia:** 6 Sharia Abd ar-Rahman Hussein, Midan Gomhuria, Cairo (Dokki); tel. (2) 3353696; fax (2) 3353699; Ambassador: KONGIT SINEGIORGIS.

**Finland:** 3 Sharia Abou el-Feda, Cairo (Zamalek); tel. (2) 3411487; fax (2) 3405170; Ambassador: AAPO POLHO.

**France:** POB 1777, 29 Sharia Charles de Gaulle, Cairo (Giza); tel. (2) 5703916; fax (2) 5710276; Ambassador: FRANÇOIS DOPFFER.

**Gabon:** 15 Sharia Mossadek, Cairo (Dokki); tel. (2) 702963; Ambassador: MAMBO JACQUES.

**Germany:** 8B Sharia Hassan Sabri, Cairo (Zamalek); tel. (2) 3399600; fax (2) 3410530; e-mail germemb@idsc.gov.eg; internet www.german-embassy.org.eg; Ambassador: PETER MICHAEL DINGENS.

**Ghana:** 1 Sharia 26 July, Cairo (Zamalek); tel. (2) 3444000; Ambassador: BON OHANE KWAPONG.

**Greece:** 18 Sharia Aicha at-Taimouria, Cairo (Garden City); tel. (2) 3555915; fax (2) 3563903; Ambassador: GEORGE ASIMAKOPOULOS.

**Guatemala:** POB 346, 11 Sharia 10, Maadi, Cairo; tel. (2) 3752914; fax (2) 3752915; e-mail guatemb@infinity.com.eg; Ambassador: JUAN ALFREDO RENDÓN.

**Guinea:** 46 Sharia Muhammad Mazhar, Cairo (Zamalek); tel. (2) 3408109; fax (2) 3411446; Ambassador: MOHAMED TSSIOGA KOUROUMA.

**Guinea-Bissau:** 37 Sharia Lebanon, Madinet el-Mohandessin, Cairo (Dokki).

**Holy See:** Apostolic Nunciature, Safarat al-Vatican, 5 Sharia Muhammad Mazhar, Cairo (Zamalek); tel. (2) 3402250; fax (2) 3406152; e-mail nunteg@rite.com; Apostolic Nuncio: Most Rev. PAOLO GIGLIO, Titular Archbishop of Tindari.

**Hungary:** 29 Sharia Muhammad Mazhar, Cairo (Zamalek); tel. (2) 3400659; fax (2) 3408648; e-mail huembcai@commnet.com.eg; Ambassador: LÁSZLÓ KÁDÁR.

**India:** 5 Sharia Aziz Abaza, Cairo (Zamalek); tel. (2) 3413051; fax (2) 3414038; e-mail indiaemb@idsc.gov.eg; Ambassador: KENWAL GIBAL; also looks after Iraqi interests at 5 Aziz Abaza St, Cairo (Zamalek) (tel. (2) 3409815).

**Indonesia:** POB 1661, 13 Sharia Aicha at-Taimouria, Cairo (Garden City); tel. (2) 3547200; fax (2) 3562495; Ambassador: Dr BOER MAUNA.

**Iraq:** *Interests served by India.*

**Ireland:** POB 2681, 3 Sharia Abou el-Feda, Cairo (Zamalek); tel. (2) 3408264; fax (2) 3412863; e-mail irishemb@rite.com; Ambassador: PETER GUNNING.

**Israel:** 6 Sharia Ibn el-Malek, Cairo (Giza); tel. (2) 3610545; fax (2) 3610414; Ambassador: ZVI MAZEL.

**Italy:** 1079 Corniche en-Nil, Cairo (Garden City); tel. (2) 3543194; Ambassador: FRANCESCO ALOISI DE LARDEREL.

**Japan:** Cairo Centre Bldg, 2nd and 3rd Floors, 2 Sharia Abd al-Kader Hamza or 106 Sharia Qasr el-Eini, Cairo (Garden City); tel. (2) 3553962; fax (2) 3546347; e-mail center@embjapan.org.eg; Ambassador: TAKESHI OHARA.

**Jordan:** 6 Sharia Juhaini, Cairo; tel. (2) 3487543; Ambassador: NABIH AN-NIMR.

**Kazakhstan:** 4 Sharia 256, New Maadi, Cairo; tel. (2) 3508471; fax (2) 3521900; Ambassador: BOLATKHAN K. TAIZHANOV.

**Kenya:** POB 362, 7 Sharia el-Mohandes Galal, Cairo (Dokki); tel. (2) 3453628; fax (2) 3443400; Ambassador: MUHAMMAD M. MAALIM.

**Korea, Democratic People's Republic:** 6 Sharia as-Saleh Ayoub, Cairo (Zamalek); tel. (2) 650970; Ambassador: PAEK YONG-HO.

**Korea, Republic:** Cairo; Ambassador YIM SUNG-JOON.

**Kuwait:** 12 Sharia Nabil el-Wakkad, Cairo (Dokki); tel. (2) 701611; ABD AR-RAZAK ABD AL-KADER AL-KANDRI.

**Lebanon:** 22 Sharia Mansour Muhammad, Cairo (Zamalek); tel. (2) 3322823; fax (2) 3322818; Ambassador: HISHAM DIMASHKIEH.

**Liberia:** 3 Midan Amman, Cairo (Dokki); tel. (2) 3367046; fax (2) 3365701; Ambassador: Dr BRAHIMA D. KABA.

**Libya:** 7 Sharia as-Saleh Ayoub, Cairo (Zamalek); tel. (2) 3401864; Secretary of People's Bureau: AHMAD GADDAF'ADDAM.

**Malaysia:** 29 Sharia Taha Hussein, Cairo (Zamalek); tel. (2) 3410863; Ambassador: Dato RAJA MANSUR RAZMAN.

**Mali:** 3 Sharia al-Kawsar, Cairo (Dokki); tel. (2) 3371641; fax (2) 3371841; Ambassador: ALLAYE ALPHADY CISSÉ.

**Malta:** 25 Sharia 12, Maadi, Cairo; tel. (2) 3754451; fax (2) 3754452; e-mail maltaemb@idsc.gov.eg; Ambassador: GAETAN NAUDI ACIS.

**Mauritania:** 114 Mohi ed-Din, Abou-el Ezz, Mohandessin, Cairo; tel. (2) 3490671; MUHAMMAD LEMINE OULD.

**Mauritius:** 156 Sharia es-Sudan, Mohandessin, Cairo; tel. (2) 3618102; fax (2) 3618101; e-mail embamaurathe@wayout.net; Ambassador: (vacant).

**Mexico:** 5th Floor, 17 Sharia Port Said, 11431 Cairo (Maadi); tel. (2) 3500258; fax (2) 3511887; e-mail mexemb@idsc.gov.eg; Ambassador: HÉCTOR CÁRDENAS.

**Mongolia:** 3 Midan en-Nasr, Cairo (Dokki); tel. (2) 3460670; Ambassador: SONOMDORJIN DAMBADARJAA.

**Morocco:** 10 Sharia Salah ed-Din, Cairo (Zamalek); tel. (2) 3409849; fax (2) 3411937; e-mail morocemb@idsc.gov.eg; Ambassador: ABD AL-LATIF MOULINE.

**Myanmar:** 24 Sharia Muhammad Mazhar, Cairo (Zamalek); tel. (2) 3404176; fax (2) 3416793; Ambassador: U AUNG GYI.

**Nepal:** 9 Sharia Tiba, Cairo (Dokki); tel. (2) 3603426; fax (2) 704447; Ambassador: JITENDRA RAJ SHARMA.

**Netherlands:** 36 Sharia Muhammad Mazhar, Cairo (Zamalek); tel. (2) 3406434; fax (2) 3415249; e-mail nlgovkai@access.com.eg; internet www.hollandemb.org.eg; Ambassador: RONALD H. LOUDON.

**Niger:** 101 Sharia Pyramids, Cairo (Giza); tel. (2) 3865607; Ambassador: MAMANE OUMAROU.

**Nigeria:** 13 Sharia Gabalaya, Cairo (Zamalek); tel. (2) 3406042; Chargé d'affaires a.i.: P. S. O. EROMOBOR.

**Norway:** 8 Sharia el-Gezireh, Cairo (Zamalek); tel. (2) 3403340; fax (2) 3420709; e-mail noembcai@intouch.com; Ambassador: METTE RAVN.

**Oman:** 52 Sharia el-Higaz, Mohandessin, Cairo; tel. (2) 3035942; Ambassador: ABDULLAH BIN HAMED AL-BUSAIDI.

**Pakistan:** 8 Sharia es-Salouli, Cairo (Dokki); tel. (2) 3487677; fax (2) 3480310; Ambassador: GUL HANEEF.

**Panama:** POB 62, 4A Sharia Ibn Zanki, 11211 Cairo (Zamalek); tel. (2) 3411093; fax (2) 3411092; Chargé d'affaires a.i.: ROY FRANCISCO LUNA GONZÁLEZ.

**Peru:** 8 Sharia Kamel esh-Shenawi, Cairo (Garden City); tel. (2) 3562973; fax (2) 3557985; Ambassador: MANUEL VERAMENDI I. SERRA.

**Philippines:** 5 Sharia Ibn el-Walid, Cairo (Dokki); tel. (2) 3480396; fax (2) 3480393; Ambassador: MENANDRO P. GALENZOGA.

**Poland:** 5 Sharia el-Aziz Osman, Cairo (Zamalek); tel. (2) 3417456; Ambassador: ROMAN CZYZYCKI.

**Portugal:** 57 Sharia el-Giza, Cairo (Giza); tel. (2) 3363950; fax (2) 3363952; Ambassador: MANUEL TAVARES DE SOUSA.

**Qatar:** 10 Sharia ath-Thamar, Midan an-Nasr, Madinet al-Mohandessin, Cairo; tel. (2) 704537; Ambassador: BADIR AD-DAFA.

**Romania:** 4 Sharia Aziz Abaza, Cairo (Zamalek); tel. (2) 3410107; fax (2) 3410851; Ambassador: RADU ONOFREI.

**Russia:** 95 Sharia Giza, Cairo (Giza); tel. (2) 3489353; fax (2) 3609074; Ambassador: VLADIMIR GOUDEV.

**Rwanda:** 23 Sharia Babel, Mohandessin, Cairo (Dokki); tel. (2) 3461126; fax (2) 3461079; Ambassador: CÉLESTIN KABANDA.

**Saudi Arabia:** 2 Sharia Ahmad Nessim, Cairo (Giza); tel. (2) 3490775; Ambassador: ASSAD ABD AL-KAREM ABOU AN-NASR.

**Senegal:** 46 Sharia Abd al-Moneim Riad, Mohandessin, Cairo (Dokki); tel. (2) 3460946; fax 3461039; Ambassador: MAMADOU SOW.

**Sierra Leone:** *Interests served by Saudi Arabia.*

**Singapore:** POB 356, 40 Sharia Babel, Cairo (Dokki); tel. (2) 704744; fax (2) 3481682; Ambassador: V. K. RAJAN.

**Slovakia:** 3 Sharia Adel Hussein Rostom, Cairo (Giza); tel. (2) 3358240; fax (2) 3355810; e-mail zukahira@gega.net; Ambassador: (vacant).

**Slovenia:** 5 es-Saraya el-Kobra Sq., Cairo (Garden City); tel. (2) 3555798; Ambassador: ANDREJ ŽLEBNIK.

**Somalia:** 27 Sharia es-Somal, Cairo (Dokki), Giza; tel. (2) 704038; Ambassador: ABDALLA HASSAN MAHMOUD.

**South Africa:** 18th Floor, Nile Tower Bldg, 21–23 Sharia Giza, Cairo; tel. (2) 5717238; fax (2) 5717241; Ambassador: JUSTUS DE GOEDE.

**Spain:** 41 Sharia Ismail Muhammad, Cairo (Zamalek); tel. (2) 3406397; fax (2) 3405829; e-mail spainemb@idsc.gov.eg; Ambassador: JUAN ALFONSO ORTIZ.

**Sri Lanka:** POB 1157, 8 Sharia Sri Lanka, Cairo (Zamalek); tel. (2) 3400047; fax (2) 3417138; e-mail srilanka@idsc.gov.eg; Ambassador: H. K. J. R. BANDARA.

**Sudan:** 4 Sharia el-Ibrahimi, Cairo (Garden City); tel. (2) 3549661; Ambassador: AHMAD ABD AL-HALIM.

**Sweden:** POB 131, 13 Sharia Muhammad Mazhar, Cairo (Zamalek); tel. (2) 3414132; fax 3404357; e-mail sveamcai@link.com.eg; Ambassador: CHRISTER SYLVÉN.

**Switzerland:** POB 633, 10 Sharia Abd al-Khalek Sarwat; Cairo; tel. (2) 5758284; fax (2) 5745236; e-mail vertretung@cai.rep.admin.ch; Ambassador: BLAISE GODET.

**Syria:** 18 Sharia Abd ar-Rehim Sabry, POB 435, Cairo (Dokki); tel. (2) 3358806; fax (2) 3377020; Ambassador: Dr ISSA DARWISH.

**Tanzania:** 9 Sharia Abd al-Hamid Lotfi, Cairo (Dokki); tel. (2) 704155; Ambassador: MUHAMMAD A. FOUM.

**Thailand:** 2 Sharia al-Malek el-Afdal, Cairo (Zamalek); tel. (2) 3410094; fax (2) 3400340; e-mail thaiemb@idsc.gov.eg; Ambassador: BUNTHAM BAIRAJ-VINICHAI.

**Tunisia:** 26 Sharia el-Jazirah, Cairo (Zamalek); tel. (2) 3404940; Ambassador: ABD AL-HAMID AMMAR.

**Turkey:** 25 Sharia Felaki, Cairo (Bab el-Louk); tel. and fax (2) 3548885; Ambassador: YAŞAR YAKIŞ.

**Uganda:** 9 Midan el-Messaha, Cairo (Dokki); tel. (2) 3485544; fax (2) 3485980; Ambassador: IBRAHIM MUKIIBI.

**United Arab Emirates:** 4 Sharia Ibn Sina, Cairo (Giza); tel. (2) 3609721; e-mail uaeembassyca@online.com.eg; Ambassador: AHMAD AL-MAHMOUD MUHAMMAD.

**United Kingdom:** 7 Sharia Ahmad Raghab, Cairo (Garden City); tel. (2) 3540852; fax (2) 3540859; e-mail registry@cairocl.mail.fco.gov.uk; Ambassador: GRAHAM BOYCE.

**USA:** 8 Sharia Kamal ed-Din, Cairo (Garden City); tel. (2) 3557371; fax (2) 3573000; Ambassador: DANIEL KURTZER.

**Uruguay:** 6 Sharia Lotfallah, Cairo (Zamalek); tel. (2) 3415137; fax (2) 3418123; Ambassador: JULIO CÉSAR FRANZINI.

**Venezuela:** 15A Sharia Mansour Muhammad, Cairo (Zamalek); tel. (2) 3413517; fax (2) 3417373; e-mail eov@idsc.gov.eg; Ambassador: DARIO BAUDER.

**Viet Nam:** 39 Sharia Kambiz, Cairo (Dokki); tel. (2) 3371494; fax (2) 3496597; Ambassador: NGUYEN LE BACH.

**Yemen:** 28 Sharia Amean ar-Rafai, Cairo (Dokki); tel. (2) 3604806; Ambassador: ABD AL-GHALIL GHILAN AHMAD.

**Yugoslavia:** 33 Sharia Mansour Muhammad, Cairo (Zamalek); tel. (2) 3404061; Ambassador: Dr IVAN IVEKOVIĆ.

**Zambia:** 6 Abd ar-Rahman Hussein, Mohandessin, Cairo (Dokki); tel. (2) 3610282; fax (2) 3610833; Ambassador: Dr ANGEL ALFRED MWENDA.

**Zimbabwe:** 36 Sharia Wadi en-Nil, Mohandessin, Cairo; tel. (2) 3471217; fax (2) 3474872; Ambassador: Dr HENRY MOYANA.

## Judicial System

The Courts of Law in Egypt are principally divided into two juridical court systems: Courts of General Jurisdiction and Administrative Courts. Since 1969 the Supreme Constitutional Court has been at the top of the Egyptian judicial structure.

### THE SUPREME CONSTITUTIONAL COURT

The Supreme Constitutional Court is the highest court in Egypt. It has specific jurisdiction over: (i) judicial review of the constitutionality of laws and regulations; (ii) resolution of positive and negative jurisdictional conflicts and determination of the competent court between the different juridical court systems, e.g. Courts of General Jurisdiction and Administrative Courts, as well as other bodies exercising judicial competence; (iii) determination of disputes over the enforcement of two final but contradictory judgments rendered by two courts each belonging to a different juridical court system; (iv) rendering binding interpretation of laws or decree laws in the event of a dispute in the application of said laws or decree laws, always provided that such a dispute is of a gravity requiring conformity of interpretation under the Constitution.

### COURTS OF GENERAL JURISDICTION

The Courts of General Jurisdiction in Egypt are basically divided into four categories, as follows: (i) The Court of Cassation; (ii) The Courts of Appeal; (iii) The Tribunals of First Instance; (iv) The District Tribunals; each of the above courts is divided into Civil and Criminal Chambers.

**(i) Court of Cassation:** Is the highest court of general jurisdiction in Egypt. Its sessions are held in Cairo. Final judgments rendered by Courts of Appeal in criminal and civil litigation may be petitioned to the Court of Cassation by the Defendant or the Public Prosecutor in criminal litigation and by any of the parties in interest in civil litigation on grounds of defective application or interpretation of the law as stated in the challenged judgment, on grounds of irregularity of form or procedure, or violation of due process, and on grounds of defective reasoning of judgment rendered. The Court of Cassation is composed of the President, 41 Vice-Presidents and 92 Justices.

**President:** Hon. ABD AL-BORHAN NOOR.

**(ii) The Courts of Appeal:** Each has geographical jurisdiction over one or more of the governorates of Egypt. Each Court of Appeal is divided into Criminal and Civil Chambers. The Criminal Chambers try felonies, and the Civil Chambers hear appeals filed against such judgment rendered by the Tribunals of First Instance where the law so stipulates. Each Chamber is composed of three Superior Judges. Each Court of Appeal is composed of President, and sufficient numbers of Vice-Presidents and Superior Judges.

**(iii) The Tribunals of First Instance:** In each governorate there are one or more Tribunals of First Instance, each of which is divided into several Chambers for criminal and civil litigations. Each Chamber is composed of: (a) a presiding judge, and (b) two sitting judges. A Tribunal of First Instance hears, as an Appellate Court, certain litigations as provided under the law.

**(iv) District Tribunals:** Each is a one-judge ancillary Chamber of a Tribunal of First Instance, having jurisdiction over minor civil and criminal litigations in smaller districts within the jurisdiction of such Tribunal of First Instance.

### PUBLIC PROSECUTION

Public prosecution is headed by the Attorney-General, assisted by a number of Senior Deputy and Deputy Attorneys-General, and a sufficient number of chief prosecutors, prosecutors and assistant prosecutors. Public prosecution is represented at all levels of the Courts of General Jurisdiction in all criminal litigations and also in certain civil litigations as required by the law. Public prosecution controls and supervises enforcement of criminal law judgments.

**Attorney-General:** MAHIR ABD AL-WAHID.

**Prosecutor-General:** MUHAMMAD ABD AL-AZIZ EL-GINDI.

### ADMINISTRATIVE COURTS SYSTEM (CONSEIL D'ETAT)

The Administrative Courts have jurisdiction over litigations involving the state or any of its governmental agencies. The Administrative Courts system is divided into two courts: the Administrative Courts and the Judicial Administrative Courts, at the top of which is the High Administrative Court. The Administrative Prosecutor investigates administrative crimes committed by government officials and civil servants.

**President of Conseil d'Etat:** Hon. MUHAMMAD HILAL QASIM.

**Administrative Prosecutor:** Hon. RIFA'AT KHAFAGI.

### THE STATE COUNCIL

The State Council is an independent judicial body which has the authority to make decisions in administrative disputes and disciplinary cases within the judicial system.

### THE SUPREME JUDICIAL COUNCIL

The Supreme Judicial Council was reinstituted in 1984, having been abolished in 1969. It exists to guarantee the independence of the judicial system from outside interference and is consulted with regard to draft laws organizing the affairs of the judicial bodies.

## Religion

According to the 1986 census, some 94% of Egyptians are Muslims (and almost all of these follow Sunni tenets). According to government figures published in the same year, there are about 2m. Copts (a figure contested by Coptic sources, whose estimates range between 6m. and 7m.), forming the largest religious minority, and about 1m. members of other Christian groups. There is also a small Jewish minority.

### ISLAM

There is a Higher Council for the Isamic Call, on which sit: the Grand Sheikh of al-Azhar (Chair); the Minister of Awqaf (Islamic Endowments); the President and Vice-President of Al-Azhar University; the Grand Mufti of Egypt; and the Secretary-General of the Higher Council for Islamic Affairs.

**Grand Sheikh of al-Azhar:** Sheikh MUHAMMAD SAYED ATTIYAH TANTAWI.

**Grand Mufti of Egypt:** NASR WASSEL.

### CHRISTIANITY

#### Orthodox Churches

**Armenian Apostolic Orthodox Church:** 179 Sharia Ramses, Cairo, POB 48-Faggalah; tel. (2) 5901385; fax (2) 906671; Archbishop ZAVEN CHINCHINIAN; 7,000 mems.

**Coptic Orthodox Church:** St Mark Cathedral, POB 9035, Anba Ruess, 222 Sharia Ramses, Abbassia, Cairo; fax (2) 2825983; f. AD 61; Leader Pope SHENOUDA III; c. 10m. followers in Egypt, Sudan, other African countries, the USA, Canada, Australia, Europe and the Middle East.

**Greek Orthodox Patriarchate:** POB 2006, Alexandria; tel. (3) 4835839; fax (3) 4835684; e-mail goptalex@tecmina.com; internet www.greece.org/goptalex; f. AD 64; Pope and Patriarch of Alexandria and All Africa His Beatitude PETROS VII; 350,000 mems.

#### The Roman Catholic Church

*Armenian Rite*

The Armenian Catholic diocese of Alexandria, with an estimated 1,149 adherents at 31 December 1997, is suffragan to the Patriarchate of Cilicia. The Patriarch is resident in Beirut, Lebanon.

**Bishop of Alexandria:** (vacant), Patriarcat Arménien Catholique, 36 Sharia Muhammad Sabri Abou Alam, Cairo; tel. (2) 3938429; fax (2) 3932025.

*Chaldean Rite*

The Chaldean Catholic diocese of Cairo had an estimated 500 adherents at 31 December 1997.

**Bishop of Cairo:** YOUSUF IBRAHIM SARRAF, Evêché Chaldéen, Basilique-Sanctuaire Notre Dame de Fatima, 141 Sharia Nouzha, 11361 Cairo (Heliopolis); tel. and fax (2) 2455718.

*Coptic Rite*

Egypt comprises the Coptic Catholic Patriarchate of Alexandria and five dioceses. At 31 December 1997 there were an estimated 87,500 adherents in the country.

**Patriarch of Alexandria:** His Beatitude STEPHANOS II (ANDREAS GHATTAS), Patriarcat Copte Catholique, POB 69, 34 Sharia Ibn Sandar, Koubbeh Bridge, 11712 Cairo; tel. (2) 2571740; fax (2) 4545766.

*Latin Rite*

Egypt comprises the Apostolic Vicariate of Alexandria (incorporating Heliopolis and Port Said), containing an estimated 6,500 adherents at 31 December 1997.

**Vicar Apostolic:** Fr EGIDIO SAMPIERI (Titular Bishop of Ida in Mauretania), 10 Sharia Sidi el-Metwalli, Alexandria; tel. (3) 4836065; fax (3) 4838169; also at 2 Sharia Banque Misr, Cairo; tel. (2) 41280.

*Maronite Rite*

The Maronite diocese of Cairo had an estimated 5,000 adherents at 31 December 1997.

**Bishop of Cairo:** JOSEPH DERGHAM, Evêché Maronite, 15 Sharia Hamdi, Daher, 11271 Cairo; tel. (2) 5939610.

*Melkite Rite*

His Beatitude MAXIMOS V HAKIM (resident in Damascus, Syria) is the Greek-Melkite Patriarch of Antioch, of Alexandria and of Jerusalem.

**Patriarchal Exarchate of Egypt and Sudan:** Patriarcat Grec-Melkite Catholique, 16 Sharia Daher, 11271 Cairo; tel. (2) 5905790; 6,500 adherents (31 December 1997); Exarch Patriarchal Mgr PAUL ANTAKI, Titular Archbishop of Nubia.

*Syrian Rite*

The Syrian Catholic diocese of Cairo had an estimated 1,772 adherents at 31 December 1997.

**Bishop of Cairo:** JOSEPH HANNOUCHE, Evêché Syrien Catholique, 46 Sharia Daher, 11271 Cairo; tel. (2) 5901234.

#### The Anglican Communion

The Anglican diocese of Egypt, suspended in 1958, was revived in 1974 and became part of the Episcopal Church in Jerusalem and the Middle East, formally inaugurated in January 1976. The Province has four dioceses: Jerusalem, Egypt, Cyprus and the Gulf, and Iran, and its President is the Bishop in Egypt. The Bishop in Egypt has jurisdiction also over the Anglican chaplaincies in Algeria, Djibouti, Eritrea, Ethiopia, Libya, Somalia and Tunisia.

**Bishop in Egypt:** Most Rev. GHAIS ABD AL-MALIK, Diocesan Office, POB 87, 5 Sharia Michel Lutfalla, Cairo (Zamalek); tel. (2) 3320313; fax (2) 3408941; e-mail diocese@intouch.com.

#### Other Christian Churches

**Protestant Churches of Egypt:** POB 1304, Cairo 11511; tel. (2) 5903925; f. 1902, independent since 1926; 200,000 mems (1985); Gen. Sec. (vacant).

Other denominations active in Egypt include the Coptic Evangelical Church (Synod of the Nile) and the Union of the Armenian Evangelical Churches in the Near East.

### JUDAISM

The 1986 census recorded 794 Jews in Egypt.

**Jewish Community:** Office of the Community, President ESTHER WEINSTEIN, 13 Sharia Sebil el-Khazindar, Abbassia, Cairo; tel. (2) 4824613; internet www.geocities.com/rain/forest/vines/5855.

## The Press

Despite a fairly high illiteracy rate in Egypt, the country's press is well developed. Cairo is one of the region's largest publishing centres.

All newspapers and magazines are supervised, according to law, by the Supreme Press Council. The four major publishing houses of al-Ahram, Dar al-Hilal, Dar Akhbar al-Yawm and Dar at-Tahrir operate as separate entities and compete with each other commercially.

The most authoritative daily newspaper is the very long-established *Al-Ahram*.

### DAILIES

#### Alexandria

**Bareed ach-Charikat** (Companies' Post): POB 813, Alexandria; f. 1952; Arabic; evening; commerce, finance, insurance and marine affairs; Editor S. BENEDUCCI; circ. 15,000.

**Al-Ittihad al-Misri** (Egyptian Unity): 13 Sharia Sidi Abd ar-Razzak, Alexandria; f. 1871; Arabic; evening; Propr ANWAR MAHER FARAG; Dir HASSAN MAHER FARAG.

**Le Journal d'Alexandrie:** 1 Sharia Rolo, Alexandria; French; evening; Editor CHARLES ARCACHE.

**La Réforme:** 8 Passage Sherif, Alexandria; French.

**As-Safeer** (The Ambassador): 4 Sharia as-Sahafa, Alexandria; f. 1924; Arabic; evening; Editor MUSTAFA SHARAF.

**Tachydromos-Egyptos:** 4 Sharia Zangarol, Alexandria; tel. (3) 35650; f. 1879; Greek; morning; liberal; Publr PENNY KOUTSOUMIS; Editor DINOS KOUTSOUMIS; circ. 2,000.

#### Cairo

**Al-Ahram** (The Pyramids): Sharia al-Galaa, Cairo 11511; tel. (2) 5801600; fax (2) 5786023; f. 1875; Arabic; morning, incl. Sundays (international edition published in London, England; North American edition published in New York, USA); Editor and Chair. IBRAHIM NAFEH; circ. 900,000 (weekdays), 1.1m. (Friday).

**Al-Ahram al-Misaa'** (The Evening *Al-Ahram*): Sharia al-Galaa, Cairo 11511; Arabic; evening; Editor-in-Chief MORSI ATALLAH.

**Al-Ahrar:** 58 Manshyet as-Sadr, Kobry al-Kobba, Cairo; tel. (2) 4823046; fax (2) 4823027; f. 1977; organ of Liberal Socialist Party; Editor-in-Chief SALAH QABADAYA.

**Al-Akhbar** (The News): Dar Akhbar al-Yawm, 6 Sharia as-Sahafa, Cairo; tel. (2) 5782600; fax (2) 5782520; f. 1952; Arabic; Chair. IBRAHIM ABU SADAH; Man. Editor GALAL DEWIDAR; circ. 780,000.

**Arev:** 3 Sharia Sulayman Halabi, Cairo; tel. (2) 754703; f. 1915; Armenian; evening; official organ of the Armenian Liberal Democratic Party; Editor AVEDIS YAPOUDJIAN.

**The Egyptian Gazette:** 24–26 Sharia Zakaria Ahmad, Cairo; tel. (2) 5783333; fax (2) 5781110; e-mail 100236.3241@compuserve.com; f. 1880; English; morning; Chair. SAMIR RAGAB; Editor-in-Chief MUHAMMAD ALI IBRAHIM; circ. 90,000.

**Al-Gomhouriya** (The Republic): 24 Sharia Zakaria Ahmad, Cairo; tel. (2) 5783333; fax (2) 5781717; f. 1953; Arabic; morning; mainly economic affairs; Chair. and Editor-in-Chief SAMIR RAGAB; circ. 900,000.

**Al-Misaa'** (The Evening): 24 Sharia Zakaria Ahmad, Cairo; tel. (2) 5781010; fax (2) 5784747; f. 1956; Arabic; evening; political, social and sport; Editor-in-Chief MUHAMMAD FOUDAH; Man. Dir ABD AL-HAMROSE; circ. 450,000.

**Phos:** 14 Sharia Zakaria Ahmad, Cairo; f. 1896; Greek; morning; Editor S. PATERAS; Man. BASILE A. PATERAS; circ. 20,000.

**Le Progrès Egyptien:** 24 Sharia Zakaria Ahmad, Cairo; tel. (2) (2) 5783333; fax (2) 5781110; f. 1890; French; morning including Sundays; Chair. SAMIR RAGAB; Editor-in-Chief KHALED ANWAR BAKIR; circ. 60,000.

**Al-Wafd:** 1 Sharia Boulos Hanna, Cairo (Dokki); tel. (2) 3482079; fax (2) 3602007; f. 1984; organ of the New Wafd Party; Editor-in-Chief GAMAL BADAWI; circ. 360,000.

### PERIODICALS

#### Alexandria

**Al-Ahad al-Gedid** (New Sunday): 88 Sharia Said M. Koraim, Alexandria; tel. (3) 807874; f. 1936; Editor-in-Chief and Publr GALAL M. KORAITEM; circ. 60,000.

**Alexandria Medical Journal:** 4 G. Carducci, Alexandria; tel. (3) 4829001; fax (3) 4833076; internet www.who.sci.eg; f. 1922; English, French and Arabic; quarterly; publ. by Alexandria Medical Asscn; Editor Prof. TOUSSOUN ABOUL AZM.

**Amitié Internationale:** 59 ave el-Hourriya, Alexandria; tel. (3) 23639; f. 1957; publ. by Asscn Egyptienne d'Amitié Internationale; Arabic and French; quarterly; Editor Dr ZAKI BADAOUI.

**L'Annuaire des Sociétés Egyptiennes par Actions:** 23 Midan Tahrir, Alexandria; f. 1930; annually in Dec.; French; Propr ELIE I. POLITI; Editor OMAR ES-SAYED MOURSI.

**L'Echo Sportif:** 7 Sharia de l'Archevêché, Alexandria; French; weekly; Propr MICHEL BITTAR.

**Egyptian Cotton Gazette:** POB 433, 12 Sharia Tala'at Nooman, Alexandria 21111; tel. (3) 4806971; fax (3) 4833002; e-mail alcotexa@idsc.gov.eg; internet www.welcome.to/alcotexa; f. 1947; organ of the Alexandria Cotton Exporters' Association; English; 2 a year; Chief Editor GALAL REFAI.

**Informateur des Assurances:** 1 Sharia Sinan, Alexandria; f. 1936; French; monthly; Propr ELIE I. POLITI; Editor SIMON A. BARANIS.

**La Réforme Illustré:** 8 Passage Sherif, Alexandria; French; weekly; general.

**Sina 'at en-Nassig** (L'Industrie Textile): 5 rue de l'Archevêché, Alexandria; Arabic and French; monthly; Editor PHILIPPE COLAS.

**Voce d'Italia:** 90 Sharia Farahde, Alexandria; Italian; fortnightly; Editor R. AVELLINO.

### Cairo

**Al-Ahali** (The People): Sharia Kareem ad-Dawli, Tala'at Harb Sq., Cairo; tel. (2) 7786583; fax (2) 3900412; f. 1978; weekly; publ. by the National Progressive Unionist Party; Chair. LOTFI WAKID; Editor-in-Chief ABD AL-BAKOURY.

**Al-Ahram al-Arabi:** Sharia al-Galaa, Cairo 11511; f. 1997; Arabic; weekly; political, social and economic affairs; Chair. IBRAHIM NAFIE; Editor-in-Chief OSAMA SARAYA.

**Al-Ahram Hebdo:** POB 1057, Sharia al-Galaa, Cairo 11511; tel. (2) 5783104; fax (2) 5782631; e-mail hebdo@ahram.org.eg; internet www.ahram.org.eg/hebdo; f. 1993; French; weekly; Editor-in-Chief MUHAMMAD SALMAWI.

**Al-Ahram al-Iqtisadi** (The Economic *Al-Ahram*): Sharia al-Galaa, Cairo 11511; tel. (2) 5786100; fax (2) 5786833; Arabic; weekly (Monday); economic and political affairs; owned by Al-Ahram publrs; Chief Editor ISSAM RIFA'AT; circ. 84,189.

**Al-Ahram Weekly** (The Pyramids): Al-Ahram Bldg, Sharia al-Galaa, Cairo 11511; tel. (2) 5786100; fax (2) 5786833; f. 1989; English; weekly; publ. by Al-Ahram publications; Editor-in-Chief HOSNI GUINDY; circ. 150,000.

**Akhbar al-Adab:** 6 Sharia as-Sahafa, Cairo; tel. (2) 5782500; fax (2) 5782510; f. 1993; literature and arts for young people; Editor-in-Chief GAMAL AL-GHITANI.

**Akhbar al-Hawadith:** 6 Sharia as-Sahafa, Cairo; tel. (2) 5782600; fax (2) 5782510; f. 1993; weekly; crime reports; Editor-in-Chief MUHAMMAD BARAKAT.

**Akhbar al-Nogoome:** 6 Sharia as-Sahafa, Cairo; tel. (2) 5782600; fax (2) 5782510; f. 1991; weekly; theatre and film news; Editor-in-Chief AMAL OSMAN.

**Akhbar ar-Riadah:** 6 Sharia as-Sahafa, Cairo; tel. (2) 5782600; fax (2) 5782510; f. 1990; weekly; sport; Editor-in-Chief IBRAHIM HEGAZY.

**Akhbar al-Yaum** (Daily News): 6 Sharia as-Sahafa, Cairo; tel. (2) 5782600; fax (2) 5782520; f. 1944; Arabic; weekly (Saturday); Chair. and Editor-in-Chief IBRAHIM ABU SEDAH; circ. 1,184,611.

**Akher Sa'a** (Last Hour): Dar Akhbar al-Yawm, Sharia as-Sahafa, Cairo; tel. (2) 5782600; fax (2) 5782530; f. 1934; Arabic; weekly (Sunday); independent; consumer and news magazine; Editor-in-Chief MAHMOUD SALAH; circ. 150,000.

**Aqidaty** (My Faith): 24–26 Sharia Zakaria Ahmad, Cairo; tel. (2) 5783333; fax (2) 5781110; weekly; Muslim religious newspaper; Editor-in-Chief ABD AR-RAOUF ES-SAYED; circ. 300,000.

**Al-Arabi an-Nassiri:** Cairo; f. 1993; publ. by the Nasserist Party; Editor-in-Chief MAHMOUD EL-MARAGHI.

**Al-Azhar:** Idarat al-Azhar, Sharia al-Azhar, Cairo; f. 1931; Arabic; Islamic monthly; supervised by the Egyptian Council for Islamic Research of Al-Azhar University; Dir MUHAMMAD FARID WAGDI.

**Al-Bitrul** (Petroleum): Cairo; monthly; publ. by the Egyptian General Petroleum Corporation.

**Cairo Today:** POB 2098, 1079 Corniche en-Nil, Cairo (Garden City); monthly.

**Computerworld Middle East:** World Publishing Ltd (Egypt), 41A Masaken al-Fursan Bldg, Sharia Kamal Hassan Ali, Cairo 11361; tel. (2) 3460601; fax (2) 3470118; English; monthly; specialist computer information.

**Contemporary Thought:** University of Cairo, Cairo; quarterly; Editor Dr Z. N. MAHMOUD.

**Ad-Da'wa** (The Call): Cairo; Arabic; monthly; organ of the Muslim Brotherhood.

**Ad-Doctor:** 8 Sharia Hoda Sharawi, Cairo; f. 1947; Arabic; monthly; Editor Dr AHMAD M. KAMAL; circ. 30,000.

**Droit al-Haqq:** Itihad al-Mohameen al-Arab, 13 Sharia Itihad, Cairo; publ. by the Arab Lawyers' Union; 3 a year.

**Echos:** 1–5 Sharia Mahmoud Bassiouni, Cairo; f. 1947; French; weekly; Dir and Propr GEORGES QRFALI.

**The Egyptian Mail:** 24–26 Sharia Zakaria Ahmad; weekly; Sat. edn of *The Egyptian Gazette*; English; circ. 40,000.

**El-Elm Magazine** (Sciences): 24 Sharia Zakaria Ahmad, Cairo; tel. (2) 5781010; fax (2) 5784747; f. 1976; Arabic; monthly; publ. with the Academy of Scientific Research in Egypt; circ. 70,000.

**Al-Fusoul** (The Seasons): 17 Sharia Sherif Pasha, Cairo; Arabic; monthly; Propr and Chief Editor SAMIR MUHAMMAD ZAKI ABD AL-KADER.

**Al-Garidat at-Tigariyat al-Misriya** (The Egyptian Business Paper): 25 Sharia Nubar Pasha, Cairo; f. 1921; Arabic; weekly; circ. 7,000.

**Hawa'a** (Eve): Dar al-Hilal, 16 Sharia Muhammad Ezz el-Arab, Cairo 11511; tel. (2) 3625450; fax (2) 3625469; f. 1892; women's magazine; Arabic; weekly (Sat.); Chief Editor EKBAL BARAKA; circ. 210,502.

**Al-Hilal Magazine:** Dar al-Hilal, 16 Sharia Muhammad Ezz el-Arab, Cairo; tel. (2) 3625450; fax (2) 3625469; f. 1895; Arabic; literary monthly; Editor MOUSTAFA NABIL.

**Horreyati:** 24 Sharia Zakaria Ahmad, Cairo; tel. (2) 5781010; fax (2) 5784747; f. 1990; weekly; social, cultural and sport; Editor-in-Chief MUHAMMAD NOUR ED-DIN; circ. 250,000.

**Huwa wa Hiya** (He and She): Middle East Foundation Ltd, POB 525, Cairo 11511; tel. (2) 3506752; fax (2) 3508604; f. 1977; monthly; news, leisure, sport, health, religion, women's issues; Dir GEORGE TAWFIK.

**Industrial Egypt:** POB 251, 26A Sharia Sherif Pasha, Cairo; tel. (2) 3928317; fax (2) 3928075; f. 1924; quarterly bulletin and year book of the Federation of Egyptian Industries in English and Arabic; Editor ALI FAHMY.

**Informateur Financier et Commercial:** 24 Sharia Sulayman Pasha, Cairo; f. 1929; weekly; Dir HENRI POLITI; circ. 15,000.

**Al-Iza'a wat-Television** (Radio and Television): 16 Sharia Muhammad Ezz el-Arab, Cairo 11511; tel. (2) 3643314; fax (2) 3543030; f. 1935; Arabic; weekly; Man. Editor MAHMOUD ALI; circ. 80,000.

**Al-Kerazeh** (The Sermon): Cairo; Arabic; weekly newspaper of the Coptic Orthodox Church.

**Al-Kawakeb** (The Stars): Dar al-Hilal, 16 Sharia Muhammad Ezz el-Arab, Cairo 11511; tel. (2) 3625450; fax (2) 3625469; f. 1952; Arabic; weekly; film magazine; Editor-in-Chief RAGAA AN-NAKKASH; circ. 86,381.

**Kitab al-Hilal:** Dar al-Hilal, 16 Sharia Muhammad Ezz el-Arab, Cairo; tel. (2) 3625450; fax (2) 3625469; monthly; Founders EMILE and SHOUKRI ZEIDAN; Editor MOUSTAFA NABIL.

**Al-Kora wal-Malaeb** (Football and Playgrounds): 24 Sharia Zakaria Ahmad, Cairo; tel. (2) 5783333; fax (2) 5784747; f. 1976; Arabic; weekly; sport; circ. 150,000.

**Al-Liwa' al-Islami** (Islamic Standard): 11 Sharia Sherif Pasha, Cairo; f. 1982; Arabic; weekly; govt paper to promote official view of Islamic revivalism; Propr AHMAD HAMZA; Editor MUHAMMAD ALI SHETA; circ. 30,000.

**Lotus Magazine:** 104 Sharia Qasr el-Eini, Cairo; f. 1992; English, French and Arabic; quarterly; computer software magazine; Editor BEREND HARMENS.

**Magallat al-Mohandessin** (The Engineer's Magazine): 28 Sharia Ramses, Cairo; f. 1945; publ. by The Engineers' Syndicate; Arabic and English; 10 a year; Editor and Sec. MAHMOUD SAMI ABD AL-KAWI.

**Al-Magallat az-Zira'ia** (The Agricultural Magazine): Cairo; monthly; agriculture; circ. 30,000.

**Mayo** (May): Sharia al-Galaa, Cairo; f. 1981; weekly; organ of National Democratic Party; Chair. ABDULLAH ABD AL-BARY; Chief Editor SAMIR RAGAB; circ. 500,000.

**Medical Journal of Cairo University:** Manyal University Hospital, Sharia Qasr el-Eini, Cairo; f. 1933; Qasr el-Eini Clinical Society; English; quarterly.

**MEN Economic Weekly:** Middle East News Agency, 4 Sharia Hoda Sharawi, Cairo; tel. (2) 3933000; fax 3935055.

**The Middle East Observer:** 41 Sharia Sherif, Cairo; tel. (2) 3926919; fax (2) 3939732; e-mail fouda@soficom.com.eg; f. 1954; English; weekly; specializing in economics of Middle East and African markets; also publishes supplements on law, foreign trade and tenders; agent for IMF, UN and IDRC publications, distributor of World Bank publications; Man. Owner AHMAD FODA; Chief Editor MUHAMMAD ABDULLAH HESHAM A. RAOUF; circ. 20,000.

**Middle East Times Egypt:** 2 Sharia el-Malek el-Afdal, Cairo (Zamalek); tel. (2) 3419930; fax (2) 3413725; e-mail met@ritsec1.com.eg; f. 1983; English; weekly; Man. Editor ROD CRAIG; circ. 6,000.

**Al-Musawar:** Dar al-Hilal, 16 Sharia Muhammad Ezz el-Arab, Cairo 11511; tel. (2) 3625450; fax (2) 3625469; f. 1924; Arabic; weekly; news; Chair. and Editor-in-Chief MAKRAM MUHAMMAD AHMAD; circ. 130,423.

**Nesf ad-Donia:** Sharia al-Galaa, Cairo 11511; tel. (2) 5786100; f. 1990; weekly; women's magazine; publ. by Al-Ahram Publications; Editor-in-Chief SANAA AL-BESI.

**October:** 1119 Sharia Corniche en-Nil, Cairo; tel. (2) 5777077; fax (2) 5744999; f. 1976; weekly; Chair. and Editor-in-Chief RAGAB AL-BANA; circ. 140,500.

**Al-Omal** (The Workers): 90 Sharia al-Galaa, Cairo; publ. by the Egyptian Trade Union Federation: Arabic; weekly; Chief Editor AHMAD HARAK.

**PC World Middle East:** World Publishing Ltd (Egypt), 41A Masaken al-Fursan Bldg, Sharia Kamal Hassan Ali, Cairo 11361; tel. (2) 34606; fax (2) 3470118; monthly; computers.

**Le Progrès Dimanche:** 24 Sharia al-Galaa, Cairo; tel. (2) 5781010; fax (2) 5784747; French; weekly; Sunday edition of *Le Progrès Egyptien*; Editor-in-Chief KHALED ANWAR BAKIR; circ. 35,000.

**Rose al-Yousuf:** 89A Sharia Qasr el-Eini, Cairo; tel. (2) 3540888; fax (2) 3556413; f. 1925; Arabic; weekly; political; circulates

# External Trade

**PRINCIPAL COMMODITIES** (distribution by SITC, US $ '000)

| Imports c.i.f. | 1994 | 1995 | 1996 |
|---|---|---|---|
| **Food and live animals** | 257,479 | 290,851 | 358,543 |
| Cereals and cereal preparations | 100,130 | 99,598 | 128,677 |
| **Crude materials (inedible) except fuels** | 81,713 | 67,373 | 95,198 |
| **Mineral fuels, lubricants, etc.** | 215,378 | 243,278 | 325,330 |
| Petroleum, petroleum products, etc. | 201,482 | 226,570 | 299,666 |
| Crude petroleum | 112,014 | 94,816 | 121,505 |
| Refined petroleum products | 86,799 | 128,553 | 175,137 |
| Gas oils | 56,592 | — | — |
| Residual fuel oils | 381 | 92,743 | 113,974 |
| **Animal and vegetable oils, fats and waxes** | 59,562 | 74,367 | 76,142 |
| **Chemicals and related products** | 373,017 | 441,416 | 455,390 |
| Medicinal and pharmaceutical products | 97,022 | 110,796 | 109,695 |
| Medicaments | 79,530 | 88,723 | 89,801 |
| Perfumes and cleansing preparations, etc. | 53,457 | 69,907 | 70,580 |
| Plastic materials, etc. | 73,765 | 93,299 | 85,124 |
| Products of polymerization, etc. | 61,605 | 80,117 | 71,764 |
| **Basic manufactures** | 399,796 | 487,189 | 435,396 |
| Paper, paperboard and manufactures | 81,585 | 127,458 | 90,293 |
| Paper and paperboard | 67,452 | 103,546 | 68,324 |
| Textile yarn, fabrics, etc. | 54,355 | 59,168 | 45,841 |
| Iron and steel | 81,979 | 80,719 | 98,974 |
| Other metal manufactures | 62,286 | 81,007 | 71,054 |
| **Machinery and transport equipment** | 695,697 | 790,051 | 700,060 |
| Power-generating machinery and equipment | 55,610 | 34,299 | 58,046 |
| Machinery specialized for particular industries | 84,403 | 106,030 | 87,180 |
| General industrial machinery, equipment and parts | 71,168 | 92,378 | 85,130 |
| Office machines and automatic data-processing equipment | 45,378 | 55,137 | 57,605 |
| Telecommunications and sound equipment | 68,168 | 73,865 | 68,458 |
| Other electrical machinery, apparatus, etc. | 81,942 | 94,295 | 94,091 |
| Road vehicles | 279,463 | 322,818 | 237,122 |
| Passenger motor cars (except buses) | 96,376 | 120,843 | 78,913 |
| Lorries and trucks | 106,218 | 119,985 | 88,935 |
| **Miscellaneous manufactured articles** | 163,486 | 214,729 | 204,714 |
| **Total** (incl. others) | 2,261,800 | 2,627,670 | 2,670,097 |

Source: UN, *International Trade Statistics Yearbook.*

**1997** (US $ million): *Imports:* Non-durable consumer goods 768.7; Durable consumer goods 149.2; Primary materials for agriculture 133.0; Primary materials for industry 866.7; Crude petroleum 120.0; Construction materials 162.2; Capital goods 744.8 (Industry 229.0, Transport 287.9, Construction 69.9); Total (incl. others) 2,973.4.

**1998** (US $ million, preliminary figures): *Imports:* Non-durable consumer goods 787.9; Durable consumer goods 140.7; Primary materials for agriculture 115.1; Primary materials for industry 180.3; Capital goods 826.4 (Industry 239.2, Transport 321.1, Construction 78.5); Total (incl. others) 3,109.7.

| Exports f.o.b. | 1994 | 1995 | 1996 |
|---|---|---|---|
| **Food and live animals** | 399,022 | 540,467 | 509,078 |
| Fish, crustaceans and molluscs | 31,257 | 30,233 | 43,603 |
| Fresh, chilled, frozen, salted or dried crustaceans and molluscs | 25,014 | 27,415 | 40,883 |
| Cereals and cereal preparations | 17,113 | 34,713 | 19,501 |
| Cereal preparations, etc. | 15,772 | 31,054 | 17,516 |
| Sugar, sugar preparations and honey | 44,058 | 49,856 | 53,086 |
| Sugar and honey | 35,894 | 43,398 | 45,671 |
| Sugars, beet and cane (raw, solid) | 27,690 | 36,272 | 31,510 |
| Coffee, tea, cocoa, etc. | 268,710 | 396,203 | 341,863 |
| Coffee and coffee substitutes | 267,767 | 373,005 | 339,909 |
| Coffee (incl. husks and skins) and substitutes containing coffee | 263,920 | 371,763 | 339,013 |
| Miscellaneous edible products and preparations | 20,329 | 9,187 | 28,315 |
| **Chemicals and related products** | 97,482 | 110,649 | 141,127 |
| Medicinal and pharmaceutical products | 34,412 | 40,445 | 49,652 |
| Medicaments | 32,568 | 37,439 | 45,679 |
| Perfumes and cleansing preparations, etc. | 27,919 | 36,546 | 48,392 |
| Soap, etc. | 22,047 | 24,887 | 33,783 |
| **Basic manufactures** | 171,078 | 189,212 | 188,579 |
| Paper, paperboard and manufactures | 56,576 | 58,124 | 56,970 |
| Shaped or cut articles of paper and paperboard | 43,929 | 42,958 | 40,584 |
| Boxes, bags, packing containers, etc. | 29,393 | 25,751 | 19,795 |
| Textile yarn, fabrics, etc. | 61,638 | 64,285 | 67,255 |
| Textile yarn | 21,884 | 18,629 | 22,069 |
| Iron and steel | 9,639 | 16,092 | 21,506 |
| Non-ferrous metals | 19,306 | 26,709 | 20,933 |
| Aluminium | 18,435 | 26,316 | 20,693 |
| Aluminium and alloys (unwrought) | 18,408 | 26,316 | 20,692 |
| Other metal manufactures | 18,154 | 17,534 | 15,846 |
| **Machinery and transport equipment** | 24,781 | 27,504 | 35,292 |
| Electrical machinery, apparatus, etc. (excl. telecommunications and sound equipment) | 20,288 | 21,697 | 29,106 |
| **Miscellaneous manufactured articles** | 89,585 | 81,595 | 77,266 |
| Clothing and accessories | 37,509 | 33,017 | 27,480 |
| **Total** (incl. others) | 812,718 | 985,202 | 1,024,266 |

Source: UN, *International Trade Statistics Yearbook.*

**1997** (US $ million): *Exports:* Coffee 517.9; Sugar 48.9; Shrimp 28.9; Total (incl. others) 1,349.2.

**1998** (US $ million, preliminary figures): *Exports:* Coffee 322.0; Sugar 63.7; Shrimp 31.7; Total (incl. others) 1,245.8.

**PRINCIPAL TRADING PARTNERS**
(US $ million)

| Imports c.i.f. | 1996 | 1997 | 1998* |
|---|---|---|---|
| Brazil | 29.4 | 23.7 | 26.0 |
| Costa Rica | 101.7 | 116.8 | 115.1 |
| Germany | 97.8 | 93.9 | 90.3 |
| Guatemala | 279.8 | 325.0 | 346.8 |
| Honduras | 70.3 | 85.4 | 87.8 |
| Italy | 31.2 | 31.2 | 31.6 |
| Japan | 114.1 | 91.6 | 145.1 |
| Mexico | 172.3 | 236.3 | 238.3 |
| Netherlands | 30.4 | 18.2 | 27.2 |
| Nicaragua | 54.1 | 51.3 | 49.5 |
| Panama† | 175.8 | 102.8 | 106.1 |
| Spain | 24.1 | 39.7 | 49.0 |
| USA | 1,021.9 | 1,209.0 | 1,178.7 |
| Venezuela | 59.6 | 63.8 | 41.8 |
| **Total** (incl. others) | 2,671.2 | 2,973.4 | 3,109.7 |

* Preliminary figures.
† Including Colón Free Zone.

| Exports f.o.b. | 1996 | 1997 | 1998* |
|---|---|---|---|
| Belgium-Luxembourg | 60.6 | 61.2 | 23.9 |
| Costa Rica | 93.3 | 111.8 | 110.3 |
| France | 4.7 | 16.9 | 14.0 |
| Germany | 158.9 | 238.4 | 139.9 |
| Guatemala | 210.6 | 265.2 | 282.5 |
| Honduras | 97.5 | 136.6 | 148.8 |
| Japan | 10.3 | 14.1 | 12.5 |
| Mexico | 12.6 | 17.9 | 17.3 |
| Netherlands | 31.3 | 29.2 | 21.9 |
| Nicaragua | 53.7 | 64.8 | 75.0 |
| Panama† | 24.5 | 24.6 | 24.3 |
| United Kingdom | 9.9 | 30.1 | 19.4 |
| USA | 190.8 | 255.3 | 265.1 |
| **Total** (incl. others) | 1,024.3 | 1,349.2 | 1,245.8 |

* Preliminary figures.
† Including Colón Free Zone.

# Transport

**RAILWAYS** (traffic)

| | 1993 | 1994 | 1995 |
|---|---|---|---|
| Passenger-km (million) | 6 | 6 | 5 |
| Net ton-km (million) | 35 | 30 | 13 |

Source: UN, *Statistical Yearbook.*

**ROAD TRAFFIC** (motor vehicles in use at 31 December)

| | 1995 | 1996 | 1997 |
|---|---|---|---|
| Passenger cars | 151,081 | 168,234 | 177,488 |
| Buses and coaches | 29,293 | 32,238 | 33,087 |
| Lorries and vans | 125,101 | 142,916 | 151,772 |
| Motorcycles and mopeds | 28,888 | 38,330 | 27,476 |

Source: IRF, *World Road Statistics.*

**SHIPPING**
**Merchant Fleet** (registered at 31 December)

| | 1996 | 1997 | 1998 |
|---|---|---|---|
| Number of vessels | 12 | 12 | 12 |
| Total displacement ('000 grt) | 1.5 | 1.5 | 1.5 |

Source: Lloyd's Register of Shipping, *World Fleet Statistics.*

**CIVIL AVIATION** (traffic on scheduled services)

| | 1993 | 1994 | 1995 |
|---|---|---|---|
| Kilometres flown (million) | 19 | 20 | 21 |
| Passengers carried ('000) | 1,242 | 1,617 | 1,698 |
| Passenger–km (million) | 1,763 | 1,978 | 2,077 |
| Total ton-km (million) | 200 | 216 | 227 |

Source: UN, *Statistical Yearbook.*

# Tourism

**TOURIST ARRIVALS BY COUNTRY OF ORIGIN**
(excluding Salvadorean nationals residing abroad)

| | 1994 | 1995 | 1996 |
|---|---|---|---|
| Canada | 5,238 | 9,735 | 8,855 |
| Colombia | 2,785 | 3,641 | 5,745 |
| Costa Rica | 9,794 | 12,464 | 19,497 |
| Germany | 3,648 | 4,086 | 5,163 |
| Guatemala | 34,385 | 33,050 | 54,210 |
| Honduras | 17,837 | 13,102 | 20,644 |
| Mexico | 8,582 | 11,481 | 11,276 |
| Nicaragua | 9,603 | 9,521 | 14,104 |
| Panama | 3,518 | 3,800 | 9,050 |
| Spain | 4,617 | 6,759 | 8,242 |
| USA | 58,240 | 99,229 | 88,905 |
| **Total** (incl. others) | 181,332 | 235,364 | 282,835 |

**Receipts from tourism** (US $ million): 29 in 1994; 41 in 1995; 44 in 1996.

Source: World Tourism Organization, *Yearbook of Tourism Statistics.*

# Communications Media

| | 1994 | 1995 | 1996 |
|---|---|---|---|
| Radio receivers ('000 in use) | 2,500 | 2,600 | 2,670 |
| Television receivers ('000 in use) | n.a. | 3,900 | 3,910 |
| Telephones ('000 main lines in use) | 236 | 285 | n.a. |
| Mobile cellular telephones (subscribers) | 6,480 | 13,475 | n.a. |
| Daily newspapers: | | | |
| Number | 6 | 6 | 5 |
| Total circulation ('000) | 284 | 280 | 278 |
| Non-daily newspapers: | | | |
| Number | n.a. | 6 | 6 |
| Total circulation ('000) | n.a. | 48 | 52 |

Source: mainly UNESCO, *Statistical Yearbook.*

# Education

(1996)

| | Institutions | Teachers | Students | | |
|---|---|---|---|---|---|
| | | | Males | Females | Total |
| Pre-primary | 3,679 | 6,009 | 74,286 | 76,463 | 150,749 |
| Primary | 5,025 | 34,496 | 576,985 | 553,915 | 1,130,900 |
| Secondary | n.a. | 9,255 | 68,227 | 75,361 | 143,588 |
| Tertiary: | | | | | |
| University level | n.a. | 5,610 | 52,921 | 54,292 | 107,213 |
| Other higher | n.a. | 309 | 2,747 | 2,044 | 4,791 |

Source: UNESCO, *Statistical Yearbook.*

# Directory

## The Constitution

The Constitution of the Republic of El Salvador came into effect on 20 December 1983.

The Constitution provides for a republican, democratic and representative form of government, composed of three Powers—Legislative, Executive, and Judicial—which are to operate independently. Voting is a right and duty of all citizens over 18 years of age. Presidential and congressional elections may not be held simultaneously.

The Constitution binds the country, as part of the Central American Nation, to favour the total or partial reconstruction of the Republic of Central America. Integration in a unitary, federal or confederal form, provided that democratic and republican principles are respected and that basic rights of individuals are fully guaranteed, is subject to popular approval.

### LEGISLATIVE ASSEMBLY

Legislative power is vested in a single chamber, the Asamblea Nacional, whose members are elected every three years and are eligible for re-election. The Asamblea's term of office begins on 1 May. The Asamblea's duties include the choosing of the President and Vice-President of the Republic from the two citizens who shall have gained the largest number of votes for each of these offices, if no candidate obtains an absolute majority in the election. It also selects the members of the Supreme and subsidiary courts; of the Elections Council; and the Accounts Court of the Republic. It determines taxes; ratifies treaties concluded by the Executive with other States and international organizations; sanctions the Budget; regulates the monetary system of the country; determines the conditions under which foreign currencies may circulate; and suspends and reimposes constitutional guarantees. The right to initiate legislation may be exercised by the Asamblea (as well as by the President, through the Council of Ministers, and by the Supreme Court). The Asamblea may override, with a two-thirds majority, the President's objections to a Bill which it has sent for presidential approval.

### PRESIDENT

The President is elected for five years, the term beginning and expiring on 1 June. The principle of alternation in the presidential office is established in the Constitution, which states the action to be taken should this principle be violated. The Executive is responsible for the preparation of the Budget and its presentation to the Asamblea; the direction of foreign affairs; the organization of the armed and security forces; and the convening of extraordinary sessions of the Asamblea. In the event of the President's death, resignation, removal or other cause, the Vice-President takes office for the rest of the presidential term; and, in case of necessity, the Vice-President may be replaced by one of the two Designates elected by the Asamblea.

### JUDICIARY

Judicial power is exercised by the Supreme Court and by other competent tribunals. The Magistrates of the Supreme Court are elected by the Legislature, their number to be determined by law. The Supreme Court alone is competent to decide whether laws, decrees and regulations are constitutional or not.

## The Government

### HEAD OF STATE

**President:** FRANCISCO FLORES PÉREZ (assumed office 1 June 1999).

**Vice-President:** CARLOS QUINTANILLA.

### COUNCIL OF MINISTERS

(February 2000)

**Minister of Foreign Affairs:** MARÍA EUGENIA BRIZUELA DE AVILA.

**Minister of the Interior:** MARIO ACOSTA OERTEL.

**Minister of Justice and Public Security:** FRANCISCO BERTRAND GALINDO.

**Minister of the Economy:** MIGUEL E. LACAYO.

**Minister of Education:** ANA EVELYN JACIR DE LOVO.

**Minister of National Defence:** Gen. JUAN ANTONIO MARTÍNEZ VARELA.

**Minister of Labour and Social Security:** JORGE NIETO MENÉNDEZ.

**Minister of Public Health and Social Welfare:** JOSÉ LÓPEZ BELTRÁN.

**Minister of the Treasury:** JOSÉ LUIS TRIGUEROS.

**Minister of Agriculture and Livestock:** SALVADOR URRUTIA LOUCEL.

**Minister of Public Works:** JOSÉ ANGEL QUIROZ.

**Minister of the Environment and Natural Resources:** ANA MARÍA MAJANO GUERRERO.

### MINISTRIES

**Ministry for the Presidency:** Avda Cuba, Calle Darió González 806, Barrio San Jacinto, San Salvador; tel. 221-8483; fax 771-0950.

**Ministry of Agriculture and Livestock:** Alameda Roosevelt, San Salvador; tel. 779-1579; fax 779-1941.

**Ministry of the Economy:** 1A Calle Poniente 2310, Col. Escalón, San Salvador; tel. 224-2159; fax 998-1965.

**Ministry of Education:** Dirección de Publicaciones, 17 Avda Sur 430, San Salvador; tel. 222-0665; fax 271-1071.

**Ministry of the Environment and Natural Resources:** Edif. Torre El Salvador, 3°, Alameda Roosevelt y 55 Avda Norte, San Salvador; tel. 260-8900; fax 260-3117; e-mail marn@vianet.com.sv; internet www.marn.gob.sv.

**Ministry of Foreign Affairs:** Alameda Dr Manuel Enrique Araújo, Km 6, Carretera a Santa Tecla, San Salvador; tel. 243-3805; fax 243-3710.

**Ministry of the Interior:** Centro de Gobierno, Alameda Juan Pablo II, San Salvador; tel. 298-5000.

**Ministry of Justice:** Avda Masferrer 612B, Col. Escalón, San Salvador; tel. 998-5413; fax 998-5232.

**Ministry of Labour and Social Security:** Avda La Capilla 223, Col. San Benito, San Salvador; tel. 779-0388; fax 779-0877.

**Ministry of National Defence:** Alameda Dr Manuel Enrique Araújo, Km 5, Carretera a Santa Tecla, San Salvador; tel. 223-0233; fax 998-2005.

**Ministry of Public Health and Social Welfare:** Calle Arce 827, San Salvador; tel. 771-0008.

**Ministry of Public Security:** 6A Col. Antiguo, Local Policia Nacional, San Salvador; tel. 245-2667; fax 245-2660.

**Ministry of Public Works:** 1A Avda Sur 603, San Salvador; tel. 222-1505; fax 771-2881.

**Ministry of the Treasury:** Edif. Las Tres Torres, San Salvador; tel. 771-0250; fax 771-0591.

## President and Legislature

### PRESIDENT

**Election, 7 March 1999**

| Candidates | % of votes cast |
|---|---|
| FRANCISCO FLORES PÉREZ (ARENA) | 51.96 |
| FACUNDO GUARDADO (FMLN/USC) | 29.05 |
| RUBÉN IGNACIO ZAMORA (CD) | 7.50 |
| RODOLFO PARKER (PDC) | 5.68 |
| RAFAEL HERNÁN CONTRERAS (PCN) | 3.82 |
| SALVADOR NELSON GARCÍA (LIDER) | 1.63 |
| FRANCISCO AYALA DE PAZ (PUNTO) | 0.36 |
| **Total** | 100.0 |

### ASAMBLEA NACIONAL

**President:** JUAN DUCH (ARENA).

**General Election, 16 March 1997**

| Party | Seats |
|---|---|
| Alianza Republicana Nacionalista (ARENA) | 28 |
| Frente Farabundo Martí para la Liberación Nacional (FMLN) | 27 |
| Partido de Conciliación Nacional (PCN) | 11 |
| Partido Demócrata Cristiano (PDC) | 7 |
| PDC/Partido Demócrata (PD) coalition | 3 |
| Partido de Renovación Social Cristiano (PRSC) | 3 |
| Convergencia Democrática (CD) | 2 |
| Partido Liberal Democrático (PLD) | 2 |
| Movimiento de Unidad (MU) | 1 |
| **Total** | 84 |

## Political Organizations

**Alianza Republicana Nacionalista (ARENA):** San Salvador; f. 1981; right-wing; Leader ALFREDO CRISTIANI BURKARD.

**Frente Farabundo Martí para la Liberación Nacional (FMLN):** 27 Calle Poniente 1316 y 9a Avda Norte 229, San Salvador; tel. 225-2961; f. 1980 (see below), achieved legal recognition 1992; left-wing; Co-ordinator FABIO CASTILLO.

**Liga Democrática Republicana (LIDER):** San Salvador; republican.

**Movimiento Auténtico Cristiano (MAC):** San Salvador; f. 1988; Leader JULIO ADOLFO REY PRENDES.

**Movimiento Estable Republicano Centrista (MERECEN):** San Salvador; f. 1982; centre party; Sec.-Gen. JUAN RAMÓN ROSALES Y ROSALES.

**Partido Acción Democrática (AD):** Apdo 124, San Salvador; f. 1981; centre-right; observer mem. of Liberal International; Leader RICARDO GONZÁLEZ CAMACHO.

**Partido Acción Renovadora (PAR):** San Salvador; f. 1944; advocates a more just society; Leader ERNESTO OYARBIDE.

**Partido Auténtico Institucional Salvadoreño (PAISA):** San Salvador; f. 1982; formerly right-wing majority of the PCN; Sec.-Gen. Dr ROBERTO ESCOBAR GARCÍA.

**Partido de Conciliación Nacional (PCN):** Calle Arce 1128, San Salvador; f. 1961; right-wing; Pres. CIRO ZEPEDA; Leader FRANCISCO JOSÉ GUERRERO; Sec.-Gen. RAFAEL MORÁN CASTANEDA.

**Partido Demócrata (PD):** San Salvador; f. 1995 by ERP, RN, MNR and a dissident faction of the PDC; centre-left.

**Partido Demócrata Cristiano (PDC):** 3a Calle Poniente 836, San Salvador; tel. 222-1815; fax 998-1526; f. 1960; 150,000 mems; anti-imperialist, advocates self-determination and Latin American integration; Sec.-Gen. RONALD UMAÑA.

**Partido de Orientación Popular (POP):** San Salvador; f. 1981; extreme right-wing.

**Partido Liberal Democrático (PLD):** San Salvador; f. 1994; right-wing; Leader KIRIO WALDO SALGADO.

**Partido Popular Salvadoreño (PPS):** Apdo 425, San Salvador; tel. 224-5546; fax 224-5523; f. 1966; right-wing; represents business interests; Sec.-Gen. FRANCISCO QUIÑÓNEZ AVILA.

**Partido Unionista Centroamericana (PUCA):** San Salvador; advocates reunification of Central America; Pres. Dr GABRIEL PILOÑA ARAÚJO.

**Pueblo Unido Nuevo Trato (PUNTO):** San Salvador.

**Unión Social Cristiana (USC):** f. 1997 by merger of Movimiento de Unidad, Partido de Renovación Social Cristiano and Movimiento de Solidaridad Nacional; Leader ABRAHAM RODRÍGUEZ.

Other parties include Partido Centrista Salvadoreño (f. 1985; Leader TOMÁS CHAFOYA MARTÍNEZ); Partido de Empresarios, Campesinos y Obreros (ECO, Leader Dr LUIS ROLANDO LÓPEZ) and Partido Independiente Democrático (PID, f. 1985; Leader EDUARDO GARCÍA TOBAR); Partido de la Revolución Salvadoreña (Sec.-Gen. JOAQUÍN VILLALOBOS); Patria Libre (f. 1985; right-wing; Leader HUGO BARRERA); Partido Social Demócrata (PSD, f. 1987; left-wing; Sec.-Gen. MARIO RENI ROLDÁN); Partido Liberal Democrático (PLD, f. 1994; right-wing; Leader KIRIO WALDO SALGADO); Expresión Renovadora del Pueblo (ERP, f. 1994; left-wing; Leader JOAQUÍN VILLALOBOS); Resistencia Nacional (RN, f. 1994; left-wing; Leader EDUARDO SANCHO).

The following groups were active during the internal disturbances of the 1980s and early 1990s:

### OPPOSITION GROUPING

**Frente Democrático Revolucionario-Frente Farabundo Martí para la Liberación Nacional (FDR-FMLN):** San Salvador; f. 1980 as a left-wing opposition front to the PDC-military coalition Government; the FDR was the political wing and the FMLN was the guerrilla front; military operations were co-ordinated by the Dirección Revolucionaria Unida (DRU); Leader RUBÉN ZAMORA RIVAS; General Command (FMLN) FERMÁN CIENFUEGOS, ROBERTO ROCA, JOAQUÍN VILLALOBOS, LEONEL GONZÁLEZ, SHAFIK JORGE HANDAL; the front comprised *c.* 20 groups, of which the principal were:

**Bloque Popular Revolucionario (BPR):** guerrilla arm: Fuerzas Populares de Liberación (FPL; Leader 'Commander GERÓNIMO'); based in Chalatenango; First Sec. LEONEL GONZÁLEZ; Second Sec. DIMAS RODRÍGUEZ.

**Frente de Acción Popular Unificado (FAPU):** guerrilla arm: Fuerzas Armadas de la Resistencia Nacional (FARN); Leaders FERMÁN CIENFUEGOS, SAÚL VILLALTA.

**Frente Pedro Pablo Castillo:** f. 1985.

**Ligas Populares del 28 de Febrero (LP-28):** guerrilla arm: Ejército Revolucionario Popular (ERP); Leaders JOAQUÍN VILLALOBOS, ANA GUADALUPE MARTÍNEZ.

**Movimiento Nacional Revolucionario (MNR):** Blvd María Cristina 128, Urbanización La Esperanza, San Salvador; tel. 226-4194; fax 225-3166; f. 1967; Sec.-Gen. Dr VÍCTOR MANUEL VALLE.

**Movimiento Obrero Revolucionario Salvado Cayetano Carpio (MOR).**

**Movimiento Popular Social Cristiano (MPSC):** formed by dissident members of PDC; Leader RUBÉN ZAMORA RIVAS.

**Partido Comunista Salvadoreño (PCS):** guerrilla arm: Fuerzas Armadas de Liberación (FAL); Leader SHAFIK JORGE HANDAL; Deputy Leader AMÉRICO ARAÚJO RAMÍREZ.

**Partido Revolucionario de los Trabajadores Centroamericanos (PRTC):** Leaders ROBERTO ROCA, MARÍA CONCEPCIÓN DE VALLADARES (alias Commdr NIDIA DÍAZ).

**Unión Democrática Nacionalista (UDN):** f. 1969; Communist; Sec.-Gen. MARIO AGUINADA CARRANZA.

In November 1987 the PSD, MNR and MPSC united to form a left-wing alliance, the **Convergencia Democrática** (CD; Leader VINICIO PEÑATE). The MNR and MPSC, however, remained as members of the FDR-FMLN. In December 1994 the Expresión Renovadora del Pueblo (fmrly the Ejército Revolucionario Popular—the guerrilla arm of the LP-28) and the Resistencia Nacional (fmrly the Fuerzas Armadas de la Resistencia Nacional—the guerrilla arm of the FAPU) announced their withdrawal from the FMLN, and subsequently formed the Partido Demócrata (PD). In August 1995 the PRTC and the PCS announced their dissolution and absorption by the FMLN.

### OTHER GROUPS

**Partido de Liberación Nacional (PLN):** political-military organization of the extreme right; the military wing was the Ejército Secreto Anti-comunista (ESA); Sec.-Gen. and C-in-C AQUILES BAIRES.

The following guerrilla groups were dissident factions of the Fuerzas Populares de Liberación (FPL):

**Frente Clara Elizabeth Ramírez:** f. 1983; Marxist-Leninist group.

**Movimiento Laborista Cayetano Carpio:** f. 1983.

There were also several right-wing guerrilla groups and 'death squads', including the Fuerza Nacionalista Roberto D'Aubuisson (FURODA), not officially linked to any of the right-wing parties.

## Diplomatic Representation

### EMBASSIES IN EL SALVADOR

**Argentina:** 79 Avda Norte 704, Col. Escalón, Apdo 384, San Salvador; tel. 224-4238; Ambassador: JUAN CARLOS IBÁÑEZ.

**Brazil:** Edif. la Centroamericana, 5°, Alameda Roosevelt 3107, San Salvador; tel. 998-2751; fax 779-3934; Ambassador: FRANCISCO DE LIMA E SILVA.

**Chile:** Pasaje Belle Vista 121, Entre 9a C.P. y 9a C.P. bis, Col. Escalón, San Salvador; tel. 223-7132; Ambassador: RENÉ PÉREZ NEGRETE.

**China (Taiwan):** 89a Avda Norte 335, Col. Escalón, Apdo 956, San Salvador; tel. 298-3464; Ambassador: Gen. LO YU-LUM.

**Colombia:** Edif. Inter-Capital, 2°, Paseo General Escalón y Calle La Ceiba, Col. Escalón, San Salvador; tel. 223-0126; Ambassador: Dr LUIS GUILLERMO VÉLEZ TRUJILLO.

**Costa Rica:** Edif. La Centroamericana, 3°, Alameda Roosevelt 3107, San Salvador; tel. 279-0303; fax 279-3079; Ambassador: FERNANDO JIMÉNEZ MAROTO.

**Dominican Republic:** San Salvador; tel. 223-6636; Ambassador: ALBERTO EMILIO DESPRADEL CABRAL.

**Ecuador:** 77 Avda Norte 208, Col. Escalón, San Salvador; tel. 223-1279; fax 779-3098; Ambassador: Dr LUIS GALLEGOS.

**France:** 1 Calle Poniente 3718, Col. Escalón, Apdo 474, San Salvador; tel. 279-4016; fax 298-1536; e-mail ambafrance@es.com.sv; Ambassador: LYDIE GAZARIAN.

**Germany:** 7a Calle Poniente 3972 esq. 77a Avda Norte, Col. Escalón, Apdo 693, San Salvador; tel. 223-6140; fax 298-3368; Ambassador: RICHARD GIESEN.

**Guatemala:** 15 Avda Norte 135, San Salvador; tel. 221-6097; Ambassador: Brig.-Gen. LUIS FEDERICO FUENTES CORADO.

**Holy See:** 87a Avda Norte y 7a Calle Poniente, Col. Escalón, Apdo 01-95, San Salvador (Apostolic Nunciature); tel. 263-2931; fax 263-3010; e-mail nunapes@es.com.sv; Apostolic Nuncio: Most Rev. GIACINTO BERLOCO, Titular Archbishop of Fidene.

**Honduras:** 7a Calle Poniente 4326, Col. Escalón, San Salvador; tel. 223-3856; fax 779-0545; Ambassador: FRANCISCO ZEPEDA ANDINO.

**Israel:** 85 Avda Norte 619, Col. Escalón, Apdo 1776, San Salvador; tel. 298-5331; Ambassador: YOSEF LIVNE.

**Italy:** Calle la Reforma 158, Col. San Benito, Apdo 0199, San Salvador; tel. 223-7325; fax 778-3050; Ambassador: Dr MARIO FORESTI (also represents the interests of Somalia).

**Japan:** Avda La Capilla 615, Col. San Benito, San Salvador; tel. 24-4597; Chargé d'affaires: HIROYUKI KIMOTO.

**Mexico:** Calle Circunvalación y Pasaje 12, Col. San Benito, Apdo 432, San Salvador; tel. 243-3190; fax 243-0437; Ambassador: Lic. JOSÉ IGNACIO PIÑA.

**Nicaragua:** 71a Avda Norte y 1a Calle Poniente 164, Col. Escalón, San Salvador; tel. 223-7729; fax 223-7201; Ambassador: ROBERTO FERREY ECHAVERRY.

**Panama:** Alameda Roosevelt 2838 y Avda Norte 55, Apdo 104, San Salvador; tel. 260-5452; fax 260-5453; Ambassador: MIRIAM BERMÚDEZ.

**Paraguay:** Avda La Capilla 414, Col. San Benito, San Salvador; tel. 223-5951; Ambassador: JUAN ALBERTO LLÁNEZ.

**Peru:** Edif. La Centroamericana, 2°, Alameda Roosevelt 3107, Apdo 1579, San Salvador; tel. 223-0008; fax 223-5672; Ambassador: GUSTAVO TEIXEIRA.

**Spain:** 51a Avda Norte 138, entre 1a Calle Poniente y Alameda Roosevelt, San Salvador; tel. 223-7961; fax 998-0402; Ambassador: RICARDO PEIDRÓ CONDE.

**United Kingdom:** Edif. Inter Inversión, Paseo General Escalón 4828, Apdo 1591, San Salvador; tel. 298-1763; fax 298-3328; Ambassador: PATRICK MORGAN.

**USA:** Blvd Santa Elena Sur, Antiguo Cuscatlán, La Libertad; tel. 278-4444; fax 278-6011; Ambassador: ANNE W. PATTERSON.

**Uruguay:** Edif. Gran Plaza, 4°, Blvd del Hipódromo San Benito, San Salvador; tel. and fax 279-1626; Ambassador: Dr ENRIQUE DELGADO GENTA.

**Venezuela:** Calle La Mascota 319, Col. La Mascota, San Salvador; tel. 223-5809; Ambassador: Dra ELSA BOCCHECIAMPE.

# Judicial System

**Supreme Court of Justice:** Centro de Gobierno José Simeón Cañas, San Salvador; tel. 771-3511; fax 771-3379; f. 1824; composed of 14 Magistrates, one of whom is its President. The Court is divided into four chambers: Constitutional Law, Civil Law, Penal Law and Litigation.

**President:** JOSÉ DOMINGO MÉNDEZ.

**Chambers of 2nd Instance:** 14 chambers composed of two Magistrates.

**Courts of 1st Instance:** 12 courts in all chief towns and districts.

**Courts of Peace:** 99 courts throughout the country.

**Attorney-General:** ROBERTO MENDOZA JEREZ.

**Secretary-General:** ERNESTO VIDAL RIVERA GUZMÁN.

**Attorney-General of the Poor:** Dr VICENTE MACHADO SALGADO.

# Religion

Roman Catholicism is the dominant religion, but other denominations are also permitted. In 1982 there were about 200,000 Protestants. Seventh-day Adventists, Jehovah's Witnesses, the Baptist Church and the Church of Jesus Christ of Latter-day Saints (Mormons) are represented.

## CHRISTIANITY

### The Roman Catholic Church

El Salvador comprises one archdiocese and seven dioceses. About 85% of the country's inhabitants are adherents.

**Bishops' Conference:** Conferencia Episcopal de El Salvador, 15 Avda Norte 1420, Col. Layco, Apdo 1310, San Salvador; tel. 225-8997; fax 226-5330; f. 1974; Pres. Most Rev. FERNANDO SÁENZ LACALLE, Archbishop of San Salvador.

**Archbishop of San Salvador:** Most Rev. FERNANDO SÁENZ LACALLE, Arzobispado, Calle San José y Avda Las Américas, Apdo 2253, San Salvador; tel. 226-0501; fax 226-4979.

### The Anglican Communion

El Salvador comprises one of the five dioceses of the Iglesia Anglicana de la Región Central de América.

**Bishop of El Salvador:** Rt Rev. MARTÍN DE JESÚS BARAHONA PASCACIO, 47 Avda Sur, 723 Col. Flor Blanca, Apdo 01-274, San Salvador; tel. 223-2252; fax 223-7952; e-mail martinba@gbm.net.

### The Baptist Church

**Baptist Association of El Salvador:** Avda Sierra Nevada 922, Col. Miramonte, Apdo 347, San Salvador; tel. 226-6287; f. 1933; Exec. Sec. Rev. CARLOS ISIDRO SÁNCHEZ.

# The Press

## DAILY NEWSPAPERS

### San Miguel

**Diario de Oriente:** Avda Gerardo Barrios 406, San Miguel.

### San Salvador

**Co Latino:** 23a Avda Sur 225, Apdo 96, San Salvador; tel. 271-0671; fax 271-0971; e-mail colatino@es.com.sv; f. 1890; evening; Editor FRANCISCO ELÍAS VALENCIA; circ. 15,000.

**El Diario de Hoy:** 11 Calle Oriente 271, Apdo 495, San Salvador; tel. 271-0100; fax 271-2040; e-mail comedh@es.com.sv; internet www.elsavador.com; f. 1936; morning; independent; Dir ENRIQUE ALTAMIRANO MADRIZ; circ. 115,000.

**Diario Oficial:** 4a Calle Poniente 829, San Salvador; tel. 221-9101; f. 1875; Dir LUD DREIKORN LÓPEZ; circ. 2,100.

**El Mundo:** 2a Avda Norte 211, Apdo 368, San Salvador; tel. 771-4400; fax 771-4342; internet www.sadecu.com/el-mundo; f. 1967; evening; Dir CRISTÓBAL IGLESIAS; circ. 58,032 (weekdays), 61,822 (Sundays).

**La Noticia:** Edif. España, Avda España 321, San Salvador; tel. 222-7906; fax 771-1650; f. 1986; evening; general information; independent; Dir CARLOS SAMAYOA MARTÍNEZ; circ. 30,000 (weekdays and Saturdays).

**La Prensa Gráfica:** 3a Calle Poniente 130, San Salvador; tel. 271-1010; fax 271-4242; e-mail lpg@gbm.net; internet www.gbm.net/la-prensa-grafica; f. 1915; general information; conservative, independent; Editor RODOLFO DUTRIZ; circ. 97,312 (weekdays), 115,564 (Sundays).

### Santa Ana

**Diario de Occidente:** 1a Avda Sur 3, Santa Ana; tel. 441-2931; f. 1910; Editor ALEX E. MONTENEGRO; circ. 6,000.

## PERIODICALS

**Anaqueles:** 8a Avda Norte y Calle Delgado, San Salvador; review of the National Library.

**Cultura:** Concultura, Ministerio de Educación, 17 Avda Sur 430, San Salvador; tel. 222-0665; fax 271-1071; quarterly; educational; Dir Dr RICARDO ROQUE BALDOVINOS.

**El Salvador Filatélico:** Avda España 207, Altos Vidrí Panades, San Salvador; f. 1940; publ. quarterly by the Philatelic Society of El Salvador.

**Orientación:** 1a Calle Poniente 3412, San Salvador; tel. 998-6838; fax 224-5099; f. 1952; Catholic weekly; Dir P. FABIAN AMAYA TORRES; circ. 8,000.

**Proceso:** Universidad Centroamericana, Apdo 01-575, San Salvador; tel. 224-0011; fax 273-3556; f. 1980; weekly newsletter, published by the Documentation and Information Centre of the Universidad Centroamericana José Simeón Cañas; Dir LUIS ARMANDO GONZÁLEZ.

**Revista del Ateneo de El Salvador:** 13a Calle Poniente, Centro de Gobierno, San Salvador; tel. 222-9686; f. 1912; 3 a year; official organ of Salvadorean Athenaeum; Pres. Lic JOSÉ OSCAR RAMÍREZ PÉREZ; Sec.-Gen. Lic. RUBÉN REGALADO SERMEÑO.

**Revista Económica:** Avda Bernal, Pasaje Recinos, Miramonte, San Salvador.

**Revista Judicial:** Centro de Gobierno, San Salvador; tel. 222-4522; organ of the Supreme Court; Dir Dr MANUEL ARRIETA GALLEGOS.

## PRESS ASSOCIATIONS

**Asociación de Corresponsales Extranjeros en El Salvador:** Edif. Montecristo, 3°, Frente a Salvador del Mundo, comienzo del Paseo Gral Escalón, San Salvador; tel. 224-5507; Dir CRISTINA HASBÚN.

**Asociación de Periodistas de El Salvador** (Press Association of El Salvador): Edif. Casa del Periodista, Paseo General Escalón 4130, San Salvador; tel. 223-8943; Pres. JORGE ARMANDO CONTRERAS.

## FOREIGN NEWS AGENCIES

**Agencia EFE** (Spain): Edif. OMSA, 2°, Of. 1, 21 Calle Poniente, San Salvador; tel. 226-0110; Bureau Chief CRISTINA HASBÚN DE MERINO.

**Agenzia Nazionale Stampa Associata (ANSA)** (Italy): Edif. 'Comercial 29', 29 Calle Poniente y 11 Avda Norte, San Salvador; tel. 226-8008; fax 774-5512; Bureau Chief RENÉ ALBERTO CONTRERAS.

**Associated Press (AP)** (USA): Hotel Camino Real, Suite 201, Blvd de Los Héroes, San Salvador; tel. 224-4885; Correspondent ANA LEONOR CABRERA.

**Deutsche Presse-Agentur (dpa)** (Germany): Avda España 225, 2°, Of. 1, Apdo 150, San Salvador; tel. 222-2640; Correspondent JORGE ARMANDO CONTRERAS.

**Inter Press Service (IPS)** (Italy): Apdo 05152, San Salvador; tel. 998-0760; Correspondent PABLO IACUB.

**Reuters** (United Kingdom): 7 Calle Poniente 3921, Col. Escalón, San Salvador; tel. 223-4736; Bureau Chief ALBERTO BARRERA.

**United Press International (UPI)** (USA): Calle y Pasaje Palneral, Col. Toluca, Apdo 05-185, San Salvador; tel. 225-4033; Correspondent (vacant).

# Publishers

**CENITEC (Centro de Investigaciones Tecnológicas y Científicas):** 85 Avda Norte 905 y 15c Pte, Col. Escalón, San Salvador; tel. 223-7928; f. 1985; politics, economics, social sciences; Dir IVO PRÍAMO ALVARENGA.

**Clásicos Roxsil, SA de CV:** 4a Avda Sur 2–3, Nueva San Salvador; tel. 228-1832; fax 228-1212; f. 1976; textbooks, literature; Dir ROSA VICTORIA SERRANO DE LÓPEZ.

**Editorial Delgado:** Universidad 'Dr José Matías Delgado', Km 8.5, Carretera a Santa Tecla, Ciudad Merliot; tel. 278-1011; f. 1984; Dir LUCÍA SÁNCHEZ.

**Editorial Universitaria:** Ciudad Universitaria de El Salvador, Apdo 1703, San Salvador; tel. 226-0017; f. 1963; Dir TÍRSO CANALES.

**D'TEXE (Distribuidora de Textos Escolares):** Edif. C, Col., Paseo y Condominio Miralvalle, San Salvador; tel. 274-2031; f. 1985; educational; Dir JORGE A. LÓPEZ HIDALGO.

**Dirección de Publicaciones e Impresos:** Ministerio de Educación, 17a Avda Sur 430, San Salvador; tel. 222-0665; fax 271-1071; e-mail dpi@netcomsa.com; f. 1953; educational and general; Dir MIGUEL HUEZO MIXCO.

**UCA Editores:** Apdo 01-575, San Salvador; tel. 273-4400; fax 273-3556; f. 1975; social science, religion, economy, literature and textbooks; Dir RODOLFO CARDENAL.

### PUBLISHERS' ASSOCIATIONS

**Asociación Salvadoreña de Agencias de Publicidad:** Centro Profesional Presidente Loc. 33a, Col. San Benito, San Salvador; tel. 243-3535; f. 1962; Dir ANA ALICIA DE GONZÁLEZ.

**Cámara Salvadoreña del Libro:** 4a Avda Sur 2–3, Apdo 2296, Nueva San Salvador; tel. 228-1832; fax 228-1212; f. 1974; Pres. ADELA CELARIÉ.

# Broadcasting and Communications

### TELECOMMUNICATIONS

**Compañía de Telecomunicaciones de El Salvador (CTE):** San Salvador; tel 771-7171; fax 221-5456; terrestrial telecommunications network, frmly part of Administración Nacional de Telecomunicaciones which was divested in 1998; 51% owned by France Télécom.

**Internacional de Telecomunicaciones (Intel):** San Salvador: manages sale of telecommunications frequencies, frmly part of Administración Nacional de Telecomunicaciones which was divested in 1998; controlling interest owned by Telefónica de España.

**Superintendencia General de Electricidad y Telecomunicaciones (SIGET):** Centro Financiero SISA, Edif. 4, 1°, Carretera a Nueva San Salvador; tel. 288-0066; internet www.siget.gob.sv/index.htm; f. 1996.

### RADIO

**Asociación Salvadoreña de Radiodifusores (ASDER):** Avda Izalco, Bloco 6 No 33, Residencial San Luis, San Salvador; tel. 222-0872; fax 274-6870; f. 1965; Pres. JOSÉ ANDRÉS ROVIRA CANALES.

**YSS Radio Nacional de El Salvador:** Dirección General de Medios, Calle Monserrat, Plantel Ex-IVU, San Salvador; tel. 773-4170; non-commercial cultural station; Dir-Gen. ALFONSO PÉREZ GARCÍA.

There are 64 commercial radio stations. Radio Venceremos and Radio Farabundo Martí, operated by the former guerrilla group FMLN, were legalized in April 1992. A new station, Radio Mayavisión (operated by FMLN supporters), began broadcasting in November 1993.

### TELEVISION

**Canal 2, SA:** Carretera a Nueva San Salvador, Apdo 720, San Salvador; tel. 223-6744; fax 998-6565; commercial; Pres. BORIS ESERSKI; Gen. Man. SALVADOR I. GADALA MARÍA.

**Canal 4, SA:** Carretera a Nueva San Salvador, Apdo 444, San Salvador; tel. 224-4555; commercial; Pres. BORIS ESERSKI; Man. RONALD CALVO.

**Canal 6, SA:** Km 6, Alameda Dr Manuel Enrique Araújo, Apdo 06-1801, San Salvador; tel. 243-3966; fax 243-3818; e-mail tv6@gbm.net; f. 1972; commercial; Exec. Dir JUAN CARLOS ESERSKI; Man. DR PEDRO LEONEL MORENO MONGE.

**Canal 8 and 10 (Televisión Cultural Educativa):** Avda Robert Baden Powell, Apdo 104, Nueva San Salvador; tel. 228-0499; fax 228-0973; f. 1964; government station; Dir TOMÁS PANAMEÑO.

**Canal 12:** Urb. Santa Elena 12, Antiguo Cuscatlán, San Salvador; tel. 278-0622; fax 278-0722; f. 1984; Pres. RICARDO SALINAS PLIEGO.

**Canal 15:** 4a Avda Sur y 5a Calle Oriente 301, San Miguel; tel 661-3298; fax 661-3298; f. 1994; Gen. Man. JOAQUÍN APARICIO.

**Canal 19 Sistemas de Video y Audio INDESI:** Final Calle Los Abetos 1, Col. San Francisco, San Salvador; Gen. Man. MARIO CAÑAS.

**Canal 21 (Megavisión):** Final Calle Los Abetos 1, Col San Francisco, Apdo 2789, San Salvador; tel. 298-5311; fax 298-6492; f. 1993; Pres. OSCAR ANTONIO SAFIE; Dir HUGO ESCOBAR.

**Canal 25 (Auvisa de El Salvador):** Final Calle Libertad 100, Nueva San Salvador; commercial; Gen. Man. MANUEL BONILLA.

**Canal 33 (Teleprensa):** Istmania 262, Col Escalón, San Salvador; tel. 224-6040; fax 224-3193; f. 1957; Dir and Gen. Man. GUILLERMO DE LEÓN.

# Finance

(cap. = capital; p.u. = paid up; res = reserves; dep. = deposits; m. = million; brs = branches; amounts in colones unless otherwise stated)

### BANKING

The banking system was nationalized in March 1980. In October 1990 the Government announced plans to return the banking system to private ownership. In June 1991 the Government initiated the transfer to private ownership of six banks and seven savings and loans institutions, as part of a programme of economic reform.

#### Supervisory Body

**Superintendencia del Sistema Financiero:** 7a Avda Norte 240, Apdo 2942, San Salvador; tel. 281-2444; fax 279-1819; internet www.ssf.gob.sv/princip.htm; Supt Lic. FRANCISCO RODOLFO BERTRÁND GALINDO.

#### Central Bank

**Banco Central de Reserva de El Salvador:** Alameda Juan Pablo II y 17 Avda Norte, Apdo 01-106, San Salvador; tel. 281-8069; fax 281-8072; e-mail comunicaciones@bcr.gob.sv; internet www.bcr.gob.sv; f. 1934; nationalized Dec. 1961; sole right of note issue; cap. 800.0m., res 830.9m., dep. 9,639.5m. (Dec. 1996); Pres. RAFAEL BARRAZA; First Vice-Pres. CARMEN ELENA DE ALEMÁN.

#### Commercial and Mortgage Banks

**Banco Agrícola Comercial de El Salvador:** Paseo General Escalón y 69 Avda Sur 3635, Col. Escalón, San Salvador; tel. 771-2666; fax 223-6516; f. 1955; privately owned; cap. 30m., res 13.1m., dep. 1,113.8m. (June 1987); Pres. RODOLFO SANTOS MORALES; 8 brs.

**Banco de Comercio de El Salvador:** Alameda Roosevelt y 43 Avda Norte, Apdo 237, San Salvador; tel. 224-3238; fax 224-0890; f. 1949; scheduled for transfer to private ownership in 1993; cap. 102m., dep. 497.6m. (June 1990); Pres. Lic. RAMÓN AVILA QUEHL; Gen. Man. Lic. MARCO TULIO MEJÍA; 23 brs.

**Banco de Construcción y Ahorro, SA (BANCASA):** 75 Avda Sur 209, Col. Escalón, Apdo 2215, San Salvador; tel. 263-5641; fax 263-5506; f. 1964; saving and building finance; cap. 289m., dep. 39,305m. (April 1999); Pres. JOSÉ LUIS ZABLAH; 37 brs.

**Banco Cuscatlán:** Edif. Pirámide Cuscatlán, La Libertad, Km 10, Carretera a Santa Tecla, Apdo 626, San Salvador; tel. 228-7777; fax 229-2168; e-mail cuscatlan@bancocuscatlan.com; f. 1972; partially privatized in 1992; cap. 400.0m., res 655.9m., dep. 10,457.9m. (June 1999); Pres. MAURICIO SAMAYOA RIVAS; 28 brs.

**Banco Desarrollo, SA:** 67 Avda Norte, Blvd Constitución y 1A Calle Poniente, San Salvador; tel. 245-7000; e-mail mail@bancodesarrollo.com; internet www.bancodesarrollo.com; f. 1978; cap. 36.57m., dep. 445.71m. (March 1999); Pres. Lic. JOSÉ ANTONIO SALAVERRÍA BORJA; 50 brs.

**Banco Hipotecario:** Pasaje Senda Florida Sur, Col. Escalón, Apdo 999, San Salvador; tel. 223-3753; fax 298-0447; f. 1935; state-owned commercial bank; cap. 104.0m., dep. 1,852m. (Dec. 1998); Pres. Lic. BENJAMÍN VIDES DÉNEKE; Exec. Dir Lic. JOSÉ DIMAS QUINTANILLA; 24 brs.

**Banco Salvadoreño, SA:** Edif. Centro Financiero, Avda Olímpica 3550, Apdo 06-73, San Salvador; tel. 298-4444; fax 298-0102;

internet www.gbm.net/bancosal; f. 1885; privatization announced in 1992; cap. 145m., res 23.6m., dep. 2,957.9m. (Aug. 1993); Pres. Lic. FÉLIX SIMÁN J.; Vice-Pres. Ing. MOISÉS CASTRO MACEDA; 61 brs.

### Public Institutions

**Banco de Fomento Agropecuario:** Km 10.5, Carretera al Puerto de la Libertad, Nueva San Salvador; tel. 228-5199; fax 229-2930; e-mail rgprieto@gbm.net; f. 1973; cap. 605.0m., dep. 872.0m. (Oct. 1997); Pres. RAÚL GARCÍA PRIETO; Gen. Man. JUAN A. MARTÍNEZ; 27 brs.

**Financiera Nacional de la Vivienda (FNV):** 49 Avda Sur 820, San Salvador; tel. 223-8822; fax 223-9985; national housing finance agency; f. 1963 to improve housing facilities through loan and savings associations; cap. 5.2m., res 20.8m. (June 1990); Pres. Lic. RICARDO F. J. MONTENEGRO PALOMO; Man. Lic. ADALBERTO ELÍAS CAMPOS.

### Savings and Loan Associations

**Asociación de Ahorro y Préstamo, SA (ATLACATL):** 55 Avda Sur 221, San Salvador; tel. 779-0033; fax 224-4278; f. 1964; savings and loan association; cap. 19.2m., dep. 305.4m. (June 1987); Pres. Ing. GASTÓN DE CLAIRMONT DUEÑAS; 17 brs.

**Ahorro, Préstamos e Inversiones, SA (APRISA):** Edif. Metroplaza, Oficina Central, San Salvador; tel. 998-0411; fax 224-1288; f. 1977; cap. 3.1m., res 0.7m., dep. 105.8m. (June 1987); Pres. Lic. GINO ROLANDO BETTAGLIO; 9 brs.

**Ahorros Metropolitanos, SA (AHORROMET):** Paseo General Escalón, Contiguo a CURACAO, Salvador del Mundo, Edif. Ahorromet, San Salvador; tel. 771-0888; fax 224-2884; f. 1972; cap. 4.5m., res 0.5m., dep. 187.9m. (June 1987); Pres. Lic. JUAN FEDERICO SALAVERRIA; 12 brs.

**La Central de Ahorros, SA:** 43 Avda Sur, Alameda Roosevelt, San Salvador; tel. 224-4840; fax 223-3783; f. 1979; cap. 5m., dep. 60m. (June 1989); Pres. Lic. GUILLERMO ALFARO CASTILLO; 7 brs.

### Banking Associations

**Federación de Asociaciones Cooperativas de Ahorro y Crédito de El Salvador, de Responsabilidad Limitada (FEDECACES DE R.L.):** 23 Avda Norte y 25 Calle Poniente 1301, Col. San Jorge, Apdo 156, San Salvador; tel. 226-9014; fax 226-8925; e-mail fedecaces.gcia@ejje.com; f. 1966; Pres. MARCOS ANTONIO GONZÁLEZ ARÉVALO; Gen. Man. HÉCTOR DAVID CÓRDOVA ARTEAGA.

**Federación de Cajas de Crédito (FEDECREDITO):** 25a Avda Norte y 23 Calle Poniente, San Salvador; tel. 225-5922; fax 226-7059; f. 1943; Pres. MARCO TULIO RODRÍGUEZ MENA; Gen. Man. RODOLFO ELÍAS SEGOVIA BAIRES.

## STOCK EXCHANGE

**Mercado de Valores de El Salvador, SA de CV (Bolsa de Valores):** Alameda Roosevelt 3107, 6°, Edif. La Centroamericana, San Salvador; tel. 298-4244; fax 223-2898; Pres. GUILLERMO HIDALGO-QUEHL.

## INSURANCE

**AIG Unión y Desarrollo, SA:** Calle Loma Linda 265, Col. San Benito, Apdo 92, San Salvador; tel. 298-5455; fax 298-5084; e-mail jorge.guirola@uni-desa.com; f. 1998 following merger of Unión y Desarrollo, SA and AIG; Exec. Dir RAMÓN AVILA.

**American Life Insurance Co.:** Edif. Omnimotores, 2°, Km 4½, Carretera a Santa Tecla, Apdo 169, San Salvador; tel. 223-4925; f. 1963; Man. CARLOS F. PEREIRA.

**Aseguradora Agrícola Comercial, SA:** Alameda Roosevelt 3104, Apdo 1855, San Salvador; tel. 260-3344; fax 260-5592; f. 1973; Pres. LUIS ALFREDO ESCALANTE; Gen. Man. FEDERICO PERAZA F.

**Aseguradora Popular, SA:** Paseo General Escalón 5338, Col. Escalón, San Salvador; tel. 998-0700; fax 224-6866; f. 1975; Exec. Pres. Dr CARLOS ARMANDO LAHÚD.

**Aseguradora Salvadoreña:** Alameda Dr Manuel Enrique Araújo y Calle Nueva 2, Edif. Omnimotores, 2°, San Salvador; tel. 224-3816; fax 224-5990; f. 1974; Pres. JOSÉ MAURICIO LOUCEL.

**Aseguradora Suiza Salvadoreña, SA:** Calle la Reforma, Col. San Benito, Apdo 1490, San Salvador; tel. 298-5222; fax 298-5060; f. 1969; Pres. MAURICIO M. COHEN; Gen. Man. RODOLFO SCHILDKNECHT.

**Internacional de Seguros, SA:** 79A Avda Norte 521, Col. Escalón, San Salvador; tel. 224-6935; fax 224-6935; f. 1958; Pres. FÉLIX JOSÉ SIMÁN JACIR; Gen. Man. ALEJANDRO CABRERA RIVAS.

**La Centro Americana, SA, Cía Salvadoreña de Seguros:** Alameda Roosevelt 3107, Apdo 527, San Salvador; tel. 223-6666; fax 223-2687; f. 1915; Pres. TOMÁS TRIGUEROS ALCAINE; Gen. Man. RUFINO GARAY.

**Compañía Anglo Salvadoreña de Seguros, SA:** Paseo General Escalón 3848, San Salvador; tel. 224-2399; fax 224-4394; f. 1976; Pres. Lic. RICARDO BARRIENTOS; Vice-Pres. JULIO E. PAYES.

**Compañía General de Seguros, SA:** Calle Loma Linda 223, Col. San Benito, Apdo 1004, San Salvador; tel. 779-2777; fax 998-2870; f. 1955; Pres. Lic. ANTONIO PERLA BUSTAMENTE; Gen. Man. Lic. HERIBERTO PÉREZ AGUIRRE.

**Seguros e Inversiones, SA (SISA):** Alameda Dr Manuel Enrique Araújo 3530, Apdo 1350, San Salvador; tel. 998-1199; fax 998-2882; f. 1962; Pres. JACOBO ESTEBAN NASSER.

**Seguros Universales, SA:** Paseo Escalón y 81 Avda Norte 205, Col. Escalón, San Salvador; tel. 779-3533; fax 779-1830; Pres. Dr ENRIQUE GARCÍA PRIETO.

# Trade and Industry

## GOVERNMENT AGENCIES AND DEVELOPMENT ORGANIZATIONS

**Consejo Nacional de Ciencia y Tecnología (CONACYT):** Urb. Isidro Menéndez, Pasaje San Antonio 51, San Salvador; f. 1992; formulation and guidance of national policy on science and technology; Exec. Dir CARLOS FEDERICO PAREDES CASTILLO.

**Corporación de Exportadores de El Salvador (COEXPORT):** Condomínios del Mediterráneo, Edif. 'A', No 23, Col. Jardines de Guadalupe, San Salvador; tel. 243-1328; fax 243-3159; e-mail service@coexport.com; internet www.coexport.com; f. 1973 to promote Salvadorean exports; Exec. Dir Lic. SILVIA M. CUÉLLAR.

**Corporación Salvadoreña de Inversiones (CORSAIN):** 1a Calle Poniente, entre 43 y 45 Avda Norte, San Salvador; tel. 224-4242; fax 224-6877; Pres. Lic. MARIO EMILIO REDAELLI.

**Fondo de Financiamiento y Garantía para la Pequeña Empresa (FIGAPE):** 9a Avda Norte 225, Apdo 1990, San Salvador; tel. 771-1994; f. 1994; government body to assist small-sized industries; Pres. Lic. MARCO TULIO GUARDADO.

**Fondo de Garantía para el Crédito Educativo (EDUCREDITO):** Avda España 726, San Salvador; tel. 222-2181; f. 1973.

**Fondo Social para la Vivienda (FSV):** Calle Rubén Darío y 17 Avda Sur 455, San Salvador; tel. 271-1662; fax 271-2910; internet www.fsv.gob.sv; f. 1973; Pres. EDGAR RAMIRO MENDOZA JEREZ; Gen. Man. FRANCISCO ANTONIO GUEVARA.

**Instituto Salvadoreño de Transformación Agraria (ISTA):** Km 5½, Carretera a Santa Tecla, San Salvador; tel. 224-6000; fax 224-0259; f. 1976 to promote rural development; empowered to buy inefficiently cultivated land; Pres. JOSÉ ROBERTO MOLINA MORALES.

**Instituto de Vivienda Urbana (IVU):** Avda Don Bosco, Centro Urbano Libertad, San Salvador; tel. 225-3011; f. 1950; government housing agency, transferred to private ownership in 1991; Pres. Lic. PEDRO ALBERTO HERNÁNDEZ P.

## CHAMBER OF COMMERCE

**Cámara de Comercio e Industria de El Salvador:** 9a Avda Norte y 5a Calle Poniente, Apdo 1640, San Salvador; tel. 771-2055; fax 771-4461; f. 1915; 1,800 mems; Pres. RICARDO SIMÁN; Exec. Dir Ing. FRANCISCO CASTRO FUNES; Gen. Man. ALBERO PADILLA; branch offices in San Miguel, Santa Ana and Sonsonate.

## INDUSTRIAL AND TRADE ASSOCIATIONS

**Asociación Cafetalera de El Salvador (ACES):** 67 Avda Norte 116, Col. Escalón, San Salvador; tel. 223-3024; fax 223-7471; f. 1930; coffee growers' asscn; Pres. Ing. EDUARDO E. BARRIENTOS.

**Asociación de Ganaderos de El Salvador:** 1a Avda Norte 1332, San Salvador; tel. 225-7208; f. 1932; livestock breeders' asscn; Pres. Lic. CARLOS ARTURO MUYSHONDT.

**Asociación Salvadoreña de Beneficiadores y Exportadores de Café (ABECAFE):** 87a Avda Norte 720, Col. Escalón, Apdo A, San Salvador; tel. 223-3292; fax 223-3292; coffee producers' and exporters' asscn; Pres. VICTORIA DALTÓN DE DÍAZ.

**Asociación Salvadoreña de Industriales:** Calles Roma y Liverpool, Col. Roma, Apdo 48, San Salvador; tel. 279-2488; fax 279-2070; e-mail asi@asi.com.sv; internet www.asi.com.sv; f. 1958; 400 mems; manufacturers' asscn; Pres. LEONEL MEJÍA; Exec. Dir Lic. JORGE ARRIAZA.

**Cooperativa Algodonera Salvadoreña, Ltda:** 7a Avda Norte 418, Apdo 616, San Salvador; tel. 222-0399; fax 222-7359; f. 1940; 185 mems; cotton growers' asscn; Pres. ULISES FERNANDO GONZÁLEZ; Gen. Man. Lic. MANUEL RAFAEL ARCE.

**Instituto Nacional del Azúcar:** Paseo General Escalón y 87a Avda Norte, San Salvador; tel. 224-6044; fax 224-5132; national sugar institute, scheduled for privatization; Pres. Lic. JAIME ALVAREZ GOTÁN.

**Instituto Nacional del Café (INCAFE):** 6a Avda Sur 133, San Salvador; tel. 771-3311; f. 1942; national coffee institute, scheduled for privatization; Pres. ROBERT SUÁREZ SUAY; Gen. Man. MIGUEL ÁNGEL AGUILAR.

**UCAFES:** San Salvador; union of coffee-growing co-operatives; Pres. FRANCISCO ALFARO CASTILLO.

### EMPLOYERS' ORGANIZATIONS

There are several business associations, the most important of which is the Asociación Nacional de Empresa Privada (National Private Enterprise Association).

### UTILITIES

#### Electricity

**Comisión Ejecutiva Hidroeléctrica del Río Lempa (CEL):** 9a Calle Poniente 950, San Salvador; tel. 271-0855; fax 228-1911; state energy agency dealing with electricity generation and transmission, and non-conventional energy sources; scheduled for privatization; Pres. GUILLERMO A. SOL BANG.

**Superintendencia General de Electricidad y Telecomunicaciones (SIGET):** Centro Financiero SISA, Edif. 4, 1°, Carretera a Nueva San Salvador; tel. 288-0066; internet www.siget.gob.sv /index.htm; f. 1996.

#### Water

**Administración Nacional de Acueductos y Alcantarillados (ANDA):** Edif. ANDA, Final Avda Don Bosco, Col Libertad, San Salvador; tel. 225-3534; fax 225-3152; f. 1961; maintenance of water supply and sewerage systems; Pres. CARLOS AUGUSTO PERLA.

### TRADE UNIONS

**Asociación de Sindicatos Independientes—ASIES** (Association of Independent Trade Unions): San Salvador.

**Central de Trabajadores Democráticos—CTD** (Democratic Workers' Confederation): 6 Avda Sur y 8 Calle Oriente 438, San Salvador; tel. 221-5405; Pres. SALVADOR CARAZO.

**Central de Trabajadores Salvadoreños—CTS** (Salvadorean Workers' Confederation): Calle Darío González 616, Barrio San Jacinto, San Salvador; f. 1966; Christian Democratic; 35,000 mems; Sec.-Gen. MIGUEL ANGEL VÁSQUEZ.

**Confederación General de Sindicatos—CGS** (General Confederation of Unions): 3a Calle Oriente 226, San Salvador; f. 1958; admitted to ICFTU/ORIT; 27,000 mems.

**Confederación General del Trabajo—CGT** (General Confederation of Workers): 2a Avda Norte 619, San Salvador; tel. 222-5980; f. 1983; 20 affiliated unions; Sec.-Gen. JOSÉ LUIS GRANDE PREZA; 85,000 mems.

**Coordinadora de Solidaridad de los Trabajadores—CST** (Workers' Solidarity Co-ordination): San Salvador; f. 1985; conglomerate of independent left-wing trade unions.

**Federación Campesina Cristiana de El Salvador-Unión de Trabajadores del Campo—FECCAS-UTC** (Christian Peasant Federation of El Salvador—Union of Countryside Workers): Universidad Nacional, Apdo 4000, San Salvador; allied illegal Christian peasants' organizations.

**Federación Nacional de Sindicatos de Trabajadores de El Salvador (FENASTRAS)** (Salvadorean Workers' National Union Federation): San Salvador; f. 1975; left-wing; 35,000 mems in 16 affiliates.

**Federación Revolucionaria de Sindicatos** (Revolutionary Federation of Unions): San Salvador; Sec.-Gen. SALVADOR CHÁVEZ ESCALANTE.

**Federación Unitaria Sindical Salvadoreña—FUSS** (United Salvadorean Union Federation): Centro de Gobierno, Apdo 2226, San Salvador; tel. and fax 225-3756; f. 1965; left-wing; Sec.-Gen. JUAN EDITO GENOVEZ.

**MUSYGES** (United Union and Guild Movement): San Salvador; labour federation previously linked to FDR; 50,000 mems (est.).

**Unión Comunal Salvadoreña—UCS** (Salvadorean Communal Union): 4a Calle Oriente 6-4, Santa Tecla, La Libertad; tel. 284-836; peasants' association; 100,000 mems; Gen. Sec. GUILLERMO BLANCO.

**Unidad Nacional de Trabajadores Salvadoreños—UNTS** (National Unity of Salvadorean Workers): San Salvador; f. 1986; largest trade union conglomerate; Leader MARCO TULIO LIMA; affiliated unions include:

> **Unidad Popular Democrática—UPD** (Popular Democratic Unity): San Salvador; f. 1980; led by a committee of 10; 500,000 mems.

**Unión Nacional Obrera-Campesina—UNOC** (Worker-Peasant National Union): San Salvador; f. 1986; centre-left labour organization; 500,000 mems.

Some unions, such as those of the taxi drivers and bus owners, are affiliated to the Federación Nacional de Empresas Pequeñas Salvadoreñas—Fenapes, the association of small businesses.

## Transport

**Comisión Ejecutiva Portuaria Autónoma (CEPA):** Edif. Torre Roble, Blvd de Los Héroes, Apdo 2667, San Salvador; tel. 224-1133; fax 224-0907; f. 1952; operates and administers the ports of Acajutla (on Pacific coast) and Cutuco (on Gulf of Fonseca) and the El Salvador International Airport, as well as Ferrocarriles Nacionales de El Salvador; Pres. RUY CÉSAR MIRANDA; Gen. Man. Lic. ARTURO GERMÁN MARTÍNEZ.

### RAILWAYS

There are about 674 km of railway track in the country. The main track links San Salvador with the ports of Acajutla and Cutuco and with San Jerónimo on the border with Guatemala. The International Railways of Central America run from Anguiatú on the El Salvador–Guatemala border to the Pacific ports of Acajutla and Cutuco and connect San Salvador with Guatemala City and the Guatemalan Atlantic ports of Puerto Barrios and Santo Tomás de Castilla.

A project to connect the Salvadorean and Guatemalan railway systems between Santa Ana and Santa Lucia (in Guatemala) is under consideration.

**Ferrocarriles Nacionales de El Salvador (FENADESAL):** Avda Peralta 903, Apdo 2292, San Salvador; tel. 271-5632; fax 271-5650; 562 km open; in 1975 Ferrocarril de El Salvador and the Salvadorean section of International Railways of Central America (429 km open) were merged and are administered by the Railroad Division of CEPA (see above); Gen. Man. TULIO O. VERGARA.

### ROADS

The country's highway system is well integrated with its railway services. There were some 15,120 km of roads in 1994, including: the Pan-American Highway: 306 km; paved highways: 1,739 km; improved roads: 7,999 km; dry-weather roads: 2,692 km. A coastal highway, with interconnecting roads, was under construction in the early 1990s.

### SHIPPING

The ports of Acajutla and Cutuco are administered by CEPA (see above). Services are also provided by foreign lines.

### CIVIL AVIATION

**AESA Aerolíneas de El Salvador, SA de CV:** Avda Las Palmas 129, Col. San Benito, Apdo 1830, San Salvador; tel. 224-6166; fax 224-6588; cargo and mail service between San Salvador and Miami; Pres. E. CORNEJO LÓPEZ; Gen. Man. JOSÉ ROBERTO SANTANA.

**TACA International Airlines:** Edif. Caribe, 2°, Col. Escalón, San Salvador; tel. 339-9155; fax 223-3757; f. 1939; passenger and cargo services to Central America and the USA; Pres. FEDERICO BLOCH; Gen. Man. BEN BALDANZA.

## Tourism

El Salvador was one of the centres of the ancient Mayan civilization, and the ruined temples and cities are of great interest. The volcanoes and lakes of the uplands provide magnificent scenery, while there are fine beaches along the Pacific coast. The civil war, from 1979 to 1992, severely affected the tourism industry. The number of tourist arrivals increased from 181,332 in 1994 to 282,835 in 1996.

**Buró de Convenciones y Visitantes de la Ciudad de San Salvador:** Edif. Olimpic Plaza, 73 Avda Sur 28, 2°, San Salvador; tel. 224-0819; fax 223-4912; f. 1973; assists in organization of national and international events; Pres. (vacant); Exec. Dir ROSY MEJÍA DE MARCHESINI.

**Cámara Salvadoreña de Turismo:** Hotel El Salvador, 89 Avda Norte y 11 Calle Poniente, Col. Escalón, San Salvador; tel. 223-9992; Pres. ARNOLDO JIMÉNEZ; co-ordinates:

> **Comité Nacional de Turismo (CONATUR):** San Salvador; tel. 223-4566; comprises hotels, restaurants, tour operators, airlines and Instituto Salvadoreño de Turismo; Sec. MERCEDES MELÉNDEZ.
>
> **Feria Internacional de El Salvador (FIES):** Km 6, Carretera a Santa Tecla, San Salvador; tel. 998-5644; fax 998-5388; Pres. MIGUEL ANGEL SALAVERRIA.
>
> **Instituto Salvadoreño de Turismo (ISTU)** (National Tourism Institute): Calle Rubén Darío 619, San Salvador; tel. 222-0960; fax 222-1208; f. 1950; Pres. CARLOS HIRLEMANN; Dir EDUARDO LÓPEZ RIVERA.

# EQUATORIAL GUINEA

## Introductory Survey

### Location, Climate, Language, Religion, Flag, Capital

The Republic of Equatorial Guinea consists of the islands of Bioko (formerly Fernando Póo and subsequently renamed Macías Nguema Biyogo under the regime of President Macías), Corisco, Great Elobey, Little Elobey and Annobón (previously known also as Pagalu), and the mainland region of Río Muni (previously known also as Mbini) on the west coast of Africa. Cameroon lies to the north and Gabon to the east and south of Río Muni, while Bioko lies off shore from Cameroon and Nigeria. The small island of Annobón lies far to the south, beyond the islands of São Tomé and Príncipe. The climate is hot and humid, with average temperatures higher than 26°C (80°F). The official languages are Spanish and French. In Río Muni the Fang language is spoken, as well as those of coastal tribes such as the Combe, Balemke and Bujeba. Bubi is the indigenous language on Bioko, although Fang is also widely used, and Ibo is spoken by the resident Nigerian population. An estimated 90% of the population are adherents of the Roman Catholic Church, although traditional forms of worship are also followed. The national flag (proportions 3 by 2) has three equal horizontal stripes, of green, white and red, with a blue triangle at the hoist and the national coat of arms (a silver shield, containing a tree, with six yellow stars above and a scroll beneath) in the centre of the white stripe. The capital is Malabo (formerly Santa Isabel).

### Recent History

Portugal ceded the territory to Spain in 1778. The mainland region and the islands were periodically united for administrative purposes. In July 1959 Spanish Guinea, as the combined territory was known, was divided into two provinces: Río Muni, on the African mainland, and Fernando Póo (now Bioko), with other nearby islands. From 1960 the two provinces were represented in the Spanish legislature. In December 1963 they were merged again, to form Equatorial Guinea, with a limited measure of self-government.

After 190 years of Spanish rule, independence was declared on 12 October 1968. Francisco Macías Nguema, Equatorial Guinea's first President, formed a coalition Government from all the parties represented in the new National Assembly. In March 1969 the Minister for Foreign Affairs, Atanasio Ndongo Miyone, was killed by security forces during a failed coup attempt.

In February 1970 the President outlawed all existing political parties and formed the Partido Unico Nacional (PUN), which later became the Partido Unico Nacional de los Trabajadores (PUNT). Macías appointed himself Life President in July 1972. A new Constitution, giving absolute powers to the President was adopted in July 1973. Macías controlled both radio and press and all citizens were forbidden to leave the country, although many fled during his rule. During 1975–77 there were many arrests and executions. Nigerian workers were repatriated in 1976, following reports of maltreatment and forced labour. The Macías regime maintained close relations with the Soviet bloc.

In August 1979 President Macías was overthrown in a coup led by his nephew, Lt-Col (later Brig.-Gen.) Teodoro Obiang Nguema Mbasogo, hitherto the Deputy Minister of Defence. (Obiang Nguema subsequently ceased to use his forename.) Macías was found guilty of treason, genocide, embezzlement and violation of human rights, and was executed in September. The Spanish Government, which admitted prior knowledge of the coup, was the first to recognize the new regime, and remained a major supplier of financial and technical aid. Obiang Nguema appointed civilians to the Government for the first time in December 1981. In August 1982 he was reappointed President for a further seven years, and later that month a new Constitution, which provided for an eventual return to civilian government, was approved by 95% of voters in a referendum. At legislative elections held in August 1983 some 41 candidates, who had been nominated by the President, were elected (unopposed) to a new House of Representatives.

The imposition, from 1979 to 1991, of a ban on organized political activity within Equatorial Guinea, and persistent allegations against the Obiang Nguema regime of human rights abuses and corruption, resulted in the development of a substantial opposition in exile. Opposition coalitions were formed in Spain and France during the 1980s. In 1991 the Coordinación Democrática de los Partidos de Oposición de Guinea Ecuatorial was established in Libreville, Gabon, and in 1999 unregistered opposition parties exiled in Spain formed the Coordinadora de la Oposición Conjunta (see below).

During the 1980s Obiang Nguema's rule was threatened on a number of occasions. Attempted coups were reported in April 1981, May 1983 and November 1983. In January 1986 the President reinforced his control by assuming the post of Minister of Defence. An attempt in July by senior civilian and military officials to occupy the presidential palace in Malabo was quelled by loyalist forces. In the following month the alleged leader of the coup attempt, Eugenio Abeso Mondu (a former diplomat and a member of the House of Representatives), was sentenced to death and executed, while prison sentences were imposed on 12 others who had been convicted of complicity in the plot, including two government ministers and the national director of the Banque des Etats de l'Afrique Centrale. In August 1987 Obiang Nguema announced the establishment of a 'governmental party', the Partido Democrático de Guinea Ecuatorial (PDGE), while continuing to reject demands for the legalization of opposition parties. At legislative elections held in July 1988, 99.2% of voters endorsed a single list of candidates who had been nominated by the President. In September severe sentences of imprisonment were imposed on nine civilians and military officers who had been convicted of plotting to overthrow Obiang Nguema; these included the Secretary-General of the Partido del Progreso de Guinea Ecuatorial, José Luis Jones. Jones was, however, released in January 1989, prior to an official visit to Spain by Obiang Nguema.

In June 1989, at the first presidential election to be held since independence, Obiang Nguema, the sole candidate, reportedly received the support of more than 99% of the electorate. Opposition groupings criticized the conduct of the election and declared the result invalid. Following his success, the President appealed to dissidents to return to Equatorial Guinea and declared an amnesty for political prisoners. However, Obiang Nguema reiterated his opposition to the establishment of a multi-party system, and in December 1990 it was reported that about 30 advocates of the introduction of a plural political system had been imprisoned. The human rights organization Amnesty International has frequently reiterated accusations against the Equato-Guinean authorities of detaining and torturing political opponents.

In April 1991 opposition groups in exile in Gabon formed a coalition, the Coordinación Democrática de los Partidos de Oposición de Guinea Ecuatorial. In early August the ruling PDGE held its first national extraordinary congress, at which delegates demanded the introduction of a new democratic constitution, the legalization of other political parties and the removal of restrictions on the media. Nevertheless, in mid-August a prominent opposition leader in exile was refused a passport to travel to Equatorial Guinea in order to campaign for democracy, and shortly afterwards it was reported that the Equato-Guinean Ambassador to Spain had been arrested during a return visit to Equatorial Guinea, for allegedly liaising with opposition movements. In the following month Amnesty International claimed that torture was 'accepted practice' in Equatorial Guinea, and reported the deaths in custody of at least six Equato-Guineans since 1988. Later in September the Government announced the formation of a human rights commission.

A new Constitution, containing provisions for a multi-party political system, was approved by an overwhelming majority of voters at a national referendum in November 1991. However, opposition movements rejected the Constitution, owing to the inclusion of clauses exempting the President from any judicial procedures arising from his tenure of office and prohibiting citizens who had not been continuously resident in Equatorial Guinea for 10 years from standing as election candidates, while requiring all political parties to submit an excessively large deposit (which could not be provided by funds from abroad) as a condition of registration. In addition, there was inadequate provision for the upholding of human rights. In January 1992 a transitional Government was formed (comprising only members of the PDGE), and, during that month, a general amnesty was extended to all political exiles. The UN published a report in January which adversely criticized the human rights record of the Equato-Guinean authorities and some of the provisions incorporated in the new Constitution. Throughout 1992 the security forces continued to arrest members of opposition parties. In early November two Spanish businessmen were charged with plotting a coup against the Government; they were found guilty later in the month and sentenced to 12 years' imprisonment, but were pardoned on the same day. During November a new alliance of opposition organizations, the Plataforma de la Oposición Conjunta (POC), was created.

In January 1993 an electoral law was promulgated. In February the UN released another report in which it alleged a serious disregard for human rights by the Obiang Nguema regime. During February and March the Government and several opposition organizations negotiated a national pact which established conditions for the conduct of legislative elections that were due to take place in 1993, including the freedom to organize political activity and the provision of equal access to the media for all political parties. However, the Government was soon accused of violating the pact, and further arrests and mistreatment of its political opponents were reported. During August violent clashes occurred on the island of Annobón between anti-Government demonstrators and the security forces. Accusations by the Equato-Guinean authorities that Spain had incited the unrest were strongly denied by the Spanish Government.

Multi-party legislative elections took place in November 1993. The elections were, however, boycotted by most of the parties in the POC, in protest at Obiang Nguema's refusal to review contentious clauses of the electoral law or to permit impartial international observers to inspect the electoral register. The UN declined a request by the Equato-Guinean authorities to monitor the elections, contending that correct electoral procedures were evidently being infringed. Representatives of the OAU were present and estimated that 50% of the electorate participated. The PDGE won 68 of the 80 seats in the House of Representatives, while, of the six opposition parties that presented candidates, the Convención Socialdemocrática Popular obtained six seats, the Unión Democrática y Social de Guinea Ecuatorial won five seats and the Convención Liberal Democrática secured one. Widespread electoral irregularities were alleged to have occurred and, prior to the elections, opposition politicians were reportedly subjected to intimidation by the security forces. In early December the Government announced that all party political gatherings would henceforth be subject to prior official authorization. In mid-December Silvestre Siale Bileka, hitherto Prime Minister of the interim Government,was appointed Prime Minister of the new administration. Shortly afterwards Bileka nominated a Council of Ministers, which included no opposition representatives.

In April 1994 Severo Moto Nsa, the founding leader of one of the most influential exiled opposition parties, the Partido del Progreso de Guinea Equatorial (PPGE), based in Spain, returned to Equatorial Guinea. In June, in response to pressure from international aid donors, the Government agreed to amend the controversial electoral law and to conduct a preliminary electoral census prior to the holding of local elections. In September, however, the authorities began to compile a full population census, instead of preparing for the local elections, which had been scheduled for November. The census was boycotted by opposition parties, and many people were arrested in ensuing clashes with the security forces. The local elections were postponed. In October the Speaker and Deputy Speaker of the National Assembly resigned, accusing the Obiang Nguema administration of incompetence and disregard for human rights. In early November Moto Nsa alleged that the Government had sanctioned the assassination of Vicente Moto, who was his brother and a senior figure in the POC.

In early 1995 the Constitution and electoral law were amended to reduce from 10 to five the minimum number of years required for candidates to have been resident in Equatorial Guinea. In February several leading members of the PPGE, including Moto Nsa, were arrested for allegedly plotting to overthrow Obiang Nguema; in April they were found guilty by a military court and sentenced to terms of imprisonment. (Moto Nsa received a sentence of 28 years.) The convictions and sentences were widely condemned by foreign Governments and in August, following representations by President Chirac of France, Obiang Nguema unexpectedly pardoned all the convicted PPGE members.

Local elections (which had been postponed in 1994—see above) were staged, on a multi-party basis, in September 1995. According to the official results, the ruling PDGE won an overall victory, securing a majority of the votes cast in two-thirds of local administrations. Allegations by the opposition (which claimed to have obtained 62% of the votes) that serious electoral malpractice had occurred were supported by the Spanish Ambassador to Equatorial Guinea. A monitoring team of international observers agreed that some electoral irregularities had taken place.

At a presidential election held in February 1996 Obiang Nguema was returned to office, reportedly securing more than 90% of the votes cast. However, influential opposition leaders boycotted the contest, in protest at alleged electoral irregularities and official intimidation. In late March Obiang Nguema appointed a new Prime Minister, Angel Serafin Seriche Dougan (hitherto a Deputy Minister); an enlarged Council of Ministers was announced in early April. Representatives of opposition parties had declined a presidential invitation to participate in the new administration. During March the POC was dissolved.

In August 1996 Obiang Nguema awarded himself the military rank of General. In November a military court found 11 army officers guilty of conspiring to overthrow the Government; all were sentenced to terms of imprisonment.

In April 1997 representatives of the Government and of 13 opposition parties concluded a new national pact. During the following month Moto Nsa was arrested by the Angolan authorities with a consignment of arms, which were reportedly intended for use in a planned coup in Equatorial Guinea. Following his release in June, Moto Nsa was granted refuge in Spain. Meanwhile, the PPGE was banned; the party subsequently divided into two factions, of which one was led by Moto Nsa. During June Obiang Nguema dismissed two cabinet ministers. In August Moto Nsa and 11 others were convicted *in absentia* of treason; Moto Nsa was sentenced to 101 years' imprisonment. In September the Government protested strongly to Spain over its offer of political asylum to Moto Nsa. Shortly afterwards French was declared the second official national language. During September representatives of opposition parties attended a national economic conference on the management of Equatorial Guinea's soaring petroleum revenues.

In January 1998 the Government resigned. Shortly afterwards Seriche Dougan was re-appointed as Prime Minister, and a new, enlarged Council of Ministers was formed. In the following month a new electoral law was approved by the House of Representatives; this banned political coalitions, and was expected to disadvantage the opposition at the next legislative elections.

In late January 1998 armed protesters launched three successive attacks against military targets on Bioko, killing four soldiers and three civilians. The terrorist action was alleged to have been perpetrated by members of the secessionist Movimiento para la Autodeterminación de la Isla de Bioko (MAIB), which was founded in 1993 by ethnic Bubis (the original inhabitants of the island, who, following independence, had become outnumbered by the mainland Fang). Subsequently hundreds of Bubis and resident Nigerians were arrested; many were reportedly also severely tortured. In late May 1998 some 116 detainees were tried by a military court in connection with the January attacks, on charges including terrorism and treason. Fifteen of the defendants were found guilty of the most serious charges and sentenced to death; in response to international pressure, however, the death sentences were commuted to sentences of life imprisonment in September. More than 70 of the alleged separatists were found guilty of lesser offences and sentenced to terms of imprisonment varying from six to 27 years. In July Martin Puye, a prominent MAIB leader who had been sentenced to 27 years in prison following the May trial, died in detention, arousing widespread international condemnation of the conditions of imprisonment in Equatorial Guinea.

During early 1999 six unregistered opposition parties exiled in Spain, including the MAIB and Moto Nsa's faction of the PPGE, formed a new alliance, the Coordinadora de la Oposición Conjunta. Equatorial Guinea's second multi-party legislative elections took place in early March amid allegations of electoral malpractice and of the systematic intimidation of opposition candidates by the security forces. The elections were contested by 13 parties (excluding the divided PPGE, which had been banned in 1997—see above), and some 99% of the electorate was estimated to have voted. According to the official results, the ruling PDGE obtained more than 90% of the votes, increasing its representation from 68 to 75 of the 80 seats in the House of Representatives. Two opposition parties, the Unión Popular (UP) and the Convergencia para la Democracia Social (CPDS), secured four seats and one seat respectively. Both parties, however, refused to participate in the new administration, in protest at alleged violations of the electoral law. The UP, CPDS and five other opposition organizations subsequently campaigned, without success, to have the election results annulled. Following the election, Seriche Dougan was reappointed to the premiership and, in late July, a new Council of Ministers was announced. In early September Plácido Micó Abogo, the Secretary-General of the CPDS, was briefly detained by the security forces. It was reported during late 1999 that Obiang Nguema was seriously ill.

Equatorial Guinea enjoyed exceptionally high revenues from petroleum exports during the late 1990s; allegations emerged, however, that members of the Obiang Nguema regime were accruing private profits from national petroleum exports.

While Spain (the former colonial power) has traditionally been a major trading partner and aid donor, Equatorial Guinea's entry in 1983 into the Customs and Economic Union of Central Africa (replaced in 1999 by the Communauté économique et monétaire de l'Afrique centrale—see p. 201) represented a significant move towards a greater integration with neighbouring francophone countries. In 1985 Equatorial Guinea joined the Franc Zone (see p. 200), with financial assistance from France. Obiang Nguema has regularly attended Franco-African summit meetings. In late 1988 Obiang Nguema postponed a visit to Spain, following allegations, in the Spanish legislature, of the misappropriation of Spanish development aid to the former colony; the visit was, however, eventually undertaken in January 1989, when the continuation of bilateral links between the two countries was confirmed and the Spanish Government agreed to cancel one-third of Equatorial Guinea's public debt to Spain. In 1991 Spain cancelled a further one-third of the bilateral debt, and in November of that year the Prime Minister of Spain made an official visit to Equatorial Guinea. From mid-1993, however, Equato-Guinean-Spanish relations deteriorated, and in January 1994 the Spanish Government withdrew one-half of its aid to Equatorial Guinea in retaliation for the expulsion in December 1993 of a Spanish diplomat whom the Equato-Guinean authorities had accused of interfering in the country's internal affairs. In November 1994 the Equato-Guinean Government accused Spain of sponsoring the passage of a resolution adopted by the European Parliament condemning violations of human rights in Equatorial Guinea. In September 1997 the Obiang Nguema administration protested strongly to the Spanish Government over Spain's offer of political asylum to the opposition leader Severo Moto Nsa (see above). Later in that month it was announced that French would henceforth be the second national official language. On several occasions in 1998 the Equato-Guinean Government accused Spain of attempting to destabilize Equatorial Guinea by providing funds to opposition organizations. In October 1999 the Spanish Government agreed to resume full assistance to its former colony. During the 1990s the European Union withdrew financial aid to Equatorial Guinea, and the United Nations Development Programme suspended some projects.

Despite Equatorial Guinea's close military links with Nigeria, relations between the two countries became strained in 1988, when evidence emerged that Equatorial Guinea, keen to attract foreign investment, had formed links with South Africa. However, reciprocal official visits in 1990 by the Equato-Guinean and Nigerian Heads of State heralded an improvement in relations between the two countries. In November 1999 Equatorial Guinea, Angola, Cameroon, the Republic of the Congo, Gabon, Nigeria and São Tomé and Príncipe established an international committee to demarcate maritime borders in the Gulf of Guinea. The development of petroleum reserves in the region during the 1990s had revived long-standing frontier disputes.

## Government

In November 1991 a new Constitution was approved in a referendum, providing for the introduction of multi-party democracy. Executive power is vested in the President, whose seven-year term of office is renewable indefinitely. The President is immune from prosecution for offences committed before, during or after his tenure of the post. Legislative power is held by an 80-member House of Representatives, which serves for a term of five years. Both the President and the House of Representatives are directly elected by universal adult suffrage. The President appoints a Council of Ministers, headed by a Prime Minister, from among the members of the House of Representatives.

## Defence

In August 1999 there were 1,100 men in the army, 120 in the navy and 100 in the air force. There was also a paramilitary force, trained by French military personnel. Military service is voluntary. The estimated defence budget for 1999 was 4,000m. francs CFA. Spain has provided military advisers and training since 1979, and military aid has also been received from the USA.

## Economic Affairs

In 1997, according to estimates by the World Bank, Equatorial Guinea's gross national product (GNP), measured at average 1995–97 prices, was US $444m., equivalent to $1,060 per head. During 1990–97, it was estimated, GNP per head increased, in real terms, at an average annual rate of 12.1%. Over the same period, the population increased by an average of 2.5% per year. Equatorial Guinea's GNP totalled $647m. in 1998, equivalent to $1,500 per head. Equatorial Guinea's gross domestic product (GDP) increased, in real terms, by an average of 22.9% annually during 1992–98. Real GDP grew by 29.1% in 1996, by 71.2% in 1997 and by an estimated 22.0% in 1998.

Agriculture (including hunting, forestry and fishing) contributed an estimated 21.8% of GDP in 1998 (compared with 51.6% of GDP in 1995). The sector employed an estimated 71.4% of the labour force in 1998. The principal cash crop is cocoa, which contributed an estimated 1.5% of export earnings in 1998. Coffee is also a traditional export. The Government is encouraging the production of bananas, spices (vanilla, black pepper and coriander) and medicinal plants for export. The main subsistence crops are cassava and sweet potatoes. Exploitation of the country's vast forest resources (principally of okoumé and akoga timber) provided an estimated 9.2% of export revenue in 1998. Almost all industrial fishing activity is practised by foreign fleets, notably by those of countries of the EU.

Industry (including mining, manufacturing, construction and power) contributed an estimated 66.4% of GDP in 1998 (compared with 27.3% of GDP in 1995).

Extractive activities were minimal during the 1980s, and the mining sector employed less than 0.2% of the working population in 1983. However, the development of onshore and offshore reserves of petroleum and of offshore deposits of natural gas led to unprecedented economic growth during the 1990s. Exports of petroleum commenced in 1992 and provided an estimated 85.9% of total export earnings by 1998. In that year exports of natural gas (which commenced in 1997) accounted for an estimated 1.6% of export earnings. The petroleum sector contributed an estimated 61.8% of GDP in 1998 (compared with 18.2% of GDP in 1995). The existence of deposits of gold, uranium, iron ore, tantalum and manganese has also been confirmed.

The manufacturing sector contributed only an estimated 0.4% of GDP in 1998. Wood-processing constitutes the main commercial manufacturing activity.

A total of 20m. kWh of electric energy was generated in 1995. Bioko is supplied by a 3.6-MW hydroelectric installation, constructed on the Riaba river. There is a further 3.6-MW installation on the mainland. Imports of fuel products comprised 7.7% of the value of total imports in 1990.

The services sector contributed an estimated 11.8% of GDP in 1998. The dominant services are trade, restaurants and hotels, and government services.

In 1996 there was a visible trade deficit of US $116.73m., while the deficit on the current account of the balance of payments was $344.04m. In 1998 the USA was both the principal source of imports (35.4%) and the main market for exports (62.0%). Other major trading partners were Spain, France, Cameroon and the People's Republic of China. In 1990 re-exported ships and boats, wood, textile fibres and waste and cocoa constituted the principal sources of export revenue, while the principal imports were ships and boats, petroleum and related products and food and live animals.

In 1998 there was a budgetary deficit estimated at 3,754m. francs CFA. Equatorial Guinea's external debt was US $283.2m. at the end of 1997, of which $208.6m. was long-term public debt. In that year the cost of debt-servicing was equivalent to 1.4% of the value of exports of goods and services. The rate of

# ESTONIA

## Introductory Survey

**Location, Climate, Language, Religion, Flag, Capital**

The Republic of Estonia (formerly the Estonian Soviet Socialist Republic) is situated in north-eastern Europe. The country is bordered to the south by Latvia, and to the east by the Russian Federation. Estonia's northern coastline is on the Gulf of Finland and its territory includes more than 1,520 islands, mainly off its western coastline in the Gulf of Riga and the Baltic Sea. The largest of the islands are Saaremaa and Hiiumaa, in the Gulf of Riga. The climate is influenced by Estonia's position between the Eurasian land mass and the Baltic Sea and the North Atlantic Ocean. The mean January temperature in Tallinn is −0.6°C (30.9°F); in July the mean temperature is 17.1°C (62.8°F). Average annual precipitation is 568 mm. The official language is Estonian, which is a member of the Baltic-Finnic group of the Finno-Ugric languages; it is written in the Latin script and is closely related to Finnish. Many of the Russian residents, who comprise nearly 30% of the total population, do not speak Estonian. Most of the population profess Christianity and, by tradition, Estonians belong to the Evangelical Lutheran Church. Smaller Protestant sects and the Eastern Orthodox Church are also represented. The national flag (proportions 11 by seven) consists of three equal horizontal stripes, of blue, black and white. The capital is Tallinn.

**Recent History**

The Russian annexation of Estonia, formerly under Swedish rule, was formalized in 1721. During the latter half of the 19th century, as the powers of the dominant Baltic German nobility declined, Estonians experienced a national cultural revival, which culminated in political demands for autonomy during the 1905 Russian Revolution, and for full independence after the beginning of the First World War. On 30 March 1917 the Provisional Government in Petrograd (St Petersburg), which had taken power after the abdication of Tsar Nicholas II in February, approved autonomy for Estonia. A Land Council was elected as the country's representative body. However, in October the Bolsheviks staged a coup in Tallinn, and declared the Estonian Soviet Executive Committee as the sole government of Estonia. As German forces advanced towards Estonia, in early 1918, the Bolshevik troops were forced to leave. The major Estonian political parties united to form the Estonian Salvation Committee, and on 24 February 1918 an independent Republic of Estonia was proclaimed. A Provisional Government, headed by Konstantin Päts, was formed, but Germany refused to recognize Estonia's independence and the country was occupied by German troops until the end of the First World War. Following the capitulation of Germany in November 1918, the Provisional Government assumed power. After a period of armed conflict between Soviet and Estonian troops, the Republic of Estonia and Soviet Russia signed the Treaty of Tartu on 2 February 1920, under the terms of which the Soviet Government recognized Estonia's independence and renounced any rights to its territory. Estonian independence was recognized by the major Western powers in January 1921, and Estonia was admitted to the League of Nations.

This period of independence lasted until 1940. During most of this time the country had a liberal-democratic political system, in which the Riigikogu (State Assembly) was the dominant political force. Significant social, cultural and economic advances were made in the 1920s, including radical land reform. However, the decline in trade with Russia and the economic depression of the 1930s, combined with the political problems of a divided parliament, caused public dissatisfaction with the regime. In March 1934 the Prime Minister, Konstantin Päts, seized power in a bloodless coup and introduced a period of authoritarian rule. The Riigikogu and political parties were disbanded, but in 1938 a new Constitution was adopted, which provided for a presidential system of government, with a bicameral legislature. In April 1938 Päts was elected President.

In August 1939 the USSR and Germany signed a non-aggression treaty (the Nazi-Soviet or Molotov-Ribbentrop Pact). The secret supplementary protocol to the treaty provided for the occupation of Estonia by the USSR. In September Estonia was forced to sign an agreement which permitted the USSR to base Soviet troops in Estonia. In June 1940 the Government, in accordance with a Soviet ultimatum, resigned, and a new administration was appointed by the Soviet authorities, with Johannes Vares-Barbarus as Prime Minister. In July elections were held, in which only candidates approved by the Soviet authorities were permitted to participate. On 21 July the Estonian Soviet Socialist Republic was proclaimed by the new legislature, and on 6 August the republic was formally incorporated into the USSR.

Soviet rule in Estonia lasted less than a year, before German forces occupied the country. In that short period, Soviet policy resulted in mass deportations of Estonians to Siberia, the expropriation of property, severe restrictions on cultural life and the introduction of Soviet-style government in the republic.

German forces entered Estonia in July 1941 and remained in occupation until September 1944. After a short-lived attempt to reinstate Estonian independence, Soviet troops occupied the whole of the country, and the process of 'sovietization' was continued. By the end of 1949 most Estonian farmers had been forced to join collective farms. Heavy industry was expanded, with investment concentrated on electricity generation and the chemical sector. Structural change in the economy was accompanied by increased political repression, with deportations of Estonians continuing until the death of Stalin, in 1953. The most overt form of opposition to Soviet rule was provided by the 'forest brethren' (*metsavennad*), a guerrilla movement, which continued to conduct armed operations against Soviet personnel and institutions until the mid-1950s. In the late 1960s, as in other Soviet republics, more traditional forms of dissent appeared, concentrating on cultural issues, provoked by the increasing domination of the republic by immigrant Russians and other Slavs.

During the late 1970s and the 1980s the issues of 'russification' and environmental degradation became subjects of intense debate in Estonia. The policy of *glasnost,* introduced by the Soviet leader, Mikhail Gorbachev, in 1986, allowed such discussion to spread beyond dissident groups. The first major demonstrations of the 1980s were organized in protest against plans to escalate the scale of open-cast phosphorite mining in north-eastern Estonia. The public opposition to the plans caused the Soviet Government to reconsider its proposals, and this success prompted further protests. In August 1987 a demonstration, attended by some 2,000 people, commemorated the anniversary of the signing of the Nazi-Soviet Pact. Following the demonstration, an Estonian Group for the Publication of the Molotov-Ribbentrop Pact (MRP-AEG) was formed. During 1988 the Nazi-Soviet Pact was duly published, and the MRP-AEG re-formed as the Estonian National Independence Party (ENIP), proclaiming the restoration of Estonian independence as its political objective. Another opposition group, the Estonian Popular Front (EPF), which had been established in April, was formally constituted at its first congress, in October, and included many members of the ruling Communist Party of Estonia (CPE). The EPF was more cautious than the ENIP in its approach, advocating the transformation of the USSR into a confederal system. The CPE itself was forced to adapt its policies to retain a measure of public support. On 16 November the Estonian Supreme Soviet (legislature) adopted a declaration of sovereignty, which included the right to annul all-Union (USSR) legislation. The Presidium of the USSR Supreme Soviet declared the sovereignty legislation unconstitutional, but the Estonian Supreme Soviet affirmed its decision in December.

The adoption of Estonian as the state language was accepted by the Supreme Soviet in January 1989, and the tricolour of independent Estonia was also reinstated as the official flag. Despite the successes of the opposition, differing political tactics were employed by the radical ENIP and the EPF. The ENIP refused to nominate candidates for elections to the all-Union Congress of People's Deputies in March. Instead, the ENIP leadership announced plans for the registration by citizens' committees of all citizens of the pre-1940 Republic of Estonia and their descendants. Voters on an electoral register, thus compiled, would elect a Congress of Estonia as the legal suc-

Home alliance, and Lennart Meri, a former Minister of Foreign Affairs, who was supported by Isamaa. In early October 1992 the Riigikogu, now dominated by members or supporters of Isamaa, elected Meri to be Estonia's President, by 59 votes to 31.

A new coalition Government, with a large representation of Isamaa members, as well as members of the Moderates electoral alliance and the ENIP, was announced in mid-October 1992. Earlier in the month Mart Laar, a 32-year-old historian and the leader of Isamaa, had been chosen as Prime Minister. Laar indicated that the principal objectives of his administration would be to negotiate the withdrawal of all Russian troops remaining in Estonia, as well as to accelerate the country's privatization programme. In late November four of the five constituent parties of the Isamaa alliance united to form the National Fatherland Party (NFP), with Laar as its Chairman. In the same month the CPE was renamed the Estonian Democratic Labour Party.

The NFP suffered a considerable loss of support at local elections held in October 1993. In Tallinn the party secured only five of the 64 seats on the city council. In the following month Laar survived a vote of 'no confidence', proposed to the Riigikogu by opposition deputies, who accused the Prime Minister of incompetence and 'strategic errors in foreign affairs'. In January 1994 Laar reshuffled four key portfolios in the Council of Ministers (finance, economy, defence and foreign affairs), overcoming initial opposition by President Meri to two of the nominees. Meanwhile, in November 1993, the EPF was disbanded; it was stated that the party had largely fulfilled its aims.

The NFP continued to lose popular support in early 1994. At the same time the governing coalition, led by the NFP, was increasingly afflicted by internal divisions, largely prompted by what was perceived as Laar's authoritarian style of leadership. In May–June four members of the Council of Ministers resigned from their posts. Defections from the Isamaa faction within the Riigikogu resulted in supporters of Laar retaining control of only 19 seats in the legislature by early September. Following the revelation, in that month, that Laar had secretly contravened an agreement with the International Monetary Fund (IMF), a vote of 'no confidence in the Prime Minister' was endorsed by 60 members of the Riigikogu (with 27 votes against). In late October Andres Tarand, hitherto Minister of the Environment, was appointed to replace Laar. A new Council of Ministers—which included representatives of the Isamaa and Moderates groups, the ENIP, and liberal and right-wing parties—was announced in the following month.

In early January 1995 seven electoral alliances and eight parties were registered to participate in the general election scheduled for 5 March. The result of the election reflected widespread popular dissatisfaction with the parties of the governing coalition. The largest number of seats in the Riigikogu (41 of the total of 101) was won by an alliance of the centrist Estonian Coalition Party (ECP, led by the former Prime Minister, Tiit Vähi) and the Rural Union (comprising various agrarian parties, most prominently Arnold Rüütel's Estonian Country People's Party). A coalition of the newly-established Estonian Reform Party (ERP, led by Siim Kallas, the President of the Bank of Estonia) and liberal groups obtained 19 seats, followed by Edgar Savisaar's Estonian Centre Party (16). The NFP (in coalition with the ENIP) won only eight seats, while the Moderates alliance (which included Andres Tarand) gained six seats. The 'Estonia is Our Home' pact (which united three new parties representing the Russian-speaking minority) also won six seats; this development was broadly welcomed as a potentially stabilizing factor in both the domestic and foreign affairs of the country. The remaining five seats were taken by a coalition of right-wing parties. The electoral turnout was almost 70%.

In late March 1995 Tiit Vähi was nominated by President Meri to form a new Council of Ministers. Vähi was confirmed as Prime Minister by the legislature in early April, and the new Government—a coalition of the ECP/Rural Union and the Estonian Centre Party—was appointed later in the month. Vähi stated that his Government's main priorities were to further the reforms undertaken by the preceding administration, to seek full membership of the EU and to improve relations with the Russian Federation (see below).

The Government survived only until early October 1995, when it was revealed that Edgar Savisaar, the Minister of the Interior, had made secret tape and video recordings of conversations that he had held with other politicians, following the Riigikogu election in March, concerning the formation of a new coalition government. In the ensuing scandal, Savisaar was dismissed from his post by Vähi; however, the Estonian Centre Party (of which Savisaar was the leader) refused to accept his dismissal. As a result of the effective collapse of the coalition, Vähi and the remaining members of the Council of Ministers tendered their resignations. In mid-October President Meri reappointed Vähi as Prime Minister and charged him with the formation of a new Government. This emerged in late October, and represented a coalition of the ECP/Rural Union and Siim Kallas's ERP. Meanwhile, Savisaar resigned as Chairman of the Estonian Centre Party; he also announced his departure from political activity. In December the NFP and the ENIP, which had campaigned jointly in the legislative election in March, merged to form the Pro Patria (Fatherland) Union. In March 1996 tension within the Estonian Centre Party, following the scandal surrounding Savisaar, resulted in the emergence of two factions: Andra Veidemann, the Chairman of the party, and six deputies from the Riigikogu established the New Democratic Association, subsequently to become the liberal-centrist Development Party, while Savisaar was re-elected as Chairman of the Estonian Centre Party. Criminal proceedings were initiated against Savisaar in May, for conducting illegal investigative activities, but these were later abandoned.

A presidential election was held in the Riigikogu on 26 August 1996, and was contested by the incumbent, Lennart Meri, and Arnold Rüütel of the Estonian Country People's Party. A further two rounds of voting took place on the following day, since neither candidate had secured the requisite 68 votes; however, these were also inconclusive. A larger electoral college, comprising the 101 deputies of the legislature and 273 representatives of local government, was therefore convened on 20 September. Five candidates contested the first round, but, as none of the contenders secured an overall majority of the votes, a second round of voting was held to choose between the leading candidates, Meri and Rüütel. The election was won by Meri, with some 52% of the votes, and in October he was duly sworn in as President for a second term in office.

In October 1996 local government elections were held, in which the ERP gained control of Tallinn city council. In the following month the ECP concluded a co-operation agreement with the Estonian Centre Party (which had been forced to leave the Government in October 1995), pledging to seek to involve the centrists in the governing coalition. Disagreements among the coalition partners led to the collapse of the Tallinn council leadership, and Savisaar was appointed as the new Chairman of the council, replacing the newly-elected ERP candidate. The ERP threatened to leave the Government unless the co-operation agreement with the Estonian Centre Party was cancelled, and on 22 November 1996 six ministers, including Siim Kallas, the Minister for Foreign Affairs, resigned, thus causing the collapse of the ruling coalition. Negotiations to form a new coalition were conducted by the ECP with the Estonian Centre Party and the Development Party, who between them commanded 16 seats in the Riigikogu, but no agreement was reached. A minority Government, comprising the ECP, the Rural Union and independent members, which had the support of 41 deputies, was therefore appointed in early December. In early 1997 a series of allegations, concerning the abuse of his office, were made against Tiit Vähi. A legislative motion of 'no confidence in the Prime Minister', presented by the leaders of four opposition parties (the Pro Patria—Fatherland—Union, the Reform Party, the Moderates' Party and the Republican Party) in early February, was defeated by a narrow margin, but Vähi nevertheless tendered his resignation at the end of that month, while denying the allegations made against him. Mart Siimann, the leader of the ECP parliamentary faction, was appointed Prime Minister, having received the support of the majority of parliamentary deputies, and was asked to form a new Government (the resignation of the Prime Minister automatically entailed that of the Government). In mid-March a new minority Government, which comprised a coalition of the ECP, the Rural Union and independent members, was appointed. Siimann immediately declared the new Government's commitment to continue to seek economic growth through reform initiatives pursued by the previous administration. In April Robert Lepikson, a former Mayor of Tallinn, was appointed Minister of Internal Affairs, replacing Riivo Sinijärv who was dismissed allegedly for his failure to address reports of abuses of official privileges at the ministry. In September Siimann refused offers to resign tendered by both the Minister of Defence,

Andrus Öövel, and the Commander of the Armed Forces, Maj.-Gen. Johannes Kert, following an accident in which 14 Estonian soldiers of the Baltic Peace-keeping Battalion drowned, in adverse weather conditions, during a military training exercise in the Kurkse strait, off the north-western coast. A commission of inquiry into the incident, headed by the Minister of Justice, Paul Varul, concluded that 'management error' had contributed to the tragedy. Also in September, former Prime Minister Tiit Vähi announced his resignation from the ECP and his retirement from political life. His position as Chairman of the ECP was assumed by Prime Minister Siimann. In late January 1998 Robert Lepikson was dismissed as Minister of Internal Affairs, following harsh criticism, proceeding largely from Siimann, of his outspoken opinions of other members of the Government; Lepikson was replaced by independent Olari Taal.

Meanwhile, during 1998 there was considerable political consolidation and realignment in preparation for legislative elections, expected in the following year. In January the Rural Union entered into a co-operation agreement with the opposition Estonian Centre Party, while in April the smaller Estonian Farmers' Party (to which the formerly independent Minister of Foreign Affairs, Toomas Hendrik Ilves, pledged his political allegiance in December 1997) and People's Party of Republicans and Conservatives merged to form the People's Party, with Ilves as leader. The new party immediately concluded a co-operation agreement with the governing ECP, although the People's Party did not enter the governing coalition. In May, in an attempt to broaden the appeal of both political platforms, the Estonian Green Party was absorbed by the Estonian Centre Party. Meanwhile, the six members of the Riigikogu representing the three major Russian-speaking minority parties announced that they were setting aside former differences in order to present a united front in the legislature, in support of their common interests. In late September, following repeated criticism of his leadership of a party not represented in the governing coalition or the legislature, Ilves resigned the foreign affairs portfolio. As a result, the co-operation agreement concluded between the People's Party and the ECP in April was abandoned. In October an independent former diplomat, Raul Malk, was appointed as Ilves's successor. In November, in an attempt to rationalize and simplify the forthcoming election campaign, the Riigikogu voted to proscribe the formation of formal political alliances. It was expected that the legislation would make the efforts of smaller parties to gain legislative representation increasingly difficult; many members of the parties participating in the incumbent coalition Government abstained from or opposed the vote. In early December President Meri announced that elections to the Riigikogu would be conducted on 7 March 1999.

In early March 1999 Siim Kallas, leader of the ERP and the former President of the Bank of Estonia, was acquitted by the Tallinn municipal court of charges in connection with the disappearance of US $10m. from the North Estonia Bank. At the general election held on 7 March the Estonian Centre Party won 28 of the 101 seats in the legislature, the ERP and the Pro Patria (Fatherland) Union each secured 18 seats, the Moderates (in alliance with the People's Party) claimed 17 seats, the Estonian Country People's Party received seven seats and the United People's Party of Estonia won six seats. According to official sources, the level of participation was a mere 57.4% of the electorate. Although the Estonian Centre Party obtained the largest number of seats, it was unable to form a majority coalition. A centre-right coalition Government was thus formed by the ERP, the Pro Patria Union and the Moderates, with each party receiving five ministerial posts; Mart Laar, leader of the Pro Patria Union, was appointed Prime Minister (a post that he had held in 1992–94). The new Government pledged to continue the policy of free-market reforms and confirmed its objective to obtain EU membership by 2003. In May 1999 it was announced that non-native Estonians (numbering an estimated 300,000) were to be allowed to participate in local elections to be held in October. Later in May large demonstrations took place in the mainly Russian-speaking border town of Narva, in protest at rising unemployment in the region.

In October 1999 the Estonian Centre Party unsuccessfully presented a motion of 'no confidence' in the Minister of Internal Affairs, Juri Mois. At the local elections held later that month the governing ERP/Pro Patria (Fatherland) Union/Moderates coalition gained control in 13 of the 15 counties in Estonia. Following prolonged negotiations, the ERP/Pro Patria (Fatherland) Union/Moderates alliance joined with four members of the People's Trust Party and one member of the People's Choice bloc, who both represented the Russian-speaking population, to take control of Tallinn city council. Rein Voog of the ERP was elected Chairman of the council, and Juri Mois was appointed Mayor of Tallinn after resigning as Minister of Internal Affairs; he was replaced by Tarmo Loodus. Following the local elections, the Estonian Rural People's Party and the Estonian Rural Union completed their proposed merger and formed the Estonian Rural People's Union. A further political merger took place in November when the Moderates' Party and the People's Party combined to form the People's Party Moderates. Meanwhile, later in October draft legislation proposed by the Estonian Centre Party to institute direct presidential elections was defeated in the Riigikogu.

Since the restoration of Estonian independence in 1991, the republic's relations with its eastern neighbour, the Russian Federation, have been strained by a number of issues, most notably the presence of former Soviet troops (under Russian jurisdiction) and the rights of the large Russian minority in Estonia. Under the Citizenship Law of 1992 (a modified version of that adopted in 1938), non-ethnic Estonians who settled in the republic after its annexation by the USSR in 1940 were obliged to apply for naturalization (as were their descendants). Many of the requirements for naturalization—including two years' residency in Estonia as well as an examination in the Estonian language—were criticized by the Russian Government as being excessively stringent, and discriminatory against the Russian-speaking minority. A new citizenship law, adopted in January 1995, extended the residency requirement to five years. Non-citizens were given until 12 July 1995 to apply for residence and work permits, by which time almost 330,000 people (more than 80% of the total) had submitted applications. The deadline was extended until 30 November 1996, following which non-citizens were required to hold either an alien's passport (which served as an international travel document) or a residence permit. (Former Soviet passports were valid for identification purposes within Estonia until the relevant documents had been issued.) By October 1996 some 110,000 people had taken Russian citizenship, while continuing to live in Estonia. In May 1997 the Ministry of Internal Affairs announced that Soviet passports were no longer valid in Estonia. An amendment to the Language Law, adopted by the Riigikogu in November 1997, provoked outrage among the Russian-speaking minority. Under the terms of the amended law, parliamentary deputies and local government officials who had not received elementary education at an Estonian language school were to be required to demonstrate their knowledge of the language. The amendment was denounced by ethnic Russian members of the legislature (who had opposed the legislation) as unconstitutional, and the amendment was vetoed by President Meri in December 1997 and in January 1998. Meri's objections to the legislation were upheld by a ruling of the Supreme Court in early February. However, revised legislation requiring elected officials to demonstrate sufficient command of Estonian to participate in the basic bureaucratic procedures of office was approved by the Riigikogu in mid-December 1998, despite opposition from the OSCE, which had urged President Meri to veto the law. The legislation became effective in May 1999. On 1 July 1999 a further amendment to the Language Law came into force, which stipulated that all people employed in the services sector be able to communicate with clients in Estonian. In early August 1999 the leader of the Tallinn Union of Russian Citizens in Estonia, Oleg Morozov, was arrested and charged with violating Estonian residency laws. He was subsequently sentenced to 20 days' imprisonment, whereupon he commenced a hunger strike and demanded recognition as a political prisoner. Morozov had refused to obtain a residency permit, owing to the fact that he had been born in Estonia and had been resident there all his life. In protest at the sentence, another member of the Union, Eduard Shaumyan, began a hunger strike in front of the Russian embassy in Tallinn; a member of the Russian legislature, Sergei Glotov, appealed to the Parliamentary Assembly of the Council of Europe to take measures to prevent further alleged violations of the Russian-speaking minority's civil rights. Officials of the Russian Ministry of Foreign Affairs, however, urged Morozov to end his protest. Following his release, Morozov was informed that he would be placed under administrative supervision and be obliged to legalize his stay by 30 January 2000 or leave the country. In late December 1999 Petr Rozhok, another prominent member of the group, was arrested and notified that, if acquitted of extortion charges, he would also be required to obtain a residency permit or leave Estonia. Meanwhile, in September it was announced that only 34 parents had applied for Estonian citizenship on behalf of their children, following the introduction of legislation in mid-July which entitled non-citizens' children under the age of 15, who were born in Estonia, to full Estonian citizenship. Estimates had indicated that some 6,000 children would be eligible to apply.

With the dissolution of the USSR in 1991, several thousand former Soviet troops remained stationed (under Russian command) on Estonian territory. Their withdrawal was commenced in 1992, but the Russian leadership increasingly linked the progress of the troop withdrawals with the question of the citizenship, and other rights, of the Russian-speaking minority in Estonia. Withdrawals of the troops were suspended temporarily on several occasions in response to allegations of violations of the Russian minority's rights. In November 1993 a resolution by the UN General Assembly demanded a complete withdrawal of the ex-Soviet troops, and the Russian Government proposed 31 August 1994 as the final deadline for the withdrawals. Negotiations continued in 1994 on the terms for the withdrawal of the troops, but were complicated by Russian demands that the 12,000 retired Russian military servicemen (and their dependants) living in Estonia be granted unqualified citizenship rights and social guarantees. In July talks were held in Moscow between President Meri and President Yeltsin of the Russian Federation, at which Meri pledged that civil and social rights would be guaranteed to all Russian military pensioners in Estonia, while Yeltsin confirmed that Russia would remove its military presence by the end of August. The withdrawal of former Soviet troops from Estonia was finally completed on 29 August 1994. The agreements on the withdrawal of troops and on Russian military pensioners were ratified by the Russian and Estonian legislatures in 1995, despite opposition from many Estonian politicians who argued that, as Russia had been an occupying force, its servicemen should not be allowed to retire in Estonia. By December 1996 the Estonian Government had granted residence permits to over 20,000 retired servicemen and their dependants.

A further cause of tension in Estonian-Russian relations concerned Estonia's demand for the return of some 2,000 sq km (770 sq miles) of territory that had been ceded to Russia in 1944. This matter remained unresolved at inter-governmental talks held in 1992–93, with Estonia insisting that the Russian-Estonian state border be determined by the terms of the Treaty of Tartu of 1920, in which Russia recognized Estonia's independence. In June 1994 President Yeltsin ordered the unilateral demarcation of Russia's border with Estonia according to the Soviet boundary, although no agreement with Estonia had been concluded. During 1995 Estonia abandoned its demand for the return of the disputed territories. Instead, during Russian-Estonian border negotiations, the Estonian Government appealed only for minor amendments to be made to the existing line of demarcation in order to improve border security; more importantly, it insisted that Russia recognize the Treaty of Tartu as the basis of future relations between the two countries. However, the Russian Government maintained that the Treaty had lost its legal force, having been superseded by the declaration on bilateral relations signed by Russia and Estonia in 1991.

Relations between Russia and Estonia deteriorated in 1996. The re-establishment of the Estonian Apostolic Orthodox Church (see section on Religion) was perceived by Russia as a threat to the rights of the Russian-speaking minority in Estonia, and the assertion of jurisdiction in Estonia by the Ecumenical Patriarch of Constantinople in February led to a temporary break in relations with the Moscow Patriarchate. Relations were restored in May, when it was agreed that congregations should be permitted to decide which Patriarchate they wished to support. Tensions increased later in that month when Russia expelled an Estonian diplomat, allegedly for espionage; Estonia retaliated by expelling a Russian diplomat from Tallinn. Negotiations concerning the adoption of the border agreement were held at intervals throughout 1996, but Russia continued to reject the inclusion in the agreement of the Treaty of Tartu, fearing that it would legitimize Estonia's claims on Russian territory (despite the fact that Estonia had abandoned such claims). In November it was announced that Estonia was prepared to omit the Treaty of Tartu from the border agreement. The Estonian Government approved the draft agreement in late November, and declared that it would be signed by Estonia and Russia at the Lisbon summit of the OSCE in December. However, the Russian Government refused to sign the agreement until other issues had been addressed, in particular the rights of the Russian-speaking minority in Estonia. Further constructive talks on the delimitation of the border were conducted in Moscow in August 1998. By January 2000 the agreement had still not been signed, although President Meri commented on a gradual improvement in relations between the two countries in mid-1999.

Estonia actively pursues close relations with its Baltic neighbours, Latvia and Lithuania. In late 1991 the three states established a consultative interparliamentary body, the Baltic Assembly, with the aim of developing political and economic co-operation. In early 1992 it was agreed to abolish almost all trade restrictions between the three countries and to introduce a common visa policy, and a tripartite agreement on free trade and regional security was signed in late 1993. A customs agreement came into force in June 1996, which constituted the first stage of the establishment of a unified customs system. At two separate meetings during November 1997 the three countries agreed to reject Russian overtures to provide unilateral security guarantees, and to remove all non-tariff customs barriers between them, thus reiterating hopes for complete customs union by mid-1998. At a meeting in Silgulda (Latvia) in July 1998 the three countries' premiers agreed further to harmonize their respective customs procedures and labour movement regulations. In January 1998 the Presidents of the three states met President Clinton of the USA in Washington, DC, and all parties signed a Charter of Partnership. The charter, which contained no specific military provision, was described as a framework for the development of closer political and economic ties. Estonia is a member of the Council of Baltic Sea States (established in March 1992). In July 1996 the member states signed a programme of co-operation aimed at encouraging economic development and integration between the countries of the Council. Further agreements on regional co-operation were concluded by the premiers of member nations of the Council at a summit meeting which took place in January 1998 in Riga, Latvia. The summit also marked the first meeting for more than two years of the Prime Ministers of Estonia and Russia. In July 1999 the Estonian, Latvian and Lithuanian Prime Ministers met in Palanga, Lithuania. Following discussions, they agreed to develop the Baltic Common Economic Area and to remove obstacles to the further implementation of trilateral agreements on free trade. The three premiers also stressed the need to prepare for the signing of the agreement on free movement of services between the countries by 1 July 2000.

An important focus of Estonia's foreign policy is the attainment of full membership of the European Union (EU). In July 1995 Estonia became an associate member of the EU, and in December it officially applied for full membership. At a meeting of the European Council of Ministers convened in Luxembourg in December 1997, the EU confirmed that Estonia was among six states with which it wished to begin bilateral negotiations on accession in April 1998. A number of political and economic agreements concluded between the EU and the Baltic states in 1995, with the aim of facilitating their membership of the EU, came into effect on 1 February 1998. In March, in accordance with the European Convention on Human Rights and Fundamental Freedoms, the Riigikogu voted to abolish the death penalty. Among the EU states, Estonia enjoys particularly cordial relations with Finland (its largest trading partner), with which it shares close cultural and linguistic ties. Estonia is also a member of the Council of Europe (see p. 158), holding the Presidency for six months from May 1996. In addition, Estonia pursues the goal of membership of NATO (Estonia joined NATO's 'Partnership for Peace' programme of military co-operation in 1994). Despite Russian opposition to the expansion of NATO into eastern Europe and, particularly, into the former USSR, Estonia hoped to obtain full NATO membership by 2002.

## Government

Legislative authority resides with the Riigikogu (State Assembly), which has 101 members, elected by universal adult suffrage for a four-year term. The Riigikogu elects the President (Head of State) for a term of five years. The President is also Supreme Commander of Estonia's armed forces. Executive power is held by the Council of Ministers, which is headed by the Prime Minister, who is nominated by the President. For administrative purposes, Estonia is divided into 15 counties (*maakond*) and six towns. The counties are subdivided into communes (*vald*).

## Defence

Before regaining independence in 1991, Estonia had no armed forces separate from those of the USSR. Following the establishment of its own Ministry of Defence in April 1992, Estonia began to form an independent army. By August 1999 total armed forces numbered 4,800 (army 4,320, navy 340, air force 140). There was also a reserve militia of some 14,000. There is a paramilitary border guard numbering 2,800 troops, under the command of the Ministry of the Interior. Military service is for 12 months. In February 1994 Estonia joined NATO's 'Partnership for Peace' programme of military co-operation (see p. 228). In 1998 the Baltic states agreed to establish a joint airspace observation system (BALTNET), a defence college and a peacekeeping battalion (BALTBAT). A Baltic naval unit (BALTRON) was established in mid-1998. Full NATO membership was scheduled to be achieved by 2002 and Estonia is implementing measures to increase its defence expenditure, in line with NATO requirements that countries aspiring to membership should assign at least 2.0% of annual GDP for defence. Central government expenditure on defence in 1998 totalled 969.4m. kroons, which represented 4.0% of total central government spending and was equivalent to 1.5% of GDP in that year. Projected budgetary expenditure on defence for 1999 was 1,134m. kroons.

## Economic Affairs

In 1997, according to the World Bank, Estonia's gross national product (GNP), measured at average 1995–97 prices, was US $4,899m., equivalent to $3,360 per head. During 1990–97, it was estimated, GNP per head declined, in real terms, at an average annual rate of 2.8%. Over the same period the population was estimated to have declined by an annual average of 1.1%. In 1998 total GNP was estimated at $4,900m., equivalent to $3,390 per head. Estonia's gross domestic product (GDP) was estimated to have increased, in real terms, by an average of 2.2% per year during 1980–90, but to have decreased by an annual average of 2.1% during 1990–98. According to the IMF, real GDP decreased by 2.0% in 1994, but increased by 4.3% in 1995, by 4.0% in 1996, by 10.6% in 1997 and by 4.0% in 1998.

Agriculture (including forestry and fishing) contributed 6.2% of GDP in 1998. In 1996 the sector provided some 10.0% of employment. Animal husbandry is the main activity in the agricultural sector. Some 27.4% of Estonia's land is cultivable. The principal crops are grains, potatoes and cabbages. Forestry products are also important. During 1990–98, according to the World Bank, agricultural GDP declined at an average annual rate of 4.3%. The value of gross agricultural output increased, in real terms, by 2.9% in 1995, but decreased by 2.2% in 1996. However, it increased by 4.8% in 1997 and by 1.3% in 1998.

Industry (including mining and quarrying, manufacturing, construction and power) contributed 26.3% of GDP in 1998. In 1996 the sector provided 33.5% of employment. The sector is dominated by machine-building, electronics and electrical engineering. During 1990–98, according to the World Bank, industrial GDP declined at an average annual rate of 5.9%. However, following declines of 18.6% in 1993 and 3.1% in 1994, industrial production (excluding construction) increased by 1.9% in 1995, by 2.9% in 1996, by 14.7% in 1997 and by 1.8% in 1998.

Mining and quarrying contributed 1.2% of GDP in 1998, and provided 1.4% of employment in 1996. Estonia's principal mineral resource is oil-shale, and there are also deposits of peat and phosphorite ore. There are total estimated reserves of oil-shale of some 4,000 metric tons. Annual extraction of oil-shale reached 31m. metric tons in 1980, but had decreased to 13.5m. tons in 1995. Phosphorite ore is processed to produce phosphates for use in agriculture, but development of the industry has been accompanied by increasing environmental problems. The value of mining GDP decreased, in real terms, by 6.0% in 1994 and by 6.8% in 1995, but increased by 7.4% in 1996 and by 13.4% in 1997. However, in 1998 it decreased by 11.8%.

In 1998 the manufacturing sector accounted for 15.3% of GDP and engaged an estimated 23.9% of the employed labour force in 1996. The sector is based on products of food- and beverage-processing (especially dairy products), textiles and clothing, fertilizers and other chemical products, and wood and timber products (particularly furniture). The value of manufacturing GDP decreased, in real terms, by 3.4% in 1994, but increased by 10.0% in 1995, by 2.7% in 1996, by 18.1% in 1997 and by 2.8% in 1998.

The country relies on oil-shale for about 65% of its energy requirements. Some 50% of electricity produced in this way is exported. In 1996 imports of fuel and energy products accounted for an estimated 9% of total imports. In 1999 Estonia imported some 700m. cu m of natural gas from Russia.

Estonia's services sector was the most developed in the former USSR. The sector accounted for 67.5% of GDP in 1998, and engaged 56.4% of the employed population in 1996. Although services GDP declined by an average of 27.1% per year in 1990–94, the sector subsequently expanded considerably, in response to increased tourism and Western investment. Services GDP increased by an estimated 5.0%, in real terms, in 1996, by 8.0% in 1997 and by 5.4% in 1998.

In 1998 Estonia recorded a visible trade deficit of US $1,114.8m., while there was a deficit of $477.9m. on the current account of the balance of payments. Of all the former republics of the USSR, Estonia experienced the most rapid reorientation of its trade after 1991: trade with Western countries, particularly Scandinavia, increased considerably, while trade with former Soviet republics declined from about 90% of the pre-1991 total to some 30% in 1995. In 1998 Finland was Estonia's principal trading partner, accounting for 22.6% of imports and 18.7% of exports; other important trading partners were Russia, Sweden, Germany and Latvia. In 1998 the principal exports were machinery and electrical goods (19.7% of total export revenue), timber products (12.7%), textiles (11.5%), base metals (8.5%), prepared foodstuffs (8.2%), chemical products (7.2%) and live animals (6.2%). The principal imports were machinery and electrical goods (25.5%), plastic and rubber articles (9.4%), base metals (9.3%), prepared foodstuffs (8.7%), chemical products (8.1%), textiles (7.5%) and mineral products (6.3%).

In 1998, according to official sources, there was a general consolidated budget deficit of 67.5m. kroons. Estonia's external debt totalled US $658.4m. at the end of 1997, of which $213.5m. was long-term public debt. In 1997 the cost of debt-servicing was equivalent to 1.4% of the value of exports of goods and services. The annual rate of inflation averaged 3.3% in 1980–89, rising to 17% in 1990, to 202% in 1991 and to as high as 1,069% in 1992. However, in 1993, following a programme of radical monetary reform, the average annual rate of inflation was reduced to 89%. During 1992–97 the annual rate of inflation averaged 37.6%. Consumer prices increased by an average of 23.1% in 1996, by 11.2% in 1997 and by 8.2% in 1998. Some 29,933 people (approximately 3.4% of the labour force) were officially registered as unemployed in June 1999.

In 1992 Estonia became a member of the IMF and the World Bank. It also joined the European Bank for Reconstruction and Development (see p. 168). In 1994 Estonia signed a free-trade agreement with the EU; in June 1995 Estonia became an associate member of the EU, and in December it applied for full membership. In November 1999 Estonia became a member of the World Trade Organization (WTO, see p. 274).

Even before it regained independence in mid-1991, Estonia had begun a transition to a market economic system, which included the nationalization of formerly Soviet-controlled enterprises and the establishment of a central bank as well as a private banking system. Further far-reaching economic reforms were continued in the early 1990s. Despite Estonia's relative prosperity during the Soviet period, the collapse of the USSR and its internal economic system resulted in serious economic difficulties. An annual decline in output was recorded in all sectors in 1991 and 1992. However, a rapid rise in the volume of exports and growing foreign investment in the country helped to reverse this trend from 1993 onwards. In June 1992 Estonia introduced a new currency, the kroon, which has remained pegged at a rate of 8:1 against the Deutsche Mark since its inception, thus further enhancing international financial confidence in Estonia. By October 1997 it was estimated that total investment from abroad since independence amounted to some US $700m. Inflation has decreased considerably since 1993. Budget proposals for 2000, approved by the Riigikogu in December 1999, were based on a projected average rate of inflation of 3.3% for the coming year. In 1999 Estonia suffered a number of set-backs as economic growth slowed to just 0.1%, compared with 4.0% in the previous year. The Government was forced to implement expenditure cuts equivalent to 1.2% of GDP in a supplementary budget announced in June 1999. Unemployment rose dramatically, by 40.8% in the 12 months to October 1999, and the rate of unemployment was forecast to reach 13.7% by 2002. Nevertheless, the Estonian Government projected GDP growth for 2000 at 4%, and the Riigikogu approved a balanced budget for that year in December 1999. In January 2000 the Government announced that it had established an advisory group to analyse the possible adoption of the euro as Estonia's currency by 2002.

### Social Welfare

In pre-1940 Estonia health care was provided by both state and private facilities. A comprehensive state-funded health system was introduced under Soviet rule. This system was restructured in the early 1990s. Social security is administered by the state and provided through specialized agencies, while social assistance and social services are the responsibility of local municipalities. The system of social security comprises pensions insurance (introduced in 1993), health insurance (1991), family benefits (1994), unemployment benefits (1995) and funeral grants (1993). Under the social assistance programme, subsistence cash benefits are paid according to means-testing. In early 1998 an estimated 366,876 Estonians were receiving state pensions totalling a monthly average of 1,096m. kroons. There is a relatively high number of physicians, equivalent to 31 per 10,000 inhabitants in 1997, but a shortage of auxiliary staff. There were 79 hospitals and 74 hospital beds per 10,000 inhabitants in 1997. In 1998 central government expenditure on health amounted to 3,948.6m. kroons, equivalent to 16.4% of central government spending. In the same year local government expenditure on health totalled 108.7m. kroons, which represented 1.7% of total local government spending. Central government expenditure on social security and welfare totalled 7,384.9m. kroons in that year, equivalent to 30.6% of total central government spending. Local government expenditure on social security and welfare was 738.6m. kroons in 1998, which represented 11.5% of total local government spending.

### Education

The Estonian education system consists of pre-school, primary, secondary, vocational, university/higher, and adult education. Compulsory education begins at the age of seven and lasts for nine years: primary school (Grades 1–6) and lower secondary (Grades 7–9). Students may then attend either general secondary school (Grades 10–12) or vocational school. In 1998 there were 35 universities in Estonia, including Tartu University (founded in 1632) and the Tallinn Technical University, with a total of 34,542 students enrolled in courses. The language of instruction at all levels is either Estonian or Russian. In 1998 29% of students at general day schools took classes with Russian as the language of instruction. In 1992/93 the proportion of students instructed in Estonian was: primary and lower secondary 64%, upper secondary 76%, vocational and technical 65% and higher 81%. In 1995 the total enrolment at primary and secondary schools was equivalent to 97% of the school-age population (95% of boys, 98% of girls). In 1989, according to census results, only 0.3% of the adult population were illiterate. Central government expenditure on education totalled 2,066.5m. kroons and represented 8.6% of total central government expenditure in 1998. In the same year local government expenditure on education amounted to 2,564.7m. kroons, equivalent to 39.9% of total local government spending.

### Public Holidays

**2000:** 1 January (New Year's Day), 24 February (Independence Day), 21 April (Good Friday), 1 May (Labour Day), 23 June (Victory Day, anniversary of the Battle of Võnnu in 1919), 24 June (Midsummer Day), 25–26 December (Christmas).

**2001:** 1 January (New Year's Day), 24 February (Independence Day), 13 April (Good Friday), 1 May (Labour Day), 23 June (Victory Day, anniversary of the Battle of Võnnu in 1919), 24 June (Midsummer Day), 25–26 December (Christmas).

### Weights and Measures

The metric system is in force.

# Statistical Survey

Source (unless otherwise stated): State Statistical Office, Endla 15, Tallinn 0100; tel. 625-9202; fax (2) 625-9370; e-mail stat@stat.ee; internet www.stat.ee.

## Area and Population

**AREA, POPULATION AND DENSITY**

| | |
|---|---|
| Area (sq km) | 45,227* |
| Population (census results)† | |
| 17 January 1979 | 1,464,476 |
| 12 January 1989 | |
| Males | 731,392 |
| Females | 834,270 |
| Total | 1,565,662 |
| Population (official estimates at 1 January)† | |
| 1997 | 1,462,130 |
| 1998 | 1,453,844 |
| 1999 | 1,445,580 |
| Density (per sq km) at 1 January 1999 | 32.0 |

* 17,462 sq miles.

† Figures refer to permanent inhabitants. The *de facto* total at the 1989 census was 1,572,916.

**POPULATION BY NATIONALITY**
(estimated permanent inhabitants at 1 January 1999)

| | Number | % |
|---|---|---|
| Estonian | 942,526 | 65.2 |
| Russian | 406,049 | 28.1 |
| Ukrainian | 36,659 | 2.5 |
| Belarusian | 21,363 | 1.5 |
| Finnish | 13,027 | 0.9 |
| Tatar | 3,246 | 0.2 |
| Latvian | 2,658 | 0.2 |
| Jewish | 2,338 | 0.2 |
| Polish | 2,324 | 0.2 |
| Lithuanian | 2,206 | 0.2 |
| German | 1,250 | 0.1 |
| Others | 11,934 | 0.8 |
| **Total** | 1,445,580 | 100.0 |

**POPULATION BY ADMINISTRATIVE COUNTY**
(estimated permanent inhabitants at 1 January 1999)

| | | | |
|---|---|---|---|
| Harjumaa | 535,131 | Raplamaa | 40,137 |
| Hiiumaa | 11,798 | Saaremaa | 40,111 |
| Ida-Virumaa | 195,460 | Tartumaa | 151,010 |
| Jõgevamaa | 41,377 | Valgamaa | 38,668 |
| Järvamaa | 43,144 | Viljandimaa | 62,336 |
| Läänemaa | 31,850 | Võrumaa | 43,029 |
| Lääne-Virumaa | 75,819 | **Total** | 1,445,580 |
| Põlvamaa | 35,610 | | |
| Pärnumaa | 100,100 | | |

**PRINCIPAL TOWNS**
(estimated population, excluding suburbs, at 1 January 1997)

| | | | |
|---|---|---|---|
| Tallinn (capital) | 420,500 | Kohtla-Järve | 53,500 |
| Tartu | 101,900 | Pärnu | 51,800 |
| Narva | 75,200 | | |

**BIRTHS, MARRIAGES AND DEATHS**

| | Registered live births | | Registered marriages | | Registered deaths | |
|---|---|---|---|---|---|---|
| | Number | Rate (per 1,000) | Number | Rate (per 1,000) | Number | Rate (per 1,000) |
| 1991 | 19,320 | 12.3 | 10,292 | 6.6 | 19,705 | 12.6 |
| 1992 | 18,006 | 11.7 | 8,878 | 5.7 | 20,115 | 13.0 |
| 1993 | 15,170 | 10.0 | 7,745 | 5.1 | 21,267 | 14.0 |
| 1994 | 14,178 | 9.5 | 7,378 | 4.9 | 22,150 | 14.8 |
| 1995 | 13,560 | 9.1 | 7,006 | 4.7 | 20,872 | 14.1 |
| 1996 | 13,291 | 9.1 | 5,517 | 3.8 | 19,019 | 13.0 |
| 1997 | 12,626 | 8.7 | 5,589 | 3.8 | 18,566 | 12.7 |
| 1998 | 12,269 | 8.5 | 5,430 | 3.7 | 19,446 | 13.4 |

**Expectation of life** (years at birth, 1998): males 64.4; females 75.5.

**EMPLOYMENT**
(labour force sample surveys, annual averages, '000 persons aged 15 years and over, excl. armed forces)

| | 1994 | 1995 | 1996 |
|---|---|---|---|
| Agriculture, hunting and forestry | 87.5 | 63.0 | 59.7 |
| Fishing | 13.5 | 6.0 | 5.0 |
| Mining and quarrying | 11.2 | 9.1 | 8.9 |
| Manufacturing | 143.2 | 162.9 | 154.4 |
| Electricity, gas and water supply | 19.5 | 15.8 | 16.4 |
| Construction | 49.9 | 35.6 | 36.8 |
| Wholesale and retail trade | 88.1 | 82.7 | 85.8 |
| Hotels and restaurants | 18.7 | 18.0 | 17.8 |
| Transport, storage and communications | 58.2 | 65.8 | 64.7 |
| Financial intermediation | 7.9 | 7.1 | 6.6 |
| Real estate, renting and business activities | 29.9 | 32.2 | 32.3 |
| Public administration and defence | 36.4 | 35.7 | 35.0 |
| Education | 48.2 | 55.8 | 56.3 |
| Health and social work | 47.0 | 36.5 | 35.9 |
| Other community, social and personal service activities | 27.0 | 29.3 | 28.8 |
| Activities not adequately defined | 6.5 | 0.5 | 1.2 |
| **Total employed** | 692.6 | 656.1 | 645.6 |

**1989 census** ('000 persons aged 15 years and over): Total labour force 856 (males 428; females 428).

**1998** (labour force sample survey, '000 persons aged 15 years and over, excl. armed forces): Total employed 640.2; unemployed 70.2.

# Agriculture

**PRINCIPAL CROPS** ('000 metric tons)

| | 1996 | 1997 | 1998 |
|---|---|---|---|
| Wheat | 101 | 111 | 111 |
| Barley | 317 | 312 | 347 |
| Rye | 62 | 72 | 45 |
| Oats | 115 | 115 | 81 |
| Other cereals | 48 | 40 | 27 |
| Potatoes | 500 | 437 | 315 |
| Cabbages | 22 | 20 | 21 |
| Tomatoes | 3 | 3 | 3 |
| Cucumbers and gherkins | 4 | 5 | 3 |
| Carrots | 10 | 9 | 8 |
| Other vegetables | 16 | 6 | 6 |
| Fruits and berries | 19 | 31 | 17 |

Source: FAO, *Production Yearbook*.

**LIVESTOCK** ('000 head)

| | 1996 | 1997 | 1998* |
|---|---|---|---|
| Cattle | 343.0 | 325.6 | 311.6 |
| Pigs | 298.4 | 306.3 | 328.8 |
| Sheep and goats | 39.2 | 35.6 | 34.0 |
| Poultry | 2,324.9 | 2,602.0 | n.a. |

* Preliminary figures.

**LIVESTOCK PRODUCTS**
('000 metric tons, unless otherwise indicated)

| | 1996 | 1997 | 1998 |
|---|---|---|---|
| Beef and veal | 22 | 19 | 19 |
| Mutton and lamb | 1 | n.a. | n.a. |
| Pig meat | 32 | 30 | 32 |
| Poultry meat | 4 | 4 | 8 |
| Cows' milk | 675 | 717 | 733 |
| Butter | 21 | 18* | 18* |
| Cheese | 18 | 15* | 15* |
| Poultry eggs | 19 | 18* | 20 |
| Honey (metric tons) | 335 | n.a. | n.a. |

* FAO estimate.
Source: mainly FAO, *Production Yearbook*.

# Forestry

**ROUNDWOOD REMOVALS** ('000 cu m, excl. bark)

| | 1995 | 1996 | 1997 |
|---|---|---|---|
| Sawlogs, veneer logs and logs for sleepers | 1,413 | 1,490 | 2,300 |
| Pulpwood | 1,528 | 1,611 | 2,200 |
| Other industrial wood | 196 | 196 | 196 |
| Fuel wood | 573 | 604 | 1,100 |
| **Total** | 3,710 | 3,901 | 5,796 |

Source: FAO, *Yearbook of Forest Products*.

**SAWNWOOD PRODUCTION** ('000 cu m, incl. railway sleepers)

| | 1995 | 1996 | 1997 |
|---|---|---|---|
| Coniferous (softwood) | 315 | 360 | 610 |
| Broadleaved (hardwood) | 35 | 40 | 40* |
| **Total** | 350 | 400 | 650 |

* FAO estimate.
Source: FAO, *Yearbook of Forest Products*.

# Fishing

('000 metric tons, live weight)

| | 1995 | 1996 | 1997 |
|---|---|---|---|
| Blue whiting | 13.7 | 11.0 | 5.7 |
| Atlantic redfishes | 17.7 | 7.1 | 3.7 |
| Cape horse mackerel | 28.7 | — | — |
| Atlantic herring | 43.9 | 45.3 | 52.4 |
| European sprat | 13.1 | 22.5 | 39.7 |
| Chub mackerel | 3.0 | 4.5 | 2.0 |
| Atlantic mackerel | 2.3 | 3.7 | 6.3 |
| Other fishes (incl. unspecified) | 7.4 | 8.7 | 8.8 |
| **Total fish** | 129.6 | 102.8 | 118.6 |
| Northern prawn | 2.4 | 3.2 | 5.0 |
| Other aquatic animals | — | 2.4 | — |
| **Total catch** | 132.0 | 108.4 | 123.6 |

Source: FAO, *Yearbook of Fishery Statistics*.

# Mining

('000 metric tons)

| | 1994 | 1995 | 1996* |
|---|---|---|---|
| Oil-shale | 14,530 | 13,310 | 14,735 |
| Peat | 645 | 583 | 629 |

* Provisional.

# Industry

**SELECTED PRODUCTS** ('000 metric tons, unless otherwise indicated)

| | 1994 | 1995 | 1996* |
|---|---|---|---|
| Wine and spirits ('000 hectolitres) | 123 | 173 | 84 |
| Beer ('000 hectolitres) | 477 | 492 | 454 |
| Soft drinks ('000 hectolitres) | 368 | 435 | 571 |
| Textile fabrics (million sq metres) | 78 | 94 | 124 |
| Footwear ('000 pairs) | 800 | 682 | 897 |
| Plywood ('000 cubic metres) | 9.9 | 11.2 | 18 |
| Paper | — | 5.9 | 19.5 |
| Paperboard | 0.3 | 0.4 | 0.9 |
| Building bricks (million) | 48 | 31 | 24 |
| Cement | 403 | 418 | 388 |
| Electric energy (million kWh) | 9,152 | 8,693 | 9,102 |

* Provisional.

# Finance

**CURRENCY AND EXCHANGE RATES**

**Monetary Units**

100 cents = 1 kroon.

**Sterling, Dollar and Euro Equivalents** (30 September 1999)

£1 sterling = 24.12 kroons;
US $1 = 14.65 kroons;
€1 = 15.62 kroons;
1,000 kroons = £41.47 = $68.27 = €64.02.

**Average Exchange Rate** (kroons per US $)

1996 12.034
1997 13.882
1998 14.075

Note: In June 1992 Estonia reintroduced its national currency, the kroon, replacing the rouble of the former USSR, initially at a rate of one kroon per 10 roubles (for details of the rouble, see the chapter on the Russian Federation).

**BUDGET** (million kroons)*

| Revenue† | 1997 | 1998 | 1999 |
|---|---|---|---|
| Tax revenue | 19,592.0 | 21,913.4 | 21,505.2 |
| Taxes on income, profits and capital gains | 3,544.1 | 4,675.7 | 4,508.9 |
| Individual | 2,315.7 | 2,761.6 | 2,870.1 |
| Corporate | 1,228.4 | 1,914.1 | 1,638.8 |
| Social security contributions | 6,867.4 | 7,937.5 | 7,793.8 |
| Domestic taxes on goods and services | 9,179.6 | 9,300.1 | 9,202.5 |
| General sales, turnover or value-added taxes | 6,686.2 | 6,413.4 | 6,418.9 |
| Excises | 2,400.9 | 2,789.2 | 2,686.5 |
| Other current revenue | 2,190.6 | 1,344.1 | 1,155.3 |
| Entrepreneurial and property income | 682.0 | 457.2 | 269.0 |
| Administrative fees and charges, non-industrial and incidental sales | 741.9 | 696.8 | 764.6 |
| Capital revenue | 577.9 | 749.0 | 209.0 |
| Sales of land and intangible assets | 468.7 | 676.8 | 141.1 |
| **Total** | 22,360.5 | 24,006.5 | 22,869.5 |

| Expenditure‡ | 1996 | 1997 | 1998 |
|---|---|---|---|
| General public services | 1,141.2 | 1,183.2 | 1,191.6 |
| Defence | 845.5 | 944.5 | 969.4 |
| Public order and safety | 1,503.2 | 1,811.1 | 1,769.3 |
| Education | 1,808.5 | 2,087.1 | 2,066.5 |
| Health | 2,944.2 | 3,232.0 | 3,948.6 |
| Social security and welfare | 5,743.4 | 6,581.5 | 7,384.9 |
| Housing and community amenities | 50.8 | 82.9 | 10.0 |
| Recreational, cultural and religious affairs and services | 841.2 | 899.8 | 1,061.0 |
| Economic affairs and services | 2,153.7 | 2,300.9 | 3,069.0 |
| Agriculture, forestry, fishing and hunting | 859.4 | 885.9 | 1,442.5 |
| Transport and communications | 1,106.3 | 1,173.1 | 1,444.2 |
| Other purposes | 682.0 | 1,428.8 | 2,633.0 |
| **Total** | 17,713.7 | 20,551.8 | 24,103.3 |
| Current§ | 16,114.6 | 18,695.8 | 22,020.3 |
| Capital | 1,599.1 | 1,856.0 | 2,083.0 |

* Figures represent a consolidation of the operations of the central Government, comprising the Republican Budget, the Medical Insurance Fund, the Social Security Fund and various extrabudgetary funds.

† Excluding grants received (million kroons): 25.0 in 1997; 124.0 in 1998; 29.5 in 1999.

‡ Excluding lending minus repayments (million kroons): 205.5 in 1996; 281.4 in 1997; 94.7 in 1998.

§ Including interest payments (million kroons): 208.1 in 1996; 211.6 in 1997; 225.5 in 1998.

**INTERNATIONAL RESERVES**
(US $ million at 31 December)

| | 1996 | 1997 | 1998 |
|---|---|---|---|
| Gold* | 3.03 | 2.39 | 2.37 |
| IMF special drawing rights | 0.17 | 0.01 | 0.07 |
| Reserve position in IMF | 0.01 | 0.01 | 0.01 |
| Foreign exchange | 636.64 | 757.70 | 810.51 |
| **Total** | 639.85 | 760.11 | 812.96 |

* National valuation.

Source: IMF, *International Financial Statistics*.

**MONEY SUPPLY** (million kroons at 31 December)

| | 1996 | 1997 | 1998 |
|---|---|---|---|
| Currency outside banks | 4,270.5 | 4,588.5 | 4,538.6 |
| Demand deposits at banks | 6,513.9 | 8,582.5 | 8,207.7 |
| **Total money** (incl. others) | 10,786.0 | 13.223.3 | 12,750.0 |

Source: IMF, *International Financial Statistics*.

**COST OF LIVING** (Consumer price index; base: 1991 = 100)

| | 1995 | 1996 | 1997 |
|---|---|---|---|
| Food (incl. beverages) | 2,837.5 | 3,354.8 | 3,540.1 |
| Fuel and light | 23,117 | 27,750 | 31,957 |
| Clothing (incl. footwear) | 2,791.7 | 3,215.5 | 3,614.0 |
| Rent | 22,215 | 26,515 | 27,753 |
| **All items** (incl. others) | 4,251.5 | 5,231.9 | 5,816.9 |

Source: ILO, *Yearbook of Labour Statistics*.

**1998** (1997 = 100): Food 104.9; All items 108.2 (Source: UN, *Monthly Bulletin of Statistics*).

**NATIONAL ACCOUNTS** (million kroons at current prices)

**Expenditure on the Gross Domestic Product**

| | 1995 | 1996 | 1997 |
|---|---|---|---|
| Government final consumption expenditure | 10,349.9 | 12,632.3 | 14,878.8 |
| Non-profit institutions | 207.0 | 353.0 | 404.4 |
| Private final consumption expenditure | 23,752.2 | 31,491.5 | 37,586.0 |
| Increase in stocks | 304.6 | 563.8 | 2,193.3 |
| Gross fixed capital formation | 10,576.4 | 14,015.3 | 17,226.6 |
| **Total domestic expenditure** | 45,190.1 | 59,055.9 | 72,289.1 |
| Exports of goods and services f.o.b. | 29,451.1 | 35,186.2 | 50,238.1 |
| *Less* Imports of goods and services f.o.b. | 32,736.3 | 41,229.4 | 57,661.1 |
| Statistical discrepancy | −1,199.8 | −566.8 | 213.8 |
| **GDP in purchasers' values** | 40,705.1 | 52,445.9 | 65,079.9 |
| **GDP at constant 1995 prices** | 40,705.1 | 42,326.0 | 47,145.5 |

**Gross Domestic Product by Economic Activity**

| | 1996 | 1997 | 1998 |
|---|---|---|---|
| Agriculture and forestry | 3,333 | 3,621 | 3,791 |
| Fishing | 203 | 278 | 288 |
| Mining and quarrying | 728 | 829 | 763 |
| Manufacturing | 7,784 | 9,386 | 10,038 |
| Electricity, gas and water supply | 1,899 | 1,984 | 2,517 |
| Construction | 2,735 | 3,314 | 3,999 |
| Trade | 8,035 | 9,737 | 11,765 |
| Hotels and restaurants | 589 | 676 | 1,053 |
| Transport and communications | 5,070 | 6,928 | 8,900 |
| Finance and insurance | 2,227 | 2,798 | 2,536 |
| Real estate, renting and business activities | 4,495 | 5,560 | 6,983 |
| Public administration | 2,185 | 2,579 | 2,853 |
| Education | 2,611 | 3,082 | 3,619 |
| Health and social care | 1,955 | 2,187 | 2,290 |
| Other services | 3,112 | 3,879 | 4,415 |
| **Sub-total** | 46,959 | 56,857 | 65,807 |
| *Less* Imputed bank service charge | 1,131 | 1,170 | 1,000 |
| **GDP at factor cost** | 45,828 | 55,687 | 64,807 |
| Net indirect taxes | 6,618 | 8,637 | 8,406 |
| **GDP in purchasers' values** | 52,446 | 64,324 | 73,213 |

Source: IMF, *Republic of Estonia: Selected Issues and Statistical Appendix* (August 1999).

**BALANCE OF PAYMENTS** (US $ million)

| | 1996 | 1997 | 1998 |
|---|---|---|---|
| Exports of goods f.o.b. | 1,812.3 | 2,291.3 | 2,690.1 |
| Imports of goods f.o.b. | −2,831.5 | −3,415.6 | −3,804.9 |
| **Trade balance** | −1,019.2 | −1,124.3 | −1,114.8 |
| Exports of services | 1,108.3 | 1,318.0 | 1,479.6 |
| Imports of services | −589.8 | −726.6 | -910.1 |
| **Balance on goods and services** | -500.7 | −532.9 | −545.3 |
| Other income received | 112.2 | 115.1 | 133.5 |
| Other income paid | −110.3 | −260.8 | −214.5 |
| **Balance on goods, services and income** | -498.8 | −678.6 | −626.3 |
| Current transfers received | 116.8 | 135.3 | 172.9 |
| Current transfers paid | −16.3 | −18.6 | −24.5 |
| **Current balance** | -398.3 | -561.9 | −477.9 |
| Capital account (net) | −0.7 | −0.2 | 1.8 |
| Direct investment abroad | −40.1 | −136.6 | −6.3 |
| Direct investment from abroad | 150.2 | 266.2 | 580.5 |
| Portfolio investment assets | −52.7 | −165.0 | −10.9 |
| Portfolio investment liabilities | 198.1 | 427.5 | 1.1 |
| Other investment assets | −7.3 | −334.2 | −168.5 |
| Other investment liabilities | 292.6 | 744.8 | 112.1 |
| Net errors and omissions | −35.6 | −24.9 | 5.3 |
| **Overall balance** | 106.3 | 215.9 | 37.3 |

Source: IMF, *International Financial Statistics*.

# External Trade

**PRINCIPAL COMMODITIES**
(million kroons)

| Imports | 1994 | 1995 | 1996 |
|---|---|---|---|
| Vegetable products | 585.7 | 896.4 | 1,267.6 |
| Prepared foodstuffs, beverages, spirits, vinegar and tobacco | 2,135.0 | 2,190.2 | 3,252.1 |
| Mineral products | 3,034.7 | 3,341.3 | 3,791.7 |
| Products of the chemical or allied industries | 1,627.1 | 2,333.9 | 3,554.6 |
| Plastics, rubber and articles thereof | 843.1 | 1,319.8 | 1,711.1 |
| Wood pulp, paper and paperboard | 570.3 | 973.5 | 1,259.0 |
| Textiles and textile articles | 2,217.3 | 3,023.5 | 3,618.8 |
| Footwear, headgear, etc. | 339.8 | 383.0 | 464.1 |
| Pearls, precious or semi-precious stones, precious metals and articles thereof | 57.7 | 82.4 | 71.7 |
| Base metals and articles of base metal | 1,278.5 | 2,059.9 | 3,015.0 |
| Machinery (incl. electrical) and parts | 4,242.1 | 6,280.6 | 8,448.4 |
| Transport equipment | 1,849.5 | 2,307.2 | 2,877.5 |
| Miscellaneous manufactured articles | 596.5 | 850.6 | 1,057.4 |
| **Total** (incl. others) | 21,509.3 | 29,111.9 | 38,552.6 |

**Revised totals** (million kroons): 21,484.8 in 1994; 29,117.5 in 1995; 38,885.5 in 1996.

| Exports | 1994 | 1995 | 1996 |
|---|---|---|---|
| Live animals and animal products | 1,300.1 | 1,616.4 | 1,559.1 |
| Animal or vegetable fats, oil and waxes | 78.9 | 103.8 | 85.3 |
| Prepared foodstuffs, beverages, spirits, vinegar and tobacco | 2,077.5 | 1,472.5 | 1,952.0 |
| Mineral products | 1,382.9 | 1,707.4 | 1,799.7 |
| Products of the chemical or allied industries | 1,148.0 | 1,593.5 | 2,200.4 |
| Plastics, rubber and articles thereof | 302.5 | 559.8 | 545.1 |
| Raw hides and skins, leather, furskins and articles thereof | 208.6 | 239.3 | 310.7 |
| Wood and cork products, etc. | 1,730.1 | 2,622.6 | 2,857.6 |
| Wood pulp, paper and paperboard | 139.6 | 246.2 | 490.6 |
| Textiles and textile articles | 2,324.8 | 2,842.4 | 3,563.8 |
| Footwear, headgear, etc. | 249.2 | 304.9 | 393.9 |
| Base metals and articles of base metal | 1,350.1 | 1,437.1 | 1,596.5 |
| Machinery (incl. electrical) and parts | 1,572.2 | 2,741.1 | 3,355.2 |
| Vehicles, aircraft, vessels and associated transport equipment | 1,287.2 | 1,455.5 | 1,587.2 |
| Miscellaneous manufactured articles | 918.5 | 1,194.3 | 1,497.7 |
| **Total** (incl. others) | 16,924.4 | 21,048.8 | 24,988.3 |

**Revised totals** (million kroons): 16,927.3 in 1994; 21,071.6 in 1995; 25,024.6 in 1996.

**PRINCIPAL TRADING PARTNERS** (million kroons)

| Imports | 1996 | 1997 | 1998 |
|---|---|---|---|
| Denmark | 1,095.6 | 1,592.8 | 1,858.2 |
| Finland | 11,322.8 | 14,420.4 | 15,222.6 |
| France | 786.1 | 1,384.8 | 1,677.6 |
| Germany | 3,877.5 | 6,191.6 | 7,301.6 |
| Italy | 1,261.8 | 1,838.4 | 2,193.0 |
| Japan | 785.5 | 2,074.9 | 3,314.2 |
| Latvia | 753.2 | 1,080.8 | 1,362.4 |
| Netherlands | 1,107.1 | 1,582.9 | 1,729.4 |
| Russia | 5,286.3 | 8,888.5 | 7,479.0 |
| Sweden | 3,170.5 | 5,607.9 | 6,091.9 |
| United Kingdom | 1,282.6 | 1,893.6 | 2,001.4 |
| USA | 895.6 | 2,293.0 | 3,120.9 |
| **Total** (incl. others) | 38,885.5 | 61,654.9 | 67,363.8 |

| Exports | 1996 | 1997 | 1998 |
|---|---|---|---|
| Belarus | 487.7 | 559.4 | 417.7 |
| Denmark | 883.2 | 1,302.9 | 1,655.7 |
| Finland | 4,586.0 | 6,386.9 | 8,539.2 |
| Germany | 1,763.9 | 2,264.0 | 2,512.6 |
| Latvia | 2,064.9 | 3,511.9 | 4,295.5 |
| Lithuania | 1,433.6 | 2,477.8 | 2,125.7 |
| Netherlands | 737.5 | 1,374.2 | 1,002.4 |
| Norway | 377.6 | 659.9 | 939.1 |
| Russia | 4,131.5 | 7,663.8 | 6,089.2 |
| Sweden | 2,891.7 | 5,498.1 | 7,597.4 |
| Ukraine | 1,253.6 | 2,032.7 | 2,268.9 |
| United Kingdom | 865.9 | 1,494.6 | 1,941.0 |
| USA | 552.3 | 745.8 | 874.8 |
| **Total** (incl. others) | 25,024.6 | 40,729.7 | 45,551.4 |

# Transport

**DOMESTIC PASSENGER TRAFFIC** (million passenger-kilometres)

| | 1996 | 1997 | 1998 |
|---|---|---|---|
| Railway traffic | 309 | 262 | 236 |
| Road traffic (bus traffic) | 2,091 | 2,238 | 2,265 |
| Sea traffic | 272 | 302 | 372 |
| Air traffic | 158 | 209 | 227 |
| **Total public transport** | 2,830 | 3,011 | 3,100 |

**DOMESTIC FREIGHT TRAFFIC** (million ton-kilometres)

| | 1996 | 1997 | 1998 |
|---|---|---|---|
| Railway traffic | 4,198 | 5,102 | 6,079 |
| Road traffic | 1,897 | 2,773 | 3,791 |
| Sea traffic | 28,918 | 26,524 | 24,764 |
| Air traffic | 2 | 5 | 3.2 |
| **Total public transport** | 35,015 | 34,404 | 34,637.2 |

**ROAD TRAFFIC** ('000 motor vehicles in use at 31 December)

| | 1996 | 1997 | 1998 |
|---|---|---|---|
| Passenger cars | 406.6 | 427.7 | 451.0 |
| Buses and coaches | 6.7 | 6.5 | 6.3 |
| Lorries and vans | 71.3 | 76.6 | 80.6 |

**SHIPPING**

**Merchant Fleet** (registered at 31 December)

| | 1996 | 1997 | 1998 |
|---|---|---|---|
| Number of vessels | 220 | 229 | 239 |
| Total displacement ('000 grt) | 545 | 602 | 522 |

Source: Lloyd's Register of Shipping.

**International Sea-borne Freight Traffic** ('000 metric tons)

| | 1996 | 1997 | 1998 |
|---|---|---|---|
| Goods loaded | 11,465 | 18,756 | 23,459 |
| Goods unloaded | 3,993 | 4,656 | 4,597 |

Source: UN, *Monthly Bulletin of Statistics*.

**CIVIL AVIATION** (traffic on scheduled services)

| | 1993 | 1994 | 1995 |
|---|---|---|---|
| Kilometres flown (million) | 4 | 3 | 4 |
| Passengers carried ('000) | 109 | 157 | 167 |
| Passenger-km (million) | 82 | 92 | 106 |
| Total ton-km (million) | 8 | 9 | 10 |

Source: UN, *Statistical Yearbook*.

**1998:** Passengers carried 324,200; Freight carried (incl. mail) 4,700 metric tons; Passenger-km 227.3m.

# Tourism

| | 1996 | 1997 | 1998 |
|---|---|---|---|
| Foreign tourist arrivals | 1,354,101 | 1,099,448 | 1,467,441 |

# Communications Media

(At 1 January)

| | 1994 | 1995 | 1996 |
|---|---|---|---|
| Telefax stations* | 10,000 | 13,000 | n.a. |
| Mobile cellular telephones (subscribers)* | 13,774 | 30,452 | n.a. |
| Books published (titles)† | 2,291 | 2,635 | 2,628 |
| Books published ('000 copies)† | 8,592 | 7,930 | 6,662 |
| Daily newspapers (number) | 15 | 19 | 15 |

* Source: UN, *Statistical Yearbook*.

† Including pamphlets (689 titles in 1996).

Radio receivers in use: 221,000 in 1996.

Television receivers in use: 455,000 in 1996.

Telephones (main lines) in use: 439,000 in 1997.

# Education

(1997/98)

| | Institutions | Teachers* | Students |
|---|---|---|---|
| Pre-primary | 670 | 8,070† | 56,300 |
| Primary | 450 | 16,628 (Primary, General secondary and Special combined) | 185,800 |
| General secondary | 232 | | 38,300 |
| Special | 48 | | n.a. |
| Vocational and professional | 90 | 1,634‡ | 31,316§ |
| Universities, etc. | 35 | 3,052 | 34,542§ |

* Figures refer to 1996/97.

† Including staff in child care and pre-school institutions (Source: UNESCO, *Statistical Yearbook*).

‡ Full-time teachers only.

§ Including students enrolled in evening and correspondence courses.

# Directory

## The Constitution

A new Constitution, based on that of 1938, was adopted by a referendum held on 28 June 1992. It took effect on 3 July. The following is a summary of its main provisions:

### FUNDAMENTAL RIGHTS, LIBERTIES AND DUTIES

Every child with one parent who is an Estonian citizen has the right, by birth, to Estonian citizenship. Anyone who, as a minor, lost his or her Estonian citizenship has the right to have his or her citizenship restored. The rights, liberties and duties of all persons, as listed in the Constitution, are equal for Estonian citizens as well as for citizens of foreign states and stateless persons who are present in Estonia.

All persons are equal before the law. No one may be discriminated against on the basis of nationality, race, colour, sex, language, origin, creed, political or other persuasions. Everyone has the right to the protection of the state and the law. Guaranteeing rights and liberties is the responsibility of the legislative, executive and judicial powers, as well as of local government. Everyone has the right to appeal to a court of law if his or her rights or liberties have been violated.

The state organizes vocational education and assists in finding work for persons seeking employment. Working conditions are under state supervision. Employers and employees may freely join unions and associations. Estonian citizens have the right to engage in commercial activities and to form profit-making associations. The property rights of everyone are inviolable. All persons legally present in Estonia have the right to freedom of movement and choice of abode. Everyone has the right to leave Estonia.

Everyone has the right to health care and to education. Education is compulsory for school-age children. Everyone has the right to instruction in Estonian.

The official language of state and local government authorities is Estonian. In localities where the language of the majority of the population is other than Estonian, local government authorities may use the language of the majority of the permanent residents of that locality for internal communication.

### THE PEOPLE

The people exercise their supreme power through citizens who have the right to vote by: i) electing the Riigikogu (legislature); ii) participating in referendums. The right to vote belongs to every Estonian citizen who has attained the age of 18 years.

### THE RIIGIKOGU

Legislative power rests with the Riigikogu (State Assembly). It comprises 101 members, elected every four years in free elections on the principle of proportionality. Every citizen entitled to vote who has attained 21 years of age may stand as a candidate for the Riigikogu.

The Riigikogu adopts laws and resolutions; decides on the holding of referendums; elects the President of the Republic; ratifies or rejects foreign treaties; authorizes the candidate for Prime Minister to form the Council of Ministers; adopts the national budget and approves the report on its execution; may declare a state of emergency, or, on the proposal of the President, declare a state of war, order mobilization and demobilization.

The Riigikogu elects from among its members a Chairman (Speaker) and two Deputy Chairmen to direct the work of the Riigikogu.

### THE PRESIDENT

The President of the Republic is the Head of State of Estonia. The President represents Estonia in international relations; appoints and recalls, on the proposal of the Government, diplomatic representatives of Estonia and accepts letters of credence of diplomatic representatives accredited to Estonia; declares regular (and early) elections to the Riigikogu; initiates amendments to the Constitution; nominates the candidate for the post of Prime Minister; and is the Supreme Commander of Estonia's armed forces.

The President is elected by secret ballot of the Riigikogu for a term of five years. No person may be elected to the office for more than two consecutive terms. Any Estonian citizen by birth, who is at least 40 years of age, may stand as a candidate for President.

Should the President not be elected after three rounds of voting, the Speaker of the Riigikogu convenes, within one month, an Electoral Body to elect the President.

### THE GOVERNMENT

Executive power is held by the Government of the Republic (Council of Ministers). The Government implements national, domestic and foreign policies; directs and co-ordinates the work of government institutions; organizes the implementation of legislation, the resolutions of the Riigikogu, and the edicts of the President; submits draft legislation to the Riigikogu, as well as foreign treaties; prepares a draft of the national budget and presents it to the Riigikogu; administers the implementation of the national budget; and organizes relations with foreign states.

The Government comprises the Prime Minister and Ministers. The President of the Republic nominates a candidate for Prime Minister, who is charged with forming a new government.

### JUDICIAL SYSTEM

Justice is administered solely by the courts. They are independent in their work and administer justice in accordance with the Constitution and laws. The court system is comprised of rural and city, as well as administrative, courts (first level); district courts (second level); and the Supreme Court of the Republic of Estonia (the highest court in the land).

## The Government

### HEAD OF STATE

**President:** LENNART MERI (elected 5 October 1992, re-elected 20 September 1996).

### COUNCIL OF MINISTERS
(February 2000)

A coalition of the Estonian Reform Party (ERP), the Pro Patria (Fatherland) Union and the People's Party Moderates.

**Prime Minister:** MART LAAR (Pro Patria (Fatherland) Union).

**Minister of Internal Affairs:** TARMO LOODUS (Pro Patria (Fatherland) Union).

**Minister of Foreign Affairs:** TOOMAS HENDRIK ILVES (Moderates).

**Minister of Justice:** MÄRT RASK (ERP).

**Minister of Economic Affairs:** MIKHEL PÄRNOJA (Moderates).

**Minister of Finance:** SIIM KALLAS (ERP).

**Minister of Transport and Communications:** TOIVO JÜRGENSON (Pro Patria (Fatherland) Union).

**Minister of the Environment:** HEIKI KRANICH (ERP).

**Minister of Culture:** SIGNE KIVI (ERP).

**Minister of Education:** TÕNIS LUKAS (Pro Patria (Fatherland) Union).

**Minister of Agriculture:** IVARI PADAR (Moderates).

**Minister of Social Affairs:** EIKI NESTOR (Moderates).

**Minister of Defence:** JÜRI LUIK (Pro Patria (Fatherland) Union).

**Minister without Portfolio (responsible for Ethnic Issues):** KATRIN SAKS (Moderates).

**Minister without Portfolio (responsible for Regional Affairs):** TOIVO ASMER (ERP).

**Secretary of State of the State Chancellery:** AINO LEPIK VON WIRÉN.

### MINISTRIES

**Office of the Prime Minister:** Lossi plats 1A, Tallinn 15161; tel. 631-6701; fax 631-6704; e-mail valitsus@rk.ee; internet www.gov.ee.

**State Chancellery:** Lossi plats 1A, Tallinn 15161; tel. 631-6860; fax 631-6914; e-mail riik@rk.ee; internet www.rk.ee.

**Ministry of Agriculture:** Lai 39/41, Tallinn 15056; tel. 625-6101; fax 625-6200; e-mail pm@agri.ee; internet www.agri.ee.

**Ministry of Culture:** Suur Karja 23, Tallinn 15076; tel. 628-2222; fax 628-2200; e-mail info@kul.ee; internet www.kul.ee.

**Ministry of Defence:** Sakala 1, Tallinn 10141; tel. 640-6000; fax 640-6001; e-mail info@kmin.ee; internet www.riik.ee/ministeries/kaitseministeerium.html.

**Ministry of Economic Affairs:** Harju 11, Tallinn 10141; tel. 625-6304; fax 631-3660; e-mail info@mineco.ee; internet www.mineco.ee.

**Ministry of Education:** Tõnismägi 9/11, Tallinn 15192; tel. 628-1212; fax 631-1213; e-mail hm@hm.ee; internet www.hm.ee.

**Ministry of the Environment:** Toompuiestee 24, Tallinn 10149; tel. 626-2800; fax 626-2801; e-mail min@ekm.envir.ee; internet www.envir.ee.

**Ministry of Finance:** Suur-Ameerika 1, Tallinn 15006; tel. 611-3445; fax 631-7810; e-mail info@fin.ee; internet www.fin.ee.

**Ministry of Foreign Affairs:** Rävala 9, Tallinn 15049; tel. 631-7000; fax 631-7099; e-mail vminfo@vm.ee; internet www.vm.ee.

**Ministry of Internal Affairs:** Pikk 61, Tallinn 15065; tel. 612-5010; fax 612-5077; e-mail sisemin@sisemin.gov.ee; internet www.riik.ee/siseministeerum/index.cgi.

**Ministry of Justice:** Tõnismägi 5A, Tallinn 15191; tel. 620-8100; fax 620-8109; e-mail sekretar@just.ee; internet www.just.ee.

**Ministry of Social Affairs:** Gonsiori 29, Tallinn 15027; tel. 626-9700; fax 626-7909; e-mail webmaster@fsl.sm.ee; internet www.sm.ee/.

**Ministry of Transport and Communications:** Viru 9, Tallinn 10140; tel. 639-7613; fax 639-7606; e-mail info@tsm.ee; internet www.tsm.ee/tsm.

# President and Legislature

## PRESIDENT

The presidential election was held on 26–27 August 1996 in the Riigikogu. LENNART MERI and ARNOLD RÜÜTEL were the contenders. A two-thirds' majority (68 votes) was needed, but, in three rounds of voting, neither contender achieved this. A larger electoral college, comprising the 101 parliamentary deputies and 273 representatives from local government, was convened on 20 September. Five candidates contested the first round of the election and, as no candidate achieved the necessary 188 votes, the leading two candidates, LENNART MERI and ARNOLD RÜÜTEL, proceeded to the second round of voting. The election was won by LENNART MERI, with 196 votes.

**Election, 20 September 1996**

| Candidate | Votes: First Round | Votes: Second Round* |
|---|---|---|
| LENNART MERI | 139 | 196 |
| ARNOLD RÜÜTEL | 85 | 126 |
| TUNNE KELAM | 76 | — |
| ENN TOUGU | 47 | — |
| SIIRI OVIIR | 25 | — |

* There were 44 abstentions and six invalid votes, with two electors absent.

## RIIGIKOGU

(State Assembly)

**Speaker:** TOOMAS SAVI.

**Deputy Speakers:** TUNNE KELAM, SIIRI OVIIR.

**General Election, 7 March 1999**

| Parties | % of votes | Seats |
|---|---|---|
| Estonian Centre Party | 23.41 | 28 |
| Pro Patria (Fatherland) Union | 16.09 | 18 |
| Estonian Reform Party | 15.92 | 18 |
| Moderates*† | 15.21 | 17 |
| Estonian Coalition Party*‡ | 7.58 | 7 |
| Estonian Country People's Party | 7.27 | 7 |
| United People's Party of Estonia*§ | 6.13 | 6 |
| Others | 8.39 | 0 |
| **Total** | 100.00 | 101 |

* As political parties require a minimum of 5% of the votes cast to obtain representation in the Riigikogu, several smaller parties formed informal alliances (formal alliances were proscribed in November 1998) and campaigned on the same electoral list under one party's name.

† Nine seats were won by the People's Party and eight by the Moderates. The two parties subsequently merged to form the People's Party Moderates in November 1999.

‡ Three seats were won by the Estonian Coalition Party, two by the Estonian Rural Union and two by the Estonian Pensioners' and Families' Party.

§ Two seats were won by the Estonian Social-Democratic Labour Party and the remaining four seats were taken by the United People's Party of Estonia and the Russian Unity Party.

# Political Organizations

**Estonian Blue Party** (Eesti Sinine Erakond): Ahtri 6–112, Tallinn 10151; tel. 625-9895; fax 625-9810; e-mail sinine.erakond@mail.ee; internet www.gaia.gi.ee/ese/ese2.html; Sec.-Gen. ANNELI MILISTVER.

**Estonian Centre Party** (Eesti Keskerakond): POB 3737, Tallinn 0090; tel. (2) 499-304; fax (2) 493-881; e-mail keskerakand@teleport.ee; internet www.keskerakond.ee; absorbed the Estonian Green Party in mid-1998; f. 1991; Chair. EDGAR SAVISAAR.

**Estonian Christian People's Party** (Eesti Kristlik Rahvapartei): Narva mnt. 51, Tallinn 10152; tel. 627-5730; fax 527-5708; e-mail ekrpkesk@uninet.ee; internet www.ekrpi.ee/sisu.htm.

**Estonian Coalition Party (ECP)** (Eesti Koonderakond): Raekoja plats 16, Tallinn 10146; tel. 631-4161; fax 631-4041; internet www.koonderakond.ee; f. 1991; Chair. ANDRUS OOBEL; Sec.-Gen. ANTS LEEMETS.

**Estonian National Progressive Party:** Tallinn; f. 1993; Chair. ANTS ERM.

**Estonian Pensioners' and Families' Party** (Eesti Pensionäride ja Perede Erakond): Estonia pst. 15A, 1 Korrus; Tallinn; tel. 645-5049; f. 1991; Chair. MAI TREIAL.

**Estonian Reform Party (ERP)** (Eesti Reformierakond): Tõnismagi 3A–15, Tallinn 0001; tel. 640-8740; fax 640-8741; internet www.reform.ee; f. 1994; Gen. Sec. HEIKI KRANICH; Chair. SIIM KALLAS.

**Estonian Royalist Party** (Eesti Rojalistlik Partei): POB 300, Tartu 2400; tel. (7) 432-986; fax (7) 431-466; f. 1989; advocates the establishment of a Kingdom of Estonia; Chair. KALLE KULBOK.

**Estonian Rural People's Union** (Eesti Maahrava Liit): Marja 4D, Tallinn 10617; tel. 611-2909; fax 611-2908; f. 1999 by merger of the Estonian Country People's Party and the Estonian Rural Union; Chair. ARVO SIRENDI.

**Estonian Social-Democratic Labour Party** (Eesti Sotsiaaldemokraatlik Tööpartei): Central Post Office, POB 4102, Tallinn 10111; tel. (2) 493-965; fax (2) 472-147; f. 1920 as the Communist Party of Estonia; renamed Estonian Democratic Labour Party in 1992 and as above in 1998; Chair. TIIT TOOMSALU; Dep. Chair. ENDEL PAAP; 1,041 mems (1998).

**Farmers' Union** (Põllumeeste Kogu): POB 543, Tallinn 0010; tel. (2) 437-733; f. 1992; Chair. ELDUR PARDER.

**Moderates' Women's Assembly** (Moodukad Naiskogu): Tallinn; e-mail moodukad@dafanet.ee; f. 1996 to encourage women to take part in politics; Pres. HELSO PIKHOF.

**People's Party Moderates:** Rahukohtu 1–15, Tallinn 0001; POB 3437, Tallinn 0090; tel. (6) 316-651; fax (6) 316-653; internet www.moodukad.ee; f. 1999 by merger of the People's Party and the Moderates' Party; Chair. ANDRES TARAND; Sec.-Gen. TONU KOIV.

**Progressive Party** (Arengupartei): Narva mnt. 9, Tallinn 10117; e-mail arengupartei@online.ee; internet www.arengupartei.ee; f. 1996 following a split in the Estonian Centre Party; Chair. ANDRA VEIDEMANN; Sec.-Gen. TOIVO KEVA; 1,300 mems.

**Pro Patria (Fatherland) Union** (Isamaaliit): Endla 4A, Tallinn 10142; tel. (6) 263-325; fax (6) 263-324; e-mail isamaa@ngonet.ee; internet www.isamaaliit.ee; f. 1995 by merger of the National Fatherland Party (Isamaa, f. 1992) and the Estonian National Independence Party (f. 1988); Chair. MART LAAR; 2,490 mems.

**Russian Christian Union:** Tallinn; f. 1996; represents Russians in Estonia; Founder BORIS PILAR.

**Russian Democratic Movement:** Mere pst. 5, Tallinn 0001; tel. (2) 440-421; fax (2) 441-237; f. 1991 to promote domestic peace and mutual understanding between Estonians and Russians living in Estonia.

**Russian Party of Estonia:** c/o Riigikogu, Lossi plats 1A, Tallinn 0100; f. 1994; merged with the Russian People's Party of Estonia in early 1996; part of the Our Home is Estonia alliance; represents the Russian-speaking minority in Estonia; Chair. NIKOLAI MASPANOV; 1,250 mems.

**Russian Unity Party (RUP):** Tallinn; f. 1997 by former members of the Russian Party of Estonia; Leader IGOR SEDASHEV.

**United People's Party of Estonia:** Estonia pst. 3/5, Tallinn 10143; tel. 645-5335; fax 645-5336; e-mail euzp@stv.ee; f. 1994; represents the Russian-speaking minority in Estonia; Chair. VIKTOR ANDREYEV.

# Diplomatic Representation

## EMBASSIES IN ESTONIA

**China, People's Republic:** Narva mnt. 98, Tallinn 0001; tel. 641-9041; fax 641-9044; Ambassador: SUN DADONG.

**Denmark:** Wismari 5, Tallinn 15047; tel. 630-6400; fax 630-6421; e-mail dan.emb@online.ee; internet www.denmark.ee; Ambassador: SVEND ROED NIELSEN.

**Finland:** Kohtu 4, Tallinn 15180; tel. 610-3200; fax 610-3281; internet www.finemb.ee; Ambassador: PEKKA OINONEN.

**France:** Toom-Kuninga 20, Tallinn 0100; tel. 631-1492; fax 631-1385; internet www.viabalt.ee/estfra/; Ambassador: JACQUES FAURE.

**Germany:** Toom-Kuninga 11, Tallinn 15048; tel. 627-5300; fax 627-5304; e-mail saksasaa@online.ee; Ambassador: Dr GERHARD ENVER SCHRÖMBGENS.

**Italy:** Vizu 1–Vene 4, Tallinn 10140; tel. 625-6444; fax 631-1370; e-mail italemb1@online.ee; internet www.online.ee/italemb; Ambassador: LUCHINO CORTESE.

**Japan:** Harju 6, Tallinn 15069; tel. 631-0531; fax 631-0533; e-mail jaapansk@online.ee; Chargé d'affaires a.i.: RYUTARO FUJII.

**Latvia:** Tõnismägi 10, Tallinn 0100; tel. 646-1313; fax 631-1366; Ambassador: ANDRIS PIEBALGS.

**Lithuania:** Uustn 15, Tallinn 0001; tel. 631-4030; fax 641-2013; Ambassador: RIMANTAS TOMKUNAS.

**Norway:** Pärnu mnt. 8, Tallinn 0100; tel. (2) 448-014; fax 631-3003; Ambassador: Dr KAI OLAF LIE.

**Poland:** Pärnu mnt. 8, Tallinn 10503; tel. 627-8206; fax 644-5221; e-mail ambrptal@netexpress.ee; internet www.online.ee/~poolabrh; Ambassador: JAKUB WOLASIEWICZ.

**Russia:** Pikk 19, Tallinn 0100; tel. 646-4175; fax 646-4178; Ambassador: ALEKSEI GLOUKHOV.

**Sweden:** Pikk 28, Tallinn 15055; tel. 640-5600; fax 640-5695; Ambassador: ELISABET BORSIIN BONNIER.

**Ukraine:** Endla 8, Tallinn; tel. 631-1555; Ambassador: YURI OLENENKO.

**United Kingdom:** Wismari 6, Tallinn 10136; tel. 667-4700; fax 667-4714; e-mail uk.talli@netexpress.ee; Ambassador: TIMOTHY JAMES CRADDOCK.

**USA:** Kentmanni 20, Tallinn 0001; tel. 631-2021; fax 631-2025; Chargé d'affaires: WALTER ANDRUSYSZYN.

# Judicial System

**Supreme Court of the Republic of Estonia:** Lossi 17, Tartu 50093; tel. (7) 441-411; fax (7) 441-433; e-mail nc@nc.ee; internet www.nc.ee.

**Chief Justice:** UNO LÕHMUS.

**Chairman of the Constitutional Review Chamber:** UNO LÕHMUS.

**Chairman of the Civil Chamber:** JAANO ODAR.

**Chairman of the Criminal Chamber:** JÜRI ILVEST.

**Chairman of the Administrative Law Chamber:** TÕNU ANTON.

**Legal Chancellor's Office:** Tõnismägi 16, Tallinn 15193; tel. 631-6582; fax 631-6583; e-mail info@lc.gov.ee; internet www.gov.ee/estno/oiguskantsler.html; f. 1993; reviews general application of legislative and executive powers and of local governments for conformity with the constitution, supervises activities of state agencies in guaranteeing constitutional rights and freedoms; Legal Chancellor EERIK JUHAN TRUUVÄLI.

**Public Prosecutor's Office:** Wismari 7, Tallinn 15188; tel. 631-3002; fax 645-1475; e-mail riigiprok@rprok.just.ee; internet www.just.ee/prokuratuur/index.html; State Prosecutor-Gen. RAIVO SEPP.

# Religion

## CHRISTIANITY

### Protestant Churches

**Consistory of the Estonian Evangelical Lutheran Church of Estonia:** Kiriku plats 3, Tallinn 10130; tel. 627-7350; fax 627-7352; e-mail eelk@eelk.ee; internet www.zzz.ee/eelk; Archbishop JAAN KIIVIT.

**Estonian Conference of Seventh-day Adventists:** Lille 18, Tartu 51010; tel. (7) 343-211; fax (7) 343-389; f. 1917; e-mail advent@uninet.ee; Chair. TÕNU JUGAR.

**Union of Evangelical Christian and Baptist Churches of Estonia:** Pargi 9, Tallinn 11620; tel. 670-0698; fax 650-6008; e-mail eekbl@ekklesia.ee; Pres. HELARI PUU.

**United Methodist Church in Estonia:** Apteegi 3, Tallinn 10146; tel. (2) 445-447; fax 631-3482; e-mail keskus@emk.edu.ee; f. 1907; Superintendent OLAV PÄRNAMETS.

### The Eastern Orthodox Church

Between 1923 and 1940 the Estonian Apostolic Orthodox Church (EAOC) was subordinate to the Constantinople Ecumenical Patriarchate (based in Istanbul, Turkey). Following the Soviet occupation of Estonia in 1940, the EAOC was banned and its churches and communities were placed under the jurisdiction of the Moscow Patriarchate. The leaders of the EAOC went into exile in Stockholm (Sweden). After the restoration of Estonian independence in 1991, negotiations were held between the Constantinople and Moscow Patriarchates over the status of the more than 50 of Estonia's 84 Orthodox congregations that wished to return to Constantinople's jurisdiction. As no agreement was reached, in February 1996 the Constantinople Patriarchate decided unilaterally to restore the EAOC to its jurisdiction. In response, the Russian Orthodox Church suspended relations with Constantinople. The Estonian Government stated that freedom of worship would be guaranteed to the (predominantly Russian-speaking) congregations that wished to remain under the jurisdiction of the Moscow Patriarchate. Relations with Constantinople were restored in May 1996, when the holy synods of the two churches agreed that congregations should be permitted to decide under which jurisdiction they wished to remain.

**Estonian Apostolic Orthodox Church:** Tallinn; Chair. of Synod NIKOLAI SUURESOOT.

**Estonian Orthodox Church of Moscow Patriarchy:** Pikk 64/4, Tallinn 10133; tel. 641-1301; fax 641-1302; Archbishop KORNELIUS.

### The Roman Catholic Church

At 31 December 1996 there were an estimated 4,000 Roman Catholic adherents in Estonia.

**Office of the Apostolic Administrator:** Jaan Poska 47, Tallinn 0001; tel. (2) 423-147; fax (2) 426-440; Apostolic Administrator Most Rev. ERWIN JOSEF ENDER (Titular Archbishop of Germania in Numidia), Apostolic Nuncio to Lithuania, Estonia and Latvia (resident in Vilnius, Lithuania).

**Roman Catholic Parish of St Peter and St Paul in Tallinn:** Vene 18, Tallinn 0001; tel. (2) 6446-367; fax (2) 6444-678; Parish Priest Fr ZBIGNIEW PIŁAT.

**Tallinn Parish of the Ukrainian Catholic (Uniate) Church:** Võrgu 13–6, Tallinn; tel. 632-4306; Chair. of Bd ANATOLII LYUTYUK.

## ISLAM

**Estonian Islamic Congregation:** Sütiste tee 52–76, Tallinn 0034; tel. (2) 522-403; f. 1928; Chair. of Bd TIMUR SEIFULLEN.

## JUDAISM

**Hineirry Jewish Progressive Community of Narva:** Narva Partisani 2, Narva 2000; tel. (35) 409-97; Chair. of Bd YEVGENII BORINSKII.

**Jewish Community of Estonia:** POB 3576, Tallinn 0090; tel. and fax (2) 438-566; Chair. CILJA LAUD.

**Jewish Progressive Community in Tallinn:** POB 200, Tallinn; Chair. of Bd DAVID SLOMKA.

# The Press

In 1997 there were 102 officially-registered newspapers published in Estonia, including 74 in Estonian, and 572 periodicals, including 496 in Estonian. There were 15 daily newspapers in 1997, including 11 in Estonian.

## PRINCIPAL NEWSPAPERS

In Estonian except where otherwise stated.

**Äripäev** (Business Daily): Tulika 19, Tallinn 0006; tel. 650-5111; fax 654-1095; e-mail mbp@mbp.ee; internet www.mbp.ee; f. 1989; five days a week; business and finance; Editor-in-Chief IGOR RÕTOV; circ. 14,200.

**Den za Dujan** (Day After Day): Pärnu mnt. 67A, Tallinn 10134; tel. 646-3710; fax 646-1139; e-mail estonia@online.ee; f. 1991; weekly; in Russian; Editor-in-Chief JANA LITVINOVA; circ. 16,500.

**Eesti Ekspress** (Estonian Express): Narva mnt. 11E, Tallinn 10151; tel. 669-8080; fax 669-8154; e-mail ekspress@ekspress.ee; f. 1989; weekly; Editor-in-Chief AAVO KOKK; circ. 56,500.

**Eesti Kirik** (Estonian Church): Ülikooli, Tartu 2400; tel. (7) 431-437; fax (7) 441-231; f. 1923; weekly; Editor-in-Chief SIRJE SEMM; circ. 3,000.

**Eesti Päevaleht** (Estonian Daily): POB 433, Pärnu mnt. 67A, Tallinn 0090; tel. 646-1294; fax 631-1162; e-mail epl@epl.zzz.ee; f. 1905; daily; Editor-in-Chief KALLE MUULI; circ. 35,300.

**Estonia:** Mere pst. 5, Tallinn 10111; tel. 641-8400; fax 641-8402; e-mail vesting@teleport.ee; internet www.vesti.ee; f. 1940; five days a week in Russian (with Estonian edn Mon.); Editor-in-Chief VLADIMIR VELMAN; circ. 12,000.

**Kultuurileht** (Cultural Gazette): Pärnu mnt. 8, Tallinn 0001; tel. (2) 448-868; fax (2) 449-247; f. 1940; weekly; Editor-in-Chief TIINA TAMMER; circ. 3,400.

**Maaleht** (Country News): Toompuiestee 16, Tallinn 10137; tel. 645-3521; fax 645-2902; e-mail ml@maaleht.ee; internet www.maaleht.ee; f. 1987; weekly; problems and aspects of politics, culture, agriculture and country life; Editor-in-Chief SULEV VALNER; circ. 42,000.

**ME:** Kentmanni 18–44, Tallinn, tel. and fax 646-1623; e-mail moles@infonet.ee; Editor-in-Chief SERGEI SERGEYEV; circ. 7,000.

**Meie Meel** (Our Mind): POB 104, Tallinn 0090; tel. (2) 681-253; fax 646-1625; e-mail meiemeel@zzz.ee; f. 1991; weekly; youth paper; Editor-in-Chief MARE VETEMAA; circ. 20,700.

**Õhtuleht** (Evening Gazette): POB 106, Narva mnt. 13, Tallinn 10151; tel. (2) 614-4000; fax 614-4001; e-mail ohtuleht@oleht.ee; internet www.oleht.ee; f. 1944; daily; in Estonian; Editor-in-Chief PRIIT HÕBE-MÄGI; circ. 50,000.

**Postimees** (Postman): Gildi 1, Tartu 2400; tel. (7) 432-126; fax (7) 433-348; e-mail postimees@postimees.ee; f. 1857; daily; Editor-in-Chief VAHUR KALMRE; circ. 59,200.

**Sõnumileht** (Reports Newspaper): Vana-Lõuna 37, Tallinn 0001; tel. 640-8930; fax 640-8911; e-mail sleht@ruuter.sl.ee; f. 1995; daily; Editor-in-Chief MART LUIK; circ. 30,000.

### PRINCIPAL PERIODICALS

**Akadeemia:** Ülikooli 21, Tartu 2400; tel. (7) 431-117; fax (7) 431-373; e-mail akadeemia@tortu.astronet.ee; f. 1989; monthly; journal of the Union of Writers; Editor-in-Chief AIN KAALEP; circ. 2,800.

**Eesti Arst** (Estonian Physician): Piiskopi 3, Tallinn 0001; tel. (2) 444-370; f. 1922; 2 a month; Editor-in-Chief OKU TAMM.

**Eesti Loodus** (Estonian Nature): POB 100, Veski 4, Tartu 50002; tel. (7) 421-186; fax (7) 427-432; e-mail toimetus@el.loodus.ee; internet www.loodus.ee/el; f. 1933; monthly; popular science; illustrated; Editor-in-Chief UNO SIITAN; circ. 5,200.

**Eesti Naine** (Estonian Woman): Tartu mnt. 31, Tallinn 10128; tel. 641-9211; fax 641-9212; e-mail katrin@eestiajakirjad.ee; internet www.eestiajakirjad.ee; f. 1924; monthly; Editor-in-Chief KATRIN STREIMANN; circ. 22,000.

**Horisont** (Horizon): Narva mnt. 5, Tallinn 0001; tel. 641-8055; fax 641-8033; e-mail horisont@datanet.ee; f. 1967; 8 a year; popular scientific; Editor-in-Chief INDREK ROHTMETS; circ. 4,800.

**Keel ja Kirjandus** (Language and Literature): Roosikrantsi 6, Tallinn 10119; tel. 644-9228; fax 644-1800; e-mail kk@eki.ee; f. 1958; monthly; joint edition of the Academy of Sciences and the Union of Writers; Editor-in-Chief MART MERI; circ. 1,500.

**Kodukiri** (Your Home): Regati 1–129A, Tallinn 0019; tel. 639-8083; fax 639-6715; e-mail kodukiri@spin.ee; f. 1992; monthly; Editor-in-Chief KATRIN KUUSEMÄE; circ. 50,000.

**Linguistica Uralica:** Roosikrantsi 6, Tallinn 10119; tel. 644-0745; e-mail lu@eki.ee; internet www.gaid.gi.ee/eap/l.-u.htm; f. 1965; Editor-in-Chief VÄINO KLAUS; circ. 400.

**Looming** (Creation): Harju 1, Tallinn 0090; tel. (2) 441-365; f. 1923; journal of the Union of Writers; fiction, poetry, literary criticism; Editor-in-Chief ANDRES LANGEMETS; circ. 2,800.

**Loomingu Raamatukogu** (Library of Creativity): Harju 1, Tallinn 10502; tel. 644-9254; f. 1957; journal of the Union of Writers; poetry, fiction and non-fiction by Estonian and foreign authors; Editor-in-Chief TOOMAS HAUG; circ. 1,500.

**Maakodu** (Country Home): Lai 39, Tallinn 10133; tel. 641-1161; e-mail maakodu@online.ee; f. 1989; monthly; Editor-in-Chief ARVO SIRENDI; circ. 5,000.

**Noorus** (Youth): Narva mnt. 11A, Tallinn 0001; tel. 646-6284; fax 640-8399; f. 1946; monthly; youth issues, contemporary life in Estonia and worldwide, fashion, music, culture, business, cinema, essays, etc.; Editor-in-Chief SIIM NESTOR; circ. 8,000.

**Oil Shale:** Estonia pst. 7, Tallinn 10143; tel. 646-7512; fax 646-6026; e-mail aili@argus.chemnet.ee; internet gaia.gi.ee/oilshale; f. 1984; quarterly; geology, chemistry, mining, oil-shale industry; Editor-in-Chief JÜRI KANN; circ. 500.

**Põllumajandus** (Agriculture): Lai 39, Tallinn 0001; tel. 641-1161; f. 1932; monthly; Editor-in-Chief ARVO SIRENDI; circ. 1,000.

**Täheke** (Little Star): Pärnu mnt. 67A, Tallinn 0007; tel. (2) 681-495; f. 1960; illustrated; for 6–10-year-olds; Editor-in-Chief ELJU SILD; circ. 10,000.

**Teater, Muusika, Kino** (Theatre, Music, Cinema): POB 3200, Narva mnt. 5, Tallinn 0090; tel. (2) 440-472; fax (2) 434-172; f. 1982; monthly; Editor-in-Chief JÜRI AARMA; circ. 2,000.

**Vikerkaar** (Rainbow): Pikk 2, Tallinn 0001; tel. (2) 601-318; f. 1986; monthly; fiction, poetry, critical works; in Estonian and Russian; Editor-in-Chief MÄRT VÄLJATAGA; circ. 2,700.

### NEWS AGENCIES

**BNS** (Baltic News Service): Pärnu mnt. 105, Tallinn; tel. 610-8800; fax 610-8811; e-mail bns@bns.ee; internet www.bns.ee; f. 1990; Dir ALLAN MARTINSON.

**ETA** (Estonian News Agency): Pärnu 67A, Tallinn 10134; tel. 630-0800; fax 630-0816; e-mail eta@www.ee; internet www.ee/eta; f 1918; Dir NEEME BRUS.

### PRESS ORGANIZATIONS

**Estonian Journalists' Union:** Pärnu mnt. 67A, Tallinn 0001; tel. 646-1005; fax 631-1210; e-mail eall@netexpress.ee; f. 1919; Chair. TOIVO TOOTSEN.

**Estonian Newspaper Association:** Pärnu mnt. 67A, Tallinn 10134; tel. 646-1005; fax 631-1210; e-mail eall@netexpress.ee; internet www.netexpress.ee/eall; f. 1990; 47 mem. newspapers; Man. Dir TARMU TAMMERK.

## Publishers

**Eesti Raamat** (Estonian Book): Laki t 26, Tallinn 12915; tel. and fax (2) 658-7889; f. 1940; fiction; Dir ANNE-ASTRI KASK.

**Estonian Encyclopaedia Publishers Ltd:** Mustamäe tee 5, Tallinn 10616; tel. 625-9415; fax 656-6542; e-mail encyclo@online.ee; f. 1991; Man. Dir TÕNU KOGER.

**Koolibri:** Pärnu mnt. 10, Tallinn 10148; tel. (2) 445-223; fax (2) 446-813; e-mail as@koolibri.ee; internet www.koolibri.ee; f. 1991; textbooks, dictionaries, children's books; Dir ANTS LANG.

**Kunst** (Fine Art): Lai 34, Tallinn 10133; POB 105, Tallinn 10502; tel. 641-1764; fax 641-1762; e-mail kunst.lai@mail.ee; f. 1957; fine arts, fiction, tourism, history, biographies; Dir SIRJE HELME.

**Kupar:** Pärnu mnt. 67A, Tallinn 10134; tel. 628-6174; fax 646-2076; e-mail kupar@netexpress.ee; f. 1987; contemporary fiction; Chair. of Bd MIHKEL MUTT.

**Logos:** Siili 21-72, Tallinn 0034; tel. (2) 525-522; fax 631-1501; f. 1991; religious publications; Chair. INGMAR KURG.

**Monokkel:** POB 311, Tallinn 0001; tel. 6501-6307; f. 1988; history, fiction; Dir ANTS ÕÕBIK.

**Olion:** Pikk 2, Tallinn 10502; tel. 644-5403; fax 644-3488; e-mail olion@eol.ee; f. 1989; politics, economics, history, law; Dir HEINO KÄÄN.

**Õllu:** Harju 1, Tallinn 0001; tel. (2) 522-038; fiction; Chair. of Bd HEINO KIIK.

**Olympia:** Ümera 2–85, Tallinn 0001; tel. (2) 442-549; fax 634-4777; sports; Editor-in-Chief PAAVO KIVINE.

**Perioodika** (Periodicals): Pärnu mnt. 8, POB 107, Tallinn 10502; tel. 644-1262; fax (2) 442-484; f. 1964; newspapers, guidebooks, periodicals, fiction, children's books in foreign languages; Dir UNO SILLAJÕE.

**Tartu University Press:** Tiigi 78, Tartu 50410; tel. (7) 375-961; fax (7) 375-944; e-mail tyk@psych.ut.ee; internet www.psych.ut.ee/tup; f. 1958; science, textbooks, etc; Chair. VAIKO TIGANE.

**Tiritamm:** Laki 15, Tallinn 12915; tel. and fax 656-3616; e-mail sirje.saimre@mail.ee; f. 1991; children's books; Dir SIRJE SAIMRE.

**Valgus:** Tulika tn. 19, Tallinn 10613; tel. 650-5027; fax 650-5104; f. 1965; popular science, dictionaries, medicine, engineering, etc.; Man. Dir ANTS SILD.

### PUBLISHERS' ASSOCIATION

**Estonian Publishers' Association:** Laki 17, Tallinn 0006; POB 3366, Tallinn 0090; tel. 650-5592; fax 650-5590; f. 1991; unites 31 publishing houses; Chair. of Bd TÕNU KOGER.

## Broadcasting and Communications

### TELECOMMUNICATIONS

#### Regulatory Authority

**Estonian Communication Board:** Adala 4D, Tallinn 10614; tel. 639-1154; fax 639-1155; e-mail postbox@sa.ee; internet www.sa.ee; Dir JÜRI JÕEMA.

#### Major Provider

**Eesti Telecom** (Estonian Telecom): Endia 16, Tallinn 0001; tel. (2) 631-1212; fax (2) 631-1224; e-mail etcom@estnet.ee; internet www.et.ee; f. 1992 as Eesti Telefon; operates national telecommunications system; Dir-Gen. TOOMAS SOMERA; Chief Exec. HEINAR TAMMET.

### BROADCASTING

#### Radio

**Eesti Raadio** (Estonian Radio): Gonsiori 21, Tallinn 15020; tel. 611-4115; fax 611-4457; e-mail raadio@er.ee; internet www.er.ee; f. 1926; four 24-hour channels (three in Estonian, one in Russian); external service in English and Esperanto; Dir-Gen. AIN SAARNA.

#### Television

**Eesti Televisioon** (Estonian Television): Faehlmanni 12, Tallinn 15029; tel. 628-4113; fax 628-4155; e-mail etv@etv.ee; internet www.etv.ee; f. 1955; one channel; programmes in Estonian and Russian; Dir-Gen. TOOMAS LEPP.

**EVTV:** Peterburi 81, Tallinn 0014; tel. 632-8228; fax 632-3650; commercial station; Chair. VICTOR SIILATS.

**Kanal Kaks (Channel 2):** Harju 9, Tallinn 0001; tel. (2) 442-356; fax (2) 446-862; Commercial Station; Chair. ILMAR TASKA.

**Reklaamitelevisioon Tallinn** (Tallinn Commercial Television): Endla 3, Tallinn 0106; tel. (2) 666-743; fax 631-1077; f. 1992; one channel in Estonian and Russian.

**TIPP TV:** Regati pst. 1–6, Tallinn 0019; tel. (2) 238-535; fax (2) 238-555; Commercial Station; Pres. JURI MAKAROV.

# Finance

(cap. = capital; res = reserves; dep. = deposits; m. = million; brs = branches; amounts in kroons, unless otherwise stated)

## BANKING

The bank of Estonia was re-established in 1990, as was a private banking system. During a crisis in the financial sector in 1992 a number of weaker banks collapsed and others merged. New legislation was subsequently enacted to strengthen the sector, with increased supervision. A currency board became responsible for monetary supervision in 1992.

### Central Bank

**Bank of Estonia** (Eesti Pank): Estonia pst. 13, Tallinn 0100; tel. 668-0719; fax 631-0836; e-mail info@epbe.ee; internet www.ee/epbe; f. 1918, re-established 1990; central bank of Estonia; bank of issue; cap. and res. 1,428.7m., dep. 3,467.7m. (Dec. 1997); Pres. VAHUR KRAFT.

### Commercial Banks

**Estonian Credit Bank** (Eesti Krediidipank): Narva mnt. 4, Tallinn 15014; tel. 640-5000; fax 661-6037; e-mail krediidipank@ekp.ee; f. 1992; cap. 82.5m., res 11.8m., dep. 360m. (Oct. 1998); Pres. REIN OTSASON; Vice-Pres. ANDRUS KLUGE; 12 brs.

**Esttexbank:** Sakala 1, Tallinn 0100; tel.(2) 666-657; fax (2) 444-102; f. 1989; Chair. MART SILD; 30 employees.

**EVEA Bank:** Pronski 19, Tallinn 10124; tel. 667-1300; fax 667-1033; e-mail info@evb.ee; internet www.evb.ee; f. 1989; cap. 61.0m., res 14.7m., dep. 653.1m. (Dec. 1997); Pres. and Chief Exec. BORIS SHPUNGIN; 12 brs.

**Hansabank:** Liivalaia 8, Tallinn 15040; tel. 613-1310; fax 613-1410; e-mail webmaster@hansa.ee; internet www.hansa.ee; f. 1991; cap. 787.6m., res. 3,103.9m., dep. 15,698.5m. (Dec. 1998); merger with Estonian Savings Bank (Eesti Hoiupank) approved in July 1998; Chair. of Bd INDREK NEIVELT; 130 brs.

**Land Bank of Estonia** (Eesti Maapank): Narva mnt 11A, Tallinn 0001; tel. 640-8300; fax 640-8301; f. 1989 as Virumaa Kommertspank, current name adopted in 1996; cap. 72.0m., res 7.1m., dep. 932.8m. (Dec. 1996); Chair. MALLE EENMAA.

**Optiva Bank:** Narva mnt. 11, Tallinn 15015; tel. 630-2100; fax 630-2200; e-mail bank@optiva.ee; internet www.optiva.ee; f. 1992; cap. 473.2m., res 49.5m., dep. 2,497.8m. (Dec. 1998); Chair. HÄRMO VÄRK; 7 brs.

**Tallinn Business Bank Ltd** (Tallinna Äripanga Aktsiaselts): Estonia pst. 3–5, Tallinn 15097; tel. 645-5349; fax 660-4868; e-mail tbb@uninet.ee; f. 1991; cap. 63.4m., dep. 172.2m. (Dec. 1998); Pres. NEEME ROOSIMÄGI.

**Union Bank of Estonia** (Eesti Ühispank): Tornimäe 2, Tallinn 15010; tel. 665-5100; fax 665-5102; e-mail postkast@eyp.ee; internet www.eyp.ee; f. 1992; cap. 661.5m., res 298.5m., dep. 8,108.3m. (Feb. 1999); merged with North Estonian Bank Jan. 1997 and with Tallinna Pank in July 1998; Pres. AIN HANSCHMIDT; 90 brs.

### Foreign Bank

**Merita Bank Ltd** (Finland): Hobujaama 4, Tallinn 10051; tel. 628-3200; fax 628-3201; e-mail merita@estpak.ee; f. 1995; Gen. Man. HEIKKI VIITANEN.

### Banking Association

**Estonian Banking Association** (Eesti Pangaliit): Ahtri 12, Tallinn 10151; tel. 611-6567; fax 611-6568; e-mail post@pangaliit.ee; internet www.pangaliit.ee; f. 1992; Chair. HÄRMO VÄRK; Man. Dir VIKTOR HÜTT.

## STOCK EXCHANGE

**Tallinn Stock Exchange:** Pärnu mnt. 12, Tallinn 10148; tel. 640-8840; fax 640-8801; e-mail tse@tse.ee; internet www.tse.ee; f. 1995; Chair. GERT TIIVAS.

## INSURANCE

**Insurance Supervisory Authority of Estonia:** Lauteri 5, Tallinn 10114; tel. 610-6700; fax 610-6701; e-mail secretary@eisa.ee; internet www.eisa.ee; f. 1993; Dir-Gen. ELLEN RIDASTE.

Principal non-life companies include Balti Kindlustus (BICO) Ltd, Eesti Varakindlustus Ltd, ETAS Kindlustus Ltd, Hansa Kindlustus Ltd, Inges Kindlustus Ltd, Kalju Ltd, Leks Kindlustus Ltd, Nordika Kindlustus Ltd, Polaris-Vara Ltd, Salva Kindlustus Ltd, Sampo Kindlustus Ltd, Seesam Rahvusvaheline Kindlustus Ltd and Ühiskindlustus.

Principal life companies include AB Elukindlustus Ltd, Bico Elukindlustus Ltd, Eesti Elukindlustus Ltd, Hansapanga Kindlustus Ltd, Leks Elukindlustus Ltd, Nordika Elukindlustus Ltd, Polaris-Elu Ltd and Seesam Elukindlustus Ltd.

# Trade and Industry

## GOVERNMENT AGENCIES

**Consumer Protection Board:** Kiriku 4, Tallinn 15071; tel. 620-1700; fax 620-1701; e-mail info@consumer.ee; Dir-Gen. HELLE ARUNIIT.

**Estonian Export Agency:** Rävala pst 6–602B, Tallinn 0001; tel. 631-3851; fax 641-0312; Dir KRISTJAN KIVIPALU.

**Estonian Grain Board:** Hobujaama 1, Tallinn 0001; tel. (2) 432-815; fax 641-9075; Dir-Gen. AGO SOOTS.

**Estonian Investment Agency:** Rävala pst 6–602B, Tallinn 0001; tel. 641-0166; fax 641-0312; e-mail info@eia.ee; internet www.eia.ee; Dir AGU REMMELG.

**Estonian Privatization Agency** (Eesti Erastamisagentuur): Rävala 6, Tallinn 0105; tel. 630-5600; fax 630-5699; e-mail eea@eea.ee; internet www.eea.ee/; Dir-Gen. VÄINO SARNET.

**Estonian Trade Council:** Kiriku 2, Tallinn 0100; tel. (2) 444-703; fax 631-4117; f. 1991; Dir AARE PUUR.

**National Standards Board of Estonia:** Aru 10, Tallinn 10317; tel. 651-9200; fax 651-9220; e-mail info@evs.ee; Dir-Gen. ARNO UNIVER.

**Trade and Investment Board:** Rävala pst. 6– 602B, Tallinn 0001; tel. 631-3850; fax 641-0312; e-mail info@eia.ee; internet www.eia.ee; Dir-Gen. JURI SAKKEUS.

## CHAMBER OF COMMERCE

**Estonian Chamber of Commerce and Industry (ECCI):** Toom-Kooli 17, Tallinn 10130; tel. 646-0244; fax 646-0245; e-mail koda@koda.ee; internet www.koda.ee; f. 1925; Pres. TOOMAS LUMAN; Gen. Dir MART RELVE.

## INDUSTRIAL AND TRADE ASSOCIATIONS

**Association of Construction Material Producers of Estonia** (Eesti Ehitusmaterjalide Tootjate Liit): Kiriku 6, Tallinn 10130; tel. 620-1918; fax 620-1935; e-mail eetl@index.ee; internet www.hot.ee/eetl; Pres. VAMBOLA JUURMANN.

**Association of Estonian Electrotechnical and Electronic Industry:** Pirita tee 20, Tallinn 0001; tel. (2) 238-981; fax (2) 237-827; Pres. GUNNAR TOOMSOO.

**Association of Estonian Food Industry:** Gonsiori 29, Tallinn 10147; tel. (2) 422-246; fax 631-2718; e-mail ettl@online.ee; internet www.online.ee/~ettl; f. 1993; Man. Dir HELVE REMMEL.

**Association of Estonian International Road Carriers** (Eesti Rahvusvaheliste Autovedajate Assotsiatsioon): Narva mnt. 91, Tallinn 10127; tel. 627-3740; fax 627-3741; e-mail info@eraa.ee; internet www.eraa.ee; Sec.-Gen. TOLBO KULDUEPP.

**Association of Estonian Local Industry:** Gonsiori 29, Tallinn 0100; tel (2) 422-367; fax (2) 424-962; Chair. HEINO VASAR.

**Estimpex Foreign Trade Association:** Uus 32/34, Tallinn 0101; tel. (2) 601-462; fax (2) 602-184; import and export of household fixtures, foodstuffs, souvenirs and oil-based products; Gen. Dir OSVALD KALDRE.

**Estonian Agricultural Producers Central Union** (Eestimaa Pollumajandustootjate Keskliit): Lai 39/41, Tallinn 0100; tel. (2) 602-045; fax (2) 440-601; Chair. of Bd HEINO PRIIMÄGI.

**Estonian Asphalt Pavement Association** (Eesti Asfaldiliit): Ristiku põik 8, Tallinn 10612; tel. 651-7646; fax 654-1351; f. 1991; coordinates Estonian asphalt paving and mixing companies; Chair. of Bd ALEKSANDER KALDAS.

**Estonian Association of Construction Entrepreneurs** (Eesti Ehitusettevõtjate Liit): Rävala pst. 8, Tallinn 10143; tel. and fax 660-4688; e-mail eeel@eeel.ee; Man. Dir ILMAR LINK.

**Estonian Association of Small and Medium-sized Enterprises (EVEA):** Pronksi 3, Tallinn 10124; tel. 640-3935; fax 631-2451; e-mail sme@evea.ee; internet www.evea.ee; f. 1988; Pres. RIIVO SINIJÄRV; Man. Dir MARGIT KALLASTE.

**Estonian Clothing and Textile Association** (Eesti Rõivaja Tekstiililiit): Tartu mnt. 63, Tallinn 10115; tel. 611-5567; fax 611-5568; e-mail ertl@online.ee; internet www.online.ee/~ertl; Chair. MADIS VÕÕRAS.

**Estonian Dairy Association** (Eesti Piimaliit): Vilmsi 53, Tallinn 10147; tel. (2) 430-715; fax (2) 643-0418 Chair. ENN SOKK.

**Estonian Fisheries Association:** Liivalaia 14, Tallinn 0100; tel. (2) 683-442; fax (2) 682-283; Chair. HEINO PALU.

**Estonian Forest Federation** (Eesti Metsaliit): Gonsiori 29, Tallinn 0001; tel. (2) 421-559; fax (2) 423-739; Pres. MART ERIK.

**Estonian Gas Association** (Eesti Gaasiliit): Liivalaia 9, Tallinn 0001; tel. 646-1571; fax 631-4340; Chair. of Bd ANDRES SAAR.

**Estonian Hotel and Restaurant Association** (Easti Hotellide Ja Restoranide Liit): Pikk 71, Tallinn 0001; tel. (2) 602-433; fax (2) 601-907; Chair. of Bd TOOMAS SILDMÄE.

**Estonian Meat Association** (Eesti Lihaliit): Lai 39/41, Tallinn 10133; tel. and fax 641-1035; f. 1989; 29 mem. companies (1999); Chair. of Bd PEETER MASPANOV.

**Estonian Union of Automobile Enterprises** (Eesti Autoettevõtete Liit): Magasini 31, Tallinn 0001; tel. (2) 439-476; fax (2) 443-345; Pres. MATI MÄGI.

**ETK Managers' Club:** Narva mnt. 7, Tallinn 10117; tel. (2) 438-242; fax 630-2333; f. 1991; Pres. GEORG ILVEST.

**Federation of Estonian Chemical Industries:** Tulika 19, Tallinn 0006; tel. and fax 659-1040; 24 mem. enterprises; Chair. REIN REILE.

**Federation of Estonian Engineering Industry:** Mustamäe tee 4, Tallinn 10621; tel. 611-5893; fax 656-6640; e-mail eml@ltnet.ee; f. 1991; 80 mem. enterprises; Chair. of Bd MIHKEL PIKNER.

**Union of Estonian Breweries** (Eesti Õlletootjate Liit): Tähtvere 58/62, Tartu 2400; tel. (7) 434-330; fax (7) 431-193; Chair. of Bd MADIS PADDAR.

**Union of Estonian Paper Manufacturers** (Eesti Paberitööstuse Liit): Tööstuse 19, Kohila 3420; tel. (48) 33-564; fax (48) 32-132; e-mail kohila pv@netexpress.ee; Chair. of Bd HENNO PAVELSON.

**Union of Estonian Wine Producers** (Eesti Veinitootjate Liit): Karksi, Polli vald 2944; tel. and fax (43) 31-533; Chair. of Bd JÜRI KERT.

### EMPLOYERS' ORGANIZATION

**Confederation of Estonian Industry and Employers:** Gonsiori 29, Tallinn 0100; tel. (2) 422-235; fax (2) 424-962; f. 1991 as Confederation of Estonian Industry, name changed as above 1995; Man. Dir VILJAR VESKIVÄLI.

### UTILITIES

#### Electricity

**Eesti Energia AS** (Estonian Energy Ltd): Estonia pst 1, Tallinn 10143; tel. 625-2222; fax 625-2200; e-mail kaja.malts@energia.ee; f. 1939; producer of thermal and electric energy; manufacture of electric motors; electrical engineering; 10,444 employees.

#### Gas

**Eesti Gaas** (Estonian Gas): Liivalaia 9, Tallinn 10118; tel. 630-3003; fax 631-3884; e-mail info@egaas.online.ee; internet www.gaas.ee; purchases and transports natural gas, constructs pipelines, calibrates gas meters; Chair. AARNE SAAR.

#### Water

**Tallinn Water Ltd:** Adala 10, POB 174, Tallinn 10502; tel. 626-2202; fax 626-2302; e-mail tvesi@tvesi.ee; f. 1867; supply and treatment of water; collection and treatment of waste water; Chair. KALLE TIITER.

### TRADE UNIONS

**Association of Estonian Trade Unions:** Rävala 4, Tallinn 10143; tel. 661-2383; fax 661-2542; e-mail eakl@eakl.ee; f. 1990; Chair. RAIVO PAAVO.

**Association of Estonian Chemical Industry Workers' Trade Unions:** Järveküla tee 40, Kohtla-Järve 30328; tel. (33) 478-28; fax (33) 457-98; f. 1990; Chair. MIHKEL ISKÜL.

**Association of Estonian Radio and Electronics Industry Workers' Trade Unions:** Rävala 4, Tallinn 0100; tel. (2) 432-318; Chair. LYUBOV SEROVA.

**Confederation of Estonian Food and Landworkers' Unions:** 32 Raua Str, Tallinn 10152; tel. and fax 641-0249; f. 1989; Chair. AARE-LEMBIT NEEVE.

**Estonian Light Industry Workers' Trade Union:** Rävala 4, Tallinn 0100; tel. and fax (2) 431-640; Chair. EVI JAAGURA.

**Trade Union of Estonian Engineering Workers:** Rävala 4, Tallinn 0100; tel. (2) 430-879; Chair. MAIT-TOOMAS REIMANN.

**Trade Union of Estonian Forest Industry Workers:** Rävala 4, Tallinn 0001; tel. (2) 421-333; fax (2) 422-369; f. 1990; Chair. JÜRI MINJAJEV.

**Trade Union of Oil-Shale Industry Workers:** Jaama 10, Jõhvi 41502; tel. (33) 70575; e-mail ental@en.ee; Chair. ENDEL PAAP.

## Transport

### RAILWAYS

In 1998 there were 1,018 km of railway track in use, of which 132 km were electrified. Main lines link Tallinn with Narva and St Petersburg (Russia), Tartu and Pskov (Russia), Tartu and Valga (Latvia), and Pärnu and Rīga (Latvia).

**Estonian Railways Ltd**(AS Eesti Raudtee): Pikk 36, Tallinn 15073; tel. 615-8610; fax 615-8710; e-mail raudtee@evr.ee; internet www.evr.ee; f. 1918; freight carriers; Chair. PARBO JUCHNEWITSCH; 5,000 employees.

### ROADS

In 1998 Estonia had 16,430 km of state roads. In 1997 Estonia had 15,304 km of state roads, of which 1,190 km were main roads, 2,666 km secondary roads and 11,448 km local roads. The motorway network totalled 64 km. About 53% of the total road network was asphalted.

**Estonian Road Administration:** Pärnu Road 24, Tallinn 10141; tel. 611-9300; fax 611-9360; e-mail estroad@mnt.ee; internet www.mnt.ee; Gen. Dir RIHO SÕRMUS.

### SHIPPING

Tallinn is the main port for freight transportation. There are regular passenger services between Tallinn and Helsinki (Finland). A service between Tallinn and Stockholm (Sweden) was inaugurated in 1991.

**Estonian National Maritime Board:** Sadama 29, Terminal B, Tallinn 10111; tel. 620-5500; fax 620-5506; e-mail eva@enmb.ee; internet www.enmb.ee; f. 1990; administers and implements state maritime safety policies, ship-control, pilot, lighthouse and hydrography services; Gen. Dir Capt. KALLE PEDAK; 500 employees.

#### Shipowning Company

**Estonian Shipping Company Ltd** (AS Eesti Merelaevardus): Estonia Blvd 3/5, Tallinn 15096; tel. 640-9500; fax 640-9595; f. 1991; transferred to private ownership in mid-1997; liner services, ship chartering and cargo shipping; Chair. ENN PANT; Dir-Gen. TOIVO NINNAS; 2,380 employees.

#### Shipowners' Association

**Estonian Shipowners' Association** (Eesti Laevaomanike Liit): Luise 1A, Tallinn 10142; tel. and fax 646-0109; e-mail reeder@teleport.ee; Pres. REIN MERISALU.

#### Port Authority

**Port of Tallinn:** Sadama 25, Tallinn 15051; tel. 631-8002; fax 631-8166; e-mail portoftallinn@ts.ee; internet www.ts.ee; Harbour Master E. HUNT.

### CIVIL AVIATION

Estonia has air links with several major cities in the former USSR, including Moscow and St Petersburg (Russia), Kiev (Ukraine), Minsk (Belarus), Rīga (Latvia) and Vilnius (Lithuania), and with several western European destinations.

**Estonian Civil Aviation Administration:** Pärnu mnt. 6, Tallinn 10148; tel. 631-3620; fax 631-2681; e-mail ecaa@trenet.ee; f. 1990; Dir Gen. EDUARD TÜÜR.

**Elk Airways** (Estonian Aviation Company Ltd): Eesti Vabariik, Majaka 26, Tallinn 11416; tel. 638-0972; fax 638-0975; e-mail elk@infonet.ee; internet www.elk.ee; f. 1992; international and domestic passenger and cargo flights to Europe and the CIS; Man. Dir VLADIMIR SLONTCHEVSH.

**Estonian Air:** Lennujaama tee 2, Tallinn 0011; tel. 640-1101; fax 631-2740; f. 1991; passenger and cargo flights to Europe and the CIS; Chair. MADIS ÜÜRIKE.

## Tourism

Estonia has a wide range of attractions for tourists, including the historic towns of Tallinn and Tartu, extensive nature reserves and coastal resorts. In 1990 the National Tourism Board was established to develop facilities for tourism in Estonia. In 1998 there were an estimated 1.5m. visitors to Estonia, with Finland the main source of tourists.

**Estonian Association of Travel Agents** (Eesti Turismifirmade Liit): Kiriku 6, Tallinn 10130; tel. 631-3013; fax 631-3622; e-mail info@etfl.ee; internet www.etfl.ee; f. 1990; Pres. DAISY JÄRVA.

**Estonian Hotel and Restaurant Association:** Kiriku 6, Tallinn 10130; tel. 641-1428; fax 641-1425; e-mail info@ehrl.ee; internet www.ehrl.ee; Man. Dir DONALD VISNAPUU.

**Estonian Marine Tourism Association:** Regati pst. 1, 6K, Tallinn 11911; tel. 639-8933; fax 639-8899; f. 1990; Man. Dir HELLE HALLIKA.

**Estonian Tourist Board:** Mundi tn. 2, Tallinn 10146; tel. 641-1420; fax 641-1432; e-mail info@turism.ee; internet www.turism.ee; f. 1990; govt agency; Dir-Gen. SILVI BLJUMOVITŠ.

# ETHIOPIA

## Introductory Survey

### Location, Climate, Language, Religion, Flag, Capital

The Federal Democratic Republic of Ethiopia is a land-locked country in eastern Africa; it has a long frontier with Somalia near the Horn of Africa. Sudan lies to the west, Eritrea to the north, Djibouti to the north-east and Kenya to the south. The climate is mainly temperate because of the high plateau terrain, with an average annual temperature of 13°C (55°F), abundant rainfall in some years and low humidity. The lower country and valley gorges are very hot and subject to recurrent drought. The official language is Amharic, but many other local languages are also spoken. English is widely used in official and commercial circles. The Ethiopian Orthodox (Tewahido) Church, an ancient Christian sect, has a wide following in the north and on the southern plateau. In much of the south and east the inhabitants include Muslims and followers of animist beliefs. The national flag (proportions 3 by 2) has three equal horizontal stripes, of green, yellow and red. The capital is Addis Ababa.

### Recent History

Ethiopia was dominated for more than 50 years by Haile Selassie, who became Regent in 1916, King in 1928 and Emperor in 1930. He continued his autocratic style of rule (except during the Italian occupation of 1936–41) until September 1974, when he was deposed by the armed forces. Haile Selassie died, a captive of the military regime, in August 1975.

The 1974 revolution was organized by an Armed Forces Co-ordinating Committee, known popularly as the Dergue (Shadow), which established a Provisional Military Administrative Council (PMAC), led by Brig.-Gen. Teferi Benti. In December Ethiopia was declared a socialist state, and in 1975 land, financial institutions and large industrial companies were nationalized. The regime introduced a radical programme of social and economic reforms, which led to widespread unrest, despite promises by the Dergue to return to civilian rule at an unspecified date. In February 1977, following disagreements within the Dergue, Lt-Col Mengistu Haile Mariam executed Teferi and his closest associates, and replaced him as Chairman of the PMAC and as Head of State.

During 1977–78, in an attempt to end opposition to the regime, the Government imprisoned or killed thousands of its opponents. Political power was consolidated in a Commission for Organizing the Party of the Working People of Ethiopia (COPWE), largely dominated by military personnel. In September 1984, at the COPWE's third congress, the Workers' Party of Ethiopia (WPE) was formally inaugurated. Lt-Col Mengistu was unanimously elected Secretary-General of the party, which modelled itself on the Communist Party of the Soviet Union. In mid-1986, in preparation for the eventual transfer of power from the PMAC to a civilian government, a draft Constitution was published. In February 1987 it was endorsed by a referendum, obtaining the support of some 81% of the votes cast. In June national elections were held to an 835-seat legislature, the National Shengo (Assembly). In September, at the inaugural meeting of the new legislature, the PMAC was abolished, and the People's Democratic Republic of Ethiopia was declared. The National Shengo unanimously elected Lt-Col Mengistu as President of the Republic, and a 24-member Council of State was also elected, to act as the Shengo's permanent organ.

Numerous insurgent groups, encouraged by the confusion resulting from the 1974 revolution, launched a number of armed insurgencies against the Government. Of these, the most effective were based in the Ogaden, Eritrea and Tigrai regions. Somalia laid claim to the Ogaden, which is populated mainly by ethnic Somalis. Regular Somali troops supported incursions by forces of the Western Somali Liberation Front, and in 1977 the Somalis made major advances in the Ogaden. In 1978, however, they were forced to retreat, and by the end of 1980 Ethiopian forces had gained control of virtually the whole of the Ogaden region, although armed clashes continued.

The former Italian colony of Eritrea was merged with Ethiopia, in a federal arrangement, in September 1952, and annexed to Ethiopia as a province in November 1962. A secessionist movement, the Eritrean Liberation Front (ELF), was founded in Egypt in 1958. In the late 1960s and early 1970s the ELF enjoyed considerable success against government troops, but was weakened by internal dissension. It eventually split into several rival factions, the largest of which was the Eritrean People's Liberation Front (EPLF). In 1978 government troops re-established control in much of Eritrea, and the EPLF was forced to retreat to the remote northern town of Nakfa. In 1982 a military offensive by government troops failed to capture Nakfa, and in 1984 the EPLF made several successful counter-attacks. In mid-1985 the Government launched a large-scale offensive in Eritrea and made significant gains. The EPLF, however, continued to attack strategic targets, and in mid-1986 government forces abandoned the north-east coast to the rebels.

An insurgent movement also emerged in Tigrai province in the late 1970s. The Tigrai People's Liberation Front (TPLF) was armed and trained by the EPLF, but relations between the two groups deteriorated sharply in the mid-1980s. The TPLF was weakened by conflict with other anti-Government groups, and in 1985 and 1986 government forces had considerable success against the TPLF.

The conflict in the north of the country during 1984–85 compounded difficulties being experienced in areas of Ethiopia already severely affected by famine. In 1984 the rains failed for the third consecutive crop season, and in May it was estimated that 7m. people could suffer starvation. Emergency food aid was received from many Western nations, but distribution was hampered, both by the continuing conflict and by the inadequacy of Ethiopia's infrastructure. Some rainfall in 1985 eased the drought in the northern provinces, but there were further fears of famine in 1987, when the crops failed again.

In September 1987 the newly-elected National Shengo announced that five areas, including Eritrea and Tigrai, were to become 'autonomous regions' under the new Constitution. Eritrea was granted a considerable degree of self-government, but both the EPLF and the TPLF rejected the proposals. In March 1988 EPLF forces captured the town of Afabet, and claimed to have killed one-third of all Ethiopian troops in Eritrea. Following the town's capture, the TPLF took advantage of the movement of government forces from Tigrai to Eritrea and overran all the garrisons in north-western and north-eastern Tigrai. In May the Government declared a state of emergency in Eritrea and Tigrai, and in June government troops regained control of some of the captured garrison towns in Tigrai, suffering heavy losses in the process. However, in early 1989, following major defeats in north-west Tigrai, government forces abandoned virtually the whole region to the TPLF.

In May 1989 the Government acted to pre-empt an attempted *coup d'état*, which had been planned by numerous senior army officers, including the Chief of Staff, the Commander of the Air Force, and the Commander of the Army in Eritrea. The failed coup and the subsequent reorganization of the military command structure hindered attempts by government forces (already weakend by heavy losses and low morale) to launch counter-offensives in Eritrea and Tigrai. Nevertheless, while the EPLF and the TPLF continued their military campaigns during 1989, both groups agreed to negotiate with the Government, in an attempt to facilitate a diplomatic solution to the conflict.

US-sponsored negotiations held in late 1989 between representatives of the Ethiopian Government and the EPLF proved inconclusive. Negotiations between the TPLF and the Ethiopian Government, in late 1989 and early 1990, were also unsuccessful. A third round of negotiations, held in Rome, Italy, in March 1990, collapsed over the TPLF's insistence that substantive negotiations should involve a joint delegation of the TPLF and their allies, the Ethiopian People's Democratic Movement (EPDM).

Severe drought in 1989 threatened widespread famine, and the UN estimated that some 4m. people in northern areas would require food aid in 1990. Substantial aid was supplied by Western governments and non-governmental organizations, but its distribution to the most needy areas remained difficult, owing to the disruption of supply convoys by both rebel and government forces. The recurrent food crises prompted further criticism of the Mengistu Government's commitment to collectivist agricultural policies and its 'villagization' programme (combining several villages in single administrative units, mainly for security reasons).

Following the capture of Massawa port by the EPLF in February 1990 (presenting a direct threat to the continued survival of the Ethiopian army in Eritrea), President Mengistu was obliged to make further concessions. In March Ethiopian socialism was virtually abandoned, when the ruling WPE was renamed the Ethiopian Democratic Unity Party, and membership was opened to non-Marxists. Mengistu began introducing elements of a market economy and dismantling many of the economic structures that had been established after the 1974 revolution. However, heavy defeats of government forces continued during 1990 and early 1991. Peace negotiations held in the USA in February 1991 between representatives of the EPLF and the Ethiopian Government failed to end the military conflict.

By late April 1991, troops of the Ethiopian People's Revolutionary Democratic Front (EPRDF—an alliance of the TPLF and the EPDM, formed in September 1989) had captured Ambo, a town 130 km west of Addis Ababa, while EPLF forces were 50 km north of Assab, Ethiopia's principal port. On 21 May, faced with the prospect of the imminent defeat of his army, Mengistu fled the country. Lt-Gen. Tesfaye, the Vice-President, assumed control. On 28 May, following the failure of negotiations in the United Kingdom, and with the public support of the USA, units of the EPRDF entered Addis Ababa. They encountered little resistance, and the EPRDF established an interim Government, pending the convening, in July, of a multiparty conference, which was to elect a transitional government. Meanwhile, the EPLF had gained control of the Eritrean capital, Asmara, and announced the establishment of a provisional Government to administer Eritrea until the holding of a referendum, within two years, on the issue of independence.

A national conference in July 1991, organized by the EPRDF, was attended by some 20 political and ethnic organizations. The conference adopted amendments to a national charter, presented by the EPRDF, and elected an 87-member Council of Representatives, which was to govern for a transitional period of two years, after which free national elections were to be held. The national charter provided guarantees for freedom of association and expression, and for self-determination for Ethiopia's various ethnic groups. The EPLF was not officially represented at the conference, but came to an agreement with the EPRDF, whereby the EPRDF accepted the formation of the EPLF's provisional Government of Eritrea and the determination by referendum of the future of the region.

In late July 1991 the Council of Representatives established a commission to draft a new constitution and elected Meles Zenawi, the leader of the EPRDF (and of the TPLF), as Chairman of the Council, a position which made him President of the transitional Government and Head of State, and in August it appointed a Council of Ministers. However, violent conflict continued in many parts of the country in the latter half of the year. There were armed clashes between troops of the EPRDF and forces of the Ethiopian People's Revolutionary Party in the Gojam and Gondar regions, and in August and September supporters of the EPRDF clashed with those of the Oromo Liberation Front (OLF), despite co-operation between these two groups at government level. EPRDF troops (who are mainly Tigraian) also encountered violent opposition from the Afar, Issa and Gurgureh ethnic groups.

In November 1991, in accordance with the national charter's promise of self-determination for Ethiopia's peoples, the transitional Government announced the division of the country into 14 regional administrations, which would have autonomy in matters of regional law and internal affairs. A transitional economic policy, designed to accelerate economic reform, was also approved.

In early 1992 skirmishes continued between forces of the EPRDF and the OLF in the south and east of the country, severely hampering the distribution of food aid to some 6.5m. people affected by drought and to a further 1.4m. people displaced during the continuing conflict. In April a cease-fire between the two sides was agreed upon, under the auspices of the USA and the EPLF. Local elections were held in many parts of the country in April and May, and regional elections in June. These latter elections were boycotted by the OLF and other political groups, amid widespread allegations of intimidation of opposition candidates by the EPRDF. (There was also evidence, however, that the OLF had harassed civilians and election officials.) An international observer group, including representatives of the UN, the Organization of African Unity (OAU) and the European Community (EC, now the European Union—EU), indicated that claims of electoral malpractice by the EPRDF in many areas were, at least in part, justified. Shortly after the elections, in which the EPRDF and associated parties obtained 90% of the votes cast, the OLF withdrew its support from the transitional Government. In July 10 political organizations which were signatories to the national charter of July 1991 demanded the annulment of the results of the regional elections. The transitional Government established a board 'to correct election errors' at the end of the month, but by late August the regional councils were functioning in all parts of the country except the Afar and Somali areas, where the elections had been postponed. Hopes that the transitional Government had truly democratic intentions were also undermined by reports from the Ethiopian Human Rights Council (EHRCO), which by mid-1992 had documented more than 2,000 cases of people who had been detained without being charged, of whom the majority were political opponents of the EPRDF. The EHRCO also reported 13 extra-judicial executions.

In June 1992 OLF troops reportedly captured the town of Asbe Teferi, about 150 km from Addis Ababa; the EPRDF's numerically greatly superior forces, however, ensured that the transitional Government's control of the capital was secure. In October talks between the EPRDF and the OLF ended in failure, with the OLF continuing to demand that the results of the June elections be annulled, while the EPRDF urged the OLF to rejoin the transitional Government. Hostilities between the two sides continued in various parts of the country, with the EPRDF taking prisoners in massive numbers: by mid-December there were an estimated 20,000 OLF prisoners of war being held.

Throughout 1992 people in many parts of the country continued to suffer acute food shortages, caused by drought and ineffective distribution of aid: in August it was estimated that 13.5m. people were affected. In the following year inadequate rainfall resulted in widespread crop failure in southern, northern and eastern Ethiopia.

Meanwhile the provisional Government of Eritrea announced in November 1992 that a UN-supervised referendum on the area's status would be held in April 1993. The Sudanese Government expressed its readiness to assist the Eritrean Referendum Commission in conducting a plebiscite among some 250,000 Eritrean refugees still residing in Sudan. The referendum revealed overwhelming support for Eritrean independence, which was duly proclaimed on 24 May 1993.

In January 1993 the Ethiopian security forces brutally suppressed a student demonstration at Addis Ababa University protesting against the UN's involvement in the Eritrean independence process (see below). There was at least one death, and more than 30 demonstrators were injured.

In July 1993 the EPRDF experienced serious internal unrest when its executive committee issued a statement denouncing an undisclosed number of party members. It was believed that a purge was under way of middle-ranking TPLF members who had criticized the Government's policy of ethnic regionalization and the slow pace of economic liberalization. Delays in the dispatch of humanitarian aid in early 1994 resulted in the deaths (from hunger and disease) of some 5,000 people in southern Ethiopia. By August relief food was reaching those in need, and by October the threat of famine had been brought under control with help from international donors.

Elections to a Constituent Assembly were conducted in June 1994, in which the EPRDF won 484 of the 547 seats. The elections were boycotted by the All-Amhara People's Organization, the recently-formed Coalition of Alternative Forces for Peace and Democracy in Ethiopia (CAFPDE—incorporating 30 opposition groups) and the OLF, whose leaders alleged that the Meles administration had intimidated their supporters and refused opposition parties permission to open offices. The Constituent Assembly was inaugurated in October to debate a draft Constitution, which it ratified in December. The new Constitution provided for the establishment of a federal government and the division of the country (renamed the Federal Democratic Republic of Ethiopia) into nine states and two chartered cities. It provided for regional autonomy, including the right of secession. A new legislature, the Federal Parliamentary Assembly, was to be established, comprising two chambers: the Council of People's Representatives (consisting of 548 directly-elected members) and the Council of the Federation (composed of 117 deputies, elected by the new state assemblies).

The EPRDF and its allies won an overwhelming victory in elections to the Council of People's Representatives and state assemblies in May 1995. In Tigrai region the TPLF won all the seats in both the federal and state assemblies; EPRDF parties were equally successful in Amhara and Oromia regions. The EPRDF itself won all 92 local assembly seats in Addis Ababa. The largest opposition party to participate in the elections, the Ethiopian National Democratic Movement, contested 80 seats, but none of its candidates was elected. Elections in Afar and Somali regions, where opposition to the EPRDF was strong, were postponed until June, when pro-EPRDF parties won narrow victories. Most opposition parties boycotted the poll. International observers at the elections accepted that the polls were conducted in a largely free and fair manner. In July EU ambassadors to Ethiopia expressed concern that the overwhelming victory of the EPRDF would impede the further development of political pluralism in the country.

On 21 August 1995 legislative power was transferred from the transitional Council of Representatives to the Federal Parliamentary Assembly. On 22 August the transitional administration was terminated, and the country's new Constitution and designation as the Federal Democratic Republic of Ethiopia were formally instituted. Later on the same day Dr Negasso Gidada (formerly the Minister of Information), a member of the Oromo People's Democratic Organization (OPDO, which is in alliance with the EPRDF) and the nominee of the EPRDF, was elected President of the Federal Republic. A new Prime Minister, ex-President Meles Zenawi, was elected from among the members of the Council of People's Representatives; Meles nominated a 17-member Council of Ministers, which was duly approved by the Federal Parliamentary Assembly.

During late 1995 and early 1996 the Meles administration was criticized for its harsh treatment of opposition activists. In June 1996 Dr Taye Wolde Semayat, the Secretary-General of the Ethiopian Teachers' Association, was arrested with several associates and accused of leading a clandestine political organization (the Ethiopian National Patriotic Front — ENPF), which, allegedly, had been responsible for several terrorist acts. The arrests were strongly criticized by human rights groups, which claimed that the detainees were guilty only of expressing discontent at certain government policies. Meanwhile, the Somali-based al-Ittihad al-Islam (Islamic Union Party—which has sought independence for Ethiopia's Ogaden province) claimed responsibility for bomb explosions at hotels in Addis Ababa and Dire Dawa in early 1996, and for the attempted assassination in July of Dr Abdul-Mejid Hussen, the Minister of Transport and Communications and current Chairman of the Ethiopian Somali Democratic League. Government forces launched reprisal attacks on al-Ittihad bases in Somalia on numerous occasions during 1996–98, resulting in the deaths of several hundred al-Ittihad members.

In September 1996 the authorities announced a campaign to address the problem of corruption, which reportedly had become endemic in the country. In the following month Tamirat Layne was accused of 'indiscipline' (he was later implicated in corrupt activities) and removed from the post of Deputy Prime Minister and Minister of Defence; he was also dismissed as Secretary-General of the Amhara National Democratic Movement (as the EPDM had been renamed in 1994), and ejected from its central committee. Hundreds of officials from regional administrations were arrested or dismissed during 1996–97 following EPRDF-organized peace, democracy and development conferences.

In late 1996 the Government announced plans to establish a 25,000-strong Afar military force (under the command of the Afar People's Democratic Organization) to counter an increase in armed attacks on government troops by militant members of the Afar Revolutionary Democratic Unity Front (ARDUF). The authorities subsequently withdrew government forces from sensitive Afar regions and granted concessions regarding political prisoners in an attempt to persuade the ARDUF to cease its military activities. In August 1997 the ARDUF reportedly agreed to renounce the use of violence in its campaigning.

In February 1997 two people were killed and nine were injured in a grenade attack on a hotel in Harar. Similar attacks in Addis Ababa in April and September resulted in as many as 100 casualties, including three fatalities. The authorities attributed the incidents to the OLF, and in December 31 OLF members stood trial for crimes including terrorism and illegally amassing weapons. Six of the accused were allegedly implicated in the grenade attacks. In mid-1998, moreover, the authorities accused the OLF of conspiring with al-Ittihad and the Eritrean leadership to undermine the Ethiopian regime.

Attempts by the authorities to stifle the opposition continued during 1997–98, with the arrest of numerous journalists and the closure of several independent periodicals. In September, meanwhile, some 30 delegates attended a meeting in Paris, France, of Ethiopian opposition movements, during which eight groups agreed to establish a new bloc, the Coalition of Ethiopian Opposition Political Organizations (CEOPO). At the conclusion of the meeting, the delegates (who included representatives of the CAFPDE, the Southern Ethiopian People's Democratic Coalition (SEPDC), the ARDUF and Ethiopians in exile) urged the Ethiopian authorities to facilitate national dialogue. A CEOPO-organized demonstration held in Addis Ababa in late January 1999 was attended by some 5,000 people.

In June 1999 Dr Taye Wolde Semayat, head of the banned ENPF, was sentenced to 15 years' imprisonment for destabilizing public order after allegedly raiding state economic, military and security institutions. In July severe drought once again threatened to cause wide-scale famine, and the UN appealed for US $50m. to help to alleviate the most severe case of starvation since 1984.

In August 1999 it was announced that elections for the Council of the Federation and the Council of People's Representatives were to be held on 14 May 2000, and registration for political parties began. Following this, there were several attempts by coalition groups to form a united opposition to the ruling EPRDF alliance; however, meetings in Frankfurt am Main, Germany, and Washington, DC, in September 1999, organized by the CEOPO and the ENC respectively, merely led to greater divisions. In late October the SEPDC withdrew from the CEOPO, and in early November the CAFPDE split into two rival factions. The office of the national electoral board reported that there were 56 legally certified political parties in October, of which 33 were in opposition to the EPRDF.

The trial of 69 former government officials, including Mengistu, opened in Addis Ababa in December 1994, although proceedings were adjourned on numerous occasions. The defendants, 23 of whom were being tried *in absentia* (including Mengistu, who was in exile in Zimbabwe) and five of whom had died while awaiting trial, were accused of crimes against humanity and of genocide, perpetrated during 1974–91. In February 1997 the office of the Special Prosecutor announced that an additional 5,198 people would be indicted for war crimes and genocide, of whom nearly 3,000 would be tried *in absentia*. In November 1999 South Africa refused a request from the Ethiopian Government to extradite ex-President Mengistu, after it emerged that he was receiving medical treatment in that country.

Ethiopia's foreign affairs after Mengistu's coup in 1977 were dominated by relations with the USSR, which replaced the USA as the principal supplier of armaments to Ethiopia and provided military advisers and economic aid. In the late 1980s, however, changes in Soviet foreign policy weakened the relationship, and the Soviet Government began to urge a political, rather than military, solution to Ethiopia's regional conflicts.

In April 1989 Ethiopia sought to upgrade its diplomatic relations with the USA, receiving a cautious initial response. The USA subsequently encouraged the EPRDF's seizure of power in May 1991 and expressed its approval of proposals for a transition to a multi-party democratic system. In late 1993 representatives of Ethiopia and the USA signed an agreement on economic and technical co-operation, the first such agreement for 17 years. In October 1996 the US Secretary of State, Warren Christopher, and the OAU Secretary-General, Salim Ahmed Salim, held talks with Prime Minister Meles in Ethiopia, who reportedly welcomed a US initiative to establish an African crisis reaction force.

Relations with Somalia have been problematic since the Ogaden War of 1977–78. However, in April 1988 Ethiopia and Somalia agreed to re-establish diplomatic relations, to withdraw troops from their common border and to exchange prisoners of war. During 1988–91 an estimated 600,000 Somali refugees entered Ethiopia from northern Somalia, of whom more than 150,000 arrived in the first half of 1991. The transitional Government of Ethiopia declared a policy of non-interference in the affairs of neighbouring states and adopted a neutral stance in Somalia's civil conflict. During 1993–98 Ethiopia hosted reconciliation conferences between Somalia's warring factions. In August 1998 Ethiopia's Minister of Foreign Affairs held discussions with Hussein Aidid, the leader of the Somali National

Alliance (SNA), on resolving Somalia's conflict. Aidid was also requested to cease providing support to al-Ittihad and Oromo organizations opposed to the Ethiopian administration. In February 1999 tensions escalated when Aidid accused the Ethiopian Government of interfering in Somali affairs and supplying arms to three anti-SNA factions. In April heavily-armed Ethiopian forces, which claimed to be pursuing OLF insurgents, entered Somalia. Aidid appealed to the UN and the OAU to take action against Ethiopia. Meanwhile, more than 20,000 Somali refugees were reported to have fled to Ethiopia during the previous two months. In early June the Somali-based Rahawin Resistance Army (RRA), assisted by some 3,000 Ethiopian troops, captured the town of Baidoa, which had been controlled by Aidid, after heavy fighting. Aidid's continuing support of the Eritrean Government and Ethiopian insurgent groups led many observers to believe that the conflict between Eritrea and Ethiopia was in danger of spreading elsewhere in the Horn of Africa. The Ethiopian Government claimed, however, that its actions were merely attempts to protect the border from attacks initiated by Somali-based rebel opposition groups. Following mediation attempts involving the two sides in October, Ethiopia withdrew its forces from Somalia, although the Ethiopian Government reiterated its demand that the SNA sever its connections with Eritrea and the Oromo rebels.

Following the military coup in Sudan in April 1985 (which deposed President Nimeri), full diplomatic relations were restored between Ethiopia and Sudan. Relations between the two countries were strained, however, by the influx into Ethiopia, in the late 1980s, of thousands of Sudanese refugees, fleeing from famine and civil war in southern Sudan. The vast majority of an estimated 380,000 refugees were reported to have returned to Sudan by early 1991, as a result of the civil war in Ethiopia. The change of government in Ethiopia in May 1991 led to a considerable improvement in relations between Ethiopia and Sudan. In October President Meles and Sudan's leader, Lt-Gen. al-Bashir, signed an agreement on friendship and co-operation. Bilateral relations deteriorated again in January 1994, when the Ethiopian Minister of Foreign Affairs accused the Sudanese National Islamic Front of supporting Islamic extremists in Ethiopia. In September 1995 the Ethiopian administration adopted a number of sanctions against Sudan, including the suspension of air flights between the two countries and a reduction in Sudanese diplomatic representation in Ethiopia, after the Sudanese authorities refused to extradite to Ethiopia three men allegedly involved in an assassination attempt on President Mubarak of Egypt in Addis Ababa in June. In December there were reports of military clashes between Ethiopian and Sudanese forces in the border region. Accusations of border incursions intensified during 1996–97. Although attacks against Sudanese positions were known to have been launched by the Sudan People's Liberation Army (SPLA), operating from Ethiopia, the Ethiopian authorities denied any knowledge of their activities. Relations between the two countries subsequently improved, and in late October 1998 Ethiopia reportedly resumed air flights to Sudan. The Ethiopian authorities were also reported to have closed the SPLA offices in western Ethiopia, while Sudan closed the OLF base in Khartoum. In November 1999 Prime Minister Meles received Lt-Gen. al-Bashir in Addis Ababa, where they discussed the possible reactivation of the Ethio-Sudan Joint Ministerial Commission and announced their intent to form closer economic ties between the two countries.

In November 1991 the leaders of Ethiopia and Kenya signed a co-operation agreement, although in October 1992 it was reported that the Kenyan Government was secretly giving asylum to Ethiopian dissidents. In April 1997 the two countries agreed to strengthen border controls following an attack by Ethiopian tribesmen in Kenya's frontier region; 41 civilians and 16 security personnel were killed during the incident. Additional security measures were agreed in late 1998, following an incursion by Ethiopian tribesmen into Kenya, which resulted in some 140 fatalities. In March 1999 Kenyan security forces exchanged fire with Ethiopian troops pursuing OLF rebels across the border. Kenya accused Ethiopia of violating international law, and relations between the two countries became further strained after Ethiopian soldiers attacked villages along the border.

Relations with many Arab states improved substantially following the collapse of the Mengistu regime in 1991. In November 1993 Ethiopia removed all remaining sanctions against South Africa and announced that normal financial, trade and investment relations between the two countries would now be possible.

In 1984 some 13,000 Falashas, a Jewish group in Ethiopia, reached Sudan, from where they were flown to Israel in a secret airlift. Following the renewal of formal diplomatic relations (severed in 1973) between Ethiopia and Israel in 1989, the Ethiopian Government removed restrictions on Falashas' leaving the country, and Israel began to provide Ethiopia with more armaments and anti-guerrilla training. In May 1991 Israel evacuated a further 14,000 Falashas from Addis Ababa; some 10,000 Falashmura (Ethiopian Christians whose forefathers had converted from Judaism) were subsequently granted Israeli citizenship on humanitarian grounds. In mid-1998 the Israeli authorities closed an aid camp in Addis Ababa for Ethiopians claiming Jewish descent, and officially ended the airlifts from Ethiopia. In March 1999 the Israeli Prime Minister, Binyamin Netanyahu, pledged to examine the possibility of bringing the 19,000 Jews remaining in Ethiopia to Israel. In June, following negotiations between the Israeli Minister of Foreign Affairs and the Ethiopian ambassador to Israel, a first group of around 70 Jews, of a total of 4,000 stranded in refugee camps in the Quara region of Ethiopia, was airlifted to Israel. The process was expected to last for as long as 40 weeks.

After May 1991 the EPLF governed Eritrea as a *de facto* independent state and conducted its affairs with foreign countries accordingly. Ethiopia and the newly-independent Eritrea signed a treaty of co-operation during a visit by the Eritrean President, Issaias Afewerki, to Addis Ababa in July 1993. The agreement included provisions on the joint utilization of resources and co-operation in the energy, transport, defence and education sectors. A further agreement, signed in late 1994, provided for the free movement of goods between the two countries without payment of customs dues.

In late 1997 relations with Eritrea deteriorated, following that country's adoption of a new currency (to replace the Ethiopian birr) and the subsequent disruption of cross-border trade. Fighting between Ethiopian and Eritrean troops erupted in the border region in early May 1998, with both countries accusing the other of having invaded their territory. It was estimated that some 100 people were killed in offensives launched around the towns of Badme and Sheraro; many more casualties were reported in June during clashes near Badme, Assab and Zelambessa. Eritrea rejected a peace plan drafted by the USA and Rwanda in early June, as it refused to comply with a precondition to withdraw its troops from the disputed region. The US-Rwandan plan had also envisaged the demilitarization of the border region and the dispatch of an observer mission to Badme. In mid-June the USA and Italy successfully mediated an aerial cease-fire, but a resolution passed by the UN Security Council later that month, demanding that Ethiopia and Eritrea cease hostilities forthwith, was ignored. The OAU established a mediation committee in June in an attempt to end the dispute, and in July an OAU delegation visited the two countries. The committee presented its report to the Ethiopian and Eritrean Ministers of Foreign Affairs at a meeting in Ouagadougou, Burkina Faso, in August. The OAU proposals, which endorsed the US-Rwandan peace plan, were rejected by Eritrea, necessitating the convening of a special meeting of the mediation committee in Ouagadougou in November. Prime Minister Meles and President Afewerki attended different sessions of the meeting, at which the Heads of State of Burkina Faso, Djibouti and Zimbabwe were also present. Ethiopia welcomed the committee's proposals, which stressed the need to demilitarize and demarcate the disputed region, but Eritrea rejected the plans and accused Djibouti of favouring Ethiopia in the conflict. Other international mediation attempts continued in late 1998 (including that of Anthony Lake, a former US national security adviser), but failed to resolve the dispute.

In early 1999 there were reports that Ethiopia and Eritrea were massing troops and armaments in the region of their common border, and in early February hundreds of people were killed during armed clashes in the disputed territory. Each side accused the other of having broken the aerial cease-fire and of escalating the conflict. After two weeks of intense fighting, Ethiopia recaptured the disputed town of Badme and the Eritrean Government announced that it had accepted the OAU peace plan that it had previously rejected in late 1998. However, Ethiopia appeared eager to maximize this opportunity to secure access to the coast, and ignored appeals by the UN Security Council for an immediate cease-fire. Fighting erupted again in March 1999, as the two sides continued to blame each other for obstructing the OAU's peace efforts. Ethiopia insisted on Eritrea's unilateral withdrawal from its territory; however,

Eritrea repeatedly rejected this demand and insisted that it did not form part of the OAU peace agreement. Mutual distrust persisted on both sides, and Ethiopia claimed that Eritrea had accepted the OAU agreement (which Ethiopia had accepted in November 1998) only in order to regroup its forces, and was actually continuing to attack Ethiopian troops stationed on the border. In late April 1999 Prime Minister Meles once again demanded Eritrean withdrawal from all Ethiopian territory, while Eritrea accused Ethiopia of carrying out air raids on its territory. Although Eritrea had announced its formal acceptance of the OAU peace plan, the two sides had differing interpretations of the word 'withdrawal', thus inhibiting attempts at progress. The deadlock continued into May as Eritrea steadfastly refused to withdraw from the territory that it occupied, and, despite the UN Security Council's repeated insistence on an immediate cessation of fighting, Ethiopian military aircraft bombed the Eritrean port of Massawa.

In mid-July 1999 the Algerian President, Abdelaziz Bouteflika, attempted to mediate between Ethiopia and Eritrea at the OAU summit meeting in Algiers. The deadlock appeared to have been broken when the two warring countries confirmed their commitment to the OAU peace proposals, under which both sides would withdraw from all territory captured since the outbreak of the conflict, thus effectively returning both sides to their pre-war frontiers. However, the situation was complicated by Eritrean demands for war reparations and Ethiopian requests for clarification of the technical arrangements regarding the withdrawal of troops from the disputed territory. In August Eritrea formally accepted the latest OAU peace plan; however, in the following month Ethiopia announced that it had rejected the proposals because, in its opinion, the technical arrangements were inconsistent with the other elements (the framework agreement and the modalities) of the peace propositions and did not guarantee a return to the *status quo ante.* Both sides remained distrustful of each other and were reported to be re-arming on a large scale. In October Eritrea claimed Zelambessa as its sovereign territory, and, while both sides publicly insisted that they were intent on finding a peaceful solution to the conflict, their mutual reluctance to make concessions meant that the situation remained deadlocked. Meanwhile, it was estimated that as many as 65,000 Ethiopians had been forced to leave Eritrea since July 1998, and in June 1999 the Ethiopian Government announced that more than 500,000 people had been displaced during the conflict with Eritrea.

### Government

In August 1995 the Council of Representatives, a body established in 1991 to govern the country during the transitional period after the overthrow of the Mengistu regime, formally transferred power to a newly-elected legislature, the Federal Parliamentary Assembly. Under the provisions of a new Constitution, adopted in December 1994, the country became a federation, consisting of nine states and two chartered cities, the capital, Addis Ababa, and Dire Dawa. The states have their own parliamentary assemblies, which also elect representatives to the Council of the Federation, the upper chamber of the Federal Parliamentary Assembly. The lower chamber, the Council of People's Representatives, consists of 548 directly elected deputies. The Federal Parliamentary Assembly elects a President as Head of State. However, the President fulfils mainly ceremonial functions, executive power being the preserve of the Prime Minister. The Prime Minister, who is elected by the Council of People's Representatives, appoints the Council of Ministers (subject to approval by the legislature), and acts as Commander-in-Chief of the armed forces. Elections to the Council of People's Representatives and to the state assemblies took place in May and June 1995.

### Defence

In December 1991 Ethiopia's transitional Government announced that a 'national defence army', based on already active EPRDF troops, would constitute Ethiopia's armed forces during the transitional period. In October 1993 the Minister of Defence announced that preparations were under way to create a 'multi-ethnic defence force', comprising members of all the different ethnic groups in Ethiopia. Extensive demobilization of former members of the TPLF has since taken place. In September 1996 the Government sold its naval assets. Owing to the ongoing war with Eritrea, there has been a large increase in the size, of the armed forces and in defence expenditure. In August 1999 Ethiopia's armed forces numbered an estimated 325,000 in active service. The defence budget for 1999 was estimated at 3,500m. birr, compared with 995m. birr in 1998.

### Economic Affairs

In 1997, according to estimates by the World Bank, the gross national product (GNP) of Ethiopia, measured at average 1995–97 prices, was US $6,507m., equivalent to $110 per head: one of the lowest recorded levels of GNP per caput for any country in the world. During 1990–97, it was estimated, GNP per head increased, in real terms, at an average annual rate of 2.2%. Over the same period, the population also increased by an average of 2.2% per year. In 1998 GNP was estimated at $6,100m. ($100 per head). Ethiopia's gross domestic product (GDP) increased, in real terms, by an average of 4.9% per year during 1990–98. Measured at factor cost, real GDP rose by 5.2% in 1996/97, but declined by 0.5% in 1997/98.

Agriculture (including forestry and fishing) contributed 45.7% of GDP (at constant 1980/81 prices) in 1997/98, and employed an estimated 83.2% of the economically active population in 1998. The principal cash crop is coffee (which accounted for 70.7% of export earnings in 1997/98). The principal subsistence crops are cereals (barley, maize, sorghum and teff) and sugar cane. During 1990–98 agricultural GDP increased by an average of 2.8% per year. It rose by 3.4% in 1996/97, but declined by 10.3% in 1997/98. In 1995 the Government initiated a five-year programme (supported by the World Bank), which aimed to make Ethiopia self-sufficient in food production. In 1998 agricultural production declined by 8.3%, compared with the previous year, while the cereal harvest declined by 26.3% as a result of drought and severe flooding.

Industry (including mining, manufacturing, construction and power) employed 2.0% of the labour force in 1995, and provided 11.6% of GDP (at constant prices) in 1997/98. During 1990–98 industrial GDP increased by an average of 6.5% per year. It rose by 6.8% in 1996/97 and by 6.3% in 1997/98.

Mining contributed only 0.5% of GDP in 1997/98, and employed less than 0.1% of the labour force in 1995. During 1989/90–94/95 mining GDP increased by an average of 16.8% per year. It rose by 13.0% in 1996/97 and by 10.1% in 1997/98. Ethiopia has reserves of petroleum, although these have not been exploited, and there are also deposits of copper and potash. Gold, tantalite, soda ash, kaolin, dimension stones, precious metals and gemstones, salt, and industrial and construction materials are mined.

Manufacturing employed only 1.6% of the labour force in 1995 and contributed 6.7% of GDP in 1997/98. During 1989/90–94/95 manufacturing GDP increased by an average of 0.9% per year. It rose by 5.9% in 1996/97 and by 5.8% in 1997/98. Measured by the value of output, the principal branches of manufacturing in 1996/97 were beverages and food products (accounting for 37.2% of the total), textiles (11.%), non-metallic mineral manufactures (8.7%), leather tanning, dressing and processing (8.1%) and cement, lime and plaster (6.0%).

Services, which consisted mainly of wholesale and retail trade, public administration and defence, and transport and communications, employed 9.5% of the labour force in 1995, and contributed 42.7% of GDP (at constant prices) in 1997/98. The combined GDP of the service sectors increased, in real terms, at an average rate of 6.4% per year during 1990–98. It rose by 7.1% in 1996/97, and by 10.4% in 1997/98.

In years of normal rainfall, energy is derived principally from Ethiopia's massive hydroelectric power resources. Imports of mineral fuels accounted for an estimated 16.2% of the cost of total imports in 1997/98. In 1993 agreement was reached with the World Bank on the financing of a project to construct a liquefied gas unit to exploit gas reserves in the Ogaden. In late 1995 the Government announced plans to develop geothermal energy sources at 15 sites in various regions of the country. In 1996 plans were announced to double the country's electricity generating capacity (to 756 MW) by 2002.

In 1998 Ethiopia recorded a visible trade deficit of US $473.9m., while there was a surplus of $134.0m. on the current account of the balance of payments. In 1997 the principal source of imports (10.5%) was Japan, and in 1998 the principal market for exports (24.8%) was Germany. Other major trading partners were Saudi Arabia, Italy, the USA, Djibouti, the United Kingdom and India. The principal exports in 1997/98 were coffee, leather and leather products, and oilseeds. The principal imports in that year were machinery and transport equipment, basic manufactures, and mineral fuels and related products.

In the fiscal year 1997/98 it was estimated that Ethiopia's budgetary deficit reached 1,787m. birr (equivalent to 4.0% of

GDP). Ethiopia is the principal African recipient of concessionary funding, and the largest recipient of EU aid (US $387m. for the first five years of the period covered by the Lomé IV Convention). At the end of 1997 Ethiopia's total external debt was $10,079m., of which $9,427m. was long-term public debt. In that year the cost of debt-servicing was equivalent to an estimated 9.5% of total earnings from the export of goods and sevices. In late 1992 debts repayable to various countries and international organizations amounting to $595m., including interest, were cancelled. Commercial debts worth $250m. were cancelled in early 1996. The annual rate of inflation averaged 7.7% in 1990–97. Although the rate rose considerably in 1991 (to 35.7%), in the following years it remained constant at about 10%, and in 1996 and 1997 consumer prices declined by 5.1% and 3.7%, respectively. In 1998, however, consumer prices rose by 0.9%. There were 28,350 persons registered as applicants for work in the 12 months to June 1996.

Ethiopia is a member of the African Development Bank (see p. 117) and the Common Market for Eastern and Southern Africa (see p. 142), and adheres to the Lomé Convention of the EU (see p. 196).

Ethiopia's economy continues to suffer from the effects of recurrent, catastrophic drought, which severely disrupts agricultural production (the country's economic base). During 1991–95 the transitional Government adopted many elements of a market economy, resulting in a greater readiness on the part of developed countries to provide economic assistance to Ethiopia, and the resumption of relations with the World Bank in September 1991. As part of the economic reform programme that was agreed with the World Bank and the IMF, in October 1992 the transitional Government raised interest rates and devalued the birr by 57%. The IMF approved a three-year loan in 1992 to support the programme. The privatization of 176 state-owned enterprises, which began in 1993, raised US $333m., and in April 1999 the Government announced plans to dispose of its interests in a further 120 of the remaining 163 state-owned companies over the next three years. The Ethiopian economy remains heavily dependent on assistance and grants from abroad, particularly in times of drought, and during 1999 Ethiopia, which remains one of the six poorest countries in the world, received substantial foreign aid, notably from the World Food Programme, UNICEF and the African Development Bank. Within the framework of its heavily indebted poor countries (HIPC) debt-reduction initiative, the World Bank conducted a preliminary assessment of Ethiopia in 1999; finalization of the proposed assistance package of $636m. was postponed, however, owing to the hostilities between Ethiopia and Eritrea. The conflict has had a detrimental effect on the Ethiopian economy, as, apart from the consequent suspension of economic assistance from the USA and the World Bank for the duration of the hostilities, Ethiopia's expenditure on the war has eliminated the benefits of an estimated 6.7% increase in GDP in 1998/99. Ethiopia's maritime trade, previously conducted through the Eritrean ports of Massawa and Assab, has been re-routed through Djibouti and Mombasa (Kenya), and the authorities have appealed for further international aid to assist the estimated 500,000 Ethiopians displaced or wounded as a result of the conflict.

## Social Welfare

The scope of modern health services has been greatly extended since 1960, but they still reach only a small section of the population. In 1977 free medical care for the needy was introduced. In 1980 Ethiopia had 86 hospital establishments. During 1974–87 26 new hospitals were built. By 1987 there were a total of 11,400 hospital beds, while 1,204 physicians and 3,105 nurses were working in the health service. Relative to the size of the population, the provision of hospital beds and physicians was the lowest among African countries. By 1987 there were also 2,095 clinics and 159 health centres. It was estimated that in the early 1990s there were four doctors and eight nurses per 100,000 people. With foreign assistance, health centres and clinics are steadily expanding into the rural areas. In times of famine, however, Ethiopian health services are totally inadequate. In late 1998 the World Bank announced that it would lend Ethiopia US $100m. to finance the first five-year phase of an ambitious government programme to improve health services. It was envisaged that more than 400 health centres and hospitals would be built or restored during the 20-year project. The 1997/98 budget allocated an estimated 6.0% (677.3m. birr) of total expenditure to public health.

## Education

Education in Ethiopia is available free of charge, and, after a rapid growth in numbers of schools, it became compulsory between the ages of seven and 13 years. Since 1976 most primary and secondary schools have been controlled by local peasant associations and urban dwellers' associations. In 1994 Ethiopia adopted a new Education and Training Policy and Strategy (ETPS), which restructured the education system and aimed to improve the quality of education. Primary education begins at seven years of age and lasts for eight years. Secondary education, beginning at 15 years of age, lasts for a further four years, comprising two cycles of two years each, the second of which provides preparatory education for entry to the tertiary level. A system of vocational and technical education also exists parallel to the preparatory programme. In 1995 total enrolment at primary schools was equivalent to 37% of children in the appropriate age-group (47% of boys; 27% of girls); enrolment at secondary schools was equivalent to 11% of children in the relevant age-group (13% of boys; 10% of girls). The 1997/98 budget allocated an estimated 13.8% (1,563.6m. birr) of total expenditure to education. In 1995, according to UNESCO estimates, the rate of adult illiteracy stood at 64.5% (males 54.5%; females 74.7%). There are 17 institutions of higher education in Ethiopia, including two universities (in Addis Ababa and Dire Dawa).

## Public Holidays

**2000:** 7 January* (Christmas), 8 January†‡ (Id al-Fitr, end of Ramadan), 19 January* (Epiphany), 2 March (Battle of Adowa), 16 March† (Id al-Adha/Arafat), 28 April* (Good Friday), 1 May (Easter Monday* and May Day), 5 May (Patriots' Victory Day), 28 May (Downfall of the Dergue), 15 June† (Mouloud, Birth of the Prophet), 11 September (New Year's Day), 27 September* (Feast of the True Cross), 28 December†‡ (Id al-Fitr, end of Ramadan).

**2001:** 7 January* (Christmas), 19 January* (Epiphany), 2 March (Battle of Adowa), 6 March† (Id al-Adha/Arafat), 13 April* (Good Friday), 16 April* (Easter Monday), 1 May (May Day), 5 May (Patriots' Victory Day), 28 May (Downfall of the Dergue), 4 June† (Mouloud, Birth of the Prophet), 11 September (New Year's Day), 27 September* (Feast of the True Cross), 17 December† (Id al-Fitr, end of Ramadan).

* Coptic holidays.

† These holidays are dependent on the Islamic lunar calendar and may vary by one or two days from the dates given.

‡ This festival will occur twice (in the Islamic years AH 1420 and 1421) within the same Gregorian year.

Note: Ethiopia uses its own solar calendar; the Ethiopian year 1992 began on 11 September 1999.

## Weights and Measures

The metric system is officially in use. There are also many local weights and measures.

# Statistical Survey

Source (unless otherwise stated): Central Statistical Authority, POB 1143, Addis Ababa; tel. (1) 553010; fax (1) 550334.

Note: Unless otherwise indicated, figures in this Survey refer to the territory of Ethiopia after the secession of Eritrea in May 1993.

## Area and Population

**AREA, POPULATION AND DENSITY**

| | |
|---|---|
| Area (sq km) | 1,133,380* |
| Population (census results) | |
| 9 May 1984† | 39,868,501 |
| 11 October 1994 | |
| Males | 26,910,698 |
| Females | 26,566,567 |
| Total | 53,477,265 |
| Population (official estimates at mid-year) | |
| 1997 | 58,117,000 |
| 1998 | 59,880,000 |
| 1999 | 61,672,000 |
| Density (per sq km) at mid-1999 | 54.4 |

* 437,600 sq miles.

† Including an estimate for areas not covered by the census.

**ADMINISTRATIVE DIVISIONS** (estimated population at mid-1999)

| | Population ('000) | | |
|---|---|---|---|
| | Males | Females | Total |
| Regional States | | | |
| 1 Tigrai | 1,767 | 1,826 | 3,593 |
| 2 Afar | 667 | 521 | 1,188 |
| 3 Amhara | 7,938 | 7,912 | 15,850 |
| 4 Oromia | 10,833 | 10,861 | 21,694 |
| 5 Somali | 1,952 | 1,650 | 3,602 |
| 6 Benishangul/Gumuz | 264 | 259 | 523 |
| 7 Southern Nations, Nationalities and Peoples | 6,029 | 6,103 | 12,132 |
| 8 Gambela | 105 | 101 | 206 |
| 9 Harari | 78 | 76 | 154 |
| Chartered Cities | | | |
| 1 Dire Dawa | 154 | 152 | 306 |
| 2 Addis Ababa | 1,169 | 1,255 | 2,424 |
| **Total** | 30,956 | 30,716 | 61,672 |

**PRINCIPAL TOWNS** (census results of October 1994)

| | |
|---|---|
| Addis Ababa (capital) | 2,084,588 |
| Dire Dawa | 164,851 |
| Nazret | 127,842 |
| Harar | 122,932 |
| Mekele | 119,779 |
| Jimma | 119,717 |
| Dessie | 117,268 |
| Bahir Dar | 115,531 |
| Debrezit | 105,963 |

Source: UN, *Demographic Yearbook*.

**BIRTHS AND DEATHS** (UN estimates, annual averages)

| | 1980–85 | 1985–90 | 1990–95 |
|---|---|---|---|
| Birth rate (per 1,000) | 48.0 | 49.0 | 46.5 |
| Death rate (per 1,000) | 22.1 | 20.0 | 19.2 |

**Expectation of life** (UN estimates, years at birth, 1990–95): 45.2 (males 43.9; females 46.7).

Source: UN, *World Population Prospects: The 1998 Revision*.

**ECONOMICALLY ACTIVE POPULATION** (official estimates, ISIC Major Divisions, persons aged 10 years and over, mid-1995)*

| | Males | Females | Total |
|---|---|---|---|
| Agriculture, hunting, forestry and fishing | 12,681,037 | 8,924,280 | 21,605,317 |
| Mining and quarrying | 12,114 | 4,426 | 16,540 |
| Manufacturing | 224,106 | 160,889 | 384,995 |
| Electricity, gas and water | 14,799 | 2,267 | 17,066 |
| Construction | 55,906 | 5,326 | 61,232 |
| Trade, restaurants and hotels | 335,353 | 600,584 | 935,937 |
| Transport, storage and communications | 87,975 | 15,179 | 103,154 |
| Financing, insurance, real estate and business services | 14,513 | 4,938 | 19,451 |
| Community, social and personal services | 777,907 | 474,317 | 1,252,224 |
| **Total labour force** | 14,203,710 | 10,192,206 | 24,395,916 |

* The figures exclude persons seeking work for the first time, totalling 210,184 (males 100,790; females 109,394), but include other unemployed persons.

Source: ILO, *Yearbook of Labour Statistics*.

**Mid-1998** (estimates in '000): Agriculture, etc. 21,788; Total labour force 26,175 (Source: FAO, *Production Yearbook*).

## Agriculture

**PRINCIPAL CROPS** ('000 metric tons)

| | 1996 | 1997 | 1998 |
|---|---|---|---|
| Wheat | 1,162 | 1,093 | 1,143 |
| Barley | 1,125 | 1,062 | 1,095 |
| Maize | 3,164 | 2,987 | 2,344 |
| Oats | 84 | 67 | 56 |
| Millet (Dagusa) | 244 | 296 | 260 |
| Sorghum | 1,808 | 2,040 | 1,083 |
| Other cereals | 1,792 | 1,928 | 1,216 |
| Potatoes* | 360 | 360 | 365 |
| Sweet potatoes* | 159 | 159 | 160 |
| Yams* | 265 | 265 | 266 |
| Other roots and tubers* | 1,270 | 1,270 | 1,275 |
| Dry beans* | 400 | 400 | 410 |
| Dry peas* | 160 | 160 | 165 |
| Dry broad beans* | 284 | 284 | 285 |
| Chick-peas* | 127 | 127 | 128 |
| Lentils* | 36 | 36 | 37 |
| Other pulses* | 131 | 131 | 133 |
| Sugar cane* | 1,600 | 1,600 | 1,650 |
| Soybeans* | 23 | 23 | 24 |
| Groundnuts (in shell)* | 56 | 56 | 57 |
| Castor beans* | 15 | 15 | 15 |
| Rapeseed* | 82 | 82 | 83 |
| Sesame seed* | 33 | 33 | 34 |
| Linseed* | 32 | 32 | 33 |
| Safflower seed* | 35 | 35 | 36 |
| Cottonseed† | 30 | 30 | 30 |
| Cotton (lint)† | 15 | 15 | 15 |
| Vegetables and melons* | 590 | 589 | 596 |
| Bananas* | 80 | 80 | 81 |
| Other fruit (excl. melons)* | 149 | 149 | 150 |
| Tree nuts* | 68 | 68 | 69 |
| Coffee (green)† | 230 | 228 | 204 |
| Tobacco (leaves) | 4† | 4† | 4* |
| Fibre crops (excl. cotton)* | 17 | 17 | 18 |

* FAO estimate(s). † Unofficial figure(s).

Source: FAO, *Production Yearbook*.

**LIVESTOCK** (FAO estimates, '000 head, year ending September)

| | 1996 | 1997 | 1998 |
|---|---|---|---|
| Cattle | 29,900 | 29,900 | 29,900 |
| Sheep | 21,800 | 21,850 | 21,850 |
| Goats | 16,800 | 16,850 | 16,850 |
| Asses | 5,200 | 5,200 | 5,200 |
| Horses | 2,750 | 2,750 | 2,750 |
| Mules | 630 | 630 | 630 |
| Camels | 1,020 | 1,030 | 1,030 |
| Pigs | 22 | 23 | 23 |

Poultry (FAO estimates, million): 55 in 1996; 55 in 1997; 55 in 1998.

Source: FAO, *Production Yearbook*.

**LIVESTOCK PRODUCTS** (FAO estimates, '000 metric tons)

| | 1996 | 1997 | 1998 |
|---|---|---|---|
| Beef and veal | 236 | 236 | 236 |
| Mutton and lamb | 80 | 80 | 80 |
| Goat meat | 63 | 63 | 63 |
| Pig meat | 1 | 1 | 1 |
| Poultry meat | 73 | 73 | 73 |
| Other meat | 134 | 134 | 134 |
| Cows' milk | 740 | 740 | 740 |
| Goats' milk | 93 | 93 | 93 |
| Sheep's milk | 55 | 55 | 55 |
| Butter | 10 | 10 | 10 |
| Cheese | 3 | 3 | 3 |
| Hen eggs | 74 | 74 | 74 |
| Honey | 31 | 31 | 31 |
| Wool: | | | |
| greasy | 12 | 12 | 12 |
| clean | 6 | 6 | 6 |
| Cattle hides | 47 | 47 | 47 |
| Sheepskins | 14 | 14 | 14 |
| Goatskins | 13 | 13 | 13 |

Source: FAO, *Production Yearbook*.

## Forestry

**ROUNDWOOD REMOVALS** ('000 cubic metres, excl. bark)

| | 1995 | 1996 | 1997 |
|---|---|---|---|
| Sawlogs, veneer logs and logs for sleepers | 16 | 92 | 60 |
| Pulpwood | 23 | 7 | 7 |
| Other industrial wood | 2,266 | 2,340 | 2,416 |
| Fuel wood | 46,727 | 48,251 | 49,827 |
| **Total** | 49,032 | 50,690 | 52,310 |

Source: FAO, *Yearbook of Forest Products*.

**SAWNWOOD PRODUCTION**
('000 cubic metres, incl. railway sleepers)

| | 1995 | 1996 | 1997 |
|---|---|---|---|
| **Total** | 33 | 33 | 33 |

Source: FAO, *Yearbook of Forest Products*.

## Fishing

('000 metric tons, live weight)

| | 1995 | 1996 | 1997 |
|---|---|---|---|
| **Total catch** (freshwater fishes) | 6.3 | 8.8 | 10.4 |

Source: FAO, *Yearbook of Fishery Statistics*.

## Mining

('000 metric tons, unless otherwise indicated)

| | 1993 | 1994 | 1995 |
|---|---|---|---|
| Gold (kilograms) | 3,404 | 2,370*† | 4,500*† |
| Salt (unrefined)† | 53 | 5 | 5 |
| Limestone ('000 cu metres)† | 100 | 261 | n.a. |
| Kaolin† | 1* | 0* | n.a. |
| Gypsum† | 3 | 31 | 54 |
| Clay† | 1 | 0 | n.a. |
| Marble ('000 sq metres)† | n.a. | n.a. | 184 |

**Gold** (kilograms): 5,000*† in 1996.

* Provisional figure.

† Data from US Bureau of Mines.

Source: UN, *Industrial Commodity Statistics Yearbook*.

## Industry

**SELECTED PRODUCTS**
('000 metric tons, unless otherwise indicated; year ending 7 July)

| | 1992/93* | 1993/94 | 1994/95 |
|---|---|---|---|
| Edible oils | 4.0 | 4.2 | 5.6 |
| Wheat flour | 62.3 | 74.7 | 116.0 |
| Flour of other cereals | 0.3 | 2.3 | 1.6 |
| Macaroni and pasta | 5.7 | 11.2 | 19.1 |
| Raw sugar | 136.7 | 123.3 | 129.3 |
| Wine ('000 hectolitres) | 68.9 | 57.3 | 70.9 |
| Beer ('000 hectolitres) | 522.3 | 634.4 | 723.5 |
| Mineral waters ('000 hectolitres) | 159.3 | 199.3 | 298.4 |
| Soft drinks ('000 hectolitres) | 553.8 | 546.2 | 710.5 |
| Cigarettes (million) | 1,932.0 | 1,468.4 | 1,582.8 |
| Cotton yarn (metric tons) | 3,448 | 5,669 | 4,934 |
| Woven cotton fabrics ('000 sq metres) | 36,423 | 60,591 | 50,016 |
| Nylon fabrics ('000 sq metres) | 3,840 | 3,752 | 4,910 |
| Leather footwear ('000 pairs) | 928.8 | 1,999.2 | 1,159.4 |
| Canvas and rubber footwear ('000 pairs) | 2,030.9 | 1,609.4 | 2,196.3 |
| Plastic footwear ('000 pairs) | 123.5 | 62.3 | 395.7 |
| Paper | — | — | 7.1 |
| Soap | 17.3 | 15.0 | 15.2 |
| Tyres ('000) | 99.8 | 171.3 | 167.5 |
| Clay building bricks ('000) | 19.8 | 19.5 | 19.3 |
| Quicklime | 3.7 | 2.7 | 4.9 |
| Cement | 377.1 | 464.4 | 609.3 |

* Including Eritrea.

**Electricity** (estimates, million k Wh): 1,399 in 1993; 1,302 in 1994; 1,328 in 1995; 1,316 in 1996 (Source: UN, *Industrial Commodity Statistics Yearbook*).

**1996** ('000 metric tons; data from FAO): Wheat flour 185; Raw sugar 182 (Source: UN, *Industrial Commodity Statistics Yearbook*).

## Finance

**CURRENCY AND EXCHANGE RATES**

**Monetary Units**

100 cents = 1 birr.

**Sterling, Dollar and Euro Equivalents** (30 September 1999)

£1 sterling = 13.371 birr;
US $1 = 8.121 birr;
€1 = 8.661 birr;
1,000 birr = £74.79 = $123.14 = €115.46.

**Average Exchange Rate** (birr per US $)

1996 6.3517
1997 6.7093
1998 7.1159

**GENERAL BUDGET** (million birr, year ending 7 July)

| Revenue* | 1995/96 | 1996/97† | 1997/98† |
|---|---|---|---|
| Taxation | 4,723.3 | 5,358.2 | 5,261.1 |
| Taxes on income and profits | 1,848.8 | 1,745.3 | 1,849.5 |
| Personal income | 337.4 | 366.3 | 429.3 |
| Business profits | 1,222.3 | 1,264.7 | 1,088.6 |
| Domestic indirect taxes | 1,155.6 | 1,289.9 | 1,180.6 |
| Sales/excise taxes | 955.3 | 1,067.9 | 942.2 |
| Alcohol and tobacco | 359.2 | 397.9 | 356.1 |
| Import duties | 1,694.4 | 2,025.1 | 2,037.2 |
| Customs duties | 889.1 | 1,066.9 | 1,012.4 |
| Excise taxes | 805.3 | 958.2 | 1,024.8 |
| Export duties | 119.5 | 138.5 | 181.2 |
| Other revenue | 2,242.9 | 2,519.3 | 3,139.1 |
| Government investment income | 822.4 | 1,118.5 | 1,400.4 |
| Reimbursements and property sales | 177.4 | 116.4 | 92.2 |
| Proceeds from privatization | — | 347.0 | 312.5 |
| **Total** | 6,966.2 | 7,877.5 | 8,400.2 |

* Excluding grants received from abroad (million birr): 1,096.8 in 1995/96; 1,504.0† in 1996/97; 1,273.3† in 1997/98.

† Estimate(s).

| Expenditure | 1995/96 | 1996/97* | 1997/98* |
|---|---|---|---|
| Current expenditure | 5,582.2 | 5,717.4 | 7,094.9 |
| General services | 1,949.5 | 1,860.2 | 287.5 |
| Organs of state | 343.1 | 239.2 | 287.5 |
| Judiciary | 66.6 | 220.2 | 258.9 |
| Defence | 771.9 | 334.7 | 2,083.5 |
| Public order and security | 347.4 | 185.2 | 216.4 |
| Economic services | 620.5 | 661.0 | 659.9 |
| Agriculture and natural resources | 378.6 | 408.0 | 486.5 |
| Social services | 1,422.0 | 1,488.4 | 1,723.1 |
| Education | 941.0 | 1,025.7 | 1,126.8 |
| Health | 328.1 | 331.5 | 400.4 |
| Pension payments | 290.6 | 303.4 | 308.7 |
| Interest and charges | 922.5 | 918.7 | 835.6 |
| External assistance (grants)† | 142.7 | 256.5 | 160.0 |
| Capital expenditure | 3,562.6 | 4,299.8 | 4,265.1 |
| Economic development | 2,618.8 | 3,000.4 | 2,451.1 |
| Agriculture and settlement | 357.7 | 277.2 | 370.2 |
| Water and natural resources | 422.2 | 513.2 | 464.0 |
| Mining and energy | 384.4 | 796.0 | 429.0 |
| Industry | 358.3 | 288.1 | 93.2 |
| Road construction | 670.6 | 742.1 | 898.5 |
| Transport and communications | 218.0 | 385.5 | 194.7 |
| Financial agencies | 207.1 | n.a. | n.a. |
| Social development | 712.0 | 843.5 | 1,013.4 |
| Education | 441.9 | 421.9 | 436.8 |
| Public health | 153.9 | 251.8 | 276.9 |
| Urban development and housing | 116.2 | 169.8 | 299.7 |
| General services and compensation | 231.8 | 355.9 | 305.6 |
| External assistance (grants)† | n.a. | 100.0 | 495.0 |
| Equity contribution | 1,049.2 | — | 100.0 |
| **Total** | 10,194.0 | 10,017.2 | 11,460.1 |

* Estimates.

† Imputed value of goods and services provided mainly in kind.

Source: National Bank of Ethiopia.

**NATIONAL BANK RESERVES** (US $ million, at 31 December)

| | 1996 | 1997 | 1998 |
|---|---|---|---|
| Gold* | 0.4 | 0.4 | 0.4 |
| IMF special drawing rights | — | 0.1 | 0.1 |
| Reserve position in IMF | 10.1 | 9.5 | 10.0 |
| Foreign exchange | 722.0 | 491.4 | 501.0 |
| **Total** | 732.6 | 501.5 | 511.5 |

* National valuation.

Source: IMF, *International Financial Statistics*.

**MONEY SUPPLY** (million birr, at 31 December)

| | 1996 | 1997 | 1998 |
|---|---|---|---|
| Currency outside banks | 5,401 | 4,964 | 3,978 |
| Demand deposits at commercial banks | 3,872 | 5,123 | 5,326 |
| **Total money** | 9,273 | 10,087 | 9,304 |

Source: IMF, *International Financial Statistics*.

**COST OF LIVING** (General Index of Retail Prices for Addis Ababa, excluding rent; base: 1990 = 100)

| | 1993 | 1994 | 1995 |
|---|---|---|---|
| Food | 160.4 | 176.7 | 198.6 |
| Fuel, light and soap* | 133.1 | 134.1 | 142.4 |
| Clothing | 189.9 | 170.3 | 175.8 |
| **All items** (incl. others) | 155.3 | 167.1 | 183.9 |

* Including certain kitchen utensils.

Source: ILO, *Yearbook of Labour Statistics*.

**All items:** 174.6 in 1996; 168.1 in 1997 (Source: IMF, *International Financial Statistics*).

**1998** (including rent; base: 1997 = 100): Food 101.8; All items 100.9 (Source: UN, *Monthly Bulletin of Statistics*).

**NATIONAL ACCOUNTS**

(million birr at current prices; year ending 7 July)

**Expenditure on the Gross Domestic Product**

| | 1995/96 | 1996/97 | 1997/98 |
|---|---|---|---|
| Government final consumption expenditure | 4,158.1 | 4,585.3 | 5,108 |
| Private final consumption expenditure | 31,290.7 | 33,439.4 | 36,037 |
| Gross capital formation | 7,246.1 | 7,919.8 | 9,134 |
| **Total domestic expenditure** | 42,694.9 | 45,944.5 | 50,279 |
| Exports of goods and services | 4,961.7 | 6,441.3 | 7,284 |
| *Less* Imports of goods and services | 9,719.0 | 10,920.7 | 12,358 |
| **GDP in purchasers' values** | 37,937.6 | 41,465.1 | 45,204 |

Sources: National Bank of Ethiopia; IMF, *International Financial Statistics*.

**Gross Domestic Product by Economic Activity**

(at constant 1980/81 factor cost)

| | 1995/96 | 1996/97 | 1997/98 |
|---|---|---|---|
| Agriculture, hunting, forestry and fishing | 7,206.2 | 7,453.9 | 6,687.0 |
| Mining and quarrying | 55.4 | 62.6 | 68.9 |
| Manufacturing | 881.0 | 932.8 | 986.9 |
| Electricity, gas and water | 203.2 | 215.1 | 223.1 |
| Construction | 349.3 | 379.6 | 412.1 |
| Trade, hotels and restaurants | 1,115.5 | 1,208.9 | 1,263.3 |
| Transport, storage and communications | 799.2 | 853.2 | 907.8 |
| Finance, insurance and real estate | 879.7 | 954.5 | 999.2 |
| Public administration and defence | 1,391.5 | 1,483.4 | 1,848.3 |
| Education | 298.0 | 311.1 | 327.0 |
| Health | 154.0 | 160.1 | 175.9 |
| Domestic and other services | 654.1 | 694.7 | 731.5 |
| **Total** | 13,987.1 | 14,709.9 | 14,631.0 |

Source: IMF, *Ethiopia: Recent Economic Developments* (September 1999).

**BALANCE OF PAYMENTS** (US $ million)

| | 1996 | 1997 | 1998 |
|---|---|---|---|
| Exports of goods f.o.b. | 417.5 | 588.3 | 568.3 |
| Imports of goods f.o.b. | −1,002.2 | −1,018.7 | −1,042.2 |
| **Trade balance** | −584.7 | −430.5 | −473.9 |
| Exports of services | 377.2 | 390.7 | 431.3 |
| Imports of services | −349.8 | −396.2 | −418.5 |
| **Balance on goods and services** | −557.2 | −436.0 | −461.1 |
| Other income received | 51.3 | 37.2 | 47.8 |
| Other income paid | −76.1 | −67.0 | −59.6 |
| **Balance on goods, services and income** | −582.0 | −465.8 | −472.9 |
| Current transfers received | 679.0 | 450.4 | 627.9 |
| Current transfers paid | −7.5 | −7.6 | −21.0 |
| **Current balance** | 89.4 | −23.0 | 134.0 |
| Investment assets | −306.8 | 318.5 | 45.1 |
| Investment liabilities | −192.8 | −77.3 | −68.6 |
| Net errors and omissions | −56.6 | −646.7 | −493.5 |
| **Overall balance** | −466.7 | −428.6 | −383.1 |

Source: IMF, *International Financial Statistics*.

# External Trade

**PRINCIPAL COMMODITIES** (distribution by SITC, US $ '000)

| Imports c.i.f. | 1994 | 1995 | 1996 |
|---|---|---|---|
| **Food and live animals** | 150,811 | 123,677 | 26,783 |
| Cereals and cereal preparations | 121,279 | 84,432 | 19,287 |
| **Mineral fuels, lubricants, etc.** | n.a. | 124,378 | 119,455 |
| Crude petroleum oils, etc. | 80,274 | 67,197 | 47,285 |
| Refined petroleum products | 65,795 | 57,000 | 71,822 |
| **Chemicals and related products** | n.a. | n.a. | n.a. |
| Medicinal and pharmaceutical products | 32,622 | 29,561 | 26,634 |
| Medicaments | n.a. | 27,499 | 22,282 |
| Manufactured fertilizers | 8,821 | 60,967 | 66,171 |
| **Basic manufactures** | n.a. | n.a. | n.a. |
| Rubber manufactures | 33,962 | 36,033 | 51,258 |
| Textile yarn, fabrics, etc. | 31,688 | 47,121 | 52,761 |
| Iron and steel | n.a. | 58,530 | 80,544 |
| Universals, plates and sheets | n.a. | 45,714 | 55,910 |
| **Machinery and transport equipment** | n.a. | n.a. | n.a. |
| Electrical machinery, apparatus, etc.* | n.a. | 53,255 | 69,459 |
| Road vehicles and parts† | 146,467 | 198,335 | 194,946 |
| Passenger motor cars (excl. buses) | n.a. | 43,304 | 57,066 |
| Motor vehicles for goods transport, etc. | n.a. | 102,023 | 94,397 |
| Parts and accessories for cars, buses, lorries, etc.† | n.a. | 23,373 | 22,097 |
| **Total** (incl. others) | 918,589 | 1,121,297 | 1,117,884 |

* Excluding telecommunications and sound equipment.

† Excluding tyres, engines and electrical parts.

| Exports f.o.b. | 1994 | 1995 | 1996 |
|---|---|---|---|
| **Food and live animals** | n.a. | n.a. | n.a. |
| Vegetables and fruit | 2,561 | 16,111 | 3,495 |
| Coffee, tea, cocoa and spices | n.a. | 270,829 | 278,485 |
| Coffee and coffee substitutes | 218,430 | 270,707 | 278,485 |
| **Crude materials (inedible) except fuels** | n.a. | n.a. | n.a. |
| Raw hides, skins and furskins | 48,315 | 56,450 | 71,078 |
| Raw hides and skins (excl. furs) | 48,315 | 56,450 | 71,078 |
| Cattle hides | n.a. | 8,809 | 4,559 |
| Sheep skins | n.a. | 24,301 | 50,114 |
| **Mineral fuels, lubricants, etc.** | 17,409 | 11,842 | 13,701 |
| Petroleum, petroleum products, etc. | 17,409 | 11,842 | 13,701 |
| **Total** (incl. others) | 334,894 | 414,483 | 417,411 |

**Exports f.o.b.** (US $ '000, 1997): Vegetables and fruit 23,576; Coffee, tea, cocoa and spices 382,703 (Coffee and coffee substitutes 382,314); Raw hides, skins and furskins 60,590 (Raw hides and skins, excl. furs 60,590); Total (incl. others) 557,376.

**Exports f.o.b.** (US $ '000, 1998): Vegetables and fruit 39,958; Coffee, tea, cocoa and spices 420,313 (Coffee and coffee substitutes 419,763); Raw hides, skins and furskins 49,572 (Raw hides and skins, excl. furs 49,572); Total (incl. others) 593,393.

Source: National Bank of Ethiopia.

**PRINCIPAL TRADING PARTNERS** (million birr)

| Imports c.i.f. | 1995 | 1996 | 1997* |
|---|---|---|---|
| Belgium-Luxembourg | 217.4 | 160.2 | 114.4 |
| China, People's Repub. | 163.4 | 207.5 | 366.1 |
| Denmark | 66.3 | 83.4 | n.a. |
| Djibouti | 174.3 | 186.5 | 40.0 |
| France | 183.7 | 130.2 | 149.5 |
| Germany | 539.6 | 504.9 | 749.5 |
| India | 177.2 | 243.8 | 430.6 |
| Italy | 863.8 | 863.9 | 726.7 |
| Japan | 588.5 | 565.9 | 796.8 |
| Kenya | 214.9 | 211.3 | 154.9 |
| Korea, Repub. | 155.6 | 200.6 | 358.5 |
| Netherlands | 194.1 | 342.2 | 344.9 |
| Saudi Arabia | 828.4 | 724.7 | 735.2 |
| Sweden | 198.7 | 188.6 | n.a. |
| Turkey | 36.6 | 83.7 | 121.3 |
| United Kingdom | 417.5 | 321.6 | 454.7 |
| USA | 910.4 | 374.5 | 358.5 |
| **Total** (incl. others) | 7,041.7 | 7,103.1 | 7,615.1 |

* Preliminary estimates.

| Exports f.o.b. | 1996 | 1997 | 1998* |
|---|---|---|---|
| Belgium-Luxembourg | 54.7 | 142.5 | 176.2 |
| Djibouti | 230.9 | 298.9 | 147.0 |
| France | 94.2 | 127.5 | 144.0 |
| Germany | 827.1 | 811.9 | 984.4 |
| Israel | 8.8 | 18.9 | 56.1 |
| Italy | 206.7 | 307.8 | 270.3 |
| Japan | 333.6 | 441.0 | 479.5 |
| Netherlands | 35.9 | 57.5 | 73.8 |
| Saudi Arabia | 296.3 | 337.1 | 392.5 |
| Switzerland | 21.9 | 62.6 | 22.8 |
| United Kingdom | 86.6 | 115.0 | 98.1 |
| USA | 169.9 | 448.0 | 271.2 |
| **Total** (incl. others) | 2,783.1 | 3,941.3 | 3,966.0 |

* Preliminary estimates.

Source: IMF, *Ethiopia: Recent Economic Developments* (September 1999).

# Transport

**RAILWAYS** (traffic, year ending 7 July)*

| | 1995/96 | 1996/97 | 1997/98 |
|---|---|---|---|
| Addis Ababa–Djibouti: | | | |
| Passenger-km (million) | 166 | 157 | 167 |
| Freight (million net ton-km) | 104 | 106 | 90 |

* Including traffic on the section of the Djibouti–Addis Ababa line which runs through the Republic of Djibouti. Data pertaining to freight include service traffic.

Source: Ministry of Transport and Communications, Addis Ababa.

**ROAD TRAFFIC** (motor vehicles in use, year ending 7 July)

| | 1995/96 | 1996/97 | 1997/98 |
|---|---|---|---|
| Cars | 39,584 | 42,318 | 48,307 |
| Buses and coaches | 20,058 | 22,460 | 21,959 |
| Lorries and vans | 23,199 | 24,367 | 26,000 |
| Motorcycles and mopeds | 1,709 | 1,151 | 1,172 |
| Road tractors | 6,391 | 5,888 | 5,445 |
| **Total** | 90,941 | 96,184 | 102,883 |

Source: Ministry of Transport and Communications, Addis Ababa.

**SHIPPING**

**Merchant Fleet** (registered at 7 July)

| | 1996 | 1997 | 1998 |
|---|---|---|---|
| Number of vessels | 15 | 11 | 11 |
| Displacement (grt) | 86,009 | 86,592 | 81,508 |

Source: Ethiopian Shipping Lines Corporation.

**International Sea-borne Shipping** (freight traffic, '000 metric tons, year ending 7 July)

| | 1995/96 | 1996/97 | 1997/98 |
|---|---|---|---|
| Goods loaded | 165 | 242 | 201 |
| Goods unloaded | 1,304 | 777 | 1,155 |

Source: Ministry of Transport and Communications, Addis Ababa.

**CIVIL AVIATION** (traffic on scheduled services, year ending 7 July)

| | 1995/96 | 1996/97 | 1997/98 |
|---|---|---|---|
| Kilometres flown (million) | 26 | 28 | n.a. |
| Passengers carried ('000) | 730 | 808 | 807 |
| Passenger-km (million) | 1,838 | 1,915 | 1,944 |
| Total ton-km (million) | 112 | 129 | 149 |

Source: Ministry of Transport and Communications, Addis Ababa.

# Tourism

**TOURIST ARRIVALS BY COUNTRY OF ORIGIN**

| | 1994 | 1995 | 1996 |
|---|---|---|---|
| Canada | 1,863 | 3,306 | 3,811 |
| Djibouti | 3,433 | 5,004 | 4,247 |
| France | 3,235 | 3,266 | 4,029 |
| Germany | 4,217 | 4,753 | 5,554 |
| India | 1,961 | 2,172 | 2,069 |
| Italy | 5,787 | 6,820 | 7,621 |
| Japan | 1,666 | 2,168 | 2,830 |
| Kenya | 2,844 | 6,893 | 5,336 |
| Netherlands | 2,060 | 2,274 | 2,504 |
| Russia | 3,756 | 3,513 | 3,702 |
| Saudi Arabia | 1,472 | 3,484 | 4,246 |
| Sudan | 3,137 | 5,035 | 3,485 |
| Switzerland | 1,961 | 3,245 | 3,159 |
| United Kingdom | 4,609 | 5,994 | 6,424 |
| USA | 5,883 | 7,545 | 8,819 |
| Yemen | 1,274 | 2,923 | 3,920 |
| **Total** (incl. others)* | 98,070 | 103,336 | 108,885 |

* Including Ethiopian nationals residing abroad.

**Receipts from tourism** (US $ million): 25 in 1994; 26 in 1995; 28 in 1996.

Source: World Tourism Organization, *Yearbook of Tourism Statistics*.

# Communications Media

| | 1994 | 1995 | 1996 |
|---|---|---|---|
| Telephones ('000 main lines in use)* | 138 | 142 | n.a. |
| Telefax stations (number in use)* | 1,057 | 1,445 | n.a. |
| Radio receivers ('000 in use) | 10,550 | 10,900 | 11,300 |
| Television receivers ('000 in use) | 230 | 250 | 300 |
| Daily newspapers: | | | |
| Number | 4 | 4 | 4 |
| Average circulation ('000 copies) | 81† | 92† | 86 |

* Year ending 30 June.

† Estimate.

**Book production:** 240 titles (including 93 pamphlets) in 1991.

**Non-daily newspapers:** 17 in 1995 (average combined circulation 159,000).

Source: mainly UNESCO, *Statistical Yearbook*.

# Education

(1998/99)

| | Institutions | Teachers | Students |
|---|---|---|---|
| Pre-primary | 793 | 2,487 | 90,321 |
| Primary | 11,051 | 112,405 | 5,702,223 |
| Secondary: | | | |
| General | 386 | 13,078 | 521,728 |
| Teacher-training | 12 | 273 | 5,378 |
| Vocational | 16 | 548 | 3,374 |
| University level | 4 | 1,674 | 40,936 |
| Other higher | 13 | 823 | 19,083 |

Source: Ministry of Education, Addis Ababa.

# Directory

## The Constitution

In July 1991 a national conference elected a transitional Government and approved a charter under the provisions of which the Government was to operate until the holding of democratic elections. The charter provided guarantees for freedom of association and expression, and for self-determination for Ethiopia's different ethnic constituencies. The transitional Government was to be responsible for drafting a new constitution to replace that introduced in 1987. A Constituent Assembly, dominated by representatives of the EPRDF, was elected in June 1994. It ratified the draft Constitution (already approved by the transitional Council of Representatives) in December. The Constitution of the Federal Democratic Republic of Ethiopia provides for the establishment of a federal government and the division of the country into nine states and two chartered cities. It also provides for regional autonomy, including the right of secession. Simultaneous elections of deputies to the federal and state parliaments were conducted on 7 May 1995. The new Constitution came into effect on 22 August 1995.

## The Government

### HEAD OF STATE

**President:** Dr NEGASSO GIDADA (took office 22 August 1995).

### COUNCIL OF MINISTERS

(February 2000)

**Prime Minister:** MELES ZENAWI.

**Deputy Prime Minister and Head of Economic Affairs:** Dr KASSA YLALA.

**Deputy Prime Minister and Minister of Defence:** TEFERA WALWA.

**Minister of Foreign Affairs:** SEYOUM MESFIN.

**Minister of Health:** Dr ADEM IBRAHIM.

**Minister of Energy and Mines:** EZEDIN ALI.

**Minister of Economic Development and Co-operation:** GIRMA BIRU.

**Minister of Information and Culture:** WOLDE MIKAEL CHAMO.

**Minister of Education:** GENET ZEWDE.

**Minister of Agriculture:** Dr SEIFU KEFEMA.

**Minister of Commerce and Industry:** KASAHUN AYELE.

**Minister of Finance:** SUFYAN AHMED.

**Minister of Justice:** WEREDE WOLDU WOLDE.

**Minister of Works and Urban Development:** HAILE SELASSIE ASEGIDE.

**Minister of Labour:** HASAN ABDELA.

**Minister of Water Resources:** SHIFERAW JARSO.

**Minister and Head of the Revenue Collectors Board:** DESTA AMARE.

**Minister of Transport and Communications:** MOHAMOUD DIRIR GHEDDI (acting).

### MINISTRIES AND COMMISSIONS

**Office of the Prime Minister:** POB 1013, Addis Ababa; tel. (1) 552044.

**Ministry of Agriculture:** POB 62347, Addis Ababa; tel. (1) 152816; fax (1) 512984.

**Ministry of Commerce and Industry:** POB 704, Addis Ababa; tel. (1) 518025; fax (1) 515411.

**Ministry of Defence:** POB 125, Addis Ababa; tel. (1) 445555.

**Ministry of Economic Development and Co-operation:** POB 2559, Addis Ababa; tel. (1) 552800.

**Ministry of Education:** POB 1367, Addis Ababa; tel. (1) 553133.

**Ministry of Energy and Mines:** POB 486, Addis Ababa; tel. (1) 518250; fax (1) 517874.

**Ministry of Finance:** POB 1905, Addis Ababa; tel. (1) 552400; fax (1) 551355.

**Ministry of Foreign Affairs:** POB 393, Addis Ababa; tel. (1) 447345; fax (1) 514300.

**Ministry of Health:** POB 1234, Addis Ababa; tel. (1) 518031; fax 519366.

**Ministry of Information and Culture:** POB 1020, Addis Ababa; tel. (1) 517020.

**Ministry of Justice:** POB 1370, Addis Ababa; tel. (1) 517390.

**Ministry of Labour:** POB 2056, Addis Ababa; tel. (1) 517080.

**Ministry of Transport and Communications:** POB 1238, Addis Ababa; tel. (1) 516166; fax (1) 515665.

**Ministry of Water Resources:** POB 5744, Addis Ababa, tel. (1) 611111; fax (1) 610885.

**Ministry of Works and Urban Development:** POB 3386, Addis Ababa; tel. (1) 150000.

## Regional Governments

Ethiopia comprises nine regional governments and two chartered cities, which are vested with authority for self-administration. The executive bodies are respectively headed by Presidents and Chairmen.

### PRESIDENTS

**Tigrai:** ASRAT GEBRU.
**Afar:** ESMAEL ALISERO.
**Amhara:** ADDISO LEGGESE.
**Oromia:** KUMA DEMEKSA.
**Somali:** MUHAMMED MUALIN ALI.
**Benishangul/Gumuz:** YAREGAL AYSHESHIM.
**Southern Nations, Nationalities and Peoples:** ABATE KISHO.
**Gambela:** OKALO GNIGELO.
**Harari:** ABDULAHI IDRIS IBRAHIM.

### CHAIRMEN

**Dire Dawa:** SOLOMON HAILU.
**Addis Ababa:** ALI ABDO.

## Legislature

### FEDERAL PARLIAMENTARY ASSEMBLY

The legislature comprises an upper house, the Council of the Federation, with 117 seats (members are selected by state assemblies and are drawn one each from 22 minority nationalities and one from each professional sector of the remaining nationalities), and a lower house of 548 directly elected members, the Council of People's Representatives.

At elections held on 7 May 1995 the EPRDF secured 483 of the 537 confirmed seats, while 46 were won by regional political groupings and eight were won by independent candidates. The Federal Parliamentary Assembly assumed formal legislative power from the transitional Council of Representatives on 21 August 1995.

**Speaker of the Council of the Federation:** WEIZERO ALMAZ MEKO.

**Speaker of the Council of People's Representatives:** DAWIT YOHANES.

## Political Organizations

**Afar People's Democratic Organization (APDO):** fmrly Afar Liberation Front (ALF); based in fmr Hararge and Wollo Admin. Regions; supported the Ethiopian transitional Govt; Leader ISMAIL ALI SIRRO.

**Coalition of Alternative Forces for Peace and Democracy in Ethiopia (CAFPDE):** f. 1993 as a broadly-based coalition of groups opposing the EPRDF; split into two factions in Dec. 1999, led by former Vice-Chairman KIFLE TIGNEH ABATE and by Dr BEYENE PETROS.

**Coalition of Ethiopian Democratic Forces (COEDF):** f. 1991 in the USA by the Ethiopian People's Revolutionary Party–EPRP (the dominant member), together with a faction of the Ethiopian Democratic Union (EDU) and the Ethiopian Socialist Movement (MEISON); opposes the EPRDF; Chair. MERSHA YOSEPH.

**Coalition of Ethiopian Opposition Political Organizations (CEOPO):** f. 1998 in France as a coalition of groups opposing the EPRDF; Chair. NEGEDE GOBEZIE; Chair. (Ethiopia) KIFLEH TIGNEH ABATE.

**Ethiopian Democratic Unity Party (EDUP):** Addis Ababa; f. 1984 as Workers' Party of Ethiopia; adopted present name in 1990, when its Marxist-Leninist ideology was relaxed and membership opened to non-Marxist and opposition groups; sole legal political party until May 1991; Sec.-Gen. Lt-Gen. TESFAYE GEBRE KIDAN.

**Tuvalu:** 16 Gorrie St, POB 14449, Suva; tel. 300697; fax 301023; High Commissioner: ENELE SOSENE SOPOAGA.

**United Kingdom:** Victoria House, 47 Gladstone Rd, POB 1355, Suva; tel. 311033; fax 301406; e-mail ukinfo@bhc.org.fj; internet www.ukinthepacific.bhc.org.fj; High Commissioner: MICHAEL DIBBEN.

**USA:** 31 Loftus Rd, POB 218, Suva; tel. 314466; fax 300081; e-mail usembsuva@is.com.fj; internet www.amembassy-fiji.gov; Chargé d'affaires: OSMAN SIDDIQUE.

# Judicial System

Justice is administered by the Supreme Court, the Fiji Court of Appeal, the High Court and the Magistrates' Courts. The Supreme Court of Fiji is the superior court of record presided over by the Chief Justice. The Chief Justice and six senior judges were removed from office on 15 October 1987, following the military coup of 25 September. In January 1988 the former Chief Justice, Sir Timoci Tuivaga, resumed his post in a newly-constituted judicial system and a further three High Court judges were appointed. Many judicial appointees come from overseas. Since the 1987 coups about two-thirds of Fiji's lawyers have left the country. The current judicial arrangements were regularized by the 1990 Constitution. This also provided for the establishment of Fijian customary courts and declared as final decisions of the Native Lands Commission in cases involving Fijian custom, etc.

**Supreme Court:** Suva; tel. 211481; fax 300674.

**Chief Justice:** Sir TIMOCI TUIVAGA.

**President of the Fiji Court of Appeal:** JAI RAM REDDY.

**Director of Public Prosecutions:** KENNETH WILKINSON (acting).

**Solicitor-General:** NAINENDRA NAND.

# Religion

## CHRISTIANITY

Most ethnic Fijians are Christians. Methodists are the largest Christian group, followed by Roman Catholics. In the census of 1986 about 53% of the population were Christian (mainly Methodists).

**Fiji Council of Churches:** POB 2300, Government Bldgs, Suva; tel. (1) 313798; f. 1964; seven mem. churches; Pres. Most Rev. PETERO MATACA (Roman Catholic Archbishop of Suva); Gen. Sec. EMI FRANCES.

### The Anglican Communion

In April 1990 Polynesia, formerly a missionary diocese of the Church of the Province of New Zealand, became a full and integral diocese. The diocese of Polynesia is based in Fiji but also includes Wallis and Futuna, Tuvalu, Kiribati, French Polynesia, Cook Islands, Tonga, Samoa and Tokelau.

**Bishop of Polynesia:** Rt Rev. JABEZ LESLIE BRYCE, Bishop's House, 7 Disraeli Rd, POB 35, Suva; tel. 302553; fax 302687.

### The Roman Catholic Church

Fiji comprises a single archdiocese. At 31 December 1997 there were an estimated 82,082 adherents in the country.

**Bishops' Conference:** Episcopal Conference of the Pacific Secretariat (CEPAC), 14 Williamson Rd, POB 289, Suva; tel. 300340; fax 303143; e-mail cepac@is.com.fj; f. 1968; 17 mems; Pres. Most Rev. MICHEL MARIE CALVET, Archbishop of Nouméa, New Caledonia; Gen. Sec. Rev. ARTHUR TIERNEY.

**Regional Appeal Tribunal for CEPAC:** 14 Williamson Rd, POB 289, Suva; tel. 300340; fax 303143; e-mail cepac@is.com.fj; f. 1980; 17 mems; Judicial Vicar Rev. THEO KOSTER.

**Archbishop of Suva:** Most Rev. PETERO MATACA, Archdiocesan Office, Nicolas House, Pratt St, POB 109, Suva; tel. 301955; fax 301565.

### Other Christian Churches

**Methodist Church in Fiji (Lotu Wesele e Viti):** Epworth Arcade, Nina St, POB 357, Suva; tel. 311477; fax 303771; f. 1835; autonomous since 1964; 214,697 mems (1995); Pres. Rev. Dr ILAITIA TUWERE; Gen. Sec. Rev. TOMASI KANAILAGI.

Other denominations active in the country include the Assembly of God (with c. 7,000 mems), the Baptist Mission, the Congregational Christian Church and the Presbyterian Church.

## HINDUISM

Most of the Indian community are Hindus. According to the census of 1986, 38% of the population were Hindus.

## ISLAM

In 1993 some 8% of the population were Muslim. There are several Islamic organizations:

**Fiji Muslim League:** POB 3990, Samabula, Suva; tel. 384566; fax 370204; f. 1926; Pres. Haji FAZAL KHAN; Gen. Sec. MASUM ALI BUKSH; 26 brs and 3 subsidiary orgs.

## SIKHISM

**Sikh Association of Fiji:** Suva; Pres. HARKEWAL SINGH.

## BAHÁ'Í FAITH

**National Spiritual Assembly:** National Office, POB 639, Suva; tel. 387574; fax 387772; e-mail nsafijiskm@suva.is.com.fj; mems resident in 490 localities; national headquarters for consultancy and co-ordination.

# The Press

## NEWSPAPERS AND PERIODICALS

**Coconut Telegraph:** POB 249, Savusavu, Vanua Levu; f. 1975; monthly; serves widely-scattered rural communities; Editor LEMA LOW.

**Fiji Calling:** POB 12095, Suva; tel. 305916; fax 301930; publ. by Associated Media Ltd; every 6 months; English; Publr YASHWANT GAUNDER.

**Fiji Cane Grower:** POB 12095, Suva; tel. 305916; fax 305256.

**Fiji Daily Post:** 10–16 Toorak Rd, POB 2071, Govt Bldgs, Suva; f. 1987 as *Fiji Post*, daily from 1989; English; 45% govt-owned; Gen. Man. ANURA BANDARA (acting); Editor JALE MOALA.

**Fiji Islands Business:** 46 Gordon St, POB 12718; Suva; tel. 303108; fax 301423; e-mail editor@ibi.com.fj; monthly; English; Editor-in-Chief PETER LOMAS.

**Fiji Magic:** POB 12095, Suva; tel. 305916; fax 301930; e-mail review-@is.com.fj; publ. by The Review Ltd; monthly; English; Publr YASHWANT GAUNDER.

**Fiji Republic Gazette:** Printing Dept, POB 98, Suva; tel. 385999; fax 370203; f. 1874; weekly; English.

**Fiji Sun:** Suva; re-established 1999; daily; Editor MARK GARRET.

**Fiji Times:** 20 Gordon St, POB 1167, Suva; tel. 304111; fax 301521; f. 1869; publ. by Fiji Times Ltd; daily; English; Man. Dir ALAN ROBINSON; Editor SAMISONI KAKAIUALU; circ. 34,000.

**Fiji Trade Review:** The Rubine Group, POB 12511, Suva; tel. 313944; monthly; English; Publr GEORGE RUBINE; Editor MABEL HOWARD.

**Islands Business:** 46 Gordon St, POB 12718, Suva; tel. 303108; fax 301423; e-mail editor@ibi.com.fj; f. 1980; regional monthly news and business magazine; English; Publr ROBERT KEITH-REID; Editor-in-Chief PETER LOMAS; circ. 11,950.

**Na Tui:** 422 Fletcher Rd, POB 2071, Govt Bldgs, Suva; f. 1988; weekly; Fijian; Publr TANIELA BOLEA; Editor SAMISONI BOLATAGICI; circ. 7,000.

**Nai Lalakai:** 20 Gordon St, POB 1167, Suva; tel. 304111; fax 301521; e-mail fijitimes@is.com.fj; f. 1962; publ. by Fiji Times Ltd; weekly; Fijian; Editor SAMISONI KAKAIVALU; circ. 18,000.

**Pacific Business:** POB 12095, Suva; tel. 305916; fax 301930; publ. by Associated Media Ltd; monthly; English; Publr YASHWANT GAUNDER.

**Pacific Islands Monthly:** 177 Victoria Parade, POB 1167, Suva; tel. 304111; fax 303809; e-mail pim@fijitimes.com.fj; internet www.pim.-com.fj; f. 1930; publ. by Fiji Times Ltd; monthly; English; political, economic and cultural affairs in the Pacific Islands; Publr ALAN ROBINSON; Editor SOPHIE FOSTER HILDEBRAND.

**Pacific Telecom:** POB 12095, Suva; tel. 300591; fax 302852; e-mail review@is.com.fj; publ. by Associated Media Ltd; monthly; English; Publr YASHWANT GAUNDER.

**Pactrainer:** PMB, Suva; tel. 303623; fax 303943; e-mail pina@is.com.fj; monthly; newsletter of Pacific Journalism Development Centre; Editor PETER LOMAS.

**PINA Nius:** Pacific Islands News Association, 46 Gordon St, PMB, Suva; tel. 303623; fax 303943; e-mail pina@is.com.fj; internet www.pressasia.org/pfa/; monthly newsletter of Pacific Islands News Association; Editor NINA RATULELE.

**The Review:** POB 12095, Suva; tel. 305916; fax 301930; e-mail review@is.com.fj; publ. by Associated Media Ltd; monthly; English; Publr YASHWANT GAUNDER.

**Sartaj:** John Beater Enterprises Ltd, Raiwaqa, POB 5141, Suva; f. 1988; weekly; Hindi; Editor S. DASO; circ. 15,000.

**Shanti Dut:** 20 Gordon St, POB 1167, Suva; f. 1935; publ. by Fiji Times Ltd; weekly; Hindi; Editor M. C. VINOD; circ. 8,000.

**Top Shot:** Suva; f. 1995; golf magazine; monthly.

**Volasiga:** 10–16 Toorak Rd, POB 2071, Suva; f. 1988; weekly; Fijian; Gen. Man. ANURA BANDARA (acting); Editor SAMISONI BOLATAGICI.

**The Weekender:** 2 Dension Rd, POB 15652, Suva; tel. 315477; fax 305346; publ. by Media Resources Ltd; weekly; English; Publr JOSEFATA NATA.

### PRESS ASSOCIATIONS

**Fiji Islands Media Association:** c/o Vasiti Ivaqa, POB 12718, Suva; tel. 303108; fax 301423; national press assen; operates Fiji Press Club and Fiji Journalism Training Institute; Sec. NINA RATULELE.

**Pacific Islands News Association:** 46 Gordon St, PMB, Suva; tel. 303623; fax 303943; e-mail pina@is.com.fj; internet www.pressasia.org/pfa/; regional press assen; defends freedom of information and expression, promotes professional co-operation, provides training and education; Administrator NINA RATULELE; Pres. WILLIAM PARKINSON.

## Publishers

**Fiji Times Ltd:** POB 1167, Suva; tel. 304111; fax 302011; f. 1869; Propr News Corpn Ltd; largest newspaper publr; also publrs of books and magazines; Man. Dir ALAN ROBINSON.

**Lotu Pasifika Productions:** POB 2401, Suva; tel. 301314; fax 301183; f. 1973; cookery, education, poetry, religion; Gen. Man. SERU L. VEREBALAVU.

**University of the South Pacific:** University Media Centre, POB 1168, Suva; tel. 313900; fax 301305; e-mail farkas_g@nsp.ac.fj; f. 1986; education, natural history, regional interests.

### Government Publishing House

**Printing and Stationery Department:** POB 98, Suva; tel. 385999; fax 370203.

## Broadcasting and Communications

### TELECOMMUNICATIONS

**Fiji International Telecommunicatons Ltd (FINTEL):** 158 Victoria Parade, POB 59, Suva; tel. 312933; fax 305606; e-mail fintel@is.com.fj; 51% govt-owned; Gen. Man. PHILIP RICHARDS.

**Telcom Fiji Ltd:** Private Mail Bag, Suva; tel. 304019; fax 301765; Chair. LIONEL YEE; CEO WINSTON THOMPSON.

**Vodafone Fiji Ltd:** Private Mail Bag, Suva; tel. 312000; fax 312007; 51% owned by Telecom Fiji, 41% by Vodafone Holdings Australia; Man. Dir ASLAM KHAN.

### BROADCASTING

#### Radio

**Fiji Broadcasting Commission—FBC (Radio Fiji):** Broadcasting House, POB 334, Suva; tel. 314333; fax 301643; f. 1954; statutory body; jointly funded by govt grant and advertising revenue; Chair. OLOTA ROKOVUNISEI; Gen. Man. BARRY FERBER.

Radio Fiji 1 broadcasts nationally on AM in English and Fijian.

Radio Fiji 2 broadcasts nationally on AM in English and Hindi.

Radio Fiji Gold broadcasts nationally on AM and FM in English.

104 FM and Radio Rajdhani 98 FM, mainly with musical programmes, broadcast in English and Hindi respectively, but are received only on Viti Levu.

Bula FM, musical programmes, broadcasts in Fijian, received only on Viti Levu.

**Communications Fiji Ltd:** 231 Waimanu Rd, PMB, Suva; tel. 314766; fax 303748; e-mail cfl@fm96.com.fj; f. 1985; operates three commercial stations; Man. Dir WILLIAM PARKINSON; Gen. Man. IAN JACKSON.

FM 96, f. 1985, broadcasts 24 hours per day, on FM, in English.

Navtarang, f. 1989, broadcasts 24 hours per day, on FM, in Hindi.

Viti FM, f. 1996, broadcasts 24 hours per day, on FM, in Fijian.

**Radio Light:** Shop 11B, Pacific Harbour Culture Centre, POB 319, Pacific Harbour; tel. and fax 450007; e-mail radiolights@is.com.fj; f. 1990; non-profit religious organization; broadcasts on FM 100 and FM 93.6; Station Man. and Programmes Dir DOUGLAS ROSE.

**Radio Pasifik:** POB 1168, University of the South Pacific, Suva; tel. 313900; fax 312591; e-mail schuster_a@usp.ac.fj; Gen. Man. ALFRED SCHUSTER.

#### Television

**Film and Television Unit (FTU):** c/o Ministry of Information, Govt Bldgs, POB 2225, Suva; tel. 314688; fax 300196; video library; production unit established by Govt and Hanns Seidel Foundation (Germany); a weekly news magazine and local documentary programmes.

**Fiji Television Ltd:** 20 Gorrie St, POB 2442, Suva; tel. 305100; fax 305077; e-mail fijitv@is.com.fj; f. 1994; operates two services, Fiji 1, a free channel, and Sky Fiji, a three-channel subscription service; Chair. ISOA KALOUMAIRA; CEO KEN CLARK; Head of Programmes CAROLYN JALAL.

**Fiji Vision Ltd:** Suva; f. 1997; subscription television; jointly-owned by Yasana Holdings Ltd and a Hawaiian consortium.

In 1990 two television stations were constructed at Suva and Monsavu, with aid from the People's Republic of China. A permanent television station became operational in July 1994.

## Finance

In 1996 the Ministry of Finance announced that it had secured financial assistance for the undertaking of a study to investigate the possibility of developing an 'offshore' financial centre in Fiji.

### BANKING

(cap. = capital; res = reserves; dep. = deposits; m. = million; brs = branches; amounts in Fiji dollars)

#### Central Bank

**Reserve Bank of Fiji:** PMB, Suva; tel. 313611; fax 301688; e-mail rbf@is.com.fj; f. 1984 to replace Central Monetary Authority of Fiji; bank of issue; administers Office of Commissioner of Insurance; cap. 2m., res 146.3m., dep. 125.7m. (Dec. 1998); Chair. and Gov. Ratu JONE YAVALA KUBUABOLA; Dep. Gov. SADA SIVAN REDDY.

#### Commercial Bank

**Colonial National Bank:** 33 Ellery St, POB 1166, Suva; tel. 303499; fax 302190; f. 1974; fmrly National Bank of Fiji; 51% acquired from Fiji Govt by Colonial Ltd in 1999; cap. 9.2m. res 2.3m., dep. 115.2m. (June 1997); Chair. LIONEL YEE; Chief Man. KENNETH MCARTHUR; 13 brs; 66 agencies.

#### Development Bank

**Fiji Development Bank:** 360 Victoria Parade, POB 104, Suva; tel. 314866; fax 314886; f. 1967; finances the development of natural resources, agriculture, transportation and other industries and enterprises; statutory body; cap. 50.8m., res 14.0m., dep. 182.6m. (June 1993); Chair. CHARLES WALKER; 9 brs.

#### Merchant Banks

**Merchant Bank of Fiji Ltd:** 231 Waimanu Rd, POB 14213, Suva; tel. 314955; fax 300026; f. 1986; owned by the Fijian Holdings Ltd; Man. Dir LAISENIA QARASE; 4 brs.

**National MBf Finance (Fiji) Ltd:** Burns Philp Bldg, 2nd Floor, POB 13525, Suva; tel. 302232; fax 305915; e-mail mbf@is.com.fj; f. 1991; 51% owned by the National Bank of Fiji, 49% by MBf Asia Capital Corpn Holding Ltd (Hong Kong); Chief Operating Officer SIEK KART; 4 brs.

#### Foreign Banks

**Agence Française de Développement (ADF)** (France): Suva; licensed to operate in Fiji in 1997.

**Australia and New Zealand (ANZ) Banking Group Ltd:** ANZ House, 25 Victoria Parade, POB 179, Suva; tel. 302144; fax 300267; bought Bank of New Zealand in Fiji (8 brs) in 1990; Gen. Man. (Fiji) DAVID BELL; 17 brs; 9 agencies.

**Bank of Baroda** (India): Bank of Baroda Bldg, Marks St, POB 57, Suva; tel. 311400; fax 302510; f. 1908; CEO S. K. BAGCHI; 7 brs; 2 agencies.

**Bank of Hawaii** (USA): 67–69 Victoria Parade, POB 273, Suva; tel. 312144; fax 312464; f. 1993; Man. ROBERT HO CHEE; 3 brs.

**Habib Bank** (Pakistan): Narsey's Bldg, Renwick Rd, POB 108, Suva; tel. 304011; fax 304835; Chief Man. (Fiji) ABDUL MATIN; licensed to operate in Fiji 1990; 3 brs.

**Westpac Banking Corporation** (Australia): 1 Thomson St, Suva; tel. 300666; fax 301813; Chief Man. (Pacific Islands region) TREVOR WISEMANTEL; 12 brs; 9 agencies.

### STOCK EXCHANGE

**Suva Stock Exchange:** Level 2, Plaza One, Provident Plaza, 33 Ellery St, POB 11689, Suva; tel. 304130; fax 304145; e-mail suvastockex@is.com.fj; internet www.suvastockex.com; name to be changed to South Pacific Stock Exchange in early 2000; Chair. FOANA T. NEMANI; Man. MESAKE NAWARI.

### INSURANCE

**Blue Shield (Pacific) Ltd:** Parade Bldg, POB 15137, Suva; tel. 311733; fax 300318; Fijian co; subsidiary of Colonial Mutual Life Assurance Society Ltd; medical and life insurance; Chief Exec. SIALENI VUETAKI.

**Colonial Mutual Life Assurance Society Ltd:** CMLA Bldg, PMB, Suva; tel. 314400; fax 303448; f. 1876; inc in Australia; life; Gen. Man. SILON SWANSON.

**Dominion Insurance Ltd:** Civic House, POB 14468, Suva; tel. 311055; fax 303475; partly owned by Flour Mills of Fiji Ltd; general insurance; Man. Dir GARY S. CALLAGHAN.

**FAI Insurance (Fiji) Ltd:** Suva.

**Fiji Reinsurance Corpn Ltd:** RBF Bldg, POB 12704, Suva; tel. 313471; fax 305679; 20% govt-owned; reinsurance; Chair. Ratu JONE Y. KUBUABOLA; Man. PETER MARIO.

**Fijicare Mutual Assurance:** 41 Loftus St, POB 15808, Suva; tel. 302717; fax 302119; f. 1992; CEO JEFF PRICE.

**Insurance Trust of Fiji:** Loftus St, POB 114; Suva; tel. 311242; fax 302541; Man. SAMUEL KRISHNA.

**National Insurance Co of Fiji Ltd:** McGowan Bldg, Suva; tel. 315955; fax 301376; owned by New Zealand interests; Gen. Man. GEOFF THOMPSON.

**New India Assurance Co Ltd:** Harifam Centre, POB 71, Suva; tel. 313488; fax 302679; Man. MILIND A. KHARAT.

**Queensland Insurance (Fiji) Ltd:** Queensland Insurance Center, Victoria Parade, POB 101, Suva; tel. 315455; fax 300285; owned by Australian interests; Gen. Man. PETER J. NICHOLLS.

There are also two Indian insurance companies operating in Fiji.

# Trade and Industry

## GOVERNMENT AGENCIES

**Fiji National Training Council (FNTC):** Beaumont Rd, POB 6890, Nasinu; tel. 392000; fax 340184; e-mail gen-enq@fntc.ac.fj; internet www.fntc.ac.fj; Dir-Gen. NELSON DELAILOMALOMA.

**Fiji Trade and Investment Board:** Civic House, 6th Floor, Victoria Parade, Suva; tel. 315988; fax 301783; e-mail ftibinfo@ftib.org.fj; internet www.ftib.org.fj; f. 1980, restyled 1988, to promote and stimulate foreign and local economic development investment; Chair. JAMES DATTA; CEO JESONI VITUSAGAVULU.

**Mineral Resources Department:** Private Mail Bag; Suva; tel. 381611; fax 370039; internet www.mrd.gov.fj/index.html.

## DEVELOPMENT ORGANIZATIONS

**Fiji Development Company Ltd:** POB 161, FNPF Place, 350 Victoria Parade, Suva; tel. 304611; fax 304171; e-mail hfc@is.com.fj; f. 1960; subsidiary of the Commonwealth Development Corpn; Man. F. KHAN.

**Fiji-United States Business Council:** CI-FTIB; POB 2303; Suva; f. 1998 to develop and expand trade links between the two countries; Pres. RAMENDRA NARAYAN.

**Fijian Development Fund Board:** POB 122, Suva; tel. 312601; fax 302585; f. 1951; funds derived from payments of $F20 a metric ton from the sales of copra by indigenous Fijians; deposits receive interest at 2.5%; funds used only for Fijian development schemes; Chair. Minister for Fijian Affairs; CEO VINCENT TOVATA.

**Land Development Authority:** c/o Ministry for Agriculture, Fishery and Forestry, POB 358, Suva; tel. 311233; fax 302478; f. 1961 to co-ordinate development plans for land and marine resources; Chair. Ratu Sir JOSAIA TARAIQIA.

## CHAMBERS OF COMMERCE

**Ba Chamber of Commerce:** POB 99, Ba; tel. 670134; fax 670132; Pres. DIJENDRA SINGH.

**Labasa Chamber of Commerce:** POB 121, Labasa; tel. 811262; fax 813009; Pres. SHIVLAL NAGINDAS.

**Lautoka Chamber of Commerce:** POB 366, Lautoka; tel. 661834; fax 662379; Pres. NATWARLAL VAGH.

**Levuka Chamber of Commerce:** POB 85, Levuka; tel. 440248; fax 440252; Pres. ISHRAR ALI.

**Nadi Chamber of Commerce:** POB 2735, Nadi; tel. 701704; fax 702314; e-mail arunkumar@is.com.fj; Pres. VENKAT RAMANI AIYER.

**Nausori Chamber of Commerce:** POB 228, Nausori; tel. 478235; fax 400134; Pres. ROBERT RAJ KUMAR.

**Sigatoka Chamber of Commerce:** POB 882, Sigatoka; tel. 500064; fax 520006; Pres. NATWAR SINGH.

**Suva Chamber of Commerce:** 29 Ackland St, Vatuwara, POB 337, Suva; tel. 303854; fax 300475; f. 1902; Pres. NAVIN CHANDRA; 150 mems.

**Tavua-Vatukoula Chamber of Commerce:** POB 698, Tavua; tel. 680390; fax 680390; Pres. SOHAN SINGH.

**Vanua Chamber of Commerce:** 26 Carem St, Flagstaff, POB 13132, Suva; tel. 311022; fax 304818; f. 1988; Pres. PENI VEREKAUTA (acting); Sec. LITIA K. VAKAREWAKOBAU.

## INDUSTRIAL AND TRADE ASSOCIATIONS

**Fiji Forest Industries (FFI):** Suva; Deputy Chair. Ratu SOSO KATONIVERE.

**Fiji National Petroleum Co Ltd:** Suva; f. 1991; govt-owned, distributor of petroleum products.

**Fiji Sugar Corporation Ltd:** 2nd and 3rd Floors, Western House, Cnr of Bila and Vidilo St, PMB, Lautoka; tel. 662655; fax 664685; nationalized 1974; buyer of sugar-cane and raw sugar mfrs; Chair. HAFIZUD D. KHAN; Man. Dir JONETANI K. GALUINADI.

**Fiji Sugar Marketing Co Ltd:** Dominion House, 5th Floor, Thomson St, POB 1402, Suva; tel. 311588; fax 300607; Man. Dir JONETANI GALUINADI.

**Mining and Quarrying Council:** 42 Gorrie St, Suva; tel. 302188; fax 302183; e-mail employer@is.com.fj.

**National Trading Corporation Ltd:** POB 13673, Suva; tel. 315211; fax 315584; f. 1992; a govt-owned body set up to develop markets for agricultural and marine produce locally and overseas; processes and markets fresh fruit, vegetables and ginger products; CEO APIAMA CEGUMALINA.

**Native Lands Trust Board:** Suva; manages holdings of ethnic Fijian landowners; Gen. Man. Ratu MOSESE VOLAVOLA.

**Pacific Fishing Co:** Suva; fish-canning; govt-owned.

**Sugar Cane Growers' Council:** Canegrowers' Bldg, 3rd Floor, 75 Drasa Ave, Lautoka; tel. 650466; fax 650624; f. 1985; aims to develop the sugar industry and protect the interests of registered growers; CEO GRISH MAHARAJ; Chair. RUSIATE MUSUDROKA.

**Sugar Commission of Fiji:** Dominion House, 4th Floor, Thomson St, Suva; tel. 315488; fax 301488; Chair. GERALD BARRACK.

## EMPLOYERS' ORGANIZATIONS

**Fiji Employers' Federation:** 42 Gorrie St, POB 575, Suva; tel. 313188; fax 302183; e-mail employer@is.com.fj; represents 187 major employers; Pres. K. J. CLEMENS; CEO KENNETH A. J. ROBERTS.

**Fiji Manufacturers' Association:** POB 1308, Suva; tel. 212223; fax 302567; e-mail volau-m@usp.ac.fj; internet www.fijibusiness.com; f. 1902; Pres. DESMOND WHITESIDE; 55 mems.

**Local Inter-Island Shipowners' Association:** POB 152, Suva; fax 303389; Pres. VITI G. WHIPPY.

**Textile, Clothing and Footwear Council:** POB 10015, Nabua; tel. 384777; fax 370446; Sec. R. DUNSTAN.

## UTILITIES

### Electricity

**Fiji Electricity Authority (FEA):** PMB, Suva; tel. 311133; fax 311882; f. 1966; govt-owned; responsible for the generation, transmission and distribution of electricity throughout Fiji.

### Water

**Water and Sewerage Section:** Public Works Department, Ministry of Works and Energy, Nasilivata House, Kings Rd, PMB, Samabula; tel. 211250; fax 303146; e-mail fkau@info.gov.fj; Dir RAM SUMER SHANDIL.

## TRADE UNIONS

**Fiji Trades Union Congress (FTUC):** 32 Des Voeux Rd, POB 1418, Suva; tel. 315377; fax 300306; e-mail ftucl@is.com.fj; f. 1951; affiliated to ICFTU and ICFTU–APRO; 35 affiliated unions; more than 42,000 mems; Pres. DANIEL URAI; Gen. Sec. PRATAP CHAND. Principal affiliated unions:

**Association of USP Staff:** POB 1168, Suva; tel. 313900; fax 301305; f. 1977; Pres. GANESH CHAND; Sec. D. R. RAO.

**Building Construction and Timber Workers' Union of Fiji:** POB 928, Lautoka; tel. 666353; e-mail feawu@is.com.fj; Pres. LEPANI KADI; Sec. TANGAVELLU PILLAY.

**Federated Airline Staff Association:** Nadi Airport, POB 9259, Nadi; tel. 722877; fax 790068; Sec. RAM RAJEN.

**Fiji Aviation Workers' Association:** FTUC Complex, 32 Des Voeux Rd, POB 5351, Raiwaqa; tel. 303184; fax 311805; Pres. VALENTINE SIMPSON; Gen. Sec. ATTAR SINGH.

**Fiji Bank Employees' Union:** 101 Gordon St, POB 853, Suva; tel. 301827; fax 301956; Gen. Sec. DIWAN C. SHANKER.

**Fiji Garment, Textile and Allied Workers' Union:** c/o FTUC, Raiwaqa; f. 1992.

**Fiji Nurses' Association:** POB 1364, Suva; tel. 312841; Gen. Sec. KITI VATANIMOTO.

**Fiji Public Service Association:** 298 Waimanu Rd, POB 1405, Suva; tel. 311922; fax 301099; e-mail fpsa@is.com.fj; f. 1943; 3,434 mems; Pres. AISEA BATISARESARE; Gen. Sec. M. P. CHAUDHRY.

**Fiji Sugar and General Workers' Union:** 84 Naviti St, POB 330, Lautoka; tel. 660746; fax 664888; 25,000 mems; Pres. SHIU LINGAM; Gen. Sec. FELIX ANTHONY.

**Fiji Teachers' Union:** 1–3 Berry Rd, Govt Bldgs, POB 2203, Suva; tel. 314099; fax 305962; e-mail ftu@is.com.fj; f. 1930; 3,520 mems; Pres. BALRAM; Gen. Sec. AGNI DEO SINGH.

**Fijian Teachers' Association:** POB 14464, Suva; tel. 315099; Pres. JIUTA VOLATABU; Gen. Sec. ERONI BIUKOTO.

**Insurance Officers' Association:** POB 71, Suva; tel. 313488; Pres. JAGDISH KHATRI; Sec. DAVID LEE.

**Mineworkers' Union of Fiji:** POB 876, Tavua; f. 1986; Pres. HENNESY PETERS; Sec. KAVEKINI NAVUSO.

**National Farmers' Union:** POB 522, Labasa; tel. 811838; 10,000 mems (sugar-cane farmers); Pres. DEWAN CHAND; Gen. Sec. M. P. CHAUDHRY; CEO MOHAMMED LATIF SUBEDAR.

**National Union of Factory and Commercial Workers:** POB 989, Suva; tel. 311155; 3,800 mems; Pres. CAMA TUILEVEUKA; Gen. Sec. JAMES R. RAMAN.

**National Union of Hotel and Catering Employees:** Nadi Airport, POB 9426, Nadi; tel. 70906; fax 700181; Pres. EMOSI DAWAI; Sec. TIMOA NAIVAHIWAQA.

**Public Employees' Union:** POB 781, Suva; tel. 304501; 6,752 mems; Pres. SEMI TIKOICINA; Gen. Sec. FILIMONE BANUVE.

**Transport and Oil Workers' Union:** POB 903, Suva; tel. 302534; f. 1988; following merger of Oil and Allied Workers' Union and Transport Workers' Union; Pres. J. BOLA; Sec. MICHAEL COLUMBUS.

There are several independent trade unions, including Fiji Registered Ports Workers' Union (f. 1947; Pres. JIOJI TAHOLOSALE).

# Transport

### RAILWAYS

**Fiji Sugar Corporation Railway:** Rarawai Mill, POB 155, Ba; tel. 674044; fax 670505; for use in cane-harvesting season, May–Dec.; 595 km of permanent track and 225 km of temporary track (gauge of 600 mm), serving cane-growing areas at Ba, Lautoka and Penang on Viti Levu and Labasa on Vanua Levu; Gen. Man. ADURU KUVA.

### ROADS

At the end of 1995 there were some 3,370 km of roads in Fiji, of which 49.1% were paved. A 500-km highway circles the main island of Viti Levu.

### SHIPPING

There are ports of call at Suva, Lautoka, Levuka and Savusavu. The main port, Suva, handles more than 800 ships a year, including large passenger liners. Lautoka handles more than 300 vessels and liners and Levuka, the former capital of Fiji, mainly handles commercial fishing vessels. In 1996 a feasibility study into the possible establishment of a free port at Suva was commissioned. In May 1997 the Government approved 14 new ports of entry in the northern, western and central eastern districts of Fiji.

**Maritime and Ports Authority of Fiji (MPAF):** Administration Bldg, Princes Wharf, POB 780, Suva; tel. 312700; fax 300064; corporatized in 1998; Chair. DANIEL ELISHA; Port Master Capt. GEORGE MACOMBER.

**Ports Terminals Ltd:** Suva; f. 1998, following corporatization of Ports Authority of Fiji (now MPAF, see above).

**Burns Philp Shipping (Fiji) Ltd:** Rodwell Rd, POB 15832, Suva; tel. 313068; fax 301127; e-mail burshipfiji@is.com.fj; shipping agents, customs agents and international forwarding agents; Gen. Man. MARTIN BYRNE.

**Consort Shipping Line Ltd:** Muaiwalu Complex, Rona St, Walubay, POB 152, Suva; tel. 313344; fax 303389; CEO HECTOR SMITH; Man. Dir JUSTIN SMIT.

**Fiji Maritime Services Ltd:** c/o Fiji Ports Workers and Seafarers Union, 36 Edinburgh Drive, Suva; f. 1989 by PAF and the Ports Workers' Union; services between Lautoka and Vanua Levu ports.

**Inter-Ports Shipping Corpn Ltd:** 25 Eliza St, Walu Bay; POB 152, Suva; tel. 313638; f. 1984; Man. Dir JUSTIN SMITH.

**Transcargo Express Fiji Ltd:** POB 936, Suva; f. 1974; Man. Dir LEO B. SMITH.

**Wong's Shipping Co Ltd:** Suite 647, Epworth House, Nina St, POB 1269, Suva; tel. 311867.

### CIVIL AVIATION

There is an international airport at Nadi (about 210 km from Suva), a domestic airport at Nausori (Suva) and 15 other airfields. Nadi is an important transit airport in the Pacific and in 1990 direct flights to Japan also began. In early 1998 the Government announced plans to establish a second international air service between Nadi and London (United Kingdom), via Singapore and Mumbai (Bombay, India); however these plans were suspended after India refused to grant landing rights in early 1999.

**Airports Fiji Ltd:** Nadi International Airport, Nadi; Chair. DINESH SHANKAR; CEO NORMAN YEE (acting).

**Air Fiji Ltd:** 219 Victoria Parade, POB 1259, Suva; tel. 314666; fax 300771; operates 46 scheduled services a week to 13 domestic destinations; daily service to Tonga commenced in 1999; charter operations, aerial photography and surveillance also conducted; partly owned by the Fijian Govt; Chair. DOUG HAZARD; CEO DAVID A. YOUNG.

**Air Pacific Ltd:** Air Pacific Centre, POB 9266, Nadi International Airport, Nadi; tel. 720777; fax 720512; e-mail www.airpacific.com; f. 1951 as Fiji Airways, name changed in 1971; domestic services from Nausori Airport (serving Suva) to Nadi and international services to Tonga, Solomon Islands, Vanuatu, Samoa, Japan, Australia, New Zealand, Canada and the USA; 78% govt-owned, 21% owned by Qantas (Australia); Chair. GERALD BARRACK; Man. Dir and CEO MICHAEL MCQUAY.

**Fijian Airways International:** POB 10138, Nadi International Airport, Nadi; tel. 724702; fax 724654; f. 1997; service to London via Singapore and Mumbai (India) planned (see above); Chair. NEIL UNDERHILL; CEO ALAN LINDREA.

**Hibiscus Air Ltd:** Nadi International Airport, Nadi; domestic airline operating charter and non-scheduled flights around Fiji.

**Sunflower Airlines Ltd:** POB 9452, Nadi International Airport, Nadi; tel. 723555; fax 720085; f. 1980; domestic airline; scheduled flights to 15 destinations, also charter services; Man. Dir DON IAN COLLINGWOOD.

**Vanua Air Charters:** Labasa; f. 1993; provides domestic charter and freight services; Proprs Ratu Sir KAMISESE MARA, CHARAN SINGH.

# Tourism

Scenery, climate, fishing and diving attract visitors to Fiji, where tourism is an important industry. The number of foreign tourist arrivals increased by 3.3% (compared with the previous year) in 1998, when 371,342 people visited the country (excluding cruise-ship passengers). Receipts from tourism, however, declined from some US $294.4m. in 1997 to US $284.1m.in 1998. Tourist arrivals from Japan and the Republic of Korea declined dramatically in 1998, owing to the Asian financial crisis. In that year some 27.1% of visitors came from Australia, 18.5% from Europe (with 10.6% from the United Kingdom alone), 19.1% from New Zealand, 13.0% from the USA and 9.6% from Japan. A total of 5,745 rooms in large hotels were available in 1998. Fijian hotels recorded an annual turnover of some $F267m. in 1998. The Tourism Council of the South Pacific (to become the South Pacific Tourism Organization) is based in Suva. In 1998 the Government announced its intention further to develop the tourist industry in Fiji through the establishment of the Fiji Tourism Development Plan: 1998–2005. In April 1999 construction began on a new luxury resort at Korotoga, situated half-way between Suva and Nadi.

**Fiji Hotel Association (FHA):** 42 Gorrie St, POB 13560, Suva; tel. 302980; fax 300331; e-mail fha@is.com.fj; represents 72 hotels; Pres. ROBERT WADE; Chief Exec. OLIVIA PARETI.

**Fiji Visitors' Bureau:** POB 92, Suva; tel. 302433; fax 300970; e-mail infodesk@fijifvb.gov.fj; internet www.bulafiji.com; f. 1923; Chair. WILLIAM G. J. CRUICKSHANK; Chief Exec. SITIVENI YAQONA; Dir of Tourism RAJESHWAR SINGH.

# FINLAND

## Introductory Survey

### Location, Climate, Language, Religion, Flag, Capital

The Republic of Finland lies in northern Europe, bordered to the far north by Norway and to the north-west by Sweden. Russia adjoins the whole of the eastern frontier. Finland's western and southern shores are washed by the Baltic Sea. The climate varies sharply, with warm summers and cold winters. The mean annual temperature is 5°C (41°F) in Helsinki and –0.4°C (31°F) in the far north. There are two official languages: 93.4% of the population speak Finnish and 5.9% speak Swedish. There is a small Lapp population in the north. Almost all of the inhabitants profess Christianity, and about 85.4% belong to the Evangelical Lutheran Church. The national flag (proportions 18 by 11) displays an azure blue cross (the upright to the left of centre) on a white background. The state flag has, at the centre of the cross, the national coat of arms (a yellow-edged red shield containing a golden lion and nine white roses). The capital is Helsinki.

### Recent History

Finland formed part of the Kingdom of Sweden until 1809, when it became an autonomous Grand Duchy under the Russian Empire. During the Russian revolution of 1917 the territory proclaimed its independence. Following a brief civil war, a democratic Constitution was adopted in 1919. The Soviet regime which came to power in Russia attempted to regain control of Finland but acknowledged the country's independence in 1920.

Demands by the USSR for military bases in Finland and for the cession of part of the Karelian isthmus, in south-eastern Finland, were rejected by the Finnish Government in November 1939. As a result, the USSR attacked Finland, and the two countries fought the 'Winter War', a fiercely contested conflict lasting 15 weeks, before Finnish forces were defeated. Following its surrender, Finland ceded an area of 41,880 sq km (16,170 sq miles) to the USSR in March 1940. In the hope of recovering the lost territory, Finland joined Nazi Germany in attacking the USSR in 1941. However, a separate armistice between Finland and the USSR was concluded in 1944.

In accordance with a peace treaty signed in February 1947, Finland agreed to the transfer of about 12% of its pre-war territory (including the Karelian isthmus and the Petsamo area on the Arctic coast) to the USSR, and to the payment of reparations, which totalled about US $570m. when completed in 1952. Meanwhile, in April 1948 Finland and the USSR signed the Finno-Soviet Treaty of Friendship, Co-operation and Mutual Assistance (the YYA treaty), which was extended for periods of 20 years in 1955, 1970 and again in 1983. A major requirement of the treaty was that Finland repel any attack made on the USSR by Germany, or its allies, through Finnish territory. (The treaty was replaced by a non-military agreement in 1992, see below.)

Since independence in 1917, the politics of Finland have been characterized by coalition governments (including numerous minority coalitions) and the development of consensus between parties. The Finnish Social Democratic Party (Suomen Sosialidemokraattinen Puolue, SDP) and the Finnish Centre Party (Suomen Keskusta—Kesk) have usually been the dominant participants in government. The conservative opposition gained significant support at a general election in March 1979, following several years of economic crises. A new centre-left coalition Government was formed in May, however, by Dr Mauno Koivisto, a Social Democratic economist and former Prime Minister. This four-party Government, comprising Kesk, the SDP, the Swedish People's Party (Svenska folkpartiet, SFP) and the Finnish People's Democratic League (Suomen Kansan Demokraattinen Liitto, SKDL—an electoral alliance, which included the communists), continued to pursue deflationary economic policies, although there were disagreements within the Council of State (Cabinet) in 1981, over social welfare policy and budgetary matters.

Dr Urho Kekkonen, President since 1956, resigned in October 1981. Dr Koivisto was elected President in January 1982. He was succeeded as head of the coalition by a former Prime Minister, Kalevi Sorsa, a Social Democrat. Towards the end of 1982 the SKDL refused to support austerity measures or an increase in defence spending. This led to the re-formation of the coalition in December, without the SKDL, until the general election of March 1983.

At this election the SDP won 57 of the 200 seats in the Eduskunta (Parliament), compared with 52 in the 1979 election; while the conservative opposition National Coalition Party (Kansallinen Kokoomus—Kok) lost three seats. In May Sorsa formed another centre-left coalition, comprising the SDP, the SFP, Kesk and the Finnish Rural Party (Suomen Maaseudun Puolue, SMP): the coalition parties held a total of 122 parliamentary seats.

At a general election held in March 1987, the combined non-socialist parties gained a majority in the Eduskunta for the first time since the election of 1945. Although the SDP remained the largest single party, losing one seat and retaining 56, the system of modified proportional representation enabled Kok to gain an additional nine seats, winning a total of 53, while increasing its share of the votes cast by only 1%. The communist parties (Suomen Kommunistinen Puolue, SKP, and SKP—Y) suffered a decline in popularity: although the SKDL retained all of its 16 seats, the number of seats held by the Democratic Alternative was reduced from 10 to four. President Koivisto eventually invited Harri Holkeri, a former Chairman of Kok, to form a coalition Government comprising Kok, the SDP, the SFP and the SMP, thus avoiding a polarization of the political parties within the Eduskunta. The four parties controlled 131 of the 200 seats. Holkeri became the first conservative Prime Minister since 1946, and Kesk joined the opposition for the first appreciable length of time since independence.

In February 1988 Koivisto retained office after the first presidential election by direct popular vote (in accordance with constitutional changes adopted in the previous year). He campaigned for a reduction in presidential power. He did not win the required absolute majority, however, and an electoral college was convened. Koivisto was re-elected after an endorsement by the Prime Minister, Holkeri, who was third in terms of direct votes (behind Paavo Väyrynen, the leader of Kesk).

At a general election held in March 1991, Kesk obtained 55 of the 200 seats in the Eduskunta, the SDP gained 48 seats, and Kok 40 seats. In April a coalition Government, comprising Kesk, Kok, the SFP and the Finnish Christian Union (Suomen Kristillinen Liitto, SKL), took office. The new coalition constituted the country's first wholly non-socialist Government for 25 years. The Chairman of Kesk, Esko Aho, became Prime Minister. In March 1993 President Koivisto announced that he would not present himself as a candidate for a third term in the forthcoming presidential election. In the first stage of the election, which took place in January 1994, the two most successful candidates were Martti Ahtisaari (the SDP candidate and a senior United Nations official), with 25.9% of the votes, and Elisabeth Rehn (the SFP candidate and Minister of Defence), with 22%. The Kesk candidate (Paavo Väyrynen) obtained 19.5% of the votes, and the Kok candidate 15.2%. Both of the leading candidates were firm supporters of Finland's application for membership of the European Union (EU), as the European Community (EC) had been restyled in late 1993. In accordance with constitutional changes adopted since the previous election (stipulating that, if no candidate gained more than 50% of the votes, the electorate should choose between the two candidates with the most votes), a second stage of the election took place on 6 February 1994. It was won by Ahtisaari (with 53.9% of the votes), who took office on 1 March.

In June 1994 Pertti Salolainen, the Deputy Prime Minister, resigned from his duties as Chairman of Kok, following criticism of his role in negotiations for Finland's planned entry into the EU. In the same month the Government survived a parliamentary vote of 'no confidence' on the issue of accession to the EU, and the SKL withdrew from the coalition since it opposed EU membership.

At a general election held on 19 March 1995, the SDP obtained 63 of the 200 seats in the Eduskunta, Kesk secured 44 seats, Kok 39 seats, and the Left Alliance (Vasemmistoliitto–Vänsterförbundet, formed in 1990 by a merger of the SKP, the SKP–Y and the SKDL) 22 seats. A new coalition Government was formed in April, comprising the SDP, Kok, the SFP, the Left Alliance and the Green League (Vihreä Liitto). Paavo Lipponen, the leader of the SDP, replaced Aho as Prime Minister, and Sauli Niinistö, the Chairman of Kok, was appointed Deputy Prime Minister. The first election of Finnish representatives to the parliament of the EU was held in October 1996. The SDP performed relatively poorly, securing 21.5% of the votes cast, compared with 28.3% at the 1995 election to the Finnish Parliament, while Kesk achieved 24.6% (19.9% in 1995) and Kok 20.2% (17.9% in 1995). The disappointing result for the SDP was attributed, in part, to the Government's decision, a week earlier, to commit Finland to entering the exchange rate mechanism (ERM, see Economic Affairs, below) of the EU's European Monetary System.

In August 1997 the Government announced further reductions in expenditure and increased taxes on fuels, following the disclosure that an unforeseen statistical discrepancy had resulted in a budget deficit for 1996 which was incompatible with the agreed economic criteria for European economic and monetary union. The draft budget for 1998, presented in September 1997, further reflected the Government's determination to reduce the fiscal deficit. A new junior finance minister with particular responsibility for taxation was appointed in October.

In January 1999 the Minister of Transport and Communications, Matti Aura, resigned from his post, following the revelation of a scandal surrounding the flotation of 20% of the state-owned Finnish telecommunications operator, Sonera Ltd; Aura also withdrew his candidacy for the forthcoming parliamentary elections, which were scheduled to be held in March.

Following a general election held on 21 March 1999, the SDP remained the largest party in the Eduskunta, gaining 51 of the 200 seats. Kesk won 48 seats and Kok 46 in an election that was characterized by the second lowest rate of voter participation—68%—since 1945. In April the five parties of the outgoing Government—the SDP, Kok, the SFP, the Left Alliance and the Green League—agreed to form a new coalition. The terms of the new coalition agreement stipulated that the SDP leader, Paavo Lipponen, should remain in office as Prime Minister, while the leader of Kok, Sauli Niinistö, was reappointed as Minister of Finance. The remaining portfolios of the Council of State were redistributed among the coalition partners. Another element of the coalition agreement was that there should be no increase (in real terms) in public expenditure during the term in office of the new legislature.

Presidential elections were held in January and February 2000, at which Ahtisaari did not seek re-election. In mid-January seven candidates contested the first round of the ballot, which was won by Tarja Halonen (the SDP candidate and Minister of Foreign Affairs), who received 40% of votes cast; the second largest share of the vote (34.4%) was obtained by Esko Aho (the Kesk candidate). As Halonen had failed to win 50% of the vote, a second round of voting was held on 6 February, contested by Halonen and Aho. This second stage of the election was won by Halonen (with 51.6% of the votes), who took office on 1 March. Following the conclusion of the elections, a minor reorganization of the Council of State was effected, in which Halonen was replaced as Minister of Foreign Affairs by Erkki Tuomioja, the former Minister of Trade and Industry.

A new Constitution entered into force on 1 March 2000, under the provisions of which the executive power of the President was significantly reduced while the real authority of the Parliament was increased, with the power of decision-making being divided more equally between the Parliament, the Council of State and the President. According to the 1919 Constitution, the President appointed the Prime Minister and the other ministers; however, under the new Constitution, the Parliament elects the Prime Minister (who is then officially appointed by the President) and the other government ministers are appointed by the President on the basis of nominations by the Prime Minister. In addition, according to new constitutional provisions, the President was to co-operate more closely with the Council of States with regard to issues of foreign policy.

In foreign affairs, Finland has traditionally maintained a neutral stance, although the pursuance of friendly relations with the USSR has generally been regarded as a priority. In October 1989 Mikhail Gorbachev became the first Soviet Head of State to visit Finland since 1975, and recognized Finland's neutral status. The 1948 Finno-Soviet Treaty of Friendship, Co-operation and Mutual Assistance, which bound Finland to a military defence alliance with the USSR and prevented the country from joining any international organization (including the EU) whose members posed a military threat to the USSR, was replaced in January 1992 by a 10-year agreement, signed by Finland and Russia, which involved no military commitment. The agreement was to be automatically renewed for five-year periods unless annulled by either signatory. The new treaty also included undertakings by the two countries not to use force against each other and to respect the inviolability of their common border and each other's territorial integrity. In 1998 a Russian diplomat to Finland, reportedly involved in an incident of espionage, left the country at the request of the Finnish authorities; a second Russian diplomat, also allegedly involved in the incident, left the country voluntarily, while an official from the Finnish Ministry of Foreign Affairs was suspended. During 1992 Finland established diplomatic relations with the former Soviet republics. A customs agreement was signed with Poland in November 1997, and in May 1998 President Aleksander Kwaśniewski of Poland made a three-day official visit to Finland.

Finland joined the United Nations and the Nordic Council (see p. 222) in 1955 but became a full member of EFTA (see p. 291) only in 1986. In 1989 Finland joined the Council of Europe (see p. 158). A free-trade agreement between Finland and the EC took effect in 1974. In March 1992 the Finnish Government formally applied to join the EC, despite opposition from farmers, who feared the impact of membership on Finland's strongly-protected agricultural sector. In a referendum on the question of Finland's accession to membership of the EU, which was held on 16 October 1994, 56.9% of the votes cast were in favour of membership, and in November the treaty of accession was ratified after protracted debate in Parliament. Opponents of EU membership highlighted the benefits of Finland's traditional policy of neutrality, particularly with regard to Russian national security considerations, and warned that the country would now be increasingly forced to identify with Western security policy. The Government declared, however, that Finland's neutral stance would not be compromised either by joining the EU or by its stated intention to participate in NATO's 'partnership for peace' programme, and announced that it would not seek full membership of NATO (see p. 226) or WEU (see p. 268). The decision not to apply for membership of NATO was reiterated in May 1995 by the new Prime Minister, Paavo Lipponen. Finland left EFTA and joined the EU, as scheduled, on 1 January 1995.

Finland has proved its commitment to European integration. For instance, the so-called 'rainbow coalition', formed in 1995 and renewed in 1999, ensured the country's adherence to the economic 'convergence' criteria for Stage III of economic and monetary union (EMU), which commenced on 1 January 1999. In June Finland assumed the presidency of the EU for the first time. During its six-month incumbency the Government had intended to promote economic and cultural links in the so-called 'Northern Dimension'—the Nordic countries, the Baltic states and Russia. In the event, this agenda was superseded by the conflict over the Serbian region of Kosovo and Metohija in Yugoslavia, which led to Western military intervention from March. Finland was deemed to have distinguished itself through its diplomacy, in particular the role of the Finnish President, which was important in securing an end to the hostilities in Yugoslavia.

## Government

Finland has a republican Constitution, under the provisions of which executive power is divided between the Parliament (Eduskunta), the Council of State (Cabinet) and the President. The unicameral Parliament has 200 members, elected by universal adult suffrage for four years on the basis of proportional representation. The President is elected for six years by direct popular vote. Legislative power is exercised by Parliament. The Parliament elects the Prime Minister, who is then appointed by the President. The other government ministers are appointed by the President on the basis of nominations by the Prime Minister. Finland has 12 provinces, each administered by an appointed Governor, and is divided into 452 municipalities. The province of Ahvenanmaa (the Åland Islands) has rights of legislation in internal affairs (see separate section at end of chapter).

**Defence**

In August 1999 the armed forces of Finland numbered 31,700 (of whom 23,100 were conscripts serving up to 12 months), comprising an army of 24,000 (19,000 conscripts), an air force of 2,700 (1,500 conscripts) and a navy of 5,000 (2,600 conscripts). There were also some 540,000 reserves and 3,400 frontier guards. The proposed defence budget for 2000 was 9,808m. markkaa (equivalent to 4.9% of total proposed budgetary expenditure).

**Economic Affairs**

In 1997, according to estimates by the World Bank, Finland's gross national product (GNP), measured at average 1995–97 prices, was US $127,398m., equivalent to US $24,790 per head. During 1990–97, it was estimated, GNP per head increased, in real terms, at an average annual rate of 0.9%. Over the same period, the population increased by an average of 0.4% per year. In 1998, according to preliminary World Bank data, Finland's GNP was about $124,300m. ($24,110 per head). The country's gross domestic product (GDP) increased, in real terms, by an average of 2.0% per year in 1990–98. Real GDP declined rapidly during 1991–93, but rose by 4.6% in 1994, by 5.0% in 1995, by 3.6% in 1996 and by 6.0% in 1997.

Agriculture (including hunting, forestry and fishing) contributed an estimated 3.7% of GDP in 1998 and employed 6.5% of the working population in that year. Forestry is the most important branch of the sector, with products of the wood and paper industries providing about 30% of export earnings in 1998. Animal husbandry is the predominant form of farming. The major crops are barley, sugar beet and oats. During 1980–90 agricultural GDP decreased, in real terms, by an average of 0.2% per year, while no significant movement was recorded during 1990–95, on the same terms. Agricultural production increased by 1.3% in 1996 and by 3.3% in 1997. In 1998, however, it declined by 0.2%.

Industry (including mining, manufacturing, construction and power), provided 32.3% of GDP in 1998 and employed 27.6% of the working population in the same year. Industrial GDP increased, in real terms, by an average of 3.3% per year during 1980–90. Industrial production (excluding construction) grew by an average of 2.7% per year during 1990–95, by 3.6% in 1996, by 9.4% in 1997 and by 7.6% in 1998.

Mining and quarrying contributed 0.3% of GDP in 1998 and employed 0.3% of the working population in the same year. The GDP of the mining sector increased, in real terms, at an average rate of 5.7% per year during 1980–90. Mining output increased by an average of 1.1% annually in 1990–95. It grew by 0.7% in 1996 and by 22.9% in 1997, but declined by 25% in 1998. Gold is the major mineral export, and zinc ore, copper ore and lead ore are also mined in small quantities.

Manufacturing provided 24.9% of GDP in 1998 and in the same year employed 20.1% of the working population. In 1996 the most important branches of manufacturing, measured by value added in production, were metal products and electrical and transport equipment (accounting for 39.5% of the total), and food and beverages (9.3%). The GDP of the manufacturing sector increased, in real terms, at an average rate of 3.4% per year during 1980–90. The sector's output increased by an average of 2.8% annually in 1990–95. It grew by 3.0% in 1996, by 10.1% in 1997 and by 8.7% in 1998.

Of total energy consumed in 1996, 28.6% was provided by petroleum, 16.6% by wood fuel, 16.4% by nuclear power, 14.6% by coal, 9.9% by natural gas and 7.0% by peat. At the end of 1996 there were four nuclear reactors in operation , and nuclear power provided 28.1% of total electricity generated. Imports of mineral fuels comprised 7.4% of the total cost of imports in 1998.

Services engaged 65.6% of the employed labour force in 1998 and provided 63.9% of GDP in that year. In real terms, the combined GDP of the service sectors increased at an average rate of 3.7% per year during 1980–90, but declined by 4.0% in 1991 and by 4.8% in 1992. Growth in the sector's GDP was recorded at 3.1% in 1994 and 4.5% in 1995.

In 1998 Finland recorded a visible trade surplus of US $12,304m., and there was a surplus of US $7,324m. on the current account of the balance of payments. In 1998 the principal sources of imports were Germany (15.1%), Sweden (11.6%) and the USA (8.2%). The principal customers for exports in the same year were Germany (11.7%), Sweden (9.5%) and the United Kingdom (9.2%). The EU accounted for some 49.2% of exports and 56.3% of imports in 1998. The principal exports in 1998 were machinery and transport equipment, basic manufactures (mainly paper, paperboard and manufactures) and crude materials (mainly wood and pulp). The principal imports were machinery and transport equipment, basic manufactures, chemicals and related products and miscellaneous manufactured articles.

Finland's overall budget deficit for 1998 was 7,042m. markkaa (equivalent to 1.0% of GDP). A deficit of 5,610m. markkaa was forecast for 1999, while another, of 6,335m. markkaa, was proposed for 2000. At the end of September 1997 Finland's gross public debt amounted to some 426,000m. markkaa. The average annual rate of inflation was 1.4% during 1991–98. The rate declined from 1.1% in 1994 and 1.0% in 1995 to only 0.6% in 1996. Consumer prices increased by an average of 1.2% in 1997, and 1.4% in 1998. Unemployment increased from an average of 13.1% of the labour force in 1992 to 17.9% in 1993 and to 18.4% in 1994; however, the rate of unemployment declined to an average of 15.4% in 1995, to 14.6% in 1996, to 12.6% in 1997 and to 11.4% in 1998.

Finland is a member of the Nordic Council (see p. 222) and the Organisation for Economic Co-operation and Development (p. 232). In January 1995 it left the European Free Trade Association and joined the European Union (EU, see p. 172).

In the early 1990s the Finnish economy was characterized by recession and crisis in the financial sector. In the mid-1990s, however, recovery commenced as industrial production and exports improved and Finland's membership of the EU helped stimulate investment in the economy. By late 1999 that recovery appeared to have been consolidated. The central bank reported a high degree of confidence regarding future economic developments at the level of both households and businesses. The bank forecast that total economic output would increase by an average of some 4% annually in 1999–2001. The prevailing low rate of inflation was expected to lead to growth in private consumption and private investment. However, inflation was forecast to rise gradually over the bank's reference period, to about 2%, owing to higher prices for imports and higher unit labour costs. The financial surplus of the private sector was expected to move into deficit as a result of the strength of both household and business investment. Conversely, the financial position of the general government was expected to strengthen, producing a substantial surplus. In the view of the bank, this sanguine prognosis for balanced growth was at risk from three eventualities. First, the recovery in world economic growth might cause the prices of imports to rise more quickly than anticipated, resulting in a larger-than-expected increase in the inflation differential between Finland and other parts of the euro zone. Balanced growth might also be prejudiced by excessive wage increases. Finally, the bank regarded as probable the continuation of prevailing pressures in the housing and credit markets, owing to low interest rates and strong income expectations. The IMF concurred in the view of the central bank that Finland's tax burden would have to be reduced substantially if further prospects for economic growth were to be realized. Taxation remains high when compared with the levels prevailing in similarly advanced economies, and its reduction is regarded as crucial to any attempt to reduce unemployment, which averaged 11.4% in 1998—about twice the long-term, pre-recession average, according to the IMF. At the same time as the reduction in taxation, there will have to be a corresponding adjustment in public expenditure in order to accommodate a lower tax ratio.

**Social Welfare**

Benefits are paid to compensate for loss of income owing to sickness, unemployment, maternity, old age, disability and death of a family's principal source of income. Child allowances and living allowances are also paid. Pension coverage consists of a basic pension scheme, covering all persons who are permanently resident in Finland, and earnings-related pension schemes. Some 90% of employees are members of unemployment insurance funds. All children under seven years of age are entitled to day care provided by local authorities. (In 1995 about one-half of children of that age were exercising their entitlement.) All children under the age of three are entitled to public day care. The public health services (including both primary and specialized health care) cover the whole population, and are financed mainly by the state and local authorities. The National Health Act of 1972 provided for the establishment of health centres in every municipality. In 1994 Finland had 46,400 hospital beds and there were 14,500 physicians working in the country. Of total budgetary expenditure by the central Government in 1999, 43,513m. markkaa (23.1%) was allocated to the Ministry of Social Welfare and Health. The percentage of total expenditure devoted to health and social welfare was forecast to decrease slightly, to 21.6%, in 2000.

### Education

Compulsory education was introduced in 1921. By the 1977/78 school year, the whole country had transferred to a new comprehensive education system. Tuition is free and the core curriculum is the same for all students. Compulsory attendance lasts for nine years, and is divided into a six-year lower stage, beginning at the age of seven, and a three-year upper stage (or lower secondary stage), beginning at the age of 13. After comprehensive school, the pupil may continue his or her studies, either at a general upper secondary school, or a vocational upper secondary school. Courses leading to basic vocational qualifications take between two and three years to complete. The matriculation examination taken at the end of three years of general upper secondary school gives eligibility for a university education as do tertiary vocational diplomas. In August 1998 there were 20 universities, 20 permanent and 33 temporary AMK institutions (polytechnics) and a number of vocational colleges providing higher education. Of total budgetary expenditure by the central Government in 1999, 26,640m. markkaa (14.1%) was allocated to the Ministry of Education. The percentage of total expenditure devoted to education was forecast to decrease slightly, to 14.0%, in 2000.

### Public Holidays

**2000:** 1 January (New Year's Day), 6 January (Epiphany), 21 April (Good Friday), 24 April (Easter Monday), 30 April–1 May (May Day), 1 June (Ascension Day), 11 June (Whitsun), 23–24 June (Midsummer Day), 4 November (All Saints' Day), 6 December (Independence Day), 24–26 December (Christmas).

**2001:** 1 January (New Year's Day), 6 January (Epiphany), 13 April (Good Friday), 16 April (Easter Monday), 30 April–1 May (May Day), 24 May (Ascension Day), 2 June (Whitsun), 25–26 June (Midsummer Day), 1 November (All Saints' Day), 6 December (Independence Day), 24–26 December (Christmas).

### Weights and Measures

The metric system is in force.

# Statistical Survey

Source (unless otherwise specified): Statistics Finland, 00022 Helsinki; tel. (9) 17342220; fax (9) 17342279.

Note: Figures in this Survey include data for the autonomous Åland Islands.

## Area and Population

**AREA, POPULATION AND DENSITY**

| | |
|---|---|
| Area (sq km) | |
| Land | 304,529 |
| Inland water | 33,615 |
| Total | 338,145* |
| Population (census results) | |
| 31 December 1990 | 4,998,478 |
| 31 December 1995 | |
| Males | 2,491,701 |
| Females | 2,625,125 |
| Total | 5,116,826 |
| Population (official estimates at 31 December) | |
| 1996 | 5,132,320 |
| 1997 | 5,147,349 |
| 1998 | 5,159,646 |
| Density (per sq km) at 31 December 1998† | 16.9 |

* 130,559 sq miles.

† Excluding inland waters.

**REGIONS** (estimated population at 31 December 1998)*

| | Land Area (sq km)† | Population | Density (per sq km) |
|---|---|---|---|
| Uusimaa (Nyland) | 6,366 | 1,274,475 | 200.2 |
| Itä-Uusimaa (Östra Nyland) | 2,747 | 88,159 | 32.1 |
| Varsinais-Suomi (Egentliga Finland) | 10,623 | 443,050 | 41.7 |
| Satakunta | 8,290 | 240,821 | 29.0 |
| Kanta-Häme (Egentliga Tavastland) | 5,204 | 164,914 | 31.7 |
| Pirkanmaa (Birkaland) | 12,605 | 444,505 | 35.3 |
| Päijät-Häme (Päijänne-Tavastland) | 5,133 | 197,443 | 38.5 |
| Kymenlaakso (Kymmenedalen) | 5,106 | 189,802 | 37.2 |
| Etelä-Karjala (Södra Karelen) | 5,674 | 138,104 | 24.3 |
| Etelä-Savo (Södra Savolax) | 14,436 | 170,348 | 11.8 |
| Pohjois-Savo (Norra Savolax) | 16,510 | 255,234 | 15.5 |
| Pohjois-Karjala (Norra Karelen) | 17,782 | 173,664 | 9.8 |
| Keski-Suomi (Mellersta Finland) | 16,248 | 260,135 | 16.0 |
| Etelä-Pohjanmaa (Södra Österbotten) | 13,458 | 197,703 | 14.7 |
| Pohjanmaa (Österbotten) | 7,675 | 174,099 | 22.7 |
| Keski-Pohjanmaa (Mellersta Österbotten) | 5,286 | 72,094 | 13.6 |
| Pohjois-Pohjanmaa (Norra Österbotten) | 35,291 | 360,753 | 10.2 |
| Kainuu (Kajanaland) | 21,567 | 92,071 | 4.3 |
| Lappi (Lappland) | 93,003 | 196,647 | 2.1 |
| Ahvenanmaa (Åland) | 1,527 | 25,625 | 16.8 |
| **Total** | 304,529 | 5,159,646 | 16.9 |

* A revised regional division of Finland was introduced on 1 September 1997.

† Excluding inland waters, totalling 33,615 sq km.

**PRINCIPAL TOWNS** (estimated population at 31 December 1998)

| | |
|---|---|
| Helsinki (Helsingfors) (capital) | 546,317 |
| Espoo (Esbo) | 204,962 |
| Tampere (Tammerfors) | 191,254 |
| Vantaa (Vanda) | 173,860 |
| Turku (Åbo) | 170,931 |
| Oulu (Uleåborg) | 115,493 |
| Lahti | 96,227 |
| Kuopio | 86,203 |
| Jyväskylä | 76,948 |
| Pori (Björneborg) | 76,375 |
| Lappeenranta (Villmanstrand) | 57,374 |
| Vaasa (Vasa) | 56,587 |
| Kotka | 55,551 |
| Joensuu | 51,113 |
| Hämeenlinna (Tavastehus) | 45,555 |

**BIRTHS, MARRIAGES AND DEATHS**

| | Registered live births* | | Registered marriages† | | Registered deaths* | |
|---|---|---|---|---|---|---|
| | Number | Rate (per 1,000) | Number | Rate (per 1,000) | Number | Rate (per 1,000) |
| 1990 | 65,549 | 13.1 | 24,997 | 5.0 | 50,058 | 10.0 |
| 1991 | 65,395 | 13.0 | 24,732 | 5.0 | 49,294 | 9.8 |
| 1992 | 66,877 | 13.2 | 23,093 | 4.6 | 49,523 | 9.8 |
| 1993 | 64,826 | 12.8 | 24,660 | 4.9 | 50,488 | 10.1 |
| 1994 | 65,231 | 12.8 | 24,898 | 4.9 | 48,000 | 9.4 |
| 1995 | 63,067 | 12.3 | 23,737 | 4.6 | 49,280 | 9.6 |
| 1996 | 60,723 | 11.8 | 24,464 | 4.8 | 49,167 | 9.6 |
| 1997 | 59,329 | 11.5 | 23,444 | 4.6 | 49,108 | 9.6 |
| 1998 | 57,108 | 11.1 | 24,023 | 4.7 | 49,262 | 9.6 |

* Including Finnish nationals temporarily outside the country.

† Data relate only to marriages in which the bride was domiciled in Finland.

**Expectation of life** (years at birth, 1996): males 73.0; females 80.5.

**ECONOMICALLY ACTIVE POPULATION***
(annual averages, '000 persons aged 15 to 74 years)

| | 1996 | 1997 | 1998 |
|---|---|---|---|
| Agriculture, forestry and fishing | 159 | 153 | 144 |
| Mining and quarrying | 4 | 6 | 6 |
| Manufacturing | 433 | 436 | 447 |
| Electricity, gas and water | 23 | 22 | 22 |
| Construction | 118 | 130 | 139 |
| Trade, restaurants and hotels | 316 | 329 | 339 |
| Transport, storage and communications | 160 | 164 | 170 |
| Finance, insurance, real estate and business services | 241 | 240 | 249 |
| Community, social and personal services | 667 | 684 | 700 |
| Activities not adequately defined | 6 | 5 | 6 |
| **Total employed** | 2,127 | 2,169 | 2,222 |
| Unemployed | 363 | 314 | 285 |
| **Total labour force** | 2,490 | 2,484 | 2,507 |

* Excluding persons on compulsory military service (31,000 in 1996, 25,000 in 1997, 25,000 in 1998).

# Agriculture

**PRINCIPAL CROPS**
('000 metric tons; farms with arable land of 1 hectare or more)

| | 1996 | 1997 | 1998 |
|---|---|---|---|
| Wheat | 459 | 464 | 397 |
| Barley | 1,860 | 2,004 | 1,316 |
| Rye | 87 | 47 | 49 |
| Oats | 1,261 | 1,243 | 975 |
| Mixed grain | 42 | 49 | 35 |
| Potatoes | 766 | 754 | 591 |
| Rapeseed | 89 | 93 | 64 |
| Sugar beet | 897 | 1,360 | 892 |

**LIVESTOCK**
('000 head at 1 May; farms with arable land of 1 hectare or more)

| | 1996 | 1997 | 1998 |
|---|---|---|---|
| Horses* | 52.0 | 53.1 | 55.2 |
| Cattle | 1,146.0 | 1,142.4 | 1,117.1 |
| Sheep | 150.0 | 150.1 | 128.3 |
| Reindeer | 213.0 | 203.0 | 196.0 |
| Pigs† | 1,395.0 | 1,467.0 | 1,401.0 |
| Poultry | 5,429.0 | 5,439.3 | 4,986.5 |
| Beehives‡ | 42.0 | 40.0 | 42.0 |

* Including horses not on farms.

† Including piggeries of dairies. ‡ '000 hives.

**LIVESTOCK PRODUCTS** ('000 metric tons)

| | 1996 | 1997 | 1998 |
|---|---|---|---|
| Beef | 96.4 | 99.2 | 93.5 |
| Veal | 0.2 | 0.4 | 0.3 |
| Pig meat | 171.8 | 179.7 | 184.5 |
| Poultry meat | 49.4 | 52.7 | 61.1 |
| Cows' milk* | 2,261.0 | 2,301.0 | 2,293.7 |
| Butter† | 54.2 | 56.5 | 57.3 |
| Cheese‡ | 89.7 | 82.9 | 87.7 |
| Hen eggs | 70.8 | 66.7 | 63.9 |

* Million litres.

† Including amount of butter in vegetable oil mixture.

‡ Excluding curd.

# Forestry

**ROUNDWOOD REMOVALS** ('000 cu m, excl. bark)

| | 1995 | 1996 | 1997 |
|---|---|---|---|
| Sawlogs, veneer logs and logs for sleepers | 21,697 | 20,267 | 23,332 |
| Pulpwood | 22,968 | 20,968 | 22,312 |
| Other industrial wood | 325 | 325 | 325 |
| Fuel wood | 4,095 | 4,094 | 4,094 |
| **Total** | 49,085 | 45,654 | 50,063 |

Source: FAO, *Yearbook of Forest Products*.

**SAWNWOOD PRODUCTION** ('000 cu m, incl. railway sleepers)

| | 1995 | 1996 | 1997 |
|---|---|---|---|
| Coniferous (softwood) | 9,400 | 9,300 | 10,600 |
| Broadleaved (hardwood) | 80 | 70 | 70* |
| **Total** | 9,480 | 9,370 | 10,670 |

* FAO estimate.

Source: FAO, *Yearbook of Forest Products*.

# Fishing*

('000 metric tons, live weight)

| | 1996 | 1997 | 1998 |
|---|---|---|---|
| Baltic herring | 93.3 | 90.3 | 85.5 |
| Sprat | 14.3 | 19.9 | 27.0 |
| Cod | 3.1 | 1.5 | 1.0 |
| **Total catch** (incl. others) | 121.2 | 122.2 | 118.8 |
| Freshwater | 4.6 | 4.6 | n.a. |
| Marine | 116.6 | 117.6 | 118.8 |

* Figures refer to commercial fisheries only. Including recreational fishing, the total catch ('000 metric tons) was: 179.1 in 1996; 180.1 in 1997 (Source: FAO, *Yearbook of Fishery Statistics*).

# Mining

('000 metric tons, unless otherwise indicated)

| | 1994 | 1995 | 1996† |
|---|---|---|---|
| Copper ore* | 13.2 | 9.8 | 9.2 |
| Zinc ore* | 3.7 | 16.4 | 26.3 |
| Silver (metric tons) | 0.2 | — | — |
| Gold (kilograms) | 963 | 1,459 | 1,670 |

* Figures refer to metal content.
† Figures are provisional.

# Industry

**SELECTED PRODUCTS** ('000 metric tons, unless otherwise indicated)

| | 1995 | 1996 | 1997* |
|---|---|---|---|
| Cellulose | 5,678 | 5,818 | 6,613 |
| Machine pulp (for sale) | 120 | 116† | n.a. |
| Newsprint | 1,352 | 1,603 | 1,479 |
| Other paper, boards and cardboards | 8,021 | 7,608 | 10,713 |
| Plywoods and veneers ('000 cubic metres) | 720 | 850 | 707 |
| Cement | 907 | 975 | 1,099 |
| Pig iron and ferro-alloys | 2,242 | 2,457 | 2,786 |
| Electricity (million kWh) | 60,541 | 66,357 | 65,973 |
| Cotton yarn (metric tons) | 2,794 | 2,064 | n.a. |
| Cotton fabrics (metric tons) | 2,691 | 3,099 | n.a. |
| Sugar | 259 | 254 | 161 |
| Rolled steel products (metric tons) | 3,244 | 3,272 | 3,351 |
| Copper cathodes (metric tons) | 73,665 | 110,715 | 116,328 |
| Cigarettes (million) | 6,542 | 5,915 | n.a. |

* Preliminary data.
† Net.

# Finance

**CURRENCY AND EXCHANGE RATES**

**Monetary Units**

100 penniä (singular: penni) = 1 markka (Finnmark).

**Sterling, Dollar and Euro Equivalents** (30 September 1999)

£1 sterling = 9.1792 markkaa;
US $1 = 5.5750 markkaa;
€1 = 5.9457 markkaa;
100 markkaa = £10.89 = $17.94 = €16.82.

**Average Exchange Rate** (markkaa per US $)

1996 4.5936
1997 5.1914
1998 5.3441

**BUDGET** (million markkaa)*

| Revenue | 1998 | 1999† | 2000‡ |
|---|---|---|---|
| Taxes and other levies | 148,000 | 153,559 | 165,831 |
| on income and property | 56,631 | 57,840 | 66,091 |
| on turnover | 49,660 | 52,500 | 55,280 |
| Excise duties | 26,233 | 27,650 | 28,190 |
| Miscellaneous revenues | 39,250 | 29,329 | 26,731 |
| **Sub-total** | 187,250 | 182,888 | 192,562 |
| Interest on investments and profits received | 5,315 | 3,419 | 4,235 |
| Loans receivable | 776 | 2,192 | 2,106 |
| Borrowing (net) | 6,334 | — | — |
| **Total** | 199,675 | 188,499 | 198,903 |

| Expenditure | 1998 | 1999† | 2000‡ |
|---|---|---|---|
| President of the Republic | 49 | 46 | 40 |
| Parliament | 304 | 330 | 355 |
| Council of State | 196 | 211 | 220 |
| Ministry of Foreign Affairs | 3,347 | 3,536 | 3,635 |
| Ministry of Justice | 2,894 | 3,129 | 3,137 |
| Ministry of the Interior | 6,518 | 6,243 | 7,042 |
| Ministry of Defence | 10,473 | 8,988 | 9,808 |
| Ministry of Finance | 28,468 | 28,063 | 29,672 |
| Ministry of Education | 26,581 | 26,640 | 27,787 |
| Ministry of Agriculture and Forestry | 12,657 | 12,022 | 13,213 |
| Ministry of Transport and Communications | 7,723 | 7,287 | 7,261 |
| Ministry of Trade and Commerce | 5,036 | 4,536 | 4,783 |
| Ministry of Social Welfare and Health | 42,998 | 43,513 | 42,992 |
| Ministry of Labour | 13,557 | 11,539 | 11,403 |
| Ministry of the Environment | 3,753 | 3,554 | 3,747 |
| Public debt | 29,738 | 28,862 | 33,800 |
| **Total** | 194,292 | 188,498 | 198,897 |

* Figures refer to the General Budget only, excluding the operations of the Social Insurance Institution and of other social security funds with their own budgets.
† Projections.
‡ Proposals.

**INTERNATIONAL RESERVES** (US $ million at 31 December)

| | 1996 | 1997 | 1998 |
|---|---|---|---|
| Gold* | 375.1 | 321.4 | 427.8 |
| IMF special drawing rights | 289.9 | 326.1 | 348.5 |
| Reserve position in IMF | 421.1 | 558.8 | 837.8 |
| Foreign exchange | 6,205.3 | 7,531.7 | 8,508.2 |
| **Total** | 7,291.4 | 8,738.0 | 10,122.3 |

* Valued at market-related prices.

Source: IMF, *International Financial Statistics.*

**MONEY SUPPLY** (million markkaa at 31 December)

| | 1996 | 1997 | 1998 |
|---|---|---|---|
| Currency outside banks | 13,645 | 14,517 | 14,803 |
| Demand deposits at deposit money banks | 191,188 | 201,557 | 211,632 |
| **Total money** | 204,833 | 216,074 | 226,435 |

Source: IMF, *International Financial Statistics.*

**COST OF LIVING** (Consumer Price Index; base: 1995 = 100)

| | 1996 | 1997 | 1998 |
|---|---|---|---|
| Food | 98.2 | 99.6 | 101.3 |
| Beverages and tobacco | 102.6 | 104.6 | 106.0 |
| Clothing and footwear | 100.5 | 99.9 | 98.5 |
| Rent, heating and lighting | 100.3 | 102.5 | 104.8 |
| Furniture, household equipment | 100.7 | 101.0 | 101.2 |
| **All items** | 100.6 | 101.8 | 103.2 |

**NATIONAL ACCOUNTS** (million markkaa at current prices)

**National Income and Product**

| | 1996 | 1997 | 1998* |
|---|---|---|---|
| Compensation of employees | 293,581 | 308,407 | 331,516 |
| Operating surplus | 126,246 | 141,993 | 159,400 |
| **Domestic factor incomes** | 419,827 | 450,400 | 490,916 |
| Consumption of fixed capital | 87,632 | 106,286 | 110,936 |
| **Gross domestic product at factor cost** | 507,459 | 556,686 | 601,852 |
| Indirect taxes | 83,211 | 94,669 | 100,838 |
| *Less* Subsidies | 16,643 | 15,823 | 15,948 |
| **GDP in purchasers' values** | 574,027 | 635,532 | 686,742 |
| Factor income received from abroad | 15,895 | −12,700 | −15,409 |
| *Less* Factor income paid abroad | 35,203 | | |
| Indirect taxes from the rest of the world (net) | −984 | — | — |
| **Gross national product** | 553,735 | 622,832 | 671,333 |
| *Less* Consumption of fixed capital | 87,632 | 106,286 | 110,936 |
| **National income in market prices** | 466,103 | 516,546 | 560,397 |

* Provisional figures.

**Expenditure on the Gross Domestic Product**

| | 1996 | 1997 | 1998* |
|---|---|---|---|
| Government final consumption expenditure | 126,457 | 142,641 | 149,201 |
| Private final consumption expenditure | 313,690 | 323,564 | 345,644 |
| Increase in stocks | −2,169 | 2,781 | 7,723 |
| Gross fixed capital formation | 92,035 | 114,300 | 127,446 |
| Statistical discrepancy | −3,360 | 398 | 4,459 |
| **Total domestic expenditure** | 526,563 | 583,684 | 625,555 |
| Exports of goods and services | 218,929 | 248,306 | 267,851 |
| *Less* Imports of goods and services | 171,555 | 196,458 | 206,664 |
| **GDP in purchasers' values** | 574,027 | 635,532 | 686,742 |

* Provisional figures.

**Gross Domestic Product by Economic Activity**

| | 1996 | 1997 | 1998 |
|---|---|---|---|
| Agriculture, hunting, forestry and fishing | 20,207 | 23,480 | 22,732 |
| Mining and quarrying | 1,857 | 1,717 | 1,585 |
| Manufacturing | 126,264 | 136,736 | 151,501 |
| Electricity, gas and water | 13,641 | 13,291 | 13,885 |
| Construction | 29,236 | 25,723 | 29,834 |
| Trade, restaurants and hotels | 55,474 | 68,157 | 72,341 |
| Transport, storage and communication | 44,567 | 55,311 | 60,492 |
| Finance, insurance and business services | 19,619 | 51,092 | 58,952 |
| Owner-occupied dwellings | 46,377 | 51,353 | 54,686 |
| Public administration and welfare | 96,170 | 103,296 | 107,456 |
| Other community, social and personal services | 58,546 | 32,566 | 34,988 |
| **Sub-total** | 511,958 | 562,722 | 608,452 |
| *Less* Imputed bank service charge | 13,347 | 14,858 | 15,965 |
| **GDP in basic values** | 498,611 | 547,864 | 592,487 |
| Commodity taxes | 81,164 | 93,359 | 99,354 |
| *Less* Commodity subsidies | 5,748 | 5,691 | 5,099 |
| **GDP in purchasers' values** | 574,027 | 635,532 | 686,742 |

**BALANCE OF PAYMENTS** (US $ million)

| | 1996 | 1997 | 1998 |
|---|---|---|---|
| Exports of goods f.o.b. | 40,623 | 41,060 | 43,093 |
| Imports of goods f.o.b. | −29,406 | −29,599 | −30,790 |
| **Trade balance** | 11,216 | 11,460 | 12,304 |
| Exports of services | 7,634 | 7,168 | 6,828 |
| Imports of services | −8,887 | −8,377 | −8,154 |
| **Balance on goods and services** | 9,963 | 10,252 | 10,977 |
| Other income received | 2,783 | 3,944 | 4,603 |
| Other income paid | −6,645 | −6,680 | −7,190 |
| **Balance on goods, services and income** | 6,101 | 7,516 | 8,391 |
| Current transfers received | 1,144 | 1,210 | 1,063 |
| Current transfers paid | −2,242 | −2,062 | −2,130 |
| **Current balance** | 5,004 | 6,664 | 7,324 |
| Capital account (net) | 56 | 247 | 167 |
| Direct investment abroad | −3,583 | −5,260 | −19,880 |
| Direct investment from abroad | 1,118 | 2,129 | 10,949 |
| Portfolio investment assets | −4,147 | −4,666 | −3,688 |
| Portfolio investment liabilities | 1,479 | 3,957 | 4,864 |
| Other investment assets | −4,683 | −2,563 | −127 |
| Other investment liabilities | 2,099 | 3,301 | 4,546 |
| Net errors and omissions | −377 | −1,504 | −3,859 |
| **Overall balance** | −3,036 | 2,304 | 296 |

Source: IMF, *International Financial Statistics.*

# External Trade

**PRINCIPAL COMMODITIES** (distribution by SITC, million markkaa)

| Imports c.i.f. | 1996 | 1997 | 1998 |
|---|---|---|---|
| **Food and live animals** | 7,855.1 | 9,008.7 | 9,242.9 |
| **Crude materials (inedible) except fuels** | 9,544.4 | 10,935.8 | 11,142.7 |
| Metalliferous ores and metal scrap | — | 4,948.7 | 4,613.8 |
| **Mineral fuels, lubricants, etc.** | 14,800.0 | 15,080.2 | 12,812.8 |
| Petroleum, petroleum products, etc. | 10,378.1 | 10,006.6 | 8,073.7 |
| Crude petroleum oils, etc. | 7,155.3 | 6,971.5 | 5,860.2 |
| Refined petroleum products | 3,070.1 | 2,892.0 | 2,098.8 |
| **Chemicals and related products** | 16,060.5 | 18,658.6 | 19,248.6 |
| Chemical elements and compounds | 2,412.9 | 3,181.6 | 2,780.2 |
| Plastic materials, etc. | 2,682.3 | 3,242.2 | 3,411.1 |
| **Basic manufactures** | 18,798.2 | 21,551.7 | 22,479.4 |
| Textile yarn, fabrics, etc. | 2,772.6 | 3,016.4 | 3,215.8 |
| Iron and steel | 5,139.0 | 5,569.9 | 5,645.3 |
| **Machinery and transport equipment** | 55,223.1 | 62,418.2 | 74,971.1 |
| Non-electric machinery | 22,880.2 | 25,075.8 | 29,573.9 |
| Electrical machinery, apparatus, etc. | 18,918.1 | 22,701.3 | 26,946.5 |
| Transport equipment | 13,424.9 | 14,641.1 | 18,450.7 |
| Road vehicles and parts* | 9,785.8 | 11,382.6 | 14,019.2 |
| Passenger motor cars (excl. buses) | 4,912.0 | 5,506.2 | 7,185.2 |
| **Miscellaneous manufactured articles** | 15,156.0 | 17,595.4 | 18,156.9 |
| Scientific instruments, watches, etc. | 3,594.1 | 3,995.4 | 4,195.7 |
| **Total** (incl. others) | 140,996.3 | 159,191.7 | 172,314.7 |

* Excluding tyres, engines and electrical parts.

| Exports f.o.b. | 1996 | 1997 | 1998 |
|---|---|---|---|
| **Food and live animals** | 4,436.1 | 5,175.4 | 4,452.5 |
| **Crude materials (inedible) except fuels** | 14,174.6 | 17,044.6 | 16,031.1 |
| Wood, lumber and cork | 7,176.8 | 9,107.9 | 8,974.8 |
| Shaped or simply worked wood | 6,768.2 | 8,649.7 | 8,516.5 |
| Sawn coniferous lumber | 6,495.2 | 8,361.5 | 8,238.2 |
| Pulp and waste paper | 3,479.3 | 4,202.9 | 3,822.8 |
| Chemical wood pulp | 3,306.4 | 3,971.5 | 3,580.2 |

| Exports f.o.b. — *continued* | 1996 | 1997 | 1998 |
|---|---|---|---|
| **Mineral fuels, lubricants, etc.** | 5,702.3 | 4,728.7 | 4,292.0 |
| Petroleum, petroleum products, etc. | 4,794.6 | 4,415.0 | 4,136.4 |
| Refined petroleum products | 4,724.7 | 4,332.3 | 4,096.3 |
| **Chemicals and related products** | 11,472.4 | 13,615.3 | 14,243.7 |
| **Basic manufactures** | 65,537.1 | 73,371.2 | 78,684.2 |
| Wood and cork manufactures (excl. furniture) | 4,092.5 | 4,752.2 | 4,850.4 |
| Paper, paperboard and manufactures | 39,164.4 | 43,325.1 | 48,312.4 |
| Paper and paperboard | 53,211.8 | 38,919.7 | 44,023.6 |
| Newsprint paper | 3,371.4 | 3,272.1 | 3,404.5 |
| Other printing and writing paper in bulk | 20,580.7 | 23,335.4 | 27,847.4 |
| Kraft paper and paperboard | 2,487.9 | 2,613.0 | 2,583.4 |
| Iron and steel | 9,467.8 | 9,669.3 | 10,402.8 |
| Non-ferrous metals | 4,683.2 | 6,064.8 | 5,294.2 |
| **Machinery and transport equipment** | 71,187.0 | 82,444.0 | 95,300.9 |
| Non-electric machinery | 29,819.6 | 34,506.8 | 35,606.0 |
| Electrical machinery, apparatus, etc. | 27,985.5 | 35,872.7 | 46,327.1 |
| Transport equipment | 13,380.3 | 12,064.4 | 13,367.8 |
| Ships and boats | 7,548.4 | 4,735.6 | 5,578.2 |
| **Miscellaneous manufactured articles** | 11,096.3 | 12,981.0 | 13,677.2 |
| **Total** (incl. others) | 185,797.7 | 211,694.7 | 229,233.0 |

**PRINCIPAL TRADING PARTNERS** (million markkaa)*

| Imports c.i.f. | 1996 | 1997 | 1998 |
|---|---|---|---|
| Austria | 1,556.1 | 1,702.4 | 1,893.7 |
| Belgium/Luxembourg | 4,136.0 | 4,408.4 | 4,543.6 |
| China, People's Republic | 2,072.4 | 2,844.4 | 3,167.4 |
| Denmark | 4,949.9 | 5,458.5 | 6,164.2 |
| Estonia | 1,658.4 | 2,187.8 | 3,044.8 |
| France | 6,348.5 | 7,734.0 | 8,412.6 |
| Germany | 21,269.0 | 23,147.2 | 26,096.4 |
| Italy | 5,732.3 | 6,460.8 | 7,147.2 |
| Japan | 7,254.9 | 8,586.3 | 9,763.2 |
| Netherlands | 4,999.4 | 6,437.3 | 7,284.1 |
| Norway | 5,889.3 | 5,898.5 | 6,067.2 |
| Poland | 1,300.5 | 1,794.2 | 1,523.4 |
| Russia | 10,231.5 | 12,521.7 | 11,341.7 |
| Spain | 1,958.0 | 2,274.8 | 3,065.5 |
| Sweden | 16,749.4 | 19,088.3 | 20,043.5 |
| Switzerland | 2,428.6 | 2,668.5 | 2,686.0 |
| United Kingdom | 12,437.1 | 12,163.7 | 12,428.1 |
| USA | 10,294.0 | 11,719.1 | 14,203.2 |
| **Total** (incl. others) | 140,996.3 | 159,191.7 | 172,314.7 |

| Exports f.o.b. | 1996 | 1997 | 1998 |
|---|---|---|---|
| Belgium/Luxembourg | 4,691.9 | 4,889.7 | 5,748.8 |
| China, People's Republic | — | 3,814.4 | 6,764.2 |
| Denmark | 5,679.3 | 6,493.8 | 6,429.9 |
| Estonia | 5,072.6 | 6,719.5 | 7,573.8 |
| France | 7,855.9 | 8,862.3 | 11,704.5 |
| Germany | 22,451.2 | 23,225.9 | 26,830.3 |
| Italy | 4,767.8 | 6,289.5 | 8,795.2 |
| Netherlands | 7,372.3 | 8,675.4 | 10,400.9 |
| Norway | 5,283.2 | 6,345.3 | 7,541.6 |
| Russia | 11,306.6 | 15,462.5 | 13,796.7 |
| Spain | 3,978.1 | 4,594.4 | 5,786.5 |
| Sweden | 19,798.6 | 20,830.2 | 21,674.2 |
| United Kingdom | 18,980.1 | 21,107.8 | 21,194.4 |
| USA | 14,696.3 | 14,732.7 | 16,845.6 |
| **Total** (incl. others) | 185,797.7 | 211,694.7 | 229,223.0 |

* Imports by country of production; exports by country of consumption.

# Transport

**RAILWAYS** (traffic)

| | 1996 | 1997 | 1998 |
|---|---|---|---|
| Passenger-km (million) | 3,254 | 3,376 | 3,377 |
| Freight ton-km (million) | 8,806 | 9,856 | 9,885 |

**ROAD TRAFFIC** (registered motor vehicles at 31 December)

| | 1996 | 1997 | 1998 |
|---|---|---|---|
| Passenger cars | 1,942,752 | 1,948,126 | 2,021,116 |
| Buses and coaches | 8,233 | 8,450 | 9,040 |
| Lorries and vans | 258,697 | 266,944 | 280,610 |

**SHIPPING**

**Merchant Fleet** (registered at 31 December)

| | 1996 | 1997 | 1998 |
|---|---|---|---|
| Number of vessels | 274 | 277 | 284 |
| Total displacement ('000 grt) | 1,511 | 1,559 | 1,629 |

Source: Lloyd's Register of Shipping, *World Fleet Statistics*.

**International Sea-borne Freight Traffic**

| | 1996 | 1997 | 1998 |
|---|---|---|---|
| Number of vessels entered | 22,891 | 25,203 | 26,255 |
| Goods ('000 metric tons): | | | |
| Loaded | 33,345 | 36,164 | 37,524 |
| Unloaded | 36,944 | 39,018 | 39,070 |

**CANAL TRAFFIC**

| | 1996 | 1997 | 1998 |
|---|---|---|---|
| Vessels in transit | 69,318 | 74,963 | 49,319 |
| Timber rafts in transit | 1,424 | 2,422 | 1,181 |
| Goods carried ('000 metric tons) | 4,444 | 5,471 | 4,493 |
| Passengers carried ('000) | 329 | 356 | n.a. |

**CIVIL AVIATION** (traffic on scheduled services, '000)

| | 1996 | 1997 | 1998 |
|---|---|---|---|
| Kilometres flown | 88,000 | 105,000 | 108,000 |
| Passenger-kilometres | 10,710,000 | 11,924,000 | 13,096,000 |
| Cargo ton-kilometres | 253,314 | 312,596 | 295,654 |

# Tourism

**NUMBER OF NIGHTS AT ACCOMMODATION FACILITIES**

| Country of Domicile | 1996 | 1997 | 1998 |
|---|---|---|---|
| France | 112,999 | 118,523 | 122,914 |
| Germany | 511,510 | 453,953 | 458,235 |
| Italy | 100,560 | 103,971 | 119,736 |
| Japan | 119,478 | 132,385 | 120,541 |
| Netherlands | 109,279 | 122,308 | 142,637 |
| Norway | 138,364 | 164,280 | 168,803 |
| Russia | 454,891 | 549,104 | 540,337 |
| Sweden | 540,869 | 626,451 | 570,640 |
| United Kingdom | 223,860 | 248,470 | 290,572 |
| USA | 187,032 | 198,754 | 201,037 |
| **Total** (incl. others) | 3,284,644 | 3,645,854 | 3,700,396 |

## Communications Media

| | 1996 | 1997 | 1998 |
|---|---|---|---|
| Telephone lines ('000) | 2,842 | 2,861 | 2,855 |
| Mobile cellular telephones ('000 subscribers) | 1,502 | 2,163 | 2,947 |
| Television receivers ('000 in use)* | 3,100 | n.a. | n.a. |
| Radio receivers ('000 in use)* | 7,100 | n.a. | n.a. |
| Book production: titles | 13,104 | 12,717 | 12,887 |
| Newspapers and periodicals | 5,107 | 5,238 | 5,298 |

* Source: UNESCO, *Statistical Yearbook*.

## Education

(1997)

| | Institutions | Teachers | Students |
|---|---|---|---|
| Comprehensive schools* | 4,319 | 40,663 | 595,900 |
| Senior secondary schools | 457 | 6,173 | 134,900 |
| Vocational and professional institutions | 421 | 14,624 | 242,000 |
| Polytechnics | 16 | 2,069 | 46,500 |
| Universities | 20 | 7,213 | 138,300 |

* Comprising six-year primary stage and three-year lower secondary stage.
Source: Ministry of Education.

# Directory

## The Constitution

The Constitution of Finland entered into force on 1 March 2000, amending the Constitution of July 1919. Its main provisions are summarized below:

### FUNDAMENTAL PROVISIONS

Finland is a sovereign republic. The powers of the State are vested in the people, who are represented by the Parliament. Legislative power is exercised by the Parliament, which also decides on state finances, governmental power is held by the President of the Republic and the Council of State, and judicial power is exercised by independent courts of law. The basic rights and liberties of the individual are guaranteed in the Constitution.

### PARLIAMENT

The unicameral Parliament comprises 200 representatives, who are elected for a term of four years by a direct, proportional and secret vote. For the parliamentary elections the country is divided, on the basis of the number of Finnish citizens, into at least 12 and at most 18 constituencies. In addition, the Åland Islands form their own constituency for the election of one representative. Registered political parties, and groups of persons who have the right to vote, are entitled to nominate candidates in parliamentary elections. The President of the Republic, in response to a proposal by the Prime Minister, may order that extraordinary parliamentary elections be held. The Parliament elects from among its members a Speaker and two Deputy Speakers for each parliamentary session. The proposal for the enactment of legislation is initiated in the Parliament either by the Government or through a motion submitted by a representative.

### PRESIDENT

The President of the Republic is elected by a direct vote for a term of six years (with the same person restricted to a maximum of two consecutive terms in office). The President will be a native-born Finnish citizen. The candidate who receives more than one-half of the votes cast in the election will be elected President. If none of the candidates receives a majority of the votes cast, a further election will be held between the two candidates who have received the most votes. The right to nominate a candidate in the presidential election is held by any registered political party from which at least one representative was elected to the Parliament in the most recent elections, as well as by any group of 20,000 persons who have the right to vote. The President of the Republic makes decisions on the basis of proposals submitted by the Council of State. The foreign policy of Finland is directed by the President of the Republic in co-operation with the Council of State.

### COUNCIL OF STATE

The Council of State comprises the Prime Minister and the necessary number of ministers. The Parliament elects the Prime Minister, who is thereafter appointed to the office by the President of the Republic. The President appoints the other ministers on the basis of nominations made by the Prime Minister.

### JUDICIARY

The Supreme Court, the Courts of Appeal and the District Courts are the general courts of law. The Supreme Administrative Court and the regional Administrative Courts are the general courts of administrative law. Justice in civil, commercial and criminal matters in the final instance is administered by the Supreme Court, while justice in administrative matters in the final instance is administered by the Supreme Administrative Court. The High Court of Impeachment deals with charges brought against a member of the Government, the Chancellor of Justice, the Parliamentary Ombudsman or a member of the supreme courts for unlawful conduct in office. Tenured judges are appointed by the President of the Republic.

### ADMINISTRATION AND SELF-GOVERNMENT

In addition to the Government, the civil administration of the State may consist of agencies, institutions and other bodies. The Åland Islands are guaranteed self-government. Finland is divided into municipalities, which are guaranteed self-government, and are entitled to levy tax. In their native region the Sami have linguistic and cultural autonomy.

## The Government

(March 2000)

### HEAD OF STATE

**President:** TARJA HALONEN (elected 6 February 2000 and took office on 1 March 2000).

### COUNCIL OF STATE
(Valtioneuvosto)

A coalition of the Social Democratic Party (SDP), National Coalition Party (Kok), Swedish People's Party (SFP), Left Alliance (V) and Green League (VL), with one independent (Ind.).

**Prime Minister:** PAAVO LIPPONEN (SDP).

**Deputy Prime Minister and Minister of Finance:** SAULI NIINISTÖ (Kok).

**Minister of Foreign Affairs:** ERKKI TUOMIOJA (SDP).

**Minister of the Interior:** KARI HÄKÄMIES (Kok).

**Minister of Regional and Municipal Affairs:** MATTI KORHONEN (V).

**Minister of Defence:** JAN-ERIK ENESTAM (SFP).

**Minister at the Ministry of Finance:** SUVI-ANNE SIIMES (V).

**Minister of Education:** MAIJA RASK (SDP).

**Minister of Culture:** SUVI LINDEN (Kok).

**Minister of Agriculture and Forestry:** KALEVI HEMILÄ (Ind.).

**Minister of Transport:** OLLI-PEKKA HEINONEN (Kok).

**Minister of Trade and Industry:** SINIKKA MÖNKÄRE (SDP).

**Minister of Social Affairs and Health:** MAIJA PERHO (Kok).

**Minister of Health and Social Services:** EVA BIAUDET (SFP).

**Minister for Foreign Trade:** KIMMO SASI (Kok).

**Minister of Justice:** JOHANNES KOSKINEN (SDP).
**Minister of Labour:** TARJA FILATOV (SDP).
**Minister of the Environment:** SATU HASSI (VL).

### MINISTRIES

**Prime Minister's Office:** Aleksanterinkatu 3D, 00170 Helsinki; tel. (9) 1601; fax (9) 1602099.

**Ministry of Agriculture and Forestry:** Hallituskatu 3A, 00170 Helsinki; tel. (9) 1601; fax (9) 1602190.

**Ministry of Defence:** Fabianinkatu 2, POB 31, 00130 Helsinki; tel. (9) 1601; fax (9) 653254.

**Ministry of Education:** Meritullinkatu 10, POB 293, 00171 Helsinki; tel. (9) 134171; fax (9) 1359335; e-mail pia.ekqvist@minedu.fi; internet www.minedu.fi.

**Ministry of the Environment:** Kasarmikatu 25, POB 380, 00131 Helsinki; tel. (9) 19911; fax (9) 19919545.

**Ministry of Finance:** Snellmaninkatu 1A, 00170 Helsinki; tel. (9) 1601; fax (9) 1603090; internet www.vn.fi/vm/index.html.

**Ministry of Foreign Affairs:** Merikasarmi, POB 176, 00161 Helsinki; tel. (9) 134151; fax (9) 13415070.

**Ministry of the Interior:** Kirkkokatu 12, 00170 Helsinki; tel. (9) 1601; fax (9) 1602927.

**Ministry of Justice:** Eteläesplanadi 10, POB 1, 00131 Helsinki; tel. (9) 18251; fax (9) 18257730.

**Ministry of Labour:** Eteläesplanadi 4, POB 524, 00101 Helsinki; tel. (9) 18561; fax (9) 1857950.

**Ministry of Social Affairs and Health:** Snellmaninkatu 4–6, POB 267, 00170 Helsinki; tel. (9) 1601; fax (9) 1604716.

**Ministry of Trade and Industry:** Aleksanterinkatu 4, POB 230, 00171 Helsinki; tel. (9) 1601; fax (9) 1603666; internet www.vn.fi/ktm.

**Ministry of Transport and Communications:** Eteläesplanadi 16–18, POB 235, 00131 Helsinki; tel. (9) 1601; fax (9) 1602596; e-mail info@mintc.fi; internet www.mintc.fi.

# President and Legislature

### PRESIDENT

**Elections of 16 January and 6 February 2000**

| | Popular vote (%) First Round | Popular vote (%) Second Round |
|---|---|---|
| TARJA HALONEN (SDP) | 40.0 | 51.6 |
| ESKO AHO (Kesk) | 34.4 | 48.4 |
| RIITTA UOSUKAINEN (Kok) | 12.8 | – |
| MÄRTA ELISABETH REHN (SFP) | 7.9 | – |
| HEIDI HAUTALA (VL) | 3.3 | – |
| ILKKA HAKALEHTO (PS) | 1.0 | – |
| RISTO KUISMA (REM) | 0.6 | – |
| **Total** | 100.0 | 100.0 |

### EDUSKUNTA
(Parliament)

**Speaker:** RIITTA UOSUKAINEN (Kok).
**Secretary-General:** SEPPO TIITINEN.

**General Election, 21 March 1999**

| | % of votes | Seats |
|---|---|---|
| Finnish Social Democratic Party | 22.9 | 51 |
| Finnish Centre Party | 22.4 | 48 |
| National Coalition Party | 21.0 | 46 |
| Left Alliance | 10.9 | 20 |
| Green League | 7.5 | 11 |
| Swedish People's Party | 5.1 | 11 |
| Finnish Christian Union | 4.2 | 10 |
| True Finns | 1.0 | 1 |
| Independents | 1.1 | 1 |
| Others | 4.2 | 1 |
| **Total** | 100.0 | 200 |

# Political Organizations

**Eco-Diverse Party:** Mannerheimintie 40A, 00100 Helsinki; tel. (9) 4323566; fax (9) 4322717; Chair. PERTTI VIRTANEN; Sec. JUKKA WALLENIUS.

**Kansallinen Kokoomus (Kok)** (National Coalition Party): Kansakoulukuja 3, 00100 Helsinki; tel. (9) 69381; fax (9) 6943736; e-mail firstname.lastname@kokoomus.fi; internet www.kokoomus.fi; f. 1918; moderate conservative political ideology; Chair. SAULI NIINISTÖ; Sec.-Gen. MATTI KANKARE; Chair. Parliamentary Group BEN ZYSKOWICZ; 50,000 mems.

**Liberaalinen Kansanpuolue (LKP)** (Liberal People's Party): Fredrikinkatu 58A, 00100 Helsinki; tel. (9) 440227; fax (9) 440771; e-mail liberal@pp.iaf.fi; f. 1965 as a coalition of the Finnish People's Party and the Liberal Union; Chair. ALTTI MAJAVA; Sec.-Gen. KAARINA TALOLA; 4,000 mems.

**Perussuomalaiset-Sannfinländarna rp** (True Finns): Mannerheimintie 40B, 00100 Helsinki; tel. (9) 4540411; fax (9) 4540466; e-mail perussuomalaiset@kolumbus.fi; internet www.kolumbus.fi/perussuomalaiset/; Chair. TIMO SOINI; Sec. ROLF SORMO.

**Reform Group:** Mannerheimintie 40A, 00100 Helsinki; tel. (9) 4143352; fax (9) 645379; Chair. RISTO KUISMA; Sec. SEIJA LAHTI.

**Suomen Keskusta (Kesk)** (Finnish Centre Party): Pursimiehenkatu 15, 00150 Helsinki; tel. (9) 172721; fax (9) 693263; f. 1906; a radical centre party founded to promote the interests of the rural population, now a reformist 'green' movement favouring individual enterprise, equality and decentralization; Chair. ESKO AHO; Sec.-Gen. EERO LANKIA; Chair. Parliamentary Group MAURI PEKKARINEN; 270,000 mems.

**Suomen Kristillinen Liitto (SKL)** (Finnish Christian Union): Mannerheimintie 40D, 00100 Helsinki; tel. (9) 34882200; fax (9) 34882228; e-mail merja.erapolku@eduskunta.fi; internet www.skl.fi; f. 1958; Chair. BJARNE KALLIS; Sec. MILLA KALLIOMAA; Chair. Parliamentary Group JOUKO JÄÄSKELÄINEN; 16,500 mems.

**Suomen Maaseudun Puolue (SMP)** (Finnish Rural Party): Hämeentie 157, 00560 Helsinki; tel. (9) 790299; fax (9) 790299; f. 1959; non-socialist programme; represents lower-middle-class elements, small farmers, small enterprises etc.; Chair. RAIMO VISTBACKA; Sec. TIMO SOINI; Chair. Parliamentary Group LEA MÄKIPÄÄ.

**Suomen Sosialidemokraattinen Puolue (SDP)** (Finnish Social Democratic Party): Saariniemenkatu 6, 00530 Helsinki; tel. (9) 478988; fax (9) 712752; e-mail palaute@sdp.fi; internet www.sdp.fi; f. 1899; constitutional socialist programme; mainly supported by the urban working and middle classes; Chair. PAAVO LIPPONEN; Gen. Sec. KARI LAITINEN; Chair. Parliamentary Group ERKKI TUOMIOJA; 72,000 mems.

**Svenska folkpartiet (SFP)** (Swedish People's Party): Simonsgatan 8A, 00100 Helsinki; tel. (9) 693070; fax (9) 6931968; internet www.sfp.fi; f. 1906; a liberal party representing the interests of the Swedish-speaking minority; Chair. JAN-ERIK ENESTAM; Sec. PETER HEINSTRÖM; Chair. Parliamentary Group ULLA-MAJ WIDEROOS; 42,000 mems.

**Vasemmistoliitto Vänsterförbundet** (Left Alliance): Siltasaarenkatu 6, 7th Floor, 00530 Helsinki; tel. (9) 774741; fax (9) 77474200; e-mail vas@vasemmistoliitto.fi; internet www.vasemmistoliitto.fi/english.html; f. 1990 as a merger of the Finnish People's Democratic League (f. 1944), the Communist Party of Finland (f. 1918), the Democratic League of Finnish Women, and left-wing groups; Chair. SUVI-ANNE SIIMES; Sec.-Gen. RALF SUND; Chair. Parliamentary Group MARTTI KORHONEN; 14,000 mems.

**Vihreä Liitto (VL)** (Green League): Runeberginkatu 5B, 00100 Helsinki; tel. (9) 58604160; fax (9) 58604161; e-mail vihreat@vihrealiitto.fi; internet www.vihrealiitto.fi; f. 1988; Chair. SATU HASSI; Sec. ARI HEIKKINEN.

**Young Finns:** Lönnrotinkatu 23A, 00180 Helsinki; tel. (9) 6856211; fax (9) 6856233; Chair. RISTO E. J. PENTTILÄ; Sec. MARITA VUORINEN.

# Diplomatic Representation

### EMBASSIES IN FINLAND

**Argentina:** Bulevardi 5A 11, 00120 Helsinki; tel. (9) 607630; fax (9) 646788; Ambassador: HUGO AUGUSTO URTUBEY.

**Austria:** Keskuskatu 1A, 00100 Helsinki; tel. (9) 171322; fax (9) 665084; e-mail austrian.embassy@pp.kolumbus.fi; Ambassador: Dr WENDELIN ETTMAYER.

**Belgium:** Kalliolinnantie 5, 00140 Helsinki; tel. (9) 170412; fax (9) 628842; Ambassador: LOUIS MOURAUX.

**Brazil:** Itäinen puistotie 4B, 00140 Helsinki; tel. (9) 177922; fax (9) 650084; e-mail brasemb.helsinki@kolumbus.fi; Ambassador: JOSÉ RACHE DE ALMEIDA.

**Bulgaria:** Kuusisaarentie 2B, 00340 Helsinki; tel. (9) 4584055; fax (9) 4584550; e-mail bulembfi@icon.fi; Ambassador: PLAMEN PETKOV.

**Canada:** Pohjoisesplanadi 25B, 00100 Helsinki; tel. (9) 171141; fax (9) 601060; internet www.canada.fi; Ambassador: CRAIG MACDONALD.

**Chile:** Erottajankatu 11, 00130 Helsinki; tel. (9) 6126780; fax (9) 61267825; e-mail echilefi@kolumbus.fi; Ambassador: MONTSERRAT PALOU.

# FINNISH EXTERNAL TERRITORY

# THE ÅLAND ISLANDS

## Introductory Survey

### Location, Language, Religion, Flag, Capital

The Åland Islands are a group of 6,554 islands (of which some 60 are inhabited) in the Gulf of Bothnia, between Finland and Sweden. About 95% of the inhabitants are Swedish-speaking, and Swedish is the official language. The majority profess Christianity and belong to the Evangelical Lutheran Church of Finland. The flag displays a red cross, bordered with yellow, on a blue background, the upright of the cross being to the left of centre. The capital is Mariehamn, which is situated on Åland, the largest island in the group.

### History and Government

For geographical and economic reasons, the Åland Islands were traditionally associated closely with Sweden. In 1809, when Sweden was forced to cede Finland to Russia, the islands were incorporated into the Finnish Grand Duchy. However, following Finland's declaration of independence from the Russian Empire, in 1917, the Ålanders demanded the right to self-determination and sought to be reunited with Sweden. Their demands were supported by the Swedish Government and people. In 1920 Finland granted the islands autonomy but refused to acknowledge their secession, and in 1921 the Åland question was referred to the League of Nations. In June the League granted Finland sovereignty over the islands, while directing that certain conditions pertaining to national identity be included in the autonomy legislation offered by Finland and that the islands should be a neutral and non-fortified region. Elections were held in accordance with the new legislation, and the new provincial parliament (Landsting) held its first plenary session on 9 June 1922. The revised Autonomy Act of 1951 provided for independent rights of legislation in internal affairs and for autonomous control over the islands' economy. This Act could not be amended or repealed by the Finnish Eduskunta without the consent of the Åland Landsting.

In 1988 constitutional reform introduced the principle of a majority parliamentary government, to be formed by the Lantrådskandidat, the member of the Landsting nominated to conduct negotiations beween the parties. These negotiations may yield two alternative outcomes: either the nominee will submit a proposal to create a new government or the nominee will fail to reach agreement on a new government (in which case renewed negotiations will ensue). The first formal parliamentary government and opposition were duly established. The governing coalition consisted of the three largest parties that had been elected to the Landsting in October 1987 (the Centre Party, the Liberals and the Moderates), which together held 22 seats in the 30-member legislature.

At a general election held on 20 October 1991 the Centre Party increased its share of the seats in the Landsting to 10, while the Liberal Party secured seven seats and the Moderates and Social Democrats won six and four seats respectively. The parties forming the new coalition Government included the Centre and Moderate Parties, as before, while the Liberal Party was replaced by the Social Democratic Party.

A revised Autonomy Act, providing Åland with a greater degree of autonomous control, was adopted in 1991 and took effect on 1 January 1993. The rules regarding legislative authority were modernized, and the right of the Åland legislature (henceforth known as the Lagting) to enact laws was extended. Åland was given greater discretion with respect to its budget, and the revised Act also introduced changes in matters such as right of domicile, land ownership regulations and administrative authority. The Autonomy Act contains a provision that, in any treaty which Finland may conclude with a foreign state and to which Åland is a party, the Lagting must consent to the statute implementing the treaty in order for the provision to enter into force in Åland. This procedure gave Åland the opportunity not to consent to membership of the European Union (EU). A referendum on the issue of Åland's proposed accession to membership of the EU in 1995 was held in November 1994, immediately after similar referendums in Finland and Sweden had shown a majority in favour of membership. (A small majority of Åland citizens had supported Finland's membership.) Despite low participation in the referendum, 73.7% of the votes cast supported membership and Åland duly joined the EU, together with Finland and Sweden, on 1 January 1995. Under the terms of the treaty of accession, Åland was accorded special exemption from tax union with the EU in order to stimulate the ferry and tourist industries. (In 1998 two of Europe's largest ferry operators, Silja and Viking—both Finnish—re-routed their major services via Åland in order to continue to conduct duty-free sales, which were later abolished within the rest of the EU.)

A general election was held on 15 October 1995. The Centre Party secured nine seats and the Liberal Party won eight seats, while the Moderates and Social Democrats maintained the representation that they had achieved in the previous parliament. The new coalition Government was composed of members of the Centre and Moderate Parties and one independent.

At a general election held on 17 October 1999 the Centre Party and the Liberal Party each won nine seats. The Moderate Party, meanwhile, gained only four seats, compared with six at the previous election, while the Social Democrats maintained its level of representation with 3 seats. Independents grouped together in the Obunden samling won four seats.

### Economic Affairs

In 1996 the gross domestic product (GDP) of the Åland Islands, measured at current prices, was 4,052m. marks. Forests cover most of the islands, and only 8% of the total land area is arable. The principal crops are cereals, sugar-beet, potatoes and fruit. Dairy-farming and sheep-rearing are also important.

Since 1960 the economy of the islands has expanded and diversified. Fishing has declined as a source of income, and shipping (particularly the operation of ferry services between Finland and Sweden), trade and tourism have become the dominant economic sectors. In 1996 services engaged 72.8% of the employed labour force. The transport sector, including shipping, employed 19.4%. The political autonomy of the islands and their strategic location between Sweden and Finland have contributed to expanding banking and trade sectors, which employed 19.7% of the working population in 1996. Unemployment stood at 4.2% in 1997.

### Education and Social Welfare

The education system is similar to that of Finland, except that Swedish is the language of instruction and Finnish an optional subject. In 1997 government medical services included two hospitals, with a total of 151 beds, and 51 physicians.

## Statistical Survey

Source: Government of Åland, Department of Statistics and Economic Research, POB 60, 22101 Mariehamn; tel. (18) 25000; fax (18) 19495.

### AREA, POPULATION AND DENSITY

**Area:** 1,552 sq km (599 sq miles), of which 25 sq km (9.7 sq miles) is inland waters.

**Population** (31 December 1998): 25,625.

**Density** (1998): 16.8 per sq km.

**Births and Deaths** (1998): Registered live births 311 (birth rate 12.2 per 1,000); Deaths 253 (death rate 10.0 per 1,000).

**Economically Active Population** (1996): Agriculture 968; Manufacturing 1,142; Construction 573; Trade 1,436; Transport 2,260; Financial services 860; Other services 3,924; Statistical discrepancy 489; Total employed 11,652.

**Labour Force** (1995): Males 6,466; Females 5,905; Total 12,371.

### FINANCE

**Currency:** Finnish currency: 100 penniä (singular: penni) = 1 markka.

**Government Accounts** ('000 markkaa, 1998): Revenue 1,319,909; Expenditure 1,123,954.

**Cost of Living** (consumer price index; base: 1985 = 100): 141.0 in 1996; 143.3 in 1997; 146.0 in 1998.

**Gross Domestic Product** (million markkaa at current prices): 3,799 in 1994; 3,842 in 1995; 4,052 in 1996.

### EXTERNAL TRADE

**1996** (million marks): Imports 3,473; Exports 4,250.

### TRANSPORT AND TOURISM

**Shipping** (1999): Merchant fleet 39 vessels; total displacement 397,400 grt.

**Tourist Arrivals** (1998): 1,628,881.

# Directory

## Government and Legislature

The Governor of Åland represents the Government of Finland and is appointed by the Finnish President (with the agreement of the Speaker of the Åland legislature). The legislative body is the Lagting, comprising 30 members, elected every four years on a basis of proportional representation. All Ålanders over the age of 18 years, possessing Åland regional citizenship, have the right to vote and to seek election. An executive council (Landskapsstyrelse), consisting of five to seven members, is elected by the Lagting, and its Chairman (Lantråd) is the highest-ranking politician in Åland after the Speaker (Talman) of the Lagting. The President has the right to veto Lagting decisions only when the Lagting exceeds its legislative competence, or when there is a threat to the security of the country.

**Governor:** HENRIK GUSTAFSSON.

### LANDSKAPSSTYRELSE
(February 2000)

The governing coalition comprises members of the Centre Party, the Moderate Party and the Independents.

**Chairman (Lantråd):** ROGER NORDLUND (Centre Party).

**Deputy Chairman:** OLOF SALMEN (Independents).

**Members:** DANNE SUNDMAN (Independents), RUNAR KARLSSON (Centre Party), HARRIET LINDEMAN (Moderate Party), ROGER JANSSON (Moderate Party), GUN CARLSSON (Centre Party).

### LAGTING

**Speaker (Talman):** SUNE ERIKSSON.

**Election, 17 October 1999**

| | % of votes cast | Seats |
|---|---|---|
| Liberalerna på Åland (Liberal Party) | 28.7 | 9 |
| Åländsk Center (Centre Party) | 27.3 | 9 |
| Frisinnad samverkan (Moderate Party) | 14.5 | 4 |
| Obunden samling (Independents) | 12.8 | 4 |
| Ålands socialdemokrater (Social Democratic Party) | 11.8 | 3 |
| Ålands Framstegsgrupp (Progress Group) | 4.8 | 1 |
| **Total** | 100.0 | 30 |

## Political Organizations

Unless otherwise indicated, the address of each of the following organizations is: Ålands Lagting, POB 69, 22101 Mariehamn; tel. (18) 25000; fax (18) 13302; internet www.lagtinget.aland.fi.

**Åländsk Center** (Centre Party): e-mail centern@lagtinget.aland.fi.; Chair. ROGER NORDLUND; Leader JAN-ERIK MATTSSON; Sec. ROBERT BRANÉR.

**Ålands Framstegsgrupp** (Progress Group).

**Ålands socialdemokrater** (Social Democratic Party): Leader BARBRO SUNDBACK; Chair. ANNE-HELENA SJÖBLOM.

**Frisinnad samverkan** (Moderate Party): Chair. HARRIET LINDEMAN; Leader MAX SIRÉN; Sec.-Gen. NINA DANIELSSON.

**Liberalerna på Åland** (Liberal Party): tel. (18) 25362; fax (18) 16075; e-mail liberalerna@lagtinget.aland.fi; Chair. OLOF ERLAND; Leader LISBETH ERIKSSON; Gen. Sec. BIRGITTA GUSTAVSSON.

**Obunden samling** (Independents): Chair. BERIT HAMPF; Leader ERIK TUDEER.

## The Press

**Åland:** POB 50, 22101 Mariehamn; tel. (18) 26026; fax (18) 15505; 5 a week; circ. 10,705.

**Nya Åland:** POB 21, 22101 Mariehamn; tel. (18) 23444; fax (18) 23449; 4 a week; circ. 7,768.

## Broadcasting and Communications

### RADIO

**Ålands Radio och TV:** POB 140, 22101 Mariehamn; tel. (18) 26060; fax (18) 26520; broadcasts 115 hours a week; Man. Dir PIA ROTHBERG-OLOFSSON; Editor-in-Chief ASTRID OLHAGEN.

## Finance

### BANKS

(cap. = capital; res = reserves; dep. = deposits; m. = million; amounts in markkaa; brs = branches)

**Ålandsbanken Ab** (Bank of Åland Ltd): Nygatan 2, POB 3, 22101 Mariehamn; tel. (18) 29011; fax (18) 29228; f. 1919 as Ålands Aktiebank; name changed as above in 1980; merged with Ålands Hypoteksbank Ab in November 1995; cap. 72m., res 155.5m., dep. 3,208.0m. (Dec. 1995); Man. Dir FOLKE HUSELL; 25 brs.

**Andelsbanken för Åland:** POB 34, 22101 Mariehamn; tel. (18) 26000; Dirs HÅKAN CLEMES, ROLAND KARLSSON.

**Lappo Andelsbank:** 22840 Lappo; tel. (18) 56621; fax (18) 56699; Dir TORSTEN NORDBERG.

**Merita Bank:** Torggatan 10, 22100 Mariehamn; tel. (18) 5330; fax (18) 12499; Dirs ERLING GUSTAFSSON, JAN-ERIK RASK.

**Postbanken:** Leonia, Torggatan 4, 22100 Mariehamn; tel. (18) 6360; fax (18) 636608.

### INSURANCE

**Alandia Group:** Ålandsvägen 31, POB 121, 22101 Mariehamn; tel. (18) 29000; fax (18) 12290; e-mail mhamn@alandiabolagen.com; f. 1938; life, non-life and marine; comprises three subsidiaries; Gen. Man. JOHAN DAHLMAN.

**Ålands Ömsesidiga Försäkringsbolag** (Åland Mutual Insurance Co): Köpmansgatan 6, POB 64, 22101 Mariehamn; tel. (18) 27600; fax (18) 27610; f. 1866; property; Man. Dir BJARNE OLOFSSON.

**Cabanco Insurance Co Ltd:** Köpmansgatan 6, POB 64, 22101 Mariehamn; tel. (18) 27690; fax (18) 27699; Man. Dir BO-STURE SJÖLUND.

**Hamnia Reinsurance Co Ltd:** Köpmansgatan 6, POB 64, 22101 Mariehamn; tel. (18) 27690; fax (18) 27699; Man. Dir BO-STURE SJÖLUND.

## Trade and Industry

### CHAMBER OF COMMERCE

**Ålands Handelskammare:** Nygatan 9, 22100 Mariehamn; tel. (18) 29029; fax (18) 21129; internet www.hk.aland.fi; f. 1945; Chair. TAGE SILANDER; Man. Dir AGNETA ERLANDSSON-BJÖRKLUND.

### TRADE ASSOCIATION

**Ålands Företagareförening** (Åland Business Asscn): Nygatan 9, 22100 Mariehamn; tel. (18) 29033; fax (18) 21129; f. 1957; Chair. SIGVARD PERSSON; Sec. BO HELENIUS.

### EMPLOYERS' ORGANIZATIONS

**Ålands Arbetsgivareförening** (Åland Employers' Asscn): Nygatan 9, 22100 Mariehamn; tel. (18) 291474; fax (18) 21129; f. 1969; Chair. ERIK SUNDBLOM; Man. Dir ANDERS KULVES.

**Ålands Fiskodlarförening:** (Åland Fish Farmers' Asscn): Storagatan 14, 22100 Mariehamn; tel. (18) 17834; fax (18) 17833; e-mail al.fishfarm@pb.alcom.aland.fi; Chair. MARCUS ERIKSSON; Sec. OLOF KARLSSON.

**Ålands köpmannaförening** (Åland Businessmen's Asscn): Ålandsvägen 34, 22100 Mariehamn; tel. (18) 13650; f. 1927; Chair. TOM FORSBOU; Sec. TOMAS HELLÉN.

**Ålands producentförbund** (Åland Agricultural Producers' Asscn): Ålands Landsbygdscentrum, 22150 Jomala; tel. (18) 329640; fax (18) 329639; e-mail henry.lindstrom@landsbygd.aland.fi; f. 1946; Chair. LOUISE KARLSSON; Man. Dir HENRY LINDSTROM.

**Utrikesfartens Småtonnageförening** (Shipowners Asscn for Smaller Ships in Foreign Trade): Norragatan 7A, 22100 Mariehamn; tel. (18) 23662; fax (18) 23644; e-mail small.ton@aland.net; Chair. OLOF WIDÉN.

### TRADE UNIONS

**AKAVA-Åland** (Professional Asscn): Storagatan 14, 22100 Mariehamn; tel. (18) 16348; fax (18) 12125; e-mail akava-a@aland.net; Chair. PEKKA ERÄMETSÄ; Gen. Sec. MARIA HAGMAN.

**FFC/SAK; s Lokalorganisation på Åland** (SAK Regional Trade Union in Åland): POB 108, 22101 Mariehamn; tel. (18) 16207; fax (18) 17207; e-mail kurt.gustafsson@sak.fi; internet www.facket.aland.fi; Chair. HELGE FREDRIKSSON; Gen. Sec. KURT GUSTAFSSON.

**Fackorgan för offentliga arbetsomraden på Åland (FOA-Å)** (Joint Organization of Civil Servants and Workers (VTY) in Åland): Ålandsvägen 55, 22100 Mariehamn; tel. (18) 16976; Chair. ULLA ANDERSSON; Gen. Sec. ULLA BRITT DAHL.

**Tjänstemannaorganisationerna på Åland, TCÅ r.f.** (Union of Salaried Employees in Åland): Strandgatan 23, 22100 Mariehamn;

tel. (18) 16210; e-mail tca@aland.net; Chair. ANNE SJÖLUND; Gen. Sec. TUULA MATTSSON.

## Transport

The islands are linked to the Swedish and Finnish mainlands by ferry services and by air services from Mariehamn airport.

### SHIPPING

**Ålands Redarförening r.f.** (Åland Shipowners' Association): Hamngatan 8, 22100 Mariehamn; tel. (18) 13430; fax (18) 22520; e-mail info@alship.aland.fi; f. 1934; Chair. JAN HANSES; Man. Dir HANS AHLSTRÖM.

#### Principal Companies

**Birka Line Abp:** POB 175, 22101 Mariehamn; tel. (18) 27027; fax (18) 27343; e-mail info@birkaline.com; internet www.kryssa.nu; f. 1971; shipping service; Chair. K.J. HAGMAN; Man. Dir WIKING JOHANSSON.

**Lundqvist Rederierna:** Norra Esplanadgatan 9B, 22100 Mariehamn; tel. (18) 26050; fax (18) 26428; e-mail info@lundqvist.aland.fi; f. 1927; tanker and ro-ro services; Pres. BEN LUNDQVIST; total tonnage 1.0m. dwt.

**Rederi Ab Lillgaard:** Nygatan 5, POB 136, 22101 Mariehamn; tel. (18) 13120; fax (18) 17220.

**Rederiaktiebolaget Gustaf Erikson:** POB 49, 22101 Mariehamn; tel. (18) 27070; fax (18) 12670; e-mail gustaf.erikson@geson.aland.fi; f. 1913; Man. Dir GUN ERIKSON-HJERLING; manages dry cargo and refrigerated vessels.

**United Shipping Ltd Ab:** Storagatan 11, POB 175, 22101 Mariehamn; tel. (18) 27320; fax (18) 23223.

**Viking Line Abp:** Norragatan 4, 22100 Mariehamn; tel. (18) 27000; fax (18) 12099; f. 1963; Chair. BEN LUNDQVIST; Man. Dir NILS-ERIK EKLUND; 6 car/passenger vessels; total tonnage 205,860 grt.

**Viking Line Marketing Ab Oy:** Storagatan 2, POB 35, 22101 Mariehamn; tel. (18) 26011; fax (18) 15811; internet www.vikingline.fi; Man. Dir BORIS EKMAN.

## Tourism

**Ålands TuristFörbund** (Åland Tourist Asscn): Storagatan 8, 22100 Mariehamn; tel. (18) 24000; fax (18) 24265; internet www.info.aland.fi; f. 1989; Chair. LASSE WIKLÖF; Man. Dir GUNILLA G. NORDLUND.

# FRANCE

## Introductory Survey

### Location, Climate, Language, Religion, Flag, Capital

The French Republic is situated in western Europe. It is bounded to the north by the English Channel (la Manche), to the east by Belgium, Luxembourg, Germany, Switzerland and Italy, to the south by the Mediterranean Sea and Spain, and to the west by the Atlantic Ocean. The island of Corsica is part of metropolitan France, while four overseas departments, two overseas 'collectivités territoriales' and four overseas territories also form an integral part of the Republic. The climate is temperate throughout most of the country, but in the south it is of the Mediterranean type, with warm summers and mild winters. Temperatures in Paris are generally between 0°C (32°F) and 24°C (75°F). The principal language is French, which has numerous regional dialects, and small minorities speak Breton and Basque. Almost all French citizens profess Christianity, and about 78% are adherents of the Roman Catholic Church. Other Christian denominations are represented, and there are also Muslim and Jewish communities. The national flag (proportions three by two) has three equal vertical stripes, of blue, white and red. The capital is Paris.

### Recent History

In September 1939, following Nazi Germany's invasion of Poland, France and the United Kingdom declared war on Germany, thus entering the Second World War. In June 1940 France was forced to sign an armistice, following a swift invasion and occupation of French territory by German forces. After the liberation of France from German occupation in 1944, a provisional Government took office under Gen. Charles de Gaulle, leader of the 'Free French' forces during the wartime resistance. The war in Europe ended in May 1945, when German forces surrendered at Reims. In 1946, following a referendum, the Fourth Republic was established and Gen. de Gaulle announced his intention to retire from public life.

France had 26 different Governments from 1946 until the Fourth Republic came to an end in 1958 with an insurrection in Algeria (then an overseas department) and the threat of civil war. In May 1958 Gen. de Gaulle was invited by the President, René Coty, to form a government. In June he was invested as Prime Minister by the National Assembly, with the power to rule by decree for six months. A new Constitution was approved by referendum in September and promulgated in October; thus the Fifth Republic came into being, with Gen. de Gaulle taking office as its first President in January 1959. The new system provided a strong, stable executive. Real power rested in the hands of the President, who strengthened his authority through direct appeals to the people in national referendums.

France was a founder member of the European Community (EC, now EU—see p. 172) and of NATO (see p. 226). In 1966 it withdrew from the integrated military structure of NATO, desiring a more self-determined defence policy, but remained a member of the alliance (see below).

The early years of the Fifth Republic were overshadowed by the Algerian crisis. De Gaulle suppressed a revolt of French army officers and granted Algeria independence in 1962, withdrawing troops and repatriating French settlers. A period of relative tranquillity was ended in May 1968, when dissatisfaction with the Government's authoritarian policies on education and information, coupled with discontent at low wage rates and lack of social reform, fused into a serious revolt of students and workers. For a time the republic appeared threatened, but the student movement collapsed and the general strike was settled by large wage rises. In April 1969 President de Gaulle resigned after defeat in a referendum on regional reform.

Georges Pompidou, de Gaulle's Prime Minister between April 1962 and July 1968, was elected President in June 1969. The Gaullist hold on power was, however, undermined by the Union of the Left, formed in 1972 by the Parti Socialiste (PS) and the Parti Communiste Français (PCF). Leaders of the PS and the PCF agreed a common programme for contesting legislative elections. At a general election for the National Assembly in March 1973, the government coalition was returned with a reduced majority. Pompidou died in April 1974. Valéry Giscard d'Estaing, formerly leader of the Républicains Indépendants (RI), supported by the Gaullist Union des Démocrates pour la République (UDR) and the centre parties, was elected President in May, narrowly defeating François Mitterrand, the First Secretary of the PS and the candidate of the Union of the Left (which was disbanded in 1977). A coalition Government was formed from members of the RI, the UDR and the centre parties. In August 1976 Jacques Chirac resigned as Prime Minister; he was replaced by Raymond Barre, hitherto Minister of External Trade. Chirac undertook the transformation of the UDR into a new Gaullist party, the Rassemblement pour la République (RPR). In February 1978 the non-Gaullist parties in the Government formed the Union pour la Démocratie Française (UDF), to compete against RPR candidates in the National Assembly elections held in March, when the governing coalition retained a working majority.

In the April/May 1981 presidential elections, Mitterrand, the candidate of the PS, defeated Giscard d'Estaing, with the support of communist voters. Pierre Mauroy was appointed Prime Minister forming the Fifth Republic's first left-wing Council of Ministers. At elections for a new Assembly, held in June, the PS and associated groups, principally the Mouvement des Radicaux de Gauche (MRG), won an overall majority of the seats. The Government was reorganized to include four members of the PCF in the Council of Ministers. The new Government introduced a programme of social and labour reforms; several major industrial enterprises and financial institutions were brought under state control; and administrative and financial power was transferred from government-appointed Préfets to locally-elected departmental assemblies.

An election to the National Assembly (now enlarged from 491 to 577 seats) took place in March 1986. A system of proportional representation, with voters choosing from party lists in each department or territory, replaced the previous system of single-member constituencies. The PS remained the largest single party in the new Assembly, but the centre-right RPR-UDF alliance was able to command a majority of seats, with the support of other right-wing parties. The PCF suffered a severe decline in support, while the extreme right-wing Front National (FN) won seats in the Assembly for the first time. An unprecedented period of political 'cohabitation' ensued as the socialist Mitterrand (whose presidential term of office did not expire until 1988) invited the RPR leader, Chirac, to form a new Council of Ministers.

In April 1986 Chirac introduced controversial legislation that allowed his Government to legislate by decree on economic and social issues and on the proposed reversion to a single-seat majority voting system for elections to the National Assembly. However, Mitterrand insisted on exercising the presidential right to withhold approval of decrees that reversed the previous Government's social reforms. Chirac thus resorted to the 'guillotine' procedure (setting a time-limit for consideration of legislative proposals) to gain parliamentary consent for contentious legislation, which, if approved by the predominantly right-wing Senate and the Constitutional Council, the President would be legally bound to approve. In July this procedure was used to enact legislation for the transfer to the private sector of 65 state-owned companies.

Mitterrand was returned for a further term as President in May 1988, defeating Chirac (with 54% of the votes cast) at the second round of voting. Michel Rocard succeeded Chirac as Prime Minister. However, his PS-dominated Government failed to command a reliable majority in the National Assembly, which was dissolved: a general election took place in June, with voting based on the single-seat majority system that had been reintroduced by Chirac. The PS in alliance with the MRG, together secured a total of 276 seats. The RPR and the UDF contesting the election jointly (with some other right-wing candidates) as the Union du Rassemblement et du Centre (URC), won 272. The PCF won 27 seats, and the FN one. Rocard reappointed Prime Minister, formed an administration in which the principal portfolios were retained by members of the previous Government, although six UDF members and a number of independents were also included.

Rocard resigned in May 1991, weakened by disunity within the PS and by his failure, in the previous month, to negotiate majority support in the National Assembly for three government bills. He was succeeded by Edith Cresson, France's first female Prime Minister. Cresson, who had resigned eight months previously from her post as Minister of European Affairs, in protest at Rocard's economic policies and the pace of their implementation, undertook to increase government control over economic and industrial planning.

Meanwhile, issues of urban deprivation, immigration and race relations featured increasingly in political debate. Certain politicians of the RPR, UDF and FN made public statements about immigration that were interpreted as inflammatory, and violent incidents in a number of cities exacerbated a widespread climate of hostility towards immigrants. In June 1991 Cresson announced emergency measures designed to provide training opportunities for young people in poor areas, while law-enforcement measures in suburban areas were to be strengthened. In July the Government announced that more stringent measures would be taken against illegal immigrants and that stricter criteria would be applied in the consideration of requests for asylum. In October the National Assembly approved legislation imposing heavy penalties on those convicted of employing illegal immigrants or conducting them into France.

In April 1992, in response to very poor results recorded by the PS at recent regional and cantonal elections, Mitterrand replaced Edith Cresson as Prime Minister with Pierre Bérégovoy, hitherto the Minister of State for the Economy, Finance and the Budget. Bérégovoy declared the Government's priority to be a reduction in the rate of unemployment, which had reached 9.9% of the labour force in February. In June Bérégovoy's Government narrowly defeated a motion of 'no confidence', introduced in the National Assembly by the RPR and the UDF in protest at the Government's support for a reform of the EC's Common Agricultural Policy (CAP, see p. 180). In the same month the Assembly approved constitutional changes allowing French ratification of the EC's Treaty on European Union (the 'Maastricht Treaty') to be subject to approval in a national referendum. In the referendum, held in September, 69.7% of the electorate voted, of whom 51.05% were in favour of the ratification of the Treaty.

In September 1992 Henri Emmanuelli, the President of the National Assembly and a former treasurer of the PS, was charged with complicity in illegal party fund-raising during the electoral campaigns of at least 20 PS members of the National Assembly. (Emmanuelli, by now First Secretary of the PS, was given an 18-month suspended prison sentence in May 1995 and excluded from public office for a period of two years.) In December 1992 the National Assembly adopted new legislation aimed at preventing political corruption and ensuring freedom of information on the funds donated to political parties. Meanwhile, in October two senior health service officials received prison sentences, following the discovery that unscreened blood infected with the human immunodeficiency virus (HIV) had been used in transfusions. It was estimated that more than 1,200 haemophiliacs had been infected with the virus (of whom more than 200 had since died) as a result of blood transfusions performed in 1985. Public pressure mounted to have three former government members—including the PS leader, Laurent Fabius, who had been Prime Minister in 1984–86—indicted for their alleged part in the scandal. In December 1992 the Senate voted by an overwhelming majority to endorse the decision of the National Assembly that the three should be brought to trial before the Conseil d'Etat.

As widely predicted, elections to the National Assembly in March 1993 resulted in a resounding defeat for the PS, mainly attributable to the high level of unemployment and to the recent succession of scandals in which members of the ruling party had been implicated. Several government ministers failed to retain their seats, as did Michel Rocard. In the first round of voting the RPR and the UDF (which had presented joint candidates, as the Union pour la France, in some 500 constituencies) together received 39.5% of the total votes cast, while the PS obtained 17.6%. However, as a result of voting in the second round, the RPR won 247 of the 577 seats in the Assembly, the UDF 213, and the PS only 54. Although they polled well at the first round of voting, neither the FN nor the alliance of the two main environmental parties, Les Verts and Génération Ecologie, won any seats. Chirac, the leader of the RPR, now the largest party in the legislature, had made it known that he was not available for the post of Prime Minister (since he intended to concentrate on his candidacy in the 1995 presidential election). Mitterrand therefore asked another RPR member, Edouard Balladur (Minister of Finance in the previous 'cohabitation' Government of 1986–88), to form a government. Balladur's centre-right coalition enacted stricter laws on immigration and the conferral of French citizenship during 1993–94, together with controversial legislation giving the police wider powers to make random security checks.

In the first round of presidential voting, on 23 April 1995, Lionel Jospin, the candidate of the PS, won 23% of the votes, while Chirac and Balladur, both representing the RPR, took 21% and 19% respectively. Jean-Marie Le Pen, the leader of the FN, won 15%. In the second round, on 7 May, Chirac (with 53% of the votes) defeated Jospin. Balladur resigned as Prime Minister, and Chirac appointed Alain Juppé (Minister of Foreign Affairs in the previous Government) as his successor. Juppé formed an administration in which the principal portfolios were evenly shared between the RPR and the UDF. In October Juppé was elected President of the RPR, while Jospin was elected First Secretary of the PS, replacing Emmanuelli.

In June 1995 Chirac announced that France was to end a moratorium on nuclear testing imposed by Mitterrand in 1992. Eight tests were to be conducted on Mururoa and Fangataufa atolls in French Polynesia, in the Pacific Ocean, between September 1995 and May 1996 (although this was later reduced to six). The announcement caused almost universal outrage in the international community, and was condemned for its apparent disregard for South Pacific regional opinion, as well as for undermining the considerable progress made by Western nations towards a world-wide ban on nuclear-weapons tests.

A series of strikes and demonstrations by public-sector workers in late 1995, in protest at government proposals for welfare reforms, wage restrictions and amendments to pension arrangements in the public sector, caused widespread disruption to the public transport system. In November Juppé announced a major reorganization of the Council of Ministers, reportedly following internal disagreements over the proposed reforms. The following month Juppé agreed to abandon the pension reforms and the strikes subsided. None the less, throughout 1996 the Juppé Government continued to suffer frequent criticism of its economic austerity measures, which were designed to enable France to fulfil its requirements for economic and monetary union (EMU—see p. 189) within the EU.

In May 1996 the Government approved proposals submitted by President Chirac to restructure the armed forces. The restructuring was to take place in two stages and was scheduled to be completed by 2015. The first stage, covering the period 1997–2002, envisaged a 30% reduction in military personnel and the elimination of compulsory military service. The defence budget was to be restricted to 185,000m. francs per year during this period, and state-owned companies in the defence industry were to be reorganized and sold to the private sector.

In February 1997 immigration legislation approved in the National Assembly provoked a demonstration by some 100,000 people in Paris. The protests were widely believed to have resulted in the Government's decision to exclude a controversial clause in the bill, requiring French citizens to register the arrival and departure of any foreign guests with the local authorities. Renewed controversy surrounding the conduct of French institutions during the Second World War arose in early 1997, following reports that French banks had failed to transfer the deposits of Jews killed in the Holocaust to the State, as required by law. Similar revelations that museums in France, including the Louvre, continued to hold some 2,000 valuable works of art seized from Jews under the Vichy regime (1940–44) prompted the Government to announce the creation of a commission to trace and catalogue the misappropriated property.

In April 1997 Chirac announced that legislative elections would take place in May–June. His decision to organize the elections some 10 months earlier than required was widely viewed as an attempt to secure a mandate for a number of important policies relating to EMU. In the first round of voting, held on 25 May, the PS secured 23.5% of total votes, and the RPR 15.7%. The FN was the third most successful party, obtaining 14.9% of the votes, followed by the UDF with 14.2%. As a result of voting in the second round on 1 June, the PS secured 241 seats, the RPR 134, the UDF 108 and the PCF 38. Despite its strong performance in the first round, the FN won only one seat.

The unexpected victory of the PS, which signalled the beginning of a further period of 'cohabitation', was widely attributed to dissatisfaction with Juppé's administration and the imposition of economic austerity measures necessitated under the terms ('convergence criteria') of EMU. (Juppé resigned as leader of the RPR and was subsequently replaced by Philippe Séguin.) The PS leader, Lionel Jospin, became Prime Minister, forming a coalition with several left-wing and ecologist parties. The new Government's stated objectives included the reduction of youth unemployment by the creation of some 700,000 new jobs and the shortening of the maximum working week from 39 to 35 hours. A further priority was the reform of immigration law. In August 1997 the Government announced that some 54,000 people had responded to its offer to grant residence permits to immigrants unsure of their legal status (the so-called '*sans-papiers*'), 14,000 more than had been expected. The initiative fuelled criticism by right-wing groups, who claimed that it would encourage illegal immigration and increase unemployment.

In October 1997 the trial of Maurice Papon, a former civil servant and senior official in the pro-Nazi Vichy regime, opened in Bordeaux. Papon was accused of deporting some 1,500 Jews to Germany, where almost all were killed in Nazi concentration camps, in 1943–44. Defence lawyers for Papon, who denied the charges against him, argued that their client was unfit to stand trial, owing to ill health. Proceedings were suspended on several occasions when Papon was deemed too unwell to appear in court. As a result of evidence heard at the trial, the Government announced an inquiry into the killing of Algerian demonstrators during a protest march in Paris in 1961. According to official reports, two people were killed in clashes with riot police during the demonstration, which took place during Papon's tenure as chief of the Paris police. Historians and independent witnesses, however, estimated that as many as 300 people had been killed. Police records subsequently uncovered during the inquiry revealed that the bodies of at least 90 demonstrators had been recovered from the river Seine. In April 1998 Papon was found guilty of complicity in crimes against humanity for his role in deporting Jews to Nazi concentration camps and was sentenced to 10 years' imprisonment. Many of Papon's opponents expressed outrage at the lenient sentence, while others accepted it as a symbolic punishment. Pending an appeal, Papon was exempt from imprisonment, on the grounds of ill health. In October 1999, however, on the eve of his appeal, it became clear that Papon, who had been due to surrender into custody, had absconded. He had thus forfeited any right to appeal. An international warrant was issued for his arrest, and Papon was subsequently apprehended and expelled from Switzerland, where he had been in hiding, and returned to begin sentence in France. A subsequent request that Papon be pardoned, owing to his ill health, was rejected.

In December 1997 a series of demonstrations began in Marseille, in protest at the Government's perceived failure to address adequately the problem of unemployment. The demonstrations soon spread to other parts of the country, and in many towns erupted into violence as unemployed youths attacked public-service workers (leading to strikes by public transport operators), clashed with police and set fire to buildings and vehicles. Meanwhile, protesters began an occupation of welfare offices across the country (which lasted several weeks), demanding a review of the benefits system. Measures announced by the Government in January 1998, which aimed to placate the demonstrators, were rejected by groups representing the unemployed. Furthermore, the support of communist and ecologist members of the Government for the protests highlighted divisions within the governing coalition on the matter. In February legislation shortening the maximum working week from 39 to 35 hours was approved by 316 votes to 254 in the National Assembly. The reform, central to the Government's job-creation policy, was to come into effect from 2000 for private companies with more than 20 employees and from 2002 for those with fewer than 20.

At regional council elections held in March 1998, the governing socialist coalition won 39.4% of the total vote, the centre-right opposition secured 35.6%, and the FN 15.5%. A subsequent offer by the FN to form alliances with the RPR and the UDF in order to secure control of a number of councils caused much controversy. Both parties instructed their members to ignore the proposal; however, five members of the UDF party defied the orders of their leadership and consequently obtained council presidencies. Two later resigned, while the remaining three were expelled from the party; one of these, Charles Millon, subsequently formed a new political organization called La Droite. A further two senior UDF members left the party in protest at the expulsions, amid serious criticism of party president François Léotard's management of the crisis. Further divisions within the political right wing were revealed in April, when 12 members of the RPR who had joined a new right-wing grouping on the Paris city council were dismissed by the mayor of Paris, Jean Tiberi. In an attempt to counteract the increasing fragmentation of the country's political centre right, the RPR and the UDF announced the formation in May of a loose umbrella organization called Alliance. Moreover, in late June the National Assembly voted to reform the system of regional elections, largely as a result of the problems experienced following the elections in March. The changes, which aimed to ensure coherent majorities in the regional councils, included the replacement of the previous one-round system with a two-round poll in which a party with an outright majority in the first round of voting would automatically receive 25% of the seats available.

Meanwhile, the FN experienced a number of reversals. At a by-election in May 1998 the party narrowly lost its only seat in the National Assembly to the PS. Moreover, in April a court in Versailles had banned Le Pen from holding or seeking public office for two years (reduced to one year on appeal) and given him a three-month suspended prison sentence after finding him guilty of physical assault on a socialist candidate in the 1997 general elections. The selection of a potential replacement for Le Pen, necessitated by the ban, to lead the FN list of candidates in the following year's elections to the European Parliament (of which the FN leader was a member), resulted in a major dispute within the party and the creation of two rival factions. Le Pen's decision to nominate his wife, Jany Le Pen, as his replacement (or, in the event of a further appeal against his conviction permitting him to stand for re-election himself, Charles de Gaulle, the grandson of the former President, as second on the list) infuriated supporters of Bruno Mégret, the party's second most senior member. Deepening divisions between supporters of the two rivals led, in December, to Mégret's suspension, and later expulsion, from the party, together with six other senior party officials. In January 1999 Mégret launched his own party, the Front National—Mouvement National (FN—MN).

During 1998 a number of serious political scandals threatened to tarnish the reputations of several prominent public figures. Early in the year the home and offices of Roland Dumas, the former Minister of Foreign Affairs and current president of the Constitutional Council, were raided by police as part of an ongoing investigation into the alleged fraudulent handling of commission payments, put at some US $500m., on the sale of six frigates to Taiwan in 1991. In May 1998 allegations of corruption emerged involving the inclusion of 300 fictitious employees on the payroll of the Paris city council, under Chirac's tenure as mayor. It was claimed that the payroll included friends and relatives of council members, RPR supporters and unsuccessful RPR candidates. A number of senior public officials, including Jean Tiberi, Chirac's successor as mayor of Paris, who had been responsible for the payroll during the period in question, and Alain Juppé, the former Prime Minister, who was placed under formal investigation for his role as the city's financial director, were implicated in the affair. (In January 1999 the Constitutional Council deemed Chirac to be immune from prosecution for the duration of his presidential term.) At the same time an appeals court dismissed embezzlement charges against Juppé, although he was to remain under investigation for his role in the affair. In March 1999, despite the disclosure of documentation purporting to show that he had been aware of the bogus employees' scheme, Chirac's immunity was upheld by a Paris public prosecutor. Also in March, Dumas was obliged to stand down temporarily as President of the Constitutional Council, following revelations by his former mistress that he had knowingly accepted inducements from the petroleum company Elf Aquitaine during his time as Minister of Foreign Affairs. Moreover, in June Tiberi was placed under formal investigation as part of the inquiry into the activities of employees of the Paris city council. Tiberi's wife also came under investigation, accused of accepting payment for a fictitious job, offered to her by an associate of her husband; however, the charges were later dismissed on legal technicalities. In early March 2000 Dumas stood down as President of the Constitutional Council.

The trial began in February 1999 of former Prime Minister Laurent Fabius and two cabinet ministers from his administration on charges of manslaughter and criminal negligence, following a lengthy investigation into the case of HIV-infected blood transfusions in 1985 (see above). It was estimated that some 4,300 people had been infected with HIV, of whom more than 1,000 had since died. In March 1999 Fabius and the former Minister of Social Affairs and National Solidarity, Georgina Dufoix, were acquitted, while the Secretary of State for Health at the time, Edmond Hervé, was convicted on two counts but released without sentence. In May it was recommended that a number of civil servants and advisers to Fabius be ordered to stand trial.

In February 1999 the Alliance umbrella group collapsed, following the UDF's decision to present a separate list of candidates for the forthcoming elections to the European Parliament. The RPR suffered a further reverse as one of the party's co-founders, Charles Pasqua, announced that he wished to distance himself from the RPR to pursue more anti-European policies (he formed the Rassemblement pour la France—RPF, in June, following his success at the European parliamentary elections). In April Philippe Séguin resigned as President of the RPR, asserting that he was dissatisfied with what he termed Chirac's political manoeuvrings. He was replaced, on an interim basis, by party secretary Nicolas Sarkozy, who in turn resigned in June, following disappointing results at the elections to the European Parliament. At the elections the RPR, in alliance with Alain Madelin's Democratie Libérale, took only 12.8% of the votes cast. The PS, by contrast, won 22.0%. The UDF secured 9.3%, while the FN, apparently weakened by the recent divisions, took 5.7%. In December Michèle Alliot-Marie was elected President of the RPR.

The Minister of the Economy, Finance and Industry, Dominique Strauss-Kahn, resigned in November 1999, in response to allegations that he had received 603,000 francs in payments from the MNEF (a students' mutual fund) in respect of a fictitious job. He was subsequently placed under investigation for fraud and use of fraud. Strauss-Kahn was replaced by the former Secretary of State for the Budget, Christian Sautter.

In late 1999 there were protests in Paris by employers critical of the Government's 35-hour working week policy, due to enter effect in early 1999 (see above). Employers claimed that the scheme, aimed at lowering unemployment levels, would harm smaller businesses unable to cope with the reduction in working hours. In response to criticism by employers and trade unions alike, the Government abandoned plans to draw on social security surpluses to fund the scheme, undertaking instead to divert funds from taxes on alcohol. As part of continued resistance to the policy, the main employers' group, Mouvement des Entreprises de France (MEDEF), voted in January 2000 to abandon its co-management of state social security funds, and French haulage companies blockaded border posts throughout France.

Proposed legislation, designated the civil solidarity pact (PACS), that aimed to give legal and fiscal rights to unmarried couples, including those in same-sex relationships, was presented to the National Assembly in late 1998. The bill was approved in November by 299 votes to 233, following lengthy debate characterized by a stark polarization between left- and right-wing groups. In January 1999 representatives of the church and other religious organizations joined right-wing groups in organizing an anti-PACS demonstration, attended by some 98,000 people. The legislation was rejected, without examination, by the Senate in May. The PACS was, none the less, approved at a final reading in the National Assembly in October, despite continuing strong opposition by right-wing parties, and was validated by the Constitutional Council in November. Chirac had, meanwhile, expressed personal opposition to the PACS.

As a result of the decentralization legislation of 1982, Corsica was elevated from regional status to that of a 'collectivité territoriale', with its own directly-elected 61-seat Assembly, and an administration with greater executive powers in economic, social and other spheres. However, this measure failed to pacify the pro-independence Front de Libération Nationale de la Corse (FLNC) and the Consulte des Comités Nationalistes (CCN), which were banned in 1983, following a terrorist campaign. A new independence movement, the Mouvement Corse pour l'Autodétermination (MCA), was immediately formed by members of the banned CCN, and terrorist activities continued from 1984. In January 1987 the MCA, which had six members in the Corsican Assembly in alliance with the Union du Peuple Corse (UPC), was banned after police investigations suggested links with the FLNC, and the UPC later suspended the alliance. In November 1990 the French Government proposed legislation that would grant greater autonomy to Corsica. The proposals, known as the Joxe Plan (after the Minister of the Interior, Pierre Joxe), envisaged the formation of an executive council comprising seven members, chosen from a 51-member Corsican assembly, to be elected in 1992. The Joxe Plan was opposed both by militant Corsican separatists, and by right-wing members of the National Assembly. Despite a bombing campaign and a series of assassinations in December 1990 and January 1991, the legislation was adopted in April 1991. In the early 1990s, however, an unprecedented series of armed robberies, bombings and deliberately raised forest fires threatened to undermine the Corsican tourist industry. In January 1996 the FLNC announced a suspension of terrorist attacks: the truce was ended in August. In October a faction of the FLNC (the FLNC—Canal Historique) admitted responsibility for the bombing, earlier in the month, of the town hall in Bordeaux. The attack was deemed to be in reprisal for assertions made by Prime Minister Juppé that his Government would never negotiate with terrorists (Juppé was also Mayor of Bordeaux and had presided over a meeting in the town hall on the day of the explosion). In February 1997 an unprecedented series of explosions in Corsica followed the arrest, earlier in the month, of several high-profile separatists. In one of the most serious incidents of violence on Corsica in its recent history, the prefect of the island, Claude Erignac, was assassinated in early February 1998. The killing was condemned by the FLNC, leading observers to speculate that the assassination had been carried out by a splinter group (Sampieru), which had admitted responsibility for the kidnapping of a police-officer in September 1997. In May 1998 the FLNC claimed responsibility for a bomb attack, which caused serious damage to the regional council building in Marseille. (Proposals to declare Corsica a 'free zone' during 1997–2001, exempt from customs duty and tax, were approved by the EU in October 1996. The zone came into force on 1 January 1997.)

In January 1999 the FLNC declared a cease-fire, on Corsican territory only, in an apparent attempt to prevent further attacks from damaging the separatist cause in anticipation of regional assembly elections secheduled to take place on the island in March. The elections strengthened the position of the Corsican nationalist parties, with Corsica Nazione winning almost 17% of votes cast. An arson attack on a bar in the island's capital, Ajaccio, in April led to the arrest and dismissal of the island's prefect, Bernard Bonnet. The anti-terrorist unit (GPS) that had been established after the murder of Erignac was also disbanded. Bonnet's arrest was made after revelations by three police-officers that they had been ordered to carry out the attack on the bar by the head of the GPS, Henri Mazères. In May, following the arrest of four Corsican nationalists in connection with the murder of Erignac in May, the Jospin Government narrowly avoided a motion of censure, proposed by the opposition parties in protest at the Government's handling of the situation on the island. In late 1999 two explosions in public buildings in Ajaccio injured six people. These followed a visit to Corsica by Jospin, during which he had reiterated that an end to the violence was a necessary precondition for the development of negotiations on increased autonomy. Talks involving the Government and representatives of the island, including two Corsican nationalists, commenced in Paris in December.

During the 1980s indigenous Melanesian (Kanak) separatists also campaigned for the independence of the Pacific overseas territory of New Caledonia, in conflict with the wishes of settlers of European origin (see French Overseas Possessions, p. 1518). In 1988 it was agreed that, from July 1989, a high commissioner should administer the territory, assisted by three elected provincial assemblies, until the holding of a referendum on self-determination in 1998. At the referendum, which took place in November, a gradual transfer of powers to local institutions over a period of between 15 and 20 years (as detailed in the Nouméa Accord) was approved. In October 1999 the Senate approved legislation granting French Polynesia the new status of 'pays d'outre-mer'. By March 2000, however, the constitutional amendment was still awaiting final ratification.

France granted independence to most of its former colonies after the Second World War. In Indo-China, after prolonged fighting, Laos, Cambodia and Viet Nam became fully independent in 1954. In Africa most of the French colonies in the West and Equatorial regions attained independence in 1960, but retained their close economic and political ties with France (particularly within the framework of the Franc Zone: see

p. 200). During the second half of the 1990s, however, France was active in promoting the establishment of regional peace-keeping forces for Africa, and the reorganization of the French armed forces notably entailed a reduction in military commitments in its former African colonies.

In the early 1990s a contingent of French troops was dispatched to Rwanda to train forces of the Rwandan Government and to supply military equipment, following the outbreak of armed conflict between the Government and the opposition Rwandan Patriotic Front (FPR). In April 1994 French troops re-entered Rwanda to establish a 'safe humanitarian zone' for refugees fleeing the civil war. Although France declared its presence to be restricted to a transitional period prior to the arrival of UN peace-keeping forces, the FPR accused France of using the operation secretly to transport alleged war criminals out of the country. In November 1996 the French Government rejected allegations that France had continued to supply arms to the Rwandan Government following the imposition, in May 1994, of a UN embargo on the delivery of military equipment to any party in the Rwandan conflict. In January 1998 new evidence in support of allegations that France had sold arms to Rwanda during the massacres in 1994 emerged. The Government again denied the accusations. A commission of inquiry was established to investigate the affair, during which former Prime Minister Edouard Balladur and two other former ministers, François Léotard and Alain Juppé, were questioned. The findings of the commission, published in December, effectively cleared France of any blame in the matter but implicated the international community (and particularly the USA) for failing to provide adequate support for UN forces in the country. The findings were rejected by the Rwandan Government.

In September 1994, following the killing by Islamist terrorists of five French officials at the French embassy in Algiers, the French Government initiated an extensive security operation, the results of which included the detention and subsequent expulsion from France of a number of alleged Islamic fundamentalist activists. In December members of the French security forces killed four Islamist terrorists on board an Air France aircraft, which had been hijacked in Algiers and flown to Marseille. The following day four Catholic priests, three of them French citizens, were killed in Algeria, in apparent reprisal for the actions of the French security forces. Eight people were killed in the second half of 1995 in a series of bombings in Paris and Lyon, for which the Armed Islamic Group (GIA), an extremist Algerian terrorist organization, was widely believed to be responsible. Although a number of arrests followed, terrorist activity resumed in December 1996 when four people were killed and many injured in an explosion on a crowded commuter train in Paris. Although no organization claimed responsibility for the attack it was speculated that the bombing might be in protest against the imminent trial in Paris of 30 young men of north African extraction who were accused of involvement in terrorist activities in Morocco in 1994. In December 1996 the GIA warned that it would continue its terrorist campaign in France, unless the French Government undertook to sever ties with the Algerian Government. France has been accused by Islamist groups in Algeria of providing covert military assistance to the Algerian Government following the suspension of the 1992 general election in Algeria (q.v.). France continued to resist increasing pressure to intervene in the ongoing atrocities in Algeria during 1997 and early 1998. In February 1998 36 Islamist militants were sentenced to up to 10 years' imprisonment for providing logistical support to the GIA during its bombing campaign in 1995. In September 1998 the trial of 138 suspected Islamist militants opened in Paris; 24 of the suspects were found guilty. In late 1999 24 Islamist militants, allegedly linked to the GIA, were found guilty of a series of bombings, perpetrated in 1995, in which 10 people died. Diplomatic contacts between Algerian President Abdelaziz Bouteflika and the French Minister of Foreign Affairs resulted in the reopening of a number of French consulates in Algeria, and in the resumption of flights to the country by Air France for the first time since their suspension in 1994.

In mid-1999 six Libyan intelligence agents were convicted *in absentia* of the bombing of a French airliner over Niger in 1989, in which all 170 passengers and crew were killed. The Libyan Government, which had refused to extradite the defendants, assured the French Government that it would abide by the verdict.

Relations with the People's Republic of China (PRC) were severely prejudiced in 1993 by France's decision to sell armaments to China (Taiwan). In January 1994 France suspended further sales of military equipment to Taiwan and announced the renewal of normal working relations with the PRC. In April the French Prime Minister visited Beijing, and in July the President of the PRC signed a trade agreement in Paris. Demonstrations took place in Paris in late 1999 in protest at the visit of the Chinese President Jiang Zemin. The visit of the Iranian President Muhammad Khatami to France caused similar rallies against the country's human rights record.

In October 1999 France refused to revoke its ban on imports of British beef, despite the formal ending in July of the ban imposed in 1996 by the EU. The French Government disregarded warnings that it would be in breach of EU policy were it to continue to block imports of British beef. The British Government also threatened to take legal action against France. The situation was further complicated when a report published by the European Commission in late October revealed the presence of human waste and sewage in French animal feed. In response to action by British farmers trying to prevent imports of French products, French farmers blockaded British trucks in Calais. In December the EU announced that it was to give France five days (subsequently extended by one week) to lift its ban, or it would commence legal proceedings against it. The French Government responded by stating that it would take the European Commission to court for failing to revise its decision to remove the ban on British beef earlier that year, and neglecting to protect public health. Legal action against France began in January 2000, but was expected to take as long as 18 months to be settled.

The imposition by the US Government of 100% import duties on a number of French products, in retaliation for a ban by the EU on hormone-treated beef, led to numerous protests throughout France in September 1999. The demonstrations, aimed, notably, at a US fast food chain, were triggered by the arrest of farmer and peace activist José Bové, following the destruction of a US fast food restaurant. Protesters denounced low prices, modern technologies and genetically-modified foods.

In late 1999 the European Commission announced that it was to take legal action against France because of the country's failure to open up its electricity markets to outside competition. France responded by pledging to end the monopoly of Electricité de France by mid-February 2000.

In January 1988 France and the Federal Republic of Germany signed new agreements on defence and economic co-operation (including the formation of a joint military brigade) to commemorate the 25th anniversary of the Franco-German treaty of friendship. In September 1990 France announced plans to withdraw all of its 50,000 troops stationed in Germany over the next few years. In May 1992 France and Germany announced that they would establish a joint defence force of 50,000 troops, the 'Eurocorps', which was intended to provide a basis for a European army under the aegis of Western European Union (WEU, see p. 268) and which became operational on 30 November 1995. Belgium, Spain and Luxembourg also agreed to participate in the force. In January 1993 an agreement was signed between NATO and the French and German Governments, establishing formal links between the corps and NATO's military structure. In December 1995 it was announced that France would rejoin the military structure of NATO, although it would not initially become a full member of NATO's integrated military command and would retain control of its independent nuclear forces. France's re-entry into the integrated military command was delayed in 1996, following a dispute with the USA over command of the alliance troops in southern Europe (a division of the alliance which includes the US sixth fleet). France has repeatedly insisted that the division be under the command of a European officer, and the dispute has undermined efforts to restructure NATO.

### Government

Under the 1958 Constitution, legislative power is held by the bicameral Parliament, comprising a Senate and a National Assembly. The Senate has 321 members (296 for metropolitan France, 13 for the overseas departments, 'collectivités territoriales' and territories, and 12 for French nationals abroad). Senators are elected for a nine-year term by an electoral college composed of the members of the National Assembly, delegates from the Councils of the Departments and delegates from the Municipal Councils. One-third of the Senate is renewable every three years. The National Assembly has 577 members, with 555 for metropolitan France and 22 for overseas departments, 'collectivités territoriales' and territories. Members of the

Assembly are elected by universal adult suffrage, under a single-member constituency system of direct election, using a second ballot if the first ballot failed to produce an absolute majority for any one candidate. The Assembly's term is five years, subject to dissolution. Executive power is held by the President. Since 1962 the President has been directly elected by popular vote (using two ballots if necessary) for seven years. The President appoints a Council of Ministers, headed by the Prime Minister, which administers the country and is responsible to Parliament.

Metropolitan France comprises 21 administrative regions containing 96 departments. Under the decentralization law of March 1982, administrative and financial power in metropolitan France was transferred from the Préfets, who became Commissaires de la République, to locally-elected departmental assemblies (Conseils généraux) and regional assemblies (Conseils régionaux). The special status of a 'collectivité territoriale' was granted to Corsica, which has its own directly-elected legislative Assembly. There are four overseas departments (French Guiana, Guadeloupe, Martinique and Réunion), two overseas 'collectivités territoriales' (Mayotte and St Pierre and Miquelon) and four overseas territories (French Polynesia, the French Southern and Antarctic Territories, New Caledonia and the Wallis and Futuna Islands), all of which are integral parts of the French Republic (see p. 1481). Each overseas department is administered by an elected Conseil général and Conseil régional, each 'collectivité territoriale' by an appointed government commissioner, and each overseas territory by an appointed high commissioner.

### Defence

French military policy is decided by the Supreme Defence Council. Military service is currently compulsory and lasts for 10 months, although proposals to create fully professional armed forces were submitted to the National Assembly in 1996. The cessation of conscription and decreased defence expenditure were expected to result in a reduction in the number of military personnel of some 25% by 2002. In August 1999 the total active armed forces numbered 317,300 (including 103,500 conscripts), including an army of 178,500, a navy of 62,600 and an air force of 76,400. In addition, there was a paramilitary gendarmerie of 94,300 (including 13,700 conscripts). Total reserves stood at 419,000 (army 242,500; navy 97,000; air force 79,500). Government expenditure on defence in 1998 amounted to 240,000m. francs. Defence expenditure was estimated at 190,000m. francs for 1999, and was projected at 185,000m. francs per year until 2002. Although a member of NATO, France withdrew from its integrated military organization in 1966, and possesses its own nuclear weapons. In 1995, however, it was announced that France was to rejoin NATO's defence committee, and in 1996 President Chirac declared France's intention to rejoin NATO's integrated military command.

### Economic Affairs

In 1997, according to estimates by the World Bank, France's gross national product (GNP), measured at average 1995–97 prices, was US $1,541,630m., equivalent to $26,300 per head. During 1990–97, it was estimated, GNP per head expanded, in real terms, at an average annual rate of 1.0%. Over the same period, the population increased by an average of 0.5% per year. France's gross domestic product (GDP) increased, in real terms, by an average of 2.3% per year in 1980–90, and by an average of 1.3% per year in 1990–97. Real GDP grew by 2.4% in 1997, by an estimated 3.2% in 1998 and was forecast to increase by 2.5% in 1999 and 3.0% in 2000.

Agriculture (including forestry and fishing) contributed 2.5% of GDP in 1994, and engaged 3.7% of the economically active population in 1998. The principal crops are wheat, sugar beet, maize and barley. Livestock, dairy products and wine are also important. Agricultural production increased by an average of 2.0% per year in 1980–90 and by an average of 0.6% per year in 1990–98.

Industry (including mining, manufacturing, construction and power) provided 27.6% of GDP, and employed 26.6% of the working population, in 1994. Industrial GDP, measured at constant prices, increased by an average of 1.1% per year during 1980–90, but declined by 1.0% in 1991, before increasing by 0.3% in 1992. Industrial production (excluding construction) increased at an average annual rate of 1.0% during 1990–98. It rose by 3.9% in 1997 and by 4.4% in 1998.

Mining and quarrying contributed 0.4% of GDP and employed 0.3% of the working population in 1994. Coal is the principal mineral produced, while petroleum and natural gas are also extracted. In addition, metallic minerals, including iron ore, copper and zinc, are mined. In real terms, the GDP of the mining sector declined at an average annual rate of 2.6% in 1980–90. It increased by 13.8% in 1991, by 5.5% in 1992 and by 9.5% in 1993, but declined by 8.4% in 1994.

Manufacturing provided 20.0% of GDP and employed 18.8% of the working population in 1994. Production in the manufacturing sector increased at an average rate of 0.9% per year in 1990–98. It rose by 4.7% in 1997 and by 4.9% in 1998. Measured by the value of output, the most important branches of manufacturing in 1995 were machinery and transport equipment (accounting for 31% of the total), food, beverages and tobacco (17%), chemicals (10%) and fabricated metal products (6%).

In 1997 nuclear power provided 78.2% of total electricity production, hydroelectric power 13.9% and thermal power 7.9%. Imports of mineral fuels comprised 8.3% of the value of total imports in 1996.

Services accounted for 69.9% of GDP, and employed 68.7% of the working population, in 1994. The combined GDP of all service sectors increased, in real terms, at an average rate of 3.0% per year in 1980–90, and by 1.5% per year in 1990–94.

In 1998 France recorded a trade surplus of US $26,170m., and there was a surplus of $40,160m. on the current account of the balance of payments. In 1997 the principal source of imports (16.6%) was Germany, which was also the principal market for exports (15.9%). Other major trading partners were Italy (9.8% of imports; 9.3% of exports), Belgium and Luxembourg (8.0% of imports; 8.1% of exports), the USA (8.7% of imports; 6.6% of exports) and the United Kingdom (8.5% of imports; 10.1% of exports). The EU as a whole provided 61.2% of imports in 1997 and took 62.8% of exports. The principal exports in 1997 were machinery and transport equipment, basic manufactures, chemicals and food and live animals. The principal imports were machinery and transport equipment, basic manufactures and miscellaneous manufactured articles.

The budget deficit for 1997 amounted to an estimated 275,887m. francs, equivalent to 3.7% of GDP, and was forecast to be equivalent to some 4.5% of GDP in 1998. A deficit of 236,600m. francs was forecast for 1999. In 1998 gross state debt amounted to an estimated 59.9% of annual GDP. The average annual rate of inflation in 1990–98 was 1.9%. In 1998 the rate was 0.7% (the lowest annual average for more than 40 years), and in 1999 it fell to only 0.5%. The average rate of unemployment decreased from 12.4% of the labour force in 1997 to 11.8% in 1998.

France is a member of the European Union (EU, see p. 172) and of the Organisation for Economic Co-operation and Development (see p. 232), and presides over the Franc Zone (see p. 200).

As one of the initial 11 member countries of the EU that had chosen to participate in a single currency under economic and monetary union (EMU, see p. 189), France adopted the euro on 1 January 1999 as a single currency unit for transactions throughout the euro zone and as an internationally traded currency. The euro was not expected to become legal tender in France until 1 July 2002. Among the stated economic priorities of the Jospin administration has been the reduction of the country's persistently high rate of unemployment. Notably, legislation was approved in February 1998 to reduce the duration of the working week from 39 to 35 hours. The programme of privatization of a number of major state-owned corporations (initiated in 1993) was delayed, and in some cases suspended. In 1997, however, the Government announced the transfer of more than 30% of France Télécom to the private sector, and in 1999 Crédit Lyonnais was privatized. The merger of Société Générale and Banque Paribas in February created the fourth largest banking group in the world. Moreover, the mergers of Aerospatiale and Matra, and of TotalFina and Elf Aquitaine formed, respectively, the third largest defence group and the fourth largest petroleum company in the world. Unemployment declined to 10.8% in November 1999, the lowest level since 1992, and was expected to fall to less than 10% by the end of 2000. The strong position of the economy, which was forecast to grow by 2.5% in 1999 and by 3.0% in 2000, was an important factor in lowering unemployment. Moreover, according to government sources, the shorter working week successfully created or preserved up to 120,000 jobs in 1999. However, some reservations were expressed by the IMF, notably over the funding of the new policy. The budget for 2000 included measures aimed at reducing the budget deficit (targeted at 1.8% of GDP for 2000), in accordance with the requirements of the Stability Growth Pact necessary for entry into EMU. Other measures included curbing public spending (in particular reducing expenditure on social security), and lowering taxes. Severe storms in mainland France at the end of December 1999 caused considerable material damage, the cost of which was estimated to be as high as US $75m.

### Social Welfare

France has evolved a comprehensive system of social security, which is compulsory for all wage-earners and self-employed people. A national minimum hourly wage is in force, and is periodically adjusted in accordance with fluctuations in the cost of living. State insurance of wage-earners requires contributions from both employers and employees, and provides for sickness, unemployment, maternity, disability through industrial accident, and substantial allowances for large families. War veterans receive pensions and certain privileges, and widows the equivalent of three months' salary and pension. About 95% of all medical practitioners adhere to the state scheme. The patient pays directly for medical treatment and prescribed medicines, and then obtains reimbursement for all or part of the cost. Sickness benefits and pensions are related to the insured person's income, age and the length of time for which he or she has been insured. Plans for the reform of the state pension system and the encouragement of private pension schemes became law in 1994. Proposed budgetary expenditure by the central Government in 1998 included 73,163m. francs for social services and health (4.6% of total budgetary spending). Of total government expenditure (including disbursements by government-controlled social security funds) in 1992, about 487,700m. francs (15.5%) was for health, and a further 1,419,900m. francs (45.1%) for social security and welfare. The Caisse d'Amortissement de la Dette Sociale (CADES), a financial institution created in 1996, is responsible for eliminating the deficit in the social services sector (estimated at 120,000m. francs in 1994–95 and projected at 17,000m. francs for 1996). CADES is funded by a special income tax, levied since 1996. In 1997 France had 4,186 hospital establishments (of which 1,063 were public), with a total of 659,539 beds (459,792 of which were in public establishments). In 1996 there were 144,759 physicians registered in France.

### Education

France is divided into 27 educational districts, called Académies, each responsible for the administration of education, from primary to higher levels, in its area. Education is compulsory and free for children aged six to 16 years. Primary education begins at six years of age and lasts for five years. At the age of 11 all pupils enter the first cycle of the Enseignement secondaire, with a four-year general course. At the age of 15 they may then proceed to the second cycle, choosing a course leading to the baccalauréat examination after three years or a course leading to vocational qualifications after two or three years, with commercial, administrative or industrial options. In 1963 junior classes in the Lycées were gradually abolished in favour of new junior comprehensives, called Collèges. Alongside the collèges and lycées, technical education is provided in the Lycées professionnels and the Lycées techniques. About 17% of children attend France's 10,000 private schools, most of which are administered by the Roman Catholic Church.

Educational reforms, introduced in 1980, aimed to decentralize the state school system: the school calendar now varies according to three zones, and the previously rigid and formal syllabus has been replaced by more flexibility and choice of curricula. Further decentralization measures included, from 1986, the transfer of financial responsibility for education to the local authorities.

The minimum qualification for entry to university faculties is the baccalauréat. There are three cycles of university education. The first level, the Diplôme d'études universitaires générales (DEUG), is reached after two years of study, and the first degree, the Licence, is obtained after three years. The master's degree (Maîtrise) is obtained after four years of study, while the doctorate requires six or seven years' study and the submission of a thesis. The prestigious Grandes Ecoles complement the universities; entry to them is by competitive examination, and they have traditionally supplied France's administrative élite. The 1968 reforms in higher education aimed to increase university autonomy and to render teaching methods less formal. Enrolment at schools in 1993 included 99% of children in the relevant age-group for primary education and 92% for secondary education. Expenditure on education by all levels of government in 1997 totalled an estimated 591,889m. francs (7.3% of GNP). Proposed budgetary expenditure on education by the central Government amounted to 334,378m. francs in 1998 (21.1% of total budgetary expenditure). Primary teachers are trained in Ecoles Normales. Secondary teachers must have been awarded either the Certificat d'Aptitude au Professorat d'Enseignement Général des Collèges (CAPEGC), the Certificat d'Aptitude au Professorat de l'Enseignement du Second Degré (CAPES) or the Agrégation.

### Public Holidays

**2000:** 1 January (New Year's Day), 24 April (Easter Monday), 1 May (Labour Day), 8 May (Liberation Day), 1 June (Ascension Day), 12 June (Whit Monday), 14 July (National Day, Fall of the Bastille), 15 August (Assumption), 1 November (All Saints' Day), 11 November (Armistice Day), 25 December (Christmas Day).

**2001:** 1 January (New Year's Day), 16 April (Easter Monday), 1 May (Labour Day), 8 May (Liberation Day), 24 May (Ascension Day), 4 June (Whit Monday), 14 July (National Day, Fall of the Bastille), 15 August (Assumption), 1 November (All Saints' Day), 11 November (Armistice Day), 25 December (Christmas Day).

### Weights and Measures

The metric system is in force.

# Statistical Survey

Unless otherwise indicated, figures in this survey refer to metropolitan France, excluding Overseas Departments and Territories.
Source (unless otherwise stated): Institut national de la statistique et des études économiques, 18 boulevard Adolphe Pinard, 75675 Paris Cédex 14; tel. 1-45-17-50-50.

## Area and Population

### AREA, POPULATION AND DENSITY

| | |
|---|---|
| Area (sq km) | 543,965* |
| Population (census results, *de jure*)† | |
| 5 March 1990‡ | |
| Males | 27,553,788 |
| Females | 29,080,511 |
| Total | 56,634,299 |
| 8 March 1999 | 58,416,500 |
| Density (per sq km) at 1999 census | 107.4 |

* 210,026 sq miles.
† Excluding professional soldiers and military personnel outside the country with no personal residence in France.
‡ Figures include double counting. The revised total is 56,615,155.

### NATIONALITY OF THE POPULATION
(numbers resident in France at 1990 census*)

| Country of citizenship | Population | % |
|---|---|---|
| France | 53,026,709 | 93.63 |
| Algeria | 619,923 | 1.09 |
| Belgium | 59,705 | 0.11 |
| Germany | 51,483 | 0.09 |
| Italy | 253,679 | 0.45 |
| Morocco | 584,708 | 1.03 |
| Poland | 46,283 | 0.08 |
| Portugal | 645,578 | 1.14 |
| Spain | 216,015 | 0.38 |
| Tunisia | 207,496 | 0.37 |
| Turkey | 201,480 | 0.36 |
| Yugoslavia | 51,697 | 0.09 |
| Others | 669,543 | 1.18 |
| **Total** | 56,634,299 | 100.00 |

* Figures include double counting. The revised total is 56,615,155.

### REGIONS (estimated population at 1 January 1996)

| | Area (sq km) | Population (rounded) | Density (per sq km) |
|---|---|---|---|
| Ile-de-France | 12,012.3 | 11,027,200 | 918.0 |
| Champagne–Ardenne | 25,605.8 | 1,351,800 | 52.8 |
| Picardie (Picardy) | 19,399.5 | 1,863,300 | 96.0 |
| Haute-Normandie | 12,317.4 | 1,781,500 | 144.6 |
| Centre | 39,150.9 | 2,442,700 | 62.4 |
| Basse-Normandie | 17,589.3 | 1,415,900 | 80.5 |
| Bourgogne (Burgundy) | 31,582.0 | 1,624,200 | 51.4 |
| Nord–Pas-de-Calais | 12,414.1 | 4,001,700 | 322.4 |
| Lorraine | 23,547.4 | 2,311,700 | 98.2 |
| Alsace | 8,280.2 | 1,702,200 | 205.6 |
| Franche-Comté | 16,202.3 | 1,115,800 | 68.9 |
| Pays de la Loire | 32,081.8 | 3,155,600 | 98.4 |
| Bretagne (Brittany) | 27,207.9 | 2,860,900 | 105.1 |
| Poitou–Charentes | 25,809.5 | 1,622,800 | 62.9 |
| Aquitaine | 41,308.4 | 2,877,200 | 69.7 |
| Midi–Pyrénées | 45,347.9 | 2,505,900 | 55.3 |
| Limousin | 16,942.3 | 717,600 | 42.4 |
| Rhône–Alpes | 43,698.2 | 5,608,200 | 128.3 |
| Auvergne | 26,012.9 | 1,314,700 | 50.5 |
| Languedoc–Roussillon | 27,375.8 | 2,244,200 | 82.0 |
| Provence–Alpes–Côte d'Azur | 31,399.6 | 4,452,100 | 141.8 |
| Corse (Corsica) | 8,679.8 | 260,700 | 30.0 |
| **Total** | 543,965.4 | 58,258,100 | 107.1 |

### PRINCIPAL TOWNS* (population at 1999 census)

| | | | |
|---|---|---|---|
| Paris (capital) | 2,115,757 | Brest | 149,748 |
| Marseille (Marseilles) | 797,700 | Le Mans | 145,867 |
| Lyon (Lyons) | 416,263 | Clermont-Ferrand | 136,583 |
| Toulouse | 390,712 | Amiens | 136,062 |
| Nice | 341,016 | Limoges | 133,591 |
| Nantes | 268,683 | Tours | 133,194 |
| Strasbourg | 263,896 | Nîmes | n.a. |
| Montpellier | 224,856 | Aix-en-Provence | 132,970 |
| Bordeaux | 214,940 | Metz | 123,164 |
| Rennes | 205,865 | Villeurbanne | 121,986 |
| Le Havre | 190,650 | Besançon | 117,261 |
| Reims (Rheims) | 187,149 | Caen | 113,591 |
| Lille | 182,228 | Orléans | 112,824 |
| Saint-Etienne | 179,708 | Perpignan | n.a. |
| Toulon | 160,406 | Mulhouse | 109,733 |
| Grenoble | 151,847 | Rouen | 106,029 |
| Angers | 151,107 | Boulogne-Billancourt | 105,682 |
| Dijon | 150,173 | Nancy | 102,587 |

* Figures refer to the population of communes.

### BIRTHS, MARRIAGES AND DEATHS*

| | Registered live births | | Registered marriages | | Registered deaths | |
|---|---|---|---|---|---|---|
| | Number | Rate (per 1,000) | Number | Rate (per 1,000) | Number | Rate (per 1,000) |
| 1989 | 765,473 | 13.6 | 279,900 | 5.0 | 529,283 | 9.4 |
| 1990 | 762,407 | 13.4 | 287,099 | 5.1 | 526,201 | 9.3 |
| 1991 | 759,056 | 13.3 | 280,175 | 4.9 | 524,685 | 9.2 |
| 1992 | 743,658 | 13.0 | 271,427 | 4.7 | 521,530 | 9.1 |
| 1993 | 711,610 | 12.3 | 255,190 | 4.4 | 532,263 | 9.2 |
| 1994 | 710,993 | 12.3 | 253,746 | 4.4 | 519,965 | 9.0 |
| 1995 | 729,609 | 12.5 | 254,651 | 4.4 | 531,618 | 9.1 |
| 1996† | 735,300 | 12.6 | 280,600 | 4.8 | 536,800 | 9.2 |

* Including data for national armed forces outside the country.
† Provisional figures.

**1997** (provisional figures): 725,000 registered live births; 284,500 registered marriages; 534,000 registered deaths.

**1998** (provisional figures): 740,300 registered live births (birth rate 12.6 per 1,000); 540,400 registered deaths (death rate 9.2 per 1,000).

**Expectation of life** (years at birth, 1997, provisional figures): Males 74.2; Females 82.1.

**ECONOMICALLY ACTIVE POPULATION***
(annual averages, '000 persons aged 15 years and over)

| | 1992 | 1993 | 1994 |
|---|---|---|---|
| Agriculture, hunting, forestry and fishing | 1,150.3 | 1,100.8 | 1,048.4 |
| Mining and quarrying | 72.0 | 69.9 | 65.9 |
| Manufacturing | 4,479.0 | 4,269.3 | 4,162.2 |
| Electricity, gas and water | 204.0 | 204.9 | 203.7 |
| Construction | 1,568.3 | 1,487.8 | 1,443.1 |
| Trade, restaurants and hotels | 3,715.2 | 3,680.5 | 3,715.7 |
| Transport, storage and communications | 1,418.4 | 1,403.1 | 1,397.0 |
| Financing, insurance, real estate and business services | 2,295.2 | 2,265.1 | 2,340.4 |
| Community, social and personal services† | 7,405.4 | 7,596.2 | 7,733.8 |
| **Total employed** | 22,307.6 | 22,078.2 | 22,110.0 |
| Persons on compulsory military service | 221.1 | 219.9 | 212.4 |
| Unemployed | 2,590.7 | 2,929.0 | 3,163.8 |
| **Total labour force** | 25,119.4 | 25,227.1 | 25,486.2 |

* Figures are provisional. The revised totals (in '000) are: Employed 22,306.0 in 1992, 22,052.7 in 1993, 22,043.8 in 1994; Persons on compulsory military service 225.0 in 1992; Unemployed 2,590.0 in 1992, 2,929.4 in 1993, 3,117.0 in 1994; Labour force 25,121.0 in 1992, 25,202.0 in 1993, 25,373.2 in 1994.

† Figures include regular members of the armed forces, officially estimated at 304,200 (males 286,000; females 18,200) in 1986.

Source: mainly ILO, *Yearbook of Labour Statistics*.

**1995** (annual averages, '000 persons aged 15 years and over): Total employed 22,190.0; Persons on compulsory military service 206.1; Unemployed 2,930.9; Total labour force 25,327.0 (males 14,027.9, females 11,299.1).

**1996** (annual averages, '000 persons aged 15 years and over): Total employed 22,246,7; Persons on compulsory military service 199.9; Unemployed 3,137.2; Total labour force 25,583.8 (males 14,176.7, females 11,407.1).

**1997** (annual averages, '000 persons aged 15 years and over, provisional): Total employed 22,327.2; Persons on compulsory military service 169.4; Unemployed 3,192.0; Total labour force 25,688.6 (males 14,236.6, females 11,452.0).

# Agriculture

**PRINCIPAL CROPS** ('000 metric tons)

| | 1996 | 1997 | 1998 |
|---|---|---|---|
| Wheat | 35,949 | 33,847 | 39,862 |
| Rye | 221 | 197 | 216 |
| Barley | 9,519 | 10,126 | 10,569 |
| Oats | 622 | 567 | 633 |
| Maize* | 14,530 | 16,832 | 14,426 |
| Sorghum | 343 | 455 | 397 |
| Rice (paddy) | 115 | 121 | 113 |
| Sugar beet | 31,211 | 34,311 | 31,407 |
| Potatoes | 6,249 | 6,686 | 6,200† |
| Pulses | 2,629 | 3,121 | 3.383 |
| Soybeans | 230 | 269 | 282 |
| Sunflower seed | 1,996 | 1,995 | 1,736 |
| Rapeseed | 2,902 | 3,495 | 3,756 |
| Tobacco (leaves) | 28 | 25 | 25† |
| Artichokes | 75 | 76 | 75† |
| Cabbages | 244 | 237 | 240† |
| Carrots | 644 | 675 | 670† |
| Cauliflowers | 502 | 509 | 500† |
| Cucumbers and gherkins | 140 | 140 | 135† |
| Melons | 315 | 278 | 280† |
| Onions (dry) | 324 | 337 | 340† |
| Garlic | 46 | 45 | 46† |
| Beans (green) | 104 | 114 | 115† |
| Peas (green) | 575 | 550 | 450† |
| Tomatoes | 776 | 805 | 800† |
| Apples | 2,446 | 2,445 | 2,500† |
| Apricots | 176 | 151 | 160† |
| Grapes | 7,701 | 7,162 | 7,000† |
| Peaches and nectarines | 464 | 469 | 470† |
| Pears | 367 | 271 | 256‡ |
| Plums | 351 | 211 | 210‡ |

* Figures refer to main, associated and catch crops.

† FAO estimate.

‡ Unofficial figure.

Source: FAO, *Production Yearbook*.

**LIVESTOCK** ('000 head, year ending 30 September)

| | 1996 | 1997 | 1998 |
|---|---|---|---|
| Cattle | 20,661 | 20,664 | 20,389 |
| Pigs | 14,530 | 14,976 | 15,430 |
| Sheep | 10,556 | 10,463 | 10,305 |
| Goats | 1,188 | 1,202 | 1,200 |
| Horses | 338 | 340 | 347 |
| Asses* | 25 | 25 | 25 |
| Mules | 14 | 14 | 14* |
| Chickens (million) | 221 | 231 | 238 |
| Ducks (million) | 21 | 23 | 23* |
| Turkeys (million) | 40 | 42 | 42* |

* FAO estimate(s).

Source: FAO, *Production Yearbook*.

**LIVESTOCK PRODUCTS** ('000 metric tons)

| | 1996 | 1997 | 1998 |
|---|---|---|---|
| Beef and veal | 1,735 | 1,718 | 1,595 |
| Mutton and lamb | 146 | 141 | 138* |
| Goat meat | 7 | 8 | 7* |
| Pig meat | 2,183 | 2,220 | 2,300* |
| Horse meat | 11 | 11 | 11† |
| Poultry meat | 2,194 | 2,134 | 2,176 |
| Other meat | 298 | 286 | 280 |
| Cows' milk | 25,109 | 24,916 | 24,500* |
| Sheep's milk | 237 | 243 | 243† |
| Goats' milk | 472 | 486 | 480† |
| Butter | 473 | 475 | 465* |
| Cheese | 1,605 | 1,630 | 1,625 |
| Honey | 20 | 28 | 25† |
| Hen eggs | 994 | 1,009 | 954* |
| Wool: | | | |
| greasy | 22* | 22* | 22† |
| clean | 12* | 12* | 12† |
| Cattle hides† | 164 | 163 | 153 |
| Sheepskins† | 16 | 17 | 16 |

* Unofficial figure. † FAO estimate(s).

Source: FAO, mainly *Production Yearbook*.

# Forestry

**ROUNDWOOD REMOVALS** ('000 cubic metres, excluding bark)

| | 1995 | 1996 | 1997 |
|---|---|---|---|
| Sawlogs, veneer logs and logs for sleepers | 21,698 | 20,498 | 20,498 |
| Pulpwood | 11,414 | 9,698 | 9,698 |
| Other industrial wood | 460 | 447 | 447 |
| Fuel wood | 10,460 | 10,460 | 10,466 |
| **Total** | 44,032 | 41,103 | 41,109 |

Source: FAO, *Yearbook of Forest Products*.

**SAWNWOOD PRODUCTION**
('000 cubic metres, including railway sleepers)

| | 1995 | 1996 | 1997 |
|---|---|---|---|
| Coniferous (softwood) | 6,827 | 6,506 | 6,900 |
| Broadleaved (hardwood) | 3,021 | 3,094 | 3,100 |
| **Total** | 9,848 | 9,600 | 10,000 |

Source: FAO, *Yearbook of Forest Products*.

# Fishing*

('000 metric tons, live weight)

| | 1995 | 1996 | 1997 |
|---|---|---|---|
| Atlantic cod | 17.7 | 16.2 | 16.2 |
| Saithe (Pollock) | 19.9 | 19.6 | 19.6 |
| Whiting | 27.8 | 21.5 | 21.3 |
| European hake | 16.3 | 12.3 | 10.3 |
| Angler (Monk) | 18.2 | 18.2 | 18.5 |
| Atlantic herring | 33.2 | 17.4 | 20.4 |
| European pilchard (sardine) | 24.6 | 16.9 | 17.0 |
| European anchovy | 15.8 | 18.8 | 20.7 |
| Skipjack tuna | 72.8 | 55.1 | 44.4 |
| Yellowfin tuna | 70.7 | 72.7 | 63.2 |
| Bigeye tuna | 13.8 | 18.1 | 13.7 |
| Atlantic mackerel | 23.6 | 19.4 | 25.4 |
| Sharks, rays, skates, etc. | 21.6 | 22.1 | 22.5 |
| Other fishes (incl. unspecified) | 147.4 | 162.7 | 160.4 |
| **Total fish** | 523.5 | 490.9 | 473.7 |
| Crustaceans | 22.1 | 21.3 | 21.3 |
| Oysters | 0.1 | 0.1 | 0.1 |
| Blue mussel | 8.9 | 0.2 | 0.2 |
| Mediterranean mussel | 1.9 | 0.5 | 1.1 |
| Cuttlefishes and bobtail squids | 14.6 | 14.7 | 14.5 |
| Other molluscs | 39.2 | 33.8 | 31.5 |
| Other marine animals | 0.1 | 0.1 | 0.1 |
| **Total catch** | 610.3 | 561.6 | 542.4 |
| Inland waters | 4.5 | 4.5 | 4.5 |
| Mediterranean and Black Sea | 38.0 | 27.8 | 33.0 |
| Atlantic Ocean | 468.1 | 443.4 | 430.5 |
| Indian Ocean | 99.7 | 85.8 | 74.3 |

* Figures exclude aquatic plants ('000 metric tons): 75.6 in 1995; 84.4 in 1996; 75.5 in 1997. Also excluded are corals, sponges and the products of fish-farming.

Source: FAO, *Yearbook of Fishery Statistics*.

# Mining

('000 metric tons, unless otherwise indicated)

| | 1994 | 1995 | 1996 |
|---|---|---|---|
| Hard coal | 7,538 | 7,645 | 7,314 |
| Brown coal (incl. lignite) | 1,501 | 1,400 | n.a. |
| Iron ore: | | | |
| gross weight | 2,418 | 1,497 | n.a. |
| metal content | 708 | 433 | 348 |
| Crude petroleum | 2,769 | 2,503 | 2,257 |
| Potash salts* | 936 | 869 | 812 |
| Salt (unrefined) | 4,764 | 4,500 | n.a. |
| Zinc concentrates (metric tons)† | — | — | — |
| Natural gas (petajoules) | 94.4 | 130 | 112 |

* Figures refer to recovered quantities of $K_2O$.

† Figures refer to the metal content of concentrates.

Source: mainly UN, *Industrial Commodity Statistics Yearbook*.

# Industry

**SELECTED PRODUCTS**

('000 metric tons, unless otherwise indicated)

| | 1994 | 1995 | 1996 |
|---|---|---|---|
| Margarine and other prepared fats | 134.8 | 131.2 | 138.3 |
| Wheat flour* | 5,186 | 5,282 | 5,400 |
| Raw sugar† | 4,014 | 4,198 | 4,179 |
| Wine ('000 hectolitres) | 54,850 | n.a. | n.a. |
| Beer ('000 hectolitres) | 17,688 | 18,311 | 17,140 |
| Cigarettes (million) | 48,188 | 46,361 | 46,931 |
| Cotton yarn—pure (metric tons)[1] | 110,400 | n.a. | n.a. |
| Woven cotton fabrics—pure and mixed (metric tons) | 87,000 | n.a. | n.a. |
| Wool yarn—pure and mixed (metric tons) | 15,800 | n.a. | n.a. |
| Woven woollen fabrics—pure and mixed (metric tons) | 25,850 | n.a. | n.a. |
| Non-cellulosic continuous filaments (metric tons) | 63,100 | n.a. | n.a. |
| Non-cellulosic discontinuous fibres (metric tons) | 61,600 | n.a. | n.a. |
| Woven fabrics of non-cellulosic (synthetic) fibres (metric tons) | 14,028 | n.a. | n.a. |
| Mechanical wood pulp | 886 | 934 | 757 |
| Chemical wood pulp‡ | 1,901 | 1,884 | 1,758 |
| Newsprint | 844 | 890 | 783 |
| Other printing and writing paper | 3,268 | 3,096 | 3,141 |
| Other paper and paperboard | 4,589 | 4,633 | 4,632 |
| Synthetic rubber | 518.4 | 619.4 | n.a. |
| Rubber tyres ('000)[2] | 66,744 | n.a. | n.a. |
| Sulphuric acid | 2,227 | 2,382 | n.a. |
| Caustic soda (Sodium hydroxide) | 1,561 | 1,501 | n.a. |
| Nitrogenous fertilizers (a)[3,4] | 1,720 | n.a. | n.a. |
| Phosphate fertilizers (b)[3] | 936 | n.a. | n.a. |
| Potash fertilizers (c)[3,4] | 870 | n.a. | n.a. |
| Liquefied petroleum gas[5] | 2,488 | 2,459 | n.a. |
| Motor spirit (petrol) | 17,696 | 17,946 | n.a. |
| Jet fuels | 5,297 | 5,649 | n.a. |
| Kerosene | 51 | 45 | n.a. |
| Distillate fuel oils | 30,501 | 30,877 | 32,568 |
| Residual fuel oils | 10,668 | 9,427 | n.a. |
| Petroleum bitumen (asphalt) | 3,348 | 3,132 | n.a. |
| Coke-oven coke | 5,880 | 5,566 | n.a. |
| Cement | 20,184 | 19,896 | n.a. |
| Pig-iron | 12,444 | 12,876 | 11,547 |
| Crude steel | 18,242 | 18,101 | 17,633 |
| Aluminium (unwrought): | | | |
| primary | 481.5 | 364.5 | 380.1 |
| secondary (incl. alloys) | 227.4 | 253.6 | 236.8 |
| Refined copper—unwrought (metric tons) | 51,600 | 54,000 | 62,000 |
| Lead (unwrought): | | | |
| primary | 105.3 | 128.7 | 139.1 |
| secondary | 75.4 | 168.0 | 162.0 |
| Zinc (unwrought): | | | |
| primary | 293.0 | 290.0 | 320.0 |
| Secondary | 29.3 | | |
| Radio receivers ('000) | 2,804 | n.a. | n.a. |
| Television receivers ('000) | 2,796 | n.a. | n.a. |
| Merchant ships launched ('000 gross reg. tons) | 172 | 70 | 124 |
| Passenger motor cars ('000) | 3,176 | n.a. | n.a. |
| Lorries and vans ('000) | 453.3 | n.a. | n.a. |
| Electric energy (million kWh) | 475,622 | 492,609 | 511,376 |

* Deliveries.

† Estimated production during crop year ending 30 September.

‡ Including semi-chemical pulp, but excluding dissolving grades.

1 Including tyre-cord yarn.

2 Tyres for road motor vehicles other than bicycles and motor cycles.

3 Production of fertilizers is in terms of plant nutrients: (a) nitrogen; (b) phosphoric acid; or (c) potassium oxide.

4 Figures refer to output during the 12 months ending 30 June of year stated.

5 Excluding production in natural gas processing plants ('000 metric tons): 228 in 1994; 203 in 1995.

Source: mainly UN, *Industrial Commodity Statistics Yearbook*.

# Finance

**CURRENCY AND EXCHANGE RATES**

**Monetary Units:**

100 centimes = 1 French franc.

**Sterling, Dollar and Euro Equivalents** (30 September 1999)

£1 sterling = 10.1269 francs;
US $1 = 6.1506 francs;
€1 = 6.5596 francs;
1,000 French francs = £98.75 = $162.59 = €152.45.

**Average Exchange Rate** (francs per US $)

1996 5.1155
1997 5.8367
1998 5.8995

**GENERAL BUDGET** (estimates, million francs)

| Revenue | 1996 | 1997 | 1998* |
|---|---|---|---|
| Tax revenue | 1,620,124 | 1,671,051 | 1,725,035 |
| Income tax | 314,136 | 290,000 | 296,550 |
| Corporation tax | 171,700 | 203,100 | 220,200 |
| Value-added tax | 728,244 | 753,000 | 776,770 |
| Stamp duty, etc.† | 85,443 | 91,850 | 91,750 |
| Other taxes | 320,601 | 333,101 | 339,765 |
| Non-tax revenue | 138,989 | 137,449 | 140,857 |
| **Sub-total** | 1,759,113 | 1,808,500 | 1,865,892 |
| Tax relief and reimbursements | −260,788 | −267,400 | −278,330 |
| Other deductions, e.g. EU | −243,016 | −252,970 | −255,724 |
| **Total** | 1,255,309 | 1,288,130 | 1,331,838 |

* Projected figures.

† Including registration duties and tax on stock exchange transactions.

| Expenditure | 1997 | 1998* |
|---|---|---|
| General non-salary disbursements (net) | 336,323 | 339,587 |
| Education | 324,218 | 334,378 |
| Culture and communications | 15,126 | 15,109 |
| Social services and health | 70,930 | 73,163 |
| Employment | 150,381 | 155,812 |
| Agriculture and fisheries | 35,244 | 35,172 |
| Housing | 40,348 | 39,834 |
| Transport, tourism and public works | 83,663 | 85,194 |
| Financial services | 45,844 | 46,547 |
| Industry | 25,158 | 16,367 |
| Home affairs | 76,195 | 77,829 |
| Foreign affairs | 14,462 | 14,387 |
| Defence† | 243,344 | 238,265 |
| Judiciary | 23,903 | 24,867 |
| Research and development | 28,909 | 39,611 |
| Other purposes | 49,969 | 49,185 |
| **Total** | 1,564,017 | 1,585,307 |

* Projected figures.

† Including expenditure allocated for retired personnel.

Source: Ministère du Budget.

**INTERNATIONAL RESERVES** (US $ million at 31 December)*

| | 1996 | 1997 | 1998 |
|---|---|---|---|
| Gold† | 30,368 | 25,002 | 29,871 |
| IMF special drawing rights | 981 | 971 | 1,107 |
| Reserve position in IMF | 2,695 | 2,859 | 4,452 |
| Foreign exchange | 23,120 | 27,097 | 38,753 |
| **Total** | 57,164 | 55,929 | 74,183 |

* Excluding deposits made with the European Monetary Institute (now the European Central Bank).

† Valued at market-related prices.

Source: IMF, *International Financial Statistics*.

**MONEY SUPPLY** ('000 million francs at 31 December)

| | 1995 | 1996 | 1997 |
|---|---|---|---|
| Currency outside banks | 258 | 260 | 263 |
| Demand deposits at banking institutions | 1,557 | 1,554 | 1,670 |
| **Total money** (incl. others) | 1,819 | 1,817 | 1,937 |

Source: IMF, *International Financial Statistics*.

**COST OF LIVING** (Consumer Price Index for Urban Households, average of monthly figures; base: 1990 = 100)

| | 1995 | 1996 | 1997 |
|---|---|---|---|
| Food (incl. beverages) | 105.8 | 107.1 | 109.0 |
| Fuel and light | 103.6 | 106.5 | 107.3 |
| Clothing and household linen | 107.3 | 108.3 | 108.8 |
| Rent | 121.5 | 124.1 | 125.8 |
| **All items** (incl. others) | 111.6 | 113.8 | 115.2 |

Source: ILO, *Yearbook of Labour Statistics*.

**NATIONAL ACCOUNTS**

**National Income and Product** (million francs at current prices)

| | 1991 | 1992* | 1993* |
|---|---|---|---|
| Compensation of employees | 3,531,792 | 3,669,277 | 3,723,188 |
| Operating surplus | 1,513,219 | 1,572,768 | 1,572,457 |
| **Domestic factor incomes** | 5,045,011 | 5,242,045 | 5,295,645 |
| Consumption of fixed capital | 880,117 | 907,100 | 925,227 |
| **Gross domestic product (GDP) at factor cost** | 5,925,128 | 6,149,145 | 6,220,872 |
| Indirect taxes | 995,345 | 1,015,855 | 1,036,157 |
| *Less* Subsidies | 144,242 | 154,460 | 174,239 |
| **GDP in purchasers' values** | 6,776,231 | 7,010,540 | 7,082,790 |
| Factor income received from abroad | 329,004 | 345,525 | 394,368 |
| *Less* Factor income paid abroad | 367,291 | 402,655 | 449,683 |
| **Gross national product (GNP)** | 6,737,944 | 6,953,410 | 7,027,475 |
| *Less* Consumption of fixed capital | 880,117 | 907,100 | 925,227 |
| **National income in market prices** | 5,857,827 | 6,046,310 | 6,102,248 |
| Other current transfers from abroad | 171,448 | 166,376 | 180,637 |
| *Less* Other current transfers paid abroad | 193,977 | 195,086 | 208,844 |
| **National disposable income** | 5,835,298 | 6,017,600 | 6,074,041 |

* Figures are provisional. Revised totals (in '000 million francs) are: GDP in purchasers' values 6,999.6 in 1992, 7,077.1 in 1993; GNP 6,918.4 in 1992, 7,022.9 in 1993; National income 6,012.5 in 1992, 6,097.1 in 1993.

Source: mainly UN, *National Accounts Statistics*.

**Expenditure on the Gross Domestic Product**
('000 million francs at current prices)

| | 1996 | 1997 | 1998 |
|---|---|---|---|
| Government final consumption expenditure | 1,971.1 | 2,026.5 | 2,070.7 |
| Private final consumption expenditure | 4,392.5 | 4,464.2 | 4,658.7 |
| Increase in stocks* | −19.4 | −1.5 | 27.8 |
| Gross fixed capital formation* | 1,475.1 | 1,493.4 | 1,581.8 |
| **Total domestic expenditure** | 7,819.3 | 7,982.6 | 8,339.0 |
| Exports of goods and services | 1,835.1 | 2,093.6 | 2,225.0 |
| *Less* Imports of goods and services | 1,703.1 | 1,851.3 | 1,999.8 |
| **GDP in purchasers' values** | 7,951.4 | 8,224.9 | 8,564.7 |
| **GDP at constant 1995 prices** | 7,837.9 | 7,992.2 | 8,245.0 |

* Construction of non-residential buildings is included in 'Increase in stocks'.

Source: IMF, *International Financial Statistics*.

**Gross Domestic Product by Economic Activity**
(provisional, million francs at current prices)

| | 1992 | 1993 | 1994 |
|---|---|---|---|
| Agriculture, hunting, forestry and fishing | 198,285 | 165,023 | 177,196 |
| Mining and quarrying | 33,415 | 31,965 | 31,271 |
| Manufacturing | 1,426,063 | 1,379,540 | 1,415,399 |
| Electricity, gas and water | 164,957 | 171,904 | 176,232 |
| Construction | 357,036 | 344,028 | 335,104 |
| Trade, restaurants and hotels | 1,054,344 | 1,069,494 | 1,107,233 |
| Transport, storage and communications | 417,515 | 414,816 | 427,520 |
| Finance, insurance, real estate and business services* | 1,530,308 | 1,612,689 | 1,704,649 |
| Government services† | 1,146,242 | 1,214,479 | 1,270,319 |
| Other community, social and personal services | 414,046 | 432,031 | 446,240 |
| **Sub-total** | 6,742,211 | 6,835,969 | 7,091,163 |
| Value-added tax and import duties | 531,523 | 525,446 | 553,333 |
| *Less* Imputed bank service charges | 263,193 | 278,625 | 268,446 |
| **Total** | 7,010,540 | 7,082,790 | 7,376,050 |

* Including imputed rents of owner-occupied dwellings.
† Including private non-profit services to households.

Source: UN, *National Accounts Statistics*.

**BALANCE OF PAYMENTS** (US $ '000 million)*

| | 1996 | 1997 | 1998 |
|---|---|---|---|
| Exports of goods f.o.b. | 281.85 | 284.20 | 301.70 |
| Imports of goods f.o.b. | −266.91 | −256.13 | −275.53 |
| **Trade balance** | 14.94 | 28.07 | 26.17 |
| Exports of services | 83.53 | 81.14 | 85.42 |
| Imports of services | −67.28 | −63.65 | −66.72 |
| **Balance on goods and services** | 31.19 | 45.56 | 44.88 |
| Other income received | 47.55 | 52.76 | 62.39 |
| Other income paid | −50.25 | −50.06 | −58.01 |
| **Balance on goods, services and income** | 28.48 | 48.25 | 49.26 |
| Current transfers received | 22.76 | 20.99 | 20.97 |
| Current transfers paid | −30.68 | −29.77 | −30.07 |
| **Current balance** | 20.56 | 39.47 | 40.16 |
| Capital account (net) | 1.23 | 1.48 | 1.47 |
| Direct investment abroad | −30.36 | −35.48 | −40.80 |
| Direct investment from abroad | 21.97 | 23.04 | 28.00 |
| Portfolio investment assets | −53.10 | −70.54 | −119.31 |
| Portfolio investment liabilities | −7.55 | 45.46 | 68.54 |
| Other investment assets | 26.31 | −51.86 | 25.94 |
| Other investment liabilities | 20.38 | 49.48 | 7.00 |
| Net errors and omissions | 0.79 | 4.89 | 8.82 |
| **Overall balance** | 0.24 | 5.94 | 19.82 |

* Figures refer to transactions of metropolitan France, Monaco and the French Overseas Departments and Territories with the rest of the world.

Source: IMF, *International Financial Statistics*.

# External Trade

Note: Figures refer to the trade of metropolitan France and Monaco with the rest of the world, excluding trade in war materials, goods exported under the off-shore procurement programme, war reparations and restitutions and the export of sea products direct from the high seas. The figures include trade in second-hand ships and aircraft, and the supply of stores and bunkers for foreign ships and aircraft.

**PRINCIPAL COMMODITIES** (distribution by SITC, US $ million)

| Imports c.i.f. | 1994 | 1995 | 1996 |
|---|---|---|---|
| **Food and live animals** | 21,435.4 | 24,605.8 | 23,611.1 |
| Vegetables and fruit | 5,431.2 | 6,318.5 | 6,062.9 |
| **Crude materials (inedible) except fuels** | 8,067.6 | 10,009.7 | 8,697.3 |
| **Mineral fuels, lubricants, etc.** (incl. electric current) | 17,592.4 | 18,633.5 | 22,857.6 |
| Petroleum, petroleum products, etc. | 13,166.4 | 13,814.1 | 17,691.3 |
| Crude petroleum oils, etc. | 8,784.1 | 9,614.6 | 12,746.4 |
| **Chemicals and related products** | 26,758.2 | 33,559.1 | 32,862.7 |
| Organic chemicals | 6,235.3 | 7,571.1 | 7,431.9 |
| Medicinal and pharmaceutical products | 4,203.5 | 5,626.2 | 5,723.0 |
| Artificial resins, plastic materials, etc. | 5,882.2 | 7,499.2 | 6,938.5 |
| **Basic manufactures** | 37,072.2 | 46,502.6 | 42,980.6 |
| Paper, paperboard and manufactures | 5,573.8 | 7,317.0 | 6,790.0 |
| Textile yarn, fabrics, etc. | 6,621.2 | 7,542.8 | 7,083.5 |
| Iron and steel | 7,001.9 | 9,370.5 | 8,010.3 |
| Non-ferrous metals | 4,934.4 | 6,787.0 | 5,766.6 |
| Other metal manufactures | 5,188.7 | 6,422.3 | 6,395.7 |
| **Machinery and transport equipment** | 80,445.2 | 96,726.1 | 99,648.4 |
| Power-generating machinery and equipment | 7,053.7 | 6,821.6 | 6,713.4 |
| Machinery specialized for particular industries | 5,440.1 | 7,132.8 | 7,501.3 |
| General industrial machinery, equipment and parts | 9,018.1 | 11,412.3 | 11,801.2 |
| Office machines and automatic data-processing equipment | 10,796.3 | 13,215.0 | 13,342.5 |
| Automatic data-processing machines and units | 6,416.1 | 7,566.2 | 7,936.0 |
| Telecommunications and sound equipment | 5,282.2 | 6,422.3 | 6,686.5 |
| Other electrical machinery, apparatus, etc. | 13,544.4 | 17,221.2 | 17,339.1 |
| Road vehicles and parts* | 22,030.9 | 27,490.4 | 28,485.8 |
| Passenger motor cars (excl. buses) | 12,638.1 | 14,589.8 | 16,043.7 |
| Parts and accessories for cars, buses, lorries, etc.* | 4,587.1 | 5,731.2 | 5,617.9 |
| Other transport equipment and parts* | 5,997.0 | 5,268.2 | 5,852.0 |
| **Miscellaneous manufactured articles** | 32,574.9 | 38,089.4 | 38,828.2 |
| Clothing and accessories (excl. footwear) | 9,128.4 | 10,292.2 | 10,897.8 |
| **Total** | 228,281.6 | 273,387.4 | 274,913.8 |

* Excluding tyres, engines and electrical parts.

| Exports f.o.b. | 1994 | 1995 | 1996 |
|---|---|---|---|
| **Food and live animals** | 26,054.3 | 30,460.6 | 29,974.7 |
| Cereals and cereal preparations | 6,128.9 | 7,483.7 | 7,600.2 |
| **Beverages and tobacco** | 7,365.6 | 8,332.9 | 8,378.7 |
| Beverages | 7,145.2 | 8,064.6 | 8,086.9 |
| Alcoholic beverages | 6,398.1 | 7,193.6 | 7,328.4 |
| **Crude materials (inedible) except fuels** | 5,564.6 | 6,305.5 | 6,081.8 |
| **Mineral fuels, lubricants, etc.** (incl. electric current) | 5,784.0 | 6,854.3 | 7,429.3 |

| Exports f.o.b. — *continued* | 1994 | 1995 | 1996 |
|---|---|---|---|
| **Chemicals and related products** | 33,269.4 | 35,794.0 | 40,217.5 |
| Organic chemicals | 7,004.9 | 5,770.0 | 8,732.1 |
| Medicinal and pharmaceutical products | 5,415.4 | 6,864.4 | 7,244.7 |
| Essential oils, perfume materials and cleansing preparations | 6,287.0 | 7,557.3 | 7,636.7 |
| Perfumery, cosmetics and toilet preparations (excl. soaps) | 4,836.7 | 5,782.2 | 5,877.3 |
| Artificial resins, plastic materials, etc. | 5,642.4 | 6,113.6 | 6,883.0 |
| Products of polymerization, etc. | 5,106.0 | 5,389.6 | 6,208.6 |
| **Basic manufactures** | 38,359.9 | 46,603.8 | 45,742.1 |
| Paper, paperboard and manufactures | 4,897.1 | 6,368.7 | 5,924.7 |
| Textile yarn, fabrics, etc. | 6,541.6 | 7,911.8 | 7,644.7 |
| Iron and steel | 8,800.9 | 10,575.5 | 10,343.3 |
| Other metal manufactures | 4,882.1 | 6,108.9 | 5,990.1 |
| **Machinery and transport equipment** | 91,760.6 | 112,492.0 | 115,326.8 |
| Machinery specialized for particular industries | 6,007.5 | 7,279.7 | 7,497.4 |
| General industrial machinery, equipment and parts | 10,009.9 | 12,597.0 | 13,292.7 |
| Office machines and automatic data-processing equipment | 6,766.1 | 8,964.1 | 9,815.4 |
| Automatic data-processing machines and units | 3,882.9 | 5,714.2 | 6,496.9 |
| Telecommunications and sound equipment | 4,682.6 | 6,327.8 | 6,797.2 |
| Other electrical machinery, apparatus, etc. | 14,935.3 | 19,400.9 | 20,307.3 |
| Thermionic valves, tubes, etc. | 3,738.9 | 5,641.7 | 6,113.8 |
| Road vehicles and parts* | 26,647.9 | 31,377.0 | 31,618.6 |
| Passenger motor cars (excl. buses) | 13,789.5 | 15,212.2 | 15,803.8 |
| Parts and accessories for cars, buses, lorries, etc.* | 9,294.3 | 10,323.6 | 10,346.5 |
| Other transport equipment and parts* | 13,035.5 | 15,970.3 | 15,577.3 |
| Aircraft, associated equipment and parts* | 11,080.1 | 13,548.4 | 13,223.9 |
| **Miscellaneous manufactured articles** | 23,918.7 | 28,166.6 | 28,201.2 |
| Clothing and accessories (excl. footwear) | 4,975.4 | 5,622.4 | 5,529.8 |
| **Total** | 233,307.3 | 284,045.7 | 283,901.3 |

* Excluding tyres, engines and electrical parts.

**PRINCIPAL TRADING PARTNERS** (million francs)*

| Imports c.i.f. | 1995 | 1996 | 1997 |
|---|---|---|---|
| Belgium and Luxembourg | 124,936 | 121,416 | 125,885 |
| China, People's Republic | 26,499 | 31,119 | 38,855 |
| Germany | 259,197 | 249,540 | 259,973 |
| Ireland | 17,822 | 19,989 | 24,036 |
| Italy | 141,238 | 147,032 | 153,400 |
| Japan | 48,877 | 46,223 | 52,185 |
| Netherlands | 76,293 | 74,869 | 79,001 |
| Norway | 19,048 | 23,775 | 28,407 |
| Portugal | 15,811 | 16,704 | 17,358 |
| Russia | 17,449 | 20,656 | 20,355 |
| Saudi Arabia | 12,943 | 14,877 | 15,399 |
| Spain (excl. Canary Is.) | 90,689 | 99,242 | 104,230 |
| Sweden | 20,655 | 20,263 | 22,680 |
| Switzerland | 35,399 | 34,999 | 39,928 |
| United Kingdom | 111,223 | 119,888 | 132,822 |
| USA | 110,750 | 115,235 | 136,482 |
| **Total** (incl. others) | 1,399,744 | 1,436,689 | 1,567,983 |

| Exports f.o.b. | 1995 | 1996 | 1997 |
|---|---|---|---|
| Algeria | 14,236 | 12,591 | 13,359 |
| Austria | 16,701 | 16,218 | 17,367 |
| Belgium and Luxembourg | 122,868 | 125,110 | 134,205 |
| China, People's Republic | 13,186 | 12,406 | 20,026 |
| Germany | 251,849 | 252,817 | 264,305 |
| Hong Kong | 18,737 | 18,001 | 17,181 |
| Italy | 137,632 | 135,937 | 154,157 |
| Japan | 27,961 | 27,437 | 28,540 |
| Netherlands | 67,232 | 67,365 | 77,969 |
| Portugal | 20,076 | 20,262 | 23,481 |
| Spain (excl. Canary Is.) | 103,988 | 116,406 | 133,393 |
| Sweden | 18,459 | 20,978 | 24,233 |
| Switzerland | 55,038 | 56,622 | 58,084 |
| Turkey | 9,150 | 13,080 | 16,699 |
| United Kingdom | 132,286 | 138,569 | 167,967 |
| USA | 83,746 | 88,528 | 110,510 |
| **Total** (incl. others) | 1,409,505 | 1,460,010 | 1,663,727 |

* Based on revised figures for 1995 and 1996.

Source: Ministère de l'Économie, des Finances et de l'Industrie, Direction générale des Douanes et des Droits indirects.

# Transport

**RAILWAYS** (traffic)

| | 1991 | 1992 | 1993 |
|---|---|---|---|
| Paying passengers ('000 journeys) | 837,000 | 830,000 | 823,000 |
| Freight carried ('000 metric tons) | 141,100 | 137,300 | 121,490 |
| Passenger-km (million) | 62,290 | 62,870 | 58,430 |
| Freight ton-km (million)* | 51,480 | 50,370 | 45,860 |

* Including passengers' baggage.

**1994:** Passenger-km (million) 58,930; Freight ton-km (million) 49,720.

**1995:** Passenger-km (million) 55,560; Freight ton-km (million) 46,560.

**1996:** Passenger-km (million) 59,770; Freight ton-km (million) 48,310.

**1998:** Paying passengers ('000 journeys) 823,000; Freight carried ('000 metric tons) 136,100; Passenger-km (million) 64,500; Freight ton-km (million) 53,800.

Source: mainly Société Nationale des Chemins de fer Français, Paris.

**ROAD TRAFFIC** ('000 motor vehicles in use at 31 December)

| | 1995 | 1996 | 1997 |
|---|---|---|---|
| Passenger cars | 25,100 | 25,500 | 25,900 |
| Lorries and vans | 4,926 | 4,976 | 5,057 |
| Buses | 79 | 82 | 82 |

Source: IRF, *World Road Statistics*.

**INLAND WATERWAYS**

| | 1994 | 1995 | 1996 |
|---|---|---|---|
| Freight carried ('000 metric tons) | 53,306 | 54,884 | 50,672 |
| Freight ton-km (million) | 5,606 | 5,865 | 5,745 |

Source: Voies navigables de France.

**SHIPPING**

**Merchant Fleet** (vessels registered at 30 June)

| | Displacement ('000 gross reg. tons) | | |
|---|---|---|---|
| | 1995 | 1996 | 1997 |
| Oil tankers | 2,370 | 2,440 | 2,560 |
| **Total** (incl. others) | 4,080 | 4,163 | 4,119 |

Source: Direction de la Flotte de Commerce (Ministère de l'Equipement, du Logement, des Transports et du Tourisme).

**Sea-borne Freight Traffic** ('000 metric tons)

| | 1994 | 1995 | 1996 |
|---|---|---|---|
| Goods loaded (excl. stores) | 86,071 | 81,250 | 82,382 |
| International | 76,903 | 73,615 | n.a. |
| Coastwise | 9,168 | 7,635 | n.a. |
| Goods unloaded (excl. fish) | 217,406 | 215,433 | 215,916 |
| International | 204,628 | 205,145 | n.a. |
| Coastwise | 12,778 | 10,288 | n.a. |

Source: Ministère de l'Equipement, du Logement, des Transports et du Tourisme, Direction des Ports et de la Navigation Maritimes.

**CIVIL AVIATION** (revenue traffic on scheduled services)*

| | 1993 | 1994 | 1995 |
|---|---|---|---|
| Kilometres flown (million) | 471 | 512 | 513 |
| Passengers carried ('000) | 35,221 | 38,121 | 34,796 |
| Passenger-km (million) | 60,056 | 68,212 | 67,531 |
| Total ton-km (million) | 9,808 | 11,408 | 11,510 |

* Including data for airlines based in French Overseas Departments and Territories.

Source: UN, *Statistical Yearbook*.

# Tourism

**FOREIGN TOURIST ARRIVALS BY COUNTRY OF ORIGIN** ('000)

| | 1995 | 1996 | 1997 |
|---|---|---|---|
| Belgium and Luxembourg | 7,307 | 7,375 | 8,395 |
| Germany | 10,602 | 13,378 | 14,593 |
| Italy | 5,047 | 5,299 | 5,533 |
| Japan | 966 | 578 | 641 |
| Netherlands | 5,387 | 8,115 | 9,008 |
| Spain | 3,870 | 2,759 | 2,935 |
| Switzerland | 3,111 | 3,737 | 3,715 |
| United Kingdom and Ireland | 11,173 | 9,926 | 10,497 |
| USA | 2,187 | 2,603 | 2,746 |
| **Total** (incl. others) | 60,110 | 62,406 | 67,310 |

Source: Ministère de l'Equipement, du Logement, des Transports et du Tourisme, Direction du Tourisme.

**Net earnings from tourism** (million francs): 55,894 (receipts 137,389, expenditure 81,495) in 1995; 54,287 (receipts 145,076, expenditure 90,789) in 1996; 66,732 (receipts 163,488, expenditure 96,756) in 1997; 71,615 (receipts 176,562, expenditure 104,947) in 1998.

## Communications Media

| | 1993 | 1994 | 1995 |
|---|---|---|---|
| Radio receivers ('000 in use) | 51,200 | 51,450 | 52,000 |
| Television receivers ('000 in use) | n.a. | 34,100 | 34,250 |
| Book production (titles)* | 41,234 | 45,311 | 34,766 |
| Telephones ('000 main lines in use) | 30,900 | 31,600 | 32,400 |
| Mobile cellular telephones ('000 subscribers) | 572 | 883 | 1,379 |
| Telefax stations ('000 in use) | 1,221 | 1,600 | 1,900 |

* Including pamphlets (about 32% of all titles produced in 1984).

Sources: UN, *Statistical Yearbook*; UNESCO, *Statistical Yearbook*.

**Daily newspapers** (estimates, 1996): 117 titles (combined circulation 12,700,000 copies per issue).

**Non-daily newspapers** (1995): 278 titles (circulation 1,714,000 copies in 1995).

**Other periodicals** (1993): 2,683 titles (circulation 120,018,000 copies in 1991).

## Education

(1995/96, unless otherwise indicated)

| | Institutions | Teachers | Students |
|---|---|---|---|
| Pre-primary | 18,989* | 105,925 | 2,500,867 |
| Primary | 41,244* | 216,938 | 4,065,005 |
| Secondary† | 11,212* | 478,592 | 5,980,518 |
| Higher*: | | | |
| Universities | n.a. | 46,196 | 1,395,103 |
| Other | n.a. | 6,467 | 688,129 |

* Figures are for 1993/94.

† Including vocational education (1,716,101 students).

Source: partly UNESCO, *Statistical Yearbook*.

# Directory

## The Constitution

The Constitution of the Fifth Republic was adopted by referendum on 28 September 1958 and promulgated on 6 October 1958.

### PREAMBLE

The French people hereby solemnly proclaims its attachment to the Rights of Man and to the principles of national sovereignty as defined by the Declaration of 1789, confirmed and complemented by the Preamble of the Constitution of 1946.

By virtue of these principles and that of the free determination of peoples, the Republic hereby offers to the Overseas Territories that express the desire to adhere to them, new institutions based on the common ideal of liberty, equality and fraternity and conceived with a view to their democratic evolution.

Article 1. The Republic and the peoples of the Overseas Territories who, by an act of free determination, adopt the present Constitution thereby institute a Community.

The Community shall be based on the equality and the solidarity of the peoples composing it.

### I. ON SOVEREIGNTY

Article 2. France shall be a Republic, indivisible, secular, democratic and social. It shall ensure the equality of all citizens before the law, without distinction of origin, race or religion. It shall respect all beliefs.

The national emblem shall be the tricolour flag, blue, white and red.

The national anthem shall be the 'Marseillaise'.

The motto of the Republic shall be 'Liberty, Equality, Fraternity'.

Its principle shall be government of the people, by the people, and for the people.

Article 3. National sovereignty belongs to the people, who shall exercise this sovereignty through their representatives and through the referendum.

No section of the people, nor any individual, may arrogate to themselves or himself the exercise thereof.

Suffrage may be direct or indirect under the conditions stipulated by the Constitution. It shall always be universal, equal and secret.

All French citizens of both sexes who have reached their majority and who enjoy civil and political rights may vote under the conditions to be determined by law.

Article 4. Political parties and groups are instrumental in the exercise of suffrage. They may form and carry on their activities freely. They must respect the principles of national sovereignty and of democracy.

### II. THE PRESIDENT OF THE REPUBLIC*

Article 5. The President of the Republic shall see that the Constitution is respected. He shall ensure, by his arbitration, the regular functioning of the governmental authorities, as well as the continuity of the State.

He shall be the guarantor of national independence, of the integrity of the territory, and of respect for Community agreements and for treaties.

Article 6. (As amended by referendum of 28 October 1962.) The President of the Republic shall be elected for seven years by direct universal suffrage. The method of implementation of the present article shall be determined by an organic law.

Article 7. (As amended by referendum of 28 October 1962 and by legislation of 18 June 1976.) The President of the Republic shall be elected by an absolute majority of the votes cast. If such a majority is not obtained at the first ballot, a second ballot shall take place on the second following Sunday. Those who may stand for the second ballot shall be only the two candidates who, after the possible withdrawal of candidates with more votes, have gained the largest number of votes on the first ballot.

Voting shall begin at the summons of the Government. The election of the new President of the Republic shall take place not less than 20 days and not more than 35 days before the expiry of the powers of the President in office. In the event that the Presidency of the Republic has been vacated for any reason whatsoever, or impeded in its functioning as officially declared by the Constitutional Council, after the matter has been referred to it by the Government and which shall give its ruling by an absolute majority of its members, the functions of the President of the Republic, with the exception of those covered by Articles 11 and 12 hereunder, shall be temporarily exercised by the President of the Senate or, if the latter is in his turn unable to exercise his functions, by the Government.

In the case of vacancy or when the impediment is declared to be permanent by the Constitutional Council, the voting for the election of the new President shall take place, except in case of force majeure officially noted by the Constitutional Council, not less than 20 days and not more than 35 days after the beginning of the vacancy or of the declaration of the final nature of the impediment.

If, in the seven days preceding the latest date for the lodging of candidatures, one of the persons who, at least 30 days prior to that date, publicly announced his decision to be a candidate dies or is impeded, the Constitutional Council may decide to postpone the election.

If, before the first ballot, one of the candidates dies or is impeded, the Constitutional Council orders the postponement of the election.

In the event of the death or impediment, before any candidates have withdrawn, of one of the two candidates who received the greatest number of votes in the first ballot, the Constitutional Council shall declare that the electoral procedure must be repeated in full; the same shall apply in the event of the death or impediment of one of the two candidates standing for the second ballot.

All cases shall be referred to the Constitutional Council under the conditions laid down in paragraph 2 of article 61 below, or under those determined for the presentation of candidates by the organic law provided for in Article 6 above.

The Constitutional Council may extend the periods stipulated in paragraphs 3 and 5 above provided that polling shall not take place more than 35 days after the date of the decision of the Constitutional Council. If the implementation of the provisions of this paragraph results in the postponement of the election beyond the expiry of the powers of the President in office, the latter shall remain in office until his successor is proclaimed.

Articles 49 and 50 and Article 89 of the Constitution may not be put into application during the vacancy of the Presidency of the

Republic or during the period between the declaration of the final nature of the impediment of the President of the Republic and the election of his successor.

Article 8. The President of the Republic shall appoint the Prime Minister. He shall terminate the functions of the Prime Minister when the latter presents the resignation of the Government.

At the suggestion of the Prime Minister, he shall appoint the other members of the Government and shall terminate their functions.

Article 9. The President of the Republic shall preside over the Council of Ministers.

Article 10. The President of the Republic shall promulgate laws within 15 days following the transmission to the Government of the finally adopted law.

He may, before the expiry of this time limit, ask Parliament for a reconsideration of the law or of certain of its articles. This reconsideration may not be refused.

Article 11. The President of the Republic, on the proposal of the government during [Parliamentary] sessions, or on joint motion of the two Assemblies published in the *Journal Officiel*, may submit to a referendum any bill dealing with the organization of the governmental authorities, entailing approval of a Community agreement, or providing for authorization to ratify a treaty that, without being contrary to the Constitution, might affect the functioning of the institutions.

When the referendum decides in favour of the bill, the President of the Republic shall promulgate it within the time limit stipulated in the preceding article.

Article 12. The President of the Republic may, after consultation with the Prime Minister and the Presidents of the Assemblies, declare the dissolution of the National Assembly.

A general election shall take place 20 days at the least and 40 days at the most after the dissolution.

The National Assembly shall convene by right on the second Thursday following its election. If this meeting takes place between the periods provided for ordinary sessions, a session shall, by right, be opened for a 15-day period.

There may be no further dissolution within a year following this election.

Article 13. The President of the Republic shall sign the ordinances and decrees decided upon in the Council of Ministers.

He shall make appointments to the civil and military posts of the State.

Councillors of State, the Grand Chancellor of the Legion of Honour, Ambassadors and Envoys Extraordinary, Master Councillors of the Audit Court, prefects, representatives of the Government in the Overseas Territories, general officers, rectors of academies [regional divisions of the public educational system] and directors of central administrations shall be appointed in meetings of the Council of Ministers.

An organic law shall determine the other posts to be filled by decision of the Council of Ministers, as well as the conditions under which the power of the President of the Republic to make appointments to office may be delegated by him to be exercised in his name.

Article 14. The President of the Republic shall accredit Ambassadors and Envoys Extraordinary to foreign powers; foreign Ambassadors and Envoys Extraordinary shall be accredited to him.

Article 15. The President of the Republic shall be commander of the armed forces. He shall preside over the higher councils and committees of national defence.

Article 16. When the institutions of the Republic, the independence of the nation, the integrity of its territory or the fulfilment of its international commitments are threatened in a grave and immediate manner and the regular functioning of the constitutional governmental authorities is interrupted, the President of the Republic shall take the measures required by these circumstances, after official consultation with the Prime Minister and the Presidents of the Assemblies, and the Constitutional Council.

He shall inform the nation of these measures in a message.

These measures must be prompted by the desire to ensure to the constitutional governmental authorities, in the shortest possible time, the means of accomplishing their mission. The Constitutional Council shall be consulted with regard to such measures.

Parliament shall meet by right.

The National Assembly may not be dissolved during the exercise of exceptional powers.

Article 17. The President of the Republic shall have the right of pardon.

Article 18. The President of the Republic shall communicate with the two Assemblies of Parliament by means of messages, which he shall cause to be read, and which shall not be the occasion for any debate.

Between sessions, the Parliament shall be convened especially to this end.

Article 19. Official decisions of the President of the Republic, other than those provided for under Articles 8 (first paragraph), 11, 12, 16, 18, 54, 56 and 61, shall be counter-signed by the Prime Minister and, where applicable, by the appropriate ministers.

* On 31 July 1995 legislation was enacted to permit the President to hold referendums on reforms affecting the economic and social policy of the nation and the regulation of public services.

### III. THE GOVERNMENT

Article 20. The Government shall determine and conduct the policy of the nation.

It shall have at its disposal the administration and the armed forces.

It shall be responsible to the Parliament under the conditions and according to the procedures stipulated in Articles 49 and 50.

Article 21. The Prime Minister shall direct the operation of the Government. He shall be responsible for national defence. He shall ensure the execution of the laws. Subject to the provisions of Article 13, he shall have regulatory powers and shall make appointments to civil and military posts.

He may delegate certain of his powers to the ministers.

He shall replace, should the occasion arise, the President of the Republic as the Chairman of the councils and committees provided for under Article 15.

He may, in exceptional instances, replace him as the chairman of a meeting of the Council of Ministers by virtue of an explicit delegation and for a specific agenda.

Article 22. The official decisions of the Prime Minister shall be counter-signed, when circumstances so require, by the ministers responsible for their execution.

Article 23. The functions of Members of the Government shall be incompatible with the exercise of any parliamentary mandate, with the holding of any office, at the national level, in business, professional or labour organizations, and with any public employment or professional activity.

An organic law shall determine the conditions under which the holders of such mandates, functions or employments shall be replaced.

The replacement of the members of Parliament shall take place in accordance with the provisions of Article 25.

### IV. THE PARLIAMENT

Article 24. The Parliament shall comprise the National Assembly and the Senate.

The deputies to the National Assembly shall be elected by direct suffrage.

The Senate shall be elected by indirect suffrage. It shall ensure the representation of the territorial units of the Republic. French nationals living outside France shall be represented in the Senate.

Article 25. An organic law shall determine the term for which each Assembly is elected, the number of its members, their emoluments, the conditions of eligibility, and the offices incompatible with membership of the Assemblies.

It shall likewise determine the conditions under which, in the case of a vacancy in either Assembly, persons shall be elected to replace the deputy or senator whose seat has been vacated until the holding of new complete or partial elections to the Assembly concerned.

Article 26. No Member of Parliament may be prosecuted, subjected to inquiry, arrested, detained or tried as a result of the opinions expressed or votes cast by him in the exercise of his functions.

No Member of Parliament may, during parliamentary session, be prosecuted or arrested for criminal or minor offences without the authorization of the Assembly of which he is a member except in the case of *flagrante delicto*.

When Parliament is not in session, no Member of Parliament may be arrested without the authorization of the Secretariat of the Assembly of which he is a member, except in the case of *flagrante delicto*, of authorized prosecution or of final conviction.

The detention or prosecution of a Member of Parliament shall be suspended if the assembly of which he is a member so demands.

Article 27. Any compulsory vote shall be null and void.

The right to vote of the members of Parliament shall be personal.

An organic law may, under exceptional circumstances, authorize the delegation of a vote. In this case, no member may be delegated more than one vote.

Article 28. (As amended by legislation of 31 July 1995.) Parliament shall convene by right in one ordinary session a year.

The session shall open on 2 October and last for not more than 120 days.

If 2 October is a public holiday, the session shall begin on the first working day thereafter.

Article 29. Parliament shall convene in extraordinary session at the request of the Prime Minister or of the majority of the members comprising the National Assembly, to consider a specific agenda.

When an extraordinary session is held at the request of the members of the National Assembly, the closure decree shall take effect as soon as the Parliament has exhausted the agenda for which it was called, and at the latest 12 days from the date of its meeting.

Only the Prime Minister may ask for a new session before the end of the month following the closure decree.

Article 30. Apart from cases in which Parliament meets by right, extraordinary sessions shall be opened and closed by decree of the President of the Republic.

Article 31. The members of the Government shall have access to the two Assemblies. They shall be heard when they so request.

They may call for the assistance of Commissioners of the Government.

Article 32. The President of the National Assembly shall be elected for the duration of the legislature. The President of the Senate shall be elected after each partial re-election [of the Senate].

Article 33. The meetings of the two Assemblies shall be public. An *in extenso* report of the debates shall be published in the *Journal Officiel*.

Each Assembly may sit in secret committee at the request of the Premier or of one-tenth of its members.

## V. ON RELATIONS BETWEEN PARLIAMENT AND THE GOVERNMENT

Article 34. Laws shall be voted by Parliament.

Legislation shall establish the regulations concerning:

Civil rights and the fundamental guarantees granted to the citizens for the exercise of their public liberties; the obligations imposed by the national defence upon the person and property of citizens;

Nationality, status and legal capacity of persons; marriage contracts, inheritance and gifts;

Determination of crimes and misdemeanours as well as the penalties imposed therefor; criminal procedure; amnesty; the creation of new juridical systems and the status of magistrates;

The basis, the rate and the methods of collecting taxes of all types; the issue of currency.

Legislation likewise shall determine the regulations concerning:

The electoral system of the Parliamentary Assemblies and the local assemblies;

The establishment of categories of public institutions;

The fundamental guarantees granted to civil and military personnel employed by the State;

The nationalization of enterprises and the transfers of the property of enterprises from the public to the private sector.

Legislation shall determine the fundamental principles of:

The general organization of national defence;

The free administration of local communities, of their competencies and their resources;

Education;

Property rights, civil and commercial obligations;

Legislation pertaining to employment unions and social security.

The financial laws shall determine the financial resources and obligations of the State under the conditions and with the reservations to be provided for by an organic law.

Laws pertaining to national planning shall determine the objectives of the economic and social action of the State.

The provisions of the present article may be detailed and supplemented by an organic law.

Article 35. Parliament shall authorize the declaration of war.

Article 36. Martial law shall be decreed in a meeting of the Council of Ministers.

Its extension beyond 12 days may be authorized only by Parliament.

Article 37. Matters other than those that fall within the domain of law shall be of a regulatory character.

Legislative texts concerning these matters may be modified by decrees issued after consultation with the Council of State. Those legislative texts which shall be passed after the entry into force of the present Constitution shall be modified by decree only if the Constitutional Council has stated that they have a regulatory character as defined in the preceding paragraph.

Article 38. The Government may, in order to carry out its programme, ask Parliament for authorization to take through ordinances, during a limited period, measures that are normally within the domain of law.

The ordinances shall be enacted in meetings of Ministers after consultation with the Council of State. They shall come into force upon their publication but shall become null and void if the bill for their ratification is not submitted to Parliament before the date set by the enabling act.

At the expiry of the time limit referred to in the first paragraph of the present article, the ordinances may be modified only by the law in respect of those matters which are within the legislative domain.

Article 39. The Prime Minister and the Members of Parliament alike shall have the right to initiate legislation.

Government bills shall be discussed in the Council of Ministers after consultation with the Council of State and shall be filed with the secretariat of one of the two Assemblies. Finance bills shall be submitted first to the National Assembly.

Article 40. Private members' bills and amendments shall be inadmissible when their adoption would have as a consequence either a diminution of public financial resources or an increase in public expenditure.

Article 41. If it shall appear in the course of the legislative procedure that a Parliamentary bill or an amendment is not within the domain of law or is contrary to a delegation granted by virtue of Article 38, the Government may declare its inadmissibility.

In case of disagreement between the Government and the President of the Assembly concerned, the Constitutional Council, upon the request of one or the other, shall rule within a time limit of eight days.

Article 42. The discussion of bills shall pertain, in the first Assembly to which they have been referred, to the text presented by the Government.

An Assembly given a text passed by the other Assembly shall deliberate on the text that is transmitted to it.

Article 43. Government and private members' bills shall, at the request of the Government or of the Assembly concerned, be sent for study to committees especially designated for this purpose.

Government and private members' bills for which such a request has not been made shall be sent to one of the permanent committees, the number of which is limited to six in each Assembly.

Article 44. Members of Parliament and of the Government have the right of amendment.

After the opening of the debate, the Government may oppose the examination of any amendment which has not previously been submitted to committee.

If the Government so requests, the Assembly concerned shall decide, by a single vote, on all or part of the text under discussion, retaining only the amendments proposed or accepted by the Government.

Article 45. When, as a result of disagreement between the two Assemblies, it has been impossible to adopt a Government or private member's bill after two readings by each Assembly, or, if the Government has declared the matter urgent, after a single reading by each of them, the Prime Minister shall have the right to bring about a meeting of a joint committee composed of an equal number from both Assemblies charged with the task of proposing a text on the matters still under discussion.

The text elaborated by the joint committee may be submitted by the Government for approval of the two Assemblies. No amendment shall be admissible except by agreement with the Government.

If the joint committee does not succeed in adopting a common text, or if this text is not adopted under the conditions set forth in the preceding paragraph, the Government may, after a new reading by the National Assembly and by the Senate, ask the National Assembly to rule definitively. In this case, the National Assembly may reconsider either the text elaborated by the joint committee, or the last text voted by it, modified when circumstances so require by one or several of the amendments adopted by the Senate.

Article 46. The laws that the Constitution characterizes as organic shall be passed and amended under the following conditions:

A Government or private member's bill shall be submitted to the deliberation and to the vote of the first Assembly notified only at the expiration of a period of 15 days following its introduction;

The procedure of Article 45 shall be applicable. Nevertheless, lacking an agreement between the two Assemblies, the text may be adopted by the National Assembly on final reading only by an absolute majority of its members;

The organic laws relative to the Senate must be passed in the same manner by the two Assemblies;

The organic laws may be promulgated only after a declaration by the Constitutional Council on their constitutionality.

Article 47. The Parliament shall pass finance bills under the conditions to be stipulated by an organic law.

Should the National Assembly fail to reach a decision on first reading within a time limit of 40 days after a bill has been filed, the Government shall refer it to the Senate, which must rule within a time limit of 15 days. The procedure set forth in Article 45 shall then be followed.

Should Parliament fail to reach a decision within a time limit of 70 days, the provisions of the bill may be enforced by ordinance.

Should the finance bill establishing the resources and expenditures of a fiscal year not be filed in time for it to be promulgated before the beginning of that fiscal year, the Government shall urgently request Parliament for authorization to collect taxes and shall make available by decree the funds needed to meet the Government commitments already voted.

The time limits stipulated in the present article shall be suspended when the Parliament is not in session.

The Audit Court shall assist Parliament and the Government in supervising the implementation of the finance laws.

Article 48. The discussion of the bills tabled or agreed upon by the Government shall have priority on the agenda of the Assemblies in the order determined by the Government.

One meeting a week shall be reserved, by priority, for questions asked by Members of Parliament and for answers by the Government.

Article 49. The Prime Minister, after deliberation by the Council of Ministers, shall make the Government responsible, before the National Assembly, for its programme or, should the occasion arise, for a declaration of general policy.

The National Assembly may challenge the responsibility of the Government by a motion of censure. Such a motion is admissible only if it is signed by at least one-tenth of the members of the National Assembly. The vote may not take place before 48 hours after the motion has been filed. Only the votes that are favourable to a motion of censure shall be counted; the motion of censure may be adopted only by a majority of the members comprising the Assembly. Should the motion of censure be rejected, its signatories may not introduce another motion of censure during the same session, except in the case provided for in the paragraph below.

The Prime Minister may, after deliberation by the Council of Ministers, make the Government responsible before the National Assembly for the adoption of a bill. In this case, the text shall be considered as adopted unless a motion of censure, filed during the twenty-four hours that follow, is carried under the conditions provided for in the preceding paragraph.

The Prime Minister shall have the right to request the Senate for approval of a declaration of general policy.

Article 50. When the National Assembly adopts a motion of censure, or when it disapproves the programme or a declaration of general policy of the Government, the Prime Minister must hand the resignation of the Government to the President of the Republic.

Article 51. The closure of ordinary or extraordinary sessions shall by right be delayed, should the occasion arise, in order to permit the application of the provisions of Article 49.

## VI. ON TREATIES AND INTERNATIONAL AGREEMENTS

Article 52. The President of the Republic shall negotiate and ratify treaties.

He shall be informed of all negotiations leading to the conclusion of an international agreement not subject to ratification.

Article 53. Peace treaties, commercial treaties, treaties or agreements relative to international organization, those that commit the finances of the State, those that modify provisions of a legislative nature, those relative to the status of persons, those that call for the cession, exchange or addition of territory may be ratified or approved only by a law.

They shall go into effect only after having been ratified or approved.

No cession, no exchange, or addition of territory shall be valid without the consent of the populations concerned.

Article 54. If the Constitutional Council, the matter having been referred to it by the President of the Republic, by the Prime Minister, or by the President of one or the other Assembly, shall declare that an international commitment contains a clause contrary to the Constitution, the authorization to ratify or approve this commitment may be given only after amendment of the Constitution.

Article 55. Treaties or agreements duly ratified or approved shall, upon their publication, have an authority superior to that of laws, subject, for each agreement or treaty, to its application by the other party.

## VII. THE CONSTITUTIONAL COUNCIL

Article 56. The Constitutional Council shall consist of nine members, whose mandates shall last nine years and shall not be renewable. One-third of the membership of the Constitutional Council shall be renewed every three years. Three of its members shall be appointed by the President of the Republic, three by the President of the National Assembly, three by the President of the Senate.

In addition to the nine members provided for above, former Presidents of the Republic shall be members *ex officio* for life of the Constitutional Council.

The President shall be appointed by the President of the Republic. He shall have the deciding vote in case of a tie.

Article 57. The office of member of the Constitutional Council shall be incompatible with that of minister or Member of Parliament. Other incompatibilities shall be determined by an organic law.

Article 58. The Constitutional Council shall ensure the regularity of the election of the President of the Republic.

It shall examine complaints and shall announce the results of the vote.

Article 59. The Constitutional Council shall rule, in the case of disagreement, on the regularity of the election of deputies and senators.

Article 60. The Constitutional Council shall ensure the regularity of the referendum procedure and shall announce the results thereof.

Article 61. (As amended by legislation of 29 October 1974.) Organic laws, before their promulgation, and regulations of the parliamentary Assemblies, before they come into application, must be submitted to the Constitutional Council, which shall rule on their constitutionality.

To the same end, laws may be submitted to the Constitutional Council, before their promulgation, by the President of the Republic, the Prime Minister, the President of the National Assembly, the President of the Senate, or any 60 deputies or 60 senators.

In the cases provided for by the two preceding paragraphs, the Constitutional Council must make its ruling within a time limit of one month. Nevertheless, at the request of the Government, in case of urgency, this period shall be reduced to eight days.

In these same cases, referral to the Constitutional Council shall suspend the time limit for promulgation.

Article 62. A provision declared unconstitutional may not be promulgated or implemented.

The decisions of the Constitutional Council may not be appealed to any jurisdiction whatsoever. They shall be binding on the governmental authorities and on all administrative and juridical authorities.

Article 63. An organic law shall determine the rules of organization and functioning of the Constitutional Council, the procedure to be followed before it, and in particular of the periods of time allowed for laying disputes before it.

## VIII. ON JUDICIAL AUTHORITY

Article 64. The President of the Republic shall be the guarantor of the independence of the judicial authority.

He shall be assisted by the High Council of the Judiciary.

An organic law shall determine the status of the judiciary.

Judges may not be removed from office.

Article 65. The High Council of the Judiciary shall be presided over by the President of the Republic. The Minister of Justice shall be its Vice-President *ex officio*. He may preside in place of the President of the Republic.

The High Council shall, in addition, include nine members appointed by the President of the Republic in conformity with the conditions to be determined by an organic law.

The High Council of the Judiciary shall present nominations for judges of the Court of Cassation and for First Presidents of courts of appeal. It shall give its opinion under the conditions to be determined by an organic law on proposals of the Minister of Justice relative to the nominations of the other judges. It shall be consulted on questions of pardon under conditions to be determined by an organic law.

The High Council of the Judiciary shall act as a disciplinary council for judges. In such cases, it shall be presided over by the First President of the Court of Cassation.

Article 66. No one may be arbitrarily detained.

The judicial authority, guardian of individual liberty, shall ensure the respect of this principle under the conditions stipulated by law.

## IX. THE HIGH COURT OF JUSTICE

Article 67. A High Court of Justice shall be instituted.

It shall be composed, in equal number, of members elected, from among their membership, by the National Assembly and by the Senate after each general or partial election to these Assemblies. It shall elect its President from among its members.

An organic law shall determine the composition of the High Court, its rules, as well as the procedure to be applied before it.

Article 68. The President of the Republic shall not be held accountable for actions performed in the exercise of his office except in the case of high treason. He may be indicted only by the two Assemblies ruling by identical vote in open balloting and by an absolute majority of the members of said Assemblies. He shall be tried by the High Court of Justice.

The members of the Government shall be criminally liable for actions performed in the exercise of their office and rated as crimes or misdemeanours at the time they were committed. The procedure defined above shall be applied to them, as well as to their accomplices, in case of a conspiracy against the security of the State. In the cases provided for by the present paragraph, the High Court shall be bound by the definition of crimes and misdemeanours, as well as by the determination of penalties, as they are established by the criminal laws in force when the acts are committed.

[This article was amended in July 1993 to allow any person believing himself injured by a crime or misdemeanour committed by a member of the Government in the exercise of his functions to bring a complaint before a Commission of Requests.]

## X. THE ECONOMIC AND SOCIAL COUNCIL

Article 69. The Economic and Social Council, at the referral of the Government, shall give its opinion on the Government bills, draft ordinances and decrees, as well as on the private members' bills submitted to it.

A member of the Economic and Social Council may be designated by the Council to present, before the Parliamentary Assemblies, the opinion of the Council on the Government or private members' bills that have been submitted to it.

Article 70. The Economic and Social Council may likewise be consulted by the Government on any problem of an economic or social character of interest to the Republic or to the Community. Any plan, or any bill dealing with a plan, of an economic or social character shall be submitted to it for advice.

Article 71. The composition of the Economic and Social Council and its rules of procedure shall be determined by an organic law.

## XI. ON TERRITORIAL UNITS

Article 72. The territorial units of the Republic shall be the communes, the Departments, and the Overseas Territories. Any other territorial unit shall be created by law.

These units shall be free to govern themselves through elected councils and under the conditions stipulated by law.

In the Departments and the Territories, the Delegate of the Government shall be responsible for the national interests, for administrative supervision, and for seeing that the laws are respected.

Article 73. Measures of adjustment required by the particular situation of the Overseas Departments may be taken with regard to the legislative system and administrative organization of those Departments.

Article 74. The Overseas Territories of the Republic shall have a particular organization, taking account of their own interests within the general interests of the Republic. This organization shall be defined and modified by law after consultation with the Territorial Assembly concerned.

Article 75. Citizens of the Republic who do not have ordinary civil status, the only status referred to in Article 34, may keep their personal status as long as they have not renounced it.

Article 76. The Overseas Territories may retain their status within the Republic.

If they express the desire to do so by decision of their Territorial Assemblies taken within the time limit set in the first paragraph of Article 91, they shall become either Overseas Departments of the Republic or, organized into groups among themselves or singly, member States of the Community.

## XII. ON THE COMMUNITY

Article 77. In the Community instituted by the present Constitution, the States shall enjoy autonomy; they shall administer themselves and, democratically and freely, manage their own affairs.

There shall be only one citizenship in the Community.

All citizens shall be equal before the law, whatever their origin, their race and their religion. They shall have the same duties.

Article 78. The Community shall have jurisdiction over foreign policy, defence, the monetary system, common economic and financial policy, as well as the policy on strategic raw materials.

In addition, except by special agreement, control of justice, higher education, the general organization of external and common transport, and telecommunications shall be within its jurisdiction.

Special agreements may establish other common jurisdictions or regulate the transfer of jurisdiction from the Community to one of its members.

Article 79. The member States shall benefit from the provisions of Article 77 as soon as they have exercised the choice provided for in Article 76.

Until the measures required for implementation of the present title go into force, matters within the common jurisdiction shall be regulated by the Republic.

Article 80. The President of the Republic shall preside over and represent the Community.

The Community shall have, as organs, an Executive Council, a Senate and a Court of Arbitration.

Article 81. The member States of the Community shall participate in the election of the President according to the conditions stipulated in Article 6.

The President of the Republic, in his capacity as President of the Community, shall be represented in each State of the Community.

Article 82. The Executive Council of the Community shall be presided over by the President of the Community. It shall consist of the Prime Minister of the Republic, the heads of Government of each of the member States of the Community, and the ministers responsible for the common affairs of the Community.

The Executive Council shall organize the co-operation of members of the Community at Government and administrative levels.

The organization and procedure of the Executive Council shall be determined by an organic law.

Article 83. The Senate of the Community shall be composed of delegates whom the Parliament of the Republic and the legislative assemblies of the other members of the Community shall choose from among their own membership. The number of delegates of each State shall be determined, taking into account its population and the responsibilities it assumes in the Community.

The Senate of the Community shall hold two sessions a year, which shall be opened and closed by the President of the Community and may not last more than one month each.

The Senate of the Community, upon referral by the President of the Community, shall deliberate on the common economic and financial policy, before laws in these matters are voted upon by the Parliament of the Republic, and, should circumstances so require, by the legislative assemblies of the other members of the Community.

The Senate of the Community shall examine the acts and treaties or international agreements, which are specified in Articles 35 and 53, and which commit the Community.

The Senate of the Community shall take enforceable decisions in the domains in which it has received delegation of power from the legislative assemblies of the members of the Community. These decisions shall be promulgated in the same form as the law in the territory of each of the States concerned.

An organic law shall determine the composition of the Senate and its rules of procedure.

Article 84. A Court of Arbitration of the Community shall rule on litigations occurring among members of the Community.

Its composition and its competence shall be determined by an organic law.

Article 85. By derogation from the procedure provided for in Article 89, the provisions of the present title that concern the functioning of the common institutions shall be amendable by identical laws passed by the Parliament of the Republic and by the Senate of the Community.

The provisions of the present title may also be revised by agreements concluded between all states of the Community: the new provisions are enforced in the conditions laid down by the Constitution of each state.

Article 86. (As amended by legislation of 4 June 1960.) A change of status of a member State of the Community may be requested, either by the Republic, or by a resolution of the legislative assembly of the State concerned confirmed by a local referendum, the organization and supervision of which shall be ensured by the institutions of the Community. The procedures governing this change shall be determined by an agreement approved by the Parliament of the Republic and the legislative assembly concerned.

Under the same conditions, a Member State of the Community may become independent. It shall thereby cease to belong to the Community.

A Member State of the Community may also, by means of agreement, become independent without thereby ceasing to belong to the Community.

An independent State which is not a member of the Community may, by means of agreements, adhere to the Community without ceasing to be independent.

The position of these States within the Community is determined by the agreements concluded for that purpose, in particular the agreements mentioned in the preceding paragraphs as well as, where applicable, the agreements provided for in the second paragraph of Article 85.

Article 87. The particular agreements made for the implementation of the present title shall be approved by the Parliament of the Republic and the legislative assembly concerned.

## XIII. ON AGREEMENTS OF ASSOCIATION

Article 88. The Republic or the Community may make agreements with States that wish to associate themselves with the Community in order to develop their own civilizations.

## XIV. ON AMENDMENT

Article 89. The initiative for amending the Constitution shall belong both to the President of the Republic on the proposal of the Prime Minister and to the Members of Parliament.

The Government or private member's bill for amendment must be passed by the two Assemblies in identical terms. The amendment shall become definitive after approval by a referendum.

Nevertheless, the proposed amendment shall not be submitted to a referendum when the President of the Republic decides to submit it to Parliament convened in Congress; in this case, the proposed amendment shall be approved only if it is accepted by a three-fifths majority of the votes cast. The Secretariat of the Congress shall be that of the National Assembly.

No amendment procedure may be undertaken or followed if it is prejudicial to the integrity of the territory.

The republican form of government shall not be the object of an amendment.

### XV. TEMPORARY PROVISIONS

Article 90. The ordinary session of Parliament is suspended. The mandate of the members of the present National Assembly shall expire on the day that the Assembly elected under the present Constitution convenes.

Until this meeting, the Government alone shall have the authority to convene Parliament.

The mandate of the members of the Assembly of the French Union shall expire at the same time as the mandate of the members of the present National Assembly.

Article 91. The institutions of the Republic, provided for by the present Constitution, shall be established within four months counting from the time of its promulgation.

This period shall be extended to six months for the institutions of the Community.

The powers of the President of the Republic now in office shall expire only when the results of the election provided for in Articles 6 and 7 of the present Constitution are proclaimed.

The Member States of the Community shall participate in this first election under the conditions derived from their status at the date of the promulgation of the Constitution.

The established authorities shall continue in the exercise of their functions in these States according to the laws and regulations applicable when the Constitution goes into force, until the establishment of the authorities provided for by their new regimes.

Until its definitive constitution, the Senate shall consist of the present members of the Council of the Republic. The organic laws that shall determine the definitive constitution of the Senate must be passed before 31 July 1959.

The powers conferred on the Constitutional Council by Articles 58 and 59 of the Constitution shall be exercised, until the establishment of this Council, by a committee composed of the Vice-President of the Council of State, as Chairman, the First President of the Court of Cassation, and the First President of the Audit Court.

The peoples of the member States of the Community shall continue to be represented in Parliament until the entry into force of the measures necessary to the implementation of Chapter XII.

Article 92. The legislative measures necessary to the establishment of the institutions and, until they are established, to the functioning of the public powers, shall be taken in meetings of the Council of Ministers, after consultation with the Council of State, in the form of ordinances having the force of law.

During the time limit set in the first paragraph of Article 91, the Government shall be authorized to determine, by ordinances having the force of law and passed in the same way, the system of elections to the Assemblies provided for by the Constitution.

During the same period and under the same conditions, the Government may also adopt measures, in all domains, which it may deem necessary to the life of the nation, the protection of citizens or the safeguarding of liberties.

### ELECTORAL LAW, JULY 1986

The 577 Deputies of the National Assembly are to be directly elected under the former single-member constituency system (in force before the implementation of a system of proportional representation imposed by the electoral law of 1985). Participating parties can nominate only one candidate and designate a reserve candidate, who can serve as a replacement if the elected Deputy is appointed a Minister or a member of the Constitutional Council, or is sent on a government assignment scheduled to last more than six months, or dies. A candidate must receive an absolute majority and at least one-quarter of registered votes in order to be elected to the National Assembly. If these conditions are not fulfilled, a second ballot will be held a week later, for voters to choose between all candidates receiving 12.5% of the total votes on the first ballot. The candidate who receives a simple majority of votes on the second ballot will then be elected. Candidates polling less than 5% of the votes will lose their deposit.

# The Government

### HEAD OF STATE

**President:** JACQUES CHIRAC (took office 17 May 1995).

### COUNCIL OF MINISTERS
(February 2000)

A coalition of the Parti Socialiste (PS), the Parti Communiste Français (PCF), the Parti Radical Socialiste (PRS), the Mouvement des Citoyens (MDC) and Les Verts (Green).

**Prime Minister:** LIONEL JOSPIN (PS).

**Minister of Employment and Solidarity:** MARTINE AUBRY (PS).

**Minister of Justice:** ELISABETH GUIGOU (PS).

**Minister of National Education, Research and Technology:** CLAUDE ALLÈGRE (PS).

**Minister of Defence:** ALAIN RICHARD (PS).

**Minister of Capital Works, Transport and Housing:** JEAN-CLAUDE GAYSOTT (PCF).

**Minister of Foreign Affairs:** HUBERT VÉDRINE (PS).

**Minister of the Interior:** JEAN-PIERRE CHEVÈNEMENT (MDC).

**Minister of the Economy, Finance and Industry:** CHRISTIAN SAUTTER (PS).

**Minister of Relations with Parliament:** DANIEL VAILLANT (PS).

**Minister of Town and Country Planning and the Environment:** DOMINIQUE VOYNET (Green).

**Minister of Culture and Communications and Government Spokesperson:** CATHÉRINE TRAUTMANN (PS).

**Minister of Agriculture and Fisheries:** JEAN GLAVANY (PS).

**Minister of Youth and Sport:** MARIE-GEORGE BUFFET (PCF).

**Minister of the Civil Service, Administrative Reform and Decentralization:** EMILE ZUCCARELLI (PRS).

There are also four Ministers-Delegate and 10 Secretaries of State.

### MINISTRIES

**Office of the President:** Palais de l'Elysée, 55–57 rue du Faubourg Saint Honoré, 75008 Paris; tel. 1-42-92-81-00; fax 1-47-42-24-65.

**Office of the Prime Minister:** Hôtel Matignon, 57 rue de Varenne, 75007 Paris; tel. 1-42-75-80-00; fax 1-42-75-75-04; internet www.premier-ministre-gouv.fr.

**Ministry of Agriculture and Fisheries:** 78 rue de Varenne, 75007 Paris; tel. 1-49-55-49-55; fax 1-49-55-40-39; internet www.agriculture.gouv.fr.

**Ministry of Capital Works, Transport and Housing:** 246 blvd Saint-Germain, 75007 Paris; tel. 1-40-81-21-22; internet www.equipement.gouv.fr.

**Ministry of the Civil Service:** 72 rue de Varenne, 75007 Paris; tel. 1-42-75-80-00; fax 1-47-05-93-32; internet www.fonction-publique.gouv.fr.

**Ministry of Culture:** 3 rue de Valois, 75001 Paris; tel. 1-40-15-80-00; fax 1-42-61-35-77; internet www.culture.gouv.fr.

**Ministry of Defence:** 14 rue Saint Dominique, 75007 Paris; tel. 1-42-19-30-11; fax 1-47-05-40-91; internet www.defense.gouv.fr.

**Ministry of the Economy, Finance and Industry:** 139 rue de Bercy, 75572 Paris Cédex 12; tel. 1-40-04-04-04; fax 1-43-43-75-97; internet www.finances.gouv.fr.

**Ministry of Employment and Solidarity:** 127 rue de Grenelle, 75007 Paris; tel. 1-44-38-38-38; fax 1-40-56-67-60; internet www.travail.gouv.fr.

**Ministry of Foreign Affairs:** 37 quai d'Orsay, 75007 Paris Cédex 07; tel. 1-43-17-53-53; fax 1-43-17-52-03; internet www.diplomatie.gouv.fr.

**Ministry of the Interior:** place Beauvau, 75008 Paris; tel. 1-49-27-49-27; fax 1-43-59-89-50; e-mail sirp@club-internet.fr; internet www.interieur.gouv.fr.

**Ministry of Justice:** 13 place Vendôme, 75042 Paris Cédex 01; tel. 1-42-75-80-00; fax 1-44-77-70-20; internet www.justice.gouv.fr.

**Ministry of National Education, Research and Technology:** 110 rue de Grenelle, 75007 Paris; tel. 1-49-55-10-10; fax 1-45-51-53-63; internet www.education.gouv.fr.

**Ministry of Relations with Parliament:** 69 rue de Varenne, 75007 Paris; tel. 1-42-75-80-00; fax 1-42-75-87-93.

**Ministry of Town and Country Planning and the Environment:** 20 ave de Ségur, 75302 Paris Cédex 07; tel. 1-42-19-20-21; internet www.environment.gouv.fr.

**Ministry of Youth and Sport:** 78 rue Olivier de Serres, 75015 Paris; tel. 1-40-45-90-00; fax 1-42-50-42-49; internet www.jeunesse-sports.gouv.fr.

# President and Legislature

## PRESIDENT

**Elections of 23 April and 7 May 1995**

| | First ballot | Second ballot |
|---|---|---|
| EDOUARD BALLADUR (Rassemblement pour la République) | 5,658,796 | – |
| JACQUES CHEMINADE (Fédération pour une nouvelle solidarité) | 84,959 | – |
| JACQUES CHIRAC (Rassemblement pour la République) | 6,348,375 | 15,763,027 |
| ROBERT HUE (Parti Communiste Français) | 2,632,460 | – |
| LIONEL JOSPIN (Parti Socialiste) | 7,097,786 | 14,180,644 |
| ARLETTE LAGUILLER (Lutte Ouvrière) | 1,615,552 | – |
| JEAN-MARIE LE PEN (Front National) | 4,570,838 | – |
| PHILIPPE DE VILLIERS (Mouvement pour la France) | 1,443,186 | – |
| DOMINIQUE VOYNET (Les Verts) | 1,010,681 | – |

## PARLEMENT

(Parliament)

### Assemblée Nationale

(National Assembly)

**President:** LAURENT FABIUS.

**General Election, 25 May and 1 June 1997**

| Party | % of votes cast in first ballot | % of votes cast in second ballot* | Seats |
|---|---|---|---|
| Parti Socialiste (PS) | 23.53 | 38.05 | 241 |
| Rassemblement pour la République (RPR) | 15.70 | 22.82 | 134 |
| Union pour la Démocratie Française (UDF) | 14.22 | 20.77 | 108 |
| Parti Communiste Français (PCF) | 9.94 | 3.84 | 38 |
| Parti Radical Socialiste (PRS) | 1.45 | 2.19 | 12 |
| Front National (FN) | 14.94 | 5.60 | 1 |
| Various ecologist candidates | 6.81 | 1.62 | 7 |
| Various right-wing candidates | 6.70 | 2.45 | 14 |
| Various left-wing candidates | 5.32 | 2.55 | 21 |
| Others | 1.39 | 0.11 | 1 |
| **Total** | 100.00 | 100.00 | 577 |

* Held where no candidate had won the requisite overall majority in the first ballot, between candidates who had received at least 12.5% of the votes in that round.

### Sénat

(Senate)

**President:** CHRISTIAN PONCELET.

Members of the Senate are indirectly elected for a term of nine years, with one-third of the seats renewable every three years.

After the most recent election, held on 27 September 1998, the Senate had 321 seats: 296 for metropolitan France; 13 for the overseas departments and territories; and 12 for French nationals abroad. The strength of the parties was as follows:

| | Seats |
|---|---|
| Groupe du Rassemblement pour la République | 99 |
| Groupe socialiste | 78 |
| Groupe de l'Union centriste des Démocrates de Progrès | 52 |
| Groupe de l'Union des Républicains et des Indépendants | 47 |
| Groupe du Rassemblement démocratique et européen | 22 |
| Groupe communiste, républicain et citoyen | 16 |
| Non-attached | 7 |
| **Total** | 321 |

# Political Organizations

**Alliance Populaire:** Paris; extreme right-wing; Pres. JEAN-FRANÇOIS TOUZÉ.

**Les Alternatifs:** 40 rue de Malte, 75011 Paris; tel. 1-43-57-44-80; fax 1-43-57-64-50; e-mail alternatifs@wanadoo.fr; internet www.perso.wanadoo.fr/alternatifs; f. 1998 to replace Alternative Rouge et Verte (f. 1993); left-wing ecologist party; Leaders JEAN-JACQUES BUISLAROUSSIE, MATHIEU COLLOGHAN, MARIE-FRANÇOISE PIROT, ROGER WINTERHALTER.

**Centre National des Indépendants et Paysans (CNI):** 6 rue Quentin Bauchart, 75008 Paris; tel. 1-46-05-62-40; fax 1-45-56-02-63; f. 1949; right-wing; Pres. JEAN PERRIN; Sec.-Gen. ANNICK DU ROSCOAT.

**Démocratie Libérale (DL):** 113 rue de l'Université, 75007 Paris; tel. 1-40-62-30-30; fax 1-40-62-30-40; internet www.democratie-liberale-asso.fr. formed May 1977 as Parti Républicain, a grouping of the Fédération Nationale des Républicains Indépendants (FNRI) and three smaller 'Giscardian' parties, name changed as above in 1997; Leader ALAIN MADELIN.

**La Droite:** Paris, f. 1998 by breakaway faction of UDF; Leader CHARLES MILLON.

**Front National (FN):** BP 290, 4 rue Vauguyon, 92212 Saint Cloud; tel. 1-41-12-10-18; fax 1-41-12-10-86; e-mail euronat@club-internet.fr; f. 1972; extreme right-wing nationalist; Pres. JEAN-MARIE LE PEN; Sec.-Gen. CARL LANG.

**Front National—Mouvement National (FN—MN):** f. 1999 by breakaway faction of FN; Leader BRUNO MÉGRET.

**Génération Ecologie:** 73 ave Paul Doumer, 75016 Paris; tel. 1-45-03-82-82; fax 1-45-03-82-80; f. 1990; emphasis on environmental matters; Leader BRICE LALONDE.

**Ligue Communiste Révolutionnaire (LCR):** c/o Rouge, 2 rue Richard Lenoir, 93108 Montreuil; tel. 1-48-70-42-30; fax 1-48-59-23-28; internet www.lcr.rouge.org; f. 1974; Trotskyist; French section of the Fourth International; 1,500 mems (1996); Leader ALAIN KRIVINE.

**Lutte Ouvrière (LO):** BP 233, 75865 Paris Cédex 18; Trotskyist; Leaders ARLETTE LAGUILLER, F. DUBURG, J. MORAND.

**Mouvement des Citoyens:** 9 rue du Faubourg Poissonnière, 75009 Paris; internet www.mdc-france.org; f. 1956; sceptical of increased European integration; Leader JEAN-PIERRE CHEVÈNEMENT.

**Mouvement des Démocrates:** Paris; tel. 1-47-54-06-57; fax 1-47-63-27-58; f. 1974; Leader MICHEL JOBERT.

**Mouvement Ecologiste Indépendent:** 7 rue de Verbois, 75003 Paris; tel. 1-40-27-85-36; fax 1-40-27-85-44; internet www.novomundi.com/mei; f. 1994; emphasis on environmental matters; 3,000 mems; Pres. ANTOINE WAECHTER; Nat. Sec. GÉRARD MONNIER-BESOMBES.

**Mouvement des Réformateurs (MR):** 7 rue de Villersexel, 75007 Paris; tel. 1-45-44-61-50; fax 1-45-44-91-90; f. 1992; centrist; formed by merger of Association des Démocrates, France Unie and Performance et Partage; Sec.-Gen. JEAN-PIERRE SOISSON.

**Nouvelle Union pour la Démocratie Française (UDF):** 133 rue de l'Université, 75007 Paris; tel. 1-53-59-20-00; fax 1-53-59-20-59; internet www.udf.fr; formed in 1978 to unite for electoral purposes non-Gaullist 'majority' candidates; has frequently formed electoral alliances with RPR (q.v.); Pres. FRANÇOIS BAYROU; Sec.-Gen. PIERRE-ANDRÉ WILTZER.

Affiliated parties:

**Parti Populaire pour la Démocratie Française (PPDF):** 250 blvd Saint Germain, 75007 Paris; tel. 1-42-22-69-51; fax 1-42-22-59-49; f. 1965, present name since 1995; Leader HERVÉ DE CHARETTE.

**Parti Radical:** 1 place de Valois, 75001 Paris; tel. 1-42-61-56-32; fax 1-42-61-49-65; f. 1901; Pres. THIERRY CORNILLET; Sec.-Gen. AYMERI DE MONTESQUIOU.

**Parti social-démocrate (PSD):** 191 rue de l'Université, 75007 Paris; tel. 1-47-53-84-41; fax 1-47-05-73-53; f. 1973 as Mouvement des démocrates socialistes de France, name changed 1982; Pres. MAX LEJEUNE; Sec.-Gen. ANDRÉ SANTINI.

**Parti Communiste Français (PCF):** 2 place du Colonel Fabien, 75940 Paris Cédex 19; tel. 1-40-40-12-12; fax 1-40-40-13-56; internet www.pcf.fr/index2.htm; subscribed to the common programme of the United Left (with the Parti Socialiste) until 1977; aims to follow the democratic path to socialism and advocates an independent foreign policy; national bureau of 22 mems; Nat. Sec. ROBERT HUE.

**Parti Radical de Gauche (PRG):** 13 rue Duroc, 75007 Paris; tel. 1-45-66-67-68; fax 1-45-66-47-93; e-mail prg-nat@club-internet.fr; internet www.radical-gauche.asso.fr; f. 1972 by fmr members of Parti Radical Socialiste; left-wing; Pres. JEAN-MICHEL BAYLET.

**Parti Socialiste (PS):** 10 rue de Solférino, 75333 Paris Cédex 07; tel. 1-45-56-77-00; fax 1-47-05-15-78; internet www.partisocialiste.fr; f. 1971; subscribed to the common programme of the United Left (with the Parti Communiste) until 1977; advocates solidarity, full employment and the eventual attainment of socialism through a mixed economy; 109,000 mems (1996); First Sec. FRANÇOIS HOLLANDE.

**Rassemblement pour la France:** 159 ave Charles de Gaulle, 92521 Neuilly-sur-Seine; f. 1994; opposes terms of the Maastricht Treaty; Pres. CHARLES PASQUA; Gen-Sec. JEAN JACQUES GUILLET.

**Rassemblement pour la République (RPR):** 123 rue de Lille, 75007 Paris; tel. 1-49-55-63-00; fax 1-45-51-44-79; internet www.rpr.org; f. 1976 from the Gaullist party Union des Démocrates pour la République; has frequently formed electoral alliances with UDF (q.v.); 150,000 mems ; Pres. MICHÈLE ALLIOT-MARIE; Sec.-Gen. ADRIEN GOUTEYRON.

**Les Verts:** 107 ave Parmentier, 75011 Paris; tel. 1-43-55-10-01; fax 1-43-55-16-15; e-mail secretar@verts.imaginet.fr; f. 1984; ecologist party; Spokespersons MARTINE BILLARD, DENIS BAUPIN, STÉPHANE POCRAIN, MARYSE ARDITI; National Sec. JEAN-LUC BENNAHMIAS.

# Diplomatic Representation

## EMBASSIES IN FRANCE

**Afghanistan:** 32 ave Raphaël, 75016 Paris; tel. and fax 1-45-25-05-29; e-mail ambassade.afg@worldonline.fr; Chargé d'affaires: MEHRABODIN MASSTAN.

**Albania:** 57 ave Marceau, 75116 Paris; tel. 1-47-24-31-00; fax 1-47-23-59-85; e-mail ambalbpa@aol.com; Ambassador: LUAN RAMA.

**Algeria:** 50 rue de Lisbonne, 75008 Paris; tel. 1-53-93-20-20; fax 1-42-25-10-25; Ambassador: HOCINE DJOUDI.

**Andorra:** 30 rue d'Astorg, 75008 Paris; tel. 1-40-06-03-30; fax 1-40-06-03-64; e-mail emenduina@andorra.ad; internet www .blue-brain.com/embassy/andorre/fsom.htm/; Ambassador: IMMA TOR FAUS.

**Angola:** 19 ave Foch, 75116 Paris; tel. 1-45-01-58-20; fax 1-45-00-33-71; e-mail anginfos@club-internet.fr; internet www.angolainfos .org; Ambassador: ASSUNÇÃO DOS ANJOS.

**Antigua and Barbuda:** 43 ave de Friedland, 75008 Paris; tel. 1-53-96-93-96; fax 1-53-96-93-97; Ambassador: RONALD MICHAEL SANDERS.

**Argentina:** 6 rue Cimarosa, 75116 Paris; tel. 1-44-05-27-00; fax 1-45-53-46-33; Ambassador: JUAN ARCHIBALDO LANUS.

**Armenia:** 9 rue Viète, 75017 Paris; tel. 1-42-12-98-01; fax 1-42-12-98-03; Ambassador: VAHAN PAPAZIAN.

**Australia:** 4 rue Jean Rey, 75724 Paris Cédex 15; tel. 1-40-59-33-00; fax 1-40-59-33-10; internet www.austgov.fr; Ambassador: JOHN SPENDER.

**Austria:** 6 rue Fabert, 75007 Paris; tel. 1-40-63-30-63; fax 1-45-55-63-65; e-mail ambaut@worldnet.fr; internet www.bmaa.gv.at/ embassy/fr/index.html.fr; Ambassador: FRANZ CESKA.

**Azerbaijan:** 209 rue de l'Université, 75007 Paris; tel. 1-44-18-60-20; Ambassador: ELÉONORA GOUSSEINOVA.

**Bahrain:** 3 bis place des Etats Unis, 75116 Paris; tel. 1-47-23-48-68; fax 1-47-20-55-75; Ambassador: Sheikh HAYYA BIN RASHID AL-KHALIFA.

**Bangladesh:** 39 rue Erlanger, 75116 Paris; tel. 1-46-51-90-33; fax 1-46-51-90-35; e-mail bdootpar@club-internet.fr; Ambassador: SYED MUAZZEM ALI.

**Belarus:** 38 blvd Suchet, 75016 Paris; tel. 1-44-14-69-79; fax 1-44-14-69-70; Ambassador: VLADIMIR SENKO.

**Belgium:** 9 rue de Tilsitt, 75017 Paris; tel. 1-44-09-39-39; fax 1-47-54-07-64; Ambassador: ALAIN RENS.

**Benin:** 87 ave Victor Hugo, 75116 Paris; tel. 1-45-00-98-82; fax 1-45-01-82-02; Ambassador: ANDRÉ-GUY OLOGOUDOU.

**Bolivia:** 12 ave Président Kennedy, 75016 Paris; tel. 1-42-24-93-44; fax 1-45-25-86-23; Ambassador: GONZALO CAMPERO PAZ.

**Bosnia and Herzegovina:** 174 rue de Courcelles, 75017 Paris; tel. 1-42-67-34-22; fax 1-40-53-85-22; Ambassador: NIKOLA KOVAČ.

**Brazil:** 34 cours Albert 1er, 75008 Paris; tel. 1-45-61-63-00; fax 1-42-89-03-45; e-mail azambuja@bresil.org; internet www.bresil.org; Ambassador: MARCOS CASTRISTO DE AZAMBUJA.

**Brunei:** 7 rue de Presbourg, 75116 Paris; tel. 1-53-64-67-60; fax 1-53-64-67-83; Ambassador: Pengiran Hajah MASRAINAH BINTI Pengiran Haji AHMAD.

**Bulgaria:** 1 ave Rapp, 75007 Paris; tel. 1-45-51-85-90; fax 1-45-51-18-68; Ambassador: STÉPHANE TAFRON.

**Burkina Faso:** 159 blvd Haussmann, 75008 Paris; tel. 1-43-59-90-63; fax 1-42-56-50-07; Ambassador: FILIPPE SAWADOGO.

**Burundi:** 24 rue Raynouard, 75016 Paris; tel. 1-45-20-60-61; fax 1-45-20-03-11; Ambassador: JEAN-BAPTISTE MBONYINGINGO.

**Cambodia:** 4 rue Adolphe Yvon, 75116 Paris; tel. 1-45-03-47-20; fax 1-45-03-47-40; Ambassador: PRAK SOKHONN.

**Cameroon:** 73 rue d'Auteuil, 75116 Paris; tel. 1-47-43-98-33; fax 1-46-51-24-52; Ambassador: PASCAL BILOA TANG.

**Canada:** 35 ave Montaigne, 75008 Paris; tel. 1-44-43-29-00; fax 1-44-43-29-99; Ambassador: JACQUES ROY.

**Cape Verde:** 80 rue Jouffroy d'Abbans, 75017 Paris; tel. 1-42-12-73-50; Ambassador: RUI ALBERTO DE FIGUEIREDO SOARES.

**Central African Republic:** 30 rue des Perchamps, 75116 Paris; tel. 1-42-24-42-56; fax 1-42-88-98-95; Ambassador: JEAN POLOKO.

**Chad:** 65 rue des Belles Feuilles, 75116 Paris; tel. 1-45-53-36-75; fax 1-45-53-16-09; Ambassador: MAHAMAT AHMAD ALHABO.

**Chile:** 2 ave de la Motte Picquet, 75007 Paris; tel. 1-44-18-59-60; fax 1-44-18-59-61; e-mail echilefr@iway.fr; Ambassador: FABIO VIO UGARTE.

**China, People's Republic:** 11 ave George V, 75008 Paris; tel. 1-47-23-34-45; fax 1-47-20-24-22; Ambassador: CAI FANGBO.

**Colombia:** 22 rue de l'Elysée, 75008 Paris; tel. 1-42-65-46-08; fax 1-42-66-18-60; e-mail embcolombia@wanadoo.fr; Ambassador: ADOLFO CARVAJAL.

**Comoros:** 20 rue Marbeau, 75116 Paris; tel. 1-40-67-90-54; fax 1-40-67-72-96; Ambassador: SAID HASSAN SAID HACHIM.

**Congo, Democratic Republic:** 32 cours Albert 1er, 75008 Paris; tel. 1-42-25-57-50; fax 1-42-89-80-09; Ambassador: (vacant).

**Congo, Republic :** 37 bis rue Paul Valéry, 75116 Paris; tel. 1-45-00-60-57; Ambassador: HENRI LOPES.

**Costa Rica:** 78 ave Emile Zola, 75015 Paris; tel. 1-45-78-96-96; fax 1-45-78-99-66; Ambassador: EDGAR MOHS.

**Côte d'Ivoire:** 102 ave Raymond Poincaré, 75116 Paris; tel. 1-53-64-62-62; fax 1-45-00-47-97; e-mail bureco-fr@cotedivoire.com; internet www.cotedivoire.com/indexfr.htm; Ambassador: JEAN-MARIE KALOU-GERVAIS.

**Croatia:** 39 ave Georges Mandel, 75116 Paris; tel. 1-53-70-02-80; fax 1-53-70-02-90; Ambassador: SMILJAN ŠIMAC.

**Cuba:** 16 rue de Presles, 75015 Paris; tel. 1-45-67-55-35; fax 1-45-66-80-92; e-mail embacu@club-internet.fr; Ambassador: EUMELIO CABALLERO RODRÍGUEZ.

**Cyprus:** 23 rue Galilée, 75116 Paris; tel. 1-47-20-86-28; fax 1-40-70-13-44; e-mail embrecyp@worldnet.fr; Ambassador: ANDRÉAS D. MAVROYIANNIS.

**Czech Republic:** 15 ave Charles Floquet, 75343 Paris; tel. 1-40-65-13-00; fax 1-47-83-50-78; Ambassador: PETR JANYŠKA.

**Denmark:** 77 ave Marceau, 75116 Paris; tel. 1-44-31-21-21; fax 1-44-31-21-88; e-mail adanemark@infonie.fr; internet www .amb-danemark.fr; Ambassador: HANS HENRIK BRUUN.

**Djibouti:** 26 rue Emile Ménier, 75116 Paris; tel. 1-47-27-49-22; fax 1-45-53-50-53; e-mail webmaster@amb-djibouti.org; internet www .amb-djibouti.org; Ambassador: DJAMA OMAR IDLEH.

**Dominican Republic:** 45 rue de Courcelles, 75008 Paris; tel. 1-53-53-95-95; fax 1-45-63-35-63; e-mail embajadom@wanadoo.fr; internet www.amba-dominicaine-paris.com; Ambassador: GUILLERMO PINA CONTRERAS.

**Ecuador:** 34 ave de Messine, 75008 Paris; tel. 1-45-61-10-21; fax 1-42-89-22-09; e-mail ambecuad@infonie.fr; Ambassador: JUAN CUEVA JARAMILLO.

**Egypt:** 56 ave d'Iéna , 75116 Paris; tel. 1-53-67-88-30; fax 1-47-23-06-43; Ambassador: ALY MAHER EL-SAYED.

**El Salvador:** 12 rue Galilée, 75116 Paris; tel. 1-47-20-42-02; fax 1-40-70-01-95; Ambassador: RAMIRO ZEPEDA ROLDAN.

**Equatorial Guinea:** 6 rue Alfred de Vigny, 75008 Paris; tel. 1-47-66-44-33; fax 1-47-64-94-52; Ambassador: LINO SIMO EKUA AVOMO.

**Estonia:** 46 rue Pierre Charron, 75008 Paris; tel. 1-56-62-22-00; fax 1-49-52-05-65; Ambassador: RUTH LAUSMA LUIK.

**Ethiopia:** 35 ave Charles Floquet, 75007 Paris; tel. 1-47-83-83-95; fax 1-43-06-52-14; Ambassador: MULUGETTA ETAFFA.

**Finland:** 1 place de Finlande, 75007 Paris; tel. 1-44-18-19-20; e-mail sanomat.par@formin.fi; internet www.info.finlande.fr; Ambassador: ANTTI HYNNINEN.

**Gabon:** 26 bis ave Raphaël, 75116 Paris; tel. 1-42-24-79-60; fax 1-42-24-62-42; Ambassador: HONORINE DOSSOU-NAKI.

**The Gambia:** 117 rue St Lazare, 75008 Paris; tel. 1-42-94-09-30; fax 1-42-94-11-91; Ambassador: JOHN P. BOJANG.

**Georgia:** 104 ave Raymond Poincaré, 75116 Paris; tel. 1-45-02-16-16; Ambassador: GOTCHA TCHOGOVADZE.

**Germany:** 13–15 ave Franklin D. Roosevelt, 75008 Paris; tel. 1-53-83-45-75; fax 1-53-83-45-06; e-mail ambassade@amb-allemagne.fr; internet www.amb-allemagne.fr; Ambassador: Dr PETER HARTMANN.

**Ghana:** 8 Villa Saïd, 75116 Paris; tel. 1-45-00-09-50; fax 1-45-00-81-95; Ambassador: HARRY OSEI BLAVO.

**Greece:** 17 rue Auguste Vacquerie, 75116 Paris; tel. 1-47-23-72-28; fax 1-47-23-73-85; Ambassador: ELIAS CLIS.

**Guatemala:** 73 rue de Courcelles, 75008 Paris; tel. 1-42-27-78-63; fax 1-47-54-02-06; e-mail embguafr@easynet.fr; Ambassador: GLORIA REGINA MONTENEGRO PASSARELLI DE CHIROUZE.

**Guinea:** 51 rue de la Faisanderie, 75116 Paris; tel. 1-47-04-81-48; fax 1-47-04-57-65; e-mail isylla@club-internet.fr; Ambassador: IBRAHIMA SYLLA.

**Guinea-Bissau:** 94 rue Saint Lazare, 75009 Paris; tel. 1-45-26-18-51; fax 1-42-81-24-90; Ambassador: FALI EMBALO.

**Haiti:** 10 rue Théodule Ribot, 75017 Paris; tel. 1-47-63-47-78; fax 1-42-27-02-05; e-mail haiti01@francophonie.org; Ambassador: MARC A. TROUILLOT.

**Holy See:** 10 ave du Président Wilson, 75116 Paris (Apostolic Nunciature); tel. 1-53-23-01-50; fax 1-47-23-65-44; e-mail noncapfr@worldnet.fr; Apostolic Nuncio: Most Rev. FORTUNATO BALDELLI, Titular Archbishop of Bevagna.

**Honduras:** 8 rue Crevaux, 75116 Paris; tel. 1-47-55-86-45; fax 1-47-55-86-48; e-mail ambassade.honduras@wanadoo.fr; Ambassador: ENRIQUE ORTEZ COLINDRES.

**Hungary:** 80 bis ave Foch, 75116 Paris; tel. 1-56-36-07-54; fax 1-56-36-02-68; e-mail ambassade-de-hongrie@wanadoo.fr; internet www.hongrie.org; Ambassador: DEZSŐ KÉKESSY.

**Iceland:** 8 ave Kléber, 75116 Paris; tel. 1-44-17-32-85; fax 1-40-67-99-96; e-mail icemb.paris@utn.stjr.is; Ambassador: SIGRIDUR A. SNAEVARR.

**India:** 15 rue Alfred Dehodencq, 75016 Paris; tel. 1-40-50-70-70; fax 1-40-50-09-96; e-mail administra@amb-inde.fr; internet www.amb-inde.fr; Ambassador: KANWAL SIBAL.

**Indonesia:** 47–49 rue Cortambert, 75116 Paris; tel. 1-45-03-07-60; fax 1-45-04-50-32; Ambassador: SATRIO B. JOEDONO.

**Iran:** 4 ave d'Iéna, 75116 Paris; tel. 1-40-69-79-00; fax 1-40-70-01-57; Ambassador: (vacant).

**Iraq:** see Morocco.

**Ireland:** 4 rue Rude, 75116 Paris; tel. 1-44-17-67-00; fax 1-44-17-67-60; Ambassador: PATRICK O'CONNOR.

**Israel:** 3 rue Rabelais, 75008 Paris; tel. 1-40-76-55-00; fax 1-40-76-55-55; e-mail info@amb-israel.fr; internet www.amb-israel.fr; Ambassador: ELIAHU BEN ELISSAR.

**Italy:** 51 rue de Varenne, 75007 Paris; tel. 1-49-54-03-00; fax 1-45-49-35-81; Ambassador: SERGIO VENTO.

**Japan:** 7 ave Hoche, 75008 Paris; tel. 1-48-88-62-00; fax 1-42-27-50-81; e-mail scijap@pratique.fr; internet www.amb-japon.fr; Ambassador: (vacant).

**Jordan:** 11 rue Alfred Dehodencq, 75016 Paris; tel. 1-55-74-73-73; fax 1-55-74-73-74; Ambassador: AL-SHARIF SHARAF FAWAZ.

**Kazakhstan:** 59 rue Pierre Charron, 75008 Paris; tel. 1-45-61-52-00; fax 1-45-61-52-01; Ambassador: AKMARAL ARYSTANBEKOVA.

**Kenya:** 3 rue Freycinet, 75116 Paris; tel. 1-56-62-25-25; fax 1-47-20-44-41; Ambassador: STEVEN A. LOYATUM.

**Korea, Republic:** 142 rue de Grenelle, 75007 Paris; tel. 1-47-53-01-01; fax 1-47-53-00-41; Ambassador: KWON IN-HYUK.

**Kuwait:** 2 rue de Lübeck, 75116 Paris; tel. 1-47-23-54-25; fax 1-47-20-33-59; Ambassador: AHMAD AL-EBRAHIM.

**Laos:** 74 ave Raymond Poincaré, 75116 Paris; tel. 1-45-53-02-98; fax 1-47-57-27-89; Ambassador: KHAMPHAN SIMMALAVONG.

**Latvia:** 6, villa Saïd, 75016 Paris; tel. 1-53-64-58-10; fax 1-53-64-58-19; Ambassador: SANDRA KALNIETE.

**Lebanon:** 3 villa Copernic, 75116 Paris; tel. 1-40-67-75-75; fax 1-40-67-16-42; e-mail ambliban@club-internet.fr; Ambassador: RAYMOND BAAKLINI.

**Liberia:** 12 place du Général Catroux 75017 Paris; tel. 1-47-63-58-55; fax 1-42-12-76-14; Ambassador: AARON GEORGE.

**Libya** (People's Bureau): 2 rue Charles Lamoureux, 75116 Paris; tel. 1-47-04-71-60; fax 1-47-55-96-25; Sec. of People's Bureau: Dr ALI A. TREIKI.

**Lithuania:** 14 blvd Montmartre, 75009 Paris; tel. 1-48-01-00-33; fax 1-48-01-03-31; e-mail amb.lituanie@wanadoo.fr; Ambassador: SKAISGIRYTE LIAUŠKIENE.

**Luxembourg:** 33 ave Rapp, 75007 Paris; tel. 1-45-55-13-37; fax 1-45-51-72-29; Ambassador: JEAN-MARC HOSCHEIT.

**Macedonia, former Yugoslav republic:** 21 rue Sébastian Mercier, 75015 Paris; tel. 1-45-77-10-50; fax 1-45-77-14-84; Ambassador: LUAN STAROVA.

**Madagascar:** 4 ave Raphaël, 75016 Paris; tel. 1-45-04-62-11; fax 1-45-03-58-70; Ambassador: MALALA-ZO RAOLISON.

**Malawi:** 20 rue Euler, 75008 Paris; tel. 1-47-20-20-27; fax 1-47-23-62-48; Ambassador: AUGUSTINE W. MNTHAMBALA.

**Malaysia:** 2 bis rue Bénouville, 75116 Paris; tel. 1-45-53-11-85; fax 1-47-27-34-60; Ambassador: Dr RAJMAH HUSSAIN.

**Mali:** BP 175, 89 rue du Cherche-Midi, 75263 Paris; tel. 1-45-48-58-43; fax 1-45-48-55-34; Ambassador: MADINA LY-TALL.

**Malta:** 92 ave des Champs Elysées, 75008 Paris; tel. 1-56-59-75-90; fax 1-45-62-00-36; Ambassador: Prof. SALVINO BUSCUTTIL.

**Mauritania:** 5 rue de Montévidéo, 75116 Paris; tel. 1-45-04-88-54; fax 1-40-72-82-96; Ambassador: DAH OULD ABDI.

**Mauritius:** 127 rue de Tocqueville, 75017 Paris; tel. 1-42-27-30-19; fax 1-40-53-02-91; e-mail amb-maurice-paris@gofornet.com; Ambassador: MARIE-FRANCE ROUSSETY.

**Mexico:** 9 rue de Longchamp, 75116 Paris; tel. 1-53-70-27-70; fax 1-47-55-65-29; e-mail embamex-francia@wanadoo.fr; Ambassador: SANDRA FUENTES BERAIN.

**Moldova:** 1 rue de Sfax, 75116 Paris; tel. 1-40-67-11-20; fax 1-40-67-11-23; e-mail ambassade.moldavie@free.fr; Ambassador: MIHAI POPOV.

**Monaco:** 22 blvd Suchet, 75116 Paris; tel. 1-45-04-74-54; fax 1-45-04-45-16; Ambassador: CHRISTIAN ORSETTI.

**Mongolia:** 5 ave Robert Schuman, 92100 Boulogne-Billancourt; tel. 1-46-05-28-12; fax 1-46-05-30-16; e-mail 106513.2672@compuserve.com; Ambassador: GOTOUDORJIIN LOUSAN.

**Morocco:** 3–5 rue Le Tasse, 75116 Paris; tel. 1-45-20-69-35; fax 1-45-20-22-58; Ambassador: MOHAMED BERRADA; Iraqi Interests Section: Head: AHMAD EL-AZZAWI.

**Mozambique:** 82 rue Laugier, 75017 Paris; tel. 1-47-64-91-32; fax 1-44-15-90-13; e-mail embamocparis@compuserve.com; Ambassador: JOSÉ RUI MOTA DO AMARAL.

**Myanmar:** 60 rue de Courcelles, 75008 Paris; tel. 1-42-25-56-95; fax 1-42-56-49-41; Ambassador: U NYUNT TIN.

**Namibia:** 80 ave Foch, 75016 Paris; tel. 1-44-17-32-65; fax 1-44-17-32-73; e-mail namparis@club-internet.fr; Ambassador: LEONARD IIPUMBU.

**Nepal:** 45 bis rue des Acacias, 75017 Paris; tel. 1-46-22-48-67; fax 1-42-27-08-65; e-mail nepal@worldnet.fr; Ambassador: INDRA BAHADUR SINGH.

**Netherlands:** 7–9 rue Eblé, 75007 Paris; tel. 1-40-62-33-00; fax 1-40-62-34-56; e-mail nlgovpar@worldnet.fr; internet www.amb-pays-bas.fr; Ambassador: RONALD VAN BEUGE.

**New Zealand:** 7 ter rue Léonard de Vinci, 75116 Paris; tel. 1-45-00-24-11; fax 1-45-01-26-39; e-mail nzembassy-paris@wanadoo.fr; Ambassador: Dr RICHARD GRANT.

**Nicaragua:** 34 ave Bugeaud, 75116 Paris; tel. 1-44-05-90-42; fax 1-44-05-92-42; e-mail 106115-464@compuserve.com; internet www.blue-brain.com/embassy/nicaragua; Ambassador: JOAQUÍN GÓMEZ.

**Niger:** 154 rue de Longchamp, 75116 Paris; tel. 1-45-04-80-60; fax 1-45-04-62-26; Ambassador: MARIAMA HIMA.

**Nigeria:** 173 ave Victor Hugo, 75116 Paris; tel. 1-47-04-68-65; fax 1-47-04-47-54; Ambassador: E. A. AINA.

**Norway:** 28 rue Bayard, 75008 Paris; tel. 1-53-67-04-00; fax 1-53-67-04-40; e-mail ambassade-paris@ud.dep.telemax.no; Ambassador: ROLF TROLLE ANDERSEN.

**Oman:** 50 ave d'Iéna, 75116 Paris; tel. 1-47-23-01-63; fax 1-47-23-02-25; Ambassador: JAIFER SALIM AL-SAID.

**Pakistan:** 18 rue Lord Byron, 75008 Paris; tel. 1-45-62-23-32; fax 1-45-62-89-15; e-mail parep-paris@compuserve.com; Ambassador: SAIDULLA DEHLAVI.

**Panama:** 145 ave de Suffren, 75015 Paris; tel. 1-47-83-23-32; fax 1-45-67-99-43; e-mail panaemba@worldnet.fr; internet http://.services.worldnet.net/panaemba; Ambassador: ARÍSTIDES ROYO.

**Papua New Guinea:** 25 ave George V, 75008 Paris; tel. 1-53-23-96-00; fax 1-53-23-96-09; e-mail pngemb@microking.net; Chargé d'affaires: KAPPA YAMKA.

**Paraguay:** 1 rue St Dominique, 75007 Paris; tel. 1-42-22-85-05; fax 1-42-22-83-57; Ambassador: RUBÉN BAREIRO SAGUIER.

**Peru:** 50 ave Kléber, 75116 Paris; tel. 1-53-70-42-00; fax 1-47-55-98-30; e-mail perou@easynet.fr; Ambassador: MARÍA LUISA FEDERICI SOTO.

**Philippines:** 4 hameau de Boulainvilliers, 75016 Paris; tel. 1-44-14-57-00; fax 1-46-47-56-00; e-mail ambaphil-paris@compuserve.com; Ambassador: HECTOR K. VILLARROEL.

**Poland:** 1–5 rue de Talleyrand, 75343 Paris Cédex 07; tel. 1-45-51-60-80; fax 1-45-55-72-02; e-mail 106033.3056@compuserve.com; Ambassador: STEFAN MELLER.

**Portugal:** 3 rue de Noisiel, 75116 Paris; tel. 1-47-27-35-29; fax 1-47-55-00-40; internet www.embaixada-portugal-fr.org; Ambassador: LEONARDO MATHIAS.

**Qatar:** 57 quai d'Orsay, 75007 Paris; tel. 1-45-51-90-71; fax 1-45-51-77-07; Ambassador: ABDUL RAHMAN M. AL-KHULAIFI.

**Romania:** 5 rue de l'Exposition, 75007 Paris; tel. 1-40-62-22-05; fax 1-45-56-97-47; e-mail amb.paris.ro@francophonie.org; Ambassador: DUMITRU CIAUSU.

**Russia:** 40-50 blvd Lannes, 75116 Paris; tel. 1-45-04-05-50; fax 1-45-04-17-65; e-mail rusembfr@club-internet.fr; Ambassador: NIKOLAI AFANASSIEVSKII.

**Rwanda:** 12 rue Jadin, 75017 Paris; tel. 1-42-27-36-31; fax 1-42-27-74-69; Chargé d'affaires a.i.: MODESTE RUTABAYIRU.

**San Marino:** 21 rue Auguste Vacquerie, 75116 Paris; tel. 1-47-23-77-32; fax 1-47-23-78-05; Ambassador: Countess ISA CORINALDI DE BENEDETTI.

**Saudi Arabia:** 5 ave Hoche, 75008 Paris; tel. 1-56-79-40-00; fax 1-56-79-40-01; e-mail ambsaudi@club-internet.fr; Ambassador: FAISAL ABDULAZIZ ALHEGELAN.

**Senegal:** 14 ave Robert Schuman, 75007 Paris; tel. 1-47-05-39-45; fax 1-45-56-04-30; Ambassador: KÉBA BIRANE CISSÉ.

**Seychelles:** 51 ave Mozart, 75016 Paris; tel. 1-42-30-57-47; fax 1-42-30-57-40; e-mail ambsey@aol.com;Ambassador: CALLIXTE D'OFFAY.

**Singapore:** 12 Square de l'ave Foch, 75116 Paris; tel. 1-45-00-33-61; fax 1-45-00-61-79; Ambassador: THAMBYNATHAN JASUDASEN.

**Slovakia:** 125 rue du Ranelagh, 75016 Paris; tel. 1-44-14-51-20; fax 1-42-88-76-53; e-mail zuparis@wanadoo.fr; Ambassador: VLADIMIR VALACH.

**Slovenia:** 21 rue Bouquet de Longchamp, 75116 Paris; tel. 1-47-55-65-90; fax 1-47-55-60-05; Ambassador: JOŽEF KUNIČ.

**Somalia:** 26 rue Dumont d'Urville, 75116 Paris; tel. 1-45-00-76-51; Ambassador: Said Hagi MUHAMMAD FARAH.

**South Africa:** 59 quai d'Orsay, 75343 Paris Cédex 07; tel. 1-53-59-23-23; fax 1-53-59-23-68; Ambassador: BARBARA JOYCE R. MASEKELA.

**Spain:** 22 ave Marceau, 75008 Paris; tel. 1-44-43-18-00; fax 1-47-20-56-69; internet www.amb-espagne.fr; Ambassador: CARLOS DE BENAVIDES Y SALAS.

**Sri Lanka:** 15 rue d'Astorg, 75008 Paris; tel. 1-42-66-35-01; fax 1-40-07-00-11; Ambassador: SUMITRA PERIES.

**Sudan:** 56 ave Montaigne, 75008 Paris; tel. 1-42-25-55-71; fax 1-54-63-66-73; Ambassador: EL TIGANI SALIH FIDAIL.

**Sweden:** 17 rue Barbet de Jouy, 75007 Paris; tel. 1-44-18-88-00; fax 1-44-18-88-40; e-mail presseinfo@amb-suede.fr; internet www.amb-suede.fr; Ambassador: ÖRJAN BERNER.

**Switzerland:** 142 rue de Grenelle, 75007 Paris; tel. 1-49-55-67-00; fax 1-45-51-34-77; Ambassador: BENEDIKT VON TSCHARNER.

**Syria:** 20 rue Vaneau, 75007 Paris; tel. 1-40-62-61-00; fax 1-47-05-92-73; Ambassador: ELIAS NEJMÉH.

**Tanzania:** 13 ave Raymond Poincaré, 75116 Paris; tel. 1-53-70-63-66; fax 1-47-55-05-46; e-mail tanzanie@infonie.fr; Ambassador: KASSIM M. J. MWAWADO.

**Thailand:** 8 rue Greuze, 75116 Paris; tel. 1-56-26-50-50; fax 1-56-26-04-46; e-mail thaipar@micronet.fr; Ambassador: TEJ BUNNAG.

**Togo:** 8 rue Alfred Roll, 75017 Paris; tel. 1-43-80-12-13; fax 1-43-80-91-71; Ambassador: KONDI CHARLES MADJOME AGBA.

**Tunisia:** 25 rue Barbet de Jouy, 75007 Paris; tel. 1-45-55-95-98; fax 1-45-56-02-64; Ambassador: MONGI BOUSNINA.

**Turkey:** 16 ave de Lamballe, 75016 Paris; tel. 1-53-92-72-11; fax 1-45-20-41-91; e-mail ambtrparis@cie.fr; Ambassador: TANSUG BLEDA.

**Turkmenistan:** 13 rue Picot, 75116 Paris; tel. 1-47-55-05-36; fax 1-47-55-05-68; e-mail turkmenamb@aol.com; Ambassador: TCHARY G. NIIAZOV.

**Uganda:** 13 ave Raymond Poincaré, 75116 Paris; tel. 1-53-70-62-70; fax 1-53-70-85-15; Ambassador: DAVID KAZUNGU.

**Ukraine:** 21 ave de Saxe, 75007 Paris; tel. 1-43-06-07-37; fax 1-43-06-02-94; Ambassador: YURI KOCHUBEY.

**United Arab Emirates:** 3 rue de Lota, 75116 Paris; tel. 1-44-34-02-00; fax 1-47-55-61-04; Ambassador: ABDUL AZIZ N. R. AL-SHAMSI.

**United Kingdom:** 35 rue du Faubourg Saint Honoré, 75383 Paris Cédex 08; tel. 1-44-51-31-00; fax 1-44-51-32-88; internet www.amb-grandebretagne.fr; Ambassador: Sir MICHAEL JAY.

**USA:** 2 ave Gabriel, 75382 Paris Cédex 08; tel. 1-43-12-22-22; fax 1-42-66-97-83; internet www.amb-usa.fr/pagefr.htm; Ambassador: FELIX ROHATYN.

**Uruguay:** 15 rue Le Sueur, 75116 Paris; tel. 1-45-00-81-37; fax 1-45-01-25-17; Ambassador: HÉCTOR GROS ESPIELL.

**Uzbekistan:** 22 rue d'Aguesseau, 75008 Paris; tel. 1-53-30-03-53; Ambassador: TOKHIRJON MAMAJANOV.

**Venezuela:** 11 rue Copernic, 75116 Paris; tel. 1-45-53-29-98; fax 1-47-55-64-56; e-mail embavzla@club-internet.fr; internet www.embavenez-paris.com; Ambassador: HIRAM GAVIRIA.

**Viet Nam:** 62 rue Boileau, 75016 Paris; tel. 1-44-14-64-00; fax 1-45-24-39-48; Ambassador: NGUYÊN CHIÊN THANG.

**Yemen:** 25 rue Georges Bizet, 75116 Paris; tel. 1-47-23-61-76; fax 1-47-23-69-41; Ambassador: ABDULLAH AL-ERYANI.

**Yugoslavia:** 54 rue de la Faisanderie, 75116 Paris; tel. 1-40-72-24-24; fax 1-40-72-24-11; Ambassador: BOGDAN TRIFUNOVIĆ.

**Zimbabwe:** 12 rue Lord Byron, 75008 Paris; tel. 1-56-88-16-00; fax 1-56-88-16-09; Ambassador: JOEY MAZORODZE BIMHA.

# Judicial System

The Judiciary is independent of the Government. Judges of the Court of Cassation and the First President of the Court of Appeal are appointed by the executive from nominations of the High Council of the Judiciary.

Subordinate cases are heard by Tribunaux d'instance, of which there are 471, and more serious cases by Tribunaux de grande instance, of which there are 181. Parallel to these Tribunals are the Tribunaux de commerce, for commercial cases, composed of judges elected by traders and manufacturers among themselves. These do not exist in every district. Where there is no Tribunal de commerce, commercial disputes are judged by Tribunaux de grande instance.

The Conseils de Prud'hommes (Boards of Arbitration) consist of an equal number of workers or employees and employers ruling on the differences which arise over Contracts of Work.

The Tribunaux correctionnnels (Correctional Courts) for criminal cases correspond to the Tribunaux de grande instance for civil cases. They pronounce on all graver offences (délits), including those involving imprisonment. Offences committed by juveniles of under 18 years go before specialized tribunals for children.

From all these Tribunals appeal lies to the Cours d'appel (Courts of Appeal).

The Cours d'assises (Courts of Assize) have no regular sittings, but are called when necessary to try every important case, for example, murder. They are presided over by judges who are members of the Cours d'appel, and are composed of elected judges (jury). Their decision is final, except where shown to be wrong in law, and then recourse is had to the Cour de cassation (Court of Cassation). The Cour de cassation is not a supreme court of appeal but a higher authority for the proper application of the law. Its duty is to see that judgments are not contrary either to the letter or the spirit of the law; any judgment annulled by the Court involves the trying of the case anew by a court of the same category as that which made the original decision.

Plans for extensive reforms in the judicial system were announced in late 1997. The proposed reforms aimed to reduce political control of the Judiciary and to increase citizens' rights.

## COUR DE CASSATION

Palais de Justice, 5 quai de l'Horloge, 75001 Paris; tel. 1-44-32-50-50; fax 1-44-32-78-28.

**First President:** GUY CANIVET.

**Presidents of Chambers:** PIERRE BÉZARD (Chambre commerciale), JACQUES LEMONTEY (1ère Chambre civile), GÉRARD GÉLINEAU-LARRIVE T (Chambre sociale), ROGER BEAUVOIS (3ème Chambre civile), PAUL GOMEZ (Chambre criminelle), JEAN-PIERRE DUMAS (2ème Chambre civile).

**Solicitor-General:** JEAN-FRANÇOIS BURGELIN.

There are 85 Counsellors, one First Attorney-General and 22 Attorneys-General.

**Chief Clerk of the Court:** MARLENE TARDI.

**Council of Advocates at Court of Cassation:** Pres. JEAN BARTHÉLÉMY.

## COUR D'APPEL DE PARIS

Palais de Justice, blvd du Palais, 75001 Paris; tel. 1-44-32-52-52.

**First President:** JEAN-MARIE COULON.

There are also 69 Presidents of Chambers.

**Solicitor-General:** ALEXANDRE BENMAKHLOUF.

There are also 121 Counsellors, 24 Attorneys-General and 38 Deputies.

## TRIBUNAL DE GRANDE INSTANCE DE PARIS

Palais de Justice, blvd du Palais, 75001 Paris; fax 1-43-29-12-55.

**President:** JEAN-CLAUDE MAGENDIE.

**Solicitor of Republic:** GABRIEL BESTARD.

## TRIBUNAL DE COMMERCE DE PARIS

1 quai de Corse, 75181 Paris Cédex 04.

**President:** JEAN-PIERRE MATTEÏ.

## TRIBUNAUX ADMINISTRATIFS

Certain cases arising between civil servants (when on duty) and the Government, or between any citizen and the Government are judged by special administrative courts.

The Tribunaux administratifs, of which there are 22, are situated in the capital of each area; the Conseil d'Etat (see below) has its seat in Paris.

asscn for young entrepreneurs (under 45 years of age); Pres. DIDIER LIVIO; Sec.-Gen. YVES PINAUD; 2,500 mems.

**Chambre Syndicale de l'Ameublement, Négoce de Paris et de l'Ile de France:** 15 rue de la Cerisaie, 75004 Paris; tel. 1-42-72-13-79; fax 1-42-72-02-36; f. 1860; furnishing; Chair. NICOLE PHILIBERT; 350 mems.

**Chambre Syndicale des Céramistes et Ateliers d'Art:** 62 rue d'Hauteville, 75010 Paris; tel. 1-47-70-95-83; fax 1-47-70-10-54; f. 1937; ceramics and arts; Chair. M. LUBRANO; 1,200 mems.

**Chambre Syndicale des Constructeurs de Navires:** 47 rue de Monceau, 75008 Paris; tel. 1-53-89-52-01; fax 1-53-89-52-15; shipbuilding; Chair. ALAIN GRILL; Gen. Man. FABRICE THEOBALD.

**Chambre Syndicale des Industries Transformatrices de Fibres Techniques:** 10 rue de la Pépinière, 75008 Paris; tel. 1-45-22-12-34; fax 1-40-08-01-99; f. 1898; asbestos; Chair. CYRIL X. LATTY; 15 mems.

**Comité Central de la Laine et des Fibres Associées** (Groupement Général de l'Industrie et du Commerce Lainiers Français): BP 121, 37–39 rue de Neuilly, 92113 Clichy; tel. 1-47-56-31-41; fax 1-47-37-06-20; f. 1922; manufacture of wool and associated textiles; Chair. CAMILLE AMALRIC; Vice-Chairs OLIVIER TOULEMONDE, CHRISTIAN DEWAVRIN; 250 mems.

**Comité Central des Armateurs de France:** 47 rue de Monceau, 75008 Paris; tel. 1-53-89-52-52; fax 1-53-89-52-53; e-mail ccaf@ccaf.asso.fr; internet ww.ccaf.asso.fr; f. 1903; shipping; Pres. MARC CHEVALLIER; Delegate-Gen. EDOUARD BERLET; 110 mems.

**Comité des Constructeurs Français d'Automobiles:** 2 rue de Presbourg, 75008 Paris; tel. 1-47-23-54-05; fax 1-47-23-74-73; f. 1909; motor manufacturing; Chair. RAYMOND RAVENEL; 9 mems.

**Comité National des Pêches Maritimes et des Elevages Marins:** 51 rue Salvador Allende, 92027 Nanterre Cédex; tel. 1-47-75-01-01; fax 1-49-00-06-02; marine fisheries.

**Comité Professionnel du Pétrole:** Tour Corosa, 3 rue Eugène et Armand Peugeot, BP 282, 92505 Rueil-Malmaison Cédex; tel. 1-47-16-94-60; fax 1-47-08-10-57; e-mail cpdp@cpdp.org; internet www.cpdp.org; petroleum industry.

**Commissariat à l'Energie Atomique (CEA)** (Atomic Energy Commission): 31-33 rue de la Fédération, 75752 Paris Cedex 15; tel. 1-40-56-10-00; fax 1-40-56-25-38; internet www.cea.fr; f. 1945; promotes the uses of nuclear energy in science, industry and national defence; involved in production of nuclear materials; reactor development; fundamental research; innovation and transfer of technologies; military applications; bio-technologies; robotics; electronics; new materials; radiological protection and nuclear safety; Gen. Administrator YANNICK D'ESCATHA; High Commissioner RENÉ PELLAT.

**Confédération des Commerçants-Détaillants de France:** 21 rue du Château d'Eau, 75010 Paris; tel. 1-42-08-17-15; retailers; Chair. M. FOUCAULT.

**Confédération des Industries Céramiques de France:** 15 ave Victor Hugo, 75116 Paris; tel. 1-45-00-18-56; fax 1-45-00-47-56; e-mail ceramique@wanadoo.fr; f. 1937; ceramic industry; Chair. JACQUES RUSSEIL; Man. Dir FRANÇOIS DE LA TOUR; 111 mems, 7 affiliates.

**Confédération Générale des Petites et Moyennes Entreprises:** 10 Terrasse Bellini, 92806 Puteaux Cédex; tel. 1-47-62-73-73; fax 1-47-73-08-86; f. 1945; small and medium-sized enterprises; Chair. LUCIEN REBUFFEL; 3,500 affiliated asscns.

**Fédération des Chambres Syndicales de l'Industrie du Verre:** 3 rue la Boétie, 75008 Paris; tel. 1-42-65-60-02; e-mail leverre@compuserve.com; internet www.verre-avenir.org; f. 1874; glass industry; Chair. JACQUES DEMARTY.

**Fédération des Chambres Syndicales des Minerais, Minéraux Industriels et Métaux non-Ferreux:** 30 ave de Messine, 75008 Paris; tel. 1-45-63-02-66; fax 1-45-63-61-54; e-mail fmmnfx@aol.com; f. 1945; minerals and non-ferrous metals; Chair. JEAU CHOUVEL; Delegate-Gen. G. JOURDAN; 16 affiliated syndicates.

**Fédération des Exportateurs des Vins et Spiritueux de France:** 95 rue de Monceau, 75008 Paris; tel. 1-45-22-75-73; fax 1-45-22-94-16; e-mail fevsegvf@club-internet.fr; f. 1921; exporters of wines and spirits; Pres. BERTRAND DEVILLARD; Delegate-Gen. LOUIS RÉGIS AFFRE; 450 mems.

**Fédération Française de l'Acier:** Immeuble Pacific, 11-13 Cours Valmy, 92070 Paris La Défense; tel. 1-41-25-58-00; fax 1-41-25-59-8; e-mail ffa@ffa.fr; f. 1945; steel-making; Chair. FRANCIS MER; Delegate-Gen. J.-C. GEORGES FRANÇOIS.

**Fédération Française du Bâtiment:** 33 ave Kléber, 75784 Paris Cédex 16; tel. 1-40-69-51-00; e-mail ffbbox@ffb.fr; f. 1906; building trade; Chair. ALAIN SIONNEAU; Dir-Gen. BERTRAND SABLIER; 52,000 mems.

**Fédération Française de la Bijouterie, Joaillerie, Orfèvrerie du Cadeau, Diamants, Pierres et Perles et Activités qui s'y rattachent (BJOC):** 58 rue du Louvre, 75002 Paris; tel. 1-42-33-61-33; fax 1-40-26-29-51; jewellery, gifts and tableware; Chair. DIDIER ROUX; 1,200 mems.

**Fédération Française de l'Industrie Cotonnière:** BP 121, 37+39 rue de Neuilly, 92113 Clichy Cédex; tel. 1-47-56-30-40; fax 1-47-56-30-49; e-mail ffic@fedcoton-laine.com; f. 1902; cotton manufacturing; Chair. DOMINIQUE MEILLASSOUX; Vice-Chair. DENIS CHAIGNE; mems 71 (spinning), 153 (weaving).

**Fédération Française du Négoce de Bois d'Oeuvre et Produits Dérivés:** 251 blvd Pereire, 75852 Paris Cédex 17; tel. 1-45-72-55-50; fax 1-45-72-55-56; timber trade; Pres. ANDRÉ TALON; Dir-Gen. LIONEL THOMAS D'ANNEBAULT.

**Fédération Française de la Tannerie-Mégisserie:** 122 rue de Provence, 75008 Paris; tel. 1-45-22-96-45; fax 1-42-93-37-44; e-mail fftm@leatherfrance.com; internet www.leatherfrance.com; f. 1885; leather industry; 100 mems.

**Fédération de l'Imprimerie et de la Communication Graphique:** 68 blvd Saint Marcel, 75005 Paris; tel. 1-44-08-64-46; fax 1-43-36-09-51; e-mail fic@ficg.fr; internet www.ficg.fr; printing; Pres. JACQUES SCHOR.

**Fédération des Industries de la Parfumerie (France):** 33 Champs Elysées, 75008 Paris; tel. 1-56-69-67-89; fax 1-56-69-67-90; makers of perfume, cosmetics and toiletries.

**Fédération des Industries Electriques et Electroniques (FIEE):** 11–17 rue Hamelin, 75783 Paris Cédex 16; tel. 1-45-05-70-70; fax 1-45-53-03-93; f. 1925; electrical and electronics industries; Chair. HENRI STARCK; Delegate-Gen. JEAN-CLAUDE KARPELÈS; c. 1,000 mems.

**Fédération des Industries Mécaniques:** 39–41 rue Louis Blanc, 92400 Courbevoie; tel. 1-47-17-60-00; fax 1-47-17-64-99; e-mail fim@club.internet.fr; f. 1840; mechanical and metal-working; Chair. MARTINE CLÉMENT; Man. Dir MARC BAY.

**Fédération des Industries Nautiques:** Port de Javel Haut, 75015 Paris; tel. 1-44-37-04-00; fax 1-45-77-21-88; e-mail export@france-nautic.com; internet www.france-nautic.com; f. 1965; pleasure-boating; Pres. ANNETTE ROUX; Man. Dir TIBOR SILLINGER; 500 mems.

**Fédération Nationale du Bois:** 1 place André Malraux, 75001 Paris; tel. 1-42-60-30-27; fax 1-42-60-58-94; timber and wood products; Chair. R. LESBATS; Dir PIERRE VERNERET; 2,000 mems.

**Fédération Nationale de l'Industrie Hôtelière (FNIH):** 22 rue d'Anjou, 75008 Paris; tel. 1-44-94-19-94; fax 1-42-65-16-21; e-mail fnih@imagenet.fr; Chair. ANDRÉ DAGUIN.

**Fédération Nationale de l'Industrie Laitière:** 140 blvd Haussmann, 75008 Paris; tel. 1-45-62-96-60; dairy products.

**Fédération Nationale des Industries Électrométallurgiques, Éléctrochimiques et Connexes:** 30 ave de Messine, 75008 Paris; tel. 1-45-61-06-63; fax 1-45-63-61-54; Chair. JACQUES GANI.

**Fédération Nationale de la Musique:** 62 rue Blanche, 75009 Paris; tel. 1-48-74-09-29; fax 1-42-81-19-87; f. 1964; includes Chambre Syndicale de la Facture Instrumentale, Syndicat National de l'Edition Phonographique and other groups; musical instruments, publications and recordings; Chair. PIERRE HENRY; Sec.-Gen. FRANÇOIS WELLEBROUCK.

**Groupe Intersyndical de l'Industrie Nucléaire (GIIN):** 15 rue Beaujon, 75008 Paris; tel. 1-42-67-30-68; f. 1959; aims to promote the interests of the French nuclear industry; over 200 member firms.

**Groupement des Industries Françaises Aéronautiques et Spatiales (GIFAS):** 4 rue Galilée, 75782 Paris Cédex 16; tel. 1-44-43-17-52; fax 1-40-70-91-41; aerospace industry; Pres. JEAN PAUL BÉCHAT; Delegate-Gen. GUY RUPIED.

**Syndicat Général des Cuirs et Peaux Bruts:** Bourse de Commerce, 2 rue de Viarmes, 75040 Paris Cédex 01; tel. 1-45-08-08-54; fax 1-40-39-97-31; f. 1977; untreated leather and hides; Chair. PIERRE DUBOIS; 60 mems.

**Syndicat Général des Fabricants d'Huile et de Tourteaux de France:** 118 ave Achille Peretti, 92200 Neuilly-sur-Seine; tel. 1-46-37-22-06; fax 1-46-37-15-60; f. 1928; edible oils; Pres. HENRI RIEUX; Sec.-Gen. JEAN-CLAUDE BARSACQ.

**Syndicat Général des Fondeurs de France:** 45 rue Louis Blanc, 92038 Paris La Défense Cédex; tel. 1-43-34-76-30; fax 1-43-34-76-31; e-mail sgff@wanadoo.fr; internet www.sgff.org; f. 1897; metal casting; Chair. FRANÇOIS DELACHAUX; Man. Dir OLIVIER DUCRU.

**Syndicat de l'Imprimerie et de la Communicatiòn Graphique de l'Ile-de-France:** 8 rue de Berri, 75008 Paris; tel. 1-42-25-04-35; fax 1-42-25-04-32; f. 1991; printers' asscn; 700 mems; Chair. JOËL CARDINAL.

**Syndicat National de l'Industrie Pharmaceutique (SNIP):** 88 rue de la Faisanderie, 75782 Paris Cédex 16; tel. 1-45-03-88-88; fax 1-45-04-47-71; pharmaceuticals; Chair. BERNARD MESURÉ.

**Union des Armateurs à la Pêche de France:** 59 rue des Mathurins, 75008 Paris; tel. 1-42-66-32-60; fax 1-47-42-91-12; f. 1945; fishing-vessels; Chair. PATRICK SOISSON; Delegate-Gen. MICHEL DION.

**Union des Fabricants de Porcelaine de Limoges:** 7 bis rue du Général Cérez, 87000 Limoges; tel. 5-55-77-29-18; fax 5-55-77-36-81; porcelain manufacturing; Chair. MICHEL BERNARDAUD; Sec.-Gen. MARIE-THÉRÈSE PASQUET.

**Union des Industries Chimiques:** Cédex 5, 92080 Paris La Défense; tel. 1-47-78-50-00; f. 1860; chemical industry; Chair. J.-C. ACHILLE; Dir-Gen. C. MARTIN; 58 affiliated unions.

**Union des Industries Métallurgiques et Minières:** 56 ave de Wagram, 75017 Paris; tel. 1-40-54-20-20; fax 1-47-66-22-74; metallurgy and mining; Chair. ARNAUD LEENHARDT.

**Union des Industries Papetières pour les Affaires Sociales (UNIPAS):** 154 blvd Haussmann, 75008 Paris; tel. 1-53-89-25-25; fax 1-53-89-25-26; e-mail unipas@aol.com; f. 1864; paper, cardboard and cellulose; Chair. MICHEL SORIANO; Gen. Man. DANIEL PLOIX; 500 firms affiliated.

**Union des Industries Textiles (Production):** BP 121, 37–39 rue de Neuilly, 92113 Clichy Cédex; tel. 1-47-56-31-00; fax 1-47-30-25-28; internet www.textile.fr; f. 1901; Chair. GEORGES JOLLÈS; 2,500 mems.

**Union Parisienne des Syndicats Patronaux de l'Imprimerie:** 8 rue de Berri, 75008 Paris; tel. 1-42-25-04-35; fax 1-42-25-04-32; f. 1923; Chair. JACQUES NOULET.

## EMPLOYERS' ORGANIZATIONS

**Association des Grandes Entreprises Françaises (AGREF):** 63 rue la Boétie, 75008 Paris; tel. 1-43-59-65-35; fax 1-43-59-81-17.

**Centre des Jeunes Dirigeants d'Entreprise (CJD):** 13 rue Duroc, 75007 Paris; tel. 1-47-83-42-28; fax 1-42-73-32-90.

**Centre Français du Patronat Chrétien (CFPC):** 24 rue Hamelin, 75016 Paris; tel. 1-45-53-09-01; fax 1-47-27-43-32; e-mail cfpc@cfpc.org; internet www.cfpc.org; asscn of Christian employers.

**Confédération Générale des Petites et Moyennes Entreprises (CGPME):** 10 terrasse Bellini, 92806 Puteaux Cédex; tel. 1-47-62-73-73; fax 1-47-73-08-86; small and medium-sized cos.

**Mouvement des Entreprises de France (Medef):** 31 ave Pierre Ier de Serbie, 75784 Paris Cédex 16; tel. 1-40-69-44-44; fax 1-47-23-47-32; f. 1946 as Conseil National du Patronat Français, name changed as above in 1998; an employers' organization grouping 1.5m. companies from all sectors of activity; Chair. ERNEST-ANTOINE SEILLIÈRE DE LABORDE; Exec. Vice-Chair. DENIS KESSLER.

## UTILITIES

### Electricity

**Alcatel:** 54 rue la Boétie, 75382 Paris Cedex 08; tel. 1-40-76-10-10; fax 1-40-76-14-00; internet www.alcatel.com; f. 1898; energy, nuclear energy and electrical contracting (also involved in industrial process control, telecommunications and business systems, cables and batteries, transportation); 125,000 employees; Chair. SERGE TCHURUT.

**Charbonnages de France (CdF):** Tour Albert 1er, 65 ave de Colmar, 92507 Rueil-Malmaison Cédex; tel. 1-47-52-35-00; fax 1-47-51-31-63; established under the Nationalization Act of 1946; responsible for coal mining, sales and research in metropolitan France; there are also engineering and informatics divisions; 15,010 employees; Chair. and Dir-Gen. PHILIPPE DE LADOUCETTE.

**Electricité de France:** 2 rue Louis Murat, 75008 Paris; tel. 1-40-42-53-33; established under the Electricity and Gas Industry Nationalization Act of 1946; responsible for generating and supplying electricity for distribution to consumers in metropolitan France; 120,000 employees; Chair. FRANÇOIS ROUSSELY.

**Fédération Nationale des Producteurs Indépendants d'Electricité (EAF):** 9 blvd Lannés, 75116 Paris; tel. 1-45-04-08-21; fax 1-45-04-51-99; association of producers and distributors of electricity; 800 mems; Pres. PIERRE DUMONS; Delegate-Gen. ANNE MARY ROUSSEL.

### Gas

**Gaz de France:** 23 rue Philibert Delorme, 75840 Paris Cédex 17; tel. 1-47-54-20-20; fax 1-47-54-21-87; established under the Electricity and Gas Industry Nationalization Act of 1946; responsible for distribution of gas in metropolitan France; about 10% of gas was produced in France (Aquitaine) in 1993 and the rest imported from Algeria, the Netherlands, Norway and the territories constituting the former USSR; Chair. PIERRE GADONNEIX; Dir-Gen. CLAUDE MANDIL.

### Water

**Suez-Lyonnaise des Eaux:** Paris; internet www.suez-lyonnaise-eaux.com; Pres. and CEO GÉRARD MESTRALLET.

**Vivendi:** ave Friedland, Paris; fmrly Compagnie Générale des Eaux; provides water and other environmental services, as well as telecommunications and construction; Chair. JEAN-MARIE MESSIER.

## TRADE UNIONS

In late 1995 it was estimated that some 8% of the French labour force belonged to trade unions (compared with 18% in 1980).

There are three major trade union organizations:

**Confédération Générale du Travail (CGT):** Complexe Immobilier Intersyndical CGT, 263 rue de Paris, 93516 Montreuil Cédex; tel. 1-48-18-80-00; fax 1-49-88-18-57; e-mail internat@cgt.fr; f. 1895; National Congress is held every three years; Sec.-Gen. BERNARD THIBAULT; 650,000 mems.

Affiliated unions:

**Agroalimentaire et Forestière (FNAF):** 263 rue de Paris, 93100 Montreuil Cédex; Sec.-Gen. FREDDY HUCK.

**Bois Ameublement** (Woodworkers): 263 rue de Paris, Case 414, 93514 Montreuil Cédex; tel. 1-48-18-81-61; fax 1-48-51-59-91; Sec.-Gen. HENRI SANCHEZ.

**Cheminots CGT** (Railway Workers): BP 546, 263 rue de Paris, 93515 Montreuil Cédex; Sec.-Gen. DIDIER LERESTE.

**Construction** (Building): 263 rue de Paris, 93100 Montreuil Cédex; tel. 1-48-18-81-60; fax 1-48-59-10-37; Sec.-Gen. ROBERT BRUN.

**Equipement et l'Environnement:** 263 rue de Paris, Case 543, 93515 Montreuil Cédex; tel. 1-48-18-82-81; fax 1-48-51-62-50; e-mail equipement.cgt@wanadoo.fr; Sec.-Gen. DENIS GLASSON.

**Fédération Nationale de l'Energie:** 16 rue de Candale, 93507 Pantin Cédex; tel. 1-49-91-86-00; fax 1-49-91-87-40; f. 1905; Sec.-Gen. DENIS COHEN; 65,000 mems.

**Finances:** 263 rue de Paris, 93100 Montreuil Cédex; tel. 1-48-18-82-21; Sec.-Gen. PIERRETTE CROSEMARIE.

**Fonctionnaires** (Civil Servants): 263 rue de Paris, 93515 Montreuil Cédex; tel. 1-48-18-82-31; groups National Education, Finance, Technical and Administrative, Civil Servants, Police, etc.; mems about 70 national unions covered by six federations; Sec.-Gen. BERNARD LHUBERT.

**Industries Chimiques** (Chemical Industries): 263 rue de Paris, Case 429, 93514 Montreuil Cédex; tel. 1-48-18-80-36; fax 1-48-18-80-35; e-mail fnic@cgt.fr; internet www.fnic.cgt.fr; Sec.-Gen. GEORGES HERVO.

**Industries du Livre du Papier et de la Communication (FIL PAC)** (Printing and Paper Products): 263 rue de Paris, Case 426, 93514 Montreuil Cédex; tel. 1-48-18-80-24; Sec.-Gen. MICHEL MULLER.

**Ingénieurs, Cadres et Techniciens** (Engineers, Managerial Staff and Technicians): 263 rue de Paris, Case 408, 93514 Montreuil Cédex; tel. 1-48-18-81-25; fax 1-48-51-64-57; f. 1963; Sec.-Gen. GÉRARD DELAHAYE.

**Journalistes:** 263 rue de Paris, Case 570, 93514 Montreuil Cédex; tel. 1-48-18-81-78; fax 1-48-51-58-08; Sec.-Gen. MICHEL DIARD.

**Marine Marchande** (Merchant Marine): Fédération des Officiers CGT, Cercle Franklin, Cours de la République, 76600 Le Havre; tel. 2-35-25-04-81; fax 2-35-24-23-77; Sec.-Gen. CHARLES NARELLI.

**Fédération des Travailleurs de la Métallurgie** (Metalworkers): 263 rue de Paris, 93514 Montreuil Cédex; tel. 1-48-18-21-21; fax 1-48-59-80-66; e-mail ftm@ftm.cgt.fr; f. 1891; Sec.-Gen. DANIEL SANCHEZ.

**Organismes Sociaux:** 263 rue de Paris, 93100 Montreuil Cédex; tel. 1-48-18-83-56; fax 1-48-59-24-75; Sec.-Gen. PHILIPPE HOURCADE.

**Personnels du Commerce, de la Distribution et des Services:** 263 rue de Paris, Case 425, 93514 Montreuil Cédex; tel. 1-48-18-83-11; Sec.-Gen. JACQUELINE GARCIA.

**Police:** 263 rue de Paris, Case 550, 93514 Montreuil Cédex; tel. 1-48-18-81-85; fax 1-48-59-30-56; f. 1906; Sec.-Gen. PASCAL MARTINI.

**Ports et Docks:** 263 rue de Paris, 93100 Montreuil Cédex; Sec.-Gen. DANIEL LEFÈVRE.

**Postes et Télécommunications:** 263 rue de Paris, 93100 Montreuil Cédex; Sec.-Gen. MARYSE DUMAS.

**Santé, Action Sociale, CGT** (Health and Social Services): 263 rue de Montreuil, Case 538, 93515 Montreuil Cédex; tel. 1-48-18-20-70; fax 1-48-18-80-93; e-mail santeas@cgt.fr; internet www.cgt.fr/santeas; f. 1907; Sec.-Gen. JEAN-LUC GIBELIN.

**Secteurs Financiers:** 263 rue de Paris, 93515 Montreuil Cédex; tel. 1-48-18-83-40; fax 1-49-88-16-36; Sec.-Gen. JEAN DOMINIQUE SIMONPOLI.

**Services Publics** (Community Services): 263 rue de Paris, Case 547, 93515 Montreuil Cédex; tel. 1-48-18-83-74; fax 1-48-51-98-20; Sec.-Gen. VINCENT DEBEIR.

**Sous-sol** (Miners): 263 rue de Paris, Case 535, 93515 Montreuil Cédex; Sec.-Gen. JACKY BERNARD.

**Spectacle, Audio-Visuel et Action Culturelle** (Theatre, Media and Culture): 14-16 rue des Lilas, 75019 Paris; tel. 1-48-03-87-60; Sec.-Gen. JEAN VOIRIN.

**Syndicats Maritimes** (Seamen): 263 rue de Paris, Case 420, 93514 Montreuil Cédex; tel. 1-48-18-84-21; fax 1-48-51-59-21; Sec.-Gen. ROBERT BILLIEN.

**Tabac et Allumettes** (Tobacco and Matches): 263 rue de Paris, 93100 Montreuil Cédex; Sec.-Gen. BERTRAND PAGE.

**THC** (Textiles): 263 rue de Paris, 93100 Montreuil Cédex; Sec.-Gen. CHRISTIAN LAROSE.

**Transports:** 263 rue de Paris, 93100 Montreuil Cédex; Sec.-Gen. ALAIN RENAULT.

**Travailleurs de l'Etat** (State Employees): 263 rue de Paris, 93100 Montreuil Cédex; Sec.-Gen. JEAN LOUIS NAUDET.

**Union Nationale des Syndicats de l'Education Nationale:** 263 rue de Paris, Case 544, 93515 Montreuil Cédex; tel. 1-48-18-82-44; fax 1-49-88-07-43; e-mail unsen@cgt.fr; internet www.ferc.cgt.fr; Sec.-Gen. DENIS BAUDEQUIN.

**Verre et Céramique** (Glassworkers and Ceramics): 263 rue de Paris, Case 417, 93514 Montreuil Cédex; tel. 1-48-18-80-13; fax 1-48-18-80-11; Sec.-Gen. JACQUES BEAUVOIR.

**Voyageurs-Représentants, Cadres et Techniciens de la Vente** (Commercial Travellers): Bourse du Travail, 3 rue du Château d'eau, 75010 Paris; tel. 1-44-84-50-00; Sec.-Gen. ALAIN SERRE.

**Force Ouvrière:** 141 ave du Maine, 75680 Paris Cédex 14; tel. 1-40-52-82-00; fax 1-40-52-82-02; f. 1947 by breakaway from the more left-wing CGT (above); Force Ouvrière is a member of ICFTU and of the European Trade Union Confederation; Sec.-Gen. MARC BLONDEL; c. 1m. mems.

Affiliated federations:

**Action Sociale:** 7 passage Tenaille, 75680 Paris Cédex 14; tel. 1-40-52-85-80; fax 1-40-52-85-79; Sec. MICHEL PINAUD.

**Administration Générale de l'État:** 46 rue des Petites Ecuries, 75010 Paris; tel. 1-42-46-40-19; fax 1-42-46-19-57; f. 1948; Sec.-Gen. FRANCIS LAMARQUE; 20,000 mems.

**Agriculture, Alimentation et Tabacs** (Agriculture, Food and Tobacco): 7 passage Tenaille, 75680 Paris Cédex 14; tel. 1-40-52-85-10; fax 1-40-52-85-12; Sec.-Gen. GÉRARD FOSSÉ.

**Bâtiment, Travaux Publics, Bois, Céramique, Papier Carton et Matériaux de Construction** (Building, Public Works, Wood, Ceramics, Paper, Cardboard and Building Materials): 170 ave Parmentier, 75010 Paris; tel. 1-42-01-30-00; fax 1-42-39-50-44; Sec.-Gen. ALAIN EMILE.

**Union des Cadres et Ingénieurs (UCI)** (Engineers): 2 rue de la Michodière, 75002 Paris; tel. 1-47-42-39-69; fax 1-47-42-03-53; Sec.-Gen. HUBERT BOUCHET.

**Fédération Syndicaliste Force Ouvrière des Cheminots** (Railway Workers): 61 rue de la Chapelle, 75018 Paris; tel. 1-55-26-94-00; fax 1-55-26-94-01; e-mail force.ouvriere.fdcheminots@wanadoo.fr; f. 1948; Sec.-Gen. ERIC FALEMPIN; 10,000 mems.

**Coiffeurs, Esthétique et Parfumerie** (Hairdressers, Beauticians and Perfumery): 3 rue de la Croix Blanche, 18350 Nerondes; tel. 1-48-74-89-32; fax 1-48-74-81-26; Sec.-Gen. MICHEL BOURLON.

**Cuirs, Textiles, Habillement** (Leather, Textiles and Clothing): 7 passage Tenaille, 75680 Paris Cédex 14; tel. 1-40-52-83-00; fax 1-40-52-82-99; Sec.-Gen. JEAN-CLAUDE HUMEZ.

**Défense, Industries de l'Armement et Secteurs Assimilés** (Defence, Arms Manufacture and Related Industries): 46 rue des Petites Ecuries, 75010 Paris; tel. 1-42-46-00-05; fax 1-45-23-12-89; Sec.-Gen. (vacant).

**Employés et Cadres** (Managerial Staff): 28 rue des Petits Hôtels, 75010 Paris; tel. 1-48-01-91-91; fax 1-48-01-91-92; Sec.-Gen. ROSE BOUTARIC.

**Energie Electrique et Gaz** (Gas and Electricity): 60 rue Vergniaud, 75640 Paris Cédex 13; tel. 1-44-16-86-20; fax 1-44-16-86-32; f. 1947; Sec.-Gen. GABRIEL GAUDY; 22,000 mems.

**Enseignement, Culture et Formation Professionnelle** (Teaching, Culture and Professional Training): 7 passage Tenaille, 75680 Paris Cédex 14; tel. 1-40-52-85-30; fax 1-40-52-85-35; Sec.-Gen. FRANÇOIS CHAINTRON; 50,000 mems.

**Equipement, Transports et Services** (Transport and Public Works): 46 rue des Petites Ecuries, 75010 Paris; tel. 1-42-46-36-63; fax 1-48-24-38-32; f. 1932; Sec.-Gen. YVES VEYRIER; 50,000 mems.

**Finances:** 46 rue des Petites Ecuries, 75010 Paris; tel. 1-42-46-75-20; fax 1-47-70-23-92; Sec. JACKY LESUEUR.

**Fonctionnaires** (Civil Servants): 46 rue des Petites Ecuries, 75010 Paris; tel. 1-44-83-65-55; fax 1-42-46-97-80; Sec. ROLAND GAILLARD.

**Industries Chimiques** (Chemical Industries): 60 rue Vergniaud, 75640 Paris Cédex 13; tel. 1-45-80-14-90; fax 1-45-80-08-03; f. 1948; Sec.-Gen. FRANÇOIS GRANDAZZI.

**Livre** (Printing Trades): 7 passage Tenaille, 75680 Paris Cédex 14; tel. 1-40-52-85-00; fax 1-40-52-85-01; Sec.-Gen. MAURICE ROSSAT.

**Métaux** (Metals): 9 rue Baudouin, 75013 Paris; tel. 1-53-94-54-00; fax 1-45-83-78-87; internet www.fo.metaux.org; Sec.-Gen. MICHEL HUC.

**Mineurs, Miniers et Similaires** (Mine Workers): 7 passage Tenaille, 75014 Paris; tel. 1-40-52-85-50; fax 1-40-52-85-48; e-mail fo.mineurs@wanadoo.fr; Sec.-Gen. BERNARD FRAYSSE.

**Personnels des Services des Départements et Régions** (Local Public Services): 46 rue des Petites Ecuries, 75010 Paris; tel. 1-42-46-50-52; fax 1-47-70-26-06; Sec.-Gen. MICHÈLE SIMONNIN.

**Pharmacie** (Pharmacists): 7 passage Tenaille, 75680 Paris Cédex 14; tel. 1-40-52-85-60; fax 1-40-52-85-61; Sec.-Gen. BERNARD DEVY.

**Police:** 6 rue Albert Bayet, 75013 Paris; tel. 1-45-82-28-08; fax 1-45-82-64-24; f. 1948; Sec. JEAN JACQUES PENIN; 11,000 mems.

**Postes et Télécommunications** (Posts and Telecommunications): 60 rue Vergniaud, 75640 Paris Cédex 13; tel. 1-40-78-31-50; fax 1-40-78-30-58; f. 1947; Sec.-Gen. JACQUES LEMERCIER.

**Services Publics et de Santé** (Health and Public Services): 153–155 rue de Rome, 75017 Paris; tel. 1-44-01-06-00; fax 1-42-27-21-40; f. 1947; Sec.-Gen. CAMILLE ORDRONNEAU; 130,000 mems.

**Syndicats des Arts des Spectacles de l'Audiovisuel et de la Presse et de la Communication F.O. (FASAPFO)** (Theatre and Cinema Performers, Press and Broadcasting): 2 rue de la Michodière, 75002 Paris; tel. 1-47-42-35-86; fax 1-47-42-39-45; Sec.-Gen. BERTRAND BLANC.

**Transports:** 7 passage Tenaille, 75680 Paris Cédex 14; tel. 1-40-52-85-45; fax 1-40-52-85-09; Sec. ROGER POLETTI.

**Voyageurs-Représentants-Placiers** (Commercial Travellers): 6 rue Albert Bayet, 75013 Paris; tel. 1-45-82-28-28; fax 1-45-70-93-69; f. 1930; Sec. MICHEL BOUTELEUX.

**Confédération Française Démocratique du Travail (CFDT):** 4 blvd de la Villette, 75955 Paris Cédex 19; tel. 1-42-03-80-00; fax 1-42-03-81-44; e-mail internationale@cfdt.fr; internet www.cfdt.fr; constituted in 1919 as Confédération Française des Travailleurs Chrétiens—CFTC, present title and constitution adopted in 1964; moderate; co-ordinates 2,200 trade unions, 102 departmental and overseas unions and 18 affiliated professional federations, all of which are autonomous. There are also 22 regional orgs; 723,500 mems (1998); affiliated to European Trade Union Confederation and to CISL; Sec.-Gen. NICOLE NOTAT; Nat. Secs JEAN-MARIE SPAETH, JEAN-FRANÇOIS TROGRLIC, ANNIE THOMAS, JACKY BONTENU, MICHEL JALMAIN, MICHEL CARON, JEAN-MARIE TOULISSE, REMY JOUAN.

Principal affiliated federations:

**Agroalimentaire (FGA):** 47/49 ave Simon Bolivar, 75950 Paris Cédex 19; tel. 1-53-38-12-12; fax 1-53-38-12-00; f. 1980; Sec.-Gen. ODILE BELLOUIN.

**Banques (Fédération des Syndicats CFDT de Banques et Sociétés Financières)** (Banking): 47/49 ave Simon Bolivar, 75950 Paris Cédex 19; tel. 1-44-52-71-20; fax 1-44-52-71-21; Sec.-Gen. BERNARD DUFIL.

**Chimie-Energie (FCE-CFDT):** 47/49 ave Simon Bolivar, 75950 Paris Cédex 19; tel. 1-44-84-86-00; fax 1-44-84-86-05; f. 1946; Sec.-Gen. BRUNO LÉCHEVIN.

**Communication et Culture (FTILAC):** 47/49 ave Simon Bolivar, 75950 Paris Cédex 19; tel. 1-44-52-52-70; fax 1-42-02-59-74; e-mail ftilac-cftd@wanadoo.fr; Sec.-Gen. DANIÈLE RIVED.

**Construction-Bois (FNCB):** 47/49 ave Simon Bolivar, 75950 Paris Cédex 19; tel. 1-53-72-87-20; fax 1-53-72-87-21; e-mail fncb@cfdt.fr; internet www.cfdt-construction-bois.fr; f. 1934; Sec.-Gen. JOSEPH MURGIA.

**Education Nationale (SGEN-CFDT)** (National Education): 47/49 ave Simon Bolivar, 75950 Paris Cédex 19; tel. 1-40-03-37-00; fax 1-42-02-50-97; internet www.sgen-cfdt.org; f. 1937; Sec.-Gen. JEAN-LUC VILLENEUVE.

**Etablissements et Arsenaux de l'Etat:** 47/49 ave Simon Bolivar, 75950 Paris Cédex 19; tel. 1-42-02-44-62; fax 1-42-02-08-81; Sec.-Gen. JEAN-PIERRE LE VELLY.

**Fédération Unifiée des Postes et des Télécommunications CFDT (FUPT-CFDT)** (Post, Telegraph and Telephone Workers): 47/49 ave Simon Bolivar, 75950 Paris Cédex 19; tel. 1-44-84-30-30; fax 1-42-02-42-10; e-mail fupt@cfdt.fr; Sec.-Gen. MARIE-PIERRE LIBOUTET.

**Finances et Affaires Economiques** (Finance): 47/49 ave Simon Bolivar, 75950 Paris Cédex 19; tel. 1-53-72-73-00; fax 1-42-02-49-91; f. 1936; civil servants and workers within government financial departments; Sec.-Gen. PHILIPPE LECLEZIO.

**Fonctionnaires et Assimilés (UFFA-CFDT)** (Civil Servants): 47/49 ave Simon Bolivar, 75950 Paris Cédex 19; tel. 1-42-02-44-70; fax 1-42-02-38-77; f. 1932; Sec.-Gen. MICHEL PÉRIER.

**Formation et Enseignement Privés** (Non-State education): 47/49 ave Simon Bolivar, 75950 Paris Cédex 19; tel. 1-40-18-53-53; fax 1-40-40-99-14; e-mail contact@fep-cfdt.fr; internet fep-cfdt.fr; Sec.-Gen. PHILIPPE LEPEU.

**Habillement, Cuir et Textile (HACUITEX-CFDT):** 47/49 ave Simon Bolivar, 75950 Paris Cédex 19; tel. 1-44-52-71-10; fax 1-42-01-02-98; e-mail hacuitex@cfdt.fr; f. 1963; Sec.-Gen. MARTIAL VIDET.

**Ingénieurs et Cadres (UCC-CFDT):** 47 ave Simon Bolivar, 75950 Paris Cédex 19; tel. 1-42-02-44-43; fax 1-42-02-48-58; e-mail ucc-cfdt@ucc-cfdt.fr; Sec.-Gen. MARIE ODILE PAULET.

**Justice:** 47 ave Simon Bolivar, 75019 Paris; tel. 1-42-38-64-10; fax 1-42-38-18-15; Sec.-Gen. JEAN-MARIE LIGIER.

**Mines et Métallurgie** (Miners and Metal Workers): 47/49 ave Simon Bolivar, 75950 Paris Cédex 19; tel. 1-44-52-20-20; fax 1-44-52-20-52; Sec.-Gen. ROBERT BONNAND.

**Personnel du Ministère de l'Intérieur et des Collectivités Locales (INTERCO-CFDT):** 47/49 ave Simon Bolivar, 75950 Paris Cédex 19; tel. 1-40-40-85-50; fax 1-42-06-86-86; Sec.-Gen. ALEXIS GUÉNÉGO.

**Protection Sociale, Travail, Emploi** (Social Security): 47/49 ave Simon Bolivar, 75950 Paris Cédex 19; tel. 1-40-18-77-77; fax 1-40-18-77-79; Sec.-Gen. JEAN-LOUIS TARDIVAUN.

**Santé et Services Sociaux** (Hospital and Social Workers): 47/49 ave Simon Bolivar, 75950 Paris Cédex 19; tel. 1-40-40-85-00; fax 1-42-02-48-08; e-mail santesociaux@efdt.fr; Sec.-Gen. FRANÇOIS CHEREQUE.

**Services:** 47/49 ave Simon Bolivar, 75950 Paris Cédex 19; tel. 1-42-02-50-48; fax 1-42-02-56-55; Sec.-Gen. RÉMY JOUAN.

**Transports et Equipement:** 47/49 ave Simon Bolivar, 75950 Paris Cédex 19; tel. 1-44-84-29-50; fax 1-42-02-49-96; f. 1977; Sec.-Gen. GÉRARD BALBASTRE.

**Union Confédérale des Retraités (UCR):** 47/49 ave Simon Bolivar, 75950 Paris Cédex 19; tel. 1-44-52-12-90; fax 1-42-02-34-51; Sec.-Gen. JACQUES SENSE.

**Confédération Française de l'Encadrement (CGC):** 30 rue de Gramont, 75002 Paris; tel. 1-44-55-77-77; fax 1-42-96-45-97; f. 1944; organizes managerial staff, professional staff and technicians; co-ordinates unions in every industry and sector; Chair. MARC VILBENOÎT; Sec.-Gen. CLAUDE CAMBUS; 300,000 mems.

**Confédération Française des Travailleurs Chrétiens (CFTC):** 13 rue des Ecluses Saint Martin, 75483 Paris Cédex 10; tel. 1-44-52-49-00; fax 1-44-52-49-18; e-mail secretariat@cftc.fr; f. 1919; present form in 1964 after majority CFTC became CFDT (see above); mem. European Trade Union Confederation; Chair. ALAIN DELEU; Gen. Sec. JACQUES VOISIN; 250,000 mems.

**Confédération des Syndicats Libres (CSL)** (formerly Confédération française du Travail): 37 rue Lucien Sampaix, 75010 Paris; tel. 1-55-26-12-12; fax 1-55-26-12-00; e-mail csl.syndicats.libres@hol.fr; internet www.perso.hol.fr/csl; f. 1947; right-wing; Sec.-Gen. GÉRARD FOURMAL; 250,000 mems.

**Fédération de l'Education Nationale (FEN):** 48 rue La Bruyère, 75440 Paris Cédex 09; tel. 1-42-85-71-01; fax 1-40-16-05-92; f. 1948; federation of teachers' unions; Sec.-Gen. HERVÉ BARO.

**Fédération Nationale des Syndicats Autonomes:** 19 blvd Sébastopol, 75001 Paris; f. 1952; groups unions in the private sector; Sec.-Gen. MICHEL-ANDRÉ TILLIÈRES.

**Fédération Nationale des Syndicats d'Exploitants Agricoles (FNSEA)** (National Federation of Farmers' Unions): 11 rue de la Baume, 75008 Paris; tel. 1-53-83-47-47; fax 1-53-83-48-48; e-mail yves.salmon@fnsea.fr; internet www.fnsea.fr; f. 1946; divided into 92 departmental federations and 30,000 local unions; Chair. LUC GUYAU; Dir-Gen. YVES SALMON; 700,000 mems.

**Fédération Syndicale Unitaire (FSU):** 3–5 rue de Metz, 75010 Paris; tel. 1-44-79-90-30; fax 1-48-01-02-52; e-mail fsu.nationale@wanadoo.fr; f. 1993, following split in FEN (see above); federation of 19 teachers' unions; Sec.-Gen. MONIQUE VUAILLAT; 150,000 mems.

**Syndicat National Unitaire des Instituteurs (SNUIPP):** 128 blvd Blanqui, 75013 Paris; e-mail snuipp@snuipp.fr; f. 1993; primary-school teachers; Secs-Gen. DANIEL LE BRET, LAURENT ZAPPI, NICOLE GENEIX.

# Transport

## RAILWAYS

Most of the French railways are controlled by the Société Nationale des Chemins de fer Français (SNCF) which took over the activities of the five largest railway companies in 1937. In 1997 the Réseau Ferré National was created to manage track and infrastructure. The SNCF is divided into 23 régions (areas), all under the direction of a general headquarters in Paris. In 1993 the SNCF operated 32,579 km of track, of which 13,572 km were electrified. By 1998 total track length had been reduced to 31,770 km and was forecast to fall to 26,000 km by 2000. High-speed services (trains à grande vitesse—TGV) operate between Paris and Lyon (TGV Sud-Est), Paris and Bordeaux (TGV Atlantique) and Paris and Calais (TGV Nord). The TGV network covered 1,281 km of track in 1998. The Parisian transport system is controlled by a separate authority, the Régie Autonome des Transports Parisiens (RATP, see below). A number of small railways in the provinces are run by independent organizations. In 1994 a rail link between France and the United Kingdom was opened, including a tunnel under the English Channel (la Manche), from Calais to Folkestone. The rail link was constructed and operated by the Anglo-French Eurotunnel Consortium. In 1998 some 6.9m. passengers used the link, compared with 3.3m. in 1995. The Paris-Calais TGV line, via Lille, completed in 1993, is to form the main artery of a high-speed rail network serving Belgium, the Netherlands, Germany and France. In 1996 it was announced that the TGV network was to be extended to link Strasbourg with Paris. TGV Méditerranée, which will link Valence, Marseille and Nîmes, was expected to become operational in June 2001. In June 1999 plans were announced for the creation of a high-speed rail link between the airports of Charles de Gaulle (Paris) and Heathrow (London).

**Réseau Ferré de France (RFF):** Tour Pascal, 92045 Paris La Défense; tel. 1-46-96-90-00; fax 1-46-96-90-73; f. 1977 to assume ownership and financial control of national rail infrastructure, previously the responsibility of SNCF; state-owned; Pres. C. MARTINAUD; Gen. Man. E. GISSLER.

**Société Nationale des Chemins de fer Français (SNCF):** 34 rue du Commandant Mouchotte, 75699 Paris Cédex 14; tel. 1-53-25-60-00; fax 1-53-25-61-08; e-mail webcom@sncf.fr; internet www.sncf.fr; f. 1937; formerly 51% state-owned, wholly nationalized 1983; 173,400 employees; Chair. LOUIS GALLOIS; Sec.-Gen. PAUL MINGASSON.

### Metropolitan Railways

**Régie Autonome des Transports Parisiens (RATP):** 54 quai de la Rapée, 75599 Paris Cédex 12; tel. 1-44-68-20-20; fax 1-44-68-31-60; f. 1948; state-owned; operates the Paris underground and suburban railways (totalling 333 km in 1999), and buses; Chair. and Dir-Gen. JEAN-PAUL BAILLY.

Three provincial cities also have underground railway systems: Marseille, Lyon and Lille. In 1996 it was announced that an underground railway system was to be built in Rennes.

## ROADS

At 31 December 1997 there were 9,900 km of motorways (autoroutes). There were also 28,000 km of national roads (routes nationales), 355,000 km of secondary roads and 500,000 km of major local roads. In 1993 the Government announced its intention to construct a further 2,600 km of motorways by 2003.

**Fédération Nationale des Transports Routiers (FNTR):** 6 rue Paul Valéry, 75116 Paris; tel. 1-45-53-92-88; road transport; Chair. RENÉ PETIT.

## INLAND WATERWAYS

At 31 December 1996 there were 8,500 km of navigable waterways, of which 1,686 km were accessible to craft of 3,000 tons. In 1995 it was announced that a company had been formed to construct a 230-km canal linking the Rivers Rhône and Rhine. The canal was scheduled to be completed by 2010 at a projected cost of 17,000m. francs.

**Voies navigables de France:** 175 rue Ludovic Boutleux, BP 820, 62408 Béthune Cédex; tel. 3-21-63-24-42; internet www.vnf.fr; f. 1991; management and development of France's inland waterways; Pres. F. BORDRY; Gen. Man. C. PARENT.

## SHIPPING

At 1 January 1997 the French merchant shipping fleet numbered 210 cargo-carrying vessels (excluding supply ships), with a total displacement of 4,084,343 gross tons (not including vessels of less than 100 tons, or the fishing fleet). Of this tonnage, 9.6% comprised passenger vessels, 32.8% cargo vessels and 57.6% petroleum carriers. In 1998 the principal ports, in terms of quantity of cargo, were Marseille, Le Havre and Dunkerque, and the principal passenger port was Calais. The six major seaports (Marseille, Le Havre, Dunkerque, Rouen, Nantes-Saint-Nazaire and Bordeaux) are operated by autonomous authorities, although the State retains supervisory powers.

**Conseil National des Communautés Portuaires:** 3 Square Desaise, 75007 Paris; tel. 1-40-81-86-11; f. 1987; central independent consultative and co-ordinating body for ports and port authorities; over 50 mems including 10 trade union mems; Pres. JACQUES DUPUY-DAUBY; Sec.-Gen. M. DE ROCQUIGNY DU FAYEL.

### Principal Shipping Companies

Note: Not all the vessels belonging to the companies listed below are registered under the French flag.

**Bretagne-Angleterre-Irlande (BAI):** Port du Bloscon, BP 72, 29688 Roscoff Cédex; tel. 2-98-29-28-00; fax 2-98-29-27-00; internet www.brittany-ferries.fr; transport between France, Ireland, Spain and the United Kingdom; Chair. ALEXIS GOURVENNEC; Man. Dir JEAN-MICHEL MASSON; displacement 122,068 grt.

**CETRAMAR, Consortium Européen de Transports Maritimes:** 87 ave de la Grande Armée, 75782 Paris Cédex 16; tel. 1-40-66-11-11; fax 1-45-00-77-35; tramping; Chair. PHILIPPE POIRIER D'ANGÉ D'ORSAY; Man. Dir ANDRÉ MAIRE; displacement 564,291 grt.

**Compagnie de Navigation UIM:** 93–95 rue de Provence, 75009 Paris; tel. 1-42-85-19-00; fax 1-45-26-13-02; Chair. MICHEL DUVAL; Man. Dir JEAN-YVES THOMAS.

**Compagnie Générale Maritime:** 22 quai Galliéni, 92158 Suresnes Cédex; tel. 1-46-25-70-00; fax 1-46-25-78-00; f. 1976 by merger; 99.9% state-owned (1995); privatization initiated in 1996; freight services to USA, Canada, West Indies, Central and South America, northern and eastern Europe, the Middle East, India, Australia, New Zealand, Indonesia and other Pacific and Indian Ocean areas; sales totalled 4,794m. Frs in 1994; Chair. C. ABRAHAM; displacement 653,405 grt.

**Compagnie Maritime d'Affrètement:** Immeuble le Mirabeau, 4 quai d'Arenc, 13215 Marseille Cédex 02; tel. 4-91-39-30-00; fax 4-91-39-30-95; Mediterranean, Middle East and Far East freight services; Chair. JACQUES R. SAADÉ; Man. Dir FARID T. SALEM; displacement 590,985 grt.

**Compagnie Nationale de Navigation:** 128 blvd Haussmann, 75008 Paris; tel. 1-53-04-20-00; fax 1-53-04-20-14; f. 1930 as Compagnie Navale Worms; merged with Compagnie Nationale de Navigation and Société Française de Transports Maritimes, and changed name to Compagnie Nationale de Navigation in 1986; holding co with subsidiaries: Société Française de Transports Pétroliers, Cie Morbihannaise et Nantaise de Navigation, Héli-Union and other subsidiaries abroad; Chair. PATRICK MOLIS; Deputy Man. Dir MARIE-LAURE BREARD; displacement 2,221,546 grt.

**Esso SAF:** 2 rue des Martinets, 92569 Rueil-Malmaison Cédex; tel. 1-47-10-60-00; fax 1-47-10-60-44; Chair., Man. Dir JEAN VERRÉ; Marine Man. PIERRE LANGE; 5 petroleum tankers, displacement 428,431 grt.

**Louis-Dreyfus Armateurs (SNC):** 87 ave de la Grande Armée, 75782 Paris Cédex 16; tel. 1-40-66-11-11; fax 1-45-00-23-97; gas and bulk carriers; CEO PHILIPPE POIRIER D'ANGÉ D'ORSAY; Man. Dir PHILIPPE LOUIS-DREYFUS.

**MARFRET (Compagnie Maritime Marfret):** 13 quai de la Joliette, 13002 Marseille; tel. 4-91-56-91-00; fax 4-91-56-91-01; e-mail mfmedsea@marfret.fr; Mediterranean, South American and northern Europe freight services; Chair. RAYMOND VIDIL; displacement 8,711 grt.

**Mobil Oil Française:** Tour Septentrion, 92081 Paris La Défense Cédex; tel. 1-41-45-42-41; fax 1-41-45-42-93; bulk petroleum transport; refining and marketing of petroleum products; Chair. G. DUPASQUIER; displacement 281,489 grt.

**Navale Française SA:** 8 blvd Victor Hugo, 34000 Montpellier; tel. 4-67-58-82-12; fax 4-67-92-98-34; Chair. MARC CHEVALLIER.

**Société d'Armement et de Transport (SOCATRA):** 9 Allées de Tourny, 33000 Bordeaux; tel. 5-56-00-00-47; fax 5-56-48-51-23; Chair. F. BOZZONI; Man. Dir. M. DUBOURG.

**Société Européenne de Transport Maritime:** 9 allées de Tourny, 33000 Bordeaux; tel. 5-56-00-00-56; fax 5-56-48-51-23; Man. Dirs GILLES BOUTHILLIER, FERNAND BOZZONI; displacement 53,261 grt.

**Société Française de Transports Pétroliers:** 128 blvd Haussmann, 75008 Paris; tel. 1-53-04-20-00; fax 1-53-04-20-14; long-distance petroleum transport; Chair., Man. Dir FRANÇOIS ARRADOU; displacement 236,907 grt.

**Société Nationale Maritime Corse-Méditerranée:** 61 blvd des Dames, BP 1963, 13226 Marseille Cédex 02; tel. 4-91-56-32-00; fax 4-91-56-34-94; passenger and roll on/roll off ferry services between France and Corsica, Sardinia, North Africa; Chairs CLAUDE ABRAHAM, G. MARAIS; Man. Dir BERNARD ANNE; displacement 141,454 grt.

**Société Navale Caennaise:** 24 rue Dumont d'Urville, 14000 Caen; tel. 2-31-72-54-00; fax 2-31-78-04-94; f. 1901; cargo services to Europe and West Africa; Chair., Man. Dir A. LABAT; displacement 59,680 grt.

**Société Nouvelle d'Armement Transmanche (SNAT):** 3 rue Ambroise-Paré, 75010 Paris; tel. 1-49-95-58-92; fax 1-48-74-62-37; vehicle and passenger services between France and the United Kingdom; Chair. MICHEL FÈVE; Man. Dir DIDIER BONNET; displacement 29,251 grt.

**Société Services et Transports:** route du Hoc Gonfreville-L'Orcher, 76700 Harfleur; tel. 2-35-24-72-00; fax 2-35-53-36-25; petroleum and gas transport, passenger transport; Chair. YVES ROUSIER; Man. Dir JACQUES CHARVET; displacement 118,274 grt.

**Total Transport Maritime:** Tour Aurore, 18 Place des Reflets, 92080 Paris La Défense Cédex 05; tel. 1-41-35-52-00; fax 1-47-78-59-99; f. 1931; petroleum tankers; Chair. PHILIPPE GUÉRIN; displacement 273,542 grt.

**Van Ommeren Tankers:** 5 ave Percier, 75008 Paris; tel. 1-42-99-66-66; fax 1-42-99-66-20; e-mail patrick.decavele@vanommeren.com; oil product and chemical coastal tankers and tramping; Man. Dir PATRICK DECAVELE; displacement 251,000 grt.

## CIVIL AVIATION

There are international airports at Orly, Roissy and Le Bourget (Paris), Bordeaux, Lille, Lyon, Marseille, Nice, Strasbourg and Toulouse.

**Aéroports de Paris:** 291 blvd de Raspail, 75675 Paris Cédex 14; tel. 1-43-35-70-00; fax 1-43-35-72-19; state authority in charge of Paris airports; in 1996 it was announced that a third airport was to be constructed in the Paris area, near Chartres, designed to be operational by 2005; Chair. JEAN FLEURY; Man. Dir JEAN-CLAUDE ALBOUY.

### National Airlines

**Air France:** 45 rue de Paris, 95747 Roissy Cédex; tel. 1-41-56-78-00; fax 1-41-56-70-29; internet www.airfrance.fr; f. 1933; 63.4% state-owned; international, European and inter-continental services; flights to Africa, Americas, Middle and Far East and West Indies; sales totalled 59,700m. Frs in 1998; 35.6m. passengers carried in 1998; Chair. JEAN-CYRIL SPINETTA; Pres. P. H. GOURGEUN.

**Air France Europe:** 1 ave du Maréchal Devaux, 91551 Paray Vieille Poste Cédex; tel. 1-46-75-12-12; fax 1-46-75-20-00; f. 1954; fmrly Air Inter; operates internal freight and passenger services; 15.5m. passengers carried in 1996; Man. Dir MARC VÉRON; Exec. Vice-Pres. PATRICK ALEXANDRE.

### Private Airlines

**Air Liberté:** 3 rue du Pont des Halles, Rungis Cédex 94656; tel. 1-49-79-23-00; fax 1-46-86-50-95; f. 1987; operates international, regional and domestic passenger and cargo services; 70%-owned by British Airways, 30%-owned by Banque Rivaud; 2.4m. passengers carried in 1996; Chair. MARC ROCHET; CEO FRANCIS BEAUJARD.

**Air Littoral:** Le Millénaire II, 417 rue Samuel Morse, 34961 Montpellier Cédex 2; tel. 4-67-20-67-20; fax 4-67-64-10-61; f. 1972; merged with Compagnie Aérienne du Languedoc in 1988; operates international, regional and domestic passenger and cargo services; 0.6m. passengers carried in 1996; Chair. MARC DUFOUR; Gen. Man. PASCAL FULLA.

**AOM French Airlines:** 13-15 rue du Pont des Halles, Rungis Cédex; tel. 4-66-70-72-05; fax 4-66-70-04-13; internet www.aom.ch; f. 1992 by merger of Air Outre Mer and Minerve; services to the USA, West Indies and Far East; 2.6m. passengers carried in 1996; Chair. and CEO MARC ROCHET.

**Brit Air:** Aérodrome de Ploujean, BP 156, 29204 Morlaix; tel. 2-98-62-10-22; fax 2-98-62-77-66; f. 1973; operates some 200 daily European flights on more than 30 routes; 0.8m. passengers carried in 1996; Chair. XAVIER LECLERCQ; Dir JACQUES PELLERIN.

**Euralair International:** Aéroport du Bourget, 93350 Paris; tel. 1-49-34-62-00; fax 1-49-34-63-00; f. 1964; international services to Europe and the Mediterranean region; Pres. ANTOINE DE SIZEMONT; Chair. ALEXANDRE COUVELAIRE.

**Hex Air:** Aéroport Le Puy, 43320 Loudes; tel. 4-71-08-62-28; fax 4-71-08-04-10; f. 1991; operates domestic scheduled and charter services; Pres. BERNARD GUICHON.

**TAT European Airlines:** 47 rue Christiaan Huygens, BP 7237, 37072 Tours Cédex 02; tel. 2-47-42-30-00; fax 2-47-54-29-50; f. 1968; fmrly Transport Aérien Transrégional; took over Air Alpes 1981; took over Air Alsace routes following its demise in 1982; wholly-owned by British Airways since 1996; regional charter services; Pres. RODOLPHE MARCHAIS; Chair. MARC ROCHET.

### Airlines Associations

**Chambre Syndicale du Transport Aérien (CSTA):** 28 rue de Chateaudun, 75009 Paris; tel. 1-45-26-23-24; f. 1946 to represent French airlines at national level; Chair. XAVIER LECLERCQ; Delegate-Gen. JEAN-PIERRE LE GOFF; 13 mems.

**Fédération Nationale de l'Aviation Marchande (FNAM):** 28 rue de Chateaudun, 75009 Paris; tel. 1-45-26-23-24; f. 1991; Chair. XAVIER LECLERCQ; Delegate-Gen. JEAN-PIERRE LE GOFF.

# Tourism

France attracts tourists from all over the world. Paris is famous for its boulevards, historic buildings, theatres, art treasures, fashion houses, restaurants and night clubs. The Mediterranean and Atlantic coasts and the French Alps are the most popular tourist resorts. Among other attractions are the many ancient towns, the châteaux of the Loire, the fishing villages of Brittany and Normandy, and spas and places of pilgrimage, such as Vichy and Lourdes. The theme park, Euro Disney, also attracts large numbers of tourists. There were 67,310,000 tourist arrivals in 1997, when estimated tourist receipts totalled US $66,732m. Most visitors are from the United Kingdom, Germany, Belgium, the Netherlands and Italy.

**Direction du Tourisme:** 2 rue Linois, 75740 Paris Cédex 15; tel. 1-44-37-36-00; fax 1-44-37-36-36; Dir PHILIPPE BOISADAM.

**Maison de la France:** 20 ave de l'Opéra, 75041 Paris Cédex 01; tel. 1-42-96-70-00; fax 1-42-96-70-11; internet www.maison-de-la-france.com; f. 1987; Pres. GILBERT TRIGANO.

**Observatoire National du Tourisme:** 2 rue Linois, 75015 Paris Cédex 15; tel. 1-44-37-36-49; fax 1-44-37-38-51; f. 1991; conducts studies and publishes information on all aspects of tourism in France; Pres. MAURICE BERNADET; Dir ALAIN MONFERRAND.

There are Regional Tourism Committees in the 23 regions and 4 overseas départements. There are more than 3,200 Offices de Tourisme and Syndicats d'Initiative (tourist offices operated by the local authorities) throughout France.

# FRENCH OVERSEAS POSSESSIONS

**Ministry of Overseas Departments and Territories:** 27 rue Oudinot, 75358 Paris 07 SP, France; tel. 1-53-69-20-00; fax 1-43-06-60-30.

**Minister of State responsible for Overseas Departments and Territories:** JEAN-JACK QUEYRANNE.

The national flag of France, proportions three by two, with three equal vertical stripes, of blue, white and red, is used in the Overseas Possessions.

# French Overseas Departments

The four Overseas Departments (départements d'outre-mer) are French Guiana, Guadeloupe, Martinique and Réunion. They are integral parts of the French Republic. Each Overseas Department is administered by a Prefect, appointed by the French Government, and the administrative structure is similar to that of the Departments of metropolitan France. Overseas Departments, however, have their own Courts of Appeal. In 1974 each of the Overseas Departments was granted the additional status of a Region (a unit devised for the purpose of economic and social planning, presided over by a Regional Council). Under the decentralization law of March 1982, the executive power of the Prefect in each Overseas Department was transferred to the locally-elected General Council. A proposal to replace the General Council and the indirectly-elected Regional Council by a single assembly was rejected by the French Constitutional Council in December 1982. As a compromise between autonomy and complete assimilation into France, the Regional Councils' responsibility for economic, social and cultural affairs was increased in 1983. In February of that year the first direct elections for the Regional Councils were held. Proposals regarding the institutional future and socio-economic development of the Departments were to be presented to the Council of Ministers in early 2000 and examined by the legislature by the end of June. Changes proposed by the French Government included the creation on Réunion of a second department; the establishment on French Guiana, Guadeloupe and Martinique of congresses of the Regional and General Councils, which would discuss issues of common interest and formulate proposals concerning institutional reform and economic and social development; the transfer to the Regions of responsibilities in areas such as roads, territorial development, water resources and housing; and measures to increase the Departments' autonomy in conducting relations with neighbouring countries and territories. The Overseas Departments continue to send elected representatives to the French National Assembly and to the Senate in Paris, and also to the European Parliament in Strasbourg.

# FRENCH GUIANA

## Introductory Survey

### Location, Climate, Language, Religion, Capital

French Guiana (Guyane) lies on the north coast of South America, with Suriname to the west and Brazil to the south and east. The climate is humid, with a season of heavy rains from April to July and another short rainy season in December and January. Average temperature at sea-level is 27°C (85°F), with little seasonal variation. French is the official language, but a creole patois is also spoken. The majority of the population belong to the Roman Catholic Church, although other Christian churches are represented. The capital is Cayenne.

### Recent History

French occupation commenced in the early 17th century. After brief periods of Dutch, English and Portuguese rule, the territory was finally confirmed as French in 1817. The colony steadily declined, after a short period of prosperity in the 1850s as a result of the discovery of gold in the basin of the Approuague river. French Guiana, including the notorious Devil's Island, was used as a penal colony and as a place of exile for convicts and political prisoners before the practice was halted in 1937. The colony became a Department of France in 1946.

French Guiana's reputation as an area of political and economic stagnation was dispelled by the growth of pro-independence sentiments, and the use of violence by a small minority, compounded by tensions between the Guyanais and large numbers of immigrant workers. In 1974 French Guiana was granted regional status, as part of France's governmental reorganization, thus acquiring greater economic autonomy. In that year, none the less, demonstrations against unemployment, the worsening economic situation and French government policy with regard to the Department led to the detention of leading trade unionists and pro-independence politicians. In 1975 the French Government announced plans to increase investment in French Guiana, but these were largely unsuccessful, owing partly to the problems of developing the interior (about 90% of the territory is covered by forest). Further industrial and political unrest in the late 1970s prompted the Parti Socialiste Guyanais (PSG), then the strongest political organization, to demand greater autonomy for the Department. In 1980 there were several bomb attacks against 'colonialist' targets by an extremist group, Fo nou Libéré la Guyane. Reforms introduced by the French Socialist Government in 1982–83 devolved some power over local affairs to the new Regional Council. In May 1983 French Guiana was the target for bombings by the Alliance Révolutionnaire Caraïbe, an extremist independence movement based in Guadeloupe.

In the February 1983 elections to the Regional Council the left-wing parties gained a majority of votes, but not of seats, and the balance of power was held by the separatist Union des Travailleurs Guyanais (UTG), the political wing of which became the Parti National Populaire Guyanais (PNPG) in November 1985. At elections to the General Council held in March 1985, the PSG and left-wing independents secured 13 seats out of a total of 19.

For the general election to the French National Assembly in March 1986, French Guiana's representation was increased from one to two deputies. The incumbent PSG deputy was re-elected, the other seat being won by the Gaullist Rassemblement pour la République (RPR). At simultaneous elections to the Regional Council, the PSG increased its strength on the Council from 14 to 15 members, and Georges Othily of the PSG was re-elected President of the Council. The RPR won nine seats, and the centre-right Union pour la Démocratie Française (UDF) three, while the remaining four seats were secured by Action Démocratique Guyanaise.

Of the votes cast in the Department at the 1988 French presidential election, the incumbent François Mitterrand of the Parti Socialiste (PS) obtained 52% in the first round, and 60% in the second round—against Jacques Chirac of the RPR. In the legislative elections held in June, the RPR none the less retained a seat in the National Assembly. In September–October the left-wing parties won 14 of the 19 seats at elections to the General Council. In September 1989 Othily, the President of the Regional Council, was elected to take French Guiana's seat in the French Senate. Othily had recently been expelled from the PSG for having worked too closely with the opposition parties. However, he attracted support from those who regarded the party's domination of French Guiana as corrupt, and his victory over the incumbent senator, a PSG member, was believed to reflect the level of dissatisfaction within the party.

In September 1991 an agreement signed between the state Bureau d'études géologiques et minières and a South African mining group, providing for the joint exploitation of gold deposits in French Guiana, provoked opposition from the local political parties, who united in appealing to the central Government to reconsider its position, accusing the French of colonialism. A general strike was organized in the Department, and the two organizations withdrew from the agreement in October, citing the strength of local opposition to the project.

In March 1992 elections were held to both the General and Regional Councils. In the former, the PSG retained 10 seats, while other left-wing candidates took five seats. The PSG leader, Elie Castor, retained the presidency of the General Council. The party also won 16 seats in the Regional Council, and the PSG Secretary-General, Antoine Karam, was subsequently elected as the body's President, defeating Othily (whose party, the Forces Démocratiques Guyanaises, had secured 10 seats). In a referendum in September, 67.3% of voters in French Guiana approved ratification of the Treaty on European Union (see p. 172), although an abstention rate of 81.4% was recorded.

In October 1992 the Mouvement Syndical Unitaire organized demonstrations and a widely-observed general strike, to protest against France's perceived indifference to the Department's worsening economic crisis. The strike was terminated after one week, following the signing of an accord between the French Government and professional and trade union organizations. The agreement included provisions for the reduction of redundancies and for the financing of a programme of infrastructural improvements, as well as social and educational measures.

At the March 1993 elections to the French National Assembly Léon Bertrand of the RPR was re-elected in the Kourou, Saint-Laurent-du-Maroni constituency, taking 52.1% of the valid votes. Christiane Taubira-Delannon the founder of the independent left-wing Walawari movement and an outspoken critic of existing policies for the management of French Guiana's natural resources, was elected in the Cayenne, Macouria constituency (traditionally a PSG stronghold), winning 55.5% of the votes; she subsequently joined the République et liberté grouping in the National Assembly.

The PSG's representation in the General Council declined to eight seats following the March 1994 cantonal elections; none the less, one of its members, Stéphan Phinéra-Horth, was subsequently elected President of the Council (Elie Castor having left the party). Taubira-Delannon, defeated by Karam, failed to secure election, although another member of the Walawari movement did enter the Council. Taubira-Delannon was elected to the European Parliament in June, as a representative of the Energie radicale grouping—which secured the greatest percentage of the votes (36.3%) in the Department, ahead of the government list and a combined list of the parties of the left of the four Overseas Departments. An abstention rate of 80.4% was recorded.

At the first round of voting in the 1995 presidential elections, on 23 April, there was a considerable increase in support in French Guiana for Chirac, who took 39.8% of the votes cast, at the expense of the candidate of the PS, Lionel Jospin, who received the support of 24.2% of voters. The level of support for Jean-Marie Le Pen, of the extreme right-wing Front National, almost doubled (to 8.1%), compared with that at the 1988 election. At the second round, on 7 May 1995, Chirac won 57.4% of the valid votes cast. The rate of participation by voters at this round was 48.0%. At municipal elections in June the PSG retained control of the Cayenne council, although with reduced support.

With effect from the beginning of 1996 the social security systems of the Overseas Departments were aligned with those of metropolitan France. In February of that year more than 300 representatives of the Overseas Departments' political, economic, trade union and professional organizations attended the National Assizes of Social Equality and Development, a meeting held in Paris at the instigation of Jean-Jacques de Peretti, the Minister-Delegate responsible for the Overseas Departments and Territories.

Beginning in late October 1996 a boycott of classes by secondary-school pupils, who were demanding improved conditions of study, escalated in the following month into a crisis that was regarded as exemplifying wider social tensions between the Department and metropolitan France. The refusal of the Prefect, Pierre Dartout, to receive schools' representatives prompted protests in Cayenne, which swiftly degenerated into rioting and looting, apparently as the protesters were joined by disaffected youths from deprived areas. Considerable material damage was caused to government and commercial property during two nights of violence. One pupil sustained gunshot wounds and several gendarmes were injured in clashes between rioters and security forces; a dead body was, moreover, subsequently discovered in a building that had been destroyed by fire. The central Government dispatched anti-riot police to assist the local security forces (reinforcements numbered about 200 by mid-November), and it was announced that de Peretti and the Minister of National Education, François Bayrou, would visit French Guiana. However, the conviction, shortly afterwards, of several people implicated in the rioting provoked further protests and clashes with security forces, and a one-day general strike in Cayenne, organized by the UTG, resulted in the closure of most businesses and government departments. The extent of the security forces' actions in suppressing the demonstrations was criticized both by those involved in the schools' protest and by local politicians, while the competence of the Department's administrators in their approach to the crisis was the focus of considerable scrutiny. Local officials, meanwhile, denounced the role in the violence not only of unemployed youths but also of separatist groups, alleging that the latter were seeking to exploit the crisis for their own ends. Differences also emerged between the Department's education inspector, Jean-Marcel Coteret, and the Rector of the Antilles-Guyane Academy, Michèle Rudler, as Coteret openly criticized Rudler for remaining in Martinique (the seat of the Academy) throughout the crisis. Bayrou and de Peretti subsequently arrived in Cayenne to meet those involved in the crisis. Local administrators and schools' representatives had already reached agreement on the students' material demands, but, to considerable local acclaim, the ministers announced the establishment, effective from the beginning of 1997, of separate Academies for French Guiana, Guadeloupe and Martinique. The creation was also announced of additional primary educational facilities for some 3,000 children, and a programme was declared to improve academic standards in secondary schools. In all, the measures were to cost the French Government more than 500m. francs. The removal from his post of Coteret, in December 1996, and the appointment of a new Prefect in January 1997 were perceived as indicative of the central Government's desire to assuage tensions in French Guiana.

Elie Castor died in France in June 1996; prior to his death he had been under investigation in connection with allegations including fraud and abuse of influence during his time in public office. In May 1997 further details of irregularities in the General Council's administration of French Guiana during Elie Castor's presidency were revealed in a letter from the Antilles–Guyane Chambre régionale des comptes (responsible for monitoring public finances in the region) to Phinéra-Horth, Castor's successor as President of the Council.

In April 1997 violent incidents followed the arrest of five pro-independence activists suspected of setting fire to the home of the public prosecutor during the disturbances of November 1996. Five others, including leading members of the UTG and the PNPG, were subsequently detained in connection with the arson incident. The transfer of all 10 detainees to Martinique (termed a deportation by separatist organizations) prompted further violent protests in Cayenne. Police reinforcements were dispatched by the central Government to help suppress the violence, as nine gendarmes reportedly received gunshot wounds during two nights of rioting. In July one of the detainees, Jean-Victor Castor, a prominent member of the UTG and the pro-independence Mouvement pour la Décolonisation et l'Emancipation Sociale (MDES), who had been released the previous month, was rearrested and accused of assaulting a policeman during the April riots. Following the announcement, in August, that Castor was to remain in custody, some 200 demonstrators clashed with riot police in Cayenne. Castor was released shortly afterwards, and in September a further four separatists, who had been held on remand since April, were also freed.

In late May and early June 1997 Léon Bertrand, securing 63.3% of votes cast, and Christiane Taubira-Delannon, winning 64.8% of votes, were both re-elected to the French National Assembly in elections that were marked by a high rate of abstention. Candidates from pro-independence parties notably gained increased support, winning slightly more than 10% of the votes cast in both constituencies.

Elections to the Regional and General Councils were held in March 1998. The PSG's representation in the Regional Council declined to 11 seats, with other left-wing candidates securing a further 11 seats (including two won by Walawari). Antoine Karam was re-elected to the presidency of the Council, again defeating Senator Othily, as in 1992. The PSG also lost seats in the General Council, retaining only five of the 19 seats, while other left-wing candidates took a further five, and independent candidates won seven seats. André Lecante, an independent left-wing councillor, was elected as the body's President, defeating the incumbent, Phinéra-Horth. In late September 1998 Othily was re-elected to the French Senate.

In January 1999 representatives of 10 separatist organizations from French Guiana, Guadeloupe and Martinique, including the MDES and the PNPG, signed a joint declaration denouncing 'French colonialism', in which they stated their intention to campaign for the reinstatement of the three American Overseas Departments on a UN list of territories to be decolonized. The political future of the Overseas Departments provoked much debate during 1999. In February members of the Regional and General Councils held a congress to discuss the political, economic and social future of French Guiana; the participants proposed the replacement of the two Councils with a single body, to which responsibility in several areas, such as economic development, health and education, would be transferred. Several RPR councillors boycotted the meeting. In October, however, during a visit to Guadeloupe and Martinique, Lionel Jospin, the Prime Minister, precluded from future legislation any merger of the Regional and General Councils. Following a series of meetings held in late 1999, in December the Presidents of the Regional Councils of French Guiana, Guadeloupe and Martinique signed a joint declaration in Basse-Terre, Guadeloupe, affirming their intention to propose, to the President and the Government, a legislative amendment, possibly constitutional, aimed at creating a new status of overseas region, despite an earlier statement by Jospin indicating that the Government did not envisage a change in status for the Departments. Further meetings of the three regional Presidents were held in January and February 2000. Proposals regarding the institutional future and socio-economic development of the Departments (see p. 1481) were to be considered by the Council of Ministers in early 2000 and examined by the legislature by the end of June.

In 1986–87 French Guiana's relations with neighbouring Suriname deteriorated as increasing numbers of Surinamese refugees fled across the border to escape rebel uprisings in their own country. In late 1986 additional French troops were brought in to patrol the border, as a result of which the Surinamese Government accused the French Government of preparing an invasion of Suriname via French Guiana. It was also reported that Surinamese rebels were using French Guiana as a conduit for weapons and supplies. In 1989 there was an escalation in violent crime, which was generally attributed to the immigrant and refugee population. In August a 24-hour strike, in protest against the high rate of crime, was called by the Chamber of Commerce. The strike was widely supported by trade unions and business proprietors alike. In response to demands for more effective policing, the French Government dispatched 100 riot police from France as reinforcements for the Department's regular police. In 1992 the French Government implemented a programme under which all of the refugees from Suriname were to be repatriated by the end of September. By July of that year 2,500 of the 5,900 registered Surinamese refugees had accepted financial incentives from the French administration and returned to Suriname.

### Government

France is represented in French Guiana by an appointed Prefect. There are two Councils with local powers: the General Council, with 19 members, and the Regional Council, with 31 members. Both are elected by universal adult suffrage for a period of six years. French Guiana elects two representatives to the French National Assembly in Paris, and sends one elected representative to the French Senate. French Guiana is also represented at the European Parliament.

### Defence

At 1 August 1999 France maintained military forces of 2,200 in French Guiana, as well as a gendarmerie of 600.

### Economic Affairs

In 1989, according to estimates by the UN, French Guiana's gross domestic product (GDP), measured at current prices, was US $266m., equivalent to $2,800 per head. Between 1980 and 1985, it was estimated, GDP increased, in real terms, at an average rate of 0.8% per year, and in 1985–89 the average annual growth rate increased to 3.6%. During 1980–86 GDP per head declined by an average of 2.8% annually. GDP in 1994 was 8,231m. French francs, equivalent to 57,160 francs per head. Between the censuses of 1990 and 1999, according to provisional figures, the population increased at an average annual rate of 3.6%.

Agriculture engaged about 11.4% of the employed labour force at the time of the 1990 census. The dominant activities are fisheries and forestry, although the contribution of the latter to export earnings has declined in recent years. In 1997 exports of shellfish (particularly shrimps) provided some 19.4% of total export earnings. The principal crops for local consumption are cassava, vegetables and rice, and sugar cane is grown for making rum. Rice, pineapples and citrus fruit are cultivated for export. Agricultural GDP increased at an average annual rate of 2.1% in 1980–85, and 1.6% in 1985–89.

Industry, including mining, manufacturing, construction and power, engaged about 20.7% of the employed labour force in 1990. The mining sector is dominated by the extraction of gold, which involves small-scale alluvial operations as well as larger local and multinational mining concerns. Exploration activity intensified in the mid-1990s, and the proposed construction of a major new road into the interior of the Department was expected to encourage further development. Officially-recorded gold exports contributed some 27.4% of total export earnings in 1997: actual production levels and sales are believed to be higher than published levels. Crushed rock for the construction industry is the only other mineral extracted in significant quantities, although exploratory drilling of known diamond deposits began in 1995. Deposits of bauxite, columbo-tantalite and kaolin are also present.

There is little manufacturing activity, except for the processing of fisheries products (mainly shrimp-freezing) and the distillation of rum. Manufacturing GDP declined at an average annual rate of 10.6% in 1980–85, and by an average of 1.8% per year in 1985–89.

French Guiana was heavily dependent on imported fuels for the generation of energy prior to the flooding of the Petit-Saut hydroelectric dam on the River Sinnamary, in 1994. Together with existing generating plants, the 116-MW dam was expected to satisfy the territory's electrical energy requirements for about 30 years. Imports of mineral fuels accounted for 5.3% of total imports in 1995.

The services sector engaged 67.9% of the employed labour force in 1990. The European Space Agency's satellite-launching centre at Kourou (established in 1964 and to be expanded during the 1990s) has provided a considerable stimulus to the economy, most notably the construction sector. Some 1,100 people were employed at the centre in 1991. In 1996 15 satellites were launched from 10 *Ariane-4* rockets, although the explosion of the new *Ariane-5* rocket, in July of that year, delayed the centre's programme. In October 1997 the *Ariane-5* rocket was successfully launched, and its first commercial mission was accomplished in December 1999. The tourist sector expanded during the 1980s, although its potential is limited by the lack of infrastructure away from the coast. In 1999 68,211 visitor arrivals were recorded.

In 1997 French Guiana recorded a trade deficit of 2,724.7m. French francs. In 1997 the principal source of imports was metropolitan France (which supplied 51.9% of total imports in that year); the Department's other major suppliers were the USA and Trinidad and Tobago. Metropolitan France was also the principal market for exports in that year (62.0%); other important purchasers were Switzerland, Spain, Guadeloupe and Brazil. The principal imports in 1995 were machinery and transport equipment, food and live animals, manufactured articles, chemicals, mineral fuels and lubricants, and beverages and tobacco. The principal exports in 1997 were gold, parts for air and space vehicles, shellfish and rice.

In 1992 there was a combined deficit on the budgets of French Guiana's government authorities (state, regional, departmental and communal) of 974m. French francs. Under the 1997 regional budget it was envisaged that expenditure would total 447m. French francs. By September 1988 French Guiana's external debt had reached US $1,200m. The annual rate of inflation averaged 1.6% in 1990–98; consumer prices increased by an average of 0.5% in 1998. Unemployment in 1998 was estimated at 21.4% of the total labour force. However, there is a shortage of skilled labour, offset partly by immigration.

As an integral part of France, French Guiana is a member of the European Union (EU—see p. 172). The French Overseas Departments were to receive a total of ECU 1,500m. from EU regional funds during 1994–2000.

Economic development in French Guiana has been hindered by the Department's location, poor infrastructure away from the coast and lack of a skilled indigenous labour force, although there is considerable potential for further growth in the fishing, forestry and tourism (notably 'eco-tourism') sectors. A particular concern throughout the 1990s was the rapid rise in the rate of unemployment; youth unemployment and related social problems were widely interpreted as having contributed to the violence in Cayenne in late 1996 (see Recent History). French Guiana's geographical characteristics—large parts of the territory are accessible only by river—have resulted in difficulties in regulating key areas of the economy, such as gold-mining and forestry. Considerable concern has been expressed regarding the ecological consequences of such a lack of controls; moreover, the flooding of a large area of forest (some 340 sq km), as part of the Petit-Saut barrage project, has prompted disquiet among environmental groups, as has uncertainty regarding the ecological implications of the satellite-launching programme at Kourou. A national park, covering a proposed 2.5m. ha of the south of French Guiana, was expected to be created in 2000, with the aim of protecting an expanse of equatorial forest; efforts were being made to reconcile ecological concerns with economic priorities and the needs of the resident communities. The budget deficit represents a significant obstacle to growth, while high demand for imported consumer goods (much of which is generated by relatively well-remunerated civil servants, who constitute about two-thirds of the working population) undermines progress in reducing the trade deficit.

### Social Welfare

In 1997 there were two hospital complexes, a medical centre and three private clinics. In addition, each of the 22 communes has a health centre. There were 223 doctors, 41 dental surgeons and 48 pharmacists in 1998. The Institut Pasteur, in Cayenne, undertakes research into malaria and other tropical diseases. Welfare payments and the statutory minimum wage in the Overseas Departments are aligned with those of metropolitan France.

### Education

Education is modelled on the system in metropolitan France, and is compulsory for 10 years between the ages of six and 16 years. Primary education begins at six years of age and lasts for five years. Secondary education, beginning at 11 years of age, lasts for up to seven years, comprising a first cycle of four years and a second of three years. Education at state schools (which accounted for more than 90% of total enrolment in 1992/93) is provided free of charge. Between 1980 and 1993 the number of children attending primary schools increased by more than 70%, and the number of pupils at secondary schools by 87%, although such expansion has placed considerable strain on existing facilities. Higher education in law, administration and French language and literature is provided by a branch of the Université Antilles-Guyane in Cayenne (the university as a whole had 15,810 enrolled students in the 1995/96 academic year), and one department of a technical institute opened at Kourou in 1988. There is also a teacher-training college and an agricultural college. Total government expenditure on education amounted to 851m. French francs in 1993. An Academy for French Guiana was established in January 1997. In 1982 the average rate of adult illiteracy was 17.0% (males 16.4%; females 17.7%).

### Public Holidays

**2000:** 1 January (New Year's Day), 6–7 March (Lenten Carnival), 21–24 April (Easter), 1 May (Labour Day), 1 June (Ascension Day), 12 June (Whit Monday), 14 July (National Day), 11 November (Armistice Day), 25 December (Christmas Day).

**2001:** 1 January (New Year's Day), 26–27 February (Lenten Carnival), 13–16 April (Easter), 1 May (Labour Day), 24 May (Ascension Day), 4 June (Whit Monday), 14 July (National Day), 11 November (Armistice Day), 25 December (Christmas Day).

### Weights and Measures

The metric system is in use.

# Statistical Survey

Sources (unless otherwise stated): Institut national de la statistique et des études économiques, 1 rue Maillard-Dumesle, BP 6017, 97306 Cayenne; tel. 31-56-03; fax 30-87-89; Ministère des départements et territoires d'outre-mer, 27 rue Oudinot, 75358 Paris 07 SP; tel. 1-53-69-20-00; fax 1-43-06-60-30; internet http://www.outre-mer.gouv.fr.

## AREA AND POPULATION

**Area:** 83,534 sq km (32,253 sq miles).

**Population:** 73,012 at census of 9 March 1982; 114,808 (males 59,799, females 55,009) at census of 15 March 1990; 157,277 (provisional figure) at census of 8 March 1999.

**Density** (at 1999 census): 1.9 per sq km.

**Principal Towns** (population at 1990 census): Cayenne (capital) 41,067; Kourou 13,873; Saint-Laurent-du-Maroni 13,616; Remire-Montjoly 11,709; Matoury 10,152.

**Births, Marriages and Deaths** (1996, provisional figures): Registered live births 4,367 (birth rate 27.3 per 1,000); Registered marriages 566 (marriage rate 3.5 per 1,000); Registered deaths 543 (death rate 3.4 per 1,000).

**Economically Active Population** (persons aged 15 years and over, 1990 census): Agriculture, hunting, forestry and fishing 4,177; Industry and energy 3,130; Construction 4,440; Trade 3,152; Transport and telecommunications 1,857; Financial services 408; Other marketable services 7,352; Non-marketable services 12,068; Total civilians employed 36,584; Military personnel 417; Unemployed 11,722. Total labour force 48,723 (males 30,110, females 18,613).

## AGRICULTURE, ETC.

**Principal Crops** (FAO estimates, '000 metric tons, 1998): Sugar cane 5; Cassava 10; Other roots and tubers 4; Rice (paddy) 31. Source: FAO, *Production Yearbook*.

**Livestock** (FAO estimates, '000 head, year ending September 1998): Cattle 9; Pigs 11; Sheep 3; Goats 1. Source: FAO, *Production Yearbook*.

**Livestock Products** (metric tons, unless otherwise indicated, 1997): Beef and veal 318; Pig meat 1,148; Mutton, lamb and goat meat 28; Poultry meat 463; Cows' milk (hl) 2,425; Eggs ('000) 9,003.

**Forestry** ('000 cu m, 1997): *Roundwood removals* (excl. bark): Sawlogs, veneer logs and logs for sleepers 51; Other industrial wood 9; Fuel wood 72; Total 132. *Sawnwood production* (incl. railway sleepers): Total 15. Source: FAO, *Yearbook of Forest Products*.

**Fishing** (metric tons, live weight, 1997): Marine fishes 3,600; Shrimps and prawns 4,102; Total catch 7,702. Source: FAO, *Yearbook of Fishery Statistics*.

## MINING

**Production:** Gold (metal content of ore, metric tons) 2.8 in 1998 (Source: Gold Fields Mineral Services Ltd, *Gold Survey 1999*); Sand and gravel ('000 metric tons) 3,000 in 1994 (Source: UN, *Industrial Commodity Statistics Yearbook*).

## INDUSTRY

**Production:** Rum 2,600 hl in 1996; Electric energy 450 million kWh (estimate) in 1995 (Source: UN, *Industrial Commodity Statistics Yearbook*).

## FINANCE

**Currency and Exchange Rates:** 100 centimes = 1 French franc. *Sterling, Dollar and Euro Equivalents* (30 September 1999): £1 sterling = 10.1269 francs; US $1 = 6.1506 francs; €1 = 6.5596 francs; 1,000 French francs = £98.75 = $162.59 = €152.45. *Average Exchange Rate* (French francs per US dollar): 5.1155 in 1996; 5.8367 in 1997; 5.8995 in 1998.

**Budget** (million French francs, 1992): *French Government:* Revenue 706; Expenditure 1,505. *Regional Government:* Revenue 558; Expenditure 666. *Departmental Government:* Revenue 998; Expenditure 803. *Communes:* Revenue 998; Expenditure 982. **1997** (million French francs): *Regional Budget:* Expenditure 447.

**Money Supply** (million French francs at 31 December 1996): Currency outside banks 3,000; Demand deposits at banks 1,621; Total money 4,621.

**Cost of Living** (Consumer Price Index for Cayenne; base: 1990 = 100): 111.8 in 1996; 112.9 in 1997; 113.5 in 1998. Source: UN, *Monthly Bulletin of Statistics*.

**Expenditure on the Gross Domestic Product** (million French francs at current prices, 1994): Government final consumption expenditure 3,041; Private final consumption expenditure 4,828; Increase in stocks 177; Gross fixed capital formation 2,829; *Total domestic expenditure* 10,875; Exports of goods and services 5,174; *Less* Imports of goods and services 7,818; *GDP in purchasers' values* 8,231.

**Gross Domestic Product by Economic Activity** (million French francs at current prices, 1992): Agriculture, hunting, forestry and fishing 578; Mining, quarrying and manufacturing 726; Electricity, gas and water 47; Construction 868; Trade, restaurants and hotels 961; Transport, storage and communications 921; Finance, insurance, real estate and business services 1,185; Government services 1,856; Other community, social and personal services 835; Other services 74; *Sub-total* 8,052; Import duties 383; *Less* Imputed bank service charge 458; *GDP in purchasers' values* 7,976. Source: UN, *National Accounts Statistics*.

## EXTERNAL TRADE

**Principal Commodities:** *Imports c.i.f.* (US $ million, 1995): Food and live animals 104.3 (Meat and meat preparations 29.6, Dairy products and birds' eggs 15.6); Beverages and tobacco 39.0 (Beverages 34.3); Mineral fuels, lubricants, etc. 41.9 (Petroleum and petroleum products 40.5); Chemicals and related products 58.0 (Medicinal and pharmaceutical products 17.2); Basic manufactures 92.5; Machinery and transport equipment 330.0 (Power-generating machinery and equipment 27.0, General industrial machinery, equipment and parts 28.0, Office machines and automatic data-processing machines 22.2, Telecommunications and sound equipment 27.6, Road vehicles and parts 88.6, Other transport equipment 88.6); Miscellaneous manufactured articles 97.0 (Professional, scientific and controlling instruments, etc. 15.6); Total (incl. others) 783.3. Source: UN, *International Trade Statistics Yearbook*. *Exports f.o.b.:* (million French francs, 1997): Crustaceans 177.4; Rice 51.8; Parts for air and space vehicles 220.5; Gold 250.9; Total (incl. others) 915.7.

**Principal Trading Partners** (million French francs, 1997): *Imports c.i.f.:* Belgium-Luxembourg 42.2; France (metropolitan) 1,889.9; Germany 58.3; Italy 72.2; Japan 59.0; Netherlands 66.5; Trinidad and Tobago 218.9; USA 519.9; Total (incl. others) 3,640.4. *Exports f.o.b.:* Brazil 47.6; France (metropolitan) 567.3; Guadeloupe 49.6; Martinique 44.5; Spain 54.8; Switzerland 66.5; USA 21.4; Total (incl. others) 915.7.

## TRANSPORT

**Road Traffic** ('000 motor vehicles in use, 1993): Passenger cars 29.1; Commercial vehicles 10.6. Source: UN, *Statistical Yearbook*.

**International Sea-borne Shipping** (traffic, 1998): Vessels entered 231 (1996); Goods loaded 75,000 metric tons; Goods unloaded 501,400 metric tons; Passengers carried 275,300.

**Civil Aviation** (1998): Freight carried 6,600 metric tons; Passengers carried 422,100.

## TOURISM

**Tourist Arrivals** (1999): 68,211. Source: Comité du Tourisme de la Guyane.

## COMMUNICATIONS MEDIA

**Radio Receivers** ('000 in use) 96 in 1996; **Television Receivers** ('000 in use) 27 in 1996; **Telephones** ('000 main lines in use) 40 in 1994; **Telefax Stations** (number in use) 185 in 1990; **Daily Newspaper** 1 in 1996 (average circulation 2,000 copies). Sources: UNESCO, *Statistical Yearbook*; UN, *Statistical Yearbook*.

### EDUCATION

**Pre-primary** (1995/96): 42 institutions (1993/94); 9,098 students.

**Primary** (1995/96): 78 institutions (1993/94); 802 teachers; 17,006 students.

**Secondary** (1995/96): 1,085 teachers (875 general, 210 vocational); 15,989 students (13,585 general, 2,404 vocational).

Source: UNESCO, *Statistical Yearbook*.

**Higher** (1992): 427 students.

# Directory

## The Government

(February 2000)

**Prefect:** HENRI MASSE, Préfecture, rue Fiedmont, BP 7008, 97307 Cayenne Cédex; tel. 39-45-00; fax 30-02-77.

**President of the General Council:** ANDRÉ LECANTE (Independent left), Hôtel du Département, place Léopold, BP 5021, 97307 Cayenne Cédex; tel. 29-55-00; fax 29-55-25.

**Deputies to the French National Assembly:** CHRISTIANE TAUBIRA-DELANNON (Independent left), LÉON BERTRAND (RPR).

**Representative to the French Senate:** GEORGES OTHILY (FDG).

### REGIONAL COUNCIL

Conseil Regional, 66 ave du Général de Gaulle, BP 7025, 97307 Cayenne Cédex; tel. 29-20-20; fax 31-95-22.

**President:** ANTOINE KARAM (PSG).

**Election, 15 March 1998**

| | Seats |
|---|---|
| Parti Socialiste Guyanais (PSG) | 11 |
| Rassemblement pour la République (RPR) | 6 |
| Walawari | 2 |
| Others | 12* |
| **Total** | 31 |

* Three independents and nine left-wing candidates.

## Political Organizations

**Action Démocratique Guyanaise (ADG):** Cayenne; Leader ANDRÉ LECANTE.

**Forces Démocratiques Guyanaises (FDG):** Cayenne; f. 1989 by a split in the PSG; Leader GEORGES OTHILY.

**Mouvement pour la Décolonisation et l'Emancipation Sociale (MDES):** pro-independence party; Sec.-Gen. MAURICE PINDARD.

**Parti National Populaire Guyanais (PNPG):** Cayenne; f. 1985; pro-independence party; Leader JEAN-CLAUDE RINGUET.

**Parti Socialiste:** Cayenne; tel. 37-81-33; local branch of the national party; Leader PIERRE RIBARDIÈRE.

**Parti Socialiste Guyanais (PSG):** 1 Cité Césaire, Cayenne; f. 1956; Sec.-Gen. ANTOINE KARAM.

**Rassemblement pour la République (RPR):** Cayenne; tel. 31-66-60; f. 1946; local branch of the national party; Gaullist; Leader ROLAND HO-WEN-SZE.

**Union pour la Démocratie Française (UDF):** Cayenne; tel. 31-17-10; f. 1979; local branch of the national party; centre-right; Leader R. CHOW-CHINE.

**Union Socialiste Démocratique (USD):** Cayenne; Leader THÉODORE ROUMILLAC.

**Walawari:** Cayenne; left-wing; Leader CHRISTIANE TAUBIRA-DELANNON.

## Judicial System

**Courts of Appeal:** see Judicial System, Martinique.

**Tribunal de Grande Instance:** Palais de Justice, 9 ave du Général de Gaulle, 97300 Cayenne; Pres. J. FAHET; Procurator-Gen. ANNE KAYANAKIS.

## Religion

### CHRISTIANITY

#### The Roman Catholic Church

French Guiana comprises the single diocese of Cayenne, suffragan to the archdiocese of Fort-de-France, Martinique. At 31 December 1997 there were an estimated 120,000 adherents in French Guiana, representing some 75% of the total population. French Guiana participates in the Antilles Episcopal Conference, currently based in Port of Spain, Trinidad and Tobago.

**Bishop of Cayenne:** Rt Rev. LOUIS SANKALÉ, Evêché, 24 rue Madame-Payé, BP 378, 97328 Cayenne Cédex; tel. 31-01-18; fax 30-20-33.

#### The Anglican Communion

Within the Church in the Province of the West Indies, French Guiana forms part of the diocese of Guyana. The Bishop is resident in Georgetown, Guyana.

#### Other Churches

**Assembly of God:** 16 route La Madeleine, 97300 Cayenne; tel. 31-09-14; fax 35-23-05; Pres. JACQUES RHINO.

**Church of Jesus Christ of Latter-day Saints (Mormons):** chemin Constant Chlore, 97354 Rémire-Montjoly; tel. 30-55-92; Br. Pres. FRANÇOIS PRATIQUE, allée des Cigales, route de Montabo, 97300 Cayenne; tel. 31-21-86.

**Quadrangular Gospel Church:** 97300 Cayenne; tel. 37-84-81.

**Seventh-day Adventist Church:** Mission Adventiste, 39 rue Schoëlcher, 97300 Cayenne Cédex; tel. 30-30-64; fax 37-93-02.

The Jehovah's Witnesses are also represented.

## The Press

**France-Guyane:** 88 bis ave du Général de Gaulle, 97300 Cayenne; tel. 29-85-86; fax 31-11-57; daily; Dir PHILIPPE HERSANT; circ. 5,500.

**La Presse de Guyane:** 26 rue du Lieutenant Brassé, BP 6012, 97300 Cayenne; tel. 29-59-90; 4 a week; circ. 1,000.

## Broadcasting and Communications

### TELECOMMUNICATIONS

**France Telecom:** 76 ave Voltaire, 97300 Cayenne; tel. 39-91-14; fax 39-93-02; local branch of national telecommunications co.

### BROADCASTING

**Réseau France Outre-mer (RFO):** 43 rue du Dr Devèze, BP 7013, 97305 Cayenne; tel. 30-15-00; fax 30-26-49; e-mail rfosaf@nplus.gf; internet www.rfo.fr; fmrly Société Nationale de Radio-Télévision Française d'Outre-mer, renamed as above 1998; Radio-Guyane Inter: broadcasts 18 hours daily; Téléguyane: 2 channels, 32 hours weekly; Pres. ANDRÉ-MICHEL BESSE; Regional Dir GEORGES CHOW TOUN.

#### Radio

Six private FM radio stations are in operation.

**Cayenne FM:** 88 ave Général de Gaulle, BP 428, 97300 Cayenne; tel. 31-37-38; private radio station broadcasting 126 hours weekly.

**Radio Nou Men:** private station; broadcasts in Creole and Boni.

**Radio Tout Moune:** rue des Mandarines, 97300 Cayenne; tel. 31-80-74; fax 30-91-19; f. 1982; private station; broadcasts 24 hours a day; Pres. R. BATHILDE; Dir GUY SAINT-AIME.

#### Television

**Antenne Créole:** 31 ave Louis Pasteur, 97300 Cayenne; tel. 31-20-20; private television station.

**Canal Plus Guyane:** Cayenne; private 'coded' television station.

## Finance

(cap. = capital; res = reserves; dep. = deposits; m. = million; brs = branches; amounts in French francs)

### BANKING

#### Central Bank

**Institut d'Emission des Départements d'Outre-mer (IEDOM):** 8 rue Christophe Colomb, BP 6016, 97306 Cayenne Cédex; tel. 29-36-50; fax 30-02-76.

#### Commercial Banks

**Banque Française Commerciale Antilles–Guyane (BFC Antilles Guyane):** 8 pl. des Palmistes, 97300 Cayenne (see chapter on Guadeloupe).

**Banque Nationale de Paris–Guyane (BNP Guyane):** 2 pl. Victor Schoëlcher, BP 35, 97300 Cayenne; tel. 39-63-00; fax 30-23-08; f. 1855; cap. 71.7m., res 100.0m., dep. 2,007m. (Dec. 1994); Chair. of Bd (Cayenne) VINCENT DE ROUX; 5 brs.

**Crédit Populaire Guyanais:** Caisse de Crédit Mutuel, 93 rue Lallouette, BP 818, 97338 Cayenne; tel. 30-15-23; fax 30-17-65.

#### Development Bank

**Société financière pour le développement économique de la Guyane (SOFIDEG):** PK 3, route de Baduel, BP 860, 97339 Cayenne Cédex; tel. 29-94-29; fax 30-60-44; f. 1982; Dir FRANÇOIS CHEVILLOTTE.

## Trade and Industry

### GOVERNMENT AGENCY

**Direction Régionale de l'Industrie, de la Recherche et de l'Environnement (DRIRE):** impasse Buzaré, BP 7001, 97307 Cayenne; tel. 29-75-00; fax 29-07-34; e-mail drire.antilles.guyane@wanadoo.fr; mining authority; responsible for assessing applications for and awarding exploration and exploitation rights; Regional Dir JEAN-CLAUDE BARA.

### DEVELOPMENT ORGANIZATION

**Agence Française de Développement (AFD):** Cayenne; tel. 31-41-33; fmrly Caisse Française de Développement; Dir CLAUDE ALBINA.

### CHAMBERS OF COMMERCE

**Chambre Départementale de Commerce et d'Industrie:** Hôtel Consulaire, pl. de l'Esplanade, BP 49, 97321 Cayenne Cédex; tel. 29-96-00; fax 29-96-34; internet www.guyane.cci.fr; Pres. JEAN-PIERRE PRÉVÔT.

**Chambre de Métiers de Guyane:** Jardin Botanique, blvd de la République, BP 176, 97324 Cayenne Cédex; tel. 30-21-80; Pres. RICHARD HO-A-SIM.

**Jeune Chambre Economique de Cayenne:** Cité A. Horth, route de Montabo, BP 683, Cayenne; tel. 31-62-99; fax 31-76-13; f. 1960; Pres. FRANCK VERSET.

### EMPLOYERS' ORGANIZATIONS

**Organisation des Producteurs Guyanais de Crevettes (OPG):** Kourou; tel. 32-27-26; fax 32-19-18; shrimp producers' asscn and export business; Man. ROBERT COTONNEC.

**Syndicat des Exploitants Forestiers et Scieurs de la Guyane (SEFSEG):** Macouria; tel. 31-72-50; fax 30-08-27; f. 1987; asscn of 14 forestry developers (450 employees); timber processers; Man. M. POMIES.

**Syndicat des Exportateurs de la Guyane:** Z. I. de Dégrad-des-Cannes, 97354 Rémire-Montjoly; tel. 35-40-78; Pres. JEAN PATOZ.

**Union Patronale de la Guyane (UPDG):** c/o SOFIDEG, km 3 route de Baduel, BP 820, 97338 Cayenne Cédex; tel. 31-17-71; fax 30-32-13; e-mail updg@nplus.gf; Pres. ALAIN CHAUMET.

### TRADE UNIONS

**Centrale Démocratique des Travailleurs de la Guyane (CDTG):** 113 rue Christophe Colomb, BP 383, Cayenne; tel. 31-02-32; Sec.-Gen. RENÉ SYDALZA.

**Force Ouvrière (FO):** 107 rue Barthélemy, Cayenne; Sec.-Gen. M. XAVERO.

**SE/FEN (Syndicat des enseignants):** 52 rue F. Arago, Cayenne; Sec.-Gen. GEORGINA JUDICK-PIED.

**Union des Travailleurs Guyanais (UTG):** 7 ave Ronjon, Cayenne; tel. 31-26-42; Sec.-Gen. PAUL CÉCILIEN.

## Transport

### RAILWAYS

There are no railways in French Guiana.

### ROADS

In 1988 there were 1,137 km (707 miles) of roads in French Guiana, of which 371 km were main roads. Much of the network is concentrated along the coast, although proposals for a major new road into the interior of the Department were under consideration in late 1997.

### SHIPPING

Dégrad-des-Cannes, on the estuary of the river Mahury, is the principal port, handling 80% of maritime traffic in 1989. There are other ports at Le Larivot, Saint-Laurent-du-Maroni and Kourou. Saint-Laurent is used primarily for the export of timber, and Larivot for fishing vessels. There are river ports on the Oyapock and on the Approuague. There is a ferry service across the Maroni river between Saint-Laurent and Albina, Suriname. The rivers provide the best means of access to the interior, although numerous rapids prevent navigation by large vessels.

**Direction Départementale des Affaires Maritimes:** 2 bis rue Mentel, BP 307, 97305 Cayenne Cédex; tel. 31-00-08; Dir PIERRE-YVES ANDRIEUX.

**Somarig:** Z. I. de Dégrad-des-Cannes, Remire, BP 81, 97322 Cayenne Cédex; tel. 35-42-00; fax 35-53-44; joint venture between the Compagnie Générale Maritime and Delmas; Dir DANIEL DOURET.

### CIVIL AVIATION

Rochambeau International Airport, situated 17.5 km (11 miles) from Cayenne, is equipped to handle the largest jet aircraft. Access to remote inland areas is frequently by helicopter.

**Air Guyane:** Aéroport de Rochambeau, 97300 Matoury; tel. 35-65-55; operates internal services.

**Guyane Aéro Services:** Aéroport de Rochambeau, 97307 Matoury; tel. 35-65-55; f. 1980; fmrly Guyane Air Transport; Pres. PIERRE PRÉVÔT; Dir PATRICK LENCLOE.

## Tourism

The main attractions are the natural beauty of the tropical scenery and the Amerindian villages of the interior. In 1999 there were 30 hotels with 1,200 rooms, and 68,211 tourist arrivals were recorded.

**Comité du Tourisme de la Guyane:** Pavillon du Tourisme, Jardin Botanique, 12 rue Lallouette, BP 801, 97338 Cayenne Cédex; tel. 29-65-00; fax 29-65-01; internet www.tourisme-guyane.gf.

**Délégation Régionale au Tourisme, au Commerce et à l'Artisanat pour la Guyane:** BP 7008, 97307 Cayenne; tel. 31-01-04; fax 31-84-91; e-mail drtguyan@nplus.gf; Delegate PATRICE MALLET.

**Fédération des Offices de Tourisme et Syndicats de l'Initiative de la Guyane (FOTSIG):** 12 rue Lallouette, 97300 Cayenne; tel. 30-96-29; fax 31-23-43; e-mail fotsig@nplus.gf; internet www.guyane.net.

# GUADELOUPE

## Introductory Survey

**Location, Climate, Language, Religion, Capital**

Guadeloupe is the most northerly of the Windward Islands group in the West Indies. Dominica lies to the south, and Antigua and Montserrat to the north-west. Guadeloupe is formed by two large islands, Grande-Terre and Basse-Terre, separated by a narrow sea channel (but linked by a bridge), with a smaller island, Marie-Galante, to the south-east, and another, La Désirade, to the east. There are also a number of small dependencies, mainly Saint-Barthélemy and the northern half of Saint-Martin (the remainder being part of the Netherlands Antilles), among the Leeward Islands. The climate is tropical, with an average temperature of 26°C (79°F), and a more humid and wet season between June and November. French is the official language, but a creole patois is widely spoken. The majority of the population profess Christianity, and belong to the Roman Catholic Church. The capital is the town of Basse-Terre; the other main town and the principal commercial centre is Pointe-à-Pitre, on Grande-Terre.

**Recent History**

Guadeloupe was first occupied by the French in 1635, and has remained French territory, apart from a number of brief occupations by the British in the 18th and early 19th centuries. It gained departmental status in 1946.

The deterioration of the economy and an increase in unemployment provoked industrial and political unrest during the 1960s and 1970s, including outbreaks of serious rioting in 1967. Pro-independence parties (which had rarely won more than 5% of the total vote at elections in Guadeloupe) resorted, in some cases, to violence as a means of expressing their opposition to the economic and political dominance of white, pro-French landowners and government officials. In 1980 and 1981 there was a series of bomb attacks on hotels, government offices and other targets by a group called the Groupe Libération Armée, and in 1983 and 1984 there were further bombings by a group styling itself the Alliance Révolutionnaire Caraïbe (ARC), which was also responsible for bomb attacks in French Guiana and Martinique at this time. The Government responded by outlawing the ARC and reinforcing the military and police presence throughout Guadeloupe. (The ARC merged with the Mouvement Populaire pour une Guadeloupe Indépendante—MPGI—in 1984). Further sporadic acts of violence continued into 1985, but in October of that year the ARC suspended its bombing campaign prior to the holding of legislative elections. A further series of bomb attacks began in November 1986, and in January 1988 responsibility for bomb explosions in various parts of the territory was claimed by a previously unknown pro-independence group, the Organisation Révolutionnaire Armée.

In 1974 Guadeloupe was granted the status of a Region, and an indirectly-elected Regional Council was formed. In direct elections to a new Regional Council in February 1983, held as a result of the recent decentralization reforms, the centre-right coalition succeeded in gaining a majority of the seats and control of the administration. In January 1984 Lucette Michaux-Chevry, the President of the General Council, formed a new conservative centre party, Le Parti de la Guadeloupe, which remained in alliance with the right-wing Rassemblement pour la République (RPR). However, at the elections for the General Council held in March 1985, the left-wing combination of the Parti Socialiste (PS) and the Parti Communiste Guadeloupéen (PCG) gained a majority of seats on the enlarged (42-member) Council, and the PS leader, Dominique Larifla, was elected its President. In July demonstrations and a general strike, organized by pro-separatist activists in order to obtain the release of a leading member of the MPGI, quickly intensified into civil disorder and rioting in the main commercial centre, Pointe-à-Pitre.

For the March 1986 general election to the French National Assembly, Guadeloupe's representation was increased from three to four deputies. The local branches of the RPR and the centre-right Union pour la Démocratie Française (UDF), which had campaigned jointly at the 1981 general election and the 1983 regional elections, presented separate candidates. Ernest Moutoussamy and Frédéric Jalton, respectively the incumbent PCG and PS members of the Assembly, were re-elected, but the UDF deputy was not; the two remaining seats were won by RPR candidates (Michaux-Chevry and Henri Beaujean). In the concurrent elections for the 41 seats on the Regional Council, the two left-wing parties together won a majority of seats, increasing their combined strength from 20 to 22 members (PS 12, PCG 10). As a result, José Moustache of the RPR was replaced as President of the Council by Félix Proto of the PS. In September 1986 the publication of a report (prepared at Proto's request) criticizing the management of finances by the former RPR-UDF majority on the Regional Council, led by Moustache, caused disruption within the Council and had repercussions on the indirect elections for the two Guadeloupe members of the French Senate later in the month: there was a decline in support for centre-right candidates, and, as before, two left-wing Senators were elected (one from the PCG and one from the PS).

At the 1988 French presidential elections the incumbent President François Mitterrand of the PS received 55% of the votes cast in Guadeloupe in the first round, and 69% in the second round against Jacques Chirac of the RPR. At elections to the French National Assembly in June, Larifla (for the PS) defeated Beaujean, while the three other deputies to the National Assembly retained their seats. In September–October the left-wing parties won 26 of the 42 seats at elections to the General Council, and Larifla was re-elected President of the Council.

In April 1989 the separatist Union Populaire pour la Libération de la Guadeloupe (UPLG) organized protests in Port Louis to demand the release of 'political prisoners', which led to violent clashes with the police. A number of activists of the now disbanded ARC (including its leader, Luc Reinette) staged a hunger strike while awaiting trial in Paris, accused in connection with politically-motivated offences in the Overseas Departments. In the following month the Comité Guadeloupéen de Soutien aux Prisonniers Politiques united 11 organizations in demonstrations against the Government. Demands included the release of the prisoners held in France, a rejection of the Single European Act and the granting of a series of social demands. In June the French National Assembly approved legislation granting an amnesty for crimes that had taken place before July 1988, and that were intended to undermine the authority of the French Republic in the Overseas Departments. The agreement of those seeking greater independence in Guadeloupe to work within the democratic framework had gained parliamentary support for the amnesty. However, when the freed activists returned to Guadeloupe in July 1989, they urged increased confrontation with the authorities in order to achieve autonomous rule. In March 1990 the UPLG declared that it would henceforth participate in elections, and would seek associated status (rather than full independence) for Guadeloupe.

In March 1992 concurrent elections were held to the General and Regional Councils. Larifla was re-elected as President of the General Council, despite his refusal to contest as part of the local official PS list of candidates and his leadership of a group of 'dissident' PS members. (The division was not recognized at national level.) In the elections to the Regional Council the official PS list (headed by Jalton) secured nine seats and the dissident PS members seven. Former members of the PCG, who had formed a new organization, the Parti Progressiste Démocratique Guadeloupéen (PPDG) in September 1991, won five seats, compared with only three for the PCG. The RPR, the UDF and other right-wing candidates formed an electoral alliance, Objectif Guadeloupe, to contest the elections, together securing 15 of the 41 seats in the Regional Council. Jalton's refusal to reach an agreement with the 'dissident' PS members prompted Larifla's list to support the presidential candidacy of Michaux-Chevry. Thus, despite an overall left-wing majority in the Regional Council, the right-wing Michaux-Chevry was elected as President with 21 votes. In December 1992, however, the French Conseil d'Etat declared the election to the Regional Council invalid, owing to the failure of Larifla's list to pay a deposit on each seat prior to the registration of its candidates. Seven other heads of lists, including Moutoussamy of the PPDG, were subsequently found to have submitted incomplete documents to the election commission, and (although malpractice was discounted) the electoral code necessitated that they be declared ineligible for election to the Regional Council for one year. Fresh elections took place in January 1994, at which Objectif Guadeloupe took 22 seats, while the PS and 'dissident' PS retained a total of only 10 seats.

In a referendum on 20 September 1992 67.5% of voters in Guadeloupe endorsed ratification of the Treaty on European Union (see p. 172), although an abstention rate of 83.4% was recorded. In November banana growers in Guadeloupe and Martinique suspended economic activity in their respective Departments by obstructing access to ports and airports and blocking roads, in protest at the threatened loss of special advantages under the Single European Act. Order was restored, however, following assurances that subsidies would be maintained and that products such as bananas (Guadeloupe's main export) would be protected under new proposals.

The persistence of divisions between the socialists was evident at the March 1993 elections to the French National Assembly. Michaux-Chevry of the RPR was re-elected, as were Moutoussamy (for the PPDG) and Jalton (representing the anti-Larifla faction of the PS). Larifla, meanwhile, was defeated by Edouard Chammougon, a candidate of the independent right, who was elected (despite his implication in several corruption scandals—see below) with the assistance of votes in the second round of those socialists who resented Larifla's support for Michaux-Chevry in 1992. Michaux-Chevry was appointed to the position of Minister-Delegate, with responsibility for human rights and humanitarian action, in Edouard Balladur's centre-right coalition Government.

The left retained control of the General Council following cantonal elections in March 1994: Jalton's PS won eight seats, and the 'dissident' PS and PPDG six each. Larifla was subsequently re-elected President of the Council. At elections to the European Parliament in June, a combined list of parties of the left of the French Overseas Departments, including the PPDG (the list was headed by Moutoussamy), won the greatest share of the votes cast (37.2%) in Guadeloupe; an abstention rate of 85.4% was recorded.

Meanwhile, local political affairs were dominated by scandals involving prominent public figures. Twice during 1993 the Antilles-Guyane Chambre régionale des comptes—the body responsible for overseeing public finances in the region—rejected budget figures submitted by Guadeloupe's Regional Council, deeming that the Council's deficit projections were severely underestimated. In January 1994 an administrative tribunal in Basse-Terre ruled that Michaux-Chevry had been unjustified in dismissing (following the first rejection of the budget) the Regional Council's director of finances, who had submitted departmental accounts, as required by law, to the Chambre régional des comptes; this judgment was upheld at an appeal in Paris in April 1995. In January 1993 Chammougon, the Mayor of Baie-Mahault, was sentenced to three years' imprisonment, fined and deprived of his civic and civil rights for 10 years, following his conviction on corruption charges dating as far back as 1980. He remained at liberty pending an appeal and also, after March 1993, benefited from parliamentary immunity; the prison sentence was suspended and the fine lowered in November 1993, and in October 1994 a higher appeal reduced the deprivation of rights to five years. In September 1993 an investigation of alleged corruption among several of Chammougon's close associates resulted in the deputy's implication in further charges of 'passive corruption' and the abuse and misappropriation of public funds. Civil proceedings were also pending against him in respect of a bank loan disbursed in 1989 for a municipal construction contract in Baie-Mahault that was never undertaken. In November 1994 the French Constitutional Council revoked Chammougon's membership of the National Assembly, and the former deputy was subsequently detained briefly in Pointe-à-Pitre, in connection with the failure to honour a security of 1m. francs arising from an earlier detention. In January 1995 Chammougon's wife (elected in the previous month to replace him as Mayor of Baie-Mahault) was elected to succeed him in the General Council, although Léo Andy, the candidate of the 'dissident' PS, was elected to the vacant seat in the National Assembly, defeating (at the second round) the candidate supported by both Chammougon and Michaux-Chevry.

The rate of abstention in Guadeloupe (64.5%) at the first round of the 1995 presidential election, held on 23 April, was the highest recorded at a presidential contest since 1965. Chirac emerged as the leading candidate, with 38.2% of the valid votes cast, ahead of the PS candidate, Lionel Jospin, who took 35.1%. At the second round, on 7 May 1995, Jospin secured 55.1% of the votes, having benefited from the expressed support of all the parties of the left. The level of abstention at this round was 55.2%. At municipal elections in June, Michaux-Chevry became mayor of Basse-Terre, defeating the incumbent PPDG candidate. Jalton, who was supplanted as mayor of Les Abymes by a candidate of the 'dissident' PS, died in November. Michaux-Chevry and Larifla were elected to the Senate in September; the defeat of one of the incumbents, Henri Bangou of the PPDG, was attributed to the continuing divisions within the left. Philippe Chaulet of the RPR was subsequently elected to take Michaux-Chevry's seat in the National Assembly.

Hurricanes Luis and Marilyn struck the islands in September 1995, causing widespread devastation. The former, which resulted in at least two deaths, affected in particular Saint-Martin and Saint-Barthélemy, where a natural catastrophe was declared. The destruction on Saint-Martin of the dwellings of some 7,000 illegal immigrants (many of whom were Haitians employed for many years in the construction and tourist industries) was apparently used by the island's authorities as a pretext for the repatriation of the immigrants: the rebuilding of shanty towns was forbidden, and it was stated that, should an insufficient number fail to take advantage of incentives to leave the island, compulsory repatriations would ensue.

With effect from the beginning of 1996 the social security systems of the Overseas Departments were aligned with those of metropolitan France. In February delegates from Guadeloupe were among more than 300 representatives of the Overseas Departments' political, economic, trade union and professional organizations who attended a meeting in Paris, entitled the National Assizes of Social Equality and Development, held at the instigation of Jean-Jacques de Peretti, the Minister-Delegate responsible for the Overseas Departments and Territories.

At elections to the French National Assembly in late May and early June 1997, Moutoussamy, Andy and Chaulet all retained their seats, while Daniel Marsin, a candidate of the independent left, was elected in the constituency of Les Abymes, Pointe-à-Pitre. An abstention rate of 52.5% was recorded. The RPR performed strongly in elections to the Regional Council in March 1998, securing 25 of the 41 seats, while the PS won 12; Michaux-Chevry was re-elected as President of the Council. The composition of the General Council remained largely unchanged following concurrent cantonal elections, with the left retaining a majority of 28 seats, although the RPR doubled its representation to eight seats; Marcellin Lubeth, of the PPDG, was elected to the presidency, defeating Larifla.

In January 1999 representatives of 10 separatist organizations from French Guiana, Guadeloupe and Martinique, including the UPLG, signed a joint declaration denouncing 'French colonialism', in which they stated their intention to campaign for the reinstatement of the three American Overseas Departments on a UN list of territories to be decolonized.

Social and industrial unrest intensified in Guadeloupe in late October 1999, prior to a two-day visit by Lionel Jospin, the Prime Minister. Demonstrations escalated into rioting in Pointe-à-Pitre, following the sentencing of Armand Toto, a leading member of the Union Générale des Travailleurs de la Guadeloupe (UGTG), to four months' imprisonment for assaulting two policemen and threatening to kill another while occupying the premises of a motor vehicle company in support of a dismissed worker. Further protests ensued a few days later when an appeal against Toto's sentence failed. Moreover, banana producers demonstrated around the port of Basse-Terre, demanding the disbursement of 100m. French francs, and additional assistance for the restructuring of their businesses, as compensation for a significant decline in banana prices on the European market. Meanwhile, an indefinite strike by hospital workers, organized by the UGTG, affected Guadeloupe's 16 private clinics. However, calls issued by several trade union and political organizations for a 48-hour general strike during Jospin's visit were largely ignored, and the Prime Minister announced an emergency plan for the banana sector.

Also in October 1999, 61 Chinese emigrants were rescued by French naval forces when the shrimp boat in which they were apparently attempting to reach the USA encountered difficulties off the coast of Guadeloupe. In December the French authorities refused to consider asylum claims made by 53 of the emigrants, despite a petition, signed by nearly 7,000 people, including Marcellin Lubeth and the Department's four deputies, urging the Government to give residence and work permits to the refugees. Two bodies were recovered from the sea in January 2000, following a failed attempt by 26 of the emigrants to leave Guadeloupe secretly by boat for an unknown destination

The institutional future of the Overseas Departments provoked much discussion in 1999. Following a series of meetings, in December 1999 the Presidents of the Regional Councils of French Guiana, Guadeloupe and Martinique signed a joint declaration in Basse-Terre, affirming their intention to propose, to the President and the Government, a legislative amendment, possibly constitutional, aimed at creating a new status of overseas region, despite an earlier statement by Jospin indicating that the Government did not envisage a change in status for the Departments. Further meetings of the three regional Presidents were held in January and February 2000. Proposals regarding the institutional future and socio-economic development of the Departments (see p. 1481) were to be considered by the Council of Ministers in early 2000 and were to be examined by the legislature by the end of June.

## Government

France is represented in Guadeloupe by an appointed prefect. There are two councils with local powers: the 42-member General Council and the 41-member Regional Council. Both are elected by universal adult suffrage for a period of up to six years. Guadeloupe elects four deputies to the French National Assembly in Paris, and sends two indirectly-elected representatives to the Senate. The Department is also represented at the European Parliament.

## Defence

At 1 August 1999 France maintained a military force of 2,200 and a gendarmerie of 860 in the Antilles, with headquarters in Fort-de-France (Martinique).

## Economic Affairs

In 1995, according to UN estimates, Guadeloupe's gross domestic product (GDP), measured at current prices, was US $3,877m., equivalent to $9,145 per head. During 1990–95 GDP declined, in real terms, at an average annual rate of 0.1%; GDP increased by 1.9% in 1994, but declined by 2.9% in 1995. Between the censuses of 1990 and 1999, according to provisional figures, the population increased at an average annual rate of 1.0%.

Agriculture, hunting, forestry and fishing contributed 6.7% of GDP in 1992, and engaged an estimated 3.8% of the labour force in 1998. The principal cash crops are bananas and sugar cane; exports of the former provided 21.9% of total export earnings in 1997, while exports of raw sugar accounted for 23.7% of the total in that year. Yams, sweet potatoes and plantains are the chief subsistence crops. Fishing, mostly at an artisanal level, fulfilled about two-thirds of domestic requirements in the mid-1990s; shrimp-farming was developed during the 1980s. Agricultural GDP increased at an average annual rate of 4.9% in 1980–85, and by an average of 3.9% per year in 1985–89. Agricultural production increased at an average rate of 2.6% per year during 1990–98. It rose by 25.8% in 1997, but declined by 5.0% in 1998.

The industrial sector (including manufacturing, construction and power) contributed 15.1% of GDP in 1992, and engaged about 20.1% of the employed labour force at the time of the 1990 census. Manufacturing and mining provided 6.9% of GDP in 1992. The main manufacturing activity is food processing, particularly sugar production, rum distillation, and flour-milling. The sugar industry was in decline in the 1990s, owing to deteriorating equipment and a reduction in the area planted with sugar cane (from 20,000 ha in 1980 to 16,000 ha in 1990 and to only 9,600 ha in 1999). Industrial GDP increased at an average annual rate of 2.7% in 1980–85, and by an average of 1.8% per year in 1985–89.

Of some 700,000 tons of petroleum imported annually, about one-third is used for the production of electricity. Efforts are currently being concentrated on the use of renewable energy resources—notably solar, geothermal and wind power—for energy production; there is also thought to be considerable potential for the use of sugar cane as a means of generating energy in Guadeloupe. Imports of mineral fuels accounted for 5.8% of total expenditure on imports in 1995.

The services sector engaged 72.8% of the employed labour force in 1990 and provided 78.2% of GDP in 1992. Tourism superseded sugar production in 1988 as the Department's principal source of income, and there is significant potential for the further development of the sector, particularly 'eco-tourism'. In 1998 tourist arrivals totalled 693,000, and receipts from tourism amounted to US $496m. in 1996.

In 1997 Guadeloupe recorded a trade deficit of 9,417.2m. French francs. In 1997 the principal source of imports (62.9%) was metropolitan France, which was also the principal market for exports (60.7%). Martinique, the USA and Germany are also important trading partners. The principal exports in 1997 were sugar, bananas, boats and rum. The principal imports in 1995 were machinery and transport equipment (mainly road vehicles), food and live animals, miscellaneous manufactured articles, basic manufactures and chemicals.

Guadeloupe's budget deficit was estimated by the metropolitan authorities to amount to some 800m. French francs (including arrears) in 1993. Under the 1997 regional budget it was envisaged that expenditure would total 1,700m. French francs. The annual rate of inflation averaged 2.1% in 1990–97; consumer prices increased by an average of 1.1% in 1997. Some 28.8% of the labour force were unemployed in 1998.

As an integral part of France, Guadeloupe belongs to the European Union (EU—see p. 172). Guadeloupe and the other French Overseas Departments were to receive a total of ECU 1,500m. from EU regional funds in 1994–2000.

Economic growth in Guadeloupe has been restricted by certain inherent problems: its location; the fact that the domestic market is too narrow to stimulate the expansion of the manufacturing base; the lack of primary materials; and the inflated labour and service costs compared with those of neighbouring countries. Economic activity was severely disrupted in September 1989, when Hurricane Hugo struck the islands, causing widespread devastation. The French Government undertook to provide more than 2,000m. French francs for reconstruction, and additional aid for the modernization of the sugar industry. The banana-growing sector and the tourist industry, both of which were particularly adversely affected, had recovered well by the early 1990s. However, Hurricanes Luis and Marilyn, which struck in September 1995, caused severe infrastructural damage, destroyed banana plantations, hotels and public buildings, and threatened the 1996 sugar crop. In the late 1990s Guadeloupe's banana sector was adversely affected by declining prices on the European market, while an ongoing dispute between the USA and four major Latin American producers and the EU over the latter's banana import regime also threatened the sector. Furthermore, increasing social and industrial unrest also disrupted economic activity in 1998–99.

### Social Welfare

In 1997 there were seven hospital complexes (including one for psychiatric care), two local hospitals, a physiotherapy clinic and 16 private clinics. In addition, each of the 34 communes has a clinic. In 1998 there were 760 doctors, 230 pharmacists and 135 dental surgeons in Guadeloupe. The social security legislation of metropolitan France is applicable in Guadeloupe. With effect from 1 January 1996 welfare payments and the statutory minimum wage in the Overseas Departments were aligned with those of metropolitan France.

### Education

The education system is similar to that of metropolitan France (see chapter on French Guiana). In 1996 secondary education was provided at 40 junior comprehensives, or collèges, 10 vocational lycées, 10 general and technological lycées and one agricultural lycée. A branch of the Université Antilles-Guyane, at Pointe-à-Pitre, has faculties of law, economics, sciences, medicine and Caribbean studies. The university in Guadeloupe had 5,800 enrolled students in 1997. There is also a teacher training college. An Academy for Guadeloupe was established in January 1997. Total government expenditure on education amounted to 2,776m. French francs in 1993. In 1982 the average rate of adult illiteracy was 10.0% (males 10.4%; females 9.6%).

### Public Holidays

**2000:** 1 January (New Year's Day), 6–7 March (Lenten Carnival), 21–24 April (Easter), 1 May (Labour Day), 8 May (Victory Day), 1 June (Ascension Day), 12 June (Whit Monday), 14 July (National Day), 21 July (Victor Schoëlcher Day), 15 August (Assumption), 1 November (All Saints' Day), 11 November (Armistice Day), 25 December (Christmas Day).

**2001:** 1 January (New Year's Day), 26–27 February (Lenten Carnival), 13–16 April (Easter), 1 May (Labour Day), 8 May (Victory Day), 24 May (Ascension Day), 4 June (Whit Monday), 14 July (National Day), 21 July (Victor Schoëlcher Day), 15 August (Assumption), 1 November (All Saints' Day), 11 November (Armistice Day), 25 December (Christmas Day).

### Weights and Measures

The metric system is in use.

# Statistical Survey

Sources (unless otherwise stated): Institut national de la statistique et des études économiques, ave Paul Lacavé, BP 96, 97102 Basse-Terre; tel. 81-17-86; fax 81-07-15; Ministère des départements et territoires d'outre-mer, 27 rue Oudinot, 75700 Paris 07 SP; tel. 1-53-69-20-00; fax 1-43-06-60-30; internet www.outre-mer.gouv.fr.

## AREA AND POPULATION

**Area:** 1,705 sq km (658.3 sq miles), incl. dependencies (La Désirade, Les Saintes, Marie-Galante, Saint-Barthélemy, Saint-Martin).

**Population:** 327,002 (males 160,112, females 166,890) at census of 9 March 1982; 387,034 (males 189,187, females 197,847) at census of 15 March 1990; 422,496 (provisional figure) at census of 8 March 1999.

**Density** (at 1999 census): 247.8 per sq km.

**Principal Towns** (population at 1990 census): Basse-Terre (capital) 14,003; Les Abymes 62,605; Saint-Martin 28,518; Pointe-à-Pitre 26,069; Le Gosier 20,688; Capesterre/Belle-Eau 19,012.

**Births, Marriages and Deaths** (1996, provisional figures): Registered live births 7,256 (birth rate 17.1 per 1,000); Registered marriages 1,869 (marriage rate 4.4 per 1,000); Registered deaths 2,457 (death rate 5.8 per 1,000).

**Expectation of Life** (UN estimates, years at birth, 1990–95): 75.9 (males 72.4, females 80.1). Source: UN, *World Population Prospects: The 1998 Revision*.

**Economically Active Population** (persons aged 15 years and over, 1990 census): Agriculture, hunting, forestry and fishing 8,391; Industry and energy 9,630; Construction and public works 13,967; Trade 15,020; Transport and telecommunications 6,950; Financial services 2,802; Other marketable services 26,533; Non-marketable services 34,223; Total employed 117,516 (males 68,258, females 49,258); Unemployed 54,926 (males 25,691, females 29,235); Total labour force 172,442 (males 93,949, females 78,493).

## AGRICULTURE, ETC.

**Principal Crops** (FAO estimates, '000 metric tons, 1998): Sweet potatoes 3; Yams 9; Cassava 1; Other roots and tubers 4; Vegetables 23; Melons and watermelons 4; Pineapples 7; Bananas 141; Plantains 6; Sugar cane 638. Source: FAO, *Production Yearbook*.

**Livestock** (FAO estimates, '000 head, year ending September 1998): Cattle 80; Goats 63; Pigs 15; Sheep 4. Source: FAO, *Production Yearbook*.

**Livestock Products** (FAO estimates, '000 metric tons, 1998): Beef and veal 3; Pig meat 1; Poultry meat 1; Hen eggs 2. Source: FAO, *Production Yearbook*.

**Forestry:** Roundwood removals ('000 cu m, excl. bark, 1997): Total (fuel wood) 15. Source: FAO, *Yearbook of Forest Products*.

**Fishing** (metric tons, live weight, 1998): Marine fishes 8,400; Crustaceans 134; Molluscs 550; Total catch 9,084.

## MINING

**Production** ('000 metric tons, 1995): Pozzolan 210.0. Source: UN, *Industrial Commodity Statistics Yearbook*.

## INDUSTRY

**Production:** Raw sugar 38,400 metric tons in 1998; Rum 62,679 hl in 1998; Cement 283,000 metric tons in 1996; Electric energy (million kWh) 1,014 (estimate) in 1995 (Source: UN, *Industrial Commodity Statistics Yearbook*).

## FINANCE

**Currency and Exchange Rates:** French currency is used (see French Guiana).

**Budget** (million French francs): *State budget* (1990): Revenue 2,494; Expenditure 4,776. *Regional budget* (1997): Expenditure 1,700. *Departmental budget* (1989): Revenue 1,617; Expenditure 1,748.

**Money Supply** (million French francs at 31 December 1996): Currency outside banks 1,148; Demand deposits at banks 6,187; Total money 7,335.

**Cost of Living** (Consumer Price Index for urban areas; base: 1990 = 100): 112.4 in 1995; 114.0 in 1996; 115.3 in 1997. Source: ILO, *Yearbook of Labour Statistics*.

**Expenditure on the Gross Domestic Product** (million French francs at current prices, 1994): Government final consumption expenditure 5,721; Private final consumption expenditure 16,779;

highest number of votes on Mayotte (although Chirac subsequently won the election).

Following a further coup attempt by mercenaries in the Comoros, which took place in September 1995 (see p. 1070), the French Government dispatched additional troops to Mayotte, prior to staging a military intervention. In elections to the Senate in September, the incumbent MPM representative, Marcel Henry, was returned by a large majority. During a visit to Mayotte in October, the French Secretary of State for Overseas Departments and Territories pledged that a referendum on the future status of the island would be conducted by 1999. In October 1996 he confirmed that two commissions, based in Paris and Mayotte, were preparing a consultation document, which would be presented in late 1997, and announced that the resulting referendum would take place before the end of the decade.

Partial elections to fill nine seats in the General Council were held in March 1997; the MPM secured three seats (losing two that it had previously held), the RPR won three seats, the local PS one seat, and independent right-wing candidates two seats. In elections to the French National Assembly Jean-Baptiste, representing the alliance of the UDF and the Force Démocrate (FD, formerly the CDS), defeated Kamardine, securing 51.7% of votes cast in the second round of voting, which took place in June.

In July 1997 the relative prosperity of Mayotte was believed to have prompted separatist movements on the Comoran islands of Nzwani and Mwali to demand the restoration of French rule, and subsequently to declare their independence in August (see p. 1071). In September, following an unsuccessful military intervention, mounted by the Comoran Government in an attempt to quell the insurrection, many of those injured in the fighting were taken to Mayotte for medical treatment. Illegal immigration from the Comoros continued to prove a major concern for the authorities on Mayotte; during January–February 1997 some 6,000 Comorans were expelled from the island, with many more agreeing to leave voluntarily.

Meanwhile, uncertainty remained over the future status of Mayotte. In April 1998 one of the commissions charged with examining the issue submitted its report, which concluded that the present status of Collectivité Territoriale was no longer appropriate, but did not advocate an alternative. In May the MPM declared its support for an adapted form of departmental administration, and urged the French authorities to decide on a date for a referendum. In July Pierre Bayle succeeded Philippe Boisadam as Prefect. In December two rounds of preparatory talks on the island's future constitutional status took place between local political organizations and senior French government officials. However, further negotiations, which were planned to be held in February 1999, were suspended, owing to France's concerns over the political instability in the Comoros. In May Bamana made an appeal that the inhabitants of Mayotte be allowed to organize their own vote on their future, and later that month Jean-Baptiste introduced a draft piece of legislation to the French National Assembly, which proposed the holding of a referendum regarding the island's future before the end of 1999. In August, following negotiations between the French Secretary of State for Overseas Departments and Territories, Jean-Jack Queyranne, and island representatives, Mayotte members of the RPR and the PS and Bamana (the leader of the MPM) signed a draft document providing for the transformation of Mayotte into a Collectivité Départementale, if approved at a referendum. However, both Henry and Jean-Baptiste rejected the document. The two politicians subsequently announced their departure from the MPM and formed a new political party entitled the Mouvement Départementaliste Mahorais (MDM), whilst repeating their demands that Mayotte be granted full overseas departmental status. Following the approval of Mayotte's proposed new status by the General Council (by 14 votes to five) and the municipal councils, an accord to this effect was signed by Queyranne and political representatives of Mayotte on 27 January 2000. The inhabitants of the island were expected to vote on the proposed new status of Mayotte in late July.

(For further details of the recent history of the island, see the chapter on the Comoros, p. 1067.)

## Government

The French Government is represented in Mayotte by an appointed Prefect. There is a General Council, with 19 members, elected by universal adult suffrage. Mayotte elects one deputy to the French National Assembly, and one representative to the Senate. Mayotte is also represented at the European Parliament.

## Defence

At 1 August 1999 there were 2,850 French troops stationed in Mayotte and Réunion.

## Economic Affairs

Mayotte's gross domestic product (GDP) per head in 1991 was estimated at 4,050 French francs. Between the censuses of 1991 and 1997 the population of Mayotte increased at an average annual rate of 5.7%.

The economy is based mainly on agriculture. In 1997 18.6% of the employed labour force were engaged in this sector. The principal export crops are ylang-ylang and vanilla. Rice, cassava and maize are cultivated for domestic consumption. Livestock-rearing and fishing are also important activities. However, Mayotte imports large quantities of foodstuffs, which comprised 22.8% of the value of total imports in 1997.

Industry (which is dominated by the construction sector) engaged 21.5% of the employed population in 1997. There are no mineral resources on the island. Imports of mineral products comprised 5.0%, and metals 10.3%, of the value of total imports in 1997.

Services engaged 59.8% of the employed population in 1997. The annual total of tourist arrivals (excluding cruise-ship passengers) increased from 6,700 in 1995 to 11,400 in 1998.

In 1998 Mayotte recorded a trade deficit of 896m. French francs. The principal source of imports in 1997 was France (60%); the other major supplier was South Africa. France was also the principal market for exports (taking 68% of exports in that year); the other significant purchaser was Réunion. The principal exports in 1997 were oil of ylang-ylang, transport equipment and foodstuffs. The principal imports in 1997 were foodstuffs, electrical machinery, apparatus and appliances, transport equipment and metals.

In 1986 Mayotte's external assets totalled 203.8m. French francs, and banking aid reached 6.3m. francs. In 1997 Mayotte's total budgetary revenue was estimated at 1,022.4m. French francs, while total expenditure was estimated at 964.2m. French francs. Official debt was 435.7m. French francs at 31 December 1995. The rate of inflation in the year to December 1997 was 2.1%. Some 41.2% of the labour force were unemployed in 1997.

Mayotte suffers from a persistently high trade deficit, owing to its reliance on imports, and is largely dependent on French aid. From the late 1980s the French Government granted substantial aid to finance a number of construction projects, in an attempt to encourage the development of tourism on the island. Mayotte's remote location, however, continued to prove an impediment to the development of the tourist sector. A five-year Development Plan (1986–91) included measures to improve infrastructure and to increase investment in public works; the Plan was subsequently extended to the end of 1993. In April 1995 an economic and social development agreement was signed with the French Government for the period 1995–99. Later that year Mayotte received credit from France to finance further investment in infrastructure, particularly in the road network. As Mayotte's labour force has continued to increase (mostly owing to a high birth rate and continued illegal immigration), youth unemployment has caused particular concern. In 1997 37.8% of the unemployed population were under 25 years of age. Falling prices and increased competition on international markets led to a significant decline in exports of ylang-ylang and vanilla in 1997–98.

## Social Welfare

Medical services on Mayotte are available free of charge. The island is divided into six sectors, each of which is allocated a doctor or medical worker. In 1997 Mayotte had two hospitals, situated at Mamoudzou and at Dzaoudzi, which provided a total of 186 beds. In that year there were 57 physicians, four dentists and 131 qualified nurses working in Mayotte.

## Education

Education is compulsory for children aged six to 15 years, and comprises five years' primary and five years' secondary schooling. In 1997 there were 99 primary schools on the island. In 1997 there were 14 secondary schools, comprising 12 collèges (junior comprehensives) and two lycées. There were also two vocational and technical institutions. In the same year 5,663 pre-primary school pupils, 24,681 primary school pupils and 10,616 secondary school pupils were enrolled. A further 1,449 students were enrolled at the vocational and technical institutions. In December 1996 the Caisse Française de Développement (now Agence Française de Développement) provided 21.6m. French francs for the construction of pre-primary and primary schools on Mayotte.

## Public Holidays

The principal holidays of metropolitan France are observed.

## Statistical Survey

Source (unless otherwise indicated): Institut National de la Statistique et des Etudes Economiques; 51 hauts des Jardins du Collège, BP 1362, 97600 Mamoudzou.

### AREA AND POPULATION

**Area:** 374 sq km (144 sq miles).

**Population:** 67,167 (census of August 1985); 94,410 (census of August 1991); 131,368 (males 66,600; females 64,768) at census of August 1997; 142,000 (official estimate) at 1 January 1998. *Principal towns* (population of communes at 1997 census): Dzaoudzi (capital) 10,792, Mamoudzou 32,733, Koungou 10,165.

**Density** (1 January 1998): 379.7 per sq km.

**Births and Deaths** (1997): Registered live births 5,326 (birth rate 40.6 per 1,000); Death rate 5.6 per 1,000.

**Economically Active Population** (persons aged between 15 and 64 years, census of August 1997): Agriculture and fishing 4,672; Electricity, gas and water 399; Industry 1,164; Construction and engineering 3,843; Wholesale and retail trade 2,717; Transport and telecommunications 1,563; Other marketable services 1,530; Finance and insurance 97; Other non-marketable services 9,108; Total employed 25,093 (males 18,200, females 6,893); Persons on compulsory military service 143 (males 139, females 4); Unemployed 17,660 (males 8,982, females 8,678); Total labour force 42,896 (males 27,321, females 15,575).

### AGRICULTURE, ETC.

**Livestock** (1995): Cattle 15,000; Sheep 2,700; Goats 23,000.

**Fishing** (metric tons, live weight): Total catch 646 in 1995; 1,217 in 1996; 1,531 in 1997. Source: FAO, *Yearbook of Fishery Statistics*.

### FINANCE

**Currency and Exchange Rates:** French currency is used (see French Guiana).

**Budget** (million French francs, 1997): Total revenue 1,022.4 (current 783.7, capital 238.7); Total expenditure 964.2 (current 725.4, capital 238.7).

**Money Supply** (million French francs at 31 December 1997): Currency outside banks 789; Demand deposits 266; Total money 1,055.

**Cost of Living** (Consumer Price Index; base: December 1996 = 100). 102.1 in December 1997.

### EXTERNAL TRADE

**Total Trade** (million French francs): *Imports:* 915 in 1998. *Exports:* 19 in 1998.

**Principal Commodities** (million French francs, 1997): *Imports:* Foodstuffs 188.1 (Beef and veal 19.2, Poultry and rabbit meat 26.4, Rice 33.6); Mineral products 41.0 (Hydraulic cements 31.4); Chemicals and related products 63.1 (Medicinal and pharmaceutical products 21.6); Plastic materials, ethers and resins 29.1; Wood, charcoal and wickerwork 25.5 (Sawnwood 16.2); Paper-making material, paper and paper products 20.8; Textiles 22.9; Base metals and metal products 84.6; Electrical machinery, apparatus and appliances 168.5; Transport equipment 101.1 (Passenger motor cars 44.3, Road motor vehicles for goods transport 25.2); Optical and photographic apparatus 21.4; Miscellaneous goods 20.1; Total (incl. others) 823.4. *Exports:* Foodstuffs 2.4 (Vanilla 0.8); Chemicals and related products 5.8 (Ylang-ylang 5.6); Paper-making materials, paper and paper products 1.5; Base metals and metal products 1.9; Electrical machinery, apparatus and appliances 2.2; Transport equipment 4.6 (Passenger motor cars 1.0, Road motor vehicles for goods transport 1.9); Total (incl. others) 20.2.

**Principal Trading Partners** (percentage of trade, 1997): *Imports:* France 60%; South Africa 8%. *Exports:* France 68%; Réunion 7%.

### TRANSPORT

**Road Traffic** (1998): Motor vehicles in use 8,213.

**Shipping:** *Traffic* (metric tons, 1998): Goods unloaded 21,102; Goods loaded 8,165.

**Civil Aviation** (1998): *Passenger arrivals:* 42,260; *Passenger departures:* 45,774; *Freight carried:* 1,012 metric tons.

### TOURISM

**Visitor Arrivals** (excluding cruise-ship passengers): 7,300 in 1996; 9,500 in 1997; 11,400 in 1998.

### COMMUNICATIONS MEDIA

**Telephones** (1997): 9,314 subscribers.

### EDUCATION

**Pre-primary** (1997): 42 schools; 5,663 pupils.

**Primary** (1997): 99 schools; 24,681 pupils.

**General Secondary** (1997): 14 schools; 10,616 pupils.

**Vocational and Technical** (1997): 2 institutions; 1,449 students.

## Directory

## The Constitution

Under the status of Collectivité Territoriale, which was adopted in December 1976, Mayotte has an elected General Council, comprising 19 members, which assists the Prefect in the administration of the island. A referendum on the proposed transformation of Mayotte into a Collectivité Départementale was expected to be held in late July 2000.

## The Government

Représentation du Gouvernement, 97610 Dzaoudzi; tel. 60-10-54; fax 60-18-50.

(February 2000)

**Prefect:** Pierre Bayle.

**Secretary-General:** Jean-Pierre Laflaquière.

**Deputy to the French National Assembly:** Henry Jean-Baptiste (MDM).

**Representative to the French Senate:** Marcel Henry (MDM).

### GENERAL COUNCIL

Conseil Général, 8 rue de l'Hôpital, 97600 Mamoudzou; tel. 61-12-33; fax 61-10-18.

The General Council comprises 19 members. At elections in March 1994, the Mouvement Populaire Mahorais (MPM) secured 12 seats, the Fédération de Mayotte du Rassemblement pour la République four seats, and independent candidates three seats. As a result of by-elections held in March 1997, the MPM holds eight seats, the Fédération de Mayotte du Rassemblement pour la République five seats, independent right-wing candidates five seats, and the Parti Socialiste one seat.

**President of the General Council:** Younoussa Bamana.

## Political Organizations

**Fédération de Mayotte du Rassemblement pour la République:** 97610 Dzaoudzi; local branch of the French (Gaullist) Rassemblement pour la République (RPR); Sec.-Gen. Mansour Kamardine.

**Mouvement Départementaliste Mahorais (MDM):** 97610 Dzaoudzi; f. 1999 by former members of the MPM; seeks full overseas departmental status for Mayotte; Leader Henry Jean-Baptiste.

**Mouvement Populaire Mahorais (MPM):** 97610 Dzaoudzi; seeks departmental status for Mayotte; Leader Younoussa Bamana.

**Parti pour le Rassemblement Démocratique des Mahorais (PRDM):** 97610 Dzaoudzi; f. 1978; seeks unification with the Federal Islamic Republic of the Comoros; Leader Darouèche Maoulida.

**Parti Socialiste:** Dzaoudzi; local branch of the French party of the same name; Leader Ibrahim Abubacar.

## Judicial System

**Tribunal Supérieur d'Appel:** 97600 Mamoudzou, tel. 61-12-65; fax 61-19-63; Pres. JEAN-BAPTISTE FLORI; Prosecutor JEAN-LOUIS BEC.

**Procureur de la République:** PATRICK BROSSIER.

**Tribunal de Première Instance:** Pres. ARLETTE MEALLONNIER-DUGUE.

## Religion

Muslims comprise about 98% of the population. Most of the remainder are Christians, mainly Roman Catholics.

### CHRISTIANITY

#### The Roman Catholic Church

Mayotte is within the jurisdiction of the Apostolic Administrator of the Comoros.

**Office of the Apostolic Administrator:** BP 1012, 97600 Mamoudzou; tel. and fax 61-11-53.

## The Press

**L'Insulaire:** Immeuble Villa Bourhani, rue du Collège, BP 88, 97600 Mamoudzou; tel. 61-37-85; fax 61-37-86; weekly.

**Le Kwezi:** BP 5, 97600 Mamoudzou; tel. 61-30-00; fax 61-19-91; e-mail kwezi@wanadoo.fr; f. 1996; biweekly; Dir ZAÏDOU BAMANA; Editor-in-Chief LAURENT CANAVATE.

## Broadcasting and Communications

### RADIO AND TELEVISION

**Société Nationale de Radio-Télévision Française d'Outre-mer (RFO):** BP 103, 97610 Dzaoudzi; tel. 60-10-17; fax 60-18-52; e-mail jrv@wanadoo.fr; internet www.rfo.fr; f. 1977; govt-owned; radio broadcasts in French and Mahorian; television transmissions began in 1986; plans for a satellite service were announced in 1998; Pres. ANDRÉ-MICHEL BESSE; Dir-Gen. GEROGES CHOW-TOUN.

## Finance

### BANKS

#### Issuing Authority

**Institut d'Emission des Départements d'Outre-mer:** BP 500, 97600 Mamoudzou; tel. 61-10-38; fax 61-05-02.

#### Commercial Bank

**Banque Française Commerciale Océan Indien:** BP 322, 97600 Mamoudzou; tel. 61-10-91; fax 61-17-40; br. at Dzaoudzi.

## Transport

### ROADS

In 1984 the main road network totalled approximately 93 km, of which 72 km were bituminized. There were 137 km of local roads, of which 40 km were tarred, and 54 km of minor tracks (unusable during the rainy season).

### SHIPPING

Coastal shipping is provided by locally-owned small craft. There is a deep-water port at Longoni.

### CIVIL AVIATION

There is an airfield at Dzaoudzi, serving four-times weekly commercial flights to Réunion, twice-weekly services to Madagascar, Njazidja, Nzwani and Mwali, and a weekly service to Kenya. A direct service to Paris, expected to commence in 1999, was postponed, owning to the inadequacy of facilities at the island's airfield.

## Tourism

Tropical scenery provides the main tourist attraction. In 1999 the island had six hotels, providing 118 rooms, five guest houses and eight apartments and lodges. Excluding cruise-ship passengers, Mayotte received 11,400 visitors in 1998.

**Comité du Tourisme de Mayotte:** rue de la Pompe, BP 1169, 97600 Mamoudzou; tel. 61-09-09; fax 61-03-46; e-mail comite-du-tourisme-mayotte@wanadoo.fr; internet www.mayotte-island.com.

# ST PIERRE AND MIQUELON

## Introductory Survey

**Location, Climate, Language, Religion, Capital**

The territory of St Pierre and Miquelon (Iles Saint-Pierre-et-Miquelon) consists of a number of small islands which lie about 25 km (16 miles) from the southern coast of Newfoundland, Canada, in the North Atlantic Ocean. The principal islands are St Pierre, Miquelon (Grande Miquelon) and Langlade (Petite Miquelon)—the last two being linked by an isthmus of sand. Winters are cold, with temperatures falling to –20°C (–4°F), and summers are mild, with temperatures averaging between 10° and 20°C (50° and 68°F). The islands are particularly affected by fog in June and July. The language is French, and the majority of the population profess Christianity and belong to the Roman Catholic Church. The capital is Saint-Pierre, on the island of St Pierre.

**Recent History**

The islands of St Pierre and Miquelon are the remnants of the once extensive French possessions in North America. They were confirmed as French territory in 1816, and gained departmental status in July 1976. The departmentalization proved unpopular with many of the islanders, since it incorporated the territory's economy into that of the European Community (EC, now European Union, see p. 172), and was regarded as failing to take into account the islands' isolation and dependence on Canada for supplies and transport links. In March 1982 socialist and other left-wing candidates, campaigning for a change in the islands' status, were elected unopposed to all seats in the General Council. St Pierre and Miquelon was excluded from the Mitterrand administration's decentralization reforms, undertaken in 1982.

In 1976 Canada imposed an economic interest zone extending to 200 nautical miles (370 km) around its shores. Fearing the loss of traditional fishing areas and thus the loss of the livelihood of the fishermen of St Pierre, the French Government claimed a similar zone around the islands. Hopes of discovering valuable reserves of petroleum and natural gas in the area heightened the tension between France and Canada.

In December 1984 legislation was approved giving the islands the status of a Collectivité Territoriale with effect from 11 June 1985. This was intended to allow St Pierre and Miquelon to receive the investment and development aid suitable for its position, while allaying Canadian fears of EC exploitation of its offshore waters. Local representatives, however, remained apprehensive about the outcome of negotiations between the French and Canadian Governments to settle the dispute over coastal limits. (France continued to claim a 200-mile fishing and economic zone around St Pierre and Miquelon, while Canada wanted the islands to have only a 12-mile zone.) In January 1987 it was decided that the dispute should be submitted to international arbitration. Discussions began in March, and negotiations to determine quotas for France's catch of Atlantic cod over the period 1988–91 were to take place simultaneously. In the mean time, Canada and France agreed on an interim fishing accord, which would allow France to increase its cod quota. The discussions collapsed in October, however, and French trawlers were prohibited from fishing in Canadian waters. In February 1988 Albert Pen and Gérard Grignon, St Pierre's elected representatives to the French legislature, together with two members of the St Pierre administration and 17 sailors, were arrested for fishing in Canadian waters. This episode, and the arrest of a Canadian trawler captain in May for fishing in St Pierre's waters, led to an unsuccessful resumption of negotiations in September. In November the President of the Inter-American Development Bank was appointed as mediator in the dispute, and agreement was reached on fishing rights in March 1989, whereby France's annual quotas for Atlantic cod and other species were determined for the period until the end of 1991. (Further quotas were subsequently stipulated for the first nine months of 1992.) At the same time the Governments agreed upon the composition of an international arbitration tribunal which would delineate the disputed maritime boundaries and exclusive economic zones.

Meanwhile, in January 1989 two factory fishing ships from metropolitan France sailed to the area to catch the fish under agreed quotas, but there were protests by the islanders, who feared that damage might be caused to fishing stocks by the factory ships. After discussions with the French Prime Minister, it was agreed that one of the factory ships would return to France. In October 1990 the islanders protested to the Government concerning illegal fishing in their waters by a metropolitan-based company.

In July 1991 the international arbitration tribunal began its deliberations in New York, USA. The tribunal's ruling, issued in June 1992, was generally deemed to be favourable to Canada. France was allocated an exclusive economic zone around the territory totalling 2,537 square nautical miles (8,700 sq km), compared with its demand for more than 13,000 square nautical miles. The French authorities claimed that the sea area granted would be insufficient to sustain the islands' fishing community. Canadian and French officials met in Canada in the following month to negotiate new fishing quotas for the area off Newfoundland; however, the talks failed, and, in the absence of a new agreement, industrial fishing in the area was effectively halted until November 1994, when the Governments of the two countries signed an accord specifying new quotas for a period of 10 years. In the following month deputies in the French National Assembly expressed concern that the terms of the agreement would be detrimental to St Pierre and Miquelon's interests, although the Government asserted that the accord recognized the islanders' historic fishing rights in Canadian waters. Meanwhile, in January of that year St Pierre and Miquelon protested at what it alleged was an unauthorized entry into the islands' waters by Canadian coastguards (who had been attempting to intercept goods being smuggled from Saint-Pierre to Newfoundland), and appealed to France to intensify its efforts to protect the islands' territorial integrity.

At the March 1986 election to the French National Assembly the islands' incumbent deputy, Albert Pen of the Parti Socialiste (PS), was re-elected. Pen was also the sole candidate at the indirect election to choose the islands' representative in the French Senate in September. A fresh election for a deputy to the National Assembly was held in November, when Gérard Grignon, representing the centre-right Union pour la Démocratie Française (UDF), was elected. At the 1988 French presidential election Jacques Chirac of the right-wing Rassemblement pour la République (RPR) received 56% of the votes cast by the islanders in the second round, in May, against the successful PS incumbent, François Mitterrand. In June Grignon was re-elected to the National Assembly, taking 90.3% of the valid votes. In September–October, however, the parties of the left won a majority at elections to the General Council, securing 13 of the 19 seats.

In September 1992 64.2% of voters approved ratification of the Treaty on European Union (see p. 172), although only a small percentage of the electorate participated in the referendum. Grignon was re-elected to the National Assembly in March 1993; some 83% of the electorate participated in the poll. At the 1995 presidential election Chirac received the greatest proportion of the votes cast at the first round on 23 April (33.97%), and was the winning candidate at the second round on 7 May, taking 66.86% of the votes cast. The rate of abstention at the second round was 33.2%. At elections to the Senate in September, Pen was narrowly defeated at a second round of voting by Victor Reux of the RPR, since 1994 the Secretary of the islands' Economic and Social Council. Grignon was re-elected to the National Assembly at a second round of voting on 1 June 1997, with 52.34% of the votes cast.

A number of government proposals regarding the socio-economic development of the Overseas Departments, which were to be debated by the French legislature by the end of June 2000, were also to be applied to St Pierre and Miquelon. In addition, the draft legislation envisaged increased financial autonomy for the islands' communes.

### Government

The French Government is represented in St Pierre by an appointed Prefect. There is a General Council, with 19 members (15 for St Pierre and four for Miquelon), elected by adult universal suffrage for a period of six years. St Pierre and Miquelon elects one deputy to the French National Assembly and one representative to the Senate in Paris.

### Defence

France is responsible for the islands' defence.

### Economic Affairs

The soil and climatic conditions of St Pierre and Miquelon do not favour agricultural production, which is mainly confined to smallholdings, except for market-gardening and the production of eggs and chickens.

The principal economic activity of the islands is traditionally fishing and related industries, which employed some 18.5% of the working population in 1996. However, the sector has been severely affected by disputes with Canada regarding territorial waters and fishing quotas; the absence of quotas in 1992–94 effectively halted industrial fishing. New arrangements have been to the detriment of St Pierre and Miquelon, although there is some optimism regarding potential for the exploitation of shellfish, notably mussels and scallops, in the islands' waters.

Processing of fish provides the basis for industrial activity, which engages about 41% of the labour force. It is dominated by one major company, which produces frozen and salted fish, and fish meal for fodder. In 1988 the industry recorded a sharp decrease in production (to 3,710 metric tons), compared with preceding years; total production increased to 5,457 tons in 1990. Much of the fish processed is now imported. Electricity is generated by two thermal power stations, with a combined capacity of 23 MW. In 1999 plans were well advanced for the construction of a wind power station, which it was hoped would generate some 40% of the islands' electricity requirements.

The replenishment of ships' (mainly trawlers') supplies was formerly an important economic activity, but has now also been adversely affected by the downturn in the industrial fishing sector. During the late 1980s efforts were made to promote tourism, and the opening of the St Pierre–Montréal air route in 1987 led to an increase in air traffic. Tourist arrivals in 1998 were estimated at 11,994. In 1999 the completion of a new airport capable of accommodating larger aircraft further improved transport links.

In 1997 St Pierre and Miquelon recorded a trade deficit of 356m. French francs; total exports were 29m. francs. Most trade is with Canada and France and other countries of the European Union. The only significant exports are fish and fish meal. The principal imports in 1994 were fuel, building supplies and food from Canada. Items such as clothing and other consumer goods are generally imported from France.

The annual rate of inflation averaged 6.3% in 1981–91, and consumer prices increased by an average of 2.1% per year between December 1991 and December 1996. Some 9.5% of the labour force were unemployed in the late 1990s.

Given the decline of the fishing sector, the development of the port of Saint-Pierre and the expansion of tourism (particularly from Canada and the USA) are regarded by St Pierre and Miquelon as the principal means of maintaining economic progress. The islands will, none the less, remain highly dependent on budgetary assistance from the French central Government.

### Social Welfare

In 1997 there was one hospital complex, which included a retirement home and a centre for the handicapped. Citizens of St Pierre and Miquelon benefit from similar social security provisions to those of metropolitan France.

### Education

The education system is modelled on the French system, and education is compulsory for children between the ages of six and 16 years. In 1997 there were nine primary schools, three secondary schools (one of which is private and has a technical school annex) and one technical school.

### Public Holidays

**2000:** 1 January (New Year's Day), 21–24 April (Easter), 1 May (Labour Day), 1 June (Ascension Day), 12 June (Whit Monday), 14 July (National Day), 11 November (Armistice Day), 25 December (Christmas Day).

**2001:** 1 January (New Year's Day), 13–16 April (Easter), 1 May (Labour Day), 24 May (Ascension Day), 4 June (Whit Monday), 14 July (National Day), 11 November (Armistice Day), 25 December (Christmas Day).

### Weights and Measures

The metric system is in use.

## Statistical Survey

Source: Préfecture, Place du Lieutenant-Colonel Pigeaud, BP 4200, 97500 Saint-Pierre; tel. 41-10-10; fax 41-25-46.

#### AREA AND POPULATION

**Area:** 242 sq km (93.4 sq miles): St Pierre 26 sq km; Miquelon-Langlade 216 sq km.

**Population:** 6,392 at census of 15 March 1990: Saint-Pierre 5,683, Miquelon-Langlade 709; 6,700 (estimate) at 31 December 1997.

**Density** (1997): 27.7 per sq km.

**Births, Marriages and Deaths** (1997): Live births 92; Marriages 36; Deaths 51.

**Economically Active Population** (1992): Fish and fish-processing 540; Construction 333; Transport 192; Dockers 44; Trade 409; Restaurants and hotels 154; Business services 417; Government employees 727; Activities not adequately defined 106; Total labour force 2,922.

### FISHING

**Total Catch** (metric tons, live weight): 89 in 1997.

### FINANCE

**Currency and Exchange Rates:** French currency is used (see French Guiana).

**Expenditure by Metropolitan France** (1997): 280 million francs.

**Budget** (estimates, million francs, 1997): Expenditure 244 (current 128; capital 116).

**Money Supply** (million francs at 31 December 1997): Currency outside banks 281; Demand deposits at banks 897; Total money 1,178.

**Cost of Living** (Consumer price index; base: 1981 = 100): 183.0 in 1989; 189.6 in 1990; 196.5 in 1991.

### EXTERNAL TRADE

**Total** (million francs, 1997): *Imports:* 385; *Exports:* 29. Most trade is with Canada, France (imports), other countries of the European Union (exports) and the USA.

### TRANSPORT

**Road Traffic** (1997): 3,876 motor vehicles in use.

**Shipping** (1995): Ships entered 884; Freight entered 20,400 metric tons. *1997*: Ships entered 918.

**Civil Aviation** (1997): Passengers carried 30,341, Freight carried 105 metric tons.

### TOURISM

**Tourist Arrivals** (estimate, 1998): 11,994. Source: Agence Régionale du Tourisme.

### COMMUNICATIONS MEDIA

**Radio Receivers** (estimate, '000 in use): 5.0 in 1997.

**Television Receivers** (estimate, '000 in use): 3.5 in 1997.

### EDUCATION

**Primary** (1997): 9 institutions; 50 teachers (1987); 877 students.

**Secondary** (1997): 3 institutions; 55 teachers (1987); 562 students.

**Technical** (1997): 1 institution; 194 students.

# Directory

## The Government

(February 2000)

**Prefect:** FRANCIS SPITZER.

**Deputy to the French National Assembly:** GÉRARD GRIGNON (UDF-CDS).

**Representative to the French Senate:** VICTOR REUX (RPR).

### GENERAL COUNCIL

Place de l'Eglise, 97500 Saint-Pierre; tel. 41-46-22; fax 41-22-97.

The General Council has 19 members (St Pierre 15, Miquelon four).

**President of the General Council:** BERNARD LESOAVEC.

## Political Organizations

**Centre des Démocrates Sociaux (CDS):** 97500 Saint-Pierre.

**Parti Socialiste (PS):** BP 984, 97500 Saint-Pierre; tel. 41-35-74; fax 41-78-90; e-mail psspm@altavista.net; f. 1996.

**Rassemblement pour la République (RPR):** BP 113, 97500 Saint-Pierre; tel. 41-35-73; fax 41-29-97; Gaullist.

**Union pour la Démocratie Française (UDF):** 97500 Saint-Pierre; centrist.

## Judicial System

**Tribunal Supérieur d'Appel:** 97500 Saint-Pierre; tel. 41-47-26; fax 41-49-45; Pres. FRANÇOIS BILLON.

**Tribunal de Première Instance:** 14 rue Emile Sasco, BP 4215, 97500 Saint-Pierre; tel. 41-47-26; fax 41-49-45; e-mail tsaspm@cancom.net; Presiding Magistrate PASCAL MATHIS.

## Religion

Almost all of the inhabitants are adherents of the Roman Catholic Church.

### CHRISTIANITY

#### The Roman Catholic Church

The islands form the Apostolic Vicariate of the Iles Saint-Pierre et Miquelon. At 31 December 1997 there were an estimated 6,215 adherents.

**Vicar Apostolic:** FRANÇOIS JOSEPH MAURER (Titular Bishop of Chimaera), Vicariat Apostolique, BP 4245, 97500 Saint-Pierre; tel. 41-20-35; fax 41-47-09.

## The Press

**L'Echo des Caps Hebdo:** rue Georges Daguerre, BP 4213, 97500 Saint-Pierre; tel. 41-41-01; fax 41-49-33; e-mail echohebd@cancom.net; f. 1982; weekly; circ. 2,500.

**Recueil des Actes Administratifs:** 4 rue du Général Leclerc, BP 4233, 97500 Saint-Pierre; tel. 41-24-50; fax 41-20-85; f. 1866; monthly; Dir E. DEROUET.

**Trait d'Union:** BP 113, 97500 Saint-Pierre; tel. 41-35-73; fax 41-29-97; six a year; organ of the local branch of the RPR.

**Le Vent de la Liberté:** 1 rue Amiral Muselier, BP 1179, 97500 Saint-Pierre; tel. 41-42-19; fax 41-48-06; e-mail archipel@cancom.net; weekly; circ. 350; Dir GÉRARD GRIGNON.

## Broadcasting and Communications

### RADIO AND TELEVISION

**Réseau France Outre-mer (RFO):** BP 4227, 97500 Saint-Pierre; tel. 41-11-11; fax 41-22-19; internet www.rfo.fr; fmrly Société Nationale de Radio-Télévision Française d'Outre-mer, renamed as above 1998; broadcasts 24 hours of radio programmes daily and 195 hours of television programmes weekly on two channels; Pres. ANDRÉ-MICHEL BESSE; Dir JEAN-MICHEL CAMBIANICA.

**Radio Atlantique:** BP 1282, 97500 Saint-Pierre; e-mail adrian@cancom.net; private; broadcasts 24 hours of radio programmes daily; Pres. and Dir ROGER GUICHOT.

## Finance

(cap. = capital, res = reserves, dep. = deposits; m. = million; amounts in French francs)

### MAJOR BANKS

**Banque des Iles Saint-Pierre-et-Miquelon:** rue Jacques Cartier, BP 4223, 97500 Saint-Pierre; tel. 41-22-17; fax 41-25-31; f. 1889; cap. 25m., res 2.7m., dep. 262m. (Dec. 1997); Pres. and Gen. Man. GUILLAUME DE CHALUS; Man. BERNARD DURDILLY.

**Crédit Saint Pierrais:** 20 place du Général de Gaulle, BP 4218, 97500 Saint-Pierre; tel. 41-22-49; fax 41-25-96; f. 1962; cap. 36.5m., res 3m., dep. 286m. (Dec. 1998); Pres. GUY SIMON; Man. PIERRE SPIETH.

### PRINCIPAL INSURANCE COMPANIES

**Mutuelle des Iles:** 5 rue Maréchal Foch, BP 1112, 97500 Saint-Pierre; tel. 41-28-69; fax 41-51-13.

**Paturel Assurances SARL, Agence PFA Athéna:** 31 rue Maréchal Foch, BP 4288, 97500 Saint-Pierre; tel. 41-32-98; fax 41-51-65; Gen. Agent GUY PATUREL; Man. NATHALIE PATUREL.

## Trade and Industry

### GOVERNMENT AGENCY

**Comité Economique et Social:** 4 rue Borda, 97500 Saint-Pierre; tel. 41-45-50; fax 41-42-45.

### DEVELOPMENT ORGANIZATION

**SODEPAR:** Palais Royal, rue Borda, BP 4365, 97500 Saint-Pierre; tel. 41-15-15; fax 41-15-16; e-mail sodepar@cancom.net; internet www.cancom.net/~sodepar; f. 1989; economic development agency; Chair. BERNARD LESOAVEC; Dir GÉRARD MERCHER.

### CHAMBER OF COMMERCE

**Chambre de Commerce, d'Industrie et de Métiers:** 4 blvd Constant-Colmay, BP 4207, 97500 Saint-Pierre; tel. 41-45-12; fax 41-32-09; Pres. JEAN LEBAILLY.

### TRADE UNIONS

**Union Interprofessionnelle CFDT—SPM:** BP 4352, 97500 Saint-Pierre; tel. 41-23-20; fax 41-27-99; affiliated to the Confédération Française Démocratique du Travail; Sec.-Gen. PHILIPPE GUILLAUME.

**Union Interprofessionnelle CFTC:** BP 1117, 97500 Saint-Pierre; tel. 41-37-19; affiliated to the Confédération Française des Travailleurs Chrétiens.

**Union Intersyndicale CGT de Saint-Pierre et Miquelon:** 97500 Saint-Pierre; tel. 41-41-86; affiliated to the Confédération Générale du Travail; Sec.-Gen. RONALD MANET.

**Union des Syndicats CGT-FO de Saint-Pierre et Miquelon;** 15 rue Dr Dunan, BP 4241, 97500 Saint-Pierre; tel. 41-25-22; fax 41-46-55; affiliated to the Confédération Générale du Travail-Force Ouvrière; Sec.-Gen. MAX OLAISOLA.

## Transport

### SHIPPING

Packet boats and container services operate between Saint-Pierre, Halifax, Nova Scotia, and Boston, MA. The seaport at Saint-Pierre has three jetties and 1,200 metres of quays.

### CIVIL AVIATION

There is an airport on St Pierre, served by airlines linking the territory with France and Canada. Construction of a new airport, able to accommodate larger aircraft and thus improve air links, was completed in 1999.

**Air Saint-Pierre:** 18 rue Albert Briand, Saint-Pierre, BP 4225, 97500 Saint-Pierre; tel. 41-47-18; fax 41-23-36; e-mail asp@cancom.net; f. 1964; connects the territory directly with Newfoundland, Nova Scotia and Québec; Pres. RÉMY L. BRIAND; Man. THIERRY BRIAND.

## Tourism

There were an estimated 11,994 tourist arrivals in 1998.

**Agence Régionale du Tourisme:** 22 place du Général de Gaulle, BP 4274, 97500 Saint-Pierre; tel. 41-22-22; fax 41-33-55; e-mail tourispm@cancom.net; internet www.209.205.50.254./encyspmweb/; f. 1989; Pres. BERNARD LESOAVEC; Dir JEAN-HIGUES DETCHEVERRY.

# French Overseas Territories

The four Overseas Territories (territoires d'outre-mer) are French Polynesia, the French Southern and Antarctic Territories, New Caledonia, and the Wallis and Futuna Islands. They are integral parts of the French Republic. Each is administered by a High Commissioner or Chief Administrator, who is appointed by the French Government. Each permanently inhabited Territory also has a Territorial Assembly or Congress, elected by universal adult suffrage. Certain members of the Territorial Assembly or Congress sit in the French National Assembly and the Senate of the Republic in Paris. The Territories have varying degrees of internal autonomy.

# FRENCH POLYNESIA

## Introductory Survey

### Location, Climate, Language, Religion, Flag, Capital

French Polynesia comprises several scattered groups of islands in the south Pacific Ocean, lying about two-thirds of the way between the Panama Canal and New Zealand. Its nearest neighbours are the Cook Islands, to the west, and the Line Islands (part of Kiribati), to the north-west. French Polynesia consists of the following island groups: the Windward Islands (Iles du Vent—including the islands of Tahiti and Moorea) and the Leeward Islands (Iles Sous le Vent—located about 160 km north-west of Tahiti) which, together, constitute the Society Archipelago; the Tuamotu Archipelago, which comprises 78 islands scattered east of the Society Archipelago in a line stretching north-west to south-east for about 1,500 km; the Gambier Islands, located 1,600 km south-east of Tahiti; the Austral Islands, lying 640 km south of Tahiti; and the Marquesas Archipelago, which lies 1,450 km north-east of Tahiti. There are 120 islands in all. The average monthly temperature throughout the year varies between 20°C (68°F) and 29°C (84°F), and most rainfall occurs between November and April, the average annual precipitation being 1,625 mm (64 ins). The official language is French, and Polynesian languages are spoken by the indigenous population. The principal religion is Christianity; about 55% of the population are Protestant and some 34% Roman Catholic. The official flag is the French tricolour. Subordinate to this, there is a territorial flag (proportions 3 by 2), comprising three horizontal stripes, of red, white (half the depth) and red, with, in the centre, the arms of French Polynesia, consisting of a representation in red of a native canoe, bearing a platform supporting five stylized persons, on a circular background (five wavy horizontal dark blue bands, surmounted by 10 golden sunrays). The capital is Papeete, on the island of Tahiti.

### Recent History

Tahiti, the largest of the Society Islands, was declared a French protectorate in 1842, and became a colony in 1880. The other island groups were annexed during the last 20 years of the 19th century. The islands were governed from France under a decree of 1885 until 1957, when French Polynesia became an Overseas Territory, administered by a Governor in Papeete. A Territorial Assembly and a Council of Government were elected to advise the Governor.

Between May 1975 and May 1982 a majority in the Territorial Assembly sought independence for French Polynesia. Following pressure by Francis Sanford, leader of the largest autonomist party in the Assembly, a new Constitution for the Territory was negotiated with the French Government and approved by a newly-elected Assembly in 1977. Under the provisions of the new statute, France retained responsibility for foreign affairs, defence, monetary matters and justice, but the powers of the territorial Council of Government were increased, especially in the field of commerce. The French Governor was replaced by a High Commissioner, who was to preside over the Council of Government and was head of the administration, but had no vote. The Council's elected Vice-President, responsible for domestic affairs, was granted greater powers. An Economic, Social and Cultural Council, responsible for all development matters, was also created, and French Polynesia's economic zone was extended to 200 nautical miles (370 km) from the islands' coastline.

Following elections to the Territorial Assembly in May 1982, the Gaullist Tahoeraa Huiraatira, led by Gaston Flosse, which secured 13 of the 30 seats, formed successive ruling coalitions, first with the Ai'a Api party and in September with the Pupu Here Ai'a Te Nunaa Ia Ora party. Seeking greater (but not full) independence from France, especially in economic matters, elected representatives of the Assembly held discussions with the French Government in Paris in 1983, and in September 1984 a new statute was approved by the French National Assembly. This allowed the territorial Government greater powers, mainly in the sphere of commerce and development; the Council of Government was replaced by a Council of Ministers, whose President was to be elected from among the members of the Territorial Assembly. Flosse became the first President of the Council of Ministers.

At elections held in March 1986 the Tahoeraa Huiraatira gained the first outright majority to be achieved in the Territory, winning 24 of the 41 seats in the Territorial Assembly. Leaders of opposition parties subsequently expressed dissatisfaction with the election result, claiming that the Tahoeraa Huiraatira victory had been secured only as a result of the allocation of a disproportionately large number of seats in the Territorial Assembly to one of the five constituencies. The constituency at the centre of the dispute was that comprising the Mangareva and Tuamotu islands, where the two French army bases at Hao and Mururoa constituted a powerful body of support for Flosse and the Tahoeraa Huiraatira, which, in spite of winning a majority of seats, had obtained a minority of individual votes in the election. At the concurrent elections for French Polynesia's two seats in the National Assembly in Paris, Flosse and Alexandre Léontieff, the candidates of the Rassemblement pour la République (RPR—to which Tahoeraa Huiraatira is affiliated), were elected, Flosse subsequently ceding his seat to Edouard Fritch. Later in March the French Prime Minister, Jacques Chirac, appointed Flosse to a post in the French Council of Ministers, assigning him the portfolio of Secretary of State for South Pacific Affairs.

In April 1986 Flosse was re-elected President of the Council of Ministers. However, he faced severe criticism from leaders of the opposition for his allegedly inefficient and extravagant use of public funds, and was accused, in particular, of corrupt electoral practice. Flosse resigned as President of the Territory's Council of Ministers in February 1987, and was replaced by Jacques Teuira.

Unrest among dock-workers led to serious rioting in October 1987 and the declaration of a state of emergency by the authorities. In December, amid growing discontent over his policies, Teuira and the entire Council of Ministers resigned and were replaced by a coalition of opposition parties and the Te Tiaraama party (a breakaway faction of the Tahoeraa Huiraatira) under the presidency of Alexandre Léontieff. The Léontieff Government survived several challenges in the Territorial Assembly to its continuation in office during 1988–89. Amendments to the Polynesian Constitution, which were approved by the French Parliament and enacted by July 1990, augmented the powers of the President of the Territorial Council of Ministers and increased the competence of the Territorial Assembly. In addition, five consultative Archipelago Councils were established, comprising Territorial and municipal elected representatives. The major purpose of these amendments was to clarify the areas of responsibility of the State, the Territory and the judiciary, which was considered particularly necessary following various disputes about the impending single market of the European Community (EC—now European Union, EU, see p. 172). In June 1989, in protest, 90% of the electorate had refused to vote in the elections to the European Parliament.

At territorial elections in March 1991 the Tahoeraa Huiraatira won 18 of the 41 seats. Flosse then formed a coalition with the Ai'a Api, thereby securing a majority of 23 seats in the Territorial Assembly. Emile Vernaudon, leader of the Ai'a Api, was elected President of the Assembly and Flosse was elected President of the Council of Ministers. In September Flosse announced the end of the coalition between his party and the Ai'a Api, accusing Vernaudon of disloyalty, and signed a new alliance with the Pupu Here Ai'a Te Nunaa Ia Ora led by Jean Juventin.

In April 1992 Flosse was found guilty of fraud (relating to an illegal sale of government land to a member of his family) and there were widespread demands for his resignation. In November Juventin and Léontieff were charged with 'passive' corruption, relating to the construction of a golf course by a Japanese company. In the following month the French Court of Appeal upheld the judgment against Flosse, who received a six-month, suspended prison sentence. The case provoked a demonstration by more than 3,000 people in January 1993, demanding the resignation of Flosse and Juventin. In September 1994 Flosse succeeded in having the conviction overturned, on a procedural issue, in a second court of appeal. In October 1997, however, Léontieff was found guilty of accepting substantial bribes in order to facilitate a business venture and was sentenced to three years in prison (half of which was to be suspended). In May 1998 Léontieff was sentenced to a further three years' imprisonment (two of which were to be suspended) for corruption.

The approval by the Territorial Assembly in September 1994 of a new version of the fiscal law, the Contribution de Solidarité Territoriale (first introduced in July 1993), provoked widespread popular unrest and led to a six-day general strike and demonstrations by up to 10,000 people, who blocked the port and major roads around the capital.

French presidential elections took place in April/May 1995. During the second round of voting in the Territory, the socialist candidate, Lionel Jospin, received 39% of the total votes, while the RPR candidate, Jacques Chirac, won 61%. (Chirac was elected to the presidency with 52.6% of votes cast throughout the republic.)

In November 1995 the Territorial Assembly adopted a draft statute of autonomy, which proposed the extension of the Territory's powers to areas such as fishing, mining and shipping rights, international transport and communications, broadcasting and the offshore economic zone. France, however, would retain full responsibility for defence, justice and security in the islands. Advocates of independence for French Polynesia criticized the statute for promising only relatively cosmetic changes, while failing to increase the democratic rights of the islanders. The statute was approved by the French National Assembly in December and came into force in April 1996.

At territorial elections held on 13 May 1996 the Gaullist Tahoeraa Huiraatira achieved an outright majority, although the principal pro-independence party, Tavini Huiraatira/Front de Libération de la Polynésie, made considerable gains throughout the Territory (largely owing to increased popular hostility towards France since the resumption of nuclear-weapons tests at Mururoa Atoll—see below). Tahoeraa Huiraatira secured 22 of the 41 seats in the Territorial Assembly, with 38.7% of total votes cast, while Tavini Huiraatira won 10 seats, with 24.8% of votes. Other anti-independence parties won a total of eight seats and an additional pro-independence grouping secured one seat. Flosse defeated the independence leader, Oscar Temaru, by 28 votes to 11 to remain as President of the Council of Ministers later in the month, and Justin Arapari was elected President of the Territorial Assembly. Allegations of voting irregularities led to legal challenges, which overturned the results in 11 constituencies. Following by-elections in May 1998 for the 11 seats, Tahoeraa Huiraatira increased its representation by one seat. Tavini Huiraatira again claimed that the elections had not been fairly conducted.

At elections for French Polynesia's two seats in the French National Assembly in May 1997 Michel Buillard and Emile Vernaudon, both supporters of the RPR, were elected with 52% and 59% of total votes cast, respectively. However, the pro-independence leader, Oscar Temaru, was a strong contender for the western constituency seat, securing 42% of the votes. Flosse was re-elected as the Territory's representative to the French Senate in September 1998.

A state of natural disaster was declared in Tahiti in December 1998, following severe flooding which destroyed some 900 homes on the island and killed several people.

In March 1999 proposals for an increase in French Polynesia's autonomy, as part of constitutional reforms, were announced in Paris. These proposals followed an initial agreement between the Territory and the French Government in late 1998, on the future of French Polynesia. In October 1999 the French Senate adopted a constitutional amendment granting French Polynesia a greater degree of autonomy. According to the bill (which had also been approved by the National Assembly in June), the status of the islands was to be changed from that of overseas territory to overseas country, and a new Polynesian citizenship was to be created. Although France was to retain control over areas such as foreign affairs, defence, justice and electoral laws, French Polynesia would have the power to negotiate with other Pacific countries and sign its own international treaties. The constitutional amendment was presented to a joint session of the French Senate and National Assembly for final ratification in late January 2000. However, no decision was taken on the matter and the issue was unlikely to be addressed again before May 2001.

In November 1999 Flosse was found guilty of corruption, on charges of accepting $A500,000 in bribes from the owner of an illegal casino, allegedly to help fund his party. Flosse was expected to appeal against the sentence, which comprised a two-year suspended prison term, a large fine, and a one-year ban on seeking office. Demonstrations, organized by the pro-independence Tavini Huiraatira/Front de Libération de la Polynésie, took place in Tahiti, in protest at Flosse's refusal to resign from his post as President of the Territorial Council of Ministers.

The testing of nuclear devices by the French Government began in 1966 at Mururoa Atoll, in the Tuamotu Archipelago. In 1983, in spite of strong protests by many Pacific nations, the Government indicated that tests would continue for a number of years. In October 1983 Australia, New Zealand and Papua New Guinea accepted a French invitation jointly to send scientists to inspect the test site. The team subsequently reported definite evidence of environmental damage, resulting from the underground explosions, which had caused subsidence by weakening the rock structure of the atoll. Significant levels of radioactivity were also detected.

A series of tests in May and June 1985, involving bigger explosions than hitherto, prompted a renewed display of opposition. In July the trawler *Rainbow Warrior*, the flagship of the anti-nuclear environmentalist group Greenpeace, which was to have led a protest flotilla to Mururoa, was sunk in Auckland Harbour, New Zealand, in an explosion that killed one crew member. Two agents of the French secret service, the Direction générale de sécurité extérieure (DGSE), were subsequently convicted of manslaughter and imprisoned in New Zealand. In July 1986, however, they were transferred to Hao Atoll, in the Tuamoto Archipelago, after a ruling by the UN Secretary-General (acting as mediator), which effectively reduced the agents' sentences from 10 to three years' imprisonment, in return for a French payment of $NZ 7m. in compensation to the New Zealand Government. Relations between France and New Zealand deteriorated still further in 1987, when the French Prime Minister, Jacques Chirac, approved the removal of one of the prisoners to Paris, owing to illness. By the terms of the UN ruling, 'mutual consent' by both Governments was to be necessary for any such repatriation. In 1988 the other prisoner was also flown back to Paris after she became pregnant (see chapter on New Zealand for further details). In May 1991, during a visit to New Zealand, the French Prime Minister, Michel Rocard, formally apologized for the bombing of the *Rainbow Warrior*; however, in July tension between France and the region was exacerbated by the French Government's decision to award a medal for 'distinguished service' to one of the agents convicted for his role in the bombing. Between 1975 and 1992 France performed 135 underground and 52 atmospheric nuclear tests in the Territory.

In April 1992 the French Government announced that nuclear tests would be suspended until the end of the year. Although the decision was welcomed throughout the South Pacific, concern was expressed in French Polynesia over the economic implications of the move, because of the Territory's dependence on income received from hosting the nuclear-test programme. Similarly, it was feared that unemployment resulting from the ban (some 1,500 people were employed at the test centre alone) would have a serious impact on the economy. A delegation of political leaders subsequently travelled to Paris to express its concerns, and in January 1993 accepted assistance worth 7,000m. francs CFP in compensation for lost revenue and in aid for development projects.

Shortly after his election in May 1995, President Jacques Chirac announced that France would resume nuclear testing, with a programme of eight tests between September 1995 and May 1996. The decision provoked almost universal outrage in the international community, and was condemned for its apparent disregard for regional opinion, as well as for undermining the considerable progress made by Western nations towards a worldwide ban on nuclear testing. Scientists also expressed concern at the announcement; some believed that further explosions at Mururoa could lead to the collapse of the atoll, which had been weakened considerably by more than 130 blast cavities. Large-scale demonstrations and protest marches throughout the region were accompanied by boycotts of French products and the suspension of several trade and defence co-operation agreements. Opposition to the French Government intensified in July 1995, when French commandos violently seized *Rainbow Warrior II*, the flagship of Greenpeace, and its crew, which had been protesting peacefully near the test site. Chirac continued to defy mounting pressure to reverse the decision from within the EU, from Japan and Russia, as well as from Australia, New Zealand and the South Pacific region. French Polynesia became the focus of world attention when the first test took place in September. The action attracted further statements of condemnation from Governments around the world, and provoked major demonstrations in many countries. In Tahiti hitherto peaceful protests soon developed into full-scale riots, as several thousand demonstrators, enraged by the French authorities' intransigent stance, rampaged through the capital, demanding an end to French rule. Faaa airport was closed, as protesters occupied the runway and destroyed adjacent buildings and vehicles. Meanwhile, violent clashes with police, and the burning of dozens of buildings in Papeete during the riots, left much of the capital in ruins. In response, the French Government drafted thousands of extra security personnel on to the island, to quell the unrest. In defiance of world opinion, a further five tests were carried out, the sixth and final one being conducted in January 1996. Work to dismantle facilities at the test site began in 1997 and was completed in July 1998.

In September 1998 the trial of more than 60 people charged with offences relating to the riots and protests of September 1995 began in Papeete. Hiro Tefaare, a pro-independence member of the Territorial Assembly and former police officer, was found guilty of instigating the riots and was sentenced to three years' imprisonment (of which 18 months were to be suspended). Furthermore, in September 1999 the French Government was ordered by the Administrative Tribunal to pay 204m. francs CFP in damage compensation for failing to maintain law and order.

In early 1999 a study by the French Independent Research and Information Commission reported that there was serious radioactive leakage into underground water, lagoons and the ocean at Mururoa and Fangataufa atolls. These claims were dismissed by a New Zealand scientist who had taken part in an earlier study by the International Atomic Energy Agency, which had claimed that radiation levels were nearly undetectable. In May a French government official admitted that fractures had been found in the coral cone at the Mururoa and Fangataufa nuclear testing sites. The reports, by Greenpeace, that the atoll was in danger of collapsing had always been previously denied by France. However, France's claim that no serious long-term damage had been done was contested by Greenpeace, which also suggested the need for an urgent independent study of the test sites.

Meanwhile, in early 1996 the French Government confirmed reports by a team of independent scientists that radioactive isotopes had leaked into the waters surrounding the atoll, but denied that they represented a threat to the environment. However, following the election of a new socialist administration in France (in mid-1997), the French Minister of the Environment demanded in August 1998 that the matter be investigated further, stating that she had not been reassured by the initial reports. The minister's demands were reiterated by church leaders in the Territory, who asked the Government to establish radiological surveillance systems at the former test sites, to conduct thorough medical studies on people exposed to radiation from the tests and to make military records accessible to the public, claiming that previous investigations had failed to address the concerns of the islanders.

## Government

The French Government is represented in French Polynesia by its High Commissioner to the Territory, and controls various important spheres of government, including defence, foreign diplomacy and justice. A local Territorial Assembly, with 41 members, is elected for a five-year term by universal adult suffrage. The Assembly may elect a President of an executive body, the Territorial Council of Ministers, who, in turn, submits a list of between six and 12 members of the Assembly to serve as ministers, for approval by the Assembly.

In addition, French Polynesia elects two deputies to the French National Assembly in Paris and one representative to the French Senate, all chosen on the basis of universal adult suffrage. French Polynesia is also represented at the European Parliament.

## Defence

France tested nuclear weapons at Mururoa Atoll, in the Tuamotu Archipelago, between 1966 and 1996. In August 1999 France maintained a force of 2,300 military personnel in the Territory, as well as a gendarmerie of 600.

## Economic Affairs

In 1998, according to official estimates, French Polynesia's gross domestic product (GDP), measured at current prices, was 422,212m. francs CFP, equivalent to 1,881,000 francs CFP per head. During 1988–96 the population increased at an average annual rate of 1.9%.

Agriculture, forestry and fishing contributed only 3.9% of GDP in 1993, but provide most of French Polynesia's exports. The sector engaged 14.6% of the employed labour force in 1996. Coconuts are the principal cash crop, and in 1998 the estimated harvest was 87,000 metric tons. Vegetables, fruit (especially pineapples and citrus fruit), vanilla and coffee are also cultivated. Most commercial fishing, principally for tuna, is conducted, under licence, by Japanese and Korean fleets. Another important activity is the production of cultured black pearls, of which the quantity exported increased from 112 kg in 1984 to 5,487 kg in 1996. In 1998 the Territory exported some 6,500kg of black pearls, earning 16,429m. francs CFP (compared with 14,658m. francs CFP and 9,591m. francs CFP in 1997 and 1995 respectively), and during the mid-1990s was estimated to have produced more than 95% of the world's cultured black pearls. Japan is the biggest importer of black pearls from the Territory, and in 1996 purchased an estimated 70% of black pearls produced in that year.

Industry (comprising mining, manufacturing, construction and utilities) engaged 15.6% of the working population in 1996, and provided 14.5% of GDP in 1993. There is a small manufacturing sector, which is heavily dependent on agriculture. Coconut oil and copra are produced, as are beer, dairy products and vanilla essence. Important deposits of phosphates and cobalt were discovered during the 1980s. The manufacturing sector (with mining and quarrying) engaged 8.6% of the employed labour force in 1996, and provided 6.7% of GDP in 1993. Construction is an important industrial activity, contributing 5.7% of GDP in 1993, and engaging 6.4% of the employed labour force in 1996.

Hydrocarbon fuels are the main source of energy in the Territory, with the Papeete thermal power station providing about three-quarters of the electricity produced. Hydroelectric and solar energy also make a significant contribution to French Polynesia's domestic requirements. Hydroelectric power dams, with the capacity to generate the electricity requirements of 45% of Tahiti's population, have been constructed.

Tourism is the Territory's major industry. In 1990 the trade, restaurants and hotels sector contributed 22.7% of GDP. In 1998 some 188,933 tourists visited French Polynesia, and receipts from tourism totalled an estimated US $390m. French Polynesia's hotel capacity, which amounted to 3,021 rooms in 1998, was expected to have doubled by 2001, as a result of several major construction projects initiated in the late 1990s. The services sectors engaged 69.8% of the employed labour force in 1996, and provided 81.6% of GDP in 1993.

In 1998 French Polynesia recorded a trade deficit of 89,893m. francs CFP. In 1997 the principal sources of imports were France (which provided 37.9% of total imports), the USA (17.0%), Australia (7.9%) and New Zealand (8.9%). The principal markets for exports in that year were Japan (accounting for 37.0% of the total) and France (32.0%). The principal imports in that year included machinery and mechanical appliances (9.7% of the total) and electrical goods (6.6%). The principal commodity exports were cultured black pearls (providing 61.6% of total export revenue).

In 1996 there was an estimated territorial budgetary surplus of 1,622m. francs CFP. In 1996 expenditure by the French State in the Territory totalled 123,774m. francs CFP, 37% of which was on the military budget. The total external debt was estimated at US $390m. in 1992. The annual rate of inflation averaged 1.3% in 1990–97 and 1.4% in 1998. A high unemployment rate (recorded at 13.2% of the labour force in 1996) is exacerbated by the predominance of young people in the population (in 1996 some 43% of the population were under the age of 20 years).

French Polynesia forms part of the Franc Zone (see p. 200), and is a member of the Pacific Community (formerly the South Pacific Commission—see p. 257), which provides technical advice, training and assistance in economic, cultural and social development to countries in the region.

French Polynesia's traditional agriculture-based economy was distorted by the presence of large numbers of French military personnel (in connection with the nuclear-testing programme which began in 1966), stimulating employment in the construction industry and services at the expense of agriculture, and encouraging migration from the outer islands to Tahiti, where 75% of the population currently reside. These dramatic changes effectively transformed French Polynesia from a state of self-sufficiency to one of import dependency in less than a generation. The development of tourism had a similar effect. In the late 1980s some 80% of the Territory's food requirements had to be imported, while exports of vanilla and coffee, formerly important cash crops, were negligible, owing to a long-term decline in investment. The Contract for Development, an agreement for metropolitan France to provide the Territory with 28,300m. francs CFP annually between 1996 and 2006, was concluded in 1995 and took effect upon completion of the last series of nuclear tests in early 1996. It was hoped that the arrangement would enable French Polynesia to establish an economy that was more reliant upon local resources and would consequently create greater employment, thereby enhancing the Territory's potential for durable independence. In an attempt to increase revenue, the Territorial Government announced the introduction of a value-added tax from October 1997. French Polynesia's steady economic growth (GDP was expected to increase by 3%–5% in 1999, according to the Bank of Hawaii) has partly been as a result of the development of the services sector, notably in hotel construction and other tourism-related services, which has led to significant employment creation. Other sectors of the economy, such as pearl farming, however, have not expanded as rapidly, principally because of regional economic conditions (notably the recession in Japan, one of the largest importers of black pearls).

### Social Welfare

In 1991 there were 34 hospitals in French Polynesia. In 1996 there was a total of 981 hospital beds, and in that year there were 369 physicians working in the Territory. All medical services are provided free of charge for the inhabitants of French Polynesia. An estimated 32,892m. francs CFP was spent on health services in the Territory in 1995.

### Education

Education is compulsory for eight years between six and 14 years of age. It is free of charge for day pupils in government schools. Primary education, lasting six years, is financed by the territorial budget, while secondary and technical education are supported by state funds. In 1996/97 there were 59 kindergartens, with 16,049 children enrolled, and 170 primary schools, with 29,415 pupils. Secondary education is provided by both church and government schools. In 1996/97 there were 28,438 pupils at general secondary schools, and 3,730 secondary pupils were enrolled at vocational institutions in 1992/93. The French University of the Pacific was established in French Polynesia in 1987. In 1995 the Papeete branch had 50 teachers and, in 1998/99, some 1,685 students. Total government expenditure on education in the Territory was 34,063m. francs CFP in 1996.

### Public Holidays

**2000:** 1 January (New Year's Day), 24 April (Easter Monday), 1 May (Labour Day), 5 May (Liberation Day), 1 June (Ascension Day), 12 June (Whit Monday), 14 July (Fall of the Bastille), 11 November (Armistice Day), 25 December (Christmas Day).

**2001:** 1 January (New Year's Day), 16 April (Easter Monday), 1 May (Labour Day), 4 May (Liberation Day), 24 May (Ascension Day), 4 June (Whit Monday), 14 July (Fall of the Bastille), 11 November (Armistice Day), 25 December (Christmas Day).

### Weights and Measures

The metric system is in force.

# Statistical Survey

Source (unless otherwise indicated): Institut Territorial de la Statistique, Immeuble Donald (2e étage), Angle rue Jeanne d'Arc et blvd Pomare, BP 395, Papeete; tel. 543232; fax 427252.

## AREA AND POPULATION

**Area:** Total 4,167 sq km (1,609 sq miles); Land area 3,521 sq km (1,359 sq miles).

**Population:** 188,814 (98,345 males, 90,469 females) at census of 6 September 1988; 219,521 (males 113,934, females 105,587) at census of 3 September 1996; 227,800 (provisional estimate) at 1 January 1999.

*Population by island group* (1996 census): Society Archipelago 189,524 (Windward Islands 162,686, Leeward Islands 276,838); Marquesas Archipelago 8,064; Austral Islands 6,563; Tuamotu-Gambier Islands 15,370.

**Density** (January 1999): 54.7 per sq km.

**Ethnic Groups** (census of 15 October 1983): Polynesian 114,280; 'Demis' 23,625 (Polynesian-European 15,851, Polynesian-Chinese 6,356, Polynesian-Other races 1,418); European 19,320; Chinese 7,424; European-Chinese 494; Others 1,610; Total 166,753. *1988 census* ('000 persons): Polynesians and 'Demis' 156.3; Others 32.5.

**Principal Towns** (population at 1983 census): Papeete (capital) 23,496; Faaa 21,927; Pirae 12,023; Uturva 2,733. *1988 census:* Papeete 23,555. *1996 census:* Papeete 25,553; Faaa 25,888.

**Births, Marriages and Deaths** (1996): Registered live births 4,852 (birth rate 22.1 per 1,000); Registered marriages 1,244 (marriage rate 5.7 per 1,000); Registered deaths 1,029 (death rate 4.7 per 1,000). *1998* (provisional): Birth rate 20.3 per 1,000; death rate 4.9 per 1,000.

**Expectation of Life** (years at birth, 1996): 71.5 (males 69.1; females 74.2).

**Economically Active Population** (persons aged 14 years and over, 1996 census): Agriculture, hunting, forestry and fishing 10,888; Mining and manufacturing 6,424; Electricity, gas and water 459; Construction 4,777; Trade, restaurants and hotels 9,357; Transport, storage and communications 3,788; Financial services 1,482; Real estate 383; Business services 3,710; Private services 9,033; Education, health and social welfare 10,771; Public administration 13,475; Total employed 74,547 (males 46,141, females 28,406); Persons on compulsory military service 1,049 (all males); Unemployed 11,525 (males 6,255, females 5,270); Total labour force 87,121 (males 53,445, females 33,676).

## AGRICULTURE, ETC.

**Principal Crops** (metric tons, 1998): Roots and tubers 16,000*; Vegetables and melons 6,000*; Pineapples 4,000*; Other fruit 3,000*; Coconuts 87,000*; Copra 11,000*; Vanilla 31; Coffee 4.9 (1996). Source: mainly FAO, *Production Yearbook*.

* FAO estimate.

**Livestock** (FAO estimates, year ending September 1998): Cattle 9,000; Horses 2,000; Pigs 42,000; Goats 16,000; Sheep (1989) 2,000. Source: FAO, *Production Yearbook*.

**Livestock Products** (FAO estimates, metric tons, 1998): Cows' milk 1,000; Pig meat 1,000; Other meat 1,000; Hen eggs 2,000. Source: FAO, *Production Yearbook*.

**Fishing** (metric tons, live weight): Total catch 9,020 in 1995; 9,910 in 1996; 11,670 in 1997. Source: FAO, *Yearbook of Fishery Statistics*.

## INDUSTRY

**Production:** Coconut oil 5,366 metric tons (1994); Oilcake 4,477 metric tons (1987); Beer 129,000 hectolitres (1992); Printed cloth 200,000 m (1979); Japanese sandals 600,000 pairs (1979); Electric energy 354.3m. kWh (1998).

## FINANCE

**Currency and Exchange Rates:** 100 centimes = 1 franc des Comptoirs français du Pacifique (franc CFP or Pacific franc). *Sterling, Dollar and Euro Equivalents* (30 September 1999): £1 sterling = 184.13 francs CFP; US $1 = 111.83 francs CFP; €1 = 119.26 francs CFP; 1,000 francs CFP = £5.431 = $8.942 = €8.385. *Average Exchange Rate* (francs CFP per US $): 93.01 in 1996; 106.12 in 1997; 107.26 in 1998. Note: The value of the franc CFP is fixed at 5.5 French centimes (1 French franc = 18.1818 francs CFP).

**Territorial Budget** (estimates, million francs CFP, 1998): *Revenue:* Current 85,671 (Indirect taxation 51,649). *Expenditure:* Current 82,769, Capital 31,374; Total 114,143.

**French State Expenditure** (million francs CFP, 1996): Civil budget 61,706 (Current 56,564, Capital 5,142); Military budget 46,119 (Current 37,160, Capital 8,959); Pensions 10,458; Total (incl. others) 123,774 (Current 109,060, Capital 14,714).

*1998* (million francs CFP): Civil budget 86,500; Military budget 35,000; Total 121,500.

**Money Supply** (million francs CFP at 31 December 1997): Currency in circulation 6,846; Demand deposits 81,141; Total money 87,987. Source: Institut National de la Statistique et des Etudes Economiques.

**Cost of Living** (Consumer Price Index; base: 1990 = 100): 108.0 in 1996; 109.4 in 1997; 110.9 in 1998. Source: Institut National de la Statistique et des Etudes Economiques.

**Gross Domestic Product** (million francs CFP at current prices): 372,168 in 1996; 385,644 in 1997; 422,212 in 1998.

**Expenditure on the Gross Domestic Product** (million francs CFP at current prices, 1993): Government final consumption expenditure 126,127; Private final consumption expenditure 202,563; Increase in stocks −536; Gross fixed capital formation 53,494; *Total domestic expenditure* 381,648; Exports of goods and services 34,523; *Less* Imports of goods and services 86,905; *GDP in purchasers' values* 329,266. Source: UN, *National Accounts Statistics*.

**Gross Domestic Product by Economic Activity** (million francs CFP at current prices, 1993): Agriculture, forestry and fishing 12,872; Manufacturing 22,034*; Electricity, gas and water 6,917*; Construction 18,735; Service industries 173,074; Government and other services 95,634; *GDP in purchasers' values* 329,266. *Manufacturing of energy-generating products is included in electricity, gas and water. Source: UN, *National Accounts Statistics*.

### EXTERNAL TRADE

**Principal Commodities** (million francs CFP, 1997): *Imports c.i.f.:* Meat and edible offal 4,886; Beverages, spirits and vinegar 1,903; Tobacco and manufactured tobacco substitutes 394; Pharmaceutical products 3,077; Articles of iron or steel 2,594; Machinery and mechanical appliances 9,591; Electrical machinery, sound and image recorders 6,605; Total (incl. others) 99,339. *Exports f.o.b.:* Vanilla 111.1; Mother of pearl 323.9; Coconut oil 391.9; Cultured pearls 14,658.0; Total (incl. others) 23,804. Source: UN, *Statistical Yearbook for Asia and the Pacific*.

(1998) *Imports c.i.f.:* 116,355. *Exports f.o.b.:* Cultured pearls 14,587; Total (incl. others) 26,462.

**Principal Trading Partners** (million francs CFP, 1997): *Imports:* Australia 7,826; France (metropolitan) 37,646; Germany 2,807; Italy 3,182; Japan 4,189; New Zealand 7,283; USA 16,893; Total (incl. others) 99,339. *Exports:* France (metropolitan) 7,615; Japan 8,816; New Caledonia 402; USA 3,734; Total (incl. others) 23,804.

Source: Institut National de la Statistique et des Etudes Economiques.

### TRANSPORT

**Road Traffic** (1987): Total vehicles registered 54,979; (1996 census): Private cars 47,300.

**Shipping** (1990): *International traffic:* Passengers carried 47,616; Freight handled 642,314 metric tons. *Domestic traffic:* Passengers carried 596,185; Freight handled 261,593 metric tons. (1998): Goods unloaded 723,740 metric tons; Goods loaded 22,997 metric tons.

**Civil Aviation** (1998): *International traffic:* Passengers carried (incl. those in transit) 528,675; Freight handled 7,024 metric tons. *Domestic traffic:* Passengers carried 691,232; Freight handled 2,518 metric tons.

### TOURISM

**Visitors** (excluding cruise passengers and excursionists): 163,774 in 1996; 180,440 in 1997; 188,933 in 1998.

### COMMUNICATIONS MEDIA

**Radio Receivers** (1996): 125,000 in use*.

**Television Receivers** (1996): 39,000 in use*.

**Telephones** (1996): 49,868 main lines in use.

**Telefax Stations** (1996): 2,280 in use.

**Daily Newspapers** (1995): 4; estimated circulation 24,000*.

* Source: UNESCO, *Statistical Yearbook*.

### EDUCATION

**Pre-primary** (1996/97): 59 schools; 408 teachers; 16,049 pupils.

**Primary** (1996/97): 170 schools; 2,811 teachers; 29,415 pupils.

**General Secondary** (1996/97): 1,897 teachers; 28,438 pupils.

**Vocational** (1992): 316 teachers; 3,730 students.

**Tertiary** (1993): 34 teachers; 892 students.

Source: partly UNESCO, *Statistical Yearbook*.

# Directory

## The Constitution

The constitutional system in French Polynesia is established under the aegis of the Constitution of the Fifth French Republic and specific laws of 1977, 1984 and 1990. The French Polynesia Statute 1984, the so-called 'internal autonomy statute', underwent amendment in a law of July 1990. A further extension of the Territory's powers under the statute was approved by the French National Assembly in December 1995. A constitutional amendment granting French Polynesia a greater degree of autonomy was presented to a joint session of the French Senate and National Assembly for final ratification in January 2000 (see Recent History). By early March, however, no decision had been taken on the matter.

French Polynesia is declared to be an autonomous Territory of the French Republic, of which it remains an integral part. The High Commissioner, appointed by the French Government, exercises the prerogatives of the State in matters relating to defence, foreign relations, the maintenance of law and order, communications and citizenship. The head of the local executive and the person who represents the Territory is the President of the Territorial Government, who is elected by the Territorial Assembly from among its own number. The Territorial President appoints and dismisses the Council of Ministers and has competence in international relations as they affect French Polynesia and its exclusive economic zone, and is in control of foreign investments and immigration. The Territorial Assembly, which has financial autonomy in budgetary affairs and legislative authority within the Territory, is elected for a term of up to five years on the basis of universal adult suffrage. There are 41 members: 22 elected by the people of the Windward Islands (Iles du Vent—Society Islands), eight by the Leeward Islands (Iles Sous le Vent—Society Islands), five by the Tuamotu Archipelago and the Gambier Islands and three each by the Austral Islands and by the Marquesas Archipelago. The Assembly elects a Permanent Commission of between seven and nine of its members, and itself meets for two ordinary sessions each year and upon the demand of the majority party, the Territorial President or the High Commissioner. Local government is conducted by the municipalities; there are five regional, consultative Archipelago Councils, comprised of all those elected to the Territorial Assembly and the municipalities by that region (the Councils represent the same areas as the five constituencies for the Territorial Assembly). There is an Economic, Social and Cultural Council (composed of representatives of professional groups, trade unions and other organizations and agencies which participate in the economic, social and cultural activities of the Territory), a Territorial Audit Office and a judicial system which includes a Court of the First Instance, a Court of Appeal and an Administrative Court. The Territory, as a part of the French Republic, also elects two deputies to the National Assembly and one member of the Senate, and has representation in the European Parliament.

## The Government

(February 2000)

**High Commissioner:** Jean Aribaud (appointed November 1997).

**Secretary-General:** Anne Boquet.

### COUNCIL OF MINISTERS

**President:** Gaston Flosse.

**Vice-President and Minister for the Sea, Outer Island Development, Ports and Post and Telecommunications:** Edouard Fritch.

**Minister for the Economy, Economic Planning, Business and Energy:** Georges Puchon.

**Minister for Health and Research:** Patrick Howell.

**Minister for Housing and Public Lands Management and Allocation:** Jean-Christophe Bouissou.

**Minister for Social Welfare and the Family:** Béatrice Vernaudon.

**Minister for Transport:** Temauri Foster.

**Minister for Public Works:** Jonas Tahuaitu.

**Minister for Land, Town Planning, Urban Affairs, Natural Disasters and Revenue:** Gaston Tong Sang.

**Minister for Agriculture and Livestock:** Patrick Bordet.

**Minister for Finance (responsible for Administrative Reforms and the Implementation of the Pacte de Progrès):** Patrick Peaucellier.

**Minister for Marine Resources and the Craft Industry:** Llewellyn Tematahotoa.

**Minister for Culture, Higher Education and Community Life:** LOUISE PELTZER.

**Minister for Education and Technical Training:** NICOLAS SANQUER.

**Minister for Employment and Professional Training (responsible for Social Dialogue and Women's Affairs):** LUCETTE TAERO.

**Minister for the Environment (responsible for Relations with the Territorial Assembly and the Economic, Social and Cultural Council):** LUCIE LUCAS.

**Minister for Youth, Youth Opportunities, Sports and Local Government:** REYNALD TEMARII.

### GOVERNMENT OFFICES

**Office of the High Commissioner of the Republic:** Bureau du Haut Commissaire, BP 115-98713, Papeete; tel. 468686; fax 468689; e-mail courrier@haut-commissariat.pf.

**Office of the President of the Territorial Government:** BP 2551, 98713 Papeete; tel. 543450; fax 419781; e-mail presid@mail.pf.

**Territorial Government of French Polynesia:** BP 2551, Papeete; tel. 543450; fax 419781; e-mail presid@mail.pf; all ministries; Delegation in Paris: 28 blvd Saint-Germain, 75005 Paris, France; tel. 1-55-42-65-10; fax 1-55-42-64-09.

**Economic, Social and Cultural Council:** BP 1657, Papeete; tel. 416500; fax 419242; Representative to National Economic and Social Council CHRISTIAN VERNAUDON.

## Legislature

### ASSEMBLÉE TERRITORIALE

**President:** JUSTIN ARAPARI.

**Territorial Assembly:** Assemblée Territoriale, BP 28, Papeete; tel. 416100; fax 416188.

**Election, 13 May 1996**

| Party | Seats |
|---|---|
| Tahoeraa Huiraatira/RPR | 22 |
| Tavini Huiraatira | 10 |
| Ai'a Api | 5 |
| Fe'tia Api | 1 |
| Te Avei'a Mau | 1 |
| Te Henua Enata Kotoa | 1 |
| Alliance 2000 | 1 |
| **Total** | 41 |

Note: Following by-elections in May 1998, Tahoeraa Huiraatira/RPR increased its representation by one seat.

### PARLEMENT

**Deputies to the French National Assembly:** EMILE VERNAUDON (Ai'a Api/RPR), MICHEL BUILLARD (Tahoeraa Huiraatira/RPR).

**Representative to the French Senate:** GASTON FLOSSE (Tahoeraa Huiraatira/RPR).

## Political Organizations

**Ai'a Api** (New Land): BP 11055, Mahina, Tahiti; tel. 481135; f. 1982 after split in Te E'a Api; Leader EMILE VERNAUDON.

**Alliance 2000:** c/o Assemblée Territoriale, BP 28, Papeete; pro-independence grouping.

**Fe'tia Api (New Star):** c/o Assemblée Territoriale, BP 28, Papeete; Leader BORIS LÉONTIEFF.

**Haere i Mua:** Leader ALEXANDRE LÉONTIEFF.

**Heiura-Les Verts:** Papeete.

**Ia Mana Te Nunaa:** rue du Commandant Destrémau, BP 1223, Papeete; tel. 426699; f. 1976; advocates 'socialist independence'; Sec.-Gen. JACQUES DROLLET.

**Polynesian Union Party:** Papeete; Leader JEAN JUVENTIN.

**Pupu Here Ai'a Te Nunaa Ia Ora:** BP 3195, Papeete; tel. 420766; f. 1965; advocates autonomy; 8,000 mems.

**Te Tiaraama:** Papeete; f. 1987 by split from the RPR; Leader ALEXANDRE LÉONTIEFF.

**Pupu Taina/Rassemblement des Libéraux:** rue Cook, BP 169, Papeete; tel. 429880; f. 1976; seeks to retain close links with France; associated with the French Union pour la Démocratie Française (UDF); Leader MICHEL LAW.

**Taatiraa Polynesia:** BP 2916, Papeete; tel. 437494; fax 422546; f. 1977; Federal Pres. ARTHUR CHUNG; Exec. Pres. ROBERT TANSEAU.

**Tahoeraa Huiraatira/Rassemblement pour la République—RPR:** rue du Commandant Destrémeau, BP 471, Papeete; tel. 429898; fax 437758; f. 1958; supports links with France, with internal autonomy; Pres. GASTON FLOSSE; Hon. Pres. JACQUES TEUIRA.

**Tavini Huiraatira/Front de Libération de la Polynésie (FLP):** independence movement; anti-nuclear; Leader OSCAR TEMARU.

**Te Avei'a Mau** (True Path): c/o Assemblée Territoriale, BP 28, Papeete; Leader TINOMANA EBB.

**Te e'a No Maohi Nui:** Leader JEAN-MARIUS RAAPOTO.

**Te Henua Enata Kotoa:** c/o Assemblée Territoriale, BP 28, Papeete; Leader LUCIEN KIMITETE.

## Judicial System

**Court of Appeal:** Cour d'Appel de Papeete, BP 101, Papeete; tel. 415500; fax 424416; Pres. PATRICK MICHAUX; Attorney-General JACK GAUTHIER.

**Court of the First Instance:** Tribunal de Première Instance de Papeete, BP 101, Papeete; tel. 415500; fax 454012; Pres. JEAN-LOUIS THIOLET; Procurator MICHEL MAROTTE; Clerk of the Court CLAUDE LY.

**Court of Administrative Law:** Tribunal Administratif, BP 4522, Papeete; tel. 509025; fax 451724 Pres. ALFRED POUPET; Cllrs RAOUL AUREILLE, PATRICK DEMARQUET, MARIE-CHRISTINE LUBRANO.

## Religion

About 54% of the population are Protestants and 30% are Roman Catholics.

### CHRISTIANITY

#### Protestant Church

**L'Eglise évangélique de Polynésie française (Etaretia Evaneria no Porinetia Farani):** BP 113, Papeete; tel. 460600; fax 419357; e-mail eepf@mail.pf; f. 1884; autonomous since 1963; c. 95,000 mems; Pres. of Council Rev. JACQUES TERAI IHORAI; Sec.-Gen. RALPH TEINAORE.

#### The Roman Catholic Church

French Polynesia comprises the archdiocese of Papeete and the suffragan diocese of Taiohae o Tefenuaenata (based in Nuku Hiva, Marquesas Is). At 31 December 1998 there were an estimated 81,600 adherents in the Territory, representing about 37% of the total population. The Archbishop and the Bishop participate in the Episcopal Conference of the Pacific, based in Fiji.

**Archbishop of Papeete:** Most Rev. HUBERT COPPENRATH, Archevêché, BP 94, Vallée de la Mission, 98713 Papeete; tel. 420251; fax 424032; e-mail catholic@mail.pf.

#### Other Churches

There are small Sanito, Church of Jesus Christ of Latter-day Saints (Mormon), and Seventh-day Adventist missions.

## The Press

**La Dépêche de Tahiti:** Société Océanienne de Communication, BP 50, Papeete; tel. 464343; fax 464350; e-mail redaction@france-antilles.pf; internet www.ladepechedetahiti.com; f. 1964; daily; French; Editor-in-Chief DANIEL PARDON; Dir-Gen. PASCAL HEEMS; circ. 15,000.

**L'Echo de Tahiti-Nui:** Papeete; tel. 439476; fax 439430; f. 1993; weekly; French; satirical, economic, social and cultural affairs; Editor JÉRÔME JANNOT; Dir BERNARD MATHIS.

**Les Nouvelles de Tahiti:** place de la Cathédrale, BP 629, Papeete; tel. 508100; fax 508109; f. 1956; daily; French; Editor MURIEL PONTAROLLO; Dir-Gen. PASCAL HEEMS; Publr PHILIPPE HERSANT; circ. 18,500.

**Le Semeur Tahitien:** BP 94, 98713 Papeete; tel. 420251; e-mail catholic@mail.pf; f. 1909; bi-monthly; publ. by the Roman Catholic Church.

**Tahiti Beach Press:** BP 887, Papeete; tel. 426850; f. 1980; weekly; English; Publr G. WARTI; circ. 3,000.

**Tahiti Matin:** place du Marché, BP 392, Papeete; tel. 481048; fax 481220; daily; Dir PIERRE MARCHESINI.

**Tahiti Pacifique Magazine:** BP 368, Maharepa, Moorea; tel. and fax 563007; e-mail tahitipm@mail.pf; monthly; Editor ALEX DU PREL.

**Tahiti Rama:** Papeete; weekly.

**Tahiti Today:** BP 887, 98713 Papeete; tel. 426850; fax 423356; f. 1996; quarterly; Publr G. WARTI; circ. 3,000.

**La Tribune Polynésienne:** place du Marché, BP 392, Papeete; tel. 481048; fax 481220; weekly; Dir LOUIS BRESSON.

**Ve'a Katorika:** BP 94, 98713 Papeete; f. 1909; monthly; publ. by the Roman Catholic Church.

**Ve'a Porotetani:** BP 113, Papeete; tel. 460623; fax 419357; e-mail eepf@mail.pf; f. 1921; monthly; French and Tahitian; publ. by the Evangelical Church; Editor Céline Hoiore; Dir Ihorai Jacques; circ. 5,000.

### Foreign Bureaux

**Agence France-Presse (AFP):** BP 629, Papeete; tel. 508100; fax 508109; e-mail international@france-antilles.pf; Correspondent Christian Bretault.

**Associated Press (AP)** (USA): BP 912, Papeete; tel. 437562; Correspondent Al Prince.

**Reuters** (UK): BP 50, Papeete; tel. 464340; fax 464350; Correspondent Daniel Pardon.

## Publishers

**Haere Po No Tahiti:** BP 1958, Papeete; fax 582333; f. 1981; travel, history, botany, linguistics and local interest.

**Scoop/Au Vent des Îles:** BP 5670, 98716 Pirae; tel. 435456; fax 426174; e-mail scooptah@mail.pf; f. 1992; Gen. Man. Robert Christian.

**Simone Sanchez:** BP 13973, Punaauia; tel. 533260; f. 1993; fiction, history, regional interests.

### Government Printer

**Imprimerie Officielle:** BP 117, 98713 Papeete; tel. 425067; fax 425261; f. 1843; printers, publrs; Dir Claudino Laurent.

## Broadcasting and Communications

### TELECOMMUNICATIONS

**Office des Postes et Télécommunications:** 8 rue de la Reine Pomare IV, Papeete; tel. 414242; fax 436767; Dir-Gen. Geffry Salmon.

**France Cables et Radio (FCR):** Télécommunications extérieures de la Polynésie française, BP 99, Papeete; tel. 415400; fax 437553; e-mail fcr@mail.pf.

### BROADCASTING

#### Radio

**Radio-Télé-Tahiti:** 410 rue Dumont d'Urville, BP 125, Papeete; tel. 430551; fax 413155; e-mail rfopolyfr@mail.pf; internet www.tahiti-explorer.com/rfo.html; f. 1951 as Radio-Tahiti; television service began 1965; operated by Société Nationale de Radio-Télévision Française d'Outre-Mer (RFO), Paris; daily programmes in French and Tahitian; Dir Claude Ruben; Dir (Programmes) Jean-Raymond Bodin.

#### Private Stations

**Kiss FM:** BP 4552, Papeete.

**Radio Maohi:** Maison des Jeunes, Pirae.

**Radio One:** Fare Ute, BP 3601, Papeete.

**Radio Papeete:** Ex Magasin Arupa, Papeete.

**Radio Soleil:** Quartier du Commerce, Papeete.

**Radio Tahiti Api:** Pirae.

**Radio Tahiti-FM:** Mahina.

**Radio Te Reo O Tefana:** BP 13069, Punaauia; privately-owned; pro-independence; operates service in Society Islands and due to begin broadcasting in Tuamotu Islands in 1997.

**Radio Tiare:** Fare Ute, Papeete.

#### Television

**Radio-Télé-Tahiti:** (see Radio).

**Canal Plus Polynésie:** Colline de Putiaoro, BP 20051, Papeete; tel. 540754; fax 540755; e-mail classagne@cplus.pf; privately-owned; Dir Christophe Lassagne.

In January 1994 a private company, Téléfenua, received authorization to transmit television programmes in seven communes.

## Finance

(cap. = capital; res = reserves; dep. = deposits; m. = million; brs = branches; amounts in CFP francs)

### BANKING

#### Commercial Banks

**Banque de Polynésie SA:** 355 blvd Pomare, BP 530, Papeete; tel. 466666; fax 466664; f. 1973; 80% owned by Société Générale (France); cap. 1,000m., res 1,506m., dep. 38,220m. (Dec. 1998); Chair. Alain Bataille; Gen. Man. Jean-Maurice Beaux; 14 brs.

**Banque de Tahiti SA:** rue François Cardella, BP 1602, Papeete; tel. 425389; fax 423376; e-mail dir.gene@bank-tahiti.pf; f. 1969; owned by Bank of Hawaii (USA—94%) and Crédit Lyonnais (France—3%); merged with Banque Paribas de Polynésie, Aug. 1998; cap. 1,336m., res 2,939m., dep. 66,923m. (Dec. 1997); Pres. J. C. Irrmann; Exec. Vice-Pres. Michel Dupieux; 16 brs.

**Banque SOCREDO—Société pour le Crédit et le Développement en Océanie:** 115 rue Dumont d'Urville, BP 130, 98713 Papeete; tel. 415123; fax 433661; f. 1959; public body; affiliated to Banque Nationale de Paris (France); cap. 7,000m. (Dec. 1993), dep. 76,610m. (Dec. 1995); Pres. Jean Vernaudon; Dir Eric Pommier; 24 brs.

**Westpac Banking Corporation** (Australia): 2 place Notre-Dame, BP 120, Papeete; tel. 467979; fax 431333; acquired operations of Banque Indosuez in French Polynesia in 1990; sale of the bank to Société Générale (France) was announced in late 1998; Gen. Man. Patrick Picard.

## Trade and Industry

### DEVELOPMENT ORGANIZATIONS

**Agence pour l'Emploi et la Formation Professionnelle:** BP 540, Papeete; tel. 426375; fax 426281.

**Conseil Economique, Social et Culturel de Polynésie Française:** ave Bruat, BP 1657, Papeete; tel. 416500; fax 419242; Dir Willy Richmond.

**Conseil Français de Développement (CFD):** BP 578, Papeete; tel. 430486; fax 434645; public body; development finance institute.

**Service de l'Artisanat Traditionnel:** BP 4451, Papeete; tel. 423225; fax 436478; e-mail artisanat@mail.pf.

**Service du Développement de l'Industrie et des Métiers:** BP 20728, 98713 Papeete; tel. 533096; fax 412645; e-mail self@economie.gov.pf; industry and small business development administration.

**Société pour le Développement de l'Agriculture et de la Pêche:** BP 1247, Papeete; tel. 836798; fax 856886; agriculture and marine industries.

**SODEP—Société pour le Développement et l'Expansion du Pacifique:** BP 4441, Papeete; tel. 429449; f. 1961 by consortium of banks and private interests; regional development and finance co.

### CHAMBERS OF COMMERCE

**Chambre de Commerce, d'Industrie, des Services et des Métiers de Polynésie Française:** 41 rue du Docteur Cassiau, BP 118, Papeete; tel. 540700; fax 540701; e-mail cci.tahiti@mail.pf; f. 1880; 36 mems; Pres. Jules Changues.

**Chambre d'Agriculture et d'Elevage (CAEP):** route de l'Hippodrome, BP 5383, Papeete; tel. 425393; f. 1886; 10 mems; Pres. Sylvain Millaud.

**Jeune Chambre Economique de Tahiti:** BP 2576, Papeete; tel. and fax 454542; internet www.jce.pf; Pres. Cathy Gourbault.

### EMPLOYERS' ORGANIZATIONS

**Chambre Syndicale des Entrepreneurs du Bâtiment et des Travaux Publics:** BP 2218, Papeete; tel. 438898; fax 423237; Pres. Georges Tramini.

**Conseil des Employeurs:** Immeuble FARNHAM, rue E. Ahnne, BP 972, Papeete; tel. 438898; fax 423237; f. 1983; Pres. Jules Changues; Sec.-Gen. Astrid Pasquier.

**Fédération Générale de Commerce (FGC):** rue Albert Leboucher, BP 1607, 98713 Papeete; tel. 429908; fax 422359; Pres. Gilles Yau.

**Fédération Polynésienne de l'Agriculture et de l'Elevage:** Papara, Tahiti; Pres. Michel Lehartel.

**Syndicat des Importateurs et des Négociants:** BP 1607, Papeete.

**Union Interprofessionnelle du Tourisme de la Polynésie Française:** BP 4560, Papeete; tel. 439114; f. 1973; 1,200 mems; Pres. Paul Maetz; Sec.-Gen. Jean Corteel.

**Union Patronale:** BP 317, Papeete; tel. 438898; fax 423237; f. 1948; 63 mems; Pres. Didier Chomer.

### UTILITES

#### Electricity

**Electricité de Tahiti:** route de Puurai, BP 8021, Faaa-Puurai; tel. 867777.

#### Water

**Société Polynésienne des Eaux et Assainissements:** Papeete, Tahiti.

**Syndicat Central de l'Hydraulique:** Tahiti.

### TRADE UNIONS

**A Tia I Mua:** Immeuble la Ora, BP 4523, Papeete; tel. 436038; fax 450245; affiliated to CFDT (France); Gen. Sec. BRUNO SANDRAS.

**Fédération des Syndicats de la Polynésie Française:** BP 1136, Papeete; Pres. MARCEL AHINI.

**Syndicat Territorial des Instituteurs et Institutrices de Polynésie:** BP 3007, Papeete; Sec.-Gen. WILLY URIMA.

**Union des Syndicats Affiliés des Travailleurs de Polynésie/Force Ouvrière-USATP/FO:** BP 1201, Papeete; tel. 426049; fax 450635; Pres. COCO TERAIEFA CHANG; Sec.-Gen. PIERRE FRÉBAULT.

**Union des Syndicats de l'Aéronautique:** Papeete; Pres. JOSEPH CONROY.

**Union des Travailleurs de Tahiti et des Iles:** rue Albert Leboucher, Papeete; tel. 437369; Pres. JOHN TEFATUA-VAIHO.

## Transport

### ROADS

French Polynesia has 792 km of roads, of which about one-third are bitumen-surfaced and two-thirds stone-surfaced.

### SHIPPING

The principal port is Papeete, on Tahiti.

**Port Authority:** Port Autonome de Papeete, Motu Uta, BP 9164, 98715 Papeete; tel. 505454; fax 421950; e-mail portppt@mail.pf; internet www.portoftahiti.com; Harbour Master Commdt CLAUDE VIGOR; Port Man. BÉATRICE CHANSIN.

**Agence Maritime Internationale de Tahiti:** BP 274, Papeete; tel. 428972; fax 432184; e-mail amitahiti@mail.pf; services to New Zealand, USA, Australia, American Samoa, Fiji, Europe and Asia.

**CGM Tour du Monde SA:** 80 rue du Général de Gaulle, BP 96, Papeete; tel. 420890; fax 436806; shipowners and agents; freight services between Europe and many international ports; Dir HENRI C. FERRAND.

**Compagnie de Développement Maritime des Tuamotu (CODEMAT):** POB 1291, Papeete.

**Compagnie Française Maritime de Tahiti:** 2 rue de Commerce, POB 368, Papeete; tel. 426393; fax 420617; Man. M. GARBUTT.

**Compagnie Maritime des Iles Sous le Vent:** BP 9012, Papeete.

**Compagnie Polynésienne de Transport Maritime:** BP 220, Papeete; tel. 426240; fax 434889; Chair. SHAN NIM ENN; Man. Dir JEAN WONG.

**Leprado Valere SARL:** POB 3917, Papeete; tel. 450030; fax 421049.

**Richmond Frères SARL:** POB 1816, Papeete.

**Société de Navigation des Australes:** BP 1890; Papeete; tel. 429367; fax 420609.

**Société de Transport Insulaire Maritime (STIM):** BP 635, Papeete; tel. 452324.

**Société de Transport Maritime de Tuamotu:** BP 11366, Mahina; tel. 422358; fax 430373.

### CIVIL AVIATION

There is one international airport, Faaa airport, 6 km from Papeete, on Tahiti, and there are about 40 smaller airstrips. International services are operated by Air France, Air New Zealand, LAN-Chile, Air Outre Mer, Air Calédonie International, Corsair and Hawaiian Airlines (USA).

**Air Moorea:** BP 6019, Faaa; tel. 864100; fax 864269; f. 1968; operates internal services between Tahiti and Moorea Island and charter flights throughout the Territory; Pres. MARCEL GALENON; Dir-Gen. FRANÇOIS MARTIN.

**Air Tahiti:** blvd Pomare, BP 314, 98713 Papeete; tel. 864000; fax 864069; e-mail rtahitim@mail.pf; f. 1953, Air Polynésie 1970–87; operates domestic services to 39 islands; Chair. CHRISTIAN VERNAUDON; Gen. Man. MARCEL GALENON.

**Air Tahiti Nui:** BP 1673, Papeete; tel. 160202; fax 460290; e-mail fly@airtahitinui.pf; internet www.tahiti-tourisme.com/webfrtt/pub/pub-ATN.html; f. 1996; commenced operations 1998; scheduled services to Los Angeles and Tokyo; Chair. NELSON LEVY; Pres. and CEO JACQUES BANKIR.

## Tourism

Tourism is an important and developed industry in French Polynesia, particularly on Tahiti, and 188,933 people visited the Territory in 1998. In that year some 29.5% of arrivals were from France, 26.5% from the USA and 7.1% from Japan. There were a total of 3,021 hotel rooms in Tahiti in 1998, and in that year the tourism industry earned an estimated US $390m..

**GIE Tahiti Tourisme:** Immeuble Paofai, bâtiment D, blvd Pomare, BP 65, 98713 Papeete; tel. 505700; fax 436619; e-mail tahiti-tourisme@mail.pf; internet www.tahiti-tourisme.com; f. 1966 as autonomous public body, transformed into private corpn in 1993; tourist promotion; CEO BRIGITTE VANIZETTE.

**Service du Tourisme:** Fare Manihini, blvd Pomare, BP 4527, Papeete; tel. 505700; fax 481275; govt dept; manages Special Fund for Tourist Development; Dir GÉRARD VANIZETTE.

**Syndicat d'Initiative de la Polynésie Française:** BP 326, Papeete; Pres. PIU BAMBRIDGE.

# FRENCH SOUTHERN AND ANTARCTIC TERRITORIES

The French Southern and Antarctic Territories (Terres australes et antarctiques françaises) form an Overseas Territory but are administered under a special statute. The territory comprises Adélie Land, a narrow segment of the mainland of Antarctica together with a number of offshore islets, and three groups of sub-Antarctic islands (the Kerguelen and Crozet Archipelagos and St Paul and Amsterdam Islands) in the southern Indian Ocean.

Under the terms of legislation approved by the French Government on 6 August 1955, the French Southern and Antarctic Territories were placed under the authority of a chief administrator, who was responsible to the Secretary of State for Overseas Departments and Territories. The Chief Administrator is assisted by a consultative council, which meets at least twice annually. The Consultative Council is composed of seven members who are appointed for five years by the Ministers of Defence and of Overseas Departments and Territories (from among members of the Office of Scientific Research and from those who have participated in scientific missions in the sub-Antarctic islands and Adélie Land) and by the Minister of Research and Technology and the Minister of Equipment, Housing, Transport and the Sea.

In 1987 certain categories of vessels were allowed to register under the flag of the Kerguelen Archipelago, provided that 25% of their crew (including the captain and at least two officers) were French. These specifications were amended to 35% of the crew and at least four officers in April 1990. At 1 January 2000 there were 166 registered vessels.

In January 1992 the French Government created a 'public interest group', the Institut Français pour la Recherche et la Technologie Polaires (IFRTP), to assume responsibility for the organization of scientific and research programmes in the French Southern and Antarctic Territories.

France is a signatory to the Antarctic Treaty (see p. 433).

## Statistical Survey

**Area** (sq km): Kerguelen Archipelago 7,215, Crozet Archipelago 515, Amsterdam Island 58, St Paul Island 8, Adélie Land (Antarctica) 432,000.

**Population** (the population, comprising members of scientific missions, fluctuates according to season, being higher in the summer; the figures given are approximate): Kerguelen Archipelago, Port-aux-Français 56; Amsterdam Island at Martin de Viviès 20; Adélie Land at Base Dumont-d'Urville 27; the Crozet Archipelago at Alfred Faure (on Ile de la Possession) 17; St Paul Island is uninhabited. Total population (January 1999): 120.

**Fishing** (catch quotas in metric tons): Crayfish (spiny lobsters) in Amsterdam and St Paul: 340 (1999/2000); fishing by French and foreign fleets in the Kerguelen Archipelago: 6,500 (1999/2000).

**Currency:** French currency is used (see French Guiana).

**Budget:** Projected at 125.0m. francs in 1999, of which official subventions comprised 47.5m. francs.

**External Trade:** Exports consist mainly of crayfish and other fish to France and Réunion. The Territories also derive revenue from the sale of postage stamps and other philatelic items.

foremost producers and exporters of manganese (which contributed an estimated 5.0% of export earnings in 1997). Significant deposits of uranium have been exploited since the late 1950s at Mounana; however, with all reserves having been exhausted, operations ceased in early 1999. Major reserves of iron ore remain undeveloped, owing to the lack of appropriate transport facilities. Small amounts of gold are extracted, and the existence of many mineral deposits, including talc, barytes, phosphates, rare earths, titanium and cadmium, has also been confirmed. In 1999 it was expected that mining of substantial niobium (columbium) reserves at Mabounie would commence in the near future.

The manufacturing sector contributed an estimated 5.8% of GDP in 1997. The principal activities are the refining of petroleum and the processing of other minerals, the preparation of timber and other agro-industrial processes. The chemicals industry is also significant. Manufacturing GDP increased at an average annual rate of 6.8% in 1985–95. The IMF estimated growth in manufacturing GDP at 8.5% in 1996.

Electrical energy is derived principally from hydroelectric installations. Imports of fuel and energy comprised an estimated 21.3% of the total value of imports in 1995.

Services engaged 18.8% of the economically active population in 1991 and provided an estimated 35.4% of GDP in 1997. The GDP of the services sector increased at an average annual rate of 3.3% in 1990–97. Growth was estimated at 3.7% in 1996.

In 1995 Gabon recorded a visible trade surplus of US $1,744.4m., and there was a surplus of $99.8m. on the current account of the balance of payments. In 1996 the principal source of imports (42.8%) was France; other major sources were the USA and Japan. The principal market for exports in that year was the USA (64.1%); France was also an important purchaser. The principal exports in 1997 were petroleum and petroleum products, timber and manganese. The principal imports in 1996 were machinery and transport equipment, basic manufactures, food products and chemicals and related products.

In 1996 there was an estimated budgetary deficit of 46,500m. francs CFA (equivalent to 1.6% of GDP). Gabon's external debt totalled US $4,285m. at the end of 1997, of which $3,671m. was long-term public debt. In that year the cost of debt-servicing was equivalent to 13.1% of the value of exports of goods and services. In 1990–97 the average annual rate of inflation was 3.3%. The annual rate of inflation increased to 36.1% in 1994, following the 50% devaluation of the CFA franc in January of that year, but had declined to 4.0% by 1997. The Government estimated about 20% of the labour force to be unemployed in 1996.

Gabon is a member of the Central African organs of the Franc Zone (see p. 200), and of the Communauté économique des états de l'Afrique centrale (CEEAC, see p. 290). In 1996 Gabon, which had been a member of OPEC (see p. 252) since 1973, withdrew from the organization.

Gabon's potential for economic growth is based upon its considerable mineral and forestry resources. In the mid-1980s, however, the country's vulnerability to fluctuations in international prices and demand for its principal commodities precipitated a decline in export and budget revenue. By the early 1990s the country's economic and financial situation had deteriorated, owing to a decline in the international price for petroleum and the accumulation of debt arrears. Following the devaluation of the CFA franc by 50% in relation to the French franc in January 1994, a programme for economic recovery, which included the further restructuring of public-sector enterprises, was agreed with the IMF in March. In November 1995 the IMF approved a further three-year credit under an extended facility, in support of the Government's programme for 1995–98, which aimed to stimulate employment through economic diversification, to liberalize the regulatory framework and further to develop the non-petroleum sector; subsequent reviews indicated that satisfactory progress had been made, although the level of unemployment remained high. In 1996 the Government adopted measures to begin the transfer of state-owned enterprises to the private sector. In 1997 the divestiture of Gabon's electricity and water services was the first major privatization project to be implemented. Although Gabon's income per caput is among the highest in sub-Saharan Africa, the country remains heavily indebted. Falling petroleum prices and the negative impact of the Asian economic crisis on timber exports forced the Government to revise budget estimates downwards in April 1999. (The 1998 budget was subjected to similar measures.) Further strain was placed on the economy by the suspension of loans from the Agence française de développement, and from March 1999 Gabon had no IMF programme.

### Social Welfare

There is a national Fund for State Insurance, and a guaranteed minimum wage. In January 1985 Gabon had 28 hospitals, 87 medical centres and 312 dispensaries, with a total of 5,156 hospital beds. In the early 1990s there were 19 physicians per 100,000 people and 56 nurses per 100,000 people working in the country. Maternal and infant health is a major priority. The 1988 budget allocated 18,000m. francs CFA (10% of total administrative spending) to health expenditure.

### Education

Education is officially compulsory for 10 years between six and 16 years of age: in 1993 89% of children in the relevant age-group attended primary and secondary schools (90% of boys; 88% of girls). Primary and secondary education is provided by state and mission schools. Primary education begins at the age of six and lasts for six years. Secondary education, beginning at 12 years of age, lasts for up to seven years, comprising a first cycle of four years and a second of three years. The Université Omar Bongo, at Libreville, had 2,741 students in 1986. The Université des Sciences et des Techniques de Masuku was opened in 1986, with an enrolment of 550 students. In 1995, according to estimates by UNESCO, adult illiteracy averaged 36.8% (males 26.3%; females 46.7%). The 1994 budget allocated 78,850m. francs CFA (19% of total administrative spending) to expenditure on education.

### Public Holidays

**2000:** 1 January (New Year's Day), 8 January*† (Id al-Fitr, end of Ramadan), 12 March (Anniversary of Renovation, foundation of the Parti démocratique gabonais), 16 March* (Id al-Adha, feast of the Sacrifice), 24 April (Easter Monday), 1 May (Labour Day), 12 June (Whit Monday), 15 June* (Mouloud, birth of Muhammad), 17 August (Anniversary of Independence), 1 November (All Saints' Day), 25 December (Christmas), 28 December*† (Id al-Fitr, end of Ramadan).

**2001:** 1 January (New Year's Day), 12 March (Anniversary of Renovation, foundation of the Parti démocratique gabonais), 16 March* (Id al-Adha, feast of the Sacrifice), 16 April (Easter Monday), 1 May (Labour Day), 4 June (Whit Monday and Mouloud, birth of Muhammad), 17 August (Anniversary of Independence), 1 November (All Saints' Day), 17 December* (Id al-Fitr, end of Ramadan), 25 December (Christmas).

* These holidays are dependent on the Islamic lunar calendar and may vary by one or two days from the dates given.

† This festival will occur twice (in the Islamic years AH 1420 and 1421) within the same Gregorian year.

### Weights and Measures

The metric system is in official use.

# Statistical Survey

**Source (unless otherwise stated):** Direction Générale de l'Economie, Ministère de la Planification, de l'Economie et de l'Administration Territoriale, Libreville.

## Area and Population

**AREA, POPULATION AND DENSITY**

| | |
|---|---|
| Area (sq km) | 267,667* |
| Population (census results) | |
| 8 October 1960–May 1961 | 448,564 |
| 31 July 1993 | |
| Males | 501,784 |
| Females | 513,192 |
| Total | 1,014,976 |
| Population (UN estimates at mid-year)† | |
| 1996 | 1,107,000 |
| 1997 | 1,137,000 |
| 1998 | 1,167,000 |
| Density (per sq km) at mid-1998 | 4.4 |

* 103,347 sq miles.

† Source: UN, *World Population Prospects: The 1998 Revision*.

**REGIONS** (1993 census, provisional)

| Region | Area (sq km) | Population* | Density (per sq km) | Chief town |
|---|---|---|---|---|
| Estuaire | 20,740 | 462,086 | 22.3 | Libreville |
| Haut-Ogooué | 36,547 | 102,387 | 2.8 | Franceville |
| Moyen-Ogooué | 18,535 | 41,827 | 2.3 | Lambaréné |
| N'Gounié | 37,750 | 77,871 | 2.1 | Mouila |
| Nyanga | 21,285 | 39,826 | 1.9 | Tchibanga |
| Ogooué-Ivindo | 46,075 | 48,847 | 1.1 | Makokou |
| Ogooué-Lolo | 25,380 | 42,783 | 2.1 | Koula-Moutou |
| Ogooué-Maritime | 22,890 | 98,299 | 4.3 | Port-Gentil |
| Woleu-N'Tem | 38,465 | 97,739 | 2.5 | Oyem |
| **Total** | 267,667 | 1,011,665 | 3.8 | |

* Excluding 45 persons in unspecified regions.

Source: UN, *Demographic Yearbook*.

**PRINCIPAL TOWNS** (population in 1988)

Libreville (capital) 352,000; Franceville 75,000; Port-Gentil 164,000

**BIRTHS AND DEATHS** (UN estimates, annual averages)

| | 1980–85 | 1985–90 | 1990–95 |
|---|---|---|---|
| Birth rate (per 1,000) | 33.1 | 35.7 | 36.6 |
| Death rate (per 1,000) | 18.1 | 17.0 | 16.1 |

**Expectation of life** (UN estimates, years at birth, 1990–95): 52.3 (males 50.8; females 54.0).

Source: UN, *World Population Prospects: The 1998 Revision*.

**ECONOMICALLY ACTIVE POPULATION**
(estimates, '000 persons, 1991)

| | Males | Females | Total |
|---|---|---|---|
| Agriculture, etc. | 187 | 151 | 338 |
| Industry | 62 | 9 | 71 |
| Services | 69 | 26 | 95 |
| **Total labour force** | 318 | 186 | 504 |

Source: UN Economic Commission for Africa, *African Statistical Yearbook*.

**Mid-1998** (estimates, '000 persons): Agriculture, etc. 216; Total 535.
Source: FAO, *Production Yearbook*.

## Agriculture

**PRINCIPAL CROPS** ('000 metric tons)

| | 1996 | 1997 | 1998 |
|---|---|---|---|
| Maize* | 30 | 31 | 31 |
| Cassava (Manioc)* | 210 | 215 | 215 |
| Yams* | 140 | 140 | 140 |
| Taro (Coco yam)* | 57 | 58 | 58 |
| Vegetables* | 33 | 34 | 34 |
| Bananas* | 10 | 11 | 11 |
| Plantains* | 260 | 260 | 260 |
| Cocoa beans† | 1 | 1 | 1 |
| Groundnuts (in shell)* | 16 | 17 | 17 |
| Sugar cane* | 173 | 175 | 173 |

* FAO estimates. † Unofficial figures.

Source: FAO, *Production Yearbook*.

**LIVESTOCK** (FAO estimates, '000 head, year ending September)

| | 1996 | 1997 | 1998 |
|---|---|---|---|
| Cattle | 39 | 39 | 39 |
| Pigs | 208 | 208 | 208 |
| Sheep | 173 | 173 | 173 |
| Goats | 86 | 86 | 86 |

Poultry (FAO estimates, million): 3 in 1996; 3 in 1997; 3 in 1998.
Source: FAO, *Production Yearbook*.

**LIVESTOCK PRODUCTS**

**1998** (FAO estimates, '000 metric tons): Meat 28; Hen eggs 2.
Source: FAO, *Production Yearbook*.

## Forestry

**ROUNDWOOD REMOVALS** ('000 cubic metres)

| | 1995 | 1996 | 1997 |
|---|---|---|---|
| Sawlogs, veneer logs and logs for sleepers | 1,990 | 1,990 | 1,990 |
| Fuel wood | 2,356 | 2,424 | 2,493 |
| **Total** | 4,346 | 4,414 | 4,483 |

Source: FAO, *Yearbook of Forest Products*.

**SAWNWOOD PRODUCTION**
('000 cubic metres, incl. railway sleepers)

| | 1995 | 1996 | 1997 |
|---|---|---|---|
| **Total** | 170 | 170 | 170 |

Source: FAO, *Yearbook of Forest Products*.

## Fishing

('000 metric tons, live weight)

| | 1995 | 1996 | 1997 |
|---|---|---|---|
| Tilapias | 2.6* | 3.6 | 4.2 |
| Torpedo-shaped catfishes | 2.0* | 2.1 | 2.1 |
| Other freshwater fishes* | 3.0 | 4.2 | 3.6 |
| Sea catfishes | 0.4 | 2.8 | 2.7 |
| Grunts, sweetlips, etc. | 0.9 | 0.8 | 0.9 |
| Bobo croaker | 1.0 | 0.9 | 0.8 |
| West African croakers | 2.1 | 4.0 | 3.1 |
| Barracudas | 0.4 | 1.1 | 0.9 |
| Lesser African threadfin | 1.9 | 3.8 | 3.2 |
| Sardinellas | 1.2 | 1.9 | 0.9 |
| Bonga shad | 11.8 | 13.0 | 14.7 |
| Other marine fishes (incl. unspecified) | 11.3 | 5.6 | 5.7 |
| **Total fish** | 39.4 | 43.9 | 42.6 |
| Southern pink shrimp | 0.9 | 1.0 | 1.4 |
| Other crustaceans and molluscs | 0.2 | 0.5 | 0.7 |
| **Total catch** | 40.4 | 45.3 | 44.7 |

* FAO estimate(s).

Source: FAO, *Yearbook of Fishery Statistics*.

## Mining

('000 metric tons, unless otherwise indicated)

| | 1994 | 1995 | 1996 |
|---|---|---|---|
| Crude petroleum | 17,214 | 18,246 | 19,250 |
| Natural gas (petajoules) | 30 | 32 | 32* |
| Uranium ore (metric tons)† | 736 | 740* | n.a. |
| Manganese ore*†‡ | 663 | 893 | 923 |
| Gold (kilograms)*†‡ | 72 | 70 | 70 |

* Provisional or estimated figure(s).

† Figures refer to the metal content of ores.

‡ Data from the US Bureau of Mines.

Source: UN, *Industrial Commodity Statistics Yearbook*.

## Industry

**PETROLEUM PRODUCTS** ('000 metric tons)

| | 1994 | 1995 | 1996* |
|---|---|---|---|
| Liquefied petroleum gas* | 8 | 8 | 9 |
| Motor spirit (petrol) | 33 | 33 | 35 |
| Kerosene* | 85 | 88 | 90 |
| Jet fuel* | 70 | 70 | 72 |
| Distillate fuel oils | 260 | 274 | 258 |
| Residual fuel oils* | 278 | 280 | 145 |
| Bitumen (asphalt) | 4 | 4 | 4 |

* Provisional or estimated figures.

Source: UN, *Industrial Commodity Statistics Yearbook*.

**SELECTED OTHER PRODUCTS**
('000 metric tons, unless otherwise indicated)

| | 1994 | 1995 | 1996 |
|---|---|---|---|
| Palm oil (crude)* | 3 | 3 | n.a. |
| Flour* | 31 | 27 | 26 |
| Cement† | 126 | 130 | n.a. |
| Electric energy (million kWh)‡ | 933 | 940 | 953 |

* Data from the FAO.

† Data from the US Bureau of Mines.

‡ Estimated production.

**Beer** ('000 hectolitres): 819 in 1990; 814 in 1991; 785 in 1992.
**Soft drinks** ('000 hectolitres): 413 in 1990; 439 in 1991; 410 in 1992.
Source: UN, *Industrial Commodity Statistics Yearbook*.

**Plywood** (FAO estimates, '000 cu metres): 25 in 1995; 25 in 1996; 25 in 1997. (Source: FAO, *Yearbook of Forest Products*).
**Veneer sheets** (FAO estimates, '000 cu metres): 2 in 1995; 5 in 1996; 10 in 1997 (Source: FAO, *Yearbook of Forest Products*).

## Finance

**CURRENCY AND EXCHANGE RATES**

**Monetary Units**

100 centimes = 1 franc de la Coopération financière en Afrique centrale (CFA).

**Sterling, Dollar and Euro Equivalents** (30 September 1999)
£1 sterling = 1,012.69 francs CFA;
US $1 = 615.06 francs CFA;
€1 = 655.96 francs CFA;
10,000 francs CFA = £9.875 = $16.259 = €15.245.

**Average Exchange Rate** (francs CFA per US $)
1996 511.55
1997 583.67
1998 589.95

Note: An exchange rate of 1 French franc = 50 francs CFA, established in 1948, remained in force until January 1994, when the CFA franc was devalued by 50%, with the exchange rate adjusted to 1 French franc = 100 francs CFA.

**BUDGET** ('000 million francs CFA)

| Revenue | 1995 | 1996* | 1997† |
|---|---|---|---|
| Petroleum revenue | 469.2 | 562.1 | 562.6 |
| Profits tax | 265.5 | 341.8 | 330.0 |
| Royalties | 155.8 | 182.7 | 192.2 |
| Production-sharing and assets | 18.0 | 22.6 | 25.4 |
| Dividends | 30.0 | 15.0 | 15.0 |
| Non-petroleum revenue | 288.2 | 306.0 | 352.0 |
| Tax revenue | 277.7 | 293.9 | 346.2 |
| Direct taxes | 76.8 | 80.2 | 100.3 |
| Company taxes | 42.7 | 45.0 | 61.2 |
| Individual taxes | 34.1 | 35.2 | 39.0 |
| Indirect taxes | 61.7 | 43.0 | 64.0 |
| Turnover taxes | 51.6 | 29.4 | 56.0 |
| Taxes on goods and services | 10.1 | 13.6 | 8.0 |
| Taxes on refined petroleum products | 4.3 | n.a. | n.a. |
| Taxes on international trade and transactions | 128.7 | 147.8 | 175.9 |
| Import duties | 110.7 | 125.2 | 148.5 |
| Export duties | 18.0 | 22.6 | 27.4 |
| Other revenue | 21.0 | 35.0 | 11.9 |
| **Total** | 757.4 | 868.1 | 914.7 |

| Expenditure | 1995 | 1996* | 1997† |
|---|---|---|---|
| Current expenditure | 514.9 | 522.2 | 540.7 |
| Wages and salaries | 178.1 | 184.8 | 189.3 |
| Other goods and services | 112.9 | 142.6 | 150.2 |
| Transfers and subsidies | 23.0 | 21.6 | 23.3 |
| Interest payments | 201.0 | 173.1 | 177.9 |
| Capital expenditure | 136.0 | 154.3 | 215.4 |
| **Sub-total** | 650.9 | 676.5 | 756.1 |
| Adjustment for payment arrears | 53.6 | 125.1 | 170.0 |
| **Total** (cash basis) | 704.5 | 801.6 | 926.1 |

* Preliminary figures.
† Estimates.
Source: IMF, *Gabon: Statistical Annex* (February 1999).

**INTERNATIONAL RESERVES** (US $ million at 31 December)

| | 1996 | 1997 | 1998 |
|---|---|---|---|
| Gold* | 4.73 | 3.74 | 3.69 |
| IMF special drawing rights | 0.03 | — | 0.01 |
| Reserve position in IMF | 0.09 | 0.09 | 0.09 |
| Foreign exchange | 248.59 | 282.51 | 15.30 |
| **Total** | 253.45 | 286.34 | 19.09 |

* Valued at market-related prices.
Source: IMF, *International Financial Statistics*.

**MONEY SUPPLY** ('000 million francs CFA at 31 December)

| | 1996 | 1997 | 1998 |
|---|---|---|---|
| Currency outside banks | 110.88 | 121.03 | 124.72 |
| Demand deposits at commercial and development banks | 159.11 | 174.41 | 156.99 |
| **Total money** (incl. others) | 276.00 | 298.25 | 283.12 |

Source: IMF, *International Financial Statistics*.

**COST OF LIVING**
(Retail Price Index for African families in Libreville; base: 1995 = 100)

| | 1996 | 1997 |
|---|---|---|
| **All items** | 100.7 | 104.7 |

Source: IMF, *International Financial Statistics*.

**NATIONAL ACCOUNTS** ('000 million francs CFA at current prices)
**Expenditure on the Gross Domestic Product**

| | 1995 | 1996* | 1997† |
|---|---|---|---|
| Government final consumption expenditure | 291.0 | 327.4 | 339.5 |
| Private final consumption expenditure | 1,064.9 | 1,174.7 | 1,217.7 |
| Increase in stocks | 24.5 | — | — |
| Gross fixed capital formation | 561.3 | 676.4 | 794.9 |
| **Total domestic expenditure** | 1,941.7 | 2,178.5 | 2,352.1 |
| Exports of goods and services | 1,455.5 | 1,780.2 | 1,923.0 |
| *Less* Imports of goods and services | 922.1 | 1,067.9 | 1,261.5 |
| **GDP in purchasers' values** | 2,475.2 | 2,890.8 | 3,013.7 |

* Preliminary figures.
† Estimates.
Source: IMF, *Gabon: Statistical Annex* (February 1999).

**Gross Domestic Product by Economic Activity**

| | 1995 | 1996* | 1997† |
|---|---|---|---|
| Agriculture, livestock, hunting and fishing | 123.7 | 130.8 | 138.8 |
| Forestry | 75.1 | 71.0 | 85.7 |
| Petroleum exploitation and research | 951.3 | 1,226.7 | 1,247.5 |
| Other mining | 51.7 | 54.2 | 58.6 |
| Manufacturing | 146.4 | 162.2 | 167.1 |
| Electricity and water | 35.4 | 38.8 | 36.4 |
| Construction and public works | 92.8 | 102.4 | 116.3 |
| Trade | 246.4 | 287.1 | 245.8 |
| Transport | 129.5 | 135.3 | 143.4 |
| Financial services | 11.9 | 11.8 | 13.0 |
| Government services | 235.1 | 245.5 | 267.1 |
| Other services | 265.2 | 300.1 | 345.4 |
| **GDP at factor cost** | 2,364.4 | 2,765.8 | 2,865.1 |
| Import duties | 110.7 | 125.0 | 148.5 |
| **GDP in purchasers' values** | 2,475.2 | 2,890.8 | 3,013.7 |

* Preliminary figures.
† Estimates.
Source: IMF, *Gabon: Statistical Annex* (February 1999).

**BALANCE OF PAYMENTS** (US $ million)

| | 1993 | 1994 | 1995 |
|---|---|---|---|
| Exports of goods f.o.b. | 2,326.2 | 2,365.3 | 2,642.9 |
| Imports of goods f.o.b. | –845.1 | –776.7 | –898.5 |
| **Trade balance** | 1,481.1 | 1,588.6 | 1,744.4 |
| Exports of services | 311.1 | 219.6 | 272.9 |
| Imports of services | –1,022.7 | –826.7 | –949.4 |
| **Balance on goods and services** | 769.5 | 981.4 | 1,067.8 |
| Other income received | 32.1 | 11.9 | 13.4 |
| Other income paid | –658.3 | –509.9 | –783.5 |
| **Balance on goods, services and income** | 143.4 | 483.4 | 297.7 |
| Current transfers received | 48.0 | 18.7 | 4.4 |
| Current transfers paid | –240.5 | –184.8 | –202.3 |
| **Current balance** | –49.1 | 317.4 | 99.8 |
| Direct investment abroad | –2.5 | — | n.a. |
| Direct investment from abroad | –113.7 | –99.6 | –113.4 |
| Other investment assets | –7.8 | –258.6 | –5.4 |
| Other investment liabilities | –265.2 | –386.7 | –293.9 |
| Net errors and omissions | –13.6 | 254.6 | –108.2 |
| **Overall balance** | –451.9 | –173.0 | –421.2 |

Source: IMF, *International Financial Statistics*.

# External Trade

### PRINCIPAL COMMODITIES

| Imports c.i.f. (US $ million)* | 1993 | 1994 | 1996 |
|---|---|---|---|
| **Food and live animals** | 131.5 | 105.8 | 145.7 |
| Meat and meat preparations | 34.8 | 32.0 | 37.8 |
| Fresh, chilled or frozen meat | 31.5 | 28.9 | 32.8 |
| Fresh or frozen bovine meat | 16.7 | 13.1 | 10.1 |
| Dairy products and birds' eggs | 16.1 | 10.7 | 15.5 |
| Fish and fish preparations | 15.4 | 8.7 | 13.6 |
| Cereals and cereal preparations | 35.5 | 32.3 | 48.4 |
| **Beverages and tobacco** | 17.7 | 15.5 | 23.1 |
| **Mineral fuels, lubricants, etc.** | 14.5 | 17.1 | 31.6 |
| Petroleum, petroleum products, etc. | 14.3 | 16.9 | 28.3 |
| Refined petroleum products | 14.2 | 16.8 | 27.4 |
| **Chemicals and related products** | 83.6 | 70.1 | 93.0 |
| Medicinal and pharmaceutical products | 30.7 | 18.4 | 33.4 |
| Medicaments (incl. veterinary) | 28.3 | 16.7 | 30.7 |
| **Basic manufactures** | 123.8 | 112.1 | 150.2 |
| Paper, paperboard and manufactures | 19.4 | 14.1 | 16.8 |
| Iron and steel | 30.9 | 27.3 | 37.3 |
| Tubes, pipes and fittings | 23.7 | 19.7 | 24.3 |
| **Machinery and transport equipment** | 316.4 | 314.3 | 351.9 |
| Power-generating machinery and equipment | 26.9 | 25.9 | 26.3 |
| Machinery specialized for particular industries | 21.0 | 46.4 | 36.9 |
| Civil engineering and contractors' plant and equipment | 12.1 | 30.9 | 23.2 |
| General industrial machinery, equipment and parts | 67.0 | 82.2 | 105.9 |
| Pumps for liquids, etc. | 10.7 | 14.1 | 10.0 |
| Other pumps, centrifuges, etc. | 14.6 | 18.5 | 35.8 |
| Office machines and automatic data-processing equipment | 15.2 | 12.3 | 19.7 |
| Telecommunications and sound equipment | 19.0 | 16.6 | 22.8 |
| Other electrical machinery, apparatus, etc. | 40.0 | 29.8 | 42.8 |
| Switchgear, etc., and parts | 15.3 | 9.1 | 11.9 |
| Road vehicles and parts | 68.7 | 57.6 | 84.2 |
| Passenger motor cars (excl. buses) | 30.8 | 18.6 | 29.4 |
| Motor vehicles for goods transport, etc. | 18.8 | 14.1 | 23.3 |
| Goods vehicles (lorries and trucks) | 17.7 | 13.2 | 19.8 |
| Other transport equipment | 57.8 | 42.8 | 12.3 |
| Ships, boats and floating structures | 50.8 | 37.9 | 4.1 |
| **Miscellaneous manufactured articles** | 77.9 | 62.3 | 89.1 |
| Professional, scientific and controlling instruments, etc. | 21.3 | 16.9 | 29.8 |
| Measuring and controlling instruments | 15.3 | 14.3 | 24.2 |
| **Total** (incl. others) | 774.9 | 707.5 | 898.1 |

* Figures for 1995 are not available.

Source: UN, *International Trade Statistics Yearbook*.

| Exports ('000 million francs CFA) | 1995 | 1996* | 1997† |
|---|---|---|---|
| Petroleum and petroleum products | 1,055.4 | 1,335.1 | 1,369.6 |
| Manganese | 66.4 | 77.6 | 88.9 |
| Timber | 172.6 | 196.0 | 257.7 |
| Uranium | 15.5 | 13.2 | 11.7 |
| **Total** (incl. others) | 1,319.2 | 1,631.6 | 1,776.3 |

* Preliminary figures.

† Estimates.

Source: IMF, *Gabon: Statistical Annex* (February 1999).

### PRINCIPAL TRADING PARTNERS (US $ million)

| Imports c.i.f.* | 1993 | 1994 | 1996 |
|---|---|---|---|
| Belgium-Luxembourg | 22.5 | 24.5 | 37.1 |
| Cameroon | 6.3 | 12.0 | 12.1 |
| Côte d'Ivoire | 6.3 | 7.6 | 13.7 |
| France (incl. Monaco) | 370.4 | 281.4 | 384.8 |
| Germany | 27.8 | 39.7 | 41.1 |
| Italy | 24.3 | 29.6 | 31.3 |
| Japan | n.a. | n.a. | 53.8 |
| Morocco | 10.1 | 4.5 | 6.6 |
| Netherlands | 36.0 | 35.1 | 40.8 |
| Panama | — | 11.3 | — |
| SACU† | 3.5 | 4.5 | 9.3 |
| Spain | 11.2 | 11.4 | 21.0 |
| Thailand | 4.3 | 3.3 | 15.3 |
| United Kingdom | 29.4 | 45.1 | 42.8 |
| USA | 71.0 | 83.5 | 93.4 |
| **Total** (incl. others) | 774.9 | 707.5 | 898.1 |

| Exports f.o.b.* | 1993 | 1994 | 1996 |
|---|---|---|---|
| Canada | 52.3 | — | — |
| Chile | 81.6 | 22.6 | 17.5 |
| China, People's Repub. | 29.4 | 54.5 | 136.2 |
| France (incl. Monaco) | 505.6 | 361.6 | 239.8 |
| Gibraltar | 17.2 | 42.0 | n.a. |
| Israel | 9.9 | 19.8 | 34.5 |
| Japan | n.a. | n.a. | 66.1 |
| Korea, Repub. | 16.1 | 35.4 | 24.2 |
| Morocco | 14.5 | 76.2 | 16.8 |
| Netherlands | 2.9 | 89.0 | 30.7 |
| Netherlands Antilles | n.a. | n.a. | 121.4 |
| Portugal | 1.9 | 91.2 | 6.3 |
| Singapore | 17.1 | 40.6 | 2.0 |
| Spain | 32.9 | 92.5 | 36.8 |
| Switzerland-Liechtenstein | 10.8 | 9.8 | 34.7 |
| United Kingdom | 93.1 | 61.8 | 7.3 |
| USA | 1,388.2 | 1,192.9 | 2,015.3 |
| **Total** (incl. others) | 2,637.0 | 2,391.0 | 3,145.6 |

* Figures for 1995 are not available.

† Southern African Customs Union, comprising Botswana, Lesotho, Namibia, South Africa and Swaziland.

Source: UN, *International Trade Statistics Yearbook*.

# Transport

### RAILWAYS (traffic)

| | 1995 | 1996* | 1997† |
|---|---|---|---|
| Passengers carried ('000) | 175.8 | 191.9 | 195.5 |
| Freight carried ('000 metric tons) | 3,012.9 | 2,973.0 | 2,959.0 |

* Preliminary figures.

† Estimates.

Source: IMF, *Gabon: Statistical Annex* (February 1999).

### ROAD TRAFFIC (estimates, motor vehicles in use)

| | 1994 | 1995 | 1996 |
|---|---|---|---|
| Passenger cars | 22,310 | 24,000 | 24,750 |
| Lorries and vans | 14,850 | 15,840 | 16,490 |

Source: IRF, *World Road Statistics*.

### INTERNATIONAL SEA-BORNE SHIPPING
(freight traffic, '000 metric tons)

| | 1988 | 1989 | 1990 |
|---|---|---|---|
| Goods loaded | 8,890 | 10,739 | 12,828 |
| Goods unloaded | 610 | 213 | 212 |

Source: UN, *Monthly Bulletin of Statistics*.

**CIVIL AVIATION** (traffic on scheduled services)

| | 1993 | 1994 | 1995 |
|---|---|---|---|
| Kilometres flown (million) | 6 | 6 | 7 |
| Passengers carried ('000) | 302 | 481 | 508 |
| Passenger-kilometres (million) | 570 | 719 | 623 |
| Total ton-kilometres (million) | 82 | 96 | 89 |

Source: UN, *Statistical Yearbook*.

# Tourism

| | 1995 | 1996 | 1997 |
|---|---|---|---|
| Tourist arrivals | 127,332 | 141,170 | 167,197 |
| Tourism receipts (US $ million) | 7 | 7 | n.a. |

Sources: Centre Gabonais de Promotion Touristique (GABONTOUR) and World Tourism Organization, *Yearbook of Tourism Statistics*.

# Communications Media

| | 1994 | 1995 | 1996 |
|---|---|---|---|
| Radio receivers ('000 in use) | 189 | 195 | 201 |
| Television receivers ('000 in use) | 49 | 51 | 60 |
| Telephones ('000 main lines in use) | 31 | 32 | n.a. |
| Telefax stations (number in use) | n.a. | 360 | n.a. |
| Mobile cellular telephones (subscribers) | 2,581 | 4,000 | n.a. |
| Daily newspapers: | | | |
| Number | 1 | 2 | 2 |
| Average circulation ('000 copies) | 20 | 30 | 33 |

Sources: UNESCO, *Statistical Yearbook*; UN, *Statistical Yearbook*.

# Education

(1996)

| | Institu-tions | Teachers | Pupils | | |
|---|---|---|---|---|---|
| | | | Males | Females | Total |
| Pre-primary* | 9 | 37 | 465 | 485 | 950 |
| Primary | 1,147 | 4,944 | 126,208 | 124,398 | 250,606 |
| Secondary: | | | | | |
| General | 88 | 1,107 | 31,318 | 28,863 | 60,181 |
| Technical | 5 | 181 | 5,521 | 1,033 | 6,554 |
| Vocational | 6 | 52 | 291 | 189 | 480 |
| University level* | 2 | 299 | 2,148 | 852 | 3,000 |
| Other higher | n.a. | 257† | 1,033‡ | 315‡ | 1,348‡ |

* 1991/92 figures. † 1983/84 figure. ‡ 1986/87 figure.

Sources: Ministère de l'Education Nationale; UNESCO, *Statistical Yearbook*.

# Directory

## The Constitution

The Constitution of the Gabonese Republic was adopted on 14 March 1991. The main provisions are summarized below:

### PREAMBLE

Upholds the rights of the individual, liberty of conscience and of the person, religious freedom and freedom of education. Sovereignty is vested in the people, who exercise it through their representatives or by means of referenda. There is direct, universal and secret suffrage.

### HEAD OF STATE*

The President is elected by direct universal suffrage for a five-year term, renewable only once. The President is Head of State and of the Armed Forces. The President may, after consultation with his ministers and leaders of the National Assembly, order a referendum to be held. The President appoints the Prime Minister, who is Head of Government and who is accountable to the President. The President is the guarantor of national independence and territorial sovereignty.

### EXECUTIVE POWER

Executive power is vested in the President and the Council of Ministers, who are appointed by the Prime Minister, in consultation with the President.

### LEGISLATIVE POWER

The National Assembly is elected by direct universal suffrage for a five-year term. It may be dissolved or prorogued for up to 18 months by the President, after consultation with the Council of Ministers and President of the Assembly. The President may return a bill to the Assembly for a second reading, when it must be passed by a majority of two-thirds of the members. If the President dissolves the Assembly, elections must take place within 40 days.

The Constitution also provides for the establishment of an upper chamber (the Senate), to control the balance and regulation of power.

### POLITICAL ORGANIZATIONS

Article 2 of the Constitution states that 'Political parties and associations contribute to the expression of universal suffrage. They are formed and exercise their activities freely, within the limits delineated by the laws and regulations. They must respect the principles of democracy, national sovereignty, public order and national unity'.

### JUDICIAL POWER

The President guarantees the independence of the Judiciary and presides over the Conseil Supérieur de la Magistrature. Supreme judicial power is vested in the Supreme Court.

* A constitutional amendment, adopted by the legislature on 18 April 1997, extended the presidential term to seven years and provided for the creation of the post of Vice-President.

## The Government

### HEAD OF STATE

**President:** El Hadj OMAR (ALBERT-BERNARD) BONGO (took office 2 December 1967, elected 25 February 1973, re-elected December 1979, November 1986, December 1993 and December 1998).

**Vice-President:** DIDJOB DIVUNGUI-DI-N'DINGUE.

### COUNCIL OF MINISTERS

(February 2000)

**Prime Minister and Head of Government:** JEAN-FRANÇOIS NTOUTOUME EMANE.

**Vice-Prime Minister, Minister of National Solidarity and Social Welfare:** EMMANUEL ONDO-METHOGO.

**Minister of State for Equipment and Construction:** ZACHARIE MYBOTO.

**Minister of State for Planning, Development and Territorial Administration:** CASIMIR OYÉ MBA.

**Minister of State for Foreign Affairs, Co-operation and Francophone Affairs:** JEAN PING.

**Minister of State for Communications, Posts and Information Technology:** JEAN-RÉMY PENDY-BOUYIKI.

**Minister of State for Labour, Employment and Professional Training:** PAULETTE MISAMBO.

**Minister of State for the Interior, Security and Decentralization:** ANTOINE MBOUMBOU MIYAKOU.

**Minister of State for Housing, Urbanization and Cadastral Services:** JACQUES ADIAHÉNOT.

**Minister of Mining, Energy and Water Resources:** PAUL TOUNGUI.

**Minister of Justice, Guardian of the Seals:** PASCAL DÉSIRÉ MISSONGO.

**Minister of Water, Forestry, Fishing, Reafforestation and the Environment:** RICHARD ONOUVIET.

**Minister of Transport and Merchant Navy:** Gen. IDRISS NGARI.

**Minister of Trade, Tourism, Industrial Development and Crafts:** ALFRED MABICKA.

**Minister of National Education and Government Spokesperson:** ANDRÉ MBA OBAME.

**Minister of National Defence:** ALI BONGO.

**Minister of Economic Affairs, Finance, the Budget and Privatization:** EMILE NDOUMBA.

**Minister of the Civil Service, Administrative Reform and Modernization of the State:** PATRICE NZIENGUI.

**Minister of Higher Education, Research and Technology:** ANDRÉ-DIEUDONNÉ BERRE.

**Minister of Public Health and Population:** FAUSTIN BOUKOUBI.

**Minister of Agriculture, Livestock and Rural Development:** FABIEN OWONO ESSONO.

**Minister of Human Rights and Relations with Constitutional Institutions:** PIERRE-CLAVER NZENG EBOME.

**Minister of Culture, the Arts, Popular Education, Youth and Sports:** DANIEL ONA-ONDO.

**Minister of Small- and Medium-sized Enterprises:** PAUL BIYOGHE-MBA.

**Minister of Family Affairs and Women:** ANGELIQUE NGOMA.

There were also eight Ministers Delegate.

### MINISTRIES

**Office of the Prime Minister:** BP 546, Libreville; tel. 77-89-81.

**Ministry of Agriculture, Livestock and Rural Development:** BP 551, Libreville; tel. 72-09-60.

**Ministry of the Civil Service, Administrative Reform and Modernization of the State:** BP 496, Libreville; tel. 76-38-86.

**Ministry of Communications, Posts and Information Technology:** Libreville.

**Ministry of Culture, the Arts and Popular Education:** BP 2280, Libreville; tel. 76-61-83.

**Ministry of Economic Affairs, Finance, the Budget and Privatization:** BP 165, Libreville; tel. 76-12-10; fax 76-59-74.

**Ministry of Equipment and Construction:** BP 49, Libreville; tel. 76-38-56; fax 74-80-92.

**Ministry of Family Affairs and Women:** BP 5684, Libreville; tel. 77-50-32.

**Ministry of Foreign Affairs, Co-operation and Francophone Affairs:** BP 2245, Libreville; tel. 73-94-65.

**Ministry of Higher Education and Research Technology:** BP 2217, Libreville; tel. 72-41-08.

**Ministry of Housing, Urbanization and Cadastral Services:** BP 512, Libreville; tel. 77-31-02.

**Ministry of Human Rights and Relations with Constitutional Institutions:** Libreville.

**Ministry of the Interior, Security and Decentralization:** BP 2110, Libreville; tel. 72-00-75.

**Ministry of Justice:** BP 547, Libreville; tel. 74-66-28; fax 72-33-84.

**Ministry of Labour, Employment and Professional Training:** BP 4577, Libreville; tel. 74-32-18.

**Ministry of Mining and Energy:** BP 576, Libreville; tel. 77-22-39.

**Ministry of National Defence:** BP 13493, Libreville; tel. 77-86-94.

**Ministry of National Education:** BP 6, Libreville; tel. 76-13-01; fax 74-14-48.

**Ministry of National Solidarity and Social Welfare:** Libreville.

**Ministry of Planning, Development and Territorial Administration:** Libreville.

**Ministry of Public Health and Population:** BP 50, Libreville; tel. 76-36-11.

**Ministry of Small- and Medium-sized Enterprises and Crafts:** BP 3096, Libreville; tel. 74-59-21.

**Ministry of Social Welfare:** Libreville.

**Ministry of Tourism and the Environment:** BP 178, Libreville; tel. 76-34-62.

**Ministry of Trade and Industrial Development:** Libreville.

**Ministry of Transport and Marine Resources:** BP 803, Libreville; tel. 74-71-96; fax 77-33-31.

**Ministry of Water, Forestry, Fishing and Reafforestation:** BP 3974, Libreville; tel. 76-01-09; fax 76-61-83.

**Ministry of Youth and Sports:** BP 2150, Libreville; tel. 74-00-19; fax 74-65-89.

## President and Legislature

### PRESIDENT

**Presidential Election, 6 December 1998**

| Candidate | % of votes |
|---|---|
| El Hadj OMAR (ALBERT-BERNARD) BONGO | 66.55 |
| PIERRE MAMBOUNDOU | 16.54 |
| Fr PAUL M'BA ABESSOLE | 13.41 |
| PIERRE-ANDRÉ KOMBILA | 1.54 |
| PIERRE-CLAVER MAGANGA MOUSSAVOU | 0.99 |
| Others | 0.97 |
| **Total** | 100.00 |

### ASSEMBLÉE NATIONALE

**President:** GUY NDZOUBA NDAMA.

**Secretary-General:** PIERRE NGUEMA-MVE.

**General Election, 15 and 29 December 1996**

| Party | Seats |
|---|---|
| Parti démocratique gabonais (PDG) | 84 |
| Rassemblement national des bûcherons (RNB) | 7 |
| Parti gabonais du progrès (PGP) | 6 |
| Independents | 4 |
| Cercle des libéraux réformateurs (CLR) | 3 |
| Union du peuple gabonais (UPG) | 2 |
| Union socialiste gabonais (USG) | 2 |
| Others | 7 |
| **Total** | 115* |

* Voting was unable to proceed normally in five constituencies, and results in a number of other constituencies were later annulled. Following subsequent by-elections, the PDG held 89 seats, the PGP nine and the RNB six.

### SÉNAT

**President:** GEORGES RAWIRI.

**Secretary-General:** LOUIS SAMBA IGAMBA.

**Election, 26 January and 9 February 1997***

| Party | Seats |
|---|---|
| Parti démocratique gabonais (PDG) | 53 |
| Rassemblement national des bûcherons (RNB) | 20 |
| Independents | 9 |
| Parti gabonais du progrès (PGP) | 4 |
| Alliance démocratique et républicaine (ADERE) | 3 |
| Cercle des libéraux réformateurs (CLR) | 1 |
| Rassemblement pour la démocratie et le progrès (RDP) | 1 |
| **Total** | 91 |

* Following the annulment of a number of results, the PDG gained a further five seats at by-elections held later in 1997.

## Political Organizations

**Alliance démocratique et républicaine (ADERE):** Pres. MBOUMBOU NGOMA; Sec.-Gen. DIDJOB DIVUNGUI-DI-N'DINGUE.

**Association pour le socialisme au Gabon (APSG).**

**Cercle des libéraux réformateurs (CLR):** f. 1993 by breakaway faction of the PDG; Leader JEAN-BONIFACE ASSELE.

**Cercle pour le renouveau et le progrès (CRP).**

**Congrès pour la démocratie et la justice.**

**Convention des forces du changement:** f. 1993 as an informal alliance of eight opposition presidential candidates.

**Coordination de l'opposition démocratique (COD):** f. 1991 as an alliance of eight principal opposition parties; Chair. SÉBASTIEN MAMBOUNDOU MOUYAMA.

**Forum africain pour la reconstruction (FAR):** f. 1992; a factional alliance within the COD; Leader Prof. LÉON MBOYEBI; comprises three political parties:

**Mouvement de redressement national (MORENA-originels):** f. 1981 in Paris, France; Leader (vacant).

**Parti socialiste gabonais (PSG):** f. 1991; Leader Prof. LÉON MBOYEBI.

**Union socialiste gabonais (USG):** Leader Dr SERGE MBA BEKALE.

**Front national (FN):** f. 1991; Leader MARTIN EFAYONG.

**Gabon Avenir:** f. 1999; Leader SYLVESTRE OYOUOMI.

**Mouvement alternatif:** f. 1996; Leader SÉBASTIEN MAMBOUNDOU MOUYAMA.

**Mouvement pour la démocratie, le développement et la reconciliation nationale (Modern):** Libreville; f. 1996; Leader GASTON MOZOGO OVONO.

**Parti démocratique gabonais (PDG):** BP 268, Libreville; tel. 70-31-21; fax 70-31-46; f. 1968; sole legal party 1968–90; Sec.-Gen. JACQUES ADIAHÉNOT.

**Parti gabonais du centre indépendent (PGCI):** Leader JEAN-PIERRE LEMBOUMBA LEPANDOU.

**Parti gabonais du progrès (PGP):** f. 1990; Pres. PIERRE-LOUIS AGONDJO-OKAWÉ; Sec.-Gen. ANSELME NZOGHE.

**Parti des libéraux démocrates (PLD):** Leader MARC SATURNIN NAN NGUEMA.

**Parti social-démocrate (PSD):** f. 1991; Leader PIERRE-CLAVER MAGANGA MOUSSAVOU.

**Parti de l'unité du peuple gabonais (PUP):** Libreville; f. 1991; Leader LOUIS GASTON MAYILA.

**Rassemblement des démocrates (RD):** f. 1993.

**Rassemblement pour la démocratie et le progrès (RDP):** Pres. (vacant).

**Rassemblement des Gaullois:** Libreville; f. 1994, registered 1998; 5,000 mems; Pres. MAX ANICET KOUBA-MBADINGA.

**Rassemblement national des bûcherons (RNB):** f. 1990 as MORENA des bûcherons; Leader Fr PAUL M'BA ABESSOLE; Sec.-Gen. Prof. VINCENT MOULENGUI BOUKOSSO.

**Union pour la démocratie et le développement Mayumba (UDD).**

**Union démocratique et sociale (UDS):** f. 1996; Leader HERVÉ OUSSAMANE.

**Union nationale pour la démocratie et le développement (UNDD):** f. 1993; supports President Bongo.

**Union du peuple gabonais (UPG):** f. 1989 in Paris, France; Leader PIERRE MAMBOUNDOU.

# Diplomatic Representation

### EMBASSIES IN GABON

**Algeria:** BP 4008, Libreville; tel. 73-23-18; fax 73-14-03; e-mail ambalgabon@tiggabon.com; Ambassador: ABDELHAMID CHEBCHOUB.

**Angola:** BP 4884, Libreville; tel. 73-04-26; Ambassador: BERNARDO DOMBELE M'BALA.

**Argentina:** BP 4065, Libreville; tel. 74-05-49; Ambassador: HUGO HURTUBEI.

**Belgium:** BP 4079, Libreville; tel. 73-29-92; Ambassador: PAUL DE WULF.

**Bénin:** BP 3851, Akebe, Libreville; tel. 73-76-66; fax 73-77-75; Ambassador: TIMOTHÉE ADANLIN.

**Brazil:** BP 3899, Libreville; tel. 76-05-35; fax 74-03-43; e-mail emblibreville@inet.ga; Ambassador: SERGIO SEABRA DE NORONHA.

**Cameroon:** BP 14001, Libreville; tel. 73-28-00; Chargé d'affaires a.i.: NYEMB NGUENE.

**Canada:** BP 4037, Libreville; tel. 74-34-64; fax 74-34-66; e-mail robert.noble@paris03.x400.gc.ca; Ambassador: ROBERT NOBLE.

**Central African Republic:** Libreville; tel. 72-12-28; Ambassador: FRANÇOIS DIALLO.

**China, People's Republic:** BP 3914, Libreville; tel. 74-32-07; Ambassador: GUO TIANMIN.

**Congo, Democratic Republic:** BP 2257, Libreville; tel. 74-32-53; Ambassador: KABANGI KAUMBU BULA.

**Congo, Republic:** BP 269, Libreville; tel. 73-29-06; Ambassador: PIERRE OBOU.

**Côte d'Ivoire:** BP 3861, Libreville; tel. 73-82-68; Ambassador: JEAN-OBEO COULIBALY.

**Egypt:** BP 4240, Libreville; tel. 73-25-38; fax 73-25-19; Ambassador: SALAH ZAKI.

**Equatorial Guinea:** BP 1462, Libreville; tel. 75-10-56; Ambassador: CRISANTOS NDONGO ABA MESSIAN.

**France:** blvd de l'Indépendance, BP 2125, Libreville; tel. 76-10-64; fax 74-48-78; e-mail ambafran@inet.ga; Ambassador: PHILIPPE SELZ.

**Germany:** blvd de l'Indépendance, BP 299, Libreville; tel. 76-01-88; fax 72-40-12; e-mail amb-allegmagne@inet.ga; Ambassador: ADALBERT RITTMÜLLER.

**Guinea:** BP 4046, Libreville; tel. 73-85-09; Chargé d'affaires a.i.: MAMADI KOLY KOUROUMA.

**Holy See:** blvd Monseigneur Bessieux, BP 1322, Libreville (Apostolic Nunciature); tel. 74-45-41; Apostolic Nuncio: Most Rev. MARIO ROBERTO CASSARI, Titular Archbishop of Tronto.

**Iran:** BP 2158, Libreville; tel. 73-05-33; Ambassador: AHMAD SOBHAM.

**Italy:** Immeuble Personnaz et Gardin, rue de la Mairie, BP 2251, Libreville; tel. 74-28-92; fax 74-80-35; e-mail ambiasciata-italia@internetgabon.com; Ambassador: VITTORIO FUMO.

**Japan:** BP 3341, Libreville; tel. 73-22-97; fax 73-60-60; Ambassador: HIDEO KAKINUMA.

**Korea, Republic:** BP 2620, Libreville; tel. 73-40-00; fax 73-00-79; Ambassador: PARK CHANG-IL.

**Lebanon:** BP 3341, Libreville; tel. 73-96-45; Ambassador: MAMLOUK ABDELLATIF.

**Mauritania:** BP 3917, Libreville; tel. 74-31-65; Ambassador: El Hadj THIAM.

**Morocco:** BP 3983, Libreville; tel. 77-41-51; fax 77-41-50; Ambassador: MOHAMED GHALI TAZI.

**Nigeria:** BP 1191, Libreville; tel. 73-22-03; Ambassador: MARINA JAMILAH MOHAMED.

**Philippines:** BP 1198, Libreville; tel. 72-34-80; Chargé d'affaires a.i.: ARCADIO HERRERA.

**Russia:** BP 3963, Libreville; tel. 72-48-68; fax 72-48-70; Ambassador: YOURI LEYZARENKO.

**São Tomé and Príncipe:** BP 489, Libreville; tel. 72-09-94; Ambassador: JOSEPH FRET LAU CHONG.

**Senegal:** BP 3856, Libreville; tel. 77-42-67; Ambassador: OUMAR WELE.

**South Africa:** Immeuble les Arcades, 142 rue des Chavannes, BP 4063, Libreville; tel. 77-45-30; fax 77-45-36; Ambassador: MONGEHI SAMUEL MONAISA.

**Spain:** Immeuble Diamant, blvd de l'Indépendance, BP 2105, Libreville; tel. 72-12-64; fax 74-88-73; Ambassador: MIGUEL ANTONIO ARIAS ESTÉVEZ.

**Togo:** BP 14160, Libreville; tel. 73-29-04; Ambassador: AHLONKO KOFFI AQUEREBURU.

**Tunisia:** BP 3844, Libreville; tel. 73-28-41; Ambassador: EZZEDINE KERKENI.

**USA:** blvd de la Mer, BP 4000, Libreville; tel. 76-20-03; Ambassador: JAMES V. LEDESMA.

**Venezuela:** BP 3859, Libreville; tel. 73-31-18; fax 73-30-67; Ambassador: VÍCTOR CROQUER-VEGA.

**Yugoslavia:** Libreville; tel. 73-30-05; Ambassador: ČEDOMIR STRBAC.

# Judicial System

**Supreme Court:** BP 1043, Libreville; tel. 72-17-00; three chambers: judicial, administrative and accounts; Pres. BENJAMIN PAMBOU-KOMBILA.

**Constitutional Court:** Libreville; tel. 72-57-17; fax 72-55-96; Pres. MARIE MADELEINE MBORANTSUO.

**Courts of Appeal:** Libreville and Franceville.

**Court of State Security:** Libreville; 13 mems; Pres. FLORENTIN ANGO.

**Conseil Supérieur de la Magistrature:** Libreville; Pres. El Hadj OMAR BONGO; Vice-Pres. Pres. of the Supreme Court (ex officio).

There are also Tribunaux de Première Instance (County Courts) at Libreville, Franceville, Port-Gentil, Lambaréné, Mouila, Oyem, Koula-Moutou, Makokou and Tchibanga.

# Religion

About 60% of Gabon's population are Christians, mainly adherents of the Roman Catholic Church. About 40% are animists, and fewer than 1% are Muslims.

### CHRISTIANITY

#### The Roman Catholic Church

Gabon comprises one archdiocese and three dioceses. At 31 December 1997 the estimated number of adherents in the country was equivalent to 50.5% of the total population.

**Bishops' Conference:** Conférence Episcopale du Gabon, BP 2146, Libreville; tel. 72-20-73; f. 1989; Pres. Most Rev. Basile Mvé Engone, Archbishop of Libreville.

**Archbishop of Libreville:** Most Rev. Basile Mvé Engone, Archevêché, Sainte-Marie, BP 2146, Libreville; tel. 72-20-73.

#### Protestant Churches

**Christian and Missionary Alliance:** active in the south of the country; 16,000 mems.

**Eglise Evangélique du Gabon:** BP 10080, Libreville; tel. 72-41-92; f. 1842; independent since 1961; 120,000 mems; Pres. Pastor Samuel Nang Essono; Sec. Rev. Emile Ntetome.

The Evangelical Church of South Gabon and the Evangelical Pentecostal Church are also active in Gabon.

# The Press

**Le Bûcheron:** BP 6424, Libreville; official publ. of the Rassemblement national des bûcherons.

**Bulletin Evangélique d'Information et de Presse:** BP 80, Libreville; monthly; religious.

**Bulletin Mensuel de la Chambre de Commerce, d'Agriculture, d'Industrie et des Mines:** BP 2234, Libreville; tel. 72-20-64; fax 74-64-77; monthly.

**Bulletin Mensuel de Statistique de la République Gabonaise:** BP 179, Libreville; monthly; publ. by Direction Générale de l'Economie.

**L'Economiste Gabonais:** BP 3906, Libreville; quarterly; publ. by the Centre gabonais du commerce extérieur.

**Gabon d'Aujourd'hui:** BP 750, Libreville; weekly; official govt publ.

**Gabon Libre:** BP 6439, Libreville; tel. 74-42-22; weekly; Dir Dzime Ekang; Editor René Nzovi.

**Gabon-Matin:** BP 168, Libreville; daily; publ. by Agence Gabonaise de Presse; Man. Hilarion Vendany; circ. 18,000.

**La Griffe:** BP 4928, Libreville; tel. 74-73-45; weekly; independent; satirical; Pres. Jérôme Okinda; Editor Ndjoumba Moussock.

**Journal Officiel de la République Gabonaise:** BP 563, Libreville; f. 1959; fortnightly; Man. Emmanuel Obamé.

**Ngondo:** BP 168, Libreville; monthly; publ. by Agence Gabonaise de Presse.

**Le Progressiste:** blvd Léon-M'Ba, Libreville; tel. 74-54-01; Dir Benoît Mouity Nzamba; Editor Jacques Mourende-Tsioba.

**La Relance:** Libreville; tel. 70-31-66; weekly; publ. of the Parti démocratique gabonais; Pres. Jacques Adiahénot; Dir René Ndemezo'o Obiang.

**Sept Jours:** BP 213, Libreville; weekly.

**L'Union:** Sonapresse, BP 3849, Libreville; tel. 73-21-84; fax 73-83-26; f. 1975; 75% state-owned; daily; official govt publ.; Man. Dir Albert Yangari; Editor Ngoyo Moussavou; circ. 40,000.

### NEWS AGENCIES

**Agence Gabonaise de Presse (AGP):** BP 168, Libreville; tel. 21-26.

**BERP International:** BP 8483, Libreville; tel. and fax 72-90-24; e-mail BERP8483@hotmail.com; Dir Antoine Lawson.

#### Foreign Bureau

**Agence France-Presse (AFP):** Immeuble Sogapal, Les Filaos, BP 788, Libreville; tel. 76-14-36; fax 72-45-31; e-mail afp-libreville@tiggabon.com; Dir Jean-Pierre Rejete.

# Publishers

**Gabonaise d'Imprimerie (GABIMP):** BP 154, Libreville; tel. 70-22-55; fax 70-31-85; f. 1973; Dir Béatrice Caillot.

**Multipress Gabon:** blvd Léon-M'Ba, BP 3875, Libreville; tel. 73-22-33; f. 1973; Chair. Paul Bory.

**Société Imprimerie de l'Ogooué (SIMO):** BP 342, Port-Gentil; f. 1977; Man. Dir Urbain Nicoue.

**Société Nationale de Presse et d'Edition (SONAPRESSE):** BP 3849, Libreville; tel. 73-21-84; f. 1975; Pres. and Man. Dir Joseph Rendjambe.

# Broadcasting and Communications

### TELECOMMUNICATIONS

**Office des Postes et des Télécommunications (OPT):** BP 20 000, Libreville; tel. 78-70-05; fax 78-67-70; scheduled for privatization during 1999; Dir-Gen. Thomas Souah.

**Société des Télécommunications Internationales Gabonaises (TIG):** BP 2261, Libreville; tel. 78-77-56; fax 74-19-09; f. 1971; cap. 3,000m. francs CFA; 61% state-owned; planning and devt of international telecommunications systems; Man. Dir A. N'Gouma Mwyumala.

### BROADCASTING

#### Radio

The national network, 'La Voix de la Rénovation', and a provincial network broadcast for 24 hours each day in French and local languages.

**Africa No. 1:** BP 1, Libreville; tel. 76-00-01; fax 74-21-33; e-mail africa1@inet.ga; internet www. africa1.com; f. 1980; 35% state-controlled; international commercial radio station; daily programmes in French and English; Pres. Louis Barthélemy Mapangou; Mans Michel Koumbangoye, François Moreau.

**Radiodiffusion-Télévision Gabonaise (RTG):** BP 150, Libreville; tel. 73-20-25; f. 1959; state-controlled; Dir-Gen. John Joseph Mbourou; Dir of Radio Gilles Terence Nzoghe.

**Radio Fréquence 3:** f. 1996.

**Radio Génération Nouvelle:** f. 1996; Dir Jean-Boniface Assele.

**Radio Mandarine:** f. 1995.

**Radio Soleil:** f. 1995; affiliated to Rassemblement national des bûcherons.

**Radio Unité:** f. 1996.

#### Television

**Radiodiffusion-Télévision Gabonaise (RTG):** BP 150, Libreville; tel. 73-21-52; fax 73-21-53; f. 1959; state-controlled; Dir-Gen. John Joseph Mbourou; Dir of Television Jules César Lekogho.

**Télé-Africa:** Libreville; tel. 76-20-33; private channel; daily broadcasts in French.

**Télédiffusion du Gabon:** f. 1995.

# Finance

(cap. = capital; res = reserves; dep. = deposits; m. = million; brs = branches; amounts in francs CFA)

### BANKING

#### Central Bank

**Banque des Etats de l'Afrique Centrale (BEAC):** BP 112, Libreville; tel. 76-13-52; fax 74-45-63; HQ in Yaoundé, Cameroon; f. 1973; bank of issue for mem. states of the Communauté économique et monétaire de l'Afrique centrale (CEMAC, fmrly Union douanière et économique de l'Afrique centrale), comprising Cameroon, the Central African Repub., Chad, the Repub. of the Congo, Equatorial Guinea and Gabon; cap. and res 218,644m., total assets 1,303,372m. (June 1998); Gov. Jean-Félix Mamalepot; Dir in Gabon Jean-Paul Leyimangoye; 3 brs in Gabon.

#### Commercial Banks

**Banque Gabonaise et Française Internationale:** BP 2253, Libreville; tel. 76-23-26; fax 74-08-94; e-mail bgfi@internetgabon.com; internet www.bgfi.com; f. 1972; 33.4% state-owned; cap. and res 23,706.5m., dep. 65,499.7m. (Dec. 1999); Chair. Patrice Otha; Dir-Gen. Henri-Claude Oyima; 3 brs.

**Banque Internationale pour le Commerce et l'Industrie du Gabon, SA (BICIG):** ave du Colonel Parant, BP 2241, Libreville; tel. 76-26-13; fax 74-64-10; f. 1973; 27.7% state-owned; cap. and res 51,777m., dep. 172,130.8m. (Dec. 1997); Pres. Etienne Guy Mouvagha Tchioba; Man. Dir Emile Doumba; 9 brs.

**Banque Internationale pour le Gabon:** Immeuble Concorde, blvd de l'Indépendance, BP 106, Libreville; tel. 76-26-26; fax 76-20-53.

**Banque Populaire du Gabon 'La Populaire':** blvd d'Indépendance, BP 6663, Libreville; tel. 72-86-88; fax 72-86-91; e-mail bapo10@

calva.com; f. 1996; cap. and res 767.8m. (Dec. 1997); Pres. JEAN-MARC EKOH NGYEMA; Dir-Gen. SAMSON NGOMO.

**Crédit Foncier du Gabon:** blvd de l'Indépendance, BP 3905, Libreville; tel. 72-47-45; fax 76-08-70; 90% state-owned; under enforced administration since June 1996; Interim Admin. FABIEN OVONO-NGOUA.

**Union Gabonaise de Banque, SA (UGB):** ave du Colonel Parant, BP 315, Libreville; tel. 77-70-00; fax 76-46-16; f. 1962; 25% state-owned; cap. and res 14,735.0m., dep. 96,659.6m. (Dec. 1997); Chair. MARCEL DOUPAMBY-MATOKA; Pres. PIERRE-PARFAIT GONDJOUT; Man. Dir JEAN-CLAUDE DUBOIS; 6 brs.

### Development Banks

**Banque Gabonaise de Développement (BGD):** rue Alfred Marche, BP 5, Libreville; tel. 76-24-29; fax 74-26-99; f. 1960; 69% state-owned; cap. and res 23,903.4m. (Dec. 1996); Pres. MICHEL ANCHOUEY; Chair. VICTOR AFENE; Dir-Gen. RICHARD ONOUVIET.

**Banque Gabonaise et Française Internationale Participations:** BP 2253, Libreville; tel. 76-23-26; fax 74-08-94; e-mail bgfi@internetgabon.com; internet www.bgfi.com; f. 1997; cap. 1,500m. (Dec. 1999); Dir-Gen. HENRI-CLAUDE OYIMA.

**Banque Nationale de Crédit Rural (BNCR):** ave Bouet, BP 1120, Libreville; tel. 72-47-42; fax 74-05-07; f. 1986; 74% state-owned; cap. 1,350m. (Dec. 1992); Pres. GÉRARD MEYO M'EMANE; Man. Dir GEORGES ISSEMBE.

**Société Nationale d'Investissement du Gabon (SONADIG):** BP 479, Libreville; tel. 72-09-22; fax 74-81-70; f. 1968; state-owned; cap. 500m.; Pres. ANTOINE OYIEYE; Dir-Gen. MASSALA TSAMBA.

### Financial Institution

**Caisse Autonome d'Amortissement du Gabon:** BP 912, Libreville; tel. 74-41-43; management of state funds; Dir-Gen. MAURICE EYAMBA TSIMAT.

## INSURANCE

**Agence Gabonaise d'Assurance et de Réassurance (AGAR):** BP 1699, Libreville; tel. 74-02-22; fax 76-59-25; f. 1987; Man. Dir LOUIS GASTON MAYILA.

**Assurances Générales Gabonaises (AGG):** ave du Colonel Parant, BP 2148, Libreville; tel. 76-09-73; f. 1974; Co-Chair. JEAN DAVIN, JACQUES NOT.

**Assureurs Conseils Franco-Africains du Gabon (ACFRA-GABON):** BP 1116, Libreville; tel. 72-32-83; Chair. FRÉDÉRIC MARRON; Dir M. GARNIER.

**Assureurs Conseils Gabonais-Faugère et Jutheau & Cie:** Immeuble Shell-Gabon, rue de la Mairie, BP 2138, Libreville; tel. 72-04-36; fax 76-04-39; represents foreign insurance cos; Dir GÉRARD MILAN.

**Groupement Gabonais d'Assurances et de Réassurances (GGAR):** Immeuble les Horizons, blvd Triomphal Omar Bongo, BP 3949, Libreville; tel. 74-28-72; f. 1985; Chair. RASSAGUIZA AKEREY; Dir-Gen. DENISE OMBAGHO.

**Mutuelle Gabonaise d'Assurances:** ave du Colonel Parant, BP 2225, Libreville; tel. 72-13-91; Sec.-Gen. M. YENO-OLINGOT.

**Omnium Gabonais d'Assurances et de Réassurances (OGAR):** 546 blvd Triomphal Omar Bongo, BP 201, Libreville; tel. 76-15-96; fax 76-58-16; f. 1976; 10% state-owned; general; Pres. MARCEL DOUPAMBY-MATOKA; Man. Dir EDOUARD VALENTIN.

**Société Nationale Gabonaise d'Assurances et de Réassurances (SONAGAR):** ave du Colonel Parant, BP 3082, Libreville; tel. 76-28-97; f. 1974; owned by l'Union des Assurances de Paris (France); Dir-Gen. JEAN-LOUIS MESSAN.

**SOGERCO-Gabon:** BP 2102, Libreville; tel. 76-09-34; f. 1975; general; Dir M. RABEAU.

**L'Union des Assurances du Gabon (UAG):** ave du Colonel Parant, BP 2141, Libreville; tel. 74-34-34; fax 74-14-53; f. 1976; Chair. ALBERT ALEWINA CHAVIOT; Dir EKOMIE AFENE.

# Trade and Industry

## GOVERNMENT AGENCY

**Conseil Economique et Social de la République Gabonaise:** BP 1075, Libreville; tel. 73-19-46; fax 73-19-44; comprises representatives from salaried workers, employers and Govt; commissions on economic, financial and social affairs and forestry and agriculture; Pres. LOUIS GASTON MAYILA.

## DEVELOPMENT ORGANIZATIONS

**Agence Française de Développement:** BP 64, Libreville; tel. 74-33-74; fax 74-51-25; fmrly Caisse Française de Développement; Dir ANTOINE BAUX.

**Agence Nationale de Promotion de la Petite et Moyenne Entreprise (PROMO-GABON):** BP 3939, Libreville; tel. 74-31-16; f. 1964; state-controlled; promotes and assists small and medium-sized industries; Pres. SIMON BOULAMATARI; Man. Dir JEAN-FIDÈLE OTANDO.

**Centre Gabonais de Commerce Extérieur (CGCE):** BP 3906, Libreville; tel. 76-11-67; promotes foreign trade and investment in Gabon; Man. Dir MICHEL LESLIE TEALE.

**Commerce et Développement (CODEV):** BP 2142, Libreville; tel. 76-06-73; f. 1976; 95% state-owned, proposed transfer to private ownership announced 1986; import and distribution of capital goods and food products; Chair. and Man. Dir JÉRÔME NGOUA-BEKALE.

**Mission Française de Coopération:** BP 2105, Libreville; tel. 76-10-56; fax 74-55-33; administers bilateral aid from France; Dir JEAN-CLAUDE QUIRIN.

**Office Gabonais d'Amélioration et de Production de Viande (OGAPROV):** BP 245, Moanda; tel. 66-12-67; f. 1971; development of private cattle farming; manages ranch at Lekedi-Sud; Pres. PAUL KOUNDA KIKI; Dir-Gen. VINCENT EYI-NGUI.

**Palmiers et Hévéas du Gabon (PALMEVEAS):** BP 75, Libreville; f. 1956; state-owned; palm-oil development.

**Société de Développement de l'Agriculture au Gabon (AGROGABON):** BP 2248, Libreville; tel. 76-40-82; fax 76-44-72; f. 1976; 92% state-owned; Man. Dir ANDRÉ PAUL-APANDINA.

**Société de Développement de l'Hévéaculture (HEVEGAB):** BP 316, Libreville; tel. 72-08-29; fax 72-08-30; f. 1981; 99.9% state-owned; development of rubber plantations in the Mitzic, Bitam and Kango regions; Chair. FRANÇOIS OWONO-NGUEMA; Man. Dir RAYMOND NDONG-SIMA.

**Société Gabonaise de Recherches et d'Exploitations Minières (SOGAREM):** blvd de Nice, Libreville; state-owned; research and development of gold mining; Chair. ARSÈNE BOUNGUENZA; Man. Dir SERGE GASSITA.

**Société Gabonaise de Recherches Pétrolières (GABOREP):** BP 564, Libreville; tel. 75-06-40; fax 75-06-47; exploration and exploitation of hydrocarbons; Chair. HUBERT PERRODO; Man. Dir P. F. LECA.

**Société Nationale de Développement des Cultures Industrielles (SONADECI):** Libreville; tel. 76-33-97; f. 1978; state-owned; agricultural development; Chair. PAUL KOUNDA KIKI; Man. Dir GEORGES BEKALÉ.

## CHAMBER OF COMMERCE

**Chambre de Commerce, d'Agriculture, d'Industrie et des Mines du Gabon:** BP 2234, Libreville; tel. 72-20-64; fax 74-64-77; f. 1935; regional offices at Port-Gentil and Franceville; Pres. JOACHIM BOUSSAMBA-MAPAGA; Sec.-Gen. DOMINIQUE MANDZA.

## EMPLOYERS' ORGANIZATIONS

**Confédération Patronale Gabonaise:** BP 410, Libreville; tel. 76-02-43; fax 74-86-52; f. 1959; represents industrial, mining, petroleum, public works, forestry, banking, insurance, commercial and shipping interests; Pres. J. C. BALOCHE; Sec.-Gen. ERIC MESSERSCHMITT.

**Conseil National du Patronat Gabonais (CNPG):** Libreville; Pres. RAHANDI CHAMBRIER; Sec.-Gen. THOMAS FRANCK EYA'A.

**Syndicat des Entreprises Minières du Gabon (SYNDIMINES):** BP 260, Libreville; Pres. ANDRÉ BERRE; Sec.-Gen. SERGE GREGOIRE.

**Syndicat des Importateurs Exportateurs du Gabon (SIMPEX):** Libreville; Pres. ALBERT JEAN; Sec.-Gen. R. TYBERGHEIN.

**Syndicat des Producteurs et Industriels du Bois du Gabon:** BP 84, Libreville; tel. 72-26-11; fax 77-44-43; Pres. HEIRIC CHENEAU.

**Syndicat Professionnel des Usines de Sciages et Placages du Gabon:** Port-Gentil; f. 1956; Pres. PIERRE BERRY.

**Union des Représentations Automobiles et Industrielles (URAI):** BP 1743, Libreville; Pres. M. MARTINENT; Sec. R. TYBERGHEIN.

**Union Nationale du Patronat Syndical des Transports Urbains, Routiers et Fluviaux du Gabon (UNAPASYFTU-ROGA):** BP 1025, Libreville; f. 1977; Pres. LAURENT BELLAL BIBANG-BI-EDZO; Sec.-Gen. MARTIN KOMBILA-MOMBO.

## UTILITIES

**Société d'Energie et d'Eau du Gabon (SEEG):** BP 2187, Libreville; tel. 72-19-11; f. 1963; 51% owned by Compagnie Générale des Eaux (France) and Electricity Supply Board International (Ireland); controls 35 electricity generation and distribution centres and 32 water production and distribution centres; Chair. of Bd FRANÇOIS OMBANDA.

## TRADE UNIONS

**Confédération Gabonaise des Syndicats Libres (CGSL):** BP 8067, Libreville; tel. 77-37-82; fax 74-45-25; f. 1991; Sec.-Gen. FRANCIS MAYOMBO; 16,000 mems.

**Confédération Syndicale Gabonaise (COSYGA):** BP 14017, Libreville; f. 1969 by the Govt, as a specialized organ of the PDG, to organize and educate workers, to contribute to social peace and economic development, and to protect the rights of trade unions; Gen. Sec. MARTIN ALLINI.

# Transport

### RAILWAYS

The construction of the Transgabonais railway, which comprises a section running from Owendo (the port of Libreville) to Booué (340 km) and a second section from Booué to Franceville (357 km), was completed in 1986. By 1989 regular services were operating between Libreville and Franceville. Some 2m. metric tons of freight and 200,000 passengers were carried on the network in 1996. In 1998 the railways were transferred to private management.

**Office du Chemin de Fer Transgabonais (OCTRA):** BP 2198, Libreville; tel. 70-24-78; fax 70-27-68; f. 1972; management transferred to the private sector in late 1998; Chair. ALEXANDRE AYO BARRO.

### ROADS

In 1996 there were an estimated 7,670 km of roads, including 30 km of motorways, 3,780 km of main roads and 2,420 km of secondary roads; about 8.2% of the road network was paved.

### INLAND WATERWAYS

The principal river is the Ogooué, navigable from Port-Gentil to Ndjolé (310 km) and serving the towns of Lambaréné, Ndjolé and Sindara.

**Compagnie de Navigation Intérieure (CNI):** BP 3982, Libreville; tel. 72-39-28; fax 74-04-11; f. 1978; state-owned; responsible for inland waterway transport; agencies at Port-Gentil, Mayumba and Lambaréné; Chair. JEAN-PIERRE MENGWANG ME NGYEMA; Dir-Gen. JEAN LOUIS POUNAH-NDJIMBI.

### SHIPPING

The principal deep-water ports are Port-Gentil, which handles mainly petroleum exports, and Owendo, 15 km from Libreville, which services mainly barge traffic. The main ports for timber are at Owendo, Mayumba and Nyanga, and there is a fishing port at Libreville. The construction of a deep-water port at Mayumba is planned. A new terminal for the export of minerals, at Owendo, was opened in 1988. In 1998 the merchant shipping fleet had a total displacement of 26,532 grt. In 1997 the Islamic Development Bank granted a loan of 11,000m. francs CFA for the rehabilitation of Gabon's ports.

**Compagnie de Manutention et de Chalandage d'Owendo (COMACO):** BP 2131, Libreville; tel. 70-26-35; f. 1974; Pres. GEORGES RAWIRI; Dir in Libreville M. RAYMOND.

**Office des Ports et Rades du Gabon (OPRAG):** BP 1051, Libreville; tel. 70-00-48; fax 70-37-35; f. 1974; state-owned; national port authority; Pres. ALI BONGO; Dir-Gen. PHILIBERT ANDZEMBE.

**SAGA Gabon:** BP 518, Port-Gentil; tel. 55-54-00; fax 55-21-71; Chair. G. COGNON; Man. Dir J. C. SIMON.

**Société Nationale d'Acconage et de Transit (SNAT):** BP 3897, Libreville; tel. 70-04-04; fax 70-13-11; f. 1976; 51% state-owned; freight transport; Dir-Gen. CLAUDE AYO-IGUENDHA.

**Société Nationale de Transports Maritimes (SONATRAM):** BP 3841, Libreville; tel. 74-06-32; fax 74-59-67; f. 1976; relaunched 1995; 51% state-owned; river and ocean cargo transport; Man. Dir RAPHAEL MOARA WALLA.

**Société du Port Minéralier d'Owendo:** f. 1987; majority holding by Cie Minière de l'Ogooué; management of a terminal for minerals at Owendo.

**SOCOPAO–Gabon:** BP 4, Libreville; tel. 70-21-40; fax 70-02-76; f. 1963; freight transport and storage; Dir HENRI LECORDIER.

### CIVIL AVIATION

There are international airports at Libreville, Port-Gentil and Franceville, 65 other public and 50 private airfields linked mostly with the forestry and petroleum industries.

**Air Affaires Gabon:** BP 3962, Libreville; tel. 73-25-13; fax 73-49-98; f. 1975; domestic passenger chartered and scheduled flights; Chair. RAYMOND BELLANGER; Dir-Gen. DIEUDONNÉ MFOUBOU MOUDHOUMA.

**Air Service Gabon (ASG):** BP 2232, Libreville; tel. 73-24-08; fax 73-60-69; f. 1965; charter flights; Chair. JEAN-LUC CHEVRIER; Gen. Man. FRANÇOIS LASCOMBES.

**Compagnie Nationale Air Gabon:** BP 2206, Libreville; tel. 73-00-27; fax 73-11-56; f. 1951 as Cie Aérienne Gabonaise; began operating international services in 1977, following Gabon's withdrawal from Air Afrique (see under Côte d'Ivoire); 80% state-owned; internal and international cargo and passenger services; Chair. MARTIN BONGO; Dir-Gen. MFOUBOU MOUDHOUMA.

**Société de Gestion de l'Aéroport de Libreville (ADL):** BP 363, Libreville; tel. 73-62-44; fax 73-61-28; e-mail adl@inet.ga; f. 1988; 26.5% state-owned; management of airport at Libreville; Pres. CHANTAL LIDJI BADINGA; Dir-Gen. PIERRE ANDRÉ COLLET.

# Tourism

Tourist arrivals were estimated at 167,197 in 1997, and receipts from tourism totalled US $7m. in 1996. The tourism sector is being extensively developed, with new hotels and associated projects and the promotion of national parks. In 1996 there were 74 hotels, with a total of 4,000 rooms.

**Centre Gabonais de Promotion Touristique (GABONTOUR):** BP 2085, Libreville; tel. 72-85-04; fax 72-85-03; e-mail gabontour@internetgabon.com; internet www.internetgabon.com; f. 1988; Dir-Gen. JOSEPH ADJEMBIMANDE.

**Office National Gabonais du Tourisme:** BP 161, Libreville; tel. 72-21-82.

# THE GAMBIA

## Introductory Survey

### Location, Climate, Language, Religion, Flag, Capital

The Republic of The Gambia is a narrow territory around the River Gambia on the west coast of Africa. Apart from a short coastline on the Atlantic Ocean, the country is a semi-enclave in Senegal. The climate is tropical, with a rainy season from July to September. Away from the river swamps most of the terrain is covered by savannah bush. Average temperatures in Banjul range from 23°C (73°F) in January to 27°C (81°F) in July, while temperatures inland can exceed 40°C (104°F). English is the official language, while the principal vernacular languages are Mandinka, Fula and Wolof. About 85% of the inhabitants are Muslims; most of the remainder are Christians, and there are a small number of animists. The national flag (proportions 3 by 2) has red, blue and green horizontal stripes, with two narrow white stripes bordering the central blue band. The capital is Banjul.

### Recent History

Formerly administered with Sierra Leone, The Gambia became a separate British colony in 1888. Party politics rapidly gained momentum following the establishment of a universal adult franchise in 1960. Following legislative elections in May 1962, the leader of the People's Progressive Party (PPP), Dr (later Sir) Dawda Kairaba Jawara, became Premier. Full internal self-government followed in October 1963. On 18 February 1965 The Gambia became an independent country within the Commonwealth, with Jawara as Prime Minister. The country became a republic on 24 April 1970, whereupon Jawara took office as President. He was re-elected in 1972 and again in 1977, as a result of overwhelming PPP victories in legislative elections.

In July 1981 a coup was attempted while Jawara was visiting the United Kingdom. Left-wing rebels formed a National Revolutionary Council, and proclaimed their civilian leader, Kukoi Samba Sanyang, as Head of State. Under the terms of a mutual defence pact, Senegalese troops assisted in suppressing the rebellion. About 1,000 people were arrested and more than 60 people were subsequently sentenced to death, although no executions took place. A state of emergency remained in force until February 1985. All those convicted of involvement in the insurrection were released by early 1991.

The first presidential election by direct popular vote was held in May 1982. Jawara was re-elected, with 72% of the votes cast; he was opposed by the leader of the National Convention Party (NCP), Sherif Mustapha Dibba (who was in detention for his alleged involvement in the abortive coup). In the concurrent legislative elections the PPP won 27 of the 35 elective seats in the House of Representatives. At legislative elections in March 1987 the PPP took 31 of the 36 directly-elected seats in the House of Representatives: the NCP won the remaining five elective seats. In the presidential election Jawara was re-elected with 59% of the votes cast; Sherif Dibba (who had been acquitted and released from detention in June 1982) received 27% of the votes, and Assan Musa Camara, a former Vice-President who had recently formed the Gambian People's Party (GPP), won 14%. Rumours of financial impropriety, corruption and the abuse of power at ministerial level persisted throughout the decade, and apparently prompted the dismissal of at least four government members between 1984 and 1990.

Plans were announced in August 1981 for a confederation of The Gambia and Senegal, to be called Senegambia. The confederal agreement came into effect on 1 February 1982; a Confederal Council of Ministers, headed by President Abdou Diouf of Senegal (with President Jawara as his deputy), held its inaugural meeting in January 1983, as did a 60-member Confederal Assembly. Agreements followed on co-ordination of foreign policy, communications, defence and security, but Senegal was critical of Jawara's reluctance to proceed towards full economic and political integration. In August 1989 Diouf announced that Senegalese troops were to leave The Gambia, apparently in protest at a request by Jawara that The Gambia be accorded more power within the confederal structures. The confederation was dissolved in the following month, and a period of tension between the two countries followed: The Gambia alleged that the Senegalese authorities had introduced trade and travel restrictions, while Senegal accused The Gambia of harbouring rebels of the Mouvement des forces démocratiques de la Casamance (MFDC), an organization seeking independence for the Casamance region—which is virtually separated from the northern segment of Senegal by the enclave of The Gambia. In January 1991 the two countries signed an agreement of friendship and co-operation. However, relations were again strained in September 1993, when Senegal unilaterally closed the border, apparently in connection with anti-smuggling operations.

The Commander of the National Gendarmerie and Army resigned in June 1991, following a brief rebellion in Banjul by soldiers who were demanding the payment of overdue allowances. A Nigerian national was subsequently appointed Commander of the Gambian armed forces, and a defence co-operation agreement was signed by the two countries in early 1992. In March 1992 seven people were arrested following a government announcement that a Libyan-backed rebel force, led by Kukoi Samba Sanyang, was preparing to invade The Gambia.

Despite an earlier announcement that he would not be seeking a sixth presidential mandate, Jawara was re-elected in April 1992, receiving 58% of the votes cast. Sherif Dibba took 22% of the votes cast. In concurrent elections to the House of Representatives the PPP lost six seats but retained a clear majority, with 25 elected members. The NCP secured six seats, the GPP two and independent candidates the remaining three. In April 1993 the House of Representatives approved the abolition of the death penalty: although a total of 87 death sentences had been imposed (mostly in cases of high treason) since independence, only one execution had taken place.

Jawara was deposed by a self-styled Armed Forces Provisional Ruling Council (AFPRC), a group of young army officers led by Lt (later Col) Yahya Jammeh, in an abrupt but bloodless coup on 22 July 1994. Jawara and members of his entourage, including several government ministers, left The Gambia aboard a US navy vessel. Jawara later took up permanent residence in the United Kingdom.

The five-member AFPRC suspended the Constitution and announced a ban on all political activity. The new regime undertook to eliminate the institutionalized corruption that it claimed had been fostered under Jawara, pledging a return to civilian rule once this had been accomplished, and also promised to recover state funds allegedly misappropriated by former public officials. Jammeh officially pronounced himself Head of State, and appointed a mixed civilian and military Government. Members of Jawara's Government who had been arrested following the coup were released shortly afterwards. Purges of the armed forces and public institutions were implemented, and several of Jawara's former ministers were twice rearrested and briefly detained during September 1994, as part of investigations into state security and financial impropriety. In November it was announced that 10 former government ministers would be tried on charges of corruption.

The AFPRC's timetable for a transition to civilian rule, published in October 1994, envisaged a programme of reform culminating in the inauguration of new elected institutions, of what was to be designated the Second Republic, in December 1998. The length of the transition period prompted criticism both internationally and, within The Gambia, from prominent judicial, religious and trade union figures. In November it was revealed that a coup attempt, involving military officers who were said by the AFPRC to wish to install an entirely military regime, had been foiled. Some 50 soldiers, including the coup leaders, were reported to have been killed during the attempt and its suppression, and several arrests were made. Later in the month some of the police and army officers who had been detained since July were released.

The coup attempt prompted the Governments of the United Kingdom, Denmark and Sweden to issue warnings that their nationals should avoid travelling to The Gambia; this advice had a devastating effect on the Gambian tourist industry in subsequent months, although warnings to tourists had been withdrawn by March 1995. At the end of November 1994 Capt.

Jammeh commissioned a National Consultative Committee (NCC) to make recommendations regarding a possible shortening of the period of transition to civilian rule. In January 1995 two members of the AFPRC (the Vice-President, Sana Sabally, and Sadibou Hydara, the Minister of the Interior), both of whom were said to be opposed to the NCC's recommendations for a curtailment of the transition period (the Committee proposed a return to civilian government in July 1996), were arrested, following an alleged attempt to seize power. Fafa Idriss M'bai, a principal instigator of the NCC, was dismissed from the Government in March 1995, and was subsequently arrested and charged with corruption.

The death penalty was restored by government decree in August 1995, reportedly in response to a recent increase in the murder rate. In October Capt. Ebou Jallow, since January the official spokesman of the AFPRC, sought asylum in Senegal; he stated that he was seeking to overthrow Jammeh, accusing the regime of complicity in murder and arbitrary arrests. For its past, the AFPRC asserted that Jallow had embezzled government funds prior to his departure and that he was conspiring with Jawara. In January 1998 a Swiss court ordered the return of US $3m. that Jallow had transferred from the Central Bank of The Gambia to a personal bank account in Geneva.

In November 1995 a government decree was issued conferring wide powers of arrest and detention on the Minister of the Interior: under its terms, the police were authorized to detain without trial for a period of up to three months any person considered to be a threat to state security. In December Sabally was sentenced by court martial to nine years' imprisonment for plotting to overthrow Jammeh. (Hydara was reported to have died of natural causes while in detention.) In January 1996 Jawara was charged *in absentia* with embezzlement, following investigations into the alleged diversion of proceeds from the sale of petroleum donated by Nigeria. In subsequent months the confiscation was ordered of the assets in The Gambia of Jawara and 11 former government members. In July the Minister of Health and Social Welfare was arrested and charged with the misappropriation of state funds.

Although the AFPRC expressed its commitment to freedom of expression, a ban on the publication of journals by political organizations was introduced shortly after the July 1994 coup. The alleged harassment of journalists in The Gambia provoked considerable international concern, as there were periodic incidents of the arrest of, or fines against, journalists, while several non-Gambian journalists were deported.

A Constitutional Review Commission was inaugurated in April 1995, and submitted its recommendations to Jammeh in November; the draft was published in early March 1996. Despite demands by the European Union (EU) and the Commonwealth, as well as by individual countries that had previously been major donors to The Gambia (most notably the United Kingdom and the USA), for an early return to civilian rule, the AFPRC continued to assert that it would adhere to its revised timetable. In April it was announced that it would be impossible to complete the return to elected civilian government by July, and in May new dates were set for the presidential and legislative elections, which would now take place in September and December, respectively. The draft Constitution was to be submitted to a national referendum in August. Opponents of the AFPRC criticized provisions of the Constitution that, they alleged, had been formulated with the specific intention of facilitating Jammeh's election to the presidency (although the Head of State had frequently asserted that he would not seek election) and of giving political advantage to his supporters.

The constitutional referendum took place on 8 August 1996. The rate of participation was high (85.9%), and 70.4% of voters endorsed the new document. A presidential decree was issued in the following week reauthorizing party political activity. Shortly afterwards, however, it was announced that the PPP, the NCP and the GPP were to be prohibited from contesting the forthcoming presidential and parliamentary elections, as were all holders of executive office in the 30 years prior to July 1994. Thus, the only parties from the Jawara era authorized to contest the elections were the People's Democratic Organization for Independence and Socialism (PDOIS) and the People's Democratic Party (PDP). The effective ban on participation in the restoration of elected institutions of all those associated with political life prior to the military takeover was strongly criticized by the Commonwealth and its Ministerial Action Group on the Harare Declaration (CMAG, see p. 145), which had hitherto made a significant contribution to the transition process. At the same time the AFPRC announced that, following consultations between the military authorities and the Provisional Independent Electoral Commission (PIEC), which had expressed concern that newly-authorized political organizations would have insufficient time to campaign for the elections, the presidential poll was to be postponed by two weeks, to 26 September 1996.

Jammeh did not formally announce his intention to contest the presidency until mid-August 1996. At the end of the month the establishment was reported of a political party supporting Jammeh, the Alliance for Patriotic Reorientation and Construction (APRC). In early September Jammeh resigned from the army, in order to contest the presidency as a civilian, as required by the Constitution. The presidential election proceeded, as scheduled, on 26 September. Three people were reportedly killed, and more than 30 injured, in violence shortly before the poll. The earliest results of voting showed a victory for Jammeh; his nearest rival among three other candidates, Ousainou Darboe (leader of the United Democratic Party—UDP), meanwhile sought refuge at the residence of the Senegalese ambassador, where he remained until the end of the month. The official results, issued by the PIEC on 27 September, confirmed Jammeh's election as President, with 55.77% of the total votes cast, ahead of Darboe, with 35.84%. The rate of participation by voters was again high, especially in rural areas. However, observers, including CMAG, expressed doubts as to the credibility of the election results. The dissolution of the AFPRC was announced the same day. Jammeh was inaugurated as President on 18 October. In November an unconditional amnesty was extended to more than 40 political detainees, among them former government ministers detained since July 1994.

An attack took place in November 1996 on an army camp at Farafenni, 100 km east of Banjul, as a result of which six people were killed and five injured. Shortly afterwards it was announced that the legislative elections, due to take place on 11 December, were to be postponed until 2 January 1997. All the registered parties presented candidates for the 45 elective seats in the new National Assembly. Voting took place as scheduled, and the Gambian authorities, opposition groups and most international observers expressed broad satisfaction at the conduct of the poll. As expected, the APRC won an overwhelming majority of the seats in the legislature. The final results, as issued by the PIEC, allocated 28 seats to Jammeh's party (additionally, the APRC had been unopposed in five constituencies), seven to the UDP, two to the National Reconciliation Party and one to the PDOIS; independent candidates took the two remaining seats. The overall rate of participation by voters (again higher in rural areas) was 73.2%. As Head of State, Jammeh was empowered by the Constitution to nominate four additional members of parliament, from whom the Speaker (and Deputy Speaker) would be chosen. The opening session of the National Assembly, on 16 January, accordingly elected Mustapha Wadda, previously Secretary-General of the APRC and Secretary at the Presidency, as Speaker. This session denoted the full entry into force of the Constitution and thus the inauguration of the Second Republic. A further 12 political detainees were released in early February.

Under the new Constitution government ministers of cabinet rank were designated Secretaries of State, and the Government was reorganized to this effect in March 1997. Isatou Njie-Saidy, Secretary of State for Health, Social Welfare and Women's Affairs, was appointed Vice-President. However, most of the responsibilities hitherto associated with this post were transferred to the Secretary of State for the Office of the President, a position now held by Edward Singhateh: although Singhateh had succeeded Sabally as AFPRC Vice-President in early 1995, he was, under the terms of the new Constitution, too young (at 27 years of age) to assume the office of Vice-President. In April 1997 the remaining four regional military governors were replaced by civilians. Among the new governors was Jawara's former head of police, who had been released from detention only two months previously.

Supporters of the new regime attributed the electoral success of Jammeh and the APRC to the popularity within The Gambia of the ambitious infrastructural projects undertaken since July 1994, citing in particular the construction of more new schools and hospitals than had been built in 30 years by the Jawara administration, as well as a new airport terminal and modernized port facilities, a television station, and plans for a national university. However, Jammeh's critics condemned what they regarded as excessive expenditure on 'prestige' projects.

In February 1997 CMAG reiterated its earlier concerns regarding the exclusion of what it termed a 'significant element' of The Gambia's political class from the process of restoring government to elected civilian institutions. In July the group again urged the immediate removal of the ban on political activities by certain parties and individuals; CMAG sought demonstration of the Jammeh administration's expressed commitment to the observance of human rights and the rule of law, and appealed to the Government to investigate allegations of the harassment of opposition activists. In September, none the less, CMAG reported signs of progress in the democratization process.

In April 1997 the trial began (in camera) of five alleged mercenaries suspected of involvement in the November 1996 attack on the Farafenni barracks. The accused apparently confirmed press reports at the time of the attack that they had formed part of a 40-strong commando group, trained in Libya and led by Kukoi Samba Sanyang, which had fought for Charles Taylor's National Patriotic Front of Liberia during the early 1990s. Four of the accused (three Gambians and one Senegalese national) were subsequently sentenced to death; the fifth defendant had died in detention in May 1997. In early October, however, the Supreme Court ruled that the convictions, on charges of treason, were not sustainable, and ordered that the four be retried on conspiracy charges. Meanwhile, the arrest of a further mercenary had been reported in mid-April; some 13 other suspects remained at large.

Responsibility for religious affairs was transferred from the Secretary of State for the Interior to the Secretary of State for Youth and Sports in early October 1997. In the previous month members of the Pakistani Ahmadi Islamic sect had left The Gambia (where they had been working for more than 20 years), accusing the incumbent Secretary of State, Momodou Bojang, of fomenting religious intolerance by describing the sect as 'infidels' and allowing Gambian Islamic leaders to deliver sermons hostile to the Ahmadi.

In early February 1998 the director and a journalist of a private radio station, Citizen FM, were detained, and the Government ordered the closure of the station and an associated newspaper, *New Citizen,* citing the station's failure to comply with new tax requirements for independent broadcasters (taxes had been doubled). However, opponents of the closure noted that the station had recently broadcast information concerning the National Intelligence Agency. The director of Citizen FM, Baboucar Gaye, subsequently launched a legal appeal against the closure of the station. In July 1999 Gaye, whose appeal had still not been heard, accused the Government of employing delaying tactics, and in January 2000 the case was again adjourned until mid-April. The depletion of independent media outlets gave further cause for concern in May 1999, when the *Daily Observer,* the only remaining newspaper that openly criticized the Government, was purchased by Amadou Samba, a Gambian businessman closely associated with Jammeh. Despite Samba's assurances that he would not interfere in editorial matters, staff who had criticized the Government were subsequently removed from their posts. In July *The Independent,* a privately-owned newspaper, which had recently been launched, was ordered to suspend publication because of alleged irregularities in its registration. It was, however, alleged that the Government had ordered the suspension following the publication of an article which repeated accusations, made by the UDP, of widespread corruption in the Jammeh regime.

Opposition activists continued to allege harassment by the Government throughout 1998 and early 1999. In May 1998 nine people were arrested in a raid on the mosque at Brikama; among those detained were the Imam, as well as a prominent critic of Jammeh, Lamine Wa Juwara. A member of the UDP, Juwara was involved in a lawsuit seeking D20m. in compensation for alleged wrongful imprisonment during the transition period. The UDP leader, Ousainou Darboe, was briefly imprisoned shortly afterwards. In July a seminar on government structures, conducted under the auspices of the Department of State for Local Government and Lands (and attended by representatives of several international organizations), was disrupted by APRC militants who forcibly removed Juwara. The Government accused Juwara of fomenting unrest, but promised to investigate the occurrence; meanwhile, critics claimed that the activities of APRC's so-called 'Action Group' were officially condoned. At the end of the month Juwara's claim for damages, arising from his 20-month imprisonment without charge following the 1994 coup, was rejected by the Supreme Court on the grounds that the Constitution contained a clause granting immunity to the former AFPRC in connection with the transition period. In May 1999 the leader of the youth wing of the UDP, Momodou Shyngle Nyassi, was reportedly abducted by the security forces and subjected to ill-treatment. He was released without charge after nearly a month, following the intervention of the Gambian High Court and diplomatic pressure from the EU.

In late October 1998 the Supreme Court sentenced three former armed forces members to death for their part in an attack on a military base at Kartong, near the Senegalese border, in July 1997, in which at least one soldier was reportedly killed and weapons had been stolen. The convicted men were alleged to have been attempting to flee to Senegal after a failed attempt to overthrow Jammeh.

In mid-January 1998 Jammeh appointed Dr Momadou Lamine Sedat Jobe as Secretary of State for External Affairs, replacing Omar Njie. As part of a cabinet reshuffle in early March Dominic Mendy, hitherto Secretary of State for Finance and Economic Affairs, and Famara Jatta, Secretary of State for Trade, Industry and Employment, exchanged portfolios. In July Awa Ceesay-Saballay was dismissed as Secretary of State for Justice and replaced by the Attorney-General, Fatou Bensouda. Four cabinet members, among them Mendy and the Secretary of State for the Interior, Momodou Bojang, were removed from office in late January 1999. At the same time the Managing Director of the National Water and Electricity Company was dismissed. No official explanation was given for the changes, although rumours circulated that a recent audit had revealed financial mismanagement in some government departments.

In September 1999 a reporter and editor were briefly detained after the publication in *The Observer* of an article suggesting that a Senegalese helicopter had flown over Jammeh's home village and exchanged gunfire with presidential guards. In late December international attention was again focused on Jammeh's attitude to the press, when staff from *The Independent* newspaper were arrested and charged with libel following the publication of an article alleging that Jammeh had divorced his wife and had remarried. The Government was further embarrassed in October by the flight to Senegal of the APRC Secretary-General, Phokay Makalo, who had allegedly embezzled party funds, while in January 2000 an MPLC deputy was detained on suspicion of drugs smuggling.

In late December 1999 Jammeh dismissed Fasainey Dumbuya as Secretary of State for Agriculture, replacing him with Abdoulie Sallah. In mid-January 2000 Jammeh again carried out a minor cabinet reshuffle, this time assigning Abdoulie Sallah the health and social welfare portfolios, which had previously been the responsibility of the Vice-President, Isatou Njie-Saidy. Hassan Sallah was appointed as Secretary of State for Agriculture.

In early January 2000 allegations of government corruption emerged after the disclosure in legal proceedings in the United Kingdom that significant sums of money generated by the sale of crude petroleum had been paid into an anonymous Swiss bank account. The crude petroleum had been granted to The Gambia for trading purposes by the Nigerian Government between August 1996 and June 1998, reportedly in recognition of Jammeh's opposition in 1995 to the imposition of sanctions by the Commonwealth against Nigeria. The UDP leader, Ousainou Darboe, subsequently alleged that Jammeh had illegally diverted more than US $1.9m. of the proceeds of the sale of the petroleum. Jammeh vigorously denied any involvement in the matter. No further comment was offered by the Government, and journalists continued to attempt to uncover the beneficiaries of the Swiss bank account.

On 15 January 2000 the security forces announced that they had forestalled an attempted military coup. It was reported that during efforts to arrest the conspirators, Lt Almamo Manneh of the State Guard had been killed, and the Commander of the State Guard, Lt Landing Sanneh, the officer in charge of security at the presidential palace, had been wounded. Another member of the State Guard was killed on the following day while attempting to evade arrest. The Secretary of State for the Interior, Ousman Badjie, strenuously denied rumours that the authorities had invented the conspiracy as a pretext to purge the State Guard and as a means of diverting press attention from the petroleum scandal. Lt Sanneh's wife continued to deny, however, that her husband had been involved in a coup attempt, while opponents of the Government demanded that it produce evidence of the existence of the plot. None the less, the Government refused to release further details on the grounds that they might prejudice any future criminal proceedings.

In the months that followed the 1994 coup The Gambia's traditional aid donors and trading partners suspended much co-operation (although vital aid projects were generally to continue). The Jammeh administration therefore sought new links: diplomatic relations with Libya, severed in 1980, were restored in November 1994 and numerous co-operation agreements ensued. Links with Taiwan, ended in 1974, were also re-established in July 1995, whereupon Taiwan became one of the Gambia's major sources of funding. In November 1999 Jammeh visited Teheran in order to establish closer bilateral relations between The Gambia and Iran.

Despite the presence in Senegal of prominent opponents of his Government, Jammeh also sought to improve relations with that country, and in January 1996 the two countries signed an agreement aimed at increasing bilateral trade and at minimizing cross-border smuggling. A further agreement, concluded in April 1997, was designed to facilitate the trans-border movement of goods destined for re-export. In June the two countries agreed to take joint measures to combat insecurity, illegal immigration, arms-trafficking and drugs-smuggling. In January 1998 the Government of Senegal welcomed an offer by Jammeh to mediate in the conflict in the southern province of Casamance: the separatist MFDC is chiefly composed of the Diola ethnic group, of which Jammeh in a member. In late June Jammeh offered to mediate in the conflict between the Government and rebel forces in Guinea-Bissau (q.v.); the rebel leader, Gen. Ansumane Mane, was a Diola of Gambian extraction. In January 1999 The Gambia agreed to provide troops for an ECOMOG (see Economic Community of West African States, p.165) peacekeeping mission in Guinea-Bissau. After the defeat of government forces in Guinea-Bissau in May 1999, the Gambian authorities secured in June the safe passage of former President Vieira to The Gambia on medical grounds, from where he departed for Portugal. In late June the interim President of Guinea-Bissau, Malam Bacai Sanha, visited Jammeh to thank him for his intervention.

### Government

The Constitution of the Second Republic of The Gambia, which was approved in a national referendum on 8 August 1996, entered into full effect on 16 January 1997. Under its terms, the Head of State is the President of the Republic, who is directly elected by universal adult suffrage (the minimum age for voters is 18 years). No restriction is placed on the number of times a President may seek re-election. Legislative authority is vested in the National Assembly, comprising 45 members elected by direct suffrage and four members nominated by the President of the Republic. The President appoints government members, who are reponsible both to the Head of State and to the National Assembly.

### Defence

In August 1999 the Gambian National Army comprised 800 men (including a marine unit of about 70 and a presidential guard) in active service. Military service has been mainly voluntary; however, the Constitution of the Second Republic, which entered into full effect in January 1997, makes provision for compulsory service. The defence budget for 1999 was estimated at D180m.

### Economic Affairs

In 1997, according to estimates by the World Bank, The Gambia's gross national product (GNP), measured at average 1995–97 prices, was US $407m., equivalent to $340 per head. During 1990–97, it was estimated, GNP per head declined, in real terms, at an average annual rate of 0.6%. During the same period the population increased at an average annual rate of 3.6%. During 1990/91–1998 (financial years, until 1997, ending 30 June), according to data published by the IMF, The Gambia's gross domestic product (GDP) increased, in real terms, at an average annual rate of an estimated 2.9%. Real GDP increased by an estimated 4.9% in 1997, and by 4.7% in 1998.

Agriculture (including forestry and fishing) contributed an estimated 27.4% of GDP in 1998. About 73.3% of the labour force were employed in the sector in that year. The dominant agricultural activity is the cultivation of groundnuts. Exports of groundnuts and related products accounted for an estimated 62.7% of domestic export earnings in 1998; however, a significant proportion of the crop is frequently smuggled for sale in Senegal. Cotton, citrus fruits, mangoes, avocados and sesame seed are also cultivated for export. The principal staple crops are rice, millet, sorghum and maize, although The Gambia remains heavily dependent on imports of rice and other basic foodstuffs. Fishing makes an important contribution both to the domestic food supply and to export earnings: exports of fish and fish products contributed an estimated 13.6% of the value of domestic exports in 1998. Agricultural GDP increased at an estimated average annual rate of 1.8% in 1990/91–1998; the sector's GDP declined by an estimated 11.1% in 1996/97 (largely reflecting a sharp fall in the groundnut crop), but increased by an estimated 8.9% in 1997 and by an estimated 2.7% in 1998.

Industry (including manufacturing, construction, mining and power) contributed an estimated 13.7% of GDP in 1998. About 9.7% of the labour force were employed in the sector at the time of the 1993 census. Industrial GDP increased at an average annual rate of 1.0% in 1990/91–1998, with growth of an estimated 5.2% in 1998.

The Gambia has no economically viable mineral resources, although seismic surveys have indicated the existence of deposits of petroleum. Deposits of kaolin and salt are currently unexploited. Manufacturing contributed an estimated 5.8% of GDP in 1998, and employed about 6.3% of the labour force in 1993. The sector is dominated by agro-industrial activities, most importantly the processing of groundnuts and fish. Beverages and construction materials are also produced for the domestic market. Manufacturing GDP increased at an average annual rate of 1.1% in 1990/91–1998; the sector's GDP increased by an estimated 2.4% in 1998.

The Gambia is highly reliant on imported energy. According to figures published by IMF, imports of petroleum products accounted for an estimated 8.5% of the value of imports for domestic use in 1998.

The services sector contributed an estimated 58.9% of GDP in 1998. The tourist industry is of particular significance as a generator of foreign exchange. Tourism contributed about 10% of annual GDP in the early 1990s, and employed about one-third of workers in the formal sector at that time. The international response to the 1994 coup and its aftermath had a severe impact on tourism to The Gambia, although the industry recovered strongly from 1996 onwards. The Jammeh administration has expressed its intention further to exploit the country's potential as a transit point for regional trade and also as a centre for regional finance and telecommunications. Re-exports contributed an estimated 84.2% of the value of total merchandise exports in 1998, according to IMF figures. The GDP of the services sector increased at an average annual rate of 3.7% in 1990/91–1998; growth in 1998 was estimated at 5.8%.

In 1997 The Gambia recorded a visible trade deficit of US $87.48m., while there was a deficit of $23.56m. on the current account of the balance of payments. In 1998 the principal source of imports was the People's Republic of China, which supplied an estimated 13.7% of total imports; other major sources were Hong Kong, the United Kingdom, France, Côte d'Ivoire and the Netherlands. The Belgo-Luxembourg Economic Union was the principal market for exports (an estimated 72.1%) in that year. The Gambia's principal domestic exports in 1998 were groundnuts and related products, fish and fish products and cotton products. The principal imports in that year were food and live animals, machinery and transport equipment, basic manufactures and mineral fuels and lubricants.

In 1996/97 there was an estimated overall budget deficit of D381.9m. (equivalent to 9.7% of that year's GDP). The Gambia's total external debt was US $430.1m. at the end of 1997, of which $406.9m. was long-term public debt. In that year the cost of debt-servicing was equivalent to 11.6% of the value of exports of goods and services. The average annual rate of inflation was 4.2% in 1991–98; consumer prices increased by an average of 1.1% in 1998. The rate of unemployment was estimated at some 26% of the labour force in mid-1994.

The Gambia is a member of the Economic Community of West African States (ECOWAS, see p. 163), of The Gambia River Basin Development Organization (OMVG, see p. 291), of the African Groundnut Council (see p. 286), of the West Africa Rice Development Association (WARDA, see p. 289), and of the Permanent Inter-State Committee on Drought Control in the Sahel (CILSS, see p. 293).

The military coup of July 1994 caused considerable economic disruption to The Gambia: the country's principal donors suspended much financial co-operation, while there was also a dramatic decline in both entrepôt trade and tourism. Despite the resultant economic adversity, the Jammeh Government undertook numerous infrastructural projects to promote its aim to establish The Gambia as a middle-income economy within 25 years. A return to growth from 1995 was, in large part, underpinned by the recovery in the tourism sector. The installation of elected civilian institutions in early 1997 prompted a return to full support by the international economic community. The World Bank resumed co-operation in late 1997, and in mid-1998 the IMF approved a three-year Enhanced Structural Adjustment Facility (ESAF) to support the Government's economic programme for 1998–2000. The programme aimed to reduce the overall fiscal deficit from 4.5% in 1998 to 2.5% in 2000, and to restrict average inflation to 2.5% per year. Another fundamental goal of the programme was to encourage further private-sector development, and considerable efforts have also been made to attract new investors to The Gambia, although investor confidence in The Gambia was weakened by the nationalization in early 1999 of the Gambia Groundnut Corporation. The Gambia's overriding dependence on the groundnut sector, which lags behind other sectors in terms of modernization and productivity, remains an obstacle to sustained growth, while concern has also been expressed at the level of borrowing incurred by the Jammeh Government to finance its infrastructural programme; the level of The Gambia's international indebtedness has risen sharply since 1995.

### Social Welfare

At the end of 1980 there were 43 government physicians, 23 private practitioners and five dentists. There were four hospitals and a network of 12 health centres, 17 dispensaries and 68 maternity and child welfare clinics throughout the country. A major programme to improve health and social welfare facilities has been undertaken by the Jammeh administration. Among the schemes is a new hospital at Farafenni, under construction at a cost of US $65m. In 1998 spending by the central Government on health was estimated at D152.9m. Estimated current spending by the central Government on social welfare in 1996/97 was D600,000, equivalent to less than 0.1% of current spending allocations.

### Education

Primary education, beginning at seven years of age, is free but not compulsory and lasts for six years. Secondary education, from 13 years of age, comprises a first cycle of five years and a second, two-year cycle. In 1997 total enrolment at primary schools was equivalent to 73% of children in the relevant age-group (61% of girls), while the comparable ratio for secondary enrolment was only 19% (13% of girls). According to UNESCO estimates, adult illiteracy in 1995 averaged 61.4% (males 47.2%; females 75.1%). The Jammeh administration has, since 1994, embarked on an ambitious project to improve educational facilities and levels of attendance and attainment. A particular aim has been to ameliorate access to schools for pupils in rural areas. Post-secondary education is available in teacher training, agriculture, health and technical subjects. Some 1,591 students were enrolled at tertiary establishments in 1994/95. The establishment of a university remains a priority, and a cost and financing study was carried out in 1998. In 1977 The Gambia introduced Koranic studies at all stages of education, and many children attend Koranic schools (daara). In 1998 education was allocated an estimated D152.9m., equivalent to almost 22% of recurrent budget expenditure.

### Public Holidays

**2000:** 1 January (New Year's Day), 8 January*† (Eid al-Fitr, end of Ramadan), 18 February (Independence Day), 16 March* (Eid al-Kebir, Feast of the Sacrifice), 21 April (Good Friday), 1 May (Workers' Day), 15 June* (Eid al-Moulid, Birth of the Prophet), 22 July (Anniversary of the Second Republic), 15 August (Assumption/St Mary's Day), 25 December (Christmas), 28 December*† (Eid al-Fitr, end of Ramadan).

**2001:** 1 January (New Year's Day), 18 February (Independence Day), 6 March* (Eid al-Kebir, Feast of the Sacrifice), 13 April (Good Friday), 1 May (Workers' Day), 4 June* (Eid al-Moulid, Birth of the Prophet), 22 July (Anniversary of the Second Republic), 15 August (Assumption/St Mary's Day), 17 December* (Eid al-Fitr, end of Ramadan), 25 December (Christmas).

* These holidays are dependent on the Islamic lunar calendar and may vary by one or two days from the dates given.

† This festival will occur twice (in the Islamic years AH 1420 and 1421) within the same Gregorian year).

### Weights and Measures

Imperial weights and measures are used. Importers and traders also use the metric system.

# Statistical Survey

Source (unless otherwise stated): Department of Information, 14 Daniel Goddard St, Banjul; tel. 225060; fax 227230.

## Area and Population

**AREA, POPULATION AND DENSITY**

| | |
|---|---|
| Area (sq km) | 11,295* |
| Population (census results) | |
| 15 April 1983 | |
| Total | 687,817 |
| 15 April 1993 | |
| Males | 514,530 |
| Females | 511,337 |
| Total | 1,025,867 |
| Population (UN estimates at mid-year)† | |
| 1996 | 1,150,000 |
| 1997 | 1,189,000 |
| 1998 | 1,229,000 |
| Density (per sq km) at mid-1998 | 108.8 |

* 4,361 sq miles.

† Source: UN, *World Population Prospects: The 1998 Revision.*

**ETHNIC GROUPS**

1993 census (percentages): Mandinka 39.60; Fula 18.83; Wollof 14.61; Jola 10.66; Serahule 8.92; Serere 2.77; Creole/Aku 0.69; Manjago 1.85; Bambara 0.84; Others 1.23.

**PRINCIPAL TOWNS** (population at 1993 census)

| | | | |
|---|---|---|---|
| Banjul (capital) | 42,326 | Lamin | 10,668 |
| Brikama | 41,761 | Gunjur | 9,983 |
| Bakau | 28,882 | Basse | 9,265 |
| Farafenni | 20,956 | Soma | 7,988 |
| Serrekunda | 18,901 | Bansang | 5,743 |
| Sukuta | 12,170 | | |

**BIRTHS AND DEATHS** (UN estimates, annual averages)

| | 1980–85 | 1985–90 | 1990–95 |
|---|---|---|---|
| Birth rate (per 1,000) | 48.2 | 46.3 | 43.3 |
| Death rate (per 1,000) | 23.1 | 21.2 | 19.2 |

**Expectation of life** (UN estimates, years at birth, 1990–95): 45.0 (males 43.4; females 46.6).

Source: UN, *World Population Prospects: The 1998 Revision.*

**ECONOMICALLY ACTIVE POPULATION***
(persons aged 10 years and over, 1993 census)

| | Total |
|---|---|
| Agriculture, hunting and forestry | 175,692 |
| Fishing | 6,060 |
| Mining and quarrying | 398 |
| Manufacturing | 21,682 |
| Electricity, gas and water supply | 1,858 |
| Construction | 9,679 |
| Wholesale and retail trade; repair of motor vehicles, motorcycles and personal and household goods | 48,741 |
| Hotels and restaurants | 5,987 |
| Transport, storage and communications | 14,203 |
| Financial intermediation | 2,415 |
| Other community, social and personal service activities | 41,254 |
| Activities not adequately defined | 17,412 |
| **Total** | 345,381† |

* Figures exclude persons seeking work for the first time.
† Males 207,310; females 138,071.

**Mid-1998** (estimates in '000): Agriculture, etc. 500; Total 682 (Source: FAO, *Production Yearbook*).

# Agriculture

**PRINCIPAL CROPS** ('000 metric tons)

| | 1996 | 1997 | 1998* |
|---|---|---|---|
| Millet | 61 | 66 | 66 |
| Sorghum | 14 | 13 | 13 |
| Rice (paddy) | 20 | 17 | 17 |
| Maize | 10 | 8 | 8 |
| Cassava (Manioc) | 6* | 6* | 6 |
| Pulses | 4* | 4* | 4 |
| Palm kernels | 2* | 2* | 2 |
| Groundnuts (in shell) | 46 | 78 | 78 |
| Vegetables | 8* | 8* | 8 |
| Fruits | 4* | 4* | 4 |
| Cottonseed | 3* | 1* | 1 |

* FAO estimate(s).

Source: FAO, *Production Yearbook*.

**LIVESTOCK** ('000 head, year ending September)

| | 1996 | 1997 | 1998* |
|---|---|---|---|
| Cattle | 323 | 346 | 346 |
| Goats | 224 | 250 | 250 |
| Sheep | 159 | 182 | 182 |
| Pigs | 14 | 14 | 14 |
| Asses | 35* | 35* | 35 |
| Horses | 19* | 19* | 19 |

Poultry (million)*: 1 in 1996; 1 in 1997; 1 in 1998.

* FAO estimate(s).

Source: FAO, *Production Yearbook*.

**LIVESTOCK PRODUCTS** (FAO estimates, '000 metric tons)

| | 1996 | 1997 | 1998 |
|---|---|---|---|
| Beef and veal | 3 | 3 | 3 |
| Goat meat | 1 | 1 | 1 |
| Mutton and lamb | 1 | 1 | 1 |
| Poultry meat | 1 | 2 | 2 |
| Other meat | 1 | 1 | 1 |
| Cows' milk | 7 | 7 | 7 |
| Poultry eggs | 1 | 1 | 1 |

Source: FAO, *Production Yearbook*.

# Forestry

**ROUNDWOOD REMOVALS**
('000 cubic metres, excluding bark)

| | 1995 | 1996 | 1997 |
|---|---|---|---|
| Sawlogs, veneer logs and logs for sleepers | 106 | 106 | 106 |
| Other industrial wood | 7 | 7 | 7 |
| Fuel wood | 1,108 | 1,114 | 1,126 |
| **Total** | 1,221 | 1,227 | 1,239 |

Source: FAO, *Yearbook of Forest Products*.

# Fishing

('000 metric tons, live weight)

| | 1995 | 1996 | 1997 |
|---|---|---|---|
| Tilapias | 1.1 | 1.2 | 1.1 |
| Other freshwater fishes | 1.5 | 1.5 | 1.5 |
| Tonguefishes | 0.9 | 0.5 | 0.3 |
| Sea catfishes | 0.8 | 0.2 | 1.2 |
| Croakers and drums | 1.4 | 1.3 | 1.0 |
| Bonga shad | 13.9 | 22.6 | 21.5 |
| Other marine fishes (incl. unspecified) | 2.8 | 3.5 | 5.4 |
| **Total fish** | 22.4 | 30.8 | 32.0 |
| Southern pink shrimp | 0.4 | 0.3 | — |
| Other crustaceans and molluscs | 0.5 | 0.5 | 0.3 |
| **Total catch** | 23.3 | 31.6 | 32.3 |
| Inland waters | 2.5 | 2.5 | 2.5 |
| Atlantic Ocean | 20.8 | 29.1 | 29.8 |

Source: FAO, *Yearbook of Fishery Statistics*.

# Industry

**SELECTED PRODUCTS**

| | 1993 | 1994 | 1995 |
|---|---|---|---|
| Salted, dried or smoked fish ('000 metric tons)* | 0.9 | 1.1 | 0.9 |
| Palm oil—unrefined ('000 metric tons)* | 3 | 3 | 3 |
| Electric energy (million kWh)† | 73 | 73 | 74 |

* Data from the FAO. † Provisional or estimated figures.

Source: UN, *Industrial Commodity Statistics Yearbook*.

**Palm oil—unrefined** (FAO estimates, '000 metric tons): 3 in 1996; 3 in 1997; 3 in 1998. Source: FAO, *Production Yearbook*.

# Finance

**CURRENCY AND EXCHANGE RATES**

**Monetary Units**
100 butut = 1 dalasi (D).

**Sterling, Dollar and Euro Equivalents** (30 September 1999)
£1 sterling = 19.19 dalasi;
US $1 = 11.66 dalasi;
€1 = 12.43 dalasi;
1,000 dalasi = £52.10 = $85.78 = €80.43.

**Average Exchange Rate** (dalasi per US $)
1996 9.789
1997 10.200
1998 10.643

**BUDGET** (million dalasi, year ending 30 June)

| Revenue* | 1996/97‡ | 1997 | 1998§ |
|---|---|---|---|
| Tax revenue | 701.2 | 714.7 | 751.1 |
| Direct taxes | 160.2 | 168.5 | 185.1 |
| Taxes on personal incomes | 61.7 | 72.3 | 76.4 |
| Taxes on corporate profits | 93.0 | 81.8 | 93.7 |
| Indirect taxes | 531.7 | 546.2 | 566.0 |
| Domestic taxes on goods and services | 75.6 | 71.5 | 65.3 |
| Domestic sales tax | 52.9 | 57.1 | 63.0 |
| Taxes on international trade | 456.1 | 266.2 | 295.0 |
| Customs duties | 110.3 | 119.7 | 145.1 |
| Sales tax on imports | 142.0 | 146.4 | 149.9 |
| Petroleum taxes | 203.5 | 208.5 | 205.8 |
| Duty | 177.0 | 178.6 | 177.3 |
| Sales tax | 26.5 | 29.9 | 28.5 |
| Other current revenue | 74.1 | 84.8 | 80.4 |
| Government services and charges | 41.4 | 40.1 | 35.1 |
| Interest, dividends and property | 12.4 | 23.0 | 38.6 |
| Central Bank profit | 17.4 | 17.4 | 4.0 |
| **Total** | 775.3 | 799.5 | 831.5 |

| Expenditure† | 1996/97‡ | 1997 | 1998§ |
|---|---|---|---|
| Current expenditure | 738.5 | 794.6 | 799.8 |
| Expenditure on goods and services | 443.2 | 470.9 | 447.5 |
| Personal emoluments, allowances and pensions | 254.4 | 269.3 | 282.9 |
| Other charges | 188.8 | 201.6 | 164.5 |
| Goods and services | 138.9 | 147.3 | 116.3 |
| Maintenance and equipment | 36.7 | 41.5 | 31.9 |
| Interest payments | 192.7 | 214.7 | 236.9 |
| Internal | 144.5 | 155.2 | 180.4 |
| External | 48.2 | 59.5 | 56.4 |
| Subsidies and current transfers | 102.5 | 109.0 | 115.4 |
| To non-profit institutions | 83.5 | 78.5 | 87.0 |
| Development expenditure | 507.4‖ | 349.9‖ | 259.9 |
| **Total** | 1,245.9 | 1,144.5 | 1,059.7 |

* Excluding grants received (million dalasi): 69.4 in 1996/97; 53.0 in 1997; 88.5 in 1998.

† Excluding lending minus repayments (million dalasi): –14.0 in 1996/97; –20.9 in 1997; –31.2 in 1998.

‡ Year ending 30 June. § Estimates.

‖ Including foreign-financed extrabudgetary expenditure (million dalasi): 150.4 in 1996/97; 60.6 in 1997.

Source: IMF, *The Gambia: Selected Issues* (August 1999).

**INTERNATIONAL RESERVES** (US $ million at 31 December)

| | 1996 | 1997 | 1998 |
|---|---|---|---|
| IMF special drawing rights | 0.29 | 0.11 | 0.42 |
| Reserve position in IMF | 2.14 | 2.00 | 2.09 |
| Foreign exchange | 99.71 | 93.92 | 103.85 |
| **Total** | 102.13 | 96.04 | 106.36 |

Source: IMF, *International Financial Statistics*.

**MONEY SUPPLY** (million dalasi at 31 December)

| | 1996 | 1997 | 1998 |
|---|---|---|---|
| Currency outside banks | 255.03 | 360.51 | 347.55 |
| Demand deposits at commercial banks | 198.46 | 268.90 | 279.02 |
| **Total money** | 453.49 | 629.41 | 626.57 |

Source: IMF, *International Financial Statistics*.

**COST OF LIVING**
(Consumer Price Index for Banjul and Kombo St Mary; base: 1990 = 100)

| | 1994 | 1995 | 1996 |
|---|---|---|---|
| Food | 126.2 | 137.1 | 138.6 |
| Fuel and light | 160.1 | 117.3 | 116.6 |
| Clothing* | 130.9 | 134.4 | 132.9 |
| Rent | 219.1 | 251.1 | 251.1 |
| **All items** (incl. others) | 128.8 | 137.8 | 139.3 |

* Including household linen.

**1997:** Food 140.6; All items 143.2.

Source: ILO, *Yearbook of Labour Statistics*.

**1998** (base: 1995 = 100): All items 105.1. Source: IMF, *International Financial Statistics*.

**NATIONAL ACCOUNTS**
(million dalasi at current prices, estimates)

**Expenditure on the Gross Domestic Product**

| | 1996/97* | 1997 | 1998 |
|---|---|---|---|
| Government final consumption expenditure | 690.3 | 735.1 | 743.2 |
| Private final consumption expenditure | 3,070.1 | 3,120.6 | 3,352.5 |
| Increase in stocks } Gross fixed capital formation } | 771.5 | 715.1 | 812.9 |
| **Total domestic expenditure** | 4,531.9 | 4,570.8 | 4,908.7 |
| Exports of goods and services | 1,844.7 | 1,883.5 | 2,262.2 |
| *Less* Imports of goods and services | 2,375.0 | 2,303.1 | 2,746.5 |
| **GDP in purchasers' values** | 4,001.6 | 4,151.2 | 4,424.3 |
| **GDP at constant 1976/77 prices** | 609.1 | 639.2 | 669.3 |

* Year ending 30 June.

**Gross Domestic Product by Economic Activity**

| | 1996/97* | 1997 | 1998 |
|---|---|---|---|
| Agriculture, hunting, forestry and fishing | 946.4 | 983.6 | 1,056.2 |
| Manufacturing | 217.4 | 223.3 | 225.7 |
| Electricity and water | 56.1 | 66.5 | 72.1 |
| Construction | 200.1 | 216.2 | 229.8 |
| Trade, restaurants and hotels | 619.4 | 671.3 | 741.5 |
| Transport and communications | 604.1 | 565.8 | 600.7 |
| Business services and housing | 274.2 | 276.0 | 299.6 |
| Government services | 368.2 | 383.9 | 407.1 |
| Other services† | 184.0 | 218.9 | 225.4 |
| **GDP at factor cost** | 3,469.9 | 3,605.5 | 3,858.3 |
| Indirect taxes, *Less* Subsidies | 531.7 | 545.7 | 566.0 |
| **GDP in purchasers' values** | 4,001.6 | 4,151.2 | 4,424.3 |

* Year ending 30 June.

† Including banking and insurance, net of imputed bank service charges.

Source: IMF, *The Gambia: Selected Issues* (August 1999).

**LIVESTOCK** ('000 head at 1 January)

| | 1996 | 1997 | 1998 |
|---|---|---|---|
| Horses | 24 | 26 | 22* |
| Cattle | 974 | 1009 | 1027 |
| Buffaloes | 20† | 18* | 18* |
| Pigs | 353 | 333 | 330 |
| Sheep | 674 | 607† | 543† |
| Goats | 51 | 45† | 41† |
| Poultry (million) | 14† | 15† | 15* |

* FAO estimate.

† Unofficial figure.

Source: FAO, *Production Yearbook*.

**LIVESTOCK PRODUCTS** ('000 metric tons)

| | 1996 | 1997 | 1998† |
|---|---|---|---|
| Beef and veal | 59 | 52* | 55 |
| Mutton and lamb | 9 | 8* | 8 |
| Pig meat | 56 | 50* | 53 |
| Poultry meat | 9 | 10* | 10 |
| Cows' milk | 530 | 600 | 600 |
| Cheese† | 3 | 3 | 3 |
| Hen eggs | 19* | 21* | 21 |

* Unofficial figure. † FAO estimates.

Source: FAO, *Production Yearbook*.

# Fishing

(metric tons, live weight)

| | 1995 | 1996 | 1997 |
|---|---|---|---|
| Common carp | — | 375 | 463 |
| Silver carp | n.a. | 117 | 145 |
| Beluga | n.a. | 76 | 85 |
| Azov sea sprat* | 117 | — | — |
| Whiting | 146 | 223 | 57 |
| Flatfishes | — | 160 | 243 |
| European pilchard | 900* | — | — |
| European sprat | 292 | 185 | 85 |
| European anchovy | 1,401* | 1,232 | 5,446 |
| Sea snails | 700 | 711 | 118 |
| **Total catch** (incl. others) | 3,741* | 3,385 | 6,933 |
| Inland waters | 219* | 595 | 734 |
| Mediterranean and Black Sea | 2,522 | 2,790 | 6,199 |
| Atlantic Ocean | 1,000* | — | — |

* FAO estimate(s).

Source: FAO, *Yearbook of Fishery Statistics*.

# Mining

('000 metric tons, unless otherwise indicated)

| | 1993 | 1994* | 1995* |
|---|---|---|---|
| Coal | 82.2 | 44.5 | 42.7 |
| Crude petroleum | 88.2 | 66.9 | 42.7 |
| Natural gas (million cu m) | 21.8 | 11.4 | 3.3 |
| Manganese ore | 36.8 | 29.3 | 41.9 |

* Data for South Ossetia and Abkhazia are not included.

# Industry

**SELECTED PRODUCTS** ('000 metric tons, unless otherwise indicated)

| | 1993 | 1994* | 1995* |
|---|---|---|---|
| Margarine | 2.3 | 0.1 | 0.1 |
| Vegetable oil | 0.5 | 0.0 | 0.0 |
| Wine ('000 hectolitres) | 1,042.5 | 436.3 | 412.3 |
| Beer ('000 hectolitres) | 120.4 | 64.8 | 67.1 |
| Cigarettes (million) | 3,600 | 3,300 | 1,900 |
| Wool yarn | 1.5 | 0.3 | 0.3 |
| Cotton yarn | 2.6 | 0.8 | 1.0 |
| Cotton fabrics (million sq metres) | 7.5 | 1.5 | 0.6 |
| Woollen fabrics (million sq metres) | 1.9 | 0.5 | 0.5 |
| Footwear (million pairs) | 1.0 | 0.2 | 0.1 |
| Paper | 0.3 | 0.1 | n.a. |
| Synthetic resins and plastics | 10.2 | 2.1 | 0.6 |
| Chemical fibres and threads | 8.0 | 0.9 | 0.2 |
| Soap | 1.4 | 1.1 | n.a. |
| Motor spirit (petrol) | 18.6 | 8.8 | 3.3 |
| Distillate fuel oil (diesel fuel) | 34.5 | 17.9 | 8.4 |
| Residual fuel oil (mazout) | 72.0 | 24.8 | 11.7 |
| Building bricks (million) | 22.8 | 9.1 | 6.4 |
| Steel | 221.7 | 121.2 | 88 |
| Electric energy (million kWh) | 9,748 | 7,039 | 7,100 |

* Data for South Ossetia and Abkhazia are not included.

# Finance

**CURRENCY AND EXCHANGE RATES**

**Monetary Units**

100 tetri = 1 lari.

**Sterling, Dollar and Euro Equivalents** (30 September 1999)

£1 sterling = 3.049 lari;
US $1 = 1.852 lari;
€1 = 1.975 lari;
100 lari = £32.79 = $54.00 = €50.63.

**Average Exchange Rate** (lari per US $)

1996 1.2628
1997 1.2975
1998 1.3898

Note: On 25 September 1995 Georgia introduced the lari, replacing interim currency coupons at the rate of 1 lari = 1,000,000 coupons. From April 1993 the National Bank of Georgia had issued coupons in various denominations, to circulate alongside (and initially at par with) the Russian (formerly Soviet) rouble. Following the dissolution of the USSR in December 1991, Russia and several other former Soviet republics retained the rouble as their monetary unit. The average interbank market rate in 1992 was $1 = 222.1 roubles. From August 1993 coupons became Georgia's sole legal tender, but their value rapidly depreciated. The transfer from coupons to the lari lasted one week, and from 2 October 1995 the lari became the only permitted currency in Georgia.

**BUDGET** (million lari)*

| Revenue† | 1995 | 1996 | 1997 |
|---|---|---|---|
| Tax revenue | 131.9 | 304.5 | 484.6 |
| Taxes on income | 20.9 | 44.5 | 76.9 |
| Taxes on profits | 28.6 | 37.9 | 38.8 |
| Value-added tax | 58.5 | 133.8 | 205.5 |
| Customs duties | 4.5 | 19.9 | 61.2 |
| Other current revenue | 16.9 | 50.0 | 67.8 |
| Extrabudgetary revenue‡ | 41.2 | 111.2 | 126.4 |
| **Total** | 189.9 | 465.7 | 678.8 |

| Expenditure§ | 1995 | 1996 | 1997 |
|---|---|---|---|
| Current expenditure | 319.2 | 736.4 | 904.8 |
| Wages and salaries | 59.5 | 103.7 | 155.5 |
| Other goods and services | 56.1 | 120.1 | 118.5 |
| Subsidies and transfers | 39.1 | 59.0 | 103.4 |
| Interest payments | 54.6 | 57.3 | 92.4 |
| Other current expenditure | 49.7 | 101.4 | 108.3 |
| Unclassified expenditure | 10.4 | 82.4 | 54.1 |
| Extrabudgetary expenditure‖ | 49.9 | 103.8 | 168.4 |
| Local government expenditure | 70.1 | 108.7 | 104.2 |
| Capital expenditure | 38.8 | 68.9 | 73.4 |
| **Total** | 428.1 | 805.3 | 978.2 |

* Figures represent a consolidation of the State Budget (covering the central Government and local administrations) and extrabudgetary funds.

† Excluding grants received (million lari): 71.0 in 1995; 71.1 in 1996; 25.6 in 1997.

‡ Comprising the revenues of the Social Security Fund, the Employment Fund, the Health Fund, the Privatization Fund and the Road Fund (established in October 1995).

§ Excluding net lending (million lari): 27.3 in 1995; –8.9 in 1996; 6.5 in 1997.

‖ Including the payment of pensions and unemployment benefit.

Source: IMF, *Georgia: Recent Economic Developments and Selected Issues* (September 1998).

**INTERNATIONAL RESERVES** (million lari at 31 December)

| | 1995 | 1996 | 1997 |
|---|---|---|---|
| Gold | 1.5 | 1.5 | 0.7 |
| Foreign exchange | 197.7 | 201.5 | 225.9 |

**MONEY SUPPLY** (million lari at 31 December)

| | 1995 | 1996 | 1997 |
|---|---|---|---|
| Currency outside banks | 131.4 | 185.6 | 254.6 |

Source: IMF, *Georgia: Recent Economic Developments and Selected Issues* (September 1998).

**COST OF LIVING** (Consumer price index for five cities; base: 1994 = 100)

| | 1995 | 1996 | 1997 |
|---|---|---|---|
| Food, beverages and tobacco | 239.9 | 319.1 | 335.3 |
| Fuel and light | 307.0* | 409.2* | 537.7 |
| Clothing (incl. footwear) | 119.6 | 174.0 | 179.4 |
| **All items** (incl. others) | 262.7 | 366.2 | 393.3 |

* Including rent.

Source: ILO, *Yearbook of Labour Statistics*.

**NATIONAL ACCOUNTS**

**Gross Domestic Product** (million lari at current prices)

| | 1995 | 1996 | 1997 |
|---|---|---|---|
| GDP in purchasers' values | 3,694 | 5,724 | 6,798 |

**Gross Domestic Product by Economic Activity** (% of total)

| | 1995 | 1996 | 1997 |
|---|---|---|---|
| Agriculture | 38.0 | 31.0 | 28.2 |
| Industry* | 14.5 | 10.3 | 9.6 |
| Construction | 4.0 | 4.6 | 4.8 |
| Transport and communications | 4.3 | 6.3 | 9.9 |
| Trade and catering | 21.4 | 22.2 | 22.0 |
| Other services | 17.8 | 25.6 | 25.5 |
| **Total** | 100.0 | 100.0 | 100.0 |

* Principally mining, manufacturing, electricity, gas and water.

Source: IMF, *Georgia: Recent Economic Developments and Selected Issues* (September 1998).

**BALANCE OF PAYMENTS** (US $ million)

| | 1995 | 1996* | 1997† |
|---|---|---|---|
| Exports of goods f.o.b. | 362.6 | 417.0 | 462.8 |
| Imports of goods f.o.b. | –700.1 | –767.9 | –946.7 |
| **Trade balance** | –337.4 | –350.9 | –483.9 |
| Exports of services | 121.8 | 93.9 | 159.7 |
| Imports of services | –104.8 | –99.1 | –244.9 |
| **Balance on goods and services** | –320.4 | –356.1 | –569.1 |
| Other income received | 1.0 | 4.9 | 99.4 |
| Other income paid | –87.3 | –67.0 | –65.0 |
| **Balance on goods, services and income** | –406.7 | –418.2 | –534.7 |
| Current transfers (net) | 189.2 | 140.5 | 187.6 |
| **Current balance** | –217.5 | –277.7 | –347.1 |
| Medium- and long-term borrowing (net) | –171.3 | 19.0 | 68.5 |
| Other capital (net) | 84.7 | 47.4 | 183.9 |
| Net errors and omissions | 0.5 | 42.5 | –7.3 |
| **Overall balance** | –303.6 | –168.7 | –102.0 |

* Estimates. † Preliminary figures.

Source: IMF, *Georgia: Recent Economic Developments and Selected Issues* (September 1998).

# External Trade

**PRINCIPAL COMMODITIES** (US $ million)

| Imports f.o.b. | 1993 | 1994 | 1995 |
|---|---|---|---|
| Live animals and animal products | 4.8 | 4.3 | 10.9 |
| Vegetable products | 4.9 | 4.2 | 24.5 |
| Animal or vegetable fats, oil and waxes | 5.5 | 3.9 | 10.5 |
| Prepared foodstuffs, beverages, spirits, vinegar and tobacco | 20.9 | 18.0 | 76.2 |
| Mineral products | 166.3 | 267.9 | 198.9 |
| Products of the chemical or allied industries | 5.2 | 2.8 | 9.9 |
| Machinery (incl. electrical) and parts | 6.8 | 10.1 | 18.5 |
| **Total** (incl. others) | 238.5 | 327.4 | 379.0 |

| Exports f.o.b. | 1993 | 1994 | 1995 |
|---|---|---|---|
| Vegetable products | 55.7 | 20.0 | 19.8 |
| Prepared foodstuffs, beverages, spirits, vinegar and tobacco | 22.8 | 11.6 | 19.2 |
| Mineral products | 20.1 | 14.6 | 21.2 |
| Products of the chemical or allied industries | 15.2 | 13.9 | 13.1 |
| Plastics, rubber and articles thereof | 1.7 | 3.7 | 1.8 |
| Textiles and textile articles | 15.5 | 13.6 | 5.2 |
| Pearls, precious or semi-precious stones, precious metals and articles thereof | 10.1 | 1.0 | 1.2 |
| Base metals and articles thereof | 66.8 | 48.4 | 56.4 |
| Machinery (incl. electrical) and parts | 8.1 | 18.1 | 7.5 |
| **Total** (incl. others) | 226.7 | 155.7 | 154.4 |

**PRINCIPAL TRADING PARTNERS** (US $ million)

| Imports f.o.b. | 1993 | 1994 | 1995 |
|---|---|---|---|
| Armenia | 4.7 | 1.0 | 11.2 |
| Austria | 1.6 | 0.3 | 12.0 |
| Azerbaijan | 2.5 | 21.9 | 43.2 |
| Bulgaria | 0.2 | 1.9 | 25.5 |
| China, People's Republic | 2.9 | 0.1 | 0.1 |
| Czech Republic | 3.9 | 0.1 | 0.4 |
| France | 6.9 | 0.3 | 1.5 |
| Germany | 1.6 | 4.3 | 10.1 |
| Netherlands | 6.2 | 0.8 | 4.4 |
| Romania | 0.0 | 3.0 | 28.2 |
| Russia | 9.7 | 24.7 | 49.3 |
| Turkey | 34.5 | 35.1 | 80.2 |
| Turkmenistan | 132.6 | 215.6 | 41.2 |
| Ukraine | 13.2 | 3.8 | 7.1 |
| United Kingdom | 4.1 | 0.3 | 10.7 |
| USA | 2.7 | 4.6 | 17.9 |
| **Total** (incl. others) | 238.5 | 327.4 | 378.9 |

| Exports f.o.b. | 1993 | 1994 | 1995 |
|---|---|---|---|
| Armenia | 10.2 | 12.9 | 18.9 |
| Azerbaijan | 14.8 | 14.7 | 12.7 |
| Belarus | 2.2 | 3.3 | 2.1 |
| Bulgaria | 3.4 | 0.1 | 5.7 |
| Czech Republic | 9.9 | 0.2 | 0.0 |
| Italy | 0.3 | 0.1 | 2.8 |
| Kazakhstan | 12.9 | 9.0 | 1.8 |
| Russia | 103.3 | 52.3 | 47.0 |
| Switzerland | 0.4 | 2.1 | 6.1 |
| Turkey | 21.9 | 23.6 | 34.9 |
| Turkmenistan | 12.4 | 15.5 | 6.9 |
| Ukraine | 12.7 | 6.1 | 5.7 |
| USA | 0.7 | 3.7 | 0.6 |
| Uzbekistan | 4.7 | 2.7 | 0.6 |
| **Total** (incl. others) | 226.7 | 155.7 | 154.4 |

# Transport

**RAILWAYS** (traffic)

| | 1991 | 1992 | 1993 |
|---|---|---|---|
| Passenger-km (million) | 2,135 | 1,210 | 1,003 |
| Freight net ton-km (million) | 9,916 | 3,677 | 1,750 |

Source: UN, *Statistical Yearbook*.

**ROAD TRAFFIC** ('000 motor vehicles in use)

| | 1994 | 1995 | 1996* |
|---|---|---|---|
| Passenger cars | 468.8 | 441.8 | 427.0 |
| Commercial vehicles | 48.7 | 42.1 | 34.7 |

* Estimates.

Source: IRF, *World Road Statistics*.

**SHIPPING**

**Merchant Fleet** (registered at 31 December)

| | 1996 | 1997 | 1998 |
|---|---|---|---|
| Number of vessels | 84 | 97 | 95 |
| Total displacement ('000 grt) | 206.0 | 128.1 | 117.8 |

Source: Lloyd's Register of Shipping, *World Fleet Statistics*.

**CIVIL AVIATION** (traffic on scheduled services)

| | 1994 | 1995 |
|---|---|---|
| Kilometres flown (million) | 4 | 4 |
| Passengers carried ('000) | 223 | 177 |
| Passenger-km (million) | 283 | 308 |
| Total ton-km (million) | 26 | 30 |

Source: UN, *Statistical Yearbook*.

# Communications Media

| | 1994 | 1995 | 1996 |
|---|---|---|---|
| Telephones ('000 main lines in use) | 526 | 554 | n.a. |
| Telefax stations (number in use) | 457 | n.a. | n.a. |
| Mobile cellular telephone subscribers | n.a. | 150 | n.a. |
| Radio receivers ('000 in use) | 3,000 | 3,005 | 3,010 |
| Television receivers ('000 in use) | 2,500 | 2,550 | 2,560 |
| Book production: | | | |
| Titles | 314* | 1,104 | 581 |
| Copies ('000) | 1,131* | 1,627 | 834 |

* Including pamphlets (53 titles and 75,000 copies).

Sources: UN, *Statistical Yearbook*; UNESCO, *Statistical Yearbook*.

# Education

(1996/97, unless otherwise indicated)

| | Institutions | Teachers | Students |
|---|---|---|---|
| Pre-primary schools | 1,322* | 9,368 | 71,407 |
| Primary schools | 3,201 | 16,542 | 293,325 |
| Secondary schools | 3,139† | 57,963 | 444,058 |
| State secondary specialized schools | 76‡ | n.a. | 30,153‡ |
| Private secondary specialized schools | 98† | n.a. | 14,200† |
| Vocational/technical schools | 115† | 2,146 | 19,593 |
| Higher schools (incl. universities) | 23‡ | 25,549 | 163,345 |

* 1995/96. † 1994/95. ‡ 1993/94.

Sources: UNESCO, *Statistical Yearbook*, and Ministry of Education, Tbilisi.

# Directory

## The Constitution

A new Constitution was approved by the Georgian legislature on 24 August 1995; it entered into force on 17 October. The Constitution replaced the Decree on State Power of November 1992 (which had functioned as an interim basic law). The following is a summary of the Constitution's main provisions:

### GENERAL PROVISIONS

Georgia is an independent, united and undivided state, as confirmed by the referendum conducted throughout the entire territory of the country (including Abkhazia and South Ossetia) on 31 March 1991, and in accordance with the Act on the Restoration of the State Independence of Georgia of 9 April 1991. The Georgian state is a democratic republic. Its territorial integrity and the inviolability of its state borders are confirmed by the republic's Constitution and laws.

All state power belongs to the people, who exercise this power through referendums, other forms of direct democracy, and through their elected representatives. The State recognizes and defends universally recognized human rights and freedoms. The official state language is Georgian; in Abkhazia both Georgian and Abkhazian are recognized as state languages. While the State recognizes the exceptional role played by the Georgian Orthodox Church in Georgian history, it declares the complete freedom of faith and religion as well as the independence of the Church from the State. The capital is Tbilisi.

### FUNDAMENTAL HUMAN RIGHTS AND FREEDOMS

Georgian citizenship is acquired by birth and naturalization. A Georgian citizen may not concurrently be a citizen of another state. Every person is free by birth and equal before the law, irrespective of race, colour, language, sex, religion, political and other views, national, ethnic and social affiliation, origin and place of residence. Every person has the inviolable right to life, which is protected by law. No one may be subjected to torture or inhuman, cruel or humiliating treatment or punishment.

Freedom of speech, thought, conscience and faith are guaranteed. The mass media are free. Censorship is prohibited. The right to assemble publicly is guaranteed, as is the right to form public associations, including trade unions and political parties. Every citizen who has attained the age of 18 has the right to participate in referendums and elections of state and local administrative bodies.

### THE GEORGIAN PARLIAMENT

The Georgian Parliament is the supreme representative body, implementing legislation and determining the basis of the country's domestic and foreign policies. It controls the activities of the Government, within the limits prescribed by the Constitution, and has other powers of implementation.

Parliament is elected on the basis of universal, equal and direct suffrage by secret ballot, for a term of four years. It is composed of 235 members: 150 elected by proportional representation (with a minimum requirement of 7% of the votes cast to secure parliamentary representation) and 85 by majority vote in single-member constituencies. Any citizen who has attained the age of 25 years and has the right to vote may be elected a member of Parliament. The instigation of criminal proceedings against a member of Parliament, and his/her detention or arrest, are only permitted upon approval by Parliament. A member of Parliament may not hold any position in state service or engage in entrepreneurial activities.

Parliament elects a Chairman and Deputy Chairmen (including one Deputy Chairman each from deputies elected in Abkhazia and Ajaria), for the length of its term of office. Members of Parliament may unite to form parliamentary factions. A faction must have no fewer than 10 members.

(Following the creation of the appropriate conditions throughout the territory of Georgia and the formation of bodies of local self-government, the Georgian Parliament will be composed of two chambers: the Council of the Republic and the Senate. The Council of the Republic will be composed of deputies elected according to the proportional system. The Senate will be composed of deputies elected in Abkhazia, Ajaria and other territorial units of Georgia, and five members appointed by the President of Georgia.)

### THE PRESIDENT OF GEORGIA AND THE GOVERNMENT

The President of Georgia is Head of State and the head of executive power. The President directs and implements domestic and foreign policy, ensures the unity and territorial integrity of the country, and supervises the activities of state bodies in accordance with the Constitution. The President is the supreme representative of Georgia in foreign relations. He/she is elected on the basis of universal, equal and direct suffrage by secret ballot, for a period of five years. The President may not be elected for more than two consecutive terms. Any citizen of Georgia who has the right to vote and who has attained the age of 35 years and lived in Georgia for no less than 15 years, is eligible to be elected President.

The President of Georgia concludes international treaties and agreements and conducts negotiations with foreign states; with the consent of Parliament, appoints and dismisses Georgian ambassadors and other diplomatic representatives; receives the credentials of ambassadors and other diplomatic representatives of foreign states and international organizations; with the consent of Parliament, appoints members of the Government and Ministers; is empowered to remove Ministers from their posts; submits to Parliament the draft state budget, after agreeing upon its basic content with parliamentary committees; in the event of an armed attack on Georgia, declares a state of war, and concludes peace; during war or mass disorders, when the country's territorial integrity is threatened, or in the event of a *coup d'état* or an armed uprising, an ecological catastrophe or epidemic, or in other instances when the bodies of state power cannot implement their constitutional powers normally, declares a state of emergency; with the consent of Parliament, has the right to halt the activities of representative bodies of self-government or territorial units (if their activities create a threat to the sovereignty and territorial integrity of the country) as well as to halt state bodies in the exercise of their constitutional powers; signs and promulgates laws; decides questions of citizenship and the granting of political asylum; grants pardons; schedules elections to Parliament and other representative bodies; has the right to revoke acts of subordinate executive bodies; is the Commander-in-Chief of the Armed Forces; and appoints members of the National Security Council, chairs its meetings, and appoints and dismisses military commanders.

The President enjoys immunity. During his/her period in office, he/she may not be arrested, and no criminal proceedings may be instigated against him/her. In the event that the President violates the Constitution, betrays the State or commits other crimes, Parliament may remove him/her from office (with the approval of the Constitutional Court or the Supreme Court).

Members of the Government are accountable to the President. They do not have the right to hold other posts (except party posts), to engage in entrepreneurial activities or to receive a wage or any other permanent remuneration for any other activities. Members of the Government may be removed from their posts by an edict of the President or by Parliament. Ministries perform state management in specific spheres of state and public life. Each Ministry is headed by a Minister, who independently adopts decisions on questions within his/her sphere of jurisdiction.

### JUDICIAL POWER

Judicial power is independent and is implemented only by the courts. Judges are independent in their activities and are subordinate only to the Constitution and the law. Court proceedings are held in public (except for certain specified instances). The decision of the court is delivered in public. Judges enjoy immunity. It is prohibited to instigate criminal proceedings against a judge or to detain or arrest him/her, without the consent of the Chairman of the Supreme Court.

The Constitutional Court is the legal body of constitutional control. It is composed of nine judges, three of whom are appointed by the President, three elected by Parliament, and three appointed by the Supreme Court. The term of office of members of the Constitutional Court is 10 years.

The Supreme Court supervises legal proceedings in general courts according to the established judicial procedure and, as the court of first instance, examines cases determined by law. On the recommendation of the President of Georgia, the Chairman and judges of the Supreme Court are elected by Parliament for a period of at least 10 years.

The Procurator's Office is an institution of judicial power which carries out criminal prosecution, supervises the preliminary investigation and the execution of a punishment, and supports the state prosecution. On the recommendation of the President of Georgia, the Procurator-General is appointed by Parliament for a term of five years. Lower-ranking procurators are appointed by the Procurator-General.

### DEFENCE OF THE STATE

Georgia has armed forces to protect the independence, sovereignty and territorial integrity of the country, and also to fulfil international obligations. The President of Georgia approves the structure of the armed forces and Parliament ratifies their numerical strength, on the recommendation of the National Security Council. The National Security Council, which is headed by the President of Georgia, carries out military organizational development and the defence of the country.

# The Government

### HEAD OF STATE

**President of Georgia:** EDUARD SHEVARDNADZE (elected by direct popular vote 5 November 1995).

### GOVERNMENT
(February 2000)

**Minister of State and Head of the State Chancellery:** VAZHA LORTKIPANIDZE.

**Minister of Agriculture and Food:** BAKUR GULUA.

**Minister of Communications and Post:** SERGO ESAKIA.

**Minister for the Control of State Property:** MIKHEIL UKLEBA.

**Minister of Culture:** VALERI ASATIANI.

**Minister of Defence:** Gen. DAVIT TEVADZE.

**Minister of the Economy:** VLADIMER PAPAVA.

**Minister of Education:** ALEKSANDZRE KARTOZIA.

**Minister of Environmental Protection and Natural Resources:** NINO CHKHOBADZE.

**Minister of Finance:** DAVIT ONOPRISHVILI.

**Minister of Foreign Affairs:** IRAKLI MENAGHARISHVILI.

**Minister of Fuel and Energy:** DAVIT MIRTSKHULAVA.

**Minister of Health:** AVTANDIL JORBENADZE.

**Minister of Industry:** BADRI SHOSHITAISHVILI.

**Minister of Internal Affairs:** KAKHA TARGAMADZE.

**Minister of Justice:** VLADIMER CHANTURIA.

**Minister of Refugees and Resettlement:** VALERI VASHAKIDZE.

**Minister of Social Security and Labour:** TENGIZ GAZDELIANI.

**Minister of State Security:** VAKHTANG KUTATELADZE.

**Minister of Trade and Foreign Economic Relations:** TAMARA BERUCHASHVILI.

**Minister of Transport:** Dr MERAB ADEISHVILI.

**Minister of Urban Affairs and Construction:** MERAB CHKHENKELI.

### MINISTRIES

**Office of the Government:** 380018 Tbilisi, Ingorokva 7; tel. (32) 93-59-07; fax (32) 98-23-54.

**Ministry of Agriculture and Food:** 380023 Tbilisi, Kostava 41; tel. (32) 99-02-72; fax (32) 93-33-00.

**Ministry of Communications and Post:** 380008 Tbilisi, 9 April 2; tel. (32) 99-95-28; fax (32) 99-11-11.

**Ministry for the Control of State Property:** 380062 Tbilisi, Chavchavadze 64; tel. (32) 29-48-75; fax (32) 22-52-09.

**Ministry of Culture:** 380008 Tbilisi, Rustaveli 37; tel. (32) 93-74-30; fax (32) 99-90-37.

**Ministry of Defence:** 380114 Tbilisi, Universitetis 2A; tel. (32) 98-39-30; fax (32) 98-39-25.

**Ministry of the Economy:** 380008 Tbilisi, Chanturia 12; tel. (32) 23-09-25; fax (32) 98-27-43.

**Ministry of Education:** 380002 Tbilisi, Uznadze 52; tel. (32) 95-88-86; fax (32) 77-00-73.

**Ministry of Environmental Protection and Natural Resources:** 380015 Tbilisi, Kostava 68A; tel. (32) 23-06-64; fax (32) 98-34-20; e-mail irisi@gmep.kneta.ge.

**Ministry of Finance:** 380062 Tbilisi, Abashidze 70; tel. (32) 22-68-05; fax (32) 29-23-68.

**Ministry of Foreign Affairs:** 380018 Tbilisi, Chitadze 4; tel. (32) 98-93-77; fax (32) 99-72-49.

**Ministry of Fuel and Energy:** 380007 Tbilisi, Lermontov 10; tel. (32) 99-60-98; fax (32) 93-35-42.

**Ministry of Health:** 380060 Tbilisi, K. Gamsakhurdia 30; tel. (32) 38-70-71; fax (32) 38-98-02.

**Ministry of Industry:** 380060 Tbilisi, K. Gamsakhurdia 28; tel. (32) 38-55-49; fax (32) 94-12-91.

**Ministry of Internal Affairs:** 380014 Tbilisi, Gulua 10; tel. (32) 99-62-33; fax (32) 98-65-32.

**Ministry of Justice:** 380046 Tbilisi, Rustaveli 30; tel. (32) 93-27-21; fax (32) 99-02-25.

**Ministry of Refugees and Resettlement:** 380008 Tbilisi, Rustaveli 28; tel. (32) 94-16-11.

**Ministry of Social Security and Labour:** 380057 Tbilisi, Leonidze 7–2; tel. (32) 93-62-36; fax (32) 93-61-50.

**Ministry of State Security:** 380018 Tbilisi, 9 April 4; tel. (32) 99-95-82; fax (32) 99-57-84.

**Ministry of Trade and Foreign Economic Relations:** 380077 Tbilisi, Aleksandr Kazbegi 42; tel. (32) 22-51-86; fax (32) 23-41-34.

**Ministry of Transport:** 380060 Tbilisi, Aleksandr Kazbegi 12; tel. (32) 93-28-46; fax (32) 93-91-45.

**Ministry of Urban Affairs and Construction:** 380060 Tbilisi, Vazha Pshavela 16; tel. (32) 37-42-76; fax (32) 22-05-41.

# President and Legislature

### PRESIDENT

**Presidential Election, 5 November 1995**

| Candidates | Votes | % |
|---|---|---|
| EDUARD SHEVARDNADZE | 1,589,909 | 74.94 |
| JUMBER PATIASHVILI | 414,303 | 19.53 |
| AKAKI BAKRADZE | 31,350 | 1.48 |
| PANTELEIMON GIORGADZE | 10,697 | 0.50 |
| KARTLOS GHARIBASHVILI | 10,023 | 0.47 |
| ROIN LIPARTELIANI | 7,948 | 0.37 |
| **Total*** | 2,121,510 | 100.00 |

* Including 57,280 spoilt voting papers (2.70% of the total).

### GEORGIAN PARLIAMENT
(Sakartvelos Parlamenti)

**Chairman:** ZURAB ZHVANIA.

**Deputy Chairmen:** GIGI TSERETELI, ELDAR SHENGELAIA, GIORGI KOBAKHIDZE, VAKHTANG KHOLBAIA.

**General Election, 31 October and 14 November 1999**

| | Party lists | | Single-member | |
|---|---|---|---|---|
| Parties and blocs | % of votes* | Seats | constituency seats | Total seats |
| Citizens' Union of Georgia | 41.9 | 85 | 45 | 130 |
| Union for the Revival of Georgian bloc | 25.7 | 51 | 7 | 58 |
| Industry Will Save Georgia bloc | 7.8 | 14 | 1 | 15 |
| Georgian Labour Party | 6.7 | 0 | 2 | 2 |
| Abkhazian deputies† | — | — | 12 | 12 |
| Independent candidates | — | — | 17 | 17 |
| **Total** (incl. others) | 100.00 | 150 | 84 | 234‡ |

* In order to win seats, parties needed to obtain at least 7% of the total votes cast.

† Owing to the electoral boycott in the secessionist region of Abkhazia, the mandates of 12 deputies from Abkhazia (elected to the legislature in 1992) were renewed.

‡ One of the single-member constituency seats remained unfilled.

According to the Constitution of August 1995, the unicameral Georgian Parliament would be transformed into a bicameral body following the eventual restoration of Georgia's territorial integrity. The future Parliament would comprise a Council of the Republic and a Senate (the latter representing the various territorial units of the country).

# Political Organizations

More than 30 parties and alliances contested the legislative election of 31 October 1999. The following are among the most prominent parties in Georgia:

**Agrarian Party of Georgia:** Tbilisi; f. 1994; Chair. ROIN LIPARTELIANI.

**All-Georgian Union of Revival:** Batumi, Gogebashvili 7; tel. (200) 76-500; f. 1992; 200,000 mems; Chair. ASLAN ABASHIDZE.

**Citizens' Union of Georgia (CUG):** Tbilisi, Marshal Gelovani 4; tel. (32) 38-47-87; f. 1993; 300,000 mems; Chair. EDUARD SHEVARDNADZE; Gen. Sec. EDUARD SURMANIDZE.

**Conservative–Monarchist Party:** Tbilisi; Chair. TEIMURAZ ZHORZHOLIANI (sentenced to four years' imprisonment in June 1996 for possession of drugs and weapons).

**Georgian Labour Party:** f. 1997; main aim is the social protection of the population; 64,000 mems.

**Georgian People's Party:** Tbilisi; f. 1996 by dissident members of the National Democratic Party of Georgia.

**Georgian Social Democratic Party:** 380018 Tbilisi, Tskhra Aprilis 2; tel. (32) 99-95-50; fax (32) 98-73-89; f. 1893; ruling party 1918–21; re-established 1990; Chair. Prof. JEMAL KAKHNIASHVILI.

**Georgian Social-Realistic Party:** f. 1999; centrist party aimed at building united democratic Georgian state; Chair. Dr GURAM BEROZASHVILI.

**Georgian Union of Reformers and Agrarians:** Tbilisi; f. 1999; merger of Reformers' Union of Georgia and the Agrarian Union.

**Industry Will Save Georgia:** Tbilisi; opposition alliance; Chair. GEORGI TOPADZE.

**Liberal Democratic Party:** Tbilisi; Chair. MIKHEIL NANEISHVILI.

**Mtsvanta Partia** (Green Party of Georgia): c/o Sakartvelos Mtsvaneta Modzraoba, 380012 Tbilisi, Davit Aghmashenebeli Ave 182, Green House, Mushthaid Park; f. 1990; Leader ZURAB ZHVANIA.

**National Democratic Party of Georgia:** 380008 Tbilisi, Rustaveli 21; tel. (32) 98-31-86; fax (32) 98-31-88; f. 1981; Leader IRINA SHARISHVILI-CHANTURIA.

**National Independence Party:** Tbilisi; Chair. IRAKLI TSERETELI.

**Party for Liberation of Abkhazia:** Tbilisi; advocates the restoration of the jurisdiction of Georgia and constitutional order in Abkhazia; f. 1998; Chair. TAMAZ NADAREISHVILI.

**People's Patriotic Union of Georgia:** Tbilisi; left-wing alliance; Chair. YEVGENII DZHUGHASHVILI.

**People's Party:** Tbilisi.

**Revived Communist Party of Georgia:** f. 1997; Chair. SHALVA BERIANIDZE.

**Round Table—Free Georgia:** Tbilisi, Dgebuadze 4; tel. (32) 95-48-20; f. 1990; opposition party uniting supporters of former President Zviad Gamsakhurdia; Chair. SOSO JAJANIDZE.

**Socialist Party of Georgia:** Tbilisi, Leselidze 41; tel. (32) 98-33-67; f. 1995; Chair. TEMUR GAMTSEMLIDZE.

**Union for the Revival of Georgia:** Tbilisi; principal opposition alliance including parties loyal to the former President, Zviad Gamsakhurdia (the All-Georgian Union of Revival, the Socialist Party of Georgia, the Union of Traditionalists, the People's Party and the 21st Century bloc); Chair. ASLAN ABASHIDZE.

**Union of Georgian Realists:** f. 1997; aims to achieve political and economic stability in a united Georgia.

**Union of Traditionalists:** Tbilisi.

**United Communist Party of Georgia:** Tbilisi, Chodrishvili 45; tel. and fax (32) 95-32-16; f. 1994, uniting various successor parties to the former Communist Party of Georgia; 128,000 mems (1995); First Sec. PANTELEIMON GIORGADZE.

**United Republican Party:** Tbilisi; f. 1995; absorbed Georgian Popular Front (f. 1989); Chair. NODAR NATADZE.

# Diplomatic Representation

### EMBASSIES IN GEORGIA

**Armenia:** Tbilisi, Tetelashvili 4; tel. (32) 95-94-43; fax (32) 99-01-26; Ambassador: GEORGE KHOSROEV.

**Azerbaijan:** Tbilisi, Mukhadze 16; tel. and fax (32) 23-40-37; Ambassador: HAJAN HAJIYEV.

**China, People's Republic:** Tbilisi, Barnov 52; tel. (32) 99-80-11; fax (32) 93-12-76; Ambassador: ZHANG YONGQUAN.

**France:** Tbilisi, Gogebashvili 15; tel. (32) 93-42-10; fax (32) 95-33-75; Ambassador: MIREILLE MUSSO.

**Germany:** 380012 Tbilisi, Davit Aghmashenebeli 166; tel. (32) 95-09-36; fax (32) 95-89-10; Ambassador: Dr WOLFDIETRICH VOGEL.

**Greece:** Tbilisi, Arakishvili 5; tel. and fax (32) 93-89-91; Ambassador: SPYRIDON GEORGILES.

**Holy See:** 380086 Tbilisi, Dzhgenti 40, Nutsubidze Plateau; tel. (32) 94-13-05; fax (32) 29-39-44; e-mail nuntius@access.sanet.ge; Apostolic Nuncio: Most Rev. PETER STEPHAN ZURBRIGGEN, Titular Archbishop of Glastonia (Glastonbury).

**Iran:** Tbilisi, Zovreti 16; tel. (32) 98-69-90; fax (32) 98-69-93; Ambassador: ABOLFAZL KHAZAEE TORSHIZI.

**Israel:** 380012 Tbilisi, Davit Aghmashenebeli 61; tel. (32) 96-02-13; fax (32) 95-17-09; Ambassador: EHUD EITAM.

**Korea, Republic:** Tbilisi; Ambassador: YI CHONG-PIN.

**Poland:** Tbilisi, Brothers Zubalashvili 19; tel. (32) 92-03-98; fax (32) 92-03-97; Chargé d'affaires: PIOTR BORAWSKI.

**Romania:** Tbilisi, Lvov 7; tel. (32) 25-00-98; fax (32) 25-00-97; Ambassador: KONSTANTIN GIRBEA.

**Russia:** Tbilisi, Tsinamdzgvrishvili 90; tel. (32) 94-16-04; fax (32) 95-52-33; Ambassador: FELIKS STANEVSKII.

**Turkey:** 380012 Tbilisi, Davit Aghmashenebeli 61; tel. (32) 95-20-14; fax (32) 95-18-10; e-mail turkem_tifl@yahoo.com; Ambassador: BURAK GURSEL.

**Ukraine:** Tbilisi, Oniashvili 75; tel. and fax (32) 23-71-45; Ambassador: STEFAN VOLKOVETSKII.

**United Kingdom:** 380003 Tbilisi, Sheraton Palace Hotel; tel. and fax (32) 95-54-97; email british.embassy@caucasus.net; Ambassador: RICHARD JENKINS.

**USA:** Tbilisi, Atoneli 25; tel. (32) 98-99-67; fax (32) 93-37-59; internet www.georgia.net.ge/usis; Ambassador: KENNETH SPENCER YALOWITZ.

# Judicial System

In late 1997 the 12-member Georgian Justice Council was established, to co-ordinate the appointment of judges and their activities. It comprises four members nominated by the President, four nominated by Parliament and four nominated by the Supreme Court. Chair. MIKHEIL SAAKASHVILI.

**Chairman of the Constitutional Court:** AVTANDIL DEMETRASHVILI.

**Chairman of the Supreme Court:** MINDIA UGREKHELIDZE.

**Procurator-General:** JAMLET BABILASHVILI.

**First Deputy Procurator-General:** REVAZ KIPIANI.

# Religion

### CHRISTIANITY

#### The Georgian Orthodox Church

The Georgian Orthodox Church is divided into 15 dioceses, and includes not only Georgian parishes, but also several Russian and Greek Orthodox communities, which are under the jurisdiction of the Primate of the Georgian Orthodox Church. There are eight monasteries, a theological academy and a seminary.

**Patriarchate:** 380005 Tbilisi, Sioni 4; tel. (32) 72-27-18; Catholicos-Patriarch of All Georgia ILIYA II.

#### The Roman Catholic Church

The Apostolic Administrator of the Caucasus is the Apostolic Nuncio to Georgia, Armenia and Azerbaijan, who is resident in Tbilisi (see Diplomatic Representation, above).

### ISLAM

There are Islamic communities among the Ajarians, Abkhazians, Azerbaijanis, Kurds and some Ossetians. The country falls under the jurisdiction of the Muslim Board of Transcaucasia, based in Baku (Azerbaijan).

# The Press

**Department of the Press:** 380008 Tbilisi, Jorjiashvili 12; tel. (32) 98-70-08; govt regulatory body; Dir V. RTSKHILADZE.

### PRINCIPAL NEWSPAPERS

In Georgian, except where otherwise stated.

**Akhalgazrda Iverieli** (Young Iberian): Tbilisi, Kostava 14; tel. (32) 93-31-49; 3 a week; organ of the Georgian Parliament; Editor MERAB BALARJISHVILI.

**Droni** (Times): Tbilisi, Kostava 14; tel. (32) 99-56-54; Editor-in-Chief SOSO SIMONISHVILI.

**Eri** (Nation): Tbilisi; weekly; organ of the Georgian Parliament; Editor A. SILAGADZE.

**Ertoba:** Tbilisi; f. 1918; weekly; organ of the Georgian Social Democratic Party.

**Georgian Times:** Tbilisi, Chavchavadze 55; tel. and fax (32) 22-76-21; e-mail times@gtze.com.ge; f. 1993; daily; in English; Editor-in-Chief ZAZA GACHECHILADZE.

**Iberia Spektri** (Iberian Spectrum): Tbilisi, Machabeli 11; tel. (32) 98-73-87; fax (32) 98-73-88; Editor IRAKLI GOTSIRIDZE.

**Literaturuli Sakartvelo** (Literary Georgia): Tbilisi, Gudiashvili Sq. 2; tel. (32) 99-84-04; weekly; organ of the Union of Writers of Georgia; Editor TAMAZ TSIVTSIVADZE.

**Mamuli** (Native Land): Tbilisi; fortnightly; organ of the Rustaveli Society; Editor T. CHANTURIA.

**Respublika** (Republic): 380096 Tbilisi, Kostava 14; tel. and fax (32) 93-43-91; f. 1990; weekly; independent; Editor J. NINUA; circ. 40,000.

**Rezonansi:** Tbilisi, Davit Aghmashenebeli 89–24; tel. (32) 95-69-38; daily; Editor-in-Chief SHALVA MEGRELISHVILI.

**Sakartvelo** (Georgia): 380096 Tbilisi, Kostava 14; tel. (32) 99-92-26; 5 a week; organ of the Georgian Parliament; Editor (vacant).

**Shvidi Dghe** (Seven Days): Tbilisi, Krilov 5; tel. (32) 94-35-52; fax (32) 95-40-76; e-mail dge7@caucasus.net; internet www.opentext.org.ge_17dge; f. 1991; weekly; Dir GELA GURGENIDZE; Editor KOBA AKHALBEDASHVILI; circ. 3,000.

**Svobodnaya Gruziya** (Free Georgia): Tbilisi, Rustaveli 42; tel. and fax (32) 93-17-06; in Russian; Editor-in-Chief APOLON SILAGADZE.

**Tavisupali Sakartvelo** (Free Georgia): 380008 Tbilisi, POB W227; tel. (32) 95-48-20; weekly; organ of Round Table—Free Georgia party.

**Vestnik Gruzii** (Georgian Herald): Tbilisi; 5 a week; organ of the Georgian Parliament; in Russian; Editor V. KESHELAVA.

### PRINCIPAL PERIODICALS

**Alashara:** 394981 Sukhumi, Government House, kor. 1; tel. (300) 2-35-40; organ of Abkhazian Writers' Organization of the Union of Writers of Georgia; in Abkhazian.

**Dila** (Morning): 380096 Tbilisi, Kostava 14; tel. (32) 99-41-30; f. 1904; monthly; illustrated; for 5–10-year-olds; Editor-in-Chief REVAZ INANISHVILI; circ. 168,000.

**Drosha** (Banner): Tbilisi; f. 1923; monthly; politics and fiction; Editor O. KINKLADZE.

**Fidiyag:** Tskhinvali, Kostava 3; tel. 2-22-65; organ of the South Ossetian Writers' Organization of the Union of Writers of Georgia; in Ossetian.

**Khelovneba** (Art): Tbilisi; f. 1953, fmrly *Sabchota Khelovneba* (Soviet Art); monthly; journal of the Ministry of Culture; Editor N. GURABANIDZE.

**Kritika** (Criticism): 380008 Tbilisi, Rustaveli 42; tel. (32) 93-22-85; f. 1972; every 2 months; publ. by Merani Publishing House; journal of the Union of Writers of Georgia; literature, miscellaneous; Editor V. KHARCHILAVA.

**Literaturnaya Gruziya** (Literary Georgia): 380008 Tbilisi, Kostava 5; tel. (32) 93-65-15; f. 1957; quarterly; journal of the Union of Writers of Georgia; politics, art and fiction; in Russian; Editor Z. ABZIANIDZE.

**Metsniereba da Tekhnika** (Science and Technology): 380060 Tbilisi; f. 1949; monthly; publ. by the Metsniereba Publishing House; journal of the Georgian Academy of Sciences; popular; Editor Z. TSILOSANI.

**Mnatobi** (Luminary): 380004 Tbilisi, Rustaveli 28; tel. (32) 99-51-56; f. 1924; monthly; journal of the Union of Writers of Georgia; fiction, poetry and arts; Editor T. CHILADZE.

**Nakaduli** (Stream): Tbilisi, Kostava 14; tel. (32) 93-31-81; f. 1926; fmrly *Pioneri*; monthly; journal of the Ministry of Education; illustrated; for 10–15-year-olds; Editor V. GINCHARADZE; circ. 5,000.

**Niangi** (Crocodile): 380096 Tbilisi, Kostava 14; f. 1923; fortnightly; satirical; Editor Z. BOLKVADZE.

**Politika** (Politics): Tbilisi; theoretical, political, social sciences; Editor M. GOGUADZE.

**Sakartvelos Kali** (Georgian Woman): 380096 Tbilisi, Kostava 14; tel. (32) 99-98-71; f. 1957; popular, socio-political and literary; Editor-in-Chief NARGIZA MGELADZE; circ. 25,000.

**Sakartvelos Metsnierebata Akedemiis Matsne** (Herald of the Georgian Academy of Sciences, Biological Series): Tbilisi; f. 1975; 6 a year; in Georgian, English and Russian; Editor-in-Chief VAZHA OKUJAVA.

**Sakartvelos Metsnierebata Akedemiis Matsne** (Herald of the Georgian Academy of Sciences, Chemical Series): Tbilisi; f. 1975; quarterly; in Georgian, English and Russian; Editor-in-Chief TEIMURAZ ANDRONIKASHVILI.

**Sakartvelos Metsnierebata Akademiis Moambe** (Bulletin of Georgian Academy of Sciences): 380008 Tbilisi, Rustaveli 52; tel. (32) 99-75-93; fax (32) 99-88-23; e-mail bulletin@presid.achet.ge; f. 1940; 6 a year; in Georgian and English; Editor-in-Chief ALBERT TAVKHELIDZE.

**Saunje** (Treasure): 380007 Tbilisi, Dadiani 2; tel. (32) 72-47-31; f. 1974; 6 a year; organ of the Union of Writers of Georgia; foreign literature in translation; Editor S. NISHNIANIDZE.

**Tsiskari** (Dawn): 380007 Tbilisi, Dadiani 2; tel. (32) 99-85-81; f. 1957; monthly; organ of the Union of Writers of Georgia; fiction; Editor I. KEMERTELIDZE.

### NEWS AGENCIES

**BS Press:** Tbilisi, Rustaveli 42; tel. (32) 93-51-20; fax (32) 93-13-02; Dir DEVI IMEDASHVILI.

**Iberia:** Tbilisi, Marjanishvili 5; tel. (32) 93-64-22; Dir KAKHA GAGLOSHVILI.

**Iprinda:** Tbilisi, Rustaveli 19; tel. (32) 99-03-77; fax (32) 98-73-65; Dir KETEVAN BOKHUA.

**Kontakt:** Tbilisi, Kostava 68; tel. (32) 36-04-79; fax (32) 22-18-45; Dir DIMITRI KIKVADZE.

**Sakinform:** 380008 Tbilisi, Rustaveli 42; tel. (32) 93-19-20; fax (32) 99-92-00; e-mail gha@lberiapac.ge; f. 1921; state information agency; Dir VAKHTANG ABASHIDZE.

## Publishers

**Ganatleba** (Education): 380025 Tbilisi, Orjonikidze 50; f. 1957; educational, literature; Dir L. KHUNDADZE.

**Georgian National Universal Encyclopaedia:** Tbilisi, Tsereteli 1; Editor-in-Chief A. SAKVARELIDZE.

**Khelovneba** (Art): 380002 Tbilisi, Davit Aghmashenebeli 179; f. 1947; Dir N. JASHI.

**Merani** (Writer): 380008 Tbilisi, Rustaveli 42; tel. (32) 99-64-92; fax (32) 93-29-96; e-mail merani@caucasus.net; f. 1921; fiction; Dir G. GVERDTSITELI.

**Metsniereba** (Science): 380060 Tbilisi, Kutuzov 19; f. 1941; publishing house of the Georgian Academy of Sciences; Editor S. SHENGELIA.

**Nakaduli** (Stream): 380060 Tbilisi, Gamsakhurdia 28; f. 1938; books for children and youth; Dir O. CHELIDZE.

**Publishing House of Tbilisi State University:** 380079 Tbilisi, Chavchavadze 14; f. 1933; scientific and educational literature; Editor V. GAMKRELIDZE.

**Sakartvelo** (Georgia): 380002 Tbilisi, Marjanishvili 16; tel. (32) 95-42-01; f. 1921; fmrly *Sabchota Sakartvelo* (Soviet Georgia); political, scientific and fiction; Dir D. A. TCHARKVIANI.

## Broadcasting and Communications

**State Department of Television and Radio:** Tbilisi, Kostava 68; tel. (32) 36-81-66; e-mail gtvr@iberiapac.ge; Chair. (vacant).

### RADIO

**Georgian Radio:** 380015 Tbilisi, Kostava 68; tel.(32) 36-83-62; fax (32) 36-86-65; govt controlled; broadcasts in Georgian and Russian, with regional services for Abkhazia, Ajaria and South Ossetia; foreign service in English and German; Dir VAKHTANG NANITASHVILI.

### TELEVISION

**Georgian Television:** 380015 Tbilisi, Kostava 68; tel. (32) 36-22-94; fax (32) 36-23-19; two stations; relays from Russian television.

## Finance

(cap. = capital; res = reserves; dep. = deposits; m. = million; brs = branches; amounts in lari, unless otherwise indicated)

### BANKING

In August 1991 the Georgian Supreme Soviet adopted legislation which nationalized all branches of all-Union (USSR) banks in Georgia. Georgian branches of the USSR State Bank (Gosbank) were transferred to the National Bank of Georgia.

At the beginning of 1993 the Georgian banking system comprised the National Bank, five specialized state commercial banks (consisting of the domestic branches of the specialized banks of the former USSR) and 72 private commercial banks. However, of the last, only about one-half satisfied general legal provisions and only five properly complied with the paid-in capital requirement. As a result, in 1995 more than 50% of the commercial banks in Georgia (then numbering almost 230) were closed down. The remaining banks were to be audited by the National Bank to verify their commercial viability. In April 1995 three of the five specialized state commercial banks—Sakeksimbanki (Export-Import Bank), Industriabanki and Akhali Kartuli Banki (Savings Bank)—merged to form the United Georgian Bank. In 1996 the authorized capital requirement was raised to 5m. lari. At 31 December 1998 there were 43 commercial banks in Georgia.

#### Central Bank

**National Bank of Georgia:** 380005 Tbilisi, Leonidze 3–5; tel. (32) 99-65-05; fax (32) 99-98-85; f. 1991; cap. 1.3m., res 9.3m., dep. 298.8m., total assets 1,190m. (Dec. 1998); Pres. and Chair of Bd IRAKLI MANAGADZE.

#### Other Banks

**Absolute Bank:** 380008 Tbilisi, Ingorokva 8; tel. (32) 98-99-47; fax (32) 99-61-82; e-mail absolute@iberiapac.ge; cap. 4.5m., dep. 26.1m. (Apr. 1999); Chair. LOUIS LLOYD; Pres. LEIGH DURLAND; 4 brs.

**Agrobank:** 380005 Tbilisi, Trasury 3; tel. (32) 23-46-29; fax (32) 98-21-46; f. 1991 as specialized state commercial bank; 63 brs.

**Bank of Georgia:** 380005 Tbilisi, Pushkin 3; tel. (32) 99-77-26; fax (32) 98-32-62; e-mail info@bankofgeorgia.com.ge; internet www.bankofgeorgia.com.ge; f. 1991 as Zhilsotsbank—Social Development Bank, one of five specialized state commercial banks; renamed as above 1994; universal joint-stock commercial bank; cap. 6.9m., dep. 46m. (Dec. 1999); Pres. VLADIMER PATEISHVILI; 32 brs.

**Georgian Maritime Bank:** 384517 Batumi, Gogebashvili 60; tel. (222) 7-65-82; fax (222) 7-60-01; e-mail inter@gmb-batumi.com; f. 1993; cap. 3.6m., res 0.3m., dep. 13m. (Dec. 1998); Chair. NUGZAR MIKELADZE.

**Intellectbank:** 380064 Tbilisi, Davit Aghmashenebeli 127; tel. (32) 23-70-83; fax (32) 23-70-82; e-mail intellect@iberia.pac.ge; f. 1993; cap. 4m., dep. 21.5m. (Dec. 1998); Pres. KAKHA GIUASHVILI; Gen. Dir VLADIMER CHANISHVILI; 11 brs.

**JSC Kartu Bank:** Tbilisi, Chavchavadze 39A; tel. (32) 23-00-21; fax (32) 23-03-83; e-mail rcc_cartu@global-erty.net; f. 1996, name changed as above September 1998; cap. 14.1m., dep. 0.7m. (Dec. 1997); Chair. G. CHRDILELI.

**TBC-Bank:** 380079 Tbilisi, Chavchavadze 11; tel. (32) 22-06-61; fax (32) 22-04-06; e-mail info@tbcbank.com.ge; internet www.tbcbank.com.ge; f. 1992; cap. 2.9m., res 1.9m., dep. 17.7m. (Dec. 1998); Pres. MAMUKA KAZARADZE; Gen. Dir VAKHTANG BUTSKHRIKIDZE; 3 brs.

**TbilComBank:** 380007 Tbilisi, Dadiani 2; tel. (32) 98-85-93; f. 1990; cap. 4.0m., res 1.5m. (Dec. 1998); 7 brs.

**Tbilcreditbank:** 380002 Tbilisi, Davit Aghmashenebeli 79; tel. (32) 95-12-92; fax (32) 98-27-83; e-mail tbilcred@caucasus.net; internet www.tbilcreditbank.com; cap. 5.5m., dep. 7m. (Dec. 1999); Chair. DAVIT BUADZE.

**Tbiluniversalbank:** 380071 Tbilisi, Kostava 70; tel. (32) 99-82-92; fax (32) 98-61-68; f. 1994 as Superbank; name changed as above 1995; cap. 2.8m., dep. 1.4m. (Dec. 1998); Gen. Dir TARIEL GVALIA; Chair. NIKOLOZ TEVZADZE.

**United Georgian Bank:** 380008 Tbilisi, Uznadze 37; tel. (32) 99-70-04; fax (32) 95-60-85; e-mail head@ugb.com.ge; internet www.ugb.com.ge; f. 1995 by merger of three specialized state commercial banks; cap. 21.0m., res 1.2m., dep. 21.2m. (Dec. 1998); Gen. Dir IRAKLI KOVZANADZE; Chair. IVAN CHKHARTISHVILI; 26 brs.

### CURRENCY EXCHANGE

**Tbilisi Interbank Currency Exchange (TICEX):** 380005 Tbilisi, Galaktion Tabidze 4; tel. (32) 92-34-43; fax (32) 92-23-01; Gen. Dir DAVIT KLDIASHVILI.

## Trade and Industry

### GOVERNMENT AGENCY

**State Property Management Agency:** Tbilisi; f. 1992; responsible for divestment of state-owned enterprises.

### CHAMBER OF COMMERCE

**Chamber of Commerce and Industry of Georgia:** 380079 Tbilisi, Chavchavadze 11; tel. (32) 23-00-45; fax (32) 23-57-60; brs in Sukhumi and Batumi; Chair. GURAM D. AKHVLEDIANI.

### TRADE ASSOCIATION

**Georgian Import Export (Geoimpex):** 380008 Tbilisi, Giorgiashvili 12; tel. (32) 99-70-90; fax (32) 98-25-41; Gen. Dir T. A. GOGOBERIDZE.

### UTILITIES

#### Electricity

**Department of Power Supply:** Tbilisi, V. Vekua 1; tel. (32) 98-05-65; attached to the Ministry of Fuel and Energy.

**Sakenergo:** 380005 Tbilisi, V. Vekua 1; tel. and fax (32) 92-31-08; formerly state-owned energy supplier; in 1996 restructured into three cos (generation, transmission and distribution); transformation into joint-stock cos in progress in 1997; Gen. Dir EMZAR CHACHKHIANI.

**Sakenergogeneratsia:** 38005 Tbilisi, V. Vekua 1; tel. and fax (32) 98-98-13; state power-generating co; Gen. Dir G. BADURASHVILI.

#### Gas

**International Gas Corpn of Georgia:** joint-stock co; Chair. ALEKSANDR GOTSIRIDZE.

**Sakgazi:** 380007 Tbilisi, Lermontova 10; tel. (32) 99-18-30; fax (32) 99-60-93; gas production co.; Chair. DAVID ELIASHVILI.

**Saktransgasmretsvi:** Tbilisi, Delisi III 22; tel. (32) 93-29-81; fax (32) 53-61-93; state gas distribution co.; Gen. Dir IVAN ZAZASHVILI.

### TRADE UNIONS

**Confederation of Trade Unions of Georgia:** 380122 Tbilisi, Shartava 7; tel. (32) 38-29-95; fax (32) 22-46-63; f. 1995; comprises branch unions with a total membership of approx. 1.4m.; Chair. IRAKLI TUGUSHI.

## Transport

### RAILWAYS

In 1997 Georgia's rail network (including the sections within the secessionist republic of Abkhazia) totalled approximately 1,600 km. However, some 500 km of track was reported to be in a poor state of repair, as a result of which the capacity of some sections of the network had decreased by more than 75% since 1990. The main rail links are with the Russian Federation, along the Black Sea coast, with Azerbaijan, with Armenia and with Iran. The Georgian–Armenian railway continues into eastern Turkey. Various civil conflicts in the mid-1990s disrupted sections of the railway network. The separatist war in Abkhazia resulted in the severance of Georgia's rail connection with the Russian Federation. However, services to Moscow resumed in mid-1997, following a four-year interruption. In mid-1998 it was announced that the European Bank for Reconstruction and Development would assist with the refurbishment of the railways.

The first section of the Tbilisi Metro was opened in 1966; by 1999 the system comprised two lines with 20 stations, totalling 23 km in length, and three extensions, totalling 15 km, were under construction.

**Georgian Railways:** 380012 Tbilisi, Tsaritsa Tamara 15; tel. (32) 99-40-12; fax (32) 95-02-25; f. 1992, following the dissolution of the former Soviet Railways; Chair. AKAKI CHKHAIDZE.

**Tbilisi Metropolitena:** 380012 Tbilisi, Pl. Vokzalnaya 2; Gen. Man. I. G. MELKADZE.

### ROADS

In 1996 the total length of roads in use was an estimated 20,700 km (6,170 km of highways and 14,500 km of secondary roads), of which 93.5% were paved.

### SHIPPING

There are international shipping services with Black Sea and Mediterranean ports. The main ports are at Batumi and Sukhumi.

#### Shipowning Company

**Georgian Shipping Company:** 384517 Batumi, Gogebashvili 60; tel. (222) 14-02-312; fax (222) 73-91-114; Pres. Capt. B. VARSHANIDZE.

### CIVIL AVIATION

**Iveria:** Tbilisi; f. 1998 as a joint-stock co following merger.

**Orbi** (Georgian Airlines): 380058 Tbilisi, Tbilisi Airport; tel. (32) 98-73-28; fax (32) 49-51-51; successor to the former Aeroflot division in Georgia; charter and scheduled services to destinations in the CIS and the Middle East; CEO VASILI S. JAMILBAZISHVILI.

**Sukhumi United Aviation Detachment (Taifun—Adjal Avia):** 384962 Sukhumi, Babushara Airport; tel. (122) 22021; domestic scheduled and chartered flights; Cmmdr ZAUR K. KHAINDRAVA.

## Tourism

Prior to the disintegration of the USSR, Georgia attracted some 1.5m. tourists annually (mainly from other parts of the Soviet Union), owing to its location on the Black Sea and its favourable climate. However, following the outbreak of civil conflict in the early 1990s in South Ossetia and Abkhazia, there was an almost complete cessation in tourism. It was hoped that with the signing of ceasefire agreements with the secessionist republics, tourist numbers would increase. Efforts to regenerate the sector were made in the late 1990s, with the historic buildings of Tbilisi and the surrounding area one of the primary attractions. The ski resort at Gudauri also remained very popular with foreign tourists in the winter months. In 1998 there was just one international hotel in the capital.

**Department of Tourism:** 380062 Tbilisi, Chavchavadze 80; tel. (32) 22-61-25; fax (32) 29-40-52; Chair. KONSTANTINE SALIA.

# GERMANY

## Introductory Survey

### Location, Climate, Language, Religion, Flag, Capital

The Federal Republic of Germany, which was formally established in October 1990 upon the unification of the Federal Republic of Germany (FRG, West Germany) and the German Democratic Republic (GDR, East Germany), lies in the heart of Europe. Its neighbours to the west are the Netherlands, Belgium, Luxembourg and France, to the south Switzerland and Austria, to the east the Czech Republic and Poland, and to the north Denmark. The climate is temperate, with an average annual temperature of 9°C (48°F), although there are considerable variations between the North German lowlands and the Bavarian Alps. The language is German. There is a small Sorbian-speaking minority (numbering about 100,000 people). About 33% of the population are Protestants and a further 33% are Roman Catholics. The national flag (proportions 5 by 3) consists of three equal horizontal stripes, of black, red and gold. The capital is Berlin.

### Recent History

Following the defeat of the Nazi regime and the ending of the Second World War in 1945, Germany was divided, according to the Berlin Agreement, into US, Soviet, British and French occupation zones. Berlin was similarly divided. The former German territories east of the Oder and Neisse rivers, with the city of Danzig (now Gdańsk), became part of Poland, while the northern part of East Prussia, around Königsberg (now Kaliningrad), was transferred to the USSR. After the failure of negotiations to establish a unified German administration, the US, French and British zones were integrated economically in 1948. In May 1949 a provisional Constitution, the Grundgesetz (Basic Law), came into effect in the three zones (except in Saarland—see below), and federal elections were held in August. On 21 September 1949 a new German state, the Federal Republic of Germany (FRG), was established in the three Western zones. The FRG was governed from Bonn in Nordrhein-Westfalan. (Saarland was not incorporated into the FRG until 1957.) In October 1949 Soviet-occupied Eastern Germany declared itself the German Democratic Republic (GDR), with the Soviet zone of Berlin as its capital. This left the remainder of Berlin (West Berlin) as an enclave of the FRG within the territory of the GDR.

The FRG and GDR developed sharply divergent political and economic systems. The leaders of the GDR created a socialist state, based on the Soviet model. As early as 1945 large agricultural estates in eastern Germany were nationalized, followed in 1946 by major industrial concerns. Exclusive political control was exercised by the Sozialistische Einheitspartei Deutschlands (SED, Socialist Unity Party of Germany), which had been formed in April 1946 by the merger of the Communist Party of Germany and the branch of the Sozialdemokratische Partei Deutschlands (SPD, Social Democratic Party of Germany) in the Soviet zone. Other political parties in eastern Germany were under the strict control of the SED, and no political activity independent of the ruling party was permitted. In 1950 Walter Ulbricht was appointed Secretary-General (later restyled First Secretary) of the SED.

The transfer, as war reparations, of foodstuffs, livestock and industrial equipment to the USSR from eastern Germany had a devastating effect on the area's economy in the immediate post-war period. In June 1953 increasing political repression and severe food shortages led to uprisings and strikes, which were suppressed by Soviet troops. The continued failure of the GDR to match the remarkable economic recovery of the FRG prompted a growing number of refugees to cross from the GDR to the FRG (between 1949 and 1961 an estimated 2.5m. GDR citizens moved permanently to the FRG). Emigration was accelerated by the enforced collectivization of many farms in 1960, and in August 1961 the GDR authorities hastily constructed a guarded wall between East and West Berlin.

In May 1971 Ulbricht was succeeded as First Secretary of the SED by Erich Honecker. Ulbricht remained Chairman of the Council of State (Head of State), a post that he had held since 1960, until his death in August 1973. He was initially succeeded in this office by Willi Stoph, but in October 1976 Stoph returned to his previous post as Chairman of the Council of Ministers, and Honecker became Chairman of the Council of State. Under Honecker, despite some liberalization of relations with the FRG, there was little relaxation of repressive domestic policies. Honecker strongly opposed the political and economic reforms that began in the USSR and some other Eastern European countries in the mid-1980s.

The 1949 elections in the FRG resulted in victory for the conservative Christlich-Demokratische Union Deutschlands (CDU, Christian Democratic Union of Germany), together with its sister party in Bavaria, the Christlich-Soziale Union (CSU, Christian Social Union). The SPD was the largest opposition party. Dr Konrad Adenauer, the leader of the CDU, was elected Federal Chancellor by the Bundestag (Federal Assembly); Theodor Heuss became the first President of the Republic. Under Adenauer's chancellorship (which lasted until 1963) and the direction of Dr Ludwig Erhard, his Minister of Economics (and successor as Chancellor), the FRG rebuilt itself rapidly to become one of the most affluent and economically dynamic states in Europe, as well as an important strategic ally of other Western European states and the USA. The Paris Agreement of 1954 gave full sovereign status to the FRG from 5 May 1955, and also granted it membership of NATO.

The CDU/CSU ruled in coalition with the SPD from 1966 to 1969, under the chancellorship of Dr Kurt Kiesinger, but lost support at the 1969 general election, allowing the SPD to form a coalition Government with the Freie Demokratische Partei (FDP, Free Democratic Party), under the chancellorship of Willy Brandt, the SPD leader. Following elections in November 1972, the SPD became, for the first time, the largest party in the Bundestag. In May 1974, however, Brandt resigned as Chancellor, after the discovery that his personal assistant had been a clandestine agent of the GDR. He was succeeded by Helmut Schmidt of the SPD, hitherto the Minister of Finance. In the same month Walter Scheel, Brandt's Vice-Chancellor and Minister of Foreign Affairs, was elected Federal President in place of Gustav Heinemann. A deteriorating economic situation was accompanied by a decline in the popularity of the Government and increasing tension between the coalition partners. In the general election of October 1976 the SPD lost its position as largest party in the Bundestag, but the SPD-FDP coalition retained a slender majority. In July 1979 Dr Karl Carstens of the CDU succeeded Scheel as Federal President.

At the general election of October 1980 the SPD-FDP coalition secured a 45-seat majority in the Bundestag. However, over the next two years the coalition became increasingly unstable, with the partners divided on issues of nuclear power, defence and economic policy. In September 1982 the coalition finally collapsed when the two parties failed to agree on budgetary measures. In October the FDP formed a Government with the CDU/CSU, under the chancellorship of Dr Helmut Kohl, the leader of the CDU. This new partnership was consolidated by the results of the general election of March 1983, when the CDU/CSU substantially increased its share of the votes cast, obtaining 48.8% of the total, compared with 38.8% for the SPD, now led by Hans-Jochen Vogel. An environmentalist party, Die Grünen (The Greens), gained representation in the Bundestag for the first time. In July 1984 Carstens was succeeded as Federal President by Dr Richard von Weizsäcker, also of the CDU. The CDU/CSU-FDP coalition retained power after the general election of January 1987, although with a reduced majority; Kohl was reappointed Chancellor by the Bundestag.

During the period 1949–69 the FRG, under the CDU/CSU, remained largely isolated from Eastern Europe, owing to the FRG Government's refusal to recognize the GDR as an independent state or to maintain diplomatic relations with any other states that recognized the GDR. When Willy Brandt of the SPD became Chancellor in 1969, he adopted a more conciliatory approach to relations with Eastern Europe and, in particular, towards the GDR, a policy which came to be known as

Ostpolitik. In 1970 formal discussions were conducted between representatives of the GDR and the FRG for the first time, and there was a significant increase in diplomatic contacts between the FRG and the other countries of Eastern Europe. In 1970 treaties were signed with the USSR and Poland, in which the FRG formally renounced claims to the eastern territories of the Third Reich and recognized the 'Oder–Neisse Line' as the border between Germany (actually the GDR) and Poland. Further negotiations between the GDR and the FRG, following a quadripartite agreement on West Berlin in September 1971, clarified access rights to West Berlin and also allowed West Berliners to visit the GDR. In December 1972 the two German states signed a 'Basic Treaty', agreeing to develop normal, neighbourly relations with each other, to settle all differences without resort to force, and to respect each other's independence. The Treaty permitted both the FRG and the GDR to join the UN in September 1973, and allowed many Western countries to establish diplomatic relations with the GDR, although both German states continued to deny formal diplomatic recognition to each other.

In December 1981 the first official meeting took place between the two countries' leaders for 11 years, when Chancellor Schmidt of the FRG travelled to the GDR for discussions with Honecker. Inter-German relations deteriorated following the deployment, in late 1983, of US nuclear missiles in the FRG, and the subsequent siting of additional Soviet missiles in the GDR. Nevertheless, official contacts were maintained, and Honecker made his first visit to the FRG in September 1987.

Relations between the two German states were dramatically affected by political upheavals that occurred in the GDR in late 1989 and 1990. In the latter half of 1989 many thousands of disaffected GDR citizens emigrated illegally to the FRG, via Czechoslovakia, Poland and Hungary. The exodus was accelerated by the Hungarian Government's decision, in September 1989, to permit citizens of the GDR to leave Hungary without exit visas. Meanwhile, there was a growth in popular dissent within the GDR, led by Neues Forum (New Forum), an independent citizens' action group that had been established to encourage discussion of democratic reforms, justice and environmental issues.

In early October 1989, following official celebrations to commemorate the 40th anniversary of the foundation of the GDR, anti-Government demonstrations erupted in East Berlin and other large towns. Eventually, as the demonstrations attracted increasing popular support, intervention by the police ceased. (It was later reported that the SED Politburo had voted narrowly against the use of the armed forces to suppress the civil unrest.) In mid-October, as the political situation became more unsettled, Honecker resigned as General Secretary of the SED, Chairman of the Council of State and Chairman of the National Defence Council, ostensibly for reasons of ill health. He was replaced in all these posts by Egon Krenz, a senior member of the SED Politburo. Krenz immediately offered concessions to the opposition, initiating a dialogue with the members of Neues Forum (which was legalized in early November) and with church leaders. There was also a noticeable liberalization of the media, and an amnesty was announced for all persons who had been detained during the recent demonstrations and for those imprisoned for attempting to leave the country illegally. However, large demonstrations, to demand further reforms, continued in many towns throughout the GDR.

On 7 November 1989, in a further attempt to placate the demonstrators, the entire membership of the GDR Council of Ministers (including the Chairman, Willi Stoph) resigned. On the following day the SED Politburo also resigned. On 9 November restrictions on foreign travel for GDR citizens were ended, and all border crossings to the FRG were opened. During the weekend of 10–11 November an estimated 2m. GDR citizens crossed into West Berlin, and the GDR authorities began to dismantle sections of the wall dividing the city. Dr Hans Modrow, a leading member of the SED who was regarded as an advocate of greater reforms, was appointed Chairman of a new Council of Ministers. The new Government pledged to introduce comprehensive political and economic reforms and to hold free elections in 1990.

In early December 1989 the Volkskammer (the GDR's legislature) voted to remove provisions in the Constitution that protected the SED's status as the single ruling party. However, the mass demonstrations continued, prompted by revelations of corruption and personal enrichment by the former leadership and of abuses of power by the state security service (Staatssicherheitsdienst, known colloquially as the Stasi, which was subsequently disbanded). A special commission was established to investigate such charges, and former senior officials, including Honecker and Stoph, were expelled from the SED and placed under house arrest, pending legal proceedings. As the political situation became increasingly unstable, the entire membership of the SED Politburo and Central Committee, including Krenz, resigned, and both bodies, together with the post of General Secretary, were abolished. Shortly afterwards, Krenz also resigned as Chairman of the Council of State; he was replaced by Dr Manfred Gerlach, the Chairman of the Liberal-Demokratische Partei Deutschlands (LDPD, Liberal Democratic Party of Germany). Dr Gregor Gysi, a prominent defence lawyer who was sympathetic to the opposition, was elected to the new post of Chairman of the SED (restyled the Partei des Demokratischen Sozialismus-PDS, Party of Democratic Socialism, in February 1990).

In December 1989 and January 1990 all-party talks took place in the GDR, resulting in the formation, in early February, of a new administration, designated the Government of National Responsibility (still led by Modrow), to remain in office until elections were held. The GDR's first free legislative elections took place on 18 March 1990, with the participation of 93% of those eligible to vote. The East German CDU obtained 40.8% of the total votes cast, while the newly re-established East German SPD and the PDS secured 21.8% and 16.4% of the votes respectively. In April a coalition Government was formed, headed by Lothar de Maizière, leader of the Eastern CDU. Five parties were represented in the new Government: the CDU, the SPD, the Liga der Freien Demokraten (League of Free Democrats) and two smaller parties, the Deutsche Soziale Union (German Social Union), and Demokratische Aufschwung (Democratic Departure). The PDS was not invited to join the coalition.

As a result of the changes within the GDR and the subsequent free contact between Germans of east and west, the issue of possible unification of the two German states inevitably emerged. In November 1989 Chancellor Kohl proposed a plan for the eventual unification of the two countries by means of an interim confederal arrangement. In December Kohl made his first visit to the GDR, where he held discussions with the East German leadership. The two sides agreed to develop contacts at all levels and to establish joint economic, cultural and environmental commissions. However the GDR Government initially insisted that the GDR remain a sovereign, independent state. Nevertheless, in February 1990, in response to growing popular support among GDR citizens for unification, Modrow publicly advocated the establishment of a united Germany. Shortly afterwards, Kohl and Modrow met in Bonn, where they agreed to establish a joint commission to achieve full economic and monetary union between the GDR and the FRG. The new coalition Government of the GDR, formed in April 1990, pledged its determination to achieve German unification in the near future. In mid-May the legislatures of the GDR and the FRG approved the Treaty Between the FRG and the GDR Establishing a Monetary, Economic and Social Union; the Treaty came into effect on 1 July. Later in July the Volkskammer approved the re-establishment on GDR territory of the five Länder (states)—Brandenburg, Mecklenburg-Vorpommern (Mecklenburg-Western Pomerania), Sachsen (Saxony), Sachsen-Anhalt (Saxony-Anhalt) and Thüringen (Thuringia)—which had been abolished by the GDR Government in 1952 in favour of 14 Berzirke (districts). On 31 August the Treaty Between the FRG and the GDR on the Establishment of German Unity was signed in East Berlin by representatives of the two Governments. The treaty stipulated, *inter alia*, that the newly-restored Länder would accede to the FRG on 3 October 1990, and that the 23 boroughs of East and West Berlin would jointly form the Land (state) of Berlin.

Owing to the complex international status of the FRG and the GDR and the two countries' membership of opposing military alliances (respectively, NATO and the now-defunct Warsaw Pact), the process of German unification also included negotiations with other countries. In February 1990 representatives of 23 NATO and Warsaw Pact countries agreed to establish the so-called 'two-plus-four' talks (the FRG and the GDR, plus the four countries that had occupied Germany after the Second World War—France, the USSR, the United Kingdom and the USA) to discuss the external aspects of German unification. In June both German legislatures approved a resolution recognizing the inviolability of Poland's post-1945 borders, stressing that the eastern border of a future united Germany would remain along the Oder–Neisse line. In July, at bilateral talks in the USSR with Chancellor Kohl, the Soviet leader, Mikhail Gorbachev, agreed that a united Germany would be free to join whichever military alliance it wished, thus permitting Germany to remain a full member of NATO. The USSR also pledged to withdraw its armed forces (estimated at 370,000 in 1990) from GDR territory within four years, and it was agreed that a united Germany would reduce the strength of its armed forces to 370,000 within the same period. This agreement ensured a successful result to the 'two-plus-four' talks, which were concluded in September in Moscow, where the Treaty on the Final Settlement with Respect to Germany was signed. In late September the GDR withdrew from the Warsaw Pact.

On 1 October 1990 representatives of the four countries that had occupied Germany after the Second World War met in New York to sign a document in which Germany's full sovereignty was recognized. Finally, on 3 October, the two German states were formally unified. On the following day, at a session of the Bundestag (which had been expanded to permit the representation of former deputies of the GDR Volkskammer), five prominent politicians from the former GDR were sworn in as Ministers without Portfolio in the Federal Government.

Prior to unification, the CDU, the SPD and the FDP of the GDR had merged with their respective counterparts in the FRG to form three single parties. At state elections in the newly-acceded Länder, held in mid-October 1990, the CDU obtained an average of 41% of the total votes and won control of four Land legislatures, while the SPD received an average of 27% of the total votes and gained a majority only in Brandenburg. This surge of support for Chancellor Kohl and the CDU was confirmed by the results of elections to the Bundestag in early December (the first all-German elections since 1933). The CDU (together with the CSU) won 43.8% of the total votes cast, and thus secured a total of 319 seats in the 662-member Bundestag. The SPD achieved its poorest result in a general election since 1957, receiving 33.5% of the votes and winning 239 seats in the legislature (a result attributed, in large part, to the party's cautious stance on unification). The FDP won 11% of the total votes, and consequently 79 seats in the Bundestag, its most successful result in legislative elections since 1961. Unexpectedly, the West German Grünen lost the 42 seats that they had previously held in the legislature, having failed to obtain the necessary 5% of the votes cast in the area formerly constituting the FRG. However, as a result of a special clause in the electoral law (adopted in October 1990, and valid only for the legislative elections of December 1990), which permitted representation in the Bundestag for parties of the former GDR that received at least 5% of the total votes cast in former GDR territory, the party's eastern German counterpart, in coalition with Bündnis 90 (Alliance 90), secured eight seats in the legislature. Under the same ruling, the PDS won 17 seats in the Bundestag (having received almost 10% of the total votes cast in the area formerly constituting the GDR). At state elections in Berlin, which were held simultaneously with the general election, the CDU won the largest share of the votes (40%), while the SPD received 30%. Both environmentalist parties (West and East) won seats, but the extreme right-wing Republikaner (Republicans) lost the 11 seats that they had won at elections in West Berlin in 1983.

Dr Kohl was formally re-elected to the post of Federal Chancellor in mid-January 1991, immediately after the formation of the new Federal Government. This comprised 20 members, but included only three politicians from the former GDR. The FDP's representation was increased from four to five ministers, reflecting the party's success in the recent legislative elections.

Investigations into the abuse of power by the administration of the former GDR, conducted during the early 1990s, prompted the dismissal or resignation from government posts of several former SED politicians. In January 1991 the German authorities temporarily suspended efforts to arrest Honecker on charges of manslaughter (for complicity in the deaths of people who had been killed while attempting to escape from the GDR), owing to the severe ill health of the former GDR leader. In March it was announced that Honecker had been transferred, without the permission of the German authorities, to the USSR, and in December he took refuge in the Chilean embassy in Moscow.

One of the most serious problems confronting the Government immediately following unification was that of escalating unemployment in eastern Germany, as a result of the introduction of market-orientated reforms that were intended to integrate the economic system of the former GDR with that of the rest of the country. A substantial increase in the crime rate in eastern Germany was also recorded. A further disturbing social issue, particularly in the eastern Länder, was the resurgence of extreme right-wing and neo-Nazi groups. Moreover, there were also fears of a resurgence of political violence, following a series of terrorist acts culminating in the assassination, in April 1991, of Detlev Rohwedder, the executive head of the Treuhandanstalt (the trustee agency that had been established in March 1990 to supervise the privatization of state-owned enterprises in the former GDR). Responsibility for this and other attacks was claimed by the Rote Armee Fraktion (RAF, Red Army Faction), a terrorist organization which had been active in the FRG during the 1970s. (The RAF eventually disbanded in 1998.)

Increasing popular discontent with the Government's post-unification policies was reflected in successive victories for the SPD in Land elections in the first half of 1991, causing the SPD to regain its majority in the Bundesrat, which it had lost to the CDU/CSU–FDP coalition in October 1990. In June 1991 the Bundestag voted in favour of Berlin as the future seat of the legislature and of government; it was envisaged that the transfer of organs of government from Bonn to Berlin would be completed by 2000.

At the beginning of January 1992 some 2m. Stasi files were opened to public scrutiny. In February Erich Mielke, the former head of the Stasi, was brought to trial on charges of murder, and in September Markus Wolf, the former head of East Germany's intelligence service, was charged with espionage, treason and corruption; both were subsequently found guilty and each was sentenced to six years' imprisonment. Meanwhile, Honecker returned to Germany from Russia in July 1992. He was brought to trial in November, together with five other defendants (among them Mielke and Stoph), on charges of manslaughter and embezzlement. In April 1993, however, the charges against Honecker were suspended. (The former East German leader, who was terminally ill, had been allowed to leave for Chile in January of that year; he died in May 1994.) Stoph was also released on grounds of ill health. In May 1993 Hans Modrow was found guilty of electoral fraud at communal elections that had taken place in the former GDR in 1989; Modrow was subsequently sentenced to nine months' imprisonment (suspended).

The issue of asylum-seekers dominated domestic politics during the early 1990s. At Land elections which took place in April 1992, both the CDU and the SPD lost considerable support to right-wing extremist parties. In June the Bundestag approved controversial legislation that aimed to accelerate the processing of applications by refugees and introduced stricter rules for the granting of asylum. A six-week limit was imposed on the time that could be devoted to the consideration of each case, during which period applicants would be required to stay in special camps. Extreme nationalistic sentiment in some quarters led to an escalation in brutal attacks against asylum seekers and foreign workers during the early 1990s. In August 1992 neo-Nazi youths attacked refugee centres in more than 15 towns and bombed a memorial to the Holocaust (the Nazis' extermination of an estimated 6m. Jews) in Berlin. Sporadic attacks continued throughout Germany (though mainly in the east) in September and October. Several neo-Nazi vandals were arrested, but there was criticism of the lenient sentences imposed on those convicted. The murder in November of three Turkish immigrants in an arson attack in Mölln, Schleswig-Holstein, prompted the Government to ban several right-wing groups that were believed to have been responsible for co-ordinating attacks on foreigners. In December the main political parties reached agreement on the terms of a constitutional amendment to the law of asylum, and the new provisions, empowering immigration officials to refuse entry to economic migrants while still facilitating the granting of asylum to persons who were deemed to be political refugees, were approved by the Bundestag and the Bundesrat in May 1993. The Ministry of the Interior estimated that a record total of 438,191 people had sought asylum in Germany during 1992. By 1998, however, mainly as a result of the 1993 legislation, the number of applications had fallen to 98,644. During May 1993 the deaths of five Turkish women in an arson attack near Köln precipitated protest demonstrations throughout Germany and widespread condemnation in the international media.

In March 1992 Germany suspended sales of military equipment to Turkey, after the Government of that country admitted that armaments previously supplied by Germany had been used in actions to suppress Turkey's Kurdish minority. Revelations that tanks had been transferred to Turkey in late 1991, in contravention of a parliamentary ban on such shipments, in 1950; stands for the united action between Catholics and Protestants for rebuilding German life on a Christian-Democratic basis, while guaranteeing private property and the freedom of the individual, and for a 'free and equal Germany in a free, politically united and socially just Europe'; other objectives are to guarantee close ties with allies within NATO and the principle of self-determination; in Oct. 1990 incorporated the CDU of the former GDR; c. 640,000 mems (Aug. 1997); Chair. (vacant); Sec.-Gen. Dr ANGELA MERKEL; Parliamentary Leader CHRISTOPH MERZ.

**CSU:** 80335 München, Nymphenburger Str. 64; tel. (89) 12430; fax (89) 1243220; f. 1946; Christian Social party, aiming for a free market economy 'in the service of man's economic and intellectual freedom'; also combines national consciousness with support for a united Europe; 181,000 mems; Chair. Dr EDMUND STOIBER; Sec.-Gen. Dr THOMAS GOPPEL.

**Deutsche Kommunistische Partei (DKP)** (German Communist Party): 45127 Essen, Hoffnungstr. 18; tel. (201) 225148. fax (201) 202467; e-mail dkp.pv@t-online-de; internet www.dkp.de; 7,000 mems (1998); Chair. HEINZ STEHR.

**Deutsche Volksunion (DVU)** (German People's Union): 81204 München, Postfach 600464; tel. (89) 896085; fax (89) 8341534; internet www.dvu.net; f. 1987; right-wing, xenophobic.

**Freie Demokratische Partei (FDP)** (Free Democratic Party): 10117 Berlin, Reinhardtstr. 14; tel. (30) 2849580; fax (30) 28495822; e-mail tdh@fdp.de; internet www.fdp.de; f. 1948; represents democratic and social liberalism and makes the individual the focal point of the state and its laws and economy; in Aug. 1990 incorporated the three liberal parties of the former GDR—the Association of Free Democrats, the German Forum Party and the FDP; approx. 70,000 mems (Nov. 1999); Chair. Dr WOLFGANG GERHARDT; Deputy Chair. CORNELIA PIEPER, RAINER BRÜDERLE, Dr WALTER DÖRING; Chair. in Bundestag Dr WOLFGANG GERHARDT; Sec.-Gen. Dr GUIDO WESTERWELLE.

**Nationaldemokratische Partei Deutschlands (NPD)** (National Democratic Party of Germany): 12531 Berlin, Postfach 840157; internet www.npd.de; f. 1964; right-wing; 15,000 mems; youth organization Junge Nationaldemokraten (JN), 6,000 mems; Chair. UDO VOIGT.

**Neues Forum** (New Forum): 99089 Erfurt, Bergstr. 23; tel. (361) 2110114; fax (361) 2118123; e-mail bv@neuesforum.de; internet www.neuesforum.de; f. 1989 as a citizens' action group; played a prominent role in the democratic movement in the former GDR; Leaders KAROLIN SCHUBERT, MATTHIAS BÜCHNER, MICHAEL BONEHR.

**Partei des Demokratischen Sozialismus (PDS)** (Party of Democratic Socialism): 10178 Berlin, Kleine Alexanderstr. 28; tel. (30) 240090; fax (30) 24009425; e-mail pdspv@aol.com; internet www.pds-online.de; the dominant political force in the former GDR until late 1989; formed in 1946 as the Socialist Unity Party (SED), as a result of a unification of the Social Democratic Party and the Communist Party in Eastern Germany; in Dec. 1989 renamed the SED-PDS; adopted present name in Feb. 1990; has renounced Stalinism, opposes fascism, right-wing extremism and xenophobia, advocates international disarmament and a socially- and ecologically-orientated market economy with public ownership of the means of production; 105,000 mems (Dec, 1997); Chair. Prof. Dr LOTHAR BISKY; Chair. of Parliamentary Party Dr GREGOR GYSI; Hon. Chair. Dr HANS MODROW.

**Die Republikaner (REP)** (Republican Party): 13162 Berlin, Postfach 870210; tel. (30) 79098310; fax (30) 79098315; e-mail republikaner-bgs@t.online.de; internet www.rep.de; f. 1983; extreme right wing; approx. 25,000 mems; Chair. and Chair. in Bundestag Dr ROLF SCHLIERER.

**Sozialdemokratische Partei Deutschlands (SPD)** (Social Democratic Party of Germany): 10963 Berlin, Wilhelmstr. 141; tel. (30) 259910; fax (30) 410; e-mail parteivorstand@spd.de; internet www.spd.de; f. 1863; maintains that a vital democracy can be built only on the basis of social justice; advocates for the economy as much competition as possible, as much planning as necessary to protect the individual from uncontrolled economic interests; favours a positive attitude to national defence, while supporting controlled disarmament; rejects any political ties with Communism; in September 1990 incorporated the SPD of the former GDR; approx. 755,244 mems (Oct. 1999); Chair. GERHARD SCHRÖDER; Gen. Sec. FRANZ MÜNTEFERING.

There are also numerous other small parties, none of them represented in the Bundestag, covering all shades of the political spectrum and various regional interests.

# Diplomatic Representation

## EMBASSIES IN GERMANY*

**Afghanistan:** 53125 Bonn, Liebfrauenweg 1A; tel. (228) 251927; fax (228) 255310; Chargé d'affaires: AMANULLAH JAYHOON.

**Albania:** 53173 Bonn, Dürenstr. 35–37; tel. (228) 351045; fax (228) 351048; Ambassador: BASHKIM ZENELI.

**Algeria:** 13187 Berlin, Görschstr. 45–46; tel. (30) 4816170; fax (30) 4863137; MOHAMMED HANECHE.

**Angola:** 53111 Bonn, Kaiser-Karl-Ring 20C; tel. (228) 555708; fax (228) 690661; Ambassador: Dr JOÃO LANDOITE LOURENÇO.

**Argentina:** 53113 Bonn, Adenauerallee 50–52; tel. (228) 228010; fax (228) 2280130; internet www.argentinischebotschaft.de; Ambassador: Dr ANDRÉS GUILLERMO PESCI-BOUREL.

**Armenia:** 13467 Berlin, Hillmannstr. 5; tel. (30) 4050910; fax (30) 40509125; e-mail armemb@t-online.de; Ambassador: Dr ASHOT VOSKANIAN.

**Australia:** 10117 Berlin, Friedrichstr. 200; tel. (30) 8800880; fax (30) 880088310; Ambassador: PAUL O'SULLIVAN.

**Austria:** 10117 Berlin, Friedrichstr. 60, Quartier 203; tel. (30) 202870; fax (30) 2290569; internet www.oesterreichische-botschaft.de; Ambassador: Dr MARKUS LUTTEROTTI. (Full diplomatic relations were suspended in Feb. 2000.)

**Azerbaijan:** 53179 Bonn, Schloßallee 12; tel. (228) 943890; fax (228) 858644; Ambassador: HUSSEIN-AGA M. SSADIGOV.

**Bahrain:** 53173 Bonn, Plittersdorfestr. 91; tel. (228) 957610; fax (228) 9576199; Ambassador: Dr AHMED ABBAS AHMED.

**Bangladesh:** 10587 Berlin, Dovestr. 1; Ambassador: KAZI ANWARUL MASUD.

**Belarus:** 12345 Berlin, Am Treptower Park; tel. (30) 5363590; fax (30) 53635923; Ambassador: VLADIMIR SKWORZOW.

**Belgium:** 10117 Berlin, Friedrichstr. 95; tel. (30) 203520; fax (30) 20352200; Ambassador: DOMINICUS STRUYE DE SWIELANDE.

**Benin:** 53179 Bonn, Rüdigerstr. 10, 53132 Bonn, Postfach 200254; tel. (228) 943870; fax (228) 857192; Ambassador: CORNEILLE MEHISSOU.

**Bolivia:** 10787 Berlin, Wichmannstr. 5/6; tel. (30) 31503897; fax (30) 31503898; e-mail boliviabonn@t-online.de; Ambassador: Dr ERNESTO FERNANDO SCHILLING KRIETE.

**Bosnia and Herzegovina:** 53173 Bonn, Bürgerstr. 12; Ambassador: ANTON BALKOVIC.

**Brazil:** 53175 Bonn, Kennedyallee 74; tel. (228) 959230; fax (228) 373696; Ambassador: ROBERTO PINTO FERREIRA MAMERI ABDENUR.

**Brunei:** 10117 Berlin, Kronenstr. 55–58; tel. (30) 2060760; Ambassador: MAHADI BIN Haji WASLI.

**Bulgaria:** 10117 Berlin, Mauerstr. 11; tel. (30) 201092226; fax (30) 2086838; e-mail bulbot@aol.com; Ambassador: NIKOLAY APOSTOLOV.

**Burkina Faso:** 53179 Bonn, Wendelstadtallee 18; tel. (228) 952970; fax (228) 9529720; e-mail embassy-burkina-faso@t-online.de; Ambassador: JEAN-BAPTISTE ILBOUDO.

**Burundi:** 53179 Bonn, Mainzerstr. 174; tel. (228) 345032; fax (228) 340148; Ambassador: ALOYS MBONAYO.

**Cambodia:** 13187 Berlin, Benjamin-Vogelsdorf-Str.; Ambassador: KHEK LERANG.

**Cameroon:** 53173 Bonn, Rheinallee 76; tel. (228) 356038; fax (228) 359058; Ambassador: JEAN MELAGA.

**Canada:** 10117 Berlin, Friedrichstr. 95; tel. (30) 203120; fax (30) 20312111; Ambassador: GAËTAN LAVERTU.

**Cape Verde:** 10117 Berlin, Dorotheenstr. 43; tel. (30) 20450955; fax (30) 20450966; Ambassador: VICTOR ALFONSO G. FIDALGO.

**Central African Republic:** 53225 Bonn, Rheinaustr. 120; tel. (228) 233564; Ambassador: MARTIN-GÉRARD TEBITO.

**Chad:** 53173 Bonn, Basteistr. 80; tel. (228) 356026; fax (228) 355887; Ambassador: BINTOU MALLOUM.

**Chile:** 53173 Bonn, Kronprinzenstr. 20; tel. (228) 955840; fax (228) 9558440; e-mail echilede@t-online.de; Ambassador: RICARDO HORMAZÁBAL SÁNCHEZ.

**China, People's Republic:** 53177 Bonn, Kurfürstenallee 12; tel. (228) 955970; fax (228) 361635; Ambassador: LU QIUTAN.

**Colombia:** 10797 Berlin, Kurfürstenstr. 84; tel. (30) 2639610; fax (30) 26396125; e-mail cultura.emcol@t-online.de; Ambassador: HERNAN BELTZ-PERALTA.

**Congo, Democratic Republic:** 53179 Bonn, Im Meisengarten 133; tel. (228) 858160; fax (228) 340398; Ambassador: LHELO BOLOTO.

**Congo, Republic:** 53173 Bonn, Rheinallee 45; tel. (228) 358355; fax (228) 358355; Chargé d'affaires a.i.: SERGE MICHEL ODZOCKI.

**Costa Rica:** 53113 Bonn, Langenbachstr. 19; tel. (228) 540040; fax (228) 549053; e-mail 100730.1020@compuserve.com; Ambassador: Prof. Dr RAFAEL ANGEL HERRA.

**Côte d'Ivoire:** 53115 Bonn, Königstr. 93; tel. (228) 212098; fax (228) 217313; Ambassador: JEAN VINCENT ZINSOU.

**Croatia:** 10709 Berlin, Kurfürstendamm 72; tel. (30) 3237635; fax (30) 3237630; Ambassador: Prof. Dr ZORAN JASIC.

**Cuba:** 10439 Berlin, Stavanger Str. 20; tel. (30) 91611810; fax (30) 9164553; Ambassador: OSCAR ISRAEL MARTÍNEZ CORDOVÉS.

**Cyprus:** 10179 Berlin, Wallstr. 27; tel. (30) 27591270; fax (30) 27590454; e-mail botschaft-zypern-presse@t-online.de; Ambassador: THEOPHILOS V. THEOPHILOU.

**Czech Republic:** 10117 Berlin, Wilhelmstr. 44; tel. (30) 226380; fax (30) 2294033; e-mail berlin@embassy.mzv.cz; Ambassador: FRANTIŠEK ČERNÝ.

**Denmark:** 10789 Berlin, Rauchstr. 1, 10722 Berlin, Postfach 301245; tel. (30) 50502009; fax (30) 50502050; e-mail beramb@beramb.um.dk; internet www.daenemark.org; Ambassador: BENT HAAKONSEN.

**Dominican Republic:** 53177 Bonn, Burgstr. 87; tel. (228) 364956; fax (228) 352576; Ambassador: Prof. Dr VINICIO ALFONSO TOBAL UREÑA.

**Ecuador:** 53173 Bonn, Koblenzer Str. 37; tel. (228) 352544; fax (228) 361765; Ambassador: Dr WERNER MOELLER FRIELE.

**Egypt:** 53173 Bonn, Kronprinzenstr. 2; tel. (228) 956830; fax (228) 364304; Ambassador: MAHMOUD AHMED FATHY MOUBARAK.

**El Salvador:** 53113 Bonn, Adenauerallee 238; tel. (228) 549914; fax (228) 549814; e-mail embasalva.rfa@t-online.de; Ambassador: (vacant).

**Eritrea:** 50968 Köln, Marktstr. 8; tel. (221) 373016; fax (221) 3404128; Ambassador: PETROS TSEGGAI.

**Estonia:** 10707 Berlin, Kurfürstendamm 56; tel. (30) 32705355; fax (30) 32707263; e-mail saatkond-berlinis@berlin.estemb.de; Ambassador: MARGUS LAIDRE.

**Ethiopia:** 12207 Berlin, Boothstr. 20; Ambassador: Dr BERHANE TENSAY WOLDESENBET.

**Finland:** 10787 Berlin, Rauchstr. 1; tel. (30) 505030; fax (30) 5050333; internet www.finlandemb.de; Ambassador: ARTO OLAVI MANSALA.

**France:** 10969 Berlin, Kochstr. 6/7; tel. (30) 2063900; fax (30) 20639010; Ambassador: CLAUDE MARTIN.

**Gabon:** 53173 Bonn, Kronprinzenstr. 52; tel. (228) 365844; fax (228) 359195; Ambassador: SYLVESTRE RATANGA.

**Georgia:** 53177 Bonn, Am Kurpark 6; tel. (228) 957510; fax (228) 9575120; Ambassador: Dr KONSTANTIN GABASCHWILI.

**Ghana:** 53173 Bonn, Rheinallee 58; tel. (228) 367960; fax (228) 363498; Ambassador: GEORGE ROBERT NIPAH.

**Greece:** 10117 Berlin, Jägerstr. 54–55; tel. (30) 206260; fax (30) 20626444; internet www.griechenland-botschaft.de; Ambassador: DIMITRIOS NEZERITIS.

**Guatemala:** 53173 Bonn, Zietenstr. 16; tel. (228) 351579; fax (228) 354940; e-mail embaguate-bonn@compuserve.com; Ambassador: ANAMARÍA DIÉGUEZ.

**Guinea:** 53129 Bonn, Rochusweg 50; tel. (228) 231098; fax (228) 231097; Ambassador: NAMANKOUMBA KOUYATE.

**Haiti:** 53179 Bonn, Schlossallee 10; tel. (228) 340351; fax (228) 857700; e-mail haibot@aol.com; Ambassador: Dr ALRICH NICOLAS.

**Holy See:** 53175 Bonn, Turmstr. 29 (Apostolic Nunciature); tel. (228) 959010; fax (228) 379180; Apostolic Nuncio: Mgr GIOVANNI LAJOLO.

**Honduras:** 53173 Bonn, Ubierstr. 1; tel. (228) 356394; fax (228) 351981; e-mail embahonbn@t-online.de; Ambassador: MAX VELÁSQUEZ DÍAZ.

**Hungary:** 10117 Berlin, Markgrafenstr. 36; tel. (30) 203100; fax (30) 2291314; e-mail huembber@attmail.com; Ambassador: Dr PÉTER BALÁZS.

**Iceland:** 10787 Berlin, Rauchstr. 1; tel. (30) 50504000; fax (30) 50504300; e-mail icemb.berlin@utn.stjr.is; internet www.botschaft-island.de; Ambassador: INGIMUNDUR SIGFÚSSON.

**India:** 53113 Bonn, Adenauerallee 262–264; tel. (228) 54050; fax (228) 5405154; Ambassador: RANENDRA SEN.

**Indonesia:** 53175 Bonn, Bernkasteler Str. 2; tel. (228) 382990; fax (228) 311393; Ambassador: IZHAR IBRAHIM.

**Iran:** 14195 Berlin, Podbielskiallee 67; tel. (30) 8419180; fax (30) 8329874; Ambassador: AHMAD AZIZI.

**Iraq:** 53175 Bonn, Annaberger Str. 289; Chargé d'affaires: SHAMIL A. MOHAMMED.

**Ireland:** 10117 Berlin, Friedrichstr. 200; e-mail info@irish-embassy.de; Ambassador: NOEL FAHEY.

**Israel:** 14193 Berlin, Schinkelstr. 10; tel. (30) 89045500; fax (30) 89045222; e-mail botschaft@israel.de; Ambassador: (vacant).

**Italy:** 10963 Berlin, Dessauerstr. 28–29; tel. (30) 254400; fax (30) 25440116; e-mail ambitalia.segr@t-online.de; Ambassador: ENZO PERLOT.

**Jamaica:** 53177 Bonn, Am Kreuter 1; tel. (228) 934590; fax (228) 361890; e-mail jamaican-emb.bonn@home.ivm.de; Ambassador: PETER CARLYSLE BLACK.

**Japan:** 10787 Berlin, Kleiststr. 23–26; tel. (30) 210940; fax (30) 21094222; Ambassador: KUNISADA KUME.

**Jordan:** 53173 Bonn, Beethovenallee 21; tel. (228) 357046; fax (228) 353951; Ambassador: HUSSEIN AHMAD HAMMAMI.

**Kazakhstan:** 13156 Berlin, Nordendstr. 14/15; tel. (30) 470070; fax (30) 47007125; Ambassador: ERIK MAGSUMOVITCH ASANBAYEV.

**Kenya:** 53177 Bonn, Villichgasse 17; tel. (228) 935800; fax (228) 9358050; Ambassador: JOHN LEPI LANYASUNYA.

**Korea, Republic:** 10785 Berlin, Schöneberger Ufer 89/91; tel. (30) 260650; fax (30) 2606551; Ambassador: KICHOO LEE.

**Kuwait:** 53175 Bonn, Godesberger Allee 77-81; tel. (228) 378081; fax (228) 378936; Ambassador: ABDULAZEEZ ABDULLATIEF AL-SHARIKH.

**Kyrgyzstan:** 10585 Berlin, Otto-Suhr-Allee 146; e-mail 101477.1160@compuserve.com; Ambassador: Dr APAS DSCHMAGULOV.

**Laos:** 53639 Königswinter, Am Lessing 6; tel. (223) 21501; fax (223) 3065; Ambassador: PHANTHONG PHOMMAHAXAY.

**Latvia:** 14193 Berlin, Reinerzstr. 40–41; tel. (30) 8260020; fax (30) 82600233; Ambassador: ANDRIS TEIKMANIS.

**Lebanon:** 53173 Bonn, Rheinallee 27; tel. (228) 956800; fax (228) 357560; Ambassador: MELHEM NASRI MISTOU.

**Lesotho:** 53175 Bonn, Godesberger Allee 50; tel. (228) 308430; fax (228) 3084322; e-mail lesoembger@aol.com; Ambassador: LEBOHANG NTS'INYI.

**Liberia:** 53179 Bonn, Mainzerstr. 259; tel. (228) 340822; Ambassador: RUFUS WEBSTER SIMPSON.

**Libya:** 53173 Bonn, Beethovenallee 12A; tel. (228) 820090; fax (228) 364260; Secretary of the People's Committee: MOHAMMED ALBARANI.

**Lithuania:** 10711 Berlin, Katharinenstr. 9; tel. (30) 890681; fax (30) 890681; e-mail botschaftlitauen@t-online.de; Ambassador: Prof. Dr HABIL VAIDIEVUTIS.

**Luxembourg:** 10785 Berlin, Klingelhöfer Str. 7; tel. (30) 20253133; fax (30) 20253304; Ambassador: Dr JULIEN ALEX.

**Macedonia, former Yugoslav republic:** 14193 Berlin, Königsallee 2; tel. (30) 8906950; fax (30) 89541194; Ambassador: Dr SRGJAN KERIM.

**Madagascar:** 53179 Bonn, Rolandstr. 48; tel. (228) 953590; fax (228) 334628; e-mail madagaskar-botschaft@t-online.de; internet www.botschaft-madagaskar.de; Ambassador: ZAFERA A. RABESA.

**Malawi:** 53179 Bonn, Mainzer Str. 124; tel. (228) 943350; fax (228) 9433537; Ambassador: GEOFFREY G. CHIPUNGU.

**Malaysia:** 10707 Berlin, Kurfürstendamm 50; tel. (30) 8857490; fax (30) 88729028; Ambassador: Dato' ABDUL KADIR MOHAMED DEEN.

**Mali:** 53173 Bonn, Basteistr. 86; tel. (228) 357048; fax (228) 361922; Ambassador: OUSMANE DEMBÉLÉ.

**Malta:** 53173 Bonn, Viktoriastr. 1; tel. (228) 363017; fax (228) 363019; Ambassador: WILLIAM C. SPITERI.

**Mauritania:** 53173 Bonn, Bonnerstr. 48; tel. (228) 364024; fax (228) 361788; Ambassador: HAMOUD OULD ELY.

**Mexico:** 10709 Berlin, Kurfürstendamm 72; tel. (30) 3249047; fax (30) 32771121; e-mail rfaemb@edina.xnc.com; internet www.inf.fu-berlin.de/-mex; Ambassador: ROBERTO EMILIO FRIEDRICH HEINZE.

**Moldova:** 10439 Berlin, Gotlandstr. 16; tel. (30) 44652970; fax (30) 2835237; e-mail 113145.334@compuserve.com; Ambassador: Dr AURELIAN DÁNILÁ.

**Monaco:** 53113 Bonn, Zitelmannstr. 16; tel. (228) 232007; fax (228) 236282; Chargé d'affaires: EVA WITTENBERG.

**Mongolia:** 53844 Troisdorf-Sieglar, Siebengebirgsblick 4; tel. (2241) 402727; fax (2241) 47781; Ambassador: BAZARRAGCHA BAYARSAIHAN.

**Morocco:** 10117 Berlin, Niederwallstr. 39; tel. (30) 2061240; fax (30) 20612420; Ambassador: Dr ABDELADIM LHAFI.

**Mozambique:** 53113 Bonn, Adenauerallee 46A; tel. (228) 263921; fax (228) 213920; Ambassador: MANUEL TOMÁS LUBISSE.

**Myanmar:** 53113 Bonn, Schumann Str. 112; tel. (228) 210091; fax (228) 219316; e-mail k.oh@wunsch.com; Ambassador: U. SAN THIEN.

**Namibia:** 10787 Berlin, Friedrichstr. 60; Ambassador: HINYANGERWA PIUS ASHEEKE.

**Nepal:** 53179 Bonn, Im Hag 15; tel. (228) 343097; fax (228) 856747; Ambassador: Dr NOVEL KISHORE RAI.

**Netherlands:** 10117 Berlin, Friedrichstr. 95; tel. (30) 209560; fax (30) 20956441; e-mail nlgovbon@nlgovbon.bn.uunet.de; internet www.dutchembassy.de; Ambassador: Dr NIKOLAOS VAN DAM.

**New Zealand:** 10117 Berlin, Friedrichstr. 60; tel. (30) 206210; fax (30) 20621114; e-mail nzemb@t-online.de; Ambassador: W. A. COCHRANE.

**Nicaragua:** 53179 Bonn, Konstantinstr. 41; tel. (228) 362505; fax 354001; Ambassador: SUYAPA INDIANA PADILLA TERCERO.

**Niger:** 53173 Bonn, Dürenstr. 9; tel. (228) 3682061; fax (228) 3682062; Ambassador: ADAMOU OUMAROU.

**Nigeria:** 53177 Bonn, Goldbergweg 13; tel. (228) 322071; fax (228) 328088; Chargé d'affaires a.i.: BABA GANA WAKIL.

**Norway:** 10787 Berlin, Rauchstr. 1; tel. (30) 505050; fax (30) 505055; e-mail botschaft@norwegen.org; internet www.norwegen.org; Ambassador: MORTEN WETLAND.

**Oman:** 53173 Bonn, Lindenallee 11; tel. (228) 357031; fax (228) 357045; Ambassador: AHMED M. AL-HINAI.

**Pakistan:** 10719 Berlin, Schaper Str. 29; Ambassador: Gen. ASAD DURRANI.

**Panama:** 53173 Bonn, Lützowstr. 1; tel. (228) 361036; fax (228) 363558; Ambassador: FLOR DE MARIA MONTEVERDE.

**Papua New Guinea:** 53173 Bonn, Moltkestr. 44–46; e-mail 106555.326@compuserve.com; Chargé d'affaires: PETER RAKA.

**Paraguay:** 53173 Bonn, Uhlandstr. 32; tel. (228) 356727; fax (228) 366663; Ambassador: Dr MARCOS MARTÍNEZ MENDIETA.

**Peru:** 53175 Bonn, Godesberger Allee 125; tel. (228) 373045; fax (228) 379475; Ambassador: Dr LUIS GARCÍA SEMINARIO.

**Philippines:** 53115 Bonn, Argelanderstr. 1; tel. (228) 267990; fax (228) 221968; Ambassador: JOSÉ A. ZAIDE.

**Poland:** 10117 Berlin, Unter den Linden 72; tel. (30) 2202551; fax (30) 2290358; e-mail prasa@pol-bot.com; internet www.pol-bot.com; Ambassador: Dr ANDRZEJ BYRT.

**Portugal:** 10117 Berlin, Zimmerstr. 56; tel. (30) 590063500; fax (30) 590063600; Ambassador: Dr JOÃO DIOGO CORREIA SARAIVA NUNES.

**Qatar:** 14193 Berlin, Hagenstr. 56; Ambassador: MOHAMED HASSAN AL-JABER.

**Romania:** 53117 Bonn, Legionsweg 14; tel. (228) 68380; fax (228) 680247; Ambassador: TUDOR GAVRIL DUNCA.

**Russia:** 10117 Berlin, Unter den Linden 63–65; tel. (30) 2291110; fax (30) 2299397; e-mail russembassyg@trionet.de; Ambassador: SERGEI BORISOVICH KRYLOV.

**Rwanda:** 53173 Bonn, Beethovenallee 72; tel. (228) 355228; fax (228) 351922; e-mail ambrwabonn@aol.com; Ambassador: BERNARD MAKUZA.

**Saudi Arabia:** 10787 Berlin, Kurfürstendamm 63; Ambassador: ABBAS FAIG GHAZZAWI.

**Senegal:** 53115 Bonn, Argelanderstr. 3; tel. (228) 218008; fax (228) 217815; Ambassador: Gen. MOHAMADOU KEÏTA.

**Sierra Leone:** 53173 Bonn, Rheinallee 20; tel. (228) 352001; fax (228) 364269; Ambassador: UMARU BUNDU WURIE.

**Singapore:** 10117 Berlin, Friedrichstr. 200; tel. (30) 22634318; fax (30) 22634355; e-mail sing.emb.bonn@t-online.de; Ambassador: WALTER WOON.

**Slovakia:** 10117 Berlin, Leipziger Str. 36; tel. (30) 2044538; fax (30) 2082459; Ambassador: JÁN FOLTIN.

**Slovenia:** 10117 Berlin, Hausvogteiplatz 3–4; tel. (30) 2061450; fax (30) 20614570; Ambassador: ALFONZ NABERŽNIK.

**South Africa:** 10117 Berlin, Friedrichstr. 60; tel. (30) 220730; fax (30) 22073190; e-mail botschaft@suedafrika.org; internet www.suedafrika.org; Ambassador: Prof. Dr SIGUSISO M. B. BENGU.

**Spain:** 10785 Berlin, Schöneberger Ufer 89–91; tel. (30) 2540070; fax (30) 25799557; Ambassador: JOSÉ PEDRO SEBASTIÁN DE ERICE.

**Sri Lanka:** 14163 Berlin, Niklasstr. 19; tel. (30) 80909764; fax (30) 80909764; e-mail amb@slemb.bn.eunet.de; Ambassador: S. B. ATUGODA.

**Sudan:** 53177 Bonn, Koblenzer Str. 107; tel. (228) 933700; fax (228) 335115; Ambassador: Dr ACHOL DENG.

**Sweden:** 10787 Berlin, Rauchstr. 1; tel. (30) 505060; fax (30) 50506789; internet www.schweden.org; Ambassador: MATS HELLSTRÖM.

**Switzerland:** 10557 Berlin, Haus am Wasser, Kirchstr. 13; tel. (30) 3904000; fax (30) 3911030; Ambassador: THOMAS BORER-FIELDING.

**Syria:** 53175 Bonn, Andreas-Hermes-Str. 5; tel. (228) 819920; fax (228) 8199299; Ambassador: WALID HEZBOR.

**Tajikistan:** 10585 Berlin, Otto-Suhr-Allee 84; tel. (30) 3479300; fax (30) 34793029; Ambassador: AKBAR MIRZOYEV.

**Tanzania:** 53177 Bonn, Theaterplatz 26; tel. (228) 358051; fax (228) 358226; Ambassador: ANDREW M. DARAJA.

**Thailand:** 12163 Berlin, Lepsiusstr. 64–66; tel. (30) 794810; fax (30) 79481511; Ambassador: KASIT PIROMYA.

**Togo:** 53173 Bonn, Beethovenallee 13; tel. (228) 355091; fax (228) 351639; Ambassador: SOGOYOU K. KEGUEWE.

**Tunisia:** 53175 Bonn, Godesberger Allee 103; tel. (228) 376981; fax (228) 374223; Ambassador: SLAHEDDINE BEN M'BAREK.

**Turkey:** 10179 Berlin, Rungestr. 9; tel. (30) 275850; fax (30) 27585700; Ambassador: TUGAY ULUCEVIK.

**Turkmenistan:** 14052 Berlin, Langobardenallee 14; tel. (30) 30102452; fax (30) 30102453; Ambassador: TSCHARY TAGANOWITSCH KULIJEW.

**Uganda:** 53173 Bonn, Dürenstr. 44; tel. (228) 355027; fax (228) 351692; Ambassador: TIBAMANYA MWENE MUSHANGA.

**Ukraine:** 10117 Berlin, Albrechtstr. 26; tel. (30) 288870; fax (30) 28887163; Ambassador: Dr ANATOLIY PONOMARENKO.

**United Arab Emirates:** 53113 Bonn, Erste Fährgasse 6; tel. (228) 267070; fax (228) 2670714; Ambassador: MOHAMMAD ALI AL-ZAROUNI.

**United Kingdom:** 10117 Berlin, Unter den Linden 32–34; tel. (30) 201840; fax (30) 20184123; e-mail presse@fco.mail.gov.uk; internet www.britischebotschaft.de; Ambassador: Sir PAUL LEVER.

**USA:** 10117 Berlin, Neustädtische Kirche 4/5; tel. (30) 83052805; fax (30) 20453644; internet www.usembassy.de; Ambassador: JOHN CHRISTIAN KORNBLUM.

**Uruguay:** 53175 Bonn, Gotenstr. 1–3; tel. (228) 356570; fax (228) 361410; Ambassador: JUAN JOSÉ REAL PERRERA.

**Uzbekistan:** 53177 Bonn, Deutschherrenstr. 7; tel. (228) 953570; fax (228) 9535799; Ambassador: ALISHER SHAIKHOV.

**Venezuela:** 14469 Potsdam, Grosse Weinmeisterstr. 53; e-mail 100635.154@compuserve.com; Ambassador: ERIK BECKER BECKER.

**Viet Nam:** 53179 Bonn, Konstantinstr. 37; tel. (228) 957540; fax (228) 351866; Ambassador: LE KINH TAI.

**Yemen:** 53113 Bonn, Adenauerallee 77; tel. (228) 220273; fax (228) 229364; Ambassador: MOHY A. AL-DHABBI.

**Zambia:** 53175 Bonn, Mittelstr. 39; tel. (228) 376813; fax (228) 379536; Ambassador: ELIAS MARKO CHISHA CHIPIMO.

**Zimbabwe:** 53177 Bonn, Villichgasse 7; tel. (228) 356071; fax (228) 356309; Ambassador: GIFT PUNUNGWE.

* Owing to the transfer of several organs of state from Bonn to Berlin in 1999, many foreign embassies also relocated to the capital.

# Judicial System

The Unification Treaty, signed by the FRG and the GDR in August 1990, provided for the extension of Federal Law to the territory formerly occupied by the GDR, and also stipulated certain exceptions where GDR Law was to remain valid.

Judges are not removable except by the decision of a court. Half of the judges of the Federal Constitutional Court are elected by the Bundestag and half by the Bundesrat. A committee for the selection of judges participates in the appointment of judges of the Superior Federal Courts.

### FEDERAL CONSTITUTIONAL COURT

**Bundesverfassungsgericht** (Federal Constitutional Court): 76131 Karlsruhe, Schlossbezirk 3, 76006 Karlsruhe, Postfach 1771; tel. (721) 91010; fax (721) 9101382.

**President:** Prof. Dr JUTTA LIMBACH.

**Vice-President:** Prof. Dr HANS-JÜRGEN PAPIER.

**Director:** Dr ELKE LUISE BARNSTEDT.

**Judges of the First Senate:** Prof. Dr DIETER GRIMM, Dr JÜRGEN KÜHLING, RENATE JAEGER, Dr EVELYN HAAS, Dr DIETER HÖMIG, Prof. Dr UDO STEINER, Dr CHRISTINE HOHMANN-DENNHARDT.

**Judges of the Second Senate:** Prof. Dr PAUL KIRCHOF, KLAUS WINTER, BERTOLD SOMMER, Dr HANS-JOACHIM JENTSCH, Prof. Dr WINFRIED HASSEMER, Dr SIEGFRIED BROSS, Prof. Dr LERKE OSTERLOH.

### SUPERIOR FEDERAL COURTS

**Bundesgerichtshof** (Federal Court of Justice): 76133 Karlsruhe, Herrenstr. 45A; tel. (721) 1590; fax (721) 159830; internet www.uni-karlsruhe.de.

**President:** KARLMANN GEISS.

**Vice-President:** Dr BURKHARD JÄHNKE.

**Presidents of the Senate:** Prof. Dr WILLI ERDMANN, Dr VOLKER RÖHRICHT, Dr EBERHARD RINNE, Dr KARL BERNARD SCHMITZ, WERNER GROSS, Dr KATHARINA DEPPERT, Dr BERND PAULUSCH, RÜDGER ROGGE, Dr FRIEDRICH BLUMENRÖHR, Dr GERHARD SCHÄFER, Dr BURKHARD JÄHNKE, KLAUS KUTZER, Dr LUTZ MEYER-GOSSNER, Prof. Dr EIKE ULLMANN, GERD NOBBE, MONIKA HARMS.

**Federal Solicitor-General:** KAY NEHM.

**Federal Prosecutors:** REINER SCHULTE, VOLKHARD WACHE, Dr HANS-JOACHIM KURTH.

**Bundesverwaltungsgericht** (Federal Administrative Court): 10623 Berlin, Hardenbergstr. 31, 10593 Berlin, Postfach 120341; tel. (30) 31971; fax (30) 3123021; internet www.bverwg.de.

**President:** Dr EVERHARDT FRANSSEN.

**Vice-President:** Dr INGEBORG FRANKE.

**Presidents of the Senate:** ERICH BERMEL, WERNER MEYER, Dr NORBERT NIEHUES, FRIEDRICH SEEBASS, Dr GÜNTER GAENTZSCH, Dr HORST SÄCKER, Prof. Dr HANS-JOACHIM DRIEHAUS, Dr JOACHIM MAIWALD, Dr NIKOLAUS VOGELGESANG, Dr OSWIN MÜLLER, ECKART HIEN.

**Bundesfinanzhof** (Federal Financial Court): 81675 München, Ismaningerstr. 109, 81629 München, Postfach 860240; tel. (89) 92310; fax (89) 9231201.

**President:** Dr Iris Ebling.

**Vice-President:** (vacant).

**Presidents of the Senate:** Dr Siegfried Widmann, Dr Reinhard Sunder-Plassmann, Dr Hans Joachim Herrmann, Dr Georg Grube, Dr Gerhard Mösslang, Dr Werner Hein, Prof. Dr Walter Drenseck, Prof. Dr Franz Wassermeyer.

# Religion

## CHRISTIANITY

**Arbeitsgemeinschaft Christlicher Kirchen in Deutschland** (Council of Christian Churches in Germany): 60487 Frankfurt a.M., Ludolfusstr. 2-4, 60446 Frankfurt a.M., Postfach 900617; tel. (69) 2470270; fax (69) 24702730; e-mail ackoec@t-online.de; 21 affiliated Churches, including the Roman Catholic Church and the Greek Orthodox Metropoly.

### The Roman Catholic Church

In December 1997 Germany comprised seven archdioceses and 20 dioceses. It is estimated that about 33% of the population are adherents of the Roman Catholic Church.

**Bishops' Conference:** Deutsche Bischofskonferenz, 53113 Bonn, Kaiserstr. 163, 53019 Bonn, Postfach 2962; tel. (228) 103290; fax (228) 103335; e-mail sekretariat@dbk.de; Pres. Dr Dr Karl Lehmann, Bishop of Mainz; Sec. Pater Dr Hans Langendörfer.

**Archbishop of Bamberg:** Dr Karl Braun, 96033 Bamberg, Domplatz 3, 96049 Bamberg, Postfach 120153; tel. (951) 5020; fax (951) 502212.

**Archbishop of Berlin:** Cardinal Georg Maximilian Sterzinsky, 14057 Berlin, Wundtstr. 48–50; tel. (030) 326840; fax (030) 32684276.

**Archbishop of Freiburg im Breisgau:** Dr Oskar Saier, 79098 Freiburg i. Br., Herrenstr. 35; tel. (761) 21881; fax (761) 2188599.

**Archbishop of Hamburg:** Dr Ludwig Averkamp, 20099 Hamburg, Danzigerstr. 52a, 20013 Hamburg, Postfach 101925; tel. (40) 248770; fax (40) 24877233; e-mail egv@erzbistum-hamburg.de; internet www.erzbistum-hamburg.de.

**Archbishop of Köln:** Cardinal Dr Joachim Meisner, Generalvikariat, 50668 Köln, Marzellenstr. 32; tel. (221) 16420; fax (221) 1642700.

**Archbishop of München and Freising:** Cardinal Dr Friedrich Wetter, 80063 München, Rochhusstr. 5-7, 80079 München, Postfach 330360; tel. (89) 21370; fax (89) 21371585.

**Archbishop of Paderborn:** Dr Johannes Joachim Degenhardt, Erzbischöfliches Generalvikariat, 33098 Paderborn, Domplatz 3; tel. (5251) 1250; fax (5251) 125470.

**Commissariat of German Bishops—Catholic Office:** 53113 Bonn, Kaiser-Friedrich-Str. 9; tel. (228) 26940; fax (228) 261563; (represents the German Conference of Bishops before the Federal Govt on political issues); Leader Prälat Paul Bocklet.

**Central Committee of German Catholics:** 53175 Bonn, Hochkreuzallee 246; tel. (228) 382970; fax (228) 3829744; e-mail info@zdk.de; f. 1868; summarizes the activities of Catholic laymen and lay-organizations in Germany; Pres. Prof. Dr Hans Joachim Meyer; Gen. Sec. Dr Stefan Vesper.

### Evangelical (Protestant) Churches

About 33% of the population are members of the Evangelical Churches.

**Evangelische Kirche in Deutschland (EKD)** (Evangelical Church in Germany): 30419 Hannover, Herrenhäuser Str. 12; tel. (511) 27960; fax (511) 2796707; e-mail presse@ekd.de; internet www.ekd.de. The governing bodies of the EKD are its Synod of 120 clergy and lay members which meets at regular intervals, the Conference of member churches, and the Council, composed of 15 elected members; the EKD has an ecclesiastical secretariat of its own (the Evangelical Church Office), including a special office for foreign relations; Chair. of the Council Präses Manfred Kock; Pres. of the Office Valentin Schmidt.

**Synod of the EKD:** 30419 Hannover, Herrenhäuser Str. 12; tel. (511) 2796114; fax (511) 2796707; e-mail synode@ekd.de; Pres. Dr Jürgen Schmude.

**Deutscher Evangelischer Kirchentag** (German Evangelical Church Assembly): 36037 Fulda, Magdeburgerstr. 59, 36004 Fulda, Postfach 480; tel. (661) 969500; fax (661) 9695090; e-mail fulda@kirchentag.de; internet www.kirchentag.de; Pres. Martin Dolde; Gen. Sec. Frederike Woldt.

Churches and Federations within the EKD:

**Arnoldshainer Konferenz:** 10623 Berlin, Jebensstr. 3; tel. (30) 310010; fax (30) 31001200; e-mail akf@eku-kirche.de; internet www.eku-kirche.de; f. 1967; a loose federation of the church governments of one Lutheran, two Reformed Territorial and all United Churches, aiming at greater co-operation between them; Chair. of Council Bischof Prof. Dr Christian Zippert.

**Evangelische Kirche der Union (EKU)** (Evangelical Church of the Union): 10623 Berlin, Chancellery, Jebensstr. 3; tel. (30) 310010; fax (30) 31001200; e-mail kanzlei@eku-kirche.de; internet www.eku-kirche.de; composed of Lutheran and Reformed elements; includes the Evangelical Churches of Anhalt, Berlin-Brandenburg, Silesian Oberlausitz, Pomerania, the Rhineland, Saxony and Westphalia; Chair. of Synod Vizepräses Nikolaus Schneider; Chair. of Council Kirchenpräsident Helge Klassohn; Pres. of Administration Dr Wilhelm Hüffmeier.

**Reformierter Bund** (Reformed Alliance): 42109 Wuppertal, Vogelsangstr. 20; tel. (202) 755111; fax (202) 754202; f. 1884; unites the Reformed Territorial Churches and Congregations of Germany (with an estimated 2m. mems). The central body of the Reformed League is the 'Moderamen', the elected representation of the various Reformed Churches and Congregations; Moderator Rev. Peter Bukowski; Gen. Sec. Rev. Hermann Schaefer.

**Vereinigte Evangelisch-Lutherische Kirche Deutschlands (VELKD)** (The United Evangelical-Lutheran Church of Germany): 30177 Hannover, Richard-Wagner-Str. 26, 30634 Hannover, Postfach 510409; tel. (511) 62611; fax (511) 6261211; f. 1948; mems 11.2m.; a body uniting all but three of the Lutheran territorial Churches within the Evangelical Church in Germany; Presiding Bishop Landesbischof Horst Hirschler (Hannover).

Affiliated to the EKD:

**Bund Evangelisch-Reformierter Kirchen** (Association of Evangelical Reformed Churches): 20095 Hamburg, Ferdinandstr. 21; tel. (40) 3010040; Chair. Präses Sabine Dressler-Kromminga.

**Herrnhuter Brüdergemeine** or **Europäisch-Festländische Brüder-Unität** (Moravian Church): f. 1457; there are 25 congregations in Germany, Switzerland, Denmark, Sweden, Estonia and the Netherlands, with approximately 30,000 mems; Chair. Rev. Hans-Beat Motel; (73087 Bad Boll, Badwasen 6; tel. (7164) 94210; fax (7164) 942199).

†**Evangelical Church in Baden:** 76133 Karlsruhe, Blumenstr. 1, 76010 Karlsruhe, Postfach 2269; tel. (721) 9175100; fax (721) 9175550; Landesbischof Prof. Dr Ulrich Fischer.

***Evangelical-Lutheran Church in Bayern:** 80333 München, Meiserstr. 11-13; tel. (89) 55950; fax (89) 5595444; e-mail poep@elkb.de; internet www.bayern-evangelisch.de; Landesbischof Dr Johannes Friedrich.

†**Evangelical Church in Berlin-Brandenburg:** 10249 Berlin, Georgenkirchstr. 69/70; tel. (30) 2434400; fax (30) 24344500; e-mail kirche@ekibb.com; internet www.ekibb.com; Bischof Prof. Dr Wolfgang Huber.

**Evangelical-Lutheran Church in Braunschweig:** 38300 Wolfenbüttel Dietrich-Bonhoeffer-Str. 1; tel. (5331) 8020; fax (5331) 802707; e-mail info@luth-braunschweig.de; internet www.luth-braunschweig.de; Landesbischof Christian Krause.

†**Bremen Evangelical Church:** 28199 Bremen, Franziuseck 2–4, Postfach 106929; tel. (421) 55970; Pres. Heinz Hermann Brauer.

***Evangelical-Lutheran Church of Hannover:** 30169 Hannover, Haarstr. 6; tel. (511) 800188; fax (511) 880438; e-mail margot.kraesmann@evlka.de; internet www.evlka.de; Landesbischof Dr Margot Kässmann.

†**Evangelical Church in Hessen and Nassau:** 64276 Darmstadt, Paulusplatz 1; tel. (6151) 405284; fax (6151) 405441; Pres. Prof. Dr Peter Steinacker.

†**Evangelical Church of Kurhessen-Waldeck:** 34131 Kassel-Wilhelmshöhe, Wilhelmshöher Allee 330, 34114 Kassel, Postfach 410260; tel. (561) 937807; fax (561) 9378400; e-mail landeskirchenamt@ekkw.de; Bischof Prof. Dr Christian Zippert.

†**Church of Lippe:** 32756 Detmold, Leopoldstr. 27; tel. (5231) 97660; fax (5231) 976850; e-mail oeff@lippische-landeskirche.de; internet www.lippische-landeskirche.de; Landessuperintendent Gerrit Noltensmeier.

**Evangelical-Lutheran Church of Mecklenburg:** 19010 Schwerin, Münzstr. 8; tel. (385) 51850; fax (385) 5185170; Landesbischof Hermann Beste.

***Evangelical-Lutheran Church of North Elbe:** Bischof Dr Hans Christian Knuth (24837 Schleswig, Plessenstr. 5a; tel. (4621) 22056; fax (4621) 22194); Bischof Karl Ludwig Kohlwage (23564 Lübeck, Bäckerstr. 3–5; tel. (451) 790201); Bishop Maria Jepsen (20457 Hamburg, Neue Burg 1; tel. (40) 373050); Pres. of North Elbian Church Administration Prof. Dr Klaus Blaschke (24103 Kiel, Dänische Str. 21–23; tel. (431) 97975).

**Evangelical-Reformed Church in North-West Germany:** 26789 Leer, Saarstr. 6; tel. (491) 91980; fax (491) 9198251; e-mail info@reformiert.de; internet www.reformiert.de; Moderator GARRELT DUIN; Synod Clerks Rev. WALTER HERRENBRÜCK, ERNST-JOACHIM PAGENSTECHER.

**Evangelical-Lutheran Church in Oldenburg:** 26121 Oldenburg, Philosophenweg 1; tel. (441) 77010; fax (441) 7701299; e-mail ips@ev-kirche-oldenburg.de; internet www.ev.kirche.oldenburg.de; Bischof PETER KRUG.

**†Evangelical Church of the Palatinate:** 67346 Speyer, Domplatz 5; tel. (6232) 6670; fax (6232) 667228; e-mail evkpfalz@speyer.she.de; internet www.evpfalz.de; Pres. EBERHARD CHERDRON.

**†Evangelical Church in the Rhineland:** 40476 Düsseldorf, Hans-Böckler-Str. 7, 40403 Düsseldorf, Postfach 300339; tel. (211) 45620; fax (211) 4562490; e-mail pressestelle@ekir.de; internet www.ekir.de; Pres. MANFRED KOCK.

**Evangelical-Lutheran Church of Saxony:** 01069 Dresden, Lukasstr. 6, 01013 Dresden, Postfach 320101; tel. (351) 46920; fax (351) 4692144; e-mail kirche@evlks.de; internet www.evlks.de; Landesbischof VOLKER KRESS.

***Evangelical-Lutheran Church of Schaumburg-Lippe:** 31675 Bückeburg, Herderstr. 27; tel. (5722) 9600; e-mail lka-bueckeburg@t-online.de; Landesbischof HEINRICH HERRMANNS.

**Evangelical-Lutheran Church in Thuringia:** 99817 Eisenach, Dr-Moritz-Mitzenheim Str. 2A; tel. (3691) 67899; e-mail landeskirchenamteisenach@compuserve.com; Landesbischof ROLAND HOFFMANN.

**†Evangelical Church of Westfalen:** 33602 Bielefeld, Altstädter Kirchplatz 5; tel. (521) 5940; fax (521) 594129; e-mail landeskirchenamt@lka.ekvw.de; internet www.ekvw.de; Präses MANFRED SORG.

**†Evangelical-Lutheran Church of Württemberg:** 70184 Stuttgart, Gänsheidestr. 4, Postfach 101342; tel. (711) 21490; fax (711) 2149236; e-mail landesbischof@elk.wue.de; Landesbischof EBERHARDT RENZ.

(* Member of the VELKD; † member of the EKU)

### Other Evangelical (Protestant) Churches

**Arbeitsgemeinschaft Mennonitischer Gemeinden in Deutschland** (Asscn of Mennonite Congregations in Germany): 67677 Eukenbach-Alsenborn, Ringstr. 3; tel. (6303) 3883; fax (6303) 983739; e-mail rwrc.funck@t-online.de; f. 1886, re-organized 1990; Chair. WERNER FUNCK.

**Bund Evangelisch-Freikirchlicher Gemeinden** (Union of Evangelical Free Church Congregations; Baptists): 61350 Bad Homburg v. d. H., Friedberger Str. 101; tel. (6172) 80040; fax (6172) 800436; e-mail befg@baptisten.org; internet www.baptisten.org; f. 1849; Pres. WALTER ZESCHKY; Dirs HEINZ SAGER, Rev. ECKHARD SCHAEFER, Rev. LUTZ REICHART.

**Bund Freier evangelischer Gemeinden** (Covenant of Free Evangelical Churches in Germany): 58452 Witten, Goltenkamp 4, 58426 Witten, Postfach 4005; tel. (2302) 9370; fax (2302) 93799; e-mail kandwischer@bund.feg.de; internet www.feg.de; f. 1854; Pres. PETER STRAUCH; Administrator KLAUS KANWISCHER; 31,500 mems.

**Evangelisch-altreformierte Kirche von Niedersachsen** (Evangelical Reformed Church of Lower Saxony): 26736 Krummhörn-Campen, Ehm-Schipper-Weg 2; tel. (4927) 329; fax (4927) 912969; Sec. Rev. G. SCHRADER.

**Evangelisch-methodistische Kirche** (United Methodist Church): 60329 Frankfurt a.M., Wilhelm-Leuschner-Str. 8; tel. (69) 2425210; fax (69) 24252129; e-mail emk.kirchenkanzlei@t-online.de; f. 1968; Bishop Dr WALTER KLAIBER.

**Gemeinschaft der Siebenten-Tags-Adventisten** (Seventh-Day Adventist Church): 73760 Ostfildern, Senefelderstr. 15, 73745 Ostfildern, Postfach 4260; tel. (711) 448190; fax (711) 4481960; e-mail sdv.zentrale@adventisten.de.

**Heilsarmee in Deutschland** (Salvation Army in Germany): 50677 Köln, Salierring 23–27; tel. (221) 208190; fax (221) 2081951; e-mail heils@rmee.de; internet www.heilsarmee.de; f. 1886; Leader Col SIEGFRIED OLAUSEN.

**Mülheimer Verband Freikirchlich-Evangelischer Gemeinden:** (Pentecostal Church): 34305 Niedenstein, Hauptstr. 36, 34303 Niedenstein, Postfach 1109; tel. (5624) 775; fax (5624) 776; f. 1913.

**Selbständige Evangelisch-Lutherische Kirche** (Independent Evangelical-Lutheran Church): 30625 Hannover, Schopenhauerstr. 7; tel. (511) 557808; fax (511) 551588; e-mail selk@selk.de; f. 1972; Bishop Dr DIETHARDT ROTH; Exec. Sec. Rev. MICHAEL SCHÄTZEL.

### Other Christian Churches

**Alt-Katholische Kirche** (Old Catholic Church): 53115 Bonn, Gregor-Mendel-Str. 28; tel. (228) 232285; fax (228) 238314; e-mail info@alt-katholisch.de; internet www.alt-katholisch.de; seceded from the Roman Catholic Church as a protest against the declaration of Papal infallibility in 1870; belongs to the Utrecht Union of Old Catholic Churches; in full communion with the Anglican Communion; Pres. Bischof JOACHIM VOBBE (Bonn); 28,000 mems.

**Apostelamt Jesu Christi:** 7500 Cottbus, Otto-Grotewohl-Str. 57; tel. 713297; Pres. WALDEMAR ROHDE.

**Armenisch-Apostolische Orthodoxe Kirche in Deutschland:** 50735 Köln, Allensteiner Str. 5; tel. (221) 7126223; fax (221) 7126267; Archbishop KAREKIN BEKDJIAN.

**Griechisch-Orthodoxe Metropolie von Deutschland** (Greek Orthodox Metropoly of Germany): 53227 Bonn, Dietrich-Bonhoeffer-Str. 2, 53185 Bonn, Postfach 300555; tel. (228) 462041; fax (228) 464989.

**Religiöse Gesellschaft der Freunde (Quäker)** (Society of Friends): 10117 Berlin, Planckstr. 20; tel. 2082284; f. 1925; 340 mems.

**Russische Orthodoxe Kirche—Berliner Diözese** (Russian Orthodox Church): 10138 Berlin, Wildensteiner Str. 10, 10267 Berlin, Postfach 17; tel. (30) 5099611; fax (30) 5098153; e-mail red.stimme@snafu.de; Archbishop FEOFAN.

### ISLAM

There are an estimated 2.6m. Muslims in Germany.

### JUDAISM

The membership of Jewish synagogues in Germany numbered some 74,289 in 1998.

**Zentralrat der Juden in Deutschland** (Central Council of Jews in Germany): 10117 Berlin, Tucholskystr. 9, Leo-Baeck-Haus; tel. (30) 2844560; fax (30) 28445613; Pres. Board of Dirs PAUL SPIEGEL.

**Jüdische Gemeinde zu Berlin** (Jewish Community in Berlin): 10623 Berlin, Fasanenstr. 79–80; e-mail vorstand@jg-berlin.org; Pres. Dr ANDREAS NACHAMA.

## The Press

The German Press Council was founded in 1956 as a self-regulatory body, and is composed of publishers and journalists. It formulates guide-lines and investigates complaints against the press.

In 1968 a government commission stipulated various limits on the proportions of circulation that any one publishing group should be allowed to control: (1) 40% of the total circulation of newspapers or 40% of the total circulation of magazines; (2) 20% of the total circulation of newspapers and magazines together; (3) 15% of the circulation in one field if the proportion owned in the other field is 40%.

**Deutscher Presserat** (German Press Council): 53071 Bonn, Postfach 7160; tel. (228) 985720; fax (228) 9857299; e-mail info@presserat.de; internet www.presserat.de; Dir LUTZ TILLMANNS.

The principal newspaper publishing groups are:

**Axel Springer Verlag AG:** 10888 Berlin, Axel-Springer-Str. 65; tel. (30) 25910; fax (30) 251606; and 20350 Hamburg; 20355 Hamburg, Axel-Springer-Platz 1; tel. (40) 34700; fax (40) 345811; internet www.asv.de; f. 1946; the largest newspaper publishing group in continental Europe; includes five major dailies *(Die Welt, Hamburger Abendblatt, Bild, Berliner Morgenpost, BZ)*, three Sunday papers *(Welt am Sonntag, Bild am Sonntag, BZ am Sonntag)*, and radio, television, women's and family magazines; Chair. AUGUST A. FISCHER.

**Gruner + Jahr AG & Co Druck- und Verlagshaus:** 25524 Itzehoe, Am Vossbarg, tel. (4821) 7771; fax (4821) 777449; and 20444 Hamburg; 20459 Hamburg, Am Baumwall 11; tel. (40) 37030; fax (40) 3703600; internet www.co.guj.de; owns, amongst others, *Stern, Brigitte, Capital, Eltern, Schöner Wohnen, Hamburger Morgenpost*; *Financial Times Deutschland*, a jt venture with *Financial Times* (UK), was launched in Feb. 2000.

**Süddeutscher-Verlag GmbH:** 80331 München, Sendlingerstr. 80; tel. (89) 21830; fax (89) 2183787; internet www.sueddeutsche.de; f. 1945; owns *Süddeutsche Zeitung*, special interest periodicals.

**JahreszeitenVerlag GmbH:** 22301 Hamburg, Possmoorweg 5; tel. (40) 27170; fax (40) 27172056; f. 1948; owns, amongst others, the periodicals *Für Sie* and *Petra*; Pres. THOMAS GANSKE.

**Heinrich-Bauer-Verlag:** 20095 Hamburg, Burchardstr. 11, 20077 Hamburg, Postfach 4660; tel. (40) 30190; fax (40) 30191043; and 81737 München, Charles-de-Gaulle-Str. 8; tel. (89) 678600; fax (89) 6702033; internet www.hbv.de; owns 29 popular illustrated magazines, including *Quick* (München), *Neue Revue* (Hamburg), *Praline, Neue Post, TV Horen + Sehen* and *Bravo*; Pres. HEINRICH BAUER.

**Burda GmbH:** 81925 München, Arabellastr. 23; tel. (89) 92502745; fax (89) 92502745; internet www.burda.de; f. 1908; publs incl. *Bunte, Burda Moden, Bild+Funk, Focus, Freundin, Meine Familie & ich* and *Schweriner Volkszeitung*; 10 Mans.

## PRINCIPAL DAILIES

### Aachen

**Aachener Nachrichten:** 52068 Aachen, Dresdner Str. 3, 52002 Aaachen, Postfach 110; tel. (241) 51010; fax (241) 5101399; internet www.an-online.de; f. 1872; circ. 67,000.

**Aachener Zeitung:** 52068 Aachen, Dresdner Str. 3, 52085 Aachen, Postfach 500110; tel. (241) 51010; fax (241) 5101399; internet www.aachener-zeitung.de; f. 1946; Editor-in-Chief BERND MATHIEU; circ. 106,000.

### Ansbach

**Fränkische Landeszeitung:** 91522 Ansbach, Nürnberger Str. 9–17, 91504 Ansbach, Postfach 1362; tel. (981) 95000; fax (981) 13961; Editors-in-Chief GERHARD EGETEMAYER, PETER M. SZYMANOWSKI; circ. 50,000.

### Aschaffenburg

**Main-Echo:** 63739 Aschaffenburg a.M., Weichertstr. 20, 63736 Aschaffenburg, Postfach 548; tel. (6021) 3960; fax (6021) 396499; e-mail redaktionssekretariat@main-echo.de; internet www.main-echo.de; Editors HELMUT WEISS, Dr HELMUT TEUFEL; circ. 93,000.

### Augsburg

**Augsburger Allgemeine:** 86133 Augsburg; 86167 Augsburg, Curt-Frenzel-Str. 2; tel. (821) 7770; fax (821) 704471; internet www.augsburger-allgemeine.de; daily (Mon. to Sat.); Editors-in-Chief RAINER BONHORST, WINFRIED STRIEBEL; circ. 370,000.

### Baden-Baden

**Badisches Tagblatt:** 76530 Baden-Baden, Stefanienstr. 1–3, 76481 Baden-Baden, Postfach 120; tel (7221) 215241; fax (7221) 215240; Editors-in-Chief HARALD BESINGER, VOLKER-BODO ZANGER; circ. 41,000.

### Bamberg

**Fränkischer Tag:** 96050 Bamberg, Gutenbergstr. 1; tel. (951) 1880; fax (951) 188118; internet www.fraenkischer-tag.de; Publr Dr HELMUTH JUNGBAUER; circ. 75,800.

### Bautzen

**Serbske Nowiny:** 02625 Bautzen, Tuchmacher Str. 27; tel. (3591) 577232; e-mail serbske-nowiny@t-online.de; evening; Sorbian language paper; Editor BENEDIKT DYRLICH; circ. 1,500.

### Berlin

**Berliner Kurier:** 10178 Berlin, Karl-Liebknecht-Str. 29; tel. (30) 2442403; fax (30) 2442274; evening; publ. by Gruner + Jahr AG; circ. 186,200.

**Berliner Morgenpost:** 10888 Berlin, Axel-Springer-Str. 65; tel. (30) 25910; fax (30) 2516071; e-mail redaktion@berliner-morgenpost.de; internet www.berliner-morgenpost.de; f. 1898; publ. by Axel Springer Verlag AG; Editor-in-Chief HERBERT WESSELS; circ. 184,100.

**Berliner Zeitung:** 10178 Berlin, Karl-Liebknecht-Str. 29; tel. (2) 23279; fax (30) 23275533; internet www.berlinonline.de; f. 1945; morning; publ. by Gruner + Jahr AG; Editor DIETER SCHRÖDER; circ. 216,600.

**BZ (Berliner Zeitung):** 10888 Berlin, Axel-Springer-Str. 65; tel. (30) 25910; fax (30) 2510928; internet www.bz-berlin.de; f. 1877; publ. by Axel Springer Verlag AG; Editor WOLFGANG KRYSZOHN; circ. 313,500.

**Junge Welt:** 1080 Berlin, Mauerstr. 39-40; tel. (30) 22330; fax (30) 1302865; internet www.jungewelt.de; f. 1947; morning; Editor JENS KÖNIG; circ. 158,000.

**Neues Deutschland:** 10245 Berlin, Alt-Stralau 1–2; tel. (30) 293905; fax (30) 29390600; f. 1946; morning; independent; Editor WOLFGANG SPICKERMANN; circ. 72,400.

**Der Tagesspiegel:** 10785 Berlin, Potsdamer Str. 87, 10723 Berlin, Postfach 304330; tel. (30) 260090; fax (30) 26009332; f. 1945; circ. 130,200.

**Die Welt:** 10888 Berlin, Axel-Springer-Str. 65; tel. (30) 25910; fax (30) 251606; internet www.welt.de; f. 1946; publ. by Axel Springer Verlag AG; Editor Dr THOMAS LÖFFELHOLZ; circ. 216,800.

### Bielefeld

**Neue Westfälische:** 33595 Bielefeld; 33602 Bielefeld, Niedernstr. 21–27, 33502 Bielefeld, Postfach 100225; tel. (521) 5550; fax (521) 555520; internet www.nw-news.de; f. 1967; circ. 219,850.

**Westfalen-Blatt:** 33611 Bielefeld, Südbrackstr. 14–18, 33531 Bielefeld, Postfach 8740; tel. (521) 5850; fax (521) 585370; internet www.westfalen-blatt.de; f. 1946; Editor CARL-W. BUSSE; circ. 147,400.

### Bonn

**General-Anzeiger:** 53100 Bonn; 53121 Bonn, Justus-von-Liebig-Str. 15; tel. (228) 66880; fax (228) 6688170; internet www.general-anzeiger-bonn.de; f. 1725; independent; Publrs HERMANN NEUSSER, Hermann Neusser, Jr, MARTIN NEUSSER; Editor Dr HELMUT HERLES; circ. 90,000.

### Braunschweig

**Braunschweiger Zeitung:** 38114 Braunschweig, Hamburger Str. 277, 38022 Braunschweig, Postfach 3263; tel. (531) 39000; fax (531) 3900610; internet www.newsclick.de; circ. 170,400.

### Bremen

**Bremer Nachrichten:** 28189 Bremen; 28195 Bremen, Martinistr. 43, 28078 Bremen, Postfach 107801; tel. (421) 36710; fax (421) 3379233; f. 1743; Publr HERBERT C. ORDEMANN; Editor DIETRICH IDE; circ. 44,000.

**Weser-Kurier:** 28189 Bremen; 28195 Bremen, Martinistr. 43, 28078 Bremen, Postfach 107801; tel. (421) 36710; fax (421) 3379233; internet www.weser-kurier.de; f. 1945; Publr HERBERT C. ORDEMANN; Editor VOLKER WEISE; circ. 185,000.

### Bremerhaven

**Nordsee-Zeitung:** 27576 Bremerhaven 1, Hafenstr. 140, 27512 Bremerhaven, Postfach 27512; tel. (471) 5970; fax (471) 597551; internet www.nordsee-zeitung.de; Chief Editor JÖRG JUNG; circ. 77,500.

### Chemnitz

**Freie Presse:** 09111 Chemnitz, Brückenstr. 15, Postfach 261; tel. (371) 6560; fax (371) 643042; internet www.freiepresse.de; f. 1963; morning; Editor DIETER SOIKA; circ. 461,900.

### Cottbus

**Lausitzer Rundschau:** 03050 Cottbus, Str. der Jugend 54, 03002 Cottbus, Postfach 100279; tel. (355) 4810; fax (355) 481245; internet www.lr-online.de; independent; morning; Chief Officers FRANK LÜDECKE, J. FRIEDRICH ORTHS; circ. 190,000.

### Darmstadt

**Darmstädter Echo:** 64295 Darmstadt, Holzhofallee 25–31, 64276 Darmstadt, Postfach 100155; tel. (6151) 3871; fax (6151) 387448; internet www.echo-online.de; f. 1945; Publrs Dr HANS-PETER BACH, HORST BACH; Editor-in-Chief ROLAND HOF; circ. 87,300.

### Dortmund

**Ruhr-Nachrichten:** 44128 Dortmund; 44137 Westenhellweg 86–88, 44047 Dortmund, Postfach 105051; internet www.westline.de; f. 1949; Editor FLORIAN LENSING-WOLFF; circ. 215,400.

**Westfälische Rundschau:** 44135 Dortmund, Brüderweg 9, 44047 Dortmund, Postfach 105067; tel. (201) 8040; fax (201) 8042841; internet www.westfaelische-rundschau.de; Editor FRANK BÜNTE; circ. 250,000.

### Dresden

**Dresdner Morgenpost:** 01067 Dresden, Ostra-Allee; tel. (51) 4864; fax (51) 4951116; circ. 126,700.

**Dresdner Neueste Nachrichten/Union:** 01075 Dresden; 01097 Dresden, Hauptstr. 21; tel. (351) 8075210; fax (351) 8075212; morning; Editor-in-Chief DIRK BIRGEL; circ. 39,000.

**Sächsische Zeitung:** 01067 Dresden, Ostra-Allee 20, Haus der Presse; tel. (351) 48640; fax (351) 48642354; e-mail redaktion@sz-online.de; internet www.sz-online.de; f. 1946; morning; publ. by Gruner + Jahr AG; Editor-in-Chief PETER CHRIST; circ. 397,700.

### Düsseldorf

**Düsseldorf Express:** 40212 Düsseldorf, Königsallee 27, 40002 Düsseldorf, Postfach 1132; tel. (211) 13930; fax (211) 324835.

**Handelsblatt:** 40213 Düsseldorf, Kasernenstr. 67, 40018 Düsseldorf, Postfach 102741; tel. (211) 8870; fax (211) 329954; internet www.handelsblatt.de; 5 a week; Publr DIETER VON HOLTZBRINCK; circ. 156,473.

**Rheinische Post:** 40196 Düsseldorf; 40549 Düsseldorf, Zülpicherstr. 10; tel. (211) 5050; fax (211) 5052575; internet www.rp-online.de; f. 1946; Editor ULRICH REITZ; circ. 349,200.

**Westdeutsche Zeitung:** 40212 Düsseldorf, Königsallee 27, 40002 Düsseldorf, Postfach 101132; tel. (211) 83820; fax (211) 822225; internet www.wz-newsline.de; Editor-in-Chief MICHAEL HARTMANN; Publr Dr M. GIRARDET; circ. 176,800.

### Erfurt

**Thüringer Allgemeine:** 99092 Erfurt, Gottstedter Landstr. 6; tel. (361) 2274; fax (361) 2275144; f. 1946; morning; Editor-in-Chief SERGEJ LOCHTHOFEN; circ. 330,000.

### Essen

**Neue Ruhr Zeitung:** 45123 Essen; 45128 Essen, Friedrichstr. 34–38; tel. (201) 8042605; fax (201) 8042121; Editor-in-Chief Dr RICHARD KIESSLER; circ. 215,000.

**Westdeutsche Allgemeine Zeitung:** 45123 Essen; 45128 Essen, Friedrichstr. 34–38; tel. (201) 8040; fax (201) 8042841; Editor RALF LEHMANN; circ. 650,000.

### Flensburg

**Flensburger Tageblatt:** 24937 Flensburg, Nikolaistr. 7, 25804 Flensburg, Postfach 1553; tel. (461) 8080; fax (461) 8082121.

### Frankfurt am Main

**Frankfurter Allgemeine Zeitung:** 60267 Frankfurt a.M.; 60327 Frankfurt a.M., Hellerhofstr. 2–4, tel. (69) 75910; fax (69) 75911743; internet www.faz.de; f. 1949; Editors JÜRGEN JESKE, Dr HUGO MÜLLER-VOGG, Dr GÜNTHER NONNENMACHER, Dr FRANK SCHIRRMACHER; circ. 400,400.

**Frankfurter Neue Presse:** 60268 Frankfurt a.M.; 60327 Frankfurt a.M., Frankenallee 71–81, 60008 Frankfurt a.M., Postfach 100801; tel. (69) 75010; fax (69) 75014330; internet www.fnp.de; independent; Editor GERHARD MUMME; circ. 110,440.

**Frankfurter Rundschau:** 60266 Frankfurt a.M.; 60313 Frankfurt a.M., Grosse Eschenheimer Str. 16–18; tel. (69) 21991; fax (69) 2199328; internet www.fr-aktuell.de; Editor RODERICH REIFENRATH; circ. 189,000.

### Frankfurt an der Oder

**Märkische Oderzeitung:** 15230 Frankfurt a.d. Oder, Kellenspring 6, 15201 Frankfurt a.d. Oder, Postfach 178; tel. (335) 55300; fax (335) 23214; morning; Editor Dr FRANZ KADELL; circ. 150,633.

### Freiburg im Breisgau

**Badische Zeitung:** 79115 Freiburg i. Br., Pressehaus, Basler Str. 88; tel. (761) 4960; fax (761) 4965008; e-mail redaktion@badische-zeitung.de; internet www.badische-zeitung.de; f. 1946; Editor Dr JÜRGEN BUSCHE; circ. 171,005.

### Gera

**Ostthüringer Zeitung:** 6500 Gera, De-Smit-Str. 18; tel. (70) 6120; fax (70) 51233; morning; Editor-in-Chief ULLRICH ERZIGKEIT; circ. 237,537.

### Göttingen

**Göttinger Tageblatt:** 37079 Göttingen, Dransfelder Str. 1, 37009 Göttingen, Postfach 1953; tel. (551) 9011; fax (551) 901229; f. 1889; Man. Dir MANFRED DALLMANN; Editor-in-Chief HORST STEIN; circ. 50,200.

### Hagen

**Westfalenpost:** 58097 Hagen, Schürmannstr. 4; tel. (2331) 9170; fax (2331) 9174263; e-mail westfalenpost@cityweb.de; f. 1946; Chief Editor BODO ZAPP; circ. 160,000.

### Halle

**Haller Kreisblatt:** 33788 Halle; 33790 Halle, Gutenbergstr. 2, 33779 Halle, Postfach 1452.

### Hamburg

**Bild:** 20350 Hamburg; 20355 Hamburg, Axel-Springer-Platz 1; tel. (40) 34700; fax (40) 345811; internet www.bild.de; f. 1952; publ. by Axel Springer Verlag AG; Chief Editor UDO RÖBEL; circ. 4,412,200.

**Hamburger Abendblatt:** 20350 Hamburg; 20355 Hamburg, Axel-Springer-Platz 1; tel. (40) 34700; fax (40) 345811; internet www.abendblatt.de; publ. by Axel Springer Verlag AG; Editor-in-Chief KLAUS KRUSE; circ. 315,600.

**Hamburger Morgenpost:** 22751 Hamburg; 22763 Hamburg, Griegstr. 75, 22751 Hamburg; tel. (40) 8830303; fax (40) 88303237; e-mail iamedien@www.mopo.de; internet www.mopo.de; publ. by Gruner + Jahr AG; circ. 140,700.

### Hannover

**Hannoversche Allgemeine Zeitung:** 30148 Hannover; 30559 Hannover, Bemeroder Str. 58; tel. (511) 5180; fax (511) 527328; internet www.niedersachsen.com; circ. 269,600.

**Neue Presse:** 30148 Hannover; 30559 Hannover, Bemeroder Str. 58, 30001 Hannover, Postfach 149; tel. (511) 51010; fax (511) 524554.

### Heidelberg

**Rhein-Neckar-Zeitung:** 69117 Heidelberg, Hauptstr. 23, 69035 Heidelberg, Postfach 104560; tel. (6221) 5191; fax (6221) 519217; internet www.rnz-online.de; f. 1945; morning; Publrs Dr LUDWIG KNORR, WINFRIED KNORR, Dr DIETER SCHULZE; circ. 104,600.

### Heilbronn

**Heilbronner Stimme:** 74072 Heilbronn, Allee 2; tel. (7131) 6150; fax (7131) 615200; e-mail gl@stimme.de; internet www.stimme.de; f. 1946; Editor-in-Chief Dr WOLFGANG BOK; circ. 102,500.

### Hof-Saale

**Frankenpost:** 95028 Hof-Saale, Poststr. 9–11, 95012 Hof-Saale, Postfach 1320; tel. (9281) 8160; fax (9281) 816283; e-mail fp-redaktion@frankenpost.de; internet www.frankenpost.de; Publr Frankenpost Verlag GmbH; Editor-in-Chief MALTE BUSCHBECK; circ 100,000.

### Ingolstadt

**Donaukurier:** 85051 Ingolstadt, Stauffenbergstr. 2A, 85002 Ingolstadt, Postfach 100259; tel. (841) 96660; fax (841) 9666255; e-mail redaktion@donaukurier.de; internet www.donaukurier.de; f. 1872; Publr ELIN REISSMÜLLER; circ. 84,700.

### Kassel

**Hessische/Niedersächsische Allgemeine:** 34111 Kassel; 34121 Kassel, Frankfurter Str. 168, 34010 Kassel, Postfach 101009; tel. (561) 20300; fax (561) 2032116; internet www.hna.de; f. 1959; independent; circ. 189,200.

### Kempten

**Allgäuer Zeitung:** 87437 Kempten, Heisinger Str. 14, 87440 Kempten, Postfach 3155; tel. (831) 2060; fax (831) 206379; internet www.all-in.de; f. 1968; Publrs GEORG Fürst VON WALDBURG-ZEIL, GÜNTER HOLLAND; circ. 117,900.

### Kiel

**Kieler Nachrichten:** 24103 Kiel, Fleethörn 1–7, 24100 Kiel, Postfach 1111; tel. (431) 9030; fax (431) 903935; internet www.kn.online.de; Publ. by Axel Springer Verlag; Chief Editor JÜRGEN HEINEMANN; circ. 113,400.

### Koblenz

**Rhein-Zeitung:** 56070 Koblenz, August-Horch-Str. 28, Postfach 1540; tel. (261) 89200; fax (261) 892476; internet www.rhein-zeitung.de; Editor MARTIN LOHMANN; circ. 246,100.

### Köln

**Express:** 50590 Köln; 50667 Köln, Breite Str. 70, 50450 Köln, Postfach 100410; tel. (221) 2240; fax (211) 2242524; internet www.express.de; f. 1964; Publr ALFRED NEVEN DUMONT; circ. 370,000.

**Kölner Stadt-Anzeiger:** 50590 Köln; 50667 Köln, Breite Str. 70, 50450 Köln, Postfach 100410; tel. (221) 2240; fax (221) 2242524; internet www.ksta.de; f. 1876; Publr ALFRED NEVEN DUMONT; Editor DIETER JEPSEN-FÖGE; circ. 294,400.

**Kölnische Rundschau:** 50667 Köln, Stolkgasse 25–45, 50461 Köln, Postfach 102145; tel. (221) 16320; fax (221) 1632491; internet www.rundschau-online.de; f. 1946; Publr HELMUT HEINEN; Editor-in-Chief DIETER BREUERS; circ. 155,100.

### Konstanz

**Südkurier:** 78467 Konstanz, Max-Stromeyer-Str. 178, 78420 Konstanz, Presse- und Druckzentrum, Postfach 102001; tel. (7531) 9990; fax (7531) 999485; e-mail redaktion@suedkurier.de; internet www.skol.de; f. 1945; circ. 148,990.

### Leipzig

**Leipziger Volkszeitung:** 04088 Leipzig; 04107 Leipzig, Peterssteinweg 19; tel. (341) 21811; fax (341) 310992; internet www.lvz-online.de; f. 1894; morning; publ. by Axel Springer Verlag AG; circ. 264,000.

### Leutkirch im Allgäu

**Schwäbische Zeitung:** 88299 Leutkirch im Allgäu, Rudolf-Roth-Str. 18, 88291 Leutkirch im Allgäu, Postfach 1145; tel. (7561) 800; fax (7561) 80134; e-mail redaktion@schwäbische.de; internet www.schwaebische-zeitung.de; f. 1945; Editor JOACHIM UMBACH; circ. 196,000.

### Lübeck

**Lübecker Nachrichten:** 23543 Lübeck; 23556 Lübeck, Herrenholz 10-12; tel. (451) 1440; fax (451) 1441022; internet www.ln-online.de; f. 1945; publ. by Axel Springer Verlag AG; Chief Editor THOMAS LUBOWSKI; circ. 115,900.

### Ludwigshafen

**Die Rheinpfalz:** 67059 Ludwigshafen, Amtsstr. 5–11, 67011 Ludwigshafen, Postfach 211147; tel. (621) 590201; fax (621) 5902336; Dir Dr THOMAS SCHAUB; circ. 249,410.

### Magdeburg

**Magdeburger Volksstimme:** 39104 Magdeburg, Bahnhofstr. 17; tel. (391) 59990; fax (391) 388400; f. 1890; morning; publ. by Magde-

### ROADS

In January 1998 there were 11,309 km of motorway, 41,419 km of other main roads and 178,346 km of secondary roads. There were some 641,866 km of classified roads in January 1996.

### INLAND WATERWAYS

There are 7,467 km of navigable inland waterways, including the Main-Danube Canal, linking the North Sea and the Black Sea, which was opened in September 1992. Inland shipping accounts for about 20% of total freight traffic.

#### Associations

**Bundesverband der Deutschen Binnenschiffahrt eV:** 47119 Duisburg, Dammstr. 15–17; tel. (203) 800060; fax (203) 8000621; f. 1948; central Inland Waterway Association to further the interests of operating firms; Pres. WILHEIM MÜNNING; 5 Mans.

**Bundesverband Öffentlicher Binnenhäfen eV:** 41460 Neuss, Hammer Landstr. 3; tel. (2131) 21624; fax (2131) 908282; e-mail boeb@binnenhafen.de; internet www.binnenhafen.de; Chair. ERICH STAAKE.

**Bundesverband der selbstständigen Abteilung Binnenschiffahrt eV;** 53175 Bonn, Hochkreuzallee 89; tel. (228) 318162; fax (228) 318163; Man. Dir ANDREA BECKSCHÄFER.

**Deutsche Binnenreederei Binnenschiffahrt Spedition Logistik GmbH:** 10245 Berlin, Alt Stralau 55–58; tel. (30) 293760; fax (30) 29376201; e-mail reichelt@online-now-de; internet www.binnenreederei.de; f. 1949; Dir-Gen. HANS-WILHELM DÜNNER.

**Hafenschiffahrtsverband Hamburg eV:** 20457 Hamburg, Mattentwiete 2; tel. (40) 361280; fax (40) 36128292.

**Verein für europäische Binnenschiffahrt und Wasserstrassen eV (VBW):** 47119 Duisburg, Dammstr. 15–17; tel. (203) 8000627; fax (203) 8000628; represents all branches of the inland waterways; Pres. Prof. D. SCHRÖDER; Dir G. DÜTEMEYER.

### SHIPPING

The principal seaports for freight are Bremen, Hamburg, Rostock-Überseehafen and Wilhelmshaven. Some important shipping companies are:

**Argo Reederei Richard Adler & Söhne:** 28075 Bremen, Postfach 107529; tel. (421) 363070; fax (421) 321575; Finland, UK; Propr MAX ADLER.

**Aug. Bolten, Wm. Miller's Nachfolger GmbH & Co:** 20457 Hamburg, Mattentwiete 8; tel. (40) 36011; fax (40) 3601423; tramp; Man. Dir DIETER OSTENDORF.

**Bugsier- Reederei- und Bergungs-Gesellschaft mbH & Co:** 20459 Hamburg, Johannisbollwerk 10, 20422 Hamburg, Postfach 112273; tel. (40) 311110; fax (40) 313693; salvage, towage, tugs, ocean-going heavy lift cranes, submersible pontoons, harbour tugs; Man. Dirs B. J. SCHUCHMANN, J. W. SCHUCHMANN, A. HUETTMANN.

**Christian F. Ahrenkiel GmbH & Co. KG:** 20099 Hamburg, An der Alster 45, Postfach 100220; tel. (40) 248380; fax (40) 24838346; operators, shipowners and managers.

**DAL Deutsche Afrika-Linien GmbH & Co:** 22767 Hamburg, Palmaille 45; tel. (40) 380160; fax (40) 38016663; Europe and South Africa; Man. Dirs H. VON RANTZAU, DR E. VON RANTZAU.

**Deutsche Seereederei Rostock GmbH:** Rostock; tel. (381) 4580; fax (381) 4582215; container ships, general cargo ships, bulk carriers, cargo trailer ships, railway ferries, special tankers.

**Döhle, Peter, Schiffahrts-KG (GmbH & Co):** 22767 Hamburg, Palmaille 33, 22767 Hamburg, Postfach 500440; tel. (40) 381080; fax (40) 38108255; internet www.doehle.de; Man. Dir JOCHEN DÖHLE; shipbrokers, chartering agent, shipowners.

**Egon Oldendorff:** 2400 Lübeck, Fünfhausen 1; tel. (451) 15000; fax (451) 73522; Dirs H. OLDENDORFF, G. ARNDT, W. DRABERT, T. WEBER, U. BERTHEAU.

**Ernst Russ GmbH:** 20354 Hamburg, Alsterufer 10; tel. (40) 414070; fax (40) 41407111; f. 1893; worldwide.

**F. Laeisz Schiffahrtsgesellschaft mbH + Co:** 20457 Hamburg, Trostbrücke 1, 20411 Hamburg, Postfach 111111; tel. (40) 368080; fax (40) 364876; e-mail info@laeiszline.de; internet www.laeiszline.de; f. 1983; Dirs NIKOLAUS W. SCHÜES, GERHARD HEYENGA, H. NIKOLAUS SCHÜES.

**Fisser & v. Doornum GmbH & Co:** 20148 Hamburg, Feldbrunnenstr. 43, Postfach 130365; tel. (40) 441860; fax (40) 4108050; f. 1879; tramp; Man. Dirs CHRISTIAN FISSER, DR MICHAEL FISSER.

**Hamburg-Südamerikanische Dampfschiffahrts-Gesellschaft Eggert & Amsinck:** 20457 Hamburg, Ost-West-Str. 59–61 tel. (40) 37050; fax (40) 37052400; e-mail central@hsdgham.hamburg-sued.com; internet www.hamburg-sued.com; f. 1871; worldwide service.

**Hapag-Lloyd AG:** 20095 Hamburg, Ballindamm 25; tel. (40) 30010; fax (40) 336432; f. 1970; North, Central and South America, Middle East, Asia, Australasia; Chair. BERND WREDE; Dir ALBRECHT METZE.

**John T. Essberger GmbH & Co:** 22767 Hamburg, Palmaille 49, Postfach 500429; tel. (40) 380160; fax (40) 38016579; f. 1924; Man. Dirs Dr E. VON RANTZAU, H. VON RANTZAU.

**Oldenburg-Portugiesische Dampfschiffs-Rhederei GmbH & Co KG:** 20459 Hamburg, Kajen 10, 20408 Hamburg, Postfach 110869; tel. (40) 361580; fax (40) 36158200; f. 1882; Spain, Portugal, Madeira, North Africa, Canary Islands; Man. Dirs G. KEMPF, J. BERGMANN.

**Rhein-, Maas und See-Schiffahrtskontor GmbH:** 47119 Duisburg, Krausstr. 1a; tel. (203) 8040; fax (203) 804-330; e-mail rms-team@rheinmaas.de; internet www.rheinmaas.de; f. 1948.

**Sloman Neptun Schiffahrts-AG:** 28195 Bremen, Langenstr. 44, 28014 Bremen, Postfach 101469; tel. (421) 17630; fax (421) 1763-200; f. 1873; Scandinavia, North-western Europe, Mediterranean, North Africa; gas carriers; agencies, stevedoring; Mans SVEN-MICHAEL EDYE, DIRK LOHMANN.

**Walther Möller & Co:** 22767 Hamburg, Thedestr. 2; tel. (40) 3803910; fax (40) 38039199; e-mail chartering@wmco.de.

#### Shipping Organizations

**Verband Deutscher Küstenschiffseigner** (German Coastal Shipowners' Association): Hamburg-Altona; tel. (40) 313435; fax (40) 315925; f. 1896; Pres. PETER TH. HAUSEN; Man. KLAUS KÖSTER.

**Verband Deutscher Reeder eV** (German Shipowners' Association): 20354 Hamburg, Esplanade 6, 20317 Hamburg, Postfach 305580; tel. (40) 350970; fax (40) 35097211; Pres. FRANK LEONHARDT; Man. Dir Dr BERND KRÖGER.

**Zentralverband der Deutschen Seehafenbetriebe eV** (Federal Association of German Seaport Operators): Hamburg; tel. (40) 366377; fax (40) 366377; e-mail zds-seehafen@t-online.de; f. 1932; Chair. PETER DIETRICH; 246 mems.

### CIVIL AVIATION

There are three international airports in the Berlin region and further international airports at Köln-Bonn, Dresden, Düsseldorf, Frankfurt, Hamburg, Hannover, Leipzig, München and Stuttgart. Plans were under way in 2000 for the construction of a major new international airport to serve Berlin.

**Aero Lloyd Flugreisen Luftverkehrs-KG:** 61440 Oberursel, Lessingstr. 7–9, Postfach 2029; tel. (6171) 62501 fax (6171) 625109; f. 1981; charter services; Gen. Mans Dr W. SCHNEIDER, WOLFGANG JOHN.

**Condor Flugdienst GmbH:** 65440 Kelsterbach, Am Greunen Weg 3; tel. (6107) 9390; fax (6107) 939440; internet www.condor.de; f. 1955, wholly-owned subsidiary of Lufthansa; charter and inclusive-tour services; Man. Dirs DIETER HEINEN, GERHARD SCHMID.

**Deutsche Lufthansa AG:** 50679 Köln, Von-Gablenz-Str. 2–6; tel. (221) 8260; fax (221) 8263818; f. 1953; extensive world-wide network; Chair. Supervisory Bd Dr WOLFGANG RÖLLER; Chair. Exec. Bd JÜRGEN WEBER.

**Germania Flug-GmbH:** 51129 Köln, Flughafen; tel. (2203) 402375; fax (2203) 504490; f. 1978; charter and inclusive-tour services; Man. Dr HENRICH BISCHOFF.

**Hapag-Lloyd Flug-GmbH:** 30855 Langenhagen, Flughafenstr. 10, Box 420240; tel. (511) 97270; fax (511) 9727739; e-mail info@hlf.de; internet www.hlf.de; f. 1972; charter and scheduled passenger services; Man. Dirs WOLFGANG KURTH, DIETER SCHENK.

**LTU Lufttransport-Unternehmen GmbH:** 40474 Düsseldorf, Flughafen, Halle 8; tel. (211) 9418888; fax (211) 9418881; f. 1955; charter and scheduled services; Man. Dir PETER HASLEBACHER.

**Lufthansa Cargo AG:** 65441 Kelsterbach, Langer Kornweg 34; tel. (6107) 777615; fax (6107) 777888; f. 1993; wholly-owned subsidiary of Lufthansa; freight-charter world-wide; Man. Dirs WALTER GEHL, JEAN-PETER JANSEN, STEFAN LAUER.

**Lufthansa Cityline GmbH:** 51147 Köln, Flughafen Köln-Bonn, Heinrich-Steinmann-Str.; tel. (2203) 5960; fax (2203) 596801; scheduled services; Man. Dir GEORG STEINBACHER.

## Tourism

Germany's tourist attractions include spas, summer and winter resorts, mountains, medieval towns and castles, and above all a variety of fascinating cities. The North and Baltic Sea coasts, the Rhine Valley, the Black Forest, the mountains of Thuringia, the Erzgebirge and Bavaria are the most popular areas. In 1998 there were 54,247 hotels and guesthouses in Germany, with 2,404,688 beds available for tourists. Overnight stays by foreign tourists totalled about 34,467,500 in 1998, when the total number of foreign visitors was 15,593,800.

**Deutsche Zentrale für Tourismus eV (DZT)** (German National Tourist Board): 60325 Frankfurt a.M., Beethovenstr. 69; tel. (69) 974640; fax (69) 751903; e-mail gnto-fra@compuserve.com; internet www.germany-tourism.de; f. 1948; Dir URSULA SCHÖRCHER.

# GHANA

## Introductory Survey

### Location, Climate, Language, Religion, Flag, Capital

The Republic of Ghana lies on the west coast of Africa, with Côte d'Ivoire to the west and Togo to the east. It is bordered by Burkina Faso to the north. The climate is tropical, with temperatures generally between 21°C and 32°C (70°–90°F) and average annual rainfall of 2,000 mm (80 ins) on the coast, decreasing inland. English is the official language, but there are eight major national languages. Many of the inhabitants follow traditional beliefs and customs. Christians comprise an estimated 42% of the population. The national flag (proportions 3 by 2) has three equal horizontal stripes, of red, yellow and green, with a five-pointed black star in the centre of the yellow stripe. The capital is Accra.

### Recent History

Ghana was formed as the result of a UN-supervised plebiscite in May 1956, when the British-administered section of Togoland, a UN Trust Territory, voted to join the Gold Coast, a British colony, in an independent state. Ghana was duly granted independence, within the Commonwealth, on 6 March 1957, and thus became the first British dependency in sub-Saharan Africa to achieve independence under majority rule. Dr Kwame Nkrumah, the Prime Minister of the former Gold Coast since 1952, became Prime Minister of the new state. Ghana became a republic on 1 July 1960, with Nkrumah as President. In 1964 the Convention People's Party, led by Nkrumah, was declared the sole authorized party.

In February 1966 Nkrumah, whose repressive policies and financial mismanagement had caused increasing resentment, was deposed by a military coup, whose leaders established a governing National Liberation Council (NLC), led by Gen. Joseph Ankrah. In April 1969, following disputes within the NLC, Ankrah was replaced by Brig. (later Lt-Gen.) Akwasi Afrifa, and a new Constitution was introduced. Power was returned in October to an elected civilian Government, led by Dr Kofi Busia. However, in reaction to increasing economic and political difficulties, the army again seized power in January 1972, under the leadership of Lt-Col (later Gen.) Ignatius Acheampong. Some improvement in Ghana's economic situation was achieved by the military, which announced in 1977 that it intended to relinquish power to a new government following a general election to take place in 1979. These plans, however, were forstalled in July 1978 by Acheampong's deputy, Lt-Gen. Frederick Akuffo, who assumed power in a bloodless coup. Tensions within the army became evident in May 1979, when junior military officers staged an unsuccessful coup attempt. The alleged leader of the conspirators, Flight-Lt Jerry Rawlings, was imprisoned, but was subsequently released by other officers. On 4 June he and his associates successfully seized power, amid popular acclaim, established the Armed Forces Revolutionary Council (AFRC), led by Rawlings, and introduced measures to eradicate corruption. Acheampong and Akuffo were among nine senior officers who were convicted on charges of corruption and executed.

The AFRC indicated that its assumption of power was temporary, and the elections took place in June 1979, as scheduled, although the return to civilian rule was postponed until September. The People's National Party (PNP), led by Dr Hilla Limann, emerged with the largest number of parliamentary seats and formed a coalition Government with support from the smaller United National Convention. Dr Limann took office as President in September. However, dissatisfaction with measures taken by the Government to improve the economy provoked widespread strikes and riots.

On 31 December 1981 Rawlings seized power for a second time, and established a governing Provisional National Defence Council (PNDC), with himself as Chairman. The Council of State was abolished, the Constitution suspended, the legislature dissolved and political parties banned. In 1982 city and district councils were replaced by People's Defence Committees (PDC), which were designed to allow popular participation in local government. In 1984 the PDC were redesignated as Committees for the Defence of the Revolution (CDR).

The PNDC's policies initially received strong support, but discontent with the regime and with the apparent ineffectiveness of its economic policies was reflected by a series of coup attempts and widespread student unrest; between 1984 and 1987 some 34 people were executed for their alleged involvement in plots to overthrow the Government. In August 1986 a former government minister and presidential candidate, Victor Owusu, was arrested for alleged subversion. In June 1987 it was announced that several people had been arrested and that weapons had been seized, following the discovery of a further conspiracy to overthrow the PNDC. In November the Government detained a further seven people, including leaders of two opposition movements, the New Democratic Movement (NDM) and the Kwame Nkrumah Revolutionary Guards (KNRG).

In July 1987 the PNDC announced that elections for district assemblies, scheduled for mid-1987, were to be postponed until late 1988, and that the ban on political parties was to remain. By April 1988 more than 89% of the electorate had been registered to vote in the forthcoming elections. In that month there was an extensive government reshuffle, in which a new post to co-ordinate the work of the CDR was created. During 1988 the number of districts was increased from 65 to 110, and in October districts were grouped within three electoral zones. Elections for the district assemblies in each zone were held in stages between December 1988 and February 1989. Although one-third of the 7,278 members of the district assemblies were appointed by the PNDC, the establishment of the assemblies was envisaged as the first stage in the development of a new political system of national democratic administration.

On 24 September 1989 a coup attempt was staged, led by a close associate of Rawlings, Maj. Courage Quashigah. Shortly afterwards Lt-Gen. Arnold Quainoo was dismissed as Commander of the Armed Forces, although he remained a member of the PNDC. (Rawlings himself assumed control of the armed forces until June 1990, when Maj.-Gen. Winston Mensah-Wood was appointed Commander.) In October 1989 five senior members of the security forces, including Quashigah, were arrested on charges of conspiring to assassinate Rawlings. The predominance of the Ewe ethnic group in government positions and other important posts, which had provoked discontent among other factions, was initially considered to be the cause of the revolt. In November, however, a board of inquiry, which investigated the allegations of treason, concluded that most of the conspirators were motivated by personal grievances and ambition. In January 1990 five more arrests were made in connection with the coup attempt. In August the human rights organization, Amnesty International, criticized the continued detention of Quashigah and six other members of the security forces, and claimed that they were imprisoned for political dissension.

In July 1990, in response to pressure from Western aid donors to introduce further democratic reforms, the PNDC announced that a National Commission for Democracy (NCD), under the chairmanship of Justice Daniel Annan (the Vice-Chairman of the PNDC), would organize a series of regional debates to consider Ghana's political and economic future. (Ten such debates took place between July and October 1992.) In August a newly-formed political organization, the Movement for Freedom and Justice (MFJ), criticized the NCD, claiming that it was too closely associated with the PNDC. The MFJ also demanded the abolition of legislation prohibiting political associations, the release of all political prisoners, the cessation of press censorship and the holding of a national referendum on the restoration of a multi-party system. In September the MFJ accused the PNDC of intimidation, after an inaugural meeting of the MFJ was suppressed by security forces. In October the PNDC pledged to accept the conclusions of any national consensus on future democracy in the country.

In December 1990 Rawlings announced proposals for the introduction of a constitution by the end of 1991; the PNDC was to consider recommendations presented by the NCD, and subsequently to convene a consultative body to determine constitutional reform. However, the MFJ, the Christian Council of Ghana and the Ghana Bar Association objected to the proposals, on the grounds that no definite schedule for political reform had been presented, and that no criteria had been established for the composition of the consultative body.

In March 1991 the NCD presented a report on the democratic process, which recommended the election of an executive President for a fixed term, the establishment of a legislature and the creation of the post of Prime Minister. Rawlings announced that the PNDC would consider the report and submit recommendations to a national consultative body later that year. In May, however, the PNDC endorsed the restoration of a multi-party system and approved the NCD's recommendations, although it was emphasized that the formation of political associations remained prohibited. The MFJ immediately disputed the veracity of the PNDC's announcement, causing the state-controlled press to accuse the MFJ of planning subversive activity. Later in May the Government announced the establishment of a 260-member Consultative Assembly, which was to present a draft constitution to the PNDC by the end of 1991. The new Constitution was subsequently to be submitted for endorsement by a national referendum. The Government appointed a nine-member committee of constitutional experts, who were to submit recommendations for a draft constitution to the Consultative Assembly by the end of July.

In June 1991 the Government reiterated denials that a number of political prisoners were detained in Ghana. In the same month the PNDC announced an amnesty for political exiles, which did not, however, include persons who were implicated in acts of subversion against the Government. In early August a newly-formed alliance of eleven opposition movements, human rights organizations and trade unions, including the MFJ, the NDM and the KNRG, known as the Co-ordinating Committee of Democratic Forces of Ghana, demanded that a constitutional conference be convened to determine a schedule for the transition to a democratic system. In the same month the committee of constitutional experts submitted a series of recommendations for reform, which included the establishment of a parliament and a council of state. It was proposed that the President, who would also be Commander-in-Chief of the Armed Forces, would be elected by universal suffrage for a four-year term of office, while the leader of the party which commanded a majority in the legislature would be appointed to the post of Prime Minister. However, the subsequent review of the draft Constitution by the Consultative Assembly was impeded by opposition demands for a boycott, on the grounds that the number of government representatives in the Assembly was too high. Later in August Rawlings announced that presidential and legislative elections were to take place in late 1992.

In early December 1991 Rawlings ordered the arrest of the Secretary-General of the MFJ, John Ndebugre, for allegedly failing to stand when the national anthem was played. Amnesty International subsequently reiterated claims that a number of prisoners in Ghana were detained for political dissension. In the same month the Government established an Interim National Electoral Commission (INEC), which was to be responsible for the demarcation of electoral regions and the supervision of elections and referendums. In January 1992 the Government extended the allocated period for the review of the draft Constitution to the end of March 1992. In March Rawlings announced a programme for transition to a multi-party system, which was to be completed on 7 January 1993. Later in March 1992 the Government granted an amnesty to 17 prisoners who had been convicted of subversion, including Quashigah.

At the end of March 1992 the Consultative Assembly approved the majority of the constitutional recommendations that had been submitted to the PNDC. However, the proposed creation of the post of Prime Minister was rejected by the Assembly; executive power was to be vested in the President, who would appoint a Vice-President. Opposition groups subsequently objected to a provision in the draft Constitution that members of the Government be exempt from prosecution for human rights violations allegedly committed during the PNDC's rule. At a national referendum on 28 April, however, the adoption of the draft Constitution was approved by 92% of votes cast, with 43.7% of the electorate voting.

On 18 May 1992 the Government introduced legislation permitting the formation of political associations (opposition groups had previously demanded that a multi-party system be adopted prior to the constitutional referendum); political parties were henceforth required to apply to the INEC for legal recognition. Under the terms of the legislation, however, emergent parties were not permitted to use names or slogans associated with 21 former political organizations that remained proscribed; in addition, individual monetary contributions to political parties were restricted. Later in May the High Court rejected an application for an injunction against the legislation by opposition leaders, who claimed that it was biased in favour of the PNDC. At the end of May it was reported that some 63 people had been killed in clashes between the Gonja and Nawuri ethnic groups in northern Ghana.

In June 1992 a number of political associations were established, many of which were identified with supporters of former President Nkrumah; six opposition movements, including the People's National Convention (PNC), led by ex-President Limann, were subsequently granted legal recognition. In the same month a coalition of pro-Government organizations, the National Democratic Congress (NDC), was formed to contest the forthcoming elections on behalf of the PNDC. However, an existing alliance of Rawlings' supporters, the Eagle Club, refused to join the NDC, and created its own political organization, the Eagle Party (later known as the EGLE—Every Ghanaian Living Everywhere—Party). In July Rawlings denied that he was associated with the Eagle Club, and rejected the EGLE Party's nomination as its candidate for the presidential election. In August the Government promulgated a new electoral code, which included a provision that in the event that no presidential candidate received more than 50% of votes cast the two candidates with the highest number of votes would contest a second round within 21 days. In September Rawlings officially retired from the air force (although he retained the post of Commander-in-Chief of the Armed Forces in his capacity as Head of State), in compliance with a stipulation in the new Constitution, and accepted a nomination to contest the presidential election as a candidate of the NDC. The NDC, the EGLE Party and the National Convention Party (NCP) subsequently formed a pro-Government electoral coalition, known as the Progressive Alliance.

In early October 1992 legislation that permitted indefinite detention without trial was repealed, in response to repeated protests by human rights organizations and opposition groups. However, new legislation, providing for the detention of individuals suspected of certain crimes for a period of up to 14 days was promulgated, and a special review court, which was empowered to extend the initial 14-day detention period, was established. Later in October the High Court dismissed an application by the MFJ for an injunction to prevent Rawlings from contesting the presidential election, on the grounds that he was not a Ghanaian national (his father was British), and that he remained accountable for charges of treason in connection with the coups that he had led.

In the presidential election, which took place on 3 November 1992, Rawlings secured 58.3% of votes cast, thereby obviating the necessity for a second round of voting. The four opposition parties that had presented candidates, the PNC, the New Patriotic Party (NPP), the National Independence Party (NIP) and the People's Heritage Party (PHP), claimed that there had been widespread electoral malpractice, although international observers maintained that the election had been conducted fairly (despite isolated irregularities). A curfew was subsequently imposed in Kumasi, in the district of Ashanti, following riots by supporters of the NPP in protest at the election results; a series of bombings in Tema and Accra were also attributed to members of the opposition. Later in November the NPP, the PNC, the NIP and the PHP withdrew from the forthcoming legislative elections (scheduled for 8 December), in protest at the Government's refusal to comply with their demands that a new electoral register be compiled and that allegations of misconduct during the presidential election be investigated. As a result, the legislative elections were postponed until 22 December (and subsequently by a further week) to allow time for the nomination of new candidates. In December the opposition claimed that many of its members had left Ghana, as a result of widespread intimidation by the Government. In the legislative elections, which duly took place on 29 December, the NDC secured 189 of the 200 seats in the Parliament, while the NCP obtained eight seats, the EGLE Party one seat and independent candidates the remaining two. (The NDC, the NCP and the EGLE Party were obliged to present separate candidates, following the withdrawal of the opposition parties.) According to official figures, however, only 29% of the electorate voted in the legislative elections.

On 7 January 1993 Rawlings was sworn in as President of what was designated the Fourth Republic, and the PNDC was officially dissolved; on the same day the new Parliament was inaugurated, and Justice Daniel Annan was elected as its Speaker. Later in January the NPP, the PNC, the NIP and the PHP formed an alliance, known as the Inter-party Co-ordinating Committee, and announced that they were to act as an official opposition to the Government, despite their lack of representation in the Parliament. At the end of January Rawlings began to submit nominations for members of the Council of Ministers and the Council of State for approval by the Parliament. However, he announced that members of the existing Government were to remain in office in an interim capacity, pending the appointment of a Council of Ministers and other officials. The opposition subsequently criticized the delay in the formation of a new government, and protested that the new Constitution did not permit members of the former PNDC to remain in office. In March the nomination of a number of ministers was approved by the Parliament. Later that month legislation was promulgated to exempt from prosecution perpetrators of offences that had been committed under the auspices of the former PNDC Government.

In April 1993 elections took place for the regional seats in the Council of State. In May a 17-member Council of Ministers, which included several ministers who had served in the former PNDC administration, was inaugurated. Substantial pledges of assistance for Ghana, made in July at a meeting of donor nations (under the aegis of the World Bank), indicated Western support for the new Government. In the same month the Supreme Court upheld a motion by the NPP that certain existing legislation was in contravention of the Constitution. In August the NPP (which, together with other principal opposition parties, had hitherto continued to contest the results of the presidential election) announced that it was prepared to recognize the legitimacy of the Government. In October the Minister of Justice, who (in his capacity as public prosecutor) had failed to win several trials in the Supreme Court, resigned after a state-owned newspaper questioned his competence. In November a 20-member National Security Council, chaired by the Vice-President, Kow Nkensen Arkaah, was inaugurated. In December the PHP, the NIP and a faction of the PNC, all of which comprised supporters of ex-President Nkrumah, merged to form a new organization, known as the People's Convention Party (PCP). In the same month, following a further appeal by the NPP, the Supreme Court ruled that the anniversary of the December 1981 coup should no longer be observed as a public holiday.

In February 1994 long-standing hostility between the Konkomba ethnic group, which originated in Togo, and the land-owning Nanumba intensified, following demands by the Konkomba for traditional status that would entitle them to own land; some 500 people were killed in clashes between the two factions in the Northern Region. The Government subsequently dispatched troops to restore order and imposed a state of emergency in seven districts for a period of three months. Nevertheless, skirmishes continued in the region, with several other ethnic groups becoming involved in the conflict, and it was reported that some 6,000 Konkomba had fled to Togo. In early March 12 people were killed at Tamale (the capital of the Northern Region), when security forces fired on demonstrators belonging to the Dagomba ethnic group, who had allegedly attacked a number of Konkomba.

In March 1994 a minor government reorganization was effected. Later that month elections to the District Assemblies took place (except in the seven districts subject to the state of emergency). Negotiations between representatives of the various ethnic groups involved in the conflict in the Northern Region were initiated in April, under the aegis of the Government. In the same month the authorities claimed that reported threats to kill Quashigah (the instigator of the coup attempt in 1989) and editors of two privately-owned newspapers were part of a conspiracy to destabilize the Government. In May a further minor reorganization of the Government took place. Meanwhile, the state of emergency in force in the Northern Region (where a total of 1,000 people had been killed, and a further 150,000 displaced) was extended for one month. In early June, however, the ethnic factions involved in the hostilities signed a peace agreement that provided for the imposition of an immediate cease-fire and renounced violence as a means of settling disputes over land-ownership. The Government subsequently announced that troops were to be permanently stationed in the Northern Region in order to prevent further conflict, and established a negotiating team which was to attempt to resolve the inter-ethnic differences. The state of emergency was extended for a further month in June, and again in July; in early August, however, the Government announced that order had been restored in the Northern Region, and officially ended the state of emergency.

In September 1994 five civilians, who had allegedly conspired to overthrow the Government, were charged with treason. In October two men were arrested by security forces, after attempting to transport armaments illicitly to the Northern Region; an increase in tension in the region was reflected by further arrests, in connection with violent incidents in which several people had been killed. Following a joint rally of the NPP, the PNC and the PCP in November, the parties announced that they would present a single candidate to contest the presidential election in 1996. Meanwhile, rumours emerged of ill-feeling between Rawlings and Arkaah. In January 1995 Arkaah officially refuted speculation that Rawlings was responsible for allegations, which had appeared in an independent newspaper, of an illicit relationship between Arkaah and a minor, and attributed blame to subversive elements. In the same month, however, the Government denied a reported statement by Arkaah that he had refused a request by Rawlings for his resignation.

In March 1995 the Government imposed a curfew in the Northern Region following renewed ethnic violence, in which about 100 people were killed. In April a joint commission, comprising prominent members of the Konkomba and Nanumba ethnic groups, was established, in an effort to resolve the conflict. Meanwhile, the imposition, in February, of value-added tax (VAT) under the budget for 1995 prompted widespread protests, while civil servants threatened to initiate strike action; a series of demonstrations, which was organized by a grouping of opposition leaders, Alliance for Change, culminated in May, when five people were killed in clashes between government supporters and protesters. (The Government subsequently agreed to suspend VAT, although it was reintroduced, at a lower rate, in 1999.) Later in May the National Executive Committee of the NCP decided to withdraw the party from the government coalition, claiming that the NDC had dominated the alliance. However, Arkaah (a member of the NCP) subsequently announced that he was to retain the office of Vice-President on the grounds that his mandate remained valid. In July the long-serving Minister of Finance, Kwesi Botchwey, resigned (apparently in response to the failure of government efforts to impose VAT); a minor reorganization of the Council of Ministers ensued. At a by-election in the same month, the vacant seat was secured by a joint candidate of the PNC, NPP, NCP and PCP. In October the Chairman of the NCP resigned, following dissent within the party. In November the Commission on Human Rights and Administrative Justice (CHRAJ) commenced investigations into allegations of corruption on the part of government ministers and civil servants. In January 1996 an alleged incident in which Rawlings assaulted Arkaah during a meeting of the Council of Ministers prompted further speculation of animosity between the President and Vice-President; opposition parties subsequently demanded that Rawlings resign. In February three journalists were arraigned after publishing a report alleging the Government's complicity in a case of drugs-trafficking involving a Ghanaian diplomat based in Geneva, Switzerland. In the same month the NCP and PCP merged to form a single party, known as the Convention People's Party. Rawlings reshuffled his Council of Ministers in March.

In April 1996 presidential and parliamentary elections were scheduled for 10 December, although this was later changed to 7 December to meet constitutional requirements. Nominations of candidates were to take place in September. In May Kwame Pianim, prospective presidential candidate for the NPP, was disqualified from the elections on the grounds of his conviction for treason in 1982. In the same month it was announced that the Popular Party for Democracy and Development (PPDD), a group formed in 1992 by supporters of Nkrumah, was to merge with the PCP. The PPDD also announced its support for unity with the NPP. In June Thomas Appiah resigned for personal reasons as Chairman of the NCP and Vice-Chairman of the PCP. In July the NCP announced that it had removed Kow Nkensen Arkaah as its leader, following his selection as presidential candidate by the PCP. In August the NPP and PCP announced their formation of an electoral coalition, to be known as the Great Alliance; it was subsequently announced that John Kufuor, of the NPP, was to be the Great Alliance's presidential candidate, with Arkaah, of the PCP, as the candidate for the vice-presidency. The NCP stated that it would support the NDC in the forthcoming elections, while the PNC announced its intention to contest the elections alone; Edward Mahama was subsequently selected as the PNC's presidential candidate. In September Rawlings was nominated as the NDC's presidential candidate. By 18 September, the official deadline for the nomination of candidates, only the Progressive Alliance (the NDC, the EGLE party and the Democratic People's Party—DPP), the Great Alliance and the PNC had succeeded in having their nomination papers accepted. In early October the NCP, which, according to the National Electoral Commission, had not presented the appropriate papers, declared its intention to take legal action against the Commission. In mid-October the Electoral Commission denied accusations that it had shown bias against the NCP. The selection of common candidates provoked a lengthy dispute between the NPP and the PCP, with the parties contradicting each other regarding previous agreements on the distribution of seats. In late October at least 20 people were wounded in clashes between NDC and NPP militant supporters in Tamale (in the north) and Kibi (in the north-east). In November a network of Domestic Election Observers (including religious councils, the Trades Union Congress, and civil servants' and journalists' associations), was created to oversee the December elections. The resignation of the Minister of the Interior in October was followed, in November, by the resignations of the Minister of Trade and Industry and the Presidential Aide on Cocoa Affairs, following corruption allegations against them.

In the presidential election, which took place on 7 December 1996, Rawlings was re-elected by 57.2% of votes cast, while Kufuor secured 39.8% of the votes. In the parliamentary elections the NDC's representation was reduced to 133 seats, while the NPP won 60 seats, the PCP five and the PNC one seat. Voting was postponed in the constituency of Afigya Sekyere East, in Ashanti, because of a legal dispute concerning the eligibility of candidates. (The seat was subsequently won by the NPP in a by-election in June 1997.) Despite opposition claims of malpractice, international observers declared that the elections had been conducted fairly, and a high electoral turn-out of 76.8% was reported. Following the announcement of the election results, about 15 people were injured in clashes between NDC and opposition supporters in Bimbila, south-east of Tamale. At the end of December the PCP announced that its electoral alliance with the NPP had broken down. On 7 January 1997 Rawlings was sworn in as President.

The lengthy process of appointing a new Council of Ministers led to a protracted dispute between the NDC and the opposition, prompting a series of parliamentary boycotts by the NPP, which insisted that all ministerial appointees be approved by the parliamentary appointments committee prior to assuming their duties. In late February 1997 opposition parties sought a Supreme Court ruling to prevent Kwame Peprah, the reappointed Minister of Finance, from presenting the budget. Owing to the NDC's parliamentary majority, however, procedures were approved to allow those ministers who had been retained from the previous Government to avoid the vetting process. The majority of ministerial appointments were made during March and April, although a number of posts were not filled until June. In early June the Supreme Court ruled that all presidential nominees for ministerial positions had to be approved by Parliament, even if they had served in the previous Government. Following the ruling, the NPP withdrew from the chamber on several occasions when ministers attempted to address Parliament. The Government subsequently announced that ministers who had participated in the previous administration were prepared to undergo vetting procedures.

In early September 1997 it was reported that three people had been killed, and more than 1,000 displaced, in the Brong Ahafo Region, following ethnic skirmishes which had been prompted by a dispute over land-ownership. In December violent clashes between two Muslim sects resulted in severe damage to property in Wa, in the north-west of Ghana. In the following month four people were killed, and 26 injured, in an outbreak of violence between opposing Muslim factions in Wenchi, in the Brong Ahafo Region; 57 people were subsequently arrested. In September 1998 108 people were arrested in Kumasi, following violent clashes between rival Muslim sects.

Following increasing accusations of government corruption, President Rawlings dismissed a Minister of State in February 1998, after a committee of inquiry discovered lapses of propriety regarding a sea defence project for which the Minister was responsible. In August two of Ghana's three Nkrumahist movements, the NCP and the PCP, merged to form the Convention Party. In October the NPP nominated Kufuor to stand again as its presidential candidate, in elections due to be held in 2000. In November 1998 Rawlings effected a government reshuffle. At an NDC congress in December 1998 the party constitution was amended to create the position of 'life chairman' of the party for Rawlings. He then confirmed he would comply with the terms of the constitution and not attempt to stand for a third term as President. He subsequently announced in April 1999 that the incumbent Vice-President, Prof. John Evans Atta Mills, was to contest the election on behalf of the NDC.

In March 1999 ECOMOG forces in Sierra Leone arrested a Ghanaian officer, Capt. James Owoo, who had allegedly been involved in attempts to remove the PNDC administration in the 1980s. He was subsequently taken to Accra where he was charged with conspiring to overthrow the Rawlings Government in 1998. In June 1999, owing to dissatisfaction within the NDC at the changes carried out at the party congress and at Rawlings' announcement regarding his successor, a disaffected group of party members broke away to form a new political organization, the National Reform Party (NRP). In mid-August student demonstrations in protest at a rise in tuition fees developed into violent clashes between police and protesters, resulting in injuries to several students. All five of the country's universities were temporarily closed; however, demonstrations were renewed in Accra in mid-September. In early November Queen Elizabeth II visited Ghana for the first time since 1961. An opposition demonstration scheduled to take place shortly before the Queen's arrival was postponed until the end of the month. Rawlings carried out three government reshuffles in late 1999 and early 2000.

Following a military coup in Burkina Faso in October 1987, which was condemned by the Ghanaian Government (relations between Rawlings and the deposed Burkinabè leader, Capt. Thomas Sankara, had been close), links between the two countries were temporarily strained, but improved following meetings between Rawlings and Capt. Blaise Compaoré, the Burkinabè leader, in early 1988. In December 1989, however, Ghana was accused by Burkina Faso of involvement in an attempt to overthrow the Burkinabè Government. In mid-January 1990 120 Ghanaians were deported from Burkina Faso without official explanation. In March 1998 Ghana and Burkina Faso agreed to establish a joint commission to manage water resources. Tensions had previously arisen over Burkinabè plans to build hydroelectric dams on a major tributory of the Volta river. Further agreements on co-operation were signed in August during a visit to Ghana by Compaoré.

In 1986 relations between Ghana and Togo became strained, following subversive activity by Ghanaian dissidents based in Togo, and an attempted coup in Togo, which was allegedly initiated from Ghanaian territory. The common border between the two countries was closed in October, but was reopened by Togo in February 1987, and by Ghana in May. Between December 1988 and January 1989 more than 130 Ghanaians were deported from Togo, where they were alleged to be residing illegally. In October 1991 the Governments of Ghana and Togo signed an agreement on the free movement of goods and persons between the two countries. In October 1992, however, Ghana denied claims by the Togolese Government that it was implicated in subversive activity by Togolese dissidents based in Ghana. In November Rawlings formally protested to the Togolese Government, after five Ghanaians were killed by Togolese security forces on the border between the two countries.

In March 1993 the Rawlings administration denied allegations, made by the Togolese Government, of Ghanaian complicity in an armed attack on the residence of Togo's President. In January 1994 relations with Togo further deteriorated, following an attempt to overthrow the Togolese Government, which was said by the Togolese authorities to have been staged by armed dissidents based in Ghana. The Ghanaian Chargé d'affaires in Togo was arrested, and Togolese forces killed 12 Ghanaians and bombarded a customs post at Aflao and several villages near the border. Ghana, however, denied the accusations of involvement in the coup attempt, and threatened to retaliate against further acts of aggression. In May allegations by the Togolese Government that Ghana had been responsible (owing to lack of border security) for bomb attacks in Togo resulted in further tension between the two nations. In August the Togolese Government protested to Ghana, following an article in a privately-owned Ghanaian newspaper to the effect that Togolese rebels based in Ghana were preparing to launch an offensive to overthrow the Eyadéma administration. Later that year, however, relations between the two countries improved, and in November full diplomatic links were formally restored. In the following month Togo's border with Ghana (which had been closed in January 1994) was reopened. After discussions between Eyadéma and Rawlings in July 1995, an agreement was reached, providing for the reconstitution of the Ghana-Togo joint commission for economic, social and technical co-operation and the Ghana-Togo border demarcation commission. In August the Togolese Government denied involvement in the assassination of a political opponent who had taken refuge in Ghana. In February 1996 both Parliaments established friendship groups to examine ways of easing tensions. By the end of that year some 48,000 Togolese refugees were estimated to have received payment for voluntary repatriation. Eyadéma and Rawlings met again in Accra in May 1998, amid an easing of relations between the two countries. In mid-August of that year a joint operation was mounted to arrest a group of armed men from Ghana who had attacked military posts in Togo. In August 1999, following recent Togolese incursions into Ghanaian territory and airspace, delegations from the two countries met in Ghana's Volta Region for talks regarding the border situation, after which both sides expressed their desire for peace and harmony between the two countries. In September the Ghanaian Government proposed that the Ghana-Togo border demarcation commission resume its work.

During the conflict in Liberia, which commenced in December 1989 (see Liberia, Vol. II), Ghana contributed troops to the Monitoring Group (ECOMOG) of the Economic Community of West African States (ECOWAS, see p. 163). In August 1994 Rawlings, who in that month replaced President Nicéphore Soglo of Benin as Chairman of the ECOWAS Conference of Heads of State and Government, indicated that Ghana was to consider the withdrawal of troops from ECOMOG. However, it subsequently appeared that the Ghanaian contingent was to remain in ECOMOG until peace was achieved, while Rawlings (in his capacity as Chairman) mediated protracted negotiations between the warring Liberian factions. Ghana granted temporary asylum to some 2,000 Liberian war refugees in May 1996, but insisted that no more could be accepted in the future. By mid-1997, however, some 17,000 Liberian refugees had arrived in Ghana. In August Rawlings was the first foreign leader to visit Liberia following its return to civilian rule. In January 1999 Ghanaian ECOMOG troops began to leave Liberia. Meanwhile, in June 1997 Ghana, together with Côte d'Ivoire, Guinea and Nigeria, became a member of the 'committee of four', which was established by ECOWAS to monitor the situation in Sierra Leone, following the staging of a military coup in the previous month; troops were dispatched to participate in a peace-keeping force deployed in that country. It was reported in February 1998 that Ghana had opposed the use of force by the Nigerian contingent of this peace-keeping unit to overthrow the military government in Sierra Leone. Following the reinstatement of the democratically-elected Government in March, ECOMOG units remained in the country and continued to launch attacks against rebel forces, which still retained control of a number of areas. In August 1999 it was estimated that Ghanaian troops in Sierra Leone numbered some 500.

In March 1998 US President Clinton visited Ghana during a tour of six African countries. At the end of August, following the bombing of its embassies in Kenya and Tanzania, the USA temporarily closed its embassy in Accra for security reasons.

## Government

Under the terms of the Constitution, which was approved by national referendum on 28 April 1992, Ghana has a multi-party political system. Executive power is vested in the President, who is the Head of State and Commander-in-Chief of the Armed Forces. The President is elected by direct universal suffrage for a maximum of two four-year terms of office. Legislative power is vested in a 200-member unicameral Parliament, which is elected by direct universal suffrage for a four-year term. The President appoints a Vice-President, and nominates a Council of Ministers, subject to approval by the Parliament. The Constitution also provides for a 25-member Council of State, principally comprising regional representatives and presidential nominees, and a 20-member National Security Council, chaired by the Vice-President, which act as advisory bodies to the President.

Ghana has 10 regions, each headed by a Regional Minister, who is assisted by a regional co-ordinating council. The regions constitute 110 administrative districts, each with a District Assembly, which is headed by a District Chief Executive. Regional colleges, which comprise representatives selected by the District Assemblies and by regional Houses of Chiefs, elect a number of representatives to the Council of State.

## Defence

At 1 August 1999 Ghana had total armed forces of 7,000 (army 5,000, navy 1,000 and air force 1,000). The defence budget for 1999 was 150,000m. cedis. The headquarters of the Defence Commission of the OAU is in Accra.

## Economic Affairs

In 1997, according to estimates by the World Bank, Ghana's gross national product (GNP), measured at average 1995–97 prices, was US $6,982m., equivalent to $390 per head. During 1990–97, it was estimated, GNP per head increased, in real terms, at an average annual rate of 1.4%, while the population increased at an average annual rate of 2.7% over the same period. GNP was estimated at $7,200m. in 1998, equivalent to $390 per head. Ghana's gross domestic product (GDP) increased, in real terms, at an average annual rate of 4.2% in 1990–98; in 1997 GDP increased by 4.8%, and, according to the IMF, it increased by 4.7% in 1998.

Agriculture (including forestry and fishing) contributed 40.1% of GDP in 1997. An estimated 57.4% of the labour force were employed in the sector in 1998. The principal cash crops are cocoa beans (Ghana being one of the world's leading producers, and exports of which accounted for 29.9% of total exports in 1998), coffee, bananas, cassava, oil palm, coconuts, limes, kola nuts and shea-nuts (karité nuts). Timber production is also important, with the forestry sector accounting for 3.8% of GDP in 1997 and 9.4% of total export earnings in 1998. Fishing satisfies more than three-quarters of domestic requirements. During 1990–98, according to the World Bank, agricultural GDP increased at an average average rate of 2.8%. According to the IMF, agricultural GDP increased by 4.3% in 1997.

Industry (including mining, manufacturing, construction and power) contributed 28.7% of GDP in 1997, and employed 12.8% of the working population in 1984. According to the World Bank, industrial GDP increased at an average annual rate of 4.4% in 1990–98. According to the IMF, industrial GDP increased by 6.4% in 1997.

Mining contributed 5.7% of GDP in 1997, and employed 0.5% of the working population in 1984. Gold and diamonds are the major minerals exported, although Ghana also exploits large reserves of bauxite and manganese ore. According to IMF figures, the GDP of the mining sector increased by an average of 5.1% per year in 1993–97, and by 5.6% in 1997.

Manufacturing contributed 10.1% of GDP in 1997, and employed 10.9% of the working population in 1984. The most important sectors are food processing, textiles, vehicles, cement, paper, chemicals and petroleum. According to IMF figures, manufacturing GDP increased at an average annual rate of 3.5% in 1993–97, and by 7.3% in 1997.

The Akosombo and Kpong hydroelectric plants supply 90% of Ghana's electricity; thermal power provides an alternative source of energy. Low rainfall resulted in a severe energy crisis in 1998, however, prompting the Government to accelerate plans for the further development of thermal power. The construction of a nuclear reactor at Kwabenya, near Accra, was completed in January 1995. In August 1999 the Governments of Ghana, Benin, Togo and Nigeria agreed jointly to finance the West African Gas Pipeline (WAGP), which was to supply natural gas from Nigeria to the three recipient countries. The project was scheduled to be completed in 2002. Imports of mineral fuels comprised 4.8% of the total value of imports in 1998. Electricity is exported to Benin and Togo.

The services sector contributed 31.2% of GDP in 1997, and engaged 26.1% of the working population in 1984. According to the World Bank, the GDP of the services sector increased at an average annual rate of 5.6% in 1993–98. According to the IMF the GDP of the services sector increased by 6.5% in 1997.

In 1998 Ghana recorded a visible trade deficit of US $532.8m., while there was a deficit of $349.8m. on the current account of the balance of payments. In 1998 the principal source of imports was the USA (11.7%); other major sources were the United Kingdom and Germany. Switzerland was the principal market for exports (taking 23.6% of the total) in that year; other important purchasers were the United Kingdom, the Netherlands and Germany. The principal exports in 1998 were gold (which accounted for 37.5% of total export earnings), cocoa beans and timber and timber products. The principal imports in 1998 were machinery and transport equipment and food and live animals.

Ghana's overall budget deficit for 1997 was 1,292,700m. cedis (equivalent to 9.2% of GDP). Ghana's external debt totalled US $5,982m. at the end of 1997, of which $4,691m. was long-term public debt. In the same year the cost of debt-servicing was equivalent to 29.5% of exports of goods and services. In 1995–98 the average annual rate of inflation was 29.0%. In 1998 consumer prices increased by 14.6%. In 1995 some 41,000 people were registered as unemployed in Ghana.

Ghana is a member of the Economic Community of West African States (ECOWAS, see p. 163), of the International Cocoa Organization (ICCO, see p. 287) and of the International Coffee Organization (ICO, see p. 287).

With the continuing support and assistance of international donors, Ghana's economy has made steady progress since the transfer to civilian rule in 1992. However, it remains vulnerable to unfavourable weather conditions and to fluctuations in international commodity prices. In 1999 a combination of a fall in cocoa prices, a turbulent gold market and a steep rise in the price of petroleum placed a severe strain on government finances. This was further aggravated by a shortfall in foreign assistance. In May, however, the IMF approved a three-year Enhanced Structural Adjustment Facility (ESAF), equivalent to US $209.4m., to support the Government's economic reform programme. Nevertheless, despite the re-introduction of value-added tax, at 10%, in January and the continued reduction in the rate of inflation, the country's economy appeared likely to be faced with a testing future. There have been delays in the Government's privatization programme, the cedi depreciated by 17.9% against the US dollar between January and October 1999, and GDP growth targets for 1999 were not met, thus jeopardizing President Rawlings' 'Vision 2020' project, an ambitious development programme, which aims to achieve middle-income status for Ghana by that year.

### Social Welfare

The Government provides hospitals and medical care at nominal rates, and there is a government pension scheme. In 1992 government health facilities included 49 general hospitals and about 300 rural health clinics; religious missions operated 41 hospitals and 64 clinics, while there were an additional 400 private clinics. In that year there were about 800 physicians and 11,000 nurses working in the public sector, with about 300 physicians working in private practice. In 1995 the Government allocated 73,600m. cedis for health services (5.7% of total government expenditure).

### Education

Education is officially compulsory for nine years between the ages of six and 16. Primary education begins at the age of six and lasts for six years. Secondary education, beginning at the age of 12, lasts for a further six years, comprising two three-year cycles. Following three years of junior secondary education, pupils are examined to determine admission to senior secondary school courses, or to technical and vocational courses. In 1991 primary enrolment was equivalent to 76% of children in the relevant age-group (boys 83%; girls 70%), while the comparable ratio for secondary enrolment was 37% (boys 45%; girls 29%). It was estimated that 52,000 students were enrolled in higher education in 1992, with about 10,700 students attending the country's five universities. Tertiary institutions also included 38 teacher-training colleges, seven diploma-awarding colleges, 21 technical colleges and six polytechnics. Expenditure on education by the central Government in 1995 was 258,700m. cedis (20.1% of total spending). According to UNESCO estimates, the average rate of adult illiteracy in 1995 was 35.5% (males 24.1%; females 46.5%).

### Public Holidays

**2000:** 1 January (New Year's Day), 6 March (Independence Day), 21–24 April (Easter), 1 May (Labour Day), 1 July (Republic Day), 1 December (National Farmers' Day), 25–26 December (Christmas).

**2001:** 1 January (New Year's Day), 6 March (Independence Day), 13–16 April (Easter), 1 May (Labour Day), 1 July (Republic Day), 1 December (National Farmers' Day), 25–26 December (Christmas).

### Weights and Measures

The metric system is in force.

# Statistical Survey

Source (except where otherwise stated): Central Bureau of Statistics, POB 1098, Accra; tel. (21) 66512.

## Area and Population

**AREA, POPULATION AND DENSITY**

| | |
|---|---|
| Area (sq km) | 238,537* |
| Population (census results) | |
| 1 March 1970 | 8,559,313 |
| 11 March 1984 | |
| Males | 6,063,848 |
| Females | 6,232,233 |
| Total | 12,296,081 |
| Population (UN estimates at mid-year)† | |
| 1996 | 18,154,000 |
| 1997 | 18,656,000 |
| 1998 | 19,162,000 |
| Density (per sq km) at mid-1998 | 80.3 |

* 92,100 sq miles.

† Source: UN, *World Population Prospects: The 1998 Revision*.

**POPULATION BY REGION** (1984 census)

| | |
|---|---|
| Western | 1,157,807 |
| Central | 1,142,335 |
| Greater Accra | 1,431,099 |
| Eastern | 1,680,890 |
| Volta | 1,211,907 |
| Ashanti | 2,090,100 |
| Brong-Ahafo | 1,206,608 |
| Northern | 1,164,583 |
| Upper East | 772,744 |
| Upper West | 438,008 |
| **Total** | 12,296,081 |

**Principal ethnic groups** (1991 estimates, percentage of total population): Akan 52.4, Mossi 15.8, Ewe 11.9, Ga-Adangme 7.8, Guan 11.9, Gurma 3.3%, Yoruba 1.3%.

**PRINCIPAL TOWNS** (population at 1984 census)

| | | | |
|---|---|---|---|
| Accra (capital) | 867,459 | Takoradi | 61,484 |
| Kumasi | 376,249 | Cape Coast | 57,224 |
| Tamale | 135,952 | Sekondi | 31,916 |
| Tema | 131,528 | | |

**BIRTHS AND DEATHS** (UN estimates, annual averages)

| | 1980–85 | 1985–90 | 1990–95 |
|---|---|---|---|
| Birth rate (per 1,000) | 45.0 | 43.1 | 40.1 |
| Death rate (per 1,000) | 13.1 | 11.9 | 10.6 |

**Expectation of life** (UN estimates, years at birth, 1990–95): 58.0 (males 56.3; females 59.7).

Source: UN, *World Population Prospects: The 1998 Revision.*

**ECONOMICALLY ACTIVE POPULATION** (1984 census)

| | Males | Females | Total |
|---|---|---|---|
| Agriculture, hunting, forestry and fishing | 1,750,024 | 1,560,943 | 3,310,967 |
| Mining and quarrying | 24,906 | 1,922 | 26,828 |
| Manufacturing | 198,430 | 389,988 | 588,418 |
| Electricity, gas and water | 14,033 | 1,404 | 15,437 |
| Construction | 60,692 | 3,994 | 64,686 |
| Trade, restaurants and hotels | 111,540 | 680,607 | 792,147 |
| Transport, storage and communications | 117,806 | 5,000 | 122,806 |
| Financing, insurance, real estate and business services | 19,933 | 7,542 | 27,475 |
| Community, social and personal services | 339,665 | 134,051 | 473,716 |
| **Total employed** | 2,637,029 | 2,785,451 | 5,422,480 |
| Unemployed | 87,452 | 70,172 | 157,624 |
| **Total labour force** | 2,724,481 | 2,855,623 | 5,580,104 |

Source: ILO, *Yearbook of Labour Statistics*.

**Mid-1998** (estimates in '000): Agriculture, etc. 5,212; Total 9,086 (Source: FAO, *Production Yearbook*).

# Agriculture

**PRINCIPAL CROPS** ('000 metric tons)

| | 1996 | 1997 | 1998 |
|---|---|---|---|
| Maize | 1,008 | 996 | 1,015 |
| Millet | 193 | 114 | 162 |
| Sorghum | 353 | 333 | 355 |
| Rice (paddy) | 216 | 197 | 281 |
| Sugar cane* | 110 | 110 | 110 |
| Cassava (Manioc) | 7,111 | 7,000 | 7,172 |
| Yams | 2,275 | 2,408 | 2,703 |
| Taro (Coco yam) | 1,552 | 1,530 | 1,577 |
| Onions* | 25 | 25 | 25 |
| Tomatoes* | 160 | 160 | 160 |
| Green chillies and peppers* | 70 | 70 | 70 |
| Eggplants (Aubergines)* | 6 | 6 | 6 |
| Pulses* | 15 | 16 | 16 |
| Oranges* | 50 | 50 | 50 |
| Lemons and limes* | 30 | 30 | 30 |
| Mangoes* | 4 | 4 | 4 |
| Bananas* | 4 | 4 | 4 |
| Plantains | 1,823 | 1,878 | 1,878* |
| Pineapples* | 35 | 35 | 35 |
| Palm kernels | 35† | 35* | 35* |
| Groundnuts (in shell) | 133 | 135* | 135* |
| Coconuts* | 240 | 240 | 240 |
| Copra* | 10 | 10 | 10 |
| Coffee (green) | 6 | 6* | 6* |
| Cocoa beans | 403 | 400† | 380† |
| Tobacco (leaves) | 1† | 2* | 2* |

* FAO estimate(s). † Unofficial figure.

Source: FAO, *Production Yearbook.*

**LIVESTOCK** ('000 head, year ending September)

| | 1996 | 1997 | 1998 |
|---|---|---|---|
| Horses* | 2 | 2 | 2 |
| Asses* | 13 | 13 | 13 |
| Cattle | 1,248 | 1,150* | 1,150* |
| Pigs | 318 | 395* | 395* |
| Sheep | 2,207 | 2,100* | 2,100* |
| Goats | 2,340 | 2,200* | 2,200* |

Poultry (million): 13 in 1996; 13* in 1997; 13* in 1998.

* FAO estimate(s).

Source: FAO, *Production Yearbook.*

**LIVESTOCK PRODUCTS** (FAO estimates, '000 metric tons)

| | 1996 | 1997 | 1998 |
|---|---|---|---|
| Beef and veal | 21 | 20 | 20 |
| Mutton and lamb | 6 | 6 | 7 |
| Goat meat | 5 | 6 | 6 |
| Pig meat | 8 | 9 | 9 |
| Poultry meat | 12 | 12 | 13 |
| Other meat | 91 | 91 | 89 |
| Cows' milk | 28 | 27 | 27 |
| Hen eggs | 14 | 14 | 14 |
| Cattle hides | 3 | 3 | 2 |

Source: FAO, *Production Yearbook.*

# Forestry

**ROUNDWOOD REMOVALS** ('000 cubic metres, excl. bark)

| | 1995 | 1996 | 1997 |
|---|---|---|---|
| Sawlogs, veneer logs and logs for sleepers | 1,194 | 1,166 | 1,166 |
| Other industrial wood | 89 | 89 | 89 |
| Fuel wood | 25,190 | 25,190 | 25,190 |
| **Total** | 26,473 | 26,445 | 26,445 |

Source: FAO, *Yearbook of Forest Products.*

**SAWNWOOD PRODUCTION** ('000 cubic metres, incl. railway sleepers)

| | 1995 | 1996 | 1997 |
|---|---|---|---|
| Coniferous (softwood)* | 54 | 54 | 54 |
| Broadleaved (hardwood) | 558 | 550 | 550* |
| **Total** | 612 | 604 | 604 |

* FAO estimate(s).

Source: FAO, *Yearbook of Forest Products.*

# Fishing

('000 metric tons, live weight)

| | 1995 | 1996 | 1997 |
|---|---|---|---|
| Freshwater fishes | 60.0 | 73.6 | 70.0 |
| Bigeye grunt | 14.8 | 13.6 | 19.8 |
| Jack and horse mackerels | 9.5 | 10.9 | 17.5 |
| Round sardinella | 67.8 | 118.4 | 49.4 |
| Madeiran sardinella | 13.2 | 13.6 | 14.2 |
| Other sardinellas | 14.1 | 20.1 | 36.0 |
| Bonga shad | 1.1 | 1.2 | 9.8 |
| European anchovy | 65.5 | 98.3 | 82.7 |
| Skipjack tuna | 18.6 | 21.4 | 28.5 |
| Yellowfin tuna | 9.3 | 11.4 | 18.4 |
| Chub mackerel | 12.5 | 15.6 | 19.9 |
| Other marine fishes (incl. unspecified) | 61.3 | 73.4 | 74.5 |
| Crustaceans and molluscs | 5.6 | 5.1 | 5.8 |
| **Total catch** | 353.3 | 476.6 | 446.5 |
| Inland waters | 60.0 | 73.6 | 70.0 |
| Atlantic Ocean | 293.3 | 403.0 | 376.5 |

Source: FAO, *Yearbook of Fishery Statistics.*

# Mining

('000 metric tons, unless otherwise indicated)

| | 1995 | 1996* | 1997* |
|---|---|---|---|
| Gold ('000 kilograms)† | 51.3 | 48.3 | 53.5 |
| Diamonds ('000 carats) | 622.7 | 714.3 | 585.5 |
| Manganese ore‡ | 100.0 | 266.8 | 333.4 |
| Bauxite | 513.0 | 383.4 | 500.7 |

* Estimates.

† Figures refer to the metal content of ores.

‡ Figures refer to gross weight. The estimated manganese content was 101,000 metric tons in 1996.

Source: IMF, *Ghana: Selected Issues* (January 1999).

# Industry

**SELECTED PRODUCTS** ('000 metric tons, unless otherwise indicated)

| | 1994 | 1995 | 1996 |
|---|---|---|---|
| Groundnut oil* | 25 | 21 | 17 |
| Coconut oil* | 6 | 6 | 6 |
| Palm oil* | 100 | 100 | 105 |
| Palm kernel oil* | 9 | 9 | 9 |
| Motor spirit (petrol)* | 215 | 218 | 218 |
| Kerosene* | 125 | 127 | 128 |
| Diesel and gas oil* | 214 | 215 | 215 |
| Cement | 1,350† | 1,400† | 1,575 |
| Aluminium (unwrought)‡§ | 140.7 | 135.4 | 137.0 |
| Electric energy (million kWh)* | 6,155 | 6,159 | 6,036 |

* Provisional or estimated figures.

† Data from US Bureau of Mines.

‡ Primary metal only.

§ Data from *World Metal Statistics* (London).

**1997 and 1998** (estimates, '000 metric tons): Groundnut oil 18, Coconut oil 6, Palm oil 100, Palm kernel oil 10.

Sources: FAO, *Quarterly Bulletin of Statistics;* UN, *Industrial Commodity Statistics Yearbook.*

# Finance

**CURRENCY AND EXCHANGE RATES**

**Monetary Units**

100 pesewas = 1 new cedi.

**Sterling, Dollar and Euro Equivalents** (30 September 1999)

£1 sterling = 4,450.0 cedis;
US $1 = 2,702.7 cedis;
€1 = 2,882.4 cedis;
10,000 cedis = £2.247 = $3.700 = €3.469.

**Average Exchange Rate** (cedis per US $)

1996 1,637.23
1997 2,050.17
1998 2,314.15

**GENERAL BUDGET** ('000 million new cedis)

| Revenue* | 1995 | 1996 | 1997 |
|---|---|---|---|
| Tax revenue | 1,138.5 | 1,710.6 | 2,070.0 |
| Taxes on income, profits and capital gains | 275.0 | 433.3 | 606.4 |
| Individual | 80.8 | 131.1 | 225.1 |
| Corporate | 157.2 | 242.3 | 293.1 |
| Other unallocated taxes on income | 37.0 | 59.9 | 88.3 |
| Domestic taxes on goods and services | 503.7 | 732.4 | 833.4 |
| General sales, turnover or value-added tax | 210.1 | 329.6 | 407.4 |
| Excises (excl. petroleum) | 69.6 | 112.6 | 111.6 |
| Petroleum revenue | 224.0 | 290.2 | 314.3 |
| Taxes on international trade and transactions | 359.9 | 544.9 | 630.2 |
| Import duties | 202.6 | 267.2 | 364.3 |
| Export duties | 157.2 | 277.7 | 265.9 |
| Non-tax revenue | 446.1 | 287.0 | 376.7 |
| **Total** | 1,584.6 | 1,997.5 | 2,446.7 |

| Expenditure† | 1993 | 1994‡ | 1995‡ |
|---|---|---|---|
| General public services | 83.9 | 145.4 | 93.6 |
| Defence | 39.5 | 30.9 | 34.5 |
| Public order and safety | 30.8 | 23.9 | 42.9 |
| Education | 179.2 | 207.6 | 258.7 |
| Health | 56.6 | 58.6 | 73.6 |
| Social security and welfare | 57.8 | 112.3 | 138.8 |
| Housing and community amenities | 12.4 | 16.8 | 48.7 |
| Other community and social services | 10.1 | 20.6 | — |
| Economic services | 129.7 | 137.3 | 199.3 |
| Agriculture, forestry and fishing | 28.4 | 26.8 | 18.5 |
| Mining, manufacturing and construction | 11.0 | 18.5 | 24.6 |
| Utilities | 7.0 | 12.8 | 21.5 |
| Transport and communications | 79.5 | 75.5 | 116.7 |
| Other economic services | 3.8 | 3.7 | 18.0 |
| Other purposes | 162.7 | 338.9 | 342.7 |
| Interest payments | 134.8 | 230.1 | 328.8 |
| **Sub-total** | 762.7 | 1,092.3 | 1,232.8 |
| Special efficiency payments§ | 50.8 | 64.0 | 51.4 |
| **Total** | 813.5 | 1,156.3 | 1,284.2 |
| Current | 694.3 | n.a. | n.a. |
| Capital | 135.3 | n.a. | n.a. |
| Adjustment for payment arrears‖ | –16.0 | n.a. | n.a. |

* Excluding grants received ('000 million new cedis): 280.1 in 1995; 291.1 in 1996; 262.2 in 1997. Also excluded are the proceeds from the divestiture of state-owned enterprises ('000 million new cedis): 106.2 in 1995; 143.5 in 1996; 105.7 in 1997.

† Excluding lending minus repayments ('000 million new cedis): 8.0 in 1993; 8.3 in 1994; 15.8 in 1995. Also excluded is capital expenditure resulting from foreign financing ('000 million new cedis): 286.9 in 1993; 456.0 in 1994; 564.8 in 1995.

‡ Excluding unallocable expenditure.

§ Including provision for redeployment, retraining and relocation of public-sector employees.

‖ Minus sign indicates an increase in arrears.

Source: IMF, *Ghana: Selected Issues* (January 1999).

**INTERNATIONAL RESERVES** (US $ million at 31 December)

| | 1996 | 1997 | 1998 |
|---|---|---|---|
| Gold* | 77.2 | n.a. | 77.8 |
| IMF special drawing rights | 2.2 | 3.4 | 59.7 |
| Reserve position in IMF | 25.0 | 23.4 | 24.5 |
| Foreign exchange | 801.5 | n.a. | 292.8 |
| **Total** | 905.9 | n.a. | 454.8 |

* National valuation.

Source: IMF, *International Financial Statistics.*

**MONEY SUPPLY** ('000 million new cedis at 31 December)

| | 1996 | 1997 | 1998 |
|---|---|---|---|
| Currency outside banks | 723.99 | 981.82 | 1,083.63 |
| Deposits of non-financial public enterprises | 7.87 | 6.32 | 3.17 |
| Demand deposits at deposit money banks | 482.14 | 776.54 | 982.53 |
| **Total money** (incl. others) | 1,215.72 | 1,767.26 | 2,073.12 |

Source: IMF, *International Financial Statistics.*

**COST OF LIVING** (Consumer Price Index; base: 1995 = 100)

| | 1996 | 1997 | 1998 |
|---|---|---|---|
| **All items** | 146.6 | 187.4 | 214.8 |

Source: IMF, *International Financial Statistics.*

**NATIONAL ACCOUNTS** ('000 million new cedis at current prices)

**National Income and Product**

| | 1995 | 1996 | 1997 |
|---|---|---|---|
| **GDP in purchasers' values** | 7,418.0 | 10,633.1 | 14,113.4 |
| Net factor income from abroad | −155.1 | −220.0 | 273.9 |
| **Gross national product** | 7,262.9 | 10,413.1 | 13,839.5 |
| *Less* Consumption of fixed capital | 359.8 | 560.5 | 996.7 |
| **National income in market prices** | 6,903.1 | 9,852.6 | 12,842.8 |

Source: IMF, *International Financial Statistics.*

**Expenditure on the Gross Domestic Product**

| | 1995 | 1996 | 1997 |
|---|---|---|---|
| Government final consumption expenditure | 921.7 | 1,345.0 | 1,743.8 |
| Private final consumption expenditure | 6,108.1 | 8,800.3 | 11,267.0 |
| Increase in stocks | 5.4 | 6.2 | 127.3 |
| Gross fixed capital formation | 1,028.1 | 1,464.2 | 3,338.2 |
| **Total domestic expenditure** | 8,063.3 | 11,615.7 | 16,476.3 |
| Exports of goods and services | 1,898.9 | 2,537.6 | 2,794.6 |
| *Less* Imports of goods and services | 2,544.2 | 3,520.1 | 5,157.5 |
| **GDP in purchasers' values** | 7,418.0 | 10,633.1 | 14,113.4 |
| **GDP at constant 1990 prices** | 2,530.3 | 2,661.1 | 2,796.7 |

Source: IMF, *International Financial Statistics.*

**Gross Domestic Product by Economic Activity**

| | 1995 | 1996 | 1997 |
|---|---|---|---|
| Agriculture and livestock | 2,351.0 | 3,440.0 | 3,848.7 |
| Forestry and logging | 211.0 | 297.0 | 477.2 |
| Fishing | 444.0 | 680.0 | 724.2 |
| Mining and quarrying | 371.0 | 536.0 | 719.8 |
| Manufacturing | 723.0 | 979.0 | 1,277.5 |
| Electricity, water and gas | 206.0 | 302.0 | 425.7 |
| Construction | 582.0 | 856.0 | 1,199.6 |
| Transport, storage and communications | 303.0 | 423.0 | 580.4 |
| Wholesale and retail trade | 465.0 | 654.0 | 917.0 |
| Finance, real estate and business services | 302.6 | 430.0 | 586.6 |
| Public administration, defence and other government services | 825.0 | 1,124.0 | 1,377.0 |
| Other community, social and personal services | 185.0 | 249.0 | 341.6 |
| Private non-profit services | 72.0 | 97.0 | 133.2 |
| **GDP at factor cost** | 7,040.6 | 10,067.0 | 12,608.5 |
| Indirect taxes, *less* subsidies | 712.0 | 1,272.0 | 1,504.9 |
| **GDP in purchasers' values** | 7,752.6 | 11,339.0 | 14,113.4 |

Source: IMF, *Ghana: Selected Issues* (January 1999).

**BALANCE OF PAYMENTS** (US $ million)

| | 1996 | 1997 | 1998 |
|---|---|---|---|
| Exports of goods f.o.b. | 1,570.1 | 1,489.9 | 1,813.2 |
| Imports of goods f.o.b. | −1,937.0 | −2,128.2 | −2,346.0 |
| **Trade balance** | −366.9 | −638.3 | −532.8 |
| Exports of services | 156.8 | 164.9 | 175.9 |
| Imports of services | −456.4 | −505.0 | −540.5 |
| **Balance on goods and services** | −666.5 | −978.4 | −897.4 |
| Other income received | 23.5 | 26.7 | 26.7 |
| Other income paid | −163.4 | −158.1 | −163.0 |
| **Balance on goods, services and income** | −806.4 | −1,109.8 | −1,033.7 |
| Current transfers received | 497.9 | 576.5 | 701.0 |
| Current transfers paid | −16.2 | −16.4 | −17.1 |
| **Current balance** | −324.7 | −549.7 | −349.8 |
| Capital account (net) | −1.0 | −1.0 | −1.0 |
| Direct investment from abroad | 120.0 | 82.6 | 55.8 |
| Other investment assets | −179.4 | 33.1 | 87.9 |
| Other investment liabilities | 344.5 | 378.1 | 215.3 |
| Net errors and omissions | 20.2 | 83.7 | 99.6 |
| **Overall balance** | −20.4 | 26.7 | 107.8 |

Source: IMF, *International Financial Statistics.*

# External Trade

**PRINCIPAL COMMODITIES** (US $ million)

| Imports | 1996 | 1997 | 1998 |
|---|---|---|---|
| Food and live animals | 267.4 | 361.1 | 536.2 |
| Rice | 53.8 | 46.5 | 106.0 |
| Mineral fuels, lubricants, etc. | 55.4 | 341.8 | 159.5 |
| Crude petroleum | 21.5 | 139.1 | 97.1 |
| Petroleum products | 30.6 | 200.7 | 52.0 |
| Chemicals | 100.7 | 110.6 | 100.7 |
| Machinery and transport equipment | 876.7 | 1,270.8 | 1,293.0 |
| Passenger cars (incl. buses) | 127.7 | 114.5 | 154.9 |
| Lorries and trucks | 134.7 | 224.0 | 229.8 |
| Miscellaneous manufactured articles | 105.9 | 116.1 | 40.3 |
| **Total** (incl. others) | 2,839.7 | 3,033.6 | 3,329.8 |

| Exports | 1996 | 1997 | 1998 |
|---|---|---|---|
| Cocoa beans | 494.7 | 384.8 | 541.6 |
| Cocoa products | 73.2 | 92.7 | 78.2 |
| Timber and timber products | 147.8 | 170.5 | 171.0 |
| Gold | 681.6 | 545.1 | 679.4 |
| Electricity | 58.2 | 67.6 | 40.9 |
| **Total** (incl. others) | 1,698.0 | 1,753.7 | 1,811.6 |

Source: Ministry of Trade and Industry, Accra.

**PRINCIPAL TRADING PARTNERS** (US $ million)

| Imports | 1996 | 1997 | 1998 |
|---|---|---|---|
| Belgium | 68.1 | 87.7 | 136.7 |
| China, People's Repub. | 96.7 | 76.0 | 105.8 |
| France | 123.6 | 118.5 | 129.2 |
| Germany | 341.6 | 237.6 | 277.4 |
| India | 72.2 | 61.7 | 77.5 |
| Italy | 108.6 | 130.3 | 152.7 |
| Japan | 176.0 | 167.0 | 159.9 |
| Korea, Republic | 59.8 | 68.3 | 110.2 |
| Netherlands | 108.9 | 146.6 | 153.2 |
| Nigeria | 262.5 | 163.6 | 44.9 |
| South Africa | 48.1 | 70.5 | 90.6 |
| Spain | 82.1 | 77.4 | 102.2 |
| United Kingdom | 453.1 | 472.8 | 383.8 |
| USA | 360.7 | 395.2 | 390.0 |
| **Total** (incl. others) | 2,839.7 | 3,033.6 | 3,329.8 |

| Exports | 1996 | 1997 | 1998 |
|---|---|---|---|
| Belgium | 32.3 | 35.3 | 65.4 |
| France | 60.5 | 80.5 | 77.8 |
| Germany | 142.6 | 117.8 | 93.8 |
| Italy | 44.8 | 49.7 | 57.0 |
| Japan | 58.4 | 75.1 | 55.3 |
| Netherlands | 165.3 | 211.8 | 202.4 |
| South Africa | 6.1 | 3.2 | 41.3 |
| Spain | 31.3 | 31.9 | 31.9 |
| Switzerland | 486.3 | 437.1 | 418.0 |
| Togo | 19.0 | 14.9 | 60.0 |
| United Kingdom | 369.5 | 284.4 | 364.5 |
| USA | 49.2 | 33.8 | 69.2 |
| **Total** (incl. others) | 1,639.8 | 1,586.1 | 1,770.6 |

Source: Ministry of Trade and Industry, Accra.

# Transport

**RAILWAYS** (traffic)

| | 1996 |
|---|---|
| Passengers carried ('000) | 2,100 |
| Freight carried ('000 metric tons) | 857 |
| Passenger-km (million) | 208 |
| Net ton-km (million) | 152.8 |

Source: *Railway Directory*.

**ROAD TRAFFIC** ('000 motor vehicles in use at 31 December)

| | 1994 | 1995* | 1996* |
|---|---|---|---|
| Passenger cars | 90.0 | 90.0 | 90.0 |
| Lorries and vans | 44.7 | 45.0 | 45.0 |

* Estimates.

Source: International Road Federation, *World Road Statistics*.

**SHIPPING**

**Merchant Fleet** (registered at 31 December)

| | 1996 | 1997 | 1998 |
|---|---|---|---|
| Number of vessels | 195 | 206 | 205 |
| Total displacement ('000 grt) | 134.7 | 129.7 | 115.5 |

Source: Lloyd's Register of Shipping.

**International Sea-borne Freight Traffic**
(estimates, '000 metric tons)

| | 1991 | 1992 | 1993 |
|---|---|---|---|
| Goods loaded | 2,083 | 2,279 | 2,424 |
| Goods unloaded | 2,866 | 2,876 | 2,904 |

Source: UN Economic Commission for Africa, *African Statistical Yearbook*.

**CIVIL AVIATION** (traffic on scheduled services)

| | 1993 | 1994 | 1995 |
|---|---|---|---|
| Kilometres flown (million) | 4 | 5 | 5 |
| Passengers carried ('000) | 152 | 182 | 186 |
| Passenger-km (million) | 387 | 478 | 611 |
| Total ton-km (million) | 61 | 72 | 86 |

Source: UN, *Statistical Yearbook*.

# Tourism

**ARRIVALS BY NATIONALITY**

| | 1994 | 1995 | 1996 |
|---|---|---|---|
| Côte d'Ivoire | 13,044 | 13,750 | 14,657 |
| France | 9,804 | 10,334 | 11,016 |
| Germany | 13,090 | 13,799 | 14,709 |
| Liberia | 7,116 | 7,500 | 7,995 |
| Netherlands | 6,568 | 6,924 | 7,380 |
| Nigeria | 37,238 | 39,254 | 41,842 |
| Togo | 8,120 | 8,560 | 9,124 |
| United Kingdom | 23,490 | 24,762 | 26,395 |
| USA | 17,896 | 18,864 | 20,108 |
| **Total** (incl. others)* | 271,310 | 286,000 | 304,860 |

* Includes Ghanaian nationals resident abroad: 73,851 in 1994; 77,850 in 1995; 82,984 in 1996.

Source: World Tourism Organization, *Yearbook of Tourism Statistics*.

**Receipts from tourism** (US $ million): 228 in 1994; 233 in 1995; 248 in 1996 (Source: mainly UN, *Statistical Yearbook*).

**1997:** Tourist arrivals 325,000; Receipts from tourism US $266m. (Source: Ghana Tourist Board).

## Communications Media

| | 1994 | 1995 | 1996 |
|---|---|---|---|
| Radio receivers ('000 in use) | 3,880 | 4,000 | 4,250 |
| Television receivers ('000 in use) | 1,500 | 1,600 | 1,650 |
| Telephones ('000 main lines in use) | 50 | 60 | n.a. |
| Telefax stations (number in use) | 4,500 | n.a. | n.a. |
| Mobile cellular telephones (subscribers) | 3,336 | 6,200 | n.a. |
| Daily newspapers | | | |
| Number | 4 | 4 | 4 |
| Average circulation ('000 copies) | 310* | 310* | 250,000 |

* Provisional or estimated figure.

Sources: UNESCO, *Statistical Yearbook*; UN, *Statistical Yearbook*.

## Education

(1989/90, unless otherwise indicated)

| | Institutions | Teachers | Students |
|---|---|---|---|
| Pre-primary | 4,735 | 15,152 | 323,406 |
| Primary[1] | 11,064 | 72,925[2] | 2,011,602 |
| Secondary | | | |
| General (public only) | n.a. | 39,903[3] | 841,722[1] |
| Teacher training | 38[4] | 1,001 | 15,723 |
| Vocational (public only) | 20[5] | 1,247 | 22,578[1] |
| University | 3[5] | 700[6] | 9,609[3] |

[1] 1991/92 figure(s).
[2] Provisional figure.
[3] 1990/91 figure.
[4] 1988 figure.
[5] 1988/89 figure.
[6] Excluding the University of Ghana.

Source: mainly UNESCO, *Statistical Yearbook*.

**1992:** *Primary* 10,623 institutions, 1,800,000 students (estimate); *Junior secondary* 5,136 institutions, 569,000 students (estimate); *Senior secondary* 404 institutions, 147,000 students (estimate); *Higher* 52,000 students.

Source: African Development Bank.

# Directory

## The Constitution

Under the terms of the Constitution of the Fourth Republic, which was approved by national referendum on 28 April 1992, Ghana has a multi-party political system. Executive power is vested in the President, who is Head of State and Commander-in-Chief of the Armed Forces. The President is elected by universal adult suffrage for a term of four years, and appoints a Vice-President. The duration of the President's tenure of office is limited to two four-year terms. It is also stipulated that, in the event that no presidential candidate receives more than 50% of votes cast, a new election between the two candidates with the highest number of votes is to take place within 21 days. Legislative power is vested in a 200-member unicameral Parliament, which is elected by direct adult suffrage for a four-year term. The Council of Ministers is appointed by the President, subject to approval by the Parliament. The Constitution also provides for a 25-member Council of State, principally comprising presidential nominees and regional representatives, and a 20-member National Security Council (chaired by the Vice-President), both of which act as advisory bodies to the President.

## The Government

### HEAD OF STATE

**President and Commander-in-Chief of the Armed Forces:** Flt-Lt (retd) JERRY JOHN RAWLINGS (assumed power as Chairman of Provisional National Defence Council 31 December 1981; elected President 3 November 1992; re-elected 7 December 1996).

**Vice-President:** Prof. JOHN EVANS ATTA MILLS.

### COUNCIL OF MINISTERS

(February 2000)

**Minister of Defence:** Lt-Col ENOCH K. T. DONKOH.

**Minister of National Security:** KOFI TOTOBI-QUAKYI.

**Minister of Finance:** RICHARD KWAME PEPRAH.

**Minister of Parliamentary Affairs:** Dr KWABENA ADJEI.

**Minister of Foreign Affairs:** JAMES VICTOR GBEHO.

**Attorney-General and Minister of Justice:** Dr OBED ASAMOAH.

**Minister of Local Government:** CECILIA JOHNSON.

**Minister of Education:** EKWOW SPIO-GARBRAH.

**Minister of the Interior:** NII OKAIDJA ADAMAFIO.

**Minister of Food and Agriculture:** J. H. OWUSU-ACHEAMPONG.

**Minister of Health:** Dr KWAME DANSO-BUAFO.

**Minister of Roads and Transport:** EDWARD SALIA.

**Minister of Tourism:** MIKE GIZO.

**Minister of Trade and Industry:** DAN ABODAKPI.

**Minister of Youth and Sports:** ENOCH T. MENSAH.

**Minister of Lands and Forestry:** Dr CHRISTINA AMOAKO-NUAMA.

**Minister of Works and Housing:** ISAAC ADJEI-MENSAH.

**Minister of Communications:** JOHN MAHAMA.

**Minister of Employment and Social Welfare:** Alhaji MOHAMMED MUMUNI.

**Minister of the Environment, Science and Technology:** CLETUS APUL AVOKA.

**Minister of Mines and Energy:** Dr JOHN EBU.

**Minister of State for Planning and Regional Economic Co-operation and Integration:** KWAMENA AHWOI.

**Minister of State at the Presidency responsible for Chieftancy Affairs and State Protocol:** D. O. AGYEKUM.

**Presidential Staffer:** JOHN E. AFFUL.

### REGIONAL MINISTERS

(February 2000)

**Ashanti:** KOJO YANKAH.

**Brong Ahafo:** DAVID OSEI-WUSU.

**Central:** JACOB ARTHUR.

**Eastern:** PATIENCE AIDOW.

**Greater Accra:** JOSHUA ALABI.

**Northern:** Alhaji SEIDU IDDI.

**Upper East:** DONALD ADABRE.

**Upper West:** Alhaji AMIDU SULEMANA.

**Volta:** Lt-Col CHARLES K. AGBENAZA.

**Western:** ESTHER LILY NKANSAH.

### MINISTRIES

**Office of the President:** POB 1627, Osu, Accra.

**Ministry of Communications:** POB M41, Accra; tel. (21) 228011; fax (21) 229786.

**Ministry of Defence:** Burma Camp, Accra; tel. (21) 777611; fax (21) 773951.

**Ministry of Education:** POB M45, Accra; tel. (21) 665421; fax (21) 664067.

**Ministry of Employment and Social Welfare:** POB M84, Accra; tel. (21) 665421; fax (21) 667251.

**Ministry of the Environment, Science and Technology:** POB M232, Accra; tel. (21) 662626; fax (21) 666828; e-mail barnes@africaonline.com.gh.

**Ministry of Finance:** POB M40, Accra; tel. (21) 665441; fax (21) 667069; internet www.finance.gov.gh.

**Ministry of Food and Agriculture:** POB M37, Accra; tel. (21) 665421; fax (21) 663250; e-mail mofa@africaonline.com.gh.

**Ministry of Foreign Affairs:** POB M53, Accra; tel. (21) 664951; fax (21) 665363.

**Ministry of Health:** POB M44, Accra; tel. (21) 665421; fax (21) 663810.

**Ministry of the Interior:** POB M42, Accra; tel. (21) 665421; fax (21) 667450.

**Ministry of Justice:** POB M60, Accra.

**Ministry of Lands and Forestry:** POB M212, Accra; tel. (21) 665421; fax (21) 666801.

**Ministry of Local Government:** POB M50, Accra; tel. (21) 665421; fax (21) 661015.

**Ministry of Mines and Energy:** POB M212, Accra; tel. (21) 667151; fax (21) 668262.

**Ministry of National Security:** Accra.

**Ministry of Parliamentary Affairs:** Parliament House, Accra; tel. (21) 664716.

**Ministry of Roads and Transport:** POB M38, Accra; tel. (21) 665421; fax (21) 668340.

**Ministry of Tourism:** POB 4386, Accra; tel. (21) 666701; fax (21) 666182.

**Ministry of Trade and Industry:** POB M85, Accra; tel. (21) 665421; fax (21) 664115.

**Ministry of Works and Housing:** POB M43, Accra; tel. (21) 665421; fax (21) 663268.

**Ministry of Youth and Sports:** POB 1272, Accra; tel. (21) 665421; fax (21) 663927.

# President and Legislature

### PRESIDENT

**Presidential Election, 7 December 1996**

| Candidates | % of votes |
|---|---|
| Flt-Lt (retd) JERRY RAWLINGS (NDC) | 57.2 |
| JOHN KUFUOR (Great Alliance*) | 39.8 |
| EDWARD MAHAMA (PNC) | 3.0 |
| **Total** | 100 |

* An electoral coalition comprising the New Patriotic Party (NPP) and the People's Convention Party (PCP).

### PARLIAMENT

**Speaker:** Justice DANIEL F. ANNAN.

**Legislative Election, 7 December 1996**

| | Seats |
|---|---|
| National Democratic Congress (NDC) | 133 |
| New Patriotic Party (NPP) | 60 |
| People's Convention Party (PCP)* | 5 |
| People's National Convention (PNC) | 1 |
| **Total†** | 200 |

* Merged with the non-parliamentary National Convention Party to form the Convention Party in August 1998.

† Voting in one constituency was postponed. At a by-election in June 1997 the seat was won by the NPP.

### COUNCIL OF STATE

**Chairman:** Alhaji MUMUNI BAWUMIA.

# Political Organizations

**Convention Party (CP):** Accra; f. 1998 by merger of the National Convention Party (f. 1992) and the People's Convention Party (f. 1993); Nkrumahist.

**Democratic People's Party (DPP):** Accra; f. 1992; Chair. T. N. WARD-BREW.

**EGLE (Every Ghanaian Living Everywhere) Party:** Accra; pro-Govt alliance; Co-Chair. OWORAKU AMOFA, Capt. NII OKAI.

**Ghana Democratic Republican Party (GDRP):** Accra; f. 1992; Leader Dr KOFI AMOAH.

**Great Consolidated People's Party (GCPP):** Leader DAN LARTEY; Chair. E. B. MENSAH.

**National Democratic Congress (NDC):** Tamale; f. 1992; pro-Govt alliance; Leader Flt-Lt (retd) JERRY JOHN RAWLINGS; Chair. Alhaji ISSIFU ALI; Sec.-Gen. Alhaji HUUDU YAHAYA.

**National Reform Party (NRP):** Accra; f. June 1999 by a breakaway group of the National Democratic Congress; Nat. Chair. PETER KPORDUGBE (acting); Nat. Sec. KYERETWIE OPOKU (acting).

**New Patriotic Party (NPP):** Private Mail Bag, Accra-North; tel. (21) 227951; fax (21) 224418; e-mail npp@africaonline.com.gh; f. 1992 by supporters of the fmr Prime Minister, Dr Kofi Busia, and Dr J. B. Danquah; Chair SAMUEL ARTHUR ODOI-SYKES; Sec.-Gen. DANIEL BOTWE.

**People's National Convention (PNC):** Accra; f. 1992 by supporters of the fmr Pres., Dr Kwame Nkrumah; Chair. EDWARD MAHAMA; Pres. JOHN EDWIN.

**United Ghana Movement (UGM):** Accra.

# Diplomatic Representation

### EMBASSIES AND HIGH COMMISSIONS IN GHANA

**Algeria:** 22 Josif Broz Tito Ave, POB 2747, Accra; tel. (21) 776719; fax (21) 776828; Ambassador: HASSANE RABEHI.

**Benin:** 19 Volta St, Second Close, Airport Residential Area, POB 7871, Accra; tel. (21) 774860; fax (21) 774889; Ambassador: SÊDJORO THÉOPHILE HOUESSINON.

**Brazil:** 24 Sir Arku Korsah Rd, Roman Ridge Ambassadorial Area, POB CT 3859, Accra; tel. (21) 774921; fax (21) 778566; e-mail brasemb@ighmail.com; Ambassador: PAULO AMÉRICO V. WOLOWSKI.

**Bulgaria:** 3 Kakramadu Rd, East Cantonments, POB 3193, Accra; tel. (21) 772404; fax (21) 774231; e-mail bulembgh@ghana.com; Chargé d'affaires: GEORGE MITEV.

**Burkina Faso:** 772/3, Asylum Down, off Farrar Ave, POB 651, Accra; tel. (21) 221988; Ambassador: EMILE GOUBA.

**Canada:** No. 46, Independence Ave, POB 1639, Accra; tel. (21) 228555; fax (21) 773792; High Commissioner: (vacant).

**China, People's Republic:** No. 7, Agostinho Neto Rd, Airport Residential Area, POB 3356, Accra; tel. (21) 774527; Ambassador: LI ZUPEI.

**Côte d'Ivoire:** F710/2 18th Lane, off Cantonments Rd, POB 3445, Christiansborg, Accra; tel. (21) 774611; fax (21) 773516; Ambassador: AMON TANOE EMMANUEL.

**Cuba:** 20 Amilcar Cabral Rd, Airport Residential Area, POB 9163 Airport, Accra; tel. (21) 775868; Ambassador: JUAN CARRETERO.

**Czech Republic:** C260/5, Kanda High Rd No. 2, POB 5226, Accra-North; tel. (21) 223540; fax (21) 225337; e-mail accraczemb@ighmail.com; Ambassador: JINDŘICH JUNEK.

**Denmark:** 67 Dr Isert Rd, 8th Ave Extension, North Ridge, POB C596, Accra; tel. (21) 226972; fax (21) 228061; e-mail accamb@accamab.um.dk; Ambassador: OLE BLICHER-OLSEN.

**Egypt:** 27 Fetreke St, Roman Ridge Ambassadorial Estate, POB 2508, Accra; tel. (21) 776925; fax (21) 776795; Ambassador: MOHAMED EL-ZAYAT.

**Ethiopia:** 6 Adiembra Rd, East Cantonments, POB 1646, Accra; tel. (21) 775928; fax (21) 776807; Ambassador: Dr KUWANG TUTILAM.

**France:** 12th Rd, off Liberation Ave, POB 187, Accra; tel. (21) 774480; fax (21) 778321; Ambassador: DIDIER FERRAND.

**Germany:** Valdemosa Lodge, Ridge Rd No. 6, North Ridge, POB 1757, Accra; tel. (21) 221311; fax (21) 221347; Ambassador: CHRISTIAN NAKONZ.

**Guinea:** 11 Osu Badu St, Dzorwulu, POB 5497, Accra-North; tel. (21) 777921; fax (21) 760961; Ambassador: DORE DIALE DRUS.

**Holy See:** 8 Drake Ave, Airport Residential Area, POB 9675, Accra; tel. (21) 777759; fax (21) 774019; Apostolic Nuncio: Most Rev. ANDRÉ DUPUY, Titular Archbishop of Selsea (Selsey).

**Hungary:** 14 West Cantonments, off Switchback Rd, POB 3072, Accra; tel. (21) 777234; Chargé d'affaires a.i.: IMRE SOSOVICSKA.

**India:** 9 Ridge Rd, Roman Ridge, POB 3040, Accra; tel. (21) 775601; fax (21) 772176; High Commissioner: DILJIT SINGH PANNUN.

**Iran:** 12 Sir Arku Korsah St, Roman Ridge, POB 12673, Accra North; tel. (21) 777043; Ambassador: KIUMARS FOTUHI-QIYAM.

**Italy:** Jawaharlal Nehru Rd, POB 140, Accra; tel. (21) 775621; e-mail ambital@ghana.com; Ambassador: MARIO FUGAZZOLA.

**Japan:** 5th Ave Extension, West Cantonments, POB 1637, Accra; tel. (21) 765066; fax (21) 762553; Ambassador: SHOSUKE ITO.

**Korea, Democratic People's Republic:** 139 Nortei Ababio Loop, Ambassadorial Estate, POB 13874, Accra; tel. (21) 777825; Ambassador: RI JAE SONG.

**Korea, Republic:** 3 Abokobi Rd, East Cantonments, POB 13700, Accra North; tel. (21) 776157; Ambassador: HWANG PU-HONG.

**Lebanon:** F864/1 off Cantonments Rd, OSU, POB 562, Accra; tel. (21) 776727; fax (21) 764290; e-mail lebanon@ighmail.com; Ambassador: CHARBEL AOUN.

**Liberia:** 10 West Cantonments, off Jawaharlal Nehru Rd, POB 895, Accra; tel. (21) 775641; Ambassador: ELWOOD GREAVES.

**Libya:** 14 Sixth St, Airport Residential Area, POB 9665, Accra; tel. (21) 774820; Secretary of People's Bureau: Dr FATIMA MAGAME.

**Mali:** Agostino Neto Rd, Airport Residential Area, POB 1121, Accra; tel. (21) 666423; Ambassador: MUPHTAH AG HAIRY.

**Netherlands:** 89 Liberation Rd, Thomas Sankara Circle, POB 3248, Accra; tel. (21) 773644; fax (21) 773655; Ambassador: HELN C. R. M. PRINCEN.

**Niger:** E104/3 Independence Ave, POB 2685, Accra; tel. (21) 224962; Ambassador: OUMAROU YOUSSOUFOU.

**Nigeria:** Josif Broz Tito Ave, POB 1548, Accra; tel. (21) 776158; High Commissioner: T. A. OLU-OTUNLA.

**Pakistan:** 11 Ring Rd East, Danquah Circle, POB 1114, Accra; tel. (21) 776059; High Commissioner: Dr ABDUL KABIR.

**Poland:** 2 Akosombo St, Airport Residential Area, POB 2552, Accra; tel. (21) 775972; fax (21) 776108; Chargé d'affaires a.i.: KAZIMIERZ MAURER.

**Romania:** North Labone, Ward F, Block 6, House 262, POB 3735, Accra; tel. (21) 774076; Chargé d'affaires a.i.: GHEORGHE V. ILIE.

**Russia:** 856/1, 13th Lane, Ring Rd East, Osu, POB 1634, Accra; tel. (21) 775611; fax (21) 772699; e-mail russia@ghana.com; Ambassador: PAVEL D. PAVLOV.

**Saudi Arabia:** 10 Noi Fetreke St, Roman Ridge, Airport Residential Area, POB 670, Accra; tel. (21) 774311; Chargé d'affaires a.i.: ANWAR ABDUL FATTAH ABDRABBUH.

**South Africa:** 10 Klottey Crescent, Labone North, POB 298, Accra; tel. (21) 762380; fax (21) 762381; e-mail sahcgh@africaonline.com.gh; High Commissioner: JOSIAH MOTSEPE.

**Spain:** Drake Ave Extension, Airport Residential Area, POB 1218, Accra; tel. (21) 774004; fax (21) 776217; Ambassador: FERNANDO CORRAL.

**Switzerland:** 9 Water Rd S.I., North Ridge Area, POB 359, Accra; tel. (21) 228125; fax (21) 223583; Ambassador: PETER SCHWEIZER.

**Togo:** Togo House, near Cantonments Circle, POB C120, Accra; tel. (21) 777950; fax (21) 777961; Ambassador: ASSIONGBOR FOLIVI.

**United Kingdom:** Osu Link, off Gamel Abdul Nasser Ave, POB 296, Accra; tel. (21) 221665; fax (21) 7010655; e-mail high.commission@accra.mail.fco.gov.uk; High Commissioner: IAN W. MACKLEY.

**USA:** Ring Road East, POB 194, Accra; tel. (21) 775347; fax (21) 776008; internet www.usia.gov/posts/ghana; Ambassador: KATHRYN DEE ROBINSON.

**Yugoslavia:** 47 Senchi St, Airport Residential Area, POB 1629, Accra; tel. (21) 775761; Ambassador: LAZAR COVIĆ.

# Judicial System

The civil law in force in Ghana is based on the Common Law, doctrines of equity and general statutes which were in force in England in 1874, as modified by subsequent Ordinances. Ghanaian customary law is, however, the basis of most personal, domestic and contractual relationships. Criminal Law is based on the Criminal Procedure Code, 1960, derived from English Criminal Law, and since amended. The Superior Court of Judicature comprises a Supreme Court, a Court of Appeal, a High Court and a Regional Tribunal; Inferior Courts include Circuit Courts, Circuit Tribunals, Community Tribunals and such other Courts as may be designated by law.

**Supreme Court:** Consists of the Chief Justice and not fewer than nine other Justices. It is the final court of appeal in Ghana and has jurisdiction in matters relating to the enforcement or interpretation of the Constitution.

**Chief Justice:** ISAAC KOBINA ABBAN.

**Court of Appeal:** Consists of the Chief Justice and not fewer than five Judges of the Court of Appeal. It has jurisdiction to hear and determine appeals from any judgment, decree or order of the High Court.

**High Court:** Comprises the Chief Justice and not fewer than 12 Justices of the High Court. It exercises original jurisdiction in all matters, civil and criminal, other than those for offences involving treason. Trial by jury is practised in criminal cases in Ghana and the Criminal Procedure Code, 1960, provides that all trials on indictment shall be by a jury or with the aid of Assessors.

**Circuit Courts:** Exercise original jurisdiction in civil matters where the amount involved does not exceed C100,000. They also have jurisdiction with regard to the guardianship and custody of infants, and original jurisdiction in all criminal cases, except offences where the maximum punishment is death or the offence of treason. They have appellate jurisdiction from decisions of any District Court situated within their respective circuits.

**District Courts:** To each magisterial district is assigned at least one District Magistrate who has original jurisdiction to try civil suits in which the amount involved does not exceed C50,000. District Magistrates also have jurisdiction to deal with all criminal cases, except first-degree felonies, and commit cases of a more serious nature to either the Circuit Court or the High Court. A Grade I District Court can impose a fine not exceeding C1,000 and sentences of imprisonment of up to two years and a Grade II District Court may impose a fine not exceeding C500 and a sentence of imprisonment of up to 12 months. A District Court has no appellate jurisdiction, except in rent matters under the Rent Act.

**Juvenile Courts:** Jurisdiction in cases involving persons under 17 years of age, except where the juvenile is charged jointly with an adult. The Courts comprise a Chairman, who must be either the District Magistrate or a lawyer, and not fewer than two other members appointed by the Chief Justice in consultation with the Judicial Council. The Juvenile Courts can make orders as to the protection and supervision of a neglected child and can negotiate with parents to secure the good behaviour of a child.

**National Public Tribunal:** Considers appeals from the Regional Public Tribunals. Its decisions are final and are not subject to any further appeal. The Tribunal consists of at least three members and not more than five, one of whom acts as Chairman.

**Regional Public Tribunals:** Hears criminal cases relating to prices, rent or exchange control, theft, fraud, forgery, corruption or any offence which may be referred to them by the Provisional National Defence Council.

**Special Military Tribunal:** Hears criminal cases involving members of the armed forces. It consists of between five and seven members.

# Religion

At the 1960 census the distribution of religious groups was: Christians 42.8%, traditional religions 38.2%, Muslims 12.0%, unclassified 7.0%.

## CHRISTIANITY

**Christian Council of Ghana:** POB 919, Accra; tel. (21) 776725; f. 1929; advisory body comprising 14 Protestant churches; Chair. (vacant); Gen. Sec. Rev. DAVID A. DARTEY.

### The Anglican Communion

Anglicans in Ghana are adherents of the Church of the Province of West Africa, comprising 12 dioceses, of which seven are in Ghana.

**Archbishop of the Province of West Africa and Bishop of Koforidua:** Most Rev. ROBERT OKINE, POB 980, Koforidua; tel. (81) 2329.

**Bishop of Accra:** Rt Rev. JUSTICE OFEI AKROFI, Bishopscourt, POB 8, Accra; tel. (21) 669125.

**Bishop of Cape Coast:** Rt Rev. KOBINA QUASHIE, Bishopscourt, POB A233, Cape Coast; tel. (42) 2637.

**Bishop of Kumasi:** Rt Rev. DANIEL YINKAH SARFO, Bishop's Office, POB 144, Kumasi; tel. and fax (51) 24117.

**Bishop of Sekondi:** (vacant), POB 85, Sekondi; tel. (21) 6048; fax (21) 669125.

**Bishop of Sunyani:** Rt Rev. THOMAS AMPAH BRIENT, Bishop's House, POB 23, Sunyani; fax (61) 7023; e-mail deegyab@ighmail.com.

**Bishop of Tamale:** Rt Rev. EMMANUEL ARONGO, POB 110, Tamale; tel. (71) 2018; fax (71) 22849.

### The Roman Catholic Church

Ghana comprises three archdioceses and 15 dioceses. At 31 December 1997 there were 2,341,401 adherents in the country, equivalent to 13.1% of the total population.

**Ghana Bishops' Conference:** National Catholic Secretariat, POB 9712, Airport, Accra; tel. (21) 500491; fax (21) 500493; f. 1960; Pres. Most Rev. PETER K. APPIAH-TURKSON, Archbishop of Cape Coast.

**Archbishop of Accra:** Most Rev. DOMINIC KODWO ANDOH, Chancery Office, POB 247, Accra; tel. (21) 222728; fax (21) 231619.

**Archbishop of Cape Coast:** Most Rev. PETER KODWO APPIAH-TURKSON, Archbishop's House, POB 112, Cape Coast; tel. (42) 33471; fax (42) 33473.

**Archbishop of Tamale:** Most Rev. GREGORY EBO KPIEBAYA, Gumbehini Rd, POB 163, Tamale; tel. (71) 22425; fax (71) 22425.

### Other Christian Churches

**African Methodist Episcopal Zion Church:** Sekondi; Pres. Rev. Dr ZORMELO.

**Christian Methodist Episcopal Church:** POB 3906, Accra; Pres. Rev. YENN BATA.

**Evangelical-Lutheran Church of Ghana:** POB 197, Kaneshie; tel. (21) 223487; fax (21) 223353; Pres. Rt Rev. Dr PAUL KOFI FYNN; 21,700 mems.

**Evangelical-Presbyterian Church:** POB 18, Ho; tel. (91) 755; f. 1847; Moderator Rt Rev. D. A. KORANTENG; 295,000 mems.

**Ghana Baptist Convention:** POB 1979, Kumasi; tel. (51) 5215; f. 1963; Pres. Rev. FRED DEEGBE; Sec. Rev. FRANK ADAMS.

**Mennonite Church:** POB 5485, Accra; fax (21) 220589; f. 1957; Moderator Rev. Dr TEI-KWABLA; Sec. ISAAC K. QUARTEY; 4,800 mems.

**Methodist Church of Ghana:** Liberia Rd, POB 403, Accra; tel. (21) 228120; fax (21) 227008; Pres. Rt Rev. Dr SAMUEL ASANTE ANTWI; Sec. Rev. MACLEAN AGYIRI KUMI; 341,000 mems.

**Presbyterian Church of Ghana:** POB 1800, Accra; tel. (21) 662511; fax (21) 665594; f. 1828; Moderator Rt Rev. ANTHONY ANTWI BEEKO; Sec. Rev. Dr D. N. A. KPOBI; 422,500 mems.

**Seventh-day Adventists:** POB 1016, Accra; tel. (21) 223720. 1943; Pres. P. K. ASAREH; Sec. SETH A. LARYEA.

The African Methodist Episcopal Church, the F'Eden Church and the Society of Friends (Quakers) are also active in Ghana.

### ISLAM

There is a substantial Muslim population in the Northern Region. The majority are Malikees.

**Chief Imam:** CHEICK USMAN NUBUSHARABUTU.

## The Press

### DAILY NEWSPAPERS

**Daily Graphic:** Graphic Rd, POB 742, Accra; tel. (21) 228911; fax (21) 669886; f. 1950; state-owned; Editor ELVIS ARYEH; circ. 100,000.

**Evening News:** POB 7505, Accra; tel. (21) 229416; Man. Editor OSEI POKU; circ. 30,000.

**The Ghanaian Times:** New Times Corpn, Ring Rd West, POB 2638, Accra; tel. (21) 228282; fax (21) 229398; e-mail newtimes@ghana.com; internet www.gtimes.com.gh; f. 1958; state-owned; Editor BOB BENTIL (acting); circ. 45,000.

**The Pioneer:** Abura Printing Works Ltd, POB 325, Kumasi; tel. (51) 2204; f. 1939; Editor JOHNSON GYAMPOH; circ. 100,000.

### PERIODICALS

#### Weekly

**Bombshell:** Crossfire Publications , POB 376, Sakumono, Accra; tel. (21) 234750; fax (21) 233172; Editor BEN ASAMOAH.

**Business and Financial Times:** POB 2157, Accra; tel. and fax (21) 223334; e-mail BFT@africaonline.com.gh; internet www.bftgh.com; f. 1989; Man. Editor JOHN HANSON; Editor WALLY ODOOM; circ. 20,000.

**Catholic Standard:** Accra.

**Champion:** POB 6828, Accra-North; tel. (21) 229079; Man. Dir MARK D. N. ADDY; Editor FRANK CAXTON WILLIAMS; circ. 300,000.

**Christian Chronicle:** Accra; English; Editor GEORGE NAYKENE.

**The Democrat:** Democrat Publications, POB 13605, Accra; tel. (21) 76804; Editor L. K. NYAHO.

**Echo:** POB 5288, Accra; f. 1968; Sun.; Man. Editor M. K. FRIMPONG; circ. 40,000.

**Entertaining Eye:** Kad Publications, POB 125, Darkuman-Accra; Editor NANA KWAKYE YIADOM; circ. 40,000.

**Evening Digest:** News Media Ltd, POB 7082, Accra; tel. (21) 221071; Editor P. K. ANANTITETTEH.

**Experience:** POB 5084, Accra-North; Editor ALFRED YAW POKU; circ. 50,000.

**Free Press:** Tommy Thompson Books Ltd, POB 6492, Accra; tel. (21) 225994; independent; English; Editor EBEN QUARCOO.

**Ghana Life:** Ghana Life Publications, POB 11337, Accra; tel. (21) 229835; Editor NIKKI BOA-AMPONSEM.

**Ghana Palaver:** Palaver Publications, POB 15744, Accra-North; tel. (21) 232495; Editor BRUCE QUANSAH.

**Ghanaian Chronicle:** General Portfolio Ltd, Private Mail Bag, Accra-North; tel. (21) 227789; fax (21) 775895; Editor EBO QUANSAH; circ. 60,000.

**Ghanaian Dawn:** Dawn Publications, POB 721, Mamprobi, Accra; Editor MABEL LINDSAY.

**The Ghanaian Voice:** Newstop Publications, POB 514, Mamprobi, Accra; Editor DAN K. ANSAH; circ. 100,000.

**The Gossip:** Gossip Publications, POB 5355, Accra-North; Editor C. A. ACHEAMPONG.

**Graphic Sports:** Graphic Rd, POB 742, Accra; tel. (21) 228911; state-owned; Editor JOE AGGREY; circ. 60,000.

**The Guide:** Western Publications Ltd, POB 8253, Accra-North; tel. (21) 232760; Editor KWEKU BAAKO Jnr.

**The Independent:** Accra.

**The Mirror:** Graphic Rd, POB 742, Accra; tel. (21) 228911; fax (21) 669886; f. 1953; state-owned; Sat.; Editor E. N. V. PROVENCAL; circ. 90,000.

**The New Ghanaian:** Tudu Publishing House, POB 751, Tamale; tel. (71) 22579; Editor RAZAK EL-ALAWA.

**New Nation:** POB 6828, Accra-North; Editor S. N. SASRAKU; circ. 300,000.

**Private Eye:** Kad Life Books Channels, POB 125, Accra; tel. (21) 230684; Editor AWUKU AGYEMANG-DUAH.

**Public Agenda:** P. A. Communications, POB 5564, Accra-North; tel. (21) 238821; fax (21) 231687; e-mail isodec@ncs.com.gh; f. 1994; Editor YAO GRAHAM; circ. 12,000.

**Sporting News:** POB 5481, Accra-North; f. 1967; Man. Editor J. OPPONG-AGYARE.

**The Standard:** Standard Newspapers & Magazines Ltd, POB 765, Accra; tel. (21) 220165; Editor ISAAC FRITZ ANDOH; circ. 10,000.

**Statesman:** Kinesic Communications, POB 846, Accra; tel. and fax (21) 233242; official publ. of the New Patriotic Party; Editor HARUNNA ATTAH.

**Voice:** Accra.

**The Weekend:** Newstop Publications, POB 514, Mamprobi, Accra; tel. and fax (21) 226943; Editor EMMANUEL YARTEY; circ. 40,000.

**Weekly Events:** Clear Type Image Ltd, 29 Olympic Street (Enterprise House), Kokomlemle, POB 7634, Accra-North; tel. (21) 223085; Editor JORIS JORDAN DODOO.

**Weekly Insight:** Militant Publications Ltd, POB K272, Accra New Town, Accra; tel. (21) 660148; f. 1993; independent; English; Editor KWESI PRATT Jnr.

**Weekly Spectator:** New Times Corpn, Ring Road West, POB 2638, Accra; tel. (21) 228282; fax (21) 229398; state-owned; f. 1963; Sun.; Editor WILLIE DONKOR; circ. 165,000.

#### Other

**Africa Flamingo:** Airport Emporium Ltd, POB 9194, Accra; monthly; Editor FELIX AMANFU; circ. 50,000.

**African Observer:** POB 1171, Kaneshie, Accra; tel. (012) 231459; bi-monthly; Editor STEVE MALLORY.

**African Woman:** Ring Rd West, POB 1496, Accra; monthly.

**AGI Newsletter:** c/o Asscn of Ghana Industries, POB 8624, Accra-North; tel. (21) 777283; e-mail agi@ighmail.com; f. 1974; quarterly; Editor (vacant); circ. 1,500.

**Akwansosem:** Ghana Information Services, POB 745, Accra; tel. (21) 228011; quarterly; in Akuapim Twi, Asanti Twi and Fante; Editor KATHLEEN OFOSU-APPIAH.

**Armed Forces News:** General Headquarters, Directorate of Public Relations, Burma Camp, Accra; tel. (21) 776111; f. 1966; quarterly; Editor ADOTEY ANKRAH-HOFFMAN; circ. 4,000.

**Boxing and Football Illustrated:** POB 8392, Accra; f. 1976; monthly; Editor NANA O. AMPOMAH; circ. 10,000.

**Business and Financial Concord:** Sammy Tech Consult Enterprise, POB 5677, Accra-North; tel. (21) 232446; fortnightly; Editor KWABENA RICHARDSON.

**Chit Chat:** POB 7043, Accra; monthly; Editor ROSEMOND ADU.

**Christian Messenger:** Presbyterian Book Depot Bldg, POB 3075, Accra; tel. and fax (21) 662415; f. 1883; English; also **The Presbyterian** (in Twi and Ga); quarterly; Editor G. B. K. OWUSU; circ. 40,000.

**Drum:** POB 1197, Accra; monthly; general interest.

**Ghana Journal of Science:** Ghana Science Asscn, POB 7, Legon; monthly; Editor Dr A. K. AHAFIA.

**Ghana Official News Bulletin:** Information Services Dept, POB 745, Accra; English; political, economic, investment and cultural affairs.

**Ideal Woman** (Obaa Sima): POB 5737, Accra; tel. (21) 221399; f. 1971; fortnightly; Editor KATE ABBAM.

**Independent:** Trans Afrika News Ltd, POB 4031, Accra; tel. (21) 661091; bi-weekly; Editor KABRAL BLAY-AMIHERE.

**Insight and Opinion:** POB 5446, Accra; quarterly; Editorial Sec. W. B. OHENE.

**Legon Observer:** POB 11, Legon; fax (21) 774338; f. 1966; publ. by Legon Society on National Affairs; fortnightly; Chair. J. A. DADSON; Editor EBOW DANIEL.

**Police News:** Police HQ, Accra; monthly; Editor S. S. APPIAH; circ. 20,000.

**The Post:** Ghana Information Services, POB 745, Accra; tel. (21) 228011; f. 1980; monthly; current affairs and analysis; circ. 25,000.

**Radio and TV Times:** Ghana Broadcasting Corpn, Broadcasting House, POB 1633, Accra; tel. (21) 221161; f. 1960; quarterly; Editor SAM THOMPSON; circ. 5,000.

**The Scope:** POB 8162, Tema; monthly; Editor EMMANUEL DOE ZIORKLUI; circ. 10,000.

**Students World:** POB M18, Accra; tel. (21) 774248; fax (21) 778715; e-mail aframpub@ighmail.com; f. 1974; monthly; educational; Man. Editor ERIC OFEI; circ. 10,000.

**The Teacher:** Ghana National Asscn of Teachers, POB 209, Accra; tel. (21) 221515; fax (21) 226286; f. 1931; quarterly; circ. 30,000.

**Truth and Life:** Gift Publications, POB 11337, Accra-North; monthly; Editor Pastor KOBENA CHARM.

**The Watchman:** Watchman Gospel Ministry, POB GP 4521, Accra; tel. (21) 502011; fax (21)507428; e-mail sonlife@africaonline.com.gh; fortnightly; Pres. and CEO DIVINE P. KUMAH; Chair. Dr E. K. OPUNI.

### NEWS AGENCIES

**Ghana News Agency:** POB 2118, Accra; tel. (21) 665136; fax 669841; e-mail ghnews@ncs.com.gh; f. 1957; Gen. Man. SAM B. QUAICOE; 10 regional offices and 110 district offices.

#### Foreign Bureaux

**Associated Press (AP)** (USA): Accra; Bureau Chief P. K. COBBINAH-ESSEM.

**Xinhua (New China) News Agency** (People's Republic of China): 2 Seventh St, Airport Residential Area, POB 3897, Accra; tel. (21) 772042.

Deutsche Presse-Agentur (Germany) and Reuters (UK) are also represented.

## Publishers

**Advent Press:** POB 0102, Osu, Accra; tel. (21) 777861; f. 1937; Gen. Man. EMMANUEL C. TETTEH.

**Adwinsa Publications (Ghana) Ltd:** Advance Press Bldg, 3rd Floor, School Rd, POB 92, Legoh Accra; tel. (21) 221654; f. 1977; general, educational; Man. Dir KWABENA AMPONSAH.

**Afram Publications:** 9 Ring Rd East, POB M18, Accra; tel. (21) 774248; fax (21) 778715; e-mail aframpub@ighmail.com; f. 1974; textbooks and general; Man. Dir ERIC OFEI.

**Africa Christian Press:** POB 30, Achimota; tel. (21) 244147; fax (21) 220271; f. 1964; religious, fiction, theology, children's; Gen. Man. RICHARD A. B. CRABBE.

**Allgoodbooks Ltd:** POB AN10416, Accra-North; tel. (21) 665629; fax (21) 302993; e-mail allgoodbooks@hotmail.com; f. 1968; children's; Man. MARY ASIRIFI.

**Asempa Publishers:** POB GP919, Accra; tel. (21) 233084; fax (21) 235140; e-mail asempa@ncs.com.gh; f. 1970; religion, social issues, African music, fiction, children's; Gen. Man. Rev. EMMANUEL B. BORTEY.

**Baafour and Co:** POB K189, Accra New Town; f. 1978; general; Man. B. KESE-AMANKWAA.

**Benibengor Book Agency:** POB 40, Aboso; fiction, biography, children's and paperbacks; Man. Dir J. BENIBENGOR BLAY.

**Black Mask Ltd:** 17 Watson Ave, Adabraka, Accra; tel. (21) 234577; f. 1979; textbooks, plays, novels, handicrafts; Man. Dir YAW OWUSU ASANTE.

**Editorial and Publishing Services:** POB 5743, Accra; general, reference; Man. Dir M. DANQUAH.

**Educational Press and Manufacturers Ltd:** POB 9184, Airport-Accra; tel. (21) 220395; f. 1975; textbooks, children's; Man. G. K. KODUA.

**Encyclopaedia Africana Project:** POB 2797, Accra; tel. (21) 776939; f. 1962; reference; Dir J. O. VANDERPUYE.

**Frank Publishing Ltd:** POB MB414, Accra; tel. (21) 240711; f. 1976; secondary school textbooks; Man. Dir FRANCIS K. DZOKOTO.

**Ghana Publishing Corpn:** PMB Tema; tel. (221) 2921; f. 1965; textbooks and general fiction and non-fiction; Man. Dir F. K. NYARKO.

**Ghana Universities Press:** POB GP4219, Accra; tel. (21) 500300; fax (21) 501930; f. 1962; scholarly and academic; Dir K. M. GANU.

**Golden Wings Publications:** 26 Mantse Kwao St, POB 1337, Accra; educational and children's; Man. Editor GREGORY ANKRAH.

**Miracle Bookhouse:** POB 7487, Accra-North; tel. (21) 226684; f. 1977; general; Man. J. APPIAH-BERKO.

**Moxon Paperbacks:** POB M160, Accra; tel. (21) 761175; fax (21) 777971; f. 1967; travel and guide books, fiction and poetry, Africana, telephone directory; Man. Dir JAMES MOXON.

**Sam-Woode Ltd:** A.979/15 Dansoman High Street, POB 12719, Accra-North; tel. (21) 305287; fax (021) 310482; internet www.samwoode@africaonline.com.gh; educational and children's; Chair. KWESI SAM-WOODE.

**Sedco Publishing Ltd:** Sedco House, 5 Tabon St, North Ridge, POB 2051, Accra; tel. (21) 221332; fax (21) 220107; e-mail sedco@africaonline.com.gh; f. 1975; educational; Man. Dir COURAGE K. SEGBAWU.

**Sheffield Publishing Co:** Accra; tel. (21) 667480; fax (21) 665960; f. 1970; religion, politics, economics, science, fiction; Publr RONALD MENSAH.

**Unimax Publishers Ltd:** 42 Ring Rd South Industrial Area, POB 10722, Accra-North; tel. (21) 227443; fax (21) 225215; e-mail unimax@africanonline.com.gh; atlases, educational and children's; Dir EDWARD ADDO.

**Waterville Publishing House:** POB 195, Accra; tel. (21) 663124; f. 1963; general fiction and non-fiction, textbooks, paperbacks, Africana; Man. Dir H. W. O. OKAI.

**Woeli Publishing Services:** POB NT601, Accra New Town; tel. and fax (21) 229294; f. 1984; children's, fiction, academic; Dir W. A. DEKUTSEY.

### PUBLISHERS' ASSOCIATIONS

**Ghana Book Development Council:** POB M430, Accra; tel. (21) 229178; f. 1975; govt-financed agency; promotes and co-ordinates writing, production and distribution of books; Exec. Dir D. A. NIMAKO.

**Ghana Book Publishers' Association:** c/o Africa Christian Press, POB 430, Achimota; Sec. E. B. BORTEY.

**Private Newspaper Publishers' Association of Ghana (PRINPAG):** POB 125, Darkuman, Accra; Gen. Sec. K. AGYEMANG DUAH.

## Broadcasting and Communications

### TELECOMMUNICATIONS

**Ghana Telecommunication Co Ltd:** Posts and Telecommunications Bldg, Accra-North; tel. (21) 221001; fax (21) 667979; f. 1995; 30% transferred to private ownership in 1997; Dir-Gen. JOSEPH AGGREY-MENSAH; Man. Dir ADNAN ROFIEE.

### BROADCASTING

There are internal radio broadcasts in English, Akan, Dagbani, Ewe, Ga, Hausa and Nzema, and an external service in English and French. There are three transmitting stations, with a number of relay stations. There is a total of eight main colour television transmitters. In 1995 36 private companies were granted authorization to operate radio and television networks. The Ghana Frequency Registration and Control Board gave approval for 10 new community radio stations in 1996.

**Ghana Broadcasting Corporation:** Broadcasting House, POB 1633, Accra; tel. (21) 221161; fax (21) 221153; e-mail gtv@ncs.com.gh; f. 1935; Dir-Gen. Dr KOFI FRIMPONG; Dir of TV Prof. MARK DUODU; Dir of Radio CRIS TACKIE.

## Finance

(cap. = capital; res = reserves; dep. = deposits; m. = million; brs = branches; amounts in cedis)

### BANKING

The commercial banking sector comprised nine commercial banks, four development banks and four merchant banks in 1998. There were also 130 rural banks and several non-banking financial institutions.

#### Central Bank

**Bank of Ghana:** High Street, Thorpe Rd, POB 2674, Accra; tel. (21) 666902; fax (21) 662996; e-mail secretary@bog.gov.gh; f. 1957; bank of issue; cap. and res 200,504m., dep. 696,921m. (Dec. 1997); Chair. and Gov. KWABENA DUFFOUR.

#### Commercial and Development Banks

**Agricultural Development Bank:** Cedi House, Liberia Rd, POB 4191, Accra; tel. (21) 662758; fax (21) 662846; e-mail adb@africaonline.com.gh; internet www.ghanaclassifieds.com/adb; f. 1965; 79% state-owned; credit facilities for farmers and commercial banking; cap. and res 77,658.4m., dep. 119,463.0m. (Dec. 1997); Chair. NATHAN QUAO; Man. Dir PERCIVAL A. KURANCHIE; 34 brs.

**Bank for Housing and Construction (BHC):** Okofoh House, 24 Kwame Nkrumah Ave, POB M1, Adabraka, Accra; tel. (21) 220033; fax (21) 229631; e-mail bhc@ghana.com; f. 1973; 50% state-owned;

cap. 1,000m. (Dec. 1995); Chair. K. TWUM BOAFO; Man. Dir L. A. ADJAIDOO.

**Ghana Commercial Bank Ltd:** POB 134, Accra; tel. (21) 664914; fax (21) 662168; e-mail gcbmail@ncs.com.gh; f. 1953; 59.1% state-owned; cap. and res 101,613m., dep. 555,607m. (Dec. 1997); Chair. JOHN SEY; Man. Dir WILLIAM PANFORD BRAY (acting); 145 brs.

**Ghana Co-operative Bank Ltd:** Kwame Nkrumah Ave, POB 5292, Accra-North; tel. (21) 663131; fax (21) 662359; f. 1970; 81% state-owned; cap. 2,913.7m. (Dec. 1994); Chair. W. E. INKUMSAH (acting); Man. Dir S. A. DONKOR; 21 brs.

**Leasafric Ghana Ltd:** 7 Main St, Tesano, POB C2430, Accra; tel. (21) 240140; fax (21) 228375; e-mail leasafric@africaonline.com.gh; cap. 893m. (Dec. 1996); Chair. JOHN KOBINA RISHCARDSON; Man. Dir SETH K. DEI.

**National Investment Bank Ltd (NIB):** 37 Kwame Nkrumah Ave, POB 3726, Accra; tel. (21) 669301; fax (21) 240030; f. 1963; 86.5% state-owned; provides long-term investment capital, jt venture promotion, consortium finance man. and commercial banking services; cap. 3,259.7m., dep. 58,867.5m. (Dec. 1997); Chair. NICHOLAS AKPEBU; Man. Dir MAHMOUD HANTOUR; 11 brs.

**National Trust Holding Co Ltd:** Martco House, Okai Mensah Link, off Kwame Nkrumah Ave, POB 9563 KIA, Airport, Accra; tel. (21) 238492; fax (21) 229975; e-mail nthc@ghana.com; internet www.nthcghana.com; f. 1976 to finance Ghanaian acquisitions of indigenous cos; also assists in their development and expansion, and provides financial advisory services; cap. 500m. (1999); Chair. JACOB BRUCE YIRERONG; Acting Man. Dir PAUL EFFAH OTENG.

**Prudential Bank Ltd:** Kingsway Stores Bldg, 34 Kwame Nkrumah Ave, POB 9820, Accra; tel. (21) 226322; fax (21) 226803; f. Aug. 1996; Chair. and Man. Dir JOHN SACKAH ADDO.

**Social Security Bank Ltd (SSB):** POB 13119, Accra; tel. (21) 221726; fax (21) 220713; e-mail ssb@ghana.com; internet www.ssb.com.gh; f. 1976; cap. 6,734.5m., dep. 277,309.1m. (Dec. 1996); Chair. FRANCIS E. Y. ATTIPOE; Man. Dir PRYCE K. THOMPSON.

**Trust Bank Ghana Ltd:** 68 Kwame Nkrumah Ave, POB 1862, Accra; tel. (21) 240049; fax (21) 240056; e-mail trust@gh.com; f. 1996; cap. and res 15,347.2m., dep. 60,078.9m. (Dec. 1997); Chair. ALEX AWUKU; Man. Dir JEAN-MARIE MARQUEBREUCQ; 6 brs.

### Merchant Banks

**CAL Merchant Bank Ltd:** 45 Independence Ave, POB 14596, Accra; tel. (21) 221056; fax (21) 231913; e-mail calbank@calbankgh.com; internet www.africaonline.com.gh/cal/; f. 1990 as Continental Acceptances Ltd; cap. and res 17,816.1m., dep. 45,795.2m. (Dec. 1998); Chair. LOUIS CASELY-HAYFORD; Man. Dir JUDE KOFI BUCKNOR.

**Ecobank Ghana Ltd (EBG):** 19 Seventh Ave, Ridge West, Accra; tel. (21) 229532; fax (21) 667127; e-mail ecobank@ghana.com; internet www.ghanaclassifieds.com/ecobank; f. 1989; 93.7% owned by Ecobank Transnational Inc (operating under the auspices of the Economic Community of West African States); cap. and res 33,861.4m., dep. 215,878.3m. (Dec. 1997); Chair. EDWARD PATRICK LARBI GYAMPOH; Man. Dir JEAN N. AKA.

**First Atlantic Merchant Bank Ltd:** Atlantic Place, 1 Seventh Ave, Ridge West, POB C1620, Cantonments, Accra; tel. (21) 231433; fax (21) 231399; e-mail fambl@ghana.com; f. 1995; cap. and res 4,563.9m., dep. 35,307.6m. (Dec. 1998); Chair. SAM JONAH; Man. Dir JUDE ARTHUR.

**Merchant Bank (Ghana) Ltd:** Merban House, 44 Kwame Nkrumah Ave, POB 401, Accra; tel. (21) 666331; fax (21) 667305; e-mail merban-services@ighmail.com; internet www.ghanaclassifieds.com/merchantbank; f. 1972; cap. and res 17,497.0m., dep. 166,828.0m. (Dec. 1998); Chair. Dr JOHN RICHARDSON; Man. Dir CHRIS N. NARTEY; 4 brs.

### Foreign Banks

**Barclays Bank of Ghana Ltd** (UK): High St, POB 2949, Accra; tel. (21) 664901; fax (21) 667420; e-mail barclays@africaonline.com.gh; f. 1917; 10% state-owned; cap. and res 58,628m., dep. 485,302m. (Dec. 1998); Chair. NANA WEREKO AMPEM; Man. Dir K. QUANSAH; 25 brs.

**Standard Chartered Bank Ghana Ltd** (UK): 3rd Floor, Accra, High St Building, POB 768, Accra; tel. (21) 664591; fax (21) 667751; e-mail dzaney@scb.ghana.nhs.compuserve.com; f. 1896; cap. and res 87,861.0m., dep. 715,188.0m. (Dec. 1998); Chair. DAVID ANDOH; CEO VISHNU MOHAN; 28 brs.

## STOCK EXCHANGE

**Ghana Stock Exchange (GSE):** Cedi House, 5th Floor, Liberia Rd, POB 1849, Accra; tel. (21) 669908; fax (21) 669913; e-mail stockex@ncs.com.gh; internet www.gse.com.gh; 52 mems; Man. Dir YEBOAH AMOAH.

## INSURANCE

**Ghana Union Assurance Co Ltd:** POB 1322, Accra; tel. (21) 664421; fax (21) 664988; f. 1973; Man. Dir KWADWO DUKU.

**The Great African Insurance Co Ltd:** POB 12349, Accra North; tel. (21) 227459; fax (21) 228905; f. 1980; Man. Dir KWASI AKOTO.

**The State Insurance Corporation of Ghana:** POB 2363, Accra; tel. (21) 666961; fax (21) 662205; f. 1962; state-owned; all classes of insurance; Man. Dir B. K. QUASHIE.

**Social Security and National Insurance Trust:** Pension House, POB M149, Accra; tel. (21) 667742; fax (21) 662226; f. 1972; covers over 650,000 contributors; Dir-Gen. HENRY G. DEI.

**Vanguard Assurance Co Ltd:** Insurance Hall, Derby House, Derby Ave, POB 1868, Accra; tel. (21) 666485; fax (21) 668610; f. 1974; general accident, marine, motor and life insurance; Man. Dir NANA AWUAH-DARKO AMPEM; 7 brs.

Several foreign insurance companies operate in Ghana.

# Trade and Industry

## GOVERNMENT AGENCIES

**Divestiture Implementation Committee:** F35/5 Ring Road East, North Labone; POB CT102, Cantonments, Accra; tel. (21) 772049; fax (21) 773126; e-mail dicgh@ncs.com.gh; f. 1988; Exec. Sec. EMMANUEL AGBODO.

**Food Production Corporation:** POB 1853, Accra; f. 1971; state corpn providing employment for youth in large-scale farming enterprises; controls 76,900 ha of land (16,200 ha under cultivation); operates 87 food farms on a co-operative and self-supporting basis, and rears poultry and livestock.

**Ghana Export Promotion Council (GEPC):** Republic House, Tudu, POB M146, Accra; tel. (21) 228813; fax (21) 668263; e-mail gepc@ighmail.com; f. 1974; Exec. Sec. TAWIA AKYEA.

**Ghana Food Distribution Corporation:** POB 4245, Accra; tel. (21) 228428; f. 1971; buys, stores, preserves, distributes and retails foodstuffs through 10 regional centres; Man. Dir E. H. K. AMANKWA.

**Ghana Free Zones Board:** POB M626, Accra; tel. (21) 780532; fax (21) 670536; e-mail gfzb@ighmail.com; internet www.africaonline.com.gfzb; f. 1996; approves establishment of cos in export processing zones; Exec. Sec. GEORGE ABOAGYE.

**Ghana Industrial Holding Corporation (GIHOC):** POB 2784, Accra; tel. (21) 664998. 1967; controls and manages 26 state enterprises, including steel, paper, bricks, paint, pharmaceuticals, electronics, metals, canneries, distilleries and boat-building factories; also has three subsidiary cos and four jt ventures; Chair. J. E. K. MOSES; Man. Dir J. K. WILLIAMS.

**Ghana Investment Promotion Centre:** Central Ministerial Area, POB M193, Accra; tel. (21) 665125; fax (21) 663801; e-mail gipc@ghana.com; internet www.gipc.org.gh; f. 1981; negotiates new investments, approves projects, registers foreign capital and decides extent of govt participation; Chair. P. V. OBENG.

**Ghana National Trading Corporation (GNTC):** POB 67, Accra; tel. (21) 664871; f. 1961; organizes exports and imports of selected commodities; over 500 retail outlets in 12 admin. dists.

**Ghana Standards Board:** c/o POB M245, Accra; tel. (21) 500065; fax (21) 500092; f. 1967; establishes and promulgates standards; promotes standardization, industrial efficiency and development and industrial welfare, health and safety; operates certification mark scheme; 403 mems; Dir Rev. Dr E. K. MARFO.

**National Board for Small-scale Industries:** Ministry of Trade and Industry, POB M85, Accra; f. 1985; promotes small and medium-scale industrial and commercial enterprises by providing credit, advisory services and training.

**State Farms Corporation:** Accra; undertakes agricultural projects in all regions but Upper Region; Man. Dir E. N. A. THOMPSON (acting).

**State Housing Construction Co:** POB 2753, Accra; f. 1982 by merger; oversees govt housing programme.

## CHAMBER OF COMMERCE

**Ghana National Chamber of Commerce:** POB 2325, Accra; tel. (21) 662427; fax (21) 662210; e-mail gncc@ncs.com.gh; f. 1961; promotes and protects industry and commerce, organizes trade fairs; 2,500 individual mems and 8 mem. chambers; Pres. ATO AMPIAH; Exec. Dir SAL D. AMEGAVIE.

## INDUSTRIAL AND TRADE ASSOCIATIONS

**Best Fibres Development Board:** POB 1992, Kumasi; f. 1970; promotes the commercial cultivation of best fibres and their processing, handling and grading.

**Ghana Cocoa Board (COCOBOD):** POB 933, Accra; tel. (21) 221212; fax (21) 667104; e-mail cocobod@africaonline.comigh; f. 1985; monopoly purchaser of cocoa until 1993; responsible for purchase, grading and export of cocoa, coffee and shea nuts; also encourages production and scientific research aimed at improving quality and yield of these crops; controls all exports of cocoa; CEO JOHN NEWMAN.

**Grains and Legumes Development Board:** POB 4000, Kumasi; tel. (51) 4231; f. 1970; state-controlled; promotes and develops production of cereals and leguminous vegetables.

**Minerals Commission:** 9 Switch Rd, Residential Area, Cantonments, POB M248, Accra; tel. (21) 772783; fax (21) 773324; e-mail mincom@ncs.com.gh; f. 1984; supervises, promotes and co-ordinates the minerals industry; CEO KOFI ANSAH.

**Timber Export Development Board:** POB 515, Takoradi; tel. (31) 22921; fax (31) 23339; f. 1985; promotes the sale and export of timber; CEO SAMUEL KWESI APPIAH.

### EMPLOYERS' ORGANIZATION

**Ghana Employers' Association:** 122 Kojo Thompson Rd, POB 2616, Accra; tel. (21) 228455; fax (21) 228405; f. 1959; 400 mems; Pres. ISHMAEL E. YAMSON; Vice-Pres. ATO AMPIAH.

#### Affiliated Bodies

**Association of Ghana Industries:** Trade Fair Centre, POB 8624, Accra-North; tel. and fax (21) 779793; e-mail agi@ghana.com; internet www.agi-org.gh; f. 1957; Pres. Prince KOFI KLUDJESON; Exec. Dir ANDREW E. QUAYSON.

**Ghana Booksellers' Association:** POB 10367, Accra-North; tel. (21) 773002; fax (21) 773242; Pres. SAMPSON BRAKO; Gen. Sec. FRED J. REIMMER.

**The Ghana Chamber of Mines:** 2nd Floor, Diamond House, POB 991, Accra; tel. (21) 665355; fax (21) 662926; f. 1928; Pres. PETER BRADFORD; Exec. Dir GEORGE M. OSEI (acting).

**Ghana Electrical Contractors' Association:** POB 1858, Accra.

**Ghana National Association of Teachers:** POB 209, Accra; tel. (21) 221515; fax (21) 226286; f. 1931; Pres. G. N. NAASO; Gen. Sec. PAUL OSEI-MENSAH.

**Ghana National Contractors' Association:** c/o J. T. Osei and Co, POB M11, Accra.

**Ghana Timber Association (GTA):** POB 246, Takoradi; f. 1952; promotes, protects and develops timber industry; Chair. TETTEH NANOR.

### UTILITIES

#### Electricity

**Electricity Corporation of Ghana (ECG):** Electro-Volta House, POB 521, Accra; tel. (21) 664941; fax (21) 666262; Man. Dir JOHN HAGAN.

**Ghana Atomic Energy Commission:** POB 80, Legon/Accra; tel. (21) 400310; fax (21) 400807; e-mail secgaec@ncs.com.gh; f. 1963; promotes, develops and utilizes nuclear techniques; construction of a research reactor at Kwabenya, near Accra, which was begun in 1964, was completed in 1995; Chair. Prof. KWAME SARPONG.

**Volta River Authority:** POB MB77, Accra; tel. (21) 664941; fax (21) 662610; e-mail orgsrv@accra.rva.com; f. 1965; controls the generation and distribution of electricity; Chair. and CEO E. A. K. KALITSI.

#### Water

**Ghana Water and Sewerage Corporation:** POB M194, Accra; tel. (21) 666781; f. 1966 to provide, distribute and conserve water supplies for public, domestic and industrial use, and to establish, operate and control sewerage systems; Man. Dir T. B. F. ACQUAH.

### CO-OPERATIVES

In 1998 there were 11,154 registered co-operative societies, grouped into four sectors: industrial, financial, agricultural and service.

**Department of Co-operatives:** POB M150, Accra; tel. (21) 666212; fax (21) 772789; f. 1944; govt-supervised body, responsible for registration, auditing and supervision of co-operative socs; Registrar R. BUACHIE-APHRAM.

**Ghana Co-operatives Council Ltd:** POB 4034, Accra; tel. (21) 232195; f. 1951; co-ordinates activities of all co-operative socs; comprises five active nat. asscns and two central organizations; Sec.-Gen. THOMAS ANDOH.

The five national associations and two central organizations include the Ghana Co-operative Marketing Asscn Ltd, the Ghana Co-operative Credit Unions Asscn Ltd, the Ghana Co-operative Distillers and Retailers Asscn Ltd, and the Ghana Co-operative Poultry Farmers Asscn Ltd.

### TRADE UNIONS

**Ghana Trades Union Congress (GTUC):** Hall of Trade Unions, POB 701, Accra; tel. (21) 662568; fax (21) 667161; f. 1945; 17 affiliated unions; all activities of the GTUC were suspended in 1982; Chair. Interim Man. Cttee E. K. ABOAGYE; Sec.-Gen. CHRISTIAN APPIAH-AGYEI.

## Transport

### RAILWAYS

Ghana has a railway network of 1,300 km, which connects Accra, Kumasi and Takoradi.

**Ghana Railway Corporation:** POB 251, Takoradi; tel. (31) 22181; fax (31) 23797; f. 1977; responsible for the operation and maintenance of all railways; Man. Dir M. K. ARTHUR.

### ROADS

In 1996 Ghana had an estimated total road network of 37,800 km, including 30 km of motorways, 5,230 km of main roads, and 9,620 km of secondary roads; some 24.1% of the road network was paved. A five-year Road Sector Expenditure Programme, costing US $259m., commenced in 1995.

**Ghana Highway Authority:** POB 1641, Accra; tel. (21) 666591; fax (21) 665571; f. 1974 to plan, develop, administer and maintain trunk roads and related facilities; CEO B. L. T. SAKIBU.

**State Transport Corporation:** Ring Rd West, POB 7384, Accra; tel. (21) 221912. 1965; Man. Dir Lt-Col AKYEA-MENSAH.

### SHIPPING

The two main ports are Tema (near Accra) and Takoradi, both of which are linked with Kumasi by rail. A project to upgrade facilities at both ports, at a cost of US $365m., was to commence in 1998. In 1996 some 6.7m. metric tons of goods were handled at the two ports.

**Ghana Ports and Harbour Authority:** POB 150, Tema; tel. (22) 202631; fax (22) 202812; e-mail ghpa@ghana.com; holding co for the ports of Tema and Takoradi; Dir Gen. K. T. DOVLO.

**Alpha (West Africa) Line Ltd:** POB 451, Tema; operates regular cargo services to west Africa, the UK, the USA, the Far East and northern Europe; shipping agents; Man. Dir AHMED EDGAR COLLINGWOOD WILLIAMS.

**Black Star Line Ltd:** 4th Lane, Kuku Hill Osu, POB 248, Accra; tel. (21) 2888; fax (21) 2889; f. 1957; state-owned; transfer to private sector pending in 1997; operates passenger and cargo services to Europe, the UK, Canada, the USA, the Mediterranean and west Africa; shipping agents; Chair. MAGNUS ADDICO; Man. Dir Capt. V. N. ATTUQUAYEFIO.

**Bunktrad Shipping and Trading Ltd:** 4th Floor, Trust Towers, POB 14801, Accra; tel. (21) 238401; fax (21) 236121; e-mail bunktrad @africaonline.com.gh; charters tankers.

**Holland West-Afrika Lijn NV:** POB 269, Accra; POB 216, Tema; and POB 18, Takoradi; cargo services to and from North America and the Far East; shipping agents.

**Liner Agencies and Trading (Ghana) Ltd:** POB 214, Tema; tel. (22) 202187; fax (22) 202189; international freight services; shipping agents; Dir J. OSSEI-YAW.

**Remco Shipping Lines Ltd:** POB 3898, Accra; tel. (21) 224609.

**Scanship (Ghana) Ltd:** CFAO Bldg, High St, POB 1705, Accra; tel. (21) 664314; shipping agents.

#### Association

**Ghana Shippers' Council:** Enterprise House, 5th Floor, opp. Barclay's Bank, High St, POB 1321, Accra; tel. (21) 666915; fax (21) 668768; e-mail shippers@ncs.com.gh; f. 1974; represents interests of c. 3,000 registered Ghanaian shippers; also provides cargo-handling and allied services; CEO M. T. ADDICO.

### CIVIL AVIATION

The main international airport is at Kotoka (Accra). There are also airports at Takoradi, Kumasi, Sunyani, Tamale and Wa. The construction of a dedicated freight terminal at Kotoka Airport was completed in 1994.

**Ghana Civil Aviation Authority:** Kotoka International Airport, Accra; tel. (21) 776171; fax (21) 773293; e-mail centre-gcaa@ ighmail.com; internet www.gcaa.com.gh.

**Gemini Airlines Ltd:** America House, POB 7328, Accra-North; tel. (21) 665785; f. 1974; operates weekly cargo flight between Accra and London; Dir V. OWUSU; Gen. Man. P. F. OKINE.

**Ghana Airways Ltd.:** Plot 9, Ghana Airways Avenue, Ghana Airways House, POB 1636, Accra; tel. (21) 773321; fax (21) 773316; e-mail ghanaairways@ighmail.com; internet www.ghanaairways.com;

**Union of Democratic Centre Party (Enossi Dimokratikou Kentrou—EDIK):** Odos Charilaou Trikoupi 18, 106 79 Athens; tel. (1) 3612792; fax (1) 3634412; f. 1974; democratic socialist party, merging Centre Union (f. 1961 by Georgios Papandreou) and New Political Forces (f. 1974 by Prof. Ioannis Pesmazoglou and Prof. G. A. Mangakis); favours a united Europe; Chair. Prof. NEOKLIS SARRIS.

Other parties include the People's Militant Unity Party (f. 1985 by PASOK splinter group), the Progressive Party (f. 1979, right-wing), the (Maoist) Revolutionary Communist Party of Greece (EKKE), the Panhellenic Unaligned Party of Equality (PAKI, f. 1988; Leader KHARALAMBOS ALOMA TAMONTSIDES), Olympianism Party (pacifist, Leader GIORGIOS ZOE), and the left-wing United Socialist Alliance of Greece (ESPE, f. 1984).

Terrorist organizations include the left-wing 17 November Revolutionary Organization (f. 1975; opposed to Western capitalism and the continuing existence of US military bases in Greece), the 1 May Revolutionary Organization, the Revolutionary People's Struggle (ELA), People's Revolutionary Solidarity, the Anti-State Struggle group, the Christos Tsoutsouvis Revolutionary Organization, the Revolutionary Praxis, Fighting Guerilla Faction and Autonomous Cells of Rebel Action.

# Diplomatic Representation

## EMBASSIES IN GREECE

**Albania:** Odos Karachristou 1, Kolonaki, 115 21 Athens; tel. (1) 7234412; fax (1) 7231972; Ambassador: KASTRIOT ROBO.

**Algeria:** Leoforos Vassileos Konstantinou 14, 116 35 Athens; tel. (1) 7564191; fax (1) 7018681; e-mail ambdzath@otenet.gr; Ambassador: KAMEL HOUHOU.

**Argentina:** Leoforos Vassilissis Sofias 59, Athens; tel. (1) 7224753; fax (1) 7227568; Ambassador: JORGE DE BELAUSTEGUI.

**Armenia:** Leoforos Sygrou 159, 171 21 Athens; tel. (1) 9345727; fax (1) 9318100; e-mail armemb@hol.gr; Ambassador: ARMEN PETROSSIAN.

**Australia:** Odos Dimitriou Soutsou 37/Odos Tsoha, Athens; tel. (1) 6447303; Ambassador: R. BURNS.

**Austria:** Leoforos Alexandras 26, 106 83 Athens; tel. (1) 8216800; fax (1) 8219823; e-mail austria@ath.forthnet.gr; Ambassador: Dr HANS SABADITSCH.

**Belgium:** Odos Sekeri 3, 106 71 Athens; tel. (1) 3617886; fax (1) 3604289; e-mail athens@diplobel.org; Ambassador: CLAUDE RIJMENANS.

**Brazil:** Plateia Philikis Etairias 14, 106 73 Athens; tel. (1) 7213039; Ambassador: ALCIDES DA COSTA GUIMARÃES FILHO.

**Bulgaria:** Odos Stratigou Kallari 33A, Palaio Psychiko, 154 52 Athens; tel. (1) 6478105; fax (1) 6478130; Ambassador: BRANIMIR PETROV.

**Canada:** Odos Ioannou Ghennadiou 4, 115 21 Athens; tel. (1) 7254011; Ambassador: DEREK R. T. FRASER.

**Chile:** Leoforos Vasilissis Sofias 25, 106 74 Athens; tel. (1) 7252574; fax (1) 7252536; e-mail echile@compulink.gr; Ambassador: MARCIA COVARRUBIAS.

**China, People's Republic:** Odos Krinon 2A, Paleo Psychiko, 154 52 Athens; tel. (1) 6723282; fax (1) 6723819; Ambassador: YANG GUANGSHENG.

**Congo, Democratic Republic:** Athens; tel. (1) 6847013; Ambassador: BOMOLO LOKOKA.

**Cuba:** Odos Sofokleou 5, Filothei, 152 37 Athens; tel. (1) 6842807; fax (1) 6849590; Ambassador: ANA MARÍA GONZÁLEZ SUÁREZ.

**Cyprus:** Odos Herodotou 16, 106 75 Athens; tel. (1) 7232727; fax (1) 7231927; Ambassador: KHARALAMBOS CHRISTOFOROU.

**Czech Republic:** Odos Georgiou Seferis 6, Palaio Psychiko, 154 52 Athens; tel. (1) 6713755; fax (1) 6710675; e-mail athens@embassy.mzv.cz; Ambassador: VLADIMÍR ZAVÁZAL.

**Denmark:** Leoforos Vassilissis Sofias 11, 106 71 Athens; tel. (1) 3608315; fax (1) 3636163; e-mail athamb@athamb.um.dk; Ambassador: HANS GRUNNET.

**Egypt:** Leoforos Vassilissis Sofias 3, 106 71 Athens; tel. (1) 3618612; fax (1) 3603538; Ambassador: MUHAMMAD EL-AMIR KHALIL.

**Estonia:** Patriarchou Ioakeim 48, 106 76 Athens; tel. (1) 7229803; fax (1) 7229804; e-mail estemb@otenet.gr; Chargé d'affaires a.i.: JÜRI ARUSOO.

**Finland:** Odos Eratosthenous 1, 116 35 Athens; tel. (1) 7010444; Ambassador: ARTO TANNER.

**France:** Leoforos Vassilissis Sofias 7, 106 71 Athens; tel. (1) 3391000; fax (1) 3391009; e-mail ambafran@hol.gr; internet www.ambafran.gr; Ambassador: BERNARD KESSEDJIAN.

**Georgia:** Odos Agiou Dimitriou 24, 154 52 Paleo Psihio, Athens; tel. (1) 6716737; fax (1) 6716722; Ambassador: ALEKSANDRE CHIKVAIDZE.

**Germany:** Odos Karaoli and Dimitriou 3, 106 75 Athens; tel. (1) 7285111; fax (1) 7251205; e-mail boathens@compulink.gr; internet www.germanembassy.gr; Ambassador: KARL-HEINZ ALBERT KUHNA.

**Holy See:** POB 65075; Odos Mavili 2, Palaio Psychiko, 154 52 Athens; tel. (1) 6743598; fax (1) 6742849; e-mail nunate@mail.otenet.gr; Apostolic Nuncio: Most Rev. PAUL FOUAD TABET, Titular Archbishop of Sinna.

**Honduras:** 5, K, Servicios FT Costella, 185 33 Piraeus; tel. (1) 4118850; fax (1) 4116105; Chargé d'affaires a.i.: TEODOLINDA BANEGAS DE MAKRIS.

**Hungary:** Odos Kalvou 16, Palaio Psychiko, 154 52 Athens; tel. (1) 6725337; Ambassador: ISTVÁN PATAKI.

**India:** Odos Kleanthous 3, 106 74 Athens; tel. (1) 7216227; fax (1) 7211252; Ambassador: AFTAB SETH.

**Indonesia:** Odos Papanastasidu 55, Palaio Psychiko, 154 52 Athens; tel. (1) 6712737; Ambassador: SAMSUBAHRI SIREGAR.

**Iran:** Odos Kalari 16, Palaio Psychiko, Athens; tel. (1) 6471436; Ambassador: MAHDI KHANDAGH ABADI.

**Iraq:** Odos Mazaraki 4, Palaio Psychiko, Athens; tel. (1) 6715012; Ambassador: FETAH AL-KHEZREJI.

**Ireland:** Leoforos Vassileos Konstantinou 7, Athens; tel. (1) 7232771; fax (1) 7240217; Ambassador: EAMON RYAN.

**Israel:** Odos Marathonodromou 1, Palaio Psychiko, 154 52 Athens; tel. (1) 6719530; fax (1) 6479510; Ambassador: DAVID SASSON.

**Italy:** Odos Sekeri 2, 106 74 Athens; tel. (1) 3617260; fax (1) 3617330; Ambassador: ENRICO PIETROMARCHI.

**Japan:** 21st Floor, Athens A Tower, Leoforos Messoghion 2–4, Pirgas Athinon, 115 27 Athens; tel. (1) 7758101; fax (1) 7758206; Ambassador: KAZUO MATSUMOTO.

**Jordan:** Odos Panagi Zervou 30, Palaio Psychiko, 154 10 Athens; tel. (1) 6474161; fax (1) 6470578; Ambassador: AMJAD MAJALI.

**Korea, Republic:** Odos Eratosthenous 1, 116 35 Athens; tel. (1) 7012122; Ambassador: NAM KYUN PARK.

**Kuwait:** Odos Marathonodromou 27, Palaio Psychiko, 154 52 Athens; tel. (1) 6473593; fax (1) 6875875; Ambassador: ALI FAHED AZ-ZAID.

**Lebanon:** Odos Maritou 25, Palaio Psychiko, 154 52 Athens; tel. (1) 6855873; fax (1) 6855612; Ambassador: ELIAS GHOSN.

**Libya:** Odos Vironos 13, Palaio Psychiko, 154 52 Athens; tel. (1) 6472120; Secretary of the People's Bureau: AYAD M. TAYARI.

**Mexico:** Plateia Philikis Etairias 14, 106 73 Athens; tel. (1) 7294780; fax (1) 7294783; e-mail embamex2@compulink.gr; Ambassador: ARIEL BUIRA.

**Morocco:** Odos Mousson 14, Palaio Psychiko, 154 52 Athens; tel. (1) 6744209; fax (1) 6749480; Ambassador: NOUREDDINE SEFIANI.

**Netherlands:** Leoforos Vassileos Konstantinou 5–7, 106 74 Athens; tel. (1) 7239701; fax (1) 7248900; e-mail nlgovath@dutchembassy.gr; Ambassador: P. R. BROUWER.

**New Zealand:** Leoforos Kifissias 268, 152 32 Halandri, Athens; tel. (1) 6874700; fax (1) 6874444; e-mail costas.cotsilinis@gr.pwcglobal.com; Ambassador: PETER BENNETT.

**Norway:** Leoforos Vassilissis Sofias 23, 106 74 Athens; tel. (1) 7246173; fax (1) 7244989; e-mail norwemba@socrates.netplan.gr; Ambassador: JAN WESSEL HEGG.

**Pakistan:** Odos Loukianou 6, Kolonaki, 106 75 Athens; tel. (1) 7290122; fax (1) 7247231; Ambassador: AMIN JAN NAIM.

**Peru:** Leoforos Vassilissis Sofias 105, Athens; tel. (1) 6411221; fax (1) 6411321; Ambassador: MARTÍN YRIGOYEN-YRIGOYEN.

**Poland:** Odos Chryssanthemon 22, Palaio Psychiko, 154 52 Athens; tel. (1) 6716917; Ambassador: JANUSZ LEWANDOWSKI.

**Portugal:** Leoforos Vassilissis Sofias 23, 106 74 Athens; tel. (1) 7290096; fax (1) 7245122; e-mail embportg@otenet.gr; Ambassador: ANTÓNIO SYDER SANTIAGO.

**Romania:** Odos Emmanuel Benaki 7, Palaio Psychiko, Athens; tel. (1) 6728875; fax (1) 6728883; Ambassador: DAN RĂDULESCU.

**Russia:** Odos Nikiforou Litra 28, Palaio Psychiko, Athens; tel. (1) 6725235; Ambassador: VALERY D. NIKOLAYENKO.

**Saudi Arabia:** Odos Marathonodromou 71, Palaio Psychiko, 154 52 Athens; tel. (1) 6716911; Ambassador: Sheikh ABDULLAH ABDUL-RAHMAN AL-MALHOOQ.

**Slovakia:** Odos Georgiou Seferis 4, Palaio Psychiko, 154 52 Athens; tel. (1) 6776757; fax (1) 6776760; e-mail zuateny@compulink.gr; Ambassador: MILAN DUBČEK.

**South Africa:** Leoforos Kifissias 60, 151 25 Athens; tel. (1) 6106645; fax (1) 6106640; e-mail embassy@southafrica.gr; Ambassador: DAVID JACOBS.

**Spain:** Odos D. Areapagitou 21, 117 42 Athens; tel. (1) 9213123; fax (1) 9213264; e-mail emb-esp@otenet.gr; Ambassador: JAVIER JIMÉNEZ-UGARTE.

**Sweden:** Leoforos Vassileos Konstantinou 7, 106 74 Athens; tel. (1) 7290421; fax (1) 7229953; e-mail ambassaden.athens@foreign.ministry.se; Ambassador: BJÖRN ELMÉR.

**Switzerland:** Odos Iassiou 2, 115 21 Athens; tel. (1) 7230364; Ambassador: CHARLES STEINHÄUSLIN.

**Syria:** Odos Marathonodromou 79, Palaio Psychiko, Athens; tel. (1) 6725577; Ambassador: SHAHIN FARAH.

**Thailand:** Odos Taigetou 23, Palaio Psychiko, 154 52 Athens; tel. (1) 6717969; fax (1) 6479508; Ambassador: SUKHUM RASMIDATTA.

**Tunisia:** Odos Anthéon 2, Palaio Psychiko, 154 52 Athens; tel. (1) 6717590; fax (1) 6713432; Ambassador: YOUSSEF BEN HAHA.

**Turkey:** Odos Vassileos Gheorghiou B 8, 106 74 Athens; tel. (1) 7245915; fax (1) 7221778; Ambassador: ALI TUYGAN.

**United Kingdom:** Odos Ploutarchou 1, 106 75 Athens; tel. (1) 7272600; fax (1) 7272734; e-mail britania@hol.gr; internet www.british-embassy.gr; Ambassador: DAVID MADDEN.

**USA:** Leoforos Vassilissis Sofias 91, 106 60 Athens; tel. (1) 7212951; fax (1) 7226724; Ambassador: NICHOLAS BURNS.

**Uruguay:** Odos Likavitou I G, 106 72 Athens; tel. (1) 3613549; Ambassador: ULYSSES PEREIRA REVERBEL.

**Venezuela:** Leoforos Vassilissis Sofias 112, Athens; tel. (1) 7708769; Ambassador: OLGA LUCILA CARMONA.

**Yugoslavia:** Leoforos Vassilissis Sofias 106, Athens; tel. (1) 7774344; Ambassador: DRAGMIR VUČIČEVIĆ.

# Judicial System

The Constitution of 1975 provides for the establishment of a Special Supreme Tribunal. Other provisions in the Constitution provided for a reorganization of parts of the judicial system to be accomplished through legislation.

### SUPREME ADMINISTRATIVE COURTS

**Special Supreme Tribunal:** Odos Patision 30, Athens; has final jurisdiction in matters of constitutionality.

**Council of State:** Odos Panepistimiou 47, 105 64 Athens; tel. (1) 3223830; fax (1) 3231154; has appellate powers over acts of the administration and final rulings of administrative courts; has power to rule upon matters of judicial review of laws.

**President:** VASSILIS BOTOPOULOS.

### SUPREME JUDICIAL COURT

**Supreme Court:** Leoforos Alexandros 121, 115 22 Athens; tel. (1) 6411845; supreme court in the State, having also appellate powers; consists of six sections, four Civil and two Penal, and adjudicates in quorum.

**President:** STEPHANOS MATHIAS.

### COURTS OF APPEAL

There are 12 Courts of Appeal with jurisdiction in cases of Civil and Penal Law of second degree, and, in exceptional penal cases, of first degree.

### COURTS OF FIRST INSTANCE

There are 59 Courts of First Instance with jurisdiction in cases of first degree, and in exceptional cases, of second degree. They function both as Courts of First Instance and as Criminal Courts. For serious crimes the Criminal Courts function with a jury.

In towns where Courts of First Instance sit there are also Juvenile Courts. Commercial Tribunals do not function in Greece, and all commercial cases are tried by ordinary courts of law. There are, however, Tax Courts in some towns.

### OTHER COURTS

There are 360 Courts of the Justice of Peace throughout the country. There are 48 Magistrates' Courts (or simple Police Courts).

In all the above courts, except those of the Justice of Peace, there are District Attorneys. In Courts of the Justice of Peace the duties of District Attorney are performed by the Public Prosecutor.

# Religion

## CHRISTIANITY

### The Eastern Orthodox Church

**The Orthodox Church of Greece:** Odos Ioannou Gennadiou 14, 115 21 Athens; tel. (1) 7218381; f. 1850; 78 dioceses, 8,335 priests, 84 bishops, 9,025,000 adherents (1985).

The Greek branch of the Holy Eastern Orthodox Church is the officially established religion of the country, to which nearly 97% of the population profess adherence. The administrative body of the Church is the Holy Synod of 12 members, elected by the bishops of the Hierarchy.

**Primate of Greece:** Archbishop CHRISTODOULOS of Athens.

Within the Greek State there is also the semi-autonomous Church of Crete, composed of seven Metropolitans and the Holy Archbishopric of Crete. The Church is administered by a Synod consisting of the seven Metropolitans under the Presidency of the Archbishop; it is under the spiritual jurisdiction of the Oecumenical Patriarchate of Constantinople, which also maintains a degree of administrative control.

**Archbishop of Crete:** Archbishop TIMOTHEOS (whose See is in Heraklion).

There are also four Metropolitan Sees of the Dodecanese, which are spiritually and administratively dependent on the Oecumenical Patriarchate and, finally, the peninsula of Athos, which constitutes the region of the Holy Mountain (Mount Athos) and comprises 20 monasteries. These are dependent on the Oecumenical Patriarchate of Constantinople, but are autonomous and are safeguarded constitutionally.

### The Roman Catholic Church

Latin Rite

Greece comprises four archdioceses (including two directly responsible to the Holy See), four dioceses and one Apostolic Vicariate. At December 1997 there were an estimated 59,828 adherents in the country.

**Bishop's Conference:** Conferentia Episcopalis Graeciae, Odos Homirou 9, 106 72 Athens; tel. (1) 3624311; fax (1) 3618632; f. 1967; Pres. Most Rev. NIKOLAOS FÓSKOLOS, Archbishop of Athens.

**Archdiocese of Athens:** Archbishopric, Odos Homirou 9, 106 72 Athens; tel. (1) 3624311; fax (1) 3618632; Archbishop Most Rev. NIKOLAOS FÓSKOLOS.

**Archdiocese of Rhodes:** Archbishopric, Odos I. Dragoumi 5A, 851 00 Rhodes; tel. (241) 21845; fax (241) 26688; Apostolic Administrator Most Rev. NIKOLAOS FÓSKOLOS (Archbishop of Athens).

**Metropolitan Archdiocese of Corfu, Zante and Cefalonia:** Archbishopric, Montzenikhov 3, 491 00 Kerkyra; tel. and fax (661) 30277; Archbishop Mgr ANTONIOS VARTHALITIS.

**Metropolitan Archdiocese of Naxos, Andros, Tinos and Mykonos:** Archbishopric, 842 00 Tinos; tel. (283) 22382; fax (283) 24769; e-mail karcntam@thn.forthnet.gr; also responsible for the suffragan diocese of Chios; Archbishop Mgr NIKOLAOS PRINTESIS

**Apostolic Vicariate of Salonika (Thessaloniki):** Leoforos Vassilissis Olgas 120B, 546 45 Thessaloniki; tel. (31) 835780; Apostolic Administrator Archbishop Mgr VARTHALITIS of Corfu.

Byzantine Rite

**Apostolic Exarchate for the Byzantine Rite in Greece:** Odos Akarnon 246, 112 53 Athens; tel. (1) 8670170; fax (1) 8677039; 2 parishes (Athens and Jannitsa, Macedonia); 7 secular priests, 2,300 adherents (Dec. 1997); Exarch Apostolic Mgr ANARGHYROS PRINTESIS, Titular Bishop of Gratianopolis.

Armenian Rite

**Exarchate for the Armenian Catholics in Greece:** Odos René Piot 2, 117 44 Athens; tel. (1) 9014089; fax (1) 9012109; 600 adherents (Dec. 1997); Exarch Archpriest NICHAN KARAKEHEYAN.

### Protestant Church

**Greek Evangelical Church (Reformed):** Odos Markon Botsari 24, 117 41 Athens; tel. (1) 9222684; internet www.gec.gr; f. 1858; comprises 30 organized churches; 5,000 adherents (1996); Moderator Rev. JOANNIS YPHANTIDES.

## ISLAM

The law provides as religious head of the Muslims a Chief Mufti; the Muslims in Greece possess a number of mosques and schools.

## JUDAISM

The Jewish population of Greece, estimated in 1943 at 75,000 people, was severely reduced as a result of the German occupation. In 1994 there were about 5,000 Jews in Greece.

**Central Board of the Jewish Communities of Greece:** Odos Voulis 36, 105 57 Athens; tel. (1) 3244315; fax (1) 3313852; e-mail hhkis@hellasnet.gr; f. 1945; officially recognized representative body of the communities of Greece; Pres. MOSES KONSTANTINIS.

**Jewish Community of Athens:** Odos Melidoni 8, 105 53 Athens; tel. (1) 3252823; fax (1) 3220761; Rabbi JACOB D. ARAR.

**Jewish Community of Larissa:** Odos Kentavrou 27, Larissa; tel. (41) 220762; Rabbi ELIE SABETAI.

**Jewish Community of Thessaloniki:** Odos Tsimiski 24, 546 24 Thessaloniki; tel. (31) 275701; Pres. ANDREAS SEFIHA; Rabbi ITZHAK DAYAN.

# The Press

## PRINCIPAL DAILY NEWSPAPERS

Morning papers are not published on Mondays, nor afternoon papers on Sundays. Afternoon papers are more popular than morning ones; in 1990 about 73,644 papers were sold each morning and up to 784,474 each afternoon.

### Athens

**Acropolis:** Leoforos Ionias 166, 111 44 Athens; tel. (1) 2114594; fax (1) 2114594; f. 1881; morning; Independent-Conservative; Acropolis Publications SA; Publr G. LEVIDES; Dir MARNIS SKOUNDRIDAKIS; circ. 50,819.

**Apogevmatini** (The Afternoon): Odos Phidiou 12, 106 78 Athens; tel. (1) 6430011; fax (1) 3609876; f. 1956; independent; Publr GEORGIOS HATZIKONSTANTINOU; Editor P. KARAYANNIS; circ. 67,257.

**Athens Daily Post:** Odos Stadiou 57, Athens; tel. (1) 3249504; f. 1952; morning; English; Owner G. SKOURAS.

**Athens News:** Odos Christou Lada 3, 102 37 Athens; tel. (1) 3333161; fax (1) 3231384; e-mail athnews@dolnet.gr; internet athensnews.dolnet.gr; f. 1952; morning; English; Publr CHRISTOS D. LAMBRAKIS; circ. 6,500.

**Athlitiki Icho** (Athletics Echo): Odos Aristonos 5-7, 104 41 Athens; tel. (1) 5232201; fax (1) 5232433; f. 1945; morning; Editor K. GEORGALAS; circ. 40,000.

**Avghi** (Dawn): Odos Ag. Konstantiou 12, 104 31 Athens; tel. (1) 5231831; fax (1) 5231830; f. 1952; morning; independent newspaper of the left; Dir and Editor L. VOUTSAS; circ. 5,400.

**Avriani** (Tomorrow): Odos Dimitros 11, 177 78 Athens; tel. (1) 3424090; fax (1) 3452190; f. 1980; evening; Publr GEORGE KOURIS; circ. 51,317.

**Dimokratikos Logos** (Democratic Speech): Odos Dimitros 11, 177 78 Athens; tel. (1) 3424023; fax (1) 3452190; f. 1986; morning; Dir and Editor KOSTAS GERONIKOLOS; circ. 7,183.

**Eleftheri Ora:** Odos Akademias 32, 106 72 Athens; tel. (1) 3621868; fax (1) 3603258; f. 1981; evening; Editor G. MIHALOPOULOS; circ. 1,026.

**Eleftheros Typos** (Free Press): Iroos Matsi, Ano Kalamaki, Athens; tel. (1) 9942431; f. 1983; evening; Dir. and Editor CH. PASALARIS; circ. 167,186.

**Eleftherotypia** (Press Freedom): Odos Minoou 10–16, 117 43 Athens; tel. (1) 9296001; fax (1) 9028311; f. 1974; evening; Publr CHR. TEGOPOULOS; Dir S. FYNDANIDIS; circ. 115,000.

**Estia** (Vesta): Odos Anthimou Gazi 7, 105 61 Athens; tel. (1) 3230650; fax (1) 3243071; e-mail estianews@otenet.gr; f. 1894; afternoon; Publr and Editor KOINONIA ASTIKOU DIKAIOU; circ. 60,000.

**Ethnos** (Nation): Odos Benaki 152, Metamorfosi Chalandriou, 152 35 Athens; tel. (1) 6580640; fax (1) 6396515; f. 1981; evening; Publr GEORGE BOBOLAS; Dir TH. KALOUDIS; circ. 84,735.

**Express:** Odos Halandriou 39, Paradissos Amaroussiou, 151 25 Athens; tel. (1) 6850200; fax (1) 6852202; f. 1963; morning, financial; Publr Hellenews Publications; Editor D. G. KALOFOLIAS; circ. 28,000.

**Filathlos:** Odos Dimitros 11, 177 78 Athens; tel. (1) 3424090; f. 1982; morning; Dir NICK KARAGIANNIDIS; Publr and Editor G. A. KOURIS; circ. 40,000.

**Imerissia** (Daily): Odos Benaki & Ag. Nektariou, Metamorfosi Chalandriou, 152 35 Athens; tel. (1) 6061729; fax (1) 6016563; e-mail imerissia@pegasus.gr; internet www.pegasus.gr; f. 1947; morning; Publr PETROS ANTONIADIS; Man. Editor ANONIS DALIPIS; circ. 26,000.

**Kathimerini** (Every Day): Odos Sokrateous 57, Athens; tel. (1) 5231001; fax (1) 5247685; f. 1919; morning; Conservative; Editor A. KARKAYANNIS; circ. 34,085.

**Kerdos** (Profit): Leoforos Kifissias 178, Halandri, 152 31 Athens; tel. (1) 6473384; fax (1) 6472003; f. 1985; morning; Publr TH. LIAKOUNAKOS; Man. Editor SERAFIM KONSTANDINIDIS; circ. 18,000.

**Messimvrini** (Midday): El Venizelou 10, 106 71 Athens; tel. (1) 3646019; fax (1) 3636125; f. 1980; evening; Publr and Dir PANOS LOUKAKOS; circ. 17,451.

**Naftemboriki** (Daily Journal): Odos Lenorman 205, 104 42 Athens; tel. (1) 5130605; fax (1) 5146013; f. 1923; morning; non-political journal of finance, commerce and shipping; Dir N. ATHANASSIADIS; circ. 35,000.

**Niki** (Victory): Odos Sina 14 and Akademias, Athens; tel. (1) 3613301; fax (1) 3627270; f. 1989; Editor MARIA LOUDAROU.

**Onoma:** Odos Theatrou 3, 105 52 Athens; tel. (1) 3313167; fax (1) 3313174; Publr MAKIS PSOMIADIS.

**Ora Gia Spor** (Time for Sport): Athens; tel. (1) 9251200; fax (1) 9226167; f. 1991; sport; Editor EVANGELOS SEMBOS.

**Rizospastis** (Radical): Odos Irakliou 145, Perissos, 142 31 Athens; tel. (1) 2522002; fax (1) 2529480; f. 1974; morning; pro-Soviet Communist; Dir T. TSIGAS; Editor G. TRIKALINOS; circ. 28,740.

**Ta Nea** (News): Odos Christou Lada 3, 102 37 Athens; tel. (1) 3250611; fax (1) 3228797; f. 1944; liberal; evening; Dir L. KARAPANAYIOTIS; Editor CHRISTOS LAMBRAKIS; circ. 135,000.

**Vradyni** (Evening Press): Athens; tel. (1) 5231001; f. 1923; evening; right-wing; Gen. Man. H. ATHANASIADOU; circ. 71,914.

### Patras

**Peloponnesos:** Maizonos 206, 262 22 Patras; tel. (61) 312530; fax (61) 312535; f. 1886; independent conservative; Publr and Editor S. DOUKAS; circ. 7,000.

### Thessaloniki

**Ellinikos Vorras** (Greek North): Odos Grammou-Vitsi 19, 551 34 Thessaloniki; tel. (31) 416621; f. 1935; morning; Publr TESSA LEVANTIS; Dir N. MERGIOS; circ. 14,467.

**Thessaloniki:** Odos Monastiriou 85, 546 27 Thessaloniki; tel. (31) 521621; f. 1963; evening; Propr Publishing Co of Northern Greece SA; Dir LAZAROS HADJINAKOS; Editor KATERINA VELLIDI; circ. 36,040.

## SELECTED PERIODICALS

**Agora** (Market): Leoforos Kifissias 178, Halandri, 151 31 Athens; tel. (1) 6473384; fax (1) 6477893; f. 1987; fortnightly; politics, finance; Dir ANT. KEFALAS; circ. 20,000.

**Aktines:** Odos Karytsi 14, 105 61 Athens; tel. (1) 3235023; f. 1938; monthly; current affairs, science, philosophy, arts; aims to promote a Christian civilization; Publr Christian Union; circ. 10,000.

**Athèmes:** Athens; monthly; French; cultural; Chief Editor EMMANUEL ADELY; circ. 5,000.

**The Athenian:** Athens; tel. (1) 3222802; fax (1) 3223052; e-mail the-athenian@hol.gr; internet www.hol.gr; f. 1974; monthly; English; Publr KONSTANTINOS GEROU; Editor JOANNA STAVROPOULOS; circ. 14,000.

**Auto Express:** Odos Halandriou 39, Halandri, 152 32 Athens; tel. (1) 6816906; fax (1) 6825858; Dir D. KALOFOLIAS; circ. 18,828.

**Cosmopolitan:** Leoforos Marathonas 14, Pallini, 153 00 Athens; tel. (1) 6667312; f. 1979; monthly; women's magazine; Publr P. ROKANAS; Dir K. KOSTOULIAS; circ. 39,471.

**Deltion Diikiseos Epichiriseon Euro-Unial**(Business Administration Bulletin Euro-Unial): Odos Rhigillis 26, 106 74; Athens; tel. (1) 7235736; fax (1) 7240000; monthly; Editor I. PAPAMICHALAKIS; circ. 26,000.

**Demosiografiki** (Journalism): Procopiou 7–9, 171 24 Athens; tel. (1) 9731338; fax (1) 7470463; e-mail odeg@ath.forthnet.gr; f. 1987; quarterly; Dir JOHN MENOÚNOS; circ. 4,000.

**Ekonomicos Tachydromos** (Financial Courier): Odos Christou Lada 3, 102 37 Athens; tel. (1) 3333630; fax (1) 3238740; e-mail oikonomikos@dolnet.gr; f. 1926; weekly; illustrated magazine; Man. Editor DENIS ANTIPAS; circ. 23,000.

**Ena** (One): Odos Voukourestiou 15, 106 71 Athens; tel. (1) 3644151; f. 1983; weekly; Dir S. TSIHLIAS; circ. 34,124.

**Epiloghi:** Odos Stadiou 4, 105 64 Athens; tel. (1) 3238427; fax (1) 3235160; e-mail epilogi@mail.hol.gr; f. 1962; weekly; economics; Editor GEORGE MALOUHOS.

**Greece's Weekly for Business and Finance:** Athens; tel. (1) 7707280; weekly; English; finance; Dir V. KORONAKIS.

**Gynaika** (Women): Odos Fragoklissias 7, Marousi, 151 25 Athens; tel. (1) 6199149; fax (1) 6104707; f. 1950; monthly; fashion, beauty, cookery, social problems, news; Publr CHRISTOS TERZOPOULOS; circ. 45,000.

**Hellenews:** Odos Halandriou 39, Marousi, 151 25 Athens; tel. (1) 6899400; fax (1) 6899430; weekly; English; finance and business; Publr Hellenews Publications; Editor J. M. GERMANOS.

**Hellenic Business:** Odos Ravine 12, 115 21 Athens; fax (1) 7217519; Greek and English; circ. 20,000.

**Makedoniki Zoi** (Macedonian Life): Thessaloniki; tel. (31) 277700; fax (31) 266908; monthly; Editor N. J. MERTZOS; circ. 70,000.

**48 Ores** (48 Hours): Leoforos Alexandras 19, 114 73 Athens; tel. (1) 6430313; fax (1) 6461361; weekly; Dir and Editor SP. KARATZAFERIS; circ. 9,127.

**Pantheon:** Odos Christou Lada 3, 102 37 Athens; tel. (1) 3230221; fax (1) 3228797; fortnightly; Publr and Dir N. THEOFANIDES; circ. 23,041.

**Politika Themata:** Odos Ypsilantou 25, 106 75 Athens; tel. (1) 7218421; weekly; Publr J. CHORN; Dir C. KYRKOS; circ. 2,544.

**Pontiki** (Mouse): Odos Massalias 10, 106 81 Athens; tel. (1) 3609531; weekly; humour; Dir and Editor K. PAPAIOANNOU.

**Radiotileorassi** (Radio-TV): Odos Mourouzi 16, 106 74 Athens; tel. (1) 7224811; weekly; circ. 134,626.

**Technika Chronika** (Technical Times): Odos Karageorgi Servias 4, 105 62 Athens; tel. (1) 3234751; f. 1952; monthly; general edition on technical and economic subjects; Editor D. ROKOS; circ. 12,000.

**Tilerama:** Odos Voukourestiou 18, 106 71 Athens; tel. (1) 3607160; fax (1) 3607032; f. 1977; weekly; radio and television; circ. 189,406.

**To Vima** (Tribune): Odos Christou Lada 3, 102 37 Athens; tel. (1) 3333103; fax (1) 3239097; f. 1922; weekly; liberal; Dir and Editor STAVROS R. PSYCHARIS; circ. 250,000.

**La Tribune hellénique:** Athens; bimonthly; French; politics, economics; Dir THEODORE BENAKIS; circ. 3,000.

**Viomichaniki Epitheorissis** (Industrial Review): Odos Zalokosta 4, 106 71 Athens; tel. (1) 3627218; fax (1) 3626388; e-mail viomep@acci.gr; f. 1934; monthly; industrial and economic review; Publr A.C. VOVOLINI-LASKARIDIS; Editor D. KARAMANOS; circ. 25,000.

### NEWS AGENCIES

**Athens News Agency (ANA):** Odos Tsoha 36, 115 21 Athens; tel. (1) 6400560; fax (1) 6400581; e-mail ape@ana.gr; internet www.ana.gr; f. 1895; correspondents in leading capitals of the world and towns throughout Greece; Gen. Dir ANDREAS CHRISTODOULIDES.

#### Foreign Bureaux

**Agence France-Presse (AFP):** Athens; tel. (1) 3633388; Bureau Chief JEAN-PIERRE ALTIER.

**Agencia EFE** (Spain): Athens; tel. (1) 3635826; Bureau Chief D. MARÍA-LUISA RUBIO; Correspondent JUAN JOSÉ FERNÁNDEZ ELORRIAGA.

**Agenzia Nazionale Stampa Associata (ANSA)** (Italy): Odos Kanari 9, 106 71 Athens; tel. (1) 3605285; fax (1) 3635367; Correspondent FRANCESCO INDRACCOLO.

**Associated Press (AP)** (USA): Leoforos Amalias 52, 105 52 Athens; tel. (1) 3310802; fax (1) 3310804.

**Deutsche Presse-Agentur (dpa)** (Germany): Miniati 1, 116 36 Athens; tel. (1) 9247774; fax (1) 9222185; Correspondent HILDEGARD HÜLSENBECK.

**Informatsionnoye Telegrafnoye Agentstvo Rossii—Telegrafnoye Agentstvo Suverennykh Stran (ITAR—TASS)** (Russia): Odos Gizi 39, Palaio Psychiko, 15 452 Athens; tel. and fax (1) 6713069; Bureau Chief VLADIMIR V. MALYSHEV.

**Novinska Agencija Tanjug** (Yugoslavia): Evrou 94–96, Ambelokipi, Athens; tel. (1) 7791545.

**Reuters Hellas SA** (UK): 7th Floor, Kolokotroni 1/Leoforos Stadiou, 105 62 Athens; tel. (1) 3647610; fax (1) 3604490; Man. Dir WILLIAM CAIRLEY.

**Rossiiskoye Informatsionnoye Agentstvo—Novosti (RIA—Novosti)** (Russia): Odos Irodotou 9, 138 Athens; tel. (1) 7291016; Bureau Chief BORIS KOROLYOV; Correspondent J. KURIZIN.

**Xinhua (New China) News Agency** (People's Republic of China): Odos Amarilidos 19, Palaio Psychiko, Athens; tel. (1) 6724997; Bureau Chief XIE CHENGHAO.

### PRESS ASSOCIATIONS

**Enosis Antapokriton Xenou Tipou** (Foreign Press Association of Greece): Odos Akademias 23, 106 71 Athens; tel. (1) 3637318; fax (1) 3605035.

**Enosis Syntakton Imerission Ephimeridon Athinon** (Journalists' Union of Athens Daily Newspapers): Odos Akademias 20, 106 71 Athens; tel. (1) 3632601; fax (1) 3632608; f. 1914; Pres. DIMITRIOS MATHIOPOULOS; Gen. Sec. MANOLIS MATHIOUDAKIS; 1,400 mems.

**Enosis Syntakton Periodikou Tipou** (Journalists' Union of the Periodical Press): Odos Valaoritou 9, 106 71 Athens; tel. (1) 3636039; fax (1) 3644967; e-mail espt@magazinepress.gr; internet www magazinepress.gr; Pres. ATHENESE PAPANDROPOULOS; 600 mems.

## Publishers

**Agkyra Publications:** Leoforos Kifisou 85, Egaleo, 122 41 Athens; tel. (1) 3455276; fax (1) 3474732; f. 1890; general; Man. Dir DIMITRIOS PAPADIMITRIOU.

**Agritas:** Odos Efessou 24, 171 21 Athens; tel. (1) 9334685; fax (1) 9311436; e-mail akritaspublications@ath.forthnet.gr; f. 1979; history, spirituality, children's books.

**D. I. Arsenidis & Co:** Odos Akademias 57, 106 79 Athens; tel. (1) 3629538; fax (1) 3618707; biography, literature, children's books, history, philosophy, social sciences; Man. Dir JOHN ARSENIDIS.

**Boukoumanis Editions:** Odos Mavromichali 1, 106 79 Athens; tel. (1) 3618502; fax (1) 3630669; f. 1967; history, politics, sociology, psychology, belles-lettres, educational, arts, children's books, ecology; Man. ELIAS BOUKOUMANIS.

**Dorikos Publishing House:** Odos Charalabou Sotiriou 9–11, 114 72 Athens; tel. (1) 6454726; fax (1) 3301866; f. 1958; literature, fiction, history, politics; Editor ROUSSOS VRANAS.

**Ekdotike Athenon, SA:** Odos Omirou 11, 106 72 Athens; tel. (1) 3608911; fax (1) 3606157; f. 1961; history, archaeology, art; Man. Dirs GEORGE A. CHRISTOPOULOS, JOHN C. BASTIAS.

**G. C. Eleftheroudakis, SA:** Odos Panepistimiou 17, 105 64 Athens; tel. (1) 3314180; fax (1) 3239821; e-mail elebooks@netor.gr; f. 1915; general, technical and scientific; Man. Dir VIRGINIA ELEFTHEROUDAKIS-GREGOU.

**Exandas Publrs:** Odos Didotou 57, 106 81 Athens; tel. (1) 3804885; fax (1) 3813065; f. 1974; fiction, literature, social sciences; Pres. MAGDA N. KOTZIA.

**Govostis Publishing, SA:** Zoodohou Pigis 21, 106 81 Athens; tel. (1) 3815433; fax (1) 3816661; e-mail cotsos@compulink.gr; f. 1926; arts, fiction, politics; Pres. COSTAS GOVOSTIS.

**Denise Harvey:** Katounia, 340 05 Limmi, Evia; tel. and fax (227) 31154; f. 1972; modern Greek literature and poetry, belles-lettres, theology, translations, selected general list (English and Greek); Man. Dir DENISE HARVEY.

**Hestia-I.D. Kollaros & Co, SA:** Odos Solonos 60, 106 72 Athens; tel. (1) 3615077; fax (1) 3606759; f. 1885; literature, history, politics, architecture, philosophy, travel, religion, psychology, textbooks, general; Gen. Dir MARINA KARAITIDIS.

**Kastaniotis Editions, SA:** Odos Zalogou 11, 106 78 Athens; tel. (1) 3301208; fax (1) 3822530; e-mail kastaniotis@ath.forthnet.gr; f. 1969; arts, fiction, social sciences; Man. Dir ATHANASIOS KASTANIOTIS.

**Kritiki Publishing:** Odos Koletti 25, 106 77 Athens; tel. (1) 3622390; fax (1) 3621367; e-mail kritiki@hol.gr; f. 1987; economics, politics, literature; Pres. THEMIS MINOGLOU.

**Kronos:** Odos Egnatia 33, 546 26 Thessaloniki; tel. (31) 532077; fax (31) 538158; Dir TH. GIOTAS.

**Lambrakis Press, SA:** Odos Christou Lada 3, 102 37 Athens; tel. (1) 3333555; fax (1) 3228797; internet www.dolnet.gr; newspapers and magazines; 18 titles.

**Livani Publishing Org.:** Odos Solonos 98, 106 80 Athens; tel. (1) 3610589; fax (1) 3617791; e-mail glykeria@livanis.gr; general; Publr A. A. LIVANI.

**Minoas Ilias Konstantaropoulos & Co, OE:** Odos Possidonos 1, 141 21 Athens; tel. (1) 2776814; fax (1) 2711056; e-mail info@minoas.gr; internet www.minoas.gr; f. 1954; fiction, art, history; Man. Dir YANNIS KONSTANTAROPOULOS.

**Odos Panos:** Odos Didotou 39, 106 08 Athens; tel. and fax (1) 3616782; poetry, drama, biography.

**Papazissis Publishers:** Nikitara 2, 106 78 Athens; tel. (1) 3822496; fax (1) 3809150; e-mail papazisi@otenet.gr; internet www.papzisi.gr; f. 1929; economics, politics, law, history, school books; Man. Dir VICTOR PAPAZISSIS.

**Patakis Publications:** Odos Valtetsiou 14, 106 80 Athens; tel. (1) 3638362; fax (1) 3628950; art, reference, literature, educational, philosophy, psychology, sociology, religion, music, children's books, educational toys, CD-Rom and audiobooks; Pres. STEFANOS PATAKIS.

**Pontiki Publications SA:** Odos Massalias 10, 106 80 Athens; tel. (1) 3609531; fax (1) 3645406; f. 1979; govt, history, political science; Man. Dir KOSTAS TABANIS.

**John Sideris:** Odos Stadiou 44, 105 64 Athens; tel. (1) 3229638; fax (1) 3245052; f. 1898; school textbooks, general; Man. J. SIDERIS.

**J. G. Vassiliou:** Odos Hippokratous 15, 106 79 Athens; tel. (1) 3623382; fax (1) 3623580; f. 1913; fiction, history, philosophy, dictionaries and children's books; Pres. J. VASSILIOU.

#### Government Publishing House

**Government Printing House:** Odos Kapodistriou 34, 104 32 Athens; tel. (1) 5248320.

### PUBLISHERS' FEDERATIONS

**Hellenic Federation of Publishers and Booksellers:** Odos Themistokleus 73, 106 83 Athens; tel. (1) 3300924; fax (1) 3301617; e-mail poev@otenet.gr; f. 1961; Pres. GEORGE DARDANOS; Gen. Sec. STEFANOS VASILOPOULOS.

**Publishers' and Booksellers' Association of Athens:** Odos Themistokleus 73, 106 83 Athens; tel. (1) 3303268; fax (1) 3823222; Pres. VASSILIS CHATZIAKOVOU; Sec. ELENI KAVIAKI.

## Broadcasting and Communications

### TELECOMMUNICATIONS

**National Telecommunications Commission (NTC):** Leoforos Kifissias 60, 151 25 Athens; tel. (1) 6805040; fax (1) 6805049; e-mail alouk@eet.gr; internet www.eet.gr; regulatory body; Chair. A. LAMBRINOPOULOS.

**Organismos Telepikoinonion tis Elladas, SA (OTE)** Hellenic Telecommunications Organization): Leoforos Kifissias 99, 151 24 Maroussi, Athens; tel. (1) 8827015; fax (1) 6115825; e-mail ote@ote.gr; internet www.ote.gr; f. 1949; owned 51% by the Government, 49% by public shareholders; 5.6m. lines in service; Man. Dir GEORGE SYMEONIDIS.

**Cosmote:** Leoforos Kifissias 44, 151 25 Athens; tel. (1) 6177700; fax (1) 6177594; e-mail customercare@cosmote.gr; internet www.cosmote.gr; OTE subsidiary, 30%-owned by Telenor; mobile services; Man. Dir NIKOS MANASSIS.

**Maritel:** Odos Egaleo 8, 185 45 Piraeus; tel. (1) 4599500; fax (1) 4599600; e-mail maritel@maritel.gr; internet www.maritel.gr; OTE subsidiary; marine telecommunications; Chair. THEODOROS VENIAMIS; Man. Dir MICHALIS MICHAELIDES.

**Panafon SA:** Leoforos Messoghion 2, 115 27 Athens; tel. (1) 7483601; e-mail webmaster@panafon.gr; internet www.panafon.gr; mobile telecommunications.

**Telestet Hellas SA:** Leoforos Alex. Papagoy 8, 157 71 Athens; tel. (1) 7772033; internet www.telestet.gr; 75%-owned by STET International; mobile network; Man. Dir GIACINTO CICCHESE.

### RADIO

**Elliniki Radiophonia Tileorassi (ERT, SA)** (Greek Radio-Television): Leoforos Messoghion 432, 153 42 Athens; tel. (1) 6066835; fax (1) 6009325; e-mail pxristofylakou@ert.gr; state-controlled since 1938; Chair. and Man. Dir PANAGHIOTIS PANAGHIOTOU.

**Elliniki Radiophonia-ERA** (Greek Radio): POB 60019, Leoforos Messoghion 432, 153 42 Aghia Paraskevi, Athens; tel. (1) 6066815; fax (1) 6009425; e-mail ijanetakos@ert.gr; Dir YANNIS TZANNETAKOS.

**Macedonia Radio Station:** Odos Angelaki 2, 546 21 Thessaloniki; tel. (31) 299400; fax (31) 299451; e-mail ert3rd@compulink.gr; internet www.ert3.gr.

### TELEVISION

A television network of 17 transmitters is in operation. The State's monopoly of television broadcasting ended in 1990, and by 1998 there were 17 private broadcasters.

#### State stations

**Elliniki Radiophonia Tileorassi (ERT, SA)** (Greek Radio-Television): (see Radio).

**Elliniki Tileorassi** (Greek Television) **1 (ET1):** Leoforos Messoghion 136, 115 27 Athens; tel. (1) 7758824; fax (1) 7797776; e-mail kalavanos@ert.gr; Dir-Gen. KONSTANTINOS ALAVANOS.

**ET2:** Leoforos Messoghion 136; 115 25 Athens; tel. (1) 7701911; fax (1) 7797776; Dir-Gen. PANAYOTIS PANAYOTOU.

**ET3:** Aggelaki 2, 546 21 Thessaloniki; tel. (31) 299400; fax (31) 299655; e-mail ert3pl@compulink.gr; internet www.ert3.gr; Dir-Gen. MICHALIS ALEXANDRIDIS.

#### Private stations

**Antenna TV:** Leoforos Kifissias 10-12, Maroussi, 151 25 Athens; tel. (1) 688600; fax (1) 6834349; e-mail webmaster@antenna.gr; internet www.antenna.gr.

**Argo TV:** Metamorphosseos 9, 551 32 Kalamaria, Thessaloniki; tel. (31) 351733; fax (31) 351739.

**Channel Seven-X:** Leoforos Kifissias 64, Athens; tel. (1) 68976042; fax (1) 6897608.

**City Channel:** Leoforos Kastoni 14, 41223 Larissa; tel. (41) 232839; fax (41) 232013.

**Jeronimo Groovy TV:** Ag konstantin 40, 151 24 Athens; tel. (1) 6896360; fax (1) 6896950.

**Mega Channel:** Leoforos Messoghion 117, 115 26 Athens; tel. (1) 6903000; fax (1) 6983600; e-mail ngeorgiou@megatv.com; internet www.megatv.com; f. 1989; Man. Dir ELIAS TSIGAS.

**Neo Kanali SA:** Pireos 9-11, 105 52 Athens; tel. (1) 5238230; fax (1) 5247325.

**Serres TV:** Nigritis 27, 62124 Serres.

**Skai TV:** Phalereos & Ethnarchou 2, Macaroiu, N. Phaliro.

**Star Channel:** Dimitras 37, 1178 Tayros, Athens; tel. (1) 3450626; fax (1) 3452190.

**Tele City:** Praxitelous 58, 17674 Athens; tel (1) 9429222; fax (1) 9413589.

**Teletora:** Lycabetous 17, 10672 Athens; tel. (1) 3617285; fax (1) 3638712.

**Traki TV:** Central Square, 67100 Xanthi; tel. (541) 20670; fax (541) 27368.

**TRT:** Odos Zachou 5, 38333 Volos; tel. (421) 288013; fax (421) 36888.

**TV Macedonia:** Nea Egnatia 222, 54642 Thessaloniki; tel. (31) 850512; fax (31) 850513.

**TV Plus:** Athens; tel. (1) 9028707; fax (1) 9028310.

**TV-100:** Odos Aggelaki 16, 54621 Thessaloniki; tel. (31) 265828; fax (31) 267532.

# Finance

(cap. = capital; p.u. = paid up; res = reserves; dep. = deposits; dre = drachmae; m. = million; br. = branch)

### BANKING

#### Central Bank

**Bank of Greece:** Leoforos E. Venizelos 21, 102 50 Athens; tel. (1) 3201111; fax (1) 3232239; e-mail bogsecr@ath.forthnet.gr; f. 1927; state bank of issue; cap. dre 13,905.4m., res dre 114,970.2m., dep. dre 7,801,693.3m. (Dec. 1997); Gov. LUKAS PAPADEMOS; 27 brs.

#### Commercial Banks

**Agricultural Bank of Greece:** Odos Panepistimiou 23, 105 64 Athens; tel. (1) 3230521; fax (1) 3234386; f. 1929; wholly-owned by State; cap. dre 160,007.0m., res dre 46,660.0m., dep. dre 3,495,028.9m. (Dec. 1997); Gov. and Chair. PETROS LAMBROU, 437 brs.

**Alpha Credit Bank:** Odos Stadiou 40, 102 52 Athens; tel. (1) 3260000; fax (1) 3265438; e-mail secretariat@alpha.gr; internet www.alpha.gr; f. 1879, renamed 1972; cap. dre 88,000.0m., res dre 255,523.8m., dep. dre 3,713,484.2m. (Dec. 1998); Chair. and Gen. Man. YANNIS S. COSTOPOULOS; 214 brs.

**Bank of Attica:** Odos Omirou 23, 106 72 Athens; tel. (1) 3646910; fax (1) 3646115; e-mail info@bankofattica.gr; internet www .bankofattica.gr; f. 1925; affiliated to the Commercial Bank of Greece; cap. dre 3,387.2m., res dre 15,058.8m., dep. dre 172,951.0m. (Dec. 1998); Chair. CHRISTOS APOSTOLOPOULOS; 39 brs.

**Bank of Crete, SA:** Odos Voukourestiou 22, 106 71 Athens; tel. (1) 3606511; fax (1) 3644832; f. 1924 (reformed 1973); privatized in 1998; cap. dre 41,874m., res dre 1,076.5m., dep. dre 359,784.5m. (Dec. 1997); Dir KOSTAS GEORGAKOPOULOS; 87 brs.

**Commercial Bank of Greece:** Odos Sophokleous 11, 102 35 Athens; tel. (1) 3284000; fax (1) 3253746; e-mail pubrel@combank.gr; internet www.combank.gr; f. 1907; cap. dre 140,995.5m., res dre 187,265.8m., dep. dre 2,897,391.0m. (Nov. 1999); Chair. and Man. Dir KONSTANTINOS GEORGOUTSAKOS; Gen. Man. GEORGE MICHELIS; 380 brs.

**Dorian Bank, SA:** Odos Fragoklissias 5, Maroussi, 151 25 Athens; tel. (1) 6896960; fax (1) 689191; e-mail dorianbank@otenet.gr; f. 1990; cap. dre 8,860.0m., res dre 3,980.0m., dep. dre 68,988.0m. (Dec. 1998); Chair. PANOS TSOUPIDES; 3 brs.

**EFG Eurobank SA:** Odos Othonos 8, 105 57 Athens; tel. (1) 3371062; fax (1) 3337256; internet www.eurobank.gr; f. 1990 as Euromerchant Bank SA (Eurobank), renamed as above 1997, merged with Bank of Athens in 1999; cap. dre 16,500m., res dre 6,980m., dep. dre 263.327m. (Dec. 1996); Chair. GEORGE GONTIKAS; Man. Dir NIKOLAS NANOPOULOS; 5 brs.

**Egnatia Bank:** Odos Danaidon 4, 546 26 Thessaloniki; tel. (31) 598600; fax (31) 598675; e-mail pr@egnatiabank.gr; internet www.egnatiabank.gr; f. 1991; merged with Bank of Central Greece in 1999; Pres. VASSILLOS THEOCHARAKIS; Man. Dir and Gen. Man. VASSILLIS KELTSOPOULOS; 49 brs.

**Ergobank, SA:** Kolokotroni and Voulis 3, 105 62 Athens; tel. (1) 3221345; fax (1) 3253308; internet www.ergobank.gr; f. 1975; cap. dre 22,240.7m., res dre 97,478.7m., dep. dre 1,491,659.6m. (Dec. 1998); Chair. Gen. X. C. NICKITAS; Man. Dir A. G. BIBAS; 124 brs.

**European Popular Bank SA:** Odos Panepistimiou 13, 105 64 Athens; tel. (1) 3550000; fax (1) 3313305; f. 1992; cap. dre 5,500m.; res dre 1,202.3m; dep. dre 68,599.4m. (Dec. 1995); Chair. KIKIS LAZARIDES; Dep. Gen. Man. CHRISTOS STYLANIDES; 13 brs.

**General Bank of Greece SA:** Odos Panepistimiou 9, 102 29 Athens; tel. (1) 33250300; fax (1) 3222271; e-mail epithesistomellon@geniki.gr; f. 1937 as Bank of the Army Share Fund, renamed General Hellenic Bank in 1966, and as above in 1997; cap. dre 16,972.1m., res dre 21,484.2m., dep. dre 470,009.6m. (Dec. 1998); Chair. GEORGIOS P. DASKALAKIS; Gen. Man. N. BERETANOS; 91 brs.

**Ionian and Popular Bank of Greece, SA:** Odos Panepistimiou 45, 105 64 Athens; tel. (1) 3225501; fax (1) 3222882; internet www.ionianbank.gr; f. 1958 by merger; cap. dre 19,602.0m., res dre 40,694.2m., dep. dre 1,769,744.8m. (Dec. 1998); Chair. and Man. Dir YANNIS S. COSTOPOULOS; Gen. Man. DIMITRIOS P. MANTZOUNIS; 216 local brs, 2 overseas.

**Macedonia Thrace Bank, SA:** Odos Ionos Dragoumi 5, 546 25 Thessaloniki; tel. (31) 539644; fax (31) 547323; e-mail mtbinfo@mathrabank.gr; internet www.mathrabank.gr; f, 1979; to merge with Piraeus Bank and Xiosbank by June 2000; cap. dre 17,369.5m., res dre 42,185.4m., dep. dre 577,642.0m. (Dec. 1998); Chair. MICHALIS SALLAS; Man. Dir DAVID WATSON; 74 brs.

**National Bank of Greece, SA:** Odos Aeolou 86, 102 32 Athens; tel. (1) 3441000; fax (1) 3346550; internet www.ethniki.gr; f. 1841; cap. dre 205,330.1m., res dre 253,034.2m., dep. dre 11,140,623.2m. (Dec. 1998); Gov. THEODOROS KARATZAS; 610 brs.

**Piraeus Bank, SA:** Leoforos Amalias 20, 105 57 Athens; tel. (1) 3335000; fax (1) 3335030; internet www.piraeusbank.gr; f. 1916; to merge with Macedonia Thrace Bank and Xiosbank by June 2000; cap. dre 39,960.0m. res 44,299.8m., dep. dre 535,942.6m. (Dec. 1998); Chair. M. SALLAS; Man. Dir D. WATSON; 36 brs.

**Piraeus Prime Bank, SA:** Leoforos Vassilissis Sofias 75, 115 21 Athens; tel. (1) 7250323; fax (1) 7210134; f. 1981 as Banque Franco-Hellenique de Commerce International et Maritime SA, renamed Credit Lyonnais Grèce 1994 and as above 1998; dre 8,300m., res dre 5,075.7m., dep. dre 69,149.9m. (Dec. 1997); Pres. ALFRED BOUCKAERT; Man. Dir BAUDOUIN MERLET; 1 br.

**Xiosbank, SA:** Leoforos Vassilissis Sofias 11, 106 71 Athens; tel. (1) 3288888; fax (1) 3244909; e-mail xiosbank@netor.gr; internet www.xiosbank.gr; f. 1990; to merge with Macedonia Thrace Bank and Piraeus Bank by June 2000; cap. dre 12,068.3m., res dre 15,001.5m., dep. dre 461,543.9m. (Dec. 1998); Chair. VARDIS I. VARDINOYANNIS; Gen. Man. IOANNIS G. PEHLIVANIDIS; 34 brs.

### Development Banks

**Hellenic Industrial Development Bank, SA:** Leoforos Syngrou 87, 117 45 Athens; tel. (1) 9241425; fax (1) 9241513; f. 1964; state-owned limited liability banking company; the major Greek institution in the field of industrial investment; cap. dre 245,890.0m., res dre 44,424.3m., dep. dre 502,897.6m. (Dec. 1996); Chair. and Gov. GEORGE KASMAS; 11 brs.

**National Investment Bank for Industrial Development, SA:** Leoforos Amalias 12-14, 102 36 Athens; tel. (1) 3242651; fax (1) 3296211; f. 1963; cap. dre 8,156.2m., res dre 23,653.7m., dep. dre 58,950.0m. (Dec. 1996); long-term loans, equity participation, promotion of co-operation between Greek and foreign enterprises; Chair. NIKOLAOS KARAMOUZIS; Man. Dir DEMETRIOS PAVLAKIS.

## STOCK EXCHANGE

**Athens Stock Exchange:** Odos Sophokleous 10, 105 59 Athens; tel. (1) 3211301; fax (1) 3213938; internet www.ase.gr; f. 1876; Pres. SPIROS KOUNIAKIS; Vice-Pres. THEODOROS PANTOLAKIS.

## PRINCIPAL INSURANCE COMPANIES

**Agrotiki Hellenic Insurance Co:** Leoforos Syngrou 163, 171 21 Athens; tel. (1) 9379100; fax (1) 9358924; Gen. Man. TR. LISIMACHOU.

**Alpha Insurance:** Leoforos Kifissias 44, 151 25 Maroussi, Athens; tel. (1) 6162000; fax (1) 6162810; f. 1940; Chair. PHOTIS P. COSTOPOULOS; Gen. Man. JOHN L. GALANOPOULOS.

**Apollon Insurance Co:** Leoforos Syngrou 39, 117 43 Athens; tel. (1) 9236362; fax (1) 9236916; f. 1976; Gen. Man. E. PANANIDIS.

**Aspis Pronia General Insurance SA:** Leoforos Kifissias 62, Maroussi, 151 25 Athens; tel. (1) 6804480; fax (1) 6898990; f. 1941; Pres. and CEO PAUL PSOMIADES.

**Astir:** Odos Merlin 6, 106 71 Athens; tel. (1) 3604111; fax (1) 3633333; f. 1930; Gen. Man. B. CHARDALIAS.

**Atlantiki Enosis:** Odos Messoghion 71, 115 26 Athens; tel. (1) 7799211; fax (1) 7794446; f. 1970; Gen. Man. N. LAPATAS.

**Dynamis, SA:** Leoforos Syngrou 106, 117 41 Athens; tel. (1) 9227255; fax (1) 9237768; f. 1977; Man. Dir NIKOLAS STAMATOPOULOS.

**Egnatia Co:** Odos Fragon 1, 546 26 Thessaloniki; tel. (31) 523325; fax (31) 523555; Rep. P. MIGAS.

**Emporiki:** Odos Philhellinon 6, 105 57 Athens; tel. (1) 3240093; fax (1) 3223835; f. 1940; Chair. PHOTIS P. KOSTOPOULOS; Exec. Dir MICHAEL P. PSALIDAS.

**Estia Insurance and Reinsurance Co, SA:** Odos Parnonos 3, 151 25 Maroussi, Athens; tel. (1) 6127540; fax (1) 6127559; f. 1943; Chair. ALKIVIADIS CHIONIS; Gen. Man. D. GIANNIOS.

**Ethniki Hellenic General Insurance Co:** Odos Karageorgi Servias 8, 102 10 Athens; tel. (1) 3299000; fax (1) 3236101; f. 1891; Gen. Man. C. PHILIPOU.

**Eurogroup Insurance and Reinsurance Co:** Leoforos Syngrou 247, 171 22 Athens; tel. (1) 9425094; fax (1) 9411919.

**Galaxias:** Leoforos Syngrou 40–42, 117 42 Athens; tel. (1) 9241082; fax (1) 9241698; f. 1967; Gen. Man. I. TSOUPRAS.

**Geniki Epagelmatiki:** Odos Panepistimiou 56, 106 78 Athens; tel. (1) 3636910; fax (1) 3606848; f. 1967; Gen. Man. A. FILIPPATOS.

**Gothaer Hellas, SA:** Odos Michalakopoulou 174, 115 27 Athens; tel. (1) 7750801; fax (1) 7757094; Gen. Man. S. GALANIS.

**Hellas:** Leoforos Kifissias 119, 151 24 Marousi; tel. (1) 6124286; fax (1) 8027189; f. 1973; Gen. Man. N. NARDIS.

**Hellenic Reliance General Insurances, SA:** Leoforos Kifissias 304, 152 32 Halandri; tel. (1) 6843733; fax (1) 6843734; f. 1990; Man. Dir S. F. TRIANTAFYLLAKIS.

**Hellenobretanniki General Insurances, SA:** Leoforos Messogion 2–4, 115 27 Athens; tel. (1) 7755301; fax (1) 7714768; f. 1988.

**Helvetia General Insurance Co:** Leoforos Kifissias 124, 115 26 Athens; tel. (1) 6980840; fax (1) 6923446; f. 1943; Gen. Man. J. DELENDAS.

**Horizon Insurance Co, SA:** Leoforos Amalias 26A, 105 57 Athens; tel. (1) 3227932; fax (1) 3225540; f. 1965; Gen. Mans THEODORE ACHIS, CHR. ACHIS.

**Hydrogios:** Odos Solonos 137, 176 75 Athens; tel. (1) 9401300; fax (1) 9407072; Gen. Man. A. KASKARELIS.

**Ikonomiki:** Odos Kapodistriou 38, 104 32 Athens; tel. (1) 5243374; fax (1) 5234962; f. 1968; Gen. Man. D. NIKOLAIDIS.

**Imperial Hellas, SA:** Leoforos Syngrou 253, 171 22 Athens; tel. (1) 9426352; fax (1) 9426202; f. 1971; Gen. Man. G. JANIS.

**Interamerican Hellenic Life Insurance Co:** Interamerican Plaza, Leoforos Kifissias 117, 151 80 Maroussi, Athens; tel. (1) 6191111; fax (1) 6191877; e-mail tzoumass@interamerican.gr; f. 1971; Pres. and Man. Dir DIMITRI KONTOMINAS.

**Interamerican Property and Casualty Insurance Co:** Leoforos Kifissias 117, 151 80 Maroussi, Athens; tel. (1) 6191111; fax (1) 8060820; e-mail tzoumas@interamerican.gr; f. 1974; Man. Dir C. BERTSIAS.

**Kykladiki:** Leoforos Syngrou 80–88, 117 41 Athens; tel. (1) 9247664; fax (1) 9247344; f. 1919; Gen. Man. PAN. KATSIKOSTAS.

**Laiki Insurance Company, SA:** Leoforos Syngrou 135, 171 21 N. Smyrni; tel. (1) 9332911; fax (1) 9335949; f. 1942; Gen. Man. N. MOURTZOUKOS.

**National Insurance Institution of Greece:** Odos Agiou Konstantinou 6, 104 31 Athens; tel. (1) 5223300; fax (1) 5239754; Rep. J. KYRIAKOS.

**Olympic-Victoria General Insurance Co, SA:** Odos Tsimiski 21, 546 22 Thessaloniki; tel. (31) 239331; fax (31) 239264; f. 1972; Man. Dir G. ANDONIADIS.

**Panellinios:** Leoforos Syngrou 171, 171 21 Athens; tel. (1) 9352003; fax (1) 9352451; f. 1918; Gen. Man. A. VALYRAKIS.

**Pegasus Insurance Co:** Odos Stadiou 5, 105 62 Athens; tel. (1) 3227357; fax (1) 3246728; Gen. Man. M. PARASKAKIS.

**Phoenix-General Insurance Co of Greece, SA:** Odos Omirou 2, 105 64 Athens; tel. (1) 3295111; fax (1) 3239135; f. 1928; general insurance; Rep. G. KOTSALOS.

**Poseidon:** Odos Karaiskou 163, 185 35 Piraeus; tel. (1) 4522685; fax (1) 4184337; f. 1972; Gen. Man. THANOS J. MELAKOPIDES.

**Proodos:** Leoforos Syngrou 198, 176 71 Kallithea; tel. (1) 9593302; fax (1) 9592992; f. 1941; Gen. Man. P. KARALIS.

**Propontis–Merimna A.E.A.:** Odos Agiou Konstantinou 6, 104 31 Athens; tel. (1) 5223300; fax (1) 5239754; f. 1917; Man. Dirs E. BALA-HILL, M. ARTAVANIS.

**Sideris Insurance Co, SA:** Odos Lekka 3–5, 105 63 Athens; tel. (1) 3224484; fax (1) 3231066; Dir G. SIDERIS.

**Syneteristiki:** Leoforos Syngrou 367, 175 64 Athens; tel. (1) 9491280; fax (1) 9403148; Gen. Man. D. ZORBAS.

**United Insurance Co SA:** Leoforos Kifissias 250–254, 152 31 Athens; tel. (1) 6742411; fax (1) 6741826; e-mail united@atheneos.com; f. 1977; Pres. D. DASKALOPOULOS; Man. Dir P. ATHENEOS.

A large number of foreign insurance companies also operate in Greece.

### Insurance Association

**Association of Insurance Companies:** Odos Xenophontos 10, 105 57 Athens; tel. (1) 3334100; fax (1) 3334149; e-mail eaee@eaee.gr; internet www.eaee.gr; 149 mems; Gen. Dir MARGARITA ANTONAKI.

# Trade and Industry

## GOVERNMENT AGENCY

**Organismos Anasinkrotiseos Epicheiriseon** (Industrial Reconstruction Organization): Athens; f. 1982; reconstruction and sale of Greek businesses under state receivership.

## CHAMBERS OF COMMERCE

**Athens Chamber of Commerce & Industry:** Odos Akademias 7, 106 71 Athens; tel. (1) 3602411; fax (1) 3616464; e-mail info@acci.gr; internet www.acci.gr; f. 1919; Pres. JOHN PAPATHANASSIOU; Sec.-Gen. DRACOULIS FOUNDOUKAKOS; 50,000 mems.

**Athens Chamber of Small and Medium-Sized Industries:** Odos Akademias 18, 106 71 Athens; tel. (1) 3635313; fax (1) 3614726; f.

1940; Pres. G. KYRIOPOULOS; Sec.-Gen. STERGIOS VASSILIOU; c. 60,000 mems.

**Handicraft Chamber of Piraeus:** Odos Karaiscou 111, 185 32 Piraeus; tel. (1) 4174152; f. 1925; Pres. KONSTANTINOS MOSCHOLIOS; Sec.-Gen. PANTELIS ANTONIADIS; 18,500 mems.

**Piraeus Chamber of Commerce & Industry:** Odos Loudovikou 1, 185 31 Piraeus; tel. (1) 4177241; fax (1) 4178680; f. 1919; Pres. GEORGE KASSIMATIS; Sec.-Gen. KONSTANTINOS SARANTOPOULOS.

**Thessaloniki Chamber of Commerce and Industry:** Odos Tsimiski 29, 546 24 Thessaloniki; tel. (31) 224438; fax (31) 230237; f. 1919; Pres. PANTELIS KONSTANTINIDIS; Sec.-Gen. EMMANUEL VLACHOYANNIS; 14,500 mems.

### INDUSTRIAL AND TRADE ASSOCIATIONS

**Association of Industries of Northern Greece:** Morihovou 1, 546 35 Thessaloniki; tel. (31) 539817; fax (31) 546244; f. 1914; Pres. NIKOLAOS EFTHIMIADES.

**Federation of Greek Industries (SEV):** Odos Xenophontos 5, 105 57 Athens; f. 1907; Pres. JASON STRATOS; 950 mems.

**Hellenic Cotton Board:** Leoforos Syngrou 150, 176 71 Athens; tel. (1) 9225011; fax (1) 9249656; f. 1931; state organization; Pres. P. K. MYLONAS.

**Hellenic Organization of Small and Medium-size Industries and Handicrafts:** Odos Xenias 16, 115 28 Athens; tel. (1) 7491370; fax (1) 7491146; e-mail interel@eommex.gr; Pres. GEORGE FRANTZESKAKIS.

### UTILITIES

#### Electricity

**Public Power Corpn (DEH):** Odos Xalkokondyli 30, 104 32 Athens; tel. (1) 5230301; fax (1) 5238445; e-mail webmaster@dei.gr; internet www.dei.gr; f. 1950; generating capacity 9,372 MW; generation, transmission and distribution of electricity in Greece; Chair. G. BIRDIMIRIS; Gen. Man. A. PAPATHANASIOU.

#### Gas

**Public Gas Corpn (DEPA):** Leoforos Messoghian 207, 115 25 Athens; tel. (1) 6749106; fax (1) 6749504; e-mail dimep@otenet.gr; internet www.depa.gr; owned by Public Petroleum Corpn (DEH); began gas imports 1997; initially for industrial use.

#### Water

In 1980 a law was passed under which Municipal Enterprises for Water Supply and Sewerage (DEYA) were created to manage drinking water and sewerage throughout Greece. Since then some 90 DEYA have been established.

**The Hellenic Union of Municipal Enterprises for Water Supply and Sewerage (EDEYA):** Odos Anthimou Gaza 3, 441 22 Larissa; internet www.edeya.gr; f. 1989; 67 mems; co-ordinates activities of DEYA and represents them to the Government.

### TRADE UNIONS

There are about 5,000 registered trade unions, grouped together in 82 federations and 86 workers' centres, which are affiliated to the Greek General Confederation of Labour (GSEE).

**Greek General Confederation of Labour (GSEE):** Odos Patission 69, Athens; tel. (1) 8834611; fax (1) 8229802; f. 1918; Pres. CHRISTOS PROTOPAPAS; Gen. Sec. IOANNIS THEONAS; 700,000 mems.

**Pan-Hellenic Federation of Seamen's Unions (PNO):** Livanos Bldg, Akti Miaouli 47–49, 185 36 Piraeus; tel. (1) 4292960; fax (1) 4293040; f. 1920; confederation of 14 marine unions; Pres. YANNIS CHELAS; Gen. Sec. JOHN HALAS.

## Transport

### RAILWAYS

**Ilektriki Sidirodromi Athinon–Pireos (ISAP)** (Athens–Piraeus Electric Railways): Odos Athinas 67, 105 52 Athens; tel. (1) 3248311; fax (1) 3223935; internet www.isap.gr; 26 km of electrified track; Man. Dir KOSTAS M. VASSILIADIS.

**Organismos Sidirodromon Ellados (OSE)** (Hellenic Railways Organization Ltd): Odos Karolou 1–3, 104 37 Athens; tel. (1) 5248395; fax (1) 5243290; f. 1971; state railways; total length of track: 2,600 km (1995); Chair. CHR. PAPAGEORGIOU; Dir Gen. A. LAZARIS.

A five-year programme to upgrade the Greek rail network was initiated in 1996, supported by 350m. drachmae from EU structural funds. The major undertaking was to electrify the 500-km Athens-Thessaloniki line and to extend services to the Bulgarian border. Construction of a 26.3-km electrified extension to the Athens Piraeus line, in order to provide a 3-line urban railway system for Athens, was scheduled to be completed by October 1998.

### ROADS

In 1995 there were an estimated 116,440 km of roads in Greece. Of this total, an estimated 9,120 km were main roads, and 420 km were motorways.

### INLAND WATERWAYS

There are no navigable rivers in Greece.

**Corinth Canal:** built 1893; over six km long, links the Corinthian and Saronic Gulfs; shortens the journey from the Adriatic to the Piraeus by 325 km; spanned by three single-span bridges, two for road and one for rail; can be used by ships of a maximum draught of 22 ft and width of 60 ft.

### SHIPPING

In 1998 the Greek merchant fleet totalled 1,545 vessels amounting to 25,224,543 grt. Greece controls one of the largest merchant fleets in the world. The principal ports are Piraeus, Patras and Thessaloniki.

**Union of Greek Shipowners:** Akti Miaouli 85, 185 38 Piraeus; Pres. JOHN GOUMAS.

#### Port Authorities

**Port of Patras:** Patras Port Authority, Central Port Office, Patras; tel. (61) 341002; fax (61) 327136; Harbour Master Capt. NIKOLAS RAFAILOVITS.

**Port of Piraeus:** Port of Piraeus Authority, Odos Merarchias 2, 185 35 Piraeus; tel. (1) 4520910; fax (1) 4520852; Gen. Man. SPIROS STALIAS; Harbour Master Capt. EMMANUEL PELOPONNESIOS.

**Port of Thessaloniki:** Thessaloniki Port Authority, 541 10 Thessaloniki; tel. (31) 593911; fax (31) 510500; Gen. Man. D. PAPADOPOULOS.

Among the largest shipping companies are:

**Anangel Shipping Enterprises, SA:** Akti Miaouli 25, 185 10 Piraeus; tel. (1) 4224500; fax (1) 4224819; Man. Dir J. PLATSIDAKIS.

**Attika Shipping Co.:** Odos Voucourestion 16, 10671 Athens; tel. (1) 3609631; fax (1) 3601439; Dir G. PRIOVOLOS.

**Bilinder Marine Corpn, SA:** Odos Igias 1-3 and Akti Themistokleos, 185 36 Piraeus; tel. (1) 4287300; fax (1) 4287355; Gen. Man. V. ARMOGENI.

**Ceres Hellenic Shipping Enterprises Ltd:** Akti Miaouli 69, 185 37 Piraeus; tel. (1) 4591000; fax (1) 4283552; e-mail chse@ceres.gr; Dir NICK FISTES.

**Chandris (Hellas) Inc:** POB 80067, Akti Miaouli 95, 185 38 Piraeus; tel. (1) 4290300; fax (1) 4290256; e-mail chandris@19080845.multimessage.com; Man. Dirs A. C. PIPERAS, M. G. SKORDIAS.

**Costamare Shipping Co, SA:** Odos Zephyrou 60 and Leoforos Syngrou, 175 64 Athens; tel. (1) 9390000; fax (1) 9409051; Pres. Capt. V. C. KONSTANTAKOPOULOS; Man. Dir Capt. G. SARDIS.

**European Navigation Inc:** Odos Artemissiou 2 and Fleming Sq., 166 75 Athens; tel. (1) 8981581; fax (1) 8946777; Dir P. KARNESSIS.

**Glafki (Hellas) Maritime Co:** Odos Mitropoleos 3, 105 57 Athens; tel. (1) 3244991; fax (1) 3228944; Dirs M. FRAGOULIS, G. PANAGIOTOU.

**Golden Union Shipping Co, SA:** Odos Aegales 8, 185 45 Piraeus; tel. (1) 4329900; fax (1) 4627933; Man. Dir THEODORE VENIAMIS.

**M. Koutlakis and Co Ltd:** Makras Stoas 5, 185 31 Piraeus; tel. (1) 4129428; fax (1) 4178755; Dir M. KOUTLAKIS.

**Laskaridis Shipping Co Ltd:** Odos Chimaras 5, Maroussi, 151 25 Athens; tel. (1) 6899090; fax (1) 6806762; e-mail athens@laskship.cc.cwmail.com; Man. Dirs P. C. LASKARIDIS, A. C. LASKARIDIS.

**Marmaras Navigation Ltd:** Odos Filellinon 4–6, Okeanion Bldg, 185 36 Piraeus; tel. (1) 4294226; fax (1) 4294304; Dir D. DIAMANTIDES.

**Minoan Lines Shipping SA:** Odos 25 August 17, 712 02 Iraklion; tel. (81) 330301; fax (81) 330308; internet www.minoan.gr; Pres. KONSTANTINOS KLIRONOMAS.

**Naftomar Shipping and Trading Co Ltd:** Leoforos Alkyonidon 243, 166 73 Voula; tel. (1) 9670220; fax (1) 9670237; e-mail naftomar@naftomar.gr; Man. Dir RIAD ZEIN.

**Strintzis Lines Maritime S.A.:** Odos Akti Possidonos 26, 185 31 Piraeus; (1) 4225000; fax (1) 4225265; Man. Dir G. STRINTZIS.

**Thenamaris (Ships Management) Inc:** Odos Athinas 16, Kavouri, 166 71 Athens; tel. (1) 8969111; fax (1) 8969653; e-mail sg.gd@thenamaris.gr; Dir K. MARTINOS.

**Tsakos Shipping and Trading, SA:** Leoforos Syngrou 367, Faliro, 175 64 Athens; tel. (1) 9380700; fax (1) 9480710; Dirs P. N. TSAKOS, E. SAROGLOU.

**United Shipping and Trading Co of Greece, SA:** Odos Iassonos 6, 185 37 Piraeus; tel. (1) 4283660; fax (1) 4283630; Dir CH. TSAKOS.

**Varnima Corporation International, SA:** Odos Irodou Attikou 12A, Maroussi, 151 24 Athens; tel. (1) 8093000; fax (1) 8093222; e-mail john_k@attglobal.net; Gen. Man. S. V. SPANOUDAKIS.

### CIVIL AVIATION

There are international airports at Athens, Thessaloniki, Alexandroupolis, Corfu, Lesbos, Andravida, Rhodes, Kos and Heraklion/Crete, and 24 domestic airports (of which 13 are authorized to receive international flights). Construction of a new international airport at Spata, some 25 km east of Athens, was finally approved in 1995. The airport was expected to become operational in 2000, with a handling capacity of 16m. passengers per year.

**Cronus Airlines:** Leoforos Vauliogmenis 500, 174 56 Alimos; tel. (1) 9956400; fax (1) 9956405; f. 1995; charter services to United Kingdom, East Africa and Middle East; Chair. IOANNIS TH. MANETAS.

**Olympic Airways, SA:** Leoforos Syngrou 96–100, 117 41 Athens; tel. (1) 9269111; fax (1) 9267154; e-mail olyair10@otenet.gr; internet www.olympic-airways.gr; f. 1957; 51% state-owned, 49% of shares offered for transfer to private ownership in 1990; domestic services linking principal cities and islands in Greece, and international services to Singapore, Thailand, South Africa and the USA, and throughout Europe and the Middle East; Chair. GIORGOS ZIGOYANNIS; CEO ROD LYNCH.

**Olympic Aviation:** Leoforos Syngrou 96–100, 117 41 Athens; tel. (1) 9269111; fax (1) 9884059; wholly-owned subsidiary of Olympic Airways; independent operator of scheduled domestic and regional services; Chair. STERGIOS PAPASIS; CEO PETROS STEFANOU.

## Tourism

The sunny climate, the natural beauty of the country and its great history and traditions attract tourists to Greece. There are numerous islands and many sites of archaeological interest. The number of tourists visiting Greece increased from 1m. in 1968 to 10.6m. in 1997. Receipts from tourism, which totalled US $120m. in 1968, reached $5,186m. in 1998.

**Ellinikos Organismos Tourismou (EOT)** (Greek National Tourist Organization): Odos Amerikis 2B, 105 64 Athens; tel. (1) 3223111; fax (1) 3252895; Pres. IOANNIS STEFANIDES; Vice-Pres. IOANNIS ROUBATIS.

# GRENADA

## Introductory Survey

### Location, Climate, Language, Religion, Flag, Capital

Grenada, a mountainous, heavily-forested island, is the most southerly of the Windward Islands, in the West Indies. The country also includes some of the small islands known as the Grenadines, which lie to the north-east of Grenada. The most important of these are the low-lying island of Carriacou and its neighbour, Petit Martinique. The climate is semi-tropical, with an average annual temperature of 28°C (82°F) in the lowlands. Annual rainfall averages about 1,500 mm (60 ins) in the coastal area and 3,800 mm to 5,100 mm (150–200 ins) in mountain areas. Most of the rainfall occurs between June and December. The majority of the population speak English, although a French patois is sometimes spoken. According to the census of 1991, 82% of Grenada's population were of African descent, while 13% were of mixed ethnic origins. Most of the population profess Christianity, and the main denominations are Roman Catholicism (to which 53% of the population adhered at the time of the 1991 census) and Anglicanism (about 14% of the population). The national flag (proportions 2 by 1) consists of a diagonally-quartered rectangle (yellow in the upper and lower segments, green in the right and left ones) surrounded by a red border bearing six five-pointed yellow stars (three at the upper edge of the flag, and three at the lower edge). There is a red disc, containing a large five-pointed yellow star, in the centre, and a representation of a nutmeg (in yellow and red) on the green segment near the hoist. The capital is St George's.

### Recent History

Grenada was initially colonized by the French but was captured by the British in 1762. British control was recognized in 1783 by the Treaty of Versailles. Grenada continued as a British colony until 1958, when it joined the Federation of the West Indies, remaining a member until the dissolution of the Federation in 1962. Full internal self-government and statehood in association with the United Kingdom were achieved in March 1967. During this period, the political life of Grenada was dominated by Herbert Blaize, the leader of the Grenada National Party (GNP), and Eric Gairy, a local trade union leader, who in 1950 founded the Grenada United Labour Party (GULP), with the support of an associated trade union. Gairy became Premier after the elections of 1967 and again after those of 1972, which he contested chiefly on the issue of total independence. Grenada became independent, within the Commonwealth, on 7 February 1974, with Gairy as Prime Minister. Domestic opposition to Gairy was expressed in public unrest, and the formation by the three opposition parties – the GNP, the United People's Party and the New Jewel Movement (NJM) – of the People's Alliance, which contested the 1976 general elections and reduced GULP's majority in the Lower House.

The rule of Sir Eric Gairy, as he became in June 1977, was regarded by the opposition as increasingly autocratic and corrupt, and on 13 March 1979 he was replaced in a bloodless coup by the leader of the left-wing NJM, Maurice Bishop. The new People's Revolutionary Government (PRG) suspended the 1974 Constitution and announced the imminent formation of a People's Consultative Assembly to draft a new constitution. Meanwhile, Grenada remained a monarchy, with the British Queen as Head of State, represented in Grenada by a Governor-General. During 1980–81 there was an increase in repression, against a background of mounting anti-Government violence and the PRG's fears of an invasion by US forces.

By mid-1982 relations with the USA, the United Kingdom and the more conservative members of the Caribbean Community and Common Market (CARICOM—see p. 136) were becoming increasingly strained: elections had not been arranged, restrictions against the privately-owned press had been imposed, many detainees were still awaiting trial, and Grenada was aligning more closely with Cuba and the USSR. Cuba was contributing funds and construction workers for the airport at Point Salines, a project which further strengthened the US Government's conviction that Grenada was to become a centre for Soviet manoeuvres in the area.

In March 1983 the armed forces were put on alert, in response to renewed fears that the USA was planning to invade. (The USA strenuously denied any such plans.) In June Bishop sought to improve relations with the USA, and announced the appointment of a commission to draft a new constitution. This attempt at conciliation was denounced by the more left-wing members of the PRG as an ideological betrayal. A power struggle developed between Bishop and his deputy, Bernard Coard, the Minister of Finance and Planning. In October Bishop was placed under house arrest, allegedly for his refusal to share power with Coard. The commander of the People's Revolutionary Army (PRA), Gen. Austin Hudson, subsequently announced that Bishop had been expelled from the NJM. On 19 October thousands of Bishop's supporters stormed the house, freed Bishop, and demonstrated outside the PRA headquarters. PRA forces responded by firing into the crowd. Later in the day, Bishop, three of his ministers and two trade unionists were executed by the PRA. The Government was replaced by a 16-member Revolutionary Military Council (RMC), led by Gen. Austin and supported by Coard and one other minister. The remaining NJM ministers were arrested and imprisoned, and a total curfew was imposed.

Regional and international outrage at the assassination of Bishop, in addition to fears of a US military intervention, were so intense that after four days the RMC relaxed the curfew, reopened the airport and promised a swift return to civilian rule. However, the Organisation of Eastern Caribbean States (OECS, see p. 000) resolved to intervene in an attempt to restore democratic order, and asked for assistance from the USA, which readily complied. (It is unclear whether the decision to intervene preceded or followed a request for help to the OECS by the Grenadian Governor-General, Sir Paul Scoon.) On 25 October 1983 some 1,900 US military personnel invaded the island, accompanied by 300 troops from Jamaica, Barbados and member countries of the OECS. Fighting continued for some days, and the USA gradually increased its troop strength, with further reinforcements waiting off shore with a US naval task force. The RMC's forces were defeated, while Coard, Austin and others who had been involved in the coup were detained.

On 9 November 1983 Scoon appointed a non-political interim Council to assume responsibility for the government of the country until elections could be held. Nicholas Brathwaite, a former Commonwealth official, was appointed Chairman of this Council in December. The 1974 Constitution was reinstated (with the exception that the country did not rejoin the East Caribbean Supreme Court), and an electoral commission was created. By mid-December the USA had withdrawn all its forces except 300 support troops, military police and technicians who were to assist the 430 members of Caribbean forces who remained on the island. A 550-member police force, trained by the USA and the United Kingdom, was established, including a paramilitary body that was to be the new defence contingent.

Several political parties that had operated clandestinely or from exile during the rule of the PRG re-emerged and announced their intention of contesting the elections for a new House of Representatives. Sir Eric Gairy returned to Grenada in January 1984 to lead GULP, but stated that he would not stand as a candidate himself. In May three former NJM ministers formed the Maurice Bishop Patriotic Movement (MBPM) to contest the elections. A number of centrist parties emerged or re-emerged, including Blaize's GNP. Fears that a divided opposition would allow GULP to win a majority of seats in the new House resulted in an agreement by several of these organizations, in August 1984, to form the New National Party (NNP), led by Blaize.

At the general election held in December 1984 the NNP achieved a convincing victory by winning 14 of the 15 seats in the House of Representatives, with 59% of the popular votes. Both GULP (which won 36% of the votes cast) and the MBPM claimed that the poll had been fraudulent, and the one successful GULP candidate, Marcel Peters, initially refused to take his seat in protest. He subsequently accepted the seat, but was expelled from the party and formed the Grenada Democratic Labour Party (GDLP). Blaize became Prime Minister, and appointed a Cabinet. US and Caribbean troops remained in Grenada, at Blaize's request, until September 1985.

The trial before the Grenada High Court of 19 detainees (including Coard, his wife, Phyllis, and Gen. Austin), accused of murder and conspiracy against Bishop and six of his associates, opened in November 1984. However, repeated adjournments postponed the trial of 18 of the detainees until April 1986. One of the detainees agreed to give evidence for the State in return for a pardon. Eventually, verdicts on 196 charges of murder and conspiracy to murder were returned by the jury in December. Fourteen of the defendants were sentenced to death, three received prison sentences of between 30 and 45 years, and one was acquitted.

Differences between its component groupings gradually led to the disintegration of the NNP. In 1986 the parliamentary strength of the NNP was reduced to 12 seats, following the resignation of two members who subsequently formed the Democratic Labour Congress (DLC). Three more government members resigned in April 1987, and joined forces with the DLC and the GDLP in July to form a united opposition, with six seats in the House of Representatives. In October they formally launched a new party, the National Democratic Congress (NDC), led by George Brizan, who had earlier been appointed parliamentary opposition leader. In January 1989 Brizan resigned as leader of the NDC in order to allow the election of Nicholas Brathwaite (head of the interim Government of 1983–84) to that post.

During 1988–89 the actions of the Blaize Government, under provisions of the controversial Emergency Powers Act of 1987, gave rise to concerns both within the opposition and among regional neighbours. Deportation orders and bans were enforced by the administration against prominent left-wing politicians and journalists from the region, and a variety of books and journals were proscribed.

Meanwhile, a deterioration in Blaize's health coincided with a growing challenge to his administration from within the NNP during 1988. In January 1989 Blaize was replaced as leader of the ruling party by his cabinet colleague, Dr Keith Mitchell, although he remained Prime Minister. In July, however, following allegations of corruption by the NDC, Blaize announced the dismissal of Mitchell and the Chairman of the NNP, accusing them of violating the principles of cabinet government. Amid uncertainty as to whether the Blaize faction had formed a separate party, two more members of the Government resigned, thus reducing support for the Blaize Government to only five of the 15 members of the House of Representatives. Blaize did not officially announce the formation of a new party, the National Party (TNP), until late August, by which time he had advised the acting Governor-General to prorogue Parliament. (The Government thereby avoided being defeated in a motion of 'no confidence', the immediate dissolution of Parliament and the prospect of an early general election.) The term of the Parliament was due to expire at the end of December, and a general election had to be held within three months. However, Blaize died in mid-December, and the Governor-General appointed Ben Jones, Blaize's former deputy and the new leader of TNP, as Prime Minister. At the general election, held in March 1990, no party achieved an absolute majority in the House of Representatives. The NDC won seven of the 15 seats, GULP (which had held no seats in the previous Parliament) won four, while TNP won only two, as did the NNP. The NDC achieved a working majority in Parliament when one of GULP's successful candidates announced his defection to the NDC. Brathwaite subsequently became Prime Minister and appointed a new Cabinet.

In July 1991 the Court of Appeal upheld the original verdicts that had been imposed in 1986 on the defendants in the Bishop murder trial, and further pleas for clemency were rejected. Preparations for the imminent hanging of the 14, however, provoked international outrage, and in August Brathwaite announced that the death sentences were to be commuted to terms of life imprisonment. His decision (which was contrary to prevailing public opinion on Grenada) was considered to have been influenced by intense pressure from politicians and human rights organizations, together with the detrimental effect that the executions may have had on the country's important tourist industry.

A series of strikes by public-sector and port workers during 1992–93 caused considerable disruption, and prompted the approval by Parliament in mid-1993 of legislation aimed at restricting the right of trade unions to take industrial action.

Brathwaite resigned as leader of the NDC in September 1994; George Brizan won the subsequent leadership election, defeating the Attorney-General, Francis Alexis (who, like Brizan, had been a founder member of the NDC following their resignation from the NNP Government in 1987). In February 1995 Brathwaite resigned as Prime Minister, and was succeeded by Brizan.

At the general election held in June 1995, the NNP won 32.7% of total votes cast, securing eight of the 15 seats in the House of Representatives, while the NDC's representation was reduced to five seats. The remaining two seats were secured by GULP. Dr Keith Mitchell, leader of the NNP, became Prime Minister and appointed a Cabinet. The NNP subsequently undertook negotiations with GULP in an attempt to strengthen its single-seat majority and to secure the two-thirds' majority required to amend the Constitution. In July Alexis resigned as deputy leader of the NDC, alleging that an NDC member of Parliament had been unfairly treated by the party prior to the election. In November Alexis and three other former NDC members announced the formation of a new opposition group, the Democratic Labour Party (DLP).

The appointment in August 1996 of Daniel (later Sir Daniel) Williams to the position of Governor-General provoked considerable controversy because of Williams' connections with the NNP (he had been deputy leader of the party during the 1980s) and his previous role as a cabinet minister in the Government of Herbert Blaize. In protest at his appointment, opposition members staged a walk-out at his inauguration ceremony. Later in August Parliament approved a motion claiming that the Leader of the Opposition, Brizan, had been guilty of contempt of Parliament and disrespect to Queen Elizabeth II (as Head of State) by leading the protest; Brizan was duly suspended from the House of Representatives for one month.

An extensive cabinet reorganization in September 1996 included the appointment of a GULP member, Clarence Rapier, in recognition of the informal alliance between that party and the NNP. However, relations between the two parties became strained in November when Rapier was dismissed following an incident involving a British bar proprietor.

Concern that the Government was attempting to restrict media freedom was heightened during 1996, following a series of apparently politically-motivated personnel changes at the state-owned Grenada Broadcasting Corporation. Local and regional press associations criticized the appointment, in April, of a senior NNP official as chief news editor and the dismissal, in July, of four experienced journalists (for allegedly failing to report an event staged by the ruling party). In January 1997 the Chairman of the corporation was similarly dismissed for failing to broadcast the budget debate in its entirety.

In late February 1997 Mitchell removed the Minister of Health, Housing and the Environment, Grace Duncan, from the post of Deputy Prime Minister, announcing the abolition of the deputy premiership. Earlier in the month Duncan had boycotted the NNP's annual convention, citing minor grievances with the Prime Minister. Duncan did not resign from the Government, but was dismissed in mid-July for making what were termed 'vulgar' remarks about Mitchell and for disclosing confidential information about government affairs, as well as allegedly disseminating misinformation, to the media. The dismissed minister subsequently stated that she had warned Mitchell of an internal party plot to undermine his administration. Meanwhile, in May GULP joined with the NDC, TNP, DLP and MBPM to announce a strategy of co-operation in opposing the Government on major national issues, accusing Mitchell of a lack of consultation and of 'growing dictatorship'. In the previous month an opposition motion of 'no confidence' in the Government had been rejected by the House of Representatives, as had a motion against the chamber's Speaker, Sir Curtis Strachan. At the end of June the establishment was announced of an eighth political party, the Grenada Progressive Party, led by Prescott Williams.

In March 1997 the Government's Mercy Committee rejected a request made by the Conference of Churches of Grenada for the release, on the grounds of their deteriorating physical and mental health, of Phyllis Coard and another of those serving terms of life imprisonment for the murder of Maurice Bishop. None the less, the Committee gave assurances that the detainees' medical requirements would receive attention, and that conditions at the prison where they were being held would be improved. Also in March Mitchell announced plans for the establishment of a national commission to investigate the 1979–83 revolutionary period.

Sir Eric Gairy, the founder and leader of GULP, died in August 1997. A lengthy power struggle within the party ensued, but a convention to elect Gairy's successor was eventually held in April/May 1998; in a controversial vote, Herbert Preudhomme (a former Deputy Prime Minister) narrowly defeated his opponent, who subsequently launched a protest against alleged electoral fraud.

In January 1998 Mitchell announced a cabinet reorganization and the creation of a new ministry, of Carriacou and Petit Martinique affairs, which was to be headed by Elvin Nimrod. In September the NDC and GULP announced that they had begun a working dialogue to seek to unseat the Government; the NDC accused Mitchell of being 'corrupt and incapable'. In late November the Minister of Foreign Affairs, Raphael Fletcher, resigned from the Government and NNP in order to join GULP. Fletcher declared his 'growing disenchantment and disagreement' with Mitchell and was reportedly critical of government moves to obtain US $100m. of loans from foreign business executives (including a wealthy Czech entrepreneur who had been charged with fraud in the Czech Republic). Fletcher's resignation resulted in the dissolution of Parliament on 2 December (and the postponement of the presentation of the 1999 budget proposals); a general election was called for January 1999, although constitutionally it was not due until mid-2000. The DLP and GULP agreed to contest the election together in an informal alliance known as United Labour.

At the general election held on 18 January 1999 (in which 56.5% of the electorate voted), the NNP achieved a comprehensive victory, receiving 62.2% of total votes cast and obtaining all of the 15 seats in the House of Representatives. The NDC won 24.9% of the votes, while the United Labour alliance received only 11.6%. Keith Mitchell retained his position as Prime Minister and appointed a new Cabinet. Several ministers retained their portfolios, while Mitchell himself replaced Fletcher as Minister of Foreign Affairs. The NNP's return to power constituted the first time in the country's history that a political party had been given two successive terms in government. In its electoral campaign the party had highlighted its recent successes in maintaining strong economic growth and reducing unemployment.

In late September and early October 1999 two leading journalists were arrested on separate charges of alleged criminal libel. One of the detainees was the editor of *Grenada Today*, which had published a letter accusing Mitchell of having bribed voters during the last general election campaign. Opposition parties, human rights organizations and media associations claimed that the Government was seeking to intimidate independent journalists.

Also in early October 1999 Bernard Coard, the former Deputy Prime Minister serving a term of life imprisonment with 16 others for the 1983 murder of Prime Minister Maurice Bishop and a number of his associates (see above), read a statement issued from the prison. In the statement Coard, for the first time, accepted full responsibility for the crimes; it was, however, unclear as to whether he was speaking on behalf of all 17 prisoners. In early January 2000 it was announced that the bodies of Bishop and his cabinet colleagues may have been discovered (although their murderers still claimed that US troops removed the bodies following their invasion of Grenada in 1983).

On 1 November 1999 Mitchell announced a cabinet reorganization in which he ceded the Foreign Affairs and Finance portfolios to Mark Isaac and Anthony Boatswain respectively.

As a member of the OECS, Grenada has been involved in discussions concerning the possible formation of a political union. In 1988 Grenada, Dominica, Saint Lucia and Saint Vincent and the Grenadines decided to proceed with their own plans for a political union. At a meeting held by representatives of the four countries in St George's in late 1990, it was agreed that a Windward Islands Regional Constituent Assembly (RCA) would be convened to discuss the economic and political feasibilities of creating a federation. In late 1992 members of Grenada's House of Representatives fully endorsed a continuation of progress towards political unity. In 1995 the newly-elected Mitchell Government expressed its commitment to increased political and economic integration between the four countries.

In May 1996 Grenada signed two treaties with the USA, relating to mutual legal assistance and extradition, as part of a regional campaign to combat drugs-trafficking. Improved relations with Cuba, which had been severely strained since 1983, resulted in offers of assistance with education, health and agriculture in Grenada in early 1997. Prime Minister Mitchell led a delegation to Cuba in April of that year; at the same time an aircraft of Cuba's national airline, carrying representatives of the Cuban Government, landed at Point Salines for the first time since the downfall of the revolution. In August 1998 President Fidel Castro Ruz of Cuba visited Grenada at Mitchell's invitation, provoking protest from GULP and the DLP, which demanded the release of political prisoners from Cuban jails and the implementation by Cuba of certain human rights agreements. Diplomatic relations between Grenada and Cuba (which had been suspended in 1983) were restored in December 1999.

## Government

Grenada has dominion status within the Commonwealth. The British monarch is Head of State and is represented locally by a Governor-General. Executive power is held by the Cabinet, led by the Prime Minister. Parliament comprises the Senate, made up of 13 Senators appointed by the Governor-General on the advice of the Prime Minister and the Leader of the Opposition, and the 15-member House of Representatives, elected by universal adult suffrage. The Cabinet is responsible to Parliament.

## Defence

A regional security unit was formed in late 1983, modelled on the British police force and trained by British officers. A paramilitary element, known as the Special Service Unit and trained by US advisers, acts as the defence contingent and participates in the Regional Security System, a defence pact with other East Caribbean states.

## Economic Affairs

In 1997, according to estimates by the World Bank, Grenada's gross national product (GNP), measured at average 1995–97 prices, was US $300m., equivalent to US $3,140 per head. In 1990–97, it was estimated, the country's GNP per head increased, in real terms, by an average of 1.3% annually. Over the same period Grenada's population increased at an average rate of 0.3% per year. In 1998 GNP, measured in current prices, totalled US $305m. (US $3,170 per head). Gross domestic product (GDP) increased, in real terms, at an average annual rate of 2.5% in 1990–97. Real GDP increased by 3.1% in 1996, by 4.6% in 1997, and by an estimated 5.8% in 1998; growth was projected at 4.5% for 1999.

Agriculture (including forestry and fishing) contributed 7.9% of GDP in 1997. The sector engaged 17.1% of the employed labour force in 1995. Grenada, known as the Spice Island of the Caribbean, is the largest producer of nutmeg after Indonesia (which produces some 75% of the world's total), and in 1987 it supplied 23% of the world's nutmeg. In 1997, according to IMF data, sales of nutmeg and mace (the pungent red membrane around the nut) accounted for 33.8% of Grenada's domestic export earnings. The other principal cash crops are bananas and other fruit and cocoa. Exports of bananas were suspended in early 1997 by the Windward Islands Banana Development and Exporting Company (WIBDECO) because of poor quality, but were permitted to resume in late 1998, following a rehabilitation programme. Nevertheless, exports of bananas were still greatly reduced in 1999. In 1996 a US company conducted a feasibility study into the development of large-scale vanilla cultivation on Grenada. Livestock production, for domestic consumption, is important on Carriacou. There are extensive timber reserves on the island of Grenada; forestry development is strictly controlled and involves a programme of reafforestation. Exports of fish contributed 15.6% of domestic export earnings in 1997. Agricultural GDP declined at an average annual rate of 2.5% in 1990–97. The sector's GDP contracted by 6.8% in 1996, and by a further 1.3% in 1997, owing to a reduction in output of cocoa and bananas. However, agricultural GDP grew by some 2.4% in 1998, largely owing to increased cocoa production.

Industry (mining, manufacturing, construction and utilities) provided 18.7% of GDP in 1997, and engaged 22.4% of the employed labour force in 1995. The mining sector accounted for only 0.5% of employment in 1995 and the same percentage of GDP in 1997. However, in 1996 a US company announced plans to conduct exploration for oil and gas deposits off the southern coast of Grenada. Manufacturing, which contributed 6.2% of GDP in 1997 and employed 7.6% of the working population in 1995, consists mainly of the processing of agricultural products and of cottage industries producing garments and spice-based items. A nutmeg oil distillation plant commenced production in

1995, and exports of the oil earned some EC $2m. in that year. Rum is the only significant industrial export, but soft drinks, paints and varnishes, household paper products and the tyre-retreading industries are also important. Manufacturing GDP increased by an average of 3.5% per year in 1990–97. The sector's GDP increased by 5.6% in 1996, but by only 0.8% in 1997, owing to a lack of competitiveness; growth in manufacturing was, however, estimated at 14.1% in 1998. Overall, industrial GDP increased by an average of 4.0% annually in 1990–97.

Grenada is dependent upon imports for its energy requirements, and in 1997 mineral fuels, lubricants, etc. accounted for 7.9% of the total cost of imports.

The services sector contributed 73.4% of GDP in 1997, when the hotels and restaurants sector accounted for some 7.4% of GDP. Tourism receipts totalled around EC$219m. in 1997. Since 1984 the number of stop-over arrivals and cruise-ship visitors has more than doubled. In 1998 the tourism industry recovered after experiencing several difficulties in 1997; in 1998 stop over arrivals increased by 4.6%, while cruise-ship arrivals rose by 7.8% and cruise-ship calls by 1.5%. Of total stop-over visitors (excluding non-resident Grenadians) in 1997, 31.2% were from the USA, 17.5% from Caribbean countries and 22.7% from the United Kingdom. In 1997 18.1% of all stop-over arrivals were Grenadians resident abroad. The GDP of the services sector increased at an average annual rate of 3.0% in 1990–97.

In 1997 Grenada recorded a visible trade deficit of EC $372.8m. and there was a deficit of EC $207.8m. on the current account of the balance of payments. In 1995 the principal source of imports was the USA, accounting for 41.1% of the total. The United Kingdom is the principal market for exports, taking 22.7% of the total in 1991. The United Kingdom also provided 13.8% of imports in 1991 (and 10.5% of imports in 1995). Trinidad and Tobago provided 20.2% of imports in 1995 and received 13.1% of Grenada's exports in 1991. The principal exports are agricultural, notably nutmeg. The principal imports in 1997 were machinery and transport equipment, foodstuffs, and basic manufactures. The trade deficit is partly offset by earnings from tourism, capital receipts and remittances from Grenadians working abroad.

In 1998 there was a current budgetary surplus of EC $5.8m., but an overall deficit of EC $37.2m. Grenada's total external debt was US $105.3m. at the end of 1997, of which US $92.4m. was long-term public debt. In 1996 (when the external debt totalled US $120.1m.) the cost of debt-servicing was equivalent to 5.7% of the value of exports of goods and services. The average annual rate of inflation was 2.6% in 1990–97, and consumer prices increased by 2.0% in 1996 and by 1.3% in 1997. Inflation was estimated at 1.4% in 1998. According to government figures, an estimated 14% of the labour force were unemployed at the end of 1999.

Grenada is a member of CARICOM (see p. 136), and secured limited protection for some of its products when tariff barriers within the organization were removed in 1988. It is also a member of the Economic Commission for Latin America and the Caribbean (ECLAC, see p. 29), the Organization of American States (OAS, see p. 245), the Organisation of Eastern Caribbean States (OECS, see p. 292) and is a signatory of the Lomé Conventions between the African, Caribbean and Pacific (ACP) countries and the European Union (see p. 196).

Grenada's economy remains largely dependent upon agriculture, which is vulnerable to adverse weather conditions and infestation by pests. Furthermore, the economy's susceptibility to the fluctuations in international commodity prices was demonstrated in 1990, when the price of nutmeg on the world market decreased by 30%, following the breakdown of Grenada's cartel agreement with Indonesia (signed in 1987). The two countries have since concluded several informal agreements in an attempt to stabilize the world nutmeg market through closer co-operation. From 1997 a decline in production of nutmeg in Indonesia resulted in higher prices on the external market, stimulating a significant increase in Grenada's output. In the year to June 1999 the country earned US $9.2m. from exports of nutmeg, compared with US $5.5m. for the same period in 1998. (However, a fall in world prices was predicted for 2000, as production levels were projected to increase in Indonesia.) The need for further economic diversification has recently been underscored by the potential loss of preferential access to European markets for banana producers of the ACP countries. In the late 1990s the Government hoped to diversify the economy partly through the expansion of the 'offshore' financial sector. Since the introduction of legislation in 1997, some 900 offshore financial companies (including 21 banks) have been registered in Grenada; in September 1999 the creation of a regulatory body, the International Business and Finance Corporation, was announced. The most promising sector of the economy is tourism, from which revenue more than doubled between 1992 and 1996. Growth in the tourism sector has, in turn, stimulated the construction sector, the GDP of which expanded by some 16.9% in 1998. About 5,000 new jobs were expected to be created in tourism and construction in 1998–99, while from 1997 public-sector jobs were created under the Micro-Enterprise Development programme. In the budget proposals for 1999 the Government introduced no new taxation, but promised to increase spending on infrastructure, agriculture and tourism. Meanwhile, some 95% of taxpayers were effectively exempted from personal income tax obligations after April 1996, when the Government raised significantly the income threshold for liability for this tax. The reintroduction of a value-added tax (abolished in 1990) was under consideration in 1999. In that year the IMF urged the Grenadian Government to tighten fiscal policy in order to improve the state of public finances (which continue to suffer from sizeable internal and external debts), warning that otherwise the high economic growth of recent years would become unsustainable. Growth in GDP of 4.5% was forecast for 1999.

### Social Welfare

There was no system of social security payments in Grenada prior to 1979. New initiatives launched in that year included the Youth for Reconstruction Programme, to provide basic para-medical services and assistance to the elderly and disabled, a national milk distribution programme and the establishment of community-directed day care centres. A National Insurance Scheme was inaugurated in 1983. In 1997 there was one hospital bed for every 178 people and one physician per 1,244 inhabitants. There are three main hospitals in St. George's, St. Andrew's and on Carriacou, as well as six local health centres, all in the main towns. The Ministry of Health also finances free weekly clinics in each district. A mental hospital, destroyed by military action in 1983, was rebuilt with US financial aid. Projected budgetary expenditure on health was EC $27.5m. in 1997 (equivalent to 13.3% of total recurrent expenditure).

### Education

Education is free and compulsory for children between the ages of five and 16 years. Primary education begins at five years of age and lasts for seven years. Secondary education, beginning at the age of 12, lasts for a further five years. In 1995 a total of 23,256 children received public primary education in 57 schools. There were 19 public secondary schools, with 7,260 pupils registered, in that year. Technical Centres have been established in St Patrick's, St David's and St John's, and the Grenada National College, the Mirabeau Agricultural School and the Teachers' Training College have been incorporated into the Technical and Vocational Institute in St George's. The Extra-Mural Department of the University of the West Indies has a branch in St George's. A School of Medicine has been established at St George's University (SGU), where a School of Arts and Sciences was also founded in 1997, while there is a School of Fishing at Victoria. The rate of adult literacy was estimated at around 96% in the late 1990s. In 1997 the World Bank agreed to finance a US $7.6m. loan for improvements to schools. Projected budgetary expenditure on education was EC $25m. in 1998 (equivalent to 11.5% of total recurrent expenditure).

### Public Holidays

**2000:** 3 January (for New Year's Day), 7 February (Independence Day), 21 April (Good Friday), 24 April (Easter Monday), 1 May (Labour Day), 12 June (Whit Monday), 22 June (Corpus Christi), 7–8 August (Emancipation Holidays), 25 October (Thanksgiving Day), 25–26 December (Christmas).

**2001:** 1 January (New Year's Day), 7 February (Independence Day), 13 April (Good Friday), 16 April (Easter Monday), 7 May (Labour Day), 4 June (Whit Monday), 14 June (Corpus Christi), 6–7 August (Emancipation Holidays), 25 October (Thanksgiving Day), 25–26 December (Christmas).

### Weights and Measures

The metric system is in use.

# Statistical Survey

Source (unless otherwise stated): Central Statistical Office, Ministry of Finance, Lagoon Rd, St George's; tel. 440-2731; fax 440-4115.

## AREA AND POPULATION

**Area:** 344.5 sq km (133.0 sq miles).

**Population:** 89,088 at census of 30 April 1981; 94,806 (males 46,637; females 48,169) at census of 12 May 1991 (excluding 537 persons in institutions and 33 persons in the foreign service); 99,500 (official estimate) at mid–1997.

**Density** (mid–1997): 288.8 per sq km.

**Principal Town:** St George's (capital), population 4,439 (1991 census).

**Births and Deaths** (1996): Registered live births 2,096 (birth rate 21.3 per 1,000); Registered deaths 782 (death rate 7.9 per 1,000).

**Expectation of Life** (years at birth, 1997): Males 69; Females 72. Source: IMF, *Grenada: Statistical Annex* (May 1999).

**Employment** (employees only, 1995): Agriculture, hunting, forestry and fishing 4,223; Mining and quarrying 126; Manufacturing 1,881; Electricity, gas and water 350; Construction 3,168; Wholesale and retail trade 4,299; Restaurants and hotels 850; Transport, storage and communications 1,614; Financing, insurance, real estate and business services 866; Community, social and personal services 4,980; Other services 1,334; Activities not adequately defined 959; Total employed 24,650 (males 15,194; females 9,456).

## AGRICULTURE, ETC.

**Principal Crops** (FAO estimates, '000 metric tons, 1998): Roots and tubers 4; Pulses 1; Coconuts 7; Vegetables 2; Sugar cane 7; Apples 1; Plums 1; Oranges 1; Grapefruit and pomelos 2; Other citrus fruits 1; Avocados 2; Mangoes 2; Bananas 4; Plantains 1; Other fruits 3; Cocoa beans 1 (unofficial figure). Source: FAO, *Production Yearbook*.

*Official Estimates* ('000 lb, 1997): Cocoa beans 2,617; Bananas 223; Nutmeg 5,287; Mace 449. Source: IMF, *Grenada: Statistical Annex* (May 1999).

**Livestock** (FAO estimates, '000 head, year ending September 1998): Cattle 4; Pigs 5; Sheep 13; Goats 7; Asses 1. Source: FAO, *Production Yearbook*.

**Livestock Products** (FAO estimates, '000 metric tons, 1998): Meat 1; Cows' milk 1; Hen eggs 1. Source: FAO, *Production Yearbook*.

**Fishing** (metric tons, live weight): Total catch 1,486 in 1995; 1,280 in 1996; 1,408 in 1997. Source: FAO, *Yearbook of Fishery Statistics*.

## INDUSTRY

**Production** (1994): Rum 3,000 hectolitres; Beer 24,000 hectolitres; Wheat flour 4,000 metric tons (1996); Cigarettes 15m.; Electric energy 87.5 million kWh (1995). Source: partly UN, *Industrial Commodity Statistics Yearbook*.

## FINANCE

**Currency and Exchange Rates:** 100 cents = 1 Eastern Caribbean dollar (EC $). *Sterling, US Dollar and Euro Equivalents* (30 September 1999): £1 sterling = EC $4.446; US $1 = EC $2.700; €1 = EC $2.880; EC $100 = £22.49 = US $37.04 = €34.73. *Exchange Rate:* Fixed at US $1 = EC $2.70 since July 1976.

**Budget** (EC $ million 1998): *Revenue:* Tax revenue 205.1 (Taxes on income and profits 24.7, Taxes on domestic goods and services 42.6, Taxes on international trade and transactions 132.0); Other current revenue 23.6; Capital revenue 4.7; Total 233.4, excluding grants received (31.7). *Expenditure:* Current expenditure 222.9 (Personal emoluments 103.4, Goods and services 52.3, Interest payments 18.6, Transfers and subsidies 48.6); Capital expenditure 79.4; Total 302.3. Source: Eastern Caribbean Central Bank, *Report and Statement of Accounts*.

*1999* (projections, EC $ million): *Revenue:* Total 300.9 (Recurrent 289.0; Capital 11.9), excl. grants (65.8). *Expenditure:* Total 438.8 (Recurrent 253.8; Capital 185.0).

**International Reserves** (US $ million at 31 December 1998): IMF special drawing rights 0.04; Foreign exchange 46.80; Total 46.84. Source: IMF, *International Financial Statistics*.

**Money Supply** (EC $ million at 31 December 1998): Currency outside banks 64.08; Demand deposits at deposit money banks 114.31; Total money 178.38. Source: IMF, *International Financial Statistics*.

**Cost of Living** (Consumer Price Index; base: 1995 = 100): 100.0 in 1995; 102.0 in 1996; 103.3 in 1997. Source: IMF, *International Financial Statistics*.

**Expenditure on the Gross Domestic Product** (EC $ million at current prices, 1997): Government final consumption expenditure 146.6; Private final consumption expenditure 562.3; Gross capital formation 324.3; *Total domestic expenditure* 1,033.2; Exports of goods and services, *less* Imports of goods and services –179.0; *GDP in purchasers' values* 854.2. Source: IMF, *Grenada: Statistical Annex* (May 1999).

**Gross Domestic Product by Economic Activity** (EC $ million at current prices, 1997): Agriculture, hunting, forestry and fishing 58.2; Mining and quarrying 3.3; Manufacturing 45.7; Electricity and water 33.8; Construction 56.0; Wholesale and retail trade 81.7; Restaurants and hotels 59.5; Transport and communications 164.7; Finance and insurance 63.8; Real estate 27.3; Government services 126.4; Other community, social and personal services 19.9; *Sub-total* 740.3; *Less* Imputed bank service charge 41.1; *GDP at factor cost* 699.2. Source: Eastern Caribbean Central Bank, *Statistical Digest 1998*.

**Balance of Payments** (EC $ million, 1997): Exports of goods f.o.b. 78.09; Imports of goods f.o.b. –450.85; *Trade balance* –372.76; Exports of services 306.76; Imports of services –149.86; *Balance on goods and services* –215.87; Other income received 12.71; Other income paid –57.77; *Balance on goods, services and income* –260.93; Current transfers received 63.97; Current transfers paid –10.83; *Current balance* –207.79; Capital account (net) 92.21; Direct investment (net) 95.41; Portfolio investment (net) –0.06; Other investments (net) 58.34; Net errors and omissions –19.25; *Overall balance* 18.85. Source: Eastern Caribbean Central Bank, *Balance of Payments 1998*.

## EXTERNAL TRADE

**Principal Commodities** (US $ million, 1997): *Imports:* Food and live animals 37.6; Crude materials (inedible) except fuels 5.5; Mineral fuels, lubricants, etc. 13.7; Chemicals 12.9; Basic manufactures 32.5; Machinery and transport equipment 45.0; Miscellaneous manufactured articles 24.1; Total (incl. others) 174.3 (excl. unrecorded imports). *Exports:* Cocoa 1.9; Nutmeg 6.8; Mace 1.2; Fresh fruit and vegetables 0.3; Fish 3.7; Clothing 1.4; Total (incl. others) 23.7 (excl. re-exports 2.3). Source: IMF, *Grenada: Statistical Annex* (May 1999).

**Principal Trading Partners** (EC $ million, 1991): *Imports c.i.f.:* Barbados 11.1; Canada 16.5; Japan 22.3; Trinidad and Tobago 50.3; United Kingdom 43.7; USA 98.9; Total (incl. others) 316.5. *Exports f.o.b.:* Belgium-Luxembourg 3.7; Canada 7.2; Germany 5.9; Netherlands 5.1; Trinidad and Tobago 7.1; United Kingdom 12.3; USA 7.7; Total (incl. others) 54.1.

*1995* (EC $ million): *Imports c.i.f.:* Barbados 9.2; Canada 13.8; Japan 11.4; Trinidad and Tobago 70.7; United Kingdom 36.7; USA 143.7; Total (incl. others) 349.7.

## TRANSPORT

**Road Traffic** (1991): Motor vehicles registered 8,262.

**Shipping:** *Merchant Fleet* (registered at 31 December 1998): 5 vessels (total displacement 887 grt). Source: Lloyd's Register of Shipping, *World Fleet Statistics*. *International Sea-borne Freight Traffic* (estimates, '000 metric tons, 1995): Goods loaded 21.3; Goods unloaded 193.0. *Ship Arrivals* (1991): 1,254. *Fishing vessels* (registered, 1987): 635.

**Civil Aviation** (aircraft arrivals, 1995): 11,310.

## TOURISM

**Visitor Arrivals:** 369,346 in 1995; 386,013 in 1996; 368,417 (110,748 stop-overs, 246,612 cruise-ship passengers, 11,057 excursionists) in 1997. Source: Eastern Caribbean Central Bank, *Balance of Payments 1998*.

*1998:* 115,794 stop-overs, 265,875 cruise-ship passengers. Source: Eastern Caribbean Central Bank, *Report and Statement of Accounts*.

**Cruise-ship Calls:** 328 in 1998.

**Receipts from Tourism** (EC $ million): 205.8 in 1995; 212.3 in 1996; 219.0 in 1997. Source: Eastern Caribbean Central Bank, *Balance of Payments 1998*.

# Directory

## The Constitution*

In December 1984 the Constituent Assembly drafted a new Constitution (based on that of 1965), which was approved in May 1985 and came into effect in January 1986. Its main provisions are summarized below:

Guatemala has a republican representative democratic system of government and power is exercised equally by the legislative, executive and judicial bodies. The official language is Spanish. Suffrage is universal and secret, obligatory for those who can read and write and optional for those who are illiterate. The free formation and growth of political parties whose aims are democratic is guaranteed. There is no discrimination on grounds of race, colour, sex, religion, birth, economic or social position or political opinions.

The State will give protection to capital and private enterprise in order to develop sources of labour and stimulate creative activity.

Monopolies are forbidden and the State will limit any enterprise which might prejudice the development of the community. The right to social security is recognized and it shall be on a national, unitary, obligatory basis.

Constitutional guarantees may be suspended in certain circumstances for up to 30 days (unlimited in the case of war).

### CONGRESS

Legislative power rests with Congress, which is made up of 116 deputies, 87 of whom are elected directly by the people through universal suffrage. The remaining 29 deputies are elected on the basis of proportional representation. Congress meets on 15 January each year and ordinary sessions last four months; extraordinary sessions can be called by the Permanent Commission or the Executive. All Congressional decisions must be taken by absolute majority of the members, except in special cases laid down by law. Deputies are elected for five years; they may be re-elected after a lapse of one session, but only once. Congress is responsible for all matters concerning the President and Vice-President and their execution of their offices; for all electoral matters; for all matters concerning the laws of the Republic; for approving the budget and decreeing taxes; for declaring war; for conferring honours, both civil and military; for fixing the coinage and the system of weights and measures; for approving, by two-thirds' majority, any international treaty or agreement affecting the law, sovereignty, financial status or security of the country.

### PRESIDENT

The President is elected by universal suffrage, by absolute majority for a non-extendable period of five years. Re-election or prolongation of the presidential term of office are punishable by law. The President is responsible for national defence and security, fulfilling the Constitution, leading the armed forces, taking any necessary steps in time of national emergency, passing and executing laws, international policy, nominating and removing Ministers, officials and diplomats, co-ordinating the actions of Ministers of State. The Vice-President's duties include presiding over Congress and taking part in the discussions of the Council of Ministers.

### ARMY

The Guatemalan Army is intended to maintain national independence, sovereignty and honour, territorial integrity and peace within the Republic. It is an indivisible, apolitical, non-deliberating body and is made up of land, sea and air forces.

### LOCAL ADMINISTRATIVE DIVISIONS

For the purposes of administration the territory of the Republic is divided into Departments and these into Municipalities, but this division can be modified by Congress to suit interests and general development of the Nation without loss of municipal autonomy.

### JUDICIARY

Justice is exercised exclusively by the Supreme Court of Justice and other tribunals. Administration of Justice is obligatory, free and independent of the other functions of State. The President of the Judiciary, judges and other officials are elected by Congress for six years. The Supreme Court of Justice is made up of at least seven judges. The President of the Judiciary is also President of the Supreme Court. The Supreme Court nominates all other judges. Under the Supreme Court come the Court of Appeal, the Administrative Disputes Tribunal, the Tribunal of Second Instance of Accounts, Jurisdiction Conflicts, First Instance and Military, the Extraordinary Tribunal of Protection. There is a Court of Constitutionality presided over by the President of the Supreme Court.

* A series of changes to the Constitution, which were approved by referendum on 30 January 1994 and concerned the election of a new Congress (to serve until 14 January 1996), the appointment of members of a new Supreme Court and the reduction in the term of office of the President, legislature and municipal authorities (from five to four years), and of Supreme Court justices (from six to five years), took effect in April 1994. In addition, the number of deputies in Congress was reduced from 116 to 80, of whom 64 are elected according to departmental representation and 16 by national listing. (The number of deputies was later revised by the Supreme Electoral Tribunal for the legislative election of 7 November 1999 when 113 seats were contested, 91 according to departmental representation and 22 by national listing).

Under the terms of an accord, signed with the URNG in September 1996, concerning civilian power and the role of the armed forces, the Government undertook to revise the Constitution to relieve the armed forces of responsibility for internal security. This role would be assumed by a new National Civilian Police force.

## The Government

### HEAD OF STATE

**President:** ALFONSO ANTONIO PORTILLO CABRERA (took office 14 January 2000).

**Vice-President:** FRANCISCO REYES.

### CABINET
(February 2000)

**Minister of Foreign Affairs:** GABRIEL ORELLANA ROJAS.

**Minister of the Interior:** GUILLERMO RUIZ WONG.

**Minister of National Defence:** Col JUAN DE DIOS ESTRADA VELÁSQUEZ.

**Minister of Economy:** EDUARDO WEYMANN.

**Minister of Public Finance:** MANUEL HIRAM MAZA CASTELLANOS.

**Minister of Public Health and Social Welfare:** MARIO BOLAÑOS.

**Minister of Communications, Transport and Public Works:** LUIS RABBE.

**Minister of Agriculture, Livestock and Food:** ROGER VALENZUELA.

**Minister of Education:** MARIO TORRES.

**Minister of Employment and Social Security:** JUAN FRANCISCO ALFARO.

**Minister of Energy and Mines:** RAÚL ARCHILA.

**Minister of Culture and Sport:** OTILIA LUX DE COTI.

### MINISTRIES

**Ministry of Agriculture, Livestock and Food:** Palacio Nacional, 6a Calle y 7a Avda, Zona 1, Guatemala City; tel. 28-6696; fax 253-6807.

**Ministry of Communications, Transport and Public Works:** Palacio Nacional, 6a Calle y 7a Avda, Zona 1, Guatemala City; tel. 22-1212; fax 28-1613.

**Ministry of Culture and Sport:** 24a Calle 3-81, Zona 1, Guatemala City; tel. 230-0718; fax 230-0758.

**Ministry of Economy:** Palacio Nacional, 6a Calle y 7a Avda, Zona 1, Guatemala City.

**Ministry of Education:** Palacio Nacional, 6a Calle y 7a Avda, Zona 1, Guatemala City; tel. 22-0162; fax 253-7386.

**Ministry of Employment and Social Security:** Edif. NASA, 14 Calle 5+49, Zona 1, Guatemala City; tel. 230-1364; fax 251-3559.

**Ministry of Energy and Mines:** Diagonal 17, 29–78, Zona 11, Guatemala City; tel. 276-0679; fax 276-3175.

**Ministry of Foreign Affairs:** Palacio Nacional, 6a Calle y 7a Avda, Zona 1, Guatemala City; tel. 22-1212; fax 251-6745.

**Ministry of the Interior:** Palacio Nacional, 6a Calle y 7a Avda, Zona 1, Guatemala City; tel. 22-1212; fax 251-5368.

**Ministry of National Defence:** Palacio Nacional, 6a Calle y 7a Avda, Zona 1, Guatemala City; tel. 22-1212; fax 28-1613.

**Ministry of Public Finance:** Edif. de Fianzas, Centro Cívico, 8a Avda y Calle 21, Zona 1, Guatemala City; tel. 251-1380; fax 251-0987.

**Ministry of Public Health and Social Welfare:** Palacio Nacional, 6a Calle y 7a Avda, Zona 1, Guatemala City; tel. 22-1212; fax 22-2736.

# President and Legislature

## PRESIDENT

**Election, 7 November 1999**

| | Percentage of votes cast |
|---|---|
| ALFONSO ANTONIO PORTILLO CABRERA (FRG) | 47.8 |
| ÓSCAR BERGER PERDOMO (PAN) | 30.3 |
| ÁLVARO COLOM CABALLEROS (ANN) | 12.3 |
| ACISCLO VALLADARES MOLINA (PLP) | 3.1 |
| JUAN FRANCISCO BIANCHI CASTILLO (ARDE) | 2.1 |
| ANA CATALINA SOBERANIS REYES (FDNG) | 1.3 |
| JOSÉ ENRIQUE ASTURIAS RUDEKE (LOV) | 1.1 |
| DANILO JULIÁN ROCA BARILLAS (UCN) | 1.0 |
| **Total** (incl. others) | 100.0 |

Since none of the candidates achieved the required 50% of the votes necessary to win outright, a second round of voting was held on 26 December 1999. At this election ALFONSO ANTONIO PORTILLO CABRERA (FRG) received 68.3% of the valid votes cast, while ÓSCAR BERGER PERDOMO (PAN) won the remaining 31.7%.

## CONGRESO NACIONAL

**President:** Gen. (retd) JOSÉ EFRAÍN RÍOS MONTT.

**Election, 7 November 1999**

| | Seats |
|---|---|
| Frente Republicano Guatemalteco (FRG) | 63 |
| Partido de Avanzada Nacional (PAN) | 37 |
| Alianza Nueva Nación (ANN) | 9 |
| Partido Democracia Cristiana Guatemalteca (PDCG) | 2 |
| Partido Liberal Progresista (PLP) | 1 |
| La Organización Verde (LOV) | 1 |
| **Total** | 113 |

# Political Organizations

**Acción Reconciliadora Democrática (ARDE):** 4a Avda 14-53, Zona 1, Guatemala City; tel. 232-0591; fax 251-4076; centre-right; Sec.-Gen. HERLINDO ALVAREZ DEL CID.

**Alianza Democrática:** Guatemala City; f. 1983; centre party; Leader LEOPOLDO URRUTIA.

**Alianza Nueva Nación (ANN):** electoral alliance comprising:

**Desarrollo Integral Auténtico (DIA):** 12a Calle 'A' 2-18, Zona 1, Guatemala City; left-wing party; Sec.-Gen. FRANCISCO ROLANDO MORALES CHÁVEZ.

**Unidad de Izquierda Democrática (UNID):** Guatemala City; left-wing party.

**Unidad Revolucionaria Nacional Guatemalteca (URNG):** (see below).

**Alianza Popular Cinco (AP5):** 6a Avda 3-23, Zona 1, Guatemala City; tel. 231-6022; Sec.-Gen. MAX ORLANDO MOLINA NARCISO.

**Central Auténtica Nacionalista (CAN):** 15a Avda 4-31, Zona 1, Guatemala City; tel. 251-2992; f. 1980 from the CAO (Central Arañista Organizado); Leader HÉCTOR MAYORA DAWE; Sec.-Gen. JORGE ROBERTO ARANA ESPAÑA.

**Comité Guatemalteca de Unidad Patriota (CGUP):** f. 1982; opposition coalition consisting of:

**Frente Democrático Contra la Represión (FDCR):** Leader RAFAEL GARCÍA.

**Frente Popular 31 de Enero (FP-31):** f. 1980; left-wing amalgamation of student, peasant and trade union groups.

**Frente de Avance Nacional (FAN):** 3a Calle 'A' 1-66, Zona 10, Guatemala City; tel. 231-8036; right-wing group; Sec.-Gen. FEDERICO ABUNDIO MALDONADO GULARTE.

**Frente Cívico Democrático (FCD):** Guatemala City; Leader JORGE GONZÁLEZ DEL VALLE.

**Frente Demócrata Guatemalteco:** Leader CLEMENTE MARROQUÍN ROJAS.

**Frente Democrático Nueva Guatemala (FDNG):** left-wing faction of Partido Revolucionario; Pres. JORGE GONZÁLEZ DEL VALLE; Sec.-Gen. RAFAEL ARRIAGA.

**Frente Republicano Guatemalteco (FRG):** 6a Avda 'A' 3-18, Zona 1, Guatemala City; tel. 250-1778; right-wing group; leader Gen. (retd) JOSÉ EFRAÍN RÍOS MONTT.

**Frente de Unidad Nacional (FUN):** 6a Avda 5-18, Zona 12, Guatemala City; tel. 271-4048; f. 1971; nationalist group; Leader GABRIEL GIRÓN ORTIZ.

**Fuerza Demócrata Popular:** 11a Calle 4-13, Zona 1, Guatemala City; tel. 251-5496; f. 1983; democratic popular force; Sec. Lic. FRANCISCO REYES IXCAMEY.

**Fuerza Nueva:** Leader CARLOS RAFAEL SOTO.

**La Organización Verde (LOV):** electoral coalition comprising:

**Unidad Social Demócrata.**

**Unión Democrática (UD):** 10a Avda 11-27, Zona 1, Guatemala City; tel. 251-7687; Sec.-Gen. JOSÉ LUIS CHEA URRUELA.

**Movimiento de los Descamisados (MD):** Avda J. R. Barrios L. 896 Sta Luisa, Zona 6, Guatemala City; Sec.-Gen. ENRIQUE MORALES PÉREZ.

**Movimiento Humanista de Integración Demócrata:** Guatemala City; f. 1983; Leader VICTORIANO ALVAREZ.

**Movimiento de Liberación Nacional (MLN):** 5a Calle 1–20, Zona 1, Guatemala City; tel. 22-6528; f. 1960; extreme right-wing; 95,000 mems; Leader Lic. MARIO SANDÓVAL ALARCÓN; Sec.-Gen. EDGAR ANTONIO FIGUEROA MUÑOZ.

**Movimiento 20 de Octubre:** Leader MARCO ANTONIO VILLAMAR CONTRERAS.

**Pantinamit:** f. 1977; represents interests of Indian population; Leader FERNANDO TEZAHUIC TOHÓN.

**Partido de Avanzada Nacional (PAN):** 6a Calle 7-70, Zona 9, Guatemala City; tel. 231-7431; Leader ALVARO ENRIQUE ARZÚ IRIGOYEN; Gen. Sec. HÉCTOR CIFUENTES MENDOZA.

**Partido Democracia Cristiana Guatemalteca (PDCG):** Avda Elena 20-66, Zona 3, Guatemala City; tel. 28-4988; f. 1968; 130,000 mems; Sec.-Gen. LUIS ALFONSO CABRERA HIDALGO.

**Partido Demócrata Guatemalteco (PDG):** 5a Calle 3-30, Zona 9, Guatemala City; tel. 231-2550; Sec.-Gen. JORGE ANTONIO REYNA CASTILLO.

**Partido Institucional Democrático (PID):** 2a Calle 10–73, Zona 1, Guatemala City; tel. 28-5412; f. 1965; 60,000 mems; moderate conservative; Sec.-Gen. OSCAR HUMBERTO RIVAS GARCÍA; Dir DONALDO ALVAREZ RUIZ.

**Partido Liberal Progresista (PLP):** Diagonal 16, 11-188, Zona 1, Quetzaltenango; Sec.-Gen. ISMAEL MUÑOZ PÉREZ.

**Partido Petenero:** Guatemala City; f. 1983; defends regional interests of El Petén.

**Partido Progresista (PP):** 1a Calle 6-77, Zona 2, Guatemala City; Sec.-Gen. JOSÉ RAMÓN FERNÁNDEZ GONZÁLEZ.

**Partido Reformador Guatemalteco (PREG):** 3a Calle 9-59, Zona 1, Guatemala City; tel. 22-8759; Sec.-Gen. MIGUEL ANGEL MONTEPEQUE CONTRERAS.

**Partido Revolucionario de los Trabajadores Centro-americanos (PRTC):** Guatemala City.

**Partido Social Cristiano (PSC):** P. Savoy, Of. 113, 8°, 8a Calle 9-41, Zona 1, Guatemala City; tel. 274-0577; f. 1983; Sec.-Gen. ALFONSO ALONZO BARILLAS.

**Partido Socialista Democrático (PSD):** 12a Calle 10-37, Zona 1, 01001, Apdo 1279, Guatemala City; tel. 253-3219; fax 273-7036; f. 1978; Sec.-Gen. SERGIO ALEJANDRO PÉREZ CRUZ.

**Partido de Unificación Anticomunista (PUA):** Guatemala City; right-wing party; Leader LEONEL SISNIEGA OTERO.

**Unidad Nacionalista Organizada (UNO):** Calzada Aguilar Batres 17-14, Zona 11, Guatemala City; Sec.-Gen. MARIO ROBERTO ARMANDO PONCIANO CASTILLO.

**Unión del Centro Nacional (UCN):** 12a Calle 2-45, Zona 1, Guatemala City; tel. 253-6211; f. 1984; centre party; Sec.-Gen. EDMOND MULET.

**Unión Reformista Social (URS):** 5a Calle 'A' 0-64, Zona 3, Guatemala City; Sec.-Gen. MARCOS EMILIO RECINOS ALVAREZ.

In February 1982 the principal guerrilla groups unified to form the **Unidad Revolucionaria Nacional Guatemalteca (URNG)** (Guatemalan National Revolutionary Unity), which has links with the PSD. The political wing of the URNG was the **Representación Unitaria de la Oposición Guatemalteca (RUOG).** At the end of 1996 the URNG consisted of:

**Ejército Guerrillero de los Pobres (EGP):** f. 1972; draws main support from Indians of western highlands; works closely with the **Comité de Unidad Campesina (CUC)** (Committee of Peasant Unity) and radical Catholic groups; mems 4,000 armed, 12,000 unarmed.

**Fuerzas Armadas Rebeldes (FAR):** formed early 1960s; originally military commission of CGTG; associated with the CNT and CONUS trade unions; based in Guatemala City, Chimaltenango and El Petén; Commdr JORGE ISMAEL SOTO GARCÍA ('PABLO MONSANTO').

**Organización del Pueblo en Armas (ORPA):** f. 1979; military group active in San Marcos province; originally part of FAR; Commdr RODRIGO ASTURIAS ('GASPAR ILOM').

**Partido Guatemalteco del Trabajo (PGT):** communist party; divided into three armed factions: PGT-Camarilla (began actively participating in war in 1981); PGT-Núcleo de Conducción y Dirección; PGT-Comisión Nuclear; Gen. Sec. RICARDO ROSALES ('CARLOS GONZÁLEZ').

In December 1996 the Government and the URNG signed a definitive peace treaty, bringing the 36-year conflict to an end. The demobilization of the URNG guerrillas began in March 1997 and was completed by early May. In June the URNG registered as a political party in formation. In August the movement held elections to a provisional executive committee. The URNG applied for formal recognition as a political party in October 1998 and was formally registered in December. In May 1999 the URNG formed an alliance, the Alianza Nueva Nación, with the FDNG (which later withdrew from the alliance), the UNID and the DIA in order to contest legislative elections, scheduled to be held in November 1999.

# Diplomatic Representation

### EMBASSIES IN GUATEMALA

**Argentina:** 2a Avda 11-04, Zona 10, Guatemala City; Ambassador: Dr ANGEL FERNANDO GIRARDI.

**Austria:** 6a Avda 20-25, Zona 10, Guatemala City; tel. 368-1134; fax 333-6180; Ambassador: GABRIEL KRAMARICS.

**Belgium:** Avda de la Reforma 13-70, Zona 9, Apdo 3725, Guatemala City; tel. 225-6633; Ambassador: MICHEL DELFOSSE.

**Belize:** Edif. El Reformador, Suite 803, 8°, Avda de la Reforma 1-50, Zona 9, Guatemala City; tel. 334-5531; fax 334-5536; Ambassador: MIKE MENA.

**Bolivia:** 12a Avda 15-37, Zona 10, Guatemala City; Chargé d'affaires a.i.: Dr JOSÉ GABINA VILLANUEVA G.

**Brazil:** 18a Calle 2-22, Zona 14, Apdo 196-A, Guatemala City; tel. 337-0949; fax 337-3475; e-mail brasilgua@gua.gbm.net; Ambassador: SÉRGIO DAMASCENO VIEIRA.

**Canada:** Edyma Plaza, 13a Calle 8-44210, 8 Nivel, Guatemala City; tel. 333-6102; fax 333-6189; Ambassador: DANIEL LIVERMORE.

**Chile:** 13a Calle 7-85, Zona 10, Guatemala City; Ambassador: SILVIO SALGADO RAMÍREZ.

**China (Taiwan):** 4a Avda 'A' 13–25, Zona 9, Apdo 1646, Guatemala City; tel. 239-0711; Ambassador: WU JEN-HSIU.

**Colombia:** Edif. Gemini 10, 12a Calle, 1a Avda, Zona 10, Guatemala City; tel. 232-0604; Ambassador: LAURA OCHOA DE ARDILLA.

**Costa Rica:** Edif. Galerías Reforma, Of. 701, Avda de la Reforma 8-60, Zona 9, Guatemala City; tel. 232-1522; Ambassador: YOLANDA INGIANNA-MAINIERI.

**Dominican Republic:** 7a Calle 'A' 4-28, Zona 10, Guatemala City; Ambassador: PEDRO PABLO ALVAREZ BONILLA.

**Ecuador:** Of. 602, Avda de la Reforma 12-01, Zona 10, Guatemala City; tel. 231-2439; Ambassador: DIEGO PAREDES-PEÑA.

**Egypt:** Avda de la Reforma 7-89, Zona 10, Guatemala City; tel. 231-5315; fax 232-6055; Ambassador: MOHAMED FADEL WEHEBA.

**El Salvador:** 12a Calle 5-43, Zona 9, Guatemala City; tel. 262-9385; Ambassador: AGUSTÍN MARTÍNEZ VARELA.

**France:** Edif. Marbella, 16a Calle 4-53, Zona 10, Guatemala City; tel. 237-3639; Ambassador: SERGE PINOT.

**Germany:** Edif. Plaza Marítima, 6a Avda 20-25, Zona 10, Guatemala City; tel. 337-0028; Ambassador: Dr JOACHIM NEUKIRCH.

**Holy See:** 10a Calle 4-47, Zona 9, Guatemala City (Apostolic Nunciature); tel. 332-4274; fax 334-1918; e-mail nuntius@gua.net; Apostolic Nuncio: Most Rev. RAMIRO MOLINER INGLÉS, Titular Archbishop of Sarda.

**Honduras:** 16a Calle 8-27, Zona 10, Apdo 730-A, Guatemala City; tel. 237-3919; fax 233-4629; Ambassador: GUILLERMO BOQUÍN V.

**Israel:** 13a Avda 14-07, Zona 10, Guatemala City; Ambassador: JACQUES YAACOV DECKEL.

**Italy:** 5a Avda 8-59, Zona 14, Guatemala City; tel. 337-4557; fax 337-0795; e-mail embitaly@guatenet.net.gt; Ambassador: ALESSANDRO SERAFINI.

**Japan:** Ruta 6, Zona 4, Apdo 531, Guatemala City; tel. 331-9666; fax 331-5462; Ambassador: HISATO MURAYAMA.

**Korea, Republic:** 15a Avda 24-51, Zona 13, Apdo 1649, Guatemala City; tel. 232-1578; fax 234-7037; Ambassador: WUNG-SIK KANG.

**Mexico:** 16a Calle 0-51, Zona 14, Guatemala City; tel. 268-0769; Ambassador: ABRAHAM TALAVERA LÓPEZ.

**Nicaragua:** 10a Avda 14-72, Zona 10, Guatemala City; Ambassador: RICARDO ZAMBRANA.

**Paraguay:** 7a Avda 7-78, 8°, Zona 4, Guatemala City; tel. 334-2981; fax 331-5048.

**Peru:** 2a Avda 9-67, Zona 9, Guatemala City; Ambassador: JULIO FLORIÁN ALEGRE.

**Portugal:** 5a Avda 12-60, Zona 9, Guatemala City; Ambassador: ANTÓNIO CABRITA MATIAS.

**Spain:** 6a Calle 6-48, Zona 9, Guatemala City; tel. 334-3757; fax 332-2456; Ambassador: VÍCTOR LUIS FAGILDE GONZÁLEZ.

**Sweden:** 8a Avda 15-07, Zona 10, Guatemala City; tel. 333-6536; fax 333-7607; Ambassador: STAFFAN WRIGSTAD.

**Switzerland:** 4a Calle 7-73, Zona 9, Apdo 1426, Guatemala City; tel. 234-0743; fax 231-8524; Ambassador: WILLY HOLD.

**United Kingdom:** Edif. Torre Internacional, 11°, 16a Calle 00-55, Zona 10, Guatemala City; tel. 367-5425; fax 367-5430; e-mail embassy@infovia.com.gt; Ambassador: ANDREW J. F. CAIE.

**USA:** Avda de la Reforma 7-01, Zona 10, Guatemala City; tel. 231-1541; Ambassador: DONALD J. PLANTY.

**Uruguay:** 20a Calle 8–00, Zona 10, Guatemala City; Chargé d'affaires: HÉCTOR L. PEDETTI A.

**Venezuela:** 8a Calle 0-56, Zona 9, Guatemala City; Ambassador: Dr ROGELIO ROSAS GIL.

# Judicial System

**Corte Suprema:** Centro Cívico, 21a Calle y 7a Avda, Guatemala City; tel. 284323.

There are 13 members of the Supreme Court, appointed by the Congress.

**President of the Supreme Court:** JOSÉ ROLANDO QUESADA FERNÁNDEZ.

**Civil Courts of Appeal:** 10 courts, 5 in Guatemala City, 2 in Quezaltenango, 1 each in Jalapa, Zacapa and Antigua. The two Labour Courts of Appeal are in Guatemala City.

**Judges of the First Instance:** 7 civil and 10 penal in Guatemala City, 2 civil each in Quezaltenango, Escuintla, Jutiapa and San Marcos, 1 civil in each of the 18 remaining Departments of the Republic.

# Religion

Almost all of the inhabitants profess Christianity, with a majority belonging to the Roman Catholic Church. In recent years the Protestant Churches have attracted a growing number of converts.

### CHRISTIANITY

#### The Roman Catholic Church

For ecclesiastical purposes, Guatemala comprises two archdioceses, 10 dioceses and the Apostolic Vicariates of El Petén and Izabal. At 31 December 1997 adherents represented about 90% of the total population.

**Bishops' Conference:** Conferencia Episcopal de Guatemala, Secretariado General del Episcopado, Km 15, Calzada Roosevelt 4-54, Zona 7, Mixco, Apdo 1698, Guatemala City; tel. 593-1831; fax 593-1834; f. 1973; Pres. VÍCTOR HUGO MARTÍNEZ CONTRERAS, Archbishop of Los Altos, Quetzaltenango-Totonicapán.

**Archbishop of Guatemala City:** PRÓSPERO PEÑADOS DEL BARRIO, Arzobispado, 7a Avda 6-21, Zona 1, Apdo 723, Guatemala City; tel. 232-1071; fax 238-0004.

**Archbishop of Los Altos, Quetzaltenango—Totonicapán:** VÍCTOR HUGO MARTÍNEZ CONTRERAS, Arzobispado, 11a Avda 6-27, Zona 1, Apdo 11, Quezaltenango; tel. (961) 2840; fax (961) 6049.

#### The Anglican Communion

Guatemala comprises one of the five dioceses of the Iglesia Anglicana de la Región Central de América.

**Bishop of Guatemala:** Rt Rev. ARMANDO GUERRA SORIA; Avda Castellana 40–06, Zona 8, Apdo 58-A, Guatemala City; tel. 272-0852; fax 472-0764; e-mail diocesis@infovia.com.gt; diocese founded 1967.

#### Protestant Churches

**The Baptist Church:** Convention of Baptist Churches of Guatemala, 12a Calle 9–54, Zona 1, Apdo 322, Guatemala City; tel. 22-4227; f. 1946; Pres. Lic. JOSÉ MARROQUÍN R.

**Church of Jesus Christ of Latter-day Saints:** 12a Calle 3–37, Zona 9, Guatemala City; 17 bishoprics, 9 chapels; Regional Rep. GUILLERMO ENRIQUE RITTSCHER.

**Lutheran Church:** Consejo Nacional de Iglesias Luteranas, Apdo 1111, Guatemala City; tel. 22-3401; 3,077 mems; Pres. Rev. DAVID RODRÍGUEZ U.

**Presbyterian Church:** Iglesia Evangélica Presbiteriana Central, 6a Avda 'A' 4–68, Zona 1, Apdo 655, Guatemala City; tel. 22-0791; f. 1882; 36,000 mems; Pastors: Rev. JUAN RENÉ GIRÓN T., Rev. JULIO CÉSAR PAZ PORTILLO, Rev. JOSÉ RAMIRO BOLAÑOS R.

**Union Church:** 12a Calle 7–37, Plazuela España, Zona 9, Apdo 150-A, Guatemala City; tel. 331-6904; f. 1943; Pastor: BRENT C. WILLIAMS.

### BAHÁ'Í FAITH

**National Spiritual Assembly of the Bahá'ís:** 3a Calle 4–54, Zona 1, Guatemala City; tel. 232-9673; fax 232-9673; e-mail aenguate@emailgua.com; mems resident in 464 localities; Sec. MARVIN E. ALVARADO E.

## The Press

### PRINCIPAL DAILIES

**Al Día:** Avda La Reforma 6–64, Zona 9, Guatemala City; tel. 339-0870; fax 339-1276; f. 1996; Pres. LIONEL TORIELLO NÁJERA; Dir GERARDO JIMÉNEZ ARDÓN.

**Diario de Centroamérica:** 18a Calle 6–72, Zona 1, Guatemala City; tel. 22-4418; f. 1880; morning; official; Dir LUIS MENDIZÁBAL; circ. 15,000.

**La Hora:** 9a Calle 'A' 1–56, Zona 1, Apdo 1593, Guatemala City; tel. 232-6864; fax 251-7084; e-mail lahora@tikal.net.gt; f. 1920; evening; independent; Dir OSCAR MARROQUÍN ROJAS; circ. 18,000.

**Impacto:** 9a Calle 'A' 1-56, Apdo 1593, Guatemala City; tel. 22-6864; fax 251-7084; daily.

**Imparcial:** 7a Calle 10-54, Zona 1, Guatemala City; tel. 251-4723; daily; circ. 25,000.

**La Nación:** 1a Avda 11-12, Guatemala City.

**El Periódico:** 15a Avda 24–51, Zona 13, Guatemala City; tel. 362-0242; fax 332-9761; e-mail periodic@gold.guate.net; f. 1996; morning; independent; Pres. JOSÉ RUBÉN ZAMORA; Editors JUAN LUIS FONT, SYLVIA GEREDA; circ. 50,000.

**Prensa Libre:** 13a Calle 9–31, Zona 1, Apdo 2063, Guatemala City; tel. 230-5096; fax 251-8768; e-mail econtrer@infovia.com.gt; internet www.prensalibre.com; f. 1951; morning; independent; Gen. Man. EDGAR CONTRERAS MOLINA; Editor GONZALO MARROQUÍN GODOY; circ. 120,000.

**Siglo Veintiuno:** 7a Avda 11-63, Zona 9, Guatemala City; tel. 360-6704; fax 331-9145; e-mail buzon21@sigloxxi.com; internet www.sigloxxi.com; f. 1990; morning; Pres. LIONEL TORIELLO NÁJERA; circ. 65,000.

**La Tarde:** 14a Avda 4-33, Guatemala City.

### PERIODICALS

**AGA:** 9a Calle 3–43, Zona 1, Guatemala City; monthly; agricultural.

**Crónica Semanal:** Edif. Torre Profesional II, Of. 312, 6a Avda 0-60, Guatemala City; tel. 235-2155; fax 235-2360; f. 1988; weekly; politics, economics, culture; Publr FRANCISCO PÉREZ.

**Gerencia:** La Asociación de Gerentes de Guatemala, Edif. Aseguradora General, 7°, 10a Calle 3-17, Guatemala City; tel. 231-1644; fax 231-1646; f. 1967; monthly; official organ of the Association of Guatemalan Managers; Editor MARGARITA SOLOGUREN.

**El Industrial:** 6a Ruta 9-21, Zona 4, Guatemala City; monthly; official organ of the Chamber of Industry.

**Inforpress Centroamericana:** Guatemala City; f. 1972; weekly; Spanish; regional political and economic news and analysis; Dir ARIEL DE LEÓN.

**Panorama Internacional:** 13a Calle 8-44, Zona 9, Apdo 611-A, Guatemala City; tel. 233-6367; fax 233-6203; weekly; politics, economics, culture.

### PRESS ASSOCIATIONS

**Asociación de Periodistas de Guatemala (APG):** 14a Calle 3-29, Zona 1, Guatemala City; tel. 232-1813; fax 238-2781; f. 1947; Pres. JULIO RAFAEL MENDIZÁBAL GUZMÁN; Sec. ALVARO ENRIQUE PALMA SANDOVAL.

**Cámara Guatemalteca de Periodismo (CGP):** Guatemala City; Pres. EDUARDO DÍAZ REINA.

**Círculo Nacional de Prensa (CNP):** Guatemala City; Pres. ISRAEL TOBAR ALVARADO.

### NEWS AGENCIES

**Inforpress Centroamericana:** 7a Avda 2-05, Zona 1, Guatemala City; tel. and fax 232-9034; f. 1972; independent news agency; publishes two weekly news bulletins, in English and Spanish.

### Foreign Bureaux

**ACAN-EFE** (Central America): Edif. El Centro, 8°, Of. 8-21, 9a Calle y 7a Avda, Zona 1, Of. Guatemala City; tel. 251-9454; fax 251-9484: Man. ANA CAROLINA ALPÍREZ A.

**Agenzia Nazionale Stampa Associata (ANSA)** (Italy): Torre Norte, Edif. Geminis 10, Of. 805, 12a Calle 1-25, Zona 10, Guatemala City; tel. 235-3039; Chief ALFONSO ANZUETO LÓPEZ.

**Deutsche Presse-Agentur (dpa)** (Germany): 5a Calle 4-30, Zona 1, Apdo 2333, Guatemala City; tel. 251-7505; fax 251-7505; Correspondent JULIO CÉSAR ANZUETO.

**Inter Press Service (IPS)** (Italy): Edif. El Centro, 3°, Of. 13, 7a Avda 8-56, Zona 1, Guatemala City; tel. 253-8837; fax 251-4736; Correspondent GEORGE RODRÍGUEZ-OTEIZA.

**United Press International (UPI)** (USA): 6a Calle 4-17, Zona 1, Guatemala City; tel. and fax 251-4258; Correspondent AMAFREDO CASTELLANOS.

## Publishers

**Ediciones América:** 12a Avda 14-55B, Zone 1, Guatemala City; tel. 251-4556; Man. Dir RAFAEL ESCOBAR ARGÜELLO.

**Ediciones Gama:** 5a Avda 14-46, Zone 1, Guatemala City; tel. 234-2331; Man. Dir SARA MONZÓN DE ECHEVERRÍA.

**Ediciones Legales 'Commercio e Industria':** 12a Avda 14-78, Zone 1, Guatemala City; tel. 253-5725; Man. Dir LUIS EMILIO BARRIOS.

**Editorial Impacto:** Via 6, 3-14, Zone 4, Guatemala City; tel. 232-2887; Man. Dir IVÁN CARPIO.

**Editorial del Ministerio de Educación:** 15a Avda 3-22, Zona 1, Guatemala City.

**Editorial Nueva Narrativa:** Edificio El Patio, Of. 106, 7a Avda 7-07, Zona 4, Guatemala City; Man. Dir MAX ARAÚJO A.

**Editorial Oscar de León Palacios:** 6a Calle 'A' 10-12, Zone 11, Guatemala City; tel. 272-1636; educational texts; Man. Dir OSCAR DE LEÓN CASTILLO.

**Editorial Palo de Hormigo:** O Calle 16-40, Zone 15, Col. El Maestro, Guatemala City; tel. 269-2080; fax 231-5928; Man. Dir JUAN FERNANDO CIFUENTES.

**Editorial Universitaria:** Edif. de la Editorial Universitaria, Universidad de San Carlos de Guatemala, Ciudad Universitaria, Zona 12, Guatemala City; tel. 276-0790; literature, social sciences, health, pure and technical sciences, humanities, secondary and university educational textbooks; Editor IVANOVA ALVARADO DE ANCHETA.

**Piedra Santa:** 5a Calle 7-55, Zona 1, Guatemala City; tel. 220-1524; fax 323-9053; f. 1947; children's literature, text books; Man. Dir IRENE PIEDRA SANTA.

**Seminario de Integración Social Guatemalteco:** 11a Calle 4-31, Zona 1, Guatemala City; tel. 22-9754; f. 1956; sociology, anthropology, social sciences, educational textbooks.

## Broadcasting and Communications

### TELECOMMUNICATIONS

**Superintendencia de Telecomunicaciones de Guatemala:** Edif. Murano Center, 16°, 14a Calle 3-51, Zona 10, Guatemala City; tel. 366-5880; fax 366-5890; e-mail supertel@sit.gob.gt; Superintendent JOSÉ TOLEDO ORDÓÑEZ.

**Empresa Guatemalteca de Telecomunicaciones (Guatel):** 7a Avda 12-39, Zona 1, Guatemala City; 95% share transferred to private ownership in 1998; Dir ALFREDO GUZMÁN.

### BROADCASTING

**Dirección General de Radiodifusión y Televisión Nacional:** Edif. Tipografía Nacional, 3°, 18 de Septiembre 6-72, Zona 1, Guatemala City; tel. 253-2539; f. 1931; government supervisory body; Dir-Gen. ENRIQUE ALBERTO HERNÁNDEZ ESCOBAR.

#### Radio

There are five government and six educational stations, including:

**La Voz de Guatemala:** 18a Calle 6-72, Zona 1, Guatemala City; tel. 253-2539; government station; Dir ARTURO SOTO ECHEVERRÍA.

**Radio Cultural TGN:** 4a Avda 30-09, Zona 3, Apdo 601, Guatemala City; tel. 471-4378; fax 440-0260; e-mail ssywulka@guate.net; f. 1950; religious and cultural station; programmes in Spanish and English, Cakchiquel and Kekchí; Dir ESTEBAN SYWULKA; Man. ANTHONY WAYNE BERGER.

There are some 80 commercial stations, of which the most important are:

**Emisoras Unidas de Guatemala:** 4a Calle 6-84, Zona 13, Guatemala City; tel. 440-5133; fax 440-5159; e-mail rboileau@tikal.net.gt;

f. 1964; Pres. JORGE EDGARDO ARCHILA MARROQUÍN; Vice-Pres. ROLANDO ARCHILA MARROQUÍN.

**Radio Cinco Sesenta:** 14a Calle 4-73, Zona 11, Guatemala City; Dir EDNA CASTILLO OBREGÓN.

**Radio Continental:** 15a Calle 3-45, Zona 1, Guatemala City; Dir ROBERTO VIZCAÍNO R.

**Radio Nuevo Mundo:** 6a Avda 10-45, Zona 1, Apdo 281, Guatemala City; fax 232-2036; f. 1947; Man. ALFREDO GONZÁLEZ GAMARRA.

**Radio Panamericana:** 1a Avda 35-48, Zona 7, Guatemala City; Dir JAIME J. PANIAGUA.

**La Voz de las Américas:** 11a Calle 2-43, Zona 1, Guatemala City; Dir AUGUSTO LÓPEZ S.

### Television

**Canal 3—Radio-Televisión Guatemala, SA:** 30a Avda 3-40, Zona 11, Apdo 1367, Guatemala City; tel. 292-2491; fax 294-7492; f. 1956; commercial station; Pres. Lic. MAX KESTLER FARNÉS; Vice-Pres. J. F. VILLANUEVA.

**Canal 5—Televisión Cultural y Educativa, SA:** 4a Calle 18-38, Zona 1, Guatemala City; tel. 238-1781; fax 232-7003; f. 1980; cultural and educational programmes; Dir ALFREDO HERRERA CABRERA.

**Teleonce:** 20a Calle 5-02, Zona 10, Guatemala City; tel. 368-2595; fax 337-0861; f. 1968; commercial; Gen. Dir JUAN CARLOS ORTIZ.

**Televisiete, SA:** Blvr Vista Hermosa 18-07, Zona 15, Apdo 1242, Guatemala City; tel. 369-0033; fax 369-1393; f. 1988; commercial station channel 7; Dir ABDÓN RODRÍGUEZ ZEA.

**Trecevisión, SA:** 3a Calle 10-70, Zona 10, Guatemala City; tel. 26-3266; commercial; Dir Ing. PEDRO MELGAR R.; Gen. Man. GILDA VALLADARES ORTIZ.

# Finance

(cap. = capital; p.u. = paid up; res = reserves; dep. = deposits; m. = million; brs = branches; amounts in quetzales)

## BANKING

**Superintendencia de Bancos:** 9a Avda 22-00, Zona 1, Apdo 2306, Guatemala City; tel. 232-0001; fax 232-5301; e-mail sibcos@guate.net; f. 1946; Superintendent ROBERTO A. GUTIÉRREZ NÁJERA.

### Central Bank

**Banco de Guatemala:** 7a Avda 22-01, Zona 1, Apdo 365, Guatemala City; tel. 230-6222; fax 253-4035; internet www.banguat.gob.gt; f. 1946; cap. and res 603.2m., dep. 12,040.6m. (Dec. 1997); Pres. LIZARDO SOSA; Man. EDWIN GIOVANNI VERBENA DE LEÓN; 8 brs.

### State Commercial Bank

**Crédito Hipotecario Nacional de Guatemala:** 7a Avda 22-77, Zona 1, Apdo 242, Guatemala City; tel. 238-0742; fax 238-2041; e-mail jpedchn@infovia. com.gt; f. 1930; government-owned; Pres. FABIÁN PIRA ARRIVILLAGA; Gen. Man. SERGIO DURINI CÁRDENAS; 35 agencies.

### Private Commercial Banks

Guatemala City

**Banco Agrícola Mercantil, SA:** 7a Avda 7-30, Zona 9, Guatemala City; tel. 362-3141; fax 251-0780; e-mail interbam@guate.net; internet www.bamguatemala.com; f. 1948; cap. 84.1m., res 2.5m., dep. 974.1m. (Dec. 1996); Gen. Man. ALFONSO VILLA DE VOTO; 2 brs, 8 agencies.

**Banco del Agro, SA:** 9a Calle 5-39, Zona 1, Apdo 1443, Guatemala City; tel. 251-4026; fax 232-4566; f. 1956; cap. 10.0m., res 19.4m., dep. 374.9m. (June 1991); Pres. JOSÉ MARÍA VALDÉS GARCÍA; Gen. Man. HÉCTOR ESTUARDO PIVARAL; 25 brs.

**Banco del Café, SA:** Avda de la Reforma 9-30, Zona 9, Apdo 831, Guatemala City; tel. 361-3645; fax 331-1418; e-mail mercadeo@bancafe.com.gt; internet www.bancafe.com.gt; f. 1978; cap. 63.2m., res 11.9m., dep. 1,431.4m. (Dec. 1997); Pres. EDUARDO MANUEL GONZÁLEZ RIVERA; Asst Gen. Man. INGO HABERLAND HAESLOOP.

**Banco de la Construcción, SA:** 12a Calle 4-17, Zona 1, Apdo 999, Guatemala City; tel. 230-2824; fax 230-6150; internet www.construcredit.gua.net; f. 1983; cap. 55.0m., dep. 491.1m. (Dec. 1997); Pres. LUIS ROBERTO COBAR CIFUENTES; Gen. Man. JOSÉ LUIS RODAS PALACIOS.

**Banco del Ejército, SA:** 7a Avda 3-73, Zona 9, Apdo 1797, Guatemala City; tel. 362-7042; fax 362-7117; e-mail baneje@gua.net; f. 1972; cap. 72.2m., res 22.2m., dep. 735.9m. (Dec. 1997); Pres. Col GUIDO FERNANDO ABDALA PEÑAGOS; 14 brs.

**Banco de Exportación, SA:** Avda de la Reforma 11-49, Zona 10, Guatemala City; tel. 231-9861; fax 232-2879; f. 1985; cap. 71.8m., res 30.0m., dep. 731.3m. (Dec. 1993); Pres. DR FRANCISCO MANSILLA CÓRDOVA; Man. Ing. RAFAEL VIEJO RODRÍGUEZ.

**Banco Granai y Townson, SA:** 7a Avda 1-86, Zona 4, Apdo 654, Guatemala City; tel. 331-2333; fax 332-9083; internet www.gyt.com.gt; f. 1962; cap. 33.0m., res 37.5m., dep. 1,405.8m. (Dec. 1993); Pres. MARIO GRANAI ARÉVALO; Gen. Man. GERARDO TOWNSON RINCÓN; 40 brs.

**Banco Industrial, SA (BAINSA):** Edif. Centro Financiero, Torre 1, 7a Avda 5-10, Zona 4, Apdo 744, Guatemala City; tel. 234-5111; fax 232-1712; f. 1964 to promote industrial development; cap. and res 119.1m., dep. 1,709.7m. (June 1994); Pres. JUAN MIGUEL TORREBIARTE LANTZENDORFFER; Gen. Man. Lic. NORBERTO RODOLFO CASTELLANOS DÍAZ.

**Banco Inmobilario, SA:** 7a Avda 11-59, Zona 9, Apdo 1181, Guatemala City; tel. 332-1950; fax 332-2325; e-mail info@bancoinmob.com.gt; internet www.bcoinmob.com.gt; f. 1958; cap. 45.0m., res 6.2m., dep. 532.3m. (June 1992); Pres. EMILIO ANTONIO PERALTA PORTILLO; Man. MARCO ANTONIO OVANDO; 15 brs.

**Banco Internacional, SA:** Torre Internacional, Avda Reforma 15-85, Zona 10, Apdo 2588, Guatemala City; tel. 366-6666; fax 366-6743; e-mail binter60@gua.gbm.net; internet www.bcointer.com/gt; f. 1976; cap. 50.0m., res 15.4m., dep. 822.6m. (Dec. 1997); Pres. JUAN SKINNER-KLÉE; Gen. Man. JOSÉ MANUEL REQUEJO SÁNCHEZ; 28 brs.

**Banco Metropolitano, SA:** 5a Avda 8-24, Zona 1, Apdo 2688, Guatemala City; tel. 325-3609; fax 28-4073; f. 1978; cap. 39.4m., res 9.4m., dep. 410.6m. (Dec. 1994); Pres. Ing. FRANCISCO ALVARADO MACDONALD; Man. EBERTO CÉSAR SIGÜENZA LÓPEZ.

**Banco Promotor, SA:** 10a Calle 6-47, Zona 1, Apdo 930, Guatemala City; tel. 251-2928; fax 251-3387; f. 1986; cap. 15.0m., dep. 174.0m. (June 1994); Pres. Lic. JULIO VALLADARES CASTILLO; Gen. Man. Lic. JOSÉ LUIS URÍZAR NORIEGA; 6 brs.

**Banco del Quetzal, SA:** Edif. Plaza El Roble, 7a Ave 6-26, Zona 9, Apdo 1001-A, Guatemala City; tel. 231-8333; fax 232-6937; f. 1984; cap. 37.4m., dep. 342.7m. (July 1994); Pres. Lic. MARIO ROBERTO LEAL PIVARAL; Gen. Man. ALFONSO VILLA DEVOTO.

**Banco de los Trabajadores:** 8a Avda 9-41, Zona 1, Apdo 1956, Guatemala City; tel. 22-4651; fax 251-8902; f. 1966; deals with loans for establishing and improving small industries as well as normal banking business; Pres. Lic. CÉSAR AMILCAR BÁRCENAS; Gen. Man. Lic. OSCAR H. ANDRADE ELIZONDO.

Quezaltenango

**Banco de Occidente, SA:** 7a Ave 11-15, Zona 1, Quezaltenango; tel. (961) 53-1333; fax (961) 30-0970; f. 1881; cap. 10.0m., res 118.9m., dep. 1,227.8m. (Dec. 1993); Pres. DR LUIS BELTRANENA VALLADARES; Gen. Man. Ing. JOSÉ E. ASCOLI CÁCERES; 29 brs.

### State Development Banks

**Banco Nacional de Desarrollo Agrícola—BANDESA:** 9a Calle 9-47, Zona 1, Apdo 350, Guatemala City; tel. 253-5222; fax 253-7927; f. 1971; agricultural development bank; Pres. Minister of Agriculture, Livestock and Food; Gen. Man. GUSTAVO ADOLFO LEAL CASTELLANOS.

**Banco Nacional de la Vivienda—BANVI:** 6a Avda 1-22, Zona 4, Apdo 2632, Guatemala City; tel. 332-5777; fax 236-6592; f. 1973; Pres. JOAQUÍN MARTÍNEZ.

### Finance Corporations

**Corporación Financiera Nacional—CORFINA:** 11a Avda 3-14, Zona 1, Guatemala City; tel. 253-4550; fax 22-5805; f. 1973; provides assistance for the development of industry, mining and tourism; Pres. Lic. SERGIO A. GONZÁLEZ NAVAS; Gen. Man. Lic. MARIO ARMANDO MARTÍNEZ ZAMORA.

**Financiera Guatemalteca, SA—FIGSA:** 1a Avda 11-50, Zona 10, Apdo 2460, Guatemala City; tel. 232-1423; fax 231-0873; f. 1962; investment agency; Pres. CARLOS GONZÁLEZ BARRIOS; Gen. Man. Ing. ROBERTO FERNÁNDEZ BOTRÁN.

**Financiera Industrial y Agropecuaria, SA—FIASA:** Plaza Continental, 3°, 6a Avda 9-08, Zona 9, Guatemala City; tel. 239-1951; fax 239-2089; f. 1968; private development bank; medium- and long-term loans to private industrial enterprises in Central America; cap. 2.5m., res 27.1m. (Dec. 1994); Pres. JORGE CASTILLO LOVE; Gen. Man. Lic. ALEJANDRO MEJÍA AVILA.

**Financiera Industrial, SA (FISA):** Centro Financiero, Torre 2, 7a Avda 5-10, Zona 4, Apdo 744, Guatemala City; tel. 232-1750; fax 231-1773; f. 1981; cap. 3m., res 6.2m. (Aug. 1991); Pres. CARLOS ARÍAS MASSELLI; Gen. Man. Lic. ELDER F. CALDERÓN REYES.

**Financiera de Inversión, SA:** 11a Calle 7-44, Zona 9, Guatemala City; tel. 332-4020; fax 332-4320; f. 1981; investment agency; cap. 15.0m. (June 1997); Pres. Lic. MARIO AUGUSTO PORRAS GONZÁLEZ; Gen. Man. Lic. JOSÉ ROLANDO PORRAS GONZÁLEZ.

### Foreign Bank

**Lloyds TSB Group PLC:** Edif. Gran Vía, 6a Avda 9-51, Zona 9, Guatemala City; tel. 332-7580; fax 332-7641; f. 1959; cap. 13m., dep. 159.1m. (1990); Man. N. M. A. HUBBARD; 8 brs.

### Banking Association

**Asociación de Banqueros de Guatemala:** Edif. Quinta Montúfar, 2°, 12a Calle 4-74, Zona 9, Guatemala City; tel. 231-8211; fax 231-9477; f. 1961; represents all state and private banks; Pres. Ing. RAFAEL VIEJO RODRÍGUEZ.

## STOCK EXCHANGE

**Guatemala Stock Exchange:** 4a Calle 6-55, Zona 9, Guatemala City; tel. 234-2479; fax 231-4509; f. 1987; the exchange is commonly owned (one share per associate) and trades stocks from private companies, government bonds, letters of credit and other securities.

## INSURANCE

### National Companies

**Aseguradora General, SA:** 10a Calle 3-17, Zona 10, Guatemala City; tel. 332-5933; fax 334-2093; f. 1968; Pres. JUAN O. NIEMANN; Man. ENRIQUE NEUTZE A.

**Aseguradora Guatemalteca, SA:** 5a Avda 6-06, Zona 1, Guatemala City; tel. 251-9795; fax 234-2093; f. 1978; Pres. Gen. CARLOS E. PINEDA CARRANZA; Man. CÉSAR A. RUANO SANDOVAL.

**Cía de Seguros Generales Granai & Townson, SA:** 2a Ruta, 2-39, Zona 4, Guatemala City; tel. 334-1361; fax 332-2993; f. 1947; Pres. ERNESTO TOWNSON R.; Exec. Man. MARIO GRANAI FERNÁNDEZ.

**Cía de Seguros Panamericana, SA:** Avda de la Reforma 9-00, Zona 9, Guatemala City; tel. 232-5922; fax 231-5026; f. 1968; Pres. JOHN ROBERTS; Gen. Man. Lic. SALVADOR ORTEGA.

**Cía de Seguros El Roble, SA:** Torre 2, 7a Avda 5-10, Zona 4, Guatemala City; tel. 332-1702; fax 332-1629; f. 1973; Pres. FEDERICO KÖNG VIELMAN; Man. Ing. RICARDO ERALES CÓBAR.

**Comercial Aseguradora Suizo-Americana, SA:** 7a Avda 7-07, Zona 9, Apdo 132, Guatemala City; tel. 332-0666; fax 331-5495; f. 1946; Pres. WILLIAM BICKFORD B.; Gen. Man. MARIO AGUILAR.

**Departamento de Seguros y Previsión del Crédito Hipotecario Nacional:** 7a Avda 22-77, Zona 1, Centro Cívico, Guatemala City; tel. 250-0271; fax 253-8584; f. 1935; Pres. FABIÁN PIRA; Man. SERGIO DURINI.

**Empresa Guatemalteca Cigna de Seguros, SA:** Edif. Plaza Marítima 10, 6a Avda 20-25, Zona 10, Guatemala City; tel. 337-2285; fax 337-0121; f. 1951; Gen. Man. Lic. RICARDO ESTRADA DARDÓN.

**La Seguridad de Centroamérica, SA:** Avda de la Reforma 12-01, Zona 10, Guatemala City; tel. 231-7566; fax 231-7580; f. 1967; Pres. EDGARDO WAGNER D.; Vice-Pres. RICARDO CAU MARTÍNEZ.

**Seguros Alianza, SA:** Edif. Etisa, 6°, Plazuela España, Zona 9, Guatemala City; tel. 331-5475; fax 331-0023; f. 1968; Pres. LUIS FERNANDO SAMAYOA; Gen. Man. DAVID LEMUS PIVARAL.

**Seguros de Occidente, SA:** 7a Calle 'A' 7-14, Zona 9, Guatemala City; tel. 231-1222; fax 234-1413; f. 1979; Pres. Lic. PEDRO AGUIRRE; Gen. Man. CARLOS LAINFIESTA.

**Seguros Universales, SA:** 4a Calle 7-73, Zona 9, Apdo 1479, Guatemala City; tel. 234-0733; fax 232-3372; f. 1962; Pres. MARÍA AUGUSTA VALLS DE SICILIA.

### Insurance Association

**Asociación Guatemalteca de Instituciones de Seguros—AGIS:** Edif. Torre Profesional I, Of. 411, 4°, 6a Avda 0-60, Zona 4, Guatemala City; tel. 235-1657; fax 235-2021; f. 1953; 12 mems; Pres. ENRIQUE NUETZE A.; Man. Lic. FERNANDO RODRÍGUEZ TREJO.

# Trade and Industry

## DEVELOPMENT ORGANIZATIONS

**Comisión Nacional Petrolera:** Diagonal 17, 29-78, Zona 11, Guatemala City; tel. 276-0680; fax 276-3175; f. 1983; awards petroleum exploration licences.

**Consejo Nacional de Planificación Económica:** 9a Calle 10-44, Zona 1, Guatemala City; tel. 251-4549; fax 253-3127; e-mail mrayo@ns.concyt.gob.gt; f. 1954; prepares and supervises the implementation of the national economic development plan; Sec.-Gen. MARIANO RAYO MUÑOZ.

**Corporación Financiera Nacional—CORFINA:** see under Finance.

**Empresa Nacional de Fomento y Desarrollo Económico de El Petén (FYDEP):** 11a Avda 'B' 32-46, Zona 5, Guatemala City; tel. 231-6834; f. 1959; attached to the Presidency; economic development agency for the Department of El Petén; Dir FRANCISCO ANGEL CASTELLANOS GÓNGORA.

**Instituto de Fomento de Hipotecas Aseguradas (FHA):** 6a Avda 0-60, Zona 4, Guatemala City; f. 1961; insured mortgage institution for the promotion of house construction; Pres. Lic. HOMERO AUGUSTO GONZÁLEZ BARILLAS; Man. Lic. JOSÉ SALVADOR SAMAYOA AGUILAR.

**Instituto Nacional de Administración Pública (INAP):** 5a Avda 12-65, Zona 9, Apto 2753, Guatemala City; tel. 26-6339; f. 1964; provides technical experts to assist all branches of the Government in administrative reform programmes; provides in-service training for local and central government staff; has research programmes in administration, sociology, politics and economics; provides post-graduate education in public administration; Gen. Man. Dr ARIEL RIVERA IRÍAS.

**Instituto Nacional de Transformación Agraria (INTA):** 14a Calle 7-14, Zona 1, Guatemala City; tel. 28-0975; f. 1962 to carry out agrarian reform; current programme includes development of the 'Faja Transversal del Norte'; Pres. Ing. NERY ORLANDO SAMAYOA; Vice-Pres Ing. SERGIO FRANCISCO MORALES-JUÁREZ, ROBERTO EDMUNDO QUIÑÓNEZ LÓPEZ.

## CHAMBERS OF COMMERCE AND INDUSTRY

**Comité Coordinador de Asociaciones Agrícolas, Comerciales, Industriales y Financieras (CACIF):** Edif. Cámara de Industria de Guatemala, 6a Ruta 9-21, Zona 4, Guatemala City; tel. 231-0651; co-ordinates work on problems and organization of free enterprise; mems: 6 chambers; Pres. JORGE BRIZ; Sec.-Gen. RAFAEL POLA.

**Cámara de Comercio de Guatemala:** 10a Calle 3-80, Zona 1, Guatemala City; tel. 28-2681; fax 251-4197; f. 1894; Gen. Man. EDGARDO RUIZ.

**Cámara de Industria de Guatemala:** 6a Ruta 9-21, 12°, Zona 4, Apdo 214, Guatemala City; tel. 334-0850; fax 334-1090; f. 1958; Pres. JUAN JOSÉ URRUELA KONG; Gen. Man. CARLOS PERALTA.

## INDUSTRIAL AND TRADE ASSOCIATIONS

**Asociación de Agricultores Productores de Aceites Esenciales:** 6a Calle 1-36, Zona 10, Apdo 272, Guatemala City; tel. 234-7255; f. 1948; essential oils producers' asscn; 40 mems; Pres. FRANCISCO RALDA; Gen. Man. CARLOS FLORES PAGAZA.

**Asociación de Azucareros de Guatemala—ASAZGUA:** Edif. Tívoli Plaza, 6a Calle 6-38, Zona 9, Guatemala City; fax 231-8191; f. 1957; sugar producers' asscn; 19 mems; Gen. Man. Lic. ARMANDO BOESCHE.

**Asociación de Exportadores de Café:** 11a Calle 5-66, 3°, Zona 9, Guatemala City; coffee exporters' asscn; 37 mems; Pres. EDUARDO GONZÁLEZ RIVERA.

**Asociación General de Agricultores:** 9a Calle 3-43, Zona 1, Guatemala City; f. 1920; general farmers' asscn; 350 mems; Pres. DAVID ORDÓÑEZ; Man. PEDRO ARRIVILLAGA RADA.

**Asociación Nacional de Avicultores—ANAVI:** Edif. Galerías Reforma, Torre 2, 9°, Of. 904, Avda de la Reforma 8-60, Zona 9, Guatemala City; tel. 231-1381; fax 234-7576; f. 1964; national asscn of poultry farmers; 60 mems; Pres. Lic. FERNANDO ROJAS; Dir Dr MARIO A. MOTTA GONZÁLEZ.

**Asociación Nacional de Fabricantes de Alcoholes y Licores (ANFAL):** Km 16½, Carretera Roosevelt, Zona 10, Apdo 2065, Guatemala City; tel. 292-0430; f. 1947; distillers' asscn; Pres. FELIPE BOTRÁN MERINO; Man. Lic. JUAN GUILLERMO BORJA MOGOLLÓN.

**Asociación Nacional del Café—Anacafé:** Edif. Etisa, Plazuela España, Zona 9, Guatemala City; tel. 236-7180; fax 234-7023; f. 1960; national coffee asscn; Pres. WILLIAM STIXRUD.

**Cámara del Agro:** 15a Calle 'A' 7-65, Zona 9, Guatemala City; tel. 26-1473; f. 1973; Man. CÉSAR BUSTAMANTE ARAÚZ.

**Consejo Nacional del Algodón:** 11a Calle 6-49, Zona 9, Guatemala City; tel. 234-8390; fax 234-8393; f. 1964; consultative body for cultivation and classification of cotton; 119 mems; Pres. ROBERTO MARTÍNEZ R.; Man. ALFREDO GIL SPILLARI.

**Gremial de Huleros de Guatemala:** Edif. Centroamericano, Of. 406, 7a Avda 7-78, Zona 4, Guatemala City; tel. 231-4917; f. 1970; rubber producers' guild; 125 mems; Pres. JOSÉ LUIS RALDA; Man. Lic. CÉSAR SOTO.

## UTILITIES

### Electricity

**Empresa Eléctrica de Guatemala, SA:** 6a Avda 8-14, Zona 1, Guatemala City; state electricity producer; 80% share transferred to private ownership in 1998; Pres. OSCAR MARTÍNEZ AMAYA.

**Instituto Nacional de Electrificación (INDE):** Edif. La Torre, 7a Avda 2-29, Zona 9, Guatemala City; tel. (2) 34-5711; fax (2) 34-5811; f. 1959; former state agency for the generation and distribution of hydroelectric power; principal electricity producer; privatized in 1998; Pres. GUILLERMO RODRÍGUEZ.

## CO-OPERATIVES

**Instituto Nacional de Cooperativas (INACOP):** 4a Calle 4-37, Zona 9, 01001 Guatemala City; tel. 234-1097; fax 234-7536; technical and financial assistance in planning and devt of co-operatives; Man. CÉSAR AGUSTO MASSELLA BARRERA.

### TRADE UNIONS

**Frente Nacional Sindical (FNS)** (National Trade Union Front): Guatemala City; f. 1968 to achieve united action in labour matters; affiliated are two confederations and 11 federations, which represent 97% of the country's trade unions and whose General Secretaries form the governing council of the FNS. The affiliated organizations include:

**Comité Nacional de Unidad Sindical Guatemalteca—CONUS:** Leader MIGUEL ANGEL SOLÍS; Sec.-Gen. GERÓNIMO LÓPEZ DÍAZ.

**Confederación General de Sindicatos** (General Trade Union Confederation): 18a Calle 5-50, Zona 1, Apdo 959, Guatemala City.

**Confederación Nacional de Trabajadores** (National Workers' Confederation): Guatemala City; Sec.-Gen. MIGUEL ANGEL ALBIZÚREZ.

**Consejo Sindical de Guatemala** (Guatemalan Trade Union Council): 18a Calle 5-50, Zona 1, Apdo 959, Guatemala City; f. 1955; admitted to ICFTU and ORIT; Gen. Sec. JAIME V. MONGE DONIS; 30,000 mems in 105 affiliated unions.

**Federación Autónoma Sindical Guatemalteca** (Guatemalan Autonomous Trade Union Federation): Guatemala City; Gen. Sec. MIGUEL ANGEL SOLÍS.

**Federación de Obreros Textiles** (Textile Workers' Federation): Edif. Briz, Of. 503, 6a Avda 14-33, Zona 1, Guatemala City; f. 1957; Sec.-Gen. FACUNDO PINEDA.

**Federación de Trabajadores de Guatemala (FTG)** (Guatemalan Workers' Federation): 5a Calle 4-33, Zona 1, Guatemala City; tel. 22-6515; Promoter ADRIAN RAMÍREZ.

A number of unions exist without a national centre, including the Union of Chicle and Wood Workers, the Union of Coca-Cola Workers and the Union of Workers of the Enterprise of the United Fruit Company.

**Central General de Trabajadores de Guatemala (CGTG):** 3a Avda 12-22, Zona 1, Guatemala City; tel. 232-9234; fax 251-3212; f. 1987; Sec.-Gen. JOSÉ E. PINZÓN SALAZAR.

**Central Nacional de Trabajadores (CNT):** 9a Avda 4-29, Zona 1, Apdo 2472, Guatemala City; f. 1972; cover all sections of commerce, industry and agriculture including the public sector; clandestine since June 1980; Sec.-Gen. JULIO CELSO DE LEÓN; 23,735 mems.

**Unidad de Acción Sindical y Popular (UASP):** f. 1988; broad coalition of leading labour and peasant organizations; includes:

**Comité de la Unidad Campesina (CUC)** (Committee of Peasants' Unity).

**Confederación de Unidad Sindical de Trabajadores de Guatemala (CUSG):** 5a Calle 4-33, Zona 1, Guatemala City; tel. 22-6515; f. 1983; Sec.-Gen. FRANCISCO ALFARO MIJANGOS.

**Federación Nacional de Sindicatos de Trabajadores del Estado de Guatemala (Fenasteg):** Sec. ARMANDO SÁNCHEZ.

**Sindicato de Trabajadores de la Educación Guatemaltecos (STEG).**

**Sindicato de Trabajadores de la Industria de la Electricidad (STINDE).**

**Sindicato de Trabajadores del Instituto Guatemalteco de Seguro Social (STIGSS).**

**Unidad Sindical de Trabajadores de Guatemala (UNSITRAGUA).**

## Transport

### RAILWAYS

**Ferrocarriles de Guatemala—FEGUA:** 9a Avda 18-03, Zona 1, Guatemala City; tel. 28-3030; fax 251-2006; f. 1968; 50-year concession to rehabilitate and operate railway awarded in 1997 to the US Railroad Devt Corpn; 782 km from Puerto Barrios and Santo Tomás de Castilla on the Atlantic coast to Tecún Umán on the Mexican border, via Zacapa, Guatemala City and Santa María. Branch lines: Santa María–San José; Las Cruces–Champerico. From Zacapa another line branches southward to Anguiatú, on the border with El Salvador; owns the ports of Barrios (Atlantic) and San José (Pacific); first 65-km section, Guatemala City – El Chile, reopened mid-1999; further 300-km section, extending to Barrios, due to reopen in late 1999; Administrator ANDRÉS PORRAS CASTILLO.

There are 102 km of plantation lines.

### ROADS

In 1996 there were an estimated 13,100 km of roads, of which 3,616 km were paved. The Guatemalan section of the Pan-American highway is 518.7 km long and totally asphalted.

### SHIPPING

Guatemala's major ports are Santo Tomás de Castilla and Puerto Quetzal.

**Armadora Marítima Guatemalteca, SA:** 14a Calle 8-14, Zona 1, Apdo 1008, Guatemala City; tel. 230-4686; fax 253-7464; cargo services; Pres. and Gen. Man. L. R. CORONADO CONDE.

**Empresa Portuaria 'Quetzal':** Edif. 74, 6°, 7a Avda 3-74, Zona 9, Guatemala City; tel. 331-4824; fax 334-8152; port and shipping co; Man. Ing. LUIS FERNANDO PAIZ.

**Empresa Portuaria Nacional Santo Tomás de Castilla:** Edif. Mini, 6a Avda 1-27, Zone 4, Guatemala City; tel. 232-3685; fax 232-6894; Man. ENRIQUE SALAZAR.

**Flota Mercante Gran Centroamericana, SA:** Edif. Canella, 5°, 1a Calle 7-21, Zona 9, Guatemala City; tel. 231-6666. 1959; services from Europe (in association with WITASS), Gulf of Mexico, US Atlantic and East Coast Central American ports; Pres. R. S. RAMÍREZ; Gen. Man. J. E. A. MORALES.

**Líneas Marítimas de Guatemala, SA:** Edif. Plaza Marítima, 8°, 6a Avda 20-25, Zona 10, Guatemala City; tel. 237-0166; cargo services; Pres. J. R. MATHEAU ESCOBAR; Gen. Man. F. HERRERÍAS.

Several foreign lines link Guatemala with Europe, the Far East and North America.

### CIVIL AVIATION

There are two international airports, 'La Aurora' in Guatemala City and at Santa Elena Petén.

**Aerolíneas de Guatemala—AVIATECA:** Avda Hincapié 12-22, Aeropuerto 'La Aurora', Zona 13, Guatemala City; tel. 231-8261; fax 231-7412; internet www.flylatinamerica.com; f. 1945; internal services and external services to the USA, Mexico, and within Central America; transferred to private ownership in 1989; Pres. Ing. JULIO OBOLS GOMES; Gen. Man. ENRIQUE BELTRONERA.

**Aeroquetzal:** Avda Hincapié y 18a Calle, Lado Sur, Aeropuerto 'La Aurora', Zona 13, Guatemala City; tel. 231-8282; fax 232-1491; scheduled domestic passenger and cargo services, and external services to Mexico.

**Aerovías:** Avda Hincapié 4 y 18a Calle, Aeropuerta 'La Aurora', Zona 13, Guatemala City; tel. 232-5686; fax 234-7470; operates scheduled and charter cargo services; Pres. FERNANDO ALFONSO CASTILLO R.; Vice-Pres. NELSON C. PUENTE.

**Aviones Comerciales de Guatemala (Avcom):** Avda Hincapié, Aeropuerto 'La Aurora', Zona 13, Guatemala City; tel. 231-5821; fax 232-4946; domestic charter passenger services.

## Tourism

As a result of violence in the country, the annual total of tourist arrivals declined from 504,000, in 1979, when tourist receipts were US $201m., to 192,000, in 1984 (receipts $56.6m.). After 1985, however, the number of arrivals recovered and were recorded as some 600,000 in 1998, when receipts were an estimated $364m.

**Instituto Guatemalteco de Turismo (INGUAT)** (Guatemala Tourist Commission): Centro Cívico, 7a Avda 1-17, Zona 4, Guatemala City; tel. 331-1333; fax 331-8893; e-mail inguat@guate.net; internet www.guatemala.travel.com.gt; f. 1967; policy and planning council: 13 mems representing the public and private sectors; Pres. LAURA DE ESTRADA; Dir CLAUDIA ARENAS BIANCHI.

**Asociación Guatemalteca de Agentes de Viajes (AGAV)** (Guatemalan Association of Travel Agents): 6a Avda 8-41, Zona 9, Apdo 2735, Guatemala City; tel. 231-0320; Pres. MARÍA DEL CARMEN FERNÁNDEZ O.

# GUINEA

## Introductory Survey

**Location, Climate, Language, Religion, Flag, Capital**

The Republic of Guinea lies on the west coast of Africa, with Sierra Leone and Liberia to the south, Senegal and Guinea-Bissau to the north, and Mali and Côte d'Ivoire inland to the east. The climate on the coastal strip is hot and moist, with temperatures ranging from about 32°C (90°F) in the dry season to about 23°C (73°F) in the wet season (May–October). The interior is higher and cooler. The official language is French, but Soussou, Manika and six other national languages are widely spoken. Most of the inhabitants are Muslims, but some follow traditional animist beliefs. Around 2% are Roman Catholics. The national flag (proportions 3 by 2) consists of three equal vertical stripes, of red, yellow and green. The capital is Conakry.

**Recent History**

The Republic of Guinea (formerly French Guinea, part of French West Africa) became independent on 2 October 1958, after 95% of voters rejected the Constitution of the Fifth Republic under which the French colonies became self-governing within the French Community. The new state was the object of punitive reprisals by the outgoing French authorities: all aid was withdrawn, and the administrative infrastructure destroyed. The Parti démocratique de Guinée—Rassemblement démocratique africain (PDG—RDA) became the basis for the construction of new institutions. Its leader, Ahmed Sekou Touré, became President, and the PDG—RDA the sole political party.

Sekou Touré, formerly a prominent trade unionist, pursued vigorous policies of socialist revolution, with emphasis on popular political participation. Opposition was ruthlessly crushed, and Sekou Touré perpetuated rumours of a 'permanent conspiracy' by foreign powers to overthrow his regime. By 1983 almost 2m. Guineans were estimated to have fled the country. Several coup attempts were alleged during the 1960s, and an abortive invasion by Portuguese troops and Guinean exiles in 1970 prompted the execution of many of those (including several foreigners) convicted of involvement.

All private trade was forbidden in 1975: transactions were conducted through official co-operatives under the supervision of an 'economic police'. In August 1977 demonstrations by women in Conakry, in protest against the abolition of the traditional market and the abuse of power by the 'economic police', provoked rioting in other towns, as a result of which three state governors were killed. Sekou Touré subsequently disbanded the 'economic police', and allowed limited private trading to recommence in July 1979. Meanwhile, in November 1978 it was announced that the functions of the PDG—RDA and the State were to be merged, and the country was renamed the People's Revolutionary Republic of Guinea. There was, none the less, a general move away from rigid Marxism and a decline in relations with the USSR, as Guinea sought a political and economic *rapprochement* with its African neighbours, with France and with other Western powers. In December 1978 Valéry Giscard d'Estaing made the first visit by a French President to independent Guinea.

At legislative elections in January 1980 voters endorsed the PDG—RDA's list of 210 candidates for a new Assemblée nationale (to replace the Assemblée législative elected in December 1974). In May 1982 Sekou Touré was returned unopposed to the presidency for a fourth seven-year term of office, reportedly receiving 100% of the votes cast. He made his first official visit to France in September of that year.

In January 1984 a plot to overthrow the Government was disclosed when a group of mercenaries was arrested in southern Senegal. Thousands of Guineans were reportedly detained, accused of complicity in the affair. In March Sekou Touré died while undergoing surgery in the USA. On 3 April, before a permanent successor had been chosen by the ruling party, the armed forces seized power in a bloodless coup. A Comité militaire de redressement national (CMRN) was appointed, headed by Col (later Gen.) Lansana Conté, hitherto commander of the Boké region. The PDG—RDA and the legislature were dissolved, and the Constitution was suspended. The CMRN pledged to restore democracy and to respect human rights; some 250 political prisoners were released, and a relaxation of press restrictions was announced. In May the country was renamed the Second Republic of Guinea. The Prime Minister, Col Diarra Traoré, toured the region to rally support from Guinea's neighbours, and also visited Europe in an effort to attract foreign investment and to consolidate relations, particularly with France. By mid-1984 an estimated 200,000 Guinean exiles had returned to the country.

Trials of former associates of Sekou Touré, most of whom had been detained since the coup, began in November 1984. In December President Conté assumed the posts of Head of Government and Minister of Defence; the post of Prime Minister was abolished, and Traoré was demoted to a lesser post. In July 1985 Traoré attempted to seize power while Conté was out of the country. Troops loyal to the President suppressed the revolt, and Traoré was arrested, along with many members of his family and more than 200 suspected sympathizers. A series of attacks was subsequently aimed at the Malinke ethnic group, of which both Traoré and the late President Sekou Touré were members. (Conté's opponents have frequently claimed that the regime has unduly favoured his own Soussou ethnic group.) In May 1987 it was announced that 58 people, including nine former government ministers, had been sentenced to death following secret trials of more than 200 Guineans detained either for crimes committed under Sekou Touré or in the aftermath of the 1985 coup attempt. The announcement did little to allay suspicions of international observers that many detainees had already been executed in the aftermath of the abortive coup, and in December 1987 Conté admitted publicly that Traoré had died in the hours following his arrest. In January 1988 an amnesty was announced for 67 political prisoners, including Sekou Touré's widow and son.

In October 1985 Conté began to implement radical economic reforms, demanded by the World Bank and IMF as preconditions for the provision of structural aid. In December the Council of Ministers was reorganized to include a majority of civilians. In October 1988 Conté proposed the establishment of a committee to draft a new constitution. One year later he announced that, following a national referendum on the document, the CMRN would be replaced by a Comité transitoire de redressement national (CTRN). The joint civilian and military CTRN would oversee a transitional period of not more than five years, at the end of which civilian rule, with an executive and legislature directly elected in the context of a two-party system, would be established. The draft Constitution of what was designated the Third Republic was endorsed by 98.7% of those who voted (some 97.4% of the electorate) in a referendum on 23 December 1990, and in February 1991 the 36-member CTRN was inaugurated under Conté's chairmanship.

In November 1990, meanwhile, Conté made an appeal to political exiles to return to Guinea. Alpha Condé, the leader of the Rassemblement populaire guinéen (RPG—an unofficial political organization whose activities had been suppressed by the authorities), returned to Guinea in May 1991, after a long period of exile in France and Senegal. Three arrests were made when a meeting of his supporters was dispersed by security forces, and a ban was subsequently imposed on unauthorized meetings and demonstrations. In June one person was killed when security forces opened fire on a group of demonstrators who had gathered outside the police headquarters in Conakry, to where Condé had been summoned in connection with the seizure of allegedly subversive materials. As many as 60 people were reported to have been arrested; Condé sought refuge in the Senegalese embassy, and was subsequently granted political asylum in Senegal. In October three people were killed during anti-Government riots in Kankan.

In October 1991 Conté announced that an 'organic law' authorizing the registration of an unlimited number of political parties would come into effect in April 1992, and that legislative elections, in the context of a full multi-party political system, would take place before the end of 1992. The Constitution was promulgated on 23 December 1991, and in January 1992 Conté ceded the presidency of the CTRN (whose membership was, at the same time, reduced to 15), in conformity with the constitutional separation of the powers of the executive and the legislature. In the following month a major reorganization of the Council of Ministers entailed the departure of most military officers and of those who had returned from exile after the 1984 coup (known as *Guinéens de l'extérieur*), as well as the abolition of resident regional ministries.

The 'organic law' entered into force on 3 April 1992, whereupon 17 political parties were legalized. Among these was the RPG, and Condé again returned to Guinea in June. However, a lack of cohesion among opposition parties undermined attempts to persuade the Government to convene a national conference in advance of the electoral programme. Moreover, it was widely rumoured that the pro-Conté Parti pour l'unité et le progrès (PUP), established by prominent *Guinéens de l'extérieur*, was benefiting from state funds. Conté reportedly escaped an assassination attempt in October, when gunmen opened fire on the vehicle in which he was travelling. In early December the Government announced the indefinite postponement of the legislative elections, which had been scheduled for the end of that month, stating that preparations were incomplete. Subsequent indications that the parliamentary elections would not take place until after a presidential election caused resentment among the opposition, which had hoped to present a single candidate (from the party that had performed best in the legislative elections) for the presidency.

In September 1993 the Government imposed a ban on all street demonstrations, following violent incidents when police opened fire on anti-Government protesters in Conakry, as a result of which, according to official figures, as many as 18 people were killed. In October, at the first meeting between Conté and opposition leaders since the legalization of political parties, it was reportedly agreed to establish an independent electoral commission (a principal demand of the opposition), although Conté rejected demands for the establishment of a transitional government. Controversy subsequently arose regarding the composition of the electoral commission, as well as the Government's decision to place the commission under the jurisdiction of the Minister of the Interior and Security.

In October 1993 the Supreme Court approved eight candidates for the presidential election, scheduled for 5 December. Among Conté's main rivals for the presidency were Condé, representing the RPG, together with Mamadou Boye Bâ of the Union pour la nouvelle République (UNR) and Siradiou Diallo of the Parti pour le renouveau et le progrès (PRP). Opposition candidates subsequently demanded that the election be postponed, citing irregularities in the compilation of electoral lists as well as delays in the issuing of voting cards and in the appointment of the electoral commission. In late November the Government announced a two-week postponement of the presidential election. At least four deaths were recorded in pre-election violence involving PUP supporters and opposition activists in Conakry and in the interior, and there were six deaths in Conakry as voting proceeded on 19 December. Although several opposition candidates were reported to have withdrawn from the presidential contest prior to the election, the rate of participation by voters was high (78.5%, according to official figures), with supporters of all candidates voting. Preliminary results indicated that Conté had secured an absolute majority of the votes cast, thus obviating the need for a second round of voting. Opposition claims that the poll had been fraudulent and the result manipulated in favour of Conté intensified when the Supreme Court annulled the outcome of voting in the Kankan and Siguiri prefectures (in both of which the RPG leader had won more than 95% of the votes), owing to irregularities in the conduct of the polls. According to the official results of the election, confirmed by the Court in early January 1994, Conté was elected with 51.70% of the votes cast; Condé took 19.55% of the votes, Bâ 13.37% and Diallo 11.86%.

Conté, who had resigned from the army in order to contest the election as a civilian, was inaugurated as President on 29 January 1994. He identified as priorities for his presidency the strengthening of national security and the promotion of economic growth. A major restructuring of the Council of Ministers was implemented in August, with a particular emphasis on economic reform and the development of the primary sector.

In May 1994 Bâ, asserting his lack of confidence in the Guinean opposition, announced the UNR's intention to support Conté as the country's legitimately elected Head of State. However, relations between the Government and the opposition remained generally strained, and the RPG in particular alleged the harassment of its supporters by the security forces. The brief detention, in June, of eight senior armed forces officers, including the Deputy Chief of Staff of the air force, prompted rumours of a coup plot. The Government confirmed that several members of the military had participated in a 'political' meeting, in contravention of their terms of service, but denied the existence of any conspiracy. The announcement that there would be no facilities abroad to allow expatriate Guineans to vote in the forthcoming legislative elections (following violent disturbances at polling stations outside Guinea at the presidential election) provoked criticism by opposition parties and by members of the electoral commission, who stated that the disenfranchisement of Guineans abroad was in contravention of both the Constitution and the electoral code. The UNR condemned the policy and withdrew its support for Conté. Earlier in the year the Association guinéenne des droits de l'homme (AGDH) had alleged a recent increase in the ill-treatment of prisoners in Guinea, together with attempts by the authorities to deny basic rights and freedoms.

In December 1994 the Government announced new measures aimed at combating organized crime and other serious offences. As well as the creation of a special police unit to counter banditry, the enforcement of the death penalty was envisaged, together with stricter policies governing immigration and asylum for refugees—the Conté administration frequently attributed the increase in insecurity to the presence of large numbers of refugees (see below) in Guinea. In January 1996 human rights organizations expressed concern at the recent rejection of appeals against six death penalties.

Meanwhile, in February 1995 Conté readopted his military title. The legislative election finally took place on 11 June. Prior to the elections opposition leaders alleged that efforts were being made to prevent campaigning in areas where support for the opposition was likely to be strong. They also denounced the use by the PUP of portraits of Conté on campaign posters and literature, protesting that the President was constitutionally required to distance himself from party politics. A total of 846 candidates, from 21 parties, contested the 114 seats in the Assemblée nationale. As preliminary results indicated that the PUP had won an overwhelming majority in the legislature, the so-called 'radical' opposition parties (the RPG, the PRP and the UNR) protested that voting had been conducted fraudulently, stating that they would take no further part in the electoral process and announcing their intention to boycott the assembly. According to the final results, which were verified by the Supreme Court in July (whereupon the Assemblée nationale officially superseded the CTRN), the PUP won 71 seats—having taken 30 of the 38 single-member constituencies and 41 of the 76 seats allocated by a system of national proportional representation. Eight other parties won representation, principal among them the RPG, which took 19 seats, the PRP and the UNR, both of which won nine seats. Some 63% of the registered electorate were reported to have voted. At municipal elections in late June the PUP won control of 20 of the country's 36 municipalities, while the RPG, the PRP and the UNR, which had presented a co-ordinated campaign, took 10. Once again, the opposition protested of electoral fraud. In July the three radical opposition parties joined forces with nine other organizations in a Coordination de l'opposition démocratique (Codem). Codem indicated its willingness to enter into a dialogue with the authorities; however, at a meeting between a representative of Codem and the Minister of the Interior, Alsény René Gomez, the latter rejected what Codem had presented as evidence of electoral fraud as not affecting the overall credibility of the results. The official inauguration of the Assemblée nationale, on 30 August, was, none the less, attended by representatives of all the elected parties. Boubacar Biro Diallo, of the PUP, was elected (unopposed) as the new parliament's Speaker.

In February 1996 elements of the military opposed to Conté's regime apparently took advantage of protests by soldiers in Conakry who were demanding increased pay and improved allowances. Disaffected soldiers seized control of the airport and offices of the state broadcasting service, and shelling around the presidential palace caused severe damage. Conté was reportedly seized as he attempted to flee the palace, and was held by rebels for some 15 hours until he made concessions including a doubling of salaries and immunity from prosecution for those involved in the mutiny. The Minister of Defence, Col Abdourahmane Diallo, was dismissed, and Conté assumed personal responsibility for defence. It was estimated that about 50 people (some of them civilians) were killed and at least 100 injured as rebels clashed with forces loyal to the Conté regime. In all, as many as 2,000 soldiers, including members of the Presidential Guard, were believed to have joined the rebellion. Despite Conté's undertaking that there would be no punitive action, several officers were arrested shortly afterwards, and both Conté and Gomez stated that any legal proceedings would be a matter for the judiciary.

In late February 1996 Codem withdrew from a parliamentary commission that had been established to investigate the circumstances surrounding the coup attempt, in protest at Conté's allusions to opposition links with anti-Government elements within the military. The initial recommendations of the commission included that there should be a complete depoliticization of the military, accompanied by the demilitarization of political life; the need to restore discipline within the armed forces was particularly emphasized. Meanwhile, the opposition warned that avoidance of further insurrection could be guaranteed only by full observance of the agreement reached by Conté and the military during the rebellion. In late March, none the less, it was announced that eight members of the military (four of them senior officers) had been charged with undermining state security in connection with the coup attempt. A reinforcement of security measures followed the assassination of the commander of the military camp where the February rebellion had begun. Calm was quickly restored, and Conté left his barracks for the first time since early February to meet President Alpha Oumar Konaré of Mali, who arrived in Conakry to discuss terms for the release into Guinean custody of one of the alleged perpetrators of the coup attempt, who had taken refuge in the Malian embassy. (In the following month, however, Mali recalled its ambassador from Conakry, protesting that Guinean forces had stormed the embassy to arrest the officer.)

The armed forces Chief of Staff and the military Governor of Conakry, both of whom had been regarded as close associates of Conté, were replaced in April 1996, apparently in accordance with the President's expressed commitment to a restructuring of both the civilian and military administration. In July Conté announced (for the first time under the Third Republic) the appointment of a Prime Minister. The premiership was assigned to a non-partisan economist, Sydia Touré. A comprehensive reorganization of the Government included the departure of Gomez and the division of the Ministry of the Interior into two separate departments (one responsible for territorial administration and decentralization, the other for security), as well as the appointment of a new Minister of Justice. Touré responded to criticism by opposition leaders that there was no constitutional provision for the post of Prime Minister by stating that his appointment was in accordance with the article of the Constitution empowering the President of the Republic to appoint ministers and to delegate part of his functions. During August 1996 40 of those detained in connection with the February mutiny were released from custody; charges remained against three suspects, including Cmmdr Joseph Gbago Zoumanigui, allegedly a main conspirator, who was believed to have fled the country.

Touré announced that his Government's priorities were to be economic recovery and the combating of institutionalized corruption, with the aim of securing new assistance from the international financial community, and also of attracting increased foreign investment. A new financing programme was agreed with the IMF in January 1997. In the following month Touré relinquished control of the economy portfolio to his two ministers-delegate, who now became Minister of Planning and Co-operation and Minister of the Economy and Finance.

In June 1997 it was announced that a State Security Court was to be established to deal with matters of exceptional jurisdiction, and that its first task would be to try the alleged leaders of the 1996 mutiny. The establishment of the court provoked strong criticism both by the opposition parties and the Guinean lawyers' association, which expressed particular concern that there was no constitutional provision for such a court, and that its members were to be personally appointed by Conté; the announcement that the mutiny trial was to be held in camera caused further disquiet. Furthermore, the political opposition again warned that Conté should beware of reneging on his earlier pledge that there would be no reprisals for those involved in the rebellion. Rumours circulated, meanwhile, that Guinean dissidents were conspiring with rebels in neighbouring Sierra Leone and Liberia to overthrow Conté, and that Zoumanigui was attempting to recruit mercenaries for a planned invasion. However, opposition parties asserted that the Conté regime itself was the source of such rumours.

The Ministers of Security and of Planning and Co-operation left the Government in October 1997, as part of a reorganization of portfolios in which a new Minister of the Interior and Decentralization, Zaïnoul Abidine Sanoussi, was appointed. Dorank Diasség Assifat, hitherto Minister of Territorial Administration and Decentralization, was transferred to the higher education and scientific research portfolio, but shortly afterwards was appointed Minister of National Defence (thereby becoming the first civilian to hold this post since the 1984 *coup d'état*).

In a report published in October 1997 the AGDH accused the Guinean security forces of daily atrocities, alleging the systematic ill-treatment of detainees. The association expressed particular concern at the continued detention of civilians related to the suspects in the 1996 mutiny, and at the detention without trial, in solitary confinement, of Liberian and Sierra Leonean nationals. The detention (since early 1997) of three Belgian nationals, with a Guinean associate, was similarly condemned. In November 1997 it was revealed that 53 soldiers, in custody since the mutiny, had in a joint letter to the Assemblée nationale alleged that they had been tortured following their arrest and complained of their conditions of detention. Agence France-Presse subsequently reported that the same soldiers had alleged that many senior military officers remained in post despite their active or passive complicity in the mutiny. Among the officers identified by the detainees were the present and former chiefs of staff of the armed forces.

A total of 96 defendants were brought before the State Security Court in February 1998, to answer charges related to the attempted coup two years earlier; hearings were immediately adjourned, after defence lawyers complained that they had had no access to their clients for the past four months. Reportedly among the defendants was the former Minister of Defence dismissed by Conté on the second day of the mutiny. Hearings resumed in March; however, it was reported that defence lawyers were refusing to represent their clients, whose rights were, they alleged, being infringed by the State Security Court. Trials were again adjourned, and the Court did not reconvene until September. At the end of that month 38 of the accused received custodial sentences ranging from seven months to 15 years, some with hard labour (Zoumanigui was sentenced *in absentia*). A further 51 defendants were acquitted.

In March 1998 Bâ and two other deputies of the UNR were arrested, following the deaths of nine people as a result of violence in a suburb of Conakry which was a stronghold of the party. The authorities alleged that Islamist extremists were implicated in the unrest, although other observers stated that ethnic rivalries had exacerbated confrontations between members of the security forces and residents whose homes were threatened with demolition. The brief detention, in early April, of two RPG deputies who had attended a political rally in eastern Guinea further exacerbated tensions, and deputies of the Codem parties boycotted the opening ceremony of the new session of the Assemblée nationale. Bâ was released in June, and in September his two UNR colleagues resumed their seats in the legislature, having been released from custody. In October the Speaker of the Assemblée nationale was suspended from the PUP, after he denounced what he termed 'atrocious and inhuman torture' of detainees, notably those held in connection with the 1996 mutiny; Diallo subsequently issued a further statement regretting the PUP's 'insolent contempt for the law'.

Meanwhile, Codem denounced preparations for the forthcoming presidential election, notably proposals for the establishment of what was designated the Haut conseil aux affaires électorales (HCE), which was to act in conjunction with the Ministry of the Interior and Decentralization in preparing and supervising the poll. The 68-member HCE was to comprise representatives of the presidential majority, as well as opposition delegates, ministerial representatives and members of the civic society. As at the 1993 election, the opposition alleged that the PUP was abusing the state apparatus in support of Conté's re-election campaign, while the other candidates were disadvantaged by a ban imposed on public demonstrations. Conté was challenged by four candidates: Mamadou Boye Bâ, representing the Union pour le progrès et le renouveau (formed in September 1998 by a merger of the UNR and the PRP), Alpha Condé (who had been out of the country since April 1997, owing to fears for his personal safety) for the RPG, Jean-Marie Doré for the Union pour le progrès de Guinée, and Charles-Pascal Tolno (a former education minister who had been dismissed from the Government in 1993) for the Parti du peuple de Guinée. Despite violent incidents during the election campaign—including, in late November 1998, the lynching of a local government official who had fired shots on an RPG rally in Farannah—voting proceeded, according to schedule, on 14 December. However, the arrest near the border with Côte d'Ivoire, two days after the poll, of Condé, who was accused of seeking to leave the country illegally and of plotting against the state, provoked further violence. By the end of the month at least 12 people were reported to have been killed as a result of violence in Conakry, Kankan, Siguiri and Baro. In late December Condé was formally charged with having recruited mercenaries with the aim of overthrowing the Conté regime. In the mean time, opposition representatives denounced the conduct of the election as fraudulent, and withdrew from the HCE. The official results, as issued by the HCE on 17 December, and confirmed by the Supreme Court two weeks later, confirmed a decisive victory for the incumbent, with 56.1% of the valid votes cast. Bâ took 24.6% and Condé 16.6%. The rate of participation by voters was 71.4% of the registered electorate.

At his inauguration, on 30 January 1999, Conté asserted that his new term of office would witness a period of economic growth and social progress for all sectors of society. He emphasized that his administration would ensure the defence of individual freedoms and security, and gave an undertaking that all abuses, including those commited by the security forces, would be severely punished. In early March Lamine Sidimé, hitherto Chief Justice of the Supreme Court, was appointed Prime Minister. Ibrahima Kassory Fofana was reappointed Minister of the Economy and Finance, although it had been widely rumoured that he would himself be awarded the premiership. Assifat, now Minister at the Presidency, retained the national defence portfolio, while Sanoussi was redesignated Minister at the Presidency, in charge of Foreign Affairs; he was succeeded as Minister of Territorial Administration and Decentralization by Moussa Solano. Maurice Zogbelemou Togba became Minister of Justice. An apparent purge of the military high command, in mid-March, included the removal from office of former Chief of Staff Col Oumar Sanko; in all, 18 officers were dismissed, accused of high treason, and 13 retired early, on the grounds of what were termed 'serious faults' arising from the 1996 mutiny.

Impending local government elections were postponed in early June 1999. In mid-June Codem denounced government proposals to extend the mandate of the President of the Republic from five years to seven, although assurances were given that, if adopted, the measure would take effect from the presidential election due in 2003, and would not be applied retroactively.

Opposition groups and human rights organizations campaigned throughout 1999 for the release of Alpha Condé and other activists arrested at the time of the 1998 presidential election. Condé's defence counsel withdrew from the case in February 1999, citing serious violations of the rule of law and exercise of legal practice on the part of the authorities. Lawyers complained in particular of being denied free access to their client (who was being held in solitary confinement), and that a French defence lawyer had been denied entry to Guinea; in addition, they denounced the 'politicization' of the case. However, the lawyers resumed their defence in April. In mid-July, shortly before a visit to Guinea by the French President, Jacques Chirac, it was announced that Condé's trial would begin in early September; however, a decree published in mid-August stating that the RPG leader would be tried by the State Security Court provoked further controversy. Moreover, it was reported that Condé would not be allowed foreign lawyers. In the event, Condé's trial did not proceed, and his lawyers protested that neither defence counsel nor the prosecution lawyers had received any documentation relating to the trial.

Trials of other opposition activists were pursued in the mean time. In mid-March 1999 13 RPG officials in Kankan were sentenced to four months' imprisonment, convicted of disturbing public order, but they were released at the President's behest; 15 others were sentenced *in absentia* to five years' detention. The trial began in mid-July of 20 of those (mainly RPG supporters) arrested following the death of the local official in Farannah in late 1998. Some 50 people were charged in connection with this incident, but most had since absconded.

It was reported in mid-1999 that the Government had agreed to release some 10,000m. FG in order to pay soldiers who were threatening a rebellion against the regime. Rumours of disaffection in some quarters of the military continued to circulate, frequently linked to the insecurity in the region of Guinea's borders with Sierra Leone and Liberia: in August reports circulated that dissident Guinean soldiers in Sierra Leone were planning an imminent offensive against the Conté regime, with the support of Sierra Leonean rebel elements. Following student unrest in mid-October, as a result of which at least two people were killed, the Guinean Government issued a statement blaming the violence on 'external elements'. In late September, meanwhile, the authorities had launched a campaign to register all foreigners in the capital.

Relations with both the Government of France and with private French interests have strengthened considerably in recent years: official assistance from, and trade with, France is of great importance to the Guinean economy, as is French participation in the mining sector and in newly-privatized organizations. Visiting Guinea in July 1999, President Jacques Chirac stated that he had been given to understand that the Guinean authorities intended to pursue a swift investigation and 'transparent' trial of the RPG leader, Alpha Condé. As a member of the Organization of the Islamic Conference (see p. 249) Guinea has also forged links with other Islamic states, notably signing several co-operation agreements with Iran in the 1990s. The People's Republic of China provided funds for the construction of a new presidential palace following the unrest of early 1996.

In August 1990 Guinean armed forces were deployed along the border with Liberia, following a series of violent incursions by deserters from the Liberian army. Guinean army units also participated in the ECOMOG cease-fire monitoring group, deployed in Liberia in that month (see the Economic Community of West African States—ECOWAS, p. 164), and in April 1991 it was announced that a Guinean contingent was to be dispatched to Sierra Leone to assist that country in repelling violations of its territory by Charles Taylor's National Patriotic Front of Liberia (NPFL). In October 1992 the Guinean Government admitted for the first time that Liberian forces were being trained in Guinea; it was stated that those receiving instruction were to constitute the first Liberian government forces following an eventual restoration of peace in that country. Efforts were undertaken from early 1994 to reinforce security along Guinea's borders, following recent incursions by fighters of both the NPFL and the anti-Taylor United Liberation Movement of Liberia for Democracy (ULIMO).

Following the *coup d'état* in Sierra Leone in April 1992, ex-President Momoh of that country was granted asylum in Guinea, although the Conté administration expressed its wish to establish 'normal' relations with the new regime led by Capt. Valentine Strasser and announced that Guinean forces would remain in Sierra Leone. Strasser, like his predecessor, took refuge in Guinea after he was deposed in January 1996. None the less, close co-operation was developed with the new regime, and President Ahmed Tejan Kabbah made several visits to Guinea both before and after his election to the presidency in March of that year. Kabbah, in turn, fled to Guinea in May 1997, following the seizure of power in Sierra Leone by forces led by Maj. Johnny Paul Koroma, and established a government-in-exile in Conakry. Military reinforcements were deployed to protect Guinea's border, and 1,500 Guinean troops were dispatched in support of the Nigerian-led ECOMOG force in Sierra Leone. Guinea joined other members of the international community in condemning the subversion of constitutional order in Sierra Leone, and became a member of the 'Committee of Four' (with Côte d'Ivoire, Ghana and Nigeria) charged with ensuring the implementation of decisions and recommendations pertaining to the situation in Sierra Leone. In June 1998 Guinea dispatched troops to Guinea-Bissau, in support of the Government of President João Vieira following the outbreak of a military rebellion in that country; by early July there were an estimated 500 Guinean troops in Guinea-Bissau. Guinea's Minister of Foreign Affairs additionally became a member of the ECOWAS 'Committee of Seven', which was to co-ordinate a regional response to the crisis in Guinea-Bissau.

It was reported in June 1999 that the Guinean army was conducting an offensive in the border region with Sierra Leone, with the aim of curbing the activities of the Sierra Leone People's Army, a guerrilla group held responsible for a recent series of raids in southern Guinea to procure food and livestock. Some 20 people, including five Guinean soldiers, were said to have been killed in the raids. (In April it had been reported that a refugee camp at Mollah had been sacked by local residents following an attack, blamed on rebels harboured at the camp, in which two people had been killed). Meanwhile, the Liberian

Government delivered a formal note of protest to Guinea in April, in response to what it termed an invasion from Guinea of the border town of Voinjama, in Lofa County, by a rebel group which had briefly held hostage aid workers and foreign diplomats before being repelled by the Liberian armed forces. The Guinean Government expressed indignation at the Liberian regime's actions, reiterating that Guinea had never been, and would never be, used as a base for destabilization of another country, and emphasizing its commitment to the pursuit of peace in the sub-region. In August, however, the Liberian Government declared a state of emergency, again claiming that an invasion force had entered Liberia from Guinea. The border between the two countries was closed with immediate effect. Guinea again denied involvement, and urged international observers to visit the border area to verify that incursions were not originating from Guinea. In late August ECOWAS ministers responsible for foreign affairs agreed to establish a commission in an effort to resolve the issue of border insecurity in this region. In the following month Guinea protested to the Organization of African Unity, the UN and ECOWAS, after 28 people were allegedly killed in attacks by Liberian troops on villages in the Macenta region. An extraordinary summit meeting involving eight ECOWAS leaders proceeded none the less in Abuja, Nigeria, in mid-September, at which Presidents Conté and Taylor made pledges of good neighbourliness and non-aggression. A communiqué issued at the end of the session did not apportion blame for the insecurity nor identify the perpetrators of the raids, but condemned the attacks as likely to threaten the peace and stability of both countries, and potentially to destabilize the region. The functions of the Mano River Union (see p. 292) were to be reactivated, with its members—Guinea, Liberia and Sierra Leone—directed to exchange among themselves information on suspected perpetrators of subversive activities, and to establish a joint committee to monitor and ensure the security of their common borders. The summit also urged the international community to assist in addressing the humanitarian crisis resulting from the attacks. Liberia reopened the border in February 2000.

The protracted conflicts in Liberia and Sierra Leone, and more recently the instability in Guinea-Bissau, have resulted in the presence in Guinea of large numbers of refugees from these countries—variously estimated to number some 5%–10% of the total population. The office of the UN High Commissioner for Refugees (UNHCR) assessed the total number of refugees in Guinea at 413,700 at the end of 1998, compared with 663,900 two years previously. The conclusion of a peace accord for Liberia in 1995, culminating in the installation of elected organs of government (under the presidency of Charles Taylor) in 1997, facilitated a programme for the voluntary repatriation of refugees, under UNHCR auspices. By mid-1999 some 80,000 refugees had left Guinea for Liberia, of a total of 120,000 seeking to return voluntarily; a further 40,000 had chosen to remain in Guinea. However, repatriations were effectively halted from August of that year, as a result of the closure of the Guinea–Liberia border (see above). Meanwhile, continuing insecurity in Sierra Leone during 1999 was unlikely to expedite the return of some 366,000 refugees from Guinean territory.

## Government

Under the terms of the Constitution promulgated on 23 December 1991, and amended by an 'organic law' of 3 April 1992, the President of the Republic, who is Head of State, is elected for five years by universal adult suffrage, in the context of a multi-party political system. The 114-member Assemblée nationale, which holds legislative power, is elected by universal suffrage with a five-year mandate. The President of the Republic is also Head of Government, and in this capacity appoints the other members of the Council of Ministers.

Local administration is based on eight administrative entities—the city of Conakry and seven administrative regions—each under the authority of an appointed Governor; the country is sub-divided into 34 regions, including Conakry (which is divided into three communes).

## Defence

In August 1999 Guinea's active armed forces totalled 9,700, comprising an army of 8,500, a navy of 400 and an air force of 800. Paramilitary forces comprised a Republican Guard of 1,600 and a 1,000-strong gendarmerie, as well as a reserve 'people's militia' of 7,000. Military service is compulsory (conscripts were estimated at some 7,500 in 1999) and lasts for two years. The defence budget for 1999 was estimated at 75,000m. FG.

## Economic Affairs

In 1997, according to estimates by the World Bank, Guinea's gross national product (GNP), measured at average 1995–97 prices, was US $3,830m., equivalent to $550 per head. During 1990–97, it was estimated, GNP per head increased, in real terms, at an average annual rate of 2.7%. Over the same period the population increased by an annual average of 2.6%. GNP was estimated at $3,800m. in 1998, equivalent to $540 per head. Guinea's gross domestic product (GDP) increased, in real terms, at an average annual rate of 5.0% in 1990–98; growth in 1998 was estimated at 4.5%.

Agriculture (including hunting, forestry and fishing) contributed an estimated 22% of GDP in 1998. About 84.6% of the labour force were employed in the agricultural sector in that year. The principal cash crops are fruits, oil palm, groundnuts and coffee. Important staple crops include cassava, rice and other cereals and vegetables. The attainment of self-sufficiency in rice and other basic foodstuffs remains a priority. The food supply is supplemented by the rearing of cattle and other livestock. The Government has made efforts towards the commercial exploitation of Guinea's forest resources (forests cover about two-thirds of the country's land area) and substantial fishing stocks. During 1990–98 agricultural GDP increased by an estimated annual average of 4.4%.

Industry (including mining, manufacturing, construction and power) contributed an estimated 35% of GDP in 1998. Less than 2% of the employed labour force were engaged in the industrial sector at the time of the 1983 census. Industrial GDP increased by an estimated annual average of 1.6% in 1990–98.

Measured at constant 1994 prices, mining contributed 16.6% of GDP in 1996. Only 0.7% of the employed labour force were engaged in extractive activities in 1983. Guinea is the world's foremost exporter of bauxite and the second largest producer of bauxite ore, possessing between one-quarter and one-third of known reserves of the mineral. In 1996, according to estimates published by the IMF, exports of bauxite and alumina provided 61.4% of export earnings. Gold and diamonds are also mined: recorded exports of these contributed, respectively, 13.3% and 7.8% of total export revenue in 1996. The eventual exploitation of valuable reserves of high-grade iron ore at Mt Nimba, near the border with Liberia, is envisaged. Of Guinea's other known mineral deposits, only granite is exploitable on a commercial scale. The GDP of the mining sector declined by 1.2% in 1994, but increased by 7.5% in 1995 and by 11.7% in 1996.

The manufacturing sector remains largely undeveloped, contributing only an estimated 4% of GDP in 1998. In 1983 only 0.6% of the employed labour force were engaged in the manufacturing sector. Other than the country's one alumina smelter, most industrial companies are involved in import-substitution, including the processing of agricultural products and the manufacture of construction materials. Manufacturing GDP increased by an annual average of 0.8% in 1990–97.

Electricity generation is, at present, insufficient to meet demand, and power failures outside the mining and industrial sectors (in which the largest operators generate their own power supplies) have been frequent. However, Guinea possesses considerable hydroelectric potential. The 75-MW Garafiri dam project was inaugurated in 1999, and a further major scheme, at Kaléta, is scheduled for completion in 2002. In the mean time, some 600,000 metric tons of hydrocarbons are imported annually, and in 1996 imports of petroleum products accounted for 5.5% of the value of total imports.

The services sector contributed an estimated 42% of GDP in 1998. During 1990–98 the average rate of growth in the sector's GDP was estimated at 7.8% per year.

In 1998 Guinea recorded a visible trade surplus of US $120.9m., while there was a deficit of $118.5m. on the current account of the balance of payments. Excluding trade with countries of the former USSR, the principal suppliers of imports in 1996 were France (which supplied an estimated 18.5% of the total) and Côte d'Ivoire (15.9%); other major suppliers were the Belgo-Luxembourg Economic Union, the USA and Japan. The principal market for exports in the same year was the USA (which took an estimated 30.9% of exports); other major purchasers included Spain, Ireland, France and Canada. Ukraine is notable as a market for Guinean bauxite. The principal exports in 1996 were bauxite, alumina, gold and diamonds. The principal imports include manufactured goods, mineral fuels and foodstuffs.

In 1997 Guinea's overall budget deficit was estimated at 179,200m. FG, equivalent to 4.2% of GDP in that year. The country's total external debt was US $3,520m. at the end of 1997, of which $3,008m. was long-term public debt. In that year the cost of debt-servicing was equivalent to 21.5% of the value of exports of goods and services. Annual inflation averaged 9.2% in 1990–96; consumer prices increased by an annual average of 3.0% in 1996.

Guinea is a member of the Economic Community of West African States (ECOWAS, see p. 163), of the Gambia River Basin Development Organization (OMVG, see p. 291), of the International Coffee Organization (see p. 287), of the West Africa Rice Development Association (WARDA, see p. 289) and of the Mano River Union (see p. 292).

Guinea's potential for the attainment of wealth is substantial, owing to its valuable mineral deposits, water resources and generally favourable climate; however, the economy remains over-dependent on revenue from bauxite reserves and on external assistance, the country's infrastructure is vastly inadequate and its manufacturing base narrow. The recent insecurity in neighbouring Liberia and Sierra Leone, and the consequent presence in Guinea of large numbers of refugees, have, furthermore, strained the country's resources. Since 1985 economic liberalization measures have been undertaken, as advocated by the IMF and the World Bank, and by the late 1990s, despite frequent difficulties in implementing reforms, growth in overall GDP was considerable; success had been achieved in reducing the rate of inflation, foreign-exchange reserves had increased, as had private investment in the economy. The depression in world mineral prices during 1999 resulted in a sharp decline in revenue from sales of bauxite and alumina, and also hampered efforts to sell a majority stake in the Friguia alumina plant to private interests. Furthermore, considerable strain was placed on Guinea's budgetary resources by continuing regional instability, requiring substantial financial commitments to Guinea's role in peace-keeping forces and to strengthening security in the region of Guinea's borders with Liberia and Sierra Leone. Slower growth, of 3.7%, was forecast for 1999. Meanwhile, the IMF expressed concern at weaknesses particularly in fiscal revenue collection, and annual funding under the Enhanced Structural Adjustment Facility (ESAF) originally agreed in early 1997 was delayed until the end of 1999, when support under the Poverty Reduction and Growth Facility (the successor to the ESAF) was granted. Fiscal reform and the elimination of administrative inefficiency and corruption were to remain priorities for 2000, together with efforts to foster private investment, notably in the mining sector, and to restructure or liquidate unprofitable public enterprises. Increased budgetary resources were to be allocated to improving education, health and other social welfare provisions. None the less, the preservation of political stability, and thus the maintenance of investor confidence (as well as donor support), was to remain essential to the pursuit of economic reform.

## Social Welfare

Wages are fixed according to the Government Labour Code. A maximum working week of 48 hours is in force for industrial workers. In 1988 there were 2,945 physicians, and there were 18,674 hospital beds. The extension of basic health care to low-income groups forms a significant element of the Government's structural adjustment efforts. Private medical care has been legally available since 1984. Budget estimates for 1997 allocated 20,400m. FG to health (representing 2.8% of total budgetary expenditure).

## Education

Education is provided free of charge at every level in state institutions. Primary education, which begins at seven years of age and lasts for six years, is officially compulsory. In 1995/96, however, enrolment at primary schools was equivalent to only 48% of children in the relevant age-group (boys 63%; girls 31%). As part of government plans to extend the provision of basic education, it was aimed to increase the rate of primary enrolment to 53% by 2000. Secondary education, from the age of 13, lasts for seven years, comprising a first cycle (collège) of four years and a second (lycée) of three years. Enrolment at secondary schools in 1995/96 was equivalent to only 12% of children in the appropriate age-group (boys 18%; girls 6%). There are universities at Conakry and Kankan, and other tertiary institutions at Maneah, Boké and Faranah. In 1993, according to the national literacy service, the average rate of adult illiteracy was 72% (males 61%; females 83%). UNESCO estimated average adult illiteracy at 64.1% in 1995 (males 50.1%; females 78.1%). Private schools, which had been banned for 23 years under the Sekou Touré regime, were legalized in 1984. Budget estimates for 1997 allocated 67,400m. FG to education (equivalent to 9.2% of total budgetary expenditure).

## Public Holidays

**2000:** 1 January (New Year's Day), 8 January*† (Id al-Fitr, end of Ramadan), 24 April (Easter Monday), 1 May (Labour Day), 15 June* (Mouloud, birth of Muhammad), 27 August (Anniversary of Women's Revolt), 28 September (Referendum Day), 2 October (Republic Day), 1 November (All Saints' Day), 22 November (Day of 1970 Invasion), 25 December (Christmas); 28 December*† (Id al-Fitr, end of Ramadan).

**2001:** 1 January (New Year's Day), 16 April (Easter Monday), 1 May (Labour Day), 4 June* (Mouloud, birth of Muhammad), 27 August (Anniversary of Women's Revolt), 28 September (Referendum Day), 2 October (Republic Day), 1 November (All Saints' Day), 22 November (Day of 1970 Invasion), 17 December* (Id al-Fitr, end of Ramadan), 25 December (Christmas).

* These holidays are determined by the Islamic lunar calendar and may vary by one or two days from the dates given.

† This festival will occur twice (in the Islamic years AH 1420 and 1421) within the same Gregorian year.

## Weights and Measures

The metric system is in force.

# Statistical Survey

Source (unless otherwise stated): Service de la Statistique Générale, Conakry; tel. 44-21-48.

## Area and Population

**AREA, POPULATION AND DENSITY**

| | |
|---|---|
| Area (sq km) | 245,857* |
| Population (census results) | |
| 4–17 February 1983 | 4,533,240† |
| 31 December 1996‡ | |
| Males | 3,496,150 |
| Females | 3,668,673 |
| Total | 7,164,823 |
| Density (per sq km) at census of 1996 | 29.1 |

* 94,926 sq miles.

† Excluding adjustment for underenumeration.

‡ Provisional figure, including refugees from Liberia and Sierra Leone (estimated at 640,000).

**PRINCIPAL TOWNS** (population at December 1972)

Conakry (capital) 525,671 (later admitted to be overstated); Kankan 60,000.

**BIRTHS AND DEATHS** (UN estimates, annual averages)

| | 1980–85 | 1985–90 | 1990–95 |
|---|---|---|---|
| Birth rate (per 1,000) | 51.3 | 47.3 | 44.1 |
| Death rate (per 1,000) | 23.8 | 22.0 | 19.4 |

**Expectation of life** (UN estimates, years at birth, 1990–95): 44.5 (males 44.0; females 45.0).

Source: UN, *World Population Prospects: The 1998 Revision*.

**ECONOMICALLY ACTIVE POPULATION**
(persons aged 10 years and over, census of 1983, provisional)

| | Males | Females | Total |
|---|---|---|---|
| Agriculture, hunting, forestry and fishing | 856,971 | 566,644 | 1,423,615 |
| Mining and quarrying | 7,351 | 4,890 | 12,241 |
| Manufacturing | 6,758 | 4,493 | 11,251 |
| Electricity, gas and water | 1,601 | 1,604 | 3,205 |
| Construction | 5,475 | 3,640 | 9,115 |
| Trade, restaurants and hotels | 22,408 | 14,901 | 37,309 |
| Transport, storage and communications | 17,714 | 11,782 | 29,496 |
| Finance, insurance, real estate and business services | 2,136 | 1,420 | 3,556 |
| Community, social and personal services | 82,640 | 54,960 | 137,600 |
| Activities not adequately defined* | 101,450 | 54,229 | 155,679 |
| **Total labour force** | 1,104,504 | 718,563 | 1,823,067 |

* Includes 18,244 unemployed persons (not previously employed), whose distribution by sex is not available.

Source: ILO, *Yearbook of Labour Statistics*.

**Mid-1998** (estimates in '000): Agriculture, etc. 3,091; Total labour force 3,655 (Source: FAO, *Production Yearbook*).

## Agriculture

**PRINCIPAL CROPS** ('000 metric tons)

| | 1996 | 1997 | 1998 |
|---|---|---|---|
| Maize | 82 | 85 | 89 |
| Millet | 8 | 8* | 8* |
| Sorghum | 6 | 5* | 5* |
| Rice (paddy) | 673 | 716 | 764 |
| Other cereals | 110 | 118* | 117* |
| Sweet potatoes | 132* | 135* | 135 |
| Cassava (Manioc) | 667 | 732 | 812 |
| Yams | 90* | 95* | 89 |
| Taro (Coco yam) | 24 | 27 | 29 |
| Pulses* | 60 | 60 | 60 |
| Coconuts* | 18 | 18 | 18 |
| Cottonseed | 5 | 9* | 14* |
| Cotton (lint) | 6 | 10 | 16 |
| Vegetables | 476* | 476* | 476 |
| Sugar cane* | 220 | 220 | 220 |
| Citrus fruits* | 205 | 215 | 215 |
| Bananas | 150* | 150* | 150 |
| Plantains | 435* | 430* | 429 |
| Mangoes | 76 | 75* | 85 |
| Pineapples | 65* | 67* | 72 |
| Other fruits* | 44 | 46 | 45 |
| Palm kernels | 52 | 52* | 52* |
| Groundnuts (in shell) | 145 | 158 | 174 |
| Coffee (green) | 23 | 20* | 21 |
| Cocoa beans | 5† | 6† | 6* |
| Tobacco (leaves)* | 2 | 2 | 2 |

* FAO estimate(s). † Unofficial figure.

Source: FAO, *Production Yearbook*.

**LIVESTOCK** ('000 head, year ending September)

| | 1996 | 1997 | 1998 |
|---|---|---|---|
| Cattle | 2,246 | 2,291 | 2,337 |
| Sheep | 631 | 650 | 669 |
| Goats | 758 | 788 | 820 |
| Pigs | 48 | 51 | 53 |
| Horses* | 3 | 3 | 3 |
| Asses* | 2 | 2 | 2 |

* FAO estimates.

Poultry (million): 7 in 1996; 8 in 1997; 9 in 1998.

Source: FAO, *Production Yearbook*.

**LIVESTOCK PRODUCTS** (FAO estimates, '000 metric tons)

| | 1996 | 1997 | 1998 |
|---|---|---|---|
| Beef and veal | 15 | 15 | 15 |
| Poultry meat | 2 | 3 | 3 |
| Mutton and lamb | 1 | 2 | 2 |
| Goat meat | 3 | 3 | 3 |
| Other meat | 6 | 4 | 5 |
| Cows' milk | 50 | 55 | 59 |
| Goats' milk | 5 | 5 | 5 |
| Sheep's milk | 2 | 2 | 2 |
| Poultry eggs | 8 | 8 | 8 |
| Cattle hides | 2 | 2 | 3 |

Source: FAO, *Production Yearbook*.

# Forestry

**ROUNDWOOD REMOVALS** ('000 cubic metres, excl. bark)

| | 1995 | 1996 | 1997 |
|---|---|---|---|
| Sawlogs, veneer logs and logs for sleepers | 170 | 170 | 170 |
| Other industrial wood | 512 | 524 | 531 |
| Fuel wood | 4,541 | 4,642 | 4,700 |
| **Total** | 5,223 | 5,336 | 5,401 |

Source: FAO, *Yearbook of Forest Products*.

**SAWNWOOD PRODUCTION** ('000 cubic metres, incl. railway sleepers)

| | 1995 | 1996 | 1997 |
|---|---|---|---|
| **Total** (all broadleaved) | 85 | 85* | 85* |

* FAO estimate.

Source: FAO, *Yearbook of Forest Products*.

# Fishing

('000 metric tons, live weight)

| | 1995 | 1996 | 1997 |
|---|---|---|---|
| Freshwater fishes | 3.1 | 2.8 | 3.6 |
| Tonguefishes | 2.5 | 2.1 | 4.3 |
| Sea catfishes | 4.8 | 4.4 | 4.0 |
| Bobo croaker | 4.4 | 3.8 | 6.7 |
| West African croakers | 5.7 | 4.4 | 6.9 |
| Porgies and seabreams | 5.4 | 4.8 | 5.1 |
| Mullets | 1.8 | 1.9 | 1.3 |
| Carangids | 3.0 | 8.1 | 6.5 |
| Sardinellas | 4.5 | 5.3 | 4.6 |
| Bonga shad | 23.6 | 26.1 | 29.6 |
| Chub mackerel | 0.3 | 1.3 | 2.2 |
| Other marine fishes (incl. unspecified) | 11.2 | 10.1 | 19.3 |
| **Total fish** | 70.2 | 75.1 | 94.0 |
| Panaeus shrimps | 1.0 | 1.0 | 1.6 |
| Cuttlefish and bobtail squids | 6.4 | 5.7 | 6.5 |
| Other crustaceans and molluscs | 0.7 | 0.5 | 0.5 |
| **Total catch** | 78.4 | 82.3 | 102.6 |

Source: FAO, *Yearbook of Fishery Statistics*.

# Mining

| | 1990 | 1991 | 1992 |
|---|---|---|---|
| Bauxite ('000 metric tons) | 15,341 | 14,862 | 13,625 |
| Diamonds ('000 carats)* | 127 | 97 | 95 |

**Bauxite** ('000 metric tons): 14,784 in 1993; 13,761 in 1994; 13,761 in 1995; 17,733† in 1995; 18,393† in 1996.

* Data from the US Bureau of Mines.

† Source: *World Metal Statistics* (London).

Source: UN, *Industrial Commodity Statistics Yearbook*.

**Gold** (Mineral content of ore, metric tons): 4.5 in 1991; 4.2 in 1992; 3.8 in 1993; 4.3 in 1994; 6.5 in 1995; 7.0 in 1996; 7.1 in 1997; 13.1 in 1998 (Source: Gold Fields Mineral Services Ltd, *Gold Survey 1999*).

# Industry

**SELECTED PRODUCTS** ('000 metric tons, unless otherwise indicated)

| | 1994 | 1995 | 1996 |
|---|---|---|---|
| Salted, dried or smoked fish* | 11.0 | 11.0 | n.a. |
| Raw sugar* | 19 | 19 | 19 |
| Alumina (calcined equivalent)† | 640 | 566 | 600 |
| Electric energy (million kWh)‡ | 532 | 537 | n.a. |

* Data from FAO.

† Data from the US Bureau of Mines.

‡ Provisional or estimated figures.

Source: UN, *Industrial Commodity Statistics Yearbook*.

**Palm oil** (unrefined): 50 in 1994; 50 (estimate) in 1995; 55 in 1996; 55 (estimate) in 1997; 50 in 1998 (Source: FAO, *Production Yearbook*).

# Finance

**CURRENCY AND EXCHANGE RATES**

**Monetary Units**

100 centimes = 1 franc guinéen (FG or Guinean franc).

**Sterling and Dollar Equivalents** (31 July 1998)

£1 sterling = 2,032.5 Guinean francs;
US $1 = 1,241.0 Guinean francs;
10,000 Guinean francs = £4.920 = $8.058.

**Average Exchange Rate** (Guinean francs per US $)

1996 1,004.0
1997 1,095.3
1998 1,236.8

**BUDGET** ('000 million Guinean francs)

| Revenue* | 1995 | 1996 | 1997† |
|---|---|---|---|
| Mining-sector revenue | 110.7 | 106.8 | 123.0 |
| Special tax on mining products | 100.2 | 101.5 | 116.1 |
| Other revenue | 290.8 | 291.8 | 353.0 |
| Tax revenue | 265.6 | 266.0 | 320.5 |
| Taxes on income and profits | 36.6 | 43.5 | 46.0 |
| Personal | 20.9 | 26.0 | 26.1 |
| Corporate | 10.7 | 8.9 | 9.5 |
| Taxes on domestic production and trade | 171.0 | 166.2 | 200.6 |
| Value-added tax (VAT)‡ | 52.4 | 58.0 | 108.8 |
| Excise surcharge | 13.8 | 11.1 | 9.0 |
| Petroleum excise tax | 72.6 | 66.7 | 63.9 |
| Taxes on international trade | 58.0 | 56.3 | 74.0 |
| Import duties | 54.8 | 49.6 | 71.1 |
| **Total** | 401.5 | 398.6 | 475.9 |

| Expenditure§ | 1995 | 1996 | 1997† |
|---|---|---|---|
| Current expenditure | 332.8 | 350.7 | 377.4 |
| Wages and salaries | 154.9 | 173.4 | 171.7 |
| Other goods and services | 73.1 | 75.0 | 83.9 |
| Subsidies and transfers | 52.2 | 50.3 | 54.3 |
| Interest payments | 52.5 | 52.1 | 67.4 |
| Public investment programme | 313.9 | 289.7 | 349.1 |
| Domestically financed | 51.2 | 48.7 | 39.7 |
| Externally financed | 262.7 | 241.0 | 309.4 |
| **Sub-total** | 646.9 | 640.4 | 734.0 |
| Adjustment for payments arrears ‖ | 52.1 | –9.1 | 56.6 |
| **Total** (cash basis) | 699.0 | 631.3 | 790.6 |

* Excluding grants received ('000 million Guinean francs): 146.3 in 1995; 122.5 in 1996; 135.4† in 1997.

† Estimate(s).

‡ VAT, introduced in August 1996, replaced the turnover tax. Includes VAT (turnover tax before 1996) on imports.

§ Excluding lending minus repayments ('000 million Guinean francs): 0.2† in 1995.

‖ Minus sign indicates an increase in arrears.

Source: IMF, *Guinea: Statistical Annex* (June 1998).

**Ministry of Defence and Freedom Fighters:** Amura, Bissau; tel. 213297.

**Ministry of Economic and Social Reconstruction:** Bissau.

**Ministry of Economy and Finance:** CP 67, Bissau; tel. 201967; fax 201626.

**Ministry of Education, Science and Technology:** Rua Areolino Cruz, Bissau; tel. 202244.

**Ministry of Foreign Affairs and International Co-operation:** Rua General Omar Torrijo, Bissau; tel. 202752; fax 202378.

**Ministry of Health:** CP 50, Bissau; tel. 201107; fax 201701.

**Ministry of Internal Administration:** Avda Unidade Africana, Bissau; tel. 201527.

**Ministry of Justice:** Avda Amílcar Cabral, CP 17, Bissau; tel. 202187.

**Ministry of Natural Resources and the Environment:** Bissau.

**Ministry of Social Infrastructure:** CP 14, Bissau; tel. 202466; fax 201137.

**Ministry of War Veterans:** Bissau.

# President and Legislature

## PRESIDENT

**Presidential Election, First Ballot, 28 November 1999**

| Candidate | % of Votes |
|---|---|
| KUMBA IALA (PRS) | 38.8 |
| MALAM BACAI SANHA (PAIGC) | 23.4 |
| FAUSTINO IMBALI (PUSD/RGB—MB) | 8.2 |
| FERNANDO GOMES (Independent) | 7.0 |
| JOÃO TATIS SÁ (Independent) | 6.5 |
| ABUBACAR BALDÈ (UNDP) | 5.4 |
| **Total** (incl. others) | 100.0 |

**Second Ballot, 16 January 2000**

| Candidate | % of Votes |
|---|---|
| KUMBA IALA (PRS) | 72.0 |
| MALAM BACAI SANHA (PAIGC) | 28.0 |
| **Total** | 100.0 |

## NATIONAL PEOPLE'S ASSEMBLY

**General Election, 28 November 1999**

| | Seats |
|---|---|
| Partido para a Renovação Social (PRS) | 38 |
| Resistência da Guiné-Bissau—Movimento Bah-Fatah (RGB–MB) | 28 |
| Partido Africano da Independência da Guiné e Cabo Verde (PAIGC) | 24 |
| Aliança Democrática (AD) | 4 |
| União para a Mudança (UM) | 3 |
| Partido Social Democrático (PSD) | 3 |
| Frente Democrática Social (FSD) | 1 |
| União Nacional para a Democracia e o Progresso (UNDP) | 1 |
| **Total** (incl. others) | 102 |

# Political Organizations

**Aliança Democrática (AD):** Bissau.

**Foro Cívico da Guiné (FCG):** Bissau; Leader ANTONIETA ROSA GOMES.

**Frente Democrática Social (FDS):** Bissau; f. 1991; legalized in Dec. 1991; Leader RAFAEL BARBOSA.

**Frente da Luta para a Libertação da Guiné (FLING):** Bissau; f. 1962 as an external opposition movement; legally registered in May 1992; Leader FRANÇOIS KANKOILA MENDY.

**Liga Guineense de Protecção Ecológica (LIPE):** Bairro Missirá 102, CP 1290, Bissau; tel. and fax 252309; f. 1991; ecology party; Pres. Alhaje BUBACAR DJALÓ.

**Partido Africano da Independência da Guiné e Cabo Verde (PAIGC):** CP 106, Bissau; f. 1956; fmrly the ruling party in both Guinea-Bissau and Cape Verde; although Cape Verde withdrew from the PAIGC following the coup in Guinea-Bissau in Nov. 1980, Guinea-Bissau has retained the party name and initials; Pres. FRANCISCO BENANTE; Perm. Sec. FLAVIO PROENÇA.

**Partido da Convergência Democrática (PCD):** Bissau; Leader VÍTOR MANDINGA.

**Partido para a Renovação Social (PRS):** Bissau; f. 1992 by four mems of the Frente Democrática Social; officially registered in Oct. 1992; Leader KUMBA IALA.

**Partido Social Democrático (PSD):** Bissau; f. 1995 by breakaway faction of RGB–MB; Leader JOAQUIM BALDÉ; Sec.-Gen. GASPAR FERNANDES.

**Partido Unido Social Democrático (PUSD):** Bissau; f. 1991; officially registered in Jan. 1992; Leader (vacant).

**Resistência da Guiné-Bissau–Movimento Bah-Fatah (RGB–MB):** Bissau; f. 1986 in Lisbon, Portugal, as Resistência da Guiné-Bissau–Movimento Bafatá; adopted present name prior to official registration in Dec. 1991; maintains offices in Paris (France), Dakar (Senegal) and Praia (Cape Verde); Chair. HELDER VAZ LOPES.

**União para a Mudança (UM):** Bissau; f. 1994 as coalition to contest presidential and legislative elections, re-formed April 1995; comprises following parties:

**Frente Democrática (FD):** Bissau; f. 1991; officially registered in Nov. 1991; Pres. CANJURA INJAI; Sec.-Gen. MARCELINO BATISTA.

**Movimento para a Unidade e a Democracia (MUDE):** Bissau; officially registered in Aug. 1992; Leader FILINTO VAZ MARTINS.

**Partido Democrático do Progresso (PDP):** Bissau; f. 1991; officially registered in Aug. 1992; Pres. of Nat. Council AMINE MICHEL SAAD.

**Partido de Renovação e Desenvolvimento (PRD):** Bissau; f. 1992 as the 'Group of 121' by PAIGC dissidents; officially registered in Oct. 1992; Leaders MANUEL RAMBOUT BARCELOS, AGNELO REGALA.

**União Nacional para a Democracia e o Progresso (UNDP):** Bissau; f. 1998; Leader ABUBACAR BALDÈ.

# Diplomatic Representation

## EMBASSIES IN GUINEA-BISSAU

**Brazil:** Rua São Tomé, Bissau; tel. 201327; fax 201317; Ambassador: LUIZ FERNANDO NAZARETH.

**China (Taiwan):** Avda Amílcar Cabral 35, CP 66, Bissau; tel. 201501; fax 201466.

**Cuba:** Rua Joaquim N'Com 1, Bissau; tel. 213579; Ambassador: DIOSDADO FERNÁNDEZ GONZÁLEZ.

**Egypt:** Avda Omar Torrijos, Rua 15, CP 72, Bissau; tel. 213642; Ambassador: MOHAMED REDA FARAHAT.

**France:** Avda 14 de Novembro, Bairro de Penha, Bissau; tel. 201610; fax 253142; Ambassador: FRANÇOIS CHAPPELLET.

**Guinea:** Rua 14, no. 9, CP 396, Bissau; tel. 212681; Ambassador: MOHAMED LAMINÉ FODÉ.

**Libya:** Rua 16, CP 362, Bissau; tel. 212006; Representative: DOKALI ALI MUSTAFA.

**Portugal:** Rua Cidade de Lisboa 6, Apdo 276, Bissau; tel. 201261; fax 201269; Ambassador: FRANCISCO HENRIQUES DA SILVA.

**Russia:** Avda 14 de Novembro, Bissau; tel. 251036; fax 251050; Ambassador: VIKTOR M. ZELENOV.

**Senegal:** Avda Omar Torrijos 43A, Bissau; tel. 211561; Ambassador: MAMADOU NIANG.

**USA:** CP 297, 1067 Bissau; tel. 252273; fax 252282; Ambassador: PEGGY BLACKFORD.

# Judicial System

Judges of the Supreme Court are appointed by the Conselho Superior da Magistratura.

**President of the Supreme Court:** MAMADU SALIU DJALO PIRES.

# Religion

According to the 1991 census, 45.9% of the population are Muslims, 39.7% are animists and 14.4% are Christians, mainly Roman Catholics.

## CHRISTIANITY

### The Roman Catholic Church

Guinea-Bissau comprises a single diocese, directly responsible to the Holy See. The Bishop participates in the Episcopal Conference of Senegal, Mauritania, Cape Verde and Guinea-Bissau, currently based in Senegal. At 31 December 1997 there were an estimated 132,000 adherents in the country.

**Bishop of Bissau:** (vacant), CP 20, 1001 Bissau; tel. 251057; fax 251058.

### The Anglican Communion

Anglicans in Guinea-Bissau are adherents of the Church of the Province of West Africa, comprising 12 dioceses.

**Bishop of Guinea and Guinea-Bissau:** (vacant), BP 1187, Conakry, Guinea.

# The Press

**Baguerra:** Bissau; owned by the Partido da Convergência Democrática.

**Banobero:** Bissau; weekly; Dir FERNANDO JORGE PEREIRA.

**Nô Pintcha:** Bissau; daily; Dir Sra CABRAL; circ. 6,000.

### NEWS AGENCY

**Agência Noticiosa da Guinea (ANG):** CP 248, Bissau; tel. 212151.

# Broadcasting and Communications

### TELECOMMUNICATIONS

**Guiné-Telecom:** Bissau; 49% state-owned.

### RADIO AND TELEVISION

An experimental television service began transmissions in 1989. Regional radio stations were to be established at Bafatá, Cantchungo and Catió in 1990. In 1990 Radio Freedom, which broadcast on behalf of the PAIGC during Portuguese rule and had ceased operations in 1974, resumed transmissions.

**Radiodifusão Nacional da República da Guiné-Bissau:** CP 191, Bissau; govt-owned; broadcasts in Portuguese on short-wave, MW and FM; Dir FRANCISCO BARRETO.

**Rádio Bombolom:** f. 1996; independent; Dir AGNELO REGALA.

**Rádio Pidjiguiti:** f. 1995; independent.

# Finance

(cap. = capital; res = reserves; m. = million; brs = branches; amounts in francs CFA unless otherwise indicated)

### BANKING

#### Central Bank

**Banque Centrale des Etats de l'Afrique de l'Ouest (BCEAO):** Avda Amílcar Cabral, CP 38, Bissau; tel. 215548; fax 201305; HQ in Dakar, Senegal; f. 1955; bank of issue for the mem states of the Union économique et monétaire ouest-africaine (UEMOA, comprising Benin, Burkina Faso, Côte d'Ivoire, Guinea-Bissau, Mali, Niger, Senegal and Togo); cap. and res 806,918m., total assets 4,084,464m.; (Dec. 1998); Gov. CHARLES KONAN BANNY; Dir in Guinea-Bissau LUÍS CÂNDIDO LOPES RIBEIRO.

#### Other Banks

**Banco Internacional da Guiné-Bissau:** Avda Amílcar Cabral, CP 74, Bissau; tel. 213744; fax 201033; e-mail big@solgtelecom.gw; f. 1989; cap. 3,260m. Guinea pesos (Dec. 1993); 26% state-owned, 25% by Guinea-Bissau enterprises and private interests, 49% by Crédito Predial Português (Portugal); Chair. FILINTO E. BARROS; Gen. Man. JOSÉ ANTÓNIO TAVARES DA CRUZ.

**Banco Totta e Açores** (Portugal): Rua 19 de Setembro 15, CP 618, Bissau; tel. 214794; fax 201591; Gen. Man. CARLOS MADEIRA.

**Caixa de Crédito da Guiné:** Bissau; govt savings and loan institution.

**Caixa Económica Postal:** Avda Amílcar Cabral, Bissau; tel. 212999; postal savings institution.

### STOCK EXCHANGE

In 1998 a regional stock exchange, the Bourse Régionale des Valeurs Mobilières, was established in Abidjan, Côte d'Ivoire, to serve the member states of the UEMOA.

### INSURANCE

In 1979 it was announced that a single state-owned insurer was to replace the Portuguese company Ultramarina.

# Trade and Industry

The Government has actively pursued a policy of small-scale industrialization to compensate for the almost total lack of manufacturing capacity. Following independence, it adopted a comprehensive programme of state control, and in 1976 acquired 80% of the capital of a Portuguese company, **Ultramarina**, a large firm specializing in a wide range of trading activities, including ship-repairing and agricultural processing. The Government also held a major interest in the **CICER** brewery (until its privatization in 1996) and created a joint-venture company with the Portuguese concern **SACOR** to sell petroleum products. Since 1975 three fishing companies have been formed with foreign participation: **GUIALP** (with Algeria), **Estrela do Mar** (with the former USSR) and **SEMAPESCA** (with France), all of which were awaiting divestment in 1998. In December 1976 **SOCOTRAM**, an enterprise for the sale and processing of timber, was inaugurated. It operates a factory in Bissau for the production of wooden tiles and co-ordinates sawmills and carpentry shops throughout the country. In 1998 SOCOTRAM was in the process of being divested through separate sales of its regional operational divisions. The restructuring of several further public enterprises was proceeding in the late 1990s, as part of the Government's programme to attract private investment.

**Empresa Nacional de Pesquisas e Exploração Petrolíferas e Mineiras (PETROMINAS):** Rua Eduardo Mondlane 58, Bissau; tel. 212279; state-owned; regulates all prospecting for hydrocarbons and other minerals; Dir-Gen. ANTÓNIO CARDOSO.

### CHAMBER OF COMMERCE

**Associação Comercial, Industrial e Agrícola da Guiné-Bissau:** Bissau; f. 1987; Pres. CANJURA INJAI.

### UTILITIES

#### Electricity and Water

**EAGB:** Bissau; operated under contract by private management co.

### TRADE UNION

**União Nacional dos Trabalhadores da Guiné (UNTG):** 13 Avda Ovai di Vievra, CP 98, Bissau; tel. 212094; Pres. DEFEJADO LIMA DA COSTA; Sec.-Gen. MÁRIO MENDES CORREA.

Legislation permitting the formation of other trade unions was approved by the National People's Assembly in 1991.

# Transport

### RAILWAYS

There are no railways in Guinea-Bissau. In March 1998 Guinea-Bissau and Portugal signed an agreement providing for the construction of a railway linking Guinea-Bissau with Guinea.

### ROADS

In 1996, according to International Road Federation estimates, there were about 4,400 km of roads, of which 453 km were paved. A major road rehabilitation scheme is proceeding, and an international road, linking Guinea-Bissau with The Gambia and Senegal, is planned. In 1989 the Islamic Development Bank granted more than US $2m. towards the construction of a 111-km road linking north and south and a 206-km road between Guinea-Bissau and Guinea.

### SHIPPING

Under a major port modernization project, the main port at Bissau was to be renovated and expanded, and four river ports were to be upgraded to enable barges to load and unload at low tide. The total cost of the project was estimated at US $47.4m., and finance was provided by the World Bank and Arab funds. In 1986 work began on a new river port at N'Pungda, which was to be partly funded by the Netherlands.

### CIVIL AVIATION

There is an international airport at Bissau, which there are plans to expand, and 10 smaller airports serving the interior.

**Transportes Aéreos da Guiné-Bissau (TAGB):** Aeroporto Osvaldo Vieira, CP 111, Bissau; tel. 201277; fax 251536; f. 1977; domestic services and flights to France, Portugal, the Canary Islands (Spain), Guinea and Senegal; Dir Capt. EDUARDO PINTO LOPES .

# Tourism

**Centro de Informação e Turismo:** CP 294, Bissau; state tourism and information service.

# GUYANA

## Introductory Survey

**Location, Climate, Language, Religion, Flag, Capital**

The Co-operative Republic of Guyana lies on the north coast of South America, between Venezuela to the west and Suriname to the east, with Brazil to the south. The narrow coastal belt has a moderate climate with two wet seasons, from April to August and from November to January, alternating with two dry seasons. Inland, there are tropical forests and savannah, and the dry season lasts from September to May. The average annual temperature is 27°C (80°F), with average rainfall of 1,520 mm (60 ins) per year inland, rising to between 2,030 mm (80 ins) and 2,540 mm (100 ins) on the coast. English is the official language but Hindi, Urdu and Amerindian dialects are also spoken. The principal religions are Christianity (which is professed by about 50% of the population), Hinduism (about 33%) and Islam (less than 10%). The national flag (proportions 5 by 3 when flown on land, but 2 by 1 at sea) is green, with a white-bordered yellow triangle (apex at the edge of the fly) on which is superimposed a black-bordered red triangle (apex in the centre). The capital is Georgetown.

**Recent History**

Guyana was formerly British Guiana, a colony of the United Kingdom, formed in 1831 from territories finally ceded to Britain by the Dutch in 1814. A new Constitution, providing for universal adult suffrage, was introduced in 1953. The elections of April 1953 were won by the left-wing People's Progressive Party (PPP), led by Dr Cheddi Bharat Jagan. In October, however, the British Government, claiming that a communist dictatorship was threatened, suspended the Constitution. An interim administration was appointed. The PPP split in 1955, and in 1957 some former members founded a new party, the People's National Congress (PNC), under the leadership of Forbes Burnham. The PNC drew its support mainly from the African-descended population, while PPP support came largely from the (Asian-descended) 'East' Indian community.

A revised Constitution was introduced in December 1956 and fresh elections were held in August 1957. The PPP won and Dr Jagan became Chief Minister. Another Constitution, providing for internal self-government, was adopted in July 1961. The PPP won the elections in August and Dr Jagan was appointed Premier in September. In the elections of December 1964, held under the system of proportional representation that had been introduced in the previous year, the PPP won the largest number of seats in the Legislative Assembly, but not a majority. A coalition Government was formed by the PNC and The United Force (TUF), with Burnham as Prime Minister. This coalition led the colony to independence, as Guyana, on 26 May 1966.

The PNC won elections in 1968 and in 1973, although the results of the latter, and every poll thenceforth until the defeat of the PNC in 1992, were disputed by the opposition parties. Guyana became a co-operative republic on 23 February 1970, and Arthur Chung was elected non-executive President in March. In 1976 the PPP, which had boycotted the National Assembly since 1973, offered the Government its 'critical support'. Following a referendum in July 1978 that gave the Assembly power to amend the Constitution, elections to the Assembly were postponed for 15 months. The legislature assumed the role of a constituent assembly, established in November 1978, to draft a new constitution. In October 1979 elections were postponed for a further year. In October 1980 Forbes Burnham declared himself executive President of Guyana, and a new Constitution was promulgated.

Internal opposition to the PNC Government had increased after the assassination in June 1980 of Dr Walter Rodney, leader of the Working People's Alliance (WPA). The Government was widely believed to have been involved in the incident; an official inquest into Rodney's death was finally ordered in November 1987, but in 1988 it produced a verdict, rejected by the opposition, of death by misadventure. All opposition parties except the PPP and TUF urged their supporters to boycott the December 1980 elections to the National Assembly. The PNC, under Burnham, received 77.7% of the votes, according to official results, and won 41 of the 53 elective seats, although allegations of substantial electoral malpractice were made, both within the country and by international observers. None the less, Burnham was formally inaugurated as President in January 1981.

In 1981 arrests and trials of opposition leaders continued, and in 1982 the Government's relations with human rights groups, and especially the Christian churches, deteriorated further. Editors of opposition newspapers were threatened, political violence increased, and the Government was accused of interference in the legal process. Industrial unrest and public discontent continued in 1983, as Guyana's worsening economic situation increased opposition to the Government, and led to growing disaffection within the trade union movement and the PNC. There were more strikes in 1984, and in December Burnham announced some concessions, including a rise in the daily minimum wage (virtually the only increase since 1979).

Burnham died in August 1985 and was succeeded as President by Desmond Hoyte, hitherto the First Vice-President and Prime Minister. President Hoyte's former posts were assumed by Hamilton Green, previously the First Deputy Prime Minister. At a general election in December the PNC won 78% of the votes and 42 of the elective seats in the National Assembly. Hoyte was declared President-elect. Opposition groups, including the PPP and WPA, denounced the poll as fraudulent. In January 1986 five of the six opposition parties formed the Patriotic Coalition for Democracy (PCD).

During 1988 the opposition expressed fears about the independence of the judiciary. The opposition also claimed that the Government's continued recourse to the laws of libel against its critics was an abuse of the legal system. Social unrest and industrial disruption in 1988 continued to hamper government efforts to reform the economy, while the Government's hold on power was further compromised, following a division within the trade union movement. Seven unions withdrew from the Trades Union Congress (TUC) in September, alleging that elections for TUC officials were weighted in favour of PNC-approved candidates. The seven independent unions formed a separate congress, the Federation of Independent Trade Unions in Guyana (FITUG), in October. However, the Government refused to negotiate with the FITUG, accusing it of being politically motivated. Furthermore, the severity of austerity measures contained in the budget of March 1989, which included a devaluation of the currency, prompted a six-week strike in the sugar and bauxite industries.

Outside the formal opposition of the political parties, the Government also experienced pressure from members of the Guyana Human Rights Association, business leaders and prominent religious figures. This culminated, in January 1990, in the formation of a movement for legal and constitutional change, Guyanese Action for Reform and Democracy (Guard), which initiated a series of mass protests, urging the Government to accelerate the process of democratic reform. To counter this civic movement, the PNC began mobilizing its own newly-established Committees to Re-elect the President (Creeps). Guard accused the Creeps of orchestrating violent clashes at Guard's rallies, and of fomenting racial unrest in the country in an attempt to regain support from the Afro-Guyanese population.

In October 1990 the former US President, Jimmy Carter, visited President Hoyte to discuss matters related to electoral reform. Following discussions, it was agreed that a new electoral register would be compiled. However, the date of the forthcoming general election was postponed, following the approval of legislation by the PNC in January 1991, extending the term of office of the National Assembly by two months after its official dissolution date of 2 February 1991. In March a further two-month extension of the legislative term provoked the resignation of TUF and PPP members from the National Assembly (in addition to the WPA members, who had resigned a month earlier). Similar extensions followed in May and July, owing to alleged continuing problems relating to electoral reforms. The National Assembly was finally dissolved in late September. The publication of the revised electoral register in that month, however, revealed widespread inaccuracies, including the omission of an estimated 100,000 eligible voters. In November several opposition parties announced a boycott of the general election, which had been rescheduled for mid-December. However, on 28 November Hoyte declared a state of emergency in order to legitimize a further postponement of the election (which, according to the Constitution, was due to take place by 28 December). Legislation restoring the opposition seats in the National Assembly followed, and the Assembly was reconvened. In mid-December the state of emergency was extended until June 1992. A further revised electoral register was published in that month, and was finally approved by the Elections Commission in August. The election took place on 5 October and resulted in a narrow victory for the PPP in alliance with the CIVIC movement (a social and political movement of businessmen and professionals), which secured 32 of the 65 elective seats in the National Assembly (53.5% of the votes), while the PNC secured 31 (42.3% of the votes). The result, which signified an end to the PNC's 28-year period in government, provoked riots by the mainly Afro-Guyanese PNC supporters in Georgetown, in which two people were killed. International observers were, however, satisfied that the elections had been fairly conducted, and on 9 October Dr Cheddi Bharat Jagan took office as President. On the following day Jagan appointed Samuel Hinds, an industrialist who was not a member of the PPP, as Prime Minister.

Following a joint conference in September 1993, the unions belonging to the TUC and the FITUG agreed to reunify as the TUC. In May 1994 a strike, organized by four public-sector unions in support of demands for pay increases, causing considerable disruption, was ended after ten days when the Government agreed to a 35% increase in the minimum wage.

At municipal and local government elections held in August 1994, the first to be contested since 1970, the PPP/CIVIC alliance secured control of 49 of the 71 localities concerned. However, the important post of mayor of Georgetown was won by Hamilton Green, representing Good and Green Georgetown, a party founded specifically to contest the election in the capital. In December, Green, who was expelled from the PNC in 1993, announced the establishment of a new nationwide political movement entitled Good and Green Guyana.

In December 1994 the National Assembly approved a proposal, drafted by the PPP, for the creation of a select parliamentary committee to review the Constitution, with a view to adopting reforms prior to the next general election, due in 1997. However, the PNC, whose support would be required to gain the two-thirds' majority necessary for constitutional amendments, voted against the proposal, favouring instead the appointment of a constituent assembly.

In August 1995 a serious environmental incident resulted in the temporary closure of Omai Gold Mines Ltd (OGML). The company, which began production in the Omai District of Essequibo province in 1993, was responsible for an increase of some 400% in Guyana's gold production in subsequent years and was Guyana's largest foreign investor. However, in August 1995 a breach in a tailings pond (a reservoir where residue from the gold extraction process is stored) resulted in the spillage of some 3.5m. cu m of cyanide-tainted water, of which a large volume flowed into the Omai river, a tributary of the Essequibo river. Environmental warnings were issued to residents of the Essequibo region, and the National Assembly approved a resolution to close the mine for an indefinite period pending an inquiry into the incident. In January 1996 a commission of inquiry appointed by the Government submitted a report recommending that OGML be permitted to resume operations subject to the prior implementation of certain environmental safeguards. OGML resumed operations in the following month.

In February 1996, amid growing public concern at an increase in criminal violence, Guyana resumed judicial executions with the hanging of a convicted murderer. The execution, the first for more than five years, provoked protest from human rights organizations.

In March 1997, following the death of Dr Cheddi Bharat Jagan, Prime Minister Hinds succeeded to the Presidency, in accordance with the provisions of the Constitution. Hinds subsequently appointed Janet Jagan, the widow of the former President, to the post of Prime Minister. In September the PPP/CIVIC alliance formally adopted Jagan as its presidential candidate for the forthcoming general election.

At the general election of 15 December 1997 delays in the verification of votes prompted protest by PNC supporters who accused the Government of electoral fraud, and eleven protesters were injured during clashes with the security forces. With some 90% of the votes counted, the Chairman of the Elections Commission, Doudnauth Singh, declared that Jagan had established an unassailable lead, and on 19 December she was inaugurated as President. Singh's actions were strongly criticized as being premature by opposition parties, and the PNC expressed its intention to appeal to the High Court to have Jagan's appointment annulled. In the following days PNC supporters began a series of public demonstrations in protest at the alleged electoral fraud and at Jagan's appointment. On 31 December the final election results were declared. With two legislative seats remaining to be decided by the National Congress of Local Democratic Organs (see The Constitution), the PPP/CIVIC alliance secured 34 seats, the PNC won 26, and TUF, the Alliance for Guyana and the Guyana Democratic Party each obtained one seat. (In February 1998 the remaining two seats were declared to have been won by the PPP/CIVIC alliance.)

In January 1998, in the light of continued unrest being fomented by opposition supporters, the Government accepted a proposal by private-sector leaders for an international audit of the election to be conducted. The PNC, however, rejected the proposal and demanded instead the holding of fresh elections. In mid-January, in rejection of an appeal by the PNC, the Chief Justice ruled that it was beyond the jurisdiction of the High Court to prohibit Jagan from exercising her presidential functions pending a judicial review of the election. The ruling provoked serious disturbances in Georgetown, which, in turn, prompted the Government to introduce a one-month ban on public assemblies and demonstrations in the capital. Nevertheless, public protests by PNC supporters continued in defiance of the ban, resulting in confrontation with the security forces. However, in mid-January, following mediation by a three-member CARICOM commission, headed by a former Minister of Foreign Affairs of Barbados, Sir Henry Forde, it was announced that an agreement (the Herdmanston Agreement) had been signed by Jagan and PNC leader Desmond Hoyte, which provided for the organization of fresh elections within 36 months and the creation of a constitutional commission to make recommendations on constitutional reform, subsequently to be submitted to a national referendum and a National Assembly vote. The agreement also made provision for an independent audit of the December election, and in February the PPP/CIVIC alliance and the PNC agreed on the legal procedures necessary for the audit, which was to be conducted by a CARICOM electoral team, to be authorized. Meanwhile, although the PNC had submitted the names of 22 deputies who would represent the party in an emergency, the PNC continued to boycott the National Assembly. In early June the CARICOM commission upheld the published results of the December poll, declaring that there had been only minor procedural irregularities. While both the PPP and the PNC were bound to abide by the findings of the commission (under the terms of the Herdmanston Agreement), Hoyte continued publicly to question the legitimacy of the Jagan administration. Later in the month, mounting political frustration, arising from the National Assembly's informing the PNC that its deputies had effectively forfeited their legislative seats (having failed to attend six consecutive sittings), erupted onto the streets of Georgetown. PNC supporters congregated in the capital, where violent demonstrations against the Government escalated into riot conditions that were dispersed by the security forces with rubber bullets and tear gas. However, renewed CARICOM mediation between the PPP and the PNC, at the CARICOM annual summit in St Lucia in early July, produced fresh commitments from both sides to restore peaceful political dialogue, renew discussions on constitutional reform and reinstate full legislative participation. Legislation designed to enable the PNC deputies to recover their seats in the legislature was subsequently formulated by both sides, and the PNC (with the exception of Hoyte—who continued to deny the legitimacy of Jagan's authority) rejoined the National Assembly on 14 July.

In August 1998 the National Assembly announced a 14-member select committee on constitutional reform, entrusted with establishing the terms of reference and composition of a national reform commission. The select committee comprised eight members of the PPP/CIVIC alliance, four from the PNC and one each from the TUF and the AFG. In January 1999 the 20-member Constitutional Reform Commission was created, comprising representatives of the country's principal political parties and community groups. The Commission had until the end of July 1999 to formulate recommendations for constitutional reform. Also in January, Ronald Gajraj, a former head of the national police commission, relieved the Prime Minister of the home affairs portfolio, following mounting concern at a recent sharp increase in violent crimes in the business community.

In February 1999 Hoyte, who had alleged that the PPP/CIVIC alliance was not interested in achieving a lasting political solution, announced that the PNC was to withdraw from discussions and was to resume public protests. In response, President Jagan warned that she would not 'succumb to unreasonableness and uncompromising stances'. In March, however, Maurice King, the facilitator appointed by CARICOM, announced that Hoyte and Jagan had agreed to meet privately, and in May the parties agreed to resume dialogue.

In April 1999 the Constitutional Reform Commission began public consultations. The PPP/CIVIC alliance submitted proposals suggesting that the country should be renamed the Republic of Guyana, and that the President should be limited to two consecutive terms of office. The PPP/CIVIC also proposed the deletion of the clause in the Constitution whereby the President is empowered to dissolve the National Assembly should he/she be censured by the Assembly. These proposals were subsequently adopted in the report published by the Commission in July. The Commission further proposed that the President should no longer have the power to dismiss a public officer in the public interest, and the President and Cabinet should be collectively responsible to the National Assembly and should resign if defeated in a vote of 'no confidence'.

In late April 1999 the Guyana Public Service Union (GPSU) called a general strike after the Government had offered a pay rise of between 3% and 4.5% in response to the union's demand for an increase of at least 40%. Other public-sector unions, including the Federation of Government Employees and the Guyana Teachers' Union, later joined the GPSU in taking industrial action, and much of the country was paralysed. Tension was exacerbated following the serving of legal summonses to three prominent union leaders for having organized protest marches in defiance of a government ban, while in mid-May the police opened fire (with pellet guns) on an allegedly violent crowd of strikers, injuring 17 people. After 56 days of industrial action, an agreement was finally reached between the unions and the authorities in late June, which granted public-sector workers an interim pay rise of 4.6% prior to the full settlement of their claim by an arbitration tribunal. Many members of the GPSU were reported to be dissatisfied with the agreement, and the headquarters of the union were subsequently attacked, while the Minister for Public Service, George Fung-On, was assaulted in his car. In September the arbitration tribunal awarded public-sector workers an increase of 31.6% in 1999 and 26.7% in 2000. The Government, however, announced that it would only be bound by the tribunal's findings if it could be proved that the tribunal had followed the correct procedures, and it also warned the unions that the cost of the pay rises might necessitate redundancies.

In early August 1999 President Jagan announced her retirement on the grounds of ill health. Jagan was replaced as President by the erstwhile Minister of Finance, Bharrat Jagdeo. The appointment of Jagdeo, whose relative youth (he was 35 years of age at the time of his appointment), reported willingness to reach across the political divide, and strong background in economics all contributed to his popularity, was widely welcomed in Guyana and by the international community. Jagdeo, who announced that he was to continue the largely market-orientated policies of the Jagan administration, reappointed Samuel Hinds as Prime Minister (Hinds had earlier resigned in accordance with the requirements of the Constitution), and announced that there was to be no cabinet reorganization in the immediate future. There was, however, controversy at the absence of Hoyte and other PNC representatives from the President's inauguration ceremony; Hoyte, who had refused to recognize Jagan as President, was reported to have declined to recognize any successor nominated by her. In late November Saisnarine Kowlessar, the head of the University of Guyana's Department of Management, was appointed Minister in the Office of the President with responsibility for Finance, a portfolio previously held by the President. The President also appointed Geoffrey Da Silva as the new Minister of Trade, Industry and Tourism, replacing Michael Shree Chan, who had retired on the grounds of ill health.

In December 1999 the National Assembly approved the establishment of a committee to supervise the revision of the Constitution prior to the legislative elections scheduled for mid-January 2001. Two 'task forces' were also established by the National Assembly; one was to deal with electoral reform and the other was to establish an Ethnic Relations Commission.

Guyana has border disputes with its neighbours, Venezuela and Suriname, although relations with Brazil have continued to improve through trade and military agreements. Suriname restored diplomatic representation in Guyana in 1979 and bilateral meetings were resumed at the end of the year. In 1983 relations improved further as a result of increased trade links between the countries. In late 1998 it was announced that a joint border commission, created to negotiate the settlement of a territorial dispute between Suriname and Guyana, was to be revived, after a two-year suspension. The two countries were also expected to conclude an agreement on fishing rights.

In 1962 Venezuela renewed its claim to 130,000 sq km (50,000 sq miles) of land west of the Essequibo river (nearly two-thirds of Guyanese territory). The area was accorded to Guyana in 1899, on the decision of an international tribunal, but Venezuela based its claim on a papal bull of 1493, referring to Spanish colonial possessions. The Port of Spain Protocol of 1970 put the issue in abeyance until 1982. Guyana and Venezuela referred the dispute to the UN in 1983, and, after a series of UN efforts and a visit to Venezuela by President Hoyte, the two countries agreed to a mutually acceptable intermediary, suggested by the UN Secretary-General, in August 1989. In March 1999 Guyana and Venezuela established a joint commission, the High Level Binational Commission, which was intended to expedite the resolution of the territorial dispute and to promote mutual co-operation. However, in September the Venezuelan Government alleged that the Guyanese authorities had granted concessions to petroleum companies within the disputed areas, and in October President Chávez of Venezuela, speaking on the 100th anniversary of the international tribunal's decision, announced his Government's intention to reopen its claim to the territory. Reports of Venezuelan troop movements near the border area caused alarm in Guyana, but were described by the Venezuelan authorites as part of a campaign against drugs-traffickers. The Venezuelan Government subsequently reaffirmed its commitment to seek a peaceful solution to the dispute, and in December an agreement was reached between the two countries on co-operation in the fisheries sector. In January 2000 the Guyanese Government approved a donation of US $100,000 to Venezuela to assist humanitarian efforts following the severe flooding in that country.

During the early 1990s Hoyte committed Guyana to closer integration with the Caribbean Community and Common Market (CARICOM, see p. 136), and CARICOM played an active role in attempts to achieve a peace agreement between the PPP and PNC in the late 1990s.

### Government

Under the 1980 Constitution, legislative power is held by the unicameral National Assembly, with 65 members: 53 elected for five years by universal adult suffrage, on the basis of proportional representation, and 12 regional representatives. Executive power is held by the President, who leads the majority party in the Assembly and holds office for its duration. The President appoints and heads a Cabinet, which includes the Prime Minister, and may include Ministers who are not elected members of the Assembly. The Cabinet is collectively responsible to the National Assembly. Guyana comprises 10 regions, each having a regional democratic council which returns a representative to the National Assembly.

### Defence

In August 1999 the Combined Guyana Defence Force consisted of some 1,600 men (of whom 1,400 were in the army, 100 were in the air force and some 100 in the navy). One-third of the combined forces are civilian personnel. A paramilitary force, the People's Militia, totalled 1,500. Defence expenditure was budgeted at $ G900m. for 1999.

### Economic Affairs

According to estimates by the World Bank, in 1997 Guyana's gross national product (GNP), measured at average 1995–97 prices, was US $677m. GNP per head, equivalent to $800 in 1997, was estimated to have increased at an average rate of 12.9% per year, in real terms, during 1990–97. Over the same period, the population increased at an average annual rate of 0.7%. Total GNP was estimated to be $660m. in 1998, equivalent to $770 per head. Guyana's gross domestic product (GDP) increased, in real terms, by an average of 6.0% per year during 1990–98, although a decline of 1.5% was estimated in GDP in 1998.

Agriculture (including forestry and fishing) provided an estimated 34.7% of GDP in 1998, according to preliminary figures, and employed an estimated 18.7% of the economically active population in that year. The principal cash crops are sugar cane (sugar providing an estimated 23.6% of the value of total domestic exports in 1998) and rice (13.3%). The sugar industry alone accounted for an estimated 10.4% of GDP in 1998, and, it was estimated, employed about one-half of the agricultural labour force in 1988. Vegetables and fruit are cultivated for the local market, and livestock-rearing is being developed. Fishing (particularly for shrimp) is also important, and accounted for an estimated 6.6% of GDP in 1998. Agricultural production increased at an average annual rate of 8.4% during 1990–98. Agricultural GDP increased, in real terms, by 4.0% in 1997, but declined by an estimated 5.1% in 1998.

Timber resources in Guyana are extensive and underdeveloped. According to FAO estimates, some 77% of the country's total land area consisted of forest and woodland in 1994. In 1998 timber shipments provided only an estimated 2.4% of total domestic exports. Although foreign investment in Guyana's largely undeveloped interior continues to be encouraged by the Government, there is much popular concern at the extent of the exploitation of the rainforest. Timber production, which increased rapidly in the early and mid-1990s, declined by an estimated 21.8% in 1998.

Industry (including mining, manufacturing and construction) provided an estimated 32.5% of GDP in 1998, according to preliminary figures, and engaged 24.0% of the employed labour force at the time of the 1980 census. Industrial GDP declined at an average annual rate of 7.8% in 1990–98. Industrial GDP increased, in real terms, by 9.6% in 1997, but declined by an estimated 1.0% in 1998.

Mining contributed an estimated 16.0% of GDP in 1998, and employed 4.8% of the total working population in 1980. Bauxite, which is used for the manufacture of aluminium, is one of Guyana's most valuable exports, and accounted for an estimated 14.3% of total domestic exports in 1998. The registered production of gold (accounting for an estimated 22.7% of domestic exports in 1998) has increased considerably since 1986. There are also significant diamond resources and some petroleum reserves. The GDP of the mining sector was estimated to have increased by an average of 12.0% per year in 1991–94, before declining in 1995 by 11.4%, owing to the temporary closure of Omai Gold Mines Ltd. The sector's GDP increased, in real terms, by 15.2% in 1996, by 15.0% in 1997 and by an estimated 2.7% in 1998.

Manufacturing accounted for an estimated 10.9% of GDP in 1998, and, according to the 1980 census, employed 14.4% of the total working population. The main activities are the processing of bauxite, sugar, rice and timber. Manufacturing GDP increased at an average annual rate of 5.7% in 1990–98. Manufacturing GDP increased by 2.4% in 1997, but decreased by an estimated 8.9% in 1998.

Energy requirements are almost entirely met by imported hydrocarbon fuels. In 1998, according to preliminary figures, fuels and lubricants constituted 12.0% of the total value of imports (mainly from Venezuela and Trinidad and Tobago).

The services sector contributed an estimated 32.8% of GDP in 1998, and engaged 43.2% of the employed labour force in 1980. The GDP of the services sector increased by an average of 3.4% per year in 1990–98. Services GDP increased, in real terms, by 5.3% in 1997 and by an estimated 0.7% in 1998.

In 1995 Guyana recorded a visible trade deficit of US $40.8m. and a deficit of US $134.8m. on the current account of the balance of payments. In 1983 the principal source of imports was Trinidad and Tobago (30.0%), mainly on account of petroleum imports, and Venezuela also became an important trading partner during the 1980s. The USA and the United Kingdom are other important suppliers of imports. The United Kingdom is the principal market for exports (35.9% of total exports in 1989); the USA, Canada and Japan are also significant recipients. The principal exports are gold, sugar and bauxite, and the principal imports are fuels and lubricants and consumer goods.

In 1997 the overall budget deficit was $ G6,611m. (equivalent to 6.2% of GDP). By the end of 1997 Guyana's external debt totalled US $1,611m., of which US $1,345m. was long-term public debt. The cost of debt-servicing in 1997 was equivalent to 17.6% of the value of exports of goods and services. The average annual rate of inflation in 1995–98 was 5.1%. Urban consumer prices increased by 3.6% in 1997 and by 4.6% in 1998. An estimated 13.5% of the labour force were unemployed in 1991.

Guyana is a founder member of CARICOM (see p. 136). It is also a member of the UN Economic Commission for Latin America and the Caribbean (ECLAC, see p. 29) and of the International Sugar Organization (see p. 288).

In 1988, in response to serious economic decline, the Government introduced an extensive recovery programme of adjustment measures and structural reforms, directing policy away from state control towards a market-orientated economy. Funds made available under a three-year Enhanced Structural Adjustment Facility (ESAF), approved by the IMF in 1990, contributed to the considerable success of this recovery programme, and in 1994 the IMF approved a further three-year ESAF to support the Government's economic programme, while in 1996 negotiations with the 'Paris Club' of creditor nations and Trinidad and Tobago resulted in the cancellation of 67% of Guyana's bilateral debt with five creditor nations (a total reduction of US $395m.). In 1998, however, Guyana was severely affected by a substantial period of drought, resulting from aberrant climatic conditions (associated with the periodic warming of the tropical Pacific Ocean, known as El Niño), which undermined the production of export crops, thus diminishing foreign exchange earnings and exacerbating the economic difficulties arising from a decline in world gold prices. As a consequence, real GDP in 1998 declined by 1.5%, while the rate of inflation in that year increased to 4.6%. In late July 1998 the Government announced that it had secured a new three-year ESAF with the IMF, and in May 1999 the IMF and the World Bank declared that Guyana had become eligible for some US $410m. in nominal debt-service relief under the Initiative for Highly Indebted Poor Countries (HIPC Initiative). It was hoped that a reduction in the external debt burden would permit increased budgetary spending on education and social welfare. However, following industrial action by public-sector workers in mid-1999 (see Recent History), the Government was obliged to grant salary increases of 31.6%, thereby reducing the funds available for development expenditure. In an attempt to stimulate development, the Jagdeo administration has sought to attract foreign investment in Guyana and to restore investor confidence, damaged by the political and social unrest of the late 1990s.

## Social Welfare

Health services are provided by the Government, partly through the National Insurance Scheme, by non-governmental organizations, by the private sector, and by state-owned companies for their work force. The 1994 version of the National Health Plan identified as a priority the control of malaria, acute respiratory infections and sexually transmitted diseases, while the National Development Strategy of 1997 emphasized health promotion and improved access to health services, in particular for geographically isolated Amerindian communities. In 1998, according to IMF estimates, there was one physician per 2,326 inhabitants and one hospital bed per 236 inhabitants. In 1997, as well as the Georgetown Public Hospital, the Government operated three specialist hospitals, four regional hospitals, 18 district hospitals, 39 health posts and 194 health centres. In addition, there were six private hospitals and five company hospitals. In 1996 the Government spent D$2.88m. on health, equivalent to 6.3% of the national budget.

## Education

Education is officially compulsory, and is provided free of charge, for eight years between six and 14 years of age. Primary education begins at six years of age and lasts for at least six years. Secondary education, beginning at 12 years of age, lasts for up to five years, comprising a first cycle of three years and a second cycle of two years. Enrolment at all primary schools in 1995 was equivalent to 87% of the school-age population. Gross secondary enrolment in that year was equivalent to an estimated 75% of children in the relevant age-group (boys 73%; girls 78%). There are also 14 technical, vocational, special and higher educational institutions. These include the University of Guyana in Georgetown and a teacher training college. In 1995, according to estimates by UNESCO, the average rate of adult illiteracy was only 1.9% (males 1.4%; females 2.5%), one of the lowest in the Western hemisphere. Expenditure on education by the central Government in 1996 was estimated at $ G4,590m., and represented 10.0% of total government expenditure in that year.

### Public Holidays

**2000:** 1 January (New Year's Day), 8 January* (Id al-Fitr, end of Ramadan†), 23 February (Mashramani, Republic Day), 16 March* (Id al-Adha, feast of the Sacrifice), 21 April (Good Friday), 24 April (Easter Monday), 1 May (Labour Day), 5 May (Indian Heritage Day), 15 June* (Yum an-Nabi, birth of the Prophet), 26 June (Caribbean Day), 7 August (Freedom Day), 25–26 December (Christmas), 28 December* (Id al-Fitr, end of Ramadan†).

**2001:** 1 January (New Year's Day), 23 February (Mashramani, Republic Day), 6 March* (Id al-Adha, feast of the Sacrifice), 13 April (Good Friday), 16 April (Easter Monday), 1 May (Labour Day), 5 May (Indian Heritage Day), 4 June* (Yum an-Nabi, birth of the Prophet), 25 June (Caribbean Day), 6 August (Freedom Day), 17 December* (Id al-Fitr, end of Ramadan), 25–26 December (Christmas).

* These holidays are dependent on the Islamic lunar calendar and may vary by one or two days from the dates given.

† This festival will occur twice (in the Islamic years AH 1420 and 1421) within the same Gregorian year.

In addition, the Hindu festivals of Holi Phagwah (usually in March) and Divali (October or November) are celebrated. These festivals are dependent on sightings of the moon and their precise date is not known until two months before they take place.

### Weights and Measures

The metric system has been introduced.

# Statistical Survey

Source (unless otherwise stated): Bank of Guyana, 1 Church St and Ave of the Republic, POB 1003, Georgetown; tel. (2) 63261; fax (2) 72965.

## AREA AND POPULATION

**Area:** 214,969 sq km (83,000 sq miles).

**Population:** 758,619 (males 375,481, females 382,778) at census of 12 May 1980; 773,400 at mid-1998 (official estimate).

**Density** (mid-1998): 3.6 per sq km.

**Ethnic Groups** (1980 census): 'East' Indians 389,760, Africans 231,330, Portuguese 2,975, Chinese 1,842, Amerindians 39,867, Mixed 83,763, Others 9,082; Total 758,619.

**Capital:** Georgetown, population 72,049 (metropolitan area 187,056) at mid-1976 (estimate).

**Births and Deaths:** Birth rate 29.9 per 1,000 in 1980–85, 26.5 per 1,000 in 1985–90, 25.2 per 1,000 in 1990–95; Crude death rate 8.8 per 1,000 in 1980–85, 8.2 per 1,000 in 1985–90, 8.0 per 1,000 in 1990–95. Source: UN, *World Population Prospects: The 1998 Revision*.

**Expectation of Life** (UN estimates, years at birth, 1990–95): 62.9 (males 59.8; females 66.4). Source: UN, *World Population Prospects: The 1998 Revision*.

**Economically Active Population** (persons between 15 and 65 years of age, 1980 census): Agriculture, forestry and fishing 48,603; Mining and quarrying 9,389; Manufacturing 27,939; Electricity, gas and water 2,772; Construction 6,574; Trade, restaurants and hotels 14,690; Transport, storage and communications 9,160; Financing, insurance, real estate and business services 2,878; Community, social and personal services 57,416; Activities not adequately defined 15,260; Total employed 194,681 (males 153,645; females 41,036); Unemployed 44,650 (males 26,439, females 18,211); Total labour force 239,331 (males 180,084, females 59,247). **Mid-1998** (estimates): Agriculture, etc. 68,000; Total labour force 364,000 (Source: FAO, *Production Yearbook)*.

## AGRICULTURE, ETC.

**Principal Crops** ('000 metric tons, 1998): Rice (paddy) 532 (unofficial figure); Maize 3; Roots and tubers 42; Coconuts 56; Sugar cane 2,600 (unofficial figure) Pulses 2 (FAO estimate); Vegetables 9; Oranges 3; Bananas 11; Plantains 14 (FAO estimate); Other fruit 12. Source: FAO, *Production Yearbook*.

**Livestock** (FAO estimates, '000 head, year ending September 1998): Cattle 220; Pigs 20; Sheep 130; Goats 79; Chickens 12,000. Source: FAO, *Production Yearbook*.

**Livestock Products** (FAO estimates, '000 metric tons, 1998): Beef and veal 3; Mutton and lamb 1; Pig meat 1; Poultry meat 11; Cows' milk 13; Hen eggs 7. Source: FAO, *Production Yearbook*.

**Forestry** ('000 cubic metres, 1997): Roundwood removals: Sawlogs, veneer logs and logs for sleepers 522, Pulpwood 2, Other industrial wood 17, Fuel wood 15, Total 556; Sawnwood production: Total 89. Source: FAO, *Yearbook of Forest Products*.

**Fishing** (metric tons, live weight): Total catch 47,900 (FAO estimate) in 1995; 48,585 in 1996; 57,209 in 1997.
Source: FAO, *Yearbook of Fishery Statistics*.

## MINING

**Production** (preliminary figures, 1996): Bauxite 2,475,000 metric tons; Gold 312,000 troy oz; Diamonds 46,700 metric carats. Source: IMF, *Guyana: Statistical Appendix* (February 1998).

## INDUSTRY

**Selected Products** (preliminary figures, 1996): Raw sugar 257,000 metric tons; Rum 237,000 hectolitres; Beer 112,000 hectolitres; Cigarettes 400.2m.; Electric energy 328m. kWh. Sources: UN, *Industrial Commodity Statistics Yearbook*; IMF, *Guyana: Statistical Appendix* (February 1998).

## FINANCE

**Currency and Exchange Rates:** 100 cents = 1 Guyana dollar ($ G). *Sterling, US Dollar and Euro Equivalents* (30 September 1999): £1 sterling = $ G295.96; US $1 = $ G179.75; €1 = $G191.70; $ G1,000 = £3.379 = US $5.563 = €5.216. *Average Exchange Rate:* ($ G per US $): 140.4 in 1996; 142.4 in 1997; 150.5 in 1998.

**Budget** (preliminary figures, $ G million, 1998): *Revenue:* Tax revenue 31,075 (Income tax 11,854, Consumption tax 11,445, Taxes on international trade 4,481, Sugar levy 2,000); Other current revenue 1,954; Total 33,028. *Expenditure:* Current expenditure 28,177 (Personnel emoluments 9,124, Other goods and services 6,253, Interest 8,677, Transfers 4,123); Capital expenditure 13,656; Total 41,833. Source: IMF, *Guyana: Recent Economic Developments* (June 1999).

**International Reserves** (US $ million at 31 December 1998): IMF special drawing rights 0.24, Foreign exchange 276.36; Total 276.6. Source: IMF, *International Financial Statistics*.

**Money Supply** ($ G million at 31 December 1998): Currency outside banks 11,334, Demand deposits at commercial banks 7,639; Total money (including also private-sector deposits at the Bank of Guyana) 18,980. Source: IMF, *International Financial Statistics*.

**Cost of Living** (Urban Consumer Price Index; base: 1995 = 100): 107.1 in 1996; 110.9 in 1997; 116.0 in 1998. Source: IMF, *International Financial Statistics*.

**Expenditure on the Gross Domestic Product** (estimates, $ G million at current prices, 1998): Government final consumption expenditure 19,114; Private final consumption expenditure 70,843; Gross fixed capital formation 31,144; *Total domestic expenditure* 121,101; Exports of goods and services 103,920; *Less* Imports of goods and services, 116,557; *GDP in purchasers' values* 108,465. Source: IMF, *Guyana: Recent Economic Developments* (June 1999).

**Gross Domestic Product by Economic Activity** (estimates, $ G million at current factor cost, 1998): Agriculture (incl. forestry and fishing) 31,949; Mining and quarrying 14,752; Manufacturing (incl. power) 10,220; Construction 4,926; Distribution 4,202; Transport and communication 6,168; Rented dwellings 3,629; Financial services 3,087; Other services 1,407; Government 11,662; GDP at factor cost 92,002; Indirect taxes, *less* subsidies 16,464; GDP at market prices 108,465. Source: IMF, *Guyana: Recent Economic Developments* (June 1999).

**Balance of Payments** (US $ million, 1995): Exports of goods f.o.b. 495.7; Imports of goods f.o.b. –536.5; *Trade balance* –40.8; Exports of services 133.5; Imports of services –171.8; *Balance on goods and services* –79.2; Other income received 12.2; Other income paid –129.9; *Balance on goods, services and income* –196.8; Current transfers received 67.4; Current transfers paid –5.3; *Current balance* –134.8; Capital account (net) 9.5; Direct investment from abroad 74.4; Portfolio investment liabilities 3.2; Other investment assets –8.9; Other investment liabilities 2.3; Net errors and omissions 11.2; *Overall balance* –43.0. Source; IMF, *International Financial Statistics*.

### EXTERNAL TRADE

**Principal Commodities** (preliminary figures, US $ million, 1998): *Imports c.i.f.*: Capital goods 162.6; Consumer goods 193.7; Fuel and lubricants 72.0; Other intermediate goods 172.4; Total (incl. others) 601.2. *Exports f.o.b.*: Bauxite 78; Sugar 129; Rice 73; Gold 124, Total (incl. others) 547 (excl. re-exports 22). Source: IMF, *Guyana: Recent Economic Developments* (June 1999).

**Principal Trading Partners** (US $ million, 1983): *Imports:* Brazil 5.8; Canada 6.6; German Democratic Republic 1.6; Germany, Federal Republic 8.0; Jamaica 5.1; Japan 3.9; Netherlands 9.3; Trinidad and Tobago 73.8; United Kingdom 27.9; USA 53.4; Total (incl. others) 246.1. *Exports:* Barbados 5.2; Canada 24.0; France 18.7; German Democratic Republic 14.9; Germany, Federal Republic 4.9; Italy 6.0; Jamaica 5.3; Japan 30.2; Mexico 4.2; Spain 4.2; Trinidad and Tobago 48.8; United Kingdom 103.3; USA 65.4; Venezuela 18.7; Total (incl. others) 375.8. Source: UN, *International Trade Statistics Yearbook.*

**1989** ($ G million): *Exports:* Canada 1,312.4; Japan 530.9; United Kingdom 3,659.9; USA 1,900.9; Total (incl. others) 10,207.7.

### TRANSPORT

**Road Traffic** ('000 vehicles in use, 1993): Passenger cars 24.0; Commercial vehicles 9.0. Source: UN, *Statistical Yearbook.*

**Shipping** (international sea-borne freight traffic, estimates in '000 metric tons, 1990): Goods loaded 1,730; Goods unloaded 673. Source: UN, *Monthly Bulletin of Statistics. Merchant Fleet* (at 31 December 1998): Vessels 62; Displacement 16,260 grt. (Source: Lloyd's Register of Shipping, *World Fleet Statistics*).

**Civil Aviation** (traffic on scheduled services, 1995): Kilometres flown (million) 2; passengers carried ('000) 121; passenger-km (million) 235; total ton-km (million) 25. Source: UN, *Statistical Yearbook.*

### TOURISM

**Visitor Arrivals** ('000): 105.5 in 1995; 91.9 in 1996; 78.9 in 1997.

**Tourist Receipts** (US $ million): 47 in 1994; 47 in 1995; 38 in 1996.

Source: mainly World Tourism Organization, *Yearbook of Tourism Statistics.*

### COMMUNICATIONS MEDIA

**Radio Receivers** (1996): 415,000 in use*.

**Television Receivers** (1996): 45,000 in use*.

**Telephones** (1995): 45,000 main lines in use†.

**Telefax Stations** (1990): 195 in use.

**Mobile Cellular Telephones** (1995): 1,243 subscribers.

**Daily Newspapers** (1996): 2; estimated circulation 42,000*.

**Non-daily Newspapers** (1988): 6 (estimate); estimated circulation 84,000*.

**Book Production** (school textbooks, 1994): 32 titles.

* Source: UNESCO, *Statistical Yearbook.*

† Source: UN, *Statistical Yearbook.*

### EDUCATION

**Pre-primary** (1997/98): Institutions 305; Teachers 1,976; Students 33,366.

**Primary** (1997/98): Institutions 418; Teachers 3,710; Students 100,998.

**General Secondary** (1997/98): Institutions 416; Teachers 3,028; Students 61,253.

**Special Education** (1997/98): Institutions 6; Teachers 28; Students 585.

**Technical and Vocational** (1997/98): Institutions 6; Teachers 168; Students 3,307.

**Teacher Training** (1997/98): Institutions 1; Teachers 70; Students 1,235.

**University** (1997/98): Institutions 1; Teachers 383; Students 4,671.

**Private Education** (1997/98): Institutions 5; Teachers 138; Students 1,590.

Source: Ministry of Education, Georgetown.

# Directory

## The Constitution

Guyana became a republic, within the Commonwealth, on 23 February 1970. A new Constitution was promulgated on 6 October 1980. Its main provisions are summarized below:

The Constitution declares the Co-operative Republic of Guyana to be an indivisible, secular, democratic sovereign state in the course of transition from capitalism to socialism. The bases of the political, economic and social system are political and economic independence, involvement of citizens and socio-economic groups, such as co-operatives and trade unions, in the decision-making processes of the State and in management, social ownership of the means of production, national economic planning and co-operativism as the principle of socialist transformation. Personal property, inheritance, the right to work, with equal pay for men and women engaged in equal work, free medical attention, free education and social benefits for old age and disability are guaranteed. Individual political rights are subject to the principles of national sovereignty and democracy, and freedom of expression to the State's duty to ensure fairness and balance in the dissemination of information to the public. Relations with other countries are guided by respect for human rights, territorial integrity and non-intervention.

### THE PRESIDENT

The President is the supreme executive authority, Head of State and Commander-in-Chief of the armed forces, elected for a term of office, usually of five years' duration, with no limit on re-election. The successful presidential candidate is the nominee of the party with the largest number of votes in the legislative elections. The President may prorogue or dissolve the National Assembly (in the case of dissolution, fresh elections must be held immediately) and has discretionary powers to postpone elections for up to one year at a time for up to five years. The President may be removed from office on medical grounds, or for violation of the Constitution (with a two-thirds' majority vote of the Assembly), or for gross misconduct (with a three-quarters' majority vote of the Assembly if allegations are upheld by a tribunal).

The President appoints a First Vice-President and Prime Minister who must be an elected member of the National Assembly, and a Cabinet of Ministers, which may include non-elected members and is collectively responsible to the legislature. The President also appoints a Minority Leader, who is the elected member of the Assembly deemed by the President most able to command the support of the opposition.

### THE LEGISLATURE

The legislative body is a unicameral National Assembly of 65 members; 53 members are elected by universal adult suffrage in a system of proportional representation, 10 members are elected by the 10 Regional Democratic Councils and two members are elected by the National Congress of Local Democratic Organs. The Assembly passes bills, which are then presented to the President, and may pass constitutional amendments.

### LOCAL GOVERNMENT

Guyana is divided into 10 Regions, each having a Regional Democratic Council elected for a term of up to five years and four months, although it may be prematurely dissolved by the President. Local councillors elect from among themselves deputies to the National Congress of Democratic Organs. This Congress and the National Assembly together form the Supreme Congress of the People of Guyana, a deliberative body which may be summoned, dissolved or prorogued by the President and is automatically dissolved along with the National Assembly.

### OTHER PROVISIONS

Impartial commissions exist for the judiciary, the public service and the police service. An Ombudsman is appointed, after consultation between the President and the Minority Leader, to hold office for four years.

## The Government

### HEAD OF STATE

**President:** BHARRAT JAGDEO (sworn in 11 August 1999).

### CABINET

(February 2000)

**President:** BHARRAT JAGDEO.

**Prime Minister and Minister of Public Works:** SAMUEL A. HINDS.

**Head of the Presidential Secretariat, Secretary to the Cabinet:** Dr ROGER LUNCHEON.

**Minister of Home Affairs:** RONALD GAJRAJ.

**Attorney-General and Minister of Legal Affairs:** CHARLES RAMSON.

**Minister in the Office of the President with responsibility for Finance:** SAISNARINE KOWLESSAR.

**Minister of Foreign Affairs:** CLEMENT ROHEE.

**Minister of Information:** MOSES NAGAMOOTOO.

**Minister of Agriculture and Parliamentary Affairs:** REEPU DAMAN PERSAUD.

**Minister of Public Service:** GEORGE FUNG-ON.

**Minister of Education:** Dr DALE BISNAUTH.

**Minister of Amerindian Affairs:** VIBERT DE SOUZA.

**Adviser to the President on Science, Technology and Environment:** NAVIN CHANDARPAL.

**Minister of Local Government:** HARRIPERSAUD NOKTA.

**Minister in the Ministry of Local Government:** CLINTON COLLYMORE.

**Political Adviser to the President:** KELLAWAN LALL.

**Minister of Trade, Industry and Tourism:** GEOFFREY DA SILVA.

**Minister of Transport and Hydraulics:** ANTHONY XAVIER.

**Minister of Labour and Health:** Dr HENRY JEFFREY.

**Minister of Human Services and Social Security:** INDRANIE CHANDARPAL.

**Minister of Culture, Youth and Sports:** GAIL TEIXEIRA.

**Minister of Fisheries, Crops and Livestock:** SATYADEOW SAWH.

**Minister of Housing and Water:** SHAIK BAKSH.

**MINISTRIES**

**Office of the President:** New Garden St and South Rd, Georgetown; tel. (2) 51330; fax (2) 63395.

**Office of the Prime Minister:** Wights Lane, Georgetown; tel. (2) 73101; fax (2) 67563.

**Office of Amerindian Affairs:** see Ministry of Public Works and Communications.

**Ministry of Agriculture:** POB 1001, Regent and Vlissingen Rds, Georgetown; tel. (2) 61565; fax (2) 73638; e-mail guyagri@hotmail.com; internet www.sdnp.org.gy/minagri.

**Ministry of Culture, Youth and Sports:** 71 Main St, North Cummingsburg; tel. (2) 60142; fax (2) 65067.

**Ministry of Education:** 26 Brickdam, Stabroek, POB 1014, Georgetown; tel. (2) 63094; fax (2) 58511; internet www.sdnp.org.gy/minedu.

**Ministry of Finance:** Main and Urquhart Sts, Georgetown; tel. (2) 71114; fax (2) 61284.

**Ministry of Fisheries, Crops and Livestock:** see Ministry of Agriculture.

**Ministry of Foreign Affairs:** Takuba Lodge, 254 South Rd and New Garden St, Georgetown; tel. (2) 56467; fax (2) 59192; e-mail minfor@sdnp.org.gy; internet www.sdnp.org.gy/minfor.

**Ministry of Home Affairs:** 6 Brickdam, Stabroek, Georgetown; tel. (2) 57270; fax (2) 62740.

**Ministry of Housing and Water:** Homestretch Ave, Durban Park; tel. (2) 54991.

**Ministry of Human Services and Social Security:** 1 Water St, Stabroek; tel. (2) 68996; fax (2) 71308.

**Ministry of Information:** Area B, Homestretch Ave; tel. (2) 68849; fax (2) 68853.

**Ministry of Labour and Health:** Brickdam, Stabroek, Georgetown; tel. (2) 61560; fax (2) 56958; internet www.sdnp.org.gy/moh.

**Ministry of Legal Affairs and Office of Attorney-General:** 95 Carmichael St, Georgetown; tel. (2) 53607; fax (2) 50732.

**Ministry of Local Government:** De Winkle Bldgs, Fort St, Kingston, Georgetown; tel. (2) 58621.

**Ministry of Public Works and Communications:** Wight's Lane, Kingston, Georgetown; tel. (2) 72365; fax (2) 56954.

**Ministry of Trade, Tourism and Industry:** 229 South Rd, Lacytown, Georgetown; tel. (2) 62505; fax (2) 54310; e-mail mintrade@sdnp.org.gy; internet www.sdnp.org.gy/mtti.

**Ministry of Transport and Hydraulics:** Georgetown.

# President and Legislature

**NATIONAL ASSEMBLY**

**Speaker:** Dr DEREK JAGAN.

**Election, 15 December 1997**

| Party | No. of Seats: Regional | National | Total |
|---|---|---|---|
| People's Progressive Party (PPP)–CIVIC | 7 | 29 | 36 |
| People's National Congress (PNC) | 4 | 22 | 26 |
| Alliance For Guyana (AFG) | – | 1 | 1 |
| The United Force (TUF) | – | 1 | 1 |
| Guyana Democratic Party (GDP) | 1 | – | 1 |
| **Total** | 12 | 53 | 65 |

Under Guyana's system of proportional representation, the nominated candidate of the party receiving the most number of votes was elected to the presidency. In the 1997 elections the PPP (candidate, JANET JAGAN), which was in alliance with the CIVIC movement, won 48% of the votes cast, compared with 35% for the PNC (HUGH DESMOND HOYTE).

# Political Organizations

**Alliance For Guyana (AFG):** Georgetown; f. 1997; electoral alliance comprising following two parties:

**Guyana Labour Party (GLP):** Georgetown; f. 1992 by members of Guyanese Action for Reform and Democracy (see below).

**Working People's Alliance (WPA):** Walter Rodney House, Lot 80, Croal St, Stabroek, Georgetown; tel. (2) 36624; internet saxakali.com/wpa; originally popular pressure group, became political party 1979; independent Marxist; Collective Leadership: EUSI KWAYANA, Dr CLIVE THOMAS, Dr RUPERT ROOPNARINE, WAZIR MOHAMED.

**CIVIC:** New Garden St, Georgetown; social/political movement of businessmen and professionals; allied to PPP; Leader SAMUEL ARCHIBALD ANTHONY HINDS.

**Guyana Democratic Party (GDP):** Georgetown; f. 1996; Leaders ASGAR ALLY, NANDA K. GOPAUL.

**Guyana People's Party (GPP):** Georgetown; f. 1996; Leader MAX MOHAMED.

**Guyana Republican Party (GRP):** Paprika East Bank, Essequibo; f. 1985; right-wing; Leader LESLIE PRINCE (resident in the USA).

**National Republican Party (NRP):** Georgetown; f. 1990 after a split with URP; right-wing; Leader ROBERT GANGADEEN.

**Patriotic Coalition for Democracy (PCD):** Georgetown; f. 1986 by five opposition parties; the PCD campaigns for an end to alleged electoral malpractices; principal offices, including the chair of the collective leadership, rotate among the parties; now comprises the following three parties:

**Democratic Labour Movement (DLM):** 34 Robb and King Sts, 4th Floor, Lacytown, POB 10930, Georgetown; f. 1983; democratic-nationalist; Pres. PAUL NEHRU TENNASSEE.

**People's Democratic Movement (PDM):** Stabroek House, 10 Croal St, Georgetown; tel. (2) 64707; fax (2) 63002; f. 1973; centrist; Leader LLEWELLYN JOHN.

**People's Progressive Party (PPP):** Freedom House, 41 Robb St, Lacytown, Georgetown; tel. (2) 72095; fax (2) 72096; e-mail ppp@guyana.net.gy; internet www.pppcivic.org; f. 1950; Marxist-Leninist; Leader JANET JAGAN; Gen. Sec. DONALD RAMOTAR.

**People's National Congress (PNC):** Congress Place, Sophia, POB 10330, Georgetown; tel. (2) 57852; fax 56055; e-mail peoples_national_congress@yahoo.com; internet www.guyana-pnc.org; f. 1955 after a split with the PPP; Leader HUGH DESMOND HOYTE; Gen. Sec. OSCAR CLARKE.

**The United Force (TUF):** 96 Robb St, Bourda, Georgetown; tel. (2) 62596; f. 1960; right-wing; advocates rapid industrialization through govt partnership and private capital; Leader MANZOOR NADIR.

**United Republican Party (URP):** Georgetown; f. 1985; right-wing; advocates federal govt; Leader Dr LESLIE RAMSAMMY.

**United Workers' Party (UWP):** Georgetown; f. 1991; Leader WINSTON PAYNE.

# Diplomatic Representation

**EMBASSIES AND HIGH COMMISSIONS IN GUYANA**

**Brazil:** 308 Church St, Queenstown, POB 10489, Georgetown; tel. (2) 57970; fax (2) 69063; e-mail bragetown@solutions2000.net; Ambassador: CLAUDIO LYRA.

**Canada:** High and Young Sts, POB 10880, Georgetown; tel. (2) 72081; fax (2) 58380; e-mail grgtn@dfait-maecl.gc.ca; High Commissioner: JACQUES CRÊTE.

**China, People's Republic:** 108 Duke St, Kingston, Georgetown; tel. (2) 71651; tel. (2) 2251; Ambassador: WANG FUYUAN.

**Colombia:** 306 Church and Peter Rose Sts, Queenstown, POB 10185, Georgetown; tel. (2) 71410; fax (2) 58198; e-mail embcolguy@solutions2000.net; Ambassador: Dr LUIS GUILLERMO MARTÍNEZ FERNÁNDEZ.

**Cuba:** 46 High St, Kingston, Georgetown; tel. (2) 66732; Ambassador: RICARDO GARCIA DIAZ.

**India:** Bank of Baroda Bldg, 10 Ave of the Republic, POB 101148, Georgetown; tel. (2) 63996; fax 57012; High Commissioner: Dr PRAKASH V. JOSHI.

**Korea, Democratic People's Republic:** 88 Premniranjan Place, Georgetown; tel. (2) 60266; Ambassador: CHON HYUN CHAN.

**Russia:** 3 Public Rd, Kitty, Georgetown; tel. (2) 69773; fax (2) 72975; Ambassador: TAHIR BYASHIMOVICH DURDIYEV.

**Suriname:** 304 Church St, POB 10508, Georgetown; tel. (2) 67844; Ambassador: HUMPHREY ABDUL RAFIK HASRAT.

**United Kingdom:** 44 Main St, POB 10849, Georgetown; tel. (2) 65881; fax (2) 53555; High Commissioner: EDWARD GLOVER.

**USA:** Duke and Young Sts, Georgetown; tel. (2) 54900; fax (2) 58497; Ambassador: JAMES F. MACK.

**Venezuela:** 296 Thomas St, Georgetown; tel. (2) 61543; Ambassador: Dr HECTOR AZOCAR.

# Judicial System

The Judicature of Guyana comprises the Supreme Court of Judicature, which consists of the Court of Appeal and the High Court (both of which are superior courts of record), and a number of Courts of Summary Jurisdiction.

The Court of Appeal, which came into operation in 1966, consists of the Chancellor as President, the Chief Justice, and such number of Justices of Appeal as may be prescribed by the National Assembly.

The High Court of the Supreme Court consists of the Chief Justice as President of the Court and Puisne Judges. Its jurisdiction is both original and appellate. It has criminal jurisdiction in matters brought before it on indictment. A person convicted by the Court has a right of appeal to the Guyana Court of Appeal. The High Court of the Supreme Court has unlimited jurisdiction in civil matters and exclusive jurisdiction in probate, divorce and admiralty and certain other matters. Under certain circumstances, appeal in civil matters lies either to the Full Court of the High Court of the Supreme Court, which is composed of not less than two judges, or to the Guyana Court of Appeal.

A magistrate has jurisdiction to determine claims where the amount involved does not exceed a certain sum of money, specified by law. Appeal lies to the Full Court.

**Chancellor of Justice:** CECIL KENNARD.

**Chief Justice:** DESIRÉE BERNARD.

**Attorney-General:** CHARLES RAMSON.

# Religion

## CHRISTIANITY

**Guyana Council of Churches:** 71 Murray St, Georgetown; tel. (2) 66610; f. 1967 by merger of the Christian Social Council (f. 1937) and the Evangelical Council (f. 1960); 15 mem. churches, 1 assoc. mem.; Chair. Rt Rev. RANDOLPH OSWALD GEORGE (Anglican Bishop of Guyana); Sec. MICHAEL MCCORMACK.

### The Anglican Communion

Anglicans in Guyana are adherents of the Church in the Province of the West Indies, comprising eight dioceses. The Archbishop of the Province is the Bishop of the North Eastern Caribbean and Aruba, resident in St John's, Antigua. The diocese of Guyana also includes French Guiana and Suriname. In 1986 the estimated membership in the country was 125,000.

**Bishop of Guyana:** Rt Rev. RANDOLPH OSWALD GEORGE, Austin House, Georgetown; tel. (2) 64183; fax (2) 63353.

### The Baptist Church

**The Baptist Convention of Guyana:** POB 10149, Georgetown; tel. (2) 60428; Chair. Rev. ALFRED JULIEN.

### The Lutheran Church

**The Lutheran Church in Guyana:** 28–29 North and Alexander Sts, Lacytown, Georgetown; tel. (2) 64227; 14,147 mems; Pres. JAMES LOCHAN.

### The Roman Catholic Church

Guyana comprises the single diocese of Georgetown, suffragan to the archdiocese of Port of Spain, Trinidad and Tobago. At 31 December 1997 adherents of the Roman Catholic Church comprised about 10.9% of the total population. The Bishop participates in the Antilles Episcopal Conference Secretariat, currently based in Port of Spain, Trinidad.

**Bishop of Georgetown:** G. BENEDICT SINGH, Bishop's House, 27 Brickdam, POB 10720, Stabroek, Georgetown; tel. (2) 64469; fax (2) 58519; e-mail rcbishop@solutions2000.net.

### Other Christian Churches

Other denominations active in Guyana include the African Methodist Episcopal Church, the African Methodist Episcopal Zion Church, the Church of God, the Church of the Nazarene, the Ethiopian Orthodox Church, the Guyana Baptist Mission, the Guyana Congregational Union, the Guyana Presbyterian Church, the Hallelujah Church, the Methodist Church in the Caribbean and the Americas, the Moravian Church and the Presbytery of Guyana.

## HINDUISM

**Hindu Religious Centre:** Maha Sabha, 162 Lamaha St, POB 10576, Georgetown; tel. (2) 57443; f. 1934; Hindus account for about one-third of the population; Pres. RAMRAJ JAGNANDAN; Gen. Sec. CHRISHNA PERSAUD.

## ISLAM

**The Central Islamic Organization of Guyana (CIOG):** M.Y.O. Bldg, Woolford Ave, Thomas Lands, POB 10245, Georgetown; tel. (2) 58654; fax (2) 57313; e-mail ciog@sdnp.org.gy; internet www.ali.on.ca/ciog; Pres. Alhaji FAZEEL M. FEROUZ: Gen. Sec. MUJTABA NASIR.

**Guyana United Sad'r Islamic Anjuman:** 157 Alexander St, Kitty, POB 10715, Georgetown; tel. (2) 69620; f. 1936; 120,000 mems; Pres. Haji A. H. RAHAMAN; Sec. YACOOB HUSSAIN.

# The Press

## DAILIES

**Guyana Chronicle:** 2A Lama Ave, Bel Air Park, POB 11, Georgetown; tel. (2) 63243; fax (2) 75208; e-mail khan@guyana.net.gy; internet chronicle.guyana.net.gy; f. 1881; govt-owned; also produces weekly *Sunday Chronicle* (tel. (2) 63243); Editor-in-Chief SHARIEF KHAN; circ. 23,000 (weekdays), 43,000 (Sundays).

**Stabroek News:** 46–47 Robb St, Lacytown, Georgetown; tel. (2) 57473; fax (2) 54637; e-mail stabroeknews@stabroeknews.com; internet www.stabroeknews.com; f. 1986; liberal independent; Editor-in-Chief DAVID DE CAIRES; circ. 24,000 (weekdays), 40,000 (Sundays).

## WEEKLIES AND PERIODICALS

**The Catholic Standard:** 293 Oronoque St, Queenstown, POB 10720, Georgetown; tel. (2) 61540; f. 1905; weekly; Editor COLIN SMITH; circ. 10,000.

**Diocesan Magazine:** 144 Almond and Oronoque Sts, Queenstown, Georgetown; quarterly.

**Guyana Business:** 156 Waterloo St, POB 10110, Georgetown; tel. (2) 56451; f. 1889; organ of the Georgetown Chamber of Commerce and Industry; quarterly; Editor C. D. KIRTON.

**Guynews:** Georgetown; monthly.

**Kaieteur News:** 24 Saffon St, Charlestown; tel. (2) 58452; fax (2) 58473; f. 1994; independent weekly; Editor W. HENRY SKERRETT; circ. 30,000.

**Labour Advocate:** Georgetown; weekly.

**Mirror:** Lot 8, Industrial Estate, Ruimveldt, Greater Georgetown; tel. (2) 62471; fax (2) 62472; owned by the New Guyana Co Ltd; Sundays and Wednesdays; Editor JANET JAGAN; circ. 25,000.

**New Nation:** Congress Place, Sophia, Georgetown; tel. (2) 67891; f. 1955; organ of the People's National Congress; weekly; Editor FRANCIS WILLIAMS; circ. 26,000.

**The Official Gazette of Guyana:** Guyana National Printers Ltd, Lot 1, Public Road, La Penitence; weekly; circ. 450.

**Ratoon:** Georgetown; monthly.

**Thunder:** Georgetown; f. 1950; organ of the People's Progressive Party; quarterly; Editor RALPH RAMKARRAN; circ. 5,000.

## NEWS AGENCY

**Guyana Information Services:** Office of the President, New Garden St and South Rd, Georgetown; tel. (2) 63389; fax (2) 64003; f. 1993; Dir MILTON DREPAUL.

#### Foreign Bureaux

**Inter Press Service** (Italy): Georgetown; tel. (2) 53213.

**United Press International (UPI)** (USA): Georgetown; tel. (2) 65153.

**Xinhua (New China) News Agency** (People's Republic of China): 52 Brickdam, Stabroek, Georgetown; tel. (2) 69965.

Associated Press (USA) and Informatsionnoye Telegrafnoye Agentstvo Rossii—Telegrafnoye Agentstvo Suverennykh Stran (ITAR—TASS) (Russia) are also represented.

### PRESS ASSOCIATION

**Guyana Press Association:** Georgetown; revived in 1990; Pres. ENRICO WOOLFORD.

## Publishers

**Guyana Free Press:** POB 10386, Georgetown; tel. 63239; fax 73465; e-mail guyrev@networksgy.com; books and learned journals.

**Guyana National Printers Ltd:** 1 Public Rd, La Penitence, POB 10256, Greater Georgetown; tel. (2) 53623; f. 1939; govt-owned printers and publishers; privatization pending in 2000; Gen. Man. NOVEAR DEFREITAS.

**Guyana Publications Inc.:** 46/47 Robb St, Lacytown, Georgetown; tel. (2) 57473; fax (2) 54637.

## Broadcasting and Communications

### TELECOMMUNICATIONS

**Caribbean Wireless Telecom (CWT):** Georgetown; f. 1999; intends to launch a mobile cellular telephone service by 2001; CEO EARL SINGH.

**Guyana Telephones and Telegraph Company (GT & T):** 79 Brickdam, POB 10628, Georgetown; tel. (2) 67840; fax (2) 62457; f. 1991; formerly state-owned Guyana Telecommunications Corpn; 80% ownership by Atlantic Tele-Network (USA); Gen. Man. ANAND PERSAUD.

### BROADCASTING

#### Radio

**Guyana Broadcasting Corporation (GBC):** Broadcasting House, 44 High St, POB 10760, Georgetown; tel. (2) 58734; fax (2) 58756; f. 1979; operates channels GBC 1 (Coastal Service) and GBC 2 (National Service); Gen. Man. M. FAZIL AZEEZ.

**Radio Roraima:** Georgetown.

**Voice of Guyana:** Georgetown.

#### Television

**Guyana Television:** 68 Hadfield St, Georgetown; tel. (2) 69231; f. 1993; fmrly Guyana Television Corporation; govt-owned; limited service; Dir A. BREWSTER.

Two private stations relay US satellite television programmes.

## Finance

(dep. = deposits; m. = million; brs = branches; amounts in Guyana dollars)

### BANKING

#### Central Bank

**Bank of Guyana:** 1 Church St and Ave of the Republic, POB 1003, Georgetown; tel. (2) 63250; fax (2) 72965; e-mail boglib@guyana.net.gy; internet www.bankofguyana.org.gy; f. 1965; cap. 1,000m., res 10,138m., dep. 86,717m. (Dec. 1998); central bank of issue; acts as regulatory authority for the banking sector; Gov. DOLLY S. SINGH; Dir LESLIE GLEN.

#### Commercial Banks

**Demerara Bank Ltd:** 230 Camp and South Sts, Georgetown; tel. (2) 50610; fax (2) 50601; e-mail banking@demerarabank.com; internet www.demerarabank.com; f. 1994; cap. 450m., res 52m., dep. 4,949m. (Sept. 1998); Chair. YESU PERSAUD; Man. AHMED M. KHAN.

**Guyana Bank for Trade and Industry Ltd:** 47–48 Water St, POB 10280, Georgetown; tel. (2) 68431; fax (2) 71612; e-mail gbti@solutions2000.net; f. 1987 to absorb the operations of Barclays Bank; cap. 800m., dep. 14,411m., total assets 19,310m. (1996); Pres. and CEO PAUL GEER; 5 brs.

**Guyana National Co-operative Bank:** 1 Lombard and Cornhill Sts, POB 10400, Georgetown; tel. (2) 57810; fax (2) 60231; f. 1970; merged with Guyana Co-operative Agricultural and Industrial Development Bank in 1995; state-owned; Gen. Man. ROSALIE A. ROBERTSON; 11 brs.

**National Bank of Industry and Commerce (NBIC):** 38–40 Water St, POB 10440, Georgetown; tel. (2) 64091; fax (2) 72921; 51% owned by Republic Bank, Trinidad and Tobago; Man. Dir CONRAD PLUMMER; 5 brs.

#### Foreign Banks

**Bank of Baroda** (India): 10 Regent St and Ave of the Republic, POB 10768, Georgetown; tel. (2) 69105; fax (2) 51691; f. 1908; Chief Man. DIPANKAR MUKERJEE.

**Bank of Nova Scotia** (Canada): Regent and Hincks Sts; Georgetown; tel. (2) 64031; fax (2) 59309; Man. J. F. I. COOPER; 2 brs.

**Citizens' Bank Ltd** (Jamaica): 201 Camp and Charlotte Sts, Lacytown, Georgetown; tel. (2) 61705; fax (2) 78251; internet citizens-carib.com/guyana.htm; f. 1994; Chair. DENNIS LALOR.

### INSURANCE

In mid-1999 there were six insurance companies licensed to operate in Guyana.

**Demerara Mutual Life Assurance Society Ltd:** Demerara Life Bldg, 61–62 Robb St and Ave of the Republic, POB 10409, Georgetown; tel. (2) 58991; fax (2) 58288; f. 1891; Chair. RICHARD B. FIELDS; Gen. Man. EAWAN E. DEVONISH.

**Guyana Co-operative Insurance Service:** 46 Main St, Georgetown; tel. (2) 59153; f. 1976; 67% share offered for private ownership in 1996; Chair. G. A. LEE; Gen. Man. PAT BENDER.

**Guyana and Trinidad Mutual Life Insurance Co Ltd:** Lots 27–29, Robb and Hincks Sts, Georgetown; tel. (2) 57910; fax (2) 59397; e-mail gtmgroup@guyana.net.org; f. 1925; Chair. HAROLD B. DAVIS; Man. Dir R. E. CHEONG; affiliated company: Guyana and Trinidad Mutual Fire Insurance Co Ltd.

**Hand-in-Hand Mutual Fire and Life Group:** 1–4 Ave of the Republic, POB 10188, Georgetown; tel. (2) 50462; fax (2) 57519; f. 1865; fire and life insurance; Chair. J. A. CHIN; Gen. Man. K. A. EVELYN.

#### Insurance Association

**Insurance Association of Guyana:** 54 Robb St, Bourda, POB 10741, Georgetown; tel. (2) 63514; f. 1968.

### STOCK EXCHANGE

In July 1989 the Government announced that it intended to establish a national securities exchange, with a view to becoming a member of the proposed regional stock exchange.

## Trade and Industry

### GOVERNMENT AGENCIES

**Guyana Agency for the Environment:** Georgetown; tel. (2) 57523; fax (2) 57524; f. 1988; formulates, implements and monitors policies on the environment; Dir Dr WALTER CHIN.

**Guyana Marketing Corporation:** 87 Robb and Alexander Sts, Georgetown; tel. (2) 68255; fax (2) 74114; Chair. CHANDRABALLI BISHESWAR; Gen. Man. ROXANNE GREENIDGE.

**Guyana Public Communications Agency:** Georgetown; tel. (2) 72025; f. 1989; Exec. Chair. KESTER ALVES.

### DEVELOPMENT ORGANIZATIONS

**Guyana Office for Investment (Go-Invest):** 237 Camp St, Cummingsburg, Georgetown: tel. (2) 56710; fax (2) 54310; internet www.sdnp.org.gy/goinvest; f. 1994; provision of investment promotion service for foreign and local cos; under control of the Office of the President; Dir. KHELLAWAN LALL.

**State Planning Commission:** 229 South St, Lacytown, Georgetown; tel. (2) 68093; fax (2) 72499; Chief Planning Officer CLYDE ROOPCHAND.

### CHAMBER OF COMMERCE

**Georgetown Chamber of Commerce and Industry:** 156 Waterloo St, Cummingsburg, POB 10110, Georgetown; tel. (2) 55846; fax (2) 63519; f. 1889; 122 mems; Pres. JOHN S. DEFREITAS; Chief Exec. G. C. FUNG-ON.

### INDUSTRIAL AND TRADE ASSOCIATIONS

**Bauxite Industry Development Company Ltd:** 71 Main St, Georgetown; tel. (2) 57780; fax (2) 67413; f. 1976; Chair. J. I. F. BLACKMAN.

**Guyana Rice Development Board:** 117 Cowan St, Georgetown; tel. (2) 58717; fax (2) 56486; e-mail grdb@gol.net.gy; f. 1994 to assume operations of Guyana Rice Export Board and Guyana Rice Grading Centre; Chair. and CEO CHARLES KENNARD.

**Livestock Development Co Ltd:** 58 High St, Georgetown; tel. (2) 61601.

### EMPLOYERS' ORGANIZATIONS

**Consultative Association of Guyanese Industry Ltd:** 157 Waterloo St, POB 10730, Georgetown; tel. (2) 64603; f. 1962; 193 mems, 3 mem. asscns, 159 assoc. mems; Chair. DAVID KING; Exec. Dir DAVID YANKANA.

**Forest Products Association of Guyana:** 157 Waterloo St, Georgetown; tel. (2) 69848; f. 1944; 47 mems; Pres. L. J. P. WILLEMS; Exec. Officer WARREN PHOENIX.

**Guyana Manufacturers' Association Ltd:** 62 Main St, Cummingsburg, Georgetown; tel. (2) 74295; fax (2) 70670; f. 1967; 190 members; Pres. KIM KISSOON; Exec. Sec. TREVOR SHARPLES.

**Guyana Rice Producers' Association:** Lot 104, Regent St, Lacytown, Georgetown; tel. (2) 64411; f. 1946; c. 35,000 families; Pres. BUDRAM MAHADEO.

### UTILITIES

#### Electricity

**Guyana Power and Light Inc:** 40 Main St, POB 10390, Georgetown; tel. (2) 54618; fax (2) 71978; f. 1999; fmrly Guyana Electricity Corpn.; 50% state-owned; 50% owned by the Commonwealth Devt Corpn and the Electricity Supply Bd International; Chair. ADAM HEDAYAT; CEO NOEL HATCH.

#### Water

**Guyana Water Authority (GUYWA):** Georgetown; CEO KARAN SINGH.

### CO-OPERATIVE SOCIETIES

**Chief Co-operatives Development Officer:** Ministry of Labour, Human Services and Social Security, 1 Water and Cornhill Sts, Georgetown; tel. (2) 58644; fax (2) 53477; f. 1948; A. HENRY.

In October 1996 there were 1,324 registered co-operative societies, mainly savings clubs and agricultural credit societies, with a total membership of 95,950.

### TRADE UNIONS

**Trades Union Congress (TUC):** Critchlow Labour College, Woolford Ave, Non-pareil Park, Georgetown; tel. (2) 61493; fax (2) 70254; f. 1940; national trade union body; 22 affiliated unions; merged with the Federation of Independent Trade Unions in Guyana in 1993; Pres. LAURIE LEWIS; Gen. Sec. JOSEPH H. POLLYDORE.

**Amalgamated Transport and General Workers' Union:** 46 Urquhart St, Georgetown; tel. (2) 66243; Pres. RICHARD SAMUELS.

**Clerical and Commercial Workers' Union (CCWU):** Clerico House, 140 Quamina St, South Cummingsburg, POB 101045, Georgetown; tel. (2) 70611; Gen. Sec. BIRCHMORE PHILADELPHIA.

**Federative Union of Government Employees (FUGE):** Georgetown.

**General Workers' Union:** 79 New North Rd, Georgetown; tel. (2) 64879; f. 1954; terminated affiliation to People's National Congress in 1989; Pres. NORRIS WITTER; Gen. Sec. EDWIN JAMES; 3,000 mems.

**Guyana Agricultural and General Workers' Union (GAWU):** 104–106 Regent St, Lacytown, Georgetown; tel. (2) 72091; allied to the PPP; Gen. Sec. KOMAL CHAND; 20,000 mems.

**Guyana Bauxite Supervisors' Union:** Linden; Gen. Sec. LINCOLN LEWIS.

**Guyana Labour Union:** 198 Camp St, Georgetown; tel. (2) 71196; Pres.-Gen. HUGH DESMOND HOYTE; 6,000 mems.

**Guyana Mine Workers' Union:** 56 Wismar St, Wismar; tel. (4) 2822; Pres. ASHTON ANGEL; Gen. Sec. CHRISTOPHER JAMES; 5,800 mems.

**Guyana Postal and Telecommunication Workers' Union:** 310 East St, POB 10352, Georgetown; tel. (2) 65255; fax (2) 51633; Pres. MAUREEN WALCOTT-FORTUNE; Gen. Sec. DIAN PRINCE-JOHNSON.

**Guyana Public Service Union (GPSU):** 160 Regent Rd and New Garden St, Georgetown; tel. (2) 61770; Pres. PATRICK YARDE; Gen. Sec. RANDOLPH KIRTON; 11,600 mems.

**Guyana Teachers' Union:** Georgetown.

**National Association of Agricultural, Commercial and Industrial Employees:** 64 High St, Kingston, Georgetown; tel. (2) 72301; f. 1946; Pres. B. KHUSIEL; c. 2,000 mems.

**Printing Industry and Allied Workers' Union:** Georgetown; Gen. Sec. LESLIE REECE.

**University of Guyana Workers' Union:** Turkeyen, Georgetown; supports Working People's Alliance; Pres. DR CLIVE THOMAS.

## Transport

### RAILWAY

There are no public railways in Guyana.

**Linmine Railway:** Mackenzie, Linden; tel. (4) 2484; fax (4) 2795; bauxite transport; 48 km of line, Itumi to Linden; Superintendent G. RUTHERFORD FELIX.

### ROADS

The coastal strip has a well-developed road system. In 1996 there were an estimated 7,970 km (4,859 miles) of paved and good-weather roads and trails.

**Guyana Transport Services Ltd:** Georgetown; tel. (2) 58261; f. 1971; privately owned; provides road haulage and bus services; Gen Man. R. VAN VELZEN.

### SHIPPING

Guyana's principal ports are at Georgetown and New Amsterdam. A ferry service is operated between Guyana and Suriname. Communications with the interior are chiefly by river, although access is hindered by rapids and falls. There are 1,077 km (607 miles) of navigable rivers. The main rivers are the Mazaruni, the Potaro, the Essequibo, the Demerara and the Berbice.

**Transport and Harbours Department:** Battery Rd, Kingston, Georgetown; tel. (2) 59350; e-mail t&hd@solutions2000.net; Gen. Man. IVOR B. ENGLISH; Harbour Master STEPHEN THOMAS.

**Shipping Association of Guyana Inc:** 24 Water St, Georgetown; tel. (2) 61505; fax (2) 61881; e-mail ferna@guyana.net.gy; f. 1952; Pres. CHRISTOPHER FERNANDES; Sec. and Man. W. V. BRIDGEMOHAN; members:

**Caribbean Molasses Co Inc:** 1–2 Water St, POB 10208, Kingston, Georgetown; tel. (2) 69238; fax 71327; e-mail cmc@networksgy.com; subsidiary of British co Tate and Lyle PLC; exporters of molasses in bulk; Man. Dir D. P. WALLACE.

**Guyana National Industrial Company Inc.:** 2–9 Lombard St, Charlestown, POB 10520, Georgetown; tel. (2) 58428; fax (2) 58526; metal foundry, ship building and repair, agents for a number of international transport cos; Man. Dir and CEO CLAUDE SAUL.

**Guyana National Shipping Corporation Ltd:** 5–9 Lombard St, La Penitence, POB 10988, Georgetown; tel. (2) 61732; fax (2) 53815; e-mail gnsc@guyana.net.gy; internet www.gnsc.com; govt-owned; Exec. Chair. DESMOND MOHAMED; Man. Dir M. F. BASCOM.

**John Fernandes Ltd:** 24 Water St, POB 10211, Georgetown; tel. (2) 56294; fax (2) 61881; e-mail chris@jf-ltd.com; ship agents, pier operators and stevedore contractors; Man. Dir C. J. FERNANDES.

### CIVIL AVIATION

The main airport is Timehri International, 42 km (26 miles) from Georgetown. The more important settlements in the interior have airstrips.

**Guyana Airways 2000:** 32 Main St, POB 10223, Georgetown; tel. (2) 57337; fax (2) 60032; internet www.turq.com/guyana/guyanair.html; f. 1939 as British Guiana Airways; renamed as Guyana Airways Corpn 1963; state-owned until 1999 when 51% share sold and renamed as above; operates internal scheduled services and external services to the USA and Canada; Chair. ANTHONY MEKDECI.

There is a weekly flight, via Georgetown, from Caracas (Venezuela) to Port of Spain (Trinidad and Tobago) and Suriname.

## Tourism

Despite the beautiful scenery in the interior of the country, Guyana has limited tourist facilities, and began encouraging tourism only in the late 1980s. Guyana has considerable potential as an eco-tourism destination. The total number of visitors to Guyana in 1997 was 78,872. Tourism receipts totalled US $38m. in 1996.

**Tourism Association of Guyana:** Georgetown; e-mail info@interknowledge.com; internet www.interknowledge.com; f. 1991; Dir TONY THORNE.

# HAITI

## Introductory Survey

**Location, Climate, Language, Religion, Flag, Capital**

The Republic of Haiti occupies the western part of the Caribbean island of Hispaniola (the Dominican Republic occupies the remaining two-thirds) and some smaller offshore islands. Cuba, to the west, is less than 80 km away. The climate is tropical but the mountains and fresh sea winds mitigate the heat. Temperatures vary little with the seasons, and the annual average in Port-au-Prince is about 27°C (80°F). The rainy season is from May to November. The official languages are French and Creole. About 70% of the population belong to the Roman Catholic Church, the country's official religion, and other Christian churches are also represented. The folk religion is voodoo, a fusion of beliefs originating in West Africa involving communication with the spirit-world through the medium of trance. The national flag (proportions variable) has two equal vertical stripes, of dark blue and red. The state flag (proportions 5 by 3) has, in addition, a white rectangular panel, containing the national coat of arms (a palm tree, surmounted by a Cap of Liberty and flanked by flags and cannons), in the centre. The capital is Port-au-Prince.

**Recent History**

Haiti was first colonized in 1659 by the French, who named the territory Saint-Domingue. French sovereignty was formally recognized by Spain in 1697. Following a period of internal unrest, a successful uprising, begun in 1794 by African-descended slaves, culminated in 1804 with the establishment of Haiti as an independent state, ruled by Jean-Jacques Dessalines, who proclaimed himself Emperor. Hostility between the negro population and the mulattos continued throughout the 19th century until, after increasing economic instability, the USA intervened militarily and supervised the government of the country from 1915 to 1934. Mulatto interests retained political ascendancy until 1946, when a negro President, Dumarsais Estimé, was installed following a military coup. Following the overthrow of two further administrations, Dr François Duvalier, a country physician, was elected President in 1957.

The Duvalier administration soon became a dictatorship, maintaining its authority by means of a notorious private army, popularly called the Tontons Macoutes (Creole for 'Bogeymen'), who used extortion and intimidation to crush all possible opposition to the President's rule. In 1964 Duvalier became President-for-Life, and at his death in April 1971 he was succeeded by his 19-year-old son and designated successor Jean-Claude Duvalier.

At elections held in February 1979 for the 58-seat National Assembly, 57 seats were won by the official government party, the Parti de l'Unité Nationale. The first municipal elections for 25 years, which took place in 1983, were overshadowed by allegations of electoral fraud and Duvalier's obstruction of opposition parties. No opposition candidates were permitted to contest the elections for the National Assembly held in February 1984.

In April 1985 Duvalier announced a programme of constitutional reforms, including the eventual appointment of a Prime Minister and the formation of political parties, subject to certain limiting conditions. In September Roger Lafontant, the minister most closely identified with the Government's acts of repression, was dismissed. However, protests organized by the Roman Catholic Church and other religious groups gained momentum, and further measures to curb continued disorder were adopted in January 1986. The university and schools were closed indefinitely, and radio stations were forbidden to report on current events. Duvalier imposed a state of siege and declared martial law.

In February 1986, following intensified public protests, Duvalier and his family fled from Haiti to exile in France, leaving a five-member National Council of Government (Conseil National Gouvernemental—CNG), led by the Chief of Staff of the army, Gen. Henri Namphy, to succeed him. The interim military-civilian Council announced the appointment of a new Cabinet. The National Assembly was dissolved, and the Constitution was suspended. Later in the month, the Tontons Macoutes were disbanded. Prisoners from Haiti's largest gaol were freed under a general amnesty. However, renewed rioting occurred to protest against the inclusion in the new Government of known supporters of the former dictatorship. In March 1986 there was a cabinet reshuffle, following the resignations of three Duvalierist members of the CNG (only one of whom was replaced). The new three-member CNG comprised Gen. Namphy, Col (later Brig.-Gen.) Williams Régala (Minister of the Interior and National Defence) and Jacques François (then Minister of Finance).

In April 1986 Gen. Namphy announced a proposed timetable for elections to restore constitutional government by February 1988. The first of these elections, to select 41 people (from 101 candidates) who would form part of the 61-member Constituent Assembly which was to revise the Constitution, took place in October 1986. However, the level of participation at the election was only about 5%.

The new Constitution was approved by 99.8% of voters in a referendum held on 29 March 1987. An estimated 50% of the electorate voted. An independent Provisional Electoral Council (Conseil Electoral Provisoire—CEP) was appointed to supervise the presidential and legislative elections, which were scheduled for 29 November.

On 29 November 1987 the elections were cancelled three hours after voting had begun, owing to renewed violence and killings, for which former members of the Tontons Macoutes were believed to be responsible. The Government dissolved the CEP and took control of the electoral process. In December a new CEP was appointed by the Government, and elections were rescheduled for 17 January 1988. Leslie Manigat of the Rassemblement des Démocrates Nationaux Progressistes (RDNP), with 50.3% of the total votes cast, was declared the winner of the presidential election. Legislative and municipal elections were held concurrently. It was officially estimated that 35% of the electorate had voted in the elections, although opposition leaders claimed that only 5% had participated, and alleged that there had been extensive fraud and malpractice.

The Manigat Government took office in February 1988, but was overthrown by disaffected members of the army in June. Gen. Namphy, whom Manigat had attempted to replace as army Chief of Staff, assumed the presidency and appointed a Cabinet comprising members of the armed forces. The Constitution of 1987 was abrogated, and Duvalier's supporters returned to prominence, as did the Tontons Macoutes.

On 18 September 1988 Gen. Namphy was ousted in a coup, led by Brig.-Gen. Prosper Avril (who became President) and non-commissioned officers from the presidential guard, who advocated the introduction of radical reforms. In November an independent electoral body, the Collège Electoral d'Haïti (CEDA), was established to supervise future elections, to draft an electoral law and to ensure proper registration of voters.

In March 1989 President Avril partially restored the Constitution of 1987 and restated his intention to hold democratic elections. In the following month the Government survived two coup attempts by the Leopard Corps, the country's élite anti-subversion squadron, and the Dessalines battalion, based in Port-au-Prince. Both battalions were subsequently disbanded.

In September 1989 Avril published a timetable for elections that had been drafted by the CEP. It provided for local and regional elections to be held in April 1990, followed by national and legislative elections, in two rounds, in July and August. The presidential election, also in two rounds, was scheduled to take place in October and November 1990. (These arrangements were revised under the interim presidency of Ertha Pascal-Trouillot—see below.) In August 1989 the conservative former Minister of Finance, Marc Bazin, and the leader of the Parti Nationaliste Progressiste Révolutionnaire (PANPRA), Serge Gilles, established the Alliance Nationale pour la Démocratie et le Progrès (ANDP).

In early January 1990, during the President's absence abroad on official business, the Rassemblement National, a broadly-based opposition coalition including conservative and left-wing political organizations, initiated a series of strikes and demonstrations to protest against the Government's economic policies. On 20 January, following his return to Haiti, Avril imposed a

# HONDURAS

## Introductory Survey

**Location, Climate, Language, Religion, Flag, Capital**

The Republic of Honduras lies in the middle of the Central American isthmus. It has a long northern coastline on the Caribbean Sea and a narrow southern outlet to the Pacific Ocean. Its neighbours are Guatemala to the west, El Salvador to the south-west and Nicaragua to the south-east. The climate ranges from temperate in the mountainous regions to tropical in the coastal plains: temperatures in the interior range from 15°C (59°F) to 24°C (75°F), while temperatures in the coastal plains average about 30°C (86°F). There are two rainy seasons in upland areas, May–July and September–October. The national language is Spanish. Almost all of the inhabitants profess Christianity, and the overwhelming majority are adherents of the Roman Catholic Church. The national flag (proportions 2 by 1) has three horizontal stripes, of blue, white and blue, with five blue five-pointed stars, arranged in a diagonal cross, in the centre of the white stripe. The capital is Tegucigalpa.

**Recent History**

Honduras was ruled by Spain from the 16th century until 1821 and became a sovereign state in 1838. From 1939 the country was ruled as a dictatorship by Gen. Tiburcio Carías Andino, leader of the Partido Nacional (PN), who had been President since 1933. In 1949 Carías was succeeded as President by Juan Manuel Gálvez, also of the PN. In 1954 the leader of the Partido Liberal (PL), Dr José Ramón Villeda Morales, was elected President, but was immediately deposed by Julio Lozano Díaz, himself overthrown by a military Junta in 1956. The Junta organized elections in 1957, when the PL secured a majority in Congress and Villeda was re-elected President. He was overthrown in 1963 by Col (later Gen.) Oswaldo López Arellano, the Minister of Defence, who, following elections held on the basis of a new Constitution, was appointed President in June 1965.

A presidential election in March 1971 was won by Dr Ramón Ernesto Cruz Uclés, the PN candidate. In December 1972, however, Cruz was deposed in a bloodless coup, led by former President López. In March 1974, at the instigation of the Consejo Superior de las Fuerzas Armadas (Supreme Council of the Armed Forces), President López was replaced as Commander-in-Chief of the Armed Forces by Col (later Gen.) Juan Melgar Castro, who was appointed President in April 1975. President Melgar was forced to resign by the Consejo Superior de las Fuerzas Armadas in August 1978, and was replaced by a military Junta. The Commander-in-Chief of the Armed Forces, Gen. Policarpo Paz García, assumed the role of Head of State, and the Junta promised that elections would take place.

Military rule was ended officially when, in April 1980, elections to a Constituent Assembly were held. The PL won 52% of the votes but was unable to assume power. Gen. Paz was appointed interim President for one year. At a general election in November 1981 the PL, led by Dr Roberto Suazo Córdova, gained an absolute majority in the National Assembly. Suazo was sworn in as President in January 1982. However, real power lay in the hands of Col (later Gen.) Gustavo Alvarez Martínez, who was appointed Head of the Armed Forces in the same month. In November Gen. Alvarez became Commander-in-Chief of the Armed Forces, having brought about an amendment to the Constitution in that month, whereby the posts of President and Commander-in-Chief of the Armed Forces, which had been merged under the rule of the military Junta, were separated. During 1982 and 1983 Gen. Alvarez suppressed increasing political unrest by authorizing the arrests of trade union activists and left-wing sympathizers; 'death squads' were allegedly also used to eliminate 'subversive' elements of the population. In March 1984 Gen. Alvarez was deposed as Commander-in-Chief of the Armed Forces by a group of army officers.

At the November 1985 presidential election the leading candidate of the PN, Rafael Leonardo Callejas Romero, obtained 42% of the individual votes cast, but the leading candidate of the PL, José Simeón Azcona del Hoyo (who had obtained only 27% of the individual votes cast), was declared the winner because, in accordance with a new electoral law, the combined votes of the PL's candidates secured the requisite majority of 51% of the total votes cast.

In February 1988 a report by a human rights organization, Amnesty International, gave evidence of an increase in violations of human rights by the armed forces and by right-wing 'death squads'. In August of that year, and again in 1989, the Inter-American Court of Human Rights (an organ of the Organization of American States—OAS, see p. 245) found the Honduran Government guilty of the 'disappearances' of Honduran citizens between 1981 and 1984, and ordered that compensation be paid to the families involved. In January 1989 Gen. Alvarez was killed by left-wing guerrillas in Tegucigalpa. The PL gained a majority of seats in the National Assembly at legislative elections held in November, while Callejas of the PN won the concurrent presidential election, receiving 51% of the votes cast. Callejas assumed office in January 1990. The new administration promptly adopted economic austerity measures, which provoked widespread social unrest.

In May 1991 units of the armed forces were implicated in the massacre of nine farmers during a dispute over land ownership. In the following month Amnesty International published a report alleging the mistreatment, torture and killing of detainees by members of the Honduran security forces, and the International Confederation of Free Trade Unions accused the security forces of complicity in the assassinations of several trade union organizers during 1990 and early 1991. In January 1992 the Government announced the creation of a special commission to investigate numerous accusations of corruption against government officials.

In March 1993, in response to increasing pressure by human rights organizations and criticism by the State Department of the USA, the Government established a special commission to investigate allegations of human rights violations by the armed forces and to evaluate the need for a reform of the security forces and the judiciary. In its report, the commission recommended the replacement of the armed forces' much-criticized secret counter-intelligence organization, the División Nacional de Investigaciones (DNI), with a body under civilian control. Other recommendations included the establishment of a fully independent Public Ministry office headed by a democratically-elected Attorney-General.

At presidential and legislative elections held in November 1993, Carlos Roberto Reina Idiaquez, the candidate of the PL, was elected President, winning 52% of the votes cast; Osvaldo Ramos Soto, the PN candidate, took 41% of the votes. The PL also obtained a clear majority in the National Assembly, with 71 seats, while the PN secured 55 seats and the Partido Innovación y Unidad—Social Democracia (PINU) won the remaining two seats. Legislation replacing the DNI with a new ministry, the Dirección de Investigación Criminal (DIC), was approved in December 1993. On taking office in January 1994 Reina, a former President of the Inter-American Court of Human Rights, expressed his commitment to the reform of the judicial system, which had failed to act effectively against those responsible for human rights violations. In addition he promised to redefine the role of the armed forces, reducing its size and sphere of influence. In that month, following the release by the National Commission for the Protection of Human Rights of a report incriminating the armed forces in the disappearance of 184 people in the previous decade, the head of the Commission, Leo Valladares Lanza, demanded the resignation of the Commander-in-Chief of the Armed Forces, Gen. Luis Alonso Discua Elvir. At the time of the disappearances Discua had been the Commander of Battalion 3-16, the army intelligence unit widely regarded as responsible for the murder of left-wing political activists. As a result of the report, the Supreme Court ordered an investigation of the allegations.

In April 1994 an apparent attempt to assassinate Reina was thwarted when one of three Nicaraguan hired assassins revealed the plot to the Honduran authorities. The Nicaraguans reportedly had been offered US $400,000 by a Honduran, Luis Hernández Sosa, to conduct the killing. Reina dismissed suggestions of a political motive for the attempt, attributing it instead to the work of criminals opposed to his efforts to suppress drug trafficking in Honduras. In that month demonstrations were organized in the capital in protest at the deterioration of living standards caused by the Government's economic austerity policies. Demonstrations also occurred in the department of Copán where peasant organizations blocked the Pan-American Highway in support of demands for Reina to honour election commitments to reduce the severity of the economic policies of the previous administration.

In May 1994 the National Assembly approved a proposal for a reform of the Constitution to abolish compulsory military service. Subject to ratification by the National Assembly in 1995, military service was to be voluntary from that year. Also approved was the transfer of the police from military to civilian control. In that month measures initiated by the Callejas administration for the establishment of a Public Ministry were officially completed. The new ministry was to be supervised by the DIC, which was inaugurated in January 1995. The DNI was officially disbanded in June 1994.

In July 1994, following protracted demonstrations in the capital, 4,000 members of indigenous organizations occupied the National Assembly building and succeeded in securing an agreement with the Government granting rights and social assistance to the country's indigenous community, including the creation of the first indigenous municipality in Yamaranguila, Intibucá. The following months were characterized by growing social and political tension, including several bomb attacks. Concern was raised by human rights organizations that the climate of instability was being fomented by the armed forces in an attempt to stem the rapid diminution of its powers. In August however, Reina conceded the temporary reintroduction of compulsory conscription in order to fill some 7,000 vacancies which the armed forces complained were impairing military efficiency. In the same month Reina ordered an investigation into charges of corruption and drug trafficking in the air force. Widespread concern at the possibility that growing tension between the Government and the armed forces might result in a military coup prompted Gen. Discua to issue a public statement denying any such intentions and reaffirming military support for the civilian authorities. In mid-August an increase in the incidence of crime and violent demonstrations resulting from the accumulating effect of austerity measures, a worsening energy crisis and food shortages, forced the Government to declare a state of national emergency and to deploy the armed forces to maintain order.

In November 1994 public-sector unions organized strikes in protest at low pay, poor working conditions and the Government's failure to honour earlier pay agreements. The disputes were resolved, however, following government promises of concessions, to be awarded once new loans had been disbursed to Honduras by international lending agencies. In late November corruption charges were filed by the public prosecutor's office against former President Callejas and 12 of his former ministers.

In April 1995 the National Assembly ratified the constitutional amendment abolishing compulsory military service. Sustained protests by members of indigenous organizations, in support of demands that the Government honour its commitments of July 1994 to the indigenous community, culminated in July 1995 in a 2,000-strong demonstration in the capital. The protests resulted in renewed pledges by the Government to provide social assistance and grant land titles to the indigenous population. In September the PL, PN, PINU and Partido Demócrata Cristiano de Honduras (PDCH) established the Consejo Nacional de Convergencia (National Convergence Council) in order to seek a consensus on political, social and economic issues.

In July 1995, in an unprecendented development in the Government's efforts to investigate past human rights violations, a civilian court issued indictments against 10 senior officers of the security services who had been involved in the activities of Battalion 3-16 during the 1980s. The charges concerned the kidnapping, torture and attempted murder in 1982 of six left-wing students. However, the officers refused to appear in court, invoking an amnesty granted in 1991 which, they claimed, afforded them immunity from prosecution. In October a warrant was issued for the arrest of several of the officers, who promptly went into hiding. In January 1996 the Supreme Court ruled that the officers were not entitled to protection under the 1991 amnesty law, overturning an earlier decision by the Court of Appeal. Information concerning the activities of Battalion 3-16, which had been financed and trained by the US Central Intelligence Agency, was being sought from the US Government by Valladares to support the prosecution of this and other human rights cases.

In January 1996 Col. Mario Raúl Hung Pacheco succeeded Gen. Discua as Commander-in-Chief of the Armed Forces, and was subsequently promoted to the rank of General. In the following month, in an apparent demonstration of his control over the military high command, Reina ignored the nominations for a new Minister of National Defence and Public Security proposed by Gen. Hung, appointing his own candidate instead. In the following month a grenade was thrown into the grounds of the presidential residence, prompting speculation that the armed forces had been responsible for the attack.

In mid-1996 there was widespread protest at the Government's policies of wage restraint and the implementation of public-sector redundancies. Public-sector workers conducted strikes in support of demands for salary increases, a reform of the labour code and price controls. Following negotiations, the Government granted concessions, including payments totalling US $12.2m. in answer to salary demands.

In July 1996 the Human Rights Defence Committee (Codeh) claimed that the extrajudicial execution of five former military intelligence agents had occurred in recent months, and alleged that the killings were the responsibility of military officers who were attempting to prevent evidence of human rights violations from coming to light. Later that month four officers of the armed forces were arrested for allegedly conspiring to overthrow the Commander-in-Chief of the Armed Forces. Gen. Hung claimed, however, that the incident had been exaggerated and that it merely reflected the discontent within the ranks at low pay and reductions in the defence budget.

In early October 1996 a bomb exploded, without causing injury, at the parliament building in the capital. A further device was defused outside the headquarters of the PL. Responsibility for the attacks was claimed later that month by a previously unknown organization describing itself as 'Hambre' (Hunger), which claimed to be acting in response to recent rises in fuel prices. However, the President of Codeh, Ramón Custodio, expressed the popular suspicion that the attacks had been perpetrated by the armed forces in an attempt to pressurize the civilian authorities into reversing the decline in military influence in the country. In mid-October, Custodio's home in San Pedro Sula was the target of a grenade attack. A further such attack was conducted in early November on a central court building in Tegucigalpa, resulting in one fatality. In response, the Government deployed some 3,000 troops to patrol the capital and San Pedro Sula. An organization known as 'Justa C.' claimed responsibility for the attack and issued a communiqué threatening the lives of several judges involved in the investigation of cases concerning official corruption and human rights abuses by the armed forces.

In late October 1996 a judge ordered the arrest of an entire former Cabinet which had served during the Callejas administration. It was alleged that the politicians were implicated in the illicit trade of passport documents in 1993.

In early 1997 the legislature approved a constitutional reform providing for control of the police force to be transferred from the military to the civilian authorities. The Fuerza de Seguridad Pública, which had been under military control since 1963 and was widely suspected of perpetrating human rights abuses, was to be replaced by a new force, the Policía Nacional. The official transfer occurred in May 1998.

In February 1997 demonstrations by thousands of public-sector employees, who were protesting in support of demands for salary increases, culminated in violent clashes between demonstrators and the security forces. As a result of sustained unrest the Government subsequently signed a social pact with labour leaders, which included commitments to increased social spending and price controls on basic goods. In May, following the killing of two ethnic minority leaders in the previous month, more than 3,000 members of the indigenous community conducted a march from the western departments of Copán and Ocotepeque to the capital to protest outside the presidential palace. As a result Reina signed an agreement to conduct a full investigation into the killings and to accelerate the distribution of some 7,000 ha of land to the indigenous community. However, the killing of a further two ethnic minority leaders later that month led to accusations by human rights groups that attempts were being made to eliminate minority autonomous organizations.

During August 1997 attention was drawn to a serious crisis in the national prison system following a series of riots by prison inmates who were protesting at overcrowding and poor conditions. Several prisons were destroyed by fire and hundreds of inmates escaped.

In September 1997 Reina announced that in 1998 the post of Commander-in-Chief of the Armed Forces was to be abolished and its responsibilities assumed by the Minister of National Defence and Public Security. In the following month the National Assembly unanimously approved a constitutional amendment providing for the reduction of the legislature from 128 to 80 seats. In order to be adopted, the legislation would have to be ratified by the succeeding National Assembly, following the forthcoming general election.

At the general election held on 30 November 1997 Carlos Roberto Flores Facussé, the candidate of the ruling PL, was elected President, winning 52.7% of the votes cast; Alba Nora Gúnera de Melgar, the PN candidate, took 42.7% of the votes. The PL also obtained a majority in the National Assembly, with 67 seats, while the PN secured 55 seats, the PINU won three, the PDCH two and the left-wing Partido de Unificación Democrática obtained the remaining seat. In December Flores announced his intention to conduct a restructuring of the armed forces, incorporating the reform announced by Reina in September. Flores was inaugurated on 27 January 1998.

In September 1998 the National Assembly approved a constitutional amendment abolishing the post of Commander-in-Chief of the Armed Forces and transferring its responsibilities to the Minister of National Defence and Public Security. The amendment remained to be ratified by the following session of the National Assembly, which was due to begin in January 1999, before it could take effect. In October 1998, in the wake of a serious escalation in the incidence of violent crime in Tegucigalpa and San Pedro Sula, and in response to increasing pressure, in particular from business groups concerned at the effect of growing public insecurity on investment, Flores deployed the armed forces to reinforce the efforts of the police in those two cities.

In November 1998, in the wake of the devastation caused by 'Hurricane Mitch', which struck the country in late October, causing losses estimated at more than US $4,000m., Flores declared a state of emergency and imposed a curfew in order to combat widespread looting. As many as 7,000 people were estimated to have died, and many thousands more were reported missing, as a result of the storms, which left some 2.13m. homeless and caused widespread damage to the country's infrastructure, as well as destroying principal export crops.

In January 1999 Flores conducted a major cabinet reorganization in an apparent attempt to eradicate corruption and inefficiency. Later in that month the National Assembly ratified the constitutional amendment placing the armed forces directly under civilian control. In addition, the military's ruling body, the Consejo Superior de las Fuerzas Armadas, was disbanded. Edgardo Dumas Rodríguez was subsequently appointed to the defence portfolio. In July, acting on intelligence reports of a plot by senior-ranking military officers to overthrow the Government, Flores implemented a number of changes to the military high command. Notably, the Head of the Joint Chiefs of Staff, Col Eugenio Romero Eucedo, who was suspected of being one of the principal instigators of the coup plot, was replaced by the head of the presidential guard, Col Daniel López Carballo, who was considered to be loyal to the presidency. The plot itself was believed to have been prompted by resentment in the officer corps at the determination of Dumas to exert civilian control over the armed forces, and in particular at his plans to investigate military expenditure and supervise the armed forces' extensive business activities. The potential for further military unrest developed in August following the decision by the Attorney-General to investigate a series of clandestine cemeteries discovered in that month at the disused El Aguacate airbase, situated some 130 km east of the capital. The base had been used by Nicaraguan Contras and the Honduran military in the 1980s.

From the early 1980s former members of the Nicaraguan National Guard, regarded by the left-wing Sandinista Government of Nicaragua as counter-revolutionaries ('Contras'), established bases in Honduras, from which they conducted raids across the border between the two countries, allegedly with support from the Honduran armed forces. In 1983, when Honduran foreign policy was controlled by the pro-US Gen. Alvarez (the Commander-in-Chief of the Armed Forces), US involvement in Honduras increased substantially. In February 1983 the USA and Honduras initiated 'Big Pine', a series of joint military manoeuvres on Honduran territory; these exercises continued throughout the 1980s, thus enabling the USA to construct permanent military installations in Honduras. In return for considerable military assistance from the USA, the Honduran Government permitted US military aid to be supplied to the Contras based in Honduras.

Following the overthrow of Gen. Alvarez in March 1984, public opposition to the US military presence in Honduras increased, causing a temporary deterioration in relations between Honduras and the USA. In mid-1984 the Suazo Government indicated that it would review its policy of co-operation with the USA. In 1985 the USA declined to enter into a security pact with Honduras, but confirmed that it would take 'appropriate' measures to defend Honduras against any Communist aggression. In August of that year the Honduran Government announced that it would prevent the US Government from supplying further military aid to the Contras through Honduras. However, following a visit by President Azcona to the USA in 1986, the supply of aid was believed to have resumed.

In 1986 relations with Nicaragua deteriorated sharply, when Honduran troops were mobilized in an attempt to curb alleged border incursions by Nicaraguan government forces. In December, however, following revelations that the USA had secretly sold weapons to the Government of Iran and that the proceeds had been used to finance the activities of the Contra rebels, President Azcona requested the departure of the Contras from Honduras.

In August 1987 Honduras, Costa Rica, El Salvador, Guatemala and Nicaragua signed a Central American peace plan, known as the 'Esquipulas agreement', the crucial provisions of which were the implementation of simultaneous cease-fires in Nicaragua and El Salvador, a halt to foreign assistance to rebel groups, democratic reform in Nicaragua, a ban on the use of foreign territory as a base for attack, and the establishment of national reconciliation commissions in each of the Central American nations. However, the commitment of the Honduran Government to the accord appeared to be only partial. Claiming that it no longer permitted the Nicaraguan Contras to maintain bases on its territory, the Honduran Government opposed a clause in the agreement providing for the establishment of a committee to monitor the dismantling of Contra bases in Honduras.

In March 1988 several thousand US troops were temporarily deployed in Honduras, in response to an incursion into Honduran territory by the Nicaraguan army. Further violations of the border between Honduras and Nicaragua occurred during that year, as Nicaraguan troops forced at least 12,000 Contra rebels, based in the border area, into Honduras. In November President Azcona declared his opposition to the presence of the Contras in his country. In the following month it was announced that the International Court of Justice (ICJ) would consider an application that had been submitted by the Nicaraguan Government in 1986, in which Nicaragua contended that Honduras had breached international law by allowing the Contras to operate from its territory. In response, the Honduran Government threatened to withdraw support from the Esquipulas agreement.

In February 1989 a summit meeting of the five Central American Presidents was convened at Costa del Sol, El Salvador. An agreement was reached whereby the Nicaraguan Contra forces encamped in Honduras would demobilize, while President Ortega of Nicaragua guaranteed that free and fair elections would take place in his country by February 1990. At a further summit meeting, held in August at Tela, Honduras, the conditions for the demobilization of the Contras were expanded. The Honduran Government agreed to the establishment by the UN and the OAS of an international commission to oversee the voluntary repatriation or removal to a third country of the rebel forces by December 1989; in return, the Nicaraguan Government agreed to abandon the action that it had initiated against Honduras at the ICJ.

Despite the initiatives towards peace which emerged during 1989, the Contra rebels continued to launch attacks against Nicaraguan troops during the latter part of that year, maintaining their positions in Honduras beyond the December deadline. In February 1990, following national elections in Nicaragua, the outgoing President Ortega of Nicaragua ordered his forces to observe an immediate unilateral cease-fire with the Contras. Contra raids into Nicaragua continued during early 1990; however, the rebel units officially disbanded and left Honduras in June.

In June 1995 Honduras and Nicaragua signed an accord providing for the visible demarcation of each country's territorial waters in the Gulf of Fonseca, and the establishment of a joint naval patrol to police the area. The agreement followed frequent disputes concerning fishing rights in the Gulf, which occurred as a consequence of inefficient demarcation. In May a Nicaraguan naval patrol boat had seized Honduran fishing vessels that were alleged to have been operating illegally in Nicaraguan waters. An armed confrontation between naval units of both countries had ensued. Despite the June agreement, however, conflict continued, and the demarcation process did not begin until May 1998.

In December 1999 a further dispute arose with Nicaragua, prompting it to sever commercial ties with, and impose import taxes on, Honduras, in direct contravention of Central American free-trade undertakings. The dispute stemmed from the Caribbean Sea Maritime Limits Treaty, which Honduras had signed with Colombia in 1986 and had finally ratified in late November 1999, thereby formally recognizing a frontier with Colombia the demarcation of which granted Colombia territorial rights to areas of the Caribbean historically claimed by Nicaragua.

A long-standing dispute between Honduras and El Salvador, regarding the demarcation of the two countries' common border and rival claims to three islands in the Gulf of Fonseca, caused hostilities to break out between the two countries in 1969. Although armed conflict soon subsided, the Honduran and Salvadorean Governments did not sign a peace treaty until 1980. In 1982 the Honduran armed forces were engaged against guerrilla forces in El Salvador, indicating an improvement in Honduran-Salvadorean relations. Honduran troops were also reportedly responsible for the deaths of several hundred Salvadorean refugees in Honduras during that year. In 1984 the Government of Honduras suspended the training of Salvadorean troops by Honduran-based US military advisers, pending agreement on the disputed territory. In 1986, however, the Governments of Honduras and El Salvador agreed that their conflicting territorial claims should be examined by the ICJ. During 1989 several border clashes occurred between Honduran and Salvadorean troops. In September 1992 the ICJ awarded Honduras sovereignty over some two-thirds of the disputed mainland territory and over one of the disputed islands in the Gulf of Fonseca. However, in subsequent years disputes continued to arise concerning the legal rights of those people resident in the reallocated territory, particularly with regard to land ownership. Following protracted negotiation, a convention governing the acquired rights and nationality of those people was finally signed by the Presidents of both countries in January 1998. An agreement was also signed providing for the demarcation of the countries' common border to be undertaken within one year.

In November 1991 the Presidents of Honduras and El Salvador signed an agreement to establish a free-trade zone on their common border, and subsequently to seek economic union. In May 1992 the Governments of Honduras, El Salvador and Guatemala agreed to promote trade and investment between the three countries. A further agreement, concluded by Honduras, El Salvador and Guatemala in October of that year, provided for the eventual establishment of a Central American political federation.

### Government

Under the provisions of the Constitution approved by the National Assembly in 1982, the President is elected by a simple majority of the voters. The President holds executive power and has a single four-year mandate. Legislative power is vested in the National Assembly, with 128 members elected by universal adult suffrage for a term of four years. The country is divided into 18 local Departments.

In October 1997 the National Assembly approved a constitutional amendment providing for the reduction of the legislature from 128 to 80 members. In order to be adopted, the amendment would have to be ratified by the succeeding National Assembly, which was elected in November 1997.

### Defence

Military service is voluntary. Active service lasts eight months, with subsequent reserve training. In August 1999 the armed forces totalled 8,300 men, of whom 5,500 were in the army, 1,000 in the navy and 1,800 in the air force. Paramilitary forces numbered 6,000 men. In 1999 government expenditure on defence was budgeted at 500m. lempiras. In 1990 US military aid to Honduras was almost halved, compared with the previous year, to US $20.2m. By 1993 annual assistance from the USA had been reduced to $2.7m. In mid-1998 some 719 US troops were based in Honduras.

### Economic Affairs

In 1997, according to estimates by the World Bank, Honduras' gross national product (GNP), measured at average 1995–97 prices, was US $4,426m., equivalent to $740 per head. During 1990–97, it was estimated, GNP per head increased, in real terms, at an average annual rate of 1.0%. Over the same period the population increased at an average annual rate of 2.9%. In 1998 GNP was estimated at $4,500m. ($730 per head). Honduras' gross domestic product (GDP) increased, in real terms, at an average annual rate of 3.7% in 1990–98, and by 3.0% in 1998.

Agriculture (including hunting, forestry and fishing) contributed an estimated 20.3% of GDP and employed 33.5% of the economically active population in 1998. The principal cash crops are coffee and bananas (which contributed, respectively, an estimated 28.0% and 11.5% of all export earnings in 1998), while the main subsistence crops include maize, plantains, beans, rice, sugar cane and citrus fruit. Exports of shellfish make a significant contribution to foreign earnings (supplying 10.3% of total export earnings in 1998), and timber production is also important. Agricultural GDP increased at an average annual rate of 1.9% during 1991–98, but declined by an estimated 7.0% in 1998.

Industry (including mining, manufacturing, construction and power) contributed an estimated 30.9% of GDP in 1998, and employed 22.0% of the economically active population in 1997. Industrial GDP increased at an average annual rate of 4.9% during 1991–98, and by an estimated 9.0% in 1998.

Mining contributed an estimated 1.8% of GDP in 1998, and employed 0.1% of the economically active population in 1997. Lead, zinc and silver are the major mineral exports. Gold, copper and low-grade iron ore are also mined. In addition, small quantities of petroleum derivatives are exported. The GDP of the mining sector increased by an average of 6.4% per year in 1991–98, and by an estimated 7.4% in 1998.

Manufacturing contributed an estimated 18.3% of GDP in 1998, and employed 17.3% of the economically active population in 1997. In 1996, the most important branches, measured by gross value of output, were food products (providing 37.5% of the total), beverages, apparel, chemical products, non-metallic mineral products and wood products. Manufacturing GDP increased at an average annual rate of 4.6% during 1991–98, and by an estimated 5.8% in 1998.

Energy is derived principally from hydroelectric power, which accounted for some 55% of energy consumption in the late 1990s. Imports of mineral fuels and lubricants accounted for an estimated 8.6% of the value of total imports in 1998. Fuel wood remains a prime source of domestic energy.

The services sector contributed an estimated 48.8% of GDP in 1998, and engaged 41.0% of the working population in 1997. The GDP of the services sector increased by an average of 4.5% per year in 1991–98, and an estimated 5.9% in 1998.

In 1998 Honduras recorded a visible trade deficit of US $323.1m., while there was a deficit of $332.9m. on the current account of the balance of payments. In 1997 the principal source of imports (48.1%) was the USA; other major suppliers were Guatemala, Mexico and El Salvador. The USA was also the principal market for exports (42.4%) in that year; other significant purchasers were Germany, Nicaragua and Belgium. The principal exports in 1998 were coffee, bananas and shellfish. The principal imports in 1998 were crude materials for industry, non-durable consumer goods, capital goods for industry, capital goods for transport, and mineral fuels and lubricants.

In 1998 there was a budgetary deficit of 1,654.9m. lempiras (equivalent to 2.3% of GDP in that year). Honduras' external debt totalled US $4,698m. at the end of 1997, of which $3,910m. was long-term public debt. In that year the cost of debt-servicing was equivalent to 20.9% of the value of exports of goods and services. The annual rate of inflation averaged 20.0% in 1990–98. Consumer prices increased by an annual average of 13.7% in 1998. An estimated 3.2% of the labour force were unemployed in 1997.

Honduras is a member of the Central American Common Market (CACM, see p. 141).

In terms of average income, Honduras is among the poorest nations in the Western hemisphere, with some 80% of the population living below the poverty line. In October 1998 the Honduran economy was devastated by the effects of 'Hurricane Mitch'. Much of the country's infrastructure was destroyed, and as many as 2.13m. people left homeless. Losses in agricultural production were estimated at US $200m. for 1998, rising to more than $500m. for 1999, while the total cost to the economy of the hurricane damage was estimated at more than $4,000m. The Government's 'National Reconstruction and Transformation Plan' estimated that some $5,000m. would be required to finance the rehabilitation of the country. In May 1999 the Consultative Group for Honduras of international financial agencies and donor countries agreed to provide $1,100m. for the reconstruction process. In March the IMF approved a three-year Enhanced Structural Adjustment Facility (ESAF) totalling $215m. in support of the Government's economic programme for 1999–2001. In the following month the 'Paris Club' of creditor governments agreed to suspend Honduras' bilateral debt-service payments for a period of three years, and offered a 67% reduction in its debt of $1,170m. on the condition that it complied with the terms of the ESAF. These included commitments by the Government to reduce public expenditure, rationalize state bureaucracy, and sustain its privatization programme. The successful implementation of these measures was also expected to facilitate further debt relief under the Heavily Indebted Poor Countries initiative of the World Bank. In late 1999 there were indications of a gradual upturn in the economy based on a recovery in the banana sector, robust growth in the *maquiladora* (assembly plant) sector and investment in reconstruction projects. Real GDP was expected to decline by 3% in 1999, when a fiscal deficit equivalent to some 6% of GDP was envisaged. However, the Central Bank predicted GDP growth of 6% in 2000, based on an expected increase in private-sector investment and the receipt of fresh credits related to reconstruction, in addition to proceeds from the divestment of state assets.

### Social Welfare

The state-run system of social security provides benefits for sickness, maternity, orphans, unemployment and accidents. It also provides family and old-age allowances. The Labour Code affords guarantees for employees. In 1991 the Government announced plans to transfer the provision of some social welfare services to the private sector. In the early 1990s there were 22 physicians per 100,000 inhabitants and 17 nurses per 100,000 inhabitants working in Honduras. In 1995 there were 62 hospitals (of which 33 were private), 889 health centres and 5,682 hospital beds, cots and incubators. The 1995 budget allocated 1,071.5m. lempiras to the health sector.

### Education

Primary education, beginning at seven years of age and lasting for six years, is officially compulsory and is provided free of charge. Secondary education, which is not compulsory, begins at the age of 13 and lasts for up to five years, comprising a first cycle of three years and a second of two years. On completion of the compulsory period of primary education, every person is required to teach at least two illiterate adults to read and write. In 1995, according to estimates by UNESCO, adult illiteracy averaged 27.3% (males 27.4%; females 27.3%). In 1993 the enrolment at primary schools included 90% of children in the relevant age-group (males 89%; females 91%), while enrolment at secondary schools in that year was equivalent to only 32% of children in the appropriate age-group. There are six universities, including the Autonomous National University in Tegucigalpa. For 1995 the education budget was 1,353m. lempiras (16.5% of total government expenditure).

### Public Holidays

**2000:** 1 January (New Year's Day), 14 April (Pan-American Day/Bastilla's Day), 21–24 April (Easter), 1 May (Labour Day), 15 September (Independence Day), 3 October (Morazán Day), 12 October (Discovery Day), 21 October (Army Day), 25 December (Christmas).

**2001:** 1 January (New Year's Day), 13–16 April (Easter), 14 April (Pan-American Day/Bastilla's Day), 1 May (Labour Day), 15 September (Independence Day), 3 October (Morazán Day), 12 October (Discovery Day), 21 October (Army Day), 25 December (Christmas).

### Weights and Measures

The metric system is in force, although some old Spanish measures are used, including: 25 libras = 1 arroba; 4 arrobas = 1 quintal (46 kg).

# Statistical Survey

Source (unless otherwise stated): Department of Economic Studies, Banco Central de Honduras—BANTRAL, 6a y 7a Avda, 1a Calle, Apdo 3165, Tegucigalpa; tel. 337-2270; fax 337-1876.

## Area and Population

**AREA, POPULATION AND DENSITY**

| | |
|---|---|
| Area (sq km) | 112,492* |
| Population (census results)† | |
| 6 March 1974 | 2,656,948 |
| 29 May 1988 | |
| Males | 2,110,106 |
| Females | 2,138,455 |
| Total | 4,248,561 |
| Population (official estimates at mid-year) | |
| 1995 | 5,952,585 |
| 1996 | 6,139,876 |
| 1997 | 6,338,272 |
| Density (per sq km) at mid-1997 | 56.3 |

* 43,433 sq miles.

† Excluding adjustments for underenumeration, estimated to have been 10% at the 1974 census.

**PRINCIPAL TOWNS** (estimated population, '000 at mid-1995)

| | | | |
|---|---|---|---|
| Tegucigalpa (capital) | 813.9 | Siguatepeque | 39.4 |
| San Pedro Sula | 383.9 | Puerto Cortés | 33.9 |
| La Ceiba | 89.2 | Juticalpa | 26.8 |
| El Progreso | 85.4 | Tela | 25.0 |
| Choluteca | 76.4 | Santa Rosa de Copán | 24.1 |
| Comayagua | 55.3 | | |
| Danlí | 46.2 | | |

**BIRTHS AND DEATHS** (UN estimates, annual averages)

| | 1980–85 | 1985–90 | 1990–95 |
|---|---|---|---|
| Birth rate (per 1,000) | 42.3 | 39.4 | 37.1 |
| Death rate (per 1,000) | 8.9 | 7.1 | 6.1 |

**Expectation of life** (UN estimates, years at birth, 1990–95): 67.3 (males 65.4; females 70.1).

Source: UN, *World Population Prospects: The 1998 Revision*.

**ECONOMICALLY ACTIVE POPULATION**
('000 persons aged 10 years and over, Sept. 1997)

| | Males | Females | Total |
|---|---|---|---|
| Agriculture, hunting, forestry and fishing | 722.0 | 50.7 | 772.7 |
| Mining and quarrying | 2.9 | 0.1 | 3.1 |
| Manufacturing | 170.6 | 191.1 | 361.7 |
| Electricity, gas and water | 5.6 | 1.0 | 6.7 |
| Construction | 86.7 | 1.6 | 88.3 |
| Trade, restaurants and hotels | 157.3 | 236.5 | 393.8 |
| Transport, storage and communications | 43.0 | 3.8 | 46.8 |
| Financing, insurance, real estate and business services | 26.8 | 14.6 | 41.4 |
| Community, social and personal services | 159.6 | 214.5 | 374.1 |
| **Total employed** | 1,374.5 | 714.0 | 2,088.5 |
| Unemployed | 45.4 | 23.9 | 69.4 |
| **Total labour force** | 1,420.0 | 737.9 | 2,157.8 |

# Agriculture

**PRINCIPAL CROPS** ('000 metric tons)

| | 1996 | 1997 | 1998 |
|---|---|---|---|
| Rice (paddy) | 40 | 50 | 53 |
| Maize | 658 | 610 | 623 |
| Sorghum | 86 | 96 | 99 |
| Dry beans | 55 | 55 | 76 |
| Sugar cane | 3,580 | 3,637 | 3,779 |
| Pineapples | 69* | 68* | 73 |
| Bananas | 1,022 | 946 | 947 |
| Plantains | 206 | 231 | 218 |
| Coffee (green) | 149 | 163 | 173 |
| Tobacco | 4 | 4 | 4 |

* FAO estimate.

Source: FAO, *Production Yearbook*.

**LIVESTOCK** ('000 head)

| | 1996 | 1997 | 1998 |
|---|---|---|---|
| Cattle | 2,127 | 2,200 | 1,945† |
| Pigs* | 640 | 670 | 700 |
| Horses and mules* | 244 | 244 | 244 |

Poultry (FAO estimates, million): 15 in 1996; 17 in 1997; 18 in 1998.

* FAO estimates. † Unofficial figure.

Source: FAO, *Production Yearbook*.

**LIVESTOCK PRODUCTS** ('000 metric tons)

| | 1996 | 1997 | 1998 |
|---|---|---|---|
| Beef and veal | 25* | 29 | 22* |
| Pig meat | 15 | 15 | 16 |
| Poultry meat | 54 | 58 | 54 |
| Cows' milk | 529 | 524 | 605 |
| Hen eggs | 41 | 40 | 45† |

* Unofficial figure. † FAO estimate.

Source: FAO, *Production Yearbook*.

# Forestry

**ROUNDWOOD REMOVALS** ('000 cubic metres, excluding bark)

| | 1995 | 1996 | 1997 |
|---|---|---|---|
| Sawlogs, veneer logs and logs for sleepers | 481 | 645 | 704 |
| Other industrial wood | 6 | 1 | 9 |
| Fuel wood | 5,869 | 6,038 | 6,209 |
| **Total** | 6,356 | 6,684 | 6,922 |

Source: FAO, *Yearbook of Forest Products*.

**SAWNWOOD PRODUCTION**
('000 cubic metres, incl. railway sleepers)

| | 1995 | 1996 | 1997 |
|---|---|---|---|
| Coniferous (softwood) | 230 | 321 | 357 |
| Broadleaved (hardwood) | 1 | 1 | 1 |
| **Total** | 231 | 322 | 358 |

Source: FAO, *Yearbook of Forest Products*.

# Fishing

(metric tons, live weight)

| | 1995 | 1996* | 1997* |
|---|---|---|---|
| Freshwater fishes | 127 | 98 | 100 |
| Marine fishes | 8,896 | 7,492 | 6,720 |
| Marine crustaceans | 5,703 | 2,011 | 2,190 |
| Marine molluscs | 5,027 | 4,453 | 4,500 |
| **Total catch** | 19,753 | 14,054 | 13,510 |

* FAO estimates.

Source: FAO, *Yearbook of Fishery Statistics*.

# Mining

(metal content)

| | 1991 | 1992 | 1993 |
|---|---|---|---|
| Lead ('000 metric tons) | 8.7 | 9.2 | 4.9 |
| Zinc ('000 metric tons) | 33.7 | 29.8 | 26.5 |
| Silver (metric tons)* | 43 | 35 | 24 |

**Gold** (kg): 180 in 1991; 163 in 1992; 111 in 1993; 106 in 1994; 110 in 1995; 142 in 1996 (estimate) (Source: US Bureau of Mines).
**Zinc** ('000 metric tons): 16.7 in 1994; 26.2 in 1995; 25.3 in 1996 (Source: US Bureau of Mines).
**Silver** (metric tons)*: 28 in 1994; 31 in 1995; 37 in 1996; 47 in 1997; 47 in 1998.

* Source: The Silver Institute, *World Silver Survey*.

# Industry

**SELECTED PRODUCTS**

| | 1993 | 1994 | 1995 |
|---|---|---|---|
| Raw sugar ('000 quintales) | 3,839 | 3,474 | 4,060 |
| Cement ('000 bags of 42.5 kg) | 21,961 | 23,519 | 23,413 |
| Cigarettes ('000 packets of 20) | 109,642 | 120,311 | 119,425 |
| Matches ('000 boxes of 50) | 67,640 | 83,437 | 95,888 |
| Beer ('000 12 oz bottles) | 235,436 | 217,835 | 236,252 |
| Soft drinks ('000 12 oz bottles) | 876,772 | 947,573 | 1,054,591 |
| Wheat flour ('000 quintales) | 2,284 | 2,277 | 2,161 |
| Fabric ('000 yards) | 14,259 | 11,286 | 12,731 |
| Rum ('000 litres) | 2,409 | 2,530 | 2,375 |
| Other alcoholic drinks ('000 litres) | 4,561 | 4,220 | 5,130 |
| Vegetable oil ('000 lb) | 33,730 | 21,623 | 16,887 |
| Vegetable fat ('000 lb) | 107,115 | 101,276 | 102,942 |

# Finance

## CURRENCY AND EXCHANGE RATES

**Monetary Units**
100 centavos = 1 lempira.

**Sterling, Dollar and Euro Equivalents** (30 September 1999)
£1 sterling = 23.658 lempiras;
US $1 = 14.369 lempiras;
€1 = 15.324 lempiras;
1,000 lempiras = £42.27 = $69.59 = €65.26.

**Average Exchange Rate** (lempiras per US $)
1996 11.7053
1997 13.0035
1998 13.3850

## BUDGET (million lempiras)

| Revenue | 1996 | 1997* | 1998† |
|---|---|---|---|
| Current revenue | 7,927.2 | 10,374.4 | 13,237.2 |
| Taxes | 6,972.6 | 8,652.1 | 11,973.0 |
| Direct taxes | 2,043.2 | 2,512.3 | 3,377.4 |
| Income tax | 1,909.1 | 2,293.3 | 3,110.2 |
| Property tax | 134.1 | 219.0 | 267.2 |
| Indirect taxes | 4,929.4 | 6,139.8 | 8,595.6 |
| External transactions | 1,803.1 | 2,156.1 | 2,115.5 |
| Exports | 97.5 | 88.3 | 72.3 |
| Imports | 1,705.6 | 2,067.8 | 2,043.2 |
| Internal transactions | 3,126.3 | 3,983.7 | 6,480.1 |
| Non-tax revenue | 695.9 | 1,422.1 | 949.0 |
| Transfers | 258.7 | 300.2 | 315.2 |
| Other revenue (incl. capital revenue) | 1.9 | 3.4 | 3.2 |
| **Total** | 7,929.1 | 10,377.8 | 13,240.4 |

| Expenditure | 1996 | 1997* | 1998† |
|---|---|---|---|
| Current expenditure | 7,659.5 | 10,072.2 | 12,093.5 |
| Consumption expenditure | 4,244.3 | 5,421.8 | 7,114.8 |
| Interest | 2,070.0 | 2,697.8 | 2,376.8 |
| Internal debt | 612.0 | 1,090.9 | 748.4 |
| External debt | 1,458.0 | 1,606.9 | 1,628.4 |
| Transfers | 1,345.1 | 1,952.6 | 2,601.9 |
| Capital expenditure | 2,193.6 | 2,912.8 | 4,149.4 |
| Real investment | 1,315.3 | 1,661.2 | 2,291.6 |
| Transfers | 877.3 | 1,243.2 | 1,857.6 |
| Net lending | −110.2 | −795.4 | −468.2 |
| **Total** | 9,742.8 | 12,189.6 | 15,774.7 |

* Preliminary figures. † Estimates.

## CENTRAL BANK RESERVES (US $ million at 31 December)

| | 1996 | 1997 | 1998 |
|---|---|---|---|
| Gold* | 8.03 | 6.43 | n.a. |
| IMF special drawing rights | 0.09 | 0.07 | 0.07 |
| Foreign exchange | 249.10 | 580.30 | 818.00 |
| **Total** | 257.22 | 586.80 | n.a. |

* National valuation.

Source: IMF, *International Financial Statistics*.

## MONEY SUPPLY (million lempiras at 31 December)

| | 1996 | 1997 | 1998 |
|---|---|---|---|
| Currency outside banks | 2,630 | 3,315 | 3,744 |
| Demand deposits at commercial banks | 3,074 | 4,287 | 4,841 |
| **Total money** (incl. others) | 6,053 | 8,294 | 9,344 |

Source: IMF, *International Financial Statistics*.

## COST OF LIVING (Consumer Price Index; base: 1978 = 100)

| | 1996 | 1997 | 1998 |
|---|---|---|---|
| Food | 895.4 | 1,072.4 | 1,198.1 |
| Housing | 783.7 | 904.8 | 1,005.1 |
| Clothing | 1,008.9 | 1,295.0 | 1,496.4 |
| Health care | 960.5 | 1,195.1 | 1,413.9 |
| Personal care | 751.3 | 917.0 | 1,065.0 |
| Beverages and tobacco | 1,120.5 | 1,322.2 | 1,601.5 |
| Transport | 791.4 | 948.6 | 1,068.7 |
| Education, reading matter and recreation | 1,014.9 | 1,308.3 | 1,634.1 |
| **All items** | 881.7 | 1,059.6 | 1,204.7 |

## NATIONAL ACCOUNTS (million lempiras at current prices)

**Expenditure on the Gross Domestic Product**

| | 1996 | 1997 | 1998 |
|---|---|---|---|
| Government final consumption expenditure | 4,556 | 5,118 | 7,434 |
| Private final consumption expenditure | 31,092 | 40,747 | 48,171 |
| Increase in stocks | 3,400 | 3,893 | 763 |
| Gross fixed capital formation | 11,110 | 15,187 | 20,541 |
| **Total domestic expenditure** | 50,158 | 64,945 | 76,909 |
| Exports of goods and services | 22,436 | 28,235 | 31,993 |
| *Less* Imports of goods and services | 24,821 | 31,775 | 37,006 |
| **GDP in purchasers' values** | 47,774 | 61,405 | 71,896 |
| **GDP at constant 1978 prices** | 6,374 | 6,696 | 6,900 |

Source: IMF, *International Financial Statistics*.

**Gross Domestic Product by Economic Activity**

| | 1996 | 1997* | 1998† |
|---|---|---|---|
| Agriculture, hunting, forestry and fishing | 9,188 | 12,396 | 12,637 |
| Mining and quarrying | 763 | 920 | 1,132 |
| Manufacturing | 7,455 | 9,535 | 11,397 |
| Electricity, gas and water | 2,540 | 2,946 | 3,664 |
| Construction | 1,900 | 2,297 | 3,062 |
| Wholesale and retail trade | 4,903 | 6,264 | 7,528 |
| Transport, storage and communications | 1,824 | 2,464 | 2,963 |
| Finance, insurance and real estate | 3,678 | 5,061 | 6,317 |
| Owner-occupied dwellings | 2,317 | 2,941 | 3,487 |
| Public administration and defence | 2,429 | 3,162 | 3,840 |
| Other services | 4,174 | 5,207 | 6,305 |
| **GDP at factor cost** | 41,171 | 53,193 | 62,332 |
| Indirect taxes, *less* subsidies | 6,603 | 8,212 | 9,564 |
| **GDP in purchasers' values** | 47,774 | 61,405 | 71,896 |

* Preliminary figures. † Estimates.

**BALANCE OF PAYMENTS** (US $ million)

| | 1996 | 1997 | 1998 |
|---|---|---|---|
| Exports of goods f.o.b. | 1,638.4 | 1,856.5 | 2,016.5 |
| Imports of goods f.o.b. | -1,925.8 | -2,150.4 | -2,339.6 |
| **Trade balance** | -287.4 | -293.9 | -323.1 |
| Exports of services | 283.3 | 334.9 | 370.0 |
| Imports of services | -327.8 | -360.9 | -396.0 |
| **Balance on goods and services** | -331.9 | -319.9 | -349.1 |
| Other income received | 61.2 | 70.0 | 90.5 |
| Other income paid | -292.0 | -281.8 | -266.2 |
| **Balance on goods, services and income** | -562.7 | -531.7 | -524.8 |
| Current transfers received | 271.7 | 306.8 | 268.6 |
| Current transfers paid | -44.4 | -47.3 | -76.7 |
| **Current balance** | -335.4 | -272.2 | -332.9 |
| Capital account (net) | 28.5 | 14.6 | 47.6 |
| Direct investment from abroad | 90.9 | 121.5 | 84.0 |
| Portfolio investment assets | 16.0 | — | — |
| Portfolio investment liabilities | — | — | -25.8 |
| Other investment assets | -89.4 | -53.4 | -61.7 |
| Other investment liabilities | 52.7 | 175.2 | 264.2 |
| Net errors and omissions | 157.9 | 196.5 | 22.7 |
| **Overall balance** | -78.8 | 182.2 | -1.9 |

Source: IMF, *International Financial Statistics.*

# External Trade

**PRINCIPAL COMMODITIES** (US $ million)

| Imports c.i.f. | 1996 | 1997* | 1998† |
|---|---|---|---|
| Consumer goods | 400.2 | 480.8 | 573.8 |
| Non-durable | 281.2 | 337.9 | 403.2 |
| Durable | 119.0 | 142.9 | 170.6 |
| Crude materials and intermediate products | 661.6 | 794.9 | 948.6 |
| For agriculture | 137.5 | 165.2 | 197.1 |
| For industry | 524.1 | 629.7 | 751.5 |
| Mineral fuels and lubricants | 246.2 | 233.7 | 214.4 |
| Construction materials | 56.3 | 67.6 | 80.7 |
| Capital goods | 440.2 | 528.9 | 631.2 |
| For industry | 243.8 | 293.0 | 349.6 |
| For transport | 178.0 | 213.8 | 255.2 |
| **Total** (incl. others) | 1,840.0 | 2,148.8 | 2,499.8 |

| Exports f.o.b. | 1996 | 1997* | 1998† |
|---|---|---|---|
| Bananas | 279.8 | 212.0 | 175.7 |
| Coffee | 278.9 | 326.3 | 429.8 |
| Shellfish | 178.2 | 179.1 | 158.1 |
| **Total** (incl. others) | 1,320.8 | 1,447.0 | 1,532.9 |

* Preliminary figures. † Estimates.

**PRINCIPAL TRADING PARTNERS** (US $ million)

| Imports c.i.f. | 1995 | 1996 | 1997 |
|---|---|---|---|
| Brazil | 26.3 | 20.5 | 24.2 |
| Cambodia | 18.7 | 19.0 | 16.0 |
| Costa Rica | 57.4 | 59.3 | 56.6 |
| El Salvador | 83.6 | 89.4 | 113.4 |
| France | 5.2 | 19.8 | 9.0 |
| Germany | 37.3 | 30.4 | 33.4 |
| Guatemala | 134.4 | 133.5 | 151.1 |
| Japan | 59.2 | 78.3 | 76.4 |
| Mexico | 72.2 | 90.0 | 115.2 |
| Netherlands | 55.7 | 17.8 | 9.7 |
| Spain | 27.0 | 19.9 | 20.1 |
| USA | 705.2 | 857.6 | 1,033.0 |
| Venezuela | 21.7 | 29.4 | 16.0 |
| **Total** (incl. others) | 1,642.7 | 1,840.0 | 2,148.8 |

| Exports f.o.b. | 1995 | 1996 | 1997 |
|---|---|---|---|
| Belgium | 42.4 | 63.8 | 65.7 |
| Costa Rica | 23.5 | 27.2 | 28.1 |
| El Salvador | 51.9 | 59.1 | 61.0 |
| France | 14.1 | 13.6 | 14.5 |
| Germany | 104.7 | 85.8 | 120.6 |
| Guatemala | 49.2 | 56.0 | 57.8 |
| Italy | 20.5 | 28.8 | 41.7 |
| Japan | 39.3 | 37.6 | 43.2 |
| Netherlands | 23.1 | 29.9 | 15.6 |
| Nicaragua | 56.2 | 64.0 | 66.1 |
| Spain | 38.8 | 43.5 | 49.1 |
| United Kingdom | 29.0 | 21.8 | 52.7 |
| USA | 592.3 | 590.4 | 613.0 |
| **Total** (incl. others) | 1,220.2 | 1,320.8 | 1,447.0 |

# Transport

**ROAD TRAFFIC** (motor vehicles in use)

| | 1993 | 1994 | 1995 |
|---|---|---|---|
| Passenger cars | 67,777 | 72,233 | 81,439 |
| Commercial vehicles | 146,866 | 161,757 | 170,006 |
| Motorcycles and bicycles | 18,021 | 19,427 | 22,482 |

**SHIPPING**

**Merchant Fleet** (registered at 31 December)

| | 1996 | 1997 | 1998 |
|---|---|---|---|
| Number of vessels | 1,408 | 1,339 | 1,465 |
| Total displacement ('000 grt) | 1,197.8 | 1,053.0 | 1,083.2 |

Source: Lloyd's Register of Shipping, *World Fleet Statistics.*

**International Sea-borne Freight Traffic** ('000 metric tons)

| | 1988 | 1989 | 1990 |
|---|---|---|---|
| Goods loaded | 1,328 | 1,333 | 1,316 |
| Goods unloaded | 1,151 | 1,222 | 1,002 |

Source: UN, *Monthly Bulletin of Statistics.*

**CIVIL AVIATION** (traffic on scheduled services)

| | 1993 | 1994 | 1995 |
|---|---|---|---|
| Kilometres flown (million) | 4 | 5 | 5 |
| Passengers carried ('000) | 409 | 449 | 474 |
| Passenger-km (million) | 362 | 323 | 341 |
| Total ton-km (million) | 50 | 42 | 33 |

Source: UN, *Statistical Yearbook.*

# Tourism

**VISITOR ARRIVALS BY COUNTRY OF ORIGIN**

| | 1994 | 1995 | 1996 |
|---|---|---|---|
| Canada | 5,411 | 8,265 | 7,711 |
| Costa Rica | 9,020 | 9,931 | 10,509 |
| El Salvador | 31,328 | 28,065 | 20,778 |
| Germany | 6,121 | 6,877 | 6,602 |
| Guatemala | 18,440 | 18,968 | 23,949 |
| Mexico | 6,301 | 7,683 | 7,698 |
| Nicaragua | 21,014 | 25,413 | 29,174 |
| USA | 92,783 | 109,693 | 107,389 |
| **Total** (incl. others) | 233,516 | 270,549 | 263,317 |

**Receipts from tourism** (US $ million): 72 in 1994; 80 in 1995; 115 in 1996.

Source: World Tourism Organization, *Yearbook of Tourism Statistics.*

## Communications Media

| | 1994 | 1995 | 1996 |
|---|---|---|---|
| Radio receivers ('000 in use) | 2,240 | 2,310 | 2,380 |
| Television receivers ('000 in use) | 428 | 500 | 550 |
| Telephones ('000 main lines in use) | 131 | 161 | n.a. |
| Daily newspapers | | | |
| Number | 5 | 5* | 7 |
| Average circulation ('000 copies) | 240* | 240* | 320 |

* Estimate.

Sources: partly UN, *Statistical Yearbook*, and UNESCO, *Statistical Yearbook*.

## Education

(1995)

| | Institutions | Teachers | Students |
|---|---|---|---|
| Pre-primary | 1,348 | 2,671 | 73,491 |
| Primary | 8,168 | 28,978 | 1,008,092 |
| Secondary | 661 | 12,480 | 184,589 |
| University level | 8 | 3,676 | 54,293 |

# Directory

## The Constitution

Following the elections of April 1980, the 1965 Constitution was revised. The new Constitution was approved by the National Assembly in November 1982, and amended in 1995. The following are some of its main provisions:

Honduras is constituted as a democratic Republic. All Hondurans over 18 years of age are citizens.

### THE SUFFRAGE AND POLITICAL PARTIES

The vote is direct and secret. Any political party which proclaims or practises doctrines contrary to the democratic spirit is forbidden. A National Electoral Council will be set up at the end of each presidential term. Its general function will be to supervise all elections and to register political parties. A proportional system of voting will be adopted for the election of Municipal Corporations.

### INDIVIDUAL RIGHTS AND GUARANTEES

The right to life is declared inviolable; the death penalty is abolished. The Constitution recognizes the right of habeas corpus and arrests may be made only by judicial order. Remand for interrogation may not last more than six days, and no-one may be held incommunicado for more than 24 hours. The Constitution recognizes the rights of free expression of thought and opinion, the free circulation of information, of peaceful, unarmed association, of free movement within and out of the country, of political asylum and of religious and educational freedom. Civil marriage and divorce are recognized.

### WORKERS' WELFARE

All have a right to work. Day work shall not exceed eight hours per day or 44 hours per week; night work shall not exceed six hours per night or 36 hours per week. Equal pay shall be given for equal work. The legality of trade unions and the right to strike are recognized.

### EDUCATION

The State is responsible for education, which shall be free, lay, and, in the primary stage, compulsory. Private education is liable to inspection and regulation by the State.

### LEGISLATIVE POWER

Deputies are obliged to vote, for or against, on any measure at the discussion of which they are present. The National Assembly has power to grant amnesties to political prisoners; approve or disapprove of the actions of the Executive; declare part or the whole of the Republic subject to a state of siege; declare war; approve or withhold approval of treaties; withhold approval of the accounts of public expenditure when these exceed the sums fixed in the budget; decree, interpret, repeal and amend laws, and pass legislation fixing the rate of exchange or stabilizing the national currency. The National Assembly may suspend certain guarantees in all or part of the Republic for 60 days in the case of grave danger from civil or foreign war, epidemics or any other calamity. Deputies are elected in the proportion of one deputy and one substitute for every 35,000 inhabitants, or fraction over 15,000. Congress may amend the basis in the light of increasing population.

### EXECUTIVE POWER

Executive power is exercised by the President of the Republic, who is elected for four years by a simple majority of the people. No President may serve more than one term.

### JUDICIAL POWER

The Judiciary consists of the Supreme Court, the Courts of Appeal and various lesser tribunals. The nine judges and seven substitute judges of the Supreme Court are elected by the National Assembly for a period of four years. The Supreme Court is empowered to declare laws unconstitutional.

### THE ARMED FORCES

The armed forces are declared by the Constitution to be essentially professional and non-political. The President exercises military power through a Commander-in-Chief who is designated for a period of three years by the National Assembly, and may be dismissed only by it by a two-thirds' majority.

### LOCAL ADMINISTRATION

The country is divided into 18 Departments for purposes of local administration, and these are subdivided into autonomous Municipalities; the functions of local offices shall be only economic and administrative.

## The Government

### HEAD OF STATE

**President:** CARLOS ROBERTO FLORES FACUSSÉ (assumed office 27 January 1998).

### CABINET

(February 2000)

**Minister of the Interior and Justice:** ENRIQUE FLORES VALERIANO.

**Minister in the Office of the President:** GUSTAVO ALFARO ZELAYA.

**Minister of Foreign Affairs:** ROBERTO FLORES BERMÚDEZ.

**Minister of Industry and Commerce:** OSCAR KAFATI.

**Minister of Finance:** GABRIELA NÚÑEZ LÓPEZ.

**Minister of National Defence:** EDGARDO DUMAS RODRÍGUEZ.

**Minister of Public Security:** MARÍA E. CHIUZ SIERRA.

**Minister of Labour and Social Welfare:** ROSA AMÉRICA MIRANDA DE GALO.

**Minister of Health:** PLUTARCO CASTELLANOS.

**Minister of Public Education:** RAMÓN CÁLIX FIGUEROA.

**Minister of Public Works, Transport and Housing:** TOMÁS R. LOZANO REYES.

**Minister of Culture, Art and Sports:** HERMÁN ALLAN PADGETT.

**Minister of Agriculture and Livestock:** GUILLERMO ALVARADO DOWNING.

**Minister of Natural Resources and Environment:** SILVIA XIOMARA GÓMEZ DE CABALLERO.

**Minister of Tourism:** ANA ABARCA UCLÉS.

**Minister of International Co-operation:** MOISÉS STARKMAN PINEL.

### MINISTRIES

**Office of the President:** Palacio José Cecilio del Valle, Blvd Juan Pablo II, Tegucigalpa; tel. 32-6282; fax 31-0097.

**Ministry of Agriculture and Livestock:** Tegucigalpa.

**Ministry of Culture, Art and Sports:** Avda La Paz, Tegucigalpa; tel. 36-9738; fax 36-9532.

**Ministry of Finance:** 5a Avda, 3a Calle, Tegucigalpa; tel. 22-1278; fax 38-2309.

**Ministry of Foreign Affairs:** Centro Cívico Gubernamental, Tegucigalpa; tel. 34-3297; fax 34-1484.

**Ministry of Health:** 4a Avda, 3a Calle, Tegucigalpa; tel. 22-1386; fax 38-4141.

**Ministry of Industry and Commerce:** Edif. Salame, 5a Avda, 4a Calle, Tegucigalpa; tel. 38-2025; fax 37-2836.

**Ministry of the Interior and Justice:** Palacio de los Ministerios, 2°, Tegucigalpa; tel. 22-8604; fax 37-1121.

**Ministry of International Co-operation:** Tegucigalpa.

**Ministry of Labour and Social Welfare:** 2a y 3a Avda, 7a Calle, Comayagüela, Tegucigalpa; tel. 22-8526; fax 22-3220.

**Ministry of National Defence and Public Security:** 5a Avda, 4a Calle, Tegucigalpa; tel. 22-8560; fax 38-0238.

**Ministry of Natural Resources and Environment:** Blvd Miraflores, Tegucigalpa; tel. 32-3141.

**Ministry of Public Education:** 1a Avda, 2a y 3a Calle, No 201, Comayagüela, Tegucigalpa; tel. 22-8517; fax 37-4312.

**Ministry of Public Works, Transport and Housing:** Barrio La Bolsa, Comayagüela, Tegucigalpa; tel. 33-7690; fax 25-2227.

**Ministry of Tourism:** Edif. Salame, 5a Avda, 4a Calle, Tegucigalpa; tel. 38-2025; fax 37-2836.

## President and Legislature

### PRESIDENT

**Election, 30 November 1997**

| Candidate | Votes cast | % of votes |
|---|---|---|
| CARLOS ROBERTO FLORES FACUSSÉ (PL) | 1,039,567 | 52.70 |
| ALBA NORA GÚNERA DE MELGAR (PN) | 843,154 | 42.74 |
| OLBAN F. VALLADARES (PINU) | 41,463 | 2.10 |
| ARTURO CORRALES ALVÁREZ (PDCH) | 24,717 | 1.25 |
| MATÍAS FUNES (PUD) | 23.745 | 1.20 |
| **Total** | 1,972,646 | 100.00 |

### ASAMBLEA NACIONAL

**General Election, 30 November 1997**

| Party | Votes cast | % of votes | Seats |
|---|---|---|---|
| Partido Liberal (PL) | 940,575 | 49.55 | 67 |
| Partido Nacional (PN) | 789,015 | 41.56 | 55 |
| Partido Innovación y Unidad—Social Democracia (PINU) | 78,495 | 4.13 | 3 |
| Partido Demócrata Cristiano de Honduras (PDCH) | 49,650 | 2.62 | 2 |
| Partido de Unificación Democrática (PUD) | 40,658 | 2.14 | 1 |
| **Total*** | 1,898,393 | 100.00 | 128 |

* There were, in addition, 108,635 blank votes and 55,431 spoiled votes.

## Political Organizations

**Asociación para el Progreso de Honduras (APROH):** right-wing grouping of business interests and members of the armed forces; Vice-Pres. MIGUEL FACUSSÉ; Sec. OSWALDO RAMOS SOTO.

**Francisco Morazán Frente Constitucional (FMFC):** f. 1988; composed of labour, social, political and other organizations.

**Frente Patriótico Hondureño (FPH):** left-wing alliance comprising:

**Partido de Acción Socialista de Honduras (PASOH):** Leaders MARIO VIRGILIO CARAS, ROGELIO MARTÍNEZ REINA.

**Partido Comunista de Honduras—Marxista-Leninista (PCH—ML):** f. 1954; gained legal status 1981; linked with DNU; Leader RIGOBERTO PADILLA RUSH.

**Partido Demócrata Cristiano de Honduras (PDCH):** legally recognized in 1980; Pres. EFRAÍN DÍAZ ARRIVILLAGA; Leader Dr HERNÁN CORRALES PADILLA.

**Partido Innovación y Unidad—Social Democracia (PINU):** Apdo 105, Tegucigalpa; tel. 37-1357; f. 1970; legally recognized in 1978; Leader OLBAN F. VALLADARES.

**Partido Liberal (PL):** Tegucigalpa; tel. 32-0520; f. 1980; factions within the party include the Alianza Liberal del Pueblo, the Movimiento Florista (Leader CARLOS ROBERTO FLORES FACUSSÉ), and the Movimiento Liberal Democrático Revolucionario (Pres. JORGE ARTURO REINA); Pres. CARLOS ROBERTO FLORES FACUSSÉ; Sec.-Gen. ROBERTO MICHELETTI BAIN.

**Partido Nacional (PN):** Tegucigalpa; f. 1902; traditional right-wing party; internal opposition tendencies include Movimiento Democratizador Nacionalista (MODENA), Movimiento de Unidad y Cambio (MUC), Movimiento Nacional de Reivindicación Callejista (MONARCA) and Tendencia Nacionalista de Trabajo; Pres. CARLOS URBIZO; Sec. MARIO AGUILAR GONZÁLEZ.

**Partido de Unificación Democrática (PUD):** f. 1993; left-wing coalition comprising Partido Revolucionario Hondureño, Partido Renovación Patriótica, Partido para la Transformación de Honduras and Partido Morazanista.

**Pueblo Unido en Bloque por Honduras (PuebloH):** Tegucigalpa; f. 1999; Leader RAMÓN CUSTODIO.

**Unión Revolucionaria del Pueblo (URP):** f. 1980 following split in Communist Party; peasant support.

The Dirección Nacional Unificada—Movimiento Revolucionario Hondureño (DNU—MRH) comprises the following guerrilla groups:

**Fuerzas Populares Revolucionarias (FRP) Lorenzo Zelaya.**

**Frente Morazanista para la Liberación de Honduras (FMLH).**

**Froylan Turcios.**

**Movimiento Popular de Liberación Cinchonero (MPLC).**

**Movimiento de Unidad Revolucionaria (MUR).**

**Partido Revolucionario de los Trabajadores Centroamericanos de Honduras (PRTCH).**

Other guerrilla forces include the **Alianza por Acción Anticomunista (AAA)** and the **Frente Popular de Liberación, Nueve de Mayo (FPL).**

## Diplomatic Representation

### EMBASSIES IN HONDURAS

**Argentina:** Avda José María Medina 417, Col. Rubén Darío, Apdo 3208, Tegucigalpa; tel. 32-3376; fax 31-0376; Ambassador: ADRIÁN GUILLERMO MIRSON.

**Brazil:** Col. La Reforma, Calle La Salle 1309, Apdo 341, Tegucigalpa; tel. 236-5867; fax 236-5873; e-mail brastegu@hondudata.com; Ambassador: RUBEM AMARAL Jr.

**Chile:** Edif. Interamericana frente Los Castaños, Blvd Morazán, Apdo 222, Tegucigalpa; fax 32-8853; Ambassador: GERMÁN CARRASCO.

**China (Taiwan):** Col. Lomas del Guijarro, Calle Eucaliptos 3750, Apdo 3433, Tegucigalpa; tel. 31-1484; e-mail giohon@datum.hn; Ambassador: CHING-YEN CHANG.

**Colombia:** Edif. Palmira, 4°, Col. Palmira, Apdo 468, Tegucigalpa; tel. 32-9709; fax 32-8133; Ambassador: GERMÁN RAMÍREZ BULLA.

**Costa Rica:** Residencial El Triángulo, Lomas del Guijarro, Apdo 512, Tegucigalpa; tel. 32-1768; fax 32-1876; Ambassador: MANUEL CARBALLO QUINTANA.

**Dominican Republic:** Col. La Granja 402, 4a Calle entre 4a y 5a Avda Comayagüela, Apdo 1460, Tegucigalpa; Ambassador: JUAN EMILIO CANÓ DE LA MOTA.

**Ecuador:** Col. Palmira, Avda Juan Lindo 122, Apdo 358, Tegucigalpa; tel. 36-5980; fax 36-6929; Ambassador: Dr JOSÉ IGNACIO JIJÓN FREILE.

**El Salvador:** Col. San Carlos, 2a Avda 219, Tegucigalpa; tel. 36-7344; fax 36-9403; Ambassador: Dr BYRON FERNANDO LARIOS LÓPEZ.

**France:** Col. Palmira, Avda Juan Lindo, Apdo 3441, Tegucigalpa; tel. 36-6800; fax 36-8051; Ambassador: GILLES VIDAL.

**Germany:** Edif. Paysen, 3°, Blvd Morazán, Apdo 3145, Tegucigalpa; tel. 32-3161; fax 32-9518; Ambassador: ANDREAS KULICK.

**Guatemala:** Col. Palmira, Avda Juan Lindo 313, Apdo 34-C, Tegucigalpa; tel. 32-5018; Ambassador: EUNICE LIMA.

**Holy See:** Palacio de la Nunciatura Apostólica, Col. Palmira 412, Apdo 324, Tegucigalpa; tel. 236-6613; fax 232-8280; e-mail nunciatureateg@hondudata.com; Apostolic Nuncio: Most Rev. GEORGE PANIKULAM, Titular Archbishop of Arpaia.

**Israel:** Edif. Palmira, Col. Palmira, Apdo 1187, Tegucigalpa; Ambassador: SHIMON AGOUR.

**Italy:** Col. Reforma 2062, Avda Principal, Apdo 317, Tegucigalpa; Ambassador: Dr MARIO ALBERTO MONTECALVO.

**Japan:** Col. Reforma, 2a Avda, Plaza del Guanacaste, Apdo 125-C, Tegucigalpa; Ambassador: KIICHI ITABASHI.

**Mexico:** Avda República de México 2402, Apdo 769, Tegucigalpa; tel. 32-4039; fax 32-4224; Ambassador: BENITO ANDION SANCHO.

**Nicaragua:** Col. Tepeyac, Bloque M-1, Apdo 392, Tegucigalpa; tel. 232-7224; fax 231-1412; Ambassador: Dr JOSÉ RENÉ GUTIÉRREZ HUETE.

**Panama:** Edif. Palmira, Col. Palmira, Apdo 397, Tegucigalpa; tel. 31-5441; fax 31-5441; Ambassador: JULIO E. GÓMEZ AMADOR.

**Peru:** Col. Alameda, Villeda Morales 1902, Apdo 3171, Tegucigalpa; tel. 31-5261; fax 32-0145; Ambassador: JOSÉ ARTURO MONTOYA STUVA.

**Spain:** Col. Matamoros, Calle Santander 801, Apdo 3223, Tegucigalpa; tel. 236-6875; fax 236-8682; Ambassador: CARLOS GÓMEZ-MÚGICA SANZ.

**United Kingdom:** Edif. Palmira, 3°, Col. Palmira, Apdo 290, Tegucigalpa; tel. 32-0612; fax 32-5480; Ambassador: DAVID A. OSBORNE.

**USA:** Avda La Paz, Apdo 26-C, Tegucigalpa; tel. 32-3120; fax 32-0027; Ambassador: JAMES F. CREAGAN.

**Uruguay:** Edif. Palmira, 4°, Col. Palmira, Apdo 329, Tegucigalpa; Ambassador: ALFREDO MENINI TERRA.

**Venezuela:** Col. Rubén Darío, entre Avda Las Minitas y Avda Rubén Darío, Casa 2321, Tegucigalpa; Ambassador: JESÚS ELÍAS M.

# Judicial System

Justice is administered by the Supreme Court (which has nine judges), five Courts of Appeal, and departmental courts (which have their own local jurisdiction).

Tegucigalpa has two Courts of Appeal which have jurisdiction (1) in the department of Francisco Morazán, and (2) in the departments of Choluteca Valle, El Paraíso and Olancho.

The Appeal Court of San Pedro Sula has jurisdiction in the department of Cortés. That of Comayagua has jurisdiction in the departments of Comayagua, La Paz and Intibucá; that of Santa Bárbara in the departments of Santa Bárbara, Lempira and Copán.

**Supreme Court:** Edif. Palacio de Justicia, contiguo Col. Miraflores, Centro Cívico Gubernamental, Tegucigalpa; tel. 33-9208; fax 33-6784.

**President of the Supreme Court of Justice:** OSCAR ARMANDO AVILA.

**Attorney-General:** EDMUNDO ORELLANA.

# Religion

The majority of the population are Roman Catholics; the Constitution guarantees toleration to all forms of religious belief.

## CHRISTIANITY

### The Roman Catholic Church

Honduras comprises one archdiocese and six dioceses. At 31 December 1997 some 91% of the population were adherents.

**Bishops' Conference:** Conferencia Episcopal de Honduras, Blvd Suyapa, Apdo 847, Tegucigalpa; tel. 239-1900; fax 232-7838; e-mail ceh@sdnhon.org.hn; f. 1929; Pres. Most Rev. OSCAR ANDRÉS RODRÍGUEZ MARADIAGA, Archbishop of Tegucigalpa.

**Archbishop of Tegucigalpa:** Most Rev. OSCAR ANDRÉS RODRÍGUEZ MARADIAGA, Arzobispado, 3a-2a Avda 1113, Apdo 106, Tegucigalpa; tel. 237-0353; fax 222-2337.

### The Anglican Communion

Honduras comprises a single missionary diocese, in Province IX of the Episcopal Church in the USA.

**Bishop of Honduras:** Rt Rev. LEOPOLD FRADE, Apdo 586, San Pedro Sula; tel. 556-6155; fax 556-6467; e-mail episcopal@mayanet.hn.

### The Baptist Church

**Baptist Convention of Honduras:** Apdo 868, Tegucigalpa; tel. and fax 38-3717; Pres. MISAEL MARRIAGA.

## BAHÁ'Í FAITH

**National Spiritual Assembly:** Sendero de los Naranjos 2801, Col. Castaños, Apdo 273, Tegucigalpa; tel. 232-6124; fax 231-1343; e-mail bahaihon@globenet.hn; mems resident in 667 localities.

# The Press

## DAILIES

**El Faro Porteño:** Puerto Cortés.

**La Gaceta:** Tegucigalpa; f. 1830; morning; official govt paper; Dir MARCIAL LAGOS; circ. 3,000.

**El Heraldo:** Avda los Próceres, Frente Instituto del Tórax, Barrio San Felipe, Apdo 1938, Tegucigalpa; tel. 36-6000; fax 21-0778; f. 1979; morning; independent; Dir JOSÉ FRANCISCO MORALES CÁLIX; circ. 45,000.

**El Nuevo Día:** 3a Avda, 11–12 Calles, San Pedro Sula; tel. 52-4298; fax 57-9457; e-mail elndia@hondutel.hn; f. 1994; morning; independent; Pres. ABRAHAM ANDONIE; Editor ARMANDO CERRATO; circ. 20,000.

**El Periódico:** Carretera al Batallón, Tegucigalpa; tel. 34-3086; fax 34-3090; f. 1993; morning; Pres. EMIN ABUFELE; Editor OSCAR ARMANDO MARTÍNEZ.

**La Prensa:** 3a Avda, 6a–7a Calles No 34, Apdo 143, San Pedro Sula; tel. 53-3101; fax 53-0778; e-mail laprensa@simon.intertel.hn; internet www.laprensahn.com; f. 1964; morning; independent; Pres. JORGE CANAHUATI LARACH; Editor NELSON EDGARDO FERNÁNDEZ; circ. 62,000.

**El Tiempo:** Altos del Centro Comercial Miramontes, Col. Miramontes, Tegucigalpa; tel. 31-0418; f. 1970; liberal; Dir MANUEL GAMERO; circ. 42,000.

**El Tiempo:** 1a Calle, 5a Avda 102, Santa Anita, Apdo 450, San Pedro Sula; tel. 53-3388; fax 53-4590; e-mail tiempo@simon.intertel.hn; internet www.tiempo.hn; f. 1960; morning; left-of-centre; Pres. JAIME ROSENTHAL OLIVA; Editor MANUEL GAMERO; circ. 35,000.

**La Tribuna:** Col. Santa Bárbara, Comayagüela, Apdo 1501, Tegucigalpa; tel. 33-1138; fax 33-1188; e-mail tribuna@david.intertel.hn; internet www.latribuna.hn; f. 1977; morning; independent; Dir ADÁN ELVIR FLORES; Pres. CARLOS ROBERTO FLORES FACUSSÉ; circ. 45,000.

## PERIODICALS

**Cambio Empresarial:** Apdo 1111, Tegucigalpa; tel. 37-2853; fax 37-0480; monthly; economic, political, social; Editor JOAQUÍN MEDINA OVIEDO.

**El Comercio:** Cámara de Comercio e Industrias de Tegucigalpa, Blvd Centroamérica, Apdo 3444, Tegucigalpa; tel. 32-8210; fax 31-2049; f. 1970; monthly; commercial and industrial news; Exec. Dir JOSÉ ANÍBAL MADRID.

**Cultura para Todos:** San Pedro Sula; monthly.

**Espectador:** San Pedro Sula; weekly.

**Extra:** Tegucigalpa; tel. 37-2533; f. 1965; monthly; independent; current affairs; Editor VICENTE MACHADO VALLE.

**Hablemos Claro:** Edif. Abriendo Brecha, Blvd Suyapa, Tegucigalpa; tel. 232-8058; fax 239-7008; e-mail abrecha@hondutel.hn; f. 1990; weekly; Editor RODRIGO WONG ARÉVALO; circ. 15,000.

**Hibueras:** Apdo 955, Tegucigalpa; Dir RAÚL LANZA VALERIANO.

**Presente:** Tegucigalpa; monthly.

**Revista Ideas:** Tegucigalpa; 6 a year; women's interest.

**Revista Prisma:** Tegucigalpa; quarterly; cultural; Editor MARÍA LUISA CASTELLANOS.

**Sucesos:** Tegucigalpa; monthly.

**Tribuna Sindical:** Tegucigalpa; monthly.

## PRESS ASSOCIATION

**Asociación de Prensa Hondureña:** 6a Calle (altos), Barrio Guanacaste, Apdo 893, Tegucigalpa; tel. 37-8345; f. 1930; Pres. MIGUEL OSMUNDO MEJA ERAZO.

## FOREIGN NEWS AGENCIES

**Agence France-Presse (AFP)** (France): Tegucigalpa; Correspondent WINSTON CÁLIX.

**Agencia EFE** (Spain): Edif. Jiménez Castro, 5°, Of. 505, Tegucigalpa; tel. 22-0493; Bureau Chief ARMANDO ENRIQUE CERRATO CORTÉS.

**Agenzia Nazionale Stampa Associata (ANSA)** (Italy): Edif. La Plazuela, Barrio La Plazuela, Tegucigalpa; tel. 37-7701; Correspondent RAÚL MONCADA.

**Deutsche Presse-Agentur (dpa)** (Germany): Edif. Jiménez Castro, Of. 203, 4a Calle y 5a Avda, No 405, Apdo 3522, Tegucigalpa; tel. 37-8570; Correspondent WILFREDO GARCÍA CASTRO.

**Inter Press Service (IPS)** (Italy): Apdo 228, Tegucigalpa; tel. 32-5342; Correspondent JUAN RAMÓN DURÁN.

**Reuters** (United Kingdom): Edif. Palmira, frente Honduras Maya, 5°, Col. Palmira, Tegucigalpa; tel. 31-5329.

**United Press International (UPI)** (USA): c/o El Tiempo, Altos del Centro Comercial Miramontes, Col. Miramontes, Tegucigalpa; tel. 31-0418; Correspondent VILMA GLORIA ROSALES.

# Publishers

**Compañía Editora Nacional, SA:** 5a Calle Oriente, No 410, Tegucigalpa.

**Editora Cultural:** 6a Avda Norte, 7a Calle, Comayagüela, Tegucigalpa.

**Editorial Nuevo Continente:** Tegucigalpa; tel. 22-5073; Dir LETICIA SILVA DE OYUELA.

**Editorial Paulino Valladares, Carlota Vda de Valladares:** 5a Avda, 5a y 6a Calle, Tegucigalpa.

**Guaymuras:** Apdo 1843, Tegucigalpa; tel. 237-5433; fax 237-9931; f. 1980; Dir ISOLDA ARITA MELZER; Admin. ROSENDO ANTÚNEZ.

**Industria Editorial Lypsa:** Apdo 167-C, Tegucigalpa; tel. 22-9775; Man. JOSÉ BENNATON.

**Universidad Nacional Autónoma de Honduras:** Blvd Suyapa, Tegucigalpa; tel. 31-4601; fax 31-4601; f. 1847.

# Broadcasting and Communications

### TELECOMMUNICATIONS

**Comisión Nacional de Telecomunicaciones (Conatel):** Apdo 15012, Tegucigalpa; tel. 221-3500; fax 221-0578; e-mail nhernández @conatel.hn; Pres. NORMAN ROY HERNÁNDEZ D.; Exec. Sec. WALTER DAVID SANDOVAL.

**Empresa Hondureña de Telecomunicaciones (Hondutel):** Apdo 1794, Tegucigalpa; tel. 22-2041; fax 38-4206; scheduled for privatization in 2000; Gen. Man. ARTURO MORALES FÚNEZ.

### BROADCASTING

#### Radio

**Radio América:** Col. Alameda, frente a la Droguería Mandofer, Apdo 259, Tegucigalpa; commercial station; tel. 32-7028; fax 31-4180; f. 1948; 13 relay stations; Pres. MANUEL ANDONIE FERNÁNDEZ; Gen. Man. BERNARDINO RIVERA.

**Radio Nacional de Honduras:** Zona El Olvido, Apdo 403, Tegucigalpa; tel. 38-5478; fax 37-9721; f. 1976; official station, operated by the Govt; Dir ROY ARTHURS LEYLOR.

**Radio Tegucigalpa:** Edif. Landa Blanca, Calle La Fuente, Tegucigalpa; tel. 38-3880; f. 1982; Dir NERY ARTEAGA; Gen. Man. ANTONIO CONDE MAZARIEGOS.

**La Voz de Centroamérica:** 9a Calle, 10a Avda 64, Apdo 120, San Pedro Sula; tel. 52-7660; fax 57-3257; f. 1955; commercial station; Gen. Man. NOEMI SIKAFFY.

**La Voz de Honduras:** Blvd Suyapa, Apdo 642, Tegucigalpa; commercial station; 23 relay stations; Gen. Man. NOEMI VALLADARES.

#### Television

**Centroamericana de Televisión, Canal 7 y 4:** Edif. Televicentro, Blvd Suyapa, Apdo 734, Tegucigalpa; tel. 39-2081; fax 32-0097; f. 1959; Pres. JOSÉ RAFAEL FERRARI; Gen. Man. RAFAEL ENRIQUE VILLEDA.

**Compañía Televisora Hondureña, SA:** Blvd Suyapa, Apdo 734, Tegucigalpa; tel. 232-7835; fax 232-0097; f. 1959; main station Channel 5; nine relay stations; Gen. Man. JOSÉ RAFAEL FERRARI.

**Corporación Centroamericana de Comunicaciones, SA de CV:** 9a Calle, 10a Avda 64, Barrio Guamilito, Apdo 120, San Pedro Sula; tel. 52-7660; fax 57-3257; f. 1986; Pres. BLANCA SIKAFFY.

**Voz y Imagen de Centro América:** 9a Calle, 10a Avda 64, Barrio Guamilito, Apdo 120, San Pedro Sula; tel. 52-7660; fax 57-3257; Channels 9, 2 and 13; Pres. BLANCA SIKAFFY.

**Telesistema Hondureño, SA, Canal 3:** Edif. Televicentro, Blvd Suyapa, Apdo 734, Tegucigalpa; tel. 32-7064; fax 32-5019; f. 1967; Pres. MANUEL VILLEDA TOLEDO; Gen. Man. RAFAEL ENRIQUE VILLEDA.

**Telesistema Hondureño, Canal 7:** Col. Tara, Apdo 208, San Pedro Sula; tel. 53-1229; fax 57-6343; f. 1967; Pres. MANUEL VILLEDA TOLEDO; Dir JOSÉ RAFAEL FERRARI.

**Trecevisión:** Apdo 393, Tegucigalpa; subscriber TV; one relay station in San Pedro Sula; Gen. Man. F. PON AGUILAR.

# Finance

(cap. = capital; res = reserves; dep. = deposits;
m. = million; brs = branches;
amounts in lempiras unless otherwise stated)

### BANKING

#### Central Bank

**Banco Central de Honduras—BANTRAL:** 6a y 7a Avda, 1a Calle, Apdo 3165, Tegucigalpa; tel. 237-2270; fax 237-1876; internet www.bch.hn; f. 1950; bank of issue; cap. 63.7m., res 373.5m., dep. 4,762.2m. (Dec. 1992); Pres. VICTORIA ASFURA DE DÍAZ; Man. J. ERNESTO ANARIBA; 4 brs.

#### Commercial Banks

**Banco de el Ahorro Hondureño, SA (BANCAHORRO):** Avda Colón 711, Apdo 78-C, Tegucigalpa; tel. 22-5161. 1960; Pres. and Gen. Man. FRANCISCO VILLARS; 8 brs.

**Banco Atlántida, SA (BANCATLAN):** Blvd Centroamérica, Plaza Bancatlán, Apdo 3164, Tegucigalpa; tel. 232-1742; fax 232-6120; e-mail webmaster@bancatlán.hn; internet www.bancatlán.hn; f. 1913; cap. 500.0m., dep. 4,523.5m. (Dec. 1999); Exec. Pres. GUILLERMO BUESO; First Vice-Pres. SALVADOR GÓMEZ A.; 18 brs.

**Banco La Capitalizadora Hondureña, SA (BANCAHSA):** 5a Avda, 5a Calle 508, Apdo 344, Tegucigalpa; tel. 337-1171; fax 332-2775; f. 1948; cap. and res US $16.3m., dep. $119.9m. (June 1995); Pres. and Gen. Man. JORGE ALBERTO ALVARADO; 52 brs.

**Banco del Comercio, SA (BANCOMER):** 6a Avda, Calle SO 1-2, Apdo 160, San Pedro Sula; tel. 54-3600; Pres. RODOLFO CÓRDOBA PINEDA; 4 brs.

**Banco Continental, SA (BANCON):** Edif. Continental, 3a Avda 7, entre 2a y 3a Calle, Apdo 390, San Pedro Sula; tel. 550-2942; fax 550-2750; f. 1974; cap. 100m., res 14.3m., dep. 304.5m. (Dec. 1994); Pres. JAIME ROSENTHAL OLIVA; 6 brs.

**Banco de las Fuerzas Armadas, SA (BANFFAA):** Centro Comercial Los Castaños, Blvd Morazán, Apdo 877, Tegucigalpa; tel. 331-2051; fax 331-3825; f. 1979; cap. 10m., res 33.2m., dep. 428.1m. (Dec. 1992); Pres. LUIS ALONSO DISCUA ELVIR; Gen. Man. CARLOS RIVERA XATRUCH; 15 brs.

**Banco de Honduras, SA:** Edif. Midence-Soto, frente a Plaza Morazán, Apdo 3434, Tegucigalpa; tel. 332-6122; fax 332-6167; f. 1889; cap. and res 23.4m., dep. 190m. (Dec. 1994); Gen. Man. PATRICIA FERRO; 3 brs.

**Banco Mercantil, SA:** Blvd Suyapa, frente a Emisoras Unidas, Apdo 116, Tegucigalpa; tel. 32-0006; fax 32-3137; Pres. JOSÉ LAMAS; Gen. Man. JACOBO ATALA.

**Banco de Occidente, SA (BANCOCCI):** Calle Centenario, Apdo 208, Santa Rosa de Copán; tel. 662-0159; fax 662-0692; e-mail boccipan@pty.com; f. 1951; cap. and res 69m., dep. 606m. (June 1994); Pres. and Gen. Man. JORGE BUESO ARIAS; Vice-Pres. EMILIO MEDINA R.; 6 brs.

**Banco Sogerin, SA:** 8a Avda, 1a Calle, Apdo 440, San Pedro Sula; tel. 550-3888; fax 550-2001; e-mail sogelba@hondutel.hn; f. 1969; cap. and res 132.7m., dep. 812m. (Dec. 1998); Pres. and Gen. Man. EDMOND BOGRÁN ACOSTA; 39 brs.

**Banco de los Trabajadores, SA (BANCOTRAB):** 3a Avda, 13a Calle, Paseo El Obelisco, Comayagüela, Apdo 3246, Tegucigalpa; tel. 37-8723; f. 1967; cap. and res US $6.6m., dep. $43.1m. (Dec. 1992); Pres. ROLANDO DEL CID VELÁSQUEZ; 13 brs.

#### Development Banks

**Banco Centroamericano de Integración Económica:** Apdo 772, Tegucigalpa; tel. 228-2243; fax 228-2185; f. 1960 to finance the economic development of the Central American Common Market and its mem. countries; mems Costa Rica, El Salvador, Guatemala, Honduras, Nicaragua; cap. and res US $1,005.7m. (June 1999); Exec. Pres. ALEJANDRO ARÉVALO.

**Banco Hondureño del Café, SA (BANHCAFE):** Calle República de Costa Rica, Blvd Juan Pablo II, Apdo 583, Tegucigalpa; tel. 232-8370; fax 232-8671; e-mail bancafeinf@hondutel.hn; f. 1981 to help finance coffee production; owned principally by private coffee producers; cap. 34.0m., res 17.8m., dep. 671.3m. (Dec. 1996); Pres. RAMÓN DAVID RIVERA; Gen. Man. RENÉ ARDÓN MATUTE; 2 brs.

**Banco Municipal Autónomo (BANMA):** 6a Avda, 6a Calle, Tegucigalpa; tel. 22-5963; fax 37-5187; f. 1963; Pres. JUSTO PASTOR CALDERÓN; 2 brs.

**Banco Nacional de Desarrollo Agrícola (BANADESA):** 405 Avda Comayagüela, 13a Calle, Comayagüela, Apdo 212, Tegucigalpa; tel. 337-3802; fax 337-5187; f. 1980; govt development bank (transfer to private ownership pending); loans to agricultural sector; cap. 34.5m., res 42.7m., dep. 126.9m. (March 1993); Pres. GUSTAVO A. ZELAYA CHÁVEZ; 34 brs.

**Financiera Centroamericana, SA (FICENSA):** Edif. FICENSA, Blvd Los Castaños, Apdo 1432, Tegucigalpa; tel. 38-1661; fax 38-1630; f. 1974; private org. providing finance for industry, commerce and transport; cap. and res US $5.1m., dep. $42.6m. (Dec. 1995); Pres. OSWALDO LÓPEZ ARELLANO; Gen. Man. ROQUE RIVERA RIBAS.

**Financiera Nacional de la Vivienda—FINAVI:** Apdo 1194, Tegucigalpa; f. 1975; housing development bank; Exec. Pres. Lic. ELMAR LIZARDO.

#### Foreign Bank

**Lloyds TSB Bank PLC:** Edif. Europa, Col. San Carlos, Calle República de México, Avda Ramón Ernesto Cruz, Apdo 3136, Tegucigalpa; tel. 236-6864; fax 236-6417; e-mail lloydstsb@david.intertel .hn; Man. G. JOHNS.

### Banking Association

**Asociación Hondureña de Instituciones Bancarias (AHIBA):** Blvd Suyapa contiguo a CANNON, Apdo 1344, Tegucigalpa; tel. 35-6770; fax 39-0191; f. 1956; 22 mem. banks; Pres. JACOBO ATALA Z.; Exec. Sec. GUILLERMO MATAMOROS.

### STOCK EXCHANGE

**Bolsa Hondureña de Valores:** Edif. Martínez Valenzuela, 1°, 2a Calle, 3a Avda, San Pedro Sula; tel. 553-4410; fax 553-4480; e-mail bhvsps@bhv.hn2.com; Gen. Man. MARCO TULIO LÓPEZ PEREIRA.

### INSURANCE

**American Home Assurance Co:** Edif. Los Castaños, 4°, Blvd Morazán, Apdo 3220, Tegucigalpa; tel. 232-3938; fax 232-8169; f. 1958; Mans LEONARDO MOREIRA, EDGAR WAGNER.

**Aseguradora Hondureña, SA:** Centro Comercial Plaza Miraflores, 3°, Col. Miraflores, Apdo 312, Tegucigalpa; tel. 32-2729; fax 31-0982; f. 1954; Pres. FRANÇOIS DE PEYRECAVE; Gen. Man. ALBERTO AGURCIA.

**Compañía de Seguros El Ahorro Hondureño, SA:** Edif. Trinidad, Avda Colón, Apdo 3643, Tegucigalpa; tel. 237-8219; fax 237-4780; e-mail elahorro@seguroselahorro.hn; f. 1917; Pres. JORGE A. ALVARADO.

**Interamericana de Seguros, SA:** Col. Los Castaños, Apdo 593, Tegucigalpa; tel. 32-7614; fax 32-7762; f. 1957; Pres. CAMILO ATALA FARAJ; Gen. Man. LUIS ATALA FARAJ.

**Pan American Life Insurance Co (PALIC):** Edif. PALIC, Avda República de Chile 804, Tegucigalpa; tel. 32-8774; fax 32-3907; f. 1944; Gen. Man. FERNANDO RODRÍGUEZ.

**Previsión y Seguros, SA:** Edif. Maya, Col. Palmira, Apdo 770, Tegucigalpa; tel. 31-2127; fax 32-5215; f. 1982; Pres. Gen. HÉCTOR CASTRO CABUS; Gen. Man. P. M. ARTURO BOQUÍN OSEJO.

**Seguros Atlántida:** Edif. Sonisa, Costado Este Plaza Bancatlán, Tegucigalpa; tel. 232-4014; fax 232-3688; e-mail morellana@bancatlan.hn; f. 1986; Pres. GUILLERMO BUESO; Gen. Man. JUAN MIGUEL ORELLANA.

**Seguros Continental, SA:** 3a Avda 2 y 3, 7a Calle, Apdo 320, San Pedro Sula; tel. 52-0880; fax 52-2750; f. 1968; Pres. JAIME ROSENTHAL OLIVA; Gen. Man. MARIO R. SOLÍS.

**Seguros Crefisa:** Edif. Banfinan, 6°, Avda Cervantes 602, Apdo 3774, Tegucigalpa; tel. 38-5799; fax 38-8064; f. 1993; Pres. OSWALDO LÓPEZ ARELLANO; Gen. Man. HÉCTOR EDGARDO CHAVARRÍA R.

### Insurance Association

**Cámara Hondureña de Aseguradores (CAHDA):** Edif. Los Jarros, Blvd Morazán, Local 313, Apdo 3290, Tegucigalpa; tel. 239-0342; fax 232-6020; e-mail cahda@gbm.hn; f. 1974; Man. JOSÉ LUIS MONCADA RODRÍGUEZ.

## Trade and Industry

### GOVERNMENT AGENCIES

**Fondo Hondureño de Inversión Social (FHIS):** Tegucigalpa; social investment fund; Gen. Man. MANUEL ZELAYA ROSALES.

**Fondo Social de la Vivienda (FOSOVI):** Col. Florencia, Tegucigalpa; tel. 39-1605; social fund for housing, urbanization and devt; Gen. Man. MARIO MARTÍ.

**Secretaria Técnica del Consejo Superior de Planificación Económica (CONSUPLANE):** Edif. Bancatlán, 3°, Apdo 1327, Comayagüela, Tegucigalpa; tel. 22-8738; f. 1965; national planning office; Exec. Sec. FRANCISCO FIGUEROA ZÚÑIGA.

### DEVELOPMENT ORGANIZATIONS

**Consejo Hondureño de la Empresa Privada (COHEP):** Col. Reforma, Calle Principal 2723, Apdo 3240, Tegucigalpa; f. 1968; comprises 23 private enterprises; Pres. EDUARDO FACUSSÉ.

**Corporación Financiera de Olancho:** f. 1977 to co-ordinate and manage all financial aspects of the Olancho forests project; Pres. RAFAEL CALDERÓN LÓPEZ.

**Corporación Hondureña de Desarrollo Forestal (COHDEFOR):** Salida Carretera del Norte, Zona El Carrizal, Comayagüela; Apdo 1378, Tegucigalpa; tel. 22-8810; fax 22-2653; f. 1974; semi-autonomous org. exercising control and man. of the forestry industry; transfer of all sawmills to private ownership was proceeding in 1991; Gen. Man. PORFIRIO LOBO S.

**Dirección General de Minas e Hidrocarburos** (General Directorate of Mines and Hydrocarbons): Blvd Miraflores, Apdo 981, Tegucigalpa; tel. 32-7848; fax 32-7848; Dir-Gen. MIGUEL VILLEDA VILLELA.

**Instituto Hondureño del Café (IHCAFE):** Apdo 40-C, Tegucigalpa; tel. 37-3131; f. 1970; coffee devt programme; Gen. Man. FERNANDO D. MONTES M.

**Instituto Hondureño de Mercadeo Agrícola (IHMA):** Apdo 727, Tegucigalpa; tel. 35-3193; fax 35-5719; f. 1978; agricultural devt agency; Gen. Man. TULIO ROLANDO GIRÓN ROMERO.

**Instituto Nacional Agrario (INA):** Col. La Almeda, 4a Avda, entre 10a y 11a Calles, No 1009, Apdo 3391, Tegucigalpa; tel. 32-8400; fax 32-8398; agricultural devt programmes; Exec. Dir ANÍBAL DELGADO FIALLOS.

### CHAMBERS OF COMMERCE

**Cámara de Comercio e Industrias de Cortés:** 17a Avda, 10a y 12a Calle, Apdo 14, San Pedro Sula; tel. 53-0761; f. 1931; 812 mems; Pres. ROBERTO REYES SILVA; Dir LUIS FERNANDO RIVERA.

**Cámara de Comercio e Industrias de Tegucigalpa:** Blvd Centroamérica, Apdo 3444, Tegucigalpa; tel. 232-8110; fax 232-0159; e-mail camara@ccit.hn; internet www.ccit.hn; Pres. ANTONIO TAVEL OTERO.

**Federación de Cámaras de Comercio e Industrias de Honduras (FEDECAMARA):** Edif. Castañito, 2°, Col. Los Castaños, Sur 6a Avda, Calle Jamaica, Apdo 3393, Tegucigalpa; tel. 32-6083; fax 32-1870; f. 1948; 1,200 mems; Pres. ROLIN ELI ESCOBER; Exec. Dir DELFINA MEDINA.

### INDUSTRIAL AND TRADE ASSOCIATIONS

**Asociación de Bananeros Independientes (ANBI)** (National Association of Independent Banana Producers): San Pedro Sula; tel. 22-7336; f. 1964; 62 mems; Pres. Ing. JORGE ALBERTO ALVARADO; Sec. CECILIO TRIMINIO TURCIOS.

**Asociación Hondureña de Productores de Café** (Coffee Producers' Association): 10a Avda, 6a Calle, Apdo 959, Tegucigalpa.

**Asociación Nacional de Exportadores de Honduras (ANEXHON)** (National Association of Exporters): Tegucigalpa; comprises 104 private enterprises; Pres. Dr RICHARD ZABLAH.

**Asociación Nacional de Industriales (ANDI)** (National Association of Manufacturers): Blvd Los Próceres 505, Apdo 20-C, Tegucigalpa; Pres. HÉCTOR BULNES; Exec. Sec. DORCAS DE GONZALES.

**Asociación Nacional de Pequeños Industriales (ANPI)** (National Association of Small Industries): Apdo 730, Tegucigalpa; Pres. JUAN RAFAEL CRUZ.

**Federación Nacional de Agricultores y Ganaderos de Honduras (FENAGH)** (Farmers and Livestock Breeders' Association): Tegucigalpa; tel. 31-1392; Pres. ROBERTO GALLARDO LARDIZÁBAL.

**Federación Nacional de Cooperativas Cañeras (Fenacocal)** (National Federation of Sugar Cane Co-operatives): Tegucigalpa.

### UTILITIES

#### Electricity

**Empresa Nacional de Energía Eléctrica—ENEE** (National Electrical Energy Co): Apdo 99, Tegucigalpa; tel 22-2432; state-owned electricity co; scheduled for privatization; Man. SALOMÁN ORDÓÑEZ.

### TRADE UNIONS

**Asociación Nacional de Empleados Públicos de Honduras (ANDEPH)** (National Association of Public Employees of Honduras): Plaza Los Dolores, Tegucigalpa; tel. 37-4393; Pres. OSCAR MARTÍNEZ.

**Confederación de Trabajadores de Honduras—CTH** (Workers' Confederation of Honduras): Edif. FARAJ, 5°, Avda Lempira, Barrio La Fuente, Apdo 720, Tegucigalpa; tel. 38-7859; fax 37-4243; f. 1964; affiliated to CTCA, ORIT, CIOSL, FIAET and ICFTU; Pres. JOSÉ ANGEL MEZA; Sec.-Gen. FRANCISCO GUERRERO NÚÑEZ; 200,000 mems; comprises the following federations:

**Federación Central de Sindicatos Libres de Honduras (FECESITLIH)** (Honduran Federation of Free Trade Unions): 1a Avda, 1a Calle 102, Apdo 621, Comayagüela, Tegucigalpa; tel. 37-5601; Pres. JOSÉ ANGEL MEZA.

**Federación Sindical de Trabajadores Nacionales de Honduras (FESITRANH)** (Honduran Federation of Farmworkers): 10a Avda, 11a Calle, Barrio Los Andes, San Pedro Sula; tel. 57-2539; f. 1957; Pres. MARIO QUINTANILLA.

**Sindicato Nacional de Motoristas de Equipo Pesado de Honduras (SINAMEQUIPH)** (National Union of HGV Drivers): Tegucigalpa; tel. 37-4243; Pres. ERASMO FLORES.

**Central General de Trabajadores de Honduras (CGTH)** (General Confederation of Labour of Honduras): Calle Real de Comayagüela, Apdo 1236, Tegucigalpa; tel. 37-4398; attached to Partido Demócrata Cristiano; Sec.-Gen. FELICITO AVILA.

**Federación Auténtica Sindical de Honduras (FASH):** 1a Avda, 11a Calle 1102, Comayagüela, Tegucigalpa.

**Federación de Trabajadores del Sur (FETRASUR)** (Federation of Southern Workers): Choluteca.

**Federación Unitaria de Trabajadores de Honduras (FUTH):** 2a Avda entre 11a y 12a Calle, Casa 1127, frente a BANCAFE, Apdo 1663, Comayagüela, Tegucigalpa; tel. 37-6349; f. 1981; linked to left-wing electoral alliance Frente Patriótico Hondureño; Pres. HÉCTOR HERNÁNDEZ FUENTES; 45,000 mems.

**Frente de Unidad Nacional Campesino de Honduras (FUNACAMH):** f. 1980; group of farming co-operatives and six main peasant unions as follows:

**Asociación Nacional de Campesinos Hondureños (ANACH)** (National Association of Honduran Farmworkers): 3a Avda, entre 9a y 10a Calle, Barrio Barandillas, San Pedro Sula; tel. 53-1884; f. 1962; affiliated to ORIT; Pres. ANTONIO JULÍN MÉNDEZ; 80,000 mems.

**Federación de Cooperativas Agropecuarias de la Reforma Agraria de Honduras (FECORAH):** Barrio Guanacaste, Casa 1702, Tegucigalpa; tel. 37-5391; Pres. JOSÉ NAHUM CÁLIX.

**Frente Nacional de Campesinos Independientes de Honduras.**

**Unión Nacional de Campesinos (UNC)** (National Union of Farmworkers): 1a Avda, Comayagüela, Tegucigalpa; tel. 38-2435; linked to CLAT; Pres. MARCIAL REYES CABALLERO; c. 25,000 mems.

**Unión Nacional de Campesinos Auténticos de Honduras (UNCAH).**

**Unión Nacional de Cooperativas Populares de Honduras (UNACOOPH).**

# Transport

## RAILWAYS

The railway network is confined to the north of the country and most lines are used for fruit cargo.

**Ferrocarril Nacional de Honduras** (National Railway of Honduras): 1a Avda entre 1a y 2a Calle, Apdo 496, San Pedro Sula; tel. and fax 552-8001; f. 1870; govt-owned; 595 km of track; Gen. Man. M. A. QUINTANILLA.

**Tela Railroad Co:** La Lima; tel. 56-2037; Pres. RONALD F. WALKER; Gen. Man. FREDDY KOCH.

**Vaccaro Railway:** La Ceiba; tel. 43-0511; fax 43-0091; fmrly operated by Standard Fruit Co.

## ROADS

In 1996 there were an estimated 15,400 km of roads in Honduras, of which 3,126 km were paved. Some routes have been constructed by the Instituto Hondureño del Café and COHDEFOR in order to facilitate access to coffee plantations and forestry development areas.

**Dirección General de Caminos:** Barrio La Bolsa, Comayagüela, Tegucigalpa; tel. 33-7703; fax 33-2469; f. 1915; Dir ROBERTO AVILÉS GARCÍA; highways board.

## SHIPPING

**Empresa Nacional Portuaria** (National Port Authority): Apdo 18, Puerto Cortés; tel. 55-0192; fax 55-0968; f. 1965; has jurisdiction over all ports in Honduras (Puerto Cortés, Tela, La Ceiba, Trujillo/Castilla, Roatán, Amapala and San Lorenzo); a network of paved roads connects Puerto Cortés and San Lorenzo with the main cities of Honduras, and with the principal cities of Central America; Gen. Man. ROBERTO VALENZUELA SIMÓN.

There are several minor shipping companies. A number of foreign shipping lines call at Honduran ports.

## CIVIL AVIATION

Local airlines in Honduras compensate for the deficiencies of road and rail transport, linking together small towns and inaccessible districts. There are four international airports.

**Honduras Airways:** Tegucigalpa; f. 1994; operates domestic flights and scheduled services to the USA.

**Isleña Airlines:** Avda San Isidro, frente al Parque Central, Apdo 402, La Ceiba; tel. 43-2683; fax 43-2632; e-mail islena@caribe.hn; internet www.caribe.hn; domestic service and service to Guatemala, Nicaragua and the Cayman Islands; Pres. and CEO ARTURO ALVARADO WOOD.

**Líneas Aéreas Nacionales, SA (LANSA):** Apdo 35, La Ceiba; f. 1971; scheduled services within Honduras and to Islas de Bahía; Gen. Man. OSCAR M. ELVIR.

# Tourism

Tourists are attracted by the Mayan ruins, the fishing and boating facilities in Trujillo Bay and Lake Yojoa, near San Pedro Sula, and the beaches on the northern coast. Honduras received 306,646 tourists in 1997, when tourism receipts totalled US $145.6m.

**Instituto Hondureño de Turismo:** Edif. Europa, 5°, Col. San Carlos, Tegucigalpa; tel. 222-2124; fax 222-6621; e-mail inturism@hondutel.hn; internet www.hondurastips.honduras.com; f. 1972; dept of the Secretaría de Cultura y Turismo; Dir-Gen. RICARDO MARTÍNEZ.

# HUNGARY

## Introductory Survey

### Location, Climate, Language, Religion, Flag, Capital

The Republic of Hungary (known as the Hungarian People's Republic between August 1949 and October 1989) lies in eastern Europe, bounded to the north by Slovakia, to the east by Ukraine and Romania, to the south by Yugoslavia (the Serbian province of Vojvodina) and Croatia, and to the west by Slovenia and Austria. Its climate is continental, with long, dry summers and severe winters. Temperatures in Budapest are generally between –3°C (27°F) and 28°C (82°F). The language is Hungarian (Magyar). There is a large Romany community (numbering between 500,000 and 700,000 people), and also Croat, German, Romanian, Serbian, Slovak, Slovene and Jewish minorities. Most of the inhabitants profess Christianity, and the largest single religious denomination is the Roman Catholic Church, representing about 65% of the population. Other Christian groups are the Calvinists (20%), the Lutheran Church (5%) and the Hungarian Orthodox Church. The national flag (proportions 3 by 2) consists of three equal horizontal stripes, of red, white and green. The capital is Budapest.

### Recent History

Hungary allied itself with Nazi Germany before the Second World War and obtained additional territory when Czechoslovakia was partitioned in 1938 and 1939. Having sought to break the alliance in 1944, Hungary was occupied by German forces. In January 1945 Hungary was liberated by Soviet troops and signed an armistice, restoring the pre-1938 frontiers. It became a republic in February 1946. Meanwhile, land distribution, instituted in 1945, continued. Nationalization measures began in December 1946, despite opposition from the Roman Catholic Church under Cardinal József Mindszenty. In the 1947 elections the Communists became the largest single party, with 22.7% of the vote. By the end of that year the Communist Party had emerged as the leading political force. The Communists merged with the Social Democrats to form the Hungarian Workers' Party in June 1948. A People's Republic was established in August 1949.

Mátyás Rákosi became the leading figure as First Secretary of the Workers' Party. Opposition was subsequently removed by means of purges and political trials. Rákosi became Prime Minister in 1952 but, after the death of Stalin a year later, was replaced by the more moderate Imre Nagy, and a short period of liberalization followed. Rákosi, however, remained as First Secretary of the party, and in 1955 forced Nagy's resignation. András Hegedüs, sponsored by Rákosi, was appointed Prime Minister. Dissension between the Rákosi and Nagy factions increased in 1956; in July Rákosi was forced to resign but was replaced by a close associate, Ernő Gerő.

The consequent discontent provoked demonstrations against communist domination, and in October 1956 fighting broke out. Nagy was reinstated as Prime Minister, renounced membership of the Warsaw Pact and promised various other controversial reforms. In November Soviet troops, stationed in Hungary under the 1947 peace treaty, intervened, and the uprising was suppressed. A new Soviet-supported Government, led by János Kádár, was installed. Some 20,000 participants in the uprising were arrested, of whom 2,000 were subsequently executed, including Nagy and four associates. Many opponents of the regime were deported to the USSR. Kádár, who was appointed the leader of the renamed Hungarian Socialist Workers' Party (HSWP), held the premiership until January 1958, and from September 1961 to July 1965.

The 13th HSWP Congress, held in March 1985, re-elected Kádár leader of the party, with the new title of General Secretary of the Central Committee. The Congress reaffirmed the party's commitment to the country's economic reforms, which had been introduced in 1968. Legislative elections in June 1985 were the first to be held under the revised electoral law, giving voters a wider choice of candidates under the system of mandatory multiple nominations. In June 1987 Pál Losonczi was replaced in the largely ceremonial post of President of the Presidential Council by Károly Németh, a leading member of the HSWP. Károly Grósz, a member of the Politburo, was appointed Chairman of the Council of Ministers.

At a special ideological conference of the HSWP, held in May 1988, major changes in party personnel and policy were approved. Kádár was replaced as General Secretary of the Central Committee by Károly Grósz. Kádár was promoted to the newly-created and purely ceremonial post of HSWP President, but lost his membership of the Politburo. About one-third of the members of the Central Committee (in particular, conservative associates of Kádár) were removed and replaced by younger politicians. The new Politburo included Rezső Nyers, who had been largely responsible for the economic reforms initiated in 1968, but who had been removed from the Politburo in 1975. Grósz declared his commitment to radical economic and political change, although he excluded the immediate possibility of a multi-party political system. In June 1988 Dr Brunó Ferenc Straub, who was not a member of the HSWP, was elected to the post of President of the Presidential Council, in succession to Károly Németh. In November Miklós Németh, a prominent member of the HSWP, replaced Grósz as Chairman of the Council of Ministers.

Following Grósz's appointment as leader of the HSWP, there was a relaxation of censorship laws, and independent political groups were formally established. In January 1989 the right to strike was fully legalized. In the same month the National Assembly enacted two laws guaranteeing the right to demonstrate freely and to form associations and political parties independent of the HSWP.

In February 1989 the HSWP agreed to support the transition to a multi-party system and also to abandon the clause in the Constitution upholding the party's leading role in society. In the following month an estimated 100,000 people took part in a peaceful anti-Government demonstration in Budapest, in support of demands for democracy, free elections, the withdrawal of Soviet troops from Hungary, and an official commemoration of the 1956 uprising and of the execution of Imre Nagy in 1958.

During 1989 there was increasing evidence of dissension within the HSWP between conservative and reformist members. (At least 100,000 members had tendered their resignation between late 1987 and early 1989). In April Grósz was re-elected General Secretary of the party, and the Politburo was replaced by a smaller body. In May the Council of Ministers declared its independence from the HSWP. In the same month Kádár was relieved of his post as President of the HSWP and of his membership of the Central Committee of the party, officially for health reasons. In June a radical restructuring of the HSWP was effected, following increasing dissatisfaction among members with Grósz's leadership: while Grósz remained as General Secretary of the party, the newly-elected Chairman, Rezső Nyers, effectively emerged as the party's leading figure.

In June 1989 discussions were initiated between the HSWP and representatives of opposition groups regarding the holding of multi-party elections, changes to the presidential structure, amendments to the Constitution, and economic reforms. Evidence of the opposition's increasing strength was provided at a provincial by-election in July, when a joint candidate of three main opposition groups, the centre-right Hungarian Democratic Forum (HDF), the liberal Alliance of Free Democrats (AFD) and the Federation of Young Democrats (FYD), defeated a candidate of the HSWP, thus becoming the first opposition deputy since 1947 to win representation in the legislature. Four of five further by-elections were won by opposition candidates in July–September 1989.

At the 14th HSWP Congress, held in October 1989, delegates voted to dissolve the party and to reconstitute it as the Hungarian Socialist Party (HSP). Nyers was elected Chairman of the HSP. The HSP initially failed to attract a large membership, however, and in December HSWP activists declared that their party had not been dissolved, and that it still retained a membership of around 80,000. Gyula Thürmer was elected the HSWP President.

On 23 October 1989 (the anniversary of the 1956 uprising) the Republic of Hungary was proclaimed. In preparation the National Assembly approved fundamental amendments to the Constitution, including the removal of the clause guaranteeing one-party rule. A new electoral law was approved, and the Presidential Council was replaced by the post of President of the Republic. Mátyás Szűrös, the President of the National Assembly (Speaker), was named President of the Republic, on an interim basis.

Hungary's first free multi-party elections since 1945 were held, in two rounds, on 25 March and 8 April 1990. The elections were held under a mixed system of proportional and direct representation and were contested by a total of 28 parties and groups. The HDF received the largest share of the total votes (42.7%) and won 165 of the 386 seats in the National Assembly. The Independent Smallholders' Party (ISP, which advocated the restoration to its original owners of land collectivized after 1947) and the Christian Democratic People's Party (CDPP), both of which contested the second round of the election in alliance with the HDF, secured 43 and 21 seats, respectively. The AFD obtained the second largest proportion of the total votes (23.8%), winning 92 seats in the Assembly. The FYD, which was closely aligned with the AFD, obtained 21 seats. The HSP, with 8.5% of the votes, secured 33 seats in the legislature. The HSWP failed to secure the 4% of the votes required for representation.

A coalition Government was formed in May 1990, comprising members of the HDF (which held the majority of posts), together with members of the ISP, the CDPP and three independents. József Antall, the Chairman of the HDF, had earlier been elected to chair the new Council of Ministers. Among the declared aims of the new Government was to withdraw from the Warsaw Pact (the defence grouping of the Soviet bloc), to seek membership of the European Community (now European Union—EU—see p. 172), and to effect a full transition to a western-style market economy. In August Árpád Göncz, a writer and member of the AFD, was elected President of the Republic by an overwhelming majority of the legislature. In May Gyula Horn, the Minister of Foreign Affairs in the outgoing Government, had replaced Nyers as leader of the HSP.

At elections in September and October 1990, which were designed to replace the Soviet-style council system with a system of multi-party self-governing local bodies, a coalition of the AFD and the FYD won control of Budapest and many other cities, while in rural areas independent candidates gained an overwhelming majority of the votes. The governing coalition's poor result was attributed, in large part, to its failure to redress the recent sharp increase in the rates of inflation and unemployment.

In mid-1991 the National Assembly approved legislation to compensate the former owners of land and property that had been expropriated between 1939 and 1989. Legislation was approved by parliament in November that would allow prosecution for the crimes of murder and treason committed between 1944 and 1990. It was expected that, under the new law, former communist leaders might be brought to trial, in particular in connection with the suppression of the 1956 uprising. However, Göncz refused to give assent to the bill, and in March 1992 the Constitutional Court ruled that such retroactive legislation, which held individuals responsible for the crimes of the former communist regime, was inadmissible. Nevertheless, in May the National Assembly approved legislation to compensate for persons killed, imprisoned or deported, or whose property had been expropriated, for political reasons during the period 1939–89. Further legislation was approved in early 1993 allowing for prosecutions in connection with crimes committed under the communist regime.

In February 1992 the Chairman of the ISP, József Törgyán, announced that his party was withdrawing from the government coalition, in protest at what he claimed to be a lack of political influence. However, most of the ISP's deputies in the National Assembly refused to withdraw their support for the Government, thus causing a rift in the ISP. In April as many as 20,000 people were reported to have attended an anti-Government demonstration organized by Törgyán in Budapest. The split in the party was formalized in June, when party members who remained loyal to Antall suspended Törgyán as their Chairman, and elected László Horváth to chair what subsequently became the United Historic Smallholders' Party.

Meanwhile, in June 1992 a public disagreement arose between Antall and Göncz over alleged widespread interference by the Government in the state radio and television corporations and other branches of the mass media. During 1992–93 many senior media figures were either dismissed or tendered their resignation, and in October 1993 some 10,000 people demonstrated in Budapest to demand press freedom.

In September 1992 a demonstration by some 50,000 people in Budapest against extreme right-wing figures, including the Vice-Chairman of the HDF, István Csurka, reflected public concern at the increase in extreme right-wing sentiment in the country. The Government's failure to censure Csurka prompted widespread criticism. At an HDF congress in January 1993 Antall avoided a threatened revolt and possible split in the party by accepting the election of six right-wing extremists to the party's presidium. In May Lajos Für resigned from his position as Secretary-General of the HDF, claiming that he had not been able to maintain the unity of the party, which was divided between supporters of Csurka and centrists led by Antall. In July, however, Csurka was expelled from the HDF for his increasingly unacceptable views. (He subsequently founded the Hungarian Justice and Life Party—HJLP.) Antall died in December; he was succeeded as Prime Minister by Dr Péter Boross, an independent and hitherto the Minister of the Interior, who had acted as premier while Antall was receiving medical treatment. In February 1994 Für was elected Chairman of the HDF. In that month an investigation was initiated into alleged financial irregularities at the Ministry of Defence.

In March 1994 129 employees of Hungarian Radio were dismissed, ostensibly for economic reasons. Mass demonstrations were staged in Budapest in support of freedom of the press. There were widespread accusations that the Government sought to use the state radio service for propaganda purposes, since many of the dismissed employees had been known for their anti-Government views.

Legislative elections, which took place on 8 and 29 May 1994, resulted in a clear parliamentary majority for the HSP, which received 33.0% of the votes for regional party lists and won 209 of the National Assembly's 386 seats. The AFD won 19.8% of the votes and 70 seats, while the HDF won only 11.7% of the votes and 37 seats. The Independent Smallholders' and Peasants' Party (ISPP—formerly the ISP), the CDPP and the FYD won, repectively, 26, 22 and 20 seats. Csurka's HJLP attracted only 1.6% of the votes at the first round and did not proceed to the second. Horn announced that the HSP would be willing to form a Government with the AFD, and the two parties signed a coalition agreement (whereby the HSP was to control the majority of posts in the Council of Ministers, while the AFD would have right to veto government decisions) in late June. With 279 seats in the National Assembly, the coalition held the two-thirds' majority necessary to institute constitutional reforms. Horn was invested as Prime Minister in July. At municipal elections in December the HSP won 32.3% of the votes and the AFD 15.7%.

In June 1994 the Hungarian Radio employees were reinstated. In the following month, however, the directors of Hungarian Radio and Hungarian Television were dismissed, having been accused of favouring the former HDF administration. In October the Constitutional Court declared government interference in the media to be unlawful. In January 1995 László Bekesi, the HSP Minister of Finance, resigned, following disagreements with Horn regarding the economic reform programme. In the same month the Director of the State Property Agency was dismissed, following his alleged mismanagement of the privatization of state-owned hotels. In late February Dr Lajos Bokros of the HSP was designated Minister of Finance; at the same time Horn appointed Tamás Suchman, also of the HSP, to the newly-created post of Minister for Privatization, under the jurisdiction of the Ministry of Finance, as well as a new president of the central bank. New economic austerity measures, adopted in March, prompted strong domestic criticism; the ministers responsible for public health and for national security (both members of the HSP) resigned shortly after the programme was announced, and some 10,000 people joined a demonstration in Budapest to denounce the measures.

In early May 1995 the National Assembly approved legislation which was designed to accelerate the privatization process. On 19 June Göncz was re-elected President of the Republic by an overwhelming majority in the National Assembly. In late June the HSP Minister of Trade and Industry, who had voiced criticism of the privatization of parts of the energy sector, was dismissed; he was replaced by Imre Dunai, a technocrat with no party affiliation, at the end of the month. At the end of June the Constitutional Court ruled that elements of the austerity programme announced in March (specifically those relating to welfare provisions) were unconstitutional. Accordingly, in late July the National Assembly approved new adjustments, including increases in fuel prices and reductions in government expenditure, in an attempt to mitigate losses arising from the judgment. The Court reiterated its decision in a further ruling in September.

The implementation of the economic programme continued to cause dissent within the Government. The HSP Minister of Labour tendered her resignation in early October 1995, in protest against the adverse social consequences of the austerity measures. In late November, following a ruling by the Constitutional Court against the validity of further provisions of the austerity programme, Bokros submitted his resignation, although this was rejected by Horn. In mid-February 1996, however, Bokros again tendered his resignation (which was accepted by Horn), citing a lack of support from other government members. A banker, Péter Medgyessy, who had been Deputy Chairman and Chairman of the Planning and Economic Committee in the administration of Miklós Németh, was appointed the new Minister of Finance. Medgyessy undertook to pursue the programme of austerity instigated by Bokros, although his approach to politically sensitive issues such as health and social security was expected to be less confrontational than that of his predecessor.

Division was reported in the HDF in early March 1996, following the election of Sándor Lezsák to the party leadership. Denouncing what they regarded as an increasingly nationalistic tendency within the party, a faction led by Iván Szabó (who had been Minister of Finance in the HDF Government) broke away to form a new organization, the Hungarian Democratic People's Party.

In August 1996 Imre Dunai resigned from the post of Minister of Industry and Trade, ostensibly on grounds of ill health; it was reported that he had opposed the proposed increases in fuel prices. Dunai was replaced by Tamás Suchman (who retained responsibility for the privatization portfolio). Later in August the Government announced that increases in fuel prices were to be postponed, pending a review of the energy industry by a committee of independent experts. (In January 1997 the Government finally increased fuel prices, although by far less than originally envisaged.)

In early October 1996 it emerged that the Hungarian Privatization and State Holding Company (ÁPV Rt—which had been formed in 1995 by the amalgamation of the State Property Agency and State Holding Company) had made payments for consultations to a lawyer who had not been formally contracted, in contravention of the body's internal regulations. The Government removed the directors of ÁPV Rt, after they were discovered to have endorsed the payments. Horn subsequently announced the dismissal of Suchman from the Government, on the grounds that, as Minister for Privatization, he was responsible for ÁPV Rt's violation of regulations.

In January 1997 the HDF proposed a motion expressing 'no confidence' against Horn in the National Assembly, on the grounds that he was ultimately responsible for the unauthorized payments made by ÁPV Rt. In February a parliamentary investigative committee attributed responsibility to the Government for the irregularities. (In June eight officials were charged with fraud or mismanagement in connection with the operations of ÁPV Rt.)

In March 1997 two members of the National Intelligence Bureau were dismissed, after it emerged that the service had conducted unauthorized investigations of several prominent HSP members (who were suspected of having connections with organized crime groups). The Minister responsible for National Security ordered an official inquiry, which subsequently confirmed that irregularities had taken place and recommended that the Government regulate the operations of national security organizations.

Following a NATO summit meeting, which took place in Madrid, Spain, in July 1997, Hungary was invited to enter into discussions regarding its application for membership of the organization; it was envisaged that Hungary (together with the Czech Republic and Poland) would be formally admitted to NATO by April 1999. In August 1997 the Government announced that a national referendum on the country's entry into NATO would be conducted on 16 November. Amendments to legislation regulating land ownership were also to be submitted to the electorate at the referendum (after opposition parties criticized government proposals that foreign purchasers be authorized to acquire arable land).

In September 1997 Horn rejected demands that he resign from office by a committee which had been established to investigate the past of senior politicians; the committee claimed that Horn had served with a paramilitary force which had restored communist power following the 1956 rebellion, and that he had suppressed political opposition through the security services. In early October the National Assembly approved the wording of proposals on foreign land ownership, which were to be submitted to the electorate at the consultative referendum. However, the Constitutional Court overruled the decision of the National Assembly, and favoured an alternative formation of the proposals, which had been presented by opposition parties with the support of a petition. (Under the terms of constitutional amendments, adopted in July, a referendum that had been initiated by a minimum of 200,000 eligible voters was to be given precedence to a government-proposed referendum.) Following concern that the continuing controversy would delay the holding of the referendum, however, Horn announced that the planned amendments to legislation on land ownership were to be abandoned, and that the referendum was to be conducted on the single issue of Hungary's proposed admission to NATO. In early November the National Assembly approved the removal from the referendum of the proposals on land ownership.

At the national referendum, which took place on 16 November 1997 as scheduled, Hungary's accession to NATO was approved by 85.3% of votes cast, with 49% of the electorate participating in the referendum. The National Election Committee ratified the results of the referendum (despite objections by a pacifist movement, which claimed that the low rate of voter participation invalidated the results of the referendum). In December the HDF established an electoral alliance with the Federation of Young Democrats—Hungarian Civic Party (FYD—HCP, which had been reconstituted from the FYD) and the Hungarian Christian Democratic Federation, a newly-formed association of breakaway members of the CDPP.

In March 1998 the leader of the ISPP claimed that a bomb attack at his private residence had been politically motivated. The first round of the legislative elections, which was contested by 26 parties, took place on 10 May: the HSP secured 32.3% of votes cast, while the FYD—HCP won 28.2%, and the ISPP 13.8% of the votes. Following a second round of voting on 24 May, however, the FYD—HCP, with 147 seats, obtained the highest representation in the National Assembly; the HSP received 134, the ISPP 48, the AFD 24, the HDF 18 and the HJLP 14 seats. The defeat of the HSP was widely attributed to discontent with social and economic conditions, and the increasing rate of crime in the country. At the inaugural session of the new legislature in June, a member of the FYD—HCP, János Áder, was elected President of the National Assembly. In the same month, following inter-party negotiations, the FYD—HCP signed an agreement with the HDF and the ISPP, providing for the formation of a new coalition government. (The FYD—HCP and ISPP also agreed to contest the forthcoming presidential election in the year 2000 in alliance.) In early July the Chairman of the FYD—HCP, Viktor Orbán, was elected to the office of Prime Minister by the National Assembly, which subsequently approved the installation of a new Council of Ministers, comprising 11 representatives of the FYD—HCP, four of the ISPP (later renamed the Independent Smallholders' and Civic Party), one of the HDF, and one of the Hungarian Christian Democratic Federation. The new Government presented a programme for the reduction of crime and the improvement of social and economic conditions.

In September 1998, following the resignation of Horn from the leadership of the HSP in response to the party's electoral defeat, a former minister, László Kovács, was elected Chairman. Local government elections were conducted in October: it was reported that the three government coalition parties had received 39.6% of votes cast, while the HSP and AFD won 35.1% of the votes. In December a constitutional amendment that would have empowered the Council of Ministers, rather than the legislature, to approve the deployment of foreign troops in Hungary and Hungarian troops abroad (thereby facilitating Hungary's participation in NATO) failed to obtain the requisite two-thirds' majority in the National Assembly. Later in December the HSP and AFD deputies boycotted the legislature in protest at government proposals for the appointment of new management boards of the state media supervisory bodies. In February 1999 the National Assembly approved Hungary's

**Industrial Co-operative Commercial Banking House Ltd** (Iparbankház Rt): 1052 Budapest, Gerlóczy u. 5; tel. (1) 117-6811; fax (1) 118-2209; f. 1984; cap. 2,171m., dep. 6,981m. (Dec. 1994); 12 brs; Pres. Gábor Szabó; CEO Tibor Rostás.

**ING Bank Rt:** 1061 Budapest, Andrássy ut 9; tel. (1) 268-0140; fax (1) 269-6447; f. 1992 as NMB Bank; owned by ING Bank NV (Amsterdam); cap. 4,061.9m., res 5,249.5m., dep. 111,073.9m. (Dec. 1998); Man. Dir J. J. M. van der Heijden.

**Inter-Európa Bank Ltd:** 1054 Budapest, Szabadság tér 15; tel. (1) 373-6000; fax (1) 269-2526; e-mail ieb@ieb.hu; internet www.ieb.hu; f. 1981 as INTERINVEST; associated mem. of San Paolo Group; cap. 6,608.9m., res 3,153.7m., dep. 86,616.8m. (Dec. 1998); Chair. Dr Péter Medgyessy; Man. Dir Ezio Salvai; 19 brs.

**National Savings and Commercial Bank Ltd—NSB Ltd** (Országos Takarékpénztár és Kereskedelmi Bank Rt—OTP Rt): 1051 Budapest, Nádor u. 16; tel. (1) 153-1444; fax (1) 312-6858; f. 1949; cap. 28,000m., res 36,459m., dep. 1,312.3m. (Dec. 1997); savings deposits, credits, foreign transactions; privatized in late 1996; 380 brs; Chair. and Chief Exec. Dr Sándor Csányi.

**Post Bank and Savings Bank Corporation** (Postabank és Takarékpénztár Rt): 1920 Budapest, József nádor tér 1; tel. (1) 318-0855; fax (1) 317-1369; e-mail info@postabank.hu; internet www.postabank.hu; f. 1988; cap. 20,021m., res 155,547m., dep. 283,117m. (Dec. 1998); Chair. László Madarasz; 39 brs.

**Raiffeisen Rt:** 1052 Budapest, Váci út 19–21; tel. (1) 484-4100; fax (1) 484-4444; e-mail info@raiffeisen.hu; internet www.raiffeisen.hu; f. 1986 as Unicbank Rt; name changed in 1999; cap. 8,929.3m., res 4,029m., dep. 147,259.2m. (Dec. 1998); Man. Dir Dr Péter Felcsuti; 11 brs.

### Specialized Financial Institutions

**Hungarian Export-Import Bank Ltd** (Magyar Export-Import Bank Rt): 1065 Budapest, Nagymezö u. 44; tel. (1) 269-0580; fax (1) 269-4476; Pres. Dr Kálmán Mizsei; Gen. Man. Dr Iván Nyíri.

**Kvantum Investment Bank Ltd:** 1117 Budapest, Budafoki út 79; tel. (1) 464-4085; fax (1) 161-3457; Pres. János Erös; Gen. Man. László Haás.

**Merkantil Bank Ltd:** 1051 Budapest, József Attila u. 24; tel. (1) 118-2688; fax (1) 117-2331; f. 1988; affiliated to Commercial and Creditbank Ltd; cap. 1,100m.; Chair. and Chief Exec. Ádám Kolossváry.

**Opel Bank Hungary:** 1027 Budapest, Kapás u. 11-15; tel. (1) 457-9110; Gen. Man. Jari Arjavalta.

**Porsche Bank Hungaria AG.:** 1139 Budapest, Fay u. 27; tel. (1) 465-4701; fax (1) 465-4711; e-mail r.walker@porschebank.hu; Pres. Pál Antall.

**Rákóczi Regional Development Bank Ltd** (Rákóczi Regionális Fejlesztési Bank Rt): 3530 Miskolc, Mindszent tér 1; tel. (46) 510-300; fax (46) 510-396; e-mail central@rakoczibank.hu; internet www.rakoczibank.hu; f. 1992; Gen. Man. Koszticza Kornél.

### Other Financial Institution

**Central Corporation of Banking Companies** (Pénzintézeti Központ): 1093 Budapest, Lónyay u. 38; tel. (1) 117-1255; fax (1) 215-9963; f. 1916; banking, property, rights and interests, deposits, securities, and foreign exchange management; cap. 11,127m., res 3,548m., dep. 12,289m.; Chair. and CEO Péter Király; 3 brs.

## STOCK EXCHANGE

**Budapest Stock Exchange** (Budapesti Értéktőzsde): 1052 Budapest, Deák Ferenc u. 5; tel. (1) 429-6900; fax (1) 429-6800; e-mail info@bse.hu; internet www.bse.hu; Pres. András Simor; CEO Mária Dunavölgyi.

## COMMODITY EXCHANGE

**Budapest Commodity Exchange** (Budapesti Árutőzsde): 1134 Budapest, Róbert Károly krt. 61–65; tel. (1) 465-6979; fax (1) 465-6981; Chair. Szergej Keresztesi.

## INSURANCE

In July 1986 the state insurance enterprise was divided into two companies, one of which retained the name of the former Állami Biztosító. By 1995 13 insurance companies had been established.

**Atlasz Travel Insurance Company** (Atlasz Utazási Biztosító): 1052 Budapest, Deák F. u. 23; tel. (1) 118-1999; fax (1) 117-1529; f. 1988; cap. 1,000m.; Gen. Man. Gábor Darvas.

**Garancia Insurance Company** (Garancia Biztosító Rt): 1054 Budapest, Vadász u. 12; tel. (1) 269-2533; fax (1) 269-2549; f. 1988; cap. 4,050m.; Gen. Man. and CEO Dr Zoltán Nagy; 25 brs.

**Hungária Insurance Company** (Hungária Biztosító Rt): 1054 Budapest, Bajcsy u. 52; tel. (1) 301-6565; fax (1) 301-6100; f. 1986; handles international insurance, industrial and commercial insurance and motor-car, marine, life, household, accident and liability insurance; cap. 4,266m.; Chair. and CEO Dr Mihály Patai.

**Insurance Company** (AB-AEGON Általános Biztosító Rt): 1091 Budapest, Üllői St 1; tel. (1) 218-1866; fax (1) 217-7065; f. 1949 as Állami Biztosító, reorganized 1986, present name since 1992; handles pensions, life and property insurance, insurance of agricultural plants, co-operatives, foreign insurance, etc.; Gen. Man. Dr Gábor Kepecs.

# Trade and Industry

## GOVERNMENT AGENCY

**Hungarian Privatization and State Holding Company (ÁPV Rt):** 1133 Budapest, Pozsonyi út 56; tel. (1) 237-4400; fax (1) 237-4100; e-mail apvrt@apvrt.hu; f. 1995 by merger of the State Property Agency and the State Holding Company; Chair. Gyula Gansperger.

## NATIONAL CHAMBERS OF COMMERCE AND AGRICULTURE

**Hungarian Chamber of Agriculture** (Magyar Agrárkamara): 1036 Budapest, Lajos u. 160-162; tel. (1) 368-6890; fax (1) 250-5138; e-mail agota@kozpont.agrarkamara.hu; Pres. Miklós Csikai.

**Hungarian Chamber of Commerce and Industry** (Magyar Kereskedelmi és Iparkamara): 1372 Budapest V, POB 452; tel. (1) 368-6890; fax (1) 250-5138; e-mail mkik@mail.mkik.hu; f. 1850; central organization of the 20 Hungarian county chambers of commerce and industry; based on a system of compulsory membership; over 400,000 mems. Pres. Dr Lajos Tolnay; Sec. Gen. Péter Dunai.

## REGIONAL CHAMBERS OF COMMERCE

**Bács-Kiskun County Chamber of Commerce**: 6000 Kecskemét, Árpád krt 4, POB 228; tel. (76) 501-500; fax (76) 501-538; e-mail bkmkik@mail.datanet.hu; Chair. Tamás Csongovai; Sec. László Leitner.

**Békés County Chamber of Commerce and Industry**: 5600 Békéscsaba, Penza lkt. 5; tel. (66) 451-775; fax (66) 324-976; Chair. Gábor Bangó; Man. Dir Zsolt Tóth.

**Borsod-Abaúj-Zemplén County Chamber of Commerce** (Borsod-Abaúj-Zemplén Kereskedelmi és Iparkamara): 3525Miskolc, Szentpáli u. 1; tel. (46) 328-539; fax (46) 328-722; e-mail bokik@mail.matav.hu; f. 1990; membership of 12,000 individuals, 6,000 cos; Pres. Tamás Bihall; Sec. Anna Baán.

**Budapest Chamber of Industry and Commerce** (Budapesti Kereskedelmi és Iparkamara): 1016 Budapest, Krisztina krt. 99; tel. (1) 202-5990; fax (1) 214-1807; Chair. László Koji; Sec. Gen. Péter Révész.

**Csongrád County Chamber of Commerce and Industry** : 6721 Szeged, Tisza L. krt. 2–4; tel. (62) 423-451; fax (62) 426-149; e-mail csmkik@tiszanet.hu; internet www.tiszanet.hu/kamara; Chair. István Szeri; Sec. Lajos Horváth.

**Fejér County Chamber of Commerce and Industry** (Fejér Megyei Kereskedelmi és Iparkamara): 8000 Székesfehérvár, Petőfi u. 5; tel. (22) 327-627; fax (22) 510-312; Chair. Jenô Radetzky; Sec. Gen. Dr Miklós Siska.

**Gyôr-Moson-Sopron County Chamber of Commerce and Industry**: 9001 Gyôr, Király u. 20; tel. (96) 318-485; fax (96) 319-650; Chair. Péter Jancsó; Dir József Vápár.

**Hajdú-Bihar County Chamber of Commerce and Industry**: 4025 Debrecen, Petőfi tér 10; tel. (52) 500-721; fax (52) 500-720; Chair. György Ruszkabányai; Sec. Eva Csabai.

**Heves County Chamber of Commerce and Industry**: 3300 Eger, Deák F. út 51; tel. (36) 429-612; fax (36) 312-989; Chair. József Gyetvai; Sec. Gen. Gábor Fülöp.

**Jász-Nagykun-Szolnok County Chamber of Commerce and Industry**: 5000 Szolnok, Verseghy Park 8; tel. (56) 370-005; Chair. Dr András Sziráki; Sec. Dr Imre Kerékgyártó.

**Komárom-Esztergom County Chamber of Commerce and Industry**: 2800 Tatabánya, Elôd vezér u. 17; tel. (34) 316-259; fax (34) 316-259; Chair. Dr István Horváth; Sec. Zoltán Bátor.

**Nógrád County Chamber of Commerce and Industry**: 3100 Salgótarján, Bartók Béla út 10; tel. (32) 316-476; fax (32) 316-476; Chair. Sándor Gressai; Sec. Dr Erzsébet Kurucz.

**Pécs-Baranya County Chamber of Commerce and Industry**: 7625 Pécs, Dr Majorossy I. u. 36; tel. (72) 211-592; fax (72) 211-604; Chair. Gyula Higi; Sec. Tamás Síkfôi.

**Pest County Chamber of Commerce and Industry** (Pest Megyei Kereskedelmi és Iparkamara): 1054 Budapest, Kossuth L. tér 6–8; tel. (1) 153-3009; fax (1) 153-3067; Chair. Vince Peterdy; Sec. Gen. Dr Zoltán Vereczkey.

**Somogy County Chamber of Commerce** (Somogyi Kereskedelmi és Iparkamara): 7400 Kaposvár, Anna u. 6; tel. (82) 501-000; fax

(82) 319-428; e-mail skik@skik.hu; internet www.sominfo.hu/skik; Chair. JÓZSEF VARGA; Dep. Pres. LAJOS HORVÁTH.

**Szabolcs-Szatmár-Bereg County Chamber of Commerce and Industry**: 4400 Nyíregyháza, Szarvas u. 1–3; tel. (42) 416-074; fax (42) 311-750; Chair. Dr JÁNOS VERES; Sec. Dr IMRE JAKAB.

**Tolna County Chamber of Commerce and Industry**: 7100 Szekszárd, Arany J. u. 23–25; tel. (74) 411-661; fax (74) 411-456; e-mail rostasrostas@tmkik.hu; Chair. Dr KÁLMÁN BERTHA; Sec. ILONA ROSTAS.

**Vas County Chamber of Commerce and Industry** (Vas Megyei Kereskedelmi és Iparkamara): 9700 Szombathely, Honvéd tér 2; tel. (94) 312-356; fax (94) 316-936; Chair. VINCE KOVÁCS; Sec. Gen. GYIMESI FERENC.

**Veszprém County Chamber of Commerce and Industry**: 8200 Veszprém, Budapest út 3; tel. (88) 429-008; fax (88) 412-150; e-mail vkik@infornax.hu; Chair. KÁROLY HENGER; Dir TAMÁS CSABAI.

**Zala County Chamber of Commerce and Industry** (Zalai Kereskedelmi és Iparkamara): 8900 Zalaegerszeg, Petőfi u. 24; tel. (92) 550-510; fax (92) 550-525; e-mail zmkik@zmkik.hu; Chair. IMRE FARKAS; Sec. Gen. ISTVÁN TÓTH.

## INDUSTRIAL AND TRADE ASSOCIATIONS

**HUNICOOP Foreign Trade Company Ltd for Industrial Co-operation:** 1367 Budapest 5, POB 111; tel. (1) 267-1477; fax (1) 267-1482; agency for foreign companies in Hungary, export and import.

**Interco-operation Co Ltd for Trade Promotion:** 1085 Budapest, POB 136; tel. (1) 118-9966; fax (1) 118-2161; establishment and carrying out of co-operation agreements, representation of foreign companies, brands, marketing and distribution, joint ventures and import-export deals.

**Hungarian Industrial Association** (Magyar Iparszövetség—OKISz): 1146 Budapest, Thököly u. 58–60; tel. (1) 343-5570; fax (1) 343-5521; e-mail okisz@mail.elender.hu; internet www.okiszinfo.hu; safeguards interests of over 2,000 member enterprises (all private); Pres. Dr CSABA SÜMEGHY.

**National Co-operative Council** (Országos Szövetkezeti Tanács—OSzT): 1054 Budapest, Szabadság tér 14; tel. (1) 312-7467; fax (1) 311-3647; f. 1968; Pres. ANDRÁS SZŐKE; Sec. Dr JÓZSEF PÁL.

**National Federation of Agricultural Co-operators and Producers** (Mezőgazdasági Szövetkezők és Termelők Országos Szövetsege—MOSZ): 1054 Budapest, Akadémia u. 1–3; tel. and fax (1) 353-2552; e-mail mosz@mail.tvnet.hu; internet www.msztorz.hu; f. 1990; frmly Termelő szövetkezetek Országos Tanácsa (TOT) (National Council of Agricultural Co-operatives); Pres. TAMÁS NAGY; Sec.-Gen. GÁBOR HORVÁTH; est. 1,300 member organizations.

**National Federation of Consumer Co-operatives** (Általános Fogyasztási Szövetkezetek Országos Szövetsége—ÁFEOSz): 1054 Budapest, Szabadság tér 14; tel. (1) 153-4222; fax (1) 111-3647; safeguards interests of Hungarian consumer co-operative societies; organizes co-operative wholesale activities; Pres. Dr PÁL BARTUS; 800,000 mems.

## UTILITIES

### Electricity

**Hungarian Electrical Trust** (Magyar Villamos Muvek Rt—MVM Rt): 1251 Budapest, POB 34; 1011 Budapest, Vám u. 5–7; tel. (1) 201-5455; fax (1) 202-1246; Hungarian national electricity wholesaler and power-system controller; 6 distributers and 2 generation plants privatized in 1995; remaining 5 plants privatized in 1996; Chair. GYÖRGY HATVANI.

**National Power Grid Company Ltd:** 1054 Budapest, Szabadsajto út 5.

**Paks Nuclear Plant Ltd** (Paksi Atomeromu v Pav): 7031 Paks, POB 71; tel. (75) 311222; fax (75) 355-1332; internet www.npp.hu; f. 1992; electric energy production; Plant Man. SÁNDOR NAGY; 2,800 employees.

### Gas

**Degaz—Delalfoldi Gazszolgaltato Rezvenytarsasag:** 6724 Szeged, Pulcz u. 44; tel. (62) 472-572; fax (63) 324-943; public gas supply and services; 1,327 employees.

**Hungarian Oil and Gas Company Ltd** (MOL—Magyar Olaj és Gáziparirt Rt): 1117 Budapest, Október huszonharmadika u. 18; tel. (1) 209-0000; fax (1) 209-0005; internet www.mol.hu; f. 1991 by merger of part of the National Oil and Gas Trust and a technical development co; privatized in 1995, with the state retaining a majority stake; 19,648 employees; Chair. JÁNOS CSAK; CEO GYÖRGY MOSONYI.

## TRADE UNIONS

Since 1988, and particularly after the restructuring of the former Central Council of Hungarian Trade Unions (SzOT) as the National Confederation of Hungarian Trade Unions (MSzOSz) in 1990, several new union federations have been created. Several unions are affiliated to more than one federation, and others are completely independent.

### Trade Union Federations

**Association of Hungarian Free Trade Unions** (Magyar Szabad Szakszervezetek Szövetsége): Budapest; f. 1994; 200,000 mems.

**Autonomous Trade Union Confederation** (Autonóm Szakszervezetek Svövetsége): 1068 Budapest, Benczúr út 45; tel. (1) 342-1776; Pres. LAJOS FŐCZE.

Principal affiliated unions include:

**Federation of Hungarian Chemical Industry Workers' Unions** (Magyar Vegyipari Dolgozók Szakszervezeti Szövetsége): 1068 Budapest, Benczúr út 45; tel. (1) 342-1778; fax (1) 342-9978; f. 1906; Pres. LAJOS FŐCZE; 42,000 mems.

**Democratic League of Independent Trade Unions** (Független Szakszervezetek Demokratikus Ligája—FSzDL): 1146 Budapest, Thököly út 156; tel. (1) 251-2300; fax (1) 251-2288; e-mail liga@mail.c3.hu; f. 1988; Pres. ISTVÁN GASKÓ; 98,000 mems.

Principal affiliated unions include:

**Democratic Trade Union of Scientific Workers** (Tudományos Dolgozók Demokratikus Szakszervezete—TDDSz): 1068 Budapest, Városligeti fasor 38; tel. (1) 142-8438; f. 1988; Chair. PÁL FORGACS.

**Federation of Unions of Intellectual Workers** (Értelmiségi Szakszervezeti Tömörülés—ÉSzT): 1068 Budapest, Városligeti fasor 10; tel. (1) 122-8456; Pres. Dr LÁSZLÓ KIS; Gen. Sec. Dr GÁBOR BÁNK.

**Forum for the Co-operation of Trade Unions** (Szakszervezetek Együttműködési Fóruma—SzEF): 1068 Budapest VIII, Puskin u. 4; tel. (1) 138-2651; fax (1) 118-7360; f. 1990; Pres. Dr. ENDRE SZABÓ.

Principal affiliated unions include:

**Federation of Hungarian Public Service Employees' Unions** (Közszolgálati Szakszervezetek Szövetsége): 1081 Budapest, Kiss Jozsef u. 8 II em; tel. (1) 313-5436; fax (1) 133-7223; f. 1945; Pres. PÉTER MICHALKO; Vice-Pres. Dr JUDIT BÁRDOS, Dr CSILLA NOVÁK.

**National Confederation of Hungarian Trade Unions** (Magyar Szakszervezetek Országos Szövetsége—MSzOSz): 1415 Budapest, VI. Dózsa György út 84B; tel. (1) 352-1815; fax (1) 342-1799; f. 1898, reorganized 1990; Pres. Dr LÁSZLÓ SÁNDOR; Dep. Pres. FERENC RABI; 405,000 mems in 41 member organizations.

Principal affiliated unions include:

**Commercial Employees' Trade Union** (Kereskedelmi Alkalmazottak Szakszervezete): 1066 Budapest, Jókai u. 6; tel. (1) 131-8970; fax (1) 132-3382; f. 1900; Pres. Dr JÓZSEF SÁLING; 160,000 mems.

**Confederation of Iron and Metallurgical Industry Workers' Unions** (Vas- és Fémipari Dolgozók Szakszervezeti Szövetsége): 1086 Budapest, Magdolna u. 5–7; tel. (1) 210-0130; fax (1) 333-8327; e-mail vasasszaksz@mail.datanet.hu; f. 1877; Pres. KÁROLY SZŐKE; 135,000 mems.

**Federation of Agricultural, Forestry and Water Conservancy Workers' Unions** (Mezőgazdasági, Erdészeti és Vizgazdálkodási Dolgozók Szakszervezeti Szövetsége): 1066 Budapest, Jókai u. 2–4; tel. (1) 331-4550; fax (1) 331-4568; f. 1906; Pres. (vacant); Gen. Sec. ANDRÁS BERECZKY; 21,000 mems.

**Federation of Building, Wood and Building Industry Workers' Unions** (Építő-, Fa-és Építőanyagipari Dolgozók Szakszervezeteinek Szövetsége): 1068 Budapest, Dózsa György út 84A; tel. (1) 122-9426; fax (1) 142-4395; f. 1906; Pres. JÁNOS NAGYMIHALY; Vice-Pres. ANTAL MIHALUSZ; 140,000 mems.

**Federation of Chemical Workers' Unions of Hungary, Confederation Founding Section** (Magyar Vegyipari Dolgozók Szakszervezeti Szövetsége, össz-szövetségi alapitó tagozata): 1068 Budapest, Benczúr út 45; tel. (1) 342-1778; fax (1) 342-9975; Gen. Sec. GYÖRGY PASZTERNÁK; 12,000 mems.

**Federation of Communal Service Workers' Unions** (Kommunális Dalgozók Szakszervezete): 1068 Budapest, Benczur u. 43; tel. (1) 111-6950; Gen. Sec. ZSOLT PÉK; 28,000 mems.

**Federation of Hungarian Artworkers' Unions** (Müvészeti Szakszervezetek Szövetsége): 1068 Budapest, Városligeti fasor 38; tel. (1) 342-8927; fax (1) 342-8372; e-mail eji@mail.datanet.hu; f. 1957; Pres. LÁSZLÓ GYIMESI; 32,000 mems.

**Federation of Local Industry and Municipal Workers' Unions** (Helyiipari és Városgazdasági Dolgozók Szövetségének): 1068 Budapest, Benczúr u. 43; tel. (1) 111-6950; f. 1952; Pres. JÓZSEFNÉ SVEVER; Gen. Sec. PÁL BAKÁNYI; 281,073 mems.

**Federation of Mineworkers' Unions** (Bányaipari Dolgozók Szakszervezeti Szövetsége): 1068 Budapest, Városligeti fasor 46–48; tel. (1) 322-1226; fax (1) 342-1942; f. 1913; Pres. ANTAL SCHALKHAMMER; Vice-Pres. Dr. JÁNOS HORN; 80,000 mems.

**Federation of Municipal Industries and Service Workers' Unions** (Települési Ipari és Szolgáltatási Dolgozók Szakszervezete): 1068 Budapest, Benczur u. 43; tel. (1) 111-6950; Gen. Sec. ZOLTÁN SZIKSZAI; 20,000 mems.

**Federation of Postal and Telecommunications Workers' Unions** (Postai és Hirközlési Dolgozók Szakszervezeti Szövetsége): 1146 Budapest, Cházár András u. 13; tel. (1) 142-8777; fax (1) 121-4018; f. 1945; Pres. ENIKŐ HESZKY-GRICSER; 69,900 mems.

**Federation of Transport Workers' Unions** (Közlekedési Dolgozók Szakszervezeteinek Szövetségé): 1081 Budapest, Köztársaság tér 3; tel. (1) 113-9046; f. 1898; Pres. ISTVÁN TRENKA; 8,000 mems.

**Hungarian Federation of Food Industry Workers' Unions** (Magyar Élelmezésipari Dolgozók Szakszervezeteinek Szövetsége): 1068 Budapest, Városligeti fasor 44; tel. (1) 122-5880; fax (1) 142-8568; f. 1905; Pres. GYULA SÓKI; Gen. Sec. BÉLA VANEK; 226,243 mems.

**Hungarian Graphical Workers' Union** (Nyomdaipari Dolgozók Szakszervezete): 1085 Budapest, Kölcsey u. 2; tel. (1) 266-0065; fax (1) 266-0028; f. 1862; Pres. ANDRÁS BÁRSONY; Vice-Pres JÁNOS ACZÉL, EMIL SZELEI; 17,000 mems.

**Hungarian Union of Teachers** (Magyar Pedagógusok Szakszervezete): 1068 Budapest, Városligeti fasor 10; tel. (1) 122-8456; fax (1) 142-8122; f. 1945; Gen. Sec. ISTVÁNNÉ SZÖLLŐSI; 200,000 mems.

**Hungarian Union of Textile Workers** (Magyar Textilipari Dolgozók Szakszervezete): 1068 Budapest, Rippl-Rónai u. 2; tel. (1) 428-196; fax (1) 122-5414; f. 1905; Pres. (vacant); Gen. Sec. TAMÁS KELETI; 70,241 mems.

**Textile Workers' Union** (Textilipari Dolgozók Szakszervezete): 1068 Budapest, Rippl Rónai u. 2; tel. (1) 112-3868; fax (1) 342-8169; Gen. Sec. TAMÁS KELETI; 39,500 mems.

**Union of Health Service Workers** (Egészségügyben Dolgozók Szakszervezeteinek Szövetsége): 1051 Budapest, Nádor u. 32, POB 36; tel. (1) 110-645; f. 1945; Pres. Dr ZOLTÁN SZABÓ; Gen. Sec. Dr PÁLNÉ KÁLLAY; 280,536 mems.

**Union of Leather Industry Workers** (Bőripari Dolgozók Szakszervezete): 1062 Budapest, Bajza u. 24; tel. (1) 342-9970; f. 1868; Gen. Sec. TAMÁS LAJTOS; 12,000 mems.

**Union of Clothing Workers** (Ruházatipari Dolgozók Szakszervezete (): 1077 Budapest, Almássy tér 2; tel. (1) 342-3702; fax (1) 122-6717; f. 1892; Gen. Sec. TAMÁS WITTICH; 22,000 mems.

**Union of Railway Workers** (Vasutasok Szakszervezete): 1068 Budapest, Benczúr u. 41; tel. (1) 122-1895; fax (1) 122-8818; f. 1945; Pres. PÁL PAPP; Gen. Sec. FERENC KOSZORUS; 115,000 mems.

# Transport

## RAILWAYS

In 1991 the total rail network in Hungary amounted to 10,607 km. Some 157m. passengers were carried in 1998. There is an underground railway in Budapest, which had a network of 23 km in 1989; in that year 296m. passengers were carried. Since 1996 PHARE, the EU's programme for the economic reconstruction of Eastern Europe, has financed a number of modernization projects of the rail network.

**Hungarian State Railways Ltd** (Magyar Államvasutak—MÁV): 1940 Budapest, Andrássy út 73–75; tel. (1) 322-0660; fax (1) 342-8596; f. 1868; transformed into joint-stock co in 1993; total network 7,600 km, including 2,360 km of electrified lines (1998); Pres. GYULA TAKÁCSY; Gen. Dir MÁRTON KUKELY.

**Railway of Győr–Sopron–Ebenfurt** (Győr–Sopron–Ebenfurti-Vasut—Gysev-ROeEE): 9400 Sopron, Matyas Kiraly u. 19; Hungarian-Austrian-owned railway; 101 km in Hungary, 65 km in Austria, all electrified; transport of passengers and goods; Dir-Gen. Dr JÁNOS BERÉNYI.

## ROADS

At the end of 1996 the road network totalled 158,633 km, including 420 km of motorways, 29,653 km of main or national roads and 52,683 km of secondary roads. There are extensive long-distance bus services. Road passenger and freight transport is provided by the state-owned Volán companies and by individual operators. In 1996 a section of a 42-km motorway was opened between Győr and Hegyeshalom. The road was eventually to extend from Budapest to Vienna (Austria).

**Hungarocamion:** 1442 Budapest, POB 108; tel. (1) 257-3600; fax (1) 256-6755; international road freight transport company; 17 offices in Europe and the Middle East; fleet of 1,100 units for general and specialized cargo; Gen. Man. GABRIELLA SZAKÁL; 3,800 employees.

**Centre of Volán Enterprises** (Volán Vállalatok Központja): 1391 Budapest, Erzsébet krt 96, POB 221; tel. (1) 112-4290; centre of 25 Volán enterprises for inland and international road freight and passenger transport, forwarding, tourism; fleet of 17,000 lorries, incl. special tankers for fuel, refrigerators, trailers, 8,000 buses for regular passenger transport; 3 affiliates, offices and joint-ventures in Europe; Head ELEMER SASLICS.

## SHIPPING AND INLAND WATERWAYS

At the end of 1994 the Hungarian river merchant fleet comprised 199 vessels, with a capacity totalling 223,718 dwt. At 31 December 1998 the ocean merchant fleet comprised only two vessels, with a combined displacement of 15,285 grt.

**Hungarian Shipping Co** (MAHART—Magyar Hajózási Rt): 1366 Budapest, POB 58; tel. (1) 118-1880; fax (1) 138-2421; carries passenger traffic on the Danube and Lake Balaton; cargo services on the Danube and its tributaries, Lake Balaton, and also Mediterranean and ocean-going services; operates port of Budapest (container terminal, loading, storage, warehousing, handling and packaging services); ship-building and ship-repair services; Pres. Dir-Gen. ANDRÁS FÁY.

**MAFRACHT International Shipping, Forwarding and Agency Ltd Co:** 1364 Budapest 4, POB 105; tel. (1) 266-1208; fax (1) 266-1329; shipping agency.

## CIVIL AVIATION

The Ferihegy international airport is 16 km from the centre of Budapest. Ferihegy-2 opened in 1985. Balatonkiliti airport, near Siófok in western Hungary, reopened to international traffic in 1989. Public internal air services resumed in 1993, after an interval of 20 years, between Budapest and Nyíregyháza, Debrecen, Szeged, Pécs, Szombathely and Győr.

**Air Traffic and Airport Administration** (Légiforgalmi és Repülőtéri Igazgatóság): 1675 Budapest, POB 53; tel. (1) 291-8722; fax (1) 157-6982; f. 1973; controls civil air traffic and operates Ferihegy and Siófok Airports; Dir-Gen. TAMÁS ERDEI.

**General Directorate of Civil Aviation** (Légügyi Főigazgatóság): 1400 Budapest, Dob u. 75–81, POB 87; tel. (1) 342-2544; fax (1) 322-2848; controls civil aviation; Dir-Gen. ÖDÖN SKONDA.

**Hungarian Airlines** (Magyar Légiközlekedési Részvénytársaság—MALEV Rt): 1051 Budapest, Roosevelt tér 2, POB 122; tel. (1) 235-3535; fax (1) 266-2685; f. 1946; regular services from Budapest to Europe, North Africa, North America, Asia and the Middle East; Chair. CSABA SIKLÓS; CEO Dr ANTAL PONGRÁCZ.

**LinAir Hungarian Regional Airlines:** 1675 Budapest, POB 53; tel. (1) 296-7092; fax (1) 296-7891; e-mail info@linair.hu; internet www.linair.hu; f. 1994; regional carrier; Man. Dir TAMÁS KOVÁCS.

# Tourism

Tourism has developed rapidly and is an important source of foreign exchange. Lake Balaton is the main holiday centre for boating, bathing and fishing. Hungary's cities have great historical and recreational attractions. The annual Budapest Spring Festival is held in March. Budapest has numerous swimming pools watered by thermal springs, which are equipped with modern physiotherapy facilities. In 1997 there were about 37.3m. foreign visitors (including 20.1m. visitors in transit). Revenue from tourism in 1998 totalled about US $2,504m.

**Hungarian Travel Agency** (IBUSZ—Idegenforgalmi, Beszerzési, Utazási és Szállítási Rt): 1364 Budapest, Ferenciek tér 5; tel. (1) 118-6866; fax (1) 117-7723; f. 1902; has 118 brs throughout Hungary; Gen. Man. Dr ERIKA SZEMENKÁR.

**Tourinform:** 1052 Budapest, Sütő u. 2; tel. (1) 317-9800; fax (1) 317-9656; e-mail tourinform@mail.hungarytourism.hu; internet www.hungarytourism.hu.

# ICELAND

## Introductory Survey

**Location, Climate, Language, Religion, Flag, Capital**

The Republic of Iceland comprises one large island and numerous smaller ones, situated near the Arctic Circle in the North Atlantic Ocean. The main island lies about 300 km (190 miles) south-east of Greenland, about 1,000 km (620 miles) west of Norway and about 800 km (500 miles) north of Scotland. The Gulf Stream keeps Iceland warmer than might be expected, with average temperatures ranging from 10°C (50°F) in the summer to 1°C (34°F) in winter. Icelandic is the official language. Almost all of the inhabitants profess Christianity: the Evangelical Lutheran Church is the established church and embraces about 89% of the population. The civil flag (proportions 25 by 18) displays a red cross, bordered with white, on a blue background, the upright of the cross being towards the hoist; the state flag (proportions 16 by 9) bears the same design, but has a truncated triangular area cut from the fly. The capital is Reykjavík.

**Recent History**

Iceland became independent on 17 June 1944, when the Convention that linked it with Denmark, under the Danish crown, was terminated. Iceland became a founder-member of the Nordic Council (see p. 222) in 1952, and has belonged to both NATO (see p. 226) and the Council of Europe (see p. 158) since 1949. Membership of the European Free Trade Association (EFTA, see p. 291) was formalized in 1970.

From 1959 to 1971 Iceland was governed by a coalition of the Independence Party (IP) and the Social Democratic Party (SDP). Following the general election of June 1971, Ólafur Jóhannesson, the leader of the Progressive Party (PP), formed a coalition Government with the left-wing People's Alliance (PA) and the Union of Liberals and Leftists. At the general election held in June 1974 voters favoured right-wing parties, and in August the IP and the PP formed a coalition Government, led by the IP leader, Geir Hallgrímsson. Failure adequately to address economic difficulties resulted in a decline in the coalition's popularity, however, and prompted the Government's resignation in June 1978, following extensive election gains by the PA and the SDP. Disagreements over economic measures, and over the PA's advocacy of Icelandic withdrawal from NATO, led to two months of negotiations before a new government could be formed. In September Jóhannesson formed a coalition of the PP with the PA and the SDP, but this Government, after addressing immediate economic necessities, resigned in October 1979, when the SDP withdrew from the coalition. An interim administration was formed by Benedikt Gröndal, the SDP leader. The results of a general election, held in December, were inconclusive, and in February 1980 Gunnar Thoroddsen of the IP formed a coalition with the PA and the PP.

In June 1980 Vigdís Finnbogadóttir, a non-political candidate who was favoured by left-wing groups because of her opposition to the US military airbase at Keflavík, achieved a narrow victory in the election for the mainly ceremonial office of President. She took office on 1 August 1980, becoming the world's first popularly-elected female Head of State. The coalition Government lost its majority in the Lower House of the Althing/Althingi (Parliament) in September 1982, and a general election took place in April 1983. The IP received the largest share (38.7%) of the votes, but two new parties, the Social Democratic Alliance (SDA) and the Women's List (WL), together won almost 13% of the votes. A centre-right coalition was formed by the IP and the PP, with Steingrímur Hermannsson (the PP leader and former Minister of Fisheries and Communications) as Prime Minister. Despite government efforts in 1983 to halt the sharp increase in the rate of inflation through a variety of measures (including a devaluation of the króna), there was considerable industrial unrest in 1984–85, as a result of which large increases in wages for public-sector employees and fishermen were secured. There was also a further devaluation of the króna. In June 1985, to forestall the threat of further strikes, private-sector employers secured a guarantee from the Icelandic Federation of Labour to refrain from industrial action.

In May 1985 the Althing unanimously approved a resolution declaring the country a 'nuclear-free zone', i.e. banning the entry of nuclear weapons.

A general election for an enlarged, 63-seat Althing was held in April 1987. Both parties of the outgoing coalition suffered losses: the IP's representation decreased from 24 to 18 seats, and the PP lost one of its 14 seats. The right-wing Citizens' Party (CP, which had been formed only one month earlier by Albert Guðmundsson, following his resignation from the Ministry of Energy and Industry and from the IP) won seven seats. Ten seats were won by the SDP, which included former members of the SDA (disbanded in 1986). A coalition of the IP, the PP and the SDP was formally constituted in July 1987. Thorsteinn Pálsson, the leader of the IP since November 1983 and the Minister of Finance in the outgoing Cabinet, was appointed Prime Minister.

In June 1988 President Finnbogadóttir (who had begun a second term in office, unopposed, in August 1984) was elected for a third term, receiving more than 90% of the votes. This was the first occasion on which an incumbent President seeking re-election had been challenged. In August 1992 the President began a fourth term of office, her candidacy being unopposed.

In September 1988 the SDP and the PP withdrew from the Pálsson Government, following disagreements over economic policy. Later that month, the PP leader, Steingrímur Hermannsson, became Prime Minister in a centre-left coalition with the SDP and the PA. The new Government committed itself to a series of devaluations of the króna, and introduced austerity measures, with the aim of lowering the rate of inflation and stimulating the fishing industry.

Following the resignation of Guðmundsson from the leadership of the CP in January 1989, relations between this party and the left improved, and in September a new Government, based on a coalition agreement between the PP, the SDP, the PA, the CP and the Association for Equality and Social Justice, was formed. Hermannsson, who remained as Prime Minister, affirmed that the new Government would not change its policies, emphasizing the need to reduce inflation and to stimulate economic growth, as well as reiterating an earlier declaration of the Althing that no nuclear weapons would be located in Iceland.

In March 1991 Davíð Oddsson, the mayor of Reykjavík, successfully challenged Pálsson for the leadership of the IP. At a general election in April the IP emerged as the largest single party, securing 26 seats (with 38.6% of the votes), mostly at the expense of the CP. Although the incumbent coalition would have retained an overall majority of seats, the SDP decided to withdraw from the coalition, chiefly as a result of the failure to reach agreement on Iceland's position in the discussions between EFTA and the EC with regard to the creation of a European Economic Area (EEA, see below). A new coalition Government was formed in late April by the IP and the SDP, with Oddsson as Prime Minister; the new administration promised economic liberalization and a strengthening of links with the USA and Europe (although no application for membership of the EC was envisaged), but was faced with a deteriorating economic situation (see below).

In 1991 Iceland's Constitution was amended, ending the system whereby the Althing was divided into an Upper House (one-third of the members) and a Lower House.

Although the IP secured the largest number of seats (25, with 37% of the votes) at a general election in April 1995, the SDP obtained only seven seats, three fewer than in the previous election. Later in the month a new coalition Government was formed, comprising the IP and the PP, with Oddsson continuing as Prime Minister, and Halldór Ásgrímsson, the leader of the PP, being named Minister of Foreign Affairs. Since both parties in the coalition opposed the Common Fisheries Policy of the European Union (EU, as the EC had been restyled in 1993), it was considered unlikely that Iceland would apply for full membership of the EU in the near future.

Following the decision by Finnbogadóttir not to seek re-election as President in 1996, the principal candidates were Ólafur Ragnar Grímsson, a former leader of the PA (who had previously opposed Iceland's membership of NATO), Pétur Hafstein, a justice in the Supreme Court, and Guðrún Agnarsdóttir of the WL. In the election, held on 29 June 1996, Grímsson secured 41% of the votes cast, while Hafstein won 29% and Agnarsdóttir gained 26%. Grímsson duly took office as President in August.

At a general election held on 8 May 1999 the IP obtained the largest share of the votes cast (40.7%) and won 26 seats, thereby remaining the party with the largest representation in the Althing. An electoral grouping entitled The Alliance, which was composed of the PA, the SDP, the People's Movement and the WL, received 26.8% of the votes and won 17 seats, while the PP won 18.4% (12 seats). Two new parties also secured seats in the Althing: the Left-Green Alliance, established by three former PA deputies, obtained 9.1% of the votes (six seats), while the Liberal Party, founded by the former IP minister Sverrir Hermannsson, won 4.2% (two seats). A new coalition Government, which, once again, comprised the IP and the PP, and which continued to be led by Oddsson, took office at the end of the month.

The importance of fishing to Iceland's economy, and fears of excessive exploitation of the fishing grounds near Iceland by foreign fleets, caused the Icelandic Government to extend its territorial waters to 12 nautical miles (22 km) in 1964 and to 50 nautical miles (93 km) in 1972. British opposition to these extensions resulted in two 'cod wars'. In October 1975 Iceland unilaterally introduced a fishing limit of 200 nautical miles (370 km), both as a conservation measure and to protect Icelandic interests. The 1973 agreement on fishing limits between Iceland and the United Kingdom expired in November 1975, and failure to reach a new agreement led to the third and most serious 'cod war'. Casualties occurred, and in February 1976 Iceland temporarily severed diplomatic relations with the UK, the first diplomatic break between two NATO countries. In June the two countries reached an agreement, and in December the British trawler fleet withdrew from Icelandic waters. In June 1979 Iceland declared its exclusive rights to the 200-mile fishing zone. Following negotiations between the EC and EFTA on the creation of the EEA, an agreement was reached (in October 1991) allowing tariff-free access to the EC for 97% of Iceland's fisheries products by 1997, while Iceland was to allow EC vessels to catch 3,000 metric tons of fish per year in its waters, in return for some access to EC waters. The EEA agreement was ratified by the Althing in January 1993 and entered into force in January 1994.

In August 1993 a dispute developed between Iceland and Norway over fishing rights in an area of the Barents Sea fished by Iceland, over which Norway claimed jurisdiction. The dispute continued throughout 1994, and in June the Norwegian coastguards cut the nets of Icelandic trawlers fishing for cod in the disputed region. Iceland's case was weakened in January 1995, when Canada officially recognized Norway's sovereign rights over the disputed area (a fisheries protection zone extending 200 km around the Svalbard archipelago). A similar dispute arose in August 1996 between Iceland and Denmark over fishing rights in an area of the Atlantic Ocean between Iceland and Greenland (a self-governing province of Denmark). The Danish Government claimed that an agreement had been concluded in 1988 to allow fishing boats that were in possession of a licence issued in Greenland to operate in the area. Iceland, however, denied the existence of such an agreement, and announced that Danish boats would not be permitted to fish in the disputed area.

Iceland strongly criticized the moratorium on commercial whaling, imposed (for conservation purposes) by the International Whaling Commission (IWC, see p. 284) in 1986, and continued to catch limited numbers of whales for scientific purposes until 1989, when it halted whaling, following appeals by environmental organizations for an international boycott of Icelandic products. In 1991 Iceland announced its withdrawal from the IWC (with effect from June 1992), claiming that certain species of whales were not only too plentiful to be in danger of extinction, but were also threatening Iceland's stocks of cod and other fish. In 1994 a report, commissioned by the Government, recommended that limited hunting be resumed in the future. In March 1999 the Althing voted to end the self-imposed 10-year ban on whaling and requested the Government to implement the ruling, urging a resumption of hunting as soon as possible.

## Government

According to the Constitution, executive power is vested in the President (elected for four years by universal adult suffrage) and the Cabinet, consisting of the Prime Minister and other ministers appointed by the President. In practice, however, the President performs only nominally the functions ascribed in the Constitution to this office, and it is the Cabinet alone which holds real executive power. Legislative power is held jointly by the President and the unicameral Althing (Parliament), with 63 members elected by universal suffrage for four years (subject to dissolution by the President), using a mixed system of proportional representation. The Cabinet is responsible to the Althing. Iceland has seven administrative districts.

## Defence

Apart from a 120-strong coastguard, Iceland has no defence forces of its own, but it is a member of NATO. There are units of US forces at Keflavík air base, which is used for observation of the North Atlantic Ocean, under a bilateral agreement made in 1951 between Iceland and the USA. The airfield at Keflavík is a base for the US airborne early warning system. In August 1999 a total of 1,640 US military personnel (navy 960, air force 600, marines 80) were stationed in Iceland, together with a 16-strong naval contingent from the Netherlands.

## Economic Affairs

In 1996, according to estimates by the World Bank, Iceland's gross national product (GNP), measured at 1994–96 prices, was US $7,175m., equivalent to $26,580 per head. During 1990–96, it was estimated, GNP per head increased, in real terms, at an average annual rate of 3.1%. Over the same period the population increased at an average annual rate of 1.0%. Estimated GNP in 1998 was $7,675m. ($28,010 per head). Iceland's gross domestic product (GDP) increased, in real terms, by 5.4% in both 1997 and 1998; according to preliminary data published by the Central Bank of Iceland, GDP subsequently rose by 5.8% in 1999.

Agriculture (including fishing) contributes some 12% of GDP. About 8.6% of the labour force were employed in the agricultural sector in 1998. The principal agricultural products are dairy produce and lamb, although these provided less than 1% of export earnings in 1997. Marine products accounted for 72.7% of total export earnings in 1998. During 1986–96 agricultural production declined at an estimated average annual rate of 2.3%. According to preliminary data published by the Central Bank of Iceland, the level of agricultural production remained static in 1997 but increased by 1.1% in 1998.

Industry (including mining, manufacturing, construction and power) contributed 30.2% of GDP in 1991. In 1997 25.5% of the labour force were employed in the industrial sector. Mining activity is negligible. During 1986–91 industrial production increased by 8%.

Manufacturing contributed 17.3% of GDP in 1991, and, together with mining and quarrying, employed 18.4% of the labour force in 1998. The most important sectors, measured by gross value of output (excluding fish-processing, which dominates the sector), are the production of aluminium, diatomite, fertilizer, cement and ferro-silicon. Manufacturing GDP (including that contributed by fish-processing) declined by 4.2% in 1992, but recovered in 1993 and 1994 (when real growth of 5.9% was recorded, largely owing to increased fish-processing). Growth in the sector's GDP was estimated at 2.0% for 1995.

Iceland is potentially rich in hydroelectric and geothermal power, but both energy sources are significantly underexploited. In 1996 some 85% of homes were equipped with geothermal heating. Imports of mineral fuels and lubricants comprised 4.8% of the value of merchandise imports in 1998.

In 1998 Iceland recorded a visible trade deficit of US $351m. and there was a deficit of $469m. on the current account of the balance of payments. In 1998 the principal sources of imports were Germany (11.5%), the USA (11.1%) and the United Kingdom (9.7%); the principal market for exports was the United Kingdom (19.0%), followed by Denmark (15.0%) and the USA (13.2%). In the same year EU member countries provided 58.0% of Iceland's merchandise imports and took 62.1% of exports. The principal imports in 1998 were road vehicles, electrical machinery, apparatus and appliances and industrial machinery and equipment. The principal exports in the same year were marine products (including animal feeds) and non-ferrous metals.

In 1997 there was a budgetary surplus of 800m. krónur, equivalent to 0.2% of GDP. Iceland's net external debt was equivalent to 56.3% of GDP at the end of 1998; the cost of debt-servicing was equivalent to an estimated 21.0% of export earnings in the same year. The annual rate of inflation averaged 2.2% in 1990–97; consumer prices increased by 2.3% in 1996, by 1.8% in 1997 and by 1.7% in 1998. In November 1999 1.9% of the total labour force were unemployed.

Iceland is a member of the Nordic Council (see p. 222), the Nordic Council of Ministers (see p. 223), the European Free Trade Association (EFTA, see p. 291) and the Organisation for Economic Co-operation and Development (OECD, see p. 232).

Iceland's dependence on its fisheries proved to be a disadvantage in the late 1980s and early 1990s, when catches were reduced in volume as a deliberate conservation measure, made necessary by a serious depletion of stocks, while lower prices were paid for exports of fish products. Iceland's other principal exports—aluminium and ferro-silicon—were also affected by weakness of demand and deteriorating terms of trade during the same period. However, an economic upturn, with low inflation and strong export growth, resulted in real GDP growth of 3.7% in 1994, since which year the Icelandic economy has experienced a period of rapid growth. The annual rate of growth of GDP exceeded 5% in 1996–99, while inflation remained at a moderate level, largely as a result of tight monetary and fiscal policy, and the rate of unemployment declined. Foreign investment in power-intensive industries and renewed interest in recovered fish stocks also facilitated an improvement in general economic conditions in the mid-1990s, although the sharply-increasing deficit on the current account remained a source of concern.

Government fiscal policy in the late 1990s focused on the maintenance of economic stability, and placed emphasis on the improvement of market forces, the reduction of government involvement through privatization and the liberalization of the financial market. The Government effected a significant restructuring of the financial services industry in 1998, which included the creation of a new commercial bank, the Icelandic Investment Bank, through the merger of four state credit funds, and the privatization of government assets. In the same year, the Government appeared to be attempting to avert potential future over-dependence on the EU, currently Iceland's largest trading partner, by exploring the possibility of trading relationships with other countries. According to the Ministry of Finance, GDP was forecast to grow by 2.8% in 2000; inflation was also forecast to increase, to between 3.5% and 4.0%, in the same year. Fiscal policy was to be tightened considerably in 2000, and the Ministry of Finance forecast that the economy would continue to grow in the first years of the new century, although at a slower pace.

### Social Welfare

There is a comprehensive system of social security, providing a wide range of insurance benefits, including old-age pensions, family allowances, maternity grants, widows' pensions, etc. The scheme is mainly financed by the Government. Pensions and health insurance now apply to the whole population. Accident insurance applies to all wage and salary earners and self-employed persons—unless they request exemption—and unemployment insurance to the unions of skilled and unskilled workers and seamen in all towns and villages of over 300 inhabitants, as well as to several unions in villages of fewer than 300 inhabitants. In 1997 there were 884 physicians and surgeons, 2,075 nurses and 284 dentists working in Iceland. In 1991 the country had 14 general hospitals, with about 1,000 short-term beds. In addition there are a number of long-term institutions with more than 2,000 beds. Of total expenditure by the central Government in 1996, 36,257m. krónur (23.2%) was for health, while a further 35,606m. krónur (22.8%) was for social security and welfare.

### Education

Education is compulsory and free for eight years between seven and 15 years of age (primary and lower secondary levels). Secondary education begins at 16 years of age and lasts for four years. In 1994 89% of 16-year-olds were continuing their education at a secondary school. Iceland has 10 institutions providing tertiary-level education, including two universities. Expenditure on education by the central Government in 1996 was 20,068m. krónur, representing 12.8% of total spending. Local communities contribute about 20% of the cost of compulsory and secondary education.

### Public Holidays

**2000:** 1 January (New Year's Day), 20 April (Maundy Thursday and First Day of Summer), 21 April (Good Friday), 24 April (Easter Monday), 1 May (Labour Day), 1 June (Ascension Day), 12 June (Whit Monday), 17 June (National Day), 7 August (Bank Holiday), 24–26 December (Christmas), 31 December (New Year's Eve).

**2001:** 1 January (New Year's Day), 12 April (Maundy Thursday), 13 April (Good Friday), 16 April (Easter Monday), 19 April (First Day of Summer), 1 May (Labour Day), 24 May (Ascension Day), 4 June (Whit Monday), 17 June (National Day), 6 August (Bank Holiday), 24–26 December (Christmas), 31 December (New Year's Eve).

### Weights and Measures

The metric system is in force.

# Statistical Survey

Sources (unless otherwise stated): Statistics Iceland, Skuggasundi 3, 150 Reykjavík; tel. 5609800; fax 5628865; e-mail statice@statice.is; internet www.statice.is; National Economic Institute of Iceland, Reykjavík; tel. 5699500; internet www.stjr.is/frr/thst/; Seðlabanki Íslands (Central Bank of Iceland), Kalkofnsvegur 1, 150 Reykjavík; tel. 5699600; internet sedlabanki.is.

## AREA AND POPULATION

**Area:** 103,000 sq km (39,769 sq miles).

**Population:** 204,578 at census of 1 December 1970; 275,264 (males 137,874; females 137,390) at 1 December 1998; 278,702 at 1 December 1999.

**Density** (per sq km): 2.7 (1999).

**Principal Town:** Reykjavík (capital), population 108,351 at 1 December 1998.

**Births, Marriages and Deaths** (1998): Live births 4,178 (birth rate 15.3 per 1,000); Marriages 1,529 (marriage rate 5.6 per 1,000); Deaths 1,821 (death rate 6.7 per 1,000).

**Expectation of Life** (years at birth, 1997/98): Males 77.0; Females 81.5.

**Employment** (1998): Agriculture and fishing 12,700; Manufacturing 24,800; Electricity and water supply 1,500; Construction 10,900; Trade, restaurants and hotels 25,000; Transport, storage and communications 10,800; Finance, real estate and business services 14,200; Public administration, education, health services and other services not specified 47,900; Total 147,900.

## AGRICULTURE, ETC.

**Principal Crops** (metric tons, 1998): Potatoes 11,544; Turnips 627; Roots and tubers 9,000*.

*Source: FAO, *Production Yearbook*.

**Livestock** ('000 head, 1998): Cattle 75.5; Sheep 490.0; Horses 78.4; Pigs 4.0; Poultry 166.9.

**Livestock Products** (metric tons, 1998): Mutton and lamb 8,176; Beef and veal 3,443; Pig meat 3,886; Milk 105,000 (1997); Wool (unwashed) 667; Sheepskins 1,475 (1997); Eggs 2,333 (1997).

**Fishing** ('000 metric tons, live weight, 1998): Atlantic cod 242.9; Haddock 40.8; Atlantic redfishes 116.1; Capelin 748.5; Atlantic herring 277.5; Blue whiting 68,514; Molluscs and crustaceans 83.0; Total (incl. others) 1,678.7.

## INDUSTRY

**Selected Products** ('000 metric tons, unless otherwise indicated, 1997): Frozen fish 139.3 (1996, demersal catch); Salted, dried or smoked fish 72.5 (1996); Cement 108.5; Ferro-silicon 69.9; Aluminium (unwrought) 122.3; Electric energy 5,581 million kWh.

## FINANCE

**Currency and Exchange Rates:** 100 aurar (singular: eyrir) = 1 new Icelandic króna (plural: krónur). *Sterling, Dollar and Euro Equivalents* (30 September 1999): £1 sterling = 117.91 krónur; US $1 = 71.61 krónur; €1 = 76.37 krónur; 1,000 krónur = £8.481 = $13.965 = €13.094. *Average Exchange Rate* (krónur per US $): 66.500 in 1996; 70.904 in 1997; 70.958 in 1998.

**Budget** (million krónur, 1996): *Revenue:* Tax revenue 128,895 (Taxes on income, profits and capital gains 35,034, Social security contributions 13,101, Taxes on property 6,612, Domestic taxes on goods and services 71,803); Other current revenue 20,726 (Entrepreneurial and property income 8,754, Administrative fees and charges, non-industrial and incidental sales 7,342); Capital revenue 1,195; Total 150,816. *Expenditure:* General public services 8,052; Public order and safety 6,578; Education 20,068; Health 36,257; Social security and welfare 35,606; Housing and community amenities 1,298; Recreational, cultural and religious affairs and services 4,104; Economic affairs and services 27,211 (Agriculture, forestry, fishing and hunting 8,858, Transport and communications 14,022); Other purposes 17,279 (Interest payments 15,812); Total 156,454 (current 141,917, capital 14,537), excluding lending minus repayments (−1,248). Note: Figures refer to consolidated operations of the central Government, comprising budgetary accounts and social security funds. Source: IMF, *Government Finance Statistics Yearbook*.

**1997:** Total revenue 193,600m. krónur; Total expenditure 193,700m. krónur. **1998:** Total revenue 219,200m. krónur; Total expenditure 213,600m. krónur. Note: Figures for 1997 and 1998 refer to transactions of the public sector (including local government units). Source: Central Bank of Iceland.

**International Reserves** (US $ million at 31 December 1998): Gold 2.8; Reserve position in IMF 14.8; Foreign exchange 411.6; Total 429.2. Source: IMF, *International Financial Statistics*.

**Money Supply** (million krónur at 31 December 1998): Currency outside banks 6,322; Demand deposits at commercial and savings banks 51,852; Total money 56,878. Source: IMF, *International Financial Statistics*.

**Cost of Living** (consumer price index for Reykjavík; average of monthly figures; base: May 1988 = 100): 177.1 in 1996; 180.3 in 1997; 183.3 in 1998.

**Gross Domestic Product in purchasers' values** (million krónur at current prices): 486,454 in 1996; 529,949 in 1997; 586,572 (provisional) in 1998.

**Expenditure on the Gross Domestic Product** (million krónur at current prices, 1998): Government final consumption expenditure 124,019; Private final consumption expenditure 361,593; Increase in stocks 1,143; Gross fixed capital formation 125,365; *Total domestic expenditure* 612,120; Exports of goods and services 204,659; *Less* Imports of goods and services 230,207; *Gross domestic product* 586,572.

**Balance of Payments** (US $ million, 1998): Exports of goods f.o.b. 1,927, Imports of goods f.o.b. −2,278, *Trade balance* −351; Exports of services 947, Imports of services −965, *Balance on goods and services* −369; Other income received 216, Other income paid −300, *Balance on goods, services and income* −453; Current transfers received 4, Current transfers paid −20, *Current balance* −469; Capital account (net) −5, Direct investment abroad −73, Direct investment from abroad 150, Portfolio investment assets −401, Portfolio investment liabilities 66, Other investment assets 52, Other investment liabilities 805, Net errors and omissions −93, *Overall balance* 32. Source: IMF, *International Financial Statistics*.

### EXTERNAL TRADE

**Principal Commodities** (distribution by SITC, million krónur, 1998): *Imports c.i.f.:* Fish, crustaceans, molluscs and preparations thereof 4,500; Metalliferous ores and metal scrap 5,683; Petroleum and petroleum products 8,391; Medicinal and pharmaceutical products 4,242; Paper, paperboard and articles thereof 4,365; Textile yarn, etc. 3,875; Iron and steel 3,639; Machinery specialized for particular industries 7,546; General industrial machinery and equipment 9,556; Office machines and computers 6,244; Telecommunications equipment, etc. 6,423; Electrical machinery, apparatus and appliances 12,934; Road vehicles 16,881; Other transport equipment 8,299; Furniture, mattresses, cushions, etc. 3,785; Apparel and clothing accessories 6,437; Total (incl. others) 176,072. *Exports f.o.b.:* Fish, crustaceans, molluscs and preparations thereof 85,292; Animal feeds (excl. unmilled cereals) 11,954; Animal oils and fats 4,634; Iron and steel 3,241; Non-ferrous metals 18,422; Total (incl. others) 136,592.

**Principal Trading Partners** (million krónur, country of consignment, 1998): *Imports c.i.f.:* Australia 5,485.4; Belgium 3,266.8; China, People's Republic 2,418.3; Denmark 13,519.8; Finland 2,823.3; France 6,343.3; Germany 20,175.8; Ireland 2,603.7; Italy 5,668.5; Japan 8,933.3; Korea, Republic 2,123.2; Netherlands 10,477.1; Norway 16,137.1; Poland 2,570.7; Russia 3,792.0; Spain 3,530.5; Sweden 11,154.4; Switzerland 2,624.8; United Kingdom 17,026.6; USA 19,540.2; Total (incl. others) 176,072.1. *Exports f.o.b.:* Belgium 1,716.4; Canada 2,111.3; Denmark 7,449.0; France 9,220.9; Germany 20,486.8; Italy 2,366.7; Japan 6,544.8; Netherlands 5,548.0; Norway 6,574.4; Portugal 5,236.9; Russia 1,515.8; Spain 6,867.7; Switzerland 6,298.6; United Kingdom 25,897.0; USA 18,031.4; Total (incl. others) 136,592.0.

### TRANSPORT

**Road Traffic** (registered motor vehicles at 31 December 1998): Passenger cars 140,372; Buses and coaches 1,544; Goods vehicles 16,550; Motorcycles 1,379.

**Shipping:** *Merchant fleet* (registered vessels, 31 December 1998): Fishing vessels 799 (displacement 184,728 grt); Passenger ships, tankers and other vessels 156 (displacement 52,651 grt). *International freight traffic* ('000 metric tons, 1994): Goods loaded 1,162; Goods unloaded 1,733.

**Civil Aviation** (scheduled external Icelandic traffic, '000, 1996): Kilometres flown 22,526, Passenger-kilometres 2,801,000, Cargo ton-kilometres 52,655, Mail ton-kilometres 1,987.

### TOURISM

**Foreign Visitors by Country of Origin** (1997): Denmark 20,240, France 9,320, Germany 29,782, Norway 16,669, Sweden 19,150, UK 23,210, USA 32,384; Total (incl. others) 201,655. *1998* (total) 232,219. *1999* (total) 262,605.

**Receipts from Tourists** (million krónur): 22,301 in 1997; 26,334 in 1998.

### COMMUNICATIONS MEDIA

**Radio Receivers** (1997): 99,800 licensed.

**Television Receivers** (1997): 95,800 licensed.

**Telephones** (1997): 167,600 in use.

**Telefax Stations** (1993): 4,100 in use (Source: UN, *Statistical Yearbook*).

**Mobile Cellular Telephones** (subscribers, 1997): 68,700.

**Books** (provisional, production, 1998): 1,799 titles (incl. new editions).

**Daily Newspapers** (1998): 3.

### EDUCATION

**Institutions** (1997): Pre-primary 250; Primary and secondary (lower level) 198; Secondary (higher level) 37; Tertiary (universities and colleges) 10.

**Teachers** (incl. part-time, 1997): Pre-primary 2,939; Primary and secondary (lower level) 3,877; Secondary (higher level, 1996) 1,454; Tertiary (1996) 508.

**Students:** Pre-primary 14,857 (1997); Primary 29,082 (1996); Secondary (lower level) 13,130 (1996); Secondary (higher level) 20,406 (1998); Tertiary 8,791 (1998).

# Directory

## The Constitution

A new Constitution came into force on 17 June 1944, when Iceland declared its full independence. The main provisions of the Constitution are summarized below:

### GOVERNMENT

The President is elected for four years by universal suffrage. All those qualified to vote who have reached the age of 35 years are eligible for the Presidency.

Legislative power is jointly vested in the Althing (Althingi) and the President. Executive power is exercised by the President and other governmental authorities in accordance with the Constitution and other laws of the land.

The President summons the Althing every year and determines when the session shall close. The President may adjourn meetings of the Althing but not for more than two weeks nor more than once a year. The President appoints the Ministers and presides over the State Council. The President may be dismissed only if a resolution supported by three-quarters of the Althing is approved by a plebiscite.

The President may dissolve the Althing. Elections must be held within two months and the Althing must reassemble within eight months.

The Althing is composed of 63 members, elected by eight proportionately represented constituencies for a period of four years. Substitute members are elected at the same time and in the same manner as Althing members. Until 1991 the Althing was divided into two houses, the Upper House (efri deild) and the Lower House (nedri deild); but sometimes both Houses worked together as a United Althing. The Upper House consisted of 21 of the members, whom the United Althing chose from among the representatives, the remaining 42 forming the Lower House. Each House and the United Althing elected its own Speaker. In 1991 the two houses were merged to form a unicameral Althing. The minimum voting age, both for local administrative bodies and for the Althing, is 18 years, and all citizens domiciled in Iceland may vote, provided they are considered morally and financially responsible.

Bills must be given three readings in the Althing and be approved by a simple majority before they are submitted to the President. If the President disapproves a bill, it nevertheless becomes valid but must be submitted to a plebiscite. Ministers are responsible to the Althing and may be impeached by that body, in which case they are tried by the Court of Impeachment.

### LOCAL GOVERNMENT

For purposes of local government, the country is divided into Provinces, Districts and Municipalities. The eight Urban Municipalities are governed by Town Councils, which possess considerable autonomy. The Districts also have Councils and are further grouped together to form the Provinces, over each of which a centrally appointed Chief Official presides. The franchise for municipal purposes is universal above the age of 18 years, and elections are conducted on a basis of proportional representation.

# The Government

### HEAD OF STATE

**President:** ÓLAFUR RAGNAR GRÍMSSON (took office 1 August 1996).

### THE CABINET

(February 2000)

A coalition of the Independence Party (IP) and the Progressive Party (PP).

**Prime Minister and Minister of the Statistical Bureau of Iceland:** DAVÍÐ ODDSSON (IP).

**Minister for Foreign Affairs and External Trade:** HALLDÓR ÁSGRÍMSSON (PP).

**Minister of Finance:** GEIR H. HAARDE (IP).

**Minister of Fisheries:** ÁRNI M. MATHIESEN (IP).

**Minister of Justice and Ecclesiastical Affairs:** SÓLVEIG PÉTURSDÓTTIR (IP).

**Minister of Agriculture:** GUÐNÍ ÁGÚSTSSON (PP).

**Minister for the Environment:** SIV FRIDLEIFSDÓTTIR (PP).

**Minister of Industry and Commerce:** VALGERÐUR SVERRISDÓTTIR (PP).

**Minister of Education:** BJÖRN BJARNASON (IP).

**Minister of Social Affairs:** PÁLL PÉTURSSON (PP).

**Minister of Communications:** STURLA BÖDVARSSON (IP).

**Minister of Health and Social Security:** INGIBJORG PALMADÓTTIR (PP).

### MINISTRIES

**Office of the President:** Stadastadur, Soleyjargata 1, 150 Reykjavík; tel. 5404400; fax 5624802; e-mail forseti@forseti.is.

**Prime Minister's Office:** Stjórnarráðshúsinu v/Laekjargötu, 150 Reykjavík; tel. 5609400; fax 5624014; e-mail postur@for.stjr.is; internet www.stjr.is/for.

**Ministry of Agriculture:** Sölvhólsgata 7, 150 Reykjavík; tel. 5609750; fax 5521160; e-mail postur@lan.stjr.is; internet www .stjr.is/lan.

**Ministry of Communications:** Hafnarhúsinu við Tryggvagötu, 150 Reykjavík; tel. 5609630; fax 5621702; e-mail postur@sam.stjr.is; internet www.sam.stjr.is.

**Ministry of Education:** Sölvhólsgata 4, 150 Reykjavík; tel. 5609500; fax 5623068; e-mail postur@mrn.stjr.is; internet www.mrn.stjr.is.

**Ministry for the Environment:** Vonarstraeti 4, 150 Reykjavík; tel. 5609600; fax 5624566; e-mail postur@umh.stjr.is; internet www.stjr.is/umh.

**Ministry of Finance:** Arnarhváli, 150 Reykjavík; tel. 5609200; fax 5628280; e-mail postur@fjr.stjr.is; internet www.stjr.is/fjr.

**Ministry of Fisheries:** Skúlagötu 4, 150 Reykjavík; tel. 5609670; fax 5621853; e-mail sjavar@hafro.is; internet www.stjr.is/sjr.

**Ministry for Foreign Affairs:** Raudarárstíg 25, 150 Reykjavík; tel. 5609900; fax 5622373; e-mail external@utn.stjr.is; internet www.mfa.is.

**Ministry of Health and Social Security:** Laugavegi 116, 150 Reykjavík; tel. 5609700; fax 5519165; e-mail postur@htr.stjr.is; internet www.stjr.is/htr.

**Ministry of Industry and Commerce:** Arnarhváli, 150 Reykjavík; tel. 5609070; fax 5621289; e-mail postur@ivr.stjr.is; internet www.stjr.is/ivr.

**Ministry of Justice and Ecclesiastical Affairs:** Arnarhváli, 150 Reykjavík; tel. 5609010; fax 5527340; e-mail postur@dkm.stjr.is; internet www.stjr.is/dkm.

**Ministry of Social Affairs:** Hafnarhúsinu við Tryggvagötu, 150 Reykjavík; tel. 5609100; fax 5524804; e-mail postur@fel.stjr.is.

# President and Legislature

### PRESIDENT

**Presidential Election, 29 June 1996**

| | Number of votes cast | % of votes |
|---|---|---|
| ÓLAFUR RAGNAR GRÍMSSON | 68,370 | 40.9 |
| PÉTUR K. HAFSTEIN | 48,863 | 29.2 |
| GUÐRÚN AGNARSDÓTTIR | 43,578 | 26.0 |
| ÁSTTHÓR MAGNÚSSON | 4,422 | 2.6 |

### ALTHING
### (Althingi)

**Althing:** v/Austurvöll, 150 Reykjavík; tel. 5630500; fax 5630520; e-mail parlsecalthingi.is; internet www.althingi.is.

**Speaker of the Althing:** HALLDÓR BLÖNDAL.

**Secretary-General (Clerk) of the Althing:** FRIDRIK ÓLAFSSON.

**General Election, 8 May 1999**

| | % of votes | Seats |
|---|---|---|
| Independence Party | 40.7 | 26 |
| The Alliance* | 26.8 | 17 |
| Progressive Party | 18.4 | 12 |
| Left-Green Alliance | 9.1 | 6 |
| Liberal Party | 4.2 | 2 |
| Others | 0.8 | — |
| **Total** | 100.0 | 63 |

* The Alliance (Samfylkinginn) comprises the People's Alliance, the Social Democratic Party, the People's Movement and the Women's List.

# Political Organizations

**Althýdubandalag** (People's Alliance—PA): Austurstraeti 10, 101 Reykjavík; tel. 5517500; fax 5517599; f. 1956 by amalgamation of a section of the Social Democratic Party and the Socialist Unity Party, reorganized as a socialist party 1968; twin goals of socialism and national independence; Chair. MARGRÉT FRÍMANNSDÓTTIR; Parliamentary Leader SVAVAR GESTSSON; Gen. Sec. HEIMIR MÁR PÉTURSSON.

**Althýduflokkurinn** (Social Democratic Party—SDP): Althýduhusid, Hverfisgata 8–10, 101 Reykjavík; tel. 5529244; fax 5629155; f. 1916 with a moderate socialist programme; emphasizes greater equality in the distribution of wealth and income; Chair. JÓN BALDVIN HANNIBALSSON; Parliamentary Leader ÖSSUR SKARPHÉDINSSON.

**Framsóknarflokkurinn** (Progressive Party—PP): Hverfisgata 33, POB 453, 121 Reykjavík; tel. 5624480; fax 5623325; e-mail framsokn @framsokn.is; internet www.framsokn.is; f. 1916 with a programme of social liberalism and co-operation; Chair. HALLDÓR ÁSGRÍMSSON; Parliamentary Leader KRISTINN H. GUNNARSSON; Sec.-Gen. EGILL HEIÐAR GÍSLASON.

**Frjálslindi flokkurinn** (Liberal Party): c/o v/Austurvöll, 150 Reykjavík; tel. 5630500; fax 5630520; formed by Sverrir Hermannsson, former member of the IP and cabinet minister; Leader SVERRIR HERMANNSSON.

**Samtök um kvennalista** (Women's List—WL): Hverfisgata 8–10, 101 Reykjavík; tel. 5513725; fax 5629155; e-mail kvennalistinn@ kvennalistinn.is; internet www.centrum.is/kvennalistinn/; f. 1983; a non-hierarchical feminist movement to promote the interests of women and children; parliamentary leadership rotates.

**Sjálfstædisflokkurinn** (Independence Party—IP): Háaleitisbraut 1, 105 Reykjavík; tel. 5151700; fax 5151717; e-mail xd@xd.is; internet www.xd.is; f. 1929 by an amalgamation of the Conservative and Liberal Parties; its programme is social reform within the framework of private enterprise and the furtherance of national and individual independence; Leader DAVÍÐ ODDSSON.

**Thjóðvaki—hreyfing folksins** (Awakening of the Nation—People's Movement): Hafnarstraeti 7, 101 Reykjavík; tel. 5528100; fax 5627060; f. 1994; founded by dissident mems of the SDP; Leader JÓHANNA SIGURÐARÓTTIR.

**Vinstrihreyfing-Grænt frambod** (Left-Green Alliance): c/o v/Austurvöll, 150 Reykjavík; tel. 5630500; fax 5630520; founded by three dissident members of the PA.

# Diplomatic Representation

## EMBASSIES IN ICELAND

**China, People's Republic:** Viðimelur 29, POB 580, Reykjavík; Ambassador: WANG RONGHUA.

**Denmark:** Hverfisgata 29, 101 Reykjavík; tel. 5621230; fax 5623316; e-mail ambdan@mmedia.is; Ambassador: FLEMMING MØRCH.

**Finland:** Túngata 30, 101 Reykjavík; tel. 5100100; fax 5623880; e-mail finamb@itn.is; Ambassador: TOM SÖDERMAN.

**France:** Túngata 22, 101 Reykjavík; tel. 5517621; fax 5628177; Ambassador: ROBERT CANTONI.

**Germany:** Laufásvegur 31, POB 400, 121 Reykjavík; tel. 5301100; fax 5301101; e-mail germanembassy@islandia.is; Ambassador: Dr REINHART W. EHNI.

**Norway:** Fjólugata 17, Reykjavík; tel. 5520700; fax 5529553; Ambassador: KNUT TARALDSET.

**Russia:** Garðastraeti 33, Reykjavík; tel. 5515156; fax 5620633; Ambassador: YURII RECHETOV.

**Sweden:** Box 8136, 128 Reykjavík; tel. 5201230; fax 5201235; e-mail sveamb@itn.is; Ambassador: HERMAN AF TROLLE.

**United Kingdom:** Laufásvegur 31, POB 460, 121 Reykjavík; tel. 5505100; fax 5505105; e-mail britemb@centrum.is; Ambassador: JAMES MCCULLOCH.

**USA:** Laufásvegur 21, Reykjavík; tel. 5629100; fax 5629139; Ambassador: DAY OLIN MOUNT.

# Judicial System

All cases are heard in Ordinary Courts except those specifically within the jurisdiction of Special Courts. The Ordinary Courts include both a lower division of urban and rural district courts presided over by the district magistrates, and the Supreme Court.

Justices of the Supreme Court are appointed by the President and cannot be dismissed except by the decision of a court. The Justices elect the Chief Justice for a period of two years.

## SUPREME COURT

Dómhúsið v. Arnarhól, 150 Reykjavík; tel. 5103030; fax 5623995; e-mail haestirettur@haestirettur.is; internet www.haestirettur.is.

**Chief Justice:** PÉTUR KR. HAFSTEIN.

**Justices:** ARNLJÓTUR BJÖRNSSON, GUÐRÚN ERLENDSDÓTTIR, GARÐAR GÍSLASON, GUNNLAUGUR CLAESSEN, HJÖRTUR TORFASON, HRAFN BRAGASON, MARKÚS SIGURBJÖRNSSON, HARALDUR HENRYSSON.

# Religion

## CHRISTIANITY

### Protestant Churches

**Tjodkirkja Islands:** (Evangelical Lutheran Church of Iceland): Biskupsstofa, Laugavegur 31, 150 Reykjavík; tel. 5351500; fax 5513284; e-mail kirkjan@kirkjan.is; internet www.kirkjan.is; the national Church, endowed by the State; about 89% of the population are members; Iceland forms one diocese, Reykjavík, with two suffragan sees; 284 parishes and 138 pastors; Bishop KARL SIGURBJÖRNSSON.

**Fríkirkjan í Reykjavík** (The Congregational Church in Reykjavík): POB 1671, 121 Reykjavík; tel. 5527270; fax 5527287; e-mail hjorturm@frikirkian.is; f. 1899; Free Lutheran denomination; 5,500 mems; Head CECIL HARALDSSON.

**Óhádi söfnudurinn** (Independent Congregation): Reykjavík; Free Lutheran denomination; 1,100 mems; Head Rev. THÓRSTEINN RAGNARSSON.

**Seventh-day Adventists:** Suðurhlið 36, 105 Reykjavík; tel. 5887800; fax 5887808; e-mail sda@mmedia.is; internet www.sda.is.

### The Roman Catholic Church

Iceland comprises a single diocese, directly responsible to the Holy See. At 31 December 1997 there were an estimated 2,950 adherents in the country (just over 1% of the total population).

**Bishop of Reykjavík:** Most Rev. Dr JÓHANNES M. GIJSEN, Hávallagötu 14, POB 489, 121 Reykjavík; tel. 5525388; fax 5623878.

# The Press

## PRINCIPAL DAILIES

**Althýdublaðið** (The Labour Journal): Hverfisgata 8–10, 101 Reykjavík; tel. 5625566; fax 5629244; f. 1919; organ of the Social Democratic Party; Editor HRAFN JÖKULSSON; circ. 4,000.

**DV (Dagblaðið-Visir):** Thverholt 11, POB 5380, 105 Reykjavík; tel. 5505000; fax 5505020; f. 1981; independent; Editors JÓNAS KRISTJÁNSSON, OLI BJÖRN KÁRASON; circ. 44,000.

**Dagur-Tíminn:** Strandgata 31, POB 58, 600 Akureyri; tel. 4606100; fax 4627639; f. 1918, restructured 1996; organ of the Progressive Party; Editor STEFÁN JÓN HAFSTEIN.

**Morgunblaðið** (Morning News): Kringlan 1, POB 3040, 103 Reykjavík; tel. 5691100; fax 5691181; e-mail mbl@mbl.is; internet www.mbl.is; f. 1913; independent; Editors MATTHÍAS JOHANNESSEN, STYRMIR GUNNARSSON; circ. 53,000.

## WEEKLIES

**Austri:** Tjarnarbraut 19, POB 173, 700 Egilsstaðir; tel. 4711984; e-mail austri@eldhorn.is; local newspaper; f. 1979; Editor JÓN KRISTJÁNSSON; circ. 2,000.

**Einherji:** Siglufjorður; organ of the Progressive Party.

**Fiskifréttir:** POB 1120, 121 Reykjavík; tel. 5155500; fax 5155599; e-mail fiskifrettir@frodi.is; f. 1983; weekly; for the fishing industry; Editor GUÐJÓN EINARSSON; circ. 6,000.

**Helgarpósturinn** (Weekend Post): Borgartúni 27, 101 Reykjavík; tel. 5522211; fax 5522311; f. 1994; independent; Editor PÁLL VILHJÁLMSSON; circ. 10,000.

**Íslendingur-Ísafold** (Icelander-Icecountry): Kaupangi v/Mýrarveg, 600 Akureyri; tel. 4621500; f. 1915; for North and East Iceland; Editor STEFÁN SIGTRYGGSSON.

**Séð & Heyrt:** Seljavegur 2, 101 Reykjavík; tel. 5155652; fax 5155599; showbusiness and celebrities; Editors BJARNI BRYNJOLFSSON, KRISTJAN THORVALDSSON; circ. 23,000.

**Siglfirðingur:** Siglufjorður; organ of the Independence Party.

**Skagablaðið:** Skólabraut 21, 300 Akranesi; tel. 4314222; fax 4314122; f. 1984; local newspaper; Editor SIGURÐUR SVERRISSON; circ. 1,500.

**Suðurnesjafréttir:** Hafnargötu 28, 230 Keflavík; tel. 4213800; fax 4213802; f. 1992; local newspaper; Editors EMIL PÁLL JÓNSSON, HALLDÓR LEVI BJÖRNSSON; circ. 6,500.

**Sunnlenska Fréttablaðið:** Austurvegi 1, 800 Selfoss; tel. 4823074; fax 4823084; f. 1991; local newspaper; Editor BJARNI HARÐARSON; circ. 6,300.

**Vestfirska Fréttablaðið:** Fjarðastraeti 16, 400 Ísafjörður; tel. 4564011; fax 4565225; f. 1975; local newspaper; Editors HLYNUR THÓR MAGNÚSSON, GÍSLI HJARTARSON; circ. 2,000.

**Vikublaðið** (The Weekly Paper): Austurstraeti 10A, 101 Reykjavík; tel. 5528655; fax 5517599; f. 1992; organ of People's Alliance; Editor FRIÐRIK THÓR GUÐMUNDSSON; circ. 3,000–4,000.

**Víkurblaðið:** Heðinsbraut 1, 640 Húsavík; tel. 4641780; fax 4641399; f. 1979; local newspaper; Editor JÓHANNES SIGURJÓNSSON; circ. 1,300.

**Víkurfréttir:** Vallargata 15, 230 Keflavík; tel. 4214717; fax 4212777; f. 1983; local newspaper; Editor PÁLL KETILSSON; circ. 6,400.

## OTHER PERIODICALS

**Ægir**: Skerpla, Sudurlandsbraut 10, Reykjavík; tel. 5681225; fax 5681224; f. 1905; published by the Fisheries Association of Iceland in co-operation with Athygli ehf Publishing; monthly; Editors BJARNI KR. GRÍMSSON, JÓHANN ÓLAFUR HALLDÓRSSON; circ. 2,500.

**Æskan og ABC** (The Youth and ABC): Eiríksgötu 5, 101 Reykjavík; tel. 5510248; fax 5510248; f. 1897; 9 a year; children's magazine; Editor KARL HELGASON.

**Atlantica:** Nóatún 17, 105 Reykjavík; tel. 5115700; fax 5115701; e-mail iceland@icenews.is; internet www.icenews.is; 6 a year; in-flight magazine of Icelandair; Editor HARALDUR J. HAMAR.

**AVS (Arkitektur, verktækni og skipulag):** Garðastræti 17, 101 Reykjavík; tel. 5616577; fax 5616571; e-mail skipark@centrum.is; f. 1979; 4 a year; architecture and environment; Editor GESTUR ÓLAFSSON; circ. 6,000.

**Bændablaðið:** POB 7080, 127 Reykjavík; tel. 5630300; fax 5623058; e-mail ath@bi.bondi.is; f. 1995; fortnightly; organ of the Icelandic farmers' union; Editor ÁSKELL THÓRISSON; circ. 6,400.

**Bíllinn:** Myrargata 26, 101 Reykjavík; tel. 5526090; fax 5529490; f. 1982; 3–4 a year; cars and motoring equipment; Editor LEÓ M. JÓNSSON; circ. 4,000.

**Bleikt og Blátt:** Seljavegur 2, 101 Reykjavík; tel. 5155500; fax 5155599; f. 1989; 6 a year; sex education, communication between men and women; Editor DAVÍÐ THOR JÓNSSON; circ. 11,000.

**Eiðfaxi:** Ármúli 38, POB 8133, 128 Reykjavík; tel. 5882525; fax 5882528; e-mail eidfaxi@eidfaxi.is; internet www.eidfaxi.is; f. 1977; monthly; horse-breeding and horsemanship; Man. Dir GYDA GERÐARSDÓTTIR; Editor JENS EINARSSON; circ. 7,000.

**Fasteignablaðið:** Sídumúli 10, 108 Reykjavík; tel. 5888844; fax 5888843; monthly; real estate; Editor DAVÍÐ JÓNSSON; circ. 60,000.

**Fjármálatíðindi:** Kalkofnsvegur 1, 150 Reykjavík; tel. 5699600; fax 5699605; 2 a year; economic journal published by the Central Bank; circ. 1,600.

**Freyr, búnaðarblað:** Baendahöllin við Hagatorg, POB 7080, 127 Reykjavík; tel. 5630300; fax 5623058; e-mail bbl@bi.bondi.is; internet www.bondi.is; monthly; agriculture; Editors ASKELL THORISSON, MATTHIAS EGGERTSSON; circ. 1,900.

**Frjáls Verslun** (Free Trade): Borgartún 23, 105 Reykjavík; tel. 5617575; fax 5618646; f. 1939; 10 a year; business magazine; Editor JÓN G. HAUKSSON; circ. 6,000–9,000.

**Gestgjafinn:** Seljavegur 2, 101 Reykjavík; tel. 5155500; fax 5155599; e-mail gestgjafinn@frodi.is; f. 1981; 10 a year; food and wine; Editor SOLVEIG BALDURSDOTTIR; circ. 15,000.

**Hagtíðindi** (Monthly Statistics): published by Statistics Iceland, Skuggasund 3, 150 Reykjavík; tel. 5609800; fax 5628865; e-mail statice@statice.is; internet www.statice.is; f. 1916; monthly; Dir-Gen. HALLGRIMUR SNORRASON; circ. 1,300.

**Hár og Fegurð** (Hair and Beauty Magazine): Skúlagata 54, 105 Reykjavík; tel. and fax 5628141; e-mail pmelsted@vortex.is; internet www.vortex.is/fashion; f. 1980; 3 a year; hair, beauty, fashion; Editor PÉTUR MELSTEÐ.

**Heilbrigðismál:** Skógarhlíð 8, 105 Reykjavík; tel. 5621414; fax 5621417; f. 1949; quarterly; public health; Editor JÓNAS RAGNARSSON; circ. 6,000.

**Heima Er Bezt:** Ármuli 23, 108 Reykjavík; tel. 5882400; fax 5888994; e-mail skjaldborg@islania.is; f. 1951; monthly; literary; Editor GUÐJÓN BALDVINSSON; circ. 3,500.

**Heimsmynd:** Aðalstræti 4, 101 Reykjavík; tel. 5622020; fax 5622029; f. 1986; 10 a year; general interest; Editor KARL BIRGISSON; circ. 8,000.

**Hús og Híbýli:** Seljavegur 2, 101 Reykjavík; tel. 5155500; fax 5155599; e-mail hogh@frodi.is; f. 1978; 11 a year; architecture, family and homes; Editor ÉLÍN ALBERTSDÓTTIR; circ. 11,000–13,000.

**Húsfreyjan** (The Housewife): Túngata 14, 101 Reykjavík; tel. 5517044; f. 1950; quarterly; the organ of the Federation of Icelandic Women's Societies; Editor HRAFNHILDUR VALGARÐS; circ. 4,000.

**Iceland Business:** Nóatún 17, 105 Reykjavík; tel. 5115700; fax 5115701; e-mail iceland@icenews.is; internet www.icenews.is; f. 1994; 5 a year, in English; Publr HARALDUR J. HAMAR.

**Iceland Review:** Nóatún 17, 105 Reykjavík; tel. 5115700; fax 5115701; e-mail iceland@icenews.is; internet www.icenews.is; f. 1963; quarterly, in English; general; Editor HARALDUR J. HAMAR.

**Innflutningur** (Import): Héðinsgata 1–3, 105 Reykjavík; tel. 5813411; fax 5680211; f. 1991; 3–4 a year; Editor SÓLVEIG BALDURSDÓTTIR; circ. 5,000.

**Ithróttablaðið:** Seljavegur 2, 101 Reykjavík; tel. 5155500; fax 5155599; f. 1939; 6 a year; sport; Editor JÓHANN ARNASON; circ. 6,000.

**Lisin að lifa:** Hverfisgata 105, 101 Reykjavík; tel. 5882111; fax 5882114; e-mail feb@islandia.is; f. 1986; 4 a year; for elderly people; Editor SU BJÖRGUINS; circ. 13,000–15,000.

**Mannlíf:** Seljavegur 2, 101 Reykjavík; tel. 5155555; fax 5155599; e-mail mannlif@frodi.is; f. 1984; 10 a year; general interest; Editors GERDUR KRISTNÝ GUDJÖNSDÖTTIR; circ. 16,000.

**Myndbönd mánaðarins** (Videos of the Month): Ármúli 15, 108 Reykjavík; tel. 5811280; fax 5811286; f. 1993; monthly; Editor GUÐBERGUR ÍSLEIFSSON; circ. 26,000.

**Ný menntamál:** Lágmúli 7, 108 Reykjavík; tel. 5531117; e-mail hannes@ismennt.is; f. 1983; quarterly; educational issues; Editor HANNES ÍSBERG; circ. 6,500.

**Nýtt Líf:** Seljavegur 2, 101 Reykjavík; tel. 5155660; fax 5155599; f. 1978; 10 a year; fashion; Editor GULLVEIG SÆMUNDSDÓTTIR; circ. 13,000–16,000.

**Peningamál:** Kalkofnsvegi 1, 150 Reykjavik; tel. 5699600; fax 5699608; e-mail sedlabanki@sedlabanki.is; internet www.sedlabanki.is; f. 1999; quarterly bulletin published by the Central Bank; circ. 1,600.

**Sjávarfréttir:** POB 1120, 121 Reykjavík; tel. 5155500; fax 5155599; e-mail fiskifrettir@frodi.is; f. 1973; yearly; ship registry, statistics on Icelandic fisheries; Editor GUÐJÓN EINARSSON; circ. 5,500.

**Skutull** (Harpoon): Fjarðarstræti 2, 400 Isafjörður; tel. 4563948; fax 4565148; e-mail stapi@simnet.is; f. 1923; monthly; organ of the Social Democratic Party; Editor GÍSLI HJARTARSON.

**Stúdentablaðið:** Stúdentaheimilinu v/Hringbraut, 101 Reykjavík; tel. 5700850; fax 5700855; e-mail shi@hi.is; internet www.shi.hi.is; f. 1924; 8 issues during the academic year; students' interests; Editor SIGTRYGGUR MAGNASON; circ. 7,500.

**Sveitastjórnarmál:** Háaleitisbraut 11, 128 Reykjavík; tel. 5813711; fax 5687866; f. 1941; 24 a year; publ. by the Asscn of Icelandic Municipalities: Editor UNNAR STEFÁNSSON; circ. 3,400.

**Uppeldi:** Bolholt 4, 105 Reykjavík; tel. 5680170; fax 5677215; f. 1988; quarterly; Editor KRISTÍN ELFA GUÐNADÓTTIR; circ. 10,000.

**Úrval** (Digest): Thverholt 11, 105 Reykjavík; tel. 5505000; fax 5505999; f. 1942; bi-monthly; Editor SIGURÐUR HREIÐARSSON; circ. 6,500.

**Veiðimaðurinn** (Hunter): Hédinshúsið, Seljavegur 2, 101 Reykjavík; tel. 5155500; fax 5155599; f. 1984; 3 a year; fishing and hunting; Editor MAGNÚS HREGGVIDSSON; circ. 6,000.

**Vera:** Vesturgata 3B, 101 Reykjavík; tel. 5522188; fax 5527560; f. 1982; 6 a year; feminist issues; Editor ELÍSABET THORGEIRSDÓTTIR.

**Víkingur** (Seaman): Borgartún 18, 105 Reykjavík; 10 a year; Editor SIGURJÓN VALDIMARSSON.

**Vinnan** (Work): Grensásvegur 16A, 108 Reykjavík; tel. 5813044; fax 5680093; e-mail arnar@gsi.is; 14 a year; f. 1943; publ. by Icelandic Federation of Labour; Editor ARNAR GUÐMUNDSSON: circ. 5,000.

### NEWS AGENCIES

#### Foreign Bureaux

**Agence France-Presse (AFP):** Garðastræti 13, 101 Reykjavík; tel. 5510586; Correspondent GÉRARD LEMARQUIS.

**United Press International (UPI)** (USA): Reykjavík; tel. 5539816; Correspondent BERNARD SCUDDER.

### PRESS ASSOCIATION

**Samtök bæjar- og héraðsfréttablaða** (Asscn of Local Newspapers): Bæjarhraun 16, 220 Hafnarfjörður; tel. 5651945; fax 5650745; represents 15 newspapers; Pres. FRÍÐA PROPPE.

## Publishers

**Bifröst:** Gimli, Álftanesvegi, 101 Reykjavík; tel. 5659300; fax 5653520; f. 1988; spiritual, self-help; Dir GUÐMUNDUR EINARSSON.

**Bókaútgáfa Æskunnar:** Eiríksgata 5, 101 Reykjavík; tel. and fax 5510248; Editor KARL HELGASON.

**Bókaútgáfan Bjartur:** Braeðraborgarstígur 9, 101 Reykjavík; tel. 5621826; fax 5628360; f. 1989; contemporary fiction; Man. Dir SNAEBJÖRN ARNGRÍMSSON.

**Bókaútgáfan Björk:** Birkivöllum 30, 800 Selfoss; tel. 4821394; fax 4823894; f. 1941; children's; Man. ERLENDUR DANIELSSON.

**Fjölvaútgáfan:** Njorvasundi 15a, 104 Reykjavík; tel. 5688433; fax 5688142; f. 1966; general; Dir THORSTEINN THORARENSEN.

**Forlagið:** Laugavegi 18, 101 Reykjavík; tel. 5152500; fax 5152506; e-mail forlag@mm.is; f. 1984; general; Dir JÓHANN PÁLL VALDIMARSSON.

**Frjáls fjölmiðlun:** Thverholt 11, POB 5380; 105 Reykjavík; tel. 5505000; fax 5505999; f. 1981; fiction in translation, romance; Gen. Man. EYJÓLFUR SVEINSSON.

**Fródi Ltd:** Seljavegur 2, 101 Reykjavík; tel. 5155500; fax 5155599; e-mail frodi@frodi.is; internet www.frodi.is; f. 1989; general magazines and books; Chair. and CEO MAGNUS HREGGVIDSSON; Editor STEINAR LUÐVIKSSON.

**Háskólaútgáfan** (University Publishing): Háskóli Íslands v/Suðurgötu, 101 Reykjavík; tel. 5254003; fax 5521331; e-mail hu@hi.is; f. 1988; non-fiction, science, culture, history; Man. Dir JÖRUNDUR GUÐMUNDSSON.

**Hið íslenska bókmenntafélag:** Siðumúli 21, POB 8935, 128 Reykjavík; tel. 5889060; fax 5889095; e-mail hib@islandia.is; internet www.arctic.is/hib; f. 1816; general; Pres. SIGURÐUR LÍNDAL; Dir SVERRIR KRISTINSSON.

**Hið íslenska Fornritafélag:** Siðumúli 21, POB 8935, 128 Reykjavík; tel. 5889060; fax 5889095; e-mail hib@islandia.is; internet www.arctic.is/hib; f. 1928; Pres. J. NORDAL.

**Hörpuútgáfan:** Stekkjarholti 8-10, POB 25, 300 Akranes; tel. 4312860; fax 4313309; Dir BRAGI THORÐARSON.

**Iðunn:** POB 294, 121 Reykjavík; tel. 5528555; fax 5528380; e-mail idunn@vortex.is; general; f. 1945; Man. Dir JÓN KARLSSON.

**Islendingasagnaútgáfan:** POB 488, 220 Hafnarfjordur; tel. 8985868; fax 5655868; f. 1945; poetry, fiction, children's, general non-fiction; Dir BENEDIKT KRISTJÁNSSON.

**Krydd í tilveruna:** Bakkasel 10, 109 Reykjavík; tel. 5575444; fax 5575466; f. 1989; mainly cookery; Dir ANTON ÖRN KJAERNSTED.

**Mál og menning** (Literary Book Club): Síðumúli 7 9, 108 Reykjavík; tel. 5102525; fax 5102505; e-mail klubbar@mm.is; internet www.mm.is/; f. 1937; 10,000 mems; Man. THÓRHILDUR GARÐARSDÓTTIR; Editor HALLDÓR GUÐMUNDSSON.

**Námsgagnastofnun** (National Centre for Educational Materials): POB 5020, Reykjavík 125; tel. 5528088; fax 5624137; e-mail simi@nams.is; f. 1979; Dir (Publishing House) ÁSGEIR GUÐMUNDSSON.

**Ormstunga:** Austurströnd 3, 170 Seltjarnarnes; tel. 5610055; fax 5610025; e-mail books@ormstunga.is; internet www.ormstunga.is; f. 1992; Icelandic and foreign fiction; Dir GÍSLI MÁR GÍSLASON.

**Reykholt:** POB 8950, 128 Reykjavík; tel. 5888821; fax 5888380; f. 1987; general; Dir REYNIR JÓHANNSSON.

**Setberg:** Freyjugata 14, POB 619, 101 Reykjavík; tel. 5517667; fax 5526640; fiction, cookery, juvenile, picture books, activity books and children's books; Dir ARNBJÖRN KRISTINSSON.

**Skálholtsútgáfan:** Laugavegur 31, 101 Reykjavík; tel. 5621581; fax 5621595; f. 1981; non-fiction, Christian church; Man. Dir EDDA MÖLLER.

**Skjaldborg Ltd:** Grensásvegi 14, POB 8427, 108 Reykjavík; tel. 5882400; fax 5888994; e-mail skjaldborg@skjaldborg.is; general; Dir BJÖRN EIRÍKSSON.

**Sögufélagið:** Fischersund 3, 101 Reykjavík; tel. 5514620; non-fiction, history; Dir RAGNHEIÐUR THORLÁKSDÓTTIR.

**Stofnun Arna Magnussonar:** Arnagardur v/ Sudurgotu, 101 Reykjavík; tel. 5254010; fax 5254035; e-mail rosat@hi.is; internet www.am.hi.is; f. 1972; non-fiction; Dir VÉSTEINN ÓLASON.

**Vaka-Helgafell Inc:** Siðumúli 6, 108 Reykjavík; tel. 5503000; fax 5503033; general reference, fiction, non-fiction; Dir ÓLAFUR RAGNARSSON.

### PUBLISHERS' ASSOCIATION

**Félag íslenskra bókaútgefenda** (Icelandic Publishers' Assn): Suðurlandsbraut 4A, 108 Reykjavík; tel. 5538020; fax 5888668; e-mail baekur@mmedia.is; internet this.is/baekur; f. 1889; Pres. SIGURDUR SVAVARSSON; Man. VILBORG HARÐARDÓTTIR.

# Broadcasting and Communications

### TELECOMMUNICATIONS

**Iceland Telecom Ltd:** Austurvöllur, 150 Reykjavík; tel. 5506000; fax 5506009; e-mail simi@simi.is; internet www.simi.is; f. 1998; operation of telecommunications; also operation of Skyggnir, earth station for satellite telecommunications; Pres. and CEO THORARINN V. THORARINSSON.

**Post and Telecom Administration:** Smiðjuvegur 68–70, 200 Kópavogur; tel. 5101500; fax 5101509; e-mail pta@pta.is.

### BROADCASTING

**Ríkisútvarpið** (Icelandic National Broadcasting Service): Broadcasting Centre, Efstaleiti 1, 150 Reykjavík; tel. 5153000; fax 5153010; e-mail isradio@ruv.is; internet www.ruv.is; f. 1930; Dir-Gen. MARKÚS ÖRN ANTONSSON; Chair. of Programme Board GUNNLAUGUR SÆVAR GUNNLAUGSSON.

#### Radio

**Ríkisútvarpið:** Radio Division, Efstaleiti 1, 150 Reykjavík; tel. 5153000; fax 5153010; f. 1930; Dir of Radio DORA INGVADOTTIR.

Programme 1 has two long-wave, three medium-wave and 77 FM transmitters broadcasting 127 hours a week.

Programme 2 has 67 FM transmitters broadcasting 168 hours a week.

**Aðalstöðin:** POB 46, 121 Reykjavík; tel. 5621520; fax 5620044; Head BALDVIN JÓNSSON.

**Add Ice:** Tangarhöfdi 7, 112 Reykjavík; tel. 5775500; fax 57755; e-mail addice@addice.is; internet www.addice.is; broadcasts only in Reykjanesbær; Head AXRNGRÍMUR HERMANNSSON.

**Alfa-Omega:** Evrópsk fjölmiðlun, Hlaðbae 11, 110 Reykjavík; tel. 5676111; Head ERÍKUR SIGURBJÖRNSSON.

**Brosið:** Suðurnesjabrosið hf, Hafnargata 15, 230 Keflavík; tel. 4216300; fax 4216301; broadcasts only in Reykjanesbær; Head RAGNAR ÖRN STEFÁNSSON.

**Bylgjan:** Lyngháls 5, 110 Reykjavík; tel. 5156300; fax 5156830; privately-owned by Icelandic Broadcasting Corpn.

**FM 95,7:** Útvarp FM hf, Álfabakka 8, 109 Reykjavík; tel. 5870900; fax 5870920; Head BJÖRN Á. ÁRNASON.

**Klassík FM:** Fínn Miðill EHF, Aðalstræti 6, 101 Reykjavík; tel. 5116500; fax 5116501; Head C. F. JONES.

**Lindin:** Krókháls 4, 110 Reykjavík; tel. 5671030; e-mail lindin@lindin.is; Head MICHAEL E. FITZGERALD.

**Rás Fás:** Fjölbrautarskóli Norðurlands vestra, 550 Sauðárkrókur; Head GUNNAR BÚASON.

**Stjarnan:** Islenska útvarpsfélagið-Fjölmiðlum hf, Lyngháls 5, 110 Reykjavík; Head (vacant).

**Útvarp Hafnarfjörður:** Köldukinn 2, 220 Hafnarfjörður; tel. 5651766; fax 5651796; broadcasts only in Hafnarfjörður; Head HALLDÓR ÁRNI SVEINSSON.

**Útvarp Húsavík:** Ketilsbraut 9, 640 Húsavík; tel 4642277; broadcasts only in Húsavík; Head EINAR BJÖRNSSON.

**Útvarp Kántrýbær:** Brimnes, 545 Skagaströnd; tel. 4522960; e-mail kantrybar@islandia.is; broadcasts only in Skagaströnd; Head HALLBJÖRN J. HJARTARSON.

**Útvarp Vestmannaeyjar:** Brekkugata 1, 900 Vestmannaeyjar; tel. 4811534; fax 4813475; broadcasts only in Vestmannaeyjar; Head BJARNI JÓNASSON.

**Xið:** Aflvakinn hf, Aðalstræti 16, 101 Reykjavík; tel. 5626977; fax 5620044; Head THORMÓÐUR JÓNSSON.

**Vila-Árna Útvarp:** Skipholt 6, 355 Ólafsvík; tel. 4361334; fax 4361379; Head VILHELM ÁRNASON.

#### Television

**Ríkisútvarpið—Sjónvarp** (Icelandic National Broadcasting Service—Television): Laugavegur 176, 105 Reykjavík; tel. 5153900; fax 5153842; e-mail istv@ruv.is; internet www.ruv.is; f. 1966; covers 99% of the population; broadcasts daily, total 70 hours a week; Man. Dir BJARNI GUDMUNDSSON.

**Aksjón ehf:** Strandgötu 31, 600 Akureyri; tel. 4611050; fax 4612356; e-mail aksjon@nett.is; broadcasts only in Akureyri; Head GÍSLI GUNNLAUGSSON.

**Fjölsýn:** Strandvegur 47, 900 Vestmannaeyjar; tel. 4811300; fax 4812643; e-mail siglt@eyjar.is; broadcasts only in Vestmannaeyjar; Head ÓMAR GUÐMUNDSSON.

**Íslenska Útvarpsfélagið hf** (Icelandic Broadcasting Corporation): Channel 2 and TV SYN; Lynghalsi 5, 110 Reykjavík; tel. 5156000; fax 5156860; f. 1986; privately-owned 'pay-TV' station; Pres. HREGGVIDUR JONSSON.

**Norðurljós:** Húsvísk fjölmiðlun hf, Héðinsbraut 1, 640 Húsavík; tel. 4641780; fax 4641785; broadcasts only in Húsavík; Head ÓMAR GUÐMUNDSSON.

**Omega:** Grensasvegur 8, 108 Reykjavík; tel. 5683131; fax 5683741; broadcasts only in Reykjavík; religious; Gen. Dir ERIK ERIKSSON.

**S.j.ó.l:** Sjónvarp Ólafsfjörður, Ólafsvegur 28, 625 Ólafsfjörður; tel 4662111; broadcasts only in Ólafsfjörður; Head SKÚLI PÁLSSON.

**Sjónvarp Hafnarfjarðar:** Hafnfirsk fjölmiðlun hf, Bæjarhraun 16, 220 Hafnarfjörður; tel. 5651796; broadcasts only in Hafnarfjörður; Head HALLDÓR ÁRNI SVEINSSON.

**Stöð 3:** Krokhals 6, 112 Reykjavík; tel. 5335600; fax 5335699; f. 1996; Head MAGNÚS KRISTJÁNSSON.

**Villa Video:** Skipholt 6, 335 Ólafsvík; tel. 4361563; fax 4361379; broadcasts only in Ólafsvík; Head VILHELM ÁRNASON.

The US Navy operates a radio station (24 hours a day), and a cable television service (80 hours a week), on the NATO base at Keflavík.

# Finance

(cap. = capital; p.u. = paid up; res = reserves; dep. = deposits; m. = million; kr = krónur; brs = branches)

### BANKING

Since the 1980s Iceland's banking and finance system has undergone substantial transformation. In 1989–90 the number of commercial banks was reduced from seven to three, by amalgamating four banks to form Íslandsbanki as the only remaining major commercial bank in private ownership. The 27 savings banks operate a commercial bank, Icebank, which functions as a central banking institution. In January 1995 full liberalization of foreign exchange regulations on the movement of capital was realized.

#### Central Bank

**Seðlabanki Íslands** (Central Bank of Iceland): Kalkofnsvegur 1, 150 Reykjavík; tel. 5699600; fax 5699605; e-mail sedlabanki@sedlabanki.is; internet www.sedlabanki.is; f. 1961 to take over central banking activities of Landsbanki Íslands; cap. and res 17,969m.

## NATIONAL ACCOUNTS

('000 million rupees at current prices, year ending 31 March)

### National Income and Product

| | 1995/96 | 1996/97 | 1997/98 |
|---|---|---|---|
| Domestic factor incomes* | 9,891 | 11,540 | 12,786 |
| Consumption of fixed capital | 1,141 | 1,313 | 1,481 |
| **Gross domestic product at factor cost** | 11,032 | 12,853 | 14,267 |
| Indirect taxes | 1,424 | 1,627 | 1,754 |
| *Less* Subsidies | 277 | 380 | 385 |
| **GDP in purchasers' values** | 12,179 | 14,098 | 15,635 |
| Factor income from abroad / *Less* Factor income paid abroad | −135 | −131 | −134 |
| **Gross national product** | 12,044 | 13,967 | 15,501 |
| *Less* Consumption of fixed capital | 1,141 | 1,313 | 1,481 |
| **National income in market prices** | 10,903 | 12,654 | 14,020 |
| Other current transfers from abroad | 222 | 442 | 439 |
| *Less* Other current transfers paid abroad | 1 | 2 | 1 |
| **National disposable income** | 11,124 | 13,094 | 14,458 |

* Compensation of employees and the operating surplus of enterprises.

### Expenditure on the Gross Domestic Product

| | 1995/96 | 1996/97 | 1997/98 |
|---|---|---|---|
| Government final consumption expenditure | 1,270 | 1,440 | 1,738 |
| Private final consumption expenditure | 7,517 | 8,790 | 9,548 |
| Increase in stocks | 219 | −7 | 75 |
| Gross fixed capital formation | 2,901 | 3,271 | 3,578 |
| **Total domestic expenditure** | 11,907 | 13,494 | 14,940 |
| Exports of goods and services | 1,307 | 1,453 | 1,608 |
| *Less* Imports of goods and services | 1,449 | 1,610 | 1,815 |
| Statistical discrepancy | 414 | 761 | 902 |
| **GDP in purchasers' values** | 12,179 | 14,098 | 15,635 |

### Gross Domestic Product by Economic Activity

(provisional estimates, at current factor cost)

| | 1995/96 | 1996/97 | 1997/98 |
|---|---|---|---|
| Agriculture | 2,877.0 | 3,475.0 | 3,595.9 |
| Forestry and logging | 123.7 | 135.4 | 144.7 |
| Fishing | 127.3 | 150.6 | 180.8 |
| Mining and quarrying | 245.9 | 272.1 | 293.8 |
| Manufacturing | 1,920.7 | 2,152.9 | 2,398.6 |
| Electricity, gas and water | 276.7 | 298.5 | 358.2 |
| Construction | 554.6 | 629.1 | 676.6 |
| Trade, restaurants and hotels | 1,648.7 | 1,970.9 | 2,218.1 |
| Transport, storage and communications | 777.9 | 923.7 | 1,079.0 |
| Banking and insurance | 658.9 | 770.1 | 879.6 |
| Real estate and business services | 574.8 | 621.0 | 672.5 |
| Public administration and defence | 565.9 | 646.4 | 832.8 |
| Other services | 680.5 | 807.0 | 936.2 |
| **Total** | 11,032.4 | 12,852.6 | 14,266.7 |

## BALANCE OF PAYMENTS (US $ million)

| | 1996 | 1997 | 1998 |
|---|---|---|---|
| Exports of goods f.o.b. | 33,737 | 35,702 | 34,076 |
| Imports of goods f.o.b. | −43,789 | −45,730 | −44,828 |
| **Trade balance** | −10,052 | −10,028 | −10,752 |
| Exports of services | 7,238 | 9,111 | 11,691 |
| Imports of services | −11,171 | −12,443 | −14,540 |
| **Balance on goods and services** | −13,984 | −13,360 | −13,601 |
| Other income received | 1,411 | 1,484 | 1,806 |
| Other income paid | −4,667 | −5,002 | −5,443 |
| **Balance on goods, services and income** | −17,240 | −16,878 | −17,238 |
| Current transfers received | 11,350 | 13,975 | 10,402 |
| Current transfers paid | −66 | −62 | −67 |
| **Current balance** | −5,956 | −2,965 | −6,903 |
| Direct investment abroad | −239 | −113 | −48 |
| Direct investment from abroad | 2,426 | 3,577 | 2,635 |
| Portfolio investment liabilities | 3,958 | 2,556 | −601 |
| Other investment assets | −4,710 | −4,743 | −3,239 |
| Other investment liabilities | 10,413 | 8,357 | 9,837 |
| Net errors and omissions | −1,934 | −1,348 | 1,390 |
| **Overall balance** | 3,958 | 5,321 | 3,071 |

Source: IMF, *International Financial Statistics.*

## OFFICIAL DEVELOPMENT ASSISTANCE (US $ million)

| | 1994 | 1995 | 1996 |
|---|---|---|---|
| Bilateral donors | 1,350.8 | 1,024.3 | 1,013.6 |
| Multilateral donors | 974.2 | 719.6 | 922.7 |
| **Total** | 2,325.0 | 1,743.9 | 1,936.3 |
| Grants | 1,000.2 | 994.7 | 1,024.7 |
| Loans | 1,324.8 | 749.2 | 911.6 |
| Per caput assistance (US $) | 2.6 | 1.9 | 2.1 |

Source: UN, *Statistical Yearbook for Asia and the Pacific.*

# External Trade

## PRINCIPAL COMMODITIES

(million rupees, year ending 31 March)

| Imports c.i.f. | 1995/96 | 1996/97 | 1997/98 |
|---|---|---|---|
| Manufactured fertilizers | 46,210 | 24,342 | 30,652 |
| Metalliferous ores and metal scrap | 27,510 | 29,096 | 22,960 |
| Mineral fuels, lubricants, etc. | 251,736 | 356,287 | 305,382 |
| Organic chemicals | 56,983 | 94,461 | 111,198 |
| Inorganic chemicals | 28,833 | | |
| Artificial resins, plastic materials, etc. | 26,875 | 28,257 | 25,649 |
| Pearls, precious and semi-precious stones | 70,447 | 103,836 | 116,800 |
| Iron and steel | 48,376 | 48,650 | 56,010 |
| Non-ferrous metals | 30,235 | 39,249 | 33,771 |
| Non-electrical machinery | 223,689 | 129,374 | 131,603 |
| Transport equipment | 36,967 | 52,692 | 33,681 |
| Electronic goods | 62,657 | 53,540 | 76,110 |
| **Total** (incl. others) | 1,226,781 | 1,389,190 | 1,515,440 |

Source: Ministry of Commerce.

| Exports f.o.b. | 1995/96 | 1996/97 | 1997/98 |
|---|---|---|---|
| Marine products | 33,810 | 40,080 | 43,127 |
| Tea and maté | 11,710 | 10,371 | 15,051 |
| Oil cakes | 23,490 | 34,953 | 34,036 |
| Cotton fabrics, yarn, etc. | 86,190 | 110,821 | 120,936 |
| Ready-made garments | 122,950 | 133,240 | 140,340 |
| Carpets (hand-made) | 14,060 | 15,489 | 15,061 |
| Leather and leather manufactures | 57,900 | 36,198 | 34,670 |
| Gems and jewellery | 176,450 | 168,721 | 190,136 |
| Iron ore | 17,210 | 17,064 | 17,632 |
| Engineering products | 120,580 | 143,957 | 155,845 |
| Chemicals and related products | 78,910 | 138,910 | 161,260 |
| Petroleum products | 15,180 | 17,104 | 13,110 |
| Ores and minerals (excluding iron ore, mica and coal) | 20,850 | 23,470 | 21,110 |
| Man-made textiles | 25,110 | 24,940 | 28,540 |
| Electronic goods and computer software | 25,200 | 27,820 | 26,000 |
| **Total** (incl. others) | 1,063,530 | 1,188,173 | 1,262,858 |

Source: Ministry of Commerce.

**PRINCIPAL TRADING PARTNERS**
(million rupees, year ending 31 March)

| Imports c.i.f. | 1995/96 | 1996/97 | 1997/98 |
|---|---|---|---|
| Australia | 34,180 | 46,761 | 55,611 |
| Bahrain | 28,770 | 31,880 | 22,540 |
| Belgium | 56,930 | 79,935 | 90,744 |
| Canada | 12,750 | 11,120 | 15,857 |
| France | 28,120 | 27,268 | 29,235 |
| Germany | 105,200 | 100,503 | 92,946 |
| Iran | 20,010 | 31,040 | 23,688 |
| Italy | 35,600 | 35,052 | 34,171 |
| Japan | 82,540 | 77,654 | 79,118 |
| Korea, Republic | 27,590 | 31,368 | 33,316 |
| Kuwait | 65,900 | 85,370 | 85,986 |
| Malaysia | 30,200 | 39,320 | 44,052 |
| Netherlands | 19,070 | 17,536 | 16,080 |
| Nigeria | 25,750 | 54,160 | 41,510 |
| Russia | 40,900 | 27,570 | 32,900 |
| Saudi Arabia | 67,730 | 98,322 | 93,963 |
| Singapore | 36,520 | 37,748 | 44,149 |
| Switzerland | 34,140 | 40,020 | 95,278 |
| United Arab Emirates | 53,740 | 61,630 | 64,899 |
| United Kingdom | 64,150 | 75,781 | 86,965 |
| USA | 129,160 | 130,840 | 135,096 |
| **Total** (incl. others) | 1,226,781 | 1,389,190 | 1,515,535 |

| Exports f.o.b. | 1995/96 | 1996/97 | 1997/98 |
|---|---|---|---|
| Australia | 12,570 | 13,680 | 15,817 |
| Bangladesh | 35,090 | 30,848 | 28,394 |
| Belgium | 37,480 | 38,790 | 44,264 |
| Canada | 10,220 | 12,531 | 15,489 |
| France | 24,990 | 25,424 | 27,506 |
| Germany | 66,140 | 67,204 | 68,920 |
| Hong Kong | 60,930 | 66,122 | 71,330 |
| Italy | 33,920 | 35,150 | 40,820 |
| Japan | 74,110 | 71,209 | 69,072 |
| Korea, Republic | 14,990 | 18,406 | 15,300 |
| Malaysia | 13,150 | 18,855 | 17,885 |
| Netherlands | 25,720 | 30,259 | 29,037 |
| Russia | 34,950 | 28,800 | 33,060 |
| Saudi Arabia | 16,130 | 20,490 | 25,096 |
| Singapore | 30,160 | 34,700 | 27,461 |
| Spain | 13,080 | 15,080 | 15,983 |
| Switzerland | 9,420 | 10,640 | 13,891 |
| Thailand | 15,820 | 15,871 | 12,547 |
| United Arab Emirates | 47,780 | 52,398 | 59,294 |
| United Kingdom | 67,260 | 72,665 | 75,779 |
| USA | 184,660 | 232,717 | 246,407 |
| **Total** (incl. others) | 1,063,530 | 1,188,173 | 1,262,858 |

Source: Ministry of Commerce.

# Transport

**RAILWAYS** (million, year ending 31 March)

| | 1996/97 | 1997/98 | 1998/99 |
|---|---|---|---|
| Passengers | 4,153 | 4,368 | 4,415 |
| Passenger-km | 357,012 | 370,560 | 390,976 |
| Freight (metric tons) | 409.2 | 429.6 | 420.9 |
| Freight (metric ton-km) | 277,572 | 284,124 | 282,094 |

Source: Railway Board, Ministry of Railways.

**ROAD TRAFFIC** ('000 motor vehicles in use at 31 March)

| | 1996 | 1997 | 1998* |
|---|---|---|---|
| Private cars, jeeps and taxis | 4,204 | 4,662 | 5,088 |
| Buses and coaches | 449 | 488 | 512 |
| Goods vehicles | 2,031 | 2,260 | 2,413 |
| Motor cycles and scooters | 23,252 | 25,693 | 27,919 |
| Others | 3,847 | 4,128 | 4,526 |
| **Total** | 33,783 | 37,231 | 40,458 |

* Provisional figures.

Source: Transport Research Division, Ministry of Surface Transport.

**SHIPPING**

**Merchant Fleet** (registered at 31 December)

| | 1996 | 1997 | 1998 |
|---|---|---|---|
| Vessels | 920 | 941 | 947 |
| Displacement ('000 grt) | 7,127.2 | 6,934.3 | 6,777.1 |

Source: Lloyd's Register of Shipping, *World Fleet Statistics*.

**International Sea-Borne Traffic** (year ending 31 March)

| | 1995/96 | 1996/97 | 1997/98 |
|---|---|---|---|
| Vessels* ('000 net regd tons): | | | |
| Entered | 47,857 | 48,358 | 47,052 |
| Cleared | 48,497 | 44,494 | 45,369 |
| Freight† ('000 metric tons): | | | |
| Loaded | 57,243 | 57,822 | 61,173 |
| Unloaded | 94,858 | 106,685 | 117,329 |

* Excluding minor and intermediate ports.

† Including bunkers.

Sources: Transport Research Division, Ministry of Surface Transport; Directorate General of Commercial Intelligence and Statistics.

**CIVIL AVIATION** (traffic)

| | 1995/96 | 1996/97 | 1997/98 |
|---|---|---|---|
| Kilometres flown ('000) | 155,016 | 179,532 | 175,308 |
| Passenger-km ('000) | 21,506,184 | 23,376,792 | 23,353,980 |
| Freight ton-km ('000) | 616,080 | 498,000 | 482,148 |
| Mail ton-km ('000) | 27,240 | 21,924 | 21,048 |

Source: Directorate General of Civil Aviation.

## Tourism

**FOREIGN VISITORS BY COUNTRY OF ORIGIN***

| | 1996 | 1997 | 1998 |
|---|---|---|---|
| Australia | 48,755 | 50,647 | 57,807 |
| Canada | 74,031 | 78,570 | 80,111 |
| CIS | 41,085 | 32,190 | 29,493 |
| France | 93,325 | 91,423 | 97,898 |
| Germany | 99,853 | 105,979 | 93,993 |
| Italy | 49,910 | 53,854 | 54,058 |
| Japan | 99,018 | 99,729 | 89,565 |
| Malaysia | 53,370 | 60,401 | 47,496 |
| Netherlands | 40,246 | 44,843 | 54,227 |
| Singapore | 47,136 | 52,004 | 54,328 |
| Sri Lanka | 107,351 | 122,080 | 118,292 |
| United Kingdom | 360,686 | 360,567 | 376,513 |
| USA | 228,829 | 244,239 | 244,687 |
| **Total** (incl. others) | 1,923,695 | 1,973,647 | 1,974,815 |

* Figures exclude nationals of Bangladesh and Pakistan. Including these, the total was 2,287,860 in 1996, 2,374,094 in 1997 and 2,358,629 in 1998.

Source: Ministry of Tourism and Civil Aviation.

**Receipts from tourism** (million rupees, year ending 31 March): 104,176 in 1996/97; 108,796 in 1997/98; 120,115 in 1998/99.

## Communications Media

| | 1993 | 1994 | 1995 |
|---|---|---|---|
| Television receivers ('000 in use) | n.a. | n.a. | 47,000 |
| Radio receivers ('000 in use) | 72,000 | 74,000 | 75,500 |
| Main telephone lines ('000)* | 6,796.7 | 8,025.6 | 9,795.3 |
| Telefax stations ('000 in use) | 45 | 50 | n.a. |
| Daily newspapers | 3,740 | n.a. | 4,236 |
| Net circulation (million) | 67.6 | n.a. | n.a. |
| Non-daily newspapers and other periodicals* | 28,455 | 29,872 | n.a. |

* Year ending 31 March.

**Daily newspapers:** 4,453 in 1996; 4,719 in 1997.

**1995/96** (year ending 31 March): 11,978,000 main telephone lines; 76,680 mobile cellular telephone subscribers.

**1996** ('000 in use): 57,700 television receivers; 99,000 radio receivers.

**1998:** 21,593,700 main telephone lines; 1,070,709 mobile cellular telephone subscribers.

Sources: Ministry of Communications; Registrar of Newspapers for India; Ministry of Information and Broadcasting; UNESCO, *Statistical Yearbook*; UN, *Statistical Yearbook*.

## Education

(1997/98)

| | Institutions | Teachers | Students |
|---|---|---|---|
| Primary | 610,763 | 1,871,542 | 108,781,792 |
| Middle | 185,506 | 1,211,803 | 39,487,071 |
| Secondary (High school) | 76,230 | 869,420 | 17,946,705 |
| Higher secondary (New pattern) | 26,491 | 651,766 | 6,944,069 |

Source: Planning, Monitoring and Statistics Division, Department of Education, Ministry of Human Resources Development.

# Directory

## The Constitution

The Constitution of India, adopted by the Constituent Assembly on 26 November 1949, was inaugurated on 26 January 1950. The Preamble declares that the People of India solemnly resolve to constitute a Sovereign Democratic Republic and to secure to all its citizens justice, liberty, equality and fraternity. There are 397 articles and nine schedules, which form a comprehensive document.

### UNION OF STATES

The Union of India comprises 25 states, six Union Territories and one National Capital Territory. There are provisions for the formation and admission of new states.

The Constitution confers citizenship on a threefold basis of birth, descent, and residence. Provisions are made for refugees who have migrated from Pakistan and for persons of Indian origin residing abroad.

### FUNDAMENTAL RIGHTS AND DIRECTIVE PRINCIPLES

The rights of the citizen contained in Part III of the Constitution are declared fundamental and enforceable in law. 'Untouchability' is abolished and its practice in any form is a punishable offence. The Directive Principles of State Policy provide a code intended to ensure promotion of the economic, social and educational welfare of the State in future legislation.

### THE PRESIDENT

The President is the head of the Union, exercising all executive powers on the advice of the Council of Ministers responsible to Parliament. He is elected by an electoral college consisting of elected members of both Houses of Parliament and the Legislatures of the States. The President holds office for a term of five years and is eligible for re-election. He may be impeached for violation of the Constitution. The Vice-President is the ex officio Chairman of the Rajya Sabha and is elected by a joint sitting of both Houses of Parliament.

### THE PARLIAMENT

The Parliament of the Union consists of the President and two Houses: the Rajya Sabha (Council of States) and the Lok Sabha (House of the People). The Rajya Sabha consists of 245 members, of whom a number are nominated by the President. One-third of its members retire every two years. Elections are indirect, each state's legislative quota being elected by the members of the state's legislative assembly. The Lok Sahba has 543 members elected by adult franchise; not more than 13 represent the Union Territories and National Capital Territory. Two members are nominated by the President to represent the Anglo-Indian community.

### GOVERNMENT OF THE STATES

The governmental machinery of states closely resembles that of the Union. Each of these states has a governor at its head appointed by the President for a term of five years to exercise executive power on the advice of a council of ministers. The states' legislatures consist of the Governor and either one house (legislative assembly) or two houses (legislative assembly and legislative council). The term of the assembly is five years, but the council is not subject to dissolution.

### LANGUAGE

The Constitution provides that the official language of the Union shall be Hindi. (The English language will continue to be an associate language for many official purposes.)

### LEGISLATION—FEDERAL SYSTEM

The Constitution provides that bills, other than money bills, can be introduced in either House. To become law, they must be passed by both Houses and receive the assent of the President. In financial affairs, the authority of the Lower House is final. The various subjects of legislation are enumerated on three lists in the seventh schedule of the Constitution: the Union List, containing nearly 100 entries, including external affairs, defence, communications and atomic energy; the State List, containing 65 entries, including local government, police, public health, education; and the Concurrent

List, with over 40 entries, including criminal law, marriage and divorce, labour welfare. The Constitution vests residuary authority in the Centre. All matters not enumerated in the Concurrent or State Lists will be deemed to be included in the Union List, and in the event of conflict between Union and State Law on any subject enumerated in the Concurrent List the Union Law will prevail. In time of emergency Parliament may even exercise powers otherwise exclusively vested in the states. Under Article 356, 'If the President on receipt of a report from the government of a state or otherwise is satisfied that a situation has arisen in which the Government of the state cannot be carried on in accordance with the provisions of this Constitution, the President may by Proclamation: (a) assume to himself all or any of the functions of the government of the state and all or any of the powers of the governor or any body or authority in the state other than the Legislature of the state; (b) declare that the powers of the Legislature of the state shall be exercisable by or under the authority of Parliament; (c) make such incidental provisions as appear to the President to be necessary': provided that none of the powers of a High Court be assumed by the President or suspended in any way. Unless such a Proclamation is approved by both Houses of Parliament, it ceases to operate after two months. A Proclamation so approved ceases to operate after six months, unless renewed by Parliament. Its renewal cannot be extended beyond a total period of three years. An independent judiciary exists to define and interpret the Constitution and to resolve constitutional disputes arising between states, or between a state and the Government of India.

### OTHER PROVISIONS

Other Provisions of the Constitution deal with the administration of tribal areas, relations between the Union and states, inter-state trade and finance.

### AMENDMENTS

The Constitution is flexible in character, and a simple process of amendment has been adopted. For amendment of provisions concerning the Supreme Courts and the High Courts, the distribution of legislative powers between the Union and the states, the representation of the states in Parliament, etc., the amendment must be passed by both Houses of Parliament and must further be ratified by the legislatures of not less than half the states. In other cases no reference to the state legislatures is necessary.

Numerous amendments were adopted in August 1975, following the declaration of a state of emergency in June. The Constitution (39th Amendment) Bill laid down that the President's reasons for proclaiming an emergency may not be challenged in any court. Under the Constitution (40th Amendment) Bill, 38 existing laws may not be challenged before any court on the ground of violation of fundamental rights. Thus detainees under the Maintenance of Internal Security Act could not be told the grounds of their detention and were forbidden bail and any claim to liberty through natural or common law. The Constitution (41st Amendment) Bill provided that the President, Prime Minister and state Governors should be immune from criminal prosecution for life and from civil prosecution during their term of office.

In November 1976 a 59-clause Constitution (42nd Amendment) Bill was approved by Parliament and came into force in January 1977. Some of the provisions of the Bill are that the Indian Democratic Republic shall be named a 'Democratic Secular and Socialist Republic'; that the President 'shall act in accordance with' the advice given to him by the Prime Minister and the Council of Ministers, and, acting at the Prime Minister's direction, shall be empowered for two years to amend the Constitution by executive order, in any way beneficial to the enforcement of the whole; that the term of the Lok Sabha and of the State Assemblies shall be extended from five to six years; that there shall be no limitation on the constituent power of Parliament to amend the Constitution, and that India's Supreme Court shall be barred from hearing petitions challenging constitutional amendments; that strikes shall be forbidden in the public services and the Union Government have the power to deploy police or other forces under its own superintendence and control in any state. Directive Principles are given precedence over Fundamental Rights: 10 basic duties of citizens are listed, including the duty to 'defend the country and render national service when called upon to do so'.

The Janata Party Government, which came into power in March 1977, promised to amend the Constitution during the year, so as to 'restore the balance between the people and Parliament, Parliament and the judiciary, the judiciary and the executive, the states and the centre, and the citizen and the Government that the founding fathers of the Constitution had worked out'. The Constitution (43rd Amendment) Bill, passed by Parliament in December 1977, the Constitution (44th Amendment) Bill, passed by Parliament in December 1977 and later redesignated the 43rd Amendment, and the Constitution (45th Amendment) Bill, passed by Parliament in December 1978 and later redesignated the 44th Amendment, reversed most of the changes enacted by the Constitution (42nd Amendment) Bill. The 44th Amendment is particularly detailed on emergency provisions: An emergency may not be proclaimed unless 'the security of India or any part of its territory was threatened by war or external aggression or by armed rebellion.' Its introduction must be approved by a two-thirds majority of Parliament within a month, and after six months the emergency may be continued only with the approval of Parliament. Among the provisions left unchanged after these Bills were a section subordinating Fundamental Rights to Directive Principles and a clause empowering the central Government to deploy armed forces under its control in any state without the state government's consent. In May 1980 the Indian Supreme Court repealed sections 4 and 55 of the 42nd Amendment Act, thus curtailing Parliament's power to enforce directive principles and to amend the Constitution. The death penalty was declared constitutionally valid.

The 53rd Amendment to the Constitution, approved by Parliament in August 1986, granted statehood to the Union Territory of Mizoram; the 55th Amendment, approved in December 1986, granted statehood to the Union Territory of Arunachal Pradesh; and the 57th Amendment, approved in May 1987, granted statehood to the Union Territory of Goa (Daman and Diu remain, however, as a Union Territory). The 59th Amendment, approved in March 1988, empowered the Government to impose a state of emergency in Punjab, on the grounds of internal disturbances. In December 1988 the minimum voting age was lowered from 21 to 18 years. The 71st Amendment, approved in August 1992, gave official language status to Nepali, Konkani and Manipuri.

### THE PANCHAYAT RAJ SCHEME

This scheme is designed to decentralize the powers of the Union and State Governments. It is based on the Panchayat (Village Council) and the Gram Sabha (Village Parliament) and envisages the gradual transference of local government from state to local authority. Revenue and internal security will remain state responsibilities at present. By 1978 the scheme had been introduced in all the states except Meghalaya, Nagaland and 23 out of 31 districts in Bihar. The Panchayat operated in all the Union Territories except Lakshadweep, Mizoram (which became India's 23rd state in February 1987) and Pondicherry. The 72nd Amendment, approved in late 1992, provided for direct elections to the Panchayats, members of which were to have a tenure of five years.

## The Government

**President:** Dr Kocheril Raman Narayanan (sworn in 25 July 1997).

**Vice-President:** Krishan Kant (sworn in 21 August 1997).

### COUNCIL OF MINISTERS
(February 2000)

A coalition of the Bharatiya Janata Party (BJP), the Biju Janata Dal (BJD), the Dravida Munnetra Kazhagam (DMK), the Trinamool Congress (TC), the Shiv Sena (SS), the Shiromani Akali Dal (SAD), Jammu and Kashmir National Conference, the Pattali Makkal Katchi (PMK), the Marumalarchi Dravida Munnetra Kazhagam (MDMK), the Janata Dal (United) (JD—U) and Independents (Ind.).

**Prime Minister*:** Atal Bihari Vajpayee (BJP).

**Minister of Home Affairs:** Lal Krishna Advani (BJP).

**Minister of External Affairs:** Jaswant Singh (BJP).

**Minister of Finance:** Yashwant Sinha (BJP).

**Minister of Tourism (with additional charge of Department of Culture):** Ananth Kumar (BJP).

**Minister of Environment and Forests:** T. R. Baalu (DMK).

**Minister of Railways:** Mamata Banerjee (TC).

**Minister of Defence:** George Fernandes (JD—U).

**Minister of Urban Development and Poverty Alleviation:** Jagmohan (BJP).

**Minister of Labour:** Dr Satya Narayan Jatiya (BJP).

**Minister of Law, Justice and Company Affairs:** Ram Jethmalani (Ind.).

**Minister of Heavy Industries and Public Enterprises:** Manohar Joshi (SS).

**Minister of Human Resource Development, of Ocean Development and of Science and Technology:** Dr Murli Manohar Joshi (BJP).

**Minister of Power:** P. R. Kumaramangalam (BJP).

**Minister of Parliamentary Affairs and of Information Technology:** Pramod Mahajan (BJP).

**Minister of Commerce and Industry:** Murasoli Maran (DMK).

**Minister of Petrolelum and Natural Gas:** Ram Naik (BJP).

**Minister of Surface Transport:** Rajnath Singh (BJP).

**Minister of Tribal Affairs:** JUEL ORAM (BJP).

**Minister of Communications:** RAM VILAS PASWAN (JD–U).

**Minister of Mines and Minerals:** NAVEEN PATNAIK (BJD).

**Minister of Rural Development:** SUNDERLAL PATWA (BJP).

**Minister of Chemicals and Fertilizers:** SURESH PRABHAKAR PRABHU (SS).

**Minister of Textiles:** KASHIRAM RANA (BJP).

**Minister of Consumer Affairs and Public Distribution:** SHANTA KUMAR (BJP).

**Minister of Civil Aviation:** SHARAD YADAV (JD–U).

**Minister of Water Resources:** C. P. THAKUR (BJP).

**Minister of Works and Estates (with additional charge of Department of Youth Affairs and Sports):** SUKHDEV SINGH DHINDSA (SAD).

**Minister of Agriculture:** NITISH KUMAR (JD–U).

**Minister for Disinvestment:** ARUN JAITLEY (BJP).

**Ministers of State with Independent Charge**

**Minister of State for Social Justice and Empowerment:** MANEKA GANDHI (Ind.).

**Minister of State for Information and Broadcasting:** ARUN JAITLEY (BJP).

**Minister of State for Non-Conventional Energy Sources:** K. KANNAPAN (MDMK).

**Minister of State for Steel:** DILIP RAY (BJP).

**Minister of State for Small-scale Industries and Agro and Rural Industries:** VASUNDHARA RAJE (BJP).

**Minister of State for Health and Family Welfare:** N. T. SHANMUGHAM (PMK).

There are, in addition, 37 Ministers of State without independent charge.

* The Prime Minister is also in charge of ministries and departments not allotted to others.

## MINISTRIES

**President's Office:** Rashtrapati Bhavan, New Delhi 110 004; tel. (11) 3015321; fax (11) 3017290.

**Vice-President's Office:** 6 Maulana Azad Rd, New Delhi 110 011; tel. (11) 3016344; fax (11) 3018124.

**Prime Minister's Office:** South Block, New Delhi 110 011; tel. (11) 3013040; fax (11) 3016857.

**Ministry of Agriculture:** Krishi Bhavan, Dr Rajendra Prasad Rd, New Delhi 110 001; tel. (11) 3382651; fax (11) 3386004.

**Ministry of Atomic Energy:** South Block, New Delhi 110 011; tel. (11) 3011773; fax (11) 3013843.

**Ministry of Chemicals and Fertilizers:** Shastri Bhavan, New Delhi 110 001; tel. (11) 3383695; fax (11) 3386222.

**Ministry of Civil Aviation:** Rajiv Gandhi Bhavan, Safdarjung Airport, New Delhi 110 023; tel. (11) 4610358; fax (11) 4610354.

**Ministry of Civil Supplies, Consumer Affairs and Public Distribution:** Krishi Bhavan, New Delhi 110 001; tel. (11) 3384882; fax (11) 3388302.

**Ministry of Coal:** Shram Shakti, Rafi Marg, New Delhi 110 001; tel. (11) 3384884; fax (11) 3387738.

**Ministry of Commerce and Industry:** Udyog Bhavan, New Delhi 110 011; tel. (11) 3012107; fax (11) 3014335.

**Ministry of Communications:** Sanchar Bhavan, 20 Asoka Rd, New Delhi 110 001; tel. (11) 3719898; fax (11) 3782344.

**Ministry of Defence:** South Block, New Delhi 110 011; tel. (11) 3012380.

**Ministry of Electronics:** Electronics Niketan, 6 CGO Complex, New Delhi 110 003; tel. (11) 4364041; fax (11) 4363134.

**Ministry of Environment and Forests:** Paryavaran Bhavan, CGO Complex Phase II, Lodi Rd, New Delhi 110 003; tel. (11) 4360721; fax (11) 4360678.

**Ministry of External Affairs:** South Block, New Delhi 110 011; tel. (11) 3012318; fax (11) 3010700.

**Ministry of Finance:** North Block, New Delhi 110 001; tel. (11) 3012611; fax (11) 3012477.

**Ministry of Food:** 45 Krishi Bhavan, New Delhi 110 001; tel. (11) 3382437; fax (11) 3782213.

**Ministry of Food-Processing Industries:** Panchsheel Bhavan, Khelgaon Marg, New Delhi 110 049; tel. (11) 6493225; fax (11) 6493228.

**Ministry of Health and Family Welfare:** Nirman Bhavan, New Delhi 110 011; tel. (11) 3018863; fax (11) 3014252; e-mail secyhlth@mohfw.delhi.nic.in.

**Ministry of Heavy Industries and Public Enterprises:** Udyog Bhavan, New Delhi 110 011; tel. (11) 3012433; fax (11) 3011770.

**Ministry of Home Affairs:** North Block, New Delhi 110 001; tel. (11) 3011989; fax (11) 3015750.

**Ministry of Human Resource Development:** Shastri Bhavan, New Delhi 110 001; tel. (11) 3386995; fax (11) 3384093.

**Ministry of Information and Broadcasting:** Shastri Bhavan, New Delhi 110 001; tel. (11) 3382639; fax (11) 3383513.

**Ministry of Information Technology:** New Delhi, tel. (11) 4364041.

**Ministry of Labour:** Shram Shakti Bhavan, Rafi Marg, New Delhi 110 001; tel. (11) 3710265; fax (11) 3711708.

**Ministry of Law, Justice and Company Affairs:** Shastri Bhavan, Dr Rajendra Prasad Rd, New Delhi 110 001; tel. (11) 3384777; fax (11) 3387259.

**Ministry of Mines:** Udyog Bhavan, New Delhi 110 011; tel. (11) 3385173; fax (11) 3386402.

**Ministry of Non-Conventional Energy Sources:** Block 14, CGO Complex, New Delhi 110 003; tel. (11) 4361481; fax (11) 4361298.

**Ministry of Ocean Development:** Block 12, CGO Complex, Lodi Rd, New Delhi 110 003; tel. (11) 4360874; fax (11) 4360779.

**Ministry of Parliamentary Affairs:** Parliament House, New Delhi 110 001; tel. (11) 3017663; fax (11) 3017726.

**Ministry of Personnel, Public Grievances and Pensions:** North Block, New Delhi 110 001; tel. (11) 3014848; fax (11) 3012432.

**Ministry of Petroleum and Natural Gas:** Shastri Bhavan, New Delhi 110 001; tel. (11) 3383501; fax (11) 3384787.

**Ministry of Power:** Shram Shakti Bhavan, New Delhi 110 001; tel. (11) 3710271; fax (11) 3717519.

**Ministry of Railways:** Rail Bhavan, Raisina Rd, New Delhi 110 001; tel. (11) 3384010; fax (11) 3384481; internet www.indianrailway.com.

**Ministry of Rural Development:** Krishi Bhavan, New Delhi 110 001; tel. (11) 3384467; fax (11) 3782502.

**Ministry of Science and Technology:** Technology Bhavan, New Mehrauli Rd, New Delhi 110 016; tel. (11) 6511439; fax (11) 6863847.

**Ministry of Small-scale Industries and Agro and Rural Industries:** New Delhi; tel. (11) 3013045.

**Ministry of Social Justice and Empowerment:** Shastri Bhavan, New Delhi 110 001; tel. (11) 3382683; fax (11) 3384918.

**Ministry of Statistics and Programme Implementation:** Sardar Patel Bhavan, Patel Chowk, New Delhi 110 001; tel. (11) 3732150; fax (11) 3732067.

**Ministry of Steel:** Udyog Bhavan, New Delhi 110 011; tel. (11) 3015489; fax (11) 3013236.

**Ministry of Surface Transport:** Parivahan Bhavan, 1 Sansad Marg, New Delhi 110 001; tel. (11) 3714938; fax (11) 3714324.

**Ministry of Textiles:** Udyog Bhavan, New Delhi 110 011; tel. (11) 3011769; fax (11) 3013711.

**Ministry of Tourism:** Transport Bhavan, Parliament St, New Delhi 110 001; tel. (11) 3711792; fax (11) 3710518.

**Ministry of Tribal Affairs:** Shastri Bhavan, New Delhi; tel. (11) 3381652.

**Ministry of Urban Affairs and Employment:** Nirman Bhavan, New Delhi 110 011; tel. (11) 3019377; fax (11) 3014459.

**Ministry of Water Resources:** Shram Shakti Bhavan, Rafi Marg, New Delhi 110 001; tel. (11) 3710305; fax (11) 3710253.

**Ministry of Works and Estates:** New Delhi; tel. (11) 3017444.

# Legislature

## PARLIAMENT

### Rajya Sabha

(Council of States)

Most of the members of the Rajya Sabha are indirectly elected by the State Assemblies for six years, with one-third retiring every two years. The remaining members are nominated by the President.

**Chairman:** KRISHAN KANT.

**Deputy Chairman:** NAJMA HEPPTULLAH.

**Distribution of Seats, February 1999**

| Party | Seats |
|---|---|
| Congress (I) | 67 |
| Janata Dal | 9 |
| Communist Party of India—Marxist | 17 |
| Telugu Desam | 11 |
| Bharatiya Janata Party | 44 |
| Samajwadi Party | 9 |
| Rashtriya Janata Dal | 9 |
| Dravida Munnetra Kazhagam | 7 |
| Shiromani Akali Dal | 5 |
| Biju Janata Dal | 3 |
| Tamil Maanila Congress | 3 |
| Asom Gana Parishad | 2 |
| Muslim League | 2 |
| Forward Bloc | 2 |
| All-India Anna Dravida Munnetra Kazhagam | 6 |
| Communist Party of India | 7 |
| Jammu and Kashmir National Conference (F) | 3 |
| Shiv Sena | 5 |
| Bahujan Samaj Party | 4 |
| Independents and others | 22 |
| Nominated | 8 |
| **Total** | 245 |

**Lok Sabha**
(House of the People)

**Speaker:** GANTI MOHAN CHANDRA BALAYOGI.

**General Election, 5, 11, 18 and 25 September and 3 October 1999**

| Party | Seats |
|---|---|
| National Democratic Alliance | 299 |
| Bharatiya Janata Party | 182 |
| Dravida Munnetra Kazhagam | 12 |
| Marumalarchi Dravida Munnetra Kazhagam | 4 |
| Pattali Makkal Katchi | 5 |
| Janata Dal (United) | 20 |
| Shiv Sena | 15 |
| Shiromani Akali Dal | 2 |
| Indian National League | 4 |
| Himachal Vikash Congress | 1 |
| Telugu Desam | 29 |
| Biju Janata Dal | 10 |
| Trinamool Congress | 8 |
| Sikkim Democratic Front | 1 |
| Manipur State Congress Party | 1 |
| Jammu and Kashmir National Conference | 4 |
| M.G.R. Anna D.M. Kazhagam | 1 |
| Congress (I) and allies | 134 |
| Congress (I) | 112 |
| Rashtriya Janata Dal | 7 |
| All-India Anna Dravida Munnetra Kazhagam | 10 |
| Muslim League Kerala State Committee | 2 |
| Rashtriya Lok Dal | 2 |
| Kerala Congress (M) | 1 |
| Bahujan Samaj Party | 14 |
| Comunist Party of India | 4 |
| Communist Party of India—Marxist | 32 |
| Samajwadi Party | 26 |
| Nationalist Congress Party | 7 |
| Revolutionary Socialist Party | 3 |
| Asom Gana Parishad | 1 |
| Peasants' and Workers' Party of India | 1 |
| Janata Dal (Secular) | 1 |
| Independents and others | 20 |
| Nominated | 2* |
| Vacant | 1 |
| **Total** | 545 |

* Nominated by the President to represent the Anglo-Indian community.

## State Governments

(February 2000)

**ANDHRA PRADESH**
**(Capital—Hyderabad)**

**Governor:** Dr CHAKRAVARTY RANGARAJAN.

**Chief Minister:** N. CHANDRABABU NAIDU (Telugu Desam).

**Legislative Assembly:** 294 seats (Telugu Desam 180, Congress—I 90, Communist—CPI—M 2, Bharatiya Janata Party 12, independents and others 9, vacant 1).

**ARUNACHAL PRADESH**
**(Capital—Itanagar)**

**Governor:** ARVIND DAVE.

**Chief Minister:** MUKUT MITHI (Congress—I).

**Legislative Assembly:** 60 seats (Congress—I 50, Nationalist Congress Party 4, Arunachal Congress 1, independents 2, vacant 3).

**ASSAM**
**(Capital—Dispur)**

**Governor:** ARVIND DAVE.

**Chief Minister:** PRAFULLA KUMAR MOHANTA (Asom Gana Parishad).

**Legislative Assembly:** 126 seats (Asom Gana Parishad 59, Congress—I 34, Bharatiya Janata Party 4, Communist—CPI 3, independents and others 22, vacant 4).

**BIHAR**
**(Capital—Patna)**

**Governor:** VINOD CHANDRA PANDE.

**Chief Minister:** NITISH KUMAR (BJP).

**Legislative Assembly:** 324 seats (Rashtriya Janata Dal 124, Bharatiya Janata Party 67, Congress—I 23, Samata Party 34, Janata Dal (United) 21, Jharkhand Mukti Morcha 12, Bahujan Samaj Party 5, Communist—CPI 5, Communist—CPI—M 2, Communist—Marxist-Leninist (Liberation) 6, independents and others 25).

**Legislative Council:** 96 seats.

**GOA**
**(Capital—Panaji)**

**Governor:** MOHAMMAD FAZAL.

**Chief Minister:** FRANCISCO SARDINHA (Goa Democratic Alliance) .

**Legislative Assembly:** 40 seats (Congress—I 18, Maharashtrawadi Gomantak Party 12, Bharatiya Janata Party 4, United Goans Party 3, independents and others 3).

**GUJARAT**
**(Capital—Gandhinagar)**

**Governor:** SUNDAR SINGH BHANDARI.

**Chief Minister:** KESHUBHAI PATEL (Bharatiya Janata Party).

**Legislative Assembly:** 182 seats (Bharatiya Janata Party 116, Rashtriya Janata Party 4, Congress—I 55, Janata Dal 3, independents and others 4).

**HARYANA**
**(Capital—Chandigarh)**

**Governor:** MAHABIR PRASAD.

**Chief Minister:** OM PRAKASH CHAUTALA (Indian National Lok Dal).

**Legislative Assembly:** 90 seats (Congress—I 21, Indian National Lok Dal 47, Haryana Vikas Party 2, Bharatiya Janata Party 6, independents and others 14).

**HIMACHAL PRADESH**
**(Capital—Simla)**

**Governor:** VISHNU KANT SHASTRI.

**Chief Minister:** PREM KUMAR DHUMAL (Bharatiya Janata Party).

**Legislative Assembly:** 68 seats (Congress—I 31, Bharatiya Janata Party 28, Himachal Vikas Congress 4, independents 1, vacant 4).

**JAMMU AND KASHMIR**
**(Capitals—(Summer) Srinagar, (Winter) Jammu)**

**Governor:** GIRISH CHANDRA SAXENA.

**Chief Minister:** Dr FAROOQ ABDULLAH (Jammu and Kashmir National Conference).

**Legislative Assembly:** 87 seats (Jammu and Kashmir National Conference 55, Bharatiya Janata Party 8, Congress—I 7, Janata Dal 5, Bahujan Samaj Party 4, All India Indira Congress (Tewari) 1, Communist—CPI—M 1, Awami League 1, independents 2, others 3).

**Legislative Council:** 36 seats.

**KARNATAKA**
**(Capital—Bangalore)**

**Governor:** V. S. RAMA DEVI.

**Chief Minister:** SOMANAHALLI MALLIAM KRISHNA (Congress—I).

**Legislative Assembly:** 224 seats Congress—I 132, Bharatiya Janata Party 44, Janata Dal (Secular) 19, Janata Dal (United) 9, independents and others 20).

**Legislative Council:** 75 seats.

### KERALA
### (Capital—Thiruvananthapuram)

**Governor:** SUKHDEV SINGH KANG.

**Chief Minister:** E. K. NAYANAR (Communist—CPI—M).

**Legislative Assembly:** 140 seats (Communist—CPI—M 41, Communist—CPI 18, Congress—I 37, Muslim League 13, Kerala Congress (Joseph) 6, Kerala Congress (M) 5, Congress—S 3, Janata Dal 4, Revolutionary Socialist Party 5, independents and others 8).

### MADHYA PRADESH
### (Capital—Bhopal)

**Governor:** Dr BHAI MAHAVIR.

**Chief Minister:** DIGVIJAY SINGH (Congress—I).

**Legislative Assembly:** 320 seats (Congress—I 172, Bharatiya Janata Party 119, Bahujan Samaj Party 11, Samajwadi Party 4, independents and others 14).

### MAHARASHTRA
### (Capital—Mumbai)

**Governor:** Dr P. C. ALEXANDER.

**Chief Minister:** VILASRAO DESMUKH (Congress—I).

**Legislative Assembly:** 288 seats (Congress—I 75, Shiv Sena 69, Nationalist Congress Party 58, Bharatiya Janata Party 56, Janata Dal (Secular) 2, Peasants' and Workers' Party 5, Bharatiya Bahujan Mahasangh 3, Communist—CPI—M 2, Samajwadi Party 2, independents and others 16).

**Legislative Council:** 78 seats.

### MANIPUR
### (Capital—Imphal)

**Governor:** VED P. MARWAH.

**Chief Minister:** W. NIPAMACHA SINGH (Manipur State Congress).

**Legislative Assembly:** 60 seats (Congress—I 10, Manipur Peoples' Party 4, Manipur State Congress Party 23, Federal Party 6, Bharatiya Janata Party 6, Rashtriya Janata Dal 1, Samata Party 1, Janata Dal (United) 1, Nationalist Congress Party 4, Janata Dal (Secular) 1, independents 1, vacant 2).

### MEGHALAYA
### (Capital—Shillong)

**Governor:** M. M. JACOB.

**Chief Minister:** MUKUL MITHI (United Democratic Party).

**Legislative Assembly:** 60 seats (Congress—I 16, Nationalist Congress Party 9, United Democratic Party 20, Bharatiya Janata Party 3, People's Democratic Movement 3, Hills State People's Democratic Party 3, independents and others 6).

### MIZORAM
### (Capital—Aizawl)

**Governor:** A. PADMANABHAN.

**Chief Minister:** ZORAMTHANGA (Mizo National Front).

**Legislative Assembly:** 40 seats (Mizo National Front 21, Congress—I 6, Mizo Pradesh Congress 12, others 1).

### NAGALAND
### (Capital—Kohima)

**Governor:** OM PRAKASH SHARMA.

**Chief Minister:** S. C. JAMIR (Congress—I).

**Legislative Assembly:** 60 seats (Congress—I 53, independents and others 10).

### ORISSA
### (Capital—Bhubaneswar)

**Governor:** Dr CHAKRAVARTY RANGARAJAN (acting).

**Chief Minister:** NAVEEN PATNAIK (Biju Janata Dal).

**Legislative Assembly:** 147 seats (Biju Janata Dal 68, Bharatiya Janata Party 38, Congress—I 26, Jharkhand Mukti Morcha 3, Communist—CPI 1, Communist—CPI—M 1, Janata Dal (Secular) 1, All-India Trinamool Congress 1, independents 8).

### PUNJAB
### (Capital—Chandigarh)

**Governor:** Lt-Gen. (retd) J. F. R. JACOB.

**Chief Minister:** PRAKASH SINGH BADAL (Shiromani Akali Dal).

**Legislative Assembly:** 117 seats (Shiromani Akali Dal 75, Congress—I 14, Bharatiya Janata Party 18, Communist—CPI 2, Akali Dal (Mann) 1, Bahujan Samaj Party 1, independents 6).

### RAJASTHAN
### (Capital—Jaipur)

**Governor:** ANSHUMAN SINGH.

**Chief Minister:** ASHOK GEHLOT (Congress—I).

**Legislative Assembly:** 200 seats (Congress—I 150, Bharatiya Janata Party 33, Janata Dal 3, Communist—CPI—M 1, Bahujan Samaj Party 2, independents and others 8, vacant 3).

### SIKKIM
### (Capital—Gangtok)

**Governor:** CHAUDHURY RANDHIR SINGH.

**Chief Minister:** PAWAN KUMAR CHAMLING (Sikkim Democratic Front).

**Legislative Assembly:** 32 seats (Sikkim Democratic Front 25, Sikkim Sangram Parishad 7).

### TAMIL NADU
### (Capital—Chennai)

**Governor:** M. S. FATHIMA BEEVI.

**Chief Minister:** MUTHUVEL KARUNANIDHI (Dravida Munnetra Kazhagam).

**Legislative Assembly:** 234 seats (Dravida Munnetra Kazhagam 172, Tamil Maanila Congress 39, Communist—CPI 8, AIADMK 4, independents and others 11).

### TRIPURA
### (Capital—Agartala)

**Governor:** SIDDHESWAR PRASAD.

**Chief Minister:** MANIK SARKAR (Communist—CPI—M).

**Legislative Assembly:** 60 seats (Communist—CPI—M 38, Congress—I 13, Tripura Upajati Juba Samity 4, independents and others 5).

### UTTAR PRADESH
### (Capital—Lucknow)

**Governor:** SURAJ BHAN.

**Chief Minister:** RAM PRAKASH GUPTA (Bharatiya Janata Party).

**Legislative Assembly:** 425 seats (Bharatiya Janata Party 176, Samajwadi Party 110, Bahujan Samaj Party 54, Congress—I 15, Loktantric Congress 22, Janatantric Bahujan Samaj Party 13, Janata Dal (R) 4, Janata Dal 3, Communist—CPI—M 4, Bharatiya Kisan Kamgar Party 8, independents and others 16).

**Legislative Council:** 108 seats.

### WEST BENGAL
### (Capital—Kolkata)

**Governor:** VIREN J. SHAH.

**Chief Minister:** JYOTI BASU (Communist—CPI—M).

**Legislative Assembly:** 294 seats (Communist—CPI—M 150, Congress—I 82, Forward Bloc 21, Revolutionary Socialist 18, Communist—CPI 6, others 17).

### UNION TERRITORIES

**Andaman and Nicobar Islands** (Headquarters—Port Blair):
Lt-Gov.: I. P. GUPTA.

**Chandigarh** (Headquarters—Chandigarh):
Administrator: B. K. N. CHHIBER.
Chandigarh was to be incorporated into Punjab state on 26 January 1986, but the transfer was postponed indefinitely.

**Dadra and Nagar Haveli** (Headquarters—Silvassa):
Administrator: S. P. AGGARWAL.

**Daman and Diu** (Headquarters—Daman):
Administrator: RAMESH NEGI.

**Lakshadweep** (Headquarters—Kavaratti):
Administrator: RAJEEV TALWAR.

**Pondicherry** (Capital—Pondicherry):
Lt-Gov.: Dr RAJANI RAI.
Chief Minister: R. V. JANAKIRAMAN (Dravida Munnetra Kazhagam).
Assembly: 33 seats (DMK 10, AIADMK 3, Congress—I 8, Tamil Maanila Congress 7, Communist—CPI 1, Janata Dal 1, Pattali Makkal Katchi 2, independents 1).

### NATIONAL CAPITAL TERRITORY

**Delhi** (Headquarters—Delhi):
Lt-Gov.: VIJAY KUMAR KAPOOR.
Chief Minister: SHEILA DIXIT (Congress—I).

Assembly: 70 seats (Congress—I 51, Bharatiya Janata Party 15, Janata Dal 2, independents 2, vacant 1).

# Political Organizations

### MAJOR NATIONAL POLITICAL ORGANIZATIONS

**All India Congress Committee (I):** 24 Akbar Rd, New Delhi 110 011; tel. (11) 3019080; f. 1978, as Indian National Congress (I), as a breakaway group under Indira Gandhi; Pres. SONIA GANDHI; Gen. Secs AMBIKA SONI, MOHSINA KIDWAI, MOTILAL VORA, OSCAR FERNANDES, PRABHA RAO, SUSHIL SHINDE; 35m. mems (1998).

**Bahujan Samaj Party** (Majority Society Party): promotes the rights of the *Harijans* ('Untouchables') of India; Leader KANSHI RAM; Gen. Sec. Ms MAYAWATI.

**Bharatiya Janata Party (BJP)** (Indian People's Party): 11 Ashok Rd, New Delhi 110 001; tel. (11) 3382234; fax (11) 3782163; e-mail bjpco@del3.vsnl.net.in; f. 1980 as a breakaway group from Janata Party; radical right-wing Hindu party; Pres. KUSHABHAU THAKRE; Vice-Pres. J. P. MATHUR; Gen. Secs NARENDRA MODI, SANGHA PRIYA GAUTAM, SUMITRA MAHAJAN, M. V. NAIDU, K. N. GOVINDACHARYA; 10.5m. mems.

**Communist Party of India (CPI):** Ajoy Bhavan, Kotla Marg, New Delhi 110 002; tel. (11) 3235546; fax (11) 3235543; f. 1925; advocates the establishment of a socialist society led by the working class, and ultimately of a communist society; nine-mem. central secretariat; Gen. Sec. ARDHENDU BHUSHAN BARDHAN; 558,838 mems (1997).

**Communist Party of India—Marxist (CPI—M):** A. K. Gopalan Bhavan, 27–29 Bhai Vir Singh Marg, New Delhi 110 001; tel. (11) 3747435; fax (11) 3747483; e-mail cpim@vsnl.com; internet www.del.vsnl.net.in/cpim; f. 1964 as pro-Beijing breakaway group from the CPI; declared its independence of Beijing in 1968 and is managed by a central committee of 73 mems and a politburo of 17 mems; Leaders JYOTI BASU, PRAKASH KARAT, SITARAM YECHURY, SOMNATH CHATTERJEE; Gen. Sec. HARKISHAN SINGH SURJEET; 717,645 mems (1998).

**Janata Dal** (People's Party): 7 Jantar Mantar Rd, New Delhi 110 001; tel. (11) 3368833; fax (11) 3368138; f. 1988 as a merger of parties within the Rashtriya Morcha; advocates non-alignment, the eradication of poverty, unemployment and wide disparities in wealth, and the protection of minorities; 136-mem. National Executive; Pres. SHARAD YADAV; Sec.-Gen. Dr BAPU KALDATE; split into two factions in July 1999—Janata Dal (United), headed by SHARAD YADAV, and Janata Dal (Secular), headed by H. D. DEVE GOWDA.

**Nationalist Congress Party (NCP):** New Delhi; f. 1999 as breakaway faction of Congress (I); Pres. SHARAD PAWAR.

### MAJOR REGIONAL POLITICAL ORGANIZATIONS

**Akhil Bharat Hindu Mahasabha:** Hindu Mahasabha Bhavan, Mandir Marg, New Delhi 110 001; tel. (11) 3342087; fax (11) 3363105; f. 1915; seeks the establishment of a democratic Hindu state; Pres. DINESH CHANDRA TYAGI; Gen. Sec. Dr MADANLAL GOYAL; 525,000 mems.

**All-India Anna Dravida Munnetra Kazhagam (AIADMK)** (All-India Anna Dravidian Progressive Asscn): Lloyd's Rd, Chennai 600 004; f. 1972; breakaway group from the DMK; Chair. (vacant); Gen. Sec. C. JAYALALITHA JAYARAM.

**All India Forward Bloc:** 28 Gurudwara Rakabganj Rd, New Delhi 110 001; tel. and fax (11) 3714131; e-mail dbiswas@sansad.nic.in; f. 1940 by Netaji Subhash Chandra Bose; socialist aims, including nationalization of major industries, land reform and redistribution; Chair. D. D. SHASTRI; Gen. Sec. DEBABRATA BISWAS; 900,000 mems (1999).

**Asom Gana Parishad (AGP)** (Assam People's Council): Golaghat, Assam; f. 1985; draws support from the All-Assam Gana Sangram Parishad and the All-Assam Students' Union (Pres. KESHAB MAHANTA; Gen. Sec. ATUL BORA); advocates the unity of India in diversity and a united Assam; Pres. PRAFULLA KUMAR MOHANTA; a breakaway faction formed a new central exec. committee under PULAKESH BARUA in April 1991.

**Dravida Munnetra Kazhagam (DMK):** Anna Arivalayam, Teynampet, Chennai 600 018; f. 1949; aims at full autonomy for states (primarily Tamil Nadu) within the Union, to establish regional languages as state languages and English as the official language pending the recognition of regional languages as official languages of the Union; Pres. MUTHUVEL KARUNANIDHI; Gen. Sec. K. ANBAZHAGAN; more than 4m. mems.

**Jammu and Kashmir National Conference (JKNC):** Mujahid Manzil, Srinagar 190 002; tel. 71500; fmrly All Jammu and Kashmir National Conference, f. 1931, renamed 1939, reactivated 1975; state-based party campaigning for internal autonomy and responsible self-govt; Leader Dr FAROOQ ABDULLAH; Pres. BASHIR AHMAD BHAT (acting); Gen. Sec. SHEIKH NAZIR AHMED; 1m. mems.

**Pattali Makkal Katchi:** Chennai; Leader Dr RAMADAS.

**Peasants' and Workers' Party of India:** Mahatma Phule Rd, Naigaum, Mumbai 400 014; f. 1949; Marxist; seeks to nationalize all basic industries, to promote industrialization, and to establish a unitary state with provincial boundaries drawn on a linguistic basis; Gen. Sec. DAJIBA DESAI; c. 10,000 mems.

**Rashtriya Loktantrik Morcha** (National Democratic Front): New Delhi; f. 1998; Convenor MULAYAM SINGH YADAV; includes:

**Rashtriya Janata Dal (RJD)** (National People's Party): New Delhi; f. 1997 as a breakaway group from Janata Dal; Leader LALOO PRASAD YADAV.

**Samajwadi Party** (Socialist Party): New Delhi; f. 1991 by the merger of the Janata Dal (S) and the Janata Party; National Pres. MULAYAM SINGH YADAV; Gen. Sec. AMAR SINGH.

**Republican Party of India (RPI):** Ensa Hutments, I Block, Azad Maidan, Fort, Mumbai 400 001; tel. (22) 2621888; main aim is to realize the aims and objects set out in the preamble to the 1950 Constitution; Pres. PRAKASH RAO AMBEDKAR; Gen. Sec. RAMDAS ATHAVALE; 100,000 mems.

**Samata Party:** c/o Lok Sabha, New Delhi; Pres. JAYA JAITLEY.

**Shiromani Akali Dal:** Baradan Shri Darbar Sahib, Amritsar; f. 1920; merged with Congress Party 1958–62; Sikh party composed of several factions both moderate and militant; seeks the establishment of an autonomous Sikh state of 'Khalistan'; Pres. (Shiromani Akali Dal—Badal) PRAKASH SINGH BADAL; Sec.-Gen. (Shiromani Akali Dal—Badal) GURDEV SINGH DHINDSA.

**Shiv Sena:** Shiv Sena Bhavan, Ram Ganesh Gadkari Chowk, Dadar, Mumbai 400 028; tel. (22) 4309128; e-mail senabhavan@shivsena.org; internet www.shivsena.org; f. 1966; militant Hindu group; Pres. BALASHAHEB 'BAL' THACKERAY.

**Tamil Maanila Congress:** c/o Lok Sabha, New Delhi; Pres. G. K. MOOPANAR; Gen. Sec. PETER ALPHONS.

**Tamil Rajiv Congress:** Chennai; Pres. K. RAMAMURTHY.

**Telugu Desam** (Telugu Nation): 3-5-910, Himayatnagar, Hyderabad 500 029; tel. (842) 237290; f. 1982; state-based party (Andhra Pradesh); campaigns against rural poverty and social prejudice; Pres. N. CHANDRABABU NAIDU).

**Trinamool Congress:** c/o Lok Sabha, New Delhi; Leader MAMATA BANERJEE.

# Diplomatic Representation

### EMBASSIES AND HIGH COMMISSIONS IN INDIA

**Afghanistan:** 5/50F Shanti Path, Chanakyapuri, New Delhi 110 021; tel. (11) 6886625; fax (11) 6875439; Chargé d'affaires: MASOOD KHALILI.

**Algeria:** B-3/61 Safdarjung Enclave, New Delhi 110 029; tel. (11) 6185057; fax (11) 6185062; e-mail embalg@nda.vsnl.net.in; Ambassador: ABDELHAMID SENOUCI BEREKSI.

**Argentina:** B-8/9 Vasant Vihar, Paschmi Marg, New Delhi 110 057; tel. (11) 6141345; fax (11) 6886501; e-mail eindi@giasdl01.vsnl.net.in; Ambassador: GERARDO M. BIRITOS.

**Armenia:** A-153 New Friends Colony, New Delhi 110 065; tel. (11) 6310504; fax (11) 6847548.

**Australia:** 1/50-G Shanti Path, Chanakyapuri, New Delhi 110 021; tel. (11) 6888223; fax (11) 6885199; High Commissioner: ROBERT STEPHEN LAURIE.

**Austria:** EP/13 Chandragupta Marg, Chanakyapuri, New Delhi 110 021; tel. (11) 6889037; fax (11) 6886929; e-mail aedelhi@del2.vsnl.net.in; Ambassador: Dr HERBERT TRAXL.

**Bangladesh:** 56 Ring Rd, Lajpat Nagar-III, New Delhi 110 024; tel. (11) 6834065; fax (11) 6839237; High Commissioner: MOSTAFA FAROQUE MOHAMMAD.

**Belarus:** D-6/23 Vasant Vihar, New Delhi 110 057; tel. (11) 6151202; fax (11) 6151203.

**Belgium:** 50N, Plot 4, Shanti Path, Chanakyapuri, New Delhi 110 021; tel. (11) 6889851; fax (11) 6885821; Ambassador: GUILLAUME METTEN.

**Bhutan:** Chandragupta Marg, Chanakyapuri, New Delhi 110 021; tel. (11) 6889807; fax (11) 6876710; Ambassador: Lyonpo DAGO TSHERING.

**Brazil:** 8 Aurangzeb Rd, New Delhi 110 011; tel. (11) 3017301; fax (11) 3793684; e-mail brasindi@giasdl01.vsnl.net.in; Ambassador: VERA BARROUIN MACHADO.

**Brunei:** A-42 Vasant Marg, Vasant Vihar, New Delhi 110 057; tel. (11) 6148340; fax (11) 6142101.

**Bulgaria:** 16/17 Chandragupta Marg, Chanakyapuri, New Delhi 110 021; tel. (11) 6115550; fax (11) 6876190; Ambassador: EDVIN SUGAREV.

**Cambodia:** New Delhi; tel. (11) 6423782; fax (11) 6475233; Ambassador: SIM SUONG.

**Canada:** 7/8 Shanti Path, Chanakyapuri, New Delhi 110 021; tel. (11) 6876500; fax (11) 6876579; High Commissioner: PETER F. WALKER.

**Chile:** R/7 Hauz Khas, New Delhi 110 016; tel. (11) 6850537; fax (11) 6850231; Ambassador: ULDARICIO FIGUEROA.

**China, People's Republic:** 50D Shanti Path, Chanakyapuri, New Delhi 110 021; tel. (11) 6871585; fax (11) 6885486; Ambassador: ZHOU GANG.

**Colombia:** 82D Malcha Marg, Chanakyapuri, New Delhi 110 021; tel. (11) 6110773; fax (11) 6112486; Ambassador: MARÍA CLARA BETANCUR.

**Congo, Democratic Republic:** C-56 Panchsheel Enclave, New Delhi 110 017; tel. (11) 6222796; fax (11) 6227226; Ambassador: KITENGE NKUMBI KASDNGO.

**Croatia:** 70 Ring Rd, Lajpat Nagar-III, New Delhi 110 024; tel. (11) 6924761; fax (11) 6924763; e-mail croemnd@del1.vsnl.net.in; Ambassador: Dr ZORAN ANDRIĆ.

**Cuba:** E-1/9 Vasant Vihar, New Delhi 110 057; tel. (11) 6143849; fax (11) 6143806; e-mail embcuind@ndf; Ambassador: OLGA CHAMERO TRIAS.

**Cyprus:** 106 Jor Bagh, New Delhi 110 003; tel. (11) 4697503; fax (11) 4628828; High Commissioner: REA YIORDAMLIS.

**Czech Republic:** 50M Niti Marg, Chanakyapuri, New Delhi 110 021; tel. (11) 6110205; fax (11) 6886221; e-mail newdelhi@embassy.mzv.cz; Ambassador: IVAN JESTŘÁB.

**Denmark:** 11 Aurangzeb Rd, New Delhi 110 011; tel. (11) 3010900; fax (11) 3010961; e-mail denmark@vsnl.com; Ambassador: BIRGIT STORGAARD MADSEN.

**Egypt:** 1/50M Niti Marg, Chanakyapuri, New Delhi 110 021; tel. (11) 6114096; fax (11) 6885355; e-mail egypt@del2.vsnl.net.in; Ambassador: GEHAD MADI.

**Ethiopia:** 7/50G Satya Marg, Chanakyapuri, New Delhi 110 021; tel. (11) 6119513; fax (11) 6875731; e-mail delethem@bol.net.in; Ambassador: DESTA ERIFO.

**Finland:** E–3 Nyaya Marg, Chanakyapuri, New Delhi 110 021; tel. (11) 6115258; fax (11) 6886713; e-mail finemb@del2.vsnl.net.in; Ambassador: BENJAMIN BASSIN.

**France:** 2/50E Shanti Path, Chanakyapuri, New Delhi 110 021; tel. (11) 6118790; fax (11) 6872305; Ambassador: CLAUDE BLANCHEMAISON.

**Germany:** 6 Block 50G, Shanti Path, Chanakyapuri, New Delhi 110 021; tel. (11) 6871831; fax (11) 6873117; e-mail german@del3.vsnl.net.in; internet www.germanembassy-india.org; Ambassador: Dr HEINRICH-DIETRICH DIECKMANN.

**Ghana:** 50-N Satya Marg, Chanakyapuri, New Delhi 110 021; tel. (11) 6883298; fax (11) 6883202; High Commissioner: Rear-Adm. (retd) THOMAS KWESI ANNAN.

**Greece:** 16 Sundar Nagar, New Delhi 110 003; tel. (11) 4617800; fax (11) 4601363; Ambassador: Y. A. ZEPOS.

**Holy See:** 50C Niti Marg, Chanakyapuri, New Delhi 110 021 (Apostolic Nunciature); tel. (11) 6889184; fax (11) 6874286; e-mail nuntius@bol.net.in; Pro-Nuncio: Most Rev. LORENZO BALDISSERI, Titular Archbishop of Diocletiana.

**Hungary:** Plot 2, 50M Niti Marg, Chanakyapuri, New Delhi 110 021; tel. (11) 6114737; fax (11) 6886742; Ambassador: ANDRAS DALLOS.

**Indonesia:** 50A Chanakyapuri, New Delhi 110 021; tel. (11) 6118642; fax (11) 6884402; Ambassador: GATOT SUWARDI.

**Iran:** 5 Barakhamba Road, New Delhi 110 001; tel. (11) 3329600; fax (11) 3325493; Ambassador: MIR MAHMOUD-MOUSSAVI KHAMENEH.

**Iraq:** 169–171 Jor Bagh, New Delhi 110 003; tel. (11) 4618011; fax (11) 4631547; Ambassador: MOHAMMED F. H. AL-HABOUBI.

**Ireland:** 13 Jor Bagh, New Delhi 110 003; tel. (11) 4626733; fax (11) 4697053; Ambassador: JAMES FLAVIN.

**Israel:** 3 Aurangzeb Rd, New Delhi 110 011; tel. (11) 3013238; fax (11) 3014298; e-mail israelem@vsnl.com; Ambassador: Dr YEHOYADA HAIM.

**Italy:** 50E Chandragupta Marg, Chanakyapuri, New Delhi 110 021; tel. (11) 6114355; fax (11) 6873889; Ambassador: Dr GAETANO ZUCCONI.

**Japan:** Plots 4–5, 50G Shanti Path, Chanakyapuri, New Delhi 110 021; tel. (11) 6876581; fax (11) 6885587; Ambassador: HIROSHI HIRABAYASHI.

**Jordan:** 1/21 Shanti Niketan, New Delhi 110 021; tel. and fax (11) 6883763; Ambassador: HUSHAN MUHAISEN.

**Kazakhstan:** 4 Olof Palme Marg, Vasant Vihar, New Delhi 110 057; tel. (11) 6144779; fax (11) 6144778; Ambassador: ASKAR O. SHAKIROV.

**Kenya:** E-66 Vasant Marg, Vasant Vihar, New Delhi 110 057; tel. (11) 6146537; fax (11) 6146550; High Commissioner: L. O. AMAYO.

**Korea, Democratic People's Republic:** 42/44 Sundar Nagar, New Delhi 110 003; tel. (11) 4617140; Ambassador: PAK MYONG GU.

**Korea, Republic:** 9 Chandragupta Marg, Chanakyapuri, POB 5416, New Delhi 110 021; tel. (11) 6885314; fax (11) 6884840; Ambassador: LEE CHONG-MOO.

**Kuwait:** 5A Shanti Path, Chanakyapuri, New Delhi 110 021; tel. (11) 4100791; fax (11) 6873516; Ambassador: ABDUL AL-SULEIMAN OTHMAN AL-QINAIE.

**Kyrgyzstan:**New Delhi; tel. (11) 6141682; fax (11) 6880372.

**Laos:** E53 Panchshila Park, New Delhi 110 017; tel. (11) 6497447; fax (11) 6495812; Ambassador: KIDENG THAMMAVONG.

**Lebanon:** 10 Sardar Patel Marg, Chanakyapuri, New Delhi 110 021; tel. (11) 3013174; fax (11) 3015555; e-mail lebanemb@giasdl01.vsnl.net.in; Ambassador: Dr JEAN DANIEL.

**Libya:** 22 Golf Links, New Delhi 110 003; tel. (11) 4697717; fax (11) 4633005; Secretary of People's Bureau: OMAR AHMAD JADOLLAH AL-AUKALI.

**Malaysia:** 50M Satya Marg, Chanakyapuri, New Delhi 110 021; tel. (11) 6111291; fax (11) 6881538; High Commissioner: WAN HUSSAIN WAN MUSTAPHA.

**Mauritius:** 5 Kautilya Marg, Chanakyapuri, New Delhi 110 021; tel. (11) 3011112; fax (11) 3019925; e-mail mhcnd@giasdl01.vsnl.net.in; High Commissioner: ROHIT NARAINSING GUTTEE.

**Mexico:** B-33 Friends Colony (West), New Delhi 110 065; tel. (11) 6932860; fax (11) 6932864; Ambassador: (vacant).

**Mongolia:** 34 Archbishop Makarios Marg, New Delhi 110 003; tel. (11) 4631728; fax (11) 4633240; Ambassador: TERBISHIIN CHIMEDDORJ.

**Morocco:** 33 Archbishop Makarios Marg, New Delhi 110 003; tel. (11) 4636920; fax (11) 4636925; Ambassador: MOHAMMED BELMAHI.

**Myanmar:** 3/50F Nyaya Marg, Chanakyapuri, New Delhi 110 021; tel. (11) 6889007; fax (11) 6877942; Ambassador: U TIN LATT.

**Namibia:** D-6/24 Vasant Vihar, New Delhi 110 057; tel. (11) 6144772; fax (11) 6146120; High Commissioner: JOEL KAAPANDA.

**Nepal:** Barakhamba Rd, New Delhi 110 001; tel. (11) 3328191; fax (11) 3326857; e-mail rned.ramjnki@axcess.net.in; Ambassador: Dr BHEKH B. THAPA.

**Netherlands:** 6/50F Shanti Path, Chanakyapuri, New Delhi 110 021; tel. (11) 6884951; fax (11) 6884956; e-mail nlembas@giasdl01.vsnl.net.in; Ambassador: P. F. C. KOCH.

**New Zealand:** 50N Nyaya Marg, Chanakyapuri, New Delhi 110 021; tel. (11) 6883170; fax (11) 6883165; e-mail coral.sanford@mfat.govt.nz; High Commissioner: ADRIAN SIMCOCK.

**Nigeria:** 21 Olof Palme Marg, Vasant Vihar, New Delhi 110 057; tel. (11) 6146211; fax (11) 6146647; High Commissioner: E. OLA ADEFEMIWA.

**Norway:** 50C Shanti Path, Chanakyapuri, New Delhi 110 021; tel. (11) 6873532; fax (11) 6873814; e-mail noramb@vsnl.com; Ambassador: TRULS HANEVOLD.

**Oman:** 16 Olof Palme Marg, New Delhi 110 057; tel. (11) 6144798; fax (11) 6876478; Ambassador: MOHAMMED TAHER ALAWMI AIDEED.

**Pakistan:** 2/50G Shanti Path, Chanakyapuri, New Delhi 110 021; tel. (11) 4676004; fax (11) 6872339; High Commissioner: ASHRAF JEHANGIR.

**Peru:** D-6/13C, Vasant Vihar, New Delhi 110 057; tel. (11) 6144085; fax (11) 6146427; e-mail perdelhi@giasdl01.vsnl.net.in; Ambassador: CARLOS HIGUERAS-RAMOS.

**Philippines:** 50N Nyaya Marg, Chanakyapuri, New Delhi 110 021; tel. (11) 6889091; fax (11) 6876401; Ambassador: JOSÉ P. DEL ROSARIO, Jr.

**Poland:** 5/50M Shanti Path, Chanakyapuri, New Delhi 110 021; tel. (11) 6889211; fax (11) 6871914; Ambassador: JAN KRZYSZTOF MROZIEWICZ.

**Portugal:** 13 Sundar Nagar, New Delhi 110 003; tel. (11) 4601262; fax (11) 4601252; e-mail ccpindia@giasdl01.vsnl.net.in; Ambassador: MANUEL MARCELO CURTO.

**Qatar:** G-5 Anand Niketan, New Delhi 110 021; tel. (11) 6117241; fax (11) 6882184; Ambassador: MUBARAK RASHID M. AL-BOAININ.

**Romania:** A-52 Vasant Marg, Vasant Vihar, New Delhi 110 057; tel. (11) 6140447; fax (11) 6140611; e-mail emrond@hotmail.com; Chargé d'affaires a.i.: PETRE STOÍCESCU.

**Russia:** Shanti Path, Chanakyapuri, New Delhi 110 021; tel. (11) 6873799; fax (11) 6876823; Ambassador: ALBERT SERGEYEVICH CHERNYSHOV.

**Saudi Arabia:** D-12, New Delhi South Extension Part II, New Delhi 110 049; tel. (11) 6442470; fax (11) 6449423; Ambassador: A. REHMAN N. ALOHALY.

**Senegal:** 30 Paschimi Marg, Vasant Vihar, New Delhi 110 057; tel. (11) 6143720; fax (11) 6145809; Ambassador: AHMED EL MANSOUR DIOP.

**Singapore:** E-6 Chandragupta Marg, Chanakyapuri, New Delhi 110 021; tel. (11) 6885659; fax (11) 6886798; e-mail singhnd@giasdl01.vsnl.net.in; High Commissioner: Ong Keng Yong.

**Slovakia:** 50M Niti Marg, Chanakyapuri, New Delhi 110 021; tel. (11) 6889071; fax (11) 6877941; e-mail skdelhi@giasdl01.vsnl.net.in; Ambassador: Ladislav Volko.

**Somalia:** A-17, Defence Colony, New Delhi 110 024; tel. (11) 4619559; Ambassador: Mohamed Osman Omar.

**South Africa:** B-18 Vasant Marg, Vasant Vihar, New Delhi 110 057; tel. (11) 6149411; fax (11) 6143605; High Commissioner: M. Emily Mohale.

**Spain:** 12 Prithviraj Rd, New Delhi 110 011; tel. (11) 3792085; fax (11) 3793375; Ambassador: Alberto Escudero Claramunt.

**Sri Lanka:** 27 Kautilya Marg, Chanakyapuri, New Delhi 110 021; tel. (11) 3010201; fax (11) 3015295; High Commissioner: Mangala Moonesinghe.

**Sudan:** Plot No. 3, Shanti Path, Chanakyapuri, New Delhi 110 021; tel. (11) 6873785; fax (11) 6883758; Ambassador: Awed el Karim Fadlalla.

**Sweden:** Nyaya Marg, Chanakyapuri, New Delhi 110 021; tel. (11) 6875760; fax (11) 6885401; Ambassador: K. G. Engstrom.

**Switzerland:** Nyaya Marg, Chanakyapuri, New Delhi 110 021; tel. (11) 6878372; fax (11) 6873093; Ambassador: Guy Ducrey.

**Syria:** 28 Vasant Marg, Vasant Vihar, New Delhi 110 057; tel. (11) 6140285; fax (11) 6873107; Ambassador: Saddik Saddikni.

**Tanzania:** 10/1 Sarv Priya Vihar, New Delhi 110 016; tel. (11) 6853046; fax (11) 6968408; High Commissioner: Alfred C. Tandau.

**Thailand:** 56N Nyaya Marg, Chanakyapuri, New Delhi 110 021; tel. (11) 6118103; fax (11) 6872029; Ambassador: Vichai Vannasin.

**Trinidad and Tobago:** 131 Jor Bagh, New Delhi 110 003; tel. (11) 4618186; fax (11) 4624581; High Commissioner: Ousman Ali.

**Tunisia:** 23 Olof Palme Marg, Vasant Vihar, New Delhi 110 057; tel. (11) 6145346; fax (11) 6145301; Ambassador: Mohamed Sahbi Basli.

**Turkey:** 50N Nyaya Marg, Chanakyapuri, New Delhi 110 021; tel. (11) 6889054; fax (11) 6881409; e-mail temdelhi@telz.vsnl.net.in; Ambassador: Yusuf Buluc.

**Turkmenistan:** 1/13 Shanti Niketan, New Delhi 110 021; tel. (11) 6118409; fax (11) 6118332; Ambassador: Ashir Ataev.

**Uganda:** B-3/26 Vasant Vihar, New Delhi 110 057; tel. (11) 6144413; fax (11) 6144405; e-mail ughcdl@gndel.global.ems.vsnl.net.in; High Commissioner: Joseph Tomusange.

**Ukraine:** 46 Paschimi Marg, Vasant Vihar, New Delhi 110 057; tel. (11) 6146041; fax (11) 6146043; e-mail embassy@bol.net.in; Ambassador: Valentyn V. Adomaitis.

**United Arab Emirates:** EP–12 Chandragupt Marg, New Delhi 110 021; tel. (11) 6872937; fax (11) 6873272; Ambassador: Ahmed Abdullah al-Musally.

**United Kingdom:** Shanti Path, Chanakyapuri, New Delhi 110 021; tel. (11) 6872161; fax (11) 6872882; e-mail bhcndpa@del2.vsnl.net.in; internet www.ukinindia.org; High Commissioner: Sir Robertson Young.

**USA:** Shanti Path, Chanakyapuri, New Delhi 110 021; tel. (11) 6889033; fax (11) 6872028; Ambassador: Richard F. Celeste.

**Uzbekistan:** D-4/6 Vasant Vihar, New Delhi 110 057; tel. (11) 6149026; fax (11) 6143246; Ambassador: Ilhom Nematov.

**Venezuela:** N-114 Panchshila Park, New Delhi 110 017; tel. (11) 6496913; fax (11) 6491686; Ambassador: Walter Marquez.

**Viet Nam:** 17 Kautilya Marg, Chanakyapuri, New Delhi 110 021; tel. (11) 3018059; fax (11) 3017714; Ambassador: Pham Sy Tam.

**Yemen:** B-70 Greater Kailash-I, New Delhi 110 048; tel. (11) 6414731; fax (11) 6478728; Ambassador: Ibrahim Abdulla I. Saidi.

**Yugoslavia:** 3/50G Niti Marg, Chanakyapuri, New Delhi 110 021; tel. (11) 6873661; fax (11) 6885535; Ambassador: Dr Cedomir Strabac.

**Zambia:** F 8/22 Vasant Vihar, New Delhi 110 057; tel. (11) 6145862; fax (11) 6147928; High Commissioner: S. K. Mubukwanu.

**Zimbabwe:** B-8 Anand Niketan, New Delhi 110 021; tel. (11) 6885060; fax (11) 6886073; High Commissioner: Lucia Muvingi.

# Judicial System

### THE SUPREME COURT

The Supreme Court, consisting of a Chief Justice and not more than 25 judges appointed by the President, exercises exclusive jurisdiction in any dispute between the Union and the states (although there are certain restrictions where an acceding state is involved). It has appellate jurisdiction over any judgment, decree or order of the High Court where that Court certifies that either a substantial question of law or the interpretation of the Constitution is involved. The Supreme Court can enforce fundamental rights and issue writs covering habeas corpus, mandamus, prohibition, quo warranto and certiorari. The Supreme Court is a court of record and has the power to punish for its contempt.

Provision is made for the appointment by the Chief Justice of India of judges of High Courts as ad hoc judges at sittings of the Supreme Court for specified periods, and for the attendance of retired judges at sittings of the Supreme Court. The Supreme Court has advisory jurisdiction in respect of questions which may be referred to it by the President for opinion. The Supreme Court is also empowered to hear appeals against a sentence of death passed by a State High Court in reversal of an order of acquittal by a lower court, and in a case in which a High Court has granted a certificate of fitness.

The Supreme Court also hears appeals which are certified by High Courts to be fit for appeal, subject to rules made by the Court. Parliament may, by law, confer on the Supreme Court any further powers of appeal.

The judges hold office until the age of 65 years.

**Supreme Court:** New Delhi; tel. (11) 3388942; fax (11) 3383792; internet www.caselaw.delhi.nic.in\sc-cl.

**Chief Justice of India:** Dr Adarsh Sein Anand.

**Judges of the Supreme Court:** S. P. Bharucha, S. B. Majmudar, S. Rajendra Babu, A. P. Misra, Syed Shah Mohammed Quadri, Kallupurackal T. Thomas, Dr Girish Thakorlal Nanavati, Saiyed Saghir Ahmad, Bhupinder Nath Kirpal, Namidanna Jagannadha Rao, Visheshwar Nath Khare, Devindar Pratap Wadhwa, S. P. Kurdukar, G. B. Pattanaik, Manharlal Bhikhalal Shah, Debapriya Mohapatra, Umesh Chandra Banerjee, Ramesh Chandra Lahoti, Santosh Hegde, Ram Prakash Sethi, S. N. Phukan.

**Attorney-General:** Soli J. Sorabjee.

### HIGH COURTS

The High Courts are the Courts of Appeal from the lower courts, and their decisions are final except in cases where appeal lies to the Supreme Court.

### LOWER COURTS

Provision is made in the Code of Criminal Procedure for the constitution of lower criminal courts called Courts of Session and Courts of Magistrates. The Courts of Session are competent to try all persons duly committed for trial, and inflict any punishment authorized by the law. The President and the local government concerned exercise the prerogative of mercy.

The constitution of inferior civil courts is determined by regulations within each state.

# Religion

### INDIAN FAITHS

**Buddhism:** The Buddhists in Ladakh (Jammu and Kashmir) are followers of the Dalai Lama. Head Lama of Ladakh: Kaushak Sakula, Dalgate, Srinagar, Kashmir. In 1991 there were 6.3m. Buddhists in India, representing 0.80% of the population.

**Hinduism:** 672.6m. Hindus (1991 census), representing 82.4% of the population.

**Islam:** Muslims are divided into two main sects, Shi'as and Sunnis. Most of the Indian Muslims are Sunnis. At the 1991 census Islam had 95.2m. adherents (11.2% of the population).

**Jainism:** 3.4m. adherents (1991 census), 0.4% of the population.

**Sikhism:** 16.3m. Sikhs (comprising 2.0% of the population at the 1991 census), the majority living in the Punjab.

**Zoroastrians:** More than 120,000 Parsis practise the Zoroastrian religion.

### CHRISTIANITY

According to the 1991 census, Christians represented 2.3% of the population in India.

**National Council of Churches in India:** Christian Council Lodge, Civil Lines, POB 205, Nagpur 440 001, Maharashtra; tel. (712) 531312; fax (712) 520554; e-mail nccindia@nagpur.dot.net.in; internet www.ncci.org; f. 1914; mems: 26 reformed and three orthodox churches, 14 regional Christian councils, 13 All-India ecumenical orgs and seven related agencies; represents c. 8m. mems; Pres. Dr K. Rajratnam; Gen. Sec. Rev. Dr Ipe Joseph.

#### Orthodox Churches

**Malankara Orthodox Syrian Church:** Catholicate Palace, Devalokam, Kottayam 686 038, Kerala; tel. 578500; c. 2.5m. mems (1995); 22 bishops, 21 dioceses, 1,340 parishes; Catholicos of the East and Malankara Metropolitan: HH Baselius Marthoma Mathews II; Asscn Sec. A. K. Thomas.

**Mar Thoma Syrian Church of Malabar:** Mar Thoma Sabha Office, Poolatheen, Tiruvalla 689 101, Kerala; tel. (473) 630449; fax (473) 630327; c. 800,000 mems (1997); Metropolitan: Most Rev. Dr ALEXANDER MAR THOMA; Sec. Very Rev. A. C. KURIAN.

The Malankara Jacobite Syrian Orthodox Church is also represented.

### Protestant Churches

**Church of North India (CNI):** CNI Bhavan, 16 Pandit Pant Marg, New Delhi 110 001; tel. (11) 3716513; fax (11) 3716901; e-mail gscni@nda.vsnl.net.in; internet www.cnisynod.org; f. 1970 by merger of the Church of India (fmrly known as the Church of India, Pakistan, Burma and Ceylon), the Council of the Baptist Churches in Northern India, the Methodist Church (British and Australasian Conferences), the United Church of Northern India (a union of Presbyterians and Congregationalists, f. 1924), the Church of the Brethren in India, and the Disciples of Christ; comprises 26 dioceses; c. 1.2m. mems (1999); Moderator Most Rev. VINOD A. R. PETER, Bishop of Nagpur; Gen. Sec. Dr VIDYA SAGAR LALL.

**Church of South India (CSI):** CSI Centre, 5 Whites Rd, Chennai 600 014; tel. (44) 8521566; fax (44) 8523528; e-mail csind@md3.vsnl.net.in; f. 1947 by merger of the Methodist Church in South India, the South India United Church (itself a union of churches in the Congregational and Presbyterian/Reformed traditions) and the four southern dioceses of the (Anglican) Church of India; comprises 21 dioceses (incl. one in Sri Lanka); c. 2.2m. mems (1988); Moderator Most Rev. WILLIAM MOSES, Bishop of Coimbatore; Gen. Sec. Rev. G. DYVASIRVADAM.

**Methodist Church in India:** Methodist Centre, 21 YMCA Rd, Mumbai Central, Mumbai 400 008; tel. and fax (22) 3074137; e-mail taranath@bom8.vsnl.net.in; f. 1856 as the Methodist Church in Southern Asia; 600,000 mems (1998); Gen. Sec. Rev. TARANATH S. SAGAR.

**Samavesam of Telugu Baptist Churches:** C. A. M. Compound, Nellore 524 003, Andhra Pradesh; tel. (861) 24177; f. 1962; comprises 856 independent Baptist churches; 578,295 mems (1995); Gen. Sec. Rev. Dr S. BENJAMIN.

**United Evangelical Lutheran Churches in India:** 1 First St, Haddows Rd, Chennai 600 006; tel. (44) 6421575; fax (44) 6421870; f. 1975; 11 constituent denominations: Andhra Evangelical Lutheran Church, Arcot Lutheran Church, Evangelical Lutheran Church in Madhya Pradesh, Gossner Evangelical Lutheran Church, India Evangelical Lutheran Church, Jeypore Evangelical Lutheran Church, Northern Evangelical Lutheran Church, North Western Gossner Evangelical Lutheran Church, South Andhra Lutheran Church, Good Samaritan Evangelical Lutheran Church and Tamil Evangelical Lutheran Church; c. 1.3m. mems; Pres. Rev. C. S. R. TOPNO; Exec. Sec. Dr K. RAJARATNAM.

Other denominations active in the country include the Assembly of the Presbyterian Church in North East India, the Bengal-Orissa-Bihar Baptist Convention (6,000 mems), the Chaldean Syrian Church of the East, the Convention of the Baptist Churches of Northern Circars, the Council of Baptist Churches of North East India, the Council of Baptist Churches of Northern India, the Hindustani Convent Church and the Mennonite Church in India.

### The Roman Catholic Church

India comprises 24 archdioceses and 142 dioceses. These include four archdioceses and 20 dioceses of the the Syro-Malabar rite, and one archdiocese and three dioceses of the Syro-Malankara rite. The archdiocese of Goa and Daman is also the seat of the Patriarch of the East Indies. The remaining archdioceses are metropolitan sees. In 1999 there were an estimated 16.3m. adherents of the Roman Catholic faith in the country.

**Catholic Bishops' Conference of India (CBCI):** CBCI Centre, 1 Ashok Place, Goledakkhana, New Delhi 110 001; tel. (11) 3344470; fax (11) 3364615; e-mail cbci@nda.vsnl.net.in; f. 1944; Pres. Most Rev. ALAN DE LASTIC, Archbishop of Delhi; Sec.-Gen. Rt Rev. OSWALD GRACIAS (Auxiliary Bishop of Bombay).

*Latin Rite*

**Conference of Catholic Bishops of India—Latin Rite (CCBI—LR):** CCBI Secretariat, Divya Deepti Sadan, 2nd Floor, 9–10 Bhai Vir Singh Marg, POB 680, New Delhi 110 001; tel. (11) 3364242; fax (11) 3364343; f. 1994; Pres. Most Rev. HENRY SEBASTIAN D'SOUZA, Archbishop of Calcutta.

**Patriarch of the East Indies:** Most Rev. RAUL NICOLAU GONSALVES (Archbishop of Goa and Daman), Paço Patriarcal, POB 216, Altinho, Panjim, Goa 403 001; tel. (832) 223353; fax (832) 224139.

**Archbishop of Agra:** Most Rev. VINCENT M. CONCESSAO, Cathedral House, Wazirpura Rd, Agra 282 003; tel. (562) 351318; fax (562) 353939; e-mail stpeters@nde.vsnl.net.in.

**Archbishop of Bangalore:** Most Rev. IGNATIUS PAUL PINTO, Archbishop's House, 75 Miller's Rd, Bangalore 560 046; tel. (80) 3330438; fax (80) 3330838; e-mail bgarchdi@bgl.vsnl.net.in.

**Archbishop of Bhopal:** Most Rev. PASCHAL TOPNO, Archbishop's House, 33 Ahmedabad Palace Rd, Bhopal 462 001; tel. (755) 540829; fax (755) 544737.

**Archbishop of Bombay (Mumbai):** Most Rev. IVAN DIAS, Archbishop's House, 21 Nathalal Parekh Marg, Fort, Mumbai 400 001; tel. (22) 2021093; fax (22) 2853872.

**Archbishop of Calcutta (Kolkata):** Most Rev. HENRY SEBASTIAN D'SOUZA, Archbishop's House, 32 Park St, Kolkata 700 016; tel. (33) 2471960; fax (33) 2474666; e-mail archbishop@cal.indiax.com.

**Archbishop of Chennai (Madras) and Mylapore:** Most Rev. JAMES MASILAMONY ARUL DAS, Archbishop's House, 21 San Thome High Rd, Chennai 600 004; tel. (44) 4941102; fax (44) 4941999.

**Archbishop of Cuttack-Bhubaneswar:** Most Rev. RAPHAEL CHEENATH, Archbishop's House, Satya Nagar, Bhubaneswar 751 007; tel. (674) 502234; fax (674) 501817.

**Archbishop of Delhi:** Most Rev. ALAN DE LASTIC, Archbishop's House, 1 Ashok Place, Goledakkhana, New Delhi 110 001; tel. (11) 3343457; fax (11) 3746575; e-mail archbish@ndf.vsnl.net.in.

**Archbishop of Guwahati:** Most Rev. THOMAS MENAMPARAMPIL, Archbishop's House, POB 100, Guwahati 781 001; tel. (361) 547664; fax (361) 520588; e-mail bishop@gw1.vsnl.net.in; internet www.catholicindia.org/guwahati.htm.

**Archbishop of Hyderabad:** Most Rev. SAMININI ARULAPPA, Archbishop's House, Sardar Patel Rd, Secunderabad 500 003; tel. (40) 7805545; fax (40) 7805104.

**Archbishop of Imphal:** Most Rev. JOSEPH MITTATHANY, Archbishop's House, POB 35, Imphal 795 001; tel. (385) 221170; fax (385) 220193.

**Archbishop of Madurai:** Most Rev. MARIANUS AROKIASAMY, Archbishop's House, K. Pudur, Madurai 625 007; tel. (452) 563330; fax (452) 566630.

**Archbishop of Nagpur:** Most Rev. ABRAHAM VIRUTHAKULANGARA, Archbishop's House, 25 Kamptee Rd, Mohan Nagar, Nagpur 440 001; tel. (712) 533239; fax (712) 527906.

**Archbishop of Patna:** Most Rev. BENEDICT JOHN OSTA, Archbishop's House, Bankipore, Patna 800 004; tel. (612) 673811.

**Archbishop of Pondicherry and Cuddalore:** Most Rev. Dr S. MICHAEL AUGUSTINE, Archbishop's House, Cathedral St, POB 193, Pondicherry 605 001; tel. (413) 334748; fax (413) 339911.

**Archbishop of Ranchi:** Most Rev. TELESPHORE P. TOPPO, Archbishop's House, Purulia Rd, POB 5, Ranchi 834 001; tel. (651) 204728; fax (651) 304844.

**Archbishop of Shillong:** Most Rev. DOMINIC JALA, Archbishop's House, POB 37, Shillong 793 003; tel. (364) 23355; fax (364) 211306.

**Archbishop of Verapoly:** Most Rev. DANIEL ACHARUPARAMBIL, Latin Archbishop's House, POB 2581, Kochi 682 031; tel. (484) 372892; fax (484) 360911; e-mail vpoiy@giasmd01.vsnl.net.in.

*Syro-Malabar Rite*

**Major Archbishop of Ernakulam-Angamaly:** Most Rev. VARKEY VITHAYATHIL, Major Archbishop's House, Ernakulam, POB 2580, Kochi 682 031; tel. (484) 352629; fax (484) 366028; e-mail abperang@md3.vsnl.net.in.

**Archbishop of Changanacherry:** Most Rev. JOSEPH MAR POWATHIL, Archbishop's House, POB 20, Changanacherry 686 101; tel. (481) 420040; fax (481) 422540; e-mail abpchry@md2.vsnl.net.in.

**Archbishop of Tellicherry:** Most Rev. GEORGE VALIAMATTAM, Archbishop's House, POB 70, Tellicherry 670 101; tel. and fax (497) 231058.

**Archbishop of Trichur:** Most Rev. JACOB THOOMKUZHY, Archbishop's House, Trichur 680 005; tel. (487) 333325; fax (487) 338204.

*Syro-Malankara Rite*

**Archbishop of Thiruvananthapuram:** Most Rev. CYRIL MAR BASELIOS MALANCHARUVIL, Archbishop's House, Pattom, Thiruvananthapuram 695 004; tel. (471) 541643; fax (471) 541635.

### BAHÁ'Í FAITH

**National Spiritual Assembly:** Bahá'í House, 6 Canning Rd, POB 19, New Delhi 110 001; tel. (11) 3386458; fax (11) 3782178; e-mail nsaindia@bahaindia.org; internet www.bahaindia.org; c. 2m. mems; Sec.-Gen. R. N. SHAH; Exec. Sec. A. K. MERCHANT.

## The Press

Freedom of the Press was guaranteed under the 1950 Constitution. In 1979 a Press Council was established (its predecessor was abolished in 1975), the function of which was to uphold the freedom of the press and maintain and improve journalistic standards.

The growth of a thriving press has been inhibited by cultural barriers caused by religious, social and linguistic differences. Consequently the English-language press, with its appeal to the educated middle-class urban readership throughout the states, has retained its dominance. The English-language metropolitan dailies are some of the widest circulating and most influential newspapers. The main Indian language dailies, by paying attention to rural affairs, cater for the increasingly literate non-anglophone provincial population. Most Indian-language papers have a relatively small circulation.

The majority of publications in India are under individual ownership (74% in 1995), and they claim a large part of the total circulation (49% in 1995). The most powerful groups, owned by joint stock companies, publish most of the large English dailies and frequently have considerable private commercial and industrial holdings. Four of the major groups are as follows:

**Times of India Group** (controlled by family of the late ASHOK JAIN): dailies: *The Times of India, Economic Times*, the Hindi *Navbharat Times*, the *Maharashtra Times* (Mumbai); periodicals: the English fortnightlies *Femina* and *Filmfare*.

**Indian Express Group** (controlled by the RAMNATH GOENKA family): publishes nine dailies including the *Indian Express*, the Marathi *Lokasatta*, the Tamil *Dinamani*, the Telugu *Andhra Prabha*, the Kannada *Kannada Prabha* and the English *Financial Express*; six periodicals including the English weeklies the *Indian Express* (Sunday edition), *Screen*, the Telugu *Andhra Prabha Illustrated Weekly* and the Tamil *Dinamani Kadir* (weekly).

**Hindustan Times Group** (controlled by the K. K. BIRLA family): dailies: the *Hindustan Times* (Delhi, Lucknow and Patna), *Pradeep* (Patna) and the Hindi *Hindustan* (Delhi and Patna); periodicals: the weekly *Overseas Hindustan Times* and the Hindi monthly *Nandan* and *Kadambini* (New Delhi).

**Ananda Bazar Patrika Group** (controlled by AVEEK SARKAR and family): dailies: the *Ananda Bazar Patrika* (Calcutta) and the English *The Telegraph*; periodicals include: the English weeklies *Sunday* and *Business World*, Bengali fortnightly *Desh*, Bengali monthly *Anandamela*, Bengali fortnightly *Anandalok* and the Bengali monthly *Sananda*.

## PRINCIPAL DAILIES

### Delhi (incl. New Delhi)

**The Asian Age:** New Delhi; tel. (11) 3712543; fax (11) 3755514; f. 1994; morning; English; also publ. from Bangalore, Bhubaneswar, Mumbai, Kolkata and London; Editor-in-Chief M. J. AKBAR; circ. 83,700 (New Delhi and Mumbai).

**Business Standard:** Pratap Bhavan, 5 Bahadur Shah Zafar Marg, New Delhi 110 002; tel. (11) 3720202; fax (11) 3720201; e-mail editor@business-standard.com; internet www.business-standard.com; morning; English; also publ. from Kolkata, Bangalore, Chennai and Mumbai; Editor T. N. NINAN; combined circ. 67,631.

**Daily Milap:** 8A Bahadur Shah Zafar Marg, New Delhi 110 002; tel. (11) 3317737; fax (11) 3319166; e-mail info@milap.com; internet www.milap.com; f. 1923; Urdu; nationalist; Man. Editor PUNAM SURI; Chief Editor NAVIN SURI; circ. 31,250.

**Daily Pratap:** Pratap Bhawan, 5 Bahadur Shah Zafar Marg, New Delhi 110 002; tel. (11) 3317938; fax (11) 3318276; f. 1919; Urdu; Editor K. NARENDRA; circ. 26,700.

**Delhi Mid Day:** World Trade Tower, Barakhamba Lane, New Delhi 110 001; tel. (11) 3715581; fax (11) 3350491; e-mail delhimidday@hotmail.com; f. 1989; Editor JOHN DAYAL.

**The Economic Times:** 7 Bahadur Shah Zafar Marg, New Delhi 110 002; tel. (11) 3312277; fax (11) 3323346; f. 1961; English; also publ. from Kolkata, Ahmedabad, Bangalore, Hyderabad, Chennai and Mumbai; Editor (Delhi) ARINDAM SENGUPTA; combined circ. 534,200, circ. (Delhi) 99,400.

**Financial Express:** Bahadur Shah Zafar Marg, New Delhi 110 002; tel. (11) 3311111; f. 1961; morning; English; also publ. from Ahmedabad (in Gujarati), Mumbai, Bangalore, Kolkata, Coimbatore, Kochi and Chennai; Editor R. JAGANNATHAN; combined circ. 29,400.

**The Hindu:** INS Bldg, Rafi Marg, New Delhi 110 001; tel. (11) 3715426; fax (11) 3718158; f.1878; morning; English; also publ. from Bangalore, Coimbatore, Hyderabad, Chennai, Madurai, Thiruvananthapuram and Visakhapatnam; Editor N. RAVI; combined circ. 698,000.

**Hindustan:** 18/20 Kasturba Gandhi Marg, New Delhi 110 001; tel. (11) 3361234; fax (11) 3704645; f. 1936; morning; Hindi; also publ. from Lucknow and Patna; Exec. Editor ALOK MEHTA; circ. (Delhi) 101,200, (Patna) 280,100.

**The Hindustan Times:** 18/20 Kasturba Gandhi Marg, New Delhi 110 001; tel. (11) 3361234; fax (11) 3704589; f. 1923; morning; English; also publ. from Patna and Lucknow; Editor VIR SANGHVI; circ. (Delhi) 566,600, combined circ. 594,100.

**Indian Express:** Bahadur Shah Zafar Marg, New Delhi 110 002; tel. (11) 3311111; fax (11) 3716037; f. 1953; English; also publ. from 18 other towns thoughout India; Man. Editor VIVEK GOENKA; Editor-in-Chief SHEKHAR GUPTA; combined circ. 688,878, circ. (New Delhi, Jammu and Chandigarh) 138,462.

**Janasatta:** 9/10 Bahadur Shah Zafar Marg, New Delhi 110 002; f. 1983; Hindi; tel. (11) 3311111; fax (11) 3310089; also publ. from Chandigarh, Kolkata and Mumbai; Editor-in-Chief PRABHASH JOSHI; circ. (New Delhi and Chandigarh) 45,100, combined circ. 78,700.

**National Herald:** Herald House, Bahadur Shah Zafar Marg, New Delhi 110 002; tel. (11) 3319014; fax (11) 3313458; f. 1938; English; nationalist; also publ. from Lucknow; Editor-in-Chief K. V. S. RAMA SARMA; combined circ. 80,000.

**Navbharat Times:** 7 Bahadur Shah Zafar Marg, New Delhi 110 002; tel. (11) 3712211; fax (11) 3323346; f. 1947; Hindi; also publ. from Mumbai; Editor RAMESH CHANDRA; combined circ. 438,300, circ. (Delhi) 305,700.

**The Observer of Business and Politics:** 'Vijaya', 17 Barakhamba Rd, New Delhi 110 001; tel. (11) 3713200; fax (11) 3327065; f. 1990; Chair. of Editorial Board and Editor-in-Chief R. K. MISHRA.

**The Pioneer:** Link House, 3 Bahadur Shah Zafar Marg, New Delhi 110 002; tel. (11) 3755271; fax (11) 3755275; e-mail pioneer@del2.vsnl.net.in; f. 1865; also publ. from Lucknow; Editor CHANDAN MITRA.

**Punjab Kesari:** Romesh Bhavan, 2 Printing Press Complex, nr Wazirpur DTC Depot, Ring Rd, Delhi 110 052; tel. (11) 7181133; fax (11) 7187700; Hindi; also publ. from Jalandhar and Ambala; Editor VIJAY KUMAR CHOPRA; Resident Editor ASHWINI KUMAR; circ. 318,400 (Delhi).

**Rashtriya Sahara:** Amba Deep, Kasturba Gandhi Marg, New Delhi 110 001; tel. (11) 3327727; fax (11) 3755317; morning; Hindi; also publ. from Lucknow; Resident Editor NISHIT JOSHI; circ. 104,000 (New Delhi), 105,200 (Lucknow).

**Sandhya Times:** 7 Bahadur Shah Zafar Marg, New Delhi 110 002; tel (11) 3312277; fax (11) 3323346; f. 1979; Hindi; evening; Editor SAT SONI; circ. 83,500.

**The Statesman:** Rajiv Gandhi Circus, New Delhi 110 001; tel. (11) 3315911; fax (11) 3315295; f. 1875; English; also publ. from Kolkata and Siliguri; Editor-in-Chief C. R. IRANI; combined circ. 180,000).

**The Times of India:** 7 Bahadur Shah Zafar Marg, New Delhi 110 002; tel. (11) 3312277; fax (11) 3323346; f. 1838; English; also publ. from Mumbai, Kolkata, Bangalore, Ahmedabad, Lucknow and Patna; Man. Editor RAMESH CHANDRA; circ. (Delhi and Kolkata) 546,200, combined circ. 1,429,300.

### Andhra Pradesh

Hyderabad

**Deccan Chronicle:** 36 Sarojini Devi Rd, Hyderabad 500 003; tel. (40) 7803930; fax (40) 7805256; f. 1938; English; Editor-in-Chief M. J. AKBAR; Editor A. T. JAYANTI; circ. 126,700.

**Eenadu:** Somajiguda, Hyderabad 500 082; tel. (40) 3318181; fax (40) 3318555; e-mail eenadu@hd2.vsnl.net.in; f. 1974; Telugu; also publ. from Tirupati, Anantapur, Suryapet, Nellore, Guntur, Rajahmundry, Kurnool, Srikakulam, Visakhapatnam, Karimnagar and Vijayawada; Chief Editor RAMOJI RAO; combined circ. 772,000 (weekdays), 900,000 (Sundays).

**Newstime:** 6-3-570 Somajiguda, Hyderabad 500 482; tel. (40) 318181; fax (40) 318555; f. 1984; also publ. from Vijaywada and Visakhapatnam; Editor RAMOJI RAO; circ. 60,000.

**Rahnuma-e-Deccan:** 5-3-831, Goshamahal, Hyderabad 500 012; tel. (40) 4732225; fax (40) 4616991; f. 1949; morning; Urdu; independent; Gen. Man. MIR ALI HYDER HUSSAINI; Chief Editor SYED VICARUDDIN; circ. 20,000.

**Siasat Daily:** Jawaharlal Nehru Rd, Hyderabad 500 001; tel. (40) 4603666; fax (40) 4603188; e-mail siasat@hd1.vsnl.net.in; internet www.siasat.com; f. 1949; morning; Urdu; Editor ZAHID ALI KHAN; circ. 43,505.

Vijayawada

**Andhra Jyoti:** Andhra Jyoti Bldg, POB 712, Vijayawada 520 010; tel. (866) 474532; f. 1960; Telugu; also publ. from Hyderabad, Visakhapatnam and Tirupati; Editor NANDURI RAMAMOHAN RAO; combined circ. 78,600.

**Andhra Prabha:** 16-1-28, Kolandareddy Rd, Poornanandampet, Vijayawada 520 003; tel. (866) 571351; internet www.andhraprabha.com; f. 1935; Telugu; also publ. from Bangalore, Hyderabad, Chennai and Visakhapatnam; Editor V. V. DEEKSHITULU; combined circ. 29,700.

**New Indian Express:** 16-1-28, Kolandareddy Rd, Poornanandampet, Vijayawada 520 003; tel. (866) 571351; English; also publ. from Bangalore, Belgaum, Kochi, Kozhikode, Thiruvananthapuram, Madurai, Chennai, Hyderabad, Visakhapatnam, Coimbatore and Bhubaneswar; Man. Editor MANOJ KUMAR SONTHALIA; Editor (Andhra Pradesh) P. S. SUNDARAM; combined circ. 324,200.

### Assam

Guwahati

**Asomiya Pratidin:** Maniram Dewan Rd, Guwahati 781 003; tel. (361) 540420; fax (361) 522017; morning; Assamese; circ. 77,300.

**Assam Tribune:** Tribune Bldgs, Maniram Dewan Rd, Chandmari, Guwahati 781 003; tel. (361) 541357; fax (361) 540594; e-mail webmaster@assamtribune.com; internet www.assamtribune.com; f. 1939; English; Man. Dir and Editor P. G. Baruah; circ. 47,098.

**Dainik Agradoot:** Agradoot Bhavan, Dispur, Guwahati 781 006; tel. (361) 561923; fax (361) 560655; f. 1995; Assamese; Editor K. S. Deka; circ. 50,500.

**Dainik Asam:** Tribune Bldgs, Maniram Dewan Rd, Chandmari, Guwahati 781 003; tel. (361) 541360; fax (361) 516356; e-mail webmaster@assamtribune.com; internet www.assamtribune.com; f. 1965; Assamese; Editor Anil Baruah; circ. 17,800.

Jorhat

**Dainik Janambhumi:** Nehru Park Rd, Jorhat 785 001; tel. (376) 320033; fax (376) 321713; f. 1972; Assamese; Editor Deva Kr. Borah; circ. 28,100.

### Bihar

Patna

**Aryavarta:** Mazharul Haque Path, Patna 800 001; tel. (612) 233015; fax (612) 222350; morning; Hindi; Editor Harishankar Dwivedi.

**Hindustan Times:** Buddha Marg, Patna 800 001; tel. (612) 223434; fax (612) 226120; f. 1918; morning; English; also publ. from New Delhi and Lucknow; Editor V. N. Narayanan; circ. 27,500.

**Indian Nation:** Mazharul Haque Path, Patna 800 001; tel. (612) 233015; fax (612) 222350; morning; English; Editor Harishankar Dwivedi.

**The Times of India:** Times House, Fraser Rd, Patna 800 001; tel. (612) 226301; fax (612) 233525; also publ. from New Delhi, Mumbai, Ahmedabad, Bangalore and Lucknow; Man. Editor Ramesh Chandra; circ. 30,400.

Ranchi

**Ranchi Express:** 55 Baralal St, Ranchi 834 001; tel. (651) 206320; fax (651) 203466; f. 1963; Hindi; Editor Ajay Maroo; circ. 76,700.

### Goa

Panaji

**Gomantak:** Gomantak Bhavan, St Inez, Panaji, Goa 403 001; tel. (832) 223212; fax (832) 223213; f. 1962; morning; Marathi and English edns; Editor Narayan G. Athawalay; circ. 17,500 (Marathi), 5,900 (English).

**Navhind Times:** Navhind Bhavan, Rua Ismail Gracias, POB 161, Panaji, Goa 403 001; tel. (832) 224033; fax (832) 224258; e-mail navhind@goa1.dot.net.in; f. 1963; morning; English; Editor Arun Sinha; circ. 28,283.

### Gujarat

Ahmedabad

**Gujarat Samachar:** Gujarat Samachar Bhavan, Khanpur, Ahmedabad 380 001; tel. (79) 5504010; fax (79) 5502000; f. 1930; morning; Gujarati; also publ. from Surat, Rajkot, Baroda, Mumbai and New York; Editor Shantibhai Shah; combined circ. 861,200.

**Indian Express:** Janasatta Bldg, Mirzapur Rd, Ahmedabad; tel. (79) 5507028; fax (79) 5507708; f. 1968; English; also publ. in 19 other towns throughout India; Man. Editor Vivek Goenka; Chief Editor Shekhar Gupta; circ. (Ahmedabad and Vadodara) 42,900.

**Lokasatta—Janasatta:** Mirzapur Rd, POB 188, Ahmedabad 380 001; tel. (79) 5507307; fax (79) 5507708; f. 1953; morning; Gujarati; also publ. from Rajkot and Vadodara; Man. Editor Vivek Goenka; combined circ. 28,600.

**Sandesh:** Sandesh Bhavan, Gheekanta Rd, Ahmedabad 380 001; tel. (79) 5624241; fax (79) 5624392; e-mail sandesh@adl.vsnl.net.in; f. 1923; Gujarati; also publ. from Baroda, Rajkot and Surat; Editor Falgunbhai C. Patel; combined circ. 658,600.

**The Times of India:** 139 Ashram Rd, POB 4046, Ahmedabad 380 009; tel. (79) 6582151; fax (79) 6583758; f. 1968; English; also publ. from Mumbai, Delhi, Bangalore, Patna and Lucknow; Resident Editor Kamlendra Kanwar; circ. (Ahmedabad) 94,766.

**Western Times:** 'Western House', Marutnandan Complex, Madalpur, Ahmedabad 380 006; tel. (79) 6576037; fax (79) 6577421; f. 1967; English and Gujarati edns; also publ. (in Gujarati) from Mehsana, Surendranagar, Godhra, Charotar-Nadiad, South Gujarat, Gandhinagar, Baroda and Bharuch; Man. Editor Nikunj Patel; Editor Ramu Patel; circ. (Ahmedabad) 25,364 (English), 39,359 (Gujarati); circ. 27,775 (Mehsana), 27,675 (Godhra), 21,545 (Charotar-Nadiad), 24,620 (Baroda), 27,645 (South Gujarat), 21,620 (Gandhinagar).

Bhuj

**Kutchmitra:** Kutchmitra Bhavan, nr Indirabai Park, Bhuj 370 001; tel. (2832) 52090; fax (2832) 50271; f. 1954; Propr Saurashtra Trust; Editor Kirti Khatri; circ. 31,000.

Rajkot

**Jai Hind:** Jai Hind Press Bldg, Babubhai Shah Marg, POB 59, Rajkot 360 001; tel. (281) 440511; fax (281) 448677; e-mail jaihind@satyam.net.in; f. 1948; morning and evening (in Rajkot as *Sanj Samachar*); Gujarati; also publ. from Ahmedabad; Editor Y. N. Shah; combined circ. 146,269.

**Phulchhab:** Phulchhab Bhavan, Phulchhab Chowk, Rajkot 360 001; tel. (281) 444611; fax (281) 448751; f. 1950; morning; Gujarati; Propr Saurashtra Trust; Editor Dinesh Raja; circ. 91,200.

Surat

**Gujaratmitra and Gujaratdarpan:** Gujaratmitra Bhavan, nr Old Civil Hospital, Sonifalia, Surat 395 003; tel. (261) 478703; fax (261) 478700; f. 1863; morning; Gujarati; Editor B. P. Reshamwala; circ. 88,624.

### Jammu and Kashmir

Jammu

**Himalayan Mail:** Srinagar; f. 1996; English.

**Kashmir Times:** Residency Rd, Jammu 180 001; tel. (191) 543676; fax (191) 542029; f. 1955; morning; English; Editor Ved Bhasin; circ. 67,500.

Srinagar

**Srinagar Times:** Badshah Bridge, Srinagar; f. 1969; Urdu; Editor Gulam Muhammad Sofi; circ. 14,000.

### Karnataka

Bangalore

**Deccan Herald:** 75 Mahatma Gandhi Rd, Bangalore 560 001; tel. (80) 5588999; fax (80) 5587179; f. 1948; morning; English; also publ. from Hubli-Dharwar; Editor-in-Chief K. N. Hari Kumar; combined circ. 192,300.

**Kannada Prabha:** Express Bldgs, 1 Queen's Rd, Bangalore 560 001; tel. (80) 2866893; fax (80) 2866617; e-mail bexpress@bgl.vsnl.net.in; internet www.kannadaprabha.com; f. 1967; morning; Kannada; also publ. from Belgaum and Hyderabad; Editor Y. N. Krishnamurthy; circ. 99,635.

**New Indian Express:** 1 Queen's Rd, Bangalore 560 001; tel. (80) 2256893; fax (80) 2256617; f. 1965; English; also publ. from Kochi, Hyderabad, Chennai, Madurai, Vijayawada and Vizianagaram; Man. Editor Manoj Kumar Sonthalia; Editor Shekhar Gupta; combined circ. 324,200.

**Prajavani:** 75 Mahatma Gandhi Rd, Bangalore 560 001; tel. (80) 5587292; fax (80) 5587675; internet www.prajavani.net; f. 1948; morning; Kannada; also publ. from Hubli-Dharwar; Editor-in-Chief K. N. Harikumar; combined circ. 300,000.

Hubli-Dharwar

**Samyukta Karnataka:** Koppikar Rd, Hubli 580 020; tel. (836) 364303; fax (836) 362760; e-mail info@samyuktakarnataka.com; internet www.samyuktakarnataka.com; f. 1933; Kannada; also publ. from Bangalore and Gulburga; Man. Editor K. Shama Rao; combined circ. 171,165.

Manipal

**Udayavani:** Udayavani Bldg, Press Corner, Manipal 576 119; tel. (8252) 70845; fax (8252) 70563; f. 1970; Kannada; Editor T. Satish U. Pai; circ. 138,600.

### Kerala

Kottayam

**Deepika:** POB 7, Kottayam 686 001; tel. (481) 566706; fax (481) 567947; e-mail deepika@md2.vsnl.net.in; internet www.deepika.com; f. 1887; Malayalam; independent; also publ. from Kannur, Kochi, Thiruvananthapuram and Thrissur; Dir George Jacob; combined circ. 150,000.

**Malayala Manorama:** K. K. Rd, POB 26, Kottayam 686 001; tel. (481) 563646; fax (481) 562479; e-mail editor@malayalamanorama.com; internet www.malayalamanorama.com; f. 1888; also publ. from Kozhikode, Thiruvananthapuram, Palakkad, Kannur, Kollam, Thrissur and Kochi; morning; Malayalam; Man. Dir and Editor Mammen Mathew; Chief Editor K. M. Mathew; combined circ. 1,128,401.

Kozhikode

**Deshabhimani:** 11/127 Convent Rd, Kozhikode 673 032; tel. (495) 77286; f. 1946; morning; Malayalam; publ. by the CPI—M; also publ. from Kochi and Thiruvananthapuram; Chief Editor S. Ramachandran Pillai; combined circ. 178,000.

**Mathrubhumi:** Mathrubhumi Bldgs, K. P. Kesava Menon Rd, POB 46, Kozhikode 673 001; tel. (495) 366655; fax (495) 366656; e-mail mathrelt@md2.vsnl.net.in; f. 1923; Malayalam; Editor K. K. Sreedharan Nair; also publ. from Thiruvananthapuram, Kannur, Thrissur, Kottayam and Kochi; combined circ. 712,400.

Thiruvananthapuram

**Kerala Kaumudi:** POB 77, Pettah, Thiruvananthapuram 695 024; tel. (471) 461050; fax (471) 461985; e-mail sreeni@giasmd01.vsnl.net.in; internet www.keralakaumudi.com; f. 1911; Malayalam; also publ. from Kollam, Alappuzha, Kochi, Kannur and Kozhikode; Editor-in-Chief M. S. MANI; combined circ. 243,260.

Thrissur

**Express:** POB 15, Trichur 680 001; tel. 25800; f. 1944; Malayalam; Editor K. BALAKRISHNAN; circ. 68,200.

**Madhya Pradesh**

Bhopal

**Dainik Bhaskar:** 6 Dwarka Sadan, Habibganj Rd, Bhopal 462 011; tel. (755) 551601; f. 1958; morning; Hindi; also publ. from Indore, Raipur, Jhansi, Bhopal, Bilaspur and Gwalior; Chief Editor R. C. AGARWAL; circ. 87,300 (Bhopal), 43,500 (Gwalior), 26,500 (Bilaspur), 134,300 (Indore), 70,300 (Raipur).

Indore

**Naidunia:** 60/1 Babu Labhchand Chhajlani Marg, Indore 452 009; tel. (731) 763111; fax (731) 763120; e-mail naidunia@edi.com; internet www.naidunia.com; f. 1947; morning; Hindi; Chief Editor ABHAY CHHAJLANI; circ. 122,400.

Raipur

**Deshbandhu:** Deshbandhu Complex, Ramsagarpara Layout, Raipur 492 001; tel. (771) 534911; fax (771) 534955; Hindi; also publ. from Jabalpur, Satna, Bilaspur and Bhopal; Chief Editor LALIT SURJAN; circ. 53,600 (Raipur), 19,300 (Satna), 24,240 (Bhopal), 19,637 (Jabalpur), 27,300 (Bilaspur).

**Maharashtra**

Kolhapur

**Pudhari:** 2318, 'C' Ward, Kolhapur 416 002; tel. (231) 22251; fax (231) 22256; f. 1974; Marathi; Editor P. G. JADHAV; circ. 146,000.

Mumbai

**Afternoon Despatch and Courier:** 6 Nanabhai Lane, Fort, Mumbai 400 001; tel. (22) 2871616; fax (22) 2870371; evening; English; Editor BEHRAM CONTRACTOR; circ. 65,800.

**The Daily:** Asia Publishing House, Mody Bay Estate, Calicut St, Mumbai 400 038; tel. (22) 2653104; fax (22) 2619773; f. 1981; Editor RAJIV BAJAJ; circ. 40,400.

**The Economic Times:** Times of India Bldg, Dr Dadabhai Naoroji Rd, Mumbai 400 001; tel. (22) 2620271; fax (22) 2620144; e-mail etbom@timesgroup.com; internet www.economictimes.com; f. 1961; also publ. from New Delhi, Kolkata, Ahmedabad, Hyderabad, Chennai and Bangalore; English; Exec. Editor JAIDEEP BOSE; combined circ. 351,900, circ. (Mumbai) 108,300.

**Financial Express:** Express Towers, Nariman Point, Mumbai 400 021; tel. (22) 2022627; fax (22) 2886402; e-mail iemumbai@express.indexp.co.in; f. 1961; morning; English; also publ. from New Delhi, Bangalore, Kolkata, Coimbatore, Kochi, Ahmedabad (Gujarati) and Chennai; Man. Editor VIVEK GOENKA; Editor R. JAGANNATHAN; combined circ. (English) 29,400.

**The Free Press Journal:** Free Press House, 215 Free Press Journal Rd, Nariman Point, Mumbai 400 021; tel. (22) 2874566; fax (22) 2874688; f. 1930; English; also publ. from Indore; Man. Editor G. L. LAKHOTIA; combined circ. 87,000.

**Inquilab:** 156 D. J. Dadajee Rd, Tardeo, Mumbai 400 034; tel. (22) 4942586; fax (22) 4938734; e-mail haroonr@mid-day.mailserve.net; f. 1938; morning; Urdu; Editor HAROON RASHID; circ. 33,609.

**Janmabhoomi:** Janmabhoomi Bhavan, Janmabhoomi Marg, Fort, POB 62, Mumbai 400 001; tel. (22) 2870831; fax (22) 2874097; e-mail bhoomi@bom3.vsnl.net.in; f. 1934; evening; Gujarati; Propr Saurashtra Trust; Editor KUNDAN VYAS; circ. 57,898.

**Lokasatta:** Express Towers, Nariman Point, Mumbai 400 021; tel. (22) 2022627; fax (22) 2022139; f. 1948; morning (incl. Sunday); Marathi; also publ. from Pune, Nagpur and Ahmednagar; Editor Dr AROON TIKEKAR; combined circ. 367,700.

**Maharashtra Times:** Dr Dadabhai Naoroji Rd, POB 213, Mumbai 400 001; tel. (22) 2620271; fax (22) 2620144; f. 1962; Marathi; Editor KUMAR KETKAR; circ. 189,700.

**Mid-Day:** 64 Sitaram Mills Compound, N. M. Joshi Marg, Lower Parel, Mumbai 400 011; tel. (22) 3054545; fax (22) 3054536; e-mail mid-day@giasbm01.vsnl.net.in; internet www.mid-day.com; f. 1979; daily and Sunday; English; Editor AYAZ MEMON; circ. 122,630.

**Mumbai Samachar:** Red House, Syed Abdulla Brelvi Rd, Fort, Mumbai 400 001; tel. (22) 2045531; fax (22) 2046642; f. 1822; morning and Sunday; Gujarati; political, social and commercial; Editor JEHAN D. DARUWALA; circ. 131,600.

**Navakal:** 13 Shenviwadi, Khadilkar Rd, Girgaun, Mumbai 400 004; tel. (22) 353585; f. 1923; Marathi; Editor N. Y. KHADILKAR; circ. 302,900.

**Navbharat Times:** Dr Dadabhai Naoroji Rd, Mumbai 400 001; tel. (22) 2620382; f. 1950; Hindi; also publ. from New Delhi, Jaipur, Patna and Lucknow; circ. (Mumbai) 132,600.

**Navshakti:** Free Press House, 215 Nariman Point, Mumbai 400 021; tel. (22) 2874566; f. 1932; Marathi; Editor D. B. JOSHI; circ. 65,000.

**New Indian Express:** Express Towers, Nariman Point, Mumbai 400 021; tel. (22) 2022627; fax (22) 2022139; f. 1940; English; also publ. from Pune and Nagpur; Man. Editor VIVEK GOENKA; Chief Editor SHEKHAR GUPTA; combined circ. 179,500.

**Sakal:** Sakal Bhavan, Plot No. 42-B, Sector No. 11, CBD Belapur, Navi Mumbai 400 614; tel. (22) 7574327; fax (22) 7574280; f. 1970; daily; Marathi; also publ. from Pune, Nasik and Kolhapur; Editor RADHAKRISHNA NARVEKAR; combined circ. 438,500.

**The Times of India:** The Times of India Bldg, Dr Dadabhai Naoroji Rd, Mumbai 400 001; tel. (22) 2620271; fax (22) 2620144; e-mail toieditorial@timesgroup.com; internet www.timesofindia.com; f. 1838; morning; English; also publ. from Delhi, Ahmedabad, Bangalore, Patna and Lucknow; Exec. Man. Editor DILEEP PADGAONKAR; circ. (Mumbai) 565,700, combined circ. 1,429,300.

Nagpur

**Hitavada:** Wardha Rd, Nagpur 440 012; tel. (712) 523155; fax (712) 535093; e-mail hitavada@nagpur.net.in; f. 1911; morning; English; Man. Editor BANWARILAL PUROHIT; Editor V. PHANSHIKAR; circ. 53,500.

**Lokmat:** Lokmat Bhavan, Wardha Rd, Nagpur 440 012; tel. (712) 523527; fax (712) 526923; also publ. from Jalgaon, Ahmednagar, Solapur, Nasik and Aurangabad; Marathi; **Lokmat Samachar** (Hindi) publ. from Nagpur and Aurangabad; **Lokmat Times** (English) publ. from Nagpur and Aurangabad; Editor VIJAY DARDA; combined circ. 273,700.

**Nava Bharat:** Nava Bharat Bhavan, Cotton Market, Nagpur 440 018; tel. (712) 726677; f. 1938; morning; Hindi; also publ. from Bhopal, Jabalpur, Bilaspur, Indore and Raipur; Editor-in-Chief R. G. MAHESWARI; combined circ. 443,200.

**Tarun Bharat:** 28 Farmland, Ramdaspeth, Nagpur 440 010; tel. (712) 525052; e-mail ibharat@nagpur.dot.net.in; f. 1944; Marathi; independent; also publ. from Pune and Belgaum; Chief Gen. Man. MOHAN PANDE; Editor SUDHIR PATHAK; circ. 49,695 (Nagpur).

Pune

**Kesari:** 568 Narayan Peth, Pune 411 030; tel. (20) 4459250; fax (20) 4451677; f. 1881; Marathi; also publ. from Solapur, Kolhapur, Chiplun, Ahmednagar and Sangli; Editor ARVIND VYANKATESH GOKHALE; combined circ. 150,000.

**Sakal:** 595 Budhwar Peth, Pune 411 002; tel. (20) 4455500; fax (20) 4450583; e-mail sakal@giaspn01.vsnl.net.in; f. 1932; daily; Marathi; also publ. from Mumbai, Nashik, Aurangabad and Kolhapur; Chief Editor VIJAY KUWALEKAR; Man. Dir PRATAP PAWAR; combined circ. 457,052.

**Orissa**

Bhubaneswar

**Dharitri:** B-26, Industrial Estate, Bhubaneswar 751 010; tel. (674) 480101; fax (674) 480795; morning; Oriya; Editor TATHAGATA SATPATHY; circ. 128,100.

**Pragativadi:** 178-B, Mancheswar Industrial Estate, Bhubaneswar 751 010; tel. (674) 580297; fax (674) 582636; e-mail samahitbal@hotmail.com; circ. 106,851.

Cuttack

**Prajatantra:** Prajatantra Bldgs, Behari Baug, Cuttack 753 002; tel. (671) 603071; fax (671) 603063; f. 1947; Oriya; Editor BHARTRUHARI MAHTAB; circ. 107,800.

**Samaj:** Cuttack; tel. (671) 20994; fax (671) 601044; f. 1919; Oriya; circ. 121,600.

**Punjab**

Chandigarh

**The Tribune:** Sector 29C, Chandigarh 160 020; tel. (172) 655065; fax (172) 655054; e-mail tribunet@ch1.dot.net.in; internet www.tribuneindia.com; f. 1881 (English edn), f. 1978 (Hindi and Punjabi edns); Editor (all edns) HARI JAISINGH; Editor (Hindi edn) VIJAY SAIGHAL; Editor (Punjabi edn) G. S. BHULLAR; circ. 211,907 (English), 81,989 (Hindi), 73,296 (Punjabi).

Jalandhar

**Ajit:** Ajit Bhavan, Nehru Garden Rd, Jalandhar 144 001; tel. 55960; f. 1955; Punjabi; Man. Editor S. BARJINDER SINGH; circ. 197,500.

**Hind Samachar:** Civil Lines, Jalandhar 144 001; tel. (181) 280104; fax (181) 280113; f. 1948; morning and Sunday; Urdu; also publ.

from Ambala; Editor Vijay Kumar Chopra; Jt Editor Avinash Chopra; combined circ. 43,036.

**Jag Bani:** Civil Lines, Jalandhar 144 001; tel. (181) 280104; fax (181) 280113; f. 1978; morning; Punjabi; Editor Vijay Kumar Chopra; Jt Editor Avinash Chopra; circ. 140,452.

**Punjab Kesari:** Civil Lines, Jalandhar 144 001; tel. (181) 280104; fax (181) 280113; f. 1965; morning and Sunday; Hindi; also publ. from Delhi and Ambala; Editor Vijay Kumar Chopra; Jt Editor Avinash Chopra; combined circ. 777,805.

### Rajasthan

Jaipur

**Rajasthan Patrika:** Kesargarh, Jawahar Lal Nehru Marg, Jaipur 302 004; tel. (141) 561582; fax (141) 566011; e-mail info@rajasthan_patrika.com; internet www.rajasthan_patrika.com; f. 1956; Hindi and English edns; Hindi edn also publ. from Jodhpur, Bikaner, Udaipur, Bangalore and Kota; Editor Moti Chand Kochar; combined circ. (Hindi) 573,000, (English) 3,630.

**Rashtradoot:** M.I. Rd, POB 30, Jaipur 302 001; tel. (141) 372634; fax (141) 373513; f. 1951; Hindi; also publ. from Kota, Udaipur, Ajmer and Bikaner; CEO Somesh Sharma; Chief Editor Rajesh Sharma; circ. 368,482 (Jaipur), 76,763 (Kota), 45,250 (Bikaner), 38,023 (Udaipur), 27,514 (Ajmer).

### Tamil Nadu

Chennai (Madras)

**Daily Thanthi:** 46 E.V.K. Sampath Rd, POB 467, Chennai 600 007; tel. (44) 587731; fax (44) 580069; f. 1942; Tamil; also publ. from Bangalore, Coimbatore, Cuddalore, Erode, Madurai, Nagercoil, Salem, Tiruchi, Tirunelveli, Pondicherry and Vellore; Chief Gen. Man. R. Somasundaram; Editor R. Thiruvadi; combined circ. 509,900.

**Dinakaran:** 106/107 Kutchery Rd, Mylapore, POB 358, Chennai 600 004; tel. (44) 4941006; fax (44) 4951008; e-mail dinakaran@dinakaran.com; internet www.dinakaran.com; f. 1977; Tamil; also publ. from Madurai, Tiruchirapalli, Vellore, Tirunelveli, Salem and Coimbatore; Man. Dir K. Kumaran; Editor D. Paulraj; combined circ. 351,872.

**Dinamalar:** 161 Anna Salai, Chennai 600 002; tel. (44) 8523715; f. 1951; Tamil; also publ. from Coimbatore, Erode, Madurai, Pondicherry, Tiruchirapalli, Tirunelveli and Vellore; Editor R. Krishnamoorthy; combined circ. 397,300.

**Dinamani:** Express Estates, Mount Rd, Chennai 600 002; tel. (44) 8520751; fax (44) 8524500; e-mail express@giasmd01.vsnl.net.in; internet www.dinamani.com; f. 1934; morning; Tamil; also publ. from Madurai, Coimbatore and Bangalore; Editor T. Sambandam; combined circ. 188,301.

**Financial Express:** Vasanthi Medical Center, 20 Pycrofts Garden Rd, Chennai 600 006; tel. (44) 8231112; fax (44) 8231489; internet www.financialexpress.com; morning; English; also publ. from Mumbai, Ahmedabad (in Gujarati), Bangalore, Kochi, Kolkata and New Delhi; Man. Editor Vivek Goenka; Exec. Editor R. Jagannathan; combined circ. 30,400.

**The Hindu:** Kasturi Bldgs, 859/860 Anna Salai, Chennai 600 002; tel. (44) 8413344; fax (44) 8415325; f. 1878; morning; English; independent; also publ. from Bangalore, Coimbatore, New Delhi, Visakhapatnam, Hyderabad, Thiruvananthapuram and Madurai; Publr S. Rangarajan; Editor N. Ravi; combined circ. 697,976.

**The Hindu Business Line:** 859/860 Anna Salai, Chennai 600 002; tel. (44) 8413344; fax (44) 8415325; f. 1994; morning; English; also publ. from Bangalore, Hyderabad, Madurai, Coimbatore, New Delhi, Visakhapatnam and Thiruvananthapuram; Publr S. Rangarajan; Editor N. Ram; combined circ. 27,314.

**Murasoli:** 93 Kodambakkam High Rd, Chennai 600 034; tel. (44) 470044; f. 1960; organ of the DMK; Tamil; Editor S. Selvam; circ. 54,000.

**New Indian Express:** Express Estates, Mount Rd, Chennai 600 002; tel. (44) 8520751; fax (44) 8524500; e-mail express@giasmd01.vsnl.net.in; f. 1932 as Indian Express; morning; English; also publ. from Coimbatore, Kochi, Bangalore, Kozhikode, Thiruvananthapuram, Madurai, Hyderabad, Visakhapatnam, Bhubaneswar, Belgaum and Vijayawada; Man. Editor Manoj Kumar Sonthalia; combined circ. 324,161.

### Tripura

Agartala

**Dainik Sambad:** 11 Jagannath Bari Rd, POB 2, Agartala 799 001; tel. (381) 226676; fax (381) 224845; f. 1966; Bengali; morning; Editor Bhupendra Chandra Datta Bhaumik.

### Uttar Pradesh

Agra

**Amar Ujala:** Sikandra Rd, Agra 282 007; tel. (562) 361600; fax (562) 361602; f. 1948; Hindi; also publ. from Bareilly, Allahabad, Jhansi, Kanpur, Moradabad and Meerut; Editor Ajay K. Agarwal; Dep. Gen. Man. L. K. Shrimali; circ. 127,000 (Agra), 79,500 (Bareilly), 35,200 (Moradabad), 162,000 (Meerut), 25,300 (Kanpur), 22,400 (Allahabad), 11,800 (Jhansi).

Allahabad

**Amrita Prabhat:** 10 Edmonstone Rd, Allahabad 211 001; tel. (532) 600654; f. 1977; Hindi; Editor Tamal Kanti Ghosh; circ. 44,000.

**Northern India Patrika:** 10 Edmonstone Rd, Allahabad 211 001; tel. (532) 52665; f. 1959; English; Chief Editor Tushar Kanti Ghosh; Editor Manas Mukul Das; circ. 46,000.

Kanpur

**Dainik Jagran:** 2 Sarvodaya Nagar, Kanpur 208 005; tel. (512) 216161; fax (512) 216972; e-mail jpl@jagran.com; internet www.jagran.com; f. 1942; Hindi; also publ. from Gorakhpur, Jhansi, Lucknow, Jalandhar, Meerut, Agra, Varanasi (Allahabad), Bareilly and New Delhi; Editor Narendra Mohan; combined circ. 821,981.

**Vyapar Sandesh:** 26/104 Birhana Rd, Kanpur 208 001; tel. (512) 352066; f. 1958; Hindi; commercial news and economic trends; Editor Hari Shankar Sharma; circ. 17,000.

Lucknow

**National Herald:** Lucknow; f. 1938 Lucknow, 1968 Delhi; English; Editor-in-Chief K. V. S. Rama Sharma.

**The Pioneer:** 20 Vidhan Sabha Marg, Lucknow 226 001; tel. (522) 220516; fax (522) 220466; f. 1865; English; also publ. from New Delhi; Publr Dipak Mukerji; Editor Chandan Mitra; combined circ. 136,000.

**Swatantra Bharat:** 1st Floor, Suraj Deep Complex, 1 Jopling Rd, Lucknow 226 001; tel. (522) 209301; fax (522) 209308; e-mail sbharat@lw1.vsnl.net.in; f. 1947; Hindi; also publ. from Kanpur; Editor K. K. Srivastava; circ. 66,058 (Lucknow), 48,511 (Kanpur).

Varanasi

**Aj:** Aj Bhavan, Sant Kabir Rd, Kabirchaura, Varanasi 221 001; tel. (542) 393981; fax (542) 393989; f. 1920; Hindi; also publ. from Gorakhpur, Patna, Allahabad, Ranchi, Agra, Bareilly, Lucknow, Jamshedpur, Dhanbad and Kanpur; Editor Shardul Vikram Gupta; circ. 46,700 (Agra), 39,500 (Allahabad), 41,200 (Gorakhpur), 156,500 (Kanpur), 19,800 (Jamshedpur), 52,100 (Lucknow), 141,500 (Patna), 38,500 (Ranchi), 182,400 (Varanasi), 28,300 (Bareilly).

### West Bengal

Kolkata (Calcutta)

**Aajkaal:** 96 Raja Rammohan Sarani, Kolkata 700 009; tel. (33) 3509803; fax (33) 3500877; e-mail aajkaal@cal.vsnl.net.in; f. 1981; morning; Bengali; Chief Editor Pratap K. Roy; circ. 153,300.

**Ananda Bazar Patrika:** 6 Prafulla Sarkar St, Kolkata 700 001; tel. (33) 278000; fax (33) 303240; f. 1922; morning; Bengali; Editor Aveek Sarkar; circ. 599,200.

**Banga Sambad:** 7 Old Court House St, Kolkata 700 001; tel. (33) 207618; fax (33) 206663; f. 1991; Bengali; Editor S. C. Talukdar; circ. 36,895.

**Bartaman:** 76A Acharya J.C. Bose Rd, Kolkata 700 014; tel. (33) 2448208; fax (33) 2441215; f. 1984; Editor Barun Sengupta; circ. 369,800.

**Business Standard:** Church Lane, Kolkata 700 001; tel. (33) 278000; fax (33) 2253241; f. 1975; morning; also publ. from New Delhi, Bangalore, Chennai and Mumbai; English; Editor T. N. Ninan; combined circ. 61,200.

**Dakshin Banga Sambad:** 7 Old Court House St, Kolkata 700 001; tel. (33) 207618; fax (33) 206663; f. 1991; Bengali; Editor S. C. Talukdar; circ. 36,123.

**The Economic Times:** 105/7A, S. N. Banerjee Rd, Kolkata 700 014; tel. (33) 294232; fax (33) 292400; English; also publ. from Ahmedabad, Delhi, Bangalore, Chennai, Hyderabad and Mumbai; circ. (Kolkata) 43,200.

**Financial Express:** 83 B. K. Pal Ave, Kolkata 700 005; morning; English; also publ. from Mumbai, Ahmedabad, Bangalore, Coimbatore, Kochi, Chennai and New Delhi; Man. Editor Vivek Goenka; Exec. Editor R. Jagannathan; combined circ. 29,400.

**Frontier News:** 7 Old Court House St, Kolkata 700 001; tel. (33) 207618; fax (33) 206663; f. 1992; English; Editor S. C. Talukdar; circ. 26,720.

**Ganashakti:** 74A A. J. C. Bose Rd, Kolkata 700 016; tel. (33) 2458950; fax (33) 2456263; e-mail mail@ganashakti.co.in; f. 1967; morning; Bengali; Editor Dipen Ghosh; circ. 115,300.

**Himalchuli:** 7 Old Court House St, Kolkata 700 001; tel. (33) 207618; fax (33) 206663; f. 1982; Nepali; Editor S. C. Talukdar; circ. 42,494.

**Overland:** Kolkata; f. 1991; morning; Editor Ajit Kumar Bhowal; circ. 122,000.

**Sambad Pratidin:** 20 Prafulla Sarkar St, Kolkata 700 072; tel. (33) 2445441; fax (33) 2445451; morning; Bengali; Editor SWAPAN SADHAN BASU; circ. 228,900.

**Sandhya Aajkaal:** 96 Raja Rammohan Sarani, Kolkata 700 009; tel. (33) 3509803; fax (33) 3500877; evening; Bengali; Chief Editor PRATAP K. ROY; circ. 17,500.

**Sanmarg:** 160C Chittaranjan Ave, Kolkata 700 007; tel. (33) 2413862; fax (33) 2415087; e-mail sanmarg@giascl01.vsnl.net.in; f. 1948; Hindi; Editor RAMAWATAR GUPTA; circ. 80,423.

**The Statesman:** Statesman House, 4 Chowringhee Sq., Kolkata 700 001; tel. (33) 271000; fax (33) 270118; f. 1875; morning; English; independent; also publ. from New Delhi and Siliguri; Editor-in-Chief C. R. IRANI; combined circ. 180,000.

**The Telegraph:** 6 Prafulla Sarkar St, Kolkata 700 001; tel. (33) 278000; fax (33) 2253240; e-mail thetelegraphindia@newscom.com; f. 1982; English; Editor AVEEK SARKAR; circ. 247,500.

**Uttar Banga Sambad:** 7 Old Court House St, Kolkata 700 001; tel. (33) 2207618; fax (33) 2206663; f. 1980; Bengali; Editor S. C. TALUKDAR; circ. 102,366.

**Vishwamitra:** 74 Lenin Sarani, Kolkata 700 013; tel. (33) 2441139; fax (33) 2446393; f. 1916; morning; Hindi; commercial; also publ. from Mumbai; Editor PRAKASH CHANDRA AGRAWALLA; combined circ. 76,605.

## SELECTED PERIODICALS

### Delhi and New Delhi

**Alive:** Delhi Press Bldg, E-3, Jhandewala Estate, Rani Jhansi Rd, New Delhi 110 055; tel. (11) 3529557; fax (11) 7525020; f. 1940; monthly; English; political and cultural; Editor VISHWA NATH; circ. 20,000.

**Bal Bharati:** Patiala House, Publications Division, Ministry of Information and Broadcasting, Delhi; tel. (11) 387038; f. 1948; monthly; Hindi; for children; Editor SHIV KUMAR; circ. 30,000.

**Bano:** 13/14 Asaf Ali Rd, New Delhi 110 002; tel. (11) 3232666; fax (11) 3237569; f. 1947; monthly; Urdu; women's interests; Editor SADIA DEHLVI; circ. 5,500.

**Biswin Sadi:** 3583 Netaji Subash Marg, Darya Ganj, POB 7013, New Delhi 110 002; tel. (11) 3271637; f. 1937; monthly; Urdu; Editor Z. REHMAN NAYYAR; circ. 36,000.

**Business Today:** F-26 Connaught Place, New Delhi 110 001; tel. (11) 3315801; fax (11) 3318385; e-mail btoday@giasdl01.vsnl.net.in; fortnightly; English; Editor ANAND P. RAMAN; circ. 122,800.

**Careers Digest:** 21 Shankar Market, Delhi 110 001; tel. (11) 44726; f. 1963; monthly; English; Editor O. P. VARMA; circ. 35,000.

**Catholic India:** CBCI Centre, 1 Ashok Place, Goldakkhana, New Delhi 110 001; tel. (11) 3344470; fax (11) 3364615; e-mail cbci@nda.vsnl.net.in; quarterly.

**Champak:** Delhi Press Bldg, E-3, Jhandewala Estate, Rani Jhansi Rd, New Delhi 110 055; tel. (11) 3529557; fax (11) 7525020; f. 1969; fortnightly (Hindi, English, Gujarati and Marathi edns); monthly (Kannada edn); children; Editor VISHWA NATH; combined circ. 122,600.

**Children's World:** Nehru House, 4 Bahadur Shah Zafar Marg, New Delhi 110 002; tel. (11) 3316970; fax (11) 3721090; e-mail cbtnd@vsnl.com; internet www.childrensbooktrust.com; f. 1968; monthly; English; Editor NAVIN MENON; circ. 25,000.

**Competition Refresher:** 2767, Bright House, Daryaganj, New Delhi 110 002; tel. (11) 3282226; fax (11) 3269227; e-mail psbright@ndb.vsnl.net.in; internet www.brightcareers.com; f. 1984; monthly; English; Chief Editor D. S. PHULL; Publr and Man. Dir PRITAM SINGH BRIGHT; circ. 148,693.

**Competition Success Review:** 604 Prabhat Kiran Bldg, Rajendra Place, Delhi 110 008; tel. (11) 5712898; fax (11) 5754647; monthly; English; f. 1964; Editor S. K. SACHDEVA; circ. 266,200.

**Computers Today:** Marina Arcade, G-59 Connaught Circus, New Delhi 110 001; tel. (11) 3736233; fax (11) 3725506; e-mail ctoday@india-today.com; f. 1984; Editor J. SRIHARI RAJU; circ. 49,100.

**Cricket Samrat:** L–1, Kanchan House, Najafgarh Rd, Commercial Complex, nr Milan Cinema, New Delhi 110 015; tel. (11) 5191175; fax (11) 5469581; f. 1978; monthly; Hindi; Editor ANAND DEWAN; circ. 145,000.

**Employment News:** Government of India, East Block IV, Level 5, R. K. Puram, New Delhi 110 066; tel. (11) 6193316; f. 1976; weekly; Hindi, Urdu and English edns; Gen. Man. and Chief Editor N. N. SHARMA; Editor I. K. CHARI; combined circ. 550,000.

**Filmi Duniya:** 16 Darya Ganj, New Delhi 110 002; tel. (11) 3278087; fax (11) 3279341; f. 1958; monthly; Hindi; Chief Editor NARENDRA KUMAR; circ. 143,700.

**Filmi Kaliyan:** 4675-B/21 Ansari Rd, New Delhi 110 002; tel. (11) 3272080; f. 1969; monthly; Hindi; cinema; Editor-in-Chief V. S. DEWAN; circ. 85,000.

**Global Travel Express:** 26F Indira Gandhi Chowk (Connaught Place), New Delhi 110 001; tel. (11) 3312329; f. 1993; monthly; English; travel and tourism; Chief Editor HARBHAJAN SINGH; Editor GURINDER SINGH; circ. 28,100.

**Grih Shobha:** Delhi Press Bldg, E-3 Jhandewala Estate, Rani Jhansi Rd, New Delhi 110 055; tel. (11) 3529557; fax (11) 7525020; f. 1979; monthly; Kannada, Marathi, Hindi and Gujarati edns; women's interests; Editor VISHWA NATH; circ. 117,000 (Kannada), 62,500 (Gujarati), 166,100 (Marathi), 316,100 (Hindi).

**India Perspectives:** Room 149B 'A' Wing, Shastri Bhavan, New Delhi 110 001; tel. (11) 3389471; f. 1988; Editor BHARAT BHUSHAN.

**India Today:** F 14/15, Indira Gandhi Place, New Delhi 110 001; tel. (11) 3315801; fax (11) 3316180; f. 1975; English, Tamil, Telugu, Malayalam and Hindi; weekly; Editor AROON PURIE; circ. 417,500 (English), 287,500 (Hindi), 77,600 (Tamil), 80,700 (Malayalam), 68,700 (Telugu).

**Indian Observer:** 26F Indira Gandhi Chowk (Connaught Place), New Delhi 110 001; tel. (11) 3312329; f. 1964; fortnightly; English; Editor HARBHAJAN SINGH; circ. 37,000.

**Indian Railways:** 411 Rail Bhavan, Raisina Rd, New Delhi 110 001; tel. (11) 3383540; fax (11) 3384481; f. 1956; monthly; English; publ. by the Ministry of Railways (Railway Board); Editor MANOHAR D. BANERJEE; circ. 12,000.

**Intensive Agriculture:** Ministry of Agriculture, Dept of Agriculture and Co-operation, Directorate of Extension, Krishi Vistar Bhavan, Pusa, New Delhi 110 012; tel. (11) 5723404; f. 1955; bi-monthly; English; Editor H.P.S. PATANGA; circ. 7,500.

**Journal of Industry and Trade:** Ministry of Commerce, Delhi 110 011; tel. (11) 3016664; f. 1952; monthly; English; Man. Dir A. C. BANERJEE; circ. 2,000.

**Junior Science Refresher:** 2769, Bright House, Daryaganj, New Delhi 110 002; tel. (11) 3282227; fax (11) 3269227; e-mail psbright@ndb.vsnl.net.in; internet www.brightcareers.com; f. 1987; monthly; English; Chief Editor D. S. PHULL; Publr and Man. Dir PRITAM SINGH BRIGHT; circ. 94,330.

**Kadambini:** Hindustan Times House, Kasturba Gandhi Marg, New Delhi 110 001; tel. (11) 3704581; fax (11) 3704600; f. 1960; monthly; Hindi; Editor RAJENDRA AWASTHY; circ. 100,000.

**Krishak Samachar:** Bharat Krishak Samaj, Dr Panjabrao Deshmukh Krishak Bhavan, A-1 Nizamuddin West, New Delhi 110 013; tel. (11) 4619508; f. 1957; monthly; English and Hindi edns; agriculture; Editor Dr. KRISHAN BIR CHAUDHARY; circ. (English) 5,000, (Hindi) 14,000.

**Kurukshetra:** Ministry of Rural Development, Room No. 655/661, 'A' Wing, Nirman Bhavan, New Delhi 110 011; tel. (11) 3015014; fax (11) 3386879; monthly; English; rural development; Editor P. V. RAO; circ. 14,000.

**Mainstream:** 145/1D Shahpur Jat, 1st Floor, nr Asiad Village, New Delhi 110 049; tel. (11) 6497188; English; weekly; politics and current affairs; Editor SUMIT CHAKRAVARTTY.

**Mayapuri:** A-5, Mayapuri Phase 1, New Delhi 110 064; tel. (11) 5141439; fax (11) 5138596; e-mail mayapuri@hotmail.com; f. 1974; weekly; Hindi; cinema; Editor A. P. BAJAJ; circ. 146,144.

**Mukta:** Delhi Press Bldg, E-3 Jhandewala Estate, Rani Jhansi Rd, New Delhi 110 055; tel. (11) 3529557; fax (11) 7525020; f. 1961; monthly; Hindi; youth; Editor VISHWA NATH; circ. 20,213.

**Nandan:** Hindustan Times House, Kasturba Gandhi Marg, New Delhi 110 001; tel. (11) 3361234; fax (11) 3704600; f. 1963; monthly; Hindi; Editor JAI PRAKASH BHARTI; circ. 187,000.

**New Age:** 15 Kotla Rd, Delhi 110 002; tel. (11) 3310762; f. 1953; main organ of the Communist Party of India; weekly; English; Editor PAULY V. PARAKAL; circ. 215,000.

**The North East Sun:** 8B Bahadur Shah Zafar Marg, New Delhi 110 002; tel. (11) 3316722; fax (11) 3317947; f. 1977; fortnightly; English; Editor V. B. GUPTA; circ. 26,374.

**Organiser:** 29 Rani Jhansi Marg, New Delhi 110 055; tel. (11) 7526977; fax (11) 7514876; f. 1947; weekly; English; Editor SESHADRI CHARI; circ. 44,100.

**Outlook:** AB-10 Safdarjung Enclave, New Delhi 110 029; tel. (11) 6191421; fax (11) 6191420; e-mail outlook@outlookindia.com; internet www.outlookindia.com; f. 1995; weekly; Editor-in-Chief VINOD MEHTA; circ. 191,000.

**Panchjanya:** Sanskriti Bhavan, Deshbandhu Gupta Marg, Jhandewala, New Delhi 110 055; tel. (11) 3514244; fax (11) 3558613; e-mail panch@nde.vsnl.net.in; f. 1947; weekly; Hindi; general interest; nationalist; Chair. S. N. BANSAL; Editor TARUN VIJAY; circ. 59,300.

**Proven Trade Contacts:** POB 5730, New Delhi 110 055; tel. (11) 3526402; fax (11) 3625666; e-mail tc@narang.com; internet www.narang.com/ptc; f. 1992; monthly; medical/surgical/scientific/pharmaceutical trade promotion; circ. 10,000.

**Punjabi Digest:** 209 Hemkunt House, 6 Rajendra Place, POB 2549, New Delhi 110 008; tel. (11) 5715225; f. 1971; literary monthly; Gurmukhi; Chief Editor Sardar J. B. SINGH; circ. 84,200.

**Rangbhumi:** 5A/15 Ansari Rd, Darya Ganj, Delhi 110 002; tel. (11) 3274667; f. 1941; Hindi; films; Editor S. K. GUPTA; circ. 30,000.

**Sainik Samachar:** Block L-1, Church Rd, New Delhi 110 001; tel. (11) 3019668; f. 1909; pictorial fortnightly for India's armed forces; English, Hindi, Urdu, Tamil, Punjabi, Telugu, Marathi, Kannada, Gorkhali, Malayalam, Bengali, Assamese and Oriya edns; Editor-in-Chief S. N. MISHRA; circ. 20,000.

**Saras Salil:** Delhi Press Bldg, E-3, Jhandewala Estate, Rani Jhansi Rd, New Delhi 110 055; tel. (11) 3529557; fax (11) 7525020; f. 1993; fortnightly; Hindi; Editor VISHWA NATH; circ. 963,200.

**Sarita:** Delhi Press Bldg, E-3, Jhandewala Estate, Rani Jhansi Rd, New Delhi 110 055; tel. (11) 3529557; fax (11) 7525020; f. 1945; fortnightly; Hindi; family magazine; Editor VISHWA NATH; circ. 172,800.

**Shama:** 13/14 Asaf Ali Rd, New Delhi 110 002; tel. (11) 3232674; fax (11) 3235167; f. 1939; monthly; Urdu; art and literature; Editors M. YUNUS DEHLVI, IDREES DEHLVI, ILYAS DEHLVI; circ. 58,000.

**Sher-i-Punjab:** Hemkunt House, 6 Rajendra Place, New Delhi 110 008; tel. (11) 5715225; f. 1911; weekly news magazine; Chief Editor Sardar JANG BAHADUR SINGH; circ. 15,000.

**Suman Saurabh:** Delhi Press Bldg, E-3 Jhandewala Estate, Rani Jhansi Rd, New Delhi 110 055; tel. (11) 3529557; fax (11) 7525020; f. 1983; monthly; Hindi; youth; Editor VISHWA NATH; circ. 52,600.

**The Sun:** 8B Bahadur Shah Zafar Marg, POB 7164, New Delhi 110 002; tel. (11) 3316722; fax (11) 3317947; f. 1977; fortnightly; English; Editor V. B. GUPTA; circ. 69,953.

**The Sunday Observer:** Vijaya, 17 Barakhamba Rd, New Delhi 110 001; tel. (11) 3713200; fax (11) 3327065; f. 1981; weekly; English and Hindi edns; also publ. from Mumbai; Editor-in-Chief NIKHIL LAKSHMAN; combined circ. 72,400.

**Sushama:** 13/14 Asaf Ali Rd, New Delhi 110 002; tel. (11) 3232674; fax (11) 3235167; f. 1959; monthly; Hindi; art and literature; Editors IDREES DEHLVI, ILYAS DEHLVI, YUNUS DEHLVI; circ. 30,000.

**Trade Union Record:** 24 Canning Lane, New Delhi 110 001; tel. (11) 3387320; fax (11) 3386427; f. 1930; fortnightly; English and Hindi edns; Editor SANTOSH KUMAR.

**Vigyan Pragati:** PID Bldg, Dr K. S. Krishnan Marg, New Delhi 110 012; tel. (11) 5785647; fax (11) 5731353; f. 1952; monthly; Hindi; popular science; Editor DEEKSHA BIST; circ. 100,000.

**Woman's Era:** Delhi Press Bldg, E-3, Jhandewala Estate, Rani Jhansi Rd, New Delhi 110 055; tel. (11) 3529557; fax (11) 7525020; f. 1973; fortnightly; English; Editor VISHWA NATH; circ. 95,000.

**Yojana:** Yojana Bhavan, Sansad Marg, New Delhi 110 001; tel. (11) 3710473; f. 1957; monthly; English, Tamil, Bengali, Marathi, Gujarati, Assamese, Malayalam, Telugu, Kannada, Punjabi, Urdu, Oriya and Hindi edns; Chief Editor Dr J. BHAGYALAKSHMI; circ. more than 100,000.

### Andhra Pradesh

Hyderabad

**Andhra Prabha Illustrated Weekly:** 591 Lower Tank Bund Rd, Express Centre, Domalaguda, Hyderabad 500 029; tel. (40) 233586; f. 1952; weekly; Telugu; Editor POTTURI VENKATESWARA RAO; circ. 26,100.

Secunderabad

**Andhra Bhoomi Sachitra Vara Patrika:** 36 Sarojini Devi Rd, Secunderabad 500 003; tel. (842) 7802346; fax (842) 7805256; f. 1977; weekly; Telugu; Editor T. VENKATRAM REDDY; circ. 59,000.

Vijayawada

**Andhra Jyoti Sachitra Vara Patrika:** Vijayawada 520 010; tel. (866) 474532; f. 1967; weekly; Telugu; Editor PURANAM SUBRAMANYA SARMA; circ. 59,000.

**Bala Jyoti:** Labbipet, Vijayawada 520 010; tel. (866) 474532; f. 1980; monthly; Telugu; Assoc. Editor A. SASIKANT SATAKARNI; circ. 12,500.

**Jyoti Chitra:** Andhra Jyoti Bldgs, Vijayawada 520 010; tel. (866) 474532; f. 1977; weekly; Telugu; Editor T. KUTUMBA RAO; circ. 20,100.

**Swati Saparivara Patrika:** Anil Bldgs, Suryaraopet, POB 339, Vijayawada 520 002; tel. (866) 431862; fax (866) 430433; e-mail swati@md3.vsnl.net.in; f. 1984; weekly; Telugu; Editor VEMURI BALARAM; circ. 245,692.

**Vanita Jyoti:** Labbipet, POB 712, Vijayawada 520 010; tel. (866) 474532; f. 1978; monthly; Telugu; Asst Editor J. SATYANARAYANA; circ. 13,100.

### Assam

Guwahati

**Agradoot:** Agradoot Bhavan, Dispur, Guwahati 781 006; tel. (361) 561923; fax (361) 560655; f. 1971; bi-weekly; Assamese; Editor K. S. DEKA; circ. 41,212.

**Asam Bani:** Tribune Bldg, Guwahati 781 003; tel. (361) 541356; fax (361) 540594; e-mail webmaster@assamtribune.com; internet www.assamtribune.com; f. 1955; weekly; Assamese; Editor DILIP CHANDAN; circ. 13,200.

### Bihar

Patna

**Anand Digest:** Govind Mitra Rd, Patna 800 004; tel. (612) 656557; fax (612) 225192; f. 1981; monthly; Hindi; family magazine; Editor Dr S. S. SINGH; circ. 44,500.

**Balak:** Govind Mitra Rd, POB 5, Patna 800 004; tel. (612) 650341; f. 1926; monthly; Hindi; children's; Editor S. R. SARAN; circ. 32,000.

### Gujarat

Ahmedabad

**Akhand Anand:** Anand Bhavan, Relief Rd, POB 123, Ahmedabad 380 001; tel. (79) 357482; f. 1947; monthly; Gujarati; Pres. ANAND AMIN; Editor PRAKASH N. SHAH; circ. 10,000.

**Chitralok:** Gujarat Samachar Bhavan, Khanpur, POB 254, Ahmedabad 380 001; tel. (79) 5504010; fax (79) 5502000; f. 1952; weekly; Gujarati; films; Man. Editor SHREYANS S. SHAH; circ. 20,000.

**Sakhi:** Sakhi Publications, Jai Hind Press Bldg, nr Gujarat Chamber, Ashram Rd, Navrangpura, Ahmedabad 380 009; tel. (79) 6581734; fax (79) 6587681; f. 1984; fortnightly; Gujarati; women's; Man. Editor NITA Y. SHAH; Editor Y. N. SHAH; circ. 10,000.

**Shree:** Gujarat Samachar Bhavan, Khanpur, Ahmedabad 380 001; tel. (79) 5504010; fax (79) 5502000; f. 1964; weekly; Gujarati; women's; Editor SMRUTIBEN SHAH; circ. 20,000.

**Stree:** Sandesh Bhavan, Gheekanta, POB 151, Ahmedabad 380 001; tel. (79) 5624241; fax (79) 5624392; e-mail sandesh@adl.vsnl.net.in; 1962; weekly; Gujarati; Jt Editors RITABEN PATEL, LILABEN PATEL; circ. 63,900.

**Zagmag:** Gujarat Samachar Bhavan, Khanpur, Ahmedabad 380 001; tel. (79) 22821; f. 1952; weekly; Gujarati; for children; Editor BAHUBALI S. SHAH; circ. 38,000.

Rajkot

**Amruta:** Jai Hind Publications, Jai Hind Press Bldg, Babubhai Shah Marg, Rajkot 360 001; tel. (281) 440513; fax (281) 448677; f. 1967; weekly; Gujarati; films; Editor Y. N. SHAH; circ. 27,000.

**Niranjan:** Jai Hind Publications, Jai Hind Press Bldg, Babubhai Shah Marg, Rajkot 360 001; tel. (281) 440517; fax (281) 448677; f. 1972; fortnightly; Gujarati; children's; Editor N. R. SHAH; circ. 15,000.

**Parmarth:** Jai Hind Publications, Jai Hind Press Bldg, Babubhai Shah Marg, Rajkot 360 001; tel. (281) 440511; fax (281) 448677; monthly; Gujarati; philosophy and religion; Editor Y. N. SHAH; circ. 30,000.

**Phulwadi:** Jai Hind Publications, Jai Hind Press Bldg, Babubhai Shah Marg, Rajkot 360 001; tel. (281) 440513; fax (281) 448677; f. 1967; weekly; Gujarati; for children; Editor Y. N. SHAH; circ. 27,000.

### Karnataka

Bangalore

**Mayura:** 75 Mahatma Gandhi Rd, Bangalore 560 001; tel. (80) 5588999; fax (80) 5587179; f. 1968; monthly; Kannada; Editor-in-Chief K. N. HARI KUMAR; circ. 55,300.

**New Leader:** 93 North Rd, St Mary's Town, Bangalore 560 005; f. 1887; weekly; English; Editor Rt Rev. HERMAN D'SOUZA; circ. 10,000.

**Prajamata:** North Anjaneya Temple Rd, Basavangudi, Bangalore 560 004; tel. (80) 602481; f. 1931; weekly; Kannada; news and current affairs; Chief Editor G. V. ANJI; circ. 28,377.

**Sudha:** 66 Mahatma Gandhi Rd, Bangalore 560 001; tel. (80) 5588999; fax (80) 5587179; f. 1965; weekly; Kannada; Editor-in-Chief K. N. HARI KUMAR; circ. 130,500.

Manipal

**Taranga:** Udayavani Bldg, Press Corner, Manipal 576 119; tel. (8252) 70845; fax (8252) 70563; f. 1983; weekly; Kannada; Editor S. K. GULVADY; circ. 126,100.

Mysore

**The Indian Mineralogist:** Mineralogical Society of India, Department of Geology, Manasagangotri, Mysore 570 006; tel. 514144; twice a year.

### Kerala

Kottayam

**Balarama:** MM Publications Ltd, POB 226, Erayilkadavu, Kottayam 686 001; tel. (481) 563721; fax (481) 564393; e-mail mmpubls@md3.vsnl.net.in; f. 1972; children's weekly; Malayalam; Chief Editor BINA PHILIP MATHEW; Senior Man. V. SAJEEV GEORGE; circ. 304,948.

**Malayala Manorama:** K. K. Rd, POB 26, Kottayam 686 001; tel. (481) 563646; fax (481) 562479; e-mail editor@malayalamanorama.com; internet www.malayalamanorama.com; f. 1937; weekly; Malayalam; also publ. from Kozhikode; Man. Dir and Editor MAMMEN MATHEW; Chief Editor MAMMEN VARGHESE; combined circ. 1,111,059.

**Manorajyam:** Manorajyam Bldg, M. C. Rd, Kottayam 686 039; tel. (481) 61203; f. 1967; weekly; Malayalam; Publr R. KALYANARAMAN; circ. 50,900.

**Vanitha:** MM Publications Ltd, POB 226, Erayilkadavu, Kottayam 686 001; tel. (481) 563721; fax (481) 564393; e-mail mmpubls@md3.vsnl.net.in; f. 1975; women's fortnightly; Malayalam; Chief Editor Mrs K. M. MATHEW; Senior Man. V. SAJEEV GEORGE; circ. 368,975.

**The Week:** Malayala Manorama Co Ltd, K. K. Rd, POB 26, Kottayam 686 001; tel. (481) 563646; fax (481) 562479; e-mail editor@theweek.com; internet www.the_week.com; f. 1982; weekly; English; current affairs; Chief Editor MAMMEN MATHEW; circ. 131,355.

Kozhikode

**Arogya Masika:** Mathrubhumi Bldgs, K. P. Kesava Menon Rd, Kozhikode 673 001; tel. (495) 366655; fax (495) 366656; e-mail mathrclt@md2.vsnl.net.in; monthly; Malayalam; health; Man. Editor P. V. CHANDRAN; circ. 82,200.

**Chitrabhumi:** Mathrubhumi Bldgs, K. P. Kesava Menon Rd, Kozhikode 673 001; tel. (495) 366655; fax (495) 366656; weekly; Malayalam; films; Editor M. T. VASUDEVAN NAIR; circ. 41,700.

**Grihalakshmi:** Mathrubhumi Bldgs, K. P. Kesava Menon Rd, POB 46, Kozhikode 673 001; tel. and fax (495) 366655; e-mail mathrclt@md2.vsnl.net.in; internet www.mathrubhumi.com; f. 1979; monthly; Malayalam; women's; Editor K. K. SREEDHARAN NAIR; circ. 78,500.

**Mathrubhumi Illustrated Weekly:** Mathrubhumi Bldgs, K. P. Kesava Menon Rd, POB 46, Kozhikode 673 001; tel. (495) 366655; fax (495) 56656; f. 1923; weekly; Malayalam; Editor M. T. VASUDEVAN NAIR; circ. 53,000.

**Sports Masika:** Mathrubhumi Bldgs, K. P. Kesava Menon Rd, Kozhikode 673 001; tel. (495) 366655; fax (495) 366656; monthly; Malayalam; sport; Exec. Editor V. RAJAGOPAL; circ. 44,000.

Quilon

**Karala Sabdam:** Thevally, Quilon 691 009; tel. (474) 72403; fax (474) 740710; f. 1962; weekly; Malayalam; Man. Editor B. A. RAJA KRISHNAN; circ. 66,600.

**Nana:** Therally, Quilon 691 009; tel. 2403; weekly; Malayalam; Man. Editor B. A. RAJAKRISHNAN; circ. 50,500.

Thiruvananthapuram

**Kalakaumudi:** Kaumudi Bldgs, Pettah, Thiruvananthapuram 695 024; tel. (471) 443531; fax (471) 461985; e-mail sreeni@giasmd01.vsnl.net.in; f. 1975; weekly; Malayalam; Chief Editor M. S. MANI; Gen. Man. ABRAHAM EAPEN; circ. 73,000.

**Vellinakshatram:** Kaumudi Bldgs, Pettah, Thiruvananthapuram 695 024; tel. (471) 443531; fax (471) 477870; e-mail kalakaumudi@vsnl.com; internet www.vellinakshatram.com; f. 1987; film weekly; Malayalam; Editor PRASAD LAKSHMANAN; Man. Editor SUKUMARAN MANI; circ. 55,000.

### Madhya Pradesh

Bhopal

**Krishak Jagat:** 14 Indira Press Complex, M. P. Nagar, POB 3, Bhopal 462 001; tel. (755) 768452; fax (755) 510334; f. 1946; weekly; Hindi; agriculture; Chief Editor VIJAY KUMAR BONDRIYA; Editor SUNIL GANGRADE; circ. 51,436.

### Maharashtra

Mumbai (Bombay)

**Abhiyaan:** Abhiyaan Press and Publications Ltd, 4A/B, Government Industrial Estate, Charkop, Kandivli (W), Mumbai 400 067; tel. (22) 8687515; fax (22) 8680991; f. 1986; weekly; Gujarati; Dir DILIP PATEL; Editor VINOD PANDYA; circ. 140,900.

**Arogya Sanjeevani:** C-14 Royal Industrial Estate, 5-B Naigaum Cross Rd, Wadala, Mumbai 400 031; tel. (22) 4138723; fax (22) 4133610; e-mail woman@bom3.vsnl.net.in; f. 1990; quarterly; Hindi; Editor VAIDYA MISHRA; circ. 50,098.

**Auto India:** Nirmal, Nariman Point, Mumbai 400 021; tel. (22) 2024422; fax (22) 2875671; f. 1994; monthly; circ. 102,300.

**Bhavan's Journal:** Bharatiya Vidya Bhavan, Mumbai 400 007; tel. (22) 3634462; fax (22) 3630058; f. 1954; fortnightly; English; literary; Man. Editor J. H. DAVE; Editor S. RAMAKRISHNAN; circ. 25,000.

**Blitz News Magazine:** 17/17H Cawasji Patel St, Fort, Mumbai 400 001; tel. (22) 2040720; fax (22) 2047984; f. 1941; weekly; English; Editor-in-Chief M. J. AKBAR; combined circ. 419,000.

**Bombay Samachar:** Red House, Sayed Brelvi Rd, Mumbai 400 001; tel. (22) 2045531; fax (22) 2046642; f. 1822; weekly; Gujarati; Editor JEHANBUX D. DARUWALA; circ. 140,900.

**Business India:** Nirmal, 14th Floor, Nariman Point, Mumbai 400 021; tel. (22) 2024422; fax (22) 2875671; f. 1978; fortnightly; English; Publr ASHOK ADVANI; circ. 102,100.

**Business World:** 25–28 Atlanta, 2nd Floor, Nariman Point, Mumbai 400 021; tel. (22) 2851352; fax (22) 2870310; f. 1980; weekly; English; Man. Editor PARTHASARATHI SWAMI; Exec. Editor P. G. MATHAI; circ. 89,500.

**Chitralekha:** 62 Vaju Kotak Marg, Fort, Mumbai 400 001; tel. (22) 2614730; fax (22) 2615895; e-mail jee@bom2.vsnl.net.in; f. 1950 (Gujarati), f. 1989 (Marathi); weekly; Gujarati and Marathi; Editors MADHURI KOTAK, HARKISHAN MEHTA; circ. 294,900 (Gujarati), 120,600 (Marathi).

**Cine Blitz Film Monthly:** 17/17H Cawasji Patel St, Fort, Mumbai 400 001; tel. (22) 2044143; fax (22) 2047984; f. 1974; English; Editor RITA K. MEHTA; circ. 184,100.

**Dalal Street:** DSJ Communications Ltd, 105 Shreyas Bldg, New Link Rd, Andheri (W), Mumbai 400 057; tel. (22) 6293293; fax (22) 6291105; f. 1985; fortnightly; investment; Editor PRATAP PADODE.

**Debonair:** Maurya Publications (Pvt) Ltd, 20/21, Juhu Centaur Hotel, Juhu Tara Rd, POB 18292, Mumbai 400 049; tel. (22) 6116631; fax (22) 6152677; e-mail maurya@bom3.vsnl.net.in; f. 1972; monthly; English; Publr CLEYTUS COELHO; CEO JOSEPH MASCARENHAS; circ. 110,000.

**Economic and Political Weekly:** Hitkari House, 284 Shahid Bhagatsingh Rd, Mumbai 400 001; tel. (22) 2696073; fax (22) 2696072; e-mail epw@vsnl.com; internet www.epw.org; f. 1966; English; Editor KRISHNA RAJ; circ. 132,800.

**Femina:** Times of India Bldg, Dr Dadabhai Naoroji Rd, Mumbai 400 001; tel. (22) 2620271; fax (22) 2620985; f. 1959; fortnightly; English; Editor SATHYA SARAN; circ. 132,000.

**Filmfare:** Times of India Bldg, Dr Dadabhai Naoroji Rd, Mumbai 400 001; tel. (22) 2620271; fax (22) 2620144; internet www.filmfare.com; f. 1952; fortnightly; English; Editor KHALID MOHAMED; circ. 171,300.

**G:** 62 Vaju Kotak Marg, Fort, Mumbai 400 001; tel. (22) 2614730; fax (22) 2615395; e-mail jee@bom2.vsnl.net.in; monthly; English; Editor BHAWNA SOMAYA; circ. 60,574.

**Gentleman:** Teritex Business Service Centre, B-201 Teritex Bldg, opp. Chandivli Petrol Pump, Saki Vihar Rd, Saki Naka Andheri (East), Mumbai 400 072; tel. (22) 8571490; fax (22) 8572447; e-mail gent@bom3.vsnl.net.in; internet www.wbiznetgroup.com; f. 1980; monthly; English; Editor PREMNATH NAIR (acting).

**Indian PEN:** Theosophy Hall, 40 New Marine Lines, Mumbai 400 020; tel. (22) 2032175; e-mail ambika.sirkar@gems.vsnl.net.in; f. 1934; quarterly; organ of Indian Centre of the International PEN; Editor RANJIT HOSKOTE.

**Janmabhoomi-Pravasi:** Janmabhoomi Bhavan, Janmabhoomi Marg, Fort, POB 62, Mumbai 400 001; tel. (22) 2870831; fax (22) 2874097; e-mail bhoomi@bom3.vsnl.net.in; f. 1939; weekly; Gujarati; Propr Saurashtra Trust; Editor KUNDAN VYAS; circ. 102,687.

**JEE:** 62 Vaju Kotak Marg, Fort, Mumbai 400 001; tel. (22) 2614730; fax (22) 2615895; e-mail jee@bom2.vsnl.net.in; fortnightly; Gujarati, Hindi and Marathi; Editor MADHURI KOTAK; circ. 79,100 (Gujarati), 76,127 (Hindi), 30,200 (Marathi).

**Meri Saheli:** C-14 Royal Industrial Estate, 5-B Naigaum Cross Rd, Wadala, Mumbai 400 031; tel. (22) 4182797; fax (22) 4133610; e-mail woman@bom3.vsnl.net.in; f. 1987; monthly; Hindi; Editor HEMA MALINI; circ. 267,994.

**Movie:** Mahalaxmi Chambers, 5th Floor, 22 Bhulabhai Desai Rd, Mumbai 400 026; tel. (22) 4935636; fax (22) 4938406; f. 1981; monthly; English; Editor DINESH RAHEJA; circ. 70,700.

**New Woman:** C-14 Royal Industrial Estate, 5-B Naigaum Cross Rd, Wadala, Mumbai 400 031; tel. (22) 4138723; fax (22) 4133610; e-mail woman@bom3.vsnl.net.in; f. 1996; monthly; English; Editor HEMA MALINI; circ. 77,164.

**Onlooker:** Free Press House, 215 Free Press Journal Marg, Nariman Point, Mumbai 400 021; tel. (22) 2874566; f. 1939; fortnightly; English; news magazine; Exec. Editor K. SRINIVASAN; circ. 61,000.

**Reader's Digest:** Orient House, Adi Marzban Path, Ballard Estate, Mumbai 400 001; tel. (22) 2617291; fax (22) 2613347; f. 1954; monthly; English; Publr and Editor ASHOK MAHADEVAN; circ. 389,378.

**Savvy:** Magna Publishing Co Ltd, Magna House, 100/E Old Prabhadevi Rd, Prabhadevi, Mumbai 400 025; tel. (22) 4362270; fax (22) 4306523; f. 1984; monthly; English; Editor USHA RADHAKRISHNAN; circ. 112,800.

**Screen:** D-2, Podar Chambers, Mathuradas Mill Compound, Ideal Industrial Estate, Lower Parel (W), Mumbai 400 013; tel. (22) 4046420; fax (22) 4920657; f. 1951; film weekly; English; Editor UDAYA TARA NAYAR; circ. 90,000.

**Society:** Magna Publishing Co Ltd, Magna House, 100/E Old Prabhadevi Rd, Prabhadevi, Mumbai 400 025; tel. (22) 4362270; fax (22) 4306523; f. 1979; monthly; English; Editor LALITHA GOPALAN; circ. 95,000.

**Star and Style:** Maurya Publications (Pvt) Ltd, 20/21, Juhu Centaur Hotel, Juhu Tara Rd, POB 18292, Mumbai 400 049; tel. (22) 6116632; fax (22) 6152677; e-mail maurya@bom3.vsnl.net.in; f. 1965; bimonthly; English; film; Publr/Editor NISHI PREM; circ. 60,000.

**Stardust:** Magna Publishing Co Ltd, Magna House, 100/E Old Prabhadevi Rd, Prabhadevi, Mumbai 400 025; tel. (22) 4362270; fax (22) 4306523; e-mail stardust@bom1.vsnl.net.in; f. 1985; monthly; English; Editor SONALI KOTNIS; circ. 298,300.

**Vyapar:** Janmabhoomi Bhavan, Janmabhoomi Marg, POB 62, Fort, Mumbai 400 001; tel. (22) 2870831; fax (22) 2874097; f. 1949 (Gujarati), 1987 (Hindi); Gujarati (2 a week) and Hindi (weekly); commerce; Propr Saurashtra Trust; Editor SHASHIKANT J. VASANI; circ. 33,100 (Gujarati), 19,405 (Hindi).

**Yuvdarhsan:** c/o Warsha Publications Pvt Ltd, Warsha House, 6 Zakaria Bunder Rd, Sewri, Mumbai 400 015; tel. (22) 441843; f. 1975; weekly; Gujarati; Editor and Man. Dir R. M. BHUTTA; circ. 18,600.

Nagpur

**All India Reporter:** AIR Ltd, Congress Nagar, POB 209, Nagpur 440 012; tel. (712) 34321; f. 1914; monthly; English; law journal; Chief Editor V. R. MANOHAR; circ. 36,000.

### Rajasthan

Jaipur

**Balhans:** Kesargarh, Jawahar Lal Nehru Marg, Jaipur 302 004; tel. (141) 561582; fax (141) 566011; e-mail ads@rajasthanpatrika.com; internet www.rajasthanpatrika.com; fortnightly; Hindi; circ. 60,200.

**Itwari Patrika:** Kesargarh, Jawahar Lal Nehru Marg, Jaipur 302 004; tel. (141) 561582; fax (141) 566011; weekly; Hindi; circ. 21,600.

**Rashtradoot Saptahik:** HO, M.I. Rd, POB 30, Jaipur 302 001; tel. (141) 372634; fax (141) 373513; f. 1983; Hindi; also publ. from Kota and Bikaner; Chief Editor and Man. Editor RAJESH SHARMA; CEO SOMESH SHARMA; combined circ. 167,500.

### Tamil Nadu

Chennai (Madras)

**Aishwarya:** 325 N. S. K. Salai, Chennai 600 024; tel. (44) 422064; f. 1990; weekly; Tamil; general; Editor K. NATARAJAN; circ. 20,000.

**Ambulimama:** 188 N. S. K. Salai, Vadapalani, Chennai 600 026; f. 1947; monthly; Tamil; Editor NAGI REDDI; circ. 60,000.

**Ambuli Ammavan:** 188 N. S. K. Salai, Vadapalani, Chennai 600 026; f. 1970; children's monthly; Malayalam; Editor NAGI REDDI; circ. 10,000.

**Ananda Vikatan:** 757 Anna Salai, Chennai 600 002; tel. (44) 8524054; fax (44) 8523819; e-mail editor@vikatan.com; internet www.vikatan.com; f. 1924; weekly; Tamil; Editor and Man. Dir S. BALASUBRAMANIAN; circ. 174,100.

**Chandamama:** 188 N. S. K. Salai, Vadapalani, Chennai 600 026; f. 1947; children's monthly; Hindi, Gujarati, Telugu, Kannada, English, Sanskrit, Bengali, Assamese; Editor NAGI REDDI; combined circ. 410,200.

**Chandoba:** 188 N. S. K. Salai, Vadapalani, Chennai 600 026; f. 1952; monthly; Marathi; Editor NAGI REDDI; circ. 92,000.

**Devi:** 727 Anna Salai, Chennai 600 006; tel. (44) 8521428; f. 1979; weekly; Tamil; Editor B. RAMACHANDRA ADITYAN; circ. 136,500.

**Dinamani Kadir:** Express Estate, Mount Rd, Chennai 600 002; tel. (44) 8520751; fax (44) 8524500; weekly; Editor G. KASTURI RANGAN (acting); circ. 55,000.

**Frontline:** Kasturi Bldgs, 859/860 Anna Salai, Chennai 600 002; tel. (44) 8413344; fax (44) 8415325; f. 1984; fortnightly; English; Publr S. RANGARAJAN; Editor N. RAM; circ. 64,000.

**Hindu International Edition:** 859/860 Anna Salai, Chennai 600 002; tel. (44) 8535067; fax (44) 8535325; f. 1975; weekly; English; Editor N. RAVI; circ. 4,760.

**Jahnamamu (Oriya):** 188 N. S. K. Salai, Vadapalani, Chennai 600 026; f. 1972; children's monthly; Editor NAGI REDDI; circ. 110,000.

**Junior Post:** 757 Anna Salai, Chennai 600 002; tel. (44) 8524054; fax (44) 8523819; e-mail editor@vikatan.com; internet www.vikatan.com; f. 1988; weekly; English; Editor and Man. Dir S. BALASUBRAMANIAN; circ. 35,000.

**Junior Vikatan:** 757 Anna Salai, Chennai 600 002; tel. (44) 8524054; fax (44) 8523819; e-mail editor@vikatan.com; internet www.vikatan.com; f. 1983; 2 times a week; Tamil; Editor and Man. Dir S. BALASUBRAMANIAN; circ. 209,900.

**Kalai Magal:** POB 604, Chennai 600 004; tel. (44) 843099; f. 1932; monthly; Tamil; literary and cultural; Editor R. NARAYANASWAMY; circ. 10,200.

**Kalkandu:** 151 Purasawalkam High Rd, Chennai; f. 1948; weekly; Tamil; Editor TAMIL VANAN; circ. 82,500.

**Kalki:** 47 Jawaharlal Nehru Rd, Ekkaduthangal, Chennai 600 097; tel. (44) 2345621; e-mail kalkiweekly@vsnl.com; internet www.kalkiweekly.com; f. 1941; weekly; Tamil; literary and cultural; Editor SEETHA RAVI; circ. 62,487.

**Kumudam:** 151 Purasawalkam High Rd, Chennai 600 010; tel. (44) 6422146; fax (44) 6425041; e-mail kumudam@giasmd01.vsnl.net.in; f. 1947; weekly; Tamil; Editor Dr S. A. P. JAWAHAR PALANIAPPAN; circ. 460,500.

**Kungumam:** 93A Kodambakkam High Rd, Chennai 600 034; tel. (44) 8268177; f. 1978; weekly; Tamil; Editor PARASAKTHI; circ. 159,800.

**Malaimathi:** Chennai; f. 1958; weekly; Tamil; Editor P. S. ELANGO; circ. 57,500.

**Muththaram:** 93A Kogambakkam High Rd, Chennai 600 034; tel. (44) 476306; f. 1980; weekly; Tamil; Editor Sri PARASAKTHI; circ. 30,700.

**Pesum Padam:** 325 N. S. K. Salai, Chennai 600 024; tel. (44) 422064; f. 1942; monthly; Tamil; films; Man. Editor K. NATARAJAN; circ. 34,700.

**Picturpost:** 325 N. S. K. Salai, Chennai 600 024; tel. (44) 422064; f. 1943; monthly; English; films; Man. Editor K. NATARAJAN; circ. 11,000.

**Rajam:** 325 N. S. K. Salai, Chennai 600 024; tel. (44) 422064; f. 1986; monthly; Tamil; women's interests; Man. Dir and Editor K. NATARAJAN; circ. 32,677.

**Rani Muthu:** 1091 Periyar E.V.R. High Rd, Chennai 600 007; tel. (44) 5324771; f. 1969; monthly; Tamil; Editor A. MA. SAMY; circ. 82,800.

**Rani Weekly:** 1091 Periyar E.V.R. High Rd, Chennai 600 007; tel. (44) 5324771; e-mail rani.chen@gems.vsnl.net.in; f. 1962; Tamil; Editor A. MA SAMY; circ. 198,486.

**Sportstar:** Kasturi Bldgs, 859/860 Anna Salai, Chennai 600 002; tel. (44) 8413344; fax (44) 8415325; f. 1978; weekly; English; Publr S. RANGARAJAN; Editor N. RAM; circ. 88,604.

**Thuglak:** 46 Greenways Rd, Chennai 600 028; tel. (44) 4936913; fax (44) 4936915; f. 1970; weekly; Tamil; Editor CHO S. RAMASWAMY; circ. 149,100.

Vellore

**Madha Jothidam:** 3 Arasamaram St, Vellore 632 004; f. 1949; monthly; Tamil; astrology; Editor and Publr A. K. THULASIRAMAN; circ. 8,000.

### Uttar Pradesh

Allahabad

**Alokpaat:** Mitra Prakashan (Pvt) Ltd, 281 Muthiganj, Allahabad 211 003; tel. (532) 606693; fax (532) 601156; f. 1986; monthly; Bengali; Editor ALOKE MITRA; circ. 33,700.

**Manohar Kahaniyan:** Mitra Prakashan (Pvt) Ltd, 281 Muthiganj, Allahabad 211 003; tel. (532) 606693; fax (532) 601156; f. 1940; monthly; Hindi; Editor ALOKE MITRA; circ. 301,200.

**Manorama:** Mitra Parkashan (Pvt) Ltd, 281 Muthiganj, Allahabad 211 003; tel. (532) 606694; fax (532) 606379; f. 1924 (Hindi), 1986 (Bengali); fortnightly (Hindi), monthly (Bengali); Editor ALOKE MITRA; circ. 176,000 (Hindi), 33,000 (Bengali).

**Maya:** Mitra Prakashan (Pvt) Ltd, 281 Muthiganj, Allahabad 211 003; tel. (532) 606694; fax (532) 601156; f. 1929; fortnightly; Hindi; Editor ALOKE MITRA; circ. 175,200.

**Nutan Kahaniyan:** 15 Sheo Charan Lal Rd, Allahabad 211 003; tel. (532) 400612; f. 1975; Hindi; monthly; Chief Editor K. K. BHARGAVA; circ. 167,500.

**Satyakatha:** Mitra Prakashan (Pvt) Ltd, 281 Muthiganj, Allahabad 211 003; tel (532) 606693; fax (532) 606379; f. 1974; monthly; Hindi; Editor ALOKE MITRA; circ. 98,100.

### West Bengal

Kolkata (Calcutta)

**All India Appointment Gazette:** 7 Old Court House St, Kolkata 700 001; tel. (33) 2206663; fax (33) 2296548; f. 1973; 2 a week; English; Editor S. C. TALUKDAR; circ. 158,900.

**Anandalok:** 6 Prafulla Sarkar St, Kolkata 700 001; tel. (33) 278000; f. 1975; fortnightly; Bengali; film; Editor DULENDRA BHOWMIK; circ. 49,600.

**Anandamela:** 6 Prafulla Sarkar St, Kolkata 700 001; tel. (33) 278000. 1975; monthly; Bengali; juvenile; Editor DEBASHIS BANDOPADHYAY; circ. 51,400.

**Contemporary Tea Time:** 1/2 Old Court House Corner, POB 14, Kolkata 700 001; tel. (33) 2200099; fax (33) 2203053; e-mail ctlcal@cal.vsnl.net.in; f. 1988; quarterly; English; tea industry; Exec. Editor GITA NARAYANI; circ. 5,000.

**Desh:** 6 Prafulla Sarkar St, Kolkata 700 001; tel. (33) 274880; f. 1933; fortnightly; Bengali; literary; Editor AMITABHA CHOUDHURY; circ. 69,400.

**Investment Preview:** 7 Old Court House St, Kolkata 700 001; tel. (33) 2206663; fax (33) 296548; f. 1992; weekly; English; Editor S. C. TALUKDAR; circ. 53,845.

**Khela:** 96 Raja Rammohan Sarani, Kolkata 700 009; tel. (33) 3509803; f. 1981; weekly; Bengali; sports; Editor ASOKE DASGUPTA; circ. 13,500.

**Naba Kallol:** 11 Jhamapookur Lane, Kolkata 700 009; tel. (33) 354294; f. 1960; monthly; Bengali; Editor P. K. MAZUMDAR; circ. 32,700.

**Neetee:** 4 Sukhlal Johari Lane, Kolkata; f. 1955; weekly; English; Editor M. P. PODDAR.

**Prabuddha Bharata** (Awakened India): 5 Dehi Entally Rd, Kolkata 700 014; tel. (33) 2440898; fax (33) 2450050; e-mail advaita@vsnl.com; internet www.education.vsnl.com/advaita; f. 1896; monthly; art, culture, religion and philosophy; Publr SWAMI BODHASARANANDA; circ. 8,000.

**Sananda:** 6 Prafulla Sarkar St, Kolkata 700 001; tel. (33) 278000; f. 1986; fortnightly; Bengali; Editor APARNA SEN; circ. 79,300.

**Saptahik Bartaman:** 76A J. C. Bose Rd, Kolkata 700 014; tel. (33) 2448208; fax (33) 2441215; f. 1988; weekly; Bengali; Editor BARUN SENGUPTA; circ. 106,600.

**Screen:** P-5, Kalakar St, Kolkata 700 070; f. 1960; weekly; Hindi; Editor M. P. PODDAR; circ. 58,000.

**Statesman:** Statesman House, 4 Chowringhee Sq., Kolkata 700 001; tel. (33) 271000; fax (33) 270118; f. 1875; overseas weekly; English; Editor-in-Chief C. R. IRANI.

**Suktara:** 11 Jhamapooker Lane, Kolkata 700 009; tel. (33) 355294; f. 1948; monthly; Bengali; juvenile; Editor M. MAJUMDAR; circ. 36,500.

**Sunday:** 6 Prafulla Sarkar St, Kolkata 700 001; tel. (33) 274880; f. 1973; weekly; English; Editor VIR SANGHVI; circ. 29,500.

### NEWS AGENCIES

**Press Trust of India Ltd:** 4 Parliament St, New Delhi 110 001; tel. (11) 3716621; fax (11) 3718714; f. 1947, re-established 1978; Chair. R. LAKSHMIPATHY; Gen. Man. M. K. RAZDAN.

**United News of India (UNI):** 9 Rafi Marg, New Delhi 110 001; tel. (11) 3715898; fax (11) 3716211; e-mail uninet@del2.vsnl.net.in; f. 1961; Indian language news in Hindi and Urdu; English wire service; World TV News Service (UNISCAN); photograph service; graphics service; special services covering banking and business; brs in 90 centres in India; Chair. SHOBHA SUBRAHMANYAN; Gen. Man. and Chief Editor VIRENDER MOHAN.

#### Foreign Bureaux

**Agence France-Presse (AFP):** 410 Surya Kiran Bldg, 19 Kasturba Gandhi Marg, New Delhi 110 001; tel. (11) 3712963; fax (11) 3311105; Bureau Chief PASCAL TAILLANDIER.

**Agencia EFE** (Spain): 72 Jor Bagh, New Delhi 110 003; tel. (11) 4618092; fax (11) 4615013; Correspondent ISABEL CALLEJA SOLERA.

**Agenzia Nazionale Stampa Associata (ANSA)** (Italy): C-179 Defence Colony, New Delhi 110 024; tel. (11) 4615004; fax (11) 4640190; e-mail natale@giasdl01.vsnl.net.in; Bureau Chief BENIAMINO NATALE.

**Associated Press (AP)** (USA): 6B Jor Bagh Lane, New Delhi 110 003; tel. (11) 4628506; fax (11) 4616870; Bureau Chief ARTHUR MAX.

**Deutsche Presse-Agentur (dpa)** (Germany): 39 Golf Links, New Delhi 110 003; tel. (11) 4617792; fax (11) 4635772; e-mail dpadelhi@del2.vsnl.net.in; Chief Rep. JÜRGEN HEIN.

**Informatsionnoye Telegrafnoye Agentstvo Rossii—Telegrafnoye Agentstvo Suverennykh Stran (ITAR—TASS)** (Russia): E-5/4 Vasant Vihar, New Delhi 110 057; tel. (11) 6886232; fax (11) 6876233; Bureau Chief LEONID KOTOV.

**Inter Press Service (IPS)** (Italy): 49 (F.F.) Defence Colony Market, New Delhi 110 024; tel. (11) 4634154; fax (11) 4624725.

**Islamic Republic News Agency (IRNA)** (Iran): 11 Hemkunt Colony, New Delhi 110 048; tel. (11) 6446866; fax (11) 6221529; Bureau Chief MOHD FAZELI.

**Jiji Tsushin** (Japan): Apt No. 1/B, 13 Paschimi Nagar, Vasant Vihar, New Delhi 110 057; tel. (11) 6879432; fax (11) 6113578; Correspondent RYOGO HORI.

**Kyodo News Service** (Japan): PTI Bldg, 1st Floor, 4 Parliament St, New Delhi 110 001; tel. (11) 3711954; fax (11) 3718756; Bureau Chief SHINGO KINIWA.

**Reuters** (UK): 1 Kautilya Marg, Chanakyapuri, New Delhi 110 021; tel. (11) 3012024; fax (11) 3014043; Bureau Chief JOHN CHALMERS (acting).

**United Press International (UPI)** (USA): 706, Sector 7B, Chandigarh 160 019; tel. (172) 772365; fax (172) 772366; e-mail hsnanda@ch1.dot.net.in; Bureau Chief HARBAKSH SINGH NANDA.

**Xinhua (New China) News Agency** (People's Republic of China): 50D, Shanti Path, Chanakyapuri, New Delhi 110 021; tel. (11) 601886; Chief YAN FENG.

The following agencies are also represented: Associated Press of Pakistan, A. P. Dow Jones, Bloomberg Business News, Depthnews, Knight-Ridder Financial News, Middle East News Agency and Viet Nam News Agency.

### CO-ORDINATING BODIES

**Press Information Bureau:** Shastri Bhavan, Dr Rajendra Prasad Rd, New Delhi 110 001; tel. (11) 3383643; f. 1946 to co-ordinate press affairs for the govt; represents newspaper managements, journalists, news agencies, parliament; has power to examine journalists under oath and may censor objectionable material; Prin. Information Officer N. J. KRISHNA.

**Registrar of Newspapers for India:** Ministry of Information and Broadcasting, West Block 8, Wing 2, Ramakrishna Puram, New Delhi 110 066; tel. (11) 608788; f. 1956 as a statutory body to collect press statistics; maintains a register of all Indian newspapers; Registrar G. D. BELIYA.

### PRESS ASSOCIATIONS

**All-India Newspaper Editors' Conference:** 36–37 Northend Complex, Rama Krishna Ashram Marg, New Delhi 110 001; tel. (11) 3364519; fax (11) 3716665; f. 1940; c. 400 mems; Pres. VISHWA BANDHU GUPTA; Secs MANAK CHOPRA, BISHAMBER NEWAR.

**The Foreign Correspondents' Club of South Asia:** AB-19 Mathura Rd, New Delhi 110 001; tel. (11) 3388535; 210 mems; Pres. L. E. THREUNE; Man. KIRAN KAPUR.

**Indian Federation of Working Journalists:** F-101, M.S. Apts, Kasturba Gandhi Marg, New Delhi 110 001; tel. (11) 3384956; fax (11) 3384650; f. 1950; 27,000 mems; Pres. K. VIKRAM RAO; Sec.-Gen. PARMANAND PANDEY.

**Indian Journalists' Association:** New Delhi; Pres. VIJAY DUTT; Gen. Sec. A. K. DHAR.

**Indian Languages Newspapers' Asscn:** Janmabhoomi Bhavan, Janmabhoomi Marg, POB 10029, Fort, Mumbai 400 001; tel. (22) 2870537; f. 1941; 320 mems; Pres. VIJAY KUMAR BONDRIYA; Hon. Gen. Secs PRADEEP G. DESHPANDE, KRISHNA SHEWDIKAR, LALIT SHRIMAL.

**Indian Newspaper Society:** INS Bldg, Rafi Marg, New Delhi 110 001; tel. (11) 3715401; fax (11) 3723800; e-mail indnews@nde.vsnl.net.in; f. 1939; 693 mems; Pres. SHOBHA SUBRAHMANYAM; Sec.-Gen. P. K. LAHIRI.

**Indian Small and Medium Newspapers' Federation:** New Delhi; Pres. PUSHPA PANDYA; Sec.-Gen. SUSHIL JHALANI.

**National Union of Journalists (India):** 7 Jantar Mantar Rd, 2nd Floor, New Delhi 110 001; tel. (11) 3368610; fax (11) 3368723; e-mail nujindia@ndf.vsnl.in; internet www.education.vsnl.com/nujindia; f. 1972; 12,000 mems; Pres. Dr N. K. TRIKHA; Sec.-Gen. GULAB BATRA.

**Press Institute of India:** Sapru House Annexe, Barakhamba Rd, New Delhi 110 001; tel. (11) 3318066; fax (11) 3311975; e-mail presinst@sansad.nic.in; f. 1963; 29 mem. newspapers and other orgs; Chair. NARESH MOHAN; Dir AJIT BHATTACHARJEA.

## Publishers

### Delhi and New Delhi

**Affiliated East-West Press (Pvt) Ltd:** G-1/16 Ansari Rd, Daryaganj, New Delhi 110 002; tel. (11) 3264180; fax (11) 3260538; e-mail affiliat@vsnl.com; textbooks and reference books; Dirs SUNNY MALIK, KAMAL MALIK.

**All India Educational Supply Co:** 17 Sri Ram Bldg, Jawahar Nagar, POB 2147, Delhi 110 007; tel. (11) 2914448; fax (11) 6866588; f. 1944; maps, charts and teaching aids; CEO R. D. AGGARWAL.

**Allied Publishers Ltd:** 13/14 Asaf Ali Rd, New Delhi 110 002; tel. (11) 3239001; fax (11) 3235967; e-mail aplnd@del2.vsnl.net.in; academic and general; Man. Dir S. M. SACHDEV.

**Amerind Publishing Co (Pvt) Ltd:** Oxford Bldg, N-56 Connaught Circus, New Delhi 110 001; tel. (11) 3314957; fax (11) 3322639; f. 1970; offices at Kolkata, Mumbai and New York; scientific and technical; Dirs MOHAN PRIMLANI, GULAB PRIMLANI.

**Arnold Heinman Publishers (India) Pvt Ltd:** AB/9 Safdarjung Enclave, 1st Floor, New Delhi 110 029; tel. (11) 6883422; fax (11) 6877571; f. 1969 as Arnold Publishers (India) Pvt Ltd; literature and general; Man. Dir G. A. VAZIRANI.

**Atma Ram and Sons:** 1376 Kashmere Gate, POB 1429, Delhi 110 006; tel. (11) 2523082; f. 1909; scientific, technical, humanities, medical; Man. Dir S. PURI; Dir Y. PURI.

**B.I. Publications Pvt Ltd:** 13 Daryaganj, New Delhi 110 002; tel. (11) 3274443; fax (11) 3261290; f. 1959; academic, general and professional; Man. Dir R. D. BHAGAT.

**B.R. Publishing Corpn:** A-6, Nimri Commercial Centre, nr Bharat Nagar, Ashok Vihar, Phase-IV, Delhi 110 052; tel. (11) 7430113; fax (11) 7452453; a division of BRPC (India) Ltd; Man. Dir PRAVEEN MITTAL.

**S. Chand and Co Ltd:** Ram Nagar, POB 5733, New Delhi 110 055; tel. (11) 7772080; fax (11) 7777446; e-mail schandco@giasdl01.vsnl.net.in; internet www.schandgroup.com; f. 1917; educational and general in English and Hindi; also book exports and imports; Man. Dir RAJENDRA KUMAR GUPTA.

**Children's Book House:** A-4 Ring Rd, South Extension Part I, POB 3854, New Delhi 110 049; tel. (11) 4636030; fax (11) 4636011; e-mail neeta@giasdl01.vsnl.net.in; f. 1952; educational and general; Dir R. S. GUPTA.

**Children's Book Trust:** Nehru House, 4 Bahadur Shah Zafar Marg, New Delhi 110 002; tel. (11) 3316970; fax (11) 3721090; e-mail cbtnd@vsnl.com; internet www.childrensbooktrust.com; f. 1957; children's books in English and other Indian languages; Editor C. G. R. KURUP; Gen. Man. RAVI SHANKAR.

**Clarion Books:** G.T. Rd, Dilshad Garden, Delhi 110 095; tel. (11) 2297792; fax (11) 2282332; art books, Indology, environment; Dir MADHVI MALHOTRA.

**Concept Publishing Co:** A/15-16, Commercial Block, Mohan Garden, New Delhi 110 059; tel. (11) 5648039; fax (11) 5648053; f. 1975; geography, rural and urban development, education, sociology, economics, anthropology, agriculture, religion, history, law, philosophy, information sciences, ecology; Man. Dir ASHOK KUMAR MITTAL; Man. Editor ARVIND KUMAR MITTAL.

**Eurasia Publishing House (Pvt) Ltd:** Ram Nagar, New Delhi 110 055; tel (11) 7772080; fax (11) 7777446; f. 1964; educational in English and Hindi; Man. Dir RAJENDRA KUMAR GUPTA.

**Frank Bros and Co (Publishers) Ltd:** 4675A Ansari Rd, 21 Daryaganj, New Delhi 110 002; tel. (11) 3263393; fax (11) 3269032; e-mail frank@nda.vsnl.net.in; f. 1930; children's and educational books; Chair. R. C. GOVIL.

**Global Business Press:** GT Rd, 18–19 Dilshad Garden, Delhi 110 095; tel. (11) 2297792; fax (11) 2282332; business, management and computers; Dir SHEKHAR MALHOTRA.

**Heritage Publishers:** 32 Prakash Apartments, 5 Ansari Rd, Darya Ganj, New Delhi 110 002; tel. (11) 3266258; fax (11) 3263050; e-mail heritage@nda.vsnl.net.in; f. 1973; social sciences, art and architecture, technical, medical, scientific; Propr and Dir B. R. CHAWLA.

**Hind Pocket Books (Pvt) Ltd:** 18–19 Dilshad Garden, Delhi 110 095; tel. (11) 2297792; fax (11) 2282332; f. 1958; fiction and non-fiction paperbacks in English, Hindi, Punjabi, Malayalam and Urdu; Chair DINANATH MALHOTRA; Exec. Dir SHEKHAR MALHOTRA.

**Hindustan Publishing Corpn (India):** 4805/24 Bharat Ram Rd, Daryaganj, New Delhi 110 002; tel. (11) 3254401; fax (11) 6193511; e-mail hpc@hpc.cc; archaeology, pure and applied sciences, geology, sociology, anthropology, economics; Man. Partner P. C. KUMAR.

**Inter-India Publications:** D-17, Raja Garden, New Delhi 110 015; tel. (11) 5441120; f. 1977; academic and research works; Dir MOOL CHAND MITTAL.

**Kali for Women:** B1/8 Hauz Khas, New Delhi 110 016; tel. (11) 6852530; fax (11) 6864497; women's studies, social sciences, humanities, general non-fiction, fiction, etc.; Heads of Organization URVASHI BUTALIA, RITU MENON.

**Lancers Books:** POB 4236, New Delhi 110 048; tel. (11) 6241617; fax (11) 6992063; e-mail lanbooks@aol.com; f. 1977; politics (with special emphasis on north-east India), defence; Propr S. KUMAR.

**Motilal Banarsidas Publishers (Pvt) Ltd:** 41 U.A. Bungalow Rd, Jawahar Nagar, Delhi 110 007; tel. (11) 2911985; fax (11) 2930689; e-mail gloryindia@poboxes.com; f. 1903; Indology, in English and Sanskrit; Editorial Exec. N. P. JAIN.

**Munshiram Manoharlal Publishers Pvt Ltd:** 54 Rani Jhansi Rd, POB 5715, New Delhi 110 055; tel. (11) 7771668; fax (11) 3612745; e-mail mrml@mantraonline.com; f. 1952; Indian art, architecture, archaeology, religion, music, law, medicine, dance, dictionaries, travel, history, politics, numismatics, Buddhism, philosophy, sociology, etc.; Publishing Dir DEVENDRA JAIN; Dir ASHOK JAIN.

**National Book Trust:** A-5 Green Park, New Delhi 110 016; tel. (11) 6564020; fax (11) 6851795; e-mail nbtindia@ndb.vsnl.net.in; f. 1957; autonomous organization established by the Ministry of Human Resources Development to produce and encourage the production of good literary works; Chair. SITAKANT MAHAPATRA; Dir NIRMAL KANTHI BHATACHARJEE.

**National Council of Educational Research and Training (NCERT):** Sri Aurobindo Marg, New Delhi 110 016; tel. (11) 6519154; fax (11) 6868419; e-mail dirc@glasdlo1.vsnl.net.in; f. 1961; school textbooks, teachers' guides, research monographs, journals, etc.; Dir Prof. A. K. SHARMA.

**Neeta Prakashan:** A-4 Ring Rd, South Extension Part I, POB 3853, New Delhi 110 049; tel. (11) 4636010; fax (11) 4636011; e-mail neeta@giasdl01.vsnl.net.in; f. 1960; educational, children's, general; Dir RAKESH GUPTA.

**New Age International Pvt Ltd:** 4835/24 Ansari Rd, Daryaganj, New Delhi 110 002; tel. (11) 3278348; fax (11) 3267437; f. 1966; science, engineering, technology, management, humanities, social science; Dir A. R. KUNDAJI.

**Oxford and IBH Publishing Co (Pvt) Ltd:** 66 Janpath, New Delhi 110 001; tel. (11) 3324578; fax (11) 3710090; e-mail oxford@nda.vsnl.net.in; f. 1964; science, technology and reference in English; Dir VIJAY PRIMLANI; Man. Dir MOHAN PRIMLANI.

**Oxford University Press:** YMCA Library Bldg, 1st Floor, Jai Singh Rd, POB 43, New Delhi 110 001; tel. (11) 3273841; fax (11) 3277812; e-mail mk@oupin.com; f. 1912; educational, scientific, medical, general and reference; Man. Dir MANZAR KHAN.

**Penguin Books India (Pvt) Ltd:** 11 Community Centre, Panchsheel Park, New Delhi 110 017; tel. (11) 6494401; fax (11) 6494403; e-mail penguin@del2.vsnl.net.in; f. 1987; Indian literature and general non-fiction in English; Chair. MICHAEL LYNTON; CEO and Publr DAVID DAVIDAR.

**People's Publishing House (Pvt) Ltd:** 5E Rani Jhansi Rd, New Delhi 110 055; tel. (11) 7524701; f. 1947; Marxism, Leninism, peasant movt; Dir SHAMEEM FAIZEE.

**Pitambar Publishing Co Pvt Ltd:** 888 East Park Rd, Karol Bagh, New Delhi 110 005; tel. (11) 7770067; fax (11) 7776058; e-mail pitambar@bol.net.in; internet www.pitambar.hypermart.com; academic, children's books, textbooks and general; Man. Dir ANAND BHUSHAN.

**Prentice-Hall of India (Pvt) Ltd:** M-97 Connaught Circus, New Delhi 110 001; tel. (11) 3321779; fax (11) 3717179; e-mail phi@phindia.com; internet www.phindia.com; f. 1963; university-level text and reference books; Man. Dir A. K. GHOSH.

**Pustak Mahal:** 10B Netaji Subhas Marg, Daryaganj, New Delhi 110 002; tel. (11) 3268292; fax (11) 3280567; e-mail delaad37@giasdl01.vsnl.net.in; children's, general, computers, religious, encyclopaedia; Man. Dir RAM AVTAR GUPTA; Dir (Production) VINOD KUMAR GUPTA.

**Radhakrishna Prakashan (Pvt) Ltd:** 2/38 Ansari Rd, New Delhi 110 002; tel. (11) 3279351; f. 1968; Hindi; literary; Dir ASHOK MAHESWARI.

**Rajkamal Prakashan (Pvt) Ltd:** 1B Netaji Subhas Marg, New Delhi 110 002; tel. (11) 3274463; f. 1946; Hindi; literary; also literary journal and monthly trade journal; Man. Dir ASHOK MAHESHWARI.

**Rajpal and Sons:** 1590 Madrasa Rd, Kashmere Gate, Delhi 110 006; tel. (11) 2965483; fax (11) 2967791; e-mail orienpbk@ndb.vsnl.net.in; f. 1891; humanities, social sciences, art, juvenile; Hindi; Chair VISHWANATH MALHOTRA.

**RIS (Research and Information System) Publications:** Zone IV-B, Fourth Floor, India Habitat Centre, Lodhi Rd, New Delhi 110 003; tel. (11) 4617403; fax (11) 4628068; e-mail risnodec@del2.vsnl.net.in; f. 1983; current and economic affairs involving non-aligned and developing countries; Dir-Gen. Dr V. R. PANCHAMUKHI.

**Rupa & Co:** 7/16 Makhanlal St, Ansari Rd, Daryaganj, POB 7017, New Delhi 110 002; tel. (11) 3278586; fax (11) 3277294; e-mail del.rupaco@axcess.net.in; f. 1936; Chief Exec. R. K. MEHRA.

**Sage Publications India Pvt Ltd:** 32 M-Block Market, Greater Kailash-1, POB 4215, New Delhi 110 048; tel. (11) 6485884; fax (11) 6472426; e-mail sageind@nda.vsnl.net.in; f. 1981; social science, development studies, business and management studies; Man. Dir TEJESHWAR SINGH.

**Sahitya Akademi:** Rabindra Bhavan, 35 Ferozeshah Rd, New Delhi 110 001; tel. (11) 3386626; fax (11) 3382428; e-mail secy@ndb.vsnl.net.in; f. 1956; bibliographies, translations, monographs, encyclopaedias, literary classics, etc.; Pres. RAMAKANTA RATH; Sec. Dr K. SATCHIDANANDAN.

**Scholar Publishing House (P) Ltd:** 85 Model Basti, New Delhi 110 005; tel. (11) 3541299; fax (11) 7776565; e-mail scholar@del2.vsnl.net.in; internet www.scholargroup.com; f. 1968; educational; Man. Dir Y. P. RANADE.

**Shiksha Bharati:** Madrasa Rd, Kashmere Gate, Delhi 110 006; tel. (11) 2965483; fax (11) 2967791; f. 1955; textbooks, creative literature, popular science and juvenile in Hindi and English; Editor MEERA JOHRI.

**Sterling Publishers (Pvt) Ltd:** L-10 Green Park Extension, New Delhi 110 016; tel. (11) 6191023; fax (11) 6190028; e-mail ghai@nda.vsnl.net.in; internet www.sterlingpublishers.com; f. 1965; academic books on the humanities and social sciences, children's books, computer books, management books, paperbacks; Chair. and Man. Dir S. K. GHAI; Gen. Man. A. J. SEHGAL.

**Tata McGraw-Hill Publishing Co Ltd:** 7 West Patel Nagar, New Delhi 110 008; tel. (11) 5819304; fax (11) 5819302; f. 1970; engineering, computers, sciences, management, humanities, social sciences; Chair. Dr F. A. MEHTA; Man. Dir Dr N. SUBRAHMANYAM.

**Technical and Commercial Book Co:** 75 Gokhale Market, Tis Hazari, Delhi 110 054; tel. (11) 228315; f. 1913; technical; Propr D. N. MEHRA; Man. RAMAN MEHRA.

**Vikas Publishing House (Pvt) Ltd:** 576 Masjid Rd, Jangpura, New Delhi 110 014; tel. (11) 4314605; fax (11) 4310879; e-mail orders@vikas.gobookshopping.com; internet www.gobookshopping .com; f. 1969; computers, management, commerce, sciences, engineering, textbooks; Chair. and Man. Dir CHANDER M. CHAWLA.

**A. H. Wheeler & Co Ltd:** 411 Surya Kiran Bldg, 19 K. G. Marg, New Delhi 110 001; tel. (11) 3312629; fax (11) 3357798; e-mail jeet@mantraonline.com; f. 1958; textbooks, reference books, computer science and information technology, electronics, management, telecommunications, social sciences, etc.; Exec. Pres. ALOK BANERJEE.

### Chennai (Madras)

**Higginbothams Ltd:** 814 Anna Salai, POB 311, Chennai 600 002; tel. (44) 8521841; fax (44) 834590; e-mail higginbothams@vsnl.com; f. 1844; general; Dir S. CHANDRASEKHAR.

**B. G. Paul and Co:** 4 Francis Joseph St, Chennai; f. 1923; general, educational and oriental; Man. K. NILAKANTAN.

**T. R. Publications Pvt Ltd:** PMG Complex, 2nd Floor, 57 South Usman Rd, T. Nagar, Chennai 600 017; tel. (44) 4340765; fax (44) 4348837; e-mail trgeetha@giasmd01.vsnl.net.in; internet www.trpubs.com; Chief Exec. S. GEETHA.

### Kolkata (Calcutta)

**Academic Publishers:** 12/1A Bankim Chatterjee St, POB 12341, Kolkata 700 073; tel. (33) 2414857; fax (33) 2413702; e-mail aca books@cal.vsnl.net.in; f. 1958; textbooks, management, medical, technical; Man. Partner DIPANKAR DHUR.

**Advaita Ashrama:** 5 Dehi Entally Rd, Kolkata 700 014; tel. (33) 2440898; fax (33) 2450050; e-mail advaita@vsnl.com; internet www.education, vsnl.com/advaita; f. 1899; religion, philosophy, spiritualism, Vedanta; publication centre of Ramakrishna Math and Ramakrishna Mission; Publication Man. Swami BODHASARANANDA.

**Allied Book Agency:** 18A Shyama Charan De St, Kolkata 700 073; tel. (33) 312594; general and academic; Dir B. SARKAR.

**Ananda Publishers (Pvt) Ltd:** 45 Beniatola Lane, Kolkata 700 009; tel. (33) 2414352; fax (33) 2253240; literature, general; Dir A. SARKAR; Gen. Man. D. N. BASU.

**Assam Review Publishing Co:** 27A Waterloo St, 1st Floor, Kolkata 700 069; tel. (33) 2482251; f. 1926; publrs of *Tea Plantation Directory* and *Tea News*; Partners G. L. BANERJEE, S. BANERJEE.

**Book Land (Pvt) Ltd:** Kolkata; tel. (33) 2414158; economics, politics, history and general; Dir SUBHANKAR BASU.

**Chuckervertty, Chatterjee and Co Ltd:** 15 College Sq., Kolkata 700 073; tel. (33) 2416425; Man. Dir MALA MAZUMDAR.

**Eastern Law House (Pvt) Ltd:** 54 Ganesh Chunder Ave, Kolkata 700 013; tel. (33) 2374989; fax (33) 2150491; e-mail elh@cal.vsnl .net.in; f. 1918; legal, commercial and accountancy; Dir ASOK DE; br. in New Delhi.

**Firma KLM Private Ltd:** 257B B. B. Ganguly St, Kolkata 700 012; tel. (33) 2374391; fax (33) 2217294; e-mail fklm@satyam.net.in; f. 1950; Indology, scholarly in English, Bengali, Sanskrit and Hindi, alternative medicine; Man. Dir R. N. MUKHERJI.

**Intertrade Publications (India) (Pvt) Ltd:** 55 Gariahat Rd, POB 10210, Kolkata 700 019; tel. (33) 474872; f. 1954; economics, medicine, law, history and trade directories; Man. Dir Dr K. K. ROY.

**A. Mukherjee and Co (Pvt) Ltd:** 2 Bankim Chatterjee St, Kolkata 700 073; tel. (33) 311406; fax (33) 7448172; f. 1940; educational and general in Bengali and English; Man. Dir RAJEEV NEOGI.

**Naya Prokash:** 206 Bidhan Sarani, POB 11468, Kolkata 700 006; tel. (33) 2414709; fax (33) 5382897; f. 1960; agriculture, horticulture, Indology, history, political science; Man. Dir BHUBANI MITRA; Senior Partner BARIN MITRA.

**New Era Publishing Co:** 31 Gauri Bari Lane, Kolkata 700 004; f. 1944; Propr Dr P. N. MITRA; Man. S. K. MITRA.

**W. Newman and Co Ltd:** 3 Old Court House St, Kolkata 700 069; tel. (33) 2489436; f. 1854; general; Man. K. M. BANTIA.

**Punthi Pustak:** 136/4B Bidhan Sarani, Kolkata 700 004; tel. (33) 558473; religion, history, philosophy; Propr S. K. BHATTACHARYA.

**Renaissance Publishers (Pvt) Ltd:** 15 Bankim Chatterjee St, Kolkata 700 012; f. 1949; politics, philosophy, history; Man. Dir J. C. GOSWAMI.

**Saraswati Library:** 206 Bidhan Sarani, Kolkata 700 006; tel. (33) 345492; f. 1914; history, philosophy, religion, literature; Man. Partner B. BHATTACHARJEE.

**M. C. Sarkar and Sons (Pvt) Ltd:** 14 Bankim Chatterjee St, Kolkata 700 073; tel. (33) 312490; f. 1910; reference; Dirs SUPRIYA SARKAR, SAMIT SARKAR.

**Visva-Bharati:** 6 Acharya Jagadish Bose Rd, Kolkata 700 017; tel. (33) 2479868; f. 1923; literature; Dir ASHOKE MUKHOPADHYAY.

### Mumbai (Bombay)

**Allied Publishers Ltd:** 15 J. N. Heredia Marg, Ballard Estate, Mumbai 400 001; tel. (22) 2617926; fax (22) 2617928; e-mail alliedpl@bom4.vsnl.net.in; f. 1934; economics, politics, history, philosophy, science, mathematics; Man. Dir S. M. SACHDEV.

**Bharatiya Vidya Bhavan:** Munshi Sadan, Kulapati K. M. Munshi Marg, Mumbai 400 007; tel. (22) 3634462; fax (22) 3630058; e-mail brbhavan@bom7.vsnl.net.in; f. 1938; art, literature, culture, education, philosophy, religion, history of India; various periodicals in English, Hindi, Sanskrit and other Indian languages; Pres. C. SUBRAMANIAM; Sec.-Gen. S. RAMAKRISHNAN.

**Blackie and Son (Pvt) Ltd:** Blackie House, 103–105 Walchand Hirachand Marg, POB 381, Mumbai 400 001; tel. (22) 261410; f. 1901; educational, scientific and technical, general and juvenile; Man. Dir D. R. BHAGI.

**Himalaya Publishing House:** 'Ramdoot', Dr Bhalerao Marg (Kelewadi), Girgaon, Mumbai 400 004; tel. (22) 3800170; fax (22) 3877178; e-mail himpub@bomb5.vsnl.net.in; f. 1976; textbooks and research work; Dir MEENA PANDEY; CEO D. P. PANDEY.

**India Book House Ltd:** 412 Tulsiani Chambers, Nariman Point, Mumbai 400 021; tel. (22) 2840626; fax (22) 2835099; e-mail ibhltd@bom2.vsnl.net.in; Man. Dir DEEPAK MIRCHANDANI.

**International Book House (Pvt) Ltd:** Indian Mercantile Mansions (Extension), Madame Cama Rd, Mumbai 400 001; tel. (22) 2021634; fax (22) 2851109; e-mail intbh@giasbm01.vsnl.net.in; f. 1941; general, educational, scientific and law; Man. Dir S. K. GUPTA; Exec. Dir SANJEEV GUPTA.

**Jaico Publishing House:** 127 Mahatma Gandhi Rd, opposite Mumbai University, Mumbai 400 023; tel. (22) 2676702; fax (22) 2656412; e-mail jaicopub@giasbm01.vsnl.net.in; f. 1947; general paperbacks, management, computer and engineering books, etc.; imports scientific, medical, technical and educational books; Man. Dir ASHWIN J. SHAH.

**Popular Prakashan (Pvt) Ltd:** 35c Pandit Madan Mohan Malaviya Marg, Tardeo, Popular Press Bldg, opp. Roche, Mumbai 400 034; tel. (22) 4941656; fax (22) 4945294; e-mail popular@bom7.vsnl.net.in; f. 1968; sociology, biographies, religion, philosophy, fiction, arts, music, current affairs, medicine, history, politics and administration in English and Marathi; Man. Dir R. G. BHATKAL.

**Somaiya Publications (Pvt) Ltd:** 172 Mumbai Marathi Grantha Sangrahalaya Marg, Dadar, Mumbai 400 014; tel. (22) 4130230; fax (22) 2047297; f. 1967; economics, sociology, history, politics, mathematics, sciences, language, literature, education, psychology, religion, philosophy, logic; Chair. Dr S. K. SOMAIYA; Chief Editor S. G. NENE.

**Taraporevala, Sons and Co (Pvt) Ltd D.B.:** 210 Dr Dadabhai Naoroji Rd, Fort, Mumbai 400 001; tel. (22) 2071433; f. 1864; Indian art, culture, history, sociology, scientific, technical and general in English; Chief Exec. R. J. TARAPOREVALA.

**N. M. Tripathi (Pvt) Ltd:** 164 Shamaldas Gandhi Marg, Mumbai 400 002; tel. (22) 2013651; f. 1888; general in English and Gujarati; Chair. N. M. TRIVEDI; Man. Dir KARTIK R. TRIPATHI.

### Other Towns

**Bharat Bharati Prakashan & Co:** Western Kutchery Rd, Meerut 250 001; tel. 663698; f. 1952; textbooks; Man. Dir SURENDRA AGARWAL.

**Bharati Bhawan:** Thakurbari Rd, Kadamkuan, Patna 800 003; tel. (612) 671356; fax (612) 670010; e-mail bbpdpat@giascl01.vsnl.net.in; f. 1942; educational and juvenile; Man. Partner SANJIB BOSE.

**Bishen Singh Mahendra Pal Singh:** 23A New Connaught Place, POB 137, Dehra Dun 248 001; tel. (135) 655748; fax (135) 650107; e-mail bsmps@del2.vsnl.net.in; internet www.bishensinghbooks .com; f. 1957; botany, forestry, agriculture; Dirs GAJENDRA SINGH GAHLOT, ABHIMANYU GAHLOT.

**Catholic Press:** Ranchi 834 001, Bihar; f. 1928; books and periodicals; Dir WILLIAM TIGGA.

**Chugh Publications:** 2 Strachey Rd, POB 101, Allahabad; tel. (532) 623063; sociology, economics, history, general; Propr RAMESH KUMAR CHUGH.

**Geetha Book House:** K. R. Circle, Mysore 570 001; tel. (821) 33589; f. 1959; general; Dirs M. GOPALA KRISHNA, M. GURURAJA RAO.

**Kalyani Publishers:** 1/1 Rajinder Nagar, Civil Lines, Ludhiana, Punjab; tel. (161) 745756; fax (161) 745872; textbooks; Dir RAJ KUMAR.

**Kitabistan:** 30 Chak, Allahabad 211 003; tel. (532) 653219; f. 1932; general, agriculture, govt publs in English, Hindi, Urdu, Farsi and Arabic; Partners A. U. KHAN, SULTAN ZAMAN.

**Krishna Prakashan Media (P) Ltd:** (Unit) Goel Publishing House, 11 Shivaji Rd, Meerut 250 001; tel. (121) 642946; fax (121) 645855; textbooks; Man. Dir SATYENDRA KUMAR RASTOGI; Dir ANITA RASTOGI.

**The Law Book Co (Pvt) Ltd:** 18B Sardar Patel Marg, Civil Lines, POB 1004, Allahabad 211 001; tel. (532) 624905; fax (532) 420852; e-mail baggal@nae.vsnl.net.in; f. 1929; legal texts in English; Dir ANIL BAGGA; Man. Dir L. R. BAGGA.

**Macmillan India Ltd:** 315/316 Raheja Chambers, 12 Museum Rd, Bangalore 560 001; tel. (80) 5587878; fax (80) 5588713; e-mail rberi@bgl.vsnl.net.in; school and university books in English; general; Pres. and Man. Dir RAJIV BERI; Sales Man. KAPIL RAWAL.

**Navajivan Publishing House:** PO Navajivan, Ahmedabad 380 014; tel. (79) 7540635; f. 1919; Gandhiana and related social science; in English, Hindi and Gujarati; Man. Trustee JITENDRA DESAI; Sales Man. KAPIL RAWAL.

**Nem Chand and Bros:** Civil Lines, Roorkee 247 667; tel. (1332) 72258; fax (1332) 73258; f. 1951; engineering textbooks and journals.

**Orient Longman Ltd:** 3-6-272 Himayat Nagar, Hyderabad 500 029; tel. (40) 3224305; fax (40) 3222900; e-mail orlongco@hd2.dot .net.in; f. 1948; educational, technical, general and children's in English and almost all Indian languages; Chair. SHANTA RAMESHWAR RAO; Dirs Dr NANDINI RAO, J. KRISHNADEV RAO.

**Publication Bureau:** Panjab University, Chandigarh 160 014; tel. (172) 541782; f. 1948; textbooks, academic and general; Man. H. R. GROVER.

**Publication Bureau:** Punjabi University, Patiala 147 002; tel. 282461; university-level text and reference books; Head of Bureau Dr HAZARA SINGH.

**Ram Prasad and Sons:** Hospital Rd, Agra 282 003; tel. (562) 360906; e-mail ea_08@yahoo.com; f. 1905; agricultural, arts, history, commerce, education, general, pure and applied science, economics, sociology; Dirs R. N., B. N. and RAVI AGARWAL; Man. S. N. AGARWAL.

#### Government Publishing House

**Publications Division:** Ministry of Information and Broadcasting, Govt of India, Patiala House, New Delhi 110 001; tel. (11) 3387983; fax (11) 3386879; f. 1941; culture, art, literature, planning and development, general; also 21 periodicals in English and several Indian languages; Dir SURINDER KAUR.

#### PUBLISHERS' ASSOCIATIONS

**Bombay Booksellers' and Publishers' Association:** No. 25, 6th Floor, Bldg No. 3, Navjivan Commercial Premises Co-op Society Ltd, Dr Bhadkamkar Marg, Mumbai 400 008; tel. (22) 3088691; f. 1961; 400 mems; Pres. CHANDRA PAL GUPTA; Gen. Sec. SAMSON JHIRAD.

**Delhi State Booksellers' and Publishers' Association:** 3026/7H (South Patel Nagar) Ranjit Nagar, New Delhi 110 008; tel. (11) 5786769; fax (11) 5772748; f. 1943; 400 mems; Pres. Dr S. K. BHATIA; Sec. S. K. JAIN.

**Federation of Educational Publishers in India:** 19 Rani Jhansi Rd, New Delhi 110 055; tel. (11) 3522697; f. 1987; 14 affiliated asscns; 152 mems; Pres. Prof. R. S. DHILLON; Sec.-Gen. ASHOK GOYAL.

**Federation of Indian Publishers:** Federation House, 18/1-C Institutional Area, nr JNU, New Delhi 110 067; tel. (11) 6964847; fax (11) 6864054; 18 affiliated asscns; 159 mems; Pres. S. BALWANT; Hon. Gen. Sec. ASHA RANI.

**Akhil Bharatiya Hindi Prakashak Sangh:** A-2/1, Krishan Nagar, Delhi 110 051; tel. (11) 2219398; f. 1954; 400 mems; Pres. KESHAVDEV SHARMA; Gen. Sec. ARUN KUMAR SHARMA.

**All India Urdu Publications' and Booksellers' Association:** 437 Matia Mahal, Delhi 110 006; tel. (11) 3265480; fax (11) 3257189; e-mail aakif@del3.vsnl.net.in; internet www.aakif.com; f. 1988; 150 mems; Pres. Dr KHALIQ ANJUM; Gen. Sec. S. M. ZAFAR ALI.

**Assam Publishers' Association:** College Hostel Rd, Panbazar, Guwahati 780 001; tel. (361) 43995; Pres. K. N. DUTTA BARUAH; Sec. J. N. DUTTA BARUAH.

**Booksellers' and Publishers' Association of South India:** 8, II Floor, Sun Plaza, G. N. Chetty Rd, Chennai 600 006; 158 mems; Pres. S. CHANDRASEKAR; Sec. RAVI CHOPRA.

**Gujarati Sahitya Prakashak Vikreta Mandal:** Navajivan Trust, P.O. Navajivan, Ahmedabad 380 014; tel. (79) 7540635; 125 mems; Pres. JITENDRA DESAI; Sec. K. N. MADRASI.

**Karnataka Publishers' Association:** 88 Mysore Rd, Bangalore 560 018; tel. (80) 601638; Pres. Prof. H. R. DASEGOWDA; Sec. S. V. SRINIVASA RAO.

**Kerala Publishers' and Booksellers' Association:** Piaco Bldg, Jew St, Kochi 682 011; 30 mems; Pres. D. C. KIZHAKEMURI; Sec. E. K. SEKHAR.

**Marathi Prakashak Parishad:** Mehta Publishing House, Dhanashree Apartments, 1216 Sadashiv Peth, Pune 411 030; tel. (212) 476924; fax (212) 475462; 100 mems; Pres. ANIL MEHTA.

**Orissa Publishers' and Booksellers' Association:** Binodbihari, Cuttack 753 002; f. 1973–74; 280 mems; Pres. KRISHNA CHANDRA BEHERA; Sec. BHIKARI CHARAN MOHAPATRA.

**Paschimbanga Prakasak Sabha:** 206 Bidhan Sarani, Kolkata 700 061; tel. (33) 2410176; Pres. J. SEN; Gen. Sec. T. SAHA.

**Publishers' Association of West Bengal:** 6-B, Ramanath Mazumder St, Kolkata 700 009; tel. (33) 325580; 164 mems; Pres. MOHIT KUMAR BASU; Gen. Sec. SHANKARI BHUSAN NAYAK.

**Publishers' and Booksellers' Association of Bengal:** 93 Mahatma Gandhi Rd, Kolkata 700 007; tel. (33) 2411993; f. 1912; 4,500 mems; Pres. PRASOON BASU; Gen. Sec. CHITTA SINGHA ROY.

**Punjabi Publishers' Association:** Satnam Singh, Singh Brothers, Bazar Mai Sewan, Amritsar 143 006; tel. (183) 45787; Sec. SATNAM SINGH.

**Vijayawada Publishers' Association:** 27-1-68, Karl Marx Rd, Vijayawada 520 002; tel. (866) 74500; 41 mems; Pres. DUPATI VIJAY KUMAR; Sec. U. N. YOGI.

**Federation of Publishers' and Booksellers' Associations in India:** 4833/24 Govind Lane, 1st Floor, Ansari Rd, New Delhi 110 002; tel. (11) 3272845; 17 affiliated asscns; 706 mems; Pres. C. M. CHAWLA; Sec. S. C. SETHI.

**Publishers' and Booksellers' Guild:** 5A Bhawani Dutta Lane, Kolkata 700 073; tel. (33) 2413680; fax (33) 2418248; e-mail guild@cal2.vsnl.net.in; f. 1975; 38 mems; organizes annual Kolkata Book Fair; Pres. PRABIR KUMAR MAZUMDAR; Sec. ANIL ACHARYA.

**UP Publishers' and Booksellers' Association:** 111-A/243 Ashok Nagar, Kanpur 208 012; asscn for Uttar Pradesh state.

## Broadcasting and Communications

#### TELECOMMUNICATIONS

**Telecom Regulatory Authority of India (TRAI):** 16th Floor, Jawahar Vyapar Bhavan 1, Tolstoy Marg, New Delhi 110 001; tel. (11) 3357815; fax (11) 3738708; e-mail trai@del2.vsnl.net.in; f. 1998; Chair. S. S. SODHI; Vice-Chair. BAL KRISHAN ZUTSHI.

**Bharti Telenet Ltd:** Indore; f. 1998; India's first privately-owned telephone network; Exec. Dir BHAGWAN KHURANA.

**Ericsson:** POB 10912, New Delhi 110 066.

**ITI (Indian Telephone Industries) Ltd:** 45/1 Magrath Rd, Bangalore 560 025; tel. (80) 5566366; fax (80) 5593188; f. 1948; mfrs of all types of telecommunication equipment, incl. telephones, automatic exchanges and long-distance transmission equipment; also produces optical fibre equipment and microwave equipment; will manufacture all ground communication equipment for the 22 earth stations of the Indian National Satellite; in conjunction with the Post and Telegraph Department, a newly designed 2,000-line exchange has been completed; Chair. and Man. Dir S. S. MOTIAL.

**Mahanagar Telephone Nigam Ltd (MTNL):** Jeevan Bharati Tower, 124 Connaught Circus, New Delhi 110 001; tel. (11) 3732212; fax (11) 3317344; internet www.mtnl.net.in; f. 1986; 66% state-owned; owns and operates telephone networks in Mumbai and Delhi; Chair. S. RAJAGOPALAN.

**Videsh Sanchar Nigam Ltd (VSNL):** M. G. Rd, Fort, Mumbai 400 001; tel. (22) 2624020; fax (22) 2624027; e-mail helpdesk@giaspn01.vsnl.net.in; internet www.vsnl.com; f. 1986; 65% state-owned; has had monopoly on international telecommunications services since 1994; Chair. and Man. Dir AMITABH KUMAR.

#### BROADCASTING

**Prasar Bharati** (Broadcasting Corpn of India): New Delhi; autonomous body; oversees operations of state-owned radio and television services; f. 1997; Chief Exec. R. R. SHAH.

##### Radio

**All India Radio (AIR):** Akashvani Bhavan, Parliament St, New Delhi 110 001; tel. (11) 3710006; fax (11) 3714061; broadcasting is controlled by the Ministry of Information and Broadcasting and is primarily govt-financed; operates a network of 195 stations and 302 transmitters (grouped into four zones— north, south, east and west), covering 97.3% of the population and about 90% of the total area of the country; Dir-Gen. Dr O. P. KEJRIWAL.

The News Services Division of AIR, centralized in New Delhi, is one of the largest news organizations in the world. It has 42 regional news units, which broadcast 314 bulletins daily in 24 languages and 38 dialects. One hundred and three bulletins in 19 languages are broadcast in the Home Services, 137 regional bulletins in 72 languages and dialects, and 65 bulletins in 22 languages in the External Services.

### Television

**Doordarshan India** (Television India): Mandi House, Doordarshan Bhavan, Copernicus Marg, New Delhi 110 001; tel. (11) 3387786; fax (11) 3386507; f. 1976; broadcasting is controlled by the Ministry of Information and Broadcasting and is govt-financed; programmes: 280 hours weekly; 3 main channels—the National Channel, Metro Channel and DD3—(broadcasting mostly in Hindi) and 14 other channels; Dir-Gen. K. S. SARMA; Chief Exec. K. C. C. RAJA.

In March 1999 72% of the country's area and 87% of the population were covered by the TV network. There were 1,025 transmitters in operation in that month. By 1998 42 programme production centres and nine relay centres had been established.

Satellite television was introduced in India by a Hong Kong company, Star TV, in 1991. By mid-1993 Star TV attracted an audience of about 18.8m. in India. In July 1992 the Government announced that it would permit broadcasting time to private companies on a second state channel (the Metro Channel) broadcast to major Indian cities. In August 1993 Doordarshan India launched five new satellite television channels; three of the channels were taken off the air, however, in February 1994 following the introduction of a new satellite television policy. Doordarshan International Channel commenced broadcasting (three hours daily) in March 1995; the service was extended to 18 hours daily in November 1996. In 1997 legislation was introduced to license private broadcasters and to impose a 49% limit on foreign ownership of television channels.

# Finance

(cap. = capital; p.u. = paid up; res = reserves; dep. = deposits; m. = million; brs = branches; amounts in rupees)

## BANKING

### State Banks

**Reserve Bank of India:** Central Office Bldg, Shahid Bhagat Singh Rd, POB 406, Mumbai 400 023; tel. (22) 2661602; fax (22) 2661784; e-mail rbiprd@giasbm01.vsnl.net.in; internet www.rbi.org.in; f. 1934; nationalized 1949; sole bank of issue; cap. 50m., res 65,000m., dep. 691,192.3m. (Dec. 1999); Gov. Dr BIMAL JALAN; Dep. Govs Dr Y. V. REDDY, JAGDISH CAPOOR, S. P. TALWAR; 4 offices and 14 brs.

**State Bank of India:** Madame Cama Rd, POB 10121, Mumbai 400 021; tel. (22) 2022426; e-mail gm@mumbai.cobom.sbi.co.in; internet www.sbi.co.in; f. 1955; cap. p.u. 5,263m., dep. 1,690,419.3m. (March 1999); 7 associates, 7 domestic subsidiaries/affiliates, 3 foreign subsidiaries, 4 jt ventures abroad; Chair. G. G. VAIDYA; Man. Dirs S. R. IYER, V. JANAKIRAMAN; 8,982 brs (incl. 52 overseas brs and rep. offices in 33 countries).

### State-owned Commercial Banks

Fourteen of India's major commercial banks were nationalized in 1969 and a further six in 1980. They are managed by 15-mem. boards of directors (two directors to be appointed by the central Government, one employee director, one representing employees who are not workmen, one representing depositors, three representing farmers, workers, artisans, etc., five representing persons with special knowledge or experience, one Reserve Bank of India official and one Government of India official). The Department of Banking of the Ministry of Finance controls all banking operations.

There were 64,547 branches of public-sector and other commercial banks in June 1998.

Aggregate deposits of all scheduled commercial banks amounted to Rs 7,172,710m. in March 1999.

**Allahabad Bank:** 2 Netaji Subhas Rd, Kolkata 700 001; tel. (33) 2204735; fax (33) 2214048; e-mail albfd@giascl01.vsnl.net.in; internet www.allahabadbank.com/; f. 1865; nationalized 1969; cap. p.u. 2,467m., res 6,023.7m., dep. 155,103.6m. (March 1999); Chair. and Man. Dir Dr B. SAMAL; 1,875 brs.

**Andhra Bank:** Andhra Bank Bldgs, 5-9-11 Saifabad, Hyderabad 500 004; tel. (40) 230001; fax (40) 240509; f. 1923; nationalized 1980; cap. p.u. 3,479.5m., res 1,436.2m., dep. 104,387.4m. (March 1999); Chair. and Man. Dir R. S. KAMATH; 1,006 brs and 87 extension counters.

**Bank of Baroda:** 3 Walchand Hirachand Marg, Ballard Pier, POB 10046, Mumbai 400 038; tel. (22) 2610341; fax (22) 2615065; e-mail bobio@calva.com; f. 1908; nationalized 1969; cap. 2,941.4m., res 26,043.0m., dep. 446,140.4m. (March 1999); Chair. and Man. Dir P. S. SHENOY; 2,483 brs in India, 37 brs overseas.

**Bank of India:** Express Towers, Nariman Point, POB 234, Mumbai 400 021; tel. (22) 2023020; fax (22) 2022831; e-mail cmdsect@bom3.vsnl.net.in; internet www.bankofindia.com; f. 1906; nationalized 1969; cap. 6,383.3m., res and surplus 17,683.3m., dep. 474,093.3m. (March 1999); Chair. and Man. Dir K. V. KRISHNAMURTHY; 2,476 brs in India, 17 brs overseas.

**Bank of Maharashtra:** 'Lokmangal', 1501 Shivajinagar, Pune 411 005; tel. (212) 322731; fax (212) 322581; e-mail cppd@bomco.xeepnq.xeemail.com;internet www.bank-of-maharashtra.com; f. 1935; nationalized 1969; cap. 3,305.1m., res 1,477.4m., dep. 110,647.2m. (March 1999); Chair. M. M. VAISH; Man. Dir S. C. BASU; 1,155 brs.

**Canara Bank:** 112 Jayachamarajendra Rd, POB 6648, Bangalore 560 002; tel. (812) 2221581; fax (812) 2222704; e-mail cmdsec@wipro.net.in; internet www.canbankindia.com; f. 1906; nationalized 1969; cap. 5,778.7m., res 18,349.4m., dep. 433,410.0m. (March 1999); Chair. and Man. Dir R. J. KAMATH; 2,379 brs.

**Central Bank of India:** Chandermukhi, Nariman Point, Mumbai 400 021; tel. (22) 2026428; fax (22) 2044336; f. 1911; nationalized 1969; cap. 18,054.5m., res and surplus 7,893.9m., dep. 308,006.0m. (March 1999); Chair. and Man. Dir DALBIR SINGH; 3,084 brs.

**Corporation Bank:** Mangaladevi Temple Rd, POB 88, Mangalore 575 001; tel. (824) 426416; fax (824) 441208; e-mail corpho@corpbank.com; internet www.corpbank.com; f. 1906; nationalized 1980; cap. 1,199.3m., res 8,546.2m., dep. 126,014.3m. (March 1999); Chair. and Man. Dir R. KUMAR; Exec. Dir K. R. SHENOY; 617 brs.

**Dena Bank:** Maker Towers 'E', 10th Floor, Cuffe Parade, Colaba, POB 6058, Mumbai 400 005; tel. (22) 2189151; fax (22) 2189046; f. 1938 as Devkaran Nanjee Banking Co Ltd; nationalized 1969; cap. 2,068.2m., res and surplus 4,898.7m., dep. 117,953.5m. (March 1999); Chair. and Man. Dir S. GOPALAKRISHNAN; 1,134 brs.

**Indian Bank:** 31 Rajaji Salai, POB 1866, Chennai 600 001; tel. (44) 5232939; fax (44) 5231285; e-mail indbank@giasmd01.vsnl.net.in; internet www.indian-bank.com; f. 1907; nationalized 1969; cap. 25,039.6m., res 3,946.7m., dep. 171,559.2m. (March 1999); Chair. and Man. Dir T. S. RAGHAVAN; Exec. Dir R. S. HUGAR; 1,424 brs.

**Indian Overseas Bank:** 762 Anna Salai, POB 3765, Chennai 600 002; tel. (44) 8524145; fax (44) 8523395; internet www.iob.com; f. 1937; nationalized 1969; cap. 3,336m., res 3,850.3m., dep. 219,143.1m. (March 1999); Chair. and Man. Dir R. V. SHASTRI; 1,365 brs.

**Oriental Bank of Commerce:** Harsha Bhavan, E Block, Connaught Place, POB 329, New Delhi 110 001; tel. (11) 3323444; fax (11) 3321514; f. 1943; nationalized 1980; cap. 1,925.4m., res 10,389.4m. dep. 168,048.8m. (March 1999); Chair. and Man. Dir V. S. THAKUR; 533 brs.

**Punjab and Sind Bank:** 21 Bank House, Rajendra Place, New Delhi 110 008; tel. (11) 5720849; fax (11) 5751765; f. 1908; nationalized 1980; cap. 2,430.6m., res 1,307.4m., dep. 94,966m. (March 1999); Chair. and Man. Dir SURINDER SINGH KOHLI; Exec. Dir B. D. NARANG; 811 brs.

**Punjab National Bank:** 7 Bhikaiji Cama Place, Africa Ave, POB 6, New Delhi 110 066; tel. (11) 6102303; fax (11) 6196514; f. 1895; nationalized 1969; merged with New Bank of India in 1993; cap. 2,122.4m., res 17,175.1m., dep. 409,746.1m. (March 1999); Chair. and Man. Dir RASHID JILANI; Exec. Dir K. R. CHABRIA; 3,734 brs.

**Syndicate Bank:** POB 1, Manipal 576 119; tel. (8252) 71181; fax (8252) 70266; e-mail idcb@syndicatebank.com; internet www.syndicatebank.com; f. 1925 as Canara Industrial and Banking Syndicate Ltd; name changed as above 1964; nationalized 1969; cap. 3,469.7m., res 3,514.3m., dep. 200,136.4m. (March 1999); Chair. and Man. Dir D. T. PAI; Exec. Dir J. Y. DIWANJI; 1,661 brs.

**UCO Bank:** 10 Biplabi Trailokya Maharaj Sarani (Brabourne Rd), POB 2455, Kolkata 700 001; tel. (33) 2254120; fax (33) 2253986; e-mail hoidiv.calcutta@ucobank.wiprobt.ems.vsnl.net.in; internet www.ucobank.com; f. 1943 as United Commercial Bank Ltd; nationalized 1969; name changed as above 1985; cap. 22,645.2m., res 3,696.8m., dep. 162,512.1m. (March 1999); Chair. and Man. Dir K. CHERIAN VERGHESE; Exec. Dir M. M. VAISH; 1,797 brs.

**Union Bank of India:** Union Bank Bhavan, 239 Vidhan Bhavan Marg, Nariman Point, Mumbai 400 021; tel. (22) 2023060; fax (22) 2025238; e-mail union@bom3.vsnl.net.in; internet www.unionbankofindia.com; f. 1919; nationalized 1969; cap. 3,380m., res 13,446.2m., dep. 281,356.6m. (March 1999); Chair. and Man. Dir V. LILADHAR; 2,087 brs.

**United Bank of India:** 16 Old Court House St, Kolkata 700 001; tel. (33) 2487471; fax (33) 2485852; e-mail itbihoc@giaselpi.vsnl.net.in; f. 1950; nationalized 1969; cap. 18,108.7m., res 1,618.1m., dep. 146,229.0m. (March 1999); Chair. and Man. Dir BISWAJIT CHOUDHURI; Exec. Dir G. R. SUNDARAVADIVEL; 1,333 brs.

**Vijaya Bank:** 41/2 Mahatma Gandhi Rd, Bangalore 560 001; tel. (80) 5584066; fax (80) 5584142; e-mail vijbank@bgl.vsnl.net.in; internet www.vijayabank.com; f. 1931; nationalized 1980; cap. 5,563.1m., res 1,477.1m.,dep. 98,364.9m. (March 1999); Chair. and Man. Dir N. R. NATARAJAN; 835 brs.

### Principal Private Banks

**Bank of Madura Ltd:** 'Karumuttu Nilayam', 758 Anna Salai, POB 5225, Chennai 600 002; tel. (44) 8523456; fax (44) 8523868; e-mail mdsaab34@giasmd01.vsnl.net.in; internet www.bankofmadura.com; f. 1943; cap. 117.7m., res 1,992.1m., dep. 32,255.4m. (March 1999); Chair. Dr K. M. THIAGARAJAN; Gen. Mans V. NACHIAPPAN, S. KATHIRESAN; 276 brs.

**The Bank of Rajasthan Ltd:** C-3 Sardar Patel Marg, Jaipur 302 001; tel. (141) 381222; fax (141) 381123; f. 1943; cap. p.u. 179.4m., res 1,690.4m., dep. 29,894.2m. (March 1999); Chair. PRAVIN KUMAR TAYAL; Man. Dir I. SADA SHIV GUPTA; 282 brs.

**Benares State Bank Ltd (BSB):** S-20/52 A-K Varuna Bridge, Varanasi 221 002; tel. (542) 348681; fax (542) 348680; f. 1946; cap. 621.1m., res 37.5m., dep. 6,899.9m. (March 1998); Chair. H. DINESH NAYAK; 105 brs.

**Bharat Overseas Bank Ltd:** Habeeb Towers, 756 Anna Salai, Chennai 600 002; tel. (44) 8525686; fax (44) 8524700; f. 1973; cap. 157.5m., res 674.8m., dep. 13,499.6m. (March 1999); Chair. S. SRINIVASAN; Dep. Gen. Man. G. CHANDRAN; 57 brs.

**Bombay Mercantile Co-operative Bank Ltd:** 78 Mohammed Ali Rd, Mumbai 400 003; tel. (22) 3425961; fax (22) 3433385; e-mail bmcb@bom5.vsnl.net.in; f. 1939; cap. 126m., res 1,696.6m., dep. 20,324.7m. (March 1998); Chair. A. R. KIDWAI; Man. Dir SHAMIM KAZIM; 52 brs.

**The Catholic Syrian Bank Ltd:** St Mary's College Rd, POB 502, Trichur 680 020; tel. (487) 333020; fax (487) 333435; e-mail csbho@md2.vsnl.net.in; internet www.casybank.com; f. 1920; cap. 54.1m., res 294.4m., dep. 18,971.0m. (March 1998); Chair. and CEO A. SOLOMON; Gen. Man. JOHN J. ALAPATT; 267 brs.

**Centurion Bank Ltd:** 1201 Raheja Centre, Free Press Journal Marg, Nariman Point, Mumbai 400 021; tel. (22) 2047234; fax (22) 2845860; f. 1995; cap. 1,187.2m., res 553.2m., dep. 21,408.1m. (March 1999); Pres. M. G. RAMAKRISHNA; Man. Dir and CEO V. SRINIVASAN.

**City Union Bank Ltd:** 149 TSR (Big) St, Kumbakonam 612 001; tel. (435) 32322; fax (435) 431746; e-mail cubco@md3.vsnl.net.in; internet www.cityunion.com; f. 1904; cap. 240.0m., res 670.0m., dep. 12,638.1m. (March 1999); Chair. V. NARYANAN; Chief Gen. Man. K. VENKATARAMAN; 108 brs.

**The Federal Bank Ltd:** Federal Towers, POB 103, Alwaye 683 101; tel. (484) 624061; fax (484) 622566; e-mail fednri@md2.vsnl.net.in; f. 1931; cap. 217.1m., res and surplus 3,009.0m., dep. 67,820.7m. (March 1999); Chair. K. P. PADMAKUMAR; 399 brs.

**Global Trust Bank Ltd:** 303-48-3 Sardar Patel Rd, Secunderabad 500 003; tel. (40) 7819333; fax (40) 7815892; e-mail ask@globaltrustbank.com; internet www.globaltrustbank.com; f. 1994; cap. p.u. 1,040m., res 1,862.5m., dep. 40,968m. (March 1999); Chair. and Man. Dir RAMESH GELLI; Exec. Dir SRIDHAR SUBASRI; 63 brs.

**ICICI Bank:** ICICI Towers, 4th Floor, South Tower, Bandra–Kurla Complex, Bandra (East), Mumbai 400 051; tel. (22) 6531414; fax (22) 6531167; e-mail sinorhn@icicibank.com; internet www.icicibank.com; f. 1994; cap. 1,650m., res and surplus 1,874.3m., dep. 65,797m. (Sept. 1999); Man. Dir and CEO H. N. SINOR; 62 brs.

**IndusInd Bank Ltd:** IndusInd House, 425 Dadasaheb Bhadkamkar Marg, Lamington Rd, nr Opera House, Mumbai 400 004; tel. (22) 3859901; fax (22) 3859913; e-mail glob@indusind.com; internet www.indusind.com; f. 1994; cap. 1,589.1m., res 3,707.3m., dep. 50,184.2m. (March 1999); Chair. ARJUN ASRANI; Man. Dir K. R. MAHESWARI; 22 brs.

**Jammu and Kashmir Bank Ltd:** Zum Zum Bldg, Ram Bagh, Srinagar 190 015; tel. (194) 430730; fax (194) 430247; e-mail jkbgm@nde.vsnl.net.com; internet www.jammuandkashmirbank.com; f. 1938; cap. p.u. 478.4m., res 3,805.5m., dep 66,533.3m. (March 1999); Chair. and CEO M. Y. KHAN; 389 brs.

**The Karnataka Bank Ltd:** POB 716, Kodialbail, Mangalore 575 003; tel. (824) 440751; fax (824) 441212; internet www.thekarnatakabankltd.com; f. 1924; cap. 135m., dep. 43,821.1m. (March 1999); Chair. and CEO M. S. KRISHNA BHAT; Chief Gen. Man. Mr ANANTHAKRISHNA; 346 brs.

**The Karur Vysya Bank Ltd:** Erode Rd, POB 21, Karur 639 002; tel. (4324) 32520; fax (4324) 30202; e-mail kvbid@giasmd01.vsnl.net.in; f. 1916; cap. 60.0m., res 1,886.2m., dep. 27,732.5m. (March 1999); Chair. A. D. NAVANEETHAN; Sr Gen. Man. V. DEVARAJAN; 203 brs.

**Lakshmi Vilas Bank Ltd:** Kathaparai, Salem Rd, POB 2, Karur 639 006; tel. (4324) 20051; fax (4324) 20068; f. 1926; cap. 115.1m., res 897.2m., dep. 15,910.1m. (March 1999); Chair. K. R. SHENOY; Gen. Man. R. MUNISWAMY; 205 brs.

**The Sangli Bank Ltd:** Rajwada Chowk, POB 158, Sangli 416 416; tel. (233) 73611; fax (233) 77156; f. 1916; cap. p.u. 60.2m., dep. 7,303.6m. (March 1995); Chair. and CEO SURESH D. JOSHI; Gen. Man. Dr V. PRASANNA BHAT; 178 brs.

**The South Indian Bank Ltd:** SIB House, Mission Quarters, Thrissur 680 001, Kerala; tel. (487) 420020; fax (487) 442021; e-mail head@southindianbank.com; internet www.southindianbank.com; f. 1929; cap. 354.8m., res 1,280.1m., dep. 31,225.6m. (March 1999); Chair. and CEO A. SETHUMADHAVAN; 365 brs.

**Tamilnad Mercantile Bank Ltd:** 57 Victoria Extension Rd, Tuticorin 628 002; tel. (461) 321932; fax (461) 322994; f. 1921 as Nadar Bank, name changed as above 1962; cap. 2.8m., res 1,508m., dep. 16,044m. (March 1998); Chair. S. KRISHNAMURTHY; 142 brs.

**Times Bank Ltd:** Times of India Bldg, Dr D. N. Rd, Mumbai 400 001; tel. (22) 2679951; fax (22) 2679944; f. 1994; cap. 1,000m., res 437.1m., dep. 22,143.9m. (March 1998); Chair. S. M. DATTA; Man. Dir NANI JAVERI; 38 brs.

**The United Western Bank Ltd:** 172/4 Raviwar Peth, Shivaji Circle, POB 2, Satara 415 001; tel. (2162) 20517; fax (2162) 23374; f. 1936; cap. 298.9m., res and surplus 1,608.8m., dep. 34,346.0m. (March 1999); Chair. and Chief Exec. P. N. JOSHI; Gen. Man. V. G. PALKAR; 203 brs.

**The Vysya Bank Ltd:** 72 St Marks Rd, Bangalore 560 001; tel. (80) 2272021; fax (80) 2272220; f. 1930; cap. 171.9m., res 4,206m., dep. 65,104m. (March 1999); Chair. K. R. RAMAMOORTHY; Exec. Dir G. LAXMINARAYANA; 492 brs.

### Foreign Banks

**ABN AMRO Bank NV** (Netherlands): 14 Veer Nariman Rd, Mumbai 400 023; tel. (22) 2042331; CEO FERGUS FLEMING; 6 brs.

**Abu Dhabi Commercial Bank** (UAE): Rehmat Manzil, 75-B Veer Nariman Rd, Mumbai 400 020; tel. (22) 2830235; fax (22) 2870686; Chief Exec. IBRAHIM ABDULWAHID; 1 br.

**American Express Bank Ltd** (USA): Dalamal Tower, First Floor, 211 Nariman Point, Mumbai 400 021; tel. (22) 233230; fax (22) 2872968; Country Head STEVE MARTIN; 4 brs.

**ANZ Grindlays Bank** (UK): 90 Mahatma Gandhi Rd, POB 725, Mumbai 400 023; tel. (22) 271295; fax (22) 2619903; Country Head ANUROOP SINGH; 57 brs.

**Banca Nazionale del Lavoro Spa** (Italy): 67 Maker Chambers VI, 6th Floor, Nariman Point, Mumbai 400 021; tel. (22) 2047763; fax (22) 2023482; Rep. L. S. AGARWAL.

**Bank of America National Trust and Savings Association** (USA): Hansalaya, 15 Barakhamba Rd, New Delhi 110 001; tel. (11) 3715565; fax (11) 3714754; Sr Vice-Pres. and Country Man. ARUN DUGGAL; 4 brs.

**Bank of Bahrain and Kuwait BSC:** Jolly Maker Chambers II, Ground Floor, 225 Nariman Point, Mumbai 400 021; tel. (22) 2823698; fax (22) 2044458; Gen. Man. and CEO K. S. KRISHNAKUMAR; 2 brs.

**Bank of Ceylon:** 1090 Poonamallee High Rd, Chennai 600 084; tel. (44) 6420972; fax (44) 5325590; e-mail ceybank@md3.vsnl.net.in; internet www.bocindia.com; Asst Vice-Pres. B. KARTHIK; Country Man. N. V. MOORTHY.

**Bank of Muscat International** (Oman): Empire Infantry, Infantry Rd, Bangalore 560 001; tel. (80) 2867755; fax (80) 2862214; e-mail bmiimgt@bgl.vsnl.net.in; CEO SAMIT GHOSH; 1 br.

**Bank of Nova Scotia** (Canada): Mittal Tower B, Nariman Point, Mumbai 400 021; tel. (22) 2832822; fax (22) 2873125; Sr Vice-Pres. and CEO (India) DOUGLAS H. STEWART; Vice-Pres. and Man. BHASKAR DESAI; 3 brs.

**Bank of Tokyo-Mitsubishi Ltd** (Japan): Jeevan Prakash, Sir P. Mehta Rd, Mumbai 400 001; tel. (22) 2660564; fax (22) 2661787; Regional Rep. for India and Gen. Man. KUNIHIKO NISHIHARA; 4 brs.

**Banque Nationale de Paris** (France): French Bank Bldg, 4th Floor, 62 Homji St, Fort, POB 45, Mumbai 400 001; tel. (22) 2660822; fax (22) 2660144; e-mail bnp@giasbm01.vsnl.net.in; Chief Exec. and Country Man. JONATHAN LYON; 7 brs.

**Barclays Bank PLC** (UK): 21–23 Maker Chambers VI, 2nd Floor, Nariman Point, Mumbai 400 021; tel. (22) 2044353; fax (22) 2043238; CEO KAMAL KALKAT; 2 brs.

**British Bank of the Middle East** (Hong Kong): 16 Veer Nariman Rd, Fort, POB 876, Mumbai 400 023; tel. (22) 2048203; fax (22) 2046077; Man. D. GHANSHYAMDAS; 2 brs.

**Chase Manhattan Bank:** Maker Chambers VI, 7/F, Nariman Point, Mumbai 400 021; tel. (22) 2855666; fax (22) 2027772; e-mail david.baggs@chase.com; Man. Dir and Sr Country Officer (India and South Asia) ANIL BHALLA; 1 br.

**Chinatrust Commercial Bank** (Taiwan): 21-A Janpath, New Delhi 110 001; tel. (11) 3356001; fax (11) 3731815; e-mail ctcbindd@ndf.vsnl.net.in; internet www.chinatrustindia.com; Gen. Man. and CEO JACK T. U. HSIEH; 1 br.

**Citibank, NA** (USA): Sakhar Bhavan, 230 Backbay Reclamation, Nariman Point, Mumbai 400 021; tel. (22) 2025499; CEO NANOO PAMNANI; 6 brs.

**Commerzbank AG** (Germany): Free Press House, 215 Free Press Journal Rd, Nariman Point, Mumbai 400 021; tel. (22) 2885510; fax (22) 2885524; Gen. Mans G. SHEKHAR, PETER KENYON-MUIR; 2 brs.

**Crédit Agricole Indosuez** (France): Ramon House, 169 Backbay Reclamation, Mumbai 400 020; tel. (22) 2045104; fax (22) 2049108; Sr Country Officer ALAIN BUTZBACH; Gen. Man. NIRENDU MAZUMDAR.

**Crédit Lyonnais** (France): Scindia House, 1st Floor, Narottam Morarjee Marg, Ballard Estate, Mumbai 400 038; tel. (22) 2612313; fax (22) 2612603; Chief Exec. and Country Man. JEAN-YVES LE PAULMIER; 4 brs.

**Deutsche Bank AG** (Germany): DB House, Hazarimal Somani Marg, Fort, POB 1142, Mumbai 400 001; tel. (22) 2074720; fax (22) 2075047; CEO JAVAD SHIRAZI; 5 brs.

**Development Bank of Singapore Ltd:** Maker Chambers IV, 12th Floor, Nariman Point, Mumbai 400 021; tel. (22) 2826991; fax (22) 2875602; 1 br.

**Dresdner Bank** (Germany): Hoechst House, Nariman Point, Mumbai 400 021; tel. (22) 2850009; 2 brs.

**Fuji Bank Ltd** (Japan): Maker Chambers III, 1st Floor, Jamnalal Bajaj Rd, Nariman Point, Mumbai 400 021; tel. (22) 2886638; fax (22) 2886640; CEO (India) and Gen. Man. TATSUJI TAMAKA; 1 br.

**Hongkong and Shanghai Banking Corpn Ltd** (Hong Kong): 52-60 Mahatma Gandhi Rd, POB 128, Mumbai 400 001; tel. (22) 2674921; fax (22) 2658309; CEO ZARIR J. CAMA; 21 brs.

**ING Bank** (Netherlands): Hoechst House, 7th Floor, 193 Backbay Reclamation, Nariman Point, Mumbai 400 005; tel. (22) 2029876; fax (22) 2046134; Country Head PRADEEP SAXENA; 2 brs.

**Mashreq Bank PSC** (United Arab Emirates): Air-India Bldg, Nariman Point, Mumbai 400 021; tel. (22) 2026096; fax (22) 2831278; CEO SUNEIL KUCCHAL.

**Oman International Bank S.A.O.G.** (Oman): 201 Raheja Centre, Free Press Journal Marg, Nariman Point, Mumbai 400 021; tel. (22) 2837733; fax (22) 2875626; e-mail oibind@bom3.vsnl.net.in; Country Man. ABDUL GHAFOOR AL-BULUSHI; 2 brs.

**Sanwa Bank Ltd** (Japan): Mercantile House, Upper Ground Floor, 15 Kasturba Gandhi Marg, New Delhi 110 001; tel. (11) 3318008; fax (11) 3315162; Gen. Man. KANZO MURAKAMI.

**Société Générale** (France): Maker Chambers IV, Bajaj Marg, Nariman Point, POB 11635, Mumbai 400 021; tel. (22) 2870909; fax (22) 2045459; e-mail sgbombay@giasbm01.vsnl.net.in; CEO R. KERNEIS; 4 brs.

**Sonali Bank** (Bangladesh): 15 Park St, Kolkata 700 016; tel. (33) 297998; Dep. Gen. Man. SIRAJUDDIN AHMED; 1 br.

**Standard Chartered Bank** (UK): New Excelsior Bldg, 4th Floor, A. K. Naik Marg, POB 1806, Mumbai 400 001; tel. (22) 2075409; fax (22) 2072550; e-mail vkrishn@scbindia.mhs.compuserve.com; Chief Exec. S. MARTIN FISH; 17 brs.

**State Bank of Mauritius Ltd:** 101, Raheja Centre, 1st Floor, Free Press Journal Marg, Nariman Point, Mumbai 400 021; tel. (22) 2842965; fax (22) 2842966; Gen. Man. and CEO P. THONDRAYEN; 2 brs.

**Sumitomo Bank** (Japan): 15/F Jolly Maker Chamber No. 2, 225 Nariman Point, Mumbai 400 021; tel. (22) 2880025; fax (22) 2880026; CEO and Gen. Man. KOZO OTSUBO.

**Union Bank of Switzerland:** Mumbai.

### Banking Organizations

**Indian Banks' Association:** Stadium House, 6th Floor, Block 3, Veer Nariman Rd, Churchgate, Mumbai 400 020; tel. (22) 2844999; fax (22) 2835638; 163 mems; Chair. A. T. PANEERSELVAM; Sec. M. N. DANDEKAR.

**Indian Institute of Bankers:** 'The Arcade', World Trade Centre, 2nd Floor, East Wing, Cuffe Parade, Mumbai 400 005; tel. (22) 2187003; fax (22) 2185147; f. 1928; 343,202 mems; Pres. Dr C. RANGARAJAN; Chief Sec. R. H. SARMA.

**National Institute of Bank Management:** NIBM Post Office, Kondhwe Khurd, Pune 411 048; tel. (20) 673080; fax (20) 674478; e-mail nibmweb@nibm.ernet.in; internet www.nibmindia.com; f. 1969; Dir Dr GANTI SUBRAHMANYAM.

## DEVELOPMENT FINANCE ORGANIZATIONS

**Agricultural Finance Corporation Ltd:** Dhanraj Mahal, 1st Floor, Chhatrapati Shivaji Maharaj Marg, Mumbai 400 001; tel. (22) 2028924; fax (22) 2028966; e-mail afcl@bom2.vsnl.net.in; f. 1968 by a consortium of 35 public- and private-sector commercial banks to help increase the flow of investment and credit into agriculture and rural development projects; provides project consultancy services to commercial banks, Union and State govts, public-sector corpns, the World Bank, the ADB, FAO, the International Fund for Agricultural Development and other institutions and to individuals; undertakes techno-economic and investment surveys in agriculture and agro-industries etc.; 3 regional offices and 9 br. offices; cap. p.u. 100m., res and surplus 26.6m. (March 1998); Chair. Dr. P. V. SHENOI; Man. Dir SUBHASH WADHWA.

**Export-Import Bank of India:** Centre 1, Floor 21, World Trade Centre, Cuffe Parade, Mumbai 400 005; tel. and fax (22) 2182572; e-mail eximind@vsnl.com; internet www.eximbankindia.com; f. 1982; cap. 4,999.9m., res 8,352.1m., dep. 34,239.9m. (March 1999); offices in Bangalore, Kolkata, Chennai, New Delhi, Pune, Ahmedabad, Johannesburg, Budapest, Rome, Singapore and Washington, DC; Man. Dir Y. B. DESAI; Exec. Dir T. C. VENKAT SUBRAMANIAN.

**Housing Development Finance Corpn Ltd (HDFC):** Ramon House, 169 Backbay Reclamation, Mumbai 400 020; tel. (22) 2820282; fax (22) 2046758; e-mail library@hdfcindia.com; internet www.hdfcindia.com; provides loans to individuals and corporate bodies; Chair. DEEPAK S. PAREKH; Man. Dir ADITYA PURI; 69 brs.

**Industrial Credit and Investment Corpn of India Ltd:** 163 Backbay Reclamation, Mumbai 400 020; tel. (22) 2022535; fax (22) 2046582; f. 1955 to assist industrial enterprises by providing finance in both rupee and foreign currencies in the form of long- or medium-term loans or equity participation, guaranteeing loans from other private investment sources, furnishing managerial, technological and administration advice to industry; also offers suppliers' and buyers' credit, export development capital, asset credit, technology finance, instalment sale and equipment leasing facilities, and infrastructure finance; zonal offices at Mumbai, Kolkata, Chennai, New Delhi, Vadodara, Pune, Bangalore, Hyderabad and Coimbatore; development office at Guwahati (Assam); equity share cap. 4,781.4m., res 41,921.8m. (March 1998); Chair. N. VAGHUL, Man. Dir and CEO K. V. KAMATH.

**Industrial Development Bank of India (IDBI):** IDBI Tower, WTC Complex, Cuffe Parade, Colaba, Mumbai 400 005; tel. (22) 2189111; fax (22) 2180411; e-mail s.koshy@idbi.co.in; internet www.idbi.com; f. 1964, reorg. 1976; 72.1% govt-owned; India's premier financial institution for providing direct finance, refinance of industrial loans and bills, finance to large- and medium-sized industries, and for extending financial services, such as merchant banking and forex services, to the corporate sector; 5 zonal offices and 38 br. offices; cap. 6,595.3m., res 83,065.1m., dep. 410,828.9m. (March 1999); Chair. and Man. Dir GIAN PRAKASH GUPTA; Dep. Gen. Man. SUSAN KOSHY.

**Small Industries Development Bank of India:** 10/10 Madan Mohan Malviya Marg, Lucknow 226 001; tel. (522) 209517; fax (522) 209514; e-mail nvenkat@sidbi.com; internet www.sidbi.com; f. 1990; wholly-owned subsidiary of Industrial Development Bank of India; cap. p.u. 4,500m., res 20,566m. (March 1999); Chair. G. P. GUPTA; Man. Dir Dr SAILENDRA NARAIN; 39 offices.

**Industrial Finance Corpn of India Ltd:** IFCI Tower, 61 Nehru Place, New Delhi 110 019; tel. (11) 6487444; fax (11) 6488471; e-mail ifci@giasd01.vsnl.net.in; f. 1948 to provide medium- and long-term finance to cos and co-operative socs in India, engaged in manufacture, preservation or processing of goods, shipping, mining, hotels and power generation and distribution; promotes industrialization of less developed areas, and sponsors training in management techniques and development banking; cap. p.u. 3,535.6m., res 9,361.4m. (March 1999); Chair. and Man. Dir P. V. NARASIMHAN; Exec. Dirs S. P. BANERJEE, H. C. SHARMA; 8 regional offices and 10 br. offices.

**Industrial Investment Bank of India:** 19 Netaji Subhas Rd, Kolkata 700 001; tel. (33) 2209941; fax (33) 2207182; Chair. and Man. Dir Dr G. GOSWAMI.

**National Bank for Agriculture and Rural Development:** Sterling Centre, Shivsagar Estate, Dr Annie Besant Rd, Worli, POB 6552, Mumbai 400 018; tel. (22) 4964396; fax (22) 4931621; f. 1982 to provide credit for agricultural and rural development through commercial, co-operative and regional rural banks; cap. p.u. 10,000m., res 20,505m. (March 1998); held 50% each by the cen. Govt and the Reserve Bank; Chair. P. KOTAIAH; Man. Dir SAROJ K. KALIA; 17 regional offices, 10 sub-offices and 5 training establishments.

## STOCK EXCHANGES

There are 24 stock exchanges (with a total of more than 6,250 listed companies) in India, including:

**National Stock Exchange of India Ltd:** 'A' Wing, Mahindra Towers, 1st Floor, Worli, Mumbai 400 018; tel. (22) 4960525; fax (22) 4935631; e-mail postmaster@nse.co.in; internet www.nse.co.in; f. 1994; Pres. RAMCHANDRA PATIL.

**Ahmedabad Share and Stock Brokers' Association:** Manek Chowk, Ahmedabad 380 001; tel. (79) 347149; fax (79) 340117; f. 1894; 299 mems; Pres. V. G. GAJJAR; Exec. Dir M. L. SONEJI.

**Bangalore Stock Exchange Ltd:** 51 Stock Exchange Towers, 1st Corss, J. C. Rd, Bangalore 560 027; tel. (812) 2995234; fax (80) 2995242; e-mail kamala_k_@hotmail.com; 234 mems; Pres. PANKAJ J. SHAH; Exec. Dir K. KAMALA.

**Calcutta Stock Exchange Association Ltd:** 7 Lyons Range, Kolkata 700 001; tel. (33) 2206928; fax (33) 2104492; internet www.lyonrange.com; f. 1908; 910 mems; Pres. J. M. CHOUDHARY; Exec. Dir TAPAS DUTTA.

**Delhi Stock Exchange Association Ltd:** 3/1 Asaf Ali Rd, New Delhi 110 002; tel. (11) 3292002; fax (11) 3326182; f. 1947; 379 mems; Pres. BHARAT BHUSHAN SAHNY; Exec. Dir S. S. SODHI.

market for exports (18.7%) was Japan. Other major suppliers were the USA, Singapore, Germany, Australia and the Republic of Korea; other major purchasers were the USA, Singapore, the Republic of Korea, Hong Kong and the People's Republic of China. The principal exports in 1996 were petroleum and petroleum products, machinery and transport equipment, wood and wood products (particularly plywood), natural and manufactured gas, clothing and textiles. The principal imports were machinery, transport and electrical equipment, and chemical and mineral products.

In the financial year ending 31 March 1998 there was a budgetary surplus of 8,748m. rupiahs (equivalent to 2.3% of GDP). Indonesia's total external debt totalled US $136,174m. at the end of 1997, of which $55,869m. was long-term public debt. In that year the cost of debt-servicing was equivalent to 30.0% of revenue from exports of goods and services. The annual rate of inflation averaged 8.4% in 1990–97. Consumer prices rose by an average of 6.7% in 1997 and 57.7% in 1998. In 1994 about 4.4% of the labour force were unemployed; in the same year the rate of underemployment (defined as those working less than 35 hours per week) was 39.9%.

Indonesia is a member of the Association of South East Asian Nations (ASEAN—see p. 128), which aims to accelerate economic progress in the region, and of the Organization of the Petroleum Exporting Countries (OPEC—see p. 252). As a member of ASEAN, Indonesia signed an accord in January 1992, pledging to establish a free trade zone, to be known as the ASEAN Free Trade Area (AFTA), within 15 years (subsequently reduced to 10 years), beginning in January 1993.

The rapid financial deregulation from 1988 onwards, which resulted in a massive increase in the number of banks and an unsustainable expansion of bank credit and offshore borrowing, increased Indonesia's vulnerability to the currency crisis which affected South-East Asia in the second half of 1997. In August the Government was forced to allow the flotation of the currency, which constituted an effective devaluation, causing widespread unemployment and hardship. A US $43,000m. IMF programme to restore confidence in the economy was agreed in October but Suharto failed to honour the conditions of the agreement, finally announcing a completely unrealistic budget in January 1998. The rupiah continued to decline rapidly against other currencies, notably the US dollar, the value of shares on the Jakarta Stock Exchange dropped sharply and the price of basic commodities increased rapidly. A second agreement with the IMF and a revised budget were endorsed by Suharto later in January. However, the rupiah continued to fall (partly as a result of political uncertainty owing to Suharto's failure to nominate a credible successor). Also in January the Indonesian Banking Restructuring Agency (IBRA) was established to address problems in the country's banking sector, which remained in disarray. (A number of banks were subsequently closed during 1998, and a large number of others placed under the control of the IBRA. In October four of the seven state banks were merged into a single new institution, Bank Mandiri, and in December it was announced that the Government was to recapitalize a further 70 state and private banks.) Suspension of the IMF support programme in early March weakened international confidence in the country's economy; subsequently, however, a new, third agreement with the IMF was concluded. A sharp reduction in government subsidies on fuel, energy and public transport was announced in early May, resulting in a dramatic increase in prices. The riots that ensued led to the resignation of Suharto later that month, by which time, however, international trade had declined, GDP had contracted considerably and the rate of inflation had surged. In late June a third revision of the IMF rescue programme was agreed. Subsequently, restrictions on foreign investment in the banking sector and other industries were relaxed and the planned privatization of a number of state-owned companies was announced. Approved foreign direct investment was reported to have declined by more than 50% in 1998, however, while GDP contracted by 14% in the same year. During 1999, however, the economy began to recover, although unemployment remained high: a modest expansion of GDP was recorded, inflation was reduced dramatically, interest rates were lowered and the currency appreciated. The recovery was influenced considerably by political events in the country during the course of 1999. On the day following the legislative election held in June, the benchmark Jakarta stock index rose by 12% to a 23-month high. The defeat of Habibie (still associated by many with former President Suharto) in the presidential elections held in November also strengthened the economy, increasing the confidence of potential foreign investors. The recovery process remained hampered by obstacles, however, with the banking sector in particular continuing to be burdened by high levels of non-performing loans. In March the Government announced the scheduled closure of 38 private domestic banks and the nationalization of a further seven, and also approved the recapitalization of an additional nine. In late 1999 President Wahid brought the IBRA under his control in order to ensure the independence of the Agency; the importance of the IBRA was emphasized in 1999 following a scandal involving Bank Bali, from which funds had allegedly been transferred to a company linked to the former ruling party, Golkar. (A full report on the Bank Bali scandal was released in November, and recommended that senior banking officials, including the Governor of the central bank, Sjahril Sabirin, be questioned further.) The scandal resulted in delays in the disbursement of loans worth an estimated US $4,600m. from the IMF, the World Bank and the Asian Development Bank. In January 2000 the banking sector provided further cause for concern when an independent audit revealed that the central bank might be subject to far greater losses and liabilities than previously acknowledged, prompting calls for the recapitalization of the bank. Although the economy expanded by only 0.2% in 1999, the rate of growth for the final quarter of the year measured 5.8% compared with a year earlier, encouraging optimism that the process of economic recovery would continue to gain momentum in 2000. GDP was forecast to expand by 3.8% in 2001.

## Social Welfare

Certain members of the population benefit from a state insurance scheme. Benefits include life insurance and old-age pensions. In addition, there are two social insurance schemes, administered by state corporations, providing pensions and industrial accident insurance. In 1995, according to preliminary data, Indonesia had 1,062 hospitals (with a total of 118,306 beds). In the same year, there were 7,076 public health centres in Indonesia. In March 1996 there were 30,402 physicians working in the country and 138,974 nurses and midwives. In the 1996/97 budget, according to provisional data, 1,962,000m. rupiahs, 2.5% of total expenditure, was allocated to health.

## Education

Education is mainly under the control of the Ministry of Education and Culture, but the Ministry of Religious Affairs is in charge of Islamic religious schools at the primary level. In 1987 primary education, beginning at seven years of age and lasting for six years, was made compulsory. In 1993 it was announced that compulsory education was to be expanded to nine years. Secondary education begins at 13 years of age and lasts for six years, comprising two cycles of three years each. Primary enrolment in 1994 included 97% of children in the relevant age-group (males 99%; females 95%). In the same year enrolment at secondary level included 42% of the relevant population (males 45%; females 39%). In 1997/98, according to preliminary data, there were 1,391 universities. In 1994 enrolment at tertiary level was equivalent to 11.1% of the relevant population (males 13.5%; females 8.6%). In 1996/97, according to provisional data, the Government allocated 7,040,000m. rupiahs, representing 9.0% of total expenditure, to education. In 1995, according to UNESCO estimates, the average rate of adult illiteracy was 16.2% (males 10.4%; females 22.0%).

## Public Holidays

**2000:** 1 January (New Year's Day), 8 January* (Id al-Fitr, end of Ramadan), 16 March* (Id al-Adha, Feast of the Sacrifice), 6 April* (Muharram, Islamic New Year), 21 April (Good Friday), 18 May (Vesak Day), 1 June (Ascension Day), 15 June* (Mouloud, Prophet Muhammad's Birthday), 17 August (Independence Day), 26 October* (Ascension of the Prophet Muhammad), 25 December (Christmas Day), 28 December* (Id al-Fitr, end of Ramadan).

**2001:** 1 January (New Year's Day), 6 March* (Id al-Adha, Feast of the Sacrifice), 26 March* (Muharram, Islamic New Year), 13 April (Good Friday), 24 May (Ascension Day), May (Vesak Day), 24 June* (Mouloud, Prophet Muhammad's Birthday), 17 August (Independence Day), 15 October* (Ascension of the Prophet Muhammad), 17 December* (Id al-Fitr, end of Ramadan), 25 December (Christmas Day).

* These holidays are dependent on the Islamic lunar calendar and may vary by one or two days from the dates given.

## Weights and Measures

The metric system is in force.

# Statistical Survey

Source (unless otherwise stated): Central Bureau of Statistics, Jalan Dr Sutomo 8, Jakarta 10710; tel. (21) 363360; fax (21) 3857046; e-mail elaps@mailhost.bps.go.id.

Note: Unless otherwise stated, figures for East Timor (occupied by Indonesia between July 1976 and October 1999) are not included in the tables.

## Area and Population

**AREA, POPULATION AND DENSITY**

| | |
|---|---|
| Area (sq km) | 1,922,570* |
| Population (census results) | |
| 31 October 1980 | 146,934,948 |
| 31 October 1990 | |
| Males | 89,076,606 |
| Females | 89,554,590 |
| Total | 178,631,196 |
| Population (official estimates at 31 December) | |
| 1994 | 191,390,500 |
| 1995 | 194,440,100 |
| 1996 | 197,483,200 |
| Density (per sq km) at 31 December 1996 | 102.7 |

* 742,308 sq miles.

**ISLANDS** (estimated population at 31 December 1996)*

| | Area (sq km) | Population | Density (per sq km) |
|---|---|---|---|
| Jawa (Java) and Madura | 127,499 | 116,379,200 | 912.8 |
| Sumatera (Sumatra) | 482,393 | 41,840,700 | 86.7 |
| Sulawesi (Celebes) | 191,800 | 14,019,800 | 73.1 |
| Kalimantan | 547,891 | 10,807,900 | 19.7 |
| Nusa Tenggara† | 67,502 | 7,348,600 | 108.9 |
| Bali | 5,633 | 2,924,400 | 519.2 |
| Maluku (Moluccas) | 77,871 | 2,141,700 | 27.5 |
| Irian Jaya (now West Papua) | 421,981 | 2,020,900 | 4.8 |
| **Total** | 1,922,570 | 197,483,200 | 102.7 |

* Figures refer to provincial divisions, each based on a large island or group of islands but also including adjacent small islands.

† Comprising most of the Lesser Sunda Islands, principally Flores, Lombok, Sumba, Sumbawa and part of Timor.

**PRINCIPAL TOWNS** (estimated population at 31 December 1996)

| | |
|---|---|
| Jakarta (capital) | 9,341,400 |
| Surabaya | 2,743,400 |
| Bandung | 2,429,000 |
| Medan | 1,942,000 |
| Palembang | 1,394,300 |
| Semarang | 1,366,500 |
| Ujung Pandang (Makassar) | 1,121,300 |
| Malang | 775,900 |
| Padang | 739,500 |
| Banjarmasin | 544,700 |
| Surakarta | 518,600 |
| Pontianak | 459,100 |
| Yogyakarta (Jogjakarta) | 421,000 |

**BIRTHS AND DEATHS** (UN estimates, annual averages)

| | 1980–85 | 1985–90 | 1990–95 |
|---|---|---|---|
| Birth rate (per 1,000) | 32.2 | 28.2 | 24.6 |
| Death rate (per 1,000) | 11.2 | 9.4 | 8.4 |

**Expectation of life** (UN estimates, years at birth, 1990–95): 62.6 (males 61.0; females 64.5).

Source: UN, *World Population Prospects: The 1998 Revision.*

**Birth rate** (per 1,000): 23.6 in 1995; 23.3 in 1996; 22.9 in 1997. Source: UN, *Statistical Yearbook for Asia and the Pacific.*

**Death rate** (per 1,000): 7.7 in 1995; 7.6 in 1996; 7.5 in 1997. Source: UN, *Statistical Yearbook for Asia and the Pacific.*

**EMPLOYMENT** (ISIC Major Divisions, '000 persons aged 10 years and over, survey of May 1997)*

| | Males | Females | Total |
|---|---|---|---|
| Agriculture, hunting, forestry and fishing | 21,960 | 13,889 | 35,849 |
| Mining and quarrying | 710 | 186 | 897 |
| Manufacturing | 6,189 | 5,026 | 11,215 |
| Electricity, gas and water | 214 | 19 | 233 |
| Construction | 4,050 | 150 | 4,200 |
| Trade, restaurants and hotels | 8,404 | 8,817 | 17,221 |
| Transport, storage and communications | 4,023 | 115 | 4,138 |
| Financing, insurance, real estate and business services | 447 | 209 | 657 |
| Public services | 7,972 | 4,666 | 12,637 |
| Activities not adequately defined | 2 | 2 | 3 |
| **Total employed** | 53,971 | 33,079 | 87,050 |

* Figures include East Timor.

Source: ILO, *Yearbook of Labour Statistics.*

## Agriculture

**PRINCIPAL CROPS** ('000 metric tons, incl. East Timor)

| | 1996 | 1997 | 1998 |
|---|---|---|---|
| Rice (paddy) | 51,102 | 49,377 | 48,472 |
| Maize | 9,307 | 8,771 | 10,059 |
| Potatoes | 1,100 | 813 | 840 |
| Sweet potatoes | 2,018 | 1,847 | 1,928 |
| Cassava (Manioc) | 17,002 | 15,134 | 14,728 |
| Other roots and tubers | 340 | 331 | 330 |
| Dry beans* | 860 | 870 | 870 |
| Soybeans | 1,517 | 1,357 | 1,306 |
| Groundnuts (in shell)† | 1,055 | 983 | 988 |
| Coconuts | 14,138† | 14,710† | 14,710* |
| Copra* | 1,155 | 1,360 | 1,120 |
| Palm kernels | 1,085 | 1,190 | 1,303 |
| Cabbages | 1,580 | 1,335 | 1,156 |
| Tomatoes | 337 | 277 | 261 |
| Pumpkins, squash and gourds | 145† | 145* | 145* |
| Cucumbers and gherkins* | 310 | 310 | 310 |
| Aubergines (Eggplants)* | 130 | 145 | 145 |
| Chillies and peppers (green) | 453 | 316 | 274 |
| Onions (dry) | 769 | 602 | 442 |
| Garlic | 146 | 102 | 38 |
| Green beans | 186 | 186 | 145 |
| Carrots | 270 | 227 | 260 |
| Other vegetables* | 1,540 | 1,549 | 1,548 |
| Sugar cane | 29,486 | 27,764 | 27,500† |
| Oranges | 731 | 693 | 614 |
| Avocados | 143 | 130 | 115 |
| Mangoes | 783 | 605 | 605* |
| Pineapples | 501 | 385 | 349 |
| Bananas | 3,023 | 3,025 | 3,012 |
| Papayas | 382 | 355 | 336 |
| Other fruits and berries* | 2,301 | 2,420 | 2,419 |
| Cashew nuts | 68 | 67 | 67 |
| Coffee (green) | 459 | 454 | 455 |
| Cocoa beans | 374 | 307 | 370 |
| Tea (made) | 166 | 149 | 152 |
| Tobacco (leaves) | 151 | 137 | 138 |
| Natural rubber | 1,574 | 1,549 | 1,564 |

* FAO estimate(s). † Unofficial figure(s).

Source: FAO, *Production Yearbook.*

**LIVESTOCK** ('000 head, incl. East Timor; year ending September)

| | 1996 | 1997 | 1998 |
|---|---|---|---|
| Cattle | 11,816 | 12,031 | 12,239 |
| Sheep | 7,724 | 7,700 | 8,151 |
| Goats | 13,840 | 14,308 | 15,198 |
| Pigs | 7,597 | 8,589 | 10,069 |
| Horses | 579 | 582 | 740* |
| Buffaloes | 3,171 | 3,114 | 3,145 |

Chickens (million): 980 in 1996; 1,002 in 1997; 889 in 1998.
Ducks (million): 30 in 1996; 30 in 1997; 28* in 1998.

* Unofficial figure.

Source: FAO, *Production Yearbook*.

**LIVESTOCK PRODUCTS** ('000 metric tons, incl. East Timor)

| | 1996 | 1997 | 1998 |
|---|---|---|---|
| Beef and veal | 347 | 355 | 347 |
| Buffalo meat | 49 | 47 | 53 |
| Mutton and lamb | 39 | 42 | 27 |
| Goat meat | 60 | 66 | 70 |
| Pig meat* | 600 | 616 | 759 |
| Poultry meat | 940 | 900 | 819 |
| Cows' milk | 441 | 424 | 434 |
| Sheep's milk* | 93 | 96 | 96 |
| Goats' milk* | 220 | 232 | 232 |
| Hen eggs | 629 | 613 | 429 |
| Other poultry eggs | 150 | 155 | 159 |
| Wool (greasy)* | 23 | 24 | 24 |
| Cattle and buffalo hides* | 43 | 46 | 46 |
| Sheepskins* | 9 | 9 | 8 |
| Goatskins* | 14 | 14 | 15 |

Note: Figures for meat refer to inspected production only, i.e. from animals slaughtered under government supervision.

* FAO estimates.

Source: FAO, *Production Yearbook*.

# Forestry

**ROUNDWOOD REMOVALS**
('000 cubic metres, excluding bark)

| | 1995 | 1996 | 1997 |
|---|---|---|---|
| Sawlogs, veneer logs and logs for sleepers*: | | | |
| Coniferous | 333 | 333 | 333 |
| Non-coniferous | 31,066 | 32,250 | 32,250 |
| Pulpwood* | 8,738 | 11,547 | 11,547 |
| Other industrial wood* | 3,066 | 3,113 | 3,159 |
| Fuel wood | 151,095 | 153,385 | 155,700 |
| **Total** | 194,298 | 200,627 | 202,989 |

* FAO estimates.

Source: FAO, *Yearbook of Forest Products*.

**SAWNWOOD PRODUCTION**
('000 cubic metres, including railway sleepers)

| | 1995 | 1996 | 1997 |
|---|---|---|---|
| Coniferous (softwood)* | 138 | 138 | 138 |
| Broadleaved (hardwood) | 6,500 | 7,200† | 7,100† |
| **Total** | 6,638 | 7,338 | 7,238 |

* FAO estimates.

† Unofficial figure.

Source: FAO, *Yearbook of Forest Products*.

# Fishing

('000 metric tons, live weight)

| | 1995 | 1996 | 1997 |
|---|---|---|---|
| Freshwater fishes | 308.0 | 314.9 | 317.0 |
| Ponyfishes (Slipmouths) | 66.2 | 71.4 | 69.3 |
| Scads | 247.3 | 251.3 | 250.0 |
| Other carangids | 182.5 | 184.3 | 183.2 |
| Goldstripe sardinella | 161.1 | 157.1 | 158.2 |
| Bali sardinella | 98.9 | 88.6 | 86.1 |
| 'Stolephorus' anchovies | 157.2 | 161.8 | 161.5 |
| Skipjack tuna | 159.7 | 182.1 | 209.1 |
| Yellowfin tuna | 101.7 | 115.5 | 122.8 |
| Other tunas, bonitos, billfishes, etc. | 267.7 | 300.1 | 311.4 |
| Indian mackerels | 193.9 | 188.9 | 189.1 |
| Sharks, rays, skates, etc. | 98.1 | 94.7 | 95.6 |
| Other marine fishes (incl. unspecified) | 1,011.2 | 1,106.7 | 1,110.5 |
| **Total fish** | 3,053.6 | 3,217.4 | 3,263.7 |
| Marine shrimps, prawns, etc. | 185.9 | 191.4 | 196.7 |
| Other crustaceans | 33.9 | 32.0 | 37.8 |
| Molluscs | 100.5 | 103.9 | 106.6 |
| Jellyfishes | 123.1 | 6.7 | 38.2 |
| Other aquatic animals | 6.8 | 6.2 | 6.3 |
| **Total catch** | 3,503.8 | 3,557.6 | 3,649.2 |
| Inland waters | 329.7 | 335.7 | 339.3 |
| Indian Ocean | 558.0 | 591.2 | 632.8 |
| Pacific Ocean | 2,616.0 | 2,630.7 | 2,677.1 |

Crocodiles (number): 12,362 in 1994.
Corals (metric tons): 1,700* in 1995; 1,700* in 1996; 1,500* in 1997.
Aquatic plants ('000 metric tons): 9.6 in 1995; 13.5 in 1996; 15.0 in 1997.

* FAO estimate.

Source: FAO, *Yearbook of Fishery Statistics*.

# Mining

(metric tons, unless otherwise indicated)

| | 1996 | 1997 | 1998* |
|---|---|---|---|
| Crude petroleum ('000 barrels) | 548,648 | 543,753 | n.a. |
| Natural gas (million cu ft) | 3,164,016 | 3,166,035 | n.a. |
| Bauxite | 841,976 | 808,749 | 513,396 |
| Coal | 50,332,047 | 54,797,322 | n.a. |
| Nickel ore† | 3,426,867 | 2,829,936 | 1,642,114 |
| Copper concentrate† | 1,758,910 | 1,817,880 | 2,640,040 |
| Tin ore (metal content) | 48,765 | 53,037 | 43,056 |
| Gold (kg)‡ | 83,044 | 89,069 | 118,246 |
| Silver (kg)‡ | 250,109 | 269,712 | 266,550 |

* Preliminary data.

† Figures refer to gross weight. The estimated metal content was: Nickel 3.1%; Copper 44%.

‡ Including gold and silver in copper concentrate.

Source: Department of Mines and Energy, Jakarta.

# Industry

**SELECTED PRODUCTS** ('000 metric tons, unless otherwise indicated)

| | 1993 | 1994 | 1995 |
|---|---|---|---|
| Refined sugar | 2,294 | 2,224 | 2,202 |
| Cigarettes (million) | 171,828 | 194,424 | 216,199 |
| Veneer sheets ('000 cubic metres) | 55 | 50 | 50 |
| Plywood ('000 cubic metres) | 10,050 | 9,836 | 9,500 |
| Newsprint | 54 | 150 | 71 |
| Other printing and writing paper | 844 | 992 | 1,061 |
| Other paper and paperboard* | 1,561 | 1,823 | 2,408 |
| Nitrogenous fertilizers (a)† | 2,513 | 2,357 | 2,428 |
| Phosphatic fertilizers (b)† | 1,179 | n.a. | 67 |
| Jet fuel | 576 | 686 | 838 |
| Motor spirit (petrol) | 5,330 | 5,264 | 4,942 |
| Naphthas | 1,002 | 1,138 | 1,115 |
| Kerosene | 6,197 | 6,694 | 6,193 |
| Distillate fuel oils‡ | 12,800 | 13,200 | 13,300 |
| Residual fuel oils‡ | 10,900 | 11,000 | 11,600 |
| Lubricating oils | 224 | 253 | 236 |
| Liquefied petroleum gas | 2,777 | 3,122 | 2,941 |
| Rubber tyres ('000)§ | 14,376 | 20,842 | n.a. |
| Cement | 19,610 | 24,564 | 23,136 |
| Aluminium (unwrought)‖ | 202.1 | 221.9¶ | 228.1¶ |
| Tin (unwrought, metric tons)‡‖¶ | 38,300 | 39,000 | 44,218 |
| Radio receivers ('000) | 3,882 | 3,372 | n.a. |
| Television receivers ('000) | 1,001 | 1,791 | 1,555 |
| Passenger motor cars ('000)** | 72 | 95 | 127 |
| Electric energy (million kWh)‡ | 58,888 | 64,351 | 68,804 |
| Gas from gasworks (terajoules) | 12,025 | 15,065 | 19,807 |

* Data from the FAO.
† Production in terms of (a) nitrogen or (b) phosphoric acid.
‡ Provisional or estimated production.
§ For road motor vehicles, excluding bicycles and motorcycles.
‖ Primary metal production only.
¶ Data from *World Metal Statistics*.
** Vehicles assembled from imported parts.

Source: UN, *Industrial Commodity Statistics Yearbook*.

Palm oil ('000 metric tons): 3,421 in 1993; 4,008 in 1994; 4,480 in 1995; 4,899 in 1996; 5,385 in 1997; 5,902 in 1998. Source: FAO, *Production Yearbook*.

Raw sugar (centrifugal, '000 metric tons): 2,483 in 1993; 2,454 in 1994; 2,098 in 1995; 2,160 in 1996; 2,221 in 1997; 2,050 (unofficial figure) in 1998. Source: FAO, *Production Yearbook*.

# Finance

**CURRENCY AND EXCHANGE RATES**

**Monetary Units**

100 sen = 1 rupiah (Rp.).

**Sterling, Dollar and Euro Equivalents** (30 September 1999)

£1 sterling = 13,807.5 rupiahs;
US $1 = 8,386.0 rupiahs;
€1 = 8,943.7 rupiahs;
100,000 rupiahs = £7.242 = $11.925 = €11.181.

**Average Exchange Rate** (rupiahs per US $)

| | |
|---|---|
| 1996 | 2,342.3 |
| 1997 | 2,909.4 |
| 1998 | 10,013.6 |

**BUDGET** ('000 million rupiahs, year ending 31 March)*

| Revenue† | 1994/95 | 1995/96 | 1996/97‡ |
|---|---|---|---|
| Tax revenue | 62,338 | 72,828 | 78,241 |
| Taxes on income, profits, etc. | 32,895 | 37,077 | 45,368 |
| Social security contributions | 1,380 | 4,811 | 2,431 |
| Domestic taxes on goods and services | 23,382 | 26,762 | 26,701 |
| General sales, turnover or VAT | 18,335 | 18,519 | 20,393 |
| Excises | 3,153 | 3,593 | 4,217 |
| Taxes on international trade | 4,224 | 3,215 | 2,877 |
| Import duties | 4,093 | 3,029 | 2,807 |
| Other current revenue | 7,056 | 7,584 | 12,048 |
| Entrepreneurial and property income | 5,286 | 6,210 | 8,807 |
| Administrative fees and charges, non-industrial and incidental sales | 1,623 | 928 | 1,763 |
| Capital revenue | 8 | 15 | 9 |
| **Total** | 69,402 | 80,427 | 90,298 |

| Expenditure§ | 1994/95 | 1995/96 | 1996/97‡ |
|---|---|---|---|
| General public services | 3,948 | 4,713 | 12,281 |
| Defence | 4,266 | 4,792 | 5,695 |
| Public order and safety | 1,260 | 1,912 | 2,299 |
| Education | 6,045 | 6,042 | 7,040 |
| Health | 2,011 | 1,723 | 1,962 |
| Social security and welfare | 3,259 | 4,153 | 5,643 |
| Housing and community amenities | 11,041 | 13,699 | 15,819 |
| Recreational, cultural and religious affairs and services | 1,448 | 1,610 | 1,862 |
| Economic affairs and services | 19,358 | 14,125 | 18,431 |
| Agriculture, forestry, fishing and hunting | 11,903 | 6,290 | 9,729 |
| Transport and communications | 5,230 | 5,086 | 5,720 |
| Other purposes | 9,230 | 9,612 | 6,932 |
| Interest payments | 7,565 | 7,130 | 6,426 |
| Unallocable | — | 4,342 | — |
| **Total** | 61,866 | 66,723 | 77,964 |
| Current | 31,722 | 36,037 | 46,150 |
| Capital | 30,144 | 30,686 | 31,814 |

* Figures represent a consolidation of the General Budget, the Investment Fund, the Reforestation Fund and three social security schemes.
† Excluding grants received ('000 million rupiahs): 67 in 1994/95.
‡ Figures are provisional.
§ Excluding lending minus repayments ('000 million rupiahs): 4,022 in 1994/95; 3,619 in 1995/96; 6,154 (provisional) in 1996/97.

Source: IMF, *Government Finance Statistics Yearbook*.

**1996/97** (revised totals): Revenue 92,770,000 million rupiahs; Expenditure 78,623,000 million rupiahs.
**1997/98:** Total revenue 115,922,000 million rupiahs; Total expenditure 100,024,000 million rupiahs.

Source: IMF, *International Financial Statistics*.

**INTERNATIONAL RESERVES** (US $ million at 31 December)

| | 1996 | 1997 | 1998 |
|---|---|---|---|
| Gold* | 1,030 | 809 | 803 |
| IMF special drawing rights | 2 | 499 | 312 |
| Reserve position in IMF | 429 | — | — |
| Foreign exchange | 17,820 | 16,088 | 22,401 |
| **Total** | 19,281 | 17,396 | 23,516 |

* Valued at market-related prices.

Source: IMF, *International Financial Statistics*.

**MONEY SUPPLY** ('000 million rupiahs at 31 December)

| | 1996 | 1997 | 1998 |
|---|---|---|---|
| Currency outside banks | 22,487 | 28,424 | 41,394 |
| Demand deposits at deposit money banks | 28,883 | 40,232 | 45,717 |
| **Total money** (incl. others) | 51,652 | 68,786 | 87,301 |

Source: IMF, *International Financial Statistics*.

**COST OF LIVING** (Consumer Price Index; base: 1990 = 100)

| | 1995 | 1996 | 1997 |
|---|---|---|---|
| Food (incl. beverages) | 156.3 | 171.1 | 186.2 |
| **All items** (incl.others) | 153.2 | 165.3 | 176.2 |

Source: ILO, *Yearbook of Labour Statistics*.

**All items** (base: 1995 = 100): 108.0 in 1996; 115.2 in 1997; 181.7 in 1998. (Source: IMF, *International Financial Statistics*).

**NATIONAL ACCOUNTS** ('000 million rupiahs at current prices)

**National Income and Product**

| | 1990 | 1991 | 1992 |
|---|---|---|---|
| Domestic factor incomes* | 172,393 | 201,118 | 229,946 |
| Consumption of fixed capital | 9,784 | 11,380 | 13,045 |
| **Gross domestic product (GDP) at factor cost** | 182,177 | 212,498 | 242,991 |
| Indirect taxes, *less* subsidies | 13,420 | 15,004 | 17,795 |
| **GDP in purchasers' values** | 195,597 | 227,502 | 260,786 |
| Net factor income from abroad | -9,614 | -10,899 | -12,213 |
| **Gross national product (GNP)** | 185,983 | 216,603 | 248,573 |
| *Less* Consumption of fixed capital | 9,784 | 11,380 | 13,045 |
| **National income in market prices** | 176,199 | 205,223 | 235,528 |

* Compensation of employees and the operating surplus of enterprises. The amount is obtained as a residual.

Source: UN, *National Accounts Statistics*.

**Expenditure on the Gross Domestic Product**

| | 1996 | 1997 | 1998 |
|---|---|---|---|
| Government final consumption expenditure | 40,299 | 42,952 | 54,416 |
| Private final consumption expenditure | 332,094 | 387,171 | 663,460 |
| Gross capital formation | 163,453 | 199,301 | 131,782 |
| **Total domestic expenditure** | 535,847 | 629,424 | 849,658 |
| Exports of goods and services | 137,533 | 174,871 | 506,245 |
| *Less* Imports of goods and services | 140,812 | 176,600 | 413,059 |
| **GDP in purchasers' values** | 532,568 | 627,695 | 942,843 |
| **GDP at constant 1993 prices** | 413,798 | 433,246 | 374,719 |

Source: IMF, *International Financial Statistics*.

**Gross Domestic Product by Economic Activity**

| | 1996 | 1997 | 1998 |
|---|---|---|---|
| Agriculture, forestry and fishing | 88,792 | 100,151 | 186,483 |
| Mining and quarrying | 46,088 | 54,510 | 127,217 |
| Manufacturing | 136,426 | 159,748 | 259,564 |
| Electricity, gas and water | 6,893 | 7,939 | 11,531 |
| Construction | 42,025 | 46,181 | 53,841 |
| Trade, hotels and restaurants | 87,137 | 103,763 | 147,478 |
| Transport and communications | 34,926 | 42,232 | 53,640 |
| Finance and insurance | 30,333 | 40,976 | 59,152 |
| Dwellings and real estate | 13,648 | 17,715 | 22,318 |
| Government services | 29,753 | 32,128 | 37,250 |
| Other services | 16,547 | 20,164 | 31,101 |
| **Total** | 532,568 | 625,506 | 989,573 |

Source: IMF, *Indonesia: Statistical Appendix* (May 1999).

**BALANCE OF PAYMENTS** (US $ million)

| | 1996 | 1997 | 1998 |
|---|---|---|---|
| Exports of goods f.o.b. | 50,188 | 56,298 | 50,371 |
| Imports of goods f.o.b. | 44,240 | 46,223 | 31,942 |
| **Trade balance** | 5,948 | 10,075 | 18,429 |
| Exports of services | 6,599 | 6,941 | 4,479 |
| Imports of services | 15,139 | 16,607 | 11,813 |
| **Balance on goods and services** | -2,592 | 409 | 11,095 |
| Other income received | 1,210 | 1,855 | 1,910 |
| Other income paid | -7,218 | -8,187 | 10,122 |
| **Balance on goods, services and income** | -8,600 | -5,923 | 2,883 |
| Current transfers received | 937 | 1,034 | 1,089 |
| **Current balance** | -7,663 | -4,889 | 3,972 |
| Direct investment abroad | -600 | -178 | -44 |
| Direct investment from abroad | 6,194 | 4,677 | -356 |
| Portfolio investment liabilities | 5,005 | -2,632 | -2,002 |
| Other investment liabilities | 248 | -2,470 | -7,945 |
| Net errors and omissions | 1,319 | -2,133 | 2,727 |
| **Overall balance** | 4,503 | -7,625 | -3,648 |

Source: IMF, *International Financial Statistics*.

## External Trade

**PRINCIPAL COMMODITIES** (distribution by SITC, US $ million)

| Imports c.i.f. | 1994 | 1995 | 1996 |
|---|---|---|---|
| **Food and live animals** | 1,895.6 | 3,020.0 | 3,926.5 |
| Cereals and cereal preparations | 926.6 | 1,551.5 | 2,002.5 |
| **Crude materials (inedible) except fuels** | 2,723.7 | 3,624.0 | 3,441.2 |
| Pulp and waste paper | 614.2 | 882.3 | 704.5 |
| Textile fibres and waste | 948.2 | 1,244.7 | 1,261.3 |
| Cotton | 701.3 | 923.2 | 980.6 |
| Raw cotton (excl. linters) | 700.6 | 922.3 | 980.1 |
| **Mineral fuels, lubricants, etc.** | 2,487.6 | 3,094.9 | 3,774.9 |
| Petroleum, petroleum products, etc. | 2,461.8 | 3,045.1 | 3,746.2 |
| Crude petroleum oils, etc. | 1,073.2 | 1,317.6 | 1,518.9 |
| Refined petroleum products | 1,290.5 | 1,604.8 | 2,086.1 |
| Gas oils | 582.9 | 783.6 | 963.6 |
| **Chemicals and related products** | 4,757.3 | 6,130.2 | 5,876.9 |
| Organic chemicals | 1,609.7 | 2,327.9 | 2,226.7 |
| Plastic materials, etc. | 1,145.3 | 1,390.7 | 1,166.4 |
| Products of polymerization, etc. | 754.2 | 893.5 | 740.8 |
| **Basic manufactures** | 5,386.7 | 6,855.2 | 6,844.6 |
| Textile yarn, fabrics, etc. | 1,175.3 | 1,327.1 | 1,288.3 |
| Iron and steel | 1,684.1 | 2,451.0 | 2,370.7 |
| Non-ferrous metals | 643.6 | 1,018.7 | 905.4 |

| Imports c.i.f. — *continued* | 1994 | 1995 | 1996 |
|---|---|---|---|
| **Machinery and transport equipment** | 13,426.3 | 16,257.1 | 17,458.6 |
| Power-generating machinery and equipment | 1,752.0 | 1,827.6 | 1,968.6 |
| Internal combustion piston engines and parts | 717.8 | 855.6 | 727.4 |
| Machinery specialized for particular industries | 3,014.7 | 3,891.4 | 4,118.3 |
| Textile and leather machinery | 836.9 | 1,051.3 | 740.4 |
| General industrial machinery, equipment and parts | 2,393.0 | 3,059.2 | 3,629.1 |
| Heating and cooling equipment and parts | 643.1 | 838.1 | 944.0 |
| Telecommunications and sound equipment | 759.5 | 1,086.2 | 1,766.3 |
| Other electrical machinery, apparatus, etc. | 1,758.2 | 1,965.6 | 1,868.3 |
| Switchgear, etc., and parts | 557.2 | 559.3 | 476.5 |
| Road vehicles and parts* | 2,335.2 | 2,983.7 | 2,673.5 |
| Parts and accessories for cars, buses, lorries, etc.* | 1,532.5 | 1,843.2 | 1,359.5 |
| Other transport equipment* | 800.6 | 606.1 | 533.9 |
| **Miscellaneous manufactured articles** | 967.8 | 1,282.6 | 1,215.0 |
| **Total** (incl. others) | 28,327.8 | 40,628.7 | 42,928.5 |

* Excluding tyres, engines and electrical parts.

Source: UN, *International Trade Statistics Yearbook.*

| Exports f.o.b. | 1994 | 1995 | 1996 |
|---|---|---|---|
| **Food and live animals** | 3,550.7 | 3,579.9 | 3,764.4 |
| Fish, crustaceans and molluscs | 1,581.5 | 1,665.3 | 1,676.8 |
| Crustaceans and molluscs (fresh, chilled, frozen or salted) | 1,050.9 | 1,080.8 | 1,063.6 |
| Coffee, tea, cocoa and spices | 1,296.9 | 1,250.5 | 1,275.7 |
| **Crude materials (inedible) except fuels** | 3,235.4 | 5,033.6 | 5,081.2 |
| Crude rubber (incl. synthetic and reclaimed) | 1,274.6 | 1,965.4 | 1,922.8 |
| Natural rubber and gums | 1,273.1 | 1,963.9 | 1,920.1 |
| Natural rubber (other than latex) | 1,228.3 | 1,919.3 | 1,872.9 |
| Metalliferous ores and metal scrap | 1,148.2 | 1,883.5 | 2,034.3 |
| Ores and concentrates of non-ferrous base metals | 1,133.2 | 1,870.2 | 2,019.0 |
| Copper ores and concentrates | 857.6 | 1,537.4 | 1,747.6 |
| **Mineral fuels, lubricants, etc.** | 10,523.5 | 11,508.6 | 12,860.8 |
| Coal, coke and briquettes | 829.6 | 1,043.7 | 1,123.7 |
| Coal, lignite and peat | 819.3 | 1,033.2 | 1,120.9 |
| Petroleum, petroleum products, etc. | 6,004.7 | 6,442.9 | 7,243.3 |
| Crude petroleum oils, etc. | 5,071.6 | 5,145.7 | 5,711.8 |
| Refined petroleum products | 923.3 | 1,276.4 | 1,502.1 |
| Gas (natural and manufactured) | 3,689.1 | 4,022.0 | 4,493.9 |
| Petroleum gases, etc., in the liquefied state | 3,689.1 | 4,022.0 | 4,493.9 |
| **Animal and vegetable oils, fats and waxes** | 1,374.4 | 1,383.6 | 1,567.8 |
| Fixed vegetable oils and fats | 1,132.4 | 1,040.8 | 1,343.7 |
| Fixed vegetable oils, fluid or solid, crude, refined or purified | 1,115.4 | 1,034.7 | 1,338.4 |
| **Chemicals and related products** | 1,001.2 | 1,510.1 | 1,723.6 |
| **Basic manufactures** | 9,534.9 | 10,527.2 | 10,887.9 |
| Wood and cork manufactures (excl. furniture) | 4,832.4 | 4,662.5 | 4,839.8 |
| Veneers, plywood, etc. | 4,123.9 | 3,825.5 | 3,985.8 |
| Plywood of wood sheets | 3,716.4 | 3,462.0 | 3,595.4 |
| Paper, paperboard, etc. | 595.2 | 933.1 | 947.3 |
| Textile yarn, fabrics, etc. | 2,515.9 | 2,738.1 | 2,856.8 |
| Woven fabrics of man-made fibres* | 1,115.7 | 1,179.9 | 1,150.7 |
| **Machinery and transport equipment** | 3,044.7 | 3,823.5 | 4,994.0 |
| Telecommunications and sound equipment | 1,472.5 | 1,634.3 | 2,068.2 |

| Exports f.o.b. — *continued* | 1994 | 1995 | 1996 |
|---|---|---|---|
| **Miscellaneous manufactured articles** | 7,499.9 | 7,806.1 | 8,613.7 |
| Clothing and accessories (excl. footwear) | 3,272.9 | 3,451.8 | 3,654.7 |
| Men's and boys' outer garments (excl. knitted goods) | 823.6 | 727.9 | 834.5 |
| Women's, girls' and infants' outer garments (excl. knitted goods) | 860.6 | 887.7 | 964.9 |
| Footwear | 1,848.3 | 1,998.1 | 2,135.0 |
| Footwear with leather soles | 1,511.5 | 1,601.9 | 1,662.3 |
| **Total** (incl. others) | 40,053.4 | 45,418.0 | 49,814.7 |

* Excluding narrow or special fabrics.

Source: UN, *International Trade Statistics Yearbook.*

**PRINCIPAL TRADING PARTNERS** (US $ million)*

| Imports c.i.f. | 1996 | 1997 | 1998 |
|---|---|---|---|
| Australia | 2,535.1 | 2,426.7 | 1,760.5 |
| Belgium/Luxembourg | 393.6 | 339.5 | 276.8 |
| Brazil | 412.8 | 352.3 | 203.5 |
| Canada | 785.6 | 682.4 | 504.2 |
| China, People's Republic | 1,597.6 | 1,518.0 | 906.3 |
| France | 1,006.0 | 1,016.5 | 568.1 |
| Germany | 3,001.4 | 2,628.7 | 2,365.7 |
| India | 886.2 | 697.4 | 293.0 |
| Iran | 453.6 | 444.2 | 175.0 |
| Italy | 1,212.1 | 917.9 | 480.4 |
| Japan | 8,504.0 | 8,252.3 | 4,292.4 |
| Korea, Republic | 2,411.4 | 2,321.8 | 1,527.8 |
| Malaysia | 823.7 | 864.8 | 626.6 |
| Netherlands | 493.0 | 565.9 | 338.4 |
| Russia | 378.4 | 287.3 | 30.4 |
| Singapore | 2,875.3 | 3,410.9 | 2,542.8 |
| Sweden | 718.7 | 482.0 | 235.4 |
| Switzerland | 370.1 | 335.3 | 228.0 |
| Thailand | 1,095.4 | 866.7 | 842.0 |
| United Kingdom | 1,117.8 | 1,084.4 | 920.3 |
| USA | 5,059.8 | 5,440.9 | 3,517.3 |
| **Total** (incl. others) | 42,928.5 | 41,679.8 | 27,336.9 |

| Exports f.o.b. | 1996 | 1997 | 1998 |
|---|---|---|---|
| Australia | 1,201.5 | 1,517.4 | 1,533.5 |
| Belgium/Luxembourg | 681.6 | 795.7 | 875.9 |
| China, People's Republic | 2,057.5 | 2,229.3 | 1,832.0 |
| France | 564.1 | 499.3 | 547.3 |
| Germany | 1,489.0 | 1,465.7 | 1,401.3 |
| Hong Kong | 1,624.8 | 1,785.1 | 1,865.0 |
| Italy | 743.6 | 826.1 | 858.8 |
| Japan | 12,885.2 | 12,485.0 | 9,116.0 |
| Korea, Republic | 4,823.1 | 3,462.2 | 2,567.8 |
| Malaysia | 1,109.7 | 1,357.2 | 1,358.5 |
| Netherlands | 1,666.6 | 1,842.4 | 1,512.3 |
| Philippines | 688.4 | 794.1 | 707.4 |
| Saudi Arabia | 515.6 | 579.3 | 505.9 |
| Singapore | 4,564.4 | 5,467.9 | 5,718.3 |
| Spain | 812.7 | 888.1 | 868.7 |
| Thailand | 822.6 | 848.4 | 942.5 |
| United Arab Emirates | 601.2 | 745.8 | 653.6 |
| United Kingdom | 1,192.9 | 1,238.1 | 1,143.1 |
| USA | 6,794.7 | 7,148.1 | 7,031.0 |
| **Total** (incl. others) | 49,814.8 | 53,443.6 | 48,847.6 |

* Imports by country of production; exports by country of consumption. Figures include trade in gold.

Source: *Statistical Yearbook of Indonesia.*

# Transport

**RAILWAYS** (traffic)

| | 1996 | 1997 | 1998* |
|---|---|---|---|
| Passengers embarked (million) | 154 | 159 | 169 |
| Passenger-km (million) | 15,223 | 15,518 | 16,340 |
| Freight loaded ('000 tons) | 18,481 | 19,186 | 20,290 |
| Freight ton-km (million) | 4,700 | 5,030 | 5,368 |

* Estimates.

Source: Indonesian State Railways.

**ROAD TRAFFIC** (motor vehicles registered at 31 December)

| | 1996 | 1997 | 1998* |
|---|---|---|---|
| Passenger cars | 2,409,088 | 2,653,662 | 2,734,769 |
| Lorries and trucks | 1,434,783 | 1,551,038 | 1,564,512 |
| Buses and coaches | 595,419 | 598,476 | 625,364 |
| Motor cycles | 10,090,805 | 12,028,475 | 12,718,199 |

* Estimates.

Source: State Police of Indonesia.

**SHIPPING**

**Merchant Fleet** (registered at 31 December)

| | 1996 | 1997 | 1998 |
|---|---|---|---|
| Number of vessels | 2,348 | 2,383 | 2,359 |
| Displacement ('000 grt) | 2,972.6 | 3,195.0 | 3,252.1 |

Source: Lloyd's Register of Shipping, *World Fleet Statistics*.

**Sea-borne Freight Traffic** ('000 metric tons)

| | 1995 | 1996 | 1997 |
|---|---|---|---|
| International: | | | |
| Goods loaded | 131,692.1 | 135,008.8 | 131,289.0 |
| Goods unloaded | 72,803.4 | 76,185.6 | 67,195.8 |
| Domestic: | | | |
| Goods loaded | 178,553.6 | 164,212.4 | 147,769.5 |
| Goods unloaded | 136,067.6 | 148,506.4 | 148,055.0 |

Source: Indonesian Port Administration.

**CIVIL AVIATION** (traffic on scheduled services)

| | 1996 | 1997 | 1998* |
|---|---|---|---|
| Kilometres flown (million) | 190 | 193 | 142 |
| Passengers carried ('000) | 11,571 | 11,635 | 7,891 |
| Passenger-km (million) | 20,551 | 21,190 | 13,883 |
| Total ton-km (million) | 2,552 | 2,596 | 1,691 |

* Preliminary data.

Source: *Statistical Yearbook of Indonesia*.

# Tourism

**FOREIGN VISITORS BY COUNTRY OF ORIGIN**
(excluding cruise passengers and excursionists)

| | 1996 | 1997 | 1998 |
|---|---|---|---|
| Australia | 361,234 | 458,733 | 302,425 |
| France | 89,204 | 107,228 | 86,541 |
| Germany | 191,723 | 185,661 | 186,816 |
| Italy | 62,630 | 63,884 | 57,937 |
| Japan | 632,287 | 661,214 | 555,864 |
| Korea, Republic | 224,624 | 226,327 | 151,037 |
| Malaysia | 495,478 | 546,005 | 419,304 |
| Netherlands | 117,794 | 135,209 | 132,359 |
| Philippines | 77,757 | 93,535 | 57,543 |
| Singapore | 1,199,566 | 1,354,458 | 1,092,843 |
| Sweden/Norway/Finland | 47,833 | 53,886 | 43,084 |
| Switzerland | 42,289 | 34,432 | 49,381 |
| Taiwan | 527,746 | 347,354 | 371,643 |
| Thailand | 51,453 | 57,835 | 39,265 |
| United Kingdom | 171,064 | 170,238 | 184,856 |
| USA | 257,138 | 230,394 | 194,280 |
| **Total** (incl. others) | 5,034,472 | 5,185,243 | 4,337,017 |

**Receipts from tourism** (US $ million): 6,308 in 1996; 5,321 in 1997; 3,459 in 1998.

Source: Directorate-General of Tourism, Jakarta.

# Communications Media

| | 1994 | 1995 | 1996 |
|---|---|---|---|
| Television receivers ('000 in use) | 12,000* | 13,000 | 13,500 |
| Radio receivers ('000 in use) | 28,800* | 29,500 | 31,000 |
| Telephones ('000 main lines in use) | 2,463† | 3,291† | 4,112‡ |
| Telefax stations (number in use)* | 55,000† | 85,000† | n.a. |
| Mobile cellular telephones (subscribers)† | 78,024 | 218,593 | n.a. |
| Daily newspapers: | | | |
| Number of titles | 56 | 74 | 69 |
| Average circulation ('000) | 3,800* | 4,701 | 4,665 |
| Non-daily newspapers: | | | |
| Number of titles | n.a. | 90 | 94 |
| Average circulation ('000) | n.a. | 3,895 | 4,696 |

Telephones ('000 main lines in use, 1997): 4,856‡.

* Estimate(s).

† Source: UN, *Statistical Yearbook*.

‡ Source: Central Bureau of Statistics, Jakarta.

Source (unless otherwise indicated): UNESCO, *Statistical Yearbook*.

# Education

(1997/98*)

| | Institutions | Teachers | Pupils and Students |
|---|---|---|---|
| Primary schools | 151,064 | 1,158,616 | 25,689,693 |
| General junior secondary schools | 21,157 | 434,722 | 7,956,506 |
| General senior secondary schools | 8,241 | 219,783 | 2,864,633 |
| Vocational senior secondary schools | 4,006 | 127,270 | 1,862,060 |
| Universities | 1,391 | 181,545 | 2,051,001 |

* Preliminary data.

Source: Ministry of Education and Culture.

# Directory

## The Constitution

Indonesia had three provisional Constitutions: in August 1945, February 1950 and August 1950. In July 1959 the Constitution of 1945 was re-enacted by presidential decree. The General Elections Law of 1969 supplemented the 1945 Constitution, which has been adopted permanently by the Majelis Permusyawaratan Rakyat (MPR—People's Consultative Assembly). The following is a summary of its main provisions, with subsequent amendments:

### GENERAL PRINCIPLES

The 1945 Constitution consists of 37 articles, four transitional clauses and two additional provisions, and is preceded by a preamble. The preamble contains an indictment of all forms of colonialism, an account of Indonesia's struggle for independence, the declaration of that independence and a statement of fundamental aims and principles. Indonesia's National Independence, according to the text of the preamble, has the state form of a Republic, with sovereignty residing in the People, and is based upon five fundamental principles, the *pancasila*:

1. Belief in the One Supreme God.
2. Just and Civilized Humanity.
3. The Unity of Indonesia.
4. Democracy led by the wisdom of deliberations (*musyawarah*) and consensus among representatives.
5. Social Justice for all the people of Indonesia.

### STATE ORGANS

**Majelis Permusyawaratan Rakyat—MPR** (People's Consultative Assembly)

Sovereignty is in the hands of the People and is exercised in full by the MPR as the embodiment of the whole Indonesian People. The MPR is the highest authority of the State, and is to be distinguished from the legislative body proper (Dewan Perwakilan Rakyat, see below), which is incorporated within the MPR. The MPR, with a total of 700 members (reduced from 1,000 in 1999), is composed of the 500 members of the Dewan, 135 members elected by provincial assemblies and 65 members appointed by the Komite Pemilihan Umum (General Election Committee). Elections to the MPR are held every five years. The MPR sits at least once every five years, and its primary competence is to determine the Constitution and the broad lines of the policy of the State and the Government. It also elects the President and Vice-President, who are responsible for implementing that policy. All decisions are taken unanimously in keeping with the traditions of *musyawarah*.

**The President**

The highest executive of the Government, the President, holds office for a term of five years and may be re-elected once. As Mandatory of the MPR he must execute the policy of the State according to the Decrees determined by the MPR during its Fourth General and Special Sessions. In conducting the administration of the State, authority and responsibility are concentrated in the President. The Ministers of the State are his assistants and are responsible only to him.

**Dewan Perwakilan Rakyat** (House of Representatives)

The legislative branch of the State, the Dewan Perwakilan Rakyat, sits at least once a year. It has 500 members: 38 nominated by the President (from the armed forces) and 462 directly elected. Every statute requires the approval of the Dewan. Members of the Dewan have the right to submit draft bills which require ratification by the President, who has the right of veto. In times of emergency the President may enact ordinances which have the force of law, but such Ordinances must be ratified by the Dewan during the following session or be revoked.

**Dewan Pertimbangan Agung—DPA** (Supreme Advisory Council)

The DPA is an advisory body assisting the President who chooses its members from political parties, functional groups and groups of prominent persons.

**Mahkamah Agung** (Supreme Court)

The judicial branch of the State, the Supreme Court and the other courts of law are independent of the Executive in exercising their judicial powers.

**Badan Pemeriksa Keuangan** (State Audit Board)

Controls the accountability of public finance, enjoys investigatory powers and is independent of the Executive. Its findings are presented to the Dewan.

## The Government

### HEAD OF STATE

**President:** ABDURRAHMAN WAHID (inaugurated 20 October 1999).

**Vice-President:** MEGAWATI SUKARNOPUTRI.

### CABINET

(February 2000)

**Co-ordinating Minister for Economy, Finance and Industry:** Drs KWIK KIAN GIE.

**Co-ordinating Minister for Social Welfare and Poverty Alleviation:** BASRI HASANUDDIN.

**Minister of Home Affairs and Acting Co-ordinating Minister for Political Affairs and Security:** Gen. (retd) SURYADI SUDIRJA.

**Minister of Foreign Affairs:** Dr ALWI SHIHAB.

**Minister of Defence:** Prof. Dr YUWONO SUDARSONO.

**Minister of Exploration of Marine Resources:** Ir SARWONO KUSUMAATMAJA.

**Minister of Justice:** Prof. Dr YUSRIL IHZA MAHENDRA.

**Minister of Finance:** BAMBANG SUDIBYO.

**Minister of Trade and Industry:** Drs YUSUF KALLA.

**Minister of Agriculture:** Dr M. PRAKOSA.

**Minister of Mines and Energy:** Lt-Gen. SUSILO BAMBANG YUDHOYONO.

**Minister of Forestry and Plantation:** Dr NUR MAHMUDI ISMAIL.

**Minister of Transportation:** Lt-Gen. AGUM GUMELAR.

**Minister of Workforce:** Dr BOMER PASARIBU.

**Minister of National Education:** Dr YAHYA MUHAIMIN.

**Minister of Health:** Dr AHMAD SUYUDI.

**Minister of Religious Affairs:** Drs KIAI Haji MUHAMMAD TOLKHAKH HASAN.

**Minister of Housing and Regional Development:** Ir ERNA WITULAR.

**Minister of State for Research and Technology:** Dr A. S. HIKAM.

**Minister of State for Investment and Promotion of State Enterprises:** Ir LAKSAMANA SUKARDI.

**Minister of State for Co-operatives and Development of Small- and Medium-Sized Businesses:** Drs ZARKASIH NUR.

**Minister of State for the Environment:** Dr SONNY KERAF.

**Minister of State for Regional Autonomy:** Dr RYAAS RASYID.

**Minister of State for Tourism and the Arts:** Drs Haji HIDAYAT JAILANI.

**Minister of State for Public Works:** Dr Ir RAFIQ BUDIRO SUTJIPTO.

**Minister of State for Human Rights:** Dr HASBALLAH M. SAAD.

**Minister of State for Transmigration and Population:** Ir AL HILAL HAMDI.

**Minister of State for State Apparatus Reform:** Rear-Adm. FREDDY NUMBERI.

**Minister of State for Social Affairs:** Dr ANAK Agung GDE Agung.

**Minister of State for Women's Affairs:** Dra KHOFIFAH INDAR PARAWANSA.

**Minister of State for Youth Affairs and Sports:** Drs MAHADI SINAMBELA.

Officials with the rank of Minister of State:

**Attorney-General:** MARZUKI DARUSMAN.

**Governor of Bank Indonesia:** SJAHRIL SABIRIN.

### MINISTRIES

**Office of the President:** Istana Merdeka, Jakarta; tel. (21) 3840946.

**Office of the Vice-President:** Jalan Merdeka Selatan 6, Jakarta; tel. (21) 363539.

**Office of the Attorney-General:** Jalan Sultan Hasanuddin 1, Kebayoran Baru, Jakarta; tel. (21) 7208557; fax (21) 7392576.

**Office of the Cabinet Secretary:** Jalan Veteran 18, Jakarta Pusat; tel. (21) 3810973.

**Office of the Co-ordinating Minister for Political Affairs and Security:** Jalan Medan Merdeka Barat 15, Jakarta 10110; tel. (21) 3849453; fax (21) 3450918.

**Office of the Co-ordinating Minister for Economy, Finance and Industry:** Jalan Taman Suropati 2, Jakarta 10310; tel. (21) 3849063; fax (21) 334779.

**Office of the Co-ordinating Minister for Social Welfare and Poverty Alleviation:** Jalan Merdeka Barat 3, Jakarta 10110; tel. (21) 3849845; fax (21) 3453055.

**Office of the State Secretary:** Jalan Veteran 17, Jakarta 10110; tel. (21) 3849043; fax (21) 3452685.

**Ministry of Agriculture:** Jalan Harsono R.M. 3, Ragunan, Pasar Minggu, Jakarta Selatan 12550; tel. (21) 7804086; fax (21) 7804237.

**Ministry of Defence:** Mabes TNI Cilangkap, Jakarta Timur; tel. (21) 3842679; fax (21) 3806711.

**Ministry of Finance:** Jalan Lapangan Banteng Timur 2-4, Jakarta 10710; tel. (21) 3814324; fax (21) 353710.

**Ministry of Foreign Affairs:** Jalan Taman Pejambon 6, Jakarta 10110; tel. (21) 366014; fax (21) 3805511.

**Ministry of Forestry and Plantation:** Gedung Manggala Wanabakti, Block 1, 4th Floor, Jalan Jenderal Gatot Subroto, Jakarta 10270; tel. (21) 5731820; fax (21) 5700278.

**Ministry of Health:** Jalan H. R. Rasuna Said, Block X5, Kav. 4-9, Jakarta 12950; tel. (21) 5201587; fax (21) 5201591.

**Ministry of Home Affairs:** Jalan Merdeka Utara 7, Jakarta Pusat 10110; tel. (21) 3842222; fax (21) 372812.

**Ministry of Justice:** Jalan H. R. Rasuna Said, Kav. 4–5, Kuningan, Jakarta Pusat; tel. (21) 5253004; fax (21) 5253095.

**Ministry of Mines and Energy:** Jalan Merdeka Selatan 18, Jakarta 10110; tel. (21) 3804242; fax (21) 3847461.

**Ministry of National Education:** Jalan Jenderal Sudirman, Senayan, Jakarta Pusat; tel. (21) 5731618; fax (21) 5736870.

**Ministry of Religious Affairs:** Jalan Lapangan Banteng Barat 3–4, Jakarta Pusat; tel. (21) 3811436; fax (21) 380836.

**Ministry of Trade and Industry:** Jalan Jenderal Gatot Subroto, Jakarta Selatan; tel. (21) 5256458; fax (21) 5201606.

**Ministry of Transportation:** Jalan Merdeka Barat 8, Jakarta 10110; tel. (21) 3456332; fax (21) 3451657.

**Ministry of Workforce:** Jalan Jenderal Gatot Subroto, Kav. 51, Jakarta Selatan 12950; tel. (21) 5255683; fax (21) 515669; internet www.depnaker.go.id.

**Office of the Minister of State for Co-operatives and the Development of Small- and Medium-Sized Businesses:** Jalan H. R. Rasuna Said, Kav. 3–5, POB 177, Jakarta Selatan 12940; tel. (21) 5204366; fax (21) 5204383.

**Office of the Minister of State for the Environment:** Jalan D. I. Panjaitan, Kebon Nanas Lt. II, Jakarta 134110; tel. (21) 8580103; fax (21) 8580101.

**Office of the Minister of State for Human Rights:** Jakarta.

**Office of the Minister of State for Investment/The Investment Co-ordinating Board:** Jalan Jenderal Gatot Subroto 44, Jakarta Selatan 12190; tel. (21) 5250023; fax (21) 5254945.

**Office of the Minister of State for Public Works:** Jalan Pattimura 20, Kebayoran Baru, Jakarta Selatan 12110; tel. (21) 7262805; fax (21) 7260769.

**Office of the Minister of State for Regional Autonomy:** Jakarta.

**Office of the Minister of State for Research and Technology:** Jalan M. H. Thamrin 8, Jakarta Pusat; tel. (21) 324767; fax (21) 328169.

**Office of the Minister of State for Social Affairs:** Jalan Salemba Raya 28, Jakarta Pusat 10430; tel. (21) 3103781; fax (21) 3103783.

**Office of the Minister of State for Tourism and the Arts:** Jalan Medan Merdeka Barat 17, Jakarta 10110; tel. (21) 3456705; fax (21) 3848245.

**Office of the Minister of State for Transmigration and Population:** Jalan Taman Makam Pahlawan 17, Kalibata Jakarta Selatan; tel. (21) 7989924.

**Office of the Minister of State for Women's Affairs:** Jalan Medan Merdeka Barat 15, Jakarta 10110; tel. (21) 3805563; fax (21) 3805562; e-mail birum@menperta.go.id.

**Office of the Minister of State for Youth Affairs and Sports:** Gedung Pemuda, Jalan Gerbang Pemuda 3, Jakarta Pusat; tel. (21) 5738150; fax (21) 588313.

### OTHER GOVERNMENT BODIES

**Supreme Advisory Council:** Jalan Merdeka Utara 15, Jakarta; tel. (21) 362369; Chair. ACHMAD TIRTOSUDIRO; Sec.-Gen. SUTOYO.

**Supreme Audit Board:** Jalan Gatot Subroto 31, Jakarta; tel. (21) 584081; Chair. Prof. Dr SATRIO BUDIHARDJO JUDONO; Vice-Chair. Drs BAMBANG TRIADJI.

## Legislature

### MAJELIS PERMUSYAWARATAN RAKYAT—MPR

(People's Consultative Assembly)

Jalan Gatot Subroto 6, Jakarta; tel. (21) 5801322: fax (21) 5734526.

The Majelis Permusyawaratan Rakyat (MPR—People's Consultative Assembly) consists of the 500 members of the Dewan Perwakilan Rakyat (House of Representatives) and 200 other appointees (reduced from 500 in 1999), including regional delegates and representatives of various professions.

**Speaker:** DR AMIEN RAIS.

| | Seats |
|---|---|
| Members of the Dewan Perwakilan Rakyat | 500 |
| Regional representatives | 135 |
| Professional representatives | 65 |
| **Total** | 700 |

### Dewan Perwakilan Rakyat

(House of Representatives)

Jalan Gatot Subroto 16, Jakarta; tel. (21) 586833.

Following the election of June 1999 the Dewan Perwakilan Rakyat (House of Representatives) comprised 500 members; of these, 462 were directly elected (increased from 425) and 38 were nominated by the President from the armed forces (reduced from 75).

**Speaker:** IR AKBAR TANJUNG.

**General Election, 7 June 1999**

| | Seats |
|---|---|
| Partai Demokrasi Indonesia Perjuangan (PDI—P) | 154 |
| Golongan Karya (Golkar) | 120 |
| Partai Persatuan Pembangunan (PPP) | 59 |
| Partai Kebangkitan Bangsa (PKB) | 51 |
| Partai Amanat Nasional (PAN) | 35 |
| Partai Bulan Bintang (PBB) | 13 |
| Partai Keadilan (PK) | 6 |
| Partai Keadilan dan Persatuan (PKP) | 6 |
| Partai Demokrasi Kasih Bangsa (PDKB) | 3 |
| Partai Nahdlatul Umat (PNU) | 3 |
| Partai Bhinneka Tunggal Ika | 3 |
| Partai Demokrasi Indonesia (PDI) | 2 |
| Others | 7 |
| Appointed members* | 38 |
| **Total** | 500 |

* Members of the political wing of the Indonesian National Defence Forces (TNI).

## Political Organizations

Prior to 1998, electoral legislation permitted only three organizations (Golkar, the PDI and PPP) to contest elections. Following the replacement of President Suharto in May 1998, political restrictions were relaxed and new parties were allowed to form (with the only condition being that all parties must adhere to the *pancasila* and reject communism); by early 1999, more than 200 new political parties were reported to have been established.

**Barisan Nasional** (National Front): Jakarta; f. 1998; committed to ensuring that Indonesia remains a secular state; Sec.-Gen. RACHMAT WITOELAR.

**Chinese Indonesian Reform Party:** Jakarta; f. 1998.

**Golongan Karya (Golkar)** (Functional Group): Jalan Anggrek Nelimurni, Jakarta 11480; tel. (21) 5302222; fax (21) 5303380; f. 1964; reorg. 1971; the governing alliance of groups representing farmers, fishermen and the professions; 35m. mems (1993); Pres. and Chair., Co-ordinator of Advisors Haji HARMOKO; Chair. Ir AKBAR TANJUNG; Sec.-Gen. JUSWANDI.

**Indonesian National Unity:** Jakarta; f. 1995 by fmr mems of Sukarno's National Party; seeks full implementation of 1945 Constitution; Chair. SUPENI.

**Indonesian Reform Party (PPI):** Jakarta; f. 1998; Gen. Chair. CHANDRA KUWATLI; Sec.-Gen. Dr H. ACE MULYADI.

**Islamic Indonesian Party (PII):** Jakarta; f. 1998; Pres. SUUD BAJEBER; Sec.-Gen. SYAIFUL MUNIR.

**National Brotherhood Foundation:** Jakarta; f. 1995; Chair. KHARIS SUHUD.

**New Indonesian National Party:** Jakarta; f. 1998.

**Partai Amanat Nasional (PAN)** (National Mandate Party): c/o Dewan Perwakilan Rakyat, Jalan Gatot Subroto 16, Jakarta; f. 1998; aims to achieve democracy, progress and social justice, to limit the length of the presidential term of office and to increase autonomy in the provinces; Gen. Chair. Dr AMIEN RAIS; Sec.-Gen. FAISAL BASRI.

**Partai Bhinneka Tunggal Ika:** c/o Dewan Perwakilan Rakyat, Jalan Gatot Subroto 16, Jakarta.

**Partai Bulan Bintang (PBB)** (Cresent Moon and Star Party): c/o Dewan Perwakilan Rakyat, Jalan Gatot Subroto 16, Jakarta; f. 1998; Leader YUSRIL IHZA MAHENDRA.

**Partai Demokrasi Indonesia (PDI)** (Indonesian Democratic Party): Jalan Diponegoro 58, Jakarta 10310; tel. (21) 336331; fax (21) 5201630; f. 1973 by the merger of five nationalist and Christian parties; Chair. SOERJADI (installed to replace Megawati Sukarnoputri as leader of the party in a government-orchestrated coup in 1996).

**Partai Demokrasi Indonesia Perjuangan (PDI—P)** (Indonesian Democratic Struggle Party): c/o Dewan Perwakilan Rakyat, Jalan Gatot Subroto 16, Jakarta; established by Megawati Sukarnoputri, fmr leader of the Partai Demokrasi Indonesia (PDI—see above), following her removal from the leadership of the PDI by the Government in 1996; Chair. MEGAWATI SUKARNOPUTRI.

**Partai Demokrasi Kasih Bangsa (PDKB)** (Democracy and Love for Nation Party): c/o Dewan Perwakilan Rakyat, Jalan Gatot Subroto 16, Jakarta.

**Partai Keadilan (PK)** (Justice Party): c/o Dewan Perwakilan Rakyat, Jalan Gatot Subroto 16, Jakarta; internet www.keadilan .or.id; f. 1998; Islamic; Pres. Dr NUR MAHMUDI ISMA'IL; Sec.-Gen. LUTHFI HASAN ISHAAQ.

**Partai Keadilan dan Persatuan (PKP)** (Justice and Unity Party): c/o Dewan Perwakilan Rakyat, Jalan Gatot Subroto 16, Jakarta; f. 1999; Gen. Chair. EDI SUDRADJAT.

**Partai Kebangkitan Bangsa (PKB)** (National Awakening Party): Jakarta; Islamic; f. 1998; Chair. of Exec. Council KIAI Haji MA'RUF AMIN; Chair. of Advisory Council Haji MATORI ABDUL JALIL.

**Partai Kebangkitan Umat (PKU)** (Islamic Awakening Party): c/o Dewan Perwakilan Rakyat, Jalan Gatot Subroto 16, Jakarta; f. 1998 by clerics and members of the Nahdlatul Ulama, with the aim of promoting the adoption of Islamic law in Indonesia.

**Partai Nahdlatul Umat (PNU):** c/o Dewan Perwakilan Rakyat, Jalan Gatot Subroto 16, Jakarta; Islamic party.

**Partai Pembauran** (Assimilation Party): Jakarta; f. 1998; Chinese.

**Partai Persatuan Pembangunan (PPP)** (United Development Party): Jalan Diponegoro 60, Jakarta 10310; tel. (21) 336338; fax (21) 3908070; f. 1973 by the merger of four Islamic parties; Leader: HAMZAH HAZ; Sec.-Gen. ALI MARWAN HANAN.

**Partai Rakyat Demokrasi (PRD)** (People's Democratic Party): Jakarta; Chair. BUDIMAN SUJATMIKO.

**Partai Tionghoa Indonesia** (The Indonesian-Chinese Party): Jakarta; f. 1998; Chinese.

**Partai Uni Demokrasi Indonesia (PUDI)** (United Democratic Party of Indonesia): Jakarta; f. 1996; Chair. Sri BINTANG PAMUNGKAS.

Other groups with political influence include:

**Nahdlatul Ulama** (Council of Scholars): Jalan H. Agus Salim 112, Jakarta Pusat; tel. (21) 336250; largest Muslim organization; 30m. mems; Chair. AHMAD HASYIM.

**Muhammadiyah**: Jalan Menteng Raya 62, Jakarta Pusat; tel. (21) 3903024; fax (21) 3141582; second largest Muslim organization; f. 1912; 28m. mems; Chair. (vacant).

**Syarikat Islam**: Jalan Taman Amir Hamzah Nomor 2, Jakarta; tel. (21) 31906037.

**Ikatan Cendekiawan Muslim Indonesia (ICMI)** (Association of Indonesian Muslim Intellectuals): Gedung BPPT, Jalan M.H. Thamrin 8, Jakarta; tel. (21) 3410382; f. 1990 with government support; Chair. ACHMAD TIRTOSUDIRO; Sec.-Gen. ADI SASONO.

**Masyumi Baru**: Jalan Pangkalan Asem 12, Cempaka Putih Ba, Jakarta Pusat; tel. (21) 4225774; fax (21) 7353077; Sec.-Gen. RIDWAN SAIDI.

The following groups remain in conflict with the Government:

**Gerakan Aceh Merdeka (GAM)** (Free Aceh Movement): based in Aceh; f. 1976; seeks independence from Indonesia; Leader AHMAD KANDANG.

**National Liberation Front Aceh Sumatra:** based in Aceh; f. 1989; seeks independence from Indonesia.

**Organisasi Papua Merdeka (OPM)** (Free Papua Movement): based in Irian Jaya; f. 1963; seeks unification with Papua New Guinea; Chair. MOZES WEROR; Leader KELLY KWALIK.

# Diplomatic Representation

## EMBASSIES IN INDONESIA

**Afghanistan:** Jalan Dr Kusuma Atmaja 15, Jakarta; tel. (21) 333169; Chargé d'affaires: ABDUL GHAFUR BAHER.

**Algeria:** Jalan H. R. Rasuna Said, Kav. 10-1, Kuningan, Jakarta 12950; tel. (21) 5254719; fax (21) 5254654; Ambassador: SOUFIANE MIMOUNI.

**Argentina:** Jalan Panarukan 17, Jakarta 10310; tel. (21) 338088; fax (21) 336148; Ambassador: GASPAR TABOADA.

**Australia:** Jalan H. R. Rasuna Said, Kav. C15-16, Jakarta 12940; tel. (21) 25505555; fax (21) 5227101; internet www .austembjak.or.id; Ambassador: JOHN MCCARTHY.

**Austria:** Jalan Diponegoro 44, Jakarta 10310; tel. (21) 338101; fax (21) 3904927; e-mail auambjak@rad.net.id; Ambassador: Dr VIKTOR SEGALLA.

**Bangladesh:** Jalan Denpasar Raya 3, Block A-13 Kav. 10, Kuningan, Jakarta 12950; tel. (21) 5221574; fax (21) 5261807; e-mail bdootjak@rad.net.id; Ambassador: Maj.-Gen. Dr M. AFSARUL QADER.

**Belgium:** Deutsche Bank Bldg, 16th Floor, Jalan Imam Bonjol 80, Jakarta 10310; tel. (21) 3162030; fax (21) 3162035; e-mail jakarta@diplobel.org; Ambassador: LUK DARRAS.

**Brazil:** Menara Mulia, Suite 1602, Jalan Jenderal Gatot Subroto, Kav. 9, Jakarta 12930; tel. (21) 3904056; fax (21) 3101374; Ambassador: JADIEL FERREIRA DE OLIVEIRA.

**Brunei:** Wisma BCA, 8th Floor, Jalan Jenderal Sudirman, Kav. 22–23, Jakarta Selatan 12920; tel. (21) 5712124; fax (21) 5712205; Ambassador: Dato' Paduka Haji AWANG YAHYA BIN Haji HARRIS.

**Bulgaria:** Jalan Imam Bonjol 34–36, Jakarta 10310; tel. (21) 3904049; fax (21) 3904049; Ambassador: GATYU GATEV.

**Canada:** Wisma Metropolitan I, 5th Floor, Jalan Jenderal Sudirman, Kav. 29, POB 8324/JKS, Jakarta 12920; tel. (21) 5250709; fax (21) 5712251; e-mail jkrta.gr@jkrta01.x400.gc.ca; Ambassador: KEN J. SUNQUIST.

**Chile:** Bina Mulia Bldg, 7th Floor, Jalan H. R. Rasuna Said, Kav. 10, Kuningan, Jakarta 12950; tel. (21) 5201131; fax (21) 5201955; Ambassador: FERNANDO COUSIÑO.

**China, People's Republic:** Jalan Jenderal Sudirman 69, Jakarta; tel. (21) 714897; fax (21) 7207782; Ambassador: CHEN SHIQIU.

**Colombia:** Central Plaza Bldg, 16th Floor, Jalan Jenderal Sudirman, Kav. 48, Jakarta; tel. (21) 516446; fax (21) 5207717; Ambassador: LUIS FERNANDO ANGEL.

**Croatia:** Menara Mulia, Suite 2101, Jalan Gatot Subroto, Kav. 9–11, Jakarta 12930; tel. (21) 5257822; fax (21) 5204073; e-mail croemb@rad.net.id; internet www.croatemb.or.id; Ambassador: BORIS MITROVIĆ.

**Czech Republic:** Jalan Gereja Theresia 20, POB 1319, Jakarta Pusat; tel. (21) 3904075; fax (21) 336282; e-mail Jakarta embassy.MZV.CZ; internet www.czech-embassy.or.id; Ambassador: MILAN SARAPATKA.

**Denmark:** Menara Rajawali, 25th Floor, Jalan Mega Kuningan, Lot 5.1, Jakarta 12950; tel. (21) 5761478; fax (21) 5761535; e-mail dkemb9@cbn.net.id; internet www.emb-denmark.or.id; Ambassador: MICHAEL STERNBERG.

**Egypt:** Jalan Teuku Umar 68, Jakarta 10350; tel. (21) 331141; fax (21) 3105073; Ambassador: AHMAD NABIL ELSALAWY.

**Finland:** Menara Rajawali, 9th Floor, Jalan Mega Kuningan, Kawasan Mega Kuningan, Jakarta 12950; tel. (21) 5761650; fax (21) 5761631; e-mail sanomat.jak@formin.fi; Ambassador: HANNU HIMANEN.

**France:** Jalan M. H. Thamrin 20, Jakarta 10310; tel. (21) 3142807; fax (21) 3143338; Ambassador: GÉRARD CROS.

**Germany:** Jalan M. H. Thamrin 1, Jakarta 10310; tel. (21) 323908; fax (21) 3143338; Ambassador: WALTER LEWALTER.

**Holy See:** Jalan Merdeka Timur 18, POB 4227, Jakarta Pusat (Apostolic Nunciature); tel. (21) 3841142; fax (21) 3841143; Apostolic Nuncio: Most Rev. RENZO FRATINI, Titular Archbishop of Botriana.

**Hungary:** 36 Jalan H. R. Rasuna Said, Kav. X/3, Kuningan, Jakarta 12950; tel. (21) 5203459; fax (21) 5203461; Ambassador: LAJOS TAMÁS.

**India:** Jalan H. R. Rasuna Said, Kav. S/1, Kuningan, Jakarta 12950; tel. (21) 5204150; fax (21) 5204160; e-mail eoiisi@indo.net.id; Ambassador: M. VENKATRAMAN.

**Iran:** Jalan Hos Cokroaminoto 110, Menteng, Jakarta Pusat; tel. (21) 331391; fax (21) 3107860; Ambassador: SEYED MOHSEN NABAVI.

**Iraq:** Jalan Teuku Umar 38, Jakarta 10350; tel. (21) 4214067; fax (21) 4214066; Chargé d'affaires: MUSTAFA MUHAMMAD TAWFIQ.

**Italy:** Jalan Diponegoro 45, Jakarta 10310; tel. (21) 337445; fax (21) 337422; e-mail italemba@rad.net.id; internet www.italambjkt.or.id; Ambassador: Dr CARLO MARSILI.

**Japan:** Jalan M. H. Thamrin 24, Jakarta 10350; tel. (21) 324308; fax (21) 325460; Ambassador: TAIZO WATANABE.

**Jordan:** Jalan Denpasar Raya, Blok A XIII, Kav. 1–2, Jakarta 12950; tel. (21) 5204400; fax (21) 5202447; Ambassador: LU'AY KHASHMAN.

**Korea, Democratic People's Republic:** Jalan H. R. Rasuna Said, Kav. X.5, Jakarta; tel. (21) 5210181; Ambassador: JO KYU IL.

**Korea, Republic:** Jalan Jenderal Gatot Subroto 57, Jakarta Selatan; tel. (21) 5201915; fax (21) 514159; Ambassador: YOUNG-SUP KIM.

**Kuwait:** Jalan Denpasar Raya, Blok A XII, Kuningan, Jakarta 12950; tel. (21) 5202477; fax (21) 5204359; Ambassador: JASEM M. J. AL-MUBARAKI.

**Laos:** Jalan Patra Kuningan XIV 1-A, Kuningan, Jakarta 12950; tel. (21) 5229602; fax (21) 5229601; Ambassador: SOMPHET KHOUSAKOUN.

**Libya:** Jalan Pekalongan 24, Jakarta; tel. (21) 335308; fax (21) 335726; Chargé d'affaires a.i.: TAJEDDIN A. JERBI.

**Malaysia:** Jalan H. R. Rasuna Said, Kav. X/6, Kuningan, Jakarta 12950; tel. (21) 5224947; fax (21) 5224974; Ambassador: Datuk RASTAM MOHAMMAD ISA.

**Mexico:** Menara Mulia, Suite 2306, Jalan Gatot Subroto, Kav. 9–11, Jakarta 12930; tel. (21) 5203980; fax (21) 5203978; Ambassador: SERGIO LEY-LÓPEZ.

**Morocco:** Suite 512, 5th Floor, South Tower, Kuningan Plaza, Jalan H. R. Rasuna Said C-11-14, Jakarta 12940; tel. (21) 5200773; fax (21) 5200586; Ambassador: HASSAN FASSI-FIHRI.

**Myanmar:** Jalan Haji Agus Salim 109, Jakarta Selatan; tel. (21) 320440; fax (21) 327204; Ambassador: U NYUNT TIN.

**Netherlands:** Jalan H. R. Rasuna Said, Kav. S/3, Kuningan, Jakarta 12950; tel. (21) 5251515; fax (21) 5700734; e-mail nlgovjak@-ibm.net; internet www.neth-embassy-jakarta.org; Ambassador: Baron S. VAN HEEMSTRA.

**New Zealand:** BRI II Bldg, 23rd Floor, Jalan Jenderal Sudirman, Kav. 44–46, Jakarta; tel. (21) 5709460; fax (21) 5709457; e-mail nzembjak@cbn.net.id; Ambassador: MICHAEL GREEN.

**Nigeria:** Jalan Tamam Patra xiv/11–11A, Kuningan Timur, POB 3649, Jakarta Selatan 12950; tel. (21) 5260922; fax (21) 5260924; e-mail embnig@centrin.net.id; Ambassador: SAIDU MOHAMMED.

**Norway:** Bina Mulia Bldg, 4th Floor, Jalan H. R. Rasuna Said, Kav. 10, Jakarta 12950; tel. (21) 5251990; fax (21) 5207365; Ambassador: SJUR TORGERSEN.

**Pakistan:** Jalan Teuku Umar 50, Jakarta 10350; tel. (21) 350576; e-mail pakjkt@rad.net.id; Ambassador: MATAHAR HUSEIN.

**Papua New Guinea:** Panin Bank Centre, 6th Floor, Jalan Jenderal Sudirman 1, Jakarta 10270; tel. (21) 7251218; fax (21) 7201012; e-mail kdujkt@tbn.net.id; Ambassador: TARCY ERI.

**Peru:** Menara Rajawali, 12th Floor, Jalan Mega Kuningan Lot 5.1, Kawasan Mega, Kuningan, Jakarta 12950; tel. (21) 5761820; fax (21) 5761825; e-mail embaperu@cbn.net.id; Ambassador: ELARD ESCALA.

**Philippines:** Jalan Imam Bonjol 6–8, Jakarta 10310; tel. (21) 3100334; fax (21) 3151167; e-mail phjkt@indo.net.id; Ambassador: LEONIDES T. CADAY.

**Poland:** H. R. Rasuna Said, Kav. X Blok IV/3, Jakarta Selatan 12950; tel. (21) 2525948; fax (21) 2525958; Ambassador: (vacant).

**Qatar:** Jakarta; tel. (21) 5277751; fax (21) 5277753.

**Romania:** Jalan Teuku Cik Ditiro 42A, Menteng, Jakarta Pusat; tel. (21) 3106240; fax (21) 3907759; Ambassador: DUMITRU TANCU.

**Russia:** Jalan H. R. Rasuna Said, Blok X/7, Kav. 1–2, Jakarta; tel. (21) 5222912; Ambassador: NIKOLAI SOLOVIYEV.

**Saudi Arabia:** Jalan Imam Bonjol 3, Jakarta 10310; tel. (21) 3105499; fax (21) 4214046; Ambassador: ABDULLAH A. ALIM.

**Singapore:** Jalan H. R. Rasuna Said, Blok X/4, Kav. 2, Kuningan, Jakarta 12950; tel. (21) 5201489; fax (21) 5201486; Ambassador: EDWARD LEE.

**Slovakia:** Jalan Prof. Mohammed Yamin 29, POB 1368, Jakarta Pusat; tel. (21) 3101068; fax (21) 3101180; e-mail slovemby@indo.net.id; Ambassador: MILAN LAJČIAK.

**South Africa:** Suite 705, Wisma GKBI, Jalan Jenderal Sudirman 28, Jakarta 10210; tel. (21) 5740660; fax (21) 5740661; e-mail saembjak@centrin.net.id; internet www.saembassy-jakarta.or.id; Ambassador: S. B. KUBHEKA.

**Spain:** Jalan H. Agus Salim 61, Jakarta 10350; tel. (21) 335937; fax (21) 325996; Ambassador: ANTONIO SÁNCHEZ JARA.

**Sri Lanka:** Jalan Diponegoro 70, Jakarta 10320; tel. (21) 3161886; fax (21) 3107962; e-mail lankaemb@vision.net.id; Ambassador: TISSA DIAS BANDARANAYAKE.

**Sudan:** Wisma Bank Dharmala, 7th Floor, Suite 01, Jalan Jenderal Sudirman, Kav. 28, Jakarta 12920; tel. (21) 5212075; fax (21) 5212077; e-mail sudanijk@centrin.net.id; Ambassador: HASSAN IBRAHIM GADELKARIM.

**Sweden:** Bina Mulia Bldg, 7th Floor, Jalan H. R. Rasuna Said, Kav. 10; POB 2824, Jakarta 10001; tel. (21) 5201551; fax (21) 5252652; e-mail sweden@cbn.net.id; internet www.swedemb-jakarta.com; Ambassador: HARALD SANDBERG.

**Switzerland:** Jalan H. R. Rasuna Said X-3/2, Kuningan 12950 Jakarta Selatan; tel. (21) 5256061; fax (21) 5202289; e-mail swiemjak@rad.net.id; Ambassador: GÉRARD FONJALLAZ.

**Syria:** Jalan Karang Asem I/8, Jakarta 12950; tel. (21) 515991; Ambassador: NADIM DOUAY.

**Thailand:** Jalan Imam Bonjol 74, Jakarta 10310; tel. (21) 3904052; fax (21) 3107469; e-mail thaijkt@indo.net.id; Ambassador: SOMPHAND KOKILANON.

**Tunisia:** Wisma Dharmala Sakti, Jalan Jenderal Sudirman 32, Jakarta 10220; tel. (21) 5703432; fax (21) 5700016; Ambassador: MOHAMED GHERIB.

**Turkey:** Jalan H. R. Rasuna Said, Kav. 1, Kuningan, Jakarta 12950; tel. (21) 516258; fax (21) 5226056; Ambassador: SEVINÇ DALYANOĞLU.

**United Arab Emirates:** Jalan Singaraja Blok C-4 Kav. 16-17, Jakarta Selatan; tel. (21) 5206518; fax (21) 5206526; Chargé d'affaires: HAMAD SAEED LI'ZAABI.

**United Kingdom:** Jalan M. H. Thamrin 75, Jakarta 10310; tel. (21) 3156264; fax (21) 3926263; e-mail postmaster@jakarta.mail.fco.gov.uk; internet www.british-emb-jakarta.or.id; Ambassador: Sir ROBIN CHRISTOPHER.

**USA:** Jalan Merdeka Selatan 4-5, Jakarta 10110; tel. (21) 3442211; fax (21) 3862259; internet www.usembassyjakarta.org; Ambassador: ROBERT GELBARD.

**Venezuela:** Menara Mulia, 20th Floor, Suite 2005, Jalan Jenderal Gatot Subroto, Kav. 9–11, Jakarta Selatan 12930; tel. (21) 5227547; fax (21) 5227549; Ambassador: VASCO ALTUVE FEBRES.

**Viet Nam:** Jalan Teuku Umar 25, Jakarta; tel. (21) 3100358; fax (21) 3100359; Ambassador: NGUYEN DANG QUANG.

**Yemen:** Jalan Yusuf Adiwinata 29, Jakarta; tel. (21) 3904074; fax (21) 4214946; Ambassador: ABDUL WAHAD FARAH.

**Yugoslavia:** Jalan Hos Cokroaminoto 109, Jakarta 10310; tel. (21) 3143560; fax (21) 3143613; e-mail ambajaka@rad.net.id; Chargé d'affaires: DUSAN STOJKOVIC.

# Judicial System

There is one codified criminal law for the whole of Indonesia. In December 1989 the Islamic Judicature Bill, giving wider powers to Shariah courts, was approved by the Dewan Perwakilan Rakyat (House of Representatives). The new law gave Muslim courts authority over civil matters, such as marriage. Muslims may still choose to appear before a secular court. Europeans are subject to the Code of Civil Law published in the State Gazette in 1847. Alien orientals (i.e. Arabs, Indians, etc.) and Chinese are subject to certain parts of the Code of Civil Law and the Code of Commerce. The work of codifying this law has started, but, in view of the great complexity and diversity of customary law, it may be expected to take a considerable time to achieve.

**Supreme Court** (Mahkamah Agung): Jalan Merdeka Utara 9–13, Jakarta 10110; tel. (21) 3843348; fax (21) 3811057; the final court of appeal.

**Chief Justice:** SARWATA.

**High Courts** in Jakarta, Surabaya, Medan, Ujungpandang (Makassar), Banda Aceh, Padang, Palembang, Bandung, Semarang, Banjarmasin, Menado, Denpasar, Ambon and Jayapura deal with appeals from the District Courts.

**District Courts** deal with marriage, divorce and reconciliation.

# Religion

All citizens are required to state their religion. According to a survey in 1985, 86.9% of the population were Muslims, while 9.6% were Christians, 1.9% were Hindus, 1.0% were Buddhists and 0.6% professed adherence to tribal religions.

### ISLAM

In 1993 nearly 90% of Indonesians were Muslims. Indonesia has the world's largest Islamic population.

**Majelis Ulama Indonesia (MUI)** (Indonesian Ulama Council): Komp. Masjid Istiqlal, Jalan Taman Wijaya Kesuma, Jakarta 10710; tel. (21) 3455471; fax (21) 3855412; Central Muslim organization; Chair. (vacant).

### CHRISTIANITY

**Persekutuan Gereja-Gereja di Indonesia** (Communion of Churches in Indonesia): Jalan Salemba Raya 10, Jakarta 10430; tel. (21) 3908119; fax (21) 3150457; f. 1950; 70 mem. churches; Chair. Rev. Dr SULARSO SOPATER; Gen. Sec. Rev. Dr JOSEPH M. PATTIASINA.

#### The Roman Catholic Church

Indonesia comprises eight archdioceses and 26 dioceses. At 31 December 1997 there were an estimated 5,686,450 adherents, representing 2.7% of the population.

**Bishops' Conference:** Konferensi Waligereja Indonesia (KWI), Jalan Cut Meutia 10, POB 3044, Jakarta 10002; tel. (21) 336422; fax (21) 3918527; e-mail kwi@parokinet.org; f. 1973; Pres. Rt Rev. JOSEPH SUWATAN, Bishop of Manado.

**Archbishop of Ende:** Most Rev. ABDON LONGINUS DA CUNHA, Keuskupan Agung, POB 210, Jalan Katedral 5, Ndona-Ende 86312, Flores; tel. (381) 21176; fax (381) 21606.

**Archbishop of Jakarta:** Cardinal JULIUS RIYADI DARMAATMADJA, Keuskupan Agung, Jalan Katedral 7, Jakarta 10710; tel. (21) 3813345; fax (21) 3855681.

**Archbishop of Kupang:** Most Rev. PETER TURANG, Keuskupan Agung Kupang, Jalan Thamrin, Oepoi, Kupang 85111, Timor NTT; tel. and fax (0380) 33331.

**Archbishop of Medan:** Most Rev. ALFRED GONTI PIUS DATUBARA, Jalan Imam Bonjol 39, POB 1191, Medan 20152, Sumatra Utara; tel. (61) 516647; fax (61) 545745.

**Archbishop of Merauke:** Most Rev. JACOBUS DUIVENVOORDE, Keuskupan Agung, Jalan Mandala 30, Merauke 99602, Irian Jaya; tel. (971) 21011; fax (971) 21311.

**Archbishop of Pontianak:** Most Rev. HIERONYMUS HERCULANUS BUMBUN, Keuskupan Agung, Jalan A. R. Hakin 92A, POB 1119, Pontianak 78011, Kalimantan Barat; tel. (561) 732382; fax (561) 738785; e-mail kap@pontianak.wasantara.net.id.

**Archbishop of Semarang:** Most Rev. IGNATIUS SUHARYO HARDJOATMODJO), Keuskupan Agung, Jalan Pandanaran 13, Semarang 50244; tel. (24) 411780; fax (24) 414741.

**Archbishop of Ujung Pandang:** Most Rev. JOHANNES LIKU ADA', Keuskupan Agung, Jalan Thamrin 5–7, Ujung Pandang 90111, Sulawesi Selatan; tel. (411) 315744; fax (411) 326674.

#### Other Christian Churches

**Protestant Church in Indonesia** (Gereja Protestan di Indonesia): Jalan Medan Merdeka Timur 10, Jakarta 10110; tel. (21) 3519003; consists of nine churches of Calvinistic tradition; 2,789,055 mems, 3,839 congregations, 1,963 pastors (1997); Chair. Rev. D. J. LUMENTA.

Numerous other Protestant communities exist throughout Indonesia, mainly organized on a local basis. The largest of these (1985 memberships) are: the Batak Protestant Christian Church (1,875,143); the Christian Church in Central Sulawesi (100,000); the Christian Evangelical Church in Minahasa (730,000); the Christian Protestant Church in Indonesia (210,924); the East Java Christian Church (123,850); the Evangelical Christian Church in West Irian (360,000); the Evangelical Christian Church of Sangir-Talaud (190,000); the Indonesian Christian Church/Huria Kristen Indonesia (316,525); the Javanese Christian Churches (121,500); the Kalimantan Evangelical Church (182,217); the Karo Batak Protestant Church (164,288); the Nias Protestant Christian Church (250,000); the Protestant Church in the Moluccas (575,000); the Simalungun Protestant Christian Church (155,000); and the Toraja Church (250,000).

### BUDDHISM

**All-Indonesia Buddhist Association:** Jakarta.

**Indonesian Buddhist Council:** Jakarta.

## The Press

In August 1990 the Government announced that censorship of both the local and foreign press was to be relaxed and that the authorities would refrain from revoking the licences of newspapers that violated legislation governing the press. In practice, however, there was little change in the Government's policy towards the press. In June 1994 the Government revoked the publishing licences of three principal news magazines, *Tempo, Editor* and *DeTik*. Following the resignation of President Suharto in May 1998, the new Government undertook to allow freedom of expression. *DeTik* magazine subsequently resumed publication under the new name, *DeTak,* in July; *Tempo* magazine resumed publication in October.

### PRINCIPAL DAILIES

#### Bali

**Harian Pagi Umum** (Bali Post): Jalan Kepudang 67A, Denpasar 80232; f. 1948; daily (Indonesian edn), weekly (English edn); Editor K. NADHA; circ. 25,000.

#### Java

**Angkatan Bersenjata:** Jalan Kramat Raya 94, Jakarta Pusat; tel. (21) 46071; fax (21) 366870.

**Bandung Post:** Jalan Lodaya 38A, Bandung 40264; tel. (22) 305124; fax (22) 302882; f. 1979; Chief Editor AHMAD SAELAN; Dir AHMAD JUSACC.

**Berita Buana:** Jalan Tahah Abang Dua 33–35, Jakarta, 10110; tel. (21) 5487175; fax (21) 5491555; f. 1970; relaunched 1990; Indonesian; circ. 150,000.

**Berita Yudha:** Jalan Letjenderal Haryono MT22, Jakarta; tel. (21) 8298331; f. 1971; Indonesian; Editor SUNARDI; circ. 50,000.

**Bisnis Indonesia:** Wisma Bisnis Indonesia, Jalan Letjenderal S. Parman, Kav. 12, Slipi, Jakarta; tel. (21) 5305869; fax (21) 5305868; f. 1985; Indonesian; Editor SUKAMDANI S. GITOSARDJONO; circ. 60,000.

**Harian Indonesia** (Indonesia Rze Pao): Jalan Toko Tiga Seberang 21, POB 4755, Jakarta 11120; tel. (21) 6295984; fax (21) 6297830; f. 1966; Chinese; Editor W. D. SUKISMAN; Dir HADI WIBOWO; circ. 42,000.

**Harian Terbit:** Jalan Pulogadung 15, Kawasan Industri Pulogadung, Jakarta 13920; tel. (21) 4602953; fax (21) 4602950; f. 1972; Indonesian; Editor H. R. S. HADIKAMAJAYA; circ. 125,000.

**Harian Umum AB:** CTC Bldg, 2nd Floor, Kramat Raya 94, Jakarta Pusat; f. 1965; official armed forces journal; Dir GOENARSO; Editor-in-Chief N. SOEPANGAT; circ. 80,000.

**The Indonesia Times:** Jalan Pulo Lentut 12, Jakarta Timur; tel. (21) 4611280; fax (21) 375012; f. 1974; English; Editor TRIBUANA SAID; circ. 35,000.

**Indonesian Observer:** Redtop Square, Block C-7, Jalan Pecenongan 72, Jakarta 10120; tel. (21) 3500155; fax (21) 3502417; f. 1955; English; independent; Editor (vacant); circ. 25,000.

**Jakarta Post:** Jalan Palmerah Selatan 15, Jakarta 10270; tel. (21) 5300476; fax (21) 5309066; f. 1983; English; Gen. Man. RAYMOND TORUAN; Chief Editor SUSANTO PUDJOMARTONO; circ. 50,000.

**Jawa Pos:** Jalan Kembang Jepun 167–169, Surabaya; tel. (31) 830774; fax (31) 830996; f. 1949; Indonesian; Chief Editor DAHLAN ISKAN; circ. 120,000.

**Kedaulatan Rakyat:** Jalan P. Mangkubumi 40–42, Yogyakarta; tel. (274) 65685; fax (274) 63125; f. 1945; Indonesian; independent; Editor IMAN SUTRISNO; circ. 50,000.

**Kompas:** Jalan Palmerah Selatan 26–28, Jakarta; tel. (21) 5483008; fax (21) 5305868; f. 1965; Indonesian; Editor Drs JAKOB OETAMA; circ. 523,453.

**Media Indonesia Daily:** Komplek Delta Kedoya, Jalan Pilar Mas Raya, Kav. A-D, Kedoya Selatan-Kebon Jeruk, Jakarta 11520; tel. (21) 5812088; fax (21) 5812105; e-mail redaksi@mediaindonesia.co.id; internet www.mediaindo.co.id; f. 1989; fmrly Prioritas; Indonesian; Pres. Dir SURYA PALOH; circ. 260,000.

**Merdeka:** Jalan Raya Kebayoran Lama 17, Jakarta Selatan 12210; tel. (21) 5556059; fax (21) 5556063; f. 1945; Indonesian; independent; Dir and Chief Editor B. M. DIAH; circ. 130,000.

**Neraca:** Jalan Jambrut 2–4, Jakarta; tel. (21) 323969; fax (21) 3101873.

**Pelita** (Torch): Jalan Jenderal Sudirman 65, Jakarta; f. 1974; Indonesian; Muslim; Editor AKBAR TANJUNG; circ. 80,000.

**Pewarta Surabaya:** Jalan Karet 23, POB 85, Surabaya; f. 1905; Indonesian; Editor RADEN DJAROT SOEBIANTORO; circ. 10,000.

**Pikiran Rakyat:** Jalan Asia-Afrika 77, Bandung 40111; tel. (22) 51216; f. 1950; Indonesian; independent; Editor BRAM M. DARMAPRAWIRA; circ. 150,000.

**Pos Kota:** Yayasan Antar Kota, Jalan Gajah Mada 100, Jakarta 10130; tel. (21) 6290874; f. 1970; Indonesian; Editor H. SOFYAN LUBIS; circ. 500,000.

**Republika:** Jalan Warung Buncit Raya 37, Jakarta 12510; tel. (21) 7803747; fax (21) 7800420; f. 1993; organ of ICMI; Chief Editor PARNI HADI.

**Sinar Pagi:** Jalan Letjenderal Haryono MT22, Jakarta Selatan.

**Suara Karya:** Jalan Bangka II/2, Kebayoran Baru, Jakarta Selatan; tel. (21) 7991352; fax (21) 7995261; f. 1971; Indonesian; Editor SYAMSUL BASRI; circ. 100,000.

**Suara Merdeka:** Jalan Pandanaran 30, Semarang 50241; tel. (24) 412660; fax (24) 411116; f. 1950; Indonesian; Publr Ir BUDI SANTOSO; Editor SUWARNO; circ. 200,000.

**Suara Pembaruan:** Jalan Dewi Sartika 136/D, Cawang, Jakarta 13630; tel. (21) 8093208; fax (21) 8091652; f. 1987; licence revoked in 1986 as Sinar Harapan (Ray of Hope); Chief Editor ALBERT HASIBUAN.

**Surabaya Post:** Jalan Taman Ade Irma Nasution 1, Surayaba; tel. (31) 45394; fax (31) 519585; f. 1953; independent; Publr Mrs TUTY AZIS; Editor IMAM PUJONO; circ. 115,000.

**Wawasan:** Komplek Pertokoan Simpang Lima, Blok A 10, Semarang 50241; tel. (24) 314171; fax (24) 413001; f. 1986; Indonesian; Chief Editor SOETJIPTO; circ. 65,000.

#### Kalimantan

**Banjarmasin Post:** Jalan Haryono MT 54–143, Banjarmasin; tel. (511) 53266; fax (511) 53120; f. 1971; Indonesian; Chief Editor H. J. MENTAYA; circ. 50,000.

**Gawi Manuntung:** Jalan Pangeran Samudra 97B, Banjarmasin; f. 1972; Indonesian; Editor M. ALI SRI INDRADJAYA; circ. 5,000.

**Harian Umum Akcaya:** Jalan Veteran 1, Pontianak.

**Lampung Post:** Jalan Pangkal Pinang, Lampung.

**Manuntung:** Jalan Jenderal Sudirman RT XVI 82, Balikpapan 76144; tel. (542) 35359.

### Maluku

**Pos Maluku:** Jalan Raya Pattimura 19, Ambon; tel. (911) 44614.

**Suara Maluku:** Komplex Perdagangan Mardikas, Block D3/11A, Ternate; tel. (911) 44590.

### Riau

**Riau Pos:** Pekanbaru, Riau; circ. 40,000.

### Sulawesi

**Bulletin Sulut:** Jalan Korengkeng 38, Lt II Manado, 95114, Sulawesi Utara.

**Cahaya Siang:** Jalan Kembang II 2, Manado, 95114, Sulawesi Utara; tel. (431) 61054; fax (431) 63393.

**Fajar** (Dawn): Ujung Pandang; circ. 35,000.

**Manado Post:** Jalan Yos Sudarso 73, Manado.

**Pedoman Rakyat:** Jalan H. A. Mappanyukki 28, Ujung Pandang; f. 1947; independent; Editor M. BASIR; circ. 30,000.

**Suluh Merdeka:** Jalan Haryane MT, POB 1105, Manado, 95110.

**Tegas:** Jalan Mappanyukki 28, Ujung Pandang; tel. (411) 3960.

### Sumatra

**Analisa:** Jalan Jenderal A. Yani 37–43, Medan; tel. (61) 326655; fax (61) 514031; f. 1972; Indonesian; Editor SOFFYAN; circ. 75,000.

**Harian Haluan:** Jalan Damar 59 C/F, Padang; f. 1948; Editor-in-Chief RIVAI MARLAUT; circ. 40,000.

**Harian Umum Nasional Waspada:** Jalan Brigjenderal 1 Katamso, Medan 20151; tel. (61) 550858; fax (61) 510025; e-mail waspada@indosat.net.id; internet www.waspada.com; f. 1947; Indonesian; Editor-in-Chief H. PRABUDI SAID.

**Mimbar Umum:** Merah, Medan; tel. (61) 517807; f. 1947; Indonesian; independent; Editor MOHD LUD LUBIS; circ. 55,000.

**Serambi Indonesia:** Jalan T. Nyak Arief 159, Lampriek, Banda Aceh.

**Sinar Indonesia Baru:** Jalan Brigjenderal Katamso 66, Medan 20151; tel. (61) 512530; fax (61) 510150; f. 1970; Indonesian; Chief Editor G. M. PANGGABEAN; circ. 150,000.

**Suara Rakyat Semesta:** Jalan K. H. Ashari 52, Palembang; Indonesian; Editor DJADIL ABDULLAH; circ. 10,000.

**Waspada:** Jalan Jenderal Sudirman, cnr Jalan Brigjenderal Katamso 1, Medan 20151; tel. (61) 550858; fax (61) 510025; f. 1947; Indonesian; Chief Editor ANI IDRUS; circ. 60,000 (daily), 55,000 (Sunday).

### West Papua (Irian Jaya)

**Berita Karya:** Jayapura.

**Cendrawasih Post:** Jayapura; Editor RUSTAM MADUBUN.

**Teropong:** Jalan Halmahera, Jayapura.

## PRINCIPAL PERIODICALS

**Amanah:** Jalan Garuda 69, Kemayoran, Jakarta; tel. (21) 410254; fortnightly; Muslim current affairs; Indonesian; Man. Dir MASKUN ISKANDAR; circ. 180,000.

**Berita Negara:** Jalan Pertjetakan Negara 21, Kotakpos 2111, Jakarta; tel. (21) 4207251; fax (21) 4207251; f. 1951; 2 a week; official gazette.

**Bobo:** PT Gramedia, Jalan Kebahagiaan 4-14, Jakarta 11140; tel. (21) 6297809; fax (21) 6390080; f. 1973; weekly; children's magazine; Editor TINEKE LATUMETEN; circ. 240,000.

**Bola:** Yayasan Tunas Raga, Jalan Palmerah Selatan 17, Jakarta 10270; tel. and fax (21) 5483008; 2 a week; Tue. and Fri.; sports magazine; Indonesian; Editor SUMOHADI MARSIS; circ. 715,000.

**Buana Minggu:** Jalan Tanah Abang Dua 33, Jakarta Pusat 10110; tel. (21) 364190; weekly; Sunday; Indonesian; Editor WINOTO PARARTHO; circ. 193,450.

**Business News:** Jalan H. Abdul Muis 70, Jakarta 10160; tel. (21) 3848207; fax (21) 3454280; f. 1956; 3 a week (Indonesian edn), 2 a week (English edn); Chief Editor SANJOTO SASTROMIHARDJO; circ. 15,000.

**Citra:** Gramedia Bldg, Unit 11, 5th Floor, Jalan Palmerah Selatan 24-26, Jakarta 10270; tel. (21) 5483008; fax (21) 5494035; f. 1990; weekly; TV and film programmes, music trends and celebrity news; circ. 239,000

**Depthnews Indonesia:** Jalan Jatinegara Barat III/6, Jakarta 13310; tel. (21) 8194994; fax (21) 8195501; f. 1972; weekly; publ. by Press Foundation of Indonesia; Editor SUMONO MUSTOFFA.

**Dunia Wanita:** Jalan Brigjenderal, Katamso 1, Medan; tel. (61) 550858; fax (61) 510025; e-mail waspada@indosat.net.id; f. 1949; fortnightly; Indonesian; women's magazine; Chief Editor Dr RAYATI SYAFRIN; circ. 10,000.

**Economic Review:** c/o Bank BNI, Strategic Planning Division, Jalan Jenderal Sudirman, Kav. 1, POB 2955, Jakarta 10220; tel. (21) 5728606; fax (21) 5728456; f. 1966; 4 a year; English.

**Ekonomi Indonesia:** Jalan Merdeka, Timur 11–12, Jakarta; tel. (21) 494458; monthly; English; economic journal; Editor Z. ACHMAD; circ. 20,000.

**Eksekutif:** Jalan R. S. Fatmawati 21, Jakarta 12410; tel. (21) 7502513; fax (21) 7502676.

**Femina:** Jalan H. R. Rasuna Said, Blok B, Kav. 32–33, Jakarta Selatan; tel. (21) 513816; fax (21) 513041; f. 1972; weekly; women's magazine; Publr SOFJAN ALISJAHBANA; Editor WIDARTI GUNAWAN; circ. 130,000.

**Forum:** Kebayoran Centre, 12A–14, Jalan Kebayoran Baru, Welbak, Jakarta 12240; tel. (21) 7255625; fax (21) 7255645.

**Gadis Magazine:** Jalan H. R. Rasuna Said, Blok B, Kav. 32–33, Jakarta 12910; tel. (21) 513816; fax (21) 513041; f. 1973; every 10 days; Indonesian; youth, women's interest; Editor PIA ALISJAHBANA; circ. 90,000.

**Gamma:** Jakarta; f. 1999; by fmr employees of *Tempo* and *Gatra*.

**Gatra:** Gedung Gatra, Jalan Kalibata Timur IV/15, Jakarta 12740; tel. (21) 7973535; fax (21) 79196941; e-mail gatra@gatra.com; internet www.gatra.com; f. 1994 by fmr employees of *Tempo* (banned 1994–1998); Editor-in-Chief WIDI YARMANTO; Gen. Man. YUDHISTIRA ANM MASSARDI.

**Gugat** (Accuse): Surabaya; politics, law and crime; weekly; circ. 250,000.

**Hai:** Gramedia, Jalan Palmerah Selatan 22, Jakarta 10270; tel. (21) 5483008; fax (21) 6390080; f. 1973; weekly; youth magazine; Editor ARSWENDO ATMOWILOTO; circ. 70,000.

**Indonesia Business News:** Wisma Bisnis Indonesia, Jalan Letjenderal S. Parman, Kav. 12, Slipi, Jakarta 11410; tel. (21) 5304016; fax (21) 5305868; English.

**Indonesia Business Weekly:** Jalan Letjenderal S. Parman, Kav. 12, Slipi, Jakarta 11410; tel. (21) 5304016; fax (21) 5305868; English; Editor TAUFIK DARUSMAN.

**Indonesia Magazine:** 20 Jalan Merdeka Barat, Jakarta; tel. (21) 352015; f. 1969; monthly; English; Chair. G. DWIPAYANA; Editor-in-Chief HADELY HASIBUAN; circ. 15,000.

**Intisari** (Digest): Jalan Palmerah Selatan 24, Jakarta 10270; tel. (21) 5483008; fax (21) 5494035; e-mail intisari@indomedia .com; internet www.indomedia.com/intisari; f. 1963; monthly; Indonesian; investment and trading; Editors IRAWATI, Drs J. OETAMA; circ. 141,000.

**Jakarta Jakarta:** Gramedia Bldg, Unit II, 5th Floor, Jalan Palmerah Selatan No. 24–26, Jakarta 10270; tel. (21) 5483008; fax (21) 5494035; f. 1985; weekly; food, fun, fashion and celebrity news; circ. 70,000.

**Keluarga:** Jalan Sangaji 11, Jakarta; fortnightly; women's and family magazine; Editor S. DAHONO.

**Majalah Ekonomis:** POB 4195, Jakarta; monthly; English; business; Chief Editor S. ARIFIN HUTABARAT; circ. 20,000.

**Majalah Kedokteran Indonesia** (Journal of the Indonesian Medical Asscn): Jalan Kesehatan 111/29, Jakarta 11/16; f. 1951; monthly; Indonesian, English.

**Manglé:** Jalan Lodaya 19–21, 40262 Bandung; tel. (22) 411438; f. 1957; weekly; Sundanese; Chief Editor Drs OEJANG DARAJATOEN; circ. 74,000.

**Matra:** Grafity Pers, Kompleks Buncit Raya Permai, Kav. 1, Jalan Warung, POB 3476, Jakarta; tel. (21) 515952; f. 1986; monthly; men's magazine; general interest and current affairs; Editor-in-Chief (vacant); circ. 100,000.

**Mimbar Kabinet Pembangunan:** Jalan Merdeka-Barat 7, Jakarta; f. 1966; monthly; Indonesian; publ. by Dept of Information.

**Mutiara:** Jalan Dewi Sartika 136D, Cawang, Jakarta Timur; general interest; Publr H. G. RORIMPANDEY.

**Nova:** PT Gramedia, Jalan Kebahagiaan 4-14, Jakarta 11140; tel. (21) 6297809; fax (21) 6390080; weekly; Sunday; women's interest; Indonesian; Editor EVIE FADJARI; circ. 220,000.

**Oposisi:** Jakarta; weekly; politics; circ. 400,000.

**Otomotif:** Gramedia Bldg, Unit II, 5th Floor, Jalan Palmerah Selatan 24–26, Jakarta 10270; tel. (21) 5490666; fax (21) 5494035; e-mail iklanmjl@ub.net.id; f. 1990; weekly; automotive specialist tabloid; circ. 215,763.

**Peraba:** Bintaran Kidul 5, Yogyakarta; weekly; Indonesian and Javanese; Roman Catholic; Editor W. KARTOSOEHARSONO.

**Pertani PT:** Jalan Pasar Minggu, Kalibata, POB 247/KBY, Jakarta Selatan; tel. (21) 793108; f. 1974; monthly; Indonesian; agricultural; Pres. Dir Ir RUSLI YAHYA.

**Petisi:** Surabaya; weekly; Editor CHOIRUL ANAM.

**Rajawali:** Jakarta; monthly; Indonesian; civil aviation and tourism; Dir R. A. J. LUMENTA; Man. Editor KARYONO ADHY.

**Selecta:** Kebon Kacang 29/4, Jakarta; fortnightly; illustrated; Editor SAMSUDIN LUBIS; circ. 80,000.

**Simponi:** Jakarta; f. 1994 by former employees of *DeTik* (banned 1994–98).

**Sinar Jaya:** Jakarta Selatan; fortnightly; agriculture; Chief Editor Ir SURYONO PROJOPRANOTO.

**Swasembada:** Gedung Chandra Lt 2, Jalan M. H. Thamrin 20, Jakarta 10310; tel. (21) 3103316.

**Tempo:** Gedung Tempo, 8th Floor, Jalan H.R. Rasuna Said, Kav. C-17, Kuningan, Jakarta 12940; tel. (21) 5201022; fax (21) 5200092; f. 1971; weekly; Editor GOENAWAN MOHAMAD.

**Tiara:** Gramedia Bldg, Unit 11, 5th Floor, Jalan Palmerah Selatan 24–26, Jakarta 10270; tel (21) 5483008; fax (21) 5494035; f. 1990; fortnightly; lifestyles, features and celebrity news; circ. 47,000.

**Ummat:** Jakarta; Islamic; sponsored by ICMI.

### NEWS AGENCIES

**Antara** (Indonesian National News Agency): Wisma Antara, 19th and 20th Floors, 17 Jalan Merdeka Selatan, POB 1257, Jakarta 10110; tel. (21) 364768; fax (21) 3843052; f. 1937; 2,784 commercial, 11 radio, five television and 86 newspaper subscribers in 1994; 27 brs in Indonesia, seven overseas brs; nine bulletins in Indonesian and seven in English; monitoring service of stock exchanges worldwide; photo service; Editor-in-Chief BUDIARTO DANUJAYA; Gen. Man. PARNI HADI.

**Kantorberita Nasional Indonesia** (KNI News Service): Jalan Jatinegara Barat III/6, Jakarta Timur 13310; tel. (21) 811003; fax (21) 8195501; f. 1966; independent national news agency; foreign and domestic news in Indonesian; Dir and Editor-in-Chief Drs SUMONO MUSTOFFA; Exec. Editor HARIM NURROCHADI.

#### Foreign Bureaux

**Agence France-Presse (AFP):** Jalan Indramayu 18, Jakarta Pusat 10310; tel. (21) 3336082; fax (21) 3809186; Chief Correspondent PASCAL MALLET.

**Agenzia Nazionale Stampa Associata (ANSA)** (Italy): Jalan Petogogan 1 Go-2 No, 13 Kompleks RRI, Kebayoran Baru, Jakarta Selatan; tel. (21) 7391996; fax (21) 7392247; Correspondent HERYTNO PUJOWIDAGDO.

**Associated Press (AP)** (USA): Wisma Antara, 18th Floor, Suite 1806, 17 Jalan Merdeka Selatan, Jakarta 10110; tel. (21) 3813510; fax (21) 3457690; Correspondent GHAFUR FADYL.

**Central News Agency Inc (CNA)** (Taiwan): Jalan Gelong Baru Timur 1-13, Jakarta Barat; tel. and fax (21) 5600266; Bureau Chief WU PIN-CHIANG.

**Informatsionnoye Telegrafnoye Agentstvo Rossii—Telegrafnoye Agentstvo Suverennykh Stran (ITAR—TASS)** (Russia): Jalan Surabaya 7 Menteng, Jakarta Pusat 10310; tel. and fax (21) 3155283; e-mail ab1952@indosat.net.id; Correspondent ANDREY ALEKSANDROVICH BYTCHKOV.

**Inter Press Service (IPS)** (Italy): Gedung Dewan Pers, 4th Floor, Jalan Kebon Sirih 34, Jakarta 10110; tel. (21) 3453131; fax (21) 3453175; Chief Correspondent ABDUL RAZAK.

**Jiji Tsushin** (Japan): Jalan Raya Bogor 109B, Jakarta; tel. (21) 8090509; Correspondent MARGA RAHARJA.

**Kyodo Tsushin** (Japan): Skyline Bldg, 11th Floor, Jalan M. H. Thamrin 9, Jakarta 10310; tel. (21) 345012; Correspondent MASAYUKI KITAMURA.

**Reuters** (United Kingdom): Wisma Antara, 6th Floor, Jalan Medan Merdeka Selatan 17, Jakarta 10110; tel. (21) 3846364; fax (21) 3448404; Bureau Chief JONATHAN THATCHER.

**United Press International (UPI)** (USA): Wisma Antara, 14th Floor, Jalan Medan Merdeka Selatan 17, Jakarta; tel. (21) 341056; Bureau Chief JOHN HAIL.

**Xinhua (New China) News Agency** (People's Republic of China): Jakarta.

### PRESS ASSOCIATIONS

**Alliance of Independent Journalists (AJI):** Jakarta; f. 1994; unofficial; aims to promote freedom of the press; Sec.-Gen. AHMAD TAUFIK.

**Persatuan Wartawan Indonesia** (Indonesian Journalists' Asscn): Gedung Dewan Pers, 4th Floor, Jalan Kebon Sirih 34, Jakarta 10110; tel. (21) 353131; fax (21) 353175; f. 1946; government-controlled; 5,041 mems (April 1991); Chair. TARMAN AGAM; Gen. Sec. H. SOFJAN LUBIS.

**Serikat Penerbit Suratkabar (SPS)** (Indonesian Newspaper Publishers' Asscn): Gedung Dewan Pers, 6th Floor, Jalan Kebon Sirih 34, Jakarta 10110; tel. (21) 359671; fax (21) 3862373; f. 1946; Chair. (vacant); Sec.-Gen. Drs A. BAGJO PURWANTHO.

**Yayasan Pembina Pers Indonesia** (Press Foundation of Indonesia): Jalan Jatinegara Barat III/6, Jakarta 13310; tel. (21) 8194994; f. 1967; Chair. SUGIARSO SUROYO, MOCHTAR LUBIS.

## Publishers

### Jakarta

**Aries Lima/New Aqua Press PT:** Jalan Rawagelan II/4, Jakarta Timur; tel. (21) 4897566; general and children's; Pres. TUTI SUNDARI AZMI.

**Aya Media Pustaka PT:** Wijaya Grand Centre C/2, Jalan Dharmawangsa III, Jakarta 12160; tel. (21) 7206903; fax (21) 7201401; children's; Dir Drs ARIANTO TUGIYO.

**PT Balai Pustaka:** Jalan Gunung Sahari Raya 4, POB 1029, Jakarta 10710; tel. and fax (21) 3855733; e-mail bp1917@hotmail.com; f. 1917; children's, school textbooks, literary, scientific publs and periodicals; Dir R. SISWADI.

**Bhratara Niaga Media PT:** Jalan Oto Iskandardinata III/29F, Jakarta 13340; tel. (21) 8502050; fax (21) 8191858; f. 1986; fmrly Bhratara Karya Aksara; university and educational textbooks; Man. Dir AHMAD JAYUSMAN.

**Bina Rena Pariwara PT:** Jalan Kyai Maja 227 E/1, Jakarta 12120; tel. (21) 7261179; fax (21) 7208571; f. 1988; financial, social science, economic, Islamic, children's; Dir Dra YULIA HIMAWATI.

**Bulan Bintang PT:** Jalan Kramat Kwitang 1/8, Jakarta 10420; tel. (21) 3842883; f. 1954; Islamic, social science, natural and applied sciences, art; Pres. AMRAN ZAMZAMI; Man. Dir FAUZI AMELZ.

**Bumi Aksara PT:** Jalan Sawo Raya 18, Rawamanguu, Jakarta 13220; tel. (21) 4892714; f. 1990; university textbooks; Dir H. AMIR HAMZAH.

**Cakrawala Cinta PT:** Jalan Minyak I/12B, Duren Tiga, Jakarta 12760; tel. (21) 7990725; fax (21) 7982454; f. 1984; science; Dir Drs M. TORSINA.

**Centre for Strategic and International Studies (CSIS):** Jalan Tanah Abang III/23–27, Jakarta 10160; tel. (21) 3865532; fax (21) 3847517; e-mail csis@pacific.net.id; f. 1971; political and social sciences; Dir Dr DAOED JOESOEF.

**Cipta Adi Pustaka:** Jalan Letjenderal Suprapto L20K, Cempaka Putih, Jakarta Pusat; tel. (21) 4241484; fax (21) 4208830; f. 1986; encyclopedias; Dir BUDI SANTOSO.

**Dian Rakyat PT:** Jalan Rawagelas I/4, Kaw. Industri P/Gadung, Jakarta; tel. (21) 4891809; f. 1966; general; Dir H. MOHAMMED AIS.

**Djambatan PT:** Jalan Wijaya I/39, Jakarta 12170; tel. (21) 7203199; fax (21) 7227989; f. 1954; children's, textbooks, social sciences, fiction; Dir SJARIFUDIN SJAMSUDIN.

**Dunia Pustaka Jaya:** Gedung Maya Indah, Jalan Kramat Raya 5K, Jakarta 10450; tel. (21) 3909284; f. 1971; fiction, religion, essays, poetry, drama, criticism, art, philosophy and children's; Man. A. RIVAI.

**EGC Medical Publications:** Jalan Agung Jaya III/2, Sunter Agung Podomoro, Jakarta 14350; tel. (21) 686351; fax (21) 686352; f. 1978; medical and public health, nursing, dentistry; Dir IMELDA DHARMA.

**Elex Media Komputindo:** Jalan Palmerah Selatan 22, Kompas–Gramedia Bldg 6th Floor, Jakarta 10270; tel. (21) 5483008; fax (21) 5326219; e-mail sekr_bukuanakln@elexmedia.co.id; f. 1985; computing and technology; Dir TEDDY SURIANTO.

**Erlangga PT:** Jalan H. Baping 100, Ciracas, Jakarta 13740; tel. (21) 8717006; fax (21) 8717011; e-mail mahameru@rad.net.id; f. 1952; secondary school and university textbooks; Man. Dir GUNAWAN HUTAURUK.

**Gaya Favorit Press:** Jalan H. R. Rasuna Said, Blok B, Kav. 32–33, Jakarta 12910; tel. (21) 5253816; fax (21) 5209366; f. 1971; fiction, popular science and children's; Vice-Pres. MIRTA KARTOHADIPRODJO; Man. Dir WIDARTI GUNAWAN.

**Gema Insani Press:** Jalan Kalibata Utara II/84, Jakarta 12740; tel. (21) 7988593; fax (21) 7984388; e-mail gipnet@indosat.net.id; internet www.gemainsani.co.id; f. 1986; Islamic; Dir UMAR BASYARAHIL.

**Ghalia Indonesia:** Jalan Pramuka Raya 4, Jakarta 13140; tel. (21) 8581814; fax (21) 8580842; f. 1972; children's and general science, textbooks; Man. Dir LUKMAN SAAD.

**Gramedia Widyasarana Indonesia:** Jalan Palmerah Selatan 22, Lantai IV, POB 615, Jakarta 10270; tel. (21) 5483008; fax (21) 5486085; f. 1973; university textbooks, general non-fiction, children's and magazines; Gen. Man. ALFONS TARYADI.

**Gunung Mulia PT:** Jalan Kwitang 22–23, Jakarta 10420; tel. (21) 3901208; fax (21) 3901633; e-mail bpkgm@centrin.net.id; f. 1951; general, children's, Christian; Dirs BUDI ARLIANTO, Rev. Dr SOETARMAN.

**Hidakarya Agung PT:** Jalan Kebon Kosong F/74, Kemayoran, Jakarta Pusat; tel. (21) 411074; Dir MAHDIARTI MACHMUD.

**Ichtiar:** Jalan Majapahit 6, Jakarta Pusat; tel. (21) 341226; f. 1957; textbooks, law, social sciences, economics; Dir JOHN SEMERU.

**Indira PT:** Jalan Borobudur 20, Jakarta 10320; tel. (21) 882754; f. 1953; general science and children's; Man. Dir BAMBANG P. WAHYUDI.

**Kinta CV:** Jalan Kemanggisan Ilir V/110, Pal Merah, Jakarta Barat; tel. (21) 5494751; f. 1950; textbooks, social science, general; Man. Drs MOHAMAD SALEH.

**LP 3 ES:** Jalan Letjen. S. Parman 81, Jakarta 11420; tel. (21) 5674211; fax (21) 5683785; e-mail lp3es@indo.net.id; f. 1971; general; Dir IMAM AHMAD.

**Masagung Group:** Gedung Idayu, Jalan Kwitang 13, POB 2260, Jakarta 10420; tel. (21) 3154890; fax (21) 3154889; f. 1986; general, religious, textbooks, science; Pres. H. ABDURRAHMAN MASAGUNG.

**Midas Surya Grafindo PT:** Jalan Kesehatan 54, Cijantung, Jakarta 13760; tel. (21) 8400414; fax (21) 8400270; f. 1984; children's; Dir Drs FRANS HENDRAWAN.

**Mutiara Sumber Widya PT:** Jalan Salemba Tengah 36–38, Jakarta 10440; tel. (21) 3908651; fax (21) 3160313; f. 1951; textbooks, Islamic, social sciences, general and children's; Pres. FADJRAA OEMAR.

**Penebar Swadya PT:** Jalan Gunung Sahari III/7, Jakarta Pusat; tel. (21) 4204402; fax (21) 4214821; agriculture, animal husbandry, fisheries; Dir Drs ANTHONIUS RIYANTO.

**Penerbit Universitas Indonesia:** Jalan Salemba Raya 4, Jakarta; tel. (21) 335373; f. 1969; science; Man. S. E. LEGOWO.

**Pradnya Paramita PT:** Jalan Bunga 8–8A, Matraman, Jakarta 13140; tel. (21) 8504944; f. 1973; children's, general, educational, technical and social science; Pres. Dir SOEHARDJO.

**Pustaka Antara PT:** Jalan Taman Kebon Sirih III/13, Jakarta Pusat 10250; tel. (21) 3156994; fax (21) 322745; e-mail nacelod@indonet.id; f. 1952; textbooks, political, Islamic, children's and general; Man. Dir AIDA JOESOEF AHMAD.

**Pustaka Binaman Pressindo:** Bina Manajemen Bldg, Jalan Menteng Raya 9–15, Jakarta 10340; tel. (21) 2300313; fax (21) 2302047; e-mail pustaka@bit.net.id; f. 1981; management; Dir Ir MAKFUDIN WIRYA ATMAJA.

**Pustaka Sinar Harapan PT:** Jalan Dewi Sartika 136D, Jakarta 13630; tel. (21) 8093208; fax (21) 8091652; f. 1981; general science, fiction, comics, children's; Dir ARISTIDES KATOPPO.

**Pustaka Utma Grafiti PT:** Pusat Perdagangan Senen Blok II, Lantai II, Jakarta Pusat; tel. (21) 4520747; fax (21) 4520246; f. 1981; general science; Dir ZULKIFLY LUBIS.

**Rajagrafindo Persada PT:** Jalan Pelepah Hijau IV TN-1 14–15, Kelapa Gading Permai, Jakarta 14240; tel. (21) 4520951; fax (21) 4529409; f. 1980; general science and religion; Dir Drs ZUBAIDI.

**Rineka Cipta PT:** Blok B/5, Jalan Jenderal Sudirman, Kav. 36A, Bendungan Hilir, Jakarta 10210; tel. (21) 5737646; fax (21) 5711985; f. 1990 by merger of Aksara Baru (f. 1972) and Bina Aksara; general science and university texts; Dir Drs SUARDI.

**Rosda Jayaputra PT:** Jalan Kembang 4, Jakarta 10420; tel. (21) 3904984; fax (21) 3901703; f. 1981; general science; Dir H. ROZALI USMAN.

**Sastra Hudaya:** Jalan Kalasan 1, Jakarta Pusat; tel. (21) 882321; f. 1967; religious, textbooks, children's and general; Man. ADAM SALEH.

**Tintamas Indonesia:** Jalan Kramat Raya 60, Jakarta 10420; tel. and fax (21) 3911459; f. 1947; history, modern science and culture, especially Islamic; Man. Miss MARHAMAH DJAMBEK.

**Tira Pustaka:** Jalan Cemara Raya 1, Kav. 10D, Jaka Permai, Jaka Sampurna, Bekasi 17145; tel. (21) 8841276; fax (21) 8842736; f. 1977; translations, children's; Dir ROBERT B. WIDJAJA.

**Widjaya:** Jalan Pecenongan 48C, Jakarta Pusat; tel. (21) 363446; f. 1950; textbooks, children's, religious and general; Man. DIDI LUTHAN.

**Yasaguna:** Jalan Minangkabau 44, POB 422, Jakarta Selatan; tel. (21) 8290422; f. 1964; agricultural, children's, handicrafts; Dir HILMAN MADEWA.

### Bandung

**Alma'arif:** Jalan Tamblong 48–50, Bandung; tel. (22) 4207177; f. 1949; textbooks, religious and general; Man. H. M. BAHARTHAH.

**Alumni:** Ir H. Juanda 54, Bandung 40163; tel. (22) 2501251; fax (22) 2503044; f. 1968; university and school textbooks; Dir EDDY DAMIAN.

**Angkasa:** Jalan Merdeka 6, POB 1353 BD, Bandung 40111; tel. (22) 4204795; fax (22) 439183; Dir H. FACHRI SAID.

**Armico:** Jalan Madurasa Utara 10, Bandung 40253; tel. (22) 443107; fax (22) 471972; f. 1980; school textbooks; Dir Ir ARSIL TANJUNG.

**Citra Aditya Bakti PT:** Jalan Geusanulun 17, Bandung 40115; tel. (22) 438251; f. 1985; general science; Dir Ir IWAN TANUATMADJA.

**Diponegoro Publishing House:** Jalan Mohammad Toha 44–46, Bandung 40252; tel. and fax (22) 5201215; f. 1963; Islamic, textbooks, fiction, non-fiction, general; Man. H. A. DAHLAN.

**Epsilon Grup:** Jalan Pasir Bogor Indah Q.10, Margacinta, Bandung 40287; tel. (22) 762505; f. 1985; school textbooks; Dir Drs BAHRUDIN.

**Eresco PT:** Jalan Sriwulan 26, Srimahi Baru, Bandung; tel. (22) 470977; f. 1957; scientific and general; Man. Drs ARFAN ROZALI.

**Ganeca Exact Bandung:** Jalan Kiaracondong 167, Bandung 40283; tel. (22) 701519; fax (22) 75329; f. 1982; school textbooks; Dir Ir KETUT SUARDHARA LINGGIH.

**Mizan Pustaka PT:** Jalan Yodkali 16, Bandung 40124; tel. (22) 700931; e-mail mizan@indosat.net.id; internet www.mizan.com; f. 1983; Islamic and general books; Pres. Dir HAIDAR BAGIR; Man. Dir PUTUT WIDJANARKO.

**Orba Sakti:** Jalan Pandu Dalam 3/67, Bandung; tel. (22) 614718; Dir H. HASBULLOH.

**Penerbit ITB:** Jalan Ganesa 10, Bandung 40132; tel. and fax (22) 2504257; e-mail itbpress@bdg.centrin.net.id; f. 1971; academic books; Dir EMMY SUPARKA; Chief Editor SOFIA MANSOOR-NIKSOLIHIN.

**Putra A. Bardin:** Jalan Ganesya 4, Bandung; tel. (22) 2504319; f. 1998; textbooks, scientific and general; Dir NAI A. BARDIN.

**Remaja Rosdakarya PT:** Jalan Ciateul 34–36, POB 284, Bandung 40252; tel. (22) 500287; textbooks and children's fiction; Pres. ROZALI USMAN.

**Sarana Panca Karyam PT:** Jalan Kopo 633 KM 13/4, Bandung 40014; f. 1986; general; Dir WIMPY S. IBRAHIM.

**Tarsito PT:** Jalan Guntur 20, Bandung 40262; tel. (22) 304915; fax (22) 314630; academic; Dir T. SITORUS.

### Flores

**Nusa Indah:** Jalan El Tari, Ende 86318, Flores; tel. (381) 21502; fax (381) 21645; f. 1970; religious and general; Dir HENRI DAROS.

### Kudus

**Menara Kudus:** Jalan Menara 4, Kudus 59315; tel. (291) 37143; fax (291) 36474; f. 1958; Islamic; Man. CHILMAN NAJIB.

### Medan

**Hasmar:** Jalan Letjenderal Haryono M.T. 1, POB 446, Medan 20231; tel. (61) 24181; f. 1962; primary school textbooks; Dir HASBULLAH LUBIS; Man. AMRAN SAID RANGKUTI.

**Impola:** Jalan Sisingamangaraja 104, Medan 20218; tel. (61) 23614; f. 1984; school textbooks; Dir. PAMILANG M. SITUMORANG.

**Islamiyah:** Jalan Sutomo 328–329, Kotakpos 11, Medan; tel. (61) 25426; f. 1954.

**Madju:** Jalan Sisingamangaraja Raja 25, Medan 20215; tel. (61) 711990; f. 1950; textbooks, children's and general; Pres. H. MOHAMED ARBIE; Man. Dir Drs ALFIAN ARBIE.

**Masco:** Jalan Sisingamangaraja 191, Medan 20218; tel. (61) 713375; f. 1992; school textbooks; Dir P. M. SITUMORANG.

**Monora:** Jalan Pandu 79, Medan 20212; tel. (61) 518885; f. 1968; school textbooks; Dir CHAIRIL ANWAR.

### Semarang

**Aneka Ilmu:** Jalan Pleburan VIII/64, Semarang 50242; tel. (24) 310274; f. 1983; general and school textbooks; Dir H. SUWANTO.

**Effhar COY PT:** Jalan Dorang 7, Semarang; tel. (24) 511172; fax (24) 551540; f. 1976; gen. textbooks; Dir H. DARADJAT HARAHAP.

**Intan Pariwara:** Jalan Macanan, Ketandan, Klaten, Jawa-Tengah; tel. (272) 21641; school textbooks; Pres. SOETIKNO.

**Mandira PT:** Jalan M.T. Haryono 501, Semarang 50136; tel. (24) 316150; fax (24) 415092; f. 1962; Dir Ir A. HARIYANTO.

**Mandira Jaya Abadi PT:** Jalan Kartini 48, Semarang 50124; tel. (24) 519547; fax (24) 542189; f. 1981; Dir Ir A. HARIYANTO.

**Toha Putra:** Jalan Kauman 16, Semarang; tel. (24) 24871; f. 1962; Islamic; Dir HASAN TOHA PUTRA.

### Solo

**Pabelan PT:** Jalan Raya Pajang, Kertasura KM 8, Solo 57162; tel. (271) 48811; fax (271) 41375; f. 1983; school textbooks; Dir AGUNG SASONGKO.

# Agriculture

**PRINCIPAL CROPS** ('000 metric tons)

| | 1996 | 1997 | 1998 |
|---|---|---|---|
| Wheat | 10,015 | 10,045 | 12,000* |
| Rice (paddy) | 2,685 | 2,350 | 2,600† |
| Barley | 2,736 | 2,499 | 2,300† |
| Maize | 900 | 1,000* | 1,000† |
| Potatoes | 3,140 | 3,284 | 3,300† |
| Dry beans | 135* | 110* | 110† |
| Chick-peas | 350 | 267 | 280† |
| Lentils | 159* | 130* | 130† |
| Soybeans | 140* | 145* | 145† |
| Cottonseed | 365* | 250* | 280† |
| Cotton (lint)† | 176 | 132 | 141 |
| Tomatoes | 2,975 | 2,547 | 2,700† |
| Pumpkins, squash and gourds | 500* | 500* | 500† |
| Cucumber and gherkins | 1,292 | 1,038 | 1,100† |
| Onions (dry) | 1,200 | 1,157 | 1,540 |
| Other vegetables | 3,153* | 3,911* | 3,911† |
| Watermelons | 2,061 | 2,174 | 2,200† |
| Melons | 462 | 926 | 800† |
| Grapes | 1,978 | 2,125 | 2,200† |
| Dates | 855 | 877 | 900† |
| Apples | 1,925 | 1,998 | 2,000† |
| Pears† | 170 | 172 | 175 |
| Peaches and nectarines† | 128 | 130 | 132 |
| Plums | 117 | 160 | 160† |
| Oranges | 1,670 | 1,706 | 1,800† |
| Tangerines, mandarins, clementines and satsumas | 628 | 684 | 684† |
| Lemons and limes | 754 | 940 | 1,000† |
| Other citrus fruits | 117* | 115* | 155† |
| Apricots | 215 | 198 | 198† |
| Other fruits and berries | 1,479* | 1,595* | 1,556† |
| Sugar cane | 1,833 | 2,059* | 2,059† |
| Sugar beets | 3,687 | 4,754* | 4,754† |
| Almonds | 91 | 76 | 76† |
| Pistachios | 260 | 112 | 130 |
| Tea (made) | 62 | 69 | 69† |
| Tobacco (leaves) | 17 | 20† | 20† |

* Unofficial figure. † FAO estimate(s).

Source: FAO, *Production Yearbook*.

**LIVESTOCK** ('000 head, year ending September)

| | 1996 | 1997 | 1998* |
|---|---|---|---|
| Horses* | 250 | 250 | 250 |
| Mules | 137† | 137* | 137 |
| Asses | 1,400† | 1,400* | 1,400 |
| Cattle | 8,492 | 8,600* | 8,600 |
| Buffaloes | 456 | 465 | 465 |
| Camels | 143 | 143* | 143 |
| Sheep | 51,499 | 52,000 | 53,000 |
| Goats | 25,757 | 26,000 | 27,000 |

**Chickens** (million): 202 in 1996; 210* in 1997; 230* in 1998.

* FAO estimate(s). † Unofficial figure.

Source: FAO, *Production Yearbook*.

**LIVESTOCK PRODUCTS** ('000 metric tons)

| | 1996 | 1997 | 1998 |
|---|---|---|---|
| Beef and veal | 277 | 298 | 315 |
| Buffalo meat* | 10 | 11 | 11 |
| Mutton and lamb | 280 | 301 | 309 |
| Goat meat | 100 | 105 | 109 |
| Poultry meat | 672 | 716 | 752 |
| Other meat* | 19 | 13 | 12 |
| Cows' milk | 3,809 | 3,897 | 4,075 |
| Buffaloes' milk | 160 | 190† | 169 |
| Sheep's milk | 438 | 412 | 463 |
| Goats' milk | 412 | 396 | 398 |
| Cheese* | 196 | 197 | 203 |
| Butter* | 119 | 121 | 127 |
| Poultry eggs | 520 | 486 | 625 |
| Honey* | 8 | 8 | 8 |
| Wool: | | | |
| greasy | 51 | 57 | 63 |
| clean | 28 | n.a. | n.a. |
| Cattle and buffalo hides* | 41 | 44 | 47 |
| Sheepskins* | 53 | 56 | 58 |
| Goatskins* | 18 | 19 | 20 |

* FAO estimates. † Unofficial figure.

Source: FAO, *Production Yearbook*.

# Forestry

**ROUNDWOOD REMOVALS** ('000 cubic metres, excl. bark)

| | 1995 | 1996 | 1997 |
|---|---|---|---|
| Sawlogs, veneer logs and logs for sleepers | 396 | 386 | 386 |
| Pulpwood | 509 | 509 | 509 |
| Other industrial wood | 4,007 | 4,007 | 4,007 |
| Fuel wood | 2,567 | 2,579 | 2,597 |
| **Total** | 7,469 | 7,481 | 7,499 |

Source: FAO, *Yearbook of Forest Products*.

**SAWNWOOD PRODUCTION**
('000 cubic metres, incl. railway sleepers)

| | 1995 | 1996 | 1997 |
|---|---|---|---|
| **Total** (all broadleaved) | 159 | 159* | 159* |

* FAO estimate.

Source: FAO, *Yearbook of Forest Products*.

## Fishing

('000 metric tons, live weight)

| | 1995 | 1996 | 1997 |
|---|---|---|---|
| Kutum | 8.4 | 9.2 | 7.7 |
| Silver carp | 17.0 | 17.5 | 15.8 |
| Other cyprinids | 14.8 | 19.2 | 21.5 |
| Other freshwater fishes | 0.2 | 1.9 | 1.1 |
| Caspian shads | 41.0 | 57.0 | 60.4 |
| Other diadromous fishes | 2.4 | 1.9 | 1.9 |
| Clupeoids | 8.0 | 10.0 | 10.0 |
| Narrow-barred Spanish mackerel | 11.0 | 3.6 | 2.3 |
| Kawakawa | 3.7 | 5.6 | 7.8 |
| Skipjack tuna | 2.0 | 2.5 | 8.2 |
| Longtail tuna | 27.2 | 16.5 | 17.9 |
| Yellowfin tuna | 22.5 | 28.5 | 19.9 |
| Other marine fishes | 172.0 | 170.8 | 154.5 |
| **Total fish** | 330.1 | 344.1 | 329.0 |
| Shrimps and prawns | 7.0 | 5.8 | 10.2 |
| Cephalopods | 2.5 | 1.6 | 8.6 |
| Other crustaceans and molluscs | 0.2 | 0.2 | 2.1 |
| **Total catch** | 339.8 | 351.7 | 349.9 |
| Inland waters | 88.8 | 109.3 | 111.4 |
| Indian Ocean | 251.0 | 242.4 | 238.5 |

Source: FAO, *Yearbook of Fishery Statistics*.

**Production of caviar** (metric tons, year ending 20 March): 281 in1988/89; 310 in 1989/90; 233 in 1990/91.

## Mining

**CRUDE PETROLEUM**
(net production, '000 barrels per day, year ending 20 March)

| | 1988/89 | 1989/90 | 1990/91 |
|---|---|---|---|
| Southern oilfields | 2,454 | 2,716 | 2,987 |
| Offshore oilfields | 103 | 231 | 244 |
| Doroud–Forouzan–Abouzar–Soroush | 58 | 162 | 166 |
| Salman–Rostam–Resalat | 23 | 40 | 46 |
| Sirri–Hendijan–Bahregan | 22 | 29 | 32 |
| **Total** | 2,557 | 2,947 | 3,231 |

**1991/92** ('000 barrels per day): Total production 3,366.
**1992/93** ('000 barrels per day): Total production 3,484.
**1993/94** ('000 barrels per day): Total production 3,609.
**1994/95** ('000 barrels per day): Total production 3,603.
**1995/96** ('000 barrels per day): Total production 3,600.
**1996/97** ('000 barrels per day): Total production 3,610.
**1997/98** ('000 barrels per day): Total production 3,623.
**1998/99** ('000 barrels per day): Total production 3,666.

Source: Ministry of Oil.

**NATURAL GAS** (million cu metres, year ending 20 March)*

| | 1996/97 | 1997/98 | 1998/99† |
|---|---|---|---|
| Consumption (domestic)‡ | 42,400 | 47,600 | 54,000 |
| Flared | 13,200 | 11,500 | 10,000 |
| Regional uses and wastes | 8,600 | 10,400 | 12,000 |
| **Total production** | 64,200 | 69,500 | 76,000 |

* Excluding gas injected into oil wells.
† Estimates.
‡ Includes gas for household, commercial, industrial, generator and refinery consumption.

Source IMF, *Islamic Republic of Iran: Statistical Appendix* (May 1999).

**OTHER MINERALS** ('000 metric tons, year ending 20 March)

| | 1994/95 | 1995/96 | 1996/97 |
|---|---|---|---|
| Hard coal | 980* | 1,000* | n.a. |
| Iron ore*†‡ | 4,300 | 4,500 | 4,500 |
| Copper ore†§ | 117.9 | 102.2 | 107.6 |
| Lead ore†§ | 18.3 | 15.9 | 15.7 |
| Zinc ore†§ | 72.9 | 145.1 | 76.3 |
| Manganese ore† | 13.0‡ | n.a. | n.a. |
| Chromium ore*†‡ | 39 | 39 | 39 |
| Magnesite‡ | 49.4 | 40.0 | n.a. |
| Fluorspar (Fluorite)*‡ | 10.0 | 10.0 | 10.0 |
| Barytes‡ | 139 | 150 | 150 |
| Salt (unrefined)‡ | 1,050 | 936 | 450* |
| Gypsum (crude)‡ | 8,430 | 8,230 | n.a. |

* Provisional or estimated figure(s).
† Figures refer to the metal content of ores.
‡ Data from the US Bureau of Mines.
§ Data from *World Metal Statistics* (London).

Source: UN, *Industrial Commodity Statistics Yearbook*.

## Industry

**PETROLEUM PRODUCTS**
(estimates, '000 metric tons, year ending 20 March)

| | 1993/94 | 1994/95 | 1995/96 |
|---|---|---|---|
| Liquefied petroleum gas | 2,800 | 3,100 | 3,710 |
| Naphtha | 400 | 300 | 400 |
| Motor spirit (petrol) | 6,291 | 6,200 | 6,300 |
| Aviation gasoline | 90 | 100 | 100 |
| Kerosene | 4,400 | 4,500 | 4,600 |
| White spirit | 300 | 300 | 300 |
| Jet fuel | 1,100 | 1,200 | 1,250 |
| Gas-diesel (distillate fuel) oil | 14,200 | 14,400 | 14,500 |
| Residual fuel oils | 14,300 | 14,100 | 14,100 |
| Lubricating oils | 600 | 610 | 610 |
| Petroleum bitumen (asphalt) | 2,200 | 2,100 | 2,200 |

**1996/97:** Liquefied petroleum gas 3,710.

Source: UN, *Industrial Commodity Statistics Yearbook*.

**OTHER PRODUCTS** (year ending 20 March)*

| | 1994/95 | 1995/96 | 1996/97 |
|---|---|---|---|
| Refined sugar ('000 metric tons) | 1,052 | 1,151 | 1,597 |
| Cigarettes (million) | 7,939 | 9,787 | 11,860 |
| Paints ('000 metric tons) | 36 | 32 | 33 |
| Cement ('000 metric tons) | 16,250 | 16,904 | 17,426 |
| Refrigerators ('000) | 629 | 638 | 887 |
| Gas stoves ('000) | 215 | 243 | n.a. |
| Telephone sets ('000) | 218 | 161 | 89 |
| Radios and recorders ('000) | 138 | 33 | 48 |
| Television receivers ('000) | 360 | 253 | 433 |
| Motor vehicles (assembled) ('000) | 69 | 92 | n.a. |
| Footwear (million pairs) | 17.6 | 15.8 | 16.1 |
| Carpets and rugs ('000 sq m) | 28,064 | 25,369 | 28,970 |

* Figures refer to production in large-scale manufacturing establishments with 50 workers or more.

Source: mainly UN, *Industrial Commodity Statistics Yearbook*.

**Production of Electricity** (million kWh, year ending 20 March): *Ministry of Energy:* 77,086 in 1994/95; 80,044 in 1995/96; 85,825 in 1996/97; 92,310 in 1997/98; 97,863 in 1998/99. *Private Sector:* 4,933 in 1994/95; 4,925 in 1995/96; 5,026 in 1996/97; 5,434 in 1997/98; 5,550 in 1998/99.

# Finance

## CURRENCY AND EXCHANGE RATES

**Monetary Units**

100 dinars = 1 Iranian rial (IR).

**Sterling, Dollar and Euro Equivalents** (30 September 1999)

£1 sterling = 2,869.4 rials;
US $1 = 1,742.7 rials;
€1 = 1,858.6 rials;
10,000 Iranian rials = £3.485 = $5.738 = €5.380.

**Average Exchange Rate** (rials per US $)

1996 1,750.76
1997 1,752.92
1998 1,751.86

Note: In March 1993 the multiple exchange rate system was unified, and since then the exchange rate of the rial has been market-determined. The foregoing information refers to the base rate, applicable to receipts from exports of petroleum and gas, payments for imports of essential goods and services, debt-servicing costs and imports related to large national projects. There is also an export rate, set at a mid-point of US $1 = 3,007.5 rials in May 1995, which applies to receipts from non-petroleum exports and to all other official current account transactions not effected at the base rate. The weighted average of the basic and export rates was estimated to be US $1 = 2,194.0 rials in 1996 and $1 = 2,779.5 rials in 1997. It was reported in September 1999 that the export rate would be abolished in March 2000, and that thereafter most transactions would be conducted at a 'floating' exchange rate. The free-market rate in September 1999 was about 8,500 rials per US dollar.

**BUDGET** ('000 million rials, year ending 20 March)*

| Revenue | 1996/97 | 1997/98 | 1998/99† |
|---|---|---|---|
| Oil and gas revenues | 38,153 | 37,493 | 22,979 |
| Non-oil revenues | 23,903 | 32,519 | 39,262 |
| Taxation | 12,560 | 17,345 | 18,690 |
| Income and wealth taxes | 8,971 | 11,053 | 12,426 |
| Corporate taxes | 5,378 | 6,858 | 7,585 |
| Public corporations | 2,328 | 3,197 | 3,527 |
| Private corporations | 3,050 | 3,661 | 4,058 |
| Taxes on wages and salaries | 1,586 | 1,616 | 1,708 |
| Taxes on other income | 1,408 | 1,868 | 2,337 |
| Import taxes | 2,934 | 4,289 | 4,976 |
| Customs duties | 1,536 | 2,055 | 2,740 |
| Order registration fees | 1,358 | 2,163 | 2,179 |
| Taxes on consumpton and sales | 655 | 2,003 | 1,288 |
| Non-tax revenues | 6,563 | 8,777 | 11,906 |
| Services and sales of goods | 2,132 | 2,490 | 3,100 |
| Other revenues‡ | 4,431 | 6,287 | 8,806 |
| Excises on petroleum products | 1,514 | 2,451 | 3,009 |
| Special revenues | 4,780 | 6,397 | 8,666 |
| **Total** | 62,056 | 70,012 | 62,241 |

| Expenditure§ | 1995/96 | 1996/97 | 1997/98‖ |
|---|---|---|---|
| General services | 3,149 | 4,778 | 5,478 |
| National defence | 2,774 | 4,616 | 5,800 |
| Social services | 14,556 | 21,799 | 24,652 |
| Education | 7,153 | 10,964 | 12,075 |
| Health and nutrition | 2,280 | 3,108 | 3,200 |
| Social security and welfare | 2,663 | 7,727 | 9,377 |
| Other social services | 2,460 | | |
| Economic services | 15,350 | 12,109 | 15,103 |
| Agriculture | 1,647 | 1,357 | 1,600 |
| Water resources | 1,514 | 2,045 | 2,163 |
| Petroleum, fuel and power | 5,245 | 4,756 | 7,010 |
| Transport and communication | 1,929 | 2,876 | 3,340 |
| Commerce | 4,493 | 1,075 | 990 |
| Other economic services | 522 | | |
| Other expenditure‡ | 2,774 | 10,724 | 13,634 |
| Foreign exchange obligations | 9,337 | 7,164 | 6,806 |
| Special expenditures | 3,581 | 4,780 | 6,397 |
| **Total** | 51,521 | 65,970 | 77,870 |
| Current | 38,638 | 48,578 | 58,995 |
| Capital | 12,883 | 17,392 | 18,875 |

**1998/99** (forecasts, '000 million rials): Total expenditure and net lending 78,836 (current expenditure 64,154).

* Figures refer to the consolidated accounts of the central Government, comprising the General Budget, the operations of the Social Security Organization and special (extrabudgetary) revenue and expenditure.

† Forecasts.

‡ Including operations of the Organization for Protection of Consumers and Producers, a central government unit with its own budget.

§ Excluding lending minus repayments ('000 million rials): –14 in 1995/96; –67 in 1996/97; –330 (provisional) in 1997/98.

‖ Provisional figures.

Source: IMF, mainly *Islamic Republic of Iran: Statistical Appendix* (May 1999).

**INTERNATIONAL RESERVES** (US $ million at 31 December)*

| | 1993 | 1994 | 1995 |
|---|---|---|---|
| Gold (national valuation) | 229 | 242 | 252 |
| IMF special drawing rights | 144 | 143 | 134 |
| **Total** | 373 | 385 | 386 |

* Excluding reserves of foreign exchange, for which no figures are available since 1982 (when the value of reserves was US $5,287m.).

**1996** (US $ million at 31 December): IMF special drawing rights 345.
**1997** (US $ million at 31 December): IMF special drawing rights 330.
**1998** (US $ million at 31 December): IMF special drawing rights 2.

Source: IMF, *International Financial Statistics*.

**MONEY SUPPLY** ('000 million rials at 20 December)

| | 1996 | 1997 | 1998 |
|---|---|---|---|
| Currency outside banks | 9,598 | 11,271 | 14,050 |
| Non-financial public enterprises' deposits at Central Bank | 2,639 | 2,642 | 4,662 |
| Demand deposits at commercial banks | 33,628 | 41,064 | 48,732 |
| **Total money** | 45,865 | 54,977 | 67,444 |

Source: IMF, *International Financial Statistics*.

**COST OF LIVING** (Consumer Price Index in urban areas, year ending 20 March; base: 1990/91 = 100)

| | 1996/97 | 1997/98 | 1998/99 |
|---|---|---|---|
| Food, beverages and tobacco | 499.2 | 568.4 | 709.6 |
| Clothing | 431.0 | 487.8 | 521.8 |
| Housing, fuel and light | 375.4 | 489.5 | 589.4 |
| **All items** (incl. others) | 458.8 | 538.2 | 645.6 |

Source: Bank Markazi Jomhouri Islami Iran.

**NATIONAL ACCOUNTS**

('000 million rials at current prices, year ending 20 March)

**National Income and Product**

| | 1995/96 | 1996/97 | 1997/98* |
|---|---|---|---|
| Domestic factor incomes† | 152,726.3 | 197,735.1 | 229,051.2 |
| Consumption of fixed capital | 28,073.8 | 38,026.1 | 51,335.2 |
| **Gross domestic product (GDP) at factor cost** | 180,800.1 | 235,757.2 | 280,386.4 |
| Indirect taxes / *Less* Subsidies | -1,925.1 | -524.3 | 345.0 |
| **GDP in purchasers' values** | 178,875.0 | 235,232.9 | 280,731.4 |
| Factor income from abroad / *Less* Factor income paid abroad | -1,809.4 | -2,100.4 | -1,761.3 |
| **Gross national product (GNP)** | 177,065.6 | 233,132.5 | 278,970.1 |
| *Less* Consumption of fixed capital | 28,073.8 | 38,026.1 | 51,335.2 |
| **National income in market prices** | 148,991.8 | 195,106.4 | 227,634.9 |

* Provisional figures.

† Compensation of employees and the operating surplus of enterprises.

Source: Bank Markazi Jomhouri Islami Iran.

**Expenditure on the Gross Domestic Product**

| | 1996/97 | 1997/98 | 1998/99 |
|---|---|---|---|
| Government final consumption expenditure | 31,906 | 38,365 | 43,792 |
| Private final consumption expenditure | 140,514 | 172,350 | 212,784 |
| Increase in stocks* | -11,254 | -9,829 | -412 |
| Gross fixed capital formation | 60,534 | 69,232 | 72,446 |
| **Total domestic expenditure** | 221,701 | 270,118 | 328,610 |
| Exports of goods and services | 43,535 | 36,374 | 27,144 |
| *Less* Imports of goods and services | 30,003 | 28,661 | 27,416 |
| **GDP in purchasers' values** | 235,233 | 277,831 | 328,338 |
| **GDP at constant 1982/83 prices**† | 14,661 | 15,203 | 15,479 |

* Including statistical discrepancy.

† Including adjustment for changes in terms of trade ('000 million rials): -1,498.3 in 1996/97; -1,503.8 in 1997/98; -1,572.8 (provisional) in 1998/99.

Source: mainly IMF, *International Financial Statistics*.

**Gross Domestic Product by Economic Activity** (at factor cost)

| | 1995/96 | 1996/97 | 1997/98* |
|---|---|---|---|
| Agriculture, hunting, forestry and fishing | 40,091.0 | 47,803.2 | 55,455.4 |
| Mining and quarrying† | 29,952.2 | 37,160.5 | 33,141.0 |
| Manufacturing† | 25,877.2 | 34,132.5 | 44,316.8 |
| Electricity, gas and water | 2,430.4 | 4,018.1 | 6,479.8 |
| Construction | 6,386.3 | 10,146.7 | 11,364.3 |
| Trade, restaurants and hotels | 28,988.7 | 37,437.5 | 47,386.8 |
| Transport, storage and communications | 11,368.2 | 16,986.9 | 21,108.4 |
| Finance, insurance, real estate and business services | 17,053.5 | 22,888.1 | 29,413.9 |
| Government services | 15,686.8 | 21,726.2 | 27,092.6 |
| Other services | 3,706.4 | 4,657.3 | 5,952.0 |
| **Sub-total** | 181,540.7 | 236,957.0 | 281,711.0 |
| *Less* Imputed bank service charge | 740.6 | 1,199.8 | 1,324.6 |
| **Total** | 180,800.1 | 235,757.2 | 280,386.4 |

* Provisional figures.

† Refining of petroleum is included in mining and excluded from manufacturing.

Source: Bank Markazi Jomhouri Islami Iran.

**BALANCE OF PAYMENTS** (US $ million, year ending 20 March)

| | 1996/97 | 1997/98 | 1998/99 |
|---|---|---|---|
| Exports of goods f.o.b. | 22,391 | 18,381 | 12,993 |
| Petroleum and gas | 19,271 | 15,471 | 9,900 |
| Non-petroleum and gas exports | 3,120 | 2,910 | 3,093 |
| Imports of goods f.o.b. | -14,989 | -14,123 | -13,889 |
| **Trade balance** | 7,402 | 4,258 | -896 |
| Exports of services | 860 | 1,192 | 1,121 |
| Imports of services | -3,083 | -3,371 | -2,456 |
| **Balance on goods and services** | 5,179 | 2,079 | -2,231 |
| Other income received | 488 | 466 | 238 |
| Other income paid | -898 | -725 | -731 |
| **Balance on goods, services and income** | 4,769 | 1,820 | -2,724 |
| Unrequited transfers (net) | 463 | 393 | 497 |
| **Current balance** | 5,232 | 2,213 | -2,227 |
| Long-term capital (net) | -5,246 | -3,554 | -822 |
| Short-term capital (net) | -262 | -1,268 | 2,794 |
| Net errors and omissions | 2,622 | -1,096 | -1,317 |
| **Overall balance** | 2,346 | -3,705 | -1,572 |

Source: Bank Markazi Jomhouri Islami Iran.

# External Trade

**PRINCIPAL COMMODITIES** (US $ million, year ending 20 March)

| Imports c.i.f. (distribution by SITC)* | 1995/96 | 1996/97 | 1997/98† |
|---|---|---|---|
| **Food and live animals** | 2,404 | 2,581 | 2,508 |
| Cereals and cereal preparations | 1,444 | 1,881 | 1,705 |
| Sugar, sugar preparations and honey | 376 | 335 | 405 |
| **Crude materials (inedible) except fuels** | 660 | 770 | 647 |
| **Mineral fuels, lubricants, etc.** | 228 | 377 | 265 |
| **Animal and vegetable oils and fats** | 490 | 602 | 434 |
| Vegetable oils and fats | 455 | 580 | 420 |
| **Chemicals** | 1,733 | 1,931 | 1,890 |
| Chemical elements and compounds | 430 | 571 | 494 |
| Medicinal and pharmaceutical products | 431 | 448 | n.a. |
| Plastic materials, etc. | 259 | 385 | 403 |
| **Basic manufactures** | 2,533 | 3,704 | 2,720 |
| Paper, paperboard, etc. | 527 | 569 | 392 |
| Textile yarn, fabrics, etc | 206 | 304 | 324 |
| Iron and steel | 820 | 2,049 | 1,290 |
| **Machinery and transport equipment** | 3,656 | 4,205 | 5,045 |
| Non-electric machinery | 2,285 | 2,325 | 2,672 |
| Electrical machinery, apparatus, etc. | 892 | 1,184 | 1,444 |
| Transport equipment | 479 | 696 | 929 |
| **Miscellaneous manufactured articles** | 306 | 353 | 384 |
| Scientific instruments, watches, etc. | 222 | 217 | 271 |
| **Total** (incl. others) | 12,313 | 15,117 | 14,196 |

* Including registration fee, but excluding defence-related imports.

† Provisional figures.

**1998/99** (US $ million): Total imports c.i.f. 14,507.

Source: IMF, *Islamic Republic of Iran: Statistical Appendix* (May 1999).

| Exports f.o.b.* | 1995/96 | 1996/97 | 1997/98† |
|---|---|---|---|
| **Agricultural and traditional goods** | 1,901.0 | 1,645.8 | 1,138,6 |
| Carpets | 981.1 | 642.5 | 595.1 |
| Fruit and nuts (fresh and dried) | 580.0 | 639.2 | 260.3 |
| Pistachios | 424.7 | 477.5 | 178.3 |
| Animal skins and hides, and leather | 115.0 | 98.4 | 86.2 |
| **Metal ores** | 73.4 | 46.8 | 38.3 |
| **Industrial manufactures** | 1,276.3 | 1,413.1 | 1,701.5 |
| Chemical products | 136.0 | 182.8 | 471.9 |
| Footwear | 50.8 | 61.3 | 77.3 |
| Textile manufactures | 75.0 | 75.3 | 193.0 |
| Copper bars, sheets and wire | 64.2 | 40.6 | 102.9 |
| Domestic appliances and sanitary ware | 41.6 | 59.1 | 0.4 |
| Iron and steel | 168.9 | 69.9 | 176.7 |
| Hydrocarbons (gas) | 96.8 | 112.8 | 194.6 |
| **Total** | 3,250.7 | 3,105.7 | 3,008.2 |

* Excluding exports of petroleum (US $ million): 15,103 in 1995/96; 19,271 in 1996/97; 15,464† in 1997/98.

† Provisional figures. Revised total for 1997/98 (excluding exports of petroleum) is (US $ million) 2,875.6.

**1998/99** (US $ million): Total exports f.o.b. (excluding exports of petroleum) 3,013.

Source: Bank Markazi Jomhouri Islami Iran.

**PRINCIPAL TRADING PARTNERS**
(US $ million, year ending 20 March)

| Imports c.i.f. | 1995/96 | 1996/97 | 1997/98† |
|---|---|---|---|
| Argentina | 544 | 798 | 833 |
| Australia | 412 | 741 | 522 |
| Austria | 189 | 172 | 265 |
| Azerbaijan | 210 | 252 | n.a. |
| Bahrain | 60 | 129 | n.a. |
| Belgium | 663 | 926 | 457 |
| Brazil | 227 | 349 | 294 |
| Canada | 458 | 449 | 616 |
| China, People's Republic | 232 | 242 | n.a. |
| France | 498 | 437 | 675 |
| Germany | 1,777 | 2,100 | 1,854 |
| India | 222 | 231 | n.a. |
| Indonesia | 205 | n.a. | n.a. |
| Italy | 535 | 675 | 796 |
| Japan | 886 | 844 | 882 |
| Korea, Republic | 342 | 445 | 552 |
| Netherlands | 281 | 268 | 296 |
| Pakistan | 165 | n.a. | n.a. |
| Russia | 372 | 644 | n.a. |
| South Africa | 41 | 140 | n.a. |
| Spain | 154 | 252 | 263 |
| Switzerland | 509 | 812 | 531 |
| Thailand | 225 | 405 | 173 |
| Turkey | 240 | 284 | 289 |
| United Arab Emirates | 441 | 473 | 562 |
| United Kingdom | 505 | 685 | 681 |
| USA | 476 | n.a. | n.a. |
| Viet Nam | 2 | 134 | n.a. |
| **Total** (incl. others) | 12,313 | 15,117 | 14,196 |

| Exports f.o.b. | 1995/96 | 1996/97 | 1997/98 |
|---|---|---|---|
| Azerbaijan | 169.7 | 200.0 | n.a. |
| Belgium | 524.0 | 29 | 236 |
| Brazil | 276.7 | n.a. | n.a. |
| China, People's Republic | 216.4 | 73.6 | 543 |
| France | 847.8 | 721 | 684 |
| Germany | 783.2 | 570.2 | 428 |
| Greece | 839.1 | 1,118.5 | 989 |
| Hong Kong | 5.9 | 673.4 | n.a. |
| India | 555.2 | 722 | 531 |
| Italy | 1,586.9 | 1,821.9 | 1,631 |
| Japan | 2,774.9 | 3,835 | 2,783 |
| Korea, Republic | 1,107.8 | 1,716.4 | 1,280 |
| Poland | 109.0 | n.a. | n.a. |
| Singapore | 392.4 | 586 | 695 |
| Spain | 781.4 | 748.2 | n.a. |
| Sweden | 243.4 | n.a. | n.a. |
| Switzerland | 139.5 | 86.3 | n.a. |
| Taiwan | 301.8 | 58.2 | n.a. |
| Turkey | 760.9 | 706.3 | 546 |
| Turkmenistan | 40.5 | 125.1 | n.a. |
| United Arab Emirates | 808.5 | 695 | 775 |
| United Kingdom | 1,439.0 | 3,907.6 | 3,037 |
| USA | 761.7 | n.a. | n.a. |
| Uzbekistan | 69.9 | 124.6 | n.a. |
| **Total** (incl. others) | 18,360.0 | 22,496 | 18,374 |

Source: IMF, *Islamic Republic of Iran: Statistical Appendix* (May 1999).

# Transport

**RAILWAYS** (traffic)

| | 1994 | 1995 | 1996 |
|---|---|---|---|
| Passenger-km (million) | 6,479 | 7,294 | 7,044 |
| Freight ton-km (million) | 10,700 | 11,865 | 13,638 |

**ROAD TRAFFIC** (estimates, '000 motor vehicles in use)

| | 1994 | 1995 | 1996 |
|---|---|---|---|
| Passenger cars | 1,636 | 1,714 | 1,793 |
| Lorries and vans | 626 | 657 | 692 |
| Motor-cycles and mopeds | 2,262 | 2,381 | 2,566 |

Source: International Road Federation, *World Road Statistics*.

**SHIPPING**

**Merchant Fleet** (registered at 31 December)

| | 1996 | 1997 | 1998 |
|---|---|---|---|
| Number of vessels | 414 | 417 | 382 |
| Displacement ('000 grt) | 3,566.8 | 3,553.0 | 3,347.4 |

Source: Lloyd's Register of Shipping, *World Fleet Statistics*.

**International Sea-borne Freight Traffic**
('000 metric tons)

| | 1994 | 1995 | 1996 |
|---|---|---|---|
| Goods loaded | 128,026 | 132,677 | 140,581 |
| Crude petroleum and petroleum products | 123,457 | 127,143 | 134,615 |
| Goods unloaded | 20,692 | 22,604 | 27,816 |
| Petroleum products | 6,949 | 7,240 | 7,855 |

**CIVIL AVIATION** (traffic on scheduled services)*

| | 1994 | 1995 | 1996 |
|---|---|---|---|
| Passengers carried ('000) | 5,441 | 5,809 | 5,889 |
| Passenger-km (million) | 5,055 | 5,384 | 5,840 |
| Cargo ton-km (million) | 515 | 547 | 643 |

* Figures refer only to traffic of Iran Air.

# Tourism

| | 1993 | 1994 | 1995 |
|---|---|---|---|
| Tourist arrivals ('000) | 304.1 | 362.0 | 443.2 |
| Tourism receipts (US $ million) | 131 | 153 | 160 |

Source: UN, *Statistical Yearbook*.

# Communications Media

| | 1994 | 1995 | 1996 |
|---|---|---|---|
| Radio receivers ('000 in use) | 15,550 | 15,580 | 16,600 |
| Television receivers ('000 in use) | 4,076 | 4,300 | 4,500 |
| Telephones ('000 main lines in use)* | 4,320 | 5,090 | n.a. |
| Telefax stations (number in use)* | 30,000 | n.a. | n.a. |
| Mobile cellular telephones (subscribers)* | 9,200 | 26,300 | n.a. |
| Book production: | | | |
| Titles | 10,753 | 13,031 | 15,073 |
| Copies ('000) | n.a. | 87,756 | 87,861 |
| Daily newspapers: | | | |
| Number | n.a. | 27 | 32 |
| Average circulation ('000 copies) | n.a. | 1,446 | 1,651 |

* Twelve months ending March following the year stated.

Sources: UNESCO, *Statistical Yearbook*; UN, *Statistical Yearbook*.

**Periodicals** (number): 403 in 1994; 623 in 1995.

# Education

(1996/97, unless otherwise indicated)

| | Insti-tutions | Teachers | Students | | |
|---|---|---|---|---|---|
| | | | Males | Females | Total |
| Pre-primary | 3,322 | 6,025 | 99,842 | 95,339 | 195,181 |
| Primary | 63,101 | 298,755 | 4,885,665 | 4,352,728 | 9,238,393 |
| Secondary: | | | | | |
| General* | n.a. | 228,889 | 3,974,141 | 3,310,470 | 7,284,611 |
| Teacher-training* | n.a. | 538 | 13,605 | 7,605 | 21,210 |
| Vocational* | n.a. | 19,880 | 262,952 | 84,056 | 347,008 |
| Higher: | | | | | |
| Universities, etc. | n.a. | 28,343 | 237,510 | 129,786 | 367,296 |
| Distance-learning | n.a. | 3,380 | 73,615 | 59,320 | 132,935 |
| Others | n.a. | 8,304 | 58,782 | 20,057 | 78,839 |

* 1994/95 figures. Figures for all categories of secondary education in 1996/97 were: Teachers 280,309; Students 8,776,792 (males 4,711,559; females 4,065,233).

† Excluding private universities.

Source: UNESCO, *Statistical Yearbook*.

# Directory

## The Constitution

A draft constitution for the Islamic Republic of Iran was published on 18 June 1979. It was submitted to a 'Council of Experts', elected by popular vote on 3 August 1979, to debate the various clauses and to propose amendments. The amended Constitution was approved by a referendum on 2–3 December 1979. A further 45 amendments to the Constitution were approved by a referendum on 28 July 1989.

The Constitution states that the form of government of Iran is that of an Islamic Republic, and that the spirituality and ethics of Islam are to be the basis for political, social and economic relations. Persians, Turks, Kurds, Arabs, Balochis, Turkomans and others will enjoy completely equal rights.

The Constitution provides for a President to act as chief executive. The President is elected by universal adult suffrage for a term of four years. Legislative power is held by the Majlis (Islamic Consultative Assembly), with 290 members (effective from the 2000 election) who are similarly elected for a four-year term. Provision is made for the representation of Zoroastrians, Jews and Christians.

All legislation passed by the Islamic Consultative Assembly must be sent to the Council for the Protection of the Constitution (Article 94), which will ensure that it is in accordance with the Constitution and Islamic legislation. The Council for the Protection of the Constitution consists of six religious lawyers appointed by the Faqih (see below) and six lawyers appointed by the High Council of the Judiciary and approved by the Islamic Consultative Assembly. Articles 19–42 deal with the basic rights of individuals, and provide for equality of men and women before the law and for equal human, political, economic, social and cultural rights for both sexes.

The press is free, except in matters that are contrary to public morality or insult religious belief. The formation of religious, political and professional parties, associations and societies is free, provided they do not negate the principles of independence, freedom, sovereignty and national unity, or the basis of Islam.

The Constitution provides for a Wali Faqih (religious leader) who, in the absence of the Imam Mehdi (the hidden Twelfth Imam), carries the burden of leadership. The amendments to the Constitution that were approved in July 1989 increased the powers of the Presidency by abolishing the post of Prime Minister, formerly the Chief Executive of the Government.

## The Government

### WALI FAQIH (RELIGIOUS LEADER)

Ayatollah SAYED ALI KHAMENEI.

### HEAD OF STATE

**President:** Hojatoleslam Dr SAYED MUHAMMAD KHATAMI (assumed office 3 August 1997).

**First Vice-President:** HASSAN IBRAHIM HABIBI.

**Vice-President in charge of Executive Affairs:** MUHAMMAD HASHEMI RAFSANJANI.

**Vice-President in charge of Legal and Parliamentary Affairs:** Hojatoleslam MUHAMMAD ALI SADUQI.

**Vice-President and Head of the Iranian Atomic Energy Organization:** GHOLAMREZA AGHAZADEH.

**Vice-President and Head of the Organization for the Protection of the Environment:** MA'SUMEH EBTEKAR.

**Vice-President and Head of the Plan and Budget Organization:** MUHAMMAD ALI NAJAFI.

**Vice-President and Head of the Physical Education Organization:** SAYED MOSTAFA HASHEMI-TABA.

**Vice-President and Secretary General of the Organization for Administrative and Employment Affairs:** Muhammad Baqerian.

### COUNCIL OF MINISTERS
(February 2000)

**Minister of Foreign Affairs:** Kamal Kharrazi.

**Minister of Education:** Hossein Mozafar.

**Minister of Culture and Islamic Guidance:** Ata'ollah Mohajerani.

**Minister of Information:** Hojatoleslam Ali Yunesi.

**Minister of Commerce:** Muhammad Shari'atmadari.

**Minister of Health:** Muhammad Farhadi.

**Minister of Posts, Telegraphs and Telephones:** Muhammad Reza Aref.

**Minister of Justice:** Muhammad Ismail Shoushtari.

**Minister of Defence and Logistics:** Ali Shamkhani.

**Minister of Roads and Transport:** Mahmud Hojjati.

**Minister of Industries:** Gholamreza Shafe'i.

**Minister of Higher Education:** Mostafa Mo'in.

**Minister of Mines and Metals:** Eshaq Jahangiri.

**Minister of Labour and Social Affairs:** Hossein Kamali.

**Minister of the Interior:** Hojatoleslam Sayed Abdolvahed Musavi-Lari.

**Minister of Agriculture:** Isa Kalantari.

**Minister of Housing and Urban Development:** Ali Abd al-Alizadeh.

**Minister of Energy:** Habibollah Bitaraf.

**Minister of Oil:** Bizam Namdar-Zangeneh.

**Minister of Economic Affairs and Finance:** Hossein Namazi.

**Minister of Construction Jihad:** Muhammad Sa'idi-Kia.

**Minister of Co-operatives:** Morteza Haji.

**Head of the Presidential Office:** Muhammad Ali Abtahi.

### MINISTRIES

All ministries are in Teheran.

**Ministry of Co-operatives:** 16 Bozorgmehr St, Vali-e-Asr Ave, Teheran 14169; tel. (21) 6400938; fax (21) 6417041.

**Ministry of Health and Medical Education:** POB 15655-415, 371 Shariati Ave, Averezi Station, Teheran 16139; tel. (21) 767631; fax (21) 7676733.

**Ministry of Mines and Metals:** 248 Somayeh Ave, Teheran; tel. (21) 836051.

**Ministry of Roads and Transport:** 49 Taleghani Ave, Teheran; tel. (21) 661034.

## President and Legislature

### PRESIDENT

**Election, 23 May 1997**

| Candidates | Votes | % |
|---|---|---|
| Sayed Muhammad Khatami | 20,088,338 | 69.1 |
| Ali Akbar Nateq Nouri | 7,233,568 | 24.9 |
| Sayed Reza Zavarei | 771,463 | 2.7 |
| Muhammad Muhammadi Reyshahri | 742,599 | 2.6 |
| Spoilt votes | 240,994 | 0.8 |
| **Total** | 29,076,962 | 100.0 |

### MAJLIS-E-SHURA E ISLAMI—ISLAMIC CONSULTATIVE ASSEMBLY

A first round of voting in elections to the sixth Majlis took place on 18 February 2000. According to results available at early March, 'reformist' and 'liberal' candidates were likely to control at least two-thirds of the assembly's 290 seats. A second round of voting, for some 65 undecided seats, was to take place in April.

### SHURA-YE ALI-YE AMNIYYAT-E MELLI—SUPREME COUNCIL FOR NATIONAL SECURITY

Formed in July 1989 to co-ordinate defence and national security policies, the political programme and intelligence reports, and social, cultural and economic activities related to defence and security. The Council is chaired by the President and includes two representatives of the Wali Faqih, the Head of the Judiciary, the Speaker of the Majlis, the Chief of Staff, the General Command of the Armed Forces, the Minister of Foreign Affairs, the Minister of the Interior, the Minister of Information and the Head of the Plan and Budget Organization.

### MAJLIS-E KHOBREGAN—COUNCIL OF EXPERTS

Elections were held on 10 December 1982 to appoint a Council of Experts which was to choose an eventual successor to the Wali Faqih (then Ayatollah Khomeini) after his death. The Constitution provides for a three- or five-man body to assume the leadership of the country if there is no recognized successor on the death of the Wali Faqih. The Council comprises 86 clerics. Elections to a third term of the Council were held on 23 October 1998.

**Speaker:** Ayatollah Ali Meshkini.

**First Deputy Speaker:** Hojatoleslam Ali Akbar Hashemi Rafsanjani.

**Second Deputy Speaker:** Ayatollah Ibrahim Amini Najafabadi.

**Secretaries:** Hojatoleslam Hassan Taheri-Khorramabadi, Ayatollah Qorbanali Dorri Najafabadi.

### SHURA-E-NIGAHBAN—COUNCIL OF GUARDIANS

The Council of Guardians, composed of six qualified Muslim jurists appointed by Ayatollah Khomeini and six lay Muslim lawyers, appointed by the Majlis from among candidates nominated by the Head of the Judiciary, was established in 1980 to supervise elections and to examine legislation adopted by the Majlis, ensuring that it accords with the Constitution and with Islamic precepts.

**Chairman:** Ayatollah Muhammad Muhammadi Guilani.

### SHURA-YE TASHKHIS-E MASLAHAT-E NEZAM—COMMITTEE TO DETERMINE THE EXPEDIENCY OF THE ISLAMIC ORDER

Formed in February 1988, by order of Ayatollah Khomeini, to arbitrate on legal and theological questions in legislation passed by the Majlis, in the event of a dispute between the latter and the supervisory Council of Guardians. Its permanent members, defined in March 1997, are Heads of the Legislative, Judiciary and Executive Powers, the jurist members of the Council of Guardians and the Minister or head of organization concerned with the pertinent arbitration.

**Chairman:** Hojatoleslam Ali Akbar Hashemi Rafsanjani.

### HEY'AT-E PEYGIRI-YE QANUN ASASI VA NEZARAT BAR AN—COMMITTEE FOR ENSURING AND SUPERVISING THE IMPLEMENTATION OF THE CONSTITUTION

Formed by President Khatami in November 1997; members are appointed for a four-year term.

**Members:** Dr Gudarz Eftekhar-Jahromi; Muhammad Ismail Shoushtari; Sayed Abdolvahed Musavi-Lari; Dr Hossein Mehrpur; Dr Muhammad Hossein Hashemi.

## Political Organizations

Numerous political organizations were registered in the late 1990s, following the election of President Khatami, among them several political tendencies that had formed within the Majlis. The following organizations appeared to have achieved considerable success at elections to the sixth Majlis in early 2000:

**Chekad-e Azadandishan** (Freethinkers' Front).

**Hezb-e E'tedal va Towse'eh** (Moderation and Development Party).

**Hezb-e Hambastegi-ye Iran-e Islami** (Islamic Iran Solidarity Party).

**Hezb-e Kargozaran-e Sazandegi** (Servants of Construction Party): Sec.-Gen. Gholamhossein Karbaschi.

**Jam'iyat-e Isargaran** (Society of Self-sacrificing Devotees).

**Jebbeh-ye Masharekat-e Iran-e Islami** (Islamic Iran Participation Front): Leader Muhammad Reza Khatami.

**Majma'-e Niruha-ye Khat-e Imam** (Assembly of the Followers of the Imam's Line).

Most of the following organizations are opposed to the Iranian Government:

**Anzar-e Hezbollah:** f. 1995; seeks to gain access to the political process for religious militants.

**Democratic Party of Iranian Kurdistan:** f. 1945; seeks autonomy for Kurdish area; mem. of the National Council of Resistance; 54,000 mems; Sec.-Gen. Mustapha Hassanzadeh.

**Fedayin-e-Khalq** (Warriors of the People): urban Marxist guerrillas; Spokesman Farrakh Negahdar.

**Fraksion-e Hezbollah:** f. 1996 by deputies in the Majlis who had contested the 1996 legislative elections as a loose coalition known as the Society of Combatant Clergy; Leader Ali Akbar Hossaini.

**Hezb-e-Komunist Iran** (Communist Party of Iran): f. 1979 by dissident mems of Tudeh Party; Sec.-Gen. 'AZARYUN'.

**Komala:** f. 1969; Kurdish wing of the Communist Party of Iran; Marxist-Leninist; Leader IBRAHIM ALIZADEH.

**Mujahidin-e-Khalq** (Holy Warriors of the People): Islamic guerrilla group; since June 1987 comprising the National Liberation Army; mem. of the National Council of Resistance; Leaders MASSOUD RAJAVI and MARYAM RAJAVI (in Baghdad, 1986–).

**National Democratic Front:** f. March 1979; Leader HEDAYATOLLAH MATINE-DAFTARI (in Paris, January 1982–).

**National Front** (Union of National Front Forces): comprises Iran Nationalist Party, Iranian Party, and Society of Iranian Students; Leader Dr KARIM SANJABI (in Paris, August 1978–).

**Nehzat-Azadi** (Liberation Movement of Iran): f. 1961; emphasis on basic human rights as defined by Islam; Gen. Sec. Dr IBRAHIM YAZDI; Principal Officers Prof. SAHABI, S. SADR, Dr SADR, Eng. SABAGHIAN, Eng. TAVASSOLI.

**Pan-Iranist Party:** extreme right-wing; calls for a Greater Persia; Leader Dr MOHSEN PEZESHKPOUR.

**Sazmane Peykar dar Rahe Azadieh Tabaqe Kargar** (Organization Struggling for the Freedom of the Working Class): Marxist-Leninist.

**Tudeh Party** (Communist): f. 1941; declared illegal 1949; came into open 1979, banned again April 1983; First Sec. Cen. Cttee ALI KHAVARI.

The National Council of Resistance (NCR) was formed in Paris in October 1981 by former President ABOLHASAN BANI-SADR and the Council's current leader, MASSOUD RAJAVI, the leader of the Mujahidin-e-Khalq in Iran. In 1984 the Council comprised 15 opposition groups, operating either clandestinely in Iran or from exile abroad. BANI-SADR left the Council in 1984 because of his objection to RAJAVI's growing links with the Iraqi Government. The French Government asked RAJAVI to leave Paris in June 1986 and he is now based in Baghdad, Iraq. On 20 June 1987 RAJAVI, Secretary of the NCR, announced the formation of a National Liberation Army (10,000–15,000-strong) as the military wing of the Mujahidin-e-Khalq. There is also a National Movement of Iranian Resistance, based in Paris. Dissident members of the Tudeh Party founded the Democratic Party of the Iranian People in Paris in February 1988.

# Diplomatic Representation

## EMBASSIES IN IRAN

**Afghanistan:** Dr Beheshi Ave, Pompe Benzine, Corner of 4th St, Teheran; tel. (21) 627531; Ambassador: MOHAMMAD KHEIRKHAH.

**Albania:** Teheran; Ambassador: GILANI SHEHU.

**Angola:** Teheran; Ambassador: MANUEL BERNARDO DE SOUSA.

**Argentina:** 3rd Floor, 7 Argentina Sq., Teheran; tel. (21) 8718294; fax (21) 8712583; Chargé d'affaires: EDUARDO LIONEL DE'AUP.

**Armenia:** 1 Ostad Shahriar St, Corner of Razi, Jomhouri Islami Ave, Teheran 11337; tel. (21) 674833; fax (21) 670657; Ambassador: YAHAN BAIBOURDIAN.

**Australia:** POB 15875-4334, 123 Shahid Khaled al-Islambuli Ave, Teheran 15138; tel. (21) 8724456; fax (21) 8720484; Ambassador: STUART HUME.

**Austria:** 3rd Floor, 78 Argentine Sq., Teheran; tel. (21) 8710753; fax (21) 8710778; Ambassador: Dr HELMUTH WERNER EHRLICH.

**Azerbaijan:** Teheran; tel. (21) 2280063; fax (21) 2284929; e-mail azaremb@www.dci.co.ir; Ambassador: ABBASALI K. HASANOV.

**Bahrain:** 31 Khiaban Wzra'a-Kochah, Block 16, Teheran; tel. (21) 2263381; fax (21) 2269112; Chargé d'affaires: RAMSEY JALAL.

**Bangladesh:** POB 11365-3711, Gandhi Ave, 5th St, Building No. 14, Teheran; tel. (21) 8772979; fax (21) 8778295; e-mail banglaemb@neda.net; Ambassador: TUFAIL K. HAIDER.

**Belgium:** POB 11365-115, Fayazi Ave, Shabdiz Lane, 3 Babak St, Teheran 19659; tel. (21) 2009507; Ambassador: GUILLAUME METTEN.

**Brazil:** Vanak Sq., 58 Vanak Ave, Teheran 19964; tel. (21) 8035175; fax (21) 8083348; e-mail emb.brazil@yahoo.com; Ambassador: CLAUDIO LUIZ DOS SANTOS ROCHA.

**Bulgaria:** POB 11365-7451, Vali Asr Ave, Tavanir St, Nezami Ganjavi St, No. 82, Teheran; tel. (21) 685662; Ambassador: STEFAN POLENDAKOV.

**Canada:** POB 11365-4647, 57 Shahid Sarafraz St; tel. (21) 8732623; fax 8733202; Ambassador: MICHEL DE SALABERRY.

**China, People's Republic:** Pasdaran Ave, Golestan Ave 1, No. 53, Teheran; tel. (21) 245131; Ambassador: WANG SHIJIE.

**Colombia:** Teheran; Ambassador: RAFAEL CANAL SANDOVAL.

**Congo, Democratic Republic:** Teheran; tel. (21) 222199; Chargé d'affaires a.i.: N'DJATE ESELE SASA.

**Cuba:** Teheran; tel. (21) 685030; Ambassador: ENRIQUE TRUJILLO RAPALLO.

**Cyprus:** 55 Shahid Sartip Reza Saeidi (ex Mehmandoust), Farmanieh Ave, Teheran; tel. (21) 2299795; fax (21) 2299794; Ambassador: GEORGIOS VIRYDES.

**Czech Republic:** POB 11365-4457, Mirza-ye Shirazi Ave, Ali Mirza Hassani St, No. 15, Teheran; tel. (21) 8716720; fax (21) 8717858; Chargé d'affaires: Eng. JIŘÍ DOLEŽAL.

**Denmark:** POB 19395-5358, 18 Dashti Ave, Teheran 19148; tel. (21) 261363; fax (21) 2030007; Ambassador: HUGO ØESTERGAARD-ANDERSEN.

**Ethiopia:** Teheran; Ambassador: MOHAMMED HASAN KAHIM.

**Finland:** POB 19395-1733, Elahiyeh, Agha Bozorgi St, Shirin Alley, No. 4, Teheran; tel. (21) 2230979; fax (21) 2210948; Ambassador: A. KOISTINEN.

**France:** 85 Neauphle-le-Château Ave, Teheran; tel. (21) 676005; Ambassador: PHILIPPE DE SUREMAIN.

**Gambia:** Teheran; Ambassador: OMAR JAH.

**Georgia:** POB 19575-379, Elahiyeh, Teheran; tel. (21) 2211470; fax (21) 2206848; e-mail georgia@apadana.com; Ambassador: JEMSHID GIUNASHVILI.

**Germany:** POB 11365-179, 324 Ferdowsi Ave, Teheran; tel. (21) 3114111; fax (21) 3119883; Ambassador: Dr KLAUS ZELLER.

**Ghana:** Teheran; Ambassador: Mr AL-HASSAN.

**Greece:** POB 11365-8151, Africa Expressway (Ex. Jordan Ave), Esfandiar St No. 43, Teheran 19686; tel. (21) 2050533; Ambassador: DIMITRI TSIKOURIS.

**Guinea:** POB 11365-4716, Ave Shariati, Ave Malek, No. 10, Teheran; tel. (21) 7535744; fax (21) 7535743; Ambassador: ALPHA IBRAHIMA SOW.

**Holy See:** Apostolic Nunciature, POB 11365-178, Razi Ave, No. 97, Neauphle-le-Château Ave, Teheran; tel. (21) 6403574; fax (21) 6419442; Apostolic Nuncio: Most Rev. ANGELO MOTTOLA, Titular Archbishop of Cercina.

**Hungary:** POB 6363-19395, Darrous, Hedayat Sq, Shadloo St, No. 15, Teheran; tel. (21) 2550460; fax (21) 2550503; Ambassador: Dr ISTVÁN VÁSÁRY.

**India:** POB 15875-4118, 46 Mir-Emad, Cnr of 9th St, Dr Behesti Ave, Teheran; tel. (21) 855102; fax (21) 855973; Ambassador: S. K. ARORA.

**Indonesia:** POB 11365-4564, Ghaem Magham Farahani Ave, No. 210, Teheran; tel. (21) 626865; Ambassador: BAMBANG SUDARSONO.

**Iraq:** Vali Asr Ave, No. 494, Teheran; Chargé d'affaires: ABD AS-SATTAR AR-RAWI.

**Ireland:** Farmaniyeh Ave, North Kamraniyeh St, Bonbast Nahid St, No. 8, Teheran 19369; tel. (21) 2297918; fax (21) 2286933; Ambassador: THOMAS D. LYONS.

**Italy:** POB 11365-7863, 81 Neauphle-le-Château Ave, Teheran; tel. (21) 6496955; fax (21) 6496961; Ambassador: LUDOVICO ORTONA.

**Japan:** POB 11365-814, Bucharest Ave, Corner of 5th St, Teheran; tel. (21) 8813396; Ambassador: UKERU MAGOSAKI.

**Jordan:** POB 19395-4666, No. 6, 2nd Alley, Shadavar St, Mahmoodieh Ave, Teheran; tel. (21) 291432; fax (21) 2007160; Ambassador NUH ALI SALMAN.

**Kazakhstan:** Darrus, Hedayat St, Masjed, No. 4, Teheran; tel (21) 2565933; fax (21) 2546400; Ambassador: VYACHESLAV GIZZATOV.

**Kenya:** 60 Hormoz Satari St, Africa Ave, Teheran; tel. (21) 2270795; fax (21) 2270160; Ambassador: SALIM JUMA.

**Korea, Democratic People's Republic:** Fereshteh Ave, Sarvestan Ave, No. 11, Teheran; tel. (21) 298610; Ambassador: KING YONG MU.

**Korea, Republic:** 37 Bucharest Ave, Teheran; tel. (21) 8751125; fax (21) 8737917; Ambassador: JAE-KYU KIM.

**Kuwait:** Dehkadeh Ave, 3–38 Sazman-Ab St, Teheran; tel. (21) 636712; Ambassador: ABDULLAH ABD AL-AZIZ AD-DUWAYKH.

**Kyrgyzstan:** Teheran.

**Laos:** Teheran; Ambassador: CHANPHENG SIHAPHOM.

**Lebanon:** Teheran; tel. (21) 8908451; fax (21) 8907345; Ambassador: ADNAN MANSOUR.

**Libya:** Ostad Motahhari Ave, No. 163, Teheran; tel. (21) 859191; Sec.-Gen. Committee of People's Bureau: MAHDI AL-MABIRASH.

**Malaysia:** 72 Fereshteh Ave, Teheran; tel. (21) 2009275; fax (21) 2009143; Ambassador: MUHAMMAD KHALIS.

**Mauritania:** Teheran.

**Mexico:** POB 15875-4636, No. 24, Shabnam Alley, Africa Expressway, Teheran; tel. (21) 2225374; fax (21) 2225375; Ambassador: ANTONIO DUEÑAS PULIDO.

**Mongolia:** Teheran; Ambassador: L. KHASHOAT.

**Morocco:** Teheran; tel. (21) 2059707; fax (21) 2051872; Ambassador: MOHAMMAD AZAROUAL.

**Mozambique:** Teheran; Ambassador: MURADE ISAC MIGUIGY MURARGY.

**Myanmar:** Teheran; Ambassador: U SAW HLAING.

**Namibia:** Teheran; Ambassador: MWAILEPENI T. P. SHITILIFA.

**Nepal:** Teheran; Ambassador: Gen. ARJUN NARSING RONA.

**Netherlands:** POB 11365-138, Darrous, Shahrzad Blvd, Kamasaie St, 1st East Lane, No. 33, Teheran 19498; tel. (21) 2567005; fax (21) 2566990; e-mail nlambiran@dpi.net.ir; Ambassador: R. A. MOLLINGER.

**New Zealand:** POB 15875-4313, 57 Javad Sarafarez St, Ostad Motahhari Ave, Teheran; tel. (21) 8757052; fax (21) 8757056; Ambassador: WARWICK ALEXANDER HAWKER.

**Nigeria:** POB 11365-7148, Shahid Fayazi, Vali Asr, No. 155, Teheran; tel. (21) 2044608; Ambassador: ADO SANUSI.

**Norway:** POB 19395-5398, Pasdaran Ave, Kouhestan 8, Ekhtiarieh Shomali 412, Teheran; tel. (21) 2291333; fax (21) 2292776; Ambassador: SVEIN AASS.

**Oman:** POB 41-1586, Pasdaran Ave, Golestan 9, No. 5 and 7, Teheran; tel. (21) 286021; Chargé d'affaires a.i.: RASHID BIN MUBARAK BIN RASHID AL-ODWALI.

**Pakistan:** Dr Fatemi Ave, Jamshidabad Shomali, Mashal St, No. 1, Teheran; tel. (21) 934332; KHALID MAHMUD.

**Panama:** Teheran; Ambassador: G. MOVAGA.

**Philippines:** POB 19395-4797, 24 Golazin Blvd., Africa Ave, Zafaranieh, Teheran; tel. (21) 2055134; fax (21) 2057260; Ambassador HARON P. ALONTO.

**Poland:** Africa Expressway, Piruz St, No. 1/3, Teheran; tel. (21) 227262; Ambassador: STEFAN SZYMCZYKIEWICZ.

**Portugal:** Vali Asr Ave, Tavanir Ave, Nezami Ghanjavi Ave, No. 30, Teheran; tel. (21) 8772132; fax (21) 8777834; Ambassador: Dr MANUEL MARCELO CURTO.

**Qatar:** Africa Expressway, Golazin Ave, Parke Davar, No. 4, Teheran; tel. (21) 221255; Ambassador: ALI ABDULLAH ZAID AL-MAHMOOD.

**Romania:** Fakhrabad Ave 12, Darvaze Shemiran, Teheran; tel. (21) 7509309; fax (21) 7509841; Ambassador: CRISTIAN TEODORESCU.

**Russia:** 39 Neauphle-le-Château Ave, Teheran; tel. (21) 671163; Ambassador: KONSTANTIN SHUVALOV.

**Saudi Arabia:** 10 Saba Blvd, Africa Ave, Teheran; tel. (21) 2050081; fax (21) 2050083; Ambassador: JAMIL BIN ABDULLAH AL-JISHI.

**Slovakia:** POB 11365-4451, No. 24, Babak Markazi St, Africa Ave, Teheran; tel. (21) 2271058; fax (21) 2271057; Chargé d'affaires a.i.: ALEXANDER BAJKAI.

**South Africa:** POB 11365-7476, Yetha St 5, Vali-Asr Ave, Teheran; tel. (21) 2702866; fax (21) 2719516; Ambassador: MOOSA MOOLLA.

**Spain:** Vali-Asr Ave, 76 Sarv St, Teheran; tel. (21) 8714575; fax (21) 8724581. Chargé d'affaires: JUAN CARLOS GAFO.

**Sri Lanka:** 6 Arash St, Africa Expressway, Teheran; tel. (21) 2053902; fax (21) 2052688; Ambassador: Y. L. M. ZAWAHIR.

**Sudan:** Khaled Islambouli Ave, 23rd St, No. 10, Teheran; tel. (21) 628476; Ambassador: Dr ABDEL RAHANA MOHAMMED SAID.

**Sweden:** POB 19575-458, 2 Nastaran St, Teheran; tel. (21) 2296802; fax (21) 2286021; Ambassador: MATS MARLING.

**Switzerland:** POB 19395-4683, 13/1 Boustan Ave, 19649 Teheran; tel. (21) 268227; fax 269448; Ambassador: TIM GULDIMANN.

**Syria:** Africa Ave, 19 Iraj St, Teheran; tel. (21) 229032; Ambassador: AHMAD AL-HASSAN.

**Tajikistan:** Teheran.

**Thailand:** POB 11495-111, Baharestan Ave, Parc Amin ed-Doleh, No. 4, Teheran; tel. (21) 7531433; fax (21) 7532022; Ambassador: MAHADI WIMANA.

**Tunisia:** Teheran; Ambassador: Dr NOUREDDINE AL-HAMDANI.

**Turkey:** Ferdowsi Ave, No. 314, Teheran; tel. (21) 3115299; fax (21) 3117928; Ambassador: TURAN MORALI.

**Turkmenistan:** Teheran; Ambassador: MURAT NAZAROV.

**Ukraine:** Hefez Avenue, Teheran 487; tel. (21) 675148; Chargé d'affaires: IVAN G. MAYDAN.

**United Arab Emirates:** Zafar Ave, No. 355–7, Teheran; tel. (21) 221333; Ambassador: AHMAD MUHAMMAD BORHEIMAH.

**United Kingdom:** POB 11365-4474, 143 Ferdowsi Ave, Teheran 11344; tel. (21) 6705011; fax (21) 6708021; e-mail britemb@neda.net; Ambassador: NICHOLAS W. BROWNE.

**Uruguay:** 45 Shabnam Alley, Atefi Shargi St, Jordan Ave, Teheran; tel. (21) 2052030; Ambassador: MARCIAL BIRRIEL IGLESIAS.

**Uzbekistan:** Teheran.

**Venezuela:** POB 15875-4354, Bucharest Ave, 9th St, No. 31, Teheran; tel. (21) 625185; fax (21) 622840; Ambassador: Dr HERNÁN CALCURIAN.

**Viet Nam:** Teheran; Ambassador: VUXNAN ANG.

**Yemen:** Bucharest Ave, No. 26, Teheran; Chargé d'affaires a.i.: Dr AHMAD MUHAMMAD ALI ABDULLAH.

**Yugoslavia:** POB 11365-118, Vali Asr Ave, Fereshteh Ave, Amir Teymour Alley, No. 12, 19659 Teheran; tel. (21) 2044126; fax (21) 2044978; Chargé d'affaires: STOJAN GLIGORIĆ.

# Judicial System

In August 1982 the Supreme Court revoked all laws dating from the previous regime which did not conform with Islam. In October 1982 all courts set up prior to the Islamic Revolution were abolished. In June 1987 Ayatollah Khomeini ordered the creation of clerical courts to try members of the clergy opposed to government policy. A new system of *qisas* (retribution) was established, placing the emphasis on speedy justice. Islamic codes of correction were introduced in 1983, including the dismembering of a hand for theft, flogging for fornication and violations of the strict code of dress for women, and stoning for adultery. In 1984 there was a total of 2,200 judges. The Supreme Court has 16 branches.

**Head of the Judiciary:** Ayatollah SAYED MAHMOUD HASHEMI SHAHRUDI.

### SUPREME COURT

**Chief Justice:** Hojatoleslam MUHAMMAD MUHAMMADI GUILANI.

**Prosecutor-General:** Hojatoleslam MORTEZA MOQTADAI.

# Religion

According to the 1979 constitution, the official religion is Islam of the Ja'fari sect (Shi'ite), but other Islamic sects, including Zeydi, Hanafi, Maleki, Shafe'i and Hanbali, are valid and will be respected. Zoroastrians, Jews and Christians will be recognized as official religious minorities. According to the 1976 census, there were then 310,000 Christians (mainly Armenian), 80,000 Jews and 30,000 Zoroastrians.

### ISLAM

The great majority of the Iranian people are Shi'a Muslims, but there is a minority of Sunni Muslims. Persians and Azerbaijanis are mainly Shi'i, while the other ethnic groups are mainly Sunni.

### CHRISTIANITY

#### The Roman Catholic Church

At 31 December 1997 there were an estimated 12,750 adherents in Iran, comprising 6,250 of the Chaldean Rite, 2,500 of the Armenian Rite and 4,000 of the Latin Rite.

*Armenian Rite*

**Bishop of Isfahan:** Dr VARTAN TÉKÉYAN, Armenian Catholic Bishopric, Khiaban Ghazzali 22, Teheran; tel. (21) 677204; fax (21) 8715191.

*Chaldean Rite*

**Archbishop of Ahwaz:** HANNA ZORA, Archbishop's House, POB 61956, Naderi St, Ahwaz; tel. (61) 24890.

**Archbishop of Teheran:** (vacant), Archevêché, Forsat Ave 91, Teheran 15819; tel. (21) 8823549.

**Archbishop of Urmia (Rezayeh) and Bishop of Salmas (Shahpour):** THOMAS MERAM, Khalifagari Kaldani Katholiq, POB 338, Orumiyeh 57135; tel. (441) 22739.

*Latin Rite*

**Archbishop of Isfahan:** IGNAZIO BEDINI, Consolata Church, POB 11365-445, 75 Neauphle-le-Château Ave, Teheran; tel. (21) 673210; fax (21) 6494749.

#### The Anglican Communion

Anglicans in Iran are adherents of the Episcopal Church in Jerusalem and the Middle East, formally inaugurated in January 1976. The Rt Rev. HASSAN DEHQANI-TAFTI, the Bishop in Iran from 1961 to 1990, was President-Bishop of the Church from 1976 to 1986. He was succeeded by the Bishop of Jerusalem during 1986–96 and the Bishop of Egypt from 1996 onwards.

**Bishop in Iran:** Rt Rev. IRAJ KALIMI MOTTAHEDEH, St Luke's Church, Abbas-abad, POB 81465-135, Isfahan; tel. (31) 234675; diocese founded 1912.

**Presbyterian Church**

**Synod of the Evangelical (Presbyterian) Church in Iran:** Assyrian Evangelical Church, Khiaban-i Hanifnejad, Khiaban-i Aramanch, Teheran; Moderator Rev. ADEL NAKHOSTEEN.

### ZOROASTRIANS

There are about 30,000 Zoroastrians, a remnant of a once widespread sect. Their religious leader is MOUBAD.

### OTHER COMMUNITIES

Communities of Armenians, and somewhat smaller numbers of Jews (an estimated 30,000 in 1986), Assyrians, Greek Orthodox Christians, Uniates and Latin Christians are also found as officially recognized faiths. The Bahá'í faith, which originated in Iran, has about 300,000 Iranian adherents, although at least 10,000 are believed to have fled since 1979 in order to escape persecution. The Government banned all Bahá'í institutions in August 1983.

## The Press

Teheran dominates the media, as many of the daily papers are published there, and the bi-weekly, weekly and less frequent publications in the provinces generally depend on the major metropolitan dailies as a source of news. A press law announced in August 1979 required all newspapers and magazines to be licensed and imposed penalties of imprisonment for insulting senior religious figures. Offences against the Act will be tried in the criminal courts. Under the Constitution the press is free, except in matters that are contrary to public morality, insult religious belief or slander the honour and reputation of individuals.

### PRINCIPAL DAILIES

**Abrar** (Rightly Guided): 26 Shahid Denesh Kian Alley, Below Zartasht St, Valiassr Ave, Teheran; tel. (21) 8848270; fax (21) 8849200; f. 1985 after closure of *Azadegan* by order of the Prosecutor-General; morning; Farsi; circ. 75,000.

**Alik:** POB 11365-953, Jomhoori Islami Ave, Alik Alley, Teheran 11357; tel. (21) 676671; f. 1931; afternoon; political and literary; Armenian; Propr A. AJEMIAN; circ. 3,400.

**Bahari Iran:** Khayaban Khayham, Shiraz; tel. (71) 33738.

**Ettela'at** (Information): Ettela'at Bldg, Mirdamad Ave, South Naft St, Teheran 15499; tel. (21) 29999; fax (21) 2258022; internet www.ettela'at.com; f. 1925; evening; Farsi; political and literary; operates under the direct supervision of Wilayat-e-Faqih (religious jurisprudence); Editor S. M. DOAEI; circ. 500,000.

**Iran News:** 41 Lida St, Valiassr Ave, North Vanak Sq, tel. (21) 8880231; fax (21) 8786475; e-mail irannews@www.dci.co.ir; Teheran; English.

**Kayhan** (Universe): Ferdowsi Ave, Teheran; tel. (21) 310251. 1941; evening; Farsi; political; also publishes *Kayhan International* (f. 1959; daily and weekly; English; Editor HOSSEIN RAGHFAR), *Kayhan Arabic* (f. 1980; daily and weekly; Arabic), *Kayhan Persian* (f. 1942; daily; Persian), *Kayhan Turkish* (f. 1984; monthly; Turkish), *Kayhan Havaie* (f. 1950; weekly for Iranians abroad; Farsi), *Kayhan Andishe* (World of Religion; f. 1985; 6 a year; Farsi), *Zan-e-Ruz* (Woman Today; f. 1964; weekly; Farsi), *Kayhan Varzeshi* (World of Sport; f. 1955; weekly; Farsi), *Kayhan Bacheha* (Children's World; f. 1956; weekly; Farsi), *Kayhan Farhangi* (World of Culture; f. 1984; monthly; Farsi); *Kayhan Yearbook* (yearly; Farsi); *Period of 40 Years, Kayhan* (series of books; Farsi); owned and managed by Mostazafin Foundation from October 1979 until 1 January 1987, when it was placed under the direct supervision of Wilayat-e-Faqih (religious jurisprudence); Chief Editor HOSSEIN SHARIATMADARI; circ. 350,000.

**Khorassan:** Meshed; Head Office: Khorassan Daily Newspapers, 14 Zohre St, Mobarezan Ave, Teheran; f. 1948; Propr MUHAMMAD SADEGH TEHERANIAN; circ. 40,000.

**Rahnejat:** Darvazeh Dowlat, Isfahan; political and social; Propr N. RAHNEJAT.

**Ressallat** (The Message): Teheran; tel. (21) 8902642; fax (21) 8900587; organ of right-wing group of the same name; political, economic, social; Propr Ressallat Foundation; Man. Dir MORTEZA NABAVI; circ. 100,000.

**Salam:** 2 Shahid Reza Nayebi Alley, South Felestin St, Teheran; tel. (21) 6495831; fax (21) 6495835; f. 1991; Farsi; political, cultural, economic, social; Editor MUHAMMAD MUSAVI KHOIENI. (Closure ordered July 1999.)

**Teheran Times:** 32 Bimeh Alley, Nejatullahi Ave, Teheran 15998; tel. (21) 8810293; fax (21) 8808214; f. 1979; independent; English; Man. Dir ABBAS SALIMI NAMIN.

### PRINCIPAL PERIODICALS

**Acta Medica Iranica:** Faculty of Medicine, Teheran Medical Sciences Univ., Poursina St, Teheran 14-174; tel. (21) 6112743; fax (21) 6404377; f. 1960; quarterly; English; Editors-in-Chief A. R. DEHPOUR, M. SAMINI; circ. 2,000.

**Akhbar-e-Pezeshki:** 86 Ghaem Magham Farahani Ave, Teheran; weekly; medical; Propr Dr T. FORUZIN.

**Ashur:** Ostad Motahhari Ave, 11-21 Kuhe Nour Ave, Teheran; tel. (21) 622117; f. 1969; Assyrian; monthly; Founder and Editor Dr W. BET-MANSOUR; circ. 8,000.

**Auditor:** 77 Ferdowsi Ave North, Teheran; quarterly; financial and managerial studies.

**Ayandeh:** POB 19575-583, Niyavaran, Teheran; tel. (21) 283254; fax (21) 6406426; monthly; Iranian literary, historical and book review journal; Editor Prof. IRAJ AFSHAR.

**Bulletin of the National Film Archive of Iran:** POB 5158, Baharestan Sq., Teheran 11365; tel. 311242. 1989; English periodical; Editor M. H. KHOSHNEVIS.

**Daneshmand:** POB 15875-3649, Teheran; tel. (21) 8741323; f. 1963; monthly; scientific and technical magazine; Editor-in-Chief A. R. KARAMI.

**Daneshkadeh Pezeshki:** Faculty of Medicine, Teheran Medical Sciences University; tel. (21) 6112743; fax (21) 6404377; f. 1947; 10 a year; medical magazine; Propr Dr HASSAN AREFI; circ. 1,500.

**Donaye Varzesh:** Khayyam Ave, Ettela'at Bldg, Teheran; tel. (21) 3281; fax (21) 3115530; weekly; sport; Editor G. H. SHABANI; circ. 200,000.

**Echo of Islam:** POB 14155-3899, Teheran; tel. (21) 8758296; fax (21) 892725; e-mail editor-in-chief@www.iran-itf.com; internet www.iran-itf.com/echoofislam.html; monthly; English; published by the Islamic Thought Foundation; Man. Dir MUHAMMAD BEHESHTI; Editor-in-Chief MUHAMMAD SH. SHAKIB.

**Ettela'at Elmi:** 11 Khayyam Ave, Teheran; tel. (21) 3281; fax (21) 3115530; f. 1985; fortnightly; sciences; Editor Mrs GHASEMI; circ. 75,000.

**Ettela'at Haftegi:** 11 Khayyam Ave, Teheran; tel. (21) 3281; fax (21) 3115530; f. 1941; general weekly; Editor F. JAVADI; circ. 150,000.

**Ettela'at Javanan:** POB 15499-51199, Ettela'at Bldg, Mirdamad Ave, South Naft St, Teheran; tel. (21) 29999; fax (21) 2258022; f. 1966; weekly; youth; Editor M. J. RAFIZADEH; circ. 120,000.

**Farhang-e-Iran Zamin:** POB 19575-583, Niyavaran, Teheran; tel. (21) 283254; annual; Iranian studies; Editor Prof. IRAJ AFSHAR.

**Film International, Iranian Film Quarterly:** POB 11365-5875, Teheran; tel. (21) 6709373; fax (21) 6719971; e-mail filmmag@apadana.com; f. 1993; quarterly; English; Editor HOUSHANG GOLMAKANI; circ 20,000.

**Iran Press Digest (Economic):** POB 11365-5551, Hafiz Ave, 4 Kucheh Hurtab, Teheran; tel. (21) 668114; weekly; Editor J. BEHROUZ.

**Iran Press Digest (Political):** POB 11365-5551, Hafiz Ave, 4 Kucheh Hurtab, Teheran; tel. (21) 668114; weekly.

**Iranian Cinema:** POB 5158, Baharestan Sq., Teheran 11365; tel. 311242; f. 1985; annually; English; Editor B. REYPOUR.

**Javaneh:** POB 15875-1163, Motahhari Ave, Cnr Mofatteh St, Teheran; tel. (21) 839051; published by Soroush Press; quarterly.

**JIDA:** POB 14185-518, Teheran; tel. (21) 8269591; fax 8269592; e-mail IDA@apadna.com; f. 1963; four a year; journal of the Iranian Dental Association; Editor-in-Chief Dr ALI KOWSARI.

**Kayhan Bacheha** (Children's World): Shahid Shahsheragi Ave, Teheran; tel. (21) 310251. 1956; weekly; Editor AMIR HOSSEIN FARDI; circ. 150,000.

**Kayhan Varzeshi** (World of Sport): Ferdowsi Ave, Teheran; tel. (21) 310251. 1955; weekly; Dir MAHMAD MONSETI; circ. 125,000.

**Mahjubah:** POB 14155-3897, Teheran; tel. (21) 8000067; fax (21) 8001453; e-mail tjamshid@chamran.ut.ac.ir; Islamic family magazine; published by the Islamic Thought Foundation.

**Music Iran:** 1029 Amiriye Ave, Teheran; f. 1951; monthly; Editor BAHMAN HIRBOD; circ. 7,000.

**Negin:** Vali Asr Ave, Adl St 52, Teheran; monthly; scientific and literary; Propr and Dir M. ENAYAT.

**Salamate Fekr:** M.20, Kharg St, Teheran; tel. (21) 223034; f. 1958; monthly; organ of the Mental Health Soc.; Editors Prof. E. TCHEHRAZI, ALI REZA SHAFAI.

**Soroush:** POB 15875-1163, Motahhari Ave, Corner Mofatteh St, Teheran; tel. (21) 830771; f. 1972; two monthly magazines in Farsi, one for children and one for adolescents; Editor MEHDI FIROOZAN.

**Zan-e-Ruz** (Woman Today): Ferdowsi Ave, Teheran; tel. (21) 3911570; fax (21) 3911569; e-mail kayhan@istn.irost.com; internet www.irost.com/kayhan; f. 1964; weekly; women's; circ. over 60,000. (Closure ordered April 1999.)

### NEWS AGENCIES

**Islamic Republic News Agency (IRNA):** POB 764, 873 Vali Asr Ave, Teheran; tel. (21) 8902050; fax (21) 8905068; e-mail irna@

| Expenditure | 1981 | 1982 |
|---|---|---|
| Ordinary | 5,025.0 | 8,740.0 |
| Economic development plan | 6,742.0 | 7,700.0 |
| Autonomous government agencies | 7,982.4 | n.a. |
| **Total** | 19,750.2 | n.a. |

**1991** (ID million): General consolidated state budget expenditure 13,876; Investment budget expenditure 1,660.

**CENTRAL BANK RESERVES** (US $ million at 31 December)

| | 1975 | 1976 | 1977 |
|---|---|---|---|
| Gold | 168.0 | 166.7 | 176.1 |
| IMF special drawing rights | 26.9 | 32.5 | 41.5 |
| Reserve position in IMF | 31.9 | 31.7 | 33.4 |
| Foreign exchange | 2,500.5 | 4,369.8 | 6,744.7 |
| **Total** | 2,727.3 | 4,600.7 | 6,995.7 |

**IMF special drawing rights** (US $ million at 31 December): 132.3 in 1981; 81.9 in 1982; 9.0 in 1983; 0.1 in 1984; 7.2 in 1987.
**Reserve position in IMF** (US $ million at 31 December): 130.3 in 1981; 123.5 in 1982.

Note: No figures for gold or foreign exchange have been available since 1977.

Source: IMF, *International Financial Statistics.*

**COST OF LIVING** (Consumer Price Index; base: 1990 = 100)

| | 1991* |
|---|---|
| Food | 363.9 |
| Fuel and light | 135.4 |
| Clothing | 251.1 |
| Rent | 107.0 |
| **All items** (incl. others) | 286.5 |

* May to December only.

Source: ILO, *Yearbook of Labour Statistics.*

**NATIONAL ACCOUNTS** (ID million at current prices)

**National Income and Product**

| | 1989 | 1990 | 1991 |
|---|---|---|---|
| Compensation of employees | 6,705.2 | 7,855.4 | 8,989.9 |
| Operating surplus | 11,866.0 | 12,936.6 | 10,405.2 |
| **Domestic factor incomes** | 18,571.2 | 20,792.0 | 19,395.1 |
| Consumption of fixed capital | 1,836.7 | 2,056.3 | 1,918.2 |
| **Gross domestic product (GDP) at factor cost** | 20,407.9 | 22,848.3 | 21,313.3 |
| Indirect taxes | 1,035.0 | 1,024.8 | 485.6 |
| *Less* Subsidies | 417.1 | 576.3 | 1,859.2 |
| **GDP in purchasers' values** | 21,025.8 | 23,296.8 | 19,939.7 |
| Net factor income from the rest of the world | -704.3 | -773.9 | -650.5 |
| **Gross national product** | 20,321.5 | 22,522.9 | 19,289.2 |
| *Less* Consumption of fixed capital | 1,836.7 | 2,056.3 | 1,918.2 |
| **National income in market prices** | 18,484.8 | 20,466.6 | 17,371.0 |
| Net current transfers from abroad | -149.3 | -49.3 | 122.8 |
| **National disposable income** | 18,335.5 | 20,417.3 | 17,493.8 |

Source: UN, *National Accounts Statistics.*

**Expenditure on the Gross Domestic Product**

| | 1989 | 1990 | 1991 |
|---|---|---|---|
| Government final consumption expenditure | 5,990.1 | 6,142.0 | 7,033.3 |
| Private final consumption expenditure | 11,232.4 | 11,760.5 | 9,611.1 |
| Increase in stocks | -2,317.5 | -976.9 | -520.0 |
| Gross fixed capital formation | 6,305.5 | 6,220.0 | 3,289.1 |
| **Total domestic expenditure** | 21,210.5 | 23,145.6 | 20,453.5 |
| Exports of goods and services | 4,482.6 | 4,305.4 | 547.8 |
| *Less* Imports of goods and services | 4,667.3 | 4,154.2 | 1,061.6 |
| **GDP in purchasers' values** | 21,025.8 | 23,296.8 | 19,939.7 |

Source: UN, *National Accounts Statistics.*

**Gross Domestic Product by Economic Activity** (at factor cost)

| | 1989 | 1990 | 1991 |
|---|---|---|---|
| Agriculture, hunting, forestry and fishing | 3,346.1 | 4,613.3 | 6,047.0 |
| Mining and quarrying | 3,894.8 | 3,330.6 | 149.4 |
| Manufacturing | 2,694.2 | 2,058.7 | 1,273.9 |
| Electricity, gas and water* | 269.0 | 247.5 | 162.4 |
| Construction | 1,417.8 | 1,693.2 | 812.4 |
| Trade, restaurants and hotels* | 2,376.4 | 3,454.7 | 3,608.2 |
| Transport, storage and communications | 1,533.3 | 2,103.9 | 2,645.9 |
| Finance, insurance and real estate† | 2,384.8 | 2,781.2 | 3,150.4 |
| Government services | 3,599.1 | 3,823.5 | 4,845.7 |
| Other services | 305.0 | 292.2 | 489.8 |
| **Sub-total** | 21,820.5 | 24,398.8 | 23,185.1 |
| *Less* Imputed bank service charge | 1,412.6 | 1,550.5 | 1,871.8 |
| **Total** | 20,407.9 | 22,848.3 | 21,313.3 |
| **GDP at constant 1975 prices** | 6,491.8 | 6,492.9 | 2,199.8 |

* Gas distribution is included in trade.
† Including imputed rents of owner-occupied dwellings.

Source: UN, *National Accounts Statistics.*

# External Trade

**PRINCIPAL COMMODITIES** (ID million)

| Imports c.i.f. | 1976 | 1977* | 1978 |
|---|---|---|---|
| **Food and live animals** | 159.6 | 154.0 | 134.5 |
| Cereals and cereal preparations | 70.0 | 79.9 | 74.9 |
| Sugar, sugar preparations and honey | 37.2 | 24.1 | 10.2 |
| **Crude materials (inedible) except fuels** | 33.7 | 20.5 | 25.1 |
| **Chemicals** | 58.5 | 47.4 | 58.7 |
| **Basic manufactures** | 293.3 | 236.7 | 285.2 |
| Textile yarn, fabrics, etc. | 44.3 | 69.4 | 72.7 |
| Iron and steel | 127.5 | 44.3 | 73.2 |
| **Machinery and transport equipment** | 557.4 | 625.8 | 667.4 |
| Non-electric machinery | 285.4 | 352.5 | 368.1 |
| Electrical machinery, apparatus, etc. | 106.9 | 120.2 | 160.5 |
| Transport equipment | 165.2 | 153.1 | 138.8 |
| **Miscellaneous manufactured articles** | 33.2 | 49.4 | 51.7 |
| **Total** (incl. others) | 1,150.9 | 1,151.3 | 1,244.1 |

* Figures are provisional. Revised total is ID 1,323.2 million.

**Total imports** (official estimates, ID million): 1,738.9 in 1979; 2,208.1 in 1980; 2,333.8 in 1981.
**Total imports** (IMF estimates, ID million): 6,013.0 in 1981; 6,309.0 in 1982; 3,086.2 in 1983; 3,032.4 in 1984; 3,285.7 in 1985; 2,773.0 in 1986; 2,268.7 in 1987; 2,888.8 in 1988; 3,077.1 in 1989; 2,028.5 in 1990; 131.5 in 1991; 187.3 in 1992; 165.6 in 1993; 155.0 in 1994; 203.6 in 1995; 175.5 in 1996; 273.6 in 1997; 420.7 in 1998 (Source: IMF, *International Financial Statistics*).

**Total exports** (ID million): 5,614.6 (crude petroleum 5,571.9) in 1977; 6,422.7 (crude petroleum 6,360.5) in 1978; 12,522.0 (crude petroleum 12,480.0) in 1979.

**Exports of crude petroleum** (estimates, ID million): 15,321.3 in 1980; 6,089.6 in 1981; 5,982.4 in 1982; 5,954.8 in 1983; 6,937.0 in 1984; 8,142.5 in 1985; 5,126.2 in 1986; 6,988.9 in 1987; 7,245.8 in 1988.

Source: IMF, *International Financial Statistics.*

**PRINCIPAL TRADING PARTNERS** (US $ million)

| Imports c.i.f. | 1988 | 1989 | 1990 |
|---|---|---|---|
| Australia | 153.4 | 196.2 | 108.7 |
| Austria | n.a. | 1.1 | 50.9 |
| Belgium and Luxembourg | 57.6 | 68.2 | 68.3 |
| Brazil | 346.0 | 416.4 | 139.5 |
| Canada | 169.9 | 225.1 | 150.4 |
| China, People's Republic | 99.2 | 148.0 | 157.9 |
| France | 278.0 | 410.4 | 278.3 |
| Germany | 322.3 | 459.6 | 389.4 |
| India | 32.3 | 65.2 | 57.5 |
| Indonesia | 38.9 | 122.7 | 104.9 |
| Ireland | 150.4 | 144.9 | 31.6 |
| Italy | 129.6 | 285.1 | 194.0 |
| Japan | 533.0 | 621.1 | 397.2 |
| Jordan | 164.3 | 210.0 | 220.3 |
| Korea, Republic | 98.5 | 123.9 | 149.4 |
| Netherlands | 111.6 | 102.6 | 93.8 |
| Romania | 113.3 | 91.1 | 30.1 |
| Saudi Arabia | 37.2 | 96.5 | 62.5 |
| Spain | 43.4 | 129.0 | 40.5 |
| Sri Lanka | 50.1 | 33.5 | 52.3 |
| Sweden | 63.0 | 40.6 | 64.8 |
| Switzerland | 65.7 | 94.4 | 126.6 |
| Thailand | 22.3 | 59.2 | 68.9 |
| Turkey | 874.7 | 408.9 | 196.0 |
| USSR | 70.7 | 75.7 | 77.9 |
| United Kingdom | 394.6 | 448.5 | 322.1 |
| USA | 979.3 | 1,001.7 | 658.4 |
| Yugoslavia | 154.5 | 182.0 | 123.1 |
| **Total** (incl. others) | 5,960.0 | 6,956.2 | 4,833.9 |

| Exports f.o.b. | 1988 | 1989 | 1990* |
|---|---|---|---|
| Belgium and Luxembourg | 147.5 | 249.6 | n.a. |
| Brazil | 1,002.8 | 1,197.2 | n.a. |
| France | 517.4 | 623.9 | 0.8 |
| Germany | 122.0 | 76.9 | 1.7 |
| Greece | 192.5 | 189.4 | 0.3 |
| India | 293.0 | 438.8 | 14.7 |
| Italy | 687.1 | 549.7 | 10.6 |
| Japan | 712.1 | 117.1 | 0.1 |
| Jordan | 28.4 | 25.2 | 101.6 |
| Netherlands | 152.9 | 532.3 | 0.2 |
| Portugal | 120.8 | 125.8 | n.a. |
| Spain | 370.0 | 575.7 | 0.7 |
| Turkey | 1,052.6 | 1,331.0 | 83.5 |
| USSR | 835.7 | 1,331.7 | 8.9 |
| United Kingdom | 293.1 | 167.0 | 4.4 |
| USA | 1,458.9 | 2,290.8 | 0.2 |
| Yugoslavia | 425.4 | 342.0 | 10.4 |
| **Total** (incl. others) | 10,268.3 | 12,333.7 | 392.0 |

* Excluding exports of most petroleum products.

Source: UN, *International Trade Statistics Yearbook*.

# Transport

**RAILWAYS** (traffic)

| | 1995* | 1996† | 1997† |
|---|---|---|---|
| Passenger-km (million) | 2,198 | 1,169 | 1,169 |
| Freight ton-km (million) | 1,120 | 931 | 956 |

* Source: UN, *Statistical Yearbook*.

† Source: Railway Gazette International, *Railway Directory*.

**ROAD TRAFFIC** ('000 motor vehicles in use)

| | 1993 | 1994 | 1995 |
|---|---|---|---|
| Passenger cars | 672.4 | 678.5 | 680.1 |
| Commercial vehicles | 309.3 | 317.2 | 319.9 |

Source: UN, *Statistical Yearbook*.

**SHIPPING**

**Merchant Fleet** (registered at 31 December)

| | 1996 | 1997 | 1998 |
|---|---|---|---|
| Number of vessels | 113 | 102 | 99 |
| Total displacement ('000 grt) | 856.9 | 572.0 | 511.1 |

Source: Lloyd's Register of Shipping, *World Fleet Statistics*.

**CIVIL AVIATION** (revenue traffic on scheduled services)

| | 1991 | 1992 | 1994* |
|---|---|---|---|
| Kilometres flown (million) | 0 | 0 | 0 |
| Passengers carried ('000) | 28 | 53 | 31 |
| Passenger-km (million) | 17 | 35 | 20 |
| Freight ton-km (million) | 0 | 3 | 2 |

* Figures for 1993 unavailable.

Source: UN, *Statistical Yearbook*.

# Tourism

| | 1993 | 1994 | 1995 |
|---|---|---|---|
| Tourist arrivals ('000)* | 400 | 330 | 340 |
| Tourist receipts (US $ million) | 15 | 12 | 13 |

* Including same-day visitors.

Source: UN, *Statistical Yearbook*.

## Communications Media

| | 1994 | 1995 | 1996 |
|---|---|---|---|
| Radio receivers ('000 in use) | 4,335 | 4,500 | 4,760 |
| Television receivers ('000 in use) | 1,500 | 1,600 | 1,700 |
| Daily newspapers | | | |
| Number | 4 | 4 | 4* |
| Average circulation ('000 copies) | 532 | 530 | 407 |

* Estimate.

Non-daily newspapers: 12 in 1988.

Source: UNESCO, *Statistical Yearbook*.

Telephones ('000 main lines in use): 674 in 1987; 678 in 1988; 675 (estimate) in 1989 (Source: UN, *Statistical Yearbook*).

## Education

| | Teachers | | Pupils/Students | |
|---|---|---|---|---|
| | 1990 | 1992* | 1990 | 1992* |
| Pre-primary | 4,908 | 4,778 | 86,508 | 90,836 |
| Primary | 134,081 | 131,271 | 3,328,212 | 2,857,467 |
| Secondary: | | | | |
| General | 44,772 | 48,496 | 1,023,710 | 992,617 |
| Teacher training | n.a. | 1,303 | n.a. | 22,018 |
| Vocational | n.a. | 9,318 | n.a. | 130,303 |

* Figures for 1991 are unavailable.

**Schools:** Pre-primary: 646 in 1990; 578 in 1992. Primary: 8,917 in 1990; 8,003 in 1992.

**Higher education** (1988): Teachers 11,072; Students 209,818.

**1995:** Pre-primary: 571 schools; 4,841 teachers; 85,024 pupils. Primary: 8,145 schools; 145,455 teachers; 2,903,923 pupils.

Source: UNESCO, *Statistical Yearbook*.

# Directory

## The Constitution

The following are the principal features of the Provisional Constitution, issued on 22 September 1968:

The Iraqi Republic is a popular democratic and sovereign state. Islam is the state religion.

The political economy of the State is founded on socialism.

The State will protect liberty of religion, freedom of speech and opinion. Public meetings are permitted under the law. All discrimination based on race, religion or language is forbidden. There shall be freedom of the Press, and the right to form societies and trade unions in conformity with the law is guaranteed.

The Iraqi people is composed of two main nationalities: Arabs and Kurds. The Constitution confirms the nationalistic rights of the Kurdish people and the legitimate rights of all other minorities within the framework of Iraqi unity.

The highest authority in the country is the Council of Command of the Revolution (or Revolutionary Command Council—RCC), which will promulgate laws until the election of a National Assembly. The Council exercises its prerogatives and powers by a two-thirds majority.

Two amendments to the Constitution were announced in November 1969. The President, already Chief of State and Head of the Government, also became the official Supreme Commander of the Armed Forces and President of the RCC. Membership of the latter body was to increase from five to a larger number at the President's discretion.

Earlier, a Presidential decree replaced the 14 local government districts by 16 governorates, each headed by a governor with wide powers. In April 1976 Tikrit (Salah ad-Din) and Karbala became separate governorates, bringing the number of governorates to 18, although three of these are designated Autonomous Regions.

The 15-article statement which aimed to end the Kurdish war was issued on 11 March 1970. In accordance with this statement, a form of autonomy was offered to the Kurds in March 1974, but some of the Kurds rejected the offer and fresh fighting broke out. The new Provisional Constitution was announced in July 1970. Two amendments were introduced in 1973 and 1974, the 1974 amendment stating that 'the area whose majority of population is Kurdish shall enjoy autonomy in accordance with what is defined by the Law'.

The President and Vice-President are elected by a two-thirds majority of the Council. The President, Vice-President and members of the Council will be responsible to the Council. Vice-Presidents and Ministers will be responsible to the President.

Details of a new, permanent Constitution were announced in March 1989. The principal innovations proposed in the permanent Constitution, which was approved by the National Assembly in July 1990, were the abolition of the RCC, following a presidential election, and the assumption of its duties by a 50-member Consultative Assembly and the existing National Assembly; and the incorporation of the freedom to form political parties. The new, permanent Constitution is to be submitted to a popular referendum for approval.

In September 1995 an interim constitutional amendment was endorsed by the RCC whereby the elected Chairman of the RCC will assume the Presidency of the Republic subject to the approval of the National Assembly and endorsement by national referendum.

In July 1973 President Bakr announced a National Charter as a first step towards establishing the Progressive National Front. A National Assembly and People's Councils are features of the Charter. A law to create a 250-member National Assembly and a 50-member Kurdish Legislative Council was adopted on 16 March 1980, and the two Assemblies were elected in June and September 1980 respectively.

## The Government

### HEAD OF STATE

**President:** SADDAM HUSSAIN (assumed power 16 July 1979; according to official results, at a national referendum conducted on 15 October 1995, 99.96% of Iraq's 8.4m. electorate recorded its endorsement of President Saddam Hussain's continuance in office for a further seven years).

**Vice-Presidents:** TAHA YASSIN RAMADAN, TAHA MOHI ED-DIN MARUF.

### REVOLUTIONARY COMMAND COUNCIL

**Chairman:** SADDAM HUSSAIN.

**Vice-Chairman:** TAHA YASSIN RAMADAN.

**Other Members:**

IZZAT IBRAHIM AD-DURI
TAREQ AZIZ
Gen. SULTAN HASHIM AHMAD
MUHAMMAD HAMZAH AZ-ZUBAYDI
TAHA MOHI ED-DIN MARUF
SA'ADOUN HAMMADI MAZBAN KHADR HADI

### COUNCIL OF MINISTERS

(February 2000)

**Prime Minister:** SADDAM HUSSAIN.

**Deputy Prime Ministers:** TAREQ AZIZ, TAHA YASSIN RAMADAN, MUHAMMAD HAMZAH AZ-ZUBAYDI.

**Deputy Prime Minister and Minister of Finance:** HIKMAT MIZBAN IBRAHIM.

**Minister of the Interior:** MUHAMMAD ZIMAN ABD AR-RAZZAQ.

**Minister of Defence:** Gen. SULTAN HASHIM AHMAD.

**Minister of Foreign Affairs:** MUHAMMAD SAEED AS-SAHAF.

**Minister of Agriculture:** ABDULLAH HAMEED MAHMOUD SALEH.

**Minister of Culture and Information:** HUMAM ABD AL-KHALIQ ABD AL-GHAFUR.

**Minister of Justice:** SHABIB AL-MALKI.

**Minister of Irrigation:** MAHMOUD DIYAB AL-AHMAD.

**Minister of Industry and Minerals:** ADNAN ABD AL-MAJID JASSIM.

**Minister of Oil:** Gen. AMIR MUHAMMAD RASHID.

**Minister of Education:** FAHD SALIM ASH-SHAKRAH.

**Minister of Health:** UMEED MADHAT MUBARAK.

**Minister of Labour and Social Affairs:** Gen. SAADI TUMA ABBAS.

**Minister of Planning:** SAMAL MAJID FARAJ.

**Minister of Higher Education and Scientific Research:** ABD AL-JABBAR TAWFIQ MUHAMMAD.

**Minister of Housing and Construction:** MAAN ABDULLAH SARSAM.

**Minister of Transport and Communications:** Dr AHMAD MURTADA AHMAD KHALIL.

**Minister of Awqaf (Religious Endowments) and Religious Affairs:** Dr ABD AL-MUNIM AHMAD SALIH.

**Minister of Trade:** MUHAMMAD MAHDI SALIH.

**Minister of State for Military Affairs:** Gen. ABD AL-JABBAR KHALIL ASH-SHANSHAL.

**Ministers of State:** ARSHAD MUHAMMAD AHMAD MUHAMMAD AZ-ZIBARI, ABD AL-WAHHAB UMAR MIRZA AL-ATRUSHI.

**Presidential Advisers:** WATBAN IBRAHIM AL-HASSAN, SAFA HADI JAWAD, ABD AS-SATTAR AHMAD AL-MAINI, ABD AL-WAHHAB ABDULLAH AS-SABBAGH, ABDULLAH FADEL-ABBAS, AMER HAMMADI AS-SAADI HATIM AL-AZAWI, NIZAR JUMAH ALI AL-QASIR.

### MINISTRIES

**Office of the President:** Presidential Palace, Karradat Mariam, Baghdad.

**Ministry of Agriculture and Irrigation:** Khulafa St, Khullani Sq., Baghdad; tel. (1) 887-3251.

**Ministry of Awqaf (Religious Endowments) and Religious Affairs:** North Gate, St opposite College of Engineering, Baghdad; tel. (1) 888-9561.

**Ministry of Culture and Information:** Nr an-Nusoor Sq., fmrly Qasr as-Salaam Bldg, Baghdad; tel. (1) 551-4333.

**Ministry of Defence:** North Gate, Baghdad; tel. (1) 888-9071.

**Ministry of Education:** POB 258, Baghdad; tel. (1) 886-0000.

**Ministry of Finance:** Khulafa St, Nr ar-Russafi Sq., Baghdad; tel. (1) 887-4871.

**Ministry of Foreign Affairs:** Opposite State Org. for Roads and Bridges, Karradat Mariam, Baghdad; tel. (1) 537-0091.

**Ministry of Health, Labour and Social Affairs:** Khulafa St, Khullani Sq., Baghdad; tel. (1) 887-1881.

**Ministry of Industry and Minerals:** Nidhal St, Nr Sa'adoun Petrol Station, Baghdad; tel. (1) 887-2006.

**Ministry of Local Government:** Karradat Mariam, Baghdad; tel. (1) 537-0031.

**Ministry of Oil:** POB 6178, al-Mansour, Baghdad; tel. (1) 443-0749.

**Ministry of Planning:** Karradat Mariam, ash-Shawaf Sq., Baghdad; tel. (1) 537-0071.

**Ministry of Trade:** Khulafa St, Khullani Sq., Baghdad; tel. (1) 887-2682.

**Ministry of Transport and Communications:** Nr Martyr's Monument, Karradat Dakhil, Baghdad; tel. (1) 776-6041.

### KURDISH AUTONOMOUS REGION

**Executive Council:** Chair. MUHAMMAD AMIN MUHAMMAD (acting).

**Legislative Council:** Chair. AHMAD ABD AL-QADIR AN-NAQSHABANDI.

In May 1992, in the absence of a negotiated autonomy agreement with the Iraqi Government, the KIF (see below) organized elections to a 105-member Kurdish National Assembly. The DPK and the PUK were the only parties to achieve representation in the new Assembly and subsequently agreed to share seats equally between them. Elections held at the same time as those to the National Assembly, to choose an overall Kurdish leader, were inconclusive and were to be held again at a later date.

## Legislature

### NATIONAL ASSEMBLY

No form of National Assembly existed in Iraq between the 1958 revolution, which overthrew the monarchy, and June 1980. (The existing provisional Constitution, introduced in 1968, contains provisions for the election of an assembly at a date to be determined by the Government. The members of the Assembly are to be elected from all political, social and economic sectors of the Iraqi people.) In December 1979 the RCC invited political, trade union and popular organizations to debate a draft law providing for the creation of a 250-member National Assembly (elected from 56 constituencies) and a 50-member Kurdish Legislative Council, both to be elected by direct, free and secret ballot. Elections for the first National Assembly took place on 20 June 1980, and for the Kurdish Legislative Council on 11 September 1980, 13 August 1986 and 9 September 1989. The Assembly was dominated by members of the ruling Baath Party.

Elections for the fourth National Assembly were held on 24 March 1996. Some 689 candidates contested 220 of the Assembly's 250 seats, while the remaining 30 seats (reserved for representatives of the Autonomous Regions of Arbil, D'hok and As-Sulaimaniya) were filled by presidential decree. According to official sources, 93.5% of Iraq's 8m.-strong electorate participated in the elections. Elections to the fifth National Assembly will be held in March 2000.

**Chairman:** Dr SA'ADOUN HAMMADI.

**Chairman of the Kurdish Legislative Council:** AHMAD ABD AL-QADIR AN-NAQSHABANDI.

## Political Organizations

**National Progressive Front:** Baghdad; f. July 1973, when Arab Baath Socialist Party and Iraqi Communist Party signed a joint manifesto agreeing to establish a comprehensive progressive national and nationalistic front. In 1975 representatives of Kurdish parties and organizations and other national and independent forces joined the Front; the Iraqi Communist Party left the National Progressive Front in mid-March 1979; Sec.-Gen. NAIM HADDAD (Baath).

**Arab Baath Socialist Party:** POB 6012, al-Mansour, Baghdad; revolutionary Arab socialist movement founded in Damascus in 1947; has ruled Iraq since July 1968, and between July 1973 and March 1979 in alliance with the Iraqi Communist Party in the National Progressive Front; founder MICHEL AFLAQ; Regional Command Sec.-Gen. SADDAM HUSSAIN; Deputy Regional Command Sec.-Gen. IZZAT IBRAHIM; mems of Regional Command: TAHA YASSIN RAMADAN, TAREQ AZIZ, MUHAMMAD HAMZAH AZ-ZUBAYDI, ABD AL-GHANI ABD AL-GHAFUR, SA'ADOUN HAMMADI MAZBAN KHADR HADI, ALI HASSAN AL-MAJID, KAMIL YASSIN RASHID, MUHAMMAD ZIMAM ABD AR-RAZZAQ, MUHAMMAD YOUNIS AL-AHMAD, KHADER ABD AL-AZIZ HUSSAIN, ABD AR-RAHMAN AHMAD ABD AR-RAHMAN, NOURI FAISAL SHAHIR, MIZHER MATNI AL-AWWAD, FAWZI KHALAF, LATIF NUSAYYIF JASIM, ADEL ADBULLAH MEHDI; approx. 100,000 mems.

**Kurdistan Revolutionary Party:** f. 1972; succeeded Democratic Kurdistan Party; admitted to National Progressive Front 1974; Sec.-Gen. ABD AS-SATTAR TAHER SHAREF.

There are several illegal opposition groups, including:

**Ad-Da'wa al-Islamiya** (Voice of Islam): f. 1968; based in Teheran; mem. of the Supreme Council of the Islamic Revolution in Iraq (see below); guerrilla group; Leader Sheikh AL-ASSEFIE.

**Iraqi Communist Party:** Baghdad: f. 1934; became legally recognized in July 1973 on formation of National Progressive Front; left National Progressive Front March 1979; proscribed as a result of its support for Iran during the Iran–Iraq War; First Sec. AZIZ MUHAMMAD.

**Umma (Nation) Party:** f. 1982; opposes Saddam Hussain's regime; Leader SAAD SALEH JABR.

There is also a breakaway element of the Arab Baath Socialist Party represented on the Iraqi National Joint Action Cttee (see below); the Democratic Gathering (Leader SALEH DOUBLAH); the Iraqi Socialist Party (ISP; Leader Gen. HASSAN AN-NAQUIB); the Democratic Party of Kurdistan (DPK; f. 1946; Leader MASOUD BARZANI); the Patriotic Union of Kurdistan (PUK; f. 1975; Leader JALAL TALIBANI); the Socialist Party of Kurdistan (SPK; f. 1975; Leader RASSOUL MARMAND); the United Socialist Party of Kurdistan (USPK; Leader MAHMOUD OSMAN), a breakaway group from the PUK; the Kurdistan People's Democratic Party (KPDP; Leader SAMI ABD AR-RAHMAN); the Kurdish Workers' Party (PKK); the Islamic League of Kurdistan (ILK, also known as the Islamic Movement of Iraqi Kurdistan (IMIK) ); the Kurdish Hezbollah (Party of God; f. 1985; Leader Sheikh MUHAMMAD KALED), a breakaway group from the DPK and a member of the Supreme Council of the Islamic Revolution in Iraq (SCIRI), which is based in Teheran under the leadership of the exiled Iraqi Shi'ite leader, Hojatoleslam MUHAMMAD BAQIR AL-HAKIM, and has a military wing, the Badr Brigade; the Iraqi National Accord (INA; Leader SALAH ESH-SHEIKHLI); and Hizb al-Watan or Homeland Party (Leader MISHAAN AL-JUBOURI).

Various alliances of political and religious groups have been formed to oppose the regime of Saddam Hussain in recent years. They include the Kurdistan Iraqi Front (KIF; f. 1988), an alliance of the DPK, the PUK, the SPK, the KPDP and other, smaller Kurdish groups; the Iraqi National Joint Action Cttee, formed in Damascus in 1990 and grouping together the SCIRI, the four principal Kurdish parties belonging to the KIF, Ad-Da'wa al-Islamiya, the Movement of the Iraqi Mujahidin (based in Teheran; Leaders Hojatoleslam MUHAMMAD BAQIR AL-HAKIM and SAID MUHAMMAD AL-HAIDARI), the Islamic Movement in Iraq (Shi'ite group based in Teheran; Leader Sheikh MUHAMMAD MAHDI AL-KALISI), Jund al-Imam (Imam Soldiers; Shi'ite; Leader ABU ZAID), the Islamic Action Organization (based in Teheran; Leader Sheikh TAQI MODARESSI), the Islamic Alliance (based in Saudi Arabia; Sunni; Leader ABU YASSER AL-ALOUSI), the Independent Group, the Iraqi Socialist Party, the Arab

Socialist Movement, the Nasserite Unionist Gathering and the National Reconciliation Group. There is also the London-based Iraqi National Congress (INC), which has sought to unite the various factions of the opposition. At a conference held in London in April 1999 a new collegiate leadership, under SALAH ESH-SHEIKHLI of the INA, was appointed. In November some 300 delegates to a national assembly, held in New York, USA, elected a 65-member central council and a new, seven-member collegiate leadership (AYAD ALLAWI, INA; RIYAD AL-YAWAR, independent; Sharif ALI BIN AL-HUSSAIN, Movement for Constitutional Monarchy; AHMAD CHALABI, independent; Sheikh MOHAMMED MOHAMMED ALI, independent; LATIF RASHID, PUK; HOSHYAR ZIBARI, DPK). In September 1992 the KPDP, the SPK and the Kurdish Democratic Independence Party were reported to have merged to form the Kurdistan Unity Party (KUP).

# Diplomatic Representation

## EMBASSIES IN IRAQ

**Albania:** Baghdad; Ambassador: GYLANI SHEHU.

**Algeria:** ash-Shawaf Sq., Karradat Mariam, Baghdad; tel. (1) 537-2181; Ambassador: AL-ARABI SI AL-HASSAN.

**Argentina:** POB 2443, Hay al-Jamia District 915, St 24, No. 142, Baghdad; tel. (1) 776-8140; Ambassador: GERÓNIMO CORTES-FUNES.

**Australia:** POB 661, Masba 39B/35, Baghdad; tel. (1) 719-3434; Ambassador: P. LLOYD (embassy temporarily closed).

**Bahrain:** POB 27117, al-Mansour, Hay al-Watanabi, Mahalla 605, Zuqaq 7, House 4/1/44, Baghdad; tel. (1) 542-3656; Ambassador: ABD AR-RAHMAN AL-FADHIL.

**Bangladesh:** 75/17/929 Hay Babel, Baghdad; tel. (1) 719-6367; Ambassador: MUFLEH R. OSMARRY.

**Belgium:** Hay Babel 929/27/25, Baghdad; tel. (1) 719-8297; Ambassador: MARC VAN RYSSELBERGHE.

**Brazil:** 609/16 al-Mansour, Houses 62/62–1, Baghdad; tel. (1) 541-1365; Ambassador: MAURO SERGIO CONTO.

**Bulgaria:** POB 28022, Ameriya, New Diplomatic Quarter, Baghdad; tel. (1) 556-8197; Ambassador: ASSEN ZLATANOV.

**Canada:** 47/1/7 al-Mansour, Baghdad; tel. (1) 542-1459; Ambassador: DAVID KARSGAARD.

**Central African Republic:** 208/406 az-Zawra, Harthiya, Baghdad; tel. (1) 551-6520; Chargé d'affaires: RENÉ BISSAYO.

**Chad:** POB 8037, 97/4/4 Karradat Mariam, Baghdad; tel. (1) 537-6160; Ambassador: MAHAMAT DJIBER AHNOUR.

**China, People's Republic:** New Embassy Area, International Airport Rd, Baghdad; tel. (1) 556-2741; fax (1) 541-7628; Ambassador: SUN BIGAN.

**Cuba:** St 7, District 929 Hay Babel, al-Masba Arrasat al-Hindi; tel. 776-5324; Ambassador: LUIS MARISY FIGUEREDO.

**Czech Republic:** Dijlaschool St, No. 37, Mansour, Baghdad; tel. (1) 541-7136; fax (1) 543-0275; Chargé d'affaires: MIROSLAV BELICA.

**Djibouti:** POB 6223, al-Mansour, Baghdad; tel. (1) 551-3805; Ambassador: ABSEIA BOOH ABDULLA.

**Finland:** POB 2041, Alwiyah, Baghdad; tel. (1) 776-6271; Ambassador: (vacant).

**Greece:** 63/3/913 Hay al-Jamia, al-Jadiriya, Baghdad; tel. (1) 776-6572; Ambassador: EPAMINONDAS PEYOS.

**Holy See:** POB 2090, as-Sa'adoun St 904/2/46, Baghdad (Apostolic Nunciature); tel. (1) 719-5183; fax (1) 224-5411; Apostolic Nuncio: Most Rev. GIUSEPPE LAZZAROTTO, Titular Archbishop of Numana.

**Hungary:** POB 2065, Abu Nuwas St, az-Zuwiya, Baghdad; tel. (1) 776-5000; Ambassador: TAMÁS VARGA; also represents Italian interests.

**India:** POB 4114, House No. 6, Zuqaq 25, Mahalla 306, Hay al-Magrib, Baghdad; tel. (1) 422-2014; fax (1) 422-9549; Ambassador: ARIF QAMARAIN.

**Indonesia:** 906/2/77 Hay al-Wahda, Baghdad; tel. (1) 719-8677; Ambassador: A. A. MURTADHO.

**Iran:** Karradat Mariam, Baghdad; Ambassador: Chargé d'affaires: HOSSEIN NIKNAM.

**Ireland:** 913/28/101 Hay al-Jamia, Baghdad; tel. (1) 776-8661; Ambassador: PATRICK MCCABE.

**Japan:** 929/17/70 Hay Babel, Masba, Baghdad; tel. (1) 719-5156; fax (1) 719-6186; Ambassador: TAIZO NAKAMARA.

**Jordan:** POB 6314, House No. 1, St 12, District 609, al-Mansour, Baghdad; tel. (1) 541-2892; Ambassador: HILMI LOZI.

**Korea, Republic:** 915/22/278 Hay al-Jamia, Baghdad; tel. (1) 776-5496; Ambassador: BONG RHUEM CHEI.

**Libya:** Baghdad; Head of the Libyan People's Bureau: ABBAS AHMAD AL-MASSRATI (acting).

**Malaysia:** 6/14/929 Hay Babel, Baghdad; tel. (1) 776-2622; Ambassador: K. N. NADARAJAH.

**Malta:** 2/1 Zuqaq 49, Mahalla 503, Hay an-Nil, Baghdad; tel. (1) 772-5032; Chargé d'affaires a.i.: NADER SALEM RIZZO.

**Mexico:** 601/11/45 al-Mansour, Baghdad; tel. (1) 719-8039; Chargé d'affaires: VÍCTOR M. DELGADO.

**Morocco:** POB 6039, Hay al-Mansour, Baghdad; tel. (1) 552-1779; Ambassador: ABOLESLAM ZENINED.

**Netherlands:** POB 2064, 29/35/915 Jadiriya, Baghdad; tel. (1) 776-7616; Ambassador: Dr N. VAN DAM.

**New Zealand:** POB 2350, 2D/19 az-Zuwiya, Jadiriya, Baghdad; tel. (1) 776-8177; Ambassador: (vacant).

**Nigeria:** POB 5933, 2/3/603 Mutanabi, al-Mansour, Baghdad; tel. (1) 542-1750; Ambassador: A. G. ABDULLAHI.

**Oman:** POB 6180, 213/36/15 al-Harthiya, Baghdad; tel. (1) 551-8198; Ambassador: KHALIFA BIN ABDULLA BIN SALIM AL-HOMAIDI.

**Pakistan:** 14/7/609 al-Mansour, Baghdad; tel. (1) 541-5120; fax (1) 542-8707; Ambassador: MANZAR SHAFIQ.

**Philippines:** Hay Babel, Baghdad; tel. (1) 719-3228; Ambassador: RONALDO BARONCA.

**Poland:** POB 2051, 30 Zuqaq 13, Mahalla 931, Hay Babel, Baghdad; tel. (1) 719-0296; Ambassador: KRZYSZTOF SLOMINSKI.

**Portugal:** POB 2123, 66/11 al-Karada ash-Sharqiya, Hay Babel, Sector 925, St 25, No. 79, Alwiya, Baghdad; tel. (1) 718-7524; Ambassador: (vacant).

**Qatar:** 152/406 Harthiya, Hay al-Kindi, Baghdad; tel. (1) 551-2186; Ambassador: MUHAMMAD RASHID KHALIFA AL-KHALIFA.

**Romania:** Arassat al-Hindia, Hay Babel, Zuqaq 31, Mahalla 929, No 452/A, Baghdad; tel. (1) 776-2860; Chargé d'affaires: GHEORGHE TSARLESCU.

**Russia:** 4/5/605 al-Mutanabi, Baghdad; tel. (1) 541-4749; Ambassador: ALEKSANDR PETROVICH CHEVIN.

**Senegal:** 569/5/10, Hay al-Mansour Baghdad; tel. (1) 542-0806; Ambassador: DOUDOU DIOP.

**Slovakia:** POB 238, Jamiyah St, No. 94, Jadiriyah, Baghdad; tel. (1) 776-7367.

**Somalia:** 603/1/5 al-Mansour, Baghdad; tel. (1) 551-0088; Ambassador: ISSA ALI MOHAMMED.

**Spain:** POB 2072, ar-Riyad Quarter, District 908, Street No. 1, No. 21, Alwiya, Baghdad; tel. (1) 719-2852; Ambassador: JUAN LÓPEZ DE CHICHERI.

**Sri Lanka:** POB 1094, House No. 22, Zukak 29, Mahalla 903, Hay al-Karada, Baghdad; tel. (1) 719-3040; Ambassador: N. NAVARATNARAJAH.

**Sudan:** 38/15/601 al-Imarat, Baghdad; tel. (1) 542-4889; Ambassador: ALI ADAM MUHAMMAD AHMAD.

**Sweden:** 15/41/103 Hay an-Nidhal, Baghdad; tel. (1) 719-5361; Ambassador: HENRIK AMNEUS.

**Switzerland:** POB 2107, Hay Babel, House No. 41/5/929, Baghdad; tel. (1) 719-3091.

**Thailand:** POB 6062, 1/4/609, al-Mansour, Baghdad; tel. (1) 541-8798; Ambassador: CHEUY SUETRONG.

**Tunisia:** POB 6057, Mansour 34/2/4, Baghdad; tel. (1) 551-7786; Ambassador: LARBI HANTOUS.

**Turkey:** POB 14001, 2/8 Waziriya, Baghdad; tel. (1) 422-2768; Ambassador: SÖNMEZ KÖKSAL.

**Uganda:** 41/1/609 al-Mansour, Baghdad; tel. (1) 551-3594; Ambassador: SWAIB M. MUSOKE.

**United Arab Emirates:** al-Mansour, 50 al-Mansour Main St, Baghdad; tel. (1) 551-7026; Ambassador: HILAL SA'ID HILAL AZ-ZU'ABI.

**Venezuela:** al-Mansour, House No. 12/79/601, Baghdad; tel. (1) 552-0965; Ambassador: FREDDY RAFAEL ALVAREZ YANES.

**Viet Nam:** 29/611 Hay al-Andalus, Baghdad; tel. (1) 551-1388; Ambassador: TRAN KY LONG.

**Yemen:** Jadiriya 923/28/29, Baghdad; tel. (1) 776-0647; Ambassador: MUHAMMAD ABDULLAH ASH-SHAMI.

**Yugoslavia:** POB 2061, 16/35/923 Hay Babel, Jadiriya, Baghdad; tel. (1) 776-7887; fax (1) 217-1069; Chargé d'affaires a.i.: JOVAN KOSTIĆ.

# Judicial System

Courts in Iraq consist of the following: The Court of Cassation, Courts of Appeal, First Instance Courts, Peace Courts, Courts of Sessions, *Shari'a* Courts and Penal Courts.

**The Court of Cassation:** This is the highest judicial bench of all the Civil Courts; it sits in Baghdad, and consists of the President and a number of vice-presidents and not fewer than 15 permanent judges, delegated judges and reporters as necessity requires. There are four bodies in the Court of Cassation, these are: (*a*) the General body, (*b*) Civil and Commercial body, (*c*) Personal Status body, (*d*) the Penal body.

**Courts of Appeal:** The country is divided into five Districts of Appeal: Baghdad, Mosul, Basra, Hilla, and Kirkuk, each with its Court of Appeal consisting of a president, vice-presidents and not fewer than three members, who consider the objections against the decisions issued by the First Instance Courts of first grade.

**Courts of First Instance:** These courts are of two kinds: Limited and Unlimited in jurisdiction.

**Limited Courts** deal with Civil and Commercial suits, the value of which is 500 Iraqi dinars and less; and suits, the value of which cannot be defined, and which are subject to fixed fees. Limited Courts consider these suits in the final stage and they are subject to Cassation.

**Unlimited Courts** consider the Civil and Commercial suits irrespective of their value, and suits the value of which exceeds 500 Iraqi dinars with first grade subject to appeal.

First Instance Courts consist of one judge in the centre of each *Liwa*, some *Qadhas* and *Nahiyas*, as the Minister of Justice judges necessary.

**Courts of Sessions:** There is in every District of Appeal a Court of Sessions which consists of three judges under the presidency of the President of the Court of Appeal or one of his vice-presidents. It considers the penal suits prescribed by Penal Proceedings Law and other laws. More than one Court of Sessions may be established in one District of Appeal by notification issued by the Minister of Justice mentioning therein its headquarters, jurisdiction and the manner of its establishment.

**Shari'a Courts:** A *Shari'a* Court is established wherever there is a First Instance Court; the Muslim judge of the First Instance Court may be a *Qadhi* to the *Shari'a* Court if a special *Qadhi* has not been appointed thereto. The *Shari'a* Court considers matters of personal status and religious matters in accordance with the provisions of the law supplement to the Civil and Commercial Proceedings Law.

**Penal Courts:** A Penal Court of first grade is established in every First Instance Court. The judge of the First Instance Court is considered as penal judge unless a special judge is appointed thereto. More than one Penal Court may be established to consider the suits prescribed by the Penal Proceedings Law and other laws.

One or more Investigation Court may be established in the centre of each *Liwa* and a judge is appointed thereto. They may be established in the centres of *Qadhas* and *Nahiyas* by order of the Minister of Justice. The judge carries out the investigation in accordance with the provisions of Penal Proceedings Law and the other laws.

There is in every First Instance Court a department for the execution of judgments presided over by the Judge of First Instance if a special president is not appointed thereto. It carries out its duties in accordance with the provisions of Execution Law.

# Religion

## ISLAM

About 95% of the population are Muslims, more than 50% of whom are Shi'ite. The Arabs of northern Iraq, the Bedouins, the Kurds, the Turkomans and some of the inhabitants of Baghdad and Basra are mainly of the Sunni sect, while the remaining Arabs south of the Diyali belong to the Shi'i sect.

## CHRISTIANITY

There are Christian communities in all the principal towns of Iraq, but their principal villages lie mostly in the Mosul district. The Christians of Iraq comprise three groups: (*a*) the free Churches, including the Nestorian, Gregorian and Syrian Orthodox; (*b*) the churches known as Uniate, since they are in union with the Roman Catholic Church, including the Armenian Uniates, Syrian Uniates and Chaldeans; (*c*) mixed bodies of Protestant converts, New Chaldeans and Orthodox Armenians.

### The Assyrian Church

Assyrian Christians, an ancient sect having sympathies with Nestorian beliefs, were forced to leave their mountainous homeland in northern Kurdistan in the early part of the 20th century. The estimated 550,000 members of the Apostolic Catholic Assyrian Church of the East are now exiles, mainly in Iraq, Syria, Lebanon and the USA. Their leader is the Catholicos Patriarch, His Holiness MAR DINKHA IV.

### The Orthodox Churches

**Armenian Apostolic Church:** Bishop AVAK ASADOURIAN, Primate of the Armenian Diocese of Iraq, POB 2280, Younis as-Saba'awi Sq., Baghdad; tel. (1) 885-1853; fax (1) 885-1857; nine churches (four in Baghdad); 18,000 adherents, mainly in Baghdad.

**Syrian Orthodox Church:** about 12,000 adherents in Iraq.

The Greek Orthodox Church is also represented in Iraq.

### The Roman Catholic Church

*Armenian Rite*

At 31 December 1997 the archdiocese of Baghdad contained an estimated 2,200 adherents.

**Archbishop of Baghdad:** Most Rev. PAUL COUSSA, Archevêché Arménien Catholique, Karrada Sharkiya, POB 2344, Baghdad; tel. (1) 719-1827.

*Chaldean Rite*

Iraq comprises the patriarchate of Babylon, five archdioceses (including the patriarchal see of Baghdad) and five dioceses (all of which are suffragan to the patriarchate). Altogether, the Patriarch has jurisdiction over 21 archdioceses and dioceses in Iraq, Egypt, Iran, Lebanon, Syria, Turkey and the USA, and the Patriarchal Vicariate of Jerusalem. At 31 December 1997 there were an estimated 190,000 Chaldean Catholics in Iraq (including 150,000 in the archdiocese of Baghdad).

**Patriarch of Babylon of the Chaldeans:** His Beatitude RAPHAËL I BIDAWID, POB 6112, Patriarcat Chaldéen Catholique, Baghdad; tel. (1) 887-9604; fax (1) 884-9967.

**Archbishop of Arbil:** Most Rev. JACQUES ISHAQ, Archevêché Catholique Chaldéen, Ainkawa, Arbil; tel. (665) 24701.

**Archbishop of Baghdad:** the Patriarch of Babylon (see above).

**Archbishop of Basra:** Most Rev. DJIBRAIL KASSAB, Archevêché Chaldéen, POB 217, Ahsar-Basra; tel. (40) 210323.

**Archbishop of Kirkuk:** Most Rev. ANDRÉ SANA, Archevêché Chaldéen, Kirkuk; tel. (50) 213978.

**Archbishop of Mosul:** Most Rev. GEORGES GARMO, Archevêché Chaldéen, Mayassa, Mosul; tel. (60) 762022; fax (60) 772460.

*Latin Rite*

The archdiocese of Baghdad, directly responsible to the Holy See, contained an estimated 3,000 adherents at 31 December 1997.

**Archbishop of Baghdad:** Most Rev. PAUL DAHDAH, Archevêché Latin, Hay al-Wahda—Mahalla 904, rue 8, Imm. 44, POB 35130, Baghdad; tel. (1) 719-9537; fax (1) 717-2471.

*Melkite Rite*

The Greek-Melkite Patriarch of Antioch (MAXIMOS V HAKIM) is resident in Damascus, Syria.

**Patriarchal Exarchate of Iraq:** Rue Asfar, Karrada Sharkiya, Baghdad; tel. (1) 719-1082; 600 adherents (31 December 1995); Exarch Patriarchal: Archimandrite NICOLAS DAGHER.

*Syrian Rite*

Iraq comprises two archdioceses, containing an estimated 53,000 adherents at 31 December 1997.

**Archbishop of Baghdad:** Most Rev. ATHANASE MATTI SHABA MATOKA, Archevêché Syrien Catholique, Baghdad; tel. (1) 719-1850; fax (1) 719-0168.

**Archbishop of Mosul:** Most Rev. CYRILLE EMMANUEL BENNI, Archevêché Syrien Catholique, Mosul; tel. (60) 762160.

### The Anglican Communion

Within the Episcopal Church in Jerusalem and the Middle East, Iraq forms part of the diocese of Cyprus and the Gulf. Expatriate congregations in Iraq meet at St George's Church, Baghdad (Hon. Sec. GRAHAM SPURGEON). The Bishop in Cyprus and the Gulf is resident in Cyprus.

## JUDAISM

Unofficial estimates assess the present size of the Jewish community at 2,500, almost all residing in Baghdad.

## OTHERS

About 30,000 Yazidis and a smaller number of Turkomans, Sabeans and Shebeks reside in Iraq.

**Sabean Community:** 20,000 adherents; Head Sheikh DAKHIL, Nasiriyah; Mandeans, mostly in Nasiriyah.

**Yazidis:** 30,000 adherents; Leader TASHIN BAIK, Ainsifni.

# The Press

## DAILIES

**Al-Baath ar-Riyadhi:** Baghdad; sports; Propr and Editor UDAY SADDAM HUSSAIN.

**Babil** (Babylon): Baghdad; f. 1991; Propr and Editor UDAY SADDAM HUSSAIN.

**Baghdad Observer:** POB 624, Karantina, Baghdad; f. 1967; tel. (1) 416-9341; English; state-sponsored; Editor-in-Chief NAJI AL-HADITHI; circ. 22,000.

**Al-Iraq:** POB 5717, Baghdad; f. 1976; Kurdish; formerly *Al-Ta'akhi*; organ of the National Progressive Front; Editor-in-Chief SALAHUDIN SAEED; circ. 30,000.

**Al-Jumhuriya** (The Republic): POB 491, Waziriya, Baghdad; f. 1963, refounded 1967; Arabic; Editor-in-Chief SAMI MAHDI; circ. 150,000.

**Al-Qadisiya:** Baghdad; organ of the army.

**Ar-Riyadhi** (Sportsman): POB 58, Jadid Hassan Pasha, Baghdad; f. 1971; Arabic; published by Ministry of Youth; circ. 30,000.

**Tariq ash-Sha'ab** (People's Path): as-Sa'adoun St, Baghdad; Arabic; organ of the Iraqi Communist Party; Editor ABD AR-RAZZAK AS-SAFI.

**Ath-Thawra** (Revolution): POB 2009, Aqaba bin Nafi's Square, Baghdad; tel. (1) 719-6161; f. 1968; Arabic; organ of Baath Party; Editor-in-Chief HAMEED SAEED; circ. 250,000.

### WEEKLIES

**Alif Baa** (Alphabet): POB 8063, Ministry of Education Bldg, Baghdad; tel. (1) 886-2948; fax (1) 884-3799; Arabic; Editor-in-Chief AMIR AL-HILOU; circ. 25,000.

**Al-Idaa'a wal-Television** (Radio and Television): Iraqi Broadcasting and Television Establishment, Karradat Mariam, Baghdad; tel. (1) 537-1161; radio and television programmes and articles; Arabic; Editor-in-Chief KAMIL HAMDI ASH-SHARQI; circ. 40,000.

**Majallati:** Children's Culture House, POB 8041, Baghdad; Arabic; children's newspaper; Editor-in-Chief RAAD BENDER; circ. 35,000.

**Ar-Rased** (The Observer): Baghdad; Arabic; general.

**Sabaa Nisan:** Baghdad; f. 1976; Arabic; organ of the General Union of the Youth of Iraq.

**Sawt al-Fallah** (Voice of the Peasant): Karradat Mariam, Baghdad; f. 1968; Arabic; organ of the General Union of Farmers Societies; circ. 40,000.

**Waee ul-Ummal** (The Workers' Consciousness): Headquarters of General Federation of Trade Unions in Iraq, POB 2307, Gialani St, Senak, Baghdad; Arabic; Iraq Trades Union organ; Chief Editor KHALID MAHMOUD HUSSEIN; circ. 25,000.

### PERIODICALS

**Afaq Arabiya** (Arab Horizons): POB 2009, Aqaba bin Nafi's Sq., Baghdad; monthly; Arabic; literary and political; Editor-in-Chief Dr MOHSIN J. AL-MUSAWI.

**Al-Aqlam** (Pens): POB 4032, Adamiya, Baghdad; tel. (1) 443-3644. 1964; publ. by the Ministry of Culture and Information; monthly; Arabic; literary; Editor-in-Chief Dr ALI J. AL-ALLAQ; circ. 7,000.

**Bagdad:** Dar al-Ma'mun for Translation and Publishing, POB 24015, Karradat Mariam, Baghdad; tel. (1) 538-3171; fortnightly; French; cultural and political.

**Al-Funoon al-Ida'iya** (Fields of Broadcasting): Cultural Affairs House, Karradat Mariam, Baghdad; quarterly; Arabic; supervised by Broadcasting and TV Training Institute; engineering and technical; Chief Editor MUHAMMAD AL-JAZA'RI.

**Gilgamesh:** Dar al-Ma'mun for Translation and Publishing, POB 24015, Karradat Mariam, Baghdad; tel. (1) 538-3171; quarterly; English; cultural.

**Hurras al-Watan:** Baghdad; Arabic.

**L'Iraq Aujourd'hui:** POB 2009, Aqaba bin Nafi's Sq., Baghdad; f. 1976; bi-monthly; French; cultural and political; Editor NADJI AL-HADITHI; circ. 12,000.

**Iraq Oil News:** POB 6178, al-Mansour, Baghdad; tel. (1) 541-0031. 1973; monthly; English; publ. by the Information and Public Relations Div. of the Ministry of Oil.

**The Journal of the Faculty of Medicine:** College of Medicine, University of Baghdad, Jadiriya, Baghdad; tel. (1) 93091; f. 1935; quarterly; Arabic and English; medical and technical; Editor Prof. YOUSUF D. AN-NAAMAN.

**Majallat al-Majma' al-'Ilmi al-'Iraqi** (Journal of the Academy of Sciences): POB 4023, Waziriya, Baghdad; tel. (1) 422-1733; fax (1) 425-4523; f. 1950; quarterly; Arabic; scholarly magazine on Arabic Islamic culture; Editor-in-Chief Dr NAJIH M. K. EL-RAWI.

**Majallat ath-Thawra az-Ziraia** (Magazine of Iraq Agriculture): Baghdad; quarterly; Arabic; agricultural; published by the Ministry of Agriculture and Irrigation.

**Al-Maskukat** (Coins): Dept of Antiquities and Heritage, Karkh, Salihiya St, Baghdad; tel. (1) 884-0875; f. 1969; annually; numismatics; Chair. of Ed. Board RABI' AL-QAISI.

**Al-Masrah wal-Cinema:** Iraqi Broadcasting, Television and Cinema Establishment, Salihiya St, Baghdad; monthly; Arabic; artistic, theatrical and cinema.

**Al-Mawrid:** POB 2009, Aqaba bin Nafi's Sq., Baghdad; f. 1971; monthly; Arabic; cultural.

**Al-Mu'allem al-Jadid:** Ministry of Education, al-Imam al-A'dham St, A'dhamaiya, Nr Antar Sq., Baghdad; tel. (1) 422-2594. 1935; quarterly; Arabic; educational, social, and general; Editor-in-Chief KHALIL I. HAMASH; circ. 190,000.

**An-Naft wal-Aalam** (Oil and the World): Ministry of Oil, POB 6178, Baghdad; f. 1973; monthly; Arabic; Editor-in-Chief Gen. AMIR MUHAMMAD RASHID.

**Sawt at-Talaba** (The Voice of Students): al-Maghreb St, Waziriya, Baghdad; f. 1968; monthly; Arabic; organ of National Union of Iraqi Students; circ. 25,000.

**As-Sina'a** (Industry): POB 5665, Baghdad; every 2 months; Arabic and English; publ. by Ministry of Industry and Minerals; Editor-in-Chief ABD AL-QADER ABD AL-LATIF; circ. 16,000.

**Sumer:** Dept of Antiquities and Heritage, Karkh, Salihiya St, Baghdad; tel. (1) 884-0875; f. 1945; annually; archaeological, historical journal; Chair. of Ed. Board RABI' AL-QAISI.

**Ath-Thaquafa** (Culture): Place at-Tahrir, Baghdad; f. 1970; monthly; Arabic; cultural; Editor-in-Chief SALAH KHALIS; circ. 5,000.

**Ath-Thaquafa al-Jadida** (The New Culture): Baghdad; f. 1969; monthly; pro-Communist; Editor-in-Chief SAFA AL-HAFIZ; circ. 3,000.

**At-Turath ash-Sha'abi** (Popular Heritage): POB 2009, Aqaba bin Nafi's Sq., Baghdad; monthly; Arabic; specializes in Iraqi and Arabic folklore; Editor-in-Chief LUTFI AL-KHOURI; circ. 15,000.

**Al-Waqai al-Iraqiya** (Official Gazette of Republic of Iraq): Ministry of Justice, Baghdad; f. 1922; Arabic and English weekly editions; circ. Arabic 4,000, English 400; Dir HASHIM N. JAAFER.

### PRESS ORGANIZATIONS

**The General Federation of Journalists:** POB 6017, Baghdad; tel. (1) 541-3993.

**Iraqi Journalists' Union:** POB 14101, Baghdad; tel. (1) 537-0762.

### NEWS AGENCIES

**Iraqi News Agency (INA):** POB 3084, 28 Nissan Complex—Baghdad, Sadoun; tel. (1) 8863024. 1959; Dir-Gen. UDAI EL-TAIE.

#### Foreign Bureaux

**Agence France-Presse (AFP):** POB 190, Apt 761-91-97, Baghdad; tel. (1) 551-4333; Correspondent FAROUQ CHOUKRI.

**Agenzia Nazionale Stampa Associata (ANSA)** (Italy): POB 5602, Baghdad; tel. (1) 776-2558; Correspondent SALAH H. NASRAWI.

**Associated Press (AP)** (USA): Hay al-Khadra 629, Zuqaq No. 23, Baghdad; tel. (1) 555-9041; Correspondent SALAH H. NASRAWI.

**Deutsche Presse-Agentur (dpa)** (Germany): POB 5699, Baghdad; Correspondent NAJHAT KOTANI.

**Informatsionnoye Telegrafnoye Agentstvo Rossii—Telegrafnoye Agentstvo Suverennykh Stran (ITAR—TASS)** (Russia): 67 Street 52, Alwiya, Baghdad; Correspondent ANDREI OSTALSKY.

**Reuters** (UK): House No. 8, Zuqaq 75, Mahalla 903, Hay al-Karada, Baghdad; tel. (1) 719-1843; Correspondent SUBHY HADDAD.

**Xinhua (New China) News Agency** (People's Republic of China): al-Mansour, Adrus District, 611 Small District, 5 Lane No. 8, Baghdad; tel. (1) 541-8904; Correspondent ZHU SHAOHUA.

## Publishers

**National House for Publishing, Distribution and Advertising:** Ministry of Culture and Information, POB 624, al-Jumhuriya St, Baghdad; tel. (1) 425-1846. 1972; publishes books on politics, economics, education, agriculture, sociology, commerce and science in Arabic and other Middle Eastern languages; sole importer and distributor of newspapers, magazines, periodicals and books; controls all advertising activities, inside Iraq as well as outside; Dir-Gen. M. A. ASKAR.

**Afaq Arabiya Publishing House:** POB 4032, Adamiya, Baghdad; tel. (1) 443-6044; fax (1) 444-8760; publisher of literary monthlies, *Al-Aqlam* and *Afaq Arabiya*, periodicals, *Foreign Culture, Art, Folklore,* and cultural books; Chair. Dr MOHSIN AL-MUSAWI.

**Dar al-Ma'mun for Translation and Publishing:** POB 24015, Karradat Mariam, Baghdad; tel. (1) 538-3171; publisher of newspapers and magazines including: the *Baghdad Observer* (daily newspaper), *Bagdad* (monthly magazine), *Gilgamesh* (quarterly magazine).

**Al-Hurriyah Printing Establishment:** Karantina, Sarrafia, Baghdad; tel. (1) 69721. 1970; largest printing and publishing establishment in Iraq; state-owned; controls *Al-Jumhuriyah* (see below).

**Al-Jamaheer Press House:** POB 491, Sarrafia, Baghdad; tel. (1) 416-9341; fax (1) 416-1875; f. 1963; publisher of a number of newspapers and magazines, *Al-Jumhuriyah, Baghdad Observer, Alif Baa, Yord Weekly*; Pres. SAAD QASSEM HAMMOUDI.

**Al-Ma'arif Ltd:** Mutanabi St, Baghdad; f. 1929; publishes periodicals and books in Arabic, Kurdish, Turkish, French and English.

**Al-Muthanna Library:** Mutanabi St, Baghdad; f. 1936; booksellers and publishers of books in Arabic and oriental languages; Man. ANAS K. AR-RAJAB.

**An-Nahdah:** Mutanabi St, Baghdad; politics, Arab affairs.

**Kurdish Culture Publishing House:** Baghdad; f. 1976; attached to the Ministry of Culture and Information.

**Ath-Thawra Printing and Publishing House:** POB 2009, Aqaba bin Nafi's Sq., Baghdad; tel. (1) 719-6161. 1970; state-owned; Chair. TAREQ AZIZ.

**Thnayan Printing House:** Baghdad.

# Broadcasting and Communications

### TELECOMMUNICATIONS

**Iraqi Telecommunications and Posts:** POB 2450, Karrada Dakhil, Baghdad; tel. (1) 718-0400; fax (1) 718-2125; Dir-Gen. Eng. MEZHER M. HASAN.

### BROADCASTING

**State Enterprise for Communications and Post:** f. 1987 from State Org. for Post, Telegraph and Telephones, and its subsidiaries.

**State Organization for Broadcasting and Television:** Broadcasting and Television Bldg, Salihiya, Karkh, Baghdad; tel. (1) 537-1161.

**Iraqi Broadcasting and Television Establishment:** Salihiya, Baghdad; tel. (1) 884-4412; fax (1) 541-0480; f. 1936; radio broadcasts began 1936; home service broadcasts in Arabic, Kurdish, Syriac and Turkoman; foreign service in French, German, English, Russian, Azeri, Hebrew and Spanish; there are 16 medium-wave and 30 short-wave transmitters; Dir-Gen. SABAH YASEEN.

#### Radio

**Idaa'a Baghdad** (Radio Baghdad): f.1936; 22 hours daily.

**Idaa'a Sawt al-Jamahir:** f. 1970; 24 hours.

Other stations include **Idaa'a al-Kurdia, Idaa'a al-Farisiya** (Persian).

**Radio Iraq International:** POB 8145, Baghdad.

#### Television

**Baghdad Television:** Ministry of Culture and Information, Iraqi Broadcasting and Television Establishment, Salihiya, Karkh, Baghdad; tel. (1) 537-1151. 1956; government station operating daily on two channels for 9 hours and 8 hours respectively; Dir-Gen. Dr MAJID AHMAD AS-SAMARRIE.

**Kirkuk Television:** f. 1967; government station; 6 hours daily.

**Mosul Television:** f. 1968; government station; 6 hours daily.

**Basra Television:** f. 1968; government station; 6 hours daily.

**Missan Television:** f. 1974; government station; 6 hours daily.

**Kurdish Television:** f. 1974; government station; 8 hours daily.

There are 18 other TV stations operating in the Iraqi provinces.

# Finance

(cap. = capital; dep. = deposits; res = reserves; brs = branches; m. = million; amounts in Iraqi dinars)

All banks and insurance companies, including all foreign companies, were nationalized in July 1964. The assets of foreign companies were taken over by the State. In May 1991 the Government announced its decision to end the State's monopoly in banking, and by mid-1992 three private banks had commenced operations.

### BANKING

#### Central Bank

**Central Bank of Iraq:** POB 64, Rashid St, Baghdad; tel. (1) 886-5171. 1947 as National Bank of Iraq; name changed as above 1956; has the sole right of note issue; cap. and res 125m. (Sept. 1988); Gov. SUBHI N. FRANKOOL; brs in Mosul and Basra.

#### Nationalized Commercial Banks

**Rafidain Bank:** New Banks St, Baghdad; tel. (1) 415-8001. 1941; state-owned; cap. 500m., res 1,703.5m., dep. 196,595.0m., total assets 221,132.4m. (Dec. 1996); Pres. DHIA HABIB AL-KHAYYOON; 152 brs in Iraq, 9 brs abroad.

**Rashid Bank:** BOP 7177, Haifa St, Baghdad; tel. (1) 885-3411. 1988; state-owned; cap. 1,000m., res 1.5m., dep. 236.1m. (1999); Chair. and Gen. Man. FAIQ M. AL-OBAIDY; 133 brs.

#### Private Commercial Banks

**Baghdad Bank:** POB 64, Rashid St, Baghdad; tel. (1) 717-5007; fax (1) 717-3487; f. 1992; cap. 100m.; Chair. HASSAN AN-NAJAFI.

**Commercial Bank of Iraq SA:** POB 5639, 902/14/13 Al-Wahda St, Baghdad; tel. (1) 707-0049, fax (1) 718-4312; f. 1992; cap. 800m. (1998); Chair. MUHAMMAD H. DRAGH.

#### Specialized Banks

**Al-Ahli Bank for Agricultural Investment and Financing:** Al-Huria Sq., Al-Ahh, Baghdad.

**Agricultural Co-operative Bank of Iraq:** POB 2421, Rashid St, Baghdad; tel. (1) 886-4768; fax (1) 886-5047; f. 1936; state-owned; cap. 295.7m., res 14m., dep. 10.5m., total assets 351.6m. (Dec. 1988); Dir-Gen. HDIYA H. AL-KHAYOUN; 32 brs.

**Industrial Bank of Iraq:** POB 5825, as-Sinak, Baghdad; tel. (1) 887-2181; fax (1) 888-3047; f. 1940; state-owned; cap. 59.7m., dep. 77.9m. (Dec. 1988); Dir-Gen. BASSIMA ABD AL-HADDI ADH-DHAHIR; 5 brs.

**Investment Bank of Iraq:** POB 3724, 102/91/24 Hay as-Sadoon, Alwiya, Baghdad; tel. (1) 718-4624; fax (1) 719-8505; f. 1993; cap. 300m., res 39.2m. (Dec. 1998); Chair. THAMIR R. SHAIKHLY; Man. Dir MOWAFAQ HASAN MAHMOOD.

**Iraqi Islamic Bank SA:** POB 940, Al-Kahiay, Bab Al-Muathem, Baghdad; tel. (1) 414-0694.

**Iraqi Middle East Investment Bank:** POB 10379, Bldg 65, Hay Babel, 929 Arasat al-Hindiya, Baghdad; tel. (1) 717-3745. 1993; cap., res and dep. 3,254.8m. (1998).

**Real Estate Bank of Iraq:** POB 8118, 29/222 Haifa St, Baghdad; tel. (1) 885-3212; fax (1) 884-0980; f. 1949; state-owned; gives loans to assist the building industry; cap. 800m., res 11m., total assets 2,593.6m. (Dec. 1988); acquired the Co-operative Bank in 1970; Dir-Gen. ABD AR-RAZZAQ AZIZ; 18 brs.

### INSURANCE

**Iraq Life Insurance Co:** POB 989, Aqaba bin Nafi's Sq., Khalid bin al-Waleed St, Baghdad; tel. (1) 719-2184. 1959; state-owned; Chair. and Gen. Man. TARIQ KHALIL IBRAHIM.

**Iraq Reinsurance Co:** POB 297, Aqaba bin Nafi's Sq., Khalid bin al-Waleed St, Baghdad; tel. (1) 719-5131; fax (1) 791497; f. 1960; state-owned; transacts reinsurance business on the international market; total assets 93.2m. (1985); Chair. and Gen. Man. K. M. AL-MUDARIES.

**National Insurance Co:** POB 248, National Insurance Co Bldg, Al-Khullani St, Baghdad; tel. (1) 885-3026; fax (1) 886-1486; f. 1950; cap. 20m.; all types of general and life insurance, reinsurance and investment; Chair. and Gen. Man. MUHAMMAD HUSSAIN JAAFAR ABBAS.

### STOCK EXCHANGE

**Capital Market Authority:** Baghdad; Chair. MUHAMMAD HASSAN FAG EN-NOUR.

# Trade and Industry

### CHAMBERS OF COMMERCE

**Federation of Iraqi Chambers of Commerce:** Mustansir St, Baghdad; tel. (1) 886-1811; fax (1) 886-0283; f. 1969; all Iraqi Chambers of Commerce are affiliated to the Federation; Chair. ZUHAIR A. AL-YOUNIS; Sec.-Gen. FALIH A. AS-SALEH.

### INDUSTRIAL AND TRADE ASSOCIATIONS

In 1987 and 1988, as part of a programme of economic and administrative reform, to increase efficiency and productivity in industry and agriculture, many of the state organizations previously responsible for various industries were abolished or merged, and new state enterprises or mixed-sector national companies were established to replace them.

**Military Industries Commission (MIC):** Baghdad; attached to the Ministry of Defence; Chair. ABD AT-TAWAB ABDULLAH MULLAH HAWAISH.

State enterprises include the following:

**Iraqi State Enterprise for Cement:** f. 1987 by merger of central and southern state cement enterprises.

**National Co for Chemical and Plastics Industries:** Dir-Gen. RAJA BAYYATI.

**The Rafidain Co for Building Dams:** f. 1987 to replace the State Org. for Dams.

**State Enterprise for Battery Manufacture:** f. 1987; Dir-Gen. ADEL ABBOUD.

**State Enterprise for Construction Industries:** f. 1987 by merger of state orgs for gypsum, asbestos, and the plastic and concrete industries.

**State Enterprise for Cotton Industries:** f. 1988 by merger of State Org. for Cotton Textiles and Knitting, and the Mosul State Org. for Textiles.

**State Enterprise for Drinks and Mineral Water:** f. 1987 by merger of enterprises responsible for soft and alcoholic drinks.

**State Enterprise for the Fertilizer Industries:** f. by merger of Basra-based and central fertilizer enterprises.

**State Enterprise for Import and Export:** f. 1987 to replace the five state organizations responsible to the Ministry of Trade for productive commodities, consumer commodities, grain and food products, exports and imports.

**State Enterprise for Leather Industries:** f. 1987; Dir-Gen. MUHAMMAD ABD AL-MAJID.

**State Enterprise for Sugar Beet:** f. 1987 by merger of sugar enterprises in Mosul and Sulaimaniya.

**State Enterprise for Textiles:** f. 1987 to replace the enterprise for textiles in Baghdad, and the enterprise for plastic sacks in Tikrit.

**State Enterprise for Tobacco and Cigarettes.**

**State Enterprise for Woollen Industries:** f. by merger of state orgs for textiles and woollen textiles and Arbil-based enterprise for woollen textiles and women's clothing.

### AGRICULTURAL ORGANIZATIONS

The following bodies are responsible to the Ministry of Agriculture and Irrigation:

**State Agricultural Enterprise in Dujaila.**

**State Enterprise for Agricultural Supplies:** Dir-Gen. MUHAMMAD KHAIRI.

**State Enterprise for Developing Animal Wealth.**

**State Enterprise for Fodder.**

**State Enterprise for Grain Trading and Processing:** Dir-Gen. ZUHAIR ABD AR-RAHMAN.

**State Enterprise for Poultry (Central and Southern Areas).**

**State Enterprise for Poultry (Northern Area).**

**State Enterprise for Sea Fisheries:** POB 260, Basra; Baghdad office: POB 3296, Baghdad; tel. (1) 92023; fleet of 3 fish factory ships, 2 fish carriers, 1 fishing boat.

### PEASANT SOCIETIES

**General Federation of Peasant Societies:** Baghdad; f. 1959; has 734 affiliated Peasant Societies.

### EMPLOYERS' ORGANIZATION

**Iraqi Federation of Industries:** Iraqi Federation of Industries Bldg, al-Khullani Sq., Baghdad; f. 1956; 6,000 mems; Pres. HATAM ABD AR-RASHID.

### UTILITIES

#### Electricity

**State Enterprise for Generation and Transmission of Electricity:** f. 1987 from State Org. for Major Electrical Projects.

### PETROLEUM AND GAS

**Ministry of Oil:** POB 6178, al-Mansour City, Baghdad; tel. (1) 551-0031; solely responsible until mid-1989 for petroleum sector and activities relevant to it; since mid-1989 these responsibilities have been shared with the Technical Corpn for Special Projects of the Ministry of Industry and Military Industrialization (Ministry of Industry and Minerals from July 1991); the Ministry was merged with INOC in 1987; the state organizations responsible to the ministry for petroleum refining and gas processing, for the distribution of petroleum products, for training personnel in the petroleum industry, and for gas were simultaneously abolished, and those for northern and southern petroleum, for petroleum equipment, for petroleum and gas exploration, for petroleum tankers, and for petroleum projects were converted into companies, as part of a plan to reorganize the petroleum industry and make it more efficient; Minister of Oil Gen. AMIR MUHAMMAD RASHID.

**Iraq National Oil Co (INOC):** POB 476, al-Khullani Sq., Baghdad; tel. (1) 887-1115. in 1964 to operate the petroleum industry at home and abroad; when Iraq nationalized its petroleum industry, structural changes took place in INOC, and it became solely responsible for exploration, production, transportation and marketing of Iraqi crude petroleum and petroleum products. INOC was merged with the Ministry of Oil in 1987, and the functions of some of the organizations under its control were transferred to newly-created ministerial departments or to companies responsible to the ministry.

**Iraqi Oil Drilling Co:** f. 1990.

**Iraqi Oil Tankers Co:** POB 37, Basra; tel. (40) 319990; fmrly the State Establishment for Oil Tankers; re-formed as a company in 1987; responsible to the Ministry of Oil for operating a fleet of 17 oil tankers; Chair. MUHAMMAD A. MUHAMMAD.

**National Co for Distribution of Oil Products and Gas:** POB 3, Rashid St, South Gate, Baghdad; tel. (1) 888-9911; fmrly a state organization; re-formed as a company in 1987; fleet of 6 tankers; Dir-Gen. ALI H. IJAM.

**National Co for Manufacturing Oil Equipment:** fmrly a state organization; re-formed as a company in 1987.

**National Co for Oil and Gas Exploration:** INOC Building, POB 476, al-Khullani Sq., Baghdad; fmrly the State Establishment for Oil and Gas Exploration; re-formed as a company in 1987; responsible for exploration and operations in difficult terrain such as marshes, swamps, deserts, valleys and in mountainous regions; Dir-Gen. RADHWAN AS-SAADI.

**Northern Petroleum Co (NPC):** POB 1, at-Ta'meem Governorate; f. 1987 by the merger of the fmr Northern and Central petroleum organizations to carry out petroleum operations in northern Iraq; Dir-Gen. GHAZI SABIR ALI.

**Southern Petroleum Co (SPC):** POB 240, Basra; fmrly the Southern Petroleum Organization; re-formed as the SPC in 1987 to undertake petroleum operations in southern Iraq; Dir-Gen. ASRI SALIH (acting).

**State Co for Oil Marketing (SCOM):** Man.-Dir ZEIN SADDAM AT-TIKRITI.

**State Co for Oil Projects (SCOP):** POB 198, Oil Compound, Baghdad; tel. (1) 416-8040; fax (1) 286-9432; fmrly the State Org. for Oil Projects; re-formed as a company in 1987; responsible for construction of petroleum projects, mostly inside Iraq through direct execution, and also for design supervision of the projects and contracting with foreign enterprises, etc.; Dir-Gen. Dr TALA'AT HATTAB.

**State Enterprise for Oil and Gas Industrialization in the South:** f. 1988 by merger of enterprises responsible for the gas industry and petroleum refining in the south.

**State Enterprise for Petrochemical Industries.**

**State Establishment for Oil Refining in the Central Area:** Dir-Gen. KAMIL AL-FATLI.

**State Establishment for Oil Refining in the North:** Dir-Gen. TAHA HAMOUD.

**State Establishment for Pipelines:** Dir-Gen. SABAH ALI JOUMAH.

### TRADE UNIONS

**General Federation of Trade Unions of Iraq (GFTU):** POB 3049, Tahrir Sq., Rashid St, Baghdad; tel. (1) 887-0810; fax (1) 886-3820; f. 1959; incorporates six vocational trade unions and 18 local trade union federations in the governorates of Iraq; the number of workers in industry is 536,245, in agriculture 150,967 (excluding peasants) and in other services 476,621 (1986); GFTU is a member of the International Confederation of Arab Trade Unions and of the World Federation of Trade Unions; Pres. FADHIL MAHMOUD GHAREB.

**Union of Teachers:** Al-Mansour, Baghdad; Pres. Dr ISSA SALMAN HAMID.

**Union of Palestinian Workers in Iraq:** Baghdad; Sec.-Gen. SAMI ASH-SHAWISH.

There are also unions of doctors, pharmacologists, jurists, artists, and a General Federation of Iraqi Women (Chair. MANAL YOUNIS).

## Transport

### RAILWAYS

The metre-gauge line runs from Baghdad, through Khanaqin and Kirkuk, to Arbil. The standard gauge line covers the length of the country, from Rabia, on the Syrian border, via Mosul, to Baghdad (534 km), and from Baghdad to Basra and Umm Qasr (608 km), on the Arabian Gulf. A 404-km standard-gauge line linking Baghdad to Husaibah, near the Iraqi-Syrian frontier, was completed in 1983. The 638-km line from Baghdad, via al-Qaim (on the Syrian border), to Akashat, and the 252-km Kirkuk–Baiji–Haditha line, which was designed to serve industrial projects along its route, were opened in 1986. The 150-km line linking the Akashat phosphate mines and the fertilizer complex at al-Qaim was formally opened in January 1986 but had already been in use for two years. Lines totalling some 2,400 km were planned at the beginning of the 1980s, but by 1988 only 800 km had been constructed. All standard-gauge trains are now hauled by diesel-electric locomotives, and all narrow-gauge (one-metre) line has been replaced by standard gauge (1,435 mm). As well as the internal service, there is a regular international service between Baghdad and İstanbul. A rapid transit transport system is to be established in Baghdad, with work to be undertaken as part of the 1987–2001 development plan for the city.

Responsibility for all railways, other than the former Iraq Republic Railways (see below), and for the design and construction of new railways, which was formerly the province of the New Railways Implementation Authority, was transferred to the newly created State Enterprise for Implementation of Transport and Communications Projects.

**State Enterprise for Iraqi Railways:** Baghdad Central Station Bldg, Damascus Sq., Baghdad; tel. (1) 543-4404; fax (1) 884-0480; fmrly the Iraqi Republic Railways, under the supervision of State Org. for Iraqi Railways; re-formed as a State Enterprise in 1987, under the Ministry of Transport and Communications; total length of track (1996): 2,029 km, consisting of 1,496 km of standard gauge, 533 km of one-metre gauge; Dir-Gen. Dr Yousuf Abd al-Wahid Jassim.

**New Railways Implementation Authority:** POB 17040, al-Hurriya, Baghdad; tel. (1) 537-0021. to design and construct railways to augment the standard-gauge network and to replace the metre-gauge network; Sec.-Gen. R. A. al-Umari.

### ROADS

At the end of 1996, according to the International Road Federation, there was an estimated total road network of 47,400 km, of which approximately 40,760 km were paved.

The most important roads are: Baghdad–Mosul–Tel Kotchuk (Syrian border), 521 km; Baghdad–Kirkuk–Arbil–Mosul-Zakho (border with Turkey), 544 km; Kirkuk–Sulaimaniya, 160 km; Baghdad–Hilla–Diwaniya–Nasiriya–Basra, 586 km; Baghdad–Kut-Nasirya, 186 km; Baghdad–Ramadi–Rurba (border with Syria), 555 km; Baghdad–Kut–Umara–Basra–Safwan (border with Kuwait), 660 km; Baghdad–Baqaba–Kanikien (border with Iran). Most sections of the six-lane 1,264-km international Express Highway, linking Safwan (on the Kuwaiti border) with the Jordanian and Syrian borders, had been completed by June 1990. Studies have been completed for a second, 525-km Express Highway, linking Baghdad and Zakho on the Turkish border. The estimated cost of the project is more than US $4,500m. and is likely to preclude its implementation in the immediate future. An elaborate network of roads was constructed behind the war front with Iran in order to facilitate the movement of troops and supplies during the 1980–88 conflict.

**Iraqi Land Transport Co:** Baghdad; f. 1988 to replace State Organization for Land Transport; fleet of more than 1,000 large trucks; Dir Gen. Aysar as-Safi.

**Joint Land Transport Co:** Baghdad; joint venture between Iraq and Jordan; operates a fleet of some 750 trucks.

**State Enterprise for Implementation of Expressways:** f. 1987; Dir-Gen. Faiz Muhammad Said.

**State Enterprise for Roads and Bridges:** POB 917, Karradat Mariam, Karkh, Baghdad; tel. (1) 32141; responsible for road and bridge construction projects to the Ministry of Housing and Construction.

### SHIPPING

The ports of Basra and Umm Qasr are usually the commercial gateway of Iraq. They are connected by various ocean routes with all parts of the world, and constitute the natural distributing centre for overseas supplies. The Iraqi State Enterprise for Maritime Transport maintains a regular service between Basra, the Gulf and north European ports. There is also a port at Khor az-Zubair, which came into use during 1979.

At Basra there is accommodation for 12 vessels at the Maqal Wharves and accommodation for seven vessels at the buoys. There is one silo berth and two berths for petroleum products at Muftia and one berth for fertilizer products at Abu Flus. There is room for eight vessels at Umm Qasr. There are deep-water tanker terminals at Khor al-Amaya and Faw for three and four vessels respectively. The latter port, however, was abandoned during the early part of the Iran–Iraq War.

For the inland waterways, which are now under the control of the General Establishment for Iraqi Ports, there are 1,036 registered river craft, 48 motor vessels and 105 motor boats.

**General Establishment for Iraqi Ports:** Maqal, Basra; tel. (40) 413211. 1987, when State Org. for Iraqi Ports was abolished; Dir-Gen. Abd ar-Razzaq Abd al-Wahab.

**State Enterprise for Iraqi Water Transport:** POB 23016, Airport St, al-Furat Quarter, Baghdad. 1987 when State Org. for Iraqi Water Transport was abolished; responsible for the planning, supervision and control of six nat. water transportation enterprises, incl.:

**State Enterprise for Maritime Transport (Iraqi Line):** POB 13038, al-Jadiriya al-Hurriya Ave, Baghdad; tel. (1) 776-3201; Basra office: 14 July St, POB 766, Basra; tel. 210206. 1952; Dir-Gen. Jaber Q. Hassan; Operations Man. M. A. Ali.

#### Shipping Company

**Arab Bridge Maritime Navigation Co:** Aqaba, Jordan; tel. (03) 316307; fax (03) 316313; f. 1987; joint venture by Egypt, Iraq and Jordan to improve economic co-operation; an expansion of the company that established a ferry link between the ports of Aqaba, Jordan, and Nuweibeh, Egypt, in 1985; cap. US $6m.; Chair. Nabeeh al-Abwah.

### CIVIL AVIATION

There are international airports near Baghdad, at Bamerni, and at Basra. A new airport, Saddam International, is under construction at Baghdad. Internal flights connect Baghdad to Basra and Mosul. Civilian, as well as military, airports sustained heavy damage during the war with the multinational force in 1991. Basra airport reopened in May 1991.

**National Co for Civil Aviation Services:** al-Mansour, Baghdad; tel. (1) 551-9443. 1987 following the abolition of the State Organization for Civil Aviation; responsible for the provision of aircraft, and for airport and passenger services.

**Iraqi Airways Co:** Saddam International Airport, Baghdad; tel. (1) 887-2400; fax (1) 887-5808; f. 1948; Dir-Gen. Nour ed-Din as-Safi Hammadi; formerly Iraqi Airways, prior to privatization in September 1988; operates limited domestic services.

## Tourism

The Directorate-General for Tourism was abolished in 1988 and the various bodies under it and the services that it administered were offered for sale or lease to the private sector. The directorate was responsible for 21 summer resorts in the north, and for hotels and tourist villages throughout the country. These were to be offered on renewable leases of 25 years or sold outright. In 1995 an estimated 340,000 tourists visited Iraq. Tourist receipts in that year were estimated at US $13m.

# IRELAND

## Introductory Survey

### Location, Climate, Language, Religion, Flag, Capital

The Republic of Ireland consists of 26 of the 32 counties which comprise the island of Ireland. The remaining six counties, in the north-east, form Northern Ireland, which is part of the United Kingdom. Ireland lies in the Atlantic Ocean, about 80 km (50 miles) west of Great Britain. The climate is mild and equable, with temperatures generally between 0°C (32°F) and 21°C (70°F). Irish is the official first language, but its use as a vernacular is now restricted to certain areas, collectively known as the Gaeltacht, mainly in the west of Ireland. English is universally spoken. Official documents are printed in English and Irish. The vast majority of the inhabitants profess Christianity: of these about 95% are Roman Catholics and 5% Protestants. The national flag (proportions 2 by 1) consists of three equal vertical stripes, of green, white and orange. The capital is Dublin.

### Recent History

The whole of Ireland was formerly part of the United Kingdom. In 1920 the island was partitioned, the six north-eastern counties remaining part of the United Kingdom, with their own government. In 1922 the 26 southern counties achieved dominion status, under the British Crown, as the Irish Free State. The dissolution of all remaining links with Great Britain culminated in 1937 in the adoption, by plebiscite, of a new constitution, which gave the Irish Free State full sovereignty within the Commonwealth. Formal ties with the Commonwealth were ended in 1949, when the 26 southern counties became a republic. The partition of Ireland remained a contentious issue, and in 1969 a clandestine organization, calling itself the Provisional Irish Republican Army (IRA—see Northern Ireland, Vol. II), initiated a violent campaign to achieve reunification.

In the general election of February 1973, the Fianna Fáil (FF) party, which had held office, with only two interruptions, since 1932, was defeated. Jack Lynch, who had been Prime Minister since 1966, resigned, and Liam Cosgrave formed a coalition between his own party, Fine Gael (FG), and the Labour Party (LP). The Irish Government remained committed to power-sharing in the six counties, but opposed any British military withdrawal from Northern Ireland (see Northern Ireland, Vol. II).

Following the assassination of the British Ambassador to Ireland by the Provisional IRA in July 1976, the Irish Government introduced stronger measures against terrorism. FF won the general election of June 1977 and Jack Lynch again became Prime Minister. In December 1979 Lynch resigned as Prime Minister and was succeeded by Charles Haughey. In June 1981, following an early general election, Dr Garret FitzGerald, a former Minister for Foreign Affairs, became Prime Minister in a coalition government between his own party, FG, and the LP. However, the rejection by the Dáil of the coalition's budget proposals precipitated a further general election in February 1982. Haughey was returned to power, with the support of three members of the Workers' Party (WP) and two independents. The worsening economic situation, however, made the FF Government increasingly unpopular, and in November Haughey lost the support of the independents over proposed reductions in public expenditure. In the subsequent general election FF failed to gain an overall majority, and in December FitzGerald took office as Prime Minister in a coalition with the LP.

During 1986 FitzGerald's coalition lost popular support, partly due to the formation of a new party, the Progressive Democrats (PD), by disaffected members of FF. In early June a controversial government proposal to end a 60-year constitutional ban on divorce was defeated by national referendum, and shortly afterwards, as a result of a series of defections, the coalition lost its parliamentary majority. In January 1987 the LP refused to support FG's budget proposals envisaging reductions in planned public expenditure, and the coalition collapsed. FF, led by Charles Haughey, won 81 of the 166 seats in the Dáil at the general election held in February. FF formed a minority government, which initially retained popular support, despite instituting a programme of unprecedented economic austerity.

In May 1989, following the Government's sixth parliamentary defeat over a minor policy issue, Haughey called a general election for 15 June. FG and the PD subsequently concluded an electoral pact to oppose FF. Although the Haughey administration had achieved significant economic improvements, severe reductions in public expenditure and continuing problems of unemployment and emigration adversely affected FF's electoral support, and it obtained only 77 of the 166 seats in the Dáil, while FG won 55 seats and the PD six seats. The LP and the WP both made significant gains.

At the end of June 1989 the Dáil reconvened to elect the Prime Minister. The PD voted in favour of Alan Dukes, the leader of FG, in accordance with their pre-election pact, and Haughey was defeated by 86 votes to 78. Dukes and Dick Spring, the leader of the LP, also failed to be elected. Haughey was forced to resign (on the insistence of the opposition parties, who claimed that his remaining as Prime Minister would be unconstitutional), although continuing to lead an interim administration. After nearly four weeks of negotiations, however, FF formed an 'alliance' with the PD and included two of the latter's members in a new cabinet. In mid-July 1989 Haughey became Prime Minister in an FF–PD coalition.

In October 1990 Brian Lenihan, the Deputy Prime Minister and Minister for Defence, was accused of having approached the President in an attempt to avert a general election following the collapse in 1982 of the FG–LP coalition. Lenihan denied the accusation, despite the subsequent release of tape-recordings in which he was heard to refer to the alleged incident. The opposition parties proposed a motion of 'no confidence' in Lenihan and the Government. The PD demanded Lenihan's resignation in return for its continued support. Following the resultant dismissal of Lenihan, the coalition Government defeated the no-confidence motion by 83 votes to 80. Lenihan was retained as the FF candidate in the forthcoming presidential election, which took place in November 1990, but was defeated by Mary Robinson, an independent candidate supported by the LP and the WP. Robinson, a liberal lawyer who specialized in issues of human rights, took office as President in December. Following FG's poor performance in the presidential election, Alan Dukes resigned the party leadership and was replaced by the party's deputy leader, John Bruton.

In October 1991 the Government, whose popularity had been adversely affected by economic recession, won a vote of confidence in the Dáil by 84 votes to 81. The motion of 'no confidence' had been introduced following a series of financial scandals involving public officials. Although members of FF were critical of Haughey's management of these affairs, which resulted in the resignation of five senior executives of state-owned and -subsidized enterprises, they were reluctant to precipitate a general election, owing to the party's decline in popularity. The narrow government victory was secured with the support of the PD, following an agreement between FF and the PD on a programme of tax reforms (which were implemented in the 1992 budget). In November 1991, however, a group of FF deputies proposed a motion demanding Haughey's removal as leader of the party. Albert Reynolds, the Minister for Finance and a former close associate of Haughey, and Padraig Flynn, the Minister for the Environment, announced their intention of supporting the motion, and were immediately dismissed from office. In the event the attempt to depose Haughey was defeated by a substantial majority of the FF parliamentary grouping.

In January 1992 a former Minister for Justice, Seán Doherty, alleged that, contrary to Haughey's previous denials, the Prime Minister had been aware of the secret monitoring, in 1982, of the telephone conversations of two journalists perceived to be critical of the Government. The PD made its continued support of the Government (without which a general election would have been necessary) conditional on Haughey's resignation. In February Reynolds was elected as leader of FF and assumed the office of Prime Minister, following Haughey's resignation. Reynolds extensively reshuffled the Cabinet, but retained the two representatives of the PD, in an attempt to preserve the coalition Government.

In June 1992 the leader of the PD, Desmond O'Malley, criticized Reynolds' conduct as Minister for Industry and Commerce in a parliamentary inquiry, which had been established in June 1991 to investigate allegations of fraud and political favouritism in the beef industry during 1987–88. In October 1992, in his testimony to the inquiry, the Prime Minister accused O'Malley of dishonesty. Following Reynolds' refusal to withdraw the allegations, in early November the PD left the coalition, and the Government was defeated on the following day in a motion of 'no confidence', proposed in the Dáil by the LP. It was subsequently announced that a general election was to take place on 25 November, concurrently with three constitutional referendums on abortion. FF suffered a substantial loss of support, securing 68 of the 166 seats in the Dáil and 39% of the votes cast (compared with 77 seats and 44% of the votes in 1989). FG also obtained a reduced number of seats (45, compared with 55 in 1989). In contrast, the LP attracted substantial support, more than doubling its number of seats (33, compared with 15 in 1989), while the PD increased its representation from six seats in 1989 to 10. In the concurrent referendums on abortion two of the proposals (on the right to seek an abortion in another EC state and the right to information on abortion services abroad) were approved by about two-thirds of the votes cast. The third proposal—on the substantive issue of abortion, permitting the operation only in cases where the life (not merely the health) of the mother was threatened—was rejected, also by a two-thirds' majority.

Since no party had secured an overall majority in the general election, an extended period of consultations ensued, during which the four major parties negotiated on the composition of a governing coalition. In January 1993 FF and the LP reached agreement on a joint policy programme and formed a coalition Government which took office on 12 January. Albert Reynolds retained the premiership, while Dick Spring received the foreign affairs portfolio, as well as the post of Deputy Prime Minister. Labour members of the Dáil were given five further ministerial portfolios, including those for the newly-created Departments of Enterprise and Employment, and of Equality and Law Reform. In June the Government began the introduction of a number of important social reforms. The Dáil approved legislation to provide for the legalized sale of prophylactics, despite opposition from the Roman Catholic Church, and decriminalized homosexual acts between consenting adults over the age of 17 years. Legislation was approved in March 1995 to give effect to the decision of the 1992 referendum to allow the distribution of information on foreign abortion services. However, other controversial social issues, in particular the legalization of divorce, remained unresolved.

In November 1994 serious differences arose within the coalition Government over the insistence by FF that the Attorney-General, Harry Whelehan, be appointed to a senior vacancy that had arisen in the High Court. Although such promotions accorded with past precedent, Whelehan's conservative record on social issues, particularly in relation to abortion, was unacceptable to the LP, whose specific objection to Whelehan's appointment was based on his alleged obstruction, as Attorney-General, of the processing of an extradition warrant for a Roman Catholic priest sought by the authorities in Northern Ireland on charges of the sexual abuse of children. (During the seven months taken to process the extradition request, the accused had returned voluntarily to Northern Ireland, where he was tried and imprisoned.) It was alleged by the LP that the transfer of Whelehan to the presidency of the High Court was intended by FF to protect him from public accountability for his conduct as Attorney-General. However, Reynolds and the FF members of the Cabinet approved the appointment in the absence of the LP ministers.

On 15 November 1994 Reynolds admitted to the Dáil that there was no satisfactory explanation for the delay in processing the extradition warrant, but denied that the matter affected the suitability of Whelehan for judicial office. On the following day, after consultations with the new Attorney-General, Reynolds conceded that there had been unnecessary delays in the extradition procedure, and that Whelehan's promotion had been ill-advised. Spring, however, accused Reynolds of having earlier deliberately withheld information, and Whelehan of having lied. The LP withdrew from the coalition, and on the following day the Government resigned. Reynolds, while remaining as Prime Minister of a 'caretaker' Government, relinquished the FF leadership on 19 November and was succeeded by the Minister for Finance, Bertie Ahern. Whelehan, meanwhile, resigned as President of the High Court.

The desire of all the major political parties to avoid immediate general elections led to protracted efforts to form a new coalition administration. Discussions between Spring and Ahern, however, failed to produce an agreement, and, following extensive negotiations between the LP and other parties, a new coalition, led by John Bruton of FG, and with Spring again the Deputy Prime Minister and Minister for Foreign Affairs, took office on 15 December 1994. A third coalition partner, the DL, obtained the social welfare portfolio.

The coalition Government experienced few apparent internal stresses during 1995. In May, however, the Minister for Defence and for the Marine, Hugh Coveney, resigned following allegations of an attempt by him to obtain a state consultancy contract for his former business interests. In November a referendum on the termination of the constitutional ban on divorce (which had been heavily defeated in 1986) resulted in a narrow majority (50.3% to 49.7%) in favour of legalizing the dissolution of marriage. The proposal was supported by all the major political parties, but strongly opposed by the Roman Catholic Church. The outcome of the referendum was the subject of an unsuccessful legal challenge in the Supreme Court in 1996, and the first divorce under the revised constitutional arrangements was granted in January 1997 (although legislation to implement the reform did not come into effect until February).

In June 1996 a journalist who had been investigating organized criminal activities for a national newspaper was shot dead in Dublin. The murder of Veronica Guerin focused national concern on an escalation of organized drugs-related crime in Ireland and prompted widespread criticism of the Government for having failed to implement adequate restraints to uphold law and order. The Government subsequently announced proposals to tighten the law on bail and to curtail the right of silence of people suspected of drugs-trafficking, and endorsed legislative measures, proposed by FF, to enable the courts to freeze personal assets thought to have been illegally obtained, for a period of up to five years. A constitutional referendum, on proposals to permit courts to refuse bail in certain circumstances to defendants in criminal proceedings, was conducted in November. These changes, which were supported by all of the main political parties, were approved in a low turn-out (29% of eligible voters).

In November 1996 the Minister for Transport, Energy and Communications, Michael Lowry, resigned following allegations that he had received personal financial gifts from an Irish business executive, Ben Dunne. Alan Dukes was named as Lowry's successor. During 1997 an inquiry into other political donations by Dunne, chaired by Justice Brian McCracken, revealed that payments totalling some IR£1.3m. had been made to the former Irish Prime Minister, Charles Haughey, during his term in office. Haughey later admitted the allegations, although insisting that he had no knowledge of the donations until he resigned his premiership; however, McCracken's report, published in August, condemned Haughey's earlier misleading evidence given to the tribunal and recommended further legal investigation. The Government, at that time led by Bertie Ahern of FF following a general election (see below), endorsed the results of the inquiry and agreed to establish a new tribunal to investigate further payments made to politicians and the sources of specific 'offshore' bank accounts that had been used by Haughey. In December 1998 it was revealed that a tax liability on some IR£2m. of personal financial gifts received by Haughey, including those made by Dunne, had been cancelled by the Revenue Commission. Opposition criticism of the decision intensified following the disclosure that the tax appeals commissioner responsible for the concession was a brother-in-law of Ahern. Ahern denied that he had influenced the decision.

In May 1997 Prime Minister Bruton called a general election, relying on strong economic growth figures and the negative impact of allegations concerning financial donations to former FF leader Charles Haughey to secure victory for FG's coalition with the LP and DL, despite public opinion polls revealing a significant shortfall in support for the Government over the opposition FF. In the election, which was conducted on 6 June, none of the main political parties secured an overall majority in the Dáil. FG increased its representation from 45 seats to 54, having won 27.9% of the first-preference votes cast, while FF secured 77 seats with 39.3% of the votes. Support for the LP, however, declined substantially and the party won just 17 seats (compared with 33 in the 1992 parliament). Sinn Féin won its first ever seat in the Dáil at the election. John Bruton conceded that he could not form a majority coalition administration, and Bertie Ahern, the FF leader, undertook to form a new government, in alliance with the PD, which had won four parliamentary seats, and with the support of independents. A new administration, with Ahern as Prime Minister, was formally approved in the Dáil at the end of June. Mary Harney of the PD was appointed as Deputy Prime Minister, the first woman ever to hold that position, while the other Cabinet positions were taken by FF.

In early October 1997 the Minister for Foreign Affairs, Ray Burke, resigned, owing to allegations of political favours granted in return for financial gifts (received in 1989) and the improper sale of Irish passports to Saudi Arabian business executives. In the resulting Cabinet reorganization David Andrews was awarded the foreign affairs portfolio and Michael Smith was appointed as Andrews's successor, responsible for defence and European affairs.

In September 1997 President Robinson resigned her position in order to assume her new functions as the United Nations High Commissioner for Human Rights. All the main parties put forward candidates to contest the ensuing presidential election; however, internal divisions within FF were revealed following the failure of Albert Reynolds, the former Prime Minister, to secure that party's nomination. Controversy arose during the election campaign when private documents were supplied to a newspaper, with the intention of undermining support for the FF candidate, Dr Mary McAleese, by emphasizing her sympathies with the republican movement. A former FG political adviser was later arrested in connection with the leaked information. In the election, conducted on 30 October, McAleese won 45.2% of the first-preference votes cast, compared with 29.3% for Mary Banotti of FG. McAleese was inaugurated on 11 November, and became the country's first President to be from Northern Ireland.

In early November 1997 the LP leader, Dick Spring, resigned, owing to his party's poor electoral performances. He was replaced by Ruairí Quinn, who had been Minister for Finance in the previous FG-LP administration.

In January 1999 the Government was undermined by revelations of a financial scandal involving its Commissioner to the EU, Padraig Flynn. It was alleged that, in 1989, Flynn, who held the environment portfolio at that time, had misappropriated a political donation made to his party, Fianna Fail, by a property developer. In October Ahern and three former finance ministers were required to give evidence to the public accounts committee of the Dáil. The committee was conducting an inquiry into widespread avoidance of a deposit interest tax introduced in 1986. The introduction of the tax, which was payable on deposits made by Irish residents, had prompted a sudden increase in non-resident accounts. A report by the Comptroller-General's office estimated that, as of November 1998, more than IR£3,000m. (equivalent to 30% of the deposit base of the country's four major clearing banks) was held in non-resident accounts, and that as many as half of these could be bogus accounts opened by Irish residents using foreign addresses in order to avoid paying tax. According to evidence given by the Governor of the Central Bank, the problem was widely recognized but the authorities had failed to act for fear that intervention would precipitate a flight of capital.

In October 1999 the Irish Nurses' Organization began an indefinite strike in support of demands for salary increases and improved working conditions. The Government refused to concede to the demands stating that they amounted to a 35% increase in basic salary, a figure far higher than that stipulated in the 'Partnership 2000' agreement between the unions, businesses and the Government under which unions had agreed to voluntary pay restraint in exchange for tax cuts and an influence on economic policy. It was feared that a concession to the nurses would precipitate similar demands from other unions.

Regular discussions between the British and Irish heads of government, initiated in May 1980, led to the formation in November 1981 of an Anglo-Irish Intergovernmental Council, intended to meet at ministerial and official levels. Consultations between the United Kingdom and Ireland on the future of Northern Ireland resulted in November 1985 in the signing of the Anglo-Irish Agreement, which provided for regular participation in Northern Ireland affairs by the Irish Government on political, legal, security and cross-border matters. The involvement of the Government of Ireland was to be through an Intergovernmental Conference. The Agreement maintained that no change in the status of Northern Ireland would be made without the assent of the majority of its population. The terms of the Agreement were approved by both the Irish and the British Parliaments, despite strong opposition by many Protestants in Northern Ireland.

Under the provisions of the Anglo-Irish Agreement, the Irish Government pledged co-operation in the implementation of new measures to improve cross-border security, in order to suppress IRA operations. It also promised to participate in the European Convention on the Suppression of Terrorism, which it signed in February 1986 and ratified in December 1987, when legislation amending the 1965 Extradition Act came into effect. In the same month the Government introduced controversial measures (without consulting the British Government) granting the Irish Attorney-General the right to approve or reject warrants for extradition of suspected IRA terrorists to the United Kingdom. In January 1988, however, the Irish Supreme Court ruled that members of the IRA could not be protected from extradition to Northern Ireland on the grounds that their offences were politically motivated. In December, however, the Irish Attorney-General refused to grant the extradition of an alleged terrorist who had been repatriated to Ireland in November, following a similar refusal by the Belgian authorities. The Irish decision was based on allegations that the accused man would not receive a fair trial in the United Kingdom because publicity had prejudiced his case.

Relations between the Irish and British Governments in 1988 were also strained when Irish confidence in the impartiality of the British legal system was severely undermined by proposed legislation to combat terrorism in Northern Ireland and by the decision, in January, not to prosecute members of the Royal Ulster Constabulary (RUC) allegedly implicated in a policy of shooting terrorist suspects, without attempting to apprehend them, in Northern Ireland in 1982. Difficult relations with the United Kingdom did not, however, present a threat to the Anglo-Irish Agreement, and the co-ordination between the Garda Síochána (Irish police force) and the RUC, established under the agreement, resulted in an unprecedentedly high level of co-operation on cross-border security. In February 1989 a permanent joint consultative assembly, comprising 25 British and 25 Irish MPs, was established. The representatives were selected in October. The assembly's meetings, the first of which began in February 1990, were to take place twice a year, alternately in Dublin and London.

In July 1990 an IRA member who had been charged with terrorist offences in the United Kingdom, lost his appeal against extradition in the High Court in Dublin. It was the first case to be considered under the 1987 Extradition Act, based on the European Convention on the Suppression of Terrorism. In November the Supreme Court upheld the ruling, and the alleged terrorist, Desmond Ellis, was extradited to stand trial in the United Kingdom. In November 1991 the Supreme Court upheld the extradition to the United Kingdom of an IRA member convicted of murder, who had escaped from detention in Belfast. At the same time, however, the Supreme Court overturned an order for extradition to the United Kingdom of two other IRA members who had similarly escaped, ruling that their convictions of possession of non-automatic fire-arms did not constitute an extraditable offence. This prompted assurances from the Minister of Justice that this omission in the legislation on extradition would be rectified. The Irish Government, however, also requested changes in British legislation to ensure that defendants could be tried in the United Kindom only for the offences for which they had been extradited. In January 1994 the Irish Cabinet approved draft legislation to remove the argument of 'political offence', and subsequent exemption from extradition, to persons charged with the use or possession of non-automatic weapons.

In January 1990 the British Secretary of State for Northern Ireland, Peter Brooke, launched an initiative to convene meetings between representatives from the major political parties in Northern Ireland, and the British and Irish Governments, to discuss devolution in Northern Ireland. In response to demands from Northern Ireland's Unionist parties, the Irish and British Governments publicly stated that they were prepared to consider an alternative to the Anglo-Irish Agreement. In March the Irish Supreme Court rejected an attempt by Ulster Unionists to have the Anglo-Irish Agreement declared contrary to Ireland's Constitution, which claims jurisdiction over Northern Ireland. In May the Unionists agreed to hold direct discussions with the Irish Government, a concession previously withheld because it lent credence to the Irish claim to a right to be involved in Northern Ireland's affairs. Disagreement remained, however, on the timing and conditions of Ireland's entry to the talks. Following extensive negotiations (see Northern Ireland, Vol. II), discussions between the Northern Ireland parties, which were a prelude to the inclusion of the Irish Government, commenced in June 1991. In early July, however, Brooke announced that the talks were to be discontinued, with no substantive progress having been made. This resulted from the Unionists' refusal to continue negotiations if the meeting of the Anglo-Irish Conference scheduled for July took place. The Irish and British Governments were both unwilling to postpone the Conference. In September Brooke announced an attempt to revive discussions on Northern Ireland, and in January 1992 presented an amended plan for negotiations (see Northern Ireland, Vol. II).

In February 1992 President Robinson met Brooke in Belfast, thus becoming the first Irish Head of State to visit Northern Ireland in an official capacity. In June 1993, during a visit by the President to Belfast, a brief meeting with Gerry Adams, the leader of Sinn Féin (the political wing of the IRA), was strongly opposed by the British Government and by Unionist politicians. An official visit to Britain by Robinson took place in June 1996.

In April 1992 confidential discussions between the four major parties in Northern Ireland recommenced. No agreement was reached on the principal issue of devolved government for the province, but in June the Unionists agreed, for the first time, to a meeting to discuss the agenda for the second element of the talks, which were to involve the Irish Government in the process for the first time. The Irish and British Governments agreed on an agenda for the third element of the negotiating process in July, comprising the discussion of the future of the Anglo-Irish Agreement (although this remained unaddressed, owing to the subsequent failure of the second stage of the talks). When the second stage of talks reopened in September in Belfast, the principal point of contention was the Unionists' demand that Ireland hold a referendum on Articles 2 and 3 of its Constitution, which lay claim to the territory of Northern Ireland. Ireland was unwilling to make such a concession except as part of an overall settlement. The Democratic Unionist Party (DUP) left the talks over this issue and boycotted the meeting in Dublin that was held later in the month. The Ulster Unionist Party (UUP), however, attended the meeting: the first official Unionist deputation to visit the Republic since 1922. At the end of September, following a statement from Reynolds suggesting that the constitutional articles were not negotiable, the DUP returned to the talks to confront the Irish delegation. With no progress made on this question, nor on the subject of Ireland's role in the administration of Northern Ireland, the negotiations formally ended in November, and the Anglo-Irish Conference resumed.

In January 1993 the British Secretary of State for Northern Ireland, Sir Patrick Mayhew, challenged the incoming FF–LP Irish Government to review the controversial articles of the Constitution, in order to give a new impetus to the stalled negotiating process. Dick Spring, the new Minister for Foreign Affairs, expressed the opinion that constitutional changes were necessary, although he gave no outright commitment to undertake such measures. The first meeting of the Anglo-Irish Conference with the new Irish administration was convened in February. Unionist leaders, however, refused to participate in the negotiations, which made little progress.

In September 1993 the British and Irish Governments agreed to renew efforts to recommence negotiations. A further meeting of the Anglo–Irish Conference, that had been scheduled for the end of October, was cancelled following the explosion of an IRA bomb in a loyalist district of Belfast, killing 10 people. The Irish Government condemned the close relationship of Sinn Féin to those responsible for the attack and distanced itself from a peace initiative which Adams had negotiated with the leader of Northern Ireland's Social Democratic and Labour Party (SDLP), John Hume.

At the end of October 1993 Albert Reynolds and John Major issued a joint statement setting out the principles on which future negotiations were to be based. The statement emphasized the precondition that Sinn Féin permanently renounce violence before being admitted to the negotiations. In December the Prime Ministers made a joint declaration, known as the 'Downing Street Declaration', which provided a specific framework for a peace settlement. The Declaration referred to the possibility of a united Ireland and accepted the legitimacy of self-determination, but insisted on majority consent within Northern Ireland. While the Sinn Féin and Unionist parties considered their response to the Declaration, Reynolds received both groups' conditional support for his proposal to establish a 'Forum for Peace and Reconciliation', which was to encourage both sides to end violent action. In January 1994, in an apparently conciliatory approach to Sinn Féin's repeated requests for a 'clarification' of the Declaration, Spring and Mayhew agreed to expand on this theme in public speeches, but declined to participate in direct meetings with Sinn Féin. In the following month, despite the increasing impatience of the Irish Government for a definitive response by Sinn Féin, Reynolds informed Mayhew that substantive negotiations could not proceed without the participation of Sinn Féin. In January 1994 the Irish Cabinet relaxed a ban (that had operated since 1976) forbidding the broadcast of interviews and speeches by persons deemed to be paramilitary supporters.

In April 1994 the IRA declared a temporary cease-fire over the Easter period. Despite a subsequent resumption of operations negotiations culminated in an announcement on 31 August by the IRA that it had ceased all military operations. This was followed in October by a similar suspension on the part of its counterpart loyalist organizations. In late 1994 and early 1995 the Irish authorities granted early release to more than 15 prisoners convicted of IRA terrorist offences. Despite misgivings that the political crisis during November and early December 1994 (see above) might impede the progress of inter-governmental talks, consultations were effectively maintained, resulting in the publication, in February 1995, of a 'Joint Framework' document, in which the Irish Government undertook to support the withdrawal of the Republic's constitutional claim to jurisdiction over Northern Ireland. The document's proposals, which included detailed arrangements for cross-border institutions and economic programmes which would operate on an all-island basis (see Northern Ireland, Vol. II), were stated by the British Government to be intended to provide a basis for public discussion and not as a definitive statement of government policy.

During 1995 the Irish Government expressed its increasing concern at the delay in initiating substantive all-party negotiations on the formulation of a permanent settlement of the conflict in Northern Ireland. The insistence of the British Government that the IRA decommission its weapons as a precondition to such talks received strong support from the Unionists, but was denounced by Sinn Féin as a 'delaying tactic', and was also opposed by the SDLP and the Irish Government. In June 1995 Sinn Féin issued a warning that the peace process was 'losing momentum', and in the following month Bruton and Hume, with the support of Adams, appealed for the urgent initiation of all-party talks. The Irish Government, meanwhile, had continued its programme of the early release of certain IRA prisoners, freeing four in April 1995 and a further 12 in July. Joint proposals in August by the British and Irish Governments for the formation of an international panel to consider the merits of decommissioning paramilitary weaponry in Northern Ireland received the full support of the US Government; President Clinton additionally urged the British authorities to accelerate their programme of releases of IRA prisoners, and requested the IRA to negotiate on the question of decommissioning weapons. Clinton reinforced these proposals in meetings with political leaders during a visit in November/December to Dublin and Northern Ireland. The international panel, under the chairmanship of George Mitchell (a former US Senator and close political associate of President Clinton), began work in December, in a series of private meetings with representatives of the contending political interests. Its findings, announced in January 1996, recommended that the decommissioning of arms should take place in parallel with all-party talks, and that their destruction should be monitored by an independent commission. The report additionally called on all groups to renounce violence and commit themselves to peaceful and democratic means. The British and Irish Governments accepted the recommendations of the report, but new controversy arose over proposals by the British Cabinet to hold elections for a Northern Ireland assembly which was to provide the framework for all-party negotiations. Although broadly acceptable to Unionist interests, this plan was rejected outright by the SDLP and Sinn Féin, and declared unacceptable by the Irish Government.

In February 1996, following a bomb explosion in London, the IRA announced that the cease-fire had been terminated. Official contacts with Sinn Féin were suspended by the British and Irish Governments, pending acceptable assurances that the IRA had discontinued all violence. It was announced at the end of February that plans were proceeding for an all-party meeting in June, at which Sinn Féin representation would be conditional on the restoration of the IRA cease-fire and on the willingness of Sinn Féin to participate in negotiations on the decommissioning of weapons. The multi-party meetings, which commenced in June without Sinn Féin participation, were overshadowed in July by violent confrontations in Northern Ireland between the RUC and nationalists opposed to the routing of loyalist parades through predominantly nationalist districts. The Irish Government formally protested to the British Government over the conduct of the RUC, both in failing to re-route the processions and in its methods of suppressing the ensuing public disorders. The multi-party talks were suspended in March 1997, pending the outcome of a general election in the United Kingdom. In May a meeting of Bruton with the newly-elected British Prime Minister, Anthony (Tony) Blair, and the new Secretary of State for Northern Ireland, Dr Marjorie Mowlam, generated speculation that significant progress could be achieved in furthering a political agreement. In June the two Governments announced a new initiative to proceed with the decommissioning of paramilitary weapons, on the basis of the Mitchell report, at the same time as pursuing political negotiations for a constitutional settlement. In early July the newly-elected Irish Prime Minister, Bertie Ahern, confirmed his commitment to the peace initiative during a meeting with Blair in London, and declared his support for the efforts of the British administration to prevent violence during the sectarian marching season in Northern Ireland. On 19 July the IRA announced a restoration of its cease-fire. A few days later the Irish and British Governments issued a joint statement that all-party negotiations would commence in mid-September with the participation of Sinn Féin. At the same time, however, the Unionist parties rejected the measures for weapons decommissioning that had been formulated by the two Governments. At the end of July the Irish Government restored official contacts with Sinn Féin and resumed the policy of considering convicted IRA activists for early release from prison.

In September 1997 Sinn Féin endorsed the so-called Mitchell principles, which committed participants in the negotiations to accepting the outcome of the peace process and renouncing violence as a means of punishment or resolving problems, providing for the party's participation in all-party talks when they resumed in the middle of that month. However, the Unionist parties failed to attend the opening session of the talks, owing partly to a statement by the IRA undermining Sinn Féin's endorsement of the Mitchell principles. A procedural agreement to pursue negotiations in parallel with the decommissioning of weapons (which was to be undertaken by a separate commission, the Independent International Commission on Decommissioning (IICD), led by Gen. John de Chastelain of Canada) was signed by all the main parties later in September. Substantive negotiations commenced in October; however, the UUP withdrew from discussions concerning relations between Northern Ireland and Ireland on the issue of Ireland's constitutional claim to the six counties. The new Irish Minister for Foreign Affairs, David Andrews, confirmed that the constitutional Articles would be discussed during the talks but could not commit the Government to repealing them in advance of a final settlement or a popular referendum. In November Ahern met the UUP leader, David Trimble, to strengthen relations between the two sides and facilitate progress in the negotiations. The all-party talks were adjourned in mid-December without agreement on an agenda for the next session of discussions. In mid-January 1998 the two Governments published a document outlining a framework for negotiations and specified that they hoped to achieve a settlement by May. The so-called Propositions on Heads of Agreement provided for 'balanced constitutional change' by both Governments and incorporated proposals for a Northern Ireland assembly, a joint North/South Ministerial Council and an inter-governmental British-Irish Council, that was to comprise representatives of the British and Irish Governments and of the assemblies in Northern Ireland, Scotland and Wales, under the framework of a new British-Irish Agreement.

In March 1998 Mitchell set a deadline of 9 April for the conclusion of the peace talks. On 10 April the two Governments and eight political parties involved in the talks signed a comprehensive political accord, the Good Friday (or Belfast) Agreement, at Stormont Castle. Immediately thereafter the two Governments signed a new British-Irish Agreement, replacing the Anglo-Irish Agreement of November 1985, committing them to put the provisions of the multi-party agreement into effect, subject to approval of the Good Friday Agreement by a referendum to be held in the whole of Ireland in May. The peace settlement provided for changes to the Irish Constitution and to British constitutional legislation to enshrine the principle that a united Ireland could be achieved only with the consent of the majority of the people of both Ireland and Northern Ireland. Under the terms of the Good Friday Agreement the new Northern Ireland Assembly was to have devolved legislative powers over areas of social and economic policy, while security, justice, taxation and foreign policy were to remain under the authority of the British Government. Executive authority was to be discharged by an Executive Committee, comprising a First Minister, Deputy First Minister and as many as 10 ministers of government departments. The Assembly, which was to be elected in June, was to operate in transitional mode, without legislative or executive powers, until the establishment of the North/South and British-Irish institutions. In addition, provision was made for the release of paramilitary prisoners affiliated to organizations that established a complete and unequivocal cease-fire. All qualifying prisoners were to be released within two years of the commencement of the scheme, which was due to begin in June. The decommissioning of paramilitary weapons was to be completed within two years of the approval by referendum of the Good Friday Agreement. On 22 April the Dáil overwhelmingly approved the peace agreement.

In early May 1998 Sinn Féin conducted a special conference in Dublin at which its delegates voted to endorse the peace agreement and to participate in the new Northern Ireland Assembly. At the referendums held simultaneously on 22 May the people of Ireland and Northern Ireland voted in support of the Good Friday Agreement. In Ireland 94.4% voted to allow the Government to become party to the agreement, while in Northern Ireland 71.1% voted to approve the accord. The two Governments and the political parties in Northern Ireland subsequently began the task of implementing the agreement and establishing the institutions for which it provided.

At elections to the 108-member Northern Ireland Assembly, conducted on 25 June 1998, those parties opposed to the Good Friday Agreement, headed by Rev. Dr Ian R. K. Paisley's DUP, failed to secure a sufficient number of seats to impede the functioning of the Assembly. In July the Assembly convened for the first time and elected the leader of the UUP, David Trimble, as Northern Ireland's First Minister to head the Executive Committee. However, that month sectarian violence threatened to disrupt the peace process following confrontations between the security forces and members of the loyalist Orange Order, who, in defiance of a ban imposed by the Northern Ireland Parades Commission, sought to march its traditional route along the predominantly Roman Catholic Garvaghy Road in Drumcree, County Armagh. In August the peace process again came under threat following an atrocity in Omagh, County Tyrone. In the worst single incident in Northern Ireland since the beginning of the conflict, 29 people were killed when an explosive device, planted by a Republican splinter group, the Real IRA, was detonated. Later that month Ahern announced a series of anti-terrorist measures, including restrictions on the right to silence and an extension to the maximum period of detention allowable for suspected terrorists, in an effort to facilitate convictions against terrorists based in Ireland.

Progress in the peace process continued to be obstructed throughout late 1998 by a dispute between Unionists and Sinn Féin concerning the decommissioning of paramilitary weapons, with Trimble insisting that the admittance of Sinn Féin representatives to the Executive Committee be conditional on progress in the demilitarization of the IRA. As a result of the dispute the deadline for the formation of the Executive Committee and the North/South body, specified as 21 October by the Good Friday Agreement, was not met. In November both Ahern and Blair held talks with Sinn Féin and the UUP in an effort to end the deadlock. In December Blair asserted that the release of convicted terrorists under the accelerated prisoner release programme, which began in September, would continue despite demands made by Unionists for the release of nationalist prisoners to be linked with progress on decommissioning by the IRA. In mid-December agreement was finally reached on the responsibilities of the 10 government departments of the Executive Committee and of six North/South 'implementation' bodies. This was endorsed by the Northern Ireland Assembly in February 1999. However, the dispute concerning decommissioning remained unresolved and Unionists continued to demand Sinn Féin's exclusion from the Executive Committee until the IRA had begun disarming. In that month Ahern appeared to support the Unionists' demands when he publicly declared that Sinn Féin's membership of the Executive Committee was 'incompatible' with the absence of progress in decommissioning. In early March the date for the devolution of powers to the new Northern Ireland institutions, envisaged as 10 March in the Good Friday Agreement, was postponed until 2 April (Good Friday). However, despite strenuous efforts by Blair and Ahern to end the impasse, the April deadline was not met. An 'absolute' deadline for the devolution of powers was subsequently set for 30 June 1999, after which date, Blair asserted, he would suspend the Northern Ireland Assembly if agreement had not been reached. On 25 June the two Prime Ministers presented a compromise plan which envisaged the immediate establishment of the Executive Committee prior to the surrender of paramilitary weapons, with the condition that Sinn Féin guarantee that the IRA complete decommissioning by May 2000. Negotiations continued beyond the June deadline but effectively collapsed in mid-July when Trimble announced that the UUP would not participate in a devolved administration with Sinn Féin until some decommissioning had taken place. Consequently the devolution of powers from Westminster was postponed until after the summer recess. A review of the peace process, headed by George Mitchell, began in early September. In early October Peter Mandelson succeeded Mowlam as the British Secretary of State for Northern Ireland. During that month police in the Republic made a series of arrests and seized weaponry in an effort to prevent a renewed offensive by republican terrorists.

In November 1999 Mitchell concluded the review of the peace process and succeeded in producing an agreement providing for the devolution of powers to the Executive Committee. The agreement followed a statement by the IRA that it would appoint a representative to enter discussions with the IICD. At a meeting of the ruling council of the UUP held in late November Trimble persuaded his party to vote in favour of the agreement. However, approval was only given on the condition that the council meet again on 12 February 2000 to review the decommissioning process; it was expected that the UUP would withdraw from the executive if the IRA had failed to begin submitting its weapons. On 29 November 1999 the Northern Ireland Assembly convened to appoint the 10-member Executive Committee. On 2 December power was officially transferred from Westminster to the new Northern Ireland executive at Stormont Castle. On the same day, in accordance with the Good Friday Agreement, the Irish Government removed from the Constitution the Republic's territorial claim over Northern Ireland. In mid-December the Cabinet of the Republic attended the inaugural meeting, in Armagh, of the North/South Ministerial Council. The British-Irish Council met for the first time later that month. However, in late January 2000 Adams dismissed the possibility of imminent IRA decommissioning and a report by the IICD confirmed that there had been no disarmament. With the prospect of the collapse of the peace process the British and Irish Governments engaged in intensive negotiations. On 1 February the IRA released a statement giving assurances that its cease-fire would not be broken and expressing support for the peace process. On 4 February the IRA were given until 11 February to begin decommissioning. However, it failed to comply and legislation came into effect on that day suspending the new executive, legislative and co-operative institutions and returning Northern Ireland to direct rule. The IRA subsequently announced its withdrawal from discussions with the IICD, raising serious doubts about the future of its cease-fire. In addition, Adams refused to participate in any further review of the peace process until the suspended institutions had been restored. At a republican rally held at the end of February Adams announced that Sinn Féin had abandoned its special role of attempting to persuade the IRA to decommission. In early March Blair and Ahern agreed a timetable for renewed talks. The principal parties were to meet in Washington, USA, on 17 March.

Ireland became a member of the European Community (EC, now the European Union (EU)—see p. 172) in 1973. In May 1987 the country affirmed its commitment to the EC when, in a referendum, 69.9% of Irish voters supported adherence to the Single European Act, which provided for closer economic and political co-operation between EC member-states (including the creation of a single Community market by 1993). In December 1991, during the EC summit conference at Maastricht, in the Netherlands, Ireland agreed to the the far-reaching Treaty on European Union. Ireland secured a special provision within the Treaty (which was signed by all parties in February 1992), guaranteeing that Ireland's constitutional position on abortion would be unaffected by any future EC legislation. The four major political parties in Ireland united in support of the ratification of the Treaty prior to a referendum on the issue, which took place in June. Despite opposition, from both pro- and anti-abortion campaigners, to the special provision within the Treaty and the threat to Ireland's neutrality inherent in the document's proposals for a common defence policy, ratification of the Treaty was endorsed by 68.7% of the votes cast (57.3% of the electorate participated in the referendum). In a referendum conducted in May 1998, 62% of Irish voters endorsed the Amsterdam Treaty, which had been signed by EU ministers in October 1997, amending the Treaty on European Union.

## Government

Legislative power is vested in the bicameral National Parliament, comprising the Senate (with restricted powers) and the House of Representatives. The Senate (Seanad Éireann) has 60 members, including 11 nominated by the Prime Minister (Taoiseach) and 49 indirectly elected for five years. The House of Representatives (Dáil Éireann) has 166 members (Teachtaí Dála), elected by universal adult suffrage for five years (subject to dissolution) by means of the single transferable vote, a form of proportional representation.

The President (Uachtarán) is the constitutional Head of State, elected by direct popular vote for seven years. Executive power is effectively held by the Cabinet, led by the Prime Minister, who is appointed by the President on the nomination of the Dáil. The President appoints other Ministers on the nomination of the Prime Minister with the previous approval of the Dáil. The Cabinet is responsible to the Dáil.

## Defence

At 1 August 1999 the regular armed forces totalled 11,500. The army comprised 9,300, the navy 1,100 and the air force 1,100. There was also a reserve of 14,800. Defence was allocated IR£586m. in the 1999 budget. Military service is voluntary.

## Economic Affairs

In 1997, according to estimates by the World Bank, Ireland's gross national product (GNP), measured at average 1995–97 prices, was US $65,137m., equivalent to $17,790 per head. During 1990–97, it was estimated, GNP per head increased, in real terms, at an average rate of 5.6% per year. Over the same period, the population increased by an average of 0.6% per year. In 1998 GNP was estimated at $67,500m. ($18,340 per head). Ireland's gross domestic product (GDP) increased, in real terms, by an average of 7.5% per year in 1990–98. GDP rose by 10.7% in 1997 and by 8.9% in 1998.

Agriculture (including forestry and fishing) contributed 5.1% of GDP (at factor cost) in 1998. An estimated 8.5% of the working population were employed in the sector in 1999. Beef and dairy production dominate Irish agriculture (in 1998 meat and meat preparations accounted for 2.6% of total exports while dairy products and birds' eggs accounted for 1.8%). Principal crops include barley, sugar beet, potatoes and wheat. Agricultural GDP increased by an average of 0.5% per year during 1991–97, and by an estimated 1.4% in 1997.

Industry (comprising mining, manufacturing, construction and utilities) provided 37.6% of GDP in 1998, and employed an estimated 28.3% of the working population in 1999. Industrial GDP increased by an average of 9.6% per year during 1991–97, by 16.2% in 1995, 8.3% in 1996 and by an estimated 15.2% in 1997.

Mining (including quarrying and turf production) provided employment to 0.4% of the working population in 1997. Ireland possesses substantial deposits of lead-zinc ore and recoverable peat, both of which are exploited. Natural gas, mainly from the Kinsale field, and small quantities of coal are also extracted. A significant natural gas deposit discovered in 1999 was expected to yield sufficient gas to meet more than half of the country's current average demand. Offshore reserves of petroleum have been located and several licences awarded to foreign-owned enterprises to undertake further exploration. During 1980–90 mining production decreased by an annual average of 1.7%.

Manufacturing was estimated to employ 20.3% of the working population in 1997. The manufacturing sector comprises many high-technology, largely foreign-owned, capital-intensive enterprises. The electronics industry accounted for 32.6% of the value of exports in 1996. During 1992–96 manufacturing production increased by an average of 10.1% per year.

Energy is derived principally from petroleum, which provided 51% of total requirements in 1996, while coal provided 18%, natural gas 18%, peat 11%, and hydroelectric power 2%. In 1998 imports of mineral fuels were 2.5% (by value) of total merchandise imports.

Service industries (including commerce, finance, transport and communications, and public administration) contributed an estimated 57.3% of GDP in 1998, and employed 63.1% of the working population in 1999. The financial sector is of increasing importance to Ireland. An International Financial Services Centre in Dublin was opened in 1990; by January 1998 more than 400 companies were participating in the Centre, many of which were foreign concerns attracted by tax concessions offered by the Irish Government. Tourism is one of the principal sources of foreign exchange. Revenue from the tourism and travel sector amounted to IR£2,105m. in 1997. The GDP of the services sector increased by an average of 4.3% per year during 1991–97, and by an estimated 6.2% in 1997.

In 1998, according to IMF statistics, Ireland recorded a visible trade surplus of US $23,381m. and there was a surplus of $806m. on the current account of the balance of payments. In that year the principal source of imports (33.9%) was the United Kingdom, which was also the principal market for exports (22.6%). Other major trading partners were the USA, Germany and France. In 1998 principal imports included office equipment and other electrical machinery, chemical products and other manufactured items. Principal exports included electronic goods, chemicals and beef and dairy products.

In 1999 it was projected that there would be a budgetary surplus of IR£954m. The 1998 budget recorded a deficit of IR£220m. (equivalent to 0.4% of GDP). At the end of 1996 Ireland's total national debt was estimated to be IR£29,912m., and in that year the cost of servicing the debt amounted to an estimated IR£2,560m. In 1994 the ratio of debt interest to GNP was 2.4%. The annual rate of inflation averaged 2.3% in 1990–98. The rate increased from 1.5% in 1997 to 2.4% in 1998. An estimated 10.3% of the labour force were unemployed in 1997, compared with 11.6% in 1996, 12.3% in 1995 and 14.3% in 1994.

Ireland became a member of the European Community (EC) (see European Union, EU, p. 172) in 1973, and of the EC's Exchange Rate Mechanism (ERM) in 1979.

In 1991–92, the Irish economy was affected by recessionary trends, particularly in its principal market, the United Kingdom. The crisis in the ERM during the latter half of 1992, during which the United Kingdom withdrew from the mechanism, threatened the value of the punt within the system and had a serious impact on Irish industry. The Central Bank of Ireland was forced to raise interest rates to protect the punt, and in January 1993 the Government was obliged to devalue the Irish currency by 10%. The Government has subsequently undertaken adjustments to the value of the currency as necessary, in order to secure its position within the ERM. Between 1993–98 the economy enjoyed an unprecedentedly high rate of growth with GDP increasing by an annual average of 8.5%. This was attributable to a number of factors including prudent fiscal and monetary management and an expanding, well-qualified labour force. In addition government policies offering financial incentives to foreign-owned enterprises resulted in a substantial increase in direct foreign investment and steady expansion, particularly in the financial services and electronic manufacturing industries. (By 1998 Ireland had become the world's second largest exporter of computer software, after the USA.) Continued growth was facilitated by an agreement, reached in December 1996 and covering the period 1997–99, between the Government, trade unions and industrial and agricultural organizations. The accord, entitled 'Partnership 2000', provided for wage moderation under a centralized wage policy in exchange for reductions in corporate and personal rates of taxation and increased social welfare payments. In addition to supporting efforts to contain inflation, wage restraint also improved competitiveness, contributing to increased exports. However, in 1999 'Partnership 2000' came under increasing strain owing to industrial action by the Irish Nurses' Organization (see Recent History). A new three-year agreement was to be negotiated in 2000. Continued strong economic growth was envisaged in 1999 and 2000, with projected real GDP growth of 7.5% and 6.7%, respectively. In those years inflation was expected to remain below 2.5%. However, the announcement of budget plans for 2000, including income tax cuts and a 26% increase in expenditure on public infrastructure, raised concerns among economists of potential inflationary pressures, and prompted the IMF and the Organisation for Economic Co-operation and Development to urge fiscal restraint.

### Social Welfare

Social welfare benefits in Ireland may be grouped broadly in three categories: contributory (social) insurance payments, which are made on the basis of pay-related social insurance contributions; non-contributory (social assistance) payments, which are made on the basis of claimants' satisfying the criteria of a means test; and universal services, such as child benefit and free travel. Child benefit is payable to all households for each child.

Social insurance is compulsory for both employees and the self-employed. The social insurance scheme provides for orphans' benefits, widows', retirement and old-age pensions; unemployment, disability, maternity, invalidity, death grants and occupational injury, dental and optical benefits. The cost of the social insurance scheme is shared by the employer, the employee, the self-employed and the State. Varying rates of social insurance are payable, and the rate payable determines the range of benefits available. Private-sector employees contribute the highest rate and have cover for all benefits; the contributions of the self-employed provide funds for old age, and survivors' benefits and orphans' contributory allowance; permanent and pensionable employees in the state sector have cover mainly for widows'/widowers' (contributory) pensions, orphans' (contributory) allowance and limited occupational injury benefits.

People of inadequate means who are not entitled to benefit under these contributory schemes may receive non-contributory pensions or other benefits from the State or other public funds. These benefits include one-parent family payments, old-age and blindness pensions, carers' allowance, orphans' (non-contributory) pension, supplementary welfare allowance, unemployment assistance and family income supplement. The central Government's budgetary expenditure on social welfare services in 1999 was projected at IR£5,100m. (equivalent to 28.3% of total expenditure).

Health services are provided by eight health boards, administered by the Department of Health and Children. There are two categories of entitlement, with people on low incomes qualifying for the full range of health services free of charge, and people on higher incomes qualifying for fewer free services.

Drugs and medicines are available free of charge to all people suffering from specified long-term ailments. Hospital in-patient and out-patient services are free of charge to all children under 16 years of age, suffering from specified long-term ailments. Immunization and diagnostic services, as well as hospital services, are free of charge to everyone suffering from an infectious disease. A maintenance allowance is also payable in certain cases. The central Government's budgetary expenditure on health was projected at IR£3,369m. in 1999 (18.7% of total spending). In addition, there are various community welfare services for the chronically sick, the elderly, the disabled and families under stress. In 1995 Ireland had 104 publicly-funded hospitals, with a total of 13,557 beds. In 1995 there were 8,233 physicians resident in the country.

### Education

The State in Ireland has constitutional responsibility for the national education system. Irish schools are owned, not by the State, but by community groups, traditionally religious groups. It is in general an aided system: the State does not itself operate the schools (with a few minor exceptions) but assists other bodies, usually religious, to do so.

Education in Ireland is compulsory for nine years between six and 15 years of age. Primary education may begin at the age of four and lasts for eight years. Aided primary schools account for the education of 98.5% of children in the primary sector, who attend until the age of 12, when they transfer to a post-primary school.

Post-primary education lasts for up to six years, comprising a junior cycle of three years and a senior cycle of two or three years. The Junior Certificate examination is taken after three years in post-primary (second-level) education. In senior cycle there is an optional one-year Transition Year Programme, followed by a two-year course leading to the Leaving Certificate at 17 or 18. In 1997/98 there were 435 secondary schools and a further 246 vocational schools, providing primary school leavers

year trial period of Israeli-Syrian 'normalization' would ensue. The proposals were rejected by President Assad; however, he did state his willingness, in an address to the Syrian People's Assembly, to work towards peace with Israel. In late September Rabin and King Hussein held talks in Aqaba with the aim of devising a timetable for a full Israeli-Jordanian peace treaty. The following day the six members of the Co-operation Council for the Arab States of the Gulf (the Gulf Co-operation Council, see p. 153) announced their decision to revoke the subsidiary elements of the Arab economic boycott of Israel.

A World Bank-sponsored conference of international donors, held in Paris in September 1994, collapsed almost immediately, owing to a dispute between Israel and the Palestinians over Palestinian investment plans to fund projects in East Jerusalem. Israel regarded such plans as compromising negotiations on the final status of Jerusalem which, under the terms of the Declaration of Principles, were not due to begin before May 1996. Meeting in Oslo, Norway, shortly afterwards, Arafat and Peres negotiated a 15-point agreement aimed at accelerating economic aid to the PNA. In late September 1994 Arafat and Rabin met at the Erez crossing point between Gaza and Israel to discuss the future Palestinian elections in the Gaza Strip and the West Bank. The PLO reportedly sought to elect a 100-member Palestinian Council, while Israel insisted that its size should be restricted to 25 members. Israel rejected Arafat's proposal for elections on 1 November as unrealistic; it was, however, agreed to meet again in October to negotiate a compromise. At the same time, Arafat agreed to 'take all measures' to prevent attacks on Israeli targets by opponents of the Declaration of Principles.

In late September 1994 Rabin approved a plan to construct some 1,000 new housing units at a Jewish settlement about 3 km inside the West Bank, in an apparent reversal of the moratorium he had imposed on new construction in 1992 in return for US loan guarantees. The PLO claimed that this contravened both the letter and the spirit of the Declaration of Principles. In early October 1994 Hamas claimed responsibility for an attack in Jerusalem in which an Israeli soldier and a Palestinian civilian died. On the same day another Israeli soldier was abducted by Hamas fighters near Tel-Aviv, who subsequently demanded that Israel release the detained Hamas leader, Sheikh Ahmad Yassin, and other Palestinian prisoners in exchange for his life. Despite Palestinian action to detain some 300 Hamas members in the Gaza Strip, the kidnapped soldier was killed in the West Bank in mid-October. Shortly afterwards an attack by a Hamas suicide bomber in Tel-Aviv, in which 22 people died, prompted Israel to close its borders with the West Bank and the Gaza Strip for an indefinite period.

On 26 October 1994 Israel and Jordan signed a formal peace treaty, defining the border between the two countries and providing for a normalization of relations. The peace treaty was denounced by the Syrian Government, all elements of Palestinian opinion, and by some Islamists in Jordan.

In November 1994 a member of Islamic Jihad was killed in a car bomb attack in Gaza. The attack was blamed on the Israeli security forces by many Palestinians opposed to the Declaration of Principles. Three Israeli soldiers were subsequently killed in a suicide bombing near a Jewish settlement in the Gaza Strip; Islamic Jihad claimed responsibility for the attack. It became clear in December 1994 that Israel's concern about security would continue to delay the redeployment of its armed forces in the West Bank and the holding of Palestinian elections, as Rabin stated that the elections would either have to take place in the continued presence of Israeli armed forces, or be postponed for a year. At the end of the month it was reported that there had been a 10% increase in the number of Jewish settlers in the occupied West Bank during 1994. In January 1995 a suicide bombing (responsibility for which was claimed by Islamic Jihad) at Beit Lid, in which 21 Israeli soldiers and civilians died, and more than 60 were injured, seriously jeopardized the peace process. The Government again closed Israel's borders with the Gaza Strip and the West Bank, and postponed the planned release of some 5,500 Palestinian prisoners. In early February an emergency meeting of the leaders of Egypt, Israel, Jordan and the PLO was convened in Cairo; a communiqué issued at the conclusion of the meeting condemned acts of terror and violence, and expressed support for the Declaration of Principles and the wider peace process. US President Clinton subsequently held a meeting with the Israeli and the Egyptian Ministers of Foreign Affairs and the Palestinian (PNA) Minister of Planning and Economic Co-operation in Washington, DC. After the meeting, Peres was reported to have stated that any further expansion of Palestinian self-rule in the West Bank was conditional upon real progress by the PNA in suppressing terrorism. On 9 February, meanwhile, Israeli armed forces completed their withdrawal from Jordanian territories, in accordance with the peace treaty concluded by the two countries in October 1994.

In March 1995 Yasser Arafat and Shimon Peres agreed, at talks in Gaza, to adopt 1 July as the date by which an agreement on the expansion of Palestinian self-rule in the West Bank should be concluded. Later in March it was announced that Israel and Syria had agreed to resume peace negotiations for the first time since February 1994. In May Syria and Israel were reported to have concluded a 'framework understanding on security arrangements', intended to facilitate negotiations on security issues. Peres subsequently indicated that Israel had proposed that its forces should withdraw from the Golan Heights over a four-year period; Syria, however, had insisted that the withdrawal be effected over 18 months.

In April 1995 seven Israeli soldiers were killed, and more than 50 people injured, in two suicide bomb attacks in the Gaza Strip. The Palestinian police force was subsequently reported to have arrested as many as 300 members of Hamas and Islamic Jihad, which claimed responsibility for the attacks.

The Likud party appeared to suffer a serious division in June 1995, when one of its most prominent members, David Levy (who had opposed Netanyahu's election as party leader in 1993), announced that he was to form a new party to contest the legislative elections scheduled for 1996. The division was reportedly the result of Levy's opposition to new selection procedures within Likud for general election candidates. Levy's new political movement, Gesher, was formally inaugurated in mid-June, although Levy himself remained a member of Likud.

Despite intensive negotiations, it proved impossible to conclude an agreement on the expansion of Palestinian self-rule in the West Bank by the target date of 1 July 1995. The principal obstacles to an agreement were the question of precisely to where Israeli troops in the West Bank would redeploy; and the exact nature of security arrangements for the approximately 130,000 Jewish settlers who were to remain in the West Bank. In August Hamas claimed responsibility for a suicide bomb attack on a bus in Jerusalem, which killed six people. On 28 September 1995 the Israeli-Palestinian Interim Agreement on the West Bank and the Gaza Strip was finally signed by Israel and the PLO. Its main provisions were the withdrawal of Israeli armed forces from a further six West Bank towns (Nablus, Ramallah, Jenin, Tulkaram, Kakilya and Bethlehem), and a partial redeployment away from the town of Hebron; national Palestinian legislative elections to an 82-member Palestinian Council, and for a Palestinian Executive President; and the release, in three phases, of Palestinians detained by Israel. In anticipation of a violent reaction against the Interim Agreement by so-called 'rejectionist' groups within the West Bank and the Gaza Strip, Israel immediately announced the closure of its borders with the Gaza Strip and the West Bank. Meanwhile, right-wing elements within Israel denounced the agreement, believing that too much had been conceded to the Palestinians.

On 4 November 1995 Itzhak Rabin was assassinated in Tel-Aviv by a Jewish law student opposed to the peace process, in particular the Israeli withdrawal from the West Bank. The assassination caused a further marginalization of those on the extreme right wing of Israeli politics who had advocated violence as a means of halting the implementation of the Declaration of Principles, and provoked criticism of Likud, which, it was widely felt, had not sufficiently distanced itself from such extremist elements. Following the assassination, the Minister of Foreign Affairs, Shimon Peres, became acting Prime Minister, and in mid-November, with the agreement of the opposition Likud, Peres was invited to form a new government. The members of the outgoing administration—Labour, Meretz and Yi'ud—subsequently signed a new coalition agreement, and a new Cabinet was formally approved by the Knesset in late November. In February Peres announced that elections to the Knesset and—for the first time—the direct election of the Prime Minister would take place in May 1996.

In spite of the assassination, Israeli armed forces completed their withdrawal from the West Bank town of Jenin on 13 November 1995, and during December they withdrew from Tulkaram, Nablus, Kakilya, Bethlehem and Ramallah. With regard to Hebron, Israel and the PNA signed an agreement transferring jurisdiction in some 17 areas of civilian affairs from

Israel to the PNA. At talks with Arafat at Erez in December, Peres confirmed that Israel would release some 1,000 Palestinian prisoners before the Palestinian legislative and presidential elections scheduled for January 1996.

Peace negotiations between Israel and Syria resumed in December 1995 in Maryland, USA, followed by a second round in January 1996. Also in January King Hussein made a public visit to Tel-Aviv, during the course of which Israel and Jordan signed a number of agreements relating to the normalization of economic and cultural relations.

Palestinian legislative and presidential elections were held in late January 1996, leading in principle to the final stage of the peace process, when Palestinian and Israeli negotiators would address such issues as Jerusalem, the rights of Palestinian refugees, the status of Jewish settlements in the Palestinian Autonomous Areas, and the extent of that autonomy. In February and March, however, suicide bomb attacks in Jerusalem, Ashkelon and Tel-Aviv caused the death of more than 50 Israelis and led to a further suspension of talks. Israel again ordered the indefinite closure of the borders of the West Bank and the Gaza Strip, and demanded that the Palestinian authorities suppress the activities of Hamas and Islamic Jihad in the areas under their control. A hitherto unknown group, the 'Yahya Ayyash Units', claimed responsibility for the attacks, to avenge the assassination—allegedly by Israeli agents—of Ayyash, a leading member of Hamas, in January 1996. Yasser Arafat, now the elected Palestinian President, condemned the bombings, and in late February more than 200 members of Hamas were reported to have been detained by the Palestinian security forces. The bomb attacks led Israel to impose even more stringent security measures, notably asserting the right of its armed forces to enter the areas under Palestinian jurisdiction when Israeli security was at stake. Furthermore, an agreement to redeploy troops from Hebron by 20 March was rescinded. For their part, the Palestinian authorities were reported to have held emergency talks with the leadership of Hamas and Islamic Jihad, and to have outlawed the armed wings of these and other, unspecified Palestinian paramilitary groups.

The suicide bomb attacks also affected the talks taking place between Israeli and Syrian representatives in the USA, and in March the Israeli negotiators returned to Israel. Syria and Lebanon both declined an invitation to attend a summit meeting, held in the Egyptian town of Sharm esh-Sheikh in mid-March, at which some 27 Heads of State expressed their support for the Middle East peace process and pledged to redouble their efforts to combat terrorism. In April 1996 Israel and Turkey signed a number of military co-operation agreements, one of which provided for the establishment of a joint organization for research and strategy. Syria condemned the agreement as a threat to its own security and to that of all Arab and Islamic countries.

In April 1996 Israeli armed forces began a sustained campaign of intense air and artillery attacks on alleged Hezbollah positions in southern Lebanon and the southern suburbs of Beirut. The declared aim of the Israeli operation (code-named 'Grapes of Wrath') was to achieve the complete cessation of rocket attacks by Hezbollah on settlements in northern Israel. Some 400,000 Lebanese were displaced northwards, after the Israeli military authorities warned that they would be endangered by the offensive against Hezbollah. Moreover, the shelling by Israeli forces of a base of the UN peace-keeping force at Qana resulted in the death of more than 100 Lebanese civilians who had been sheltering there, and of four members of the UN force. A cease-fire 'understanding' took effect in late April 1996, after more than two weeks of hostilities. This was effectively a compromise confining the conflict to the area of the security zone in southern Lebanon, recognizing both Hezbollah's right to resist Israeli occupation and Israel's right to self-defence; the 'understanding' also envisaged the establishment of an Israel-Lebanon Monitoring Group (ILMG), comprising Israel, Lebanon, Syria, France and the USA, to supervise the cease-fire. A UN report on the killing of Lebanese civilians at Qana, presented to the Security Council in May, concluded that it was 'unlikely' that the shelling of the UN base had, as claimed by Israel, been the result of 'gross technical and/or procedural errors'.

Israel welcomed the decision of the Palestinian National Council in late April 1996 to amend the Palestinian National Charter (or PLO Covenant), removing all clauses demanding the destruction of Israel: the Israeli Government had demanded that the Covenant be amended by 7 May 1996 as a precondition for participation in the final stage of peace negotiations with the PLO.

In the months following the assassination of Itzhak Rabin the victory of the Labour Party and Shimon Peres in the legislative and prime ministerial elections scheduled for 29 May 1996 was generally expected, even after the suicide bomb attacks of February and March led to increased public support for Likud and other right-wing political groups. In the event, no party gained an outright majority of the 120 seats in the elections to the Knesset, but the Likud leader, Binyamin Netanyahu, achieved a marginal victory over Peres in the direct election of the Prime Minister. (The Likud and Labour leaders were the only candidates.) Prior to the legislative election a formal alliance between Likud, the Tzomet Party and the newly-formed Gesher had been announced. This alliance secured 32 seats, and Labour 34. The success of the ultra-orthodox Shas and the National Religious Party (NRP), with 10 seats and nine, respectively, was the key factor in determining that the new Government would be formed by Likud. Some 79.7% of the 3.9m.-strong Israeli electorate were reported to have participated in the elections.

In June 1996 Netanyahu signed a series of agreements between the Likud alliance and Shas, the NRP, Israel B'Aliyah, United Torah Judaism and the Third Way, to form a coalition which would command the support of 66 deputies in the Knesset. Moledet also agreed to support the Government, but did not formally enter the coalition. On 18 June the new Government received the approval of the Knesset. Its statement of policy excluded the possibility of granting Palestinian statehood or, with regard to Syria, of relinquishing *de facto* sovereignty of the occupied Golan Heights.

The election of a Likud-led Government appeared to have grave implications for the future of the Israeli-Palestinian peace negotiations: during the election campaign the Likud alliance had explicitly stated that it would never agree to the establishment of a Palestinian state, and even seemed to indicate that it was prepared to renege on some aspects of agreements already concluded with the Palestinians. In late May 1996 the Palestinian Council of Ministers (formed after the Palestinian legislative elections in January) and the Executive Committee of the PLO held a joint meeting in Gaza, at which they urged the incoming Israeli Government to implement all previous agreements and to commence the final stage of the peace negotiations. In late June, in response to Likud's electoral victory, a summit meeting of the leaders of all Arab countries (with the exception of Iraq) was convened in Cairo. The meeting's final communiqué reiterated Israel's withdrawal from all occupied territories (including East Jerusalem) as a basic requirement for a comprehensive Middle East peace settlement.

In June 1996 it was reported that Netanyahu had postponed further discussion of the withdrawal of Israeli armed forces from the West Bank town of Hebron—where they remained in order to provide security for some 400 Jewish settlers. Furthermore, Netanyahu made clearer his refusal to meet the Palestinian President. In July the likely stance of the new Government was underlined by the incorporation into the Cabinet, as Minister of Infrastructure, of Ariel Sharon—who had played a leading role in the creation and expansion of Jewish settlements in the West Bank. The PNA organized a short general strike at the end of the month, in protest at the refusal of the Israeli authorities to allow Palestinian Muslims to participate in Friday prayers at the Al-Aqsa mosque in Jerusalem, and also at a decision by the Israeli Government to expand existing Jewish settlements in the West Bank. On 4 September, none the less, Netanyahu and Arafat did meet, for the first time, at the Erez crossing point, and they confirmed their commitment to the implementation of the Interim Agreement.

In September 1996 it was announced that the Israeli Ministry of Defence had approved plans to construct some 1,800 new housing units at existing Jewish settlements in the West Bank. By late September many observers agreed that the new Israeli Government had effectively halted the peace process by either abandoning or postponing many of the commitments which it had inherited from its predecessor. Violent confrontations began between Palestinian security forces, Palestinian civilians and the Israeli armed forces, in which at least 50 Palestinians and 18 Israelis were killed and hundreds wounded. The West Bank town of Ramallah was the initial point of confrontation, and the direct cause of the disturbances was attributed to the decision of the Israeli Government to open the north end of the Hasmonean tunnel which ran beneath the Al-Aqsa mosque in East Jerusalem. Most observers, however, viewed the violence as the inevitable culmination of Palestinian frustration at the Israeli Government's failure to implement agreements it had signed with the PNA, and there were fears of a new Palestinian *intifada*. The Israeli military authorities declared a state of emergency in the Gaza Strip and the West Bank, and threatened military intervention to suppress the disturbances. A special session of the UN Security Council was convened, and intense international diplomacy led to the holding of a crisis summit meeting in Washington, DC, hosted by US President Clinton and attended by Binyamin Netanyahu, Yasser Arafat and King Hussein of Jordan. The meeting reportedly achieved nothing, but in early October it was announced that, following further US mediation, Israel had agreed to resume negotiations on the partial withdrawal of its armed forces from Hebron. Netanyahu subsequently stated that once the question of the redeployment from Hebron had been settled Israel would reopen its borders with the West Bank and the Gaza Strip—which had remained closed since February—and move quickly towards seeking a final settlement with the Palestinians.

In January 1997 Israel and the PNA finally concluded an agreement on the withdrawal of Israeli armed forces from Hebron. The principal terms of the US-brokered agreement were that Israeli armed forces should withdraw from 80% of the town of Hebron within 10 days, and that the first of three subsequent redeployments from the West Bank should take place six weeks after the signing of the agreement, and the remaining two by August 1998. With regard to security arrangements for Jewish settlers in central Hebron, Palestinian police patrols would be armed only with pistols in areas close to the Jewish enclaves, while joint Israeli-Palestinian patrols would secure the heights above the enclaves. The 'final status' negotiations on borders, the Jerusalem issue, Jewish settlements and Palestinian refugees were to commence within two months of the signing of the agreement on Hebron. As guarantor of the agreement, the USA undertook to obtain the release of some Palestinian prisoners, and to ensure that Israel continued to engage in negotiations for a Palestinian airport in the Gaza Strip and on safe passage between the West Bank and the Gaza Strip for Palestinians. The USA also undertook to ensure that the Palestinians would continue to combat terrorism, complete the revision of the Palestinian National Charter and consider Israeli requests to extradite Palestinians suspected of involvement in attacks in Israel.

The conclusion of the agreement regarding Hebron marked the first significant progress in the peace process since Netanyahu's election as Prime Minister in May 1996. Negotiations with Syria, however, remained suspended. In late January 1997 Netanyahu urged Syria to exert pressure on Hezbollah to cease hostilities in Israel's self-declared security zone in southern Lebanon. In February, however, he denied speculation that Israel was considering a unilateral withdrawal from the security zone, which had intensified as a result of the deaths, in a helicopter accident, of 73 Israeli soldiers travelling to southern Lebanon.

In February 1997 the progress achieved through the agreement on Hebron was severely undermined when Israel announced that it was to proceed with the construction of 6,500 housing units at Har Homa in East Jerusalem. Tensions escalated during March, after Israel unilaterally decided to withdraw its armed forces from only 9% of the West Bank. Yasser Arafat denounced the decision and King Hussein accused Netanyahu of intentionally destroying the peace process. Increasing anti-Israeli sentiment reportedly motivated a Jordanian soldier to murder seven Israeli schoolgirls in Nayarim, an enclave between Israel and Jordan. Israeli intransigence over the Har Homa settlement prompted Palestinians to abandon the 'final status' talks, scheduled to begin on 17 March, and on the following day construction at the site began. Riots among Palestinians erupted immediately, and shortly afterwards Hamas carried out a bomb attack in Tel-Aviv, killing four and wounding more than 60 people. In response, the Israeli Government once again ordered the closure of Israel's borders with the West Bank and the Gaza Strip. In late March the Arab League voted to resume its economic boycott of Israel, suspend moves to establish diplomatic relations, and withdraw from multilateral peace talks. (Jordan, the PNA and Egypt were excluded from the resolution, owing to their binding bilateral agreements with Israel.)

In early April 1997 Netanyahu met with US President Clinton in Washington, DC, but reiterated that he would not suspend the programme of construction. Rioting erupted in Hebron the following day, after a Palestinian was allegedly murdered by Jewish settlers. The disturbances subsided at the end of the month, and the borders with the Gaza Strip and the West Bank were reopened. During May the USA's chief peace process negotiator, Dennis Ross, failed to achieve any progress towards a resumption of peace talks despite a nine-day mediation attempt.

In April 1997, meanwhile, police investigators recommended that the Prime Minister be charged with fraud and breach of trust for his appointment, in January, of Roni Bar-On as Attorney-General. Bar-On had resigned within 12 hours of his appointment after it was alleged that his promotion had been made in order to facilitate a plea bargain for Aryeh Der'i, leader of the Shas party, who was the subject of separate corruption charges. It was suggested that, in return for Bar-On's appointment, Der'i had pledged the support of his party for the Cabinet's decision regarding the withdrawal from Hebron. In May Der'i was indicted for obstruction of justice, but charges against Netanyahu were dismissed owing to lack of evidence. However, the Prime Minister's authority was further undermined by the subsequent resignation of the Minister of Finance, Dan Meridor. Yaacov Ne'eman was appointed Minister of Finance in July. In June Ehud Barak, a former government minister and army chief of staff, was elected to replace Peres as Labour Party Chairman.

In June 1997 the US House of Representatives voted in favour of recognizing Jerusalem as the undivided capital of Israel and of transferring the US embassy there, from Tel-Aviv. The decision coincided with violent clashes between Palestinian civilians and Israeli troops in both Gaza and Hebron. Meanwhile, Yasser Arafat, fearing Israeli reoccupation of Hebron, assigned 200 police-officers to patrol the area.

In July 1997 a series of meetings between US Under-Secretary of State, Thomas Pickering, and Israeli and Palestinian officials secured an agreement to resume peace talks the following month. At the end of July, however, on the eve of a visit to Israel by Dennis Ross, two Hamas suicide bombers killed 14 civilians and wounded more than 150 others in Jerusalem. Ross cancelled his visit temporarily and Israel suspended payment of tax revenues to the PNA and closed off the Gaza Strip and the West Bank. Netanyahu insisted that the restrictions would remain until the Palestinians demonstrated a commitment to combat terrorism. In August Yasser Arafat convened a forum of Palestinian groups, during which he publicly embraced Hamas leaders and urged them, together with Islamic Jihad, to unite with the Palestinian people against Israeli policies. Israel reopened borders with the West Bank and the Gaza Strip in early September, but restrictions were reimposed three days later after suicide bombings in West Jerusalem killed eight people and wounded more than 150 others. The security crisis cast doubt on the viability of a planned visit by Madeleine Albright, the US Secretary of State, who was to tour the Middle East in mid-September. However, Albright's visit was positively received; Israel released further Palestinian assets (one-third of tax revenues owed to the PNA had been released in mid-August), while the Palestinians announced the closure of 17 institutions affiliated to Hamas. In early October, Netanyahu and Arafat met for the first time in eight months. Israel announced plans to release further dues to the PNA and to reopen the sealed borders. However, Israel failed to participate in a second round of negotiations, scheduled for mid-October, to accelerate the 'final status' talks, and Netanyahu stated that further redeployments would not take place until Palestinians made further efforts to combat terrorism.

Meanwhile, relations between Jordan and Israel deteriorated in September 1997, after members of the Israeli intelligence force, Mossad, attempted to assassinate a Hamas leader, Khalid Meshaal in Amman. In an attempt to preserve relations, intensive diplomatic negotiations took place between Netanyahu, Crown Prince Hassan of Jordan and US officials. Several agreements regarding the release of prisoners ensued: in early October Israel released one of the founders of Hamas, Sheikh Ahmad Yassin, in return for the release by Jordan of two Mossad agents arrested in connection with the attack on Meshaal. A further 12 Mossad agents were expelled by the Jordanian authorities following the release of 23 Jordanian and 50 Palestinian prisoners by Israel.

Bilateral negotiations between Israel and Palestinian negotiators resumed in November 1997. Israel offered to decelerate its construction of Jewish settlements in return for Palestinian approval of a plan to delay further redeployments of Israeli troops from the West Bank. At the same time, the Israeli Government announced plans to build 900 new housing units in the area. This virtual stalemate in the peace process prompted several Arab states to boycott the Middle East and North Africa economic conference, held in Doha, Qatar, in mid-November, which an Israeli delegation was scheduled to attend. Separate peace talks involving Albright, Netanyahu and Arafat were inconclusive. At the end of November the Israeli Cabinet agreed in principle to a partial withdrawal from the West Bank, but specified neither its timing nor its scale. Conflicting opinions within the Cabinet meant that Netanyahu failed to produce a conclusive redeployment plan to present at talks with Albright in Paris in December. Furthermore, the Israeli Government had recently prevented PNA officials from conducting a census in East Jerusalem. Israeli and Palestinian officials none the less demonstrated their commitment to peace by signing a security memorandum.

Strong opposition within the coalition Government to proposals by Netanyahu for a reform of the system for the selection of Likud candidates for the Knesset obliged the Prime Minister, in November 1997, to retract the plan. Evidence of further divisions within the coalition emerged at the end of December prior to the 1998 budget vote, effectively a demonstration of confidence in the Prime Minister. In order to muster the necessary support, Netanyahu granted concessions to various parties, in particular to right-wing members of the coalition. Opposition parties claimed that the Prime Minister had bribed coalition members in order to remain in power. In early January 1998 David Levy, the leader of Gesher, withdrew from the Government, citing dissatisfaction with the budget and with the slow rate of progress in the peace talks. Gesher's departure reduced Netanyahu's majority to only two votes, although the budget secured the approval of the Knesset. In mid-January Netanyahu survived a vote of 'no-confidence'. Nevertheless, the Prime Minister remained in a precarious position, since several parties threatened to leave the Government if their demands for troop redeployment were not met. Since right-wing members opposed redeployment and moderates advocated a withdrawal, Netanyahu was left with the challenge of satisfying all members of the coalition in order to remain in power, while, at the same time, fulfilling Israel's obligations to the Declaration of Principles.

Meanwhile, Netanyahu announced that he would not make any further decisions regarding the peace process until the Palestinians had demonstrated further efforts to combat terrorism, reduced their security forces from 40,000 to 24,000 and amended their National Charter to recognize Israel's right to exist. The announcement was condemned by the PNA, which claimed that it had taken action to reduce terrorist activity. Later in January 1998 again Netanyahu failed to present a plan of redeployment in talks with President Clinton in Washington, DC. The Israeli Prime Minister did express interest in a US proposal to withdraw troops from at least 10% of the land in several stages, but this was decisively rejected by Arafat. In response to the continuing stalemate, Madeleine Albright reportedly informed Netanyahu in early February that the USA was considering abandoning its mediation attempts unless Israel adopted a more conciliatory attitude towards the peace process.

Renewed hostilities erupted in northern Israel in August 1997 after Hezbollah launched a rocket attack on civilians in Kiryat Shmona. The attack, made in retaliation for attacks by Israeli commandos in which five Hezbollah members were killed, prompted further air strikes by Israel in southern Lebanon. Violence escalated, and in mid-August the SLA shelled the Lebanese port of Sidon, killing at least six and wounding more than 30 civilians. Israeli claims that the attack was the sole initiative of the SLA were rejected by Hezbollah. In early September 12 Israeli marines, who were allegedly planning to assassinate Shi'ite leaders, were killed in the village of Insariyeh, south of Sidon, reportedly by the joint forces of Hezbollah and Amal, and Lebanese soldiers. The death toll was the highest to occur in a single incident since 1985, when Israeli troops withdrew to the buffer zone, and domestic pressure on the Israeli Government to withdraw from southern Lebanon increased.

During February 1998 several meetings between Israeli and Palestinian officials failed to break the deadlock over further redeployments of Israeli troops from the West Bank. At the end of the month Arafat rejected Netanyahu's appeals for a peace summit, stating that he would hold talks only after Israel had agreed to further redeployment and had fully implemented existing agreements. Progress had been further frustrated in early February, when the Ministry of the Interior approved plans to construct a new, 132-home Jewish settlement in East Jerusalem.

In late February 1998 Itzhak Levi, who had recently become leader of the NRP, was appointed Minister of Education and Culture, and of Religious Affairs. Shaul Yahalom replaced Levi as Minister of Transport and Energy. On 4 March the Knesset re-elected Ezer Weizman to a second presidential term; Weizman was challenged by the Likud candidate, Shaul Amor, who had been endorsed by Netanyahu.

In mid-March 1998 the British Secretary of State for Foreign and Commonwealth Affairs, Robin Cook, toured the Middle East in order to promote a European Union (EU) peace initiative. Cook's visit to Israel became highly controversial when he announced his intention of visiting, with a Palestinian official, the Har Homa settlement (the construction of which had brought about the collapse of the peace process in March 1997). In late March 1998 the UN Secretary-General, Kofi Annan, addressed the Knesset, urging Israel to end 'provocative acts' towards the Palestinians, including the building of new Jewish settlements. Meanwhile, the US envoy, Dennis Ross, visited the region, briefing Netanyahu, Arafat and President Mubarak of Egypt on a US peace proposal whereby Israel would redeploy from 13.1% of the West Bank over a 12-week period, in exchange for specific security guarantees from the Palestinians. The proposal failed to revive the peace process, however, with Israel reportedly agreeing only to a phased redeployment from 9% of the territory. Meanwhile, violence re-erupted on the West Bank, following an incident earlier in March in which three Palestinians were killed by Israeli soldiers near Hebron. Moreover, the assassination—allegedly by the Israeli secret services—of a senior member of Hamas in late March precipitated widespread protests among Palestinians. Netanyahu warned that the risk of reprisal attacks on Israeli citizens would prevent further redeployments of Israeli troops from the Occupied Territories. The release from detention in Israel, after agreeing to renounce terrorism and violence, of two senior members of the Popular Front for the Liberation of Palestine (PFLP) in mid-April prompted speculation that a deal had been struck between the PFLP and Israel's security service, Shin Bet. One of the released men had been held, without trial, since 1992.

In late April 1998 Netanyahu and President Mubarak held their first meeting since May 1997, in Cairo. Mubarak reportedly advised Netanyahu to 'respond positively' to the US peace initiative. However, the Israeli Prime Minister rejected the proposal, which was publicly accepted by Arafat the following day. In early May 1998 US Secretary of State Albright held separate rounds of talks with Netanyahu and Arafat in London, United Kingdom, with the aim of reviving negotiations on redeployments. The talks were inconclusive, and further meetings held in Washington, DC, in mid-May similarly failed to achieve a breakthrough. Meanwhile, celebrations to commemorate the 50th anniversary of the founding of the State of Israel provoked widespread rioting in the Occupied Territories.

In May 1998 the UN Committee Against Torture ruled for a second successive year that Shin Bet's interrogation methods were in contravention of the 1984 UN Convention against Torture and Other Cruel, Inhuman or Degrading Treatment or Punishment (which Israel had ratified in 1991). Shortly afterwards proceedings began at the Israeli Supreme Court in an unprecedented appeal case, brought by Palestinian detainees and two human rights groups, questioning the legality of Shin Bet's use of torture.

Details of the US peace plan were published in the Israeli newspaper Ha'aretz in early June 1998. Following reports in mid-June that Netanyahu was seriously accepting the proposals, several Jewish settler groups threatened a campaign of civil disobedience in protest at any further redeployments from the West Bank. It became apparent, however, that Netanyahu was under increasing pressure to accept the US initiative. Public opinion was reportedly shifting in favour of further redeployments, there was speculation of a possible referendum on the issue, and in late June President Weizman angered Netanyahu by publicly demanding the dissolution of the Knesset and early elections so that Israelis might choose the future direction of peace negotiations. Meanwhile, further controversy arose when the Cabinet approved Netanyahu's draft plan to extend the municipal boundaries of Jerusalem to incorporate seven Jewish settlements in the West Bank. Under the plan, a 'Greater Jerusalem' would cover six times the current area of the city. Arab leaders, including King Hussein, President

Mubarak and Arafat, accused Netanyahu of seeking formally to annex parts of the West Bank, and the UN Security Council called on Israel to abandon the proposals. Arafat stated that the peace process was 'completely deadlocked', and that Palestinians could make no further concessions beyond those outlined in the US plan. Relations between Israel and the EU also deteriorated in June, after the European Commission instructed Israel to end the practice of labelling goods produced in Jewish settlements in the Occupied Territories as 'made in Israel'.

During July 1998 Netanyahu was the subject of allegations, made by a Labour Knesset member, that he had intervened in the trial of Nahum Manbar, an Israeli business executive who had in June been convicted of supplying toxic and chemical weapons material to Iran. Netanyahu denied claims that he had directly contacted the trial judge to demand a harsh sentence for Manbar, who in mid-July was sentenced to 16 years' imprisonment. Shortly afterwards the Ministry of Justice initiated an investigation into the affair. Netanyahu's domestic political standing was further undermined in late July, when the Labour Party secured a preliminary vote seeking the dissolution of the Knesset and early elections. Some members of Netanyahu's coalition supported the motion, citing disillusionment with the stalled peace process.

The first substantive senior-level meetings for several months between Israeli and Palestinian negotiators took place in Jerusalem in mid-July 1998. The negotiations failed when Arafat withdrew his delegates in protest at what he described as Israel's 'obscure formulations' on the US peace plan. Israel had reportedly offered a compromise package, proposing redeployment from 10%, and partial redeployment from 3%, of the West Bank. By the end of August 1998 there were indications that the so-called '10+3' compromise plan for redeployment might lead to a revival of peace negotiations. However, the assassination of a settler rabbi in Hebron increased tensions on the West Bank; the Israeli Government sealed off the town for several days, while settlers threatened to avenge the killing. In late August a bomb attack in the centre of Tel-Aviv, believed to have been perpetrated by Hamas, injured some 18 people. In mid-September Israel closed its borders with the West Bank and Gaza, following warnings of imminent terrorist attacks in retaliation for the fatal shooting, by Israeli troops, of two leading Hamas members.

Meanwhile, in early September 1998 Israel's public sector was paralysed by a four-day general strike involving members of the powerful Histadrut workers' federation, after Netanyahu announced a 'freeze' on senior officials' salaries. The strike ended when a compromise was reached between the Ministry of Finance and Histradrut.

A report published by a prominent human rights organization, Amnesty International, in early September 1998 condemned both the Israeli and Palestinian authorities for alleged widespread human rights abuses. The report's demands included an end to imprisonment without trial, to judicial killings and to the legalized torture of detainees.

Addressing the UN General Assembly in New York in September 1998, Netanyahu reiterated warnings that the unilateral declaration of an independent Palestinian state by Arafat would fundamentally violate the Oslo accords and bring about the collapse of the peace process. (Arafat reasserted throughout 1998 his right to declare a Palestinian state on 4 May 1999, the expiry date of the interim stage defined in Oslo.) A US-mediated meeting between Netanyahu and Arafat held at the end of September in Washington, DC, resulted in an agreement by the two leaders to attend a peace summit in mid-October, with the aim of finalizing agreement on further Israeli redeployments.

In early October 1998 Ariel Sharon was redesignated Minister of Foreign Affairs and National Infrastructure. (The foreign affairs portfolio had been assumed by Netanyahu following David Levy's resignation in January.) Sharon's promotion was widely regarded as an attempt by Netanyahu to secure the support of right-wing nationalists and settler groups, since he was known to be opposed to redeployment from a further 13% of the West Bank.

On 23 October 1998, after nine days of intensive talks with President Clinton at the Wye Plantation, Maryland, USA, Netanyahu and Arafat finally signed an agreement that effectively outlined a three-month timetable for the implementation of the 1995 Interim Agreement and signalled the start of 'final status' talks, which were due to have begun in May 1996. The signing of the Wye River Memorandum broke a 19-month stalemate in the Israeli-Palestinian track of the Middle East peace process; it was achieved despite a Palestinian grenade attack in Beersheba, in which at least 60 people were injured, which had threatened to bring about the collapse of negotiations. However, with the mediation of Clinton and King Hussein of Jordan, Israel agreed to redeploy its troops from 13.1% of the West Bank, while the Palestinians agreed to intensify measures to prevent terrorism and to rewrite the Palestinian National Charter. On Netanyahu's return to Israel, Jewish settlers held demonstrations in the West Bank to protest against the signing of the Wye Memorandum. In an effort to reassure settler groups, Netanyahu gave assurances that the construction of 1,025 new homes at the Har Homa settlement would proceed.

On 11 November 1998, after the postponement of four scheduled meetings (due to a bombing by Islamic Jihad in Jerusalem and Israeli fears of further terrorist attacks), the Israeli Cabinet approved the land-for-security deal agreed at Wye Plantation by a majority of eight votes to four. Netanyahu subsequently reiterated that a number of conditions would first have to be met by the Palestinians (primarily an annulment of clauses in the Palestinian National Charter demanding Israel's destruction), and threatened effective Israeli annexation of areas of the West Bank if a Palestinian state were to be declared on 4 May 1999. In mid-November 1998 Arafat retracted a previous warning that the PLO would renew its armed struggle against Israel. On 17 November the Knesset ratified the Wye Memorandum by 75 votes to 19. Three days later the Israeli Government implemented the first stage of renewed redeployment from the West Bank, also releasing 250 Palestinian prisoners and signing a protocol allowing for the opening of an international airport at Gaza.

During December 1998 it became increasingly evident that divisions within Netanyahu's coalition over implementation of the Wye Memorandum were making government untenable. Attempts to rescue the coalition (and thereby avoid an early general election) by offering to reappoint David Levy to the Government were frustrated when the Gesher leader refused the terms proposed by Netanyahu. Moreover, in mid-December Yaacov Ne'eman, the Minister of Finance, announced his resignation, stating that Netanyahu's coalition was no longer functioning. Shortly afterwards the Knesset voted to hold elections to the legislature and premiership in the spring of 1999; a general election was subsequently scheduled for 17 May 1999. The ensuing election campaign further undermined the political stability of Israel, prompting the emergence of several new political parties and the realignment of political allegiances. Netanyahu's leadership was challenged by senior members of Likud, including Binyamin Begin, who left to form the New Herut party. In mid-January 1999 Netanyahu appointed Shaul Amor as Minister without Portfolio, with responsibility for social and economic issues. Later in January Netanyahu dismissed Itzhak Mordechai as Minister of Defence, amid speculation that the latter intended to leave Likud; Moshe Arens was subsequently appointed Minister of Defence, while Mordechai launched the new Centre Party, along with other former allies of Netanyahu. In late February Meir Shitrit, Likud's Knesset leader, became Minister of Finance.

Meanwhile, unrest in the West Bank and Gaza increased prior to a visit by President Clinton in mid-December 1998. Palestinians demonstrated in support of almost 700 of their prisoners who began a nine-day hunger strike to protest against Israel's failure to honour commitments agreed at Wye Plantation to release Palestinians detained on political charges. On 14 December Clinton attended a meeting of the PLO's Palestine National Council (PNC), at which the removal from the Palestinian National Charter of all clauses seeking Israel's destruction was reaffirmed. At a meeting between Clinton, Arafat and Netanyahu at the Erez checkpoint during Clinton's visit, Netanyahu reiterated accusations that the Palestinians had not adequately addressed their security commitments and announced that he would not release Palestinian prisoners considered to have 'blood on their hands'. Netanyahu also demanded that Arafat renounce his intention to declare Palestinian statehood in May 1999. Arafat, for his part, reasserted demands for a 'freeze' on the construction of Jewish settlements in disputed territory. Following the meeting Netanyahu announced that the second phase of Israeli troop deployment envisaged by the Wye Memorandum, scheduled for 18 December, would not be undertaken. On 20 December the Knesset voted to suspend implementation of the Wye Memorandum, which effectively led to a suspension of the peace process.

In early January 1999 it was reported that US Secretary of State Albright would refuse to meet Ariel Sharon during a visit to the USA, owing to US frustration with Israel's 'freezing' of peace negotiations. However, the stalemate appeared likely to continue as violent clashes between Israelis and Palestinians again broke out on the West Bank. (In late December 1998 Arafat had freed the Hamas leader, Sheikh Ahmad Yassin, from house arrest, leading to further Israeli claims that agreed anti-terrorism measures were not being implemented.) The US Government threatened to withhold US $1,200m. promised to Israel to fund its redeployment in the West Bank unless it complied with the terms of the Wye Memorandum. President Clinton refused, for several months, to hold a private meeting with Netanyahu, while agreeing to meet Arafat in late March to discuss Arafat's threatened unilateral declaration of Palestinian statehood on 4 May. (The declaration was postponed on 29 April, following intense international pressure.) Meanwhile, relations between Israel and the EU deteriorated, owing to continuing disagreement over Likud's settlement expansion programme and the status of Jerusalem. In mid-March 1999 the EU strongly condemned Israeli instructions to foreign delegations not to visit the PLO's *de facto* headquarters in Jerusalem. Earlier in March the EU had provoked condemnation from Israeli officials by reaffirming that it regarded Jerusalem as a *corpus separatum* (in accordance with UN Resolution 181), which was outside Israeli sovereignty.

In mid-February 1999 some 200,000 ultra-Orthodox Jews demonstrated in Jerusalem over recent judicial rulings which, they claimed, would reduce the influence of Orthodoxy in many areas of civil law. Secular Jews held a counter-demonstration, prompting concerns that divisions between the two groups might erupt into open conflict. In mid-April the Chairman of the Shas party, Aryeh Der'i (a close associate of Netanyahu), was sentenced to four years' imprisonment, having been found guilty of bribery, fraud and breach of public trust; however, his sentence was suspended until after the outcome of an appeal, thus enabling Der'i to campaign in the general election. In mid-June, however, Der'i resigned as the Shas leader.

By mid-May 1999 Netanyahu and Ehud Barak were the only remaining candidates for the premiership, four others having withdrawn their candidacy. Following a decision by Itzhak Mordechai to transfer his support to Barak, who in March had established the 'One Israel' movement including Gesher and the moderate Meimad party, victory for the Labour leader seemed certain. On 17 May Ehud Barak was elected Prime Minister, gaining 56.1% of the total votes cast, compared with 43.9% for Netanyahu. In the elections to the Knesset, Barak's One Israel secured 26 seats, while Likud's strength declined from 32 seats to 19. Shas, meanwhile, increased its representation to 17 seats. The new Knesset contained an unprecedented 15 factions. Some 78.8% of Israel's 4.3m.-strong electorate were reported to have participated in the elections. Netanyahu subsequently resigned from both the Knesset and the Likud leadership, and in early September Ariel Sharon was elected as Likud's new Chairman.

Although Ehud Barak had received a clear mandate to form a government that would attempt to restart the stalled Middle East peace process, Israel's Prime Minister-Elect committed himself only to seek a formula for regional peace. In his victory speech on 18 May 1999, Barak stated that he would observe four 'security red lines' concerning negotiations with the Palestinians: Jerusalem would remain under Israeli sovereignty; there would be no return to the pre-1967 borders; most West Bank settlers would remain in settlements under Israeli sovereignty; and no 'foreign armies' would be based west of the river Jordan. On 6 July 1999 Barak presented his Cabinet to the Knesset. Following lengthy negotiations, he had formed a broad coalition, granting ministerial portfolios to the Centre Party, Shas, Meretz, Israel B'Aliyah and the NRP (talks with Likud having collapsed). However, Barak reserved the most influential posts for himself (he was also appointed Minister of Defence) and for loyalists such as David Levy, who became Minister of Foreign Affairs. Itzhak Mordechai was made one of three Deputy Prime Ministers and assigned the transport portfolio, while Shimon Peres became the Minister of Regional Co-operation. In early August legislation to expand the cabinet from 18 to 23 ministers was adopted. Barak, however, received criticism from women's groups and Arab Israelis, since the new Cabinet included only two women and no Arab Israelis (although one subsequently became Deputy Foreign Minister). In July the Speaker of the Palestinian Legislative Council became the first senior Palestinian official to be invited to address the Knesset.

Having formed his Cabinet, Prime Minister Barak held a series of summit meetings with Arab and European leaders, culminating in direct discussions with US President Clinton in mid-July 1999. The first direct talks between Yasser Arafat and Barak were held at the Erez checkpoint in Gaza on 11 July, during which both leaders reaffirmed their commitment to peace. By late July, however, relations had deteriorated, after Barak expressed the desire to combine the Israeli land withdrawals agreed under the terms of the Wye Memorandum with 'final status' negotiations. The Palestinians were angered by this proposed delay in implementing the Wye agreement. In early August Palestinian negotiators walked out of discussions after Barak accused them of refusing to compromise. However, in mid-August negotiations resumed after Israel agreed to withdraw its demand to postpone further land withdrawals.

On 4 September 1999, during a visit to the region by US Secretary of State Albright, Israel and the PNA signed the Sharm esh-Sheikh Memorandum (or Wye Two accords). The Memorandum outlined a revised timetable for implementation of the outstanding provisions of the original Wye Memorandum. However, the success of the deal was immediately threatened by two suicide bomb attacks in northern Israel. On 8 September the Knesset ratified the Wye Two accords by 54 votes to 23 (with two abstentions). On the following day, under the terms of the Wye agreement, Israel released some 200 Palestinian 'security' prisoners, and on 10 September a further 7% of the West Bank was transferred to Palestinian civilian control. A ceremony marking the launch of 'final status' negotiations between Israel and the Palestinians was held at the Erez checkpoint on 13 September, and a few days later it was reported that Barak and Arafat had held a secret meeting to discuss an agenda for such talks. Also in mid-September Israel signed an agreement with the USA to purchase 50 F-16 fighter aircraft.

In early September 1999 the Israeli Supreme Court ruled that the use of 'physical force' by Shin Bet during the interrogation of suspects was illegal. The ruling invalidated a 1987 decision which allowed the use of 'moderate physical pressure' against those accused of plotting terrorist attacks against Israel; it was praised by human rights groups, although certain members of the Cabinet claimed that it would hinder the prevention of terrorism. In mid-September 1999 former Prime Minister Netanyahu and his wife were questioned by police following allegations, published in the daily newspaper, *Yediot Aharanot*, that they had charged extensive private work on their residence to the Prime Minister's Office while Netanyahu was in power. Further allegations of the misuse of public funds emerged, and in late October police reportedly seized several official gifts from Netanyahu's home and offices. The Netanyahus were also accused of having sought to pervert the course of justice. In late September the Shas and Likud parties anounced that they were to co-ordinate their policies on issues of national importance; however, Shas denied rumours that the party was about to join the opposition. (An ongoing dispute between Shas and the Government over the amount of funds to be allocated for Shas' education system regularly threatened Barak's new coalition; however, the crisis appeared to have been resolved after the announcement of the 2000 budget in December.) Meanwhile, Eliyahu Yishai, the Minister of Labour and Social Affairs, replaced Aryeh Der'i as Chairman of Shas.

In the autumn of 1999 Prime Minister Barak faced severe criticism by left-wing groups and Palestinians over his Government's apparent intention to continue to approve the expansion of Jewish settlements in the West Bank. (Since coming to power, the new Government had issued tenders for some 2,600 new homes in such settlements.) Barak subsequently ruled that several of the 42 'outpost settlements' established in the West Bank under the Likud Government had been built illegally. After reaching a compromise with angry settler groups, 12 of the 'outposts' were dismantled in late October.

Israel released a further 151 Palestinian prisoners, under the terms of the Wye Two accords, on 15 October 1999. On 25 October a 'safe passage' for Palestinians travelling between Gaza and Hebron was finally opened, under the terms of the Wye Memorandum. In late October Mauritania became the third member of the Arab League (after Egypt and Jordan) to establish full diplomatic relations with Israel, generating protests in several Arab states. In early November Arafat, Barak and US President Clinton held talks in Oslo, Norway, after a ceremony to mark the fourth anniversary of Itzhak

Rabin's assassination. 'Final status' peace negotiations between Israel and the PNA commenced on 8 November 1999 in the West Bank city of Ramallah; further rounds of talks were held during November and December. Prior to the discussions, three bombs had exploded in the Israeli town of Netanya, wounding at least 33 people. Although no group claimed responsibility for the attack, it followed an alleged warning by the military wing of Hamas of an escalation of violence in protest at Israeli settlement policies. The redeployment of Israeli armed forces from a further 5% of the West Bank (due on 15 November) was delayed owing to a dispute over which areas were to be transferred. Relations between Israel and the Palestinians deteriorated again in early December, following an announcement that the Israeli Government had issued tenders for a further 500 Jewish homes to be built in the West Bank. However, Barak, probably bowing to US pressure, subsequently refused to authorize the construction. In late November the Israeli Government recommended legislation to phase out the country's 51-year-old state of emergency. In late December Barak and Arafat held discussions in Palestinian territory for the first time. At the end of the month Israel released some 26 Palestinian security prisoners as a goodwill gesture, while on 5 January 2000 Israeli troops withdrew from a further 5% of the West Bank. However, in mid-January Israel announced the postponement of a third redeployment agreed under the Wye Two accords until Barak had returned from talks with Syria in the USA. Meanwhile, 20 people were reportedly wounded in a bomb explosion in northern Israel, believed to have been carried out by Palestinian militants. In early February Palestinian negotiators suspended peace negotiations with Israel, following the decision by the Israeli Cabinet to withdraw its armed forces from a sparsely-populated 6.1% of the West Bank.

In mid-January 2000 a criminal investigation began into the financial affairs of the Israeli President, Ezer Weizman, following allegations that he had accepted some US $450,000m. in donations from a French friend while serving as a member of the Knesset. In late January the State Comptroller, Eliezer Goldberg, accused the One Israel campaign team for the 1999 general election of serious financial irregularities. The Attorney-General subsequently ordered a criminal investigation into the financial activities of One Israel and several other parties.

Hostilities between Israeli forces and Hezbollah in southern Lebanon continued during 1998. In that year some 23 Israeli soldiers were killed, and there was increasing pressure on Netanyahu, from public opinion and some Likud ministers, for a unilateral withdrawal from the territory. On 1 April the Israeli Security Cabinet voted unanimously to adopt UN Resolution 425 (which called for an immediate withdrawal of Israeli troops from all Lebanese territory), provided that the Lebanese army gave security guarantees. However, both Lebanon and Syria demanded an unconditional withdrawal. At the end of May fighting in southern Lebanon was at its most intense for several months. In late June, however, the first Israeli-Lebanese exchange of prisoners and bodies since July 1996 took place. Fighting escalated when, in late August 1998, Hezbollah launched rocket attacks on northern Israel in retaliation for an Israeli helicopter attack in which a senior Lebanese military official died. In two attacks in November seven Israeli soldiers died, leading Netanyahu to curtail a European tour in order to hold an emergency cabinet meeting on a possible withdrawal. At the end of December an Israeli air attack in which eight Lebanese civilians died provoked condemnation from the ILMG, which declared it to be a violation of the cease-fire 'understanding' reached in April 1996. Following several Hezbollah attacks, in early January 1999 Netanyahu reiterated previous warnings that in the event of further attacks, Israeli troops would attack Lebanon's infrastructure.

In February 1999 three Israeli army officers were killed during fighting with Hezbollah. A few days later the commander of the Israeli army unit for liaison with the SLA was killed in a bomb attack—the most senior Israeli officer to be killed in southern Lebanon since 1982. Israel responded by launching its heaviest air raids against Lebanon since the 1996 'Grapes of Wrath' operation, and the two sides appeared close to another major conflict. However, Israel's Minister of Defence, Moshe Arens, stated that Israel had no intention of escalating the conflict as long as Syria refrained from encouraging Hezbollah rocket attacks on northern Israel. Meanwhile, in mid-February 1999 it was reported that Israeli forces had annexed the Lebanese village of Arnoun. Although Arnoun was subsequently 'liberated' by Lebanese students, in mid-April Israel was reported to have annexed it again. In mid-May, for the first time, senior Israeli commanders in southern Lebanon urged an immediate Israeli withdrawal. (Prime Minister-Elect Barak had made a pre-election pledge that he would remove Israeli troops from Lebanon by July 2000.) In early June 1999 the SLA completed a unilateral withdrawal from the Jezzine enclave. However, in late June Barak was reportedly angered when the outgoing Netanyahu administration launched a series of air attacks on Lebanon, destroying Beirut's main power station and other infrastructure. The raids were undertaken in response to Hezbollah rocket attacks on northern Israel. In July Barak announced that he would propose to his Cabinet a unilateral withdrawal from Lebanon if no peace accord had been reached (in the context of an agreement with Syria over the Golan Heights) within one year. In mid-December Israel apologized for an attack in which some 18 Lebanese schoolchildren were injured. The incident followed an increase in Hezbollah military action after the announcement of a resumption of Israeli-Syrian peace negotiations (see below). In late December it was reported that Israel and Syria had reached an understanding in principle to limit the fighting in southern Lebanon; the informal cease-fire did not last, however, and in late January 2000 a senior SLA commander became the first Israeli soldier to be killed there for five months. At the end of January the deaths of another three Israeli soldiers led Israel to declare that peace talks with Syria would not resume until Syria took action to restrain Hezbollah. Attacks by Hezbollah escalated, however, and in early February Israel retaliated by carrying out a massive series of bombing raids on Lebanese infrastructure, and by attacking a Hezbollah command post. Since Israel announced a unilateral withdrawal from the 1996 'cease-fire' agreement, the two countries appeared once again to be on the brink of a major conflict. Following the killing of a further three Israeli soldiers by Hezbollah, in mid-February 2000 the Israeli Security Cabinet approved wide powers for the Prime Minister to order immediate retaliatory bombing raids into Lebanon.

Although in March 1998 Ariel Sharon announced publicly that Israel still planned to assassinate the Hamas leader Khalid Meshaal, there were signs of an improvement in Israeli-Jordanian relations during 1998. In March Netanyahu and Crown Prince Hassan signed a series of bilateral trade agreements. In mid-April King Hussein and the Israeli Prime Minister met for the first time since the assassination attempt which had strained relations in 1997. In December 1998 Israel agreed to allow foreign airlines en route to Jordan to use Israeli airspace. There was widespread apprehension about the future of Israel's relations with Jordan following the death, in February 1999, of King Hussein (whose funeral was attended by Netanyahu). Nevertheless, the Israeli Government expected 'continuity' in its relations with Jordan under the new King Abdullah. During 1999 an ongoing dispute over Israel's proposals to reduce, by 40%, its supply of water to Jordan (in contravention of the terms of the 1994 peace treaty), owing to a shortage in Israel, contributed to a slight deterioration in relations. In September 1999 Israel commended the Jordanian authorities for their arrest of Khalid Meshaal and two other Hamas leaders.

In July 1998 it was reported that Israel and Syria might resume talks on the disputed Golan Heights. Both countries had reportedly agreed to a French initiative whereby Israel would accept a 'land-for-peace' formula in return for Syrian acceptance of Israel's security needs. However, in late July the Knesset approved preliminary legislation seeking a majority parliamentary vote and a referendum before Israel would withdraw from the territory. The vote was condemned in Syria, and tensions between the two countries increased in September when Israel stated publicly, for the first time, its intention to enter a military alliance with Turkey. Syria welcomed the election of Ehud Barak as Israel's Prime Minister. At the inauguration of his Cabinet on 6 July 1999, Barak undertook to negotiate a bilateral peace with Syria, based on UN Resolutions 242 and 338. (This was interpreted as a signal of his intention to return most of the occupied Golan Heights in exchange for peace and normalized relations.) On 20 July Syria ordered a 'cease-fire' with Israel. However, diplomatic efforts made by the USA and France failed to produce a suitable formula for renewed peace talks. In October, during a visit by Barak to Turkey, Turkish leaders were reported to have offered to mediate between Israel and Syria. In early December the two sides agreed to a resumption of negotiations from the point at which they had broken off, reportedly as a result of diplomacy by President Clinton and agreements reached during secret meetings between Israeli and Syrian officials. The Knesset subsequently approved the decision to resume talks (by 47 votes to 31), while Barak reasserted that any agreement concluded with Syria would be put to a national referendum.

On 15 December 1999 President Clinton inaugurated the first round of discussions between Barak and the Syrian Minister of Foreign Affairs, Farouk ash-Shara', in Washington, DC, USA. The talks commenced amid rising tensions in southern Lebanon and resulted only in an agreement to resume discussions in January 2000. Barak, meanwhile, faced growing opposition in Israel to a possible return of the Golan Heights to Syria. In late December 1999 it was reported that Israel and Syria had agreed an informal 'cease-fire' to curb hostilities in Lebanon. Further high-level discussions between Israel and Syria were held on 3–9 January 2000 in Shepherdstown, near Washington, DC. The talks (in which President Clinton played an active role) only began after it was agreed that four committees would be established to discuss simultaneously the issues of borders, security, normalization of relations and water sharing. When further discussions proved inconclusive, the US Government presented a 'draft working document' to both sides, which was to act as the basis for a framework agreement. However, Syria announced that it required a commitment from Israel to withdraw from the Golan Heights before negotiations could resume. Israel, meanwhile, demanded the personal involvement of President Assad in the peace process. In early January a demonstration was held in Tel-Aviv by some 10,000 Israelis in order to oppose any withdrawal from the Golan Heights, while both Israel B'Aliyah and the NRP threatened to leave Barak's coalition in any such event. On 17 January peace talks between Israel and Syria were postponed indefinitely.

## Government

Supreme authority in Israel rests with the Knesset (Assembly), with 120 members elected by universal suffrage for four years (subject to dissolution), on the basis of proportional representation. The President, a constitutional Head of State, is elected by the Knesset for five years. Executive power lies with the Cabinet, led by a directly-elected Prime Minister. The Cabinet takes office after receiving a vote of confidence in the Knesset, to which it is responsible. Ministers are usually members of the Knesset, but non-members may be appointed.

The country is divided into six administrative districts. Local authorities are elected at the same time as elections to the Knesset. There are 31 municipalities (including two Arab towns), 115 local councils (46 Arab and Druze) and 49 regional councils (one Arab) comprising representatives of 700 villages.

## Defence

The Israel Defence Forces consist of a small nucleus of commissioned and non-commissioned regular officers, a contingent enlisted for national service, and a large reserve. Men are enlisted for 36 months of military service, and women for 21 months. Military service is compulsory for Jews and Druzes, but voluntary for Christians, Circassians and Muslims. Total regular armed forces numbered 173,500 (including 107,500 conscripts) in August 1999, and full mobilization to 598,500 can be quickly achieved with reserves of 425,000. The armed forces are divided into an army of 130,000, a navy estimated at 6,500 and an air force of 37,000. The defence budget for 1999 was 27,600m. new shekels (US $6,700m.).

## Economic Affairs

In 1997, according to estimates by the World Bank, Israel's gross national product (GNP), measured at average 1995–97 prices, was US $94,402m., equivalent to $16,180 per head. During 1990–97, it was estimated, GNP per head increased, in real terms, at an average rate of 2.6% per year. Over the same period, the population increased by an average of 3.2% per year. In 1998 total GNP was an estimated US $95,200m., equivalent to $15,940 per head. Israel's gross domestic product (GDP) increased, in real terms, by an average of 3.5% per year in 1980–90 and 5.4% in 1990–98. Real GDP increased by 4.6% in 1996, by 2.2% in 1997 and by an estimated 1.7% in 1998.

Agriculture (including hunting, forestry and fishing) contributed 4.2% of the GDP of the business sector in 1994, and in 1997 employed 2.4% of the working population, the majority of whom lived in large co-operatives (*kibbutzim*), of which there were 268 at December 1997, or co-operative smallholder villages (*moshavim*), of which there were 455. Israel is largely self-sufficient in foodstuffs. Citrus fruits constitute the main export crop. Other important crops are vegetables (particularly potatoes and tomatoes), wheat, melons and apples. The export of exotic fruits, winter vegetables and flowers has increased significantly in recent years. Poultry, livestock and fish production are also important. Agricultural output declined at an average annual rate of 0.5% in 1990–98.

Industry (manufacturing and mining) contributed 29% of the GDP of the business sector in 1994, and employed 19.5% of the working population in 1997. The State plays a major role in all sectors of industry, and there is a significant co-operative sector. Industrial production increased by an average 5.9% annually in 1988–95.

The mining and quarrying sector employed about 0.2% of the working population in 1997. There were some 33 producing oil wells in 1995, and some natural gas is produced. In 1999 the discovery of potential oil reserves in central Israel was reported. Potash, bromides, magnesium and other salts are mined. Israel is the world's largest exporter of bromine. There are also proven reserves of 20m. metric tons of low-grade copper ore, and gold, in potentially commercial quantities, was discovered in 1988.

Manufacturing employed 19.3% of the working population in 1997. The principal branches of manufacturing, measured by gross revenue, in 1992 were food products, beverages and tobacco (accounting for 18.7% of the total), electrical machinery (15.6%), chemical, petroleum and coal products (11.6%), metal products (9.7%) and transport equipment (5.6%). Diamond polishing is also an important activity. In 1980–90 manufacturing production increased, on average, by 2.8% each year.

Construction contributed 9.1% of the GDP of the business sector in 1994, and in 1997 the sector employed 7.2% of the working population.

The power sector (water and electricity) contributed 4% of the GDP of the business sector in 1994. In 1997 electricity, gas and water employed 0.9% of the working population. Energy is derived principally from imported petroleum and petroleum products. Imports of mineral fuels comprised 5.2% of the total value of imports in 1998.

Tourism is an important source of revenue. However, the sector has been damaged by regional instability and a series of bomb attacks carried out by Islamic extremist groups in the late 1990s. In 1998 almost 2m. tourists visited Israel, while receipts from tourism totalled US $2,657m. in that year.

The Israeli banking system is highly developed. The subsidiaries of the three major Israeli bank-groups are represented in many parts of the world.

In 1998 Israel recorded a visible trade deficit of US $3,226m., and there was a deficit of $668m. on the current account of the balance of payments. In 1998 the principal source of imports was the USA, which was also the principal market for exports. Other major trading partners are the United Kingdom, Germany, Belgium, the Netherlands, Italy and Switzerland. The principal exports in 1998 were worked diamonds, machinery and parts, chemical products, and clothing. The principal imports were machinery and parts, rough diamonds, chemicals and related products, crude petroleum and petroleum products and vehicles.

The budget for 1995 set revenue and expenditure to balance at 149,393m. new shekels. Government revenue each year normally includes some US $3,000m. in economic and military aid from the USA. At 31 December 1998 Israel's gross foreign debt amounted to $54,595m., of which $27,401m. was government debt. In that year the cost of debt-servicing was $5,150m., equivalent to 17.9% of revenue from exports of goods and services. During 1990–97 consumer prices rose by an annual average rate of 12.0%. At the end of 1998 the unemployment rate stood at 8.5%.

The most significant factor affecting the Israeli economy in the 1990s was the mass influx of Jews from the former USSR. Large-scale immigration led to a substantial increase in the population, additional flexibility in the labour market and growth in construction. In 1996, however, a period of economic slowdown began, reflecting an end to the demand boom and reduced tourism revenues following an increase in Islamist violence. By mid-1999 Israel was experiencing a growth rate recession and unemployment of about 9%; the Central Bureau of Statistics described 1999 as the worst economic year for a decade. By late 1999, however, a recovery was under way, with a significant improvement in activity reported, and an increase in foreign investment. Moreover, inflation, at 1.3%, was at its lowest level since 1967, representing a considerable success for the monetary policies of the previous Government, after years of double-digit inflation. In May 1998 foreign-exchange restrictions were ended, allowing the shekel to become fully convertible. Budget proposals for 2000 were aimed at reducing government expenditure and debt, and expanding infrastructural investment, by means of an ambitious package of structural reforms. The progress that had been achieved in the Middle East peace process had led to an improvement in relations with neighbouring states (notably Jordan and the Gulf states) prior to 1997, when Israel's plans for settlement construction in East Jerusalem brought an effective halt to peace talks and undermined any economic *rapprochement*. Following the election of Ehud Barak in May 1999 and the subsequent revival of the peace process, the prospects for regional peace improved significantly. Should talks between Israel and Syria eventually result in a comprehensive, and enduring, Middle East peace settlement, Israel would be in a far better position to achieve its long-term economic growth potential.

### Social Welfare

There is a highly advanced system of social welfare. Under the National Insurance Law, the State provides retirement pensions, benefits for industrial injury and maternity, and allowances for large families. The Histadrut (General Federation of Labour), to which about 85% of all Jewish workers in Israel belong, provides sickness benefits and medical care. The Ministry of Social Welfare provides for general assistance, relief grants, child care and other social services. In 1983 Israel had 11,895 physicians, equivalent to one for every 339 inhabitants, one of the best doctor-patient ratios in the world. In 1998 there were 317 hospitals (of which 122 were private) and 36,411 beds. Of total budgetary expenditure by the central Government in 1999, 12,253m. new shekels (5.5%) was allocated to the Ministry of Health, and a further 20,039m. new shekels (8.9%) was given to the Ministry of Labour and Social Welfare.

### Education

Israel has high standards of literacy and educational services. Free compulsory education is provided for all children between five and 15 years of age. Primary education is provided for all children between five and 10 years of age. There is also secondary, vocational and agricultural education. Post-primary education is also free, and it lasts six years, comprising two cycles of three years. Enrolment at primary and secondary schools in 1993 was equivalent to 96% of children aged six to 17. There are six universities, one institute of technology (the Technion) and one institute of science (the Weizmann Institute), which incorporates a graduate school of science. In 1999 budgetary expenditure on education, culture and sports by the central Government was 24,831m. new shekels (11.1% of total spending). In early 1999 legislation was passed which will allow for the introduction of free education for pre-primary children.

### Public Holidays

The Sabbath starts at sunset on Friday and ends at nightfall on Saturday. The Jewish year 5761 begins on 30 September 2000, and the year 5762 on 18 September 2001.

**2000:** 20–26 April (Passover—public holidays on first and last days of festival), 10 May (Independence Day), 9 June (Shavuot), 30 September–1 October (Rosh Hashanah, Jewish New Year), 9 October (Yom Kippur), 14–20 October (Succot).

**2001:** 8–14 April (Passover, see 2000), 28 April (Independence Day), 28 May (Shavuot), 18–19 September (Rosh Hashanah, Jewish New Year), 27 September (Yom Kippur), 2–8 October (Succot).

(The Jewish festivals and fast days commence in the evening of the dates given.)
Islamic holidays are observed by Muslim Arabs, and Christian holidays by the Christian Arab community.

### Weights and Measures

The metric system is in force.

1 dunum = 1,000 sq metres.

# Statistical Survey

Source: Central Bureau of Statistics, POB 13015, Hakirya, Romema, Jerusalem 91130; tel. 2-553553; fax 2-553325; e-mail yael@cbs.gov.il; internet www.cbs.gov.il.

## Area and Population

**AREA, POPULATION AND DENSITY**

| | |
|---|---|
| Area (sq km) | |
| Land | 21,671 |
| Inland water | 474 |
| Total | 22,145* |
| Population (*de jure*; census results)† | |
| 20 May 1972 | 3,147,683 |
| 4 June 1983 | |
| Males | 2,011,590 |
| Females | 2,026,030 |
| Total | 4,037,620 |
| Population (*de jure*; official estimates at mid-year)† | |
| 1996 | 5,685,100 |
| 1997 | 5,828,900 |
| 1998 | 5,970,700 |
| Density (per sq km) at mid-1998† | 269.6 |

* 8,550 sq miles. Area includes East Jerusalem, annexed by Israel in June 1967, and the Golan sub-district (1,154 sq km), annexed by Israel in December 1981.

† Including the population of East Jerusalem and Israeli residents in certain other areas under Israeli military occupation since June 1967. Beginning in 1981, figures also include non-Jews in the Golan sub-district, an Israeli-occupied area of Syrian territory. Census results exclude adjustment for underenumeration.

**1999** (estimate at 31 December): 6,220,000

**POPULATION BY RELIGION** (estimates, 31 December 1999)

| | Number | % |
|---|---|---|
| Jews | 4,900,000 | 78.78 |
| Muslims | 936,000 | 15.05 |
| Christians | 131,000 | 2.11 |
| Druze | 101,000 | 1.62 |
| Unclassified | 152,000 | 2.44 |
| **Total** | 6,220,000 | 100.00 |

**DISTRICTS** (31 December 1998)

| | Area (sq km)* | Population† | Density (per sq km) |
|---|---|---|---|
| Jerusalem‡ | 652 | 717,000 | 1,099.7 |
| Northern§ | 4,478 | 1,026,700 | 229.3 |
| Haifa | 863 | 788,600 | 913.8 |
| Central | 1,276 | 1,358,200 | 1,064.4 |
| Tel-Aviv | 171 | 1,138,700 | 6,659.1 |
| Southern | 14,231 | 840,000 | 59.0 |
| **Total** | 21,671 | 6,041,400 | 278.8 |

* Excluding lakes, with a total area of 474 sq km.

† Excluding Israelis residing in Jewish localities in the West Bank and Gaza Strip, totalling 172,200.

‡ Including East Jerusalem, annexed by Israel in June 1967.

§ Including the Golan sub-district (area 1,154 sq km, population 33,000 at 31 December 1998), annexed by Israel in December 1981.

**PRINCIPAL TOWNS** (estimated population at 31 December 1998)

| | | | |
|---|---|---|---|
| Jerusalem (capital) | 633,700* | Petach-Tikva | 159,400 |
| Tel-Aviv—Jaffa | 348,100 | Netanya | 154,900 |
| Haifa | 265,700 | Bat Yam | 137,000 |
| Rishon LeZiyyon | 188,200 | Ashdod | 155,800 |
| Holon | 163,100 | Bene Beraq | 133,900 |
| Beersheba | 163,700 | Ramat Gan | 126,900 |

* Including East Jerusalem, annexed in June 1967.

**BIRTHS, MARRIAGES AND DEATHS***

| | Registered live births | | Registered marriages | | Registered deaths | |
|---|---|---|---|---|---|---|
| | Number | Rate (per 1,000) | Number | Rate (per 1,000) | Number | Rate (per 1,000) |
| 1991 | 105,725 | 21.4 | 32,291 | 6.5 | 31,266 | 6.3 |
| 1992 | 110,062 | 21.5 | 32,769 | 6.4 | 33,327 | 6.5 |
| 1993 | 112,330 | 21.3 | 34,856 | 6.6 | 33,027 | 6.3 |
| 1994 | 114,543 | 21.2 | 36,035 | 6.7 | 33,535 | 6.2 |
| 1995 | 116,886 | 21.1 | 35,990 | 6.5 | 35,348 | 6.4 |
| 1996 | 121,333 | 21.3 | 36,081 | 6.3 | 34,658 | 6.1 |
| 1997 | 124,478 | 21.4 | 37,611 | 6.5 | 36,106 | 6.2 |
| 1998† | 130,080 | 21.8 | 38,449 | 6.6 | 36,919 | 6.2 |

* Including East Jerusalem. † Provisional figures.

**Expectation of life** (years at birth, 1997): Males 75.9; Females 80.1.

**IMMIGRATION***

| | 1996 | 1997 | 1998 |
|---|---|---|---|
| Immigrants: | | | |
| on immigrant visas | 60,671 | 56,070 | 48,537 |
| on tourist visas† | 9,525 | 9,756 | 8,081 |
| Potential immigrants: | | | |
| on potential immigrant visas | 36 | 24 | 9 |
| on tourist visas† | 687 | 371 | 95 |
| **Total** | 70,919 | 66,221 | 56,722 |

* Excluding immigrating citizens (4,040 in 1996; 3,905 in 1997; 3,255 in 1998) and Israeli residents returning from abroad.

† Figures refer to tourists who changed their status to immigrants or potential immigrants.

**ECONOMICALLY ACTIVE POPULATION** (sample surveys, '000 persons aged 15 years and over, excluding armed forces)*

| | 1995 | 1996 | 1997 |
|---|---|---|---|
| Agriculture, hunting and forestry; Fishing | 57.4 | 51.0 | 48.9 |
| Mining and quarrying | 6.2 | 4.7 | 5.1 |
| Manufacturing | 397.9 | 400.4 | 393.1 |
| Electricity, gas and water supply | 19.1 | 18.5 | 18.8 |
| Construction | 140.6 | 150.0 | 146.2 |
| Wholesale and retail trade; repair of motor vehicles, motorcycles and personal and household goods | 248.6 | 255.3 | 263.1 |
| Hotels and restaurants | 81.0 | 75.9 | 75.5 |
| Transport, storage and communications | 114.9 | 124.3 | 124.4 |
| Financial intermediation | 67.7 | 67.6 | 73.6 |
| Real estate, renting and business activities | 176.3 | 193.6 | 204.4 |
| Public administration and defence; compulsory social security | 107.4 | 108.1 | 113.7 |
| Education | 235.8 | 243.0 | 246.2 |
| Health and social work | 172.4 | 179.4 | 184.2 |
| Other community, social and personal service activities | 92.3 | 95.3 | 96.4 |
| Private households with employed persons | 32.6 | 33.8 | 32.4 |
| Extra-territorial organizations and bodies | 1.3 | 1.0 | 1.3 |
| Not classifiable by economic activity | 13.5 | 10.8 | 12.9 |
| **Total employed** | 1,965.0 | 2,012.7 | 2,040.2 |
| Unemployed | 145.0 | 144.1 | 169.8 |
| **Total labour force** | 2,110.0 | 2,156.7 | 2,210.0 |
| Males | 1,197.2 | 1,217.7 | 1,240.0 |
| Females | 912.8 | 939.0 | 970.0 |

* Figures are estimated independently, so the totals may not be the sum of the component parts.

Source: ILO, *Yearbook of Labour Statistics*.

# Agriculture

**PRINCIPAL CROPS** ('000 metric tons)

| | 1996 | 1997 | 1998 |
|---|---|---|---|
| Wheat | 185 | 116 | 116* |
| Barley | 2 | 1 | 1* |
| Potatoes | 353 | 271 | 271* |
| Groundnuts (in shell) | 23 | 23 | 23* |
| Cottonseed | 96 | 98 | 98* |
| Olives | 41 | 19 | 19* |
| Cabbages | 61 | 52 | 52* |
| Tomatoes | 491 | 386 | 386* |
| Pumpkins, squash and gourds* | 25 | 30 | 30 |
| Cucumbers* | 95 | 100 | 100 |
| Peppers (green) | 76 | 75 | 75* |
| Onions (dry) | 94 | 69 | 69* |
| Carrots | 81 | 68 | 68* |
| Watermelons | 254 | 260 | 260* |
| Melons* | 76 | 74 | 74 |
| Grapes | 90 | 90 | 90* |
| Apples | 98 | 111 | 111* |
| Peaches | 47 | 48 | 48* |
| Oranges | 366 | 325 | 325* |
| Tangerines, mandarins, clementines and satsumas | 115 | 125 | 125* |
| Lemons and limes | 27 | 21 | 21* |
| Grapefruit | 348 | 364 | 364* |
| Avocados | 76 | 80 | 80* |
| Bananas | 98 | 112 | 112* |
| Strawberries | 13 | 14 | 14* |
| Cotton (lint) | 51 | 54 | 54* |

* FAO estimate.

Source: FAO, *Production Yearbook*.

tion in Jerusalem with additional studios in Tel-Aviv and Haifa. IBA broadcasts six programmes for local and overseas listeners on medium, shortwave and VHF/FM in 16 languages; Hebrew, Arabic, English, Yiddish, Ladino, Romanian, Hungarian, Moghrabi, Persian, French, Russian, Bucharian, Georgian, Portuguese, Spanish and Amharic; Chair. MICHA YINON; Dir-Gen. URI PORAT; Dir of Radio (vacant); Dir External Services VICTOR GRAJEWSKY.

**Galei Zahal:** MPOB 01005, Zahal; tel. 3-5126666; fax 3-5126750; e-mail galatz@glz.co.il; internet www.glz.co.il; f. 1950; Israeli Defence Force broadcasting station, Tel-Aviv, with studios in Jerusalem; broadcasts news, current affairs, music and cultural programmes on medium-wave and FM stereo, 24-hour in Hebrew; Dir MOSHE SHLENSKY; Dir Dr ZE'EV DRORI.

**Kol Israel (The Voice of Israel):** POB 1082, 21 Heleni Hamalka, Jerusalem 91010; tel. 2-6248715; fax 2-5383173; internet www.artificia.com/html/news.cgi; broadcasts music, news, and multilingual programmes for immigrants in Hebrew, Arabic, French and English on medium wave and FM stereo; Dir and Prog. Dir AMNON NADAV.

### Television

**Israel Broadcasting Authority (IBA):** POB 7139, Jerusalem 91071; tel. 2-5301333; fax 2-292944; broadcasts began in 1968; station in Jerusalem with additional studios in Tel-Aviv; one colour network (VHF with UHF available in all areas); one satellite channel; broadcasts in Hebrew, Arabic and English; Dir-Gen URI PORAT; Dir of Television YAIR STERN; Dir of Engineering RAFI YEOSHUA.

**Cable Television Council:** 23 Jaffa Rd, Jerusalem 94229; tel. 2-6702200; fax 2-6706373; Chair. MICHAEL RAPHAELI; Man. Dir AVI AL-KALAI.

**Israel Educational Television:** Ministry of Education, 14 Klausner St, Tel-Aviv; tel. 3-6415270; fax 3-6427091; f. 1966 by Hanadiv (Rothschild Memorial Group) as Instructional Television Trust; began transmission in 1966; school programmes form an integral part of the syllabus in a wide range of subjects; also adult education; Gen. Man. AHUVA FAINMESSE ; Dir of Engineering S. KASIF.

**Second Channel TV and Radio Administration:** 3 Kanfi Nesharim St, POB 34112, Jerusalem 95464; tel. 2-6556222; fax 2-6556287; e-mail channel2@netvision.net.il. f. 1991. Chair. Prof. GIDEON DORON; Man. Dir NACHMAN SHAI.

In 1986 the Government approved the establishment of a commercial radio and television network to be run in competition with the state system.

## Finance

(cap. = capital; p.u. = paid up; dep. = deposits; m. = million; res = reserves; brs = branches; amounts in shekels)

### BANKING

During 1991–98 the Government raised some US $3,995m. through privatization and the issuance of shares and convertible securities in the banking sector.

#### Central Bank

**Bank of Israel:** POB 780, Bank of Israel Bldg, Kiryat Ben-Gurion, Jerusalem 91007; tel. 2-6552211; fax 2-6528805; e-mail webmaster@bankisrael.gov.il; internet www.bankisrael.gov.il; f. 1954 as the Central Bank of the State of Israel; cap. 60m., res 260m., dep. 94,838m. (Dec. 1998); Gov. DAVID KLEIN; 2 brs.

#### Principal Israeli Banks

**Bank Hapoalim BM:** POB 27, 50 Rothschild Blvd, Tel-Aviv 66883; tel. 3-5673333; fax 3-5607028; e-mail international@bnhp.co.il; internet www.bankhapoalim.co.il; f. 1921 as the Workers' Bank, name changed as above 1961; American-Israel Bank merged into the above 1999; 12.3% state-owned; total assets 187,101m., dep. 157,418m. (Dec. 1998); Chair. Bd of Man. and CEO AMIRAM SIVAN; 364 brs in Israel and abroad.

**Bank Leumi le-Israel BM:** POB 2, 24–32 Yehuda Halevi St, Tel-Aviv 65546; tel. 3-5148111; fax 3-5661872; internet www.bankleumi.com; f. 1902 as Anglo-Palestine Co; renamed Anglo-Palestine Bank 1930; reincorporated as above 1951; 50% state-owned; total assets 175,153m., dep. 154,134m. (Dec. 1998); Chair. EITAN RAFF; Pres. and CEO GALIA MAOR; 228 brs.

**Euro-Trade Bank Ltd:** POB 37318, 41 Rothschild Blvd, Tel-Aviv 66883; tel. 3-5643838; fax 3-5602483; e-mail eurotra@ibm.net; f. 1953; total assets 231,747m., dep. 177,889m. (Dec. 1998); Chair. REUVEN KOKOLEVITZ; Man. Dir MENAHEM WEBER.

**First International Bank of Israel Ltd:** POB 29036, Shalom Mayer Tower, 9 Ahad Ha'am St, Tel-Aviv 62251; tel. 3-5196111; fax 3-5100316; e-mail yuvall@fibi.co.il; internet www.fibi.co.il; f. 1972 as a result of a merger between Foreign Trade Bank Ltd and Export Bank Ltd; total assets 48,912m., cap. 2,577m., dep. 40,698m. (Sept. 1999); Chair. YIGAL ARNON; Man. Dir and CEO SHLOMO PIOTRKOWSKY; 90 brs.

**Industrial Development Bank of Israel Ltd:** POB 33580, Asia House, 4 Weizman, Tel-Aviv 61334; tel. 3-6972727; fax 3-6972893; f. 1957; total assets 11,648.8m., dep. 10,460.0m. (Dec. 1998); Chair. SHLOMO BOROCHEV; Gen. Man. YEHOSHUA ICHILOV.

**Investec Clali Bank Ltd:** POB 677, 38 Rothschild Blvd, Tel-Aviv 61006; tel. 3-5645645; fax 3-5645210; e-mail irroni@igb.co.il; internet www.igb.co.il; f. 1934 as Palestine Credit Utility Bank Ltd, renamed Israel General Bank Ltd 1964; ownership transferred to Investec Bank Ltd (South Africa) in 1996; name changed as above 1999; total assets 4,366.4m., dep. 3,855.3m. (Dec. 1998); Chair. HUGH SYDNEY HERMAN; Man. Dir and CEO JONATHON IRRONI; 3 brs.

**Israel Continental Bank Ltd:** POB 37406, 65 Rothschild Blvd, Tel-Aviv 61373; tel. 3-5641616; fax 3-6200399; f. 1974; capital held jointly by Bank Hapoalim BM (62.5%) and Bank für Gemeinwirtschaft AG (37.5%); total assets 1,315.9m., res 247.6m., dep. 1,041.6m. (Dec. 1998); Chair. AMIRAM SIVAN; Man. Dir P. HOREV; 3 brs.

**Israel Discount Bank Ltd:** 27 Yehuda Halevi St, Tel-Aviv 65136; tel. 3-5145555; fax 3-5145346; e-mail contact@discountbank.net; internet www.israel-discount-bank.co.il; f. 1935; 59.65% state-owned; cap p.u. 93m., dep. 96,080m. (Sept. 1999); Chair. ARIE MIENTKAVICH; Pres. and CEO DAVID GRANOT; some 162 brs in Israel and abroad.

**Leumi Industrial Development Bank Ltd:** POB 2, 35 Yehuda Halevi St, Tel-Aviv 61000; tel. 3-5149908; fax 3-5179514; f. 1944; subsidiary of Bank Leumi le-Israel BM; cap. and res 81m. (Dec. 1997); Chair. B. NAVEH; Gen. Man. M. ZIV.

**Maritime Bank of Israel Ltd:** POB 29373, 35 Ahad Ha'am St, Tel-Aviv 61293; tel. 3-5642222; fax 3-5642323; f. 1962; total assets 896.1m., cap. 5.9m., res 168.6m., dep. 621.1m. (Dec. 1998); Chair. SHIMON TOPOR; CEO DAVID LEVON.

**Mercantile Discount Bank Ltd:** POB 1292, 24 Rothschild Blvd, Tel-Aviv 61012; tel. 3-5647333; fax 3-5647205; e-mail mercant@netvision.net.il; f. as Barclays Discount Bank Ltd in 1971 by Barclays Bank International Ltd and Israel Discount Bank Ltd to incorporate Israel brs of Barclays; Israel Discount Bank Ltd became the sole owner in February 1993; name changed as above April 1993; absorbed Mercantile Bank of Israel Ltd in 1997; total assets 10,864m., cap. 47.2m., res 25.6m., dep. 10,003.8m. (Dec. 1998); Chair. of Bd ARIE MIENTKAVICH; Gen. Man. MOSHE GAVISH; 75 brs.

**Union Bank of Israel Ltd:** POB 2428, 6–8 Ahuzat Bayit St, Tel-Aviv 65143; tel. 3-5191111; fax 3-5191274; internet www.unionbank.co.il; f. 1951; 19.5% state-owned; total assets 14,660.2m., dep. 13,171.5m. (Dec. 1998); Chair. D. FRIEDMANN; Gen. Man. and CEO B. OSHMAN; 28 brs.

**United Mizrahi Bank Ltd:** POB 309, 13 Rothschild Blvd, Tel-Aviv 61002; tel. 3-5679211; fax 3-5604780; e-mail info@mizrahi.co.il; internet www.mizrahi.co.il; f. 1923 as Mizrahi Bank Ltd; 1969 absorbed Hapoel Hamizrahi Bank Ltd and name changed as above; 6.7% state-owned; total assets 51,689.3m., dep. 46,688.1m. (Dec. 1998); Pres. and CEO VICTOR MEDINA; 91 brs.

#### Mortgage Banks

**Discount Mortgage Bank Ltd:** POB 2844, 16–18 Simtat Beit Hashoeva, Tel-Aviv 61027; tel. 3-5643311; fax 3-5661704; f. 1959; subsidiary of Israel Discount Bank Ltd; cap. p.u. 1.3m., res 463.6m. (Dec. 1997); Chair. ARIE MIENTKAVICH; Man. M. ELDAR.

**First International Mortgage Bank Ltd.:** 39 Montefiore St, Tel-Aviv 65201; tel. 3-5643311; fax 3-5643321; f. 1922 as the Mortgage and Savings Bank, name changed as above 1996; subsidiary of First International Bank of Israel Ltd; cap. and res 334m. (Dec. 1996); Chair. S. PIOTRKOWSKY; Man. Dir P. HAMO; 50 brs.

**Leumi Mortgage Bank Ltd:** POB 69, 31–37 Montefiore St, Tel-Aviv 65201; tel. 3-5648444; fax 3-5648334; f. 1921; subsidiary of Bank Leumi le-Israel BM; total assets 20,955.6m., dep. 18,504.5m. (Dec. 1998); Chair. A. ZELDMAN; Gen. Man. R. ZABAG; 6 brs.

**Mishkan-Hapoalim Mortgage Bank Ltd:** POB 1610, 2 Ibn Gvirol St, Tel-Aviv 61015; tel. 3-6970505; fax 3-6961379; f. 1950; subsidiary of Bank Hapoalim BM; total assets 8,289m., dep. 10,268.3m. (Dec. 1993); Chair. M. OLENIK; Man. Dir A. KROIZER; 131 brs.

**Tefahot, Israel Mortgage Bank Ltd:** POB 93, 9 Heleni Hamalka St, Jerusalem 91902; tel. 2-6755222; fax 2-6755344; f. 1945; subsidiary of United Mizrahi Bank Ltd; cap. and res 1,181m., total assets 18,973m. (Dec. 1994); Chair. DAVID BRODET; Man. Dir URI WÜRZBURGER; 60 brs.

### STOCK EXCHANGE

**Tel-Aviv Stock Exchange:** POB 29060, 54 Ahad Ha'am St, Tel-Aviv 65202; tel. 3-5677411; fax 3-5105379; e-mail spokesperson@tase.co.il; internet www.tase.co.il; f. 1953; Chair. Prof. YAIR E. ORGLER; Gen. Man. SAUL BRONFELD.

### INSURANCE

The Israel Insurance Asscn lists 35 companies, a selection of which are listed below; not all companies are members of the association.

**Ararat Insurance Co Ltd:** Ararat House, 13 Montefiore St, Tel-Aviv 65164; tel. 3-640888; f. 1949; Co-Chair. AHARON DOVRAT, PHILIP ZUCKERMAN; Gen. Man. PINCHAS COHEN.

**Aryeh Insurance Co of Israel Ltd:** 9 Ahad Ha'am St, Tel-Aviv 65251; tel. 3-5141777; fax 3-5179337; e-mail aryeh@isdn.net.il; f. 1948; Chair. AVIGDOR KAPLAN.

**Clal Insurance Co Ltd:** POB 326, 42 Rothschild Blvd, Tel-Aviv 61002; tel. 3-627711; fax 3-622666; f. 1962; Man. Dir RIMON BEN-SHAOUL.

**Hassneh Insurance Co of Israel Ltd:** POB 805, 115 Allenby St, Tel-Aviv 61007; tel. 3-5649111; f. 1924; Man. Dir M. MICHAEL MILLER.

**Israel Phoenix Assurance Co Ltd:** 30 Levontin St, Tel-Aviv 65116; tel. 3-7141111; fax 3-5601242; e-mail yoni@phoenix.co.il; internet www.phoenix.co.il; f. 1949; Chair. of Bd JOSEPH D. HACKMEY; Man. Dir Dr ITAMAR BOROWITZ.

**Maoz Insurance Co Ltd:** Tel-Aviv; f. 1945; formerly Binyan Insurance Co Ltd; Chair. B. YEKUTIELI.

**Menorah Insurance Co Ltd:** Menorah House, 73 Rothschild Blvd, Tel-Aviv 65786; tel. 3-5260771; fax 3-5618288; f. 1935; Gen. Man. SHABTAI ENGEL.

**Migdal Insurance Co Ltd:** POB 37633, 26 Sa'adiya Ga'on St, Tel-Aviv 61375; tel. 3-5637637; part of Bank Leumi Group; f. 1934; Chair. S. GROFMAN; CEO U. LEVY.

**Palglass Palestine Plate Glass Insurance Co Ltd:** Tel-Aviv 65541; f. 1934; Gen. Man. AKIVA ZALZMAN.

**Sahar Israel Insurance Co Ltd:** POB 26222, Sahar House, 23 Ben-Yehuda St, Tel-Aviv 63806; tel. 3-5140311; f. 1949; Chair. G. HAMBURGER.

**Samson Insurance Co Ltd:** POB 33678, Avgad Bldg, 5 Jabotinsky St, Ramat-Gan, Tel-Aviv 52520; tel. 3-7521616; fax 3-7516644; f. 1933; Chair. E. BEN-AMRAM; Gen. Man. GIORA SAGI.

**Sela Insurance Co Ltd:** Tel-Aviv; tel. 3-61028; f. 1938; Man. Dir E. SHANI.

**Shiloah Insurance Co Ltd:** 3 Abba-Hillel St, Ramat-Gan, Tel-Aviv 52118; f. 1933; Gen. Man. Dr S. BAMIRAH; Man. Mme BAMIRAH.

**Zion Insurance Co Ltd:** POB 1425, 41–45 Rothschild Blvd, Tel-Aviv 61013; f. 1935; Chair. A. R. TAIBER.

## Trade and Industry

### CHAMBERS OF COMMERCE

**Federation of Bi-National Chambers of Commerce and Industry with and in Israel:** POB 50196, 29 Hamered St, Tel-Aviv 61500; tel. 3-5173261; fax 3-5173283; federates: Israel-British Chamber of Commerce; Australia-Israel Chamber of Commerce; Chamber of Commerce and Industry Israel-Asia; Chamber of Commerce Israel-Belgique-Luxembourg; Canada-Israel Chamber of Commerce and Industry; Israel-Denmark Chamber of Commerce; Chambre de Commerce Israel-France; Chamber of Commerce and Industry Israel-Germany; Camera di Commercio Israeli-Italia; Israel-Japan Chamber of Commerce; Israel-Latin America, Spain and Portugal Chamber of Commerce; Netherlands-Israel Chamber of Commerce; Israel-Greece Chamber of Commerce; Israel-Bulgaria Chamber of Commerce; Israel-Ireland Chamber of Commerce; Handelskammer Israel-Schweiz; Israel-South Africa Chamber of Commerce; Israel-Sweden Chamber of Commerce; Israel-Hungary Chamber of Commerce; Israel-Romania Chamber of Commerce; Israel-Russia Chamber of Commerce; Israel-Poland Chamber of Commerce; Israel-Austria Chamber of Commerce; Israel-Ukraine Chamber of Commerce; Israel-Africa Chamber of Commerce; Israel-Jordan Chamber of Commerce; Israel-Egypt Chamber of Commerce; Israel-Morocco Chamber of Commerce; Israel-Moldova Chamber of Commerce; Israel-Norway Chamber of Commerce; Israel-Slovakia Chamber of Commerce; Israel-Portugal Chamber of Commerce; Israel-Finland Chamber of Commerce; Israel-Kazakhstan Chamber of Commerce; Israel-Turkey Chamber of Commerce; Israel-Thailand Chamber of Commerce; Chair. G. PROPPER.

**Federation of Israeli Chambers of Commerce:** POB 20027, 84 Hahashmonaim St, Tel-Aviv 67011; tel. 3-5631010; fax 3-5619025; e-mail chamber@tlv-chamber.org.il; internet www.tlv-chamber.org.il; co-ordinates the Tel-Aviv, Jerusalem, Haifa and Beersheba Chambers of Commerce; Pres. DAN GILLERMAN.

**Haifa Chamber of Commerce and Industry** (Haifa and District): POB 33176, 53 Haatzmaut Rd, Haifa 31331; tel. 4-8626364; fax 4-8645428; e-mail main@haifachamber.org.il; internet www.haifachamber.com; f. 1921; 700 mems; Pres. S. GANTZ; Man. Dir D. MAROM.

**Israel-British Chamber of Commerce:** POB 50321, 29 Hamered St, Tel-Aviv 61502; tel. 3-5109424; fax 3-5109540; e-mail isrbrit@netvision.net.il; f. 1951; 350 mems; Chair. AMNON DOTAN; Exec. Dir FELIX KIPPER.

**Jerusalem Chamber of Commerce:** POB 2083, 10 Hillel St, Jerusalem 91020; tel. 2-6254333; fax 2-6254335; e-mail jerccom@inter.net.il; internet www.jerccom.co.il; f. 1908; c. 300 mems; Pres. JOSEPH PERLMAN.

**Tel-Aviv-Jaffa Chamber of Commerce:** POB 20027, 84 Hahashmonaim St, Tel-Aviv 61200; tel. 3-5631010; fax 3-5619025; f. 1919; 1,800 mems; Pres. DAN GILLERMAN.

### INDUSTRIAL AND TRADE ASSOCIATIONS

**Agricultural Export Co (AGREXCO):** Tel-Aviv; state-owned agricultural marketing organization; Dir-Gen. AMOTZ AMIAD.

**The Agricultural Union:** Tel-Aviv; consists of more than 50 agricultural settlements and is connected with marketing and supplying organizations, and Bahan Ltd, controllers and auditors.

**The Centre for International Agricultural Development Cooperation (CINADCO):** Ministry of Agriculture and Rural Development, POB 7011, Kiryat Ben-Gurion, Tel-Aviv 61070; tel. 3-6971709; fax 3-6971677; e-mail cinadco@netvision.net.il.

**Citrus Marketing Board:** POB 80, Beit Dagan 50250; tel. 3-9683811; fax 3-9683838; e-mail cmbi@netvision.net.il; f. 1942; the central co-ordinating body of citrus growers and exporters in Israel; represents the citrus industry in international organizations; licenses private exporters; controls the quality of fruit; has responsibility for Jaffa trademarks; mounts advertising and promotion campaigns for Jaffa citrus fruit worldwide; carries out research and development of new varieties of citrus fruit, and 'environmentally friendly' fruit; Chair. D. KRITCHMAN; Gen. Man. M. DAVIDSON.

**Farmers' Union of Israel:** POB 209, 8 Kaplan St, Tel-Aviv; tel. 3-69502227; fax 3-6918228; f. 1913; membership of 7,000 independent farmers, citrus and winegrape growers; Pres. PESACH GRUPPER; Dir-Gen. SHLOMO REISMAN.

**Fruit Board of Israel:** POB 20117, 119 Rehov Hahashmonaim, Tel-Aviv 61200; tel. 3-5612929; fax 3-5614672; Dir-Gen. SHALOM BLAYER.

**General Asscn of Merchants in Israel:** 6 Rothschild Blvd, Tel-Aviv; the organization of retail traders; has a membership of 30,000 in 60 brs.

**Israel Cotton Production and Marketing Board Ltd:** POB 384, Herzlia B'46103; tel. 9-9509491; fax 9-9509159.

**Israel Diamond Exchange Ltd:** POB 3222, Ramat-Gan, Tel-Aviv; tel. 3-5760211; fax 3-5750652; f. 1937; production, export, import and finance facilities; net exports (1998) US $3,635m.; Pres. SHMUEL SCHNITZER.

**Israel Export Institute:** POB 50084, 29 Hamered St, Tel-Aviv 68125; tel. 3-5142830; fax 3-5142902; e-mail library@export.gov.il; internet www.export.gov.il; Dir-Gen. AMIR HAYEK.

**Israel Journalists' Asscn Ltd:** 4 Kaplan St, Tel-Aviv 64734; tel. 3-6956141; Sec. YONA SHIMSHI.

**Kibbutz Industries' Asscn:** 8 Rehov Shaul Hamelech, Tel-Aviv 64733; tel. 3-6955413; fax 3-6951464; e-mail kiak@kia.co.il; liaison office for marketing and export of the goods produced by Israel's kibbutzim; Pres. GIORA MASAD.

**Manufacturers' Asscn of Israel:** POB 50022, Industry House, 29 Hamered St, Tel-Aviv 61500; tel. 3-5198787; fax 3-5162026; e-mail gendiv@industry.org.il; internet www.industry.org.il; 1,700 mem.-enterprises employing nearly 85% of industrial workers in Israel; Pres. DAN PROPPER.

**National Federation of Israeli Journalists:** POB 7009, 4 Kaplan St, Tel-Aviv 64734; tel. 3-6956141; fax 3-6951438.

### UTILITIES

**The Israel Electric Corporation** and the **Mekorot Water Co** are two of Israel's largest state-owned companies, with total assets valued at US $10,832m. and US $1,978m., respectively, at the end of 1997.

**Israel Electric Corporation (IEC):** 2 Ha 'Haganah St, Haifa 31086; tel. 4-8548548; fax 4-8548545; Chair. GAD YA'ACOBI; Dir-Gen. RAFI PELED.

**Mekorot Water Co:** 7th Floor, Department Hall, 9 Lincoln St Development, Tel-Aviv 61201; tel. 3-6230772; fax 3-6230598.

## The Histadrut

**Hahistadrut Haklalit shel Haovdim Beeretz Israel (General Federation of Labour in Israel):** 93 Arlosoroff St, Tel-Aviv 62098; tel. 3-6921111; fax 3-6969906; e-mail histint@netvision.net.il; f. 1920.

The General Federation of Labour in Israel, usually known as the Histadrut, is the largest voluntary organization in Israel, and the most important economic body in the state. It is open to all workers, including the self-employed, members of co-operatives and of the liberal professions, as well as housewives, students, pensioners and the unemployed. Members of two small religious labour organizations, Histadrut Hapoel Hamizrahi and Histadrut Poale Agudat Israel, also belong to the trade union section and social services of the Histadrut, which thus extend to *c.* 85% of all workers. Dues—between 3.6% and 5.8% of wages—cover all its trade union, health insurance and social service activities. The Histadrut engages in four main fields of activity: trade union organization (with some 50 affiliated trade unions and 65 local labour councils operating throughout the country); social services (including a comprehensive health insurance scheme 'Kupat Holim', pension and welfare funds, etc.); educational and cultural activities (vocational schools, workers' colleges, theatre and dance groups, sports clubs, youth movement); and economic development (undertaken by Hevrat Haovdim (Labour Economy), which includes industrial enterprises partially or wholly owned by the Histadrut, agricultural and transport co-operatives, workers' bank, insurance company, publishing house etc.). A women's organization, Na'amat, which also belongs to the Histadrut, operates nursery homes and kindergartens, provides vocational education and promotes legislation for the protection and benefit of working women. The Histadrut is a member of the ICFTU and its affiliated trade secretariats, APRO, ICA and various international professional organizations.

**Chair:** AMIR PERETZ.

**Secretary-General:** HAIM RAMON.

### ORGANIZATION

In 1989 the Histadrut had a membership of 1,630,000. In addition some 110,000 young people under 18 years of age belong to the Organization of Working and Student Youth, a direct affiliate of the Histadrut.

All members take part in elections to the Histadrut Convention (Veida), which elects the General Council (Moetsa) and the Executive Committee (Vaad Hapoel). The latter elects the 41-member Executive Bureau (Vaada Merakezet), which is responsible for day-to-day implementation of policy. The Executive Committee also elects the Secretary-General, who acts as its chairman as well as head of the organization as a whole and chairman of the Executive Bureau. Nearly all political parties are represented on the Histadrut Executive Committee.

The Executive Committee has the following departments: Trade Union, Organization and Labour Councils, Education and Culture, Social Security, Industrial Democracy, Students, Youth and Sports, Consumer Protection, Administration, Finance and International.

### TRADE UNION ACTIVITIES

Collective agreements with employers fix wage scales, which are linked with the retail price index; provide for social benefits, including paid sick leave and employers' contributions to sick and pension and provident funds; and regulate dismissals. Dismissal compensation is regulated by law. The Histadrut actively promotes productivity through labour management boards and the National Productivity Institute, and supports incentive pay schemes.

There are unions for the following groups: clerical workers, building workers, teachers, engineers, agricultural workers, technicians, textile workers, printing workers, diamond workers, metal workers, food and bakery workers, wood workers, government employees, seamen, nurses, civilian employees of the armed forces, actors, musicians and variety artists, social workers, watchmen, cinema technicians, institutional and school staffs, pharmacy employees, medical laboratory workers, X-ray technicians, physiotherapists, social scientists, microbiologists, psychologists, salaried lawyers, pharmacists, physicians, occupational therapists, truck and taxi drivers, hotel and restaurant workers, workers in Histadrut-owned industry, garment, shoe and leather workers, plastic and rubber workers, editors of periodicals, painters and sculptors and industrial workers.

**Histadrut Trade Union Department:** Dir SHLOMO SHANI.

### ECONOMIC ACTIVITIES AND SOCIAL SERVICES

These include Hevrat Haovdim (employing 260,000 workers in 1983), Kupat Holim (the Sick Fund, covering almost 77% of Israel's population), seven pension funds, and Na'amat (see above).

#### Other Trade Unions

**General Federation of West Bank Trade Unions:** Sec.-Gen. SHAHER SAAD.

**Histadrut Haovdim Haleumit** (National Labour Federation): 23 Sprintzak St, Tel-Aviv 64738; tel. 3-6958351; fax 3-6961753; f. 1934; 170,000 mems; Chair. HIRSHZON ABRAHAM.

**Histadrut Hapoel Hamizrahi** (National Religious Workers' Party): 166 Even Gavirol St, Tel-Aviv 62023; tel. 3-5442151; fax 3-5468942; 150,000 mems in 85 settlements and 15 kibbutzim; Sec.-Gen. ELIEZER ABTABI.

**Histadrut Poale Agudat Israel** (Agudat Israel Workers' Organization): POB 11044, 64 Frishman St, Tel-Aviv; tel. 3-5242126; fax 3-5230689; has 33,000 members in 16 settlements and 8 educational insts.

## Transport

### RAILWAYS

Freight traffic consists mainly of grain, phosphates, potash, containers, petroleum and building materials. Rail service serves Haifa and Ashdod ports on the Mediterranean Sea, while a combined rail-road service extends to Eilat port on the Red Sea. Passenger services operate between the main towns: Nahariya, Haifa, Tel-Aviv and Jerusalem. In 1988 the National Ports Authority assumed responsibility for the rail system, although Israel Railways was expected to become a separate state concern in 1999. Bids to construct the first line of a US $1,400m. light railway network in Jerusalem (to be launched in 2004) were expected in 2000.

**Israel Railways:** POB 18085, Central Station, Tel-Aviv 61180; tel. 3-6937401; fax 3-6937480; the total length of main line is 530 km and there are 170 km of branch line; gauge 1,435 mm; Dir-Gen. A. UZANI; Gen. Man. EHUD HADAR.

#### Underground Railway

**Haifa Underground Funicular Railway:** 122 Hanassi Ave, Haifa 34633; tel. 04-8376861; fax 04-8376875; opened 1959; 2 km in operation; Man. AVI TELLEM.

### ROADS

In 1997 there were 15,464 km of paved roads, of which 56 km were motorways, 5,647 km highways, main or national roads and 10,361 km other roads.

**Ministry of National Infrastructure:** POB 13198, Public Works Dept, Jerusalem; tel. 2-584711; fax 2-823532.

### SHIPPING

At 31 December 1998 Israel's merchant fleet consisted of 53 vessels amounting to 751,614 grt.

Haifa and Ashdod are the main ports in Israel. The former is a natural harbour, enclosed by two main breakwaters and dredged to 45 ft below mean sea-level. In 1965 the deep water port was completed at Ashdod which had a capacity of about 8.6m. tons in 1988.

The port of Eilat is Israel's gateway to the Red Sea. It is a natural harbour, operated from a wharf. Another port, to the south of the original one, started operating in 1965.

**Israel Ports and Railways Authority:** POB 20121, 74 Petach Tikva Rd, Tel-Aviv 61201; tel. 3-5657000; fax 3-5617142; e-mail dovf@israports.org.il; internet www.israports.org.il; f. 1961; to plan, build, develop, maintain and operate Israel's commercial ports and Israel Railways. In 1999 a US $1,000m.-development plan was under way at Haifa and Ashdod ports. Cargo traffic in 1998 amounted to 33.8m. tons (oil excluded); Chair. AZRIEL FEUCHTWANGER; Dir-Gen. GIDEON SHAMIR.

**Ofer Brothers (Management) Ltd:** POB 1755, Haifa 31000; tel. 4-8610610; fax 4-8675666; runs cargo and container services; operates some 15 vessels; Chair. Y. OFER; Man. Dir E. ANGEL.

**ZIM Israel Navigation Co Ltd:** POB 1723, 7–9 Pal-Yam Ave, Haifa 31000; tel. 4-8652111; fax 4-8652956; e-mail zimpress@zim.co.il; internet www.zim.co.il; f. 1945; provides cargo and container services in the Mediterranean and northern Europe, North, South and Central America, the Far East, Africa and Australia; operates some 81 vessels (75 of which are container vessels); total cargo carried: 1,180,000 TEUs in 1999; Chair. U. ANGEL; Pres. and CEO Dr YORAM SEBBA.

### CIVIL AVIATION

**Israel Airports Authority:** Ben-Gurion International Airport, Tel-Aviv; tel. 3-9712804; fax 3-9712436; Dir-Gen. AVI KOSTELITZ.

**El Al Israel Airlines Ltd:** POB 41, Ben-Gurion International Airport, Tel-Aviv 70100; tel. 3-9716111; fax 3-9716040; internet www.elal.com; f. 1948; 100% state-owned; total assets US $980m. (Dec. 1997); daily services to most capitals of Europe; over 20 flights weekly to New York; services to the USA, Canada, China, Egypt, India, Kenya, South Africa, Thailand and Turkey; Chair. JOSEPH CIECHANOVER; Pres. JOEL FELDSCHUH.

**Arkia Israeli Airlines Ltd:** POB 39301, Sde-Dov Airport, Tel-Aviv 61392; tel. 3-6902222; fax 3-6991390; e-mail income@arkia.co.il; internet www.arkia.co.il; f. 1980 through merger of Kanaf-Arkia Airlines and Aviation Services; scheduled passenger services linking Tel-Aviv, Jerusalem, Haifa, Eilat, Rosh Pina, Kiryat Shmona and Yolveta; charter services to European destinations; Chair. and CEO Prof. ISRAEL BOROVICH.

## Tourism

In 1998 some 1,941,600 tourists visited Israel. Tourist receipts in that year totalled US $2,657m.

**Ministry of Tourism:** POB 1018, 24 Rehov King George, Jerusalem 91009; tel. 2-6754811; fax 2-6733593; Minister of Tourism AMNON LIPKIN-SHAHAK; Dir-Gen. DAVID LITVAK.

# Occupied Territories

## THE GOLAN HEIGHTS

### Location, Climate

The Golan Heights, a mountainous plateau which formed most of Syria's Quneitra Province (1,710 sq km) and parts of Dera'a Province, was occupied by Israel after the 1967 Arab–Israeli War. Following the Disengagement Agreement of 1974, Israel continued to occupy some 70% of the territory (1,176 sq km), valued for its strategic position and abundant water resources (the headwaters of the Jordan river have their source on the slopes of Mount Hermon). The average height of the Golan is approximately 1,200 m above sea-level in the northern region and about 300 m above sea-level in the southern region, near Lake Tiberias (the Sea of Galilee). Rainfall ranges from about 1,000 mm per year in the north to less than 600 mm per year in the southern region.

### Administration

Prior to the Israeli occupation, the Golan Heights were incorporated by Syria into a provincial administration of which the city of Quneitra, with a population at the time of 27,378, was capital. The disengagement agreement that was mediated in 1974 by the US Secretary of State, Henry Kissinger, after the 1973 Arab–Israeli War, provided for the withdrawal of Israeli forces from Quneitra. Before they withdrew, however, Israeli army engineers destroyed the city. In December 1981 the Israeli Knesset enacted the Golan Annexation Law, whereby Israeli civilian legislation was extended to the territory of Golan, now under the administrative jurisdiction of the Commissioner for the Northern District of Israel. The Arab-Druze community of the Golan immediately responded by declaring a strike and appealed to the UN Secretary-General to force Israel to rescind the annexation decision. At the seventh round of multilateral talks between Israeli and Arab delegations in Washington in August 1992, the Israeli Government of Itzhak Rabin for the first time accepted that UN Security Council Resolution 242, adopted in 1967, applied to the Golan Heights. In January 1999 the Knesset passed legislation which stated that any transfer of land under Israeli sovereignty (referring to the Golan Heights and East Jerusalem) was conditional on the approval of at least 61 of the 120 Knesset members and of the Israeli electorate in a subsequent national referendum. Following the election of Ehud Barak as Israel's Prime Minister in May 1999, peace negotiations between Israel and Syria were resumed in mid-December. However, in January 2000 the talks were postponed indefinitely after Syria demanded a written commitment from Israel to withdraw from the Golan Heights. The withdrawal of Israel from the disputed territory is one of President Assad of Syria's primary objectives in any future peace agreement with Israel.

### Demography and Economic Affairs

As a consequence of the Israeli occupation, an estimated 93% of the ethnically diverse Syrian population of 147,613, distributed across 163 villages and towns and 108 individual farms, was expelled. The majority were Arab Sunni Muslims, but the population also included Alawite and Druze minorities and some Circassians, Turcomen, Armenians and Kurds. Approximately 9,000 Palestinian refugees from the 1948 Arab–Israeli War also inhabited the area. At the time of the occupation, the Golan was a predominantly agricultural province, 64% of the labour force being employed in agriculture. Only one-fifth of the population resided in the administrative centres. By 1991 the Golan Heights had a Jewish population of approximately 12,000 living in 21 Jewish settlements (four new settlements had been created by the end of 1992), and a predominantly Druze population of approximately 16,000 living in the only six remaining villages, of which Majd ash-Shams is by far the largest. According to official figures, at the end of 1998 the Golan Heights had a total population of 33,000 (including 14,400 Jews, 16,400 Druze and 1,700 Muslims). The Golan Heights have remained predominantly an agricultural area, and, although many of the Druze population now work in Israeli industry in Eilat, Tel-Aviv and Jerusalem, the indigenous economy relies almost solely on the cultivation of apples, for which the area is famous. The apple orchards benefit from a unique combination of fertile soils, abundance of water and a conducive climate.

## EAST JERUSALEM

### Location, Climate

Greater Jerusalem includes Israeli West Jerusalem (99% Jewish), the Old City and Mount of Olives, East Jerusalem (the Palestinian residential and commercial centre), Arab villages declared to be part of Jerusalem by Israel in 1967 and Jewish neighbourhoods constructed since 1967, either on land expropriated from Arab villages or in areas requisitioned as 'government land'. Although the area of the Greater Jerusalem district is 627 sq km, the Old City of Jerusalem covers just 1 sq km.

### Administration

Until the 1967 Arab–Israeli War, Jerusalem had been divided into the new city of West Jerusalem—captured by Jewish forces in 1948—and the old city, East Jerusalem, which was part of Jordan. Israel's victory in 1967, however, reunited the city under Israeli control. Two weeks after the fighting had ended, on 28 June, Israeli law was applied to East Jerusalem and the municipal boundaries were extended by 45 km (28 miles). Jerusalem had been, in effect, annexed. Israeli officials, however, still refer to the 'reunification' of Jerusalem.

### Demography and Economic Affairs

In June 1993 the Deputy Mayor of Jerusalem, Avraham Kahila, declared that the city now 'had a majority of Jews', based on population projections which estimated the Jewish population at 158,000 and the Arab population at 155,000. This was a significant moment for the Israeli administration, as this had been a long-term objective. Immediately prior to the June 1967 Arab–Israeli War, East Jerusalem and its Arab environs had an Arab population of approximately 70,000, and a small Jewish population in the old Jewish quarter of the city. By contrast, Israeli West Jerusalem had a Jewish population of 196,000. As a result of this population imbalance, in the Greater Jerusalem district as a whole the Jewish population was in the majority even prior to the occupation of the whole city in 1967. Israeli policy following the occupation of East Jerusalem and the West Bank consisted of encircling the eastern sector of the city with Jewish settlements. In contrast to the more politically sensitive siting of Jewish settlements in the old Arab quarter of Jerusalem, the Government of Itzhak Rabin concentrated on the outer circle of settlement building. Official statistics for the end of 1998 reported that Greater Jerusalem had a total population of 633,700, of whom 433,600 (68%) were Jews.

The Old City, within the walls of which are found the ancient quarters of the Jews, Christians, Muslims and Armenians, has a population of approximately 25,500 Arabs and 2,600 Jews. In addition, there are some 600 recent Jewish settlers in the Arab quarter.

Many imaginative plans have been submitted with the aim of finding a solution to the problem of sharing Jerusalem between Arabs and Jews, including the proposal that the city be placed under international trusteeship, under the auspices of the UN. However, to make the implementation of such plans an administrative as well as a political quagmire, the Israeli administration, after occupying the whole city in June 1967, began creating 'facts on the ground'. Immediately following the occupation, all electricity, water and telephone grids in West Jerusalem were extended to the east. Roads were widened and cleared, and the Arab population immediately in front of the 'Wailing Wall' was forcibly evicted. Arabs living in East Jerusalem became 'permanent residents' and could apply for Israeli citizenship if they wished (in contrast to Arabs in the West Bank and Gaza Strip). However, few chose to do so. None the less, issued with identity cards (excluding the estimated 25,000 Arabs from the West Bank and Gaza Strip living illegally in the city), the Arab residents were taxed by the Israeli authorities, and their businesses and banks became subject to Israeli laws and business regulations. Now controlling approximately one-half of all land in East Jerusalem and the surrounding Palestinian villages (previously communally, or privately, owned by Palestinians), the Israeli authorities allowed Arabs to construct buildings on only 10%–15% of the land in the city; and East Jerusalem's commercial district has been limited to three streets. The Palestinian economy was quite seriously affected by the fall in tourism during the *intifada* and by curfews, enforced tax collections and confiscations of property exercised by the Israeli authorities.

Since the 1993 signing of the Declaration of Principles on Palestinian Self-Rule, the future status of Jerusalem and the continuing expansion of Jewish settlements in East Jerusalem have emerged as two of the most crucial issues affecting the peace process. In May 1999 the Israeli Government announced its refusal to grant Israeli citizenship to several hundred Arabs living in East Jerusalem, regardless of their compliance with the conditions stipulated under the Citizenship Law. In October Israel ended its policy of revoking the right of Palestinians to reside in Jerusalem if they had spent more than seven years outside the city.

# EMERGING PALESTINIAN AUTONOMOUS AREAS

## Introductory Survey

### Location, Climate, Language, Religion, Flag, Capital

The Emerging Palestinian Autonomous Areas are located in the West Bank and the Gaza Strip. (For a more detailed description of the location of the Palestinian territories, see Government, below.) The West Bank lies in western Asia to the west of the Jordan river and the Dead Sea. To the north and south is the State of Israel, to the west the State of Israel and the Gaza Strip. The Interim Agreement of September 1995 (see below) provides for the creation of a corridor, or safe passage, linking the Gaza Strip with the West Bank. Including East Jerusalem, the West Bank covers an area of 5,633 sq km (2,175 sq miles). The West Bank can be divided into three major sub-regions: the Mount Hebron massif, the peaks of which rise to between 700 m and 1,000 m above sea-level; the Jerusalem mountains, which extend to the northernmost point of the Hebron-Bethlehem massif; and the Mount Samaria hills, the central section of which—the Nablus mountains—reaches heights of up to 800 m before descending to the northern Jenin hills, of between 300 m and 400 m. The eastern border of the West Bank is bounded by the valley of the Jordan river, leading to the Dead Sea (part of the Syrian-African rift valley), into which the Jordan drains. The latter is 400 m below sea-level. Precipitation ranges between 600 mm and 800 mm on the massif and 200 mm in the Jordan Valley. Apart from the urban centres of Bethlehem (Beit Lahm) and Hebron (Al-Khalil) to the south, the majority of the Palestinian population is concentrated in the northern localities around Ramallah (Ram Allah), Nablus (Nabulus), Jenin (Janin) and Tulkarm.

The Gaza Strip, lying beside the Mediterranean Sea and Israel's border with Egypt, covers an area of 364 sq km (140.5 sq miles). Crossed only by two shallow valleys, the Gaza Strip is otherwise almost entirely flat, and has no surface water. Annual average rainfall is 300 mm. Gaza City is the main population centre and the centre of administration for the Palestinian National Authority (PNA).

The language of the Palestinians of the West Bank and the Gaza Strip is Arabic. The majority of the Palestinian population of the territories are Muslims. A Christian minority represents about 2% of the Palestinian population of the West Bank and the Gaza Strip. This minority, in turn, represents about 45% of all Palestinian Christians.

In November 1988 the Palestine National Council (PNC) proclaimed Jerusalem as the capital of the newly-declared independent State of Palestine. In fact, West Jerusalem has been the capital of the State of Israel since 1950. In 1967 East Jerusalem was formally annexed by the Israeli authorities, although the annexation has never been recognized by the UN. The permanent status of Jerusalem remains subject to negotiation in the context of the Interim Agreement of September 1995.

### Recent History

Until the end of the 1948 Arab–Israeli War, the West Bank formed part of the British Mandate of Palestine, before becoming part of the Hashemite Kingdom of Jordan under the Armistice Agreement of 1949. It remained under Jordanian sovereignty, despite Israeli occupation in 1967, until King Hussein of Jordan formally relinquished legal and administrative control on 31 July 1988. Under Israeli military occupation the West Bank was administered by a military government, which divided the territory into seven subdistricts. The Civil Administration, as it was later termed, did not extend its jurisdiction to the many Israeli settlements that were established under the Israeli occupation; settlements remained subject to the Israeli legal and administrative system. By July 1998 approximately 26% of the West Bank was under Israeli military control, with responsibility for civil administration transferred to the Palestinian authorities; about 2% was under full Palestinian control; and the remainder under complete Israeli control.

An administrative province under the British Mandate of Palestine, Gaza was transferred to Egypt after the 1949 armistice and remained under Egyptian administration until June 1967, when it was invaded and occupied by Israel. Following Israeli occupation the Gaza Strip, like the West Bank, became an 'administered territory'. Until the provisions of the Declaration of Principles on Palestinian Self-Rule (see below) began to take effect, the management of day-to-day affairs was the responsibility of the area's Israeli military commander. Neither Israeli laws nor governmental and public bodies—including the Supreme Court—could review or alter the orders of the military command to any great extent. In 1993 it was estimated that about 50% of the land area was under Israeli control, either through the establishment of Jewish settlements or through the closure of areas by the military authorities.

In accordance with the Declaration of Principles on Palestinian Self-Rule of September 1993, and the Cairo Agreement on the Gaza Strip and Jericho of May 1994, the Palestine Liberation Organization (PLO) assumed control of the Jericho area of the West Bank, and of the Gaza Strip, on 17 May 1994. In November and December 1995, under the terms of the Israeli-Palestinian Interim Agreement on the West Bank and the Gaza Strip (the 'Oslo accords') signed by Israel and the PLO on 28 September 1995, Israeli armed forces withdrew from the West Bank towns of Nablus, Ramallah, Jenin, Tulkarm, Qalqilya and Bethlehem. In late December the PLO assumed responsibility in some 17 areas of civil administration in the town of Hebron. Under the terms of the Oslo accords, the PLO was eventually to assume full responsibility for civil affairs in the 400 surrounding villages, but the Israeli armed forces were to retain freedom of movement to act against potential hostilities there. In Hebron Israel effected a partial withdrawal of its armed forces in January 1997, but the Israeli authorities retained responsibility for the security of some 400 Jewish settlers occupying about 15% of the town. Responsibility for security in the rest of Hebron passed to the Palestinian police force, but Israel retained responsibility for security on access roads. Under the terms of the Oslo accords, Israel was to retain control over a large area of the West Bank (including Jewish settlements, rural areas, military installations and the majority of junctions between Palestinian roads and those used by Israeli troops and settlers until July 1997. Following the first phase of the redeployment and the holding, on its completion, of elections to a Palestinian Legislative Council and for a Palestinian executive president, Israel was to carry out a second redeployment from rural areas, to be completed by July 1997. The Israeli occupation was to be maintained in Jewish settlements, military installations, East Jerusalem and the Jewish settlements around Jerusalem until the conclusion of 'final status' negotiations between Israel and the Palestinians, scheduled for May 1999.

Subsequent postponements, and further negotiations within the context of the Oslo accords, resulted in a new timetable for Israeli redeployment which envisaged two phases, subsequent to the Hebron withrawal, to be completed by October 1997 and August 1998. 'Final status' negotiations on borders, the Jerusalem issue, Jewish settlements and Palestinian refugees were to commence within two months of the signing of the agreement on Hebron. As guarantor of the agreements, the USA undertook to obtain the release of some Palestinian prisoners, and to ensure that Israel continued to engage in negotiations for the establishment of a Palestinian airport in the Gaza Strip and for safe passage for Palestinians between the West Bank and the Gaza Strip. The USA also undertook to ensure that the Palestinians would continue to combat terrorism, complete the revision of the Palestinian National Charter (or PLO Covenant), adopted in 1964 and amended in 1968, and consider Israeli requests to extradite Palestinians suspected of involvement in attacks in Israel. By July 1998, however, conflicting interpretations of the extent of both the phased and total final redeployment (90% of the East Bank according to the Palestinians; less than 50% according to Israel) had resulted in a seemingly intractable impasse in the Oslo peace process.

By July 1998 progress on the redeployment of Israeli armed forces had been impeded for some 15 months. This paralysis emerged from the decision of the Israeli Government, announced in February 1997, to begin the construction of a new Jewish settlement on Jabal Abu Ghunaim (Har Homa in Hebrew), near Beit Sahur. Construction in this area was particularly controversial because, if completed, the new settlement would make it impossible to reach East Jerusalem from the West Bank without crossing Israeli territory, thereby prejudicing 'final status' negotiations concerning Jerusalem. In response, the Palestinians withdrew from 'final status' talks which had been scheduled to commence on 17 March. The beginning of construction work at Jabal Abu Ghunaim on 18 March provoked rioting among Palestinians and a resumption of attacks by the military wing of the Islamic Resistance Movement (Hamas) on Israeli civilian targets. The Israeli Cabinet responded by ordering a general closure of the West Bank and the Gaza Strip.

Both the Jabal Abu Ghunaim (Har Homa) construction and Israel's unilateral decision to redeploy its armed forces from only 9% of West Bank territory (announced in March 1997) were regarded by many observers as a vitiation of both the Oslo and the subsequent post-Hebron agreements. These were further undermined by the publication, in the Israeli daily newspaper, *Ha'aretz*, of the results of a US study which claimed that more than 25% of Jewish settlers' homes in the Gaza Strip and the West Bank were uninhabited (a claim rejected by the Israeli Central Bureau of Statistics which argued that only 12% of the settlements were unoccupied). The same newspaper later reported that Israeli plans, evolved within the framework of the Oslo accords, to relinquish 90% of the West Bank, had been revised in a new proposal—the so-called 'Allon plus' plan—to a 40% redeployment.

In June 1997 the US House of Representatives voted in favour of recognizing Jerusalem as the undivided capital of Israel and of transferring the US embassy to the city from Tel-Aviv. US President Bill Clinton was reported to have strongly disapproved of the vote, owing to its possible implications for the peace process. The decision coincided with violent clashes between Palestinian civilians and Israeli troops in both Gaza and Hebron, which reached a climax in Hebron at the end of the month.

At the beginning of July 1997 a series of meetings were held between the US Under-Secretary of State for Political Affairs, Thomas Pickering, and Israeli and Palestinian officials, with the aim of resuming negotiations between the Palestinian National Authority (PNA) and the Israeli Government. On 28 July both sides announced that peace talks were to be resumed in early August. However, on 30 July, on the eve of Dennis Ross's visit to reactivate the negotiations, Hamas carried out a 'suicide bomb' attack at a Jewish market in Jerusalem, in which 14 civilians were killed and more than 150 injured. Ross cancelled his visit and the Israeli Government immediately halted payment of tax revenues to the PNA and closed the Gaza Strip and the West Bank. In the aftermath of the bombing the Palestinian authorities commenced a campaign to detain members of Hamas and Islamic Jihad.

At the beginnning of September 1997, in anticipation of a visit to the region in mid-September by the US Secretary of State, Madeleine Albright, the Israeli authorities relaxed the closure they had imposed on the Gaza Strip and the West Bank in July. On 4 September, however, a further 'suicide bomb' attack in Jerusalem in which eight people died (including the bombers themselves), led to the reimposition of Israeli sanctions. Hamas claimed responsibility for the attack, and the Israeli Prime Minister, Binyamin Netanyahu, immediately renewed his demand that the Palestinian authorities should take effective action against terrorism.

The visit to the Middle East in September 1997 by the US Secretary of State failed to reactivate the peace process. During her visit, Albright reportedly stated that Israel should halt the construction of Jewish settlements on Arab lands, cease confiscations of land and the demolition of Arab dwellings, and end its policy of confiscating Palestinian identity documents. At the same time, she endorsed Netanyahu's demand that the PNA should take more effective measures to suppress the military wing of Hamas. Impatience within the US Administration at the Israeli Government's apparently provocative acts was demonstrated by Albright's criticism of Netanyahu's decision, announced in late September 1997, to permit the construction of 300 new homes for Jewish settlers in Efrat in the West Bank.

On 28 September 1997 it was announced that, as a result of US diplomacy, Israeli and Palestinian officials had agreed to resume negotiations in early October. The first round of talks, scheduled to commence on 6 October, would reportedly focus on the outstanding issues of the Oslo accords, in particular the opening of an airport and seaport facilities in the Gaza Strip, the establishment of a safe corridor linking the Gaza Strip with the West Bank and the release of Palestinian prisoners being detained in Israel. A second round of talks was to commence on 13 October, in order to address the issues of security co-operation between the Palestinian and the Israeli authorities; the long-delayed redeployment of Israeli armed forces from the West Bank; Israeli expansion and construction of settlements; and questions pertaining to 'final status' negotiations.

The attempted assassination in Amman, in late September 1997, of Khalid Meshaal, the head of the Hamas political bureau in Jordan, provoked warnings of retaliation both before and after official confirmation that agents of the Israeli security service, Mossad, had been responsible for the attack. In order to secure the release of its agents by the Jordanian authorities, Israel was obliged, on 1 October, to free (together with other Arab political prisoners) Sheikh Ahmad Yassin, the founder and spiritual leader of Hamas, who had been sentenced to life imprisonment in Israel in 1989 for complicity in attacks on Israeli soldiers. The release of Sheikh Yassin into Jordanian custody was swiftly followed by his return, on 6 October, to Gaza, where his presence further complicated co-operation between the Israeli and the Palestinian authorities on security issues.

On 7 October 1997 talks resumed between Palestinian and Israeli negotiators on the outstanding issues of the Oslo accords, and on the following day the Palestinian President and the Israeli Prime Minister held their first meeting for eight months.

In December 1997, following further US pressure, it was reported that the Israeli Cabinet had agreed in principle to withdraw troops from an unspecified area of West Bank territory. Some two weeks later, however, it remained uncertain whether Netanyahu would be able to persuade intransigent elements within his Government to endorse this decision. In early January 1998 the US special envoy to the Middle East, Dennis Ross, visited Israel in a further attempt to break the deadlock regarding the redeployment. However, in the second week of January the Israeli Government reiterated that it would not conduct such a redeployment until the Palestinian authorities had fulfilled a series of conditions. Among these were requirements that the Palestinian leadership should adopt effective measures to counter terrorism; that it should reduce the strength of its security forces from 40,000 to 24,000; and that the Palestinian National Charter should be revised to recognize explicitly Israel's right to exist. Palestinian officials maintained that these conditions had already been met when the agreement regarding the withdrawal of Israeli armed forces from Hebron was concluded one year earlier. There was further evidence of a hardening of the Israeli position prior to a summit meeting, scheduled to take place in Washington, DC, in late January. The Israeli Cabinet issued a communiqué detailing 'vital and national interests' in the West Bank (amounting to some 60% of the entire territory) which it was not prepared to relinquish. The document asserted that Israel would, among other areas, retain control of the territory surrounding the Jerusalem region.

On 20 January 1998 US President Bill Clinton held talks with the Israeli Prime Minister in Washington, DC. It was reported that the USA was seeking to persuade Israel to effect a second withdrawal of its armed forces from some 12% of the West Bank over a period of 80 days, in exchange for increased co-operation on security issues by the Palestinian authorities. On 25 January, however, it was announced that direct contacts between the Palestinian delegation and the Israeli Prime Minister had collapsed. President Arafat was reported to be seeking to convene an Arab summit meeting on the deadlocked Middle East peace process.

In late March 1998 it emerged that the USA planned to present new proposals regarding the withdrawal of Israeli armed forces at separate meetings between the US Secretary of State and Arafat and Netanyahu in Europe. On 26 March Dennis Ross arrived in Jerusalem in order to present details of the latest US initiative. Although no details had been published, it appeared that the US proposals would involve an Israeli withdrawal from slightly more than 13% of West Bank territory, and a suspension of settlement construction in return for further efforts by the PNA to combat organizations, such as Hamas, engaged in campaigns of violence against Israeli targets. President Arafat sought an Israeli withdrawal from a further 30% of West Bank territory, but there were indications that he might be prepared to accept an initial withdrawal from some 13% of the West Bank. However, it was evident that, even if agreement could be reached between the two sides, the issue of whether a subsequent withdrawal should take place prior to the commencement of 'final status' negotiations remained far more contentious. In any case, the Israeli Cabinet rejected the reported details of the new US initiative. At the end of March US Secretary of State Albright stated that the peace process was on the verge of collapse, and indicated that the USA was considering ending its involvement as a mediator.

In late April 1998 it emerged that the EU was seeking to play a greater role in the stalled Middle East peace process. It was reported that, during a visit to Gaza City, the British Prime Minister, Tony Blair, had obtained the agreement of President Arafat to attend a conference in London, based on the most recent US initiative for restarting the peace process. A summit meeting, hosted by Blair and attended by Netanyahu, Arafat and the US Secretary of State, took place in early May. At its conclusion Albright invited Netanyahu and Arafat to attend a summit meeting with US President Clinton in Washington, DC, on 12 May. The USA had reportedly proposed that the parties could proceed to 'final status' negotiations as soon as the scope of the next Israeli withdrawal from the West Bank had been agreed. However, the Israeli Government subsequently rejected the US initiative in advance of Clinton's direct participation. Further discussions in mid-May, involving the US Secretary of State, achieved no progress.

In early June 1998 details of the latest US initiative were unofficially disclosed in the Israeli press. Israel would have to agree to 'no significant expansion' of Jewish settlements and relinquish slightly more than 13% of West Bank territory over a period of 12 weeks in exchange for increased Palestinian co-operation. The adoption by the Israeli Cabinet in late June 1998 of a plan to extend the boundaries of Jerusalem and construct homes there for a further 1m. people prompted incredulity at the US Department of State and accusations by Palestinian officials that it amounted to a *de facto* annexation of territories that were officially subject to 'final status' negotiations. It was subsequently reported that the Israeli Government was considering holding a popular referendum on a further withdrawal of Israeli armed forces from West Bank territory.

On 7 July 1998 the United Nations General Assembly, in defiance of objections from the USA and Israel, approved a resolution, by a vote of 124–4, to upgrade the status of the PLO at the UN. The new provision allowed the PLO to participate in debates, to co-sponsor resolutions, and to raise points of order during discussions of Middle Eastern affairs.

On 19–22 July 1998 Israeli and Palestinian delegations held direct negotiations for the first time since March 1997. They discussed the most recent US initiative to reactivate the peace process, which had been disclosed in June, but the proposal was deemed unacceptable by Israel. In late August Netanyahu was reported to have presented a compromise plan to his Cabinet, whereby Israel would effect a full redeployment from a further 10% of the West Bank and a partial withdrawal from 3% of the Judaean desert. Arafat gave a cautious welcome to the compromise plan on the following day. In late September Netanyahu and Arafat met for the first time since October 1997, at the White House in Washington, DC, and agreed to participate in a peace conference in the USA in the following month. The summit meeting, also attended by US President Bill Clinton, commenced at the Wye Plantation, Maryland, USA, on 15 October 1998, and culminated in the signing, on 23 October, of the Wye River Memorandum, which was intended to facilitate the implementation of the Oslo accords of September 1995.

Under the terms of the Wye Memorandum, which was to be implemented within three months of its signing, Israel was to transfer a further 13.1% of West Bank territory from exclusive Israeli control to joint Israeli-Palestinian control. An additional 14% of the West Bank was to be transferred from joint Israeli-Palestinian control to exclusive Palestinian control. The Wye Memorandum also stipulated that negotiations with regard to a third Israeli redeployment under the Oslo accords should proceed concurrently with 'final status' negotiations; that the Palestinians should reinforce anti-terrorism measures under the supervision of the US Central Intelligence Agency (CIA); that the strength of the Palestinian police force should be reduced by 25%; that the Palestinians should arrest 30 suspected terrorists; that Israel should carry out the phased release of 750 Palestinian prisoners (including political detainees); that the Palestine National Council (PNC) should annul those clauses of the PLO Covenant deemed to be anti-Israeli; that Gaza International Airport was to become operational with an Israeli security presence; and that an access corridor between the West Bank and the Gaza Strip should be opened.

The Memorandum was endorsed by the Israeli Cabinet on 11 November 1998, and was approved by the Knesset on 17 November. Three days later Israel redeployed its armed forces from about 500 sq km of the West Bank. Of this area, some 400 sq km came under exclusive Palestinian control for both civil and security affairs. In the remaining 100 sq km the PNA assumed responsibility for civil affairs, while Israel retained control over security. At the same time, Israel released some 250 Palestinian prisoners (although a majority were non-political prisoners) and signed a protocol for the opening of Gaza International Airport. Israel retained the right to decide which airlines could use the airport, which was officially inaugurated by President Arafat on 24 November. However, implementation of the Wye Memorandum did not proceed smoothly, with mutual accusations of failure to observe its terms.

In the weeks prior to a visit to Israel and the Gaza Strip by the US President on 12–15 December 1998, violent clashes erupted in the West Bank between Palestinians and the Israeli security forces. One cause of the unrest was a decision by the Israeli Cabinet to suspend further releases of Palestinian prisoners under the terms of the Wye Memorandum, and its insistence that Palestinians convicted of killing Israelis, and members of Hamas and Islamic Jihad, would not be released. On 14 December, meanwhile, in the presence of President Clinton, the PNC voted to annul articles of the Palestinian National Charter which were deemed to be anti-Israeli. While the Israeli Prime Minister welcomed the vote, he insisted that several further conditions had to be met before Israel would expedite the implementation of the Wye Memorandum. At a summit meeting between the US President, Netanyahu and Arafat at the Erez checkpoint between Israel and the Gaza Strip on 15 December, Netanyahu reiterated Israel's stance regarding the release of Palestinian prisoners (see above). He further demanded that the Palestinians should cease incitement to violence and formally relinquish plans to declare unilaterally Palestinian statehood on 4 May 1999, the original deadline as established by the Oslo accords. (In November 1998 Arafat had reasserted his intention to declare statehood on that date, which in 1999 he repeatedly insisted was 'sacred'). At the conclusion of the meeting Netanyahu announced that Israel would not proceed with the second scheduled redeployment of its armed forces (under the Wye Memorandum) on 18 December 1998, claiming once again that the Palestinians had failed to honour their commitments. On 20 December the Israeli Cabinet voted to suspend implementation of the Wye Memorandum.

In January 1999 President Arafat came under intense international pressure, notably from the USA, EU countries, Egypt and Jordan, to postpone any unilateral declaration of Palestinian statehood, at least until after the Israeli elections, scheduled for 17 May. Moreover, Arafat apparently considered that making such a declaration prior to the elections might actually improve Netanyahu's chances of re-election. In late January Arafat indicated that he might postpone a declaration of independence if he received certain assurances from Israel and the international community (particularly the USA and EU) regarding the issue of settlement expansion. During a tour of several European countries, Arafat was advised by EU governments that a declaration of statehood was likely to result in victory in the Israeli elections for those parties which opposed the Oslo accords. In a further attempt to influence Arafat, in February the German Vice-Chancellor and Minister of Foreign Affairs, Joseph Fischer, led an EU delegation to the Palestinian territories; the visit coincided with mounting controversy over the provision of EU funding to the PNA. (In late April the European Parliament accused the PNA of financial mismanagement, while the European Commission denied reports that funds intended for housing projects in Gaza had been used to build luxury apartments for associates of Arafat.) Meanwhile, at the end of January it was reported that more than 80% of PLC deputies were opposed to a unilateral declaration of Palestinian statehood on 4 May. In mid-March the Palestinian leader embarked on a further round of intensive diplomacy, visiting Gulf states and several European capitals. On 23 March he held a private meeting with President Clinton in Washington, DC. Meanwhile, at a summit meeting in Berlin, Germany, on 26 March, EU leaders issued their firmest commitment to date to support the creation of an independent Palestinian state. During April President Arafat visited, among other countries, Canada, Turkey, Russia, China, India, Egypt and Jordan. In late April PLO chief negotiators Mahmud Abbas and Saeb Erekat visited Washington, DC, in order to secure certain assurances from the USA in return for an extension of the 4 May deadline. On 27 April the PLO Central Council, together with Hamas representatives, met in Gaza; two days later the Council announced a postponement of a declaration on Palestinian statehood until after the Israeli elections. Despite being welcomed by Israel, the USA, the EU and Arab states, the PLO's decision provoked violent demonstrations among many Palestinians.

Palestinians cautiously welcomed Ehud Barak's victory in the Israeli premiership elections of 17 May 1999 (see chapter on Israel). PNA officials immediately urged Barak to break the deadlock in the Middle East peace process. However, in his victory address on 18 May, the new Israeli Prime Minister disappointed Palestinians by insisting that he would not offer them any fundamental concessions. After the elections there emerged a Palestinian consensus that a halt to Israel's programme of settlement expansion in the Israeli-occupied territories (which Palestinians view as part of an attempt to predetermine the 'final status' borders) must be a precondition for any meaningful resumption of the peace process. On 3 June Palestinians in the West Bank declared a 'day of rage' against continuing settlement expansion there; the mass protests, which were particularly violent in Hebron, followed an announcement in late May that the population of the West Bank's largest Jewish settlement, Ma'aleh Edomin, was to be expanded from 25,000 to 50,000 settlers.

The first direct meeting between Prime Minister Barak and Arafat was held at the Erez checkpoint on 11 July 1999. Both leaders repeated their commitment to restarting the peace process; however, Arafat was reportedly alarmed by Barak's apparent opposition to full implementation of the Wye Memorandum and his seeming preoccupation with the Syrian component of the peace process (see below). During the second meeting between the two leaders on 27 July at Erez, Barak angered Palestinians by seeking to win Arafat's approval to postpone implementation of the Wye Memorandum until it could be combined with 'final status' negotiations (thereby implying a 15-month delay in further Israeli troop redeployments). On 1 August Barak promised to bring forward the release of 250 Palestinian prisoners if Arafat agreed to a postponement. On the same day, however, discussions between the two delegations broke down when Arafat rejected the Israeli stance. Discussions were resumed in mid-August, when Israel agreed to pursue implementation of the Wye Memorandum, and on 4 September Barak and Arafat signed the Sharm esh-Sheikh Memorandum (or Wye Two accords). Under the terms of the Memorandum (which outlined a revised timetable for implementation of the outstanding provisions of the original Wye Memorandum), on 9 September Israel released some 200 Palestinian 'security' prisoners; on the following day Israel transferred a further 7% of the West Bank to PNA control.

A ceremonial opening of 'final status' negotiations between Israel and the Palestinians took place at the Erez checkpoint on 13 September 1999; shortly afterwards details emerged of a secret meeting between the Israeli and Palestinian leaders to discuss an agenda for such talks. However, in early October the Palestinians' chief negotiator, Yasser Abd ar-Rabbuh, warned that the PNA would boycott 'final status' talks unless Israel ended its settlement expansion programme. In mid-October Barak, also under pressure from left-wing groups in Israel, responded by dismantling 12 'settlement outposts' in the West Bank which he deemed to be illegal. Meanwhile, on 15 October Israel released a further 151 Palestinian prisoners, under the terms of the Wye Two agreement. The inauguration of the first 'safe passage' between the West Bank and Gaza Strip took place on 25 October. The opening had been delayed by almost a month owing to a dispute between the Israeli and Palestinian authorities over security arrangements for the 44 km-route, which linked the Erez checkpoint in the Gaza Strip to Hebron in the West Bank. Israel asserted that it would maintain almost complete control over the so-called 'southern route', as well as deciding which Palestinians would be permitted to use it. In late October the killing of a Palestinian by Israeli soldiers resulted in several days of violence between Palestinians and Israeli security forces in the West Bank town of Bethlehem.

'Final status' negotiations between Israel and the PNA commenced in Ramallah on 8 November 1999, following a summit meeting, held earlier in the month in Oslo, Norway, between Arafat, Barak and President Clinton. The opening of 'final status' talks had been threatened when three bombs exploded in northern Israel. (Israel claimed that Hamas was responsible, since the attack followed an alleged warning by the organization's military wing that it would intensify its activities in protest at Israel's settlement policies.) A further redeployment of Israeli armed forces from 5% of the West Bank, scheduled for 15 November, was postponed owing to disagreement over the areas to be transferred. Relations between the two sides worsened when, on 6 December, Palestinian negotiators walked out of 'final status' talks after demanding that Israel should end immediately its policy of settlement expansion. The announcement came amid reports that settlement activity had intensified under Barak. The Israeli Prime Minister, apparently in response to US pressure, subsequently announced a halt to settlement construction, at least during the negotiations regarding a framework agreement. On 21 December Arafat held talks in Ramallah with Barak, who was the first Israeli premier to hold peace discussions in Palestinian territory. At the end of the month Israel released some 26 Palestinian 'security' prisoners as a 'gesture of goodwill'. On 5 January 2000 Israeli armed forces withdrew from a further 5% of the West Bank; however, Israel announced in mid-January that a third redeployment from some 6% of the territory (scheduled to take place on 20 January, according to Wye Two) would be postponed until Barak had returned from peace talks with Syria in the USA. During a meeting with Arafat on 18 January, Barak was reported to have proposed that the deadline for reaching a framework 'final status' agreement be postponed for two months. The approval by the Israeli Cabinet of a withdrawal of its troops from a sparsely-populated area of the West Bank led Palestinian negotiators to break off the negotiations in early February.

Since Barak's victory in May 1999, one of Arafat's principal concerns has been the Israeli concentration of efforts on the Lebanese and, especially, Syrian elements of the Middle East peace process. Any possibility of a breakthrough in Israeli-Syrian negotiations (which resumed in early December) would leave the Palestinians in a position of isolation. In mid-June Arafat was reported to have accused both the Jordanian and Syrian leaders of having abandoned the PNA. In August a political crisis developed after the Syrian Deputy Prime Minister and Minister of Defence, Maj.-Gen. Mustafa Tlass, was reported to have made highly insulting remarks about Yasser Arafat—including a claim that Arafat had 'sold Jerusalem and the Arab nation' in peace deals concluded with Israel since 1993—leading to Palestinian demands for Tlass' resignation, and the issuing, by Fatah, of a death warrant for him.

Palestinians reacted to the death of King Hussein of Jordan on 7 February 1999 with public grief—about 65% of the Kingdom's inhabitants are believed to be of Palestinian origin—especially in the West Bank, which King Hussein ruled for 15 years until June 1967. For Arafat, the death of Hussein was a political disaster since the King had frequently supported him when the peace process with Israel appeared to be on the verge of collapse. Arafat subsequently surprised many Jordanians by proposing the establishment of a Palestinian-Jordanian confederation. The proposal (which had been put forward as part of a peace initiative in 1985, but was rejected by King Hussein) was not welcomed in Jordan, where it was considered to be premature while the West Bank was still largely under Israeli occupation.

Elections to a Palestinian Legislative Council (PLC) took place on 20 January 1996. Some 75% of the estimated 1m. eligible Palestinian voters were reported to have participated in the elections, returning 86 deputies to the 89-seat Council. Of the remaining three seats, one was automatically reserved for the president of the Council's executive body—the Palestinian President. The remaining two seats were not filled at the elections of January 1996 and one seat remained vacant in early 2000. The election of a Palestinian Executive President was held at the same time as the elections to the PLC. Yasser Arafat, who was opposed by one other candidate, received 88.1% of the votes cast in the election and took office as President on 12 February 1996. Deputies returned to the PLC automatically became members of the PNC, the existing 483 members of which were subsequently permitted to return from exile by the Israeli authorities. The PLC held its first session in Gaza City on 7 March, electing Ahmed Quray as its Speaker.

At the 21st session of the PNC, held in Gaza City on 22–24 April 1996, the PNC voted to amend the Palestinian National Charter by annulling those clauses that sought the destruction of the State of Israel. The PNC also voted to amend all clauses contained within the Charter that were not in harmony with an agreement of mutual recognition concluded by Israel and the PLO in September 1993. On 24 April the PNC elected a new Executive Committee, and in May President Arafat appointed the members of a Palestinian Cabinet. The appointments were approved by the PLC in July.

In April 1997 President Arafat's audit office announced the misappropriation by PNA ministers of some US $326m. of public funds. Khalid al-Qidram, the General Prosecutor of the PNA who resigned in response to the findings, was reportedly placed under house arrest in June. At the end of July a parliamentary committee, appointed by Arafat to conduct an inquiry into the affair, concluded that the Cabinet should be dissolved and that some of its members should be prosecuted. In early August the Cabinet submitted its resignation, but this was not accepted by the President until December. The Cabinet was to remain in office in a provisional capacity until new ministerial appointments were made in early 1998.

In addition to persistent allegations of corruption within the PNA, President Arafat himself has been the target of criticism from within the Palestinian leadership, which has accused him of autocracy. In October 1997 Haider Abd ash-Shafi, who had played a prominent role in the peace negotiations with Israel and who was reportedly held in high popular esteem, resigned in protest at the style of Arafat's leadership and at the way in which talks with Israel were being conducted. It was reported in November that potential successors to Arafat had initiated political manoeuvres amid enduring rumours that the President was in poor health. Among those cited as possible candidates to replace him were Djibril Rajoub, the head of the Palestinian preventive security services in the West Bank, and Muhammad Dahlan, his counterpart in the Gaza Strip.

It has frequently been claimed that the Palestinian security forces resort to intimidation and torture in their treatment of Palestinian detainees. Such allegations were contained in a report published by a prominent human rights organization, Human Rights Watch, in 1998. In February, in its annual report, the Palestinian Independent Commission for Citizens' Rights accused Palestinian security personnel of the mistreatment of prisoners. In the same month the results of the first census conducted by the Palestinian authorities, in December 1997, were released.

In February 1998 President Arafat instigated firm action to suppress popular demonstrations in support of Iraq, which had exposed itself to threats of military action by the USA in a dispute over weapons inspections by the UN. It was reported that many members of Arafat's own political movement, Fatah, had been arrested for flouting a ban on such protests, and that the publication and broadcasting of reports in support of President Saddam Hussain of Iraq had been forbidden.

In March 1998 the PLC threatened to hold a vote of 'no-confidence' in President Arafat's leadership in protest at alleged corruption within the PNA, the prolonged delay in approval of budget proposals for 1998 and at the failure to hold local government elections. There was speculation that the PNA had postponed these elections because it feared that they would reveal widespread dissatisfaction at the way in which peace negotiations with Israel were being conducted. The PLC renewed its threat in mid-1998, when it issued an ultimatum to President Arafat and the Cabinet, demanding that they should respond to allegations of corruption and mismanagement and approve the 1998 budget within two weeks.

US officials were reported to have confirmed, in March 1998, that the US CIA was assisting the Palestinian security forces in the spheres of espionage, information-gathering and interrogation in an attempt to reassure the Israeli Government of their ability to take effective action against groups involved in attacks on Israeli targets. Later in March the death of a senior member of Hamas provoked a serious deterioration in relations between the Islamist organization and the PNA. Hamas accused the PNA of collaboration with the Israeli authorities in the killing of Muhi ad-Din Sharif, and its threats to wreak revenge on Israeli citizens prompted the PNA to arrest many of its members. In April, however, Hamas's political leader in Jordan retracted the allegation that the PNA had collaborated with Israel. In the same month it was reported that Hamas had become the dominant political force in Palestinian universities, where the organization claimed to command the allegiance of some 40% of students.

In June 1998 the Cabinet resigned, apparently in order to obstruct an attempt by the PLC to pass a vote of 'no-confidence' in it (see above). A new Cabinet, appointed by Arafat on 5 August, included several new ministers, but only one minister of the outgoing Cabinet was actually dismissed. On the following day, two prominent ministers resigned on the grounds that the Cabinet reshuffle had failed adequately to address the shortcomings of the PNA. The new Cabinet was also criticized by officials of the principal international organizations granting funds to the PNA. In November, nevertheless, donors agreed to grant the PNA more than US $3,000m., to be disbursed over the next five years.

During September 1998 the chief negotiator at the peace talks and Minister of Local Government, Saeb Erekat, and the Minister of State for the Environment, Yousuf Abu Saffieh, were both persuaded by Arafat to withdraw their resignations, tendered in protest at inefficiency and incompetence within the PNA. In mid-October the PNA faced allegations of financial mismanagement, after some US $70m. collected in customs revenues at border crossings allegedly failed to be deposited in the PNA treasury.

In late October 1998, shortly after the signing of the Wye Memorandum, the PNA detained 11 journalists for attempting to obtain an interview with the spiritual leader of Hamas, Sheikh Ahmad Yassin (who was subsequently placed under house arrest); they also arrested an outspoken cleric and Islamic Jihad's chief spokesman for publicly criticizing the Wye agreement. In subsequent weeks there was a steady erosion of press freedom in the West Bank and the Gaza Strip: several radio and television stations, as well as press offices, were closed down by the PNA, and journalists were imprisoned on various charges. There was also a marked increase in self-censorship in the pro-government printed and electronic media and at the state-controlled radio and television stations.

The PNA's dubious human rights record remained a major concern for Palestinians in 1999. In January the PLC approved a motion urging an end to political detention and the release of all those imprisoned on exclusively political charges. (The motion demanded the formation of a special committee to assess the case of every political prisoner in the Palestinian territories and to recommend which prisoners should be released; the committee was duly appointed on 15 February, under the chairmanship of the Minister of Justice.) The PNA responded to the PLC's immediate demands by releasing 37 political prisoners. However, in late January many detainees linked to Hamas and Islamic Jihad began a hunger strike in Jericho and Nablus, in protest at their continued detention without trial. During February thousands of Palestinians—mostly Hamas supporters—demonstrated in support of the detainees. On 6 February some 3,000 protesters marched to the PNA headquarters, accusing the PNA of 'subservience to Israel and the CIA'. (Under the terms of the Wye Memorandum, the US CIA was charged with monitoring the PNA's compliance with the security provisions as part of a trilateral committee involving the PNA and Israel.)

In February 1999 a Gaza-based police chief, known to be an opponent of Hamas, alleged that the organization had received some US $35m. from Iran in order to carry out 'suicide bombings' against Israeli targets, and thus assist Netanyahu's May 1999 election campaign (see chaprter on Israel). Both Iran and Hamas leaders strongly denied the allegations. Relations between the PNA and Hamas were further strained following the murder of a Palestinian intelligence officer in Rafah. In March a security agent and former member of Hamas' military wing was sentenced to death for the attack, while two accomplices received lengthy prison sentences. The verdict provoked serious clashes between Palestinian police and protesters in the Gaza Strip, during which two teenagers were shot dead by police; Arafat was forced to curtail an official visit to Jordan to address the domestic security crisis.

Throughout May 1999 lawyers and jurists in the West Bank and the Gaza Strip organized a series of strikes and protests against the alleged 'virtual collapse of the Palestinian judicial system'. The protests followed an appeal made to Yasser Arafat by the head of the Palestinian Bar Association to resolve the problem of continuing lawlessness in Palestinian society, to increase the number of lawyers in the territories and improve their training, and to appoint a new General Prosecutor of the PNA (the post having been vacant for many months). In mid-June Zuheir as-Surani was appointed General Prosecutor.

In early June 1999 security surrounding Yasser Arafat was tightened, after a group of Palestinian dissidents calling themselves 'the Free Officers and the Honest People of Palestine' released a statement in which they accused leading Palestinian officials of corruption and of collaboration with Israel, and indirectly threatened to assassinate the President; nine arrests were subsequently made by the security forces. On 1 August a Palestinian national dialogue conference was held in Cairo, Egypt, and included representatives of Fatah and the Popular Front for the Liberation of Palestine (PFLP). On 22–23 August Arafat and the Secretary-General of the Democratic Front for the Liberation of Palestine (DFLP), Naif Hawatmeh, met, in Cairo, for the first time since 1993. At the end of the month representatives of nine Palestinian political factions, meeting in Ramallah, agreed on an agenda for a comprehensive national dialogue; Hamas and Islamic Jihad, however, refused to enter the dialogue. (In late August 1999 the Palestinian authorities were reported to have arrested several suspected activists of these two organizations in the West Bank and the Gaza Strip, while the Jordanian authorities closed Hamas' offices in Amman.) Meanwhile, it was reported in early September that the leader of the PFLP, George Habash, had resigned. In late September the organization's deputy leader, Abu Ali Moustafa, was permitted by the Israeli Government to return to the West Bank from exile in Jordan, in order to participate in reconciliation talks with Arafat. However, although in late October Israel had also reportedly granted an entry permit to the DFLP leader, the Israeli authorities subsequently cancelled Hawatmeh's right of return. On 10 October the Chairman of the Palestinian Public Control Commission was granted ministerial status, under the terms of a presidential decree issued by Yasser Arafat.

In November 1999 a statement was issued by 20 leading Palestinian intellectuals (including members of the PLC), in which they criticized the corruption, mismanagement and abuse of power within the PNA, and accused Palestinian officials of ineffectiveness in the peace talks with Israel. The authorities responded by launching a crackdown on Arafat's critics, detaining several of the document's signatories or placing them under house arrest. In December a PLC member, who had signed the anti-corruption manifesto, was wounded by unidentified gunmen in Nablus, in an apparent attempt to silence criticism of Arafat's administration. Meanwhile, in late 1999 the US-based organization, Human Rights Watch, issued a letter to Arafat, in which it urged the President to take action in order to increase press freedom.

## Government

In accordance with the Declaration of Principles on Palestinian Self-Rule of September 1993, and the Cairo Agreement on the Gaza Strip and Jericho, the PLO assumed control of the Jericho area of the West Bank and of the Gaza Strip on 17 May 1994. In November and December 1995, under the terms of the Israeli-Palestinian Interim Agreement on the West Bank and the Gaza Strip (the 'Oslo accords') signed by Israel and the PLO on 28 September 1995, Israeli armed forces withdrew from the West Bank towns of Nablus, Ramallah, Jenin, Tulkarm, Qalqilya and Bethlehem. In late December the PLO assumed responsibility in some 17 areas of civil administration in the town of Hebron. The Oslo accords divided the West Bank into three zones: Areas A, B and C. As of July 1998, the PNA had sole jurisdiction and security control in Area A (2% of the West Bank), but Israel retained authority over movement into and out of the Area. In Area B (26% of the West Bank) the PNA had some limited authority while Israel maintained a security presence and 'overriding security responsibility'. Area C, the remaining 72% of the West Bank, was under Israeli military occupation. In accordance with the Wye Memorandum of October 1998 (see Recent History, above), Israel effected a further redeployment of its armed forces from approximately 500 sq km of West Bank territory in November 1998. Of this, about 400 sq km became Area A territory and the remainder Area B territory. After full implementation of the Wye Memorandum Area A will constitute 17.2% of the West Bank, Area B 23.9% and Area C 58.9%. The total area of the West Bank over which the PNA will eventually assume control, and the extent of its jurisdiction there, remain subject to 'final status' negotiations with Israel.

## Defence

Paramilitary forces in the Gaza Strip and in the areas of the West Bank where the PNA has assumed responsibility for security totalled an estimated 35,000 in August 1999. They included a Public Security Force of 14,000 (Gaza 6,000, West Bank 8,000); a Civil Police Force of 10,000 (Gaza 4,000, West Bank 6,000); a Preventive Security Force of 3,000 (Gaza 1,200, West Bank 1,800); a General Intelligence Force of 3,000; a Military Intelligence Force of 500; and a Presidential Security Force of 3,000. In addition, there are small forces belonging to Coastal Police, Civil Defence, Air Force, a Customs and Excise Police Force and a University Security Service. Units of the Palestine National Liberation Army (PNLA) are garrisoned in various countries in the Middle East and North Africa. The security budget of the Gaza Strip and the Palestinian Autonomous Areas of the West Bank was estimated at US $500m. in 1999.

## Economic Affairs

In 1997, according to the Palestinian Central Bureau of Statistics (PCBS), the gross national product (GNP) of the West Bank and the Gaza Strip, measured in current prices, was US $4,906m., equivalent to $1,763 per head. Expressed in Israeli new shekels at constant 1986 prices, the IMF estimates that the GNP of the West Bank and the Gaza Strip declined at an average annual rate of 0.8%, and that GNP per head declined at an average annual rate of 5.4%, in 1995–97. Over the same period the population increased by an estimated annual average rate of 5.0%. The IMF estimates that in 1995–97, again expressed in Israeli new shekels at constant 1986 prices, the gross domestic product (GDP) of the West Bank and the Gaza Strip declined at an average annual rate of 1.3%. According to the Ministry of Finance, GDP increased by 4.2% in 1998, and was forecast to grow by 4.5% in 1999.

According to the PCBS, agriculture and fishing contributed 7.2% of the GDP of the West Bank and the Gaza Strip in 1997. At the census conducted by the Palestinian authorities in December 1997, agriculture, hunting, forestry and fishing were reported to employ 10.7% of the total labour force of the West Bank (excluding East

Jerusalem) and the Gaza Strip. Although the agricultural sector is focused mainly on supplying local needs, about one-half of Palestinian exports are derived from agricultural production. Citrus fruits are the principal export crop, and horticulture also makes a significant contribution to trade. Other important crops are olives, tomatoes, cucumbers, grapes and potatoes. It was reported that a drought during the 1998/99 season had seriously affected the Palestinian economy.

Industry (mining and quarrying, manufacturing, electricity and water supply and construction) contributed 30.0% of the GDP of the West Bank and the Gaza Strip in 1997. At the census conducted in December 1997 the industrial sectors (including gas utilities) employed 40.9% of the total labour force of the West Bank (excluding East Jerusalem) and the Gaza Strip. Construction alone employed 25.6% of the total labour force.

Mining and quarrying contributed 1.1% of the GDP of the West Bank and the Gaza Strip in 1997. At the census conducted in December 1997 the sector employed 0.4% of the total labour force of the West Bank (excluding East Jerusalem) and the Gaza Strip.

Manufacturing contributed 17.8% of the GDP of the West Bank and the Gaza Strip in 1997. At the census conducted in December 1997 the sector employed 14.8% of the total labour force of the West Bank (excluding East Jerusalem) and the Gaza Strip. Palestinian manufacturing is characterized by small-scale enterprises which typically engage in food-processing and the production of textiles and footwear.

The power sector—electricity and water supply—contributed 0.9% of the GDP of the West Bank and the Gaza Strip in 1997. At the census conducted in December 1997, electricity, gas and water utilities employed 0.2% of the total labour force of the West Bank (excluding East Jerusalem) and the Gaza Strip. In the West Bank there is no utility supplying electric power apart from the Jerusalem District Electric Company, which supplies Jerusalem, Bethlehem, Ramallah and Al-Birah. Most municipalities in the Gaza Strip purchase electricity from the Israel Electric Corporation.

In 1997 the services sector contributed 63% of the GDP of the West Bank and the Gaza Strip. Within the services sector, real estate and business services contributed 16.0% of GDP, and wholesale and retail trade 13.4%. At the census conducted in December 1997 the services sector employed 48.3% of the total labour force of the West Bank (excluding East Jerusalem) and the Gaza Strip. The census reported that 13.7% of the total labour force were employed in the wholesale and retail trade and repair branch of the services sector, and almost 12% in public administration and defence and compulsory social security.

According to the Palestine Monetary Authority, in 1997 the West Bank and the Gaza Strip recorded a trade deficit of an estimated US $1,775m. and a deficit of $755m. on the current account of the balance of payments. In that year, according to PCBS figures, the value of exports (f.o.b.) to Israel was estimated at $358m., while the value of imports from Israel amounted to an estimated $1,803m. In the absence of seaport facilities and of an airport (Gaza International Airport was not opened until November 1998) foreign trade (in terms of value) has been conducted almost exclusively with Israel since occupation. Most Palestinian exports are of agricultural or horticultural products. One notable feature of this trade is that Palestinian goods have often in the past been exported to Israel, and subsequently re-exported as originating in Israel.

In 1999 the budget of the Palestinian National Authority forecast revenues totalling US $1,589m. and expenditure of $1,740m. In 2000, for the first time, a balanced budget was forecast, with both revenue and expenditure set at $1,360m. Since 1998 the aim of the Palestinian Authority has been to achieve current budget surpluses, and to focus public expenditure on health, education and on investment in infrastructure. From 1998 capital expenditure under the Palestinian public investment programme is included in the PNA's budget. A draft Palestinian Development Plan envisages investment expenditure of $3,500m. in 1998–2000. For 1999 donor countries pledged to commit aid worth some $770m., although by September only $174m. had been received. The annual rate of inflation in the West Bank and the Gaza Strip averaged 5.6% in 1998 and 5.5% in 1999. Official figures estimated that 14.4% of the labour force were unemployed in 1998.

The salient feature of the Palestinian economies of the West Bank and the Gaza Strip since the Israeli occupation has been and remains their dependence on Israel. The prospects for an improvement in economic conditions in the Emerging Palestinian Autonomous Areas are therefore inextricably linked to the full implementation of the Oslo accords (see Recent History, above) and the outcome of 'final status' negotiations between the PNA and Israel. The two most striking examples of this economic dependency are the large number of Palestinian workers who find employment in Israel; and the reliance of the trade sector on Israel as a market for exports and source of imports, and—to a lesser extent—as a conduit for exports to and imports from other trading partners. Economic conditions in the Palestinian areas of the West Bank and in the Gaza Strip have deteriorated markedly since 1993, largely as a result of punitive border closures enforced by the Israeli authorities in response to terrorist attacks by groups such as Hamas and Islamic Jihad, which reject the Oslo accords. Such closures lead to an immediate rise in the already high rate of unemployment among Palestinians, increase transportation costs for Palestinian goods and, at worst, halt trade entirely. The Oslo accords provide for the development of seaport facilities, the opening of Gaza International Airport and the opening of a safe passage linking the Gaza Strip with the West Bank. By February 2000 the provision for a seaport at Gaza had still not been implemented.

The frequent closure of the West Bank and the Gaza Strip by the Israeli authorities in 1993–99 has prompted the development of free-trade industrial zones on the Palestinian side of the boundaries separating Israel from the West Bank and the Gaza Strip. Israeli and Palestinian enterprises can continue to take advantage of low-cost Palestinian labour at times of closure, and the zones also benefit from tax exemptions and export incentives. Small and medium-sized enterprises dominate production in the three Gazan and six West Bank industrial zones. In January 1998 the World Bank announced a loan of US $10m. to the PNA for the development of the Gaza Industrial Estate project. In September 1999 the World Bank pledged a further $15m. to assist with further improvements to Palestinian electricity networks. In early 2000 the PNA announced the creation of a Palestinian Investment Fund and a Higher Council for Development, the latter being charged with the preparation of a comprehensive privatization strategy by May. The underdevelopment of Palestinian agriculture and industry is a legacy of the Israeli occupation, when Palestinian investment became orientated towards residential construction at their expense. Agriculture remains focused mainly on meeting local demand, although the sector supplies the bulk of Palestinian exports and there is proven demand for Palestinian products beyond the Israeli market. The expansion of Palestinian agriculture is also limited by problems with irrigation: access to water supplies is subject to 'final status' negotiations with Israel.

### Social Welfare

Programmes operated by the United Nations Relief and Works Agency for Palestine Refugees in the Near East (UNRWA) form the basis of the social welfare system in the West Bank and the Gaza Strip, since about 41% of the population there are registered refugees. UNRWA assists refugee families by providing direct material and financial support (including food) to those in special hardship. UNRWA also engages in projects initiated in response to identified needs or in support of wider political and socio-economic objectives. Following the signing of the Declaration of Principles on Palestinian Self-Rule in 1993, UNRWA introduced a Peace Implementation Programme (PIP) in order to improve infrastructure, create employment and improve conditions among Palestinian refugees. An Income Generation Programme (IGP) provides working capital at commercial rates to small enterprises to assist in the creation of sustainable employment and in the elimination of poverty. In the Gaza Strip, where UNRWA's income-generation efforts are concentrated, the programme is the largest and most successful of its kind.

Palestinians working for Israeli employers are required to participate in Israel's national social security scheme. However, taxes deducted from Palestinian workers finance only very limited benefits to Palestinians as residency in Israel is a requirement to qualify for most Israeli schemes.

UNRWA provides primary health care through 34 facilities in the West Bank and 17 in the Gaza Strip. Health staff number 665 in the West Bank and 915 in the Gaza Strip. Primary services include outpatient care, disease prevention and control, maternal and child health care and family planning. UNRWA also assists with secondary care by means of contractual agreements with non-governmental and private hospitals, or through the partial reimbursement of treatment costs. UNRWA operates a 43-bed hospital in Qalqilya, West Bank. According to the PCBS, there are nine PNA-operated hospitals in the West Bank, and five in the Gaza Strip.

Health services are also provided by the Israeli Civil Administration (excluding those areas where civil jurisdiction has been transferred to the PNA), private voluntary organizations and private, profit-seeking organizations. Institutions operated by the Israeli Civil Administration in the West Bank derive from Jordanian systems. Until 1974, when a government health insurance scheme was introduced, residents of the West Bank were entitled to free health care from these facilities. Now only members of the government health insurance scheme may receive comprehensive care at government facilities without charge. Prenatal care and preventive services are provided by the Civil Administration free of charge to all children under the age of three years.

### Education

Since 1950 UNRWA has provided education services to all Palestinian refugees. The focus of UNRWA's education programme is basic primary and junior secondary schooling, offered free of charge to all refugee children and youth in accordance with local systems.

In the 1997/98 school year UNRWA operated 267 schools in the West Bank and the Gaza Strip. The number of pupils receiving education through the UNRWA programme in that year was 200,886. Education personnel numbered 3,682. In addition, UNRWA operated four vocational training centres and provided 410 university scholarships.

In 1996/97, according to UNESCO, 69,134 pupils in total attended 705 pre-primary institutions, and 656,353 attended 1,118 primary institutions. The number of teachers at pre-primary institutions was 2,377 and that at primary institutions 15,903. In the same year, 56,467 students attended secondary institutions, at which the number of teachers was 7,950. The number of students attending universities or equivalent third-level institutions was 36,921, while teachers numbered 1,966.

**Public Holidays**

**2000:** 1 January (Fatah Day), 8 January*† (Id al-Fitr, end of Ramadan), 16 March* (Id al-Adha, Feast of the Sacrifice), 15 November (Independence Day), 28 December*† (Id al-Fitr, end of Ramadan).

**2001:** 1 January (Fatah Day), 6 March* (Id al-Adha, Feast of the Sacrifice), 15 November (Independence Day).

* These holidays are dependent on the Islamic lunar calendar and may vary by one or two days from the dates given.

† This festival will occur twice (in the Islamic years AH 1420 and 1421) within the same Gregorian year.

Christian holidays are observed by the Christian Arab community.

# Statistical Survey of the West Bank and the Gaza Strip

Source (unless otherwise indicated): Palestinian Central Bureau of Statistics (PCBS), POB 1647, Ramallah, West Bank, Palestine; tel. 2-2986340; fax 2-2986343; internet www.pcbs.org.

Note: Unless otherwise indicated, data include East Jerusalem, annexed by Israel in 1967.

## Area and Population

**AREA, POPULATION AND DENSITY**

| | |
|---|---|
| Area (sq km) | 5,997* |
| Population (census of 9 December 1997)† | |
| Males | 1,470,506 |
| Females | 1,425,177 |
| Total | 2,895,683 |
| Density (per sq km) in December 1997† | 482.9 |

* 2,315.5 sq miles. The total comprises: West Bank 5,633 sq km (2,175 sq miles); Gaza Strip 364 sq km (140.5 sq miles).

† Figures include an estimate of 210,209 for East Jerusalem and an adjustment of 83,805 for estimated underenumeration. The total comprises 1,873,476 (males 951,693; females 921,783) in the West Bank (including East Jerusalem) and 1,022,207 (males 518,813; females 503,394) in the Gaza Strip. The data exclude Jewish settlers. According to official Israeli estimates, the population of Israelis residing in Jewish localities in the West Bank (excluding East Jerusalem) and Gaza Strip was 146,900 at 31 December 1996.

**GOVERNORATES** (census of December 1997)

| | Area (sq km) | Population* | Density (per sq km) |
|---|---|---|---|
| *West Bank* | | | |
| Janin (Jenin) | 578 | 203,026 | 351.3 |
| Tubas | 221 | 36,609 | 165.7 |
| Tulkarm | 244 | 134,110 | 549.6 |
| Qalqilya | 165 | 72,007 | 436.4 |
| Salfit | 205 | 48,538 | 236.8 |
| Nabulus (Nablus) | 848 | 261,340 | 308.2 |
| Ram Allah (Ramallah) and Al-Birah | 850 | 213,582 | 251.3 |
| Al-Quds (Jerusalem) | 338 | 328,601 | 972.2 |
| Ariha (Jericho) | 544 | 32,713 | 60.1 |
| Beit Lahm (Bethlehem) | 625 | 137,286 | 219.7 |
| Al-Khalil (Hebron) | 1,015 | 405,664 | 399.7 |
| *Gaza Strip* | | | |
| North Gaza | 364 (all Gaza Strip) | 183,373 | 2,808.3 (all Gaza Strip) |
| Gaza | | 367,388 | |
| Deir al-Balah | | 147,877 | |
| Khan Yunus (Khan Yunis) | | 200,704 | |
| Rafah | | 122,865 | |
| **Total** | 5,997 | 2,895,683 | 482.9 |

* Figures exclude Jewish settlers. The data include an estimate for East Jerusalem and an adjustment for estimated underenumeration.

**PRINCIPAL LOCALITIES***
(population at 9 December 1997, excluding Jewish settlers)

| | | | |
|---|---|---|---|
| *West Bank* | | | |
| Al-Quds (Jerusalem) | 210,209† | Beit Lahm (Bethlehem) | 21,947 |
| Al-Khalil (Hebron) | 119,401 | Adh-Dhahiriya | 20,548 |
| Nabulus (Nablus) | 100,231 | Ar-Ram | 18,967 |
| Tulkarm | 33,949 | Ram Allah (Ramallah) | 18,017 |
| Qalqilya | 31,772 | Halhul | 15,682 |
| Yattah (Yatta) | 30,823 | Dura | 15,503 |
| Al-Birah | 27,972 | Ariha (Jericho) | 14,744 |
| Janin (Jenin) | 26,681 | Qabatiya | 14,694 |
| *Gaza Strip* | | | |
| Ghazzah (Gaza) | 353,632‡ | Beit Lahya | 38,460 |
| Khan Yunus (Khan Yunis) | 123,175‡ | Al-Braij Camp | 25,180 |
| | | Bani Suhaylah | 23,031 |
| Jabalyah | 113,901‡ | Beit Hanun | 20,791 |
| Rafah | 92,020‡ | Tel as-Sultan Camp | 17,154 |
| Al-Insairat Camp | 44,722 | Al-Maghazi Camp | 16,858 |
| Deir al-Balah | 42,870‡ | | |

* Except for Jerusalem, figures refer to census results, excluding adjustment for underenumeration.

† Estimated population. The figure refers only to the eastern sector of the city.

‡ Including the population of an associated refugee camp.

**BIRTHS AND DEATHS** (excluding East Jerusalem)*

| | 1991 | 1992 | 1993 |
|---|---|---|---|
| Live births (reported) | | | |
| West Bank | 46,456 | 46,853 | 49,045 |
| Gaza Strip | 37,018 | 37,599 | 39,436 |
| Deaths (estimated) | | | |
| West Bank | 6,200 | 6,900 | 7,100 |
| Gaza Strip | 4,100 | 4,400 | 4,400 |

* Excluding Jewish settlers.

Source: Israeli Central Bureau of Statistics.

**MARRIAGES** (number registered)*

| | 1996 | 1997 | 1998 |
|---|---|---|---|
| West Bank | 13,613 | 15,883 | 16,285 |
| Gaza Strip | 7,123 | 7,609 | 8,115 |

* Including marriages registered in *Shari'a* courts and churches.

**ECONOMICALLY ACTIVE POPULATION***
(persons aged 10 years and over, census of December 1997, excluding East Jerusalem)

| | Males | Females | Total |
|---|---|---|---|
| Agriculture, hunting and forestry | 51,890 | 7,132 | 59,022 |
| Fishing | 895 | — | 895 |
| Mining and quarrying | 2,189 | 19 | 2,208 |
| Manufacturing | 73,941 | 8,427 | 82,368 |
| Electricity, gas and water supply | 1,045 | 31 | 1,076 |
| Construction | 142,373 | 187 | 142,560 |
| Wholesale and retail trade; repair of motor vehicles, motorcycles and personal and household goods | 74,266 | 2,242 | 76,508 |
| Hotels and restaurants | 9,049 | 191 | 9,240 |
| Transport, storage and communications | 24,557 | 340 | 24,897 |
| Financial intermediation | 3,618 | 1,089 | 4,707 |
| Real estate, renting and business activities | 6,570 | 1,231 | 7,801 |
| Public administration and defence; compulsory social security | 60,777 | 5,925 | 66,702 |
| Education | 24,531 | 20,050 | 44,581 |
| Health and social work | 9,951 | 6,667 | 16,618 |
| Other community, social and personal service activities | 8,219 | 1,626 | 9,845 |
| Private households with employed persons | 54 | 183 | 237 |
| Extra-territorial organizations and bodies | 2,022 | 537 | 2,559 |
| Activities not adequately defined | 5,199 | 648 | 5,847 |
| **Total labour force** | 501,146 | 56,525 | 557,671 |
| West Bank | 336,655 | 43,523 | 380,178 |
| Gaza Strip | 164,491 | 13,002 | 177,493 |

* Figures refer to Palestinians only. The data exclude persons seeking work for the first time, totalling 44,421, but include other unemployed persons, totalling 63,314.

# Agriculture

**PRINCIPAL CROPS** ('000 metric tons, year ending September)

| | 1994/95 | 1995/96 | 1996/97 |
|---|---|---|---|
| Wheat | 40.7 | 30.9 | 28.3 |
| Barley | 24.9 | 20.4 | 14.2 |
| Maize | 4.3 | 7.5 | 9.0 |
| Potatoes | 50.0 | 54.6 | 45.0 |
| Olives | 44.5 | 130.5 | 50.7 |
| Cabbages | 9.2 | 10.7 | 14.5 |
| Tomatoes | 135.5 | 122.5 | 140.7 |
| Cauliflower | 16.8 | 16.0 | 15.2 |
| Squash | 39.2 | 41.5 | 44.3 |
| Cucumbers | 87.7 | 91.3 | 106.6 |
| Aubergines (Eggplants) | 30.9 | 30.7 | 43.0 |
| Hot pepper | 10.5 | 11.4 | 15.7 |
| Onions | 43.1 | 23.3 | 39.6 |
| Okra | 7.1 | 9.5 | 4.3 |
| Jew's mallow | 19.4 | 16.3 | 11.9 |
| Watermelons | 11.6 | 7.6 | 15.5 |
| Musk-melons | 8.3 | 4.0 | 11.8 |
| Grapes | 47.1 | 57.0 | 52.8 |
| Plums | 17.3 | 12.4 | n.a. |
| Oranges* | 96.7 | 117.1 | 114.6 |
| Mandarins and clementines | 25.4 | 23.9 | 20.8 |
| Lemons | 17.8 | 15.9 | 24.5 |
| Grapefruit | 9.1 | 6.6 | 8.5 |
| Bananas | 18.4 | 19.8 | n.a. |
| Figs | 10.2 | 8.6 | 6.5 |
| Guava | 17.5 | 14.7 | n.a. |
| Almonds | 11.9 | 8.4 | 6.5 |

* Valencia, Shamouti and navel oranges.

**LIVESTOCK** ('000 head, year ending September)*

| | 1994/95 | 1995/96 | 1996/97 |
|---|---|---|---|
| Cattle | 18.0 | 19.3 | 21.0 |
| Sheep | 445.2 | 634.5 | 504.9 |
| Goats | 252.2 | 272.6 | 267.1 |
| Chickens | 29,977 | 27,196 | 37,481 |

* Including estimates for the Gaza Strip.

# Fishing

**Gaza Strip** (metric tons, live weight)

| | 1995 | 1996 | 1997 |
|---|---|---|---|
| Marine fishes | 1,057 | 2,281 | 3,477 |
| Crustaceans | 116 | 127 | 186 |
| Molluscs | 56 | 85 | 128 |
| **Total catch** | 1,229 | 2,493 | 3,791 |

Source: FAO, *Yearbook of Fishery Statistics*.

# Finance

**CURRENCY AND EXCHANGE RATES**

At present there is no domestic Palestinian currency in use. The Israeli shekel, the Jordanian dinar and the US dollar all circulate within the West Bank and the Gaza Strip.

**BUDGET OF THE PALESTINIAN AUTHORITY**
(estimates, US $ million)

| Revenue | 1995 | 1996 | 1997 |
|---|---|---|---|
| Domestic revenue | 158.5 | 264.6 | 331.8 |
| Tax revenue | 108.2 | 178.8 | 209.8 |
| Income tax | 44.4 | n.a. | n.a. |
| Value-added tax | 55.8 | n.a. | n.a. |
| Other receipts | 50.3 | 85.8 | 122.0 |
| Revenue clearances* | 266.4 | 419.6 | 484.2 |
| Value-added tax | 191.9 | n.a. | n.a. |
| Petroleum excise | 33.5 | n.a. | n.a. |
| **Total** | 424.9 | 684.2 | 816.0 |

| Expenditure† | 1995 | 1996 | 1997 |
|---|---|---|---|
| Current expenditure | 492.0 | 780.1 | 866.0 |
| Wages and salaries | 304.3 | 403.0 | 495.0 |
| Civil service | 193.8 | 246.5 | 296.0 |
| Police force | 110.5 | 156.5 | 199.0 |
| Other purposes | 187.7 | 377.0 | 371.0 |
| Capital expenditure | 190.0 | n.a.‡ | n.a. |
| **Total** | 682.0 | n.a. | n.a. |

* Figures refer to an apportionment of an agreed pool of selected tax revenues arising as a result of the *de facto* customs union between Israel and the Palestinian territories. Israel is the collecting agent for these receipts and periodically makes transfers to the Palestinian Authority.

† Excluding the cost of foreign-financed employment programmes (estimates, US $ million): 49.2 in 1996; 8.6 in 1997.

‡ Projected capital expenditure in 1996 was US $160 million.

Source: IMF.

**1999** (estimates, US $ million): Total revenue 1,589; Total expenditure 1,740.

**2000** (estimates, US $ million): Total revenue 1,360; Total expenditure 1,360.

**COST OF LIVING**
(Consumer Price Index; base: 1996 = 100)

| | 1997 | 1998 | 1999 |
|---|---|---|---|
| Food | 106.2 | 113.9 | 119.3 |
| Beverages and tobacco | 109.6 | 117.1 | 126.9 |
| Textiles, clothing and footwear | 112.8 | 121.9 | 123.2 |
| Housing | 105.5 | 109.4 | 116.7 |
| **All items** (incl. others) | 107.6 | 113.6 | 119.9 |

**NATIONAL ACCOUNTS**
(estimates, US $ million at current prices)

**Expenditure on the Gross Domestic Product**

| | 1995 | 1996 | 1997 |
|---|---|---|---|
| Government final consumption expenditure | 484.9 | 780.2 | 902.4 |
| Private final consumption expenditure | 3,640.6 | 4,230.5 | 4,375.6 |
| Increase in stocks | 65.6 | 86.3 | 138.4 |
| Gross fixed capital formation | 1,178.5 | 1,091.1 | 1,432.9 |
| Statistical discrepancy* | −239.7 | −364.5 | 134.1 |
| **Total domestic expenditure** | 5,129.8 | 5,823.6 | 6,983.3 |
| Exports of goods and services | 806.3 | 859.2 | 1,069.6 |
| *Less* Imports of goods and services | 2,361.3 | 2,786.0 | 3,879.7 |
| **GDP in purchasers' values** | 3,574.9 | 3,896.8 | 4,173.1 |

* Referring to the difference between the sum of the expenditure components and official estimates of GDP, compiled from the production approach.

**Gross Domestic Product by Economic Activity**

| | 1995 | 1996 | 1997 |
|---|---|---|---|
| Agriculture and fishing | 405.2 | 476.2 | 266.6 |
| Mining and quarrying | 32.1 | 28.3 | 41.3 |
| Manufacturing | 540.6 | 510.9 | 657.9 |
| Electricity and water supply | 42.8 | 29.9 | 35.0 |
| Construction | 292.1 | 297.7 | 371.7 |
| Wholesale and retail trade | 509.8 | 471.7 | 495.5 |
| Hotels and restaurants | 65.4 | 64.0 | 57.7 |
| Transport, storage and communications | 150.3 | 158.1 | 202.6 |
| Financial intermediation | 61.2 | 80.0 | 100.7 |
| Real estate and business services* | 574.1 | 592.0 | 591.4 |
| Government services | 423.9 | 536 | 865.5 |
| Other community, social and personal services | 48.9 | 53.7 | |
| Private non-profit services to households | 196.1 | 220.8 | |
| Domestic services of households | 5.6 | 6.5 | |
| **Sub-total** | 3,348.0 | 3,525.8 | 3,685.9 |
| Customs duties | 57.0 | 206.1 | 285.9 |
| Value-added tax on imports (net) | 205.7 | 228.9 | 286.2 |
| *Less* Imputed bank service charges | 35.8 | 64.1 | 85.0 |
| **GDP in purchasers' values** | 3,574.9 | 3,896.8 | 4,173.1 |

* Including imputed rents of owner-occupied dwellings (estimated at 66% in 1995 and 70% in 1996).

**BALANCE OF PAYMENTS**
(provisional, US $ million, excluding East Jerusalem)

| | 1995 | 1996 |
|---|---|---|
| Exports of goods f.o.b. | 417.7 | 449.5 |
| Imports of goods f.o.b. | −1,783.7 | −2,123.2 |
| **Trade balance** | −1,366.0 | −1,673.7 |
| Exports of services | 132.0 | 132.7 |
| Imports of services | −228.7 | −244.8 |
| **Balance on goods and services** | −1,462.6 | −1,785.8 |
| Other income received | 550.4 | 487.7 |
| Other income paid | −15.7 | −18.8 |
| **Balance on goods, services and income** | −927.9 | −1,316.9 |
| Current transfers received | 439.7 | 532.2 |
| Current transfers paid | −85.7 | −71.5 |
| **Current balance** | −573.9 | −856.2 |
| Capital account (net) | 237.2 | 271.3 |
| Direct investment abroad | n.a. | −52.4 |
| Direct investment from abroad | n.a. | 199.5 |
| Portfolio investment assets | n.a. | −19.2 |
| Portfolio investment liabilities | n.a. | 3.0 |
| Other investment (net) | n.a. | 96.5 |
| Net errors and omissions | n.a. | 440.4 |
| **Overall balance** | n.a. | 83.0 |

# External Trade

**PRINCIPAL COMMODITIES** (US $ '000)

| Imports c.i.f. | 1996 | 1997 |
|---|---|---|
| Food and live animals | 422,863 | 479,930 |
| Beverages and tobacco | 107,576 | 70,461 |
| Crude materials (inedible) except fuels | 68,117 | 75,667 |
| Mineral fuels, lubricants, etc. | 384,609 | 329,041 |
| Animal and vegetable oils and fats | 22,870 | 23,880 |
| Chemicals | 158,038 | 169,015 |
| Basic manufactures | 462,829 | 577,746 |
| Machinery and transport equipment | 251,261 | 274,138 |
| Miscellaneous manufactured articles | 133,085 | 150,374 |
| Other commodities and transactions | 5,013 | 13,785 |
| **Total** | 2,016,261 | 2,164,037 |

| Exports f.o.b. | 1996 | 1997 |
|---|---|---|
| Food and live animals | 48,626 | 57,240 |
| Beverages and tobacco | 15,400 | 19,639 |
| Crude materials (inedible) except fuels | 23,316 | 17,237 |
| Mineral fuels, lubricants, etc. | 8,276 | 6,175 |
| Animal and vegetable oils and fats | 8,930 | 7,907 |
| Chemicals | 23,692 | 22,701 |
| Basic manufactures | 138,041 | 165,578 |
| Machinery and transport equipment | 20,314 | 21,715 |
| Miscellaneous manufactured articles | 51,997 | 56,878 |
| Other commodities and transactions | 875 | 5,354 |
| **Total** | 339,467 | 380,524 |

**EMIGRATION**

| Destination | 1994 | 1995 | 1996 |
|---|---|---|---|
| Belgium | 3,845 | 2,177 | 1,870 |
| France | 5,181 | 3,371 | 3,448 |
| Germany | 21,407 | 10,816 | 10,805 |
| Switzerland | 10,449 | 4,560 | 5,149 |
| United Kingdom | 3,515 | 2,787 | 3,666 |
| Other European countries | 6,380 | 6,780 | 8,049 |
| Argentina | 1,936 | 1,592 | 1,478 |
| Brazil | 636 | 641 | 770 |
| Canada | 1,082 | 693 | 706 |
| USA | 4,135 | 3,043 | 3,939 |
| Venezuela | 632 | 433 | 484 |
| Oceania | 866 | 692 | 656 |
| Other countries | 5,484 | 5,718 | 6,590 |
| **Total** | 65,548 | 43,303 | 47,610 |

**ECONOMICALLY ACTIVE POPULATION***
(annual averages, '000 persons aged 15 years and over)

| | 1996 | 1997 | 1998 |
|---|---|---|---|
| Agriculture, forestry, hunting and fishing | 1,277 | 1,245 | 1,201 |
| Energy and water, and industrial transformations† | 5,125 | 5,096 | 5,186 |
| Construction | 1,568 | 1,564 | 1,544 |
| Trade, restaurants and hotels | 3,934 | 3,925 | 3,942 |
| Transport, storage and communications | 1,076 | 1,099 | 1,097 |
| Financing, insurance, real estate and business services | 1,718 | 1,800 | 1,890 |
| Community, social and personal services | 5,427 | 5,479 | 5,575 |
| **Total employed** | 20,125 | 20,207 | 20,435 |
| Persons seeking work for the first time | 1,111 | 1,121 | 1,151 |
| Other unemployed | 1,542 | 1,567 | 1,593 |
| **Total labour force** | 22,778 | 22,895 | 23,180 |
| Males | 14,289 | 14,309 | 14,403 |
| Females | 8,489 | 8,586 | 8,777 |

* Figures exclude permanent members of institutional households (134,031 in 1991) and persons on compulsory military service (194,000 in 1996; 206,000 in 1997; 183,000 in 1998).

† Mining and manufacturing.

# Agriculture

**PRINCIPAL CROPS** ('000 metric tons)

| | 1997 | 1998 | 1999* |
|---|---|---|---|
| Wheat | 6,758 | 8,338 | 8,063 |
| Rice (paddy) | 1,442 | 1,309 | n.a. |
| Barley | 1,180 | 1,379 | 1,329 |
| Maize | 10,005 | 9,031 | 9,231 |
| Oats | 311 | 378 | 346 |
| Potatoes | 2,020 | 2,194 | 2,107 |
| Dry beans | 22 | 21 | 22 |
| Dry broad beans | 70 | 65 | 59 |
| Soybeans (Soya beans) | 1,146 | 1,231 | 960 |
| Olives | 3,591 | 2,549 | 3,045 |
| Cabbages | 111 | 123 | 134 |
| Artichokes | 521 | 509 | 472 |
| Tomatoes | 5,575 | 5,852 | 6,782 |
| Cauliflowers | 494 | 526 | 448 |
| Pumpkins, squash and gourds | 465 | 465 | 285 |
| Aubergines (Egg-plants) | 361 | 341 | 266 |
| Onions (dry) | 447 | 451 | 462 |
| Green beans | 193 | 193 | 198 |
| Green peas† | 130‡ | 130§ | n.a. |
| Carrots | 458 | 505 | 470 |
| Watermelons† | 590‡ | 590§ | n.a. |
| Melons | 520 | 476 | 381 |
| Grapes | 8,058 | 9,208 | 9,732 |
| Sugar beet | 13,803 | 13,006 | n.a. |
| Apples | 1,967 | 2,116 | 2,311 |
| Pears | 589 | 965 | 843 |
| Peaches and nectarines | 1,158 | 1,429 | 1,741 |
| Oranges | 1,824 | 1,294 | 1,993 |
| Lemons and limes | 574 | 610 | 564 |
| Almonds (in the shell) | 105 | 88 | 115 |
| Tobacco | 131 | 133 | n.a. |

* Provisional figures.

† Source: FAO, *Production Yearbook*.

‡ Unofficial figure. § FAO estimate.

**LIVESTOCK** ('000 head, year ending September)

| | 1996 | 1997 | 1998 |
|---|---|---|---|
| Horses | 312 | 313 | 300 |
| Mules | 9 | 8 | 8 |
| Asses | 25 | 22 | 18 |
| Cattle | 7,163 | 7,166 | 7,150 |
| Buffaloes | 172 | 162 | 170* |
| Pigs | 8,171 | 8,281 | 8,225* |
| Sheep | 10,947 | 10,890 | 10,770* |
| Goats | 1,419 | 1,347 | 1,365* |

* Provisional figure.

**Chickens** (FAO estimates, million, year ending September): 138 in 1996; 138 in 1997; 138 in 1998.

**Turkeys** (FAO estimates, million, year ending September): 22 in 1996; 23 in 1997; 23 in 1998.

Source (for Chickens and Turkeys): FAO, *Production Yearbook*.

**LIVESTOCK PRODUCTS** ('000 metric tons)

| | 1996 | 1997 | 1998 |
|---|---|---|---|
| Beef and veal | 1,182 | 1,161 | 1,113 |
| Mutton and lamb | 74 | 72 | 70 |
| Goat meat | 4 | 4 | 3 |
| Pig meat | 1,410 | 1,396 | 1,412 |
| Horse meat | 54 | 53 | 56 |
| Poultry meat | 1,119 | 1,139 | 1,158 |
| Other meat | 237 | 240 | 241 |
| Cows' milk | 10,799 | 10,876* | 11,250* |
| Buffaloes' milk | 120 | 144 | 93* |
| Sheep's milk | 802 | 759 | 600* |
| Goats' milk | 97 | 91 | 89* |
| Butter | 117 | 142 | 137* |
| Cheese | 985 | 949 | 1,057* |
| Hen eggs | 697 | 703 | 706 |
| Wool: greasy | 12 | 11 | 12 |

* Provisional figure.

# Forestry

**ROUNDWOOD REMOVALS** ('000 cubic metres, excl. bark)

| | 1997 | 1998 |
|---|---|---|
| Sawlogs, veneer logs and logs for sleepers | 2,169 | 2,533 |
| Pulpwood | 820 | 984 |
| Other industrial wood | 799 | 871 |
| Fuel wood | 5,140 | 5,183 |
| **Total** | 8,928 | 9,570 |

**SAWNWOOD PRODUCTION**
('000 cubic metres, incl. railway sleepers)

| | 1995 | 1996 | 1997 |
|---|---|---|---|
| Coniferous (softwood) | 800 | 750 | 788 |
| Broadleaved (hardwood) | 1,050 | 900 | 963 |
| **Total** | 1,850 | 1,650 | 1,751 |

Source: FAO, *Yearbook of Forest Products.*

# Fishing

('000 metric tons, live weight)

| | 1995 | 1996 | 1997 |
|---|---|---|---|
| Freshwater fishes | 6.4 | 5.3 | 6.1 |
| European hake | 38.1 | 30.7 | 18.0 |
| Surmullets (Red mullets) | 9.4 | 11.3 | 7.5 |
| European pilchard (sardine) | 36.8 | 42.1 | 38.2 |
| European anchovy | 42.7 | 40.5 | 53.4 |
| Scomber mackerels | 6.9 | 8.0 | 7.9 |
| Other fishes | 125.7 | 99.3 | 99.2 |
| **Total fish** | 266.2 | 237.4 | 230.3 |
| Deepwater rose shrimp | 7.8 | 7.1 | 16.7 |
| Other crustaceans | 16.6 | 17.2 | 15.7 |
| Mediterranean mussel | 21.4 | 22.2 | 21.4 |
| Striped venus | 32.6 | 36.7 | 28.6 |
| Cuttlefishes | 12.5 | 9.0 | 9.4 |
| Squids | 11.0 | 10.5 | 6.8 |
| Octopuses | 12.5 | 11.3 | 11.1 |
| Other molluscs | 13.3 | 11.2 | 9.8 |
| **Total catch** | 394.0 | 362.5 | 349.7 |
| Inland waters | 10.0 | 9.0 | 10.4 |
| Mediterranean and Black Sea | 373.2 | 349.0 | 331.2 |
| Atlantic Ocean | 9.1 | 3.9 | 7.2 |
| Indian Ocean | 1.7 | 0.7 | 0.9 |

Source: FAO, *Yearbook of Fishery Statistics.*

# Mining

('000 metric tons)

| | 1996 | 1997 | 1998 |
|---|---|---|---|
| Lead concentrates* | 21.0 | 17.6 | 10.1 |
| Zinc concentrates* | 20.1 | 15.4 | 4.5 |
| Barytes | 80.5 | 26.3 | 36.0 |
| Fluorspar | 103.0 | 105.8 | 107.0 |
| Petroleum | 5,430.0 | 5,400.0 | 5,600.0 |
| Natural gas (million cu m) | 20,200.0 | 19,500.0 | 19,160.0 |
| Lignite | 223.0 | 203.1 | 83.7 |
| Salt | 2,941.0 | 3,507.0 | 3,354.0 |
| Talc | 136.0 | 141.0 | 138.0 |

* Figures refer to gross weight of ores and concentrates.

Source: Mining Annual Review 1999.

# Industry

**SELECTED PRODUCTS**
('000 metric tons, unless otherwise indicated)

| | 1994 | 1995 | 1996 |
|---|---|---|---|
| Wine ('000 hectolitres) | 59,280 | 56,200 | 60,000 |
| Pig iron | 11,160.9 | 11,677.7 | 10,324.3 |
| Steel | 25,933.7 | 27,771.1 | 24,284.9 |
| Rolled iron | 23,509.0 | 24,825.3 | 22,431.0 |
| Other iron and steel-finished manufactures | 879.6 | 1,032.4 | 982.3 |
| Iron alloys and *spiegel-eisen* special pig irons | 121 | 145 | n.a. |
| Fuel oil | 18,408.1 | 17,281.3 | 16,828.9 |
| Synthetic ammonia | 612.5 | 592.2 | 524.6 |
| Sulphuric acid at 50° Bé | 1,975.5 | 2,161.8 | 2,214.0 |
| Synthetic organic dyes | 24.2 | 23.0 | 23.7 |
| Tanning materials | 35.5 | 33.2 | 30.3 |
| Caustic soda | 952.9 | 922.1 | 875.7 |
| Cotton yarn | 262.5 | 260.1 | 262.0 |
| Natural methane gas (million cu m) | 20,341.4 | 20,383.5 | 20,047.5 |
| Passenger motor cars ('000) | 1,340.5 | 1,422.3 | 1,318.0 |
| Lorries (Trucks) ('000) | 194.1 | 245.7 | 227.6 |
| Hydroelectric power (million kWh)* | 47,731 | 41,907 | 47,072 |
| Thermoelectric power (million kWh)* | 173,071 | 187,904 | 184,921 |

* Net production.

# Finance

**CURRENCY AND EXCHANGE RATES**

**Monetary Units**

100 centèsimi (singular: centèsimo) = 1 Italian lira (plural: lire).

**Sterling, Dollar and Euro Equivalents** (30 September 1999)

£1 sterling = 2,989.3 lire;
US $1 = 1,815.5 lire;
€1 = 1,936.3 lire;
10,000 lire = £3.345 = $5.508 = €5.165.

**Average Exchange Rate** (lire per US $)

1996 1,542.9
1997 1,703.1
1998 1,736.2

**STATE BUDGET** ('000 million lire)*

| Revenue† | 1995 | 1996 | 1997 |
|---|---|---|---|
| Taxation | 678,635 | 760,405 | 824,001 |
| Taxes on income, profits, etc. | 240,606 | 266,400 | 304,318 |
| Social security contributions | 225,478 | 276,648 | 291,328 |
| Domestic taxes on goods and services | 187,158 | 189,958 | 199,823 |
| Other current revenue | 51,862 | 38,406 | 48,501 |
| Entrepreneurial and property income | 26,447 | 12,304 | 19,955 |
| Capital revenue | 7,384 | 3,033 | 1,627 |
| Adjustment | 4,038 | 11 | — |
| **Total** | 741,919 | 801,855 | 874,129 |

| Expenditure‡ | 1995 | 1996 | 1997 |
|---|---|---|---|
| Current expenditure | 815,416 | 876,233 | 885,081 |
| Expenditure on goods and services | 126,496 | 172,657 | 176,045 |
| Wages and salaries | 96,066 | 132,571 | 137,949 |
| Interest payments | 202,284 | 191,036 | 177,927 |
| Subsidies and other current transfers | 486,636 | 512,540 | 531,109 |
| Capital expenditure | 44,765 | 51,271 | 48,497 |
| Acquisition of fixed capital assets | 11,153 | 11,591 | 11,440 |
| Capital transfers | 33,612 | 39,680 | 37,057 |
| Domestic | 33,355 | 39,402 | 36,809 |
| **Total** | 860,181 | 927,504 | 933,578 |

* Figures represent the consolidated operations of the Central Government, comprising the General Account Budget and the budgets of three autonomous agencies and 12 social security institutions. Data exclude the accounts of the Deposit and Loan Fund and miscellaneous extrabudgetary agencies.

† Excluding grants received ('000 million lire): 6,937 in 1995; 2,923 in 1996; 14,477 in 1997.

‡ Excluding lending minus repayments ('000 million lire): 23,069 in 1995; 16,363 in 1996; 15,783 in 1997.

Source: IMF, *Government Finance Statistics Yearbook*.

**INTERNATIONAL RESERVES** (US $ million at 31 December)*

| | 1996 | 1997 | 1998 |
|---|---|---|---|
| Gold† | 25,369 | 21,806 | 24,711 |
| IMF special drawing rights | 29 | 67 | 111 |
| Reserve position in IMF | 1,855 | 2,241 | 4,330 |
| Foreign exchange | 44,064 | 53,431 | 25,447 |
| **Total** | 71,317 | 77,545 | 54,599 |

* Excluding deposits made with the European Monetary Institute (now the European Central Bank).

† Valued at market-related prices.

Source: IMF, *International Financial Statistics*.

**MONEY SUPPLY** ('000 million lire at 31 December)*

| | 1996 | 1997 | 1998 |
|---|---|---|---|
| Currency outside banks | 115,440 | 122,940 | 126,540 |
| Demand deposits at commercial banks | 498,870 | 531,720 | 601,150 |
| **Total money** | 614,310 | 654,660 | 727,690 |

* Figures are rounded to the nearest 10,000 million lire.

Source: IMF, *International Financial Statistics*.

**COST OF LIVING** (Consumer Price Index; base: 1990 = 100)

| | 1995 | 1996 | 1997 |
|---|---|---|---|
| Food (incl. beverages) | 125.6 | 130.9 | 130.9 |
| Fuel and light | 128.8 | 130.2 | 132.8 |
| Clothing (incl. footwear) | 123.4 | 128.3 | 131.7 |
| Rent | 141.5 | 153.2 | 163.4 |
| **All items** (incl. others) | 127.7 | 132.8 | 135.5 |

Source: ILO, *Yearbook of Labour Statistics*.

**NATIONAL ACCOUNTS** ('000 million lire at current prices)

**National Income and Product**

| | 1994 | 1995 | 1996 |
|---|---|---|---|
| Compensation of employees | 698,174 | 727,779 | 768,358 |
| Operating surplus | 572,440 | 637,567 | 676,120 |
| **Domestic factor incomes** | 1,270,614 | 1,365,346 | 1,444,478 |
| Consumption of fixed capital | 203,398 | 219,629 | 231,781 |
| **Gross domestic product (GDP) at factor cost** | 1,474,012 | 1,584,975 | 1,676,259 |
| Indirect taxes | 204,154 | 221,181 | 234,685 |
| *Less* Subsidies | 39,500 | 35,138 | 37,450 |
| **GDP in purchasers' values** | 1,638,666 | 1,771,018 | 1,873,494 |
| Factor income received from abroad | 46,355 | 55,657 | 59,574 |
| *Less* Factor income paid abroad | 73,697 | 81,526 | 83,790 |
| **Gross national product** | 1,611,324 | 1,745,149 | 1,849,278 |
| *Less* Consumption of fixed capital | 203,398 | 219,629 | 231,781 |
| **National income in market prices** | 1,407,926 | 1,525,520 | 1,617,497 |
| Other current transfers from abroad | 19,774 | 21,455 | 22,109 |
| *Less* Other current transfers paid abroad | 31,072 | 29,173 | 33,659 |
| **National disposable income** | 1,396,628 | 1,517,802 | 1,605,947 |

**Expenditure on the Gross Domestic Product***

| | 1996 | 1997 | 1998 |
|---|---|---|---|
| Government final consumption expenditure | 352,400 | 367,600 | 381,800 |
| Private final consumption expenditure | 1,119,000 | 1,177,000 | 1,224,900 |
| Increase in stocks | 6,400 | 16,700 | 27,800 |
| Gross fixed capital formation | 344,200 | 354,600 | 372,600 |
| **Total domestic expenditure** | 1,822,000 | 1,915,900 | 2,007,100 |
| Exports of goods and services | 451,100 | 481,300 | 491,700 |
| *Less* Imports of goods and services | 377,000 | 422,600 | 441,000 |
| **GDP in purchasers' values** | 1,896,100 | 1,974,600 | 2,057,800 |
| **GDP at constant 1995 prices** | 1,802,700 | 1,829,500 | 1,853,900 |

* Figures are rounded to the nearest 100,000 million lire.

Source: IMF, *International Financial Statistics*.

**Gross Domestic Product by Economic Activity**

| | 1994 | 1995 | 1996 |
|---|---|---|---|
| Agriculture, forestry, hunting and fishing | 47,527 | 50,843 | 53,302 |
| Energy and water | 95,920 | 103,575 | 107,174 |
| Industrial transformations* | 331,792 | 366,359 | 382,228 |
| Construction | 84,721 | 88,310 | 92,943 |
| Trade, restaurants and hotels† | 301,889 | 327,928 | 345,357 |
| Transport, storage and communications | 105,342 | 113,958 | 118,754 |
| Other private services | 428,610 | 466,415 | 502,037 |
| Government services | 203,439 | 209,229 | 225,873 |
| Other producers | 16,394 | 17,923 | 19,022 |
| **Sub-total** | 1,615,634 | 1,774,540 | 1,846,690 |
| Import duties | 95,839 | 104,924 | 107,994 |
| *Less* Imputed bank service charge | 72,807 | 78,446 | 81,190 |
| **GDP in purchasers' values** | 1,638,666 | 1,771,018 | 1,873,494 |

* Mining and manufacturing, excluding energy.

† Including repair services.

**BALANCE OF PAYMENTS** (US $ million)

| | 1996 | 1997 | 1998 |
|---|---|---|---|
| Exports of goods f.o.b. | 252,039 | 240,404 | 242,572 |
| Imports of goods f.o.b. | -197,921 | -200,527 | -206,941 |
| **Trade balance** | 54,118 | 39,878 | 35,631 |
| Exports of services | 65,660 | 66,991 | 67,549 |
| Imports of services | -57,605 | -59,227 | -63,636 |
| **Balance on goods and services** | 62,173 | 47,642 | 39,801 |
| Other income received | 40,142 | 45,734 | 51,319 |
| Other income paid | -55,101 | -56,936 | -63,636 |
| **Balance on goods, services and income** | 47,213 | 36,440 | 27,483 |
| Current transfers received | 14,320 | 15,552 | 14,402 |
| Current transfers paid | -21,535 | -19,588 | -21,887 |
| **Current balance** | 39,999 | 32,403 | 19,998 |
| Capital account (net) | 66 | 3,434 | 2,358 |
| Direct investment abroad | -8,697 | -10,414 | -12,407 |
| Direct investment from abroad | 3,546 | 3,700 | 2,635 |
| Portfolio investment assets | -26,607 | -62,975 | -109,913 |
| Portfolio investment liabilities | 75,927 | 74,649 | 113,027 |
| Other investment assets | -68,358 | -25,541 | -21,232 |
| Other investment liabilities | 16,206 | 13,703 | 9,816 |
| Net errors and omissions | -20,176 | -15,810 | -25,754 |
| **Overall balance** | 11,907 | 13,150 | -21,472 |

Source: IMF, *International Financial Statistics*.

# External Trade

Note: Data refer to the trade of Italy (excluding San Marino and the commune of Campione). The figures include trade in second-hand ships, and stores and bunkers for foreign ships and aircraft, but exclude manufactured gas, surplus military equipment, war reparations and repayments and gift parcels by post. Also excluded are imports of military goods and exports of fish landed abroad directly from Italian vessels.

**PRINCIPAL COMMODITIES** (distribution by SITC, '000 million lire)

| Imports c.i.f. | 1996 | 1997 | 1998 |
|---|---|---|---|
| **Food and live animals** | 30,539.6 | 31,866.6 | 32,601.5 |
| **Crude materials (inedible) except fuels** | 21,544.9 | 23,462.4 | 23,082.9 |
| **Mineral fuels and lubricants** | 26,875.6 | 28,124.4 | 20,853.1 |
| Petroleum and petroleum products | 24,505.6 | 25,293.4 | 18,406.2 |
| Crude petroleum | 17,383.1 | 18,631.8 | 13,720.6 |
| Refined petroleum products | 6,584.6 | 5,869.4 | 3,958.2 |
| **Chemicals and related products** | 41,769.7 | 46,461.8 | 48,270.0 |
| Organic chemicals | 12,346.6 | 13,583.4 | 13,650.9 |
| Medicinal and pharmaceutical products | 7,137.5 | 8,160.4 | 9,431.6 |
| Artificial resins and plastic materials, and cellulose esters and ethers | 8,865.6 | 9,840.8 | 9,742.8 |
| Products of polymerization etc. | 7,183.6 | 7,817.2 | 7,830.0 |
| **Basic manufactures** | 51,918.3 | 58,235.8 | 62,254.6 |
| Textile yarn, fabrics, etc. | 9,497.0 | 11,048.2 | 11,446.1 |
| Iron and steel | 12,219.0 | 13,894.9 | 15,784.7 |
| Non-ferrous metals | 8,189.8 | 9,489.0 | 9,782.7 |
| **Machinery and transport equipment** | 96,782.3 | 110,505.2 | 126,302.0 |
| Machinery specialized for particular industries | 7,324.8 | 7,594.6 | 8,975.1 |
| Office machines and automatic data-processing equipment | 11,568.8 | 12,159.8 | 13,270.1 |
| Telecommunications and sound recording and reproducing apparatus and equipment | 7,013.6 | 9,709.1 | 11,588.7 |
| Other electrical machinery, apparatus, etc. | 17,118.6 | 18,281.0 | 18,984.7 |
| Road vehicles and parts | 31,517.4 | 38,855.8 | 44,055.7 |
| Passenger motor cars (excl. buses) | 22,309.3 | 28,665.8 | 31,385.2 |
| **Miscellaneous manufactured articles** | 30,786.4 | 35,456.0 | 38,197.4 |
| Clothing and accessories (excl. footwear) | 7,761.7 | 9,129.5 | 10,146.9 |
| **Special transactions and commodities not classified according to kind** | 15,043.7 | 16,893.1 | 16,489.3 |
| **Gold, non-monetary (excluding gold ores and concentrates)** | 6,264.3 | 7,181.9 | 7,140.6 |
| **Total** (incl. others) | 321,285.8 | 357,586.7 | 374,283.1 |

| Exports f.o.b. | 1996 | 1997 | 1998 |
|---|---|---|---|
| **Food and live animals** | 20,334.6 | 21,168.9 | 21,645.1 |
| **Chemicals and related products** | 30,510.5 | 33,770.4 | 35,073.4 |
| **Basic manufactures** | 82,784.9 | 87,742.9 | 89,893.5 |
| Textile yarn, fabrics, etc. | 20,370.6 | 22,119.4 | 22,635.7 |
| Non-metallic mineral manufactures | 13,870.5 | 14,713.3 | 15,073.4 |
| Iron and steel | 11,806.0 | 12,523.1 | 12,639.7 |
| Other manufactures of metals | 15,732.2 | 16,384.4 | 17,105.0 |
| **Machinery and transport equipment** | 148,904.3 | 154,589.7 | 164,055.2 |
| Machinery specialized for particular industries | 28,209.9 | 30,245.0 | 28,929.6 |
| General industrial machinery and equipment | 39,811.8 | 41,526.6 | 44,094.4 |
| Electrical machinery, apparatus, etc. (excl. telecommunications and sound equipment) | 23,297.2 | 24,107.8 | 24,837.1 |
| Domestic electrical equipment | 8,449.8 | 8,974.3 | 9,194.1 |
| Road vehicles and parts | 30,939.2 | 31,633.5 | 33,994.5 |
| Passenger motor cars (excl. buses) | 12,109.9 | 10,993.6 | 11,956.8 |
| **Miscellaneous manufactured articles** | 87,867.8 | 91,424.8 | 91,026.5 |
| Furniture and parts thereof | 13,766.3 | 2,630.5 | 2,273.1 |
| Clothing and accessories (excl. footwear) | 24,946.8 | 25,543.9 | 25,643.4 |
| Outer garments and other articles, knitted or crocheted, not elastic nor rubberized | 23,482.8 | 24,023.4 | 24,150.5 |
| Footwear | 13,838.1 | 14,009.1 | 13,490.1 |
| Jewellery, goldsmiths' and silversmiths' wares, etc. | 7,637.5 | 8,205.1 | 8,237.4 |
| **Total** (incl. others) | 388,885.1 | 409,128.3 | 420,764.1 |

**PRINCIPAL TRADING PARTNERS** ('000 million lire)*

| Imports c.i.f. | 1996 | 1997 | 1998 |
|---|---|---|---|
| Algeria | 4,188.5 | 5,053.0 | 4,442.1 |
| Austria | 7,414.2 | 8,313.9 | 8,976.2 |
| Belgium-Luxembourg | 15,429.9 | 16,750.4 | 18,023.6 |
| China, People's Republic | 6,225.3 | 7,515.5 | 8,407.1 |
| France | 43,585.7 | 47,580.3 | 49,274.3 |
| Germany | 59,513.3 | 64,640.9 | 70,403.5 |
| Japan | 6,136.2 | 7,180.3 | 8,222.1 |
| Libya | 6,987.4 | 7,592.4 | 5,515.1 |
| Netherlands | 19,309.4 | 22,063.3 | 23,113.9 |
| Russia | 7,249.5 | 7,280.1 | 6,461.5 |
| Saudi Arabia | 2,915.3 | 3,662.3 | 2,411.6 |
| Spain | 13,374.1 | 17,037.7 | 16,987.4 |
| Sweden | 4,455.1 | 5,029.5 | 5,725.9 |
| Switzerland | 13,642.6 | 13,745.7 | 15,184.7 |
| United Kingdom | 21,242.5 | 24,115.4 | 24,072.3 |
| USA | 15,697.7 | 17,382.7 | 18,895.2 |
| **Total** (incl. others) | 321,285.8 | 357,586.7 | 374,283.1 |

| Exports f.o.b. | 1996 | 1997 | 1998 |
|---|---|---|---|
| Austria | 9,201.8 | 9,323.9 | 9,624.1 |
| Belgium-Luxembourg | 10,774.6 | 11,141.8 | 11,469.8 |
| Brazil | 4,802.5 | 5,988.0 | 5,727.2 |
| China, People's Republic | 4,425.1 | 4,305.5 | 3,567.5 |
| France | 48,801.8 | 50,071.6 | 53,681.5 |
| Germany | 68,009.5 | 67,388.1 | 69,422.8 |
| Greece | 7,376.6 | 8,055.1 | 8,356.2 |
| Hong Kong | 6,770.2 | 6,817.5 | 5,350.8 |
| Japan | 8,613.6 | 8,028.0 | 7,022.0 |
| Netherlands | 11,473.1 | 11,714.5 | 12,087.1 |
| Poland | 5,287.3 | 6,347.0 | 6,715.8 |
| Portugal | 5,170.6 | 5,479.3 | 5,913.5 |
| Russia | 5,735.0 | 6,556.8 | 5,245.2 |
| Spain | 19,122.9 | 21,334.4 | 24,376.5 |
| Switzerland | 14,213.1 | 13,901.9 | 14,682.9 |
| Turkey | 6,608.7 | 7,481.0 | 7,104.6 |
| United Kingdom | 25,182.8 | 29,272.2 | 30,315.1 |
| USA | 28,389.5 | 32,191.2 | 36,044.4 |
| **Total** (incl. others) | 388,885.1 | 409,128.3 | 420,764.1 |

* Imports by country of production; exports by country of consumption.

# Transport

**STATE RAILWAYS** (traffic)

| | 1996 | 1997 | 1998 |
|---|---|---|---|
| Passenger journeys ('000) | 468,300 | 461,000 | 440,500 |
| Passenger-km (million) | 50,300 | 49,500 | 47,285 |
| Freight ton-km (million) | 23,314 | 25,228 | 24,704 |

**ROAD TRAFFIC** (vehicles in use at 31 December)

| | 1995 | 1996 | 1997 |
|---|---|---|---|
| Passenger motor cars | 30,301,424 | 30,467,173 | 30,741,953 |
| Buses and coaches | 75,023 | 83,182 | 84,177 |
| Goods vehicles | 2,788,432 | 3,094,563 | 3,169,538 |

**SHIPPING**

**Merchant Fleet** (registered at 31 December)

| | 1996 | 1997 | 1998 |
|---|---|---|---|
| Number of vessels | 1,348 | 1,324 | 1,329 |
| Displacement ('000 grt) | 6,594 | 6,194 | 6,819 |

Source: Lloyd's Register of Shipping, *World Fleet Statistics*.

**International Sea-borne Freight Traffic**

| | 1993 | 1994 | 1995 |
|---|---|---|---|
| Vessels entered ('000 nrt) | 168,545 | 180,175 | n.a. |
| Vessels cleared ('000 nrt) | 84,044 | 91,288 | n.a. |
| Goods loaded ('000 metric tons) | 51,420 | 50,247 | 48,250 |
| Goods unloaded ('000 metric tons) | 222,060 | 226,220 | 234,120 |

Source: UN, *Statistical Yearbook* and *Monthly Bulletin of Statistics*.

**1996** ('000 metric tons): Goods loaded 59,218; Goods unloaded 248,063.

**CIVIL AVIATION** (traffic on scheduled services)

| | 1995 | 1996 | 1997 |
|---|---|---|---|
| Kilometres flown (million) | 260 | 293 | 326 |
| Passengers carried ('000) | 23,396 | 25,868 | 27,241 |
| Passenger-km (million) | 33,264 | 36,140 | 37,734 |

# Tourism

| | 1995 | 1996 | 1997 |
|---|---|---|---|
| Foreign tourist arrivals* | 55,706,188 | 56,300,496 | 56,370,381 |
| Amount spent (million lire) | 44,717,611 | 46,249,264 | n.a. |

* Including excursionists and cruise passengers. Arrivals at accommodation establishments were 27,581,077 in 1995; 29,324,237 in 1996; 29,963,670 in 1997; 30,941,982 in 1998.

**Number of hotel beds:** 1,772,096 in 1997; 1,782,382 in 1998.

**TOURIST ARRIVALS BY COUNTRY OF ORIGIN*** (including excursionists)

| | 1995 | 1996 | 1997 |
|---|---|---|---|
| Austria | 5,962,422 | 6,147,073 | 5,872,836 |
| France | 8,405,889 | 9,303,490 | 9,726,229 |
| Germany | 8,806,197 | 8,752,281 | 8,441,385 |
| Netherlands | 1,145,502 | 933,549 | 838,532 |
| Switzerland | 8,982,815 | 8,374,527 | 8,164,696 |
| United Kingdom | 1,688,530 | 1,659,319 | 1,858,828 |
| USA | 1,384,006 | 1,309,113 | 1,322,589 |
| Yugoslavia (former) | 8,703,774 | 9,461,235 | 9,083,232 |
| **Total** (incl. others) | 55,706,188 | 56,300,496 | 56,370,381 |

* The collection of data relevant to tourist arrivals by country of origin was suspended from 1 April 1998 as a result of the lack of information on passengers from those EU countries which adhered to the Schengen Agreement on cross border travel.

## Communications Media

| | 1993 | 1994 | 1995 |
|---|---|---|---|
| Telephone subscriptions | 24,166,572 | 24,542,000 | 24,854,000 |
| Telefax stations (number in use) | 202,000 | n.a. | n.a. |
| Mobile cellular telephones (subscribers) | 1,207,000 | 2,239,740 | 3,864,000 |
| Radio receivers ('000 in use) | 45,800 | 45,850 | 47,000 |
| Television receivers ('000 in use) | 24,500 | 25,000 | 25,500 |
| Book production (titles) | 30,110 | 32,673 | 34,470 |
| Daily newspapers: | | | |
| Number of titles | 79 | 74 | 76 |
| Average circulation ('000) | 6,366 | 5,985 | 5,722 |
| Non-daily newspapers: | | | |
| Number of titles | n.a. | 231 | 274 |
| Average circulation ('000) | n.a. | 1,428 | 2,132 |

**1996:** Book production (titles) 35,236; Daily newspapers: Number of titles 78, Average circulation ('000) 5,960.

Source: mainly UNESCO, *Statistical Yearbook*.

## Education

(1995/96)

| | Schools | Teachers | Students |
|---|---|---|---|
| Pre-primary | 26,249 | 121,520 | 1,573,308 |
| Primary | 20,442 | 289,055 | 2,825,838 |
| Secondary: | | | |
| Scuola Media | 9,278 | 214,861 | 1,907,024 |
| Secondaria Superiore | 7,888 | 313,001 | 2,661,760 |
| of which: | | | |
| Technical | 2,966 | 139,392 | 1,113,794 |
| Vocational | 1,690 | 68,957 | 507,125 |
| Teacher training | 762 | 22,317 | 200,305 |
| Art Licei | 312 | 13,481 | 93,429 |
| Classical, linguistic and scientific Licei | 2,158 | 68,854 | 747,107 |
| Higher* | 56 | 34,724 | 1,660,747 |

* Data refer to the 1994/95 academic year.

Source: Ministry of Education.

**1996/97:** *Pre-primary:* 26,047 schools; 117,125 teachers; 1,580,414 students. *Primary:* 20,006 schools; 262,246 teachers; 2,801,407 students. *Secondary—Scuola Media:* 9,215 schools; 210,965 teachers; 1,893,476 students. *Secondary—Secondaria Superiore:* 7,875, schools; 2,644,291 students.

# Directory

## The Constitution*

The Constitution of the Italian Republic was approved by the Constituent Assembly on 22 December 1947 and came into force on 1 January 1948 (and was amended in April 1993). The fundamental principles are declared in Articles 1–12, as follows:

Italy is a democratic republic based on the labour of the people.

The Republic recognizes and guarantees as inviolable the rights of its citizens, either as individuals or in a community, and it expects, in return, devotion to duty and the fulfilment of political, economic and social obligations.

All citizens shall enjoy equal status and shall be regarded as equal before the law, without distinction of sex, race, language or religion, and without regard to the political opinions which they may hold or their personal or social standing.

It shall be the function of the Republic to remove the economic and social inequalities which, by restricting the liberty of the individual, impede the full development of the human personality, thereby reducing the effective participation of the citizen in the political, economic and social life of the country.

The Republic recognizes the right of all citizens to work and shall do all in its power to give effect to this right.

The Republic, while remaining one and indivisible, shall recognize and promote local autonomy, fostering the greatest possible decentralization in those services which are administered by the State, and subordinating legislative methods and principles to the exigencies of decentralized and autonomous areas.

The State and the Catholic Church shall be sovereign and independent, each in its own sphere. Their relations shall be governed by the Lateran Pact (Patti Lateranensi), and any modification in the pact agreed upon by both parties shall not necessitate any revision of the Constitution.

All religious denominations shall have equal liberty before the law, denominations other than the Catholic having the right to worship according to their beliefs, in so far as they do not conflict with the common law of the country.

The Republic shall do all in its power to promote the development of culture and scientific and technical research. It shall also protect and preserve the countryside and the historical and artistic monuments which are the inheritance of the nation.

The juridical system of the Italian Republic shall be in conformity with the generally recognized practice of international law. The legal rights of foreigners in the country shall be regulated by law in accordance with international practice.

Any citizen of a foreign country who is deprived of democratic liberty such as is guaranteed under the Italian Constitution, has the right of asylum within the territory of the Republic in accordance with the terms of the law, and his extradition for political offences will not be granted.

Italy repudiates war as an instrument of offence against the liberty of other nations and as a means of resolving international disputes. Italy accepts, under parity with other nations, the limitations of sovereignty necessary for the preservation of peace and justice between nations. To that end, it will support and promote international organizations.

The Constitution is further divided into Parts I and II, in which are set forth respectively the rights and responsibilities of the citizen and the administration of the Republic.

### PART ONE

#### Civic Clauses

Section I (Articles 13–28). The liberty of the individual is inviolable and no form of detention, restriction or inspection is permitted unless it be for juridical purposes and in accordance with the provisions of the law. The domicile of a person is likewise inviolable and shall be immune from forced inspection or sequestration, except according to the provisions of the law. Furthermore, all citizens shall be free to move wheresoever they will throughout the country, and may leave it and return to it without let or hindrance. Right of public meeting, if peaceful and without arms, is guaranteed. Secret organizations of a directly or indirectly political or military nature are, however, prohibited.

Freedom in the practice of religious faith is guaranteed.

The Constitution further guarantees complete freedom of thought, speech and writing, and lays down that the Press shall be entirely free from all control or censorship. No person may be deprived of civic or legal rights on political grounds.

The death penalty is not allowed under the Constitution except in case of martial law. The accused shall be considered 'not guilty' until he is otherwise proven. All punishment shall be consistent with humanitarian practice and shall be directed towards the re-education of the criminal.

#### Ethical and Social Clauses

Section II (Articles 29–34). The Republic regards the family as the fundamental basis of society and considers the parents to be responsible for the maintenance, instruction and education of the children. The Republic shall provide economic assistance for the family, with special regard to large families, and shall make provision for maternity, infancy and youth, subject always to the liberty and freedom of choice of the individuals as envisaged under the law.

Education, the arts and science shall be free, the function of the State being merely to indicate the general lines of instruction. Private entities and individuals shall have the right to conduct educational institutions without assistance from the State, but such non-state institutions must ensure to their pupils liberty and instruction equal to that in the state schools. Institutions of higher culture, universities and academies shall be autonomous within the limitations prescribed by the law.

Education is available to all and is free and obligatory for at least eight years. Higher education for students of proven merit shall be aided by scholarships and other allowances made by the Republic.

**Economic Clauses**

Section III (Articles 35–47). The Republic shall safeguard the right to work in all its aspects, and shall promote agreement and co-operation with international organizations in matters pertaining to the regulation of labour and the rights of workers. The rights of Italian workers abroad shall be protected.

All workers shall be entitled to remuneration proportionate to the quantity and quality of their work, and in any case shall be ensured of sufficient to provide freedom and a dignified standard of life for themselves and their families.

The maximum working hours shall be fixed by law, and the worker shall be entitled to a weekly day of rest and an annual holiday of nine days with pay.

Women shall have the same rights and, for equal work, the same remuneration as men. Conditions of work shall be regulated by their special family requirements and the needs of mother and child. The work of minors shall be specially protected.

All citizens have the right to sickness, unemployment and disability maintenance.

Liberty to organize in trade unions is guaranteed and any union may register as a legal entity, provided it is organized on a democratic basis. The right to strike is admitted within the limitations of the relevant legislation.

Private enterprise is permitted in so far as it does not run counter to the well-being of society nor constitute a danger to security, freedom and human dignity.

Ownership of private property is permitted and guaranteed within the limitations laid down by the law regarding the acquisition, extent and enjoyment of private property. Inheritance and testamentary bequests shall be regulated by law.

Limitation is placed by law on private ownership of land and on its use, with a view to its best exploitation for the benefit of the community.

The Republic recognizes the value of mutual co-operation and the right of the workers to participate in management.

The Republic shall encourage all forms of saving, by house purchase, by co-operative ownership and by investment in the public utility undertakings of the country.

**Political Clauses**

Section IV (Articles 48–54). The electorate comprises all citizens, both men and women, who have attained their majority. Voting is free, equal and secret, and its exercise is a civic duty. All citizens have the right to associate freely together in political parties, and may also petition the Chambers to legislate as may be deemed necessary.

All citizens of both sexes may hold public office on equal terms.

Defence of one's country is a sacred duty of the citizen, and military service is obligatory within the limits prescribed by law. Its fulfilment shall in no way prejudice the position of the worker nor hinder the exercise of political rights. The organization of the armed forces shall be imbued with the spirit of democracy.

All citizens must contribute to the public expenditure, in proportion to their capacity.

All citizens must be loyal to the Republic and observe the terms of the law and the Constitution.

**PART TWO**

Sections I, II and III (Articles 55–100). These sections are devoted to a detailed exposition of the Legislature and legislative procedure of the Republic.

Parliament shall comprise two Chambers, namely the Chamber of Deputies (Camera dei Deputati) and the Senate of the Republic (Senato).

The Chamber of Deputies is elected by direct universal suffrage, the number of Deputies being 630. All voters who on the day of the elections are 25 years of age, may be elected Deputies.

Three-quarters of the seats are allocated on the basis of a simple plurality and the remaining one-quarter by proportional representation.

The Senate of the Republic is elected on a regional basis, the number of eligible Senators being 315. No region shall have fewer than seven Senators. Valle d'Aosta has only one Senator.

Three-quarters of the seats are allocated on the basis of a simple plurality and the remaining one-quarter by proportional representation.

The Chamber of Deputies and the Senate of the Republic are elected for five years.

The term of each House cannot be extended except by law and only in the case of war.

Members of Parliament shall receive remuneration fixed by law.

The President of the Republic must be a citizen of at least fifty years of age and in full enjoyment of all civic and political rights. The person shall be elected for a period of seven years (Articles 84–85).

The Government shall consist of the President of the Council and the Ministers who themselves shall form the Council. The President of the Council, or Prime Minister, shall be nominated by the President of the Republic, who shall also appoint the ministers on the recommendation of the Prime Minister (Article 92).

Section IV (Articles 101–113). Sets forth the judicial system and procedure.

Section V (Articles 114–133). Deals with the division of the Republic into regions, provinces and communes, and sets forth the limits and extent of autonomy enjoyed by the regions. Under Article 131 the regions are enumerated as follows:

| | |
|---|---|
| Piemonte (Piedmont) | Marche |
| Lombardia (Lombardy) | Lazio |
| Veneto | Abruzzo |
| Liguria | Molise |
| Emilia-Romagna | Campania |
| Toscana (Tuscany) | Puglia |
| Umbria | Basilicata |
| Calabria | Trentino-Alto Adige† |
| Sicilia (Sicily)† | Friuli-Venezia Giulia† |
| Sardegna (Sardinia)† | Valle d'Aosta† |

The final articles provide for the establishment of the Corte Costituzionale to deal with constitutional questions and any revisions which may be found necessary after the Constitution has come into operation.

* In June 1997 a parliamentary commission on constitutional reform, which had been established in January, announced its recommendations, which included: a directly-elected President for a six-year term with responsibility for foreign and defence policy; a reduction of the Chamber of Deputies from 630 to 400 members and of the Senate from 315 to 200 members; greater financial autonomy for the regions; and a second round of voting for seats allocated on the basis of a simple plurality. The recommendations required approval by both the Chamber of Deputies and the Senate prior to endorsement at a national referendum.

† These five regions have a wider form of autonomy, based on on constitutional legislation specially adapted to their regional characteristics (Article 116). Each region shall be administered by a Regional Council, in which is vested the legislative power and which may make suggestions for legislation to the Chambers, and the Giunta regionale, which holds the executive power (Article 121).

# The Government

(January 2000)

## HEAD OF STATE

**President of the Republic:** CARLO AZEGLIO CIAMPI (inaugurated 18 May 1999).

## COUNCIL OF MINISTERS

A coalition of the Democratici di Sinistra (DS), the Partito Popolare Italiano (PPI), I Democratici per l'Ulivo (Democratici), the Partito dei Comunisti Italiani (PdCI), the Federazione dei Verdi (FV), the Rinnovamento Italiano (RI), the Unione Democratica per la Repubblica (UDR), the Unione Democratici per l'Europa (UDEUR) and Independents (Ind.).

**Prime Minister:** MASSIMO D'ALEMA (DS).

**Minister of Foreign Affairs:** Prof. LAMBERTO DINI (RI).

**Minister of the Interior:** ENZO BIANCO (Democratici).

**Minister of Justice:** OLIVIERO DILIBERTO (PdCI).

**Minister of the Treasury and of the Budget:** GIULIANO AMATO (Ind.).

**Minister of Finance:** VINCENZO VISCO (DS).

**Minister of Defence:** SERGIO MATTARELLA (PPI).

**Minister of Education:** LUIGI BERLINGUER (DS).

**Minister of Public Works:** WILLER BORDON (Democratici).

**Minister of Culture:** GIOVANNA MELANDRI (DS).

**Minister of Agriculture:** PAOLO DE CASTRO (Ind.).

**Minister of Transport:** PIER LUIGI BERSANI (DS).

**Minister of Communications:** SALVATORE CARDINALE (UDR).

**Minister of Industry, Commerce and Handicrafts:** ENRICO LETTA (PPI).

**Minister of Employment and Social Welfare:** CESARE SALVI (DS).

**Minister of Foreign Trade:** PIERO FASSINO (DS).

**Minister of Health:** ROSY BINDI (PPI).

**Minister of the Environment:** EDO RONCHI (FV).

**Minister of Universities and Scientific Research:** ORTENSIO ZECCHINO (PPI).

**Ministers without Portfolio:**

**Institutional Reforms:** ANTONIO MACCANICO (Democratici).

**Social Solidarity:** LIVIA TURCO (DS).

**Equal Opportunities:** LAURA BALBO (FV).

**Public Administration:** FRANCO BASSANINI (DS).

**Regional Affairs:** KATIA BELILLO (PdCI).

**European Policies:** PATRIZIA TOIA (PPI).

**Relations with Parliament:** AGAZIO LOIERO (UDEUR).

**MINISTRIES**

**Office of the President:** Palazzo del Quirinale, 00187 Rome; tel. (06) 46991.

**Office of the Prime Minister:** Palazzo Chigi, Piazza Colonna 370, 00187 Rome; tel. (06) 67791; fax (06) 6783998.

**Ministry of Agriculture:** Via XX Settembre, 00187 Rome; tel. (06) 46651; fax (06) 4742314.

**Ministry of Communications:** Viale America 201, 00144 Rome; tel. (06) 54441; fax (06) 5407728; e-mail mincom@tin.it; internet www.comunicazioni.it.

**Ministry of Culture:** Via del Collegio Romano 27, 00186 Rome; tel. (06) 67231; fax (06) 6793156; internet www.beniculturali.it.

**Ministry of Defence:** Via XX Settembre 8, 00187 Rome; tel. (06) 4882126; fax (06) 4747775.

**Ministry of Education:** Viale Trastevere 76A, 00153 Rome; tel. (06) 58491; fax (06) 5803381; internet www.istruzione.it.

**Ministry of Employment and Social Welfare:** Via Flavia 6, 00187 Rome; tel. (06) 4683; fax (06) 47887174; internet www.minlavoro.it.

**Ministry of the Environment:** Piazza Venezia 11, 00187 Rome; tel. (06) 70361; fax (06) 6790130; internet www.scn.minambiente.it.

**Ministry of Finance:** Viale America 242, 00144 Rome; tel. (06) 59648826; fax (06) 5910993; internet www.finanze.it.

**Ministry of Foreign Affairs:** Piazzale della Farnesina 1, 00194 Rome; tel. (06) 36911; fax (06) 3236210; internet www.esteri.it.

**Ministry of Foreign Trade:** Viale America 341, 00144 Rome; tel. (06) 59931; fax (06) 59647531; internet www.mincomes.it.

**Ministry of Health:** Viale dell'Industria 20, 00144 Rome; tel. (06) 59941; fax (06) 59647749; internet www.sanita.it.

**Ministry of Industry, Commerce and Handicrafts:** Via Vittorio Veneto 33, 00187 Rome; tel. (06) 47051; fax (06) 47052215; internet www.minindustria.it.

**Ministry of the Interior:** Piazzale del Viminale, 00184 Rome; tel. (06) 46671; fax (06) 4825792; internet www.mininterno.it.

**Ministry of Justice:** Via Arenula 71, 00186 Rome; tel. (06) 68851; fax (06) 6875419; internet www.giustizia.it.

**Ministry of Public Works:** Piazza Porta Pia 1, 00198 Rome; tel. (06) 84821; fax (06) 867187; internet www.llpp.it.

**Ministry of Transport:** Piazza della Croce Rossa 1, 00161 Rome; tel. (06) 84901; fax (06) 8415693; internet www.trasportinavigazione.it.

**Ministry of the Treasury and of the Budget:** Via XX Settembre 97, 00187 Rome; tel. (06) 59931; fax (06) 5913751; internet www.tesoro.it.

**Ministry of Universities and Scientific Research:** Piazza J. F. Kennedy 20, 00144 Rome; tel. (06) 59911; fax (06) 59912967; internet www.murst.it.

# Legislature

**PARLAMENTO**
(Parliament)

**Senato**
(Senate)

**President:** NICOLA MANCINO.

**General Election, 21 April 1996**

| Parties/Alliances | Percentage of votes for seats elected by proportional representation* | Total seats |
|---|---|---|
| L'Ulivo† | 41.2 | 157 |
| Polo per le Libertà‡ | 37.3 | 116 |
| Lega Nord | 10.4 | 27 |
| Rifondazione Comunista (RC) | 2.9 | 10 |
| Liste Autonomiste§ | 1.8 | 3 |
| Movimento Sociale Fiamma Tricolore | 2.3 | 1 |
| Lista Pannella-Sgarbi | 1.6 | 1 |
| Socialisti Italiani (SI) | 0.9 | – |
| Others | 1.6 | – |
| **Total** | 100.0 | 315‖ |

* Figures refer to seats elected by proportional representation (25% of the total); percentages for the remaining 75% of seats, elected by majority vote, are not available.

† Centre-left alliance comprising the Partito Democratico della Sinistra (PDS, renamed the Democratici di Sinistra in 1998), the Partito Popolare Italiano (PPI), the Südtiroler Volkspartei (SVP), the Partito Repubblicano Italiano (PRI), the Unione Democratica (UD), the Lista Romano Prodi, the Rinnovamento Italiano (RI) and the Federazione dei Verdi (FV).

‡ Centre-right grouping including Forza Italia, the Alleanza Nazionale (AN), the Centro Cristiano Democratico (CCD) and the Cristiani Democratici Uniti (CDU).

§Autonomous (regionalist) lists.

‖ In addition to the 315 elected members, there are 10 life members.

**Camera dei Deputati**
(Chamber of Deputies)

**President:** LUCIANO VIOLANTE.

**General Election, 21 April 1996**

| Parties/Alliances | Percentage of votes for seats elected by proportional representation* | Total seats |
|---|---|---|
| L'Ulivo | 34.8 | 284 |
| Partito Democratico della Sinistra (PDS)† | 21.1 | |
| Partito Popolare Italiano (PPI), Lista Romano Prodi | 6.8 | |
| Rinnovamento Italiano (RI) | 4.3 | |
| Federazione dei Verdi (FV) | 2.5 | |
| Others | 0.1 | |
| Polo per le Libertà e del Buon Governo | 44.0 | 246 |
| Forza Italia | 20.6 | |
| Alleanza Nazionale (AN) | 15.7 | |
| Centro Cristiano Democratico (CCD) Cristiani Democratici Uniti (CDU)‡ | 5.8 | |
| Others | 1.9 | |
| Lega Nord | 10.1 | 59 |
| Rifondazione Comunista (RC) | 8.6 | 35 |
| Others | 2.5 | 6 |
| **Total** | 100.0 | 630 |

* Figures refer to seats elected by proportional representation (25% of the total); percentages for the remaining 75% of seats, elected by majority vote, are not available.

† Renamed the Democratici di Sinistra in 1998.

‡ The CDU left the Polo per le Libertà in February 1998.

# Political Organizations

**Alleanza Nazionale (AN)** (National Alliance): Via della Scrofa 39, 00186 Rome; tel. (06) 68803014; fax (06) 6548256; internet www.alleanza-nazionale.it; f. 1994; in early 1995 absorbed the neo-fascist Movimento Sociale Italiano-Destra Nazionale (MSI-DN, f. 1946); Sec.-Gen. GIANFRANCO FINI; 400,000 mems.

**Centro Cristiano Democratico (CCD)** (Christian-Democratic Centre): Via dei Due Macelli 66, Rome; tel. (06) 69791001; fax (06) 6795940; e-mail direzione@ccd.it; internet www.ccd.it; advocates centre-right policies; Pres. SANDRO FONFANA.

**Cristiani Democratici Uniti (CDU)** (United Christian Democrats): Piazza del Gesù 46, 00186 Rome; tel. (06) 67751; e-mail cdu@wmail.axnet.it; internet www.axnet.it/cdu/web_cdu.html;

f. 1995 after split with Partito Popolare Italiano; advocates centre-right policies; Sec.-Gen. ROCCO BUTTIGLIONE.

**I Democratici per l'Ulivo** (The Democrats for the Olive Tree): Piazza SS Apostoli 73, Rome; internet www.democraticiperlulivo.it; f. 1999; Pres. ROMANO PRODI; Exec. Vice-Pres. ARTURO PARISI.

**Democratici di Sinistra (DS)** (Democrats of the Left): Via delle Botteghe Oscure 4, 00186 Rome; tel. (06) 67111; fax (06) 6792085; e-mail posta@democraticidisinistra.it; internet www.democraticidisinistra.it; f. 1921 as the Partito Comunista Italiano (PCI) (Italian Communist Party); name changed to Partito Democratico della Sinistra 1991; name changed as above 1998; advocates a democratic and libertarian society; Gen. Sec. WALTER VELTRONI; approx. 1.4m. mems.

**Federazione dei Verdi (FV)** (Green Party): Via Antonio Salandra 6, 00187 Rome; tel. (06) 4203061; e-mail federazione@verdi.it; f. 1986; advocates environmentalist and anti-nuclear policies; branch of the European Green movement; Leader GRAZIA FRANCESCATO.

**Forza Italia** (Come on, Italy!): Via dell'Umiltà 48, 00187 Rome; tel. (06) 67311; fax (06) 69941315; e-mail lettere@forza-italia.it; internet www.forza-italia.it; f. 1993; advocates principles of market economy; Leader SILVIO BERLUSCONI.

**Lega Nord** (Northern League): Via C. Bellerio 41, 20161 Milan; tel. (02) 662341; fax (02) 66802766; e-mail webmaster@leganord.org; internet www.leganord.org; f. 1991; advocates federalism and transfer of control of resources to regional govts; in 1996 declared the 'Independent Republic of Padania'; opposes immigration; Sec. UMBERTO BOSSI.

**Movimento Sociale Fiamma Tricolore** (Social Movement of the Tricolour Flame): Corso Vittorio Emanuele 39, 00186 Rome; tel. (06) 69200129; fax (06) 69200129; e-mail fiamma@msifiammatric.it; internet www.msifiammatric.it; f. 1996; electoral alliance incorporating former mems of neo-fascist Movimento Sociale Italiano-Destra Nazionale; Nat. Sec. PINO RAUTI.

**Partito dei Comunisti Italiani (PdCI)** (Party of Italian Communists): Corso Vittorio Emanuele II 209, 00186 Rome; tel. (06) 6862721; fax (06) 68627230; e-mail direzionenazionale@comunisti-italiani.it; internet www.comunisti-italiani.it; f. 1998; Chair. ARMANDO COSSUTTA.

**Partito Liberale Italiano (PLI)** (Liberal Party): Via Frattina, 00187 Rome; tel. (06) 6796951; f. 1848 by Cavour, its chief aim is the realization of the principle of freedom in all public and private matters; Sec.-Gen. RAFFAELE COSTA; 153,000 mems.

**Partito Popolare Italiano (PPI)** (Italian People's Party): Central Office: Piazza del Gesù 46, 00186 Rome; tel. (06) 699591; fax (06) 69959327; e-mail ppidirnaz@pronet.it; f. 1994 as the successor to the Partito della Democrazia Cristiana (DC) (Christian Democrat Party; f. 1943); while extending its appeal to voters of all classes, the party attempts to maintain a centre position; Pres. GERARDO BIANCO; Sec.-Gen. FRANCO MARINI.

**Partito Radicale (PR)** (Radical Party): Via di Torre Argentina 76, 00186 Rome; tel. (06) 689791; fax (06) 68805396; campaigns on civil rights issues; Leader MARCO PANNELLA; 42,463 mems.

**Partito Repubblicano Italiano (PRI)** (Italian Republican Party): Piazza dei Caprettari 70, 00186 Rome; tel. (06) 6834037; f. 1897; followers of the principles of Mazzini (social justice in a modern free society) and modern liberalism; Pres. BRUNO VISENTINI; 110,000 mems.

**Partito della Rifondazione Comunista (PRC)** (Reconstructed Communism): Viale del Policlinico 131, 00161 Rome; tel. (06) 441821; fax (06) 44239490; e-mail direzione.prc@rifondazione.it; internet www.rifondazione.it; f. 1991 by former members of the Partito Comunista Italiano (Italian Communist Party); Pres. (vacant); Sec.-Gen. FAUSTO BERTINOTTI.

**Patto Segni** (Segni's Pact): Via Belsiana 100, 00187 Rome; tel. (06) 69941838; fax (06) 6789890; e-mail edpatto@tin.it; internet www.pattosegni.it; f. 1993; liberal party, advocating institutional reform; Leader MARIO SEGNI.

**Polo per le Libertà e del Buon Governo** (Freedom Alliance): Rome; f. 1994; centre-right alliance; including Forza Italia, the Alleanza Nazionale and the Centro Cristiano Democratico; Leader SILVIO BERLUSCONI.

**La Rete** (The Network): Via Marianna Dionigi 29, 00193 Rome; tel. (06) 36001302; f. 1991; anti-Mafia party; Leader LEOLUCA ORLANDO.

**Rinnovamento Italiano** (Italian Renewal): Via di Ripetta 142, 00186 Rome; tel. (06) 68808480; e-mail informa@rinnovamento.it; internet www.rinnovamento.it; f. 1996; centrist; Leader Prof. LAMBERTO DINI.

**Socialisti Democratici Italiani (SDI)** (Italian Democratic Socialists): Piazza S. Lorenzo in Lucina 26, 00186 Rome; tel. (06) 68307666; fax (06) 6872218; e-mail socialisti@nexus.it; internet www.socialisti.org; f. 1892 as Partito Socialista Italiano (PSI); in 1966 merged with the Social Democratic Party to form the United Socialist Party, but in 1969 the Social Democrats broke away; name changed to Socialisti Italiani in 1994; in 1998 re-merged with Social Democratic Party, name changed as above; centre-left; it adheres to the Socialist International and believes that socialism is inseparable from democracy and individual freedom; Pres. ENRICO BOSSELLI.

**Südtiroler Volkspartei (SVP)** (South Tyrol People's Party): Brennerstrasse 7A, 39100 Bozen/Bolzano; tel. (0471) 304000; fax (0471) 981473; regional party of the German and Ladin-speaking people in the South Tyrol; Pres. SIEGFRIED BRUGGER; Gen. Sec. THOMAS WIDMANN.

**L'Ulivo** (The Olive Tree): Via della Dogana Vecchia 27, 00186 Rome; tel. (06) 68808860; f. 1995; centre-left alliance comprising the Partito Democratico della Sinistra (renamed Democratici di Sinistra in 1998), the Partito Popolare Italiano, the Südtiroler Volkspartei, the Unione Democratica, the Lista Romano Prodi, the Rinnovamento Italiano and the Federazione dei Verdi; Leader Prof. ROMANO PRODI.

**Unione Democratica per la Repubblica (UDR)** (Democratic Union for the Republic): Rome; e-mail info@udr.org; internet www.udr.org; f. 1998; moderate; centre-left; Leader FRANCESCO COSSIGA.

**Unione Democratici per l'Europa (UDEUR)** (Union of Democrats for Europe): Largo Arenula 34, 00186 Rome; tel. (06) 684241; fax (06) 6872593; e-mail udeur@udeur.org; internet www.udeur.org; f. 1999; Pres. IRENE PIVETTI; Sec. CLEMENTE MASTELLA.

There are also numerous small political parties, including the following: **Union Valdôtaine** (regional party for the French minority in the Valle d'Aosta); **Partito Sardo d'Azione** (Sardinian autonomy party); **Democrazia Proletaria** (left-wing); and **Lotta Continua** (left-wing).

# Diplomatic Representation

## EMBASSIES IN ITALY

**Afghanistan:** Via Nomentana, 120, 00161 Rome; tel. (06) 8611009; fax (06) 86322939; Chargé d'affaires a.i.: HAMIDULLAH NASSER ZIA.

**Albania:** Via Asmara 9, 00199 Rome; tel. (06) 86218214; fax (06) 86216005; Ambassador: LEONTIEV ÇUÇI.

**Algeria:** Via Barnaba Oriani 26, 00197; Rome; tel. (06) 80687620; fax (06) 8083436; Ambassador: HOCINE MEGHAR.

**Angola:** Via Filippo Bernardini 21, 00165 Rome; tel. (06) 39366902; fax (06) 634960; Ambassador: BOAVENTURA DA SILVA CARDOSO.

**Argentina:** Piazza dell'Esquilino 2, 00185 Rome; tel. (06) 4742551; fax (06) 4744756; Chargé d'affaires a.i.: MARÍA ISABEL RENDON.

**Armenia:** Via dei Colli della Farnesina 174, 00194 Rome; tel. (06) 3296638; fax (06) 3297763; e-mail gaghikb@tin.it; Ambassador: GAGHIK BAGHDASSARIAN.

**Australia:** Via Alessandria 215, 00198 Rome; tel. (06) 852721; fax (06) 85272300; e-mail pbaffairs@australian_embassy.it; internet www.australian-embassy.it; Ambassador: WILLIAM RORY STEELE.

**Austria:** Via G. B. Pergolesi 3, 00198 Rome; tel. (06) 8558241; fax (06) 8543286; e-mail austrianembassyrome@rmnet.it; internet www.austria.it; Ambassador: GÜNTER BIRBAUM.

**Bangladesh:** Via Antonio Bertoloni 14, 00197 Rome; tel. (06) 8083595; fax (06) 8084853; Ambassador: MUHAMMAD ZAMIR.

**Belarus:** Via della Giuliana 113, 0195 Rome; tel. (06) 39741268; fax (06) 3724634; Ambassador: NATALYA DROZD.

**Belgium:** Via dei Monti Parioli 49, 00197 Rome; tel. (06) 3609511; fax (06) 3226935; Ambassador: PATRICK NOTHOMB.

**Bolivia:** Via Brenta 2A, 00198 Rome; tel. (06) 8841001; fax (06) 8840740; Ambassador: JAVIER ZUAZO CHÁVEZ.

**Bosnia and Herzegovina:** Via G. Bazzoni 3, 00195 Rome; tel. (06) 3728509; fax (06) 3728526; Ambassador: MIROSLAV PALAMETA.

**Brazil:** Palazzo Pamphili, Piazza Navona 14, 00186 Rome; tel. (06) 683981; fax (06) 6867858; internet www.web.tin.it/brasile; Ambassador: PAULO TARSO FLECHA DE LIMA.

**Bulgaria:** Via Pietro P. Rubens 21, 00197 Rome; tel. (06) 3224640; fax (06) 3226122; Ambassador: DIMITAR LASAROV.

**Burkina Faso:** Via Alessandria 26, 00198 Rome; tel. (06) 44250052; fax (06) 44250042; internet www.airafrique.it/burkinafaso.htm; Ambassador: NOELLIE MARIE BEATRICE DAMIBA.

**Cameroon:** Via Siracusa 4–6, 00161 Rome; tel. (06) 44291285; fax (06) 44291323; Ambassador: MICHAEL TABONG KIMA.

**Canada:** Via G. B. de Rossi 27, 00161 Rome; tel. (06) 445981; fax (06) 44598750; e-mail rome@dfaitmaeci.gc.ca; internet www.canada.it; Ambassador: JEREMY K. B. KINSMAN.

**Cape Verde:** Via Giosuè Carducci 4, 00187 Rome; tel. (06) 4744678; fax (06) 4744643; Ambassador: ELVIO GONÇALVES NAPOLEÃO FERNANDES.

**Chile:** Via Po 23, 00198 Rome; tel. (06) 8841449; fax (06) 8812348; e-mail embachite.italia@flashnet.it; Ambassador: ALVARO BRIONES.

**China, People's Republic:** Via Bruxelles 56, 00198 Rome; tel. (06) 8848186; fax (06) 85352891; Ambassador: CHENG WENDONG.

**Colombia:** Via Giuseppe Pisanelli 4, 00196 Rome; tel. (06) 3612131; fax (06) 3225798; Ambassador: CARLOS EDUARDO MARTÍNEZ SIMAHAN.

**Congo, Democratic Republic:** Via Tuscolana 979, 00174 Rome; tel. (06) 7480240; Ambassador: EDOUARD UMBA ILUNGA.

**Congo, Republic:** Salita San Nicola da Tolentino 1/B, 00187 Rome; tel. (06) 4746216; fax (06) 4826311; Ambassador: MAMADOU KAMARA DEKAMO.

**Costa Rica:** Via B. Eustachio 22, 00161 Rome; tel. (06) 44251046; fax (06) 44251048; internet www.mix.it/utenti/embcosta; Ambassador: MANUEL HERNÁNDEZ GUTIÉRREZ.

**Côte d'Ivoire:** Via Lazzaro Spallanzani 4–6, 00161 Rome; tel. (06) 44231129; fax (06) 4402619; Ambassador: KOUASSI E. A. NOUAMA.

**Croatia:** Via L. Bodio 74–76, 00191 Rome; tel. (06) 36307650; fax (06) 36303405; Ambassador: DAVORIN RUDOLF.

**Cuba:** Via Licinia 7, 00153 Rome; tel. (06) 5755984; fax (06) 5745445; internet www.elabora95.it/ambasciatadicuba; Ambassador: MARIO RODRÍGUEZ MARTÍNEZ.

**Cyprus:** Via Francesco Denza 15, 00197 Rome; tel. (06) 8088365; fax (06) 8088338; e-mail ciproamb@tin.it; Ambassador: MYRNA Y. KLEOPAS.

**Czech Republic:** Via dei Gracchi 322, 00192 Rome; tel. (06) 3244459; fax (06) 3244466; Ambassador: HANA ŠEVEČÍKOVÁ.

**Denmark:** Via dei Monti Parioli 50, 00197 Rome; tel. (06) 3200441; fax (06) 3610290; e-mail ambadane@iol.it; Ambassador: GUNNAR RIBERHOLDT.

**Dominica:** Via Laurentina 767, 00143 Rome; tel. and fax (06) 5010643; Ambassador: HANNELORE BENJAMIN.

**Dominican Republic:** Via Domenico Chelini 10, 00197 Rome; tel. (06) 8074665; fax (06) 8074791; Ambassador: RAFAEL CALVENTI.

**Ecuador:** Via Guido d'Arezzo 14, 00198 Rome; tel. (06) 8541784; fax (06) 85354434; Ambassador: JOSÉ PARRA GIL.

**Egypt:** 119 Roma Villa Savoia, Via Salaria 267, 00199 Rome; tel. (06) 8440191; fax (06) 8554424; Ambassador: NEHAD IBRAHIM ABD AL-LATIF.

**El Salvador:** Via Castellini 13, 00197 Rome; tel. (06) 8076605; fax (06) 8079726; Chargé d'affaires a.i.: MARÍA EULALIA JIMÉNEZ ZEPEDA.

**Eritrea:** Via Boncompagni 16B, 00187 Rome; tel. (06) 42741293; fax (06) 42086806; Ambassador: PIETROS FESSAHAZION.

**Estonia:** Via Po 24, 00198 Rome; tel. (06) 8417595; fax (06) 8550192; e-mail saatkond@rooma.vm.ee; Ambassador: JAAK JÕERÜÜT.

**Ethiopia:** Via Andrea Vesalio 16–18, 00161 Rome; tel. (06) 4402602; fax (06) 5040546; Ambassador: HALIMA MOHAMMED.

**Finland:** Via Lisbona 3, 00198 Rome; tel. (06) 852231; fax (06) 8540362; e-mail ambasciata.di.finlandia@interbusiness.it; internet www.finland.it; Ambassador: DIETER VITZTHUM.

**France:** Piazza Farnese 67, 00186 Rome; tel. (06) 686011; fax (06) 68601360; internet www.france-italia.it; Ambassador: JACQUES BLOT.

**Gabon:** Via Mercalli 25, 00197 Rome; tel. (06) 80691390; fax (06) 80691504; Ambassador: MARCEL IBINGA-MAGWANGU.

**Georgia:** Palazzo Pierret, Piazza di Spagna 20, 00187 Rome; tel. (06) 69941972; fax (06) 69941942; Ambassador: RUSSUSLAN LORTKIPANIDZE.

**Germany:** Via San Martino della Battaglia 4, 00185 Rome; tel. (06) 49213; fax (06) 4452672; internet www.ambgermania.it; Ambassador: FRITJOF VON NORDENSKJÖLD.

**Ghana:** Via Ostriana 4, 00199 Rome; tel. (06) 86217191; fax (06) 86325762; Ambassador: AANAA NAMUA ENIN.

**Greece:** Via Mercadente 36, 00198 Rome; tel. (06) 8549630; fax (06) 8415927; e-mail gremroma@tin.it; Ambassador: ALEXANDROS SANDIS.

**Guatemala:** Via dei Colli della Farnesina 128, 00194 Rome; tel. (06) 36307392; Ambassador: JOSEFINA MORALES FIGUEROA.

**Guinea:** Via Adelaide Ristori 9/13, 00197 Rome; tel. (06) 8078989; fax (06) 8075569; Chargé d'affaires a.i.: MACKA KEITA.

**Haiti:** 1st floor, Via Ottaviano 32, 00192 Rome; tel. (06) 39723362; fax (06) 33269214; Chargé d'affaires a.i.: JEAN-WALNARD DORNEVAL.

**Holy See:** Via Po 27–29, 00198 Rome; tel. (06) 8546287; fax (06) 8549725; Apostolic Nuncio: Most Rev. ANDREA CORDERO LANZA DI MONTEZEMOLO, Titular Archbishop of Tuscania.

**Honduras:** Via Giambattista Vico 40, 00196 Rome; tel. (06) 3207236; fax (06) 3207973; e-mail ambhond@tin.it; Ambassador: SALOMONE CASTELLANOS.

**Hungary:** Via dei Villini 14, 00161 Rome; tel. (06) 44230567; fax (06) 4403270; internet www.web.tin.it/huembit; Ambassador: ENIKI GYORI.

**India:** Via XX Settembre 5, 00187 Rome; tel. (06) 4884642; fax (06) 4819539; Ambassaor: KALARICKAL PRANCHU FABIAN.

**Indonesia:** Via Campania 55, 00187 Rome; tel. (06) 4825951; fax (06) 4880280; Ambassador: SOENDROE RACHMAD.

**Iran:** Via Nomentana 361, 00162 Rome; tel. (06) 86328485; fax (06) 86215287; e-mail embassiran_rome@hotmail.com; Ambassador: ALI AHANI.

**Ireland:** Piazza di Campitelli 3, 00186 Rome; tel. (06) 6979121; fax (06) 6792354; Ambassador: JOSEPH SMALL.

**Israel:** Via M. Mercati 14, 00197 Rome; tel. (06) 36198500; fax (06) 36198555; e-mail israel.roma@agora.stm.it; internet www.israel.amb.it; Ambassador: YEHUDA MILLO.

**Japan:** Via Quintino Sella 60, 00187 Rome; tel. (06) 487991; fax (06) 4873316; internet www.ambasciatajp.it; Ambassador: HIROMOTO SEKI.

**Jordan:** Via G. Marchi 1B, 00161 Rome; tel. (06) 86205303; fax (06) 8606122; Ambassador: SAMIR MASARWEH.

**Kazakhstan:** Piazza Farnese 101, 00186 Rome; tel. (06) 68808640; fax (06) 68891360; Ambassador: OLZHAS SULEYMENOV.

**Kenya:** Via Archimede 164, 00197 Rome; tel. (06) 8082714; fax (06) 8082707; Ambassador: BOB F. JALANG'O.

**Korea, Republic:** Via Barnaba Oriani 30, 00197 Rome; tel. (06) 8088769; fax (06) 80687794; Ambassador: CHUNG TAE-IK.

**Kuwait:** Via Archimede 124, 00197 Rome; tel. (06) 8078415; fax (06) 8076651; Ambassador: GHAZI AR-RAYES.

**Latvia:** Viale Liegi 42, 00189 Rome; tel. (06) 8841227; fax (06) 8841239; e-mail segrom@ricanet.it; Ambassador: MARTINS PERTS.

**Lebanon:** Via Giacomino Carissimi 38, 00198 Rome; tel. (06) 8557119; fax (06) 8411794; Ambassador: SAMIR EL-KHOURY.

**Lesotho:** Via Serchio 8, 00198 Rome; tel. (06) 8542496; fax (06) 8542527; e-mail les.rome@flashnet.it; Ambassador: RACHEL R. MATHABO NTSINYI.

**Liberia:** Via A. Vivaldi 13, 00199 Rome; tel. (06) 86205754; fax (06) 86205754; Chargé d'affaires a.i.: KRONYANH MOSES WEEFUR.

**Libya:** Via Nomentana 365, 00162 Rome; tel. (06) 86320951; fax (06) 86205473; Ambassador: ABDULATI IBRAHIM ALOBIDI.

**Lithuania:** Viale di Villa Grazioli 9, 00198 Rome; tel. (06) 8559052; fax (06) 8559053; e-mail ltemb@tin.it; Ambassador: ROMANAS PODAGÉLIS.

**Luxembourg:** Via S. Croce in Gerusalemme 90, 00185 Rome; tel. (06) 77201177; fax (06) 77201055; Ambassador: PAUL FABER.

**Macedonia, former Yugoslav republic:** Via Bruxelles 73–75, 00198 Rome; tel. (06) 84241109; fax (06) 84241131; e-mail repmaced@ats.it; Ambassador: VIKTOR GABER.

**Madagascar:** Via Riccardo Zandonai 84A, 00194 Rome; tel. (06) 36307797; fax (06) 3294306; Ambassador: GEORGES RUPHIN.

**Malaysia:** Via Nomentana 297, 00162 Rome; tel. (06) 8415764; fax (06) 8555040; Ambassador: R. VENGADESAN.

**Mali:** Via Nomentana 13, 00100 Rome; Ambassador: IBRAHIM BOCAR DAGA.

**Malta:** Lungotevere Marzio 12, 00186 Rome; tel. (06) 6879990; fax (06) 6892687; Ambassador: JOSEPH CASSAR.

**Mauritania:** Via Giovanni Paisiello 26, 00198 Rome; tel. (06) 85351530; fax (06) 85351441; Ambassador: MELANINE OULD MOCTAR NECHE.

**Mexico:** Via Lazzaro Spallanzani 16, 00161 Rome; tel. (06) 441151; fax (06) 4403876; e-mail messico@target.it; internet www.target.it/messico; Ambassador: MARIO MOYA PALENCIA.

**Moldova:** Via Montebello 8, 00185 Rome; tel. and fax (06) 47881092; Ambassador: VALENTIN CIUMAC.

**Monaco:** Via Bertoloni 36, 00197 Rome; tel. (06) 8083361; fax (06) 8077692; Ambassador: RENÉ NOVELLA.

**Morocco:** Via Lazzaro Spallanzani 8, 00161 Rome; tel. (06) 4402524; fax (06) 4402695; Ambassador: AZIZ MEKOUAR.

**Mozambique:** Via Filippo Corridoni 14, 00195 Rome; tel. (06) 37514852; fax (06) 37514699; Chargé d'affaires a.i.: ANANIAS BENJAMIN SIGAUQUE.

**Myanmar:** Via Gioacchino Rossini 18, 00198 Rome; tel. (06) 8549374; fax (06) 8413167; Ambassador: MYINT U PHONE.

**Netherlands:** Via Michele Mercati 8, 00197 Rome; tel. (06) 3221141; fax (06) 3221440; e-mail rom@rom.minbuza.nl; Ambassador: M. Y. KRÖNER.

**New Zealand:** Via Zara 28, 00198 Rome; tel. (06) 4417171; fax (06) 4402984; e-mail nzemb.rom@flashnet.it; Ambassador: PETER ROBERT BENNETT.

**Nicaragua:** Via Brescia 16, 00198 Rome; tel. (06) 8413471; fax (06) 8841695; Ambassador: ALEJANDRO MEJA FERRETTI.

**Niger:** Via Antonio Baiamonti 10, 00195 Rome; tel. and fax (06) 3729013; Ambassador: ADAMOU SEYKOU.

**Nigeria:** Via Orazio 14–18, 00193 Rome; tel. (06) 6896243; fax (06) 6832528; Ambassador: GABRIEL SAM AKUNWAFOR.

**Norway:** Via delle Terme Deciane 7, 00153 Rome; tel. and fax (06) 5717031; Ambassador: GEIR GRUNG.

**Oman:** Via della Camilluccia 625, 00135 Rome; tel. (06) 36300517; fax (06) 3296802; Ambassador: SAID KHALIFA MUHAMMAD AL-BUSAIDI.

**Pakistan:** Via della Camilluccia 682, 00135 Rome; tel. (06) 36301775; fax (06) 36301936; e-mail pareprom@forobit.it; Ambassador: ARIF AYUB.

**Panama:** Viale Regina Margherita 239, 00198 Rome; tel. (06) 44252113; fax (06) 44252237; Ambassador: ROBERTO ALFARO EDTRIPEAUT.

**Paraguay:** Via Salaria 237B, 00199 Rome; tel. (06) 8848150; fax (06) 8558739; Ambassador: LILIA ROMERO PEREIRA.

**Peru:** Via Siacci 4, 00197 Rome; tel. (06) 80691510; fax (06) 8073216; e-mail amb.peru@agora.stm.it; Ambassador: ANA MARÍA DEUSTUA.

**Philippines:** Viale delle Medaglie d'Oro 112, 00136 Rome; tel. (06) 39746621; fax (06) 39740872; e-mail ph1@agora.it; Ambassador: PHILIPPE J. LHUILLIER.

**Poland:** Via Pietro Paolo Rubens 20, 00197 Rome; tel. (06) 3224455; fax (06) 3217895; Ambassador: MACIEJ GORSKI.

**Portugal:** Viale Liegi 21–23, 00198 Rome; tel. (06) 844801; fax (06) 8542262; Ambassador: JOSÉ CESAR PAULOURO DAS NEVES.

**Qatar:** Via Antonio Bosio 14, 00161 Rome; tel. (06) 44249450; fax (06) 44245273; Ambassador: AHMED ALI AHMED AL-ANSARI.

**Romania:** Via Nicolò Tartaglia 36, 00197 Rome; tel. (06) 8084529; fax (06) 8084995; Ambassador: SERBAN STATI.

**Russia:** Via Gaeta 5, 00185 Rome; tel. (06) 4941680; fax (06) 491031; Ambassador: NIKOLAI NIKOLAYEVICH SPASSKII.

**San Marino:** Via Eleonora Duse 35, 00197 Rome; tel. (06) 8084567; fax (06) 8070072; Ambassador: BARBARA PARA.

**Saudi Arabia:** Via G. B. Pergolesi 9, 00198 Rome; tel. (06) 844851; fax (06) 8557633; internet www.arabia-saudita.it; Ambassador: MUHAMMAD BIN NAWAF BIN ABD AL-AZIZ AS-SAUD.

**Senegal:** Via Giulia 66, 00186 Rome; tel. (06) 6872381; fax (06) 6865212; Ambassador: MAME BALLA SY.

**Slovakia:** Via dei Colli della Farnesina 144, 00194 Rome; tel. (06) 36308741; fax (06) 36308617; Ambassador: RUDOLF ZELENAY.

**Slovenia:** Via Leonardo Pisano 10, 00197 Rome; tel. (06) 8081075; fax (06) 8081471; Ambassador: PETER ANDREJ BEKEŠ.

**South Africa:** Via Tanaro 14, 00198 Rome; tel. (06) 852541; fax (06) 85254300; e-mail sae@flashnet.it; internet www.sudafrica.it; Ambassador: ANTHONY LE CLERK MONGALO.

**Spain:** Palazzo Borghese, Largo Fontenella Borghese 19, 00186 Rome; tel. (06) 6878172; fax (06) 6872256; e-mail embaspagna.roma@pronet.it; Ambassador: JUAN PRAT COLL.

**Sri Lanka:** Via Adige 2, 00198 Rome; tel. (06) 8554360; fax (06) 84241670; e-mail mc7785@mclink.it; Ambassador: THELMUTH HARRIS WILHELM WOUTERSZ.

**Sudan:** Via Lazzaro Spallanzani 24, 00161 Rome; tel. (06) 4403609; fax (06) 4402358; Ambassador: ANDREW MAKUR THOU.

**Sweden:** Piazza Rio de Janeiro 3, 00161 Rome; tel. (06) 441941; fax (06) 44194760; Ambassador: ROLF GORAN KRISTOFFER BERG.

**Switzerland:** Via Barnaba Oriani 61; 00197 Rome; tel. (06) 809571; fax (06) 8088510; Ambassador: ALEXEI LAUTENBERG.

**Syria:** Piazza dell'Ara Coeli, 00186 Rome; tel. (06) 6797791; fax (06) 6794989; Chargé d'affaires a.i.: NAJDI ALJAZZAR.

**Tanzania:** Via C. Becaria 88, 00196 Rome; tel. (06) 36005234; fax (06) 3216611; Chargé d'affaires a.i.: ALBANO LUMBE TENEKU ASMANI.

**Thailand:** Via Nomentana 132, 00162 Rome; tel. (06) 86204381; fax (06) 86208399; e-mail thai.em.rome@pn.itnet.it; Ambassador: SOMBOON SANGIAMBUT.

**Tunisia:** Via Asmara 7, 00199 Rome; tel. (06) 8603060; fax (06) 86218204; Ambassador: AZOUZ ENNIFAR.

**Turkey:** Via Palestro 28, 00185 Rome; tel. (06) 4469933; fax (06) 4941526; Ambassador: NECATI UTKAN.

**Uganda:** Via Ennio Quirino Visconti 8, 00193 Rome; tel. (06) 3225220; fax (06) 3203174; Ambassador; VINCENT KIRABOKYAMARIA.

**Ukraine:** Via Guido d'Arezzo 9, 00198 Rome; tel. (06) 8412630; fax (06) 8547539; Ambassador: VOLODYMYR YEVTUKH.

**United Arab Emirates:** Via della Camilluccia 551, 00135 Rome; tel. (06) 36306100; fax (06) 36306155; Ambassador: MUHAMMAD FAHD ADH-DHAIM.

**United Kingdom:** Via XX Settembre 80A, 00187 Rome; tel. (06) 4825551; fax (06) 4873324; e-mail info@rome.mail.fco.gov.uk; internet www.britain.it; Ambassador: JOHN SHEPHERD.

**USA:** Via Vittorio Veneto 119A, 00187 Rome; tel. (06) 46741; fax (06) 46742356; internet www.usis.it; Ambassador: THOMAS FOGLIETTA.

**Uruguay:** Via Vittorio Veneto 183, 00187 Rome; tel. (06) 4821776; fax (06) 4823695; Ambassador: CARLOS BRUGNINI.

**Uzbekistan:** Via Tolmino 12, 00198 Rome; tel. (06) 8542456; fax (06) 8541020; e-mail uzbembass@tiskalinet.it; internet www.uzbekistanitalia.com; Chargé d'affaires a.i.: KHURSHID M. BABASHEV.

**Venezuela:** Via Nicolò Tartaglia 11, 00197 Rome; tel. (06) 8079464; fax (06) 8084410; Chargé d'affaires a.i.: AMADEO VOLPE GIACOBONI.

**Viet Nam:** Via Clitunno 34–36, 00198 Rome; tel. (06) 8543223; fax (06) 8548501; Ambassador: TRAN MINH QUOE.

**Yemen:** Viale Regina Margherita 1, 00198 Rome; tel. (06) 8416711; fax (06) 8416801; Ambassador: MUHAMMAD ABDULLAH ELWAZIR.

**Yugoslavia:** Via dei Monti Parioli 20, 00197 Rome; tel. (06) 3200796; fax (06) 3200868; Chargé d'affaires a.i.: SLAVKO NJEGOMIR.

**Zimbabwe:** Via Virgilio 8, 00193 Rome; tel. (06) 68807781; fax (06) 68308324; Ambassador: MARY MARGARET MULCHADA.

# Judicial System

The Constitutional Court was established in 1956 and is an autonomous constitutional body, standing apart from the judicial system. Its most important function is to pronounce on the constitutionality of legislation both subsequent and prior to the present Constitution of 1948. It also judges accusations brought against the President of the Republic or ministers.

At the base of the system of penal jurisdiction are the Preture (District Courts), where offences carrying a sentence of up to four years' imprisonment are tried. Above the Preture are the Tribunali (Tribunals) and the Corti di Assise presso i Tribunali (Assize Courts attached to the Tribunals), where graver offences are dealt with. From these courts appeal lies to the Corti d'Appello (Courts of Appeal) and the parallel Corti di Assise d'Appello (Assize Courts of Appeal). Final appeal may be made, on juridical grounds only, to the Corte Suprema di Cassazione.

Civil cases may be taken in the first instance to the Giudici Conciliatori (Justices of the Peace), Preture or Tribunali, according to the economic value of the case. Appeal from the Giudici Conciliatori lies to the Preture, from the Preture to the Tribunali, from the Tribunali to the Corti d'Appello, and finally, as in penal justice, to the Corte Suprema di Cassazione on juridical grounds only.

Special divisions for cases concerning labour relations are attached to civil courts. Cases concerned with the public service and its employees are tried by Tribunali Amministrativi Regionali and the Consiglio di Stato. Juvenile courts have criminal and civil jurisdiction.

A new penal code was introduced in late 1989.

**Consiglio Superiore della Magistratura (CSM):** Piazza dell'Indipendenza 6, 00185 Rome; f. 1958; tel. (06) 444911; supervisory body of judicial system; 33 mems.

**President:** The President of the Republic.

### CONSTITUTIONAL COURT

**Corte Costituzionale:** Palazzo della Consulta, Piazza del Quirinale 41, 00187 Rome; tel. (06) 46981; fax (06) 4825706; e-mail c.costit@mclink.it; internet www.cortecostituzionale.it; consists of 15 judges, one-third appointed by the President of the Republic, one-third elected by Parliament in joint session, one-third by the ordinary and administrative supreme courts.

**President:** CESARE MIRABELLI.

### ADMINISTRATIVE COURTS

**Consiglio di Stato:** Palazzo Spada, Piazza Capo di Ferro 13, 00186 Rome; tel. (06) 67771; established in accordance with Article 10 of the Constitution; has both consultative and judicial functions.

**President:** GIORGIO CRISCO.

**Corte dei Conti:** Via Baiamonti 25, Rome; tel. (06) 48951, and Via Barberini 38, Rome; functions as the court of public auditors for the state.

**President:** GIUSEPPE CARBONE.

### SUPREME COURT OF APPEAL

**Corte Suprema di Cassazione:** Palazzo di Giustizia, 00100 Rome; tel. (06) 68831; fax (06) 6883420; supreme court of civil and criminal appeal.

**First President:** FERDINANDO ZUCCONI GALLI FONSECA.

# Religion

More than 90% of the population of Italy are adherents of the Roman Catholic Church. Under the terms of the Concordat formally ratified in June 1985, Roman Catholicism was no longer to be the state religion, compulsory religious instruction in schools was abolished and state financial contributions reduced. The Vatican City's sovereign rights as an independent state, under the terms of the Lateran Pact of 1929, were not affected.

Several Protestant churches also exist in Italy, with a total membership of about 50,000. There is a small Jewish community, and in 1987 an agreement between the State and Jewish representatives recognized certain rights for the Jewish community, including the right to observe religious festivals on Saturdays by not attending school or work.

### CHRISTIANITY

#### The Roman Catholic Church

For ecclesiastical purposes, Italy comprises the Papal See of Rome, the Patriarchate of Venice, 58 archdioceses (including six directly responsible to the Holy See), 157 dioceses (including seven within the jurisdiction of the Pope, as Archbishop of the Roman Province, and 17 directly responsible to the Holy See), two territorial prelatures (including one directly responsible to the Holy See) and seven territorial abbacies (including four directly responsible to the Holy See). Almost all adherents follow the Latin rite, but there are two dioceses and one abbacy (all directly responsible to the Holy See) for Catholics of the Italo-Albanian (Byzantine) rite.

**Bishops' Conference:** Conferenza Episcopale Italiana, Circonvallazione Aurelia 50, 00165 Rome; tel. (06) 663981; fax (06) 6623037; f. 1985; Pres. HE Cardinal CAMILLO RUINI, Vicar-General of Rome.

**Primate of Italy, Archbishop and Metropolitan of the Roman Province and Bishop of Rome:** His Holiness Pope JOHN PAUL II.

**Patriarch of Venice:** HE Cardinal MARCO CÉ.

**Archbishops:**

Acerenza: Most Rev. MICHELE SCANDIFFIO.
Amalfi-Cava de'Tirreni: (vacant).
Ancona-Osimo: Most Rev. FRANCO FESTORAZZI.
Bari-Bitonto: Most Rev. FRANCESCO CACUCCI.
Benevento: Most Rev. SERAFINO SPROVIERI.
Bologna: HE Cardinal GIACOMO BIFFI.
Brindisi-Ostuni: Most Rev. SETTIMIO TODISCO.
Cagliari: Most Rev. OTTORINO PIETRO ALBERTI.
Camerino-San Severino Marche: Most Rev. ANGELO FAGIANI.
Campobasso-Boiano: Most Rev. ETTORE DI FILIPPO.
Capua: Most Rev. BRUNO SCHETTINO.
Catania: Most Rev. LUIGI BOMMARITO.
Catanzaro-Squillace: Most Rev. ANTONIO CANTISANI.
Chieti-Vasto: Most Rev. EDOARDO MENICHELLI.
Cosenza-Bisignano: Most Rev. GIUSEPPE AGOSTINO.
Crotone-Santa Severina: Most Rev. ANDREA MUGIONE.
Fermo: Most Rev. GENNARO FRANCESCHETTI.
Ferrara-Comacchio: Most Rev. CARLO CAFFARRA.
Florence: HE Cardinal SILVANO PIOVANELLI.
Foggia-Bovino: Most Rev. DOMENICO UMBERTO D'AMBROSIO.
Gaeta: Most Rev. PIER LUIGI MAZZONI.
Genoa: HE Cardinal DIONIGI TETTAMANZI.
Gorizia: Most Rev. DINO DE ANTONI.
Lanciano-Ortona: Most Rev. ENZIO D'ANTONIO.
L'Aquila: Most Rev. GIUSEPPE MOLINARI.
Lecce: Most Rev. COSMO FRANCESCO RUPPI.
Lucca: Most Rev. BRUNO TOMMASI.
Manfredonia-Vieste: Most Rev. VINCENZO D'ADDARIO.
Matera-Irsina: Most Rev. ANTONIO CILIBERTI.
Messina-Lipari-Santa Lucia del Mela: Most Rev. GIOVANNI MARRA.
Milan: HE Cardinal CARLO MARIA MARTINI.
Modena-Nonantola: Most Rev. BENITO COCCHI.
Monreale: Most Rev. PIO VITTORIO VIGO.
Naples: HE Cardinal MICHELE GIORDANO.
Oristano: Most Rev. PIER GIULIANO TIDDIA.
Otranto: (vacant).
Palermo: HE Cardinal SALVATORE DE GIORGI.
Perugia-Città della Pieve: Most Rev. GIUSEPPE CHIARETTI.
Pescara-Penne: Most Rev. FRANCESCO CUCCARESE.
Pisa: Most Rev. ALESSANDRO PLOTTI.
Potenza-Muro Lucano-Marsico Nuovo: Most Rev. ENNIO APPIGNANESI.
Ravenna-Cervia: Most Rev. LUIGI AMADUCCI.
Reggio Calabria-Bova: Most Rev. VITTORIO LUIGI MONDELLO.
Rossano-Cariati: Most Rev. ANDREA CASSONE.
Salerno-Campagna-Acerno: Most Rev. GERARDO PIERRO.
Sant'Angelo dei Lombardi-Conza-Nusco-Bisaccia: Most Rev. SALVATORE NUNNARI.
Sassari: Most Rev. SALVATORE ISGRÓ.
Siena-Colle di Val d'Elsa-Montalcino: Most Rev. GAETANO BONICELLI.
Sorrento-Castellammare di Stabia: Most Rev. FELICE CECE.
Spoleto-Norcia: Most Rev. RICCARDO FONTANA.
Syracuse: Most Rev. GIUSEPPE COSTANZO.
Taranto: Most Rev. BENIGNO LUIGI PAPA.
Trani-Barletta-Bisceglie: Most Rev. GIOVANNI BATTISTA PICHIERRI.
Trento: Most Rev. LUIGI BRESSAN.
Turin: Most Rev. SEVERINO POLETTO.
Udine: Most Rev. ALFREDO BATTISTI.
Urbino-Urbania-Sant'Angelo in Vado: (vacant).
Vercelli: Most Rev. ENRICO MASSERONI.

**Azione Cattolica Italiana (ACI)** (Catholic Action): Via della Conciliazione 1, 00193 Rome; tel. (06) 6868751; fax (06) 68802088; in Italy there are numerous apostolic lay organizations, prominent among which is Italian Catholic Action, which has a total membership of 1m.; National Presidency is the supreme executive body and co-ordinator of the different branches of Catholic Action; Pres. Avv. GIUSEPPE GERVASIO; Sec.-Gen. AURELIANO INGLESI.

#### Protestant Churches

**Federazione delle Chiese Evangeliche in Italia** (Federation of the Protestant Churches in Italy): Via Firenze 38, 00184 Rome; tel. (06) 4825120; fax (06) 4828728; e-mail fed.evangelica@agora.stm.it; the Federation was formed in 1967; total mems more than 50,000; Pres. Pastor DOMENICO TOMASETTO; Sec. LUCA MARIA NEGRO; includes the following organizations:

**Chiesa Apostolica d'Italia**

**Chiesa Evangelica Luterana in Italia** (Lutheran Church): Via Toscana 7, 00187 Rome; tel. (06) 4880394; fax (06) 4874506; Dean JÜRGEN ASTFALK; 20,100 mems.

**Chiesa Evangelica Metodista in Italia** (Evangelical Methodist Church): Via Firenze 38, 00184 Rome; tel. (06) 4743695; fax (06) 47881267; e-mail metodismo@tin.it; f. 1861; Pres. Pastor VALDO BENECCHI; 4,000 mems.

**Comunione delle Chiese Libere**

**Comunità Ecumenica di Ispra-Varese**

**Comunità Evangelica di Confessione Elvetica**

**Esercito della Salvezza** (Salvation Army): Via degli Apuli 39, 00185 Rome; tel. (06) 4462614; fax (06) 490078; Officer Commanding for Italy Lt-Col DAVID ARMISTEAD; 15 regional centres.

**Fiumi di Vita**

**Tavola Valdese** (Waldensian Church): Via Firenze 38, 00184 Rome; tel. (06) 4745537; fax (06) 47885308; e-mail tvmode@tin.it; internet www.chiesavaldese.org; Moderator GIANNI ROSTAN; Sec.-Treas. ROSELLA PANZIRONI; 22,000 mems.

**Unione Cristiana Evangelica Battista d'Italia** (Italian Baptist Union): Piazza San Lorenzo in Lucina 35, 00186 Rome; tel. (06) 6876124; fax (06) 6876185; e-mail ucebit@tin.it; f. 1873; Pres. Dott. RENATO MAIOCCHI; Admin. Sec. ALDO CASONATO; 5,000 mems.

#### Associated Organization

**Seventh-day Adventists:** Lungotevere Michelangelo 7, 00192 Rome; tel. (06) 3609591; fax (06) 36095952; e-mail uicca@avventisti.org; internet www.avventisti.org; f. 1929; represents 90 communities in Italy and Malta; Supt VINCENZO MAZZA; Sec. DANIELE BENINI.

### JUDAISM

The number of Jews was estimated at 30,000 in 1997.

**Union of Italian Jewish Communities:** Lungotevere Sanzio 9, 00153 Rome; tel. (06) 5803667; fax (06) 5899569; f. 1930; represents 21 Jewish communities in Italy; Pres. AMOS LUZZATTO; Chief Rabbi of Rome Dott. ELIO TOAFF.

**Rabbinical Council:** Chief Rabbi Dott. ELIO R. TOAFF (Via Catalana 1A, Rome), Rabbi Dott. GIUSEPPE LARAS (Via Guastalla 19, Milan), Rabbi Dott. ELIA RICHETTI (Via Guastalla 19, Milan).

### BAHÁ'Í FAITH

**Assemblea Spirituale Nazionale:** Via Stoppani 10, 00197 Rome; tel. (06) 8079647; fax (06) 8070184; e-mail segretaria@bahai.it; internet www.bahai.it; mems resident in 330 localities.

## The Press

Relative to the size of Italy's population, the number of daily newspapers is rather small (78 in 1996). The average total circulation of daily newspapers in 1996 was 5,960,000 copies per issue; sales in the north and centre of the country accounted for 80% of this figure, and those in the south for 20%.

Rome and Milan are the main press centres. The most important national dailies are *Corriere della Sera* in Milan and Rome and *La Repubblica* in Rome, followed by Turin's *La Stampa*, *Il Sole 24 Ore* in Milan, the economic and financial newspaper with the highest circulation in Europe, *Il Messaggero* in Rome, *Il Resto del Carlino* in Bologna, *La Nazione* in Florence, and *Il Giornale* and *Il Giorno*, which circulate mainly in the north.

In 1993 there were about 10,000 periodical titles, with a combined annual circulation of some 4,036m. Many illustrated weekly papers and magazines maintain very high levels of circulation, with *TV Sorrisi e Canzoni* and *Famiglia Cristiana* enjoying the highest figures. Other very popular general-interest weeklies are *Gente* and *Oggi*. Among the serious and influential magazines are *Panorama* and *L'Espresso*.

## PRINCIPAL DAILIES

### Ancona

**Corriere Adriatico:** Via Berti 20, 60100 Ancona; tel. (071) 4581; fax (071) 42980; f. 1860; Dir Dott. PAOLO BIAGI; circ. 29,349.

### Bari

**La Gazzetta del Mezzogiorno:** Viale Scipione l'Africano 264, 70124 Bari; tel. (080) 5470200; fax (080) 5470488; f. 1928; independent; Man. Dir LINO PATRUNO; circ. 82,398.

### Bergamo

**L'Eco di Bergamo:** Viale Papa Giovanni XXIII 118, 24121 Bergamo; tel. (035) 386111; fax (035) 386217; e-mail redazione@eco.bg.it; internet www.eco.bg.it; f. 1880; Catholic; Man. Dr SERGIO BORSI; circ 68,449.

### Bologna

**Il Resto del Carlino:** Via Enrico Mattei 106, 40138 Bologna; tel. (051) 536111; fax (051) 6570099; f. 1885; independent; Dir MARCO LEONELLI; circ. 232,866.

### Bolzano/Bozen

**Alto Adige:** Via Volta 10, 39100 Bozen; tel. (0471) 904111; fax (0471) 9042663; e-mail altoadi@tin.it; internet www.altoadige.it; f. 1945; independent; Dir FRANCO DE BATTAGLIA; circ. 53,674.

**Dolomiten:** Weinbergweg 7, 39100 Bozen; tel. (0471) 925111; fax 925440; e-mail dolomiten@athesia.it; internet www.dolomiten.it; f. 1926; independent; German language; Dir Dr TONI EBNER; circ. 56,500.

### Brescia

**Bresciaoggi Nuovo:** Via Eritrea 20, 25126 Brescia; tel. (030) 22941; fax (030) 2294229; f. 1974; Dir MINO ALLIONE; circ. 18,500.

**Il Giornale di Brescia:** Via Solferino 22, 25121 Brescia; tel. (030) 37901; fax (030) 292226; f. 1945; Editor GIAN BATTISTA LANZANI; Man. Dir FRANCESCO PASSERINI GLAZEL; circ. 72,301.

### Cagliari

**L'Unione Sarda:** Viale Regina Elena 14, 09124 Cagliari; tel. (070) 60131; e-mail unione@unionesarda.it; internet www.unionesarda.it; f. 1889; independent; Dir ANTONANGELO LIORI; circ. 81,810.

### Catania

**La Sicilia:** Viale Odorico da Pordenone 50, 95126 Catania; tel. (095) 330544; fax (095) 253316; f. 1945; independent; Dir Dott. MARIO CIANCIO SANFILIPPO; circ. 87,942.

### Como

**La Provincia di Como:** Via Anzani 52, 22100 Como; tel. (031) 31211; e-mail laprovincia@laprovincia.it; f. 1892; independent; Dir LUIGI DARIO; circ. 49,711.

### Cremona

**La Provincia di Cremona:** Via delle Industrie 2, 26100 Cremona; tel. (0372) 4981; fax (0372) 28487; f. 1946; independent; Pres. MARIO MAESTRONI; Man. Editor ROBERTO GELMINI; circ. 26,777.

### Ferrara

**La Nuova Ferrara:** Viale Cavour 129, 44100 Ferrara; tel. (0532) 200777; fax (0532) 47689; internet www.lanuovaferrara.it; f. 1989; independent; Man. Dir ENRICO PIRONDINI; circ. 11,886.

### Florence

**La Nazione:** Via Ferdinando Paolieri 2, 50121 Florence; tel. (055) 24851; f. 1859; independent; Dir RICCARDO BERTI; circ. 258,794.

### Genoa

**L'Avvisatore Marittimo:** Piazza Piccapietra 21, 16121 Genoa; tel. (010) 562929; fax (010) 566415; e-mail avvmar@tin.it; f. 1925; shipping and financial; Editor SANDRO GRIMALDI; circ. 2,400.

**Corriere Mercantile:** Via Archimede 169, 16142 Genoa; tel. (010) 53691; fax (010) 504148; f. 1824; political and financial; independent; Editor MIMMO ANGELI; circ. 17,000.

**Il Secolo XIX:** Via Varese 2, 16122 Genoa; tel. (010) 53881; f. 1886; independent; Dir GAETANO RIZZUTO; circ. 181,617.

### Lecce

**Quotidiano di Lecce/Brindisi/Taranto:** Viale degli Studenti (Palazzo Casto), 73100 Lecce; tel. (0832) 300897; f. 1979; Man. Editor VITTORIO BRUNO STAMERRA; circ. 26,502.

### Leghorn/Livorno

**Il Tirreno:** Viale Alfieri 9, 57124 Livorno; tel. (0586) 401141; fax (0586) 416671; e-mail iltirreno@petrurianet.it; internet www.iltirreno.it; f. 1978; independent; Editor ENNIO SIMEONE; circ. 130,000.

### Mantua

**Gazzetta di Mantova:** Via Fratelli Bandiera 32, 46100 Mantua; tel. (0376) 303270; internet www.gazzettadimantova.it; f. 1664; independent; Man. Editor SERGIO BARALDI; circ. 42,684.

### Messina

**Gazzetta del Sud:** Uberto Bonino 15C, 98100 Messina; tel. (090) 2261; internet www.gazzettadelsud.it; f. 1952; independent; Dir NINO CALARCO; circ. 92,722.

### Milan

**Avvenire:** Piazza Carbonari 3, 20125 Milan; tel. (02) 67801; internet www.avvenire.it; f. 1968; Catholic; Man. Dir DINO BOFFO; circ. 138,000.

**Corriere della Sera:** Via Solferino 28, 20121 Milan; tel. (02) 6339; fax (02) 29009668; internet www.rcs.it/corriere; f. 1876; independent; contains weekly supplement, *Sette*; Dir PAOLO MIELI; circ. 720,239.

**La Gazzetta dello Sport:** Via Solferino 28, 20121 Milan; tel. (02) 6353; fax (02) 29009668; e-mail gasport@rcs.it; internet www.gazzetta.it; f. 1896; sport; Dir CANDIDO CANNAVÒ; circ. 426,000.

**Il Giornale:** Via Gaetano Negri 4, 20123 Milan; tel. (02) 85661; fax (02) 8566327; e-mail segretaria@ilgiornale.it; internet www.ilgiornale.com; f. 1974; independent, controlled by staff; Editor MARIO CERVI; circ. 210,000.

**Il Giorno:** Piazza Cavour 2, 20121 Milan; tel. (02) 77681; e-mail ilgiorno@ilgiorno.it; internet www.ilgiorno.it; Man. Dir ENZO CATANIA; circ. 255,377.

**Il Sole 24 Ore:** Via Paolo Lomazzo 52, 20154 Milan; tel. (02) 30221; fax (02) 312055; internet www.ilsole24ore.it; f. 1865; financial, political, economic; Dir ERNESTO AUCI; circ. 400,000.

### Modena

**Nuova Gazzetta di Modena:** Via del Taglio 22, 41100 Modena; tel. (059) 247311; internet www.nuovagazzettadimodena.it; Dir ANTONIO MASCOLO; circ. 14,710.

### Naples

**Il Giornale di Napoli:** Piazza M. Serao 19, 80132 Naples; tel. (081) 2458111; f. 1985; Editor ROBERTO TUMBARELLO; circ. 11,000.

**Il Mattino:** Via Chiatamone 65, 80121 Naples; tel. (081) 7947111; f. 1892, reformed 1950; independent; Dir PAOLO GRALDI; circ. 207,040.

### Padua

**Il Mattino di Padova:** Via Pelizzo 3, 35128 Padua; tel. (049) 8292611; f. 1978; Dir ALBERTO STATERA; circ. 37,252.

### Palermo

**Giornale di Sicilia:** Via Lincoln 21, 90133 Palermo; tel. (091) 6165355; internet www.gds.it; f. 1860; independent; Dir ANTONIO ARDIZZONE; circ. 89,880.

### Parma

**Gazzetta di Parma:** Via Emilio Casa 5A, 43100 Parma; tel. (0521) 2251; fax (0521) 285515; f. 1735; Pres. ACHILLE BORRINI; Dir BRUNO ROSSI; circ. 59,710.

### Pavia

**La Provincia Pavese:** Viale Canton Ticino 16–18, 27100 Pavia; tel. (0382) 434511; fax (0382) 473875; e-mail info@laprovincia.pv.it; internet www.laprovincia.pv.it; f. 1870; independent; Editor FRANCO MANZITTI; circ. 33,793.

### Perugia

**Corriere dell'Umbria:** Via Pievaiola km 5.8, 06132 Perugia; tel. (075) 52731; fax (075) 5273264; f. 1983; independent; Editor SEBASTIANO BOTTA; circ. 23,000.

### Pescara

**Il Centro:** Corso Vittorio Emanuele 372, 65122 Pescara; tel. (085) 20521; fax (085) 4214568; e-mail ilcentro@micso.it; internet www.ilcentro.it; f. 1986; independent; Editor PIER VITTORIO BUFFA; circ. 38,655.

### Piacenza

**Libertà:** Via Benedettine 68, 29100 Piacenza; tel. (0523) 393939; fax (0523) 26396; e-mail info@liberta.it; internet www.liberta.it; f. 1883; Dir ERNESTO LEONE; circ. 37,445.

### Reggio Emilia

**Gazzetta di Reggio:** Via Sessi 1, 42100 Reggio Emilia; tel. (0552) 501511; fax (0522) 454279; internet www.gazzettadireggio.it; f. 1860; Dir UMBERTO BONAFINI; circ. 19,563.

### Rome

**Corriere dello Sport:** Piazza Indipendenza 11B, 00185 Rome, tel. (06) 49921; fax (06) 4992690; f. 1924; 13 regional editions; Editor ITALO UCI; circ. 270,307.

**Il Fiorino:** Via Parigi 11, 00185 Rome; tel. (06) 47490; f. 1969; business; Editor LUIGI D'AMATO; circ. 4,500.

**Il Giornale d'Italia:** Via Parigi 11, 00185 Rome; tel. (06) 47490; Dir LUIGI D'AMATO; circ. 25,000.

**Il Manifesto:** Via Tomacelli 146, 00186 Rome; tel. (06) 6867029; fax (06) 6892600; e-mail redazione@ilmanifesto.mir.it; internet www.mir.it; f. 1971; splinter communist; Man. Editor VALENTINO PARLATO; circ. 55,000.

**Il Messaggero:** Via del Tritone 152, 00187 Rome; tel. (06) 47201; fax (06) 4720300; internet www.ilmessaggero.it; f. 1878; independent; Editor GIULIO ANSELMI; circ. 260,000.

**L'Opinione:** Via del Leone 13, 00186 Rome; tel. (06) 6861172; fax (06) 6832659; f. 1977; independent; Man. Editor ARTURO DIACONALE; circ. 5,000.

**Ore 12 Il Globo:** Via Alfana 39, 00191 Rome; tel. (06) 3331418; fax (06) 333199; financial; independent; Dir ENZO CARETTI; circ. 2,000.

**Il Popolo:** Piazza delle 5 Lune 113, 00186 Rome; tel. (06) 68251; fax (06) 6893724; f. 1944; organ of the PPI; Editor SERGIO MATTARELLA; circ. 6,000.

**La Repubblica:** Piazza dell'Indipendenza 11B, 00185 Rome; tel. (06) 49821; fax (06) 49822923; e-mail larepubblica@repubblica.it; internet www.repubblica.it; f. 1976; left-wing; Publr Editoriale L'Espresso; Editor-in-Chief EZIO MAURO; circ. 662,000.

**Il Secolo d'Italia:** Via della Scrofa 43, 00187 Rome; tel. (06) 6833987; fax (06) 6861598; f. 1951; organ of the AN; Editor GENNARO MALGIERI; circ. 15,000.

**Il Tempo:** Piazza Colonna 366, 00187 Rome; tel. (06) 675881; f. 1944; right-wing; Editor GIOVANNI MOTTOLA; circ. 100,000.

**L'Unità:** Via dei Due Macelli 23/13, 00187 Rome; tel. (06) 699961; fax (06) 69996217; e-mail unitaedi@unita.it; f. 1924; Dir MINO FUCCILLO; circ. 137,000.

**La Voce Repubblicana:** Piazza dei Capprettari 70, 00186 Rome; tel. (06) 68300802; fax (06) 6542990; f. 1921; organ of the PRI; Dir GIORGIO LA MALFA; circ. 18,000.

### Sassari

**La Nuova Sardegna:** Via Porcellana 9, 07100 Sassari; tel. (079) 222400; fax (079) 236246; internet www.lanuovasardegna.it; f. 1892; independent; Editor LIVIO LIUZZI; circ. 65,000.

### Taranto

**Corriere del Giorno di Puglia e Lucania:** Piazza Dante 5, Zona 'Bestat', 74100 Taranto; tel. (099) 3591; f. 1947; Dir CLEMENTE SELVAGGIO; circ. 3,500.

### Trent

**l'Adige:** Via Missioni Africane 17, 38100 Trent; tel. (0461) 886111; fax (0461) 886262; f. 1946; independent; Dir Dott. PAOLO GHEZZI: circ. 25,450.

### Treviso

**La Tribuna di Treviso:** Corso del Popolo 44, 31100 Treviso; tel. (0422) 410001; fax (0422) 579212; f. 1978; independent; Dir ALBERTO STATERA; circ. 25,641.

### Trieste

**Il Piccolo (Giornale di Trieste):** Via Guido Reni 1, 34122 Trieste; tel. (040) 3733111; fax (040) 3733312; e-mail piccolo@ilpiccolo.it; internet www.ilpiccolo.it; f. 1881; independent; Dir MARIO QUAIA; circ. 52,544.

**Primorski Dnevnik:** Via dei Montecchi 6, 34137 Trieste; tel. (040) 7796600; fax (040) 772418; e-mail redakcija@primorski.it; internet www.primorski.it; f. 1945; Slovene; Editor-in-Chief BOJAN BREZIGAR; circ. 10,000.

### Turin

**La Stampa:** Via Marenco 32, 10126 Turin; tel. (011) 65681; fax (011) 655306; e-mail lettere@lastampa.it; internet www.lastampa.it; f. 1868; independent; Dir PAOLO PALOSCHI; circ. 500,000.

**Tuttosport:** Corso Svizzera 185, 10147 Turin; tel. (011) 77731; f. 1945; sport; Dir FRANCO COLOMBO; circ. 102,000.

### Udine

**Messaggero Veneto:** Viale Palmanova 290, 33100 Udine; tel. (0432) 5271; e-mail messven@messaggeroveneto.it; internet www.messaggeroveneto.it; f. 1946; Editor SERGIO GERVASUTTI; circ. 60,309.

### Varese

**La Prealpina:** Viale Tamagno 13, 21100 Varese; tel. (0332) 275700; e-mail prealpina@betanet.it; internet www.laprealpinagiorn.it; f. 1888; Dir MINO DURAND; circ. 38,000.

### Venice

**Il Gazzettino:** Via Torino 110, 30175 Venezia-Mestre; tel. (041) 665111; fax (041) 665386; f. 1887; independent; Dir GIULIO GIUSTINIANI; circ. 139,000.

**La Nuova Venezia:** Via Verdi 30/32, Castello, 5620 Rialto, 30175 Venice; tel. (041) 2403011; Dir ALBERTO STATERA; circ. 13,000.

### Verona

**L'Arena:** Viale del Lavoro 11, 37036 S. Martino Buon Albergo, Verona; tel. (045) 8094000; fax (045) 994527; f. 1866; independent; Editor-in-Chief Dr MINO ALLIONE; Man. Dir Ing. ALESSANDRO ZELGER; circ. 67,746.

### Vicenza

**Il Giornale di Vicenza:** Viale S. Lazzaro 89, 36100 Vicenza; tel. (0444) 564533; f. 1946; Editor MINO ALLIONE; circ. 47,000.

## SELECTED PERIODICALS

### Fine Arts

**Casabella:** Via Trentacoste 7, 20134 Milan; tel. (02) 215631; fax (02) 21563260; e-mail casabella@mondadori.it; f. 1938; 10 a year; architecture and interior design; Editor FRANCESCO DAL CO; circ. 43,000.

**Domus:** Via A. Grandi 5/7, 20089 Rozzano, Milan; tel. (02) 824721; fax (02) 82472386; e-mail domus@edidomus.it; internet www .edidomus.it; f. 1928; 11 a year; architecture, interior design and art; Editor FRANÇOIS BURKHARDT; circ. 53,000.

**Il Fotografo:** Via Rivoltana 8, 20090 Segrate, Milan; tel. (02) 75421; monthly; photography; Dir GIORGIO COPPIN.

**Graphicus:** Via Morgari 36B, 10125 Turin; tel. (011) 6690577; fax (011) 6689200; e-mail graphicus@arpnet.it; internet www.arpnet.it/prograf; f. 1911; 10 a year; printing and graphic arts; Dir ANGELO DRAGONE; Editor LUCIANO LOVERA; circ. 7,200.

**L'Illustrazione Italiana:** Via Nino Bixio 30, 20129 Milan; tel. (02) 2043941; fax (02) 2046507; f. 1873; quarterly; fine arts; Editor MASSIMO CAPRARA.

**Interni:** Via Trentacoste 7, 20134 Milan; tel. (02) 215631; fax (02) 26410847; e-mail interni@mondadori.it; monthly; interior decoration and design; Editor GILDA BOLARDI; circ. 40,000.

**Lotus International:** Via Trentacoste 7, 20134 Milan; tel. (02) 21563240; fax (02) 26410847; e-mail lotus@mondadori.it; f. 1963; quarterly; architecture, town-planning; Editor PIERLUIGI NICOLIN.

**Rivista Italiana di Musicologia:** Leo S. Olschki, Viuzzo del Pozzetto, 50126 Florence; tel. (055) 6530684; fax (055) 6530214; f. 1966; twice a year; musicology; Editor ENRICO FUBINI.

**Il Saggiatore Musicale:** Leo S. Olschki, Viuzzo del Pozzetto, 50126 Florence; tel. (055) 6530684; fax (055) 6530214; f. 1994; twice a year; musicology: Editor GIUSEPPINA LA FACE BIANCONI.

**Storia dell'Arte:** Viale Carso 46, 00195 Rome; tel. (0361) 3729220; fax (0361) 3251055; f. 1969; quarterly; art history; Dirs MAURIZIO CALVESI, ORESTE FERRARI, ANGIOLA M. ROMANINI: circ. 1,200.

**Studi Musicali:** Leo S. Olschki, Viuzzo del Pozzetto, 50126 Florence; tel. (055) 6530684; fax (055) 6530214; f. 1972; twice a year; musicology; Editor BRUNO CAGLI.

### General, Literary and Political

**Archivio Storico Italiano:** Leo S. Olschki, Viuzzo del Pozzetto, 50126 Florence; tel. (055) 6530684; fax (055) 6530214; f. 1842; quarterly; history; Editor GIULIANO PINTO.

**Belfagor:** Leo S. Olschki, Viuzzo del Pozzetto, 50126 Florence; tel. (055) 6530684; fax (055) 6530214; f. 1946; every 2 months; historical and literary criticism; Editor CARLO FERDINANDO RUSSO; circ. 2,500.

**La Bibliofilia:** Leo S. Olschki, Viuzzo del Pozzetto, 50126 Florence; tel. (055) 6530684; fax (055) 6530214; f. 1899; every 4 months; bibliography, history of printing; Editor LUIGI BALSAMO.

**Epoca:** Arnoldo Mondadori Editore SpA, Via Marconi 27, 20090 Segrate, Milan; tel. (02) 7542; f. 1950; illustrated; topical weekly; Dir CARLO ROGNONI; circ. 211,000.

**L'Espresso:** Via Po 12, 00198 Rome; tel. (06) 84781; e-mail segred@espresso.it; internet www.espressoedit.it; weekly; independent left; political; illustrated; Editor CLAUDIO RINALDI; circ. 381,000.

**Famiglia Cristiana:** Via Giotto 36, 20145 Milan; tel. (02) 48071; fax (02) 48008247; e-mail famigliacristiana@stpauls.it; internet www.stpauls.it; f. 1931; weekly; Catholic; illustrated; Dir FRANCO PIERINI; circ. 1,053,240.

**Francofonia:** Leo S. Olschki, Viuzzo del Pozzetto, 50126 Florence; tel. (055) 6530684; fax (055) 6530214; f. 1981; twice a year; French language; Editor ADRIANO MARCHETTI.

**Gazzetta del Lunedì:** Via Archimede 169, 16142 Genoa; tel. (010) 53691; f. 1945; weekly; political; Dir MIMMO ANGELI; circ. 83,315.

**Gente:** Viale Sarca 235, 20126 Milan; tel. (02) 27751; f. 1957; weekly; illustrated political, cultural and current events; Editor Dott. RENDINI; circ. 789,906.

**Giornale della Libreria:** Viale Vittorio Veneto 24, 20124 Milan; tel. (02) 29006965; fax (02) 654624; e-mail bibliografica@alice.it; f. 1888; monthly; organ of the Associazione Italiana Editori; bibliographical; Editor FEDERICO MOTTA; circ. 5,000.

**Lettere Italiane:** Leo S. Olschki, POB 66, 50100 Florence; tel. (055) 6530684; fax (055) 6530214; f. 1949; quarterly; literary; Dirs VITTORE BRANCA, CARLO OSSOLA.

**Mondo Economico:** Via Paolo Lomazzo 51, 20154 Milan; tel. (02) 331211; fax (02) 316905; f. 1948; weekly; economics; business, finance; Editor ENRICO SASSOON; circ. 85,752.

**Il Mulino:** Strada Maggiore 37, 40125 Bologna; tel. (051) 222419; fax (051) 6486014; e-mail ilmulino@mulino.it; internet www.mulino.it; f. 1951; every 2 months; culture and politics; Editor ALESSANDRO CAVALLI.

**Oggi:** Gruppo Rizzoli, Corso Garibaldi 86, 20121 Milan; tel. (02) 665941; f. 1945; weekly; topical, literary; illustrated; Dir WILLY MOLCO; circ. 727,965.

**Panorama:** Arnoldo Mondadori Editore SpA, Via Marconi 27, 20090 Segrate, Milan; tel. (02) 7542; fax (02) 75422769; f. 1962; weekly; current affairs; Editor GIULIANO FERRARA; circ. 540,000.

**Il Pensiero Politico:** Leo S. Olschki, Viuzzo del Pozzetto, 50126 Florence, tel. (055) 6530684; fax (055) 6530214; f. 1968; every 4 months; political and social history; Editor SALVO MASTELLONE.

**Rassegna Storica Toscana:** Leo S. Olschki, Viuzzo del Pozzetto, 50126 Florence; tel. (055) 6530684; fax (055) 6530214; f. 1955; twice a year; Tuscan history; Editor LUIGI LOTTI.

**Rivista di Storia della Filosofia:** Via Albricci 9, 20122 Milan; tel. (02) 8052538; fax (02) 8053948; f. 1946; quarterly; philosophy.

**Scuola e Didattica:** Via L. Cadorna 11, 25186 Brescia; tel. (030) 29931; e-mail lascuola@tin.it; 19 a year; education; Editor GIUSEPPE VICO.

**Selezione dal Reader's Digest:** Via Alserio 10, 20173 Milan; tel. (02) 69871; fax (02) 66800070; e-mail readerd@hbox.vol.it; internet www.readersdigest.com; monthly; Editor-in-Chief CLAUDIO PINA (acting); circ. 521,432.

**Visto:** Via Rizzoli 4, 20132 Milan; tel. (02) 2588; fax (02) 25843683; f. 1989; illustrated weekly review; Editor-in-Chief MARCELLO MINERBI; circ. 342,850.

**Zett-Volksbole:** Weinbergweg 7, 39100 Bozen; tel. (0471) 200400; fax (0471) 200462; e-mail zett@athesia.it; f. 1989; German language; circ. 34,000.

### Religion

**Città di Vita:** Piazza Santa Croce 16, 50122 Florence; tel. and fax (055) 242783; e-mail cittadivita@dada.it; internet www.casa.dada.it/cittadivita; f. 1946; every 2 months; cultural review of religious research in theology, art and science; Dir P. M. GIUSEPPE ROSITO; circ. 2,000.

**La Civiltà Cattolica:** Via di Porta Pinciana 1, 00187 Rome; tel. (06) 6979201; fax (06) 69792022; f. 1850; fortnightly; Catholic; Editor GIAN PAOLO SALVINI.

**Humanitas:** Via G. Rosa 71, 25121 Brescia; tel. (030) 46451; fax (030) 2400605; f. 1946; every 2 months; religion, philosophy, science, politics, history, sociology, literature, etc.; Dir STEFANO MINELLI.

**Protestantesimo:** Via Pietro Cossa 42, 00193 Rome; tel. (06) 3210789; fax (06) 3201040; e-mail s.rostagno@agora.stm.it; f. 1946; quarterly; theology and current problems, book reviews; Prof. SERGIO ROSTAGNO.

**La Rivista del Clero Italiano:** Largo Gemelli 1, 20123 Milan; tel. (02) 72342335; fax (02) 72342260; f. 1920; monthly; Dir BRUNO MAGGIONI.

**Rivista di Storia della Chiesa in Italia:** c/o Herder Editrice e Libreria, Piazza Montecitorio 117, 00187 Rome; f. 1947; twice a year; Editor PIETRO ZERBI.

**Rivista di Storia e Letteratura Religiosa:** Leo S. Olschki, Viuzzo del Pozzetto, 50126 Florence; tel. (055) 6530684; fax (055) 6530214; f. 1965; every 4 months; religious history and literature; Dir FRANCO BOLGIANI.

### Science and Technology

**L'Automobile:** Viale Regina Margherita 290, 00198 Rome; tel. (06) 441121; fax (06) 44231160; e-mail lea.srl@iol.it; f. 1945; monthly; motor mechanics, tourism; Dir CARLO LUNA; circ. 1,083,210.

**Gazzetta Medica Italiana-Archivio per le Scienze Mediche:** Corso Bramante 83–85, 10126 Turin; tel. (011) 678282; fax (011) 674502; e-mail minmed@tin.it; internet www.medialog.it/minmed; six a year; medical science; Dir ALBERTO OLIARO; circ. 2,900.

**Il Medico d'Italia:** Rome; tel. (06) 36000710; fax (06) 6876739; weekly; medical science; Editor-in-Chief Dott. ANDREA SERMONTI.

**Minerva Medica:** Corso Bramante 83–85, 10126 Turin; tel. (011) 678282; fax (011) 674502; e-mail minmed@tin.it; internet www.minervamedica.it; 10 a year, medical science; Dir ALBERTO OLIARO; circ. 4,900.

**Monti e Boschi:** Via Emilia Levante 31/2, 40139 Bologna; tel. (051) 492211; internet www.agriline.it/edagri; f. 1949; 2 a month; ecology and forestry; Publr Edagricole; Editor UMBERTO BAGNARESI; circ. 16,700.

**Motor:** Piazza Antonio Mancini 4G, 00196 Rome; tel. (06) 3233195; fax (06) 3233309; f. 1942; monthly; motor mechanics; Dir S. FAVIA DEL CORE; circ. 12,500.

**Nuncius:** Leo S. Olschki, Viuzzo del Pozzetto, 50126 Florence; tel. (055) 6530684; fax (055) 6530214; f. 1976; twice a year; history of science; Dir P. GALLUZZI.

**Physis:** Leo S. Olschki, Viuzzo del Pozzetto, 50126 Florence; tel. (055) 6530684; fax (055) 6530214; f. 1959; twice a year; history of science; Editors V. CAPPELLETTI, G. CIMINO.

**Rivista Geografica Italiana:** Via Curtatone 1, 50123 Florence; tel. (055) 2710445; fax (055) 2710424; f. 1894; quarterly geographical review; Editor PAOLO DOCCIOLI.

### Women's Publications

**Amica:** Via Rizzoli 2, 20132 Milan; tel. (02) 2588; f. 1962; weekly; Editor G. MAZZETTI; circ. 196,244.

**Anna:** Via Civitavecchia 102, Milan; tel. (02) 25843213; f. 1932; weekly; Editor M. VENTURI; circ. 549,227.

**Confidenze:** Arnoldo Mondadori Editore SpA, Via Mondadori, 20090 Segrate, Milan; tel. (02) 75421; fax (02) 75422806; f. 1946; weekly; Dir GIORDANA MASOTTO; circ. 303,178.

**Gioia:** Viale Sarca 235, 20126 Milan; tel. (02) 66191; fax (02) 66192717; f. 1938; weekly; Dir VERA MONTANARI; circ. 432,326.

**Grazia:** Arnoldo Mondadori Editore SpA, Via Marconi 27, 20090 Segrate, Milan; tel. (02) 75422390; fax (02) 75422515; e-mail grazia@mondadori; f. 1938; weekly; Dir CARLA VANNI; circ. 377,804.

**Intimità della Famiglia:** Via Borgogna 5, 20122 Milan; tel. (02) 781051; weekly; published by Cino del Duca; Dir G. GALLUZZO; circ. 424,946.

**Vogue Italia:** Piazza Castello 27, 20121 Milan; tel. (02) 85611; fax (02) 870686; monthly; Editor FRANCA SOZZANI; circ. 73,773.

### Miscellaneous

**Annali della Scuola Normale Superiore di Pisa:** Scuola Normale Superiore, Pisa; tel. (050) 509111; fax (050) 563513; f. 1871; quarterly; mathematics, philosophy, philology, history, literature; Editor (Mathematics) Prof. EDOARDO VESENTINI; Editor (literature and philosophy) Prof. GIUSEPPE NENCI; circ. 1,300.

**Cooperazione Educativa:** La Nuova Italia, Via dei Piceni 16, 00185 Rome; tel. (06) 4457228; fax (06) 4460386; f. 1952; monthly; education; Dir MIRELLA GRIEG.

**Lares:** Leo S. Olschki, Viuzzo del Pozzeto, 50126 Florence; tel. (055) 6530684; fax (055) 6530214; f. 1912; quarterly; folklore; Editor GIOVANNI BATTISTA BRONZINI.

**Il Maestro:** Clivo Monte del Gallo 48, 00165 Rome; tel. (06) 634651; fax (06) 39375903; f. 1945; monthly; Catholic teachers' magazine; Dir MARIANGELA PRIORESCHI; circ. 40,000.

**Quattroruote:** Via A. Grandi 5/7, 20089 Rozzano, Milan; tel. (02) 824721; fax (02) 57500416; f. 1956; motoring; monthly; Editor MAURO COPPINI; circ. 662,000.

## NEWS AGENCIES

**Agenzia Giornalistica Italia (AGI):** Via Nomentana 92, 00161 Rome; tel. (06) 84361; fax (06) 8416072; Editor FRANCO ANGRISANI.

**Agenzia Nazionale Stampa Associata (ANSA):** Via della Dataria 94, 00187 Rome; tel. (06) 6774310; fax (06) 6782408; e-mail webmaster@ansa.it; internet www.ansa.it; f. 1945; 22 regional offices in Italy and 90 brs all over the world; service in Italian, Spanish, French, English; Pres. UMBERTO CUTTICA; Man. Dir and Gen. Man. ALFREDO ROMA; Chief Editor BRUNO CASELLI.

**Inter Press Service (IPS):** Via Panisperna 207, 00184 Rome; tel. (06) 485692; fax (06) 4817877; e-mail romadir@ips.org; internet

# Agriculture

**PRINCIPAL CROPS** ('000 metric tons)

| | 1996 | 1997 | 1998* |
|---|---|---|---|
| Sweet potatoes | 33 | 23 | 23 |
| Cassava | 20 | 14 | 14 |
| Yams | 253 | 213 | 213 |
| Other roots and tubers | 60 | 57 | 57 |
| Coconuts | 115* | 115* | 115 |
| Pumpkins, squash and gourds | 42 | 42* | 42 |
| Other vegetables and melons | 177 | 135 | 135 |
| Sugar cane | 2,624 | 2,413 | 2,413 |
| Oranges | 72* | 72* | 72 |
| Lemons and limes | 24* | 24* | 24 |
| Grapefruit and pomelo | 42* | 42* | 42 |
| Bananas | 130* | 130* | 130 |
| Plantains | 34 | 34* | 34 |
| Other fruit | 115 | 113 | 113 |
| Coffee (green) | 3 | 3 | 2 |
| Cocoa beans | 1 | 2 | 2 |
| Tobacco (leaves) | 2* | 2* | 2 |

* FAO estimate(s).

Source: FAO, *Production Yearbook*.

**LIVESTOCK** (FAO estimates, '000 head, year ending September)

| | 1996 | 1997 | 1998 |
|---|---|---|---|
| Horses | 4 | 4 | 4 |
| Mules | 10 | 10 | 10 |
| Asses | 23 | 23 | 23 |
| Cattle | 420 | 400 | 400 |
| Pigs | 180 | 180 | 180 |
| Sheep | 2 | 2 | 2 |
| Goats | 440 | 440 | 440 |

Poultry (FAO estimates, million): 9 in 1996; 10 in 1997; 10 in 1998.

Source: FAO, *Production Yearbook*.

**LIVESTOCK PRODUCTS** ('000 metric tons)

| | 1996 | 1997 | 1998 |
|---|---|---|---|
| Beef and veal | 16 | 16 | 15* |
| Goat meat* | 2 | 2 | 2 |
| Pig meat | 7 | 7 | 7* |
| Poultry meat | 55 | 59 | 59* |
| Cows' milk* | 53 | 53 | 53 |
| Poultry eggs* | 28 | 28 | 28 |

* FAO estimate(s).

Source: FAO, *Production Yearbook*.

# Forestry

**ROUNDWOOD REMOVALS** ('000 cubic metres, excl. bark)

| | 1995 | 1996 | 1997 |
|---|---|---|---|
| Sawlogs, veneer logs and logs for sleepers | 42 | 42 | 42 |
| Other industrial wood | 1 | 1 | 1 |
| Fuel wood | 312 | 312 | 312 |
| **Total** | 355 | 355 | 355 |

Source: FAO, *Yearbook of Forest Products*.

**SAWNWOOD PRODUCTION** ('000 cubic metres, incl. railway sleepers)

| | 1995 | 1996 | 1997 |
|---|---|---|---|
| **Total** | 12 | 12 | 12 |

Source: FAO, *Yearbook of Forest Products*.

# Fishing

('000 metric tons, live weight)

| | 1995 | 1996 | 1997 |
|---|---|---|---|
| **Total catch** | 10.5* | 12.8 | 8.4 |

* FAO estimate.

Source: FAO, *Yearbook of Fishery Statistics*.

# Mining

('000 metric tons)

| | 1996 | 1997 | 1998 |
|---|---|---|---|
| Bauxite* | 11,757 | 11,987 | 12,675 |
| Alumina | 3,365 | 3,394 | 3,440 |
| Crude Gypsum | 251 | 132 | 154 |

* Dried equivalent of crude ore.

# Industry

**SELECTED PRODUCTS**

| | 1996 | 1997 | 1998 |
|---|---|---|---|
| Edible oil ('000 litres) | 10,824 | 13,712 | 14,038 |
| Flour (metric tons) | 141,131 | 147,961 | 135,859 |
| Sugar (metric tons) | 236,027 | 232,798 | 182,761 |
| Molasses (metric tons) | 95,247 | 92,158 | 97,865 |
| Rum ('000 litres) | 20,435 | 22,362 | 22,171 |
| Beer and stout ('000 litres) | 68,973 | 67,434 | 66,933 |
| Animal feed (metric tons) | 174,213 | 186,955 | 191,765 |
| Fertilizers (metric tons) | n.a. | n.a. | 27,918 |
| Fuel oil ('000 litres) | 349,803 | 382,134 | 399,018 |
| Asphalt ('000 litres) | 4,524 | 15,722 | 3,708 |
| Gasoline (petrol) ('000 litres) | 109,709 | 143,061 | 146,224 |
| Kerosene, turbo and jet fuel ('000 litres) | 69,904 | 72,486 | 52,690 |
| Auto diesel oil ('000 litres) | 160,987 | 159,013 | 150,109 |
| Cement ('000 metric tons) | 559,304 | 588,118 | 588,001 |
| Electric energy (million kWh) | 6,038 | n.a. | n.a. |

# Finance

**CURRENCY AND EXCHANGE RATES**

**Monetary Units**

100 cents = 1 Jamaican dollar (J $).

**Sterling, US Dollar and Euro Equivalents** (30 September 1999)

£1 sterling = J $65.617;
US $1 = J $39.852;
€1 = J $42.503;
J $1,000 = £15.24 = US $25.09 = €23.53.

**Average Exchange Rate** (J $ per US $)

1996 37.120
1997 35.404
1998 36.550

**BUDGET** (J $ million, year ending 31 March)*

| Revenue† | 1995/96 | 1996/97 | 1997/98‡ |
|---|---|---|---|
| Tax revenue | 50,263 | 55,191 | 58,878 |
| Taxes on income and profits | 18,889 | 21,646 | 23,297 |
| Taxes on production and consumption | 15,469 | 17,139 | 18,415 |
| Taxes on international trade | 15,428 | 16,006 | 17,167 |
| Bauxite levy | 2,795 | 2,798 | 2,872 |
| Other current revenue | 3,585 | 3,310 | 3,097 |
| Capital revenue | 700 | 727 | 508 |
| **Total** | 57,343 | 62,026 | 65,355 |

| Expenditure | 1995/96 | 1996/97 | 1997/98‡ |
|---|---|---|---|
| Current expenditure | 44,442 | 64,225 | 72,113 |
| Wages and salaries | 15,806 | 24,043 | 28,842 |
| Other goods and services | 5,157 | 12,902 | 18,708 |
| Pensions | 1,222 | | |
| Other current transfers | 4,286 | | |
| Interest payments | 17,971 | 27,280 | 24,564 |
| Capital expenditure | 11,201 | 13,498 | 13,128 |
| Unallocated expenditure (net) | 925 | 329 | 2,275 |
| **Total** | 54,718 | 78,052 | 87,516 |

* Figures refer to budgetary transactions of the central Government, excluding the operations of the National Insurance Fund and other government units with individual budgets.

† Excluding grants received (J $ million): 1,181 in 1995/96; 1,060 in 1996/97; 725‡ in 1997/98.

‡ Preliminary.

Source: IMF, *Jamaica: Selected Issues* (January 1999).

**INTERNATIONAL RESERVES** (US $ million, at 31 December)

| | 1996 | 1997 | 1998 |
|---|---|---|---|
| IMF special drawing rights | 0.1 | 0.2 | 0.7 |
| Foreign exchange | 879.9 | 681.9 | 708.8 |
| **Total** | 880.0 | 682.1 | 709.5 |

Source: IMF, *International Financial Statistics*.

**MONEY SUPPLY** (J $ million at 31 December)

| | 1996 | 1997 | 1998 |
|---|---|---|---|
| Currency outside banks | 10,760 | 12,449 | 13,504 |
| Demand deposits at commercial banks | 22,788 | 22,022 | 23,160 |
| **Total money** | 33,548 | 34,470 | 36,664 |

Source: IMF, *International Financial Statistics*.

**COST OF LIVING** (Consumer Price Index; base: January 1988 = 100)

| | 1995 | 1996 | 1997* |
|---|---|---|---|
| Food (incl. beverages) | 841.5 | 1,045.7 | 1,127.9 |
| Fuel and household supplies | 643.3 | 941.5 | 12,029.2 |
| Clothing (incl. footwear) | 750.1 | 946.9 | 1,103.1 |
| Rent and household operation | 579.4 | 686.5 | 767.6 |
| **All items** (incl. others) | 762.1 | 963.4 | 1,056.5 |

* Preliminary.

Source: IMF, *Jamaica: Selected Issues* (January 1999).

**NATIONAL ACCOUNTS** (J $ million at current prices)

**Expenditure on the Gross Domestic Product**

| | 1996 | 1997 | 1998 |
|---|---|---|---|
| Government final consumption expenditure | 31,836 | 39,741 | 44,641 |
| Private final consumption expenditure | 143,289 | 154,946 | 167,030 |
| Increase in stocks | 372 | 605 | 425 |
| Gross fixed capital formation | 70,022 | 76,494 | 72,519 |
| **Total domestic expenditure** | 245,519 | 271,786 | 284,615 |
| Exports of goods and services | 106,090 | 103,466 | 107,162 |
| *Less* Imports of goods and services | 133,943 | 137,264 | 140,655 |
| **GDP in purchasers' values** | 217,667 | 237,987 | 251,122 |
| **GDP at constant 1986 prices** | 18,064 | 17,692 | 17,566 |

Source: IMF, *International Financial Statistics*.

**Gross Domestic Product by Economic Activity**

| | 1995 | 1996 | 1997* |
|---|---|---|---|
| Agriculture, forestry and fishing | 15,447 | 16,893 | 17,637 |
| Mining and quarrying | 11,712 | 11,915 | 12,281 |
| Manufacturing | 28,871 | 33,976 | 35,906 |
| Electricity and water | 4,102 | 4,599 | 4,402 |
| Construction | 21,187 | 23,598 | 24,833 |
| Wholesale and retail trade | 38,420 | 45,812 | 50,674 |
| Hotels, restaurants and clubs | 3,234 | 3,746 | 4,214 |
| Transport, storage and communication | 17,703 | 21,876 | 24,743 |
| Finance, insurance, real estate and business services | 22,795 | 28,383 | 28,375 |
| Producers of government services | 15,171 | 23,053 | 26,695 |
| Household and private non-profit services | 1,084 | 1,341 | 1,484 |
| Other community, social and personal services | 3,226 | 4,229 | 4,963 |
| **Sub-total** | 182,952 | 219,421 | 236,307 |
| Value-added tax | 14,397 | 16,965 | 18,334 |
| *Less* Imputed bank service charge | 12,820 | 16,311 | 15,649 |
| **GDP in purchasers' values** | 184,530 | 220,074 | 238,890 |

* Preliminary.

Source: IMF, *Jamaica: Selected Issues* (January 1999).

**BALANCE OF PAYMENTS** (US $ million)

| | 1996 | 1997 | 1998 |
|---|---|---|---|
| Exports of goods f.o.b. | 1,721.0 | 1,700.3 | 1,613.4 |
| Imports of goods f.o.b. | −2,715.2 | −2,832.6 | −2,710.1 |
| **Trade balance** | −994.2 | −1,132.3 | −1,096.7 |
| Exports of services | 1,624.5 | 1,714.6 | 1,769.9 |
| Imports of services | −1,140.8 | −1,225.8 | −1,260.0 |
| **Balance on goods and services** | −510.5 | −643.5 | −586.8 |
| Other income received | 141.8 | 147.3 | 156.3 |
| Other income paid | −366.5 | −440.9 | −459.8 |
| **Balance on goods, services and income** | −735.2 | −937.1 | −890.3 |
| Current transfers received | 709.3 | 705.7 | 732.1 |
| Current transfers paid | −85.7 | −80.9 | −97.1 |
| **Current balance** | −111.6 | −312.3 | −255.3 |
| Capital account (net) | 37.7 | 16.9 | 15.5 |
| Direct investment abroad | −93.3 | −56.6 | −82.0 |
| Direct investment from abroad | 183.7 | 203.3 | 369.1 |
| Portfolio investment (net) | — | 5.7 | 7.0 |
| Other investment assets | −13.8 | −92.4 | −38.6 |
| Other investment liabilities | 212.0 | 108.9 | 71.8 |
| Net errors and omissions | 56.7 | −43.9 | −43.6 |
| **Overall balance** | 271.4 | −170.4 | 43.9 |

Source: IMF, *International Financial Statistics*.

## External Trade

**PRINCIPAL COMMODITIES** (US $ million, year ending 31 March)

| Imports c.i.f. | 1995/96 | 1996/97 | 1997/98* |
|---|---|---|---|
| Consumer goods | 738 | 748 | 951 |
| Foods | 200 | 221 | 288 |
| Non-durable goods | 235 | 230 | 290 |
| Durable goods | 303 | 297 | 373 |
| Fuels | 406 | 467 | 356 |
| Raw materials | 1,281 | 1,150 | 1,175 |
| Capital goods | 502 | 577 | 621 |
| Construction materials | 148 | 131 | 174 |
| Transport equipment | 90 | 171 | 188 |
| Other machinery | 263 | 275 | 259 |
| **Total** | 2,926 | 2,942 | 3,104 |

| Exports f.o.b. | 1995/96 | 1996/97 | 1997/98* |
|---|---|---|---|
| Agricultural products | 86 | 89 | 85 |
| Bananas | 46 | 44 | 44 |
| Coffee | 27 | 33 | 31 |
| Minerals | 722 | 665 | 743 |
| Bauxite | 72 | 79 | 72 |
| Alumina | 651 | 586 | 671 |
| Manufactures | 380 | 389 | 334 |
| Sugar | 95 | 122 | 81 |
| Clothing | 264 | 241 | 224 |
| Other | 249 | 226 | 236 |
| **Total** | 1,438 | 1,369 | 1,397 |

* Estimates.

Source: IMF, *Jamaica: Selected Issues* (January 1999).

**PRINCIPAL TRADING PARTNERS** (US $ million)

| Imports c.i.f. | 1995 | 1996 | 1997 |
|---|---|---|---|
| Canada | 100 | 88 | 94 |
| Japan | 185 | 164 | 215 |
| Trinidad and Tobago | 218 | 243 | 253 |
| United Kingdom | 115 | 116 | 116 |
| USA | 1,429 | 1,514 | 1,482 |
| Venezuela | 57 | 66 | 67 |
| **Total** (incl. others) | 2,832 | 2,916 | 3,107 |

| Exports f.o.b. | 1995 | 1996 | 1997 |
|---|---|---|---|
| Canada | 154 | 164 | 195 |
| Japan | 27 | 32 | 31 |
| Norway | 109 | 91 | 84 |
| United Kingdom | 192 | 184 | 186 |
| USA | 522 | 511 | 462 |
| **Total** (incl. others) | 1,430 | 1,387 | 1,388 |

Source: IMF, *Jamaica: Selected Issues* (January 1999).

# Transport

**RAILWAYS** (traffic)

| | 1988 | 1989 | 1990 |
|---|---|---|---|
| Passenger-km ('000) | 36,146 | 37,995 | n.a. |
| Freight ton-km ('000) | 115,076 | 28,609 | 1,931 |

Source: Jamaica Railway Corporation.

**ROAD TRAFFIC** ('000 motor vehicles in use)

| | 1992 | 1993 | 1994 |
|---|---|---|---|
| Passenger cars | 73.0 | 81.1 | 86.8 |
| Commercial vehicles | 30.5 | 36.2 | 41.3 |

Source: UN, *Statistical Yearbook*.

**SHIPPING**

**Merchant Fleet** (registered at 31 December)

| | 1996 | 1997 | 1998 |
|---|---|---|---|
| Number of vessels | 11 | 12 | 9 |
| Total displacement ('000 grt) | 9.3 | 9.6 | 3.6 |

Source: Lloyd's Register of Shipping, *World Fleet Statistics*.

**International Sea-borne Freight Traffic** (estimates, '000 metric tons)

| | 1989 | 1990 | 1991 |
|---|---|---|---|
| Goods loaded | 7,711 | 8,354 | 8,802 |
| Goods unloaded | 5,167 | 5,380 | 5,285 |

Source: Port Authority of Jamaica.

**CIVIL AVIATION** (traffic on scheduled services)

| | 1993 | 1994 | 1995 |
|---|---|---|---|
| Kilometres flown (million) | 13 | 13 | 13 |
| Passengers carried ('000) | 1,038 | 1,011 | 1,126 |
| Passenger-km (million) | 1,488 | 1,430 | 1,592 |
| Total ton-km (million) | 155 | 150 | 166 |

Source: UN, *Statistical Yearbook*.

# Tourism

(year ending 31 March)

| | 1995/96 | 1996/97 | 1997/98* |
|---|---|---|---|
| Visitor arrivals ('000) | 1,667 | 1,751 | 1,779 |
| Stop-overs | 1,044 | 1,056 | 1,088 |
| Cruise-ship passengers and armed forces | 623 | 695 | 691 |
| Tourist expenditure (US $ million) | 1,086 | 1,103 | 1,140 |

* Preliminary figures.

Source: IMF, *Jamaica: Selected Issues* (January 1999).

Hotel rooms (1995): 29,376.

# Communications Media

| | 1994 | 1995 | 1996 |
|---|---|---|---|
| Radio receivers ('000 in use) | 1,060 | 1,080 | 1,200 |
| Television receivers ('000 in use) | 345 | 400 | 450 |
| Telephones (main lines in use, '000)* | 251 | 292 | n.a. |
| Mobile cellular telephones (subscribers)* | 26,106 | 45,178 | n.a. |
| Daily newspapers (number) | 3 | 3 | 3 |
| Circulation (estimates, '000) | 160 | 160 | 158 |

**Telefax stations** (number in use)*: 1,567 in 1992.

* Year beginning 1 April.

Sources: UNESCO, *Statistical Yearbook*, and UN, *Statistical Yearbook*.

# Education

(1992/93)

| | Institutions | Teachers | Students |
|---|---|---|---|
| Pre-primary | 1,668* | 4,158†‡ | 114,427‡ |
| Primary | n.a. | 9,512‡ | 293,863‡ |
| Secondary | — | 10,931§ | 235,071§ |
| Tertiary | — | 395* | 15,891* |
| University | 1§ | 418‖ | 8,434¶ |

* Figure for 1991/92.

† Figure for 1990/91.

‡ Public sector only.

§ Figure for 1992/93.

‖ Figure for 1995/96.

¶ Provisional or estimated figure.

Source: mainly UNESCO, *Statistical Yearbook*.

# Directory

## The Constitution

The Constitution came into force at the independence of Jamaica on 6 August 1962. Amendments to the Constitution are enacted by Parliament, but certain entrenched provisions require ratification by a two-thirds majority in both chambers of the legislature, and some (such as a change of the head of state) require the additional approval of a national referendum.

### HEAD OF STATE

The Head of State is the British monarch, who is locally represented by a Governor-General, appointed on the recommendation of the Jamaican Prime Minister.

### THE LEGISLATURE

The Senate or Upper House consists of 21 Senators of whom 13 will be appointed by the Governor-General on the advice of the Prime Minister and eight by the Governor-General on the advice of the Leader of the Opposition. (Legislation enacted in 1984 provided for eight independent Senators to be appointed, after consultations with the Prime Minister, in the eventuality of there being no Leader of the Opposition.)

The House of Representatives consists of 60 elected members called Members of Parliament.

A person is qualified for appointment to the Senate or for election to the House of Representatives if he or she is a citizen of Jamaica or other Commonwealth country, of the age of 21 or more and has been ordinarily resident in Jamaica for the immediately preceding 12 months.

### THE PRIVY COUNCIL

The Privy Council consists of six members appointed by the Governor-General after consultation with the Prime Minister, of whom at least two are persons who hold or who have held public office. The functions of the Council are to advise the Governor-General on the exercise of the Royal Prerogative of Mercy and on appeals on disciplinary matters from the three Service Commissions.

### THE EXECUTIVE

The Prime Minister is appointed from the House of Representatives by the Governor-General as the person who, in the Governor-General's judgement, is best able to command the support of the majority of the members of that House.

The Leader of the Opposition is appointed by the Governor-General as the member of the House of Representatives who, in the Governor-General's judgement, is best able to command the support of the majority of those members of the House who do not support the Government.

The Cabinet consists of the Prime Minister and not fewer than 11 other ministers, not more than four of whom may sit in the Senate. The members of the Cabinet are appointed by the Governor-General on the advice of the Prime Minister.

### THE JUDICATURE

The Judicature consists of a Supreme Court, a Court of Appeal and minor courts. Judicial matters, notably advice to the Governor-General on appointments, are considered by a Judicial Service Commission, the Chairman of which is the Chief Justice, members being the President of the Court of Appeal, the Chairman of the Public Service Commission and three others.

### CITIZENSHIP

All persons born in Jamaica after independence automatically acquire Jamaican citizenship and there is also provision for the acquisition of citizenship by persons born outside Jamaica of Jamaican parents. Persons born in Jamaica (or persons born outside Jamaica of Jamaican parents) before independence who immediately prior to independence were citizens of the United Kingdom and colonies also automatically become citizens of Jamaica.

Appropriate provision is made which permits persons who do not automatically become citizens of Jamaica to be registered as such.

### FUNDAMENTAL RIGHTS AND FREEDOMS

The Constitution includes provisions safeguarding the fundamental freedoms of the individual, irrespective of race, place of origin, political opinions, colour, creed or sex, subject only to respect for the rights and freedoms of others and for the public interest. The fundamental freedoms include the rights of life, liberty, security of the person and protection from arbitrary arrest or restriction of movement, the enjoyment of property and the protection of the law, freedom of conscience, of expression and of peaceful assembly and association, and respect for private and family life.

## The Government

**Head of State:** HM Queen ELIZABETH II (succeeded to the throne 6 February 1952).

**Governor-General:** Sir HOWARD FELIX HANLAN COOKE (appointed 1 August 1991).

### PRIVY COUNCIL OF JAMAICA

Dr VERNON LINDO, EWART FORREST, G. OWEN, W. H. SWABY, Dr DOUGLAS FLETCHER.

### CABINET
(February 2000)

**Prime Minister:** PERCIVAL J. PATTERSON.

**Deputy Prime Minister and Minister of Land and the Environment:** SEYMOUR MULLINGS.

**Minister of Finance and Planning:** Dr OMAR DAVIES.

**Minister of Labour and Social Security:** DONALD BUCHANAN.

**Minister of Tourism and Sport:** PORTIA SIMPSON-MILLER.

**Minister of Local Government, Youth and Community Development:** ARNOLD BERTRAM.

**Minister of National Security and Justice:** KEITH (K.D.) KNIGHT.

**Minister of Agriculture:** ROGER CLARKE.

**Minister of Foreign Affairs:** Dr PAUL ROBERTSON.

**Minister of Foreign Trade:** ANTHONY HYLTON.

**Minister of Mining and Energy:** ROBERT PICKERSGILL.

**Minister of Health:** JOHN JUNOR.

**Minister of Education and Culture:** BURCHELL WHITEMAN.

**Minister of Transportation and Works:** Dr PETER PHILLIPS.

**Minister of Water and Housing:** Dr KARL BLYTHE.

**Minister of Industry, Commerce and Technology:** PHILLIP PAULWELL.

**Minister of Information:** MAXINE HENRY-WILSON.

### MINISTRIES

**Office of the Governor-General:** King's House, Hope Rd, Kingston 10; tel. 927-6424.

**Office of the Prime Minister:** Jamaica House, 1 Devon Rd, POB 272, Kingston 6; tel. 927-9941; fax 929-0005; e-mail jamhouse@cwjamaica.com.

**Ministry of Agriculture:** Hope Gardens, Kingston 6; tel. 927-1731; fax 927-1904.

**Ministry of Commerce and Technology:** 36 Trafalgar Rd, Kingston 10; tel. 929-8990; fax 960-1623; e-mail crhone@mct.gov.jm; internet www.mct.gov.jm.

**Ministry of Education and Culture:** 2 National Heroes Circle, Kingston 4; tel. 922-1400; fax 967-1837; e-mail moec@educateja.edu.jm; internet www.educateja.edu.jm.

**Ministry of the Environment and Housing:** 2 Hagley Park Rd, Kingston 10; tel. 926-1590; fax 926-2591; e-mail mehsys@hotmail.com.

**Ministry of Finance and Planning:** 30 National Heroes Circle, Kingston 4; tel. 922-8600; fax 922-8804; internet www.mof.gov.jm.

**Ministry of Foreign Affairs and Foreign Trade:** 21 Dominica Drive, POB 624, Kingston 5; tel. 926-4220; fax 929-6733; e-mail mfaftjam@cwjamaica.com.

**Ministry of Health:** Oceana Hotel Complex, 2 King St, Kingston; tel. 967-1092; fax 926-9234; internet www.moh.gov.jm.

**Ministry of Industry and Investment:** PCJ Bldg, 36 Trafalgar Rd, Kingston 10; tel. 929-8990; fax 929-8196; e-mail gojmii@infochan.com; internet www.milgov.jm.

**Ministry of Labour and Social Security:** 1F North St, POB 10, Kingston; tel. 922-9500; fax 922-6902.

**Ministry of Local Government, Youth and Community Development:** 85 Hagley Park Rd, Kingston 10; tel. 754-0994; fax 960-0725.

**Ministry of Mining and Energy:** PCJ Bldg, 36 Trafalgar Rd, Kingston 10; tel. 926-9170; fax 968-2082; e-mail hmme@cwjamaica.com.

**Ministry of National Security and Justice:** 12 Ocean Blvd, Kingston Mall, Kingston 10; tel. 922-0080; fax 922-6950 (Justice), 922-6028 (National Security); e-mail inform@infochan.com; internet www.minsj.gov.jm.

**Ministry of Tourism and Sport:** 64 Knutsford Blvd, Kingston 5; tel. 920-4956; fax 920-4944; e-mail opmt@cwjamaica.com.

**Ministry of Transportation and Works:** IC Pawsey Place, Kingston; tel. 754-1900; fax 927-8763; internet www.mtw.gov.jm.

**Ministry of Water:** 7th Floor, Island Life Bldg, 6 St Lucia Ave, Kingston 5; tel. 754-0973; fax 754-0975; e-mail prumow@cwjamaica.com.

# Legislature

### PARLIAMENT

**Houses of Parliament:** Gordon House, Duke St, Kingston; tel. 922-0200.

#### Senate

**President:** SYRINGA MARSHALL-BURNETT.

The Senate has 20 other members.

#### House of Representatives

**Speaker:** VIOLET NEILSON.

**General Election, 18 December 1997**

| | Votes cast | Seats |
|---|---|---|
| People's National Party (PNP) | 441,739 | 50 |
| Jamaica Labour Party (JLP) | 312,471 | 10 |
| National Democratic Movement (NDM) | 38,430 | — |
| **Total** | 792,640 | 60 |

# Political Organizations

**Jamaica Labour Party (JLP):** 20 Belmont Rd, Kingston 5; tel. 929-1183; fax 968-0873; e-mail jlp@colis.com; internet www.thejlp.com; f. 1943; supports free enterprise in a mixed economy and close co-operation with the USA; Leader EDWARD SEAGA; Deputy Leader DWIGHT NELSON.

**National Democratic Movement (NDM):** NDM House, 3 Easton Ave, Kingston 5; e-mail mail@ndmjamaica.org; internet www.ndmjamaica.org; f. 1995; advocates a clear separation of powers between the central executive and elected representatives; supports private investment and a market economy; Pres. BRUCE GOLDING; Chair. STAFFORD HAUGHTON.

**People's National Party (PNP):** 89 Old Hope Rd, Kingston 5; tel. 978-1337; fax 927-4389; internet www.pnp.org.jm; f. 1938; socialist principles; affiliated with the National Workers' Union; Leader PERCIVAL J. PATTERSON; Gen. Sec. MAXINE HENRY-WILSON; First Vice-Pres. PETER PHILLIPS.

In 1999 a pressure group, **Citizens for a Civil Society (CCS)**, was formed by Daryl Vaz to lobby the Government on specific issues.

# Diplomatic Representation

### EMBASSIES AND HIGH COMMISSIONS IN JAMAICA

**Argentina:** Dyoll Bldg, 40 Knutsford Blvd, Kingston 5; tel. 926-5588; fax 926-0580; e-mail embargen@kasnet.com; Ambassador: ALFREDO ALCORTA.

**Brazil:** PCMB Bldg, 3rd Floor, 64 Knutsford Blvd, Kingston 5; tel. 929-8607; fax 929-1259; e-mail brasking@infochan.com; Ambassador: SÉRGIO ARRUDA.

**Canada:** 3 West Kings House Rd, POB 1500, Kingston 10; tel. 926-1500; e-mail kngtn@dfait-maeci.gc.ca; High Commissioner: JOHN ROBINSON.

**Chile:** 1 Holborn Rd, Kingston 10; tel. 968-0260; Ambassador: JAIME JANA.

**China, People's Republic:** 8 Seaview Ave, Kingston 10; tel. 927-0850; Ambassador: LI SHANGSHENG.

**Colombia:** Victoria Mutual Bldg, 3rd Floor, 53 Knutsford Blvd, Kingston 5; tel. 929-1702; fax 929-1701; Ambassador: RICARDO VARGAS TAYLOR.

**Costa Rica:** Belvedere House, Beverly Drive, Kingston 5; tel. 927-5988; fax 978-3946; e-mail cr_emb_jam@hotmail.com; Ambassador: RODRIGO CASTRO ECHEVERRIA.

**Cuba:** 9 Trafalgar Rd, Kingston 5; tel. 978-0931; fax 978-5372; Ambassador: DARÍO DE URRA.

**France:** 13 Hillcrest Ave, POB 93, Kingston 6; e-mail albert.salon@diplomatie.fr; Ambassador: ALBERT SALON.

**Germany:** 10 Waterloo Rd, POB 444, Kingston 10; tel. 926-6728; fax 929-8282; e-mail germanemb@cwjamaica.com; Ambassador: ADOLF EDERER.

**Haiti:** 2 Monroe Rd, Kingston 6; tel. 927-7595; Chargé d'affaires: ANDRÉ L. DORTONNE.

**India:** 4 Retreat Ave, POB 446, Kingston 6; tel. 927-0486; fax 978-2801; High Commissioner: V. B. SONI.

**Italy:** 10 Rovan Drive, Kingston 6; tel. 978-1273; fax 978-0675; Ambassador: RAMIRO RUGGIERO.

**Japan:** Mutual Life Centre, North Tower, 6th Floor, 2 Oxford Rd, Kingston 10; tel. 929-3338; fax 968-1373; Ambassador: TAKASHI MATSUMOTO.

**Mexico:** PCJ Bldg, 36 Trafalgar Rd, Kingston 10; tel. 926-4242; fax 929-7995; e-mail mexico.j@cwjamaica.com; Ambassador: JOSE LUIS VALLARTA MARRON.

**Netherlands:** Victoria Mutual Bldg, 53 Knutsford Blvd, Kingston 5; tel. 926-2026; fax 926-1248; e-mail rnekst@cwjamaica.com; Ambassador: E. W. P. KLIPP.

**Nigeria:** 5 Waterloo Rd, Kingston 10; tel. 926-6400; fax 968-7371; High Commissioner: EMMANUEL UGOCHUKWU.

**Panama:** Suite B-4, 1 Braemar Ave, Kingston 10; tel. and fax 978-1953; Chargé d'affaires: ERNESTO LOZANO LÓPEZ.

**Russia:** 22 Norbrook Drive, Kingston 8; tel. 924-1048; Ambassador: IGOR YAKOVLEV.

**Spain:** 25 Dominica Drive, 10th Floor, Kingston 5; tel. 929-6710; Ambassador: FERNANDO DE LA SERNA INCIARTE.

**Trinidad and Tobago:** Pan Jamaican Bldg, 3rd Floor, 60 Knutsford Blvd, Kingston 5; tel. 926-5730; fax 926-5801; e-mail t&thckgn@infochan.com; High Commissioner: PEARL WILSON.

**United Kingdom:** 28 Trafalgar Rd, POB 575, Kingston 10; tel. 926-9050; fax 929-7869; e-mail bhcjamaica@toj.com; High Commissioner: ANTONY SMITH.

**USA:** Mutual Life Centre, 2 Oxford Rd, Kingston 5; tel. 929-4850; Ambassador: STANLEY L. MCLELLAND.

**Venezuela:** Petroleum Corpn of Jamaica Bldg, 3rd Floor, 36 Trafalgar Rd, Kingston 10; tel. 926-5510; fax 926-7442; Chargé d'affaires a.i.: NÉSTOR CASTELLANOS.

# Judicial System

The Judicial System is based on English common law and practice. Final appeal is to the Judicial Committee of the Privy Council in the United Kingdom, although in 1994 the Jamaican Government announced plans to establish a Caribbean Court of Appeal to fulfil this function.

Justice is administered by the Privy Council, Court of Appeal, Supreme Court (which includes the Revenue Court and the Gun Court), Resident Magistrates' Court (which includes the Traffic Court), two Family Courts and the Courts of Petty Sessions.

**Judicial Service Commission:** Office of the Services Commissions, 63–67 Knutsford Blvd, Kingston 5; advises the Governor-General on judicial appointments, etc.; chaired by the Chief Justice.

**Attorney-General:** ARNOLD J. NICHOLSON.

### SUPREME COURT

POB 491, Kingston; tel. 922-8300; fax 967-0669; e-mail CJ@infochan.com; internet www.sc.gov.jm.

**Chief Justice:** LENSLEY H. WOLFE.

**Senior Puisne Judge:** LLOYD B. ELLIS.

**Master:** CAROL BESWICK.

**Registrar:** CHRISTINE MCDONALD.

### COURT OF APPEAL

POB 629, Kingston; tel. 922-8300.

**President:** R. CARL RATTRAY.

**Registrar:** G. P. LEVERS.

# Religion

### CHRISTIANITY

There are more than 100 Christian denominations active in Jamaica. According to the 1982 census, the largest religious bodies were the Church of God, Baptists, Anglicans and Seventh-day Adventists. Other denominations include the Methodist and Congregational Churches, the Ethiopian Orthodox Church, the Disciples of Christ, the Moravian Church, the Salvation Army and the Society of Friends (Quakers).

**Jamaica Council of Churches:** 14 South Ave, POB 30, Kingston 10; tel. 926-0974; f. 1941; 11 member churches and seven agencies; Pres. Rev. STANLEY CLARKE; Gen. Sec. CYNTHIA CLAIR.

### The Anglican Communion

Anglicans in Jamaica are adherents of the Church in the Province of the West Indies, comprising eight dioceses. The Archbishop of the Province is the Bishop of the North East Caribbean and Aruba. The Bishop of Jamaica, whose jurisdiction also includes Grand Cayman (in the Cayman Islands), is assisted by three suffragan Bishops (of Kingston, Mandeville and Montego Bay). The 1982 census recorded 154,548 Anglicans.

**Bishop of Jamaica:** Rt Rev. NEVILLE WORDSWORTH DE SOUZA, Church House, 2 Caledonia Ave, Kingston 5; tel. 926-6609; fax 968-0618.

### The Roman Catholic Church

Jamaica comprises the archdiocese of Kingston in Jamaica (also including the Cayman Islands), and the dioceses of Montego Bay and Mandeville. At 31 December 1997 the estimated total of adherents in Jamaica and the Cayman Islands was 96,645, representing about 7% of the total population. The Archbishop and Bishops participate in the Antilles Episcopal Conference (currently based in Port of Spain, Trinidad and Tobago).

**Archbishop of Kingston in Jamaica:** Most Rev. EDGERTON ROLAND CLARKE, Archbishop's Residence, 21 Hopefield Ave, POB 43, Kingston 6; tel. 927-9915; fax 927-4487; e-mail rcabkgn@cwjamaica.com.

### Other Christian Churches

**Assembly of God:** Evangel Temple, 3 Friendship Park Rd, Kingston 3; tel. 928-2728; Pastor WILSON.

**Baptist Union:** 6 Hope Rd, Kingston 10; tel. 926-1395; fax 968-7832; e-mail jbuaid@infochan.com; Pres. Rev. JEFFREY MCKENZIE; Gen. Sec. Rev. KARL HENLIN (acting).

**Church of God in Jamaica:** 35A Hope Rd, Kingston 10; tel. 927-8128; 400,379 adherents (1982 census).

**First Church of Christ, Scientist:** 17 National Heroes Circle, C.S.O., Kingston 4.

**Methodist Church (Jamaica District):** 143 Constant Spring Rd, POB 892, Kingston 8; tel. and fax 924-2560; f. 1789; 18,284 mems; Chair. Rev. BRUCE B. SWAPP; Synod Sec. Rev. GILBERT G. BOWEN.

**Moravian Church in Jamaica:** 3 Hector St, POB 8369, Kingston 5; tel. 928-1861; fax 928-8336; f. 1754; 30,000 mems; Pres. Rev. STANLEY G. CLARKE.

**Seventh-day Adventist Church:** 56 James St, Kingston; tel. 922-7440; f. 1901; 150,722 adherents (1982 census); Pastor Rev. E. H. THOMAS.

**United Church in Jamaica and the Cayman Islands:** 12 Carlton Cres., POB 359, Kingston 10; tel. 926-8734; fax 929-0826; f. 1965 by merger of the Congregational Union of Jamaica (f. 1877) and the Presbyterian Church of Jamaica and Grand Cayman to become United Church of Jamaica and Grand Cayman; merged with Disciples of Christ in Jamaica in 1992 when name changed as above; 20,000 mems; Gen. Sec. Rev. MAITLAND EVANS.

### RASTAFARIANISM

Rastafarianism is an important influence in Jamaican culture. The cult is derived from Christianity and a belief in the divinity of Ras (Prince) Tafari Makonnen (later Emperor Haile Selassie) of Ethiopia. It advocates racial equality and non-violence, but causes controversy in its use of 'ganja' (marijuana) as a sacrament. The 1982 census recorded 14,249 Rastafarians (0.7% of the total population). Although the religion is largely unorganized, there are some denominations.

**Royal Ethiopian Judah Coptic Church:** Kingston; not officially incorporated, on account of its alleged use of marijuana; Leader ABUNA S. WHYTE.

### BAHÁ'Í FAITH

**National Spiritual Assembly:** 208 Mountain View Ave, Kingston 6; tel. 927-7051; fax 978-2344; incorporated in 1970; 6,300 mems resident in 368 localities.

### ISLAM

At the 1982 census there were 2,238 Muslims.

### JUDAISM

The 1991 census recorded 250 Jews.

**United Congregation of Israelites:** 92 Duke St, Kingston; tel. 927-7948; fax 978-6240; f. 1655; c. 250 mems; Spiritual Leader and Sec. ERNEST H. DE SOUZA; Pres. WALLACE R. CAMPBELL.

## The Press

### DAILIES

**Daily Gleaner:** 7 North St, POB 40, Kingston; tel. 922-3400; fax 922-2058; e-mail ads@jamaica-gleaner.com; internet www.jamaica-gleaner.com; f. 1834; morning; independent; Chair. and Man. Dir OLIVER CLARKE; Editor-in-Chief WYVOLYN GAGER; circ. 44,000.

**Daily Star:** 7 North St, POB 40, Kingston; tel. 922-3400; evening; Editor LEIGHTON LEVY; circ. 49,500.

**Jamaica Herald:** 29 Molynes Rd, Kingston 10; tel. 968-7721; fax 968-7722; Man. Editor FRANKLIN MCKNIGHT.

**Jamaica Observer:** 2 Fagan Ave, Kingston 8; tel. 931-5188; fax 931-5190; internet www.jamaicaobserver.com; f. 1993; Chair. GORDON 'BUTCH' STEWART; CEO Dr GEORGE T. PHILLIP.

### PERIODICALS

**Caribbean Challenge:** 55 Church St, POB 186, Kingston; tel. 922-5636; f. 1957; monthly; Editor JOHN KEANE; circ. 18,000.

**Caribbean Shipping:** Creative Communications Inc, Kingston; tel. 968-7279; fax 926-2217; 2 a year.

**Catholic Opinion:** 21 Hopefield Ave, POB 43, Kingston 6; tel. 927-9915; fax 927-4487; e-mail rcabkgn@cwjamaica.com; 6 a year; religious; Editor Rev. MICHAEL LEWIS.

**Children's Own:** 7 North St, POB 40, Kingston; weekly during term time; circ. 120,188.

**Government Gazette:** POB 487, Kingston; f. 1868; Govt Printer RALPH BELL; circ. 1,350.

**Inquirer:** 7 11 West St, Kingston; tel. 922-3952; weekly; current affairs.

**Jamaica Churchman:** 2 Caledonia Ave, Kingston 5; tel. 926-6608; quarterly; Editor BARBARA GLOUDON; circ. 7,000.

**Jamaica Journal:** 4 Camp Rd, Kingston 4; tel. 929-4048; fax 926-8817; f. 1967; 3 a year; literary, historical and cultural review; publ. by Instit. of Jamaica Publs Ltd; Man. Dir PATRICIA ROBERTS; Editor LEETA HEARNE.

**Jamaica Weekly Gleaner:** 7 North St, POB 40, Kingston; tel. 922-3400; weekly; overseas; Chair. and Man. Dir OLIVER CLARKE; circ. 13,599.

**New Kingston Times:** Kingston; tel. 929-4595.

**The Siren:** 1 River Bay Rd, PO Box 614, Montego Bay, St James; tel. 952-0997; f. 1990; weekly.

**Sunday Gleaner:** 7 North St, POB 40, Kingston; tel. 922-3400; weekly; Editor-in-Chief WYVOLYN GAGER; circ. 100,000.

**Sunday Herald:** 86 Hagley Park Rd, Kingston 10; tel. 901-5022; fax 937-7313; f. 1997; weekly; Editor FRANKLYN MCKNIGHT; circ. 20,000.

**Swing:** 102 East St, Kingston; f. 1968; monthly; entertainment and culture; Editor ANDELL FORGIE; circ. 12,000.

**The Vacationer:** POB 614, Montego Bay; tel. 952-6006; f. 1987; monthly; Man. Editor EVELYN L. ROBINSON; circ. 8,000.

**The Visitor Vacation Guide:** 82 Barnett St, POB 1258, Montego Bay; tel. 952-5253; fax 952-6513; weekly; Editor LLOYD B. SMITH.

**Weekend Star:** 7 North St, POB 40, Kingston; tel. 922-3400; weekly; Editor LOLITA TRACEY-LONG; circ. 100,000.

**The Western Mirror:** 82 Barnett St, POB 1258, Montego Bay; tel. 952-5253; fax 952-6513; f. 1980; 2 a week; Man. Dir and Editor LLOYD B. SMITH; circ. 16,000.

**West Indian Medical Journal:** Faculty of Medical Sciences, University of the West Indies, Kingston 7; tel. 927-1846; fax 927-2556; f. 1951; quarterly; Editor-in-Chief W. N. GIBBS; circ. 2,000.

### PRESS ASSOCIATION

**Press Association of Jamaica (PAJ):** 5 East Ave, Kingston; tel. 926-7584; f. 1943; 240 mems; Pres. DESMOND ALLEN; Sec. MONICA DIAS.

### NEWS AGENCIES

**Jampress Ltd:** 3 Chelsea Ave, Kingston 10; tel. 926-8428; fax 929-6727; e-mail jamnews@infochan.com; f. 1984; govt news agency; Exec. Dir DESMOND ALLEN.

### Foreign Bureaux

**Inter Press Service (IPS)** (Italy): Suite 1G, 2-6 Melmac Ave, Kingston 5; tel. 960-0604; fax 929-6889; Regional Editor CORINNE BARNES.

Associated Press (USA) and CANA (Caribbean News Agency) are also represented.

## Publishers

**Caribbean Publishing Co Ltd:** Kingston; tel. 925-3228.

**Jamaica Publishing House Ltd:** 97 Church St, Kingston; tel. 922-1385; fax 922-3257; f. 1969; wholly-owned subsidiary of Jamaica Teachers' Asscn; educational, English language and literature, mathematics, history, geography, social sciences, music; Chair. WOODBURN MILLER; Man. ELAINE R. STENNETT.

**Kingston Publishers Ltd:** 7 Norman Road, Suite 10, LOJ Industrial Complex, Kingston CSO; tel. 928-8898; fax 928-5719; f. 1970; educational textbooks, general, travel, atlases, fiction, non-fiction, children's books; Chair. L. MICHAEL HENRY.

**Western Publishers Ltd:** 82 Barnett St, POB 1258, Montego Bay; tel. 952-5253; fax 952-6513; f. 1980; Man. Dir and Editor-in-Chief LLOYD B. SMITH.

### Government Publishing House

**Jamaica Printing Services:** 77 Duke St, Kingston; tel. 967-2250; Chair. EVADNE STERLING; Man. RALPH BELL.

# Broadcasting and Communications

## TELECOMMUNICATIONS

In September 1999 the Government announced a three-year transition period to a fully competitive telecommunications sector. The sector was to be regulated by the Office of Utilities Regulation (see Utilities).

**Cable & Wireless Jamaica Ltd:** 7 Cecilio Ave, Kingston 10; tel. 926-9450; fax 929-9530; f. 1989; in 1995 merged with Jamaica Telephone Co Ltd and Jamaica International Telecommunications Ltd, name changed as above 1995; 79% owned by Cable & Wireless; Pres. E. MILLER.

**Cellular One Caribbean:** Kingston; mobile cellular telephone operator; license granted Dec. 1999.

**Mossel Ltd:** Kingston; mobile cellular telephone operator; Irish owned; license granted Jan. 2000.

## BROADCASTING

### Television

**Television Jamaica Limited (TVJ):** 5–9 South Odeon Avenue, POB 100, Kingston 10; tel. 926-5620; fax 929-0129; e-mail tvj@radiojamaica.com; internet www.radiojamaica.com; f. 1959 as Jamaica Broadcasting Corporation; privatized 1997, name changed as above; island-wide VHF transmission, 24 hrs a day; Gen. Man. MARCIA FORBES.

### Radio

**Educational Broadcasting Service:** Multi-Media Centre, 37 Arnold Road, Kingston 4; tel. 922-9370; f. 1964; radio broadcasts during school term; Pres. OUIDA HYLTON-TOMLINSON.

**Independent Radio:** 6 Bradley Ave, Kingston 10; tel. 968-4880; fax 968-9165; commercial radio station; broadcasts 24 hrs a day on FM; Gen. Man. NEWTON JAMES.

**IRIE FM:** Coconut Grove, POB 282, Ocho Rios; tel. 974-5043; fax 974-5943; f. 1991; commercial radio station.

**Island Broadcasting Services Ltd:** 41B Half Way Tree Rd, Kingston 5; tel. 929-1344; fax 929-1345; commercial; broadcasts 24 hrs a day on FM; Exec. Chair. NEVILLE JAMES.

**KLAS-FM:** 81 Knutsford Blvd, Kingston 5; f. 1991; commercial radio station.

**Radio Jamaica Ltd (RJR):** Broadcasting House, 32 Lyndhurst Rd, POB 23, Kingston 5; tel. 926-1100; fax 929-7467; e-mail rjr@radiojamaica.com; internet www.radiojamaica.com; f. 1947; commercial, public service; three channels:

**RJR Supreme '94:** broadcasts on AM and FM, island-wide, 24 hrs a day; Exec. Prod. NORMA BROWN-BELL.

**FAME FM:** broadcasts on FM, island-wide, 24 hrs a day; Exec. Prod. FRANCOIS ST. JUSTE.

**Radio 2:** broadcasts on FM, island-wide, 24 hrs a day; Media Services Man. DONALD TOPPING.

# Finance

(cap. = capital; p.u. = paid up; res = reserves; dep. = deposits; m. = million; brs = branches; amounts in Jamaican dollars)

## BANKING

### Central Bank

**Bank of Jamaica:** Nethersole Place, POB 621, Kingston; tel. 922-0752; fax 922-0854; e-mail info@boj.org.jm; internet www.boj.org.jm; f. 1960; cap. 4.0m., res 159.9m., dep. 51,793.3m. (Dec. 1998); Gov. DERICK LATIBEAUDIÈRE.

### Commercial Banks

**Bank of Nova Scotia Jamaica Ltd** (Canada): Scotiabank Centre Bldg, cnr Duke and Port Royal Sts, POB 709, Kingston; tel. 922-1000; fax 924-9294; f. 1967; cap. 1,463.6m., res 4,114.0m., dep. 47,628.4m. (Dec. 1998); Chair. BRUCE R. BIRMINGHAM; Man. Dir WILLIAM E. CLARKE; 36 brs.

**CIBC Jamaica Ltd** (Canada): CIBC Centre, 23–27 Knutsford Blvd, POB 762, Kingston 5; tel. 929-9310; fax 929-7751; 57% owned by Canadian Imperial Bank of Commerce; cap. 96.7m., res 516.2m., dep. 8,153.1m. (Oct. 1997); Man. Dir A. W. WEBB; 12 brs.

**Citibank, NA** (USA): 63–67 Knutsford Blvd, POB 286, Kingston 5; tel. 926-3270; fax 929-3745.

***Citizens Bank Ltd:** 17 Dominica Drive, Kingston 5; tel. 960-1350; fax 960-2332; f. 1967 as Jamaica Citizens Bank Ltd, name changed 1993; cap. 95.10m., res 379.9m., dep. 5,729.8m. (Dec. 1996); Chair. Dr OWEN JEFFERSON; Man. Dir MICHAEL WRIGHT; 14 brs.

***Eagle Commercial Bank Ltd:** 20–22 Trinidad Terrace, Kingston 5; tel. 968-7007; Man. Dir LLOYD O. WIGGAN.

***Island Victoria Bank Ltd:** 6 St Lucia Ave, Kingston 5; tel. 968-5800; Chair. FAYDEN MCMORRIS.

**National Commercial Bank Jamaica Ltd:** 'The Atrium', 32 Trafalgar Rd, POB 88, Kingston 10; tel. 929-9050; fax 929-8399; internet www.jncb.com; f. 1977; merged with Mutual Security Bank in 1996; cap. 433.0m., res 1,811.6m., dep. 67,471.9m. (Sept. 1998); Chair GLORIA D. KNIGHT; Man. Dir REX JAMES; 33 brs.

**Trafalgar Commercial Bank Ltd:** 60 Knutsford Blvd, Kingston 5; tel. 968-5119.

***Workers' Savings and Loan Bank:** 12 Trafalgar Rd, Kingston 10; tel. 927-3540. 1973; cap. p.u. 83m., res 11m., dep. 3,700m. (1996); Gen. Man. HOWARD MCINTOSH; CEO and Chair. DELROY LINDSAY; 12 brs.

* Under the control of FINSAC Ltd (see below); merger pending as Union Bank of Jamaica Ltd.

### Development Banks

**Jamaica Mortgage Bank:** 33 Tobago Ave, POB 950, Kingston 5; tel. 929-6350; fax 968-5428; f. 1971 by the Jamaican Govt and the US Agency for Int. Devt; govt-owned statutory org. since 1973; intended to function primarily as a secondary market facility for home mortgages and to mobilize long-term funds for housing dvts in Jamaica; also insures home mortgage loans made by approved financial institutions, thus transferring risk of default on a loan to the Govt; Chair. PETER THOMAS; Man. Dir EVERTON HANSON.

**National Development Bank of Jamaica Ltd:** 11A–15 Oxford Rd, POB 8309, Kingston 5; tel. 929-6124; fax 929-6996; e-mail ndb@ndbjam.com; internet www.ndbjam.com; replaced Jamaica Development Bank, f. 1969; provides funds for medium- and long-term devt-orientated projects in the tourism, industrial, agro-industrial and mining sectors through financial intermediaries; Pres. NATAN RICHARDS; Chair. HUNTLEY MANHERTZ.

**Agricultural Credit Bank of Jamaica:** 11A–15 Oxford Rd, POB 466, Kingston 5; tel. 929-4010; fax 929-6055; f. 1981; provides loans to small farmers through co-operative banks; Man. Dir KINGSLEY THOMAS; Chair. ARTHUR BARRET.

**Trafalgar Development Bank:** The Towers, 3rd Floor, 25 Dominica Drive, Kingston 5; tel. 929-4760; e-mail tdbhrgen@cwjamaica.com.

### Other Banks

**National Export-Import Bank of Jamaica Ltd:** 48 Duke St, POB 3, Kingston; tel. 922-9690; fax 922-9184; e-mail eximjam@cwjamaica.com; replaced Jamaica Export Credit Insurance Corpn; Chair. Dr OWEN JEFFERSON.

**National Investment Bank of Jamaica Ltd:** 11 Oxford Rd, POB 889, Kingston 5; tel. 960-9691; fax 920-0379; e-mail nibj@infochan.com; Chair. DAVID COORE; Pres. Dr GAVIN CHEN.

### Banking Association

**Jamaica Bankers' Association:** POB 1079, Kingston; tel. 929-9050; fax 929-8399; Pres. PETER MOSES.

### Financial Sector Adjustment Company

**FINSAC Ltd:** 76 Knutsford Blvd, POB 54, Kingston 5; tel. 906-1809; fax 906-1822; e-mail info@FINSAC.com; internet finsac.com; f. 1997; state-owned; intervenes in the banking and insurance sectors to restore stability in the financial sector.

## STOCK EXCHANGE

**Jamaica Stock Exchange Ltd:** 40 Harbour St, Kingston; tel. 967-3271; fax 922-6966; f. 1968; 50 listed cos (1995); Chair. RITA HUMPHRIES-LEWIN; Gen. Man. C. WAIN ITON.

## INSURANCE

**Office of the Superintendent of Insurance:** 51 St Lucia Ave, POB 800, Kingston 5; tel. 926-1790; fax 968-4346; f. 1972; regulatory body; Superintendent YVONNE BLENMAN (acting).

**Jamaica Association of General Insurance Companies:** 58 Half Way Tree Rd, POB 459, Kingston 10; tel. 929-8404; Man. GLORIA M. GRANT; Chair. ERROL T. ZIADIE.

### Principal Companies

**British Caribbean Insurance Co Ltd:** 36 Duke St, POB 170, Kingston; tel. 922-1260; fax 922-4475; internet www.bcicdirect.com; f. 1962; general insurance; Gen. Man. LESLIE W. CHUNG.

**First Life Insurance Group:** 60 Knutsford Blvd, Kingston 5; tel. 926-3700; fax 929-8523; e-mail info@firstlife.com.jm; internet www.firstlife.com.jm; division of the Pan-Jamaican Investment Trust Group; all branches.

**Globe Insurance Co of the West Indies Ltd:** 17 Dominica Drive, POB 401, Kingston 5; tel. 926-3720; fax 929-2727; Gen. Man. R. E. D. THWAITES.

**Guardian Holdings:** Kingston; pension and life policies.

**Insurance Co of the West Indies Ltd (ICWI):** 2 St Lucia Ave, POB 306, Kingston 5; tel. 926-9182; fax 929-6641; Chair. DENNIS LALOR; CEO KENNETH BLAKELEY.

**Island Life Insurance Co:** Kingston; 64% owned by Barbados Mutual Life Assurance Co; 26% owned by FINSAC.

**Jamaica General Insurance Co Ltd:** 9 Duke St, POB 408, Kingston; tel. 922-6420; fax 922-2073; Man. Dir A. C. LEVY.

**Life of Jamaica Ltd:** 28–48 Barbados Ave, Kingston 5; tel. 929-8920; fax 929-4730; f. 1970; life and health insurance, pensions; Pres. R. D. WILLIAMS.

**NEM Insurance Co (Jamaica) Ltd:** NEM House, 9 King St, Kingston; tel. 922-1460; fax 922-4045; fmrly the National Employers' Mutual General Insurance Asscn; Gen. Man. NEVILLE HENRY.

## Trade and Industry

### GOVERNMENT AGENCIES

**Jamaica Commodity Trading Co Ltd:** 8 Ocean Blvd, POB 1021, Kingston; tel. 922-0971. 1981 as successor to State Trading Corpn; oversees all importing on behalf of state; Chair. DAVID GAYNAIR; Man. Dir ANDREE NEMBHARD.

**Jamaica Information Service (JIS):** 58A Half Way Tree Rd, POB 2222, Kingston 10; tel. 926-3741; fax 926-6715; e-mail jis@jis.gov.jm; internet www.jis.gov.jm; f. 1963; information agency for govt policies and programmes, ministries and public sector agencies; Exec. Dir GLORIA ROYALE-DAVIS.

### DEVELOPMENT ORGANIZATIONS

**Agricultural Development Corpn (ADC) Group of Companies:** Mais House, Hope Rd, POB 552, Kingston; tel. 977-4412; fax 977-4411; f. 1989; manages and develops breeds of cattle, provides warehousing, cold storage, offices and information for exporters and distributors of non-traditional crops and ensures the proper utilization of agricultural lands under its control; Chair. Dr ASTON WOOD; Gen. Man. DUDLEY IRVING.

**Coffee Industry Development Co:** Marcus Garvey Drive, Kingston 15; tel. 923-5645; fax 923-7587; e-mail cofeboard-jam@cwjamaica.com; f. 1981; to implement coffee devt and rehabilitation programmes financed by international aid agencies; Sec. JOYCE CHANG.

**Jamaica Promotions (JAMPRO) Ltd:** 35 Trafalgar Rd, Kingston 10; tel. 929-7190; fax 924-9650; e-mail jampro@investjamaica.com; f. 1988 by merger of Jamaica Industrial Development Corpn, Jamaica National Export Corpn and Jamaica National Investment Promotion Ltd; economic devt agency; Pres. PATRICIA FRANCIS; Chair. JOSEPH A. MATALON.

**National Development Agency Ltd:** Kingston; tel. 922-5445.

**Planning Institute of Jamaica:** 8 Ocean Blvd, Kingston Mall; tel. 967-3690; fax 967-3688; e-mail doccen@mail.colis.com; f. 1955 as the Central Planning Unit; adopted current name in 1984; monitoring performance of the economy and the social sector; publishing of devt plans and social surveys; Dir-Gen. WESLEY HUGHES.

**Urban Development Corpn:** The Office Centre, 8th Floor, 12 Ocean Blvd, Kingston; tel. 922-8310; fax 922-9326; f. 1968; responsibility for urban renewal and devt within designated areas; Chair. Dr VINCENT LAWRENCE; Gen. Man. IVAN ANDERSON.

### CHAMBERS OF COMMERCE

**Associated Chambers of Commerce of Jamaica:** 7–8 East Parade, POB 172, Kingston; tel. 922-0150; f. 1974; 12 associated Chambers of Commerce; Pres. RAY CAMPBELL.

**Jamaica Chamber of Commerce:** 7–8 East Parade, POB 172, Kingston; tel. 922-0150; fax 924-9056; f. 1779; 450 mems; Pres. HOWARD HAMILTON.

### INDUSTRIAL AND TRADE ASSOCIATIONS

**Cocoa Industry Board:** Marcus Garvey Drive, POB 68, Kingston 15; tel. 923-6411; fax 923-5837; f. 1957; has statutory powers to regulate and develop the industry; owns and operates four central fermentaries; Chair. JOSEPH SUAH; Man. and Sec. NEVILLE CONDAPPA.

**Coconut Industry Board:** 18 Waterloo Rd, Half Way Tree, Kingston 10; tel. 926-1770; fax 968-1360; f. 1945; 9 mems; Chair. R. A. JONES; Gen. Man. JAMES S. JOYLES.

**Coffee Industry Board:** Marcus Garvey Drive, POB 508, Kingston 15; tel. 923-5850; fax 923-7587; e-mail coffeeboard@jamaicancoffee.gov.jm; internet www.jamaicancoffee.gov.jm; f. 1950; 9 mems; has wide statutory powers to regulate and develop the industry; Chair. RICHARD DOWNER; CEO GONZALO HERNANDEZ.

**Jamaica Bauxite Institute:** Hope Gardens, POB 355, Kingston 6; tel. 927-2073; fax 927-1159; f. 1975; adviser to the Govt in the negotiation of agreements, consultancy services to clients in the bauxite/alumina and related industries, laboratory services for mineral and soil-related services, Pilot Plant services for materials and equipment testing, research and development; Gen. Man. PARRIS A. LYEW-AYEE.

**Jamaica Export Trading Co Ltd:** 6 Waterloo Rd, POB 645, Kingston 10; tel. 929-4390; fax 926-1608; e-mail jetcoja@infochan.com; f. 1977; export trading in non-traditional products, incl. spices, fresh produce, furniture, garments, processed foods, etc.; Chair. JOSEPH A. MATALON; Man. Dir HERNAL HAMILTON.

**Sugar Industry Authority:** 5 Trevennion Park Rd, POB 127, Kingston 10; tel. 926-5930; fax 929-6149; e-mail sia@netcomm-jm.com; f. 1970; statutory body under portfolio of Ministry of Agriculture; responsible for regulation and control of sugar industry and sugar marketing; conducts research through Sugar Industry Research Institute; Exec. Chair. ANDRÉE NEMBHARD.

**Trade Board:** 107 Constant Spring Rd, Kingston 10; tel. 969-0478; Admin. JEAN MORGAN.

### EMPLOYERS' ORGANIZATIONS

**All-Island Banana Growers' Association Ltd:** Banana Industry Bldg, 10 South Ave, Kingston 4; tel. 922-5492; fax 922-5497; f. 1946; 1,500 mems (1997); Chair. BOBBY POTTINGER; Sec. I. CHANG.

**All-Island Jamaica Cane Farmers' Association:** 4 North Ave, Kingston 4; tel. 922-3010; fax 922-2077; f. 1941; registered cane farmers; 27,000 mems; Chair. KENNETH A. HAUGHTON; Man. DAVID BELINFANTI.

**Banana Export Co (BECO):** 1A Braemar Ave, Kingston 10; tel. 927-3402; fax 978-6096; f. 1985 to replace Banana Co of Jamaica; oversees the devt of the banana industry; Chair. Dr MARSHALL HALL.

**Citrus Growers' Association Ltd:** Kingston; tel. 922-8230; fax 922-2774; f. 1944; 13,000 mems; Chair. IVAN H. TOMLINSON.

**Jamaica Exporters' Association (JEA):** 13 Dominica Drive, POB 9, Kingston 5; tel. 960-1675; fax 960-1465; e-mail sbed@cwjamaica.com; internet www.exportjamaica.org; Pres. KARL JAMES; Exec. Dir PAULINE GRAY.

**Jamaica Livestock Association:** Newport East, POB 36, Kingston; f. 1941; tel. 922-7130; fax 923-5046; 7,316 mems; Chair. Dr JOHN MASTERTON; Man. Dir and CEO HENRY J. RAINFORD.

**Jamaica Manufacturers' Association Ltd:** 85A Duke St, Kingston; tel. 922-8869; fax 922-0051; e-mail jma@toj.com; f. 1947; 400 mems; Pres. SAMEER YOUNIS.

**Jamaica Producers' Group Ltd:** 6A Oxford Rd, POB 237, Kingston 5; tel. 926-3503; fax 929-3636; e-mail cosecretary@jpjamaica.com; f. 1929; fmrly Jamaica Banana Producers' Asscn; Chair. C. H. JOHNSTON; Man. Dir Dr MARSHALL HALL.

**Jamaican Association of Sugar Technologists:** c/o Sugar Industry Research Institute, Mandeville; tel. 962-2241; fax 962-1288; f. 1936; 265 mems; Pres. MICHAEL HYLTON; Hon. Sec. H. M. THOMPSON.

**Private Sector Organization of Jamaica (PSOJ):** 39 Hope Rd, POB 236, Kingston 10; tel. 927-6238; fax 927-5137; federative body of private business individuals, cos and asscns; Pres. CLIFTON CAMERON; Exec. Dir CHARLES A. ROSS.

**Small Businesses' Association of Jamaica (SBAJ):** 2 Trafalgar Rd, Kingston 5; tel. 927-7071; fax 978-2738; Pres. ALBERT GRAY; Exec. Dir ESME L. BAILEY.

**Sugar Manufacturing Corpn of Jamaica Ltd:** 5 Trevennion Park Rd, Kingston 5; tel. 926-5930; fax 926-6149; established to represent the sugar manufacturers in Jamaica; deals with all aspects of the sugar industry and its by-products; provides liaison between the Govt, the Sugar Industry Authority and the All-Island Jamaica Cane Farmers' Asscn; 9 mems; Chair. CHRISTOPHER BOVELL; Gen. Man. DERYCK T. BROWN.

### UTILITIES

#### Regulatory Authority

**Office of Utilities Regulation (OUR):** PCJ Resource Centre, 36 Trafalgar Rd, Kingston 10; tel. 960-6474; fax 968-8703; e-mail office.our@cwjamaica.com; internet www.cwjamaica.com/~office.our; f. 1995; regulates provision of services in the following sectors: water, electricity, telecommunications, public passenger transportation, sewerage; Dir-Gen. WINSTON HAY.

#### Electricity

**Jamaica Public Service Co (JPSCo):** Dominion Life Bldg, 6 Knutsford Blvd, POB 54, Kingston 5; tel. 926-3190; fax 968-3337; responsible for the generation and supply of electricity to the island; plans for divestment suspended in late 1996; Chair. GORDON SHIRLEY; Man. Dir DERRICK DYER.

### Water

**National Water Commission:** 4A Marescaux Rd, Kingston 5; tel. 929-3540; internet www.nwcjamaica.com; statutory body; provides potable water and waste water services.

**Water Resources Authority:** Hope Gardens, POB 91, Kingston 7; tel. 927-0077; fax 977-0179; internet www.wra-ja.org; f. 1996; manages, protects and controls allocation and use of water supplies.

### TRADE UNIONS

**Bustamante Industrial Trade Union (BITU):** 98 Duke St, Kingston; tel. 922-2443; fax 967-0120; f. 1938; Pres. HUGH SHEARER; Gen. Sec. GEORGE FYFFE; 60,000 mems.

**National Workers' Union of Jamaica (NWU):** 130–132 East St, Kingston 16; tel. 922-1150; e-mail nwyou@toj.com; f. 1952; affiliated to the International Confederation of Free Trade Unions, etc.; Pres. CLIVE DOBSON; Gen. Sec. LLOYD GOODLEIGH; 10,000 mems.

**Trades Union Congress of Jamaica:** 25 Sutton St, POB 19, Kingston; tel. 922-5313; fax 922-5468; affiliated to the Caribbean Congress of Labour and the International Confederation of Free Trade Unions; Pres. E. SMITH; Gen. Sec. HOPETON CRAVEN; 20,000 mems.

### Principal Independent Unions

**Dockers' and Marine Workers' Union:** 48 East St, Kingston 16; tel. 922-6067; Pres. MILTON A. SCOTT.

**Industrial Trade Union Action Council:** 2 Wildman St, Kingston; Pres. RODERICK FRANCIS; Gen. Sec. KEITH COMRIE.

**Jamaica Federation of Musicians' and Artistes' Unions:** POB 1125, Montego Bay 1; tel. 952-3238; f. 1958; Pres. HEDLEY H. G. JONES; Sec. CARL AYTON; 2,000 mems.

**Jamaica Local Government Officers' Union:** c/o Public Service Commission, Knutsford Blvd, Kingston 5; Pres. E. LLOYD TAYLOR.

**Jamaica Teachers' Association:** 97 Church St, Kingston; tel. 922-1385; fax 922-3257; e-mail jta@toj.com; Pres. PATRICK SMITH.

**Master Printers' Association of Jamaica:** Kingston; f. 1943; 44 mems; Pres. HERMON SPOERRI; Sec. RALPH GORDON.

**National Union of Democratic Teachers (NUDT):** Kingston; tel. 922-3902; f. 1978; Pres. and Gen. Sec. HOPETON HENRY.

**Union of Schools, Agricultural and Allied Workers (USAAW):** 2 Wildman St, Kingston; tel. 967-2970; f. 1978; Pres. IAN HINES.

**United Portworkers' and Seamen's Union:** Kingston.

**University and Allied Workers' Union (UAWU):** Students' Union, University of West Indies, Mona; tel. 927-7968; affiliated to the WPJ; Gen. Sec. Dr TREVOR MUNROE.

There are also 35 associations registered as trade unions.

## Transport

### RAILWAYS

There are about 339 km (211 miles) of railway, all standard gauge, in Jamaica. Most of the system is operated by the Jamaica Railway Corpn, which is subsidized by the Government. The main lines are from Kingston to Montego Bay and Spanish Town to Ewarton and Port Antonio. Passenger services were suspended in 1992; operations were scheduled to resume in 2000. There are four railways for the transport of bauxite.

**Jamaica Railway Corpn (JRC):** 142 Barry St, POB 489, Kingston; tel. 922-6620; fax 922-4539; f. 1845 as Jamaica Railway Co, the earliest British colonial railway; transferred to JRC in 1960; govt-owned, but autonomous, statutory corpn until 1990, when it was partly leased to Alcan Jamaica Co Ltd as the first stage of a privatization scheme; 207 km of railway; Chair. W. TAYLOR; Gen. Man. OWEN CROOKS.

**Alcoa Railroads:** Alcoa Minerals of Jamaica Inc, May Pen PO; tel. 986-2561; fax 986-2026; 43 km of standard-gauge railway; transport of bauxite; Superintendent RICHARD HECTOR; Man. FITZ CARTY (Railroad Operations and Maintenance).

**Kaiser Jamaica Bauxite Co Railway:** Discovery Bay PO, St Ann; tel. 973-2221; 25 km of standard-gauge railway; transport of bauxite; Gen. Man. GENE MILLER.

### ROADS

Jamaica has a good network of tar-surfaced and metalled motoring roads. According to estimates by the International Road Federation, there were 19,000 km of roads in 1996, of which 70.7% were paved. A five-year programme to improve the condition of all arterial and secondary roads and 30% of minor roads was to begin in 1999. In September 1999 plans were announced for a 290 km-highway system linking major cities.

### SHIPPING

The principal ports are Kingston, Montego Bay and Port Antonio. The port at Kingston has four container berths, and is a major transhipment terminal for the Caribbean area. Jamaica has interests in the multi-national shipping line WISCO (West Indies Shipping Corpn—based in Trinidad and Tobago). Services are also provided by most major foreign lines serving the region.

**Port Authority of Jamaica:** 15–17 Duke St, Kingston; tel. 922-0290; fax 924-9437; e-mail pajmktg@infochan.com; f. 1966; Govt's principal maritime agency; responsible for monitoring and regulating the navigation of all vessels berthing at Jamaican ports, for regulating the tariffs on public wharves, and for the devt of industrial Free Zones in Jamaica; Pres. and Chair. NOEL HYLTON; Exec. Vice-Pres. KENNETH GARRICK.

**Kingston Free Zone Co Ltd:** 27 Shannon Drive, POB 1025, Kingston 15; tel. 923-5274; fax 923-6023; f. 1976; subsidiary of Port Authority of Jamaica; management and promotion of an export-orientated industrial free trade zone for cos from various countries; Gen. Man. OWEN HIGGINS.

**Montego Bay Export Free Zone:** c/o Port Authority of Jamaica, 15–17 Duke St, Kingston; tel. 922-0290.

**Shipping Association of Jamaica:** 4 Fourth Ave, Newport West, POB 1050, Kingston 15; tel. 923-3491; fax 923-3421; e-mail shipping.assoc@cwjamaica.com; f. 1939; 63 mems; an employers' trade union which regulates the supply and management of stevedoring labour in Kingston; represents members in negotiations with govt and trade bodies; Pres. GRANTLEY STEPHENSON; Gen. Man. ALVIN C. HENRY.

### Principal Shipping Companies

**Jamaica Freight and Shipping Co Ltd (JFS):** 80–82 Second St, Port Bustamante, POB 167, Kingston 13; tel. 923-9371; fax 923-4091; e-mail cshaw@toj.com; cargo services to and from the USA, Caribbean, Central and South America, the United Kingdom, Japan and Canada; Exec. Chair. CHARLES JOHNSTON; Man. Dir GRANTLEY STEPHENSON.

**Petrojam Ltd:** 96 Marcus Garvey Drive, POB 241, Kingston; tel. 923-8727; fax 923-5698; Man. Dir STEPHEN WEDDERBURN (acting).

**Portcold Ltd:** 122 Third St, Newport West, Kingston 13; tel. 923-7425; fax 923-5713; Chair. and Man. Dir ISHMAEL E. ROBERTSON.

### CIVIL AVIATION

There are two international airports linking Jamaica with North America, Europe, and other Caribbean islands. The Norman Manley International Airport is situated 22.5 km (14 miles) outside Kingston. The Donald Sangster International Airport is 5 km (3 miles) from Montego Bay. In May 1999 a J $800m.-programme to expand and improve the latter was announced.

**Air Jamaica Ltd:** 72–76 Harbour St, Kingston; tel. 922-3460; fax 922-0107; internet www.airjamaica.com; f. 1968; privatized in 1994; services within the Caribbean and to Canada (in asscn with Air Canada), the USA and the United Kingdom; Chair. GORDON 'BUTCH' STEWART; CEO ANDREW GRAY.

**Air Jamaica Express:** Tinson Pen Aerodrome, Kingston 11; tel. 923-6664; fax 937-3807; previously known as Trans-Jamaican Airlines; internal services between Kingston, Montego Bay, Negril, Ocho Rios and Port Antonio; Chair. GORDON 'BUTCH' STEWART; Man. Dir PAULO MOREIRA.

**Airports Authority of Jamaica:** Victoria Mutual Bldg, 53 Knutsford Blvd, POB 567, Kingston 5; tel. 926-1622; fax 929-8171; Chair. CEZLEY SAMPSON; Pres. LUCIEN RATTRAY.

**Civil Aviation Department:** Kingston; tel. 926-9115.

## Tourism

Tourists, mainly from the USA, visit Jamaica for its beaches, mountains, historic buildings and cultural heritage. In 1997/98 there were an estimated 1,779,000 visitors (of whom 1,088,000 were 'stopover' visitors and 691,000 were cruise-ship passengers). Tourist receipts were estimated to be US $1,140m. in that year.

**Jamaica Tourist Board (JTB):** ICWI Bldg, 2 St Lucia Ave, Kingston 5; tel. 929-9200; fax 929-9375; internet www.jamaicatravel.com; f. 1955; a statutory body set up by the Govt to develop all aspects of the tourist industry through marketing, promotional and advertising efforts; Chair. ADRIAN ROBINSON; Dir of Tourism FAY PICKERSGILL.

**Jamaica Hotel and Tourist Association (JHTA):** 2 Ardenne Rd, Kingston 10; tel. 926-2796; fax 929-1054; e-mail jhta@colis.com; f. 1961; trade asscn for hoteliers and other cos involved in Jamaican tourism; Pres. JAMES SAMUELS; Exec. Dir CAMILLE NEEDHAM.

# JAPAN

## Introductory Survey

**Location, Climate, Language, Religion, Flag, Capital**

Japan lies in eastern Asia and comprises a curved chain of more than 3,000 islands. Four large islands, named (from north to south) Hokkaido, Honshu, Shikoku and Kyushu, account for about 98% of the land area. Hokkaido lies just to the south of Sakhalin, a large Russian island, and about 1,300 km (800 miles) east of Russia's mainland port of Vladivostok. Southern Japan is about 150 km (93 miles) east of the Republic of Korea. Although summers are temperate everywhere, the climate in winter varies sharply from cold in the north to mild in the south. Temperatures in Tokyo range from –6°C (21°F) to 30°C (86°F). Typhoons and heavy rains are common in summer. The language is Japanese. The major religions are Shintoism and Buddhism, and there is a Christian minority. The national flag (proportions 10 by 7) is white, with a red disc (a sun without rays) in the centre. The capital is Tokyo.

**Recent History**

Following Japan's defeat in the Second World War, Japanese forces surrendered in August 1945. Japan signed an armistice in September, and the country was placed under US military occupation. A new democratic constitution, which took effect from May 1947, renounced war and abandoned the doctrine of the Emperor's divinity. Following the peace treaty of September 1951, Japan regained its independence on 28 April 1952, although it was not until 1972 that the last of the US-administered outer islands were returned to Japanese sovereignty.

In November 1955 rival conservative groups merged to form the Liberal-Democratic Party (LDP). Nobusuke Kishi, who became Prime Minister in February 1957, was succeeded by Hayato Ikeda in July 1960. Ikeda was replaced by Eisaku Sato in November 1964. Sato remained in office until July 1972, when he was succeeded by Kakuei Tanaka.

Tanaka's premiership was beset by problems, leading to his replacement by Takeo Miki in December 1974. Tanaka was subsequently accused of accepting bribes from the Marubeni Corporation, and he was arrested in July 1976. The LDP lost its overall majority in the House of Representatives (the lower house of the Diet) at a general election held in December. Miki resigned and was succeeded by Takeo Fukuda. However, Mayayoshi Ohira defeated Fukuda in the LDP presidential election of November 1978, and replaced him as Prime Minister in December. Ohira was unable to win a majority in the lower house at elections in October 1979. In May 1980 the Government was defeated in a motion of 'no confidence', proposed by the Japan Socialist Party (JSP), forcing Ohira to dissolve the lower house. Ohira died before the elections in June, when the LDP won 284 of the 511 seats, although obtaining only a minority of the votes cast. In July Zenko Suzuki, a relatively little-known compromise candidate, was elected President of the LDP, and subsequently appointed Prime Minister. In November 1981 Suzuki reorganized the Cabinet, distributing major posts among the five feuding LDP factions. The growing factionalism of the LDP and the worsening economic crisis prompted Suzuki's resignation as Prime Minister and LDP President in October 1982. He was succeeded by Yasuhiro Nakasone.

At elections in June 1983 for one-half of the seats in the House of Councillors (the upper house of the Diet), a new electoral system was used. Of the 126 contested seats, 50 were filled on the basis of proportional representation. As a result, two small parties entered the House of Councillors for the first time. The LDP increased its strength from 134 to 137 members in the 252-seat chamber. This result was seen as an endorsement of Nakasone's policies of increased expenditure on defence, closer ties with the USA and greater Japanese involvement in international affairs.

In October 1983 former Prime Minister Tanaka was found guilty of accepting bribes. However, Tanaka refused to resign from his legislative seat (he had already resigned from the LDP), and, as a result of this and his continuing influence within the LDP, the opposition parties led a boycott of the Diet, forcing Nakasone to call a premature general election in December 1983. The Komeito (Clean Government Party), the Democratic Socialist Party (DSP) and the JSP gained seats, at the expense of the Communists and the New Liberal Club (NLC). The LDP, which had performed badly in the election, formed a coalition with the NLC (which had split from the LDP over the Tanaka affair in 1976) and several independents. Nakasone remained President of the LDP, after promising to reduce Tanaka's influence. Following the trial of Tanaka, reforms were introduced, whereby cabinet members were required to disclose the extent of their personal assets. In November 1984 Nakasone was re-elected as President of the LDP, and became the first Prime Minister to serve a second term since Sato.

Nakasone called another premature general election for July 1986, which coincided with elections for one-half of the seats in the House of Councillors. In the election to the House of Representatives, the LDP obtained 49.4% of the votes, its highest level of electoral support since 1963, and won a record 304 of the 512 seats. The increased LDP majority was achieved largely at the expense of the JSP and the DSP. The LDP, therefore, was able to dispense with its coalition partner, the NLC (which disbanded in August and rejoined the LDP). The new Cabinet was composed entirely of LDP members. In September the leaders of the LDP agreed to alter by-laws to allow party presidents one-year extensions beyond the normal limit of two terms of two years each. Nakasone was thus able to retain the posts of President of the LDP and Prime Minister until 30 October 1987.

In July 1987 the Secretary-General of the LDP, Noboru Takeshita, left the Tanaka faction, with 113 other members, and announced the formation of a major new grouping within the ruling party. In the same month Tanaka's political influence was further weakened when the Tokyo High Court upheld the decision, taken in 1983, which found him guilty of accepting bribes. (In February 1995 this ruling was upheld by the Supreme Court.)

In October 1987 Nakasone nominated Takeshita as his successor. On 6 November the Diet was convened and Takeshita was formally elected as Prime Minister. In the new Cabinet, Takeshita maintained a balance among the five major factions of the LDP, retaining only two members of Nakasone's previous Cabinet, but appointing four members of the Nakasone faction to senior ministerial posts (including Nakasone's staunch ally, Sosuke Uno, as Minister of Foreign Affairs).

The implementation of a programme of tax reforms was one of the most important issues confronting Takeshita's Government. In June 1988 the LDP's tax deliberation council proposed the introduction of a new indirect tax (a general consumption tax, or a form of value-added tax), which was to be levied at a rate of 3%. This proposal, however, encountered widespread opposition. In the same month, the Prime Minister and the LDP suffered a serious set-back when several leading figures in the party, including Nakasone, Shintaro Abe, Kiichi Miyazawa and Takeshita himself, were alleged to have been indirectly involved in share-trading irregularities with the Recruit Cosmos Company. In November, shortly after the LDP had agreed to establish a committee to investigate the Recruit scandal, the House of Representatives approved proposals for tax reform (which constituted the most wide-ranging revision of the tax system for 40 years). Three cabinet ministers and the Chairman of the DSP were subsequently forced to resign, owing to their alleged involvement in the Recruit affair.

In January 1989 Emperor Hirohito, who had reigned since 1926, died after a long illness, thus ending the Showa era. He was succeeded by his son, Akihito, and the new era was named Heisei ('achievement of universal peace').

In April 1989, as the allegations against politicians widened to include charges of bribery and malpractice, Takeshita announced his resignation. He was subsequently found to have accepted donations worth more than 150m. yen from the Recruit organization. Takeshita nominated Sosuke Uno as his successor. Uno was elected Prime Minister by the Diet on 2 June; a new Cabinet was appointed on the same day. Uno thus became the first Japanese Prime Minister since the foundation of the LDP not to command his own political faction. In May, following an eight-month investigation undertaken by the LDP's special committee, public prosecutors indicted 13 people. Nakasone resigned from his faction and from the LDP, assuming complete moral responsibility for the Recruit affair, since it had occurred during his administration, but did not resign his seat in the Diet.

Within a few days of Uno's assumption of office, a Japanese magazine published allegations of sexual impropriety involving the Prime Minister, which precipitated demands for his resignation. Serious losses suffered by the LDP in Tokyo's municipal elections in July 1989 further discredited Uno. As a result of a considerable increase in support for the JSP, led by Takako Doi (who emphasized her opposition to the unpopular consumption tax), the LDP lost its majority in the upper house for the first time in its history. The JSP received 35% of the total votes, while the LDP obtained only 27%. Uno offered to resign as soon as the LDP had decided on a suitable successor, and in August the LDP chose the relatively unknown Toshiki Kaifu, a former Minister of Education, to replace Uno as the party's President and as the new Prime Minister. Although the House of Councillors' ballot rejected Kaifu as the new Prime Minister in favour of Takako Doi, the decision of the lower house was adopted, in accordance with stipulations embodied in the Constitution. This was the first time in 41 years that the two houses of the Diet had disagreed over the choice of Prime Minister. Kaifu's popularity increased as a result of a successful visit to North America and Mexico, and his attempts to address the issue of the consumption tax, and in October he was re-elected as President of the LDP for a further two-year term.

At a general election, held on 18 February 1990, the LDP was returned to power with an unexpectedly large measure of support, receiving 46.1% of the votes cast and securing 275 of the 512 seats in the lower house. Despite substantial gains by the JSP (which won 136 seats), the LDP's strength was considered sufficient for it to elect its nominees to preside over all 18 standing committees of the lower house and thus ensure the smooth passage of future legislation.

In May 1990 Kaifu announced his commitment to the implementation of electoral reforms that had been proposed in April by the Election System Council, an advisory body to the Prime Minister. Although the proposals were presented as an attempt to counter electoral corruption and to end factionalism within the LDP itself, opposition supporters expressed fears that the changes would invest more power in party committees responsible for nominating candidates and therefore increase the possibility of bribery.

In October 1990 Hisashi Shinto, the former chairman of the Nippon Telegraph and Telephone Corporation, became the first person to be convicted in the Recruit scandal trial; his sentence was subsequently suspended owing to his age. In December Toshiyuki Inamura, a former cabinet minister, resigned from the LDP after charges of large-scale tax evasion and complicity in a new stock-manipulation scandal were brought against him. A prison sentence with hard labour, which he received in November 1991, was regarded as a deterrent to other politicians from engaging in financial corruption.

In January 1991 the JSP changed its English name to the Social Democratic Party of Japan (SDPJ) and in July Makato Tanabe replaced Takako Doi as Chairman of the party. In September senior LDP officials forced Kaifu to abandon proposals for electoral reform and the Takeshita faction of the LDP subsequently withdrew its support for the Prime Minister. Sponsored by the Takeshita faction, the former Minister of Finance, Kiichi Miyazawa, was elected President of the LDP in October, and in November the Diet endorsed his appointment as Prime Minister. New allegations of involvement in the Recruit affair, publicized by the SDPJ in December 1991, seriously undermined Miyazawa's position. Only by abandoning draft legislation to authorize the participation of Japanese forces in United Nations (UN) peace-keeping operations could Miyazawa apparently quell SDPJ demands that he should testify under oath in the Diet.

In early 1992 public disgust at official corruption was registered at two prefectural by-elections to the upper house, when the LDP lost seats, which had previously been considered secure, to Rengo-no-kai (the political arm of RENGO, the trade union confederation). However, the anti-Government alliance, which had supported Rengo-no-kai, disintegrated in May over the issue of Japanese involvement in UN peace-keeping operations. The SDPJ attempted to obstruct the vote in the lower house on the approved modified bill by submitting their resignations *en masse*. The Speaker, however, ruled that they could not be accepted during the current Diet session. The successful passage through the Diet of the legislation on international peace-keeping improved the Government's standing, and in elections to the upper house in July the LDP performed much better than expected, gaining 69 of the 127 seats contested. The SDPJ, by contrast, lost 25 of its 46 seats in the upper house; the Komeito increased its total strength from 20 to 24 seats, but Rengo-no-kai failed to win any seats, owing to the dissolution of the informal coalition it had facilitated between the SDPJ and the DSP. The Japan New Party (JNP), founded only two months prior to the election by LDP dissidents, gained four seats in the upper house.

In December 1992 Miyazawa instituted a cabinet reorganization, retaining only the Ministers of Foreign Affairs and Agriculture. The reshuffle coincided with an announcement that a formal split in the Takeshita faction was to take place. Miyazawa sought to counter public criticism of factional domination within the ruling party by allocating fewer (and less important) portfolios to the two halves of the dividing leading faction, although the appointments still reflected the power of each of the factions. The new faction was to be led nominally by Tsutomu Hata, the Minister of Finance, although it was widely recognized that Ichiro Ozawa held the real power in the grouping.

Electoral reform was again a major political issue in the first half of 1993. While the LDP favoured a single-member constituency system, the opposition parties proposed various forms of proportional representation. Since the LDP did not have a majority in the upper house, it was unable to enforce any reforms without the agreement of the opposition parties. Within the LDP itself there was conflict between those, led by Ozawa and Hata, who wished the LDP to reach a compromise with opposition parties, and senior LDP members who opposed any form of co-operation. In June the lower house adopted a motion of 'no confidence' against the Government, after the LDP refused to modify its reform proposals to meet opposition demands. Thirty-nine LDP members voted against the Government, while 16 others abstained. The Ozawa-Hata group, comprising 44 former LDP members, immediately established a new party, the Shinseito (Japan Renewal Party, JRP), in order to contest the forthcoming general election. Another new party, the New Party Sakigake, was also formed by LDP Diet members. In the election to the House of Representatives, held on 18 July, only 67.2% of the electorate participated. The LDP won 223 of the 511 seats, and was thus 33 seats short of a majority. Miyazawa resigned as Prime Minister and a coalition Government, composed of members of seven opposition parties, including a number of independents, was formed. On 6 August Morihiro Hosokawa, the leader of the JNP, was elected Prime Minister, defeating the new President of the LDP, Yohei Kono.

In late 1993 it was reported that local government officials and Diet members had received payments from construction companies in return for awarding building contracts. Three senior politicians were implicated—Noboru Takeshita, Ichiro Ozawa and Kishiro Nakamura, a former Minister of Construction. Ozawa claimed that the payments were legal, since none had exceeded 1.5m. yen. In January 1994 the Public Prosecutor's office began investigations into bribery allegations against Nakamura and Hideo Watanabe, the former Minister of Posts and Telecommunications.

In November 1993 the Government presented four items of electoral reform legislation to the House of Representatives. The bills, which were passed by a majority of 270 to 226 votes (they were opposed by the LDP), altered the multi-seat constituency system to one of a combination of single-seat constituencies and seats allocated through proportional representation. All political donations exceeding 50,000 yen were to be disclosed, and any politician found guilty of corruption would be prohibited from holding further office. In January 1994 the reform bills were defeated in the upper house. A few days later, however, Hosokawa, who had threatened to resign if the legislation were not passed, reached agreement with the LDP on modifications to the reform bills (see below).

Hosokawa resigned as Prime Minister in April 1994, following allegations of irregularity in his personal financial affairs. Later in that month the coalition appointed Tsutomu Hata as Prime Minister of a minority Government, which excluded the SDPJ and the New Party Sakigake. Hata was obliged to resign in June, however, owing to his continued failure to command a viable majority in the Diet, and a new coalition of the SDPJ, the LDP and the New Party Sakigake took office. Tomiichi

Murayama, the leader of the SDPJ, became Prime Minister, and Kono was appointed Deputy Prime Minister and Minister of Foreign Affairs.

In July 1994 Murayama recognized the constitutional right to the existence of Japan's Self-Defence Forces (SDF, the armed forces), thereby effectively contradicting official SDPJ policy on the issue. (The SDPJ amended its policy to accord with Murayama's statement in September.) In December nine opposition parties, including the JNP, the JRP, the DSP and the Komeito, amalgamated to form a new political party, the Shinshinto (New Frontier Party, NFP). A faction of Komeito remained outside the new party and was renamed Komei. Kaifu, the former LDP Prime Minister, was elected leader of the NFP, defeating Hata and Takashi Yonezawa, the former leader of the DSP. Ozawa, who was believed to have been pivotal to the formation of the new party, was appointed Secretary-General.

The creation of the NFP was widely perceived to be a response to the approval by the Diet in November 1994 of the electoral reform bills first proposed in 1993, which appeared to favour larger political parties. Under the terms of the new law, the House of Representatives was to be reduced to 500 seats, comprising 300 single-seat constituencies and 200 seats determined by proportional representation; the proportional-representation base was to be divided into 11 regions, and a party would qualify for a proportional-representation seat if it gained a minimum of 2% of the vote; donations amounting to 500,000 yen annually per private sector corporation to individual politicians were permitted, but this was to be phased out after five years; restrictions on corporate donations would be subsidized by the State; door-to-door campaigning was to be permitted and an independent body would draw up new electoral boundaries. In June 1995 a total of 29,900m. yen was awarded in the first distribution of public money to political parties.

On 18 January 1995 a massive earthquake in the Kobe region resulted in the deaths of more than 6,300 people and caused severe infrastructural damage. In the aftermath of the earthquake, the Government was severely criticized (and subsequently acknowledged responsibility) for the poor co-ordination of the relief operation. In March a poisonous gas, sarin, was released into the Tokyo underground railway system, killing 12 people and injuring more than 5,000. A religious sect, Aum Shinrikyo, was accused of perpetrating the attack. Following a further gas attack in Yokohama in April, a number of sect members were detained by the authorities. In June Shoko Asahara, the leader of Aum Shinrikyo, was indicted on a charge of murder. The sect was declared bankrupt in March 1996 and the trial of Asahara opened in the following month. In September Asahara and two other members of the sect were instructed to pay some US $7.3m. in compensation to victims of the Tokyo incident. Attempts by the Ministry of Justice to outlaw the sect, on the grounds that it had engaged in anti-subversive activities, were unsuccessful; however, the sect was denied legal status as a religious organization.

Only 44.5% of the electorate took part in the elections to the House of Councillors, held in July 1995. With one-half of the 252 seats being contested, the LDP won only 49 seats, the SDPJ 16 and the New Party Sakigake three, whereas the NFP, benefiting from the support of the Soka Gakkai religious organization, won 40 seats. In response to the coalition's poor performance, Murayama undertook a major reorganization of the Cabinet. In September Ryutaro Hashimoto, the Minister of International Trade and Industry, was elected leader of the LDP, after Yohei Kono announced that he would not seek re-election.

In October 1995 the Minister of Justice was obliged to resign, following allegations that he had accepted an undisclosed loan of 200m. yen from a Buddhist group. His resignation was followed by that of the Director-General of the Management and Co-ordination Agency in November, owing to controversy arising from his suggestion that Japanese colonial rule over Korea had been of some benefit to the Koreans.

Conflict in the Diet escalated between February and June 1995 over government plans, announced in June 1994, to issue a resolution to commemorate the 50th anniversary of the ending of the Second World War. The resolution was to constitute an apology to countries whose citizens had suffered from the actions of the Japanese army during the war. The New Party Sakigake threatened to withdraw from the coalition if an apology was not made, while a group of 160 LDP Diet members, led by Seisuke Okuno, objected to the labelling of Japan as an aggressor. A resolution was finally passed in June 1995, despite a boycott of the vote by the NFP.

In December 1995 Toshiki Kaifu announced that he would not be seeking re-election as leader of the NFP. He was succeeded by Ichiro Ozawa, who defeated Tsutomu Hata at the leadership election. Ozawa appointed Takashi Yonezawa as Secretary-General of the NFP.

In January 1996 Tomiichi Murayama resigned as Prime Minister; he was, however, re-elected Chairman of the SDPJ. The LDP leader, Ryutaro Hashimoto, was elected Prime Minister on 11 January, winning 288 votes to Ozawa's 167. A coalition Cabinet, largely dominated by the LDP, was formed. Hashimoto's first task was to gain legislative approval for the 1996/97 draft budget, which included an unpopular proposal to use public expenditure to liquidate housing loan companies (*jusen*). Shinshinto organized a 'sit-in' in the parliament building to obstruct the House of Representatives' budget committee meetings. Deliberations resumed after three weeks, however, when the Government agreed to Shinshinto's demand for an inquiry into the alleged receipt of illegal political contributions by the LDP Secretary-General, Koichi Kato. No action was taken against Kato as a result of this inquiry and the draft budget was eventually approved in May 1996 with little revision.

In March 1996 the New Socialist Party (NSP) was formed by left-wing defectors from the SDPJ, who disapproved of the latter's transformation under Murayama's leadership into a moderate liberal party. Osamu Yatabe was elected Chairman of the NSP and Tetsuo Yamaguchi was appointed Secretary-General. In mid-1996, in an attempt to strengthen their electoral bases, particularly in the new single-member districts, there was a further realignment of political parties. In August Shoichi Ide and Hiroyuki Sonoda were elected Leader and Secretary-General, respectively, of the New Party Sakigake following the resignations of Masayoshi Takemura and Yukio Hatoyama. Hatoyama left the party and founded the Democratic Party of Japan (DPJ), with other dissident members of the New Party Sakigake and individual members of the SDPJ and NFP.

A general election was held on 20 October 1996. The LDP won the election, gaining 239 of the 500 seats, while the NFP secured 156, the DPJ 52, the Japan Communist Party (JCP) 26, the SDPJ 15, and the New Party Sakigake two seats. Four deputies, including Hajime Funada, who were elected as independents, subsequently formed a new party called the 21st Century. On 7 November Ryutaro Hashimoto was re-elected Prime Minister for a second term, and formed the first single-party Cabinet since 1993 (the SDPJ and Sakigake had agreed to support the minority Government but chose not to re-enter a coalition).

Almost immediately after the election, public attention was again focused on corruption scandals: 10 politicians, including the Ministers of Finance, and Health and Welfare, and the LDP Secretary-General, Koichi Kato, were accused of receiving a total of 26.1m. yen in political donations from a petroleum trader, Junichi Izui. Izui was arrested and charged with tax evasion and was also placed under suspicion of questionable business dealings with some of Japan's largest petroleum companies. In December 1996 Nobuharu Okamitsu, a former Vice-Minister of Health and Welfare, was arrested and charged with accepting 60m. yen in return for granting state subsidies to a nursing-home operator; Hashimoto, himself, admitted accepting a 2m.-yen legal political donation from a hospital linen-leasing group connected to the Okamitsu scandal. In a further scandal, Morihiro Hosokawa, the former Prime Minister, returned the 30m. yen that he had received for his election campaign from the Orange Kyosai Kumiai, a mutual aid society that had posed as a savings bank, and in January 1997 Tatsuo Tomobe, an independent member of the Diet and a former member of the NFP, was arrested on charges of defrauding investors of more than 8,000,000m. yen.

In December 1996, following disagreements with Ichiro Ozawa, the NFP's President, the former Prime Minister, Tsutomu Hata, left the NFP and formed a new party, called Taiyoto (Sun Party) together with 12 other dissident NFP members. The formal appointment in late December of Takako Doi as Chairwoman of the SDPJ (she had been acting Chairwoman since the dissolution of the House of Representatives in September) prompted the resignation of the party's Secretary-General, Wataru Kubo, in January 1997; he was replaced by Shigeru Ito.

In early 1997 the Government established several commissions, charged with devising a comprehensive programme of administrative and economic reforms. A reduction in government bureaucracy and public expenditure was envisaged, and details of a series of financial deregulation measures were announced in February, including the transfer of the Ministry of Finance's supervisory role to an independent agency in mid-1998. The Government's management of the nuclear programme was comprehensively reviewed, following two accidents, in December 1995 and March 1997, at plants managed by the Power Reactor and Nuclear Fuel Development Corporation, a public organization supervised by the Science and Technology Agency. Allegations that the corporation had failed to report a further 11 radiation leaks over the previous three years served to heighten public disquiet over Japan's nuclear research and development programme.

In mid-1997 the NFP experienced a serious set-back, when Hosokawa resigned from the party, reportedly owing to dissatisfaction with Ozawa's style of leadership. (In December Hosokawa formed a new party—From Five.) In addition, the NFP failed to retain a single seat in elections to the Tokyo Metropolitan Assembly, held in July. The LDP and the JCP, by contrast, increased their representation in the Assembly. By September the LDP had regained its majority in the House of Representatives, following a series of defections by members of the NFP. In December, following further defections from the NFP, the party was dissolved. Six new parties were founded by former NFP members and a significant political realignment took place. In January 1998 six opposition parties, including the DPJ, formed a parliamentary group, Minyuren, which constituted the largest opposition bloc in the Diet. In March the parties comprising Minyuren agreed on their integration into the DPJ, formally establishing a new DPJ, with Naoto Kan as its President, in the following month.

Meanwhile, in late 1997 a series of corruption scandals, involving substantial payments to corporate racketeers by leading financial institutions, had a severe impact on the Japanese economy. The crisis was exacerbated by an increase in the rate of the unpopular consumption tax in April, from 3% to 5%, and a decrease in public expenditure (as part of the Government's fiscal reforms), which resulted in a significant weakening in consumer demand. The collapse of several prominent financial institutions in November, and the threat of further bankruptcies, deepened the economic crisis. The Government announced a series of deregulation and stimulus measures designed to encourage economic growth, including a reduction in taxes and, in a major reversal of policy, the use of public money to support the banking system. In January 1998 the Diet reconvened earlier than scheduled, in order to approve the budget for 1998/99, as well as supplementary budget proposals incorporating the tax reductions. The credibility of the Ministry of Finance was further weakened in late January 1998, when two senior officials were arrested on suspicion of accepting bribes from banks. The Minister of Finance, Hiroshi Mitsuzuka, resigned, accepting full moral responsibility for the affair. He was replaced by Hikaru Matsunaga. As more banks and other financial institutions became implicated in the bribery scandal, the central bank initiated an internal investigation into its own operations. In March the Governor resigned after a senior bank executive was arrested amid further allegations of bribery. Trials of those implicated in the financial scandals took place in 1998 and 1999.

A number of financial deregulation measures, including the liberalization of brokerage commissions and the removal of foreign-exchange controls, came into effect on 1 April 1998, as part of Japan's 'Big Bang' reform process. The economy continued to stagnate, however, despite the launch of a series of economic stimulus packages, and Hashimoto's administration was widely criticized for its slow reaction to the economic crisis. In June the SDPJ and the New Party Sakigake withdrew from their alliance with the ruling LDP. Administrative reform legislation, providing for a reduction in the number of government ministries and agencies from 22 to 13 by 2001, was approved by the Diet in June.

The LDP performed poorly in elections for one-half of the seats in the House of Councillors on 12 July 1998, retaining only 44 of its 61 seats contested, while the DPJ won 27 seats, increasing its representation to 47 seats, and the JCP became the third-largest party in the upper house, gaining 15 seats. Some 58% of the registered electorate voted. Hashimoto resigned as Prime Minister and President of the LDP and was succeeded by Keizo Obuchi, hitherto Minister for Foreign Affairs. Having comfortably defeated two rival candidates in the LDP presidential election, Obuchi was elected Prime Minister on 30 July, despite the preference of the House of Councillors for Naoto Kan, the main opposition candidate.

Obuchi's Government comprised a large number of hereditary politicians, prompting some concern regarding its commitment to comprehensive economic reform, despite its designation as an 'economic reconstruction' Cabinet. Kiichi Miyazawa, a former Prime Minister, was appointed to the position of Minister of Finance. In his inaugural policy speech before the Diet Obuchi announced the establishment of an Economic Strategy Council and promised tax cuts to the value of some 7,000,000m. yen. As Japan's economic situation worsened, political disputes over banking reform dominated the following months, with the Government reluctant to commit itself to the closure of failing banks. Japan's financial institutions had accumulated non-performing loans totalling an estimated 87,500,000 yen. Following weeks of negotiations, in October 1998 the Diet approved banking legislation which included provisions for the nationalization of failing banks, as demanded by the opposition. In November the Government presented a 24,000,000m.-yen stimulus package aimed at revitalizing the country's economy, but ruled out a reduction in the consumption tax.

Shinto Heiwa and Komei merged in November 1998 to form New Komeito, which thus became the second-largest opposition party. Also that month Fukushiro Nukaga, the Director-General of the Defence Agency, resigned from the Government to assume responsibility for a procurement scandal involving his agency. In mid-November the LDP and the Liberal Party (LP), led by Ichiro Ozawa (who had defected from the LDP in 1993), reached a basic accord on the formation of a coalition, which would still remain short of a majority in the upper house. In early January 1999, following intense discussions, agreement was reached on coalition policies, including measures to reduce the influence of bureaucrats on the legislative process. Ozawa appeared to have won concessions on a number of proposals that the LP wanted to be submitted for consideration by the Diet in forthcoming sessions, including a reduction in the number of seats determined by proportional representation in the House of Representatives from 200 to 150 and provision for an expansion of Japan's participation in UN peace-keeping operations. The Cabinet was reshuffled to include the LP, with the number of ministers reduced from 20 to 18 (excluding the Prime Minister). Takeshi Noda of the LP, the only new member of the Cabinet, was appointed as Minister of Home Affairs. Ozawa had declined Obuchi's offer of a cabinet position. At the end of January the Government adopted an administrative reform plan, which aimed to reduce further the number of cabinet ministers and public servants and to establish an economic and fiscal policy committee. Draft legislation on the implementation of the plan was introduced to the Diet in April. In March Shozaburo Nakamura resigned as Minister of Justice following allegations of repeated abuse of power.

Local elections in April 1999 were largely unremarkable; 11 of the 12 governorships contested were won by the incumbents, all standing as independents. The 19-candidate gubernatorial election for Tokyo created by far the most interest. The convincing victory of Shintaro Ishihara, a nationalist writer and a former Minister of Transport under the LDP (although now unaffiliated), was regarded as an embarrassment for the ruling party, which had supported Yasushi Akashi, a former senior UN official. Ishihara immediately provoked controversy, making a series of inflammatory comments about the 1937 Nanjing massacre and criticizing the Chinese Government, which responded angrily, prompting the Japanese Government to distance itself publicly from the new Governor's remarks. In November the Chinese Government also expressed its concern regarding an unofficial visit by Ishihara to Taiwan, which had recently suffered a major earthquake.

In June 1999 the Government voted to grant official legal status to the *de facto* national flag (*Hinomaru*) and anthem (*Kimigayo*), despite considerable opposition owing to their association with Japan's militaristic past. The necessary legislation was subsequently approved by the Diet, however, and became effective in mid-August. Also approved was controversial legislation allowing police investigators, in certain circumstances, to tap the telephones of suspected criminals. Meanwhile, in July New Komeito agreed to join the ruling LDP-LP coalition, giving the Government a new majority in the upper house and expanding its control in the lower house to more than 70% of the seats. Negotiations on policy initiatives proved difficult, however, and were still continuing in September, owing to differences over a number of contentious issues such as constitutional revision and New Komeito's opposition to a reduction in the number of seats in the lower house, as favoured by the LP. Obuchi was re-elected to the presidency of the LDP in September, defeating Koichi Kato, a former Secretary-General of the party, and Taku Yamasaki, a former policy chief. Naoto Kan, however, failed to retain the presidency of the DPJ, and was replaced by Yukio Hatoyama, hitherto Secretary-General of the party.

A new Cabinet was appointed in October 1999. The Minister of Finance, Kiichi Miyazawa, and the Director-General of the Economic Planning Agency retained their portfolios, while Michio Ochi was appointed Chairman of the Financial Reconstruction Commission. The LP and New Komeito each received one cabinet post. A basic accord on coalition policy included an agreement to seek a reduction in the number of seats in the House of Representatives, initially by 20 and subsequently by a further 30. Shingo Nishimura, a Vice-Minister at the Defence Agency, resigned only two weeks after being appointed, following widespread criticism of his suggestion that Japan should arm itself with nuclear weapons. Obuchi, whose judgement was questioned over the affair, subsequently apologized to the nation in a speech to the Diet.

In December 1999 a political crisis was averted when Ozawa was persuaded not to withdraw the LP from the ruling coalition, as he had threatened, over a delay in the proposal of legislation to reduce the number of seats in the lower house. The ruling parties had earlier agreed also to postpone the consideration of a proposal to expand Japan's participation in UN peace-keeping activities. In early 2000 the ruling coalition passed the controversial legislation on the reduction in seats through the Diet, despite an opposition boycott, which continued for some two weeks. Political observers speculated that the opposition had hoped to force Obuchi to dissolve the House of Representatives and call elections, which were due to be held by 19 October. Meanwhile, multi-party committees were established in both houses in January, which were to review the Constitution over a period of five years. In late February Michio Ochi was forced to resign from the Cabinet over remarks that suggested he would be lenient on banking reform.

At the end of September 1999 a serious accident at a uranium-processing plant at Tokaimura, which temporarily raised levels of radiation to 15 times the normal level and appeared to have been caused by human error and poor management, severely undermined public confidence in the safety of Japan's nuclear industry. Furthermore, in November it was revealed that 15 of 17 nuclear facilities recently inspected by government officials had failed to meet legal health and safety standards. In December the Diet enacted legislation aimed at preventing accidents and improving procedures for the management of any future incidents at nuclear power facilities. In February 2000 the Government announced that 439 people had been exposed to radiation in the Tokaimura accident, far more than the 69 recorded in the initial report.

Trials continued in 1997–99 of members of Aum Shinrikyo, the cult which was accused of perpetrating the sarin gas attack on the Tokyo underground railway system in March 1995. In September 1999 Masato Yokoyama, a leading member of the cult, became the first of those accused to receive the death sentence. In late 1999, as the Diet considered and subsequently enacted legislation aimed at curbing its activities, Aum Shinrikyo issued a series of statements in an apparent attempt to avert any restriction on the cult or seizure of its assets. The leaders of the cult announced a suspension of all external activites from October, and in December acknowledged its culpability for a number of crimes, including the 1995 gas attack. Moreover, in January 2000 the cult announced that it was changing its name to Aleph and renouncing its leader, Shoko Asahara, who was still being tried for his part in the gas attack.

Since the mid-1990s Japan's growing trade surplus with the USA has become a matter of increasing concern for the US authorities. In 1994 trade negotiations between Japan and the USA failed, following Japan's refusal to accept numerical targets for imports and exports. The USA initiated protectionist measures against Japan, but relations improved in October, when trade agreements in three of the four main areas under discussion were signed.

Negotiations concerning the automobile trade resulted in the signing of an agreement with the USA in June 1995. However, an increase in the export of Japanese vehicles to the USA in 1997, and a concomitant rise in the US trade deficit with Japan, caused growing tension between the two countries. Negotiations between Prime Minister Hashimoto and President Clinton of the USA in April and June focused on trade issues. In September the USA imposed large fines on three Japanese shipping companies, following complaints about restrictive harbour practices in Japan; however, an agreement to reform Japanese port operations was concluded shortly thereafter. Negotiations on increased access to airline routes were successfully concluded in January 1998. However, relations were again strained by trade disputes in 1998, with Japan's high tariffs on rice, and in the forestry and fisheries sectors, and low-priced steel exports of particular concern to the USA. Tension also arose over the USA's repeated criticism that Japan was not doing enough to stimulate its own economy and alleviate the Asian economic crisis. During a two-day visit to Japan in November 1998, President Clinton urged the Government rapidly to implement measures to encourage domestic demand, reform the banking sector and liberalize its markets, reinforcing earlier warnings that it risked provoking protectionist measures. Meanwhile, Japan's trade surplus with the USA continued to increase, growing by some 33% in 1998, to reach its highest level since 1987. In May 1999, during a six-day visit by Prime Minister Obuchi to the USA (the first such official state visit in 12 years), Clinton praised Obuchi's efforts to stimulate economic recovery and welcomed Japanese plans for further deregulation in several sectors, including telecommunications, energy, housing and financial services. Meanwhile, the dispute over Japanese steel exports had escalated. A ruling, in April 1999, by the US Department of Commerce that Japan had 'dumped' hot-rolled steel into the US market was endorsed, in June, by the US International Trade Commission, and punitive duties of up to 67% were subsequently imposed. In November Japan announced its intention to bring a complaint before the World Trade Organization against the US ruling.

Together with trade issues, Japan's bilateral security arrangements with the USA, concluded by treaty in 1951, have been the focus of US-Japanese relations. The treaty grants the use of military bases in Japan to the USA, in return for a US commitment to provide military support to Japan in the event of external aggression. During a visit to Japan by President Bush of the USA in January 1992, the 'Tokyo declaration on the US-Japan global partnership' was issued, whereby the two countries undertook to co-operate in promoting international security and prosperity. In February 1993 Japan and the USA reaffirmed their security relationship, with the USA agreeing to protect Japan from the threat posed by potential nuclear proliferation around the world.

The presence of the US forces in Japan provoked much debate in the mid-1990s. In November 1995 three US servicemen were arrested and subsequently imprisoned for the rape of a schoolgirl in Okinawa. Considerable civil unrest ensued and legal proceedings were initiated against the Governor of Okinawa, Masahide Ota, following his refusal to renew the leases for US military installations in the region. Lengthy negotiations between the two countries resulted in the USA agreeing, in December 1996, to release 21% of the land used for US military purposes in Okinawa, and to build a floating offshore helicopter base to replace the air base at Futenma. In April 1997 measures were proposed to promote economic development in Okinawa, and plans were put forward to relocate several of the US bases to other prefectures. In December 1997, in a non-binding referendum held in Nago, Okinawa, to assess public opinion concerning the construction of the offshore helicopter base, the majority of voters rejected the proposal. The Mayor of Nago, who advocated the construction of the offshore base in return for measures to stimulate the region's economy, tendered his resignation. Governor Ota stated his opposition to the proposed base, a position also adopted by the new Mayor, elected in February 1998, who had initially announced his approval of its construction. In November 1998 Keiichi Inamine defeated Ota in the Okinawa gubernatorial elections. Inamine, who had been supported by the LDP, presented an alternative solution in an attempt to gain government support for the local economy, proposing that a military-commercial airport be built in northern Okinawa and leased to the USA for a period of 15 years. In December 1998 a US military site was officially returned to the Japanese Government, the first of the 11 bases to be returned under the 1996 agreement. In December 1999 Inamine's proposal for the relocation of the Futenma air base was approved by both the local authorities and the Japanese Government, with the Henoko district of Nago chosen as the site for the new airport; at the same time funding was allocated for a 10-year development plan for northern Okinawa. Negotiations with the US Government, which opposed any time limit on its use of the airport, were to take place in early 2000; it was hoped that the issue could be fully resolved before the next summit meeting of G-8 nations, which was due to be held in Nago in July of that year.

In September 1997 revised Guidelines for Japan-US Defense Co-operation (first compiled in 1978) were issued. The Guidelines, which had been under review since the signing of the US-Japan Joint Declaration on Security in April 1996, envisaged enhanced military co-operation between the USA and Japan, not only on Japanese territory, but also in situations in unspecified areas around Japan. In April 1998 the LDP Government approved legislation on the implementation of the revised Guidelines, despite strong opposition from the SDPJ. The legislation was enacted in May 1999, prompting criticism from China and Russia. Its approval was ensured by an agreement between the LDP, its new coalition partner, the LP, and New Komeito to exclude a clause that would have allowed the inspection of unidentified foreign ships by the SDF, with the aim of enforcing economic sanctions. In August 1999 the Japanese Government formally approved a memorandum of understanding with the USA stipulating details of joint technical research on the development of a theatre missile defence system, which aims to detect and shoot down incoming ballistic missiles within a 3,000-km radius. The Defence Agency has estimated that Japan will have to allocate up to 30,000m. yen to the controversial research project over a period of five years.

Since 1982 Japan has been under continued pressure from the USA to increase its defence expenditure and to assume greater responsibility for security in the Western Pacific area. In 1986 the Japanese Government decided to exceed the self-imposed limit on defence expenditure of 1% of the gross national product (GNP), set in 1976. In December 1990 the Government announced a new five-year programme (to begin in the 1991/92 fiscal year) to develop the country's defence capability. The average annual increase in total military expenditure over the five-year period was expected to be 3%, in comparison with the 5% average annual increase during the previous five-year programme. The new programme, to be implemented at an estimated total cost of US $172,000m., also envisaged that Japan would assume a greater share of the cost of maintaining US troops stationed in Japan. In December 1992 the Government, under concerted pressure from the opposition, announced a reduction in the average annual increase during the 1991–96 defence programme to 2.1%. In November 1995 the Cabinet approved a new national defence programme, which envisaged a 20% reduction in troops and confirmed Japan's security co-operation with the USA.

In September 1990 Japan announced a US $4,000m.-contribution to the international effort to force an unconditional Iraqi withdrawal from Kuwait. A controversial LDP-sponsored Peace Co-operation Bill, which provided for the dispatch to the Persian (Arabian) Gulf area of some 2,000 non-combatant personnel, encountered severe political opposition and provoked widespread discussion on the constitutional legitimacy of the deployment of Japanese personnel (in any capacity), and in November the proposals were withdrawn. In January 1991, following repeated US demands for a greater financial commitment to the Gulf crisis (and a swifter disbursement of moneys already pledged), the Japanese Government announced plans to increase its contribution by US $9,000m. and to provide aircraft for the transportation of refugees in the region. Opposition to the proposal was again vociferous. By mid-February, however, the Government had secured the support of several centrist parties, by pledging that any financial aid from Japan would be employed in a 'non-lethal' capacity. Legislation to approve the new contribution was adopted by the Diet in March.

In June 1992 controversial legislation to permit the SDF to participate in UN peace-keeping operations was approved. Their role, however, was to be confined to logistical and humanitarian tasks, unless a special dispensation from the Diet were granted. In early September, following a request from the UN Secretary-General, the Government endorsed the dispatch of 1,800 members of the SDF to serve in the UN Transitional Authority in Cambodia (UNTAC). Japanese troops participated in further UN peace-keeping operations in Mozambique, in 1993, and, under Japanese command, on the Rwandan-Zairean border, in 1994. Legislation was approved in November 1994 to enable Japanese forces to be deployed overseas if the Government believed the lives of Japanese citizens to be at risk. In September Japan reiterated its desire to be a permanent member of the UN Security Council, particularly in view of its status as the world's largest donor of development aid and the second-largest contributor (after the USA) to the UN budget. In October 1996 the UN General Assembly voted to allocate to Japan a non-permanent seat on the Security Council, to be held for a two-year period from January 1997. In the late 1990s the Japanese Government was campaigning for a greater proportion of senior-level positions within the UN to be allocated to Japanese personnel, as a reflection of its contribution to the UN budget. Draft legislation on an expansion of SDF participation in UN peace-keeping operations was to be considered by the Japanese Diet in early 2000.

Stability in East and South-East Asia is a vital consideration in Japanese foreign policy, since Japan depends on Asia for much of its foreign trade, including imports of vital raw materials. Despite the signing of a treaty of peace and friendship with the People's Republic of China in 1978, relations deteriorated in the late 1980s after China expressed concern at Japan's increased defence expenditure and its more assertive military stance. Japanese aid to China was suspended in June 1989, following the Tiananmen Square massacre in Beijing, and was not resumed until November 1990, after the Chinese Government's declaration, in January, that a state of martial law was no longer in force. Relations between the two countries were strengthened by the visits to China by Emperor Akihito in October 1992, the first-ever Japanese imperial visit to China, and by Prime Minister Hosokawa in March 1994. However, in August of that year Japan announced the suspension of economic aid to China, following renewed nuclear testing by the Chinese Government. The provision of economic aid was resumed in early 1997, following the declaration of a moratorium on Chinese nuclear testing.

In July 1996 Japan's relations with both China and Taiwan were strained when a group of nationalists, the Japan Youth Federation, constructed a lighthouse and war memorial on the Senkaku Islands (or Diaoyu Islands in Chinese), a group of uninhabited islands situated in the East China Sea, to which all three countries laid claim. The situation was further aggravated in September by the accidental drowning of a Hong Kong citizen during a protest near the islands against Japan's claim. In October a flotilla of small boats, operated by 300 activists from Taiwan, Hong Kong and Macau, evaded Japanese patrol vessels and raised the flags of China and Taiwan on the disputed islands. The Japanese Government sought to defuse tensions with China and Taiwan by withholding official recognition of the lighthouse; it did not, however, condemn the right-wing activists who had constructed the controversial buildings. In May 1997 China expressed serious concern, when a member of the Japanese Diet landed on one of the disputed islands. The Japanese Government distanced itself from the action.

In September 1997 Hashimoto visited China to commemorate the 25th anniversary of the normalization of relations between the two countries. China expressed concern at the revised US-Japanese security arrangements, following a statement by a senior Japanese minister that the area around Taiwan might be covered under the new guidelines. Procedures for the removal of chemical weapons, deployed in China by Japanese forces during the Second World War, were also discussed. During a visit to Japan by the Chinese Premier, Li Peng, in November, a bilateral fisheries agreement was signed. In November 1998, during a six-day state visit by President Jiang Zemin, Obuchi and Zemin issued (but declined to sign) a joint declaration on friendship and co-operation, in which Japan expressed deep remorse for past aggression against China. China was reported to be displeased by the lack of a written apology, however, and remained concerned by the implications of US-Japanese defence arrangements regarding Taiwan. A subsequent US-Japanese agreement to initiate joint technical research on the development of a theatre missile defence system, followed by the Japanese Diet's approval, in May 1999, of legislation on the implementation of the revised US-Japanese defence guidelines (see above) provoked severe criticism from China, despite Japan's insistence that military co-operation with the USA was purely defensive. In July a meeting in Beijing between Obuchi and the Chinese Premier, Zhu Rongji, resulted in the formalization of a bilateral agreement on China's entry to the WTO, following several months of intense negotiations on the liberalization of trade in services.

nifty.ne.jp; f. 1958; Moderator TOHRU NUMAJIRI; Gen. Sec. KAZUO OYA; 4,819 mems.

**Japan Evangelical Lutheran Church:** 1-1, Sadowara-cho, Ichigaya, Shinjuku-ku, Tokyo 169; tel. (3) 3260-8631; fax (3) 3268-3589; f. 1893; Moderator Rev. SHOICHI ASAMI; Gen. Sec. Rev. ISAMU AOTA; 22,246 mems (March 1996).

**Korean Christian Church in Japan:** Room 52, Japan Christian Center, 2-3-18, Nishi Waseda, Shinjuku-ku, Tokyo 169-0051; tel. (3) 3202-5398; fax (3) 3202-4977; e-mail kccj@kb3.so-net.ne.jp; f. 1909; Moderator KYUNG HAE-JUNG; Gen. Sec. KANG YOUNG-IL; 10,000 mems (1994).

Among other denominations active in Japan are the Christian Catholic Church, the German Evangelical Church and the Tokyo Union Church.

### OTHER COMMUNITIES

#### Bahá'í Faith

**The National Spiritual Assembly of the Bahá'ís of Japan:** 7-2-13, Shinjuku, Shinjuku-ku, Tokyo 160-0022; tel. (3) 3209-7521; fax (3) 3204-0773; e-mail nsajpn@att.ne.jp.

#### Judaism

**Japan Jewish Centre:** Tokyo; Pres. ERNIE SALOMON.

#### Islam

Islam has been active in Japan since the late 19th century. There is a small Muslim community, maintaining several mosques, including those at Kobe, Nagoya, Chiba and Isesaki, the Arabic Islamic Institute and the Islamic Center in Tokyo. The construction of Tokyo Central mosque was ongoing in early 1999.

**Islamic Center, Japan:** 1-16-11, Ohara, Setagaya-ku, Tokyo 156-0041; tel. (3) 3460-6169; fax (3) 3460-6105; e-mail islamcpj@islamcenter.or.jp; internet www.islamcenter.or.jp; f. 1965; Chair. Dr SALIH SAMARRAI.

#### The New Religions

Many new cults have emerged in Japan since the end of the Second World War. Collectively these are known as the New Religions (Shinko Shukyo), among the most important of which are Tenrikyo, Omotokyo, Soka Gakkai, Rissho Kosei-kai, Kofuku-no-Kagaku, Agonshu and Aum Shinrikyo. (Following the indictment on charges of murder of several members of Aum Shinrikyo, including its leader, SHOKO ASAHARA, the cult lost its legal status as a religious organization in 1996. In January 2000 the cult announced its intention to change its name to Aleph.)

**Kofuku-no-Kagaku** (Institute for Research in Human Happiness): Tokyo; f. 1986; believes its founder to be reincarnation of Buddha; 8.25m. mems; Leader RYUHO OKAWA.

**Rissho Kosei-kai:** 2-11-1, Wada Suginami-ku, Tokyo 166; tel. (3) 3380-5185; fax (3) 3381-9792; f. 1938; Buddhist lay organization based on the teaching of the Lotus Sutra, active inter-faith co-operation towards peace; Pres. Rev. Dr NICHIKO NIWANO; 6.3m. mems with 245 brs world-wide (1995).

**Soka Gakkai:** 32, Shinano-machi, Shinjuku-ku, Tokyo 160-8583; tel. (3) 5360-9830; fax (3) 5360-9885; e-mail webmaster@sokagakkai.or.jp; internet www.sokagakkai.or.jp; f. 1930; society of lay practitioners of the Buddhism of Nichiren; membership of 8.12m. households (1997); group promotes activities in education, international cultural exchange and consensus-building towards peace, based on the humanist world view of Buddhism; Hon. Pres. DAISAKU IKEDA; Pres. EINOSUKE AKIYA.

## The Press

In October 1997 there were 122 daily newspapers in Japan. Their average circulation was the highest in the world, and the circulation per head of population was also among the highest, at 580 copies per 1,000 inhabitants in 1996. The large number of weekly news journals is a notable feature of the Japanese press. At December 1998 a total of 2,763 periodicals were produced, 85 of which were weekly publications. Technically the Japanese press is highly advanced, and the major newspapers are issued in simultaneous editions in the main centres.

The two newspapers with the largest circulations are the *Yomiuri Shimbun* and *Asahi Shimbun*. Other influential papers include *Mainichi Shimbun, Nihon Keizai Shimbun, Chunichi Shimbun* and *Sankei Shimbun*.

### NATIONAL DAILIES

**Asahi Shimbun:** 5-3-2, Tsukiji, Chuo-ku, Tokyo 104-8011; tel. (3) 3545-0131; fax (3) 3545-0358; f. 1879; also published by Osaka, Seibu and Nagoya head offices and Hokkaido branch office; Pres. SHINICHI HAKOSHIMA; Dir and Exec. Editor KIYOFUKU CHUMA; circ. morning 8.3m., evening 4.4m.

**Mainichi Shimbun:** 1-1-1, Hitotsubashi, Chiyoda-ku, Tokyo 100-8051; tel. (3) 3212-0321; fax (3) 3211-3598; f. 1882; also published by Osaka, Seibu and Chubu head offices, and Hokkaido branch office; Pres. AKIRA SAITO; Man. Dir and Editor-in-Chief ATSUMU KIDO; circ. morning 4.0m., evening 1.8m.

**Nihon Keizai Shimbun:** 1-9-5, Otemachi, Chiyoda-ku, Tokyo 100-8066; tel. (3) 5255-2061; fax (3) 5255-2661; internet www.nikkei.co.jp; f. 1876; also published by Osaka head office and Sapporo, Nagoya and Seibu branch offices; Pres. TAKUHIKO TSURUTA; Dir and Man. Editor MASAYUKI SHIMADA; circ. morning 1.8m., evening 953,575.

**Sankei Shimbun:** 1-7-2, Otemachi, Chiyoda-ku, Tokyo 100-8077; tel. (3) 3231-7111; internet www.sankei.co.jp; f. 1933; also published by Osaka head office; Man. Dir and Editor TAKEHIKO KIYOHARA; circ. morning 2.0m., evening 911,502.

**Yomiuri Shimbun:** 1-7-1, Otemachi, Chiyoda-ku, Tokyo 100-8055; tel. (3) 3242-1111; fax (3) 3246-0888; e-mail kokusai@yominet.ne.jp; internet www.yomiuri.co.jp/daily; f. 1874; also published by Osaka, Seibu and Chubu head offices, and Hokkaido and Hokuriku branch offices; Pres. and Editor-in-Chief TSUNEO WATANABE; circ. morning 10.2m., evening 4.3m.

### PRINCIPAL LOCAL DAILIES

#### Tokyo

**Asahi Evening News :** 5-3-2, Tsukiji, Chuo-ku, Tokyo 104-8011; tel. (3) 5540-7641; fax (3) 3542-6172; f. 1954; evening; English; Exec. Editor YOSHIO MURAKAMI; Man. Editor MANABU HARA; circ. 38,800.

**Daily Sports:** 1-20-3, Osaki, Shinagawa-ku, Tokyo 141-8585; tel. (3) 5434-1752; f. 1948; morning; Dir YOSHIHIKO SHIMOMURA; circ. 400,254.

**The Daily Yomiuri:** 1-7-1, Otemachi, Chiyoda-ku, Tokyo 100-8055; tel. (3) 3242-1111; f. 1955; morning; Editor ICHIRO TANIGUCHI; circ. 52,007.

**Dempa Shimbun:** 1-11-15, Higashi Gotanda, Shinagawa-ku, Tokyo 141-8790; tel. (3) 3445-6111; fax (3) 3444-7515; f. 1950; morning; Pres. TETSUO HIRAYAMA; Man. Editor TOSHIO KASUYA; circ. 298,000.

**Hochi Shimbun:** 4-6-49, Konan, Minato-ku, Tokyo 108-8485; tel. (3) 5479-1111; f. 1872; morning; Pres. MASARU FUSHIMI; Man. Editor JUNJI IKEJIRI; circ. 773,069.

**The Japan Times:** 4-5-4, Shibaura, Minato-ku, Tokyo 108-8071; tel. (3) 3453-5312; f. 1897; morning; English; Chair. and Pres. TOSHIAKI OGASAWARA; Dir and Editor-in-Chief YUTAKA MATAEBARA; circ. 65,925.

**The Mainichi Daily News:** 1-1-1, Hitotsubashi, Chiyoda-ku, Tokyo 100-8051; tel. (3) 3212-0321; f. 1922; morning; English; also publ. from Osaka; Man. Editor MICHIO TAKIMOTO; combined circ. 48,450.

**Naigai Times:** 1-1-15, Ariake, Koto-ku, Tokyo 135-0063; tel. (3) 5564-7021; f. 1949; evening; Pres. MITSUGU ONDA; Vice-Pres. and Editor-in-Chief MASAHIRO MORITA; circ. 298,000.

**Nihon Kaiji Shimbun** (Japan Maritime Daily): 5-19-2, Shimbashi, Minato-ku, Tokyo 105-0004; tel. (3) 3436-3221; f. 1942; morning; Man. Editor MINORU TAKASHIMIZU; circ. 55,000.

**Nihon Kogyo Shimbun:** 1-7-2, Otemachi, Chiyoda-ku, Tokyo 100-8125; tel. (3) 3231-7111; f. 1933; morning; industrial, business and financial; Man. Editor HIDETATSU FURUTATE; circ. 263,508.

**Nihon Nogyo Shimbun** (Agriculture): 2-3, Akihabara, Taito-ku, Tokyo 110-8722; tel. (3) 5295-7411; fax (3) 3253-0980; f. 1928; morning; Man. Editor ATSUSHI MATSUZAWA; circ. 433,180.

**Nihon Sen-i Shimbun** (Textile and Fashion): 1-13-12, Nihonbashi-muromachi, Chuo-ku, Tokyo 103-0022; tel. (3) 3270-1661; fax (3) 3246-1858; f. 1943; morning; Man. Editor KIYOSHIGE SEIRYU; circ. 143,060.

**Nikkan Kogyo Shimbun** (Industrial Daily News): 1-8-10, Kudan-kita, Chiyoda-ku, Tokyo 102-8181; tel. (3) 3222-7111; fax (3) 3262-6031; f. 1915; morning; Man. Editor NOBUKATSU OKAMURA; circ. 533,145.

**Nikkan Sports News:** 3-5-10, Tsukiji, Chuo-ku, Tokyo 104-8055; tel. (3) 5550-8888; fax (3) 5550-8901; f. 1946; morning; Man. Editor YUKIHIRO MORI; circ. 992,230.

**Sankei Sports:** 1-7-2, Otemachi, Chiyoda-ku, Tokyo 100-8077; tel. (3) 3231-7111; f. 1963; morning; Man. Editor YUKIO INADA; circ. 815,215.

**Shipping and Trade News:** Tokyo News Service Ltd, Tsukiji Hamarikyu Bldg, 5-3-3, Tsukiji, Chuo-ku, Tokyo 104-8004; tel. (3) 3542-6511; fax (3) 3542-5086; f. 1949; English; Man. Editor TAKASHI INOUE; circ. 14,500.

**Sports Nippon:** 2-1-30, Ecchujima, Koto-ku, Tokyo 135-8753; tel. (3) 3820-0700; f. 1949; morning; Man. Editor SUSUMU KOMURO; circ.950,675.

**Suisan Keizai Shimbun** (Fisheries): 6-8-19, Roppongi, Minato-ku, Tokyo 106-0032; tel. (3) 3404-6531; fax (3) 3404-0863; f. 1948; morning; Editor-in-Chief KOSHI TORINOUMI; circ. 61,000.

**Tokyo Chunichi Sports:** 2-3-13, Kohnan, Minato-ku, Tokyo 108-8010; tel. (3) 3471-2211; f. 1956; evening; Head Officer YASUKUNI SATO; circ. 323,951.

**Tokyo Shimbun:** 2-3-13, Kohnan, Minato-ku, Tokyo 108-8010; tel. (3) 3471-2211; fax (3) 3471-1851; f. 1942; Man. Editor KUNIHIRO TAKABA; circ. morning 665,470, evening 370,908.

**Tokyo Sports:** 2-1-30, Ecchujima, Koto-ku, Tokyo 135-8721; tel. (3) 3820-0801; f. 1959; evening; Man. Editor YASUO SAKURAI; circ. 1,397,760.

**Yukan Fuji:** 1-7-2, Otemachi, Chiyoda-ku, Tokyo 100-8077; tel. (3) 3231-7111; fax (3) 3246-0377; f. 1969; evening; Dir and Man. Editor TOMIO SAITO; circ. 268,984.

### Osaka District

**Daily Sports:** 1-18-11, Edobori, Nishi-ku, Osaka 550-0002; tel. (6) 6443-0421; f. 1948; morning; Man. Editor TOSHIAKI MITANI; circ. 562,715.

**The Mainichi Daily News:** 3-4-5, Umeda, Kita-ku, Osaka 530-8251; tel. (6) 6345-1551; f. 1922; morning; English; Man. Editor KATSUYA FUKUNAGA.

**Nikkan Sports:** 5-92-1, Hattori-kotobuki-cho, Toyonaka 561-8585; tel. (6) 6867-2811; f. 1950; morning; Man. Editor TOSHIHIDE YAMAZAKI; circ. 523,120.

**Osaka Shimbun:** 2-4-9, Umeda, Kita-ku, Osaka 530-8279; tel. (6) 6343-1221; f. 1922; evening; Man. Editor KAORU YURA; circ. 87,633.

**Osaka Sports:** Osaka Ekimae Daiichi Bldg, 4th Floor, 1-3-1-400, Umeda, Kita-ku, Osaka 530-0001; tel. (6) 6345-7657; f. 1968; evening; Head Officer KAZUOMI TANAKA; circ. 470,660.

**Sankei Sports:** 2-4-9, Umeda, Kita-ku, Osaka 530-8277; tel. (6) 6343-1221; f. 1955; morning; Man. Editor MASAKI YOSHIDA; circ. 552,519.

**Sports Nippon:** 3-4-5, Umeda, Kita-ku, Osaka 530-8278; tel. (6) 6346-8500; f. 1949; morning; Man. Editor HIDETOSHI ISHIHARA; circ. 477,300.

### Kanto District

**Chiba Nippo** (Chiba Daily News): 4-14-10, Chuo, Chuo-ku, Chiba 260-0013; tel. (43) 222-9211; f. 1957; morning; Man. Editor NOBORU HAYASHI; circ. 189,597.

**Ibaraki Shimbun:** 2-15, Kitami-machi, Mito 310-8686; tel. (292) 21-3121; f. 1891; morning; Man.Dir and Man. Editor TADANORI TOMOSUE; circ. 117,328.

**Jomo Shimbun:** 1-50-21, Furuichi-machi, Maebashi 371-8666; tel. (272) 54-9911; f. 1887; morning; Man. Editor TOSHIO MATSUMOTO; circ. 292,137.

**Joyo Shimbun:** 2-7-6, Manabe, Tsuchiura 300-0051. (298) 21-1780; f. 1948; morning; Pres. MINEO IWANAMI; circ. 20,731.

**Kanagawa Shimbun:** 6-145, Hanasaki-cho, Nishi-ku, Yokohama 220-8588; tel. (45) 411-7450; f. 1942; morning; Dir and Man. Editor TADASHI ITO; circ. 237,607.

**Saitama Shimbun:** 6-12-11, Kishi-machi, Urawa 336-8686; tel. (48) 862-3371; f. 1944; morning; Man. Editor YOTARO NUMATA; circ. 160,964.

**Shimotsuke Shimbun:** 1-8-11, Showa, Utsunomiya 320-8686; tel. (286) 25-1111; f. 1884; morning; Man. Dir and Editor-in-Chief EISUKE TODA; circ. 302,025.

### Tohoku District
(North-east Honshu)

**Akita Sakigake Shimpo:** 1-1, San-no-rinkai-cho, Akita 010-8601; tel. (188) 88-1800; fax (188) 23-1780; f. 1874; Man. Editor SHIGEAKI MAEKAWA; circ. 261,297.

**Daily Tohoku:** 1-3-12, Joka, Hachinohe 031-8601; tel. (178) 44-5111; f. 1945; morning; Man. Editor UICHI IZUMIYAMA; circ. 105,233.

**Fukushima Mimpo:** 13-17, Otemachi, Fukushima 960-8602; tel. (245) 31-4111; f. 1892; Pres. and Editor-in-Chief TSUTOMU HANADA; circ. morning 306,009, evening 9,479.

**Fukushima Minyu:** 4-29, Yanagimachi, Fukushima 960-8648; tel. (245) 23-1191; f. 1895; Dir and Man. Editor KOICHI HANZAWA; circ. morning 200,852, evening 6,260.

**Hokuu Shimpo:** 3-2, Nishi-dori-machi, Noshiro 016-0891. (185) 54-3150; f. 1895; morning; Chair. KOUICHI YAMAKI; circ. 31,470.

**Ishinomaki Shimbun:** 2-1-28, Sumiyoshi-machi, Ishinomaki 986; tel. (225) 22-3201; f. 1946; evening; Man. Editor MASATOSHI SATO; circ. 13,050.

**Iwate Nichi-nichi Shimbun:** 60, Minami-shin-machi, Ichinoseki 021-8686; tel. (191) 26-5114; f. 1923; morning; Pres. and Editor-in-Chief TAKESHI YAMAGISHI; circ. 59,697.

**Iwate Nippo:** 3-7, Uchimaru, Morioka 020-8622; tel. (196) 53-4111; f. 1928; Man. Editor HIROSHI MIURA; circ. morning 224,807, evening 224,320.

**Kahoku Shimpo:** 1-2-28, Itsutsubashi, Aoba-ku, Sendai 980-8660; tel. (22) 211-1111; fax (22) 224-7947; f. 1897; Man. Editor MASAHIKO ICHIRIKI; circ. morning 502,053, evening 142,001.

**Mutsu Shimpo:** 2-1, Shimo-shirogane-cho, Hirosaki 036-8356; tel. (172) 34-3111; f. 1946; morning; Man. Editor TAKASHI IZUMI; circ. 53,500.

**Shonai Nippo:** 8-29, Baba-cho, Tsuruoka 997-8691; tel. (235) 22-1480; f. 1946; morning; Pres. SHOJI KON-NO; Exec. Dir and Editor-in-Chief MASATOSHI MATSUNOKI; circ. 22,500.

**To-o Nippo:** 78, Kanbayashi, Yatsuyaku, Aomori 030-0180; tel. (177) 39-1111; f. 1888; Man. Editor TAKAO SHIOKOSHI; circ. morning 262,667, evening 258,426.

**Yamagata Shimbun:** 2-5-12, Hatago-cho, Yamagata 990-0047; tel. (236) 22-5271; f. 1876; Dir and Man. Editor YOUSUKE KUROSAWA; circ. 228,230.

**Yonezawa Shimbun:** 3-3-7, Monto-cho, Yonezawa 992-0039; tel. (238) 22-4411; f. 1879; morning; Man. Dir and Editor-in-Chief MAKOTO SATO; circ. 13,750.

### Chubu District
(Central Honshu)

**Chubu Keizai Shimbun:** 4-4-12, Meieki, Nakamura-ku, Nagoya 450-8561; tel. (52) 561-5215; f. 1946; morning; Man. Editor NORIMITSU INAGAKI; circ. 96,000.

**Chukyo Sports:** Chunichi Kosoku Offset Insatsu Bldg, 4-3-9, Kinjo, Naka-ku, Nagoya 460-0847; tel. (52) 982-1911; f. 1968; evening; circ. 289,430; Head Officer OSAMU SUETSUGU.

**Chunichi Shimbun:** 1-6-1, Sannomaru, Naka-ku, Nagoya 460-8511; tel. (52) 201-8811; f. 1942; Man. Editor SATORU TAJIMA; circ. morning 2.7m., evening 758,475.

**Chunichi Sports:** 1-6-1, Sannomaru, Naka-ku, Nagoya 460-8511; tel. (52) 201-8811; f. 1954; evening; Head Officer KATSUHIKO SAKAI; circ. 602,776.

**Gifu Shimbun:** 10, Imakomachi, Gifu 500-8577; tel. (582) 64-1151; f. 1879; Exec. Dir and Man. Editor TADASHI TANAKA; circ. morning 171,895, evening 31,965.

**Higashi-Aichi Shimbun:** 62, Torinawate, Shinsakae-machi, Toyohashi 441-8666; tel. (532) 32-3111; f. 1957; morning; Man. Editor HARUO INOUE; circ. 52,300.

**Nagano Nippo:** 3-1323-1, Takashima, Suwa 392-8611; tel. (266) 52-2000; f. 1901; morning; Exec. Dir and Man. Editor KENJIRO BANZAI; circ. 47,676.

**Nagoya Times:** 1-3-10, Marunouchi, Naka-ku, Nagoya 460-8530; tel. (52) 231-1331; f. 1946; evening; Man. Editor NAOKI KITO; circ. 146,137.

**Shinano Mainichi Shimbun:** 657, Minamiagata-machi, Nagano 380-8546; tel. (26) 236-3000; fax (26) 236-3197; internet www .shinmai.co.jp; f. 1873; Man. Editor SEIICHI INOMATA; circ. morning 477,000, evening 56,900.

**Shizuoka Shimbun:** 3-1-1, Toro, Shizuoka 422-8033; tel. (54) 284-8900; f. 1941; Dir and Man. Editor SEIJI HARADA; circ. morning 723,342, evening 723,431.

**Yamanashi Nichi-Nichi Shimbun:** 2-6-10, Kitaguchi, Kofu 400-8515; tel. (552) 31-3000; f. 1872; morning; Man. Editor MATSUO MORIMOTO; circ. 201,463.

### Hokuriku District
(North Coastal Honshu)

**Fukui Shimbun:** 1-1-14, Haruyama, Fukui 910-8552; tel. (776) 23-5111; f. 1899; morning; Man. Editor MITSUSHI ASANO; circ. 197,518.

**Hokkoku Shimbun:** 2-5-1, Kohrinbo, Kanazawa 920-8588; tel. (762) 63-2111; f. 1893; Man. Editor MASAYUKI ONISHI; circ. morning 289,350, evening 100,157.

**Hokuriku Chunichi Shimbun:** 2-7-15, Kohrinbo, Kanazawa 920-8573; tel. (762) 61-3111; f. 1960; Man. Editor KANJI KOMIYA; circ. morning 119,419, evening 13,442.

**Kitanippon Shimbun:** 2-14, Azumi-cho, Toyama 930-8680; tel. (764) 45-3300; f. 1940; Dir and Man. Editor RYUICHI KITAGAWA; circ. morning 221, 058, evening 29,997.

**Niigata Nippo:** 258-24, Sanban-cho, Nishibori-dori, Niigata 951-8620; tel. (25) 378-9111; f. 1942; Dir and Man. Editor GEN HOSHINO; circ. morning 493,921, evening 69,260.

**Toyama Shimbun:** 5-1, Otemachi, Toyama 930-8520; tel. (764) 91-8111; f. 1923; morning; Man. Editor SACHIO MIYAMOTO; circ. 42,988.

### Kinki District
(West Central Honshu)

**Daily Sports:** 1-5-7, Higashi-Kawasaki-cho, Chuo-ku, Kobe 650-0044; tel. (78) 362-7100; morning; Man. Editor HIROHISA KARUO.

**Ise Shimbun:** 34-6, Hon-cho, Tsu 514-0831; tel. (592) 24-0003; f. 1878; morning; Man. Editor FUJIO YAMAMOTO; circ. 100,550.

**Kii Minpo:** 100, Akitsu-machi, Tanabe 646-8660; tel. (739) 22-7171; f. 1911; evening; Vice-Pres. and Man. Editor SOH-ICHI TANIKAWA; circ. 37,792.

**Kobe Shimbun:** 1-5-7, Higashi-Kawasaki-cho, Chuo-ku, Kobe 650-8571; tel. (78) 362-7100; f. 1898; Man. Editor YASUO ISHIYAMA; circ. morning 534,172, evening 276,447.

**Kyoto Shimbun:** 239, Shoshoi-machi, Ebisugawa-agaru, Karasuma-dori, Nakagyo-ku, Kyoto 604-8577; tel. (75) 222-2111; f. 1879; Man. Editor KENZO MATSUNAGA; circ. morning 502,628, evening 324,748.

**Nara Shimbun:** 606, Sanjo-machi, Nara 630-8686; tel. (742) 26-1331; f. 1946; morning; Dir and Man. Editor SADAYUKI HAYASHI; circ. 118,064.

### Chugoku District
(Western Honshu)

**Chugoku Shimbun:** 7-1, Dobashi-cho, Naka-ku, Hiroshima 730-8677; tel. (82) 236-2111; fax (82) 236-2321; e-mail denshi@hiroshima-cdas.or.jp; internet www.hiroshima-cdas.or.jp/chugoku-np/; f. 1892; Dir and Man. Editor HIROSHI ARITA; circ. morning 738,000, evening 96,000.

**Nihonkai Shimbun:** 2-137, Tomiyasu, Tottori 680-8678; tel. (857) 21-2888; f. 1976; morning; Man. Dir and Man. Editor HISAHIRO TANAKA; circ. 78,315.

**Okayama Nichi-Nichi Shimbun:** 6-30, Hon-cho, Okayama 700-8678; tel. (86) 231-4211; f. 1946; evening; Man. Dir and Man. Editor TAKASHI ANDO; circ. 45,000.

**San-In Chuo Shimpo:** 383, Tono-machi, Matsue 690-8668; tel. (852) 32-3440; f. 1942; morning; Man. Editor MASAMI MOCHIDA; circ. 170,365.

**Sanyo Shimbun:** 2-1-23, Yanagi-machi, Okayama 700-8634; tel. (86) 231-2210; f. 1879; Dir and Man. Editor TAKAMASA KOSHIMUNE; circ. morning 451,837, evening 71,324.

**Ube Jiho:** 3-6-1, Kotobuki-cho, Ube 755-8557; tel. (836) 31-1511; f. 1912; evening; Exec. Dir and Man. Editor KAZUYA WAKI; circ. 42,550.

**Yamaguchi Shimbun:** 1-1-7, Higashi-Yamato-cho, Shimonoseki 750-8506; tel. (832) 66-3211; f. 1946; morning; Man. Editor YOJI OGOCHI; circ. 82,500.

### Shikoku Island

**Ehime Shimbun:** 1-12-1, Otemachi, Matsuyama 790-8511; tel. (899) 35-2111; f. 1941; morning; Man. Editor RYOJI YAND; circ. 318,906.

**Kochi Shimbun:** 3-2-15, Hon-machi, Kochi 780-8572; tel. (888) 22-2111; f. 1904; Dir and Man. Editor KENGO FUJITO; circ. morning 232,996, evening 146,088.

**Shikoku Shimbun:** 15-1, Nakano-machi, Takamatsu 760-8572; tel. (878) 33-1111; f. 1889; morning; Dir and Man. Editor YOSHINE YOSHIDA; circ. 211,023.

**Tokushima Shimbun:** 2-5-2, Naka-Tokushima-cho, Tokushima 770-8572; tel. (886) 55-7373; fax (866) 54-0165; f. 1941; Dir and Man. Editor HIROSHI MATSUMURA; circ. morning 249,300, evening 50,956.

### Hokkaido Island

**Doshin Sports:** 3-6, Ohdori-Nishi, Chuo-ku, Sapporo 060-8711; tel. (11) 241-1230; f. 1982; morning; Pres. YOSHIAKI KODAMA; circ. 142,451.

**Hokkai Times:** 10-6, Nishi, Minami-Ichijo, Chuo-ku, Sapporo 060; tel. (11) 231-0131; f. 1946; Man. Editor KOKI ITO; circ. morning 120,736.

**Hokkaido Shimbun:** 3-6, Ohdori-Nishi, Chuo-ku, Sapporo 060-8711; tel. (11) 221-2111; f. 1942; Man. Dir and Man. Editor KOJI UESAWA; circ. morning 1.2m., evening 751,739.

**Kushiro Shimbun:** 7-3, Kurogane-cho, Kushiro 085-8650; tel. (154) 22-1111; f. 1955; morning; Man. Dir and Editor-in-Chief KAZUO YOKOZAWA; circ. 56,095.

**Muroran Mimpo:** 1-3-16, Hon-cho, Muroran 051-8550; tel. (143) 22-5121; f. 1945; Man. Editor HIROSHI SHINPO; circ. morning 61,800, evening 52,190.

**Nikkan Sports:** 3-1-30, Higashi, Kita-3 jo, Chuo-ku, Sapporo 060-0033; tel. (11) 242-3900; fax (11) 231-5470; f. 1962; morning; Pres. SHIZUO HASEGAWA; circ. 160,199.

**Tokachi Mainichi Shimbun:** 8-2, Minami, Higashi-Ichijo, Obihiro 080-8688; tel. (155) 22-2121; fax (155) 25-2700; internet www.tokachi.co.jp; f. 1919; evening; Dir and Man. Editor MASAO MATSUDA; circ. 87,950.

**Tomakomai Mimpo:** 3-1-8, Wakakusa-cho, Tomakomai 053-8611; tel. (144) 32-5311; f. 1950; evening; Dir and Man. Editor RYUICHI KUDO; circ. 60,676.

**Yomiuri Shimbun:** 4-1, Nishi, Kita-4 jo, Chuo-ku, Sapporo 060-8656; tel. (11) 242-3111; f. 1959; Head Officer YOSHIRO KUTANI; circ. morning 260,671, evening 82,535.

### Kyushu Island

**Kagoshima Shimpo:** 7-28, Jonan-cho, Kagoshima 892-8551; tel. (99) 226-2100; f. 1959; morning; Dir and Man. Editor JUNSUKE KINOSHITA; circ. 40,045.

**Kumamoto Nichi-Nichi Shimbun:** 2-33, Kamitori-cho, Kumamoto 860-8505; tel. (96) 327-3111; f. 1942; Man. Editor HIROSHI KAWARABATA; circ. morning 385,087, evening 100,464.

**Kyushu Sports:** Fukuoka Tenjin Centre Bldg, 2-14-8, Tenjin-cho, Chuo-ku, Fukuoka 810-0001; tel. (92) 781-7401; f. 1966; morning; Head Officer HIROSHI MITOMI; circ. 471,740.

**Minami Nippon Shimbun:** 1-2, Yasui-cho, Kagoshima 892-8684; tel. (99) 225-9713; fax (99) 224-1490; e-mail tuusin@po.minc.ne.jp; internet www.minaminippon.co.jp; f. 1881; Editor KEITEN NISHIMURA; circ. morning 402,000, evening 27,800.

**Miyazaki Nichi-Nichi Shimbun:** 1-1-33, Takachihodori, Miyazaki 880-8570; tel. (985) 26-9315; f. 1940; morning; Man. Editor MASAAKI MINAMIMURA; circ. 234,109.

**Nagasaki Shimbun:** 3-1, Morimachi, Nagasaki 852-8601; tel. (958) 44-2111; f. 1889; Dir and Man. Editor KOJI UMEHARA; circ. morning 195,349.

**Nankai Nichi-Nichi Shimbun:** 10-3, Nagahama-cho, Naze 894-8601; tel. (997) 53-2121; f. 1946; morning; Man. Editor TERUMI MATSUI; circ. 24,083.

**Nishi Nippon Shimbun:** 1-4-1, Tenjin, Chuo-ku, Fukuoka 810-8721; tel. (92) 711-5555; f. 1877; Exec. Dir and Man. Editor TAKAMICHI TAMAGAWA; circ. morning 848,479, evening 190,814.

**Nishi Nippon Sports:** 1-4-1, Tenjin, Chuo-ku, Fukuoka 810; tel. (92) 711-5555; f. 1954; Man. Editor KENJI ISHIZAKI; circ. 179,089.

**Oita Godo Shimbun:** 3-9-15, Fudai-cho, Oita 870-8605; tel. (975) 36-2121; f. 1886; Dir and Man. Editor MASAKATSU TANABE; circ. morning 239,306, evening 239,287.

**Okinawa Times:** 2-2-2, Kumoji, Naha 900-8678; tel. (98) 860-3000; f. 1948; Pres. and Editor-in-Chief RYOICHI TOYOHIRA; circ. morning 200,662, evening 200,226.

**Ryukyu Shimpo:** 1-10-3, Izumisaki, Naha 900-8525; tel. (98) 865-5111; f. 1893; Man. Editor TOMOKAZU TAKAMINE; circ. 197,469.

**Saga Shimbun:** 3-2-23, Tenjin, Saga 840-8585; tel. (952) 28-2111; fax (952) 29-4829; f. 1884; morning; Man. Editor TERUHIKO WASHIZAKI; circ. 136,766.

**Yaeyama Mainichi Shimbun:** 614, Tonoshiro, Ishigaki 907-0004; tel. (9808) 2-2121; f. 1950; morning; Exec. Dir and Man. Editor YOSHIO UECHI; circ. 14,500.

## WEEKLIES

**An-An:** Magazine House, 3-13-10, Ginza, Chuo-ku, Tokyo 104-03; tel. (3) 3545-7050; fax (3) 3546-0034; f. 1970; fashion; Editor MIYOKO YODOGAWA; circ. 650,000.

**Asahi Graphic:** Asahi Shimbun Publishing Dept, 5-3-2, Tsukiji, Chuo-ku, Tokyo 104-11; tel. (3) 3545-0131; f. 1923; pictorial review; Editor KIYOKAZU TANNO; circ. 120,000.

**Diamond Weekly:** Diamond Inc, 1-4-2, Kasumigaseki, Chiyoda-ku, Tokyo 100; tel. (3) 3504-6250; f. 1913; economics; Editor YUTAKA IWASA; circ. 78,000.

**Focus:** Shincho-Sha, 71, Yaraicho, Shinjuku-ku, Tokyo 162; tel. (3) 3266-5271; fax (3) 3266-5390; politics, economics, sport; Editor KAZUMASA TAJIMA; circ. 850,000.

**Friday:** Kodan-Sha Co Ltd, 2-12-21, Otowa, Bunkyo-ku, Tokyo 112; tel. (3) 5395-3440; fax (3) 3943-8582; current affairs; Editor-in-Chief TETSU SUZUKI; circ. 1m.

**Hanako:** Magazine House, 3-13-10, Ginza, Chuo-ku, Tokyo 104-03; tel. (3) 3545-7070; fax (3) 3546-0994; f. 1988; consumer guide; Editor KOJI TOMONO; circ. 350,000.

**Nikkei Business:** Nikkei Business Publications Inc, 2-7-6, Hirakawa-cho, Chiyoda-ku, Tokyo 102; tel. (3) 5210-8111; fax (3) 5210-8112; f. 1969; Editor-in-Chief KIYOSHI OOYA; circ. 296,720.

**Shukan Asahi:** Asahi Shimbun Publishing Dept, 5-3-2, Tsukiji, Chuo-ku, Tokyo 104-11; tel. (3) 3545-0131; f. 1922; general interest; Editor-in-Chief CHIAHI OMORI; circ. 482,000.

**Shukan Bunshun:** Bungei-Shunju Ltd, 3-23, Kioicho, Chiyoda-ku, Tokyo 102; tel. (3) 3265-1211; f. 1959; general interest; Editor KIYONDO MATSUI; circ. 800,000.

**Shukan Gendai:** Kodan-Sha Co Ltd, 2-12-21, Otowa, Bunkyo-ku, Tokyo 112; tel. (3) 5395-3438; fax (3) 3943-7815; f. 1959; general; Editor MASAHIKO MOTOKI; circ. 550,000.

**Shukan Josei:** Shufu-To-Seikatsu Sha Ltd, 3-5-7, Kyobashi, Chuo-ku, Tokyo 104; tel. (3) 3563-5130; fax (3) 3563-2073; f. 1957; women's interest; Editor HIDEO KIKUCHI; circ. 638,000.

**Shukan Post:** Shogakukan Publishing Co Ltd, 2-3-1, Hitotsubashi, Chiyoda-ku, Tokyo 101-01; tel. (3) 3230-5951; f. 1969; general; Editor NORIMICHI OKANARI; circ. 696,000.

**Shukan Shincho:** Shincho-Sha, 71, Yarai-cho, Shinjuku-ku, Tokyo 162; tel. (3) 3266-5311; fax (3) 3266-5622; f. 1956; general interest; Editor HIROSHI MATSUDA; circ. 521,000.

**Shukan SPA:** Fuso-Sha Co, 1-15-1, Kaigan, Minato-ku, Tokyo 105; tel. (3) 5403-8875; f. 1952; general interest; Editor-in-Chief TOSHIHIKO SATO; circ. 400,000.

**Shukan ST:** Japan Times Ltd, 4-5-4, Shibaura, Minato-ku, Tokyo 108-0023; tel. (3) 3452-4077; fax (3) 3452-3303; e-mail shukanst@japantimes.co.jp; f. 1951; English and Japanese; Editor MITSURU TANAKA; circ. 150,000.

**Shukan Yomiuri:** Yomiuri Shimbun Publication Dept, 1-2-1, Kiyosumi, Koto-ku, Tokyo 135; tel. (3) 5245-7001; f. 1938; general interest; Editor SHINI KAGEYAMA; circ. 453,000.

**Sunday Mainichi:** Mainichi Newspapers Publishing Dept, 1-1-1, Hitotsubashi, Chiyoda-ku, Tokyo 100-51; tel. (3) 3212-0321; fax (3) 3212-0769; f. 1922; general interest; Editor KENJI MIKI; circ. 237,000.

**Tenji Mainichi:** Mainichi Newspapers Publishing Dept, 3-4-5, Umeda, Osaka; tel. (6) 6346-8386; fax (6) 6346-8385; f. 1922; in Japanese braille; Editor TADAMITSU MORIOKA; circ. 12,000.

**Weekly Economist:** Mainichi Newspapers Publishing Dept, 1-1-1, Hitotsubashi, Chiyoda-ku, Tokyo 100-51; tel. (3) 3212-0321; f. 1923; Editorial Chief NOBUHIRO SHUDO; circ. 120,000.

**Weekly Toyo Keizai:** Toyo Keizai Inc, 1-2-1, Hongoku-cho, Nihonbashi, Chuo-ku, Tokyo 103-8345; tel. (3) 3246-5470; fax (3) 3270-0159; f. 1895; business and economics; Editor TOSHIKI OTA; circ. 62,000.

## PERIODICALS

**All Yomimono:** Bungei-Shunju Ltd, 3-23, Kioicho, Chiyoda-ku, Tokyo 102; tel. (3) 3265-1211; fax (3) 3239-5481; f. 1930; monthly; popular fiction; Editor KOICHI SASAMOTO; circ. 95,796.

**Any:** 1-3-14, Hirakawa-cho, Chiyoda-ku, Tokyo 102; tel. (3) 5276-2200; fax (3) 5276-2209; f. 1989; every 2 weeks; women's interest; Editor YUKIO MIWA; circ. 380,000.

**Asahi Camera:** Asahi Shimbun Publishing Dept, 5-3-2, Tsukiji, Chuo-ku, Tokyo 104-8011; tel. (3) 3545-0131; fax (3) 5565-3286; f. 1926; monthly; photography; Editor HIROSHI HIROSE; circ. 90,000.

**Balloon:** Shufunotomo Co Ltd, 2-9, Kanda Surugadai, Chiyoda-ku, Tokyo 101; tel. (3) 3294-1132; fax (3) 3291-5093; f. 1986; monthly; expectant mothers; Dir MARIKO HOSODA; circ. 250,000.

**Brutus:** Magazine House, 3-13-10, Ginza, Chuo-ku, Tokyo 104-03; tel. (3) 3545-7000; fax (3) 3546-0034; f. 1980; every 2 weeks; men's interest; Editor KOICHI TETSUKA; circ. 250,000.

**Bungei-Shunju:** Bungei-Shunju Ltd, 3-23, Kioicho, Chiyoda-ku, Tokyo 102-8008; tel. (3) 3265-1211; fax (3) 3221-6623; f. 1923; monthly; general; Pres. MITSURU ANDO; Editor TAKAHIRO HIRAO; circ. 656,000.

**Business Tokyo:** Keizaikai Bldg, 2-13-18, Minami-Aoyama, Minato-ku, Tokyo 105; tel. (3) 3423-8500; fax (3) 3423-8505; f. 1987; monthly; Dir TAKUO IDA; Editor ANTHONY PAUL; circ. 125,000.

**Chuokoron:** Chuokoron-Sha Inc, 2-8-7, Kyobashi, Chuo-ku, Tokyo 104; tel. (3) 3563-1866; fax (3) 3561-5920; f. 1887; monthly; general interest; Chief Editor KAZUHO MIYA; circ. 100,000.

**Clique:** Magazine House, 3-13-10, Ginza, Chuo-ku, Tokyo 104-03; tel. (3) 3545-7080; fax (3) 3546-0034; f. 1989; every 2 weeks; women's interest; Editor TAKAKO NOGUCHI; circ. 250,000.

**Croissant:** Magazine House, 3-13-10, Ginza, Chuo-ku, Tokyo 104-03; tel. (3) 3545-7111; fax (3) 3546-0034; f. 1977; every 2 weeks; home; Editor MASAAKI TAKEUCHI; circ. 600,000.

**Fujinkoron:** Chuokoron-Sha Inc, 2-8-7, Kyobashi, Chuo-ku, Tokyo 104; tel. (3) 3563-1866; fax (3) 3561-5920; f. 1916; women's literary monthly; Editor YUKIKO YUKAWA; circ. 185,341.

**Geijutsu Shincho:** Shincho-Sha, 71, Yarai-cho, Shinjuku-ku, Tokyo 162-8711; tel. (3) 3266-5381; fax (3) 3266-5387; e-mail geishin@shinchosha.co.jp; f. 1950; monthly; fine arts, music, architecture, films, drama and design; Editor-in-Chief MIDORI YAMAKAWA; circ. 65,000.

**Gendai:** Kodan-Sha Ltd, 2-12-21, Otowa, Bunkyo-ku, Tokyo 112; tel. (3) 5395-3517; fax (3) 3945-9128; f. 1966; monthly; cultural and political; Editor SHUNKICHI YABUKI; circ. 250,000.

**Gunzo:** Kodan-Sha Ltd, 2-12-21, Otowa, Bunkyo-ku, Tokyo 112; tel. (3) 5395-3501; fax (3) 5395-5626; f. 1946; literary monthly; Editor KATSUO WATANABE; circ. 30,000.

**Hot-Dog Press:** Kodan-Sha Ltd, 2-12-21, Otowa, Bunkyo-ku, Tokyo 112-01; tel. (3) 5395-3473; fax (3) 3945-9128; every 2 weeks; men's interest; Editor ATSUHIDE KOKUBO; circ. 650,000.

**Ie-no-Hikari** (Light of Home): Ie-no-Hikari Asscn, 11, Ichigaya Funagawaramachi, Shinjuku-ku, Tokyo 162-8448; tel. (3) 3266-9013; fax (3) 3266-9052; e-mail hikari@mxd.meshnet.or.jp; internet www.mediagalaxy.co.jp/ienohikarinet; f. 1925; monthly; rural and general interest; Pres. SHUZO SUZUKI; Editor KAZUO NAKANO; circ. 928,000.

**Japan Company Handbook:** Toyo Keizai Inc, 1-2-1, Nihonbashi Hongoku-cho, Chuo-ku, Tokyo 103-8345; tel. (3) 3246-5655; fax (3) 3241-5543; f. 1974; quarterly; English; Editor FUSAKAZU IZUMURA; total circ. 100,000.

**Japan Quarterly:** Asahi Shimbun Publishing Co, 5-3-2, Tsukiji, Chuo-ku, Tokyo 104-8011; tel. (3) 5541-8699; fax (3) 5541-8700; e-mail jpnqtrly@mx.asahi-np.co.jp; f. 1954; English; political, economic and cultural; Editor-in-Chief JUN HAGITANI; circ. 10,000.

**Jitsugyo No Nihon:** Jitsugyo No Nihon-Sha Ltd, 1-3-9, Ginza, Chuo-ku, Tokyo 104; tel. (3) 3562-1967; fax (3) 2564-2382; f. 1897; monthly; economics and business; Editor TOSHIO KAWAJIRI; circ. 60,000.

**Junon:** Shufu-To-Seikatsu Sha Ltd, 3-5-7, Kyobashi, Chuo-ku, Tokyo 104; tel. (3) 3563-5132; fax (3) 5250-7081; f. 1973; monthly; television and entertainment; circ. 560,000.

**Kagaku** (Science): Iwanami Shoten Publishers, 2-5-5, Hitotsubashi, Chiyoda-ku, Tokyo 102; tel. (3) 5210-4070; fax (3) 5210-4073; f. 1931; Editor NOBUAKI MIYABE; circ. 29,000.

**Kagaku Asahi:** Asahi Shimbun Publishing Dept, 5-3-2, Tsukiji, Chuo-ku, Tokyo 104-8011; tel. (3) 5540-7810; fax (3) 3546-2404; f. 1941; monthly; scientific; Editor TOSHIHIRO SASAKI; circ. 105,000.

**Keizaijin:** Kansai Economic Federation, Nakanoshima Center Bldg, 6-2-27, Nakanoshima, Kita-ku, Osaka 530-6691; tel. (6) 6441-0105; fax (6) 6443-5347; internet www.kankeiren.or.jp; f. 1947; monthly; economics; Editor M. YASUTAKE; circ. 2,600.

**Lettuce Club:** SS Communications, 11-2, Ban-cho, Chiyoda-ku, Tokyo 102; tel. (3) 5276-2151; fax (3) 5276-2229; f. 1987; every 2 weeks; cookery; Editor MITSURU NAKAYA; circ. 800,000.

**Money Japan:** SS Communications, 11-2, Ban-cho, Chiyoda-ku, Tokyo 102; tel. (3) 5276-2220; fax (3) 5276-2229; f. 1985; monthly; finance; Editor TOSHIO KOBAYASHI; circ. 500,000.

**Popeye:** Magazine House, 3-13-10, Ginza, Chuo-ku, Tokyo 104-8003; tel. (3) 3545-7160; fax (3) 3546-0034; f. 1976; every 2 weeks; fashion, teenage interest; Editor SHINICHIRO ONODERA; circ. 320,000.

**President:** President Inc, Bridgestone Hirakawacho Bldg, 2-13-12, Hirakawa-cho, Chiyoda-ku, Tokyo 102; tel. (3) 3237-3737; fax (3) 3237-3748; internet www.president.co.jp; f. 1963; monthly; business; Editor KAYOKO ABE; circ. 263,308.

**Ray:** Shufunotomo Co Ltd, 2-9, Kanda Surugadai, Chiyoda-ku, Tokyo 101; tel. (3) 3294-1163; fax (3) 3291-5093; f. 1988; monthly; women's interest; Editor TATSURO NAKANISHI; circ. 450,000.

**Ryoko Yomiuri:** Ryoko Yomiuri Publications Inc, 2-2-15, Ginza, Chuo-ku, Tokyo 104; tel. (3) 3561-8911; fax (3) 3561-8950; f. 1966; monthly; travel; Editor TETSUO KINUGAWA; circ. 470,000.

**Sekai:** Iwanami Shoten Publishers, 2-5-5, Hitotsubashi, Chiyoda-ku, Tokyo 101; tel. (3) 5210-4141; fax (3) 5210-4144; internet www.iwanami.co.jp/sekai; f. 1946; monthly; review of world and domestic affairs; Editor ATSUSHI OKAMOTO; circ. 120,000.

**Shinkenchiku:** Shinkenchiku-Sha Co Ltd, 2-31-2, Yushima, Bunkyo-ku, Tokyo 113; tel. (3) 3814-2251; fax (3) 3812-8187; e-mail ja-business@japan-architecture.co.jp; internet www.japan-architect.co.jp; f. 1925; monthly; architecture; Editor YASUHIRO TERAMATSU; circ. 87,000.

**Shiso** (Thought): Iwanami Shoten Publishers, 2-5-5, Hitotsubashi, Chiyoda-ku, Tokyo 101-8002; tel. (3) 5210-4055; fax (3) 5210-4037; e-mail shiso@iwanami.co.jp; internet www.iwanami.co.jp/shiso; f. 1921; monthly; philosophy, social sciences and humanities; Editor KIYOSHI KOJIMA; circ. 20,000.

**Shosetsu Shincho:** Shincho-Sha, 71, Yarai-cho, Shinjuku-ku, Tokyo 162-8711; tel. (3) 3266-5241; fax (3) 3266-5412; internet www.shincho.net/magazines/shosetsushincho; f. 1947; monthly; literature; Editor-in-Chief TSUYOSHI MENJO; circ. 80,000.

**Shufunotomo:** Shufunotomo Co Ltd, 2-9, Kanda Surugadai, Chiyoda-ku, Tokyo 101; tel. (3) 5280-7531; fax (3) 5280-7431; f. 1917; monthly; home and lifestyle; Editor KYOKO FURUTO; circ. 450,000.

**So-en:** Bunka Publishing Bureau, 4-12-7, Hon-cho, Shibuya-ku, Tokyo 151; tel. (3) 3299-2531; fax (3) 3370-3712; f. 1936; fashion monthly; Editor KEIKO SASAKI; circ. 270,000.

## NEWS AGENCIES

**Jiji Tsushin** (Jiji Press Ltd): Shisei Bldg, 1-3, Hibiya Park, Chiyoda-ku, Tokyo 100-8568; tel. (3) 3591-1111; e-mail info@tky.jiji.co.jp; f. 1945; Pres. MASATOSHI MURAKAMI; Man. Editor KUNIJI OGURO.

**Kyodo Tsushin** (Kyodo News): 2-2-5, Toranomon, Minato-ku, Tokyo 105-8474; tel. (3) 5573-8081; fax (3) 5573-8082; e-mail kokusai@hq.kyodo.co.jp; internet www.kyodo.co.jp; f. 1945; Pres. ICHIRO SAITA; Man. Editor KAZUYOSHI SUZUKI.

**Radiopress Inc:** R-Bldg Shinjuku, 33-8, Wakamatsu-cho, Shinjuku-ku, Tokyo 162-0056; tel. (3) 5273-2171; fax (3) 5273-2180; e-mail rptokyo@oak.ocn.ne.jp; f. 1945; provides news from China, the former USSR, Democratic People's Repub. of Korea, Viet Nam and elsewhere to the press and govt offices; Pres. YOSHITOMO TANAKA.

**Sun Telephoto:** Palaceside Bldg, 1-1-1, Hitotsubashi, Chiyoda-ku, Tokyo 100-0003; tel. (3) 3213-6771; e-mail webmaster@suntele.co.jp;

internet www.suntele.co.jp; f. 1952; Pres. KOZO TAKINO; Man. Editor KIYOSHI HIRAI.

### Foreign Bureaux

**Agence France-Presse (AFP):** Asahi Shimbun Bldg, 11th Floor, 5-3-2, Tsukiji, Chuo-ku, Tokyo 104-0045; tel. (3) 3545-3061; fax (3) 3546-2594; Bureau Chief PHILIPPE RIES.

**Agencia EFE** (Spain): Kyodo Tsushin Bldg, 9th Floor, 2-2-5, Toranomon, Minato-ku, Tokyo 105-0001; tel. (3) 3585-8940; fax (3) 3585-8948; Bureau Chief CARLOS DOMÍNGUEZ.

**Agenzia Nazionale Stampa Associata (ANSA)** (Italy): Kyodo Tsushin Bldg, 9th Floor, 2-2-5, Toranomon, Minato-ku, Tokyo 105-0001; tel. (3) 3584-6667; fax (3) 3584-5114; Bureau Chief ALBERTO ZANCONATO.

**Antara** (Indonesia): Kyodo Tsushin Bldg, 9th Floor, 2-2-5, Toranomon, Minato-ku, Tokyo 105-0001; tel. (3) 3584-4234; fax (3) 3584-4591; Correspondent MARIA ANDRIANA.

**Associated Press (AP)** (USA): Asahi Shimbun Bldg, 11th Floor, 5-3-2, Tsukiji, Chuo-ku, Tokyo 104-0045; tel. (3) 3545-5902; fax (3) 3545-0895; internet www.ap.org; Bureau Chief JAMES C. LAGIER.

**Central News Agency** (Taiwan): 3-7-3-302, Shimo-meguro, Meguro-ku, Tokyo 153-0064; tel. (3) 3495-2046; fax (3) 3495-2066; Bureau Chief CHANG FANG MIN.

**Deutsche Presse-Agentur (dpa)** (Germany): Nippon Press Center, 3rd Floor, 2-2-1, Uchisaiwai-cho, Chiyoda-ku, Tokyo 100-0011; tel. (3) 3580-6629; fax (3) 3593-7888; Bureau Chief LARS NICOLAYSEN.

**Informatsionnoye Telegrafnoye Agentstvo Rossii—Telegrafnoye Agentstvo Suverennykh Stran (ITAR—TASS)** (Russia): 1-5-1, Hon-cho, Shibuya-ku, Tokyo 151-0071; tel. (3) 3377-0380; fax (3) 3378-0606; Bureau Chief VASILII GOLOVNIN.

**Inter Press Service (IPS)** (Italy): 1-15-19, Ishikawa-machi, Ota-ku, Tokyo 145-0061; tel. (3) 3726-7944; fax (3) 3726-7896; Correspondent SUVENDRINI KAKUCHI.

**Magyar Távirati Iroda (MTI)** (Hungary): 1-3-4-306, Okamoto, Setagaya-ku, Tokyo 157-0076; tel. (3) 3708-3093; fax (3) 3708-2703; Bureau Chief JÁNOS MARTON.

**Reuters** (UK): Shuwa Kamiya-cho Bldg, 5th Floor, 4-3-13, Toranomon, Minato-ku, Tokyo 105-0001; tel. (3) 3432-4141; fax (3) 3433-2921; Editor WILLIAM SPOSATO.

**Rossiiskoye Informatsionnoye Agentstvo—Novosti (RIA—Novosti)** (Russia): 3-9-13 Higashi-gotanda, Shinagawa-ku, Tokyo 141-0022; tel. (3) 3441-9241; fax (3) 3447-3538; Bureau Chief ANDREI ILIACHENKO.

**United Press International (UPI)** (USA): Ferrare Bldg, 4th Floor, 1-24-15, Ebisu, Shibuya-ku, Tokyo 150-0013; tel. (3) 5421-1333; fax (3) 5421-1339; Bureau Chief RUTH YOUNGBLOOD.

**Xinhua (New China) News Agency** (People's Republic of China): 3-35-23, Ebisu, Shibuya-ku, Tokyo 150-0013; tel. (3) 3441-3766; fax (3) 3446-3995; Bureau Chief WANG DAJUN.

**Yonhap (United) News Agency** (Republic of Korea): Kyodo Tsushin Bldg, 2-2-5, Toranomon, Minato-ku, Tokyo 105-0001; tel. (3) 3584-4681; fax (3) 3584-4021; f. 1945; Bureau Chief MOON YOUNG SHIK.

### PRESS ASSOCIATIONS

**Foreign Correspondents' Club of Japan:** 20th Floor, 1-7-1, Yuraku-cho, Chiyoda-ku, Tokyo 100-0006; tel. (3) 3211-3161; fax (3) 3211-3168; e-mail katayama@fccj.or.jp; internet www.fccj.or.jp; f. 1945; 193 companies; Pres. ROGER SCHREFFLER; Man. KENJI KATAYAMA.

**Foreign Press Center:** Nippon Press Center Bldg, 6th Floor, 2-2-1, Uchisaiwai-cho, Chiyoda-ku, Tokyo 100-0011; tel. (3) 3501-3401; fax (3) 3501-3622; internet www.nttls.co.jp/fpc; f. 1976; est. by the Japan Newspaper Publrs' and Editors' Asscn and the Japan Fed. of Economic Orgs; provides services to the foreign press; Pres. YOSHIO HATANO; Man. Dir TOKUJI HOSONO.

**Nihon Shinbun Kyokai** (The Japan Newspaper Publishers and Editors Asscn): Nippon Press Center Bldg, 2-2-1, Uchisaiwai-cho, Chiyoda-ku, Tokyo 100-8543; tel. (3) 3591-3462; fax (3) 3591-6149; e-mail s_intl@pressnet.or.jp; internet www.pressnet.or.jp; f. 1946; mems include 154 companies (110 daily newspapers, 5 news agencies and 39 radio and TV companies); Chair. TSUNEO WATANABE; Man. Dir and Sec.-Gen. SHIGEMI MURAKAMI.

**Nihon Zasshi Kyokai** (Japan Magazine Publishers Asscn): 1-7, Kanda Surugadai, Chiyoda-ku, Tokyo 101-0062; tel. (3) 3291-0775; fax (3) 3293-6239; f. 1956; 85 mems; Pres. HARUHIKO ISHIKAWA; Sec. GENYA INUI.

## Publishers

**Akane Shobo Co Ltd:** 3-2-1, Nishikanda, Chiyoda-ku, Tokyo 101-0065; tel. (3) 3263-0641; fax (3) 3263-5440; f. 1949; juvenile; Pres. MASAHARU OKAMOTO.

**Akita Publishing Co Ltd:** 2-10-8, Iidabashi, Chiyoda-ku, Tokyo 102-8101; tel. (3) 3264-7011; fax (3) 3265-9076; f. 1948; social sciences, history, juvenile; Chair. SADAO AKITA; Pres. SADAMI AKITA.

**ALC Press Inc:** 2-54-12, Eifuku, Suginami-ku, Tokyo 168-0064; tel. (3) 3323-1101; fax (3) 3327-1022; f. 1969; linguistics, educational materials, dictionary, juvenile; Pres. TERUMARO HIRAMOTO.

**Asahi Shimbun Publications Division:** 5-3-2, Tsukiji, Chuo-ku, Tokyo 100-0000; tel. (3) 3545-0131; fax (3) 3545-0311; f. 1879; general; Pres. MUNEYUKI MATSUSHITA; Dir of Publications HISAO KUWASHIMA.

**Asakura Publishing Co Ltd:** 6-29, Shin Ogawa-machi, Shinjuku-ku, Tokyo 162-8707; tel. (3) 3260-0141; fax (3) 3260-0180; e-mail edit@asakura.co.jp; internet www.asakura.co.jp; f. 1929; natural science, medicine, social sciences; Pres. KUNIZO ASAKURA.

**Baifukan Co Ltd:** 4-3-12, Kudan Minami, Chiyoda-ku, Tokyo 102-0074; tel. (3) 3262-5256; fax (3) 3262-5276; f. 1924; engineering, natural and social sciences, psychology; Pres. ITARU YAMAMOTO.

**Baseball Magazine-Sha:** 3-10-10, Misaki-cho, Chiyoda-ku, Tokyo 101-8381; tel. (3) 3238-0081; fax (3) 3238-0106; internet www.bbm-japan.com; f. 1946; sports, physical education, recreation, travel; Chair. TSUNEO IKEDA; Pres. TETSUO IKEDA.

**Bijutsu Shuppan-Sha Ltd:** Inaoka Bldg, 6th Floor, 2-36, Kanda Jimbo-cho, Chiyoda-ku, Tokyo 101-8417; tel. (3) 3234-2151; fax (3) 3234-9451; f. 1905; fine arts, graphic design; Pres. ATSUSHI OSHITA.

**Bonjinsha Co Ltd:** 1-3-13, Hirakawa-cho, Chiyoda-ku, Tokyo 102; tel. (3) 3262-4129; fax (3) 3263-6705; f. 1973; Japanese language teaching materials; Pres. HISAMITSU TANAKA.

**Bungeishunju Ltd:** 3-23, Kioi-cho, Chiyoda-ku, Tokyo 102-8008; tel. (3) 3265-1211; fax (3) 3239-5482; internet www.bunshun.topica.ne.jp; f. 1923; fiction, general literature, recreation, economics, sociology; Dir KENGO TANAKA.

**Chikuma Shobo:** Komuro Bldg, 2-5-3, Kuramae, Taito-ku, Tokyo 111-8755; tel. (3) 5687-2680; fax (3) 5687-2685; f. 1940; general literature, fiction, history, juvenile, fine arts; Pres. AKIO KIKUCHI.

**Child-Honsha Co Ltd:** 5-24-21, Koishikawa, Bunkyo-ku, Tokyo 112-0002; tel. (3) 3813-3781; fax (3) 3813-3765; f. 1930; juvenile; Pres. YOSHIAKI SHIMAZAKI.

**Chuokoron-Sha Inc:** 2-8-7, Kyobashi, Chuo-ku, Tokyo 104-0031; tel. (3) 3563-1261; fax (3) 3561-5920; f. 1886; philosophy, history, sociology, general literature; Chair. MASAKO SHIMANAKA; Pres. YUKIO SHIMANAKA.

**Corona Publishing Co Ltd:** 4-46-10, Sengoku, Bunkyo-ku, Tokyo 112-0011; tel. (3) 3941-3131; fax (3) 3447-4666; e-mail corona-3@magical.egg.or; f. 1927; electronics business publs; Pres. TATSUMI GORAI.

**Dempa Publications Inc:** 1-11-15, Higashi Gotanda, Shinagawa-ku, Tokyo 141-0022; tel. (3) 3445-6111; fax (3) 3444-7515; f. 1950; electronics, personal computer software, juvenile, trade newspapers; Pres. TETSUO HIRAYAMA.

**Diamond Inc:** 6-12-17, Jingumae, Shibuya-ku, Tokyo 150-8409; tel. (3) 5778-7203; fax (3) 5778-6612; e-mail mitachi@diamond.co.jp; internet www.diamond.co.jp; f. 1913; business, management, economics, financial; Pres. YUTAKA IWASA.

**Dohosha Ltd:** TAS Bldg, 2-5-2, Nishikanda, Chiyoda-ku, Tokyo 101-0065; tel. (3) 5276-0831; fax (3) 5276-0840; e-mail intl@doho-sha.co.jp; f. 1997; general works, architecture, art, Buddhism, business, children's education, cooking, flower arranging, gardening, medicine.

**Froebel-Kan Co Ltd:** 6-14-9, Honkomagome, Bunkyo-ku, Tokyo 113-8611; tel. (3) 5395-6614; fax (3) 5395-6627; e-mail soumu@froebel-kan.co.jp; f. 1907; juvenile, educational; Pres. KENNOSUKE ARAI; Dir HARRY IDICHI.

**Fukuinkan Shoten, Publishers Inc:** 6-6-3, Honkomagome, Bunkyo-ku, Tokyo 113-8686; tel. (3) 3942-0032; fax (3) 3942-1401; f. 1952; juvenile; Pres. SHIRO TOKITA; Chair. KATSUMI SATO.

**Gakken Co Ltd:** 4-40-5, Kamiikedai, Ohta-ku, Tokyo 145-0064; tel. (3) 3726-8111; fax (3) 3493-3338; f. 1946; juvenile, educational, art, encyclopaedias, dictionaries; Pres. KAZUHIKO SAWADA.

**Graphic-sha Publishing Co Ltd:** 1-9-12, Kudan Kita, Chiyoda-ku, Tokyo 102-0073; tel. (3) 3263-4318; fax (3) 3263-5297; e-mail info@graphicsha.co.jp; internet www.graphicsha.co.jp; f. 1963; art, design, hobbies; Pres. TOSHIRO KUZE.

**Gyosei Corpn:** 4-30-16, Ogikubo, Suginami-ku, Tokyo 167-8088; tel. (3) 5349-6666; fax (3) 5349-6677; e-mail business@gyosei.co.jp; internet www.gyosei.co.jp; f. 1893; law, education, science, politics, business, art, language, literature, juvenile; Pres. MOTOO FUJISAWA.

**Hakusui-Sha Co Ltd:** 3-24, Kanda Ogawa-machi, Chiyoda-ku, Tokyo 101-0052; tel. (3) 3291-7821; fax (3) 3291-7810; f. 1915; general literature, science and languages; Pres. KAZUAKI FUJIWARA.

**Hayakawa Publishing Inc:** 2-2, Kanda-Tacho, Chiyoda-ku, Tokyo 101-0046; tel. (3) 3252-3111; fax (3) 3254-1550; f. 1945; science fiction, mystery, autobiography, literature, fantasy; Pres. HIROSHI HAYAKAWA.

**Heibonsha Ltd Publishers:** 5-16-19, Himonya, Meguro-ku, Tokyo 152-8601; tel. (3) 5721-1241; fax (3) 5721-1249; internet www.heibonsha.co.jp; f. 1914; encyclopaedias, art, history, geography, literature, science; Pres. NAOTO SHIMONAKA.

**Hirokawa Publishing Co:** 3-27-14, Hongo, Bunkyo-ku, Tokyo 113-0033; tel. (3) 3815-3651; fax (3) 5684-7030; f. 1925; natural sciences, medicine, pharmacy, nursing, chemistry; Pres. SETSUO HIROKAWA.

**Hoikusha Publishing Co:** 1-6-12, Kawamata, Higashi, Osaka 577-0063; tel. (6) 6788-4470; fax (6) 6788-4970; internet www.hoikusha.co.jp; f. 1947; natural science, juvenile, fine arts, geography; Pres. YUKI IMAI.

**Hokuryukan Co Ltd:** 3-8-14, Takanawa, Minato-ku, Tokyo 108-0074; tel. (3) 5449-4591; fax (3) 5449-4950; e-mail hk-ns@mk1.macnet.or.jp; internet www.macnet.or.jp/co/hk-ns; f. 1891; natural science, medical science, juvenile, dictionaries; Pres. HISAKO FUKUDA.

**The Hokuseido Press:** 3-32-4, Honkomagome, Bunkyo-ku, Tokyo 113-0021; tel. (3) 3827-0551; fax (3) 3827-0567; f. 1914; regional non-fiction, dictionaries, textbooks; Pres. MASAZO YAMAMOTO.

**Ie-No-Hikari Association:** 11, Funagawara-cho, Ichigaya, Shinjuku-ku, Tokyo 162-8448; tel. (3) 3266-9000; fax (3) 3266-9048; e-mail hikari@mxd.meshnet.or.jp; internet www.mediagalaxy.co.jp/ienohikarinet; f. 1925; social science, agriculture; Chair. SHUZO SUZUKI; Pres. KATSURO KAWAGUCHI.

**Igaku-Shoin Ltd:** 5-24-3, Hongo, Bunkyo-ku, Tokyo 113-8719; tel. (3) 3817-5610; fax (3) 3815-4114; e-mail info@igaku-shoin.co; internet www.igaku-shoin.co.jp; f. 1944; medicine, nursing; Pres. YU KANEHARA.

**Institute for Financial Affairs Inc (KINZAI):** 19, Minami-Motomachi, Shinjuku-ku, Tokyo 160-0012; tel. (3) 3358-1161; fax (3) 3359-7947; e-mail JDI04072@nifty.ne.or.jp; f. 1950; finance and economics, banking laws and regulations, accounting; Pres. MASATERU YOSHIDA.

**Ishiyaku Publishers Inc:** 1-7-10, Honkomagome, Bunkyo-ku, Tokyo 113-8612; tel. (3) 5395-7600; fax (3) 5395-7606; e-mail dev-mdp@nna.so-net.or.jp; internet www.so-net.or.jp/medipro/isyk; f. 1921; medicine, dentistry, rehabilitation, nursing, nutrition and pharmaceutics; Pres. HIROSHI MIURA.

**Iwanami Shoten, Publishers:** 2-5-5, Hitotsubashi, Chiyoda-ku, Tokyo 101-8002; tel. (3) 5210-4000; fax (3) 5210-4039; internet www.iwanami.co.jp; f. 1913; natural and social sciences, literature, fine arts, juvenile, dictionaries; Pres. NOBUKAZU OTSUKA.

**Japan Broadcast Publishing Co Ltd:** 41-1, Udagawa-cho, Shibuya-ku, Tokyo 150-8081; tel. (3) 3464-7311; fax (3) 3780-3353; e-mail webmaster@npb.nhk-grp.co.jp; internet www.nhk-grp.co.jp/npb; f. 1931; foreign language textbooks, gardening, home economics, sociology, education, art, juvenile; Pres. TATSUO ANDO.

**Japan External Trade Organization (JETRO):** 2-2-5, Toranomon, Minato-ku, Tokyo 105-8466; tel. (3) 3582-5512; fax (3) 3582-5662; internet www.jetro.go.jp; f. 1958; trade, economics, investment; Pres. SHOJI ISAKI.

**Japan Publications Trading Co Ltd:** 1-2-1, Sarugaku-cho, Chiyoda-ku, Tokyo 101-0064; tel. (3) 3292-3751; fax (3) 3292-0410; e-mail jpt@po.iijnet.or.jp; internet www.jptco.co.jp; f. 1942; general works, art, health, sports; Pres. SATOMI NAKABAYASHI.

**The Japan Times Ltd:** 4-5-4, Shibaura, Minato-ku, Tokyo 108-0023; tel. (3) 3453-2013; fax (3) 3453-8023; e-mail XLM05254@nifty.ne.jp; internet www.bookclub.japantimes.co.jp; f. 1897; linguistics, culture, business; Pres. TOSHIAKI OGASAWARA.

**Japan Travel Bureau Inc:** Shibuya Nomura Bldg, 1-10-8, Dogenzaka, Shibuya-ku, Tokyo 150-8558; tel. (3) 3477-9521; fax (3) 3477-9538; internet www.jtb.co.jp; f. 1912; travel, geography, history, fine arts, languages; Vice-Pres. MITSUMASA IWATA.

**Jimbun Shoin:** 9, Nishiuchihata-cho, Takeda, Fushimi-ku, Kyoto 612-8447; tel. (75) 603-1344; fax (75) 603-1814; e-mail edjimbun@mbox.kyoto-inet.or.jp; internet www.jimbunshoin.co.jp; f. 1922; general literature, philosophy, fiction, social science, religion, fine arts; Pres. MUTSUHISA WATANABE.

**Kadokawa Shoten Publishing Co Ltd:** 2-13-3, Fujimi, Chiyoda-ku, Tokyo 102-0071; tel. (3) 3238-8611; fax (3) 3238-8612; f. 1945; literature, history, dictionaries, religion, fine arts, books on tape, compact discs, CD-ROM, comics, animation, video cassettes, computer games; Pres. TSUGUHIKO KADOKAWA.

**Kaibundo Publishing Co Ltd:** 2-5-4, Suido, Bunkyo-ku, Tokyo 112-0005; tel. (3) 5684-6289; fax (3) 3815-3953; f. 1914; marine affairs, natural science, engineering, industry; Pres. YOSHIHIRO OKADA.

**Kaiseisha Publishing Co Ltd:** 3-5, Ichigaya Sadohara-cho, Shinjuku-ku, Tokyo 162-8450; tel. (3) 3260-3229; fax (3) 3260-3540; f. 1936; juvenile; Pres. MASAKI IMAMURA.

**Kanehara & Co Ltd:** 2-31-14, Yushima, Bunkyo-ku, Tokyo 113-8687; tel. (3) 3811-7185; fax (3) 3813-0288; f. 1875; medical, agricultural, engineering and scientific; Pres. SABURO KOMURO.

**Kenkyusha Ltd:** 2-11-3, Fujimi, Chiyoda-ku, Tokyo 102-8152; tel. (3) 3288-7711; fax (3) 3288-7821; e-mail kenkyusha-hanbai@in.aix.or.jp; internet www2.aix.or.jp/kenkyusha; f. 1907; bilingual dictionaries; Pres. KATSUYUKI IKEGAMI.

**Kinokuniya Co Ltd:** 5-38-1, Sakuragaoka, Setagaya-ku, Tokyo 156-8691; tel. (3) 3439-0172; fax (3) 3439-0173; e-mail publish@kinokuniya.co.jp; internet www.kinokuniya.co.jp; f. 1927; humanities, social science, natural science; Pres. OSAMU MATSUBARA.

**Kodansha International Ltd:** 1-17-14, Otowa, Bunkyo-ku, Tokyo 112-8652; tel. (3) 3944-6492; fax (3) 3944-6323; e-mail sales@kodansha-intl.co.jp; f. 1963; art, business, cookery, crafts, gardening, language, literature, martial arts; Pres. SAWAKO NOMA.

**Kodansha Ltd:** 2-12-21, Otowa, Bunkyo-ku, Tokyo 112-8001; tel. (3) 5395-3574; fax (3) 3944-9915; f. 1909; fine arts, fiction, literature, juvenile, comics, dictionaries; Pres. SAWAKO NOMA.

**Kosei Publishing Co Ltd:** 2-7-1, Wada, Suginami-ku, Tokyo 166-8535; tel. (3) 5385-2309; fax (3) 5385-2331; e-mail kspub@ppp.bekkoame.or.jp; internet www.mediagalaxy.co.jp/kosei/index1.html; f. 1966; general works, philosophy, religion, history, pedagogy, social science, art, juvenile; Pres. TEIZO KURIYAMA.

**Kyoritsu Shuppan Co Ltd:** 4-6-19, Kohinata, Bunkyo-ku, Tokyo 112-8700; tel. (3) 3947-2511; fax (3) 3947-2539; e-mail kyoritsu@po.iijnet.or.jp; internet www.kyoritsu-pub.co.jp; f. 1926; scientific and technical; Pres. MITSUAKI NANJO.

**Maruzen Co Ltd:** 3-9-2, Nihonbashi, Chuo-ku, Tokyo 103-8244; tel. (3) 3272-0521; fax (3) 3272-0693; internet www.maruzen.co.jp; f. 1869; general works; Pres. NOBUO SUZUKI.

**Medical Friend Co Ltd:** 3-2-4, Kudan Kita, Chiyoda-ku, Tokyo 102-0073; tel. (3) 3264-6611; fax (3) 3261-6602; f. 1947; medical and allied science, nursing; Pres. KAZUHARU OGURA.

**Minerva Shobo:** 1, Tsutsumi dani-cho, Hinooka, Yamashina-ku, Kyoto 607-8494; tel. (75) 581-5191; fax (75) 581-0589; e-mail info@minervashobo.co.jp; internet www.minervashobo.co.jp; f. 1948; general non-fiction and reference; Pres. NOBUO SUGITA.

**Misuzu Shobo Ltd:** 5-32-21, Hongo, Bunkyo-ku, Tokyo 113-0033; tel. (3) 3815-9181; fax (3) 3818-8497; f. 1947; general, philosophy, history, psychiatry, literature, science, art; Pres. YUJI OGURA.

**Morikita Shuppan Co Ltd:** 1-4-11, Fujimi, Chiyoda-ku, Tokyo 102-0071; tel. (3) 3265-8341; fax (3) 3264-8709; e-mail info@morikita.co.jp; internet www.morikita.co.jp; f. 1950; natural science, engineering; Pres. HAJIME MORIKITA.

**Nakayama-Shoten Co Ltd:** 1-25-14, Hakusan, Bunkyo-ku, Tokyo 113-0001; tel. (3) 3813-1101; fax (3) 3813-1134; e-mail CZ4H-WKMT@asahi-net.or.jp; internet www.so-net.or.jp/medipro/nakayama/index.htm; f. 1948; medicine, biology, zoology; Pres. TADASHI HIRATA.

**Nanzando Co Ltd:** 4-1-11, Yushima, Bunkyo-ku, Tokyo; tel. (3) 5689-7868; fax (3) 5689-7869; e-mail info@nanzando.com; internet www.nanzando.com; medical reference, paperbacks; Pres. HAJIME SUZUKI.

**Nigensha Publishing Co Ltd:** 2-2, Kanda Jimbo-cho, Chiyoda-ku, Tokyo 101-8419; tel. (3) 5210-4733; fax (3) 5210-4723; e-mail sales@nigensha.co.jp; internet www.nigensha.co.jp; f. 1953; calligraphy, fine arts, art reproductions, cars, watches; Pres. TAKAO WATANABE.

**Nihon Keizai Shimbun Inc, Publications Bureau:** 1-9-5, Otemachi, Chiyoda-ku, Tokyo 100-0004; tel. (3) 3270-0251; fax (3) 5255-2864; f. 1876; economics, business, politics, fine arts, video cassettes, CD-ROM; Pres. MASANORI TAKEUCHI.

**Nihon Vogue Co Ltd:** 3-23, Ichigaya Honmura-cho, Shinjuku-ku, Tokyo 162-8705; tel. (3) 5261-5139; fax (3) 3269-4513; e-mail nvkanri@giganet.net; internet www.creators-guild.co.jp; f. 1954; quilt, needlecraft, handicraft, knitting, decorative painting, pressed flowers; Pres. NOBUAKI SETO.

**Nippon Jitsugyo Publishing Co Ltd:** 3-2-12, Hongo, Bunkyo-ku, Tokyo 113-0033; tel. (3) 3814-5651; fax (3) 3818-2723; e-mail nipojits@po.iijnet.or.jp; internet www.wit.or.jp/njp; f. 1950; business, management, finance and accounting, sales and marketing; Chair. and CEO YOICHIRO NAKAMURA.

**Obunsha Co Ltd:** 78, Yarai-cho, Shinjuku-ku, Tokyo 162-0805; tel. (3) 3266-6000; fax (3) 3266-6291; f. 1931; internet www.obunsha.co.jp; textbooks, reference, general science and fiction, magazines, encyclopaedias, dictionaries; software; audio-visual aids; CEO FUMIO AKAO.

**Ohm-Sha Ltd:** 3-1, Kanda Nishiki-cho, Chiyoda-ku, Tokyo 101-0054; tel. (3) 3233-0641; fax (3) 3233-2426; e-mail kaigaika@ohmsha.co.jp; internet www.ohmsha.co.jp; f. 1914; engineering, technical and scientific; Pres. SEIJI SATO; Dir M. MORI.

**Ondorisha Publishers Ltd:** 11-11, Nishigoken-cho, Shinjuku-ku, Tokyo 162-8708; tel. (3) 3268-3101; fax (3) 3235-3530; f. 1945; knitting, embroidery, patchwork, handicraft books; Pres. HIDEAKI TAKEUCHI.

**Ongaku No Tomo Sha Corpn (ONT):** 6-30, Kagurazaka, Shinjuku-ku, Tokyo 162-0825; tel. (3) 3235-2111; fax (3) 3235-2119; internet www.ongakunotomo.co.jp; f. 1941; compact discs, videograms, music magazines, music books, music data, music textbooks; Pres. JUN MEGURO.

**PHP Institute Inc:** 11, Kitanouchi-cho, Nishikujo, Minami-ku, Kyoto 601-8411; tel. (75) 681-4431; fax (75) 681-9921; internet www.php.co.jp; f. 1946; social science; Pres. MASAHARU MATSUSHITA.

**Poplar Publishing Co Ltd:** 5, Suga-cho, Shinjuku-ku, Tokyo 160-8565; tel. (3) 3357-2216; fax (3) 3351-0736; e-mail henshu@poplar.co.jp; internet www.poplar.co.jp; f. 1947; children's; Pres. HARUO TANAKA.

**Sanseido Co Ltd:** 2-22-14, Misaki-cho, Chiyoda-ku, Tokyo 101-0061; tel. (3) 3230-9411; fax (3) 3230-9547; f. 1881; dictionaries, educational, languages, social and natural science; Chair. HISANORI UENO; Pres. TOSHIO GOMI.

**Sanshusha Publishing Co Ltd:** 1-5-34, Shitaya, Taito-ku, Tokyo 110-0004; tel. (3) 3842-1711; fax (3) 3845-3965; e-mail maeda_k@sanshusha.or.jp; internet www.sanshusha.co.jp; f. 1938; languages, dictionaries, philosophy, sociology, electronic publishing (CD-ROM); Pres. KANJI MAEDA.

**Seibundo-Shinkosha Co Ltd:** 3-3-11, Hango, Bunkyo-ku, Tokyo 113-0033, tel. (3) 5800-5775; fax (3) 5800-5773; f. 1912; technical, scientific, design, general non-fiction; Pres. MINORU TAKITA.

**Sekai Bunka Publishing Inc:** 4-2-29, Kudan-Kita, Chiyoda-ku, Tokyo 102-0073; tel. (3) 3262-5111; fax (3) 3221-6843; internet www.sekaibunka.com; f. 1946; history, natural science, geography, education, art, literature, juvenile; Pres. TSUTOMU SUZUKI.

**Shincho-Sha Co Ltd:** 71, Yarai-cho, Shinjuku-ku, Tokyo 162-8711; tel. (3) 3266-5411; fax (3) 3266-5534; e-mail shinchosha@webshincho.com; internet www.webshincho.com; f. 1896; general literature, fiction, non-fiction, fine arts, philosophy; Pres. TAKANOBU SATO.

**Shinkenchiku-Sha Co Ltd:** 2-31-2, Yushima, Bunkyo-ku, Tokyo; tel. (3) 3811-7101; fax (3) 3812-8229; e-mail ja-business@japan-architect.co.jp; internet www.japan-architect.co.jp; f. 1925; architecture; Pres. YOSHIO YOSHIDA.

**Shogakukan Inc:** 2-3-1, Hitotsubashi, Chiyoda-ku, Tokyo 101-8001; tel. (3) 3230-5526; fax (3) 3288-9653; internet www.shogakukan.co.jp; f. 1922; juvenile, education, geography, history, encyclopaedias, dictionaries; Pres. MASAHIRO OHGA.

**Shokabo Publishing Co Ltd:** 8-1, Yomban-cho, Chiyoda-ku, Tokyo 102-0081; tel. (3) 3262-9166; fax (3) 3262-9130; e-mail shokabo@mail.mind.ne.jp; internet www02.so-net.ne.jp/~shokabo; f. 1895; natural science, engineering; Pres. TATSUJI YOSHINO.

**Shokokusha Publishing Co Ltd:** 25, Saka-machi, Shinjuku-ku, Tokyo 160-0002; tel. (3) 3359-3231; fax (3) 3357-3961; e-mail eigyo@shokokusha.co.jp; f. 1932; architectural, technical and fine arts; Pres. TAISHIRO YAMAMOTO.

**Shueisha Inc:** 2-5-10, Hitotsubashi, Chiyoda-ku, Tokyo 101-8050; tel. (3) 3230-6320; fax (3) 3262-1309; f. 1925; literature, fine arts, language, juvenile, comics; Pres. and CEO TAMIO KOJIMA.

**Shufunotomo Co Ltd:** 2-9, Kanda Surugadai, Chiyoda-ku, Tokyo 101; tel. (3) 5280-7567; fax (3) 5280-7568; e-mail shuf-int@ba2.so-net.or.jp; internet www.shufunotomo.co.jp; f. 1916; domestic science, fine arts, gardening, handicraft, cookery and magazines; Chair. HARUHIKO ISHIKAWA; Pres. YASUHIKO ISHIKAWA.

**Shunju-Sha:** 2-18-6, Soto-Kanda, Chiyoda-ku, Tokyo 101-0021; tel. (3) 3255-9614; fax (3) 3255-9370; f. 1918; philosophy, religion, literary, economics, music; Pres. AKIRA KANDA; Man. RYUTARO SUZUKI.

**The Simul Press Inc:** 13-9, Araki-cho, Shinjuku-ku, Tokyo 160-0007; tel. (3) 3226-2851; fax (3) 3226-2840; f. 1967; international and current issues, social science, education, literature, languages; Chair. KATSUO TAMURA.

**Taishukan Publishing Co Ltd:** 3-24, Kanda-Nishiki-cho, Chiyoda-ku, Tokyo 101-8466; tel. (3) 3294-2221; fax (3) 3295-4107; internet www.taishukan.co.jp; f. 1918; reference, Japanese and foreign languages, sports, dictionaries, audio-visual aids; Pres. SHIGEO SUZUKI.

**Tanko Weathethill Inc:** 39-1, Ichigaya Yanagi-cho, Shinjuku-ku, Tokyo 162; tel. (3) 5269-2371; fax (3) 5269-7266; f. 1962; arts, crafts, architecture, gardening, language, history, zen and Eastern philosophy, sports, travel; Pres. YOSHIHARU NAYA.

**Tankosha Publishing Co Ltd:** 19-1, Miyanishi-cho Murasakino, Kita-ku, Kyoto 603-8691; tel. (75) 432-5155; fax (75) 432-0273; e-mail tankosha@magical.egg.or.jp; internet tankosha.topica.ne.jp; f. 1949; tea ceremony, fine arts, history; Pres. YOSHIHARU NAYA.

**Teikoku-Shoin Co Ltd:** 3-29, Kanda Jimbo-cho, Chiyoda-ku, Tokyo 101-0051; tel. (3) 3262-0834; fax (3) 3262-7770; e-mail rge01236@niftyserve.or.jp; f. 1926; geography, atlases, maps, textbooks; Pres. MUTSUO SHIRAHAMA.

**Tokai University Press:** 2-28-4, Tomigaya, Shibuya-ku, Tokyo 151-0063; tel. (3) 5478-0891; fax (3) 5478-0870; f. 1962; social science, cultural science, natural science, engineering, art; Pres. TATSURO MATSUMAE.

**Tokuma Shoten Publishing Co Ltd:** 1-1-16, Higashi Shimbashi, Minato-ku, Tokyo 105-8055; tel. (3) 3573-0111; fax (3) 3573-8788; e-mail info@tokuma.com; internet www.tokuma.com; f. 1954; Japanese classics, history, fiction, juvenile; Pres. YASUYOSHI TOKUMA.

**Tokyo News Service Ltd:** Tsukiji Hamarikyu Bldg, 5-3-3, Tsukiji, Chuo-ku, Tokyo 104; tel. (3) 3542-6511; fax (3) 3545-3628; f. 1947; shipping, trade and television guides; Pres. T. OKUYAMA.

**Tokyo Shoseki Co Ltd:** 2-17-1, Horifune, Kita-ku, Tokyo 114-8524; tel. (3) 5390-7513; fax (3) 5390-7409; internet www.tokyo-shoseki.co.jp; f. 1909; textbooks, reference books, cultural and educational books; Pres. ATSUSHI CHOJI.

**Tokyo Sogen-Sha Co Ltd:** 1-5, Shin-Ogawa-machi, Shinjuku-ku, Tokyo 162-0814; tel. (3) 3268-8201; fax (3) 3268-8230; f. 1954; mystery and detective stories, science fiction, literature; Pres. YASUNOBU TOGAWA.

**Toyo Keizai Inc:** 1-2-1, Nihombashi, Hongoku-cho, Chuo-ku, Tokyo 103-8345; tel. (3) 3246-5661; fax (3) 3231-0906; internet www.mediagalaxy.co.jp/toyokeizai; f. 1895; economics, business, finance and corporate, information; Pres. JUNJI ASANO.

**Tuttle Publishing Co Inc:** RK Bldg, 2-13-10 Shimo Meguro, Meguro-ku, Tokyo 153-0064, tel. (3) 5437-0171; fax (44) 5437-0755; e-mail tuttle@gol.com; f. 1948; books on Japanese and Asian religion, history, social science, arts, languages, literature, juvenile, cookery; Pres. FRANZ STEPHAN.

**United Nations University Press:** 5-53-70, Jingumae, Shibuya-ku, Tokyo 150-8925; tel. (3) 3499-2811; fax (3) 3499-2828; f. 1975; social sciences, humanities, pure and applied natural sciences; Rector HANS J. H. VAN GINKEL.

**University of Tokyo Press:** 7-3-1, Hongo, Bunkyo-ku, Tokyo 113-0033; tel. (3) 3811-0964; fax (3) 3815-1426; e-mail XLB07031@niftyserve.or.jp; f. 1951; natural and social sciences, humanities; Japanese and English; Chair. MASARU NISHIO; Man. Dir TADASHI YAMASHITA.

**Yama-Kei Publishers Co Ltd:** 1-1-33, Shiba-Daimon, Minato-ku, Tokyo 105-0012; tel. (3) 3436-4021; fax (3) 3438-1949; f. 1930; natural science, geography, mountaineering; Pres. YOSHIMITSU KAWASAKI.

**Yohan:** 3-14-9, Okubo, Shinjuku-ku, Tokyo 169-0072; tel. (3) 3208-0181; fax (3) 3209-0288; internet www.yohan.co.jp; f. 1963; social science, language, art, juvenile, dictionary; Pres. MASANORI WATANABE.

**Yuhikaku Publishing Co Ltd:** 2-17, Kanda Jimbo-cho, Chiyoda-ku, Tokyo 101-0051; tel. (3) 3264-1312; fax (3) 3264-5030; f. 1877; social sciences, law, economics; Pres. TADATAKA EGUSA.

**Yuzankaku Shuppan:** 2-6-9, Fujimi, Chiyoda-ku, Tokyo 102; tel. (3) 3262-3231; fax (3) 3262-6938; e-mail yuzan@cf.mbn.or.jp; internet www.nepto.co.jp/yuzankaku; f. 1916; history, fine arts, religion, archaeology; Pres. KEIKO NAGASAKA.

**Zoshindo Juken Kenkyusha Co Ltd:** 2-19-15, Shinmachi, Nishi-ku, Osaka 550-0013; tel. (6) 6532-1581; fax (6) 6532-1588; e-mail zoshindo@mbox.inet-osaka.or.jp; internet www.zoshindo.co.jp; f. 1890; educational, juvenile; Pres. AKITAKA OKAMATO.

### Government Publishing House

**Government Publications' Service Centre:** 1-2-1, Kasumigaseki, Chiyoda-ku, Tokyo 100-0013; tel. (3) 3504-3885; fax (3) 3504-3889.

### PUBLISHERS' ASSOCIATIONS

**Japan Book Publishers Association:** 6, Fukuro-machi, Shinjuku-ku, Tokyo 162-0828; tel. (3) 3268-1301; fax (3) 3268-1196; f. 1957; 499 mems; Pres. TAKAO WATANABE; Exec. Dir TOSHIKAZU GOMI.

**Publishers' Association for Cultural Exchange, Japan:** 1-2-1, Sarugaku-cho, Chiyoda-ku, Tokyo 101-0064; tel. (3) 3291-5685; fax (3) 3233-3645; e-mail office@pace.or.jp; f. 1953; 135 mems; Pres. Dr TATSURO MATSUMAE; Man. Dir YASUKO KORENAGA.

## Broadcasting and Communications

### TELECOMMUNICATIONS

**DDI Corpn:** 8, Ichiban-cho, Chiyoda-ku, Tokyo 102-8401; tel. (3) 3222-0077; fax (3) 3221-9696; to merge with Nippon Idou Tsushin Corpn (IDO) and Kokusai Denshin Denwa Corpn (KDD) in Oct. 2000; Chair. YUSAI OKUYAMA; Pres. AKIRA HIOKI.

**International Digital Communications:** 5-20-8, Asakusabashi, Taito-ku, Tokyo 111; tel. (3) 5820-5080; fax (3) 5820-5363; f. 1985; 53% owned by Cable and Wireless Communications (UK); Pres. SIMON CUNNINGHAM.

**Japan Telecom Co Ltd:** 4-7-1, Hatchobori, Chuo-ku, Tokyo 104-8508; tel. (3) 5540-8417; fax (3) 5540-8485; internet www

.japan-telecom.co.jp; 30% owned by alliance of British Telecommunications PLC (UK) and American Telegraph and Telephone Corpn (USA); Pres. HARUO MURAKAMI.

**Kokusai Denshin Denwa Corpn (KDD):** KDD Bldg, 2-3-2, Nishi Shinjuku, Shinjuku-ku, Tokyo 163-03; tel. (3) 3347-7111; fax (3) 3347-6470; merged with Teleway Corpn in 1998; to merge with DDI Corpn and Nippon Idou Tsushin Corpn (IDO) in Oct. 2000; major international telecommunications carrier; Chair. TAIZO NAKAMURA; Pres. TADASHI NISHIMOTO.

**Nippon Telegraph and Telephone Corpn:** 2-3-1, Otemachi, Chiyoda-ku, Tokyo 100-0004; tel. (3) 5359-2122; e-mail hyamada@yamato.ntt.jp; operates local, long-distance and international services; largest telecommunications co in Japan; Chair. SHIGEO SAWADA; Pres. JUN-ICHIRO MIYAZU.

**Tokyo Telecommunication Network Co Inc:** 4-9-25, Shibaura, Minato-ku, Tokyo 108; tel. (3) 5476-0091; fax (3) 5476-7625.

NTT DoCoMo, DDI, Nippon Idou Tsushin Corpn (IDO), Digital Phone and Digital TU-KA operate mobile telecommunication services in Japan.

### BROADCASTING

**Nippon Hoso Kyokai, NHK** (Japan Broadcasting Corporation): 2-2-1, Jinnan, Shibuya, Tokyo 150-8001; tel. (3) 3465-1111; fax (3) 3469-8110; e-mail webmaster@www.nhk.or.jp; internet www.nhk.or.jp; f. 1925; sole public broadcaster; operates five TV channels (incl. two satellite services), three radio channels and three worldwide services, NHK World TV, NHK World Premium and NHK World Radio Japan; headquarters in Tokyo, regional headquarters in Osaka, Nagoya, Hiroshima, Fukuoka, Sendai, Sapporo and Matsuyama; Pres. KATSUJI EBISAWA.

**National Association of Commercial Broadcasters in Japan (NAB-J):** 3-23, Kioi-cho, Chiyoda-ku, Tokyo 102-8577; tel. (3) 5213-7727; fax (3) 5213-7730; internet www.nab.or.jp; f. 1951; asscn of 197 companies (133 TV cos, 106 radio cos). Among these companies, 42 operate both radio and TV, with 593 radio stations and 8,185 TV stations. Pres. SEIICHIRO UJIIE; Exec. Dir AKIRA SAKAI.

In January 1999 there were a total of 97 commercial radio broadcasting companies and 126 commercial television companies operating in Japan. Some of the most important companies are:

**Asahi Hoso—Asahi Broadcasting Corpn:** 2-2-48, Ohyodo-Minami, Kita-ku, Osaka 531-8501; tel. (6) 6458-5321; fax (6) 6458-3672; internet www.asahi.co.jp; Pres. TOSHIHARU SHIBATA.

**Asahi National Broadcasting Co Ltd—TV Asahi:** 1-1-1, Roppongi, Minato-ku, Tokyo 106; tel. (3) 3587-5412; fax (3) 3586-6369; f. 1957; Pres. KUNIO ITO.

**Bunka Hoso—Nippon Cultural Broadcasting, Inc:** 1-5, Wakaba, Shinjuku-ku, Tokyo 160-8002; tel. (3) 3357-1111; fax (3) 3357-1140; f. 1952; Pres. SHIGEKI SATO.

**Chubu-Nippon Broadcasting Co Ltd:** 1-2-8, Shinsakae, Naka-ku, Nagoya 460-8405; tel. (052) 241-8111; fax (052) 259-1303; internet www.cbc-nagoya.co.jp; Pres. KEN-ICHI YOKOYAMA.

**Fuji Television Network, Inc:** 2-4-8, Daiba, Minato-ku, Tokyo 137-8088; tel. (3) 5500-8888; fax (3) 5500-8027; f. 1958; Pres. HISASHI HIEDA.

**Kansai Telecasting Corpn:** 2-1-7, Ogimachi, Kita-ku, Osaka 530-8408; tel. (6) 6314-8888; Pres. NOBUO MAKIHATA.

**Mainichi Broadcasting System, Inc:** 17-1, Chayamachi, Kita-ku, Osaka 530-8304; tel. (6) 6359-1123; fax (6) 6359-3503; internet mbs.co.jp; Chair. and CEO MORIYOSHI SAITO; Pres. AKIRA YANASE.

**Nippon Hoso—Nippon Broadcasting System, Inc:** 2-4-8, Daiba, Minato-ku, Tokyo 137-8686; tel. (3) 5500-1234; internet www.allnightnippon.com; f. 1954; Pres. MICHIYASU KAWAUCHI.

**Nippon Television Network Corpn (NTV):** 14, Niban-cho, Chiyoda-ku, Tokyo 102-8004; tel. (3) 5275-1111; fax (3) 5275-4501; f. 1953; Pres. SEIICHIRO UJIIE.

**Okinawa Televi Hoso—Okinawa Television Broadcasting Co Ltd:** 1-2-20, Kumoji, Naha 900-8588; tel. (988) 63-2111; fax (988) 61-0193; f. 1959; Pres. KAZUO KOISO.

**Radio Tampa—Nihon Short-Wave Broadcasting Co:** 1-9-15, Akasaka, Minato-ku, Tokyo 107-8373; tel. (3) 3583-8151; fax (3) 3583-7441; internet www.tampa.co.jp; f. 1954; Pres. TAMIO IKEDA.

**Ryukyu Hoso—Ryukyu Broadcasting Co:** 2-3-1, Kumoji, Naha 900-8711; tel. (98) 867-2151; fax (98) 864-5732; internet www.cosmos.ne.jp/rbc; f. 1954; Pres. KINZO KISHIMOTO.

**Television Osaka, Inc:** 1-2-18, Otemae, Chuo-ku, Osaka 540-8519; tel. (6) 6947-0019; fax (6) 6946-9796; Pres. MAKOTO FUKAGAWA.

**Television Tokyo Channel 12 Ltd:** 4-3-12, Toranomon, Minato-ku, Tokyo 105-8012; tel. (3) 3432-1212; fax (3) 5473-3447; f. 1964; Pres. YUTAKA ICHIKI.

**Tokyo-Hoso—Tokyo Broadcasting System, Inc (TBS):** 5-3-6, Akasaka, Minato-ku, Tokyo 107-8006; tel. (3) 3746-1111; fax (3) 3588-6378; internet www.tbs.co.jp; f. 1951; Chair. HIROSHI SHIHO; Pres. YUKIO SUNAHARA.

**Yomiuri Televi Hoso—Yomiuri Telecasting Corporation:** 2-2-33, Shiromi, Chuo-ku, Osaka 540-8510; tel. (6) 6947-2111; f. 1958; 20 hrs colour broadcasting daily; Pres. TOMONARI DOI.

#### Satellite, Cable and Digital Television

In addition to the two broadcast satellite services that NHK introduced in 1989, a number of commercial satellite stations are in operation. Cable television is available in many urban areas, and in 1996/97 there were some 12.6m. subscribers to cable services in Japan. Satellite digital television services, which first became available in 1996, are provided by Japan Digital Broadcasting Services (f. 1998 by the merger of PerfecTV and JSkyB) and DirecTV. Terrestrial digital services are scheduled to be introduced by 2000.

## Finance

(cap. = capital; p.u. = paid up; res = reserves; dep. = deposits; m. = million; brs = branches; amounts in yen)

### BANKING

Japan's central bank and bank of issue is the Bank of Japan. More than one-half of the credit business of the country is handled by 136 private commercial banks, seven trust banks and three long-term credit banks, collectively designated 'All Banks'. At October 1998 the private commercial banks had total assets of 641,000,000m. yen, the trust banks had total assets of 62,000,000m. yen and the long-term credit banks had total assets of 72,000,000m. yen.

Of the former category, the most important are the city banks, of which there are 10, some of which have a long and distinguished history, originating in the time of the *zaibatsu*, the private entrepreneurial organizations on which Japan's capital wealth was built before the Second World War. Although the *zaibatsu* were abolished as integral industrial and commercial enterprises during the Allied Occupation, the several businesses and industries which bear the former *zaibatsu* names, such as Mitsubishi, Mitsui and Sumitomo, continue to flourish and to give each other mutual assistance through their respective banks and trust corporations.

Among the commercial banks, the Bank of Tokyo-Mitsubishi specializes in foreign-exchange business, while the Industrial Bank of Japan finances capital investment by industry. The Long-Term Credit Bank of Japan and Nippon Credit Bank also specialize in industrial finance; the work of these three privately-owned banks is supplemented by the government-controlled Japan Development Bank.

The Government has established a number of other specialized institutions to provide services that are not offered by the private banks. Thus the Japan Export-Import Bank advances credit for the export of heavy industrial products and the import of raw materials in bulk. A Housing Loan Corporation assists firms in building housing for their employees, while the Agriculture, Forestry and Fisheries Finance Corporation provides loans to the named industries for equipment purchases. Similar services are provided for small enterprises by the Japanese Finance Corporation for Small Business.

An important financial role is played by co-operatives and by the many small enterprise institutions. Each prefecture has its own federation of co-operatives, with the Central Co-operative Bank of Agriculture and Forestry as the common central financial institution. This bank also acts as an agent for the government-controlled Agriculture, Forestry and Fisheries Finance Corporation.

There are also two types of private financial institutions for small business. There were 342 Credit Co-operatives, with total assets of 22,000,000m. yen, and 400 Shinkin Banks (credit associations), with total assets of 113,000,000m. yen at October 1998, which lend only to members. The latter also receive deposits.

The most common form of savings is through the government-operated Postal Savings System, which collects small savings from the public by means of the post office network. Total deposits amounted to 248,000,000m. yen in November 1998. The funds thus made available are used as loan funds by government financial institutions, through the Ministry of Finance's Trust Fund Bureau.

Clearing houses operate in each major city of Japan, and total 182 institutions. The largest are those of Tokyo and Osaka.

Japan's 67 Sogo Banks (mutual loan and savings banks) converted to commercial banks in 1989.

In June 1998 the Financial Supervisory Agency was established to regulate Japan's financial institutions.

#### Central Bank

**Nippon Ginko** (Bank of Japan): 2-1-1, Hongoku-cho, Nihonbashi, Chuo-ku, Tokyo 100-8630; tel. (3) 3279-1111; fax (3) 5203-8703; internet www.boj.or.jp; f. 1882; cap. and res 3,644,305m., dep. 8,199,230m. (March 1999); Gov. MASARU HAYAMI; Dep. Govs SAKUYA FUJIWARA, YUTAKA YAMAGUCHI; 33 brs.

### Principal Commercial Banks

**Asahi Bank Ltd:** 1-1-2, Otemachi, Chiyoda-ku, Tokyo 100-8106; tel. (3) 3287-2111; fax (3) 3212-3484; internet www.asahibank.co.jp; f. 1945 as Kyowa Bank Ltd; merged with Saitama Bank Ltd (f. 1943) in 1991; adopted present name in 1992; plans to establish a jt holding co with Tokai Bank Ltd in Oct. 2000; cap. 332,845m., res 301,661m., dep. 25,196,567m. (March 1998); Chair. TADASHI TANAKA; Pres. TATSURO ITOH; 424 brs.

**Ashikaga Bank Ltd:** 4-1-25, Sakura, Utsunomiya, Tochigi 320-8610; tel. (286) 22-0111; e-mail ashigin@ssctnet.or.jp; internet www.ashikagabank.co.jp; f. 1895; cap. 58,536m., res 110,716m., dep. 5,290,397m. (March 1998); Chair. HISAO MUKAE; Pres. YOSHIO YANAGITA; 140 brs.

**Bank of Fukuoka Ltd:** 2-13-1, Tenjin, Chuo-ku, Fukuoka 810-0001; tel. (92) 723-2131; fax (92) 711-1746; f. 1945; cap. 57,365m., res 188,782m., dep. 5,989,625m. (March 1998); Chair. TOYOHIKO GOTO; Pres. RYOJI TSUKUDA; 189 brs.

**Bank of Tokyo-Mitsubishi Ltd:** 2-7-1, Marunouchi, Chiyoda-ku, Tokyo 100-8388; tel. (3) 93240-1111; fax (3) 93240-4197; internet www.btm.co.jp; f. 1996 as a result of merger between Bank of Tokyo Ltd (f. 1946) and Mitsubishi Bank Ltd (f. 1880); specializes in international banking and financial business; cap. 785,970m., res 1,441,693m., dep. 66,222,515m. (March 1999); Chair. TASUKU TAKAGAKI; Pres. SATORU KISHI; 805 brs.

**Bank of Yokohama Ltd:** 3-1-1, Minatomirai, Nishi-ku, Yokohama, Kanagawa 220-8611; tel. (45) 225-1111; fax (45) 225-1160; e-mail intldept@boy.co.jp; internet www.boy.co.jp; f. 1920; cap. 134,547m., res 124,577m., dep. 9,804,707m. (March 1998); Chair. TAKASHI TANAKA; Pres. SADAAKI HIRASAWA; 192 brs.

**Chiba Bank Ltd:** 1-2, Chiba-minato, Chuo-ku, Chiba 260-0026; tel. (43) 245-1111; e-mail 57511345@people.or.jp; internet www.chibabank.co.jp; f. 1943; cap. 106,881m., res 279,208m., dep. 6,752,309m. (March 1998); Chair. TAKASHI TAMAKI; Pres. TSUNEO HAYAKAWA; 168 brs.

**Dai-Ichi Kangyo Bank Ltd:** 1-1-5, Uchisaiwai-cho, Chiyoda-ku, Tokyo 100-0011; tel. (3) 3596-1111; fax (3) 3596-2179; internet www.dkb.co.jp; f. 1971; plans to establish a jt holding co with Fuji Bank Ltd and Nippon Kogyo Ginko by late 2000, prior to full merger by early 2002; cap. 857,760m., res 994,240m., dep. 29,594,306m. (March 1999); Pres. and CEO KATSUYUKI SUGITA; 353 brs.

**Daiwa Bank Ltd:** 2-2-1, Bingo-machi, Chuo-ku, Osaka 540-8610; tel. (6) 6271-1221; internet www.daiwabank.co.jp; f. 1918; cap. 465,158m., total funds 24,127,120m. (March 1999); Pres. TAKASHI KAIHO; 210 brs.

**Fuji Bank Ltd:** 1-5-5, Otemachi, Chiyoda-ku, Tokyo 100-0004; tel. (3) 3216-2211; internet www.fujibank.co.jp; f. 1880; plans to establish a jt holding co with Dai-Ichi Kangyo Bank Ltd and Nippon Kogyo Ginko by late 2000, prior to full merger by early 2002; cap. 1,037,832m., res 1,197,277m., dep. 37,794,332m. (March 1999); Chair. TORU HASHIMOTO; Pres. YOSHIRO YAMAMOTO; 290 brs.

**Hokuriku Bank Ltd:** 1-2-26, Tsutsumichodori, Toyama 930-8637; tel. (764) 23-7111; fax (3) 3242-0541; e-mail rikbk@po3.nsknet.or.jp; internet www.hokugin.co.jp; f. 1877; cap. 83,342m., res 101,645m., dep. 5,064,434m. (March 1999); Pres. SHINICHIRO INUSHIMA; 192 brs.

**Joyo Bank Ltd:** 2-5-5, Minamimachi, Mito-shi, Ibaraki 310-0021; tel. (29) 231-2151; fax (29) 255-6522; e-mail joyointl@po.net-ibaraki.ne.jp; internet www.joyobank.co.jp; f. 1935; cap. 85,113m., res 269,219m., dep. 6,264,855m. (March 1998); Chair. ITARU ISHIKAWA; Pres. TORANOSUKE NISHINO; 197 brs.

**Sakura Bank Ltd:** 1-3-1, Kudan-Minami, Chiyoda-ku, Tokyo 100-8611; tel. (3) 3230-3111; fax (3) 3221-1084; internet www.sakura.co.jp; f. 1990; plan to merge with Sumitomo Bank Ltd announced 1999; cap. 1,042,706m., res 967,451m., dep. 38,332,071m. (March 1999); Chair. MASAHIRO TAKASAKI; Pres. AKISHIGE OKADA; 486 brs.

**Sanwa Bank Ltd:** 3-5-6, Fushimi-machi, Chuo-ku, Osaka 541-8530; tel. (6) 6206-8111; fax (6) 6229-1066; internet www.sanwabank.co.jp; f. 1933; cap. 466,842m., res 917,126m., dep. 37,801,343m. (March 1998); Chair. HIROSHI WATANABE; Pres. K. MUROMACHI; 1,144 brs.

**Shizuoka Bank Ltd:** 1-10, Gofuku-cho, Shizuoka 420-8761; tel. (54) 345-5411; fax (3) 3246-1483; internet www.shizuokabank.co.jp; f. 1943; cap. 90,845m., res 145,729m., dep. 6,646,475m. (March 1999); Chair. SOICHIRO KAMIYA; Pres. YASUO MATSUURA; 199 brs.

**Sumitomo Bank Ltd:** 4-6-5, Kitahama, Chuo-ku, Osaka 541-0041; tel. (6) 6227-2111; internet www.sumitomobank.co.jp; f. 1895; plan to merge with Sakura Bank Ltd announced 1999; cap. 752,848m., res 795,097m., dep. 41,997,316m. (March 1999); Chair. TOSHIO MORIKAWA; Pres. YOSHIFUMI NISHIKAWA; 351 brs.

**Tokai Bank Ltd:** 3-21-24, Nishiki, Naka-ku, Nagoya 460-8660; tel. (52) 211-1111; fax (52) 211-0931; internet www.csweb.co.jp/tbkj; f. 1941; plans to establish a jt holding co with Asahi Bank Ltd in Oct. 2000; cap. 722,969m., res 809,373m., dep. 24,588,218m. (March 1999); Chair. SATORU NISHIGAKI; Pres. HIDEO OGASAWARA; 276 brs.

### Principal Trust Banks

**Chuo Trust and Banking Co Ltd:** 1-7-1, Kyobashi, Chuo-ku, Tokyo 104-8345; tel. (3) 3567-1451; fax (3) 3562-6902; internet www.chuotrust.co.jp; f. 1962; merger with Mitsui Trust and Banking Co Ltd scheduled for 2000; cap. 170,966m., res 166,207m., dep. 3,306,108m. (March 1999); Chair. HISAO MURAMOTO; Pres. SHOZO ENDOH; 110 brs.

**Mitsubishi Trust and Banking Corporation:** 1-4-5, Marunouchi, Chiyoda-ku, Tokyo 100-0005; tel. (3) 3212-1211; fax (3) 3284-1326; internet www.mitsubishi-trust.co.jp; f. 1927; cap. 192,793m., res 384,833m., dep. 10,901,853m. (March 1999); Chair. HIROSHI HAYASHI; Pres. TOYOSHI NAKANO; 54 brs.

**Mitsui Trust and Banking Co Ltd:** 2-1-1, Nihonbashi-Muromachi, Chuo-ku, Tokyo 103-0022; tel. (3) 3270-9511; fax (3) 3245-0459; internet www.mitsuitrust.co.jp; f. 1924; merger with Chuo Trust and Banking Co Ltd scheduled for 2000; cap. 383,430m., res 366,137m., total assets 29,644,025m. (March 1999); Chair. KEIU NISHIDA; Pres. KIICHIRO FURUSAWA; 55 brs.

**Sumitomo Trust and Banking Co Ltd:** 4-5-33, Kitahama, Chuo-ku, Osaka 540-8639; tel. (6) 6220-2121; fax (6) 6220-2043; e-mail ipda@sumitomotrust.or.jp; internet www.sumitomotrust.co.jp; f. 1925; cap. 277,005m., res 293,473m., dep. 7,956,439m. (March 1999); Chair. HITOSHI HURAKAMI; Pres. ATSUSHI TAKAHASHI; 57 brs.

**Toyo Trust and Banking Co Ltd:** 1-4-3, Marunouchi, Chiyoda-ku, Tokyo 100-0005; tel. (3) 3287-2211; fax (3) 3201-1448; f. 1959; cap. 115,426m., res 107,366m., dep. 4,253,224m. (March 1998); Chair. MITSUO IMOSE; Pres. J. YOKOSUGA; 56 brs.

**Yasuda Trust and Banking Co Ltd:** 1-2-1, Yaesu, Chuo-ku, Tokyo 103-0028; tel. (3) 3278-8111; fax (3) 3278-0904; f. 1925; cap. 337,231m., res 213,724m., dep. 3,663,667m. (March 1999); Chair. KAZUHIKO KASAI; Pres. and CEO TAKAHIKO KIMINAMI; 50 brs.

### Long-Term Credit Banks

**The Long-Term Credit Bank of Japan Ltd:** 2-1-8, Uchisaiwai-cho, Chiyoda-ku, Tokyo 100-8501; tel. (3) 5511-5111; fax (3) 5511-8138; internet www.ltcb.co.jp; f. 1952; nationalized Oct. 1998, sale to Ripplewood Holdings (USA) announced Sept. 1999; cap. 387,229m., res 353,922m., dep. 21,557,842m. (March 1998); Chair. MASAMOTO YASHIRO; 23 brs.

**The Nippon Credit Bank Ltd:** 1-13-10, Kudan-kita, Chiyoda-ku, Tokyo 102-8660; tel. (3) 3263-1111; fax (3) 3239-8065; e-mail pr1@magical3.egg.or.jp; internet www.ncb.co.jp; f. 1957; nationalized Dec. 1998, sale to consortium led by Softbank Corpn announced Feb. 2000; cap. 353,114m., res 114,047m., dep. 9,064,857m. (March 1999); Pres. TAKUYA FUJII; 17 brs.

**Nippon Kogyo Ginko** (The Industrial Bank of Japan Ltd): 1-3-3, Marunouchi, Chiyoda-ku, Tokyo 100-8210; tel. (3) 3214-1111; fax (3) 3201-7643; internet www.ibjbank.co.jp; f. 1902; plans to establish a jt holding co with Dai-Ichi Kangyo Bank Ltd and Fuji Bank Ltd by late 2000, prior to full merger by early 2002; medium- and long-term financing; cap. 673,605m., res 650,501m., dep. 28,041,940m. (March 1999); Pres. and CEO MASAO NISHIMURA; 23 domestic brs, 20 overseas brs.

### Co-operative Bank

**Zenshinren Bank:** 3-8-1, Kyobashi, Chuo-ku, Tokyo 104-0071; tel. (3) 3563-4111; fax (3) 3563-7554; internet www.shinzin.co.jp; f. 1950; cap. 149,998m., res 290,207m., dep. 17,170,071m. (March 1999); Chair. KEIKICHI KATO; Pres. YASUTAKA MIYAMOTO; 16 brs.

### Principal Government Credit Institutions

**Agriculture, Forestry and Fisheries Finance Corporation:** Koko Bldg, 1-9-3, Otemachi, Chiyoda-ku, Tokyo 100-0004; tel. (3) 3270-2261; e-mail afc@ny.airnet.ne.jp; internet www.afc.go.jp; f. 1953; finances mainly plant and equipment investment; Gov. TOSHIHIKO TSURUOKA; Dep. Gov. KAZUHITO FUJIWARA; 21 brs.

**Development Bank of Japan:** 1-9-1, Otemachi, Chiyoda-ku, Tokyo 100-0004; tel. (3) 3244-1770; fax (3) 3245-1938; e-mail jdbintld@gol.com; internet www.jdb.go.jp; f. 1951 as the Japan Development Bank; renamed Oct. 1999 following consolidation with the Hokkaido and Tohoku Development Finance Public Corpn; provides long-term loans; subscribes for corporate bonds; guarantees corporate obligations; invests in specific projects; borrows funds from Govt and abroad; issues external bonds and notes; provides market information and consulting services for prospective entrants to Japanese market; cap. 371,525m. (Sept. 1998), res 895,400m., dep. 15,096,100m. (March 1998); Gov. MASAMI KOGAYU; Dep. Gov. MAKOTO TANJI; 7 brs.

**Housing Loan Corporation:** 1-4-10, Koraku, Bunkyo-ku, Tokyo 112-8570; tel. (3) 3812-1111; fax (3) 5800-8257; f. 1950 to provide long-term capital for the construction of housing at low interest rates; cap. 97,200m. (1994); Pres. SUSUMU TAKAHASHI; Vice-Pres. HIROYUKI ITOU; 12 brs.

**Japan Bank for International Cooperation (JBIC):** 1-4-1, Otemachi, Chiyoda-ku, Tokyo 100-8144; internet www.japanexim.go.jp;

f. 1999 by merger of The Export-Import Bank of Japan (f. 1950) and The Overseas Economic Co-operation Fund (f. 1961); responsible for Japan's external economic policy and co-operation activities; cap. 6,367,300m. (March 1999); Gov. HIROSHI YASUDA.

**Japan Finance Corporation for Small Business:** Koko Bldg, 1-9-3, Otemachi, Chiyoda-ku, Tokyo 100-0004; tel. (3) 3270-1271; internet www.jfs.go.jp; f. 1953 to supply long-term operating funds to small businesses (capital not more than 100m., or not more than 300 employees) which are not easily secured from ordinary private financial institutions; cap. 274,915m. (Feb. 1999) wholly subscribed by Govt; Gov. TOMIO TSUTSUMI; Vice-Gov. SOHEI HIDAKA; 58 brs.

**Norinchukin Bank** (Central Co-operative Bank for Agriculture, Forestry and Fisheries): 1-13-2, Yuraku-cho, Chiyoda-ku, Tokyo 100; tel. (3) 3279-0111; fax (3) 3218-5177; internet www.nochubank.or.jp; f. 1923; main banker to agricultural, forestry and fisheries co-operatives; receives deposits from individual co-operatives, federations and agricultural enterprises; extends loans to these and to local govt authorities and public corpns; adjusts excess and shortage of funds within co-operative system; issues debentures, invests funds and engages in other regular banking business; cap. 1,124,999m., res 222,951m., dep. 38,181,177m. (March 1999); Pres. KENICHI KAKUDOH; Dep. Pres. MITSUO NAITO; 39 brs.

**The People's Finance Corporation:** Koko Bldg, 1-9-3, Otemachi, Chiyoda-ku, Tokyo 100-0004; tel. (3) 3270-1361; f. 1949 to provide business funds, particularly to small enterprises unable to obtain loans from banks and other private financial institutions; cap. 204,900m. (June 1995); Gov. MAMORU OZAKI; Dep. Gov. MASAAKI TSUCHIDA; 152 brs.

**Shoko Chukin Bank** (Central Co-operative Bank for Commerce and Industry): 2-10-17, Yaesu, Chuo-ku, Tokyo 104-0028; tel. (3) 3272-6111; fax (3) 3274-1257; e-mail JDK06560@nifty.ne.jp; internet www.shokochukin.go.jp; f. 1936 to provide general banking services to facilitate finance for smaller enterprise co-operatives and other organizations formed mainly by small- and medium-sized enterprises; issues debentures; cap. 397,165m., res 23,210m., dep. and debentures 13,220,786m. (March 1998); Pres. YUKIHARU KODAMA; Dep. Pres. YOSHINOBU TAKEUCHI; 101 brs.

Other government financial institutions include the Japan Finance Corpn for Municipal Enterprises, the Small Business Credit Insurance Corpn and the Okinawa Development Finance Corpn.

### Principal Foreign Banks

In March 1998 there were 91 foreign banks operating in Japan.

**ABN AMRO Bank NV** (Netherlands): Shiroyama J. T. Mori Bldg, 4-3-1, Toranomon, Minato-ku, Tokyo 105-6013; tel. (3) 5405-6501; fax (3) 5405-6900; Country Man. (Japan) HERMAN F. KESSELER.

**Bangkok Bank Public Co Ltd** (Thailand): Bangkok Bank Bldg, 2-8-10, Nishi Shinbashi, Minato-ku, Tokyo 105-0003; tel. (3) 3503-3333; fax (3) 3502-6420; Senior Vice-Pres. and Branch Man. THAWEE PHUANGKETKEOW; br. in Osaka.

**Bank of America NA:** Ark Mori Bldg, 34th Floor, 1-12-32, Akasaka, Minato-ku, Tokyo 107; tel. (3) 3587-3155; fax (3) 3587-3460; Sr Vice-Pres. & Regional Man. Japan, Australia and Korea ARUN DUGGAL.

**Bank of India:** Mitsubishi Denki Bldg, 2-2-3, Marunouchi, Chiyoda-ku, Tokyo 100-0005; tel. (3) 3212-0911; fax (3) 3214-8667; e-mail boitok@injapan.net; CEO (Japan) Dr N. K. KHARE; br. in Osaka.

**Bank Negara Indonesia (Persero):** Kokusai Bldg, 3-1-1, Marunouchi, Chiyoda-ku, Tokyo 100-0005; tel. (3) 3214-5621; fax (3) 3201-2633; Gen. Man. SURYO DANISWORO.

**Bank One NA** (USA): Hibiya Central Bldg, 7th Floor, 1-2-9, Nishi Shinbashi, Minato-ku, Tokyo 105; tel. (3) 3596-8700; fax (3) 3596-8744; Sr Vice-Pres. and Gen. Man. YOSHIO KITAZAWA.

**Bankers Trust Co** (USA): Kishimoto Bldg, 2-2-1, Marunouchi, Chiyoda-ku, Tokyo 100; tel. (3) 3214-7171; Man. Dir MASAYUKI YASUOKA.

**Banque Nationale de Paris SA** (France): Shiroyama JT Mori Bldg, 23rd Floor, 4-3-1, Toranomon, Minato-ku, Tokyo 105-6023; tel. (3) 5473-3520; fax (3) 5473-3510; CEO (Japan) ERIC MARTIN; br. in Osaka.

**Barclays Bank PLC** (UK): Urbannet Otemachi Bldg, 15th Floor, 2-2-2, Otemachi, Chiyoda-ku, Tokyo 100-31; tel. (3) 5255-0011; fax (3) 5255-0102; Chair. SHIJURO OGATA; Pres. YOICHI KAMINA.

**Bayerische Hypo- und Vereinsbank AG** (Germany): Otemachi 1st Sq. East Tower, 17th Floor, 1-5-1, Otemachi, Chiyoda-ku, Tokyo 100-0004; tel. (3) 3284-1341; fax (3) 3284-1370; Exec. Dirs Dr PETER BARON, KENJI AKAGI.

**Chase Manhattan Bank** (USA): Akasaka Park Bldg, 11th–13th Floors, 5-2-20, Akasaka, Minato-ku, Tokyo 107; tel. (3) 5570-7500; fax (3) 5570-7960; Man. Dir and Gen. Man. NORMAN J. T. SCOTT; br. in Osaka.

**Citibank NA** (USA): Pan Japan Bldg, 1st Floor, 3-8-17, Akasaka Minato-ku, Tokyo 107; tel. (3) 3584-6321; fax (3) 3584-2924; Country Corporate Officer MASAMOTO YASHIRO; 20 brs.

**Commerzbank AG** (Germany): Nippon Press Center Bldg, 2nd Floor, 2-2-1, Uchisaiwai-cho, Chiyoda-ku, Tokyo 100-0011; tel. (3) 3502-4371; fax (3) 3508-7545; e-mail cbkjapan@gol.com; Gen. Mans BURKHARDT FIGGE, FRANÇOIS DE BELSUNCE.

**Crédit Agricole Indosuez** (France): Indosuez Bldg, 3-29-1, Kanda Jimbo-cho, Chiyoda-ku, Tokyo 101; tel. (3) 3261-3001; fax (3) 3261-0426; Sr Country Exec. FRANÇOIS BEYER.

**Deutsche Bank AG** (Germany): Deutsche Bank Bldg, 3-12-1, Toranomon, Minato-ku, Tokyo 105; tel. (3) 5401-1971; fax (3) 5401-6530; CEO and Chief Country Officer JOHN MACFARLANE; brs in Osaka and Nagoya.

**The Hongkong and Shanghai Banking Corpn Ltd** (Hong Kong): HSBC Bldg, 3-11-1, Nihonbashi, Chuo-ku, Tokyo 103-0027; tel. (3) 5203-3000; fax (3) 5203-3039; CEO STUART PEARCE; brs in Osaka and Nagoya.

**International Commercial Bank of China** (Taiwan): Togin Bldg, 1-4-2, Marunouchi, Chiyoda-ku, Tokyo 100; tel. (3) 3211-2501; fax (3) 3216-5686; Sr Vice-Pres. and Gen. Man. SHIOW-SHYONG LAI; br. in Osaka.

**Korea Exchange Bank** (Republic of Korea): Shin Kokusai Bldg, 3-4-1, Marunouchi, Chiyoda-ku, Tokyo 100; tel. (3) 3216-3561; fax (3) 3214-4491; f. 1967; Acting Gen. Man. CHAE KYOON-JUNG; brs in Osaka and Fukuoka.

**Lloyds TSB Bank PLC** (UK): Akasaka Twin Tower New Bldg, 2-11-7, Akasaka, Minato-ku, Tokyo 107; tel. (3) 3589-7700; fax (3) 3589-7722; Principal Man. (Japan) KAH HIN LIM.

**Morgan Guaranty Trust Co of New York** (USA): Akasaka Park Bldg, 5-2-20, Akasaka, Minato-ku, Tokyo 107-6151; tel. (3) 5573-1100; Man. Dir TAKESHI FUJIMAKI.

**National Bank of Pakistan:** 20 Mori Bldg, 3rd Floor, 2-7-4, Nishi Shinbashi, Minato-ku, Tokyo 105; tel. (3) 3502-0331; fax (3) 3502-0359; f. 1949; Pres. SARDAR MUHAMMAD KHAWAJA.

**Oversea-Chinese Banking Corpn Ltd** (Singapore): Akasaka Twin Tower, 15th Floor, 2-17-22, Akasaka, Minato-ku, Tokyo 107-0052; tel. (3) 5570-3421; fax (3) 5570-3426; Gen. Man. YEO WEE GHEE.

**Paribas** (France): Yurakucho Denki Bldg North, 19th Floor, 1-7-1, Yurakucho, Chiyoda-ku, Tokyo 100; tel. (3) 5222-6400; fax (3) 5222-6150; Gen. Man. DOMINIQUE SANDRET.

**Société Générale** (France): Ark Mori Bldg, 1-12-32, Akasaka, Minato-ku, Tokyo 107; tel. (3) 5549-5800; fax (3) 5549-5729; Chief Exec. BRIAN KAYE; br. in Osaka.

**Standard Chartered Bank** (UK): Fuji Bldg, 3-2-3, Marunouchi, Chiyoda-ku, Tokyo 100; tel. (3) 3213-6541; fax (3) 3215-2448; Chief Exec. (Japan) SEISHIRO KAWAMURA.

**State Bank of India:** 352 South Tower, Yuraku-cho Denki Bldg, 1-7-1, Yuraku-cho, Chiyoda-ku, Tokyo 100; tel. (3) 3284-0085; fax (3) 3201-5750; e-mail sbitok@gol.com; CEO M. RANGARAJAN; br. in Osaka.

**UBS AG:** East Tower, Otemachi 1st Sq., 1-5-1, Otemachi, Chiyoda-ku, Tokyo 100-0004; tel. (3) 5293-3000; fax (3) 5293-3456; Man. TAKAO SANKOH.

**Union de Banques Arabes et Françaises (UBAF)** (France): Sumitomo Jimbocho Bldg, 8th Floor, 3-25, Kanda Jimbocho, Chiyoda-ku, Tokyo 101-0051; tel. (3) 3263-8821; fax (3) 3263-8820; e-mail bonin@ubaf.co.jp; Gen. Man. (Japan) PHILIPPE L. BONIN; br. in Osaka.

**Westdeutsche Landesbank** (Germany): Fukoku Seimei Bldg, 2-2-2, Uchisaiwaicho, Chiyoda-ku, Tokyo 100-0011; tel. (3) 5510-6200; fax (3) 5510-6299; Gen. Mans PETER CLERMONT, PHILLIP RUSSELL.

### Bankers' Associations

**Japanese Bankers Association:** 1-3-1, Marunouchi, Chiyoda-ku, Tokyo 100-8216; tel. (3) 3216-3761; fax (3) 3201-5608; internet www.zenginkyo.or.jp; f. 1945; fmrly Federation of Bankers Associations of Japan; 147 full mems, 38 associate mems, 72 special mems; Chair. KATSUYUKI SUGITA.

**Tokyo Bankers Association, Inc:** 1-3-1, Marunouchi, Chiyoda-ku, Tokyo 100-8216; tel. (3) 3216-3761; fax (3) 3201-5608; f. 1945; 126 mem. banks; conducts the above Association's administrative business; Chair. KATSUYUKI SUGITA; Vice-Chair. AKIRA KANNO.

**National Association of Labour Banks:** 2-5-15, Kanda Surugadai, Chiyoda-ku, Tokyo 101-0062; tel. (3) 3295-6721; fax (3) 3295-6752; Pres. TETSUEI TOKUGAWA.

**Regional Banks Association of Japan:** 3-1-2, Uchikanda, Chiyoda-ku, Tokyo 101-0047; tel. (3) 3252-5171; fax (3) 3254-8664; f. 1936; 64 mem. banks; Chair. SADAAKI HIROSAWA.

**Second Association of Regional Banks:** 5, Sanban-cho, Chiyoda-ku, Tokyo 102-0075; tel. (3) 3262-2181; fax (3) 3262-2339; f. 1989 (fmrly National Asscn of Sogo Banks); 65 commercial banks; Chair. KAZUMARO KATO.

## STOCK EXCHANGES

**Fukuoka Securities Exchange:** 2-14-2, Tenjin, Chuo-ku, Fukuoka 810-0001; tel. (92) 741-8231; Pres. FUBITO SHIMOMURA.

Wheat production is also important. The agricultural sector was severely affected by a drought during 1999. During 1990–98 agricultural GDP decreased by an average of 3.1% a year.

Industry (including mining, manufacturing, construction and power) provided an estimated 29.5% of GDP in 1996. In 1992 an estimated 21.4% of the country's active labour force were employed in the industrial sector. During 1990–98 industrial GDP increased by an average of 6.8% per year

Mining contributed an estimated 3.5% of GDP in 1996. Phosphates and potash are the major mineral exports; together they accounted for about 24.3% of total export earnings in 1996. Jordan also has reserves of oil-bearing shale, but exploitation of this resource is at present undeveloped.

Manufacturing provided an estimated 15.8% of GDP in 1996, and, together with mining, engaged about 10.3% of the total employed labour force in 1992. In 1994 the most important branches of manufacturing, measured by the value of output, were chemical products (accounting for 35.6% of the total), petroleum refineries (16.1%), food products (13.9%) and non-metallic mineral products (10.1%).

Energy is derived principally from imported petroleum, but attempts are being made to develop alternative sources of power, including wind and solar power. Imports of mineral fuels comprised 12.2% of the total value of imports in 1996.

Services (including wholesale and retail trade, restaurants and hotels, transport, financing and community, social and personal services) accounted for an estimated 65.2% of Jordan's GDP in 1996. In 1992 an estimated 71.2% of the total employed labour force were engaged in the service sector. During 1990–98 the GDP of the service sector increased by an average of 5.3% per year.

In 1998 Jordan recorded a visible trade deficit of US $1,601.6m., and there was a surplus of 14.1m. on the current account of the balance of payments. In 1996 Iraq was the principal source of imports and, in 1995, was also the principal market for exports. Other major trading partners were Germany, India, Italy, Saudi Arabia and the USA. The principal exports in 1996 were chemicals, minerals and vegetables, fruit and nuts, and the principal imports were machinery and transport equipment, food and live animals and basic manufactures.

In 1997 there was a budget deficit of JD 163.4m., equivalent to 3.3% of GDP in that year. The annual rate of inflation averaged 4.4% in 1990–97. The average rate of inflation was 3.0% in 1997 and 4.4% in 1998. Jordan's external debt totalled US $8,234m. at the end of 1997, of which US $7,020m. was long-term public debt. In that year the cost of debt-servicing was equivalent to 11.1% of the value of exports of goods and services. Unemployment was officially estimated at 16–20% of the labour force in 1998.

Jordan is a member of the Arab League (see p. 218), the Arab Co-operation Council (p. 290), the Council of Arab Economic Unity (p. 156), the Organization of the Islamic Conference (p. 249) and the Arab Monetary Fund (p. 290).

Since the early 1990s the Jordanian economy has been constrained by a heavy burden of foreign debt and by the loss, owing to the imposition of UN sanctions, of its vital Iraqi market. Nevertheless, the conclusion of a peace treaty with Israel in 1994 created new opportunities, especially for tourism, transport and banking, and boosted regional co-operation in areas such water management. Jordan has implemented an adjustment and reform programme which aims to reduce the role of the state in industry and, through privatization, raise funds to support the repayment of foreign debt. By early 2000 the restructuring of a number of state enterprises was under way, notably in the water, electricity, transport and telecommunications sectors. In collaboration with the IMF, Jordan is deemed to have brought its external debt under control; in August and October 1999 the IMF carried out favourable reviews of the country's structural reform programme, commending the Government in particular on its achievements regarding privatization, and on the recent growth in international reserves. However, the IMF has recommended a faster pace of structural reform, as well as reform of the tax system and the introduction of new banking legislation. In April 1999 the IMF approved loans to support the Government's economic and structural reform programme for 1999–2001. The loans are divided between a Compensatory and Contingency Financing Facility (CCFF), and a new extended Fund facility (EFF) credit. In May 1999 the creditor governments of the 'Paris Club' agreed to reschedule a further US $800m. of Jordan's debt, and in October the USA agreed to cancel $101.7m. of debt. In order to encourage foreign investment, in June 1997 all restrictions on the movement of foreign currency were lifted. In December 1998 Jordan and Egypt signed an agreement to provide for the establishment of a free-trade zone by 2005. In September 1999 the Jordanian parliament ratified the Jordanian-European Partnership Agreement (signed with the EU in November 1997), which allows for the creation of a duty-free zone and for import duties to be lifted over a 12-year period. On 17 December 1999 Jordan was accepted as a member of the World Trade Organization (WTO).

### Social Welfare

There is no comprehensive welfare scheme but the Government administers medical and health services. In 1985 the East Bank region had 44 hospital establishments, with 3,578 beds, and 2,576 physicians. A new Social Security Law, providing security for both employers and employees, was put into effect in 1978 and extended in 1981. In January 1999 the Government announced plans for the introduction of a national health service, scheduled for completion in 2010. Of total budgetary expenditure by the central Government in 1997, JD 172.2m. (10.2%) was for health services, and a further JD 298.9m. (17.8%) for social security and welfare. In June 1998 there were 1,463,064 refugees registered with UNRWA in Jordan and a further 555,057 in the West Bank.

### Education

Primary education is free and compulsory. It starts at the age of six years and lasts for ten years. The preparatory cycle is followed by a two-year secondary cycle. UNRWA provides schooling for Palestinian Arab refugees. In 1995/96, at the primary level, there were 51,721 teachers and 1,074,877 pupils. At the secondary level (including both general and vocational secondary education) in 1995/96, there were 10,921 teachers and 176,123 pupils. In 1995/96 there were 4,821 teachers and 99,020 pupils engaged in higher education. There are 10 universities in Jordan. Budgetary expenditure on education by the central Government in 1997 was JD 245.1m. (14.6% of total spending).

### Public Holidays

**2000:** 8 January (Id al-Fitr, end of Ramadan)*, 15 January (Arbor Day), 16 March (Id al-Adha, Feast of the Sacrifice), 22 March (Arab League Day), 6 April (Muharram, Islamic New Year), 25 May (Independence Day), 15 June (Mouloud, birth of Muhammad), 11 August (King Hussein's Accession), 26 October (Leilat al-Meiraj, ascension of Muhammad), 14 November (King Hussein's Birthday), 28 December (Id al-Fitr, end of Ramadan)*.

**2001:** 15 January (Arbor Day), 6 March (Id al-Adha, Feast of the Sacrifice), 22 March (Arab League Day), 26 March (Muharram, Islamic New Year), 25 May (Independence Day), 4 June (Mouloud, birth of Muhammad), 11 August (King Hussein's Accession), 15 October (Leilat al-Meiraj, ascension of Muhammad), 14 November (King Hussein's Birthday); 17 December (Id al-Fitr, end of Ramadan).

* This festival will occur twice (in the Islamic years AH 1420 and 1421) within the same Gregorian year.

### Weights and Measures

The metric system is in force. In Jordan the dunum is 1,000 sq m (0.247 acre).

# Statistical Survey

Source: Department of Statistics, POB 2015, Jabal Amman, 1st Circle, POB 2015, Amman; tel. 24313.

## Area and Population

**AREA, POPULATION AND DENSITY**
(East and West Banks)

| | |
|---|---|
| Area (sq km) | 97,740* |
| Population (UN estimates at mid-year)† | |
| 1996 | 5,938,000 |
| 1997 | 6,126,000 |
| 1998 | 6,304,000 |
| Density (per sq km) at mid-1998 | 64.5 |

* 37,738 sq miles.

† Source: UN, *World Population Prospects: The 1998 Revision*.

(East Bank only)

| | |
|---|---|
| Area (sq km) | 89,342* |
| Population (census results) | |
| 10–11 November 1979 | 2,100,019 |
| 10 December 1994 | |
| Males | 2,135,883 |
| Females | 1,959,696 |
| Total | 4,095,579 |
| Population (official estimates at mid-year) | |
| 1994 | 4,066,000 |
| 1995 | 4,215,000 |
| 1996 | 4,368,000 |
| Density (per sq km) at mid-1996 | 48.9 |

* 34,495 sq miles.

**GOVERNORATES**
(East Bank only; estimated population at 31 December 1996)

| | |
|---|---|
| Amman | 1,696,300 |
| Irbid | 802,200 |
| Zarqa | 687,000 |
| Balqa | 301,300 |
| Mafraq | 191,900 |
| Karak | 182,200 |
| Jarash | 132,500 |
| Madaba | 110,700 |
| Ajlun | 101,400 |
| Aqaba | 85,700 |
| Ma'an | 85,300 |
| Tafiela | 67,500 |
| **Total** | 4,444,000 |

**PRINCIPAL TOWNS** (including suburbs)

Population at 31 December 1991: Amman (capital) 965,000; Zarqa 359,000; Irbid 216,000; Russeifa 115,500.

**BIRTHS, MARRIAGES AND DEATHS** (East Bank only)*

| | Registered live births | | Registered marriages | | Registered deaths | |
|---|---|---|---|---|---|---|
| | Number | Rate (per 1,000) | Number | Rate (per 1,000) | Number | Rate (per 1,000) |
| 1989 | 115,742 | n.a. | 31,508 | n.a. | 9,695 | n.a. |
| 1990 | 116,520 | n.a. | 32,706 | n.a. | 10,569 | n.a. |
| 1991 | 120,554 | n.a. | 35,926 | n.a. | 10,605 | n.a. |
| 1992 | 125,395 | n.a. | 37,216 | n.a. | 11,820 | n.a. |
| 1993 | 134,489 | n.a. | 40,391 | n.a. | 11,915 | n.a. |
| 1994 | 140,444 | 34.5 | 36,132 | 8.9 | 12,290 | 3.0 |
| 1995 | 141,319 | 33.5 | 35,501 | 8.4 | 13,018 | 3.1 |
| 1996 | 142,404 | 32.6 | 34,425 | 7.9 | 13,302 | 3.0 |

* Data are tabulated by year of registration rather than by year of occurrence. Registration of births and marriages is reported to be complete, but death registration is incomplete. Figures exclude foreigners, but include registered Palestinian refugees.

**Expectation of life** (UN estimates, years at birth, 1990–95): Males 66.20; Females 69.80. Source: UN, *Demographic Yearbook*.

**ECONOMICALLY ACTIVE POPULATION** (Jordanians only)

| | 1990 | 1991 | 1992 |
|---|---|---|---|
| Agriculture | 38,266 | 40,848 | 44,400 |
| Mining and manufacturing | 53,468 | 56,856 | 61,800 |
| Electricity and water | 6,815 | 7,176 | 6,600 |
| Construction | 51,895 | 54,096 | 60,000 |
| Trade | 52,944 | 56,856 | 63,000 |
| Transport and communications | 44,557 | 48,576 | 52,200 |
| Financial and insurance services | 16,774 | 17,664 | 19,800 |
| Social and administrative services | 259,478 | 269,928 | 292,200 |
| **Total employed** | 524,197 | 552,000 | 600,000 |
| Unemployed | 106,000 | 128,000 | 106,000 |
| **Total civilian labour force** | 630,197 | 680,000 | 706,000 |

Source: Ministry of Labour, *Annual Report*.

## Agriculture

**PRINCIPAL CROPS** (East Bank only; '000 metric tons)

| | 1996 | 1997 | 1998 |
|---|---|---|---|
| Wheat | 43 | 57 | 55 |
| Barley | 45 | 43 | 45* |
| Potatoes | 158 | 107 | 110 |
| Olives | 129 | 82 | 75 |
| Cabbages | 26 | 28 | 28† |
| Tomatoes | 568 | 641 | 640 |
| Cauliflowers | 45 | 45 | 46 |
| Pumpkins, squash and gourds | 39 | 51 | 54 |
| Cucumbers and gherkins | 88 | 130 | 125 |
| Eggplants (Aubergines) | 86 | 73 | 70 |
| Green peppers | 17 | 19 | 19† |
| Onions (dry) | 80 | 52 | 53 |
| Green beans | 27 | 22 | 21 |
| Other vegetables | 104 | 101 | 105 |
| Watermelons | 81 | 77 | 70 |
| Melons | 9 | 15† | 15† |
| Grapes | 84 | 62 | 70† |
| Apples | 61 | 69 | 65 |
| Oranges | 36 | 29 | 40 |
| Tangerines, mandarins, clementines and satsumas | 76 | 62 | 55 |
| Lemons and limes | 44 | 46 | 40 |
| Bananas | 39 | 73 | 73† |
| Other fruits and berries | 67 | 46 | 46 |
| Tobacco (leaves) | 3 | 2 | 2† |

* Unofficial figure. † FAO estimate.

Source: FAO, *Production Yearbook*.

**LIVESTOCK**
(East Bank only; '000 head, year ending September)

| | 1996 | 1997 | 1998 |
|---|---|---|---|
| Horses* | 4 | 4 | 4 |
| Mules* | 3 | 3 | 3 |
| Asses* | 18 | 18 | 18 |
| Cattle | 62 | 62 | 65* |
| Camels* | 18 | 18 | 18 |
| Sheep | 2,375 | 2,000 | 2,000* |
| Goats | 807 | 795 | 795* |

* FAO estimates.

Poultry (million): 22 in 1996, 23 in 1997 (FAO estimate), 23 in 1998.

Source: FAO, *Production Yearbook*.

**LIVESTOCK PRODUCTS** (East Bank only; '000 metric tons)

| | 1996 | 1997 | 1998 |
|---|---|---|---|
| Beef and veal | 3 | 3 | 4* |
| Mutton and lamb | 10 | 9 | 9 |
| Goat meat | 3 | 3 | 3* |
| Poultry meat | 100 | 98 | 95 |
| Cows' milk | 107 | 108 | 116 |
| Sheep's milk | 39 | 35 | 36 |
| Goats' milk | 20 | 19 | 19* |
| Cheese* | 4 | 4 | 4 |
| Poultry eggs | 45 | 45 | 44* |
| Wool: greasy* | 5 | 4 | 4 |
| clean* | 3 | 2 | 2 |
| Sheepskins | 1 | 1 | 1 |

* FAO estimate(s).

Source: FAO, *Production Yearbook.*

## Forestry

**ROUNDWOOD REMOVALS**
('000 cubic metres, excluding bark)

| | 1995 | 1996 | 1997 |
|---|---|---|---|
| Industrial wood | 4 | 4 | 4 |
| Fuel wood | 6 | 6 | 7 |
| **Total** | 10 | 10 | 11 |

Source: FAO, *Yearbook of Forest Products.*

## Fishing

(metric tons, live weight)

| | 1995 | 1996 | 1997 |
|---|---|---|---|
| Freshwater fishes | 350 | 350 | 350 |
| Marine fishes | 2 | 2 | 2 |
| **Total catch** | 352 | 352 | 352 |

Source: FAO, *Yearbook of Fishery Statistics.*

## Mining

('000 metric tons)

| | 1994 | 1995 | 1996 |
|---|---|---|---|
| Crude petroleum | 1.2 | 1.5 | 1.9 |
| Phosphate rock | 4,216.5 | 4,983.9 | 5,424.2 |
| Potash salts* | 1,550.3 | 1,780.0 | 1,765.5 |
| Salt (unrefined) | 19 | 57 | 50 |

* Figures refer to the $K_2O$ content.

## Industry

**SELECTED PRODUCTS** ('000 metric tons, unless otherwise indicated)

| | 1993 | 1994 | 1995 |
|---|---|---|---|
| Liquefied petroleum gas | 127 | 126 | 138 |
| Motor spirit (petrol) | 430 | 471 | 483 |
| Aviation gasoline | 21 | 20* | 30 |
| Kerosene | 237 | 222 | 215 |
| Jet fuels | 220 | 198 | 244 |
| Distillate fuel oils | 880 | 859 | 872 |
| Residual fuel oils | 962 | 901 | 995 |
| Lubricating oils | 21* | 24 | 28 |
| Petroleum bitumen (asphalt) | 140 | 136 | 129 |
| Nitrogenous fertilizers (a)† | 85 | 135 | n.a. |
| Phosphate fertilizers (b)† | 470 | 750 | 729 |
| Potassic fertilizers (c)† | 822 | 930 | n.a. |
| Cement | 3,437 | 3,392 | 3,415 |
| Cigarettes (million) | 3,465 | 4,191 | 3,675 |
| Electricity (million kWh) | 4,761 | 5,075 | 5,616 |

* Estimated production.

† Production in terms of (a) nitrogen; (b) phosphoric acid; and (c) potassium oxide.

**1996** ('000 metric tons, unless otherwise indicated): Phosphate fertilizers (phosphoric acid) 671; Cement 3,512; Cigarettes (million) 4,738.

Source: mainly UN, *Industrial Commodity Statistics Yearbook.*

## Finance

**CURRENCY AND EXCHANGE RATES**

**Monetary Units**

1,000 fils = 1 Jordanian dinar (JD).

**Sterling, Dollar and Euro Equivalents** (30 September 1999)

£1 sterling = JD 1.1674;
US $1 = 709.0 fils;
€1 = 756.1 fils;
JD 100 = £85.66 = $141.04 = €132.25.

**Exchange Rate**

An official mid-point rate of US $1 = 709 fils (JD1 = $1.4104) has been maintained since October 1995.

**BUDGET** (East Bank only; JD million)*

| Revenue† | 1995 | 1996 | 1997 |
|---|---|---|---|
| Taxation | 976.4 | 1,065.3 | 979.0 |
| Taxes on income, profits and capital gains | 152.4 | 173.1 | 149.7 |
| Taxes on property | 66.8 | 63.4 | 59.0 |
| Taxes on financial and capital transactions | 65.3 | 61.6 | 57.2 |
| Domestic taxes on goods and services | 351.7 | 412.2 | 407.0 |
| Excises | 263.6 | 310.0 | 308.4 |
| Taxes on international trade and transactions | 336.4 | 355.0 | 298.2 |
| Import duties | 318.7 | 336.3 | 279.7 |
| Other current revenue | 354.7 | 298.7 | 332.8 |
| Entrepreneurial and property income | 272.7 | 203.6 | 235.6 |
| Administrative fees and charges, non-industrial and incidental sales | 41.3 | 43.9 | 48.5 |
| Capital revenue | 1.5 | 2.9 | 0.9 |
| **Total** | 1,332.6 | 1,366.9 | 1,312.6 |

| Expenditure‡ | 1995 | 1996 | 1997 |
|---|---|---|---|
| General public services | 97.8 | 97.3 | 103.4 |
| Defence | 296.0 | 283.3 | 301.0 |
| Public order and safety | 121.0 | 131.6 | 139.1 |
| Education | 227.8 | 238.5 | 245.1 |
| Health | 103.7 | 150.6 | 172.2 |
| Social security and welfare | 246.3 | 306.4 | 298.9 |
| Housing and community amenities | 26.0 | 43.1 | 34.1 |
| Recreational, cultural and religious affairs and services | 31.5 | 39.4 | 35.3 |
| Economic affairs and services | 179.5 | 217.7 | 146.4 |
| Agriculture, forestry, fishing and hunting | 65.7 | 71.3 | 63.7 |
| Transport and communications | 60.9 | 71.2 | 63.7 |
| Other purposes | 141.9 | 159.0 | 206.4 |
| Interest payments | 132.7 | 153.4 | 200.9 |
| **Sub-total§** | 1,471.5 | 1,666.9 | 1,681.9 |
| Adjustment | — | — | — |
| **Total** | 1,471.5 | 1,666.9 | 1,681.9 |

* Figures represent a consolidation of the Current, Capital and Development Plan Budgets of the central Government. The data exclude the operations of the Health Security Fund and of other government agencies with individual budgets.

† Excluding grants received from abroad (JD million): 182.8 (current 175.4, capital 7.4) in 1995; 219.9 (current 216.0, capital 3.9) in 1996; 205.0 (current 202.0, capital 3.1) in 1997.

‡ Excluding lending minus repayments (JD million): –5.4 in 1995; –13.8 in 1996; –0.9 in 1997.

§ Comprising (in JD million): current expenditure 1,187.9 in 1995; 1,333.7 in 1996; 1,399.1 in 1997; capital expenditure 283.6 in 1995; 333.2 in 1996; 282.8 in 1997.

Source: IMF, *Government Finance Statistics Yearbook*.

**INTERNATIONAL RESERVES** (US $ million at 31 December)

| | 1996 | 1997 | 1998 |
|---|---|---|---|
| Gold* | 197.7 | 200.7 | 204.3 |
| IMF special drawing rights | 0.8 | 0.2 | 0.8 |
| Foreign exchange | 1,758.5 | 2,200.1 | 1,749.6 |
| **Total** | 1,957.0 | 2,401.0 | 1,954.7 |

* National valuation.

Source: IMF, *International Financial Statistics.*

**MONEY SUPPLY** (JD million at 31 December)

| | 1996 | 1997 | 1998 |
|---|---|---|---|
| Currency outside banks | 952.1 | 987.6 | 952.8 |
| Demand deposits at commercial banks | 578.1 | 636.1 | 648.8 |
| **Total money** (incl. others) | 1,532.8 | 1,626.1 | 1,612.9 |

Source: IMF, *International Financial Statistics.*

**COST OF LIVING** (Consumer Price Index; base: 1990 = 100)

| | 1995 | 1996 | 1997 |
|---|---|---|---|
| Food (incl. beverages) | 126.3 | 135.1 | 144.1 |
| Fuel and light | 122.3 | 125.9 | 129.9 |
| Clothing (incl. footwear) | 142.5 | 156.9 | 151.3 |
| Rent | 113.1 | 116.8 | 117.5 |
| **All items** (incl. others) | 123.2 | 131.2 | 135.1 |

Source: Central Bank of Jordan.

**NATIONAL ACCOUNTS** (East Bank only; JD million at current prices)

**Expenditure on the Gross Domestic Product**

| | 1996 | 1997 | 1998 |
|---|---|---|---|
| **Government final consumption expenditure** | 1,204.1 | 1,316.8 | 1,395.7 |
| Private final consumption expenditure | 3,252.2 | 3,451.1 | 3,646.0 |
| Increase in stocks | 52.1 | –3.3 | — |
| Gross fixed capital formation | 1,445.3 | 1,325.1 | 1,308.9 |
| **Total domestic expenditure** | 5,953.7 | 6,089.7 | 6,350.6 |
| Exports of goods and services | 2,597.2 | 2,532.8 | 2,569.6 |
| *Less* Imports of goods and services | 3,839.9 | 3,676.7 | 3,683.6 |
| **GDP in purchasers' values** | 4,711.0 | 4,945.8 | 5,236.6 |
| **GDP at constant 1985 prices** | 2,758.8 | 2,819.2 | n.a. |

Source: IMF, *International Financial Statistics*

**Gross Domestic Product by Economic Activity** (provisional)

| | 1994 | 1995 | 1996 |
|---|---|---|---|
| Agriculture, hunting, forestry and fishing | 197.2 | 213.3 | 232.9 |
| Mining and quarrying | 102.4 | 128.1 | 153.6 |
| Manufacturing | 561.4 | 618.7 | 688.6 |
| Electricity, gas and water | 84.0 | 90.8 | 98.2 |
| Construction | 300.2 | 327.8 | 341.1 |
| Trade, restaurants and hotels | 377.0 | 423.3 | 480.1 |
| Transport, storage and communications | 494.0 | 531.7 | 591.8 |
| Finance, insurance, real estate and business services | 658.6 | 705.6 | 766.8 |
| Government services | 671.2 | 732.9 | 792.7 |
| Other community, social and personal services | 110.6 | 121.9 | 138.3 |
| Private non-profit services to households | 47.0 | 51.8 | 56.6 |
| Domestic services of households | 6.0 | 6.4 | 7.0 |
| **Sub-total** | 3,609.6 | 3,952.3 | 4,347.7 |
| *Less* Imputed bank service charge | 73.9 | 79.2 | 87.3 |
| **GDP at factor cost** | 3,535.7 | 3,873.1 | 4,260.4 |
| Indirect taxes<br>*Less* Subsidies } | 665.6 | 781.5 | 886.3 |
| **GDP in purchasers' values** | 4,201.3 | 4,654.6 | 5,146.7 |

**BALANCE OF PAYMENTS** (US $ million)

| | 1996 | 1997 | 1998 |
|---|---|---|---|
| Exports of goods f.o.b. | 1,816.9 | 1,835.5 | 1,802.4 |
| Imports of goods f.o.b. | –3,818.1 | –3,648.5 | –3,403.9 |
| **Trade balance** | –2,001.1 | –1,813.0 | –1,601.6 |
| Exports of services | 1,846.3 | 1,736.8 | 1,825.1 |
| Imports of services | –1,597.7 | –1,537.2 | –1,783.8 |
| **Balance on goods and services** | –1,752.6 | –1,613.4 | –1,560.2 |
| Other income received | 111.7 | 248.2 | 306.9 |
| Other income paid | –412.7 | –457.0 | –445.0 |
| **Balance on goods, services and income** | –2,053.6 | –1,822.1 | –1,698.3 |
| Current transfers received | 1,970.2 | 2,096.1 | 1,984.3 |
| Current transfers paid | –138.5 | –244.6 | –271.9 |
| **Current balance** | –221.9 | 29.3 | 14.1 |
| Capital account (net) | 157.7 | 163.8 | 81.1 |
| Direct investment abroad | 43.3 | — | — |
| Direct investment from abroad | 15.5 | 360.9 | 310.0 |
| Other investment assets | –5.9 | 16.4 | –80.3 |
| Other investment liabilities | 181.0 | –135.0 | –407.1 |
| Net errors and omissions | –357.9 | –160.8 | –454.0 |
| **Overall balance** | –188.2 | 274.6 | –536.1 |

Source: IMF, *International Financial Statistics*.

# External Trade

**PRINCIPAL COMMODITIES** (distribution by SITC, US $ million)

| Imports c.i.f. | 1994 | 1995 | 1996 |
|---|---|---|---|
| Food and live animals | 586.2 | 598.2 | 967.4 |
| Crude materials (inedible) except fuels | 102.4 | 130.0 | 130.7 |
| Mineral fuels, lubricants, etc. | 430.2 | 480.0 | 525.4 |
| Crude petroleum | 332.5 | 355.7 | n.a. |
| Animal and vegetable oils and fats | 118.1 | 135.1 | 103.9 |
| Chemicals | 400.6 | 453.3 | 464.2 |
| Basic manufactures | 618.4 | 719.2 | 722.8 |
| Machinery and transport equipment | 859.1 | 905.7 | 1,114.1 |
| Miscellaneous manufactured articles | 217.0 | 210.0 | 220.2 |
| **Total** (incl. others) | 3,380.9 | 3,696.1 | 4,292.7 |

| Exports f.o.b. | 1994 | 1995 | 1996 |
|---|---|---|---|
| Natural calcium phosphates | 143.7 | 150.5 | 179.0 |
| Natural potassic salts, crude | 132.5 | 173.5 | 177.2 |
| Chemicals | 375.5 | 431.1 | 467.0 |
| Fertilizers | 127.5 | 161.4 | n.a. |
| Cement | 39.1 | 42.2 | 58.5 |
| Vegetables, fruit and nuts | 95.4 | 97.3 | 115.7 |
| Basic manufactures | 83.8 | 95.7 | 109.1 |
| Machinery and transport equipment | 56.4 | 65.5 | 34.5 |
| Miscellaneous manufactured articles | 57.9 | 68.9 | 72.1 |
| **Total** (incl. others) | 1,136.1 | 1,433.3 | 1,466.6 |

Sources: Central Bank of Jordan and IMF, *Jordan—Statistical Appendix* (March 1997).

**PRINCIPAL TRADING PARTNERS**
(countries of consignment, US $ million)

| Imports c.i.f. | 1994 | 1995 | 1996* |
|---|---|---|---|
| Argentina | 16.1 | 48.0 | 14.0 |
| Australia | 29.8 | 40.1 | 108.2 |
| Bahrain | 22.3 | 40.4 | 28.6 |
| Belgium-Luxembourg | 100.6 | 74.2 | 61.8 |
| Brazil | 37.7 | 52.6 | 56.7 |
| China, People's Republic | 89.5 | 84.1 | 89.7 |
| Egypt | 43.0 | 46.2 | 93.0 |
| France | 159.0 | 170.0 | 210.5 |
| Germany | 263.9 | 311.6 | 341.6 |
| India | 55.7 | 69.5 | 74.3 |
| Indonesia | 35.2 | 54.8 | 50.9 |
| Iraq | 417.1 | 451.3 | 505.6 |
| Italy | 199.0 | 197.7 | 251.6 |
| Japan | 134.0 | 130.5 | 179.0 |
| Korea, Republic | 83.4 | 109.6 | 133.0 |
| Lebanon | 25.8 | 42.5 | 51.6 |
| Malaysia | 94.8 | 107.8 | 85.6 |
| Netherlands | 129.0 | 102.1 | 115.4 |
| Romania | 39.4 | 30.7 | 47.1 |
| Russia | 24.3 | 43.9 | 51.2 |
| Saudi Arabia | 102.4 | 129.5 | 129.1 |
| Spain | 54.4 | 58.1 | 48.1 |
| Switzerland | 32.2 | 38.2 | 63.1 |
| Syria | 69.1 | 78.4 | 140.3 |
| Turkey | 90.0 | 127.0 | 152.3 |
| Ukraine | 71.2 | 55.4 | 33.7 |
| United Kingdom | 162.9 | 167.1 | 187.7 |
| USA | 332.2 | 342.6 | 415.9 |
| **Total** (incl. others) | 3,368.6 | 3,664.4 | 4,292.7 |

* Source: Central Bank of Jordan.

| Exports f.o.b. | 1993 | 1994 | 1995 |
|---|---|---|---|
| Bahrain | 20.8 | 23.0 | 21.5 |
| China, People's Republic | 24.3 | 12.0 | 19.5 |
| Ethiopia | 2.5 | 5.5 | 17.0 |
| France | 21.3 | 35.5 | 30.3 |
| India | 95.8 | 126.5 | 162.9 |
| Indonesia | 54.8 | 40.0 | 39.2 |
| Iran | 14.5 | 6.4 | 27.9 |
| Iraq | 140.2 | 165.0 | 301.7 |
| Italy | 10.7 | 16.4 | 28.9 |
| Japan | 14.3 | 18.3 | 19.1 |
| Korea, Republic | 11.0 | 20.8 | 18.6 |
| Lebanon | 27.9 | 29.2 | 38.9 |
| Malaysia | 16.3 | 18.9 | 21.2 |
| Netherlands | 16.6 | 19.1 | 25.9 |
| Philippines | 4.6 | 5.6 | 21.5 |
| Qatar | 14.8 | 13.3 | 14.7 |
| Russia | 37.4 | 8.8 | 8.2 |
| Saudi Arabia | 124.7 | 110.5 | 108.2 |
| Sudan | 9.0 | 15.1 | 18.4 |
| Syria | 36.4 | 49.8 | 63.2 |
| Turkey | 20.5 | 15.7 | 30.4 |
| United Arab Emirates | 48.5 | 68.8 | 67.2 |
| United Kingdom | 13.9 | 13.8 | 20.6 |
| USA | 38.6 | 47.5 | 68.3 |
| Yemen | 17.3 | 11.1 | 15.8 |
| **Total** (incl. others) | 1,225.2 | 1,411.1 | 1,768.8 |

Source (unless otherwise indicated): UN, *International Trade Statistics Yearbook*.

# Transport

**RAILWAYS** (traffic)

| | 1993 | 1994 | 1995 |
|---|---|---|---|
| Passenger-km (million) | 2 | 2 | 1 |
| Freight ton-km (million) | 711 | 676 | 698 |

Source: UN, *Statistical Yearbook*.

**ROAD TRAFFIC** (motor vehicles in use at 31 December)

| | 1994 | 1995 | 1996 |
|---|---|---|---|
| Passenger cars | 180,453 | 188,238 | 213,874 |
| Buses and coaches | 6,943 | 7,604 | 10,309 |
| Lorries and vans | 63,163 | 69,090 | 68,844 |
| Motorcycles and mopeds | 384 | 368 | 369 |

Source: IRF, *World Road Statistics*.

**SHIPPING**

**Merchant Fleet** (registered at 31 December)

| | 1996 | 1997 | 1998 |
|---|---|---|---|
| Number of vessels | 4 | 7 | 10 |
| Displacement (grt) | 40,829 | 42,799 | 42,100 |

Source: Lloyd's Register of Shipping, *World Fleet Statistics*.

**International Sea-borne Freight Traffic** ('000 metric tons)

| | 1996 | 1997 | 1998 |
|---|---|---|---|
| Goods loaded | 616 | 628 | 609 |
| Goods unloaded | 384 | 398 | 444 |

Source: UN, *Monthly Bulletin of Statistics*.

**CIVIL AVIATION** (traffic on scheduled services)

| | 1994 | 1995 | 1996 |
|---|---|---|---|
| Kilometres flown (million) | 36 | 38 | 42 |
| Passengers carried ('000) | 1,220 | 1,270 | 1,299 |
| Passenger-km (million) | 4,155 | 4,395 | 4,750 |
| Total ton-km (million) | 627 | 695 | 731 |

Sources: Jordan Civil Aviation Authority and Royal Jordanian Airline.

## Tourism

**ARRIVALS BY NATIONALITY** ('000)*

| | 1994 | 1995 | 1996 |
|---|---|---|---|
| Bahrain | 33.4 | 40.2 | 38.5 |
| Egypt | 1,026.9 | 878.1 | 803.3 |
| France | 27.5 | 29.3 | 30.3 |
| Germany | 34.2 | 44.8 | 56.6 |
| Iraq | 246.7 | 263.9 | 187.0 |
| Kuwait | 39.3 | 46.3 | 47.5 |
| Lebanon | 77.0 | 87.8 | 67.8 |
| Syria | 699.9 | 679.2 | 688.7 |
| United Kingdom | 38.1 | 45.0 | 43.8 |
| USA | 58.1 | 83.9 | 86.1 |
| Yemen | 50.8 | 43.1 | 37.9 |
| **Total** (incl. others) | 3,224.8 | 3,277.2 | 3,163.6 |

* Including pilgrims and excursionists (same-day visitors). The total number of tourist arrivals (in '000) was: 858 in 1994; 1,074 in 1995; 1,103 in 1996.

**Tourism receipts** (US $ million): 582 in 1994; 660 in 1995; 744 in 1996.

Source: World Tourism Organization, *Yearbook of Tourism Statistics*.

## Communications Media

(East Bank only)

| | 1994 | 1995 | 1996 |
|---|---|---|---|
| Radio receivers ('000 in use) | 1,265 | 1,350 | 1,600 |
| Television receivers ('000 in use) | 395 | 430 | 480 |
| Telephones ('000 main lines in use)* | 317.3 | 328.4 | 356.2 |
| Telefax stations ('000 in use)† | 31 | 32 | n.a. |
| Mobile telephones (subscribers)† | 1,446 | 11,500 | n.a. |
| Book production: titles | n.a. | 465 | 511 |
| Daily newspapers: | | | |
| Number of titles | 4 | 4 | 4 |
| Average circulation ('000 copies) | 250 | 250 | 250 |
| Non-daily newspapers: | | | |
| Number of titles | n.a. | 34 | 41 |
| Average circulation ('000 copies) | n.a. | 90 | 95 |

* Source: Jordanian Department of Statistics.

† Source: UN, *Statistical Yearbook* (data on telefax stations are estimates).

Source (unless otherwise indicated): UNESCO, *Statistical Yearbook*.

## Education

(East Bank, 1995/96)

| | Schools | Teachers | Pupils |
|---|---|---|---|
| Pre-primary | 828 | 2,848 | 63,250 |
| Primary | 2,531 | 51,721 | 1,074,877 |
| Secondary: general | n.a. | 8,615 | 143,014 |
| Secondary: vocational | n.a. | 2,306 | 33,109 |
| Universities and equivalent | n.a. | 3,511 | 76,375 |
| Other higher education | n.a. | 1,310 | 22,645 |

# Directory

## The Constitution

The revised Constitution was approved by King Talal I on 1 January 1952.

The Hashemite Kingdom of Jordan is an independent, indivisible sovereign state. Its official religion is Islam; its official language Arabic.

### RIGHTS OF THE INDIVIDUAL

There is to be no discrimination between Jordanians on account of race, religion or language. Work, education and equal opportunities shall be afforded to all as far as is possible. The freedom of the individual is guaranteed, as are his dwelling and property. No Jordanian shall be exiled. Labour shall be made compulsory only in a national emergency, or as a result of a conviction; conditions, hours worked and allowances are under the protection of the state.

The Press, and all opinions, are free, except under martial law. Societies can be formed, within the law. Schools may be established freely, but they must follow a recognized curriculum and educational policy. Elementary education is free and compulsory. All religions are tolerated. Every Jordanian is eligible for public office, and choices are to be made by merit only. Power belongs to the people.

### THE LEGISLATIVE POWER

Legislative power is vested in the National Assembly and the King. The National Assembly consists of two houses: the Senate and the House of Representatives.

### THE SENATE

The number of Senators is one-half of the number of members of the House of Representatives. Senators must be unrelated to the King, over 40, and are chosen from present and past Prime Ministers and Ministers, past Ambassadors or Ministers Plenipotentiary, past Presidents of the House of Representatives, past Presidents and members of the Court of Cassation and of the Civil and *Shari'a* Courts of Appeal, retired officers of the rank of General and above, former members of the House of Representatives who have been elected twice to that House, etc. . . . They may not hold public office. Senators are appointed for four years. They may be reappointed. The President of the Senate is appointed for two years.

### THE HOUSE OF REPRESENTATIVES

The members of the House of Representatives are elected by secret ballot in a general direct election and retain their mandate for four years. General elections take place during the four months preceding the end of the term. The President of the House is elected by secret ballot each year by the Representatives. Representatives must be Jordanians of over 30, they must have a clean record, no active business interests, and are debarred from public office. Close relatives of the King are not eligible. If the House of Representatives is dissolved, the new House shall assemble in extraordinary session not more than four months after the date of dissolution. The new House cannot be dissolved for the same reason as the last.

### GENERAL PROVISIONS FOR THE NATIONAL ASSEMBLY

The King summons the National Assembly to its ordinary session on 1 November each year. This date can be postponed by the King for two months, or he can dissolve the Assembly before the end of its three months' session. Alternatively, he can extend the session up to a total period of six months. Each session is opened by a speech from the throne.

Decisions in the House of Representatives and the Senate are made by a majority vote. The quorum is two-thirds of the total number of members in each House. When the voting concerns the Constitution, or confidence in the Council of Ministers, 'the votes shall be taken by calling the members by name in a loud voice'. Sessions are public, though secret sessions can be held at the request of the Government or of five members. Complete freedom of speech, within the rules of either House, is allowed.

The Prime Minister places proposals before the House of Representatives; if accepted there, they are referred to the Senate and finally sent to the King for confirmation. If one house rejects a law while the other accepts it, a joint session of the House of Representatives and the Senate is called, and a decision made by a two-thirds majority. If the King withholds his approval from a law, he returns it to the Assembly within six months with the reasons for his dissent; a joint session of the Houses then makes a decision, and if the law is accepted by this decision it is promulgated. The Budget is submitted to the National Assembly one month before the beginning of the financial year.

### THE KING

The throne of the Hashemite Kingdom devolves by male descent in the dynasty of King Abdullah ibn al-Hussein. The King attains his majority on his eighteenth lunar year; if the throne is inherited by a minor, the powers of the King are exercised by a Regent or a Council of Regency. If the King, through illness or absence, cannot perform his duties, his powers are given to a Deputy, or to a Council of the Throne. This Deputy, or Council, may be appointed by Iradas (decrees) by the King, or, if he is incapable, by the Council of Ministers.

On his accession, the King takes the oath to respect and observe the provisions of the Constitution and to be loyal to the nation. As Head of State he is immune from all liability or responsibility. He approves laws and promulgates them. He declares war, concludes peace and signs treaties; treaties, however, must be approved by the National Assembly. The King is Commander-in-Chief of the navy, the army and the air force. He orders the holding of elections; convenes, inaugurates, adjourns and prorogues the House of Representatives. The Prime Minister is appointed by him, as are the President and members of the Senate. Military and civil ranks are also granted, or withdrawn, by the King. No death sentence is carried out until he has confirmed it.

### MINISTERS

The Council of Ministers consists of the Prime Minister, President of the Council, and of his ministers. Ministers are forbidden to become members of any company, to receive a salary from any company, or to participate in any financial act of trade. The Council of Ministers is entrusted with the conduct of all affairs of state, internal and external.

The Council of Ministers is responsible to the House of Representatives for matters of general policy. Ministers may speak in either House, and, if they are members of one House, they may also vote in that House. Votes of confidence in the Council are cast in the House of Representatives, and decided by a two-thirds majority. If a vote of 'no confidence' is returned, the ministers are bound to resign. Every newly-formed Council of Ministers must present its programme to the House of Representatives and ask for a vote of confidence. The House of Representatives can impeach ministers, as it impeaches its own members.

### AMENDMENTS

Two amendments were passed in November 1974 giving the King the right to dissolve the Senate or to take away membership from any of its members, and to postpone general elections for a period not to exceed a year, if there are circumstances in which the Council of Ministers feels that it is impossible to hold elections. A further amendment in February 1976 enabled the King to postpone elections indefinitely. In January 1984 two amendments were passed, allowing elections 'in any part of the country where it is possible to hold them' (effectively, only the East Bank) and empowering the National Assembly to elect deputies from the Israeli-held West Bank.

# The Government

### HEAD OF STATE

King ABDULLAH IBN AL-HUSSEIN (succeeded to the throne on 7 February 1999).

### CABINET*
(February 2000)

**Prime Minister and Minister of Defence:** ABD AR-RAOUF AR-RAWABDEH.

**Deputy Prime Ministers:** AYMEN AL-MAJALI, MARWAN ABD AL-HALEEM AL-HMUD.

**Minister of Post and Telecommunications:** Dr ABDULLAH TUQAN.

**Minister of Transport:** Eng. ISSA AYYUB.

**Minister of Awqaf (Religious Endowments) and Islamic Affairs:** Dr ABD AS-SALAM AL-ABBADI.

**Minister of Municipal, Rural and Environmental Affairs, and Minister of State for Parliamentary Affairs:** TAWFIQ KREISHAN.

**Minister of Foreign Affairs:** ABD AL-ILAH AL-KHATIB.

**Minister of Culture and of Information:** SALEH QALLAB.

**Minister of Youth and Sports:** SA'ID SHUQUM.

**Minister of Tourism and Antiquities:** AQEL BELTAJI.

**Minister of the Interior:** NAYEF AL-QADI.

**Minister of Finance:** Dr MICHEL MARTO.

**Minister of Labour:** EID AL-FAYEZ.

**Minister of Education:** Dr IZZAT JARADAT.

**Minister of Agriculture:** HASHEM SHBUL.

**Minister of Energy and Mineral Resources:** Eng. WA'IL SABRI.

**Minister of Water and Irrigation:** Dr KAMEL MAHADEEN.

**Minister of Justice:** KHALAF MASA'IDAH.

**Minister of Social Development:** Dr MUHAMMAD JUM'AH AL-WAHSH.

**Minister of Health:** Dr MUSLEH AT-TARAWNEH.

**Minister of Public Works and Housing:** HUSSNI ABU GHEIDA.

**Minister of Industry and Trade, and Minister of Planning (acting):** Dr MUHAMMAD AL-HALAIQA.

**Chief of the Royal Court:** FAYEZ AT-TARAWNEH.

* The Head of Intelligence and the Governor of the Central Bank also have full ministerial status.

### MINISTRIES

**Office of the Prime Minister:** POB 1577, 35216, Amman; tel. (6) 4641211; fax (6) 4687420; e-mail pmic@pm.gov.jo; internet www.pm.gov.jo.

**Ministry of Agriculture:** POB 961043, Amman; tel. (6) 4686151; fax (6) 4686310.

**Ministry of Awqaf (Religious Endowments) and Islamic Affairs:** POB 659, Amman; tel. (6) 5666141; fax (6) 5602254.

**Ministry of Culture:** POB 6140, Amman; tel. (6) 5604701; fax (6) 5622214.

**Ministry of Defence:** POB 1577, Amman; tel. (6) 5644361.

**Ministry of Development Affairs:** POB 1577, Amman; tel. (6) 4644361; fax (6) 4648825.

**Ministry of Education:** POB 1646, Amman 11118; tel. (6) 5607181; fax (6) 5666019; e-mail moe@amra.nic.gov.jo.

**Ministry of Energy and Mineral Resources:** POB 140027, Amman; tel. (6) 5817900; fax (6) 5818336; internet www.nic.gov.jo/memr/memr.html.

**Ministry of Finance:** POB 85, Amman 11118; tel. (6) 4636321; fax (6) 4618528; e-mail webmaster@mof.gov.jo; internet www.mof.gov.jo.

**Ministry of Foreign Affairs:** POB 1577, Amman; tel. (6) 5642359; fax (6) 5648825.

**Ministry of Health:** POB 86, Amman; tel. (6) 5665131; fax (6) 5688373.

**Ministry of Industry and Trade:** POB 2019, Amman; tel. (6) 6507191; fax (6) 5603721.

**Ministry of Information:** POB 1794, Amman; tel. (6) 4641467; fax (6) 4648825.

**Ministry of the Interior:** POB 100, Amman; tel. (6) 4653533; fax (6) 5606908.

**Ministry of Justice:** POB 6040, Amman; tel. (6) 4653533; fax (6) 4629949; e-mail moj@amra.nic.gov.jo.

**Ministry of Labour:** POB 9052, Amman; tel. (6) 5607481; fax (6) 5667193.

**Ministry of Municipal, Rural and Environmental Affairs:** POB 1799, Amman; tel. (6) 4641393; fax (6) 4649341.

**Ministry of Planning:** POB 555, Amman; tel. (6) 4644466; fax (6) 4649341.

**Ministry of Post and Telecommunications:** POB 35214, Amman; tel. (6) 5607111; fax (6) 5606233.

**Ministry of Public Works and Housing:** POB 1220, Amman; tel. (6) 5850470; fax (6) 5857590; e-mail mhpw@amra.nic.gov.jo.

**Ministry of Social Development:** POB 6720, Amman; tel. (6) 5931391; fax (6) 5931518.

**Ministry of Tourism and Antiquities:** POB 224, Amman 11118; tel. (6) 4642311; fax (6) 4648465; e-mail tourism@mota.gov.jo; internet www.mota.gov.jo.

**Ministry of Transport:** POB 35214, Amman; tel. (6) 5518111; fax (6) 5527233; e-mail mot1@go.com.jo.

**Ministry of Water and Irrigation:** Amman; tel. (6) 5689400; fax (6) 5642520.

# Legislature

**MAJLIS AL-UMMA**
(National Assembly)

**Senate**

The Senate (House of Notables) consists of 40 members, appointed by the King. A new Senate was appointed by the King on 22 November 1997.

**Speaker:** ABD AL-HADI AL-MAJALI.

**House of Representatives**

**General Election, 4 November 1997***

| Party/Group | Seats |
|---|---|
| Pro-Government† | 60 |
| Independent nationalists and leftists | 10 |
| Independent Islamists | 8 |
| National Constitutional Party (NCP) | 2 |
| **Total** | 80 |

**Speaker:** SAED HAYEL AS-SROUR.

* The 1997 general election was boycotted by all the principal opposition parties in Jordan, including the Islamic Action Front (which had emerged as the largest single party in the House of Representatives after the 1993 elections).

† Excluding NCP.

# Political Organizations

Political parties were banned before the elections of July 1963. In September 1971 King Hussein announced the formation of a Jordanian National Union, which was the only legal political organization. Communists, Marxists and 'other advocates of imported ideologies' were ineligible for membership. In March 1972 the organization was renamed the Arab National Union. In April 1974 King Hussein dissolved the executive committee of the Arab National Union, and accepted the resignation of the Secretary-General. In February 1976 the Cabinet approved a law abolishing the Union, membership of which was about 100,000. A royal commission was appointed in April 1990 to draft a National Charter, one feature of which was the legalization of political parties. In January 1991 King Hussein approved the National Charter, which was formally endorsed in June. In July 1992 the House of Representatives adopted draft legislation which formally permitted the establishment of political parties, subject to certain conditions. In the same month a joint session of the Senate and the House of Representatives was convened to debate amendments to the new legislation, proposed by the Senate. The political parties which achieved representation in the general election of November 1993 were: the Islamic Action Front (Sec.-Gen. Dr ABD AL-LATIF ARABIYAT); al-Mustaqbal; the Jordanian Arab Socialist Baath Party (Sec.-Gen. MAHMOUD AL-MA'AYITAH); al-Yakatha; al-Ahd; the Jordan National Alliance; the Jordan People's Democratic Party (Leader TAYSIR AZ-ZABRI); the Jordan Social Democratic Party; and the Jordanian Arab Democratic Party. In May 1997 nine centre parties, including Pledge and the Jordan National Alliance, announced that they had united to form the National Constitutional Party (NCP), which became Jordan's largest political grouping. The formation of the NCP, together with the establishment in 1996 of the Unionist Arab Democratic Party (a coalition of three leftist parties), reduced the total number of political parties from 24 to 14. In July 1997 the establishment of a new Jordanian political party, the Popular Democratic Pan-Arab Movement, was announced. In May 1999 the Popular Participation Bloc was established to contest the municipal elections, held in July; it was a new gouping of 13 leftist, Baathist and pan-Arab parties. The formation of two new political parties was announced in late 1999: the New Generations Party (centrist green party; Leader ZAHI KARIM) and the Jordanian Arab New Dawn Party.

# Diplomatic Representation

**EMBASSIES IN JORDAN**

**Algeria:** 3rd Circle, Jabal Amman; tel. (6) 5641271; Ambassador: ABDERRAHMAN SHRAYYET.

**Australia:** POB 35201, Amman 11180; tel. (6) 5930246; fax (6) 5932160; e-mail ausemb@nets.com.jo; Ambassador: IAN W. RUSSELL.

**Austria:** POB 830795, 36 Mithqal al-Fayez St, Jabal Amman 11183; tel. (6) 4644635; fax (6) 4612725; e-mail austemb@go.com.jo; Ambassador: Dr PHILIPP HOYOS.

**Bahrain:** Amman; tel. (6) 5664148; Ambassador: IBRAHIM ALI IBRAHIM.

**Belgium:** POB 942, Amman 11118; tel. (6) 5675683; fax (6) 5697487; Ambassador: GUIDO COURTOIS.

**Bosnia and Herzegovina:** POB 850836, Amman 11185; tel. (6) 5856921; fax (6) 5856923; Chargé d'affaires: IBRAHIM EFENDIĆ.

**Brazil:** POB 5497, Amman 11183; tel. (6) 4642183; fax (6) 4641328; e-mail jorbrem@go.com.jo; Ambassador: SERGIO HENRIQUE NABUCO DE CASTRO.

**Bulgaria:** POB 950578, Al-Mousel St 7, Amman 11195; tel. (6) 5699391; fax (6) 5699393; Ambassador: (vacant).

**Canada:** POB 815403, Pearl of Shmeisani Bldg, Shmeisani, Amman; tel. (6) 5666124; fax (6) 5689227; Ambassador: MICHAEL J. MOLLOY.

**Chile:** POB 830663, 71 Suez St, Abdoun, Amman 11183; tel. (6) 5923360; fax (6) 5924263; e-mail echilejo@go.com.jo; Chargé d'affaires: ROBERTO ALVAREZ.

**China, People's Republic:** Shmeisani, Amman; tel. (6) 5666139; Ambassador: LIU BAOLAI.

**Denmark:** POB 222, 24 Sharif Abd-al Hamid Sharaf St, Shmeisani, Amman 11118; tel. (6) 5603703; fax (6) 5672170; e-mail danish_cons@nets.com.jo; Ambassador LARS BLINKENBERG.

**Egypt:** POB 35178, Qurtuba St, Between 4th-5th Circle, Jabal Amman; tel. (6) 5605175; Ambassador: HANI RIAD ALI SULAYMAN.

**France:** POB 5348, Jabal Amman; tel. (6) 4641273; fax (6) 4659606; e-mail ambafr@joinnet.com.jo; internet www.ambafrance.org.jo; Ambassador: BERNARD EMIÉ.

**Germany:** POB 183, Benghazi St, Jabal Amman; tel. (6) 5930351; fax (6) 5932887; Ambassador: PETER MENDE.

**Greece:** POB 35069, Jabal Amman; tel. (6) 5672331; fax (6) 5696591; Ambassador: THEODOROS N. PANTZARIS.

**Holy See:** POB 142916, Amman 11814; tel. (6) 5929934; fax (6) 5929931; e-mail nuntius@nol.com.jo; Apostolic Nuncio: Most Rev. GIUSEPPE LAZZAROTTO.

**Hungary:** POB 3441, Amman 11181; tel. (6) 5925614; fax (6) 5930836; Chargé d'Affaires: Dr ATTILA SZANTO.

**India:** POB 2168, 1st Circle, Jabal Amman; tel. (6) 4622098; fax (6) 4659540; e-mail <indembjo@firstnet.com.jo>; Ambassador: HER CHARAN SINGH DHODY.

**Indonesia:** POB 811784, South Um-Uthaina, 6th Circle, Amman; tel. (6) 5513232; fax (6) 5528380; e-mail amman96@go.com.jo; Ambassador: EDDY SUMANTRI.

**Iran:** POB 173, Jabal Amman; tel. (6) 5641281; Ambassador: G. ANSARI.

**Iraq:** POB 2025, 1st Circle, Jabal Amman; tel. (6) 5639331; Ambassador: NORI AL-WAYES.

**Israel:** POB 950866, Amman 11195; tel. (6) 5524680; fax (6) 5524689; e-mail isrem@go.com.jo; Ambassador: Dr ODED ERAN.

**Italy:** POB 9800, Jabal Luweibdeh, Amman; tel. (6) 4638185; fax (6) 4659730; e-mail italemb1@go.com.jo; internet www.italembamman.org; Ambassador: FRANCESCO CERULLI.

**Japan:** POB 2835, Jabal Amman; tel. (6) 5672486; fax (6) 5672006; Ambassador: KOICHI MATSUMOTO.

**Korea, Democratic People's Republic:** Amman; tel. (6) 5666349; Ambassador: CHOE GWANG RAE.

**Korea, Republic:** POB 3060, Amman 11181; tel. (6) 5930745; fax (6) 5930280; e-mail skorea@go.com.jo; Ambassador: LEE KYUNG-WOO.

**Kuwait:** POB 2107, Jabal Amman; tel. (6) 5641235; Ambassador FAYSAL MESHA'AN.

**Lebanon:** POB 811779, 2nd Circle, Jabal Amman 11181; tel. (6) 5641381; fax (6) 5929111; Ambassador: Dr WILLIAM HABIB.

**Morocco:** Jabal Amman; tel. (6) 5641451; Chargé d'affaires: SALEM FANKHAR ASH-SHANFARI.

**Norway:** POB 830510, 25 Damascus St, Abdoun, Amman; tel. (6) 5931646; fax (6) 5931650; e-mail noremb@abn.com.jo; Ambassador JAN G. JØLLE.

**Oman:** Amman; tel. (6) 5661131; Ambassador: KHAMIS BIN HAMAD AL-BATASHI.

**Pakistan:** POB 1232, Amman; tel. (6) 5638352; fax (6) 5611633; Ambassador: TARIQ KHAN AFRIDI.

**Poland:** POB 2124, 3rd Circle, 1 Mai Zayadeh St, Jabal Amman; tel. (6) 4637153; fax (6) 4618744; e-mail polemb@nol.com.jo; Chargé d'affaires: MARIUSZ WOŹNIAK.

**Qatar:** Amman; tel. (6) 5644331; Ambassador: Sheikh HAMAD BIN MUHAMMAD BIN JABER ATH-THANI.

**Romania:** POB 2869, 21 Abdullah Bin Massoud St, Shmeisani, Amman; tel. (6) 5667738; fax (6) 5684018; Ambassador: IOAN AGAFICIOAIA.

**Russia:** Amman; tel. (6) 5641158; Ambassador: ALEKSANDR VLADIMIROVICH SALTANOV.

**Saudi Arabia:** POB 2133, 5th Circle, Jabal Amman; tel. (6) 5644154; Ambassador: ABDULLAH SUDEIRI.

**South Africa:** POB 851508, Sweifieh 11185, Amman; tel. (6) 811194; fax (6) 810080; Ambassador: H. B. B. DE BRUYN.

**Spain:** Zahran St, POB 454, Jabal Amman; tel. (6) 4614166; fax (6) 4614173; Ambassador: EUDALDO MIRAPEIX MARTÍNEZ.

**Sri Lanka:** POB 830731, Amman; tel. (6) 5820611; fax (6) 5820615; e-mail lankaemb@go.com.jo.

**Sudan:** Jabal Amman; tel. (6) 5624145; Ambassador: AHMAD DIAB.

**Sweden:** POB 830536, 4th Circle, Jabal Amman; tel. (6) 5931177; fax (6) 5930179; e-mail sweamman@go.com.jo; Ambassador: KLAS GIEROW.

**Switzerland:** Jabal Amman; tel. (6) 5931416; fax (6) 5930685; Ambassador: GIAN-FEDERICO PEDOTTI.

**Syria:** POB 1377, 4th Circle, Jabal Amman; tel. (6) 5641935; Chargé d'affaires: MAJID ABOU SALEH.

**Tunisia:** Jabal Amman; tel. (6) 5674307; fax (6) 5605790; Ambassador: HATEM BEN OTHMAN.

**Turkey:** POB 2062, Islamic College St, 2nd Circle, Jabal Amman 11181; tel. (6) 5641251; fax (6) 5612353; Ambassador: SÜHA UMAR.

**United Arab Emirates:** Jabal Amman; tel. (6) 5644369; Ambassador: AHMAD ALI AZ-ZU'ABI.

**United Kingdom:** POB 87, Abdoun, Amman; tel. (6) 5923100; fax (6) 5923759; e-mail british@nets.com.jo; Ambassador: EDWARD CHAPLIN.

**USA:** POB 354, Amman 11118; tel. (6) 5920201; fax (6) 5920121; Ambassador: WILLIAMS J. BURNS.

**Yemen:** Amman; tel. (6) 5642381; Ambassador: AHMAD AL-LOZI.

**Yugoslavia:** POB 5227, Amman; tel. (6) 5665107; Ambassador: ZORAN S. POPOVIĆ.

# Judicial System

With the exception of matters of purely personal nature concerning members of non-Muslim communities, the law of Jordan was based on Islamic Law for both civil and criminal matters. During the days of the Ottoman Empire, certain aspects of Continental law, especially French commercial law and civil and criminal procedure, were introduced. Due to British occupation of Palestine and Transjordan from 1917 to 1948, the Palestine territory has adopted, either by statute or case law, much of the English common law. Since the annexation of the non-occupied part of Palestine and the formation of the Hashemite Kingdom of Jordan, there has been a continuous effort to unify the law.

**Court of Cassation.** The Court of Cassation consists of seven judges, who sit in full panel for exceptionally important cases. In most appeals, however, only five members sit to hear the case. All cases involving amounts of more than JD 100 may be reviewed by this Court, as well as cases involving lesser amounts and cases which cannot be monetarily valued. However, for the latter types of cases, review is available only by leave of the Court of Appeal, or, upon refusal by the Court of Appeal, by leave of the President of the Court of Cassation. In addition to these functions as final and Supreme Court of Appeal, the Court of Cassation also sits as High Court of Justice to hear applications in the nature of habeas corpus, mandamus and certiorari dealing with complaints of a citizen against abuse of governmental authority.

**Courts of Appeal.** There are two Courts of Appeal, each of which is composed of three judges, whether for hearing of appeals or for dealing with Magistrates Courts' judgments in chambers. Jurisdiction of the two Courts is geographical, with the Court for the Western Region (which has not sat since June 1967) sitting in Jerusalem and the Court for the Eastern Region sitting in Amman. The regions are separated by the Jordan river. Appellate review of the Courts of Appeal extends to judgments rendered in the Courts of First Instance, the Magistrates' Courts, and Religious Courts.

**Courts of First Instance.** The Courts of First Instance are courts of general jurisdiction in all matters civil and criminal except those specifically allocated to the Magistrates' Courts. Three judges sit in all felony trials, while only two judges sit for misdemeanour and civil cases. Each of the seven Courts of First Instance also exercises appellate jurisdiction in cases involving judgments of less than JD 20 and fines of less than JD 10, rendered by the Magistrates' Courts.

**Magistrates' Courts.** There are 14 Magistrates' Courts, which exercise jurisdiction in civil cases involving no more than JD 250 and in criminal cases involving maximum fines of JD 100 or maximum imprisonment of one year.

**Religious Courts.** There are two types of religious court: The *Shari'a* Courts (Muslims): and the Ecclesiastical Courts (Eastern Orthodox, Greek Melkite, Roman Catholic and Protestant). Jurisdiction extends to personal (family) matters, such as marriage, divorce, alimony, inheritance, guardianship, wills, interdiction and, for the Muslim community, the constitution of Waqfs (Religious Endowments). When a dispute involves persons of different religious communities, the Civil Courts have jurisdiction in the matter unless the parties agree to submit to the jurisdiction of one or the other of the Religious Courts involved.

Each *Shari'a* (Muslim) Court consists of one judge (*Qadi*), while most of the Ecclesiastical (Christian) Courts are normally composed of three judges, who are usually clerics. *Shari'a* Courts apply the doctrines of Islamic Law, based on the Koran and the *Hadith* (Precepts of Muhammad), while the Ecclesiastical Courts base their law on various aspects of Canon Law. In the event of conflict between any two Religious Courts or between a Religious Court and a Civil Court, a Special Tribunal of three judges is appointed by the President of the Court of Cassation, to decide which court shall have jurisdiction. Upon the advice of experts on the law of the various communities, this Special Tribunal decides on the venue for the case at hand.

# Religion

Over 80% of the population are Sunni Muslims, and the King can trace unbroken descent from the Prophet Muhammad. There is a Christian minority, living mainly in the towns, and there are smaller numbers of non-Sunni Muslims.

### ISLAM

**Chief Justice and President of the Supreme Muslim Secular Council:** Sheikh MUHAMMAD MHELAN.

**Director of Shari'a Courts:** Sheikh SUBHI AL-MUWQQAT.

**Mufti of the Hashemite Kingdom of Jordan:** Sheikh MUHAMMAD ABDO HASHEM.

### CHRISTIANITY

#### The Roman Catholic Church

*Latin Rite*

Jordan forms part of the Patriarchate of Jerusalem (see chapter on Israel).

**Vicar-General for Transjordan:** Mgr SELIM SAYEGH (Titular Bishop of Aquae in Proconsulari), Latin Vicariate, POB 851379, Amman 11185; tel. (6) 5929546; fax (6) 5920548.

*Melkite Rite*

The Greek-Melkite archdiocese of Petra (Wadi Musa) and Philadelphia (Amman) contained 31,000 adherents at 31 December 1998.

**Archbishop of Petra and Philadelphia:** Most Rev. GEORGES EL-MURR, Archevêché Grec-Melkite Catholique, POB 2435, Jabal Amman 11181; tel. (6) 4624757; fax (6) 4628560.

*Syrian Rite*

The Syrian Catholic Patriarch of Antioch is resident in Beirut, Lebanon.

**Patriarchal Exarchate of Jerusalem:** Mont Achrafieh, POB 510393, Rue Barto, Amman; Exarch Patriarchal Mgr GRÉGOIRE PIERRE ABD AL-AHAD.

#### The Anglican Communion

Within the Episcopal Church in Jerusalem and the Middle East, Jordan forms part of the diocese of Jerusalem. The President Bishop of the Church is the Bishop in Jerusalem (see the chapter on Israel).

**Assistant Bishop in Amman:** Rt Rev. ELIA KHOURY, POB 598, Amman.

#### Other Christian Churches

The Coptic Orthodox Church, the Greek Orthodox Church (Patriarchate of Jerusalem) and the Evangelical Lutheran Church in Jordan are also active.

# The Press

**Jordan Press Association (JPA):** Amman; Pres. RAKAN AL-MAJALI; Sec.-Gen. NIDAL MANSUR.

### DAILIES

**Al-Akhbar** (News): POB 62420, Amman; f. 1976; Arabic; publ. by the Arab Press Co; Editor RACAN EL-MAJALI; circ. 15,000.

**Al-Aswaq** (Markets): POB 11117, Amman 11123; tel. (6) 5687690; fax (6) 5687292; f. 1992; Editor MUSTAFA ABU LIBDEH; circ. 40,000.

**Ad-Dustour** (The Constitution): POB 591, Amman; tel. (6) 5664153; fax (6) 5667170; e-mail dustour@go.com.jo; f. 1967; Arabic; publ. by the Jordan Press and Publishing Co; owns commercial printing facilities; Chair. KAMEL ASH-SHERIF; Editor NABIL ASH-SHARIF; Man. Dir SAIF ASH-SHARIF; circ. 100,000.

**Al-Mithaq:** Amman; f. 1993; Arabic.

**Ar-Rai** (Opinion): POB 11118, University Rd, Amman; tel. (6) 5667171; fax (6) 5676581; e-mail alrai@go.com.jo; internet www.accessme.com/al-ra'i; f. 1971; morning; Arabic; independent; published by Jordan Press Foundation; Chair. Dr KHALED AL-KARAKI; Gen. Dir MUHAMMAD AL-AMAD; Editor-in-Chief SULAYMAN QUDA; circ. 90,000.

**Arab Daily:** Amman; f. 1999; English.

**The Jordan Times:** POB 6710, University Rd, Amman; tel. (6) 5684311; fax (6) 5696183; e-mail jotimes@go.com.jo; internet www.accessme.com/JordanTimes; f. 1975; English; published by Jordan Press Establishment; Editor-in-Chief GEORGE HAWATMEH; circ. 10,000.

**Sawt ash-Shaab** (Voice of the People): POB 3037, Amman; tel. (6) 5667101; fax (6) 5667993; f. 1983; Arabic; Editor-in-Chief: HASHEM KHAISAT; circ. 30,000.

### WEEKLIES

**Al-Majd:** POB 926856, Amman 11110; tel. (6) 5530553; fax (6) 5530352; f. 1994; Editor FAHD AR-RIMAWI; circ. 10,000.

### PERIODICALS

**Akhbar al-Usbou** (News of the Week): POB 605, Amman; tel. (6) 5677881; fax (6) 5677882; f. 1959; weekly; Arabic; economic, social, political; Chief Editor and Publr ABD AL-HAFIZ MUHAMMAD; circ. 50,000.

**Al-Ghad al-Iqtisadi:** Media Services International, POB 9313, Amman 11191; tel. (6) 5645380; fax (6) 5648298; fortnightly; English; economic; Chief Editor RIAD AL-KHOURI.

**Arabia Online:** POB 91128, Amman 11191; tel. (6) 5154238; fax (6) 5154239; e-mail info@arabia.com; internet www.arabia.com; f. 1995; monthly; Arabic; information technology; Editor-in-Chief KHALDOON TABAZA.

**Huda El-Islam** (The Right Way of Islam): POB 659, Amman; tel. (6) 5666141; f. 1956; monthly; Arabic; scientific and literary; published by the Ministry of Awqaf and Islamic Affairs; Editor Dr AHMAD MUHAMMAD HULAYYEL.

**Jordan:** POB 224, Amman; f. 1969; published quarterly by Jordan Information Bureau, Washington; circ. 100,000.

**Al-Liwa'** (The Standard): POB 3067, 2nd Circle, Jabal Amman 11181; tel. (6) 5642770; fax (6) 5656324; f. 1972; weekly; Arabic; Editor-in-Chief HASSAN AT-TAL; Man. Dir MUHAMMAD H. AL; circ. 15,000.

**Military Magazine:** Army Headquarters, Amman; f. 1955; quarterly; dealing with military and literary subjects; published by Armed Forces.

**Royal Wings:** POB 302, Amman; tel. (6) 5672872; fax (6) 5672527; bi-monthly; Arabic and English; magazine for Royal Jordanian Airline; circ. 40,000.

**As-Sabah** (The Morning): POB 2396, Amman; weekly; Arabic; circ. 6,000.

**Shari'a:** POB 585, Amman; f. 1959; fortnightly; Islamic affairs; published by Shari'a College; circ. 5,000.

**Shihan:** POB 96-654, Amman; tel. (6) 5601511; fax (6) 5656324; e-mail shihan@go.com.jo; internet www.access2arabia.com/shihan; weekly; Arabic; Editor-in-Chief HASSAN AT-TAL.

**The Star:** Media Services International, POB 9313 Amman 11191; tel. (6) 5645380; fax (6) 5648298; e-mail star@arabia.com; f. 1982, formerly The Jerusalem Star; weekly; English and French; Publr and Editor-in-Chief OSAMA ASH-SHERIF; circ. 9,000.

**World Travel Gazette (WTG):** POB 658, Amman; tel. (6) 5665091; fax (6) 5667933; Arabic.

### NEWS AGENCIES

**Jordan News Agency (PETRA):** POB 6845, Amman; tel. (6) 5644455; e-mail petra@petra.gov.jo; internet www.petra.gov.jo; f. 1965; government-controlled; Dir-Gen. ABDULLAH AL-UTUM.

#### Foreign News Bureaux

**Agence France-Presse (AFP):** POB 3340, Amman 11181; tel. (6) 4642976; fax (6) 4654680; e-mail randa@afp.index.com.jo; Bureau Man. Mrs RANDA HABIB.

**Agenzia Nazionale Stampa Associata (ANSA)** (Italy): POB 35111, Amman; tel. (6) 5644092; Correspondent JOHN HALABI.

**Associated Press (AP)** (USA): POB 35111, Amman 11180; tel. (6) 4614660; fax (6) 4614661; e-mail jamal-halaby@ap.org; Correspondent JAMAL HALABY.

**Deutsche Presse Agentur (dpa)** (Germany): POB 35111, Amman; tel. (6) 5623907; Correspondent JOHN HALABI.

**Reuters** (UK): POB 667, Amman; tel. (6) 5623776; fax (6) 5619231; Bureau Chief JACK REDDEN.

**Informatsionnoye Telegrafnoye Agentstvo Rossii—Telegrafnoye Agentstvo Suverennykh Stran (ITAR—TASS)** (Russia): Jabal Amman, Nabich Faris St, Block 111/83 124, Amman; Correspondent NIKOLAI LEBEDINSKY.

Central News Agency (Taiwan), Iraqi News Agency, Kuwait News Agency (KUNA), Middle East News Agency (Egypt), Qatar News Agency, Saudi Press Agency and UPI (USA) also maintain bureaux in Amman.

## Publishers

**Alfaris Publishing and Distribution Co:** POB 9157, Petra Centre, A. H. Shoman St, Shmeisani, Amman 11191; tel. (6) 5605432; fax (6) 5685501; e-mail mkayyali@nets.com.jo; internet www.kayyalibooks.com; Dir MAHER SAID KAYYALI.

**Aram Studies Publishing and Distribution House:** POB 997, Amman 11941; tel. (6) 835015; fax (6) 835079; art, finance, health, management, science, business; Gen. Dir SALEH ABOUSBA.

**El-Nafa'es:** POB 211511, Al-Abdali, Amman 11121; tel. (6) 5693940; fax (6) 5693941; e-mail alnafaes@hotmail.com; f. 1990; education, Islamic.

**Jordan Book Centre Co Ltd:** POB 301, Al-Jubeiha, Amman 11941; tel. (6) 5151882; fax (6) 5152016; e-mail jbc@go.com.jo; f. 1982; fiction, business, economics, computer science, medicine, engineering, general non-fiction; Man. Dir J. J. SHARBAIN.

**Jordan Distribution Agency Co Ltd:** POB 375, Amman 11118; tel. (6) 4630191; fax (6) 4635152; e-mail jda@go.com.jo; f. 1951; history; Chair. and Gen. Man. RAJA ELISSA; Dir NADIA ELISSA.

**Jordan House for Publication:** POB 1121, Basman St, Amman; tel. (6) 24224; fax (6) 51062; f. 1952; medicine, nursing, dentistry; Man. Dir MURSI EL-ASHKAR.

**Jordan Press and Publishing Co Ltd:** POB 591, Amman; tel. (6) 5664153; fax (6) 5667170; e-mail dustour@go.com.jo; f. 1967 by *Al-Manar* and *Falastin* dailies; publishes *Ad-Dustour* (daily), *Ad-Dustour Sport* (weekly) and *The Star* (English weekly); Chair. KAMEL ASH-SHARIF; Dir-Gen SEIF ASH-SHERIF.

**Jordan Press Foundation:** POB 6710, Amman; tel. (6) 5667171; fax (6) 5661242; publishes *Ar-Rai* (daily) and the *Jordan Times* (daily); Chair. MAHMOUD AL-KAYED; Gen. Dir MUHAMMAD AMAD.

**At-Tanwir al-Ilmi** (Scientific Enlightenment Publishing House): POB 4237, Al-Mahatta, Amman 11131; tel. and fax (6) 4899619; e-mail taisir@yahoo.com; education,engineering, philosophy, science, sociology; Owner DR TAISIR SUBHI MAHMOUD.

Other publishers in Amman include: Dairat al-Ihsaat al-Amman, George N. Kawar, Al-Matbaat al-Hashmiya and The National Press.

## Broadcasting and Communications

### TELECOMMUNICATIONS

**Telecommunications Regulatory Commission (TRC):** POB 850967, Amman 11185; tel. (6) 5862020; fax (6) 5863641; e-mail trc@trc.gov.jo; Dir-Gen. Dr YOUSUF MANSUR.

**Jordan Mobile Telephone Services (JMTS—Fastlink):** 25 Said Abujaber St, Um-Uthaina, Amman; tel. (6) 5512010; fax (6) 5673242; e-mail jumanat@fastlink.com.jo; f. 1994; private co; since 1995 operates Jordan's first mobile telecommunications network.

**Jordan Telecommunications Company (JTC):** POB 1689, Amman 11118; tel. (6) 4638301; fax (6) 4649882; 60% govt-owned; 40% privately-owned; Chair. SHABIB AMMARI.

### BROADCASTING

#### Radio and Television

**Jordan Radio and Television Corporation (JRTV):** POB 1041, Amman; tel. (6) 773111; fax (6) 751503; e-mail general@jrtv.gov.jo; internet www.jrtv.com; f. 1968; government TV station broadcasts for 90 hours weekly in Arabic and English; in colour; advertising accepted; Dir-Gen. IHSAN RAMZI SHIKIM; Dir of Television NASSER JUDEH; Dir of Radio HASHIM KHURAYSAT.

## Finance

(cap. = capital; p.u. = paid up; dep. = deposits; m. = million; res = reserves; brs = branches; JD = Jordanian dinars)

### BANKING

#### Central Bank

**Central Bank of Jordan:** POB 37, Amman 11118; tel. (6) 4630301; fax (6) 4638889; e-mail rdep@cbj.gov.jo; internet www.cbj.gov.jo;

f. 1964; cap. JD 18m., res JD 12m., dep. JD 2,232m. (Dec. 1998); Gov. and Chair. Dr ZIAD FARIZ; Dep. Gov. AHMAD ABD AL-FATTAH; 2 brs.

### National Banks

**Arab Bank PLC:** POB 950545, Shmeisani, Amman 11195; tel. (6) 5607115; fax (6) 5606793; e-mail international@arabbank.com.jo; internet www.arabbank.com; f. 1930; cap. JD 146.9m., res JD 1,604.9m., dep. JD 15,528.9m. (Dec. 1998); Chair. and CEO ABD AL-MAJID SHOMAN; Pres. and Dep. Chair. KHALID SHUMAN; 87 brs in Jordan, 82 brs abroad.

**Bank of Jordan PLC:** POB 2140, Shmeisani, Amman; tel. (6) 5696277; fax (6) 5696291; e-mail boj@go.com.jo; f. 1960; cap. JD 21m., res JD 11.7m., dep. JD 465.7m. (Dec. 1998); Chair. TAWFIK SHAKER FAKHOURI; Gen. Man. MUHAMMAD J. QASSIM; 72 brs.

**Cairo Amman Bank:** POB 950661, Cairo Amman Bank Bldg, Wadi Saqra St, Amman 11195; tel. (6) 4616910; fax (6) 4642890; e-mail can@ca-bank.com.jo; internet www.ca-bank.com; f. 1960; cap. JD 20m., res JD 15.5m., dep. JD 772m. (Dec. 1997); Chair. KHALED MASRI; Gen. Man. YAZID MUFTI; 44 brs in Jordan, 19 brs abroad.

**Export and Finance Bank:** POB 941283, Issam Ajlouni St, Amman 11194; tel. (6) 5694250; fax (6) 5692062; e-mail info@efbank.com.jo; internet www.efbank.com.jo; f. 1995; cap. JD 22m., res JD 2.9m., dep. JD 103.6m. (Dec. 1999); Chair. and CEO ALI AL-HUSRY; Gen. Man. HAGOP BANNAYAN (acting).

**Jordan Gulf Bank:** POB 9989, Shmeisani-Al Burj Area, Amman 11191; tel. (6) 5603931; fax (6) 5664110; e-mail jgb@jgbank.com.jo; f. 1977; cap JD 28m., res JD 3.2m., dep. JD 187.2m. (Dec. 1998); Chair. NABEEL Y. BARAKAT; Gen. Man. FAYEZ R. ABUL-ENEIN.

**Jordan Islamic Bank for Finance and Investment:** POB 926225, Shmeisani, Amman 11110; tel. (6) 5677377; fax (6) 5666326; f. 1978; cap. JD 22m., res JD 29m., dep. JD 597m. (Dec. 1998); Chair. MAHMOUD HASSOUBAH; Gen. Man. MUSA A. SHIHADEH; 45 brs.

**Jordan Kuwait Bank:** POB 9776, Amman 11191; tel. (6) 5688814; fax (6) 5687452; e-mail webmaster@jkbank.com.jo; internet www.jordan-kuwait-bank.com; f. 1976; cap. JD 20m., res JD 15.9m., dep. JD 298.7m. (Dec. 1999); Chair. ABD AL-KARIM AL-KABARITI; Gen. Man. MUHAMMAD YASSER AL-ASMAR; 28 brs.

**Jordan National Bank PLC:** POB 3103, Queen Noor St, Shmeisani, Amman 11181; tel. (6) 5622282; fax (6) 5689355; e-mail jnb@go.com.jo; internet www.ahli.com; f. 1955; cap. JD 42m., res JD 29.5m., dep. JD 703.0m. (Dec. 1998); Chair. Dr RAJAI MUASHER; Man. Dir WASEF AZAR; 55 brs in Jordan, 4 brs in Lebanon, 1 br. in Cyprus and 5 brs in the West Bank.

**Middle East Investment Bank:** POB 560, 30 Prince Shaker bin Zeid St, Shmeisani, Amman 11118; tel. (6) 5695470; fax (6) 5693410; e-mail meib@meib.com; internet www.meib.com; cap. JD 10m., res 1.9m., dep. 47.1m. (Dec. 1997); Chair. ALI MANGO; Gen. Man. WALID AS-SOUS (acting).

### Foreign Banks

**ANZ Grindlays Bank:** POB 9997, Shmeisani, Amman 11191; tel. (6) 5607201; fax (6) 5679115; cap. p.u. JD 10m., dep. JD 203m., total assets JD 229m. (Dec. 1998); Gen. Man. in Jordan HUGH FERGUSON; brs in Amman (7 brs), Aqaba, Irbid (2 brs), Zerka, Northern Shouneh and Kerak.

**Arab Banking Corpn:** POB 926691, ABC Bldg, Al-Malekah Noor St, Amman 11110; tel. (6) 5664183; fax (6) 5686291; e-mail info@abc.com.jo; internet www.abc.com.jo; f. 1990; cap. p.u. JD 20m., res JD 2.5m., dep. JD 203.9m., total assets JD 239.5m. (Dec. 1998); Chair. MUHAMMAD AL-MANNAI; 21 brs.

**Arab Islamic International Bank:** Amman; f. 1997; cap p.u. JD 40m.

**Arab Land Bank** (Egypt): POB 6729, Queen Musbah St, 3rd Circle, Jabal Amman 11118; tel. (6) 4656508; fax (6) 4646274; e-mail arlb@go.com.jo; wholly-owned subsidiary of the Central Bank of Egypt; cap. JD 10m., dep. JD 103.3m., res JD 5.5m., total assets JD 136.1m. (Dec. 1997); Chair. ALA AL-ALOSSIYA; Gen. Man. SAMIR MAHDI; 19 brs in Jordan, 4 brs abroad.

**Citibank NA** (USA): POB 5055, Prince Muhammad St, Jabal Amman; tel. (6) 564227; fax (6) 5658693; cap. p.u. JD 5m., dep. JD 56.2m., total assets JD 75.4m. (Dec. 1992); Chair. and CEO JOHN S. REED.

**HSBC Bank Middle East** (United Kingdom): POB 925286, Khalid Bin Walid St, Jebel Hussein, Amman 11110; tel. (6) 5607471; fax (6) 5682047; f. 1889; cap. JD 5m., dep. JD 150m., total assets JD 169m. (Dec. 1994); Chair. Sir JOHN BOND; Area Man. J. S. GIBSON; 6 brs.

**Rafidain Bank** (Iraq): POB 1194, Amman; tel. (6) 5624365; fax (6) 5658698; f. 1941; cap. p.u. JD 5m., res JD 2.1m., dep. JD 31.4m. (Dec. 1992); Pres. and Chair. DHIA HABEEB AL-KHAYOON; 3 brs.

Bank Al-Mashrek (Lebanon) also has a branch in Amman.

### Specialized Credit Institutions

**Agricultural Credit Corporation:** POB 77, Amman; tel. (6) 5661105; fax (6) 5698365; e-mail agri-cc@nets.com.jo; f. 1959; cap. p.u. JD 24m., res JD 7.5m., total assets JD 96.4m. (Dec. 1997); Chair. MEGHIM AL-KHRIESHA; Dir-Gen. NIMER AN-NABULSI; 20 brs.

**Arab Jordan Investment Bank:** POB 8797, Arab Jordan Investment Bank Bldg, Shmeisani Commercial Area, Amman 11121; tel. (6) 5607126; fax (6) 5681482; e-mail ajib@go.com.jo; internet www.ajib.com; f. 1978; cap. JD 20m., res JD 10.4m., dep. JD 229.2m. (Dec. 1998); Chair. and CEO ABD AL-KADER AL-QADI; 10 brs in Jordan, 1 br abroad.

**Cities and Villages Development Bank:** POB 1572, Amman; tel. (6) 5668151; fax (6) 5668153; e-mail cvdb100@hotmail.com; f. 1979; cap. p.u. JD 25m., res JD 14.5m., total assets JD 66.5m. (Dec. 1998); Gen. Man. Dr IBRAHIM AN-NSOUR; 4 brs.

**Housing Bank:** POB 7693, Parliament St, Abdali, Amman 11118; tel. (6) 5607315; fax (6) 5678121; e-mail hbho@go.com.jo; f. 1973; cap. JD 100m., res JD 121.9m., dep. JD 1,056.2m. (Dec. 1998); Chair. ZUHAIR KHOURI; Gen. Man. ABDUL QADER DWEIK; 111 brs.

**Industrial Development Bank:** POB 1982, Islamic College St, Jabal Amman, Amman 11118; tel. (6) 4642216; fax (6) 4647821; e-mail idb@indevbank.com.jo; internet www.indevbank.com.jo; f. 1965; cap. JD 24m., total assets JD 147.8m. (Dec. 1998); Chair. SA'AD AT-TAL; Gen. Man. Dr MAHER WAKED; 3 brs.

**Jordan Co-operative Organization:** POB 1343, Amman; tel. (6) 5665171; f. 1968; cap. p.u. JD 5.2m., dep. JD 11.5m., res JD 6.8m. (Nov. 1992); Chair. and Dir-Gen. JAMAL AL-BEDOUR.

**Jordan Investment Corporation (JIC):** Amman; state-owned; Dir-Gen. MUHAMMAD BATAYNEH.

**Jordan Investment and Finance Bank (JIFBANK):** POB 950601, Issam Ajlouni St, Shmeisani, Amman 11195; tel. (6) 5665145; fax (6) 5681410; e-mail jifbank@index.com.jo; internet www.jifbank.com; f. 1982 as Jordan Investment and Finance Corpn, name changed 1989; cap. JD 20m., res JD 3.7m., dep. JD 238.1m. (Dec. 1998); Chair. NIZAR JARDANEH; Man. Dir BASIL JARDANEH; 5 brs.

**Social Security Corporation:** POB 926031, Amman 11110; tel. (6) 4643000; fax (6) 4610014; f. 1978; Dir-Gen. Dr SAFWAN TOQAN.

**Union Bank for Savings and Investment:** POB 35104, Prince Shaker Bin Zeid St, Shmeisani, Amman 11180; tel. (6) 5607011; fax (6) 5666149; e-mail info@unionbankjo.com; internet www.unionbankjo.com; f. 1978 as Arab Finance Corpn, named changed 1991; cap. JD 23.2m., res 5.5m., dep. 165.0m. (Dec. 1998); Chair. and Gen. Man. ISAM SALFITI; 13 brs.

## STOCK EXCHANGE

**Amman Bourse:** POB 8802, Amman; tel. (6) 5607179; fax (6) 5686830; e-mail afm@go.com.jo; f. 1978 as Amman Financial Market; name changed March 1999; privately-run; Gen. Man. WAHIB SHAIR.

## INSURANCE

**Jordan Insurance Co Ltd:** POB 279, Company's Bldg, 3rd Circle, Jabal Amman, Amman; tel. and fax (6) 4634161; e-mail jicjo@go.com.jo; f. 1951; cap. p.u. JD 5m.; Chair. KHALDUN ABU HASSAN; 6 brs (3 in Saudi Arabia, 3 in the United Arab Emirates).

**Middle East Insurance Co Ltd:** POB 1802, Shmeisani, Yaqoub Sarrouf St, Amman; tel. (6) 5605144; fax (6) 5605950; f. 1963; cap. p.u. US $3.3m.; Chair. WASEF AZAR; 1 br. in Saudi Arabia.

**National Ahlia Insurance Co:** POB 6156-2938, Sayed Qutub St, Shmeisani, Amman 11118; tel. (6) 5671169; fax (6) 5684900; e-mail info@nationalahlia.com; internet www.nationalahlia.com; f. 1965; cap. p.u. JD 2m.; Chair. MUSTAFA ABU GOURA; Gen. Man. GHALEB ABU GOURA.

**United Insurance Co Ltd:** POB 7521, United Insurance Bldg, King Hussein St, Amman; tel. (6) 4648513; fax (6) 4629417; e-mail united@go.com.jo; internet www.unitedi.com; f. 1972; all types of insurance; cap. JD 2m.; Chair. and Gen. Man. RAOUF SA'AD ABUJABER.

There are 17 local and one foreign insurance company operating in Jordan.

# Trade and Industry

## DEVELOPMENT ORGANIZATIONS

**Amman Development Corporation:** POB 926621, Amman; tel. (6) 5629471; f. 1979; development of services in the Amman municipality by constructing and running real estate; industrial and other complexes; Dir Gen. SAMI AR-RASHID.

**Jordan Valley Authority:** POB 2769, Amman; tel. (6) 5642472; projects in Stage I of the Jordan Valley Development Plan were completed in 1979. In 1988 about 26,000 ha was under intensive cultivation. Infrastructure projects also completed include 1,100 km of roads, 2,100 housing units, 100 schools, 15 health centres, 14 administration buildings, 4 marketing centres, 2 community centres, 2 vocational training centres. Electricity is now provided to all the towns and villages in the valley from the national network and domestic water is supplied to them from tube wells. Contributions to the cost of development came through loans from Kuwait Fund, Abu Dhabi Fund, Saudi Fund, Arab Fund, USAID, Fed. Germany, World Bank, EC, Italy, Netherlands, UK, Japan and OPEC Special Fund. Many of the Stage II irrigation projects are now completed or under implementation. Projects under way include the construction of the Wadi al-Arab dam, the raising of the King Talal dam and the 14.5-km extension of the 98-km East Ghor main canal. Stage II will include the irrigation of 4,700 ha in the southern Ghor. The target for the Plan is to irrigate 43,000 ha of land in the Jordan Valley. Future development in irrigation will include the construction of the Maqarin dam and the Wadi Malaha storage dam; Pres. MUHAMMAD BANI HANI; Sec.-Gen. AVEDIS SERPEKIAN.

### CHAMBERS OF COMMERCE AND INDUSTRY

**Amman Chamber of Commerce:** POB 1800, Amman 11118; tel. (6) 5666151; e-mail aci@amra.nic.gov.jo; f. 1923; Pres. HAIDER MURAD; Sec.-Gen. MUHAMMAD AL-MUHTASSEB.

**Amman Chamber of Industry:** POB 1800, Amman; tel. (6) 5643001; fax (6) 5647852; e-mail aci@aci.org.jo; internet www.aci.org.jo; f. 1962; 7,500 industrial companies registered (1999); Pres. KHALDUN ABU HASSAN; Dir.-Gen. Dr MUHAMMAD SMADI.

**Federation of the Jordanian Chambers of Commerce:** Amman; e-mail fjcc@go.com.jo; internet www.fjcc.com; Pres. HAIDER MURAD.

### UTILITIES

#### Electricity

**Jordan Electricity Authority:** POB 2310, Amman; tel. (6) 815615; fax (6) 818336; Chair. MUHAMMAD ARAFAH.

**Jordanian Electric Power Company (JEPCO):** POB 618, Amman 11118; tel. (6) 4648411; fax (6) 4648482; e-mail jepco@go.com.jo; privately-owned.

**Central Electric Power Generating Company (CEPGC):** Amman; electricity generation; govt-owned.

**Electric Power Distribution Company (EPDC):** POB 2310, Orthodox St, 7th Circle, Jabal Amman; tel. (6) 5858615; fax (6) 5818336; e-mail wadah@nepco.com.jo; electricity distribution; govt-owned.

**National Electric Power Company (NEPCO):** Amman; power transmission; govt-owned.

#### Water

**Water Authority of Jordan (WAJ):** Amman.

### TRADE UNIONS

**The General Federation of Jordanian Trade Unions:** POB 1065, Amman; tel. (6) 5675533; f. 1954; 33,000 mems; member of Arab Trade Unions Confederation; Chair. KHALIL ABU KHURMAH; Gen. Sec. ABD AL-HALIM KHADDAM.

There are also a number of independent unions, including:

**Drivers' Union:** POB 846, Amman; tel. (6) 4765637; fax (6) 4765829; Sec.-Gen. MAHMOUD ABD AL-HADI HAMMAD.

**Jordan Engineers' Association (JEA):** Amman; Sec.-Gen. LEITH SHBEILAT.

**Union of Petroleum Workers and Employees:** POB 1346, Amman; Sec.-Gen. BRAHIM HADI.

## Transport

### RAILWAYS

**Aqaba Railways Corporation (ARC):** POB 50, Ma'an; tel. (3) 2132114; fax (3) 2131861; f. 1975; length of track 292 km (1,050-mm gauge); Dir-Gen. ABDULLAH KHAWALDIH.

Formerly a division of the Hedjaz–Jordan Railway (see below), the Aqaba Railway was established as a separate entity in 1972; it retains close links with the Hedjaz but there is no regular through traffic between Aqaba and Amman. It comprises the 169-km line south of Menzil (leased from the Hedjaz–Jordan Railway) and the 115-km extension to Aqaba, opened in October 1975, which serves phosphate mines at el-Hasa and Wadi el-Abyad.

**Hedjaz–Jordan Railway** (administered by the Ministry of Transport): POB 4448, Amman; tel. (6) 895414; fax (6) 894117; f. 1902; length of track 496 km (1,050-mm gauge); Chair. A. HALASA; Dir-Gen. B. ASH-SHRYDEH.

This was formerly a section of the Hedjaz Railway (Damascus to Medina) for Muslim pilgrims to Medina and Mecca. It crosses the Syrian border and enters Jordanian territory south of Dera'a, and runs for approximately 366 km to Naqb Ishtar, passing through Zarka, Amman, Qatrana and Ma'an. Some 844 km of the line, from Ma'an to Medina in Saudi Arabia, were abandoned for over sixty years. Reconstruction of the Medina line, begun in 1965, was scheduled to be completed in 1971 at a cost of £15m., divided equally between Jordan, Saudi Arabia and Syria. However, the reconstruction work was suspended at the request of the Arab states concerned, pending further studies on costs. The line between Ma'an and Saudi Arabia (114 km) is now completed, as well as 15 km in Saudi Arabia as far as Halet Ammar Station. A new 115-km extension to Aqaba (owned by the Aqaba Railway Corporation (see above) was opened in 1975. In 1987 a study conducted by Dorsch Consult (Federal Republic of Germany) into the feasibility of reconstructing the Hedjaz Railway to high international specifications to connect Saudi Arabia, Jordan and Syria, concluded that the reopening of the Hedjaz line would be viable only if it were to be connected with European rail networks. In August 1999 an express rail link between Amman and the Syrian capital, Damascus, was launched.

### ROADS

Amman is linked by road with all parts of the kingdom and with neighbouring countries. All cities and most towns are connected by a two-lane paved road system. In addition, several thousand km of tracks make all villages accessible to motor transport. In 1996 the East Bank of Jordan had an estimated 2,940 km of main roads, 1,970 km of secondary roads (both types asphalted) and 1,740 km of other roads.

**Joint Land Transport Co:** Amman; joint venture of Govts of Jordan and Iraq; operates about 750 trucks.

**Jordanian-Syrian Land Transport Co:** POB 20686, Amman; tel. (6) 5661134; fax (6) 5669645; f. 1976; transports goods between ports in Jordan and Syria; Chair. and Gen. Man. HAMDI AL-HABASHNEH.

### SHIPPING

The port of Aqaba is Jordan's only outlet to the sea and has more than 20 modern and specialized berths, and one container terminal (540 m in length). The port has 299,000 sq m of storage area, and is used for Jordan's international trade and regional transit trade (mainly with Iraq). There is a ferry link between Aqaba and the Egyptian port of Nuweibeh.

**The Ports Corporation:** POB 115, Aqaba 77110; tel. (3) 2014040; fax (3) 2016204; e-mail ports@amra.nic.gov.jo; Dir-Gen. MUHAMMAD DALABIEH.

**Arab Bridge Maritime Co:** Aqaba; f. 1987; joint venture by Egypt, Iraq and Jordan to improve economic co-operation; an extension of the company that established a ferry link between Aqaba and the Egyptian port of Nuweibeh in 1985; Chair. Eng. KHALID SALEH AMAR; Dir-Gen. TAWFIQ GRACE AWADALLA.

**Arrow Trans Shipping SA:** POB 926567, Amman; tel. (6) 692620; fax (6) 693324.

**Assaf Shipping Co SA:** POB 2637, Irbid 21110; tel. (2) 279117; e-mail ism@go.com.jo.

**T. Gargour & Fils:** POB 419, 4th Floor, Da'ssan Commercial Centre, Wasfi at-Tal St, Amman; tel. (6) 5524142; fax (6) 5530512; e-mail tgf@tgf.com.jo; f. 1928; shipping agents and owners; Chair. JOHN GARGOUR.

**Hijezi & Ghosheh Co:** POB 183292, Amman; tel. (6) 386166.

**Jordan National Shipping Lines Co Ltd:** POB 5406, Nasir Ben Jameel St, Wadi Saqra, Amman 11183; tel. (6) 5511500; fax (6) 5515119; e-mail JNL@nets.com.jo; POB 657, Aqaba; tel. (3) 2018738; fax (3) 318738; 75% govt-owned; service from Antwerp, Bremen and Tilbury to Aqaba; daily passenger ferry service to Egypt; land transportation to destinations in Iraq and elsewhere in the region; Chair. Dr FOTI KHAMIS; Gen. Man. Y. ET-TAL.

**Amin Kawar & Sons Co W.L.L.:** POB 222, 24 Abd al-Hamid Sharaf St, Shmeisani, Amman 11118; tel. (6) 5603703; fax (6) 5672170; e-mail aks@nets.com.jo; chartering and shipping agents; Chair. TAWFIQ A. KAWAR; Gen. Man. GHASSOUB F. KAWAR; Liner Man. JAMIL SAID.

**Al-Mansour Marine Transportation and Trading Co:** POB 960359, Amman; tel. (6) 697958; fax (6) 702352.

**Orient Shipping Co Ltd:** POB 207, Amman 11118; tel. (6) 5641695; fax (6) 5651567.

**Petra Navigation and International Trading Co Ltd:** POB 8362, White Star Bldg, Amman 11121; tel. (6) 5607021; fax (6) 5601362; e-mail petra@armoush.com.jo; general cargo, ro/ro and passenger ferries; Chair. AHMAD H. ARMOUSH.

**Salam International Transport and Trading Co:** King Hussein St, Abdali, Amman 11121; tel. (6) 5607021.

**Syrian-Jordanian Shipping Co:** POB 148, rue Port Said, Latakia, Syria; tel. (41) 471635; fax (41) 470250; Chair. OSMAN LEBBADI.

### PIPELINES

Two oil pipelines cross Jordan. The former Iraq Petroleum Co pipeline, carrying petroleum from the oilfields in Iraq to Haifa, has not operated since 1967. The 1,717-km (1,067-mile) pipeline, known as the Trans-Arabian Pipeline (Tapline), carries petroleum from the oilfields of Dhahran in Saudi Arabia to Sidon on the Mediterranean seaboard in Lebanon. Tapline traverses Jordan for a distance of 177 km (110 miles) and has frequently been cut by hostile action. Tapline stopped pumping to Syria and Lebanon at the end of 1983, when it was first due to close. It was later scheduled to close in 1985, but in September 1984 Jordan renewed an agreement to receive Saudi Arabian crude oil through Tapline. The agreement can be cancelled by either party at two years' notice.

### CIVIL AVIATION

There are international airports at Amman and Aqaba. The Queen Alia International Airport at Zizya, 40 km south of Amman, was opened in 1983.

**Civil Aviation Authority:** POB 7547, Amman; tel. (6) 4892282; fax (6) 4891653; e-mail caa@amra.nic.gov.jo; f. 1950; Dir-Gen. Capt. JIHAD IRSHAID.

**Royal Jordanian Airline:** Head Office: POB 302, Housing Bank Commercial Centre, Shmeisani, Amman 11118; tel. (6) 5667618; fax (6) 5660787; internet www.rja.com.jo; f. 1963; govt-owned, but scheduled for privatization in 2000; scheduled and charter services to Middle East, North Africa, Europe, USA and Far East; Chair. WALID ASFOUR; Pres. and CEO NADER DAHABI.

**Arab Wings Co Ltd:** POB 341018, Amman; tel. (6) 4891994; fax (6) 4893902; f. 1975; subsidiary of Royal Jordanian; executive jet charter service, air ambulances, priority cargo; Man. Dir AHED QUNTAR.

**Royal Wings Co Ltd:** POB 314018, Amman 1134; tel. (6) 4875206; fax (6) 4875656; internet www.royalwings.com.jo; f. 1995; subsidiary of Royal Jordanian; operates scheduled and charter regional and domestic services; Pres. and Gen. Man. AHED QUNTAR.

## Tourism

The ancient cities of Jerash and Petra, and Jordan's proximity to biblical sites, have encouraged tourism. In the late 1990s the development of Jordan's Dead Sea coast was under way; owing to the Sea's mineral-rich waters, the growth of curative tourism is anticipated. In 1996 there were an estimated 1.1m. tourists. Income from tourism in 1996 was US $743.6m.

**Ministry of Tourism and Antiquities:** Ministry of Tourism, POB 224, Amman; tel. (6) 4642311; fax (6) 4648465; f. 1952; Minister of Tourism and Antiquities AQEL BELTAJI; Sec.-Gen. Ministry of Tourism MUHAMMAD AFFASH AL-ADWAN.

**Jordan Tourism Board:** POB 830688, Amman 11118; tel. (6) 4647951; fax (6) 4647915; f. 1997; e-mail jtb@nets.com.jo; internet www.seejordan.org.

# INDEX OF INTERNATIONAL ORGANIZATIONS

(Main reference only)

A

# Major Titles from Europa

## The European Union Encyclopedia and Directory

- The very latest information on the European Union
- Charts the Union's development from its creation, through the Treaty of Amsterdam, to present day policies and activities
- Includes an A-Z section, introductory articles, a statistical section and an extensive directory, including details of all major European Union institutes and their official bodies
- Details MEPs, their political groups and national parties, members of major committees, Directorates-General and other Commission bodies

## The Environment Encyclopedia and Directory

- Provides an A-Z section of key terms relating to the environment
- A directory section organized alphabetically by country lists main governmental and non-governmental organizations, both national and international
- A series of maps show areas of pollution, rainforest and other environmental features both regionally and world-wide
- Includes an extensive bibliography of relevant periodicals
- A Who's Who section of people actively involved with environmental organizations

## The Directory of University Libraries in Europe

- Extensive information on central and other university libraries of European universities and, where appropriate, details of attached institutes and research centres
- Almost 4,000 entries, with full contact details, including the names of chief librarians and other relevant staff, and further information such as size and composition of library holdings, on-line subscription details and details of libraries' own publications
- Fully indexed

## The Territories of the Russian Federation

- This new reference survey, the first of its kind to be published in English, provides much needed up-to-date information on the 89 constituent units of the Russian Federation
- Almost 300 pages of maps, analysis, statistics and detailed information
- Provides comprehensive individual territory surveys
- Includes a chronology of Russia, an essay on the economic perspective of the Russian federative system and an introduction to the structure of the Federal Government

## A Political & Economic Dictionary of Eastern Europe

- A new dictionary written by Alan Day
- Over 800 concise entries concerning the politics and economics of Eastern Europe, the Russian Federation and all members of the Commonwealth of Independent States
- Information is provided on the countries, regions, ethnic groups, political parties, prime ministers, presidents and other prominent politicians, business organizations, geographical features, religions and border disputes
- Includes separate articles on each country, and on its economy

## A Dictionary of Human Rights

- Over 200 mini articles, arranged alphabetically and extensively cross-referenced
- Explanations of the terms, issues, organizations and laws occuring within the subject of human rights
- Outlines the significance of eminent thinkers, such as Locke, Cardozo and Nozick
- Contains extracts of leading documents, such as the Declaration of the Rights of Man and of the Citizen and the Convention on the Rights of the Child

For further information on any of the above titles contact our marketing department on:

tel. + 44 (0) 20 7842 2110 fax. + 44 (0) 20 7842 2249

e-mail sales@europapublications.co.uk www.europapublications.co.uk

Svalbard (NORWAY)
Jan Mayen (NORWAY)
Arctic Circle
ICELAND
Faroe Is (DEN.)
RUSSIAN FEDERATION
FINLAND
SWEDEN
NORWAY
OSLO
HELSINKI
St Petersburg
STOCKHOLM
ESTONIA
LATVIA
LITHUANIA
RUSSIAN FED.
MOSCOW
UNITED KINGDOM
DENMARK
MINSK
BELARUS
DUBLIN
REPUBLIC OF IRELAND
LONDON
BERLIN
WARSAW
GERMANY
POLAND
NETH.
Essen
BEL.
LUX.
KIEV
UKRAINE
CZECH
SLOV.
PARIS
FRANCE
AUSTRIA
HUNGARY
MOLDOVA
SWITZ.
SLVN.
CROATIA
ROMANIA
MON.
S.M.
BOS. & HERZ.
BULGARIA
MAC.
ALB.
ITALY
ROME
(VAT. CITY)
PORTUGAL
SPAIN
ANDORRA
LISBON
MADRID
GREECE
ATHENS
Gibraltar (U.K.)
RABAT
ALGIERS
TUNIS
SPAN. N. AF.
MALTA
TUNISIA
TRIPOLI
MOROCCO
ALGERIA
LIBYA
EGYPT
CAIRO
Tropic of Cancer
Western Sahara
MAURITANIA
NOUAKCHOTT
MALI
NIGER
CHAD
SENEGAL
GAMBIA
BAMAKO
NIAMEY
N'DJAMENA
G.-B.
GUINEA
BURKINA
NIGERIA
GHANA
BENIN
TOGO
SIERRA LEONE
LIBERIA
CÔTE D'IVOIRE
ABUJA
Lagos
CAMEROON
C.A.R.
BANGUI
EQUATORIAL GUINEA
SÃO TOMÉ & PRÍNCIPE
GABON
CONGO REP.
CONGO, DEM. REP.
KINSHASA
Equator
ERITREA
KHARTOUM
SUDAN
DJIBOUTI
ADDIS ABABA
ETHIOPIA
SOMALIA
MOGADISHU
UGANDA
KAMPALA
KENYA
RWANDA
BURUNDI
NAIROBI
TANZANIA
DAR ES SALAAM
SEYCHELLES
COMOROS
LUANDA
ANGOLA
MALAWI
ZAMBIA
LUSAKA
HARARE
ZIMB.
MOZAMBIQUE
Mayotte (FRANCE)
ANTANANARIVO
MADAGASCAR
MAURITIUS
Réunion (FRANCE)
St Helena (U.K.)
NAMIBIA
WINDHOEK
BOTS.
GABORONE
PRETORIA
MAPUTO
SWAZILAND
Tropic of Capricorn
SOUTH AFRICA
LESOTHO
TURKEY
Istanbul
ANKARA
ARM.
AZER.
GEORGIA
CYPRUS
LEBANON
ISRAEL
SYRIA
BAGHDAD
IRAQ
TEHRAN
IRAN
JORDAN
KUWAIT
BAHRAIN
QATAR
RIYADH
U.A.E.
MUSCAT
OMAN
SAUDI ARABIA
SAN'A
YEMEN
KAZAKHSTAN
ASTANA
UZBEKISTAN
TURKMENISTAN
ASHGABAT
TASHKENT
BISHKEK
KYRGYZSTAN
DUSHANBE
TAJIKISTAN
KABUL
AFGHANISTAN
ISLAMABAD
PAKISTAN
Lahore
NEW DELHI
Karachi
NEPAL
KATHMANDU
BHUTAN
THIMPHU
BANGLADESH
DHAKA
Kolkata
INDIA
Mumbai
Hyderabad
Chennai
Bangalore
SRI LANKA
COLOMBO
MALDIVES
British Indian Ocean Territory (U.K.)
Indian Ocean
MONGOLIA
ULAN BATOR
PEOPLE'S REP. OF CHINA
BEIJING
Shenyang
Tianjin
Shanghai
Hong Kong
KOREA, D.P.R.
PYONGYANG
SEOUL
KOREA, REP.
JAPAN
TOKYO
Osaka
TAIPEI
CHINA (TAIWAN)
MYANMAR
YANGON
LAOS
VIENTIANE
VIET NAM
HANOI
THAILAND
BANGKOK
CAMBODIA
PHNOM-PENH
MANILA
PHILIPPINES
Northern Mariana Is (U.S.A.)
Guam (U.S.A.)
MICRONESIA
PALAU
BRUNEI
MALAYSIA
KUALA LUMPUR
SINGAPORE
INDONESIA
JAKARTA
EAST TIMOR
Christmas Is. (AUSTRALIA)
Cocos Is (AUSTRALIA)
PAPUA NEW GUINEA
PORT MORESBY
AUSTRALIA
CANBERRA
The Europa Publications Regional Surveys of the World
Africa South of the Sahara
Central & South Eastern Europe
Eastern Europe & Central Asia
The Far East & Australia
The Middle East & North Africa
South America, Central America & the Caribbean
The USA & Canada
Western Europe
"AFGHANISTAN": independent country
"Anguilla": non-independent dependency or territory
"ALGIERS": capital city
"Bangalore": urban agglomeration over 5m. population, but not a capital
Antarctic Circle
Antarctica